THE GENERAL COUNCIL OF THE BAR™

THE BAR
DIRECTORY

Sweet & Maxwell
1999 EDITION

Published by Sweet & Maxwell Limited of
100 Avenue Road
London NW3 3PF

Set by MPG Information Division, Woking
Printed in Great Britain by MPG Books Ltd, Bodmin, Cornwall

A CIP catalogue record for this book
is available from the British Library

ISBN 0 75200 640 1

The information in this Directory was supplied in part by chambers
and individual barristers directly to the publishers (for Parts A, B, G
and I), and in part by the General Council of the Bar Records Office
(for Parts E and F). Part H was supplied by the Institute of Barristers'
Clerks. Parts C and D are drawn from information supplied by chambers and individual barristers, supplemented where necessary with
Bar Council data.

The General Council of the Bar information on chambers dates up to
19 March 1998. Sweet & Maxwell accepted applications for bronze
entries up to 15 April 1998 and for silver and gold chambers entries
up to 30 April 1998.

The General Council of the Bar information on individual barristers
in private practice dates up to 19 March 1998. Sweet & Maxwell
accepted bronze entries up to 15 April 1998, and silver and gold
entries up to 30 April 1998.

A copy of the full Bar Directory Terms and Conditions is available
from Sweet & Maxwell upon request. The publishers have attempted
to ensure accuracy of all entries in this Directory, but cannot accept
responsibility for any errors, inconsistencies or omissions.

No natural forests were destroyed to make this product,
only naturally farmed timber was used and replanted

CONTENTS

THE SERVICES PROVIDED BY THE BAR EVOLVE AND

EXPAND CONTINUOUSLY IN RESPONSE TO THE

DEMANDS OF A MODERN SOCIETY. IT IS

INCREASINGLY IMPORTANT TO BE ABLE TO IDENTIFY

READILY THE SOURCES OF APPROPRIATE SPECIALIST

ADVICE AND ADVOCACY.

THIS DIRECTORY CONTAINS COMPREHENSIVE

INFORMATION ON CHAMBERS AND BARRISTERS. THE

ASSOCIATED WEBSITE SETS OUT SIMILAR DETAILS,

AND BOTH ALLOW THE READER TO SEARCH IN TERMS

OF SPECIALISATION, GEOGRAPHICAL AREA AND

LANGUAGES SPOKEN.

I COMMEND THIS DIRECTORY TO ALL THOSE SEEKING

TO USE THE BAR'S SERVICES.

HEATHER HALLETT QC

CHAIRMAN OF THE BAR 1998

This Directory has been compiled from information supplied in part by chambers and individual barristers directly to the publishers (for Parts A, B, G and I), and in part by the General Council of the Bar Records Office (for Parts E and F). Part H was supplied by the Institute of Barristers' Clerks. Parts C and D are drawn from information supplied by chambers and individual barristers, supplemented where necessary with Bar Council data.

The General Council of the Bar information on chambers dates up to 19 March 1998. Sweet & Maxwell accepted applications for bronze entries up to 15 April 1998 and for silver and gold chambers entries up to 30 April 1998. The General Council of the Bar information on individual barristers in private practice dates up to 19 March 1998. Sweet & Maxwell accepted bronze entries up to 15 April 1998, and silver and gold entries up to 30 April 1998.

The introductory pages include information on the Bar of England and Wales, the General Council of the Bar, the Circuits of the Bar, Specialist Bar Associations and Direct Professional Access. This information was supplied by the General Council of the Bar. The Directory is divided into nine parts as follows:

Part A Types of Work by Chambers

Part A lists chambers by the type of work they do and by the town or city where they are located. The types of work undertaken by chambers are listed in alphabetical order from Administrative to Unit Trusts. Within these main categories, chambers are listed alphabetically under the town or city in which they practise. For example, a reader wishing to locate a Birmingham-based chambers specialising in trademarks would be able to look under 'T' for Trademarks and find under that heading the details of any chambers in Birmingham which offer their services in this field. A complete list of all the types of work from which chambers were asked to select their specialisms can be found at the front of Part A. Where chambers have indicated that they practise in other areas, this information is listed within Part A.

Each listing provides the name of the Head of Chambers and chambers' telephone number. The first point of contact in each instance will be the clerk. (Details of clerks can be found in *Part C Chambers by Location.*)

Please note that if a chambers is not listed in this section, it is at their request.

The symbol ● indicates that chambers have an expanded entry in *Part C Chambers by Location.*

Part B Types of Work by Individual Barristers

Part B lists individual barristers by the types of work in which they specialise. The areas of work are listed in alphabetical order from Administrative to Unit Trusts. Within these main categories, individual barristers are listed alphabetically by surname. For example, a reader wishing to locate a particular barrister specialising in trademarks would be able to look under 'T' for Trademarks and find under that heading those barristers who offer their services in this field. A complete list of all the types of work from which individual barristers were asked to select their specialisms can be found at the front of Part B. Where individuals have indicated that they practise in other areas, this information is listed within Part B.

Each listing provides the name of the individual barrister, their chambers' address and chambers' telephone number. The first point of contact in each instance will be the clerk. (Details of clerks can be found in *Part C Chambers by Location.*)

Please note that if a barrister is not listed in this section, it is at their request.

The symbol ● indicates that a barrister has an expanded entry in *Part D Individual Barristers in Private Practice.*

Part C Chambers by Location

Part C lists chambers in England and Wales by the town or city in which they are located. The town/city names are in alphabetical order and under those main headings chambers are listed alphabetically, thus 7 King's Bench Walk would be listed before 4 Pump Court under London.

Information for each set of chambers includes full contact details with names of clerks and Head of Chambers (where provided). Chambers also provided information on their list of practising barristers including indications as to whether members are Recorders, Assistant Recorders, or Door Tenants (see below). Some chambers have opted to include additional information about themselves in this part of the Directory such as the date chambers was established, opening times, chambers' facilities, languages spoken, details regarding fees and a list of the types of work undertaken, including where supplied details of the number of counsel practising in each area. Please note that details of the types of work undertaken by those chambers which have chosen not to include this information in Part C may be found in *Part A Types of Work by Chambers*.

The following symbols indicate that barristers are:

†   Recorders
‡   Assistant Recorders
*   Door Tenants

Part D Individual Barristers in Private Practice

Part D lists barristers in private practice. Individuals are listed alphabetically by surname, and details include the chambers at which they practise, date of call to the Bar, Inn of Court and academic qualifications.

Some individual barristers have opted to include additional information about themselves in this part of the Directory, such as other qualifications, membership of foreign bars, other professional experience, languages spoken, publications, reported cases and a list of the types of work they undertake. Please note that details of the types of work undertaken by individual barristers who have chosen not to include this information in Part D may be found in *Part B Types of Work by Individual Barristers*.

Part E Individual Barristers in Employment and Non-Practising

Part E lists those barristers who are in employment and those who do not practise. Barristers are listed alphabetically by surname, and details include their date of call to the Bar, their Inn of Court and academic qualifications. Barristers who are currently employed have details of their position of employment with a full address.

The symbol ● indicates that a barrister is in employment.

Part F Individual Barristers Overseas

Part F lists barristers who are based overseas. Barristers are listed alphabetically by surname and details include their membership of other Bars where appropriate, date of call to the Bar, their Inn of Court and academic qualifications.

Part G Index of Languages Spoken

Part G is an index of languages spoken by chambers and individual barristers. The languages are listed alphabetically (from Africaans to Yoruba), as are chambers and individuals.

All chambers in this section have an expanded entry in *Part C Chambers by Location* and all individual barristers in this section have an expanded entry in *Part D Individual Barristers in Private Practice*.

Part H Qualified Members of the Institute of Barristers' Clerks

Part H lists all qualified members of the Institute of Barristers' Clerks. The listings are divided into four sections: Senior Clerks, Junior Clerks, Senior Associates and Junior Associates. The information in this section was supplied by the Institute of Barristers' Clerks. The year of qualification, if supplied, is shown in brackets. Management Committee Members and Executive Committee Members are identified by the following symbols:

* Management Committee Member
** Executive Committee Member

Part I A–Z Index of Chambers

Part I lists all the chambers from *Part C Chambers by Location* alphabetically with the Part C page reference.

Updating of Information

Information about chambers or individual barristers which needs updating should be discussed with the Records Office at the General Council of the Bar on the following number:

Tel: 0171 242 0934

Updating on the Internet should be directed in the first instance to:

The Directories Unit Manager
Sweet & Maxwell
21-27 Lamb's Conduit Street
London WC1N 3NJ
Tel: 0171 420 7500

Any comments regarding *The Bar Directory* should be directed in the first instance to:

The Directories Unit Manager
Sweet & Maxwell
21-27 Lamb's Conduit Street
London WC1N 3NJ
Tel: 0171 420 7500

Barristers are independent and objective. Their highly competitive training in litigation and advocacy, together with their specialist knowledge and experience in and out of court, can make a substantial difference to the outcome of a case, whether criminal or civil. Whatever the nature of the legal problem, it is important at an early stage to decide whether to bring in a barrister.

There are some 9,000 barristers in independent practice in England and Wales. Through them the Bar offers unparalleled expertise. Broad areas of specialisation include: Building and Construction, Commercial, Company, Criminal (including extradition), Defamation, Employment, Environment, Family, Housing, Immigration, Insolvency, Insurance, Liquidation, Personal Injury, Property, Taxation and Trusts, Wills and Estates. These can be subdivided further into more than 300 categories of expertise.

Through their grouping in chambers, or in some cases working as sole practitioners, barristers are able to operate with low overheads and to offer competitive rates. Legal aid will often cover the services of a barrister and sometimes a Queens Counsel; for those not eligible for legal aid solicitors can help the lay client by negotiating an affordable fee.

The Bar remains a referral profession, usually instructed by solicitors. However, members of certain professional bodies (see *Direct Professional Access* on page xviii) are able to seek advice direct from Counsel or may instruct counsel in non-court litigation. In some cases, members of the Bar provide their services *pro bono*, for example through Free Representation Units or the recently formed Bar Pro Bono Unit. *Pro bono* work has been undertaken also in humanitarian cases.

The era of the quill pen is long gone. The Bar recognises that it must offer excellence not only in its advocacy and specialist advisory work, but through the efficiency with which it provides its services. In addition to continued refinement of the Bar's Code of Conduct, Practice Management Standards and Guidelines for barristers and chambers have been introduced. Many chambers have taken advantage of the greatly increased efficiency which modern methods of communication, computer systems and on-line information can bring. The Bar has responded in other ways to society's changing demands, for example by improving accessibility, introducing an equality code and extending the complaints system.

The substantial increase in the size of the Bar in recent years has been accompanied by an increase in the size of chambers, as well as in their number. This reflects the need to accommodate an increasing range of specialisation. A majority of the profession continues to practise from London. But about 3,000 barristers practise from major cities and in some cases small towns outside London, offering a wide range and depth of expertise.

Lawyers took over the Inner and Middle Temples from the Order of Knights Templar, a Common Bench having been established at Westminster in the late 13th and early 14th century. Lincoln's and Gray's Inns grew from association with Henry de Lacy, Earl of Lincoln and the de Gray family respectively. From the 17th century onward, the right to practise as an advocate in the Royal Courts was restricted to members of the Inns, the Bar becoming firmly a referral profession acting on the instructions of solicitors in the 19th century.

Until 1875, discipline over the Bar was maintained by the Order of Serjeants. Thereafter, the Inns became concerned directly with the management of the profession through their Benchers. The General Council of the Bar (Bar Council) was formed in 1894 to deal with matters of professional etiquette. In 1974, the Bar Council and the governing body of the Inns, the Senate, combined to form the Senate of the Inns of Court and the Bar. However, on 1 January 1987, in line with the recommendations of a report on the Constitution of the Senate by Lord Rawlinson PC QC, a Council of the Inns of Court was re-established separately and the Courts and Legal Services Act 1990 designated the Bar Council as the authorised body for the profession.

The Courts and Legal Services Act requires the exercise of rights of audience to be dependent upon membership of a professional body which has rules governing the conduct of its members, has an effective mechanism for enforcing those rules and is likely to enforce them. Accordingly, the Bar Council provides a regulatory framework, requiring work on complaints and discipline, ethics and standards, education and training, equal opportunities and pupillage. It also publishes guidance on a range of other subjects such as practice management, health and safety, and taxation.

The Council has representational responsibilities in many areas including the administration of justice and relations with Government, the European Union, legal professions in other countries, and other organisations with common interests. It participates in the negotiation of publicly funded fees and provides advice on legal aid matters, in addition to law reform consultation. Over 200 barristers serve on a range of committees contributing to the well-being of the profession and of the public through the quality of service the profession provides. The positive involvement of so many practitioners also promotes accountability, both generally and within the work of the Secretariat.

Main Offices: 3 Bedford Row London WC1R 4DB Telephone 0171 242 0082 Records Office 0171 242 0934 Fax 0171 831 9217 DX 240 LDE
Complaints, Education & Training Departments 2/3 Cursitor Street, London EC4A 1NE Tel: 0171 440 4000 DX 325 LDE
Fax: (Complaints) 0171 440 4001 Fax: (Education & Training) 0171 440 4002
Chief Executive: Niall Morison

Though their origins lie with the birth of the assize system in the 12th century, the Circuits of the Bar have survived its passing and still form the basis for the administration of the courts system and the organisation of the Bar of England and Wales.

Over the centuries the names and boundaries have changed, but there are now six Circuits covering England and Wales. The South Eastern, with a membership of about 2,000 barristers, is the largest and includes London, the Home Counties and East Anglia. The Western Circuit runs from Portsmouth in the east to Truro in the west and includes Winchester, Bristol and Exeter. The Midland and Oxford Circuit covers central England from the east coast to the Welsh borders; Wales and Chester, with the smallest membership, covers the whole of Wales and the Cheshire plain, and the Northern and North Eastern Circuits cover northern England to the west and east of the Pennines respectively. Each of the Circuits is separately administered on the court side by a circuit administrator and a circuit office under the Lord Chancellor's Department, and on the Bar side by circuit officers, including a circuit leader and junior, and in the case of the larger Circuits, a circuit committee.

Since we said farewell to the assize system, the judges no longer travel formally from town to town on circuit, but each Circuit has its own presiding High Court judges who, with the resident circuit judges in the crown and county courts and the circuit office, are responsible for all aspects of the court system. Recent years have seen increasing numbers of important cases, civil and criminal, taking place in the major circuit centres out of London. Following wider consultation about the design and building of new courts, facilities for all, including litigants, witnesses, jurors, the legal profession and the judges, have been substantially improved in the many excellent new court buildings throughout England and Wales. Other fine old courts, for example those at Lincoln on the Midland and Oxford Circuit and Lewes on the South Eastern Circuit, have been carefully and skilfully refurbished. Some courts now have video and computer facilities and, on the Welsh Circuit, courts in the main centres have simultaneous Welsh/English translation. Increasing numbers of specialist courts are being set up on circuit to deal with the complex problems of modern litigation and, for example, a mercantile court has recently been established in Birmingham.

The Bar has seen a huge increase in its numbers in the last 30 years. As a result, chambers have increased in number and size, and many more barristers now practise outside London. This has increased the importance of effective circuit organisations and the Circuits provide through their officers and committees a wide range of services for their members, including continuing education seminars, advocacy courses, overseas visits to meet foreign lawyers and judges, and sets of law reports at courts for the use of the profession. Setting up and maintaining lines of communication with all parts of the legal system, including the courts administration, the Lord Chancellor's Department, the judiciary and The Law Society, is an important aspect of the work of the Circuits on the Bar side. The circuit leaders are consulted by the Lord Chancellor on the appointment of part- and full-time judges and Queen's Counsel, and the Circuits still play an important part in the maintenance of professional standards. As constraints on public funds increase, the Circuits have assisted in the setting-up and extension of free representation schemes in different parts of the country.

For hundreds of years the Circuits have proved their capacity to adapt and survive. With the approach of the 21st century and at a time of fundamental change in the legal profession, they continue to thrive.

Leaders of the Circuits

South Eastern Circuit
Michael Lawson QC
23 Essex Street, London WC2R 3AS
(telephone 0171 413 0353)

Midland & Oxford Circuit
James Hunt QC
36 Bedford Row, London WC1R 4JH
(telephone 0171 421 8000)

Northern Circuit
Richard Henriques QC
Deans Court Chambers, Cumberland House, Crown Square
Manchester M3 3HA
(telephone 0161 834 4097)

North Eastern Circuit
Malcolm R Swift QC
Park Court Chambers, 40 Park Cross Street, Leeds LS1 2QH
(telephone 0113 243 3277)

Wales & Chester Circuit
John Griffith Williams QC
Goldsmith Building, London EC4Y 7BL
(telephone 0171 353 7881)

Western Circuit
Nigel Pascoe QC
Pump Court Chambers, 3 Pump Court, Temple,
London EC4Y 7AJ
(telephone 0171 353 0711)

These associations are groups of barristers in independent practice in specialist fields. Their memberships often overlap. The associations concern themselves with the law and procedure in their fields, advise on law reform, look after their members' interests and help them to keep up to date with new developments. Many also provide extensive continuing professional education and many publish their own directories.

Administrative Law Bar Association (ALBA)

Members provide specialist advice to public bodies (and those who have dealings with them) on their duties and powers and the exercise of them, in the light of both the general law and the specifically applicable provisions, and also of practice. They also act as specialist advocates for and against public authorities, including the government, particularly in judicial review proceedings and on appeal.

Secretary: *Jenni Richards, 39 Essex Street, London WC2R 3AT (telephone 0171 583 1111)*

Bar European Group

Set up to promote interest in, and knowledge of, community law, this group holds a yearly conference on the Continent and a number of other conferences and day educational courses in the UK. Open to all interested, membership includes specialist community law barristers advising and appearing here or before the Luxembourg Court and the Commission.

Secretary: *Julie Anderson, Pump Court Tax Chambers, 16 Bedford Row, London WC1R 4EB (telephone 0171 414 8063)*

Chancery Bar Association

The work of the Chancery Bar involves property, business and commercial disputes, trusts and connected tax matters. It encompasses litigation, drafting, and advice covering a wide field including mortgages, landlord and tenant, companies and partnerships, insolvency, probate, pensions, intellectual property and professional negligence in these areas.

Hon Secretary: *Anthony Trace, 13 Old Square, Lincoln's Inn, London WC2A 3UA (telephone 0171 404 4800)*

Bristol and Cardiff Chancery Bar Association

The Association was formed in 1990. It is open to all members of the Bar who undertake work of a Chancery or commercial nature in the west of England and South Wales.

Chairman: *Winston Roddick QC, 10 King's Bench Walk, Temple, London EC4 7EB (telephone 0171 353 2501)*

Hon Secretary: *Paul French, Guildhall Chambers, 23 Broad Street, Bristol BS1 2HG (telephone 0117 927 3366)*

Assistant Secretary: *Andrew Keyser 9 Park Place, Cardiff CF1 3DP (telephone 01222 382731)*

Northern Chancery Bar Association

Set up in 1987 as part of the lobbying exercise which led to the appointment of a full High Court judge as Vice-Chancellor of the County Palatine of Lancaster, the Association represents barristers practising on the Northern and North-Eastern Circuits doing Chancery work. The membership is just over 100. It is not always appreciated that one in four trials in the Chancery Division takes place on circuit. Membership varies from those with highly litigious practices to those who deal with the more traditional drafting and advisory work.

Secretary: *Julie Case, Exchange Chambers, Pearl Assurance House, Derby Square, Liverpool L2 9XX (telephone 0151 236 7747)*

Commercial Bar Association (COMBAR)

COMBAR was founded in 1989 to represent and promote the interests of commercial barristers serving the specialist needs of commerce, including international commercial litigation and arbitration. Its membership comprises leading commercial chambers and individual practitioners at the Commercial Bar whose expertise extends across the fields of international trade, shipping and aviation, banking and financial services, insurance and reinsurance, commodity transactions, insolvency, oil & gas/energy law, mergers and acquisitions, competition law, intellectual property, professional negligence, licensing, judicial review of government acts, employment, European Community matters and public international law. COMBAR represents its members on the Bar Council, liaises with other specialist Bar associations on matters of common interest, comments on proposed legislation affecting the commercial field, contributes to the debate concerning the reform of the English civil justice system and offers a continuing programme of lectures and seminars and links with international Bar associations. An annual directory is published in January. COMBAR actively encourages close working links with lawyers practising in other jurisdictions, particularly in Europe, North America and the Far East.

Secretary: *Timothy Howe, The Commercial Bar Association, 222-225 Strand, The Outer Temple, London WC2R 1ND (telephone 0171 353 3502)*

Criminal Bar Association

The largest specialist association with over 2,500 members who cover all criminal cases plus extradition and human rights. The Association is consulted on many types of law reform and runs a series of eight autumn lectures on topics of current interest. There is also an annual all-day conference dedicated to a specific subject, eg forensic science.

Secretary: *Richard Carey-Hughes, 4 Brick Court, Temple, London EC4Y 9AD (telephone 0171 583 8455)*

Employment Law Bar Association

The Employment Law Bar Association was formed in April 1994. The principal aim is to be a forum of consultation on behalf of those barristers throughout the UK, in private and employed practice, who work in employment law; to assist Free Representation Units; to be consulted on Tribunal and High Court Rules and on appointments; to sit on Tribunal User Groups; to help with pupils seeking to specialise, and to be the official organ of the Bar for barristers in this field.

Secretary: *Jenny Eady, Old Square Chambers, 1 Verulam Buildings, Gray's Inn, London WC1R 5LR (telephone 0171 831 0801, e-mail: jeady@compuserve.com)*

Family Law Bar Association

Members include all barristers with any degree of family work. This includes public and private work in connection with children, financial disputes between spouses, claims of cohabitees and Inheritance Act claims, covering all courts including magistrates courts.

Secretary: *Pamela Scriven QC, 1 King's Bench Walk, Temple, London EC4Y 9DB (telephone 0171 736 1500)*

Bar Association for Local Government and the Public Service

The main objectives of the association include the protection and promotion of the professional rights and interests of barristers employed in the public sector by giving advice to barristers seeking a career in the public sector, making representations to the Bar Council and elsewhere relating to training, rights of audience, direct access to counsel and by promoting professional knowledge. Details about the Association and application forms for membership can be obtained from the Honorary Treasurer.

Hon Treasurer: *Mirza F N Ahmad, Head of Legal Services, Bolton Metropolitan Borough Council, Town Hall, Bolton BL1 1RU (telephone 01204 522311)*

IP Bar Association (formerly Patent Bar Association)

Members cover all kinds of intellectual property work, including patents, trademarks, copyright, registered designs, passing-off and breach of confidence. They appear mainly in the High Court and the Patents County Court. The main patent chambers belong *en bloc* and there are a number of individuals from elsewhere.

Secretary: *Dr Heather Lawrence, 11 South Square, Gray's Inn, London WC1R 5EU (telephone 0171 405 1222)*

London Common Law and Commercial Bar Association

The Association was formed about 30 years ago. As its name suggests, it represents London common law and commercial practitioners. Its membership stands at well over 1,000 barristers.

Secretary: *Janet Turner, 3 Verulam Buildings, Gray's Inn, London WC1R 5NT (telephone 0171 831 8441)*

Official Referees' Bar Association (ORBA)

The members appear regularly before the Official Referees who are judges specialising in building, civil engineering and other disputes whose subject-matter is technical, eg disputes about ships, aircraft, chemical plant and computers. In addition to advising and drafting pleadings, members appear in disputes in litigation and arbitration (both domestic and international) and act variously for employers, contractors and professionals, eg architects, engineers, etc.

Secretary: *Chantal-Aimée Dorries, 1 Atkin Building, Gray's Inn, London WC1R 5AT (telephone 0171 404 0102)*

Parliamentary Bar Mess

Members of this long-standing institution appear regularly before parliamentary committees at the committee stage of private and hybrid bills, either for local authorities or others promoting the bills, or for petitioners against them. Most members also do town and country planning work. The Association has assisted in the debate on the committee procedure.

Treasurer: *William Hicks QC, 1 Serjeants' Inn, London EC4Y 1NH (telephone 0171 583 1355)*

Patent Bar Association (see under IP Bar Association)

Personal Injuries Bar Association (PIBA)

PIBA was established in March 1995. Its members provide specialist advice to solicitors across the entire field of personal injuries, from road traffic accidents to industrial disease and multi-party drugs cases. PIBA currently has a membership of 1,000 spread throughout England and Wales. PIBA responds on behalf of the Personal Injuries Bar to government consultative documents, Law Commission papers and represents the Personal Injury Bar in its dealings with other bodies. The Association conducts a programme of continuing education for its members.

Secretary: *Matthias Kelly, Old Square Chambers, 1 Verulam Buildings, Gray's Inn, London WC1R 5LQ (telephone 0171 831 0801)*

Planning and Environment Bar Association (PEBA)

The Association's members regularly appear at public inquiries held under legislation dealing with town and country planning, compulsory purchase, highways, housing and related matters. Members' specialist practices frequently require them also to appear in the courts, principally in the High Court of Justice, on matters of law arising from ministerial decisions. The Lands Tribunal is also a regular forum on rating and compulsory purchase matters.

Secretary: *Suzanne Ornsby, 2 Harcourt Buildings, Temple, London EC4Y 9DB (telephone 0171 353 8415)*

Professional Negligence Bar Association

Formed in November 1990 to promote the idea of a professional negligence speciality, this Association is concerned mostly with lectures, seminars and continuing professional education generally. Members are recruited from widely different parts of the Bar, as the Association covers medical, financial, construction and legal professional negligence.

Secretary: *Andrew Goodman, 199 Strand, London WC2R 1DR (telephone 0171 379 9779)*

Revenue Bar Association

Over half the members are Chancery people who do capital taxes work. The others are pure tax specialists covering all kinds of taxation, offering advice on tax claims and problems and tax planning and appearing before General and Special Commissioners and VAT Tribunals as well as in the High Court and beyond.

Secretary: *Hugh McKay, Gray's Inn Tax Chambers, Gray's Inn, London WC1R 5JA (telephone 0171 242 2642)*

Direct Professional Access (DPA) has been in existence for more than six years. Prior to April 1989 only solicitors and a few notable exceptions, such as patent and trademark agents, could instruct counsel direct.

Members of the professional bodies listed below are now able to seek advice direct from counsel or may instruct counsel in non-court litigation. DPA does not include instructing barristers to appear in the higher courts or the county courts or Employment Appeal Tribunal. Nor is DPA allowed if at any stage a barrister considers that the interests of the lay client or the administration of justice require that a solicitor be instructed.

Approved list of DPA Bodies (as of March 1998)

The Architects Registration Council of the UK
73 Hallam Street
London W1N 6EE
(Approved November 1989)

The Architects and Surveyors Institute
St Mary House
15 St Mary Street
Chippenham
Wiltshire SN15 3WD
(Approved September 1995)

The Association of Authorised Public Accountants
10 Cornfield Road
Eastbourne
East Sussex BN21 4QE
(Approved September 1989)

The Association of Average Adjusters
HQS 'Wellington'
Temple Stairs
Victoria Embankment
London WC2R 2PN
(Approved June 1989)

Association of Consultant Architects
7 Park Street
Bristol BS1 5NF
(Approved November 1989)

Association of Taxation Technicians
12 Upper Belgrave Street
London SW1X 8BB
(Approved September 1996)

Banking Ombudsman
70 Gray's Inn Road
London WC1X 8NB
(Approved March 1990)

Building Society Ombudsman
Grosvenor Gardens House
35–37 Grosvenor Gardens
London SW1
(Approved March 1990)

The Chartered Association of Certified Accountants
29 Lincoln's Inn Fields
London WC2A 3EE
(Approved April 1989)

The Chartered Institute of Loss Adjusters
Mansfield House
376 Strand
London WC2R 0LR
(Approved July 1990)

The Chartered Institute of Management Accountants
63 Portland Place
London W1N 4AB
(Approved September 1989)

The Chartered Insurance Institute
20 Aldermanbury
London EC2V 7HY
(Approved May 1990)

Commissioner for Local Administration in England and Wales
21 Queen Annes Gate
London SW1
(Approved March 1990)

Commissioner for Local Administration in England and Wales
Derwen House
Bridge End
Mid Glamorgan CF31 1BN
(Approved March 1990)

The Faculty of Actuaries
23 St Andrews Square
Edinburgh EH2 1AQ
(Approved November 1989)

Health Service Commissioner
Church House
Great Smith Street
London SW1P 3BW
(Approved March 1990)

The Incorporated Society of Valuers & Auctioneers
3 Cadogan Gate
London SW1X 0AS
(Approved July 1989)

Insolvency Practitioners Association
Buchlet Phillips & Co
43/44 Albermarle Street
Mayfair
London W1N 4AB
(Approved September 1989)

Institute of Actuaries
Staple Inn Hall
High Holborn
London WC1V 7QJ
(Approved November 1989)

*Institute of Chartered Accountants in
England and Wales*
PO Box 433
Chartered Accountants Hall
London EC2P 2BY
(Approved April 1989)

*The Institute of Chartered Accountants in
Ireland*
Chartered Accountants House
87/89 Pembroke Road
Dublin 4
Ireland
(Approved July 1989)

*Institute of Chartered Accountants in
Scotland*
27 Queen Street
Edinburgh EH2 1LA
(Approved July 1989)

*The Institute of Chartered Secretaries and
Administrators*
19 Park Crescent
London W1N 4AH
(Approved July 1989)

The Chartered Institute of Taxation
12 Upper Belgrave Street
London SW1X 8BB
(Approved July 1989)

The Institution of Chemical Engineers
George E Davis Building
165–171 Railway Terrace
Rugby CV21 3HQ
(Approved July 1989)

The Institution of Civil Engineering Surveyors
26 Market Street,
Altrincham, Cheshire WA14 1PF
(Approved November 1997)

The Institute of Civil Engineers
Great George Street
Westminster
London SW1P 3AA
(Approved November 1989)

The Institute of Electrical Engineers
Savoy Place
London WC2R 0BL
(Approved November 1991)

The Institute of Financial Accountants
Burford House
44 London Road
Sevenoaks
Kent TN13 1AS
(Approved January 1995)

Institution of Mechanical Engineers
1 Birdcage Walk
London SW1H 9JJ
(Approved July 1989)

The Institution of Structural Engineers
11 Upper Belgrave Street
London SW1X 8BH
(Approved July 1991)

Insurance Ombudsman Bureau
31 Southampton Row
London WC1B 5HJ
(Approved July 1990)

*Parliamentary Commissioner for
Administration*
Church House
Great Smith Street
London SW1P 3BW
(Approved March 1990)

*The Personal Investment Authority
Ombudsman Bureau Ltd.*
Hertsmere House,
Hertsmere Road,
London E14 4AB
(Approved January 1998)

The Royal Institute of British Architects
66 Portland Place
London W1N 4AD
(Approved September 1989)

*The Royal Institution of Chartered
Surveyors*
12 Great George Street
Parliament Square
London SW1P 3AD
(Approved April 1989)

The Royal Town Planning Institute
26 Portland Place
London W1N 4BE
(Approved April 1989)

A

ADJUDICATION

Malvern	Resolution Chambers	01684 561279

ADMINISTRATIVE

Birmingham	• Equity Chambers	0121 233 2100
	• 5 Fountain Court	0121 606 0500
	• St Philip's Chambers	0121 246 7000
Bristol	Old Square Chambers	0117 927 7111
	St John's Chambers	0117 921 3456/929 8514
Cambridge	• Fenners Chambers	01223 368761
Cardiff	9 Park Place	01222 382731
	30 Park Place	01222 398421
Chester	40 King Street	01244 323886
Durham City	Durham Barristers' Chambers	0191 386 9199
Exeter	• Cathedral Chambers (Jan Wood Independent Barristers' Clerk)	01392 210900
Leeds	The Chambers of Philip Raynor QC	0113 242 1123
	• 30 Park Square	0113 243 6388
	• 9 Woodhouse Square	0113 245 1986
Liverpool	25-27 Castle Street	0151 227 5661/5666/236 5072
	• Exchange Chambers	0151 236 7747
	India Buildings Chambers	0151 243 6000
	• Martins Building	0151 236 5818/4919
London	Albany Chambers	0171 485 5736/38
	• Arden Chambers	0171 242 4244
	Chambers of Dr Michael Arnheim	0171 833 5093
	33 Bedford Row	0171 242 6476
	• 29 Bedford Row Chambers	0171 831 2626
	• 5 Bell Yard	0171 333 8811
	• 9-12 Bell Yard	0171 400 1800
	• Blackstone Chambers (formerly known as 2 Hare Court)	0171 583 1770
	11 Bolt Court	0171 353 2300
	• 4 Breams Buildings	0171 353 5835/430 1221
	• 4 Brick Court	0171 797 7766
	Brick Court Chambers	0171 583 0777
	Bridewell Chambers	0171 797 8800
	Cloisters	0171 827 4000
	• 1 Crown Office Row	0171 797 7500
	1 Crown Office Row	0171 583 9292
	• Devereux Chambers	0171 353 7534
	• Doughty Street Chambers	0171 404 1313
	Equity Barristers' Chambers	0181 558 8336
	• One Essex Court	0171 583 2000
	• One Essex Court	0171 936 3030
	• Essex Court Chambers	0171 813 8000
	• 20 Essex Street	0171 583 9294
	• 39 Essex Street	0171 832 1111
	• Farrar's Building	0171 583 9241
	• Chambers of Norman Palmer	0171 405 6114
	• Fountain Court	0171 583 3335
	• 2 Garden Court	0171 353 1633
	• Goldsmith Building	0171 353 7881
	Goldsworth Chambers	0171 405 7117
	• Gough Square Chambers	0171 353 0924
	• Gray's Inn Chambers	0171 831 5344
	• Gray's Inn Chambers	0171 404 1111
	• 2-3 Gray's Inn Square	0171 242 4986
	• 4-5 Gray's Inn Square	0171 404 5252
	10 - 11 Gray's Inn Square	0171 405 2576
	• 2 Harcourt Buildings	0171 583 9020
	• 2 Harcourt Buildings	0171 353 8415
	• Harcourt Chambers	0171 353 6961/7
	• Hardwicke Building	0171 242 2523
	• One Hare Court	0171 353 3171
	• 3 Hare Court	0171 353 7561
	Chambers of Harjit Singh	0171 353 1356
Harrow on the Hill	• Harrow-on-the-Hill Chambers	0181 423 7444
London	• Chambers of James Hunt QC	0171 421 8000
	• John Street Chambers	0171 242 1911
	• One King's Bench Walk	0171 936 1500

• Expanded entry in Part C

A

6 King's Bench Walk	0171 353 4931/583 0695
• 8 King's Bench Walk	0171 797 8888
• 9 King's Bench Walk	0171 353 7202/3909
The Chambers of Mr Ali Mohammad Azhar	0171 353 9564 (4 lines)
• 11 King's Bench Walk	0171 632 8500
11 King's Bench Walk	0171 353 3337/8
• 13 King's Bench Walk	0171 353 7204
• Chambers of Lord Campbell of Alloway QC	0171 353 9276
Lamb Chambers	0171 797 8300
• Littman Chambers	0171 404 4866
2 Mitre Court Buildings	0171 353 1353
2 Mitre Court Buildings	0171 583 1380
• Mitre House Chambers	0171 583 8233
• Monckton Chambers	0171 405 7211
• 12 New Square	0171 419 1212
• 22 Old Buildings	0171 831 0222
• 9 Old Square	0171 405 4682
The Chambers of Leolin Price CBE, QC	0171 405 0758/242 5002
11 Old Square	0171 242 5022
• Old Square Chambers	0171 269 0300
• 5 Paper Buildings	0171 583 9275
5 Paper Buildings	0171 583 6117
• Chambers of John L Powell QC	0171 797 8000
• 1 Pump Court	0171 583 2012/353 4341
• Pump Court Chambers	0171 353 0711
• 5 Pump Court	0171 353 2532
6 Pump Court	0171 797 8400
• 3 Raymond Buildings	0171 831 3833
No 1 Serjeants' Inn	0171 415 6666
1 Serjeants' Inn	0171 583 1355
• Stanbrook & Henderson	0171 353 0101
• 1 Temple Gardens	0171 353 0407/583 1315
3 Temple Gardens (North)	0171 353 0853/4/7222
• 14 Tooks Court	0171 405 8828
Chambers of Mohammed Hashmot Ullah	0171 377 0119
• 3 Verulam Buildings	0171 831 8441
Manchester • Central Chambers	0161 833 1774
• Cobden House Chambers	0161 833 6000/6001
• 40 King Street	0161 832 9082
• 8 King Street Chambers	0161 834 9560
Lincoln House Chambers	0161 832 5701
Chambers of Ian Macdonald QC	0161 236 1840
• St James's Chambers	0161 834 7000
Middlesbrough • Fountain Chambers	01642 217037
Newcastle upon Tyne • New Court Chambers	0191 232 1980
Norwich East Anglian Chambers	01603 617351
Nottingham Ropewalk Chambers	0115 947 2581
Oxford • King's Bench Chambers	01865 311066
Peterborough Fenners Chambers	01733 562030
Preston New Bailey Chambers	01772 258 087
Redhill Redhill Chambers	01737 780781
Richmond-upon-Thames Richmond Green Chambers	0181 940 1841
Slough 11 St Bernards Road	01753 553806/817989
Wolverhampton Claremont Chambers	01902 426222

ADMIRALTY

Leeds Chambers of Andrew Campbell QC	0113 245 5438
Liverpool • The Corn Exchange Chambers	0151 227 1081/5009
London Brick Court Chambers	0171 583 0777
• 4 Essex Court	0171 797 7970
• Essex Court Chambers	0171 813 8000
• 20 Essex Street	0171 583 9294
• 4 Field Court	0171 440 6900
• Goldsmith Building	0171 353 7881
• 9 Gough Square	0171 353 5371
2 Gray's Inn Square Chambers	0171 242 0328/405 1317
The Chambers of Mr Ali Mohammad Azhar	0171 353 9564 (4 lines)
Newcastle upon Tyne • Trinity Chambers	0191 232 1927

• Expanded entry in Part C

Types of Work by Chambers

This section lists chambers by the type of work they do and by the town or city where they are located. The types of work undertaken by chambers are listed in alphabetical order from Administrative to Unit Trusts. Within these main categories, chambers are listed alphabetically under the town or city in which they practise. For example, a reader wishing to locate a Birmingham-based chambers specialising in trademarks would be able to look under 'T' for Trademarks and find under that heading the details of any chambers in Birmingham which offer their services in this field. A complete list of all the types of work from which chambers were asked to select their specialisms can be found overleaf. Where chambers have indicated that they practise in other areas, this information is listed within Part A.

Each listing provides the name of the Head of Chambers and chambers' telephone number. The first point of contact in each instance will be the clerk. (Details of clerks can be found in *Part C Chambers by Location*).

Please note that if a chamber is not listed in this section, it is at their request.

The symbol ● indicates that chambers have an expanded entry in *Part C Chambers by Location*.

A

Types of Work

Below is a complete list of all the types of work from which chambers were asked to select their areas of specialism. If a category below does not appear within this section, it has not been selected by any chambers for this edition. Where chambers have supplied other specialisms, this information can be found within Part A.

A

Administrative
Admiralty
Agriculture
Arbitration
Asset finance
Aviation

B

Banking
Bankruptcy

C

Care proceedings
Chancery (general)
Chancery land law
Charities
Civil liberties
Commercial
Commercial litigation
Commercial property
Commodities
Common land
Common law (general)
Company & commercial
Competition
Construction
Consumer law
Conveyancing
Copyright
Corporate finance
Courts martial
Crime
Crime – corporate fraud

D

Defamation
Discrimination

E

EC & competition law
Ecclesiastical
Education
Employment
Energy
Entertainment
Environment
Equity, wills & trusts

F

Family
Family provision
Film, cable, TV
Financial services
Foreign law
Franchising

H

Housing

I

Immigration
Information technology
Insolvency
Insurance
Insurance/reinsurance
International trade
Intellectual property

L

Landlord & tenant
Licensing
Local government

M

Medical negligence
Mental health

P

Parliamentary
Partnerships
Patents
Pensions
Personal injury
Planning
Private international
Probate & administration
Professional negligence
Public international

S

Sale & carriage of goods
Share options
Shipping, admiralty
Sports

T

Tax – capital & income
Tax – corporate
Telecommunications
Town & country planning
Trademarks

U

Unit trusts

ADJUDICATION

Malvern	Resolution Chambers	01684 561279

ADMINISTRATIVE

Birmingham	• Equity Chambers	0121 233 2100
	• 5 Fountain Court	0121 606 0500
	• St Philip's Chambers	0121 246 7000
Bristol	Old Square Chambers	0117 927 7111
	St John's Chambers	0117 921 3456/929 8514
Cambridge	• Fenners Chambers	01223 368761
Cardiff	9 Park Place	01222 382731
	30 Park Place	01222 398421
Chester	40 King Street	01244 323886
Durham City	Durham Barristers' Chambers	0191 386 9199
Exeter	• Cathedral Chambers (Jan Wood Independent Barristers' Clerk)	01392 210900
Leeds	The Chambers of Philip Raynor QC	0113 242 1123
	• 30 Park Square	0113 243 6388
	• 9 Woodhouse Square	0113 245 1986
Liverpool	25-27 Castle Street	0151 227 5661/5666/236 5072
	• Exchange Chambers	0151 236 7747
	India Buildings Chambers	0151 243 6000
	• Martins Building	0151 236 5818/4919
London	Albany Chambers	0171 485 5736/38
	• Arden Chambers	0171 242 4244
	Chambers of Dr Michael Arnheim	0171 833 5093
	33 Bedford Row	0171 242 6476
	• 29 Bedford Row Chambers	0171 831 2626
	• 5 Bell Yard	0171 333 8811
	• 9-12 Bell Yard	0171 400 1800
	• Blackstone Chambers (formerly known as 2 Hare Court)	0171 583 1770
	11 Bolt Court	0171 353 2300
	• 4 Breams Buildings	0171 353 5835/430 1221
	• 4 Brick Court	0171 797 7766
	Brick Court Chambers	0171 583 0777
	Bridewell Chambers	0171 797 8800
	Cloisters	0171 827 4000
	• 1 Crown Office Row	0171 797 7500
	1 Crown Office Row	0171 583 9292
	• Devereux Chambers	0171 353 7534
	• Doughty Street Chambers	0171 404 1313
	Equity Barristers' Chambers	0181 558 8336
	• One Essex Court	0171 583 2000
	• One Essex Court	0171 936 3030
	• Essex Court Chambers	0171 813 8000
	• 20 Essex Street	0171 583 9294
	• 39 Essex Street	0171 832 1111
	• Farrar's Building	0171 583 9241
	• Chambers of Norman Palmer	0171 405 6114
	• Fountain Court	0171 583 3335
	• 2 Garden Court	0171 353 1633
	• Goldsmith Building	0171 353 7881
	Goldsworth Chambers	0171 405 7117
	• Gough Square Chambers	0171 353 0924
	• Gray's Inn Chambers	0171 831 5344
	• Gray's Inn Chambers	0171 404 1111
	• 2-3 Gray's Inn Square	0171 242 4986
	• 4-5 Gray's Inn Square	0171 404 5252
	10 - 11 Gray's Inn Square	0171 405 2576
	• 2 Harcourt Buildings	0171 583 9020
	• 2 Harcourt Buildings	0171 353 8415
	• Harcourt Chambers	0171 353 6961/7
	• Hardwicke Building	0171 242 2523
	• One Hare Court	0171 353 3171
	• 3 Hare Court	0171 353 7561
	Chambers of Harjit Singh	0171 353 1356
Harrow on the Hill	• Harrow-on-the-Hill Chambers	0181 423 7444
London	• Chambers of James Hunt QC	0171 421 8000
	• John Street Chambers	0171 242 1911
	• One King's Bench Walk	0171 936 1500

• Expanded entry in Part C

A

	6 King's Bench Walk	0171 353 4931/583 0695
	• 8 King's Bench Walk	0171 797 8888
	• 9 King's Bench Walk	0171 353 7202/3909
	The Chambers of Mr Ali Mohammad Azhar	0171 353 9564 (4 lines)
	• 11 King's Bench Walk	0171 632 8500
	11 King's Bench Walk	0171 353 3337/8
	• 13 King's Bench Walk	0171 353 7204
	• Chambers of Lord Campbell of Alloway QC	0171 353 9276
	Lamb Chambers	0171 797 8300
	• Littman Chambers	0171 404 4866
	2 Mitre Court Buildings	0171 353 1353
	2 Mitre Court Buildings	0171 583 1380
	• Mitre House Chambers	0171 583 8233
	• Monckton Chambers	0171 405 7211
	• 12 New Square	0171 419 1212
	• 22 Old Buildings	0171 831 0222
	• 9 Old Square	0171 405 4682
	The Chambers of Leolin Price CBE, QC	0171 405 0758/242 5002
	11 Old Square	0171 242 5022
	• Old Square Chambers	0171 269 0300
	• 5 Paper Buildings	0171 583 9275
	5 Paper Buildings	0171 583 6117
	• Chambers of John L Powell QC	0171 797 8000
	• 1 Pump Court	0171 583 2012/353 4341
	• Pump Court Chambers	0171 353 0711
	• 5 Pump Court	0171 353 2532
	6 Pump Court	0171 797 8400
	• 3 Raymond Buildings	0171 831 3833
	No 1 Serjeants' Inn	0171 415 6666
	1 Serjeants' Inn	0171 583 1355
	• Stanbrook & Henderson	0171 353 0101
	• 1 Temple Gardens	0171 353 0407/583 1315
	3 Temple Gardens (North)	0171 353 0853/4/7222
	• 14 Tooks Court	0171 405 8828
	Chambers of Mohammed Hashmot Ullah	0171 377 0119
	• 3 Verulam Buildings	0171 831 8441
Manchester	• Central Chambers	0161 833 1774
	• Cobden House Chambers	0161 833 6000/6001
	• 40 King Street	0161 832 9082
	• 8 King Street Chambers	0161 834 9560
	Lincoln House Chambers	0161 832 5701
	Chambers of Ian Macdonald QC	0161 236 1840
	• St James's Chambers	0161 834 7000
Middlesbrough	• Fountain Chambers	01642 217037
Newcastle upon Tyne	• New Court Chambers	0191 232 1980
Norwich	East Anglian Chambers	01603 617351
Nottingham	Ropewalk Chambers	0115 947 2581
Oxford	• King's Bench Chambers	01865 311066
Peterborough	Fenners Chambers	01733 562030
Preston	New Bailey Chambers	01772 258 087
Redhill	Redhill Chambers	01737 780781
Richmond-upon-Thames	Richmond Green Chambers	0181 940 1841
Slough	11 St Bernards Road	01753 553806/817989
Wolverhampton	Claremont Chambers	01902 426222

ADMIRALTY

Leeds	Chambers of Andrew Campbell QC	0113 245 5438
Liverpool	• The Corn Exchange Chambers	0151 227 1081/5009
London	Brick Court Chambers	0171 583 0777
	• 4 Essex Court	0171 797 7970
	• Essex Court Chambers	0171 813 8000
	• 20 Essex Street	0171 583 9294
	• 4 Field Court	0171 440 6900
	• Goldsmith Building	0171 353 7881
	• 9 Gough Square	0171 353 5371
	2 Gray's Inn Square Chambers	0171 242 0328/405 1317
	The Chambers of Mr Ali Mohammad Azhar	0171 353 9564 (4 lines)
Newcastle upon Tyne	• Trinity Chambers	0191 232 1927

• Expanded entry in Part C

A

ADR

London	• Littleton Chambers	0171 797 8600

AGRICULTURE

Birmingham	1 Fountain Court	0121 236 5721
	• 5 Fountain Court	0121 606 0500
Bristol	St John's Chambers	0117 921 3456/929 8514
Cambridge	• Fenners Chambers	01223 368761
	Regency Chambers	01223 301517
Chester	40 King Street	01244 323886
Exeter	• Cathedral Chambers (Jan Wood Independent Barristers' Clerk)	01392 210900
Leeds	• Chancery House Chambers	0113 244 6691
	• No. 6	0113 245 9763
	• 37 Park Square	0113 243 9422
Liverpool	• The Chambers of Adrian Lyon	0151 236 4421/8240/6757
London	• 4 Breams Buildings	0171 353 5835/430 1221
	Brick Court Chambers	0171 583 0777
	• Essex Court Chambers	0171 813 8000
	Falcon Chambers	0171 353 2484
	• Farrar's Building	0171 583 9241
	Goldsworth Chambers	0171 405 7117
	• Gray's Inn Chambers	0171 404 1111
	• 2 Harcourt Buildings	0171 353 8415
Harrow on the Hill	• Harrow-on-the-Hill Chambers	0181 423 7444
London	• Chambers of James Hunt QC	0171 421 8000
	2 Mitre Court Buildings	0171 583 1380
	• Monckton Chambers	0171 405 7211
	Chambers of Lord Goodhart QC	0171 405 5577
	• 9 Old Square	0171 405 4682
	• 11 Old Square	0171 430 0341
	• 4 Paper Buildings	0171 353 3366/583 7155
	1 Serjeants' Inn	0171 583 1355
	• 9 Stone Buildings	0171 404 5055
	• 3 Verulam Buildings	0171 831 8441
Manchester	• Cobden House Chambers	0161 833 6000/6001
	Deans Court Chambers	0161 834 4097
	• Chambers of John Hand QC	0161 955 9000
	• St James's Chambers	0161 834 7000
Middlesbrough	• Fountain Chambers	01642 217037
Norwich	East Anglian Chambers	01603 617351
Nottingham	Ropewalk Chambers	0115 947 2581
Peterborough	Fenners Chambers	01733 562030
	Regency Chambers	01733 315215
Preston	Deans Court Chambers	01772 555163
	New Bailey Chambers	01772 258 087
	15 Winckley Square	01772 252 828
Sheffield	Paradise Square Chambers	0114 273 8951
Sonning-on-Thames	Greenway	0118 969 2484
Swansea	Iscoed Chambers	01792 652988/9/330
	Pendragon Chambers	01792 411188

AMERICAN LAW

London	• 11 Old Square	0171 430 0341

ANCILLARY RELIEF

Leeds	• 9 Woodhouse Square	0113 245 1986

ARBITRATION

Birmingham	1 Fountain Court	0121 236 5721
	• 5 Fountain Court	0121 606 0500
	• 8 Fountain Court	0121 236 5514
	• St Philip's Chambers	0121 246 7000
Bristol	Old Square Chambers	0117 927 7111
	St John's Chambers	0117 921 3456/929 8514
Cambridge	• Fenners Chambers	01223 368761
Cardiff	30 Park Place	01222 398421
	• 33 Park Place	01222 233313
Chester	40 King Street	01244 323886

• Expanded entry in Part C

	White Friars Chambers	01244 323070
Chesterfield	26 Morley Avenue	01246 234790
Exeter	• Cathedral Chambers (Jan Wood	01392 210900
	Independent Barristers' Clerk)	
Guildford	• Guildford Chambers	01483 539131
Leeds	Chambers of Andrew Campbell QC	0113 245 5438
	11 King's Bench Walk	0113 2971 200
	The Chambers of Philip Raynor QC	0113 242 1123
	• 37 Park Square	0113 243 9422
	• Sovereign Chambers	0113 245 1841/2/3
	• 9 Woodhouse Square	0113 245 1986
Leicester	2 New Street	0116 262 5906
Liverpool	25-27 Castle Street	0151 227 5661/5666/236 5072
	19 Castle Street Chambers	0151 236 9402
	Chavasse Court Chambers	0151 707 1191
	• The Chambers of Adrian Lyon	0151 236 4421/8240/6757
London	• Arbitration Chambers	0171 267 2137
	Chambers of Dr Michael Arnheim	0171 833 5093
	Atkin Chambers	0171 404 0102
	Avondale Chambers	0181 445 9984
	9 Bedford Row	0171 242 3555
	• 29 Bedford Row Chambers	0171 831 2626
	• Blackstone Chambers (formerly known	0171 583 1770
	as 2 Hare Court)	
	11 Bolt Court	0171 353 2300
	• Bracton Chambers	0171 242 4248
	• 4 Breams Buildings	0171 353 5835/430 1221
	Brick Court Chambers	0171 583 0777
	Bridewell Chambers	0171 797 8800
	• Chambers of Mr Peter Crampin QC	0171 831 0081
	1 Crown Office Row	0171 583 9292
	• Devereux Chambers	0171 353 7534
	• Enterprise Chambers	0171 405 9471
	Equity Barristers' Chambers	0181 558 8336
	• One Essex Court	0171 583 2000
	• One Essex Court	0171 936 3030
	• 4 Essex Court	0171 797 7970
	• Essex Court Chambers	0171 813 8000
	• 20 Essex Street	0171 583 9294
	• 35 Essex Street	0171 353 6381
	• 39 Essex Street	0171 832 1111
	Chambers of Geoffrey Hawker	0171 583 8899
	Falcon Chambers	0171 353 2484
	• 4 Field Court	0171 440 6900
	• Fountain Court	0171 583 3335
	Francis Taylor Buildings	0171 353 7768/2711
	• Goldsmith Building	0171 353 7881
	Goldsmith Chambers	0171 353 6802/3/4/5
	Goldsworth Chambers	0171 405 7117
	• Gray's Inn Chambers	0171 831 5344
	• 1 Gray's Inn Square Chambers of the	0171 405 3000
	Baroness Scotland of Asthal QC	
	2 Gray's Inn Square Chambers	0171 242 0328/405 1317
	• 2-3 Gray's Inn Square	0171 242 4986
	• 4-5 Gray's Inn Square	0171 404 5252
	• 2 Harcourt Buildings	0171 583 9020
	• Hardwicke Building	0171 242 2523
	• One Hare Court	0171 353 3171
	• Keating Chambers	0171 544 2600
	S Tomlinson QC	0171 583 0404
	The Chambers of Mr Ali Mohammad	0171 353 9564 (4 lines)
	Azhar	
	• 10 King's Bench Walk	0171 353 7742
	• 12 King's Bench Walk	0171 583 0811
	• 13 King's Bench Walk	0171 353 7204
	• Chambers of Lord Campbell of Alloway	0171 353 9276
	QC	
	• Lamb Building	0171 797 7788
	Lamb Chambers	0171 797 8300
	• Littleton Chambers	0171 797 8600
	• Littman Chambers	0171 404 4866
	2 Mitre Court Buildings	0171 353 1353

• Expanded entry in Part C

A

	2 Mitre Court Buildings	0171 583 1380
	• Monckton Chambers	0171 405 7211
	• 1 New Square	0171 405 0884/5/6/7
	• 3 New Square	0171 405 1111
	5 New Square	0171 404 0404
	• 12 New Square	0171 419 1212
	Chambers of Joy Okoye	0171 405 7011
	• 9 Old Square	0171 405 4682
	The Chambers of Leolin Price CBE, QC	0171 405 0758/242 5002
	11 Old Square	0171 242 5022
	• 11 Old Square	0171 430 0341
	• 13 Old Square	0171 404 4800
	• Old Square Chambers	0171 269 0300
	• 3 Paper Buildings	0171 797 7000
	• 4 Paper Buildings	0171 583 0816
	Pepys' Chambers	0171 936 2710
	• Chambers of John L Powell QC	0171 797 8000
	2 Pump Court	0171 353 5597
	• 4 Pump Court	0171 353 2656/9
	• 5 Pump Court	0171 353 2532
	No 1 Serjeants' Inn	0171 415 6666
	• 3 Serjeants' Inn	0171 353 5537
	• 3-4 South Square	0171 696 9900
	• Stanbrook & Henderson	0171 353 0101
	• 5 Stone Buildings	0171 242 6201
	• 7 Stone Buildings	0171 405 3886/242 3546
	7 Stone Buildings	0171 242 0961
	• 9 Stone Buildings	0171 404 5055
	169 Temple Chambers	0171 583 7644
	• 2 Temple Gardens	0171 583 6041
	Trafalgar Chambers	0171 583 5858
	• 3 Verulam Buildings	0171 831 8441
	Verulam Chambers	0171 813 2400
Malvern	Resolution Chambers	01684 561279
Manchester	• Byrom Street Chambers	0161 829 2100
	• Cobden House Chambers	0161 833 6000/6001
	Deans Court Chambers	0161 834 4097
	• Chambers of John Hand QC	0161 955 9000
	• 40 King Street	0161 832 9082
	• 8 King Street Chambers	0161 834 9560
	Lincoln House Chambers	0161 832 5701
	Old Colony House	0161 834 4364
	• St James's Chambers	0161 834 7000
Meopham	West Lodge Farm	01474 812280
Middlesbrough	York House	01642 213000
Newcastle upon Tyne	• Broad Chare	0191 232 0541
	• New Court Chambers	0191 232 1980
	• Trinity Chambers	0191 232 1927
Northampton	22 Albion Place	01604 636271
	Chartlands Chambers	01604 603322
Norwich	East Anglian Chambers	01603 617351
	Octagon House	01603 623186
	Sackville Chambers	01603 613516
Nottingham	Ropewalk Chambers	0115 947 2581
Oxford	• King's Bench Chambers	01865 311066
Peterborough	Fenners Chambers	01733 562030
Plymouth	Devon Chambers	01752 661659
Preston	Deans Court Chambers	01772 555163
	New Bailey Chambers	01772 258 087
Reading	Wessex Chambers	0118 956 8856
Redhill	Redhill Chambers	01737 780781
Slough	11 St Bernards Road	01753 553806/817989
Sonning-on-Thames	Greenway	0118 969 2484
Southampton	• 17 Carlton Crescent	01703 320320
	• Eighteen Carlton Crescent	01703 639001
Stoke-on-Trent	Regent Chambers	01782 286666
Swansea	Angel Chambers	01792 464623/464648
	Gower Chambers	01792 644466
Wolverhampton	Claremont Chambers	01902 426222

ASSET FINANCE

Birmingham	• 5 Fountain Court	0121 606 0500

A

Bristol	St John's Chambers	0117 921 3456/929 8514
Liverpool	• Exchange Chambers	0151 236 7747
	• Oriel Chambers	0151 236 7191
London	Brick Court Chambers	0171 583 0777
	1 Crown Office Row	0171 583 9292
	• One Essex Court	0171 583 2000
	• Chambers of Norman Palmer	0171 405 6114
	• 2 Harcourt Buildings	0171 583 9020
	• One Hare Court	0171 353 3171
	The Chambers of Mr Ali Mohammad Azhar	0171 353 9564 (4 lines)
	Chambers of John Gardiner QC	0171 242 4017
	• 3-4 South Square	0171 696 9900
	• Stanbrook & Henderson	0171 353 0101
	Verulam Chambers	0171 813 2400
Manchester	• Chambers of John Hand QC	0161 955 9000

AVIATION

Birmingham	• St Philip's Chambers	0121 246 7000
Bristol	Assize Court Chambers	0117 926 4587
Exeter	• Cathedral Chambers (Jan Wood Independent Barristers' Clerk)	01392 210900
Leeds	• 9 Woodhouse Square	0113 245 1986
London	• 5 Bell Yard	0171 333 8811
	11 Bolt Court	0171 353 2300
	• Dr Johnson's Chambers	0171 353 4716
	Equity Barristers' Chambers	0181 558 8336
	• 4 Essex Court	0171 797 7970
	• Essex Court Chambers	0171 813 8000
	• 20 Essex Street	0171 583 9294
	• 4 Field Court	0171 440 6900
	• Fountain Court	0171 583 3335
	• 4-5 Gray's Inn Square	0171 404 5252
	2 Harcourt Buildings	0171 353 2112/2817
	The Chambers of Mr Ali Mohammad Azhar	0171 353 9564 (4 lines)
	• Chambers of Lord Campbell of Alloway QC	0171 353 9276
	• Monckton Chambers	0171 405 7211
	• 4 Pump Court	0171 353 2656/9
	• 2 Temple Gardens	0171 583 6041
	Chambers of Mohammed Hashmot Ullah	0171 377 0119
Manchester	• St James's Chambers	0161 834 7000
Newcastle upon Tyne	• New Court Chambers	0191 232 1980

BAHAMAS LAW

London	• 11 Old Square	0171 430 0341

BANKING

Birmingham	1 Fountain Court	0121 236 5721
	• 3 Fountain Court	0121 236 5854
	• 5 Fountain Court	0121 606 0500
	• St Philip's Chambers	0121 246 7000
Bristol	St John's Chambers	0117 921 3456/929 8514
Cardiff	9 Park Place	01222 382731
	30 Park Place	01222 398421
Chester	White Friars Chambers	01244 323070
Exeter	• Cathedral Chambers (Jan Wood Independent Barristers' Clerk)	01392 210900
	Rougemont Chambers	01392 410471
Leeds	Chambers of Andrew Campbell QC	0113 245 5438
	• Chancery House Chambers	0113 244 6691
	Enterprise Chambers	0113 246 0391
	The Chambers of Philip Raynor QC	0113 242 1123
	• Sovereign Chambers	0113 245 1841/2/3
Liverpool	19 Castle Street Chambers	0151 236 9402
	• Exchange Chambers	0151 236 7747
	• The Chambers of Adrian Lyon	0151 236 4421/8240/6757
London	17 Bedford Row	0171 831 7314
	• 5 Bell Yard	0171 333 8811

• Expanded entry in Part C

A

• Blackstone Chambers (formerly known as 2 Hare Court)	0171 583 1770
• Bracton Chambers	0171 242 4248
Brick Court Chambers	0171 583 0777
Bridewell Chambers	0171 797 8800
Cloisters	0171 827 4000
• Chambers of Mr Peter Crampin QC	0171 831 0081
1 Crown Office Row	0171 583 9292
• Enterprise Chambers	0171 405 9471
Equity Barristers' Chambers	0181 558 8336
• Erskine Chambers	0171 242 5532
• One Essex Court	0171 583 2000
• 4 Essex Court	0171 797 7970
• Essex Court Chambers	0171 813 8000
• 20 Essex Street	0171 583 9294
• Chambers of Norman Palmer	0171 405 6114
• 4 Field Court	0171 440 6900
• Fountain Court	0171 583 3335
• 2nd Floor, Francis Taylor Building	0171 353 9942
Francis Taylor Buildings	0171 353 7768/2711
Goldsworth Chambers	0171 405 7117
• Gough Square Chambers	0171 353 0924
• 1 Gray's Inn Square Chambers of the Baroness Scotland of Asthal QC	0171 405 3000
2 Gray's Inn Square Chambers	0171 242 0328/405 1317
• 4-5 Gray's Inn Square	0171 404 5252
• 1 Harcourt Buildings	0171 353 9421/0375
• Hardwicke Building	0171 242 2523
• One Hare Court	0171 353 3171
• Harrow-on-the-Hill Chambers	0181 423 7444
• 4 King's Bench Walk	0171 822 8822
S Tomlinson QC	0171 583 0404
The Chambers of Mr Ali Mohammad Azhar	0171 353 9564 (4 lines)
• 12 King's Bench Walk	0171 583 0811
• 13 King's Bench Walk	0171 353 7204
• Chambers of Lord Campbell of Alloway QC	0171 353 9276
• Lamb Building	0171 797 7788
Lamb Chambers	0171 797 8300
• Littleton Chambers	0171 797 8600
• Littman Chambers	0171 404 4866
• Monckton Chambers	0171 405 7211
• New Court	0171 583 5123
• 1 New Square	0171 405 0884/5/6/7
Chambers of Lord Goodhart QC	0171 405 5577
5 New Square	0171 404 0404
• 12 New Square	0171 419 1212
• Twenty-Four Old Buildings	0171 404 0946
• 9 Old Square	0171 405 4682
The Chambers of Leolin Price CBE, QC	0171 405 0758/242 5002
11 Old Square	0171 242 5022
• 11 Old Square	0171 430 0341
• 13 Old Square	0171 404 4800
• 3 Paper Buildings	0171 797 7000
• 4 Paper Buildings	0171 583 0816
• 5 Paper Buildings	0171 583 9275
5 Paper Buildings	0171 583 6117
• Chambers of John L Powell QC	0171 797 8000
• 4 Pump Court	0171 353 2656/9
• 3-4 South Square	0171 696 9900
• Stanbrook & Henderson	0171 353 0101
• 3 Stone Buildings	0171 242 4937/405 8358
4 Stone Buildings	0171 242 5524
• 5 Stone Buildings	0171 242 6201
• 7 Stone Buildings	0171 405 3886/242 3546
• 9 Stone Buildings	0171 404 5055
11 Stone Buildings	+44 (0)171 831 6381
169 Temple Chambers	0171 583 7644
• 2 Temple Gardens	0171 583 6041
• 3 Verulam Buildings	0171 831 8441
Verulam Chambers	0171 813 2400

Harrow on the Hill
London

• Expanded entry in Part C

	• Wilberforce Chambers	0171 306 0102
Manchester	• Byrom Street Chambers	0161 829 2100
	• Cobden House Chambers	0161 833 6000/6001
	Deans Court Chambers	0161 834 4097
	• Chambers of John Hand QC	0161 955 9000
	• 40 King Street	0161 832 9082
	• 8 King Street Chambers	0161 834 9560
	Manchester House Chambers	0161 834 7007
	• Merchant Chambers	0161 839 7070
	• St James's Chambers	0161 834 7000
Newcastle upon Tyne	Enterprise Chambers	0191 222 3344
	• Trinity Chambers	0191 232 1927
	Westgate Chambers	0191 261 4407/232 9785
Norwich	East Anglian Chambers	01603 617351
Oxford	• King's Bench Chambers	01865 311066
Portsmouth	• Portsmouth Barristers' Chambers	01705 831292
Preston	Deans Court Chambers	01772 555163
	New Bailey Chambers	01772 258 087
Reading	Wessex Chambers	0118 956 8856
Wolverhampton	Claremont Chambers	01902 426222

BANKRUPTCY

Birmingham	• Equity Chambers	0121 233 2100
	1 Fountain Court	0121 236 5721
	• 3 Fountain Court	0121 236 5854
	• 5 Fountain Court	0121 606 0500
	• 8 Fountain Court	0121 236 5514
	• St Philip's Chambers	0121 246 7000
Bradford	Broadway House Chambers	01274 722560
Brighton	• Crown Office Row Chambers	01273 625625
Bristol	St John's Chambers	0117 921 3456/929 8514
Cambridge	• Fenners Chambers	01223 368761
	Regency Chambers	01223 301517
Cardiff	9 Park Place	01222 382731
	30 Park Place	01222 398421
	32 Park Place	01222 397364
Chester	White Friars Chambers	01244 323070
Chichester	Chichester Chambers	01243 784538
Durham City	Durham Barristers' Chambers	0191 386 9199
Eastbourne	King's Chambers	01323 416053
Guildford	• Guildford Chambers	01483 539131
Leeds	Chambers of Andrew Campbell QC	0113 245 5438
	• Chancery House Chambers	0113 244 6691
	Enterprise Chambers	0113 246 0391
	The Chambers of Philip Raynor QC	0113 242 1123
	• 9 Woodhouse Square	0113 245 1986
Liverpool	19 Castle Street Chambers	0151 236 9402
	• Exchange Chambers	0151 236 7747
	• The Chambers of Adrian Lyon	0151 236 4421/8240/6757
	• Oriel Chambers	0151 236 7191
London	9 Bedford Row	0171 242 3555
	17 Bedford Row	0171 831 7314
	• 29 Bedford Row Chambers	0171 831 2626
	• 5 Bell Yard	0171 333 8811
	11 Bolt Court	0171 353 2300
	• Bracton Chambers	0171 242 4248
	Bridewell Chambers	0171 797 8800
	• Chambers of Mr Peter Crampin QC	0171 831 0081
	• Enterprise Chambers	0171 405 9471
	Equity Barristers' Chambers	0181 558 8336
	• One Essex Court	0171 583 2000
	• One Essex Court	0171 936 3030
	• Essex Court Chambers	0171 813 8000
	• Chambers of Norman Palmer	0171 405 6114
	• 4 Field Court	0171 440 6900
	• 2nd Floor, Francis Taylor Building	0171 353 9942
	Francis Taylor Buildings	0171 353 7768/2711
	• Goldsmith Building	0171 353 7881
	Goldsmith Chambers	0171 353 6802/3/4/5
	Goldsworth Chambers	0171 405 7117
	• Gough Square Chambers	0171 353 0924
	• Gray's Inn Chambers	0171 404 1111

• Expanded entry in Part C

	2 Gray's Inn Square Chambers	0171 242 0328/405 1317
	• 2-3 Gray's Inn Square	0171 242 4986
	10 - 11 Gray's Inn Square	0171 405 2576
	• 1 Harcourt Buildings	0171 353 9421/0375
	• Hardwicke Building	0171 242 2523
	• One Hare Court	0171 353 3171
Harrow on the Hill	• Harrow-on-the-Hill Chambers	0181 423 7444
London	• Chambers of James Hunt QC	0171 421 8000
	• 4 King's Bench Walk	0171 822 8822
	• 9 King's Bench Walk	0171 353 7202/3909
	The Chambers of Mr Ali Mohammad Azhar	0171 353 9564 (4 lines)
	10 King's Bench Walk	0171 353 7742
	• 11 King's Bench Walk	0171 632 8500
	11 King's Bench Walk	0171 353 3337/8
	• 13 King's Bench Walk	0171 353 7204
	• Chambers of Lord Campbell of Alloway QC	0171 353 9276
	• Lamb Building	0171 797 7788
	Lamb Chambers	0171 797 8300
	Lion Court	0171 404 6565
	• Littleton Chambers	0171 797 8600
	• Littman Chambers	0171 404 4866
	2 Mitre Court Buildings	0171 353 1353
	• Mitre Court Chambers	0171 353 9394
	• New Court	0171 583 5123
	• 1 New Square	0171 405 0884/5/6/7
	Chambers of Lord Goodhart QC	0171 405 5577
	5 New Square	0171 404 0404
	• 12 New Square	0171 419 1212
	Chambers of Joy Okoye	0171 405 7011
	• 22 Old Buildings	0171 831 0222
	• Twenty-Four Old Buildings	0171 404 0946
	• 9 Old Square	0171 405 4682
	The Chambers of Leolin Price CBE, QC	0171 405 0758/242 5002
	11 Old Square	0171 242 5022
	• 11 Old Square	0171 430 0341
	• 13 Old Square	0171 404 4800
	• 3 Paper Buildings	0171 797 7000
	• 4 Paper Buildings	0171 583 0816
	• 5 Paper Buildings	0171 583 9275
	2 Pump Court	0171 353 5597
	• Pump Court Chambers	0171 353 0711
	• 5 Pump Court	0171 353 2532
	• 3-4 South Square	0171 696 9900
	• 3 Stone Buildings	0171 242 4937/405 8358
	4 Stone Buildings	0171 242 5524
	• 5 Stone Buildings	0171 242 6201
	• 7 Stone Buildings	0171 405 3886/242 3546
	• 9 Stone Buildings	0171 404 5055
	11 Stone Buildings	+44 (0)171 831 6381
	169 Temple Chambers	0171 583 7644
	• 2 Temple Gardens	0171 583 6041
	• Thomas More Chambers	0171 404 7000
	Trafalgar Chambers	0171 583 5858
	Verulam Chambers	0171 813 2400
	39 Windsor Road	0181 349 9194
Manchester	• Cobden House Chambers	0161 833 6000/6001
	• Chambers of John Hand QC	0161 955 9000
	• 40 King Street	0161 832 9082
	Manchester House Chambers	0161 834 7007
	• Merchant Chambers	0161 839 7070
	• St James's Chambers	0161 834 7000
Newcastle upon Tyne	• Broad Chare	0191 232 0541
	Enterprise Chambers	0191 222 3344
	• New Court Chambers	0191 232 1980
	• Trinity Chambers	0191 232 1927
	Westgate Chambers	0191 261 4407/232 9785
Northampton	22 Albion Place	01604 636271
Norwich	East Anglian Chambers	01603 617351
Nottingham	King Charles House	0115 941 8851
	Ropewalk Chambers	0115 947 2581

Oxford	• King's Bench Chambers	01865 311066
Peterborough	Fenners Chambers	01733 562030
	Regency Chambers	01733 315215
Portsmouth	• Portsmouth Barristers' Chambers	01705 831292
Preston	4 Camden Place	01772 828300
	New Bailey Chambers	01772 258 087
	15 Winckley Square	01772 252 828
Reading	Wessex Chambers	0118 956 8856
Redhill	Redhill Chambers	01737 780781
Southampton	• Eighteen Carlton Crescent	01703 639001
Swansea	Angel Chambers	01792 464623/464648
	Gower Chambers	01792 644466
	Iscoed Chambers	01792 652988/9/330
Wolverhampton	Claremont Chambers	01902 426222

CARE PROCEEDINGS

Birmingham	• Equity Chambers	0121 233 2100
	1 Fountain Court	0121 236 5721
	• 3 Fountain Court	0121 236 5854
	• 5 Fountain Court	0121 606 0500
	6 Fountain Court	0121 233 3282
	• 8 Fountain Court	0121 236 5514
	New Court Chambers	0121 693 6656
	• St Philip's Chambers	0121 246 7000
Bournemouth	20 Lorne Park Road	01202 292102
Bradford	Broadway House Chambers	01274 722560
Brighton	• Crown Office Row Chambers	01273 625625
Bristol	Assize Court Chambers	0117 926 4587
	St John's Chambers	0117 921 3456/929 8514
Cambridge	• Fenners Chambers	01223 368761
	Regency Chambers	01223 301517
Canterbury	Stour Chambers	01227 764899
Cardiff	30 Park Place	01222 398421
	32 Park Place	01222 397364
	• 33 Park Place	01222 233313
Chester	40 King Street	01244 323886
	White Friars Chambers	01244 323070
Chichester	Chichester Chambers	01243 784538
Durham City	Durham Barristers' Chambers	0191 386 9199
Eastbourne	King's Chambers	01323 416053
Enfield	Enfield Chambers	0181 364 5627
Exeter	• Cathedral Chambers (Jan Wood Independent Barristers' Clerk)	01392 210900
	Colleton Chambers	01392 274898
	Rougemont Chambers	01392 410471
	Southernhay Chambers	01392 255777
	Walnut House	01392 279751
Guildford	• Guildford Chambers	01483 539131
Leatherhead	Pembroke House	01372 376160/376493
Leeds	Chambers of Andrew Campbell QC	0113 245 5438
	11 King's Bench Walk	0113 2971 200
	• No. 6	0113 245 9763
	The Chambers of Philip Raynor QC	0113 242 1123
	• 30 Park Square	0113 243 6388
	• 37 Park Square	0113 243 9422
	• Sovereign Chambers	0113 245 1841/2/3
	• St Paul's House	0113 245 5866
	• 9 Woodhouse Square	0113 245 1986
Liverpool	25–27 Castle Street	0151 227 5661/5666/236 5072
	19 Castle Street Chambers	0151 236 9402
	Chavasse Court Chambers	0151 707 1191
	• The Corn Exchange Chambers	0151 227 1081/5009
	• Exchange Chambers	0151 236 7747
	First National Chambers	0151 236 2098
	India Buildings Chambers	0151 243 6000
	• The Chambers of Adrian Lyon	0151 236 4421/8240/6757
	• Martins Building	0151 236 5818/4919
	• Oriel Chambers	0151 236 7191
	• Peel House Chambers	0151 236 4321
London	Avondale Chambers	0181 445 9984
	Barristers' Common Law Chambers	0171 375 3012
	9 Bedford Row	0171 242 3555

• Expanded entry in Part C

A

17 Bedford Row	0171 831 7314
• 29 Bedford Row Chambers	0171 831 2626
11 Bolt Court	0171 353 2300
• 4 Brick Court	0171 797 7766
Bridewell Chambers	0171 797 8800
Britton Street Chambers	0171 608 3765
Cloisters	0171 827 4000
1 Crown Office Row	0171 583 9292
• 3 Dr Johnson's Buildings	0171 353 4854
Equity Barristers' Chambers	0181 558 8336
• One Essex Court	0171 936 3030
• 35 Essex Street	0171 353 6381
Chambers of Geoffrey Hawker	0171 583 8899
• Chambers of Norman Palmer	0171 405 6114
• 2nd Floor, Francis Taylor Building	0171 353 9942
Francis Taylor Buildings	0171 353 7768/2711
One Garden Court Family Law Chambers	0171 797 7900
• 2 Garden Court	0171 353 1633
• Goldsmith Building	0171 353 7881
Goldsmith Chambers	0171 353 6802/3/4/5
Goldsworth Chambers	0171 405 7117
• 9 Gough Square	0171 353 5371
• Gray's Inn Chambers	0171 831 5344
• Gray's Inn Chambers	0171 404 1111
• 1 Gray's Inn Square Chambers of the Baroness Scotland of Asthal QC	0171 405 3000
• 1 Gray's Inn Square	0171 405 8946
2 Gray's Inn Square Chambers	0171 242 0328/405 1317
• 2-3 Gray's Inn Square	0171 242 4986
6 Gray's Inn Square	0171 242 1052
10 - 11 Gray's Inn Square	0171 405 2576
14 Gray's Inn Square	0171 242 0858
• 1 Harcourt Buildings	0171 353 9421/0375
• 2 Harcourt Buildings	0171 583 9020
• Harcourt Chambers	0171 353 6961/7
• Hardwicke Building	0171 242 2523
• Harrow-on-the-Hill Chambers	0181 423 7444
• Chambers of James Hunt QC	0171 421 8000
• John Street Chambers	0171 242 1911
Justice Court Chambers	0181 830 7786
• 4 King's Bench Walk	0171 822 8822
6 King's Bench Walk	0171 353 4931/583 0695
• 8 King's Bench Walk	0171 797 8888
• 9 King's Bench Walk	0171 353 7202/3909
The Chambers of Mr Ali Mohammad Azhar	0171 353 9564 (4 lines)
10 King's Bench Walk	0171 353 7742
11 King's Bench Walk	0171 353 3337/8
• 13 King's Bench Walk	0171 353 7204
• Chambers of Lord Campbell of Alloway QC	0171 353 9276
• Lamb Building	0171 797 7788
Lamb Chambers	0171 797 8300
Library Chambers	0171 404 6500
Lion Court	0171 404 6565
• Littleton Chambers	0171 797 8600
• 1 Mitre Court Buildings	0171 797 7070
2 Mitre Court Buildings	0171 353 1353
• Mitre Court Chambers	0171 353 9394
• Mitre House Chambers	0171 583 8233
• New Court	0171 583 5123
• New Court Chambers	0171 831 9500
Chambers of Joy Okoye	0171 405 7011
• 22 Old Buildings	0171 831 0222
11 Old Square	0171 242 5022
• 2 Paper Buildings	0171 353 0933
• 3 Paper Buildings	0171 583 8055
Phoenix Chambers	0171 404 7888
Plowden Buildings	0171 583 0808
• 1 Pump Court	0171 583 2012/353 4341
2 Pump Court	0171 353 5597

**Harrow on the Hill
London**

	• Pump Court Chambers	0171 353 0711
	• 5 Pump Court	0171 353 2532
	• Chambers of Kieran Coonan QC	0171 583 6013/2510
	6 Pump Court	0171 797 8400
	• Stanbrook & Henderson	0171 353 0101
	7 Stone Buildings	0171 242 0961
	• 3 Temple Gardens	0171 353 3102/5/9297
	• Thomas More Chambers	0171 404 7000
	• 14 Tooks Court	0171 405 8828
	Trafalgar Chambers	0171 583 5858
	Verulam Chambers	0171 813 2400
	Warwick House Chambers	0171 430 2323
Maidstone	Earl Street Chambers	01622 671222
	• Maidstone Chambers	01622 688592
Manchester	• Central Chambers	0161 833 1774
	• Cobden House Chambers	0161 833 6000/6001
	Deans Court Chambers	0161 834 4097
	• Chambers of John Hand QC	0161 955 9000
	Kenworthy's Chambers	0161 832 4036
	• 40 King Street	0161 832 9082
	• 8 King Street Chambers	0161 834 9560
	58 King Street Chambers	0161 831 7477
	Lincoln House Chambers	0161 832 5701
	Chambers of Ian Macdonald QC	0161 236 1840
	Manchester House Chambers	0161 834 7007
	Peel Court Chambers	0161 832 3791
	• Queen's Chambers	0161 834 6875/4738
	• St James's Chambers	0161 834 7000
	18 St John Street	0161 278 1800
	• 28 St John Street	0161 834 8418
	Young Street Chambers	0161 833 0489
Middlesbrough	Baker Street Chambers	01642 873873
	• Fountain Chambers	01642 217037
Newcastle upon Tyne	• Broad Chare	0191 232 0541
	Cathedral Chambers	0191 232 1311
	• New Court Chambers	0191 232 1980
	• Trinity Chambers	0191 232 1927
Northampton	22 Albion Place	01604 636271
	Chartlands Chambers	01604 603322
Norwich	East Anglian Chambers	01603 617351
	Octagon House	01603 623186
	Sackville Chambers	01603 613516
Nottingham	King Charles House	0115 941 8851
	Ropewalk Chambers	0115 947 2581
	St Mary's Chambers	0115 950 3503
Oxford	1 Alfred Street	01865 793736
	• King's Bench Chambers	01865 311066
	28 Western Road	01865 204911
Peterborough	Fenners Chambers	01733 562030
	Regency Chambers	01733 315215
Plymouth	Devon Chambers	01752 661659
Portsmouth	Hampshire Chambers	01705 826636
Preston	4 Camden Place	01772 828300
	Deans Court Chambers	01772 555163
	New Bailey Chambers	01772 258 087
	15 Winckley Square	01772 252 828
Reading	Dr Johnson's Chambers	01189 254221
	Wessex Chambers	0118 956 8856
Redhill	Redhill Chambers	01737 780781
Sheffield	Paradise Square Chambers	0114 273 8951
Shepperton	Abbey Chambers	01932 560913
Southampton	• 17 Carlton Crescent	01703 320320
	• College Chambers	01703 230338
	• Eighteen Carlton Crescent	01703 639001
Stoke-on-Trent	Regent Chambers	01782 286666
Swansea	Angel Chambers	01792 464623/464648
	Gower Chambers	01792 644466
	Iscoed Chambers	01792 652988/9/330
	Pendragon Chambers	01792 411188
Swindon	Pump Court Chambers	01793 539899
Winchester	Pump Court Chambers	01962 868161
	4 St Peter Street	01962 868 884

• Expanded entry in Part C

| Wolverhampton | Claremont Chambers | 01902 426222 |
| York | • York Chambers | 01904 620 048 |

CHANCERY (GENERAL)

Birmingham	• Equity Chambers	0121 233 2100
	1 Fountain Court	0121 236 5721
	• 3 Fountain Court	0121 236 5854
	• 5 Fountain Court	0121 606 0500
	• 8 Fountain Court	0121 236 5514
	• St Philip's Chambers	0121 246 7000
Bournemouth	20 Lorne Park Road	01202 292102
Bradford	Broadway House Chambers	01274 722560
Bristol	Assize Court Chambers	0117 926 4587
	Old Square Chambers	0117 927 7111
	St John's Chambers	0117 921 3456/929 8514
Cambridge	• Fenners Chambers	01223 368761
	Regency Chambers	01223 301517
Cardiff	30 Park Place	01222 398421
	• 33 Park Place	01222 233313
Chichester	Chichester Chambers	01243 784538
Eastbourne	King's Chambers	01323 416053
Exeter	• Cathedral Chambers (Jan Wood	01392 210900
	Independent Barristers' Clerk)	
	Southernhay Chambers	01392 255777
	Walnut House	01392 279751
Guildford	• Guildford Chambers	01483 539131
Leeds	Chambers of Andrew Campbell QC	0113 245 5438
	• Chancery House Chambers	0113 244 6691
	11 King's Bench Walk	0113 2971 200
	• Mercury Chambers	0113 234 2265
	• No. 6	0113 245 9763
	The Chambers of Philip Raynor QC	0113 242 1123
	• Sovereign Chambers	0113 245 1841/2/3
	• St Paul's House	0113 245 5866
	• 9 Woodhouse Square	0113 245 1986
Liverpool	19 Castle Street Chambers	0151 236 9402
	• Exchange Chambers	0151 236 7747
	• The Chambers of Adrian Lyon	0151 236 4421/8240/6757
London	Barnard's Inn Chambers	0171 242 8508
	17 Bedford Row	0171 831 7314
	• 29 Bedford Row Chambers	0171 831 2626
	• 5 Bell Yard	0171 333 8811
	• 9-12 Bell Yard	0171 400 1800
	• Blackstone Chambers (formerly known	0171 583 1770
	as 2 Hare Court)	
	11 Bolt Court	0171 353 2300
	• Bracton Chambers	0171 242 4248
	• 4 Breams Buildings	0171 353 5835/430 1221
	• 4 Brick Court	0171 797 7766
	Brick Court Chambers	0171 583 0777
	Bridewell Chambers	0171 797 8800
	Britton Street Chambers	0171 608 3765
	• Chambers of Mr Peter Crampin QC	0171 831 0081
	1 Crown Office Row	0171 583 9292
	• Dr Johnson's Chambers	0171 353 4716
	• Enterprise Chambers	0171 405 9471
	Equity Barristers' Chambers	0181 558 8336
	• One Essex Court	0171 936 3030
	Chambers of Geoffrey Hawker	0171 583 8899
	• Farrar's Building	0171 583 9241
	• Chambers of Norman Palmer	0171 405 6114
	• Fountain Court	0171 583 3335
	• 2nd Floor, Francis Taylor Building	0171 353 9942
	Francis Taylor Buildings	0171 353 7768/2711
	• Goldsmith Building	0171 353 7881
	Goldsmith Chambers	0171 353 6802/3/4/5
	Goldsworth Chambers	0171 405 7117
	• Gray's Inn Chambers	0171 831 5344
	• 1 Gray's Inn Square	0171 405 8946
	2 Gray's Inn Square Chambers	0171 242 0328/405 1317
	Gray's Inn Square	0171 242 3529
	10 - 11 Gray's Inn Square	0171 405 2576

	• 1 Harcourt Buildings	0171 353 9421/0375
	• 2 Harcourt Buildings	0171 583 9020
	• Hardwicke Building	0171 242 2523
	• One Hare Court	0171 353 3171
	Chambers of Harjit Singh	0171 353 1356
Harrow on the Hill	• Harrow-on-the-Hill Chambers	0181 423 7444
London	Justice Court Chambers	0181 830 7786
	• 4 King's Bench Walk	0171 822 8822
	6 King's Bench Walk	0171 353 4931/583 0695
	• 8 King's Bench Walk	0171 797 8888
	• 9 King's Bench Walk	0171 353 7202/3909
	The Chambers of Mr Ali Mohammad Azhar	0171 353 9564 (4 lines)
	10 King's Bench Walk	0171 353 7742
	11 King's Bench Walk	0171 353 3337/8
	• 13 King's Bench Walk	0171 353 7204
	• Lamb Building	0171 797 7788
	Lamb Chambers	0171 797 8300
	Lion Court	0171 404 6565
	• Littleton Chambers	0171 797 8600
	• Littman Chambers	0171 404 4866
	2 Mitre Court Buildings	0171 353 1353
	• Mitre Court Chambers	0171 353 9394
	• Mitre House Chambers	0171 583 8233
	• New Court	0171 583 5123
	• 1 New Square	0171 405 0884/5/6/7
	Chambers of Lord Goodhart QC	0171 405 5577
	5 New Square	0171 404 0404
	• 12 New Square	0171 419 1212
	• 22 Old Buildings	0171 831 0222
	• Twenty-Four Old Buildings	0171 404 0946
	• 9 Old Square	0171 405 4682
	The Chambers of Leolin Price CBE, QC	0171 405 0758/242 5002
	11 Old Square	0171 242 5022
	• 11 Old Square	0171 430 0341
	• 13 Old Square	0171 404 4800
	• Old Square Chambers	0171 269 0300
	• 3 Paper Buildings	0171 583 8055
	• 4 Paper Buildings	0171 583 0816
	Phoenix Chambers	0171 404 7888
	Plowden Buildings	0171 583 0808
	• Chambers of John L Powell QC	0171 797 8000
	• 1 Pump Court	0171 583 2012/353 4341
	2 Pump Court	0171 353 5597
	• 5 Pump Court	0171 353 2532
	No 1 Serjeants' Inn	0171 415 6666
	• Serle Court Chambers	0171 242 6105
	• 3-4 South Square	0171 696 9900
	• Stanbrook & Henderson	0171 353 0101
	• 3 Stone Buildings	0171 242 4937/405 8358
	• 5 Stone Buildings	0171 242 6201
	• 7 Stone Buildings	0171 405 3886/242 3546
	• 9 Stone Buildings	0171 404 5055
	11 Stone Buildings	+44 (0)171 831 6381
	169 Temple Chambers	0171 583 7644
	• 2 Temple Gardens	0171 583 6041
	• 3 Temple Gardens	0171 353 3102/5/9297
	3 Temple Gardens (North)	0171 353 0853/4/7222
	Verulam Chambers	0171 813 2400
	Warwick House Chambers	0171 430 2323
	• Wilberforce Chambers	0171 306 0102
Maidstone	Earl Street Chambers	01622 671222
Manchester	• Cobden House Chambers	0161 833 6000/6001
	Deans Court Chambers	0161 834 4097
	• Chambers of John Hand QC	0161 955 9000
	• 40 King Street	0161 832 9082
	• 8 King Street Chambers	0161 834 9560
	58 King Street Chambers	0161 831 7477
	Manchester House Chambers	0161 834 7007
	• Merchant Chambers	0161 839 7070
	• Queen's Chambers	0161 834 6875/4738
	• St James's Chambers	0161 834 7000

• Expanded entry in Part C

	18 St John Street	0161 278 1800
	• 28 St John Street	0161 834 8418
	Young Street Chambers	0161 833 0489
Middlesbrough	• Fountain Chambers	01642 217037
Milton Keynes	Milton Keynes Chambers	01908 217857
Newcastle upon Tyne	• Broad Chare	0191 232 0541
	• Trinity Chambers	0191 232 1927
	Westgate Chambers	0191 261 4407/232 9785
Northampton	22 Albion Place	01604 636271
Norwich	East Anglian Chambers	01603 617351
	Octagon House	01603 623186
Nottingham	King Charles House	0115 941 8851
	Ropewalk Chambers	0115 947 2581
	St Mary's Chambers	0115 950 3503
Oxford	1 Alfred Street	01865 793736
	• King's Bench Chambers	01865 311066
	28 Western Road	01865 204911
Peterborough	Fenners Chambers	01733 562030
	Regency Chambers	01733 315215
Portsmouth	Hampshire Chambers	01705 826636
	• Portsmouth Barristers' Chambers	01705 831292
Preston	4 Camden Place	01772 828300
	Deans Court Chambers	01772 555163
	New Bailey Chambers	01772 258 087
	15 Winckley Square	01772 252 828
Reading	Wessex Chambers	0118 956 8856
Redhill	Redhill Chambers	01737 780781
Sheffield	Paradise Square Chambers	0114 273 8951
Shepperton	Abbey Chambers	01932 560913
Sonning-on-Thames	Greenway	0118 969 2484
Southampton	• 17 Carlton Crescent	01703 320320
	• College Chambers	01703 230338
	• Eighteen Carlton Crescent	01703 639001
Stoke-on-Trent	Regent Chambers	01782 286666
Swansea	Gower Chambers	01792 644466
	Iscoed Chambers	01792 652988/9/330
	Pendragon Chambers	01792 411188
Winchester	4 St Peter Street	01962 868 884
Wolverhampton	Claremont Chambers	01902 426222

CHANCERY LAND LAW

Birmingham	• 3 Fountain Court	0121 236 5854
	• 5 Fountain Court	0121 606 0500
	• 8 Fountain Court	0121 236 5514
	• St Philip's Chambers	0121 246 7000
Bradford	Broadway House Chambers	01274 722560
Bristol	Assize Court Chambers	0117 926 4587
	St John's Chambers	0117 921 3456/929 8514
Cambridge	• Fenners Chambers	01223 368761
	Regency Chambers	01223 301517
Cardiff	9 Park Place	01222 382731
	• 33 Park Place	01222 233313
Eastbourne	King's Chambers	01323 416053
Exeter	Southernhay Chambers	01392 255777
	Walnut House	01392 279751
Guildford	• Guildford Chambers	01483 539131
Leeds	Chambers of Andrew Campbell QC	0113 245 5438
	• Chancery House Chambers	0113 244 6691
	11 King's Bench Walk	0113 2971 200
	• No. 6	0113 245 9763
	The Chambers of Philip Raynor QC	0113 242 1123
	• 9 Woodhouse Square	0113 245 1986
Liverpool	• Exchange Chambers	0151 236 7747
	• The Chambers of Adrian Lyon	0151 236 4421/8240/6757
London	Barnard's Inn Chambers	0171 242 8508
	33 Bedford Row	0171 242 6476
	• 29 Bedford Row Chambers	0171 831 2626
	• Bracton Chambers	0171 242 4248
	• 4 Breams Buildings	0171 353 5835/430 1221
	Bridewell Chambers	0171 797 8800
	• Chambers of Mr Peter Crampin QC	0171 831 0081
	• Dr Johnson's Chambers	0171 353 4716

• Expanded entry in Part C

	Equity Barristers' Chambers	0181 558 8336
	• One Essex Court	0171 936 3030
	Falcon Chambers	0171 353 2484
	• Chambers of Norman Palmer	0171 405 6114
	• 2nd Floor, Francis Taylor Building	0171 353 9942
	• Goldsmith Building	0171 353 7881
	Goldsworth Chambers	0171 405 7117
	• Gough Square Chambers	0171 353 0924
	• Gray's Inn Chambers	0171 404 1111
	2 Gray's Inn Square Chambers	0171 242 0328/405 1317
	• 1 Harcourt Buildings	0171 353 9421/0375
	• Harcourt Chambers	0171 353 6961/7
Harrow on the Hill	• Harrow-on-the-Hill Chambers	0181 423 7444
London	6 King's Bench Walk	0171 353 4931/583 0695
	The Chambers of Mr Ali Mohammad	0171 353 9564 (4 lines)
	Azhar	
	• 13 King's Bench Walk	0171 353 7204
	• Lamb Building	0171 797 7788
	Lamb Chambers	0171 797 8300
	• Littman Chambers	0171 404 4866
	• Mitre Court Chambers	0171 353 9394
	• Mitre House Chambers	0171 583 8233
	• 1 New Square	0171 405 0884/5/6/7
	Chambers of Lord Goodhart QC	0171 405 5577
	5 New Square	0171 404 0404
	• 12 New Square	0171 419 1212
	• 22 Old Buildings	0171 831 0222
	• Twenty-Four Old Buildings	0171 404 0946
	• 9 Old Square	0171 405 4682
	The Chambers of Leolin Price CBE, QC	0171 405 0758/242 5002
	11 Old Square	0171 242 5022
	• 11 Old Square	0171 430 0341
	• 13 Old Square	0171 404 4800
	• 4 Paper Buildings	0171 583 0816
	• 1 Pump Court	0171 583 2012/353 4341
	• 5 Pump Court	0171 353 2532
	No 1 Serjeants' Inn	0171 415 6666
	• Serle Court Chambers	0171 242 6105
	• 3 Stone Buildings	0171 242 4937/405 8358
	• 5 Stone Buildings	0171 242 6201
	• 7 Stone Buildings	0171 405 3886/242 3546
	• 9 Stone Buildings	0171 404 5055
	11 Stone Buildings	+44 (0)171 831 6381
	• 199 Strand	0171 379 9779
	Trafalgar Chambers	0171 583 5858
	• Wilberforce Chambers	0171 306 0102
Manchester	• Cobden House Chambers	0161 833 6000/6001
	Deans Court Chambers	0161 834 4097
	• Chambers of John Hand QC	0161 955 9000
	• 40 King Street	0161 832 9082
	• 8 King Street Chambers	0161 834 9560
	58 King Street Chambers	0161 831 7477
	Manchester House Chambers	0161 834 7007
	• Merchant Chambers	0161 839 7070
	• St James's Chambers	0161 834 7000
Middlesbrough	• Fountain Chambers	01642 217037
Milton Keynes	Milton Keynes Chambers	01908 217857
Newcastle upon Tyne	• Broad Chare	0191 232 0541
	• Trinity Chambers	0191 232 1927
	Westgate Chambers	0191 261 4407/232 9785
Northampton	22 Albion Place	01604 636271
Norwich	East Anglian Chambers	01603 617351
Nottingham	Ropewalk Chambers	0115 947 2581
	St Mary's Chambers	0115 950 3503
Oxford	• King's Bench Chambers	01865 311066
Peterborough	Fenners Chambers	01733 562030
	Regency Chambers	01733 315215
Portsmouth	• Portsmouth Barristers' Chambers	01705 831292
Preston	Deans Court Chambers	01772 555163
	New Bailey Chambers	01772 258 087
	15 Winckley Square	01772 252 828
Reading	Wessex Chambers	0118 956 8856

• Expanded entry in Part C

Sonning-on-Thames	Greenway	0118 969 2484
Southampton	• 17 Carlton Crescent	01703 320320
Stoke-on-Trent	Regent Chambers	01782 286666
Swansea	Angel Chambers	01792 464623/464648
Wolverhampton	Claremont Chambers	01902 426222

CHARITIES

Birmingham	• Equity Chambers	0121 233 2100
	• St Philip's Chambers	0121 246 7000
Bristol	St John's Chambers	0117 921 3456/929 8514
Leeds	The Chambers of Philip Raynor QC	0113 242 1123
	• 9 Woodhouse Square	0113 245 1986
Liverpool	• Exchange Chambers	0151 236 7747
	First National Chambers	0151 236 2098
London	• Bracton Chambers	0171 242 4248
	• 4 Breams Buildings	0171 353 5835/430 1221
	• Chambers of Mr Peter Crampin QC	0171 831 0081
	• Enterprise Chambers	0171 405 9471
	Equity Barristers' Chambers	0181 558 8336
	• Chambers of Norman Palmer	0171 405 6114
	Chambers of Harjit Singh	0171 353 1356
	Justice Court Chambers	0181 830 7786
	• 9 King's Bench Walk	0171 353 7202/3909
	The Chambers of Mr Ali Mohammad Azhar	0171 353 9564 (4 lines)
	11 King's Bench Walk	0171 353 3337/8
	• Mitre House Chambers	0171 583 8233
	• 1 New Square	0171 405 0884/5/6/7
	Chambers of Lord Goodhart QC	0171 405 5577
	5 New Square	0171 404 0404
	• 12 New Square	0171 419 1212
	24 Old Buildings	0171 242 2744
	• 9 Old Square	0171 405 4682
	The Chambers of Leolin Price CBE, QC	0171 405 0758/242 5002
	11 Old Square	0171 242 5022
	• 11 Old Square	0171 430 0341
	• 13 Old Square	0171 404 4800
	• 3 Stone Buildings	0171 242 4937/405 8358
	• 5 Stone Buildings	0171 242 6201
	• 7 Stone Buildings	0171 405 3886/242 3546
	• 9 Stone Buildings	0171 404 5055
	11 Stone Buildings	+44 (0)171 831 6381
	• Wilberforce Chambers	0171 306 0102
Manchester	• Cobden House Chambers	0161 833 6000/6001
	• Chambers of John Hand QC	0161 955 9000
	• 40 King Street	0161 832 9082
	• St James's Chambers	0161 834 7000
Newcastle upon Tyne	• Trinity Chambers	0191 232 1927
	Westgate Chambers	0191 261 4407/232 9785
Norwich	East Anglian Chambers	01603 617351
Wolverhampton	Claremont Chambers	01902 426222

CIVIL ACTIONS AGAINST THE POLICE

Birmingham	New Court Chambers	0121 693 6656
London	• 1 Gray's Inn Square	0171 405 8946
	• 3 Serjeants' Inn	0171 353 5537

CIVIL JURY ACTIONS FOR POLICE AUTHORITIES

| London | 5 Essex Court | 0171 410 2000 |

CIVIL LAW

| Enfield | Enfield Chambers | 0181 364 5627 |

CIVIL LIBERTIES

Birmingham	• Equity Chambers	0121 233 2100
	• 5 Fountain Court	0121 606 0500
	• 8 Fountain Court	0121 236 5514
Bristol	Old Square Chambers	0117 927 7111
	St John's Chambers	0117 921 3456/929 8514

• Expanded entry in Part C   A19

Chichester	Chichester Chambers	01243 784538
Coulsdon	Advolex Chambers	0181 763 2345
Leeds	• Sovereign Chambers	0113 245 1841/2/3
	• 9 Woodhouse Square	0113 245 1986
Liverpool	25-27 Castle Street	0151 227 5661/5666/236 5072
	19 Castle Street Chambers	0151 236 9402
	• The Corn Exchange Chambers	0151 227 1081/5009
	• The Chambers of Adrian Lyon	0151 236 4421/8240/6757
	• Martins Building	0151 236 5818/4919
London	Chambers of Dr Michael Arnheim	0171 833 5093
	• 29 Bedford Row Chambers	0171 831 2626
	• Blackstone Chambers (formerly known as 2 Hare Court)	0171 583 1770
	• 4 Brick Court	0171 797 7766
	Bridewell Chambers	0171 797 8800
	Cloisters	0171 827 4000
	• 1 Crown Office Row	0171 797 7111
	• Devereux Chambers	0171 353 7534
	• Doughty Street Chambers	0171 404 1313
	Equity Barristers' Chambers	0181 558 8336
	• One Essex Court	0171 936 3030
	• Essex Court Chambers	0171 813 8000
	• 20 Essex Street	0171 583 9294
	• 39 Essex Street	0171 832 1111
	• Farrar's Building	0171 583 9241
	• Chambers of Norman Palmer	0171 405 6114
	• 2 Garden Court	0171 353 1633
	• Goldsmith Building	0171 353 7881
	• Gray's Inn Chambers	0171 831 5344
	• 4-5 Gray's Inn Square	0171 404 5252
	10 - 11 Gray's Inn Square	0171 405 2576
	• One Hare Court	0171 353 3171
Harrow on the Hill	• Harrow-on-the-Hill Chambers	0181 423 7444
London	Justice Court Chambers	0181 830 7786
	• 4 King's Bench Walk	0171 822 8822
	• 8 King's Bench Walk	0171 797 8888
	The Chambers of Mr Ali Mohammad Azhar	0171 353 9564 (4 lines)
	10 King's Bench Walk	0171 353 7742
	• 11 King's Bench Walk	0171 632 8500
	• 13 King's Bench Walk	0171 353 7204
	• Mitre House Chambers	0171 583 8233
	• Monckton Chambers	0171 405 7211
	• New Court Chambers	0171 831 9500
	• 12 New Square	0171 419 1212
	Chambers of Joy Okoye	0171 405 7011
	• Old Square Chambers	0171 269 0300
	• 2 Paper Buildings	0171 353 0933
	• 2 Paper Buildings	0171 936 2611 (10 lines)
	5 Paper Buildings	0171 583 6117
	• 1 Pump Court	0171 583 2012/353 4341
	• 3 Raymond Buildings	0171 831 3833
	• 2 Temple Gardens	0171 583 6041
	3 Temple Gardens (North)	0171 353 0853/4/7222
	• Thomas More Chambers	0171 404 7000
	• 14 Tooks Court	0171 405 8828
	Chambers of Mohammed Hashmot Ullah	0171 377 0119
	Verulam Chambers	0171 813 2400
	Warwick House Chambers	0171 430 2323
Manchester	• Central Chambers	0161 833 1774
	• Chambers of John Hand QC	0161 955 9000
	Chambers of Ian Macdonald QC	0161 236 1840
	• St James's Chambers	0161 834 7000
	Young Street Chambers	0161 833 0489
Norwich	East Anglian Chambers	01603 617351
Nottingham	Ropewalk Chambers	0115 947 2581
Oxford	• King's Bench Chambers	01865 311066
Preston	New Bailey Chambers	01772 258 087
	15 Winckley Square	01772 252 828
Slough	11 St Bernards Road	01753 553806/817989
Swansea	Pendragon Chambers	01792 411188

       • Expanded entry in Part C

Winkleigh	Barnstaple Chambers	0183 783763
Wolverhampton	Claremont Chambers	01902 426222

CLUB LAW

London	• 13 King's Bench Walk	0171 353 7204
Oxford	• King's Bench Chambers	01865 311066

COMMERCIAL

Birmingham	• Equity Chambers	0121 233 2100
	1 Fountain Court	0121 236 5721
	• 5 Fountain Court	0121 606 0500
Bristol	Assize Court Chambers	0117 926 4587
Cardiff	9 Park Place	01222 382731
Chester	40 King Street	01244 323886
	White Friars Chambers	01244 323070
Chichester	Chichester Chambers	01243 784538
Durham City	Durham Barristers' Chambers	0191 386 9199
Eastbourne	King's Chambers	01323 416053
Exeter	• Cathedral Chambers (Jan Wood	01392 210900
	Independent Barristers' Clerk)	
	Southernhay Chambers	01392 255777
Guildford	• Guildford Chambers	01483 539131
Haverhill	Helions Chambers	01440 730523
Leeds	Chambers of Andrew Campbell QC	0113 245 5438
	11 King's Bench Walk	0113 2971 200
	• Mercury Chambers	0113 234 2265
	The Chambers of Philip Raynor QC	0113 242 1123
Liverpool	25-27 Castle Street	0151 227 5661/5666/236 5072
	19 Castle Street Chambers	0151 236 9402
	• Exchange Chambers	0151 236 7747
	• Martins Building	0151 236 5818/4919
	• Oriel Chambers	0151 236 7191
London	Barnard's Inn Chambers	0171 242 8508
	17 Bedford Row	0171 831 7314
	• 5 Bell Yard	0171 333 8811
	• Blackstone Chambers (formerly known	0171 583 1770
	as 2 Hare Court)	
	• Bracton Chambers	0171 242 4248
	Cloisters	0171 827 4000
	• Chambers of Mr Peter Crampin QC	0171 831 0081
	Equity Barristers' Chambers	0181 558 8336
	• One Essex Court	0171 936 3030
	Chambers of Geoffrey Hawker	0171 583 8899
	• 4 Field Court	0171 440 6900
	Goldsworth Chambers	0171 405 7117
	• 4-5 Gray's Inn Square	0171 404 5252
	• Harcourt Chambers	0171 353 6961/7
	• Hardwicke Building	0171 242 2523
	• One Hare Court	0171 353 3171
Harrow on the Hill	• Harrow-on-the-Hill Chambers	0181 423 7444
London	• Chambers of James Hunt QC	0171 421 8000
	Justice Court Chambers	0181 830 7786
	S Tomlinson QC	0171 583 0404
	The Chambers of Mr Ali Mohammad	0171 353 9564 (4 lines)
	Azhar	
	• Chambers of Lord Campbell of Alloway	0171 353 9276
	QC	
	• Lamb Building	0171 797 7788
	• Mitre Court Chambers	0171 353 9394
	• Monckton Chambers	0171 405 7211
	• New Court	0171 797 8999
	• New Court Chambers	0171 831 9500
	Chambers of Lord Goodhart QC	0171 405 5577
	Chambers of Joy Okoye	0171 405 7011
	• 22 Old Buildings	0171 831 0222
	• Twenty-Four Old Buildings	0171 404 0946
	• 11 Old Square	0171 430 0341
	• 13 Old Square	0171 404 4800
	• 4 Paper Buildings	0171 583 0816
	5 Paper Buildings	0171 583 6117
	Plowden Buildings	0171 583 0808

• Expanded entry in Part C

	• 4 Pump Court	0171 353 2656/9
	• 5 Pump Court	0171 353 2532
	6 Pump Court	0171 797 8400
	• 1 Raymond Buildings	0171 430 1234
	No 1 Serjeants' Inn	0171 415 6666
	• Thomas More Chambers	0171 404 7000
	Verulam Chambers	0171 813 2400
	Warwick House Chambers	0171 430 2323
	• Wilberforce Chambers	0171 306 0102
Manchester	• Byrom Street Chambers	0161 829 2100
	• Cobden House Chambers	0161 833 6000/6001
	• 40 King Street	0161 832 9082
	• 8 King Street Chambers	0161 834 9560
	Manchester House Chambers	0161 834 7007
	• Merchant Chambers	0161 839 7070
	• Queen's Chambers	0161 834 6875/4738
	• St James's Chambers	0161 834 7000
Nottingham	King Charles House	0115 941 8851
	Ropewalk Chambers	0115 947 2581
Peterborough	Fenners Chambers	01733 562030
Preston	New Bailey Chambers	01772 258 087
	15 Winckley Square	01772 252 828
Reading	Wessex Chambers	0118 956 8856
Richmond-upon-Thames	Richmond Green Chambers	0181 940 1841
Shepperton	Abbey Chambers	01932 560913
Swansea	Iscoed Chambers	01792 652988/9/330
Wolverhampton	Claremont Chambers	01902 426222

COMMERCIAL LITIGATION

Birmingham	• Equity Chambers	0121 233 2100
	1 Fountain Court	0121 236 5721
	• 3 Fountain Court	0121 236 5854
	• 5 Fountain Court	0121 606 0500
	• 8 Fountain Court	0121 236 5514
	• St Philip's Chambers	0121 246 7000
Bournemouth	20 Lorne Park Road	01202 292102
Bradford	Broadway House Chambers	01274 722560
Bristol	Old Square Chambers	0117 927 7111
	St John's Chambers	0117 921 3456/929 8514
Cambridge	• Fenners Chambers	01223 368761
	Regency Chambers	01223 301517
Cardiff	30 Park Place	01222 398421
	• 33 Park Place	01222 233313
Chichester	Chichester Chambers	01243 784538
Exeter	• Cathedral Chambers (Jan Wood	01392 210900
	Independent Barristers' Clerk)	
Leeds	Chambers of Andrew Campbell QC	0113 245 5438
	• Chancery House Chambers	0113 244 6691
	• Mercury Chambers	0113 234 2265
	• No. 6	0113 245 9763
	The Chambers of Philip Raynor QC	0113 242 1123
	• Sovereign Chambers	0113 245 1841/2/3
	• 9 Woodhouse Square	0113 245 1986
Leicester	2 New Street	0116 262 5906
Liverpool	19 Castle Street Chambers	0151 236 9402
	• The Corn Exchange Chambers	0151 227 1081/5009
	• Exchange Chambers	0151 236 7747
	India Buildings Chambers	0151 243 6000
	• The Chambers of Adrian Lyon	0151 236 4421/8240/6757
	• Oriel Chambers	0151 236 7191
London	Atkin Chambers	0171 404 0102
	Barnard's Inn Chambers	0171 242 8508
	9 Bedford Row	0171 242 3555
	33 Bedford Row	0171 242 6476
	• 29 Bedford Row Chambers	0171 831 2626
	• 5 Bell Yard	0171 333 8811
	• 9-12 Bell Yard	0171 400 1800
	11 Bolt Court	0171 353 2300
	• Bracton Chambers	0171 242 4248
	Brick Court Chambers	0171 583 0777
	Bridewell Chambers	0171 797 8800
	• Chambers of Mr Peter Crampin QC	0171 831 0081

• Expanded entry in Part C

A

1 Crown Office Row	0171 583 9292
• Two Crown Office Row	0171 797 8100
• Devereux Chambers	0171 353 7534
• Enterprise Chambers	0171 405 9471
Equity Barristers' Chambers	0181 558 8336
• One Essex Court	0171 583 2000
• One Essex Court	0171 936 3030
• 4 Essex Court	0171 797 7970
• Essex Court Chambers	0171 813 8000
• 20 Essex Street	0171 583 9294
• 35 Essex Street	0171 353 6381
• 39 Essex Street	0171 832 1111
Chambers of Geoffrey Hawker	0171 583 8899
• Farrar's Building	0171 583 9241
• Chambers of Norman Palmer	0171 405 6114
• Fountain Court	0171 583 3335
Francis Taylor Buildings	0171 353 7768/2711
• Goldsmith Building	0171 353 7881
• 9 Gough Square	0171 353 5371
• Gough Square Chambers	0171 353 0924
2 Gray's Inn Square Chambers	0171 242 0328/405 1317
• 2-3 Gray's Inn Square	0171 242 4986
10 - 11 Gray's Inn Square	0171 405 2576
• 1 Harcourt Buildings	0171 353 9421/0375
• 2 Harcourt Buildings	0171 583 9020
• Harrow-on-the-Hill Chambers	0181 423 7444
Justice Court Chambers	0181 830 7786
• Keating Chambers	0171 544 2600
• 4 King's Bench Walk	0171 822 8822
• 9 King's Bench Walk	0171 353 7202/3909
The Chambers of Mr Ali Mohammad Azhar	0171 353 9564 (4 lines)
• 11 King's Bench Walk	0171 632 8500
11 King's Bench Walk	0171 353 3337/8
• 12 King's Bench Walk	0171 583 0811
• 13 King's Bench Walk	0171 353 7204
Lamb Chambers	0171 797 8300
• Littleton Chambers	0171 797 8600
• Littman Chambers	0171 404 4866
• Monckton Chambers	0171 405 7211
5 New Square	0171 404 0404
• 12 New Square	0171 419 1212
• Twenty-Four Old Buildings	0171 404 0946
The Chambers of Leolin Price CBE, QC	0171 405 0758/242 5002
• Old Square Chambers	0171 269 0300
One Paper Buildings	0171 583 7355
• 3 Paper Buildings	0171 797 7000
• 3 Paper Buildings	0171 583 8055
• 4 Paper Buildings	0171 353 3366/583 7155
• 5 Paper Buildings	0171 583 9275
Phoenix Chambers	0171 404 7888
• Chambers of John L Powell QC	0171 797 8000
• 5 Raymond Buildings	0171 242 2902
• 3 Serjeants' Inn	0171 353 5537
• Serle Court Chambers	0171 242 6105
• 3-4 South Square	0171 696 9900
• Stanbrook & Henderson	0171 353 0101
• 3 Stone Buildings	0171 242 4937/405 8358
4 Stone Buildings	0171 242 5524
• 5 Stone Buildings	0171 242 6201
• 7 Stone Buildings	0171 405 3886/242 3546
7 Stone Buildings	0171 242 0961
• 9 Stone Buildings	0171 404 5055
11 Stone Buildings	+44 (0)171 831 6381
• 199 Strand	0171 379 9779
169 Temple Chambers	0171 583 7644
• 2 Temple Gardens	0171 583 6041
• 3 Verulam Buildings	0171 831 8441
Verulam Chambers	0171 813 2400
• Wilberforce Chambers	0171 306 0102
39 Windsor Road	0181 349 9194
• Cobden House Chambers	0161 833 6000/6001

Harrow on the Hill
London

Manchester

• Expanded entry in Part C

	Deans Court Chambers	0161 834 4097
	• Chambers of John Hand QC	0161 955 9000
	Kenworthy's Chambers	0161 832 4036
	• 40 King Street	0161 832 9082
	Manchester House Chambers	0161 834 7007
	18 St John Street	0161 278 1800
	Young Street Chambers	0161 833 0489
Middlesbrough	• Fountain Chambers	01642 217037
Milton Keynes	Milton Keynes Chambers	01908 217857
Newcastle upon Tyne	• New Court Chambers	0191 232 1980
	• Trinity Chambers	0191 232 1927
	Westgate Chambers	0191 261 4407/232 9785
Norwich	East Anglian Chambers	01603 617351
Nottingham	St Mary's Chambers	0115 950 3503
Oxford	1 Alfred Street	01865 793736
	• King's Bench Chambers	01865 311066
Peterborough	Regency Chambers	01733 315215
Portsmouth	• Portsmouth Barristers' Chambers	01705 831292
Preston	4 Camden Place	01772 828300
	Deans Court Chambers	01772 555163
Reading	Wessex Chambers	0118 956 8856
Redhill	Redhill Chambers	01737 780781
Swansea	Gower Chambers	01792 644466
Winchester	4 St Peter Street	01962 868 884
York	• York Chambers	01904 620 048

COMMERCIAL LITIGATION AND ADVISORY WORK

| London | Alban Chambers | 0171 419 5051 |

COMMERCIAL PROPERTY

Birmingham	• 5 Fountain Court	0121 606 0500
	• 8 Fountain Court	0121 236 5514
	• St Philip's Chambers	0121 246 7000
Bristol	St John's Chambers	0117 921 3456/929 8514
Cambridge	• Fenners Chambers	01223 368761
	Regency Chambers	01223 301517
Cardiff	9 Park Place	01222 382731
	• 33 Park Place	01222 233313
Chester	40 King Street	01244 323886
Exeter	• Cathedral Chambers (Jan Wood Independent Barristers' Clerk)	01392 210900
	Rougemont Chambers	01392 410471
	Southernhay Chambers	01392 255777
Leeds	Chambers of Andrew Campbell QC	0113 245 5438
	• Chancery House Chambers	0113 244 6691
	• Mercury Chambers	0113 234 2265
Liverpool	• Exchange Chambers	0151 236 7747
	• The Chambers of Adrian Lyon	0151 236 4421/8240/6757
	• Martins Building	0151 236 5818/4919
London	Barnard's Inn Chambers	0171 242 8508
	17 Bedford Row	0171 831 7314
	• 29 Bedford Row Chambers	0171 831 2626
	• 5 Bell Yard	0171 333 8811
	• Bracton Chambers	0171 242 4248
	• 4 Breams Buildings	0171 353 5835/430 1221
	Bridewell Chambers	0171 797 8800
	• Chambers of Mr Peter Crampin QC	0171 831 0081
	• Devereux Chambers	0171 353 7534
	• Enterprise Chambers	0171 405 9471
	Equity Barristers' Chambers	0181 558 8336
	• One Essex Court	0171 936 3030
	Chambers of Geoffrey Hawker	0171 583 8899
	Falcon Chambers	0171 353 2484
	• Chambers of Norman Palmer	0171 405 6114
	• 4 Field Court	0171 440 6900
	• 2nd Floor, Francis Taylor Building	0171 353 9942
	Francis Taylor Buildings	0171 353 7768/2711
	• Goldsmith Building	0171 353 7881
	• 9 Gough Square	0171 353 5371
	2 Gray's Inn Square Chambers	0171 242 0328/405 1317
	10 - 11 Gray's Inn Square	0171 405 2576

• Expanded entry in Part C

	• 1 Harcourt Buildings	0171 353 9421/0375
Harrow on the Hill	• Harrow-on-the-Hill Chambers	0181 423 7444
London	• Chambers of James Hunt QC	0171 421 8000
	• 9 King's Bench Walk	0171 353 7202/3909
	The Chambers of Mr Ali Mohammad	0171 353 9564 (4 lines)
	Azhar	
	10 King's Bench Walk	0171 353 7742
	11 King's Bench Walk	0171 353 3337/8
	Lamb Chambers	0171 797 8300
	• Littman Chambers	0171 404 4866
	2 Mitre Court Buildings	0171 353 1353
	2 Mitre Court Buildings	0171 583 1380
	• Mitre Court Chambers	0171 353 9394
	• New Court Chambers	0171 831 9500
	• 1 New Square	0171 405 0884/5/6/7
	Chambers of Lord Goodhart QC	0171 405 5577
	• 12 New Square	0171 419 1212
	• Twenty-Four Old Buildings	0171 404 0946
	• 9 Old Square	0171 405 4682
	The Chambers of Leolin Price CBE, QC	0171 405 0758/242 5002
	• 11 Old Square	0171 430 0341
	• 13 Old Square	0171 404 4800
	• 3 Paper Buildings	0171 797 7000
	• 4 Paper Buildings	0171 353 3366/583 7155
	• 4 Paper Buildings	0171 583 0816
	• 5 Pump Court	0171 353 2532
	No 1 Serjeants' Inn	0171 415 6666
	• Serle Court Chambers	0171 242 6105
	• 3-4 South Square	0171 696 9900
	• 3 Stone Buildings	0171 242 4937/405 8358
	• 5 Stone Buildings	0171 242 6201
	• 7 Stone Buildings	0171 405 3886/242 3546
	• 9 Stone Buildings	0171 404 5055
	11 Stone Buildings	+44 (0)171 831 6381
	• 2 Temple Gardens	0171 583 6041
	Trafalgar Chambers	0171 583 5858
	• 3 Verulam Buildings	0171 831 8441
	Verulam Chambers	0171 813 2400
	• Wilberforce Chambers	0171 306 0102
Manchester	• Cobden House Chambers	0161 833 6000/6001
	• Chambers of John Hand QC	0161 955 9000
	Kenworthy's Chambers	0161 832 4036
	Manchester House Chambers	0161 834 7007
	• Merchant Chambers	0161 839 7070
	• St James's Chambers	0161 834 7000
Middlesbrough	• Fountain Chambers	01642 217037
Newcastle upon Tyne	Westgate Chambers	0191 261 4407/232 9785
Norwich	East Anglian Chambers	01603 617351
Nottingham	King Charles House	0115 941 8851
	Ropewalk Chambers	0115 947 2581
Peterborough	Fenners Chambers	01733 562030
	Regency Chambers	01733 315215
Preston	New Bailey Chambers	01772 258 087
Reading	Wessex Chambers	0118 956 8856
Richmond-upon-Thames	Richmond Green Chambers	0181 940 1841
Swansea	Angel Chambers	01792 464623/464648
	Gower Chambers	01792 644466
	Iscoed Chambers	01792 652988/9/330
Wolverhampton	Claremont Chambers	01902 426222

COMMODITIES

Exeter	• Cathedral Chambers (Jan Wood	01392 210900
	Independent Barristers' Clerk)	
London	• Blackstone Chambers (formerly known	0171 583 1770
	as 2 Hare Court)	
	Brick Court Chambers	0171 583 0777
	Equity Barristers' Chambers	0181 558 8336
	• 4 Essex Court	0171 797 7970
	• Essex Court Chambers	0171 813 8000
	• 20 Essex Street	0171 583 9294
	• One Hare Court	0171 353 3171
	S Tomlinson QC	0171 583 0404

• Expanded entry in Part C

	The Chambers of Mr Ali Mohammad Azhar	0171 353 9564 (4 lines)
	• Mitre Court Chambers	0171 353 9394
	• 3-4 South Square	0171 696 9900
	• 9 Stone Buildings	0171 404 5055
	11 Stone Buildings	+44 (0)171 831 6381
	• 3 Verulam Buildings	0171 831 8441

COMMON LAND

Birmingham	• 5 Fountain Court	0121 606 0500
Bristol	Assize Court Chambers	0117 926 4587
	St John's Chambers	0117 921 3456/929 8514
Cambridge	• Fenners Chambers	01223 368761
	Regency Chambers	01223 301517
Cardiff	9 Park Place	01222 382731
Chester	40 King Street	01244 323886
Exeter	Walnut House	01392 279751
Leeds	Chambers of Andrew Campbell QC	0113 245 5438
	• 9 Woodhouse Square	0113 245 1986
Liverpool	• Exchange Chambers	0151 236 7747
	• The Chambers of Adrian Lyon	0151 236 4421/8240/6757
London	• 29 Bedford Row Chambers	0171 831 2626
	• 4 Breams Buildings	0171 353 5835/430 1221
	• 4 Brick Court	0171 797 7766
	• Chambers of Mr Peter Crampin QC	0171 831 0081
	• One Essex Court	0171 936 3030
	Chambers of Geoffrey Hawker	0171 583 8899
	• Chambers of Norman Palmer	0171 405 6114
	• Goldsmith Building	0171 353 7881
	2 Gray's Inn Square Chambers	0171 242 0328/405 1317
	10 - 11 Gray's Inn Square	0171 405 2576
	• 2 Harcourt Buildings	0171 353 8415
Harrow on the Hill	• Harrow-on-the-Hill Chambers	0181 423 7444
London	• Chambers of James Hunt QC	0171 421 8000
	The Chambers of Mr Ali Mohammad Azhar	0171 353 9564 (4 lines)
	Lamb Chambers	0171 797 8300
	2 Mitre Court Buildings	0171 583 1380
	• Mitre Court Chambers	0171 353 9394
	• 1 New Square	0171 405 0884/5/6/7
	Chambers of Lord Goodhart QC	0171 405 5577
	5 New Square	0171 404 0404
	• 12 New Square	0171 419 1212
	• Twenty-Four Old Buildings	0171 404 0946
	• 9 Old Square	0171 405 4682
	The Chambers of Leolin Price CBE, QC	0171 405 0758/242 5002
	1 Serjeants' Inn	0171 583 1355
	• 5 Stone Buildings	0171 242 6201
	• 7 Stone Buildings	0171 405 3886/242 3546
	• 9 Stone Buildings	0171 404 5055
Manchester	• Cobden House Chambers	0161 833 6000/6001
	• St James's Chambers	0161 834 7000
Newcastle upon Tyne	• Trinity Chambers	0191 232 1927
Norwich	East Anglian Chambers	01603 617351
Nottingham	Ropewalk Chambers	0115 947 2581
Peterborough	Fenners Chambers	01733 562030
	Regency Chambers	01733 315215
Preston	New Bailey Chambers	01772 258 087
Sheffield	Paradise Square Chambers	0114 273 8951
Southampton	• 17 Carlton Crescent	01703 320320
Stoke-on-Trent	Regent Chambers	01782 286666
Swansea	Angel Chambers	01792 464623/464648
	Iscoed Chambers	01792 652988/9/330
York	• York Chambers	01904 620 048

COMMON LAW (GENERAL)

Birmingham	• Equity Chambers	0121 233 2100
	1 Fountain Court	0121 236 5721
	• 3 Fountain Court	0121 236 5854
	• 5 Fountain Court	0121 606 0500
	6 Fountain Court	0121 233 3282

• Expanded entry in Part C

A

	• 8 Fountain Court	0121 236 5514
	New Court Chambers	0121 693 6656
	• St Philip's Chambers	0121 246 7000
Bournemouth	20 Lorne Park Road	01202 292102
Bradford	Broadway House Chambers	01274 722560
Brighton	• Crown Office Row Chambers	01273 625625
Bristol	Assize Court Chambers	0117 926 4587
	St John's Chambers	0117 921 3456/929 8514
Cambridge	• Fenners Chambers	01223 368761
	Regency Chambers	01223 301517
Canterbury	Stour Chambers	01227 764899
Cardiff	9 Park Place	01222 382731
	30 Park Place	01222 398421
	32 Park Place	01222 397364
	• 33 Park Place	01222 233313
Chester	40 King Street	01244 323886
	White Friars Chambers	01244 323070
Chesterfield	26 Morley Avenue	01246 234790
Chichester	Chichester Chambers	01243 784538
Coulsdon	Advolex Chambers	0181 763 2345
Durham City	Durham Barristers' Chambers	0191 386 9199
Eastbourne	King's Chambers	01323 416053
Ely	Cathedral Chambers, Ely	01353 666775
Enfield	Enfield Chambers	0181 364 5627
Exeter	• Cathedral Chambers (Jan Wood Independent Barristers' Clerk)	01392 210900
	Colleton Chambers	01392 274898
	Rougemont Chambers	01392 410471
	Southernhay Chambers	01392 255777
	Walnut House	01392 279751
Guildford	• Guildford Chambers	01483 539131
Haverhill	Helions Chambers	01440 730523
Leatherhead	Pembroke House	01372 376160/376493
Leeds	Chambers of Andrew Campbell QC	0113 245 5438
	• Chancery House Chambers	0113 244 6691
	11 King's Bench Walk	0113 2971 200
	The Chambers of Philip Raynor QC	0113 242 1123
	• 30 Park Square	0113 243 6388
	• 37 Park Square	0113 243 9422
	• St Paul's House	0113 245 5866
	• 9 Woodhouse Square	0113 245 1986
Leicester	2 New Street	0116 262 5906
Liverpool	25-27 Castle Street	0151 227 5661/5666/236 5072
	19 Castle Street Chambers	0151 236 9402
	Chavasse Court Chambers	0151 707 1191
	• The Corn Exchange Chambers	0151 227 1081/5009
	• Exchange Chambers	0151 236 7747
	First National Chambers	0151 236 2098
	• Martins Building	0151 236 5818/4919
	• Oriel Chambers	0151 236 7191
	• Peel House Chambers	0151 236 4321
London	Alban Chambers	0171 419 5051
	Albany Chambers	0171 485 5736/38
	Avondale Chambers	0181 445 9984
	Barnard's Inn Chambers	0171 242 8508
	Barristers' Common Law Chambers	0171 375 3012
	9 Bedford Row	0171 242 3555
	17 Bedford Row	0171 831 7314
	• 29 Bedford Row Chambers	0171 831 2626
	• 5 Bell Yard	0171 333 8811
	• 9-12 Bell Yard	0171 400 1800
	11 Bolt Court	0171 353 2300
	• Bracton Chambers	0171 242 4248
	• 4 Brick Court	0171 797 8910
	• 4 Brick Court	0171 797 7766
	Brick Court Chambers	0171 583 0777
	Bridewell Chambers	0171 797 8800
	Britton Street Chambers	0171 608 3765
	Cloisters	0171 827 4000
	• 1 Crown Office Row	0171 797 7500
	1 Crown Office Row	0171 583 9292
	• Two Crown Office Row	0171 797 8100

• Expanded entry in Part C

• Doughty Street Chambers	0171 404 1313
• 3 Dr Johnson's Buildings	0171 353 4854
• Dr Johnson's Chambers	0171 353 4716
Equity Barristers' Chambers	0181 558 8336
• One Essex Court	0171 936 3030
5 Essex Court	0171 410 2000
23 Essex Street	0171 413 0353
• 35 Essex Street	0171 353 6381
• 39 Essex Street	0171 832 1111
Chambers of Geoffrey Hawker	0171 583 8899
• Farrar's Building	0171 583 9241
• Chambers of Norman Palmer	0171 405 6114
• Fountain Court	0171 583 3335
• 2nd Floor, Francis Taylor Building	0171 353 9942
Francis Taylor Buildings	0171 353 7768/2711
• Goldsmith Building	0171 353 7881
Goldsmith Chambers	0171 353 6802/3/4/5
Goldsworth Chambers	0171 405 7117
• 9 Gough Square	0171 353 5371
• Gray's Inn Chambers	0171 831 5344
• Gray's Inn Chambers	0171 404 1111
• 1 Gray's Inn Square	0171 405 8946
2 Gray's Inn Square Chambers	0171 242 0328/405 1317
• 2-3 Gray's Inn Square	0171 242 4986
6 Gray's Inn Square	0171 242 1052
10 - 11 Gray's Inn Square	0171 405 2576
14 Gray's Inn Square	0171 242 0858
• 1 Harcourt Buildings	0171 353 9421/0375
• 2 Harcourt Buildings	0171 583 9020
• Hardwicke Building	0171 242 2523
• One Hare Court	0171 353 3171
Chambers of Harjit Singh	0171 353 1356
• Harrow-on-the-Hill Chambers	0181 423 7444
• Chambers of James Hunt QC	0171 421 8000
• John Street Chambers	0171 242 1911
1 Dr Johnson's Buildings	0171 353 9328
Justice Court Chambers	0181 830 7786
• One King's Bench Walk	0171 936 1500
• 4 King's Bench Walk	0171 822 8822
4 King's Bench Walk	0171 353 3581
6 King's Bench Walk	0171 353 4931/583 0695
• 8 King's Bench Walk	0171 797 8888
• 9 King's Bench Walk	0171 353 7202/3909
The Chambers of Mr Ali Mohammad Azhar	0171 353 9564 (4 lines)
10 King's Bench Walk	0171 353 7742
11 King's Bench Walk	0171 353 3337/8
• 13 King's Bench Walk	0171 353 7204
• Chambers of Lord Campbell of Alloway QC	0171 353 9276
• Lamb Building	0171 797 7788
Lamb Chambers	0171 797 8300
Library Chambers	0171 404 6500
Lion Court	0171 404 6565
• Littleton Chambers	0171 797 8600
• Mitre Court Chambers	0171 353 9394
• Mitre House Chambers	0171 583 8233
• New Court	0171 583 5123
• New Court Chambers	0171 831 9500
• 1 New Square	0171 405 0884/5/6/7
5 New Square	0171 404 0404
Chambers of Joy Okoye	0171 405 7011
• 22 Old Buildings	0171 831 0222
11 Old Square	0171 242 5022
• 11 Old Square	0171 430 0341
1 Paper Buildings	0171 353 3728/4953
• 2 Paper Buildings	0171 353 0933
• 2 Paper Buildings	0171 936 2611 (10 lines)
• 3 Paper Buildings	0171 583 8055
5 Paper Buildings	0171 583 6117
Phoenix Chambers	0171 404 7888
• Chambers of John L Powell QC	0171 797 8000

Harrow on the Hill
London

	• 1 Pump Court	0171 583 2012/353 4341
	2 Pump Court	0171 353 5597
	• Pump Court Chambers	0171 353 0711
	• 4 Pump Court	0171 353 2656/9
	• 5 Pump Court	0171 353 2532
	• Chambers of Kieran Coonan QC	0171 583 6013/2510
	6 Pump Court	0171 797 8400
	• Queen Elizabeth Building	0171 353 7181 (12 lines)
	• 3 Raymond Buildings	0171 831 3833
	No 1 Serjeants' Inn	0171 415 6666
	• 3 Serjeants' Inn	0171 353 5537
	• 3-4 South Square	0171 696 9900
	• Stanbrook & Henderson	0171 353 0101
	7 Stone Buildings	0171 242 0961
	8 Stone Buildings	0171 831 9881
	• 199 Strand	0171 379 9779
	169 Temple Chambers	0171 583 7644
	• 1 Temple Gardens	0171 353 0407/583 1315
	• 2 Temple Gardens	0171 583 6041
	• 3 Temple Gardens	0171 353 3102/5/9297
	3 Temple Gardens (North)	0171 353 0853/4/7222
	• Thomas More Chambers	0171 404 7000
	• 14 Tooks Court	0171 405 8828
	Chambers of Mohammed Hashmot Ullah	0171 377 0119
	• 3 Verulam Buildings	0171 831 8441
	Verulam Chambers	0171 813 2400
	39 Windsor Road	0181 349 9194
Maidstone	Earl Street Chambers	01622 671222
Malvern	• Maidstone Chambers	01622 688592
Manchester	Resolution Chambers	01684 561279
	• Byrom Street Chambers	0161 829 2100
	• Cobden House Chambers	0161 833 6000/6001
	Deans Court Chambers	0161 834 4097
	• Chambers of John Hand QC	0161 955 9000
	Kenworthy's Chambers	0161 832 4036
	• 40 King Street	0161 832 9082
	• 8 King Street Chambers	0161 834 9560
	58 King Street Chambers	0161 831 7477
	Chambers of Ian Macdonald QC	0161 236 1840
	Manchester House Chambers	0161 834 7007
	Peel Court Chambers	0161 832 3791
	• Queen's Chambers	0161 834 6875/4738
	• St James's Chambers	0161 834 7000
	18 St John Street	0161 278 1800
	• 28 St John Street	0161 834 8418
	Young Street Chambers	0161 833 0489
Meopham	West Lodge Farm	01474 812280
Middlesbrough	Baker Street Chambers	01642 873873
	• Fountain Chambers	01642 217037
	York House	01642 213000
Newcastle upon Tyne	• Broad Chare	0191 232 0541
	Cathedral Chambers	0191 232 1311
	• Trinity Chambers	0191 232 1927
	Westgate Chambers	0191 261 4407/232 9785
Northampton	22 Albion Place	01604 636271
	Chartlands Chambers	01604 603322
Norwich	East Anglian Chambers	01603 617351
	Octagon House	01603 623186
	Sackville Chambers	01603 613516
Nottingham	King Charles House	0115 941 8851
	Ropewalk Chambers	0115 947 2581
	St Mary's Chambers	0115 950 3503
Oxford	1 Alfred Street	01865 793736
	• King's Bench Chambers	01865 311066
	28 Western Road	01865 204911
Peterborough	Fenners Chambers	01733 562030
	Regency Chambers	01733 315215
Plymouth	Devon Chambers	01752 661659
Portsmouth	• Portsmouth Barristers' Chambers	01705 831292
Preston	4 Camden Place	01772 828300
	Deans Court Chambers	01772 555163
	New Bailey Chambers	01772 258 087

• Expanded entry in Part C

	15 Winckley Square	01772 252 828
Reading	Dr Johnson's Chambers	01189 254221
	Wessex Chambers	0118 956 8856
Redhill	Redhill Chambers	01737 780781
Richmond-upon-Thames	Richmond Green Chambers	0181 940 1841
Sheffield	Bank House Chambers	0114 275 1223
	Paradise Square Chambers	0114 273 8951
Shepperton	Abbey Chambers	01932 560913
Slough	11 St Bernards Road	01753 553806/817989
Sonning-on-Thames	Greenway	0118 969 2484
Southampton	• 17 Carlton Crescent	01703 320320
	• College Chambers	01703 230338
	• Eighteen Carlton Crescent	01703 639001
Stoke-on-Trent	Regent Chambers	01782 286666
Swansea	Angel Chambers	01792 464623/464648
	Iscoed Chambers	01792 652988/9/330
	Pendragon Chambers	01792 411188
Swindon	Pump Court Chambers	01793 539899
Winchester	Pump Court Chambers	01962 868161
	4 St Peter Street	01962 868 884
Winkleigh	Barnstaple Chambers	0183 783763
Wolverhampton	Claremont Chambers	01902 426222

COMPANY AND COMMERCIAL

Birmingham	• Equity Chambers	0121 233 2100
	1 Fountain Court	0121 236 5721
	• 3 Fountain Court	0121 236 5854
	• 5 Fountain Court	0121 606 0500
	• 8 Fountain Court	0121 236 5514
	• St Philip's Chambers	0121 246 7000
Bournemouth	20 Lorne Park Road	01202 292102
Bristol	Assize Court Chambers	0117 926 4587
	St John's Chambers	0117 921 3456/929 8514
Cambridge	• Fenners Chambers	01223 368761
Cardiff	9 Park Place	01222 382731
	30 Park Place	01222 398421
	• 33 Park Place	01222 233313
Chester	40 King Street	01244 323886
Chichester	Chichester Chambers	01243 784538
Eastbourne	King's Chambers	01323 416053
Exeter	• Cathedral Chambers (Jan Wood Independent Barristers' Clerk)	01392 210900
	Rougemont Chambers	01392 410471
	Southernhay Chambers	01392 255777
	Walnut House	01392 279751
Haverhill	Helions Chambers	01440 730523
Leeds	Chambers of Andrew Campbell QC	0113 245 5438
	• Chancery House Chambers	0113 244 6691
	Enterprise Chambers	0113 246 0391
	11 King's Bench Walk	0113 2971 200
	• Mercury Chambers	0113 234 2265
	• Park Court Chambers	0113 243 3277
	The Chambers of Philip Raynor QC	0113 242 1123
	• Sovereign Chambers	0113 245 1841/2/3
	• St Paul's House	0113 245 5866
Liverpool	25-27 Castle Street	0151 227 5661/5666/236 5072
	19 Castle Street Chambers	0151 236 9402
	• Exchange Chambers	0151 236 7747
	• The Chambers of Adrian Lyon	0151 236 4421/8240/6757
	• Martins Building	0151 236 5818/4919
London	Barnard's Inn Chambers	0171 242 8508
	Barristers' Common Law Chambers	0171 375 3012
	17 Bedford Row	0171 831 7314
	• 29 Bedford Row Chambers	0171 831 2626
	• Blackstone Chambers (formerly known as 2 Hare Court)	0171 583 1770
	11 Bolt Court	0171 353 2300
	• Bracton Chambers	0171 242 4248
	Brick Court Chambers	0171 583 0777
	Bridewell Chambers	0171 797 8800
	Cloisters	0171 827 4000
	• Chambers of Mr Peter Crampin QC	0171 831 0081

• Expanded entry in Part C

A

1 Crown Office Row	0171 583 9292
• Enterprise Chambers	0171 405 9471
Equity Barristers' Chambers	0181 558 8336
• Erskine Chambers	0171 242 5532
• One Essex Court	0171 583 2000
• One Essex Court	0171 936 3030
• Essex Court Chambers	0171 813 8000
Chambers of Geoffrey Hawker	0171 583 8899
• Chambers of Norman Palmer	0171 405 6114
• 4 Field Court	0171 440 6900
• Fountain Court	0171 583 3335
• 2nd Floor, Francis Taylor Building	0171 353 9942
• Goldsmith Building	0171 353 7881
Goldsworth Chambers	0171 405 7117
• 9 Gough Square	0171 353 5371
• Gough Square Chambers	0171 353 0924
2 Gray's Inn Square Chambers	0171 242 0328/405 1317
Gray's Inn Square	0171 242 3529
10 - 11 Gray's Inn Square	0171 405 2576
• 1 Harcourt Buildings	0171 353 9421/0375
• 2 Harcourt Buildings	0171 583 9020
• Harcourt Chambers	0171 353 6961/7
• Hardwicke Building	0171 242 2523
• One Hare Court	0171 353 3171
• Harrow-on-the-Hill Chambers	0181 423 7444
• 4 King's Bench Walk	0171 822 8822
• 9 King's Bench Walk	0171 353 7202/3909
The Chambers of Mr Ali Mohammad Azhar	0171 353 9564 (4 lines)
10 King's Bench Walk	0171 353 7742
11 King's Bench Walk	0171 353 3337/8
• 13 King's Bench Walk	0171 353 7204
• Lamb Building	0171 797 7788
Lamb Chambers	0171 797 8300
• Littleton Chambers	0171 797 8600
• Littman Chambers	0171 404 4866
2 Mitre Court Buildings	0171 353 1353
• Mitre Court Chambers	0171 353 9394
• Monckton Chambers	0171 405 7211
• 1 New Square	0171 405 0884/5/6/7
Chambers of Lord Goodhart QC	0171 405 5577
5 New Square	0171 404 0404
• 12 New Square	0171 419 1212
• 22 Old Buildings	0171 831 0222
• Twenty-Four Old Buildings	0171 404 0946
• 9 Old Square	0171 405 4682
The Chambers of Leolin Price CBE, QC	0171 405 0758/242 5002
• 11 Old Square	0171 430 0341
• 13 Old Square	0171 404 4800
• 3 Paper Buildings	0171 797 7000
• 3 Paper Buildings	0171 583 8055
• 4 Paper Buildings	0171 583 0816
• 5 Paper Buildings	0171 583 9275
Phoenix Chambers	0171 404 7888
• Chambers of John L Powell QC	0171 797 8000
• 5 Pump Court	0171 353 2532
No 1 Serjeants' Inn	0171 415 6666
• Serle Court Chambers	0171 242 6105
• 3-4 South Square	0171 696 9900
• Stanbrook & Henderson	0171 353 0101
• 3 Stone Buildings	0171 242 4937/405 8358
4 Stone Buildings	0171 242 5524
• 7 Stone Buildings	0171 405 3886/242 3546
• 9 Stone Buildings	0171 404 5055
11 Stone Buildings	+44 (0)171 831 6381
169 Temple Chambers	0171 583 7644
• 2 Temple Gardens	0171 583 6041
• Thomas More Chambers	0171 404 7000
Chambers of Mohammed Hashmot Ullah	0171 377 0119
• 3 Verulam Buildings	0171 831 8441
Verulam Chambers	0171 813 2400
Warwick House Chambers	0171 430 2323

Harrow on the Hill
London

• Expanded entry in Part C

	• Wilberforce Chambers	0171 306 0102
Maidstone	Earl Street Chambers	01622 671222
Manchester	• Cobden House Chambers	0161 833 6000/6001
	• Chambers of John Hand QC	0161 955 9000
	Kenworthy's Chambers	0161 832 4036
	• 40 King Street	0161 832 9082
	• 8 King Street Chambers	0161 834 9560
	Manchester House Chambers	0161 834 7007
	• Merchant Chambers	0161 839 7070
	• Queen's Chambers	0161 834 6875/4738
	• St James's Chambers	0161 834 7000
	• 28 St John Street	0161 834 8418
Middlesbrough	• Fountain Chambers	01642 217037
Newcastle upon Tyne	Cathedral Chambers	0191 232 1311
	Enterprise Chambers	0191 222 3344
	• Trinity Chambers	0191 232 1927
	Westgate Chambers	0191 261 4407/232 9785
Northampton	22 Albion Place	01604 636271
Norwich	East Anglian Chambers	01603 617351
Nottingham	Ropewalk Chambers	0115 947 2581
	St Mary's Chambers	0115 950 3503
Oxford	1 Alfred Street	01865 793736
	• King's Bench Chambers	01865 311066
Peterborough	Fenners Chambers	01733 562030
Portsmouth	• Portsmouth Barristers' Chambers	01705 831292
Preston	4 Camden Place	01772 828300
	New Bailey Chambers	01772 258 087
Reading	Wessex Chambers	0118 956 8856
Redhill	Redhill Chambers	01737 780781
Richmond-upon-Thames	Richmond Green Chambers	0181 940 1841
Shepperton	Abbey Chambers	01932 560913
Southampton	• College Chambers	01703 230338
	• Eighteen Carlton Crescent	01703 639001
Swansea	Angel Chambers	01792 464623/464648
	Gower Chambers	01792 644466
Winchester	4 St Peter Street	01962 868 884
Wolverhampton	Claremont Chambers	01902 426222
York	• York Chambers	01904 620 048

COMPETITION

Birmingham	1 Fountain Court	0121 236 5721
	• 5 Fountain Court	0121 606 0500
Bournemouth	20 Lorne Park Road	01202 292102
Bristol	St John's Chambers	0117 921 3456/929 8514
Guildford	• Guildford Chambers	01483 539131
Haverhill	Helions Chambers	01440 730523
Leeds	• Sovereign Chambers	0113 245 1841/2/3
London	• 5 Bell Yard	0171 333 8811
	• Blackstone Chambers (formerly known as 2 Hare Court)	0171 583 1770
	Brick Court Chambers	0171 583 0777
	Equity Barristers' Chambers	0181 558 8336
	• One Essex Court	0171 583 2000
	• Essex Court Chambers	0171 813 8000
	• 20 Essex Street	0171 583 9294
	• 4 Field Court	0171 440 6900
	Francis Taylor Buildings	0171 353 7768/2711
	• 4-5 Gray's Inn Square	0171 404 5252
	• 2 Harcourt Buildings	0171 583 9020
	• One Hare Court	0171 353 3171
Harrow on the Hill	• Harrow-on-the-Hill Chambers	0181 423 7444
London	The Chambers of Mr Ali Mohammad Azhar	0171 353 9564 (4 lines)
	Lamb Chambers	0171 797 8300
	• Littleton Chambers	0171 797 8600
	• Littman Chambers	0171 404 4866
	• Monckton Chambers	0171 405 7211
	• 1 New Square	0171 405 0884/5/6/7
	• 8 New Square	0171 405 4321
	19 Old Buildings	0171 405 2001
	• 13 Old Square	0171 404 4800
	• 3 Paper Buildings	0171 583 8055

• Expanded entry in Part C

	• 5 Paper Buildings	0171 583 9275
	Prince Henry's Chambers	0171 353 1183/1190
	• 1 Raymond Buildings	0171 430 1234
	• Stanbrook & Henderson	0171 353 0101
	11 Stone Buildings	+44 (0)171 831 6381
Manchester	• Cobden House Chambers	0161 833 6000/6001
	• 8 King Street Chambers	0161 834 9560
	Peel Court Chambers	0161 832 3791
Newcastle upon Tyne	Westgate Chambers	0191 261 4407/232 9785
Oxford	1 Alfred Street	01865 793736
Preston	New Bailey Chambers	01772 258 087
Winchester	4 St Peter Street	01962 868 884

COMPULSORY PURCHASE

London	• 2 Harcourt Buildings	0171 353 8415

CONFISCATION

London	• Furnival Chambers	0171 405 3232

CONSTRUCTION

Birmingham	• Equity Chambers	0121 233 2100
	• 5 Fountain Court	0121 606 0500
	• 8 Fountain Court	0121 236 5514
	• St Philip's Chambers	0121 246 7000
Bournemouth	20 Lorne Park Road	01202 292102
Brighton	• Crown Office Row Chambers	01273 625625
Bristol	Assize Court Chambers	0117 926 4587
	Old Square Chambers	0117 927 7111
	St John's Chambers	0117 921 3456/929 8514
Cambridge	• Fenners Chambers	01223 368761
Cardiff	9 Park Place	01222 382731
	30 Park Place	01222 398421
	• 33 Park Place	01222 233313
Chichester	Chichester Chambers	01243 784538
Exeter	• Cathedral Chambers (Jan Wood Independent Barristers' Clerk)	01392 210900
Leeds	• Chancery House Chambers	0113 244 6691
	The Chambers of Philip Raynor QC	0113 242 1123
	• Sovereign Chambers	0113 245 1841/2/3
	• 9 Woodhouse Square	0113 245 1986
Liverpool	25–27 Castle Street	0151 227 5661/5666/236 5072
	• The Corn Exchange Chambers	0151 227 1081/5009
	India Buildings Chambers	0151 243 6000
	• Martins Building	0151 236 5818/4919
London	• Arbitration Chambers	0171 267 2137
	Atkin Chambers	0171 404 0102
	Avondale Chambers	0181 445 9984
	9 Bedford Row	0171 242 3555
	• 29 Bedford Row Chambers	0171 831 2626
	• 5 Bell Yard	0171 333 8811
	• 4 Breams Buildings	0171 353 5835/430 1221
	Brick Court Chambers	0171 583 0777
	Bridewell Chambers	0171 797 8800
	• 1 Crown Office Row	0171 797 7500
	1 Crown Office Row	0171 583 9292
	• Two Crown Office Row	0171 797 8100
	• Devereux Chambers	0171 353 7534
	Equity Barristers' Chambers	0181 558 8336
	• One Essex Court	0171 936 3030
	• 4 Essex Court	0171 797 7970
	• Essex Court Chambers	0171 813 8000
	• 35 Essex Street	0171 353 6381
	• 39 Essex Street	0171 832 1111
	Chambers of Geoffrey Hawker	0171 583 8899
	• Farrar's Building	0171 583 9241
	• Chambers of Norman Palmer	0171 405 6114
	• 4 Field Court	0171 440 6900
	• Fountain Court	0171 583 3335
	Francis Taylor Buildings	0171 353 7768/2711
	Goldsworth Chambers	0171 405 7117

• Expanded entry in Part C

	2 Gray's Inn Square Chambers	0171 242 0328/405 1317
	• 2-3 Gray's Inn Square	0171 242 4986
	10 - 11 Gray's Inn Square	0171 405 2576
	• 1 Harcourt Buildings	0171 353 9421/0375
	• 2 Harcourt Buildings	0171 583 9020
	• Hardwicke Building	0171 242 2523
	• One Hare Court	0171 353 3171
Harrow on the Hill	• Harrow-on-the-Hill Chambers	0181 423 7444
London	• Keating Chambers	0171 544 2600
	• 9 King's Bench Walk	0171 353 7202/3909
	The Chambers of Mr Ali Mohammad Azhar	0171 353 9564 (4 lines)
	• 12 King's Bench Walk	0171 583 0811
	• 13 King's Bench Walk	0171 353 7204
	• Lamb Building	0171 797 7788
	Lamb Chambers	0171 797 8300
	• Littleton Chambers	0171 797 8600
	• Littman Chambers	0171 404 4866
	• Mitre Court Chambers	0171 353 9394
	• Mitre House Chambers	0171 583 8233
	• Monckton Chambers	0171 405 7211
	• 22 Old Buildings	0171 831 0222
	The Chambers of Leolin Price CBE, QC	0171 405 0758/242 5002
	11 Old Square	0171 242 5022
	• Old Square Chambers	0171 269 0300
	One Paper Buildings	0171 583 7355
	• 3 Paper Buildings	0171 797 7000
	• 3 Paper Buildings	0171 583 8055
	• 4 Paper Buildings	0171 353 3366/583 7155
	• 4 Paper Buildings	0171 583 0816
	• 5 Paper Buildings	0171 583 9275
	Pepys' Chambers	0171 936 2710
	Phoenix Chambers	0171 404 7888
	Plowden Buildings	0171 583 0808
	• Chambers of John L Powell QC	0171 797 8000
	• Pump Court Chambers	0171 353 0711
	• 4 Pump Court	0171 353 2656/9
	• 5 Pump Court	0171 353 2532
	No 1 Serjeants' Inn	0171 415 6666
	• 3 Serjeants' Inn	0171 353 5537
	• Stanbrook & Henderson	0171 353 0101
	• 2 Temple Gardens	0171 583 6041
	• 3 Verulam Buildings	0171 831 8441
Malvern	Resolution Chambers	01684 561279
Manchester	• Byrom Street Chambers	0161 829 2100
	Deans Court Chambers	0161 834 4097
	• Chambers of John Hand QC	0161 955 9000
	• 40 King Street	0161 832 9082
	• 8 King Street Chambers	0161 834 9560
	Manchester House Chambers	0161 834 7007
	• Merchant Chambers	0161 839 7070
	Peel Court Chambers	0161 832 3791
	• St James's Chambers	0161 834 7000
	Young Street Chambers	0161 833 0489
Meopham	West Lodge Farm	01474 812280
Middlesbrough	• Fountain Chambers	01642 217037
Newcastle upon Tyne	• Trinity Chambers	0191 232 1927
	Westgate Chambers	0191 261 4407/232 9785
Northampton	22 Albion Place	01604 636271
Norwich	East Anglian Chambers	01603 617351
Nottingham	Ropewalk Chambers	0115 947 2581
Oxford	1 Alfred Street	01865 793736
	• King's Bench Chambers	01865 311066
Peterborough	Fenners Chambers	01733 562030
Portsmouth	• Portsmouth Barristers' Chambers	01705 831292
Preston	Deans Court Chambers	01772 555163
	New Bailey Chambers	01772 258 087
	15 Winckley Square	01772 252 828
Reading	Wessex Chambers	0118 956 8856
Sheffield	Paradise Square Chambers	0114 273 8951
Sonning-on-Thames	Greenway	0118 969 2484
Stoke-on-Trent	Regent Chambers	01782 286666

• Expanded entry in Part C

Swansea	Gower Chambers	01792 644466
	Iscoed Chambers	01792 652988/9/330
Winchester	4 St Peter Street	01962 868 884
Wolverhampton	Claremont Chambers	01902 426222

CONSUMER LAW

Birmingham	• Equity Chambers	0121 233 2100
	• 5 Fountain Court	0121 606 0500
	• St Philip's Chambers	0121 246 7000
Bournemouth	King's Bench Chambers	01202 250025
Bristol	St John's Chambers	0117 921 3456/929 8514
Cambridge	• Fenners Chambers	01223 368761
Cardiff	9 Park Place	01222 382731
Chester	White Friars Chambers	01244 323070
Coulsdon	Advolex Chambers	0181 763 2345
Ely	Cathedral Chambers, Ely	01353 666775
Exeter	• Cathedral Chambers (Jan Wood Independent Barristers' Clerk)	01392 210900
	Rougemont Chambers	01392 410471
Leeds	Chambers of Andrew Campbell QC	0113 245 5438
	The Chambers of Philip Raynor QC	0113 242 1123
Liverpool	• Martins Building	0151 236 5818/4919
	• Oriel Chambers	0151 236 7191
London	9 Bedford Row	0171 242 3555
	• 5 Bell Yard	0171 333 8811
	Bridewell Chambers	0171 797 8800
	• Devereux Chambers	0171 353 7534
	Equity Barristers' Chambers	0181 558 8336
	Chambers of Geoffrey Hawker	0171 583 8899
	• 2nd Floor, Francis Taylor Building	0171 353 9942
	• Gough Square Chambers	0171 353 0924
	2 Gray's Inn Square Chambers	0171 242 0328/405 1317
	• 2 Harcourt Buildings	0171 583 9020
Harrow on the Hill	• Harrow-on-the-Hill Chambers	0181 423 7444
London	The Chambers of Mr Ali Mohammad Azhar	0171 353 9564 (4 lines)
	10 King's Bench Walk	0171 353 7742
	• 13 King's Bench Walk	0171 353 7204
	• Mitre Court Chambers	0171 353 9394
	• Monckton Chambers	0171 405 7211
	• 4 Paper Buildings	0171 583 0816
	5 Paper Buildings	0171 583 6117
	Phoenix Chambers	0171 404 7888
	• Stanbrook & Henderson	0171 353 0101
	• 199 Strand	0171 379 9779
	169 Temple Chambers	0171 583 7644
	3 Temple Gardens (North)	0171 353 0853/4/7222
	• Thomas More Chambers	0171 404 7000
Manchester	• Cobden House Chambers	0161 833 6000/6001
	• 40 King Street	0161 832 9082
	Chambers of Ian Macdonald QC	0161 236 1840
	Manchester House Chambers	0161 834 7007
	Peel Court Chambers	0161 832 3791
	• Queen's Chambers	0161 834 6875/4738
	• St James's Chambers	0161 834 7000
Middlesbrough	Baker Street Chambers	01642 873873
Newcastle upon Tyne	Cathedral Chambers	0191 232 1311
Norwich	Sackville Chambers	01603 613516
Nottingham	Ropewalk Chambers	0115 947 2581
Oxford	• King's Bench Chambers	01865 311066
Peterborough	Fenners Chambers	01733 562030
Preston	4 Camden Place	01772 828300
	New Bailey Chambers	01772 258 087
	15 Winckley Square	01772 252 828
Richmond-upon-Thames	Richmond Green Chambers	0181 940 1841
Stoke-on-Trent	Regent Chambers	01782 286666
Swansea	Angel Chambers	01792 464623/464648
Wolverhampton	Claremont Chambers	01902 426222

• Expanded entry in Part C

CONTRACT

London	• Hardwicke Building	0171 242 2523
	• Thomas More Chambers	0171 404 7000

CONTRACT AND COMMERCIAL

London	4 King's Bench Walk	0171 353 3581

CONVEYANCING

Birmingham	• 5 Fountain Court	0121 606 0500
	• 8 Fountain Court	0121 236 5514
	• St Philip's Chambers	0121 246 7000
Cambridge	• Fenners Chambers	01223 368761
Cardiff	9 Park Place	01222 382731
	30 Park Place	01222 398421
Exeter	Southernhay Chambers	01392 255777
Leeds	Chambers of Andrew Campbell QC	0113 245 5438
	Enterprise Chambers	0113 246 0391
	The Chambers of Philip Raynor QC	0113 242 1123
Liverpool	• Exchange Chambers	0151 236 7747
	• The Chambers of Adrian Lyon	0151 236 4421/8240/6757
London	• 29 Bedford Row Chambers	0171 831 2626
	11 Bolt Court	0171 353 2300
	• 4 Breams Buildings	0171 353 5835/430 1221
	• Chambers of Mr Peter Crampin QC	0171 831 0081
	• Enterprise Chambers	0171 405 9471
	Falcon Chambers	0171 353 2484
	• Chambers of Norman Palmer	0171 405 6114
	2 Gray's Inn Square Chambers	0171 242 0328/405 1317
	10 - 11 Gray's Inn Square	0171 405 2576
	• Hardwicke Building	0171 242 2523
Harrow on the Hill	• Harrow-on-the-Hill Chambers	0181 423 7444
London	• 9 King's Bench Walk	0171 353 7202/3909
	• 13 King's Bench Walk	0171 353 7204
	• Littman Chambers	0171 404 4866
	2 Mitre Court Buildings	0171 583 1380
	• 1 New Square	0171 405 0884/5/6/7
	Chambers of Lord Goodhart QC	0171 405 5577
	5 New Square	0171 404 0404
	• 12 New Square	0171 419 1212
	• 22 Old Buildings	0171 831 0222
	• Twenty-Four Old Buildings	0171 404 0946
	• 9 Old Square	0171 405 4682
	The Chambers of Leolin Price CBE, QC	0171 405 0758/242 5002
	11 Old Square	0171 242 5022
	• 11 Old Square	0171 430 0341
	• 13 Old Square	0171 404 4800
	• 3 Paper Buildings	0171 797 7000
	• 3 Stone Buildings	0171 242 4937/405 8358
	• 5 Stone Buildings	0171 242 6201
	• 9 Stone Buildings	0171 404 5055
Manchester	• Cobden House Chambers	0161 833 6000/6001
	• Chambers of John Hand QC	0161 955 9000
	• 40 King Street	0161 832 9082
	Manchester House Chambers	0161 834 7007
	• St James's Chambers	0161 834 7000
	• 28 St John Street	0161 834 8418
Middlesbrough	• Fountain Chambers	01642 217037
Newcastle upon Tyne	Enterprise Chambers	0191 222 3344
	• Trinity Chambers	0191 232 1927
Norwich	East Anglian Chambers	01603 617351
Nottingham	Ropewalk Chambers	0115 947 2581
Oxford	• King's Bench Chambers	01865 311066
Peterborough	Fenners Chambers	01733 562030
Redhill	Redhill Chambers	01737 780781
Southampton	• 17 Carlton Crescent	01703 320320

COPYRIGHT

Birmingham	• Equity Chambers	0121 233 2100
	1 Fountain Court	0121 236 5721
	• 5 Fountain Court	0121 606 0500

Bristol	St John's Chambers	0117 921 3456/929 8514
Cardiff	9 Park Place	01222 382731
Chester	40 King Street	01244 323886
Haverhill	Helions Chambers	01440 730523
Leeds	Chambers of Andrew Campbell QC	0113 245 5438
	• Chancery House Chambers	0113 244 6691
	11 King's Bench Walk	0113 2971 200
	The Chambers of Philip Raynor QC	0113 242 1123
	• Sovereign Chambers	0113 245 1841/2/3
Liverpool	• The Chambers of Adrian Lyon	0151 236 4421/8240/6757
London	17 Bedford Row	0171 831 7314
	• 5 Bell Yard	0171 333 8811
	• Blackstone Chambers (formerly known as 2 Hare Court)	0171 583 1770
	• Doughty Street Chambers	0171 404 1313
	Equity Barristers' Chambers	0181 558 8336
	• One Essex Court	0171 583 2000
	• 35 Essex Street	0171 353 6381
	• Chambers of Norman Palmer	0171 405 6114
	• 4 Field Court	0171 440 6900
	• Fountain Court	0171 583 3335
	Francis Taylor Buildings	0171 353 7768/2711
	• Furnival Chambers	0171 405 3232
	Goldsworth Chambers	0171 405 7117
	• 2 Harcourt Buildings	0171 583 9020
	• 9 King's Bench Walk	0171 353 7202/3909
	The Chambers of Mr Ali Mohammad Azhar	0171 353 9564 (4 lines)
	• 13 King's Bench Walk	0171 353 7204
	Lamb Chambers	0171 797 8300
	• Littleton Chambers	0171 797 8600
	2 Mitre Court Buildings	0171 353 1353
	• Mitre Court Chambers	0171 353 9394
	• Monckton Chambers	0171 405 7211
	• New Court	0171 797 8999
	• 3 New Square	0171 405 1111
	5 New Square	0171 404 0404
	• 8 New Square	0171 405 4321
	Chambers of Joy Okoye	0171 405 7011
	19 Old Buildings	0171 405 2001
	The Chambers of Leolin Price CBE, QC	0171 405 0758/242 5002
	• 11 Old Square	0171 430 0341
	• 13 Old Square	0171 404 4800
	5 Paper Buildings	0171 583 6117
	Prince Henry's Chambers	0171 353 1183/1190
	• 1 Raymond Buildings	0171 430 1234
	• 5 Raymond Buildings	0171 242 2902
	• 11 South Square	0171 405 1222
	• Stanbrook & Henderson	0171 353 0101
	• 3 Stone Buildings	0171 242 4937/405 8358
	• 9 Stone Buildings	0171 404 5055
	11 Stone Buildings	+44 (0)171 831 6381
Manchester	• Cobden House Chambers	0161 833 6000/6001
	• Chambers of John Hand QC	0161 955 9000
	• 40 King Street	0161 832 9082
	• Merchant Chambers	0161 839 7070
	• St James's Chambers	0161 834 7000
Newcastle upon Tyne	• Broad Chare	0191 232 0541
Nottingham	King Charles House	0115 941 8851
	Ropewalk Chambers	0115 947 2581
Oxford	• King's Bench Chambers	01865 311066
Preston	New Bailey Chambers	01772 258 087
Reading	Wessex Chambers	0118 956 8856
Richmond-upon-Thames	Richmond Green Chambers	0181 940 1841

CORPORATE FINANCE

Birmingham	• 5 Fountain Court	0121 606 0500
Chester	40 King Street	01244 323886
Chesterfield	26 Morley Avenue	01246 234790
Leeds	Chambers of Andrew Campbell QC	0113 245 5438
	• Chancery House Chambers	0113 244 6691
	11 King's Bench Walk	0113 2971 200

• Expanded entry in Part C

	The Chambers of Philip Raynor QC	0113 242 1123
Liverpool	• Exchange Chambers	0151 236 7747
London	• 5 Bell Yard	0171 333 8811
	• Blackstone Chambers (formerly known as 2 Hare Court)	0171 583 1770
	Bridewell Chambers	0171 797 8800
	1 Crown Office Row	0171 583 9292
	Equity Barristers' Chambers	0181 558 8336
	• Erskine Chambers	0171 242 5532
	• One Essex Court	0171 583 2000
	• Essex Court Chambers	0171 813 8000
	• Chambers of Norman Palmer	0171 405 6114
	• One Hare Court	0171 353 3171
	• 4 King's Bench Walk	0171 822 8822
	The Chambers of Mr Ali Mohammad Azhar	0171 353 9564 (4 lines)
	• 1 New Square	0171 405 0884/5/6/7
	Chambers of John Gardiner QC	0171 242 4017
	• 12 New Square	0171 419 1212
	24 Old Buildings	0171 242 2744
	The Chambers of Leolin Price CBE, QC	0171 405 0758/242 5002
	• 3-4 South Square	0171 696 9900
	4 Stone Buildings	0171 242 5524
	• 7 Stone Buildings	0171 405 3886/242 3546
	• 9 Stone Buildings	0171 404 5055
Manchester	• Chambers of John Hand QC	0161 955 9000
	• 40 King Street	0161 832 9082
	• Merchant Chambers	0161 839 7070

COURT OF PROTECTION

| London | • Chambers of Mr Peter Crampin QC | 0171 831 0081 |

COURTS MARTIAL

Birmingham	1 Fountain Court	0121 236 5721
	• 5 Fountain Court	0121 606 0500
	• St Philip's Chambers	0121 246 7000
Bournemouth	20 Lorne Park Road	01202 292102
Bristol	St John's Chambers	0117 921 3456/929 8514
Cambridge	• Fenners Chambers	01223 368761
Cardiff	32 Park Place	01222 397364
Ely	Cathedral Chambers, Ely	01353 666775
Exeter	Rougemont Chambers	01392 410471
	Walnut House	01392 279751
Guildford	• Guildford Chambers	01483 539131
Haverhill	Helions Chambers	01440 730523
Leeds	Chambers of Andrew Campbell QC	0113 245 5438
	11 King's Bench Walk	0113 2971 200
	• 30 Park Square	0113 243 6388
	• 37 Park Square	0113 243 9422
	• St Paul's House	0113 245 5866
Liverpool	25-27 Castle Street	0151 227 5661/5666/236 5072
	19 Castle Street Chambers	0151 236 9402
	First National Chambers	0151 236 2098
	• The Chambers of Adrian Lyon	0151 236 4421/8240/6757
London	9 Bedford Row	0171 242 3555
	• 9-12 Bell Yard	0171 400 1800
	• 4 Brick Court, Chambers of Anne Rafferty QC	0171 583 8455
	Bridewell Chambers	0171 797 8800
	• Dr Johnson's Chambers	0171 353 4716
	Equity Barristers' Chambers	0181 558 8336
	23 Essex Street	0171 413 0353
	• Farrar's Building	0171 583 9241
	Francis Taylor Buildings	0171 353 7768/2711
	• Furnival Chambers	0171 405 3232
	• Goldsmith Building	0171 353 7881
	• Gray's Inn Chambers	0171 831 5344
	• Gray's Inn Chambers	0171 404 1111
	6 Gray's Inn Square	0171 242 1052
	10 - 11 Gray's Inn Square	0171 405 2576
	• 2 Harcourt Buildings	0171 583 9020

         • Expanded entry in Part C

A

	2 Harcourt Buildings	0171 353 2112/2817
	• 1 Hare Court	0171 353 3982/5324
	• 3 Hare Court	0171 353 7561
	• Chambers of James Hunt QC	0171 421 8000
	• One King's Bench Walk	0171 936 1500
	• 4 King's Bench Walk	0171 822 8822
	• 8 King's Bench Walk	0171 797 8888
	• 9 King's Bench Walk	0171 353 7202/3909
	The Chambers of Mr Ali Mohammad Azhar	0171 353 9564 (4 lines)
	• Lamb Building	0171 797 7788
	Lamb Chambers	0171 797 8300
	• Mitre House Chambers	0171 583 8233
	• 2 Paper Buildings	0171 936 2611 (10 lines)
	• 3 Paper Buildings	0171 583 8055
	Phoenix Chambers	0171 404 7888
	2 Pump Court	0171 353 5597
	• Pump Court Chambers	0171 353 0711
	• Queen Elizabeth Building	0171 583 5766
	• 3 Raymond Buildings	0171 831 3833
	• Stanbrook & Henderson	0171 353 0101
	7 Stone Buildings	0171 242 0961
	• 3 Temple Gardens	0171 353 3102/5/9297
	• Thomas More Chambers	0171 404 7000
Maidstone	Earl Street Chambers	01622 671222
	• Maidstone Chambers	01622 688592
Manchester	• Cobden House Chambers	0161 833 6000/6001
	• 8 King Street Chambers	0161 834 9560
	Chambers of Ian Macdonald QC	0161 236 1840
	Manchester House Chambers	0161 834 7007
	Young Street Chambers	0161 833 0489
Middlesbrough	• Fountain Chambers	01642 217037
Newcastle upon Tyne	• Broad Chare	0191 232 0541
	• New Court Chambers	0191 232 1980
Norwich	East Anglian Chambers	01603 617351
Nottingham	King Charles House	0115 941 8851
Oxford	1 Alfred Street	01865 793736
Peterborough	Fenners Chambers	01733 562030
Preston	15 Winckley Square	01772 252 828
Reading	Dr Johnson's Chambers	01189 254221
Sheffield	Paradise Square Chambers	0114 273 8951
Shepperton	Abbey Chambers	01932 560913
Southampton	• Eighteen Carlton Crescent	01703 639001
Winchester	4 St Peter Street	01962 868 884
Winkleigh	Barnstaple Chambers	0183 783763
York	• York Chambers	01904 620 048

CRIME

Birmingham	• Equity Chambers	0121 233 2100
	1 Fountain Court	0121 236 5721
	• 3 Fountain Court	0121 236 5854
	• 5 Fountain Court	0121 606 0500
	6 Fountain Court	0121 233 3282
	• 8 Fountain Court	0121 236 5514
	New Court Chambers	0121 693 6656
	• St Philip's Chambers	0121 246 7000
Bournemouth	King's Bench Chambers	01202 250025
	20 Lorne Park Road	01202 292102
Bradford	Broadway House Chambers	01274 722560
Brandon	Thetford Lodge Farm	01842 813132
Brighton	• Crown Office Row Chambers	01273 625625
Bristol	Assize Court Chambers	0117 926 4587
	St John's Chambers	0117 921 3456/929 8514
Bromley	Bromley Chambers	0181 325 0863
Cambridge	• Fenners Chambers	01223 368761
	Regency Chambers	01223 301517
Cardiff	9 Park Place	01222 382731
	30 Park Place	01222 398421
	32 Park Place	01222 397364
	• 33 Park Place	01222 233313
Chester	40 King Street	01244 323886
	White Friars Chambers	01244 323070

Chesterfield	26 Morley Avenue	01246 234790
Chichester	Chichester Chambers	01243 784538
Durham City	Durham Barristers' Chambers	0191 386 9199
Eastbourne	King's Chambers	01323 416053
Ely	Cathedral Chambers, Ely	01353 666775
Enfield	Enfield Chambers	0181 364 5627
Exeter	• Cathedral Chambers (Jan Wood Independent Barristers' Clerk)	01392 210900
	Colleton Chambers	01392 274898
	Rougemont Chambers	01392 410471
	Walnut House	01392 279751
Guildford	• Guildford Chambers	01483 539131
Leeds	Chambers of Andrew Campbell QC	0113 245 5438
	11 King's Bench Walk	0113 2971 200
	• No. 6	0113 245 9763
	• Park Court Chambers	0113 243 3277
	The Chambers of Philip Raynor QC	0113 242 1123
	• 30 Park Square	0113 243 6388
	• 37 Park Square	0113 243 9422
	• Sovereign Chambers	0113 245 1841/2/3
	• St Paul's House	0113 245 5866
	• 9 Woodhouse Square	0113 245 1986
Leicester	2 New Street	0116 262 5906
Liverpool	25–27 Castle Street	0151 227 5661/5666/236 5072
	19 Castle Street Chambers	0151 236 9402
	Chavasse Court Chambers	0151 707 1191
	• The Corn Exchange Chambers	0151 227 1081/5009
	• Exchange Chambers	0151 236 7747
	First National Chambers	0151 236 2098
	India Buildings Chambers	0151 243 6000
	• The Chambers of Adrian Lyon	0151 236 4421/8240/6757
	• Martins Building	0151 236 5818/4919
	• Oriel Chambers	0151 236 7191
	• Peel House Chambers	0151 236 4321
London	ACHMA Chambers	0171 639 7817
	Albany Chambers	0171 485 5736/38
	Avondale Chambers	0181 445 9984
	Barnard's Inn Chambers	0171 242 8508
	Barristers' Common Law Chambers	0171 375 3012
	9 Bedford Row	0171 242 3555
	17 Bedford Row	0171 831 7314
	33 Bedford Row	0171 242 6476
	• 29 Bedford Row Chambers	0171 831 2626
	• 9–12 Bell Yard	0171 400 1800
	Bell Yard Chambers	0171 306 9292
	11 Bolt Court	0171 353 2300
	• 4 Brick Court	0171 797 8910
	• 4 Brick Court	0171 797 7766
	• 4 Brick Court, Chambers of Anne Rafferty QC	0171 583 8455
	Bridewell Chambers	0171 797 8800
	Britton Street Chambers	0171 608 3765
	Cloisters	0171 827 4000
	• 1 Crown Office Row	0171 797 7500
	• 1 Crown Office Row	0171 797 7111
	• Devereux Chambers	0171 353 7534
	• Doughty Street Chambers	0171 404 1313
	• 3 Dr Johnson's Buildings	0171 353 4854
	• Dr Johnson's Chambers	0171 353 4716
	Equity Barristers' Chambers	0181 558 8336
	• One Essex Court	0171 936 3030
	5 Essex Court	0171 410 2000
	23 Essex Street	0171 413 0353
	• 35 Essex Street	0171 353 6381
	Chambers of Geoffrey Hawker	0171 583 8899
	• Farrar's Building	0171 583 9241
	• 2nd Floor, Francis Taylor Building	0171 353 9942
	Francis Taylor Buildings	0171 353 7768/2711
	• Furnival Chambers	0171 405 3232
	• 2 Garden Court	0171 353 1633
	• Goldsmith Building	0171 353 7881
	Goldsmith Chambers	0171 353 6802/3/4/5

• Expanded entry in Part C

• 9 Gough Square	0171 353 5371
• Gray's Inn Chambers	0171 831 5344
• Gray's Inn Chambers	0171 404 1111
• 1 Gray's Inn Square Chambers of the Baroness Scotland of Asthal QC	0171 405 3000
• 1 Gray's Inn Square	0171 405 8946
2 Gray's Inn Square Chambers	0171 242 0328/405 1317
• 2-3 Gray's Inn Square	0171 242 4986
• 3 Gray's Inn Square	0171 520 5600
6 Gray's Inn Square	0171 242 1052
10 - 11 Gray's Inn Square	0171 405 2576
100E Great Portland Street	0171 636 6323
Chambers of Helen Grindrod QC	0171 404 4777
• 1 Harcourt Buildings	0171 353 9421/0375
• 2 Harcourt Buildings	0171 583 9020
2 Harcourt Buildings	0171 353 2112/2817
• Harcourt Chambers	0171 353 6961/7
• Hardwicke Building	0171 242 2523
• 1 Hare Court	0171 353 3982/5324
• 3 Hare Court	0171 353 7561
Chambers of Harjit Singh	0171 353 1356
• Harrow-on-the-Hill Chambers	0181 423 7444
• Chambers of James Hunt QC	0171 421 8000
• John Street Chambers	0171 242 1911
1 Dr Johnson's Buildings	0171 353 9328
• One King's Bench Walk	0171 936 1500
• 4 King's Bench Walk	0171 822 8822
4 King's Bench Walk	0171 353 3581
• 6 King's Bench Walk	0171 583 0410
6 King's Bench Walk	0171 353 4931/583 0695
• 8 King's Bench Walk	0171 797 8888
• 9 King's Bench Walk	0171 353 7202/3909
The Chambers of Mr Ali Mohammad Azhar	0171 353 9564 (4 lines)
10 King's Bench Walk	0171 353 7742
11 King's Bench Walk	0171 353 3337/8
• 13 King's Bench Walk	0171 353 7204
Kingsway Chambers	07000 653529
• Lamb Building	0171 797 7788
Library Chambers	0171 404 6500
Lion Court	0171 404 6565
• 1 Middle Temple Lane	0171 583 0659 (12 lines)
2 Mitre Court Buildings	0171 353 1353
• Mitre Court Chambers	0171 353 9394
• Mitre House Chambers	0171 583 8233
• New Court	0171 583 5123
Chambers of Joy Okoye	0171 405 7011
11 Old Square	0171 242 5022
1 Paper Buildings	0171 353 3728/4953
• 2 Paper Buildings	0171 353 0933
• 2 Paper Buildings	0171 936 2611 (10 lines)
2 Paper Buildings, Basement North	0171 936 2613
• 3 Paper Buildings	0171 583 8055
5 Paper Buildings	0171 583 6117
Pepys' Chambers	0171 936 2710
Phoenix Chambers	0171 404 7888
Plowden Buildings	0171 583 0808
• 1 Pump Court	0171 583 2012/353 4341
2 Pump Court	0171 353 5597
• Pump Court Chambers	0171 353 0711
• 5 Pump Court	0171 353 2532
6 Pump Court	0171 797 8400
• Queen Elizabeth Building	0171 353 7181 (12 lines)
• Queen Elizabeth Building	0171 583 5766
• 3 Raymond Buildings	0171 831 3833
• 18 Red Lion Court	0171 520 6000
Ridgeway Chambers	0181 455 2939
No 1 Serjeants' Inn	0171 415 6666
• 3 Serjeants' Inn	0171 353 5537
• Stanbrook & Henderson	0171 353 0101
7 Stone Buildings	0171 242 0961
• 1 Temple Gardens	0171 353 0407/583 1315

**Harrow on the Hill
London**

	• 3 Temple Gardens	0171 353 3102/5/9297
	3 Temple Gardens (North)	0171 353 0853/4/7222
	• Thomas More Chambers	0171 404 7000
	• 14 Tooks Court	0171 405 8828
	Trafalgar Chambers	0171 583 5858
	Chambers of Mohammed Hashmot Ullah	0171 377 0119
	Verulam Chambers	0171 813 2400
	Warwick House Chambers	0171 430 2323
Maidstone	Earl Street Chambers	01622 671222
	• Maidstone Chambers	01622 688592
Manchester	• Byrom Street Chambers	0161 829 2100
	• Central Chambers	0161 833 1774
	• Cobden House Chambers	0161 833 6000/6001
	Deans Court Chambers	0161 834 4097
	• Chambers of John Hand QC	0161 955 9000
	Kenworthy's Chambers	0161 832 4036
	• 40 King Street	0161 832 9082
	• 8 King Street Chambers	0161 834 9560
	58 King Street Chambers	0161 831 7477
	Lincoln House Chambers	0161 832 5701
	Lloyds House Chambers	0161 839 3371
	Chambers of Ian Macdonald QC	0161 236 1840
	Manchester House Chambers	0161 834 7007
	Old Colony House	0161 834 4364
	Peel Court Chambers	0161 832 3791
	• Queen's Chambers	0161 834 6875/4738
	• St James's Chambers	0161 834 7000
	18 St John Street	0161 278 1800
	• 28 St John Street	0161 834 8418
	Young Street Chambers	0161 833 0489
Middlesbrough	Baker Street Chambers	01642 873873
	• Fountain Chambers	01642 217037
Newcastle upon Tyne	• Broad Chare	0191 232 0541
	Cathedral Chambers	0191 232 1311
	• New Court Chambers	0191 232 1980
	• Trinity Chambers	0191 232 1927
	Westgate Chambers	0191 261 4407/232 9785
Northampton	22 Albion Place	01604 636271
	Chartlands Chambers	01604 603322
Norwich	East Anglian Chambers	01603 617351
	Octagon House	01603 623186
	Sackville Chambers	01603 613516
Nottingham	No. 1 High Pavement Chambers	0115 941 8218
	King Charles House	0115 941 8851
	St Mary's Chambers	0115 950 3503
Oxford	1 Alfred Street	01865 793736
	• King's Bench Chambers	01865 311066
Peterborough	Fenners Chambers	01733 562030
	Regency Chambers	01733 315215
Plymouth	Devon Chambers	01752 661659
Portsmouth	• Portsmouth Barristers' Chambers	01705 831292
Preston	4 Camden Place	01772 828300
	Deans Court Chambers	01772 555163
	New Bailey Chambers	01772 258 087
	15 Winckley Square	01772 252 828
Reading	Dr Johnson's Chambers	01189 254221
	Wessex Chambers	0118 956 8856
Redhill	Redhill Chambers	01737 780781
Richmond-upon-Thames	Richmond Green Chambers	0181 940 1841
Sheffield	Bank House Chambers	0114 275 1223
	Paradise Square Chambers	0114 273 8951
Shepperton	Abbey Chambers	01932 560913
Slough	11 St Bernards Road	01753 553806/817989
Southampton	• 17 Carlton Crescent	01703 320320
	• College Chambers	01703 230338
	• Eighteen Carlton Crescent	01703 639001
Stoke-on-Trent	Regent Chambers	01782 286666
Swansea	Angel Chambers	01792 464623/464648
	Gower Chambers	01792 644466
	Iscoed Chambers	01792 652988/9/330
	Pendragon Chambers	01792 411188
Corsham	Neston Home Chambers	01225 811909

• Expanded entry in Part C

Swindon	Pump Court Chambers	01793 539899
Winchester	Pump Court Chambers	01962 868161
	4 St Peter Street	01962 868 884
Wolverhampton	Claremont Chambers	01902 426222
York	• York Chambers	01904 620 048

CRIME - CORPORATE FRAUD

Birmingham	• Equity Chambers	0121 233 2100
	1 Fountain Court	0121 236 5721
	• 3 Fountain Court	0121 236 5854
	• 5 Fountain Court	0121 606 0500
	New Court Chambers	0121 693 6656
	• St Philip's Chambers	0121 246 7000
Brighton	• Crown Office Row Chambers	01273 625625
Bristol	St John's Chambers	0117 921 3456/929 8514
Cambridge	• Fenners Chambers	01223 368761
Cardiff	9 Park Place	01222 382731
	30 Park Place	01222 398421
	32 Park Place	01222 397364
	• 33 Park Place	01222 233313
Chester	40 King Street	01244 323886
	White Friars Chambers	01244 323070
Chichester	Chichester Chambers	01243 784538
Ely	Cathedral Chambers, Ely	01353 666775
Exeter	Colleton Chambers	01392 274898
	Walnut House	01392 279751
Guildford	• Guildford Chambers	01483 539131
Leeds	11 King's Bench Walk	0113 2971 200
	• No. 6	0113 245 9763
	The Chambers of Philip Raynor QC	0113 242 1123
	• 30 Park Square	0113 243 6388
	• Sovereign Chambers	0113 245 1841/2/3
	• St Paul's House	0113 245 5866
Leicester	2 New Street	0116 262 5906
Liverpool	25-27 Castle Street	0151 227 5661/5666/236 5072
	19 Castle Street Chambers	0151 236 9402
	• The Corn Exchange Chambers	0151 227 1081/5009
	• Exchange Chambers	0151 236 7747
	India Buildings Chambers	0151 243 6000
	• The Chambers of Adrian Lyon	0151 236 4421/8240/6757
	• Martins Building	0151 236 5818/4919
	• Oriel Chambers	0151 236 7191
London	Avondale Chambers	0181 445 9984
	Barnard's Inn Chambers	0171 242 8508
	9 Bedford Row	0171 242 3555
	• 9-12 Bell Yard	0171 400 1800
	Bell Yard Chambers	0171 306 9292
	• Blackstone Chambers (formerly known as 2 Hare Court)	0171 583 1770
	11 Bolt Court	0171 353 2300
	• Bracton Chambers	0171 242 4248
	• 4 Brick Court	0171 797 7766
	• 4 Brick Court, Chambers of Anne Rafferty QC	0171 583 8455
	Bridewell Chambers	0171 797 8800
	• 1 Crown Office Row	0171 797 7500
	• 1 Crown Office Row	0171 797 7111
	1 Crown Office Row	0171 583 9292
	• Devereux Chambers	0171 353 7534
	• Doughty Street Chambers	0171 404 1313
	Equity Barristers' Chambers	0181 558 8336
	• One Essex Court	0171 936 3030
	23 Essex Street	0171 413 0353
	• 35 Essex Street	0171 353 6381
	Chambers of Geoffrey Hawker	0171 583 8899
	Francis Taylor Buildings	0171 353 7768/2711
	• Furnival Chambers	0171 405 3232
	• 2 Garden Court	0171 353 1633
	• Goldsmith Building	0171 353 7881
	Goldsworth Chambers	0171 405 7117
	• 9 Gough Square	0171 353 5371
	• Gough Square Chambers	0171 353 0924

• Expanded entry in Part C

• Gray's Inn Chambers	0171 831 5344
• 1 Gray's Inn Square Chambers of the Baroness Scotland of Asthal QC	0171 405 3000
• 1 Gray's Inn Square	0171 405 8946
2 Gray's Inn Square Chambers	0171 242 0328/405 1317
• 3 Gray's Inn Square	0171 520 5600
• 4-5 Gray's Inn Square	0171 404 5252
6 Gray's Inn Square	0171 242 1052
10 - 11 Gray's Inn Square	0171 405 2576
100E Great Portland Street	0171 636 6323
• 1 Harcourt Buildings	0171 353 9421/0375
• 2 Harcourt Buildings	0171 583 9020
2 Harcourt Buildings	0171 353 2112/2817
• Hardwicke Building	0171 242 2523
• 1 Hare Court	0171 353 3982/5324
• One Hare Court	0171 353 3171
• 3 Hare Court	0171 353 7561

Harrow on the Hill
London

• Harrow-on-the-Hill Chambers	0181 423 7444
• Chambers of James Hunt QC	0171 421 8000
• John Street Chambers	0171 242 1911
• One King's Bench Walk	0171 936 1500
• 4 King's Bench Walk	0171 822 8822
• 6 King's Bench Walk	0171 583 0410
6 King's Bench Walk	0171 353 4931/583 0695
• 8 King's Bench Walk	0171 797 8888
• 9 King's Bench Walk	0171 353 7202/3909
The Chambers of Mr Ali Mohammad Azhar	0171 353 9564 (4 lines)
10 King's Bench Walk	0171 353 7742
11 King's Bench Walk	0171 353 3337/8
• 13 King's Bench Walk	0171 353 7204
Kingsway Chambers	07000 653529
• Lamb Building	0171 797 7788
Lion Court	0171 404 6565
• Littleton Chambers	0171 797 8600
• 1 Middle Temple Lane	0171 583 0659 (12 lines)
• Mitre Court Chambers	0171 353 9394
• Mitre House Chambers	0171 583 8233
• Monckton Chambers	0171 405 7211
• New Court	0171 583 5123
• 12 New Square	0171 419 1212
11 Old Square	0171 242 5022
• 2 Paper Buildings	0171 936 2611 (10 lines)
• 4 Paper Buildings	0171 353 3366/583 7155
5 Paper Buildings	0171 583 6117
Phoenix Chambers	0171 404 7888
• 1 Pump Court	0171 583 2012/353 4341
2 Pump Court	0171 353 5597
• Pump Court Chambers	0171 353 0711
• Chambers of Kieran Coonan QC	0171 583 6013/2510
6 Pump Court	0171 797 8400
• Queen Elizabeth Building	0171 353 7181 (12 lines)
• Queen Elizabeth Building	0171 583 5766
• 3 Raymond Buildings	0171 831 3833
• 18 Red Lion Court	0171 520 6000
Ridgeway Chambers	0181 455 2939
No 1 Serjeants' Inn	0171 415 6666
• Stanbrook & Henderson	0171 353 0101
• 9 Stone Buildings	0171 404 5055
11 Stone Buildings	+44 (0)171 831 6381
• 1 Temple Gardens	0171 353 0407/583 1315
• 3 Temple Gardens	0171 353 3102/5/9297
3 Temple Gardens (North)	0171 353 0853/4/7222
• Thomas More Chambers	0171 404 7000
Trafalgar Chambers	0171 583 5858

Manchester

• Central Chambers	0161 833 1774
• Cobden House Chambers	0161 833 6000/6001
Deans Court Chambers	0161 834 4097
• Chambers of John Hand QC	0161 955 9000
Kenworthy's Chambers	0161 832 4036
• 40 King Street	0161 832 9082
• 8 King Street Chambers	0161 834 9560

A

	58 King Street Chambers	0161 831 7477
	Lincoln House Chambers	0161 832 5701
	Chambers of Ian Macdonald QC	0161 236 1840
	Manchester House Chambers	0161 834 7007
	Peel Court Chambers	0161 832 3791
	• St James's Chambers	0161 834 7000
	18 St John Street	0161 278 1800
	• 28 St John Street	0161 834 8418
	Young Street Chambers	0161 833 0489
Middlesbrough	• Fountain Chambers	01642 217037
Norwich	East Anglian Chambers	01603 617351
Nottingham	No. 1 High Pavement Chambers	0115 941 8218
	St Mary's Chambers	0115 950 3503
Oxford	• King's Bench Chambers	01865 311066
Peterborough	Fenners Chambers	01733 562030
Plymouth	Devon Chambers	01752 661659
Preston	4 Camden Place	01772 828300
	Deans Court Chambers	01772 555163
	New Bailey Chambers	01772 258 087
	15 Winckley Square	01772 252 828
Reading	Dr Johnson's Chambers	01189 254221
Redhill	Redhill Chambers	01737 780781
Southampton	• 17 Carlton Crescent	01703 320320
Swansea	Angel Chambers	01792 464623/464648
	Gower Chambers	01792 644466
	Iscoed Chambers	01792 652988/9/330
Swindon	Pump Court Chambers	01793 539899
Winchester	Pump Court Chambers	01962 868161
Wolverhampton	Claremont Chambers	01902 426222

DEFAMATION

Birmingham	1 Fountain Court	0121 236 5721
	• 5 Fountain Court	0121 606 0500
Bristol	St John's Chambers	0117 921 3456/929 8514
Cardiff	30 Park Place	01222 398421
	32 Park Place	01222 397364
Chester	40 King Street	01244 323886
	White Friars Chambers	01244 323070
Leeds	11 King's Bench Walk	0113 2971 200
	The Chambers of Philip Raynor QC	0113 242 1123
Liverpool	25-27 Castle Street	0151 227 5661/5666/236 5072
	• The Corn Exchange Chambers	0151 227 1081/5009
	India Buildings Chambers	0151 243 6000
	• The Chambers of Adrian Lyon	0151 236 4421/8240/6757
London	Avondale Chambers	0181 445 9984
	Barristers' Common Law Chambers	0171 375 3012
	9 Bedford Row	0171 242 3555
	17 Bedford Row	0171 831 7314
	• Blackstone Chambers (formerly known as 2 Hare Court)	0171 583 1770
	1 Brick Court	0171 353 8845
	Brick Court Chambers	0171 583 0777
	Cloisters	0171 827 4000
	• 1 Crown Office Row	0171 797 7111
	1 Crown Office Row	0171 583 9292
	• Devereux Chambers	0171 353 7534
	• Doughty Street Chambers	0171 404 1313
	Equity Barristers' Chambers	0181 558 8336
	• One Essex Court	0171 936 3030
	• Farrar's Building	0171 583 9241
	• Chambers of Norman Palmer	0171 405 6114
	• 4 Field Court	0171 440 6900
	• Fountain Court	0171 583 3335
	Francis Taylor Buildings	0171 353 7768/2711
	• Goldsmith Building	0171 353 7881
	Goldsworth Chambers	0171 405 7117
	• 4-5 Gray's Inn Square	0171 404 5252
	• Hardwicke Building	0171 242 2523
Harrow on the Hill	• Harrow-on-the-Hill Chambers	0181 423 7444
London	• John Street Chambers	0171 242 1911
	• 9 King's Bench Walk	0171 353 7202/3909

A

	The Chambers of Mr Ali Mohammad Azhar	0171 353 9564 (4 lines)
	• 11 King's Bench Walk	0171 632 8500
	11 King's Bench Walk	0171 353 3337/8
	• 13 King's Bench Walk	0171 353 7204
	• Chambers of Lord Campbell of Alloway QC	0171 353 9276
	• Littleton Chambers	0171 797 8600
	2 Mitre Court Buildings	0171 353 1353
	• New Court	0171 797 8999
	• New Court Chambers	0171 831 9500
	5 Paper Buildings	0171 583 6117
	• 5 Raymond Buildings	0171 242 2902
	No 1 Serjeants' Inn	0171 415 6666
	• 3 Serjeants' Inn	0171 353 5537
	11 Stone Buildings	+44 (0)171 831 6381
	• Thomas More Chambers	0171 404 7000
	• 14 Tooks Court	0171 405 8828
Manchester	• Cobden House Chambers	0161 833 6000/6001
	• Chambers of John Hand QC	0161 955 9000
	Kenworthy's Chambers	0161 832 4036
	• 40 King Street	0161 832 9082
	Lincoln House Chambers	0161 832 5701
	• Queen's Chambers	0161 834 6875/4738
	• St James's Chambers	0161 834 7000
Newcastle upon Tyne	• Broad Chare	0191 232 0541
Norwich	East Anglian Chambers	01603 617351
Oxford	• King's Bench Chambers	01865 311066
Portsmouth	Hampshire Chambers	01705 826636
Preston	4 Camden Place	01772 828300
Sheffield	Paradise Square Chambers	0114 273 8951
Stoke-on-Trent	Regent Chambers	01782 286666

DESIGN

London	• 1 Raymond Buildings	0171 430 1234

DISCRIMINATION

Birmingham	• Equity Chambers	0121 233 2100
	1 Fountain Court	0121 236 5721
	• 5 Fountain Court	0121 606 0500
	• 8 Fountain Court	0121 236 5514
	• St Philip's Chambers	0121 246 7000
Bradford	Broadway House Chambers	01274 722560
Bristol	Old Square Chambers	0117 927 7111
	St John's Chambers	0117 921 3456/929 8514
Cambridge	• Fenners Chambers	01223 368761
Cardiff	30 Park Place	01222 398421
Chester	40 King Street	01244 323886
	White Friars Chambers	01244 323070
Coulsdon	Advolex Chambers	0181 763 2345
Durham City	Durham Barristers' Chambers	0191 386 9199
Eastbourne	King's Chambers	01323 416053
Exeter	Colleton Chambers	01392 274898
	Walnut House	01392 279751
Leeds	Chambers of Andrew Campbell QC	0113 245 5438
	The Chambers of Philip Raynor QC	0113 242 1123
	• Sovereign Chambers	0113 245 1841/2/3
Liverpool	25-27 Castle Street	0151 227 5661/5666/236 5072
	• The Corn Exchange Chambers	0151 227 1081/5009
	• The Chambers of Adrian Lyon	0151 236 4421/8240/6757
	• Peel House Chambers	0151 236 4321
London	Barnard's Inn Chambers	0171 242 8508
	Barristers' Common Law Chambers	0171 375 3012
	• 29 Bedford Row Chambers	0171 831 2626
	• 5 Bell Yard	0171 333 8811
	• Blackstone Chambers (formerly known as 2 Hare Court)	0171 583 1770
	11 Bolt Court	0171 353 2300
	• 4 Brick Court	0171 797 7766
	Bridewell Chambers	0171 797 8800
	Cloisters	0171 827 4000

• Expanded entry in Part C

A

	• Devereux Chambers	0171 353 7534
	• Doughty Street Chambers	0171 404 1313
	Equity Barristers' Chambers	0181 558 8336
	• Essex Court Chambers	0171 813 8000
	• 39 Essex Street	0171 832 1111
	• Chambers of Norman Palmer	0171 405 6114
	• 4 Field Court	0171 440 6900
	• Fountain Court	0171 583 3335
	• 2 Garden Court	0171 353 1633
	• Goldsmith Building	0171 353 7881
	• Gray's Inn Chambers	0171 831 5344
	• 1 Gray's Inn Square	0171 405 8946
	2 Gray's Inn Square Chambers	0171 242 0328/405 1317
	• 2-3 Gray's Inn Square	0171 242 4986
	• 4-5 Gray's Inn Square	0171 404 5252
	10 - 11 Gray's Inn Square	0171 405 2576
	• One Hare Court	0171 353 3171
Harrow on the Hill	• Harrow-on-the-Hill Chambers	0181 423 7444
London	• Chambers of James Hunt QC	0171 421 8000
	Justice Court Chambers	0181 830 7786
	6 King's Bench Walk	0171 353 4931/583 0695
	• 8 King's Bench Walk	0171 797 8888
	The Chambers of Mr Ali Mohammad Azhar	0171 353 9564 (4 lines)
	10 King's Bench Walk	0171 353 7742
	• 11 King's Bench Walk	0171 632 8500
	11 King's Bench Walk	0171 353 3337/8
	• Littleton Chambers	0171 797 8600
	• Littman Chambers	0171 404 4866
	• Mitre Court Chambers	0171 353 9394
	• Mitre House Chambers	0171 583 8233
	• New Court Chambers	0171 831 9500
	Chambers of Joy Okoye	0171 405 7011
	• Old Square Chambers	0171 269 0300
	• 4 Paper Buildings	0171 583 0816
	5 Paper Buildings	0171 583 6117
	• Chambers of John L Powell QC	0171 797 8000
	• 1 Pump Court	0171 583 2012/353 4341
	• 9 Stone Buildings	0171 404 5055
	3 Temple Gardens (North)	0171 353 0853/4/7222
	• Thomas More Chambers	0171 404 7000
	• 14 Tooks Court	0171 405 8828
Manchester	• Central Chambers	0161 833 1774
	• Chambers of John Hand QC	0161 955 9000
	• 40 King Street	0161 832 9082
	• 8 King Street Chambers	0161 834 9560
	Lincoln House Chambers	0161 832 5701
	Chambers of Ian Macdonald QC	0161 236 1840
	• Queen's Chambers	0161 834 6875/4738
	• St James's Chambers	0161 834 7000
Newcastle upon Tyne	Milburn House Chambers	0191 230 5511
Norwich	East Anglian Chambers	01603 617351
	Sackville Chambers	01603 613516
Peterborough	Fenners Chambers	01733 562030
Preston	4 Camden Place	01772 828300
	New Bailey Chambers	01772 258 087
Redhill	Redhill Chambers	01737 780781
Swansea	Angel Chambers	01792 464623/464648
Wolverhampton	Claremont Chambers	01902 426222

EC AND COMPETITION LAW

Birmingham	1 Fountain Court	0121 236 5721
	• 5 Fountain Court	0121 606 0500
	• St Philip's Chambers	0121 246 7000
Bournemouth	20 Lorne Park Road	01202 292102
Bristol	Old Square Chambers	0117 927 7111
	St John's Chambers	0117 921 3456/929 8514
Coulsdon	Advolex Chambers	0181 763 2345
Exeter	Rougemont Chambers	01392 410471
Guildford	• Guildford Chambers	01483 539131
Haverhill	Helions Chambers	01440 730523
Leeds	• Chancery House Chambers	0113 244 6691

• Expanded entry in Part C

A

London	The Chambers of Philip Raynor QC	0113 242 1123
	• Sovereign Chambers	0113 245 1841/2/3
	• Arden Chambers	0171 242 4244
	• 29 Bedford Row Chambers	0171 831 2626
	• 5 Bell Yard	0171 333 8811
	• Blackstone Chambers (formerly known as 2 Hare Court)	0171 583 1770
	11 Bolt Court	0171 353 2300
	• 4 Breams Buildings	0171 353 5835/430 1221
	• 4 Brick Court	0171 797 8910
	• 4 Brick Court	0171 797 7766
	Brick Court Chambers	0171 583 0777
	Cloisters	0171 827 4000
	Equity Barristers' Chambers	0181 558 8336
	• One Essex Court	0171 583 2000
	• 4 Essex Court	0171 797 7970
	• Essex Court Chambers	0171 813 8000
	• 20 Essex Street	0171 583 9294
	• 39 Essex Street	0171 832 1111
	Falcon Chambers	0171 353 2484
	• 4 Field Court	0171 440 6900
	Francis Taylor Buildings	0171 353 7768/2711
	• 2 Garden Court	0171 353 1633
	• 4-5 Gray's Inn Square	0171 404 5252
	10 - 11 Gray's Inn Square	0171 405 2576
	• 1 Harcourt Buildings	0171 353 9421/0375
	• One Hare Court	0171 353 3171
	Chambers of Harjit Singh	0171 353 1356
	• Keating Chambers	0171 544 2600
	• 4 King's Bench Walk	0171 822 8822
	4 King's Bench Walk	0171 353 3581
	The Chambers of Mr Ali Mohammad Azhar	0171 353 9564 (4 lines)
	10 King's Bench Walk	0171 353 7742
	• 11 King's Bench Walk	0171 632 8500
	Lamb Chambers	0171 797 8300
	• Littleton Chambers	0171 797 8600
	• Littman Chambers	0171 404 4866
	• Mitre House Chambers	0171 583 8233
	• Monckton Chambers	0171 405 7211
	5 New Square	0171 404 0404
	• 8 New Square	0171 405 4321
	19 Old Buildings	0171 405 2001
	24 Old Buildings	0171 242 2744
	The Chambers of Leolin Price CBE, QC	0171 405 0758/242 5002
	• 13 Old Square	0171 404 4800
	• Old Square Chambers	0171 269 0300
	• 3 Paper Buildings	0171 583 8055
	• 4 Paper Buildings	0171 353 3366/583 7155
	• 5 Paper Buildings	0171 583 9275
	Prince Henry's Chambers	0171 353 1183/1190
	• 5 Pump Court	0171 353 2532
	• 1 Raymond Buildings	0171 430 1234
	No 1 Serjeants' Inn	0171 415 6666
	• 9 Stone Buildings	0171 404 5055
	• 2 Temple Gardens	0171 583 6041
	• 3 Verulam Buildings	0171 831 8441
	Verulam Chambers	0171 813 2400
	Warwick House Chambers	0171 430 2323
Manchester	• 40 King Street	0161 832 9082
	• 8 King Street Chambers	0161 834 9560
	Peel Court Chambers	0161 832 3791
	• 28 St John Street	0161 834 8418
Norwich	East Anglian Chambers	01603 617351
Oxford	1 Alfred Street	01865 793736
Preston	New Bailey Chambers	01772 258 087
Redhill	Redhill Chambers	01737 780781
Richmond-upon-Thames	Richmond Green Chambers	0181 940 1841
Winchester	4 St Peter Street	01962 868 884

• Expanded entry in Part C

EC LAW

Cardiff	30 Park Place	01222 398421
London	• 2 Harcourt Buildings	0171 353 8415

A

ECCLESIASTICAL

Birmingham	1 Fountain Court	0121 236 5721
Bournemouth	20 Lorne Park Road	01202 292102
Bristol	St John's Chambers	0117 921 3456/929 8514
Durham City	Durham Barristers' Chambers	0191 386 9199
Leeds	• 30 Park Square	0113 243 6388
Liverpool	• The Chambers of Adrian Lyon	0151 236 4421/8240/6757
London	• 4 Breams Buildings	0171 353 5835/430 1221
	Francis Taylor Buildings	0171 353 7768/2711
	• 1 Gray's Inn Square	0171 405 8946
	• 2 Harcourt Buildings	0171 583 9020
	• 2 Harcourt Buildings	0171 353 8415
	• Harcourt Chambers	0171 353 6961/7
	• Mitre Court Chambers	0171 353 9394
	• Twenty-Four Old Buildings	0171 404 0946
	The Chambers of Leolin Price CBE, QC	0171 405 0758/242 5002
	11 Old Square	0171 242 5022
	• 11 Old Square	0171 430 0341
	• 3 Paper Buildings	0171 583 8055
	5 Paper Buildings	0171 583 6117
	• Pump Court Chambers	0171 353 0711
	• Stanbrook & Henderson	0171 353 0101
	8 Stone Buildings	0171 831 9881
Manchester	• Chambers of John Hand QC	0161 955 9000
Newcastle upon Tyne	• Broad Chare	0191 232 0541
	• New Court Chambers	0191 232 1980
Oxford	1 Alfred Street	01865 793736
	28 Western Road	01865 204911
Swindon	Pump Court Chambers	01793 539899
Winchester	Pump Court Chambers	01962 868161
	4 St Peter Street	01962 868 884
Winkleigh	Barnstaple Chambers	0183 783763

EDUCATION

Birmingham	• Equity Chambers	0121 233 2100
	1 Fountain Court	0121 236 5721
	• 3 Fountain Court	0121 236 5854
	• 5 Fountain Court	0121 606 0500
	• St Philip's Chambers	0121 246 7000
Bristol	Old Square Chambers	0117 927 7111
	St John's Chambers	0117 921 3456/929 8514
Cardiff	30 Park Place	01222 398421
Chesterfield	26 Morley Avenue	01246 234790
Durham City	Durham Barristers' Chambers	0191 386 9199
Guildford	• Guildford Chambers	01483 539131
Leeds	• Chancery House Chambers	0113 244 6691
	The Chambers of Philip Raynor QC	0113 242 1123
Liverpool	25-27 Castle Street	0151 227 5661/5666/236 5072
	• The Chambers of Adrian Lyon	0151 236 4421/8240/6757
London	9 Bedford Row	0171 242 3555
	• 29 Bedford Row Chambers	0171 831 2626
	11 Bolt Court	0171 353 2300
	• 4 Breams Buildings	0171 353 5835/430 1221
	• 4 Brick Court	0171 797 7766
	Bridewell Chambers	0171 797 8800
	Cloisters	0171 827 4000
	• Devereux Chambers	0171 353 7534
	• Doughty Street Chambers	0171 404 1313
	Equity Barristers' Chambers	0181 558 8336
	• 39 Essex Street	0171 832 1111
	Chambers of Geoffrey Hawker	0171 583 8899
	• Chambers of Norman Palmer	0171 405 6114
	One Garden Court Family Law Chambers	0171 797 7900
	• 2 Garden Court	0171 353 1633
	• Goldsmith Building	0171 353 7881

• Expanded entry in Part C

	Goldsworth Chambers	0171 405 7117
	• Gray's Inn Chambers	0171 404 1111
	• 4-5 Gray's Inn Square	0171 404 5252
	10 - 11 Gray's Inn Square	0171 405 2576
	• 2 Harcourt Buildings	0171 583 9020
	• 2 Harcourt Buildings	0171 353 8415
	• Harcourt Chambers	0171 353 6961/7
	• One Hare Court	0171 353 3171
Harrow on the Hill	• Harrow-on-the-Hill Chambers	0181 423 7444
London	Justice Court Chambers	0181 830 7786
	• One King's Bench Walk	0171 936 1500
	6 King's Bench Walk	0171 353 4931/583 0695
	• 8 King's Bench Walk	0171 797 8888
	The Chambers of Mr Ali Mohammad Azhar	0171 353 9564 (4 lines)
	• 11 King's Bench Walk	0171 632 8500
	• Chambers of Lord Campbell of Alloway QC	0171 353 9276
	• Littleton Chambers	0171 797 8600
	2 Mitre Court Buildings	0171 583 1380
	• Mitre House Chambers	0171 583 8233
	Chambers of Joy Okoye	0171 405 7011
	• 22 Old Buildings	0171 831 0222
	The Chambers of Leolin Price CBE, QC	0171 405 0758/242 5002
	11 Old Square	0171 242 5022
	• Old Square Chambers	0171 269 0300
	Phoenix Chambers	0171 404 7888
	• Chambers of John L Powell QC	0171 797 8000
	• 1 Pump Court	0171 583 2012/353 4341
	• Queen Elizabeth Building	0171 353 7181 (12 lines)
	No 1 Serjeants' Inn	0171 415 6666
	• 3 Temple Gardens	0171 353 3102/5/9297
	• 14 Tooks Court	0171 405 8828
Manchester	• Central Chambers	0161 833 1774
	Kenworthy's Chambers	0161 832 4036
	• 40 King Street	0161 832 9082
	• 8 King Street Chambers	0161 834 9560
	Chambers of Ian Macdonald QC	0161 236 1840
	• St James's Chambers	0161 834 7000
	Young Street Chambers	0161 833 0489
Norwich	East Anglian Chambers	01603 617351
Nottingham	Ropewalk Chambers	0115 947 2581
Redhill	Redhill Chambers	01737 780781
Slough	11 St Bernards Road	01753 553806/817989
Southampton	• 17 Carlton Crescent	01703 320320
York	• York Chambers	01904 620 048

EMPLOYMENT

Birmingham	• Equity Chambers	0121 233 2100
	1 Fountain Court	0121 236 5721
	• 3 Fountain Court	0121 236 5854
	• 5 Fountain Court	0121 606 0500
	6 Fountain Court	0121 233 3282
	• 8 Fountain Court	0121 236 5514
	New Court Chambers	0121 693 6656
	• St Philip's Chambers	0121 246 7000
Bournemouth	King's Bench Chambers	01202 250025
	20 Lorne Park Road	01202 292102
Bradford	Broadway House Chambers	01274 722560
Brighton	• Crown Office Row Chambers	01273 625625
Bristol	Assize Court Chambers	0117 926 4587
	Old Square Chambers	0117 927 7111
	St John's Chambers	0117 921 3456/929 8514
Cambridge	• Fenners Chambers	01223 368761
	Regency Chambers	01223 301517
Cardiff	9 Park Place	01222 382731
	30 Park Place	01222 398421
	32 Park Place	01222 397364
	• 33 Park Place	01222 233313
Chester	40 King Street	01244 323886
	White Friars Chambers	01244 323070
Chichester	Chichester Chambers	01243 784538

Coulsdon	Advolex Chambers	0181 763 2345
Durham City	Durham Barristers' Chambers	0191 386 9199
Eastbourne	King's Chambers	01323 416053
Ely	Cathedral Chambers, Ely	01353 666775
Exeter	• Cathedral Chambers (Jan Wood Independent Barristers' Clerk)	01392 210900
	Colleton Chambers	01392 274898
	Rougemont Chambers	01392 410471
	Walnut House	01392 279751
Guildford	• Guildford Chambers	01483 539131
Haverhill	Helions Chambers	01440 730523
Leatherhead	Pembroke House	01372 376160/376493
Leeds	Chambers of Andrew Campbell QC	0113 245 5438
	• Chancery House Chambers	0113 244 6691
	Enterprise Chambers	0113 246 0391
	11 King's Bench Walk	0113 2971 200
	• Mercury Chambers	0113 234 2265
	• No. 6	0113 245 9763
	The Chambers of Philip Raynor QC	0113 242 1123
	• 30 Park Square	0113 243 6388
	• 37 Park Square	0113 243 9422
	• Sovereign Chambers	0113 245 1841/2/3
	• St Paul's House	0113 245 5866
	• 9 Woodhouse Square	0113 245 1986
Liverpool	25-27 Castle Street	0151 227 5661/5666/236 5072
	19 Castle Street Chambers	0151 236 9402
	Chavasse Court Chambers	0151 707 1191
	• The Corn Exchange Chambers	0151 227 1081/5009
	• Exchange Chambers	0151 236 7747
	First National Chambers	0151 236 2098
	India Buildings Chambers	0151 243 6000
	• The Chambers of Adrian Lyon	0151 236 4421/8240/6757
	• Martins Building	0151 236 5818/4919
	• Oriel Chambers	0151 236 7191
	• Peel House Chambers	0151 236 4321
London	Albany Chambers	0171 485 5736/38
	Avondale Chambers	0181 445 9984
	Barnard's Inn Chambers	0171 242 8508
	Barristers' Common Law Chambers	0171 375 3012
	9 Bedford Row	0171 242 3555
	17 Bedford Row	0171 831 7314
	33 Bedford Row	0171 242 6476
	• 29 Bedford Row Chambers	0171 831 2626
	• 5 Bell Yard	0171 333 8811
	• Blackstone Chambers (formerly known as 2 Hare Court)	0171 583 1770
	11 Bolt Court	0171 353 2300
	• Bracton Chambers	0171 242 4248
	• 4 Breams Buildings	0171 353 5835/430 1221
	• 4 Brick Court	0171 797 7766
	Brick Court Chambers	0171 583 0777
	Bridewell Chambers	0171 797 8800
	Britton Street Chambers	0171 608 3765
	Cloisters	0171 827 4000
	1 Crown Office Row	0171 583 9292
	• Devereux Chambers	0171 353 7534
	• Doughty Street Chambers	0171 404 1313
	• Dr Johnson's Chambers	0171 353 4716
	• Enterprise Chambers	0171 405 9471
	Equity Barristers' Chambers	0181 558 8336
	• One Essex Court	0171 936 3030
	• 4 Essex Court	0171 797 7970
	• Essex Court Chambers	0171 813 8000
	23 Essex Street	0171 413 0353
	• 35 Essex Street	0171 353 6381
	• 39 Essex Street	0171 832 1111
	Chambers of Geoffrey Hawker	0171 583 8899
	• Farrar's Building	0171 583 9241
	• Chambers of Norman Palmer	0171 405 6114
	• 4 Field Court	0171 440 6900
	• Fountain Court	0171 583 3335
	• 2nd Floor, Francis Taylor Building	0171 353 9942

• Expanded entry in Part C

Francis Taylor Buildings	0171 353 7768/2711
• 2 Garden Court	0171 353 1633
• Goldsmith Building	0171 353 7881
Goldsworth Chambers	0171 405 7117
• Gough Square Chambers	0171 353 0924
• Gray's Inn Chambers	0171 831 5344
• 1 Gray's Inn Square	0171 405 8946
2 Gray's Inn Square Chambers	0171 242 0328/405 1317
• 2-3 Gray's Inn Square	0171 242 4986
• 4-5 Gray's Inn Square	0171 404 5252
6 Gray's Inn Square	0171 242 1052
10 - 11 Gray's Inn Square	0171 405 2576
• 1 Harcourt Buildings	0171 353 9421/0375
• 2 Harcourt Buildings	0171 583 9020
• Harcourt Chambers	0171 353 6961/7
• Hardwicke Building	0171 242 2523
Chambers of Harjit Singh	0171 353 1356
• Harrow-on-the-Hill Chambers	0181 423 7444
• Chambers of James Hunt QC	0171 421 8000
Justice Court Chambers	0181 830 7786
• 4 King's Bench Walk	0171 822 8822
4 King's Bench Walk	0171 353 3581
6 King's Bench Walk	0171 353 4931/583 0695
• 8 King's Bench Walk	0171 797 8888
• 9 King's Bench Walk	0171 353 7202/3909
The Chambers of Mr Ali Mohammad Azhar	0171 353 9564 (4 lines)
10 King's Bench Walk	0171 353 7742
• 11 King's Bench Walk	0171 632 8500
11 King's Bench Walk	0171 353 3337/8
• 12 King's Bench Walk	0171 583 0811
• 13 King's Bench Walk	0171 353 7204
• Chambers of Lord Campbell of Alloway QC	0171 353 9276
• Lamb Building	0171 797 7788
Lamb Chambers	0171 797 8300
Library Chambers	0171 404 6500
• Littleton Chambers	0171 797 8600
• Littman Chambers	0171 404 4866
2 Mitre Court Buildings	0171 353 1353
2 Mitre Court Buildings	0171 583 1380
• Mitre Court Chambers	0171 353 9394
• Mitre House Chambers	0171 583 8233
• Monckton Chambers	0171 405 7211
• New Court	0171 583 5123
• New Court Chambers	0171 831 9500
• 1 New Square	0171 405 0884/5/6/7
5 New Square	0171 404 0404
Chambers of Joy Okoye	0171 405 7011
• 22 Old Buildings	0171 831 0222
The Chambers of Leolin Price CBE, QC	0171 405 0758/242 5002
11 Old Square	0171 242 5022
• Old Square Chambers	0171 269 0300
• 2 Paper Buildings	0171 353 0933
2 Paper Buildings, Basement North	0171 936 2613
• 3 Paper Buildings	0171 797 7000
• 3 Paper Buildings	0171 583 8055
• 4 Paper Buildings	0171 353 3366/583 7155
• 4 Paper Buildings	0171 583 0816
Pepys' Chambers	0171 936 2710
Phoenix Chambers	0171 404 7888
Plowden Buildings	0171 583 0808
• Chambers of John L Powell QC	0171 797 8000
• 1 Pump Court	0171 583 2012/353 4341
2 Pump Court	0171 353 5597
• Pump Court Chambers	0171 353 0711
• 4 Pump Court	0171 353 2656/9
• 5 Pump Court	0171 353 2532
• Chambers of Kieran Coonan QC	0171 583 6013/2510
No 1 Serjeants' Inn	0171 415 6666
• 3 Serjeants' Inn	0171 353 5537
• Stanbrook & Henderson	0171 353 0101

**Harrow on the Hill
London**

• Expanded entry in Part C

	7 Stone Buildings	0171 242 0961
	8 Stone Buildings	0171 831 9881
	• 9 Stone Buildings	0171 404 5055
	11 Stone Buildings	+44 (0)171 831 6381
	• 199 Strand	0171 379 9779
	169 Temple Chambers	0171 583 7644
	• 1 Temple Gardens	0171 353 0407/583 1315
	• 2 Temple Gardens	0171 583 6041
	• 3 Temple Gardens	0171 353 3102/5/9297
	3 Temple Gardens (North)	0171 353 0853/4/7222
	• Thomas More Chambers	0171 404 7000
	• 14 Tooks Court	0171 405 8828
	Trafalgar Chambers	0171 583 5858
	• 3 Verulam Buildings	0171 831 8441
	Verulam Chambers	0171 813 2400
	Warwick House Chambers	0171 430 2323
	39 Windsor Road	0181 349 9194
Maidstone	Earl Street Chambers	01622 671222
	• Maidstone Chambers	01622 688592
Manchester	• Central Chambers	0161 833 1774
	• Cobden House Chambers	0161 833 6000/6001
	Deans Court Chambers	0161 834 4097
	• Chambers of John Hand QC	0161 955 9000
	Kenworthy's Chambers	0161 832 4036
	• 40 King Street	0161 832 9082
	• 8 King Street Chambers	0161 834 9560
	58 King Street Chambers	0161 831 7477
	Lincoln House Chambers	0161 832 5701
	Chambers of Ian Macdonald QC	0161 236 1840
	Manchester House Chambers	0161 834 7007
	• Merchant Chambers	0161 839 7070
	Peel Court Chambers	0161 832 3791
	• Queen's Chambers	0161 834 6875/4738
	• St James's Chambers	0161 834 7000
	• 28 St John Street	0161 834 8418
Middlesbrough	Baker Street Chambers	01642 873873
	• Fountain Chambers	01642 217037
	York House	01642 213000
Newcastle upon Tyne	• Broad Chare	0191 232 0541
	Cathedral Chambers	0191 232 1311
	Enterprise Chambers	0191 222 3344
	Milburn House Chambers	0191 230 5511
	• New Court Chambers	0191 232 1980
	• Trinity Chambers	0191 232 1927
	Westgate Chambers	0191 261 4407/232 9785
Northampton	22 Albion Place	01604 636271
	Chartlands Chambers	01604 603322
Norwich	East Anglian Chambers	01603 617351
	Octagon House	01603 623186
	Sackville Chambers	01603 613516
Nottingham	King Charles House	0115 941 8851
	Ropewalk Chambers	0115 947 2581
	St Mary's Chambers	0115 950 3503
Oxford	1 Alfred Street	01865 793736
	• King's Bench Chambers	01865 311066
Peterborough	Fenners Chambers	01733 562030
	Regency Chambers	01733 315215
Plymouth	Devon Chambers	01752 661659
Portsmouth	Hampshire Chambers	01705 826636
	• Portsmouth Barristers' Chambers	01705 831292
Preston	4 Camden Place	01772 828300
	Deans Court Chambers	01772 555163
	New Bailey Chambers	01772 258 087
	15 Winckley Square	01772 252 828
Reading	Dr Johnson's Chambers	01189 254221
	Wessex Chambers	0118 956 8856
Redhill	Redhill Chambers	01737 780781
Richmond-upon-Thames	Richmond Green Chambers	0181 940 1841
Sheffield	Paradise Square Chambers	0114 273 8951
Shepperton	Abbey Chambers	01932 560913
Slough	11 St Bernards Road	01753 553806/817989
Southampton	• 17 Carlton Crescent	01703 320320

• Expanded entry in Part C

A

	• College Chambers	01703 230338
	• Eighteen Carlton Crescent	01703 639001
Stoke-on-Trent	Regent Chambers	01782 286666
Swansea	Angel Chambers	01792 464623/464648
	Gower Chambers	01792 644466
	Iscoed Chambers	01792 652988/9/330
	Pendragon Chambers	01792 411188
Corsham	Neston Home Chambers	01225 811909
Swindon	Pump Court Chambers	01793 539899
Winchester	Pump Court Chambers	01962 868161
	4 St Peter Street	01962 868 884
Wolverhampton	Claremont Chambers	01902 426222
York	• York Chambers	01904 620 048

ENERGY

Bristol	St John's Chambers	0117 921 3456/929 8514
London	Atkin Chambers	0171 404 0102
	• Blackstone Chambers (formerly known as 2 Hare Court)	0171 583 1770
	• 4 Breams Buildings	0171 353 5835/430 1221
	• One Essex Court	0171 583 2000
	• Essex Court Chambers	0171 813 8000
	• 20 Essex Street	0171 583 9294
	• 39 Essex Street	0171 832 1111
	• Fountain Court	0171 583 3335
	Francis Taylor Buildings	0171 353 7768/2711
	• 2 Harcourt Buildings	0171 353 8415
	• Hardwicke Building	0171 242 2523
	• One Hare Court	0171 353 3171
	S Tomlinson QC	0171 583 0404
	The Chambers of Mr Ali Mohammad Azhar	0171 353 9564 (4 lines)
	• Littman Chambers	0171 404 4866
	2 Mitre Court Buildings	0171 583 1380
	• 9 Old Square	0171 405 4682
	1 Serjeants' Inn	0171 583 1355
	• 7 Stone Buildings	0171 405 3886/242 3546
Nottingham	Ropewalk Chambers	0115 947 2581
Swansea	Iscoed Chambers	01792 652988/9/330

ENTERTAINMENT

Birmingham	• Equity Chambers	0121 233 2100
	• 5 Fountain Court	0121 606 0500
	• St Philip's Chambers	0121 246 7000
Leicester	2 New Street	0116 262 5906
London	17 Bedford Row	0171 831 7314
	• 29 Bedford Row Chambers	0171 831 2626
	• 5 Bell Yard	0171 333 8811
	• Blackstone Chambers (formerly known as 2 Hare Court)	0171 583 1770
	11 Bolt Court	0171 353 2300
	Brick Court Chambers	0171 583 0777
	Bridewell Chambers	0171 797 8800
	Cloisters	0171 827 4000
	• 1 Crown Office Row	0171 797 7111
	1 Crown Office Row	0171 583 9292
	• 4 Essex Court	0171 797 7970
	• Essex Court Chambers	0171 813 8000
	• 39 Essex Street	0171 832 1111
	• Chambers of Norman Palmer	0171 405 6114
	• 4 Field Court	0171 440 6900
	• Fountain Court	0171 583 3335
	Francis Taylor Buildings	0171 353 7768/2711
	Goldsworth Chambers	0171 405 7117
	• Gough Square Chambers	0171 353 0924
	• 1 Gray's Inn Square Chambers of the Baroness Scotland of Asthal QC	0171 405 3000
	• Hardwicke Building	0171 242 2523
	• One Hare Court	0171 353 3171
	The Chambers of Mr Ali Mohammad Azhar	0171 353 9564 (4 lines)

• Expanded entry in Part C

	• 11 King's Bench Walk	0171 632 8500
	Lion Court	0171 404 6565
	• Littleton Chambers	0171 797 8600
	• New Court	0171 797 8999
	• 1 New Square	0171 405 0884/5/6/7
	• 3 New Square	0171 405 1111
	5 New Square	0171 404 0404
	• 8 New Square	0171 405 4321
	• 12 New Square	0171 419 1212
	19 Old Buildings	0171 405 2001
	• Twenty-Four Old Buildings	0171 404 0946
	The Chambers of Leolin Price CBE, QC	0171 405 0758/242 5002
	• 4 Paper Buildings	0171 353 3366/583 7155
	5 Paper Buildings	0171 583 6117
	Phoenix Chambers	0171 404 7888
	• 4 Pump Court	0171 353 2656/9
	• 1 Raymond Buildings	0171 430 1234
	• 5 Raymond Buildings	0171 242 2902
	No 1 Serjeants' Inn	0171 415 6666
	• 3 Stone Buildings	0171 242 4937/405 8358
	• 7 Stone Buildings	0171 405 3886/242 3546
	7 Stone Buildings	0171 242 0961
	• 9 Stone Buildings	0171 404 5055
	11 Stone Buildings	+44 (0)171 831 6381
	• 3 Verulam Buildings	0171 831 8441
	Verulam Chambers	0171 813 2400
Redhill	Redhill Chambers	01737 780781
Wolverhampton	Claremont Chambers	01902 426222

ENVIRONMENT

Birmingham	1 Fountain Court	0121 236 5721
	• 3 Fountain Court	0121 236 5854
	• 5 Fountain Court	0121 606 0500
	• St Philip's Chambers	0121 246 7000
Bournemouth	King's Bench Chambers	01202 250025
Bradford	Broadway House Chambers	01274 722560
Bristol	Old Square Chambers	0117 927 7111
	St John's Chambers	0117 921 3456/929 8514
Cambridge	• Fenners Chambers	01223 368761
Cardiff	9 Park Place	01222 382731
	30 Park Place	01222 398421
	• 33 Park Place	01222 233313
Chesterfield	26 Morley Avenue	01246 234790
Durham City	Durham Barristers' Chambers	0191 386 9199
Exeter	Colleton Chambers	01392 274898
	Rougemont Chambers	01392 410471
	Walnut House	01392 279751
Leeds	Chambers of Andrew Campbell QC	0113 245 5438
	11 King's Bench Walk	0113 2971 200
	• No. 6	0113 245 9763
	The Chambers of Philip Raynor QC	0113 242 1123
	• Sovereign Chambers	0113 245 1841/2/3
	• 9 Woodhouse Square	0113 245 1986
Liverpool	• The Corn Exchange Chambers	0151 227 1081/5009
	• Exchange Chambers	0151 236 7747
	• Oriel Chambers	0151 236 7191
London	• Arden Chambers	0171 242 4244
	Atkin Chambers	0171 404 0102
	Barnard's Inn Chambers	0171 242 8508
	9 Bedford Row	0171 242 3555
	• 29 Bedford Row Chambers	0171 831 2626
	• Blackstone Chambers (formerly known as 2 Hare Court)	0171 583 1770
	11 Bolt Court	0171 353 2300
	• 4 Breams Buildings	0171 353 5835/430 1221
	• 4 Brick Court	0171 797 7766
	Brick Court Chambers	0171 583 0777
	• Chambers of Mr Peter Crampin QC	0171 831 0081
	• 1 Crown Office Row	0171 797 7500
	• Devereux Chambers	0171 353 7534
	• Doughty Street Chambers	0171 404 1313
	• 4 Essex Court	0171 797 7970

• Expanded entry in Part C

• Essex Court Chambers	0171 813 8000
• 20 Essex Street	0171 583 9294
23 Essex Street	0171 413 0353
• 39 Essex Street	0171 832 1111
• 4 Field Court	0171 440 6900
• 2 Garden Court	0171 353 1633
• Goldsmith Building	0171 353 7881
• 1 Gray's Inn Square Chambers of the Baroness Scotland of Asthal QC	0171 405 3000
• 2-3 Gray's Inn Square	0171 242 4986
• 4-5 Gray's Inn Square	0171 404 5252
10 - 11 Gray's Inn Square	0171 405 2576
• 1 Harcourt Buildings	0171 353 9421/0375
• 2 Harcourt Buildings	0171 583 9020
2 Harcourt Buildings	0171 353 2112/2817
• 2 Harcourt Buildings	0171 353 8415
• One Hare Court	0171 353 3171
• Chambers of James Hunt QC	0171 421 8000
• One King's Bench Walk	0171 936 1500
• 4 King's Bench Walk	0171 822 8822
• 8 King's Bench Walk	0171 797 8888
The Chambers of Mr Ali Mohammad Azhar	0171 353 9564 (4 lines)
10 King's Bench Walk	0171 353 7742
• 11 King's Bench Walk	0171 632 8500
• 12 King's Bench Walk	0171 583 0811
Lamb Chambers	0171 797 8300
Library Chambers	0171 404 6500
• Littman Chambers	0171 404 4866
2 Mitre Court Buildings	0171 583 1380
• Mitre House Chambers	0171 583 8233
• Monckton Chambers	0171 405 7211
• 3 New Square	0171 405 1111
• 12 New Square	0171 419 1212
• 22 Old Buildings	0171 831 0222
• 9 Old Square	0171 405 4682
• Old Square Chambers	0171 269 0300
5 Paper Buildings	0171 583 6117
• Chambers of John L Powell QC	0171 797 8000
• 1 Pump Court	0171 583 2012/353 4341
• Pump Court Chambers	0171 353 0711
• 4 Pump Court	0171 353 2656/9
• 5 Pump Court	0171 353 2532
6 Pump Court	0171 797 8400
• 3 Raymond Buildings	0171 831 3833
1 Serjeants' Inn	0171 583 1355
• 3 Serjeants' Inn	0171 353 5537
• Stanbrook & Henderson	0171 353 0101
7 Stone Buildings	0171 242 0961
11 Stone Buildings	+44 (0)171 831 6381
• 199 Strand	0171 379 9779
• 2 Temple Gardens	0171 583 6041
• 3 Temple Gardens	0171 353 3102/5/9297
• 3 Verulam Buildings	0171 831 8441

Maidstone	• Maidstone Chambers	01622 688592
Manchester	• Cobden House Chambers	0161 833 6000/6001
	Deans Court Chambers	0161 834 4097
	• Chambers of John Hand QC	0161 955 9000
	• 40 King Street	0161 832 9082
	• 8 King Street Chambers	0161 834 9560
	Lincoln House Chambers	0161 832 5701
	Chambers of Ian Macdonald QC	0161 236 1840
	• St James's Chambers	0161 834 7000
	• 28 St John Street	0161 834 8418
Middlesbrough	• Fountain Chambers	01642 217037
Newcastle upon Tyne	• Broad Chare	0191 232 0541
Norwich	East Anglian Chambers	01603 617351
Nottingham	Ropewalk Chambers	0115 947 2581
Peterborough	Fenners Chambers	01733 562030
Preston	4 Camden Place	01772 828300
	Deans Court Chambers	01772 555163
	New Bailey Chambers	01772 258 087

• Expanded entry in Part C

A

Reading	Dr Johnson's Chambers	01189 254221
Redhill	Redhill Chambers	01737 780781
Richmond-upon-Thames	Richmond Green Chambers	0181 940 1841
Slough	11 St Bernards Road	01753 553806/817989
Southampton	• 17 Carlton Crescent	01703 320320
	• College Chambers	01703 230338
Swansea	Angel Chambers	01792 464623/464648
	Gower Chambers	01792 644466
	Iscoed Chambers	01792 652988/9/330
	Pendragon Chambers	01792 411188
Swindon	Pump Court Chambers	01793 539899
Winchester	Pump Court Chambers	01962 868161
Wolverhampton	Claremont Chambers	01902 426222
York	• York Chambers	01904 620 048

EQUITY, WILLS AND TRUSTS

Birmingham	• Equity Chambers	0121 233 2100
	1 Fountain Court	0121 236 5721
	• 3 Fountain Court	0121 236 5854
	• 5 Fountain Court	0121 606 0500
	• 8 Fountain Court	0121 236 5514
	• St Philip's Chambers	0121 246 7000
Bradford	Broadway House Chambers	01274 722560
Bristol	St John's Chambers	0117 921 3456/929 8514
Cambridge	• Fenners Chambers	01223 368761
	Regency Chambers	01223 301517
Cardiff	9 Park Place	01222 382731
	30 Park Place	01222 398421
	• 33 Park Place	01222 233313
Chester	White Friars Chambers	01244 323070
Chichester	Chichester Chambers	01243 784538
Eastbourne	King's Chambers	01323 416053
Exeter	Southernhay Chambers	01392 255777
Leeds	Chambers of Andrew Campbell QC	0113 245 5438
	• Chancery House Chambers	0113 244 6691
	Enterprise Chambers	0113 246 0391
	11 King's Bench Walk	0113 2971 200
	• No. 6	0113 245 9763
	The Chambers of Philip Raynor QC	0113 242 1123
	• 9 Woodhouse Square	0113 245 1986
Liverpool	• Exchange Chambers	0151 236 7747
	First National Chambers	0151 236 2098
	• The Chambers of Adrian Lyon	0151 236 4421/8240/6757
London	Barnard's Inn Chambers	0171 242 8508
	• 29 Bedford Row Chambers	0171 831 2626
	11 Bolt Court	0171 353 2300
	• Bracton Chambers	0171 242 4248
	• 4 Breams Buildings	0171 353 5835/430 1221
	Bridewell Chambers	0171 797 8800
	• Chambers of Mr Peter Crampin QC	0171 831 0081
	• Enterprise Chambers	0171 405 9471
	Equity Barristers' Chambers	0181 558 8336
	• One Essex Court	0171 936 3030
	Chambers of Geoffrey Hawker	0171 583 8899
	• Chambers of Norman Palmer	0171 405 6114
	• 2nd Floor, Francis Taylor Building	0171 353 9942
	Francis Taylor Buildings	0171 353 7768/2711
	Gray's Inn Square	0171 242 3529
	10 - 11 Gray's Inn Square	0171 405 2576
	• 1 Harcourt Buildings	0171 353 9421/0375
	• 2 Harcourt Buildings	0171 583 9020
	• Harcourt Chambers	0171 353 6961/7
	• Hardwicke Building	0171 242 2523
Harrow on the Hill	• Harrow-on-the-Hill Chambers	0181 423 7444
London	Justice Court Chambers	0181 830 7786
	• 9 King's Bench Walk	0171 353 7202/3909
	The Chambers of Mr Ali Mohammad Azhar	0171 353 9564 (4 lines)
	10 King's Bench Walk	0171 353 7742
	11 King's Bench Walk	0171 353 3337/8
	• Lamb Building	0171 797 7788
	Lamb Chambers	0171 797 8300

• Expanded entry in Part C

	Lion Court	0171 404 6565
	• Littman Chambers	0171 404 4866
	• Mitre Court Chambers	0171 353 9394
	• Mitre House Chambers	0171 583 8233
	• 1 New Square	0171 405 0884/5/6/7
	Chambers of Lord Goodhart QC	0171 405 5577
	5 New Square	0171 404 0404
	• 12 New Square	0171 419 1212
	• Twenty-Four Old Buildings	0171 404 0946
	24 Old Buildings	0171 242 2744
	• 9 Old Square	0171 405 4682
	The Chambers of Leolin Price CBE, QC	0171 405 0758/242 5002
	11 Old Square	0171 242 5022
	• 11 Old Square	0171 430 0341
	• 13 Old Square	0171 404 4800
	• 5 Paper Buildings	0171 583 9275
	• 1 Pump Court	0171 583 2012/353 4341
	No 1 Serjeants' Inn	0171 415 6666
	• Serle Court Chambers	0171 242 6105
	• Stanbrook & Henderson	0171 353 0101
	• 3 Stone Buildings	0171 242 4937/405 8358
	4 Stone Buildings	0171 242 5524
	• 5 Stone Buildings	0171 242 6201
	• 7 Stone Buildings	0171 405 3886/242 3546
	• 9 Stone Buildings	0171 404 5055
	11 Stone Buildings	+44 (0)171 831 6381
	Verulam Chambers	0171 813 2400
	• Wilberforce Chambers	0171 306 0102
Manchester	• Cobden House Chambers	0161 833 6000/6001
	Deans Court Chambers	0161 834 4097
	• 40 King Street	0161 832 9082
	58 King Street Chambers	0161 831 7477
	Manchester House Chambers	0161 834 7007
	• Merchant Chambers	0161 839 7070
	• St James's Chambers	0161 834 7000
Middlesbrough	• Fountain Chambers	01642 217037
Milton Keynes	Milton Keynes Chambers	01908 217857
Newcastle upon Tyne	• Broad Chare	0191 232 0541
	Cathedral Chambers	0191 232 1311
	Enterprise Chambers	0191 222 3344
	• New Court Chambers	0191 232 1980
	• Trinity Chambers	0191 232 1927
	Westgate Chambers	0191 261 4407/232 9785
Northampton	22 Albion Place	01604 636271
	Chartlands Chambers	01604 603322
Norwich	East Anglian Chambers	01603 617351
Nottingham	King Charles House	0115 941 8851
	Ropewalk Chambers	0115 947 2581
	St Mary's Chambers	0115 950 3503
Oxford	28 Western Road	01865 204911
Peterborough	Fenners Chambers	01733 562030
	Regency Chambers	01733 315215
Portsmouth	• Portsmouth Barristers' Chambers	01705 831292
Preston	Deans Court Chambers	01772 555163
	New Bailey Chambers	01772 258 087
	15 Winckley Square	01772 252 828
Reading	Wessex Chambers	0118 956 8856
Redhill	Redhill Chambers	01737 780781
Richmond-upon-Thames	Richmond Green Chambers	0181 940 1841
Shepperton	Abbey Chambers	01932 560913
Swansea	Gower Chambers	01792 644466
	Iscoed Chambers	01792 652988/9/330
Wolverhampton	Claremont Chambers	01902 426222
York	• York Chambers	01904 620 048

EUROPEAN LAW

London	• 4 Brick Court	0171 797 7766

EUROPEAN UNION

London	• Thomas More Chambers	0171 404 7000

• Expanded entry in Part C

A

EXTRADITION

| London | • 4 Brick Court | 0171 797 8910 |
| | • 1 Crown Office Row | 0171 797 7111 |

FACTORING

| Liverpool | • Oriel Chambers | 0151 236 7191 |

FAMILY

Birmingham	• Equity Chambers	0121 233 2100
	1 Fountain Court	0121 236 5721
	• 3 Fountain Court	0121 236 5854
	• 5 Fountain Court	0121 606 0500
	6 Fountain Court	0121 233 3282
	• 8 Fountain Court	0121 236 5514
	New Court Chambers	0121 693 6656
	• St Philip's Chambers	0121 246 7000
Bournemouth	King's Bench Chambers	01202 250025
	20 Lorne Park Road	01202 292102
Bradford	Broadway House Chambers	01274 722560
Brandon	Thetford Lodge Farm	01842 813132
Brighton	• Crown Office Row Chambers	01273 625625
Bristol	Assize Court Chambers	0117 926 4587
	St John's Chambers	0117 921 3456/929 8514
	29 Gwilliam Street	0117 966 8997
Cambridge	• Fenners Chambers	01223 368761
	Regency Chambers	01223 301517
Canterbury	Stour Chambers	01227 764899
Cardiff	9 Park Place	01222 382731
	30 Park Place	01222 398421
	32 Park Place	01222 397364
	• 33 Park Place	01222 233313
Chester	40 King Street	01244 323886
	White Friars Chambers	01244 323070
Chichester	Chichester Chambers	01243 784538
Durham City	Durham Barristers' Chambers	0191 386 9199
Eastbourne	King's Chambers	01323 416053
Ely	Cathedral Chambers, Ely	01353 666775
Enfield	Enfield Chambers	0181 364 5627
Exeter	• Cathedral Chambers (Jan Wood Independent Barristers' Clerk)	01392 210900
	Colleton Chambers	01392 274898
	Rougemont Chambers	01392 410471
	Southernhay Chambers	01392 255777
	Walnut House	01392 279751
Guildford	• Guildford Chambers	01483 539131
Leatherhead	Pembroke House	01372 376160/376493
Leeds	Chambers of Andrew Campbell QC	0113 245 5438
	11 King's Bench Walk	0113 2971 200
	• No. 6	0113 245 9763
	• Park Court Chambers	0113 243 3277
	The Chambers of Philip Raynor QC	0113 242 1123
	• 30 Park Square	0113 243 6388
	• 37 Park Square	0113 243 9422
	• Sovereign Chambers	0113 245 1841/2/3
	• St Paul's House	0113 245 5866
	• 9 Woodhouse Square	0113 245 1986
Leicester	2 New Street	0116 262 5906
Liverpool	25-27 Castle Street	0151 227 5661/5666/236 5072
	19 Castle Street Chambers	0151 236 9402
	Chavasse Court Chambers	0151 707 1191
	• The Corn Exchange Chambers	0151 227 1081/5009
	• Exchange Chambers	0151 236 7747
	First National Chambers	0151 236 2098
	India Buildings Chambers	0151 243 6000
	• The Chambers of Adrian Lyon	0151 236 4421/8240/6757
	• Martins Building	0151 236 5818/4919
	• Oriel Chambers	0151 236 7191
	• Peel House Chambers	0151 236 4321
London	ACHMA Chambers	0171 639 7817
	Alban Chambers	0171 419 5051

• Expanded entry in Part C

A

Albany Chambers	0171 485 5736/38
Barristers' Common Law Chambers	0171 375 3012
9 Bedford Row	0171 242 3555
17 Bedford Row	0171 831 7314
33 Bedford Row	0171 242 6476
• 29 Bedford Row Chambers	0171 831 2626
Bell Yard Chambers	0171 306 9292
11 Bolt Court	0171 353 2300
• Bracton Chambers	0171 242 4248
• 4 Brick Court	0171 797 8910
• 4 Brick Court	0171 797 7766
Bridewell Chambers	0171 797 8800
Cloisters	0171 827 4000
• 1 Crown Office Row	0171 797 7500
1 Crown Office Row	0171 583 9292
• 3 Dr Johnson's Buildings	0171 353 4854
• Dr Johnson's Chambers	0171 353 4716
Equity Barristers' Chambers	0181 558 8336
• One Essex Court	0171 936 3030
23 Essex Street	0171 413 0353
• 35 Essex Street	0171 353 6381
Chambers of Geoffrey Hawker	0171 583 8899
• Chambers of Norman Palmer	0171 405 6114
• 2nd Floor, Francis Taylor Building	0171 353 9942
Francis Taylor Buildings	0171 353 7768/2711
One Garden Court Family Law Chambers	0171 797 7900
• 2 Garden Court	0171 353 1633
• Goldsmith Building	0171 353 7881
Goldsmith Chambers	0171 353 6802/3/4/5
Goldsworth Chambers	0171 405 7117
• 9 Gough Square	0171 353 5371
• Gray's Inn Chambers	0171 831 5344
• Gray's Inn Chambers	0171 404 1111
• 1 Gray's Inn Square Chambers of the Baroness Scotland of Asthal QC	0171 405 3000
• 1 Gray's Inn Square	0171 405 8946
2 Gray's Inn Square Chambers	0171 242 0328/405 1317
6 Gray's Inn Square	0171 242 1052
10 - 11 Gray's Inn Square	0171 405 2576
14 Gray's Inn Square	0171 242 0858
• 1 Harcourt Buildings	0171 353 9421/0375
• 2 Harcourt Buildings	0171 583 9020
• Harcourt Chambers	0171 353 6961/7
• Hardwicke Building	0171 242 2523
Chambers of Harjit Singh	0171 353 1356
• Harrow-on-the-Hill Chambers	0181 423 7444
• Chambers of James Hunt QC	0171 421 8000
• John Street Chambers	0171 242 1911
1 Dr Johnson's Buildings	0171 353 9328
Justice Court Chambers	0181 830 7786
• One King's Bench Walk	0171 936 1500
• 4 King's Bench Walk	0171 822 8822
4 King's Bench Walk	0171 353 3581
6 King's Bench Walk	0171 353 4931/583 0695
• 8 King's Bench Walk	0171 797 8888
• 9 King's Bench Walk	0171 353 7202/3909
The Chambers of Mr Ali Mohammad Azhar	0171 353 9564 (4 lines)
10 King's Bench Walk	0171 353 7742
11 King's Bench Walk	0171 353 3337/8
• 13 King's Bench Walk	0171 353 7204
• Chambers of Lord Campbell of Alloway QC	0171 353 9276
• Lamb Building	0171 797 7788
Lamb Chambers	0171 797 8300
Library Chambers	0171 404 6500
Lion Court	0171 404 6565
• Littleton Chambers	0171 797 8600
• 1 Mitre Court Buildings	0171 797 7070
2 Mitre Court Buildings	0171 353 1353
• Mitre Court Chambers	0171 353 9394

Harrow on the Hill
London

• Expanded entry in Part C

A

• Mitre House Chambers	0171 583 8233
• New Court	0171 583 5123
• New Court Chambers	0171 831 9500
• 1 New Square	0171 405 0884/5/6/7
Chambers of Joy Okoye	0171 405 7011
• 22 Old Buildings	0171 831 0222
• Twenty-Four Old Buildings	0171 404 0946
11 Old Square	0171 242 5022
• 2 Paper Buildings	0171 353 0933
• 2 Paper Buildings	0171 936 2611 (10 lines)
2 Paper Buildings, Basement North	0171 936 2613
• 3 Paper Buildings	0171 797 7000
• 3 Paper Buildings	0171 583 8055
• 4 Paper Buildings	0171 583 0816
• 5 Paper Buildings	0171 583 9275
Pepys' Chambers	0171 936 2710
Phoenix Chambers	0171 404 7888
Plowden Buildings	0171 583 0808
• 1 Pump Court	0171 583 2012/353 4341
2 Pump Court	0171 353 5597
• Pump Court Chambers	0171 353 0711
• 5 Pump Court	0171 353 2532
• Chambers of Kieran Coonan QC	0171 583 6013/2510
6 Pump Court	0171 797 8400
• Queen Elizabeth Building	0171 353 7181 (12 lines)
No 1 Serjeants' Inn	0171 415 6666
• Stanbrook & Henderson	0171 353 0101
7 Stone Buildings	0171 242 0961
• 3 Temple Gardens	0171 353 3102/5/9297
3 Temple Gardens (North)	0171 353 0853/4/7222
• Thomas More Chambers	0171 404 7000
• 14 Tooks Court	0171 405 8828
Trafalgar Chambers	0171 583 5858
Chambers of Mohammed Hashmot Ullah	0171 377 0119
Verulam Chambers	0171 813 2400
Warwick House Chambers	0171 430 2323
Maidstone Earl Street Chambers	01622 671222
• Maidstone Chambers	01622 688592
Manchester • Central Chambers	0161 833 1774
• Cobden House Chambers	0161 833 6000/6001
Deans Court Chambers	0161 834 4097
• Chambers of John Hand QC	0161 955 9000
Kenworthy's Chambers	0161 832 4036
• 40 King Street	0161 832 9082
• 8 King Street Chambers	0161 834 9560
58 King Street Chambers	0161 831 7477
Lincoln House Chambers	0161 832 5701
Chambers of Ian Macdonald QC	0161 236 1840
Manchester House Chambers	0161 834 7007
Peel Court Chambers	0161 832 3791
• Queen's Chambers	0161 834 6875/4738
• St James's Chambers	0161 834 7000
18 St John Street	0161 278 1800
• 28 St John Street	0161 834 8418
Young Street Chambers	0161 833 0489
Middlesbrough Baker Street Chambers	01642 873873
• Fountain Chambers	01642 217037
York House	01642 213000
Newcastle upon Tyne • Broad Chare	0191 232 0541
Cathedral Chambers	0191 232 1311
• New Court Chambers	0191 232 1980
• Trinity Chambers	0191 232 1927
Westgate Chambers	0191 261 4407/232 9785
Northampton 22 Albion Place	01604 636271
Chartlands Chambers	01604 603322
Norwich East Anglian Chambers	01603 617351
Octagon House	01603 623186
Sackville Chambers	01603 613516
Nottingham King Charles House	0115 941 8851
Ropewalk Chambers	0115 947 2581
St Mary's Chambers	0115 950 3503
Oxford 1 Alfred Street	01865 793736

• Expanded entry in Part C

A

	• King's Bench Chambers	01865 311066
	28 Western Road	01865 204911
Peterborough	Fenners Chambers	01733 562030
	Regency Chambers	01733 315215
Plymouth	Devon Chambers	01752 661659
Portsmouth	Hampshire Chambers	01705 826636
	• Portsmouth Barristers' Chambers	01705 831292
Preston	4 Camden Place	01772 828300
	Deans Court Chambers	01772 555163
	New Bailey Chambers	01772 258 087
	15 Winckley Square	01772 252 828
Reading	Dr Johnson's Chambers	01189 254221
	Wessex Chambers	0118 956 8856
Redhill	Redhill Chambers	01737 780781
Richmond-upon-Thames	Richmond Green Chambers	0181 940 1841
Sheffield	Bank House Chambers	0114 275 1223
	Paradise Square Chambers	0114 273 8951
Shepperton	Abbey Chambers	01932 560913
Southampton	• 17 Carlton Crescent	01703 320320
	• College Chambers	01703 230338
	• Eighteen Carlton Crescent	01703 639001
Stoke-on-Trent	Regent Chambers	01782 286666
Swansea	Angel Chambers	01792 464623/464648
	Gower Chambers	01792 644466
	Iscoed Chambers	01792 652988/9/330
	Pendragon Chambers	01792 411188
Corsham	Neston Home Chambers	01225 811909
Swindon	Pump Court Chambers	01793 539899
Winchester	Pump Court Chambers	01962 868161
	4 St Peter Street	01962 868 884
Wolverhampton	Claremont Chambers	01902 426222

FAMILY PROVISION

Birmingham	1 Fountain Court	0121 236 5721
	• 3 Fountain Court	0121 236 5854
	• 5 Fountain Court	0121 606 0500
	• 8 Fountain Court	0121 236 5514
	• St Philip's Chambers	0121 246 7000
Bradford	Broadway House Chambers	01274 722560
Brighton	• Crown Office Row Chambers	01273 625625
Bristol	Assize Court Chambers	0117 926 4587
	St John's Chambers	0117 921 3456/929 8514
Cambridge	• Fenners Chambers	01223 368761
	Regency Chambers	01223 301517
Canterbury	Stour Chambers	01227 764899
Cardiff	9 Park Place	01222 382731
	30 Park Place	01222 398421
	32 Park Place	01222 397364
	• 33 Park Place	01222 233313
Chester	40 King Street	01244 323886
	White Friars Chambers	01244 323070
Chichester	Chichester Chambers	01243 784538
Eastbourne	King's Chambers	01323 416053
Exeter	• Cathedral Chambers (Jan Wood Independent Barristers' Clerk)	01392 210900
	Colleton Chambers	01392 274898
	Rougemont Chambers	01392 410471
	Southernhay Chambers	01392 255777
	Walnut House	01392 279751
Guildford	• Guildford Chambers	01483 539131
Leatherhead	Pembroke House	01372 376160/376493
Leeds	Chambers of Andrew Campbell QC	0113 245 5438
	11 King's Bench Walk	0113 2971 200
	• Mercury Chambers	0113 234 2265
	• No. 6	0113 245 9763
	The Chambers of Philip Raynor QC	0113 242 1123
	• 30 Park Square	0113 243 6388
	• 37 Park Square	0113 243 9422
	• Sovereign Chambers	0113 245 1841/2/3
	• St Paul's House	0113 245 5866
	• 9 Woodhouse Square	0113 245 1986
Liverpool	25-27 Castle Street	0151 227 5661/5666/236 5072

• Expanded entry in Part C

	19 Castle Street Chambers	0151 236 9402
	Chavasse Court Chambers	0151 707 1191
	• The Corn Exchange Chambers	0151 227 1081/5009
	• Exchange Chambers	0151 236 7747
	India Buildings Chambers	0151 243 6000
	• The Chambers of Adrian Lyon	0151 236 4421/8240/6757
	• Martins Building	0151 236 5818/4919
	• Oriel Chambers	0151 236 7191
	• Peel House Chambers	0151 236 4321
London	9 Bedford Row	0171 242 3555
	• 29 Bedford Row Chambers	0171 831 2626
	11 Bolt Court	0171 353 2300
	• Bracton Chambers	0171 242 4248
	• 4 Brick Court	0171 797 7766
	Bridewell Chambers	0171 797 8800
	• Chambers of Mr Peter Crampin QC	0171 831 0081
	• 1 Crown Office Row	0171 797 7500
	1 Crown Office Row	0171 583 9292
	• 3 Dr Johnson's Buildings	0171 353 4854
	• Dr Johnson's Chambers	0171 353 4716
	Equity Barristers' Chambers	0181 558 8336
	• One Essex Court	0171 936 3030
	Chambers of Geoffrey Hawker	0171 583 8899
	• Chambers of Norman Palmer	0171 405 6114
	• 2nd Floor, Francis Taylor Building	0171 353 9942
	Francis Taylor Buildings	0171 353 7768/2711
	One Garden Court Family Law Chambers	0171 797 7900
	• 2 Garden Court	0171 353 1633
	• Goldsmith Building	0171 353 7881
	• 9 Gough Square	0171 353 5371
	• Gray's Inn Chambers	0171 404 1111
	• 1 Gray's Inn Square	0171 405 8946
	2 Gray's Inn Square Chambers	0171 242 0328/405 1317
	14 Gray's Inn Square	0171 242 0858
	• 1 Harcourt Buildings	0171 353 9421/0375
	• 2 Harcourt Buildings	0171 583 9020
	• Harcourt Chambers	0171 353 6961/7
Harrow on the Hill	• Harrow-on-the-Hill Chambers	0181 423 7444
London	• Chambers of James Hunt QC	0171 421 8000
	• One King's Bench Walk	0171 936 1500
	• 4 King's Bench Walk	0171 822 8822
	6 King's Bench Walk	0171 353 4931/583 0695
	• 8 King's Bench Walk	0171 797 8888
	• 9 King's Bench Walk	0171 353 7202/3909
	The Chambers of Mr Ali Mohammad Azhar	0171 353 9564 (4 lines)
	10 King's Bench Walk	0171 353 7742
	11 King's Bench Walk	0171 353 3337/8
	• 13 King's Bench Walk	0171 353 7204
	• Lamb Building	0171 797 7788
	Lamb Chambers	0171 797 8300
	Library Chambers	0171 404 6500
	• 1 Mitre Court Buildings	0171 797 7070
	2 Mitre Court Buildings	0171 353 1353
	• Mitre Court Chambers	0171 353 9394
	• Mitre House Chambers	0171 583 8233
	• New Court	0171 583 5123
	• New Court Chambers	0171 831 9500
	Chambers of Lord Goodhart QC	0171 405 5577
	5 New Square	0171 404 0404
	• 12 New Square	0171 419 1212
	Chambers of Joy Okoye	0171 405 7011
	• 22 Old Buildings	0171 831 0222
	• Twenty-Four Old Buildings	0171 404 0946
	• 9 Old Square	0171 405 4682
	The Chambers of Leolin Price CBE, QC	0171 405 0758/242 5002
	11 Old Square	0171 242 5022
	• 11 Old Square	0171 430 0341
	• 13 Old Square	0171 404 4800
	• 2 Paper Buildings	0171 353 0933
	• 3 Paper Buildings	0171 797 7000

• Expanded entry in Part C

	• 4 Paper Buildings	0171 583 0816
	• 5 Paper Buildings	0171 583 9275
	Phoenix Chambers	0171 404 7888
	• 1 Pump Court	0171 583 2012/353 4341
	2 Pump Court	0171 353 5597
	• Pump Court Chambers	0171 353 0711
	• 4 Pump Court	0171 353 2656/9
	• 5 Pump Court	0171 353 2532
	• Chambers of Kieran Coonan QC	0171 583 6013/2510
	6 Pump Court	0171 797 8400
	No 1 Serjeants' Inn	0171 415 6666
	• Stanbrook & Henderson	0171 353 0101
	• 3 Stone Buildings	0171 242 4937/405 8358
	• 5 Stone Buildings	0171 242 6201
	7 Stone Buildings	0171 242 0961
	8 Stone Buildings	0171 831 9881
	• 9 Stone Buildings	0171 404 5055
	11 Stone Buildings	+44 (0)171 831 6381
	• 3 Temple Gardens	0171 353 3102/5/9297
	• Thomas More Chambers	0171 404 7000
	Trafalgar Chambers	0171 583 5858
	Verulam Chambers	0171 813 2400
Maidstone	• Maidstone Chambers	01622 688592
Manchester	• Central Chambers	0161 833 1774
	• Cobden House Chambers	0161 833 6000/6001
	Deans Court Chambers	0161 834 4097
	• Chambers of John Hand QC	0161 955 9000
	Kenworthy's Chambers	0161 832 4036
	• 40 King Street	0161 832 9082
	• 8 King Street Chambers	0161 834 9560
	Manchester House Chambers	0161 834 7007
	Peel Court Chambers	0161 832 3791
	• Queen's Chambers	0161 834 6875/4738
	• St James's Chambers	0161 834 7000
	• 28 St John Street	0161 834 8418
	Young Street Chambers	0161 833 0489
Middlesbrough	Baker Street Chambers	01642 873873
	• Fountain Chambers	01642 217037
	York House	01642 213000
Newcastle upon Tyne	• Broad Chare	0191 232 0541
	Cathedral Chambers	0191 232 1311
	• New Court Chambers	0191 232 1980
	• Trinity Chambers	0191 232 1927
	Westgate Chambers	0191 261 4407/232 9785
Northampton	22 Albion Place	01604 636271
	Chartlands Chambers	01604 603322
Norwich	East Anglian Chambers	01603 617351
	Octagon House	01603 623186
Nottingham	King Charles House	0115 941 8851
	Ropewalk Chambers	0115 947 2581
	St Mary's Chambers	0115 950 3503
Oxford	• King's Bench Chambers	01865 311066
	28 Western Road	01865 204911
Peterborough	Fenners Chambers	01733 562030
	Regency Chambers	01733 315215
Plymouth	Devon Chambers	01752 661659
Portsmouth	Hampshire Chambers	01705 826636
	• Portsmouth Barristers' Chambers	01705 831292
Preston	4 Camden Place	01772 828300
	Deans Court Chambers	01772 555163
	New Bailey Chambers	01772 258 087
	15 Winckley Square	01772 252 828
Reading	Dr Johnson's Chambers	01189 254221
	Wessex Chambers	0118 956 8856
Redhill	Redhill Chambers	01737 780781
Sheffield	Paradise Square Chambers	0114 273 8951
Southampton	• 17 Carlton Crescent	01703 320320
	• Eighteen Carlton Crescent	01703 639001
Stoke-on-Trent	Regent Chambers	01782 286666
Swansea	Angel Chambers	01792 464623/464648
	Gower Chambers	01792 644466
	Iscoed Chambers	01792 652988/9/330

• Expanded entry in Part C

Corsham	Neston Home Chambers	01225 811909
Swindon	Pump Court Chambers	01793 539899
Winchester	Pump Court Chambers	01962 868161
Wolverhampton	Claremont Chambers	01902 426222
York	• York Chambers	01904 620 048

FILM, CABLE, TV

Birmingham	1 Fountain Court	0121 236 5721
	• 8 Fountain Court	0121 236 5514
	• St Philip's Chambers	0121 246 7000
London	• 29 Bedford Row Chambers	0171 831 2626
	• Blackstone Chambers (formerly known as 2 Hare Court)	0171 583 1770
	11 Bolt Court	0171 353 2300
	Brick Court Chambers	0171 583 0777
	Bridewell Chambers	0171 797 8800
	• Doughty Street Chambers	0171 404 1313
	• Essex Court Chambers	0171 813 8000
	• 39 Essex Street	0171 832 1111
	• 4 Field Court	0171 440 6900
	• Fountain Court	0171 583 3335
	• One Hare Court	0171 353 3171
	• Littleton Chambers	0171 797 8600
	• Monckton Chambers	0171 405 7211
	• New Court	0171 797 8999
	• 3 New Square	0171 405 1111
	5 New Square	0171 404 0404
	• 8 New Square	0171 405 4321
	19 Old Buildings	0171 405 2001
	• 5 Raymond Buildings	0171 242 2902
	• 3 Stone Buildings	0171 242 4937/405 8358
	• 9 Stone Buildings	0171 404 5055
	11 Stone Buildings	+44 (0)171 831 6381
Redhill	Redhill Chambers	01737 780781

FINANCIAL SERVICES

Birmingham	• 5 Fountain Court	0121 606 0500
Bristol	St John's Chambers	0117 921 3456/929 8514
Cambridge	• Fenners Chambers	01223 368761
Exeter	Walnut House	01392 279751
Leeds	Chambers of Andrew Campbell QC	0113 245 5438
	The Chambers of Philip Raynor QC	0113 242 1123
London	9 Bedford Row	0171 242 3555
	17 Bedford Row	0171 831 7314
	• 29 Bedford Row Chambers	0171 831 2626
	• 5 Bell Yard	0171 333 8811
	• Blackstone Chambers (formerly known as 2 Hare Court)	0171 583 1770
	• Bracton Chambers	0171 242 4248
	Brick Court Chambers	0171 583 0777
	Cloisters	0171 827 4000
	1 Crown Office Row	0171 583 9292
	Equity Barristers' Chambers	0181 558 8336
	• Erskine Chambers	0171 242 5532
	• One Essex Court	0171 583 2000
	• One Essex Court	0171 936 3030
	• Essex Court Chambers	0171 813 8000
	• 20 Essex Street	0171 583 9294
	• Chambers of Norman Palmer	0171 405 6114
	• 4 Field Court	0171 440 6900
	• Fountain Court	0171 583 3335
	Goldsworth Chambers	0171 405 7117
	• Gough Square Chambers	0171 353 0924
	• 1 Harcourt Buildings	0171 353 9421/0375
	• 2 Harcourt Buildings	0171 583 9020
	• Hardwicke Building	0171 242 2523
	• One Hare Court	0171 353 3171
Harrow on the Hill	• Harrow-on-the-Hill Chambers	0181 423 7444
London	• 4 King's Bench Walk	0171 822 8822
	The Chambers of Mr Ali Mohammad Azhar	0171 353 9564 (4 lines)

• Expanded entry in Part C

A

• 13 King's Bench Walk	0171 353 7204
Lamb Chambers	0171 797 8300
• Littleton Chambers	0171 797 8600
• Mitre Court Chambers	0171 353 9394
Chambers of Lord Goodhart QC	0171 405 5577
• 12 New Square	0171 419 1212
• Twenty-Four Old Buildings	0171 404 0946
• 9 Old Square	0171 405 4682
The Chambers of Leolin Price CBE, QC	0171 405 0758/242 5002
• 11 Old Square	0171 430 0341
• 13 Old Square	0171 404 4800
• 3 Paper Buildings	0171 797 7000
• 5 Paper Buildings	0171 583 9275
5 Paper Buildings	0171 583 6117
• Chambers of John L Powell QC	0171 797 8000
• 4 Pump Court	0171 353 2656/9
• Queen Elizabeth Building	0171 583 5766
No 1 Serjeants' Inn	0171 415 6666
• 3-4 South Square	0171 696 9900
• Stanbrook & Henderson	0171 353 0101
• 3 Stone Buildings	0171 242 4937/405 8358
4 Stone Buildings	0171 242 5524
• 5 Stone Buildings	0171 242 6201
• 7 Stone Buildings	0171 405 3886/242 3546
• 9 Stone Buildings	0171 404 5055
11 Stone Buildings	+44 (0)171 831 6381
• 2 Temple Gardens	0171 583 6041
• Thomas More Chambers	0171 404 7000
• 3 Verulam Buildings	0171 831 8441
Verulam Chambers	0171 813 2400
• Wilberforce Chambers	0171 306 0102

Manchester	• Chambers of John Hand QC	0161 955 9000
	• 40 King Street	0161 832 9082
	• 8 King Street Chambers	0161 834 9560
	• Merchant Chambers	0161 839 7070
	• St James's Chambers	0161 834 7000
Norwich	East Anglian Chambers	01603 617351
Nottingham	Ropewalk Chambers	0115 947 2581
Oxford	• King's Bench Chambers	01865 311066
Peterborough	Fenners Chambers	01733 562030
Portsmouth	• Portsmouth Barristers' Chambers	01705 831292
Preston	New Bailey Chambers	01772 258 087
Richmond-upon-Thames	Richmond Green Chambers	0181 940 1841
Swansea	Iscoed Chambers	01792 652988/9/330
Wolverhampton	Claremont Chambers	01902 426222

FOOD

London	• Gough Square Chambers	0171 353 0924

FOREIGN LAW

Birmingham	• Equity Chambers	0121 233 2100
	• 5 Fountain Court	0121 606 0500
Bournemouth	20 Lorne Park Road	01202 292102
London	Chambers of Dr Michael Arnheim	0171 833 5093
	• Blackstone Chambers (formerly known as 2 Hare Court)	0171 583 1770
	Brick Court Chambers	0171 583 0777
	Bridewell Chambers	0171 797 8800
	1 Crown Office Row	0171 583 9292
	Equity Barristers' Chambers	0181 558 8336
	• Essex Court Chambers	0171 813 8000
	Chambers of Geoffrey Hawker	0171 583 8899
	• Chambers of Norman Palmer	0171 405 6114
	• 2 Garden Court	0171 353 1633
	Goldsworth Chambers	0171 405 7117
	• 1 Gray's Inn Square Chambers of the Baroness Scotland of Asthal QC	0171 405 3000
	10 - 11 Gray's Inn Square	0171 405 2576
	• One Hare Court	0171 353 3171
	• 3 Hare Court	0171 353 7561
	Chambers of Harjit Singh	0171 353 1356

• Expanded entry in Part C

	• Chambers of James Hunt QC	0171 421 8000
	• John Street Chambers	0171 242 1911
	Justice Court Chambers	0181 830 7786
	The Chambers of Mr Ali Mohammad Azhar	0171 353 9564 (4 lines)
	• Lamb Building	0171 797 7788
	• Mitre House Chambers	0171 583 8233
	• New Court	0171 583 5123
	• 12 New Square	0171 419 1212
	Chambers of Joy Okoye	0171 405 7011
	• 2 Paper Buildings	0171 936 2611 (10 lines)
	• 3 Paper Buildings	0171 583 8055
	• 4 Paper Buildings	0171 583 0816
	• 5 Paper Buildings	0171 583 9275
	5 Paper Buildings	0171 583 6117
	• Pump Court Chambers	0171 353 0711
	• 9 Stone Buildings	0171 404 5055
	Verulam Chambers	0171 813 2400
Norwich	East Anglian Chambers	01603 617351
Oxford	1 Alfred Street	01865 793736
Swindon	Pump Court Chambers	01793 539899
Winchester	Pump Court Chambers	01962 868161
	4 St Peter Street	01962 868 884

FRANCHISING

Birmingham	• 5 Fountain Court	0121 606 0500
	• St Philip's Chambers	0121 246 7000
Bristol	St John's Chambers	0117 921 3456/929 8514
Cardiff	30 Park Place	01222 398421
Exeter	Rougemont Chambers	01392 410471
Haverhill	Helions Chambers	01440 730523
London	• 29 Bedford Row Chambers	0171 831 2626
	1 Crown Office Row	0171 583 9292
	Equity Barristers' Chambers	0181 558 8336
	• One Essex Court	0171 583 2000
	• Essex Court Chambers	0171 813 8000
	Francis Taylor Buildings	0171 353 7768/2711
	• 2 Harcourt Buildings	0171 583 9020
	• One Hare Court	0171 353 3171
Harrow on the Hill	• Harrow-on-the-Hill Chambers	0181 423 7444
London	The Chambers of Mr Ali Mohammad Azhar	0171 353 9564 (4 lines)
	11 King's Bench Walk	0171 353 3337/8
	• New Court	0171 797 8999
	• 3 New Square	0171 405 1111
	19 Old Buildings	0171 405 2001
	Prince Henry's Chambers	0171 353 1183/1190
	• 1 Raymond Buildings	0171 430 1234
	• Stanbrook & Henderson	0171 353 0101
	11 Stone Buildings	+44 (0)171 831 6381
	• 199 Strand	0171 379 9779
Manchester	• 8 King Street Chambers	0161 834 9560
	• Merchant Chambers	0161 839 7070
	• St James's Chambers	0161 834 7000
Norwich	East Anglian Chambers	01603 617351
Nottingham	King Charles House	0115 941 8851
	Ropewalk Chambers	0115 947 2581
Preston	New Bailey Chambers	01772 258 087
Swansea	Iscoed Chambers	01792 652988/9/330

FRAUD

Bromley	Bromley Chambers	0181 325 0863
London	• Thomas More Chambers	0171 404 7000

GENERAL CIVIL

London	Bell Yard Chambers	0171 306 9292

HEALTH AND SAFETY

London	8 Stone Buildings	0171 831 9881

• Expanded entry in Part C

| | • 1 Temple Gardens | 0171 353 0407/583 1315 |
| **Slough** | 11 St Bernards Road | 01753 553806/817989 |

HIGHWAYS

| **London** | 11 Bolt Court | 0171 353 2300 |
| **Redhill** | Redhill Chambers | 01737 780781 |

HOUSING

Birmingham	• Equity Chambers	0121 233 2100
	1 Fountain Court	0121 236 5721
	• 5 Fountain Court	0121 606 0500
	• 8 Fountain Court	0121 236 5514
	New Court Chambers	0121 693 6656
	• St Philip's Chambers	0121 246 7000
Bournemouth	King's Bench Chambers	01202 250025
Bradford	Broadway House Chambers	01274 722560
Cambridge	• Fenners Chambers	01223 368761
Cardiff	30 Park Place	01222 398421
	• 33 Park Place	01222 233313
Chester	40 King Street	01244 323886
	White Friars Chambers	01244 323070
Chichester	Chichester Chambers	01243 784538
Eastbourne	King's Chambers	01323 416053
Exeter	Southernhay Chambers	01392 255777
	Walnut House	01392 279751
Guildford	• Guildford Chambers	01483 539131
Leeds	Chambers of Andrew Campbell QC	0113 245 5438
	Enterprise Chambers	0113 246 0391
	The Chambers of Philip Raynor QC	0113 242 1123
	• Sovereign Chambers	0113 245 1841/2/3
	• 9 Woodhouse Square	0113 245 1986
Liverpool	25-27 Castle Street	0151 227 5661/5666/236 5072
	19 Castle Street Chambers	0151 236 9402
	Chavasse Court Chambers	0151 707 1191
	• The Corn Exchange Chambers	0151 227 1081/5009
	• Exchange Chambers	0151 236 7747
	• The Chambers of Adrian Lyon	0151 236 4421/8240/6757
	• Oriel Chambers	0151 236 7191
London	Albany Chambers	0171 485 5736/38
	• Arden Chambers	0171 242 4244
	Chambers of Dr Michael Arnheim	0171 833 5093
	Barnard's Inn Chambers	0171 242 8508
	Barristers' Common Law Chambers	0171 375 3012
	17 Bedford Row	0171 831 7314
	33 Bedford Row	0171 242 6476
	• 29 Bedford Row Chambers	0171 831 2626
	11 Bolt Court	0171 353 2300
	• 4 Breams Buildings	0171 353 5835/430 1221
	• 4 Brick Court	0171 797 7766
	Bridewell Chambers	0171 797 8800
	Britton Street Chambers	0171 608 3765
	• Chambers of Mr Peter Crampin QC	0171 831 0081
	• Devereux Chambers	0171 353 7534
	• Doughty Street Chambers	0171 404 1313
	• 3 Dr Johnson's Buildings	0171 353 4854
	• Enterprise Chambers	0171 405 9471
	• One Essex Court	0171 936 3030
	Chambers of Geoffrey Hawker	0171 583 8899
	Falcon Chambers	0171 353 2484
	• Chambers of Norman Palmer	0171 405 6114
	• 4 Field Court	0171 440 6900
	• 2nd Floor, Francis Taylor Building	0171 353 9942
	Francis Taylor Buildings	0171 353 7768/2711
	• 2 Garden Court	0171 353 1633
	• Goldsmith Building	0171 353 7881
	Goldsmith Chambers	0171 353 6802/3/4/5
	Goldsworth Chambers	0171 405 7117
	• Gray's Inn Chambers	0171 831 5344
	• Gray's Inn Chambers	0171 404 1111
	• 1 Gray's Inn Square	0171 405 8946
	2 Gray's Inn Square Chambers	0171 242 0328/405 1317

• Expanded entry in Part C

A

	4-5 Gray's Inn Square	0171 404 5252
	6 Gray's Inn Square	0171 242 1052
	10 - 11 Gray's Inn Square	0171 405 2576
	• 1 Harcourt Buildings	0171 353 9421/0375
	• 2 Harcourt Buildings	0171 583 9020
	• 2 Harcourt Buildings	0171 353 8415
	• Hardwicke Building	0171 242 2523
	Chambers of Harjit Singh	0171 353 1356
Harrow on the Hill	• Harrow-on-the-Hill Chambers	0181 423 7444
London	• Chambers of James Hunt QC	0171 421 8000
	• John Street Chambers	0171 242 1911
	Justice Court Chambers	0181 830 7786
	• 4 King's Bench Walk	0171 822 8822
	6 King's Bench Walk	0171 353 4931/583 0695
	• 8 King's Bench Walk	0171 797 8888
	• 9 King's Bench Walk	0171 353 7202/3909
	The Chambers of Mr Ali Mohammad Azhar	0171 353 9564 (4 lines)
	10 King's Bench Walk	0171 353 7742
	• 11 King's Bench Walk	0171 632 8500
	• 12 King's Bench Walk	0171 583 0811
	• 13 King's Bench Walk	0171 353 7204
	• Chambers of Lord Campbell of Alloway QC	0171 353 9276
	• Lamb Building	0171 797 7788
	Lamb Chambers	0171 797 8300
	Lion Court	0171 404 6565
	2 Mitre Court Buildings	0171 353 1353
	• Mitre Court Chambers	0171 353 9394
	• Mitre House Chambers	0171 583 8233
	• New Court	0171 583 5123
	• 1 New Square	0171 405 0884/5/6/7
	Chambers of Joy Okoye	0171 405 7011
	• 22 Old Buildings	0171 831 0222
	11 Old Square	0171 242 5022
	• 11 Old Square	0171 430 0341
	• 2 Paper Buildings	0171 353 0933
	• 2 Paper Buildings	0171 936 2611 (10 lines)
	• 4 Paper Buildings	0171 353 3366/583 7155
	Phoenix Chambers	0171 404 7888
	• 1 Pump Court	0171 583 2012/353 4341
	2 Pump Court	0171 353 5597
	• 5 Pump Court	0171 353 2532
	• Chambers of Kieran Coonan QC	0171 583 6013/2510
	1 Serjeants' Inn	0171 583 1355
	• Stanbrook & Henderson	0171 353 0101
	7 Stone Buildings	0171 242 0961
	• 9 Stone Buildings	0171 404 5055
	• 199 Strand	0171 379 9779
	• 3 Temple Gardens	0171 353 3102/5/9297
	3 Temple Gardens (North)	0171 353 0853/4/7222
	• Thomas More Chambers	0171 404 7000
	• 14 Tooks Court	0171 405 8828
	Trafalgar Chambers	0171 583 5858
	Verulam Chambers	0171 813 2400
	Warwick House Chambers	0171 430 2323
Manchester	• Central Chambers	0161 833 1774
	• Cobden House Chambers	0161 833 6000/6001
	• Chambers of John Hand QC	0161 955 9000
	Kenworthy's Chambers	0161 832 4036
	• 40 King Street	0161 832 9082
	• 8 King Street Chambers	0161 834 9560
	58 King Street Chambers	0161 831 7477
	Chambers of Ian Macdonald QC	0161 236 1840
	Manchester House Chambers	0161 834 7007
	• Merchant Chambers	0161 839 7070
	Peel Court Chambers	0161 832 3791
	• St James's Chambers	0161 834 7000
	Young Street Chambers	0161 833 0489
Middlesbrough	Baker Street Chambers	01642 873873
	• Fountain Chambers	01642 217037
Newcastle upon Tyne	Cathedral Chambers	0191 232 1311

	Enterprise Chambers	0191 222 3344
	• Trinity Chambers	0191 232 1927
	Westgate Chambers	0191 261 4407/232 9785
Northampton	22 Albion Place	01604 636271
Norwich	East Anglian Chambers	01603 617351
Nottingham	King Charles House	0115 941 8851
	Ropewalk Chambers	0115 947 2581
Oxford	• King's Bench Chambers	01865 311066
	28 Western Road	01865 204911
Peterborough	Fenners Chambers	01733 562030
Plymouth	Devon Chambers	01752 661659
Preston	4 Camden Place	01772 828300
	New Bailey Chambers	01772 258 087
	15 Winckley Square	01772 252 828
Reading	Dr Johnson's Chambers	01189 254221
Redhill	Redhill Chambers	01737 780781
Richmond-upon-Thames	Richmond Green Chambers	0181 940 1841
Slough	11 St Bernards Road	01753 553806/817989
Southampton	• 17 Carlton Crescent	01703 320320
Stoke-on-Trent	Regent Chambers	01782 286666
Swansea	Angel Chambers	01792 464623/464648
	Gower Chambers	01792 644466
	Iscoed Chambers	01792 652988/9/330
Wolverhampton	Claremont Chambers	01902 426222

HUMAN RIGHTS

London	17 Bedford Row	0171 831 7314
	• 20 Essex Street	0171 583 9294
	• Thomas More Chambers	0171 404 7000
Slough	11 St Bernards Road	01753 553806/817989

IMMIGRATION

Birmingham	• Equity Chambers	0121 233 2100
	1 Fountain Court	0121 236 5721
	• 5 Fountain Court	0121 606 0500
	• 8 Fountain Court	0121 236 5514
	New Court Chambers	0121 693 6656
	• St Philip's Chambers	0121 246 7000
Bradford	Broadway House Chambers	01274 722560
Cardiff	30 Park Place	01222 398421
Chester	White Friars Chambers	01244 323070
Enfield	Enfield Chambers	0181 364 5627
Exeter	• Cathedral Chambers (Jan Wood	01392 210900
	Independent Barristers' Clerk)	
Leeds	Chambers of Andrew Campbell QC	0113 245 5438
	The Chambers of Philip Raynor QC	0113 242 1123
	• Sovereign Chambers	0113 245 1841/2/3
	• 9 Woodhouse Square	0113 245 1986
Liverpool	19 Castle Street Chambers	0151 236 9402
	India Buildings Chambers	0151 243 6000
	• The Chambers of Adrian Lyon	0151 236 4421/8240/6757
London	ACHMA Chambers	0171 639 7817
	Albany Chambers	0171 485 5736/38
	Chambers of Dr Michael Arnheim	0171 833 5093
	Avondale Chambers	0181 445 9984
	Barristers' Common Law Chambers	0171 375 3012
	• 29 Bedford Row Chambers	0171 831 2626
	• Blackstone Chambers (formerly known	0171 583 1770
	as 2 Hare Court)	
	11 Bolt Court	0171 353 2300
	• Bracton Chambers	0171 242 4248
	• 4 Breams Buildings	0171 353 5835/430 1221
	• 4 Brick Court	0171 797 8910
	• 4 Brick Court	0171 797 7766
	Bridewell Chambers	0171 797 8800
	Britton Street Chambers	0171 608 3765
	• Doughty Street Chambers	0171 404 1313
	Equity Barristers' Chambers	0181 558 8336
	• One Essex Court	0171 936 3030
	• Essex Court Chambers	0171 813 8000
	• 20 Essex Street	0171 583 9294

• Expanded entry in Part C

A

• 39 Essex Street	0171 832 1111
Chambers of Geoffrey Hawker	0171 583 8899
• Chambers of Norman Palmer	0171 405 6114
• 2nd Floor, Francis Taylor Building	0171 353 9942
Francis Taylor Buildings	0171 353 7768/2711
• 2 Garden Court	0171 353 1633
• Goldsmith Building	0171 353 7881
Goldsmith Chambers	0171 353 6802/3/4/5
Goldsworth Chambers	0171 405 7117
• Gray's Inn Chambers	0171 831 5344
• Gray's Inn Chambers	0171 404 1111
• 1 Gray's Inn Square Chambers of the	0171 405 3000
Baroness Scotland of Asthal QC	
• 1 Gray's Inn Square	0171 405 8946
2 Gray's Inn Square Chambers	0171 242 0328/405 1317
• 4-5 Gray's Inn Square	0171 404 5252
6 Gray's Inn Square	0171 242 1052
10 - 11 Gray's Inn Square	0171 405 2576
• 1 Harcourt Buildings	0171 353 9421/0375
2 Harcourt Buildings	0171 353 2112/2817
• One Hare Court	0171 353 3171
Chambers of Harjit Singh	0171 353 1356
• Harrow-on-the-Hill Chambers	0181 423 7444
• John Street Chambers	0171 242 1911
Justice Court Chambers	0181 830 7786
• One King's Bench Walk	0171 936 1500
• 4 King's Bench Walk	0171 822 8822
4 King's Bench Walk	0171 353 3581
6 King's Bench Walk	0171 353 4931/583 0695
• 8 King's Bench Walk	0171 797 8888
• 9 King's Bench Walk	0171 353 7202/3909
The Chambers of Mr Ali Mohammad	0171 353 9564 (4 lines)
Azhar	
10 King's Bench Walk	0171 353 7742
• 11 King's Bench Walk	0171 632 8500
• 13 King's Bench Walk	0171 353 7204
• Chambers of Lord Campbell of Alloway	0171 353 9276
QC	
Kingsway Chambers	07000 653529
• Lamb Building	0171 797 7788
Library Chambers	0171 404 6500
Lion Court	0171 404 6565
• Littman Chambers	0171 404 4866
• 1 Middle Temple Lane	0171 583 0659 (12 lines)
2 Mitre Court Buildings	0171 353 1353
• Mitre Court Chambers	0171 353 9394
• Mitre House Chambers	0171 583 8233
• Monckton Chambers	0171 405 7211
Chambers of Joy Okoye	0171 405 7011
11 Old Square	0171 242 5022
• 2 Paper Buildings	0171 353 0933
• 2 Paper Buildings	0171 936 2611 (10 lines)
• 4 Paper Buildings	0171 583 0816
• 5 Paper Buildings	0171 583 9275
5 Paper Buildings	0171 583 6117
Phoenix Chambers	0171 404 7888
Plowden Buildings	0171 583 0808
• 1 Pump Court	0171 583 2012/353 4341
2 Pump Court	0171 353 5597
• Pump Court Chambers	0171 353 0711
7 Stone Buildings	0171 242 0961
8 Stone Buildings	0171 831 9881
• 1 Temple Gardens	0171 353 0407/583 1315
3 Temple Gardens (North)	0171 353 0853/4/7222
• Thomas More Chambers	0171 404 7000
• 14 Tooks Court	0171 405 8828
Trafalgar Chambers	0171 583 5858
Chambers of Mohammed Hashmot Ullah	0171 377 0119
Verulam Chambers	0171 813 2400
Warwick House Chambers	0171 430 2323
Earl Street Chambers	01622 671222
• Maidstone Chambers	01622 688592

Harrow on the Hill
London

Maidstone

• Expanded entry in Part C

Manchester	• Central Chambers	0161 833 1774
	• Chambers of John Hand QC	0161 955 9000
	Kenworthy's Chambers	0161 832 4036
	• 40 King Street	0161 832 9082
	Lincoln House Chambers	0161 832 5701
	Chambers of Ian Macdonald QC	0161 236 1840
	Young Street Chambers	0161 833 0489
Newcastle upon Tyne	• New Court Chambers	0191 232 1980
Norwich	East Anglian Chambers	01603 617351
Oxford	• King's Bench Chambers	01865 311066
	28 Western Road	01865 204911
Portsmouth	Hampshire Chambers	01705 826636
Preston	New Bailey Chambers	01772 258 087
Reading	Dr Johnson's Chambers	01189 254221
	Wessex Chambers	0118 956 8856
Redhill	Redhill Chambers	01737 780781
Sheffield	Bank House Chambers	0114 275 1223
Slough	11 St Bernards Road	01753 553806/817989
Stoke-on-Trent	Regent Chambers	01782 286666
Swansea	Angel Chambers	01792 464623/464648
Wolverhampton	Claremont Chambers	01902 426222
York	• York Chambers	01904 620 048

INFORMATION TECHNOLOGY

Birmingham	• Equity Chambers	0121 233 2100
	• 3 Fountain Court	0121 236 5854
	• 5 Fountain Court	0121 606 0500
Coulsdon	Advolex Chambers	0181 763 2345
Leeds	11 King's Bench Walk	0113 2971 200
	The Chambers of Philip Raynor QC	0113 242 1123
Liverpool	• Oriel Chambers	0151 236 7191
London	Atkin Chambers	0171 404 0102
	9 Bedford Row	0171 242 3555
	Brick Court Chambers	0171 583 0777
	Bridewell Chambers	0171 797 8800
	• Devereux Chambers	0171 353 7534
	Equity Barristers' Chambers	0181 558 8336
	• Essex Court Chambers	0171 813 8000
	• 35 Essex Street	0171 353 6381
	• 4 Field Court	0171 440 6900
	• Fountain Court	0171 583 3335
	Francis Taylor Buildings	0171 353 7768/2711
	• 2 Garden Court	0171 353 1633
	• 2-3 Gray's Inn Square	0171 242 4986
	• 2 Harcourt Buildings	0171 583 9020
	• One Hare Court	0171 353 3171
	• Keating Chambers	0171 544 2600
	• Littleton Chambers	0171 797 8600
	• Littman Chambers	0171 404 4866
	• Mitre Court Chambers	0171 353 9394
	• New Court	0171 797 8999
	• New Court Chambers	0171 831 9500
	• 3 New Square	0171 405 1111
	5 New Square	0171 404 0404
	• 8 New Square	0171 405 4321
	• 12 New Square	0171 419 1212
	19 Old Buildings	0171 405 2001
	• 3 Paper Buildings	0171 797 7000
	• 4 Paper Buildings	0171 353 3366/583 7155
	• 4 Pump Court	0171 353 2656/9
	• 1 Raymond Buildings	0171 430 1234
	• 5 Raymond Buildings	0171 242 2902
	• 11 South Square	0171 405 1222
	• Stanbrook & Henderson	0171 353 0101
	• 9 Stone Buildings	0171 404 5055
	11 Stone Buildings	+44 (0)171 831 6381
	• 199 Strand	0171 379 9779
	• 2 Temple Gardens	0171 583 6041
	• 3 Verulam Buildings	0171 831 8441
Manchester	• Cobden House Chambers	0161 833 6000/6001
	Deans Court Chambers	0161 834 4097
	• 40 King Street	0161 832 9082

	• St James's Chambers	0161 834 7000
Norwich	East Anglian Chambers	01603 617351
Nottingham	Ropewalk Chambers	0115 947 2581
Preston	Deans Court Chambers	01772 555163
	New Bailey Chambers	01772 258 087
Southampton	• Eighteen Carlton Crescent	01703 639001

INQUESTS

London	• Dr Johnson's Chambers	0171 353 4716

INSOLVENCY

Birmingham	• Equity Chambers	0121 233 2100
	1 Fountain Court	0121 236 5721
	• 3 Fountain Court	0121 236 5854
	• 5 Fountain Court	0121 606 0500
	6 Fountain Court	0121 233 3282
	• 8 Fountain Court	0121 236 5514
	• St Philip's Chambers	0121 246 7000
Bournemouth	King's Bench Chambers	01202 250025
Bradford	Broadway House Chambers	01274 722560
Brighton	• Crown Office Row Chambers	01273 625625
Bristol	St John's Chambers	0117 921 3456/929 8514
Cambridge	• Fenners Chambers	01223 368761
Cardiff	9 Park Place	01222 382731
	30 Park Place	01222 398421
	• 33 Park Place	01222 233313
Chester	40 King Street	01244 323886
Chichester	Chichester Chambers	01243 784538
Eastbourne	King's Chambers	01323 416053
Exeter	• Cathedral Chambers (Jan Wood	01392 210900
	Independent Barristers' Clerk)	
	Rougemont Chambers	01392 410471
Leeds	Chambers of Andrew Campbell QC	0113 245 5438
	• Chancery House Chambers	0113 244 6691
	Enterprise Chambers	0113 246 0391
	11 King's Bench Walk	0113 2971 200
	• Mercury Chambers	0113 234 2265
	• No. 6	0113 245 9763
	The Chambers of Philip Raynor QC	0113 242 1123
	• Sovereign Chambers	0113 245 1841/2/3
	• St Paul's House	0113 245 5866
Liverpool	19 Castle Street Chambers	0151 236 9402
	• Exchange Chambers	0151 236 7747
	• The Chambers of Adrian Lyon	0151 236 4421/8240/6757
	• Martins Building	0151 236 5818/4919
	• Oriel Chambers	0151 236 7191
London	Barnard's Inn Chambers	0171 242 8508
	17 Bedford Row	0171 831 7314
	• 29 Bedford Row Chambers	0171 831 2626
	• 5 Bell Yard	0171 333 8811
	11 Bolt Court	0171 353 2300
	• Bracton Chambers	0171 242 4248
	Bridewell Chambers	0171 797 8800
	Cloisters	0171 827 4000
	• Chambers of Mr Peter Crampin QC	0171 831 0081
	1 Crown Office Row	0171 583 9292
	• Dr Johnson's Chambers	0171 353 4716
	• Enterprise Chambers	0171 405 9471
	Equity Barristers' Chambers	0181 558 8336
	• Erskine Chambers	0171 242 5532
	• One Essex Court	0171 583 2000
	• Essex Court Chambers	0171 813 8000
	• Chambers of Norman Palmer	0171 405 6114
	• 4 Field Court	0171 440 6900
	• Fountain Court	0171 583 3335
	• 2nd Floor, Francis Taylor Building	0171 353 9942
	Francis Taylor Buildings	0171 353 7768/2711
	• Goldsmith Building	0171 353 7881
	Goldsmith Chambers	0171 353 6802/3/4/5
	Goldsworth Chambers	0171 405 7117
	• Gough Square Chambers	0171 353 0924

A

	• 1 Gray's Inn Square	0171 405 8946
	2 Gray's Inn Square Chambers	0171 242 0328/405 1317
	10 - 11 Gray's Inn Square	0171 405 2576
	• 1 Harcourt Buildings	0171 353 9421/0375
	• Hardwicke Building	0171 242 2523
	• One Hare Court	0171 353 3171
	• 3 Hare Court	0171 353 7561
Harrow on the Hill	• Harrow-on-the-Hill Chambers	0181 423 7444
London	• 4 King's Bench Walk	0171 822 8822
	• 9 King's Bench Walk	0171 353 7202/3909
	The Chambers of Mr Ali Mohammad Azhar	0171 353 9564 (4 lines)
	11 King's Bench Walk	0171 353 3337/8
	• 13 King's Bench Walk	0171 353 7204
	• Lamb Building	0171 797 7788
	Lamb Chambers	0171 797 8300
	Lion Court	0171 404 6565
	• Littleton Chambers	0171 797 8600
	• Littman Chambers	0171 404 4866
	• Mitre Court Chambers	0171 353 9394
	• Monckton Chambers	0171 405 7211
	• New Court	0171 583 5123
	• 1 New Square	0171 405 0884/5/6/7
	Chambers of Lord Goodhart QC	0171 405 5577
	5 New Square	0171 404 0404
	• 12 New Square	0171 419 1212
	Chambers of Joy Okoye	0171 405 7011
	• 22 Old Buildings	0171 831 0222
	• Twenty-Four Old Buildings	0171 404 0946
	• 9 Old Square	0171 405 4682
	The Chambers of Leolin Price CBE, QC	0171 405 0758/242 5002
	11 Old Square	0171 242 5022
	• 11 Old Square	0171 430 0341
	• 13 Old Square	0171 404 4800
	• 3 Paper Buildings	0171 797 7000
	• 4 Paper Buildings	0171 353 3366/583 7155
	• 4 Paper Buildings	0171 583 0816
	• 5 Paper Buildings	0171 583 9275
	Phoenix Chambers	0171 404 7888
	Plowden Buildings	0171 583 0808
	• Chambers of John L Powell QC	0171 797 8000
	• Pump Court Chambers	0171 353 0711
	• 5 Pump Court	0171 353 2532
	• Serle Court Chambers	0171 242 6105
	• 3-4 South Square	0171 696 9900
	• 3 Stone Buildings	0171 242 4937/405 8358
	4 Stone Buildings	0171 242 5524
	• 5 Stone Buildings	0171 242 6201
	• 7 Stone Buildings	0171 405 3886/242 3546
	• 9 Stone Buildings	0171 404 5055
	11 Stone Buildings	+44 (0)171 831 6381
	• 199 Strand	0171 379 9779
	169 Temple Chambers	0171 583 7644
	• 2 Temple Gardens	0171 583 6041
	• Thomas More Chambers	0171 404 7000
	• 3 Verulam Buildings	0171 831 8441
	Warwick House Chambers	0171 430 2323
Manchester	• Cobden House Chambers	0161 833 6000/6001
	Deans Court Chambers	0161 834 4097
	• Chambers of John Hand QC	0161 955 9000
	• 40 King Street	0161 832 9082
	• 8 King Street Chambers	0161 834 9560
	58 King Street Chambers	0161 831 7477
	Manchester House Chambers	0161 834 7007
	• Merchant Chambers	0161 839 7070
	• Queen's Chambers	0161 834 6875/4738
	• St James's Chambers	0161 834 7000
	Young Street Chambers	0161 833 0489
Middlesbrough	• Fountain Chambers	01642 217037
Newcastle upon Tyne	• Broad Chare	0191 232 0541
	Enterprise Chambers	0191 222 3344
	• New Court Chambers	0191 232 1980

	• Trinity Chambers	0191 232 1927
	Westgate Chambers	0191 261 4407/232 9785
Northampton	22 Albion Place	01604 636271
Norwich	East Anglian Chambers	01603 617351
Nottingham	King Charles House	0115 941 8851
	Ropewalk Chambers	0115 947 2581
	St Mary's Chambers	0115 950 3503
Oxford	• King's Bench Chambers	01865 311066
Peterborough	Fenners Chambers	01733 562030
Portsmouth	Hampshire Chambers	01705 826636
	• Portsmouth Barristers' Chambers	01705 831292
Preston	4 Camden Place	01772 828300
	Deans Court Chambers	01772 555163
	New Bailey Chambers	01772 258 087
	15 Winckley Square	01772 252 828
Reading	Wessex Chambers	0118 956 8856
Redhill	Redhill Chambers	01737 780781
Southampton	• College Chambers	01703 230338
	• Eighteen Carlton Crescent	01703 639001
Stoke-on-Trent	Regent Chambers	01782 286666
Swansea	Angel Chambers	01792 464623/464648
	Gower Chambers	01792 644466
	Iscoed Chambers	01792 652988/9/330
Swindon	Pump Court Chambers	01793 539899
Winchester	Pump Court Chambers	01962 868161
Wolverhampton	Claremont Chambers	01902 426222

INSURANCE

Birmingham	• Equity Chambers	0121 233 2100
	1 Fountain Court	0121 236 5721
	• 5 Fountain Court	0121 606 0500
	• 8 Fountain Court	0121 236 5514
	• St Philip's Chambers	0121 246 7000
Bournemouth	King's Bench Chambers	01202 250025
Bristol	St John's Chambers	0117 921 3456/929 8514
Cardiff	9 Park Place	01222 382731
	30 Park Place	01222 398421
	• 33 Park Place	01222 233313
Leeds	Chambers of Andrew Campbell QC	0113 245 5438
	• Chancery House Chambers	0113 244 6691
	The Chambers of Philip Raynor QC	0113 242 1123
Liverpool	• Exchange Chambers	0151 236 7747
	India Buildings Chambers	0151 243 6000
	• The Chambers of Adrian Lyon	0151 236 4421/8240/6757
London	Barnard's Inn Chambers	0171 242 8508
	9 Bedford Row	0171 242 3555
	• 5 Bell Yard	0171 333 8811
	• Blackstone Chambers (formerly known	0171 583 1770
	as 2 Hare Court)	
	• Bracton Chambers	0171 242 4248
	Brick Court Chambers	0171 583 0777
	Bridewell Chambers	0171 797 8800
	• 1 Crown Office Row	0171 797 7500
	1 Crown Office Row	0171 583 9292
	• Two Crown Office Row	0171 797 8100
	• Devereux Chambers	0171 353 7534
	Equity Barristers' Chambers	0181 558 8336
	• One Essex Court	0171 583 2000
	• One Essex Court	0171 936 3030
	• 4 Essex Court	0171 797 7970
	• Essex Court Chambers	0171 813 8000
	• 20 Essex Street	0171 583 9294
	• 39 Essex Street	0171 832 1111
	• Chambers of Norman Palmer	0171 405 6114
	• 4 Field Court	0171 440 6900
	• Fountain Court	0171 583 3335
	• Goldsmith Building	0171 353 7881
	2 Gray's Inn Square Chambers	0171 242 0328/405 1317
	• 4-5 Gray's Inn Square	0171 404 5252
	• 1 Harcourt Buildings	0171 353 9421/0375
	• 2 Harcourt Buildings	0171 583 9020
	• Hardwicke Building	0171 242 2523

	• One Hare Court	0171 353 3171
Harrow on the Hill	• Harrow-on-the-Hill Chambers	0181 423 7444
London	• 4 King's Bench Walk	0171 822 8822
	• 8 King's Bench Walk	0171 797 8888
	The Chambers of Mr Ali Mohammad Azhar	0171 353 9564 (4 lines)
	11 King's Bench Walk	0171 353 3337/8
	• 12 King's Bench Walk	0171 583 0811
	• 13 King's Bench Walk	0171 353 7204
	Lamb Chambers	0171 797 8300
	• Littleton Chambers	0171 797 8600
	• Littman Chambers	0171 404 4866
	• Mitre Court Chambers	0171 353 9394
	• 12 New Square	0171 419 1212
	Chambers of Joy Okoye	0171 405 7011
	• 22 Old Buildings	0171 831 0222
	11 Old Square	0171 242 5022
	• 13 Old Square	0171 404 4800
	One Paper Buildings	0171 583 7355
	• 3 Paper Buildings	0171 797 7000
	• 4 Paper Buildings	0171 353 3366/583 7155
	• Chambers of John L Powell QC	0171 797 8000
	• 4 Pump Court	0171 353 2656/9
	• 5 Pump Court	0171 353 2532
	No 1 Serjeants' Inn	0171 415 6666
	• 3-4 South Square	0171 696 9900
	• Stanbrook & Henderson	0171 353 0101
	• 3 Stone Buildings	0171 242 4937/405 8358
	4 Stone Buildings	0171 242 5524
	8 Stone Buildings	0171 831 9881
	• 9 Stone Buildings	0171 404 5055
	11 Stone Buildings	+44 (0)171 831 6381
	• 199 Strand	0171 379 9779
	169 Temple Chambers	0171 583 7644
	• 1 Temple Gardens	0171 353 0407/583 1315
	• 2 Temple Gardens	0171 583 6041
	• 3 Verulam Buildings	0171 831 8441
	Warwick House Chambers	0171 430 2323
Manchester	• Byrom Street Chambers	0161 829 2100
	Deans Court Chambers	0161 834 4097
	• Chambers of John Hand QC	0161 955 9000
	• 40 King Street	0161 832 9082
	• 8 King Street Chambers	0161 834 9560
	• Merchant Chambers	0161 839 7070
	• St James's Chambers	0161 834 7000
Newcastle upon Tyne	• Trinity Chambers	0191 232 1927
Norwich	East Anglian Chambers	01603 617351
Nottingham	Ropewalk Chambers	0115 947 2581
Oxford	• King's Bench Chambers	01865 311066
Portsmouth	• Portsmouth Barristers' Chambers	01705 831292
Preston	Deans Court Chambers	01772 555163
	New Bailey Chambers	01772 258 087
	15 Winckley Square	01772 252 828
Wolverhampton	Claremont Chambers	01902 426222

INSURANCE/REINSURANCE

Birmingham	• 5 Fountain Court	0121 606 0500
Exeter	• Cathedral Chambers (Jan Wood Independent Barristers' Clerk)	01392 210900
Leeds	Chambers of Andrew Campbell QC	0113 245 5438
Liverpool	• Exchange Chambers	0151 236 7747
London	9 Bedford Row	0171 242 3555
	17 Bedford Row	0171 831 7314
	• 5 Bell Yard	0171 333 8811
	• Blackstone Chambers (formerly known as 2 Hare Court)	0171 583 1770
	Brick Court Chambers	0171 583 0777
	• Chambers of Mr Peter Crampin QC	0171 831 0081
	• 1 Crown Office Row	0171 797 7500
	1 Crown Office Row	0171 583 9292
	• Two Crown Office Row	0171 797 8100
	• Devereux Chambers	0171 353 7534

• Expanded entry in Part C

A

Equity Barristers' Chambers	0181 558 8336
• One Essex Court	0171 583 2000
• 4 Essex Court	0171 797 7970
• Essex Court Chambers	0171 813 8000
• 20 Essex Street	0171 583 9294
• 39 Essex Street	0171 832 1111
• Chambers of Norman Palmer	0171 405 6114
• 4 Field Court	0171 440 6900
• Fountain Court	0171 583 3335
2 Gray's Inn Square Chambers	0171 242 0328/405 1317
• 4-5 Gray's Inn Square	0171 404 5252
• 2 Harcourt Buildings	0171 583 9020
• One Hare Court	0171 353 3171
• Keating Chambers	0171 544 2600
• 4 King's Bench Walk	0171 822 8822
S Tomlinson QC	0171 583 0404
• 8 King's Bench Walk	0171 797 8888
The Chambers of Mr Ali Mohammad Azhar	0171 353 9564 (4 lines)
• 11 King's Bench Walk	0171 632 8500
11 King's Bench Walk	0171 353 3337/8
• 12 King's Bench Walk	0171 583 0811
• Mitre Court Chambers	0171 353 9394
• Monckton Chambers	0171 405 7211
• 1 New Square	0171 405 0884/5/6/7
• 12 New Square	0171 419 1212
11 Old Square	0171 242 5022
• 13 Old Square	0171 404 4800
One Paper Buildings	0171 583 7355
• Chambers of John L Powell QC	0171 797 8000
• 4 Pump Court	0171 353 2656/9
• 5 Raymond Buildings	0171 242 2902
No 1 Serjeants' Inn	0171 415 6666
• 3-4 South Square	0171 696 9900
• Stanbrook & Henderson	0171 353 0101
• 3 Stone Buildings	0171 242 4937/405 8358
• 9 Stone Buildings	0171 404 5055
• 2 Temple Gardens	0171 583 6041
• 3 Verulam Buildings	0171 831 8441
Warwick House Chambers	0171 430 2323

Manchester	Deans Court Chambers	0161 834 4097
	• Chambers of John Hand QC	0161 955 9000
	• 8 King Street Chambers	0161 834 9560
	• Merchant Chambers	0161 839 7070
Norwich	East Anglian Chambers	01603 617351
Nottingham	Ropewalk Chambers	0115 947 2581
Preston	Deans Court Chambers	01772 555163
	New Bailey Chambers	01772 258 087
Wolverhampton	Claremont Chambers	01902 426222

INTELLECTUAL PROPERTY

Birmingham	• Equity Chambers	0121 233 2100
	1 Fountain Court	0121 236 5721
	• 3 Fountain Court	0121 236 5854
	• 5 Fountain Court	0121 606 0500
Bristol	St John's Chambers	0117 921 3456/929 8514
Cardiff	9 Park Place	01222 382731
Chichester	Chichester Chambers	01243 784538
Haverhill	Helions Chambers	01440 730523
Leeds	Chambers of Andrew Campbell QC	0113 245 5438
	• Chancery House Chambers	0113 244 6691
	The Chambers of Philip Raynor QC	0113 242 1123
	• Sovereign Chambers	0113 245 1841/2/3
Liverpool	• The Chambers of Adrian Lyon	0151 236 4421/8240/6757
London	17 Bedford Row	0171 831 7314
	• 29 Bedford Row Chambers	0171 831 2626
	• Blackstone Chambers (formerly known as 2 Hare Court)	0171 583 1770
	• Doughty Street Chambers	0171 404 1313
	Equity Barristers' Chambers	0181 558 8336
	• One Essex Court	0171 583 2000
	• Essex Court Chambers	0171 813 8000

	• 20 Essex Street	0171 583 9294
	• 35 Essex Street	0171 353 6381
	• 4 Field Court	0171 440 6900
	• Fountain Court	0171 583 3335
	Francis Taylor Buildings	0171 353 7768/2711
	Goldsworth Chambers	0171 405 7117
	2 Gray's Inn Square Chambers	0171 242 0328/405 1317
	10 - 11 Gray's Inn Square	0171 405 2576
	• 2 Harcourt Buildings	0171 583 9020
	• Hardwicke Building	0171 242 2523
	• One Hare Court	0171 353 3171
	• 9 King's Bench Walk	0171 353 7202/3909
	The Chambers of Mr Ali Mohammad Azhar	0171 353 9564 (4 lines)
	10 King's Bench Walk	0171 353 7742
	• 11 King's Bench Walk	0171 632 8500
	11 King's Bench Walk	0171 353 3337/8
	• 13 King's Bench Walk	0171 353 7204
	Lamb Chambers	0171 797 8300
	• Littleton Chambers	0171 797 8600
	2 Mitre Court Buildings	0171 353 1353
	• Monckton Chambers	0171 405 7211
	• New Court	0171 797 8999
	• 1 New Square	0171 405 0884/5/6/7
	• 3 New Square	0171 405 1111
	5 New Square	0171 404 0404
	• 8 New Square	0171 405 4321
	• 12 New Square	0171 419 1212
	19 Old Buildings	0171 405 2001
	• 11 Old Square	0171 430 0341
	• 13 Old Square	0171 404 4800
	• 3 Paper Buildings	0171 797 7000
	• 4 Paper Buildings	0171 353 3366/583 7155
	Phoenix Chambers	0171 404 7888
	Prince Henry's Chambers	0171 353 1183/1190
	• 1 Raymond Buildings	0171 430 1234
	• 5 Raymond Buildings	0171 242 2902
	• 11 South Square	0171 405 1222
	• Stanbrook & Henderson	0171 353 0101
	• 7 Stone Buildings	0171 405 3886/242 3546
	• 9 Stone Buildings	0171 404 5055
	11 Stone Buildings	+44 (0)171 831 6381
	• 199 Strand	0171 379 9779
	• 3 Verulam Buildings	0171 831 8441
Manchester	• Byrom Street Chambers	0161 829 2100
	• Cobden House Chambers	0161 833 6000/6001
	• Chambers of John Hand QC	0161 955 9000
	• 40 King Street	0161 832 9082
	• 8 King Street Chambers	0161 834 9560
	• Merchant Chambers	0161 839 7070
	• Queen's Chambers	0161 834 6875/4738
	• St James's Chambers	0161 834 7000
	18 St John Street	0161 278 1800
Newcastle upon Tyne	Westgate Chambers	0191 261 4407/232 9785
Northampton	22 Albion Place	01604 636271
Norwich	East Anglian Chambers	01603 617351
Nottingham	King Charles House	0115 941 8851
	Ropewalk Chambers	0115 947 2581
Oxford	• King's Bench Chambers	01865 311066
Portsmouth	• Portsmouth Barristers' Chambers	01705 831292
Preston	New Bailey Chambers	01772 258 087
Reading	Wessex Chambers	0118 956 8856
Richmond-upon-Thames	Richmond Green Chambers	0181 940 1841
Southampton	• Eighteen Carlton Crescent	01703 639001
Swansea	Angel Chambers	01792 464623/464648
Wolverhampton	Claremont Chambers	01902 426222

INTERNATIONAL TRADE

Birmingham	• Equity Chambers	0121 233 2100
	• 5 Fountain Court	0121 606 0500
Leeds	• Chancery House Chambers	0113 244 6691
Liverpool	• Exchange Chambers	0151 236 7747

• Expanded entry in Part C

London
- Blackstone Chambers (formerly known as 2 Hare Court) — 0171 583 1770
- Brick Court Chambers — 0171 583 0777
- 1 Crown Office Row — 0171 583 9292
- Equity Barristers' Chambers — 0181 558 8336
- 4 Essex Court — 0171 797 7970
- Essex Court Chambers — 0171 813 8000
- 20 Essex Street — 0171 583 9294
- Chambers of Norman Palmer — 0171 405 6114
- 4 Field Court — 0171 440 6900
- Fountain Court — 0171 583 3335
- 1 Gray's Inn Square Chambers of the Baroness Scotland of Asthal QC — 0171 405 3000
- 2 Harcourt Buildings — 0171 583 9020
- One Hare Court — 0171 353 3171
- John Street Chambers — 0171 242 1911
- 4 King's Bench Walk S Tomlinson QC — 0171 822 8822 / 0171 583 0404
- The Chambers of Mr Ali Mohammad Azhar — 0171 353 9564 (4 lines)
- 11 King's Bench Walk — 0171 632 8500
- Lamb Chambers — 0171 797 8300
- Littleton Chambers — 0171 797 8600
- Littman Chambers — 0171 404 4866
- Monckton Chambers — 0171 405 7211
- New Court — 0171 797 8999
- 12 New Square — 0171 419 1212
- 5 Paper Buildings — 0171 583 9275
- 5 Raymond Buildings — 0171 242 2902
- 3-4 South Square — 0171 696 9900
- Stanbrook & Henderson — 0171 353 0101
- 9 Stone Buildings — 0171 404 5055
- 11 Stone Buildings — +44 (0)171 831 6381
- 3 Verulam Buildings — 0171 831 8441

Manchester — Byrom Street Chambers — 0161 829 2100
Preston — New Bailey Chambers — 01772 258 087

ISLAMIC LAW

London — Chambers of Dr Jamal Nasir — 0171 405 3818/9

JUDICIAL REVIEW

Liverpool — India Buildings Chambers — 0151 243 6000
London — Gray's Inn Square — 0171 242 3529
- Queen Elizabeth Building — 0171 583 5766
- Thomas More Chambers — 0171 404 7000
Manchester — Central Chambers — 0161 833 1774

LANDLORD AND TENANT

Birmingham
- Equity Chambers — 0121 233 2100
- 1 Fountain Court — 0121 236 5721
- 3 Fountain Court — 0121 236 5854
- 5 Fountain Court — 0121 606 0500
- 8 Fountain Court — 0121 236 5514
- New Court Chambers — 0121 693 6656
- St Philip's Chambers — 0121 246 7000

Bournemouth — King's Bench Chambers — 01202 250025
- 20 Lorne Park Road — 01202 292102

Bradford — Broadway House Chambers — 01274 722560
Brighton — Crown Office Row Chambers — 01273 625625
Bristol — St John's Chambers — 0117 921 3456/929 8514
Cambridge — Fenners Chambers — 01223 368761
- Regency Chambers — 01223 301517

Canterbury — Stour Chambers — 01227 764899
Cardiff — 9 Park Place — 01222 382731
- 30 Park Place — 01222 398421
- 32 Park Place — 01222 397364
- 33 Park Place — 01222 233313
- 40 King Street — 01244 323886

Chester — White Friars Chambers — 01244 323070
Chichester — Chichester Chambers — 01243 784538

Eastbourne	King's Chambers	01323 416053
Ely	Cathedral Chambers, Ely	01353 666775
Enfield	Enfield Chambers	0181 364 5627
Exeter	• Cathedral Chambers (Jan Wood Independent Barristers' Clerk)	01392 210900
	Colleton Chambers	01392 274898
	Rougemont Chambers	01392 410471
	Southernhay Chambers	01392 255777
	Walnut House	01392 279751
Guildford	• Guildford Chambers	01483 539131
Leatherhead	Pembroke House	01372 376160/376493
Leeds	Chambers of Andrew Campbell QC	0113 245 5438
	• Chancery House Chambers	0113 244 6691
	Enterprise Chambers	0113 246 0391
	11 King's Bench Walk	0113 2971 200
	• No. 6	0113 245 9763
	• Park Court Chambers	0113 243 3277
	The Chambers of Philip Raynor QC	0113 242 1123
	• 37 Park Square	0113 243 9422
	• Sovereign Chambers	0113 245 1841/2/3
	• St Paul's House	0113 245 5866
	• 9 Woodhouse Square	0113 245 1986
Liverpool	25-27 Castle Street	0151 227 5661/5666/236 5072
	19 Castle Street Chambers	0151 236 9402
	Chavasse Court Chambers	0151 707 1191
	• The Corn Exchange Chambers	0151 227 1081/5009
	• Exchange Chambers	0151 236 7747
	First National Chambers	0151 236 2098
	India Buildings Chambers	0151 243 6000
	• The Chambers of Adrian Lyon	0151 236 4421/8240/6757
	• Martins Building	0151 236 5818/4919
	• Oriel Chambers	0151 236 7191
London	Alban Chambers	0171 419 5051
	Albany Chambers	0171 485 5736/38
	• Arden Chambers	0171 242 4244
	Barnard's Inn Chambers	0171 242 8508
	Barristers' Common Law Chambers	0171 375 3012
	9 Bedford Row	0171 242 3555
	17 Bedford Row	0171 831 7314
	33 Bedford Row	0171 242 6476
	• 29 Bedford Row Chambers	0171 831 2626
	• 5 Bell Yard	0171 333 8811
	11 Bolt Court	0171 353 2300
	• Bracton Chambers	0171 242 4248
	• 4 Breams Buildings	0171 353 5835/430 1221
	• 4 Brick Court	0171 797 8910
	• 4 Brick Court	0171 797 7766
	Bridewell Chambers	0171 797 8800
	Britton Street Chambers	0171 608 3765
	• Chambers of Mr Peter Crampin QC	0171 831 0081
	• 1 Crown Office Row	0171 797 7500
	1 Crown Office Row	0171 583 9292
	• Devereux Chambers	0171 353 7534
	• Doughty Street Chambers	0171 404 1313
	• 3 Dr Johnson's Buildings	0171 353 4854
	• Dr Johnson's Chambers	0171 353 4716
	• Enterprise Chambers	0171 405 9471
	• One Essex Court	0171 936 3030
	5 Essex Court	0171 410 2000
	• 35 Essex Street	0171 353 6381
	Chambers of Geoffrey Hawker	0171 583 8899
	Falcon Chambers	0171 353 2484
	• Farrar's Building	0171 583 9241
	• Chambers of Norman Palmer	0171 405 6114
	• 4 Field Court	0171 440 6900
	• 2nd Floor, Francis Taylor Building	0171 353 9942
	Francis Taylor Buildings	0171 353 7768/2711
	• 2 Garden Court	0171 353 1633
	• Goldsmith Building	0171 353 7881
	Goldsmith Chambers	0171 353 6802/3/4/5
	Goldsworth Chambers	0171 405 7117
	• 9 Gough Square	0171 353 5371

A

• Gough Square Chambers	0171 353 0924
• Gray's Inn Chambers	0171 831 5344
• Gray's Inn Chambers	0171 404 1111
• 1 Gray's Inn Square Chambers of the Baroness Scotland of Asthal QC	0171 405 3000
• 1 Gray's Inn Square	0171 405 8946
2 Gray's Inn Square Chambers	0171 242 0328/405 1317
• 2-3 Gray's Inn Square	0171 242 4986
• 4-5 Gray's Inn Square	0171 404 5252
6 Gray's Inn Square	0171 242 1052
10 - 11 Gray's Inn Square	0171 405 2576
• 1 Harcourt Buildings	0171 353 9421/0375
• 2 Harcourt Buildings	0171 583 9020
• 2 Harcourt Buildings	0171 353 8415
• Hardwicke Building	0171 242 2523
• One Hare Court	0171 353 3171
Chambers of Harjit Singh	0171 353 1356
• Harrow-on-the-Hill Chambers	0181 423 7444
• Chambers of James Hunt QC	0171 421 8000
• John Street Chambers	0171 242 1911
Justice Court Chambers	0181 830 7786
• Keating Chambers	0171 544 2600
• 4 King's Bench Walk	0171 822 8822
4 King's Bench Walk	0171 353 3581
6 King's Bench Walk	0171 353 4931/583 0695
• 8 King's Bench Walk	0171 797 8888
• 9 King's Bench Walk	0171 353 7202/3909
The Chambers of Mr Ali Mohammad Azhar	0171 353 9564 (4 lines)
10 King's Bench Walk	0171 353 7742
11 King's Bench Walk	0171 353 3337/8
• 12 King's Bench Walk	0171 583 0811
• 13 King's Bench Walk	0171 353 7204
• Chambers of Lord Campbell of Alloway QC	0171 353 9276
• Lamb Building	0171 797 7788
Lamb Chambers	0171 797 8300
Lion Court	0171 404 6565
• Littleton Chambers	0171 797 8600
• Littman Chambers	0171 404 4866
2 Mitre Court Buildings	0171 353 1353
2 Mitre Court Buildings	0171 583 1380
• Mitre Court Chambers	0171 353 9394
• Mitre House Chambers	0171 583 8233
• New Court	0171 583 5123
• New Court Chambers	0171 831 9500
• 1 New Square	0171 405 0884/5/6/7
Chambers of Lord Goodhart QC	0171 405 5577
5 New Square	0171 404 0404
• 12 New Square	0171 419 1212
Chambers of Joy Okoye	0171 405 7011
• 22 Old Buildings	0171 831 0222
• Twenty-Four Old Buildings	0171 404 0946
• 9 Old Square	0171 405 4682
The Chambers of Leolin Price CBE, QC	0171 405 0758/242 5002
11 Old Square	0171 242 5022
• 11 Old Square	0171 430 0341
• 13 Old Square	0171 404 4800
• 2 Paper Buildings	0171 353 0933
• 2 Paper Buildings	0171 936 2611 (10 lines)
• 3 Paper Buildings	0171 797 7000
• 3 Paper Buildings	0171 583 8055
• 4 Paper Buildings	0171 353 3366/583 7155
• 4 Paper Buildings	0171 583 0816
• 5 Paper Buildings	0171 583 9275
Phoenix Chambers	0171 404 7888
• Chambers of John L Powell QC	0171 797 8000
• 1 Pump Court	0171 583 2012/353 4341
2 Pump Court	0171 353 5597
• Pump Court Chambers	0171 353 0711
• 5 Pump Court	0171 353 2532
• Chambers of Kieran Coonan QC	0171 583 6013/2510

**Harrow on the Hill
London**

	6 Pump Court	0171 797 8400
	No 1 Serjeants' Inn	0171 415 6666
	• Serle Court Chambers	0171 242 6105
	• Stanbrook & Henderson	0171 353 0101
	• 3 Stone Buildings	0171 242 4937/405 8358
	• 5 Stone Buildings	0171 242 6201
	• 7 Stone Buildings	0171 405 3886/242 3546
	7 Stone Buildings	0171 242 0961
	• 9 Stone Buildings	0171 404 5055
	11 Stone Buildings	+44 (0)171 831 6381
	• 199 Strand	0171 379 9779
	169 Temple Chambers	0171 583 7644
	• 1 Temple Gardens	0171 353 0407/583 1315
	• 2 Temple Gardens	0171 583 6041
	3 Temple Gardens (North)	0171 353 0853/4/7222
	• Thomas More Chambers	0171 404 7000
	• 14 Tooks Court	0171 405 8828
	• 3 Verulam Buildings	0171 831 8441
	Verulam Chambers	0171 813 2400
	Warwick House Chambers	0171 430 2323
	• Wilberforce Chambers	0171 306 0102
	39 Windsor Road	0181 349 9194
Maidstone	• Maidstone Chambers	01622 688592
Manchester	• Central Chambers	0161 833 1774
	• Cobden House Chambers	0161 833 6000/6001
	Deans Court Chambers	0161 834 4097
	• Chambers of John Hand QC	0161 955 9000
	Kenworthy's Chambers	0161 832 4036
	• 40 King Street	0161 832 9082
	• 8 King Street Chambers	0161 834 9560
	58 King Street Chambers	0161 831 7477
	Chambers of Ian Macdonald QC	0161 236 1840
	Manchester House Chambers	0161 834 7007
	• Merchant Chambers	0161 839 7070
	Peel Court Chambers	0161 832 3791
	• Queen's Chambers	0161 834 6875/4738
	• St James's Chambers	0161 834 7000
	18 St John Street	0161 278 1800
	• 28 St John Street	0161 834 8418
	Young Street Chambers	0161 833 0489
Middlesbrough	Baker Street Chambers	01642 873873
	• Fountain Chambers	01642 217037
Milton Keynes	Milton Keynes Chambers	01908 217857
Newcastle upon Tyne	• Broad Chare	0191 232 0541
	Cathedral Chambers	0191 232 1311
	Enterprise Chambers	0191 222 3344
	• New Court Chambers	0191 232 1980
	• Trinity Chambers	0191 232 1927
	Westgate Chambers	0191 261 4407/232 9785
Northampton	22 Albion Place	01604 636271
	Chartlands Chambers	01604 603322
Norwich	East Anglian Chambers	01603 617351
	Octagon House	01603 623186
	Sackville Chambers	01603 613516
Nottingham	King Charles House	0115 941 8851
	Ropewalk Chambers	0115 947 2581
Oxford	1 Alfred Street	01865 793736
	• King's Bench Chambers	01865 311066
	28 Western Road	01865 204911
Peterborough	Fenners Chambers	01733 562030
	Regency Chambers	01733 315215
Plymouth	Devon Chambers	01752 661659
Portsmouth	Hampshire Chambers	01705 826636
	• Portsmouth Barristers' Chambers	01705 831292
Preston	4 Camden Place	01772 828300
	Deans Court Chambers	01772 555163
	New Bailey Chambers	01772 258 087
	15 Winckley Square	01772 252 828
Reading	Dr Johnson's Chambers	01189 254221
	Wessex Chambers	0118 956 8856
Redhill	Redhill Chambers	01737 780781
Richmond-upon-Thames	Richmond Green Chambers	0181 940 1841

     • Expanded entry in Part C

Sheffield	Paradise Square Chambers	0114 273 8951
Shepperton	Abbey Chambers	01932 560913
Slough	11 St Bernards Road	01753 553806/817989
Sonning-on-Thames	Greenway	0118 969 2484
Southampton	• 17 Carlton Crescent	01703 320320
	• College Chambers	01703 230338
	• Eighteen Carlton Crescent	01703 639001
Stoke-on-Trent	Regent Chambers	01782 286666
Swansea	Angel Chambers	01792 464623/464648
	Gower Chambers	01792 644466
	Iscoed Chambers	01792 652988/9/330
Winchester	4 St Peter Street	01962 868 884
Wolverhampton	Claremont Chambers	01902 426222
York	• York Chambers	01904 620 048

LICENSING

Birmingham	• Equity Chambers	0121 233 2100
	1 Fountain Court	0121 236 5721
	• 3 Fountain Court	0121 236 5854
	• 5 Fountain Court	0121 606 0500
	6 Fountain Court	0121 233 3282
	• St Philip's Chambers	0121 246 7000
Bournemouth	King's Bench Chambers	01202 250025
	20 Lorne Park Road	01202 292102
Bradford	Broadway House Chambers	01274 722560
Brighton	• Crown Office Row Chambers	01273 625625
Bristol	St John's Chambers	0117 921 3456/929 8514
Cambridge	• Fenners Chambers	01223 368761
	Regency Chambers	01223 301517
Cardiff	30 Park Place	01222 398421
	32 Park Place	01222 397364
	• 33 Park Place	01222 233313
Chester	40 King Street	01244 323886
Eastbourne	King's Chambers	01323 416053
Ely	Cathedral Chambers, Ely	01353 666775
Exeter	• Cathedral Chambers (Jan Wood	01392 210900
	Independent Barristers' Clerk)	
	Colleton Chambers	01392 274898
	Rougemont Chambers	01392 410471
	Southernhay Chambers	01392 255777
	Walnut House	01392 279751
Guildford	• Guildford Chambers	01483 539131
Leeds	Chambers of Andrew Campbell QC	0113 245 5438
	11 King's Bench Walk	0113 2971 200
	• Park Court Chambers	0113 243 3277
	The Chambers of Philip Raynor QC	0113 242 1123
	• 30 Park Square	0113 243 6388
	• 37 Park Square	0113 243 9422
	• Sovereign Chambers	0113 245 1841/2/3
	• 9 Woodhouse Square	0113 245 1986
Leicester	2 New Street	0116 262 5906
Liverpool	25-27 Castle Street	0151 227 5661/5666/236 5072
	Chavasse Court Chambers	0151 707 1191
	• The Corn Exchange Chambers	0151 227 1081/5009
	• Exchange Chambers	0151 236 7747
	First National Chambers	0151 236 2098
	India Buildings Chambers	0151 243 6000
	• The Chambers of Adrian Lyon	0151 236 4421/8240/6757
	• Martins Building	0151 236 5818/4919
	• Oriel Chambers	0151 236 7191
	• Peel House Chambers	0151 236 4321
London	Avondale Chambers	0181 445 9984
	Barnard's Inn Chambers	0171 242 8508
	9 Bedford Row	0171 242 3555
	17 Bedford Row	0171 831 7314
	• 29 Bedford Row Chambers	0171 831 2626
	• 9-12 Bell Yard	0171 400 1800
	11 Bolt Court	0171 353 2300
	• Bracton Chambers	0171 242 4248
	• 4 Brick Court	0171 797 8910
	• 4 Brick Court	0171 797 7766
	Bridewell Chambers	0171 797 8800

A

• 1 Crown Office Row	0171 797 7111
1 Crown Office Row	0171 583 9292
• One Essex Court	0171 583 2000
• One Essex Court	0171 936 3030
23 Essex Street	0171 413 0353
Chambers of Geoffrey Hawker	0171 583 8899
• Chambers of Norman Palmer	0171 405 6114
• 4 Field Court	0171 440 6900
• 2nd Floor, Francis Taylor Building	0171 353 9942
Francis Taylor Buildings	0171 353 7768/2711
• Goldsmith Building	0171 353 7881
Goldsmith Chambers	0171 353 6802/3/4/5
• Gray's Inn Chambers	0171 831 5344
• Gray's Inn Chambers	0171 404 1111
• 1 Gray's Inn Square Chambers of the	0171 405 3000
Baroness Scotland of Asthal QC	
• 1 Gray's Inn Square	0171 405 8946
2 Gray's Inn Square Chambers	0171 242 0328/405 1317
• 2-3 Gray's Inn Square	0171 242 4986
10 - 11 Gray's Inn Square	0171 405 2576
• 1 Harcourt Buildings	0171 353 9421/0375
2 Harcourt Buildings	0171 353 2112/2817
• 2 Harcourt Buildings	0171 353 8415
• Hardwicke Building	0171 242 2523
• 1 Hare Court	0171 353 3982/5324
• 3 Hare Court	0171 353 7561
Chambers of Harjit Singh	0171 353 1356
• Chambers of James Hunt QC	0171 421 8000
• John Street Chambers	0171 242 1911
• 4 King's Bench Walk	0171 822 8822
• 8 King's Bench Walk	0171 797 8888
• 9 King's Bench Walk	0171 353 7202/3909
The Chambers of Mr Ali Mohammad	0171 353 9564 (4 lines)
Azhar	
10 King's Bench Walk	0171 353 7742
11 King's Bench Walk	0171 353 3337/8
• 13 King's Bench Walk	0171 353 7204
• Chambers of Lord Campbell of Alloway	0171 353 9276
QC	
• Lamb Building	0171 797 7788
Library Chambers	0171 404 6500
Lion Court	0171 404 6565
• 1 Middle Temple Lane	0171 583 0659 (12 lines)
• Mitre Court Chambers	0171 353 9394
• Mitre House Chambers	0171 583 8233
• New Court	0171 583 5123
• 3 New Square	0171 405 1111
Chambers of Joy Okoye	0171 405 7011
• 22 Old Buildings	0171 831 0222
11 Old Square	0171 242 5022
• 2 Paper Buildings	0171 353 0933
• 2 Paper Buildings	0171 936 2611 (10 lines)
• 3 Paper Buildings	0171 583 8055
5 Paper Buildings	0171 583 6117
Phoenix Chambers	0171 404 7888
• 1 Pump Court	0171 583 2012/353 4341
2 Pump Court	0171 353 5597
• 4 Pump Court	0171 353 2656/9
• 5 Pump Court	0171 353 2532
6 Pump Court	0171 797 8400
• Queen Elizabeth Building	0171 353 7181 (12 lines)
• Queen Elizabeth Building	0171 583 5766
• 3 Raymond Buildings	0171 831 3833
7 Stone Buildings	0171 242 0961
11 Stone Buildings	+44 (0)171 831 6381
• 3 Temple Gardens	0171 353 3102/5/9297
3 Temple Gardens (North)	0171 353 0853/4/7222
• Thomas More Chambers	0171 404 7000
Trafalgar Chambers	0171 583 5858
Verulam Chambers	0171 813 2400
Maidstone Earl Street Chambers	01622 671222
• Maidstone Chambers	01622 688592

Manchester	• Cobden House Chambers	0161 833 6000/6001
	Deans Court Chambers	0161 834 4097
	• Chambers of John Hand QC	0161 955 9000
	Kenworthy's Chambers	0161 832 4036
	• 40 King Street	0161 832 9082
	• 8 King Street Chambers	0161 834 9560
	Lincoln House Chambers	0161 832 5701
	Manchester House Chambers	0161 834 7007
	Peel Court Chambers	0161 832 3791
	• Queen's Chambers	0161 834 6875/4738
	• St James's Chambers	0161 834 7000
	• 28 St John Street	0161 834 8418
Middlesbrough	• Fountain Chambers	01642 217037
Newcastle upon Tyne	• Broad Chare	0191 232 0541
	• New Court Chambers	0191 232 1980
	• Trinity Chambers	0191 232 1927
Northampton	22 Albion Place	01604 636271
	Chartlands Chambers	01604 603322
Norwich	East Anglian Chambers	01603 617351
	Octagon House	01603 623186
	Sackville Chambers	01603 613516
Nottingham	No. 1 High Pavement Chambers	0115 941 8218
	King Charles House	0115 941 8851
	Ropewalk Chambers	0115 947 2581
	St Mary's Chambers	0115 950 3503
Oxford	1 Alfred Street	01865 793736
	• King's Bench Chambers	01865 311066
Peterborough	Fenners Chambers	01733 562030
	Regency Chambers	01733 315215
Plymouth	Devon Chambers	01752 661659
Preston	4 Camden Place	01772 828300
	Deans Court Chambers	01772 555163
	New Bailey Chambers	01772 258 087
	15 Winckley Square	01772 252 828
Reading	Dr Johnson's Chambers	01189 254221
	Wessex Chambers	0118 956 8856
Redhill	Redhill Chambers	01737 780781
Sheffield	Paradise Square Chambers	0114 273 8951
Shepperton	Abbey Chambers	01932 560913
Slough	11 St Bernards Road	01753 553806/817989
Southampton	• College Chambers	01703 230338
	• Eighteen Carlton Crescent	01703 639001
Stoke-on-Trent	Regent Chambers	01782 286666
Swansea	Angel Chambers	01792 464623/464648
	Gower Chambers	01792 644466
	Iscoed Chambers	01792 652988/9/330
	Pendragon Chambers	01792 411188
Winchester	4 St Peter Street	01962 868 884
Wolverhampton	Claremont Chambers	01902 426222
York	• York Chambers	01904 620 048

LOCAL AUTHORITY CLAIMS

London	No 1 Serjeants' Inn	0171 415 6666

LOCAL GOVERNMENT

Birmingham	• Equity Chambers	0121 233 2100
	• 3 Fountain Court	0121 236 5854
	• 5 Fountain Court	0121 606 0500
	• St Philip's Chambers	0121 246 7000
Bournemouth	King's Bench Chambers	01202 250025
Bristol	Assize Court Chambers	0117 926 4587
	St John's Chambers	0117 921 3456/929 8514
Cambridge	• Fenners Chambers	01223 368761
Cardiff	30 Park Place	01222 398421
	• 33 Park Place	01222 233313
Chester	40 King Street	01244 323886
Chesterfield	26 Morley Avenue	01246 234790
Durham City	Durham Barristers' Chambers	0191 386 9199
Exeter	• Cathedral Chambers (Jan Wood Independent Barristers' Clerk)	01392 210900
	Colleton Chambers	01392 274898

• Expanded entry in Part C

A

	Walnut House	01392 279751
Guildford	• Guildford Chambers	01483 539131
Leeds	Chambers of Andrew Campbell QC	0113 245 5438
	The Chambers of Philip Raynor QC	0113 242 1123
	• 30 Park Square	0113 243 6388
	• Sovereign Chambers	0113 245 1841/2/3
Liverpool	25-27 Castle Street	0151 227 5661/5666/236 5072
	• Exchange Chambers	0151 236 7747
	First National Chambers	0151 236 2098
London	Albany Chambers	0171 485 5736/38
	• Arden Chambers	0171 242 4244
	Chambers of Dr Michael Arnheim	0171 833 5093
	Barnard's Inn Chambers	0171 242 8508
	• 29 Bedford Row Chambers	0171 831 2626
	• 5 Bell Yard	0171 333 8811
	• 9-12 Bell Yard	0171 400 1800
	11 Bolt Court	0171 353 2300
	• Bracton Chambers	0171 242 4248
	• 4 Breams Buildings	0171 353 5835/430 1221
	• 4 Brick Court	0171 797 7766
	Brick Court Chambers	0171 583 0777
	Cloisters	0171 827 4000
	• Chambers of Mr Peter Crampin QC	0171 831 0081
	• Devereux Chambers	0171 353 7534
	• Doughty Street Chambers	0171 404 1313
	• Dr Johnson's Chambers	0171 353 4716
	Equity Barristers' Chambers	0181 558 8336
	• One Essex Court	0171 936 3030
	• 35 Essex Street	0171 353 6381
	• 39 Essex Street	0171 832 1111
	Chambers of Geoffrey Hawker	0171 583 8899
	• Chambers of Norman Palmer	0171 405 6114
	• 4 Field Court	0171 440 6900
	One Garden Court Family Law Chambers	0171 797 7900
	• 2 Garden Court	0171 353 1633
	• Goldsmith Building	0171 353 7881
	Goldsworth Chambers	0171 405 7117
	• Gray's Inn Chambers	0171 404 1111
	• 1 Gray's Inn Square Chambers of the Baroness Scotland of Asthal QC	0171 405 3000
	• 2-3 Gray's Inn Square	0171 242 4986
	• 4-5 Gray's Inn Square	0171 404 5252
	10 - 11 Gray's Inn Square	0171 405 2576
	• 1 Harcourt Buildings	0171 353 9421/0375
	• 2 Harcourt Buildings	0171 583 9020
	• 2 Harcourt Buildings	0171 353 8415
	• Harcourt Chambers	0171 353 6961/7
	• One Hare Court	0171 353 3171
	• 3 Hare Court	0171 353 7561
Harrow on the Hill	• Harrow-on-the-Hill Chambers	0181 423 7444
London	• Chambers of James Hunt QC	0171 421 8000
	• Keating Chambers	0171 544 2600
	• One King's Bench Walk	0171 936 1500
	• 8 King's Bench Walk	0171 797 8888
	The Chambers of Mr Ali Mohammad Azhar	0171 353 9564 (4 lines)
	10 King's Bench Walk	0171 353 7742
	• 11 King's Bench Walk	0171 632 8500
	11 King's Bench Walk	0171 353 3337/8
	• Chambers of Lord Campbell of Alloway QC	0171 353 9276
	• Lamb Building	0171 797 7788
	Lamb Chambers	0171 797 8300
	2 Mitre Court Buildings	0171 583 1380
	• Mitre Court Chambers	0171 353 9394
	• Mitre House Chambers	0171 583 8233
	• 1 New Square	0171 405 0884/5/6/7
	• 12 New Square	0171 419 1212
	Chambers of Joy Okoye	0171 405 7011
	• 22 Old Buildings	0171 831 0222
	• 9 Old Square	0171 405 4682

• Expanded entry in Part C

	11 Old Square	0171 242 5022
	• 1 Pump Court	0171 583 2012/353 4341
	6 Pump Court	0171 797 8400
	1 Serjeants' Inn	0171 583 1355
	• Stanbrook & Henderson	0171 353 0101
	7 Stone Buildings	0171 242 0961
	11 Stone Buildings	+44 (0)171 831 6381
	• 3 Temple Gardens	0171 353 3102/5/9297
Manchester	• Chambers of John Hand QC	0161 955 9000
	• 40 King Street	0161 832 9082
	• 8 King Street Chambers	0161 834 9560
Middlesbrough	Baker Street Chambers	01642 873873
	• Fountain Chambers	01642 217037
Newcastle upon Tyne	Milburn House Chambers	0191 230 5511
	• Trinity Chambers	0191 232 1927
	Westgate Chambers	0191 261 4407/232 9785
Norwich	East Anglian Chambers	01603 617351
Nottingham	Ropewalk Chambers	0115 947 2581
Peterborough	Fenners Chambers	01733 562030
Plymouth	Devon Chambers	01752 661659
Portsmouth	Hampshire Chambers	01705 826636
Preston	4 Camden Place	01772 828300
Reading	Dr Johnson's Chambers	01189 254221
Redhill	Redhill Chambers	01737 780781
Slough	11 St Bernards Road	01753 553806/817989
Southampton	• 17 Carlton Crescent	01703 320320
Swansea	Gower Chambers	01792 644466
	Iscoed Chambers	01792 652988/9/330
	Pendragon Chambers	01792 411188
Wolverhampton	Claremont Chambers	01902 426222

MALICIOUS PROSECUTION

London	• Dr Johnson's Chambers	0171 353 4716

MEDIA LAW

London	1 Brick Court	0171 353 8845
	• 13 Old Square	0171 404 4800

MEDIATION

London	Chambers of Dr Michael Arnheim	0171 833 5093
Malvern	Resolution Chambers	01684 561279

MEDICAL NEGLIGENCE

Bedford	Bedford Chambers	0870 733 7333
Birmingham	• Equity Chambers	0121 233 2100
	1 Fountain Court	0121 236 5721
	• 3 Fountain Court	0121 236 5854
	• 5 Fountain Court	0121 606 0500
	• 8 Fountain Court	0121 236 5514
	• St Philip's Chambers	0121 246 7000
Bournemouth	King's Bench Chambers	01202 250025
	20 Lorne Park Road	01202 292102
Bradford	Broadway House Chambers	01274 722560
Brighton	• Crown Office Row Chambers	01273 625625
Bristol	Assize Court Chambers	0117 926 4587
	Old Square Chambers	0117 927 7111
	St John's Chambers	0117 921 3456/929 8514
Cambridge	• Fenners Chambers	01223 368761
	Regency Chambers	01223 301517
Canterbury	Stour Chambers	01227 764899
Cardiff	9 Park Place	01222 382731
	30 Park Place	01222 398421
	32 Park Place	01222 397364
	• 33 Park Place	01222 233313
Chester	40 King Street	01244 323886
	White Friars Chambers	01244 323070
Chichester	Chichester Chambers	01243 784538
Coulsdon	Advolex Chambers	0181 763 2345
Eastbourne	King's Chambers	01323 416053

• Expanded entry in Part C

Exeter	• Cathedral Chambers (Jan Wood Independent Barristers' Clerk)	01392 210900
	Walnut House	01392 279751
Guildford	• Guildford Chambers	01483 539131
Leatherhead	Pembroke House	01372 376160/376493
Leeds	Chambers of Andrew Campbell QC	0113 245 5438
	• Chancery House Chambers	0113 244 6691
	11 King's Bench Walk	0113 2971 200
	• No. 6	0113 245 9763
	The Chambers of Philip Raynor QC	0113 242 1123
	• 37 Park Square	0113 243 9422
	• Sovereign Chambers	0113 245 1841/2/3
	• St Paul's House	0113 245 5866
	• 9 Woodhouse Square	0113 245 1986
Liverpool	25-27 Castle Street	0151 227 5661/5666/236 5072
	19 Castle Street Chambers	0151 236 9402
	Chavasse Court Chambers	0151 707 1191
	• The Corn Exchange Chambers	0151 227 1081/5009
	• Exchange Chambers	0151 236 7747
	First National Chambers	0151 236 2098
	India Buildings Chambers	0151 243 6000
	• The Chambers of Adrian Lyon	0151 236 4421/8240/6757
	• Martins Building	0151 236 5818/4919
	• Oriel Chambers	0151 236 7191
	• Peel House Chambers	0151 236 4321
London	Chambers of Dr Michael Arnheim	0171 833 5093
	Barnard's Inn Chambers	0171 242 8508
	Barristers' Common Law Chambers	0171 375 3012
	9 Bedford Row	0171 242 3555
	17 Bedford Row	0171 831 7314
	• 29 Bedford Row Chambers	0171 831 2626
	• 5 Bell Yard	0171 333 8811
	11 Bolt Court	0171 353 2300
	• 4 Brick Court	0171 797 8910
	• 4 Brick Court	0171 797 7766
	Bridewell Chambers	0171 797 8800
	Cloisters	0171 827 4000
	• 1 Crown Office Row	0171 797 7500
	1 Crown Office Row	0171 583 9292
	• Two Crown Office Row	0171 797 8100
	• Devereux Chambers	0171 353 7534
	• Doughty Street Chambers	0171 404 1313
	• Dr Johnson's Chambers	0171 353 4716
	Equity Barristers' Chambers	0181 558 8336
	• One Essex Court	0171 936 3030
	5 Essex Court	0171 410 2000
	• 35 Essex Street	0171 353 6381
	• 39 Essex Street	0171 832 1111
	Chambers of Geoffrey Hawker	0171 583 8899
	• Farrar's Building	0171 583 9241
	• Chambers of Norman Palmer	0171 405 6114
	• 4 Field Court	0171 440 6900
	• Fountain Court	0171 583 3335
	• 2nd Floor, Francis Taylor Building	0171 353 9942
	Francis Taylor Buildings	0171 353 7768/2711
	• 2 Garden Court	0171 353 1633
	• Goldsmith Building	0171 353 7881
	Goldsmith Chambers	0171 353 6802/3/4/5
	Goldsworth Chambers	0171 405 7117
	• 9 Gough Square	0171 353 5371
	• Gough Square Chambers	0171 353 0924
	• Gray's Inn Chambers	0171 831 5344
	• 1 Gray's Inn Square Chambers of the Baroness Scotland of Asthal QC	0171 405 3000
	• 1 Gray's Inn Square	0171 405 8946
	2 Gray's Inn Square Chambers	0171 242 0328/405 1317
	10 - 11 Gray's Inn Square	0171 405 2576
	• 1 Harcourt Buildings	0171 353 9421/0375
	• 2 Harcourt Buildings	0171 583 9020
	• Harcourt Chambers	0171 353 6961/7
	• Hardwicke Building	0171 242 2523
Harrow on the Hill	• Harrow-on-the-Hill Chambers	0181 423 7444

• Expanded entry in Part C

A

London	• Chambers of James Hunt QC	0171 421 8000
	• John Street Chambers	0171 242 1911
	Justice Court Chambers	0181 830 7786
	• One King's Bench Walk	0171 936 1500
	• 4 King's Bench Walk	0171 822 8822
	4 King's Bench Walk	0171 353 3581
	• 8 King's Bench Walk	0171 797 8888
	• 9 King's Bench Walk	0171 353 7202/3909
	The Chambers of Mr Ali Mohammad Azhar	0171 353 9564 (4 lines)
	10 King's Bench Walk	0171 353 7742
	11 King's Bench Walk	0171 353 3337/8
	• 12 King's Bench Walk	0171 583 0811
	• 13 King's Bench Walk	0171 353 7204
	• Lamb Building	0171 797 7788
	Lamb Chambers	0171 797 8300
	Lion Court	0171 404 6565
	• Littleton Chambers	0171 797 8600
	• 1 Middle Temple Lane	0171 583 0659 (12 lines)
	• Mitre Court Chambers	0171 353 9394
	• Mitre House Chambers	0171 583 8233
	• New Court	0171 583 5123
	• New Court Chambers	0171 831 9500
	• 12 New Square	0171 419 1212
	Chambers of Joy Okoye	0171 405 7011
	• 22 Old Buildings	0171 831 0222
	• Old Square Chambers	0171 269 0300
	One Paper Buildings	0171 583 7355
	• 3 Paper Buildings	0171 797 7000
	• 3 Paper Buildings	0171 583 8055
	• 4 Paper Buildings	0171 353 3366/583 7155
	• 4 Paper Buildings	0171 583 0816
	• 5 Paper Buildings	0171 583 9275
	Phoenix Chambers	0171 404 7888
	Plowden Buildings	0171 583 0808
	• Chambers of John L Powell QC	0171 797 8000
	Prince Henry's Chambers	0171 353 1183/1190
	• 1 Pump Court	0171 583 2012/353 4341
	2 Pump Court	0171 353 5597
	• Pump Court Chambers	0171 353 0711
	• 4 Pump Court	0171 353 2656/9
	• 5 Pump Court	0171 353 2532
	• Chambers of Kieran Coonan QC	0171 583 6013/2510
	6 Pump Court	0171 797 8400
	No 1 Serjeants' Inn	0171 415 6666
	• 3 Serjeants' Inn	0171 353 5537
	• Stanbrook & Henderson	0171 353 0101
	7 Stone Buildings	0171 242 0961
	8 Stone Buildings	0171 831 9881
	• 9 Stone Buildings	0171 404 5055
	11 Stone Buildings	+44 (0)171 831 6381
	• 199 Strand	0171 379 9779
	• 1 Temple Gardens	0171 353 0407/583 1315
	• 2 Temple Gardens	0171 583 6041
	• Thomas More Chambers	0171 404 7000
	• 14 Tooks Court	0171 405 8828
	• 3 Verulam Buildings	0171 831 8441
	Verulam Chambers	0171 813 2400
	Warwick House Chambers	0171 430 2323
Maidstone	• Maidstone Chambers	01622 688592
Manchester	• Byrom Street Chambers	0161 829 2100
	• Central Chambers	0161 833 1774
	• Cobden House Chambers	0161 833 6000/6001
	Deans Court Chambers	0161 834 4097
	• Chambers of John Hand QC	0161 955 9000
	Kenworthy's Chambers	0161 832 4036
	• 40 King Street	0161 832 9082
	• 8 King Street Chambers	0161 834 9560
	58 King Street Chambers	0161 831 7477
	Lincoln House Chambers	0161 832 5701
	Chambers of Ian Macdonald QC	0161 236 1840
	Manchester House Chambers	0161 834 7007

• Expanded entry in Part C

	• Merchant Chambers	0161 839 7070
	Peel Court Chambers	0161 832 3791
	• Queen's Chambers	0161 834 6875/4738
	• St James's Chambers	0161 834 7000
	18 St John Street	0161 278 1800
	• 28 St John Street	0161 834 8418
	Young Street Chambers	0161 833 0489
Middlesbrough	Baker Street Chambers	01642 873873
	• Fountain Chambers	01642 217037
Milton Keynes	Milton Keynes Chambers	01908 217857
Newcastle upon Tyne	• Broad Chare	0191 232 0541
	Cathedral Chambers	0191 232 1311
	• New Court Chambers	0191 232 1980
	• Trinity Chambers	0191 232 1927
	Westgate Chambers	0191 261 4407/232 9785
Northampton	22 Albion Place	01604 636271
Norwich	East Anglian Chambers	01603 617351
Nottingham	King Charles House	0115 941 8851
	Ropewalk Chambers	0115 947 2581
	St Mary's Chambers	0115 950 3503
Oxford	1 Alfred Street	01865 793736
	• King's Bench Chambers	01865 311066
Peterborough	Fenners Chambers	01733 562030
	Regency Chambers	01733 315215
Plymouth	Devon Chambers	01752 661659
Portsmouth	Hampshire Chambers	01705 826636
	• Portsmouth Barristers' Chambers	01705 831292
Preston	4 Camden Place	01772 828300
	Deans Court Chambers	01772 555163
	New Bailey Chambers	01772 258 087
	15 Winckley Square	01772 252 828
Reading	Wessex Chambers	0118 956 8856
Redhill	Redhill Chambers	01737 780781
Sheffield	Paradise Square Chambers	0114 273 8951
Slough	11 St Bernards Road	01753 553806/817989
Southampton	• 17 Carlton Crescent	01703 320320
	• College Chambers	01703 230338
	• Eighteen Carlton Crescent	01703 639001
Stoke-on-Trent	Regent Chambers	01782 286666
Swansea	Angel Chambers	01792 464623/464648
	Gower Chambers	01792 644466
	Iscoed Chambers	01792 652988/9/330
	Pendragon Chambers	01792 411188
Swindon	Pump Court Chambers	01793 539899
Winchester	Pump Court Chambers	01962 868161
	4 St Peter Street	01962 868 884
Wolverhampton	Claremont Chambers	01902 426222
York	• York Chambers	01904 620 048

MENTAL HEALTH

Birmingham	• Equity Chambers	0121 233 2100
	• 5 Fountain Court	0121 606 0500
	• 8 Fountain Court	0121 236 5514
	New Court Chambers	0121 693 6656
Bradford	Broadway House Chambers	01274 722560
Bristol	St John's Chambers	0117 921 3456/929 8514
Chester	40 King Street	01244 323886
Exeter	Rougemont Chambers	01392 410471
Guildford	• Guildford Chambers	01483 539131
Leeds	• 37 Park Square	0113 243 9422
	• St Paul's House	0113 245 5866
	• 9 Woodhouse Square	0113 245 1986
Liverpool	19 Castle Street Chambers	0151 236 9402
	• The Corn Exchange Chambers	0151 227 1081/5009
	• Exchange Chambers	0151 236 7747
	• The Chambers of Adrian Lyon	0151 236 4421/8240/6757
	• Martins Building	0151 236 5818/4919
London	ACHMA Chambers	0171 639 7817
	Barristers' Common Law Chambers	0171 375 3012
	9 Bedford Row	0171 242 3555
	• 29 Bedford Row Chambers	0171 831 2626
	• 5 Bell Yard	0171 333 8811

A

• 4 Brick Court	0171 797 7766
Bridewell Chambers	0171 797 8800
1 Crown Office Row	0171 583 9292
• Devereux Chambers	0171 353 7534
• Doughty Street Chambers	0171 404 1313
Equity Barristers' Chambers	0181 558 8336
5 Essex Court	0171 410 2000
• 39 Essex Street	0171 832 1111
• Chambers of Norman Palmer	0171 405 6114
Francis Taylor Buildings	0171 353 7768/2711
One Garden Court Family Law Chambers	0171 797 7900
• 2 Garden Court	0171 353 1633
• Goldsmith Building	0171 353 7881
Goldsmith Chambers	0171 353 6802/3/4/5
Goldsworth Chambers	0171 405 7117
• Gray's Inn Chambers	0171 831 5344
• 1 Gray's Inn Square Chambers of the Baroness Scotland of Asthal QC	0171 405 3000
• 1 Gray's Inn Square	0171 405 8946
6 Gray's Inn Square	0171 242 1052
10 - 11 Gray's Inn Square	0171 405 2576
2 Harcourt Buildings	0171 353 2112/2817
• Chambers of James Hunt QC	0171 421 8000
• John Street Chambers	0171 242 1911
• One King's Bench Walk	0171 936 1500
• 8 King's Bench Walk	0171 797 8888
• 9 King's Bench Walk	0171 353 7202/3909
The Chambers of Mr Ali Mohammad Azhar	0171 353 9564 (4 lines)
10 King's Bench Walk	0171 353 7742
• 13 King's Bench Walk	0171 353 7204
• Lamb Building	0171 797 7788
Lamb Chambers	0171 797 8300
• Mitre Court Chambers	0171 353 9394
• Mitre House Chambers	0171 583 8233
• New Court	0171 583 5123
• 12 New Square	0171 419 1212
Chambers of Joy Okoye	0171 405 7011
• 22 Old Buildings	0171 831 0222
• 13 Old Square	0171 404 4800
• 4 Paper Buildings	0171 583 0816
• 1 Pump Court	0171 583 2012/353 4341
• Chambers of Kieran Coonan QC	0171 583 6013/2510
• 3 Serjeants' Inn	0171 353 5537
• 5 Stone Buildings	0171 242 6201
• 1 Temple Gardens	0171 353 0407/583 1315
• 3 Temple Gardens	0171 353 3102/5/9297
• 14 Tooks Court	0171 405 8828
Trafalgar Chambers	0171 583 5858
Warwick House Chambers	0171 430 2323

	• Central Chambers	0161 833 1774
Manchester	• Chambers of John Hand QC	0161 955 9000
	Kenworthy's Chambers	0161 832 4036
	• 8 King Street Chambers	0161 834 9560
	Lincoln House Chambers	0161 832 5701
	Chambers of Ian Macdonald QC	0161 236 1840
	Manchester House Chambers	0161 834 7007
	• St James's Chambers	0161 834 7000
Northampton	22 Albion Place	01604 636271
	Chartlands Chambers	01604 603322
Norwich	East Anglian Chambers	01603 617351
Nottingham	King Charles House	0115 941 8851
Oxford	• King's Bench Chambers	01865 311066
Plymouth	Devon Chambers	01752 661659
Preston	4 Camden Place	01772 828300
	15 Winckley Square	01772 252 828
Reading	Dr Johnson's Chambers	01189 254221
Southampton	• College Chambers	01703 230338
York	• York Chambers	01904 620 048

• Expanded entry in Part C

MIDDLE EAST/PAKISTANI/ISLAMIC LAW

London	Justice Court Chambers	0181 830 7786

MINES AND MINERALS

London	• Chambers of Mr Peter Crampin QC	0171 831 0081
	• 11 Old Square	0171 430 0341

MORTGAGES AND BORROWERS

Milton Keynes	Milton Keynes Chambers	01908 217857

NATIONAL INSURANCE

London	Prince Henry's Chambers	0171 353 1183/1190

PARLIAMENTARY

Leeds	The Chambers of Philip Raynor QC	0113 242 1123
London	Chambers of Dr Michael Arnheim	0171 833 5093
	• 4 Breams Buildings	0171 353 5835/430 1221
	• Fountain Court	0171 583 3335
	• 1 Gray's Inn Square	0171 405 8946
	• 4-5 Gray's Inn Square	0171 404 5252
	• 2 Harcourt Buildings	0171 583 9020
	• 2 Harcourt Buildings	0171 353 8415
	• One Hare Court	0171 353 3171
	• One King's Bench Walk	0171 936 1500
	• Littleton Chambers	0171 797 8600
	2 Mitre Court Buildings	0171 583 1380
	• 12 New Square	0171 419 1212
	• 9 Old Square	0171 405 4682
	6 Pump Court	0171 797 8400
	1 Serjeants' Inn	0171 583 1355
	• Stanbrook & Henderson	0171 353 0101
Manchester	• 40 King Street	0161 832 9082
Norwich	East Anglian Chambers	01603 617351

PARTNERSHIPS

Birmingham	• Equity Chambers	0121 233 2100
	• 3 Fountain Court	0121 236 5854
	• 5 Fountain Court	0121 606 0500
	• 8 Fountain Court	0121 236 5514
	• St Philip's Chambers	0121 246 7000
Bradford	Broadway House Chambers	01274 722560
Bristol	St John's Chambers	0117 921 3456/929 8514
Cambridge	• Fenners Chambers	01223 368761
Cardiff	9 Park Place	01222 382731
	30 Park Place	01222 398421
	• 33 Park Place	01222 233313
	40 King Street	01244 323886
Chester	Chichester Chambers	01243 784538
Chichester	• Cathedral Chambers (Jan Wood	01392 210900
Exeter	Independent Barristers' Clerk)	
	Rougemont Chambers	01392 410471
	Southernhay Chambers	01392 255777
Leeds	Chambers of Andrew Campbell QC	0113 245 5438
	• Chancery House Chambers	0113 244 6691
	Enterprise Chambers	0113 246 0391
	11 King's Bench Walk	0113 2971 200
	• No. 6	0113 245 9763
	The Chambers of Philip Raynor QC	0113 242 1123
	• 37 Park Square	0113 243 9422
	• Sovereign Chambers	0113 245 1841/2/3
Liverpool	19 Castle Street Chambers	0151 236 9402
	• The Corn Exchange Chambers	0151 227 1081/5009
	• Exchange Chambers	0151 236 7747
	• The Chambers of Adrian Lyon	0151 236 4421/8240/6757
	• Oriel Chambers	0151 236 7191
London	9 Bedford Row	0171 242 3555
	17 Bedford Row	0171 831 7314
	48 Bedford Row	0171 430 2005

• Expanded entry in Part C

A

• 29 Bedford Row Chambers	0171 831 2626
• 5 Bell Yard	0171 333 8811
• Blackstone Chambers (formerly known as 2 Hare Court)	0171 583 1770
11 Bolt Court	0171 353 2300
• 4 Breams Buildings	0171 353 5835/430 1221
Bridewell Chambers	0171 797 8800
• Chambers of Mr Peter Crampin QC	0171 831 0081
1 Crown Office Row	0171 583 9292
• Enterprise Chambers	0171 405 9471
Equity Barristers' Chambers	0181 558 8336
• Erskine Chambers	0171 242 5532
• One Essex Court	0171 583 2000
• Essex Court Chambers	0171 813 8000
Chambers of Geoffrey Hawker	0171 583 8899
• Chambers of Norman Palmer	0171 405 6114
• 4 Field Court	0171 440 6900
• Fountain Court	0171 583 3335
• 2nd Floor, Francis Taylor Building	0171 353 9942
• Goldsmith Building	0171 353 7881
• Gough Square Chambers	0171 353 0924
• Gray's Inn Chambers	0171 404 1111
2 Gray's Inn Square Chambers	0171 242 0328/405 1317
• 2-3 Gray's Inn Square	0171 242 4986
10 - 11 Gray's Inn Square	0171 405 2576
• 1 Harcourt Buildings	0171 353 9421/0375
• 2 Harcourt Buildings	0171 583 9020
• Hardwicke Building	0171 242 2523
• One Hare Court	0171 353 3171

Harrow on the Hill

• Harrow-on-the-Hill Chambers	0181 423 7444

London

The Chambers of Mr Ali Mohammad Azhar	0171 353 9564 (4 lines)
11 King's Bench Walk	0171 353 3337/8
• 13 King's Bench Walk	0171 353 7204
• Lamb Building	0171 797 7788
Lamb Chambers	0171 797 8300
• Littleton Chambers	0171 797 8600
• Littman Chambers	0171 404 4866
2 Mitre Court Buildings	0171 353 1353
• Mitre Court Chambers	0171 353 9394
• 1 New Square	0171 405 0884/5/6/7
Chambers of Lord Goodhart QC	0171 405 5577
5 New Square	0171 404 0404
• 12 New Square	0171 419 1212
• 22 Old Buildings	0171 831 0222
• Twenty-Four Old Buildings	0171 404 0946
• 9 Old Square	0171 405 4682
The Chambers of Leolin Price CBE, QC	0171 405 0758/242 5002
• 11 Old Square	0171 430 0341
• 13 Old Square	0171 404 4800
• 3 Paper Buildings	0171 797 7000
• 4 Paper Buildings	0171 353 3366/583 7155
• 4 Paper Buildings	0171 583 0816
• Chambers of John L Powell QC	0171 797 8000
• Pump Court Chambers	0171 353 0711
• Serle Court Chambers	0171 242 6105
• 3-4 South Square	0171 696 9900
• Stanbrook & Henderson	0171 353 0101
• 3 Stone Buildings	0171 242 4937/405 8358
4 Stone Buildings	0171 242 5524
• 5 Stone Buildings	0171 242 6201
• 7 Stone Buildings	0171 405 3886/242 3546
• 9 Stone Buildings	0171 404 5055
11 Stone Buildings	+44 (0)171 831 6381
• 199 Strand	0171 379 9779
• Thomas More Chambers	0171 404 7000
Trafalgar Chambers	0171 583 5858
• 3 Verulam Buildings	0171 831 8441
Verulam Chambers	0171 813 2400
Warwick House Chambers	0171 430 2323

Manchester

• Cobden House Chambers	0161 833 6000/6001
• Chambers of John Hand QC	0161 955 9000

• Expanded entry in Part C

	• 40 King Street	0161 832 9082
	• 8 King Street Chambers	0161 834 9560
	• Merchant Chambers	0161 839 7070
	• Queen's Chambers	0161 834 6875/4738
	• St James's Chambers	0161 834 7000
	Young Street Chambers	0161 833 0489
Milton Keynes	Milton Keynes Chambers	01908 217857
Newcastle upon Tyne	Enterprise Chambers	0191 222 3344
	• Trinity Chambers	0191 232 1927
	Westgate Chambers	0191 261 4407/232 9785
Northampton	22 Albion Place	01604 636271
Norwich	East Anglian Chambers	01603 617351
Nottingham	King Charles House	0115 941 8851
	Ropewalk Chambers	0115 947 2581
	St Mary's Chambers	0115 950 3503
Oxford	• King's Bench Chambers	01865 311066
Peterborough	Fenners Chambers	01733 562030
Portsmouth	Hampshire Chambers	01705 826636
	• Portsmouth Barristers' Chambers	01705 831292
Preston	New Bailey Chambers	01772 258 087
	15 Winckley Square	01772 252 828
Reading	Dr Johnson's Chambers	01189 254221
	Wessex Chambers	0118 956 8856
Redhill	Redhill Chambers	01737 780781
Southampton	• 17 Carlton Crescent	01703 320320
	• Eighteen Carlton Crescent	01703 639001
Swansea	Iscoed Chambers	01792 652988/9/330
Swindon	Pump Court Chambers	01793 539899
Winchester	Pump Court Chambers	01962 868161
Winkleigh	Barnstaple Chambers	0183 783763
Wolverhampton	Claremont Chambers	01902 426222

PATENTS

Birmingham	• Equity Chambers	0121 233 2100
	1 Fountain Court	0121 236 5721
	• 5 Fountain Court	0121 606 0500
Bristol	St John's Chambers	0117 921 3456/929 8514
Haverhill	Helions Chambers	01440 730523
Leeds	Chambers of Andrew Campbell QC	0113 245 5438
	• Sovereign Chambers	0113 245 1841/2/3
London	Equity Barristers' Chambers	0181 558 8336
	Francis Taylor Buildings	0171 353 7768/2711
	Goldsworth Chambers	0171 405 7117
	• 2 Harcourt Buildings	0171 583 9020
	• One Hare Court	0171 353 3171
	• 9 King's Bench Walk	0171 353 7202/3909
	The Chambers of Mr Ali Mohammad Azhar	0171 353 9564 (4 lines)
	11 King's Bench Walk	0171 353 3337/8
	2 Mitre Court Buildings	0171 353 1353
	• New Court	0171 797 8999
	• 3 New Square	0171 405 1111
	5 New Square	0171 404 0404
	• 8 New Square	0171 405 4321
	19 Old Buildings	0171 405 2001
	• 3 Paper Buildings	0171 797 7000
	Prince Henry's Chambers	0171 353 1183/1190
	• 1 Raymond Buildings	0171 430 1234
	• 11 South Square	0171 405 1222
	• Stanbrook & Henderson	0171 353 0101
	Trafalgar Chambers	0171 583 5858
Manchester	• Cobden House Chambers	0161 833 6000/6001
	• Chambers of John Hand QC	0161 955 9000
	• St James's Chambers	0161 834 7000
Preston	4 Camden Place	01772 828300
	New Bailey Chambers	01772 258 087
Reading	Wessex Chambers	0118 956 8856
Wolverhampton	Claremont Chambers	01902 426222

PENSIONS

Birmingham	• 5 Fountain Court	0121 606 0500

• Expanded entry in Part C

A

	• St Philip's Chambers	0121 246 7000
Bristol	St John's Chambers	0117 921 3456/929 8514
Cambridge	• Fenners Chambers	01223 368761
Chester	White Friars Chambers	01244 323070
Durham City	Durham Barristers' Chambers	0191 386 9199
Leeds	Chambers of Andrew Campbell QC	0113 245 5438
	11 King's Bench Walk	0113 2971 200
	The Chambers of Philip Raynor QC	0113 242 1123
	• Sovereign Chambers	0113 245 1841/2/3
Liverpool	• Exchange Chambers	0151 236 7747
	• The Chambers of Adrian Lyon	0151 236 4421/8240/6757
	• Martins Building	0151 236 5818/4919
London	9 Bedford Row	0171 242 3555
	• 5 Bell Yard	0171 333 8811
	• Chambers of Mr Peter Crampin QC	0171 831 0081
	• Devereux Chambers	0171 353 7534
	Equity Barristers' Chambers	0181 558 8336
	• 35 Essex Street	0171 353 6381
	The Chambers of Mr Ali Mohammad Azhar	0171 353 9564 (4 lines)
	11 King's Bench Walk	0171 353 3337/8
	• Mitre House Chambers	0171 583 8233
	• Monckton Chambers	0171 405 7211
	• 1 New Square	0171 405 0884/5/6/7
	Chambers of Lord Goodhart QC	0171 405 5577
	5 New Square	0171 404 0404
	• 12 New Square	0171 419 1212
	• Twenty-Four Old Buildings	0171 404 0946
	24 Old Buildings	0171 242 2744
	The Chambers of Leolin Price CBE, QC	0171 405 0758/242 5002
	• 11 Old Square	0171 430 0341
	• 13 Old Square	0171 404 4800
	• 3 Paper Buildings	0171 797 7000
	• 3-4 South Square	0171 696 9900
	• 3 Stone Buildings	0171 242 4937/405 8358
	• 5 Stone Buildings	0171 242 6201
	• 7 Stone Buildings	0171 405 3886/242 3546
	• 9 Stone Buildings	0171 404 5055
	11 Stone Buildings	+44 (0)171 831 6381
	• 3 Verulam Buildings	0171 831 8441
	Verulam Chambers	0171 813 2400
	Warwick House Chambers	0171 430 2323
	• Wilberforce Chambers	0171 306 0102
Manchester	• Cobden House Chambers	0161 833 6000/6001
	• Chambers of John Hand QC	0161 955 9000
	• 40 King Street	0161 832 9082
	• 8 King Street Chambers	0161 834 9560
	Manchester House Chambers	0161 834 7007
	• St James's Chambers	0161 834 7000
	• 28 St John Street	0161 834 8418
Milton Keynes	Milton Keynes Chambers	01908 217857
Norwich	East Anglian Chambers	01603 617351
Peterborough	Fenners Chambers	01733 562030
Portsmouth	• Portsmouth Barristers' Chambers	01705 831292
Southampton	• Eighteen Carlton Crescent	01703 639001

PERSONAL INJURY

Bedford	Bedford Chambers	0870 733 7333
Birmingham	• Equity Chambers	0121 233 2100
	1 Fountain Court	0121 236 5721
	• 3 Fountain Court	0121 236 5854
	• 5 Fountain Court	0121 606 0500
	• 8 Fountain Court	0121 236 5514
	New Court Chambers	0121 693 6656
	• St Philip's Chambers	0121 246 7000
Bournemouth	King's Bench Chambers	01202 250025
	20 Lorne Park Road	01202 292102
Bradford	Broadway House Chambers	01274 722560
Brighton	• Crown Office Row Chambers	01273 625625
Bristol	Assize Court Chambers	0117 926 4587
	Old Square Chambers	0117 927 7111
	St John's Chambers	0117 921 3456/929 8514

• Expanded entry in Part C

Cambridge	• Fenners Chambers	01223 368761
	Regency Chambers	01223 301517
Canterbury	Stour Chambers	01227 764899
Cardiff	9 Park Place	01222 382731
	30 Park Place	01222 398421
	32 Park Place	01222 397364
	• 33 Park Place	01222 233313
Chester	40 King Street	01244 323886
	White Friars Chambers	01244 323070
Chichester	Chichester Chambers	01243 784538
Coulsdon	Advolex Chambers	0181 763 2345
Durham City	Durham Barristers' Chambers	0191 386 9199
Eastbourne	King's Chambers	01323 416053
Exeter	• Cathedral Chambers (Jan Wood Independent Barristers' Clerk)	01392 210900
	Rougemont Chambers	01392 410471
	Southernhay Chambers	01392 255777
	Walnut House	01392 279751
Guildford	• Guildford Chambers	01483 539131
Leatherhead	Pembroke House	01372 376160/376493
Leeds	Chambers of Andrew Campbell QC	0113 245 5438
	• Chancery House Chambers	0113 244 6691
	11 King's Bench Walk	0113 2971 200
	• Mercury Chambers	0113 234 2265
	• No. 6	0113 245 9763
	• Park Court Chambers	0113 243 3277
	The Chambers of Philip Raynor QC	0113 242 1123
	• 30 Park Square	0113 243 6388
	• 37 Park Square	0113 243 9422
	• Sovereign Chambers	0113 245 1841/2/3
	• St Paul's House	0113 245 5866
	• 9 Woodhouse Square	0113 245 1986
Leicester	2 New Street	0116 262 5906
Liverpool	25-27 Castle Street	0151 227 5661/5666/236 5072
	19 Castle Street Chambers	0151 236 9402
	Chavasse Court Chambers	0151 707 1191
	• The Corn Exchange Chambers	0151 227 1081/5009
	• Exchange Chambers	0151 236 7747
	First National Chambers	0151 236 2098
	India Buildings Chambers	0151 243 6000
	• The Chambers of Adrian Lyon	0151 236 4421/8240/6757
	• Martins Building	0151 236 5818/4919
	• Oriel Chambers	0151 236 7191
	• Peel House Chambers	0151 236 4321
London	Albany Chambers	0171 485 5736/38
	Barnard's Inn Chambers	0171 242 8508
	Barristers' Common Law Chambers	0171 375 3012
	9 Bedford Row	0171 242 3555
	17 Bedford Row	0171 831 7314
	33 Bedford Row	0171 242 6476
	• 29 Bedford Row Chambers	0171 831 2626
	• 5 Bell Yard	0171 333 8811
	• 9-12 Bell Yard	0171 400 1800
	Bell Yard Chambers	0171 306 9292
	11 Bolt Court	0171 353 2300
	• Bracton Chambers	0171 242 4248
	• 4 Brick Court	0171 797 8910
	• 4 Brick Court	0171 797 7766
	Bridewell Chambers	0171 797 8800
	Britton Street Chambers	0171 608 3765
	Cloisters	0171 827 4000
	• 1 Crown Office Row	0171 797 7500
	• 1 Crown Office Row	0171 797 7111
	1 Crown Office Row	0171 583 9292
	• Two Crown Office Row	0171 797 8100
	• Devereux Chambers	0171 353 7534
	• Doughty Street Chambers	0171 404 1313
	• Dr Johnson's Chambers	0171 353 4716
	Equity Barristers' Chambers	0181 558 8336
	• 4 Essex Court	0171 797 7970
	5 Essex Court	0171 410 2000
	23 Essex Street	0171 413 0353

    • Expanded entry in Part C

A

• 35 Essex Street	0171 353 6381
• 39 Essex Street	0171 832 1111
Chambers of Geoffrey Hawker	0171 583 8899
• Farrar's Building	0171 583 9241
• Chambers of Norman Palmer	0171 405 6114
• 4 Field Court	0171 440 6900
• Fountain Court	0171 583 3335
• 2nd Floor, Francis Taylor Building	0171 353 9942
Francis Taylor Buildings	0171 353 7768/2711
• 2 Garden Court	0171 353 1633
• Goldsmith Building	0171 353 7881
Goldsmith Chambers	0171 353 6802/3/4/5
Goldsworth Chambers	0171 405 7117
• 9 Gough Square	0171 353 5371
• Gough Square Chambers	0171 353 0924
• Gray's Inn Chambers	0171 831 5344
• Gray's Inn Chambers	0171 404 1111
• 1 Gray's Inn Square	0171 405 8946
2 Gray's Inn Square Chambers	0171 242 0328/405 1317
• 2-3 Gray's Inn Square	0171 242 4986
10 - 11 Gray's Inn Square	0171 405 2576
• 1 Harcourt Buildings	0171 353 9421/0375
• 2 Harcourt Buildings	0171 583 9020
• Harcourt Chambers	0171 353 6961/7
• Hardwicke Building	0171 242 2523
• 1 Hare Court	0171 353 3982/5324
Chambers of Harjit Singh	0171 353 1356
• Harrow-on-the-Hill Chambers	0181 423 7444
• Chambers of James Hunt QC	0171 421 8000
• John Street Chambers	0171 242 1911
1 Dr Johnson's Buildings	0171 353 9328
Justice Court Chambers	0181 830 7786
• One King's Bench Walk	0171 936 1500
• 4 King's Bench Walk	0171 822 8822
4 King's Bench Walk	0171 353 3581
6 King's Bench Walk	0171 353 4931/583 0695
• 8 King's Bench Walk	0171 797 8888
• 9 King's Bench Walk	0171 353 7202/3909
The Chambers of Mr Ali Mohammad Azhar	0171 353 9564 (4 lines)
10 King's Bench Walk	0171 353 7742
11 King's Bench Walk	0171 353 3337/8
• 12 King's Bench Walk	0171 583 0811
• 13 King's Bench Walk	0171 353 7204
• Chambers of Lord Campbell of Alloway QC	0171 353 9276
Lamb Chambers	0171 797 8300
Library Chambers	0171 404 6500
Lion Court	0171 404 6565
• Littleton Chambers	0171 797 8600
• 1 Middle Temple Lane	0171 583 0659 (12 lines)
2 Mitre Court Buildings	0171 353 1353
• Mitre Court Chambers	0171 353 9394
• Mitre House Chambers	0171 583 8233
• New Court	0171 583 5123
• New Court Chambers	0171 831 9500
• 1 New Square	0171 405 0884/5/6/7
Chambers of Joy Okoye	0171 405 7011
• 22 Old Buildings	0171 831 0222
11 Old Square	0171 242 5022
• Old Square Chambers	0171 269 0300
One Paper Buildings	0171 583 7355
• 2 Paper Buildings	0171 353 0933
2 Paper Buildings, Basement North	0171 936 2613
• 3 Paper Buildings	0171 797 7000
• 3 Paper Buildings	0171 583 8055
• 4 Paper Buildings	0171 353 3366/583 7155
• 5 Paper Buildings	0171 583 9275
5 Paper Buildings	0171 583 6117
Pepys' Chambers	0171 936 2710
Phoenix Chambers	0171 404 7888
Plowden Buildings	0171 583 0808

**Harrow on the Hill
London**

• Expanded entry in Part C

A

• Chambers of John L Powell QC	0171 797 8000
• 1 Pump Court	0171 583 2012/353 4341
2 Pump Court	0171 353 5597
• Pump Court Chambers	0171 353 0711
• 4 Pump Court	0171 353 2656/9
• 5 Pump Court	0171 353 2532
• Chambers of Kieran Coonan QC	0171 583 6013/2510
6 Pump Court	0171 797 8400
No 1 Serjeants' Inn	0171 415 6666
• 3 Serjeants' Inn	0171 353 5537
• Stanbrook & Henderson	0171 353 0101
7 Stone Buildings	0171 242 0961
8 Stone Buildings	0171 831 9881
• 9 Stone Buildings	0171 404 5055
• 199 Strand	0171 379 9779
169 Temple Chambers	0171 583 7644
• 1 Temple Gardens	0171 353 0407/583 1315
• 2 Temple Gardens	0171 583 6041
• 3 Temple Gardens	0171 353 3102/5/9297
3 Temple Gardens (North)	0171 353 0853/4/7222
• Thomas More Chambers	0171 404 7000
• 14 Tooks Court	0171 405 8828
Trafalgar Chambers	0171 583 5858
Verulam Chambers	0171 813 2400
Warwick House Chambers	0171 430 2323

Maidstone	• Maidstone Chambers	01622 688592
Manchester	• Byrom Street Chambers	0161 829 2100
	• Central Chambers	0161 833 1774
	• Cobden House Chambers	0161 833 6000/6001
	Deans Court Chambers	0161 834 4097
	• Chambers of John Hand QC	0161 955 9000
	Kenworthy's Chambers	0161 832 4036
	• 40 King Street	0161 832 9082
	• 8 King Street Chambers	0161 834 9560
	58 King Street Chambers	0161 831 7477
	Lincoln House Chambers	0161 832 5701
	Chambers of Ian Macdonald QC	0161 236 1840
	Manchester House Chambers	0161 834 7007
	Peel Court Chambers	0161 832 3791
	• Queen's Chambers	0161 834 6875/4738
	• St James's Chambers	0161 834 7000
	18 St John Street	0161 278 1800
	• 28 St John Street	0161 834 8418
	Young Street Chambers	0161 833 0489
Middlesbrough	Baker Street Chambers	01642 873873
	• Fountain Chambers	01642 217037
	York House	01642 213000
Milton Keynes	Milton Keynes Chambers	01908 217857
Newcastle upon Tyne	• Broad Chare	0191 232 0541
	Cathedral Chambers	0191 232 1311
	• New Court Chambers	0191 232 1980
	• Trinity Chambers	0191 232 1927
	Westgate Chambers	0191 261 4407/232 9785
Northampton	22 Albion Place	01604 636271
	Chartlands Chambers	01604 603322
Norwich	East Anglian Chambers	01603 617351
	Octagon House	01603 623186
	Sackville Chambers	01603 613516
Nottingham	King Charles House	0115 941 8851
	Ropewalk Chambers	0115 947 2581
	St Mary's Chambers	0115 950 3503
Oxford	1 Alfred Street	01865 793736
	• King's Bench Chambers	01865 311066
Peterborough	Fenners Chambers	01733 562030
	Regency Chambers	01733 315215
Plymouth	Devon Chambers	01752 661659
Portsmouth	Hampshire Chambers	01705 826636
	• Portsmouth Barristers' Chambers	01705 831292
Preston	4 Camden Place	01772 828300
	Deans Court Chambers	01772 555163
	New Bailey Chambers	01772 258 087
	15 Winckley Square	01772 252 828

• Expanded entry in Part C

A

Reading	Dr Johnson's Chambers	01189 254221
	Wessex Chambers	0118 956 8856
Redhill	Redhill Chambers	01737 780781
Richmond-upon-Thames	Richmond Green Chambers	0181 940 1841
Sheffield	Bank House Chambers	0114 275 1223
	Paradise Square Chambers	0114 273 8951
Shepperton	Abbey Chambers	01932 560913
Slough	11 St Bernards Road	01753 553806/817989
Southampton	• 17 Carlton Crescent	01703 320320
	• College Chambers	01703 230338
	• Eighteen Carlton Crescent	01703 639001
Stoke-on-Trent	Regent Chambers	01782 286666
Swansea	Angel Chambers	01792 464623/464648
	Gower Chambers	01792 644466
	Iscoed Chambers	01792 652988/9/330
	Pendragon Chambers	01792 411188
Swindon	Pump Court Chambers	01793 539899
Winchester	Pump Court Chambers	01962 868161
	4 St Peter Street	01962 868 884
Wolverhampton	Claremont Chambers	01902 426222
York	• York Chambers	01904 620 048

PLANNING

Birmingham	• Equity Chambers	0121 233 2100
	1 Fountain Court	0121 236 5721
	• 5 Fountain Court	0121 606 0500
	• St Philip's Chambers	0121 246 7000
Bradford	Broadway House Chambers	01274 722560
Cambridge	Regency Chambers	01223 301517
Cardiff	9 Park Place	01222 382731
Chesterfield	26 Morley Avenue	01246 234790
Ely	Cathedral Chambers, Ely	01353 666775
Exeter	• Cathedral Chambers (Jan Wood Independent Barristers' Clerk)	01392 210900
	Colleton Chambers	01392 274898
	Rougemont Chambers	01392 410471
Leeds	Chambers of Andrew Campbell QC	0113 245 5438
	11 King's Bench Walk	0113 2971 200
	• Sovereign Chambers	0113 245 1841/2/3
	• 9 Woodhouse Square	0113 245 1986
Leicester	2 New Street	0116 262 5906
Liverpool	• Exchange Chambers	0151 236 7747
London	9 Bedford Row	0171 242 3555
	• 5 Bell Yard	0171 333 8811
	11 Bolt Court	0171 353 2300
	• Bracton Chambers	0171 242 4248
	• 4 Brick Court	0171 797 8910
	• Chambers of Mr Peter Crampin QC	0171 831 0081
	Equity Barristers' Chambers	0181 558 8336
	Chambers of Geoffrey Hawker	0171 583 8899
	• Goldsmith Building	0171 353 7881
	• 2-3 Gray's Inn Square	0171 242 4986
	• 2 Harcourt Buildings	0171 353 8415
	• Hardwicke Building	0171 242 2523
Harrow on the Hill	• Harrow-on-the-Hill Chambers	0181 423 7444
London	4 King's Bench Walk	0171 353 3581
	The Chambers of Mr Ali Mohammad Azhar	0171 353 9564 (4 lines)
	10 King's Bench Walk	0171 353 7742
	11 King's Bench Walk	0171 353 3337/8
	• Pump Court Chambers	0171 353 0711
	1 Serjeants' Inn	0171 583 1355
	• Thomas More Chambers	0171 404 7000
Manchester	• Cobden House Chambers	0161 833 6000/6001
Norwich	East Anglian Chambers	01603 617351
Nottingham	Ropewalk Chambers	0115 947 2581
	St Mary's Chambers	0115 950 3503
Peterborough	Regency Chambers	01733 315215
Preston	New Bailey Chambers	01772 258 087
Reading	Dr Johnson's Chambers	01189 254221
Redhill	Redhill Chambers	01737 780781
Swansea	Gower Chambers	01792 644466

• Expanded entry in Part C

	Iscoed Chambers	01792 652988/9/330
	Pendragon Chambers	01792 411188

PRISON LAW

London	100E Great Portland Street	0171 636 6323
	• 14 Tooks Court	0171 405 8828
Manchester	Chambers of Ian Macdonald QC	0161 236 1840

PRISONERS RIGHTS

Manchester	• Central Chambers	0161 833 1774

PRIVATE CLIENT

Oxford	28 Western Road	01865 204911

PRIVATE INTERNATIONAL

Bournemouth	20 Lorne Park Road	01202 292102
Cardiff	• 33 Park Place	01222 233313
Leeds	• 9 Woodhouse Square	0113 245 1986
London	Chambers of Dr Michael Arnheim	0171 833 5093
	Barristers' Common Law Chambers	0171 375 3012
	• Blackstone Chambers (formerly known as 2 Hare Court)	0171 583 1770
	11 Bolt Court	0171 353 2300
	Brick Court Chambers	0171 583 0777
	1 Crown Office Row	0171 583 9292
	Equity Barristers' Chambers	0181 558 8336
	• 4 Essex Court	0171 797 7970
	• Essex Court Chambers	0171 813 8000
	• 20 Essex Street	0171 583 9294
	• Chambers of Norman Palmer	0171 405 6114
	• Fountain Court	0171 583 3335
	Goldsworth Chambers	0171 405 7117
	• Gough Square Chambers	0171 353 0924
	Gray's Inn Square	0171 242 3529
	• Hardwicke Building	0171 242 2523
	• One Hare Court	0171 353 3171
	Chambers of Harjit Singh	0171 353 1356
	• 4 King's Bench Walk	0171 822 8822
	The Chambers of Mr Ali Mohammad Azhar	0171 353 9564 (4 lines)
	• 11 King's Bench Walk	0171 632 8500
	• 13 King's Bench Walk	0171 353 7204
	• Littman Chambers	0171 404 4866
	• Monckton Chambers	0171 405 7211
	Chambers of Dr Jamal Nasir	0171 405 3818/9
	• 12 New Square	0171 419 1212
	The Chambers of Leolin Price CBE, QC	0171 405 0758/242 5002
	• 13 Old Square	0171 404 4800
	• 3 Paper Buildings	0171 583 8055
	• 5 Paper Buildings	0171 583 9275
	• Chambers of John L Powell QC	0171 797 8000
	No 1 Serjeants' Inn	0171 415 6666
	• 3 Stone Buildings	0171 242 4937/405 8358
	• 7 Stone Buildings	0171 405 3886/242 3546
	• 9 Stone Buildings	0171 404 5055
	11 Stone Buildings	+44 (0)171 831 6381
	• 3 Verulam Buildings	0171 831 8441
	Verulam Chambers	0171 813 2400
Manchester	• 28 St John Street	0161 834 8418
Oxford	1 Alfred Street	01865 793736
	• King's Bench Chambers	01865 311066
Redhill	Redhill Chambers	01737 780781
Winchester	4 St Peter Street	01962 868 884

PRIVY COUNCIL APPEALS

London	• Thomas More Chambers	0171 404 7000

PROBATE AND ADMINISTRATION

Birmingham	• 5 Fountain Court	0121 606 0500

• Expanded entry in Part C

A

	• 8 Fountain Court	0121 236 5514
	• St Philip's Chambers	0121 246 7000
Bristol	St John's Chambers	0117 921 3456/929 8514
Cambridge	• Fenners Chambers	01223 368761
	Regency Chambers	01223 301517
Cardiff	9 Park Place	01222 382731
	30 Park Place	01222 398421
	• 33 Park Place	01222 233313
Chester	White Friars Chambers	01244 323070
Chichester	Chichester Chambers	01243 784538
Eastbourne	King's Chambers	01323 416053
Exeter	Southernhay Chambers	01392 255777
Leeds	Chambers of Andrew Campbell QC	0113 245 5438
	Enterprise Chambers	0113 246 0391
	11 King's Bench Walk	0113 2971 200
	• No. 6	0113 245 9763
	The Chambers of Philip Raynor QC	0113 242 1123
	• 9 Woodhouse Square	0113 245 1986
Liverpool	• Exchange Chambers	0151 236 7747
	• The Chambers of Adrian Lyon	0151 236 4421/8240/6757
London	• 29 Bedford Row Chambers	0171 831 2626
	• 4 Brick Court	0171 797 7766
	Bridewell Chambers	0171 797 8800
	• Chambers of Mr Peter Crampin QC	0171 831 0081
	• Enterprise Chambers	0171 405 9471
	Equity Barristers' Chambers	0181 558 8336
	• One Essex Court	0171 936 3030
	• Chambers of Norman Palmer	0171 405 6114
	• 2nd Floor, Francis Taylor Building	0171 353 9942
	Francis Taylor Buildings	0171 353 7768/2711
	2 Gray's Inn Square Chambers	0171 242 0328/405 1317
	Gray's Inn Square	0171 242 3529
	10 - 11 Gray's Inn Square	0171 405 2576
	• 1 Harcourt Buildings	0171 353 9421/0375
	• 2 Harcourt Buildings	0171 583 9020
	• Hardwicke Building	0171 242 2523
Harrow on the Hill	• Harrow-on-the-Hill Chambers	0181 423 7444
London	• John Street Chambers	0171 242 1911
	4 King's Bench Walk	0171 353 3581
	• 9 King's Bench Walk	0171 353 7202/3909
	11 King's Bench Walk	0171 353 3337/8
	• Lamb Building	0171 797 7788
	Lion Court	0171 404 6565
	• Littman Chambers	0171 404 4866
	• Mitre Court Chambers	0171 353 9394
	• New Court	0171 583 5123
	• New Court Chambers	0171 831 9500
	• 1 New Square	0171 405 0884/5/6/7
	Chambers of Lord Goodhart QC	0171 405 5577
	5 New Square	0171 404 0404
	• 12 New Square	0171 419 1212
	• Twenty-Four Old Buildings	0171 404 0946
	• 9 Old Square	0171 405 4682
	The Chambers of Leolin Price CBE, QC	0171 405 0758/242 5002
	11 Old Square	0171 242 5022
	• 11 Old Square	0171 430 0341
	• 13 Old Square	0171 404 4800
	• 5 Paper Buildings	0171 583 9275
	• 5 Pump Court	0171 353 2532
	No 1 Serjeants' Inn	0171 415 6666
	• Stanbrook & Henderson	0171 353 0101
	• 3 Stone Buildings	0171 242 4937/405 8358
	• 5 Stone Buildings	0171 242 6201
	• 9 Stone Buildings	0171 404 5055
	11 Stone Buildings	+44 (0)171 831 6381
	Verulam Chambers	0171 813 2400
	• Wilberforce Chambers	0171 306 0102
Manchester	• Cobden House Chambers	0161 833 6000/6001
	• Chambers of John Hand QC	0161 955 9000
	• 40 King Street	0161 832 9082
	• 8 King Street Chambers	0161 834 9560
	Manchester House Chambers	0161 834 7007

• Expanded entry in Part C

	• St James's Chambers	0161 834 7000
Newcastle upon Tyne	Enterprise Chambers	0191 222 3344
	• Trinity Chambers	0191 232 1927
Northampton	22 Albion Place	01604 636271
Norwich	East Anglian Chambers	01603 617351
Oxford	28 Western Road	01865 204911
Peterborough	Fenners Chambers	01733 562030
	Regency Chambers	01733 315215
Portsmouth	Hampshire Chambers	01705 826636
Preston	New Bailey Chambers	01772 258 087
	15 Winckley Square	01772 252 828
Southampton	• 17 Carlton Crescent	01703 320320
	• Eighteen Carlton Crescent	01703 639001
Stoke-on-Trent	Regent Chambers	01782 286666
Swansea	Iscoed Chambers	01792 652988/9/330
Wolverhampton	Claremont Chambers	01902 426222

PRODUCT LIABILITY

Bristol	Old Square Chambers	0117 927 7111
London	• Old Square Chambers	0171 269 0300

PROFESSIONAL DISCIPLINARY MATTERS (SOLS) - CICB

London	• Mitre House Chambers	0171 583 8233

PROFESSIONAL NEGLIGENCE

Birmingham	• Equity Chambers	0121 233 2100
	1 Fountain Court	0121 236 5721
	• 3 Fountain Court	0121 236 5854
	• 5 Fountain Court	0121 606 0500
	• 8 Fountain Court	0121 236 5514
	• St Philip's Chambers	0121 246 7000
Bournemouth	King's Bench Chambers	01202 250025
	20 Lorne Park Road	01202 292102
Bradford	Broadway House Chambers	01274 722560
Brighton	• Crown Office Row Chambers	01273 625625
Bristol	Old Square Chambers	0117 927 7111
	St John's Chambers	0117 921 3456/929 8514
Cambridge	• Fenners Chambers	01223 368761
	Regency Chambers	01223 301517
Canterbury	Stour Chambers	01227 764899
Cardiff	9 Park Place	01222 382731
	30 Park Place	01222 398421
	• 33 Park Place	01222 233313
Chester	40 King Street	01244 323886
	White Friars Chambers	01244 323070
Chichester	Chichester Chambers	01243 784538
Coulsdon	Advolex Chambers	0181 763 2345
Exeter	• Cathedral Chambers (Jan Wood	01392 210900
	Independent Barristers' Clerk)	
	Rougemont Chambers	01392 410471
	Southernhay Chambers	01392 255777
	Walnut House	01392 279751
Guildford	• Guildford Chambers	01483 539131
Leatherhead	Pembroke House	01372 376160/376493
Leeds	Chambers of Andrew Campbell QC	0113 245 5438
	• Chancery House Chambers	0113 244 6691
	Enterprise Chambers	0113 246 0391
	11 King's Bench Walk	0113 2971 200
	• Mercury Chambers	0113 234 2265
	• No. 6	0113 245 9763
	The Chambers of Philip Raynor QC	0113 242 1123
	• 37 Park Square	0113 243 9422
	• Sovereign Chambers	0113 245 1841/2/3
	• St Paul's House	0113 245 5866
	• 9 Woodhouse Square	0113 245 1986
Leicester	2 New Street	0116 262 5906
Liverpool	25-27 Castle Street	0151 227 5661/5666/236 5072
	19 Castle Street Chambers	0151 236 9402
	Chavasse Court Chambers	0151 707 1191
	• The Corn Exchange Chambers	0151 227 1081/5009

A

	• Exchange Chambers	0151 236 7747
	India Buildings Chambers	0151 243 6000
	• The Chambers of Adrian Lyon	0151 236 4421/8240/6757
	• Martins Building	0151 236 5818/4919
	• Oriel Chambers	0151 236 7191
	• Peel House Chambers	0151 236 4321
London	Chambers of Dr Michael Arnheim	0171 833 5093
	Atkin Chambers	0171 404 0102
	Avondale Chambers	0181 445 9984
	Barnard's Inn Chambers	0171 242 8508
	Barristers' Common Law Chambers	0171 375 3012
	9 Bedford Row	0171 242 3555
	17 Bedford Row	0171 831 7314
	33 Bedford Row	0171 242 6476
	• 29 Bedford Row Chambers	0171 831 2626
	• 5 Bell Yard	0171 333 8811
	• 9-12 Bell Yard	0171 400 1800
	• Blackstone Chambers (formerly known	0171 583 1770
	as 2 Hare Court)	
	11 Bolt Court	0171 353 2300
	• Bracton Chambers	0171 242 4248
	• 4 Breams Buildings	0171 353 5835/430 1221
	• 4 Brick Court	0171 797 7766
	Brick Court Chambers	0171 583 0777
	Bridewell Chambers	0171 797 8800
	Cloisters	0171 827 4000
	• Chambers of Mr Peter Crampin QC	0171 831 0081
	• 1 Crown Office Row	0171 797 7500
	1 Crown Office Row	0171 583 9292
	• Two Crown Office Row	0171 797 8100
	• Devereux Chambers	0171 353 7534
	• Doughty Street Chambers	0171 404 1313
	• Dr Johnson's Chambers	0171 353 4716
	• Enterprise Chambers	0171 405 9471
	Equity Barristers' Chambers	0181 558 8336
	• Erskine Chambers	0171 242 5532
	• One Essex Court	0171 583 2000
	• One Essex Court	0171 936 3030
	• 4 Essex Court	0171 797 7970
	5 Essex Court	0171 410 2000
	• Essex Court Chambers	0171 813 8000
	• 20 Essex Street	0171 583 9294
	• 35 Essex Street	0171 353 6381
	• 39 Essex Street	0171 832 1111
	Chambers of Geoffrey Hawker	0171 583 8899
	Falcon Chambers	0171 353 2484
	• Farrar's Building	0171 583 9241
	• Chambers of Norman Palmer	0171 405 6114
	• 4 Field Court	0171 440 6900
	• Fountain Court	0171 583 3335
	• 2nd Floor, Francis Taylor Building	0171 353 9942
	Francis Taylor Buildings	0171 353 7768/2711
	• 2 Garden Court	0171 353 1633
	• Goldsmith Building	0171 353 7881
	Goldsworth Chambers	0171 405 7117
	• Gough Square Chambers	0171 353 0924
	• Gray's Inn Chambers	0171 831 5344
	• Gray's Inn Chambers	0171 404 1111
	• 1 Gray's Inn Square	0171 405 8946
	2 Gray's Inn Square Chambers	0171 242 0328/405 1317
	• 2-3 Gray's Inn Square	0171 242 4986
	• 4-5 Gray's Inn Square	0171 404 5252
	10 - 11 Gray's Inn Square	0171 405 2576
	• 1 Harcourt Buildings	0171 353 9421/0375
	• 2 Harcourt Buildings	0171 583 9020
	• Harcourt Chambers	0171 353 6961/7
	• Hardwicke Building	0171 242 2523
	• 1 Hare Court	0171 353 3982/5324
	• One Hare Court	0171 353 3171
Harrow on the Hill	• Harrow-on-the-Hill Chambers	0181 423 7444
London	• Chambers of James Hunt QC	0171 421 8000
	• John Street Chambers	0171 242 1911

Justice Court Chambers	0181 830 7786
• One King's Bench Walk	0171 936 1500
• 4 King's Bench Walk	0171 822 8822
4 King's Bench Walk	0171 353 3581
S Tomlinson QC	0171 583 0404
• 8 King's Bench Walk	0171 797 8888
• 9 King's Bench Walk	0171 353 7202/3909
The Chambers of Mr Ali Mohammad Azhar	0171 353 9564 (4 lines)
10 King's Bench Walk	0171 353 7742
• 11 King's Bench Walk	0171 632 8500
11 King's Bench Walk	0171 353 3337/8
• 12 King's Bench Walk	0171 583 0811
• 13 King's Bench Walk	0171 353 7204
• Chambers of Lord Campbell of Alloway QC	0171 353 9276
• Lamb Building	0171 797 7788
Lamb Chambers	0171 797 8300
• Littleton Chambers	0171 797 8600
• Littman Chambers	0171 404 4866
• 1 Mitre Court Buildings	0171 797 7070
2 Mitre Court Buildings	0171 353 1353
2 Mitre Court Buildings	0171 583 1380
• Mitre Court Chambers	0171 353 9394
• Mitre House Chambers	0171 583 8233
• Monckton Chambers	0171 405 7211
• New Court	0171 583 5123
• New Court Chambers	0171 831 9500
• 1 New Square	0171 405 0884/5/6/7
• 3 New Square	0171 405 1111
Chambers of Lord Goodhart QC	0171 405 5577
5 New Square	0171 404 0404
• 12 New Square	0171 419 1212
Chambers of Joy Okoye	0171 405 7011
• 22 Old Buildings	0171 831 0222
• Twenty-Four Old Buildings	0171 404 0946
• 9 Old Square	0171 405 4682
The Chambers of Leolin Price CBE, QC	0171 405 0758/242 5002
• 11 Old Square	0171 430 0341
• 13 Old Square	0171 404 4800
• Old Square Chambers	0171 269 0300
One Paper Buildings	0171 583 7355
• 3 Paper Buildings	0171 797 7000
• 3 Paper Buildings	0171 583 8055
• 4 Paper Buildings	0171 353 3366/583 7155
• 4 Paper Buildings	0171 583 0816
• 5 Paper Buildings	0171 583 9275
5 Paper Buildings	0171 583 6117
• Chambers of John L Powell QC	0171 797 8000
• 1 Pump Court	0171 583 2012/353 4341
2 Pump Court	0171 353 5597
• Pump Court Chambers	0171 353 0711
• 4 Pump Court	0171 353 2656/9
• 5 Pump Court	0171 353 2532
• Chambers of Kieran Coonan QC	0171 583 6013/2510
6 Pump Court	0171 797 8400
• 5 Raymond Buildings	0171 242 2902
No 1 Serjeants' Inn	0171 415 6666
• 3 Serjeants' Inn	0171 353 5537
• Serle Court Chambers	0171 242 6105
• 3–4 South Square	0171 696 9900
• Stanbrook & Henderson	0171 353 0101
• 3 Stone Buildings	0171 242 4937/405 8358
4 Stone Buildings	0171 242 5524
• 5 Stone Buildings	0171 242 6201
• 7 Stone Buildings	0171 405 3886/242 3546
8 Stone Buildings	0171 831 9881
• 9 Stone Buildings	0171 404 5055
11 Stone Buildings	+44 (0)171 831 6381
• 199 Strand	0171 379 9779
169 Temple Chambers	0171 583 7644
• 1 Temple Gardens	0171 353 0407/583 1315

	• 2 Temple Gardens	0171 583 6041
	3 Temple Gardens (North)	0171 353 0853/4/7222
	• Thomas More Chambers	0171 404 7000
	• 14 Tooks Court	0171 405 8828
	Chambers of Mohammed Hashmot Ullah	0171 377 0119
	• 3 Verulam Buildings	0171 831 8441
	Verulam Chambers	0171 813 2400
	• Wilberforce Chambers	0171 306 0102
Maidstone	• Maidstone Chambers	01622 688592
Malvern	Resolution Chambers	01684 561279
Manchester	• Byrom Street Chambers	0161 829 2100
	• Central Chambers	0161 833 1774
	• Cobden House Chambers	0161 833 6000/6001
	Deans Court Chambers	0161 834 4097
	• Chambers of John Hand QC	0161 955 9000
	Kenworthy's Chambers	0161 832 4036
	• 40 King Street	0161 832 9082
	• 8 King Street Chambers	0161 834 9560
	Lincoln House Chambers	0161 832 5701
	Chambers of Ian Macdonald QC	0161 236 1840
	Manchester House Chambers	0161 834 7007
	• Merchant Chambers	0161 839 7070
	• Queen's Chambers	0161 834 6875/4738
	• St James's Chambers	0161 834 7000
	18 St John Street	0161 278 1800
	• 28 St John Street	0161 834 8418
	Young Street Chambers	0161 833 0489
Meopham	West Lodge Farm	01474 812280
Middlesbrough	Baker Street Chambers	01642 873873
	• Fountain Chambers	01642 217037
	York House	01642 213000
Milton Keynes	Milton Keynes Chambers	01908 217857
Newcastle upon Tyne	Enterprise Chambers	0191 222 3344
	Milburn House Chambers	0191 230 5511
	• New Court Chambers	0191 232 1980
	• Trinity Chambers	0191 232 1927
	Westgate Chambers	0191 261 4407/232 9785
Northampton	22 Albion Place	01604 636271
Norwich	East Anglian Chambers	01603 617351
	Sackville Chambers	01603 613516
Nottingham	King Charles House	0115 941 8851
	Ropewalk Chambers	0115 947 2581
	St Mary's Chambers	0115 950 3503
Oxford	1 Alfred Street	01865 793736
	• King's Bench Chambers	01865 311066
Peterborough	Fenners Chambers	01733 562030
	Regency Chambers	01733 315215
Plymouth	Devon Chambers	01752 661659
Portsmouth	Hampshire Chambers	01705 826636
	• Portsmouth Barristers' Chambers	01705 831292
Preston	4 Camden Place	01772 828300
	Deans Court Chambers	01772 555163
	New Bailey Chambers	01772 258 087
	15 Winckley Square	01772 252 828
Reading	Wessex Chambers	0118 956 8856
Richmond-upon-Thames	Richmond Green Chambers	0181 940 1841
Sheffield	Paradise Square Chambers	0114 273 8951
Slough	11 St Bernards Road	01753 553806/817989
Southampton	• 17 Carlton Crescent	01703 320320
	• College Chambers	01703 230338
	• Eighteen Carlton Crescent	01703 639001
Stoke-on-Trent	Regent Chambers	01782 286666
Swansea	Angel Chambers	01792 464623/464648
	Gower Chambers	01792 644466
	Iscoed Chambers	01792 652988/9/330
Swindon	Pump Court Chambers	01793 539899
Winchester	Pump Court Chambers	01962 868161
	4 St Peter Street	01962 868 884
Winkleigh	Barnstaple Chambers	0183 783763
Wolverhampton	Claremont Chambers	01902 426222
York	• York Chambers	01904 620 048

• Expanded entry in Part C

PUBLIC CHILDCARE

Bristol	29 Gwilliam Street	0117 966 8997

PUBLIC INQUIRIES/INQUESTS

London	• 14 Tooks Court	0171 405 8828

PUBLIC INTERNATIONAL

Leeds	• 9 Woodhouse Square	0113 245 1986
London	Chambers of Dr Michael Arnheim	0171 833 5093
	• Blackstone Chambers (formerly known as 2 Hare Court)	0171 583 1770
	Brick Court Chambers	0171 583 0777
	Cloisters	0171 827 4000
	1 Crown Office Row	0171 583 9292
	Equity Barristers' Chambers	0181 558 8336
	• Essex Court Chambers	0171 813 8000
	• 20 Essex Street	0171 583 9294
	• Chambers of Norman Palmer	0171 405 6114
	Goldsworth Chambers	0171 405 7117
	• 4-5 Gray's Inn Square	0171 404 5252
	• Hardwicke Building	0171 242 2523
	• One Hare Court	0171 353 3171
	The Chambers of Mr Ali Mohammad Azhar	0171 353 9564 (4 lines)
	10 King's Bench Walk	0171 353 7742
	• 11 King's Bench Walk	0171 632 8500
	• Monckton Chambers	0171 405 7211
	Chambers of Dr Jamal Nasir	0171 405 3818/9
	• 12 New Square	0171 419 1212
	• 3 Verulam Buildings	0171 831 8441

PUBLIC PROCUREMENT

Cardiff	30 Park Place	01222 398421

RATING AND CPO

London	2 Mitre Court Buildings	0171 583 1380

REGULATORY WORK

London	23 Essex Street	0171 413 0353

RIGHTS OF LIGHT

London	• Chambers of Mr Peter Crampin QC	0171 831 0081

SALE AND CARRIAGE OF GOODS

Birmingham	• Equity Chambers	0121 233 2100
	1 Fountain Court	0121 236 5721
	• 3 Fountain Court	0121 236 5854
	• 5 Fountain Court	0121 606 0500
	• 8 Fountain Court	0121 236 5514
	• St Philip's Chambers	0121 246 7000
Bournemouth	King's Bench Chambers	01202 250025
	20 Lorne Park Road	01202 292102
Bradford	Broadway House Chambers	01274 722560
Brighton	• Crown Office Row Chambers	01273 625625
Bristol	St John's Chambers	0117 921 3456/929 8514
Cambridge	• Fenners Chambers	01223 368761
Cardiff	30 Park Place	01222 398421
Chester	White Friars Chambers	01244 323070
Chichester	Chichester Chambers	01243 784538
Eastbourne	King's Chambers	01323 416053
Exeter	• Cathedral Chambers (Jan Wood Independent Barristers' Clerk)	01392 210900
	Rougemont Chambers	01392 410471
Haverhill	Helions Chambers	01440 730523
Leeds	Chambers of Andrew Campbell QC	0113 245 5438
	• Chancery House Chambers	0113 244 6691
	The Chambers of Philip Raynor QC	0113 242 1123

Liverpool	• 9 Woodhouse Square	0113 245 1986
	25-27 Castle Street	0151 227 5661/5666/236 5072
	• The Corn Exchange Chambers	0151 227 1081/5009
	• Exchange Chambers	0151 236 7747
	• The Chambers of Adrian Lyon	0151 236 4421/8240/6757
	• Martins Building	0151 236 5818/4919
	• Oriel Chambers	0151 236 7191
London	Barnard's Inn Chambers	0171 242 8508
	9 Bedford Row	0171 242 3555
	17 Bedford Row	0171 831 7314
	• 29 Bedford Row Chambers	0171 831 2626
	• 5 Bell Yard	0171 333 8811
	• Blackstone Chambers (formerly known	0171 583 1770
	as 2 Hare Court)	
	Brick Court Chambers	0171 583 0777
	Bridewell Chambers	0171 797 8800
	• Chambers of Mr Peter Crampin QC	0171 831 0081
	• 1 Crown Office Row	0171 797 7500
	1 Crown Office Row	0171 583 9292
	• Two Crown Office Row	0171 797 8100
	• Dr Johnson's Chambers	0171 353 4716
	Equity Barristers' Chambers	0181 558 8336
	• One Essex Court	0171 936 3030
	• 4 Essex Court	0171 797 7970
	• Essex Court Chambers	0171 813 8000
	• 20 Essex Street	0171 583 9294
	• 35 Essex Street	0171 353 6381
	• 39 Essex Street	0171 832 1111
	Chambers of Geoffrey Hawker	0171 583 8899
	• Farrar's Building	0171 583 9241
	• Chambers of Norman Palmer	0171 405 6114
	• 4 Field Court	0171 440 6900
	• Fountain Court	0171 583 3335
	• 2nd Floor, Francis Taylor Building	0171 353 9942
	Francis Taylor Buildings	0171 353 7768/2711
	• Gough Square Chambers	0171 353 0924
	• 1 Gray's Inn Square Chambers of the	0171 405 3000
	Baroness Scotland of Asthal QC	
	• 1 Gray's Inn Square	0171 405 8946
	2 Gray's Inn Square Chambers	0171 242 0328/405 1317
	• 2-3 Gray's Inn Square	0171 242 4986
	• 1 Harcourt Buildings	0171 353 9421/0375
	• 2 Harcourt Buildings	0171 583 9020
	2 Harcourt Buildings	0171 353 2112/2817
	• Hardwicke Building	0171 242 2523
	• One Hare Court	0171 353 3171
Harrow on the Hill	• Harrow-on-the-Hill Chambers	0181 423 7444
London	S Tomlinson QC	0171 583 0404
	• 9 King's Bench Walk	0171 353 7202/3909
	The Chambers of Mr Ali Mohammad	0171 353 9564 (4 lines)
	Azhar	
	10 King's Bench Walk	0171 353 7742
	• 11 King's Bench Walk	0171 632 8500
	11 King's Bench Walk	0171 353 3337/8
	• 12 King's Bench Walk	0171 583 0811
	• 13 King's Bench Walk	0171 353 7204
	• Lamb Building	0171 797 7788
	Lamb Chambers	0171 797 8300
	Lion Court	0171 404 6565
	• Littleton Chambers	0171 797 8600
	• Littman Chambers	0171 404 4866
	• Mitre Court Chambers	0171 353 9394
	• Monckton Chambers	0171 405 7211
	• 3 New Square	0171 405 1111
	• 12 New Square	0171 419 1212
	• 22 Old Buildings	0171 831 0222
	The Chambers of Leolin Price CBE, QC	0171 405 0758/242 5002
	• Old Square Chambers	0171 269 0300
	• 3 Paper Buildings	0171 797 7000
	• 3 Paper Buildings	0171 583 8055
	• 4 Paper Buildings	0171 583 0816
	• 5 Paper Buildings	0171 583 9275

• Expanded entry in Part C

	5 Paper Buildings	0171 583 6117
	Phoenix Chambers	0171 404 7888
	• Chambers of John L Powell QC	0171 797 8000
	2 Pump Court	0171 353 5597
	• 4 Pump Court	0171 353 2656/9
	• 5 Pump Court	0171 353 2532
	• 5 Raymond Buildings	0171 242 2902
	No 1 Serjeants' Inn	0171 415 6666
	• 3 Serjeants' Inn	0171 353 5537
	• 3-4 South Square	0171 696 9900
	• Stanbrook & Henderson	0171 353 0101
	11 Stone Buildings	+44 (0)171 831 6381
	• 199 Strand	0171 379 9779
	169 Temple Chambers	0171 583 7644
	• 1 Temple Gardens	0171 353 0407/583 1315
	• 2 Temple Gardens	0171 583 6041
	• Thomas More Chambers	0171 404 7000
	• 3 Verulam Buildings	0171 831 8441
	Warwick House Chambers	0171 430 2323
Manchester	• Cobden House Chambers	0161 833 6000/6001
	Deans Court Chambers	0161 834 4097
	• Chambers of John Hand QC	0161 955 9000
	• 40 King Street	0161 832 9082
	• 8 King Street Chambers	0161 834 9560
	Manchester House Chambers	0161 834 7007
	• Merchant Chambers	0161 839 7070
	• Queen's Chambers	0161 834 6875/4738
	• St James's Chambers	0161 834 7000
	Young Street Chambers	0161 833 0489
Middlesbrough	Baker Street Chambers	01642 873873
	• Fountain Chambers	01642 217037
Newcastle upon Tyne	• Broad Chare	0191 232 0541
	• Trinity Chambers	0191 232 1927
Northampton	22 Albion Place	01604 636271
Norwich	East Anglian Chambers	01603 617351
	Sackville Chambers	01603 613516
Nottingham	King Charles House	0115 941 8851
	Ropewalk Chambers	0115 947 2581
Oxford	1 Alfred Street	01865 793736
	• King's Bench Chambers	01865 311066
Peterborough	Fenners Chambers	01733 562030
Plymouth	Devon Chambers	01752 661659
Portsmouth	• Portsmouth Barristers' Chambers	01705 831292
Preston	4 Camden Place	01772 828300
	Deans Court Chambers	01772 555163
	New Bailey Chambers	01772 258 087
	15 Winckley Square	01772 252 828
Reading	Wessex Chambers	0118 956 8856
Southampton	• Eighteen Carlton Crescent	01703 639001
Stoke-on-Trent	Regent Chambers	01782 286666
Swansea	Iscoed Chambers	01792 652988/9/330
Winchester	4 St Peter Street	01962 868 884
Wolverhampton	Claremont Chambers	01902 426222
York	• York Chambers	01904 620 048

SHARE OPTIONS

Birmingham	• 5 Fountain Court	0121 606 0500
Haverhill	Helions Chambers	01440 730523
Leeds	Chambers of Andrew Campbell QC	0113 245 5438
Liverpool	• Exchange Chambers	0151 236 7747
London	• 5 Bell Yard	0171 333 8811
	• Erskine Chambers	0171 242 5532
	• One Essex Court	0171 583 2000
	• Essex Court Chambers	0171 813 8000
	• Chambers of Norman Palmer	0171 405 6114
	• Fountain Court	0171 583 3335
	• One Hare Court	0171 353 3171
	• 11 King's Bench Walk	0171 632 8500
	11 King's Bench Walk	0171 353 3337/8
	• Littleton Chambers	0171 797 8600
	• 1 New Square	0171 405 0884/5/6/7
	5 New Square	0171 404 0404

A

	Chambers of John Gardiner QC	0171 242 4017
	• Twenty-Four Old Buildings	0171 404 0946
	• 3-4 South Square	0171 696 9900
	• 9 Stone Buildings	0171 404 5055
	11 Stone Buildings	+44 (0)171 831 6381
Manchester	• Chambers of John Hand QC	0161 955 9000
	• 8 King Street Chambers	0161 834 9560
	• Merchant Chambers	0161 839 7070
	• St James's Chambers	0161 834 7000

SHIPPING

| **London** | Bridewell Chambers | 0171 797 8800 |
| **Manchester** | • Byrom Street Chambers | 0161 829 2100 |

SHIPPING, ADMIRALTY

Exeter	• Cathedral Chambers (Jan Wood Independent Barristers' Clerk)	01392 210900
Leeds	Chambers of Andrew Campbell QC	0113 245 5438
Liverpool	• The Corn Exchange Chambers	0151 227 1081/5009
	• Exchange Chambers	0151 236 7747
London	• 5 Bell Yard	0171 333 8811
	Brick Court Chambers	0171 583 0777
	Bridewell Chambers	0171 797 8800
	Equity Barristers' Chambers	0181 558 8336
	• One Essex Court	0171 583 2000
	• 4 Essex Court	0171 797 7970
	• Essex Court Chambers	0171 813 8000
	• 20 Essex Street	0171 583 9294
	• 4 Field Court	0171 440 6900
	• Fountain Court	0171 583 3335
	• Goldsmith Building	0171 353 7881
	• 1 Gray's Inn Square Chambers of the Baroness Scotland of Asthal QC	0171 405 3000
	2 Gray's Inn Square Chambers	0171 242 0328/405 1317
	• 4-5 Gray's Inn Square	0171 404 5252
	• 4 King's Bench Walk	0171 822 8822
	S Tomlinson QC	0171 583 0404
	The Chambers of Mr Ali Mohammad Azhar	0171 353 9564 (4 lines)
	• 11 King's Bench Walk	0171 632 8500
	• Chambers of Lord Campbell of Alloway QC	0171 353 9276
	• Littman Chambers	0171 404 4866
	• 3 Verulam Buildings	0171 831 8441
	Verulam Chambers	0171 813 2400
	Warwick House Chambers	0171 430 2323
Portsmouth	• Portsmouth Barristers' Chambers	01705 831292

SOCIAL SERVICES

| **Slough** | 11 St Bernards Road | 01753 553806/817989 |

SOUTH ASIAN LAW

| **London** | • Essex Court Chambers | 0171 813 8000 |

SPORTS

Birmingham	• Equity Chambers	0121 233 2100
	• 5 Fountain Court	0121 606 0500
	• 8 Fountain Court	0121 236 5514
Bristol	Old Square Chambers	0117 927 7111
	St John's Chambers	0117 921 3456/929 8514
Ely	Cathedral Chambers, Ely	01353 666775
Leeds	• Sovereign Chambers	0113 245 1841/2/3
Liverpool	25-27 Castle Street	0151 227 5661/5666/236 5072
	• The Corn Exchange Chambers	0151 227 1081/5009
London	Chambers of Dr Michael Arnheim	0171 833 5093
	Barnard's Inn Chambers	0171 242 8508
	9 Bedford Row	0171 242 3555
	• 9-12 Bell Yard	0171 400 1800

• Expanded entry in Part C

• Blackstone Chambers (formerly known as 2 Hare Court)	0171 583 1770
Brick Court Chambers	0171 583 0777
Cloisters	0171 827 4000
• 1 Crown Office Row	0171 797 7111
• Devereux Chambers	0171 353 7534
• Essex Court Chambers	0171 813 8000
• 39 Essex Street	0171 832 1111
• Farrar's Building	0171 583 9241
• 4 Field Court	0171 440 6900
• Fountain Court	0171 583 3335
Francis Taylor Buildings	0171 353 7768/2711
• Goldsmith Building	0171 353 7881
• 4-5 Gray's Inn Square	0171 404 5252
• 2 Harcourt Buildings	0171 583 9020
• Hardwicke Building	0171 242 2523
• 3 Hare Court	0171 353 7561
Chambers of Harjit Singh	0171 353 1356

Harrow on the Hill
London

• Harrow-on-the-Hill Chambers	0181 423 7444
• Chambers of James Hunt QC	0171 421 8000
• One King's Bench Walk	0171 936 1500
• Chambers of Lord Campbell of Alloway QC	0171 353 9276
Kingsway Chambers	07000 653529
• Littleton Chambers	0171 797 8600
• Mitre Court Chambers	0171 353 9394
• Monckton Chambers	0171 405 7211
• New Court Chambers	0171 831 9500
• 1 New Square	0171 405 0884/5/6/7
5 New Square	0171 404 0404
• 12 New Square	0171 419 1212
• 9 Old Square	0171 405 4682
11 Old Square	0171 242 5022
• 13 Old Square	0171 404 4800
• Old Square Chambers	0171 269 0300
• 2 Paper Buildings	0171 936 2611 (10 lines)
• 4 Paper Buildings	0171 353 3366/583 7155
5 Paper Buildings	0171 583 6117
• 4 Pump Court	0171 353 2656/9
• 5 Raymond Buildings	0171 242 2902
No 1 Serjeants' Inn	0171 415 6666
• Stanbrook & Henderson	0171 353 0101
• 3 Stone Buildings	0171 242 4937/405 8358
11 Stone Buildings	+44 (0)171 831 6381
• 199 Strand	0171 379 9779

Manchester Deans Court Chambers 0161 834 4097
Nottingham Ropewalk Chambers 0115 947 2581
Preston Deans Court Chambers 01772 555163

TAX - CAPITAL AND INCOME

Birmingham

1 Fountain Court	0121 236 5721
• 5 Fountain Court	0121 606 0500
• St Philip's Chambers	0121 246 7000

Bradford Broadway House Chambers 01274 722560
Exeter • Cathedral Chambers (Jan Wood Independent Barristers' Clerk) 01392 210900

Leeds

Chambers of Andrew Campbell QC	0113 245 5438
11 King's Bench Walk	0113 2971 200
The Chambers of Philip Raynor QC	0113 242 1123
• 9 Woodhouse Square	0113 245 1986

Liverpool

• Exchange Chambers	0151 236 7747
• The Chambers of Adrian Lyon	0151 236 4421/8240/6757

London

• 5 Bell Yard	0171 333 8811
• Bracton Chambers	0171 242 4248
• 4 Breams Buildings	0171 353 5835/430 1221
• Chambers of Mr Peter Crampin QC	0171 831 0081
• Devereux Chambers	0171 353 7534
Equity Barristers' Chambers	0181 558 8336
• Fountain Court	0171 583 3335
Goldsworth Chambers	0171 405 7117
Gray's Inn Square	0171 242 3529
10 - 11 Gray's Inn Square	0171 405 2576

• Expanded entry in Part C

	Gray's Inn Tax Chambers	0171 242 2642
	• 2 Harcourt Buildings	0171 583 9020
	The Chambers of Mr Ali Mohammad Azhar	0171 353 9564 (4 lines)
	11 King's Bench Walk	0171 353 3337/8
	Chambers of Lord Goodhart QC	0171 405 5577
	Chambers of John Gardiner QC	0171 242 4017
	• 12 New Square	0171 419 1212
	24 Old Buildings	0171 242 2744
	• 9 Old Square	0171 405 4682
	The Chambers of Leolin Price CBE, QC	0171 405 0758/242 5002
	• 11 Old Square	0171 430 0341
	• 13 Old Square	0171 404 4800
	• 5 Paper Buildings	0171 583 9275
	Prince Henry's Chambers	0171 353 1183/1190
	• Queen Elizabeth Building	0171 583 5766
	• Stanbrook & Henderson	0171 353 0101
	• 3 Stone Buildings	0171 242 4937/405 8358
	• 5 Stone Buildings	0171 242 6201
	• 9 Stone Buildings	0171 404 5055
	3 Temple Gardens Tax Chambers	0171 353 7884
Manchester	• Cobden House Chambers	0161 833 6000/6001
	• Chambers of John Hand QC	0161 955 9000
	• 40 King Street	0161 832 9082
	Manchester House Chambers	0161 834 7007
	• St James's Chambers	0161 834 7000
	• 28 St John Street	0161 834 8418
Newcastle upon Tyne	Westgate Chambers	0191 261 4407/232 9785
Norwich	East Anglian Chambers	01603 617351
Portsmouth	Hampshire Chambers	01705 826636
Reading	Wessex Chambers	0118 956 8856
Swansea	Pendragon Chambers	01792 411188

TAX - CORPORATE

Birmingham	• 5 Fountain Court	0121 606 0500
	• St Philip's Chambers	0121 246 7000
Bradford	Broadway House Chambers	01274 722560
Exeter	• Cathedral Chambers (Jan Wood Independent Barristers' Clerk)	01392 210900
Leeds	Chambers of Andrew Campbell QC	0113 245 5438
	11 King's Bench Walk	0113 2971 200
	The Chambers of Philip Raynor QC	0113 242 1123
	• Sovereign Chambers	0113 245 1841/2/3
Liverpool	• Exchange Chambers	0151 236 7747
	• The Chambers of Adrian Lyon	0151 236 4421/8240/6757
London	• 5 Bell Yard	0171 333 8811
	• Bracton Chambers	0171 242 4248
	• 4 Breams Buildings	0171 353 5835/430 1221
	Equity Barristers' Chambers	0181 558 8336
	• One Essex Court	0171 583 2000
	• 4 Field Court	0171 440 6900
	Goldsworth Chambers	0171 405 7117
	Gray's Inn Square	0171 242 3529
	Gray's Inn Tax Chambers	0171 242 2642
	• 2 Harcourt Buildings	0171 583 9020
	The Chambers of Mr Ali Mohammad Azhar	0171 353 9564 (4 lines)
	11 King's Bench Walk	0171 353 3337/8
	Chambers of John Gardiner QC	0171 242 4017
	• 12 New Square	0171 419 1212
	24 Old Buildings	0171 242 2744
	The Chambers of Leolin Price CBE, QC	0171 405 0758/242 5002
	• 13 Old Square	0171 404 4800
	Prince Henry's Chambers	0171 353 1183/1190
	• Queen Elizabeth Building	0171 583 5766
	• 3-4 South Square	0171 696 9900
	• Stanbrook & Henderson	0171 353 0101
	• 3 Stone Buildings	0171 242 4937/405 8358
	• 9 Stone Buildings	0171 404 5055
	3 Temple Gardens Tax Chambers	0171 353 7884
Manchester	• Chambers of John Hand QC	0161 955 9000
	• 40 King Street	0161 832 9082

• Expanded entry in Part C

A

	Manchester House Chambers	0161 834 7007
	• St James's Chambers	0161 834 7000
Newcastle upon Tyne	Westgate Chambers	0191 261 4407/232 9785
Norwich	East Anglian Chambers	01603 617351

TAXATION AND COSTS

London	• Farrar's Building	0171 583 9241

TELECOMMUNICATIONS

London	Atkin Chambers	0171 404 0102
	Brick Court Chambers	0171 583 0777
	• Devereux Chambers	0171 353 7534
	• One Essex Court	0171 583 2000
	• Essex Court Chambers	0171 813 8000
	• Fountain Court	0171 583 3335
	Francis Taylor Buildings	0171 353 7768/2711
	• 4-5 Gray's Inn Square	0171 404 5252
	6 Gray's Inn Square	0171 242 1052
	• 2 Harcourt Buildings	0171 583 9020
	• Hardwicke Building	0171 242 2523
	• Littman Chambers	0171 404 4866
	• Mitre Court Chambers	0171 353 9394
	• Monckton Chambers	0171 405 7211
	• New Court	0171 797 8999
	• 3 New Square	0171 405 1111
	5 New Square	0171 404 0404
	• 8 New Square	0171 405 4321
	• 13 Old Square	0171 404 4800
	• 5 Raymond Buildings	0171 242 2902
	1 Serjeants' Inn	0171 583 1355
	• Stanbrook & Henderson	0171 353 0101
	7 Stone Buildings	0171 242 0961
Manchester	• Chambers of John Hand QC	0161 955 9000
	• St James's Chambers	0161 834 7000
Plymouth	Devon Chambers	01752 661659

TIMESHARE

Exeter	• Cathedral Chambers (Jan Wood Independent Barristers' Clerk)	01392 210900

TOWN AND COUNTRY PLANNING

Birmingham	• Equity Chambers	0121 233 2100
	1 Fountain Court	0121 236 5721
	• 3 Fountain Court	0121 236 5854
	• 5 Fountain Court	0121 606 0500
	• 8 Fountain Court	0121 236 5514
	• St Philip's Chambers	0121 246 7000
Bournemouth	20 Lorne Park Road	01202 292102
Bristol	St John's Chambers	0117 921 3456/929 8514
Cambridge	• Fenners Chambers	01223 368761
	Regency Chambers	01223 301517
Cardiff	9 Park Place	01222 382731
	30 Park Place	01222 398421
	• 33 Park Place	01222 233313
Chesterfield	26 Morley Avenue	01246 234790
Durham City	Durham Barristers' Chambers	0191 386 9199
Ely	Cathedral Chambers, Ely	01353 666775
Exeter	• Cathedral Chambers (Jan Wood Independent Barristers' Clerk)	01392 210900
	Colleton Chambers	01392 274898
	Rougemont Chambers	01392 410471
	Southernhay Chambers	01392 255777
	Walnut House	01392 279751
Guildford	• Guildford Chambers	01483 539131
Henley-in-Arden	Berkeley Chambers	01564 795546
Leeds	Chambers of Andrew Campbell QC	0113 245 5438
	11 King's Bench Walk	0113 2971 200
	The Chambers of Philip Raynor QC	0113 242 1123
	• 37 Park Square	0113 243 9422
	• Sovereign Chambers	0113 245 1841/2/3

• Expanded entry in Part C

	• 9 Woodhouse Square	0113 245 1986
Leicester	2 New Street	0116 262 5906
Liverpool	• Exchange Chambers	0151 236 7747
	• The Chambers of Adrian Lyon	0151 236 4421/8240/6757
	• Peel House Chambers	0151 236 4321
London	• Arden Chambers	0171 242 4244
	9 Bedford Row	0171 242 3555
	• 29 Bedford Row Chambers	0171 831 2626
	• 5 Bell Yard	0171 333 8811
	11 Bolt Court	0171 353 2300
	• 4 Breams Buildings	0171 353 5835/430 1221
	• Chambers of Mr Peter Crampin QC	0171 831 0081
	• 1 Crown Office Row	0171 797 7500
	Equity Barristers' Chambers	0181 558 8336
	Chambers of Geoffrey Hawker	0171 583 8899
	Falcon Chambers	0171 353 2484
	• Chambers of Norman Palmer	0171 405 6114
	• 2nd Floor, Francis Taylor Building	0171 353 9942
	Francis Taylor Buildings	0171 353 7768/2711
	• 2-3 Gray's Inn Square	0171 242 4986
	• 4-5 Gray's Inn Square	0171 404 5252
	10 - 11 Gray's Inn Square	0171 405 2576
	• Harcourt Chambers	0171 353 6961/7
Harrow on the Hill	• Harrow-on-the-Hill Chambers	0181 423 7444
London	• Chambers of James Hunt QC	0171 421 8000
	6 King's Bench Walk	0171 353 4931/583 0695
	The Chambers of Mr Ali Mohammad	0171 353 9564 (4 lines)
	Azhar	
	10 King's Bench Walk	0171 353 7742
	• 11 King's Bench Walk	0171 632 8500
	11 King's Bench Walk	0171 353 3337/8
	• Lamb Building	0171 797 7788
	Lamb Chambers	0171 797 8300
	• Littman Chambers	0171 404 4866
	2 Mitre Court Buildings	0171 353 1353
	2 Mitre Court Buildings	0171 583 1380
	• Mitre Court Chambers	0171 353 9394
	• 12 New Square	0171 419 1212
	• 22 Old Buildings	0171 831 0222
	• Twenty-Four Old Buildings	0171 404 0946
	The Chambers of Leolin Price CBE, QC	0171 405 0758/242 5002
	11 Old Square	0171 242 5022
	• 3 Paper Buildings	0171 797 7000
	• 3 Paper Buildings	0171 583 8055
	• Chambers of John L Powell QC	0171 797 8000
	• Pump Court Chambers	0171 353 0711
	• 5 Pump Court	0171 353 2532
	6 Pump Court	0171 797 8400
	1 Serjeants' Inn	0171 583 1355
	7 Stone Buildings	0171 242 0961
	• 9 Stone Buildings	0171 404 5055
	• 3 Temple Gardens	0171 353 3102/5/9297
	• Thomas More Chambers	0171 404 7000
Maidstone	• Maidstone Chambers	01622 688592
Manchester	• Chambers of John Hand QC	0161 955 9000
	• 40 King Street	0161 832 9082
	• Queen's Chambers	0161 834 6875/4738
	• 28 St John Street	0161 834 8418
Middlesbrough	• Fountain Chambers	01642 217037
Newcastle upon Tyne	• Trinity Chambers	0191 232 1927
Norwich	East Anglian Chambers	01603 617351
	Sackville Chambers	01603 613516
Nottingham	King Charles House	0115 941 8851
	Ropewalk Chambers	0115 947 2581
Oxford	1 Alfred Street	01865 793736
Peterborough	Fenners Chambers	01733 562030
	Regency Chambers	01733 315215
Portsmouth	Hampshire Chambers	01705 826636
Preston	4 Camden Place	01772 828300
	15 Winckley Square	01772 252 828
Reading	Dr Johnson's Chambers	01189 254221
Redhill	Redhill Chambers	01737 780781

• Expanded entry in Part C

Richmond-upon-Thames	Richmond Green Chambers	0181 940 1841
Sheffield	Paradise Square Chambers	0114 273 8951
Slough	11 St Bernards Road	01753 553806/817989
Southampton	• 17 Carlton Crescent	01703 320320
	• College Chambers	01703 230338
	• Eighteen Carlton Crescent	01703 639001
Stoke-on-Trent	Regent Chambers	01782 286666
Swansea	Angel Chambers	01792 464623/464648
	Gower Chambers	01792 644466
	Iscoed Chambers	01792 652988/9/330
Winchester	4 St Peter Street	01962 868 884
Wolverhampton	Claremont Chambers	01902 426222
York	• York Chambers	01904 620 048

TRADEMARKS

Birmingham	• Equity Chambers	0121 233 2100
	1 Fountain Court	0121 236 5721
	• 5 Fountain Court	0121 606 0500
Bristol	St John's Chambers	0117 921 3456/929 8514
Haverhill	Helions Chambers	01440 730523
Leeds	Chambers of Andrew Campbell QC	0113 245 5438
	• Chancery House Chambers	0113 244 6691
	• Sovereign Chambers	0113 245 1841/2/3
London	Equity Barristers' Chambers	0181 558 8336
	• One Essex Court	0171 583 2000
	• 4 Field Court	0171 440 6900
	• Fountain Court	0171 583 3335
	Francis Taylor Buildings	0171 353 7768/2711
	Goldsworth Chambers	0171 405 7117
	• 9 King's Bench Walk	0171 353 7202/3909
	10 King's Bench Walk	0171 353 7742
	11 King's Bench Walk	0171 353 3337/8
	Lamb Chambers	0171 797 8300
	• Littleton Chambers	0171 797 8600
	2 Mitre Court Buildings	0171 353 1353
	• Monckton Chambers	0171 405 7211
	• New Court	0171 797 8999
	• 3 New Square	0171 405 1111
	5 New Square	0171 404 0404
	• 8 New Square	0171 405 4321
	19 Old Buildings	0171 405 2001
	• 11 Old Square	0171 430 0341
	• 1 Raymond Buildings	0171 430 1234
	• 11 South Square	0171 405 1222
	11 Stone Buildings	+44 (0)171 831 6381
Manchester	• Cobden House Chambers	0161 833 6000/6001
	• St James's Chambers	0161 834 7000
Preston	New Bailey Chambers	01772 258 087
Reading	Wessex Chambers	0118 956 8856

TRADING STANDARDS

London	• Thomas More Chambers	0171 404 7000

TRAVEL

London	• New Court Chambers	0171 831 9500

TRAVEL AND HOLIDAY LAW

London	Barnard's Inn Chambers	0171 242 8508

UNIT TRUSTS

Birmingham	• 5 Fountain Court	0121 606 0500
Leeds	Chambers of Andrew Campbell QC	0113 245 5438
London	• Erskine Chambers	0171 242 5532
	11 King's Bench Walk	0171 353 3337/8
	Chambers of John Gardiner QC	0171 242 4017
	• 12 New Square	0171 419 1212
	• Chambers of John L Powell QC	0171 797 8000

VAT

Leeds	11 King's Bench Walk	0113 2971 200
London	Chambers of Geoffrey Hawker	0171 583 8899
	Chambers of John Gardiner QC	0171 242 4017
Swansea	Pendragon Chambers	01792 411188

VAT AND CUSTOMS & EXCISE

London	• 39 Essex Street	0171 832 1111
	• Monckton Chambers	0171 405 7211

A

Types of Work by Individual Barristers

This section lists individual barristers by the types of work in which they specialise. The areas of work are listed in alphabetical order from Administrative to Unit Trusts. Within these main categories, individual barristers are listed alphabetically by surname. For example, a reader wishing to locate a particular barrister specialising in trademarks would be able to look under 'T' for Trademarks and find under that heading those barristers who offer their services in this field. A complete list of all the types of work from which individual barristers were asked to select their specialisms can be found overleaf. Where individuals have indicated that they practise in other areas, this information is listed within Part B.

Each listing provides the name of the individual barrister, their chambers' address and chambers' telephone number. The first point of contact in each instance will be the clerk. (Details of clerks can be found in *Part C Chambers by Location.*)

Please note that if a barrister is not listed in this section, it is at their request.

The symbol ● indicates that a barrister has an expanded entry in *Part D Individual Barristers in Private Practice.*

B

Types of Work

Below is a complete list of all the types of work from which individual barristers were asked to select their areas of specialism. If a category below does not appear within this section, it has not been selected by any individuals for this edition. Where barristers have supplied other specialisms, this information can be found within Part B.

A

Administrative
Admiralty
Agriculture
Arbitration
Asset finance
Aviation

B

Banking
Bankruptcy

C

Care proceedings
Chancery (general)
Chancery land law
Charities
Civil liberties
Commercial
Commercial litigation
Commercial property
Commodities
Common land
Common law (general)
Company & commercial
Competition
Construction
Consumer law
Conveyancing
Copyright
Corporate finance
Courts martial
Crime
Crime – corporate law

D

Defamation
Discrimination

E

EC & competition law
Ecclesiastical
Education
Employment
Energy
Entertainment
Environment
Equity, wills & trusts

F

Family
Family provision
Film, cable, TV
Financial services
Foreign law
Franchising

H

Housing

I

Immigration
Information technology
Insolvency
Insurance
Insurance/reinsurance
International trade
Intellectual property

L

Landlord & tenant
Licensing
Local government

M

Medical negligence
Mental health

P

Parliamentary
Partnerships
Patents
Pensions
Personal injury
Planning
Private international
Probate & administration
Professional negligence
Public international

S

Sale & carriage of goods
Share options
Shipping, admiralty
Sports

T

Tax – capital & income
Tax – corporate
Telecommunications
Town & country planning
Trademarks

U

Unit trusts

ACCOUNTANCY

Barker Simon George Harry	• 13 Old Square, London	0171 404 4800

ACTIONS AGAINST THE POLICE

Abbott Francis Arthur	Pump Court Chambers, London	0171 353 0711
	Pump Court Chambers, Winchester	01962 868161
Denney Stuart Henry Macdonald	Deans Court Chambers, Manchester	0161 834 4097
	Deans Court Chambers, Preston	01772 555163

ADJUDICATION

Franklin Miss Kim	• Lamb Chambers, London	0171 797 8300

ADMINISTRATIVE

Akiwumi Anthony Sebastian Akitayo	Pump Court Chambers, London	0171 353 0711
	Pump Court Chambers, Winchester	01962 868161
Al'Hassan Khadim	Equity Chambers, Birmingham	0121 233 2100
Alesbury Alun	2 Mitre Court Buildings, London	0171 583 1380
Anderson Anthony John	2 Mitre Court Buildings, London	0171 583 1380
Bailey Mark Henry Arthur	• 6 Pump Court, London	0171 797 8400
	• 6-8 Mill Street, Maidstone	01622 688 094
Bailin Alexander	5 Paper Buildings, London	0171 583 6117
Barnes (David) Michael (William)	4 Breams Buildings, London	0171 353 5835/430 1221
Bartlett George Robert	2 Mitre Court Buildings, London	0171 583 1380
Baxter Gerald Pearson	25-27 Castle Street, Liverpool	0151 227 5661/5666/236 5072
Beal Kieron Conrad	4 Paper Buildings, London	0171 353 3366/583 7155
Beard Daniel Matthew	Monckton Chambers, London	0171 405 7211
Benson Julian Christopher Woodburn	One Essex Court, London	0171 936 3030
Bhattacharyya Ardhendu	1 Gray's Inn Square, London	0171 405 8946
	11 St Bernards Road, Slough	01753 553806/817989
Birtles William	Old Square Chambers, London	0171 269 0300
	Old Square Chambers, Bristol	0117 927 7111
Birts Peter William	• Farrar's Building, London	0171 583 9241
Boyd Phillip Joseph George	Lincoln House Chambers, Manchester	0161 832 5701
Boyle Christopher Alexander David	2 Mitre Court Buildings, London	0171 583 1380
Brunner Adrian John Nelson	Stanbrook & Henderson, London	0171 353 0101
	2 Harcourt Buildings, London	0171 583 9020
Burton Michael John	Littleton Chambers, London	0171 797 8600
Burton Nicholas Anthony	2 Mitre Court Buildings, London	0171 583 1380
Butt Michael Robert	· Pump Court Chambers, London	0171 353 0711
	Pump Court Chambers, Winchester	01962 868161
Cameron Neil St Clair	1 Serjeants' Inn, London	0171 583 1355
Cameron Miss Sheila Morag Clark	2 Harcourt Buildings, London	0171 353 8415
Carlile Alexander Charles	9-12 Bell Yard, London	0171 400 1800
	Sedan House, Chester	01244 320480/348282
Catchpole Stuart Paul	39 Essex Street, London	0171 832 1111
Caws Eian Richard Edwin	4 Breams Buildings, London	0171 353 5835/430 1221
Choudhury Akhlaq	11 King's Bench Walk, London	0171 632 8500
Clay Jonathan Roger	11 Bolt Court, London	0171 353 2300
	Redhill Chambers, Redhill	01737 780781
Collins John Morris	11 King's Bench Walk, London	0171 353 3337/8
	9 Woodhouse Square, Leeds	0113 245 1986
Colquhoun Miss Celina Daphne Marion	11 Bolt Court, London	0171 353 2300
	Redhill Chambers, Redhill	01737 780781
Davies Miss Penny May	Chambers of Harjit Singh, London	0171 353 1356
de Voghelaere Parr Adam Stephen	2 Mitre Court Buildings, London	0171 583 1380
Doggart Piers Graham	• King's Chambers, Eastbourne	01323 416053
Drabble Richard John Bloor	4 Breams Buildings, London	0171 353 5835/430 1221
Druce Michael James	2 Mitre Court Buildings, London	0171 583 1380
Edwards Philip Douglas	2 Harcourt Buildings, London	0171 353 8415
Elvin David John	4 Breams Buildings, London	0171 353 5835/430 1221
Evans Lee John	Farrar's Building, London	0171 583 9241
Fisher Jonathan Simon	• 18 Red Lion Court, London	0171 520 6000
	• Thornwood House, Chelmsford	01245 280880
Fitzgerald Edward Hamilton	Doughty Street Chambers, London	0171 404 1313
FitzGerald Michael Frederick Clive	2 Mitre Court Buildings, London	0171 583 1380
Fookes Robert Lawrence	2 Mitre Court Buildings, London	0171 583 1380
Forsdick David John	4 Breams Buildings, London	0171 353 5835/430 1221
Foster Miss Alison Lee Caroline	39 Essex Street, London	0171 832 1111
Fowler Richard Nicholas	Monckton Chambers, London	0171 405 7211

Frazer Christopher Mark	Harcourt Chambers, London	0171 353 6961/7
	Harcourt Chambers, Oxford	01865 791559
Friel John Anthony	Goldsmith Building, London	0171 353 7881
	Southsea Chambers, Portsmouth	01705 291261
Fripp Eric William Burtin	Chambers of Harjit Singh, London	0171 353 1356
Garlick Paul Richard	Pump Court Chambers, London	0171 353 0711
	Pump Court Chambers, Winchester	01962 868161
Gatty Daniel Simon	New Court Chambers, London	0171 831 9500
Gau Justin Charles	Pump Court Chambers, London	0171 353 0711
	Pump Court Chambers, Winchester	01962 868161
Giffin Nigel Dyson	11 King's Bench Walk, London	0171 632 8500
Glover Richard Michael	2 Mitre Court Buildings, London	0171 583 1380
Goodman Andrew David	199 Strand, London	0171 379 9779
Gordon Richard John Francis	39 Essex Street, London	0171 832 1111
Gore Andrew Roger	Fenners Chambers, Cambridge	01223 368761
	Fenners Chambers, Peterborough	01733 562030
Goudie James	• 11 King's Bench Walk, London	0171 632 8500
Grayson Edward	• 9-12 Bell Yard, London	0171 400 1800
Grey Miss Eleanor Mary Grace	39 Essex Street, London	0171 832 1111
Griffiths (John) Peter (Gwynne)	30 Park Place, Cardiff	01222 398421
Grodzinski Samuel Marc	39 Essex Street, London	0171 832 1111
Grundy Nicholas John	One Essex Court, London	0171 936 3030
Hall Mrs Melanie Ruth	Monckton Chambers, London	0171 405 7211
Harper Joseph Charles	4 Breams Buildings, London	0171 353 5835/430 1221
Harris Paul Best	Monckton Chambers, London	0171 405 7211
Harrison Peter John	6 Pump Court, London	0171 797 8400
	6-8 Mill Street, Maidstone	01622 688 094
Harwood Richard John	1 Serjeants' Inn, London	0171 583 1355
Hay Ms Deborah Jane	Goldsmith Building, London	0171 353 7881
Haynes Miss Rebecca	Monckton Chambers, London	0171 405 7211
Henderson Roger Anthony	Stanbrook & Henderson, London	0171 353 0101
	2 Harcourt Buildings, London	0171 583 9020
Hill Nicholas Mark	Pump Court Chambers, London	0171 353 0711
	Pump Court Chambers, Winchester	01962 868161
Hill Raymond	Monckton Chambers, London	0171 405 7211
Hill Robert Douglas	Pump Court Chambers, London	0171 353 0711
	Pump Court Chambers, Winchester	01962 868161
Hillier Andrew Charles	5 Bell Yard, London	0171 333 8811
Hockman Stephen Alexander	• 6 Pump Court, London	0171 797 8400
	• 6-8 Mill Street, Maidstone	01622 688 094
Hogg The Rt Hon Douglas Martin	4 Paper Buildings, London	0171 353 3366/583 7155
	37 Park Square, Leeds	0113 243 9422
Holgate David John	4 Breams Buildings, London	0171 353 5835/430 1221
Horton Matthew Bethell	2 Mitre Court Buildings, London	0171 583 1380
Howell John	4 Breams Buildings, London	0171 353 5835/430 1221
Hoyal Ms Jane	• 1 Pump Court, London	0171 583 2012/353 4341
Hunter William Quigley	No 1 Serjeants' Inn, London	0171 415 6666
Huskinson George Nicholas Nevil	4-5 Gray's Inn Square, London	0171 404 5252
Ivimy Ms Cecilia Rachel	11 King's Bench Walk, London	0171 632 8500
Jay Robert Maurice	39 Essex Street, London	0171 832 1111
Jones Gregory Percy	• 2 Harcourt Buildings, London	0171 353 8415
Jones Sean William Paul	11 King's Bench Walk, London	0171 632 8500
Jones Timothy Arthur	• Arden Chambers, London	0171 242 4244
	• St Philip's Chambers, Birmingham	0121 246 7000
Karas Jonathan Marcus	4 Breams Buildings, London	0171 353 5835/430 1221
Katkowski Christopher Andrew Mark	4 Breams Buildings, London	0171 353 5835/430 1221
Keen Graeme	4 Breams Buildings, London	0171 353 5835/430 1221
Kent Michael Harcourt	Two Crown Office Row, London	0171 797 8100
Kerr Tim Julian	4-5 Gray's Inn Square, London	0171 404 5252
Khan Ashraf	A K Chambers, Hull	01482 641180
King Neil Gerald Alexander	2 Mitre Court Buildings, London	0171 583 1380
Kingsland Rt Hon Lord	4 Breams Buildings, London	0171 353 5835/430 1221
Kolodynski Stefan Richard	New Court Chambers, Birmingham	0121 693 6656
Kovats Steven Laszlo	39 Essex Street, London	0171 832 1111
Laing Miss Elisabeth Mary Caroline	11 King's Bench Walk, London	0171 632 8500
Langham Richard Geoffrey	1 Serjeants' Inn, London	0171 583 1355
Lanlehin Olajide Adebola	Britton Street Chambers, London	0171 608 3765
Lasok Karol Paul Edward	Monckton Chambers, London	0171 405 7211
Leiper Richard Thomas	11 King's Bench Walk, London	0171 632 8500
Lewis Robert		
Lewsley Christopher Stanton	4 Breams Buildings, London	0171 353 5835/430 1221
Lieven Ms Nathalie Marie Daniella	4 Breams Buildings, London	0171 353 5835/430 1221

Litton John Letablere	4 Breams Buildings, London	0171 353 5835/430 1221
Lockhart-Mummery Christopher John	4 Breams Buildings, London	0171 353 5835/430 1221
Lonsdale Miss Marion Mary	Chambers of Geoffrey Hawker, London	0171 583 8899
Maclean Alan John	39 Essex Street, London	0171 832 1111
Macleod Nigel Ronald Buchanan	4 Breams Buildings, London	0171 353 5835/430 1221
	40 King Street, Manchester	0161 832 9082
Macpherson The Hon Mary Stewart	2 Mitre Court Buildings, London	0171 583 1380
Maitland Marc Claude	11 Old Square, London	0171 242 5022
Malecka Dr Mary Margaret	Goldsworth Chambers, London	0171 405 7117
Mason Ian Douglas	11 Bolt Court, London	0171 353 2300
	Redhill Chambers, Redhill	01737 780781
Mathias Miss Anna	11 Bolt Court, London	0171 353 2300
Maurici James Patrick	4 Breams Buildings, London	0171 353 5835/430 1221
Mawrey Richard Brooks	Stanbrook & Henderson, London	0171 353 0101
	2 Harcourt Buildings, London	0171 583 9020
Maxwell Miss Judith Mary Angela	The Garden House, London	0171 404 6150
McCracken Robert Henry Joy	• 2 Harcourt Buildings, London	0171 353 8415
McKenna Miss Anna Louise	Queen Elizabeth Building, London	0171 353 7181 (12 lines)
McManus Jonathan Richard	4-5 Gray's Inn Square, London	0171 404 5252
McMinn Miss Valerie Kathleen	Baker Street Chambers, Middlesbrough	01642 873873
Moore Professor Victor William Edward	2 Mitre Court Buildings, London	0171 583 1380
Morgan Jeremy	Chambers of Kieran Coonan QC, London	0171 583 6013/2510
Moriarty Gerald Evelyn	2 Mitre Court Buildings, London	0171 583 1380
Mould Timothy James	4 Breams Buildings, London	0171 353 5835/430 1221
Newcombe Andrew Bennett	• 2 Harcourt Buildings, London	0171 353 8415
Newton Miss Claire Elaine Maria Bailey	Goldsmith Building, London	0171 353 7881
Nicholls Paul Richard	11 King's Bench Walk, London	0171 632 8500
Norie-Miller Jeffrey Reginald	55 Temple Chambers, London	0171 353 7400
Ogunbiyi Oluwole Afolabi	Horizon Chambers, London	0171 242 2440
Ornsby Miss Suzanne Doreen	• 2 Harcourt Buildings, London	0171 353 8415
Ouseley Duncan Brian Walter	4-5 Gray's Inn Square, London	0171 404 5252
Paines Nicholas Paul Billot	Monckton Chambers, London	0171 405 7211
Parker Kenneth Blades	Monckton Chambers, London	0171 405 7211
Peacock Ian Christopher	12 New Square, London	0171 419 1212
	Sovereign Chambers, Leeds	0113 245 1841/2/3
Peretz George Michael John		
Peters Nigel Melvin	18 Red Lion Court, London	0171 520 6000
	Thornwood House, Chelmsford	01245 280880
Pitt-Payne Timothy Sheridan	• 11 King's Bench Walk, London	0171 632 8500
Pleming Nigel Peter	39 Essex Street, London	0171 832 1111
Purchas Robin Michael	• 2 Harcourt Buildings, London	0171 353 8415
Randall John Yeoman	7 Stone Buildings, London	0171 405 3886/242 3546
	St Philip's Chambers, Birmingham	0121 246 7000
Randle Simon Patrick	11 Bolt Court, London	0171 353 2300
	Redhill Chambers, Redhill	01737 780781
Rawlings Clive Patrick	Goldsmith Building, London	0171 353 7881
Read Lionel Frank	1 Serjeants' Inn, London	0171 583 1355
Readhead Simon John Howard	No 1 Serjeants' Inn, London	0171 415 6666
Richards Miss Jennifer	39 Essex Street, London	0171 832 1111
Robertson Aidan Malcolm David	Monckton Chambers, London	0171 405 7211
Robinson Miss Alice	4 Breams Buildings, London	0171 353 5835/430 1221
Rogers Ian Paul	1 Crown Office Row, London	0171 583 9292
Roots Guy Robert Godfrey	2 Mitre Court Buildings, London	0171 583 1380
Roth Peter Marcel	Monckton Chambers, London	0171 405 7211
Rumney Conrad William Arthur	St Philip's Chambers, Birmingham	0121 246 7000
Sharland Andrew John	4-5 Gray's Inn Square, London	0171 404 5252
Silsoe The Lord	2 Mitre Court Buildings, London	0171 583 1380
Silvester Bruce Ross	Lamb Chambers, London	0171 797 8300
Simor Miss Jessica Margaret Poppaea	Monckton Chambers, London	0171 405 7211
Simpson Edwin John Fletcher	12 New Square, London	0171 419 1212
Singh Balbir	• Equity Chambers, Birmingham	0121 233 2100
Smith David Anthony	4 Breams Buildings, London	0171 353 5835/430 1221
Smith Ms Katherine Emma	Monckton Chambers, London	0171 405 7211
Stewart Nicholas John Cameron	Hardwicke Building, London	0171 242 2523
Stilitz Daniel Malachi	11 King's Bench Walk, London	0171 632 8500

Stone Gregory	• 4-5 Gray's Inn Square, London	0171 404 5252
Straker Timothy Derrick	• 2-3 Gray's Inn Square, London	0171 242 4986
Supperstone Michael Alan	11 King's Bench Walk, London	0171 632 8500
Taylor Reuben Mallinson	2 Mitre Court Buildings, London	0171 583 1380
Thompson Rhodri William Ralph	Monckton Chambers, London	0171 405 7211
Tobin Daniel Alphonsus Joseph	Chambers of Geoffrey Hawker, London	0171 583 8899
Turner James	One King's Bench Walk, London	0171 936 1500
Turner Jonathan Richard	Monckton Chambers, London	0171 405 7211
Vajda Christopher Stephen	Monckton Chambers, London	0171 405 7211
Village Peter Malcolm	• 4-5 Gray's Inn Square, London	0171 404 5252
Vines Anthony Robert Francis	Gough Square Chambers, London	0171 353 0924
Wadsworth James Patrick	4 Paper Buildings, London	0171 353 3366/583 7155
Wallington Peter Thomas	11 King's Bench Walk, London	0171 632 8500
Ward Miss Siobhan Marie Lucia	11 King's Bench Walk, London	0171 632 8500
Ward Timothy Justin	39 Essex Street, London	0171 832 1111
Warren Rupert Miles	2 Mitre Court Buildings, London	0171 583 1380
Waters Julian William Penrose	No 1 Serjeants' Inn, London	0171 415 6666
Whybrow Christopher John	1 Serjeants' Inn, London	0171 583 1355
Widdicombe David Graham	2 Mitre Court Buildings, London	0171 583 1380
Wignall Edward Gordon	• 1 Dr Johnson's Buildings, London	0171 353 9328
	• Dr Johnson's Chambers, Reading	01189 254221
Wilken Sean David Henry	39 Essex Street, London	0171 832 1111
Williams Miss Anne Margaret	4 Breams Buildings, London	0171 353 5835/430 1221
	37 Park Square, Leeds	0113 243 9422
Williams Ms Heather Jean	Doughty Street Chambers, London	0171 404 1313
Woolley David Rorie	• 1 Serjeants' Inn, London	0171 583 1355

ADMIRALTY

Akka Lawrence Mark	20 Essex Street, London	0171 583 9294
Ambrose Miss Clare Mary Geneste	20 Essex Street, London	0171 583 9294
Charkham Graham Harold	20 Essex Street, London	0171 583 9294
Coburn Michael Jeremy Patrick	20 Essex Street, London	0171 583 9294
Collett Michael John	20 Essex Street, London	0171 583 9294
Hamblen Nicholas Archibald	20 Essex Street, London	0171 583 9294
Haven Kevin	2 Gray's Inn Square Chambers, London	0171 242 0328/405 1317
Males Stephen Martin	20 Essex Street, London	0171 583 9294
Masters Miss Sara Alayna	20 Essex Street, London	0171 583 9294
Maxwell Miss Karen Laetitia	20 Essex Street, London	0171 583 9294
Meeson Nigel Keith	4 Field Court, London	0171 440 6900
Milligan Iain Anstruther	20 Essex Street, London	0171 583 9294
Owen David Christopher	20 Essex Street, London	0171 583 9294
Saunders Nicholas Joseph	4 Field Court, London	0171 440 6900
Selvaratnam Miss Vasanti Emily Indrani	4 Field Court, London	0171 440 6900
Whiteley Miss Miranda Blyth	4 Field Court, London	0171 440 6900
Wright Colin John	4 Field Court, London	0171 440 6900

AFRICAN CUSTOMARY LAW

Adejumo Mrs Hilda Ekpo	• Temple Chambers, London	0171 583 1001 (2 lines)

AGRICULTURE

Alesbury Alun	2 Mitre Court Buildings, London	0171 583 1380
Bartlett George Robert	2 Mitre Court Buildings, London	0171 583 1380
Boyle Christopher Alexander David	2 Mitre Court Buildings, London	0171 583 1380
Burton Nicholas Anthony	2 Mitre Court Buildings, London	0171 583 1380
Cotter Miss Sara Elizabeth	• Higher Combe, Minehead	01643 862722
Cranfield Peter Anthony	3 Verulam Buildings, London	0171 831 8441
Dashwood Professor Arthur Alan	Stanbrook & Henderson, London	0171 353 0101
	2 Harcourt Buildings, London	0171 583 9020
de Voghelaere Parr Adam Stephen	2 Mitre Court Buildings, London	0171 583 1380
Dilhorne The Rt Hon Viscount	4 Breams Buildings, London	0171 353 5835/430 1221
Druce Michael James	2 Mitre Court Buildings, London	0171 583 1380
Fookes Robert Lawrence	2 Mitre Court Buildings, London	0171 583 1380
Glover Richard Michael	2 Mitre Court Buildings, London	0171 583 1380
Gore Andrew Roger	Fenners Chambers, Cambridge	01223 368761
	Fenners Chambers, Peterborough	01733 562030
Gregory John Raymond	Deans Court Chambers, Manchester	0161 834 4097
	Deans Court Chambers, Preston	01772 555163

• Expanded entry in Part D

Haynes Miss Rebecca	Monckton Chambers, London	0171 405 7211
Heywood Michael Edmundson	Chambers of Lord Goodhart QC, London	0171 405 5577
	Cobden House Chambers, Manchester	0161 833 6000/6001
Hill Raymond	Monckton Chambers, London	0171 405 7211
Hogg The Rt Hon Douglas Martin	4 Paper Buildings, London	0171 353 3366/583 7155
	37 Park Square, Leeds	0113 243 9422
Holmes Justin Francis	Chambers of Lord Goodhart QC, London	0171 405 5577
Horton Matthew Bethell	2 Mitre Court Buildings, London	0171 583 1380
Howarth Simon Stuart	Two Crown Office Row, London	0171 797 8100
Hughes Miss Mary Josephine	Chambers of Lord Goodhart QC, London	0171 405 5577
Jackson Dirik George Allan	• Chambers of Mr Peter Crampin QC, London	0171 831 0081
Jefferies Thomas Robert	Chambers of Lord Goodhart QC, London	0171 405 5577
Kealy Charles Brian	Chambers of Andrew Campbell QC, Leeds	0113 245 5438
King Neil Gerald Alexander	2 Mitre Court Buildings, London	0171 583 1380
Kingsland Rt Hon Lord	4 Breams Buildings, London	0171 353 5835/430 1221
Lamont Miss Camilla Rose	Chambers of Lord Goodhart QC, London	0171 405 5577
Lasok Karol Paul Edward	Monckton Chambers, London	0171 405 7211
Male John Martin	4 Breams Buildings, London	0171 353 5835/430 1221
Marten Richard Hedley Westwood	Chambers of Lord Goodhart QC, London	0171 405 5577
McAllister Miss Elizabeth Ann	Enterprise Chambers, London	0171 405 9471
	Enterprise Chambers, Leeds	0113 246 0391
	Enterprise Chambers, Newcastle upon Tyne	0191 222 3344
Moore Professor Victor William Edward	2 Mitre Court Buildings, London	0171 583 1380
Moriarty Gerald Evelyn	2 Mitre Court Buildings, London	0171 583 1380
Mullis Anthony Roger	Chambers of Lord Goodhart QC, London	0171 405 5577
Paines Nicholas Paul Billot	Monckton Chambers, London	0171 405 7211
Parker Kenneth Blades	Monckton Chambers, London	0171 405 7211
Parry David Julian Thomas	Chambers of Lord Goodhart QC, London	0171 405 5577
Peacocke Mrs Teresa Anne Rosen	Enterprise Chambers, London	0171 405 9471
	Enterprise Chambers, Leeds	0113 246 0391
	Enterprise Chambers, Newcastle upon Tyne	0191 222 3344
Picarda Hubert Alistair Paul	Chambers of Lord Goodhart QC, London	0171 405 5577
Roth Peter Marcel	Monckton Chambers, London	0171 405 7211
Rowell David Stewart	Chambers of Lord Goodhart QC, London	0171 405 5577
Sheridan Maurice Bernard Gerard	• 3 Verulam Buildings, London	0171 831 8441
Simor Miss Jessica Margaret Poppaea	Monckton Chambers, London	0171 405 7211
Smith Ms Katherine Emma	Monckton Chambers, London	0171 405 7211
Sydenham Colin Peter	4 Breams Buildings, London	0171 353 5835/430 1221
Taylor Reuben Mallinson	2 Mitre Court Buildings, London	0171 583 1380
Thompson Rhodri William Ralph	Monckton Chambers, London	0171 405 7211
Turner Jonathan Richard	Monckton Chambers, London	0171 405 7211
Vajda Christopher Stephen	Monckton Chambers, London	0171 405 7211
Walker Andrew Greenfield	Chambers of Lord Goodhart QC, London	0171 405 5577
Warren Rupert Miles	2 Mitre Court Buildings, London	0171 583 1380
Weatherill Bernard Richard	Chambers of Lord Goodhart QC, London	0171 405 5577

ALTERNATIVE DISPUTE RESOLUTION

Goodman Andrew David	199 Strand, London	0171 379 9779
Leigh-Morgan (David) Paul	Fenners Chambers, Cambridge	01223 368761
	Fenners Chambers, Peterborough	01733 562030
Noble Andrew	Eldon Chambers, London	0171 353 4636
	Merchant Chambers, Manchester	0161 839 7070
Whiteley Miss Miranda Blyth	4 Field Court, London	0171 440 6900

ANCILLIARY RELIEF

Bickerdike Roger John	9 Woodhouse Square, Leeds	0113 245 1986
Cross Mrs Joanna	9 Woodhouse Square, Leeds	0113 245 1986

ANGLO-US CONFLICTS OF LAW

McParland Michael Joseph	New Court Chambers, London	0171 831 9500

ANIMAL WELFARE LITIGATION

Brunton Sean Alexander McKay	Pump Court Chambers, London	0171 353 0711
	Pump Court Chambers, Winchester	01962 868161

ARBITRATION

Abbott Francis Arthur	Pump Court Chambers, London	0171 353 0711
	Pump Court Chambers, Winchester	01962 868161
Akenhead Robert	Atkin Chambers, London	0171 404 0102
Akka Lawrence Mark	20 Essex Street, London	0171 583 9294
Al'Hassan Khadim	Equity Chambers, Birmingham	0121 233 2100
Alliott George Beckles	2 Harcourt Buildings, London	0171 583 9020
Ambrose Miss Clare Mary Geneste	20 Essex Street, London	0171 583 9294
Amin Miss Farah	7 New Square, London	0171 430 1660
Anderson Anthony John	2 Mitre Court Buildings, London	0171 583 1380
Ashworth Piers	Stanbrook & Henderson, London	0171 353 0101
	2 Harcourt Buildings, London	0171 583 9020
	Priory Chambers, Birmingham	0121 236 3882/1375
Atherton Ian David	Enterprise Chambers, London	0171 405 9471
	Enterprise Chambers, Leeds	0113 246 0391
	Enterprise Chambers, Newcastle upon Tyne	0191 222 3344
Aylen Walter Stafford	Hardwicke Building, London	0171 242 2523
Baatz Nicholas Stephen	Atkin Chambers, London	0171 404 0102
Bailey Edward Henry	5 Bell Yard, London	0171 333 8811
Barker Simon George Harry	• 13 Old Square, London	0171 404 4800
Barnes (David) Michael (William)	4 Breams Buildings, London	0171 353 5835/430 1221
Barnett Andrew John	Pump Court Chambers, London	0171 353 0711
	Pump Court Chambers, Winchester	01962 868161
Barwise Miss Stephanie Nicola	Atkin Chambers, London	0171 404 0102
Berkley Michael Stuart	Rougemont Chambers, Exeter	01392 410471
Bhattacharyya Ardhendu	1 Gray's Inn Square, London	0171 405 8946
	11 St Bernards Road, Slough	01753 553806/817989
Bickford-Smith Stephen William	4 Breams Buildings, London	0171 353 5835/430 1221
Blackburn John	Atkin Chambers, London	0171 404 0102
Blair William James Lynton	3 Verulam Buildings, London	0171 831 8441
Bowdery Martin	Atkin Chambers, London	0171 404 0102
Brodie (James) Bruce	39 Essex Street, London	0171 832 1111
Brunner Adrian John Nelson	Stanbrook & Henderson, London	0171 353 0101
	2 Harcourt Buildings, London	0171 583 9020
Burr Andrew Charles	Atkin Chambers, London	0171 404 0102
Burton Michael John	Littleton Chambers, London	0171 797 8600
Cameron Jonathan James O'Grady	3 Verulam Buildings, London	0171 831 8441
Carey Jeremy Reynolds Patrick	Lamb Chambers, London	0171 797 8300
Carter Miss Lesley Ann	25-27 Castle Street, Liverpool	0151 227 5661/5666/236 5072
Charkham Graham Harold	20 Essex Street, London	0171 583 9294
Clarke Miss Alison Lee	No 1 Serjeants' Inn, London	0171 415 6666
Clarke George Robert Ivan	Chambers of Geoffrey Hawker, London	0171 583 8899
Clay Robert Charles	Atkin Chambers, London	0171 404 0102
Coburn Michael Jeremy Patrick	20 Essex Street, London	0171 583 9294
Collett Ivor William	No 1 Serjeants' Inn, London	0171 415 6666
Collett Michael John	20 Essex Street, London	0171 583 9294
Connerty Anthony Robin	Lamb Chambers, London	0171 797 8300
Cooper Adrian Edgar Mark	Stanbrook & Henderson, London	0171 353 0101
	2 Harcourt Buildings, London	0171 583 9020
Corbett James Patrick	St Philip's Chambers, Birmingham	0121 246 7000
Cranfield Peter Anthony	3 Verulam Buildings, London	0171 831 8441
Curtis Michael Alexander	Two Crown Office Row, London	0171 797 8100
Daiches Michael Salis	• 22 Old Buildings, London	0171 831 0222
Dashwood Professor Arthur Alan	Stanbrook & Henderson, London	0171 353 0101
	2 Harcourt Buildings, London	0171 583 9020
Davies Stephen Richard	8 King Street Chambers, Manchester	0161 834 9560
de Lacy Richard Michael	3 Verulam Buildings, London	0171 831 8441

• Expanded entry in Part D

Dennison Stephen Randell	Atkin Chambers, London	0171 404 0102
Dennys Nicholas Charles Jonathan	Atkin Chambers, London	0171 404 0102
Dhaliwal Miss Davinder Kaur	New Court Chambers, Birmingham	0121 693 6656
Doerries Miss Chantal-Aimee Renee Aemelia Annemarie	Atkin Chambers, London	0171 404 0102
Dumaresq Ms Delia Jane	Atkin Chambers, London	0171 404 0102
Dunn Christopher	Sovereign Chambers, Leeds	0113 245 1841/2/3
Dyer David Roger	St Philip's Chambers, Birmingham	0121 246 7000
Eastman Roger	Stanbrook & Henderson, London	0171 353 0101
	2 Harcourt Buildings, London	0171 583 9020
Edey Philip David	20 Essex Street, London	0171 583 9294
Edwards-Stuart Antony James Cobham	Two Crown Office Row, London	0171 797 8100
Evans James Frederick Meurig	3 Verulam Buildings, London	0171 831 8441
Faulks Edward Peter Lawless	No 1 Serjeants' Inn, London	0171 415 6666
Field Richard Alan	11 King's Bench Walk, London	0171 632 8500
Fookes Robert Lawrence	2 Mitre Court Buildings, London	0171 583 1380
Franklin Miss Kim	• Lamb Chambers, London	0171 797 8300
Fraser Peter Donald	Atkin Chambers, London	0171 404 0102
Frazer Christopher Mark	Harcourt Chambers, London	0171 353 6961/7
	Harcourt Chambers, Oxford	01865 791559
Freedman Sampson Clive	3 Verulam Buildings, London	0171 831 8441
Friedman David Peter	4 Pump Court, London	0171 353 2656/9
Gibson Charles Anthony Warneford	2 Harcourt Buildings, London	0171 583 9020
Gilbertson Mrs Helen Alison	Sackville Chambers, Norwich	01603 613516
Goddard Andrew Stephen	Atkin Chambers, London	0171 404 0102
Godwin William George Henry	Atkin Chambers, London	0171 404 0102
Goodchild Mrs Elizabeth Ann	Watford Chambers, Watford	01923 220553
Goodman Andrew David	199 Strand, London	0171 379 9779
Gore-Andrews Gavin Angus Russell	Stanbrook & Henderson, London	0171 353 0101
	2 Harcourt Buildings, London	0171 583 9020
Gough Miss Karen Louise	Arbitration Chambers, London	0171 267 2137
	West Lodge Farm, Meopham	01474 812280
Grantham Andrew Timothy	• Deans Court Chambers, Manchester	0161 834 4097
	• Deans Court Chambers, Preston	01772 555163
Gray Richard Paul	39 Essex Street, London	0171 832 1111
Green Patrick Curtis	Stanbrook & Henderson, London	0171 353 0101
	2 Harcourt Buildings, London	0171 583 9020
Hamblen Nicholas Archibald	20 Essex Street, London	0171 583 9294
Hamer Michael Howard Kenneth	2 Harcourt Buildings, London	0171 583 9020
	Westgate Chambers, Lewes	01273 480 510
Hamilton Graeme Montagu	Two Crown Office Row, London	0171 797 8100
Hammerton Miss Veronica Lesley	No 1 Serjeants' Inn, London	0171 415 6666
Harold Fergus Dougal	Tindal Chambers, Chelmsford	01245 267742
Harris Paul Best	Monckton Chambers, London	0171 405 7211
Harvey Jonathan Robert William	2 Harcourt Buildings, London	0171 583 9020
Harvey Michael Llewellyn Tucker	Two Crown Office Row, London	0171 797 8100
Hawker Geoffrey Fort	Chambers of Geoffrey Hawker, London	0171 583 8899
Hayes Miss Josephine Mary	Chambers of Lord Goodhart QC, London	0171 405 5577
Hayward Peter Michael	The Outer Temple, Room 26, London	0171 353 4647
Henderson Roger Anthony	Stanbrook & Henderson, London	0171 353 0101
	2 Harcourt Buildings, London	0171 583 9020
Heywood Michael Edmundson	Chambers of Lord Goodhart QC, London	0171 405 5577
	Cobden House Chambers, Manchester	0161 833 6000/6001
Hill Robert Douglas	Pump Court Chambers, London	0171 353 0711
	Pump Court Chambers, Winchester	01962 868161
Holdsworth James Arthur	Two Crown Office Row, London	0171 797 8100
Hollingworth Peter James Michael	22 Albion Place, Northampton	01604 636271
Holroyd John James	• 9 Woodhouse Square, Leeds	0113 245 1986
Horton Matthew Bethell	2 Mitre Court Buildings, London	0171 583 1380
Howells James Richard	Atkin Chambers, London	0171 404 0102
Hutton Miss Caroline	Enterprise Chambers, London	0171 405 9471
	Enterprise Chambers, Leeds	0113 246 0391
	Enterprise Chambers, Newcastle upon Tyne	0191 222 3344
Iwi Quintin Joseph	Stanbrook & Henderson, London	0171 353 0101
	2 Harcourt Buildings, London	0171 583 9020
Jarvis John Manners	3 Verulam Buildings, London	0171 831 8441
Jenkala Adrian Aleksander	11 Bolt Court, London	0171 353 2300

• Expanded entry in Part D

	Redhill Chambers, Redhill	01737 780781
Jess Digby Charles	• 8 King Street Chambers, Manchester	0161 834 9560
Jordan Andrew	Stanbrook & Henderson, London	0171 353 0101
	2 Harcourt Buildings, London	0171 583 9020
Kelly Miss Geraldine Therese		
Knight Brian Joseph	Atkin Chambers, London	0171 404 0102
Kolodziej Andrzej Jozef	• Littman Chambers, London	0171 404 4866
Lawrence Miss Rachel Camilla	One Essex Court, London	0171 936 3030
Leech Brian Walter Thomas	No 1 Serjeants' Inn, London	0171 415 6666
Legh-Jones Piers Nicholas	• 20 Essex Street, London	0171 583 9294
Lindsay Crawford Callum Douglas	No 1 Serjeants' Inn, London	0171 415 6666
Lofthouse Simon Timothy	Atkin Chambers, London	0171 404 0102
Lowenstein Paul David	Littleton Chambers, London	0171 797 8600
Lynch Terry John	22 Albion Place, Northampton	01604 636271
Macnab Alexander Andrew	Monckton Chambers, London	0171 405 7211
Male John Martin	4 Breams Buildings, London	0171 353 5835/430 1221
Malek Ali	3 Verulam Buildings, London	0171 831 8441
Males Stephen Martin	20 Essex Street, London	0171 583 9294
Mantle Peter John	Monckton Chambers, London	0171 405 7211
Masters Miss Sara Alayna	20 Essex Street, London	0171 583 9294
Mauleverer Peter Bruce	4 Pump Court, London	0171 353 2656/9
Mawrey Richard Brooks	Stanbrook & Henderson, London	0171 353 0101
	2 Harcourt Buildings, London	0171 583 9020
Maxwell Miss Karen Laetitia	20 Essex Street, London	0171 583 9294
McAllister Miss Elizabeth Ann	Enterprise Chambers, London	0171 405 9471
	Enterprise Chambers, Leeds	0113 246 0391
	Enterprise Chambers, Newcastle upon Tyne	0191 222 3344
McCredie Miss Fionnuala Mary Constance	3 Serjeants' Inn, London	0171 353 5537
McGregor Harvey	4 Paper Buildings, London	0171 353 3366/583 7155
McMinn Miss Valerie Kathleen	Baker Street Chambers, Middlesbrough	01642 873873
McMullan Manus Anthony	Atkin Chambers, London	0171 404 0102
McParland Michael Joseph	New Court Chambers, London	0171 831 9500
Meeson Nigel Keith	4 Field Court, London	0171 440 6900
Mendoza Neil David Pereira	Hardwicke Building, London	0171 242 2523
Milligan Iain Anstruther	20 Essex Street, London	0171 583 9294
Mills Simon Thomas	One Essex Court, London	0171 936 3030
Milne Michael	Chambers of Geoffrey Hawker, London	0171 583 8899
	Resolution Chambers, Malvern	01684 561279
Morgan Charles James Arthur	Enterprise Chambers, London	0171 405 9471
	Enterprise Chambers, Leeds	0113 246 0391
	Enterprise Chambers, Newcastle upon Tyne	0191 222 3344
Morgan Edward Patrick	4 King's Bench Walk, London	0171 822 8822
	Deans Court Chambers, Manchester	0161 834 4097
Morgan Richard Hugo Lyndon	13 Old Square, London	0171 404 4800
Moriarty Gerald Evelyn	2 Mitre Court Buildings, London	0171 583 1380
Muir John Henry	12 New Square, London	0171 419 1212
	Sovereign Chambers, Leeds	0113 245 1841/2/3
Munro Kenneth Stuart	5 Bell Yard, London	0171 333 8811
Nash Jonathan Scott	3 Verulam Buildings, London	0171 831 8441
Neish Andrew Graham	4 Pump Court, London	0171 353 2656/9
Noble Andrew	Eldon Chambers, London	0171 353 4636
	Merchant Chambers, Manchester	0161 839 7070
Norman Christopher John George	No 1 Serjeants' Inn, London	0171 415 6666
Norris Alastair Hubert	• 5 Stone Buildings, London	0171 242 6201
	• Southernhay Chambers, Exeter	01392 255777
Norris Paul Howard	One Essex Court, London	0171 936 3030
O'Sullivan Bernard Anthony	Stanbrook & Henderson, London	0171 353 0101
	2 Harcourt Buildings, London	0171 583 9020
Ogunbiyi Oluwole Afolabi	Horizon Chambers, London	0171 242 2440
Okoye Miss Joy Nwamala	Chambers of Joy Okoye, London	0171 405 7011
Ornsby Miss Suzanne Doreen	• 2 Harcourt Buildings, London	0171 353 8415
Ough Dr Richard Norman	• Hardwicke Building, London	0171 242 2523
Owen David Christopher	20 Essex Street, London	0171 583 9294
Parkin Miss Fiona Jane	Atkin Chambers, London	0171 404 0102
Patchett-Joyce Michael Thurston	Monckton Chambers, London	0171 405 7211
Patterson Stewart	• Pump Court Chambers, London	0171 353 0711
	• Pump Court Chambers, Winchester	01962 868161

• Expanded entry in Part D

Peacocke Mrs Teresa Anne Rosen	Enterprise Chambers, London	0171 405 9471
	Enterprise Chambers, Leeds	0113 246 0391
	Enterprise Chambers, Newcastle upon Tyne	0191 222 3344
Peglow Dr Michael Alfred Herman	Chambers of Geoffrey Hawker, London	0171 583 8899
Pelling (Philip) Mark	Monckton Chambers, London	0171 405 7211
Pershad Rohan	Two Crown Office Row, London	0171 797 8100
Phillips Stephen Edmund	3 Verulam Buildings, London	0171 831 8441
Pittaway David Michael	No 1 Serjeants' Inn, London	0171 415 6666
Planterose Rowan Michael	Littman Chambers, London	0171 404 4866
Playford Jonathan Richard	2 Harcourt Buildings, London	0171 583 9020
Powles Stephen Robert	Stanbrook & Henderson, London	0171 353 0101
	2 Harcourt Buildings, London	0171 583 9020
Prynne Andrew Geoffrey Lockyer	Stanbrook & Henderson, London	0171 353 0101
	2 Harcourt Buildings, London	0171 583 9020
Quest David Charles	3 Verulam Buildings, London	0171 831 8441
Raeside Mark Andrew	Atkin Chambers, London	0171 404 0102
Rawley Miss Dominique Jane	Atkin Chambers, London	0171 404 0102
Readhead Simon John Howard	No 1 Serjeants' Inn, London	0171 415 6666
Reese Colin Edward	Atkin Chambers, London	0171 404 0102
Robson John Malcolm	2 Gray's Inn Square Chambers, London	0171 242 0328/405 1317
	Assize Court Chambers, Bristol	0117 926 4587
Ross John Graffin	No 1 Serjeants' Inn, London	0171 415 6666
Ross Martyn John Greaves	• 5 New Square, London	0171 404 0404
	• Octagon House, Norwich	01603 623186
Rowlands Ms Catherine Janet	Victoria Chambers, Birmingham	0121 236 9900
Royce Darryl Fraser	Atkin Chambers, London	0171 404 0102
Ryan David Patrick	Chambers of Geoffrey Hawker, London	0171 583 8899
Salter Richard Stanley	3 Verulam Buildings, London	0171 831 8441
Sampson Graeme William	Chambers of Geoffrey Hawker, London	0171 583 8899
Sands Mr Philippe Joseph	3 Verulam Buildings, London	0171 831 8441
Selvaratnam Miss Vasanti Emily Indrani	4 Field Court, London	0171 440 6900
Seymour Richard William	Monckton Chambers, London	0171 405 7211
Shaikh Eur.Ing. (Jaikumar) Christopher (Samuel	Avondale Chambers, London	0181 445 9984
	Equity Chambers, Birmingham	0121 233 2100
Shepherd Philip Alexander	• 5 Bell Yard, London	0171 333 8811
Sleeman Miss Rachel Sarah Elizabeth	One Essex Court, London	0171 936 3030
Sliwinski Robert Andrew	Chambers of Geoffrey Hawker, London	0171 583 8899
Smith Matthew Robert	Sovereign Chambers, Leeds	0113 245 1841/2/3
Smith Warwick Timothy Cresswell	• Deans Court Chambers, Manchester	0161 834 4097
	• Deans Court Chambers, Preston	01772 555163
Southwell Richard Charles	One Hare Court, London	0171 353 3171
Stagg Paul Andrew	No 1 Serjeants' Inn, London	0171 415 6666
Stevenson John Melford	Two Crown Office Row, London	0171 797 8100
Stewart Alexander Joseph	5 New Square, London	0171 404 0404
Stewart Nicholas John Cameron	Hardwicke Building, London	0171 242 2523
Storey Jeremy Brian	4 Pump Court, London	0171 353 2656/9
Streatfeild-James David Stewart	Atkin Chambers, London	0171 404 0102
Symons Christopher John Maurice	3 Verulam Buildings, London	0171 831 8441
Temple Anthony Dominic	4 Pump Court, London	0171 353 2656/9
Thomas (Robert) Neville	3 Verulam Buildings, London	0171 831 8441
Tozzi Nigel Kenneth	4 Pump Court, London	0171 353 2656/9
Trace Anthony John	• 13 Old Square, London	0171 404 4800
Trotman Timothy Oliver	Deans Court Chambers, Manchester	0161 834 4097
	Deans Court Chambers, Preston	01772 555163
Tucker David William	Two Crown Office Row, London	0171 797 8100
Turner Miss Janet Mary	3 Verulam Buildings, London	0171 831 8441
Valentine Donald Graham	Atkin Chambers, London	0171 404 0102
Vaughan Terence Paul	Watford Chambers, Watford	01923 220553
Village Peter Malcolm	• 4-5 Gray's Inn Square, London	0171 404 5252
Walker Steven John	Atkin Chambers, London	0171 404 0102
Wallace Ian Norman Duncan	Atkin Chambers, London	0171 404 0102
Weatherill Bernard Richard	Chambers of Lord Goodhart QC, London	0171 405 5577

Webb Robert Stopford	• 5 Bell Yard, London	0171 333 8811
Weitzman Thomas Edward Benjamin	3 Verulam Buildings, London	0171 831 8441
West Lawrence Joseph	Stanbrook & Henderson, London	0171 353 0101
	2 Harcourt Buildings, London	0171 583 9020
White Andrew	Atkin Chambers, London	0171 404 0102
Whiteley Miss Miranda Blyth	4 Field Court, London	0171 440 6900
Widdicombe David Graham	2 Mitre Court Buildings, London	0171 583 1380
Wilmot-Smith Richard James Crosbie	39 Essex Street, London	0171 832 1111
Wilson Peter Julian		
Worsley Daniel	Stanbrook & Henderson, London	0171 353 0101
	2 Harcourt Buildings, London	0171 583 9020
Wright Colin John	4 Field Court, London	0171 440 6900
Wright Frederick George Ian	• 3 Serjeants' Inn, London	0171 353 5537
Yell Nicholas Anthony	No 1 Serjeants' Inn, London	0171 415 6666

ASSET FINANCE

Burns Peter Richard	Deans Court Chambers, Manchester	0161 834 4097
de Lacy Richard Michael	3 Verulam Buildings, London	0171 831 8441
Doyle Louis George	Chambers of Andrew Campbell QC, Leeds	0113 245 5438
Goodbody Peter James	• Oriel Chambers, Liverpool	0151 236 7191
Griffiths Peter Robert	4 Stone Buildings, London	0171 242 5524
Jarvis John Manners	3 Verulam Buildings, London	0171 831 8441
Lawson Robert John	5 Bell Yard, London	0171 333 8811
Lazarus Michael Steven	1 Crown Office Row, London	0171 583 9292
Pearson Thomas Adam Spenser	Pump Court Chambers, London	0171 353 0711
	Pump Court Chambers, Winchester	01962 868161
Reed Philip James William	5 Bell Yard, London	0171 333 8811

ASSET FORFEITURE

Pearce Ivan James	Furnival Chambers, London	0171 405 3232

AVIATION

Austins Christopher John	Assize Court Chambers, Bristol	0117 926 4587
Bailey Edward Henry	5 Bell Yard, London	0171 333 8811
Boswell Miss Lindsay Alice	4 Pump Court, London	0171 353 2656/9
Brown Miss Hannah Beatrice	5 Bell Yard, London	0171 333 8811
Colquhoun Miss Celina Daphne Marion	11 Bolt Court, London	0171 353 2300
	Redhill Chambers, Redhill	01737 780781
Dean Paul Benjamin	5 Bell Yard, London	0171 333 8811
Fisher David	5 Bell Yard, London	0171 333 8811
Forlin Gerard Emlyn	Phoenix Chambers, London	0171 404 7888
Fowler Richard Nicholas	Monckton Chambers, London	0171 405 7211
Jack Simon Michael	9 Woodhouse Square, Leeds	0113 245 1986
Jones Miss (Catherine) Charlotte	5 Bell Yard, London	0171 333 8811
Kavanagh Giles Wilfred Conor	• 5 Bell Yard, London	0171 333 8811
Kimbell John Ashley	5 Bell Yard, London	0171 333 8811
Lawson Robert John	5 Bell Yard, London	0171 333 8811
Meeson Nigel Keith	4 Field Court, London	0171 440 6900
Milligan Iain Anstruther	20 Essex Street, London	0171 583 9294
Pelling Richard Alexander	New Court Chambers, London	0171 831 9500
Perks Richard Howard	St Philip's Chambers, Birmingham	0121 246 7000
Reed Philip James William	5 Bell Yard, London	0171 333 8811
Reeve Matthew Francis	5 Bell Yard, London	0171 333 8811
Russell Robert John Finlay	5 Bell Yard, London	0171 333 8811
Saunders Nicholas Joseph	4 Field Court, London	0171 440 6900
Shepherd Philip Alexander	• 5 Bell Yard, London	0171 333 8811
Sullivan Michael Jerome	5 Bell Yard, London	0171 333 8811
Symons Christopher John Maurice	3 Verulam Buildings, London	0171 831 8441
Tedd Rex Hilary	• St Philip's Chambers, Birmingham	0121 246 7000
	• 22 Albion Place, Northampton	01604 636271
Vaughan-Neil Miss Catherine Mary Bernardine	5 Bell Yard, London	0171 333 8811
Webb Robert Stopford	• 5 Bell Yard, London	0171 333 8811
Wright Colin John	4 Field Court, London	0171 440 6900

BAHAMAS LAW

Davidson Edward Alan	• 11 Old Square, London	0171 430 0341

• Expanded entry in Part D

BANKING

Akka Lawrence Mark	20 Essex Street, London	0171 583 9294
Ambrose Miss Clare Mary Geneste	20 Essex Street, London	0171 583 9294
Amin Miss Farah	7 New Square, London	0171 430 1660
Arden Peter Leonard	Enterprise Chambers, London	0171 405 9471
	Enterprise Chambers, Leeds	0113 246 0391
	Enterprise Chambers, Newcastle upon Tyne	0191 222 3344
Baker Miss Anne Jacqueline	Enterprise Chambers, London	0171 405 9471
	Enterprise Chambers, Leeds	0113 246 0391
	Enterprise Chambers, Newcastle upon Tyne	0191 222 3344
Barker James Sebastian	Enterprise Chambers, London	0171 405 9471
	Enterprise Chambers, Leeds	0113 246 0391
	Enterprise Chambers, Newcastle upon Tyne	0191 222 3344
Barker Simon George Harry	• 13 Old Square, London	0171 404 4800
Baylis Ms Natalie Jayne	3 Verulam Buildings, London	0171 831 8441
Beaumont Marc Clifford	• Pump Court Chambers, London	0171 353 0711
	• Harrow-on-the-Hill Chambers, Harrow on the Hill	0181 423 7444
	• Pump Court Chambers, Winchester	01962 868161
	• Windsor Barristers' Chambers, Windsor	01753 648 899
Beltrami Adrian Joseph	3 Verulam Buildings, London	0171 831 8441
Berkley Michael Stuart	Rougemont Chambers, Exeter	01392 410471
Berragan (Howard) Neil	Merchant Chambers, Manchester	0161 839 7070
Bhaloo Miss Zia Kurban	Enterprise Chambers, London	0171 405 9471
	Enterprise Chambers, Leeds	0113 246 0391
	Enterprise Chambers, Newcastle upon Tyne	0191 222 3344
Bird Nigel David	Chambers of John Hand QC, Manchester	0161 955 9000
Blair William James Lynton	3 Verulam Buildings, London	0171 831 8441
Bourne Robert	• 4 Field Court, London	0171 440 6900
Brent Richard	3 Verulam Buildings, London	0171 831 8441
Brown Miss Hannah Beatrice	5 Bell Yard, London	0171 333 8811
Burton Michael John	Littleton Chambers, London	0171 797 8600
Chalmers Miss Suzanne Frances	Two Crown Office Row, London	0171 797 8100
Charman Andrew Julian	St Philip's Chambers, Birmingham	0121 246 7000
Clegg Sebastian James Barwick	Deans Court Chambers, Manchester	0161 834 4097
Collett Michael John	20 Essex Street, London	0171 583 9294
Cranbrook Alexander Douglas John	9–12 Bell Yard, London	0171 400 1800
Cranfield Peter Anthony	3 Verulam Buildings, London	0171 831 8441
Crawford Grant	11 Old Square, London	0171 430 0341
Darbyshire William Robert	Chambers of John Hand QC, Manchester	0161 955 9000
Davies Stephen Richard	8 King Street Chambers, Manchester	0161 834 9560
Davies-Jones Jonathan	3 Verulam Buildings, London	0171 831 8441
de Jehan David	St Paul's House, Leeds	0113 245 5866
de Lacy Richard Michael	3 Verulam Buildings, London	0171 831 8441
Deacock Adam Jason	Chambers of Lord Goodhart QC, London	0171 405 5577
Dougherty Nigel Peter	Erskine Chambers, London	0171 242 5532
Dowse John	Chambers of Lord Goodhart QC, London	0171 405 5577
	Chambers of John Hand QC, Manchester	0161 955 9000
Doyle Louis George	Chambers of Andrew Campbell QC, Leeds	0113 245 5438
Edwards Richard Julian Henshaw	3 Verulam Buildings, London	0171 831 8441
Elliott Nicholas Blethyn	3 Verulam Buildings, London	0171 831 8441
Evans James Frederick Meurig	3 Verulam Buildings, London	0171 831 8441
Field Richard Alan	11 King's Bench Walk, London	0171 632 8500
Francis Edward Gerald Francis	Enterprise Chambers, London	0171 405 9471
	Enterprise Chambers, Leeds	0113 246 0391
	Enterprise Chambers, Newcastle upon Tyne	0191 222 3344
Freedman Sampson Clive	3 Verulam Buildings, London	0171 831 8441
French Richard Anthony Lister	Rougemont Chambers, Exeter	01392 410471
Garcia-Miller Miss Laura	Enterprise Chambers, London	0171 405 9471

B

• Expanded entry in Part D

	Enterprise Chambers, Leeds	0113 246 0391
	Enterprise Chambers, Newcastle upon Tyne	0191 222 3344
Geering Ian Walter	3 Verulam Buildings, London	0171 831 8441
Gibaud Miss Catherine Alison Annetta	3 Verulam Buildings, London	0171 831 8441
Gilchrist David Somerled	Chambers of John Hand QC, Manchester	0161 955 9000
Godfrey Jonathan Saul	St Paul's House, Leeds	0113 245 5866
Goodhart Lord	Chambers of Lord Goodhart QC, London	0171 405 5577
Gore-Andrews Gavin Angus Russell	Stanbrook & Henderson, London	0171 353 0101
	2 Harcourt Buildings, London	0171 583 9020
Grant Thomas Paul Wentworth	New Court Chambers, London	0171 831 9500
Grantham Andrew Timothy	• Deans Court Chambers, Manchester	0161 834 4097
	• Deans Court Chambers, Preston	01772 555163
Griffiths Peter Robert	4 Stone Buildings, London	0171 242 5524
Groves Hugo Gerard	Enterprise Chambers, London	0171 405 9471
	Enterprise Chambers, Leeds	0113 246 0391
	Enterprise Chambers, Newcastle upon Tyne	0191 222 3344
Halpern David Anthony	Enterprise Chambers, London	0171 405 9471
	Enterprise Chambers, Leeds	0113 246 0391
	Enterprise Chambers, Newcastle upon Tyne	0191 222 3344
Hantusch Robert Anthony	• 3 Stone Buildings, London	0171 242 4937/405 8358
Hayes Miss Josephine Mary	Chambers of Lord Goodhart QC, London	0171 405 5577
Heywood Michael Edmundson	Chambers of Lord Goodhart QC, London	0171 405 5577
	Cobden House Chambers, Manchester	0161 833 6000/6001
Hibbert William John	Gough Square Chambers, London	0171 353 0924
Hockaday Miss Annie	3 Verulam Buildings, London	0171 831 8441
Holmes Justin Francis	Chambers of Lord Goodhart QC, London	0171 405 5577
Hughes Miss Mary Josephine	Chambers of Lord Goodhart QC, London	0171 405 5577
Hurst Brian	17 Bedford Row, London	0171 831 7314
Hutton Miss Caroline	Enterprise Chambers, London	0171 405 9471
	Enterprise Chambers, Leeds	0113 246 0391
	Enterprise Chambers, Newcastle upon Tyne	0191 222 3344
Ife Miss Linden Elizabeth	Enterprise Chambers, London	0171 405 9471
	Enterprise Chambers, Leeds	0113 246 0391
	Enterprise Chambers, Newcastle upon Tyne	0191 222 3344
James Michael Frank	Enterprise Chambers, London	0171 405 9471
	Enterprise Chambers, Leeds	0113 246 0391
	Enterprise Chambers, Newcastle upon Tyne	0191 222 3344
Jarvis John Manners	3 Verulam Buildings, London	0171 831 8441
Jefferies Thomas Robert	Chambers of Lord Goodhart QC, London	0171 405 5577
Johnson Michael Sloan	Chambers of John Hand QC, Manchester	0161 955 9000
Jory Robert John Hugh	Enterprise Chambers, London	0171 405 9471
	Enterprise Chambers, Leeds	0113 246 0391
	Enterprise Chambers, Newcastle upon Tyne	0191 222 3344
Kay Michael Jack David	3 Verulam Buildings, London	0171 831 8441
	Park Lane Chambers, Leeds	0113 228 5000
Kimbell John Ashley	5 Bell Yard, London	0171 333 8811
Kolodziej Andrzej Jozef	• Littman Chambers, London	0171 404 4866
Lamont Miss Camilla Rose	Chambers of Lord Goodhart QC, London	0171 405 5577
Lazarus Michael Steven	1 Crown Office Row, London	0171 583 9292
Leeming Ian	Lamb Chambers, London	0171 797 8300
	Chambers of John Hand QC, Manchester	0161 955 9000
Lennard Stephen Charles	Hardwicke Building, London	0171 242 2523
Lewis Miss Caroline Susannah	3 Verulam Buildings, London	0171 831 8441
Lowenstein Paul David	Littleton Chambers, London	0171 797 8600

• Expanded entry in Part D

Malek Ali	3 Verulam Buildings, London	0171 831 8441
Males Stephen Martin	20 Essex Street, London	0171 583 9294
Mann George Anthony	Enterprise Chambers, London	0171 405 9471
	Enterprise Chambers, Leeds	0113 246 0391
	Enterprise Chambers, Newcastle upon Tyne	0191 222 3344
Marks Jonathan Harold	3 Verulam Buildings, London	0171 831 8441
Marquand Charles Nicholas Hilary	Chambers of Lord Goodhart QC, London	0171 405 5577
Marten Richard Hedley Westwood	Chambers of Lord Goodhart QC, London	0171 405 5577
Masters Miss Sara Alayna	20 Essex Street, London	0171 583 9294
May Miss Juliet Mary	3 Verulam Buildings, London	0171 831 8441
McKinnell Miss Soraya Jane	Enterprise Chambers, London	0171 405 9471
	Enterprise Chambers, Leeds	0113 246 0391
	Enterprise Chambers, Newcastle upon Tyne	0191 222 3344
McQuater Ewan Alan	3 Verulam Buildings, London	0171 831 8441
Meeson Nigel Keith	4 Field Court, London	0171 440 6900
Mendoza Neil David Pereira	Hardwicke Building, London	0171 242 2523
Merriman Nicholas Flavelle	3 Verulam Buildings, London	0171 831 8441
Milligan Iain Anstruther	20 Essex Street, London	0171 583 9294
Mitchell Gregory Charles Mathew	3 Verulam Buildings, London	0171 831 8441
Mullis Anthony Roger	Chambers of Lord Goodhart QC, London	0171 405 5577
Nash Jonathan Scott	3 Verulam Buildings, London	0171 831 8441
Neville Stephen John	Gough Square Chambers, London	0171 353 0924
Odgers John Arthur	3 Verulam Buildings, London	0171 831 8441
Ogunbiyi Oluwole Afolabi	Horizon Chambers, London	0171 242 2440
Ohrenstein Dov	Chambers of Lord Goodhart QC, London	0171 405 5577
Onslow Andrew George	3 Verulam Buildings, London	0171 831 8441
Owen David Christopher	20 Essex Street, London	0171 583 9294
Padfield Ms Alison Mary	One Hare Court, London	0171 353 3171
Parry David Julian Thomas	Chambers of Lord Goodhart QC, London	0171 405 5577
Patchett-Joyce Michael Thurston	Monckton Chambers, London	0171 405 7211
Pelling (Philip) Mark	Monckton Chambers, London	0171 405 7211
Perkoff Richard Michael	Littleton Chambers, London	0171 797 8600
Pershad Rohan	Two Crown Office Row, London	0171 797 8100
Phillips Jonathan Mark	3 Verulam Buildings, London	0171 831 8441
Phillips Stephen Edmund	3 Verulam Buildings, London	0171 831 8441
Picarda Hubert Alistair Paul	Chambers of Lord Goodhart QC, London	0171 405 5577
Pickering James Patrick	Enterprise Chambers, London	0171 405 9471
	Enterprise Chambers, Leeds	0113 246 0391
	Enterprise Chambers, Newcastle upon Tyne	0191 222 3344
Pope David James	3 Verulam Buildings, London	0171 831 8441
Quest David Charles	3 Verulam Buildings, London	0171 831 8441
Reed Philip James William	5 Bell Yard, London	0171 333 8811
Reeve Matthew Francis	5 Bell Yard, London	0171 333 8811
Robson John Malcolm	2 Gray's Inn Square Chambers, London	0171 242 0328/405 1317
	Assize Court Chambers, Bristol	0117 926 4587
Rogers Ian Paul	1 Crown Office Row, London	0171 583 9292
Russell Robert John Finlay	5 Bell Yard, London	0171 333 8811
Salter Richard Stanley	3 Verulam Buildings, London	0171 831 8441
Sayer Mr Peter Edwin	Gough Square Chambers, London	0171 353 0924
Selvaratnam Miss Vasanti Emily Indrani	4 Field Court, London	0171 440 6900
Selway Dr Katherine Emma	11 Old Square, London	0171 430 0341
Seymour Richard William	Monckton Chambers, London	0171 405 7211
Sheridan Maurice Bernard Gerard	• 3 Verulam Buildings, London	0171 831 8441
Southern Professor David Boardman	• 3 Temple Gardens Tax Chambers, London	0171 353 7884
Southwell Richard Charles	One Hare Court, London	0171 353 3171
Stancombe Barry Terrence	Gough Square Chambers, London	0171 353 0924
Stewart Alexander Joseph	5 New Square, London	0171 404 0404
Storey Jeremy Brian	4 Pump Court, London	0171 353 2656/9
Sullivan Michael Jerome	5 Bell Yard, London	0171 333 8811
Sutcliffe Andrew Harold Wentworth	3 Verulam Buildings, London	0171 831 8441

• Expanded entry in Part D

Sykes (James) Richard	Erskine Chambers, London	0171 242 5532
Tedd Rex Hilary	• St Philip's Chambers, Birmingham	0121 246 7000
	• 22 Albion Place, Northampton	01604 636271
Thomas (Robert) Neville	3 Verulam Buildings, London	0171 831 8441
Tipples Miss Amanda Jane	13 Old Square, London	0171 404 4800
Tolaney Miss Sonia	3 Verulam Buildings, London	0171 831 8441
Trace Anthony John	• 13 Old Square, London	0171 404 4800
Vaughan-Neil Miss Catherine Mary Bernardine	5 Bell Yard, London	0171 333 8811
Wadsworth James Patrick	4 Paper Buildings, London	0171 353 3366/583 7155
Walker Andrew Greenfield	Chambers of Lord Goodhart QC, London	0171 405 5577
Waters Malcolm Ian	• 11 Old Square, London	0171 430 0341
Weatherill Bernard Richard	Chambers of Lord Goodhart QC, London	0171 405 5577
Whiteley Miss Miranda Blyth	4 Field Court, London	0171 440 6900
Williamson Miss Bridget Susan	Enterprise Chambers, London	0171 405 9471
	Enterprise Chambers, Leeds	0113 246 0391
	Enterprise Chambers, Newcastle upon Tyne	0191 222 3344
Wilson Ian Robert	3 Verulam Buildings, London	0171 831 8441
Wolfson David	3 Verulam Buildings, London	0171 831 8441
Wright Colin John	4 Field Court, London	0171 440 6900
Zelin Geoffrey Andrew	Enterprise Chambers, London	0171 405 9471
	Enterprise Chambers, Leeds	0113 246 0391
	Enterprise Chambers, Newcastle upon Tyne	0191 222 3344

B

BANKRUPTCY

Adamyk Simon Charles	12 New Square, London	0171 419 1212
Airey Simon Andrew	11 Bolt Court, London	0171 353 2300
	Redhill Chambers, Redhill	01737 780781
Aldridge James Hugh	13 Old Square, London	0171 404 4800
Amin Miss Farah	7 New Square, London	0171 430 1660
Angus Miss Tracey Anne	5 Stone Buildings, London	0171 242 6201
Arden Peter Leonard	Enterprise Chambers, London	0171 405 9471
	Enterprise Chambers, Leeds	0113 246 0391
	Enterprise Chambers, Newcastle upon Tyne	0191 222 3344
Atherton Ian David	Enterprise Chambers, London	0171 405 9471
	Enterprise Chambers, Leeds	0113 246 0391
	Enterprise Chambers, Newcastle upon Tyne	0191 222 3344
Ayres Andrew John William	13 Old Square, London	0171 404 4800
Baker Miss Anne Jacqueline	Enterprise Chambers, London	0171 405 9471
	Enterprise Chambers, Leeds	0113 246 0391
	Enterprise Chambers, Newcastle upon Tyne	0191 222 3344
Barber Miss Sally	5 Stone Buildings, London	0171 242 6201
Barker James Sebastian	Enterprise Chambers, London	0171 405 9471
	Enterprise Chambers, Leeds	0113 246 0391
	Enterprise Chambers, Newcastle upon Tyne	0191 222 3344
Barker Simon George Harry	• 13 Old Square, London	0171 404 4800
Barstow Stephen Royden	Harcourt Chambers, London	0171 353 6961/7
	Harcourt Chambers, Oxford	01865 791559
Baylis Ms Natalie Jayne	3 Verulam Buildings, London	0171 831 8441
Berkley Michael Stuart	Rougemont Chambers, Exeter	01392 410471
Bhaloo Miss Zia Kurban	Enterprise Chambers, London	0171 405 9471
	Enterprise Chambers, Leeds	0113 246 0391
	Enterprise Chambers, Newcastle upon Tyne	0191 222 3344
Brook Ian Stuart	Hardwicke Building, London	0171 242 2523
Browne Miss Julie Rebecca	Goldsmith Building, London	0171 353 7881
Burroughs Nigel Alfred	11 Old Square, London	0171 430 0341
Butt Miss Romasa	Goldsworth Building, London	0171 405 7117
Capon Philip Christopher William	St Philip's Chambers, Birmingham	0121 246 7000
Cawson Mark	• 12 New Square, London	0171 419 1212
	• St James's Chambers, Manchester	0161 834 7000
	• Park Lane Chambers, Leeds	0113 228 5000
Charman Andrew Julian	St Philip's Chambers, Birmingham	0121 246 7000
Clarke Miss Anna Victoria	5 Stone Buildings, London	0171 242 6201

         • Expanded entry in Part D

Clarke Ian James	Hardwicke Building, London	0171 242 2523
Collaco Moraes Francis Thomas	• 2 Gray's Inn Square Chambers, London	0171 242 0328/405 1317
Collings Matthew Glynn Burkinshaw	13 Old Square, London	0171 404 4800
Corbett James Patrick	St Philip's Chambers, Birmingham	0121 246 7000
Coulter Barry John	One Essex Court, London	0171 936 3030
Craig Kenneth Allen	Hardwicke Building, London	0171 242 2523
Crail Miss (Elspeth) Ross	12 New Square, London	0171 419 1212
	Sovereign Chambers, Leeds	0113 245 1841/2/3
Crawford Grant	11 Old Square, London	0171 430 0341
Cunningham Miss Claire Louise	St Philip's Chambers, Birmingham	0121 246 7000
Cunningham Mark James	13 Old Square, London	0171 404 4800
Darbyshire William Robert	Chambers of John Hand QC, Manchester	0161 955 9000
Davies Miss Louise	12 New Square, London	0171 419 1212
Dawson James Robert	Oriel Chambers, Liverpool	0151 236 7191
de Lacy Richard Michael	3 Verulam Buildings, London	0171 831 8441
Deacock Adam Jason	Chambers of Lord Goodhart QC, London	0171 405 5577
Dedezade Taner	Tindal Chambers, Chelmsford	01245 267742
Dodge Peter Clive	11 Old Square, London	0171 430 0341
Doyle Louis George	Chambers of Andrew Campbell QC, Leeds	0113 245 5438
Drayton Henry Alexander	2 Gray's Inn Square Chambers, London	0171 242 0328/405 1317
Elleray Anthony John	• 12 New Square, London	0171 419 1212
	• St James's Chambers, Manchester	0161 834 7000
	• Park Lane Chambers, Leeds	0113 228 5000
Evans-Gordon Mrs Jane-Anne Mary	12 New Square, London	0171 419 1212
Francis Edward Gerald Francis	Enterprise Chambers, London	0171 405 9471
	Enterprise Chambers, Leeds	0113 246 0391
	Enterprise Chambers, Newcastle upon Tyne	0191 222 3344
Garcia-Miller Miss Laura	Enterprise Chambers, London	0171 405 9471
	Enterprise Chambers, Leeds	0113 246 0391
	Enterprise Chambers, Newcastle upon Tyne	0191 222 3344
Gerald Nigel Mortimer	Enterprise Chambers, London	0171 405 9471
	Enterprise Chambers, Leeds	0113 246 0391
	Enterprise Chambers, Newcastle upon Tyne	0191 222 3344
Gibaud Miss Catherine Alison Annetta	3 Verulam Buildings, London	0171 831 8441
Godfrey Jonathan Saul	St Paul's House, Leeds	0113 245 5866
Goodhart Lord	Chambers of Lord Goodhart QC, London	0171 405 5577
Graham Thomas Patrick Henry	Lamb Chambers, London	0171 797 8300
Grantham Andrew Timothy	• Deans Court Chambers, Manchester	0161 834 4097
	• Deans Court Chambers, Preston	01772 555163
Gregory John Raymond	Deans Court Chambers, Manchester	0161 834 4097
	Deans Court Chambers, Preston	01772 555163
Griffiths Peter Robert	4 Stone Buildings, London	0171 242 5524
Groves Hugo Gerard	Enterprise Chambers, London	0171 405 9471
	Enterprise Chambers, Leeds	0113 246 0391
	Enterprise Chambers, Newcastle upon Tyne	0191 222 3344
Hall Taylor Alexander Edward	11 Old Square, London	0171 430 0341
Halpern David Anthony	Enterprise Chambers, London	0171 405 9471
	Enterprise Chambers, Leeds	0113 246 0391
	Enterprise Chambers, Newcastle upon Tyne	0191 222 3344
Hansen William Joseph	5 Bell Yard, London	0171 333 8811
Hantusch Robert Anthony	• 3 Stone Buildings, London	0171 242 4937/405 8358
Harbottle Gwilym Thomas	5 New Square, London	0171 404 0404
Hardwick Matthew Richard	Enterprise Chambers, London	0171 405 9471
	Enterprise Chambers, Leeds	0113 246 0391
	Enterprise Chambers, Newcastle upon Tyne	0191 222 3344
Hargreaves Miss Sara Jane	12 New Square, London	0171 419 1212
	Sovereign Chambers, Leeds	0113 245 1841/2/3
Harvey Miss Jayne Denise	Goldsworth Chambers, London	0171 405 7117

Haven Kevin	2 Gray's Inn Square Chambers, London	0171 242 0328/405 1317
Hayes John Allan	Chambers of Andrew Campbell QC, Leeds	0113 245 5438
Hayes Miss Josephine Mary	Chambers of Lord Goodhart QC, London	0171 405 5577
Heywood Michael Edmundson	Chambers of Lord Goodhart QC, London	0171 405 5577
	Cobden House Chambers, Manchester	0161 833 6000/6001
Hibbert William John	Gough Square Chambers, London	0171 353 0924
Hill Robert Douglas	Pump Court Chambers, London	0171 353 0711
	Pump Court Chambers, Winchester	01962 868161
Hockaday Miss Annie	3 Verulam Buildings, London	0171 831 8441
Hollingworth Peter James Michael	22 Albion Place, Northampton	01604 636271
Holmes Justin Francis	Chambers of Lord Goodhart QC, London	0171 405 5577
Hughes Miss Mary Josephine	Chambers of Lord Goodhart QC, London	0171 405 5577
Hutton Miss Caroline	Enterprise Chambers, London	0171 405 9471
	Enterprise Chambers, Leeds	0113 246 0391
	Enterprise Chambers, Newcastle upon Tyne	0191 222 3344
Ife Miss Linden Elizabeth	Enterprise Chambers, London	0171 405 9471
	Enterprise Chambers, Leeds	0113 246 0391
	Enterprise Chambers, Newcastle upon Tyne	0191 222 3344
Jack Adrian Laurence Robert	Enterprise Chambers, London	0171 405 9471
Jackson Hugh Woodward	Hardwicke Building, London	0171 242 2523
Jackson Nicholas David Kingsley	The Chambers of Adrian Lyon, Liverpool	0151 236 4421/8240/6757
James Michael Frank	Enterprise Chambers, London	0171 405 9471
	Enterprise Chambers, Leeds	0113 246 0391
	Enterprise Chambers, Newcastle upon Tyne	0191 222 3344
Jarvis John Manners	3 Verulam Buildings, London	0171 831 8441
Jefferies Thomas Robert	Chambers of Lord Goodhart QC, London	0171 405 5577
Johnson Michael Sloan	Chambers of John Hand QC, Manchester	0161 955 9000
Jory Robert John Hugh	Enterprise Chambers, London	0171 405 9471
	Enterprise Chambers, Leeds	0113 246 0391
	Enterprise Chambers, Newcastle upon Tyne	0191 222 3344
Kimbell John Ashley	5 Bell Yard, London	0171 333 8811
Kolodynski Stefan Richard	New Court Chambers, Birmingham	0121 693 6656
Kremen Philip Michael	Hardwicke Building, London	0171 242 2523
Lamont Miss Camilla Rose	Chambers of Lord Goodhart QC, London	0171 405 5577
Landes Miss Anna-Rose	St Philip's Chambers, Birmingham	0121 246 7000
Laughton Samuel Dennis	17 Old Buildings, London	0171 405 9653
Levy Benjamin Keith	Enterprise Chambers, London	0171 405 9471
	Enterprise Chambers, Leeds	0113 246 0391
	Enterprise Chambers, Newcastle upon Tyne	0191 222 3344
Levy Robert Stuart	9 Stone Buildings, London	0171 404 5055
	Assize Court Chambers, Bristol	0117 926 4587
Lowenstein Paul David	Littleton Chambers, London	0171 797 8600
Lynch Terry John	22 Albion Place, Northampton	01604 636271
Lyne Mark Hilary	One Essex Court, London	0171 936 3030
Mann George Anthony	Enterprise Chambers, London	0171 405 9471
	Enterprise Chambers, Leeds	0113 246 0391
	Enterprise Chambers, Newcastle upon Tyne	0191 222 3344
Marquand Charles Nicholas Hilary	Chambers of Lord Goodhart QC, London	0171 405 5577
Marten Richard Hedley Westwood	Chambers of Lord Goodhart QC, London	0171 405 5577
Mauger Miss Claire Shanti Andrea	Enterprise Chambers, London	0171 405 9471
McAllister Miss Elizabeth Ann	Enterprise Chambers, London	0171 405 9471
	Enterprise Chambers, Leeds	0113 246 0391
	Enterprise Chambers, Newcastle upon Tyne	0191 222 3344

• Expanded entry in Part D

McCarthy William	New Bailey Chambers, Preston	01772 258 087
McKinnell Miss Soraya Jane	Enterprise Chambers, London	0171 405 9471
	Enterprise Chambers, Leeds	0113 246 0391
	Enterprise Chambers, Newcastle upon Tyne	0191 222 3344
McQuail Ms Katherine Emma	11 Old Square, London	0171 430 0341
McQuater Ewan Alan	3 Verulam Buildings, London	0171 831 8441
Mendoza Neil David Pereira	Hardwicke Building, London	0171 242 2523
Morgan Charles James Arthur	Enterprise Chambers, London	0171 405 9471
	Enterprise Chambers, Leeds	0113 246 0391
	Enterprise Chambers, Newcastle upon Tyne	0191 222 3344
Morgan Richard Hugo Lyndon	13 Old Square, London	0171 404 4800
Mullis Anthony Roger	Chambers of Lord Goodhart QC, London	0171 405 5577
Nebhrajani Miss Mel	9 Stone Buildings, London	0171 404 5055
Neville Stephen John	Gough Square Chambers, London	0171 353 0924
Norbury Luke Edward	17 Old Buildings, London	0171 405 9653
Ohrenstein Dov	Chambers of Lord Goodhart QC, London	0171 405 5577
Parry David Julian Thomas	Chambers of Lord Goodhart QC, London	0171 405 5577
Patchett-Joyce Michael Thurston	Monckton Chambers, London	0171 405 7211
Peacock Ian Christopher	12 New Square, London	0171 419 1212
	Sovereign Chambers, Leeds	0113 245 1841/2/3
Peacock Nicholas Christopher	13 Old Square, London	0171 404 4800
Pelling Richard Alexander	New Court Chambers, London	0171 831 9500
Perkoff Richard Michael	Littleton Chambers, London	0171 797 8600
Pershad Rohan	Two Crown Office Row, London	0171 797 8100
Phillips Jonathan Mark	3 Verulam Buildings, London	0171 831 8441
Pickering James Patrick	Enterprise Chambers, London	0171 405 9471
	Enterprise Chambers, Leeds	0113 246 0391
	Enterprise Chambers, Newcastle upon Tyne	0191 222 3344
Pimentel Carlos de Serpa Alberto Legg	3 Stone Buildings, London	0171 242 4937/405 8358
Poyer-Sleeman Ms Patricia	Pump Court Chambers, London	0171 353 0711
	Pump Court Chambers, Winchester	01962 868161
Pryke Stuart	Trinity Chambers, Newcastle upon Tyne	0191 232 1927
Rees David Benjamin	5 Stone Buildings, London	0171 242 6201
Richardson Miss Sarah Jane	Enterprise Chambers, London	0171 405 9471
	Enterprise Chambers, Leeds	0113 246 0391
	Enterprise Chambers, Newcastle upon Tyne	0191 222 3344
Robson John Malcolm	2 Gray's Inn Square Chambers, London	0171 242 0328/405 1317
	Assize Court Chambers, Bristol	0117 926 4587
Ross Martyn John Greaves	• 5 New Square, London	0171 404 0404
	• Octagon House, Norwich	01603 623186
Rowell David Stewart	Chambers of Lord Goodhart QC, London	0171 405 5577
Rule Jonathan Daniel	Merchant Chambers, Manchester	0161 839 7070
Russen Jonathan Huw Sinclair	13 Old Square, London	0171 404 4800
Salter Richard Stanley	3 Verulam Buildings, London	0171 831 8441
Schaw-Miller Stephen Grant	5 Bell Yard, London	0171 333 8811
Sefton Mark Thomas Dunblane	199 Strand, London	0171 379 9779
Shah Bajul Amratlal Somchand	Twenty-Four Old Buildings, London	0171 404 0946
Sinclair-Morris Charles Robert	9 Woodhouse Square, Leeds	0113 245 1986
Singh Balbir	• Equity Chambers, Birmingham	0121 233 2100
Sisley Timothy Julian Crispin	9 Stone Buildings, London	0171 404 5055
	Westgate Chambers, Lewes	01273 480 510
Smith Miss Julia Mair Wheldon	Gough Square Chambers, London	0171 353 0924
Staddon Miss Claire Ann	12 New Square, London	0171 419 1212
	Sovereign Chambers, Leeds	0113 245 1841/2/3
Stewart Alexander Joseph	5 New Square, London	0171 404 0404
Sugar Simon Gareth	5 New Square, London	0171 404 0404
Taelor Start Miss Angharad Jocelyn	3 Verulam Buildings, London	0171 831 8441
Thomas (Robert) Neville	3 Verulam Buildings, London	0171 831 8441
Thompson Steven Lim	Twenty-Four Old Buildings, London	0171 404 0946
Tidmarsh Christopher Ralph Francis	5 Stone Buildings, London	0171 242 6201
Tipples Miss Amanda Jane	13 Old Square, London	0171 404 4800

• Expanded entry in Part D

Trace Anthony John	• 13 Old Square, London	0171 404 4800
Vane The Hon Christopher John Fletcher	Trinity Chambers, Newcastle upon Tyne	0191 232 1927
Vines Anthony Robert Francis	Gough Square Chambers, London	0171 353 0924
Walker Andrew Greenfield	Chambers of Lord Goodhart QC, London	0171 405 5577
Weatherill Bernard Richard	Chambers of Lord Goodhart QC, London	0171 405 5577
West Mark	• 11 Old Square, London	0171 430 0341
Williamson Miss Bridget Susan	Enterprise Chambers, London	0171 405 9471
	Enterprise Chambers, Leeds	0113 246 0391
	Enterprise Chambers, Newcastle upon Tyne	0191 222 3344
Wilson Ian Robert	3 Verulam Buildings, London	0171 831 8441
Zelin Geoffrey Andrew	Enterprise Chambers, London	0171 405 9471
	Enterprise Chambers, Leeds	0113 246 0391
	Enterprise Chambers, Newcastle upon Tyne	0191 222 3344

BUILDING SOCIETIES

Ovey Miss Elizabeth Helen	11 Old Square, London	0171 430 0341
Waters Malcolm Ian	• 11 Old Square, London	0171 430 0341

CARE PROCEEDINGS

Ahmed Farooq Tahir	8 King Street Chambers, Manchester	0161 834 9560
Alexander Ian Douglas Gavin	11 Bolt Court, London	0171 353 2300
	Redhill Chambers, Redhill	01737 780781
Allardice Miss Miranda Jane	Pump Court Chambers, London	0171 353 0711
	Pump Court Chambers, Winchester	01962 868161
Alomo Richard Olusoji	14 Gray's Inn Square, London	0171 242 0858
Amiraftabi Miss Roshanak	Hardwicke Building, London	0171 242 2523
Asteris Peter David	Eighteen Carlton Crescent, Southampton	01703 639001
Auld Miss Catherine Rohan	Harcourt Chambers, London	0171 353 6961/7
	Harcourt Chambers, Oxford	01865 791559
Baker Jonathan Leslie	Harcourt Chambers, London	0171 353 6961/7
	Harcourt Chambers, Oxford	01865 791559
Baldock Miss Susan Anne	2 Gray's Inn Square Chambers, London	0171 242 0328/405 1317
Bancroft Miss Anna Louise	Deans Court Chambers, Manchester	0161 834 4097
	Deans Court Chambers, Preston	01772 555163
Barlow Miss Sarah Helen	St Paul's House, Leeds	0113 245 5866
Benner Miss Lucinda Diana Kate	11 Bolt Court, London	0171 353 2300
	Redhill Chambers, Redhill	01737 780781
Bennett John Martyn	• Peel House Chambers, Liverpool	0151 236 4321
Benson Julian Christopher Woodburn	One Essex Court, London	0171 936 3030
Bergin Timothy William	Sussex Chambers, Brighton	01273 607953
Bhattacharyya Ardhendu	1 Gray's Inn Square, London	0171 405 8946
	11 St Bernards Road, Slough	01753 553806/817989
Bickerdike Roger John	9 Woodhouse Square, Leeds	0113 245 1986
Bickler Simon Lloyd	St Paul's House, Leeds	0113 245 5866
Bindloss Edward Christopher James	Chambers of Andrew Campbell QC, Leeds	0113 245 5438
Bishop Timothy Harper Paul	1 Mitre Court Buildings, London	0171 797 7070
Bloom-Davis Desmond Niall Laurence	Pump Court Chambers, London	0171 353 0711
	Pump Court Chambers, Winchester	01962 868161
Boora Jinder Singh	Regent Chambers, Stoke-on-Trent	01782 286666
Boothroyd Miss Susan Elizabeth	Westgate Chambers, Newcastle upon Tyne	0191 261 4407/232 9785
Bowcock Miss Samantha Jane	15 Winckley Square, Preston	01772 252 828
Boyle David Stuart	Deans Court Chambers, Manchester	0161 834 4097
Brasse Miss Gillian Denise	14 Gray's Inn Square, London	0171 242 0858
Brazil Dominic Thomas George	14 Gray's Inn Square, London	0171 242 0858
Brody Miss Karen Rachel	Deans Court Chambers, Manchester	0161 834 4097
	Deans Court Chambers, Preston	01772 555163
Brown David Charles	Cathedral Chambers, Newcastle upon Tyne	0191 232 1311
	Southsea Chambers, Portsmouth	01705 291261
Brown Miss Joanne	2 Gray's Inn Square Chambers, London	0171 242 0328/405 1317

Brown Miss Rebecca Jane	14 Gray's Inn Square, London	0171 242 0858
Budden Miss Caroline Rachel	One King's Bench Walk, London	0171 936 1500
Bull (Donald) Roger	One Essex Court, London	0171 936 3030
Bundred Miss Gillian Sarah	Oriel Chambers, Liverpool	0151 236 7191
Burdon Michael Stewart	St Paul's House, Leeds	0113 245 5866
Burles David John	Goldsmith Building, London	0171 353 7881
Cameron Miss Barbara Alexander	Stanbrook & Henderson, London	0171 353 0101
	2 Harcourt Buildings, London	0171 583 9020
Campbell Miss Alexis Anne	Hardwicke Building, London	0171 242 2523
Carrodus Miss Gail Caroline	New Court Chambers, London	0171 831 9500
Carter Miss Rosalyn Frances	St Philip's Chambers, Birmingham	0121 246 7000
Cave Jeremy Stephen	1 Crown Office Row, London	0171 797 7500
	Crown Office Row Chambers, Brighton	01273 625625
Cave Miss Patricia Ann	7 Stone Buildings, London	0171 242 0961
Clark Miss Hazel Anne	Fenners Chambers, Cambridge	01223 368761
	Fenners Chambers, Peterborough	01733 562030
Collinson Miss Alicia Hester	Harcourt Chambers, London	0171 353 6961/7
	Harcourt Chambers, Oxford	01865 791559
Corbett Miss Michelle Jane	14 Gray's Inn Square, London	0171 242 0858
Cottage Miss Rosina	9-12 Bell Yard, London	0171 400 1800
Coulter Barry John	One Essex Court, London	0171 936 3030
Crane Miss Suzanne Denise	New Court Chambers, Birmingham	0121 693 6656
Crookes Miss Alison Naomi		
Cross Mrs Joanna	9 Woodhouse Square, Leeds	0113 245 1986
Crosthwaite Graham Andrew	One King's Bench Walk, London	0171 936 1500
Crowley Mrs Jane Elizabeth	One Garden Court Family Law Chambers, London	0171 797 7900
	30 Park Place, Cardiff	01222 398421
Dangor Mrs Patricia Madree Trenton	14 Gray's Inn Square, London	0171 242 0858
Davidson Miss Katharine Mary	1 Mitre Court Buildings, London	0171 797 7070
Davies Miss Lindsay Jane	Fenners Chambers, Cambridge	01223 368761
	Fenners Chambers, Peterborough	01733 562030
Davies Miss Penny May	Chambers of Harjit Singh, London	0171 353 1356
De Zonie Miss Jane	14 Gray's Inn Square, London	0171 242 0858
Dhaliwal Miss Davinder Kaur	New Court Chambers, Birmingham	0121 693 6656
Dixon John Watts	Harcourt Chambers, London	0171 353 6961/7
	Harcourt Chambers, Oxford	01865 791559
Dodson Miss Joanna	14 Gray's Inn Square, London	0171 242 0858
	Park Court Chambers, Leeds	0113 243 3277
Downham Miss Gillian Celia	Rougemont Chambers, Exeter	01392 410471
Dubbery Mark Edward	Pump Court Chambers, London	0171 353 0711
Duffy Derek James	St Paul's House, Leeds	0113 245 5866
Eccles Hugh William Patrick	Harcourt Chambers, London	0171 353 6961/7
	Harcourt Chambers, Oxford	01865 791559
Edwards Anthony Howard	Oriel Chambers, Liverpool	0151 236 7191
Elvidge John Allan	1 Mitre Court Buildings, London	0171 797 7070
Emanuel Mark Pering Wolff	14 Gray's Inn Square, London	0171 242 0858
Espley Miss Susan	Fenners Chambers, Cambridge	01223 368761
	Fenners Chambers, Peterborough	01733 562030
Evans Miss Delyth Mary	2 Mitre Court Buildings, London	0171 353 1353
Evans Miss Lisa Claire	St Philip's Chambers, Birmingham	0121 246 7000
Evans Miss Suzanne Marie	Oriel Chambers, Liverpool	0151 236 7191
Everall Mark Andrew	1 Mitre Court Buildings, London	0171 797 7070
Fane Miss Angela Elizabeth	Goldsmith Building, London	0171 353 7881
Farmer Pryce Michael	1 Dr Johnson's Buildings, London	0171 353 9328
	Goldsmith Building, London	0171 353 7881
	Sedan House, Chester	01244 320480/348282
Farquharson Miss Jane Caroline	One Essex Court, London	0171 936 3030
Fenston Miss Felicia Donovan	Stanbrook & Henderson, London	0171 353 0101
	2 Harcourt Buildings, London	0171 583 9020
Ferguson Mrs Katharine Ann	Fenners Chambers, Cambridge	01223 368761
	Fenners Chambers, Peterborough	01733 562030
Fletcher Marcus Alexander	One King's Bench Walk, London	0171 936 1500
Fogarty Peter Dominic	Oriel Chambers, Liverpool	0151 236 7191
Forbes Peter George	6 Pump Court, London	0171 797 8400
	6-8 Mill Street, Maidstone	01622 688 094
Ford Gerard James	Baker Street Chambers, Middlesbrough	01642 873873
Ford Miss Monica Dorothy Patience	14 Gray's Inn Square, London	0171 242 0858
Forster Ms Sarah Judith	14 Gray's Inn Square, London	0171 242 0858
	Westgate Chambers, Lewes	01273 480 510

B

Fox Miss Anna Katherine Helen	Oriel Chambers, Liverpool	0151 236 7191
Fox Miss Nicola Susan	One Garden Court Family Law Chambers, London	0171 797 7900
Frazer Christopher Mark	Harcourt Chambers, London	0171 353 6961/7
	Harcourt Chambers, Oxford	01865 791559
Freeston Miss Lynn Roberta		
Fricker Mrs Marilyn Ann	Farrar's Building, London	0171 583 9241
	Sovereign Chambers, Leeds	0113 245 1841/2/3
Fuad Kerim	Chambers of Helen Grindrod QC, London	0171 404 4777
Furminger Michael Ashley	Michael Furminger, Brixham	01803 882293
Gibb Miss Fiona Margaret	Queen Elizabeth Building, London	0171 353 7181 (12 lines)
Gifford Miss Cynthia Alice Sophie	Verulam Chambers, London	0171 813 2400
Gilbertson Mrs Helen Alison	Sackville Chambers, Norwich	01603 613516
Gillibrand Philip Martin Mangnall	Pump Court Chambers, London	0171 353 0711
	Pump Court Chambers, Winchester	01962 868161
Godfrey John Paul	Wilberforce Chambers, Hull	01482 323 264
Godfrey Miss Louise Sarah	14 Gray's Inn Square, London	0171 242 0858
	Park Court Chambers, Leeds	0113 243 3277
Goodchild Mrs Elizabeth Ann	Watford Chambers, Watford	01923 220553
Goodwin Nicholas Alexander John	Harcourt Chambers, London	0171 353 6961/7
Gordon-Saker Mrs Liza Helen	Fenners Chambers, Cambridge	01223 368761
	Fenners Chambers, Peterborough	01733 562030
Gorna Miss Anne Christina	4 Paper Buildings, London	0171 353 3366/583 7155
	Cathedral Chambers (Jan Wood Independent Barristers' Clerk), Exeter	01392 210900
Gray Miss Jennifer	11 Old Square, London	0171 242 5022
Greene Paul Martin	Earl Street Chambers, Maidstone	01622 671222
Gregory Richard Hamilton	Harcourt Chambers, London	0171 353 6961/7
Grice Miss Joanna Harrison	One King's Bench Walk, London	0171 936 1500
Hall Miss Joanna Mary	14 Gray's Inn Square, London	0171 242 0858
Hanson Timothy Vincent Richard	St Philip's Chambers, Birmingham	0121 246 7000
Harpwood Mrs Vivienne Margaret	30 Park Place, Cardiff	01222 398421
Harrison Ms Averil	2 Harcourt Buildings, London	0171 583 9020
Hartley-Davies Paul Kevil	30 Park Place, Cardiff	01222 398421
Hayes John Allan	Chambers of Andrew Campbell QC, Leeds	0113 245 5438
Heaton Miss Frances Margaret	4 Brick Court, London	0171 797 7766
	Deans Court Chambers, Manchester	0161 834 4097
	Deans Court Chambers, Preston	01772 555163
Hilder Miss Carolyn Hayley-Jane	3 Fountain Court, Birmingham	0121 236 5854
Hodgson Ms Jane	9 Woodhouse Square, Leeds	0113 245 1986
Hogg The Rt Hon Douglas Martin	4 Paper Buildings, London	0171 353 3366/583 7155
	37 Park Square, Leeds	0113 243 9422
Hollingworth Peter James Michael	22 Albion Place, Northampton	01604 636271
Horton Miss Caroline Ann	Fenners Chambers, Cambridge	01223 368761
	Fenners Chambers, Peterborough	01733 562030
Horwood Miss Anya Louise	25-27 Castle Street, Liverpool	0151 227 5661/5666/236 5072
Howard Charles Anthony Frederick	New Court Chambers, London	0171 831 9500
Howard Graham John	Queen Elizabeth Building, London	0171 353 7181 (12 lines)
Howe Miss Penelope Anne Macgregor	Pump Court Chambers, London	0171 353 0711
Hoyal Ms Jane	• 1 Pump Court, London	0171 583 2012/353 4341
Hudson Miss Kathryn Jane	14 Gray's Inn Square, London	0171 242 0858
Hughes Miss Meryl Elizabeth	Fenners Chambers, Cambridge	01223 368761
	Fenners Chambers, Peterborough	01733 562030
Hull Leslie David	Chambers of John Hand QC, Manchester	0161 955 9000
Humberstone Mrs Pearl Edith	Verulam Chambers, London	0171 813 2400
Hunt Miss Alison Janet	St Paul's House, Leeds	0113 245 5866
Hussain Miss Frida Khanam	17 Carlton Crescent, Southampton	01703 320320
Iqbal Abdul Shaffaq	Chambers of Andrew Campbell QC, Leeds	0113 245 5438
Irving Miss Gillian	Chambers of John Hand QC, Manchester	0161 955 9000
Islam-Choudhury Mugni	11 Bolt Court, London	0171 353 2300
Iwi Quintin Joseph	Stanbrook & Henderson, London	0171 353 0101
	2 Harcourt Buildings, London	0171 583 9020
Jarman Mark Christopher	14 Gray's Inn Square, London	0171 242 0858
Jay Adam Marc	One King's Bench Walk, London	0171 936 1500
Jenkala Adrian Aleksander	11 Bolt Court, London	0171 353 2300

	Redhill Chambers, Redhill	01737 780781
John Peter Charles	One Essex Court, London	0171 936 3030
Kalsi Mrs Maninder	New Court Chambers, Birmingham	0121 693 6656
Kenward Timothy David Nelson	25–27 Castle Street, Liverpool	0151 227 5661/5666/236 5072
Ker-Reid John	Pump Court Chambers, London	0171 353 0711
	Pump Court Chambers, Winchester	01962 868161
Khan Miss Helen Mary Grace	Chambers of Lord Campbell of Alloway QC, London	0171 353 9276
Khan Saadallah Frans Hassan	55 Temple Chambers, London	0171 353 7400
King Miss Samantha Leonie	14 Gray's Inn Square, London	0171 242 0858
Kinnier Andrew John	2 Harcourt Buildings, London	0171 583 9020
Lander Charles Gideon	25–27 Castle Street, Liverpool	0151 227 5661/5666/236 5072
Langridge Ms Nicola Dawn	Hardwicke Building, London	0171 242 2523
Leigh-Morgan (David) Paul	Fenners Chambers, Cambridge	01223 368761
	Fenners Chambers, Peterborough	01733 562030
Levy Allan Edward	17 Bedford Row, London	0171 831 7314
Lewis Robert		
Litherland Miss Rebecca Jane	Fenners Chambers, Cambridge	01223 368761
	Fenners Chambers, Peterborough	01733 562030
Lloyd Miss Wendy-Jane	25–27 Castle Street, Liverpool	0151 227 5661/5666/236 5072
Lochrane Damien Horatio Ross	Pump Court Chambers, London	0171 353 0711
	Pump Court Chambers, Winchester	01962 868161
Logan Miss Maura	St John's Chambers, Hale Barns	0161 980 7379
Lunt Steven	9 Woodhouse Square, Leeds	0113 245 1986
Lynch Terry John	22 Albion Place, Northampton	01604 636271
Lyne Mark Hilary	One Essex Court, London	0171 936 3030
Lyon Stephen John	14 Gray's Inn Square, London	0171 242 0858
	Westgate Chambers, Lewes	01273 480 510
MacKillop Norman Malcolm	• Chartlands Chambers, Northampton	01604 603322
Manson Miss Julie-Ann	11 Bolt Court, London	0171 353 2300
	Redhill Chambers, Redhill	01737 780781
Marley Miss Sarah Anne	5 Pump Court, London	0171 353 2532
Marshall Philip John	One King's Bench Walk, London	0171 936 1500
Mathew Miss Nergis-Anne	2 Gray's Inn Square Chambers, London	0171 242 0328/405 1317
Mathews Deni	8 Fountain Court, Birmingham	0121 236 5514
Matthews Mrs Ann Marie	King's Bench Chambers, Bournemouth	01202 250025
McAllister Miss Eimear Jane	9 Woodhouse Square, Leeds	0113 245 1986
McFarlane Andrew Ewart	One King's Bench Walk, London	0171 936 1500
	Priory Chambers, Birmingham	0121 236 3882/1375
McGahey Miss Elizabeth Clare	30 Park Place, Cardiff	01222 398421
McGrath Miss Elizabeth Ann	St Philip's Chambers, Birmingham	0121 246 7000
McKenna Miss Anna Louise	Queen Elizabeth Building, London	0171 353 7181 (12 lines)
McLachlan David Robert		
McMinn Miss Valerie Kathleen	Baker Street Chambers, Middlesbrough	01642 873873
McNab Miss Mhairi Shuna Elspeth	14 Gray's Inn Square, London	0171 242 0858
Meachin Miss (Sarah) Vanessa Veronica	St Philip's Chambers, Birmingham	0121 246 7000
Merry Hugh Gairns	17 Carlton Crescent, Southampton	01703 320320
Miller Miss Jane Elizabeth Mackay	Pump Court Chambers, London	0171 353 0711
	Pump Court Chambers, Winchester	01962 868161
Mitchell Miss Juliana Marie	2 Harcourt Buildings, London	0171 583 9020
Moores Timothy Kieron	17 Carlton Crescent, Southampton	01703 320320
Morris Miss Brenda Alison	14 Gray's Inn Square, London	0171 242 0858
Moseley Miss Julie Ruth	St Philip's Chambers, Birmingham	0121 246 7000
Mulholland Ms Kathryn Shona	One King's Bench Walk, London	0171 936 1500
Munday Miss Anne Margaret	8 King's Bench Walk, London	0171 797 8888
	Tribune House Chambers, York	01904 630448
Murfitt Miss Catriona Anne Campbell	1 Mitre Court Buildings, London	0171 797 7070
Murray Ashley Charles	Oriel Chambers, Liverpool	0151 236 7191
Newton Miss Claire Elaine Maria Bailey	Goldsmith Building, London	0171 353 7881
Nicholls Mrs (Deborah) Jane	Oriel Chambers, Liverpool	0151 236 7191
Nicol-Gent William Philip Trahair	King's Chambers, Eastbourne	01323 416053
O'Flynn Timothy James	Pump Court Chambers, London	0171 353 0711
O'Sullivan Bernard Anthony	Stanbrook & Henderson, London	0171 353 0101
	2 Harcourt Buildings, London	0171 583 9020
Okoye Miss Joy Nwamala	Chambers of Joy Okoye, London	0171 405 7011
Ong Miss Grace Yu Mae	One Essex Court, London	0171 936 3030
Parker John	2 Mitre Court Buildings, London	0171 353 1353

Parr Ms Judith Margaret	2 Gray's Inn Square Chambers, London	0171 242 0328/405 1317
Pema Anesh Bhumin Laloo	9 Woodhouse Square, Leeds	0113 245 1986
Pithers Clive Robert	Fenners Chambers, Cambridge	01223 368761
	Fenners Chambers, Peterborough	01733 562030
Porter Miss Sarah Ruth	11 Bolt Court, London	0171 353 2300
Portnoy Leslie Reuben	Chambers of John Hand QC, Manchester	0161 955 9000
Posnansky Jeremy Ross Leon	1 Mitre Court Buildings, London	0171 797 7070
	Southernhay Chambers, Exeter	01392 255777
Posner Miss Gabrielle Jan	2 Gray's Inn Square Chambers, London	0171 242 0328/405 1317
Potter Miss Louise	1 Mitre Court Buildings, London	0171 797 7070
Poyer-Sleeman Ms Patricia	Pump Court Chambers, London	0171 353 0711
	Pump Court Chambers, Winchester	01962 868161
Priestley Ms Rebecca Janet	2 Gray's Inn Square Chambers, London	0171 242 0328/405 1317
Purdie Robert Anthony James	28 Western Road, Oxford	01865 204911
Pye Miss Margaret Jane	Sovereign Chambers, Leeds	0113 245 1841/2/3
Ramsahoye Miss Indira Kim	Hardwicke Building, London	0171 242 2523
Rayson Miss Jane Vivienne	2 Gray's Inn Square Chambers, London	0171 242 0328/405 1317
Reddish John Wilson	One King's Bench Walk, London	0171 936 1500
Reid Miss Caroline Oldcorn	14 Gray's Inn Square, London	0171 242 0858
Rice Christopher Douglas	2 Gray's Inn Square Chambers, London	0171 242 0328/405 1317
Richardson Garth Douglas Anthony	3 Paper Buildings, London	0171 583 8055
	20 Lorne Park Road, Bournemouth	01202 292102
	4 St Peter Street, Winchester	01962 868 884
Rigby Miss Charity Elizabeth	Sovereign Chambers, Leeds	0113 245 1841/2/3
Riley Miss Christine Anne	Chambers of John Hand QC, Manchester	0161 955 9000
Robinson Richard John	2 Gray's Inn Square Chambers, London	0171 242 0328/405 1317
Rodgers Miss Doris June	Harcourt Chambers, London	0171 353 6961/7
	Harcourt Chambers, Oxford	01865 791559
Rose Jonathan Lee	St Paul's House, Leeds	0113 245 5866
Ryan Miss Eithne Mary Catherine	Hardwicke Building, London	0171 242 2523
Samuels Leslie John	Pump Court Chambers, London	0171 353 0711
	Pump Court Chambers, Winchester	01962 868161
Sandiford Jonathan	St Paul's House, Leeds	0113 245 5866
Saxton Miss Nicola Helen	St Paul's House, Leeds	0113 245 5866
Scarratt Richard John	One Garden Court Family Law Chambers, London	0171 797 7900
Scott Miss Alexandra Elisabeth	2 New Street, Leicester	0116 262 5906
Scutt David Robert	11 Bolt Court, London	0171 353 2300
	Redhill Chambers, Redhill	01737 780781
Selman Miss Elizabeth	One King's Bench Walk, London	0171 936 1500
Shaikh Eur.Ing. (Jaikumar) Christopher (Samuel	Avondale Chambers, London	0181 445 9984
	Equity Chambers, Birmingham	0121 233 2100
Sheehan Malcolm Peter	Stanbrook & Henderson, London	0171 353 0101
	2 Harcourt Buildings, London	0171 583 9020
Singh Balbir	• Equity Chambers, Birmingham	0121 233 2100
Sleeman Miss Rachel Sarah Elizabeth	One Essex Court, London	0171 936 3030
Slomnicka Miss Barbara Irena	14 Gray's Inn Square, London	0171 242 0858
Somerset-Jones Miss Felicity	Oriel Chambers, Liverpool	0151 236 7191
Spain Timothy Harrisson	Trinity Chambers, Newcastle upon Tyne	0191 232 1927
Sparks Kevin Laurence	Earl Street Chambers, Maidstone	01622 671222
Spencer Miss Hannah Katya	5 Pump Court, London	0171 353 2532
	Chambers of John Hand QC, Manchester	0161 955 9000
Spollon Guy Merton	St Philip's Chambers, Birmingham	0121 246 7000
Spon-Smith Robin Witterick	1 Mitre Court Buildings, London	0171 797 7070
Staite Miss Sara Elizabeth	Stanbrook & Henderson, London	0171 353 0101
	2 Harcourt Buildings, London	0171 583 9020
Starks Nicholas Ernshaw	8 Fountain Court, Birmingham	0121 236 5514
Stead Miss Kate Rebecca	Barristers' Common Law Chambers, London	0171 375 3012
Stewart Mark Courtney	College Chambers, Southampton	01703 230338

• Expanded entry in Part D

Stonor Nicholas William	Trinity Chambers, Newcastle upon Tyne	0191 232 1927
Sutton Mrs Karoline Rosemarie	14 Gray's Inn Square, London	0171 242 0858
Temple-Bone Miss Gillian Elizabeth	7 Stone Buildings, London	0171 242 0961
Thompson Jonathan Richard	8 King Street Chambers, Manchester	0161 834 9560
Thornton Miss Anne Rebecca	9 Woodhouse Square, Leeds	0113 245 1986
Tod Jonathan Alan	7 Stone Buildings, London	0171 242 0961
Townend James Barrie Stanley	One King's Bench Walk, London	0171 936 1500
Travers Hugh	Pump Court Chambers, London	0171 353 0711
	Pump Court Chambers, Winchester	01962 868161
Trowell Stephen Mark	1 Mitre Court Buildings, London	0171 797 7070
Tucker Miss Katherine Jane Greening	St Philip's Chambers, Birmingham	0121 246 7000
Turner David George Patrick	14 Gray's Inn Square, London	0171 242 0858
Turner James	One King's Bench Walk, London	0171 936 1500
Tyack David Guy	St Philip's Chambers, Birmingham	0121 246 7000
Valks Michael	King's Chambers, Eastbourne	01323 416053
Vater John Alistair Pitt	Harcourt Chambers, London	0171 353 6961/7
Vavrecka David Paul Frank	14 Gray's Inn Square, London	0171 242 0858
Vincent Miss Ruth Carolyn	Colleton Chambers, Exeter	01392 274898
Vine Aidan James Wilson	Harcourt Chambers, London	0171 353 6961/7
	Harcourt Chambers, Oxford	01865 791559
Waddington Mrs Anne Louise	Pump Court Chambers, London	0171 353 0711
	Pump Court Chambers, Winchester	01962 868161
Waley Eric Richard Thomas	Assize Court Chambers, Bristol	0117 926 4587
Walker Miss Jane	Chambers of John Hand QC, Manchester	0161 955 9000
Walters Gareth Rupel	St Philip's Chambers, Birmingham	0121 246 7000
Warner Miss Sharan Pamela	14 Gray's Inn Square, London	0171 242 0858
Warshaw Justin Alexander Edward	1 Mitre Court Buildings, London	0171 797 7070
Watson Mark	6 Pump Court, London	0171 797 8400
	6-8 Mill Street, Maidstone	01622 688 094
White Peter-John Spencer	Pembroke House, Leatherhead	01372 376160/376493
White Mrs Tanya	Pembroke House, Leatherhead	01372 376160/376493
Whittam Ms Samantha Abigail	14 Gray's Inn Square, London	0171 242 0858
Williams Hugh David Haydn	St Philip's Chambers, Birmingham	0121 246 7000
Woodward Nicholas Frederick	White Friars Chambers, Chester	01244 323070
Woolman Andrew Paul Lander	Chambers of Andrew Campbell QC, Leeds	0113 245 5438
Woolrich Miss Sarah	Trinity Chambers, Newcastle upon Tyne	0191 232 1927
Wordsworth Mrs Philippa Lindsey	Chambers of Andrew Campbell QC, Leeds	0113 245 5438
Worrall John Raymond Guy	Chambers of Andrew Campbell QC, Leeds	0113 245 5438
Wright Gerard Henry	25-27 Castle Street, Liverpool	0151 227 5661/5666/236 5072
Wright Ms Sadie	Goldsmith Building, London	0171 353 7881
Wyatt Guy Peter James	Earl Street Chambers, Maidstone	01622 671222
Yates Nicholas Gilmore	1 Mitre Court Buildings, London	0171 797 7070
Yeung Stuart Roy	22 Albion Place, Northampton	01604 636271
Zornoza Miss Isabella	Stanbrook & Henderson, London	0171 353 0101
	2 Harcourt Buildings, London	0171 583 9020

CASES WITH A WELSH LANGUAGE ELEMENT

Bush Keith	30 Park Place, Cardiff	01222 398421

CHANCERY (GENERAL)

Abbott Alistair James Hugh	5 New Square, London	0171 404 0404
Adamyk Simon Charles	12 New Square, London	0171 419 1212
Adejumo Mrs Hilda Ekpo	• Temple Chambers, London	0171 583 1001 (2 lines)
Airey Simon Andrew	11 Bolt Court, London	0171 353 2300
	Redhill Chambers, Redhill	01737 780781
Al'Hassan Khadim	Equity Chambers, Birmingham	0121 233 2100
Aldridge James Hugh	13 Old Square, London	0171 404 4800
Alexander Ian Douglas Gavin	11 Bolt Court, London	0171 353 2300
	Redhill Chambers, Redhill	01737 780781
Amin Miss Farah	7 New Square, London	0171 430 1660
Angus Miss Tracey Anne	5 Stone Buildings, London	0171 242 6201
Arden Peter Leonard	Enterprise Chambers, London	0171 405 9471
	Enterprise Chambers, Leeds	0113 246 0391

	Enterprise Chambers, Newcastle upon Tyne	0191 222 3344
Arnfield Robert John	17 Old Buildings, London	0171 405 9653
Asplin Miss Sarah Jane	• 3 Stone Buildings, London	0171 242 4937/405 8358
Atherton Ian David	Enterprise Chambers, London	0171 405 9471
	Enterprise Chambers, Leeds	0113 246 0391
	Enterprise Chambers, Newcastle upon Tyne	0191 222 3344
Aylen Walter Stafford	Hardwicke Building, London	0171 242 2523
Ayres Andrew John William	13 Old Square, London	0171 404 4800
Baker Miss Anne Jacqueline	Enterprise Chambers, London	0171 405 9471
	Enterprise Chambers, Leeds	0113 246 0391
	Enterprise Chambers, Newcastle upon Tyne	0191 222 3344
Barber Miss Sally	5 Stone Buildings, London	0171 242 6201
Barker James Sebastian	Enterprise Chambers, London	0171 405 9471
	Enterprise Chambers, Leeds	0113 246 0391
	Enterprise Chambers, Newcastle upon Tyne	0191 222 3344
Barnes (David) Michael (William)	4 Breams Buildings, London	0171 353 5835/430 1221
Barstow Stephen Royden	Harcourt Chambers, London	0171 353 6961/7
	Harcourt Chambers, Oxford	01865 791559
Benson Julian Christopher Woodburn	One Essex Court, London	0171 936 3030
Berkley Michael Stuart	Rougemont Chambers, Exeter	01392 410471
Bhaloo Miss Zia Kurban	Enterprise Chambers, London	0171 405 9471
	Enterprise Chambers, Leeds	0113 246 0391
	Enterprise Chambers, Newcastle upon Tyne	0191 222 3344
Bird Nigel David	Chambers of John Hand QC, Manchester	0161 955 9000
Blackett-Ord Mark	• 5 Stone Buildings, London	0171 242 6201
Brannigan Peter John Sean	One Essex Court, London	0171 936 3030
Brownbill David John	Gray's Inn Square, London	0171 242 3529
Browne Miss Julie Rebecca	Goldsmith Building, London	0171 353 7881
Burroughs Nigel Alfred	11 Old Square, London	0171 430 0341
Burton Michael John	Littleton Chambers, London	0171 797 8600
Cameron Miss Barbara Alexander	Stanbrook & Henderson, London	0171 353 0101
	2 Harcourt Buildings, London	0171 583 9020
Carey Jeremy Reynolds Patrick	Lamb Chambers, London	0171 797 8300
Cawley Neil Robert Loudoun	55 Temple Chambers, London	0171 353 7400
	Milton Keynes Chambers, Milton Keynes	01908 217857
Cawson Mark	• 12 New Square, London	0171 419 1212
	• St James's Chambers, Manchester	0161 834 7000
	• Park Lane Chambers, Leeds	0113 228 5000
Charman Andrew Julian	St Philip's Chambers, Birmingham	0121 246 7000
Cherryman John Richard	4 Breams Buildings, London	0171 353 5835/430 1221
Clark Ms Julia Elisabeth	5 New Square, London	0171 404 0404
Clarke Miss Anna Victoria	5 Stone Buildings, London	0171 242 6201
Clarke Ian James	Hardwicke Building, London	0171 242 2523
Clegg Sebastian James Barwick	Deans Court Chambers, Manchester	0161 834 4097
Collaco Moraes Francis Thomas	• 2 Gray's Inn Square Chambers, London	0171 242 0328/405 1317
Collins John Morris	11 King's Bench Walk, London	0171 353 3337/8
	9 Woodhouse Square, Leeds	0113 245 1986
Conroy Miss Marian	3 Stone Buildings, London	0171 242 4937/405 8358
Cooper Adrian Edgar Mark	Stanbrook & Henderson, London	0171 353 0101
	2 Harcourt Buildings, London	0171 583 9020
Corbett James Patrick	St Philip's Chambers, Birmingham	0121 246 7000
Coulter Barry John	One Essex Court, London	0171 936 3030
Craig Kenneth Allen	Hardwicke Building, London	0171 242 2523
Crail Miss (Elspeth) Ross	12 New Square, London	0171 419 1212
	Sovereign Chambers, Leeds	0113 245 1841/2/3
Cranfield Peter Anthony	3 Verulam Buildings, London	0171 831 8441
Crawford Grant	11 Old Square, London	0171 430 0341
Creaner Paul Anthony	15 Winckley Square, Preston	01772 252 828
Cunningham Miss Claire Louise	St Philip's Chambers, Birmingham	0121 246 7000
Cunningham Mark James	13 Old Square, London	0171 404 4800
Darbyshire William Robert	Chambers of John Hand QC, Manchester	0161 955 9000
Davidson Edward Alan	• 11 Old Square, London	0171 430 0341
Davies Miss Louise	12 New Square, London	0171 419 1212

• Expanded entry in Part D

de Jehan David	St Paul's House, Leeds	0113 245 5866
Deacock Adam Jason	Chambers of Lord Goodhart QC, London	0171 405 5577
Dedezade Taner	Tindal Chambers, Chelmsford	01245 267742
Dineen Michael Laurence	Pump Court Chambers, London	0171 353 0711
	All Saints Chambers, Bristol	0117 921 1966
	Pump Court Chambers, Winchester	01962 868161
Dodge Peter Clive	11 Old Square, London	0171 430 0341
Dowse John	Chambers of Lord Goodhart QC, London	0171 405 5577
	Chambers of John Hand QC, Manchester	0161 955 9000
Doyle Louis George	Chambers of Andrew Campbell QC, Leeds	0113 245 5438
Driscoll Miss Lynn	Sovereign Chambers, Leeds	0113 245 1841/2/3
	Lancaster Buildings, Manchester	0161 661 4444
Elleray Anthony John	• 12 New Square, London	0171 419 1212
	• St James's Chambers, Manchester	0161 834 7000
	• Park Lane Chambers, Leeds	0113 228 5000
Emanuel Mark Pering Wolff	14 Gray's Inn Square, London	0171 242 0858
Evans-Gordon Mrs Jane-Anne Mary	12 New Square, London	0171 419 1212
Fawls Richard Granville	5 Stone Buildings, London	0171 242 6201
Fernandes John Piedade Amaranto Lorencio	• Arcadia Chambers, London	0171 938 1285
Ferrier Ian Gilbert Straton	Gray's Inn Square, London	0171 242 3529
Finlay Darren	Sovereign Chambers, Leeds	0113 245 1841/2/3
Francis Edward Gerald Francis	Enterprise Chambers, London	0171 405 9471
	Enterprise Chambers, Leeds	0113 246 0391
	Enterprise Chambers, Newcastle upon Tyne	0191 222 3344
Franklin Stephen Hall	5 Paper Buildings, London	0171 583 6117
	Fenners Chambers, Cambridge	01223 368761
Garcia-Miller Miss Laura	Enterprise Chambers, London	0171 405 9471
	Enterprise Chambers, Leeds	0113 246 0391
	Enterprise Chambers, Newcastle upon Tyne	0191 222 3344
Garnett Kevin Mitchell	5 New Square, London	0171 404 0404
Geering Ian Walter	3 Verulam Buildings, London	0171 831 8441
George Miss Judith Sarah	St Philip's Chambers, Birmingham	0121 246 7000
Gerald Nigel Mortimer	Enterprise Chambers, London	0171 405 9471
	Enterprise Chambers, Leeds	0113 246 0391
	Enterprise Chambers, Newcastle upon Tyne	0191 222 3344
Gibaud Miss Catherine Alison Annetta	3 Verulam Buildings, London	0171 831 8441
Gilchrist David Somerled	Chambers of John Hand QC, Manchester	0161 955 9000
Goodhart Lord	Chambers of Lord Goodhart QC, London	0171 405 5577
Gore Andrew Roger	Fenners Chambers, Cambridge	01223 368761
	Fenners Chambers, Peterborough	01733 562030
Grantham Andrew Timothy	• Deans Court Chambers, Manchester	0161 834 4097
	• Deans Court Chambers, Preston	01772 555163
Grayson Edward	• 9-12 Bell Yard, London	0171 400 1800
Gregory John Raymond	Deans Court Chambers, Manchester	0161 834 4097
	Deans Court Chambers, Preston	01772 555163
Griffiths Peter Robert	4 Stone Buildings, London	0171 242 5524
Groves Hugo Gerard	Enterprise Chambers, London	0171 405 9471
	Enterprise Chambers, Leeds	0113 246 0391
	Enterprise Chambers, Newcastle upon Tyne	0191 222 3344
Hall Taylor Alexander Edward	11 Old Square, London	0171 430 0341
Halpern David Anthony	Enterprise Chambers, London	0171 405 9471
	Enterprise Chambers, Leeds	0113 246 0391
	Enterprise Chambers, Newcastle upon Tyne	0191 222 3344
Hamer Michael Howard Kenneth	2 Harcourt Buildings, London	0171 583 9020
	Westgate Chambers, Lewes	01273 480 510
Hantusch Robert Anthony	• 3 Stone Buildings, London	0171 242 4937/405 8358
Harbottle Gwilym Thomas	5 New Square, London	0171 404 0404
Hardwick Matthew Richard	Enterprise Chambers, London	0171 405 9471
	Enterprise Chambers, Leeds	0113 246 0391

B

• Expanded entry in Part D

	Enterprise Chambers, Newcastle upon Tyne	0191 222 3344
Hargreaves Miss Sara Jane	12 New Square, London	0171 419 1212
	Sovereign Chambers, Leeds	0113 245 1841/2/3
Harrod Henry Mark	5 Stone Buildings, London	0171 242 6201
Hayes John Allan	Chambers of Andrew Campbell QC, Leeds	0113 245 5438
Hayes Miss Josephine Mary	Chambers of Lord Goodhart QC, London	0171 405 5577
Heap Gerard Miles	Sovereign Chambers, Leeds	0113 245 1841/2/3
Herbert Mark Jeremy	• 5 Stone Buildings, London	0171 242 6201
Heywood Michael Edmundson	Chambers of Lord Goodhart QC, London	0171 405 5577
	Cobden House Chambers, Manchester	0161 833 6000/6001
Holmes Justin Francis	Chambers of Lord Goodhart QC, London	0171 405 5577
Hughes Miss Mary Josephine	Chambers of Lord Goodhart QC, London	0171 405 5577
Hunter William Quigley	No 1 Serjeants' Inn, London	0171 415 6666
Hurst Brian	17 Bedford Row, London	0171 831 7314
Hutton Miss Caroline	Enterprise Chambers, London	0171 405 9471
	Enterprise Chambers, Leeds	0113 246 0391
	Enterprise Chambers, Newcastle upon Tyne	0191 222 3344
Ife Miss Linden Elizabeth	Enterprise Chambers, London	0171 405 9471
	Enterprise Chambers, Leeds	0113 246 0391
	Enterprise Chambers, Newcastle upon Tyne	0191 222 3344
Iwi Quintin Joseph	Stanbrook & Henderson, London	0171 353 0101
	2 Harcourt Buildings, London	0171 583 9020
Jack Adrian Laurence Robert	Enterprise Chambers, London	0171 405 9471
Jackson Dirik George Allan	• Chambers of Mr Peter Crampin QC, London	0171 831 0081
Jackson Nicholas David Kingsley	The Chambers of Adrian Lyon, Liverpool	0151 236 4421/8240/6757
James Michael Frank	Enterprise Chambers, London	0171 405 9471
	Enterprise Chambers, Leeds	0113 246 0391
	Enterprise Chambers, Newcastle upon Tyne	0191 222 3344
Jarvis John Manners	3 Verulam Buildings, London	0171 831 8441
Jefferies Thomas Robert	Chambers of Lord Goodhart QC, London	0171 405 5577
Jenkala Adrian Aleksander	11 Bolt Court, London	0171 353 2300
	Redhill Chambers, Redhill	01737 780781
Jennings Timothy Robin Finnegan	Enterprise Chambers, London	0171 405 9471
	Enterprise Chambers, Leeds	0113 246 0391
	Enterprise Chambers, Newcastle upon Tyne	0191 222 3344
John Peter Charles	One Essex Court, London	0171 936 3030
Johnson Michael Sloan	Chambers of John Hand QC, Manchester	0161 955 9000
Jones Geraint Martyn	Fenners Chambers, Cambridge	01223 368761
	Fenners Chambers, Peterborough	01733 562030
Jones Gregory Percy	• 2 Harcourt Buildings, London	0171 353 8415
Jory Robert John Hugh	Enterprise Chambers, London	0171 405 9471
	Enterprise Chambers, Leeds	0113 246 0391
	Enterprise Chambers, Newcastle upon Tyne	0191 222 3344
Joss Norman James	One Essex Court, London	0171 936 3030
Kirby Peter John	• Hardwicke Building, London	0171 242 2523
Knott Malcolm Stephen	New Court Chambers, London	0171 831 9500
Kolodziej Andrzej Jozef	• Littman Chambers, London	0171 404 4866
Kremen Philip Michael	Hardwicke Building, London	0171 242 2523
Lamont Miss Camilla Rose	Chambers of Lord Goodhart QC, London	0171 405 5577
Landes Miss Anna-Rose	St Philip's Chambers, Birmingham	0121 246 7000
Laughton Samuel Dennis	17 Old Buildings, London	0171 405 9653
Le Poidevin Nicholas Peter	12 New Square, London	0171 419 1212
	Sovereign Chambers, Leeds	0113 245 1841/2/3
Leeming Ian	Lamb Chambers, London	0171 797 8300
	Chambers of John Hand QC, Manchester	0161 955 9000

• Expanded entry in Part D

Legge Henry	5 Stone Buildings, London	0171 242 6201
Leiper Richard Thomas	11 King's Bench Walk, London	0171 632 8500
Levy Benjamin Keith	Enterprise Chambers, London	0171 405 9471
	Enterprise Chambers, Leeds	0113 246 0391
	Enterprise Chambers, Newcastle upon Tyne	0191 222 3344
Levy Robert Stuart	9 Stone Buildings, London	0171 404 5055
	Assize Court Chambers, Bristol	0117 926 4587
Lewis Miss Caroline Susannah	3 Verulam Buildings, London	0171 831 8441
Lobo Matthew Joseph Edwin	Fenners Chambers, Cambridge	01223 368761
	Fenners Chambers, Peterborough	01733 562030
Lonsdale Miss Marion Mary	Chambers of Geoffrey Hawker, London	0171 583 8899
Lowenstein Paul David	Littleton Chambers, London	0171 797 8600
Male John Martin	4 Breams Buildings, London	0171 353 5835/430 1221
Malecka Dr Mary Margaret	Goldsworth Chambers, London	0171 405 7117
Mann George Anthony	Enterprise Chambers, London	0171 405 9471
	Enterprise Chambers, Leeds	0113 246 0391
	Enterprise Chambers, Newcastle upon Tyne	0191 222 3344
Marten Richard Hedley Westwood	Chambers of Lord Goodhart QC, London	0171 405 5577
Mauger Miss Claire Shanti Andrea	Enterprise Chambers, London	0171 405 9471
McAllister Miss Elizabeth Ann	Enterprise Chambers, London	0171 405 9471
	Enterprise Chambers, Leeds	0113 246 0391
	Enterprise Chambers, Newcastle upon Tyne	0191 222 3344
McCarthy William	New Bailey Chambers, Preston	01772 258 087
McKinnell Miss Soraya Jane	Enterprise Chambers, London	0171 405 9471
	Enterprise Chambers, Leeds	0113 246 0391
	Enterprise Chambers, Newcastle upon Tyne	0191 222 3344
McMinn Miss Valerie Kathleen	Baker Street Chambers, Middlesbrough	01642 873873
McQuail Ms Katherine Emma	11 Old Square, London	0171 430 0341
Mendoza Neil David Pereira	Hardwicke Building, London	0171 242 2523
Morgan Charles James Arthur	Enterprise Chambers, London	0171 405 9471
	Enterprise Chambers, Leeds	0113 246 0391
	Enterprise Chambers, Newcastle upon Tyne	0191 222 3344
Morgan Edward Patrick	4 King's Bench Walk, London	0171 822 8822
	Deans Court Chambers, Manchester	0161 834 4097
Morgan Richard Hugo Lyndon	13 Old Square, London	0171 404 4800
Mullis Anthony Roger	Chambers of Lord Goodhart QC, London	0171 405 5577
Nebhrajani Miss Mel	9 Stone Buildings, London	0171 404 5055
Neville Stephen John	Gough Square Chambers, London	0171 353 0924
Newman Miss Catherine Mary	• 13 Old Square, London	0171 404 4800
Newman Ms Ingrid	Hardwicke Building, London	0171 242 2523
Nicholls John Peter	13 Old Square, London	0171 404 4800
Nicol-Gent William Philip Trahair	King's Chambers, Eastbourne	01323 416053
Noble Andrew	Eldon Chambers, London	0171 353 4636
	Merchant Chambers, Manchester	0161 839 7070
Norbury Luke Edward	17 Old Buildings, London	0171 405 9653
Norris Alastair Hubert	• 5 Stone Buildings, London	0171 242 6201
	• Southernhay Chambers, Exeter	01392 255777
Norris Paul Howard	One Essex Court, London	0171 936 3030
Nurse Gordon Bramwell William	11 Old Square, London	0171 430 0341
O'Sullivan Michael Morton	5 Stone Buildings, London	0171 242 6201
Oakley Tony	• 11 Old Square, London	0171 430 0341
Ogunbiyi Oluwole Afolabi	Horizon Chambers, London	0171 242 2440
Ohrenstein Dov	Chambers of Lord Goodhart QC, London	0171 405 5577
Ovey Miss Elizabeth Helen	11 Old Square, London	0171 430 0341
Owens Miss Hilary Jane	St Philip's Chambers, Birmingham	0121 246 7000
Parry David Julian Thomas	Chambers of Lord Goodhart QC, London	0171 405 5577
Peacock Ian Christopher	12 New Square, London	0171 419 1212
	Sovereign Chambers, Leeds	0113 245 1841/2/3
Peacock Nicholas Christopher	13 Old Square, London	0171 404 4800
Peacocke Mrs Teresa Anne Rosen	Enterprise Chambers, London	0171 405 9471
	Enterprise Chambers, Leeds	0113 246 0391

• Expanded entry in Part D

	Enterprise Chambers, Newcastle upon Tyne	0191 222 3344
Pelling Richard Alexander	New Court Chambers, London	0171 831 9500
Perkoff Richard Michael	Littleton Chambers, London	0171 797 8600
Phillips David John	199 Strand, London	0171 379 9779
	30 Park Place, Cardiff	01222 398421
Picarda Hubert Alistair Paul	Chambers of Lord Goodhart QC, London	0171 405 5577
Pickering James Patrick	Enterprise Chambers, London	0171 405 9471
	Enterprise Chambers, Leeds	0113 246 0391
	Enterprise Chambers, Newcastle upon Tyne	0191 222 3344
Pimentel Carlos de Serpa Alberto Legg	3 Stone Buildings, London	0171 242 4937/405 8358
Pryke Stuart	Trinity Chambers, Newcastle upon Tyne	0191 232 1927
Purdie Robert Anthony James	28 Western Road, Oxford	01865 204911
Quint Mrs Joan Francesca Rae	11 Old Square, London	0171 242 5022
Randall John Yeoman	7 Stone Buildings, London	0171 405 3886/242 3546
	St Philip's Chambers, Birmingham	0121 246 7000
Reed Miss Penelope Jane	9 Stone Buildings, London	0171 404 5055
Rees David Benjamin	5 Stone Buildings, London	0171 242 6201
Rich Miss Ann Barbara	5 Stone Buildings, London	0171 242 6201
Richardson Miss Sarah Jane	Enterprise Chambers, London	0171 405 9471
	Enterprise Chambers, Leeds	0113 246 0391
	Enterprise Chambers, Newcastle upon Tyne	0191 222 3344
Robson John Malcolm	2 Gray's Inn Square Chambers, London	0171 242 0328/405 1317
	Assize Court Chambers, Bristol	0117 926 4587
Ross Martyn John Greaves	• 5 New Square, London	0171 404 0404
	• Octagon House, Norwich	01603 623186
Rowell David Stewart	Chambers of Lord Goodhart QC, London	0171 405 5577
Rule Jonathan Daniel	Merchant Chambers, Manchester	0161 839 7070
Rumney Conrad William Arthur	St Philip's Chambers, Birmingham	0121 246 7000
Russell Christopher Garnet	12 New Square, London	0171 419 1212
	Sovereign Chambers, Leeds	0113 245 1841/2/3
Russen Jonathan Huw Sinclair	13 Old Square, London	0171 404 4800
Ryan David Patrick	Chambers of Geoffrey Hawker, London	0171 583 8899
Sagar (Edward) Leigh	12 New Square, London	0171 419 1212
	Sovereign Chambers, Leeds	0113 245 1841/2/3
	Newport Chambers, Newport	01633 267403/255855
Schooling Simon John	Chambers of Harjit Singh, London	0171 353 1356
Seal Julius Damien	189 Randolph Avenue, London	0171 624 9139
	3 Temple Gardens, London	0171 353 0832
Sefton Mark Thomas Dunblane	199 Strand, London	0171 379 9779
Selway Dr Katherine Emma	11 Old Square, London	0171 430 0341
Shah Bajul Amratlal Somchand	Twenty-Four Old Buildings, London	0171 404 0946
Simmonds Andrew John	5 Stone Buildings, London	0171 242 6201
Simpson Edwin John Fletcher	12 New Square, London	0171 419 1212
Sisley Timothy Julian Crispin	9 Stone Buildings, London	0171 404 5055
	Westgate Chambers, Lewes	01273 480 510
Sleeman Miss Rachel Sarah Elizabeth	One Essex Court, London	0171 936 3030
Smart Miss Jacqueline Anne	Trinity Chambers, Newcastle upon Tyne	0191 232 1927
Sparks Kevin Laurence	Earl Street Chambers, Maidstone	01622 671222
Spearman Richard	5 Raymond Buildings, London	0171 242 2902
Staddon Miss Claire Ann	12 New Square, London	0171 419 1212
	Sovereign Chambers, Leeds	0113 245 1841/2/3
Stevenson John Melford	Two Crown Office Row, London	0171 797 8100
Stewart Alexander Joseph	5 New Square, London	0171 404 0404
Stewart Nicholas John Cameron	Hardwicke Building, London	0171 242 2523
Sugar Simon Gareth	5 New Square, London	0171 404 0404
Sunnucks James Horace George	• 5 New Square, London	0171 404 0404
	• Octagon House, Norwich	01603 623186
Sutcliffe Andrew Harold Wentworth	3 Verulam Buildings, London	0171 831 8441
Sydenham Colin Peter	4 Breams Buildings, London	0171 353 5835/430 1221
Tedd Rex Hilary	• St Philip's Chambers, Birmingham	0121 246 7000
	• 22 Albion Place, Northampton	01604 636271

B

• Expanded entry in Part D

Thomas Nigel Matthew	13 Old Square, London	0171 404 4800
Thompson Steven Lim	Twenty-Four Old Buildings, London	0171 404 0946
Tidmarsh Christopher Ralph Francis	5 Stone Buildings, London	0171 242 6201
Tipples Miss Amanda Jane	13 Old Square, London	0171 404 4800
Tolaney Miss Sonia	3 Verulam Buildings, London	0171 831 8441
Trace Anthony John	• 13 Old Square, London	0171 404 4800
Tucker Miss Katherine Jane Greening	St Philip's Chambers, Birmingham	0121 246 7000
Twigger Andrew Mark	3 Stone Buildings, London	0171 242 4937/405 8358
Vane The Hon Christopher John Fletcher	Trinity Chambers, Newcastle upon Tyne	0191 232 1927
Walker Andrew Greenfield	Chambers of Lord Goodhart QC, London	0171 405 5577
Warnock-Smith Mrs Shan	5 Stone Buildings, London	0171 242 6201
Waters Malcolm Ian	• 11 Old Square, London	0171 430 0341
Weatherill Bernard Richard	Chambers of Lord Goodhart QC, London	0171 405 5577
West Mark	• 11 Old Square, London	0171 430 0341
Willer Robert Michael	Hardwicke Building, London	0171 242 2523
Wright Colin John	4 Field Court, London	0171 440 6900
Yelton Michael Paul	Fenners Chambers, Cambridge	01223 368761
	Fenners Chambers, Peterborough	01733 562030
Zelin Geoffrey Andrew	Enterprise Chambers, London	0171 405 9471
	Enterprise Chambers, Leeds	0113 246 0391
	Enterprise Chambers, Newcastle upon Tyne	0191 222 3344

CHANCERY LAND LAW

Adamyk Simon Charles	12 New Square, London	0171 419 1212
Andrews Miss Claire Marguerite	Gough Square Chambers, London	0171 353 0924
Angus Miss Tracey Anne	5 Stone Buildings, London	0171 242 6201
Arnfield Robert John	17 Old Buildings, London	0171 405 9653
Asplin Miss Sarah Jane	• 3 Stone Buildings, London	0171 242 4937/405 8358
Atherton Ian David	Enterprise Chambers, London	0171 405 9471
	Enterprise Chambers, Leeds	0113 246 0391
	Enterprise Chambers, Newcastle upon Tyne	0191 222 3344
Attala Jean Etienne	Cathedral Chambers, Newcastle upon Tyne	0191 232 1311
Ayres Andrew John William	13 Old Square, London	0171 404 4800
Baker Miss Anne Jacqueline	Enterprise Chambers, London	0171 405 9471
	Enterprise Chambers, Leeds	0113 246 0391
	Enterprise Chambers, Newcastle upon Tyne	0191 222 3344
Barber Miss Sally	5 Stone Buildings, London	0171 242 6201
Barnes (David) Michael (William)	4 Breams Buildings, London	0171 353 5835/430 1221
Beaumont Marc Clifford	• Pump Court Chambers, London	0171 353 0711
	• Harrow-on-the-Hill Chambers, Harrow on the Hill	0181 423 7444
	• Pump Court Chambers, Winchester	01962 868161
	• Windsor Barristers' Chambers, Windsor	01753 648 899
Berragan (Howard) Neil	Merchant Chambers, Manchester	0161 839 7070
Bickford-Smith Stephen William	4 Breams Buildings, London	0171 353 5835/430 1221
Bird Nigel David	Chambers of John Hand QC, Manchester	0161 955 9000
Blackett-Ord Mark	• 5 Stone Buildings, London	0171 242 6201
Bourne Charles Gregory	Stanbrook & Henderson, London	0171 353 0101
	2 Harcourt Buildings, London	0171 583 9020
Bourne Robert	• 4 Field Court, London	0171 440 6900
Brett Matthew Christopher Anthony	Harcourt Chambers, London	0171 353 6961/7
	Harcourt Chambers, Oxford	01865 791559
Brook Ian Stuart	Hardwicke Building, London	0171 242 2523
Cameron Neil Alexander	Wilberforce Chambers, Hull	01482 323 264
Campbell Oliver Edward Wilhelm	2 Harcourt Buildings, London	0171 583 9020
Cawley Neil Robert Loudoun	55 Temple Chambers, London	0171 353 7400
	Milton Keynes Chambers, Milton Keynes	01908 217857
Charman Andrew Julian	St Philip's Chambers, Birmingham	0121 246 7000
Cherryman John Richard	4 Breams Buildings, London	0171 353 5835/430 1221
Clarke Miss Anna Victoria	5 Stone Buildings, London	0171 242 6201
Clarke Ian James	Hardwicke Building, London	0171 242 2523

Clarke Peter John	Harcourt Chambers, London	0171 353 6961/7
	St Philip's Chambers, Birmingham	0121 246 7000
	Harcourt Chambers, Oxford	01865 791559
Clegg Sebastian James Barwick	Deans Court Chambers, Manchester	0161 834 4097
Collier Martin Melton	Fenners Chambers, Cambridge	01223 368761
	Fenners Chambers, Peterborough	01733 562030
Collins John Morris	11 King's Bench Walk, London	0171 353 3337/8
	9 Woodhouse Square, Leeds	0113 245 1986
Cotter Miss Sara Elizabeth	• Higher Combe, Minehead	01643 862722
Craig Kenneth Allen	Hardwicke Building, London	0171 242 2523
Crail Miss (Elspeth) Ross	12 New Square, London	0171 419 1212
	Sovereign Chambers, Leeds	0113 245 1841/2/3
Cranfield Peter Anthony	3 Verulam Buildings, London	0171 831 8441
Crawford Grant	11 Old Square, London	0171 430 0341
Cunningham Mark James	13 Old Square, London	0171 404 4800
Daiches Michael Salis	• 22 Old Buildings, London	0171 831 0222
Davies Miss Louise	12 New Square, London	0171 419 1212
de Lacy Richard Michael	3 Verulam Buildings, London	0171 831 8441
Deacock Adam Jason	Chambers of Lord Goodhart QC, London	0171 405 5577
Dedezade Taner	Tindal Chambers, Chelmsford	01245 267742
Dilhorne The Rt Hon Viscount	4 Breams Buildings, London	0171 353 5835/430 1221
Dodge Peter Clive	11 Old Square, London	0171 430 0341
Doyle Louis George	Chambers of Andrew Campbell QC, Leeds	0113 245 5438
Edwards Richard Julian Henshaw	3 Verulam Buildings, London	0171 831 8441
Elleray Anthony John	• 12 New Square, London	0171 419 1212
	• St James's Chambers, Manchester	0161 834 7000
	• Park Lane Chambers, Leeds	0113 228 5000
Elvin David John	4 Breams Buildings, London	0171 353 5835/430 1221
Evans-Gordon Mrs Jane-Anne Mary	12 New Square, London	0171 419 1212
Furber (Robert) John	4 Breams Buildings, London	0171 353 5835/430 1221
Garnett Kevin Mitchell	5 New Square, London	0171 404 0404
Gerald Nigel Mortimer	Enterprise Chambers, London	0171 405 9471
	Enterprise Chambers, Leeds	0113 246 0391
	Enterprise Chambers, Newcastle upon Tyne	0191 222 3344
Gilbert Ms Julia Jane	Trinity Chambers, Newcastle upon Tyne	0191 232 1927
Gilchrist David Somerled	Chambers of John Hand QC, Manchester	0161 955 9000
Goodhart Lord	Chambers of Lord Goodhart QC, London	0171 405 5577
Gore Andrew Roger	Fenners Chambers, Cambridge	01223 368761
	Fenners Chambers, Peterborough	01733 562030
Grant Thomas Paul Wentworth	New Court Chambers, London	0171 831 9500
Gregory John Raymond	Deans Court Chambers, Manchester	0161 834 4097
	Deans Court Chambers, Preston	01772 555163
Grundy Nicholas John	One Essex Court, London	0171 936 3030
Hall Taylor Alexander Edward	11 Old Square, London	0171 430 0341
Halpern David Anthony	Enterprise Chambers, London	0171 405 9471
	Enterprise Chambers, Leeds	0113 246 0391
	Enterprise Chambers, Newcastle upon Tyne	0191 222 3344
Hansen William Joseph	5 Bell Yard, London	0171 333 8811
Hantusch Robert Anthony	• 3 Stone Buildings, London	0171 242 4937/405 8358
Harbottle Gwilym Thomas	5 New Square, London	0171 404 0404
Hargreaves Miss Sara Jane	12 New Square, London	0171 419 1212
	Sovereign Chambers, Leeds	0113 245 1841/2/3
Harper Joseph Charles	4 Breams Buildings, London	0171 353 5835/430 1221
Hayes John Allan	Chambers of Andrew Campbell QC, Leeds	0113 245 5438
Hayes Miss Josephine Mary	Chambers of Lord Goodhart QC, London	0171 405 5577
Heywood Michael Edmundson	Chambers of Lord Goodhart QC, London	0171 405 5577
	Cobden House Chambers, Manchester	0161 833 6000/6001
Holland David Moore	29 Bedford Row Chambers, London	0171 831 2626
Holmes Justin Francis	Chambers of Lord Goodhart QC, London	0171 405 5577
Horspool Anthony Bernard Graeme	Hardwicke Building, London	0171 242 2523

Hughes Miss Mary Josephine	Chambers of Lord Goodhart QC, London	0171 405 5577
Hunter William Quigley	No 1 Serjeants' Inn, London	0171 415 6666
Jack Adrian Laurence Robert	Enterprise Chambers, London	0171 405 9471
Jackson Dirik George Allan	• Chambers of Mr Peter Crampin QC, London	0171 831 0081
Jackson Hugh Woodward	Hardwicke Building, London	0171 242 2523
Jackson Nicholas David Kingsley	The Chambers of Adrian Lyon, Liverpool	0151 236 4421/8240/6757
James Michael Frank	Enterprise Chambers, London	0171 405 9471
	Enterprise Chambers, Leeds	0113 246 0391
	Enterprise Chambers, Newcastle upon Tyne	0191 222 3344
Jefferies Thomas Robert	Chambers of Lord Goodhart QC, London	0171 405 5577
Jennings Timothy Robin Finnegan	Enterprise Chambers, London	0171 405 9471
	Enterprise Chambers, Leeds	0113 246 0391
	Enterprise Chambers, Newcastle upon Tyne	0191 222 3344
Johnson Michael Sloan	Chambers of John Hand QC, Manchester	0161 955 9000
Jones Geraint Martyn	Fenners Chambers, Cambridge	01223 368761
	Fenners Chambers, Peterborough	01733 562030
Jones Gregory Percy	• 2 Harcourt Buildings, London	0171 353 8415
Jordan Andrew	Stanbrook & Henderson, London	0171 353 0101
	2 Harcourt Buildings, London	0171 583 9020
Jory Robert John Hugh	Enterprise Chambers, London	0171 405 9471
	Enterprise Chambers, Leeds	0113 246 0391
	Enterprise Chambers, Newcastle upon Tyne	0191 222 3344
Joss Norman James	One Essex Court, London	0171 936 3030
Karas Jonathan Marcus	4 Breams Buildings, London	0171 353 5835/430 1221
Kealy Charles Brian	Chambers of Andrew Campbell QC, Leeds	0113 245 5438
Keen Graeme	4 Breams Buildings, London	0171 353 5835/430 1221
Kinnier Andrew John	2 Harcourt Buildings, London	0171 583 9020
Kremen Philip Michael	Hardwicke Building, London	0171 242 2523
Lamont Miss Camilla Rose	Chambers of Lord Goodhart QC, London	0171 405 5577
Landes Miss Anna-Rose	St Philip's Chambers, Birmingham	0121 246 7000
Laughton Samuel Dennis	17 Old Buildings, London	0171 405 9653
Le Poidevin Nicholas Peter	12 New Square, London	0171 419 1212
	Sovereign Chambers, Leeds	0113 245 1841/2/3
Leeming Ian	Lamb Chambers, London	0171 797 8300
	Chambers of John Hand QC, Manchester	0161 955 9000
Legge Henry	5 Stone Buildings, London	0171 242 6201
Levy Robert Stuart	9 Stone Buildings, London	0171 404 5055
	Assize Court Chambers, Bristol	0117 926 4587
Lochrane Damien Horatio Ross	Pump Court Chambers, London	0171 353 0711
	Pump Court Chambers, Winchester	01962 868161
Male John Martin	4 Breams Buildings, London	0171 353 5835/430 1221
Mann George Anthony	Enterprise Chambers, London	0171 405 9471
	Enterprise Chambers, Leeds	0113 246 0391
	Enterprise Chambers, Newcastle upon Tyne	0191 222 3344
Marten Richard Hedley Westwood	Chambers of Lord Goodhart QC, London	0171 405 5577
McAllister Miss Elizabeth Ann	Enterprise Chambers, London	0171 405 9471
	Enterprise Chambers, Leeds	0113 246 0391
	Enterprise Chambers, Newcastle upon Tyne	0191 222 3344
McCarthy William	New Bailey Chambers, Preston	01772 258 087
McHugh Miss Karen	4 Breams Buildings, London	0171 353 5835/430 1221
McKinnell Miss Soraya Jane	Enterprise Chambers, London	0171 405 9471
	Enterprise Chambers, Leeds	0113 246 0391
	Enterprise Chambers, Newcastle upon Tyne	0191 222 3344
McQuail Ms Katherine Emma	11 Old Square, London	0171 430 0341
Meakin Timothy William	Fenners Chambers, Cambridge	01223 368761
	Fenners Chambers, Peterborough	01733 562030
Mendoza Neil David Pereira	Hardwicke Building, London	0171 242 2523

B

Merry Hugh Gairns	17 Carlton Crescent, Southampton	01703 320320
Mitchell Miss Juliana Marie	2 Harcourt Buildings, London	0171 583 9020
Morgan Charles James Arthur	Enterprise Chambers, London	0171 405 9471
	Enterprise Chambers, Leeds	0113 246 0391
	Enterprise Chambers, Newcastle upon Tyne	0191 222 3344
Moriarty Gerald Evelyn	2 Mitre Court Buildings, London	0171 583 1380
Morshead Timothy Francis	4 Breams Buildings, London	0171 353 5835/430 1221
Mullis Anthony Roger	Chambers of Lord Goodhart QC, London	0171 405 5577
Munro Kenneth Stuart	5 Bell Yard, London	0171 333 8811
Nebhrajani Miss Mel	9 Stone Buildings, London	0171 404 5055
Newman Miss Catherine Mary	• 13 Old Square, London	0171 404 4800
Nicol-Gent William Philip Trahair	King's Chambers, Eastbourne	01323 416053
Norbury Luke Edward	17 Old Buildings, London	0171 405 9653
Norie-Miller Jeffrey Reginald	55 Temple Chambers, London	0171 353 7400
Norris Alastair Hubert	• 5 Stone Buildings, London	0171 242 6201
	• Southernhay Chambers, Exeter	01392 255777
Norris Paul Howard	One Essex Court, London	0171 936 3030
Nurse Gordon Bramwell William	11 Old Square, London	0171 430 0341
O'Sullivan Michael Morton	5 Stone Buildings, London	0171 242 6201
Oakes Miss Alison Denise	4 Breams Buildings, London	0171 353 5835/430 1221
Oakley Tony	• 11 Old Square, London	0171 430 0341
Ohrenstein Dov	Chambers of Lord Goodhart QC, London	0171 405 5577
Ornsby Miss Suzanne Doreen	• 2 Harcourt Buildings, London	0171 353 8415
Ovey Miss Elizabeth Helen	11 Old Square, London	0171 430 0341
Parry David Julian Thomas	Chambers of Lord Goodhart QC, London	0171 405 5577
Peacock Ian Christopher	12 New Square, London	0171 419 1212
	Sovereign Chambers, Leeds	0113 245 1841/2/3
Peacock Nicholas Christopher	13 Old Square, London	0171 404 4800
Peacocke Mrs Teresa Anne Rosen	Enterprise Chambers, London	0171 405 9471
	Enterprise Chambers, Leeds	0113 246 0391
	Enterprise Chambers, Newcastle upon Tyne	0191 222 3344
Perks Richard Howard	St Philip's Chambers, Birmingham	0121 246 7000
Picarda Hubert Alistair Paul	Chambers of Lord Goodhart QC, London	0171 405 5577
Pilkington Mrs Mavis Patricia	9 Woodhouse Square, Leeds	0113 245 1986
Pimentel Carlos de Serpa Alberto Legg	3 Stone Buildings, London	0171 242 4937/405 8358
Popat Prashant	Stanbrook & Henderson, London	0171 353 0101
	2 Harcourt Buildings, London	0171 583 9020
Pryke Stuart	Trinity Chambers, Newcastle upon Tyne	0191 232 1927
Quint Mrs Joan Francesca Rae	11 Old Square, London	0171 242 5022
Radevsky Anthony Eric	• 5 Bell Yard, London	0171 333 8811
Reed Miss Penelope Jane	9 Stone Buildings, London	0171 404 5055
Rees David Benjamin	5 Stone Buildings, London	0171 242 6201
Rich Miss Ann Barbara	5 Stone Buildings, London	0171 242 6201
Robson John Malcolm	2 Gray's Inn Square Chambers, London	0171 242 0328/405 1317
	Assize Court Chambers, Bristol	0117 926 4587
Ross Martyn John Greaves	• 5 New Square, London	0171 404 0404
	• Octagon House, Norwich	01603 623186
Routley Patrick	Goldsmith Building, London	0171 353 7881
Rowell David Stewart	Chambers of Lord Goodhart QC, London	0171 405 5577
Rule Jonathan Daniel	Merchant Chambers, Manchester	0161 839 7070
Rumney Conrad William Arthur	St Philip's Chambers, Birmingham	0121 246 7000
Russen Jonathan Huw Sinclair	13 Old Square, London	0171 404 4800
Ryan David Patrick	Chambers of Geoffrey Hawker, London	0171 583 8899
Sayer Mr Peter Edwin	Gough Square Chambers, London	0171 353 0924
Schaw-Miller Stephen Grant	5 Bell Yard, London	0171 333 8811
Schooling Simon John	Chambers of Harjit Singh, London	0171 353 1356
Sefton Mark Thomas Dunblane	199 Strand, London	0171 379 9779
Seifert Miss Anne Miriam	4 Breams Buildings, London	0171 353 5835/430 1221
Selway Dr Katherine Emma	11 Old Square, London	0171 430 0341
Shah Bajul Amratlal Somchand	Twenty-Four Old Buildings, London	0171 404 0946
Sheehan Malcolm Peter	Stanbrook & Henderson, London	0171 353 0101

• Expanded entry in Part D

	2 Harcourt Buildings, London	0171 583 9020
Simmonds Andrew John	5 Stone Buildings, London	0171 242 6201
Simpson Edwin John Fletcher	12 New Square, London	0171 419 1212
Sisley Timothy Julian Crispin	9 Stone Buildings, London	0171 404 5055
	Westgate Chambers, Lewes	01273 480 510
Smart Miss Jacqueline Anne	Trinity Chambers, Newcastle upon Tyne	0191 232 1927
Staddon Miss Claire Ann	12 New Square, London	0171 419 1212
	Sovereign Chambers, Leeds	0113 245 1841/2/3
Stevens-Hoare Miss Michelle	• Hardwicke Building, London	0171 242 2523
Stewart Alexander Joseph	5 New Square, London	0171 404 0404
Stewart Mark Courtney	College Chambers, Southampton	01703 230338
Stewart Nicholas John Cameron	Hardwicke Building, London	0171 242 2523
Sunnucks James Horace George	• 5 New Square, London	0171 404 0404
	• Octagon House, Norwich	01603 623186
Sydenham Colin Peter	4 Breams Buildings, London	0171 353 5835/430 1221
Taggart Nicholas	4 Breams Buildings, London	0171 353 5835/430 1221
Thomas Nigel Matthew	13 Old Square, London	0171 404 4800
Thompson Steven Lim	Twenty-Four Old Buildings, London	0171 404 0946
Tidmarsh Christopher Ralph Francis	5 Stone Buildings, London	0171 242 6201
Tipples Miss Amanda Jane	13 Old Square, London	0171 404 4800
Todd Richard Frazer	1 Mitre Court Buildings, London	0171 797 7070
Trace Anthony John	• 13 Old Square, London	0171 404 4800
Twigger Andrew Mark	3 Stone Buildings, London	0171 242 4937/405 8358
Vane The Hon Christopher John Fletcher	Trinity Chambers, Newcastle upon Tyne	0191 232 1927
Walker Andrew Greenfield	Chambers of Lord Goodhart QC, London	0171 405 5577
Warnock-Smith Mrs Shan	5 Stone Buildings, London	0171 242 6201
Waters Malcolm Ian	• 11 Old Square, London	0171 430 0341
Weatherill Bernard Richard	Chambers of Lord Goodhart QC, London	0171 405 5577
West Mark	• 11 Old Square, London	0171 430 0341
Whitaker Steven Dixon	199 Strand, London	0171 379 9779
	All Saints Chambers, Bristol	0117 921 1966
Wightwick (William) Iain	Assize Court Chambers, Bristol	0117 926 4587
Wilson Alasdair John	Fenners Chambers, Cambridge	01223 368761
	Fenners Chambers, Peterborough	01733 562030
Wonnacott Mark Andrew	199 Strand, London	0171 379 9779
Wright Colin John	4 Field Court, London	0171 440 6900

CHARITIES

Angus Miss Tracey Anne	5 Stone Buildings, London	0171 242 6201
Asplin Miss Sarah Jane	• 3 Stone Buildings, London	0171 242 4937/405 8358
Ayres Andrew John William	13 Old Square, London	0171 404 4800
Burroughs Nigel Alfred	11 Old Square, London	0171 430 0341
Clarke Miss Anna Victoria	5 Stone Buildings, London	0171 242 6201
Conroy Miss Marian	3 Stone Buildings, London	0171 242 4937/405 8358
Cracknell Douglas George	23 Warham Road, Sevenoaks	01959 522325
Cunningham Mark James	13 Old Square, London	0171 404 4800
Dodge Peter Clive	11 Old Square, London	0171 430 0341
Elleray Anthony John	• 12 New Square, London	0171 419 1212
	• St James's Chambers, Manchester	0161 834 7000
	• Park Lane Chambers, Leeds	0113 228 5000
Goodhart Lord	Chambers of Lord Goodhart QC, London	0171 405 5577
Gregory John Raymond	Deans Court Chambers, Manchester	0161 834 4097
	Deans Court Chambers, Preston	01772 555163
Hall Taylor Alexander Edward	11 Old Square, London	0171 430 0341
Hayes Miss Josephine Mary	Chambers of Lord Goodhart QC, London	0171 405 5577
Henderson Launcelot Dinadan James	• 5 Stone Buildings, London	0171 242 6201
Holmes Justin Francis	Chambers of Lord Goodhart QC, London	0171 405 5577
Jones Geraint Martyn	Fenners Chambers, Cambridge	01223 368761
	Fenners Chambers, Peterborough	01733 562030
Laughton Samuel Dennis	17 Old Buildings, London	0171 405 9653
Legge Henry	5 Stone Buildings, London	0171 242 6201
Levy Benjamin Keith	Enterprise Chambers, London	0171 405 9471
	Enterprise Chambers, Leeds	0113 246 0391

• Expanded entry in Part D

	Enterprise Chambers, Newcastle upon Tyne	0191 222 3344
Marten Richard Hedley Westwood	Chambers of Lord Goodhart QC, London	0171 405 5577
McQuail Ms Katherine Emma	11 Old Square, London	0171 430 0341
Mullis Anthony Roger	Chambers of Lord Goodhart QC, London	0171 405 5577
Nebhrajani Miss Mel	9 Stone Buildings, London	0171 404 5055
Norris Alastair Hubert	• 5 Stone Buildings, London	0171 242 6201
	• Southernhay Chambers, Exeter	01392 255777
Oakley Tony	• 11 Old Square, London	0171 430 0341
Ovey Miss Elizabeth Helen	11 Old Square, London	0171 430 0341
Picarda Hubert Alistair Paul	Chambers of Lord Goodhart QC, London	0171 405 5577
Pilkington Mrs Mavis Patricia	9 Woodhouse Square, Leeds	0113 245 1986
Pimentel Carlos de Serpa Alberto Legg	3 Stone Buildings, London	0171 242 4937/405 8358
Quint Mrs Joan Francesca Rae	11 Old Square, London	0171 242 5022
Reed Miss Penelope Jane	9 Stone Buildings, London	0171 404 5055
Rees David Benjamin	5 Stone Buildings, London	0171 242 6201
Ross Martyn John Greaves	• 5 New Square, London	0171 404 0404
	• Octagon House, Norwich	01603 623186
Rowell David Stewart	Chambers of Lord Goodhart QC, London	0171 405 5577
Selway Dr Katherine Emma	11 Old Square, London	0171 430 0341
Shah Bajul Amratlal Somchand	Twenty-Four Old Buildings, London	0171 404 0946
Stewart Alexander Joseph	5 New Square, London	0171 404 0404
Sunnucks James Horace George	• 5 New Square, London	0171 404 0404
	• Octagon House, Norwich	01603 623186
Sydenham Colin Peter	4 Breams Buildings, London	0171 353 5835/430 1221
Thomas Nigel Matthew	13 Old Square, London	0171 404 4800
Thomson Martin Haldane Ahmad	Wynne Chambers, London	0171 737 7266
Tidmarsh Christopher Ralph Francis	5 Stone Buildings, London	0171 242 6201
Walker Andrew Greenfield	Chambers of Lord Goodhart QC, London	0171 405 5577
Warnock-Smith Mrs Shan	5 Stone Buildings, London	0171 242 6201
Waters Malcolm Ian	• 11 Old Square, London	0171 430 0341
West Mark	• 11 Old Square, London	0171 430 0341

CHILD ABDUCTION

Lister Miss Caroline Jane	One King's Bench Walk, London	0171 936 1500
Ramsahoye Miss Indira Kim	Hardwicke Building, London	0171 242 2523

CHILD ABUSE

Hughes Thomas Merfyn	Goldsmith Building, London	0171 353 7881
	40 King Street, Chester	01244 323886

CHILDREN

Furminger Michael Ashley	Michael Furminger, Brixham	01803 882293

CIVIL ACTIONS AGAINST THE POLICE

Hadley Steven Frank	2 Paper Buildings, London	0171 353 0933
Millett Kenneth James	1 Hare Court, London	0171 353 3982/5324
Owen David Meurig	25-27 Castle Street, Liverpool	0151 227 5661/5666/236 5072
Reid Howard Barrington	New Court Chambers, Birmingham	0121 693 6656

CIVIL ACTIONS AGAINST THE POLICE (DEFENDING)

Perks Richard Howard	St Philip's Chambers, Birmingham	0121 246 7000

CIVIL ACTIONS FOR POLICE AUTHORITY

Studd Miss Anne Elizabeth	5 Essex Court, London	0171 410 2000

CIVIL CLAIMS FOR AND AGAINST THE POLICE

Wakeham Philip John Le Messurier	Hardwicke Building, London	0171 242 2523

       • Expanded entry in Part D

CIVIL FRAUD

Geering Ian Walter	3 Verulam Buildings, London	0171 831 8441
Phillips Stephen Edmund	3 Verulam Buildings, London	0171 831 8441

CIVIL JURY ACTIONS (FALSE IMPRISONMENT AND MALICIOUS PROSECUTION)

Barton Miss Fiona	5 Essex Court, London	0171 410 2000

CIVIL LIBERTIES

Addison Neil Patrick	Cathedral Chambers, Newcastle upon Tyne	0191 232 1311
Akiwumi Anthony Sebastian Akitayo	Pump Court Chambers, London	0171 353 0711
	Pump Court Chambers, Winchester	01962 868161
Al'Hassan Khadim	Equity Chambers, Birmingham	0121 233 2100
Bailin Alexander	5 Paper Buildings, London	0171 583 6117
Beer Jason Barrington	5 Essex Court, London	0171 410 2000
Best Stanley Philip	Bracton Chambers, London	0171 242 4248
	Westgate Chambers, Lewes	01273 480 510
	Barnstaple Chambers, Winkleigh	0183 783763
Birch Roger Allen	12 New Square, London	0171 419 1212
	Sovereign Chambers, Leeds	0113 245 1841/2/3
	Lancaster Buildings, Manchester	0161 661 4444
Breen Carlo Enrico	Chambers of John Hand QC, Manchester	0161 955 9000
Carlile Alexander Charles	9-12 Bell Yard, London	0171 400 1800
	Sedan House, Chester	01244 320480/348282
Cartwright Richard John	Queen Elizabeth Building, London	0171 353 7181 (12 lines)
Clover (Thomas) Anthony	New Court Chambers, London	0171 831 9500
Coulter Barry John	One Essex Court, London	0171 936 3030
Davies Andrew Christopher	New Court Chambers, London	0171 831 9500
Emmerson (Michael) Benedict	Doughty Street Chambers, London	0171 404 1313
Evans Lee John	Farrar's Building, London	0171 583 9241
Fitzgerald Edward Hamilton	Doughty Street Chambers, London	0171 404 1313
Florida-James Mark	• King's Bench Chambers, Bournemouth	01202 250025
Gatty Daniel Simon	New Court Chambers, London	0171 831 9500
Giffin Nigel Dyson	11 King's Bench Walk, London	0171 632 8500
Gordon Richard John Francis	39 Essex Street, London	0171 832 1111
Grey Miss Eleanor Mary Grace	39 Essex Street, London	0171 832 1111
Griffiths (John) Peter (Gwynne)	30 Park Place, Cardiff	01222 398421
Hall David Percy	9 Woodhouse Square, Leeds	0113 245 1986
Herbert Mrs Rebecca Mary	2 New Street, Leicester	0116 262 5906
Hogg The Rt Hon Douglas Martin	4 Paper Buildings, London	0171 353 3366/583 7155
	37 Park Square, Leeds	0113 243 9422
Hoyal Ms Jane	• 1 Pump Court, London	0171 583 2012/353 4341
Jack Simon Michael	9 Woodhouse Square, Leeds	0113 245 1986
Jackson Anthony Warren	3 Serjeants' Inn, London	0171 353 5537
James Simon John	Chambers of John Hand QC, Manchester	0161 955 9000
Janner Daniel Joseph Mitchell	23 Essex Street, London	0171 413 0353
Jay Robert Maurice	39 Essex Street, London	0171 832 1111
Kent Miss Georgina	5 Essex Court, London	0171 410 2000
Kerr Tim Julian	4-5 Gray's Inn Square, London	0171 404 5252
Khan Ashraf	A K Chambers, Hull	01482 641180
Kimbell John Ashley	5 Bell Yard, London	0171 333 8811
Leiper Richard Thomas	11 King's Bench Walk, London	0171 632 8500
Levy Allan Edward	17 Bedford Row, London	0171 831 7314
Maclean Alan John	39 Essex Street, London	0171 832 1111
Mason Ian Douglas	11 Bolt Court, London	0171 353 2300
	Redhill Chambers, Redhill	01737 780781
Maxwell David	Claremont Chambers, Wolverhampton	01902 426222
McManus Jonathan Richard	4-5 Gray's Inn Square, London	0171 404 5252
Middleton Miss Georgina Claire	New Court Chambers, London	0171 831 9500
Millett Kenneth James	1 Hare Court, London	0171 353 3982/5324
Moses Miss Rebecca	Barristers' Common Law Chambers, London	0171 375 3012
	Lion Court, London	0171 404 6565
Mullen Patrick Anthony	One Essex Court, London	0171 936 3030
Newman Austin Eric	9 Woodhouse Square, Leeds	0113 245 1986
Ong Miss Grace Yu Mae	One Essex Court, London	0171 936 3030
Overs Ms Estelle Fae	New Court Chambers, London	0171 831 9500

Parker Kenneth Blades	Monckton Chambers, London	0171 405 7211
Peacock Ian Christopher	12 New Square, London	0171 419 1212
	Sovereign Chambers, Leeds	0113 245 1841/2/3
Pelling Richard Alexander	New Court Chambers, London	0171 831 9500
Pitter Jason Karl	Park Court Chambers, Leeds	0113 243 3277
Pleming Nigel Peter	39 Essex Street, London	0171 832 1111
Rahman Muhammad Altafur	Barristers' Common Law Chambers, London	0171 375 3012
Richards Miss Jennifer	39 Essex Street, London	0171 832 1111
Rogers Ian Paul	1 Crown Office Row, London	0171 583 9292
Roth Peter Marcel	Monckton Chambers, London	0171 405 7211
Sadiq Tariq Mahmood	Chambers of John Hand QC, Manchester	0161 955 9000
Sarony Neville Leslie		
Sharland Andrew John	4-5 Gray's Inn Square, London	0171 404 5252
Simor Miss Jessica Margaret Poppaea	Monckton Chambers, London	0171 405 7211
Spink Peter John William	5 Essex Court, London	0171 410 2000
Stanislas Paul Junior	Somersett Chambers, London	0171 404 6701
Stewart Nicholas John Cameron	Hardwicke Building, London	0171 242 2523
Straker Timothy Derrick	• 2-3 Gray's Inn Square, London	0171 242 4986
Studd Miss Anne Elizabeth	5 Essex Court, London	0171 410 2000
Thorne Timothy Peter	33 Bedford Row, London	0171 242 6476
Tomlinson Hugh Richard Edward	New Court Chambers, London	0171 831 9500
Turner James	One King's Bench Walk, London	0171 936 1500
Ward Timothy Justin	39 Essex Street, London	0171 832 1111
Wilcox Nicholas Hugh	5 Essex Court, London	0171 410 2000
Williams Ms Heather Jean	Doughty Street Chambers, London	0171 404 1313

CO-OWNERSHIP

Brown Miss Joanne	2 Gray's Inn Square Chambers, London	0171 242 0328/405 1317

COMMERCIAL

Adamyk Simon Charles	12 New Square, London	0171 419 1212
Akka Lawrence Mark	20 Essex Street, London	0171 583 9294
Aldridge James Hugh	13 Old Square, London	0171 404 4800
Ambrose Miss Clare Mary Geneste	20 Essex Street, London	0171 583 9294
Amin Miss Farah	7 New Square, London	0171 430 1660
Arden Peter Leonard	Enterprise Chambers, London	0171 405 9471
	Enterprise Chambers, Leeds	0113 246 0391
	Enterprise Chambers, Newcastle upon Tyne	0191 222 3344
Ashworth Piers	Stanbrook & Henderson, London	0171 353 0101
	2 Harcourt Buildings, London	0171 583 9020
	Priory Chambers, Birmingham	0121 236 3882/1375
Atherton Ian David	Enterprise Chambers, London	0171 405 9471
	Enterprise Chambers, Leeds	0113 246 0391
	Enterprise Chambers, Newcastle upon Tyne	0191 222 3344
Bailey Edward Henry	5 Bell Yard, London	0171 333 8811
Baker Miss Anne Jacqueline	Enterprise Chambers, London	0171 405 9471
	Enterprise Chambers, Leeds	0113 246 0391
	Enterprise Chambers, Newcastle upon Tyne	0191 222 3344
Barker James Sebastian	Enterprise Chambers, London	0171 405 9471
	Enterprise Chambers, Leeds	0113 246 0391
	Enterprise Chambers, Newcastle upon Tyne	0191 222 3344
Beal Kieron Conrad	4 Paper Buildings, London	0171 353 3366/583 7155
Benson Julian Christopher Woodburn	One Essex Court, London	0171 936 3030
Berkley Michael Stuart	Rougemont Chambers, Exeter	01392 410471
Bhaloo Miss Zia Kurban	Enterprise Chambers, London	0171 405 9471
	Enterprise Chambers, Leeds	0113 246 0391
	Enterprise Chambers, Newcastle upon Tyne	0191 222 3344
Bird Nigel David	Chambers of John Hand QC, Manchester	0161 955 9000
Blair William James Lynton	3 Verulam Buildings, London	0171 831 8441
Breen Carlo Enrico	Chambers of John Hand QC, Manchester	0161 955 9000

• Expanded entry in Part D

Brent Richard	3 Verulam Buildings, London	0171 831 8441
Brown Geoffrey Barlow	39 Essex Street, London	0171 832 1111
Brown Miss Hannah Beatrice	5 Bell Yard, London	0171 333 8811
Burns Peter Richard	Deans Court Chambers, Manchester	0161 834 4097
Chalmers Miss Suzanne Frances	Two Crown Office Row, London	0171 797 8100
Charkham Graham Harold	20 Essex Street, London	0171 583 9294
Clarke George Robert Ivan	Chambers of Geoffrey Hawker, London	0171 583 8899
Coburn Michael Jeremy Patrick	20 Essex Street, London	0171 583 9294
Collett Michael John	20 Essex Street, London	0171 583 9294
Connerty Anthony Robin	Lamb Chambers, London	0171 797 8300
Cottrell Matthew Robert	Oriel Chambers, Liverpool	0151 236 7191
Cranfield Peter Anthony	3 Verulam Buildings, London	0171 831 8441
Darbyshire William Robert	Chambers of John Hand QC, Manchester	0161 955 9000
Dawes Gordon Stephen Knight	Goldsmith Building, London	0171 353 7881
Dawson James Robert	Oriel Chambers, Liverpool	0151 236 7191
de Jehan David	St Paul's House, Leeds	0113 245 5866
de Lacy Richard Michael	3 Verulam Buildings, London	0171 831 8441
Dowse John	Chambers of Lord Goodhart QC, London	0171 405 5577
	Chambers of John Hand QC, Manchester	0161 955 9000
Doyle Louis George	Chambers of Andrew Campbell QC, Leeds	0113 245 5438
Driscoll Miss Lynn	Sovereign Chambers, Leeds	0113 245 1841/2/3
	Lancaster Buildings, Manchester	0161 661 4444
Duffy Derek James	St Paul's House, Leeds	0113 245 5866
Eastman Roger	Stanbrook & Henderson, London	0171 353 0101
	2 Harcourt Buildings, London	0171 583 9020
Ekins Charles Wareing		
Finlay Darren	Sovereign Chambers, Leeds	0113 245 1841/2/3
Fisher David	5 Bell Yard, London	0171 333 8811
Fitzgerald John Vincent	New Court, London	0171 797 8999
Francis Edward Gerald Francis	Enterprise Chambers, London	0171 405 9471
	Enterprise Chambers, Leeds	0113 246 0391
	Enterprise Chambers, Newcastle upon Tyne	0191 222 3344
Franklin Stephen Hall	5 Paper Buildings, London	0171 583 6117
	Fenners Chambers, Cambridge	01223 368761
Freedman Sampson Clive	3 Verulam Buildings, London	0171 831 8441
French Richard Anthony Lister	Rougemont Chambers, Exeter	01392 410471
Frodsham Alexander Miles	Oriel Chambers, Liverpool	0151 236 7191
Garcia-Miller Miss Laura	Enterprise Chambers, London	0171 405 9471
	Enterprise Chambers, Leeds	0113 246 0391
	Enterprise Chambers, Newcastle upon Tyne	0191 222 3344
Gerald Nigel Mortimer	Enterprise Chambers, London	0171 405 9471
	Enterprise Chambers, Leeds	0113 246 0391
	Enterprise Chambers, Newcastle upon Tyne	0191 222 3344
Gibaud Miss Catherine Alison Annetta	3 Verulam Buildings, London	0171 831 8441
Gibson Charles Anthony Warneford	2 Harcourt Buildings, London	0171 583 9020
Gilbert Ms Julia Jane	Trinity Chambers, Newcastle upon Tyne	0191 232 1927
Glasgow Edwin John	39 Essex Street, London	0171 832 1111
Goldblatt Simon	39 Essex Street, London	0171 832 1111
Gore-Andrews Gavin Angus Russell	Stanbrook & Henderson, London	0171 353 0101
	2 Harcourt Buildings, London	0171 583 9020
Graham Thomas Patrick Henry	Lamb Chambers, London	0171 797 8300
Grantham Andrew Timothy	• Deans Court Chambers, Manchester	0161 834 4097
	• Deans Court Chambers, Preston	01772 555163
Green Patrick Curtis	Stanbrook & Henderson, London	0171 353 0101
	2 Harcourt Buildings, London	0171 583 9020
Groves Hugo Gerard	Enterprise Chambers, London	0171 405 9471
	Enterprise Chambers, Leeds	0113 246 0391
	Enterprise Chambers, Newcastle upon Tyne	0191 222 3344
Grundy Nigel Lawrence John	Chambers of John Hand QC, Manchester	0161 955 9000
Hall Mrs Melanie Ruth	Monckton Chambers, London	0171 405 7211

B

• Expanded entry in Part D

Hall Taylor Alexander Edward	11 Old Square, London	0171 430 0341
Halpern David Anthony	Enterprise Chambers, London	0171 405 9471
	Enterprise Chambers, Leeds	0113 246 0391
	Enterprise Chambers, Newcastle upon Tyne	0191 222 3344
Hamblen Nicholas Archibald	20 Essex Street, London	0171 583 9294
Hamer Michael Howard Kenneth	2 Harcourt Buildings, London	0171 583 9020
	Westgate Chambers, Lewes	01273 480 510
Hamilton Graeme Montagu	Two Crown Office Row, London	0171 797 8100
Hand John Lester	Old Square Chambers, London	0171 269 0300
	Old Square Chambers, Bristol	0117 927 7111
	Chambers of John Hand QC, Manchester	0161 955 9000
Hardwick Matthew Richard	Enterprise Chambers, London	0171 405 9471
	Enterprise Chambers, Leeds	0113 246 0391
	Enterprise Chambers, Newcastle upon Tyne	0191 222 3344
Harvey Jonathan Robert William	2 Harcourt Buildings, London	0171 583 9020
Harvey Michael Llewellyn Tucker	Two Crown Office Row, London	0171 797 8100
Hawker Geoffrey Fort	Chambers of Geoffrey Hawker, London	0171 583 8899
Henderson Roger Anthony	Stanbrook & Henderson, London	0171 353 0101
	2 Harcourt Buildings, London	0171 583 9020
Higgins Anthony Paul	Goldsmith Building, London	0171 353 7881
Hockaday Miss Annie	3 Verulam Buildings, London	0171 831 8441
Howarth Simon Stuart	Two Crown Office Row, London	0171 797 8100
Hull Leslie David	Chambers of John Hand QC, Manchester	0161 955 9000
Hurst Brian	17 Bedford Row, London	0171 831 7314
Hutton Miss Caroline	Enterprise Chambers, London	0171 405 9471
	Enterprise Chambers, Leeds	0113 246 0391
	Enterprise Chambers, Newcastle upon Tyne	0191 222 3344
Ife Miss Linden Elizabeth	Enterprise Chambers, London	0171 405 9471
	Enterprise Chambers, Leeds	0113 246 0391
	Enterprise Chambers, Newcastle upon Tyne	0191 222 3344
Ivimy Ms Cecilia Rachel	11 King's Bench Walk, London	0171 632 8500
Jack Adrian Laurence Robert	Enterprise Chambers, London	0171 405 9471
James Michael Frank	Enterprise Chambers, London	0171 405 9471
	Enterprise Chambers, Leeds	0113 246 0391
	Enterprise Chambers, Newcastle upon Tyne	0191 222 3344
Jarvis John Manners	3 Verulam Buildings, London	0171 831 8441
Jenkala Adrian Aleksander	11 Bolt Court, London	0171 353 2300
	Redhill Chambers, Redhill	01737 780781
Jennings Timothy Robin Finnegan	Enterprise Chambers, London	0171 405 9471
	Enterprise Chambers, Leeds	0113 246 0391
	Enterprise Chambers, Newcastle upon Tyne	0191 222 3344
Johnson Michael Sloan	Chambers of John Hand QC, Manchester	0161 955 9000
Jones Geraint Martyn	Fenners Chambers, Cambridge	01223 368761
	Fenners Chambers, Peterborough	01733 562030
Jordan Andrew	Stanbrook & Henderson, London	0171 353 0101
	2 Harcourt Buildings, London	0171 583 9020
Jory Robert John Hugh	Enterprise Chambers, London	0171 405 9471
	Enterprise Chambers, Leeds	0113 246 0391
	Enterprise Chambers, Newcastle upon Tyne	0191 222 3344
Joss Norman James	One Essex Court, London	0171 936 3030
Kerr Tim Julian	4-5 Gray's Inn Square, London	0171 404 5252
Khokhar Mushtaq Ahmed	Sovereign Chambers, Leeds	0113 245 1841/2/3
Kremen Philip Michael	Hardwicke Building, London	0171 242 2523
Laughton Samuel Dennis	17 Old Buildings, London	0171 405 9653
Lawson Daniel George	Goldsmith Building, London	0171 353 7881
Leeming Ian	Lamb Chambers, London	0171 797 8300
	Chambers of John Hand QC, Manchester	0161 955 9000
Legh-Jones Piers Nicholas	• 20 Essex Street, London	0171 583 9294
Leiper Richard Thomas	11 King's Bench Walk, London	0171 632 8500
Lewis Andrew William	Sovereign Chambers, Leeds	0113 245 1841/2/3

• Expanded entry in Part D

Lowenstein Paul David	Littleton Chambers, London	0171 797 8600
Macnab Alexander Andrew	Monckton Chambers, London	0171 405 7211
Maitland Jones Mark Griffith	Goldsmith Building, London	0171 353 7881
Malek Ali	3 Verulam Buildings, London	0171 831 8441
Males Stephen Martin	20 Essex Street, London	0171 583 9294
Mantle Peter John	Monckton Chambers, London	0171 405 7211
Marks Jonathan Harold	3 Verulam Buildings, London	0171 831 8441
Marquand Charles Nicholas Hilary	Chambers of Lord Goodhart QC, London	0171 405 5577
Masters Miss Sara Alayna	20 Essex Street, London	0171 583 9294
Mauger Miss Claire Shanti Andrea	Enterprise Chambers, London	0171 405 9471
Mawrey Richard Brooks	Stanbrook & Henderson, London	0171 353 0101
	2 Harcourt Buildings, London	0171 583 9020
Maxwell Miss Karen Laetitia	20 Essex Street, London	0171 583 9294
May Miss Juliet Mary	3 Verulam Buildings, London	0171 831 8441
McAllister Miss Elizabeth Ann	Enterprise Chambers, London	0171 405 9471
	Enterprise Chambers, Leeds	0113 246 0391
	Enterprise Chambers, Newcastle upon Tyne	0191 222 3344
McCall Duncan James	4 Pump Court, London	0171 353 2656/9
McCarthy William	New Bailey Chambers, Preston	01772 258 087
McGregor Harvey	4 Paper Buildings, London	0171 353 3366/583 7155
McKinnell Miss Soraya Jane	Enterprise Chambers, London	0171 405 9471
	Enterprise Chambers, Leeds	0113 246 0391
	Enterprise Chambers, Newcastle upon Tyne	0191 222 3344
McManus Jonathan Richard	4-5 Gray's Inn Square, London	0171 404 5252
McQuater Ewan Alan	3 Verulam Buildings, London	0171 831 8441
Meeson Nigel Keith	4 Field Court, London	0171 440 6900
Merriman Nicholas Flavelle	3 Verulam Buildings, London	0171 831 8441
Milligan Iain Anstruther	20 Essex Street, London	0171 583 9294
Mills Simon Thomas	One Essex Court, London	0171 936 3030
Moon Philip Charles Angus	3 Serjeants' Inn, London	0171 353 5537
Morgan Charles James Arthur	Enterprise Chambers, London	0171 405 9471
	Enterprise Chambers, Leeds	0113 246 0391
	Enterprise Chambers, Newcastle upon Tyne	0191 222 3344
Morgan Edward Patrick	4 King's Bench Walk, London	0171 822 8822
	Deans Court Chambers, Manchester	0161 834 4097
Morgan Richard Hugo Lyndon	13 Old Square, London	0171 404 4800
Naylor Jonathan Peter	King's Chambers, Eastbourne	01323 416053
Nebhrajani Miss Mel	9 Stone Buildings, London	0171 404 5055
Newman Miss Catherine Mary	• 13 Old Square, London	0171 404 4800
Nicholls John Peter	13 Old Square, London	0171 404 4800
Noble Andrew	Eldon Chambers, London	0171 353 4636
	Merchant Chambers, Manchester	0161 839 7070
Norris Paul Howard	One Essex Court, London	0171 936 3030
O'Connor Andrew McDougal	Two Crown Office Row, London	0171 797 8100
Odgers John Arthur	3 Verulam Buildings, London	0171 831 8441
Ogunbiyi Oluwole Afolabi	Horizon Chambers, London	0171 242 2440
Onslow Andrew George	3 Verulam Buildings, London	0171 831 8441
Ough Dr Richard Norman	• Hardwicke Building, London	0171 242 2523
Overs Ms Estelle Fae	New Court Chambers, London	0171 831 9500
Owen David Christopher	20 Essex Street, London	0171 583 9294
Padfield Ms Alison Mary	One Hare Court, London	0171 353 3171
Palmer James Savill	2 Harcourt Buildings, London	0171 583 9020
Parkin Jonathan	• Chambers of John Hand QC, Manchester	0161 955 9000
Patchett-Joyce Michael Thurston	Monckton Chambers, London	0171 405 7211
Peacock Ian Christopher	12 New Square, London	0171 419 1212
	Sovereign Chambers, Leeds	0113 245 1841/2/3
Peacocke Mrs Teresa Anne Rosen	Enterprise Chambers, London	0171 405 9471
	Enterprise Chambers, Leeds	0113 246 0391
	Enterprise Chambers, Newcastle upon Tyne	0191 222 3344
Pelling (Philip) Mark	Monckton Chambers, London	0171 405 7211
Pelling Richard Alexander	New Court Chambers, London	0171 831 9500
Pershad Rohan	Two Crown Office Row, London	0171 797 8100
Phillips David John	199 Strand, London	0171 379 9779
	30 Park Place, Cardiff	01222 398421
Pickering James Patrick	Enterprise Chambers, London	0171 405 9471
	Enterprise Chambers, Leeds	0113 246 0391

	Enterprise Chambers, Newcastle upon Tyne	0191 222 3344
Pope David James	3 Verulam Buildings, London	0171 831 8441
Reed Philip James William	5 Bell Yard, London	0171 333 8811
Reeve Matthew Francis	5 Bell Yard, London	0171 333 8811
Richardson Miss Sarah Jane	Enterprise Chambers, London	0171 405 9471
	Enterprise Chambers, Leeds	0113 246 0391
	Enterprise Chambers, Newcastle upon Tyne	0191 222 3344
Roe Thomas Idris	Goldsmith Building, London	0171 353 7881
Rogers Ian Paul	1 Crown Office Row, London	0171 583 9292
Routley Patrick	Goldsmith Building, London	0171 353 7881
Rule Jonathan Daniel	Merchant Chambers, Manchester	0161 839 7070
Russell Christopher Garnet	12 New Square, London	0171 419 1212
	Sovereign Chambers, Leeds	0113 245 1841/2/3
Russell Robert John Finlay	5 Bell Yard, London	0171 333 8811
Ryan David Patrick	Chambers of Geoffrey Hawker, London	0171 583 8899
Salter Richard Stanley	3 Verulam Buildings, London	0171 831 8441
Sampson Graeme William	Chambers of Geoffrey Hawker, London	0171 583 8899
Saunders Nicholas Joseph	4 Field Court, London	0171 440 6900
Schooling Simon John	Chambers of Harjit Singh, London	0171 353 1356
Selvaratnam Miss Vasanti Emily Indrani	4 Field Court, London	0171 440 6900
Seymour Richard William	Monckton Chambers, London	0171 405 7211
Sheridan Maurice Bernard Gerard	• 3 Verulam Buildings, London	0171 831 8441
Singh Balbir	• Equity Chambers, Birmingham	0121 233 2100
Sleeman Miss Rachel Sarah Elizabeth	One Essex Court, London	0171 936 3030
Smith Warwick Timothy Cresswell	• Deans Court Chambers, Manchester	0161 834 4097
	• Deans Court Chambers, Preston	01772 555163
Southwell Richard Charles	One Hare Court, London	0171 353 3171
Steinert Jonathan	New Court Chambers, London	0171 831 9500
Stevenson John Melford	Two Crown Office Row, London	0171 797 8100
Stilitz Daniel Malachi	11 King's Bench Walk, London	0171 632 8500
Sugar Simon Gareth	5 New Square, London	0171 404 0404
Sullivan Michael Jerome	5 Bell Yard, London	0171 333 8811
Symons Christopher John Maurice	3 Verulam Buildings, London	0171 831 8441
Temple Anthony Dominic	4 Pump Court, London	0171 353 2656/9
Thompson Steven Lim	Twenty-Four Old Buildings, London	0171 404 0946
Tipples Miss Amanda Jane	13 Old Square, London	0171 404 4800
Tolaney Miss Sonia	3 Verulam Buildings, London	0171 831 8441
Trace Anthony John	• 13 Old Square, London	0171 404 4800
Trotman Timothy Oliver	Deans Court Chambers, Manchester	0161 834 4097
	Deans Court Chambers, Preston	01772 555163
Tucker David William	Two Crown Office Row, London	0171 797 8100
Turner Miss Janet Mary	3 Verulam Buildings, London	0171 831 8441
Wakefield Miss Anne Prudence	3 Verulam Buildings, London	0171 831 8441
Wallington Peter Thomas	11 King's Bench Walk, London	0171 632 8500
Weitzman Thomas Edward Benjamin	3 Verulam Buildings, London	0171 831 8441
West Lawrence Joseph	Stanbrook & Henderson, London	0171 353 0101
	2 Harcourt Buildings, London	0171 583 9020
Whitaker Steven Dixon	199 Strand, London	0171 379 9779
	All Saints Chambers, Bristol	0117 921 1966
Whiteley Miss Miranda Blyth	4 Field Court, London	0171 440 6900
Williamson Miss Bridget Susan	Enterprise Chambers, London	0171 405 9471
	Enterprise Chambers, Leeds	0113 246 0391
	Enterprise Chambers, Newcastle upon Tyne	0191 222 3344
Wilmot-Smith Richard James Crosbie	39 Essex Street, London	0171 832 1111
Wilson Ian Robert	3 Verulam Buildings, London	0171 831 8441
Wolfson David	3 Verulam Buildings, London	0171 831 8441
Worsley Daniel	Stanbrook & Henderson, London	0171 353 0101
	2 Harcourt Buildings, London	0171 583 9020
Wright Colin John	4 Field Court, London	0171 440 6900
Wright Gerard Henry	25-27 Castle Street, Liverpool	0151 227 5661/5666/236 5072
Wright Ms Sadie	Goldsmith Building, London	0171 353 7881

COMMERCIAL LITIGATION

Adamyk Simon Charles	12 New Square, London	0171 419 1212

• Expanded entry in Part D

Airey Simon Andrew	11 Bolt Court, London	0171 353 2300
	Redhill Chambers, Redhill	01737 780781
Akenhead Robert	Atkin Chambers, London	0171 404 0102
Akka Lawrence Mark	20 Essex Street, London	0171 583 9294
Alexander Ian Douglas Gavin	11 Bolt Court, London	0171 353 2300
	Redhill Chambers, Redhill	01737 780781
Althaus Antony Justin	No 1 Serjeants' Inn, London	0171 415 6666
Ambrose Miss Clare Mary Geneste	20 Essex Street, London	0171 583 9294
Amin Miss Farah	7 New Square, London	0171 430 1660
Arden Peter Leonard	Enterprise Chambers, London	0171 405 9471
	Enterprise Chambers, Leeds	0113 246 0391
	Enterprise Chambers, Newcastle upon Tyne	0191 222 3344
Ashworth Piers	Stanbrook & Henderson, London	0171 353 0101
	2 Harcourt Buildings, London	0171 583 9020
	Priory Chambers, Birmingham	0121 236 3882/1375
Atherton Ian David	Enterprise Chambers, London	0171 405 9471
	Enterprise Chambers, Leeds	0113 246 0391
	Enterprise Chambers, Newcastle upon Tyne	0191 222 3344
Aylen Walter Stafford	Hardwicke Building, London	0171 242 2523
Ayres Andrew John William	13 Old Square, London	0171 404 4800
Baatz Nicholas Stephen	Atkin Chambers, London	0171 404 0102
Baker Miss Anne Jacqueline	Enterprise Chambers, London	0171 405 9471
	Enterprise Chambers, Leeds	0113 246 0391
	Enterprise Chambers, Newcastle upon Tyne	0191 222 3344
Baldry Antony Brian	No 1 Serjeants' Inn, London	0171 415 6666
Baldwin John Grant	Oriel Chambers, Liverpool	0151 236 7191
Barker James Sebastian	Enterprise Chambers, London	0171 405 9471
	Enterprise Chambers, Leeds	0113 246 0391
	Enterprise Chambers, Newcastle upon Tyne	0191 222 3344
Barker Simon George Harry	• 13 Old Square, London	0171 404 4800
Barstow Stephen Royden	Harcourt Chambers, London	0171 353 6961/7
	Harcourt Chambers, Oxford	01865 791559
Barwise Miss Stephanie Nicola	Atkin Chambers, London	0171 404 0102
Baylis Ms Natalie Jayne	3 Verulam Buildings, London	0171 831 8441
Beard Daniel Matthew	Monckton Chambers, London	0171 405 7211
Beaumont Marc Clifford	• Pump Court Chambers, London	0171 353 0711
	• Harrow-on-the-Hill Chambers, Harrow on the Hill	0181 423 7444
	• Pump Court Chambers, Winchester	01962 868161
	• Windsor Barristers' Chambers, Windsor	01753 648 899
Bellamy Jonathan Mark	39 Essex Street, London	0171 832 1111
Beltrami Adrian Joseph	3 Verulam Buildings, London	0171 831 8441
Benson Julian Christopher Woodburn	One Essex Court, London	0171 936 3030
Bergin Terence Edward	New Court Chambers, London	0171 831 9500
Berkley Michael Stuart	Rougemont Chambers, Exeter	01392 410471
Berragan (Howard) Neil	Merchant Chambers, Manchester	0161 839 7070
Bhaloo Miss Zia Kurban	Enterprise Chambers, London	0171 405 9471
	Enterprise Chambers, Leeds	0113 246 0391
	Enterprise Chambers, Newcastle upon Tyne	0191 222 3344
Bickford-Smith Stephen William	4 Breams Buildings, London	0171 353 5835/430 1221
Birch Roger Allen	12 New Square, London	0171 419 1212
	Sovereign Chambers, Leeds	0113 245 1841/2/3
	Lancaster Buildings, Manchester	0161 661 4444
Bird Nigel David	Chambers of John Hand QC, Manchester	0161 955 9000
Bishop Edward James	No 1 Serjeants' Inn, London	0171 415 6666
Blackburn John	Atkin Chambers, London	0171 404 0102
Blair William James Lynton	3 Verulam Buildings, London	0171 831 8441
Blakesley Patrick James	Two Crown Office Row, London	0171 797 8100
Boswell Miss Lindsay Alice	4 Pump Court, London	0171 353 2656/9
Bourne Robert	• 4 Field Court, London	0171 440 6900
Bowdery Martin	Atkin Chambers, London	0171 404 0102
Boyle Gerard James	No 1 Serjeants' Inn, London	0171 415 6666
Bradley Richard	Oriel Chambers, Liverpool	0151 236 7191
Brannigan Peter John Sean	One Essex Court, London	0171 936 3030
Brant Paul David	Oriel Chambers, Liverpool	0151 236 7191

• Expanded entry in Part D

Brent Richard	3 Verulam Buildings, London	0171 831 8441
Brett Matthew Christopher Anthony	Harcourt Chambers, London	0171 353 6961/7
	Harcourt Chambers, Oxford	01865 791559
Brodie (James) Bruce	39 Essex Street, London	0171 832 1111
Brook Ian Stuart	Hardwicke Building, London	0171 242 2523
Brown Geoffrey Barlow	39 Essex Street, London	0171 832 1111
Brown Miss Hannah Beatrice	5 Bell Yard, London	0171 333 8811
Browne Miss Julie Rebecca	Goldsmith Building, London	0171 353 7881
Bull (Donald) Roger	One Essex Court, London	0171 936 3030
Burns Peter Richard	Deans Court Chambers, Manchester	0161 834 4097
Burr Andrew Charles	Atkin Chambers, London	0171 404 0102
Burroughs Nigel Alfred	11 Old Square, London	0171 430 0341
Burton Michael John	Littleton Chambers, London	0171 797 8600
Capon Philip Christopher William	St Philip's Chambers, Birmingham	0121 246 7000
Carey Jeremy Reynolds Patrick	Lamb Chambers, London	0171 797 8300
Carman George Alfred	New Court Chambers, London	0171 831 9500
Cash Miss Joanne Catherine	Farrar's Building, London	0171 583 9241
Catchpole Stuart Paul	39 Essex Street, London	0171 832 1111
Cawley Neil Robert Loudoun	55 Temple Chambers, London	0171 353 7400
	Milton Keynes Chambers, Milton Keynes	01908 217857
Chalmers Miss Suzanne Frances	Two Crown Office Row, London	0171 797 8100
Charkham Graham Harold	20 Essex Street, London	0171 583 9294
Charman Andrew Julian	St Philip's Chambers, Birmingham	0121 246 7000
Cheyne Miss Phyllida Alison	4 Pump Court, London	0171 353 2656/9
Clark Ms Julia Elisabeth	5 New Square, London	0171 404 0404
Clarke Miss Alison Lee	No 1 Serjeants' Inn, London	0171 415 6666
Clarke Ian James	Hardwicke Building, London	0171 242 2523
Clay Robert Charles	Atkin Chambers, London	0171 404 0102
Clegg Sebastian James Barwick	Deans Court Chambers, Manchester	0161 834 4097
Coburn Michael Jeremy Patrick	20 Essex Street, London	0171 583 9294
Collett Ivor William	No 1 Serjeants' Inn, London	0171 415 6666
Collett Michael John	20 Essex Street, London	0171 583 9294
Collins John Morris	11 King's Bench Walk, London	0171 353 3337/8
	9 Woodhouse Square, Leeds	0113 245 1986
Connerty Anthony Robin	Lamb Chambers, London	0171 797 8300
Corbett James Patrick	St Philip's Chambers, Birmingham	0121 246 7000
Cottrell Matthew Robert	Oriel Chambers, Liverpool	0151 236 7191
Cowan Peter Sherwood McCrea	Oriel Chambers, Liverpool	0151 236 7191
Craig Kenneth Allen	Hardwicke Building, London	0171 242 2523
Crail Miss (Elspeth) Ross	12 New Square, London	0171 419 1212
	Sovereign Chambers, Leeds	0113 245 1841/2/3
Cranfield Peter Anthony	3 Verulam Buildings, London	0171 831 8441
Creaner Paul Anthony	15 Winckley Square, Preston	01772 252 828
Cross James Edward Michael	4 Pump Court, London	0171 353 2656/9
Cross (Joseph) Edward	2 Gray's Inn Square Chambers, London	0171 242 0328/405 1317
Crossley Simon Justin	9 Woodhouse Square, Leeds	0113 245 1986
Cunningham Miss Claire Louise	St Philip's Chambers, Birmingham	0121 246 7000
Cunningham Mark James	13 Old Square, London	0171 404 4800
Curtis Michael Alexander	Two Crown Office Row, London	0171 797 8100
Dallas Andrew Thomas Alastair	Chambers of Andrew Campbell QC, Leeds	0113 245 5438
Darbyshire William Robert	Chambers of John Hand QC, Manchester	0161 955 9000
Datta Mrs Wendy Patricia Mizal	Alban Chambers, London	0171 419 5051
Davidson Edward Alan	• 11 Old Square, London	0171 430 0341
Davidson Nicholas Ranking	4 Paper Buildings, London	0171 353 3366/583 7155
Davies Andrew Christopher	New Court Chambers, London	0171 831 9500
Davies Miss Louise	12 New Square, London	0171 419 1212
Davies Stephen Richard	8 King Street Chambers, Manchester	0161 834 9560
Davies-Jones Jonathan	3 Verulam Buildings, London	0171 831 8441
Dawes Gordon Stephen Knight	Goldsmith Building, London	0171 353 7881
de Jehan David	St Paul's House, Leeds	0113 245 5866
de Lacy Richard Michael	3 Verulam Buildings, London	0171 831 8441
Deacock Adam Jason	Chambers of Lord Goodhart QC, London	0171 405 5577
Dean Brian John Anthony	St Philip's Chambers, Birmingham	0121 246 7000
Dennison Stephen Randell	Atkin Chambers, London	0171 404 0102
Dennys Nicholas Charles Jonathan	Atkin Chambers, London	0171 404 0102
Dodd Christopher John Nicholas	9 Woodhouse Square, Leeds	0113 245 1986

• Expanded entry in Part D

Doerries Miss Chantal-Aimee Renee Aemelia Annemarie	Atkin Chambers, London	0171 404 0102
Doherty Bernard James	39 Essex Street, London	0171 832 1111
Dougherty Nigel Peter	Erskine Chambers, London	0171 242 5532
Dowse John	Chambers of Lord Goodhart QC, London	0171 405 5577
	Chambers of John Hand QC, Manchester	0161 955 9000
Doyle Louis George	Chambers of Andrew Campbell QC, Leeds	0113 245 5438
Driscoll Miss Lynn	Sovereign Chambers, Leeds	0113 245 1841/2/3
	Lancaster Buildings, Manchester	0161 661 4444
Dumaresq Ms Delia Jane	Atkin Chambers, London	0171 404 0102
Dunn Christopher	Sovereign Chambers, Leeds	0113 245 1841/2/3
Eastman Roger	Stanbrook & Henderson, London	0171 353 0101
	2 Harcourt Buildings, London	0171 583 9020
Edey Philip David	20 Essex Street, London	0171 583 9294
Edwards Anthony Howard	Oriel Chambers, Liverpool	0151 236 7191
Edwards Richard Julian Henshaw	3 Verulam Buildings, London	0171 831 8441
Edwards-Stuart Antony James Cobham	Two Crown Office Row, London	0171 797 8100
Ekins Charles Wareing		
Elleray Anthony John	• 12 New Square, London	0171 419 1212
	• St James's Chambers, Manchester	0161 834 7000
	• Park Lane Chambers, Leeds	0113 228 5000
Elliott Nicholas Blethyn	3 Verulam Buildings, London	0171 831 8441
Evans James Frederick Meurig	3 Verulam Buildings, London	0171 831 8441
Evans Lee John	Farrar's Building, London	0171 583 9241
Evans-Gordon Mrs Jane-Anne Mary	12 New Square, London	0171 419 1212
Evans-Tovey Jason Robert	Two Crown Office Row, London	0171 797 8100
Exall Gordon David	Chambers of Andrew Campbell QC, Leeds	0113 245 5438
Faulks Edward Peter Lawless	No 1 Serjeants' Inn, London	0171 415 6666
Field Richard Alan	11 King's Bench Walk, London	0171 632 8500
Finlay Darren	Sovereign Chambers, Leeds	0113 245 1841/2/3
Fisher David	5 Bell Yard, London	0171 333 8811
Fitzgerald John Vincent	New Court, London	0171 797 8999
Francis Edward Gerald Francis	Enterprise Chambers, London	0171 405 9471
	Enterprise Chambers, Leeds	0113 246 0391
	Enterprise Chambers, Newcastle upon Tyne	0191 222 3344
Franklin Stephen Hall	5 Paper Buildings, London	0171 583 6117
	Fenners Chambers, Cambridge	01223 368761
Fraser Peter Donald	Atkin Chambers, London	0171 404 0102
Freedman Sampson Clive	3 Verulam Buildings, London	0171 831 8441
Frodsham Alexander Miles	Oriel Chambers, Liverpool	0151 236 7191
Garcia-Miller Miss Laura	Enterprise Chambers, London	0171 405 9471
	Enterprise Chambers, Leeds	0113 246 0391
	Enterprise Chambers, Newcastle upon Tyne	0191 222 3344
Garnett Kevin Mitchell	5 New Square, London	0171 404 0404
Gatty Daniel Simon	New Court Chambers, London	0171 831 9500
Geering Ian Walter	3 Verulam Buildings, London	0171 831 8441
George Miss Judith Sarah	St Philip's Chambers, Birmingham	0121 246 7000
Gerald Nigel Mortimer	Enterprise Chambers, London	0171 405 9471
	Enterprise Chambers, Leeds	0113 246 0391
	Enterprise Chambers, Newcastle upon Tyne	0191 222 3344
Gibaud Miss Catherine Alison Annetta	3 Verulam Buildings, London	0171 831 8441
Gibson Charles Anthony Warneford	2 Harcourt Buildings, London	0171 583 9020
Giffin Nigel Dyson	11 King's Bench Walk, London	0171 632 8500
Gilchrist David Somerled	Chambers of John Hand QC, Manchester	0161 955 9000
Glasgow Edwin John	39 Essex Street, London	0171 832 1111
Goddard Andrew Stephen	Atkin Chambers, London	0171 404 0102
Godfrey Jonathan Saul	St Paul's House, Leeds	0113 245 5866
Godwin William George Henry	Atkin Chambers, London	0171 404 0102
Goldblatt Simon	39 Essex Street, London	0171 832 1111
Goodbody Peter James	• Oriel Chambers, Liverpool	0151 236 7191
Goodman Andrew David	199 Strand, London	0171 379 9779

Goose Julian Nicholas	Chambers of Andrew Campbell QC, Leeds	0113 245 5438
Gore-Andrews Gavin Angus Russell	Stanbrook & Henderson, London	0171 353 0101
	2 Harcourt Buildings, London	0171 583 9020
Goudie James	• 11 King's Bench Walk, London	0171 632 8500
Graham Thomas Patrick Henry	Lamb Chambers, London	0171 797 8300
Grant Thomas Paul Wentworth	New Court Chambers, London	0171 831 9500
Grantham Andrew Timothy	• Deans Court Chambers, Manchester	0161 834 4097
	• Deans Court Chambers, Preston	01772 555163
Green Patrick Curtis	Stanbrook & Henderson, London	0171 353 0101
	2 Harcourt Buildings, London	0171 583 9020
Greenbourne John Hugo	Two Crown Office Row, London	0171 797 8100
Grodzinski Samuel Marc	39 Essex Street, London	0171 832 1111
Groves Hugo Gerard	Enterprise Chambers, London	0171 405 9471
	Enterprise Chambers, Leeds	0113 246 0391
	Enterprise Chambers, Newcastle upon Tyne	0191 222 3344
Guggenheim Miss Anna Maeve	Two Crown Office Row, London	0171 797 8100
Gun Cuninghame Julian Arthur	• Gough Square Chambers, London	0171 353 0924
Gunning Alexander Rupert	4 Pump Court, London	0171 353 2656/9
Hall Mrs Melanie Ruth	Monckton Chambers, London	0171 405 7211
Hall Taylor Alexander Edward	11 Old Square, London	0171 430 0341
Halpern David Anthony	Enterprise Chambers, London	0171 405 9471
	Enterprise Chambers, Leeds	0113 246 0391
	Enterprise Chambers, Newcastle upon Tyne	0191 222 3344
Hamblen Nicholas Archibald	20 Essex Street, London	0171 583 9294
Hamer Michael Howard Kenneth	2 Harcourt Buildings, London	0171 583 9020
	Westgate Chambers, Lewes	01273 480 510
Hamilton Graeme Montagu	Two Crown Office Row, London	0171 797 8100
Hammerton Alastair Rolf	No 1 Serjeants' Inn, London	0171 415 6666
Hammerton Miss Veronica Lesley	No 1 Serjeants' Inn, London	0171 415 6666
Hantusch Robert Anthony	• 3 Stone Buildings, London	0171 242 4937/405 8358
Harbottle Gwilym Thomas	5 New Square, London	0171 404 0404
Hardwick Matthew Richard	Enterprise Chambers, London	0171 405 9471
	Enterprise Chambers, Leeds	0113 246 0391
	Enterprise Chambers, Newcastle upon Tyne	0191 222 3344
Harris Paul Best	Monckton Chambers, London	0171 405 7211
Harrison John Foster	St Paul's House, Leeds	0113 245 5866
Harvey Miss Jayne Denise	Goldsworth Chambers, London	0171 405 7117
Harvey Jonathan Robert William	2 Harcourt Buildings, London	0171 583 9020
Harvey Michael Llewellyn Tucker	Two Crown Office Row, London	0171 797 8100
Haven Kevin	2 Gray's Inn Square Chambers, London	0171 242 0328/405 1317
Hay Robin William Patrick Hamilton	Goldsmith Building, London	0171 353 7881
Hayes Miss Josephine Mary	Chambers of Lord Goodhart QC, London	0171 405 5577
Haynes Miss Rebecca	Monckton Chambers, London	0171 405 7211
Hayward Peter Michael	The Outer Temple, Room 26, London	0171 353 4647
Heap Gerard Miles	Sovereign Chambers, Leeds	0113 245 1841/2/3
Hegarty Kevin John	St Philip's Chambers, Birmingham	0121 246 7000
Henderson Roger Anthony	Stanbrook & Henderson, London	0171 353 0101
	2 Harcourt Buildings, London	0171 583 9020
Heywood Michael Edmundson	Chambers of Lord Goodhart QC, London	0171 405 5577
	Cobden House Chambers, Manchester	0161 833 6000/6001
Hibbert William John	Gough Square Chambers, London	0171 353 0924
Higgins Anthony Paul	Goldsmith Building, London	0171 353 7881
Hill Robert Douglas	Pump Court Chambers, London	0171 353 0711
	Pump Court Chambers, Winchester	01962 868161
Hockaday Miss Annie	3 Verulam Buildings, London	0171 831 8441
Hodgkinson Tristram Patrick	• 5 Pump Court, London	0171 353 2532
Hodgson Miss Susan Ann	Two Crown Office Row, London	0171 797 8100
Holdsworth James Arthur	Two Crown Office Row, London	0171 797 8100
Holland Charles Christopher	Trinity Chambers, Newcastle upon Tyne	0191 232 1927
Hollingworth Peter James Michael	22 Albion Place, Northampton	01604 636271
Holmes Justin Francis	Chambers of Lord Goodhart QC, London	0171 405 5577
Horspool Anthony Bernard Graeme	Hardwicke Building, London	0171 242 2523
Howells James Richard	Atkin Chambers, London	0171 404 0102

     • Expanded entry in Part D

Hughes Miss Mary Josephine	Chambers of Lord Goodhart QC, London	0171 405 5577
Hunter William Quigley	No 1 Serjeants' Inn, London	0171 415 6666
Hurst Brian	17 Bedford Row, London	0171 831 7314
Hutton Miss Caroline	Enterprise Chambers, London	0171 405 9471
	Enterprise Chambers, Leeds	0113 246 0391
	Enterprise Chambers, Newcastle upon Tyne	0191 222 3344
Ife Miss Linden Elizabeth	Enterprise Chambers, London	0171 405 9471
	Enterprise Chambers, Leeds	0113 246 0391
	Enterprise Chambers, Newcastle upon Tyne	0191 222 3344
Jack Adrian Laurence Robert	Enterprise Chambers, London	0171 405 9471
James Michael Frank	Enterprise Chambers, London	0171 405 9471
	Enterprise Chambers, Leeds	0113 246 0391
	Enterprise Chambers, Newcastle upon Tyne	0191 222 3344
Jarvis John Manners	3 Verulam Buildings, London	0171 831 8441
Jefferies Thomas Robert	Chambers of Lord Goodhart QC, London	0171 405 5577
Jenkala Adrian Aleksander	11 Bolt Court, London	0171 353 2300
	Redhill Chambers, Redhill	01737 780781
Jennings Timothy Robin Finnegan	Enterprise Chambers, London	0171 405 9471
	Enterprise Chambers, Leeds	0113 246 0391
	Enterprise Chambers, Newcastle upon Tyne	0191 222 3344
Jess Digby Charles	• 8 King Street Chambers, Manchester	0161 834 9560
Johnson Michael Sloan	Chambers of John Hand QC, Manchester	0161 955 9000
Jordan Andrew	Stanbrook & Henderson, London	0171 353 0101
	2 Harcourt Buildings, London	0171 583 9020
Jory Robert John Hugh	Enterprise Chambers, London	0171 405 9471
	Enterprise Chambers, Leeds	0113 246 0391
	Enterprise Chambers, Newcastle upon Tyne	0191 222 3344
Kavanagh Giles Wilfred Conor	• 5 Bell Yard, London	0171 333 8811
Kay Michael Jack David	3 Verulam Buildings, London	0171 831 8441
	Park Lane Chambers, Leeds	0113 228 5000
Kearl Guy Alexander	St Paul's House, Leeds	0113 245 5866
Kent Michael Harcourt	Two Crown Office Row, London	0171 797 8100
Khokhar Mushtaq Ahmed	Sovereign Chambers, Leeds	0113 245 1841/2/3
Kimbell John Ashley	5 Bell Yard, London	0171 333 8811
Kime Matthew Jonathan	• New Court, London	0171 797 8999
	• Cobden House Chambers, Manchester	0161 833 6000/6001
Knight Brian Joseph	Atkin Chambers, London	0171 404 0102
Kolodziej Andrzej Jozef	• Littman Chambers, London	0171 404 4866
Kremen Philip Michael	Hardwicke Building, London	0171 242 2523
Laing Miss Elisabeth Mary Caroline	11 King's Bench Walk, London	0171 632 8500
Lamont Miss Camilla Rose	Chambers of Lord Goodhart QC, London	0171 405 5577
Landes Miss Anna-Rose	St Philip's Chambers, Birmingham	0121 246 7000
Laughton Samuel Dennis	17 Old Buildings, London	0171 405 9653
Lawrence The Hon Patrick John Tristram	4 Paper Buildings, London	0171 353 3366/583 7155
Lawson Daniel George	Goldsmith Building, London	0171 353 7881
Lawson Robert John	5 Bell Yard, London	0171 333 8811
Lazarus Michael Steven	1 Crown Office Row, London	0171 583 9292
Leech Brian Walter Thomas	No 1 Serjeants' Inn, London	0171 415 6666
Leeming Ian	Lamb Chambers, London	0171 797 8300
	Chambers of John Hand QC, Manchester	0161 955 9000
Lees Andrew James	St Paul's House, Leeds	0113 245 5866
Leiper Richard Thomas	11 King's Bench Walk, London	0171 632 8500
Lennard Stephen Charles	Hardwicke Building, London	0171 242 2523
Leonard Charles Robert Weston	Goldsmith Building, London	0171 353 7881
Levy Benjamin Keith	Enterprise Chambers, London	0171 405 9471
	Enterprise Chambers, Leeds	0113 246 0391
	Enterprise Chambers, Newcastle upon Tyne	0191 222 3344
Levy Robert Stuart	9 Stone Buildings, London	0171 404 5055
	Assize Court Chambers, Bristol	0117 926 4587
Lewis Andrew William	Sovereign Chambers, Leeds	0113 245 1841/2/3

• Expanded entry in Part D

Lewis Miss Caroline Susannah	3 Verulam Buildings, London	0171 831 8441
Lewis Robert		
Lindsay Crawford Callum Douglas	No 1 Serjeants' Inn, London	0171 415 6666
Livingstone Simon John	11 Bolt Court, London	0171 353 2300
	Redhill Chambers, Redhill	01737 780781
Lofthouse Simon Timothy	Atkin Chambers, London	0171 404 0102
Lowenstein Paul David	Littleton Chambers, London	0171 797 8600
Lumley Nicholas James Henry	Sovereign Chambers, Leeds	0113 245 1841/2/3
Lynagh Richard Dudley	Two Crown Office Row, London	0171 797 8100
Machell Raymond Donatus	2 Pump Court, London	0171 353 5597
	Deans Court Chambers, Manchester	0161 834 4097
Maclean Alan John	39 Essex Street, London	0171 832 1111
Macnab Alexander Andrew	Monckton Chambers, London	0171 405 7211
Maitland Jones Mark Griffith	Goldsmith Building, London	0171 353 7881
Malek Ali	3 Verulam Buildings, London	0171 831 8441
Males Stephen Martin	20 Essex Street, London	0171 583 9294
Mann George Anthony	Enterprise Chambers, London	0171 405 9471
	Enterprise Chambers, Leeds	0113 246 0391
	Enterprise Chambers, Newcastle upon Tyne	0191 222 3344
Mantle Peter John	Monckton Chambers, London	0171 405 7211
Manzoni Charles Peter	39 Essex Street, London	0171 832 1111
Marks Jonathan Clive	4 Pump Court, London	0171 353 2656/9
Marquand Charles Nicholas Hilary	Chambers of Lord Goodhart QC, London	0171 405 5577
Marris Miss Sarah Selena Rixar	No 1 Serjeants' Inn, London	0171 415 6666
Marshall Paul David John	1 Crown Office Row, London	0171 583 9292
Martineau Henry Ralph Adeane	Goldsmith Building, London	0171 353 7881
Masters Miss Sara Alayna	20 Essex Street, London	0171 583 9294
Mauger Miss Claire Shanti Andrea	Enterprise Chambers, London	0171 405 9471
Mauleverer Peter Bruce	4 Pump Court, London	0171 353 2656/9
Mawrey Richard Brooks	Stanbrook & Henderson, London	0171 353 0101
	2 Harcourt Buildings, London	0171 583 9020
Maxwell David	Claremont Chambers, Wolverhampton	01902 426222
Maxwell Miss Karen Laetitia	20 Essex Street, London	0171 583 9294
Maxwell-Scott James Herbert	Two Crown Office Row, London	0171 797 8100
Mayhew Jerome Patrick Burke	Goldsmith Building, London	0171 353 7881
McAllister Miss Elizabeth Ann	Enterprise Chambers, London	0171 405 9471
	Enterprise Chambers, Leeds	0113 246 0391
	Enterprise Chambers, Newcastle upon Tyne	0191 222 3344
McCall Duncan James	4 Pump Court, London	0171 353 2656/9
McCarthy William	New Bailey Chambers, Preston	01772 258 087
McCredie Miss Fionnuala Mary Constance	3 Serjeants' Inn, London	0171 353 5537
McGregor Harvey	4 Paper Buildings, London	0171 353 3366/583 7155
McKinnell Miss Soraya Jane	Enterprise Chambers, London	0171 405 9471
	Enterprise Chambers, Leeds	0113 246 0391
	Enterprise Chambers, Newcastle upon Tyne	0191 222 3344
McManus Jonathan Richard	4-5 Gray's Inn Square, London	0171 404 5252
McMullan Manus Anthony	Atkin Chambers, London	0171 404 0102
McParland Michael Joseph	New Court Chambers, London	0171 831 9500
McQuater Ewan Alan	3 Verulam Buildings, London	0171 831 8441
Meeson Nigel Keith	4 Field Court, London	0171 440 6900
Mendoza Neil David Pereira	Hardwicke Building, London	0171 242 2523
Merriman Nicholas Flavelle	3 Verulam Buildings, London	0171 831 8441
Middleton Miss Georgina Claire	New Court Chambers, London	0171 831 9500
Milligan Iain Anstruther	20 Essex Street, London	0171 583 9294
Mitchell Gregory Charles Mathew	3 Verulam Buildings, London	0171 831 8441
Moon Philip Charles Angus	3 Serjeants' Inn, London	0171 353 5537
Morgan Charles James Arthur	Enterprise Chambers, London	0171 405 9471
	Enterprise Chambers, Leeds	0113 246 0391
	Enterprise Chambers, Newcastle upon Tyne	0191 222 3344
Morgan Richard Hugo Lyndon	13 Old Square, London	0171 404 4800
Muir John Henry	12 New Square, London	0171 419 1212
	Sovereign Chambers, Leeds	0113 245 1841/2/3
Mulcahy Miss Leigh-Ann Maria	Two Crown Office Row, London	0171 797 8100
Mullis Anthony Roger	Chambers of Lord Goodhart QC, London	0171 405 5577
Nash Jonathan Scott	3 Verulam Buildings, London	0171 831 8441

• Expanded entry in Part D

Naylor Jonathan Peter	King's Chambers, Eastbourne	01323 416053
Nebhrajani Miss Mel	9 Stone Buildings, London	0171 404 5055
Neish Andrew Graham	4 Pump Court, London	0171 353 2656/9
Nelson Vincent Leonard	39 Essex Street, London	0171 832 1111
Nesbitt Timothy John Robert	199 Strand, London	0171 379 9779
Neville Stephen John	Gough Square Chambers, London	0171 353 0924
Newman Miss Catherine Mary	• 13 Old Square, London	0171 404 4800
Newman Ms Ingrid	Hardwicke Building, London	0171 242 2523
Nicholls John Peter	13 Old Square, London	0171 404 4800
Nicholls Paul Richard	11 King's Bench Walk, London	0171 632 8500
Nicholls Peter John	5 Pump Court, London	0171 353 2532
Nicholson Jeremy Mark	4 Pump Court, London	0171 353 2656/9
Nicol-Gent William Philip Trahair	King's Chambers, Eastbourne	01323 416053
Noble Andrew	Eldon Chambers, London	0171 353 4636
	Merchant Chambers, Manchester	0161 839 7070
Norman Christopher John George	No 1 Serjeants' Inn, London	0171 415 6666
Norris Paul Howard	One Essex Court, London	0171 936 3030
Odgers John Arthur	3 Verulam Buildings, London	0171 831 8441
Ogunbiyi Oluwole Afolabi	Horizon Chambers, London	0171 242 2440
Ohrenstein Dov	Chambers of Lord Goodhart QC, London	0171 405 5577
Owen David Christopher	20 Essex Street, London	0171 583 9294
Padfield Ms Alison Mary	One Hare Court, London	0171 353 3171
Palmer James Savill	2 Harcourt Buildings, London	0171 583 9020
Paneth Miss Sarah Ruth	No 1 Serjeants' Inn, London	0171 415 6666
Parkin Miss Fiona Jane	Atkin Chambers, London	0171 404 0102
Patchett-Joyce Michael Thurston	Monckton Chambers, London	0171 405 7211
Patten Benedict Joseph	Two Crown Office Row, London	0171 797 8100
Peacock Ian Christopher	12 New Square, London	0171 419 1212
	Sovereign Chambers, Leeds	0113 245 1841/2/3
Peacock Nicholas Christopher	13 Old Square, London	0171 404 4800
Peacocke Mrs Teresa Anne Rosen	Enterprise Chambers, London	0171 405 9471
	Enterprise Chambers, Leeds	0113 246 0391
	Enterprise Chambers, Newcastle upon Tyne	0191 222 3344
Peglow Dr Michael Alfred Herman	Chambers of Geoffrey Hawker, London	0171 583 8899
Pelling (Philip) Mark	Monckton Chambers, London	0171 405 7211
Pelling Richard Alexander	New Court Chambers, London	0171 831 9500
Pema Anesh Bhumin Laloo	9 Woodhouse Square, Leeds	0113 245 1986
Peretz George Michael John		
Perkoff Richard Michael	Littleton Chambers, London	0171 797 8600
Pershad Rohan	Two Crown Office Row, London	0171 797 8100
Phillips Andrew Charles	Two Crown Office Row, London	0171 797 8100
Phillips David John	199 Strand, London	0171 379 9779
	30 Park Place, Cardiff	01222 398421
Phillips Jonathan Mark	3 Verulam Buildings, London	0171 831 8441
Phillips Stephen Edmund	3 Verulam Buildings, London	0171 831 8441
Pickering James Patrick	Enterprise Chambers, London	0171 405 9471
	Enterprise Chambers, Leeds	0113 246 0391
	Enterprise Chambers, Newcastle upon Tyne	0191 222 3344
Picton Julian Mark	4 Paper Buildings, London	0171 353 3366/583 7155
Pimentel Carlos de Serpa Alberto Legg	3 Stone Buildings, London	0171 242 4937/405 8358
Pitt-Payne Timothy Sheridan	• 11 King's Bench Walk, London	0171 632 8500
Pittaway David Michael	No 1 Serjeants' Inn, London	0171 415 6666
Pooles Michael Philip Holmes	4 Paper Buildings, London	0171 353 3366/583 7155
Pope David James	3 Verulam Buildings, London	0171 831 8441
Pryke Stuart	Trinity Chambers, Newcastle upon Tyne	0191 232 1927
Quest David Charles	3 Verulam Buildings, London	0171 831 8441
Raeside Mark Andrew	Atkin Chambers, London	0171 404 0102
Rai Amarjit Singh	St Philip's Chambers, Birmingham	0121 246 7000
Rawley Miss Dominique Jane	Atkin Chambers, London	0171 404 0102
Rawlings Clive Patrick	Goldsmith Building, London	0171 353 7881
Rea Miss Karen Marie-Jeanne	No 1 Serjeants' Inn, London	0171 415 6666
Readhead Simon John Howard	No 1 Serjeants' Inn, London	0171 415 6666
Reese Colin Edward	Atkin Chambers, London	0171 404 0102
Reeve Matthew Francis	5 Bell Yard, London	0171 333 8811
Reynold Frederic	New Court Chambers, London	0171 831 9500
Richardson Miss Sarah Jane	Enterprise Chambers, London	0171 405 9471

	Enterprise Chambers, Leeds	0113 246 0391
	Enterprise Chambers, Newcastle upon Tyne	0191 222 3344
Rigby Terence	Chambers of John Hand QC, Manchester	0161 955 9000
Rigney Andrew James	Two Crown Office Row, London	0171 797 8100
Rivalland Marc-Edouard	No 1 Serjeants' Inn, London	0171 415 6666
Robb Adam Duncan	39 Essex Street, London	0171 832 1111
Roberts Miss Catherine Ann	Erskine Chambers, London	0171 242 5532
Robson John Malcolm	2 Gray's Inn Square Chambers, London	0171 242 0328/405 1317
	Assize Court Chambers, Bristol	0117 926 4587
Roe Thomas Idris	Goldsmith Building, London	0171 353 7881
Rogers Ian Paul	1 Crown Office Row, London	0171 583 9292
Ross John Graffin	No 1 Serjeants' Inn, London	0171 415 6666
Roth Peter Marcel	Monckton Chambers, London	0171 405 7211
Routley Patrick	Goldsmith Building, London	0171 353 7881
Royce Darryl Fraser	Atkin Chambers, London	0171 404 0102
Rule Jonathan Daniel	Merchant Chambers, Manchester	0161 839 7070
Rumney Conrad William Arthur	St Philip's Chambers, Birmingham	0121 246 7000
Russell Christopher Garnet	12 New Square, London	0171 419 1212
	Sovereign Chambers, Leeds	0113 245 1841/2/3
Russell Robert John Finlay	5 Bell Yard, London	0171 333 8811
Russen Jonathan Huw Sinclair	13 Old Square, London	0171 404 4800
Salter Richard Stanley	3 Verulam Buildings, London	0171 831 8441
Sampson Graeme William	Chambers of Geoffrey Hawker, London	0171 583 8899
Sander Andrew Thomas	Goldsmith Building, London	0171 353 7881
	Oriel Chambers, Liverpool	0151 236 7191
Saunders Nicholas Joseph	4 Field Court, London	0171 440 6900
Sayer Mr Peter Edwin	Gough Square Chambers, London	0171 353 0924
Schaw-Miller Stephen Grant	5 Bell Yard, London	0171 333 8811
Selvaratnam Miss Vasanti Emily Indrani	4 Field Court, London	0171 440 6900
Seymour Richard William	Monckton Chambers, London	0171 405 7211
Shepherd Philip Alexander	• 5 Bell Yard, London	0171 333 8811
Sheridan Maurice Bernard Gerard	• 3 Verulam Buildings, London	0171 831 8441
Simor Miss Jessica Margaret Poppaea	Monckton Chambers, London	0171 405 7211
Simpson Mark Taylor	4 Paper Buildings, London	0171 353 3366/583 7155
Smith Miss Julia Mair Wheldon	Gough Square Chambers, London	0171 353 0924
Smith Ms Katherine Emma	Monckton Chambers, London	0171 405 7211
Smith Warwick Timothy Cresswell	• Deans Court Chambers, Manchester	0161 834 4097
	• Deans Court Chambers, Preston	01772 555163
Snowden John Stevenson	Two Crown Office Row, London	0171 797 8100
Soole Michael Alexander	5 Bell Yard, London	0171 333 8811
Southwell Richard Charles	One Hare Court, London	0171 353 3171
Spearman Richard	5 Raymond Buildings, London	0171 242 2902
Stagg Paul Andrew	No 1 Serjeants' Inn, London	0171 415 6666
Starcevic Petar	St Philip's Chambers, Birmingham	0121 246 7000
Stern Dr Kristina Anne	39 Essex Street, London	0171 832 1111
Stewart Alexander Joseph	5 New Square, London	0171 404 0404
Stewart Nicholas John Cameron	Hardwicke Building, London	0171 242 2523
Stilitz Daniel Malachi	11 King's Bench Walk, London	0171 632 8500
Storey Jeremy Brian	4 Pump Court, London	0171 353 2656/9
Streatfeild-James David Stewart	Atkin Chambers, London	0171 404 0102
Sullivan Michael Jerome	5 Bell Yard, London	0171 333 8811
Susman Peter Joseph	New Court Chambers, London	0171 831 9500
Sutcliffe Andrew Harold Wentworth	3 Verulam Buildings, London	0171 831 8441
Swan Ian Christopher	Two Crown Office Row, London	0171 797 8100
Symons Christopher John Maurice	3 Verulam Buildings, London	0171 831 8441
Taelor Start Miss Angharad Jocelyn	3 Verulam Buildings, London	0171 831 8441
Taylor Miss Deborah Frances	Two Crown Office Row, London	0171 797 8100
Tedd Rex Hilary	• St Philip's Chambers, Birmingham	0121 246 7000
	• 22 Albion Place, Northampton	01604 636271
Temple Anthony Dominic	4 Pump Court, London	0171 353 2656/9
Ter Haar Roger Eduard Lound	Two Crown Office Row, London	0171 797 8100
Thompson Rhodri William Ralph	Monckton Chambers, London	0171 405 7211
Thompson Steven Lim	Twenty-Four Old Buildings, London	0171 404 0946
Tobin Daniel Alphonsus Joseph	Chambers of Geoffrey Hawker, London	0171 583 8899
Tolaney Miss Sonia	3 Verulam Buildings, London	0171 831 8441

• Expanded entry in Part D

Tomlinson Hugh Richard Edward	New Court Chambers, London	0171 831 9500
Tozzi Nigel Kenneth	4 Pump Court, London	0171 353 2656/9
Trace Anthony John	• 13 Old Square, London	0171 404 4800
Tucker David William	Two Crown Office Row, London	0171 797 8100
Tucker Miss Katherine Jane Greening	St Philip's Chambers, Birmingham	0121 246 7000
Turner Miss Janet Mary	3 Verulam Buildings, London	0171 831 8441
Turner Jonathan Richard	Monckton Chambers, London	0171 405 7211
Twigger Andrew Mark	3 Stone Buildings, London	0171 242 4937/405 8358
Valentine Donald Graham	Atkin Chambers, London	0171 404 0102
Vaughan-Neil Miss Catherine Mary Bernardine	5 Bell Yard, London	0171 333 8811
Vines Anthony Robert Francis	Gough Square Chambers, London	0171 353 0924
Wadsworth James Patrick	4 Paper Buildings, London	0171 353 3366/583 7155
Walker Andrew Greenfield	Chambers of Lord Goodhart QC, London	0171 405 5577
Walker Steven John	Atkin Chambers, London	0171 404 0102
Wallace Ian Norman Duncan	Atkin Chambers, London	0171 404 0102
Ward Miss Siobhan Marie Lucia	11 King's Bench Walk, London	0171 632 8500
Ward Timothy Justin	39 Essex Street, London	0171 832 1111
Wardell John David Meredith	New Court Chambers, London	0171 831 9500
Warnock Andrew Ronald	No 1 Serjeants' Inn, London	0171 415 6666
Warrender Miss Nichola Mary	New Court Chambers, London	0171 831 9500
Waters Julian William Penrose	No 1 Serjeants' Inn, London	0171 415 6666
Weatherill Bernard Richard	Chambers of Lord Goodhart QC, London	0171 405 5577
Webb Robert Stopford	• 5 Bell Yard, London	0171 333 8811
Wedderspoon Miss Rachel Leone	Chambers of John Hand QC, Manchester	0161 955 9000
Weitzman Thomas Edward Benjamin	3 Verulam Buildings, London	0171 831 8441
West Lawrence Joseph	Stanbrook & Henderson, London	0171 353 0101
	2 Harcourt Buildings, London	0171 583 9020
West Mark	• 11 Old Square, London	0171 430 0341
Weston Clive Aubrey Richard	Two Crown Office Row, London	0171 797 8100
White Andrew	Atkin Chambers, London	0171 404 0102
Whiteley Miss Miranda Blyth	4 Field Court, London	0171 440 6900
Wilby David Christopher	• 199 Strand, London	0171 379 9779
	• Park Lane Chambers, Leeds	0113 228 5000
Wilken Sean David Henry	39 Essex Street, London	0171 832 1111
Williamson Miss Bridget Susan	Enterprise Chambers, London	0171 405 9471
	Enterprise Chambers, Leeds	0113 246 0391
	Enterprise Chambers, Newcastle upon Tyne	0191 222 3344
Wilmot-Smith Richard James Crosbie	39 Essex Street, London	0171 832 1111
Wilson Ian Robert	3 Verulam Buildings, London	0171 831 8441
Wilson Peter Julian		
Wolfson David	3 Verulam Buildings, London	0171 831 8441
Woolman Andrew Paul Lander	Chambers of Andrew Campbell QC, Leeds	0113 245 5438
Worsley Daniel	Stanbrook & Henderson, London	0171 353 0101
	2 Harcourt Buildings, London	0171 583 9020
Wright Colin John	4 Field Court, London	0171 440 6900
Wright Gerard Henry	25-27 Castle Street, Liverpool	0151 227 5661/5666/236 5072
Wright Norman Alfred	Oriel Chambers, Liverpool	0151 236 7191
Yell Nicholas Anthony	No 1 Serjeants' Inn, London	0171 415 6666
Zelin Geoffrey Andrew	Enterprise Chambers, London	0171 405 9471
	Enterprise Chambers, Leeds	0113 246 0391
	Enterprise Chambers, Newcastle upon Tyne	0191 222 3344

COMMERCIAL PROPERTY

Adamyk Simon Charles	12 New Square, London	0171 419 1212
Atherton Ian David	Enterprise Chambers, London	0171 405 9471
	Enterprise Chambers, Leeds	0113 246 0391
	Enterprise Chambers, Newcastle upon Tyne	0191 222 3344
Ayres Andrew John William	13 Old Square, London	0171 404 4800
Baker Miss Anne Jacqueline	Enterprise Chambers, London	0171 405 9471
	Enterprise Chambers, Leeds	0113 246 0391
	Enterprise Chambers, Newcastle upon Tyne	0191 222 3344

Baldry Antony Brian	No 1 Serjeants' Inn, London	0171 415 6666
Barker James Sebastian	Enterprise Chambers, London	0171 405 9471
	Enterprise Chambers, Leeds	0113 246 0391
	Enterprise Chambers, Newcastle upon Tyne	0191 222 3344
Beaumont Marc Clifford	• Pump Court Chambers, London	0171 353 0711
	• Harrow-on-the-Hill Chambers, Harrow on the Hill	0181 423 7444
	• Pump Court Chambers, Winchester	01962 868161
	• Windsor Barristers' Chambers, Windsor	01753 648 899
Bennett Gordon Irvine	5 Bell Yard, London	0171 333 8811
Bergin Terence Edward	New Court Chambers, London	0171 831 9500
Berkley Michael Stuart	Rougemont Chambers, Exeter	01392 410471
Berragan (Howard) Neil	Merchant Chambers, Manchester	0161 839 7070
Bhaloo Miss Zia Kurban	Enterprise Chambers, London	0171 405 9471
	Enterprise Chambers, Leeds	0113 246 0391
	Enterprise Chambers, Newcastle upon Tyne	0191 222 3344
Bourne Robert	• 4 Field Court, London	0171 440 6900
Boyle Christopher Alexander David	2 Mitre Court Buildings, London	0171 583 1380
Brannigan Peter John Sean	One Essex Court, London	0171 936 3030
Browne James William	Goldsworth Chambers, London	0171 405 7117
Bull (Donald) Roger	One Essex Court, London	0171 936 3030
Charman Andrew Julian	St Philip's Chambers, Birmingham	0121 246 7000
Cherryman John Richard	4 Breams Buildings, London	0171 353 5835/430 1221
Clarke Ian James	Hardwicke Building, London	0171 242 2523
Clegg Sebastian James Barwick	Deans Court Chambers, Manchester	0161 834 4097
Collier Martin Melton	Fenners Chambers, Cambridge	01223 368761
	Fenners Chambers, Peterborough	01733 562030
Crail Miss (Elspeth) Ross	12 New Square, London	0171 419 1212
	Sovereign Chambers, Leeds	0113 245 1841/2/3
Crawford Grant	11 Old Square, London	0171 430 0341
Creaner Paul Anthony	15 Winckley Square, Preston	01772 252 828
Daiches Michael Salis	• 22 Old Buildings, London	0171 831 0222
Darbyshire William Robert	Chambers of John Hand QC, Manchester	0161 955 9000
Davies Miss Louise	12 New Square, London	0171 419 1212
de Jehan David	St Paul's House, Leeds	0113 245 5866
de Voghelaere Parr Adam Stephen	2 Mitre Court Buildings, London	0171 583 1380
Deacock Adam Jason	Chambers of Lord Goodhart QC, London	0171 405 5577
Dowse John	Chambers of Lord Goodhart QC, London	0171 405 5577
	Chambers of John Hand QC, Manchester	0161 955 9000
Elleray Anthony John	• 12 New Square, London	0171 419 1212
	• St James's Chambers, Manchester	0161 834 7000
	• Park Lane Chambers, Leeds	0113 228 5000
Evans-Gordon Mrs Jane-Anne Mary	12 New Square, London	0171 419 1212
Fisher David	5 Bell Yard, London	0171 333 8811
FitzGerald Michael Frederick Clive	2 Mitre Court Buildings, London	0171 583 1380
Fookes Robert Lawrence	2 Mitre Court Buildings, London	0171 583 1380
Francis Edward Gerald Francis	Enterprise Chambers, London	0171 405 9471
	Enterprise Chambers, Leeds	0113 246 0391
	Enterprise Chambers, Newcastle upon Tyne	0191 222 3344
Furber (Robert) John	4 Breams Buildings, London	0171 353 5835/430 1221
Garcia-Miller Miss Laura	Enterprise Chambers, London	0171 405 9471
	Enterprise Chambers, Leeds	0113 246 0391
	Enterprise Chambers, Newcastle upon Tyne	0191 222 3344
Gerald Nigel Mortimer	Enterprise Chambers, London	0171 405 9471
	Enterprise Chambers, Leeds	0113 246 0391
	Enterprise Chambers, Newcastle upon Tyne	0191 222 3344
Glover Richard Michael	2 Mitre Court Buildings, London	0171 583 1380
Goodhart Lord	Chambers of Lord Goodhart QC, London	0171 405 5577
Gore Andrew Roger	Fenners Chambers, Cambridge	01223 368761
	Fenners Chambers, Peterborough	01733 562030
Grant Thomas Paul Wentworth	New Court Chambers, London	0171 831 9500

• Expanded entry in Part D

Gregory John Raymond	Deans Court Chambers, Manchester	0161 834 4097
	Deans Court Chambers, Preston	01772 555163
Groves Hugo Gerard	Enterprise Chambers, London	0171 405 9471
	Enterprise Chambers, Leeds	0113 246 0391
	Enterprise Chambers, Newcastle upon Tyne	0191 222 3344
Hall Taylor Alexander Edward	11 Old Square, London	0171 430 0341
Halpern David Anthony	Enterprise Chambers, London	0171 405 9471
	Enterprise Chambers, Leeds	0113 246 0391
	Enterprise Chambers, Newcastle upon Tyne	0191 222 3344
Hammerton Alastair Rolf	No 1 Serjeants' Inn, London	0171 415 6666
Hardwick Matthew Richard	Enterprise Chambers, London	0171 405 9471
	Enterprise Chambers, Leeds	0113 246 0391
	Enterprise Chambers, Newcastle upon Tyne	0191 222 3344
Hargreaves Miss Sara Jane	12 New Square, London	0171 419 1212
	Sovereign Chambers, Leeds	0113 245 1841/2/3
Harper Joseph Charles	4 Breams Buildings, London	0171 353 5835/430 1221
Haven Kevin	2 Gray's Inn Square Chambers, London	0171 242 0328/405 1317
Hayes Miss Josephine Mary	Chambers of Lord Goodhart QC, London	0171 405 5577
Heywood Michael Edmundson	Chambers of Lord Goodhart QC, London	0171 405 5577
	Cobden House Chambers, Manchester	0161 833 6000/6001
Holmes Justin Francis	Chambers of Lord Goodhart QC, London	0171 405 5577
Horspool Anthony Bernard Graeme	Hardwicke Building, London	0171 242 2523
Horton Matthew Bethell	2 Mitre Court Buildings, London	0171 583 1380
Hughes Miss Mary Josephine	Chambers of Lord Goodhart QC, London	0171 405 5577
Hunter William Quigley	No 1 Serjeants' Inn, London	0171 415 6666
Hutton Miss Caroline	Enterprise Chambers, London	0171 405 9471
	Enterprise Chambers, Leeds	0113 246 0391
	Enterprise Chambers, Newcastle upon Tyne	0191 222 3344
Ife Miss Linden Elizabeth	Enterprise Chambers, London	0171 405 9471
	Enterprise Chambers, Leeds	0113 246 0391
	Enterprise Chambers, Newcastle upon Tyne	0191 222 3344
Jack Adrian Laurence Robert	Enterprise Chambers, London	0171 405 9471
Jackson Dirik George Allan	• Chambers of Mr Peter Crampin QC, London	0171 831 0081
Jackson Nicholas David Kingsley	The Chambers of Adrian Lyon, Liverpool	0151 236 4421/8240/6757
James Michael Frank	Enterprise Chambers, London	0171 405 9471
	Enterprise Chambers, Leeds	0113 246 0391
	Enterprise Chambers, Newcastle upon Tyne	0191 222 3344
Jefferies Thomas Robert	Chambers of Lord Goodhart QC, London	0171 405 5577
Jennings Timothy Robin Finnegan	Enterprise Chambers, London	0171 405 9471
	Enterprise Chambers, Leeds	0113 246 0391
	Enterprise Chambers, Newcastle upon Tyne	0191 222 3344
Jones Geraint Martyn	Fenners Chambers, Cambridge	01223 368761
	Fenners Chambers, Peterborough	01733 562030
Jory Robert John Hugh	Enterprise Chambers, London	0171 405 9471
	Enterprise Chambers, Leeds	0113 246 0391
	Enterprise Chambers, Newcastle upon Tyne	0191 222 3344
King Neil Gerald Alexander	2 Mitre Court Buildings, London	0171 583 1380
Knott Malcolm Stephen	New Court Chambers, London	0171 831 9500
Kremen Philip Michael	Hardwicke Building, London	0171 242 2523
Lamont Miss Camilla Rose	Chambers of Lord Goodhart QC, London	0171 405 5577
Laughton Samuel Dennis	17 Old Buildings, London	0171 405 9653
Leeming Ian	Lamb Chambers, London	0171 797 8300
	Chambers of John Hand QC, Manchester	0161 955 9000
Levy Benjamin Keith	Enterprise Chambers, London	0171 405 9471

	Enterprise Chambers, Leeds	0113 246 0391
	Enterprise Chambers, Newcastle upon Tyne	0191 222 3344
Levy Robert Stuart	9 Stone Buildings, London	0171 404 5055
	Assize Court Chambers, Bristol	0117 926 4587
Livingstone Simon John	11 Bolt Court, London	0171 353 2300
	Redhill Chambers, Redhill	01737 780781
Lowenstein Paul David	Littleton Chambers, London	0171 797 8600
Mann George Anthony	Enterprise Chambers, London	0171 405 9471
	Enterprise Chambers, Leeds	0113 246 0391
	Enterprise Chambers, Newcastle upon Tyne	0191 222 3344
Mauger Miss Claire Shanti Andrea	Enterprise Chambers, London	0171 405 9471
McAllister Miss Elizabeth Ann	Enterprise Chambers, London	0171 405 9471
	Enterprise Chambers, Leeds	0113 246 0391
	Enterprise Chambers, Newcastle upon Tyne	0191 222 3344
McKinnell Miss Soraya Jane	Enterprise Chambers, London	0171 405 9471
	Enterprise Chambers, Leeds	0113 246 0391
	Enterprise Chambers, Newcastle upon Tyne	0191 222 3344
McManus Jonathan Richard	4-5 Gray's Inn Square, London	0171 404 5252
McQuail Ms Katherine Emma	11 Old Square, London	0171 430 0341
Meakin Timothy William	Fenners Chambers, Cambridge	01223 368761
	Fenners Chambers, Peterborough	01733 562030
Mendoza Neil David Pereira	Hardwicke Building, London	0171 242 2523
Morgan Charles James Arthur	Enterprise Chambers, London	0171 405 9471
	Enterprise Chambers, Leeds	0113 246 0391
	Enterprise Chambers, Newcastle upon Tyne	0191 222 3344
Morgan Edward Patrick	4 King's Bench Walk, London	0171 822 8822
	Deans Court Chambers, Manchester	0161 834 4097
Moriarty Gerald Evelyn	2 Mitre Court Buildings, London	0171 583 1380
Morshead Timothy Francis	4 Breams Buildings, London	0171 353 5835/430 1221
Mullis Anthony Roger	Chambers of Lord Goodhart QC, London	0171 405 5577
Munro Kenneth Stuart	5 Bell Yard, London	0171 333 8811
Nebhrajani Miss Mel	9 Stone Buildings, London	0171 404 5055
Noble Andrew	Eldon Chambers, London	0171 353 4636
	Merchant Chambers, Manchester	0161 839 7070
Norbury Luke Edward	17 Old Buildings, London	0171 405 9653
Norman Christopher John George	No 1 Serjeants' Inn, London	0171 415 6666
Norris Alastair Hubert	• 5 Stone Buildings, London	0171 242 6201
	• Southernhay Chambers, Exeter	01392 255777
Norris Paul Howard	One Essex Court, London	0171 936 3030
Oakes Miss Alison Denise	4 Breams Buildings, London	0171 353 5835/430 1221
Ohrenstein Dov	Chambers of Lord Goodhart QC, London	0171 405 5577
Palfrey Montague Mark	Hardwicke Building, London	0171 242 2523
Parry David Julian Thomas	Chambers of Lord Goodhart QC, London	0171 405 5577
Peacocke Mrs Teresa Anne Rosen	Enterprise Chambers, London	0171 405 9471
	Enterprise Chambers, Leeds	0113 246 0391
	Enterprise Chambers, Newcastle upon Tyne	0191 222 3344
Perks Richard Howard	St Philip's Chambers, Birmingham	0121 246 7000
Picarda Hubert Alistair Paul	Chambers of Lord Goodhart QC, London	0171 405 5577
Pickering James Patrick	Enterprise Chambers, London	0171 405 9471
	Enterprise Chambers, Leeds	0113 246 0391
	Enterprise Chambers, Newcastle upon Tyne	0191 222 3344
Pinder Miss Mary Elizabeth	No 1 Serjeants' Inn, London	0171 415 6666
Pryke Stuart	Trinity Chambers, Newcastle upon Tyne	0191 232 1927
Radevsky Anthony Eric	• 5 Bell Yard, London	0171 333 8811
Rai Amarjit Singh	St Philip's Chambers, Birmingham	0121 246 7000
Rees David Benjamin	5 Stone Buildings, London	0171 242 6201
Richardson Miss Sarah Jane	Enterprise Chambers, London	0171 405 9471
	Enterprise Chambers, Leeds	0113 246 0391
	Enterprise Chambers, Newcastle upon Tyne	0191 222 3344

• Expanded entry in Part D

Robson John Malcolm	2 Gray's Inn Square Chambers, London	0171 242 0328/405 1317
	Assize Court Chambers, Bristol	0117 926 4587
Roots Guy Robert Godfrey	2 Mitre Court Buildings, London	0171 583 1380
Ross Martyn John Greaves	• 5 New Square, London	0171 404 0404
	• Octagon House, Norwich	01603 623186
Rowell David Stewart	Chambers of Lord Goodhart QC, London	0171 405 5577
Rule Jonathan Daniel	Merchant Chambers, Manchester	0161 839 7070
Rumney Conrad William Arthur	St Philip's Chambers, Birmingham	0121 246 7000
Russell Christopher Garnet	12 New Square, London	0171 419 1212
	Sovereign Chambers, Leeds	0113 245 1841/2/3
Sampson Graeme William	Chambers of Geoffrey Hawker, London	0171 583 8899
Scutt David Robert	11 Bolt Court, London	0171 353 2300
	Redhill Chambers, Redhill	01737 780781
Sefton Mark Thomas Dunblane	199 Strand, London	0171 379 9779
Selvaratnam Miss Vasanti Emily Indrani	4 Field Court, London	0171 440 6900
Selway Dr Katherine Emma	11 Old Square, London	0171 430 0341
Shah Bajul Amratlal Somchand	Twenty-Four Old Buildings, London	0171 404 0946
Simpson Edwin John Fletcher	12 New Square, London	0171 419 1212
Steinert Jonathan	New Court Chambers, London	0171 831 9500
Stevens-Hoare Miss Michelle	• Hardwicke Building, London	0171 242 2523
Sydenham Colin Peter	4 Breams Buildings, London	0171 353 5835/430 1221
Taggart Nicholas	4 Breams Buildings, London	0171 353 5835/430 1221
Tidmarsh Christopher Ralph Francis	5 Stone Buildings, London	0171 242 6201
Tipples Miss Amanda Jane	13 Old Square, London	0171 404 4800
Trace Anthony John	• 13 Old Square, London	0171 404 4800
Walker Andrew Greenfield	Chambers of Lord Goodhart QC, London	0171 405 5577
Wardell John David Meredith	New Court Chambers, London	0171 831 9500
Warwick Mark Granville	• 29 Bedford Row Chambers, London	0171 831 2626
Weatherill Bernard Richard	Chambers of Lord Goodhart QC, London	0171 405 5577
West Mark	• 11 Old Square, London	0171 430 0341
Whitaker Steven Dixon	199 Strand, London	0171 379 9779
	All Saints Chambers, Bristol	0117 921 1966
Wightwick (William) Iain	Assize Court Chambers, Bristol	0117 926 4587
Williamson Miss Bridget Susan	Enterprise Chambers, London	0171 405 9471
	Enterprise Chambers, Leeds	0113 246 0391
	Enterprise Chambers, Newcastle upon Tyne	0191 222 3344
Wright Colin John	4 Field Court, London	0171 440 6900
Zelin Geoffrey Andrew	Enterprise Chambers, London	0171 405 9471
	Enterprise Chambers, Leeds	0113 246 0391
	Enterprise Chambers, Newcastle upon Tyne	0191 222 3344

COMMODITIES

Akka Lawrence Mark	20 Essex Street, London	0171 583 9294
Ambrose Miss Clare Mary Geneste	20 Essex Street, London	0171 583 9294
Charkham Graham Harold	20 Essex Street, London	0171 583 9294
Coburn Michael Jeremy Patrick	20 Essex Street, London	0171 583 9294
Collett Michael John	20 Essex Street, London	0171 583 9294
Davidson Nicholas Ranking	4 Paper Buildings, London	0171 353 3366/583 7155
Edey Philip David	20 Essex Street, London	0171 583 9294
Field Richard Alan	11 King's Bench Walk, London	0171 632 8500
Hamblen Nicholas Archibald	20 Essex Street, London	0171 583 9294
Jarvis John Manners	3 Verulam Buildings, London	0171 831 8441
Legh-Jones Piers Nicholas	• 20 Essex Street, London	0171 583 9294
Malek Ali	3 Verulam Buildings, London	0171 831 8441
Males Stephen Martin	20 Essex Street, London	0171 583 9294
Marquand Charles Nicholas Hilary	Chambers of Lord Goodhart QC, London	0171 405 5577
Masters Miss Sara Alayna	20 Essex Street, London	0171 583 9294
Maxwell Miss Karen Laetitia	20 Essex Street, London	0171 583 9294
Meeson Nigel Keith	4 Field Court, London	0171 440 6900
Milligan Iain Anstruther	20 Essex Street, London	0171 583 9294
Owen David Christopher	20 Essex Street, London	0171 583 9294
Peglow Dr Michael Alfred Herman	Chambers of Geoffrey Hawker, London	0171 583 8899

Salter Richard Stanley	3 Verulam Buildings, London	0171 831 8441
Selvaratnam Miss Vasanti Emily Indrani	4 Field Court, London	0171 440 6900
Thomas (Robert) Neville	3 Verulam Buildings, London	0171 831 8441
Wright Colin John	4 Field Court, London	0171 440 6900

COMMON LAND

Alesbury Alun	2 Mitre Court Buildings, London	0171 583 1380
Boyle Christopher Alexander David	2 Mitre Court Buildings, London	0171 583 1380
Burton Nicholas Anthony	2 Mitre Court Buildings, London	0171 583 1380
Cameron Miss Sheila Morag Clark	2 Harcourt Buildings, London	0171 353 8415
Cherryman John Richard	4 Breams Buildings, London	0171 353 5835/430 1221
Collett Gavin Charles	Rougemont Chambers, Exeter	01392 410471
	Cathedral Chambers (Jan Wood Independent Barristers' Clerk), Exeter	01392 210900
Collins John Morris	11 King's Bench Walk, London	0171 353 3337/8
	9 Woodhouse Square, Leeds	0113 245 1986
Crail Miss (Elspeth) Ross	12 New Square, London	0171 419 1212
	Sovereign Chambers, Leeds	0113 245 1841/2/3
Dineen Michael Laurence	Pump Court Chambers, London	0171 353 0711
	All Saints Chambers, Bristol	0117 921 1966
	Pump Court Chambers, Winchester	01962 868161
Druce Michael James	2 Mitre Court Buildings, London	0171 583 1380
Edwards Philip Douglas	2 Harcourt Buildings, London	0171 353 8415
Fookes Robert Lawrence	2 Mitre Court Buildings, London	0171 583 1380
Gore Andrew Roger	Fenners Chambers, Cambridge	01223 368761
	Fenners Chambers, Peterborough	01733 562030
Grundy Nicholas John	One Essex Court, London	0171 936 3030
Hall Taylor Alexander Edward	11 Old Square, London	0171 430 0341
Harwood Richard John	1 Serjeants' Inn, London	0171 583 1355
Horton Matthew Bethell	2 Mitre Court Buildings, London	0171 583 1380
Jackson Dirik George Allan	• Chambers of Mr Peter Crampin QC, London	0171 831 0081
Jones Gregory Percy	• 2 Harcourt Buildings, London	0171 353 8415
Kealy Charles Brian	Chambers of Andrew Campbell QC, Leeds	0113 245 5438
King Neil Gerald Alexander	2 Mitre Court Buildings, London	0171 583 1380
Leonard Charles Robert Weston	Goldsmith Building, London	0171 353 7881
Levy Robert Stuart	9 Stone Buildings, London	0171 404 5055
	Assize Court Chambers, Bristol	0117 926 4587
Lewis Robert		
Martineau Henry Ralph Adeane	Goldsmith Building, London	0171 353 7881
Mathews Deni	8 Fountain Court, Birmingham	0121 236 5514
Moore Professor Victor William Edward	2 Mitre Court Buildings, London	0171 583 1380
Norie-Miller Jeffrey Reginald	55 Temple Chambers, London	0171 353 7400
Pryke Stuart	Trinity Chambers, Newcastle upon Tyne	0191 232 1927
Purchas Robin Michael	• 2 Harcourt Buildings, London	0171 353 8415
Ross Martyn John Greaves	• 5 New Square, London	0171 404 0404
	• Octagon House, Norwich	01603 623186
Sefton Mark Thomas Dunblane	199 Strand, London	0171 379 9779
Simpson Edwin John Fletcher	12 New Square, London	0171 419 1212
Smart Miss Jacqueline Anne	Trinity Chambers, Newcastle upon Tyne	0191 232 1927
Thomas Nigel Matthew	13 Old Square, London	0171 404 4800
Vane The Hon Christopher John Fletcher	Trinity Chambers, Newcastle upon Tyne	0191 232 1927
Warren Rupert Miles	2 Mitre Court Buildings, London	0171 583 1380
Whybrow Christopher John	1 Serjeants' Inn, London	0171 583 1355
Wilson Andrew Robert	9 Woodhouse Square, Leeds	0113 245 1986

COMMON LAW (GENERAL)

Acton Davis Jonathan James	4 Pump Court, London	0171 353 2656/9
Airey Simon Andrew	11 Bolt Court, London	0171 353 2300
	Redhill Chambers, Redhill	01737 780781
Alexander Ian Douglas Gavin	11 Bolt Court, London	0171 353 2300
	Redhill Chambers, Redhill	01737 780781
Alldis Christopher John	Peel House Chambers, Liverpool	0151 236 4321
Alliott George Beckles	2 Harcourt Buildings, London	0171 583 9020

                                             • Expanded entry in Part D

Alomo Richard Olusoji	14 Gray's Inn Square, London	0171 242 0858
Althaus Antony Justin	No 1 Serjeants' Inn, London	0171 415 6666
Ames Geoffrey Alan	29 Bedford Row Chambers, London	0171 831 2626
Andrews Miss Claire Marguerite	Gough Square Chambers, London	0171 353 0924
Anthony Michael Guy	Two Crown Office Row, London	0171 797 8100
Ascherson Miss Isobel Ruth	23 Essex Street, London	0171 413 0353
Ashley Mark Robert	Tindal Chambers, Chelmsford	01245 267742
	Tindal Chambers, St Albans	01727 843383
Ashton Raglan Halley	New Court Chambers, Birmingham	0121 693 6656
Ashworth Piers	Stanbrook & Henderson, London	0171 353 0101
	2 Harcourt Buildings, London	0171 583 9020
	Priory Chambers, Birmingham	0121 236 3882/1375
Aslett Pepin Charles Maguire	22 Albion Place, Northampton	01604 636271
Asteris Peter David	Eighteen Carlton Crescent, Southampton	01703 639001
Attala Jean Etienne	Cathedral Chambers, Newcastle upon Tyne	0191 232 1311
Austin-Smith Michael Gerard	23 Essex Street, London	0171 413 0353
Austins Christopher John	Assize Court Chambers, Bristol	0117 926 4587
Aylen Walter Stafford	Hardwicke Building, London	0171 242 2523
Bagnall Matthew Philip Cooper	Chambers of Geoffrey Hawker, London	0171 583 8899
Bailey Edward Henry	5 Bell Yard, London	0171 333 8811
Baker Ms Rachel Mary Theresa	Hardwicke Building, London	0171 242 2523
Baldry Antony Brian	No 1 Serjeants' Inn, London	0171 415 6666
Baldwin John Grant	Oriel Chambers, Liverpool	0151 236 7191
Ball Steven James	Earl Street Chambers, Maidstone	01622 671222
Barlow Miss Sarah Helen	St Paul's House, Leeds	0113 245 5866
Barr Edward Robert	2 New Street, Leicester	0116 262 5906
Barstow Stephen Royden	Harcourt Chambers, London	0171 353 6961/7
	Harcourt Chambers, Oxford	01865 791559
Barton Miss Fiona	5 Essex Court, London	0171 410 2000
Bates Alexander Andrew	St Paul's House, Leeds	0113 245 5866
Bates John Hayward	Old Square Chambers, London	0171 269 0300
	Old Square Chambers, Bristol	0117 927 7111
Battcock Benjamin George	Stanbrook & Henderson, London	0171 353 0101
	2 Harcourt Buildings, London	0171 583 9020
Beal Kieron Conrad	4 Paper Buildings, London	0171 353 3366/583 7155
Beard Mark Christopher	6 Pump Court, London	0171 797 8400
Beaumont Marc Clifford	• Pump Court Chambers, London	0171 353 0711
	• Harrow-on-the-Hill Chambers, Harrow on the Hill	0181 423 7444
	• Pump Court Chambers, Winchester	01962 868161
	• Windsor Barristers' Chambers, Windsor	01753 648 899
Beecroft Miss Kirstie		
Beer Jason Barrington	5 Essex Court, London	0171 410 2000
Belbin Miss Heather Patricia	Oriel Chambers, Liverpool	0151 236 7191
Bendall Richard Giles	33 Bedford Row, London	0171 242 6476
Benner Miss Lucinda Diana Kate	11 Bolt Court, London	0171 353 2300
	Redhill Chambers, Redhill	01737 780781
Bennett Gordon Irvine	5 Bell Yard, London	0171 333 8811
Bennett John Martyn	• Peel House Chambers, Liverpool	0151 236 4321
Benson Julian Christopher Woodburn	One Essex Court, London	0171 936 3030
Bentwood Richard	Chambers of Geoffrey Hawker, London	0171 583 8899
Bergin Timothy William	Sussex Chambers, Brighton	01273 607953
Berkley Michael Stuart	Rougemont Chambers, Exeter	01392 410471
Best Stanley Philip	Bracton Chambers, London	0171 242 4248
	Westgate Chambers, Lewes	01273 480 510
	Barnstaple Chambers, Winkleigh	0183 783763
Bhattacharyya Ardhendu	1 Gray's Inn Square, London	0171 405 8946
	11 St Bernards Road, Slough	01753 553806/817989
Birtles William	Old Square Chambers, London	0171 269 0300
	Old Square Chambers, Bristol	0117 927 7111
Birts Peter William	• Farrar's Building, London	0171 583 9241
Bishop Edward James	No 1 Serjeants' Inn, London	0171 415 6666
Blakesley Patrick James	Two Crown Office Row, London	0171 797 8100
Bloom-Davis Desmond Niall Laurence	Pump Court Chambers, London	0171 353 0711
	Pump Court Chambers, Winchester	01962 868161

B

Boothroyd Miss Susan Elizabeth	Westgate Chambers, Newcastle upon Tyne	0191 261 4407/232 9785
Bourne Charles Gregory	Stanbrook & Henderson, London	0171 353 0101
	2 Harcourt Buildings, London	0171 583 9020
Boydell Edward Patrick Stirrup	Pump Court Chambers, London	0171 353 0711
	Pump Court Chambers, Winchester	01962 868161
Boyle David Stuart	Deans Court Chambers, Manchester	0161 834 4097
Boyle Gerard James	No 1 Serjeants' Inn, London	0171 415 6666
Bradley Miss Clodagh Maria	3 Serjeants' Inn, London	0171 353 5537
Bradley Richard	Oriel Chambers, Liverpool	0151 236 7191
Brannigan Peter John Sean	One Essex Court, London	0171 936 3030
Brant Paul David	Oriel Chambers, Liverpool	0151 236 7191
Brazil Dominic Thomas George	14 Gray's Inn Square, London	0171 242 0858
Breen Carlo Enrico	Chambers of John Hand QC, Manchester	0161 955 9000
Brett Matthew Christopher Anthony	Harcourt Chambers, London	0171 353 6961/7
	Harcourt Chambers, Oxford	01865 791559
Brook Ian Stuart	Hardwicke Building, London	0171 242 2523
Brotherton John Paul	New Court Chambers, Birmingham	0121 693 6656
Brown David Charles	Cathedral Chambers, Newcastle upon Tyne	0191 232 1311
	Southsea Chambers, Portsmouth	01705 291261
Brown Thomas Christopher Ellis	Fenners Chambers, Cambridge	01223 368761
	Fenners Chambers, Peterborough	01733 562030
Browne James William	Goldsworth Chambers, London	0171 405 7117
Browne Miss Julie Rebecca	Goldsmith Building, London	0171 353 7881
Brunner Adrian John Nelson	Stanbrook & Henderson, London	0171 353 0101
	2 Harcourt Buildings, London	0171 583 9020
Brunton Sean Alexander McKay	Pump Court Chambers, London	0171 353 0711
	Pump Court Chambers, Winchester	01962 868161
Bull (Donald) Roger	One Essex Court, London	0171 936 3030
Bundred Miss Gillian Sarah	Oriel Chambers, Liverpool	0151 236 7191
Burbidge James Michael	St Philip's Chambers, Birmingham	0121 246 7000
Burles David John	Goldsmith Building, London	0171 353 7881
Burns Peter Richard	Deans Court Chambers, Manchester	0161 834 4097
Butler Miss Judith Jane Scott	6 Pump Court, London	0171 797 8400
	6-8 Mill Street, Maidstone	01622 688 094
Cadwallader Peter	Chambers of John Hand QC, Manchester	0161 955 9000
Cameron Miss Barbara Alexander	Stanbrook & Henderson, London	0171 353 0101
	2 Harcourt Buildings, London	0171 583 9020
Cameron Neil Alexander	Wilberforce Chambers, Hull	01482 323 264
Campbell Oliver Edward Wilhelm	2 Harcourt Buildings, London	0171 583 9020
Candlin James Richard	Chambers of Geoffrey Hawker, London	0171 583 8899
Capon Philip Christopher William	St Philip's Chambers, Birmingham	0121 246 7000
Carlile Alexander Charles	9-12 Bell Yard, London	0171 400 1800
	Sedan House, Chester	01244 320480/348282
Carling Christopher James	Old Square Chambers, London	0171 269 0300
	Old Square Chambers, Bristol	0117 927 7111
Carrodus Miss Gail Caroline	New Court Chambers, London	0171 831 9500
Carron Richard Byron	11 Bolt Court, London	0171 353 2300
	Redhill Chambers, Redhill	01737 780781
Carter Miss Lesley Ann	25-27 Castle Street, Liverpool	0151 227 5661/5666/236 5072
Cartwright Richard John	Queen Elizabeth Building, London	0171 353 7181 (12 lines)
Carville Owen Brendan Neville	25-27 Castle Street, Liverpool	0151 227 5661/5666/236 5072
Casey Noel	7 Stone Buildings, London	0171 242 0961
Cash Miss Joanne Catherine	Farrar's Building, London	0171 583 9241
Cave Jeremy Stephen	1 Crown Office Row, London	0171 797 7500
	Crown Office Row Chambers, Brighton	01273 625625
Chalmers Miss Suzanne Frances	Two Crown Office Row, London	0171 797 8100
Charles Ms Deborah Ann	6 Pump Court, London	0171 797 8400
Charlwood Spike Llewellyn	4 Paper Buildings, London	0171 353 3366/583 7155
Cheyne Miss Phyllida Alison	4 Pump Court, London	0171 353 2656/9
Clargo John Paul	Hardwicke Building, London	0171 242 2523
Clark Christopher Harvey	Pump Court Chambers, London	0171 353 0711
	Westgate Chambers, Lewes	01273 480 510
	Pump Court Chambers, Winchester	01962 868161
Clarke Miss Alison Lee	No 1 Serjeants' Inn, London	0171 415 6666
Clarke George Robert Ivan	Chambers of Geoffrey Hawker, London	0171 583 8899

• Expanded entry in Part D

Clegg Sebastian James Barwick	Deans Court Chambers, Manchester	0161 834 4097
Clover Miss Sarah	2 Mitre Court Buildings, London	0171 353 1353
Clover (Thomas) Anthony	New Court Chambers, London	0171 831 9500
Cogswell Miss Frederica Natasha	Gough Square Chambers, London	0171 353 0924
Collett Gavin Charles	Rougemont Chambers, Exeter	01392 410471
	Cathedral Chambers (Jan Wood Independent Barristers' Clerk), Exeter	01392 210900
Collett Ivor William	No 1 Serjeants' Inn, London	0171 415 6666
Collins John Morris	11 King's Bench Walk, London	0171 353 3337/8
	9 Woodhouse Square, Leeds	0113 245 1986
Collinson Miss Alicia Hester	Harcourt Chambers, London	0171 353 6961/7
	Harcourt Chambers, Oxford	01865 791559
Conlin Geoffrey David	3 Serjeants' Inn, London	0171 353 5537
Connerty Anthony Robin	Lamb Chambers, London	0171 797 8300
Cooper Adrian Edgar Mark	Stanbrook & Henderson, London	0171 353 0101
	2 Harcourt Buildings, London	0171 583 9020
Cottage Miss Rosina	9-12 Bell Yard, London	0171 400 1800
Cotter Barry Paul	Old Square Chambers, London	0171 269 0300
	Old Square Chambers, Bristol	0117 927 7111
Cotter Miss Sara Elizabeth	• Higher Combe, Minehead	01643 862722
Cottrell Matthew Robert	Oriel Chambers, Liverpool	0151 236 7191
Coulter Barry John	One Essex Court, London	0171 936 3030
Cowan Peter Sherwood McCrea	Oriel Chambers, Liverpool	0151 236 7191
Cowen Miss Sally Emma	Chambers of Geoffrey Hawker, London	0171 583 8899
Craig Kenneth Allen	Hardwicke Building, London	0171 242 2523
Crane Miss Suzanne Denise	New Court Chambers, Birmingham	0121 693 6656
Crookes Miss Alison Naomi		
Cross James Edward Michael	4 Pump Court, London	0171 353 2656/9
Cross (Joseph) Edward	2 Gray's Inn Square Chambers, London	0171 242 0328/405 1317
Crosthwaite Graham Andrew	One King's Bench Walk, London	0171 936 1500
Crowley John Desmond	Two Crown Office Row, London	0171 797 8100
Crowson Howard Keith	St Paul's House, Leeds	0113 245 5866
Cunningham Miss Claire Louise	St Philip's Chambers, Birmingham	0121 246 7000
Curtis Michael Alexander	Two Crown Office Row, London	0171 797 8100
Curwen Michael Jonathan	Chambers of Kieran Coonan QC, London	0171 583 6013/2510
Daiches Michael Salis	• 22 Old Buildings, London	0171 831 0222
Dallas Andrew Thomas Alastair	Chambers of Andrew Campbell QC, Leeds	0113 245 5438
Datta Mrs Wendy Patricia Mizal	Alban Chambers, London	0171 419 5051
Davey Miss Tina Elaine	9-12 Bell Yard, London	0171 400 1800
Davidson Nicholas Ranking	4 Paper Buildings, London	0171 353 3366/583 7155
Davies Andrew	Angel Chambers, Swansea	01792 464623/464648
Davies Miss Penny May	Chambers of Harjit Singh, London	0171 353 1356
Davies Stephen Richard	8 King Street Chambers, Manchester	0161 834 9560
Davis Andrew Paul	Two Crown Office Row, London	0171 797 8100
Dawes Gordon Stephen Knight	Goldsmith Building, London	0171 353 7881
Dawson James Robert	Oriel Chambers, Liverpool	0151 236 7191
de Jehan David	St Paul's House, Leeds	0113 245 5866
Dean Paul Benjamin	5 Bell Yard, London	0171 333 8811
Dedezade Taner	Tindal Chambers, Chelmsford	01245 267742
Denton Miss Michelle Jayne	9-12 Bell Yard, London	0171 400 1800
Dhaliwal Miss Davinder Kaur	New Court Chambers, Birmingham	0121 693 6656
Dineen Michael Laurence	Pump Court Chambers, London	0171 353 0711
	All Saints Chambers, Bristol	0117 921 1966
	Pump Court Chambers, Winchester	01962 868161
Dixon David Steven	Sovereign Chambers, Leeds	0113 245 1841/2/3
Dixon Ian Frederick	Cathedral Chambers, Newcastle upon Tyne	0191 232 1311
Dodge Peter Clive	11 Old Square, London	0171 430 0341
Dogra Miss Tanyia Anita	Chambers of Harjit Singh, London	0171 353 1356
Dowokpor Jonathan Kukasi	Tollgate Mews Chambers, London	0171 511 1838
Dowse John	Chambers of Lord Goodhart QC, London	0171 405 5577
	Chambers of John Hand QC, Manchester	0161 955 9000
Doyle Peter John	9-12 Bell Yard, London	0171 400 1800
Drayton Henry Alexander	2 Gray's Inn Square Chambers, London	0171 242 0328/405 1317

Dubbery Mark Edward	Pump Court Chambers, London	0171 353 0711
Duffy Michael	Cathedral Chambers, Ely, Ely	01353 666775
Dunn Christopher	Sovereign Chambers, Leeds	0113 245 1841/2/3
Eastman Roger	Stanbrook & Henderson, London	0171 353 0101
	2 Harcourt Buildings, London	0171 583 9020
Eccles Hugh William Patrick	Harcourt Chambers, London	0171 353 6961/7
	Harcourt Chambers, Oxford	01865 791559
Edwards Anthony Howard	Oriel Chambers, Liverpool	0151 236 7191
Edwards Nigel Royston	St Paul's House, Leeds	0113 245 5866
Edwards-Stuart Antony James Cobham	Two Crown Office Row, London	0171 797 8100
Elvidge John Allan	1 Mitre Court Buildings, London	0171 797 7070
Emanuel Mark Pering Wolff	14 Gray's Inn Square, London	0171 242 0858
Evans Lee John	Farrar's Building, London	0171 583 9241
Evans Martin Alan Langham	5 Paper Buildings, London	0171 583 6117
Evans Thomas Gareth	Rougemont Chambers, Exeter	01392 410471
Evans-Tovey Jason Robert	Two Crown Office Row, London	0171 797 8100
Ewins Miss Catherine Jane	4 Paper Buildings, London	0171 353 3366/583 7155
Exall Gordon David	Chambers of Andrew Campbell QC, Leeds	0113 245 5438
Falk Miss Josephine Ruth Ann	12 Old Square, London	0171 404 0875
Farquharson Miss Jane Caroline	One Essex Court, London	0171 936 3030
Faulks Edward Peter Lawless	No 1 Serjeants' Inn, London	0171 415 6666
Fenston Miss Felicia Donovan	Stanbrook & Henderson, London	0171 353 0101
	2 Harcourt Buildings, London	0171 583 9020
Ferguson Mrs Katharine Ann	Fenners Chambers, Cambridge	01223 368761
	Fenners Chambers, Peterborough	01733 562030
Fisher Jonathan Simon	• 18 Red Lion Court, London	0171 520 6000
	• Thornwood House, Chelmsford	01245 280880
Fletcher Marcus Alexander	One King's Bench Walk, London	0171 936 1500
Forbes Peter George	6 Pump Court, London	0171 797 8400
	6-8 Mill Street, Maidstone	01622 688 094
Ford Gerard James	Baker Street Chambers, Middlesbrough	01642 873873
Forlin Gerard Emlyn	Phoenix Chambers, London	0171 404 7888
Forster Brian Clive	Trinity Chambers, Newcastle upon Tyne	0191 232 1927
Foster Charles Andrew	• Chambers of Kieran Coonan QC, London	0171 583 6013/2510
Foster Francis Alexander	St Paul's House, Leeds	0113 245 5866
Fox Miss Anna Katherine Helen	Oriel Chambers, Liverpool	0151 236 7191
Foxwell George (Augustus)	Fenners Chambers, Cambridge	01223 368761
	Fenners Chambers, Peterborough	01733 562030
Franck Richard David William	Equity Chambers, Birmingham	0121 233 2100
Franklin Stephen Hall	5 Paper Buildings, London	0171 583 6117
	Fenners Chambers, Cambridge	01223 368761
French Richard Anthony Lister	Rougemont Chambers, Exeter	01392 410471
Frodsham Alexander Miles	Oriel Chambers, Liverpool	0151 236 7191
Fuad Kerim	Chambers of Helen Grindrod QC, London	0171 404 4777
Gabb Charles Henry Escott	Pump Court Chambers, London	0171 353 0711
	Pump Court Chambers, Winchester	01962 868161
Gadney George Munro	Two Crown Office Row, London	0171 797 8100
Gallagher John David Edmund	Goldsmith Building, London	0171 353 7881
Garside Charles Roger	Chambers of John Hand QC, Manchester	0161 955 9000
Gibson Charles Anthony Warneford	2 Harcourt Buildings, London	0171 583 9020
Gilbert Ms Julia Jane	Trinity Chambers, Newcastle upon Tyne	0191 232 1927
Gilbertson Mrs Helen Alison	Sackville Chambers, Norwich	01603 613516
Gilmour Nigel Benjamin Douglas	Peel House Chambers, Liverpool	0151 236 4321
Gilroy Paul	Farrar's Building, London	0171 583 9241
	Chambers of John Hand QC, Manchester	0161 955 9000
Gittins Timothy James	Trinity Chambers, Newcastle upon Tyne	0191 232 1927
Godfrey Jonathan Saul	St Paul's House, Leeds	0113 245 5866
Goff Anthony Thomas	25-27 Castle Street, Liverpool	0151 227 5661/5666/236 5072
Goodbody Peter James	• Oriel Chambers, Liverpool	0151 236 7191
Goose Julian Nicholas	Chambers of Andrew Campbell QC, Leeds	0113 245 5438
Gordon-Dean Miss Natasha		

Gordon-Saker Mrs Liza Helen	Fenners Chambers, Cambridge	01223 368761
	Fenners Chambers, Peterborough	01733 562030
Gore-Andrews Gavin Angus Russell	Stanbrook & Henderson, London	0171 353 0101
	2 Harcourt Buildings, London	0171 583 9020
Gough Miss Karen Louise	Arbitration Chambers, London	0171 267 2137
	West Lodge Farm, Meopham	01474 812280
Grant Thomas Paul Wentworth	New Court Chambers, London	0171 831 9500
Gray Charles Anthony St John	5 Raymond Buildings, London	0171 242 2902
Gray Miss Jennifer	11 Old Square, London	0171 242 5022
Grayson Edward	• 9-12 Bell Yard, London	0171 400 1800
Green Patrick Curtis	Stanbrook & Henderson, London	0171 353 0101
	2 Harcourt Buildings, London	0171 583 9020
Greenbourne John Hugo	Two Crown Office Row, London	0171 797 8100
Greene Paul Martin	Earl Street Chambers, Maidstone	01622 671222
Gregory Richard Hamilton	Harcourt Chambers, London	0171 353 6961/7
Grice Miss Joanna Harrison	One King's Bench Walk, London	0171 936 1500
Griffin Neil Patrick Luke	9-12 Bell Yard, London	0171 400 1800
Gruffydd John	Oriel Chambers, Liverpool	0151 236 7191
Grundy Nicholas John	One Essex Court, London	0171 936 3030
Guggenheim Miss Anna Maeve	Two Crown Office Row, London	0171 797 8100
Guirguis Miss Sheren	White Friars Chambers, Chester	01244 323070
Gullick Stephen John	Sovereign Chambers, Leeds	0113 245 1841/2/3
Gunther Miss Elizabeth Ann	Pump Court Chambers, London	0171 353 0711
	Pump Court Chambers, Winchester	01962 868161
Hall Taylor Alexander Edward	11 Old Square, London	0171 430 0341
Hall-Smith Martin Clive William	Goldsmith Building, London	0171 353 7881
Hamer Michael Howard Kenneth	2 Harcourt Buildings, London	0171 583 9020
	Westgate Chambers, Lewes	01273 480 510
Hamid Mrs Beebee Nazmoon	Clapham Chambers, London	0171 978 8482/0171 642 5777
Hamilton Graeme Montagu	Two Crown Office Row, London	0171 797 8100
Hammerton Alastair Rolf	No 1 Serjeants' Inn, London	0171 415 6666
Hammerton Miss Veronica Lesley	No 1 Serjeants' Inn, London	0171 415 6666
Hand John Lester	Old Square Chambers, London	0171 269 0300
	Old Square Chambers, Bristol	0117 927 7111
	Chambers of John Hand QC, Manchester	0161 955 9000
Hanson Timothy Vincent Richard	St Philip's Chambers, Birmingham	0121 246 7000
Harbottle Gwilym Thomas	5 New Square, London	0171 404 0404
Harris Ian Robert	25-27 Castle Street, Liverpool	0151 227 5661/5666/236 5072
Harrison John Foster	St Paul's House, Leeds	0113 245 5866
Hartley-Davies Paul Kevil	30 Park Place, Cardiff	01222 398421
Harvey Miss Jayne Denise	Goldsworth Chambers, London	0171 405 7117
Harvey Jonathan Robert William	2 Harcourt Buildings, London	0171 583 9020
Harvey Michael Llewellyn Tucker	Two Crown Office Row, London	0171 797 8100
Harwood-Stevenson John Francis Richard	9-12 Bell Yard, London	0171 400 1800
	East Anglian Chambers, Norwich	01603 617351
Hatton Andrew John	Plowden Buildings, London	0171 583 0808
	Paradise Square Chambers, Sheffield	0114 273 8951
Haven Kevin	2 Gray's Inn Square Chambers, London	0171 242 0328/405 1317
Hayes John Allan	Chambers of Andrew Campbell QC, Leeds	0113 245 5438
Healy Miss Alexandra	9-12 Bell Yard, London	0171 400 1800
Henderson Lawrence Mark	11 Bolt Court, London	0171 353 2300
	Redhill Chambers, Redhill	01737 780781
Henderson Roger Anthony	Stanbrook & Henderson, London	0171 353 0101
	2 Harcourt Buildings, London	0171 583 9020
Henley Mark Robert Daniel	9 Woodhouse Square, Leeds	0113 245 1986
Herbert Mrs Rebecca Mary	2 New Street, Leicester	0116 262 5906
Higgins Anthony Paul	Goldsmith Building, London	0171 353 7881
Hill Nicholas Mark	Pump Court Chambers, London	0171 353 0711
	Pump Court Chambers, Winchester	01962 868161
Hill Robert Douglas	Pump Court Chambers, London	0171 353 0711
	Pump Court Chambers, Winchester	01962 868161
Hillier Andrew Charles	5 Bell Yard, London	0171 333 8811
Hinchliffe Philip Nicholas	Chambers of John Hand QC, Manchester	0161 955 9000
Hockman Stephen Alexander	• 6 Pump Court, London	0171 797 8400
	• 6-8 Mill Street, Maidstone	01622 688 094
Hodgson Miss Susan Ann	Two Crown Office Row, London	0171 797 8100
Hogg The Rt Hon Douglas Martin	4 Paper Buildings, London	0171 353 3366/583 7155

	37 Park Square, Leeds	0113 243 9422
Hogg Miss Katharine Elizabeth	1 Crown Office Row, London	0171 797 7500
Holdsworth James Arthur	Two Crown Office Row, London	0171 797 8100
Holland Charles Christopher	Trinity Chambers, Newcastle upon Tyne	0191 232 1927
Hollingworth Peter James Michael	22 Albion Place, Northampton	01604 636271
Horlock Timothy John	Chambers of John Hand QC, Manchester	0161 955 9000
Horspool Anthony Bernard Graeme	Hardwicke Building, London	0171 242 2523
Horton Miss Caroline Ann	Fenners Chambers, Cambridge	01223 368761
	Fenners Chambers, Peterborough	01733 562030
Horwood Miss Anya Louise	25-27 Castle Street, Liverpool	0151 227 5661/5666/236 5072
House James Michael	2 New Street, Leicester	0116 262 5906
Howard Anthony John	Chambers of John Hand QC, Manchester	0161 955 9000
Howard Graham John	Queen Elizabeth Building, London	0171 353 7181 (12 lines)
Howard-Jones Miss Sarah Rachel	8 Stone Buildings, London	0171 831 9881
Howarth Simon Stuart	Two Crown Office Row, London	0171 797 8100
Hughes William Lloyd	9-12 Bell Yard, London	0171 400 1800
Hull Leslie David	Chambers of John Hand QC, Manchester	0161 955 9000
Hunter William Quigley	No 1 Serjeants' Inn, London	0171 415 6666
Hussain Miss Frida Khanam	17 Carlton Crescent, Southampton	01703 320320
Iqbal Abdul Shaffaq	Chambers of Andrew Campbell QC, Leeds	0113 245 5438
Islam-Choudhury Mugni	11 Bolt Court, London	0171 353 2300
Iwi Quintin Joseph	Stanbrook & Henderson, London	0171 353 0101
	2 Harcourt Buildings, London	0171 583 9020
Jackson Anthony Warren	3 Serjeants' Inn, London	0171 353 5537
James Roderick Morrice	23 Essex Street, London	0171 413 0353
James Simon John	Chambers of John Hand QC, Manchester	0161 955 9000
Jarman Mark Christopher	14 Gray's Inn Square, London	0171 242 0858
Jay Adam Marc	One King's Bench Walk, London	0171 936 1500
Jenkala Adrian Aleksander	11 Bolt Court, London	0171 353 2300
	Redhill Chambers, Redhill	01737 780781
Jenkins Dr Janet Caroline	Chambers of Kieran Coonan QC, London	0171 583 6013/2510
John Peter Charles	One Essex Court, London	0171 936 3030
John Stephen Alun	9-12 Bell Yard, London	0171 400 1800
Jones Miss (Catherine) Charlotte	5 Bell Yard, London	0171 333 8811
Jones Geraint Martyn	Fenners Chambers, Cambridge	01223 368761
	Fenners Chambers, Peterborough	01733 562030
Jones Gregory Percy	• 2 Harcourt Buildings, London	0171 353 8415
Jones Rhys Charles Mansel	33 Bedford Row, London	0171 242 6476
Jones Stephen Hugh	• Farrar's Building, London	0171 583 9241
Josling William Henry Charles	Fenners Chambers, Cambridge	01223 368761
	Fenners Chambers, Peterborough	01733 562030
Joss Norman James	One Essex Court, London	0171 936 3030
Kealey Simon Thomas	Chambers of Andrew Campbell QC, Leeds	0113 245 5438
Kealy Charles Brian	Chambers of Andrew Campbell QC, Leeds	0113 245 5438
Kearl Guy Alexander	St Paul's House, Leeds	0113 245 5866
Kennedy Christopher Laurence Paul	Chambers of John Hand QC, Manchester	0161 955 9000
Kenning Thomas Patrick	New Court Chambers, Birmingham	0121 693 6656
Kent Miss Georgina	5 Essex Court, London	0171 410 2000
Kent Michael Harcourt	Two Crown Office Row, London	0171 797 8100
Kenward Timothy David Nelson	25-27 Castle Street, Liverpool	0151 227 5661/5666/236 5072
Khan Ashraf	A K Chambers, Hull	01482 641180
Khan Saadallah Frans Hassan	55 Temple Chambers, London	0171 353 7400
Kimbell John Ashley	5 Bell Yard, London	0171 333 8811
King Peter Duncan	5 Pump Court, London	0171 353 2532
	Fenners Chambers, Cambridge	01223 368761
Kinnier Andrew John	2 Harcourt Buildings, London	0171 583 9020
Kirby Peter John	• Hardwicke Building, London	0171 242 2523
Kolodynski Stefan Richard	New Court Chambers, Birmingham	0121 693 6656
Kolodziej Andrzej Jozef	• Littman Chambers, London	0171 404 4866
Kremen Philip Michael	Hardwicke Building, London	0171 242 2523
Lambert Miss Sarah Katrina	1 Crown Office Row, London	0171 797 7500
Lander Charles Gideon	25-27 Castle Street, Liverpool	0151 227 5661/5666/236 5072

B

• Expanded entry in Part D

Lawrence Miss Rachel Camilla	One Essex Court, London	0171 936 3030
Lawson Daniel George	Goldsmith Building, London	0171 353 7881
Lawson Robert John	5 Bell Yard, London	0171 333 8811
Leech Brian Walter Thomas	No 1 Serjeants' Inn, London	0171 415 6666
Lees Andrew James	St Paul's House, Leeds	0113 245 5866
Lehain Philip Peter	199 Strand, London	0171 379 9779
Leiper Richard Thomas	11 King's Bench Walk, London	0171 632 8500
Lennard Stephen Charles	Hardwicke Building, London	0171 242 2523
Lewer Michael Edward	Farrar's Building, London	0171 583 9241
Lewis Robert		
Lindsay Crawford Callum Douglas	No 1 Serjeants' Inn, London	0171 415 6666
Linstead Peter James	11 Bolt Court, London	0171 353 2300
Little Ian	Chambers of John Hand QC, Manchester	0161 955 9000
Livingstone Simon John	11 Bolt Court, London	0171 353 2300
	Redhill Chambers, Redhill	01737 780781
Logan Miss Maura	St John's Chambers, Hale Barns	0161 980 7379
Lowenstein Paul David	Littleton Chambers, London	0171 797 8600
Lynagh Richard Dudley	Two Crown Office Row, London	0171 797 8100
Lynch Terry John	22 Albion Place, Northampton	01604 636271
Lyne Mark Hilary	One Essex Court, London	0171 936 3030
Lyon Stephen John	14 Gray's Inn Square, London	0171 242 0858
	Westgate Chambers, Lewes	01273 480 510
MacDonald Iain	Gough Square Chambers, London	0171 353 0924
Machell Raymond Donatus	2 Pump Court, London	0171 353 5597
	Deans Court Chambers, Manchester	0161 834 4097
MacKillop Norman Malcolm	• Chartlands Chambers, Northampton	01604 603322
Macpherson Angus John	5 Bell Yard, London	0171 333 8811
Maitland Jones Mark Griffith	Goldsmith Building, London	0171 353 7881
Maitland Marc Claude	11 Old Square, London	0171 242 5022
Malek Ali	3 Verulam Buildings, London	0171 831 8441
Manasse Mrs Anne Katherine	Cathedral Chambers, Newcastle upon Tyne	0191 232 1311
Mandel Richard	11 Bolt Court, London	0171 353 2300
	Redhill Chambers, Redhill	01737 780781
Marks Jonathan Clive	4 Pump Court, London	0171 353 2656/9
Marley Miss Sarah Anne	5 Pump Court, London	0171 353 2532
Marris Miss Sarah Selena Rixar	No 1 Serjeants' Inn, London	0171 415 6666
Marshall Philip Derek	Farrar's Building, London	0171 583 9241
	Iscoed Chambers, Swansea	01792 652988/9/330
Martin David John	Cathedral Chambers, Newcastle upon Tyne	0191 232 1311
Martineau Henry Ralph Adeane	Goldsmith Building, London	0171 353 7881
Mason Ian Douglas	11 Bolt Court, London	0171 353 2300
	Redhill Chambers, Redhill	01737 780781
Mathews Deni	8 Fountain Court, Birmingham	0121 236 5514
Mathias Miss Anna	11 Bolt Court, London	0171 353 2300
Mawrey Richard Brooks	Stanbrook & Henderson, London	0171 353 0101
	2 Harcourt Buildings, London	0171 583 9020
Maxwell David	Claremont Chambers, Wolverhampton	01902 426222
Maxwell Miss Judith Mary Angela	The Garden House, London	0171 404 6150
Maxwell-Scott James Herbert	Two Crown Office Row, London	0171 797 8100
May Miss Juliet Mary	3 Verulam Buildings, London	0171 831 8441
Mayhew Jerome Patrick Burke	Goldsmith Building, London	0171 353 7881
McCann Simon Howard	Deans Court Chambers, Manchester	0161 834 4097
McCluggage Brian Thomas	Chambers of John Hand QC, Manchester	0161 955 9000
McGahey Miss Elizabeth Clare	30 Park Place, Cardiff	01222 398421
McGregor Harvey	4 Paper Buildings, London	0171 353 3366/583 7155
McIvor Ian Walker	334 Deansgate Chambers, Manchester	0161 834 3767
McKay Christopher Alexander	Angel Chambers, Swansea	01792 464623/464648
McKenna Miss Anna Louise	Queen Elizabeth Building, London	0171 353 7181 (12 lines)
McKeon James Patrick	Peel House Chambers, Liverpool	0151 236 4321
McLachlan David Robert		
McMinn Miss Valerie Kathleen	Baker Street Chambers, Middlesbrough	01642 873873
McParland Michael Joseph	New Court Chambers, London	0171 831 9500
Mendoza Neil David Pereira	Hardwicke Building, London	0171 242 2523
Menzies Richard Mark	8 Stone Buildings, London	0171 831 9881
Merry Hugh Gairns	17 Carlton Crescent, Southampton	01703 320320
Mills Simon Thomas	One Essex Court, London	0171 936 3030

B

Milne Michael	Chambers of Geoffrey Hawker, London	0171 583 8899
	Resolution Chambers, Malvern	01684 561279
Miskin Charles James Monckton	23 Essex Street, London	0171 413 0353
Mitchell Miss Juliana Marie	2 Harcourt Buildings, London	0171 583 9020
Moore James Anthony	2 Gray's Inn Square Chambers, London	0171 242 0328/405 1317
Moorman Miss Lucinda Claire	Farrar's Building, London	0171 583 9241
Morris Miss Brenda Alison	14 Gray's Inn Square, London	0171 242 0858
Morris-Coole Christopher	Goldsmith Building, London	0171 353 7881
Moses Miss Rebecca	Barristers' Common Law Chambers, London	0171 375 3012
	Lion Court, London	0171 404 6565
Mulcahy Miss Leigh-Ann Maria	Two Crown Office Row, London	0171 797 8100
Muller Franz Joseph	11 King's Bench Walk, London	0171 353 3337/8
	11 King's Bench Walk, Leeds	0113 2971 200
Murch Stephen James	• 11 Bolt Court, London	0171 353 2300
Murray Ashley Charles	Oriel Chambers, Liverpool	0151 236 7191
Naylor Jonathan Peter	King's Chambers, Eastbourne	01323 416053
Nesbitt Timothy John Robert	199 Strand, London	0171 379 9779
Newbury Richard Lennox	Sovereign Chambers, Leeds	0113 245 1841/2/3
Newman Austin Eric	9 Woodhouse Square, Leeds	0113 245 1986
Newman Ms Ingrid	Hardwicke Building, London	0171 242 2523
Newton-Price James Edward	Pump Court Chambers, London	0171 353 0711
	Pump Court Chambers, Winchester	01962 868161
Nicholls Mrs (Deborah) Jane	Oriel Chambers, Liverpool	0151 236 7191
Nicholls Peter John	5 Pump Court, London	0171 353 2532
Nicolson Aris Tony	23 Bracken Gardens, London	0181 748 4924
Nolan Damian Francis	25-27 Castle Street, Liverpool	0151 227 5661/5666/236 5072
Norie-Miller Jeffrey Reginald	55 Temple Chambers, London	0171 353 7400
Norman Christopher John George	No 1 Serjeants' Inn, London	0171 415 6666
Norris Paul Howard	One Essex Court, London	0171 936 3030
O'Connor Andrew McDougal	Two Crown Office Row, London	0171 797 8100
O'Sullivan Bernard Anthony	Stanbrook & Henderson, London	0171 353 0101
	2 Harcourt Buildings, London	0171 583 9020
Okoye Miss Joy Nwamala	Chambers of Joy Okoye, London	0171 405 7011
Ong Miss Grace Yu Mae	One Essex Court, London	0171 936 3030
Ough Dr Richard Norman	• Hardwicke Building, London	0171 242 2523
Outhwaite Mrs Wendy-Jane Tivnan	Stanbrook & Henderson, London	0171 353 0101
	2 Harcourt Buildings, London	0171 583 9020
Pack Miss Melissa Elizabeth Jane	Farrar's Building, London	0171 583 9241
Palfrey Montague Mark	Hardwicke Building, London	0171 242 2523
Palmer James Savill	2 Harcourt Buildings, London	0171 583 9020
Palmer Patrick John Steven	Sovereign Chambers, Leeds	0113 245 1841/2/3
Paneth Miss Sarah Ruth	No 1 Serjeants' Inn, London	0171 415 6666
Parker John	2 Mitre Court Buildings, London	0171 353 1353
Parr John Edward	8 King Street Chambers, Manchester	0161 834 9560
Pawson Robert Edward Cruickshank	Pump Court Chambers, London	0171 353 0711
	Pump Court Chambers, Winchester	01962 868161
Peacock Ian Christopher	12 New Square, London	0171 419 1212
	Sovereign Chambers, Leeds	0113 245 1841/2/3
Peirson Oliver James	Pump Court Chambers, London	0171 353 0711
	Pump Court Chambers, Winchester	01962 868161
Pelling Richard Alexander	New Court Chambers, London	0171 831 9500
Pema Anesh Bhumin Laloo	9 Woodhouse Square, Leeds	0113 245 1986
Perkoff Richard Michael	Littleton Chambers, London	0171 797 8600
Phillips Andrew Charles	Two Crown Office Row, London	0171 797 8100
Phillips David John	199 Strand, London	0171 379 9779
	30 Park Place, Cardiff	01222 398421
Pinder Miss Mary Elizabeth	No 1 Serjeants' Inn, London	0171 415 6666
Pithers Clive Robert	Fenners Chambers, Cambridge	01223 368761
	Fenners Chambers, Peterborough	01733 562030
Pittaway David Michael	No 1 Serjeants' Inn, London	0171 415 6666
Pitter Jason Karl	Park Court Chambers, Leeds	0113 243 3277
Playford Jonathan Richard	2 Harcourt Buildings, London	0171 583 9020
Pliener David Jonathan		
Popat Prashant	Stanbrook & Henderson, London	0171 353 0101
	2 Harcourt Buildings, London	0171 583 9020
Porter Miss Sarah Ruth	11 Bolt Court, London	0171 353 2300
Portnoy Leslie Reuben	Chambers of John Hand QC, Manchester	0161 955 9000
Powell Miss Debra Ann	3 Serjeants' Inn, London	0171 353 5537

• Expanded entry in Part D

Powles Stephen Robert	Stanbrook & Henderson, London	0171 353 0101
	2 Harcourt Buildings, London	0171 583 9020
Pratt Allan Duncan	New Court Chambers, London	0171 831 9500
Prynne Andrew Geoffrey Lockyer	Stanbrook & Henderson, London	0171 353 0101
	2 Harcourt Buildings, London	0171 583 9020
Pugh Michael Charles	Old Square Chambers, London	0171 269 0300
	Old Square Chambers, Bristol	0117 927 7111
Purchas Christopher Patrick Brooks	Two Crown Office Row, London	0171 797 8100
Purdie Robert Anthony James	28 Western Road, Oxford	01865 204911
Rahman Muhammad Altafur	Barristers' Common Law Chambers, London	0171 375 3012
Rahman Ms Sadeqa Shaheen	1 Crown Office Row, London	0171 797 7500
Rai Amarjit Singh	St Philip's Chambers, Birmingham	0121 246 7000
Rampersad Devan	St Philip's Chambers, Birmingham	0121 246 7000
Rankin William Peter	Oriel Chambers, Liverpool	0151 236 7191
Rawlings Clive Patrick	Goldsmith Building, London	0171 353 7881
Rayment Mr. Benedick Michael	One King's Bench Walk, London	0171 936 1500
Rea Miss Karen Marie-Jeanne	No 1 Serjeants' Inn, London	0171 415 6666
Readhead Simon John Howard	No 1 Serjeants' Inn, London	0171 415 6666
Reddish John Wilson	One King's Bench Walk, London	0171 936 1500
Rees David Benjamin	5 Stone Buildings, London	0171 242 6201
Reeve Matthew Francis	5 Bell Yard, London	0171 333 8811
Rigby Terence	Chambers of John Hand QC, Manchester	0161 955 9000
Rigney Andrew James	Two Crown Office Row, London	0171 797 8100
Riley-Smith Tobias Augustine William	2 Harcourt Buildings, London	0171 583 9020
Rivalland Marc-Edouard	No 1 Serjeants' Inn, London	0171 415 6666
Robertson Ms Alice Michelle	Chambers of Kieran Coonan QC, London	0171 583 6013/2510
Robertson Andrew James	11 King's Bench Walk, London	0171 353 3337/8
	11 King's Bench Walk, Leeds	0113 2971 200
Robinson Richard John	2 Gray's Inn Square Chambers, London	0171 242 0328/405 1317
Robson Nicholas David	Baker Street Chambers, Middlesbrough	01642 873873
Roe Thomas Idris	Goldsmith Building, London	0171 353 7881
Rogers Ian Paul	1 Crown Office Row, London	0171 583 9292
Rogers Paul John	1 Crown Office Row, London	0171 797 7500
	Crown Office Row Chambers, Brighton	01273 625625
Room Stewart	8 Stone Buildings, London	0171 831 9881
Ross John Graffin	No 1 Serjeants' Inn, London	0171 415 6666
Routley Patrick	Goldsmith Building, London	0171 353 7881
Rowlands Ms Catherine Janet	Victoria Chambers, Birmingham	0121 236 9900
Rudd Matthew Allan	11 Bolt Court, London	0171 353 2300
	Redhill Chambers, Redhill	01737 780781
Rumney Conrad William Arthur	St Philip's Chambers, Birmingham	0121 246 7000
Russell Miss Christina Martha	9-12 Bell Yard, London	0171 400 1800
Russell Robert John Finlay	5 Bell Yard, London	0171 333 8811
Ryan David Patrick	Chambers of Geoffrey Hawker, London	0171 583 8899
Sadiq Tariq Mahmood	Chambers of John Hand QC, Manchester	0161 955 9000
Samuel Glyn Ross	St Philip's Chambers, Birmingham	0121 246 7000
Samuels Leslie John	Pump Court Chambers, London	0171 353 0711
	Pump Court Chambers, Winchester	01962 868161
Sander Andrew Thomas	Goldsmith Building, London	0171 353 7881
	Oriel Chambers, Liverpool	0151 236 7191
Sandiford Jonathan	St Paul's House, Leeds	0113 245 5866
Schooling Simon John	Chambers of Harjit Singh, London	0171 353 1356
Scott Matthew John	Pump Court Chambers, London	0171 353 0711
	Pump Court Chambers, Winchester	01962 868161
Scott-Phillips Alexander James	Earl Street Chambers, Maidstone	01622 671222
Scutt David Robert	11 Bolt Court, London	0171 353 2300
	Redhill Chambers, Redhill	01737 780781
Seal Julius Damien	189 Randolph Avenue, London	0171 624 9139
	3 Temple Gardens, London	0171 353 0832
Sefton Mark Thomas Dunblane	199 Strand, London	0171 379 9779
Selway Dr Katherine Emma	11 Old Square, London	0171 430 0341
Seymour Mark William	9-12 Bell Yard, London	0171 400 1800
Shaikh Eur.Ing. (Jaikumar) Christopher (Samuel	Avondale Chambers, London	0181 445 9984

B

	Equity Chambers, Birmingham	0121 233 2100
Sharma Miss Rakhee	Kingsway Chambers, London	07000 653529
Sheehan Malcolm Peter	Stanbrook & Henderson, London	0171 353 0101
	2 Harcourt Buildings, London	0171 583 9020
Sheridan Norman Patrick	• 11 Bolt Court, London	0171 353 2300
	• Redhill Chambers, Redhill	01737 780781
Silvester Bruce Ross	Lamb Chambers, London	0171 797 8300
Sinclair-Morris Charles Robert	9 Woodhouse Square, Leeds	0113 245 1986
Singh Balbir	• Equity Chambers, Birmingham	0121 233 2100
Sisley Timothy Julian Crispin	9 Stone Buildings, London	0171 404 5055
	Westgate Chambers, Lewes	01273 480 510
Sleeman Miss Rachel Sarah Elizabeth	One Essex Court, London	0171 936 3030
Sliwinski Robert Andrew	Chambers of Geoffrey Hawker, London	0171 583 8899
Smith Jason	25-27 Castle Street, Liverpool	0151 227 5661/5666/236 5072
Smith Miss Julia Mair Wheldon	Gough Square Chambers, London	0171 353 0924
Smith Matthew Robert	Sovereign Chambers, Leeds	0113 245 1841/2/3
Smith Warwick Timothy Cresswell	• Deans Court Chambers, Manchester	0161 834 4097
	• Deans Court Chambers, Preston	01772 555163
Snowden John Stevenson	Two Crown Office Row, London	0171 797 8100
Somerset Jones Eric	Goldsmith Building, London	0171 353 7881
Somerset-Jones Miss Felicity	Oriel Chambers, Liverpool	0151 236 7191
Soole Michael Alexander	5 Bell Yard, London	0171 333 8811
Spain Timothy Harrisson	Trinity Chambers, Newcastle upon Tyne	0191 232 1927
Sparks Kevin Laurence	Earl Street Chambers, Maidstone	01622 671222
Spearman Richard	5 Raymond Buildings, London	0171 242 2902
Spencer James	11 King's Bench Walk, London	0171 353 3337/8
	11 King's Bench Walk, Leeds	0113 2971 200
Spencer Martin Benedict	4 Paper Buildings, London	0171 353 3366/583 7155
Spollon Guy Merton	St Philip's Chambers, Birmingham	0121 246 7000
St Louis Brian Lloyd	Hardwicke Building, London	0171 242 2523
Stagg Paul Andrew	No 1 Serjeants' Inn, London	0171 415 6666
Staite Miss Sara Elizabeth	Stanbrook & Henderson, London	0171 353 0101
	2 Harcourt Buildings, London	0171 583 9020
Stancombe Barry Terrence	Gough Square Chambers, London	0171 353 0924
Starcevic Petar	St Philip's Chambers, Birmingham	0121 246 7000
Starks Nicholas Ernshaw	8 Fountain Court, Birmingham	0121 236 5514
Stead Miss Kate Rebecca	Barristers' Common Law Chambers, London	0171 375 3012
Stemmer-Baldwin Marcus Stephen	8 Stone Buildings, London	0171 831 9881
Stevenson John Melford	Two Crown Office Row, London	0171 797 8100
Stewart Alexander Joseph	5 New Square, London	0171 404 0404
Stewart Mark Courtney	College Chambers, Southampton	01703 230338
Stewart Nicholas John Cameron	Hardwicke Building, London	0171 242 2523
Storey Jeremy Brian	4 Pump Court, London	0171 353 2656/9
Susman Peter Joseph	New Court Chambers, London	0171 831 9500
Sutcliffe Andrew Harold Wentworth	3 Verulam Buildings, London	0171 831 8441
Sutherland Williams Mark	4 King's Bench Walk, London	0171 822 8822
	King's Bench Chambers, Bournemouth	01202 250025
Swan Ian Christopher	Two Crown Office Row, London	0171 797 8100
Tattersall Simon Mark Rogers	Fenners Chambers, Cambridge	01223 368761
	Fenners Chambers, Peterborough	01733 562030
Taylor Andrew Peter	Fenners Chambers, Cambridge	01223 368761
	Fenners Chambers, Peterborough	01733 562030
Taylor Miss Deborah Frances	Two Crown Office Row, London	0171 797 8100
Taylor Simon Wheldon	• Cloisters, London	0171 827 4000
Tedd Rex Hilary	• St Philip's Chambers, Birmingham	0121 246 7000
	• 22 Albion Place, Northampton	01604 636271
Temple Anthony Dominic	4 Pump Court, London	0171 353 2656/9
Ter Haar Roger Eduard Lound	Two Crown Office Row, London	0171 797 8100
Thompson Jonathan Richard	8 King Street Chambers, Manchester	0161 834 9560
Thompson Lyall Norris	Tindal Chambers, Chelmsford	01245 267742
	Tindal Chambers, St Albans	01727 843383
Ticciati Oliver	4 Pump Court, London	0171 353 2656/9
Tobin Daniel Alphonsus Joseph	Chambers of Geoffrey Hawker, London	0171 583 8899
Tod Jonathan Alan	7 Stone Buildings, London	0171 242 0961
Tomlinson Hugh Richard Edward	New Court Chambers, London	0171 831 9500
Townend James Barrie Stanley	One King's Bench Walk, London	0171 936 1500

• Expanded entry in Part D

Travers Hugh	Pump Court Chambers, London	0171 353 0711
	Pump Court Chambers, Winchester	01962 868161
Trotman Timothy Oliver	Deans Court Chambers, Manchester	0161 834 4097
	Deans Court Chambers, Preston	01772 555163
Tucker David William	Two Crown Office Row, London	0171 797 8100
Tucker Miss Katherine Jane Greening	St Philip's Chambers, Birmingham	0121 246 7000
Turner James	One King's Bench Walk, London	0171 936 1500
Tyack David Guy	St Philip's Chambers, Birmingham	0121 246 7000
Vater John Alistair Pitt	Harcourt Chambers, London	0171 353 6961/7
Vaughan-Neil Miss Catherine Mary Bernardine	5 Bell Yard, London	0171 333 8811
Vincent Miss Ruth Carolyn	Colleton Chambers, Exeter	01392 274898
Waddington Nigel William James	8 Stone Buildings, London	0171 831 9881
Wadsworth James Patrick	4 Paper Buildings, London	0171 353 3366/583 7155
Wagstaffe Christopher David	Watford Chambers, Watford	01923 220553
Wakefield Miss Anne Prudence	3 Verulam Buildings, London	0171 831 8441
Walker Miss Jane	Chambers of John Hand QC, Manchester	0161 955 9000
Ward Ms Orla Mary	3 Serjeants' Inn, London	0171 353 5537
Warnock Andrew Ronald	No 1 Serjeants' Inn, London	0171 415 6666
Warrender Miss Nichola Mary	New Court Chambers, London	0171 831 9500
Waters Julian William Penrose	No 1 Serjeants' Inn, London	0171 415 6666
Watson Mark	6 Pump Court, London	0171 797 8400
	6-8 Mill Street, Maidstone	01622 688 094
Webb Geraint Timothy	2 Harcourt Buildings, London	0171 583 9020
Webb Robert Stopford	• 5 Bell Yard, London	0171 333 8811
Wedderspoon Miss Rachel Leone	Chambers of John Hand QC, Manchester	0161 955 9000
Weddle Steven Edgar	Hardwicke Building, London	0171 242 2523
West Lawrence Joseph	Stanbrook & Henderson, London	0171 353 0101
	2 Harcourt Buildings, London	0171 583 9020
West Mark	• 11 Old Square, London	0171 430 0341
Weston Clive Aubrey Richard	Two Crown Office Row, London	0171 797 8100
Wheeler Miss Marina Claire	Stanbrook & Henderson, London	0171 353 0101
	2 Harcourt Buildings, London	0171 583 9020
White Darren Paul	Cathedral Chambers (Jan Wood Independent Barristers' Clerk), Exeter	01392 210900
White Peter-John Spencer	Pembroke House, Leatherhead	01372 376160/376493
Whiteley Miss Miranda Blyth	4 Field Court, London	0171 440 6900
Whitfield Adrian	3 Serjeants' Inn, London	0171 353 5537
Wignall Edward Gordon	• 1 Dr Johnson's Buildings, London	0171 353 9328
	• Dr Johnson's Chambers, Reading	01189 254221
Wilcox Nicholas Hugh	5 Essex Court, London	0171 410 2000
Wilkinson Nigel Vivian Marshall	Two Crown Office Row, London	0171 797 8100
Willer Robert Michael	Hardwicke Building, London	0171 242 2523
Williams A John	• 13 King's Bench Walk, London	0171 353 7204
	• King's Bench Chambers, Oxford	01865 311066
Williams John Griffith	Goldsmith Building, London	0171 353 7881
	33 Park Place, Cardiff	01222 233313
Williams Rhodri John	30 Park Place, Cardiff	01222 398421
Williams Thomas Ellis	30 Park Place, Cardiff	01222 398421
Wilson Alasdair John	Fenners Chambers, Cambridge	01223 368761
	Fenners Chambers, Peterborough	01733 562030
Wilson James Mason	Fenners Chambers, Cambridge	01223 368761
	Fenners Chambers, Peterborough	01733 562030
Wilton Simon Daniel	4 Paper Buildings, London	0171 353 3366/583 7155
Wood Simon Richard Henry	Lamb Chambers, London	0171 797 8300
Woodbridge Julian Guy	One King's Bench Walk, London	0171 936 1500
Woods Jonathan	Two Crown Office Row, London	0171 797 8100
Woodward Nicholas Frederick	White Friars Chambers, Chester	01244 323070
Woolf Eliot Charles Anthony	199 Strand, London	0171 379 9779
Woolf Steven Jeremy	Hardwicke Building, London	0171 242 2523
Woolman Andrew Paul Lander	Chambers of Andrew Campbell QC, Leeds	0113 245 5438
Wordsworth Mrs Philippa Lindsey	Chambers of Andrew Campbell QC, Leeds	0113 245 5438
Worrall John Raymond Guy	Chambers of Andrew Campbell QC, Leeds	0113 245 5438
Worsley Daniel	Stanbrook & Henderson, London	0171 353 0101
	2 Harcourt Buildings, London	0171 583 9020

B

Wright Miss Clare Elizabeth	6 Pump Court, London	0171 797 8400
Wright Gerard Henry	25-27 Castle Street, Liverpool	0151 227 5661/5666/236 5072
Wright Norman Alfred	Oriel Chambers, Liverpool	0151 236 7191
Wright Ms Sadie	Goldsmith Building, London	0171 353 7881
Wyatt Guy Peter James	Earl Street Chambers, Maidstone	01622 671222
Yell Nicholas Anthony	No 1 Serjeants' Inn, London	0171 415 6666
Yelton Michael Paul	Fenners Chambers, Cambridge	01223 368761
	Fenners Chambers, Peterborough	01733 562030
Yeung Stuart Roy	22 Albion Place, Northampton	01604 636271
Zornoza Miss Isabella	Stanbrook & Henderson, London	0171 353 0101
	2 Harcourt Buildings, London	0171 583 9020

COMMUNITY CARE

Eccles Hugh William Patrick	Harcourt Chambers, London	0171 353 6961/7
	Harcourt Chambers, Oxford	01865 791559

COMPANY AND COMMERCIAL

Abbott Alistair James Hugh	5 New Square, London	0171 404 0404
Adamyk Simon Charles	12 New Square, London	0171 419 1212
Adejumo Mrs Hilda Ekpo	• Temple Chambers, London	0171 583 1001 (2 lines)
Airey Simon Andrew	11 Bolt Court, London	0171 353 2300
	Redhill Chambers, Redhill	01737 780781
Aldridge James Hugh	13 Old Square, London	0171 404 4800
Amin Miss Farah	7 New Square, London	0171 430 1660
Arden Peter Leonard	Enterprise Chambers, London	0171 405 9471
	Enterprise Chambers, Leeds	0113 246 0391
	Enterprise Chambers, Newcastle upon Tyne	0191 222 3344
Atherton Ian David	Enterprise Chambers, London	0171 405 9471
	Enterprise Chambers, Leeds	0113 246 0391
	Enterprise Chambers, Newcastle upon Tyne	0191 222 3344
Ayres Andrew John William	13 Old Square, London	0171 404 4800
Baker Miss Anne Jacqueline	Enterprise Chambers, London	0171 405 9471
	Enterprise Chambers, Leeds	0113 246 0391
	Enterprise Chambers, Newcastle upon Tyne	0191 222 3344
Barker James Sebastian	Enterprise Chambers, London	0171 405 9471
	Enterprise Chambers, Leeds	0113 246 0391
	Enterprise Chambers, Newcastle upon Tyne	0191 222 3344
Barker Simon George Harry	• 13 Old Square, London	0171 404 4800
Beaumont Marc Clifford	• Pump Court Chambers, London	0171 353 0711
	• Harrow-on-the-Hill Chambers, Harrow on the Hill	0181 423 7444
	• Pump Court Chambers, Winchester	01962 868161
	• Windsor Barristers' Chambers, Windsor	01753 648 899
Benson Julian Christopher Woodburn	One Essex Court, London	0171 936 3030
Berkley Michael Stuart	Rougemont Chambers, Exeter	01392 410471
Bhaloo Miss Zia Kurban	Enterprise Chambers, London	0171 405 9471
	Enterprise Chambers, Leeds	0113 246 0391
	Enterprise Chambers, Newcastle upon Tyne	0191 222 3344
Birch Roger Allen	12 New Square, London	0171 419 1212
	Sovereign Chambers, Leeds	0113 245 1841/2/3
	Lancaster Buildings, Manchester	0161 661 4444
Bompas Anthony George	4 Stone Buildings, London	0171 242 5524
Brannigan Peter John Sean	One Essex Court, London	0171 936 3030
Brownbill David John	Gray's Inn Square, London	0171 242 3529
Bryant Miss Ceri Jane	Erskine Chambers, London	0171 242 5532
Bull (Donald) Roger	One Essex Court, London	0171 936 3030
Burroughs Nigel Alfred	11 Old Square, London	0171 430 0341
Burton Michael John	Littleton Chambers, London	0171 797 8600
Capon Philip Christopher William	St Philip's Chambers, Birmingham	0121 246 7000
Cawson Mark	• 12 New Square, London	0171 419 1212
	• St James's Chambers, Manchester	0161 834 7000
	• Park Lane Chambers, Leeds	0113 228 5000
Charman Andrew Julian	St Philip's Chambers, Birmingham	0121 246 7000
Chivers (Tom) David	Erskine Chambers, London	0171 242 5532
Clarke Ian James	Hardwicke Building, London	0171 242 2523

• Expanded entry in Part D

Clegg Sebastian James Barwick	Deans Court Chambers, Manchester	0161 834 4097
Collaco Moraes Francis Thomas	• 2 Gray's Inn Square Chambers, London	0171 242 0328/405 1317
Collings Matthew Glynn Burkinshaw	13 Old Square, London	0171 404 4800
Cone John Crawford	Erskine Chambers, London	0171 242 5532
Corbett James Patrick	St Philip's Chambers, Birmingham	0121 246 7000
Craig Kenneth Allen	Hardwicke Building, London	0171 242 2523
Crail Miss (Elspeth) Ross	12 New Square, London	0171 419 1212
	Sovereign Chambers, Leeds	0113 245 1841/2/3
Cranfield Peter Anthony	3 Verulam Buildings, London	0171 831 8441
Crawford Grant	11 Old Square, London	0171 430 0341
Crow Jonathan Rupert	4 Stone Buildings, London	0171 242 5524
Cunningham Mark James	13 Old Square, London	0171 404 4800
Davidson Edward Alan	• 11 Old Square, London	0171 430 0341
Davies Miss Penny May	Chambers of Harjit Singh, London	0171 353 1356
Dawes Gordon Stephen Knight	Goldsmith Building, London	0171 353 7881
de Jehan David	St Paul's House, Leeds	0113 245 5866
de Lacy Richard Michael	3 Verulam Buildings, London	0171 831 8441
Deacock Adam Jason	Chambers of Lord Goodhart QC, London	0171 405 5577
Dedezade Taner	Tindal Chambers, Chelmsford	01245 267742
Dodge Peter Clive	11 Old Square, London	0171 430 0341
Dougherty Nigel Peter	Erskine Chambers, London	0171 242 5532
Doyle Louis George	Chambers of Andrew Campbell QC, Leeds	0113 245 5438
Duffy Derek James	St Paul's House, Leeds	0113 245 5866
Elleray Anthony John	• 12 New Square, London	0171 419 1212
	• St James's Chambers, Manchester	0161 834 7000
	• Park Lane Chambers, Leeds	0113 228 5000
Evans James Frederick Meurig	3 Verulam Buildings, London	0171 831 8441
Evans-Gordon Mrs Jane-Anne Mary	12 New Square, London	0171 419 1212
Foster Francis Alexander	St Paul's House, Leeds	0113 245 5866
Francis Edward Gerald Francis	Enterprise Chambers, London	0171 405 9471
	Enterprise Chambers, Leeds	0113 246 0391
	Enterprise Chambers, Newcastle upon Tyne	0191 222 3344
Franklin Stephen Hall	5 Paper Buildings, London	0171 583 6117
	Fenners Chambers, Cambridge	01223 368761
Freedman Sampson Clive	3 Verulam Buildings, London	0171 831 8441
Garcia-Miller Miss Laura	Enterprise Chambers, London	0171 405 9471
	Enterprise Chambers, Leeds	0113 246 0391
	Enterprise Chambers, Newcastle upon Tyne	0191 222 3344
George Miss Judith Sarah	St Philip's Chambers, Birmingham	0121 246 7000
Gerald Nigel Mortimer	Enterprise Chambers, London	0171 405 9471
	Enterprise Chambers, Leeds	0113 246 0391
	Enterprise Chambers, Newcastle upon Tyne	0191 222 3344
Gibaud Miss Catherine Alison Annetta	3 Verulam Buildings, London	0171 831 8441
Gillyon Philip Jeffrey	Erskine Chambers, London	0171 242 5532
Godfrey Jonathan Saul	St Paul's House, Leeds	0113 245 5866
Goodhart Lord	Chambers of Lord Goodhart QC, London	0171 405 5577
Graham Thomas Patrick Henry	Lamb Chambers, London	0171 797 8300
Grantham Andrew Timothy	• Deans Court Chambers, Manchester	0161 834 4097
	• Deans Court Chambers, Preston	01772 555163
Gregory John Raymond	Deans Court Chambers, Manchester	0161 834 4097
	Deans Court Chambers, Preston	01772 555163
Griffiths Peter Robert	4 Stone Buildings, London	0171 242 5524
Groves Hugo Gerard	Enterprise Chambers, London	0171 405 9471
	Enterprise Chambers, Leeds	0113 246 0391
	Enterprise Chambers, Newcastle upon Tyne	0191 222 3344
Hall Taylor Alexander Edward	11 Old Square, London	0171 430 0341
Halpern David Anthony	Enterprise Chambers, London	0171 405 9471
	Enterprise Chambers, Leeds	0113 246 0391
	Enterprise Chambers, Newcastle upon Tyne	0191 222 3344
Hamer Michael Howard Kenneth	2 Harcourt Buildings, London	0171 583 9020
	Westgate Chambers, Lewes	01273 480 510
Hantusch Robert Anthony	• 3 Stone Buildings, London	0171 242 4937/405 8358

B

• Expanded entry in Part D

Hardwick Matthew Richard	Enterprise Chambers, London	0171 405 9471
	Enterprise Chambers, Leeds	0113 246 0391
	Enterprise Chambers, Newcastle upon Tyne	0191 222 3344
Hargreaves Miss Sara Jane	12 New Square, London	0171 419 1212
	Sovereign Chambers, Leeds	0113 245 1841/2/3
Hayes Miss Josephine Mary	Chambers of Lord Goodhart QC, London	0171 405 5577
Heywood Michael Edmundson	Chambers of Lord Goodhart QC, London	0171 405 5577
	Cobden House Chambers, Manchester	0161 833 6000/6001
Hibbert William John	Gough Square Chambers, London	0171 353 0924
Holland Charles Christopher	Trinity Chambers, Newcastle upon Tyne	0191 232 1927
Holmes Justin Francis	Chambers of Lord Goodhart QC, London	0171 405 5577
Hughes Miss Mary Josephine	Chambers of Lord Goodhart QC, London	0171 405 5577
Hutton Miss Caroline	Enterprise Chambers, London	0171 405 9471
	Enterprise Chambers, Leeds	0113 246 0391
	Enterprise Chambers, Newcastle upon Tyne	0191 222 3344
Ife Miss Linden Elizabeth	Enterprise Chambers, London	0171 405 9471
	Enterprise Chambers, Leeds	0113 246 0391
	Enterprise Chambers, Newcastle upon Tyne	0191 222 3344
Jack Adrian Laurence Robert	Enterprise Chambers, London	0171 405 9471
James Michael Frank	Enterprise Chambers, London	0171 405 9471
	Enterprise Chambers, Leeds	0113 246 0391
	Enterprise Chambers, Newcastle upon Tyne	0191 222 3344
Jefferies Thomas Robert	Chambers of Lord Goodhart QC, London	0171 405 5577
Jenkala Adrian Aleksander	11 Bolt Court, London	0171 353 2300
	Redhill Chambers, Redhill	01737 780781
Jennings Timothy Robin Finnegan	Enterprise Chambers, London	0171 405 9471
	Enterprise Chambers, Leeds	0113 246 0391
	Enterprise Chambers, Newcastle upon Tyne	0191 222 3344
Jones Geraint Martyn	Fenners Chambers, Cambridge	01223 368761
	Fenners Chambers, Peterborough	01733 562030
Jory Robert John Hugh	Enterprise Chambers, London	0171 405 9471
	Enterprise Chambers, Leeds	0113 246 0391
	Enterprise Chambers, Newcastle upon Tyne	0191 222 3344
Kearl Guy Alexander	St Paul's House, Leeds	0113 245 5866
Kolodynski Stefan Richard	New Court Chambers, Birmingham	0121 693 6656
Kolodziej Andrzej Jozef	• Littman Chambers, London	0171 404 4866
Kosmin Leslie Gordon	Erskine Chambers, London	0171 242 5532
Kremen Philip Michael	Hardwicke Building, London	0171 242 2523
Kuschke Leon Siegfried	Erskine Chambers, London	0171 242 5532
Lamont Miss Camilla Rose	Chambers of Lord Goodhart QC, London	0171 405 5577
Laughton Samuel Dennis	17 Old Buildings, London	0171 405 9653
Lawson Daniel George	Goldsmith Building, London	0171 353 7881
Le Poidevin Nicholas Peter	12 New Square, London	0171 419 1212
	Sovereign Chambers, Leeds	0113 245 1841/2/3
Leeming Ian	Lamb Chambers, London	0171 797 8300
	Chambers of John Hand QC, Manchester	0161 955 9000
Leonard Charles Robert Weston	Goldsmith Building, London	0171 353 7881
Levy Benjamin Keith	Enterprise Chambers, London	0171 405 9471
	Enterprise Chambers, Leeds	0113 246 0391
	Enterprise Chambers, Newcastle upon Tyne	0191 222 3344
Levy Robert Stuart	9 Stone Buildings, London	0171 404 5055
	Assize Court Chambers, Bristol	0117 926 4587
Lowenstein Paul David	Littleton Chambers, London	0171 797 8600
Mabb David Michael	Erskine Chambers, London	0171 242 5532
Malek Ali	3 Verulam Buildings, London	0171 831 8441
Mann George Anthony	Enterprise Chambers, London	0171 405 9471
	Enterprise Chambers, Leeds	0113 246 0391

• Expanded entry in Part D

	Enterprise Chambers, Newcastle upon Tyne	0191 222 3344
Marten Richard Hedley Westwood	Chambers of Lord Goodhart QC, London	0171 405 5577
Martineau Henry Ralph Adeane	Goldsmith Building, London	0171 353 7881
Masters Miss Sara Alayna	20 Essex Street, London	0171 583 9294
Mawrey Richard Brooks	Stanbrook & Henderson, London	0171 353 0101
	2 Harcourt Buildings, London	0171 583 9020
Mayhew Jerome Patrick Burke	Goldsmith Building, London	0171 353 7881
McAllister Miss Elizabeth Ann	Enterprise Chambers, London	0171 405 9471
	Enterprise Chambers, Leeds	0113 246 0391
	Enterprise Chambers, Newcastle upon Tyne	0191 222 3344
McCarthy William	New Bailey Chambers, Preston	01772 258 087
McKinnell Miss Soraya Jane	Enterprise Chambers, London	0171 405 9471
	Enterprise Chambers, Leeds	0113 246 0391
	Enterprise Chambers, Newcastle upon Tyne	0191 222 3344
Mendoza Neil David Pereira	Hardwicke Building, London	0171 242 2523
Merriman Nicholas Flavelle	3 Verulam Buildings, London	0171 831 8441
Milligan Iain Anstruther	20 Essex Street, London	0171 583 9294
Moore Martin Luke	Erskine Chambers, London	0171 242 5532
Morgan Charles James Arthur	Enterprise Chambers, London	0171 405 9471
	Enterprise Chambers, Leeds	0113 246 0391
	Enterprise Chambers, Newcastle upon Tyne	0191 222 3344
Morgan Richard Hugo Lyndon	13 Old Square, London	0171 404 4800
Mullis Anthony Roger	Chambers of Lord Goodhart QC, London	0171 405 5577
Nebhrajani Miss Mel	9 Stone Buildings, London	0171 404 5055
Neville Stephen John	Gough Square Chambers, London	0171 353 0924
Newman Miss Catherine Mary	• 13 Old Square, London	0171 404 4800
Nicholls John Peter	13 Old Square, London	0171 404 4800
Norris Paul Howard	One Essex Court, London	0171 936 3030
Ogunbiyi Oluwole Afolabi	Horizon Chambers, London	0171 242 2440
Ohrenstein Dov	Chambers of Lord Goodhart QC, London	0171 405 5577
Owens Miss Hilary Jane	St Philip's Chambers, Birmingham	0121 246 7000
Parry David Julian Thomas	Chambers of Lord Goodhart QC, London	0171 405 5577
Patchett-Joyce Michael Thurston	Monckton Chambers, London	0171 405 7211
Peacock Ian Christopher	12 New Square, London	0171 419 1212
	Sovereign Chambers, Leeds	0113 245 1841/2/3
Peacock Nicholas Christopher	13 Old Square, London	0171 404 4800
Peacocke Mrs Teresa Anne Rosen	Enterprise Chambers, London	0171 405 9471
	Enterprise Chambers, Leeds	0113 246 0391
	Enterprise Chambers, Newcastle upon Tyne	0191 222 3344
Peglow Dr Michael Alfred Herman	Chambers of Geoffrey Hawker, London	0171 583 8899
Pelling (Philip) Mark	Monckton Chambers, London	0171 405 7211
Perkoff Richard Michael	Littleton Chambers, London	0171 797 8600
Pickering James Patrick	Enterprise Chambers, London	0171 405 9471
	Enterprise Chambers, Leeds	0113 246 0391
	Enterprise Chambers, Newcastle upon Tyne	0191 222 3344
Pimentel Carlos de Serpa Alberto Legg	3 Stone Buildings, London	0171 242 4937/405 8358
Potts James Rupert	Erskine Chambers, London	0171 242 5532
Potts Robin	Erskine Chambers, London	0171 242 5532
Prentice Professor Daniel David	Erskine Chambers, London	0171 242 5532
Pryke Stuart	Trinity Chambers, Newcastle upon Tyne	0191 232 1927
Rahman Ms Sadeqa Shaheen	1 Crown Office Row, London	0171 797 7500
Randall John Yeoman	7 Stone Buildings, London	0171 405 3886/242 3546
	St Philip's Chambers, Birmingham	0121 246 7000
Richards David Anthony Stewart	Erskine Chambers, London	0171 242 5532
Richardson Miss Sarah Jane	Enterprise Chambers, London	0171 405 9471
	Enterprise Chambers, Leeds	0113 246 0391
	Enterprise Chambers, Newcastle upon Tyne	0191 222 3344
Rivalland Marc-Edouard	No 1 Serjeants' Inn, London	0171 415 6666

B

• Expanded entry in Part D

Roberts Miss Catherine Ann	Erskine Chambers, London	0171 242 5532
Roe Thomas Idris	Goldsmith Building, London	0171 353 7881
Rowell David Stewart	Chambers of Lord Goodhart QC, London	0171 405 5577
Russen Jonathan Huw Sinclair	13 Old Square, London	0171 404 4800
Salter Richard Stanley	3 Verulam Buildings, London	0171 831 8441
Sampson Graeme William	Chambers of Geoffrey Hawker, London	0171 583 8899
Sayer Mr Peter Edwin	Gough Square Chambers, London	0171 353 0924
Seymour Richard William	Monckton Chambers, London	0171 405 7211
Shah Bajul Amratlal Somchand	Twenty-Four Old Buildings, London	0171 404 0946
Sleeman Miss Rachel Sarah Elizabeth	One Essex Court, London	0171 936 3030
Smith Miss Julia Mair Wheldon	Gough Square Chambers, London	0171 353 0924
Snowden Richard Andrew	Erskine Chambers, London	0171 242 5532
Southwell Richard Charles	One Hare Court, London	0171 353 3171
Staddon Miss Claire Ann	12 New Square, London	0171 419 1212
	Sovereign Chambers, Leeds	0113 245 1841/2/3
Stead Miss Kate Rebecca	Barristers' Common Law Chambers, London	0171 375 3012
Stewart Alexander Joseph	5 New Square, London	0171 404 0404
Stewart Nicholas John Cameron	Hardwicke Building, London	0171 242 2523
Stockdale Sir Thomas Minshull	Erskine Chambers, London	0171 242 5532
Stokes Miss Mary Elizabeth	Erskine Chambers, London	0171 242 5532
Stubbs William Frederick	Erskine Chambers, London	0171 242 5532
Sugar Simon Gareth	5 New Square, London	0171 404 0404
Sykes (James) Richard	Erskine Chambers, London	0171 242 5532
Taelor Start Miss Angharad Jocelyn	3 Verulam Buildings, London	0171 831 8441
Tedd Rex Hilary	• St Philip's Chambers, Birmingham	0121 246 7000
	• 22 Albion Place, Northampton	01604 636271
Thomas Nigel Matthew	13 Old Square, London	0171 404 4800
Thomas (Robert) Neville	3 Verulam Buildings, London	0171 831 8441
Thompson Andrew Richard	Erskine Chambers, London	0171 242 5532
Thompson Steven Lim	Twenty-Four Old Buildings, London	0171 404 0946
Thornton Andrew James	Erskine Chambers, London	0171 242 5532
Tipples Miss Amanda Jane	13 Old Square, London	0171 404 4800
Todd Michael Alan	Erskine Chambers, London	0171 242 5532
Tolaney Miss Sonia	3 Verulam Buildings, London	0171 831 8441
Trace Anthony John	• 13 Old Square, London	0171 404 4800
Tucker Miss Katherine Jane Greening	St Philip's Chambers, Birmingham	0121 246 7000
Twigger Andrew Mark	3 Stone Buildings, London	0171 242 4937/405 8358
Vines Anthony Robert Francis	Gough Square Chambers, London	0171 353 0924
Weatherill Bernard Richard	Chambers of Lord Goodhart QC, London	0171 405 5577
West Mark	• 11 Old Square, London	0171 430 0341
Whiteley Miss Miranda Blyth	4 Field Court, London	0171 440 6900
Williamson Miss Bridget Susan	Enterprise Chambers, London	0171 405 9471
	Enterprise Chambers, Leeds	0113 246 0391
	Enterprise Chambers, Newcastle upon Tyne	0191 222 3344
Wolfson David	3 Verulam Buildings, London	0171 831 8441
Woolf Steven Jeremy	Hardwicke Building, London	0171 242 2523
Worster David James Stewart	St Philip's Chambers, Birmingham	0121 246 7000
Wright Gerard Henry	25-27 Castle Street, Liverpool	0151 227 5661/5666/236 5072
Wright Robert Anthony Kent	Erskine Chambers, London	0171 242 5532
Wright Ms Sadie	Goldsmith Building, London	0171 353 7881
Yelton Michael Paul	Fenners Chambers, Cambridge	01223 368761
	Fenners Chambers, Peterborough	01733 562030
Zelin Geoffrey Andrew	Enterprise Chambers, London	0171 405 9471
	Enterprise Chambers, Leeds	0113 246 0391
	Enterprise Chambers, Newcastle upon Tyne	0191 222 3344

COMPANY DIRECTORS' DISQUALIFICATION

Birch Roger Allen	12 New Square, London	0171 419 1212
	Sovereign Chambers, Leeds	0113 245 1841/2/3
	Lancaster Buildings, Manchester	0161 661 4444

COMPETITION

Anderson Rupert John	Monckton Chambers, London	0171 405 7211

• Expanded entry in Part D

Beal Kieron Conrad	4 Paper Buildings, London	0171 353 3366/583 7155
Beard Daniel Matthew	Monckton Chambers, London	0171 405 7211
Beaumont Marc Clifford	• Pump Court Chambers, London	0171 353 0711
	• Harrow-on-the-Hill Chambers, Harrow on the Hill	0181 423 7444
	• Pump Court Chambers, Winchester	01962 868161
	• Windsor Barristers' Chambers, Windsor	01753 648 899
Dashwood Professor Arthur Alan	Stanbrook & Henderson, London	0171 353 0101
	2 Harcourt Buildings, London	0171 583 9020
Fowler Richard Nicholas	Monckton Chambers, London	0171 405 7211
Gregory John Raymond	Deans Court Chambers, Manchester	0161 834 4097
	Deans Court Chambers, Preston	01772 555163
Harris Paul Best	Monckton Chambers, London	0171 405 7211
Haynes Miss Rebecca	Monckton Chambers, London	0171 405 7211
Hicks Michael Charles	• 19 Old Buildings, London	0171 405 2001
Hill Raymond	Monckton Chambers, London	0171 405 7211
Hodgson Richard Andrew	New Court, London	0171 797 8999
Holman Miss Tamsin Perdita	19 Old Buildings, London	0171 405 2001
Kime Matthew Jonathan	• New Court, London	0171 797 8999
	• Cobden House Chambers, Manchester	0161 833 6000/6001
Kingsland Rt Hon Lord	4 Breams Buildings, London	0171 353 5835/430 1221
Kinnier Andrew John	2 Harcourt Buildings, London	0171 583 9020
Lasok Karol Paul Edward	Monckton Chambers, London	0171 405 7211
Macnab Alexander Andrew	Monckton Chambers, London	0171 405 7211
Mantle Peter John	Monckton Chambers, London	0171 405 7211
Masters Miss Sara Alayna	20 Essex Street, London	0171 583 9294
Mitchell Miss Juliana Marie	2 Harcourt Buildings, London	0171 583 9020
Outhwaite Mrs Wendy-Jane Tivnan	Stanbrook & Henderson, London	0171 353 0101
	2 Harcourt Buildings, London	0171 583 9020
Paines Nicholas Paul Billot	Monckton Chambers, London	0171 405 7211
Parker Kenneth Blades	Monckton Chambers, London	0171 405 7211
Pelling (Philip) Mark	Monckton Chambers, London	0171 405 7211
Peretz George Michael John		
Pickford Anthony James	Prince Henry's Chambers, London	0171 353 1183/1190
Pope David James	3 Verulam Buildings, London	0171 831 8441
Puckrin Cedric Eldred	19 Old Buildings, London	0171 405 2001
Reid Brian Christopher	19 Old Buildings, London	0171 405 2001
Robertson Aidan Malcolm David	Monckton Chambers, London	0171 405 7211
Roth Peter Marcel	Monckton Chambers, London	0171 405 7211
Shipley Norman Graham	• 19 Old Buildings, London	0171 405 2001
Simor Miss Jessica Margaret Poppaea	Monckton Chambers, London	0171 405 7211
Smith Ms Katherine Emma	Monckton Chambers, London	0171 405 7211
Thompson Rhodri William Ralph	Monckton Chambers, London	0171 405 7211
Turner Jonathan Richard	Monckton Chambers, London	0171 405 7211
Vajda Christopher Stephen	Monckton Chambers, London	0171 405 7211
Webb Robert Stopford	• 5 Bell Yard, London	0171 333 8811
West Lawrence Joseph	Stanbrook & Henderson, London	0171 353 0101
	2 Harcourt Buildings, London	0171 583 9020
Wheeler Miss Marina Claire	Stanbrook & Henderson, London	0171 353 0101
	2 Harcourt Buildings, London	0171 583 9020
Wilson Alastair James Drysdale	• 19 Old Buildings, London	0171 405 2001

COMPULSORY PURCHASE

Jones Gregory Percy	• 2 Harcourt Buildings, London	0171 353 8415
Langham Richard Geoffrey	1 Serjeants' Inn, London	0171 583 1355
Straker Timothy Derrick	• 2-3 Gray's Inn Square, London	0171 242 4986

COMPULSORY PURCHASE COMPENSATION

Purchas Robin Michael	• 2 Harcourt Buildings, London	0171 353 8415

COMPUTER CONTRACTS

Patterson Stewart	• Pump Court Chambers, London	0171 353 0711
	• Pump Court Chambers, Winchester	01962 868161

COMPUTER DISPUTES

Silverleaf Michael	• 11 South Square, London	0171 405 1222

• Expanded entry in Part D

COMPUTER SUPPLY LITIGATION

Susman Peter Joseph	New Court Chambers, London	0171 831 9500

CONSTRUCTION

Acton Davis Jonathan James	4 Pump Court, London	0171 353 2656/9
Akenhead Robert	Atkin Chambers, London	0171 404 0102
Alliott George Beckles	2 Harcourt Buildings, London	0171 583 9020
Amin Miss Farah	7 New Square, London	0171 430 1660
Atherton Ian David	Enterprise Chambers, London	0171 405 9471
	Enterprise Chambers, Leeds	0113 246 0391
	Enterprise Chambers, Newcastle upon Tyne	0191 222 3344
Aylen Walter Stafford	Hardwicke Building, London	0171 242 2523
Baatz Nicholas Stephen	Atkin Chambers, London	0171 404 0102
Bailey Edward Henry	5 Bell Yard, London	0171 333 8811
Baldry Antony Brian	No 1 Serjeants' Inn, London	0171 415 6666
Barker Simon George Harry	• 13 Old Square, London	0171 404 4800
Barstow Stephen Royden	Harcourt Chambers, London	0171 353 6961/7
	Harcourt Chambers, Oxford	01865 791559
Barwise Miss Stephanie Nicola	Atkin Chambers, London	0171 404 0102
Beal Kieron Conrad	4 Paper Buildings, London	0171 353 3366/583 7155
Bickford-Smith Stephen William	4 Breams Buildings, London	0171 353 5835/430 1221
Blackburn John	Atkin Chambers, London	0171 404 0102
Blakesley Patrick James	Two Crown Office Row, London	0171 797 8100
Boswell Miss Lindsay Alice	4 Pump Court, London	0171 353 2656/9
Bowdery Martin	Atkin Chambers, London	0171 404 0102
Bradley Richard	Oriel Chambers, Liverpool	0151 236 7191
Brannigan Peter John Sean	One Essex Court, London	0171 936 3030
Brunner Adrian John Nelson	Stanbrook & Henderson, London	0171 353 0101
	2 Harcourt Buildings, London	0171 583 9020
Bull (Donald) Roger	One Essex Court, London	0171 936 3030
Burns Peter Richard	Deans Court Chambers, Manchester	0161 834 4097
Burr Andrew Charles	Atkin Chambers, London	0171 404 0102
Bush Keith	30 Park Place, Cardiff	01222 398421
Cameron Neil Alexander	Wilberforce Chambers, Hull	01482 323 264
Catchpole Stuart Paul	39 Essex Street, London	0171 832 1111
Cawley Neil Robert Loudoun	55 Temple Chambers, London	0171 353 7400
	Milton Keynes Chambers, Milton Keynes	01908 217857
Chalmers Miss Suzanne Frances	Two Crown Office Row, London	0171 797 8100
Cheyne Miss Phyllida Alison	4 Pump Court, London	0171 353 2656/9
Clark Christopher Harvey	Pump Court Chambers, London	0171 353 0711
	Westgate Chambers, Lewes	01273 480 510
	Pump Court Chambers, Winchester	01962 868161
Clarke George Robert Ivan	Chambers of Geoffrey Hawker, London	0171 583 8899
Clay Robert Charles	Atkin Chambers, London	0171 404 0102
Clegg Sebastian James Barwick	Deans Court Chambers, Manchester	0161 834 4097
Collard Michael David	5 Pump Court, London	0171 353 2532
Connerty Anthony Robin	Lamb Chambers, London	0171 797 8300
Cooper Adrian Edgar Mark	Stanbrook & Henderson, London	0171 353 0101
	2 Harcourt Buildings, London	0171 583 9020
Creaner Paul Anthony	15 Winckley Square, Preston	01772 252 828
Cross James Edward Michael	4 Pump Court, London	0171 353 2656/9
Crowley John Desmond	Two Crown Office Row, London	0171 797 8100
Curtis Michael Alexander	Two Crown Office Row, London	0171 797 8100
Daiches Michael Salis	• 22 Old Buildings, London	0171 831 0222
Davies Richard Llewellyn	39 Essex Street, London	0171 832 1111
Davies Stephen Richard	8 King Street Chambers, Manchester	0161 834 9560
DeCamp Miss Jane Louise	Two Crown Office Row, London	0171 797 8100
Dennison Stephen Randell	Atkin Chambers, London	0171 404 0102
Dennys Nicholas Charles Jonathan	Atkin Chambers, London	0171 404 0102
Doerries Miss Chantal-Aimee Renee Aemelia Annemarie	Atkin Chambers, London	0171 404 0102
Dumaresq Ms Delia Jane	Atkin Chambers, London	0171 404 0102
Dyer David Roger	St Philip's Chambers, Birmingham	0121 246 7000
Edwards-Stuart Antony James Cobham	Two Crown Office Row, London	0171 797 8100
Evans-Tovey Jason Robert	Two Crown Office Row, London	0171 797 8100
Fisher David	5 Bell Yard, London	0171 333 8811

• Expanded entry in Part D

Foster Charles Andrew	• Chambers of Kieran Coonan QC, London	0171 583 6013/2510
Franklin Miss Kim	• Lamb Chambers, London	0171 797 8300
Franklin Stephen Hall	5 Paper Buildings, London	0171 583 6117
	Fenners Chambers, Cambridge	01223 368761
Fraser Peter Donald	Atkin Chambers, London	0171 404 0102
Freedman Sampson Clive	3 Verulam Buildings, London	0171 831 8441
Friedman David Peter	4 Pump Court, London	0171 353 2656/9
Goddard Andrew Stephen	Atkin Chambers, London	0171 404 0102
Godwin William George Henry	Atkin Chambers, London	0171 404 0102
Goff Anthony Thomas	25-27 Castle Street, Liverpool	0151 227 5661/5666/236 5072
Goldblatt Simon	39 Essex Street, London	0171 832 1111
Gough Miss Karen Louise	Arbitration Chambers, London	0171 267 2137
	West Lodge Farm, Meopham	01474 812280
Grantham Andrew Timothy	• Deans Court Chambers, Manchester	0161 834 4097
	• Deans Court Chambers, Preston	01772 555163
Gray Richard Paul	39 Essex Street, London	0171 832 1111
Green Patrick Curtis	Stanbrook & Henderson, London	0171 353 0101
	2 Harcourt Buildings, London	0171 583 9020
Greenbourne John Hugo	Two Crown Office Row, London	0171 797 8100
Grodzinski Samuel Marc	39 Essex Street, London	0171 832 1111
Grundy Nigel Lawrence John	Chambers of John Hand QC, Manchester	0161 955 9000
Guggenheim Miss Anna Maeve	Two Crown Office Row, London	0171 797 8100
Hall Mrs Melanie Ruth	Monckton Chambers, London	0171 405 7211
Hamilton Graeme Montagu	Two Crown Office Row, London	0171 797 8100
Hamilton Peter Bernard	4 Pump Court, London	0171 353 2656/9
Hantusch Robert Anthony	• 3 Stone Buildings, London	0171 242 4937/405 8358
Harper Joseph Charles	4 Breams Buildings, London	0171 353 5835/430 1221
Harris Paul Best	Monckton Chambers, London	0171 405 7211
Harvey Michael Llewellyn Tucker	Two Crown Office Row, London	0171 797 8100
Hawker Geoffrey Fort	Chambers of Geoffrey Hawker, London	0171 583 8899
Hodgson Miss Susan Ann	Two Crown Office Row, London	0171 797 8100
Holdsworth James Arthur	Two Crown Office Row, London	0171 797 8100
Holland Charles Christopher	Trinity Chambers, Newcastle upon Tyne	0191 232 1927
Holroyd John James	• 9 Woodhouse Square, Leeds	0113 245 1986
Howarth Simon Stuart	Two Crown Office Row, London	0171 797 8100
Howells James Richard	Atkin Chambers, London	0171 404 0102
Jess Digby Charles	• 8 King Street Chambers, Manchester	0161 834 9560
Jones Miss Rhiannon	Lamb Chambers, London	0171 797 8300
Jordan Andrew	Stanbrook & Henderson, London	0171 353 0101
	2 Harcourt Buildings, London	0171 583 9020
Kent Michael Harcourt	Two Crown Office Row, London	0171 797 8100
Knight Brian Joseph	Atkin Chambers, London	0171 404 0102
Knott Malcolm Stephen	New Court Chambers, London	0171 831 9500
Kolodziej Andrzej Jozef	• Littman Chambers, London	0171 404 4866
Lewsley Christopher Stanton	4 Breams Buildings, London	0171 353 5835/430 1221
Lofthouse Simon Timothy	Atkin Chambers, London	0171 404 0102
Lynagh Richard Dudley	Two Crown Office Row, London	0171 797 8100
Lynch Terry John	22 Albion Place, Northampton	01604 636271
Maclean Alan John	39 Essex Street, London	0171 832 1111
Mantle Peter John	Monckton Chambers, London	0171 405 7211
Manzoni Charles Peter	39 Essex Street, London	0171 832 1111
Mauleverer Peter Bruce	4 Pump Court, London	0171 353 2656/9
McCall Duncan James	4 Pump Court, London	0171 353 2656/9
McCredie Miss Fionnuala Mary Constance	3 Serjeants' Inn, London	0171 353 5537
McGregor Harvey	4 Paper Buildings, London	0171 353 3366/583 7155
McKinnell Miss Soraya Jane	Enterprise Chambers, London	0171 405 9471
	Enterprise Chambers, Leeds	0113 246 0391
	Enterprise Chambers, Newcastle upon Tyne	0191 222 3344
McMullan Manus Anthony	Atkin Chambers, London	0171 404 0102
Meeson Nigel Keith	4 Field Court, London	0171 440 6900
Mendoza Neil David Pereira	Hardwicke Building, London	0171 242 2523
Milne Michael	Chambers of Geoffrey Hawker, London	0171 583 8899
	Resolution Chambers, Malvern	01684 561279
Moon Philip Charles Angus	3 Serjeants' Inn, London	0171 353 5537
Morgan Charles James Arthur	Enterprise Chambers, London	0171 405 9471

	Enterprise Chambers, Leeds	0113 246 0391
	Enterprise Chambers, Newcastle upon Tyne	0191 222 3344
Mulcahy Miss Leigh-Ann Maria	Two Crown Office Row, London	0171 797 8100
Munro Kenneth Stuart	5 Bell Yard, London	0171 333 8811
Nicholson Jeremy Mark	4 Pump Court, London	0171 353 2656/9
Noble Andrew	Eldon Chambers, London	0171 353 4636
	Merchant Chambers, Manchester	0161 839 7070
Norman Christopher John George	No 1 Serjeants' Inn, London	0171 415 6666
Norris Paul Howard	One Essex Court, London	0171 936 3030
Parkin Miss Fiona Jane	Atkin Chambers, London	0171 404 0102
Patchett-Joyce Michael Thurston	Monckton Chambers, London	0171 405 7211
Patten Benedict Joseph	Two Crown Office Row, London	0171 797 8100
Patterson Stewart	• Pump Court Chambers, London	0171 353 0711
	• Pump Court Chambers, Winchester	01962 868161
Pelling (Philip) Mark	Monckton Chambers, London	0171 405 7211
Pershad Rohan	Two Crown Office Row, London	0171 797 8100
Phillips Andrew Charles	Two Crown Office Row, London	0171 797 8100
Planterose Rowan Michael	Littman Chambers, London	0171 404 4866
Powles Stephen Robert	Stanbrook & Henderson, London	0171 353 0101
	2 Harcourt Buildings, London	0171 583 9020
Raeside Mark Andrew	Atkin Chambers, London	0171 404 0102
Rawley Miss Dominique Jane	Atkin Chambers, London	0171 404 0102
Reese Colin Edward	Atkin Chambers, London	0171 404 0102
Richards Miss Jennifer	39 Essex Street, London	0171 832 1111
Rigney Andrew James	Two Crown Office Row, London	0171 797 8100
Robb Adam Duncan	39 Essex Street, London	0171 832 1111
Robson John Malcolm	2 Gray's Inn Square Chambers, London	0171 242 0328/405 1317
	Assize Court Chambers, Bristol	0117 926 4587
Ross John Graffin	No 1 Serjeants' Inn, London	0171 415 6666
Roth Peter Marcel	Monckton Chambers, London	0171 405 7211
Royce Darryl Fraser	Atkin Chambers, London	0171 404 0102
Rumney Conrad William Arthur	St Philip's Chambers, Birmingham	0121 246 7000
Ryan David Patrick	Chambers of Geoffrey Hawker, London	0171 583 8899
Salter Richard Stanley	3 Verulam Buildings, London	0171 831 8441
Sampson Graeme William	Chambers of Geoffrey Hawker, London	0171 583 8899
Seymour Richard William	Monckton Chambers, London	0171 405 7211
Shaikh Eur.Ing. (Jaikumar) Christopher (Samuel	Avondale Chambers, London	0181 445 9984
	Equity Chambers, Birmingham	0121 233 2100
Sheehan Malcolm Peter	Stanbrook & Henderson, London	0171 353 0101
	2 Harcourt Buildings, London	0171 583 9020
Silvester Bruce Ross	Lamb Chambers, London	0171 797 8300
Sliwinski Robert Andrew	Chambers of Geoffrey Hawker, London	0171 583 8899
Smith Ms Katherine Emma	Monckton Chambers, London	0171 405 7211
Smith Warwick Timothy Cresswell	• Deans Court Chambers, Manchester	0161 834 4097
	• Deans Court Chambers, Preston	01772 555163
Snowden John Stevenson	Two Crown Office Row, London	0171 797 8100
Starcevic Petar	St Philip's Chambers, Birmingham	0121 246 7000
Stevenson John Melford	Two Crown Office Row, London	0171 797 8100
Storey Jeremy Brian	4 Pump Court, London	0171 353 2656/9
Streatfeild-James David Stewart	Atkin Chambers, London	0171 404 0102
Susman Peter Joseph	New Court Chambers, London	0171 831 9500
Swan Ian Christopher	Two Crown Office Row, London	0171 797 8100
Tedd Rex Hilary	• St Philip's Chambers, Birmingham	0121 246 7000
	• 22 Albion Place, Northampton	01604 636271
Temple Anthony Dominic	4 Pump Court, London	0171 353 2656/9
Ter Haar Roger Eduard Lound	Two Crown Office Row, London	0171 797 8100
Tomlinson Hugh Richard Edward	New Court Chambers, London	0171 831 9500
Travers Hugh	Pump Court Chambers, London	0171 353 0711
	Pump Court Chambers, Winchester	01962 868161
Trotman Timothy Oliver	Deans Court Chambers, Manchester	0161 834 4097
	Deans Court Chambers, Preston	01772 555163
Tucker David William	Two Crown Office Row, London	0171 797 8100
Valentine Donald Graham	Atkin Chambers, London	0171 404 0102
Vaughan Terence Paul	Watford Chambers, Watford	01923 220553
Walker Steven John	Atkin Chambers, London	0171 404 0102
Wallace Ian Norman Duncan	Atkin Chambers, London	0171 404 0102

• Expanded entry in Part D

Ward Timothy Justin	39 Essex Street, London	0171 832 1111
Wardell John David Meredith	New Court Chambers, London	0171 831 9500
Webb Geraint Timothy	2 Harcourt Buildings, London	0171 583 9020
Weston Clive Aubrey Richard	Two Crown Office Row, London	0171 797 8100
White Andrew	Atkin Chambers, London	0171 404 0102
Wilken Sean David Henry	39 Essex Street, London	0171 832 1111
Wilkinson Nigel Vivian Marshall	Two Crown Office Row, London	0171 797 8100
Wilmot-Smith Richard James Crosbie	39 Essex Street, London	0171 832 1111
Wright Frederick George Ian	• 3 Serjeants' Inn, London	0171 353 5537

CONSUMER CREDIT

Green Patrick Curtis	Stanbrook & Henderson, London	0171 353 0101
	2 Harcourt Buildings, London	0171 583 9020
Hodgkinson Tristram Patrick	• 5 Pump Court, London	0171 353 2532
O'Sullivan Bernard Anthony	Stanbrook & Henderson, London	0171 353 0101
	2 Harcourt Buildings, London	0171 583 9020
Sayer Mr Peter Edwin	Gough Square Chambers, London	0171 353 0924
Worsley Daniel	Stanbrook & Henderson, London	0171 353 0101
	2 Harcourt Buildings, London	0171 583 9020

CONSUMER LAW

Al'Hassan Khadim	Equity Chambers, Birmingham	0121 233 2100
Althaus Antony Justin	No 1 Serjeants' Inn, London	0171 415 6666
Amin Miss Farah	7 New Square, London	0171 430 1660
Andrews Miss Claire Marguerite	Gough Square Chambers, London	0171 353 0924
Barton Miss Fiona	5 Essex Court, London	0171 410 2000
Beal Kieron Conrad	4 Paper Buildings, London	0171 353 3366/583 7155
Beaumont Marc Clifford	• Pump Court Chambers, London	0171 353 0711
	• Harrow-on-the-Hill Chambers, Harrow on the Hill	0181 423 7444
	• Pump Court Chambers, Winchester	01962 868161
	• Windsor Barristers' Chambers, Windsor	01753 648 899
Berkley Michael Stuart	Rougemont Chambers, Exeter	01392 410471
Bickford-Smith Stephen William	4 Breams Buildings, London	0171 353 5835/430 1221
Blakesley Patrick James	Two Crown Office Row, London	0171 797 8100
Bourne Robert	• 4 Field Court, London	0171 440 6900
Brant Paul David	Oriel Chambers, Liverpool	0151 236 7191
Brook Ian Stuart	Hardwicke Building, London	0171 242 2523
Carlile Alexander Charles	9-12 Bell Yard, London	0171 400 1800
	Sedan House, Chester	01244 320480/348282
Cawley Neil Robert Loudoun	55 Temple Chambers, London	0171 353 7400
	Milton Keynes Chambers, Milton Keynes	01908 217857
Chalmers Miss Suzanne Frances	Two Crown Office Row, London	0171 797 8100
Cogswell Miss Frederica Natasha	Gough Square Chambers, London	0171 353 0924
Cotter Barry Paul	Old Square Chambers, London	0171 269 0300
	Old Square Chambers, Bristol	0117 927 7111
Cowan Peter Sherwood McCrea	Oriel Chambers, Liverpool	0151 236 7191
Dawson James Robert	Oriel Chambers, Liverpool	0151 236 7191
de Jehan David	St Paul's House, Leeds	0113 245 5866
Dedezade Taner	Tindal Chambers, Chelmsford	01245 267742
Duffy Michael	Cathedral Chambers, Ely, Ely	01353 666775
Eastman Roger	Stanbrook & Henderson, London	0171 353 0101
	2 Harcourt Buildings, London	0171 583 9020
Edwards Anthony Howard	Oriel Chambers, Liverpool	0151 236 7191
Ferguson Mrs Katharine Ann	Fenners Chambers, Cambridge	01223 368761
	Fenners Chambers, Peterborough	01733 562030
Ford Gerard James	Baker Street Chambers, Middlesbrough	01642 873873
Forster Brian Clive	Trinity Chambers, Newcastle upon Tyne	0191 232 1927
French Richard Anthony Lister	Rougemont Chambers, Exeter	01392 410471
Godfrey Jonathan Saul	St Paul's House, Leeds	0113 245 5866
Goodbody Peter James	• Oriel Chambers, Liverpool	0151 236 7191
Goulding Jonathan Steven	Gough Square Chambers, London	0171 353 0924
Grantham Andrew Timothy	• Deans Court Chambers, Manchester	0161 834 4097
	• Deans Court Chambers, Preston	01772 555163
Green Patrick Curtis	Stanbrook & Henderson, London	0171 353 0101
	2 Harcourt Buildings, London	0171 583 9020

Grundy Nigel Lawrence John	Chambers of John Hand QC, Manchester	0161 955 9000
Hanson Timothy Vincent Richard	St Philip's Chambers, Birmingham	0121 246 7000
Harvey Michael Llewellyn Tucker	Two Crown Office Row, London	0171 797 8100
Henderson Lawrence Mark	11 Bolt Court, London	0171 353 2300
	Redhill Chambers, Redhill	01737 780781
Hibbert William John	Gough Square Chambers, London	0171 353 0924
Hodgkinson Tristram Patrick	• 5 Pump Court, London	0171 353 2532
Hollingworth Peter James Michael	22 Albion Place, Northampton	01604 636271
Howarth Simon Stuart	Two Crown Office Row, London	0171 797 8100
Hussain Miss Frida Khanam	17 Carlton Crescent, Southampton	01703 320320
Islam-Choudhury Mugni	11 Bolt Court, London	0171 353 2300
Kealy Charles Brian	Chambers of Andrew Campbell QC, Leeds	0113 245 5438
Kimbell John Ashley	5 Bell Yard, London	0171 333 8811
Lynch Terry John	22 Albion Place, Northampton	01604 636271
MacDonald Iain	Gough Square Chambers, London	0171 353 0924
Macpherson Angus John	5 Bell Yard, London	0171 333 8811
Maitland Marc Claude	11 Old Square, London	0171 242 5022
Mantle Peter John	Monckton Chambers, London	0171 405 7211
Marley Miss Sarah Anne	5 Pump Court, London	0171 353 2532
Mawrey Richard Brooks	Stanbrook & Henderson, London	0171 353 0101
	2 Harcourt Buildings, London	0171 583 9020
Maxwell-Scott James Herbert	Two Crown Office Row, London	0171 797 8100
McCarthy William	New Bailey Chambers, Preston	01772 258 087
McMinn Miss Valerie Kathleen	Baker Street Chambers, Middlesbrough	01642 873873
Meakin Timothy William	Fenners Chambers, Cambridge	01223 368761
	Fenners Chambers, Peterborough	01733 562030
Middleton Miss Georgina Claire	New Court Chambers, London	0171 831 9500
Murray Ashley Charles	Oriel Chambers, Liverpool	0151 236 7191
Nebhrajani Miss Mel	9 Stone Buildings, London	0171 404 5055
Neville Stephen John	Gough Square Chambers, London	0171 353 0924
Norris Paul Howard	One Essex Court, London	0171 936 3030
O'Sullivan Bernard Anthony	Stanbrook & Henderson, London	0171 353 0101
	2 Harcourt Buildings, London	0171 583 9020
Peacock Ian Christopher	12 New Square, London	0171 419 1212
	Sovereign Chambers, Leeds	0113 245 1841/2/3
Peirson Oliver James	Pump Court Chambers, London	0171 353 0711
	Pump Court Chambers, Winchester	01962 868161
Peretz George Michael John		
Pershad Rohan	Two Crown Office Row, London	0171 797 8100
Philpott Frederick Alan	Gough Square Chambers, London	0171 353 0924
Pithers Clive Robert	Fenners Chambers, Cambridge	01223 368761
	Fenners Chambers, Peterborough	01733 562030
Rigney Andrew James	Two Crown Office Row, London	0171 797 8100
Robertson Aidan Malcolm David	Monckton Chambers, London	0171 405 7211
Robson John Malcolm	2 Gray's Inn Square Chambers, London	0171 242 0328/405 1317
	Assize Court Chambers, Bristol	0117 926 4587
Roth Peter Marcel	Monckton Chambers, London	0171 405 7211
Sadiq Tariq Mahmood	Chambers of John Hand QC, Manchester	0161 955 9000
Sayer Mr Peter Edwin	Gough Square Chambers, London	0171 353 0924
Schooling Simon John	Chambers of Harjit Singh, London	0171 353 1356
Scutt David Robert	11 Bolt Court, London	0171 353 2300
	Redhill Chambers, Redhill	01737 780781
Seymour Richard William	Monckton Chambers, London	0171 405 7211
Smith Miss Julia Mair Wheldon	Gough Square Chambers, London	0171 353 0924
Somerset-Jones Miss Felicity	Oriel Chambers, Liverpool	0151 236 7191
Spain Timothy Harrisson	Trinity Chambers, Newcastle upon Tyne	0191 232 1927
Starks Nicholas Ernshaw	8 Fountain Court, Birmingham	0121 236 5514
Stewart Mark Courtney	College Chambers, Southampton	01703 230338
Stokes David Mayhew Allen	5 Paper Buildings, London	0171 583 6117
	Fenners Chambers, Cambridge	01223 368761
Treacy Colman Maurice	Chambers of James Hunt QC, London	0171 421 8000
	3 Fountain Court, Birmingham	0121 236 5854
Tucker Miss Katherine Jane Greening	St Philip's Chambers, Birmingham	0121 246 7000
Tyack David Guy	St Philip's Chambers, Birmingham	0121 246 7000
Vines Anthony Robert Francis	Gough Square Chambers, London	0171 353 0924

• Expanded entry in Part D

Wakefield Miss Anne Prudence	3 Verulam Buildings, London	0171 831 8441
Williams A John	• 13 King's Bench Walk, London	0171 353 7204
	• King's Bench Chambers, Oxford	01865 311066
Worsley Daniel	Stanbrook & Henderson, London	0171 353 0101
	2 Harcourt Buildings, London	0171 583 9020

CONTRACTS

Semple Andrew Blair	Sovereign Chambers, Leeds	0113 245 1841/2/3

CONVEYANCING

Adamyk Simon Charles	12 New Square, London	0171 419 1212
Angus Miss Tracey Anne	5 Stone Buildings, London	0171 242 6201
Atherton Ian David	Enterprise Chambers, London	0171 405 9471
	Enterprise Chambers, Leeds	0113 246 0391
	Enterprise Chambers, Newcastle upon Tyne	0191 222 3344
Attala Jean Etienne	Cathedral Chambers, Newcastle upon Tyne	0191 232 1311
Beaumont Marc Clifford	• Pump Court Chambers, London	0171 353 0711
	• Harrow-on-the-Hill Chambers, Harrow on the Hill	0181 423 7444
	• Pump Court Chambers, Winchester	01962 868161
	• Windsor Barristers' Chambers, Windsor	01753 648 899
Blackett-Ord Mark	• 5 Stone Buildings, London	0171 242 6201
Cameron Neil Alexander	Wilberforce Chambers, Hull	01482 323 264
Cherryman John Richard	4 Breams Buildings, London	0171 353 5835/430 1221
Clarke Miss Anna Victoria	5 Stone Buildings, London	0171 242 6201
Clarke Peter John	Harcourt Chambers, London	0171 353 6961/7
	St Philip's Chambers, Birmingham	0121 246 7000
	Harcourt Chambers, Oxford	01865 791559
Cranfield Peter Anthony	3 Verulam Buildings, London	0171 831 8441
Crawford Grant	11 Old Square, London	0171 430 0341
Cunningham Mark James	13 Old Square, London	0171 404 4800
Daiches Michael Salis	• 22 Old Buildings, London	0171 831 0222
Darbyshire William Robert	Chambers of John Hand QC, Manchester	0161 955 9000
Dodge Peter Clive	11 Old Square, London	0171 430 0341
Dowse John	Chambers of Lord Goodhart QC, London	0171 405 5577
	Chambers of John Hand QC, Manchester	0161 955 9000
Gerald Nigel Mortimer	Enterprise Chambers, London	0171 405 9471
	Enterprise Chambers, Leeds	0113 246 0391
	Enterprise Chambers, Newcastle upon Tyne	0191 222 3344
Gore Andrew Roger	Fenners Chambers, Cambridge	01223 368761
	Fenners Chambers, Peterborough	01733 562030
Gregory John Raymond	Deans Court Chambers, Manchester	0161 834 4097
	Deans Court Chambers, Preston	01772 555163
Hall Taylor Alexander Edward	11 Old Square, London	0171 430 0341
Hargreaves Miss Sara Jane	12 New Square, London	0171 419 1212
	Sovereign Chambers, Leeds	0113 245 1841/2/3
Hayes Miss Josephine Mary	Chambers of Lord Goodhart QC, London	0171 405 5577
Heywood Michael Edmundson	Chambers of Lord Goodhart QC, London	0171 405 5577
	Cobden House Chambers, Manchester	0161 833 6000/6001
Holmes Justin Francis	Chambers of Lord Goodhart QC, London	0171 405 5577
Horspool Anthony Bernard Graeme	Hardwicke Building, London	0171 242 2523
Hughes Miss Mary Josephine	Chambers of Lord Goodhart QC, London	0171 405 5577
Jack Adrian Laurence Robert	Enterprise Chambers, London	0171 405 9471
Jackson Dirik George Allan	• Chambers of Mr Peter Crampin QC, London	0171 831 0081
Jackson Nicholas David Kingsley	The Chambers of Adrian Lyon, Liverpool	0151 236 4421/8240/6757
Jefferies Thomas Robert	Chambers of Lord Goodhart QC, London	0171 405 5577

Johnson Michael Sloan	Chambers of John Hand QC, Manchester	0161 955 9000
Kimbell John Ashley	5 Bell Yard, London	0171 333 8811
Kremen Philip Michael	Hardwicke Building, London	0171 242 2523
Lamont Miss Camilla Rose	Chambers of Lord Goodhart QC, London	0171 405 5577
Laughton Samuel Dennis	17 Old Buildings, London	0171 405 9653
Le Poidevin Nicholas Peter	12 New Square, London	0171 419 1212
	Sovereign Chambers, Leeds	0113 245 1841/2/3
Levy Benjamin Keith	Enterprise Chambers, London	0171 405 9471
	Enterprise Chambers, Leeds	0113 246 0391
	Enterprise Chambers, Newcastle upon Tyne	0191 222 3344
Marten Richard Hedley Westwood	Chambers of Lord Goodhart QC, London	0171 405 5577
McAllister Miss Elizabeth Ann	Enterprise Chambers, London	0171 405 9471
	Enterprise Chambers, Leeds	0113 246 0391
	Enterprise Chambers, Newcastle upon Tyne	0191 222 3344
McQuail Ms Katherine Emma	11 Old Square, London	0171 430 0341
Mendoza Neil David Pereira	Hardwicke Building, London	0171 242 2523
Morgan Charles James Arthur	Enterprise Chambers, London	0171 405 9471
	Enterprise Chambers, Leeds	0113 246 0391
	Enterprise Chambers, Newcastle upon Tyne	0191 222 3344
Mullis Anthony Roger	Chambers of Lord Goodhart QC, London	0171 405 5577
Munro Kenneth Stuart	5 Bell Yard, London	0171 333 8811
Nebhrajani Miss Mel	9 Stone Buildings, London	0171 404 5055
Norie-Miller Jeffrey Reginald	55 Temple Chambers, London	0171 353 7400
Norris Alastair Hubert	• 5 Stone Buildings, London	0171 242 6201
	• Southernhay Chambers, Exeter	01392 255777
Nurse Gordon Bramwell William	11 Old Square, London	0171 430 0341
O'Sullivan Michael Morton	5 Stone Buildings, London	0171 242 6201
Oakley Tony	• 11 Old Square, London	0171 430 0341
Ohrenstein Dov	Chambers of Lord Goodhart QC, London	0171 405 5577
Ovey Miss Elizabeth Helen	11 Old Square, London	0171 430 0341
Parry David Julian Thomas	Chambers of Lord Goodhart QC, London	0171 405 5577
Perks Richard Howard	St Philip's Chambers, Birmingham	0121 246 7000
Pimentel Carlos de Serpa Alberto Legg	3 Stone Buildings, London	0171 242 4937/405 8358
Pryke Stuart	Trinity Chambers, Newcastle upon Tyne	0191 232 1927
Radevsky Anthony Eric	• 5 Bell Yard, London	0171 333 8811
Robson John Malcolm	2 Gray's Inn Square Chambers, London	0171 242 0328/405 1317
	Assize Court Chambers, Bristol	0117 926 4587
Ross Martyn John Greaves	• 5 New Square, London	0171 404 0404
	• Octagon House, Norwich	01603 623186
Sefton Mark Thomas Dunblane	199 Strand, London	0171 379 9779
Selway Dr Katherine Emma	11 Old Square, London	0171 430 0341
Smart Miss Jacqueline Anne	Trinity Chambers, Newcastle upon Tyne	0191 232 1927
Sunnucks James Horace George	• 5 New Square, London	0171 404 0404
	• Octagon House, Norwich	01603 623186
Sydenham Colin Peter	4 Breams Buildings, London	0171 353 5835/430 1221
Thomas Nigel Matthew	13 Old Square, London	0171 404 4800
Tipples Miss Amanda Jane	13 Old Square, London	0171 404 4800
Vane The Hon Christopher John Fletcher	Trinity Chambers, Newcastle upon Tyne	0191 232 1927
Walker Andrew Greenfield	Chambers of Lord Goodhart QC, London	0171 405 5577
Warnock-Smith Mrs Shan	5 Stone Buildings, London	0171 242 6201
Waters Malcolm Ian	• 11 Old Square, London	0171 430 0341
Weatherill Bernard Richard	Chambers of Lord Goodhart QC, London	0171 405 5577
West Mark	• 11 Old Square, London	0171 430 0341
Yelton Michael Paul	Fenners Chambers, Cambridge	01223 368761
	Fenners Chambers, Peterborough	01733 562030

• Expanded entry in Part D

CONVEYANCING COUNSEL OF THE COURT

Harrod Henry Mark	5 Stone Buildings, London	0171 242 6201

COPYRIGHT

Abbott Alistair James Hugh	5 New Square, London	0171 404 0404
Amin Miss Farah	7 New Square, London	0171 430 1660
Anderson Rupert John	Monckton Chambers, London	0171 405 7211
Ayres Andrew John William	13 Old Square, London	0171 404 4800
Barker Simon George Harry	• 13 Old Square, London	0171 404 4800
Bird Nigel David	Chambers of John Hand QC, Manchester	0161 955 9000
Clark Ms Julia Elisabeth	5 New Square, London	0171 404 0404
Colley Dr Peter McLean	• 19 Old Buildings, London	0171 405 2001
Cunningham Mark James	13 Old Square, London	0171 404 4800
Driscoll Miss Lynn	Sovereign Chambers, Leeds	0113 245 1841/2/3
	Lancaster Buildings, Manchester	0161 661 4444
Edwards Richard Julian Henshaw	3 Verulam Buildings, London	0171 831 8441
Elleray Anthony John	• 12 New Square, London	0171 419 1212
	• St James's Chambers, Manchester	0161 834 7000
	• Park Lane Chambers, Leeds	0113 228 5000
Fitzgerald John Vincent	New Court, London	0171 797 8999
Garnett Kevin Mitchell	5 New Square, London	0171 404 0404
Gibaud Miss Catherine Alison Annetta	3 Verulam Buildings, London	0171 831 8441
Gray Charles Anthony St John	5 Raymond Buildings, London	0171 242 2902
Grayson Edward	• 9-12 Bell Yard, London	0171 400 1800
Gregory John Raymond	Deans Court Chambers, Manchester	0161 834 4097
	Deans Court Chambers, Preston	01772 555163
Harbottle Gwilym Thomas	5 New Square, London	0171 404 0404
Harvey Miss Jayne Denise	Goldsworth Chambers, London	0171 405 7117
Henderson Roger Anthony	Stanbrook & Henderson, London	0171 353 0101
	2 Harcourt Buildings, London	0171 583 9020
Heslop Martin Sydney	1 Hare Court, London	0171 353 3982/5324
Hicks Michael Charles	• 19 Old Buildings, London	0171 405 2001
Hodgson Richard Andrew	New Court, London	0171 797 8999
Holman Miss Tamsin Perdita	19 Old Buildings, London	0171 405 2001
Johnson Michael Sloan	Chambers of John Hand QC, Manchester	0161 955 9000
Kime Matthew Jonathan	• New Court, London	0171 797 8999
	• Cobden House Chambers, Manchester	0161 833 6000/6001
Mason Ian Douglas	11 Bolt Court, London	0171 353 2300
	Redhill Chambers, Redhill	01737 780781
Norris Andrew James Steedsman	5 New Square, London	0171 404 0404
Peretz George Michael John		
Pickford Anthony James	Prince Henry's Chambers, London	0171 353 1183/1190
Puckrin Cedric Eldred	19 Old Buildings, London	0171 405 2001
Reid Brian Christopher	19 Old Buildings, London	0171 405 2001
Robertson Aidan Malcolm David	Monckton Chambers, London	0171 405 7211
Sampson Graeme William	Chambers of Geoffrey Hawker, London	0171 583 8899
Shipley Norman Graham	• 19 Old Buildings, London	0171 405 2001
Silverleaf Michael	• 11 South Square, London	0171 405 1222
Spearman Richard	5 Raymond Buildings, London	0171 242 2902
Stewart Alexander Joseph	5 New Square, London	0171 404 0404
Sugar Simon Gareth	5 New Square, London	0171 404 0404
Sullivan Rory Myles	19 Old Buildings, London	0171 405 2001
Sutcliffe Andrew Harold Wentworth	3 Verulam Buildings, London	0171 831 8441
Wilson Alastair James Drysdale	• 19 Old Buildings, London	0171 405 2001

COPYRIGHT THEFT

Hilton Alan John Howard	Queen Elizabeth Building, London	0171 583 5766
Langdale Timothy James	Queen Elizabeth Building, London	0171 583 5766
Strudwick Miss Linda Diane	Queen Elizabeth Building, London	0171 583 5766

CORONERS' INQUESTS

Beasley-Murray Mrs Caroline Wynne	Fenners Chambers, Cambridge	01223 368761
	Fenners Chambers, Peterborough	01733 562030
Fortune Malcolm Donald Porter	3 Serjeants' Inn, London	0171 353 5537
Newton-Price James Edward	Pump Court Chambers, London	0171 353 0711
	Pump Court Chambers, Winchester	01962 868161

Pollock Dr Evelyn Marian Margaret	5 Essex Court, London	0171 410 2000
Spink Peter John William	5 Essex Court, London	0171 410 2000

CORPORATE FINANCE

Barker Simon George Harry	• 13 Old Square, London	0171 404 4800
Collings Matthew Glynn Burkinshaw	13 Old Square, London	0171 404 4800
Cone John Crawford	Erskine Chambers, London	0171 242 5532
de Jehan David	St Paul's House, Leeds	0113 245 5866
de Lacy Richard Michael	3 Verulam Buildings, London	0171 831 8441
Dougherty Nigel Peter	Erskine Chambers, London	0171 242 5532
Dowse John	Chambers of Lord Goodhart QC, London	0171 405 5577
	Chambers of John Hand QC, Manchester	0161 955 9000
Doyle Louis George	Chambers of Andrew Campbell QC, Leeds	0113 245 5438
Duffy Derek James	St Paul's House, Leeds	0113 245 5866
Griffiths Peter Robert	4 Stone Buildings, London	0171 242 5524
Jarvis John Manners	3 Verulam Buildings, London	0171 831 8441
Lazarus Michael Steven	1 Crown Office Row, London	0171 583 9292
Lowenstein Paul David	Littleton Chambers, London	0171 797 8600
Malek Ali	3 Verulam Buildings, London	0171 831 8441
Marquand Charles Nicholas Hilary	Chambers of Lord Goodhart QC, London	0171 405 5577
Peglow Dr Michael Alfred Herman	Chambers of Geoffrey Hawker, London	0171 583 8899
Roberts Miss Catherine Ann	Erskine Chambers, London	0171 242 5532
Salter Richard Stanley	3 Verulam Buildings, London	0171 831 8441
Southern Professor David Boardman	• 3 Temple Gardens Tax Chambers, London	0171 353 7884
Sykes (James) Richard	Erskine Chambers, London	0171 242 5532
Weatherill Bernard Richard	Chambers of Lord Goodhart QC, London	0171 405 5577

CORRUPTION

Muller Franz Joseph	11 King's Bench Walk, London	0171 353 3337/8
	11 King's Bench Walk, Leeds	0113 2971 200

COSTS

Morgan Jeremy	Chambers of Kieran Coonan QC, London	0171 583 6013/2510

COURTS MARTIAL

Al'Hassan Khadim	Equity Chambers, Birmingham	0121 233 2100
Aldred Mark Steven	Queen Elizabeth Building, London	0171 583 5766
Alliott George Beckles	2 Harcourt Buildings, London	0171 583 9020
Barlow Miss Sarah Helen	St Paul's House, Leeds	0113 245 5866
Barnett Andrew John	Pump Court Chambers, London	0171 353 0711
	Pump Court Chambers, Winchester	01962 868161
Barnfather Miss Lydia Helen	Queen Elizabeth Building, London	0171 583 5766
Bendall Richard Giles	33 Bedford Row, London	0171 242 6476
Bennetts Philip James	Queen Elizabeth Building, London	0171 583 5766
Best Stanley Philip	Bracton Chambers, London	0171 242 4248
	Westgate Chambers, Lewes	01273 480 510
	Barnstaple Chambers, Winkleigh	0183 783763
Blackburn Luke Sebastian	7 New Square, London	0171 430 1660
Boyce William	Queen Elizabeth Building, London	0171 583 5766
Brown Edward Francis Trevenen	Queen Elizabeth Building, London	0171 583 5766
Brown Thomas Christopher Ellis	Fenners Chambers, Cambridge	01223 368761
	Fenners Chambers, Peterborough	01733 562030
Burbidge James Michael	St Philip's Chambers, Birmingham	0121 246 7000
Butt Michael Robert	Pump Court Chambers, London	0171 353 0711
	Pump Court Chambers, Winchester	01962 868161
Byers The Hon Charles William	23 Essex Street, London	0171 413 0353
Cawley Neil Robert Loudoun	55 Temple Chambers, London	0171 353 7400
	Milton Keynes Chambers, Milton Keynes	01908 217857
Collett Gavin Charles	Rougemont Chambers, Exeter	01392 410471

       • Expanded entry in Part D

	Cathedral Chambers (Jan Wood Independent Barristers' Clerk), Exeter	01392 210900
Conlin Geoffrey David	3 Serjeants' Inn, London	0171 353 5537
Coward Miss Victoria Jane	Queen Elizabeth Building, London	0171 583 5766
Darbishire Adrian Munro	Queen Elizabeth Building, London	0171 583 5766
Donne Jeremy Nigel	Queen Elizabeth Building, London	0171 583 5766
Duffy Michael	Cathedral Chambers, Ely, Ely	01353 666775
Ellison Mark Christopher	Queen Elizabeth Building, London	0171 583 5766
Evans Thomas Gareth	Rougemont Chambers, Exeter	01392 410471
Finnigan Peter Anthony	Queen Elizabeth Building, London	0171 583 5766
Fortune Malcolm Donald Porter	3 Serjeants' Inn, London	0171 353 5537
Franklin Stephen Hall	5 Paper Buildings, London	0171 583 6117
	Fenners Chambers, Cambridge	01223 368761
Fuad Kerim	Chambers of Helen Grindrod QC, London	0171 404 4777
Gabb Charles Henry Escott	Pump Court Chambers, London	0171 353 0711
	Pump Court Chambers, Winchester	01962 868161
Gore-Andrews Gavin Angus Russell	Stanbrook & Henderson, London	0171 353 0101
	2 Harcourt Buildings, London	0171 583 9020
Grey Robin Douglas	Queen Elizabeth Building, London	0171 583 5766
Gunther Miss Elizabeth Ann	Pump Court Chambers, London	0171 353 0711
	Pump Court Chambers, Winchester	01962 868161
Hallett Miss Heather Carol	23 Essex Street, London	0171 413 0353
Hatton Andrew John	Plowden Buildings, London	0171 583 0808
	Paradise Square Chambers, Sheffield	0114 273 8951
Heaton-Armstrong Anthony Eustace John	9-12 Bell Yard, London	0171 400 1800
Henry Edward Joseph Aloysius	Queen Elizabeth Building, London	0171 583 5766
Heslop Martin Sydney	1 Hare Court, London	0171 353 3982/5324
Hill Robert Douglas	Pump Court Chambers, London	0171 353 0711
	Pump Court Chambers, Winchester	01962 868161
Hogg The Rt Hon Douglas Martin	4 Paper Buildings, London	0171 353 3366/583 7155
	37 Park Square, Leeds	0113 243 9422
Horwell Richard Eric	Queen Elizabeth Building, London	0171 583 5766
James Roderick Morrice	23 Essex Street, London	0171 413 0353
Johnson Nicholas Robert	25-27 Castle Street, Liverpool	0151 227 5661/5666/236 5072
Kark Thomas Victor William	Queen Elizabeth Building, London	0171 583 5766
Kealy Charles Brian	Chambers of Andrew Campbell QC, Leeds	0113 245 5438
Kelsey-Fry John	Queen Elizabeth Building, London	0171 583 5766
Kenward Richard Francis	Watford Chambers, Watford	01923 220553
King Peter Duncan	5 Pump Court, London	0171 353 2532
	Fenners Chambers, Cambridge	01223 368761
Larkin Sean	Queen Elizabeth Building, London	0171 583 5766
Lawson Michael Henry	23 Essex Street, London	0171 413 0353
Longden Anthony Gordon	Queen Elizabeth Building, London	0171 583 5766
Lowry Miss Emma Margaret Collins	Queen Elizabeth Building, London	0171 583 5766
Mathews Deni	8 Fountain Court, Birmingham	0121 236 5514
McKinnon Warwick Nairn	Queen Elizabeth Building, London	0171 583 5766
Milne Richard James	23 Essex Street, London	0171 413 0353
Mitchell Christopher Richard	Queen Elizabeth Building, London	0171 583 5766
Morley Iain Charles	1 Hare Court, London	0171 353 3982/5324
Muller Franz Joseph	11 King's Bench Walk, London	0171 353 3337/8
	11 King's Bench Walk, Leeds	0113 2971 200
Newcombe Timothy Richard	St Paul's House, Leeds	0113 245 5866
Newton-Price James Edward	Pump Court Chambers, London	0171 353 0711
	Pump Court Chambers, Winchester	01962 868161
Oliver Michael Richard	Hardwicke Building, London	0171 242 2523
Parr John Edward	8 King Street Chambers, Manchester	0161 834 9560
Pascoe Nigel Spencer Knight	Pump Court Chambers, London	0171 353 0711
	All Saints Chambers, Bristol	0117 921 1966
	Pump Court Chambers, Winchester	01962 868161
Paton Ian Francis	Queen Elizabeth Building, London	0171 583 5766
Pawson Robert Edward Cruickshank	Pump Court Chambers, London	0171 353 0711
	Pump Court Chambers, Winchester	01962 868161
Pearce Ivan James	Furnival Chambers, London	0171 405 3232
Peirson Oliver James	Pump Court Chambers, London	0171 353 0711
	Pump Court Chambers, Winchester	01962 868161
Plaschkes Ms Sarah Georgina	Queen Elizabeth Building, London	0171 583 5766
Ramasamy Selvaraju	Queen Elizabeth Building, London	0171 583 5766
Richardson Garth Douglas Anthony	3 Paper Buildings, London	0171 583 8055

• Expanded entry in Part D

	20 Lorne Park Road, Bournemouth	01202 292102
	4 St Peter Street, Winchester	01962 868 884
Richardson (Peter) James	23 Essex Street, London	0171 413 0353
Rogers Paul John	1 Crown Office Row, London	0171 797 7500
	Crown Office Row Chambers, Brighton	01273 625625
Sparks Miss Jocelyn Margaret	Queen Elizabeth Building, London	0171 583 5766
Sparks Kevin Laurence	Earl Street Chambers, Maidstone	01622 671222
Stewart Neill Alastair	Queen Elizabeth Building, London	0171 583 5766
Still Geoffrey John Churchill	Pump Court Chambers, London	0171 353 0711
	Pump Court Chambers, Winchester	01962 868161
Strudwick Miss Linda Diane	Queen Elizabeth Building, London	0171 583 5766
Sullivan Ms Jane Teresa	Queen Elizabeth Building, London	0171 583 5766
Summers Benjamin Dylan James	Queen Elizabeth Building, London	0171 583 5766
Thorne Timothy Peter	33 Bedford Row, London	0171 242 6476
Volz Karl Andrew	Chambers of Geoffrey Hawker, London	0171 583 8899
Wakeham Philip John Le Messurier	Hardwicke Building, London	0171 242 2523
Warne Peter Lawrence	Queen Elizabeth Building, London	0171 583 5766
Wastie William Granville	Queen Elizabeth Building, London	0171 583 5766
Wilcken Anthony David Felix	Queen Elizabeth Building, London	0171 583 5766
Wilkinson Michael John	Trinity Chambers, Newcastle upon Tyne	0191 232 1927
Winter Ian David	Queen Elizabeth Building, London	0171 583 5766

CRIME

Abbott Francis Arthur	Pump Court Chambers, London	0171 353 0711
	Pump Court Chambers, Winchester	01962 868161
Acheson Robert Ian	23 Essex Street, London	0171 413 0353
Addison Neil Patrick	Cathedral Chambers, Newcastle upon Tyne	0191 232 1311
Akiwumi Anthony Sebastian Akitayo	Pump Court Chambers, London	0171 353 0711
	Pump Court Chambers, Winchester	01962 868161
Al'Hassan Khadim	Equity Chambers, Birmingham	0121 233 2100
Aldred Mark Steven	Queen Elizabeth Building, London	0171 583 5766
Alexander Ian Douglas Gavin	11 Bolt Court, London	0171 353 2300
	Redhill Chambers, Redhill	01737 780781
Archer John Francis Ashweek	Two Crown Office Row, London	0171 797 8100
Ascherson Miss Isobel Ruth	23 Essex Street, London	0171 413 0353
Ashley Mark Robert	Tindal Chambers, Chelmsford	01245 267742
	Tindal Chambers, St Albans	01727 843383
Ashman Peter Michael	22 Old Buildings, London	0171 831 0222
	Colleton Chambers, Exeter	01392 274898
Ashton Raglan Halley	New Court Chambers, Birmingham	0121 693 6656
Asteris Peter David	Eighteen Carlton Crescent, Southampton	01703 639001
Aston Maurice Charles	5 Paper Buildings, London	0171 583 6117
Austin-Smith Michael Gerard	23 Essex Street, London	0171 413 0353
Austins Christopher John	Assize Court Chambers, Bristol	0117 926 4587
Aylett Kenneth George	New Chambers, St Albans	0966 212126
Ayling Miss Tracy Jane	Farrar's Building, London	0171 583 9241
Badley Miss Pamela Hilary	25-27 Castle Street, Liverpool	0151 227 5661/5666/236 5072
Bagnall Matthew Philip Cooper	Chambers of Geoffrey Hawker, London	0171 583 8899
Bailin Alexander	5 Paper Buildings, London	0171 583 6117
Baker Harold William	30 Park Place, Cardiff	01222 398421
Baker William David	2 Paper Buildings, London	0171 353 0933
Ball Steven James	Earl Street Chambers, Maidstone	01622 671222
Barker Miss Alison	9-12 Bell Yard, London	0171 400 1800
Barlow Miss Sarah Helen	St Paul's House, Leeds	0113 245 5866
Barnett Andrew John	Pump Court Chambers, London	0171 353 0711
	Pump Court Chambers, Winchester	01962 868161
Barnett Jeremy Victor	Farrar's Building, London	0171 583 9241
	St Paul's House, Leeds	0113 245 5866
Barnfather Miss Lydia Helen	Queen Elizabeth Building, London	0171 583 5766
Barr Edward Robert	2 New Street, Leicester	0116 262 5906
Barraclough Anthony Roger	25-27 Castle Street, Liverpool	0151 227 5661/5666/236 5072
Bassra Sukhbir Singh	St Paul's House, Leeds	0113 245 5866
Bate David Christopher	Queen Elizabeth Building, London	0171 583 5766
Bates Alexander Andrew	St Paul's House, Leeds	0113 245 5866
Batty Christopher Michael	St Paul's House, Leeds	0113 245 5866
Baxter Gerald Pearson	25-27 Castle Street, Liverpool	0151 227 5661/5666/236 5072

         • Expanded entry in Part D

Beard Mark Christopher	6 Pump Court, London	0171 797 8400
Bedeau Stephen	Sovereign Chambers, Leeds	0113 245 1841/2/3
	Lancaster Buildings, Manchester	0161 661 4444
Beecroft Miss Kirstie		
Belbin Miss Heather Patricia	Oriel Chambers, Liverpool	0151 236 7191
Bendall Richard Giles	33 Bedford Row, London	0171 242 6476
Benner Miss Lucinda Diana Kate	11 Bolt Court, London	0171 353 2300
	Redhill Chambers, Redhill	01737 780781
Bennett Richard John	15 Winckley Square, Preston	01772 252 828
Bennetts Philip James	Queen Elizabeth Building, London	0171 583 5766
Benson Peter Charles	St Paul's House, Leeds	0113 245 5866
Bentwood Richard	Chambers of Geoffrey Hawker, London	0171 583 8899
Bergin Timothy William	Sussex Chambers, Brighton	01273 607953
Best Stanley Philip	Bracton Chambers, London	0171 242 4248
	Westgate Chambers, Lewes	01273 480 510
	Barnstaple Chambers, Winkleigh	0183 783763
Bevan Edward Julian	Queen Elizabeth Building, London	0171 583 5766
Bickler Simon Lloyd	St Paul's House, Leeds	0113 245 5866
Biddle Neville Leslie	25-27 Castle Street, Liverpool	0151 227 5661/5666/236 5072
Billingham Rex Richard	New Court Chambers, Birmingham	0121 693 6656
Bindloss Edward Christopher James	Chambers of Andrew Campbell QC, Leeds	0113 245 5438
Birch Roger Allen	12 New Square, London	0171 419 1212
	Sovereign Chambers, Leeds	0113 245 1841/2/3
	Lancaster Buildings, Manchester	0161 661 4444
Birnbaum Michael Ian	9-12 Bell Yard, London	0171 400 1800
	New Court Chambers, Birmingham	0121 693 6656
Birts Peter William	• Farrar's Building, London	0171 583 9241
Blackburn Luke Sebastian	7 New Square, London	0171 430 1660
Blower Graham Robert	Queen Elizabeth Building, London	0171 353 7181 (12 lines)
Bogan Paul Simon	Doughty Street Chambers, London	0171 404 1313
Boney Guy Thomas Knowles	Pump Court Chambers, London	0171 353 0711
	Harrow-on-the-Hill Chambers, Harrow on the Hill	0181 423 7444
	Pump Court Chambers, Winchester	01962 868161
Boora Jinder Singh	Regent Chambers, Stoke-on-Trent	01782 286666
Boyce William	Queen Elizabeth Building, London	0171 583 5766
Boyd Phillip Joseph George	Lincoln House Chambers, Manchester	0161 832 5701
Bradshaw David Lawrence	Chambers of Andrew Campbell QC, Leeds	0113 245 5438
Brompton Michael John	New Court Chambers, London	0171 831 9500
Brotherton John Paul	New Court Chambers, Birmingham	0121 693 6656
Brown Edward Francis Trevenen	Queen Elizabeth Building, London	0171 583 5766
Brown Thomas Christopher Ellis	Fenners Chambers, Cambridge	01223 368761
	Fenners Chambers, Peterborough	01733 562030
Browne James Nicholas	No 1 Serjeants' Inn, London	0171 415 6666
Browne James William	Goldsworth Chambers, London	0171 405 7117
Brunton Sean Alexander McKay	Pump Court Chambers, London	0171 353 0711
	Pump Court Chambers, Winchester	01962 868161
Bryant-Heron Mark Nicholas	9-12 Bell Yard, London	0171 400 1800
Burbidge James Michael	St Philip's Chambers, Birmingham	0121 246 7000
Burles David John	Goldsmith Building, London	0171 353 7881
Butler Miss Judith Jane Scott	6 Pump Court, London	0171 797 8400
	6-8 Mill Street, Maidstone	01622 688 094
Butt Michael Robert	Pump Court Chambers, London	0171 353 0711
	Pump Court Chambers, Winchester	01962 868161
Byers The Hon Charles William	23 Essex Street, London	0171 413 0353
Byrne Garrett Thomas	23 Essex Street, London	0171 413 0353
Cadwallader Peter	Chambers of John Hand QC, Manchester	0161 955 9000
Calvert-Smith David	Queen Elizabeth Building, London	0171 583 5766
Campbell Andrew Neville	Chambers of Andrew Campbell QC, Leeds	0113 245 5438
Candlin James Richard	Chambers of Geoffrey Hawker, London	0171 583 8899
Carlile Alexander Charles	9-12 Bell Yard, London	0171 400 1800
	Sedan House, Chester	01244 320480/348282
Carlisle of Bucklow The Rt Hon Lord	Queen Elizabeth Building, London	0171 583 5766
	18 St John Street, Manchester	0161 278 1800
Carman George Alfred	New Court Chambers, London	0171 831 9500

Carnes Andrew James	23 Essex Street, London	0171 413 0353
Carron Richard Byron	11 Bolt Court, London	0171 353 2300
	Redhill Chambers, Redhill	01737 780781
Carter Miss Lesley Ann	25-27 Castle Street, Liverpool	0151 227 5661/5666/236 5072
Carter Miss Rosalyn Frances	St Philip's Chambers, Birmingham	0121 246 7000
Carter William Andrew	23 Essex Street, London	0171 413 0353
Cartwright David Crispian Himley	5 Pump Court, London	0171 353 2532
Cartwright Nicholas Frederick	St Philip's Chambers, Birmingham	0121 246 7000
Carus Roderick	Chambers of John Hand QC, Manchester	0161 955 9000
Carville Owen Brendan Neville	25-27 Castle Street, Liverpool	0151 227 5661/5666/236 5072
Casey Noel	7 Stone Buildings, London	0171 242 0961
Cave Jeremy Stephen	1 Crown Office Row, London	0171 797 7500
	Crown Office Row Chambers, Brighton	01273 625625
Challinor Robert Michael	St Philip's Chambers, Birmingham	0121 246 7000
Chan Miss Abberlaine Dianne Pao Che	9-12 Bell Yard, London	0171 400 1800
Chaplin Adrian Roland	9-12 Bell Yard, London	0171 400 1800
Charles Ms Deborah Ann	6 Pump Court, London	0171 797 8400
Chawla Mukul	9-12 Bell Yard, London	0171 400 1800
Christie Simon Paul William	Peel House Chambers, Liverpool	0151 236 4321
Clark Christopher Harvey	Pump Court Chambers, London	0171 353 0711
	Westgate Chambers, Lewes	01273 480 510
	Pump Court Chambers, Winchester	01962 868161
Clarke Miss Michelle Nicola	Earl Street Chambers, Maidstone	01622 671222
Clarke Nicholas Stephen	Chambers of John Hand QC, Manchester	0161 955 9000
Clarke Peter William	Queen Elizabeth Building, London	0171 583 5766
Clover Miss Sarah	2 Mitre Court Buildings, London	0171 353 1353
Clover (Thomas) Anthony	New Court Chambers, London	0171 831 9500
Collett Gavin Charles	Rougemont Chambers, Exeter	01392 410471
	Cathedral Chambers (Jan Wood Independent Barristers' Clerk), Exeter	01392 210900
Collier Martin Melton	Fenners Chambers, Cambridge	01223 368761
	Fenners Chambers, Peterborough	01733 562030
Colman Andrew	1 Hare Court, London	0171 353 3982/5324
Conlin Geoffrey David	3 Serjeants' Inn, London	0171 353 5537
Cooke Graham Owen John	23 Essex Street, London	0171 413 0353
Copeland Andrew John	Chambers of Geoffrey Hawker, London	0171 583 8899
Corry Miss Carol Elizabeth	One Essex Court, London	0171 936 3030
Cottage Miss Rosina	9-12 Bell Yard, London	0171 400 1800
Coulter Barry John	One Essex Court, London	0171 936 3030
Coward Miss Victoria Jane	Queen Elizabeth Building, London	0171 583 5766
Cox Bryan Richard	9 Woodhouse Square, Leeds	0113 245 1986
Cranbrook Alexander Douglas John	9-12 Bell Yard, London	0171 400 1800
Crane Miss Suzanne Denise	New Court Chambers, Birmingham	0121 693 6656
Cranston-Morris Wayne	23 Essex Street, London	0171 413 0353
Crookes Miss Alison Naomi		
Crossley Simon Justin	9 Woodhouse Square, Leeds	0113 245 1986
Crosthwaite Graham Andrew	One King's Bench Walk, London	0171 936 1500
Crowley John Desmond	Two Crown Office Row, London	0171 797 8100
Crowson Howard Keith	St Paul's House, Leeds	0113 245 5866
Cutts Miss Johannah	23 Essex Street, London	0171 413 0353
Dale Julian Charles Rigby	Eastbourne Chambers, Eastbourne	01323 642102
Dallas Andrew Thomas Alastair	Chambers of Andrew Campbell QC, Leeds	0113 245 5438
Dangor Mrs Patricia Madree Trenton	14 Gray's Inn Square, London	0171 242 0858
Darbishire Adrian Munro	Queen Elizabeth Building, London	0171 583 5766
Davey Miss Tina Elaine	9-12 Bell Yard, London	0171 400 1800
Davies Andrew	Angel Chambers, Swansea	01792 464623/464648
Davies Miss Felicity Anne	Chambers of Andrew Campbell QC, Leeds	0113 245 5438
Davies Miss Penny May	Chambers of Harjit Singh, London	0171 353 1356
Davis Richard Simon	23 Essex Street, London	0171 413 0353
Davis William Easthope	St Philip's Chambers, Birmingham	0121 246 7000
Dean Brian John Anthony	St Philip's Chambers, Birmingham	0121 246 7000
Denney Stuart Henry Macdonald	Deans Court Chambers, Manchester	0161 834 4097
	Deans Court Chambers, Preston	01772 555163
Denton Miss Michelle Jayne	9-12 Bell Yard, London	0171 400 1800

• Expanded entry in Part D

Dhaliwal Miss Davinder Kaur	New Court Chambers, Birmingham	0121 693 6656
Dix-Dyer Miss Fiona Jane	St Paul's House, Leeds	0113 245 5866
Dixon David Steven	Sovereign Chambers, Leeds	0113 245 1841/2/3
Dixon Ian Frederick	Cathedral Chambers, Newcastle upon Tyne	0191 232 1311
Doggart Piers Graham	• King's Chambers, Eastbourne	01323 416053
Dogra Miss Tanyia Anita	Chambers of Harjit Singh, London	0171 353 1356
Donne Jeremy Nigel	Queen Elizabeth Building, London	0171 583 5766
Dowokpor Jonathan Kukasi	Tollgate Mews Chambers, London	0171 511 1838
Doyle Peter John	9-12 Bell Yard, London	0171 400 1800
Drayton Henry Alexander	2 Gray's Inn Square Chambers, London	0171 242 0328/405 1317
Driver Simon Gregory	25-27 Castle Street, Liverpool	0151 227 5661/5666/236 5072
Dry Nicholas David	St Paul's House, Leeds	0113 245 5866
Dubbery Mark Edward	Pump Court Chambers, London	0171 353 0711
Duffy Derek James	St Paul's House, Leeds	0113 245 5866
Duffy Michael	Cathedral Chambers, Ely, Ely	01353 666775
Dunn Christopher	Sovereign Chambers, Leeds	0113 245 1841/2/3
Durran Miss Alexia Grainne	23 Essex Street, London	0171 413 0353
Eccles Hugh William Patrick	Harcourt Chambers, London	0171 353 6961/7
	Harcourt Chambers, Oxford	01865 791559
Edwards John David	St Philip's Chambers, Birmingham	0121 246 7000
Edwards Nigel Royston	St Paul's House, Leeds	0113 245 5866
Edwards Miss Susan May	23 Essex Street, London	0171 413 0353
Egan Eugene Christopher	30 Park Place, Cardiff	01222 398421
Egan Michael Flynn John	9-12 Bell Yard, London	0171 400 1800
Ellison Mark Christopher	Queen Elizabeth Building, London	0171 583 5766
Emmerson (Michael) Benedict	Doughty Street Chambers, London	0171 404 1313
Evans David Anthony	9-12 Bell Yard, London	0171 400 1800
	Iscoed Chambers, Swansea	01792 652988/9/330
Evans David Howard	Queen Elizabeth Building, London	0171 583 5766
Evans Lee John	Farrar's Building, London	0171 583 9241
Evans Martin Alan Langham	5 Paper Buildings, London	0171 583 6117
Evans Thomas Gareth	Rougemont Chambers, Exeter	01392 410471
Farmer Pryce Michael	1 Dr Johnson's Buildings, London	0171 353 9328
	Goldsmith Building, London	0171 353 7881
	Sedan House, Chester	01244 320480/348282
Farquharson Miss Jane Caroline	One Essex Court, London	0171 936 3030
Fenhalls Mark Roydon Allen	23 Essex Street, London	0171 413 0353
Field Martin Charles	9-12 Bell Yard, London	0171 400 1800
Field Rory Dominic	Hardwicke Building, London	0171 242 2523
Finnigan Peter Anthony	Queen Elizabeth Building, London	0171 583 5766
Finucane Brendan Godfrey Eamonn	23 Essex Street, London	0171 413 0353
Fisher Jonathan Simon	• 18 Red Lion Court, London	0171 520 6000
	• Thornwood House, Chelmsford	01245 280880
Fitzgerald Edward Hamilton	Doughty Street Chambers, London	0171 404 1313
Fitzgibbon Francis George Herbert Dillon	33 Bedford Row, London	0171 242 6476
Fletcher Marcus Alexander	One King's Bench Walk, London	0171 936 1500
Florida-James Mark	• King's Bench Chambers, Bournemouth	01202 250025
Forbes Peter George	6 Pump Court, London	0171 797 8400
	6-8 Mill Street, Maidstone	01622 688 094
Forlin Gerard Emlyn	Phoenix Chambers, London	0171 404 7888
Forster Brian Clive	Trinity Chambers, Newcastle upon Tyne	0191 232 1927
Forster Ms Sarah Judith	14 Gray's Inn Square, London	0171 242 0858
	Westgate Chambers, Lewes	01273 480 510
Fortune Malcolm Donald Porter	3 Serjeants' Inn, London	0171 353 5537
Foulkes Christopher David	1 Hare Court, London	0171 353 3982/5324
Franck Richard David William	Equity Chambers, Birmingham	0121 233 2100
Franklin Stephen Hall	5 Paper Buildings, London	0171 583 6117
	Fenners Chambers, Cambridge	01223 368761
Frazer Christopher Mark	Harcourt Chambers, London	0171 353 6961/7
	Harcourt Chambers, Oxford	01865 791559
Friesner David Jonathan	Chambers of John Hand QC, Manchester	0161 955 9000
Frodsham Alexander Miles	Oriel Chambers, Liverpool	0151 236 7191
Fuad Kerim	Chambers of Helen Grindrod QC, London	0171 404 4777
Gabb Charles Henry Escott	Pump Court Chambers, London	0171 353 0711
	Pump Court Chambers, Winchester	01962 868161

Gale Michael	One King's Bench Walk, London	0171 936 1500
Gallagher John David Edmund	Goldsmith Building, London	0171 353 7881
Garlick Paul Richard	Pump Court Chambers, London	0171 353 0711
	Pump Court Chambers, Winchester	01962 868161
Garside Charles Roger	Chambers of John Hand QC, Manchester	0161 955 9000
Garth Steven David	Sovereign Chambers, Leeds	0113 245 1841/2/3
Gau Justin Charles	Pump Court Chambers, London	0171 353 0711
	Pump Court Chambers, Winchester	01962 868161
Gerry Miss Felicity Ruth	2 New Street, Leicester	0116 262 5906
Gilbertson Mrs Helen Alison	Sackville Chambers, Norwich	01603 613516
Gillette John Charles	Baker Street Chambers, Middlesbrough	01642 873873
Gillibrand Philip Martin Mangnall	Pump Court Chambers, London	0171 353 0711
	Pump Court Chambers, Winchester	01962 868161
Gittins Timothy James	Trinity Chambers, Newcastle upon Tyne	0191 232 1927
Glasgow Oliver Edwin James	1 Hare Court, London	0171 353 3982/5324
Glass Anthony Trevor	Queen Elizabeth Building, London	0171 583 5766
Glynn Miss Joanna Elizabeth	23 Essex Street, London	0171 413 0353
Godfrey Miss Louise Sarah	14 Gray's Inn Square, London	0171 242 0858
	Park Court Chambers, Leeds	0113 243 3277
Goodchild Mrs Elizabeth Ann	Watford Chambers, Watford	01923 220553
Goodwin Miss Caroline Tracy	Trinity Chambers, Newcastle upon Tyne	0191 232 1927
Goose Julian Nicholas	Chambers of Andrew Campbell QC, Leeds	0113 245 5438
Gopinathan Miss Anupama	Harrow-on-the-Hill Chambers, Harrow on the Hill	0181 423 7444
	Windsor Barristers' Chambers, Windsor	01753 648 899
Gordon Miss Catherine Anne	140 Cholmeley Road, Reading	01734 665174
Gordon David Myer	Sovereign Chambers, Leeds	0113 245 1841/2/3
Gordon Mark John	11 Bolt Court, London	0171 353 2300
	Redhill Chambers, Redhill	01737 780781
Gordon-Dean Miss Natasha		
Gorna Miss Anne Christina	4 Paper Buildings, London	0171 353 3366/583 7155
	Cathedral Chambers (Jan Wood Independent Barristers' Clerk), Exeter	01392 210900
Gower Peter John de Peauly	6 Pump Court, London	0171 797 8400
	6-8 Mill Street, Maidstone	01622 688 094
Grahame Miss Nina Stephanie	1 Hare Court, London	0171 353 3982/5324
Gray Miss Jennifer	11 Old Square, London	0171 242 5022
Grayson Edward	• 9-12 Bell Yard, London	0171 400 1800
Greaves John	9-12 Bell Yard, London	0171 400 1800
Greene Paul Martin	Earl Street Chambers, Maidstone	01622 671222
Gresty Miss Denise Lynn	Sovereign Chambers, Leeds	0113 245 1841/2/3
Grey Robin Douglas	Queen Elizabeth Building, London	0171 583 5766
Grice Miss Joanna Harrison	One King's Bench Walk, London	0171 936 1500
Griffin Miss Lynn Myfanwy	5 Paper Buildings, London	0171 583 6117
Griffin Neil Patrick Luke	9-12 Bell Yard, London	0171 400 1800
Griffin Nicholas John	5 Paper Buildings, London	0171 583 6117
Griffiths (John) Peter (Gwynne)	30 Park Place, Cardiff	01222 398421
Gruffydd John	Oriel Chambers, Liverpool	0151 236 7191
Guirguis Miss Sheren	White Friars Chambers, Chester	01244 323070
Gullick Stephen John	Sovereign Chambers, Leeds	0113 245 1841/2/3
Gunther Miss Elizabeth Ann	Pump Court Chambers, London	0171 353 0711
	Pump Court Chambers, Winchester	01962 868161
Gupta Miss Usha	New Chambers, St Albans	0966 212126
Hacking Anthony Stephen	One King's Bench Walk, London	0171 936 1500
Hadley Steven Frank	2 Paper Buildings, London	0171 353 0933
Hadrill Keith Paul	9-12 Bell Yard, London	0171 400 1800
Hall David Percy	9 Woodhouse Square, Leeds	0113 245 1986
Hall-Smith Martin Clive William	Goldsmith Building, London	0171 353 7881
Hallett Miss Heather Carol	23 Essex Street, London	0171 413 0353
Halpin Thomas Gavin	Earl Street Chambers, Maidstone	01622 671222
Hamid Mrs Beebee Nazmoon	Clapham Chambers, London	0171 978 8482/0171 642 5777
Hamilton Jaime Richard	Chambers of John Hand QC, Manchester	0161 955 9000
Hargrove Jeremy John Loveday	Trinity Chambers, Newcastle upon Tyne	0191 232 1927

• Expanded entry in Part D

Harold Fergus Dougal	Tindal Chambers, Chelmsford	01245 267742
Harris Ian Robert	25-27 Castle Street, Liverpool	0151 227 5661/5666/236 5072
Harrison John Foster	St Paul's House, Leeds	0113 245 5866
Harrison Peter John	6 Pump Court, London	0171 797 8400
	6-8 Mill Street, Maidstone	01622 688 094
Hartley-Davies Paul Kevil	30 Park Place, Cardiff	01222 398421
Harvey Colin Trevor	St Paul's House, Leeds	0113 245 5866
Harvey Miss Jayne Denise	Goldsworth Chambers, London	0171 405 7117
Harwood-Stevenson John Francis Richard	9-12 Bell Yard, London	0171 400 1800
	East Anglian Chambers, Norwich	01603 617351
Haslam Andrew Peter	Sovereign Chambers, Leeds	0113 245 1841/2/3
Hatton Andrew John	Plowden Buildings, London	0171 583 0808
	Paradise Square Chambers, Sheffield	0114 273 8951
Hawkesworth (Walter) Gareth	5 Paper Buildings, London	0171 583 6117
	Fenners Chambers, Cambridge	01223 368761
	Fenners Chambers, Peterborough	01733 562030
Haygarth Edmund Bruce	25-27 Castle Street, Liverpool	0151 227 5661/5666/236 5072
Haynes Peter	St Philip's Chambers, Birmingham	0121 246 7000
Healy Miss Alexandra	9-12 Bell Yard, London	0171 400 1800
Heaton Clive William	Chambers of Andrew Campbell QC, Leeds	0113 245 5438
Heaton-Armstrong Anthony Eustace John	9-12 Bell Yard, London	0171 400 1800
Hedworth Alan Toby	11 King's Bench Walk, London	0171 353 3337/8
	Trinity Chambers, Newcastle upon Tyne	0191 232 1927
Heer Miss Deanna Mary	Hardwicke Building, London	0171 242 2523
Hegarty Kevin John	St Philip's Chambers, Birmingham	0121 246 7000
Henderson Lawrence Mark	11 Bolt Court, London	0171 353 2300
	Redhill Chambers, Redhill	01737 780781
Henry Edward Joseph Aloysius	Queen Elizabeth Building, London	0171 583 5766
Herbert Mrs Rebecca Mary	2 New Street, Leicester	0116 262 5906
Heslop Martin Sydney	1 Hare Court, London	0171 353 3982/5324
Hick Michael Andrew	5 Paper Buildings, London	0171 583 6117
Hickey Simon Roger Greenwood	Chambers of Andrew Campbell QC, Leeds	0113 245 5438
Hill (Eliot) Michael	23 Essex Street, London	0171 413 0353
Hilton Alan John Howard	Queen Elizabeth Building, London	0171 583 5766
Hogg The Rt Hon Douglas Martin	4 Paper Buildings, London	0171 353 3366/583 7155
	37 Park Square, Leeds	0113 243 9422
Hollingworth Peter James Michael	22 Albion Place, Northampton	01604 636271
Hopkins Simeon Francis McKay	5 Pump Court, London	0171 353 2532
Horlick Lady Fiona	23 Essex Street, London	0171 413 0353
Horwell Richard Eric	Queen Elizabeth Building, London	0171 583 5766
Horwood Miss Anya Louise	25-27 Castle Street, Liverpool	0151 227 5661/5666/236 5072
Hotten Keith Robert	23 Essex Street, London	0171 413 0353
House James Michael	2 New Street, Leicester	0116 262 5906
Howard Graham John	Queen Elizabeth Building, London	0171 353 7181 (12 lines)
Hoyal Ms Jane	• 1 Pump Court, London	0171 583 2012/353 4341
Hudson Christopher John	Deans Court Chambers, Manchester	0161 834 4097
	Deans Court Chambers, Preston	01772 555163
Hughes Hywel Tudor	30 Park Place, Cardiff	01222 398421
Hughes Miss Meryl Elizabeth	Fenners Chambers, Cambridge	01223 368761
	Fenners Chambers, Peterborough	01733 562030
Hughes Thomas Merfyn	Goldsmith Building, London	0171 353 7881
	40 King Street, Chester	01244 323886
Hughes William Lloyd	9-12 Bell Yard, London	0171 400 1800
Hull Leslie David	Chambers of John Hand QC, Manchester	0161 955 9000
Humpage Miss Heather June		
Hurst Andrew Robert	23 Essex Street, London	0171 413 0353
Hussain Miss Frida Khanam	17 Carlton Crescent, Southampton	01703 320320
Iqbal Abdul Shaffaq	Chambers of Andrew Campbell QC, Leeds	0113 245 5438
Ironfield Miss Janet Ruth	Deans Court Chambers, Manchester	0161 834 4097
	Deans Court Chambers, Preston	01772 555163
Islam-Choudhury Mugni	11 Bolt Court, London	0171 353 2300
Jack Simon Michael	9 Woodhouse Square, Leeds	0113 245 1986
Jackson Anthony Warren	3 Serjeants' Inn, London	0171 353 5537
Jackson Simon Malcolm Dermot	Park Court Chambers, Leeds	0113 243 3277
James Roderick Morrice	23 Essex Street, London	0171 413 0353

B

James Simon John	Chambers of John Hand QC, Manchester	0161 955 9000
Janner Daniel Joseph Mitchell	23 Essex Street, London	0171 413 0353
Jay Adam Marc	One King's Bench Walk, London	0171 936 1500
Jayanathan Miss Shamini	30 Park Place, Cardiff	01222 398421
Jeffreys David Alfred	Queen Elizabeth Building, London	0171 583 5766
Jenkins Dr Janet Caroline	Chambers of Kieran Coonan QC, London	0171 583 6013/2510
Jenkins John David	30 Park Place, Cardiff	01222 398421
John Peter Charles	One Essex Court, London	0171 936 3030
John Stephen Alun	9-12 Bell Yard, London	0171 400 1800
Johnson Nicholas Robert	25-27 Castle Street, Liverpool	0151 227 5661/5666/236 5072
Johnson Steven	Chambers of John Hand QC, Manchester	0161 955 9000
Johnson Miss Zoe Elisabeth	Queen Elizabeth Building, London	0171 583 5766
Jones Paul Alan	One Essex Court, London	0171 936 3030
Jory Richard Norman	9-12 Bell Yard, London	0171 400 1800
Josling William Henry Charles	Fenners Chambers, Cambridge	01223 368761
	Fenners Chambers, Peterborough	01733 562030
Judge Charles Joseph	5 Paper Buildings, London	0171 583 6117
Kalsi Mrs Maninder	New Court Chambers, Birmingham	0121 693 6656
Kark Thomas Victor William	Queen Elizabeth Building, London	0171 583 5766
Karmy-Jones Miss Riel Meredith	1 Hare Court, London	0171 353 3982/5324
Katz Philip Alec Jackson	9-12 Bell Yard, London	0171 400 1800
Kealey Simon Thomas	Chambers of Andrew Campbell QC, Leeds	0113 245 5438
Kealy Charles Brian	Chambers of Andrew Campbell QC, Leeds	0113 245 5438
Kearl Guy Alexander	St Paul's House, Leeds	0113 245 5866
Keeley James Francis	Sovereign Chambers, Leeds	0113 245 1841/2/3
Kelly Miss Geraldine Therese		
Kelsey-Fry John	Queen Elizabeth Building, London	0171 583 5766
Kenning Thomas Patrick	New Court Chambers, Birmingham	0121 693 6656
Kent Alan Peter	23 Essex Street, London	0171 413 0353
Kenward Richard Francis	Watford Chambers, Watford	01923 220553
Kenward Timothy David Nelson	25-27 Castle Street, Liverpool	0151 227 5661/5666/236 5072
Khan Ashraf	A K Chambers, Hull	01482 641180
Khan Avicenna Alkindi Cornelius	55 Temple Chambers, London	0171 353 7400
Khan Miss Helen Mary Grace	Chambers of Lord Campbell of Alloway QC, London	0171 353 9276
Khan Saadallah Frans Hassan	55 Temple Chambers, London	0171 353 7400
Khokhar Mushtaq Ahmed	Sovereign Chambers, Leeds	0113 245 1841/2/3
Kinch Christopher Anthony	23 Essex Street, London	0171 413 0353
King Peter Duncan	5 Pump Court, London	0171 353 2532
	Fenners Chambers, Cambridge	01223 368761
Kinnear Jonathan Shea	9-12 Bell Yard, London	0171 400 1800
Knight Christopher Michael St John	Chambers of John Hand QC, Manchester	0161 955 9000
Kolodynski Stefan Richard	New Court Chambers, Birmingham	0121 693 6656
Kramer Stephen Ernest	• 1 Hare Court, London	0171 353 3982/5324
Kushner Miss Lindsey Joy	14 Gray's Inn Square, London	0171 242 0858
	28 St John Street, Manchester	0161 834 8418
Kyte Peter Eric	Queen Elizabeth Building, London	0171 583 5766
Lander Charles Gideon	25-27 Castle Street, Liverpool	0151 227 5661/5666/236 5072
Lane David Goodwin	11 Bolt Court, London	0171 353 2300
	All Saints Chambers, Bristol	0117 921 1966
Langdale Timothy James	Queen Elizabeth Building, London	0171 583 5766
Lanlehin Olajide Adebola	Britton Street Chambers, London	0171 608 3765
Larkin Sean	Queen Elizabeth Building, London	0171 583 5766
Law John Edward	33 Bedford Row, London	0171 242 6476
Lawrence Sir Ivan John	One Essex Court, London	0171 936 3030
Lawrence Miss Rachel Camilla	One Essex Court, London	0171 936 3030
Lawson Michael Henry	23 Essex Street, London	0171 413 0353
Lawson Rogers George Stuart	23 Essex Street, London	0171 413 0353
Leeming Michael Peter George	Chambers of John Hand QC, Manchester	0161 955 9000
Lees Andrew James	St Paul's House, Leeds	0113 245 5866
Lennon Desmond Joseph	25-27 Castle Street, Liverpool	0151 227 5661/5666/236 5072
Lewis Jeffrey Allan	9 Woodhouse Square, Leeds	0113 245 1986
Lewis Paul Keith	30 Park Place, Cardiff	01222 398421
Linstead Peter James	11 Bolt Court, London	0171 353 2300
Litherland Miss Rebecca Jane	Fenners Chambers, Cambridge	01223 368761

• Expanded entry in Part D

	Fenners Chambers, Peterborough	01733 562030
Livingstone Simon John	11 Bolt Court, London	0171 353 2300
	Redhill Chambers, Redhill	01737 780781
Llewellyn-Jones Christopher Geoffrey	Goldsmith Building, London	0171 353 7881
	9 Park Place, Cardiff	01222 382731
Lloyd Miss Wendy-Jane	25-27 Castle Street, Liverpool	0151 227 5661/5666/236 5072
Lobo Matthew Joseph Edwin	Fenners Chambers, Cambridge	01223 368761
	Fenners Chambers, Peterborough	01733 562030
Lodge John Robert	Park Court Chambers, Leeds	0113 243 3277
Loftus Miss Teresa Anne Martine	25-27 Castle Street, Liverpool	0151 227 5661/5666/236 5072
Logan Miss Maura	St John's Chambers, Hale Barns	0161 980 7379
Longden Anthony Gordon	Queen Elizabeth Building, London	0171 583 5766
Lowen Jonathan Andrew Michael	Queen Elizabeth Building, London	0171 353 7181 (12 lines)
Lowry Miss Emma Margaret Collins	Queen Elizabeth Building, London	0171 583 5766
Lumley Gerald	9 Woodhouse Square, Leeds	0113 245 1986
Lumley Nicholas James Henry	Sovereign Chambers, Leeds	0113 245 1841/2/3
Lunt Steven	9 Woodhouse Square, Leeds	0113 245 1986
MacDonald Iain	Gough Square Chambers, London	0171 353 0924
MacKillop Norman Malcolm	• Chartlands Chambers, Northampton	01604 603322
Maguire Albert Michael	Goldsmith Building, London	0171 353 7881
Maitland Jones Mark Griffith	Goldsmith Building, London	0171 353 7881
Maitland Marc Claude	11 Old Square, London	0171 242 5022
Manasse Mrs Anne Katherine	Cathedral Chambers, Newcastle upon Tyne	0191 232 1311
Manson Miss Julie-Ann	11 Bolt Court, London	0171 353 2300
	Redhill Chambers, Redhill	01737 780781
Marley Miss Sarah Anne	5 Pump Court, London	0171 353 2532
Marshall Miss Eloise Mary Katherine Selina	23 Essex Street, London	0171 413 0353
Marshall Philip Derek	Farrar's Building, London	0171 583 9241
	Iscoed Chambers, Swansea	01792 652988/9/330
Marson Geoffrey Charles	Sovereign Chambers, Leeds	0113 245 1841/2/3
Martin David John	Cathedral Chambers, Newcastle upon Tyne	0191 232 1311
Martineau Henry Ralph Adeane	Goldsmith Building, London	0171 353 7881
Mason Ian Douglas	11 Bolt Court, London	0171 353 2300
	Redhill Chambers, Redhill	01737 780781
Mathews Deni	8 Fountain Court, Birmingham	0121 236 5514
Matthews Mrs Ann Marie	King's Bench Chambers, Bournemouth	01202 250025
Maudslay Miss Diana Elizabeth		
Maxwell David	Claremont Chambers, Wolverhampton	01902 426222
May Alan	23 Essex Street, London	0171 413 0353
McAtasney Miss Philippa Mary	9-12 Bell Yard, London	0171 400 1800
McCahey Miss Catherine Anne Mary	St Philip's Chambers, Birmingham	0121 246 7000
McCartney Peter	St Philip's Chambers, Birmingham	0121 246 7000
McFarlane Andrew Ewart	One King's Bench Walk, London	0171 936 1500
	Priory Chambers, Birmingham	0121 236 3882/1375
McGuinness John Francis	9-12 Bell Yard, London	0171 400 1800
McIvor Ian Walker	334 Deansgate Chambers, Manchester	0161 834 3767
McKinnon Warwick Nairn	Queen Elizabeth Building, London	0171 583 5766
McKone Mark Desmond	Sovereign Chambers, Leeds	0113 245 1841/2/3
McLachlan David Robert		
McMinn Miss Valerie Kathleen	Baker Street Chambers, Middlesbrough	01642 873873
Meachin Miss (Sarah) Vanessa Veronica	St Philip's Chambers, Birmingham	0121 246 7000
Medland Simon Edward	23 Essex Street, London	0171 413 0353
Merz Richard James	9-12 Bell Yard, London	0171 400 1800
Miller Miss Jane Elizabeth Mackay	Pump Court Chambers, London	0171 353 0711
	Pump Court Chambers, Winchester	01962 868161
Millett Kenneth James	1 Hare Court, London	0171 353 3982/5324
Milne Richard James	23 Essex Street, London	0171 413 0353
Miskin Charles James Monckton	23 Essex Street, London	0171 413 0353
Mitchell Christopher Richard	Queen Elizabeth Building, London	0171 583 5766
Mondair Rashpal Singh	Claremont Chambers, Wolverhampton	01902 426222
Montgomery Robert Michael	Pump Court Chambers, London	0171 353 0711
	Chavasse Court Chambers, Liverpool	0151 707 1191
	Pump Court Chambers, Winchester	01962 868161
Moore James Anthony	2 Gray's Inn Square Chambers, London	0171 242 0328/405 1317

• Expanded entry in Part D

Moores Timothy Kieron	17 Carlton Crescent, Southampton	01703 320320
Moorman Miss Lucinda Claire	Farrar's Building, London	0171 583 9241
Morley Iain Charles	1 Hare Court, London	0171 353 3982/5324
Morris Christopher	New Court Chambers, Birmingham	0121 693 6656
Moses Miss Rebecca	Barristers' Common Law Chambers, London	0171 375 3012
	Lion Court, London	0171 404 6565
Moss Peter Jonathan	9-12 Bell Yard, London	0171 400 1800
Moulson Peter Charles Edward	Chambers of Andrew Campbell QC, Leeds	0113 245 5438
Mulholland Ms Kathryn Shona	One King's Bench Walk, London	0171 936 1500
Mullen Patrick Anthony	One Essex Court, London	0171 936 3030
Muller Franz Joseph	11 King's Bench Walk, London	0171 353 3337/8
	11 King's Bench Walk, Leeds	0113 2971 200
Munday Miss Anne Margaret	8 King's Bench Walk, London	0171 797 8888
	Tribune House Chambers, York	01904 630448
Murray Ashley Charles	Oriel Chambers, Liverpool	0151 236 7191
Murray John Michael Andrew	Chambers of John Hand QC, Manchester	0161 955 9000
Myatt Charles Edward	Fenners Chambers, Cambridge	01223 368761
	Fenners Chambers, Peterborough	01733 562030
Nathan Philip Gabriel	Earl Street Chambers, Maidstone	01622 671222
Nduka-Eze Chukwuemeka Cecil	New Court Chambers, Birmingham	0121 693 6656
Newbury Richard Lennox	Sovereign Chambers, Leeds	0113 245 1841/2/3
Newcombe Timothy Richard	St Paul's House, Leeds	0113 245 5866
Newman Austin Eric	9 Woodhouse Square, Leeds	0113 245 1986
Newton Miss Claire Elaine Maria Bailey	Goldsmith Building, London	0171 353 7881
Newton-Price James Edward	Pump Court Chambers, London	0171 353 0711
	Pump Court Chambers, Winchester	01962 868161
Nicholson Pratt Thomas Hycy	Hardwicke Building, London	0171 242 2523
Nicolson Aris Tony	23 Bracken Gardens, London	0181 748 4924
Nolan Damian Francis	25-27 Castle Street, Liverpool	0151 227 5661/5666/236 5072
Norie-Miller Jeffrey Reginald	55 Temple Chambers, London	0171 353 7400
Norton Miss Heather Sophia	23 Essex Street, London	0171 413 0353
Nsugbe Oba Eric	Pump Court Chambers, London	0171 353 0711
	Pump Court Chambers, Winchester	01962 868161
O'Higgins John Gerard	Chambers of Helen Grindrod QC, London	0171 404 4777
O'Neill Brian Patrick	1 Hare Court, London	0171 353 3982/5324
Ofori George Edward	Chancery Chambers, London	0171 405 6879
	ACHMA Chambers, London	0171 639 7817
Ogunbiyi Oluwole Afolabi	Horizon Chambers, London	0171 242 2440
Oke Olanrewaju Oladipupo	Kingsway Chambers, London	07000 653529
Okoye Miss Joy Nwamala	Chambers of Joy Okoye, London	0171 405 7011
Oliver Michael Richard	Hardwicke Building, London	0171 242 2523
Ong Miss Grace Yu Mae	One Essex Court, London	0171 936 3030
Orsulik Michael Anthony	9-12 Bell Yard, London	0171 400 1800
Owen David Meurig	25-27 Castle Street, Liverpool	0151 227 5661/5666/236 5072
Ozin Paul David	23 Essex Street, London	0171 413 0353
Pack Miss Melissa Elizabeth Jane	Farrar's Building, London	0171 583 9241
Palmer Patrick John Steven	Sovereign Chambers, Leeds	0113 245 1841/2/3
Paneth Miss Sarah Ruth	No 1 Serjeants' Inn, London	0171 415 6666
Pardoe Rupert Adam Corin	23 Essex Street, London	0171 413 0353
Parr John Edward	8 King Street Chambers, Manchester	0161 834 9560
Parry Charles Robert	Pump Court Chambers, London	0171 353 0711
	Pump Court Chambers, Winchester	01962 868161
Pascoe Nigel Spencer Knight	Pump Court Chambers, London	0171 353 0711
	All Saints Chambers, Bristol	0117 921 1966
	Pump Court Chambers, Winchester	01962 868161
Paton Ian Francis	Queen Elizabeth Building, London	0171 583 5766
Patterson Norman William	14 Gray's Inn Square, London	0171 242 0858
Patterson Stewart	• Pump Court Chambers, London	0171 353 0711
	• Pump Court Chambers, Winchester	01962 868161
Pawson Robert Edward Cruickshank	Pump Court Chambers, London	0171 353 0711
	Pump Court Chambers, Winchester	01962 868161
Pearce Ivan James	Furnival Chambers, London	0171 405 3232
Peirson Oliver James	Pump Court Chambers, London	0171 353 0711
	Pump Court Chambers, Winchester	01962 868161
Peters Nigel Melvin	18 Red Lion Court, London	0171 520 6000
	Thornwood House, Chelmsford	01245 280880
Phillips Frank	Iscoed Chambers, Swansea	01792 652988/9/330

• Expanded entry in Part D

Pitter Jason Karl	Park Court Chambers, Leeds	0113 243 3277
Plaschkes Ms Sarah Georgina	Queen Elizabeth Building, London	0171 583 5766
Pointon Miss Caroline Jane	Fenners Chambers, Cambridge	01223 368761
	Fenners Chambers, Peterborough	01733 562030
Porter Miss Sarah Ruth	11 Bolt Court, London	0171 353 2300
Portnoy Leslie Reuben	Chambers of John Hand QC, Manchester	0161 955 9000
Poulet Mrs Rebecca Maria	Queen Elizabeth Building, London	0171 583 5766
Power Nigel John	25-27 Castle Street, Liverpool	0151 227 5661/5666/236 5072
Powis Miss Samantha Inez	St Philip's Chambers, Birmingham	0121 246 7000
Price Albert John	23 Essex Street, London	0171 413 0353
Pulman George Frederick	• Hardwicke Building, London	0171 242 2523
	• Stour Chambers, Canterbury	01227 764899
Purnell Nicholas Robert	23 Essex Street, London	0171 413 0353
Quinlan Christopher John	30 Park Place, Cardiff	01222 398421
Rahman Muhammad Altafur	Barristers' Common Law Chambers, London	0171 375 3012
Rahman Ms Sadeqa Shaheen	1 Crown Office Row, London	0171 797 7500
Ramasamy Selvaraju	Queen Elizabeth Building, London	0171 583 5766
Rampersad Devan	St Philip's Chambers, Birmingham	0121 246 7000
Rayment Mr. Benedick Michael	One King's Bench Walk, London	0171 936 1500
Redgrave Adrian Robert Frank	No 1 Serjeants' Inn, London	0171 415 6666
Rees Gareth David	Queen Elizabeth Building, London	0171 583 5766
Reid Howard Barrington	New Court Chambers, Birmingham	0121 693 6656
Richardson Garth Douglas Anthony	3 Paper Buildings, London	0171 583 8055
	20 Lorne Park Road, Bournemouth	01202 292102
	4 St Peter Street, Winchester	01962 868 884
Richardson (Peter) James	23 Essex Street, London	0171 413 0353
Rigby Terence	Chambers of John Hand QC, Manchester	0161 955 9000
Riordan Stephen Vaughan	25-27 Castle Street, Liverpool	0151 227 5661/5666/236 5072
Robertson Ms Alice Michelle	Chambers of Kieran Coonan QC, London	0171 583 6013/2510
Robertson Andrew James	11 King's Bench Walk, London	0171 353 3337/8
	11 King's Bench Walk, Leeds	0113 2971 200
Robinson Vivian	Queen Elizabeth Building, London	0171 583 5766
Robson Nicholas David	Baker Street Chambers, Middlesbrough	01642 873873
Rogers Paul John	1 Crown Office Row, London	0171 797 7500
	Crown Office Row Chambers, Brighton	01273 625625
Rose Jonathan Lee	St Paul's House, Leeds	0113 245 5866
Rudd Matthew Allan	11 Bolt Court, London	0171 353 2300
	Redhill Chambers, Redhill	01737 780781
Rudland Martin William	Chambers of Andrew Campbell QC, Leeds	0113 245 5438
Russell Anthony Patrick	Peel Court Chambers, Manchester	0161 832 3791
Russell Miss Christina Martha	9-12 Bell Yard, London	0171 400 1800
Russell Flint Simon Coleridge	23 Essex Street, London	0171 413 0353
Russell Miss Jennifer Anne	Victoria Chambers, Birmingham	0121 236 9900
Ryan David Patrick	Chambers of Geoffrey Hawker, London	0171 583 8899
Saffian Ms Leah Susan	Queen Elizabeth Building, London	0171 583 5766
Salvesen Keith Neville	Queen Elizabeth Building, London	0171 353 7181 (12 lines)
Sampson Graeme William	Chambers of Geoffrey Hawker, London	0171 583 8899
Samuel Glyn Ross	St Philip's Chambers, Birmingham	0121 246 7000
Sandiford Jonathan	St Paul's House, Leeds	0113 245 5866
Sangster Nigel	St Paul's House, Leeds	0113 245 5866
Sarony Neville Leslie		
Savage Miss Ayisha Carol	Britton Street Chambers, London	0171 608 3765
Savill Mark Ashley	Deans Court Chambers, Manchester	0161 834 4097
Sawyer John Frederick		
Saxby Oliver Charles John	• 6 Pump Court, London	0171 797 8400
	• 6-8 Mill Street, Maidstone	01622 688 094
Scott Bell Mrs Rosalind Sara	Trinity Chambers, Newcastle upon Tyne	0191 232 1927
Scott Matthew John	Pump Court Chambers, London	0171 353 0711
	Pump Court Chambers, Winchester	01962 868161
Scott-Phillips Alexander James	Earl Street Chambers, Maidstone	01622 671222
Scutt David Robert	11 Bolt Court, London	0171 353 2300
	Redhill Chambers, Redhill	01737 780781

• Expanded entry in Part D

Seal Julius Damien	189 Randolph Avenue, London	0171 624 9139
	3 Temple Gardens, London	0171 353 0832
Semple Andrew Blair	Sovereign Chambers, Leeds	0113 245 1841/2/3
Seymour Mark William	9-12 Bell Yard, London	0171 400 1800
Shaikh Eur.Ing. (Jaikumar) Christopher (Samuel	Avondale Chambers, London	0181 445 9984
	Equity Chambers, Birmingham	0121 233 2100
Sharma Bhawani Persaud	Primrose Chambers, Alperton	0181 998 1806
Sharma Miss Rakhee	Kingsway Chambers, London	07000 653529
Shay Stephen Everett	One King's Bench Walk, London	0171 936 1500
Shorrock John Michael	Peel Court Chambers, Manchester	0161 832 3791
Sidhu-Brar Nisharn Singh	6 Gray's Inn Square, London	0171 242 1052
Sinclair-Morris Charles Robert	9 Woodhouse Square, Leeds	0113 245 1986
Singh Balbir	• Equity Chambers, Birmingham	0121 233 2100
Sleeman Miss Rachel Sarah Elizabeth	One Essex Court, London	0171 936 3030
Smith Jason	25-27 Castle Street, Liverpool	0151 227 5661/5666/236 5072
Smith Matthew Robert	Sovereign Chambers, Leeds	0113 245 1841/2/3
Smith Ms Zoe Philippa	Hardwicke Building, London	0171 242 2523
Somerset Jones Eric	Goldsmith Building, London	0171 353 7881
Sparks Miss Jocelyn Margaret	Queen Elizabeth Building, London	0171 583 5766
Sparks Kevin Laurence	Earl Street Chambers, Maidstone	01622 671222
Spencer James	11 King's Bench Walk, London	0171 353 3337/8
	11 King's Bench Walk, Leeds	0113 2971 200
Spink Peter John William	5 Essex Court, London	0171 410 2000
Spollon Guy Merton	St Philip's Chambers, Birmingham	0121 246 7000
St Louis Brian Lloyd	Hardwicke Building, London	0171 242 2523
Standfast Philip Arthur	St Paul's House, Leeds	0113 245 5866
Stanislas Paul Junior	Somersett Chambers, London	0171 404 6701
Stead Miss Kate Rebecca	Barristers' Common Law Chambers, London	0171 375 3012
Stern Ian Michael	Queen Elizabeth Building, London	0171 583 5766
Stewart Neill Alastair	Queen Elizabeth Building, London	0171 583 5766
Stilgoe Rufus Nathaniel Abbott	23 Essex Street, London	0171 413 0353
Still Geoffrey John Churchill	Pump Court Chambers, London	0171 353 0711
	Pump Court Chambers, Winchester	01962 868161
Stokes David Mayhew Allen	5 Paper Buildings, London	0171 583 6117
	Fenners Chambers, Cambridge	01223 368761
Storey Thomas Sebastian	Chambers of Andrew Campbell QC, Leeds	0113 245 5438
Strickland Miss Clare Elizabeth	23 Essex Street, London	0171 413 0353
Strudwick Miss Linda Diane	Queen Elizabeth Building, London	0171 583 5766
Stubbs Andrew James	St Paul's House, Leeds	0113 245 5866
Suckling Alan Blair	Queen Elizabeth Building, London	0171 583 5766
Sullivan Ms Jane Teresa	Queen Elizabeth Building, London	0171 583 5766
Summers Benjamin Dylan James	Queen Elizabeth Building, London	0171 583 5766
Sutherland Williams Mark	4 King's Bench Walk, London	0171 822 8822
	King's Bench Chambers, Bournemouth	01202 250025
Sutton Richard William Wallace	Chambers of Andrew Campbell QC, Leeds	0113 245 5438
Swain Miss Hannah	23 Essex Street, London	0171 413 0353
Talbot Richard Kevin Kent	Deans Court Chambers, Manchester	0161 834 4097
	Deans Court Chambers, Preston	01772 555163
Tedd Rex Hilary	• St Philip's Chambers, Birmingham	0121 246 7000
	• 22 Albion Place, Northampton	01604 636271
Temple Simon Ernest William	Chambers of John Hand QC, Manchester	0161 955 9000
Temple Victor Bevis Afamado	6 King's Bench Walk, London	0171 583 0410
Temple-Bone Miss Gillian Elizabeth	7 Stone Buildings, London	0171 242 0961
Thomas Stephen Edward Owen	St Philip's Chambers, Birmingham	0121 246 7000
Thompson Lyall Norris	Tindal Chambers, Chelmsford	01245 267742
	Tindal Chambers, St Albans	01727 843383
Thorne Timothy Peter	33 Bedford Row, London	0171 242 6476
Thornton Miss Anne Rebecca	9 Woodhouse Square, Leeds	0113 245 1986
Toal David John	Old Colony House, Manchester	0161 834 4364
Townend James Barrie Stanley	One King's Bench Walk, London	0171 936 1500
Travers Hugh	Pump Court Chambers, London	0171 353 0711
	Pump Court Chambers, Winchester	01962 868161
Treacy Colman Maurice	Chambers of James Hunt QC, London	0171 421 8000
	3 Fountain Court, Birmingham	0121 236 5854
Turner James	One King's Bench Walk, London	0171 936 1500

• Expanded entry in Part D

Turner Jonathan Chadwick	6 King's Bench Walk, London	0171 583 0410
Twana Ekwall Singh	New Court Chambers, Birmingham	0121 693 6656
Valks Michael	King's Chambers, Eastbourne	01323 416053
Vincent Miss Ruth Carolyn	Colleton Chambers, Exeter	01392 274898
Vine James Peter Stockman	Hardwicke Building, London	0171 242 2523
Volz Karl Andrew	Chambers of Geoffrey Hawker, London	0171 583 8899
Wakeham Philip John Le Messurier	Hardwicke Building, London	0171 242 2523
Waley Eric Richard Thomas	Assize Court Chambers, Bristol	0117 926 4587
Walker Allister David	5 Pump Court, London	0171 353 2532
Walters Gareth Rupel	St Philip's Chambers, Birmingham	0121 246 7000
Walters Geraint Wyn	Angel Chambers, Swansea	01792 464623/464648
Warne Peter Lawrence	Queen Elizabeth Building, London	0171 583 5766
Warner Anthony Charles Broughton	St Philip's Chambers, Birmingham	0121 246 7000
Warren Philip David Charles	Assize Court Chambers, Bristol	0117 926 4587
Wastie William Granville	Queen Elizabeth Building, London	0171 583 5766
Watson Miss Kirstie Ann	St Paul's House, Leeds	0113 245 5866
Watson Mark	6 Pump Court, London	0171 797 8400
	6-8 Mill Street, Maidstone	01622 688 094
Watts Lawrence Peter	St Philip's Chambers, Birmingham	0121 246 7000
West Michael Charles Beresford	8 Lambert Jones Mews, London	0171 638 8804
	3 & 4 Farnham Hall, Saxmundham	01728 602758
White Darren Paul	Cathedral Chambers (Jan Wood Independent Barristers' Clerk), Exeter	01392 210900
Wilcken Anthony David Felix	Queen Elizabeth Building, London	0171 583 5766
Wilkinson Michael John	Trinity Chambers, Newcastle upon Tyne	0191 232 1927
Williams Hugh David Haydn	St Philip's Chambers, Birmingham	0121 246 7000
Williams John Griffith	Goldsmith Building, London	0171 353 7881
	33 Park Place, Cardiff	01222 233313
Williams Thomas Ellis	30 Park Place, Cardiff	01222 398421
Wilson (Alan) Martin	No 1 Serjeants' Inn, London	0171 415 6666
	Priory Chambers, Birmingham	0121 236 3882/1375
Wilson Alasdair John	Fenners Chambers, Cambridge	01223 368761
	Fenners Chambers, Peterborough	01733 562030
Wilson Andrew Robert	9 Woodhouse Square, Leeds	0113 245 1986
Wilson James Mason	Fenners Chambers, Cambridge	01223 368761
	Fenners Chambers, Peterborough	01733 562030
Wilson Peter Julian		
Winter Ian David	Queen Elizabeth Building, London	0171 583 5766
Wood Michael Mure	23 Essex Street, London	0171 413 0353
Wood Nicholas Andrew	5 Paper Buildings, London	0171 583 9275
Woodbridge Julian Guy	One King's Bench Walk, London	0171 936 1500
Woodward Nicholas Frederick	White Friars Chambers, Chester	01244 323070
Woolman Andrew Paul Lander	Chambers of Andrew Campbell QC, Leeds	0113 245 5438
Wordsworth Mrs Philippa Lindsey	Chambers of Andrew Campbell QC, Leeds	0113 245 5438
Worrall John Raymond Guy	Chambers of Andrew Campbell QC, Leeds	0113 245 5438
Wright Miss Clare Elizabeth	6 Pump Court, London	0171 797 8400
Wright Gerard Henry	25-27 Castle Street, Liverpool	0151 227 5661/5666/236 5072
Wright Norman Alfred	Oriel Chambers, Liverpool	0151 236 7191
Wyatt Guy Peter James	Earl Street Chambers, Maidstone	01622 671222
Yelton Michael Paul	Fenners Chambers, Cambridge	01223 368761
	Fenners Chambers, Peterborough	01733 562030
Yeung Stuart Roy	22 Albion Place, Northampton	01604 636271

CRIME - CORPORATE FRAUD

Abbott Francis Arthur	Pump Court Chambers, London	0171 353 0711
	Pump Court Chambers, Winchester	01962 868161
Acheson Robert Ian	23 Essex Street, London	0171 413 0353
Al'Hassan Khadim	Equity Chambers, Birmingham	0121 233 2100
Aldred Mark Steven	Queen Elizabeth Building, London	0171 583 5766
Alexander Ian Douglas Gavin	11 Bolt Court, London	0171 353 2300
	Redhill Chambers, Redhill	01737 780781
Andrews Miss Claire Marguerite	Gough Square Chambers, London	0171 353 0924
Ascherson Miss Isobel Ruth	23 Essex Street, London	0171 413 0353
Austin-Smith Michael Gerard	23 Essex Street, London	0171 413 0353
Aylett Kenneth George	New Chambers, St Albans	0966 212126
Badley Miss Pamela Hilary	25-27 Castle Street, Liverpool	0151 227 5661/5666/236 5072

Barnett Andrew John	Pump Court Chambers, London	0171 353 0711
	Pump Court Chambers, Winchester	01962 868161
Barnett Jeremy Victor	Farrar's Building, London	0171 583 9241
	St Paul's House, Leeds	0113 245 5866
Barnfather Miss Lydia Helen	Queen Elizabeth Building, London	0171 583 5766
Barraclough Anthony Roger	25-27 Castle Street, Liverpool	0151 227 5661/5666/236 5072
Bassra Sukhbir Singh	St Paul's House, Leeds	0113 245 5866
Bate David Christopher	Queen Elizabeth Building, London	0171 583 5766
Bates Alexander Andrew	St Paul's House, Leeds	0113 245 5866
Bendall Richard Giles	33 Bedford Row, London	0171 242 6476
Bennetts Philip James	Queen Elizabeth Building, London	0171 583 5766
Benson Peter Charles	St Paul's House, Leeds	0113 245 5866
Bevan Edward Julian	Queen Elizabeth Building, London	0171 583 5766
Birch Roger Allen	12 New Square, London	0171 419 1212
	Sovereign Chambers, Leeds	0113 245 1841/2/3
	Lancaster Buildings, Manchester	0161 661 4444
Birnbaum Michael Ian	9-12 Bell Yard, London	0171 400 1800
	New Court Chambers, Birmingham	0121 693 6656
Blackburn Luke Sebastian	7 New Square, London	0171 430 1660
Blair William James Lynton	3 Verulam Buildings, London	0171 831 8441
Bogan Paul Simon	Doughty Street Chambers, London	0171 404 1313
Boney Guy Thomas Knowles	Pump Court Chambers, London	0171 353 0711
	Harrow-on-the-Hill Chambers, Harrow on the Hill	0181 423 7444
	Pump Court Chambers, Winchester	01962 868161
Boyce William	Queen Elizabeth Building, London	0171 583 5766
Brompton Michael John	New Court Chambers, London	0171 831 9500
Brown Edward Francis Trevenen	Queen Elizabeth Building, London	0171 583 5766
Browne James Nicholas	No 1 Serjeants' Inn, London	0171 415 6666
Bryant-Heron Mark Nicholas	9-12 Bell Yard, London	0171 400 1800
Burbidge James Michael	St Philip's Chambers, Birmingham	0121 246 7000
Butt Miss Romasa	Goldsworth Chambers, London	0171 405 7117
Byers The Hon Charles William	23 Essex Street, London	0171 413 0353
Byrne Garrett Thomas	23 Essex Street, London	0171 413 0353
Cadwallader Peter	Chambers of John Hand QC, Manchester	0161 955 9000
Calvert-Smith David	Queen Elizabeth Building, London	0171 583 5766
Carlile Alexander Charles	9-12 Bell Yard, London	0171 400 1800
	Sedan House, Chester	01244 320480/348282
Carlisle of Bucklow The Rt Hon Lord	Queen Elizabeth Building, London	0171 583 5766
	18 St John Street, Manchester	0161 278 1800
Carter William Andrew	23 Essex Street, London	0171 413 0353
Carus Roderick	Chambers of John Hand QC, Manchester	0161 955 9000
Carville Owen Brendan Neville	25-27 Castle Street, Liverpool	0151 227 5661/5666/236 5072
Challinor Robert Michael	St Philip's Chambers, Birmingham	0121 246 7000
Chawla Mukul	9-12 Bell Yard, London	0171 400 1800
Clark Christopher Harvey	Pump Court Chambers, London	0171 353 0711
	Westgate Chambers, Lewes	01273 480 510
	Pump Court Chambers, Winchester	01962 868161
Clarke Nicholas Stephen	Chambers of John Hand QC, Manchester	0161 955 9000
Clarke Peter William	Queen Elizabeth Building, London	0171 583 5766
Cottage Miss Rosina	9-12 Bell Yard, London	0171 400 1800
Coward Miss Victoria Jane	Queen Elizabeth Building, London	0171 583 5766
Cranbrook Alexander Douglas John	9-12 Bell Yard, London	0171 400 1800
Cranston-Morris Wayne	23 Essex Street, London	0171 413 0353
Crowson Howard Keith	St Paul's House, Leeds	0113 245 5866
Cutts Miss Johannah	23 Essex Street, London	0171 413 0353
Dallas Andrew Thomas Alastair	Chambers of Andrew Campbell QC, Leeds	0113 245 5438
Darbishire Adrian Munro	Queen Elizabeth Building, London	0171 583 5766
Davis Richard Simon	23 Essex Street, London	0171 413 0353
Davis William Easthope	St Philip's Chambers, Birmingham	0121 246 7000
Denney Stuart Henry Macdonald	Deans Court Chambers, Manchester	0161 834 4097
	Deans Court Chambers, Preston	01772 555163
Donne Jeremy Nigel	Queen Elizabeth Building, London	0171 583 5766
Doyle Peter John	9-12 Bell Yard, London	0171 400 1800
Duffy Derek James	St Paul's House, Leeds	0113 245 5866
Duffy Michael	Cathedral Chambers, Ely, Ely	01353 666775
Eccles Hugh William Patrick	Harcourt Chambers, London	0171 353 6961/7

         • Expanded entry in Part D

	Harcourt Chambers, Oxford	01865 791559
Edwards Miss Susan May	23 Essex Street, London	0171 413 0353
Egan Michael Flynn John	9-12 Bell Yard, London	0171 400 1800
Ellison Mark Christopher	Queen Elizabeth Building, London	0171 583 5766
Evans David Anthony	9-12 Bell Yard, London	0171 400 1800
	Iscoed Chambers, Swansea	01792 652988/9/330
Evans David Howard	Queen Elizabeth Building, London	0171 583 5766
Evans Martin Alan Langham	5 Paper Buildings, London	0171 583 6117
Fenhalls Mark Roydon Allen	23 Essex Street, London	0171 413 0353
Field Martin Charles	9-12 Bell Yard, London	0171 400 1800
Field Rory Dominic	Hardwicke Building, London	0171 242 2523
Finnigan Peter Anthony	Queen Elizabeth Building, London	0171 583 5766
Finucane Brendan Godfrey Eamonn	23 Essex Street, London	0171 413 0353
Fisher Jonathan Simon	• 18 Red Lion Court, London	0171 520 6000
	• Thornwood House, Chelmsford	01245 280880
Florida-James Mark	• King's Bench Chambers, Bournemouth	01202 250025
Forlin Gerard Emlyn	Phoenix Chambers, London	0171 404 7888
Forster Brian Clive	Trinity Chambers, Newcastle upon Tyne	0191 232 1927
Friesner David Jonathan	Chambers of John Hand QC, Manchester	0161 955 9000
Gale Michael	One King's Bench Walk, London	0171 936 1500
Gallagher John David Edmund	Goldsmith Building, London	0171 353 7881
Garlick Paul Richard	Pump Court Chambers, London	0171 353 0711
	Pump Court Chambers, Winchester	01962 868161
Garside Charles Roger	Chambers of John Hand QC, Manchester	0161 955 9000
Gau Justin Charles	Pump Court Chambers, London	0171 353 0711
	Pump Court Chambers, Winchester	01962 868161
Gillibrand Philip Martin Mangnall	Pump Court Chambers, London	0171 353 0711
	Pump Court Chambers, Winchester	01962 868161
Glass Anthony Trevor	Queen Elizabeth Building, London	0171 583 5766
Glynn Miss Joanna Elizabeth	23 Essex Street, London	0171 413 0353
Goulding Jonathan Steven	Gough Square Chambers, London	0171 353 0924
Gower Peter John de Peauly	6 Pump Court, London	0171 797 8400
	6-8 Mill Street, Maidstone	01622 688 094
Gregory John Raymond	Deans Court Chambers, Manchester	0161 834 4097
	Deans Court Chambers, Preston	01772 555163
Grey Robin Douglas	Queen Elizabeth Building, London	0171 583 5766
Griffiths (John) Peter (Gwynne)	30 Park Place, Cardiff	01222 398421
Gullick Stephen John	Sovereign Chambers, Leeds	0113 245 1841/2/3
Gupta Miss Usha	New Chambers, St Albans	0966 212126
Hacking Anthony Stephen	One King's Bench Walk, London	0171 936 1500
Hadrill Keith Paul	9-12 Bell Yard, London	0171 400 1800
Hallett Miss Heather Carol	23 Essex Street, London	0171 413 0353
Hamer Michael Howard Kenneth	2 Harcourt Buildings, London	0171 583 9020
	Westgate Chambers, Lewes	01273 480 510
Hamilton Graeme Montagu	Two Crown Office Row, London	0171 797 8100
Hamilton Jaime Richard	Chambers of John Hand QC, Manchester	0161 955 9000
Harris Ian Robert	25-27 Castle Street, Liverpool	0151 227 5661/5666/236 5072
Hatton Andrew John	Plowden Buildings, London	0171 583 0808
	Paradise Square Chambers, Sheffield	0114 273 8951
Hawkesworth (Walter) Gareth	5 Paper Buildings, London	0171 583 6117
	Fenners Chambers, Cambridge	01223 368761
	Fenners Chambers, Peterborough	01733 562030
Haygarth Edmund Bruce	25-27 Castle Street, Liverpool	0151 227 5661/5666/236 5072
Haynes Peter	St Philip's Chambers, Birmingham	0121 246 7000
Hegarty Kevin John	St Philip's Chambers, Birmingham	0121 246 7000
Henry Edward Joseph Aloysius	Queen Elizabeth Building, London	0171 583 5766
Heslop Martin Sydney	1 Hare Court, London	0171 353 3982/5324
Hibbert William John	Gough Square Chambers, London	0171 353 0924
Hill (Eliot) Michael	23 Essex Street, London	0171 413 0353
Hilton Alan John Howard	Queen Elizabeth Building, London	0171 583 5766
Hollingworth Peter James Michael	22 Albion Place, Northampton	01604 636271
Horlick Lady Fiona	23 Essex Street, London	0171 413 0353
Horwell Richard Eric	Queen Elizabeth Building, London	0171 583 5766
Hotten Keith Robert	23 Essex Street, London	0171 413 0353
Hughes Thomas Merfyn	Goldsmith Building, London	0171 353 7881
	40 King Street, Chester	01244 323886

Hull Leslie David	Chambers of John Hand QC, Manchester	0161 955 9000
Hurst Brian	17 Bedford Row, London	0171 831 7314
James Roderick Morrice	23 Essex Street, London	0171 413 0353
James Simon John	Chambers of John Hand QC, Manchester	0161 955 9000
Janner Daniel Joseph Mitchell	23 Essex Street, London	0171 413 0353
Jeffreys David Alfred	Queen Elizabeth Building, London	0171 583 5766
Johnson Steven	Chambers of John Hand QC, Manchester	0161 955 9000
Johnson Miss Zoe Elisabeth	Queen Elizabeth Building, London	0171 583 5766
Jones William John	1 Hare Court, London	0171 353 3982/5324
Kark Thomas Victor William	Queen Elizabeth Building, London	0171 583 5766
Katrak Cyrus Pesi	Gough Square Chambers, London	0171 353 0924
Katz Philip Alec Jackson	9-12 Bell Yard, London	0171 400 1800
Kearl Guy Alexander	St Paul's House, Leeds	0113 245 5866
Keeley James Francis	Sovereign Chambers, Leeds	0113 245 1841/2/3
Kelsey-Fry John	Queen Elizabeth Building, London	0171 583 5766
Kenning Thomas Patrick	New Court Chambers, Birmingham	0121 693 6656
Khan Ashraf	A K Chambers, Hull	01482 641180
Khan Miss Helen Mary Grace	Chambers of Lord Campbell of Alloway QC, London	0171 353 9276
Kinch Christopher Anthony	23 Essex Street, London	0171 413 0353
Knight Christopher Michael St John	Chambers of John Hand QC, Manchester	0161 955 9000
Kramer Stephen Ernest	• 1 Hare Court, London	0171 353 3982/5324
Kyte Peter Eric	Queen Elizabeth Building, London	0171 583 5766
Lane David Goodwin	11 Bolt Court, London	0171 353 2300
	All Saints Chambers, Bristol	0117 921 1966
Langdale Timothy James	Queen Elizabeth Building, London	0171 583 5766
Larkin Sean	Queen Elizabeth Building, London	0171 583 5766
Lawrence Sir Ivan John	One Essex Court, London	0171 936 3030
Lawson Edmund James	9-12 Bell Yard, London	0171 400 1800
Lawson Michael Henry	23 Essex Street, London	0171 413 0353
Lawson Rogers George Stuart	23 Essex Street, London	0171 413 0353
Leeming Michael Peter George	Chambers of John Hand QC, Manchester	0161 955 9000
Lees Andrew James	St Paul's House, Leeds	0113 245 5866
Lewis Paul Keith	30 Park Place, Cardiff	01222 398421
Litherland Miss Rebecca Jane	Fenners Chambers, Cambridge	01223 368761
	Fenners Chambers, Peterborough	01733 562030
Llewellyn-Jones Christopher Geoffrey	Goldsmith Building, London	0171 353 7881
	9 Park Place, Cardiff	01222 382731
Longden Anthony Gordon	Queen Elizabeth Building, London	0171 583 5766
Lowry Miss Emma Margaret Collins	Queen Elizabeth Building, London	0171 583 5766
Lynagh Richard Dudley	Two Crown Office Row, London	0171 797 8100
Mandel Richard	11 Bolt Court, London	0171 353 2300
	Redhill Chambers, Redhill	01737 780781
Manson Miss Julie-Ann	11 Bolt Court, London	0171 353 2300
	Redhill Chambers, Redhill	01737 780781
Marson Geoffrey Charles	Sovereign Chambers, Leeds	0113 245 1841/2/3
Mason Ian Douglas	11 Bolt Court, London	0171 353 2300
	Redhill Chambers, Redhill	01737 780781
McGuinness John Francis	9-12 Bell Yard, London	0171 400 1800
McIvor Ian Walker	334 Deansgate Chambers, Manchester	0161 834 3767
McKinnon Warwick Nairn	Queen Elizabeth Building, London	0171 583 5766
Medland Simon Edward	23 Essex Street, London	0171 413 0353
Merz Richard James	9-12 Bell Yard, London	0171 400 1800
Miller Miss Jane Elizabeth Mackay	Pump Court Chambers, London	0171 353 0711
	Pump Court Chambers, Winchester	01962 868161
Millett Kenneth James	1 Hare Court, London	0171 353 3982/5324
Milne Richard James	23 Essex Street, London	0171 413 0353
Miskin Charles James Monckton	23 Essex Street, London	0171 413 0353
Mitchell Christopher Richard	Queen Elizabeth Building, London	0171 583 5766
Montgomery Robert Michael	Pump Court Chambers, London	0171 353 0711
	Chavasse Court Chambers, Liverpool	0151 707 1191
	Pump Court Chambers, Winchester	01962 868161
Morley Iain Charles	1 Hare Court, London	0171 353 3982/5324
Muir John Henry	12 New Square, London	0171 419 1212
	Sovereign Chambers, Leeds	0113 245 1841/2/3
Mullen Patrick Anthony	One Essex Court, London	0171 936 3030

B

• Expanded entry in Part D

Muller Franz Joseph	11 King's Bench Walk, London	0171 353 3337/8
	11 King's Bench Walk, Leeds	0113 2971 200
Murray John Michael Andrew	Chambers of John Hand QC, Manchester	0161 955 9000
Newbury Richard Lennox	Sovereign Chambers, Leeds	0113 245 1841/2/3
Newman Miss Catherine Mary	• 13 Old Square, London	0171 404 4800
Nicholson Pratt Thomas Hycy	Hardwicke Building, London	0171 242 2523
Nicolson Aris Tony	23 Bracken Gardens, London	0181 748 4924
Norton Miss Heather Sophia	23 Essex Street, London	0171 413 0353
Nsugbe Oba Eric	Pump Court Chambers, London	0171 353 0711
	Pump Court Chambers, Winchester	01962 868161
O'Neill Brian Patrick	1 Hare Court, London	0171 353 3982/5324
Oke Olanrewaju Oladipupo	Kingsway Chambers, London	07000 653529
Oliver Michael Richard	Hardwicke Building, London	0171 242 2523
Ozin Paul David	23 Essex Street, London	0171 413 0353
Pardoe Rupert Adam Corin	23 Essex Street, London	0171 413 0353
Pascoe Nigel Spencer Knight	Pump Court Chambers, London	0171 353 0711
	All Saints Chambers, Bristol	0117 921 1966
	Pump Court Chambers, Winchester	01962 868161
Paton Ian Francis	Queen Elizabeth Building, London	0171 583 5766
Patterson Norman William	14 Gray's Inn Square, London	0171 242 0858
Patterson Stewart	• Pump Court Chambers, London	0171 353 0711
	• Pump Court Chambers, Winchester	01962 868161
Peglow Dr Michael Alfred Herman	Chambers of Geoffrey Hawker, London	0171 583 8899
Pelling (Philip) Mark	Monckton Chambers, London	0171 405 7211
Peters Nigel Melvin	18 Red Lion Court, London	0171 520 6000
	Thornwood House, Chelmsford	01245 280880
Plaschkes Ms Sarah Georgina	Queen Elizabeth Building, London	0171 583 5766
Pointon Miss Caroline Jane	Fenners Chambers, Cambridge	01223 368761
	Fenners Chambers, Peterborough	01733 562030
Portnoy Leslie Reuben	Chambers of John Hand QC, Manchester	0161 955 9000
Poulet Mrs Rebecca Maria	Queen Elizabeth Building, London	0171 583 5766
Power Nigel John	25-27 Castle Street, Liverpool	0151 227 5661/5666/236 5072
Powis Miss Samantha Inez	St Philip's Chambers, Birmingham	0121 246 7000
Price Albert John	23 Essex Street, London	0171 413 0353
Purnell Nicholas Robert	23 Essex Street, London	0171 413 0353
Ramasamy Selvaraju	Queen Elizabeth Building, London	0171 583 5766
Randall John Yeoman	7 Stone Buildings, London	0171 405 3886/242 3546
	St Philip's Chambers, Birmingham	0121 246 7000
Redgrave Adrian Robert Frank	No 1 Serjeants' Inn, London	0171 415 6666
Rees Gareth David	Queen Elizabeth Building, London	0171 583 5766
Richardson (Peter) James	23 Essex Street, London	0171 413 0353
Rigby Terence	Chambers of John Hand QC, Manchester	0161 955 9000
Robertson Andrew James	11 King's Bench Walk, London	0171 353 3337/8
	11 King's Bench Walk, Leeds	0113 2971 200
Robinson Vivian	Queen Elizabeth Building, London	0171 583 5766
Rose Jonathan Lee	St Paul's House, Leeds	0113 245 5866
Russell Anthony Patrick	Peel Court Chambers, Manchester	0161 832 3791
Russell Miss Christina Martha	9-12 Bell Yard, London	0171 400 1800
Russell Flint Simon Coleridge	23 Essex Street, London	0171 413 0353
Ryan David Patrick	Chambers of Geoffrey Hawker, London	0171 583 8899
Saffian Ms Leah Susan	Queen Elizabeth Building, London	0171 583 5766
Sampson Graeme William	Chambers of Geoffrey Hawker, London	0171 583 8899
Sangster Nigel	St Paul's House, Leeds	0113 245 5866
Sarony Neville Leslie		
Sawyer John Frederick		
Sayer Mr Peter Edwin	Gough Square Chambers, London	0171 353 0924
Scott Matthew John	Pump Court Chambers, London	0171 353 0711
	Pump Court Chambers, Winchester	01962 868161
Scutt David Robert	11 Bolt Court, London	0171 353 2300
	Redhill Chambers, Redhill	01737 780781
Seal Julius Damien	189 Randolph Avenue, London	0171 624 9139
	3 Temple Gardens, London	0171 353 0832
Seymour Richard William	Monckton Chambers, London	0171 405 7211
Shaikh Eur.Ing. (Jaikumar) Christopher (Samuel	Avondale Chambers, London	0181 445 9984
	Equity Chambers, Birmingham	0121 233 2100

Shorrock John Michael	Peel Court Chambers, Manchester	0161 832 3791
Singh Balbir	• Equity Chambers, Birmingham	0121 233 2100
Smith Ms Zoe Philippa	Hardwicke Building, London	0171 242 2523
Sparks Miss Jocelyn Margaret	Queen Elizabeth Building, London	0171 583 5766
Spencer James	11 King's Bench Walk, London	0171 353 3337/8
	11 King's Bench Walk, Leeds	0113 2971 200
Staddon Miss Claire Ann	12 New Square, London	0171 419 1212
	Sovereign Chambers, Leeds	0113 245 1841/2/3
Stancombe Barry Terrence	Gough Square Chambers, London	0171 353 0924
Stern Ian Michael	Queen Elizabeth Building, London	0171 583 5766
Stewart Neill Alastair	Queen Elizabeth Building, London	0171 583 5766
Still Geoffrey John Churchill	Pump Court Chambers, London	0171 353 0711
	Pump Court Chambers, Winchester	01962 868161
Strudwick Miss Linda Diane	Queen Elizabeth Building, London	0171 583 5766
Stubbs Andrew James	St Paul's House, Leeds	0113 245 5866
Suckling Alan Blair	Queen Elizabeth Building, London	0171 583 5766
Sullivan Ms Jane Teresa	Queen Elizabeth Building, London	0171 583 5766
Summers Benjamin Dylan James	Queen Elizabeth Building, London	0171 583 5766
Tedd Rex Hilary	• St Philip's Chambers, Birmingham	0121 246 7000
	• 22 Albion Place, Northampton	01604 636271
Temple Simon Ernest William	Chambers of John Hand QC, Manchester	0161 955 9000
Temple Victor Bevis Afamado	6 King's Bench Walk, London	0171 583 0410
Thorne Timothy Peter	33 Bedford Row, London	0171 242 6476
Treacy Colman Maurice	Chambers of James Hunt QC, London	0171 421 8000
	3 Fountain Court, Birmingham	0121 236 5854
Turner James	One King's Bench Walk, London	0171 936 1500
Turner Jonathan Chadwick	6 King's Bench Walk, London	0171 583 0410
Vine James Peter Stockman	Hardwicke Building, London	0171 242 2523
Vines Anthony Robert Francis	Gough Square Chambers, London	0171 353 0924
Wadsworth James Patrick	4 Paper Buildings, London	0171 353 3366/583 7155
Wakeham Philip John Le Messurier	Hardwicke Building, London	0171 242 2523
Walters Gareth Rupel	St Philip's Chambers, Birmingham	0121 246 7000
Warne Peter Lawrence	Queen Elizabeth Building, London	0171 583 5766
Warner Anthony Charles Broughton	St Philip's Chambers, Birmingham	0121 246 7000
Warren Philip David Charles	Assize Court Chambers, Bristol	0117 926 4587
Wastie William Granville	Queen Elizabeth Building, London	0171 583 5766
Watson Miss Kirstie Ann	St Paul's House, Leeds	0113 245 5866
Watts Lawrence Peter	St Philip's Chambers, Birmingham	0121 246 7000
Wilcken Anthony David Felix	Queen Elizabeth Building, London	0171 583 5766
Wilcox Nicholas Hugh	5 Essex Court, London	0171 410 2000
Williams John Griffith	Goldsmith Building, London	0171 353 7881
	33 Park Place, Cardiff	01222 233313
Wilson (Alan) Martin	No 1 Serjeants' Inn, London	0171 415 6666
	Priory Chambers, Birmingham	0121 236 3882/1375
Winter Ian David	Queen Elizabeth Building, London	0171 583 5766
Wood Michael Mure	23 Essex Street, London	0171 413 0353
Wood Nicholas Andrew	5 Paper Buildings, London	0171 583 9275
Woodbridge Julian Guy	One King's Bench Walk, London	0171 936 1500
Worsley Daniel	Stanbrook & Henderson, London	0171 353 0101
	2 Harcourt Buildings, London	0171 583 9020
Wright Gerard Henry	25-27 Castle Street, Liverpool	0151 227 5661/5666/236 5072
Wright Norman Alfred	Oriel Chambers, Liverpool	0151 236 7191

CRIMINAL DEFENCE

Garth Steven David	Sovereign Chambers, Leeds	0113 245 1841/2/3

CUSTOMS & EXCISE WORK

Lawson Rogers George Stuart	23 Essex Street, London	0171 413 0353

DAMAGES

McGregor Harvey	4 Paper Buildings, London	0171 353 3366/583 7155

DEFAMATION

Berragan (Howard) Neil	Merchant Chambers, Manchester	0161 839 7070
Browne James William	Goldsworth Chambers, London	0171 405 7117
Carman George Alfred	New Court Chambers, London	0171 831 9500
Cash Miss Joanne Catherine	Farrar's Building, London	0171 583 9241
Craig Kenneth Allen	Hardwicke Building, London	0171 242 2523
Donovan Joel	New Court Chambers, London	0171 831 9500

• Expanded entry in Part D

Fitzgerald John Vincent	New Court, London	0171 797 8999
Foster Charles Andrew	• Chambers of Kieran Coonan QC, London	0171 583 6013/2510
Franklin Stephen Hall	5 Paper Buildings, London	0171 583 6117
	Fenners Chambers, Cambridge	01223 368761
Gorna Miss Anne Christina	4 Paper Buildings, London	0171 353 3366/583 7155
	Cathedral Chambers (Jan Wood Independent Barristers' Clerk), Exeter	01392 210900
Graham Thomas Patrick Henry	Lamb Chambers, London	0171 797 8300
Gray Charles Anthony St John	5 Raymond Buildings, London	0171 242 2902
Harvey Miss Jayne Denise	Goldsworth Chambers, London	0171 405 7117
Heslop Martin Sydney	1 Hare Court, London	0171 353 3982/5324
Hodgson Richard Andrew	New Court, London	0171 797 8999
Hogg The Rt Hon Douglas Martin	4 Paper Buildings, London	0171 353 3366/583 7155
	37 Park Square, Leeds	0113 243 9422
Jenkala Adrian Aleksander	11 Bolt Court, London	0171 353 2300
	Redhill Chambers, Redhill	01737 780781
Kerr Tim Julian	4-5 Gray's Inn Square, London	0171 404 5252
Kolodziej Andrzej Jozef	• Littman Chambers, London	0171 404 4866
Lyne Mark Hilary	One Essex Court, London	0171 936 3030
McCahey Miss Catherine Anne Mary	St Philip's Chambers, Birmingham	0121 246 7000
Merry Hugh Gairns	17 Carlton Crescent, Southampton	01703 320320
Mondair Rashpal Singh	Claremont Chambers, Wolverhampton	01902 426222
Moorman Miss Lucinda Claire	Farrar's Building, London	0171 583 9241
Morris-Coole Christopher	Goldsmith Building, London	0171 353 7881
Moses Miss Rebecca	Barristers' Common Law Chambers, London	0171 375 3012
	Lion Court, London	0171 404 6565
Pascoe Nigel Spencer Knight	Pump Court Chambers, London	0171 353 0711
	All Saints Chambers, Bristol	0117 921 1966
	Pump Court Chambers, Winchester	01962 868161
Pearson Thomas Adam Spenser	Pump Court Chambers, London	0171 353 0711
	Pump Court Chambers, Winchester	01962 868161
Pershad Rohan	Two Crown Office Row, London	0171 797 8100
Peters Nigel Melvin	18 Red Lion Court, London	0171 520 6000
	Thornwood House, Chelmsford	01245 280880
Rahman Muhammad Altafur	Barristers' Common Law Chambers, London	0171 375 3012
Shaikh Eur.Ing. (Jaikumar) Christopher (Samuel	Avondale Chambers, London	0181 445 9984
	Equity Chambers, Birmingham	0121 233 2100
Stewart Nicholas John Cameron	Hardwicke Building, London	0171 242 2523
Tomlinson Hugh Richard Edward	New Court Chambers, London	0171 831 9500
Vater John Alistair Pitt	Harcourt Chambers, London	0171 353 6961/7
Wakefield Miss Anne Prudence	3 Verulam Buildings, London	0171 831 8441
Waters Julian William Penrose	No 1 Serjeants' Inn, London	0171 415 6666
Wright Gerard Henry	25-27 Castle Street, Liverpool	0151 227 5661/5666/236 5072

DIRECTORS' DISQUALIFICATION

Alexander Ian Douglas Gavin	11 Bolt Court, London	0171 353 2300
	Redhill Chambers, Redhill	01737 780781
Jackson Dirik George Allan	• Chambers of Mr Peter Crampin QC, London	0171 831 0081

DISCIPLINARY TRIBUNALS

Bennetts Philip James	Queen Elizabeth Building, London	0171 583 5766
Kark Thomas Victor William	Queen Elizabeth Building, London	0171 583 5766
Kelsey-Fry John	Queen Elizabeth Building, London	0171 583 5766
Kerr Tim Julian	4-5 Gray's Inn Square, London	0171 404 5252
Mitchell Christopher Richard	Queen Elizabeth Building, London	0171 583 5766
Sparks Miss Jocelyn Margaret	Queen Elizabeth Building, London	0171 583 5766
Stern Ian Michael	Queen Elizabeth Building, London	0171 583 5766
Sullivan Ms Jane Teresa	Queen Elizabeth Building, London	0171 583 5766
Winter Ian David	Queen Elizabeth Building, London	0171 583 5766

DISCRIMINATION

Al'Hassan Khadim	Equity Chambers, Birmingham	0121 233 2100
Baxter Gerald Pearson	25-27 Castle Street, Liverpool	0151 227 5661/5666/236 5072
Bendall Richard Giles	33 Bedford Row, London	0171 242 6476

Benner Miss Lucinda Diana Kate	11 Bolt Court, London	0171 353 2300
	Redhill Chambers, Redhill	01737 780781
Bhattacharyya Ardhendu	1 Gray's Inn Square, London	0171 405 8946
	11 St Bernards Road, Slough	01753 553806/817989
Birtles William	Old Square Chambers, London	0171 269 0300
	Old Square Chambers, Bristol	0117 927 7111
Bradley Miss Clodagh Maria	3 Serjeants' Inn, London	0171 353 5537
Bradley Richard	Oriel Chambers, Liverpool	0151 236 7191
Breen Carlo Enrico	Chambers of John Hand QC, Manchester	0161 955 9000
Brown Damian Robert	• Old Square Chambers, London	0171 269 0300
	• Old Square Chambers, Bristol	0117 927 7111
Cape Robert Paul	Milburn House Chambers, Newcastle upon Tyne	0191 230 5511
Carrodus Miss Gail Caroline	New Court Chambers, London	0171 831 9500
Cartwright Richard John	Queen Elizabeth Building, London	0171 353 7181 (12 lines)
Choudhury Akhlaq	11 King's Bench Walk, London	0171 632 8500
Chudleigh Miss Louise Katrina	Old Square Chambers, London	0171 269 0300
	Old Square Chambers, Bristol	0117 927 7111
Clark Miss Hazel Anne	Fenners Chambers, Cambridge	01223 368761
	Fenners Chambers, Peterborough	01733 562030
Clay Jonathan Roger	11 Bolt Court, London	0171 353 2300
	Redhill Chambers, Redhill	01737 780781
Cowen Miss Sally Emma	Chambers of Geoffrey Hawker, London	0171 583 8899
Dashwood Professor Arthur Alan	Stanbrook & Henderson, London	0171 353 0101
	2 Harcourt Buildings, London	0171 583 9020
Davies Miss Penny May	Chambers of Harjit Singh, London	0171 353 1356
Dean Paul Benjamin	5 Bell Yard, London	0171 333 8811
Dedezade Taner	Tindal Chambers, Chelmsford	01245 267742
Donovan Joel	New Court Chambers, London	0171 831 9500
Doughty Peter	17 Carlton Crescent, Southampton	01703 320320
Dowse John	Chambers of Lord Goodhart QC, London	0171 405 5577
	Chambers of John Hand QC, Manchester	0161 955 9000
Eady Miss Jennifer Jane	Old Square Chambers, London	0171 269 0300
	Old Square Chambers, Bristol	0117 927 7111
Evans Lee John	Farrar's Building, London	0171 583 9241
Fenston Miss Felicia Donovan	Stanbrook & Henderson, London	0171 353 0101
	2 Harcourt Buildings, London	0171 583 9020
Fernandes John Piedade Amaranto Lorencio	• Arcadia Chambers, London	0171 938 1285
French Richard Anthony Lister	Rougemont Chambers, Exeter	01392 410471
Fripp Eric William Burtin	Chambers of Harjit Singh, London	0171 353 1356
Galberg Marc Kay	33 Bedford Row, London	0171 242 6476
George Miss Judith Sarah	St Philip's Chambers, Birmingham	0121 246 7000
Giffin Nigel Dyson	11 King's Bench Walk, London	0171 632 8500
Gilroy Paul	Farrar's Building, London	0171 583 9241
	Chambers of John Hand QC, Manchester	0161 955 9000
Goudie James	• 11 King's Bench Walk, London	0171 632 8500
Gower Miss Helen Clare	Old Square Chambers, London	0171 269 0300
	Old Square Chambers, Bristol	0117 927 7111
Grundy Nigel Lawrence John	Chambers of John Hand QC, Manchester	0161 955 9000
Hand John Lester	Old Square Chambers, London	0171 269 0300
	Old Square Chambers, Bristol	0117 927 7111
	Chambers of John Hand QC, Manchester	0161 955 9000
Hargrove Jeremy John Loveday	Trinity Chambers, Newcastle upon Tyne	0191 232 1927
Harrison Ms Averil	2 Harcourt Buildings, London	0171 583 9020
Herbert Mrs Rebecca Mary	2 New Street, Leicester	0116 262 5906
Hillier Andrew Charles	5 Bell Yard, London	0171 333 8811
Horlock Timothy John	Chambers of John Hand QC, Manchester	0161 955 9000
Hull Leslie David	Chambers of John Hand QC, Manchester	0161 955 9000
Janner Daniel Joseph Mitchell	23 Essex Street, London	0171 413 0353
Jones Sean William Paul	11 King's Bench Walk, London	0171 632 8500

• Expanded entry in Part D

Kennedy Christopher Laurence Paul	Chambers of John Hand QC, Manchester	0161 955 9000
Kenward Timothy David Nelson	25-27 Castle Street, Liverpool	0151 227 5661/5666/236 5072
Kerr Tim Julian	4-5 Gray's Inn Square, London	0171 404 5252
Kimbell John Ashley	5 Bell Yard, London	0171 333 8811
Leiper Richard Thomas	11 King's Bench Walk, London	0171 632 8500
Lennard Stephen Charles	Hardwicke Building, London	0171 242 2523
Lewis Professor Roy Malcolm	Old Square Chambers, London	0171 269 0300
	Old Square Chambers, Bristol	0117 927 7111
Litherland Miss Rebecca Jane	Fenners Chambers, Cambridge	01223 368761
	Fenners Chambers, Peterborough	01733 562030
Marshall Philip Derek	Farrar's Building, London	0171 583 9241
	Iscoed Chambers, Swansea	01792 652988/9/330
McManus Jonathan Richard	4-5 Gray's Inn Square, London	0171 404 5252
McMinn Miss Valerie Kathleen	Baker Street Chambers, Middlesbrough	01642 873873
Mills Simon Thomas	One Essex Court, London	0171 936 3030
Moore James Anthony	2 Gray's Inn Square Chambers, London	0171 242 0328/405 1317
Nicholls Paul Richard	11 King's Bench Walk, London	0171 632 8500
Outhwaite Mrs Wendy-Jane Tivnan	Stanbrook & Henderson, London	0171 353 0101
	2 Harcourt Buildings, London	0171 583 9020
Parkin Jonathan	• Chambers of John Hand QC, Manchester	0161 955 9000
Pitt-Payne Timothy Sheridan	• 11 King's Bench Walk, London	0171 632 8500
Priestley Ms Rebecca Janet	2 Gray's Inn Square Chambers, London	0171 242 0328/405 1317
Prynne Andrew Geoffrey Lockyer	Stanbrook & Henderson, London	0171 353 0101
	2 Harcourt Buildings, London	0171 583 9020
Rahman Ms Sadeqa Shaheen	1 Crown Office Row, London	0171 797 7500
Reynold Frederic	New Court Chambers, London	0171 831 9500
Rogers Ian Paul	1 Crown Office Row, London	0171 583 9292
Sadiq Tariq Mahmood	Chambers of John Hand QC, Manchester	0161 955 9000
Schooling Simon John	Chambers of Harjit Singh, London	0171 353 1356
Segal Oliver Leon	Old Square Chambers, London	0171 269 0300
	Old Square Chambers, Bristol	0117 927 7111
Slade Miss Elizabeth Ann	• 11 King's Bench Walk, London	0171 632 8500
Soor Smair Singh	33 Bedford Row, London	0171 242 6476
Stewart Richard Paul	New Court Chambers, London	0171 831 9500
Stilitz Daniel Malachi	11 King's Bench Walk, London	0171 632 8500
Straker Timothy Derrick	• 2-3 Gray's Inn Square, London	0171 242 4986
Supperstone Michael Alan	11 King's Bench Walk, London	0171 632 8500
Thomson Martin Haldane Ahmad	Wynne Chambers, London	0171 737 7266
Tucker Miss Katherine Jane Greening	St Philip's Chambers, Birmingham	0121 246 7000
Wallington Peter Thomas	11 King's Bench Walk, London	0171 632 8500
Wedderspoon Miss Rachel Leone	Chambers of John Hand QC, Manchester	0161 955 9000
Wheeler Miss Marina Claire	Stanbrook & Henderson, London	0171 353 0101
	2 Harcourt Buildings, London	0171 583 9020
Whitcombe Mark David	Old Square Chambers, London	0171 269 0300
	Old Square Chambers, Bristol	0117 927 7111
Williams Ms Heather Jean	Doughty Street Chambers, London	0171 404 1313
Williams Thomas Ellis	30 Park Place, Cardiff	01222 398421
Wood Richard Michael	Sackville Chambers, Norwich	01603 613516
Woodwark Ms Jane Elizabeth	Milburn House Chambers, Newcastle upon Tyne	0191 230 5511

EASTERN EUROPE

Malecka Dr Mary Margaret	Goldsworth Chambers, London	0171 405 7117

EC AND COMPETITION LAW

Anderson Rupert John	Monckton Chambers, London	0171 405 7211
Beal Kieron Conrad	4 Paper Buildings, London	0171 353 3366/583 7155
Beard Daniel Matthew	Monckton Chambers, London	0171 405 7211
Brent Richard	3 Verulam Buildings, London	0171 831 8441
Colley Dr Peter McLean	• 19 Old Buildings, London	0171 405 2001
Cranfield Peter Anthony	3 Verulam Buildings, London	0171 831 8441
Dashwood Professor Arthur Alan	Stanbrook & Henderson, London	0171 353 0101
	2 Harcourt Buildings, London	0171 583 9020

Drabble Richard John Bloor	4 Breams Buildings, London	0171 353 5835/430 1221
Driscoll Miss Lynn	Sovereign Chambers, Leeds	0113 245 1841/2/3
	Lancaster Buildings, Manchester	0161 661 4444
Edwards Philip Douglas	2 Harcourt Buildings, London	0171 353 8415
Field Richard Alan	11 King's Bench Walk, London	0171 632 8500
Fowler Richard Nicholas	Monckton Chambers, London	0171 405 7211
French Richard Anthony Lister	Rougemont Chambers, Exeter	01392 410471
Gore-Andrews Gavin Angus Russell	Stanbrook & Henderson, London	0171 353 0101
	2 Harcourt Buildings, London	0171 583 9020
Grayson Edward	• 9–12 Bell Yard, London	0171 400 1800
Harris Paul Best	Monckton Chambers, London	0171 405 7211
Harvey Miss Jayne Denise	Goldsworth Chambers, London	0171 405 7117
Haynes Miss Rebecca	Monckton Chambers, London	0171 405 7211
Hicks Michael Charles	• 19 Old Buildings, London	0171 405 2001
Hill Raymond	Monckton Chambers, London	0171 405 7211
Hodgson Richard Andrew	New Court, London	0171 797 8999
Holman Miss Tamsin Perdita	19 Old Buildings, London	0171 405 2001
Jenkala Adrian Aleksander	11 Bolt Court, London	0171 353 2300
	Redhill Chambers, Redhill	01737 780781
Jones Gregory Percy	• 2 Harcourt Buildings, London	0171 353 8415
Jones Sean William Paul	11 King's Bench Walk, London	0171 632 8500
Kerr Tim Julian	4-5 Gray's Inn Square, London	0171 404 5252
Kime Matthew Jonathan	• New Court, London	0171 797 8999
	• Cobden House Chambers, Manchester	0161 833 6000/6001
Kingsland Rt Hon Lord	4 Breams Buildings, London	0171 353 5835/430 1221
Kinnier Andrew John	2 Harcourt Buildings, London	0171 583 9020
Kolodziej Andrzej Jozef	• Littman Chambers, London	0171 404 4866
Lasok Karol Paul Edward	Monckton Chambers, London	0171 405 7211
Leiper Richard Thomas	11 King's Bench Walk, London	0171 632 8500
Macnab Alexander Andrew	Monckton Chambers, London	0171 405 7211
Mantle Peter John	Monckton Chambers, London	0171 405 7211
Marks Jonathan Harold	3 Verulam Buildings, London	0171 831 8441
Masters Miss Sara Alayna	20 Essex Street, London	0171 583 9294
Mathias Miss Anna	11 Bolt Court, London	0171 353 2300
Maurici James Patrick	4 Breams Buildings, London	0171 353 5835/430 1221
McManus Jonathan Richard	4-5 Gray's Inn Square, London	0171 404 5252
Outhwaite Mrs Wendy-Jane Tivnan	Stanbrook & Henderson, London	0171 353 0101
	2 Harcourt Buildings, London	0171 583 9020
Padfield Ms Alison Mary	One Hare Court, London	0171 353 3171
Paines Nicholas Paul Billot	Monckton Chambers, London	0171 405 7211
Parker Kenneth Blades	Monckton Chambers, London	0171 405 7211
Peretz George Michael John		
Pickford Anthony James	Prince Henry's Chambers, London	0171 353 1183/1190
Pimentel Carlos de Serpa Alberto Legg	3 Stone Buildings, London	0171 242 4937/405 8358
Pope David James	3 Verulam Buildings, London	0171 831 8441
Puckrin Cedric Eldred	19 Old Buildings, London	0171 405 2001
Reid Brian Christopher	19 Old Buildings, London	0171 405 2001
Robertson Aidan Malcolm David	Monckton Chambers, London	0171 405 7211
Robinson Miss Alice	4 Breams Buildings, London	0171 353 5835/430 1221
Rogers Ian Paul	1 Crown Office Row, London	0171 583 9292
Roth Peter Marcel	Monckton Chambers, London	0171 405 7211
Sheridan Maurice Bernard Gerard	• 3 Verulam Buildings, London	0171 831 8441
Shipley Norman Graham	• 19 Old Buildings, London	0171 405 2001
Silverleaf Michael	• 11 South Square, London	0171 405 1222
Simor Miss Jessica Margaret Poppaea	Monckton Chambers, London	0171 405 7211
Smith Ms Katherine Emma	Monckton Chambers, London	0171 405 7211
Stewart Nicholas John Cameron	Hardwicke Building, London	0171 242 2523
Sullivan Rory Myles	19 Old Buildings, London	0171 405 2001
Thompson Rhodri William Ralph	Monckton Chambers, London	0171 405 7211
Tucker Miss Katherine Jane Greening	St Philip's Chambers, Birmingham	0121 246 7000
Turner Jonathan David Chattyn	• 4 Field Court, London	0171 440 6900
Turner Jonathan Richard	Monckton Chambers, London	0171 405 7211
Vajda Christopher Stephen	Monckton Chambers, London	0171 405 7211
Ward Miss Siobhan Marie Lucia	11 King's Bench Walk, London	0171 632 8500
Webb Robert Stopford	• 5 Bell Yard, London	0171 333 8811
Wheeler Miss Marina Claire	Stanbrook & Henderson, London	0171 353 0101
	2 Harcourt Buildings, London	0171 583 9020
Williams Rhodri John	30 Park Place, Cardiff	01222 398421

• Expanded entry in Part D

Wilson Alastair James Drysdale	• 19 Old Buildings, London	0171 405 2001
Yell Nicholas Anthony	No 1 Serjeants' Inn, London	0171 415 6666

EC LAW

Cameron Jonathan James O'Grady	3 Verulam Buildings, London	0171 831 8441
Sands Mr Philippe Joseph	3 Verulam Buildings, London	0171 831 8441

ECCLESIASTICAL

Best Stanley Philip	Bracton Chambers, London	0171 242 4248
	Westgate Chambers, Lewes	01273 480 510
	Barnstaple Chambers, Winkleigh	0183 783763
Briden Timothy John	• 8 Stone Buildings, London	0171 831 9881
Cameron Miss Sheila Morag Clark	2 Harcourt Buildings, London	0171 353 8415
Clark Christopher Harvey	Pump Court Chambers, London	0171 353 0711
	Westgate Chambers, Lewes	01273 480 510
	Pump Court Chambers, Winchester	01962 868161
Fookes Robert Lawrence	2 Mitre Court Buildings, London	0171 583 1380
Hands David Richard Granville	4 Breams Buildings, London	0171 353 5835/430 1221
	40 King Street, Manchester	0161 832 9082
Hill Nicholas Mark	Pump Court Chambers, London	0171 353 0711
	Pump Court Chambers, Winchester	01962 868161
Johnson Michael Sloan	Chambers of John Hand QC, Manchester	0161 955 9000
Jordan Andrew	Stanbrook & Henderson, London	0171 353 0101
	2 Harcourt Buildings, London	0171 583 9020
Leeming Ian	Lamb Chambers, London	0171 797 8300
	Chambers of John Hand QC, Manchester	0161 955 9000
McFarlane Andrew Ewart	One King's Bench Walk, London	0171 936 1500
	Priory Chambers, Birmingham	0121 236 3882/1375
Newcombe Andrew Bennett	• 2 Harcourt Buildings, London	0171 353 8415
Ough Dr Richard Norman	• Hardwicke Building, London	0171 242 2523
Pulman George Frederick	• Hardwicke Building, London	0171 242 2523
	• Stour Chambers, Canterbury	01227 764899
Purdie Robert Anthony James	28 Western Road, Oxford	01865 204911
Quint Mrs Joan Francesca Rae	11 Old Square, London	0171 242 5022
Rodgers Miss Doris June	Harcourt Chambers, London	0171 353 6961/7
	Harcourt Chambers, Oxford	01865 791559
Rule Jonathan Daniel	Merchant Chambers, Manchester	0161 839 7070
Turner David George Patrick	14 Gray's Inn Square, London	0171 242 0858

EDUCATION

Alesbury Alun	2 Mitre Court Buildings, London	0171 583 1380
Anderson Anthony John	2 Mitre Court Buildings, London	0171 583 1380
Bartlett George Robert	2 Mitre Court Buildings, London	0171 583 1380
Beaumont Marc Clifford	• Pump Court Chambers, London	0171 353 0711
	• Harrow-on-the-Hill Chambers, Harrow on the Hill	0181 423 7444
	• Pump Court Chambers, Winchester	01962 868161
	• Windsor Barristers' Chambers, Windsor	01753 648 899
Bhattacharyya Ardhendu	1 Gray's Inn Square, London	0171 405 8946
	11 St Bernards Road, Slough	01753 553806/817989
Boyle Christopher Alexander David	2 Mitre Court Buildings, London	0171 583 1380
Burton Nicholas Anthony	2 Mitre Court Buildings, London	0171 583 1380
Crowley Mrs Jane Elizabeth	One Garden Court Family Law Chambers, London	0171 797 7900
	30 Park Place, Cardiff	01222 398421
Dashwood Professor Arthur Alan	Stanbrook & Henderson, London	0171 353 0101
	2 Harcourt Buildings, London	0171 583 9020
de Voghelaere Parr Adam Stephen	2 Mitre Court Buildings, London	0171 583 1380
Drabble Richard John Bloor	4 Breams Buildings, London	0171 353 5835/430 1221
Druce Michael James	2 Mitre Court Buildings, London	0171 583 1380
Edwards Philip Douglas	2 Harcourt Buildings, London	0171 353 8415
Elvidge John Allan	1 Mitre Court Buildings, London	0171 797 7070
Faulks Edward Peter Lawless	No 1 Serjeants' Inn, London	0171 415 6666
Fookes Robert Lawrence	2 Mitre Court Buildings, London	0171 583 1380
Forster Ms Sarah Judith	14 Gray's Inn Square, London	0171 242 0858
	Westgate Chambers, Lewes	01273 480 510
Friel John Anthony	Goldsmith Building, London	0171 353 7881

• Expanded entry in Part D

	Southsea Chambers, Portsmouth	01705 291261
Giffin Nigel Dyson	11 King's Bench Walk, London	0171 632 8500
Glover Richard Michael	2 Mitre Court Buildings, London	0171 583 1380
Gordon Richard John Francis	39 Essex Street, London	0171 832 1111
Gore Andrew Roger	Fenners Chambers, Cambridge	01223 368761
	Fenners Chambers, Peterborough	01733 562030
Goudie James	• 11 King's Bench Walk, London	0171 632 8500
Grey Miss Eleanor Mary Grace	39 Essex Street, London	0171 832 1111
Hall Miss Joanna Mary	14 Gray's Inn Square, London	0171 242 0858
Hay Ms Deborah Jane	Goldsmith Building, London	0171 353 7881
Horton Matthew Bethell	2 Mitre Court Buildings, London	0171 583 1380
Howell John	4 Breams Buildings, London	0171 353 5835/430 1221
Hunter William Quigley	No 1 Serjeants' Inn, London	0171 415 6666
Jones Gregory Percy	• 2 Harcourt Buildings, London	0171 353 8415
Kerr Tim Julian	4-5 Gray's Inn Square, London	0171 404 5252
King Neil Gerald Alexander	2 Mitre Court Buildings, London	0171 583 1380
King Miss Samantha Leonie	14 Gray's Inn Square, London	0171 242 0858
Lewis Robert		
Lieven Ms Nathalie Marie Daniella	4 Breams Buildings, London	0171 353 5835/430 1221
Maclean Alan John	39 Essex Street, London	0171 832 1111
Macpherson The Hon Mary Stewart	2 Mitre Court Buildings, London	0171 583 1380
Malecka Dr Mary Margaret	Goldsworth Chambers, London	0171 405 7117
Maxwell Miss Judith Mary Angela	The Garden House, London	0171 404 6150
McManus Jonathan Richard	4-5 Gray's Inn Square, London	0171 404 5252
McMinn Miss Valerie Kathleen	Baker Street Chambers, Middlesbrough	01642 873873
Moriarty Gerald Evelyn	2 Mitre Court Buildings, London	0171 583 1380
Newton Miss Claire Elaine Maria Bailey	Goldsmith Building, London	0171 353 7881
Norie-Miller Jeffrey Reginald	55 Temple Chambers, London	0171 353 7400
Outhwaite Mrs Wendy-Jane Tivnan	Stanbrook & Henderson, London	0171 353 0101
	2 Harcourt Buildings, London	0171 583 9020
Quint Mrs Joan Francesca Rae	11 Old Square, London	0171 242 5022
Rawlings Clive Patrick	Goldsmith Building, London	0171 353 7881
Richards Miss Jennifer	39 Essex Street, London	0171 832 1111
Rowlands Ms Catherine Janet	Victoria Chambers, Birmingham	0121 236 9900
Sharland Andrew John	4-5 Gray's Inn Square, London	0171 404 5252
Spain Timothy Harrisson	Trinity Chambers, Newcastle upon Tyne	0191 232 1927
Stilitz Daniel Malachi	11 King's Bench Walk, London	0171 632 8500
Straker Timothy Derrick	• 2-3 Gray's Inn Square, London	0171 242 4986
Supperstone Michael Alan	11 King's Bench Walk, London	0171 632 8500
Tedd Rex Hilary	• St Philip's Chambers, Birmingham	0121 246 7000
	• 22 Albion Place, Northampton	01604 636271
Treacy Colman Maurice	Chambers of James Hunt QC, London	0171 421 8000
	3 Fountain Court, Birmingham	0121 236 5854
Vater John Alistair Pitt	Harcourt Chambers, London	0171 353 6961/7
Vavrecka David Paul Frank	14 Gray's Inn Square, London	0171 242 0858
Wallington Peter Thomas	11 King's Bench Walk, London	0171 632 8500
Warren Rupert Miles	2 Mitre Court Buildings, London	0171 583 1380
Whybrow Christopher John	1 Serjeants' Inn, London	0171 583 1355
Widdicombe David Graham	2 Mitre Court Buildings, London	0171 583 1380

EMPLOYMENT

Adejumo Mrs Hilda Ekpo	• Temple Chambers, London	0171 583 1001 (2 lines)
Alliott George Beckles	2 Harcourt Buildings, London	0171 583 9020
Alomo Richard Olusoji	14 Gray's Inn Square, London	0171 242 0858
Althaus Antony Justin	No 1 Serjeants' Inn, London	0171 415 6666
Baldwin John Grant	Oriel Chambers, Liverpool	0151 236 7191
Ball Steven James	Earl Street Chambers, Maidstone	01622 671222
Barlow Miss Sarah Helen	St Paul's House, Leeds	0113 245 5866
Battcock Benjamin George	Stanbrook & Henderson, London	0171 353 0101
	2 Harcourt Buildings, London	0171 583 9020
Baxter Gerald Pearson	25-27 Castle Street, Liverpool	0151 227 5661/5666/236 5072
Beaumont Marc Clifford	• Pump Court Chambers, London	0171 353 0711
	• Harrow-on-the-Hill Chambers, Harrow on the Hill	0181 423 7444
	• Pump Court Chambers, Winchester	01962 868161
	• Windsor Barristers' Chambers, Windsor	01753 648 899
Bedeau Stephen	Sovereign Chambers, Leeds	0113 245 1841/2/3
	Lancaster Buildings, Manchester	0161 661 4444

• Expanded entry in Part D

Belbin Miss Heather Patricia	Oriel Chambers, Liverpool	0151 236 7191
Bendall Richard Giles	33 Bedford Row, London	0171 242 6476
Benner Miss Lucinda Diana Kate	11 Bolt Court, London	0171 353 2300
	Redhill Chambers, Redhill	01737 780781
Bennett John Martyn	• Peel House Chambers, Liverpool	0151 236 4321
Benson Julian Christopher Woodburn	One Essex Court, London	0171 936 3030
Bentwood Richard	Chambers of Geoffrey Hawker, London	0171 583 8899
Bhattacharyya Ardhendu	1 Gray's Inn Square, London	0171 405 8946
	11 St Bernards Road, Slough	01753 553806/817989
Birtles William	Old Square Chambers, London	0171 269 0300
	Old Square Chambers, Bristol	0117 927 7111
Bourne Charles Gregory	Stanbrook & Henderson, London	0171 353 0101
	2 Harcourt Buildings, London	0171 583 9020
Boyle Gerard James	No 1 Serjeants' Inn, London	0171 415 6666
Bradley Miss Clodagh Maria	3 Serjeants' Inn, London	0171 353 5537
Bradley Richard	Oriel Chambers, Liverpool	0151 236 7191
Brant Paul David	Oriel Chambers, Liverpool	0151 236 7191
Breen Carlo Enrico	Chambers of John Hand QC, Manchester	0161 955 9000
Brown Damian Robert	• Old Square Chambers, London	0171 269 0300
	• Old Square Chambers, Bristol	0117 927 7111
Bull (Donald) Roger	One Essex Court, London	0171 936 3030
Burns Peter Richard	Deans Court Chambers, Manchester	0161 834 4097
Burton Michael John	Littleton Chambers, London	0171 797 8600
Calvert Peter Charles	Goldsmith Building, London	0171 353 7881
Cameron Neil Alexander	Wilberforce Chambers, Hull	01482 323 264
Campbell Oliver Edward Wilhelm	2 Harcourt Buildings, London	0171 583 9020
Cape Robert Paul	Milburn House Chambers, Newcastle upon Tyne	0191 230 5511
Carrodus Miss Gail Caroline	New Court Chambers, London	0171 831 9500
Cartwright Richard John	Queen Elizabeth Building, London	0171 353 7181 (12 lines)
Cawley Neil Robert Loudoun	55 Temple Chambers, London	0171 353 7400
	Milton Keynes Chambers, Milton Keynes	01908 217857
Cheyne Miss Phyllida Alison	4 Pump Court, London	0171 353 2656/9
Choudhury Akhlaq	11 King's Bench Walk, London	0171 632 8500
Chudleigh Miss Louise Katrina	Old Square Chambers, London	0171 269 0300
	Old Square Chambers, Bristol	0117 927 7111
Clark Miss Hazel Anne	Fenners Chambers, Cambridge	01223 368761
	Fenners Chambers, Peterborough	01733 562030
Clay Jonathan Roger	11 Bolt Court, London	0171 353 2300
	Redhill Chambers, Redhill	01737 780781
Clover (Thomas) Anthony	New Court Chambers, London	0171 831 9500
Collard Michael David	5 Pump Court, London	0171 353 2532
Collett Ivor William	No 1 Serjeants' Inn, London	0171 415 6666
Conlin Geoffrey David	3 Serjeants' Inn, London	0171 353 5537
Cooper Roger Bernard	Trinity Chambers, Newcastle upon Tyne	0191 232 1927
Corbett James Patrick	St Philip's Chambers, Birmingham	0121 246 7000
Coulter Barry John	One Essex Court, London	0171 936 3030
Cowen Miss Sally Emma	Chambers of Geoffrey Hawker, London	0171 583 8899
Craig Kenneth Allen	Hardwicke Building, London	0171 242 2523
Curtis Michael Alexander	Two Crown Office Row, London	0171 797 8100
Davies Stephen Richard	8 King Street Chambers, Manchester	0161 834 9560
Dawson James Robert	Oriel Chambers, Liverpool	0151 236 7191
de Jehan David	St Paul's House, Leeds	0113 245 5866
de Voghelaere Parr Adam Stephen	2 Mitre Court Buildings, London	0171 583 1380
Dean Paul Benjamin	5 Bell Yard, London	0171 333 8811
Dedezade Taner	Tindal Chambers, Chelmsford	01245 267742
Dineen Michael Laurence	Pump Court Chambers, London	0171 353 0711
	All Saints Chambers, Bristol	0117 921 1966
	Pump Court Chambers, Winchester	01962 868161
Dixon David Steven	Sovereign Chambers, Leeds	0113 245 1841/2/3
Dixon John Watts	Harcourt Chambers, London	0171 353 6961/7
	Harcourt Chambers, Oxford	01865 791559
Donovan Joel	New Court Chambers, London	0171 831 9500
Doughty Peter	17 Carlton Crescent, Southampton	01703 320320
Downs Martin John	1 Crown Office Row, London	0171 797 7500
	Crown Office Row Chambers, Brighton	01273 625625

Dowse John	Chambers of Lord Goodhart QC, London	0171 405 5577
	Chambers of John Hand QC, Manchester	0161 955 9000
Driver Simon Gregory	25-27 Castle Street, Liverpool	0151 227 5661/5666/236 5072
Dubbery Mark Edward	Pump Court Chambers, London	0171 353 0711
Duffy Michael	Cathedral Chambers, Ely, Ely	01353 666775
Eady Miss Jennifer Jane	Old Square Chambers, London	0171 269 0300
	Old Square Chambers, Bristol	0117 927 7111
Emanuel Mark Pering Wolff	14 Gray's Inn Square, London	0171 242 0858
Evans Lee John	Farrar's Building, London	0171 583 9241
Falk Miss Josephine Ruth Ann	12 Old Square, London	0171 404 0875
Fenston Miss Felicia Donovan	Stanbrook & Henderson, London	0171 353 0101
	2 Harcourt Buildings, London	0171 583 9020
Finlay Darren	Sovereign Chambers, Leeds	0113 245 1841/2/3
Fisher David	5 Bell Yard, London	0171 333 8811
Foster Francis Alexander	St Paul's House, Leeds	0113 245 5866
Foxwell George (Augustus)	Fenners Chambers, Cambridge	01223 368761
	Fenners Chambers, Peterborough	01733 562030
Franck Richard David William	Equity Chambers, Birmingham	0121 233 2100
French Richard Anthony Lister	Rougemont Chambers, Exeter	01392 410471
Friel John Anthony	Goldsmith Building, London	0171 353 7881
	Southsea Chambers, Portsmouth	01705 291261
Fripp Eric William Burtin	Chambers of Harjit Singh, London	0171 353 1356
Frodsham Alexander Miles	Oriel Chambers, Liverpool	0151 236 7191
Galberg Marc Kay	33 Bedford Row, London	0171 242 6476
Garside Charles Roger	Chambers of John Hand QC, Manchester	0161 955 9000
Gatty Daniel Simon	New Court Chambers, London	0171 831 9500
George Miss Judith Sarah	St Philip's Chambers, Birmingham	0121 246 7000
Gibson Charles Anthony Warneford	2 Harcourt Buildings, London	0171 583 9020
Giffin Nigel Dyson	11 King's Bench Walk, London	0171 632 8500
Gilbert Ms Julia Jane	Trinity Chambers, Newcastle upon Tyne	0191 232 1927
Gilbertson Mrs Helen Alison	Sackville Chambers, Norwich	01603 613516
Gilroy Paul	Farrar's Building, London	0171 583 9241
	Chambers of John Hand QC, Manchester	0161 955 9000
Goodbody Peter James	• Oriel Chambers, Liverpool	0151 236 7191
Goodwin Nicholas Alexander John	Harcourt Chambers, London	0171 353 6961/7
Goudie James	• 11 King's Bench Walk, London	0171 632 8500
Gower Miss Helen Clare	Old Square Chambers, London	0171 269 0300
	Old Square Chambers, Bristol	0117 927 7111
Graham Thomas Patrick Henry	Lamb Chambers, London	0171 797 8300
Green Patrick Curtis	Stanbrook & Henderson, London	0171 353 0101
	2 Harcourt Buildings, London	0171 583 9020
Grice Miss Joanna Harrison	One King's Bench Walk, London	0171 936 1500
Gruffydd John	Oriel Chambers, Liverpool	0151 236 7191
Grundy Nigel Lawrence John	Chambers of John Hand QC, Manchester	0161 955 9000
Hall Mrs Melanie Ruth	Monckton Chambers, London	0171 405 7211
Hall-Smith Martin Clive William	Goldsmith Building, London	0171 353 7881
Hand John Lester	Old Square Chambers, London	0171 269 0300
	Old Square Chambers, Bristol	0117 927 7111
	Chambers of John Hand QC, Manchester	0161 955 9000
Harbottle Gwilym Thomas	5 New Square, London	0171 404 0404
Hardwick Matthew Richard	Enterprise Chambers, London	0171 405 9471
	Enterprise Chambers, Leeds	0113 246 0391
	Enterprise Chambers, Newcastle upon Tyne	0191 222 3344
Hargrove Jeremy John Loveday	Trinity Chambers, Newcastle upon Tyne	0191 232 1927
Harris Paul Best	Monckton Chambers, London	0171 405 7211
Harrison Ms Averil	2 Harcourt Buildings, London	0171 583 9020
Harrison John Foster	St Paul's House, Leeds	0113 245 5866
Harvey Miss Jayne Denise	Goldsworth Chambers, London	0171 405 7117
Haslam Andrew Peter	Sovereign Chambers, Leeds	0113 245 1841/2/3
Haynes Miss Rebecca	Monckton Chambers, London	0171 405 7211
Heald Oliver	Fenners Chambers, Cambridge	01223 368761
	Fenners Chambers, Peterborough	01733 562030
Heap Gerard Miles	Sovereign Chambers, Leeds	0113 245 1841/2/3

• Expanded entry in Part D

Hendy John Giles	Old Square Chambers, London	0171 269 0300
	Old Square Chambers, Bristol	0117 927 7111
Herbert Mrs Rebecca Mary	2 New Street, Leicester	0116 262 5906
Hill Raymond	Monckton Chambers, London	0171 405 7211
Hillier Andrew Charles	5 Bell Yard, London	0171 333 8811
Hinchliffe Philip Nicholas	Chambers of John Hand QC, Manchester	0161 955 9000
Horlock Timothy John	Chambers of John Hand QC, Manchester	0161 955 9000
House James Michael	2 New Street, Leicester	0116 262 5906
Howard Anthony John	Chambers of John Hand QC, Manchester	0161 955 9000
Howe Miss Penelope Anne Macgregor	Pump Court Chambers, London	0171 353 0711
Hull Leslie David	Chambers of John Hand QC, Manchester	0161 955 9000
Ivimy Ms Cecilia Rachel	11 King's Bench Walk, London	0171 632 8500
Jack Simon Michael	9 Woodhouse Square, Leeds	0113 245 1986
Jackson Anthony Warren	3 Serjeants' Inn, London	0171 353 5537
James Michael Frank	Enterprise Chambers, London	0171 405 9471
	Enterprise Chambers, Leeds	0113 246 0391
	Enterprise Chambers, Newcastle upon Tyne	0191 222 3344
Janner Daniel Joseph Mitchell	23 Essex Street, London	0171 413 0353
Jayanathan Miss Shamini	30 Park Place, Cardiff	01222 398421
John Stephen Alun	9-12 Bell Yard, London	0171 400 1800
Jones Miss (Catherine) Charlotte	5 Bell Yard, London	0171 333 8811
Jones Geraint Martyn	Fenners Chambers, Cambridge	01223 368761
	Fenners Chambers, Peterborough	01733 562030
Jones Sean William Paul	11 King's Bench Walk, London	0171 632 8500
Josling William Henry Charles	Fenners Chambers, Cambridge	01223 368761
	Fenners Chambers, Peterborough	01733 562030
Kennedy Christopher Laurence Paul	Chambers of John Hand QC, Manchester	0161 955 9000
Kenward Timothy David Nelson	25-27 Castle Street, Liverpool	0151 227 5661/5666/236 5072
Kerr Tim Julian	4-5 Gray's Inn Square, London	0171 404 5252
Kimbell John Ashley	5 Bell Yard, London	0171 333 8811
Kinnier Andrew John	2 Harcourt Buildings, London	0171 583 9020
Kirby Peter John	• Hardwicke Building, London	0171 242 2523
Kolodziej Andrzej Jozef	• Littman Chambers, London	0171 404 4866
Laing Miss Elisabeth Mary Caroline	11 King's Bench Walk, London	0171 632 8500
Lawson Daniel George	Goldsmith Building, London	0171 353 7881
Lees Andrew James	St Paul's House, Leeds	0113 245 5866
Lehain Philip Peter	199 Strand, London	0171 379 9779
Leigh-Morgan (David) Paul	Fenners Chambers, Cambridge	01223 368761
	Fenners Chambers, Peterborough	01733 562030
Leiper Richard Thomas	11 King's Bench Walk, London	0171 632 8500
Lennard Stephen Charles	Hardwicke Building, London	0171 242 2523
Leonard Charles Robert Weston	Goldsmith Building, London	0171 353 7881
Lewis Jeffrey Allan	9 Woodhouse Square, Leeds	0113 245 1986
Lewis Robert		
Lewis Professor Roy Malcolm	Old Square Chambers, London	0171 269 0300
	Old Square Chambers, Bristol	0117 927 7111
Linstead Peter James	11 Bolt Court, London	0171 353 2300
Little Ian	Chambers of John Hand QC, Manchester	0161 955 9000
Lobo Matthew Joseph Edwin	Fenners Chambers, Cambridge	01223 368761
	Fenners Chambers, Peterborough	01733 562030
Lyne Mark Hilary	One Essex Court, London	0171 936 3030
Lyon Stephen John	14 Gray's Inn Square, London	0171 242 0858
	Westgate Chambers, Lewes	01273 480 510
Macpherson The Hon Mary Stewart	2 Mitre Court Buildings, London	0171 583 1380
Maitland Jones Mark Griffith	Goldsmith Building, London	0171 353 7881
Makey Christopher Douglas	Old Square Chambers, London	0171 269 0300
	Old Square Chambers, Bristol	0117 927 7111
Malecka Dr Mary Margaret	Goldsworth Chambers, London	0171 405 7117
Marris Miss Sarah Selena Rixar	No 1 Serjeants' Inn, London	0171 415 6666
Marshall Philip Derek	Farrar's Building, London	0171 583 9241
	Iscoed Chambers, Swansea	01792 652988/9/330
Mason Ian Douglas	11 Bolt Court, London	0171 353 2300
	Redhill Chambers, Redhill	01737 780781
Matthews Dennis Roland	5 Bell Yard, London	0171 333 8811

• Expanded entry in Part D

Maxwell David | Claremont Chambers, Wolverhampton | 01902 426222
McCann Simon Howard | Deans Court Chambers, Manchester | 0161 834 4097
McCluggage Brian Thomas | Chambers of John Hand QC, Manchester | 0161 955 9000
McCredie Miss Fionnuala Mary Constance | 3 Serjeants' Inn, London | 0171 353 5537
McGahey Miss Elizabeth Clare | 30 Park Place, Cardiff | 01222 398421
McGuinness John Francis | 9-12 Bell Yard, London | 0171 400 1800
McKenna Miss Anna Louise | Queen Elizabeth Building, London | 0171 353 7181 (12 lines)
McKeon James Patrick | Peel House Chambers, Liverpool | 0151 236 4321
McLachlan David Robert
McManus Jonathan Richard | 4-5 Gray's Inn Square, London | 0171 404 5252
McMinn Miss Valerie Kathleen | Baker Street Chambers, Middlesbrough | 01642 873873
McParland Michael Joseph | New Court Chambers, London | 0171 831 9500
Meakin Timothy William | Fenners Chambers, Cambridge | 01223 368761
| Fenners Chambers, Peterborough | 01733 562030
Merry Hugh Gairns | 17 Carlton Crescent, Southampton | 01703 320320
Mills Simon Thomas | One Essex Court, London | 0171 936 3030
Mitchell Miss Juliana Marie | 2 Harcourt Buildings, London | 0171 583 9020
Moon Philip Charles Angus | 3 Serjeants' Inn, London | 0171 353 5537
Moore James Anthony | 2 Gray's Inn Square Chambers, London | 0171 242 0328/405 1317
Moorman Miss Lucinda Claire | Farrar's Building, London | 0171 583 9241
Moriarty Gerald Evelyn | 2 Mitre Court Buildings, London | 0171 583 1380
Moses Miss Rebecca | Barristers' Common Law Chambers, London | 0171 375 3012
| Lion Court, London | 0171 404 6565
Naylor Jonathan Peter | King's Chambers, Eastbourne | 01323 416053
Nesbitt Timothy John Robert | 199 Strand, London | 0171 379 9779
Newman Austin Eric | 9 Woodhouse Square, Leeds | 0113 245 1986
Nicholls Paul Richard | 11 King's Bench Walk, London | 0171 632 8500
Ogunbiyi Oluwole Afolabi | Horizon Chambers, London | 0171 242 2440
Okoye Miss Joy Nwamala | Chambers of Joy Okoye, London | 0171 405 7011
Outhwaite Mrs Wendy-Jane Tivnan | Stanbrook & Henderson, London | 0171 353 0101
| 2 Harcourt Buildings, London | 0171 583 9020
Paines Nicholas Paul Billot | Monckton Chambers, London | 0171 405 7211
Palmer James Savill | 2 Harcourt Buildings, London | 0171 583 9020
Parkin Jonathan | • Chambers of John Hand QC, Manchester | 0161 955 9000
Patchett-Joyce Michael Thurston | Monckton Chambers, London | 0171 405 7211
Patten Benedict Joseph | Two Crown Office Row, London | 0171 797 8100
Peacock Ian Christopher | 12 New Square, London | 0171 419 1212
| Sovereign Chambers, Leeds | 0113 245 1841/2/3
Peirson Oliver James | Pump Court Chambers, London | 0171 353 0711
| Pump Court Chambers, Winchester | 01962 868161
Pershad Rohan | Two Crown Office Row, London | 0171 797 8100
Pimentel Carlos de Serpa Alberto Legg | 3 Stone Buildings, London | 0171 242 4937/405 8358
Pinder Miss Mary Elizabeth | No 1 Serjeants' Inn, London | 0171 415 6666
Pitt-Payne Timothy Sheridan | • 11 King's Bench Walk, London | 0171 632 8500
Pitter Jason Karl | Park Court Chambers, Leeds | 0113 243 3277
Powell Miss Debra Ann | 3 Serjeants' Inn, London | 0171 353 5537
Pratt Allan Duncan | New Court Chambers, London | 0171 831 9500
Priestley Ms Rebecca Janet | 2 Gray's Inn Square Chambers, London | 0171 242 0328/405 1317
Prynne Andrew Geoffrey Lockyer | Stanbrook & Henderson, London | 0171 353 0101
| 2 Harcourt Buildings, London | 0171 583 9020
Rahman Muhammad Altafur | Barristers' Common Law Chambers, London | 0171 375 3012
Rahman Ms Sadeqa Shaheen | 1 Crown Office Row, London | 0171 797 7500
Rankin William Peter | Oriel Chambers, Liverpool | 0151 236 7191
Reed Philip James William | 5 Bell Yard, London | 0171 333 8811
Reeve Matthew Francis | 5 Bell Yard, London | 0171 333 8811
Reynold Frederic | New Court Chambers, London | 0171 831 9500
Rigby Terence | Chambers of John Hand QC, Manchester | 0161 955 9000
Riley-Smith Tobias Augustine William | 2 Harcourt Buildings, London | 0171 583 9020
Robson John Malcolm | 2 Gray's Inn Square Chambers, London | 0171 242 0328/405 1317
| Assize Court Chambers, Bristol | 0117 926 4587

• Expanded entry in Part D

Robson Nicholas David	Baker Street Chambers, Middlesbrough	01642 873873
Roe Thomas Idris	Goldsmith Building, London	0171 353 7881
Rogers Ian Paul	1 Crown Office Row, London	0171 583 9292
Rogers Paul John	1 Crown Office Row, London	0171 797 7500
	Crown Office Row Chambers, Brighton	01273 625625
Room Stewart	8 Stone Buildings, London	0171 831 9881
Rudd Matthew Allan	11 Bolt Court, London	0171 353 2300
	Redhill Chambers, Redhill	01737 780781
Russell Robert John Finlay	5 Bell Yard, London	0171 333 8811
Sadiq Tariq Mahmood	Chambers of John Hand QC, Manchester	0161 955 9000
Samuels Leslie John	Pump Court Chambers, London	0171 353 0711
	Pump Court Chambers, Winchester	01962 868161
Sander Andrew Thomas	Goldsmith Building, London	0171 353 7881
	Oriel Chambers, Liverpool	0151 236 7191
Sandiford Jonathan	St Paul's House, Leeds	0113 245 5866
Schooling Simon John	Chambers of Harjit Singh, London	0171 353 1356
Scott Matthew John	Pump Court Chambers, London	0171 353 0711
	Pump Court Chambers, Winchester	01962 868161
Segal Oliver Leon	Old Square Chambers, London	0171 269 0300
	Old Square Chambers, Bristol	0117 927 7111
Semple Andrew Blair	Sovereign Chambers, Leeds	0113 245 1841/2/3
Seymour Mark William	9-12 Bell Yard, London	0171 400 1800
Shaikh Eur.Ing. (Jaikumar) Christopher (Samuel	Avondale Chambers, London	0181 445 9984
	Equity Chambers, Birmingham	0121 233 2100
Sharland Andrew John	4-5 Gray's Inn Square, London	0171 404 5252
Sheehan Malcolm Peter	Stanbrook & Henderson, London	0171 353 0101
	2 Harcourt Buildings, London	0171 583 9020
Simor Miss Jessica Margaret Poppaea	Monckton Chambers, London	0171 405 7211
Slade Miss Elizabeth Ann	• 11 King's Bench Walk, London	0171 632 8500
Sleeman Miss Rachel Sarah Elizabeth	One Essex Court, London	0171 936 3030
Smith Miss Julia Mair Wheldon	Gough Square Chambers, London	0171 353 0924
Smith Ms Katherine Emma	Monckton Chambers, London	0171 405 7211
Somerset-Jones Miss Felicity	Oriel Chambers, Liverpool	0151 236 7191
Soole Michael Alexander	5 Bell Yard, London	0171 333 8811
Soor Smair Singh	33 Bedford Row, London	0171 242 6476
Spain Timothy Harrisson	Trinity Chambers, Newcastle upon Tyne	0191 232 1927
St Louis Brian Lloyd	Hardwicke Building, London	0171 242 2523
Stancombe Barry Terrence	Gough Square Chambers, London	0171 353 0924
Starcevic Petar	St Philip's Chambers, Birmingham	0121 246 7000
Stewart Richard Paul	New Court Chambers, London	0171 831 9500
Stilitz Daniel Malachi	11 King's Bench Walk, London	0171 632 8500
Supperstone Michael Alan	11 King's Bench Walk, London	0171 632 8500
Taylor Andrew Peter	Fenners Chambers, Cambridge	01223 368761
	Fenners Chambers, Peterborough	01733 562030
Tedd Rex Hilary	• St Philip's Chambers, Birmingham	0121 246 7000
	• 22 Albion Place, Northampton	01604 636271
Thomson Martin Haldane Ahmad	Wynne Chambers, London	0171 737 7266
Thornton Miss Anne Rebecca	9 Woodhouse Square, Leeds	0113 245 1986
Tucker Miss Katherine Jane Greening	St Philip's Chambers, Birmingham	0121 246 7000
Vajda Christopher Stephen	Monckton Chambers, London	0171 405 7211
Vaughan Terence Paul	Watford Chambers, Watford	01923 220553
Vaughan-Neil Miss Catherine Mary Bernardine	5 Bell Yard, London	0171 333 8811
Wakefield Miss Anne Prudence	3 Verulam Buildings, London	0171 831 8441
Wallington Peter Thomas	11 King's Bench Walk, London	0171 632 8500
Ward Ms Orla Mary	3 Serjeants' Inn, London	0171 353 5537
Ward Miss Siobhan Marie Lucia	11 King's Bench Walk, London	0171 632 8500
Warnock Andrew Ronald	No 1 Serjeants' Inn, London	0171 415 6666
Warrender Miss Nichola Mary	New Court Chambers, London	0171 831 9500
Wedderburn of Charlton Lord	Old Square Chambers, London	0171 269 0300
	Old Square Chambers, Bristol	0117 927 7111
Wedderspoon Miss Rachel Leone	Chambers of John Hand QC, Manchester	0161 955 9000
Wheeler Miss Marina Claire	Stanbrook & Henderson, London	0171 353 0101

• Expanded entry in Part D

	2 Harcourt Buildings, London	0171 583 9020
Whitcombe Mark David	Old Square Chambers, London	0171 269 0300
	Old Square Chambers, Bristol	0117 927 7111
White Darren Paul	Cathedral Chambers (Jan Wood Independent Barristers' Clerk), Exeter	01392 210900
White Peter-John Spencer	Pembroke House, Leatherhead	01372 376160/376493
Wignall Edward Gordon	• 1 Dr Johnson's Buildings, London	0171 353 9328
	• Dr Johnson's Chambers, Reading	01189 254221
Wilken Sean David Henry	39 Essex Street, London	0171 832 1111
Williams Ms Heather Jean	Doughty Street Chambers, London	0171 404 1313
Williams Thomas Ellis	30 Park Place, Cardiff	01222 398421
Wood Richard Michael	Sackville Chambers, Norwich	01603 613516
Wood Simon Richard Henry	Lamb Chambers, London	0171 797 8300
Woodwark Ms Jane Elizabeth	Milburn House Chambers, Newcastle upon Tyne	0191 230 5511
Worrall John Raymond Guy	Chambers of Andrew Campbell QC, Leeds	0113 245 5438
Wright Gerard Henry	25-27 Castle Street, Liverpool	0151 227 5661/5666/236 5072
Yell Nicholas Anthony	No 1 Serjeants' Inn, London	0171 415 6666

ENERGY

Akenhead Robert	Atkin Chambers, London	0171 404 0102
Alesbury Alun	2 Mitre Court Buildings, London	0171 583 1380
Ambrose Miss Clare Mary Geneste	20 Essex Street, London	0171 583 9294
Anderson Anthony John	2 Mitre Court Buildings, London	0171 583 1380
Baatz Nicholas Stephen	Atkin Chambers, London	0171 404 0102
Bartlett George Robert	2 Mitre Court Buildings, London	0171 583 1380
Barwise Miss Stephanie Nicola	Atkin Chambers, London	0171 404 0102
Blackburn John	Atkin Chambers, London	0171 404 0102
Bowdery Martin	Atkin Chambers, London	0171 404 0102
Boyle Christopher Alexander David	2 Mitre Court Buildings, London	0171 583 1380
Burr Andrew Charles	Atkin Chambers, London	0171 404 0102
Burton Nicholas Anthony	2 Mitre Court Buildings, London	0171 583 1380
Clay Robert Charles	Atkin Chambers, London	0171 404 0102
de Voghelaere Parr Adam Stephen	2 Mitre Court Buildings, London	0171 583 1380
Dennison Stephen Randell	Atkin Chambers, London	0171 404 0102
Dennys Nicholas Charles Jonathan	Atkin Chambers, London	0171 404 0102
Doerries Miss Chantal-Aimee Renee Aemelia Annemarie	Atkin Chambers, London	0171 404 0102
Druce Michael James	2 Mitre Court Buildings, London	0171 583 1380
Dumaresq Ms Delia Jane	Atkin Chambers, London	0171 404 0102
FitzGerald Michael Frederick Clive	2 Mitre Court Buildings, London	0171 583 1380
Fookes Robert Lawrence	2 Mitre Court Buildings, London	0171 583 1380
Fraser Peter Donald	Atkin Chambers, London	0171 404 0102
Glasgow Edwin John	39 Essex Street, London	0171 832 1111
Glover Richard Michael	2 Mitre Court Buildings, London	0171 583 1380
Goddard Andrew Stephen	Atkin Chambers, London	0171 404 0102
Godwin William George Henry	Atkin Chambers, London	0171 404 0102
Horton Matthew Bethell	2 Mitre Court Buildings, London	0171 583 1380
Howells James Richard	Atkin Chambers, London	0171 404 0102
Jones Gregory Percy	• 2 Harcourt Buildings, London	0171 353 8415
King Neil Gerald Alexander	2 Mitre Court Buildings, London	0171 583 1380
Knight Brian Joseph	Atkin Chambers, London	0171 404 0102
Lofthouse Simon Timothy	Atkin Chambers, London	0171 404 0102
Males Stephen Martin	20 Essex Street, London	0171 583 9294
McCracken Robert Henry Joy	• 2 Harcourt Buildings, London	0171 353 8415
McMullan Manus Anthony	Atkin Chambers, London	0171 404 0102
Milligan Iain Anstruther	20 Essex Street, London	0171 583 9294
Moriarty Gerald Evelyn	2 Mitre Court Buildings, London	0171 583 1380
Ornsby Miss Suzanne Doreen	• 2 Harcourt Buildings, London	0171 353 8415
Parkin Miss Fiona Jane	Atkin Chambers, London	0171 404 0102
Raeside Mark Andrew	Atkin Chambers, London	0171 404 0102
Rawley Miss Dominique Jane	Atkin Chambers, London	0171 404 0102
Reese Colin Edward	Atkin Chambers, London	0171 404 0102
Roots Guy Robert Godfrey	2 Mitre Court Buildings, London	0171 583 1380
Royce Darryl Fraser	Atkin Chambers, London	0171 404 0102
Silsoe The Lord	2 Mitre Court Buildings, London	0171 583 1380
Streatfeild-James David Stewart	Atkin Chambers, London	0171 404 0102
Taylor Reuben Mallinson	2 Mitre Court Buildings, London	0171 583 1380
Tucker David William	Two Crown Office Row, London	0171 797 8100
Valentine Donald Graham	Atkin Chambers, London	0171 404 0102

Walker Steven John	Atkin Chambers, London	0171 404 0102
Wallace Ian Norman Duncan	Atkin Chambers, London	0171 404 0102
Warren Rupert Miles	2 Mitre Court Buildings, London	0171 583 1380
White Andrew	Atkin Chambers, London	0171 404 0102
Widdicombe David Graham	2 Mitre Court Buildings, London	0171 583 1380
Wilken Sean David Henry	39 Essex Street, London	0171 832 1111
Wilmot-Smith Richard James Crosbie	39 Essex Street, London	0171 832 1111

ENTERTAINMENT

Abbott Alistair James Hugh	5 New Square, London	0171 404 0404
Airey Simon Andrew	11 Bolt Court, London	0171 353 2300
	Redhill Chambers, Redhill	01737 780781
Barker Simon George Harry	• 13 Old Square, London	0171 404 4800
Baylis Ms Natalie Jayne	3 Verulam Buildings, London	0171 831 8441
Bennett Gordon Irvine	5 Bell Yard, London	0171 333 8811
Bergin Terence Edward	New Court Chambers, London	0171 831 9500
Brodie (James) Bruce	39 Essex Street, London	0171 832 1111
Burton Michael John	Littleton Chambers, London	0171 797 8600
Carey Jeremy Reynolds Patrick	Lamb Chambers, London	0171 797 8300
Cash Miss Joanne Catherine	Farrar's Building, London	0171 583 9241
Clark Ms Julia Elisabeth	5 New Square, London	0171 404 0404
Craig Kenneth Allen	Hardwicke Building, London	0171 242 2523
Cunningham Mark James	13 Old Square, London	0171 404 4800
Edwards Richard Julian Henshaw	3 Verulam Buildings, London	0171 831 8441
Elliott Nicholas Blethyn	3 Verulam Buildings, London	0171 831 8441
Faulks Edward Peter Lawless	No 1 Serjeants' Inn, London	0171 415 6666
Fitzgerald John Vincent	New Court, London	0171 797 8999
Freedman Sampson Clive	3 Verulam Buildings, London	0171 831 8441
Garnett Kevin Mitchell	5 New Square, London	0171 404 0404
Gibaud Miss Catherine Alison Annetta	3 Verulam Buildings, London	0171 831 8441
Goudie James	• 11 King's Bench Walk, London	0171 632 8500
Gray Charles Anthony St John	5 Raymond Buildings, London	0171 242 2902
Harbottle Gwilym Thomas	5 New Square, London	0171 404 0404
Harvey Miss Jayne Denise	Goldsworth Chambers, London	0171 405 7117
Hicks Michael Charles	• 19 Old Buildings, London	0171 405 2001
Hodgson Richard Andrew	New Court, London	0171 797 8999
Holman Miss Tamsin Perdita	19 Old Buildings, London	0171 405 2001
Kime Matthew Jonathan	• New Court, London	0171 797 8999
	• Cobden House Chambers, Manchester	0161 833 6000/6001
Lowenstein Paul David	Littleton Chambers, London	0171 797 8600
Merriman Nicholas Flavelle	3 Verulam Buildings, London	0171 831 8441
Nelson Vincent Leonard	39 Essex Street, London	0171 832 1111
Newman Ms Ingrid	Hardwicke Building, London	0171 242 2523
Norris Andrew James Steedsman	5 New Square, London	0171 404 0404
Pershad Rohan	Two Crown Office Row, London	0171 797 8100
Peters Nigel Melvin	18 Red Lion Court, London	0171 520 6000
	Thornwood House, Chelmsford	01245 280880
Puckrin Cedric Eldred	19 Old Buildings, London	0171 405 2001
Rai Amarjit Singh	St Philip's Chambers, Birmingham	0121 246 7000
Reid Brian Christopher	19 Old Buildings, London	0171 405 2001
Sampson Graeme William	Chambers of Geoffrey Hawker, London	0171 583 8899
Sayer Mr Peter Edwin	Gough Square Chambers, London	0171 353 0924
Seligman Matthew Thomas Arthur	39 Essex Street, London	0171 832 1111
Shipley Norman Graham	• 19 Old Buildings, London	0171 405 2001
Silverleaf Michael	• 11 South Square, London	0171 405 1222
Spearman Richard	5 Raymond Buildings, London	0171 242 2902
Stewart Alexander Joseph	5 New Square, London	0171 404 0404
Sugar Simon Gareth	5 New Square, London	0171 404 0404
Sullivan Rory Myles	19 Old Buildings, London	0171 405 2001
Sutcliffe Andrew Harold Wentworth	3 Verulam Buildings, London	0171 831 8441
Tucker David William	Two Crown Office Row, London	0171 797 8100
Wilson Alastair James Drysdale	• 19 Old Buildings, London	0171 405 2001
Wolfson David	3 Verulam Buildings, London	0171 831 8441

ENVIRONMENT

Akenhead Robert	Atkin Chambers, London	0171 404 0102
Alesbury Alun	2 Mitre Court Buildings, London	0171 583 1380
Allardice Miss Miranda Jane	Pump Court Chambers, London	0171 353 0711

• Expanded entry in Part D

	Pump Court Chambers, Winchester	01962 868161
Anderson Anthony John	2 Mitre Court Buildings, London	0171 583 1380
Ashworth Piers	Stanbrook & Henderson, London	0171 353 0101
	2 Harcourt Buildings, London	0171 583 9020
	Priory Chambers, Birmingham	0121 236 3882/1375
Baatz Nicholas Stephen	Atkin Chambers, London	0171 404 0102
Bailey Mark Henry Arthur	• 6 Pump Court, London	0171 797 8400
	• 6-8 Mill Street, Maidstone	01622 688 094
Barnes (David) Michael (William)	4 Breams Buildings, London	0171 353 5835/430 1221
Bartlett George Robert	2 Mitre Court Buildings, London	0171 583 1380
Barwise Miss Stephanie Nicola	Atkin Chambers, London	0171 404 0102
Bates John Hayward	Old Square Chambers, London	0171 269 0300
	Old Square Chambers, Bristol	0117 927 7111
Beard Mark Christopher	6 Pump Court, London	0171 797 8400
Bhattacharyya Ardhendu	1 Gray's Inn Square, London	0171 405 8946
	11 St Bernards Road, Slough	01753 553806/817989
Birtles William	Old Square Chambers, London	0171 269 0300
	Old Square Chambers, Bristol	0117 927 7111
Blackburn John	Atkin Chambers, London	0171 404 0102
Bowdery Martin	Atkin Chambers, London	0171 404 0102
Boyle Christopher Alexander David	2 Mitre Court Buildings, London	0171 583 1380
Bradley Richard	Oriel Chambers, Liverpool	0151 236 7191
Burr Andrew Charles	Atkin Chambers, London	0171 404 0102
Burton Nicholas Anthony	2 Mitre Court Buildings, London	0171 583 1380
Byrne Garrett Thomas	23 Essex Street, London	0171 413 0353
Cameron Jonathan James O'Grady	3 Verulam Buildings, London	0171 831 8441
Cameron Neil Alexander	Wilberforce Chambers, Hull	01482 323 264
Cameron Neil St Clair	1 Serjeants' Inn, London	0171 583 1355
Carrodus Miss Gail Caroline	New Court Chambers, London	0171 831 9500
Caws Eian Richard Edwin	4 Breams Buildings, London	0171 353 5835/430 1221
Clarke Miss Michelle Nicola	Earl Street Chambers, Maidstone	01622 671222
Clay Robert Charles	Atkin Chambers, London	0171 404 0102
Collett Gavin Charles	Rougemont Chambers, Exeter	01392 410471
	Cathedral Chambers (Jan Wood Independent Barristers' Clerk), Exeter	01392 210900
Collier Martin Melton	Fenners Chambers, Cambridge	01223 368761
	Fenners Chambers, Peterborough	01733 562030
Colquhoun Miss Celina Daphne Marion	11 Bolt Court, London	0171 353 2300
	Redhill Chambers, Redhill	01737 780781
Cottrell Matthew Robert	Oriel Chambers, Liverpool	0151 236 7191
Dashwood Professor Arthur Alan	Stanbrook & Henderson, London	0171 353 0101
	2 Harcourt Buildings, London	0171 583 9020
de Voghelaere Parr Adam Stephen	2 Mitre Court Buildings, London	0171 583 1380
DeCamp Miss Jane Louise	Two Crown Office Row, London	0171 797 8100
Dennison Stephen Randell	Atkin Chambers, London	0171 404 0102
Dennys Nicholas Charles Jonathan	Atkin Chambers, London	0171 404 0102
Doerries Miss Chantal-Aimee Renee Aemelia Annemarie	Atkin Chambers, London	0171 404 0102
Drabble Richard John Bloor	4 Breams Buildings, London	0171 353 5835/430 1221
Druce Michael James	2 Mitre Court Buildings, London	0171 583 1380
Dumaresq Ms Delia Jane	Atkin Chambers, London	0171 404 0102
Eastman Roger	Stanbrook & Henderson, London	0171 353 0101
	2 Harcourt Buildings, London	0171 583 9020
Edwards Philip Douglas	2 Harcourt Buildings, London	0171 353 8415
Edwards-Stuart Antony James Cobham	Two Crown Office Row, London	0171 797 8100
Elvin David John	4 Breams Buildings, London	0171 353 5835/430 1221
Fenhalls Mark Roydon Allen	23 Essex Street, London	0171 413 0353
FitzGerald Michael Frederick Clive	2 Mitre Court Buildings, London	0171 583 1380
Fookes Robert Lawrence	2 Mitre Court Buildings, London	0171 583 1380
Forsdick David John	4 Breams Buildings, London	0171 353 5835/430 1221
Forster Brian Clive	Trinity Chambers, Newcastle upon Tyne	0191 232 1927
Franklin Stephen Hall	5 Paper Buildings, London	0171 583 6117
	Fenners Chambers, Cambridge	01223 368761
Fraser Peter Donald	Atkin Chambers, London	0171 404 0102
Frodsham Alexander Miles	Oriel Chambers, Liverpool	0151 236 7191
Furber (Robert) John	4 Breams Buildings, London	0171 353 5835/430 1221
Glover Richard Michael	2 Mitre Court Buildings, London	0171 583 1380
Goddard Andrew Stephen	Atkin Chambers, London	0171 404 0102

• Expanded entry in Part D

Godwin William George Henry	Atkin Chambers, London	0171 404 0102
Gordon Richard John Francis	39 Essex Street, London	0171 832 1111
Gore Andrew Roger	Fenners Chambers, Cambridge	01223 368761
	Fenners Chambers, Peterborough	01733 562030
Goudie James	• 11 King's Bench Walk, London	0171 632 8500
Hall Mrs Melanie Ruth	Monckton Chambers, London	0171 405 7211
Hand John Lester	Old Square Chambers, London	0171 269 0300
	Old Square Chambers, Bristol	0117 927 7111
	Chambers of John Hand QC, Manchester	0161 955 9000
Hands David Richard Granville	4 Breams Buildings, London	0171 353 5835/430 1221
	40 King Street, Manchester	0161 832 9082
Harper Joseph Charles	4 Breams Buildings, London	0171 353 5835/430 1221
Hartley-Davies Paul Kevil	30 Park Place, Cardiff	01222 398421
Harwood Richard John	1 Serjeants' Inn, London	0171 583 1355
Haynes Peter	St Philip's Chambers, Birmingham	0121 246 7000
Haynes Miss Rebecca	Monckton Chambers, London	0171 405 7211
Heap Gerard Miles	Sovereign Chambers, Leeds	0113 245 1841/2/3
Higgins Anthony Paul	Goldsmith Building, London	0171 353 7881
Hill (Eliot) Michael	23 Essex Street, London	0171 413 0353
Hockman Stephen Alexander	• 6 Pump Court, London	0171 797 8400
	• 6-8 Mill Street, Maidstone	01622 688 094
Holgate David John	4 Breams Buildings, London	0171 353 5835/430 1221
Holroyd John James	• 9 Woodhouse Square, Leeds	0113 245 1986
Horlock Timothy John	Chambers of John Hand QC, Manchester	0161 955 9000
Horton Matthew Bethell	2 Mitre Court Buildings, London	0171 583 1380
Howell John	4 Breams Buildings, London	0171 353 5835/430 1221
Howells James Richard	Atkin Chambers, London	0171 404 0102
Huskinson George Nicholas Nevil	4-5 Gray's Inn Square, London	0171 404 5252
Jarvis John Manners	3 Verulam Buildings, London	0171 831 8441
Jones Gregory Percy	• 2 Harcourt Buildings, London	0171 353 8415
Jones Timothy Arthur	• Arden Chambers, London	0171 242 4244
	• St Philip's Chambers, Birmingham	0121 246 7000
Karas Jonathan Marcus	4 Breams Buildings, London	0171 353 5835/430 1221
Katkowski Christopher Andrew Mark	4 Breams Buildings, London	0171 353 5835/430 1221
Keen Graeme	4 Breams Buildings, London	0171 353 5835/430 1221
Kennedy Christopher Laurence Paul	Chambers of John Hand QC, Manchester	0161 955 9000
King Neil Gerald Alexander	2 Mitre Court Buildings, London	0171 583 1380
Kingsland Rt Hon Lord	4 Breams Buildings, London	0171 353 5835/430 1221
Knight Brian Joseph	Atkin Chambers, London	0171 404 0102
Langham Richard Geoffrey	1 Serjeants' Inn, London	0171 583 1355
Lewis Robert		
Lewsley Christopher Stanton	4 Breams Buildings, London	0171 353 5835/430 1221
Lieven Ms Nathalie Marie Daniella	4 Breams Buildings, London	0171 353 5835/430 1221
Litton John Letablere	4 Breams Buildings, London	0171 353 5835/430 1221
Lockhart-Mummery Christopher John	4 Breams Buildings, London	0171 353 5835/430 1221
Lofthouse Simon Timothy	Atkin Chambers, London	0171 404 0102
Lyness Scott Edward	1 Serjeants' Inn, London	0171 583 1355
Macleod Nigel Ronald Buchanan	4 Breams Buildings, London	0171 353 5835/430 1221
	40 King Street, Manchester	0161 832 9082
Macnab Alexander Andrew	Monckton Chambers, London	0171 405 7211
Macpherson The Hon Mary Stewart	2 Mitre Court Buildings, London	0171 583 1380
Makey Christopher Douglas	Old Square Chambers, London	0171 269 0300
	Old Square Chambers, Bristol	0117 927 7111
Male John Martin	4 Breams Buildings, London	0171 353 5835/430 1221
Marks Jonathan Harold	3 Verulam Buildings, London	0171 831 8441
Mathews Deni	8 Fountain Court, Birmingham	0121 236 5514
Maudslay Miss Diana Elizabeth		
Maurici James Patrick	4 Breams Buildings, London	0171 353 5835/430 1221
McCracken Robert Henry Joy	• 2 Harcourt Buildings, London	0171 353 8415
McHugh Miss Karen	4 Breams Buildings, London	0171 353 5835/430 1221
McMullan Manus Anthony	Atkin Chambers, London	0171 404 0102
Moore Professor Victor William Edward	2 Mitre Court Buildings, London	0171 583 1380
Moriarty Gerald Evelyn	2 Mitre Court Buildings, London	0171 583 1380
Morris-Coole Christopher	Goldsmith Building, London	0171 353 7881
Morshead Timothy Francis	4 Breams Buildings, London	0171 353 5835/430 1221
Mould Timothy James	4 Breams Buildings, London	0171 353 5835/430 1221
Murch Stephen James	• 11 Bolt Court, London	0171 353 2300

Nesbitt Timothy John Robert	199 Strand, London	0171 379 9779
Newcombe Andrew Bennett	• 2 Harcourt Buildings, London	0171 353 8415
O'Sullivan Bernard Anthony	Stanbrook & Henderson, London	0171 353 0101
	2 Harcourt Buildings, London	0171 583 9020
Ornsby Miss Suzanne Doreen	• 2 Harcourt Buildings, London	0171 353 8415
Ouseley Duncan Brian Walter	4-5 Gray's Inn Square, London	0171 404 5252
Ozin Paul David	23 Essex Street, London	0171 413 0353
Palfrey Montague Mark	Hardwicke Building, London	0171 242 2523
Parker Kenneth Blades	Monckton Chambers, London	0171 405 7211
Parkin Miss Fiona Jane	Atkin Chambers, London	0171 404 0102
Playford Jonathan Richard	2 Harcourt Buildings, London	0171 583 9020
Pleming Nigel Peter	39 Essex Street, London	0171 832 1111
Powles Stephen Robert	Stanbrook & Henderson, London	0171 353 0101
	2 Harcourt Buildings, London	0171 583 9020
Pugh Michael Charles	Old Square Chambers, London	0171 269 0300
	Old Square Chambers, Bristol	0117 927 7111
Purchas Robin Michael	• 2 Harcourt Buildings, London	0171 353 8415
Raeside Mark Andrew	Atkin Chambers, London	0171 404 0102
Rahman Ms Sadeqa Shaheen	1 Crown Office Row, London	0171 797 7500
Rankin William Peter	Oriel Chambers, Liverpool	0151 236 7191
Rawley Miss Dominique Jane	Atkin Chambers, London	0171 404 0102
Read Lionel Frank	1 Serjeants' Inn, London	0171 583 1355
Reese Colin Edward	Atkin Chambers, London	0171 404 0102
Richards David Wyn	Iscoed Chambers, Swansea	01792 652988/9/330
Richards Miss Jennifer	39 Essex Street, London	0171 832 1111
Robinson Miss Alice	4 Breams Buildings, London	0171 353 5835/430 1221
Roots Guy Robert Godfrey	2 Mitre Court Buildings, London	0171 583 1380
Royce Darryl Fraser	Atkin Chambers, London	0171 404 0102
Sands Mr Philippe Joseph	3 Verulam Buildings, London	0171 831 8441
Sawyer John Frederick		
Sheridan Maurice Bernard Gerard	• 3 Verulam Buildings, London	0171 831 8441
Sheridan Norman Patrick	• 11 Bolt Court, London	0171 353 2300
	• Redhill Chambers, Redhill	01737 780781
Silsoe The Lord	2 Mitre Court Buildings, London	0171 583 1380
Simor Miss Jessica Margaret Poppaea	Monckton Chambers, London	0171 405 7211
Smith David Anthony	4 Breams Buildings, London	0171 353 5835/430 1221
Smith Ms Katherine Emma	Monckton Chambers, London	0171 405 7211
Stilitz Daniel Malachi	11 King's Bench Walk, London	0171 632 8500
Stone Gregory	• 4-5 Gray's Inn Square, London	0171 404 5252
Streatfeild-James David Stewart	Atkin Chambers, London	0171 404 0102
Symons Christopher John Maurice	3 Verulam Buildings, London	0171 831 8441
Taylor Reuben Mallinson	2 Mitre Court Buildings, London	0171 583 1380
Thomas Miss Megan Moira	1 Serjeants' Inn, London	0171 583 1355
Thomas Stephen Edward Owen	St Philip's Chambers, Birmingham	0121 246 7000
Tobin Daniel Alphonsus Joseph	Chambers of Geoffrey Hawker, London	0171 583 8899
Tucker Miss Katherine Jane Greening	St Philip's Chambers, Birmingham	0121 246 7000
Turner Jonathan Richard	Monckton Chambers, London	0171 405 7211
Tyack David Guy	St Philip's Chambers, Birmingham	0121 246 7000
Valentine Donald Graham	Atkin Chambers, London	0171 404 0102
Village Peter Malcolm	• 4-5 Gray's Inn Square, London	0171 404 5252
Walker Steven John	Atkin Chambers, London	0171 404 0102
Wallace Ian Norman Duncan	Atkin Chambers, London	0171 404 0102
Warren Rupert Miles	2 Mitre Court Buildings, London	0171 583 1380
West Lawrence Joseph	Stanbrook & Henderson, London	0171 353 0101
	2 Harcourt Buildings, London	0171 583 9020
Wheeler Miss Marina Claire	Stanbrook & Henderson, London	0171 353 0101
	2 Harcourt Buildings, London	0171 583 9020
White Andrew	Atkin Chambers, London	0171 404 0102
Whybrow Christopher John	1 Serjeants' Inn, London	0171 583 1355
Widdicombe David Graham	2 Mitre Court Buildings, London	0171 583 1380
Wightwick (William) Iain	Assize Court Chambers, Bristol	0117 926 4587
Williams A John	• 13 King's Bench Walk, London	0171 353 7204
	• King's Bench Chambers, Oxford	01865 311066
Williams Miss Anne Margaret	4 Breams Buildings, London	0171 353 5835/430 1221
	37 Park Square, Leeds	0113 243 9422
Williams The Hon John Melville	• Old Square Chambers, London	0171 269 0300
	• Old Square Chambers, Bristol	0117 927 7111
Woolley David Rorie	• 1 Serjeants' Inn, London	0171 583 1355

• Expanded entry in Part D

EQUITY, WILLS AND TRUSTS

Adamyk Simon Charles	12 New Square, London	0171 419 1212
Aldridge James Hugh	13 Old Square, London	0171 404 4800
Angus Miss Tracey Anne	5 Stone Buildings, London	0171 242 6201
Arnfield Robert John	17 Old Buildings, London	0171 405 9653
Asplin Miss Sarah Jane	• 3 Stone Buildings, London	0171 242 4937/405 8358
Ayres Andrew John William	13 Old Square, London	0171 404 4800
Barber Miss Sally	5 Stone Buildings, London	0171 242 6201
Barker James Sebastian	Enterprise Chambers, London	0171 405 9471
	Enterprise Chambers, Leeds	0113 246 0391
	Enterprise Chambers, Newcastle upon Tyne	0191 222 3344
Blackett-Ord Mark	• 5 Stone Buildings, London	0171 242 6201
Brett Matthew Christopher Anthony	Harcourt Chambers, London	0171 353 6961/7
	Harcourt Chambers, Oxford	01865 791559
Brownbill David John	Gray's Inn Square, London	0171 242 3529
Cawley Neil Robert Loudoun	55 Temple Chambers, London	0171 353 7400
	Milton Keynes Chambers, Milton Keynes	01908 217857
Charman Andrew Julian	St Philip's Chambers, Birmingham	0121 246 7000
Cherryman John Richard	4 Breams Buildings, London	0171 353 5835/430 1221
Clarke Miss Anna Victoria	5 Stone Buildings, London	0171 242 6201
Clarke Ian James	Hardwicke Building, London	0171 242 2523
Clarke Peter John	Harcourt Chambers, London	0171 353 6961/7
	St Philip's Chambers, Birmingham	0121 246 7000
	Harcourt Chambers, Oxford	01865 791559
Clegg Sebastian James Barwick	Deans Court Chambers, Manchester	0161 834 4097
Collins John Morris	11 King's Bench Walk, London	0171 353 3337/8
	9 Woodhouse Square, Leeds	0113 245 1986
Collinson Miss Alicia Hester	Harcourt Chambers, London	0171 353 6961/7
	Harcourt Chambers, Oxford	01865 791559
Conroy Miss Marian	3 Stone Buildings, London	0171 242 4937/405 8358
Crail Miss (Elspeth) Ross	12 New Square, London	0171 419 1212
	Sovereign Chambers, Leeds	0113 245 1841/2/3
Cranfield Peter Anthony	3 Verulam Buildings, London	0171 831 8441
Crawford Grant	11 Old Square, London	0171 430 0341
Creaner Paul Anthony	15 Winckley Square, Preston	01772 252 828
Cross (Joseph) Edward	2 Gray's Inn Square Chambers, London	0171 242 0328/405 1317
Crosthwaite Graham Andrew	One King's Bench Walk, London	0171 936 1500
Cunningham Miss Claire Louise	St Philip's Chambers, Birmingham	0121 246 7000
Cunningham Mark James	13 Old Square, London	0171 404 4800
Darbyshire William Robert	Chambers of John Hand QC, Manchester	0161 955 9000
Davidson Edward Alan	• 11 Old Square, London	0171 430 0341
Deacock Adam Jason	Chambers of Lord Goodhart QC, London	0171 405 5577
Dilhorne The Rt Hon Viscount	4 Breams Buildings, London	0171 353 5835/430 1221
Dodge Peter Clive	11 Old Square, London	0171 430 0341
Doyle Louis George	Chambers of Andrew Campbell QC, Leeds	0113 245 5438
Elleray Anthony John	• 12 New Square, London	0171 419 1212
	• St James's Chambers, Manchester	0161 834 7000
	• Park Lane Chambers, Leeds	0113 228 5000
Fawls Richard Granville	5 Stone Buildings, London	0171 242 6201
Ferrier Ian Gilbert Straton	Gray's Inn Square, London	0171 242 3529
Francis Edward Gerald Francis	Enterprise Chambers, London	0171 405 9471
	Enterprise Chambers, Leeds	0113 246 0391
	Enterprise Chambers, Newcastle upon Tyne	0191 222 3344
Garnett Kevin Mitchell	5 New Square, London	0171 404 0404
Gerald Nigel Mortimer	Enterprise Chambers, London	0171 405 9471
	Enterprise Chambers, Leeds	0113 246 0391
	Enterprise Chambers, Newcastle upon Tyne	0191 222 3344
Gilbertson Mrs Helen Alison	Sackville Chambers, Norwich	01603 613516
Goodhart Lord	Chambers of Lord Goodhart QC, London	0171 405 5577
Gore Andrew Roger	Fenners Chambers, Cambridge	01223 368761
	Fenners Chambers, Peterborough	01733 562030
Gregory John Raymond	Deans Court Chambers, Manchester	0161 834 4097

B

• Expanded entry in Part D

	Deans Court Chambers, Preston	01772 555163
Hall Taylor Alexander Edward	11 Old Square, London	0171 430 0341
Halpern David Anthony	Enterprise Chambers, London	0171 405 9471
	Enterprise Chambers, Leeds	0113 246 0391
	Enterprise Chambers, Newcastle upon Tyne	0191 222 3344
Hantusch Robert Anthony	• 3 Stone Buildings, London	0171 242 4937/405 8358
Harbottle Gwilym Thomas	5 New Square, London	0171 404 0404
Hardwick Matthew Richard	Enterprise Chambers, London	0171 405 9471
	Enterprise Chambers, Leeds	0113 246 0391
	Enterprise Chambers, Newcastle upon Tyne	0191 222 3344
Hargreaves Miss Sara Jane	12 New Square, London	0171 419 1212
	Sovereign Chambers, Leeds	0113 245 1841/2/3
Harrod Henry Mark	5 Stone Buildings, London	0171 242 6201
Hayes Miss Josephine Mary	Chambers of Lord Goodhart QC, London	0171 405 5577
Henderson Launcelot Dinadan James	• 5 Stone Buildings, London	0171 242 6201
Herbert Mark Jeremy	• 5 Stone Buildings, London	0171 242 6201
Hess Edward John Watkin	Harcourt Chambers, London	0171 353 6961/7
	Harcourt Chambers, Oxford	01865 791559
Heywood Michael Edmundson	Chambers of Lord Goodhart QC, London	0171 405 5577
	Cobden House Chambers, Manchester	0161 833 6000/6001
Holmes Justin Francis	Chambers of Lord Goodhart QC, London	0171 405 5577
Howard Charles Anthony Frederick	New Court Chambers, London	0171 831 9500
Hughes Miss Mary Josephine	Chambers of Lord Goodhart QC, London	0171 405 5577
Hunter Anthony Charles Bryan	5 Pump Court, London	0171 353 2532
Hunter William Quigley	No 1 Serjeants' Inn, London	0171 415 6666
Iwi Quintin Joseph	Stanbrook & Henderson, London	0171 353 0101
	2 Harcourt Buildings, London	0171 583 9020
Jackson Dirik George Allan	• Chambers of Mr Peter Crampin QC, London	0171 831 0081
Jackson Nicholas David Kingsley	The Chambers of Adrian Lyon, Liverpool	0151 236 4421/8240/6757
James Michael Frank	Enterprise Chambers, London	0171 405 9471
	Enterprise Chambers, Leeds	0113 246 0391
	Enterprise Chambers, Newcastle upon Tyne	0191 222 3344
Jefferies Thomas Robert	Chambers of Lord Goodhart QC, London	0171 405 5577
Jennings Timothy Robin Finnegan	Enterprise Chambers, London	0171 405 9471
	Enterprise Chambers, Leeds	0113 246 0391
	Enterprise Chambers, Newcastle upon Tyne	0191 222 3344
Johnson Michael Sloan	Chambers of John Hand QC, Manchester	0161 955 9000
Jones Geraint Martyn	Fenners Chambers, Cambridge	01223 368761
	Fenners Chambers, Peterborough	01733 562030
Jones Rhys Charles Mansel	33 Bedford Row, London	0171 242 6476
Jory Robert John Hugh	Enterprise Chambers, London	0171 405 9471
	Enterprise Chambers, Leeds	0113 246 0391
	Enterprise Chambers, Newcastle upon Tyne	0191 222 3344
Kremen Philip Michael	Hardwicke Building, London	0171 242 2523
Lamont Miss Camilla Rose	Chambers of Lord Goodhart QC, London	0171 405 5577
Landes Miss Anna-Rose	St Philip's Chambers, Birmingham	0121 246 7000
Laughton Samuel Dennis	17 Old Buildings, London	0171 405 9653
Le Poidevin Nicholas Peter	12 New Square, London	0171 419 1212
	Sovereign Chambers, Leeds	0113 245 1841/2/3
Legge Henry	5 Stone Buildings, London	0171 242 6201
Levy Benjamin Keith	Enterprise Chambers, London	0171 405 9471
	Enterprise Chambers, Leeds	0113 246 0391
	Enterprise Chambers, Newcastle upon Tyne	0191 222 3344
Levy Robert Stuart	9 Stone Buildings, London	0171 404 5055
	Assize Court Chambers, Bristol	0117 926 4587

Lonsdale Miss Marion Mary	Chambers of Geoffrey Hawker, London	0171 583 8899
Mann George Anthony	Enterprise Chambers, London	0171 405 9471
	Enterprise Chambers, Leeds	0113 246 0391
	Enterprise Chambers, Newcastle upon Tyne	0191 222 3344
Marten Richard Hedley Westwood	Chambers of Lord Goodhart QC, London	0171 405 5577
Mauger Miss Claire Shanti Andrea	Enterprise Chambers, London	0171 405 9471
McCarthy William	New Bailey Chambers, Preston	01772 258 087
McCutcheon Barry Duff	Gray's Inn Square, London	0171 242 3529
McKay Christopher Alexander	Angel Chambers, Swansea	01792 464623/464648
McKinnell Miss Soraya Jane	Enterprise Chambers, London	0171 405 9471
	Enterprise Chambers, Leeds	0113 246 0391
	Enterprise Chambers, Newcastle upon Tyne	0191 222 3344
McQuail Ms Katherine Emma	11 Old Square, London	0171 430 0341
Middleton Miss Georgina Claire	New Court Chambers, London	0171 831 9500
Morgan Charles James Arthur	Enterprise Chambers, London	0171 405 9471
	Enterprise Chambers, Leeds	0113 246 0391
	Enterprise Chambers, Newcastle upon Tyne	0191 222 3344
Mullis Anthony Roger	Chambers of Lord Goodhart QC, London	0171 405 5577
Nebhrajani Miss Mel	9 Stone Buildings, London	0171 404 5055
Newman Miss Catherine Mary	• 13 Old Square, London	0171 404 4800
Nicol-Gent William Philip Trahair	King's Chambers, Eastbourne	01323 416053
Norbury Luke Edward	17 Old Buildings, London	0171 405 9653
Norris Alastair Hubert	• 5 Stone Buildings, London	0171 242 6201
	• Southernhay Chambers, Exeter	01392 255777
Nurse Gordon Bramwell William	11 Old Square, London	0171 430 0341
O'Sullivan Michael Morton	5 Stone Buildings, London	0171 242 6201
Oakley Tony	• 11 Old Square, London	0171 430 0341
Ohrenstein Dov	Chambers of Lord Goodhart QC, London	0171 405 5577
Ovey Miss Elizabeth Helen	11 Old Square, London	0171 430 0341
Parry David Julian Thomas	Chambers of Lord Goodhart QC, London	0171 405 5577
Peacock Nicholas Christopher	13 Old Square, London	0171 404 4800
Peacocke Mrs Teresa Anne Rosen	Enterprise Chambers, London	0171 405 9471
	Enterprise Chambers, Leeds	0113 246 0391
	Enterprise Chambers, Newcastle upon Tyne	0191 222 3344
Picarda Hubert Alistair Paul	Chambers of Lord Goodhart QC, London	0171 405 5577
Pilkington Mrs Mavis Patricia	9 Woodhouse Square, Leeds	0113 245 1986
Pimentel Carlos de Serpa Alberto Legg	3 Stone Buildings, London	0171 242 4937/405 8358
Pryke Stuart	Trinity Chambers, Newcastle upon Tyne	0191 232 1927
Purdie Robert Anthony James	28 Western Road, Oxford	01865 204911
Quint Mrs Joan Francesca Rae	11 Old Square, London	0171 242 5022
Radevsky Anthony Eric	• 5 Bell Yard, London	0171 333 8811
Randall John Yeoman	7 Stone Buildings, London	0171 405 3886/242 3546
	St Philip's Chambers, Birmingham	0121 246 7000
Reed Miss Penelope Jane	9 Stone Buildings, London	0171 404 5055
Rees David Benjamin	5 Stone Buildings, London	0171 242 6201
Rich Miss Ann Barbara	5 Stone Buildings, London	0171 242 6201
Richardson Miss Sarah Jane	Enterprise Chambers, London	0171 405 9471
	Enterprise Chambers, Leeds	0113 246 0391
	Enterprise Chambers, Newcastle upon Tyne	0191 222 3344
Robson John Malcolm	2 Gray's Inn Square Chambers, London	0171 242 0328/405 1317
	Assize Court Chambers, Bristol	0117 926 4587
Rodgers Miss Doris June	Harcourt Chambers, London	0171 353 6961/7
	Harcourt Chambers, Oxford	01865 791559
Ross Martyn John Greaves	• 5 New Square, London	0171 404 0404
	• Octagon House, Norwich	01603 623186
Rowell David Stewart	Chambers of Lord Goodhart QC, London	0171 405 5577
Rule Jonathan Daniel	Merchant Chambers, Manchester	0161 839 7070

B

• Expanded entry in Part D

Rumney Conrad William Arthur	St Philip's Chambers, Birmingham	0121 246 7000
Sagar (Edward) Leigh	12 New Square, London	0171 419 1212
	Sovereign Chambers, Leeds	0113 245 1841/2/3
	Newport Chambers, Newport	01633 267403/255855
Selway Dr Katherine Emma	11 Old Square, London	0171 430 0341
Shah Bajul Amratlal Somchand	Twenty-Four Old Buildings, London	0171 404 0946
Simmonds Andrew John	5 Stone Buildings, London	0171 242 6201
Simpson Edwin John Fletcher	12 New Square, London	0171 419 1212
Sisley Timothy Julian Crispin	9 Stone Buildings, London	0171 404 5055
	Westgate Chambers, Lewes	01273 480 510
Smart Miss Jacqueline Anne	Trinity Chambers, Newcastle upon Tyne	0191 232 1927
Soares Patrick Claude	Gray's Inn Square, London	0171 242 3529
Southern Professor David Boardman	• 3 Temple Gardens Tax Chambers, London	0171 353 7884
Staddon Miss Claire Ann	12 New Square, London	0171 419 1212
	Sovereign Chambers, Leeds	0113 245 1841/2/3
Stevens-Hoare Miss Michelle	• Hardwicke Building, London	0171 242 2523
Stewart Alexander Joseph	5 New Square, London	0171 404 0404
Stewart Nicholas John Cameron	Hardwicke Building, London	0171 242 2523
Sugar Simon Gareth	5 New Square, London	0171 404 0404
Sydenham Colin Peter	4 Breams Buildings, London	0171 353 5835/430 1221
Thomas Nigel Matthew	13 Old Square, London	0171 404 4800
Thompson Steven Lim	Twenty-Four Old Buildings, London	0171 404 0946
Tidmarsh Christopher Ralph Francis	5 Stone Buildings, London	0171 242 6201
Tipples Miss Amanda Jane	13 Old Square, London	0171 404 4800
Trace Anthony John	• 13 Old Square, London	0171 404 4800
Twigger Andrew Mark	3 Stone Buildings, London	0171 242 4937/405 8358
Vane The Hon Christopher John Fletcher	Trinity Chambers, Newcastle upon Tyne	0191 232 1927
Walker Andrew Greenfield	Chambers of Lord Goodhart QC, London	0171 405 5577
Warnock-Smith Mrs Shan	5 Stone Buildings, London	0171 242 6201
Waters Malcolm Ian	• 11 Old Square, London	0171 430 0341
Weatherill Bernard Richard	Chambers of Lord Goodhart QC, London	0171 405 5577
West Mark	• 11 Old Square, London	0171 430 0341
Whitehouse Christopher John	Gray's Inn Square, London	0171 242 3529
Williamson Miss Bridget Susan	Enterprise Chambers, London	0171 405 9471
	Enterprise Chambers, Leeds	0113 246 0391
	Enterprise Chambers, Newcastle upon Tyne	0191 222 3344
Yelton Michael Paul	Fenners Chambers, Cambridge	01223 368761
	Fenners Chambers, Peterborough	01733 562030

EUROPEAN CONVENTION ON HUMAN RIGHTS

Jones Timothy Arthur	• Arden Chambers, London	0171 242 4244
	• St Philip's Chambers, Birmingham	0121 246 7000

EUROPEAN HUMAN RIGHTS

Hoyal Ms Jane	• 1 Pump Court, London	0171 583 2012/353 4341

EXTRADITION

Saffian Ms Leah Susan	Queen Elizabeth Building, London	0171 583 5766

FACTORING

Benson Julian Christopher Woodburn	One Essex Court, London	0171 936 3030
Brannigan Peter John Sean	One Essex Court, London	0171 936 3030
Bull (Donald) Roger	One Essex Court, London	0171 936 3030
Goodbody Peter James	• Oriel Chambers, Liverpool	0151 236 7191
John Peter Charles	One Essex Court, London	0171 936 3030

FALSE IMPRISONMENT

Keeley James Francis	Sovereign Chambers, Leeds	0113 245 1841/2/3

FALSE IMPRISONMENT/MALICIOUS PROSECUTION ACTIONS

Dunn Christopher	Sovereign Chambers, Leeds	0113 245 1841/2/3

• Expanded entry in Part D

FAMILY

Adejumo Mrs Hilda Ekpo	• Temple Chambers, London	0171 583 1001 (2 lines)
Ahmed Farooq Tahir	8 King Street Chambers, Manchester	0161 834 9560
Al'Hassan Khadim	Equity Chambers, Birmingham	0121 233 2100
Alexander Ian Douglas Gavin	11 Bolt Court, London	0171 353 2300
	Redhill Chambers, Redhill	01737 780781
Allardice Miss Miranda Jane	Pump Court Chambers, London	0171 353 0711
	Pump Court Chambers, Winchester	01962 868161
Alomo Richard Olusoji	14 Gray's Inn Square, London	0171 242 0858
Ames Geoffrey Alan	29 Bedford Row Chambers, London	0171 831 2626
Amiraftabi Miss Roshanak	Hardwicke Building, London	0171 242 2523
Arthur Gavyn Farr	Harcourt Chambers, London	0171 353 6961/7
	Harcourt Chambers, Oxford	01865 791559
Ashley Mark Robert	Tindal Chambers, Chelmsford	01245 267742
	Tindal Chambers, St Albans	01727 843383
Ashton Raglan Halley	New Court Chambers, Birmingham	0121 693 6656
Asteris Peter David	Eighteen Carlton Crescent, Southampton	01703 639001
Auld Miss Catherine Rohan	Harcourt Chambers, London	0171 353 6961/7
	Harcourt Chambers, Oxford	01865 791559
Austins Christopher John	Assize Court Chambers, Bristol	0117 926 4587
Bagnall Matthew Philip Cooper	Chambers of Geoffrey Hawker, London	0171 583 8899
Baker Jonathan Leslie	Harcourt Chambers, London	0171 353 6961/7
	Harcourt Chambers, Oxford	01865 791559
Baker Ms Rachel Mary Theresa	Hardwicke Building, London	0171 242 2523
Baldock Miss Susan Anne	2 Gray's Inn Square Chambers, London	0171 242 0328/405 1317
Bancroft Miss Anna Louise	Deans Court Chambers, Manchester	0161 834 4097
	Deans Court Chambers, Preston	01772 555163
Barlow Miss Sarah Helen	St Paul's House, Leeds	0113 245 5866
Barstow Stephen Royden	Harcourt Chambers, London	0171 353 6961/7
	Harcourt Chambers, Oxford	01865 791559
Bates Alexander Andrew	St Paul's House, Leeds	0113 245 5866
Beasley-Murray Mrs Caroline Wynne	Fenners Chambers, Cambridge	01223 368761
	Fenners Chambers, Peterborough	01733 562030
Beaumont Marc Clifford	• Pump Court Chambers, London	0171 353 0711
	• Harrow-on-the-Hill Chambers, Harrow on the Hill	0181 423 7444
	• Pump Court Chambers, Winchester	01962 868161
	• Windsor Barristers' Chambers, Windsor	01753 648 899
Belbin Miss Heather Patricia	Oriel Chambers, Liverpool	0151 236 7191
Benner Miss Lucinda Diana Kate	11 Bolt Court, London	0171 353 2300
	Redhill Chambers, Redhill	01737 780781
Bennett John Martyn	• Peel House Chambers, Liverpool	0151 236 4321
Benson Julian Christopher Woodburn	One Essex Court, London	0171 936 3030
Bergin Timothy William	Sussex Chambers, Brighton	01273 607953
Bhattacharyya Ardhendu	1 Gray's Inn Square, London	0171 405 0956
	11 St Bernards Road, Slough	01753 553806/817989
Bickerdike Roger John	9 Woodhouse Square, Leeds	0113 245 1986
Bindloss Edward Christopher James	Chambers of Andrew Campbell QC, Leeds	0113 245 5438
Birch Roger Allen	12 New Square, London	0171 419 1212
	Sovereign Chambers, Leeds	0113 245 1841/2/3
	Lancaster Buildings, Manchester	0161 661 4444
Bishop Timothy Harper Paul	1 Mitre Court Buildings, London	0171 797 7070
Blair Bruce Graeme Donald	1 Mitre Court Buildings, London	0171 797 7070
Bloom-Davis Desmond Niall Laurence	Pump Court Chambers, London	0171 353 0711
	Pump Court Chambers, Winchester	01962 868161
Boney Guy Thomas Knowles	Pump Court Chambers, London	0171 353 0711
	Harrow-on-the-Hill Chambers, Harrow on the Hill	0181 423 7444
	Pump Court Chambers, Winchester	01962 868161
Boora Jinder Singh	Regent Chambers, Stoke-on-Trent	01782 286666
Booth Alan James	Deans Court Chambers, Manchester	0161 834 4097
	Deans Court Chambers, Preston	01772 555163
Boothroyd Miss Susan Elizabeth	Westgate Chambers, Newcastle upon Tyne	0191 261 4407/232 9785
Bowcock Miss Samantha Jane	15 Winckley Square, Preston	01772 252 828

Boydell Edward Patrick Stirrup	Pump Court Chambers, London	0171 353 0711
	Pump Court Chambers, Winchester	01962 868161
Boyle David Stuart	Deans Court Chambers, Manchester	0161 834 4097
Brasse Miss Gillian Denise	14 Gray's Inn Square, London	0171 242 0858
Brazil Dominic Thomas George	14 Gray's Inn Square, London	0171 242 0858
Brody Miss Karen Rachel	Deans Court Chambers, Manchester	0161 834 4097
	Deans Court Chambers, Preston	01772 555163
Brown David Charles	Cathedral Chambers, Newcastle upon Tyne	0191 232 1311
	Southsea Chambers, Portsmouth	01705 291261
Brown Miss Joanne	2 Gray's Inn Square Chambers, London	0171 242 0328/405 1317
Brown Miss Rebecca Jane	14 Gray's Inn Square, London	0171 242 0858
Brown Thomas Christopher Ellis	Fenners Chambers, Cambridge	01223 368761
	Fenners Chambers, Peterborough	01733 562030
Brunton Sean Alexander McKay	Pump Court Chambers, London	0171 353 0711
	Pump Court Chambers, Winchester	01962 868161
Budden Miss Caroline Rachel	One King's Bench Walk, London	0171 936 1500
Bull (Donald) Roger	One Essex Court, London	0171 936 3030
Bundred Miss Gillian Sarah	Oriel Chambers, Liverpool	0151 236 7191
Burdon Michael Stewart	St Paul's House, Leeds	0113 245 5866
Burles David John	Goldsmith Building, London	0171 353 7881
Butler Miss Judith Jane Scott	6 Pump Court, London	0171 797 8400
	6-8 Mill Street, Maidstone	01622 688 094
Cameron Miss Barbara Alexander	Stanbrook & Henderson, London	0171 353 0101
	2 Harcourt Buildings, London	0171 583 9020
Campbell Miss Alexis Anne	Hardwicke Building, London	0171 242 2523
Candlin James Richard	Chambers of Geoffrey Hawker, London	0171 583 8899
Carden Nicholas	1 Mitre Court Buildings, London	0171 797 7070
Carrodus Miss Gail Caroline	New Court Chambers, London	0171 831 9500
Carron Richard Byron	11 Bolt Court, London	0171 353 2300
	Redhill Chambers, Redhill	01737 780781
Carter Miss Lesley Ann	25-27 Castle Street, Liverpool	0151 227 5661/5666/236 5072
Carter Miss Rosalyn Frances	St Philip's Chambers, Birmingham	0121 246 7000
Cave Jeremy Stephen	1 Crown Office Row, London	0171 797 7500
	Crown Office Row Chambers, Brighton	01273 625625
Cave Miss Patricia Ann	7 Stone Buildings, London	0171 242 0961
Charles Ms Deborah Ann	6 Pump Court, London	0171 797 8400
Clark Miss Hazel Anne	Fenners Chambers, Cambridge	01223 368761
	Fenners Chambers, Peterborough	01733 562030
Clover Miss Sarah	2 Mitre Court Buildings, London	0171 353 1353
Collier Martin Melton	Fenners Chambers, Cambridge	01223 368761
	Fenners Chambers, Peterborough	01733 562030
Collinson Miss Alicia Hester	Harcourt Chambers, London	0171 353 6961/7
	Harcourt Chambers, Oxford	01865 791559
Cooke Graham Owen John	23 Essex Street, London	0171 413 0353
Corbett Miss Michelle Jane	14 Gray's Inn Square, London	0171 242 0858
Cottage Miss Rosina	9-12 Bell Yard, London	0171 400 1800
Cottrell Matthew Robert	Oriel Chambers, Liverpool	0151 236 7191
Coulter Barry John	One Essex Court, London	0171 936 3030
Cowen Miss Sally Emma	Chambers of Geoffrey Hawker, London	0171 583 8899
Crane Miss Suzanne Denise	New Court Chambers, Birmingham	0121 693 6656
Crookes Miss Alison Naomi		
Cross Mrs Joanna	9 Woodhouse Square, Leeds	0113 245 1986
Cross (Joseph) Edward	2 Gray's Inn Square Chambers, London	0171 242 0328/405 1317
Crossley Simon Justin	9 Woodhouse Square, Leeds	0113 245 1986
Crosthwaite Graham Andrew	One King's Bench Walk, London	0171 936 1500
Crowley Mrs Jane Elizabeth	One Garden Court Family Law Chambers, London	0171 797 7900
	30 Park Place, Cardiff	01222 398421
Cusworth Nicholas Neville Grylls	1 Mitre Court Buildings, London	0171 797 7070
Dangor Mrs Patricia Madree Trenton	14 Gray's Inn Square, London	0171 242 0858
Davey Miss Tina Elaine	9-12 Bell Yard, London	0171 400 1800
Davidson Miss Katharine Mary	1 Mitre Court Buildings, London	0171 797 7070
Davies Miss Lindsay Jane	Fenners Chambers, Cambridge	01223 368761
	Fenners Chambers, Peterborough	01733 562030
Davies Miss Penny May	Chambers of Harjit Singh, London	0171 353 1356
de Jehan David	St Paul's House, Leeds	0113 245 5866

De Zonie Miss Jane	14 Gray's Inn Square, London	0171 242 0858
Denton Miss Michelle Jayne	9-12 Bell Yard, London	0171 400 1800
Dhaliwal Miss Davinder Kaur	New Court Chambers, Birmingham	0121 693 6656
Dixon Ian Frederick	Cathedral Chambers, Newcastle upon Tyne	0191 232 1311
Dixon John Watts	Harcourt Chambers, London	0171 353 6961/7
	Harcourt Chambers, Oxford	01865 791559
Dodson Miss Joanna	14 Gray's Inn Square, London	0171 242 0858
	Park Court Chambers, Leeds	0113 243 3277
Dogra Miss Tanyia Anita	Chambers of Harjit Singh, London	0171 353 1356
Downham Miss Gillian Celia	Rougemont Chambers, Exeter	01392 410471
Dowokpor Jonathan Kukasi	Tollgate Mews Chambers, London	0171 511 1838
Drayton Henry Alexander	2 Gray's Inn Square Chambers, London	0171 242 0328/405 1317
Dubbery Mark Edward	Pump Court Chambers, London	0171 353 0711
Duffy Derek James	St Paul's House, Leeds	0113 245 5866
Duffy Michael	Cathedral Chambers, Ely, Ely	01353 666775
Dyer Nigel Ingram John	1 Mitre Court Buildings, London	0171 797 7070
Eccles Hugh William Patrick	Harcourt Chambers, London	0171 353 6961/7
	Harcourt Chambers, Oxford	01865 791559
Edwards Anthony Howard	Oriel Chambers, Liverpool	0151 236 7191
Edwards Nigel Royston	St Paul's House, Leeds	0113 245 5866
Elvidge John Allan	1 Mitre Court Buildings, London	0171 797 7070
Emanuel Mark Pering Wolff	14 Gray's Inn Square, London	0171 242 0858
Espley Miss Susan	Fenners Chambers, Cambridge	01223 368761
	Fenners Chambers, Peterborough	01733 562030
Evans Miss Delyth Mary	2 Mitre Court Buildings, London	0171 353 1353
Evans Miss Lisa Claire	St Philip's Chambers, Birmingham	0121 246 7000
Evans Miss Suzanne Marie	Oriel Chambers, Liverpool	0151 236 7191
Everall Mark Andrew	1 Mitre Court Buildings, London	0171 797 7070
Fane Miss Angela Elizabeth	Goldsmith Building, London	0171 353 7881
Farmer Pryce Michael	1 Dr Johnson's Buildings, London	0171 353 9328
	Goldsmith Building, London	0171 353 7881
	Sedan House, Chester	01244 320480/348282
Fenston Miss Felicia Donovan	Stanbrook & Henderson, London	0171 353 0101
	2 Harcourt Buildings, London	0171 583 9020
Ferguson Mrs Katharine Ann	Fenners Chambers, Cambridge	01223 368761
	Fenners Chambers, Peterborough	01733 562030
Fletcher Marcus Alexander	One King's Bench Walk, London	0171 936 1500
Fogarty Peter Dominic	Oriel Chambers, Liverpool	0151 236 7191
Forbes Peter George	6 Pump Court, London	0171 797 8400
	6-8 Mill Street, Maidstone	01622 688 094
Ford Gerard James	Baker Street Chambers, Middlesbrough	01642 873873
Ford Miss Monica Dorothy Patience	14 Gray's Inn Square, London	0171 242 0858
Forster Ms Sarah Judith	14 Gray's Inn Square, London	0171 242 0858
	Westgate Chambers, Lewes	01273 480 510
Fox Miss Anna Katherine Helen	Oriel Chambers, Liverpool	0151 236 7191
Fox Miss Nicola Susan	One Garden Court Family Law Chambers, London	0171 797 7900
Foxwell George (Augustus)	Fenners Chambers, Cambridge	01223 368761
	Fenners Chambers, Peterborough	01733 562030
Frazer Christopher Mark	Harcourt Chambers, London	0171 353 6961/7
	Harcourt Chambers, Oxford	01865 791559
Freeston Miss Lynn Roberta		
Fricker Mrs Marilyn Ann	Farrar's Building, London	0171 583 9241
	Sovereign Chambers, Leeds	0113 245 1841/2/3
Fuad Kerim	Chambers of Helen Grindrod QC, London	0171 404 4777
Furminger Michael Ashley	Michael Furminger, Brixham	01803 882293
Gibb Miss Fiona Margaret	Queen Elizabeth Building, London	0171 353 7181 (12 lines)
Gifford Miss Cynthia Alice Sophie	Verulam Chambers, London	0171 813 2400
Gilbertson Mrs Helen Alison	Sackville Chambers, Norwich	01603 613516
Gillibrand Philip Martin Mangnall	Pump Court Chambers, London	0171 353 0711
	Pump Court Chambers, Winchester	01962 868161
Godfrey John Paul	Wilberforce Chambers, Hull	01482 323 264
Godfrey Miss Louise Sarah	14 Gray's Inn Square, London	0171 242 0858
	Park Court Chambers, Leeds	0113 243 3277
Goodchild Mrs Elizabeth Ann	Watford Chambers, Watford	01923 220553
Goodwin Nicholas Alexander John	Harcourt Chambers, London	0171 353 6961/7
Gordon Mark John	11 Bolt Court, London	0171 353 2300
	Redhill Chambers, Redhill	01737 780781

B

Gordon-Dean Miss Natasha
Gordon-Saker Mrs Liza Helen | Fenners Chambers, Cambridge | 01223 368761
| Fenners Chambers, Peterborough | 01733 562030
Gorna Miss Anne Christina | 4 Paper Buildings, London | 0171 353 3366/583 7155
| Cathedral Chambers (Jan Wood Independent Barristers' Clerk), Exeter | 01392 210900
Gray Miss Jennifer | 11 Old Square, London | 0171 242 5022
Greenan Miss Sarah Octavia | • 9 Woodhouse Square, Leeds | 0113 245 1986
Gregory Richard Hamilton | Harcourt Chambers, London | 0171 353 6961/7
Gresty Miss Denise Lynn | Sovereign Chambers, Leeds | 0113 245 1841/2/3
Grice Miss Joanna Harrison | One King's Bench Walk, London | 0171 936 1500
Guirguis Miss Sheren | White Friars Chambers, Chester | 01244 323070
Hall Miss Joanna Mary | 14 Gray's Inn Square, London | 0171 242 0858
Hall-Smith Martin Clive William | Goldsmith Building, London | 0171 353 7881
Halpin Thomas Gavin | Earl Street Chambers, Maidstone | 01622 671222
Hammerton Miss Veronica Lesley | No 1 Serjeants' Inn, London | 0171 415 6666
Hanson Timothy Vincent Richard | St Philip's Chambers, Birmingham | 0121 246 7000
Harrison Ms Averil | 2 Harcourt Buildings, London | 0171 583 9020
Hartley-Davies Paul Kevil | 30 Park Place, Cardiff | 01222 398421
Harvey Miss Jayne Denise | Goldsworth Chambers, London | 0171 405 7117
Hayes John Allan | Chambers of Andrew Campbell QC, Leeds | 0113 245 5438
Heaton Clive William | Chambers of Andrew Campbell QC, Leeds | 0113 245 5438
Heaton Miss Frances Margaret | 4 Brick Court, London | 0171 797 7766
| Deans Court Chambers, Manchester | 0161 834 4097
| Deans Court Chambers, Preston | 01772 555163
Henley Mark Robert Daniel | 9 Woodhouse Square, Leeds | 0113 245 1986
Hess Edward John Watkin | Harcourt Chambers, London | 0171 353 6961/7
| Harcourt Chambers, Oxford | 01865 791559
Hilder Miss Carolyn Hayley-Jane | 3 Fountain Court, Birmingham | 0121 236 5854
Hodgson Ms Jane | 9 Woodhouse Square, Leeds | 0113 245 1986
Hogg The Rt Hon Douglas Martin | 4 Paper Buildings, London | 0171 353 3366/583 7155
| 37 Park Square, Leeds | 0113 243 9422
Hollingworth Peter James Michael | 22 Albion Place, Northampton | 01604 636271
Hollow Paul John | Fenners Chambers, Cambridge | 01223 368761
| Fenners Chambers, Peterborough | 01733 562030
Horlick Lady Fiona | 23 Essex Street, London | 0171 413 0353
Horowitz Michael | 1 Mitre Court Buildings, London | 0171 797 7070
Horton Miss Caroline Ann | Fenners Chambers, Cambridge | 01223 368761
| Fenners Chambers, Peterborough | 01733 562030
Horwood Miss Anya Louise | 25-27 Castle Street, Liverpool | 0151 227 5661/5666/236 5072
Howard Charles Anthony Frederick | New Court Chambers, London | 0171 831 9500
Howard Graham John | Queen Elizabeth Building, London | 0171 353 7181 (12 lines)
Howe Miss Penelope Anne Macgregor | Pump Court Chambers, London | 0171 353 0711
Hoyal Ms Jane | • 1 Pump Court, London | 0171 583 2012/353 4341
Hudson Miss Kathryn Jane | 14 Gray's Inn Square, London | 0171 242 0858
Hughes Miss Judith Caroline Anne | 1 Mitre Court Buildings, London | 0171 797 7070
Hughes Miss Meryl Elizabeth | Fenners Chambers, Cambridge | 01223 368761
| Fenners Chambers, Peterborough | 01733 562030
Humberstone Mrs Pearl Edith | Verulam Chambers, London | 0171 813 2400
Hunt Miss Alison Janet | St Paul's House, Leeds | 0113 245 5866
Hunter Anthony Charles Bryan | 5 Pump Court, London | 0171 353 2532
Hussain Miss Frida Khanam | 17 Carlton Crescent, Southampton | 01703 320320
Iqbal Abdul Shaffaq | Chambers of Andrew Campbell QC, Leeds | 0113 245 5438
Irving Miss Gillian | Chambers of John Hand QC, Manchester | 0161 955 9000
Islam-Choudhury Mugni | 11 Bolt Court, London | 0171 353 2300
Iwi Quintin Joseph | Stanbrook & Henderson, London | 0171 353 0101
| 2 Harcourt Buildings, London | 0171 583 9020
Jack Simon Michael | 9 Woodhouse Square, Leeds | 0113 245 1986
Jarman Mark Christopher | 14 Gray's Inn Square, London | 0171 242 0858
Jay Adam Marc | One King's Bench Walk, London | 0171 936 1500
Jenkala Adrian Aleksander | 11 Bolt Court, London | 0171 353 2300
| Redhill Chambers, Redhill | 01737 780781
Jenkins John David | 30 Park Place, Cardiff | 01222 398421
John Peter Charles | One Essex Court, London | 0171 936 3030
Jones Rhys Charles Mansel | 33 Bedford Row, London | 0171 242 6476
Josling William Henry Charles | Fenners Chambers, Cambridge | 01223 368761

• Expanded entry in Part D

	Fenners Chambers, Peterborough	01733 562030
Judd Miss Frances Jean	Harcourt Chambers, London	0171 353 6961/7
	Harcourt Chambers, Oxford	01865 791559
Kalsi Mrs Maninder	New Court Chambers, Birmingham	0121 693 6656
Kelly Geoffrey Robert	Pump Court Chambers, London	0171 353 0711
	Pump Court Chambers, Winchester	01962 868161
Kelly Miss Geraldine Therese		
Kent Miss Georgina	5 Essex Court, London	0171 410 2000
Kenward Timothy David Nelson	25-27 Castle Street, Liverpool	0151 227 5661/5666/236 5072
Ker-Reid John	Pump Court Chambers, London	0171 353 0711
	Pump Court Chambers, Winchester	01962 868161
Khan Avicenna Alkindi Cornelius	55 Temple Chambers, London	0171 353 7400
Khan Miss Helen Mary Grace	Chambers of Lord Campbell of	0171 353 9276
	Alloway QC, London	
Khan Saadallah Frans Hassan	55 Temple Chambers, London	0171 353 7400
King Peter Duncan	5 Pump Court, London	0171 353 2532
	Fenners Chambers, Cambridge	01223 368761
King Miss Samantha Leonie	14 Gray's Inn Square, London	0171 242 0858
Kingscote Geoffrey Llewelyn Woodward	1 Mitre Court Buildings, London	0171 797 7070
Kinnier Andrew John	2 Harcourt Buildings, London	0171 583 9020
Kolodynski Stefan Richard	New Court Chambers, Birmingham	0121 693 6656
Kushner Miss Lindsey Joy	14 Gray's Inn Square, London	0171 242 0858
	28 St John Street, Manchester	0161 834 8418
Lambert Miss Sarah Katrina	1 Crown Office Row, London	0171 797 7500
Lander Charles Gideon	25-27 Castle Street, Liverpool	0151 227 5661/5666/236 5072
Langridge Ms Nicola Dawn	Hardwicke Building, London	0171 242 2523
Le Grice Valentine	1 Mitre Court Buildings, London	0171 797 7070
	Southernhay Chambers, Exeter	01392 255777
Leech Brian Walter Thomas	No 1 Serjeants' Inn, London	0171 415 6666
Leonard Charles Robert Weston	Goldsmith Building, London	0171 353 7881
Levy Allan Edward	17 Bedford Row, London	0171 831 7314
Lewis Jeffrey Allan	9 Woodhouse Square, Leeds	0113 245 1986
Lister Miss Caroline Jane	One King's Bench Walk, London	0171 936 1500
Litherland Miss Rebecca Jane	Fenners Chambers, Cambridge	01223 368761
	Fenners Chambers, Peterborough	01733 562030
Lloyd Miss Wendy-Jane	25-27 Castle Street, Liverpool	0151 227 5661/5666/236 5072
Lobo Matthew Joseph Edwin	Fenners Chambers, Cambridge	01223 368761
	Fenners Chambers, Peterborough	01733 562030
Lochrane Damien Horatio Ross	Pump Court Chambers, London	0171 353 0711
	Pump Court Chambers, Winchester	01962 868161
Loftus Miss Teresa Anne Martine	25-27 Castle Street, Liverpool	0151 227 5661/5666/236 5072
Logan Miss Maura	St John's Chambers, Hale Barns	0161 980 7379
Lunt Steven	9 Woodhouse Square, Leeds	0113 245 1986
Lynch Terry John	22 Albion Place, Northampton	01604 636271
Lyne Mark Hilary	One Essex Court, London	0171 936 3030
Lyon Stephen John	14 Gray's Inn Square, London	0171 242 0858
	Westgate Chambers, Lewes	01273 480 510
MacKillop Norman Malcolm	• Chartlands Chambers, Northampton	01604 603322
Maidment Mrs Susan Rachel	One King's Bench Walk, London	0171 936 1500
Manson Miss Julie-Ann	11 Bolt Court, London	0171 353 2300
	Redhill Chambers, Redhill	01737 780781
Marley Miss Sarah Anne	5 Pump Court, London	0171 353 2532
Marshall Philip John	One King's Bench Walk, London	0171 936 1500
Martin David John	Cathedral Chambers, Newcastle upon Tyne	0191 232 1311
Mathew Miss Nergis-Anne	2 Gray's Inn Square Chambers, London	0171 242 0328/405 1317
Mathews Deni	8 Fountain Court, Birmingham	0121 236 5514
Matthews Mrs Ann Marie	King's Bench Chambers, Bournemouth	01202 250025
Maxwell David	Claremont Chambers, Wolverhampton	01902 426222
McAllister Miss Eimear Jane	9 Woodhouse Square, Leeds	0113 245 1986
McCahey Miss Catherine Anne Mary	St Philip's Chambers, Birmingham	0121 246 7000
McFarlane Andrew Ewart	One King's Bench Walk, London	0171 936 1500
	Priory Chambers, Birmingham	0121 236 3882/1375
McGahey Miss Elizabeth Clare	30 Park Place, Cardiff	01222 398421
McGrath Miss Elizabeth Ann	St Philip's Chambers, Birmingham	0121 246 7000
McKay Christopher Alexander	Angel Chambers, Swansea	01792 464623/464648
McLachlan David Robert		
McMinn Miss Valerie Kathleen	Baker Street Chambers, Middlesbrough	01642 873873

McNab Miss Mhairi Shuna Elspeth	14 Gray's Inn Square, London	0171 242 0858
Meachin Miss (Sarah) Vanessa Veronica	St Philip's Chambers, Birmingham	0121 246 7000
Merry Hugh Gairns	17 Carlton Crescent, Southampton	01703 320320
Mitchell Miss Juliana Marie	2 Harcourt Buildings, London	0171 583 9020
Moat Frank Robert	Pump Court Chambers, London	0171 353 0711
	Pump Court Chambers, Winchester	01962 868161
Moor Philip Drury	1 Mitre Court Buildings, London	0171 797 7070
Morris Miss Brenda Alison	14 Gray's Inn Square, London	0171 242 0858
Moseley Miss Julie Ruth	St Philip's Chambers, Birmingham	0121 246 7000
Moses Miss Rebecca	Barristers' Common Law Chambers, London	0171 375 3012
	Lion Court, London	0171 404 6565
Mostyn Nicholas Anthony Joseph Ghislain	1 Mitre Court Buildings, London	0171 797 7070
Mulholland Ms Kathryn Shona	One King's Bench Walk, London	0171 936 1500
Munday Miss Anne Margaret	8 King's Bench Walk, London	0171 797 8888
	Tribune House Chambers, York	01904 630448
Murfitt Miss Catriona Anne Campbell	1 Mitre Court Buildings, London	0171 797 7070
Murray Ashley Charles	Oriel Chambers, Liverpool	0151 236 7191
Newbury Richard Lennox	Sovereign Chambers, Leeds	0113 245 1841/2/3
Newton Miss Claire Elaine Maria Bailey	Goldsmith Building, London	0171 353 7881
Newton-Price James Edward	Pump Court Chambers, London	0171 353 0711
	Pump Court Chambers, Winchester	01962 868161
Nicholls Mrs (Deborah) Jane	Oriel Chambers, Liverpool	0151 236 7191
Nicol-Gent William Philip Trahair	King's Chambers, Eastbourne	01323 416053
Nicolson Aris Tony	23 Bracken Gardens, London	0181 748 4924
Nolan Damian Francis	25-27 Castle Street, Liverpool	0151 227 5661/5666/236 5072
Norris Paul Howard	One Essex Court, London	0171 936 3030
O'Flynn Timothy James	Pump Court Chambers, London	0171 353 0711
O'Sullivan Bernard Anthony	Stanbrook & Henderson, London	0171 353 0101
	2 Harcourt Buildings, London	0171 583 9020
Ofori George Edward	Chancery Chambers, London	0171 405 6879
	ACHMA Chambers, London	0171 639 7817
Okoye Miss Joy Nwamala	Chambers of Joy Okoye, London	0171 405 7011
Ong Miss Grace Yu Mae	One Essex Court, London	0171 936 3030
Ough Dr Richard Norman	• Hardwicke Building, London	0171 242 2523
Overs Ms Estelle Fae	New Court Chambers, London	0171 831 9500
Palmer Patrick John Steven	Sovereign Chambers, Leeds	0113 245 1841/2/3
Parker John	2 Mitre Court Buildings, London	0171 353 1353
Parr John Edward	8 King Street Chambers, Manchester	0161 834 9560
Parr Ms Judith Margaret	2 Gray's Inn Square Chambers, London	0171 242 0328/405 1317
Patterson Norman William	14 Gray's Inn Square, London	0171 242 0858
Pawson Robert Edward Cruickshank	Pump Court Chambers, London	0171 353 0711
	Pump Court Chambers, Winchester	01962 868161
Peirson Oliver James	Pump Court Chambers, London	0171 353 0711
	Pump Court Chambers, Winchester	01962 868161
Pithers Clive Robert	Fenners Chambers, Cambridge	01223 368761
	Fenners Chambers, Peterborough	01733 562030
Platts Miss Rachel Elizabeth	1 Mitre Court Buildings, London	0171 797 7070
Pointer Martin John	1 Mitre Court Buildings, London	0171 797 7070
Pope Mrs Heather	1 Mitre Court Buildings, London	0171 797 7070
Porter Miss Sarah Ruth	11 Bolt Court, London	0171 353 2300
Portnoy Leslie Reuben	Chambers of John Hand QC, Manchester	0161 955 9000
Posnansky Jeremy Ross Leon	1 Mitre Court Buildings, London	0171 797 7070
	Southernhay Chambers, Exeter	01392 255777
Posner Miss Gabrielle Jan	2 Gray's Inn Square Chambers, London	0171 242 0328/405 1317
Potter Miss Louise	1 Mitre Court Buildings, London	0171 797 7070
Poyer-Sleeman Ms Patricia	Pump Court Chambers, London	0171 353 0711
	Pump Court Chambers, Winchester	01962 868161
Priestley Ms Rebecca Janet	2 Gray's Inn Square Chambers, London	0171 242 0328/405 1317
Purdie Robert Anthony James	28 Western Road, Oxford	01865 204911
Pye Miss Margaret Jane	Sovereign Chambers, Leeds	0113 245 1841/2/3
Quint Mrs Joan Francesca Rae	11 Old Square, London	0171 242 5022
Rahman Muhammad Altafur	Barristers' Common Law Chambers, London	0171 375 3012
Rahman Ms Sadeqa Shaheen	1 Crown Office Row, London	0171 797 7500

B

Ramsahoye Miss Indira Kim	Hardwicke Building, London	0171 242 2523
Rankin William Peter	Oriel Chambers, Liverpool	0151 236 7191
Ratcliffe Miss Anne Kirkpatrick	5 Pump Court, London	0171 353 2532
Rayment Mr. Benedick Michael	One King's Bench Walk, London	0171 936 1500
Rayson Miss Jane Vivienne	2 Gray's Inn Square Chambers, London	0171 242 0328/405 1317
Reddish John Wilson	One King's Bench Walk, London	0171 936 1500
Reid Miss Caroline Oldcorn	14 Gray's Inn Square, London	0171 242 0858
Rice Christopher Douglas	2 Gray's Inn Square Chambers, London	0171 242 0328/405 1317
Richardson Garth Douglas Anthony	3 Paper Buildings, London	0171 583 8055
	20 Lorne Park Road, Bournemouth	01202 292102
	4 St Peter Street, Winchester	01962 868 884
Rigby Miss Charity Elizabeth	Sovereign Chambers, Leeds	0113 245 1841/2/3
Rigby Terence	Chambers of John Hand QC, Manchester	0161 955 9000
Riley Miss Christine Anne	Chambers of John Hand QC, Manchester	0161 955 9000
Ritchie Andrew George	9 Gough Square, London	0171 353 5371
Rivers Mrs Andrea Louise	2 Gray's Inn Square Chambers, London	0171 242 0328/405 1317
Robertson Ms Alice Michelle	Chambers of Kieran Coonan QC, London	0171 583 6013/2510
Robinson Richard John	2 Gray's Inn Square Chambers, London	0171 242 0328/405 1317
Rodgers Miss Doris June	Harcourt Chambers, London	0171 353 6961/7
	Harcourt Chambers, Oxford	01865 791559
Rogers Paul John	1 Crown Office Row, London	0171 797 7500
	Crown Office Row Chambers, Brighton	01273 625625
Routley Patrick	Goldsmith Building, London	0171 353 7881
Rudd Matthew Allan	11 Bolt Court, London	0171 353 2300
	Redhill Chambers, Redhill	01737 780781
Ryan Miss Eithne Mary Catherine	Hardwicke Building, London	0171 242 2523
Samuel Glyn Ross	St Philip's Chambers, Birmingham	0121 246 7000
Samuels Leslie John	Pump Court Chambers, London	0171 353 0711
	Pump Court Chambers, Winchester	01962 868161
Sandiford Jonathan	St Paul's House, Leeds	0113 245 5866
Savage Miss Ayisha Carol	Britton Street Chambers, London	0171 608 3765
Saxton Miss Nicola Helen	St Paul's House, Leeds	0113 245 5866
Scarratt Richard John	One Garden Court Family Law Chambers, London	0171 797 7900
Scott Miss Alexandra Elisabeth	2 New Street, Leicester	0116 262 5906
Scutt David Robert	11 Bolt Court, London	0171 353 2300
	Redhill Chambers, Redhill	01737 780781
Selman Miss Elizabeth	One King's Bench Walk, London	0171 936 1500
Sheehan Malcolm Peter	Stanbrook & Henderson, London	0171 353 0101
	2 Harcourt Buildings, London	0171 583 9020
Silvester Bruce Ross	Lamb Chambers, London	0171 797 8300
Singh Balbir	• Equity Chambers, Birmingham	0121 233 2100
Sleeman Miss Rachel Sarah Elizabeth	One Essex Court, London	0171 936 3030
Slomnicka Miss Barbara Irena	14 Gray's Inn Square, London	0171 242 0858
Smith Matthew Robert	Sovereign Chambers, Leeds	0113 245 1841/2/3
Smith Roger Gavin Abbey	1 Mitre Court Buildings, London	0171 797 7070
Somerset-Jones Miss Felicity	Oriel Chambers, Liverpool	0151 236 7191
Spain Timothy Harrisson	Trinity Chambers, Newcastle upon Tyne	0191 232 1927
Spencer Miss Hannah Katya	5 Pump Court, London	0171 353 2532
	Chambers of John Hand QC, Manchester	0161 955 9000
Spollon Guy Merton	St Philip's Chambers, Birmingham	0121 246 7000
Spon-Smith Robin Witterick	1 Mitre Court Buildings, London	0171 797 7070
Staite Miss Sara Elizabeth	Stanbrook & Henderson, London	0171 353 0101
	2 Harcourt Buildings, London	0171 583 9020
Starks Nicholas Ernshaw	8 Fountain Court, Birmingham	0121 236 5514
Stead Miss Kate Rebecca	Barristers' Common Law Chambers, London	0171 375 3012
Stewart Mark Courtney	College Chambers, Southampton	01703 230338
Stewart Richard Paul	New Court Chambers, London	0171 831 9500
Stonor Nicholas William	Trinity Chambers, Newcastle upon Tyne	0191 232 1927

• Expanded entry in Part D

Sutton Mrs Karoline Rosemarie	14 Gray's Inn Square, London	0171 242 0858
Tattersall Simon Mark Rogers	Fenners Chambers, Cambridge	01223 368761
	Fenners Chambers, Peterborough	01733 562030
Taylor Andrew Peter	Fenners Chambers, Cambridge	01223 368761
	Fenners Chambers, Peterborough	01733 562030
Temple-Bone Miss Gillian Elizabeth	7 Stone Buildings, London	0171 242 0961
Thomas Stephen Edward Owen	St Philip's Chambers, Birmingham	0121 246 7000
Thompson Jonathan Richard	8 King Street Chambers, Manchester	0161 834 9560
Thornton Miss Anne Rebecca	9 Woodhouse Square, Leeds	0113 245 1986
Tod Jonathan Alan	7 Stone Buildings, London	0171 242 0961
Todd Charles Louis	1 Mitre Court Buildings, London	0171 797 7070
	Trinity Chambers, Newcastle upon Tyne	0191 232 1927
Todd Mrs Elisabeth Helen Margaret	1 Mitre Court Buildings, London	0171 797 7070
Todd Richard Frazer	1 Mitre Court Buildings, London	0171 797 7070
Townend James Barrie Stanley	One King's Bench Walk, London	0171 936 1500
Travers Hugh	Pump Court Chambers, London	0171 353 0711
	Pump Court Chambers, Winchester	01962 868161
Trowell Stephen Mark	1 Mitre Court Buildings, London	0171 797 7070
Turner David George Patrick	14 Gray's Inn Square, London	0171 242 0858
Turner James	One King's Bench Walk, London	0171 936 1500
Tyack David Guy	St Philip's Chambers, Birmingham	0121 246 7000
Valks Michael	King's Chambers, Eastbourne	01323 416053
Vater John Alistair Pitt	Harcourt Chambers, London	0171 353 6961/7
Vavrecka David Paul Frank	14 Gray's Inn Square, London	0171 242 0858
Vincent Miss Ruth Carolyn	Colleton Chambers, Exeter	01392 274898
Vine Aidan James Wilson	Harcourt Chambers, London	0171 353 6961/7
	Harcourt Chambers, Oxford	01865 791559
Waddington Mrs Anne Louise	Pump Court Chambers, London	0171 353 0711
	Pump Court Chambers, Winchester	01962 868161
Wagstaffe Christopher David	Watford Chambers, Watford	01923 220553
Waley Eric Richard Thomas	Assize Court Chambers, Bristol	0117 926 4587
Walker Miss Jane	Chambers of John Hand QC, Manchester	0161 955 9000
Warner Miss Sharan Pamela	14 Gray's Inn Square, London	0171 242 0858
Warrender Miss Nichola Mary	New Court Chambers, London	0171 831 9500
Warshaw Justin Alexander Edward	1 Mitre Court Buildings, London	0171 797 7070
Watson Mark	6 Pump Court, London	0171 797 8400
	6-8 Mill Street, Maidstone	01622 688 094
White Darren Paul	Cathedral Chambers (Jan Wood Independent Barristers' Clerk), Exeter	01392 210900
White Peter-John Spencer	Pembroke House, Leatherhead	01372 376160/376493
White Mrs Tanya	Pembroke House, Leatherhead	01372 376160/376493
Whittam Ms Samantha Abigail	14 Gray's Inn Square, London	0171 242 0858
Williams Hugh David Haydn	St Philip's Chambers, Birmingham	0121 246 7000
Williams Thomas Ellis	30 Park Place, Cardiff	01222 398421
Wood Christopher Mark Bruce	1 Mitre Court Buildings, London	0171 797 7070
Wood Roderic Lionel James	One King's Bench Walk, London	0171 936 1500
Woodbridge Julian Guy	One King's Bench Walk, London	0171 936 1500
Woodward Nicholas Frederick	White Friars Chambers, Chester	01244 323070
Woolman Andrew Paul Lander	Chambers of Andrew Campbell QC, Leeds	0113 245 5438
Woolrich Miss Sarah	Trinity Chambers, Newcastle upon Tyne	0191 232 1927
Wordsworth Mrs Philippa Lindsey	Chambers of Andrew Campbell QC, Leeds	0113 245 5438
Worrall John Raymond Guy	Chambers of Andrew Campbell QC, Leeds	0113 245 5438
Wright Miss Clare Elizabeth	6 Pump Court, London	0171 797 8400
Wright Gerard Henry	25-27 Castle Street, Liverpool	0151 227 5661/5666/236 5072
Wright Ms Sadie	Goldsmith Building, London	0171 353 7881
Wyatt Guy Peter James	Earl Street Chambers, Maidstone	01622 671222
Yates Nicholas Gilmore	1 Mitre Court Buildings, London	0171 797 7070
Yelton Michael Paul	Fenners Chambers, Cambridge	01223 368761
	Fenners Chambers, Peterborough	01733 562030
Yeung Stuart Roy	22 Albion Place, Northampton	01604 636271
Zornoza Miss Isabella	Stanbrook & Henderson, London	0171 353 0101
	2 Harcourt Buildings, London	0171 583 9020

• Expanded entry in Part D

FAMILY PENSIONS

Davies Miss Lindsay Jane	Fenners Chambers, Cambridge	01223 368761
	Fenners Chambers, Peterborough	01733 562030

FAMILY PROVISION

Adamyk Simon Charles	12 New Square, London	0171 419 1212
Airey Simon Andrew	11 Bolt Court, London	0171 353 2300
	Redhill Chambers, Redhill	01737 780781
Alexander Ian Douglas Gavin	11 Bolt Court, London	0171 353 2300
	Redhill Chambers, Redhill	01737 780781
Allardice Miss Miranda Jane	Pump Court Chambers, London	0171 353 0711
	Pump Court Chambers, Winchester	01962 868161
Amiraftabi Miss Roshanak	Hardwicke Building, London	0171 242 2523
Angus Miss Tracey Anne	5 Stone Buildings, London	0171 242 6201
Arnfield Robert John	17 Old Buildings, London	0171 405 9653
Arthur Gavyn Farr	Harcourt Chambers, London	0171 353 6961/7
	Harcourt Chambers, Oxford	01865 791559
Asplin Miss Sarah Jane	• 3 Stone Buildings, London	0171 242 4937/405 8358
Auld Miss Catherine Rohan	Harcourt Chambers, London	0171 353 6961/7
	Harcourt Chambers, Oxford	01865 791559
Ayres Andrew John William	13 Old Square, London	0171 404 4800
Baker Jonathan Leslie	Harcourt Chambers, London	0171 353 6961/7
	Harcourt Chambers, Oxford	01865 791559
Baker Ms Rachel Mary Theresa	Hardwicke Building, London	0171 242 2523
Baldock Miss Susan Anne	2 Gray's Inn Square Chambers, London	0171 242 0328/405 1317
Bancroft Miss Anna Louise	Deans Court Chambers, Manchester	0161 834 4097
	Deans Court Chambers, Preston	01772 555163
Barber Miss Sally	5 Stone Buildings, London	0171 242 6201
Barker Simon George Harry	• 13 Old Square, London	0171 404 4800
Barlow Miss Sarah Helen	St Paul's House, Leeds	0113 245 5866
Barstow Stephen Royden	Harcourt Chambers, London	0171 353 6961/7
	Harcourt Chambers, Oxford	01865 791559
Beasley-Murray Mrs Caroline Wynne	Fenners Chambers, Cambridge	01223 368761
	Fenners Chambers, Peterborough	01733 562030
Beaumont Marc Clifford	• Pump Court Chambers, London	0171 353 0711
	• Harrow-on-the-Hill Chambers, Harrow on the Hill	0181 423 7444
	• Pump Court Chambers, Winchester	01962 868161
	• Windsor Barristers' Chambers, Windsor	01753 648 899
Benner Miss Lucinda Diana Kate	11 Bolt Court, London	0171 353 2300
	Redhill Chambers, Redhill	01737 780781
Bennett John Martyn	• Peel House Chambers, Liverpool	0151 236 4321
Bergin Timothy William	Sussex Chambers, Brighton	01273 607953
Bickerdike Roger John	9 Woodhouse Square, Leeds	0113 245 1986
Birch Roger Allen	12 New Square, London	0171 419 1212
	Sovereign Chambers, Leeds	0113 245 1841/2/3
	Lancaster Buildings, Manchester	0161 661 4444
Bishop Timothy Harper Paul	1 Mitre Court Buildings, London	0171 797 7070
Blackett-Ord Mark	• 5 Stone Buildings, London	0171 242 6201
Bloom-Davis Desmond Niall Laurence	Pump Court Chambers, London	0171 353 0711
	Pump Court Chambers, Winchester	01962 868161
Boora Jinder Singh	Regent Chambers, Stoke-on-Trent	01782 286666
Boothroyd Miss Susan Elizabeth	Westgate Chambers, Newcastle upon Tyne	0191 261 4407/232 9785
Bowcock Miss Samantha Jane	15 Winckley Square, Preston	01772 252 828
Boydell Edward Patrick Stirrup	Pump Court Chambers, London	0171 353 0711
	Pump Court Chambers, Winchester	01962 868161
Boyle David Stuart	Deans Court Chambers, Manchester	0161 834 4097
Brasse Miss Gillian Denise	14 Gray's Inn Square, London	0171 242 0858
Brody Miss Karen Rachel	Deans Court Chambers, Manchester	0161 834 4097
	Deans Court Chambers, Preston	01772 555163
Brown David Charles	Cathedral Chambers, Newcastle upon Tyne	0191 232 1311
	Southsea Chambers, Portsmouth	01705 291261
Brown Thomas Christopher Ellis	Fenners Chambers, Cambridge	01223 368761
	Fenners Chambers, Peterborough	01733 562030
Bull (Donald) Roger	One Essex Court, London	0171 936 3030
Bundred Miss Gillian Sarah	Oriel Chambers, Liverpool	0151 236 7191

B

• Expanded entry in Part D

Burdon Michael Stewart	St Paul's House, Leeds	0113 245 5866
Burles David John	Goldsmith Building, London	0171 353 7881
Butler Miss Judith Jane Scott	6 Pump Court, London	0171 797 8400
	6-8 Mill Street, Maidstone	01622 688 094
Cameron Miss Barbara Alexander	Stanbrook & Henderson, London	0171 353 0101
	2 Harcourt Buildings, London	0171 583 9020
Campbell Miss Alexis Anne	Hardwicke Building, London	0171 242 2523
Carrodus Miss Gail Caroline	New Court Chambers, London	0171 831 9500
Carter Miss Rosalyn Frances	St Philip's Chambers, Birmingham	0121 246 7000
Cave Jeremy Stephen	1 Crown Office Row, London	0171 797 7500
	Crown Office Row Chambers, Brighton	01273 625625
Cave Miss Patricia Ann	7 Stone Buildings, London	0171 242 0961
Clark Miss Hazel Anne	Fenners Chambers, Cambridge	01223 368761
	Fenners Chambers, Peterborough	01733 562030
Clarke Miss Anna Victoria	5 Stone Buildings, London	0171 242 6201
Clarke Peter John	Harcourt Chambers, London	0171 353 6961/7
	St Philip's Chambers, Birmingham	0121 246 7000
	Harcourt Chambers, Oxford	01865 791559
Collins John Morris	11 King's Bench Walk, London	0171 353 3337/8
	9 Woodhouse Square, Leeds	0113 245 1986
Collinson Miss Alicia Hester	Harcourt Chambers, London	0171 353 6961/7
	Harcourt Chambers, Oxford	01865 791559
Conroy Miss Marian	3 Stone Buildings, London	0171 242 4937/405 8358
Cottage Miss Rosina	9-12 Bell Yard, London	0171 400 1800
Coulter Barry John	One Essex Court, London	0171 936 3030
Crail Miss (Elspeth) Ross	12 New Square, London	0171 419 1212
	Sovereign Chambers, Leeds	0113 245 1841/2/3
Crawford Grant	11 Old Square, London	0171 430 0341
Crookes Miss Alison Naomi		
Cross Mrs Joanna	9 Woodhouse Square, Leeds	0113 245 1986
Cross (Joseph) Edward	2 Gray's Inn Square Chambers, London	0171 242 0328/405 1317
Crosthwaite Graham Andrew	One King's Bench Walk, London	0171 936 1500
Cunningham Mark James	13 Old Square, London	0171 404 4800
Davidson Miss Katharine Mary	1 Mitre Court Buildings, London	0171 797 7070
Davies Miss Lindsay Jane	Fenners Chambers, Cambridge	01223 368761
	Fenners Chambers, Peterborough	01733 562030
Deacock Adam Jason	Chambers of Lord Goodhart QC, London	0171 405 5577
Dixon John Watts	Harcourt Chambers, London	0171 353 6961/7
	Harcourt Chambers, Oxford	01865 791559
Dodge Peter Clive	11 Old Square, London	0171 430 0341
Downham Miss Gillian Celia	Rougemont Chambers, Exeter	01392 410471
Dowokpor Jonathan Kukasi	Tollgate Mews Chambers, London	0171 511 1838
Dubbery Mark Edward	Pump Court Chambers, London	0171 353 0711
Duffy Derek James	St Paul's House, Leeds	0113 245 5866
Edwards Anthony Howard	Oriel Chambers, Liverpool	0151 236 7191
Edwards Nigel Royston	St Paul's House, Leeds	0113 245 5866
Elleray Anthony John	• 12 New Square, London	0171 419 1212
	• St James's Chambers, Manchester	0161 834 7000
	• Park Lane Chambers, Leeds	0113 228 5000
Elvidge John Allan	1 Mitre Court Buildings, London	0171 797 7070
Emanuel Mark Pering Wolff	14 Gray's Inn Square, London	0171 242 0858
Evans Miss Delyth Mary	2 Mitre Court Buildings, London	0171 353 1353
Evans Miss Lisa Claire	St Philip's Chambers, Birmingham	0121 246 7000
Evans Miss Suzanne Marie	Oriel Chambers, Liverpool	0151 236 7191
Everall Mark Andrew	1 Mitre Court Buildings, London	0171 797 7070
Fane Miss Angela Elizabeth	Goldsmith Building, London	0171 353 7881
Farmer Pryce Michael	1 Dr Johnson's Buildings, London	0171 353 9328
	Goldsmith Building, London	0171 353 7881
	Sedan House, Chester	01244 320480/348282
Farquharson Miss Jane Caroline	One Essex Court, London	0171 936 3030
Fawls Richard Granville	5 Stone Buildings, London	0171 242 6201
Fenston Miss Felicia Donovan	Stanbrook & Henderson, London	0171 353 0101
	2 Harcourt Buildings, London	0171 583 9020
Ferguson Mrs Katharine Ann	Fenners Chambers, Cambridge	01223 368761
	Fenners Chambers, Peterborough	01733 562030
Fletcher Marcus Alexander	One King's Bench Walk, London	0171 936 1500
Fogarty Peter Dominic	Oriel Chambers, Liverpool	0151 236 7191
Ford Gerard James	Baker Street Chambers, Middlesbrough	01642 873873

       • Expanded entry in Part D

Forster Ms Sarah Judith	14 Gray's Inn Square, London	0171 242 0858
	Westgate Chambers, Lewes	01273 480 510
Fox Miss Anna Katherine Helen	Oriel Chambers, Liverpool	0151 236 7191
Fox Miss Nicola Susan	One Garden Court Family Law Chambers, London	0171 797 7900
Foxwell George (Augustus)	Fenners Chambers, Cambridge	01223 368761
	Fenners Chambers, Peterborough	01733 562030
Frazer Christopher Mark	Harcourt Chambers, London	0171 353 6961/7
	Harcourt Chambers, Oxford	01865 791559
Freeston Miss Lynn Roberta		
Fricker Mrs Marilyn Ann	Farrar's Building, London	0171 583 9241
	Sovereign Chambers, Leeds	0113 245 1841/2/3
Furminger Michael Ashley	Michael Furminger, Brixham	01803 882293
Galberg Marc Kay	33 Bedford Row, London	0171 242 6476
Gifford Miss Cynthia Alice Sophie	Verulam Chambers, London	0171 813 2400
Gilbertson Mrs Helen Alison	Sackville Chambers, Norwich	01603 613516
Godfrey John Paul	Wilberforce Chambers, Hull	01482 323 264
Goodchild Mrs Elizabeth Ann	Watford Chambers, Watford	01923 220553
Goodwin Nicholas Alexander John	Harcourt Chambers, London	0171 353 6961/7
Gordon Mark John	11 Bolt Court, London	0171 353 2300
	Redhill Chambers, Redhill	01737 780781
Gordon-Dean Miss Natasha		
Gordon-Saker Mrs Liza Helen	Fenners Chambers, Cambridge	01223 368761
	Fenners Chambers, Peterborough	01733 562030
Gore Andrew Roger	Fenners Chambers, Cambridge	01223 368761
	Fenners Chambers, Peterborough	01733 562030
Gray Miss Jennifer	11 Old Square, London	0171 242 5022
Gregory Richard Hamilton	Harcourt Chambers, London	0171 353 6961/7
Gresty Miss Denise Lynn	Sovereign Chambers, Leeds	0113 245 1841/2/3
Grice Miss Joanna Harrison	One King's Bench Walk, London	0171 936 1500
Guirguis Miss Sheren	White Friars Chambers, Chester	01244 323070
Hall Taylor Alexander Edward	11 Old Square, London	0171 430 0341
Hammerton Miss Veronica Lesley	No 1 Serjeants' Inn, London	0171 415 6666
Harbottle Gwilym Thomas	5 New Square, London	0171 404 0404
Hargreaves Miss Sara Jane	12 New Square, London	0171 419 1212
	Sovereign Chambers, Leeds	0113 245 1841/2/3
Harrison Ms Averil	2 Harcourt Buildings, London	0171 583 9020
Hayes John Allan	Chambers of Andrew Campbell QC, Leeds	0113 245 5438
Hayes Miss Josephine Mary	Chambers of Lord Goodhart QC, London	0171 405 5577
Heald Oliver	Fenners Chambers, Cambridge	01223 368761
	Fenners Chambers, Peterborough	01733 562030
Heaton Clive William	Chambers of Andrew Campbell QC, Leeds	0113 245 5438
Heaton Miss Frances Margaret	4 Brick Court, London	0171 797 7766
	Deans Court Chambers, Manchester	0161 834 4097
	Deans Court Chambers, Preston	01772 555163
Hess Edward John Watkin	Harcourt Chambers, London	0171 353 6961/7
	Harcourt Chambers, Oxford	01865 791559
Heywood Michael Edmundson	Chambers of Lord Goodhart QC, London	0171 405 5577
	Cobden House Chambers, Manchester	0161 833 6000/6001
Hilder Miss Carolyn Hayley-Jane	3 Fountain Court, Birmingham	0121 236 5854
Hollingworth Peter James Michael	22 Albion Place, Northampton	01604 636271
Hollow Paul John	Fenners Chambers, Cambridge	01223 368761
	Fenners Chambers, Peterborough	01733 562030
Holmes Justin Francis	Chambers of Lord Goodhart QC, London	0171 405 5577
Horton Miss Caroline Ann	Fenners Chambers, Cambridge	01223 368761
	Fenners Chambers, Peterborough	01733 562030
Howard Charles Anthony Frederick	New Court Chambers, London	0171 831 9500
Howard Graham John	Queen Elizabeth Building, London	0171 353 7181 (12 lines)
Howe Miss Penelope Anne Macgregor	Pump Court Chambers, London	0171 353 0711
Hughes Miss Mary Josephine	Chambers of Lord Goodhart QC, London	0171 405 5577
Hughes Miss Meryl Elizabeth	Fenners Chambers, Cambridge	01223 368761
	Fenners Chambers, Peterborough	01733 562030
Hull Leslie David	Chambers of John Hand QC, Manchester	0161 955 9000
Humberstone Mrs Pearl Edith	Verulam Chambers, London	0171 813 2400

Hunt Miss Alison Janet	St Paul's House, Leeds	0113 245 5866
Hunter Anthony Charles Bryan	5 Pump Court, London	0171 353 2532
Irving Miss Gillian	Chambers of John Hand QC, Manchester	0161 955 9000
Islam-Choudhury Mugni	11 Bolt Court, London	0171 353 2300
Iwi Quintin Joseph	Stanbrook & Henderson, London	0171 353 0101
	2 Harcourt Buildings, London	0171 583 9020
Jackson Dirik George Allan	• Chambers of Mr Peter Crampin QC, London	0171 831 0081
Jackson Nicholas David Kingsley	The Chambers of Adrian Lyon, Liverpool	0151 236 4421/8240/6757
Jay Adam Marc	One King's Bench Walk, London	0171 936 1500
Jefferies Thomas Robert	Chambers of Lord Goodhart QC, London	0171 405 5577
Jenkala Adrian Aleksander	11 Bolt Court, London	0171 353 2300
	Redhill Chambers, Redhill	01737 780781
John Peter Charles	One Essex Court, London	0171 936 3030
Johnson Michael Sloan	Chambers of John Hand QC, Manchester	0161 955 9000
Judd Miss Frances Jean	Harcourt Chambers, London	0171 353 6961/7
	Harcourt Chambers, Oxford	01865 791559
Kealy Charles Brian	Chambers of Andrew Campbell QC, Leeds	0113 245 5438
Kenward Timothy David Nelson	25-27 Castle Street, Liverpool	0151 227 5661/5666/236 5072
Ker-Reid John	Pump Court Chambers, London	0171 353 0711
	Pump Court Chambers, Winchester	01962 868161
Kinnier Andrew John	2 Harcourt Buildings, London	0171 583 9020
Lamont Miss Camilla Rose	Chambers of Lord Goodhart QC, London	0171 405 5577
Langridge Ms Nicola Dawn	Hardwicke Building, London	0171 242 2523
Laughton Samuel Dennis	17 Old Buildings, London	0171 405 9653
Le Grice Valentine	1 Mitre Court Buildings, London	0171 797 7070
	Southernhay Chambers, Exeter	01392 255777
Le Poidevin Nicholas Peter	12 New Square, London	0171 419 1212
	Sovereign Chambers, Leeds	0113 245 1841/2/3
Leeming Ian	Lamb Chambers, London	0171 797 8300
	Chambers of John Hand QC, Manchester	0161 955 9000
Levy Robert Stuart	9 Stone Buildings, London	0171 404 5055
	Assize Court Chambers, Bristol	0117 926 4587
Lewis Jeffrey Allan	9 Woodhouse Square, Leeds	0113 245 1986
Lister Miss Caroline Jane	One King's Bench Walk, London	0171 936 1500
Litherland Miss Rebecca Jane	Fenners Chambers, Cambridge	01223 368761
	Fenners Chambers, Peterborough	01733 562030
Logan Miss Maura	St John's Chambers, Hale Barns	0161 980 7379
Lonsdale Miss Marion Mary	Chambers of Geoffrey Hawker, London	0171 583 8899
Lynch Terry John	22 Albion Place, Northampton	01604 636271
Lyne Mark Hilary	One Essex Court, London	0171 936 3030
MacKillop Norman Malcolm	• Chartlands Chambers, Northampton	01604 603322
Manson Miss Julie-Ann	11 Bolt Court, London	0171 353 2300
	Redhill Chambers, Redhill	01737 780781
Marks Jonathan Clive	4 Pump Court, London	0171 353 2656/9
Marley Miss Sarah Anne	5 Pump Court, London	0171 353 2532
Marshall Philip John	One King's Bench Walk, London	0171 936 1500
Marten Richard Hedley Westwood	Chambers of Lord Goodhart QC, London	0171 405 5577
Mathew Miss Nergis-Anne	2 Gray's Inn Square Chambers, London	0171 242 0328/405 1317
McGahey Miss Elizabeth Clare	30 Park Place, Cardiff	01222 398421
McGrath Miss Elizabeth Ann	St Philip's Chambers, Birmingham	0121 246 7000
McKay Christopher Alexander	Angel Chambers, Swansea	01792 464623/464648
McMinn Miss Valerie Kathleen	Baker Street Chambers, Middlesbrough	01642 873873
McQuail Ms Katherine Emma	11 Old Square, London	0171 430 0341
Meachin Miss (Sarah) Vanessa Veronica	St Philip's Chambers, Birmingham	0121 246 7000
Meakin Timothy William	Fenners Chambers, Cambridge	01223 368761
	Fenners Chambers, Peterborough	01733 562030
Mitchell Miss Juliana Marie	2 Harcourt Buildings, London	0171 583 9020
Moor Philip Drury	1 Mitre Court Buildings, London	0171 797 7070
Morris Miss Brenda Alison	14 Gray's Inn Square, London	0171 242 0858

Moseley Miss Julie Ruth	St Philip's Chambers, Birmingham	0121 246 7000
Moses Miss Rebecca	Barristers' Common Law Chambers, London	0171 375 3012
	Lion Court, London	0171 404 6565
Muir John Henry	12 New Square, London	0171 419 1212
	Sovereign Chambers, Leeds	0113 245 1841/2/3
Mullis Anthony Roger	Chambers of Lord Goodhart QC, London	0171 405 5577
Munday Miss Anne Margaret	8 King's Bench Walk, London	0171 797 8888
	Tribune House Chambers, York	01904 630448
Murfitt Miss Catriona Anne Campbell	1 Mitre Court Buildings, London	0171 797 7070
Murray Ashley Charles	Oriel Chambers, Liverpool	0151 236 7191
Newbury Richard Lennox	Sovereign Chambers, Leeds	0113 245 1841/2/3
Newton Miss Claire Elaine Maria Bailey	Goldsmith Building, London	0171 353 7881
Nicholls Mrs (Deborah) Jane	Oriel Chambers, Liverpool	0151 236 7191
Nicol-Gent William Philip Trahair	King's Chambers, Eastbourne	01323 416053
Nicolson Aris Tony	23 Bracken Gardens, London	0181 748 4924
Norbury Luke Edward	17 Old Buildings, London	0171 405 9653
Norris Alastair Hubert	• 5 Stone Buildings, London	0171 242 6201
	• Southernhay Chambers, Exeter	01392 255777
Norris Paul Howard	One Essex Court, London	0171 936 3030
O'Flynn Timothy James	Pump Court Chambers, London	0171 353 0711
O'Sullivan Bernard Anthony	Stanbrook & Henderson, London	0171 353 0101
	2 Harcourt Buildings, London	0171 583 9020
O'Sullivan Michael Morton	5 Stone Buildings, London	0171 242 6201
Ohrenstein Dov	Chambers of Lord Goodhart QC, London	0171 405 5577
Okoye Miss Joy Nwamala	Chambers of Joy Okoye, London	0171 405 7011
Ong Miss Grace Yu Mae	One Essex Court, London	0171 936 3030
Ovey Miss Elizabeth Helen	11 Old Square, London	0171 430 0341
Parker John	2 Mitre Court Buildings, London	0171 353 1353
Pilkington Mrs Mavis Patricia	9 Woodhouse Square, Leeds	0113 245 1986
Pimentel Carlos de Serpa Alberto Legg	3 Stone Buildings, London	0171 242 4937/405 8358
Pithers Clive Robert	Fenners Chambers, Cambridge	01223 368761
	Fenners Chambers, Peterborough	01733 562030
Portnoy Leslie Reuben	Chambers of John Hand QC, Manchester	0161 955 9000
Posnansky Jeremy Ross Leon	1 Mitre Court Buildings, London	0171 797 7070
	Southernhay Chambers, Exeter	01392 255777
Potter Miss Louise	1 Mitre Court Buildings, London	0171 797 7070
Poyer-Sleeman Ms Patricia	Pump Court Chambers, London	0171 353 0711
	Pump Court Chambers, Winchester	01962 868161
Priestley Ms Rebecca Janet	2 Gray's Inn Square Chambers, London	0171 242 0328/405 1317
Pryke Stuart	Trinity Chambers, Newcastle upon Tyne	0191 232 1927
Purdie Robert Anthony James	28 Western Road, Oxford	01865 204911
Pye Miss Margaret Jane	Sovereign Chambers, Leeds	0113 245 1841/2/3
Rankin William Peter	Oriel Chambers, Liverpool	0151 236 7191
Ratcliffe Miss Anne Kirkpatrick	5 Pump Court, London	0171 353 2532
Reddish John Wilson	One King's Bench Walk, London	0171 936 1500
Reed Miss Penelope Jane	9 Stone Buildings, London	0171 404 5055
Rees David Benjamin	5 Stone Buildings, London	0171 242 6201
Rice Christopher Douglas	2 Gray's Inn Square Chambers, London	0171 242 0328/405 1317
Rich Miss Ann Barbara	5 Stone Buildings, London	0171 242 6201
Rigby Miss Charity Elizabeth	Sovereign Chambers, Leeds	0113 245 1841/2/3
Rigby Terence	Chambers of John Hand QC, Manchester	0161 955 9000
Riley Miss Christine Anne	Chambers of John Hand QC, Manchester	0161 955 9000
Robinson Richard John	2 Gray's Inn Square Chambers, London	0171 242 0328/405 1317
Robson John Malcolm	2 Gray's Inn Square Chambers, London	0171 242 0328/405 1317
	Assize Court Chambers, Bristol	0117 926 4587
Rodgers Miss Doris June	Harcourt Chambers, London	0171 353 6961/7
	Harcourt Chambers, Oxford	01865 791559
Ross Martyn John Greaves	• 5 New Square, London	0171 404 0404
	• Octagon House, Norwich	01603 623186

• Expanded entry in Part D

Rudd Matthew Allan	11 Bolt Court, London	0171 353 2300
	Redhill Chambers, Redhill	01737 780781
Ryan Miss Eithne Mary Catherine	Hardwicke Building, London	0171 242 2523
Sagar (Edward) Leigh	12 New Square, London	0171 419 1212
	Sovereign Chambers, Leeds	0113 245 1841/2/3
	Newport Chambers, Newport	01633 267403/255855
Samuels Leslie John	Pump Court Chambers, London	0171 353 0711
	Pump Court Chambers, Winchester	01962 868161
Sander Andrew Thomas	Goldsmith Building, London	0171 353 7881
	Oriel Chambers, Liverpool	0151 236 7191
Saxton Miss Nicola Helen	St Paul's House, Leeds	0113 245 5866
Scarratt Richard John	One Garden Court Family Law Chambers, London	0171 797 7900
Scott Miss Alexandra Elisabeth	2 New Street, Leicester	0116 262 5906
Scutt David Robert	11 Bolt Court, London	0171 353 2300
	Redhill Chambers, Redhill	01737 780781
Selman Miss Elizabeth	One King's Bench Walk, London	0171 936 1500
Selway Dr Katherine Emma	11 Old Square, London	0171 430 0341
Sheehan Malcolm Peter	Stanbrook & Henderson, London	0171 353 0101
	2 Harcourt Buildings, London	0171 583 9020
Sleeman Miss Rachel Sarah Elizabeth	One Essex Court, London	0171 936 3030
Smart Miss Jacqueline Anne	Trinity Chambers, Newcastle upon Tyne	0191 232 1927
Somerset-Jones Miss Felicity	Oriel Chambers, Liverpool	0151 236 7191
Spencer Miss Hannah Katya	5 Pump Court, London	0171 353 2532
	Chambers of John Hand QC, Manchester	0161 955 9000
Spollon Guy Merton	St Philip's Chambers, Birmingham	0121 246 7000
Spon-Smith Robin Witterick	1 Mitre Court Buildings, London	0171 797 7070
Staddon Miss Claire Ann	12 New Square, London	0171 419 1212
	Sovereign Chambers, Leeds	0113 245 1841/2/3
Staite Miss Sara Elizabeth	Stanbrook & Henderson, London	0171 353 0101
	2 Harcourt Buildings, London	0171 583 9020
Starks Nicholas Ernshaw	8 Fountain Court, Birmingham	0121 236 5514
Stewart Mark Courtney	College Chambers, Southampton	01703 230338
Stewart Nicholas John Cameron	Hardwicke Building, London	0171 242 2523
Stewart Richard Paul	New Court Chambers, London	0171 831 9500
Sugar Simon Gareth	5 New Square, London	0171 404 0404
Talbot Richard Kevin Kent	Deans Court Chambers, Manchester	0161 834 4097
	Deans Court Chambers, Preston	01772 555163
Tattersall Simon Mark Rogers	Fenners Chambers, Cambridge	01223 368761
	Fenners Chambers, Peterborough	01733 562030
Temple-Bone Miss Gillian Elizabeth	7 Stone Buildings, London	0171 242 0961
Thomas Nigel Matthew	13 Old Square, London	0171 404 4800
Thompson Jonathan Richard	8 King Street Chambers, Manchester	0161 834 9560
Tipples Miss Amanda Jane	13 Old Square, London	0171 404 4800
Tod Jonathan Alan	7 Stone Buildings, London	0171 242 0961
Todd Charles Louis	1 Mitre Court Buildings, London	0171 797 7070
	Trinity Chambers, Newcastle upon Tyne	0191 232 1927
Todd Richard Frazer	1 Mitre Court Buildings, London	0171 797 7070
Townend James Barrie Stanley	One King's Bench Walk, London	0171 936 1500
Trowell Stephen Mark	1 Mitre Court Buildings, London	0171 797 7070
Tucker Miss Katherine Jane Greening	St Philip's Chambers, Birmingham	0121 246 7000
Turner David George Patrick	14 Gray's Inn Square, London	0171 242 0858
Turner James	One King's Bench Walk, London	0171 936 1500
Vane The Hon Christopher John Fletcher	Trinity Chambers, Newcastle upon Tyne	0191 232 1927
Vater John Alistair Pitt	Harcourt Chambers, London	0171 353 6961/7
Vine Aidan James Wilson	Harcourt Chambers, London	0171 353 6961/7
	Harcourt Chambers, Oxford	01865 791559
Waddington Mrs Anne Louise	Pump Court Chambers, London	0171 353 0711
	Pump Court Chambers, Winchester	01962 868161
Wagstaffe Christopher David	Watford Chambers, Watford	01923 220553
Walker Andrew Greenfield	Chambers of Lord Goodhart QC, London	0171 405 5577
Walker Miss Jane	Chambers of John Hand QC, Manchester	0161 955 9000
Warnock-Smith Mrs Shan	5 Stone Buildings, London	0171 242 6201
Warshaw Justin Alexander Edward	1 Mitre Court Buildings, London	0171 797 7070

• Expanded entry in Part D

Watson Mark	6 Pump Court, London	0171 797 8400
	6-8 Mill Street, Maidstone	01622 688 094
Weatherill Bernard Richard	Chambers of Lord Goodhart QC, London	0171 405 5577
West Mark	• 11 Old Square, London	0171 430 0341
White Peter-John Spencer	Pembroke House, Leatherhead	01372 376160/376493
White Mrs Tanya	Pembroke House, Leatherhead	01372 376160/376493
Wilby David Christopher	• 199 Strand, London	0171 379 9779
	• Park Lane Chambers, Leeds	0113 228 5000
Woodward Nicholas Frederick	White Friars Chambers, Chester	01244 323070
Woolman Andrew Paul Lander	Chambers of Andrew Campbell QC, Leeds	0113 245 5438
Woolrich Miss Sarah	Trinity Chambers, Newcastle upon Tyne	0191 232 1927
Worrall John Raymond Guy	Chambers of Andrew Campbell QC, Leeds	0113 245 5438
Wright Colin John	4 Field Court, London	0171 440 6900
Wright Gerard Henry	25-27 Castle Street, Liverpool	0151 227 5661/5666/236 5072
Wyatt Guy Peter James	Earl Street Chambers, Maidstone	01622 671222
Yates Nicholas Gilmore	1 Mitre Court Buildings, London	0171 797 7070
Yelton Michael Paul	Fenners Chambers, Cambridge	01223 368761
	Fenners Chambers, Peterborough	01733 562030
Yeung Stuart Roy	22 Albion Place, Northampton	01604 636271
Zornoza Miss Isabella	Stanbrook & Henderson, London	0171 353 0101
	2 Harcourt Buildings, London	0171 583 9020

FAMILY PROVISION ON DEATH

Harrap Giles Thresher	• Pump Court Chambers, London	0171 353 0711
	• Pump Court Chambers, Winchester	01962 868161

FIELD SPORTS

Dineen Michael Laurence	Pump Court Chambers, London	0171 353 0711
	All Saints Chambers, Bristol	0117 921 1966
	Pump Court Chambers, Winchester	01962 868161

FILM, CABLE, TV

Cunningham Mark James	13 Old Square, London	0171 404 4800
Fitzgerald John Vincent	New Court, London	0171 797 8999
Fowler Richard Nicholas	Monckton Chambers, London	0171 405 7211
Garnett Kevin Mitchell	5 New Square, London	0171 404 0404
Hicks Michael Charles	• 19 Old Buildings, London	0171 405 2001
Hodgson Richard Andrew	New Court, London	0171 797 8999
Holman Miss Tamsin Perdita	19 Old Buildings, London	0171 405 2001
Kime Matthew Jonathan	• New Court, London	0171 797 8999
	• Cobden House Chambers, Manchester	0161 833 6000/6001
Norris Andrew James Steedsman	5 New Square, London	0171 404 0404
Peters Nigel Melvin	18 Red Lion Court, London	0171 520 6000
	Thornwood House, Chelmsford	01245 280880
Puckrin Cedric Eldred	19 Old Buildings, London	0171 405 2001
Reid Brian Christopher	19 Old Buildings, London	0171 405 2001
Robertson Aidan Malcolm David	Monckton Chambers, London	0171 405 7211
Sampson Graeme William	Chambers of Geoffrey Hawker, London	0171 583 8899
Shipley Norman Graham	• 19 Old Buildings, London	0171 405 2001
Silverleaf Michael	• 11 South Square, London	0171 405 1222
Sugar Simon Gareth	5 New Square, London	0171 404 0404
Sullivan Rory Myles	19 Old Buildings, London	0171 405 2001
Tedd Rex Hilary	• St Philip's Chambers, Birmingham	0121 246 7000
	• 22 Albion Place, Northampton	01604 636271
Thompson Rhodri William Ralph	Monckton Chambers, London	0171 405 7211
Turner Jonathan Richard	Monckton Chambers, London	0171 405 7211
Wilson Alastair James Drysdale	• 19 Old Buildings, London	0171 405 2001

FILM, TV

Barker Simon George Harry	• 13 Old Square, London	0171 404 4800

FINANCIAL SERVICES

Akka Lawrence Mark	20 Essex Street, London	0171 583 9294
Anderson Anthony John	2 Mitre Court Buildings, London	0171 583 1380

Aylett Kenneth George	New Chambers, St Albans	0966 212126
Barnett Jeremy Victor	Farrar's Building, London	0171 583 9241
	St Paul's House, Leeds	0113 245 5866
Blair William James Lynton	3 Verulam Buildings, London	0171 831 8441
Carey Jeremy Reynolds Patrick	Lamb Chambers, London	0171 797 8300
Carnes Andrew James	23 Essex Street, London	0171 413 0353
Collings Matthew Glynn Burkinshaw	13 Old Square, London	0171 404 4800
Cranbrook Alexander Douglas John	9-12 Bell Yard, London	0171 400 1800
Crow Jonathan Rupert	4 Stone Buildings, London	0171 242 5524
de Lacy Richard Michael	3 Verulam Buildings, London	0171 831 8441
Dougherty Nigel Peter	Erskine Chambers, London	0171 242 5532
Doyle Louis George	Chambers of Andrew Campbell QC, Leeds	0113 245 5438
Edwards-Stuart Antony James Cobham	Two Crown Office Row, London	0171 797 8100
Evans David Howard	Queen Elizabeth Building, London	0171 583 5766
Field Richard Alan	11 King's Bench Walk, London	0171 632 8500
Fisher Jonathan Simon	• 18 Red Lion Court, London	0171 520 6000
	• Thornwood House, Chelmsford	01245 280880
Freedman Sampson Clive	3 Verulam Buildings, London	0171 831 8441
Garcia-Miller Miss Laura	Enterprise Chambers, London	0171 405 9471
	Enterprise Chambers, Leeds	0113 246 0391
	Enterprise Chambers, Newcastle upon Tyne	0191 222 3344
Gibaud Miss Catherine Alison Annetta	3 Verulam Buildings, London	0171 831 8441
Goodhart Lord	Chambers of Lord Goodhart QC, London	0171 405 5577
Gore-Andrews Gavin Angus Russell	Stanbrook & Henderson, London	0171 353 0101
	2 Harcourt Buildings, London	0171 583 9020
Grantham Andrew Timothy	• Deans Court Chambers, Manchester	0161 834 4097
	• Deans Court Chambers, Preston	01772 555163
Griffiths Peter Robert	4 Stone Buildings, London	0171 242 5524
Hall Taylor Alexander Edward	11 Old Square, London	0171 430 0341
Hamilton Peter Bernard	4 Pump Court, London	0171 353 2656/9
Hantusch Robert Anthony	• 3 Stone Buildings, London	0171 242 4937/405 8358
Harvey Michael Llewellyn Tucker	Two Crown Office Row, London	0171 797 8100
Harwood Richard John	1 Serjeants' Inn, London	0171 583 1355
Hodgkinson Tristram Patrick	• 5 Pump Court, London	0171 353 2532
Hughes Miss Mary Josephine	Chambers of Lord Goodhart QC, London	0171 405 5577
Hurst Brian	17 Bedford Row, London	0171 831 7314
Ife Miss Linden Elizabeth	Enterprise Chambers, London	0171 405 9471
	Enterprise Chambers, Leeds	0113 246 0391
	Enterprise Chambers, Newcastle upon Tyne	0191 222 3344
Jarvis John Manners	3 Verulam Buildings, London	0171 831 8441
Jory Robert John Hugh	Enterprise Chambers, London	0171 405 9471
	Enterprise Chambers, Leeds	0113 246 0391
	Enterprise Chambers, Newcastle upon Tyne	0191 222 3344
Lewis Miss Caroline Susannah	3 Verulam Buildings, London	0171 831 8441
Ley (Nigel) Spencer	Farrar's Building, London	0171 583 9241
Lyne Mark Hilary	One Essex Court, London	0171 936 3030
Marquand Charles Nicholas Hilary	Chambers of Lord Goodhart QC, London	0171 405 5577
Masters Miss Sara Alayna	20 Essex Street, London	0171 583 9294
Mawrey Richard Brooks	Stanbrook & Henderson, London	0171 353 0101
	2 Harcourt Buildings, London	0171 583 9020
McManus Jonathan Richard	4-5 Gray's Inn Square, London	0171 404 5252
McQuater Ewan Alan	3 Verulam Buildings, London	0171 831 8441
Merriman Nicholas Flavelle	3 Verulam Buildings, London	0171 831 8441
Newman Miss Catherine Mary	• 13 Old Square, London	0171 404 4800
Norris Paul Howard	One Essex Court, London	0171 936 3030
Onslow Andrew George	3 Verulam Buildings, London	0171 831 8441
Owen David Christopher	20 Essex Street, London	0171 583 9294
Peacock Nicholas Christopher	13 Old Square, London	0171 404 4800
Pearson Thomas Adam Spenser	Pump Court Chambers, London	0171 353 0711
	Pump Court Chambers, Winchester	01962 868161
Peglow Dr Michael Alfred Herman	Chambers of Geoffrey Hawker, London	0171 583 8899
Perkoff Richard Michael	Littleton Chambers, London	0171 797 8600

         • Expanded entry in Part D

Peters Nigel Melvin	18 Red Lion Court, London	0171 520 6000
	Thornwood House, Chelmsford	01245 280880
Quest David Charles	3 Verulam Buildings, London	0171 831 8441
Rivalland Marc-Edouard	No 1 Serjeants' Inn, London	0171 415 6666
Roberts Miss Catherine Ann	Erskine Chambers, London	0171 242 5532
Salter Richard Stanley	3 Verulam Buildings, London	0171 831 8441
Sangster Nigel	St Paul's House, Leeds	0113 245 5866
Sayer Mr Peter Edwin	Gough Square Chambers, London	0171 353 0924
Stewart Alexander Joseph	5 New Square, London	0171 404 0404
Sykes (James) Richard	Erskine Chambers, London	0171 242 5532
Thomas (Robert) Neville	3 Verulam Buildings, London	0171 831 8441
Worsley Daniel	Stanbrook & Henderson, London	0171 353 0101
	2 Harcourt Buildings, London	0171 583 9020
Zelin Geoffrey Andrew	Enterprise Chambers, London	0171 405 9471
	Enterprise Chambers, Leeds	0113 246 0391
	Enterprise Chambers, Newcastle upon Tyne	0191 222 3344

FINANCIAL SERVICES CRIME

Lawson Michael Henry	23 Essex Street, London	0171 413 0353

FOOD LAW

Andrews Miss Claire Marguerite	Gough Square Chambers, London	0171 353 0924
Brown Edward Francis Trevenen	Queen Elizabeth Building, London	0171 583 5766
Hibbert William John	Gough Square Chambers, London	0171 353 0924
Philpott Frederick Alan	Gough Square Chambers, London	0171 353 0924
Vines Anthony Robert Francis	Gough Square Chambers, London	0171 353 0924

FOREIGN LAW

Al'Hassan Khadim	Equity Chambers, Birmingham	0121 233 2100
Elvidge John Allan	1 Mitre Court Buildings, London	0171 797 7070
Forlin Gerard Emlyn	Phoenix Chambers, London	0171 404 7888
Jarvis John Manners	3 Verulam Buildings, London	0171 831 8441
Jenkala Adrian Aleksander	11 Bolt Court, London	0171 353 2300
	Redhill Chambers, Redhill	01737 780781
Kingsland Rt Hon Lord	4 Breams Buildings, London	0171 353 5835/430 1221
Maurici James Patrick	4 Breams Buildings, London	0171 353 5835/430 1221
McGregor Harvey	4 Paper Buildings, London	0171 353 3366/583 7155
McParland Michael Joseph	New Court Chambers, London	0171 831 9500
Nsugbe Oba Eric	Pump Court Chambers, London	0171 353 0711
	Pump Court Chambers, Winchester	01962 868161
Oakley Tony	• 11 Old Square, London	0171 430 0341
Okoye Miss Joy Nwamala	Chambers of Joy Okoye, London	0171 405 7011
Peglow Dr Michael Alfred Herman	Chambers of Geoffrey Hawker, London	0171 583 8899
Thomson Martin Haldane Ahmad	Wynne Chambers, London	0171 737 7266
Williams Thomas Ellis	30 Park Place, Cardiff	01222 398421

FRANCHISING

Beaumont Marc Clifford	• Pump Court Chambers, London	0171 353 0711
	• Harrow-on-the-Hill Chambers, Harrow on the Hill	0181 423 7444
	• Pump Court Chambers, Winchester	01962 868161
	• Windsor Barristers' Chambers, Windsor	01753 648 899
Davies Stephen Richard	8 King Street Chambers, Manchester	0161 834 9560
Deacock Adam Jason	Chambers of Lord Goodhart QC, London	0171 405 5577
French Richard Anthony Lister	Rougemont Chambers, Exeter	01392 410471
Goodhart Lord	Chambers of Lord Goodhart QC, London	0171 405 5577
Goodman Andrew David	199 Strand, London	0171 379 9779
Grantham Andrew Timothy	• Deans Court Chambers, Manchester	0161 834 4097
	• Deans Court Chambers, Preston	01772 555163
Harvey Jonathan Robert William	2 Harcourt Buildings, London	0171 583 9020
Heywood Michael Edmundson	Chambers of Lord Goodhart QC, London	0171 405 5577
	Cobden House Chambers, Manchester	0161 833 6000/6001
Hicks Michael Charles	• 19 Old Buildings, London	0171 405 2001

Holmes Justin Francis	Chambers of Lord Goodhart QC, London	0171 405 5577
Hughes Miss Mary Josephine	Chambers of Lord Goodhart QC, London	0171 405 5577
Jefferies Thomas Robert	Chambers of Lord Goodhart QC, London	0171 405 5577
Kime Matthew Jonathan	• New Court, London	0171 797 8999
	• Cobden House Chambers, Manchester	0161 833 6000/6001
Kolodziej Andrzej Jozef	• Littman Chambers, London	0171 404 4866
Lamont Miss Camilla Rose	Chambers of Lord Goodhart QC, London	0171 405 5577
Marquand Charles Nicholas Hilary	Chambers of Lord Goodhart QC, London	0171 405 5577
Marten Richard Hedley Westwood	Chambers of Lord Goodhart QC, London	0171 405 5577
Mullis Anthony Roger	Chambers of Lord Goodhart QC, London	0171 405 5577
Nebhrajani Miss Mel	9 Stone Buildings, London	0171 404 5055
Ohrenstein Dov	Chambers of Lord Goodhart QC, London	0171 405 5577
Parry David Julian Thomas	Chambers of Lord Goodhart QC, London	0171 405 5577
Pickford Anthony James	Prince Henry's Chambers, London	0171 353 1183/1190
Steinert Jonathan	New Court Chambers, London	0171 831 9500
Sullivan Rory Myles	19 Old Buildings, London	0171 405 2001
Thompson Rhodri William Ralph	Monckton Chambers, London	0171 405 7211
Walker Andrew Greenfield	Chambers of Lord Goodhart QC, London	0171 405 5577
Weatherill Bernard Richard	Chambers of Lord Goodhart QC, London	0171 405 5577
Wilson Alastair James Drysdale	• 19 Old Buildings, London	0171 405 2001

GERMAN LAW

Peglow Dr Michael Alfred Herman	Chambers of Geoffrey Hawker, London	0171 583 8899

GHANA LAWS AND CUSTOM

Hamid Mrs Beebee Nazmoon	Clapham Chambers, London	0171 978 8482/0171 642 5777

GOVERNMENT DEPARTMENTS

Dixon David Steven	Sovereign Chambers, Leeds	0113 245 1841/2/3
Ekins Charles Wareing		

HARASSMENT

Addison Neil Patrick	Cathedral Chambers, Newcastle upon Tyne	0191 232 1311

HEALTH AND SAFETY

Bevan Edward Julian	Queen Elizabeth Building, London	0171 583 5766
Donne Jeremy Nigel	Queen Elizabeth Building, London	0171 583 5766
Heslop Martin Sydney	1 Hare Court, London	0171 353 3982/5324
Waters Julian William Penrose	No 1 Serjeants' Inn, London	0171 415 6666
Wignall Edward Gordon	• 1 Dr Johnson's Buildings, London	0171 353 9328
	• Dr Johnson's Chambers, Reading	01189 254221

HIGHWAYS

Clay Jonathan Roger	11 Bolt Court, London	0171 353 2300
	Redhill Chambers, Redhill	01737 780781
Gore Andrew Roger	Fenners Chambers, Cambridge	01223 368761
	Fenners Chambers, Peterborough	01733 562030
Lewis Robert		
Murch Stephen James	• 11 Bolt Court, London	0171 353 2300
Randle Simon Patrick	11 Bolt Court, London	0171 353 2300
	Redhill Chambers, Redhill	01737 780781
Richards David Wyn	Iscoed Chambers, Swansea	01792 652988/9/330
Simpson Edwin John Fletcher	12 New Square, London	0171 419 1212

         • Expanded entry in Part D

HONG KONG LAW

Waley Eric Richard Thomas	Assize Court Chambers, Bristol	0117 926 4587

HOUSING

Adamyk Simon Charles	12 New Square, London	0171 419 1212
Addison Neil Patrick	Cathedral Chambers, Newcastle upon Tyne	0191 232 1311
Adejumo Mrs Hilda Ekpo	• Temple Chambers, London	0171 583 1001 (2 lines)
Al'Hassan Khadim	Equity Chambers, Birmingham	0121 233 2100
Amin Miss Farah	7 New Square, London	0171 430 1660
Atherton Ian David	Enterprise Chambers, London	0171 405 9471
	Enterprise Chambers, Leeds	0113 246 0391
	Enterprise Chambers, Newcastle upon Tyne	0191 222 3344
Beal Kieron Conrad	4 Paper Buildings, London	0171 353 3366/583 7155
Bedeau Stephen	Sovereign Chambers, Leeds	0113 245 1841/2/3
	Lancaster Buildings, Manchester	0161 661 4444
Beer Jason Barrington	5 Essex Court, London	0171 410 2000
Bergin Timothy William	Sussex Chambers, Brighton	01273 607953
Bhaloo Miss Zia Kurban	Enterprise Chambers, London	0171 405 9471
	Enterprise Chambers, Leeds	0113 246 0391
	Enterprise Chambers, Newcastle upon Tyne	0191 222 3344
Bhattacharyya Ardhendu	1 Gray's Inn Square, London	0171 405 8946
	11 St Bernards Road, Slough	01753 553806/817989
Bird Nigel David	Chambers of John Hand QC, Manchester	0161 955 9000
Birks Simon Alexander	7 Stone Buildings, London	0171 242 0961
Bourne Charles Gregory	Stanbrook & Henderson, London	0171 353 0101
	2 Harcourt Buildings, London	0171 583 9020
Boyle Christopher Alexander David	2 Mitre Court Buildings, London	0171 583 1380
Brant Paul David	Oriel Chambers, Liverpool	0151 236 7191
Brazil Dominic Thomas George	14 Gray's Inn Square, London	0171 242 0858
Brett Matthew Christopher Anthony	Harcourt Chambers, London	0171 353 6961/7
	Harcourt Chambers, Oxford	01865 791559
Brook Ian Stuart	Hardwicke Building, London	0171 242 2523
Browne James William	Goldsworth Chambers, London	0171 405 7117
Burton Nicholas Anthony	2 Mitre Court Buildings, London	0171 583 1380
Campbell Oliver Edward Wilhelm	2 Harcourt Buildings, London	0171 583 9020
Carville Owen Brendan Neville	25-27 Castle Street, Liverpool	0151 227 5661/5666/236 5072
Clay Jonathan Roger	11 Bolt Court, London	0171 353 2300
	Redhill Chambers, Redhill	01737 780781
Collard Michael David	5 Pump Court, London	0171 353 2532
Copeland Andrew John	Chambers of Geoffrey Hawker, London	0171 583 8899
Cotter Miss Sara Elizabeth	• Higher Combe, Minehead	01643 862722
Cowen Miss Sally Emma	Chambers of Geoffrey Hawker, London	0171 583 8899
Creaner Paul Anthony	15 Winckley Square, Preston	01772 252 828
Crookes Miss Alison Naomi		
Crossley Simon Justin	9 Woodhouse Square, Leeds	0113 245 1986
Daiches Michael Salis	• 22 Old Buildings, London	0171 831 0222
Darbyshire William Robert	Chambers of John Hand QC, Manchester	0161 955 9000
Davey Miss Tina Elaine	9-12 Bell Yard, London	0171 400 1800
de Voghelaere Parr Adam Stephen	2 Mitre Court Buildings, London	0171 583 1380
Dedezade Taner	Tindal Chambers, Chelmsford	01245 267742
Dhaliwal Miss Davinder Kaur	New Court Chambers, Birmingham	0121 693 6656
Dodd Christopher John Nicholas	9 Woodhouse Square, Leeds	0113 245 1986
Dowse John	Chambers of Lord Goodhart QC, London	0171 405 5577
	Chambers of John Hand QC, Manchester	0161 955 9000
Edwards Philip Douglas	2 Harcourt Buildings, London	0171 353 8415
Fenston Miss Felicia Donovan	Stanbrook & Henderson, London	0171 353 0101
	2 Harcourt Buildings, London	0171 583 9020
Ford Gerard James	Baker Street Chambers, Middlesbrough	01642 873873
Foster Francis Alexander	St Paul's House, Leeds	0113 245 5866
Gerald Nigel Mortimer	Enterprise Chambers, London	0171 405 9471
	Enterprise Chambers, Leeds	0113 246 0391

	Enterprise Chambers, Newcastle upon Tyne	0191 222 3344
Giffin Nigel Dyson	11 King's Bench Walk, London	0171 632 8500
Gilchrist David Somerled	Chambers of John Hand QC, Manchester	0161 955 9000
Godfrey Jonathan Saul	St Paul's House, Leeds	0113 245 5866
Greenan Miss Sarah Octavia	• 9 Woodhouse Square, Leeds	0113 245 1986
Grundy Nicholas John	One Essex Court, London	0171 936 3030
Hargreaves Miss Sara Jane	12 New Square, London	0171 419 1212
	Sovereign Chambers, Leeds	0113 245 1841/2/3
Harper Joseph Charles	4 Breams Buildings, London	0171 353 5835/430 1221
Harrison John Foster	St Paul's House, Leeds	0113 245 5866
Henley Mark Robert Daniel	9 Woodhouse Square, Leeds	0113 245 1986
Hodgson Ms Jane	9 Woodhouse Square, Leeds	0113 245 1986
Holland Charles Christopher	Trinity Chambers, Newcastle upon Tyne	0191 232 1927
Holroyd John James	• 9 Woodhouse Square, Leeds	0113 245 1986
Howell John	4 Breams Buildings, London	0171 353 5835/430 1221
Huskinson George Nicholas Nevil	4-5 Gray's Inn Square, London	0171 404 5252
Jack Adrian Laurence Robert	Enterprise Chambers, London	0171 405 9471
John Peter Charles	One Essex Court, London	0171 936 3030
Jones Geraint Martyn	Fenners Chambers, Cambridge	01223 368761
	Fenners Chambers, Peterborough	01733 562030
Jones Miss Rhiannon	Lamb Chambers, London	0171 797 8300
Jones Stephen Hugh	• Farrar's Building, London	0171 583 9241
Joss Norman James	One Essex Court, London	0171 936 3030
Kenward Timothy David Nelson	25-27 Castle Street, Liverpool	0151 227 5661/5666/236 5072
Khan Avicenna Alkindi Cornelius	55 Temple Chambers, London	0171 353 7400
Kimbell John Ashley	5 Bell Yard, London	0171 333 8811
Kinnier Andrew John	2 Harcourt Buildings, London	0171 583 9020
Kolodynski Stefan Richard	New Court Chambers, Birmingham	0121 693 6656
Lander Charles Gideon	25-27 Castle Street, Liverpool	0151 227 5661/5666/236 5072
Lees Andrew James	St Paul's House, Leeds	0113 245 5866
Levy Robert Stuart	9 Stone Buildings, London	0171 404 5055
	Assize Court Chambers, Bristol	0117 926 4587
Lewis Robert		
Lynch Terry John	22 Albion Place, Northampton	01604 636271
Lyness Scott Edward	1 Serjeants' Inn, London	0171 583 1355
Macpherson The Hon Mary Stewart	2 Mitre Court Buildings, London	0171 583 1380
Maitland Marc Claude	11 Old Square, London	0171 242 5022
Maxwell Miss Judith Mary Angela	The Garden House, London	0171 404 6150
McAllister Miss Eimear Jane	9 Woodhouse Square, Leeds	0113 245 1986
McAllister Miss Elizabeth Ann	Enterprise Chambers, London	0171 405 9471
	Enterprise Chambers, Leeds	0113 246 0391
	Enterprise Chambers, Newcastle upon Tyne	0191 222 3344
McCarthy William	New Bailey Chambers, Preston	01772 258 087
McGahey Miss Elizabeth Clare	30 Park Place, Cardiff	01222 398421
McLachlan David Robert		
McMinn Miss Valerie Kathleen	Baker Street Chambers, Middlesbrough	01642 873873
Meakin Timothy William	Fenners Chambers, Cambridge	01223 368761
	Fenners Chambers, Peterborough	01733 562030
Mills Simon Thomas	One Essex Court, London	0171 936 3030
Mitchell Miss Juliana Marie	2 Harcourt Buildings, London	0171 583 9020
Morgan Charles James Arthur	Enterprise Chambers, London	0171 405 9471
	Enterprise Chambers, Leeds	0113 246 0391
	Enterprise Chambers, Newcastle upon Tyne	0191 222 3344
Morgan Jeremy	Chambers of Kieran Coonan QC, London	0171 583 6013/2510
Moses Miss Rebecca	Barristers' Common Law Chambers, London	0171 375 3012
	Lion Court, London	0171 404 6565
Murch Stephen James	• 11 Bolt Court, London	0171 353 2300
Nebhrajani Miss Mel	9 Stone Buildings, London	0171 404 5055
Nesbitt Timothy John Robert	199 Strand, London	0171 379 9779
Nicol-Gent William Philip Trahair	King's Chambers, Eastbourne	01323 416053
Noble Andrew	Eldon Chambers, London	0171 353 4636
	Merchant Chambers, Manchester	0161 839 7070
Nolan Damian Francis	25-27 Castle Street, Liverpool	0151 227 5661/5666/236 5072
Norbury Luke Edward	17 Old Buildings, London	0171 405 9653

• Expanded entry in Part D

Okoye Miss Joy Nwamala	Chambers of Joy Okoye, London	0171 405 7011
Palfrey Montague Mark	Hardwicke Building, London	0171 242 2523
Patterson Norman William	14 Gray's Inn Square, London	0171 242 0858
Peacock Ian Christopher	12 New Square, London	0171 419 1212
	Sovereign Chambers, Leeds	0113 245 1841/2/3
Pema Anesh Bhumin Laloo	9 Woodhouse Square, Leeds	0113 245 1986
Pithers Clive Robert	Fenners Chambers, Cambridge	01223 368761
	Fenners Chambers, Peterborough	01733 562030
Popat Prashant	Stanbrook & Henderson, London	0171 353 0101
	2 Harcourt Buildings, London	0171 583 9020
Pryke Stuart	Trinity Chambers, Newcastle upon Tyne	0191 232 1927
Purdie Robert Anthony James	28 Western Road, Oxford	01865 204911
Quint Mrs Joan Francesca Rae	11 Old Square, London	0171 242 5022
Radevsky Anthony Eric	• 5 Bell Yard, London	0171 333 8811
Rahman Muhammad Altafur	Barristers' Common Law Chambers, London	0171 375 3012
Rahman Ms Sadeqa Shaheen	1 Crown Office Row, London	0171 797 7500
Rai Amarjit Singh	St Philip's Chambers, Birmingham	0121 246 7000
Richardson Miss Sarah Jane	Enterprise Chambers, London	0171 405 9471
	Enterprise Chambers, Leeds	0113 246 0391
	Enterprise Chambers, Newcastle upon Tyne	0191 222 3344
Riley-Smith Tobias Augustine William	2 Harcourt Buildings, London	0171 583 9020
Robinson Richard John	2 Gray's Inn Square Chambers, London	0171 242 0328/405 1317
Ryan David Patrick	Chambers of Geoffrey Hawker, London	0171 583 8899
Samuel Glyn Ross	St Philip's Chambers, Birmingham	0121 246 7000
Sandiford Jonathan	St Paul's House, Leeds	0113 245 5866
Savage Miss Ayisha Carol	Britton Street Chambers, London	0171 608 3765
Schooling Simon John	Chambers of Harjit Singh, London	0171 353 1356
Scutt David Robert	11 Bolt Court, London	0171 353 2300
	Redhill Chambers, Redhill	01737 780781
Seal Julius Damien	189 Randolph Avenue, London	0171 624 9139
	3 Temple Gardens, London	0171 353 0832
Sefton Mark Thomas Dunblane	199 Strand, London	0171 379 9779
Seligman Matthew Thomas Arthur	39 Essex Street, London	0171 832 1111
Sheehan Malcolm Peter	Stanbrook & Henderson, London	0171 353 0101
	2 Harcourt Buildings, London	0171 583 9020
Smart Miss Jacqueline Anne	Trinity Chambers, Newcastle upon Tyne	0191 232 1927
Stagg Paul Andrew	No 1 Serjeants' Inn, London	0171 415 6666
Straker Timothy Derrick	• 2-3 Gray's Inn Square, London	0171 242 4986
Thomas Miss Megan Moira	1 Serjeants' Inn, London	0171 583 1355
Tobin Daniel Alphonsus Joseph	Chambers of Geoffrey Hawker, London	0171 583 8899
Tyack David Guy	St Philip's Chambers, Birmingham	0121 246 7000
Vane The Hon Christopher John Fletcher	Trinity Chambers, Newcastle upon Tyne	0191 232 1927
Webb Geraint Timothy	2 Harcourt Buildings, London	0171 583 9020
Wedderspoon Miss Rachel Leone	Chambers of John Hand QC, Manchester	0161 955 9000
Whybrow Christopher John	1 Serjeants' Inn, London	0171 583 1355
Wightwick (William) Iain	Assize Court Chambers, Bristol	0117 926 4587
Williams Ms Heather Jean	Doughty Street Chambers, London	0171 404 1313
Wilson Alasdair John	Fenners Chambers, Cambridge	01223 368761
	Fenners Chambers, Peterborough	01733 562030
Wilson Andrew Robert	9 Woodhouse Square, Leeds	0113 245 1986
Woolf Steven Jeremy	Hardwicke Building, London	0171 242 2523
Woolley David Rorie	• 1 Serjeants' Inn, London	0171 583 1355

IMMIGRATION

Adejumo Mrs Hilda Ekpo	• Temple Chambers, London	0171 583 1001 (2 lines)
Akiwumi Anthony Sebastian Akitayo	Pump Court Chambers, London	0171 353 0711
	Pump Court Chambers, Winchester	01962 868161
Al'Hassan Khadim	Equity Chambers, Birmingham	0121 233 2100
Bassra Sukhbir Singh	St Paul's House, Leeds	0113 245 5866
Bedeau Stephen	Sovereign Chambers, Leeds	0113 245 1841/2/3
	Lancaster Buildings, Manchester	0161 661 4444
Bhattacharyya Ardhendu	1 Gray's Inn Square, London	0171 405 8946
	11 St Bernards Road, Slough	01753 553806/817989

Birtles William	Old Square Chambers, London	0171 269 0300
	Old Square Chambers, Bristol	0117 927 7111
Davies Miss Penny May	Chambers of Harjit Singh, London	0171 353 1356
Dedezade Taner	Tindal Chambers, Chelmsford	01245 267742
Falk Miss Josephine Ruth Ann	12 Old Square, London	0171 404 0875
Forlin Gerard Emlyn	Phoenix Chambers, London	0171 404 7888
Foster Miss Alison Lee Caroline	39 Essex Street, London	0171 832 1111
Fripp Eric William Burtin	Chambers of Harjit Singh, London	0171 353 1356
Hamid Mrs Beebee Nazmoon	Clapham Chambers, London	0171 978 8482/0171 642 5777
Haynes Miss Rebecca	Monckton Chambers, London	0171 405 7211
Howard-Jones Miss Sarah Rachel	8 Stone Buildings, London	0171 831 9881
Kalsi Mrs Maninder	New Court Chambers, Birmingham	0121 693 6656
Khan Avicenna Alkindi Cornelius	55 Temple Chambers, London	0171 353 7400
Khan Saadallah Frans Hassan	55 Temple Chambers, London	0171 353 7400
King Peter Duncan	5 Pump Court, London	0171 353 2532
	Fenners Chambers, Cambridge	01223 368761
Lanlehin Olajide Adebola	Britton Street Chambers, London	0171 608 3765
Malecka Dr Mary Margaret	Goldsworth Chambers, London	0171 405 7117
Martin David John	Cathedral Chambers, Newcastle upon Tyne	0191 232 1311
Mathews Deni	8 Fountain Court, Birmingham	0121 236 5514
McCann Simon Howard	Deans Court Chambers, Manchester	0161 834 4097
Moses Miss Rebecca	Barristers' Common Law Chambers, London	0171 375 3012
	Lion Court, London	0171 404 6565
Nathan Philip Gabriel	Earl Street Chambers, Maidstone	01622 671222
Newman Austin Eric	9 Woodhouse Square, Leeds	0113 245 1986
Ofori George Edward	Chancery Chambers, London	0171 405 6879
	ACHMA Chambers, London	0171 639 7817
Ogunbiyi Oluwole Afolabi	Horizon Chambers, London	0171 242 2440
Oke Olanrewaju Oladipupo	Kingsway Chambers, London	07000 653529
Okoye Miss Joy Nwamala	Chambers of Joy Okoye, London	0171 405 7011
Purdie Robert Anthony James	28 Western Road, Oxford	01865 204911
Rahman Muhammad Altafur	Barristers' Common Law Chambers, London	0171 375 3012
Rogers Ian Paul	1 Crown Office Row, London	0171 583 9292
Sadiq Tariq Mahmood	Chambers of John Hand QC, Manchester	0161 955 9000
Sangster Nigel	St Paul's House, Leeds	0113 245 5866
Schooling Simon John	Chambers of Harjit Singh, London	0171 353 1356
Scott-Phillips Alexander James	Earl Street Chambers, Maidstone	01622 671222
Shaikh Eur.Ing. (Jaikumar) Christopher (Samuel	Avondale Chambers, London	0181 445 9984
	Equity Chambers, Birmingham	0121 233 2100
Smith Ms Katherine Emma	Monckton Chambers, London	0171 405 7211
Sparks Kevin Laurence	Earl Street Chambers, Maidstone	01622 671222
Stead Miss Kate Rebecca	Barristers' Common Law Chambers, London	0171 375 3012
Supperstone Michael Alan	11 King's Bench Walk, London	0171 632 8500
Wyatt Guy Peter James	Earl Street Chambers, Maidstone	01622 671222

INDUSTRIAL DISEASE

Hinchliffe Philip Nicholas	Chambers of John Hand QC, Manchester	0161 955 9000
Kennedy Christopher Laurence Paul	Chambers of John Hand QC, Manchester	0161 955 9000
Little Ian	Chambers of John Hand QC, Manchester	0161 955 9000
McCluggage Brian Thomas	Chambers of John Hand QC, Manchester	0161 955 9000

INDUSTRIAL RELATIONS

Hendy John Giles	Old Square Chambers, London	0171 269 0300
	Old Square Chambers, Bristol	0117 927 7111

INFORMATION TECHNOLOGY

Akenhead Robert	Atkin Chambers, London	0171 404 0102
Akka Lawrence Mark	20 Essex Street, London	0171 583 9294
Baatz Nicholas Stephen	Atkin Chambers, London	0171 404 0102
Barwise Miss Stephanie Nicola	Atkin Chambers, London	0171 404 0102

• Expanded entry in Part D

Blackburn John	Atkin Chambers, London	0171 404 0102
Bowdery Martin	Atkin Chambers, London	0171 404 0102
Burr Andrew Charles	Atkin Chambers, London	0171 404 0102
Clay Robert Charles	Atkin Chambers, London	0171 404 0102
Davidson Nicholas Ranking	4 Paper Buildings, London	0171 353 3366/583 7155
Davies Andrew Christopher	New Court Chambers, London	0171 831 9500
Dennison Stephen Randell	Atkin Chambers, London	0171 404 0102
Dennys Nicholas Charles Jonathan	Atkin Chambers, London	0171 404 0102
Doerries Miss Chantal-Aimee Renee Aemelia Annemarie	Atkin Chambers, London	0171 404 0102
Dumaresq Ms Delia Jane	Atkin Chambers, London	0171 404 0102
Fitzgerald John Vincent	New Court, London	0171 797 8999
Fraser Peter Donald	Atkin Chambers, London	0171 404 0102
Freedman Sampson Clive	3 Verulam Buildings, London	0171 831 8441
Friedman David Peter	4 Pump Court, London	0171 353 2656/9
Gatty Daniel Simon	New Court Chambers, London	0171 831 9500
Goddard Andrew Stephen	Atkin Chambers, London	0171 404 0102
Godwin William George Henry	Atkin Chambers, London	0171 404 0102
Goodbody Peter James	• Oriel Chambers, Liverpool	0151 236 7191
Green Patrick Curtis	Stanbrook & Henderson, London	0171 353 0101
	2 Harcourt Buildings, London	0171 583 9020
Harvey Jonathan Robert William	2 Harcourt Buildings, London	0171 583 9020
Hodgson Richard Andrew	New Court, London	0171 797 8999
Holman Miss Tamsin Perdita	19 Old Buildings, London	0171 405 2001
Howells James Richard	Atkin Chambers, London	0171 404 0102
Jackson Hugh Woodward	Hardwicke Building, London	0171 242 2523
Kime Matthew Jonathan	• New Court, London	0171 797 8999
	• Cobden House Chambers, Manchester	0161 833 6000/6001
Knight Brian Joseph	Atkin Chambers, London	0171 404 0102
Knott Malcolm Stephen	New Court Chambers, London	0171 831 9500
Lofthouse Simon Timothy	Atkin Chambers, London	0171 404 0102
Mawrey Richard Brooks	Stanbrook & Henderson, London	0171 353 0101
	2 Harcourt Buildings, London	0171 583 9020
McCall Duncan James	4 Pump Court, London	0171 353 2656/9
McMullan Manus Anthony	Atkin Chambers, London	0171 404 0102
Norris Andrew James Steedsman	5 New Square, London	0171 404 0404
Parkin Miss Fiona Jane	Atkin Chambers, London	0171 404 0102
Patterson Stewart	• Pump Court Chambers, London	0171 353 0711
	• Pump Court Chambers, Winchester	01962 868161
Portnoy Leslie Reuben	Chambers of John Hand QC, Manchester	0161 955 9000
Powles Stephen Robert	Stanbrook & Henderson, London	0171 353 0101
	2 Harcourt Buildings, London	0171 583 9020
Puckrin Cedric Eldred	19 Old Buildings, London	0171 405 2001
Raeside Mark Andrew	Atkin Chambers, London	0171 404 0102
Rawley Miss Dominique Jane	Atkin Chambers, London	0171 404 0102
Reese Colin Edward	Atkin Chambers, London	0171 404 0102
Royce Darryl Fraser	Atkin Chambers, London	0171 404 0102
Salter Richard Stanley	3 Verulam Buildings, London	0171 831 8441
Sampson Graeme William	Chambers of Geoffrey Hawker, London	0171 583 8899
Shipley Norman Graham	• 19 Old Buildings, London	0171 405 2001
Silverleaf Michael	• 11 South Square, London	0171 405 1222
Simpson Mark Taylor	4 Paper Buildings, London	0171 353 3366/583 7155
Spencer Martin Benedict	4 Paper Buildings, London	0171 353 3366/583 7155
Stewart Nicholas John Cameron	Hardwicke Building, London	0171 242 2523
Stewart Richard Paul	New Court Chambers, London	0171 831 9500
Streatfeild-James David Stewart	Atkin Chambers, London	0171 404 0102
Sullivan Rory Myles	19 Old Buildings, London	0171 405 2001
Turner Jonathan David Chattyn	• 4 Field Court, London	0171 440 6900
Valentine Donald Graham	Atkin Chambers, London	0171 404 0102
Walker Steven John	Atkin Chambers, London	0171 404 0102
Wallace Ian Norman Duncan	Atkin Chambers, London	0171 404 0102
West Lawrence Joseph	Stanbrook & Henderson, London	0171 353 0101
	2 Harcourt Buildings, London	0171 583 9020
White Andrew	Atkin Chambers, London	0171 404 0102
Wilson Alastair James Drysdale	• 19 Old Buildings, London	0171 405 2001

INHERITANCE

Fricker Mrs Marilyn Ann	Farrar's Building, London	0171 583 9241
	Sovereign Chambers, Leeds	0113 245 1841/2/3

• Expanded entry in Part D

INJUNCTIVE RELIEF

Airey Simon Andrew	11 Bolt Court, London	0171 353 2300
	Redhill Chambers, Redhill	01737 780781

INQUESTS

Jenkins Dr Janet Caroline	Chambers of Kieran Coonan QC, London	0171 583 6013/2510
Wastie William Granville	Queen Elizabeth Building, London	0171 583 5766
Wilcox Nicholas Hugh	5 Essex Court, London	0171 410 2000

INSOLVENCY

Abbott Alistair James Hugh	5 New Square, London	0171 404 0404
Adamyk Simon Charles	12 New Square, London	0171 419 1212
Airey Simon Andrew	11 Bolt Court, London	0171 353 2300
	Redhill Chambers, Redhill	01737 780781
Aldridge James Hugh	13 Old Square, London	0171 404 4800
Amin Miss Farah	7 New Square, London	0171 430 1660
Angus Miss Tracey Anne	5 Stone Buildings, London	0171 242 6201
Arden Peter Leonard	Enterprise Chambers, London	0171 405 9471
	Enterprise Chambers, Leeds	0113 246 0391
	Enterprise Chambers, Newcastle upon Tyne	0191 222 3344
Atherton Ian David	Enterprise Chambers, London	0171 405 9471
	Enterprise Chambers, Leeds	0113 246 0391
	Enterprise Chambers, Newcastle upon Tyne	0191 222 3344
Attala Jean Etienne	Cathedral Chambers, Newcastle upon Tyne	0191 232 1311
Ayres Andrew John William	13 Old Square, London	0171 404 4800
Bailey Edward Henry	5 Bell Yard, London	0171 333 8811
Baker Miss Anne Jacqueline	Enterprise Chambers, London	0171 405 9471
	Enterprise Chambers, Leeds	0113 246 0391
	Enterprise Chambers, Newcastle upon Tyne	0191 222 3344
Barber Miss Sally	5 Stone Buildings, London	0171 242 6201
Barker James Sebastian	Enterprise Chambers, London	0171 405 9471
	Enterprise Chambers, Leeds	0113 246 0391
	Enterprise Chambers, Newcastle upon Tyne	0191 222 3344
Barnett Jeremy Victor	Farrar's Building, London	0171 583 9241
	St Paul's House, Leeds	0113 245 5866
Barstow Stephen Royden	Harcourt Chambers, London	0171 353 6961/7
	Harcourt Chambers, Oxford	01865 791559
Baylis Ms Natalie Jayne	3 Verulam Buildings, London	0171 831 8441
Beltrami Adrian Joseph	3 Verulam Buildings, London	0171 831 8441
Berkley Michael Stuart	Rougemont Chambers, Exeter	01392 410471
Berragan (Howard) Neil	Merchant Chambers, Manchester	0161 839 7070
Bhaloo Miss Zia Kurban	Enterprise Chambers, London	0171 405 9471
	Enterprise Chambers, Leeds	0113 246 0391
	Enterprise Chambers, Newcastle upon Tyne	0191 222 3344
Birch Roger Allen	12 New Square, London	0171 419 1212
	Sovereign Chambers, Leeds	0113 245 1841/2/3
	Lancaster Buildings, Manchester	0161 661 4444
Bird Nigel David	Chambers of John Hand QC, Manchester	0161 955 9000
Bompas Anthony George	4 Stone Buildings, London	0171 242 5524
Brook Ian Stuart	Hardwicke Building, London	0171 242 2523
Browne Miss Julie Rebecca	Goldsmith Building, London	0171 353 7881
Bryant Miss Ceri Jane	Erskine Chambers, London	0171 242 5532
Burroughs Nigel Alfred	11 Old Square, London	0171 430 0341
Burton Michael John	Littleton Chambers, London	0171 797 8600
Butt Miss Romasa	Goldsworth Chambers, London	0171 405 7117
Capon Philip Christopher William	St Philip's Chambers, Birmingham	0121 246 7000
Carey Jeremy Reynolds Patrick	Lamb Chambers, London	0171 797 8300
Cawson Mark	• 12 New Square, London	0171 419 1212
	• St James's Chambers, Manchester	0161 834 7000
	• Park Lane Chambers, Leeds	0113 228 5000
Charman Andrew Julian	St Philip's Chambers, Birmingham	0121 246 7000
Chivers (Tom) David	Erskine Chambers, London	0171 242 5532

• Expanded entry in Part D

Clark Ms Julia Elisabeth	5 New Square, London	0171 404 0404
Clarke Miss Anna Victoria	5 Stone Buildings, London	0171 242 6201
Clarke Ian James	Hardwicke Building, London	0171 242 2523
Clegg Sebastian James Barwick	Deans Court Chambers, Manchester	0161 834 4097
Collaco Moraes Francis Thomas	• 2 Gray's Inn Square Chambers, London	0171 242 0328/405 1317
Collings Matthew Glynn Burkinshaw	13 Old Square, London	0171 404 4800
Cone John Crawford	Erskine Chambers, London	0171 242 5532
Corbett James Patrick	St Philip's Chambers, Birmingham	0121 246 7000
Craig Kenneth Allen	Hardwicke Building, London	0171 242 2523
Crail Miss (Elspeth) Ross	12 New Square, London	0171 419 1212
	Sovereign Chambers, Leeds	0113 245 1841/2/3
Cranfield Peter Anthony	3 Verulam Buildings, London	0171 831 8441
Crawford Grant	11 Old Square, London	0171 430 0341
Creaner Paul Anthony	15 Winckley Square, Preston	01772 252 828
Crow Jonathan Rupert	4 Stone Buildings, London	0171 242 5524
Cunningham Miss Claire Louise	St Philip's Chambers, Birmingham	0121 246 7000
Cunningham Mark James	13 Old Square, London	0171 404 4800
Darbyshire William Robert	Chambers of John Hand QC, Manchester	0161 955 9000
Davies Miss Louise	12 New Square, London	0171 419 1212
Dawson James Robert	Oriel Chambers, Liverpool	0151 236 7191
de Lacy Richard Michael	3 Verulam Buildings, London	0171 831 8441
Deacock Adam Jason	Chambers of Lord Goodhart QC, London	0171 405 5577
Dedezade Taner	Tindal Chambers, Chelmsford	01245 267742
Dineen Michael Laurence	Pump Court Chambers, London	0171 353 0711
	All Saints Chambers, Bristol	0117 921 1966
	Pump Court Chambers, Winchester	01962 868161
Dodge Peter Clive	11 Old Square, London	0171 430 0341
Dougherty Nigel Peter	Erskine Chambers, London	0171 242 5532
Dowse John	Chambers of Lord Goodhart QC, London	0171 405 5577
	Chambers of John Hand QC, Manchester	0161 955 9000
Doyle Louis George	Chambers of Andrew Campbell QC, Leeds	0113 245 5438
Drayton Henry Alexander	2 Gray's Inn Square Chambers, London	0171 242 0328/405 1317
Duffy Derek James	St Paul's House, Leeds	0113 245 5866
Elleray Anthony John	• 12 New Square, London	0171 419 1212
	• St James's Chambers, Manchester	0161 834 7000
	• Park Lane Chambers, Leeds	0113 228 5000
Evans-Gordon Mrs Jane-Anne Mary	12 New Square, London	0171 419 1212
Fawls Richard Granville	5 Stone Buildings, London	0171 242 6201
Finlay Darren	Sovereign Chambers, Leeds	0113 245 1841/2/3
Francis Edward Gerald Francis	Enterprise Chambers, London	0171 405 9471
	Enterprise Chambers, Leeds	0113 246 0391
	Enterprise Chambers, Newcastle upon Tyne	0191 222 3344
French Richard Anthony Lister	Rougemont Chambers, Exeter	01392 410471
Garcia-Miller Miss Laura	Enterprise Chambers, London	0171 405 9471
	Enterprise Chambers, Leeds	0113 246 0391
	Enterprise Chambers, Newcastle upon Tyne	0191 222 3344
George Miss Judith Sarah	St Philip's Chambers, Birmingham	0121 246 7000
Gerald Nigel Mortimer	Enterprise Chambers, London	0171 405 9471
	Enterprise Chambers, Leeds	0113 246 0391
	Enterprise Chambers, Newcastle upon Tyne	0191 222 3344
Gibaud Miss Catherine Alison Annetta	3 Verulam Buildings, London	0171 831 8441
Gilchrist David Somerled	Chambers of John Hand QC, Manchester	0161 955 9000
Gillyon Philip Jeffrey	Erskine Chambers, London	0171 242 5532
Goodhart Lord	Chambers of Lord Goodhart QC, London	0171 405 5577
Gore Andrew Roger	Fenners Chambers, Cambridge	01223 368761
	Fenners Chambers, Peterborough	01733 562030
Graham Thomas Patrick Henry	Lamb Chambers, London	0171 797 8300
Grant Thomas Paul Wentworth	New Court Chambers, London	0171 831 9500
Grantham Andrew Timothy	• Deans Court Chambers, Manchester	0161 834 4097

• Expanded entry in Part D

	• Deans Court Chambers, Preston	01772 555163
Gregory John Raymond	Deans Court Chambers, Manchester	0161 834 4097
	Deans Court Chambers, Preston	01772 555163
Griffiths Peter Robert	4 Stone Buildings, London	0171 242 5524
Groves Hugo Gerard	Enterprise Chambers, London	0171 405 9471
	Enterprise Chambers, Leeds	0113 246 0391
	Enterprise Chambers, Newcastle upon Tyne	0191 222 3344
Hall Taylor Alexander Edward	11 Old Square, London	0171 430 0341
Halpern David Anthony	Enterprise Chambers, London	0171 405 9471
	Enterprise Chambers, Leeds	0113 246 0391
	Enterprise Chambers, Newcastle upon Tyne	0191 222 3344
Hamer Michael Howard Kenneth	2 Harcourt Buildings, London	0171 583 9020
	Westgate Chambers, Lewes	01273 480 510
Hansen William Joseph	5 Bell Yard, London	0171 333 8811
Hantusch Robert Anthony	• 3 Stone Buildings, London	0171 242 4937/405 8358
Harbottle Gwilym Thomas	5 New Square, London	0171 404 0404
Hardwick Matthew Richard	Enterprise Chambers, London	0171 405 9471
	Enterprise Chambers, Leeds	0113 246 0391
	Enterprise Chambers, Newcastle upon Tyne	0191 222 3344
Hargreaves Miss Sara Jane	12 New Square, London	0171 419 1212
	Sovereign Chambers, Leeds	0113 245 1841/2/3
Harvey Miss Jayne Denise	Goldsworth Chambers, London	0171 405 7117
Haven Kevin	2 Gray's Inn Square Chambers, London	0171 242 0328/405 1317
Hay Robin William Patrick Hamilton	Goldsmith Building, London	0171 353 7881
Hayes John Allan	Chambers of Andrew Campbell QC, Leeds	0113 245 5438
Hayes Miss Josephine Mary	Chambers of Lord Goodhart QC, London	0171 405 5577
Heywood Michael Edmundson	Chambers of Lord Goodhart QC, London	0171 405 5577
	Cobden House Chambers, Manchester	0161 833 6000/6001
Hibbert William John	Gough Square Chambers, London	0171 353 0924
Hockaday Miss Annie	3 Verulam Buildings, London	0171 831 8441
Holland David Moore	29 Bedford Row Chambers, London	0171 831 2626
Hollingworth Peter James Michael	22 Albion Place, Northampton	01604 636271
Holmes Justin Francis	Chambers of Lord Goodhart QC, London	0171 405 5577
Horspool Anthony Bernard Graeme	Hardwicke Building, London	0171 242 2523
Hughes Miss Mary Josephine	Chambers of Lord Goodhart QC, London	0171 405 5577
Ife Miss Linden Elizabeth	Enterprise Chambers, London	0171 405 9471
	Enterprise Chambers, Leeds	0113 246 0391
	Enterprise Chambers, Newcastle upon Tyne	0191 222 3344
Jack Adrian Laurence Robert	Enterprise Chambers, London	0171 405 9471
Jackson Dirik George Allan	• Chambers of Mr Peter Crampin QC, London	0171 831 0081
Jackson Hugh Woodward	Hardwicke Building, London	0171 242 2523
Jackson Nicholas David Kingsley	The Chambers of Adrian Lyon, Liverpool	0151 236 4421/8240/6757
James Michael Frank	Enterprise Chambers, London	0171 405 9471
	Enterprise Chambers, Leeds	0113 246 0391
	Enterprise Chambers, Newcastle upon Tyne	0191 222 3344
Jarvis John Manners	3 Verulam Buildings, London	0171 831 8441
Jefferies Thomas Robert	Chambers of Lord Goodhart QC, London	0171 405 5577
Johnson Michael Sloan	Chambers of John Hand QC, Manchester	0161 955 9000
Jones Geraint Martyn	Fenners Chambers, Cambridge	01223 368761
	Fenners Chambers, Peterborough	01733 562030
Jory Robert John Hugh	Enterprise Chambers, London	0171 405 9471
	Enterprise Chambers, Leeds	0113 246 0391
	Enterprise Chambers, Newcastle upon Tyne	0191 222 3344
Kimbell John Ashley	5 Bell Yard, London	0171 333 8811
Kosmin Leslie Gordon	Erskine Chambers, London	0171 242 5532
Kremen Philip Michael	Hardwicke Building, London	0171 242 2523

• Expanded entry in Part D

Kuschke Leon Siegfried	Erskine Chambers, London	0171 242 5532
Lamont Miss Camilla Rose	Chambers of Lord Goodhart QC, London	0171 405 5577
Landes Miss Anna-Rose	St Philip's Chambers, Birmingham	0121 246 7000
Laughton Samuel Dennis	17 Old Buildings, London	0171 405 9653
Le Poidevin Nicholas Peter	12 New Square, London	0171 419 1212
	Sovereign Chambers, Leeds	0113 245 1841/2/3
Leeming Ian	Lamb Chambers, London	0171 797 8300
	Chambers of John Hand QC, Manchester	0161 955 9000
Levy Benjamin Keith	Enterprise Chambers, London	0171 405 9471
	Enterprise Chambers, Leeds	0113 246 0391
	Enterprise Chambers, Newcastle upon Tyne	0191 222 3344
Levy Robert Stuart	9 Stone Buildings, London	0171 404 5055
	Assize Court Chambers, Bristol	0117 926 4587
Lewis Miss Caroline Susannah	3 Verulam Buildings, London	0171 831 8441
Lowenstein Paul David	Littleton Chambers, London	0171 797 8600
Lynch Terry John	22 Albion Place, Northampton	01604 636271
Lyne Mark Hilary	One Essex Court, London	0171 936 3030
Mabb David Michael	Erskine Chambers, London	0171 242 5532
Mann George Anthony	Enterprise Chambers, London	0171 405 9471
	Enterprise Chambers, Leeds	0113 246 0391
	Enterprise Chambers, Newcastle upon Tyne	0191 222 3344
Marks Jonathan Harold	3 Verulam Buildings, London	0171 831 8441
Marquand Charles Nicholas Hilary	Chambers of Lord Goodhart QC, London	0171 405 5577
Marshall Paul David John	1 Crown Office Row, London	0171 583 9292
Marten Richard Hedley Westwood	Chambers of Lord Goodhart QC, London	0171 405 5577
Mauger Miss Claire Shanti Andrea	Enterprise Chambers, London	0171 405 9471
McAllister Miss Elizabeth Ann	Enterprise Chambers, London	0171 405 9471
	Enterprise Chambers, Leeds	0113 246 0391
	Enterprise Chambers, Newcastle upon Tyne	0191 222 3344
McCarthy William	New Bailey Chambers, Preston	01772 258 087
McKinnell Miss Soraya Jane	Enterprise Chambers, London	0171 405 9471
	Enterprise Chambers, Leeds	0113 246 0391
	Enterprise Chambers, Newcastle upon Tyne	0191 222 3344
McParland Michael Joseph	New Court Chambers, London	0171 831 9500
McQuail Ms Katherine Emma	11 Old Square, London	0171 430 0341
McQuater Ewan Alan	3 Verulam Buildings, London	0171 831 8441
Mendoza Neil David Pereira	Hardwicke Building, London	0171 242 2523
Merriman Nicholas Flavelle	3 Verulam Buildings, London	0171 831 8441
Mitchell Gregory Charles Mathew	3 Verulam Buildings, London	0171 831 8441
Moore Martin Luke	Erskine Chambers, London	0171 242 5532
Morgan Charles James Arthur	Enterprise Chambers, London	0171 405 9471
	Enterprise Chambers, Leeds	0113 246 0391
	Enterprise Chambers, Newcastle upon Tyne	0191 222 3344
Morgan Edward Patrick	4 King's Bench Walk, London	0171 822 8822
	Deans Court Chambers, Manchester	0161 834 4097
Morgan Richard Hugo Lyndon	13 Old Square, London	0171 404 4800
Mullis Anthony Roger	Chambers of Lord Goodhart QC, London	0171 405 5577
Nash Jonathan Scott	3 Verulam Buildings, London	0171 831 8441
Nebhrajani Miss Mel	9 Stone Buildings, London	0171 404 5055
Nesbitt Timothy John Robert	199 Strand, London	0171 379 9779
Neville Stephen John	Gough Square Chambers, London	0171 353 0924
Newman Miss Catherine Mary	• 13 Old Square, London	0171 404 4800
Nicholls John Peter	13 Old Square, London	0171 404 4800
Norbury Luke Edward	17 Old Buildings, London	0171 405 9653
Odgers John Arthur	3 Verulam Buildings, London	0171 831 8441
Ohrenstein Dov	Chambers of Lord Goodhart QC, London	0171 405 5577
Parry David Julian Thomas	Chambers of Lord Goodhart QC, London	0171 405 5577
Patchett-Joyce Michael Thurston	Monckton Chambers, London	0171 405 7211
Peacock Ian Christopher	12 New Square, London	0171 419 1212
	Sovereign Chambers, Leeds	0113 245 1841/2/3

Peacock Nicholas Christopher	13 Old Square, London	0171 404 4800
Peacocke Mrs Teresa Anne Rosen	Enterprise Chambers, London	0171 405 9471
	Enterprise Chambers, Leeds	0113 246 0391
	Enterprise Chambers, Newcastle upon Tyne	0191 222 3344
Peglow Dr Michael Alfred Herman	Chambers of Geoffrey Hawker, London	0171 583 8899
Pelling (Philip) Mark	Monckton Chambers, London	0171 405 7211
Pelling Richard Alexander	New Court Chambers, London	0171 831 9500
Perkoff Richard Michael	Littleton Chambers, London	0171 797 8600
Phillips Jonathan Mark	3 Verulam Buildings, London	0171 831 8441
Phillips Stephen Edmund	3 Verulam Buildings, London	0171 831 8441
Picarda Hubert Alistair Paul	Chambers of Lord Goodhart QC, London	0171 405 5577
Pickering James Patrick	Enterprise Chambers, London	0171 405 9471
	Enterprise Chambers, Leeds	0113 246 0391
	Enterprise Chambers, Newcastle upon Tyne	0191 222 3344
Pimentel Carlos de Serpa Alberto Legg	3 Stone Buildings, London	0171 242 4937/405 8358
Pope David James	3 Verulam Buildings, London	0171 831 8441
Potts James Rupert	Erskine Chambers, London	0171 242 5532
Potts Robin	Erskine Chambers, London	0171 242 5532
Poyer-Sleeman Ms Patricia	Pump Court Chambers, London	0171 353 0711
	Pump Court Chambers, Winchester	01962 868161
Prentice Professor Daniel David	Erskine Chambers, London	0171 242 5532
Pryke Stuart	Trinity Chambers, Newcastle upon Tyne	0191 232 1927
Randall John Yeoman	7 Stone Buildings, London	0171 405 3886/242 3546
	St Philip's Chambers, Birmingham	0121 246 7000
Rees David Benjamin	5 Stone Buildings, London	0171 242 6201
Richards David Anthony Stewart	Erskine Chambers, London	0171 242 5532
Richardson Miss Sarah Jane	Enterprise Chambers, London	0171 405 9471
	Enterprise Chambers, Leeds	0113 246 0391
	Enterprise Chambers, Newcastle upon Tyne	0191 222 3344
Roberts Miss Catherine Ann	Erskine Chambers, London	0171 242 5532
Robson John Malcolm	2 Gray's Inn Square Chambers, London	0171 242 0328/405 1317
	Assize Court Chambers, Bristol	0117 926 4587
Ross Martyn John Greaves	• 5 New Square, London	0171 404 0404
	• Octagon House, Norwich	01603 623186
Rowell David Stewart	Chambers of Lord Goodhart QC, London	0171 405 5577
Rule Jonathan Daniel	Merchant Chambers, Manchester	0161 839 7070
Russen Jonathan Huw Sinclair	13 Old Square, London	0171 404 4800
Salter Richard Stanley	3 Verulam Buildings, London	0171 831 8441
Sampson Graeme William	Chambers of Geoffrey Hawker, London	0171 583 8899
Schaw-Miller Stephen Grant	5 Bell Yard, London	0171 333 8811
Seal Julius Damien	189 Randolph Avenue, London	0171 624 9139
	3 Temple Gardens, London	0171 353 0832
Sefton Mark Thomas Dunblane	199 Strand, London	0171 379 9779
Seymour Richard William	Monckton Chambers, London	0171 405 7211
Shah Bajul Amratlal Somchand	Twenty-Four Old Buildings, London	0171 404 0946
Sheehan Malcolm Peter	Stanbrook & Henderson, London	0171 353 0101
	2 Harcourt Buildings, London	0171 583 9020
Smith Miss Julia Mair Wheldon	Gough Square Chambers, London	0171 353 0924
Snowden Richard Andrew	Erskine Chambers, London	0171 242 5532
Staddon Miss Claire Ann	12 New Square, London	0171 419 1212
	Sovereign Chambers, Leeds	0113 245 1841/2/3
Stewart Alexander Joseph	5 New Square, London	0171 404 0404
Stewart Mark Courtney	College Chambers, Southampton	01703 230338
Stewart Nicholas John Cameron	Hardwicke Building, London	0171 242 2523
Stockdale Sir Thomas Minshull	Erskine Chambers, London	0171 242 5532
Stokes Miss Mary Elizabeth	Erskine Chambers, London	0171 242 5532
Stubbs William Frederick	Erskine Chambers, London	0171 242 5532
Sugar Simon Gareth	5 New Square, London	0171 404 0404
Sykes (James) Richard	Erskine Chambers, London	0171 242 5532
Taelor Start Miss Angharad Jocelyn	3 Verulam Buildings, London	0171 831 8441
Tedd Rex Hilary	• St Philip's Chambers, Birmingham	0121 246 7000
	• 22 Albion Place, Northampton	01604 636271

• Expanded entry in Part D

Thomas (Robert) Neville	3 Verulam Buildings, London	0171 831 8441
Thompson Andrew Richard	Erskine Chambers, London	0171 242 5532
Thompson Steven Lim	Twenty-Four Old Buildings, London	0171 404 0946
Thornton Andrew James	Erskine Chambers, London	0171 242 5532
Tidmarsh Christopher Ralph Francis	5 Stone Buildings, London	0171 242 6201
Tipples Miss Amanda Jane	13 Old Square, London	0171 404 4800
Todd Michael Alan	Erskine Chambers, London	0171 242 5532
Tolaney Miss Sonia	3 Verulam Buildings, London	0171 831 8441
Trace Anthony John	• 13 Old Square, London	0171 404 4800
Tucker Miss Katherine Jane Greening	St Philip's Chambers, Birmingham	0121 246 7000
Twigger Andrew Mark	3 Stone Buildings, London	0171 242 4937/405 8358
Vane The Hon Christopher John Fletcher	Trinity Chambers, Newcastle upon Tyne	0191 232 1927
Vaughan-Neil Miss Catherine Mary Bernardine	5 Bell Yard, London	0171 333 8811
Vines Anthony Robert Francis	Gough Square Chambers, London	0171 353 0924
Walker Andrew Greenfield	Chambers of Lord Goodhart QC, London	0171 405 5577
Weatherill Bernard Richard	Chambers of Lord Goodhart QC, London	0171 405 5577
West Mark	• 11 Old Square, London	0171 430 0341
Williamson Miss Bridget Susan	Enterprise Chambers, London	0171 405 9471
	Enterprise Chambers, Leeds	0113 246 0391
	Enterprise Chambers, Newcastle upon Tyne	0191 222 3344
Wilson Ian Robert	3 Verulam Buildings, London	0171 831 8441
Wolfson David	3 Verulam Buildings, London	0171 831 8441
Worster David James Stewart	St Philip's Chambers, Birmingham	0121 246 7000
Wright Robert Anthony Kent	Erskine Chambers, London	0171 242 5532
Zelin Geoffrey Andrew	Enterprise Chambers, London	0171 405 9471
	Enterprise Chambers, Leeds	0113 246 0391
	Enterprise Chambers, Newcastle upon Tyne	0191 222 3344

INSURANCE

Akka Lawrence Mark	20 Essex Street, London	0171 583 9294
Alliott George Beckles	2 Harcourt Buildings, London	0171 583 9020
Ambrose Miss Clare Mary Geneste	20 Essex Street, London	0171 583 9294
Ashworth Piers	Stanbrook & Henderson, London	0171 353 0101
	2 Harcourt Buildings, London	0171 583 9020
	Priory Chambers, Birmingham	0121 236 3882/1375
Baylis Ms Natalie Jayne	3 Verulam Buildings, London	0171 831 8441
Beal Kieron Conrad	4 Paper Buildings, London	0171 353 3366/583 7155
Beaumont Marc Clifford	• Pump Court Chambers, London	0171 353 0711
	• Harrow-on-the-Hill Chambers, Harrow on the Hill	0181 423 7444
	• Pump Court Chambers, Winchester	01962 868161
	• Windsor Barristers' Chambers, Windsor	01753 648 899
Bishop Edward James	No 1 Serjeants' Inn, London	0171 415 6666
Blakesley Patrick James	Two Crown Office Row, London	0171 797 8100
Boyle Gerard James	No 1 Serjeants' Inn, London	0171 415 6666
Brannigan Peter John Sean	One Essex Court, London	0171 936 3030
Briden Timothy John	• 8 Stone Buildings, London	0171 831 9881
Brown Miss Hannah Beatrice	5 Bell Yard, London	0171 333 8811
Burns Peter Richard	Deans Court Chambers, Manchester	0161 834 4097
Catchpole Stuart Paul	39 Essex Street, London	0171 832 1111
Chalmers Miss Suzanne Frances	Two Crown Office Row, London	0171 797 8100
Charkham Graham Harold	20 Essex Street, London	0171 583 9294
Coburn Michael Jeremy Patrick	20 Essex Street, London	0171 583 9294
Collett Michael John	20 Essex Street, London	0171 583 9294
Cooper Adrian Edgar Mark	Stanbrook & Henderson, London	0171 353 0101
	2 Harcourt Buildings, London	0171 583 9020
Cross James Edward Michael	4 Pump Court, London	0171 353 2656/9
Crowley John Desmond	Two Crown Office Row, London	0171 797 8100
Curtis Michael Alexander	Two Crown Office Row, London	0171 797 8100
Darbyshire William Robert	Chambers of John Hand QC, Manchester	0161 955 9000
Davies Stephen Richard	8 King Street Chambers, Manchester	0161 834 9560
Davies-Jones Jonathan	3 Verulam Buildings, London	0171 831 8441
Davis Andrew Paul	Two Crown Office Row, London	0171 797 8100

• Expanded entry in Part D

DeCamp Miss Jane Louise	Two Crown Office Row, London	0171 797 8100
Eastman Roger	Stanbrook & Henderson, London	0171 353 0101
	2 Harcourt Buildings, London	0171 583 9020
Edwards-Stuart Antony James Cobham	Two Crown Office Row, London	0171 797 8100
Elliott Nicholas Blethyn	3 Verulam Buildings, London	0171 831 8441
Evans-Tovey Jason Robert	Two Crown Office Row, London	0171 797 8100
Faulks Edward Peter Lawless	No 1 Serjeants' Inn, London	0171 415 6666
Fisher David	5 Bell Yard, London	0171 333 8811
Franklin Stephen Hall	5 Paper Buildings, London	0171 583 6117
	Fenners Chambers, Cambridge	01223 368761
Freedman Sampson Clive	3 Verulam Buildings, London	0171 831 8441
Gadney George Munro	Two Crown Office Row, London	0171 797 8100
Garcia-Miller Miss Laura	Enterprise Chambers, London	0171 405 9471
	Enterprise Chambers, Leeds	0113 246 0391
	Enterprise Chambers, Newcastle upon Tyne	0191 222 3344
Gibaud Miss Catherine Alison Annetta	3 Verulam Buildings, London	0171 831 8441
Gibson Charles Anthony Warneford	2 Harcourt Buildings, London	0171 583 9020
Grace Jonathan Robert	Deans Court Chambers, Manchester	0161 834 4097
	Deans Court Chambers, Preston	01772 555163
Grantham Andrew Timothy	• Deans Court Chambers, Manchester	0161 834 4097
	• Deans Court Chambers, Preston	01772 555163
Grundy Nigel Lawrence John	Chambers of John Hand QC, Manchester	0161 955 9000
Guggenheim Miss Anna Maeve	Two Crown Office Row, London	0171 797 8100
Gunning Alexander Rupert	4 Pump Court, London	0171 353 2656/9
Hamblen Nicholas Archibald	20 Essex Street, London	0171 583 9294
Hamer Michael Howard Kenneth .	2 Harcourt Buildings, London	0171 583 9020
	Westgate Chambers, Lewes	01273 480 510
Hamilton Graeme Montagu	Two Crown Office Row, London	0171 797 8100
Hamilton Peter Bernard	4 Pump Court, London	0171 353 2656/9
Hammerton Alastair Rolf	No 1 Serjeants' Inn, London	0171 415 6666
Harvey Jonathan Robert William	2 Harcourt Buildings, London	0171 583 9020
Harvey Michael Llewellyn Tucker	Two Crown Office Row, London	0171 797 8100
Haven Kevin	2 Gray's Inn Square Chambers, London	0171 242 0328/405 1317
Henderson Roger Anthony	Stanbrook & Henderson, London	0171 353 0101
	2 Harcourt Buildings, London	0171 583 9020
Hodgson Miss Susan Ann	Two Crown Office Row, London	0171 797 8100
Holdsworth James Arthur	Two Crown Office Row, London	0171 797 8100
Holwill Derek Paul Winsor	4 Paper Buildings, London	0171 353 3366/583 7155
Horlock Timothy John	Chambers of John Hand QC, Manchester	0161 955 9000
Howarth Simon Stuart	Two Crown Office Row, London	0171 797 8100
Hurst Brian	17 Bedford Row, London	0171 831 7314
Jack Adrian Laurence Robert	Enterprise Chambers, London	0171 405 9471
Jackson Matthew David Everard	4 Paper Buildings, London	0171 353 3366/583 7155
Jarvis John Manners	3 Verulam Buildings, London	0171 831 8441
Jess Digby Charles	• 8 King Street Chambers, Manchester	0161 834 9560
Jones Geraint Martyn	Fenners Chambers, Cambridge	01223 368761
	Fenners Chambers, Peterborough	01733 562030
Kent Michael Harcourt	Two Crown Office Row, London	0171 797 8100
Kimbell John Ashley	5 Bell Yard, London	0171 333 8811
Kolodziej Andrzej Jozef	• Littman Chambers, London	0171 404 4866
Kremen Philip Michael	Hardwicke Building, London	0171 242 2523
Lawrence The Hon Patrick John Tristram	4 Paper Buildings, London	0171 353 3366/583 7155
Lawson Robert John	5 Bell Yard, London	0171 333 8811
Legh-Jones Piers Nicholas	• 20 Essex Street, London	0171 583 9294
Lindsay Crawford Callum Douglas	No 1 Serjeants' Inn, London	0171 415 6666
Lowenstein Paul David	Littleton Chambers, London	0171 797 8600
Machell Raymond Donatus	2 Pump Court, London	0171 353 5597
	Deans Court Chambers, Manchester	0161 834 4097
Males Stephen Martin	20 Essex Street, London	0171 583 9294
Masters Miss Sara Alayna	20 Essex Street, London	0171 583 9294
Matthews Dennis Roland	5 Bell Yard, London	0171 333 8811
Mauleverer Peter Bruce	4 Pump Court, London	0171 353 2656/9
Mawrey Richard Brooks	Stanbrook & Henderson, London	0171 353 0101
	2 Harcourt Buildings, London	0171 583 9020
Maxwell Miss Karen Laetitia	20 Essex Street, London	0171 583 9294

• Expanded entry in Part D

Maxwell-Scott James Herbert	Two Crown Office Row, London	0171 797 8100
May Miss Juliet Mary	3 Verulam Buildings, London	0171 831 8441
McManus Jonathan Richard	4-5 Gray's Inn Square, London	0171 404 5252
Meeson Nigel Keith	4 Field Court, London	0171 440 6900
Milligan Iain Anstruther	20 Essex Street, London	0171 583 9294
Morgan Edward Patrick	4 King's Bench Walk, London	0171 822 8822
	Deans Court Chambers, Manchester	0161 834 4097
Mulcahy Miss Leigh-Ann Maria	Two Crown Office Row, London	0171 797 8100
Nicholls Paul Richard	11 King's Bench Walk, London	0171 632 8500
Noble Andrew	Eldon Chambers, London	0171 353 4636
	Merchant Chambers, Manchester	0161 839 7070
Norman Christopher John George	No 1 Serjeants' Inn, London	0171 415 6666
Odgers John Arthur	3 Verulam Buildings, London	0171 831 8441
Owen David Christopher	20 Essex Street, London	0171 583 9294
Palmer James Savill	2 Harcourt Buildings, London	0171 583 9020
Peglow Dr Michael Alfred Herman	Chambers of Geoffrey Hawker, London	0171 583 8899
Pershad Rohan	Two Crown Office Row, London	0171 797 8100
Phillips Andrew Charles	Two Crown Office Row, London	0171 797 8100
Phillips Stephen Edmund	3 Verulam Buildings, London	0171 831 8441
Picton Julian Mark	4 Paper Buildings, London	0171 353 3366/583 7155
Pittaway David Michael	No 1 Serjeants' Inn, London	0171 415 6666
Playford Jonathan Richard	2 Harcourt Buildings, London	0171 583 9020
Pooles Michael Philip Holmes	4 Paper Buildings, London	0171 353 3366/583 7155
Powles Stephen Robert	Stanbrook & Henderson, London	0171 353 0101
	2 Harcourt Buildings, London	0171 583 9020
Prynne Andrew Geoffrey Lockyer	Stanbrook & Henderson, London	0171 353 0101
	2 Harcourt Buildings, London	0171 583 9020
Pulman George Frederick	• Hardwicke Building, London	0171 242 2523
	• Stour Chambers, Canterbury	01227 764899
Rahman Ms Sadeqa Shaheen	1 Crown Office Row, London	0171 797 7500
Readhead Simon John Howard	No 1 Serjeants' Inn, London	0171 415 6666
Reed Philip James William	5 Bell Yard, London	0171 333 8811
Reeve Matthew Francis	5 Bell Yard, London	0171 333 8811
Rigney Andrew James	Two Crown Office Row, London	0171 797 8100
Rivalland Marc-Edouard	No 1 Serjeants' Inn, London	0171 415 6666
Room Stewart	8 Stone Buildings, London	0171 831 9881
Ross John Graffin	No 1 Serjeants' Inn, London	0171 415 6666
Russell Robert John Finlay	5 Bell Yard, London	0171 333 8811
Salter Richard Stanley	3 Verulam Buildings, London	0171 831 8441
Saunt Thomas William Gatty	Two Crown Office Row, London	0171 797 8100
Selvaratnam Miss Vasanti Emily Indrani	4 Field Court, London	0171 440 6900
Sheehan Malcolm Peter	Stanbrook & Henderson, London	0171 353 0101
	2 Harcourt Buildings, London	0171 583 9020
Shepherd Philip Alexander	• 5 Bell Yard, London	0171 333 8811
Simpson Mark Taylor	4 Paper Buildings, London	0171 353 3366/583 7155
Smith Warwick Timothy Cresswell	• Deans Court Chambers, Manchester	0161 834 4097
	• Deans Court Chambers, Preston	01772 555163
Snowden John Stevenson	Two Crown Office Row, London	0171 797 8100
Soole Michael Alexander	5 Bell Yard, London	0171 333 8811
Southwell Richard Charles	One Hare Court, London	0171 353 3171
Spain Timothy Harrisson	Trinity Chambers, Newcastle upon Tyne	0191 232 1927
Steinert Jonathan	New Court Chambers, London	0171 831 9500
Stewart Nicholas John Cameron	Hardwicke Building, London	0171 242 2523
Storey Jeremy Brian	4 Pump Court, London	0171 353 2656/9
Swan Ian Christopher	Two Crown Office Row, London	0171 797 8100
Symons Christopher John Maurice	3 Verulam Buildings, London	0171 831 8441
Taylor Miss Deborah Frances	Two Crown Office Row, London	0171 797 8100
Ter Haar Roger Eduard Lound	Two Crown Office Row, London	0171 797 8100
Tozzi Nigel Kenneth	4 Pump Court, London	0171 353 2656/9
Trotman Timothy Oliver	Deans Court Chambers, Manchester	0161 834 4097
	Deans Court Chambers, Preston	01772 555163
Twigger Andrew Mark	3 Stone Buildings, London	0171 242 4937/405 8358
Wadsworth James Patrick	4 Paper Buildings, London	0171 353 3366/583 7155
Ward Miss Siobhan Marie Lucia	11 King's Bench Walk, London	0171 632 8500
Warnock Andrew Ronald	No 1 Serjeants' Inn, London	0171 415 6666
Waters Julian William Penrose	No 1 Serjeants' Inn, London	0171 415 6666
Webb Robert Stopford	• 5 Bell Yard, London	0171 333 8811
Weddle Steven Edgar	Hardwicke Building, London	0171 242 2523
Weitzman Thomas Edward Benjamin	3 Verulam Buildings, London	0171 831 8441

• Expanded entry in Part D

Weston Clive Aubrey Richard	Two Crown Office Row, London	0171 797 8100
Whiteley Miss Miranda Blyth	4 Field Court, London	0171 440 6900
Wilkinson Nigel Vivian Marshall	Two Crown Office Row, London	0171 797 8100
Wilmot-Smith Richard James Crosbie	39 Essex Street, London	0171 832 1111
Wilson Ian Robert	3 Verulam Buildings, London	0171 831 8441
Woods Jonathan	Two Crown Office Row, London	0171 797 8100
Wright Colin John	4 Field Court, London	0171 440 6900
Yell Nicholas Anthony	No 1 Serjeants' Inn, London	0171 415 6666

INSURANCE/REINSURANCE

Akka Lawrence Mark	20 Essex Street, London	0171 583 9294
Ambrose Miss Clare Mary Geneste	20 Essex Street, London	0171 583 9294
Ashworth Piers	Stanbrook & Henderson, London	0171 353 0101
	2 Harcourt Buildings, London	0171 583 9020
	Priory Chambers, Birmingham	0121 236 3882/1375
Bailey Edward Henry	5 Bell Yard, London	0171 333 8811
Baylis Ms Natalie Jayne	3 Verulam Buildings, London	0171 831 8441
Blakesley Patrick James	Two Crown Office Row, London	0171 797 8100
Block Neil Selwyn	39 Essex Street, London	0171 832 1111
Brent Richard	3 Verulam Buildings, London	0171 831 8441
Brown Geoffrey Barlow	39 Essex Street, London	0171 832 1111
Brown Miss Hannah Beatrice	5 Bell Yard, London	0171 333 8811
Burns Peter Richard	Deans Court Chambers, Manchester	0161 834 4097
Burton Michael John	Littleton Chambers, London	0171 797 8600
Butler Philip Andrew	Goldsmith Chambers, London	0171 353 6802/3/4/5
	Deans Court Chambers, Manchester	0161 834 4097
	Deans Court Chambers, Preston	01772 555163
Charkham Graham Harold	20 Essex Street, London	0171 583 9294
Cheyne Miss Phyllida Alison	4 Pump Court, London	0171 353 2656/9
Coburn Michael Jeremy Patrick	20 Essex Street, London	0171 583 9294
Collett Michael John	20 Essex Street, London	0171 583 9294
Cory-Wright Charles Alexander	39 Essex Street, London	0171 832 1111
Crowley John Desmond	Two Crown Office Row, London	0171 797 8100
Doyle Louis George	Chambers of Andrew Campbell QC, Leeds	0113 245 5438
Edey Philip David	20 Essex Street, London	0171 583 9294
Edwards-Stuart Antony James Cobham	Two Crown Office Row, London	0171 797 8100
Evans-Tovey Jason Robert	Two Crown Office Row, London	0171 797 8100
Field Richard Alan	11 King's Bench Walk, London	0171 632 8500
Freedman Sampson Clive	3 Verulam Buildings, London	0171 831 8441
Gibaud Miss Catherine Alison Annetta	3 Verulam Buildings, London	0171 831 8441
Glasgow Edwin John	39 Essex Street, London	0171 832 1111
Grantham Andrew Timothy	• Deans Court Chambers, Manchester	0161 834 4097
	• Deans Court Chambers, Preston	01772 555163
Greenbourne John Hugo	Two Crown Office Row, London	0171 797 8100
Guggenheim Miss Anna Maeve	Two Crown Office Row, London	0171 797 8100
Hamblen Nicholas Archibald	20 Essex Street, London	0171 583 9294
Hamilton Graeme Montagu	Two Crown Office Row, London	0171 797 8100
Hammerton Alastair Rolf	No 1 Serjeants' Inn, London	0171 415 6666
Harvey Jonathan Robert William	2 Harcourt Buildings, London	0171 583 9020
Harvey Michael Llewellyn Tucker	Two Crown Office Row, London	0171 797 8100
Haven Kevin	2 Gray's Inn Square Chambers, London	0171 242 0328/405 1317
Hayward Peter Michael	The Outer Temple, Room 26, London	0171 353 4647
Henderson Roger Anthony	Stanbrook & Henderson, London	0171 353 0101
	2 Harcourt Buildings, London	0171 583 9020
Hodgson Miss Susan Ann	Two Crown Office Row, London	0171 797 8100
Holdsworth James Arthur	Two Crown Office Row, London	0171 797 8100
Howarth Simon Stuart	Two Crown Office Row, London	0171 797 8100
Jarvis John Manners	3 Verulam Buildings, London	0171 831 8441
Jess Digby Charles	• 8 King Street Chambers, Manchester	0161 834 9560
Kavanagh Giles Wilfred Conor	• 5 Bell Yard, London	0171 333 8811
Kimbell John Ashley	5 Bell Yard, London	0171 333 8811
Legh-Jones Piers Nicholas	• 20 Essex Street, London	0171 583 9294
Lindsay Crawford Callum Douglas	No 1 Serjeants' Inn, London	0171 415 6666
Lynagh Richard Dudley	Two Crown Office Row, London	0171 797 8100
Mackay Colin Crichton	39 Essex Street, London	0171 832 1111
Mawrey Richard Brooks	Stanbrook & Henderson, London	0171 353 0101
	2 Harcourt Buildings, London	0171 583 9020

• Expanded entry in Part D

Maxwell Miss Karen Laetitia	20 Essex Street, London	0171 583 9294
May Miss Juliet Mary	3 Verulam Buildings, London	0171 831 8441
McManus Jonathan Richard	4-5 Gray's Inn Square, London	0171 404 5252
Meeson Nigel Keith	4 Field Court, London	0171 440 6900
Melville Richard David	39 Essex Street, London	0171 832 1111
Merriman Nicholas Flavelle	3 Verulam Buildings, London	0171 831 8441
Milligan Iain Anstruther	20 Essex Street, London	0171 583 9294
Nash Jonathan Scott	3 Verulam Buildings, London	0171 831 8441
Neish Andrew Graham	4 Pump Court, London	0171 353 2656/9
Nelson Vincent Leonard	39 Essex Street, London	0171 832 1111
Noble Roderick Grant	39 Essex Street, London	0171 832 1111
Norman Christopher John George	No 1 Serjeants' Inn, London	0171 415 6666
Owen David Christopher	20 Essex Street, London	0171 583 9294
Padfield Ms Alison Mary	One Hare Court, London	0171 353 3171
Pelling (Philip) Mark	Monckton Chambers, London	0171 405 7211
Pershad Rohan	Two Crown Office Row, London	0171 797 8100
Phillips Andrew Charles	Two Crown Office Row, London	0171 797 8100
Phillips Rory Andrew Livingstone	3 Verulam Buildings, London	0171 831 8441
Pittaway David Michael	No 1 Serjeants' Inn, London	0171 415 6666
Playford Jonathan Richard	2 Harcourt Buildings, London	0171 583 9020
Purchas Christopher Patrick Brooks	Two Crown Office Row, London	0171 797 8100
Quest David Charles	3 Verulam Buildings, London	0171 831 8441
Reed Philip James William	5 Bell Yard, London	0171 333 8811
Reeve Matthew Francis	5 Bell Yard, London	0171 333 8811
Richards Miss Jennifer	39 Essex Street, London	0171 832 1111
Rigney Andrew James	Two Crown Office Row, London	0171 797 8100
Ross John Graffin	No 1 Serjeants' Inn, London	0171 415 6666
Salter Richard Stanley	3 Verulam Buildings, London	0171 831 8441
Saunders Nicholas Joseph	4 Field Court, London	0171 440 6900
Selvaratnam Miss Vasanti Emily Indrani	4 Field Court, London	0171 440 6900
Shepherd Philip Alexander	• 5 Bell Yard, London	0171 333 8811
Snowden John Stevenson	Two Crown Office Row, London	0171 797 8100
Southwell Richard Charles	One Hare Court, London	0171 353 3171
Spearman Richard	5 Raymond Buildings, London	0171 242 2902
Storey Jeremy Brian	4 Pump Court, London	0171 353 2656/9
Swan Ian Christopher	Two Crown Office Row, London	0171 797 8100
Symons Christopher John Maurice	3 Verulam Buildings, London	0171 831 8441
Taylor Miss Deborah Frances	Two Crown Office Row, London	0171 797 8100
Temple Anthony Dominic	4 Pump Court, London	0171 353 2656/9
Ter Haar Roger Eduard Lound	Two Crown Office Row, London	0171 797 8100
Thomas (Robert) Neville	3 Verulam Buildings, London	0171 831 8441
Tozzi Nigel Kenneth	4 Pump Court, London	0171 353 2656/9
Trace Anthony John	• 13 Old Square, London	0171 404 4800
Tucker David William	Two Crown Office Row, London	0171 797 8100
Turner Miss Janet Mary	3 Verulam Buildings, London	0171 831 8441
Wadsworth James Patrick	4 Paper Buildings, London	0171 353 3366/583 7155
Webb Robert Stopford	• 5 Bell Yard, London	0171 333 8811
Weitzman Thomas Edward Benjamin	3 Verulam Buildings, London	0171 831 8441
Weston Clive Aubrey Richard	Two Crown Office Row, London	0171 797 8100
Wilken Sean David Henry	39 Essex Street, London	0171 832 1111
Wilkinson Nigel Vivian Marshall	Two Crown Office Row, London	0171 797 8100
Wright Colin John	4 Field Court, London	0171 440 6900

INTELLECTUAL PROPERTY

Abbott Alistair James Hugh	5 New Square, London	0171 404 0404
Adejumo Mrs Hilda Ekpo	• Temple Chambers, London	0171 583 1001 (2 lines)
Amin Miss Farah	7 New Square, London	0171 430 1660
Ayres Andrew John William	13 Old Square, London	0171 404 4800
Barker Simon George Harry	• 13 Old Square, London	0171 404 4800
Bird Nigel David	Chambers of John Hand QC, Manchester	0161 955 9000
Burton Michael John	Littleton Chambers, London	0171 797 8600
Clark Ms Julia Elisabeth	5 New Square, London	0171 404 0404
Clarke Ian James	Hardwicke Building, London	0171 242 2523
Colley Dr Peter McLean	• 19 Old Buildings, London	0171 405 2001
Corbett James Patrick	St Philip's Chambers, Birmingham	0121 246 7000
Cunningham Mark James	13 Old Square, London	0171 404 4800
Darbyshire William Robert	Chambers of John Hand QC, Manchester	0161 955 9000
de Jehan David	St Paul's House, Leeds	0113 245 5866

Dowse John	Chambers of Lord Goodhart QC, London	0171 405 5577
	Chambers of John Hand QC, Manchester	0161 955 9000
Driscoll Miss Lynn	Sovereign Chambers, Leeds	0113 245 1841/2/3
	Lancaster Buildings, Manchester	0161 661 4444
Edwards Richard Julian Henshaw	3 Verulam Buildings, London	0171 831 8441
Elleray Anthony John	• 12 New Square, London	0171 419 1212
	• St James's Chambers, Manchester	0161 834 7000
	• Park Lane Chambers, Leeds	0113 228 5000
Fitzgerald John Vincent	New Court, London	0171 797 8999
Garnett Kevin Mitchell	5 New Square, London	0171 404 0404
Gray Charles Anthony St John	5 Raymond Buildings, London	0171 242 2902
Grayson Edward	• 9–12 Bell Yard, London	0171 400 1800
Gregory John Raymond	Deans Court Chambers, Manchester	0161 834 4097
	Deans Court Chambers, Preston	01772 555163
Harvey Miss Jayne Denise	Goldsworth Chambers, London	0171 405 7117
Henderson Roger Anthony	Stanbrook & Henderson, London	0171 353 0101
	2 Harcourt Buildings, London	0171 583 9020
Hicks Michael Charles	• 19 Old Buildings, London	0171 405 2001
Hodgson Richard Andrew	New Court, London	0171 797 8999
Holman Miss Tamsin Perdita	19 Old Buildings, London	0171 405 2001
Johnson Michael Sloan	Chambers of John Hand QC, Manchester	0161 955 9000
Khan Saadallah Frans Hassan	55 Temple Chambers, London	0171 353 7400
Kime Matthew Jonathan	• New Court, London	0171 797 8999
	• Cobden House Chambers, Manchester	0161 833 6000/6001
Males Stephen Martin	20 Essex Street, London	0171 583 9294
Mason Ian Douglas	11 Bolt Court, London	0171 353 2300
	Redhill Chambers, Redhill	01737 780781
McCarthy William	New Bailey Chambers, Preston	01772 258 087
Merriman Nicholas Flavelle	3 Verulam Buildings, London	0171 831 8441
Norris Andrew James Steedsman	5 New Square, London	0171 404 0404
Pickering James Patrick	Enterprise Chambers, London	0171 405 9471
	Enterprise Chambers, Leeds	0113 246 0391
	Enterprise Chambers, Newcastle upon Tyne	0191 222 3344
Pickford Anthony James	Prince Henry's Chambers, London	0171 353 1183/1190
Puckrin Cedric Eldred	19 Old Buildings, London	0171 405 2001
Reid Brian Christopher	19 Old Buildings, London	0171 405 2001
Robertson Aidan Malcolm David	Monckton Chambers, London	0171 405 7211
Robson John Malcolm	2 Gray's Inn Square Chambers, London	0171 242 0328/405 1317
	Assize Court Chambers, Bristol	0117 926 4587
Sampson Graeme William	Chambers of Geoffrey Hawker, London	0171 583 8899
Shipley Norman Graham	• 19 Old Buildings, London	0171 405 2001
Silverleaf Michael	• 11 South Square, London	0171 405 1222
Stevens-Hoare Miss Michelle	• Hardwicke Building, London	0171 242 2523
Stewart Alexander Joseph	5 New Square, London	0171 404 0404
Sugar Simon Gareth	5 New Square, London	0171 404 0404
Sullivan Rory Myles	19 Old Buildings, London	0171 405 2001
Sutcliffe Andrew Harold Wentworth	3 Verulam Buildings, London	0171 831 8441
Turner Jonathan David Chattyn	• 4 Field Court, London	0171 440 6900
West Lawrence Joseph	Stanbrook & Henderson, London	0171 353 0101
	2 Harcourt Buildings, London	0171 583 9020
Wilson Alastair James Drysdale	• 19 Old Buildings, London	0171 405 2001
Wright Colin John	4 Field Court, London	0171 440 6900

INTERNATIONAL TRADE

Akka Lawrence Mark	20 Essex Street, London	0171 583 9294
Ambrose Miss Clare Mary Geneste	20 Essex Street, London	0171 583 9294
Charkham Graham Harold	20 Essex Street, London	0171 583 9294
Coburn Michael Jeremy Patrick	20 Essex Street, London	0171 583 9294
Collett Michael John	20 Essex Street, London	0171 583 9294
Connerty Anthony Robin	Lamb Chambers, London	0171 797 8300
Dashwood Professor Arthur Alan	Stanbrook & Henderson, London	0171 353 0101
	2 Harcourt Buildings, London	0171 583 9020
Driscoll Miss Lynn	Sovereign Chambers, Leeds	0113 245 1841/2/3
	Lancaster Buildings, Manchester	0161 661 4444
Edey Philip David	20 Essex Street, London	0171 583 9294
Evans James Frederick Meurig	3 Verulam Buildings, London	0171 831 8441

Field Richard Alan	11 King's Bench Walk, London	0171 632 8500
Fisher David	5 Bell Yard, London	0171 333 8811
Fitzgerald John Vincent	New Court, London	0171 797 8999
Freedman Sampson Clive	3 Verulam Buildings, London	0171 831 8441
Gore-Andrews Gavin Angus Russell	Stanbrook & Henderson, London	0171 353 0101
	2 Harcourt Buildings, London	0171 583 9020
Grantham Andrew Timothy	• Deans Court Chambers, Manchester	0161 834 4097
	• Deans Court Chambers, Preston	01772 555163
Hamblen Nicholas Archibald	20 Essex Street, London	0171 583 9294
Jarvis John Manners	3 Verulam Buildings, London	0171 831 8441
Jenkala Adrian Aleksander	11 Bolt Court, London	0171 353 2300
	Redhill Chambers, Redhill	01737 780781
Kime Matthew Jonathan	• New Court, London	0171 797 8999
	• Cobden House Chambers, Manchester	0161 833 6000/6001
Kingsland Rt Hon Lord	4 Breams Buildings, London	0171 353 5835/430 1221
Kolodziej Andrzej Jozef	• Littman Chambers, London	0171 404 4866
Lowenstein Paul David	Littleton Chambers, London	0171 797 8600
Males Stephen Martin	20 Essex Street, London	0171 583 9294
Masters Miss Sara Alayna	20 Essex Street, London	0171 583 9294
Maxwell Miss Karen Laetitia	20 Essex Street, London	0171 583 9294
Meeson Nigel Keith	4 Field Court, London	0171 440 6900
Merriman Nicholas Flavelle	3 Verulam Buildings, London	0171 831 8441
Milligan Iain Anstruther	20 Essex Street, London	0171 583 9294
Ogunbiyi Oluwole Afolabi	Horizon Chambers, London	0171 242 2440
Owen David Christopher	20 Essex Street, London	0171 583 9294
Peglow Dr Michael Alfred Herman	Chambers of Geoffrey Hawker, London	0171 583 8899
Pelling (Philip) Mark	Monckton Chambers, London	0171 405 7211
Pershad Rohan	Two Crown Office Row, London	0171 797 8100
Rigney Andrew James	Two Crown Office Row, London	0171 797 8100
Salter Richard Stanley	3 Verulam Buildings, London	0171 831 8441
Sands Mr Philippe Joseph	3 Verulam Buildings, London	0171 831 8441
Saunders Nicholas Joseph	4 Field Court, London	0171 440 6900
Selvaratnam Miss Vasanti Emily Indrani	4 Field Court, London	0171 440 6900
Thomas (Robert) Neville	3 Verulam Buildings, London	0171 831 8441
Wheeler Miss Marina Claire	Stanbrook & Henderson, London	0171 353 0101
	2 Harcourt Buildings, London	0171 583 9020
Whiteley Miss Miranda Blyth	4 Field Court, London	0171 440 6900
Wright Colin John	4 Field Court, London	0171 440 6900

ISLAMIC LAW

Thomson Martin Haldane Ahmad	Wynne Chambers, London	0171 737 7266

JUDICIAL REVIEW

Adejumo Mrs Hilda Ekpo	• Temple Chambers, London	0171 583 1001 (2 lines)
Bate David Christopher	Queen Elizabeth Building, London	0171 583 5766
Baxter Gerald Pearson	25-27 Castle Street, Liverpool	0151 227 5661/5666/236 5072
Boyce William	Queen Elizabeth Building, London	0171 583 5766
Calvert-Smith David	Queen Elizabeth Building, London	0171 583 5766
Carlisle of Bucklow The Rt Hon Lord	Queen Elizabeth Building, London	0171 583 5766
	18 St John Street, Manchester	0161 278 1800
Clarke Peter William	Queen Elizabeth Building, London	0171 583 5766
Davies The Rt Hon David John Denzil	Goldsworth Chambers, London	0171 405 7117
Ellison Mark Christopher	Queen Elizabeth Building, London	0171 583 5766
Finnigan Peter Anthony	Queen Elizabeth Building, London	0171 583 5766
Glass Anthony Trevor	Queen Elizabeth Building, London	0171 583 5766
Grey Robin Douglas	Queen Elizabeth Building, London	0171 583 5766
Heap Gerard Miles	Sovereign Chambers, Leeds	0113 245 1841/2/3
Henry Edward Joseph Aloysius	Queen Elizabeth Building, London	0171 583 5766
Horwell Richard Eric	Queen Elizabeth Building, London	0171 583 5766
Jeffreys David Alfred	Queen Elizabeth Building, London	0171 583 5766
Johnson Miss Zoe Elisabeth	Queen Elizabeth Building, London	0171 583 5766
Khan Saadallah Frans Hassan	55 Temple Chambers, London	0171 353 7400
Kyte Peter Eric	Queen Elizabeth Building, London	0171 583 5766
Larkin Sean	Queen Elizabeth Building, London	0171 583 5766
Longden Anthony Gordon	Queen Elizabeth Building, London	0171 583 5766
Malecka Dr Mary Margaret	Goldsworth Chambers, London	0171 405 7117
McKinnon Warwick Nairn	Queen Elizabeth Building, London	0171 583 5766

Parry Charles Robert	Pump Court Chambers, London	0171 353 0711
	Pump Court Chambers, Winchester	01962 868161
Paton Ian Francis	Queen Elizabeth Building, London	0171 583 5766
Plaschkes Ms Sarah Georgina	Queen Elizabeth Building, London	0171 583 5766
Poulet Mrs Rebecca Maria	Queen Elizabeth Building, London	0171 583 5766
Rees Gareth David	Queen Elizabeth Building, London	0171 583 5766
Robinson Vivian	Queen Elizabeth Building, London	0171 583 5766
Stewart Neill Alastair	Queen Elizabeth Building, London	0171 583 5766
Suckling Alan Blair	Queen Elizabeth Building, London	0171 583 5766
Wilcken Anthony David Felix	Queen Elizabeth Building, London	0171 583 5766
Wood Nicholas Andrew	5 Paper Buildings, London	0171 583 9275

LANDLORD AND TENANT

Abbott Francis Arthur	Pump Court Chambers, London	0171 353 0711
	Pump Court Chambers, Winchester	01962 868161
Adamyk Simon Charles	12 New Square, London	0171 419 1212
Adejumo Mrs Hilda Ekpo	• Temple Chambers, London	0171 583 1001 (2 lines)
Al'Hassan Khadim	Equity Chambers, Birmingham	0121 233 2100
Aldridge James Hugh	13 Old Square, London	0171 404 4800
Alomo Richard Olusoji	14 Gray's Inn Square, London	0171 242 0858
Althaus Antony Justin	No 1 Serjeants' Inn, London	0171 415 6666
Andrews Miss Claire Marguerite	Gough Square Chambers, London	0171 353 0924
Angus Miss Tracey Anne	5 Stone Buildings, London	0171 242 6201
Atherton Ian David	Enterprise Chambers, London	0171 405 9471
	Enterprise Chambers, Leeds	0113 246 0391
	Enterprise Chambers, Newcastle upon Tyne	0191 222 3344
Ayres Andrew John William	13 Old Square, London	0171 404 4800
Baker Miss Anne Jacqueline	Enterprise Chambers, London	0171 405 9471
	Enterprise Chambers, Leeds	0113 246 0391
	Enterprise Chambers, Newcastle upon Tyne	0191 222 3344
Barber Miss Sally	5 Stone Buildings, London	0171 242 6201
Barker James Sebastian	Enterprise Chambers, London	0171 405 9471
	Enterprise Chambers, Leeds	0113 246 0391
	Enterprise Chambers, Newcastle upon Tyne	0191 222 3344
Barlow Miss Sarah Helen	St Paul's House, Leeds	0113 245 5866
Barnes (David) Michael (William)	4 Breams Buildings, London	0171 353 5835/430 1221
Battcock Benjamin George	Stanbrook & Henderson, London	0171 353 0101
	2 Harcourt Buildings, London	0171 583 9020
Beal Kieron Conrad	4 Paper Buildings, London	0171 353 3366/583 7155
Beaumont Marc Clifford	• Pump Court Chambers, London	0171 353 0711
	• Harrow-on-the-Hill Chambers, Harrow on the Hill	0181 423 7444
	• Pump Court Chambers, Winchester	01962 868161
	• Windsor Barristers' Chambers, Windsor	01753 648 899
Beer Jason Barrington	5 Essex Court, London	0171 410 2000
Bendall Richard Giles	33 Bedford Row, London	0171 242 6476
Bennett Gordon Irvine	5 Bell Yard, London	0171 333 8811
Bergin Terence Edward	New Court Chambers, London	0171 831 9500
Bergin Timothy William	Sussex Chambers, Brighton	01273 607953
Berkley Michael Stuart	Rougemont Chambers, Exeter	01392 410471
Berragan (Howard) Neil	Merchant Chambers, Manchester	0161 839 7070
Bhaloo Miss Zia Kurban	Enterprise Chambers, London	0171 405 9471
	Enterprise Chambers, Leeds	0113 246 0391
	Enterprise Chambers, Newcastle upon Tyne	0191 222 3344
Bhattacharyya Ardhendu	1 Gray's Inn Square, London	0171 405 8946
	11 St Bernards Road, Slough	01753 553806/817989
Bickford-Smith Stephen William	4 Breams Buildings, London	0171 353 5835/430 1221
Bird Nigel David	Chambers of John Hand QC, Manchester	0161 955 9000
Birks Simon Alexander	7 Stone Buildings, London	0171 242 0961
Birts Peter William	• Farrar's Building, London	0171 583 9241
Blackett-Ord Mark	• 5 Stone Buildings, London	0171 242 6201
Bourne Charles Gregory	Stanbrook & Henderson, London	0171 353 0101
	2 Harcourt Buildings, London	0171 583 9020
Bourne Robert	• 4 Field Court, London	0171 440 6900
Brazil Dominic Thomas George	14 Gray's Inn Square, London	0171 242 0858
Brett Matthew Christopher Anthony	Harcourt Chambers, London	0171 353 6961/7

• Expanded entry in Part D

	Harcourt Chambers, Oxford	01865 791559
Brilliant Simon Howard	Lamb Chambers, London	0171 797 8300
Brook Ian Stuart	Hardwicke Building, London	0171 242 2523
Browne James William	Goldsworth Chambers, London	0171 405 7117
Browne Miss Julie Rebecca	Goldsmith Building, London	0171 353 7881
Burles David John	Goldsmith Building, London	0171 353 7881
Burton Nicholas Anthony	2 Mitre Court Buildings, London	0171 583 1380
Cameron Neil Alexander	Wilberforce Chambers, Hull	01482 323 264
Campbell Oliver Edward Wilhelm	2 Harcourt Buildings, London	0171 583 9020
Candlin James Richard	Chambers of Geoffrey Hawker, London	0171 583 8899
Cartwright Richard John	Queen Elizabeth Building, London	0171 353 7181 (12 lines)
Carville Owen Brendan Neville	25–27 Castle Street, Liverpool	0151 227 5661/5666/236 5072
Cave Jeremy Stephen	1 Crown Office Row, London	0171 797 7500
	Crown Office Row Chambers, Brighton	01273 625625
Cawley Neil Robert Loudoun	55 Temple Chambers, London	0171 353 7400
	Milton Keynes Chambers, Milton Keynes	01908 217857
Charles Ms Deborah Ann	6 Pump Court, London	0171 797 8400
Charlwood Spike Llewellyn	4 Paper Buildings, London	0171 353 3366/583 7155
Cherryman John Richard	4 Breams Buildings, London	0171 353 5835/430 1221
Christie-Brown Miss Sarah Louise	4 Paper Buildings, London	0171 353 3366/583 7155
Clargo John Paul	Hardwicke Building, London	0171 242 2523
Clarke Miss Anna Victoria	5 Stone Buildings, London	0171 242 6201
Clarke George Robert Ivan	Chambers of Geoffrey Hawker, London	0171 583 8899
Clarke Ian James	Hardwicke Building, London	0171 242 2523
Clegg Sebastian James Barwick	Deans Court Chambers, Manchester	0161 834 4097
Cogswell Miss Frederica Natasha	Gough Square Chambers, London	0171 353 0924
Collard Michael David	5 Pump Court, London	0171 353 2532
Collett Gavin Charles	Rougemont Chambers, Exeter	01392 410471
	Cathedral Chambers (Jan Wood Independent Barristers' Clerk), Exeter	01392 210900
Collier Martin Melton	Fenners Chambers, Cambridge	01223 368761
	Fenners Chambers, Peterborough	01733 562030
Collins John Morris	11 King's Bench Walk, London	0171 353 3337/8
	9 Woodhouse Square, Leeds	0113 245 1986
Connerty Anthony Robin	Lamb Chambers, London	0171 797 8300
Copeland Andrew John	Chambers of Geoffrey Hawker, London	0171 583 8899
Cotter Miss Sara Elizabeth	• Higher Combe, Minehead	01643 862722
Cottrell Matthew Robert	Oriel Chambers, Liverpool	0151 236 7191
Cowen Miss Sally Emma	Chambers of Geoffrey Hawker, London	0171 583 8899
Craig Kenneth Allen	Hardwicke Building, London	0171 242 2523
Crail Miss (Elspeth) Ross	12 New Square, London	0171 419 1212
	Sovereign Chambers, Leeds	0113 245 1841/2/3
Cranfield Peter Anthony	3 Verulam Buildings, London	0171 831 8441
Crawford Grant	11 Old Square, London	0171 430 0341
Crossley Simon Justin	9 Woodhouse Square, Leeds	0113 245 1986
Crosthwaite Graham Andrew	One King's Bench Walk, London	0171 936 1500
Crowson Howard Keith	St Paul's House, Leeds	0113 245 5866
Cunningham Mark James	13 Old Square, London	0171 404 4800
Daiches Michael Salis	• 22 Old Buildings, London	0171 831 0222
Darbyshire William Robert	Chambers of John Hand QC, Manchester	0161 955 9000
Datta Mrs Wendy Patricia Mizal	Alban Chambers, London	0171 419 5051
Davey Miss Tina Elaine	9–12 Bell Yard, London	0171 400 1800
Davies Miss Louise	12 New Square, London	0171 419 1212
Davis Andrew Paul	Two Crown Office Row, London	0171 797 8100
Dawes Gordon Stephen Knight	Goldsmith Building, London	0171 353 7881
de Jehan David	St Paul's House, Leeds	0113 245 5866
Deacock Adam Jason	Chambers of Lord Goodhart QC, London	0171 405 5577
Dedezade Taner	Tindal Chambers, Chelmsford	01245 267742
Denton Miss Michelle Jayne	9–12 Bell Yard, London	0171 400 1800
Dhaliwal Miss Davinder Kaur	New Court Chambers, Birmingham	0121 693 6656
Dilhorne The Rt Hon Viscount	4 Breams Buildings, London	0171 353 5835/430 1221
Dineen Michael Laurence	Pump Court Chambers, London	0171 353 0711
	All Saints Chambers, Bristol	0117 921 1966

• Expanded entry in Part D

	Pump Court Chambers, Winchester	01962 868161
Dodd Christopher John Nicholas	9 Woodhouse Square, Leeds	0113 245 1986
Dodge Peter Clive	11 Old Square, London	0171 430 0341
Doggart Piers Graham	• King's Chambers, Eastbourne	01323 416053
Dogra Miss Tanyia Anita	Chambers of Harjit Singh, London	0171 353 1356
Dowokpor Jonathan Kukasi	Tollgate Mews Chambers, London	0171 511 1838
Dowse John	Chambers of Lord Goodhart QC, London	0171 405 5577
	Chambers of John Hand QC, Manchester	0161 955 9000
Duffy Michael	Cathedral Chambers, Ely, Ely	01353 666775
Edwards Philip Douglas	2 Harcourt Buildings, London	0171 353 8415
Elleray Anthony John	• 12 New Square, London	0171 419 1212
	• St James's Chambers, Manchester	0161 834 7000
	• Park Lane Chambers, Leeds	0113 228 5000
Elvin David John	4 Breams Buildings, London	0171 353 5835/430 1221
Evans-Gordon Mrs Jane-Anne Mary	12 New Square, London	0171 419 1212
Ewins Miss Catherine Jane	4 Paper Buildings, London	0171 353 3366/583 7155
Falk Miss Josephine Ruth Ann	12 Old Square, London	0171 404 0875
Fenston Miss Felicia Donovan	Stanbrook & Henderson, London	0171 353 0101
	2 Harcourt Buildings, London	0171 583 9020
Forbes Peter George	6 Pump Court, London	0171 797 8400
	6-8 Mill Street, Maidstone	01622 688 094
Ford Gerard James	Baker Street Chambers, Middlesbrough	01642 873873
Forsdick David John	4 Breams Buildings, London	0171 353 5835/430 1221
Foster Francis Alexander	St Paul's House, Leeds	0113 245 5866
Fox Miss Anna Katherine Helen	Oriel Chambers, Liverpool	0151 236 7191
Foxwell George (Augustus)	Fenners Chambers, Cambridge	01223 368761
	Fenners Chambers, Peterborough	01733 562030
Francis Edward Gerald Francis	Enterprise Chambers, London	0171 405 9471
	Enterprise Chambers, Leeds	0113 246 0391
	Enterprise Chambers, Newcastle upon Tyne	0191 222 3344
Franklin Stephen Hall	5 Paper Buildings, London	0171 583 6117
	Fenners Chambers, Cambridge	01223 368761
Frodsham Alexander Miles	Oriel Chambers, Liverpool	0151 236 7191
Furber (Robert) John	4 Breams Buildings, London	0171 353 5835/430 1221
Galberg Marc Kay	33 Bedford Row, London	0171 242 6476
Garcia-Miller Miss Laura	Enterprise Chambers, London	0171 405 9471
	Enterprise Chambers, Leeds	0113 246 0391
	Enterprise Chambers, Newcastle upon Tyne	0191 222 3344
Gatty Daniel Simon	New Court Chambers, London	0171 831 9500
Gerald Nigel Mortimer	Enterprise Chambers, London	0171 405 9471
	Enterprise Chambers, Leeds	0113 246 0391
	Enterprise Chambers, Newcastle upon Tyne	0191 222 3344
Gibaud Miss Catherine Alison Annetta	3 Verulam Buildings, London	0171 831 8441
Gilbertson Mrs Helen Alison	Sackville Chambers, Norwich	01603 613516
Gilchrist David Somerled	Chambers of John Hand QC, Manchester	0161 955 9000
Goodhart Lord	Chambers of Lord Goodhart QC, London	0171 405 5577
Goodman Andrew David	199 Strand, London	0171 379 9779
Gore Andrew Roger	Fenners Chambers, Cambridge	01223 368761
	Fenners Chambers, Peterborough	01733 562030
Grant Thomas Paul Wentworth	New Court Chambers, London	0171 831 9500
Gray Miss Jennifer	11 Old Square, London	0171 242 5022
Greenan Miss Sarah Octavia	• 9 Woodhouse Square, Leeds	0113 245 1986
Gregory John Raymond	Deans Court Chambers, Manchester	0161 834 4097
	Deans Court Chambers, Preston	01772 555163
Grice Miss Joanna Harrison	One King's Bench Walk, London	0171 936 1500
Grundy Nicholas John	One Essex Court, London	0171 936 3030
Hall Taylor Alexander Edward	11 Old Square, London	0171 430 0341
Halpern David Anthony	Enterprise Chambers, London	0171 405 9471
	Enterprise Chambers, Leeds	0113 246 0391
	Enterprise Chambers, Newcastle upon Tyne	0191 222 3344
Hamid Mrs Beebee Nazmoon	Clapham Chambers, London	0171 978 8482/0171 642 5777
Hansen William Joseph	5 Bell Yard, London	0171 333 8811

• Expanded entry in Part D

Hantusch Robert Anthony	• 3 Stone Buildings, London	0171 242 4937/405 8358
Harbottle Gwilym Thomas	5 New Square, London	0171 404 0404
Hardwick Matthew Richard	Enterprise Chambers, London	0171 405 9471
	Enterprise Chambers, Leeds	0113 246 0391
	Enterprise Chambers, Newcastle upon Tyne	0191 222 3344
Hargreaves Miss Sara Jane	12 New Square, London	0171 419 1212
	Sovereign Chambers, Leeds	0113 245 1841/2/3
Harper Joseph Charles	4 Breams Buildings, London	0171 353 5835/430 1221
Harrison John Foster	St Paul's House, Leeds	0113 245 5866
Harrod Henry Mark	5 Stone Buildings, London	0171 242 6201
Harvey Miss Jayne Denise	Goldsworth Chambers, London	0171 405 7117
Haven Kevin	2 Gray's Inn Square Chambers, London	0171 242 0328/405 1317
Hayes Miss Josephine Mary	Chambers of Lord Goodhart QC, London	0171 405 5577
Healy Miss Alexandra	9-12 Bell Yard, London	0171 400 1800
Henley Mark Robert Daniel	9 Woodhouse Square, Leeds	0113 245 1986
Herbert Mrs Rebecca Mary	2 New Street, Leicester	0116 262 5906
Heywood Michael Edmundson	Chambers of Lord Goodhart QC, London	0171 405 5577
	Cobden House Chambers, Manchester	0161 833 6000/6001
Higgins Anthony Paul	Goldsmith Building, London	0171 353 7881
Holgate David John	4 Breams Buildings, London	0171 353 5835/430 1221
Holland Charles Christopher	Trinity Chambers, Newcastle upon Tyne	0191 232 1927
Holland David Moore	29 Bedford Row Chambers, London	0171 831 2626
Hollingworth Peter James Michael	22 Albion Place, Northampton	01604 636271
Holmes Justin Francis	Chambers of Lord Goodhart QC, London	0171 405 5577
Holroyd John James	• 9 Woodhouse Square, Leeds	0113 245 1986
Horspool Anthony Bernard Graeme	Hardwicke Building, London	0171 242 2523
Howarth Simon Stuart	Two Crown Office Row, London	0171 797 8100
Hughes Miss Mary Josephine	Chambers of Lord Goodhart QC, London	0171 405 5577
Hunter William Quigley	No 1 Serjeants' Inn, London	0171 415 6666
Huskinson George Nicholas Nevil	4-5 Gray's Inn Square, London	0171 404 5252
Hutton Miss Caroline	Enterprise Chambers, London	0171 405 9471
	Enterprise Chambers, Leeds	0113 246 0391
	Enterprise Chambers, Newcastle upon Tyne	0191 222 3344
Ife Miss Linden Elizabeth	Enterprise Chambers, London	0171 405 9471
	Enterprise Chambers, Leeds	0113 246 0391
	Enterprise Chambers, Newcastle upon Tyne	0191 222 3344
Jack Adrian Laurence Robert	Enterprise Chambers, London	0171 405 9471
Jackson Dirik George Allan	• Chambers of Mr Peter Crampin QC, London	0171 831 0081
Jackson Hugh Woodward	Hardwicke Building, London	0171 242 2523
Jackson Nicholas David Kingsley	The Chambers of Adrian Lyon, Liverpool	0151 236 4421/8240/6757
James Michael Frank	Enterprise Chambers, London	0171 405 9471
	Enterprise Chambers, Leeds	0113 246 0391
	Enterprise Chambers, Newcastle upon Tyne	0191 222 3344
Jarman Mark Christopher	14 Gray's Inn Square, London	0171 242 0858
Jefferies Thomas Robert	Chambers of Lord Goodhart QC, London	0171 405 5577
Jennings Timothy Robin Finnegan	Enterprise Chambers, London	0171 405 9471
	Enterprise Chambers, Leeds	0113 246 0391
	Enterprise Chambers, Newcastle upon Tyne	0191 222 3344
John Peter Charles	One Essex Court, London	0171 936 3030
Johnson Michael Sloan	Chambers of John Hand QC, Manchester	0161 955 9000
Jones Geraint Martyn	Fenners Chambers, Cambridge	01223 368761
	Fenners Chambers, Peterborough	01733 562030
Jones Miss Rhiannon	Lamb Chambers, London	0171 797 8300
Jones Rhys Charles Mansel	33 Bedford Row, London	0171 242 6476
Jones Stephen Hugh	• Farrar's Building, London	0171 583 9241
Jordan Andrew	Stanbrook & Henderson, London	0171 353 0101
	2 Harcourt Buildings, London	0171 583 9020

• Expanded entry in Part D

Jory Robert John Hugh	Enterprise Chambers, London	0171 405 9471
	Enterprise Chambers, Leeds	0113 246 0391
	Enterprise Chambers, Newcastle upon Tyne	0191 222 3344
Joss Norman James	One Essex Court, London	0171 936 3030
Karas Jonathan Marcus	4 Breams Buildings, London	0171 353 5835/430 1221
Kealey Simon Thomas	Chambers of Andrew Campbell QC, Leeds	0113 245 5438
Kealy Charles Brian	Chambers of Andrew Campbell QC, Leeds	0113 245 5438
Kearl Guy Alexander	St Paul's House, Leeds	0113 245 5866
Keen Graeme	4 Breams Buildings, London	0171 353 5835/430 1221
Kenward Timothy David Nelson	25-27 Castle Street, Liverpool	0151 227 5661/5666/236 5072
Khan Avicenna Alkindi Cornelius	55 Temple Chambers, London	0171 353 7400
Kimbell John Ashley	5 Bell Yard, London	0171 333 8811
Kinnier Andrew John	2 Harcourt Buildings, London	0171 583 9020
Kolodynski Stefan Richard	New Court Chambers, Birmingham	0121 693 6656
Kremen Philip Michael	Hardwicke Building, London	0171 242 2523
Lamont Miss Camilla Rose	Chambers of Lord Goodhart QC, London	0171 405 5577
Lander Charles Gideon	25-27 Castle Street, Liverpool	0151 227 5661/5666/236 5072
Laughton Samuel Dennis	17 Old Buildings, London	0171 405 9653
Law John Edward	33 Bedford Row, London	0171 242 6476
Lawson Daniel George	Goldsmith Building, London	0171 353 7881
Leeming Ian	Lamb Chambers, London	0171 797 8300
	Chambers of John Hand QC, Manchester	0161 955 9000
Lees Andrew James	St Paul's House, Leeds	0113 245 5866
Leonard Charles Robert Weston	Goldsmith Building, London	0171 353 7881
Levy Benjamin Keith	Enterprise Chambers, London	0171 405 9471
	Enterprise Chambers, Leeds	0113 246 0391
	Enterprise Chambers, Newcastle upon Tyne	0191 222 3344
Levy Robert Stuart	9 Stone Buildings, London	0171 404 5055
	Assize Court Chambers, Bristol	0117 926 4587
Lewsley Christopher Stanton	4 Breams Buildings, London	0171 353 5835/430 1221
Litton John Letablere	4 Breams Buildings, London	0171 353 5835/430 1221
Livingstone Simon John	11 Bolt Court, London	0171 353 2300
	Redhill Chambers, Redhill	01737 780781
Lochrane Damien Horatio Ross	Pump Court Chambers, London	0171 353 0711
	Pump Court Chambers, Winchester	01962 868161
Lynch Terry John	22 Albion Place, Northampton	01604 636271
Lyness Scott Edward	1 Serjeants' Inn, London	0171 583 1355
Lyon Stephen John	14 Gray's Inn Square, London	0171 242 0858
	Westgate Chambers, Lewes	01273 480 510
MacDonald Iain	Gough Square Chambers, London	0171 353 0924
Maitland Marc Claude	11 Old Square, London	0171 242 5022
Male John Martin	4 Breams Buildings, London	0171 353 5835/430 1221
Mann George Anthony	Enterprise Chambers, London	0171 405 9471
	Enterprise Chambers, Leeds	0113 246 0391
	Enterprise Chambers, Newcastle upon Tyne	0191 222 3344
Marten Richard Hedley Westwood	Chambers of Lord Goodhart QC, London	0171 405 5577
Martineau Henry Ralph Adeane	Goldsmith Building, London	0171 353 7881
Mauger Miss Claire Shanti Andrea	Enterprise Chambers, London	0171 405 9471
Maxwell Miss Judith Mary Angela	The Garden House, London	0171 404 6150
Mayhew Jerome Patrick Burke	Goldsmith Building, London	0171 353 7881
McAllister Miss Eimear Jane	9 Woodhouse Square, Leeds	0113 245 1986
McAllister Miss Elizabeth Ann	Enterprise Chambers, London	0171 405 9471
	Enterprise Chambers, Leeds	0113 246 0391
	Enterprise Chambers, Newcastle upon Tyne	0191 222 3344
McCahey Miss Catherine Anne Mary	St Philip's Chambers, Birmingham	0121 246 7000
McCarthy William	New Bailey Chambers, Preston	01772 258 087
McGahey Miss Elizabeth Clare	30 Park Place, Cardiff	01222 398421
McHugh Miss Karen	4 Breams Buildings, London	0171 353 5835/430 1221
McKenna Miss Anna Louise	Queen Elizabeth Building, London	0171 353 7181 (12 lines)
McKinnell Miss Soraya Jane	Enterprise Chambers, London	0171 405 9471
	Enterprise Chambers, Leeds	0113 246 0391
	Enterprise Chambers, Newcastle upon Tyne	0191 222 3344

B

                            • Expanded entry in Part D

McLachlan David Robert		
McMinn Miss Valerie Kathleen	Baker Street Chambers, Middlesbrough	01642 873873
McQuail Ms Katherine Emma	11 Old Square, London	0171 430 0341
Meakin Timothy William	Fenners Chambers, Cambridge	01223 368761
	Fenners Chambers, Peterborough	01733 562030
Mendoza Neil David Pereira	Hardwicke Building, London	0171 242 2523
Mills Simon Thomas	One Essex Court, London	0171 936 3030
Mitchell Miss Juliana Marie	2 Harcourt Buildings, London	0171 583 9020
Moore James Anthony	2 Gray's Inn Square Chambers, London	0171 242 0328/405 1317
Morgan Charles James Arthur	Enterprise Chambers, London	0171 405 9471
	Enterprise Chambers, Leeds	0113 246 0391
	Enterprise Chambers, Newcastle upon Tyne	0191 222 3344
Morgan Edward Patrick	4 King's Bench Walk, London	0171 822 8822
	Deans Court Chambers, Manchester	0161 834 4097
Morgan Jeremy	Chambers of Kieran Coonan QC, London	0171 583 6013/2510
Morris Miss Brenda Alison	14 Gray's Inn Square, London	0171 242 0858
Morshead Timothy Francis	4 Breams Buildings, London	0171 353 5835/430 1221
Mould Timothy James	4 Breams Buildings, London	0171 353 5835/430 1221
Mullis Anthony Roger	Chambers of Lord Goodhart QC, London	0171 405 5577
Munro Kenneth Stuart	5 Bell Yard, London	0171 333 8811
Murch Stephen James	• 11 Bolt Court, London	0171 353 2300
Nebhrajani Miss Mel	9 Stone Buildings, London	0171 404 5055
Nesbitt Timothy John Robert	199 Strand, London	0171 379 9779
Neville Stephen John	Gough Square Chambers, London	0171 353 0924
Newman Austin Eric	9 Woodhouse Square, Leeds	0113 245 1986
Nicol-Gent William Philip Trahair	King's Chambers, Eastbourne	01323 416053
Noble Andrew	Eldon Chambers, London	0171 353 4636
	Merchant Chambers, Manchester	0161 839 7070
Norbury Luke Edward	17 Old Buildings, London	0171 405 9653
Norris Alastair Hubert	• 5 Stone Buildings, London	0171 242 6201
	• Southernhay Chambers, Exeter	01392 255777
O'Sullivan Michael Morton	5 Stone Buildings, London	0171 242 6201
Oakes Miss Alison Denise	4 Breams Buildings, London	0171 353 5835/430 1221
Ogunbiyi Oluwole Afolabi	Horizon Chambers, London	0171 242 2440
Ohrenstein Dov	Chambers of Lord Goodhart QC, London	0171 405 5577
Okoye Miss Joy Nwamala	Chambers of Joy Okoye, London	0171 405 7011
Overs Ms Estelle Fae	New Court Chambers, London	0171 831 9500
Palfrey Montague Mark	Hardwicke Building, London	0171 242 2523
Parker John	2 Mitre Court Buildings, London	0171 353 1353
Parry David Julian Thomas	Chambers of Lord Goodhart QC, London	0171 405 5577
Peacock Ian Christopher	12 New Square, London	0171 419 1212
	Sovereign Chambers, Leeds	0113 245 1841/2/3
Peacock Nicholas Christopher	13 Old Square, London	0171 404 4800
Peacocke Mrs Teresa Anne Rosen	Enterprise Chambers, London	0171 405 9471
	Enterprise Chambers, Leeds	0113 246 0391
	Enterprise Chambers, Newcastle upon Tyne	0191 222 3344
Peirson Oliver James	Pump Court Chambers, London	0171 353 0711
	Pump Court Chambers, Winchester	01962 868161
Pelling Richard Alexander	New Court Chambers, London	0171 831 9500
Perks Richard Howard	St Philip's Chambers, Birmingham	0121 246 7000
Picarda Hubert Alistair Paul	Chambers of Lord Goodhart QC, London	0171 405 5577
Pickering James Patrick	Enterprise Chambers, London	0171 405 9471
	Enterprise Chambers, Leeds	0113 246 0391
	Enterprise Chambers, Newcastle upon Tyne	0191 222 3344
Pimentel Carlos de Serpa Alberto Legg	3 Stone Buildings, London	0171 242 4937/405 8358
Pithers Clive Robert	Fenners Chambers, Cambridge	01223 368761
	Fenners Chambers, Peterborough	01733 562030
Popat Prashant	Stanbrook & Henderson, London	0171 353 0101
	2 Harcourt Buildings, London	0171 583 9020
Pryke Stuart	Trinity Chambers, Newcastle upon Tyne	0191 232 1927

Purdie Robert Anthony James	28 Western Road, Oxford	01865 204911
Radevsky Anthony Eric	• 5 Bell Yard, London	0171 333 8811
Rahman Muhammad Altafur	Barristers' Common Law Chambers, London	0171 375 3012
Rahman Ms Sadeqa Shaheen	1 Crown Office Row, London	0171 797 7500
Rai Amarjit Singh	St Philip's Chambers, Birmingham	0121 246 7000
Rawlings Clive Patrick	Goldsmith Building, London	0171 353 7881
Reed Miss Penelope Jane	9 Stone Buildings, London	0171 404 5055
Rees David Benjamin	5 Stone Buildings, London	0171 242 6201
Richardson Miss Sarah Jane	Enterprise Chambers, London	0171 405 9471
	Enterprise Chambers, Leeds	0113 246 0391
	Enterprise Chambers, Newcastle upon Tyne	0191 222 3344
Riley-Smith Tobias Augustine William	2 Harcourt Buildings, London	0171 583 9020
Robinson Miss Alice	4 Breams Buildings, London	0171 353 5835/430 1221
Robson John Malcolm	2 Gray's Inn Square Chambers, London	0171 242 0328/405 1317
	Assize Court Chambers, Bristol	0117 926 4587
Roe Thomas Idris	Goldsmith Building, London	0171 353 7881
Ross Martyn John Greaves	• 5 New Square, London	0171 404 0404
	• Octagon House, Norwich	01603 623186
Routley Patrick	Goldsmith Building, London	0171 353 7881
Rowell David Stewart	Chambers of Lord Goodhart QC, London	0171 405 5577
Rule Jonathan Daniel	Merchant Chambers, Manchester	0161 839 7070
Rumney Conrad William Arthur	St Philip's Chambers, Birmingham	0121 246 7000
Russell Christopher Garnet	12 New Square, London	0171 419 1212
	Sovereign Chambers, Leeds	0113 245 1841/2/3
Ryan David Patrick	Chambers of Geoffrey Hawker, London	0171 583 8899
Sampson Graeme William	Chambers of Geoffrey Hawker, London	0171 583 8899
Samuel Glyn Ross	St Philip's Chambers, Birmingham	0121 246 7000
Schaw-Miller Stephen Grant	5 Bell Yard, London	0171 333 8811
Schooling Simon John	Chambers of Harjit Singh, London	0171 353 1356
Scutt David Robert	11 Bolt Court, London	0171 353 2300
	Redhill Chambers, Redhill	01737 780781
Seal Julius Damien	189 Randolph Avenue, London	0171 624 9139
	3 Temple Gardens, London	0171 353 0832
Sefton Mark Thomas Dunblane	199 Strand, London	0171 379 9779
Seifert Miss Anne Miriam	4 Breams Buildings, London	0171 353 5835/430 1221
Selway Dr Katherine Emma	11 Old Square, London	0171 430 0341
Shah Bajul Amratlal Somchand	Twenty-Four Old Buildings, London	0171 404 0946
Sheehan Malcolm Peter	Stanbrook & Henderson, London	0171 353 0101
	2 Harcourt Buildings, London	0171 583 9020
Simmonds Andrew John	5 Stone Buildings, London	0171 242 6201
Singh Balbir	• Equity Chambers, Birmingham	0121 233 2100
Sisley Timothy Julian Crispin	9 Stone Buildings, London	0171 404 5055
	Westgate Chambers, Lewes	01273 480 510
Sleeman Miss Rachel Sarah Elizabeth	One Essex Court, London	0171 936 3030
Smart Miss Jacqueline Anne	Trinity Chambers, Newcastle upon Tyne	0191 232 1927
Smith Miss Julia Mair Wheldon	Gough Square Chambers, London	0171 353 0924
Somerset Jones Eric	Goldsmith Building, London	0171 353 7881
Somerset-Jones Miss Felicity	Oriel Chambers, Liverpool	0151 236 7191
Sparks Kevin Laurence	Earl Street Chambers, Maidstone	01622 671222
Staddon Miss Claire Ann	12 New Square, London	0171 419 1212
	Sovereign Chambers, Leeds	0113 245 1841/2/3
Stagg Paul Andrew	No 1 Serjeants' Inn, London	0171 415 6666
Stanislas Paul Junior	Somersett Chambers, London	0171 404 6701
Starcevic Petar	St Philip's Chambers, Birmingham	0121 246 7000
Steinert Jonathan	New Court Chambers, London	0171 831 9500
Stevens-Hoare Miss Michelle	• Hardwicke Building, London	0171 242 2523
Stewart Alexander Joseph	5 New Square, London	0171 404 0404
Stewart Mark Courtney	College Chambers, Southampton	01703 230338
Stewart Nicholas John Cameron	Hardwicke Building, London	0171 242 2523
Sydenham Colin Peter	4 Breams Buildings, London	0171 353 5835/430 1221
Taelor Start Miss Angharad Jocelyn	3 Verulam Buildings, London	0171 831 8441
Taggart Nicholas	4 Breams Buildings, London	0171 353 5835/430 1221
Thomas Nigel Matthew	13 Old Square, London	0171 404 4800
Thompson Steven Lim	Twenty-Four Old Buildings, London	0171 404 0946

• Expanded entry in Part D

Tidmarsh Christopher Ralph Francis	5 Stone Buildings, London	0171 242 6201
Tipples Miss Amanda Jane	13 Old Square, London	0171 404 4800
Tobin Daniel Alphonsus Joseph	Chambers of Geoffrey Hawker, London	0171 583 8899
Tolaney Miss Sonia	3 Verulam Buildings, London	0171 831 8441
Trace Anthony John	• 13 Old Square, London	0171 404 4800
Tyack David Guy	St Philip's Chambers, Birmingham	0121 246 7000
Vane The Hon Christopher John Fletcher	Trinity Chambers, Newcastle upon Tyne	0191 232 1927
Vaughan-Neil Miss Catherine Mary Bernardine	5 Bell Yard, London	0171 333 8811
Walker Andrew Greenfield	Chambers of Lord Goodhart QC, London	0171 405 5577
Wardell John David Meredith	New Court Chambers, London	0171 831 9500
Warren Rupert Miles	2 Mitre Court Buildings, London	0171 583 1380
Warwick Mark Granville	• 29 Bedford Row Chambers, London	0171 831 2626
Waters Julian William Penrose	No 1 Serjeants' Inn, London	0171 415 6666
Weatherill Bernard Richard	Chambers of Lord Goodhart QC, London	0171 405 5577
Webb Geraint Timothy	2 Harcourt Buildings, London	0171 583 9020
West Mark	• 11 Old Square, London	0171 430 0341
Whitaker Steven Dixon	199 Strand, London	0171 379 9779
	All Saints Chambers, Bristol	0117 921 1966
White Peter-John Spencer	Pembroke House, Leatherhead	01372 376160/376493
Wightwick (William) Iain	Assize Court Chambers, Bristol	0117 926 4587
Williams Ms Heather Jean	Doughty Street Chambers, London	0171 404 1313
Williams Rhodri John	30 Park Place, Cardiff	01222 398421
Williamson Miss Bridget Susan	Enterprise Chambers, London	0171 405 9471
	Enterprise Chambers, Leeds	0113 246 0391
	Enterprise Chambers, Newcastle upon Tyne	0191 222 3344
Wilson Alasdair John	Fenners Chambers, Cambridge	01223 368761
	Fenners Chambers, Peterborough	01733 562030
Wilton Simon Daniel	4 Paper Buildings, London	0171 353 3366/583 7155
Wonnacott Mark Andrew	199 Strand, London	0171 379 9779
Wood Richard Michael	Sackville Chambers, Norwich	01603 613516
Wood Simon Richard Henry	Lamb Chambers, London	0171 797 8300
Woolf Steven Jeremy	Hardwicke Building, London	0171 242 2523
Wright Colin John	4 Field Court, London	0171 440 6900
Wright Norman Alfred	Oriel Chambers, Liverpool	0151 236 7191
Wright Ms Sadie	Goldsmith Building, London	0171 353 7881
Zelin Geoffrey Andrew	Enterprise Chambers, London	0171 405 9471
	Enterprise Chambers, Leeds	0113 246 0391
	Enterprise Chambers, Newcastle upon Tyne	0191 222 3344

LICENSING

Aldred Mark Steven	Queen Elizabeth Building, London	0171 583 5766
Alexander Ian Douglas Gavin	11 Bolt Court, London	0171 353 2300
	Redhill Chambers, Redhill	01737 780781
Ascherson Miss Isobel Ruth	23 Essex Street, London	0171 413 0353
Aston Maurice Charles	5 Paper Buildings, London	0171 583 6117
Bagnall Matthew Philip Cooper	Chambers of Geoffrey Hawker, London	0171 583 8899
Baker William David	2 Paper Buildings, London	0171 353 0933
Barnfather Miss Lydia Helen	Queen Elizabeth Building, London	0171 583 5766
Bate David Christopher	Queen Elizabeth Building, London	0171 583 5766
Bennetts Philip James	Queen Elizabeth Building, London	0171 583 5766
Bevan Edward Julian	Queen Elizabeth Building, London	0171 583 5766
Bhattacharyya Ardhendu	1 Gray's Inn Square, London	0171 405 8946
	11 St Bernards Road, Slough	01753 553806/817989
Birch Roger Allen	12 New Square, London	0171 419 1212
	Sovereign Chambers, Leeds	0113 245 1841/2/3
	Lancaster Buildings, Manchester	0161 661 4444
Boyce William	Queen Elizabeth Building, London	0171 583 5766
Bradshaw David Lawrence	Chambers of Andrew Campbell QC, Leeds	0113 245 5438
Brook Ian Stuart	Hardwicke Building, London	0171 242 2523
Brown Edward Francis Trevenen	Queen Elizabeth Building, London	0171 583 5766
Bull (Donald) Roger	One Essex Court, London	0171 936 3030
Burdon Michael Stewart	St Paul's House, Leeds	0113 245 5866
Calvert-Smith David	Queen Elizabeth Building, London	0171 583 5766

• Expanded entry in Part D

Capon Philip Christopher William	St Philip's Chambers, Birmingham	0121 246 7000
Carlisle of Bucklow The Rt Hon Lord	Queen Elizabeth Building, London	0171 583 5766
	18 St John Street, Manchester	0161 278 1800
Carman George Alfred	New Court Chambers, London	0171 831 9500
Challinor Robert Michael	St Philip's Chambers, Birmingham	0121 246 7000
Chaplin Adrian Roland	9-12 Bell Yard, London	0171 400 1800
Clarke Peter William	Queen Elizabeth Building, London	0171 583 5766
Collett Gavin Charles	Rougemont Chambers, Exeter	01392 410471
	Cathedral Chambers (Jan Wood Independent Barristers' Clerk), Exeter	01392 210900
Collier Martin Melton	Fenners Chambers, Cambridge	01223 368761
	Fenners Chambers, Peterborough	01733 562030
Corry Miss Carol Elizabeth	One Essex Court, London	0171 936 3030
Cottage Miss Rosina	9-12 Bell Yard, London	0171 400 1800
Coward Miss Victoria Jane	Queen Elizabeth Building, London	0171 583 5766
Crowson Howard Keith	St Paul's House, Leeds	0113 245 5866
Darbishire Adrian Munro	Queen Elizabeth Building, London	0171 583 5766
Davey Miss Tina Elaine	9-12 Bell Yard, London	0171 400 1800
de Jehan David	St Paul's House, Leeds	0113 245 5866
Denton Miss Michelle Jayne	9-12 Bell Yard, London	0171 400 1800
Dineen Michael Laurence	Pump Court Chambers, London	0171 353 0711
	All Saints Chambers, Bristol	0117 921 1966
	Pump Court Chambers, Winchester	01962 868161
Donne Jeremy Nigel	Queen Elizabeth Building, London	0171 583 5766
Doyle Peter John	9-12 Bell Yard, London	0171 400 1800
Drayton Henry Alexander	2 Gray's Inn Square Chambers, London	0171 242 0328/405 1317
Duffy Michael	Cathedral Chambers, Ely, Ely	01353 666775
Edwards Philip Douglas	2 Harcourt Buildings, London	0171 353 8415
Ellison Mark Christopher	Queen Elizabeth Building, London	0171 583 5766
Evans David Anthony	9-12 Bell Yard, London	0171 400 1800
	Iscoed Chambers, Swansea	01792 652988/9/330
Evans David Howard	Queen Elizabeth Building, London	0171 583 5766
Evans Thomas Gareth	Rougemont Chambers, Exeter	01392 410471
Farmer Pryce Michael	1 Dr Johnson's Buildings, London	0171 353 9328
	Goldsmith Building, London	0171 353 7881
	Sedan House, Chester	01244 320480/348282
Field Rory Dominic	Hardwicke Building, London	0171 242 2523
Finnigan Peter Anthony	Queen Elizabeth Building, London	0171 583 5766
Fletcher Marcus Alexander	One King's Bench Walk, London	0171 936 1500
Forster Brian Clive	Trinity Chambers, Newcastle upon Tyne	0191 232 1927
Fuad Kerim	Chambers of Helen Grindrod QC, London	0171 404 4777
Gillette John Charles	Baker Street Chambers, Middlesbrough	01642 873873
Glass Anthony Trevor	Queen Elizabeth Building, London	0171 583 5766
Gorna Miss Anne Christina	4 Paper Buildings, London	0171 353 3366/583 7155
	Cathedral Chambers (Jan Wood Independent Barristers' Clerk), Exeter	01392 210900
Gray Miss Jennifer	11 Old Square, London	0171 242 5022
Greaves John	9-12 Bell Yard, London	0171 400 1800
Grey Robin Douglas	Queen Elizabeth Building, London	0171 583 5766
Griffin Neil Patrick Luke	9-12 Bell Yard, London	0171 400 1800
Griffin Nicholas John	5 Paper Buildings, London	0171 583 6117
Gullick Stephen John	Sovereign Chambers, Leeds	0113 245 1841/2/3
Hadrill Keith Paul	9-12 Bell Yard, London	0171 400 1800
Hallett Miss Heather Carol	23 Essex Street, London	0171 413 0353
Hartley-Davies Paul Kevil	30 Park Place, Cardiff	01222 398421
Harvey Miss Jayne Denise	Goldsworth Chambers, London	0171 405 7117
Hatton Andrew John	Plowden Buildings, London	0171 583 0808
	Paradise Square Chambers, Sheffield	0114 273 8951
Haven Kevin	2 Gray's Inn Square Chambers, London	0171 242 0328/405 1317
Hawkesworth (Walter) Gareth	5 Paper Buildings, London	0171 583 6117
	Fenners Chambers, Cambridge	01223 368761
	Fenners Chambers, Peterborough	01733 562030
Haygarth Edmund Bruce	25-27 Castle Street, Liverpool	0151 227 5661/5666/236 5072
Haynes Peter	St Philip's Chambers, Birmingham	0121 246 7000

Heaton-Armstrong Anthony Eustace John	9-12 Bell Yard, London	0171 400 1800
Henderson Lawrence Mark	11 Bolt Court, London	0171 353 2300
	Redhill Chambers, Redhill	01737 780781
Henry Edward Joseph Aloysius	Queen Elizabeth Building, London	0171 583 5766
Heslop Martin Sydney	1 Hare Court, London	0171 353 3982/5324
Hickey Simon Roger Greenwood	Chambers of Andrew Campbell QC, Leeds	0113 245 5438
Hilton Alan John Howard	Queen Elizabeth Building, London	0171 583 5766
Holland Charles Christopher	Trinity Chambers, Newcastle upon Tyne	0191 232 1927
Horton Matthew Bethell	2 Mitre Court Buildings, London	0171 583 1380
Horwell Richard Eric	Queen Elizabeth Building, London	0171 583 5766
Hughes William Lloyd	9-12 Bell Yard, London	0171 400 1800
Islam-Choudhury Mugni	11 Bolt Court, London	0171 353 2300
Janner Daniel Joseph Mitchell	23 Essex Street, London	0171 413 0353
Jay Adam Marc	One King's Bench Walk, London	0171 936 1500
Jeffreys David Alfred	Queen Elizabeth Building, London	0171 583 5766
Johnson Miss Zoe Elisabeth	Queen Elizabeth Building, London	0171 583 5766
Jones Gregory Percy	• 2 Harcourt Buildings, London	0171 353 8415
Jory Richard Norman	9-12 Bell Yard, London	0171 400 1800
Kark Thomas Victor William	Queen Elizabeth Building, London	0171 583 5766
Kealy Charles Brian	Chambers of Andrew Campbell QC, Leeds	0113 245 5438
Kelsey-Fry John	Queen Elizabeth Building, London	0171 583 5766
Kenward Timothy David Nelson	25-27 Castle Street, Liverpool	0151 227 5661/5666/236 5072
Kyte Peter Eric	Queen Elizabeth Building, London	0171 583 5766
Lander Charles Gideon	25-27 Castle Street, Liverpool	0151 227 5661/5666/236 5072
Langdale Timothy James	Queen Elizabeth Building, London	0171 583 5766
Larkin Sean	Queen Elizabeth Building, London	0171 583 5766
Lewis Robert		
Longden Anthony Gordon	Queen Elizabeth Building, London	0171 583 5766
Lowry Miss Emma Margaret Collins	Queen Elizabeth Building, London	0171 583 5766
Lumley Gerald	9 Woodhouse Square, Leeds	0113 245 1986
Lyne Mark Hilary	One Essex Court, London	0171 936 3030
MacKillop Norman Malcolm	• Chartlands Chambers, Northampton	01604 603322
Maitland Marc Claude	11 Old Square, London	0171 242 5022
Manson Miss Julie-Ann	11 Bolt Court, London	0171 353 2300
	Redhill Chambers, Redhill	01737 780781
Marshall Philip Derek	Farrar's Building, London	0171 583 9241
	Iscoed Chambers, Swansea	01792 652988/9/330
Marson Geoffrey Charles	Sovereign Chambers, Leeds	0113 245 1841/2/3
Mason Ian Douglas	11 Bolt Court, London	0171 353 2300
	Redhill Chambers, Redhill	01737 780781
Mathew Miss Nergis-Anne	2 Gray's Inn Square Chambers, London	0171 242 0328/405 1317
McGuinness John Francis	9-12 Bell Yard, London	0171 400 1800
McKinnon Warwick Nairn	Queen Elizabeth Building, London	0171 583 5766
McLachlan David Robert		
Mitchell Christopher Richard	Queen Elizabeth Building, London	0171 583 5766
Moore James Anthony	2 Gray's Inn Square Chambers, London	0171 242 0328/405 1317
Morley Iain Charles	1 Hare Court, London	0171 353 3982/5324
Nicholls Peter John	5 Pump Court, London	0171 353 2532
Nicol-Gent William Philip Trahair	King's Chambers, Eastbourne	01323 416053
Norris Andrew James Steedsman	5 New Square, London	0171 404 0404
O'Neill Brian Patrick	1 Hare Court, London	0171 353 3982/5324
Okoye Miss Joy Nwamala	Chambers of Joy Okoye, London	0171 405 7011
Ornsby Miss Suzanne Doreen	• 2 Harcourt Buildings, London	0171 353 8415
Ozin Paul David	23 Essex Street, London	0171 413 0353
Parr John Edward	8 King Street Chambers, Manchester	0161 834 9560
Parry Charles Robert	Pump Court Chambers, London	0171 353 0711
	Pump Court Chambers, Winchester	01962 868161
Paton Ian Francis	Queen Elizabeth Building, London	0171 583 5766
Perks Richard Howard	St Philip's Chambers, Birmingham	0121 246 7000
Peters Nigel Melvin	18 Red Lion Court, London	0171 520 6000
	Thornwood House, Chelmsford	01245 280880
Phillips Frank	Iscoed Chambers, Swansea	01792 652988/9/330
Plaschkes Ms Sarah Georgina	Queen Elizabeth Building, London	0171 583 5766
Poulet Mrs Rebecca Maria	Queen Elizabeth Building, London	0171 583 5766
Purchas Robin Michael	• 2 Harcourt Buildings, London	0171 353 8415
Rahman Ms Sadeqa Shaheen	1 Crown Office Row, London	0171 797 7500

• Expanded entry in Part D

Ramasamy Selvaraju	Queen Elizabeth Building, London	0171 583 5766
Rees Gareth David	Queen Elizabeth Building, London	0171 583 5766
Robinson Vivian	Queen Elizabeth Building, London	0171 583 5766
Russell Anthony Patrick	Peel Court Chambers, Manchester	0161 832 3791
Russell Miss Christina Martha	9-12 Bell Yard, London	0171 400 1800
Ryan David Patrick	Chambers of Geoffrey Hawker, London	0171 583 8899
Saffian Ms Leah Susan	Queen Elizabeth Building, London	0171 583 5766
Salvesen Keith Neville	Queen Elizabeth Building, London	0171 353 7181 (12 lines)
Samuel Glyn Ross	St Philip's Chambers, Birmingham	0121 246 7000
Sawyer John Frederick		
Schooling Simon John	Chambers of Harjit Singh, London	0171 353 1356
Scutt David Robert	11 Bolt Court, London	0171 353 2300
	Redhill Chambers, Redhill	01737 780781
Seymour Mark William	9-12 Bell Yard, London	0171 400 1800
Shaikh Eur.Ing. (Jaikumar) Christopher (Samuel	Avondale Chambers, London	0181 445 9984
	Equity Chambers, Birmingham	0121 233 2100
Silvester Bruce Ross	Lamb Chambers, London	0171 797 8300
Singh Balbir	• Equity Chambers, Birmingham	0121 233 2100
Somerset Jones Eric	Goldsmith Building, London	0171 353 7881
Sparks Miss Jocelyn Margaret	Queen Elizabeth Building, London	0171 583 5766
St Louis Brian Lloyd	Hardwicke Building, London	0171 242 2523
Stern Ian Michael	Queen Elizabeth Building, London	0171 583 5766
Stewart Neill Alastair	Queen Elizabeth Building, London	0171 583 5766
Strickland Miss Clare Elizabeth	23 Essex Street, London	0171 413 0353
Strudwick Miss Linda Diane	Queen Elizabeth Building, London	0171 583 5766
Suckling Alan Blair	Queen Elizabeth Building, London	0171 583 5766
Sullivan Ms Jane Teresa	Queen Elizabeth Building, London	0171 583 5766
Summers Benjamin Dylan James	Queen Elizabeth Building, London	0171 583 5766
Temple Anthony Dominic	4 Pump Court, London	0171 353 2656/9
Thompson Lyall Norris	Tindal Chambers, Chelmsford	01245 267742
	Tindal Chambers, St Albans	01727 843383
Tucker David William	Two Crown Office Row, London	0171 797 8100
Tyack David Guy	St Philip's Chambers, Birmingham	0121 246 7000
Volz Karl Andrew	Chambers of Geoffrey Hawker, London	0171 583 8899
Wakeham Philip John Le Messurier	Hardwicke Building, London	0171 242 2523
Warne Peter Lawrence	Queen Elizabeth Building, London	0171 583 5766
Wastie William Granville	Queen Elizabeth Building, London	0171 583 5766
Wignall Edward Gordon	• 1 Dr Johnson's Buildings, London	0171 353 9328
	• Dr Johnson's Chambers, Reading	01189 254221
Wilcken Anthony David Felix	Queen Elizabeth Building, London	0171 583 5766
Williams A John	• 13 King's Bench Walk, London	0171 353 7204
	• King's Bench Chambers, Oxford	01865 311066
Winter Ian David	Queen Elizabeth Building, London	0171 583 5766
Wood Nicholas Andrew	5 Paper Buildings, London	0171 583 9275
Wyatt Guy Peter James	Earl Street Chambers, Maidstone	01622 671222

LIMITATION AND STRIKING OUT FOR DELAY

Gun Cuninghame Julian Arthur	• Gough Square Chambers, London	0171 353 0924

LIMITED PARTNERSHIPS

Banks Roderick Charles l'Anson	• 48 Bedford Row, London	0171 430 2005

LOCAL GOVERNMENT

Addison Neil Patrick	Cathedral Chambers, Newcastle upon Tyne	0191 232 1311
Alesbury Alun	2 Mitre Court Buildings, London	0171 583 1380
Alliott George Beckles	2 Harcourt Buildings, London	0171 583 9020
Anderson Anthony John	2 Mitre Court Buildings, London	0171 583 1380
Bailey Mark Henry Arthur	• 6 Pump Court, London	0171 797 8400
	• 6-8 Mill Street, Maidstone	01622 688 094
Barnes (David) Michael (William)	4 Breams Buildings, London	0171 353 5835/430 1221
Bartlett George Robert	2 Mitre Court Buildings, London	0171 583 1380
Bates John Hayward	Old Square Chambers, London	0171 269 0300
	Old Square Chambers, Bristol	0117 927 7111
Baxter Gerald Pearson	25-27 Castle Street, Liverpool	0151 227 5661/5666/236 5072
Beard Mark Christopher	6 Pump Court, London	0171 797 8400
Beaumont Marc Clifford	• Pump Court Chambers, London	0171 353 0711

	• Harrow-on-the-Hill Chambers, Harrow on the Hill	0181 423 7444
	• Pump Court Chambers, Winchester	01962 868161
	• Windsor Barristers' Chambers, Windsor	01753 648 899
Bhattacharyya Ardhendu	1 Gray's Inn Square, London	0171 405 8946
	11 St Bernards Road, Slough	01753 553806/817989
Birch Roger Allen	12 New Square, London	0171 419 1212
	Sovereign Chambers, Leeds	0113 245 1841/2/3
	Lancaster Buildings, Manchester	0161 661 4444
Birks Simon Alexander	7 Stone Buildings, London	0171 242 0961
Birtles William	Old Square Chambers, London	0171 269 0300
	Old Square Chambers, Bristol	0117 927 7111
Birts Peter William	• Farrar's Building, London	0171 583 9241
Boyle Christopher Alexander David	2 Mitre Court Buildings, London	0171 583 1380
Burton Nicholas Anthony	2 Mitre Court Buildings, London	0171 583 1380
Bush Keith	30 Park Place, Cardiff	01222 398421
Cameron Neil Alexander	Wilberforce Chambers, Hull	01482 323 264
Cameron Neil St Clair	1 Serjeants' Inn, London	0171 583 1355
Cameron Miss Sheila Morag Clark	2 Harcourt Buildings, London	0171 353 8415
Cape Robert Paul	Milburn House Chambers, Newcastle upon Tyne	0191 230 5511
Caws Eian Richard Edwin	4 Breams Buildings, London	0171 353 5835/430 1221
Choudhury Akhlaq	11 King's Bench Walk, London	0171 632 8500
Clay Jonathan Roger	11 Bolt Court, London	0171 353 2300
	Redhill Chambers, Redhill	01737 780781
Colquhoun Miss Celina Daphne Marion	11 Bolt Court, London	0171 353 2300
	Redhill Chambers, Redhill	01737 780781
Cooper Adrian Edgar Mark	Stanbrook & Henderson, London	0171 353 0101
	2 Harcourt Buildings, London	0171 583 9020
Cottage Miss Rosina	9-12 Bell Yard, London	0171 400 1800
Curtis Michael Alexander	Two Crown Office Row, London	0171 797 8100
Daiches Michael Salis	• 22 Old Buildings, London	0171 831 0222
Davies Miss Louise	12 New Square, London	0171 419 1212
de Voghelaere Parr Adam Stephen	2 Mitre Court Buildings, London	0171 583 1380
Denton Miss Michelle Jayne	9-12 Bell Yard, London	0171 400 1800
Drabble Richard John Bloor	4 Breams Buildings, London	0171 353 5835/430 1221
Druce Michael James	2 Mitre Court Buildings, London	0171 583 1380
Edwards Philip Douglas	2 Harcourt Buildings, London	0171 353 8415
Elvin David John	4 Breams Buildings, London	0171 353 5835/430 1221
FitzGerald Michael Frederick Clive	2 Mitre Court Buildings, London	0171 583 1380
Fookes Robert Lawrence	2 Mitre Court Buildings, London	0171 583 1380
Ford Gerard James	Baker Street Chambers, Middlesbrough	01642 873873
Forsdick David John	4 Breams Buildings, London	0171 353 5835/430 1221
Friel John Anthony	Goldsmith Building, London	0171 353 7881
	Southsea Chambers, Portsmouth	01705 291261
Gibson Charles Anthony Warneford	2 Harcourt Buildings, London	0171 583 9020
Giffin Nigel Dyson	11 King's Bench Walk, London	0171 632 8500
Gillette John Charles	Baker Street Chambers, Middlesbrough	01642 873873
Gordon Richard John Francis	39 Essex Street, London	0171 832 1111
Gore Andrew Roger	Fenners Chambers, Cambridge	01223 368761
	Fenners Chambers, Peterborough	01733 562030
Goudie James	• 11 King's Bench Walk, London	0171 632 8500
Gower Peter John de Peauly	6 Pump Court, London	0171 797 8400
	6-8 Mill Street, Maidstone	01622 688 094
Greaves John	9-12 Bell Yard, London	0171 400 1800
Gresty Miss Denise Lynn	Sovereign Chambers, Leeds	0113 245 1841/2/3
Grundy Nicholas John	One Essex Court, London	0171 936 3030
Hands David Richard Granville	4 Breams Buildings, London	0171 353 5835/430 1221
	40 King Street, Manchester	0161 832 9082
Hargreaves Miss Sara Jane	12 New Square, London	0171 419 1212
	Sovereign Chambers, Leeds	0113 245 1841/2/3
Harper Joseph Charles	4 Breams Buildings, London	0171 353 5835/430 1221
Harrison Peter John	6 Pump Court, London	0171 797 8400
	6-8 Mill Street, Maidstone	01622 688 094
Harwood Richard John	1 Serjeants' Inn, London	0171 583 1355
Haynes Peter	St Philip's Chambers, Birmingham	0121 246 7000
Healy Miss Alexandra	9-12 Bell Yard, London	0171 400 1800
Henderson Roger Anthony	Stanbrook & Henderson, London	0171 353 0101

	2 Harcourt Buildings, London	0171 583 9020
Hillier Andrew Charles	5 Bell Yard, London	0171 333 8811
Hockman Stephen Alexander	• 6 Pump Court, London	0171 797 8400
	• 6-8 Mill Street, Maidstone	01622 688 094
Holgate David John	4 Breams Buildings, London	0171 353 5835/430 1221
Horton Matthew Bethell	2 Mitre Court Buildings, London	0171 583 1380
Howell John	4 Breams Buildings, London	0171 353 5835/430 1221
Huskinson George Nicholas Nevil	4-5 Gray's Inn Square, London	0171 404 5252
Ivimy Ms Cecilia Rachel	11 King's Bench Walk, London	0171 632 8500
John Stephen Alun	9-12 Bell Yard, London	0171 400 1800
Jones Gregory Percy	• 2 Harcourt Buildings, London	0171 353 8415
Jones Sean William Paul	11 King's Bench Walk, London	0171 632 8500
Jones Timothy Arthur	• Arden Chambers, London	0171 242 4244
	• St Philip's Chambers, Birmingham	0121 246 7000
Jordan Andrew	Stanbrook & Henderson, London	0171 353 0101
	2 Harcourt Buildings, London	0171 583 9020
Joss Norman James	One Essex Court, London	0171 936 3030
Karas Jonathan Marcus	4 Breams Buildings, London	0171 353 5835/430 1221
Katkowski Christopher Andrew Mark	4 Breams Buildings, London	0171 353 5835/430 1221
Keen Graeme	4 Breams Buildings, London	0171 353 5835/430 1221
Kenward Timothy David Nelson	25-27 Castle Street, Liverpool	0151 227 5661/5666/236 5072
Kerr Tim Julian	4-5 Gray's Inn Square, London	0171 404 5252
King Neil Gerald Alexander	2 Mitre Court Buildings, London	0171 583 1380
Kingsland Rt Hon Lord	4 Breams Buildings, London	0171 353 5835/430 1221
Laing Miss Elisabeth Mary Caroline	11 King's Bench Walk, London	0171 632 8500
Langham Richard Geoffrey	1 Serjeants' Inn, London	0171 583 1355
Lawson Rogers George Stuart	23 Essex Street, London	0171 413 0353
Leiper Richard Thomas	11 King's Bench Walk, London	0171 632 8500
Levy Robert Stuart	9 Stone Buildings, London	0171 404 5055
	Assize Court Chambers, Bristol	0117 926 4587
Lewis Robert		
Lewsley Christopher Stanton	4 Breams Buildings, London	0171 353 5835/430 1221
Lieven Ms Nathalie Marie Daniella	4 Breams Buildings, London	0171 353 5835/430 1221
Litton John Letablere	4 Breams Buildings, London	0171 353 5835/430 1221
Lockhart-Mummery Christopher John	4 Breams Buildings, London	0171 353 5835/430 1221
Lyness Scott Edward	1 Serjeants' Inn, London	0171 583 1355
Maclean Alan John	39 Essex Street, London	0171 832 1111
Macleod Nigel Ronald Buchanan	4 Breams Buildings, London	0171 353 5835/430 1221
	40 King Street, Manchester	0161 832 9082
Male John Martin	4 Breams Buildings, London	0171 353 5835/430 1221
Mandel Richard	11 Bolt Court, London	0171 353 2300
	Redhill Chambers, Redhill	01737 780781
Mason Ian Douglas	11 Bolt Court, London	0171 353 2300
	Redhill Chambers, Redhill	01737 780781
Mathias Miss Anna	11 Bolt Court, London	0171 353 2300
Maurici James Patrick	4 Breams Buildings, London	0171 353 5835/430 1221
Mawrey Richard Brooks	Stanbrook & Henderson, London	0171 353 0101
	2 Harcourt Buildings, London	0171 583 9020
Maxwell Miss Judith Mary Angela	The Garden House, London	0171 404 6150
McCracken Robert Henry Joy	• 2 Harcourt Buildings, London	0171 353 8415
McHugh Miss Karen	4 Breams Buildings, London	0171 353 5835/430 1221
McManus Jonathan Richard	4-5 Gray's Inn Square, London	0171 404 5252
McMinn Miss Valerie Kathleen	Baker Street Chambers, Middlesbrough	01642 873873
Moore Professor Victor William Edward	2 Mitre Court Buildings, London	0171 583 1380
Morgan Jeremy	Chambers of Kieran Coonan QC, London	0171 583 6013/2510
Moriarty Gerald Evelyn	2 Mitre Court Buildings, London	0171 583 1380
Morshead Timothy Francis	4 Breams Buildings, London	0171 353 5835/430 1221
Mould Timothy James	4 Breams Buildings, London	0171 353 5835/430 1221
Newcombe Andrew Bennett	• 2 Harcourt Buildings, London	0171 353 8415
Norie-Miller Jeffrey Reginald	55 Temple Chambers, London	0171 353 7400
Okoye Miss Joy Nwamala	Chambers of Joy Okoye, London	0171 405 7011
Ornsby Miss Suzanne Doreen	• 2 Harcourt Buildings, London	0171 353 8415
Ouseley Duncan Brian Walter	4-5 Gray's Inn Square, London	0171 404 5252
Peacock Ian Christopher	12 New Square, London	0171 419 1212
	Sovereign Chambers, Leeds	0113 245 1841/2/3
Peters Nigel Melvin	18 Red Lion Court, London	0171 520 6000
	Thornwood House, Chelmsford	01245 280880
Pitt-Payne Timothy Sheridan	• 11 King's Bench Walk, London	0171 632 8500

Pleming Nigel Peter	39 Essex Street, London	0171 832 1111
Purchas Robin Michael	• 2 Harcourt Buildings, London	0171 353 8415
Rai Amarjit Singh	St Philip's Chambers, Birmingham	0121 246 7000
Randle Simon Patrick	11 Bolt Court, London	0171 353 2300
	Redhill Chambers, Redhill	01737 780781
Read Lionel Frank	1 Serjeants' Inn, London	0171 583 1355
Richards Miss Jennifer	39 Essex Street, London	0171 832 1111
Robb Adam Duncan	39 Essex Street, London	0171 832 1111
Robinson Miss Alice	4 Breams Buildings, London	0171 353 5835/430 1221
Roots Guy Robert Godfrey	2 Mitre Court Buildings, London	0171 583 1380
Rumney Conrad William Arthur	St Philip's Chambers, Birmingham	0121 246 7000
Seligman Matthew Thomas Arthur	39 Essex Street, London	0171 832 1111
Semple Andrew Blair	Sovereign Chambers, Leeds	0113 245 1841/2/3
Seymour Mark William	9-12 Bell Yard, London	0171 400 1800
Silsoe The Lord	2 Mitre Court Buildings, London	0171 583 1380
Silvester Bruce Ross	Lamb Chambers, London	0171 797 8300
Simpson Edwin John Fletcher	12 New Square, London	0171 419 1212
Smith David Anthony	4 Breams Buildings, London	0171 353 5835/430 1221
Stilitz Daniel Malachi	11 King's Bench Walk, London	0171 632 8500
Stone Gregory	• 4-5 Gray's Inn Square, London	0171 404 5252
Straker Timothy Derrick	• 2-3 Gray's Inn Square, London	0171 242 4986
Sunnucks James Horace George	• 5 New Square, London	0171 404 0404
	• Octagon House, Norwich	01603 623186
Supperstone Michael Alan	11 King's Bench Walk, London	0171 632 8500
Taylor Reuben Mallinson	2 Mitre Court Buildings, London	0171 583 1380
Thomas Miss Megan Moira	1 Serjeants' Inn, London	0171 583 1355
Treacy Colman Maurice	Chambers of James Hunt QC, London	0171 421 8000
	3 Fountain Court, Birmingham	0121 236 5854
Tucker Miss Katherine Jane Greening	St Philip's Chambers, Birmingham	0121 246 7000
Vater John Alistair Pitt	Harcourt Chambers, London	0171 353 6961/7
Village Peter Malcolm	• 4-5 Gray's Inn Square, London	0171 404 5252
Wallington Peter Thomas	11 King's Bench Walk, London	0171 632 8500
Ward Timothy Justin	39 Essex Street, London	0171 832 1111
Warren Rupert Miles	2 Mitre Court Buildings, London	0171 583 1380
West Lawrence Joseph	Stanbrook & Henderson, London	0171 353 0101
	2 Harcourt Buildings, London	0171 583 9020
Whybrow Christopher John	1 Serjeants' Inn, London	0171 583 1355
Widdicombe David Graham	2 Mitre Court Buildings, London	0171 583 1380
Wignall Edward Gordon	• 1 Dr Johnson's Buildings, London	0171 353 9328
	• Dr Johnson's Chambers, Reading	01189 254221
Williams Miss Anne Margaret	4 Breams Buildings, London	0171 353 5835/430 1221
	37 Park Square, Leeds	0113 243 9422
Williams Rhodri John	30 Park Place, Cardiff	01222 398421
Woodwark Ms Jane Elizabeth	Milburn House Chambers, Newcastle upon Tyne	0191 230 5511

LOCAL GOVERNMENT FINANCE

Howell John	4 Breams Buildings, London	0171 353 5835/430 1221

MASS DISASTERS

Webb Robert Stopford	• 5 Bell Yard, London	0171 333 8811

MEDIATION

Patterson Stewart	• Pump Court Chambers, London	0171 353 0711
	• Pump Court Chambers, Winchester	01962 868161

MEDICAL LAW

Levy Allan Edward	17 Bedford Row, London	0171 831 7314

MEDICAL NEGLIGENCE

Abbott Francis Arthur	Pump Court Chambers, London	0171 353 0711
	Pump Court Chambers, Winchester	01962 868161
Al'Hassan Khadim	Equity Chambers, Birmingham	0121 233 2100
Alexander Ian Douglas Gavin	11 Bolt Court, London	0171 353 2300
	Redhill Chambers, Redhill	01737 780781
Alldis Christopher John	Peel House Chambers, Liverpool	0151 236 4321
Alliott George Beckles	2 Harcourt Buildings, London	0171 583 9020
Andrews Peter John	• 199 Strand, London	0171 379 9779

• Expanded entry in Part D

	• 3 Fountain Court, Birmingham	0121 236 5854
Anthony Michael Guy	Two Crown Office Row, London	0171 797 8100
Archer John Francis Ashweek	Two Crown Office Row, London	0171 797 8100
Ashworth Piers	Stanbrook & Henderson, London	0171 353 0101
	2 Harcourt Buildings, London	0171 583 9020
	Priory Chambers, Birmingham	0121 236 3882/1375
Aslett Pepin Charles Maguire	22 Albion Place, Northampton	01604 636271
Aylen Walter Stafford	Hardwicke Building, London	0171 242 2523
Baker Ms Rachel Mary Theresa	Hardwicke Building, London	0171 242 2523
Barlow Miss Sarah Helen	St Paul's House, Leeds	0113 245 5866
Barnett Andrew John	Pump Court Chambers, London	0171 353 0711
	Pump Court Chambers, Winchester	01962 868161
Barstow Stephen Royden	Harcourt Chambers, London	0171 353 6961/7
	Harcourt Chambers, Oxford	01865 791559
Battcock Benjamin George	Stanbrook & Henderson, London	0171 353 0101
	2 Harcourt Buildings, London	0171 583 9020
Bedeau Stephen	Sovereign Chambers, Leeds	0113 245 1841/2/3
	Lancaster Buildings, Manchester	0161 661 4444
Beech Ms Jacqueline Elaine	199 Strand, London	0171 379 9779
	York Chambers, York	01904 620 048
Bendall Richard Giles	33 Bedford Row, London	0171 242 6476
Bennett John Martyn	• Peel House Chambers, Liverpool	0151 236 4321
Berkley Michael Stuart	Rougemont Chambers, Exeter	01392 410471
Bhattacharyya Ardhendu	1 Gray's Inn Square, London	0171 405 8946
	11 St Bernards Road, Slough	01753 553806/817989
Bishop Edward James	No 1 Serjeants' Inn, London	0171 415 6666
Blakesley Patrick James	Two Crown Office Row, London	0171 797 8100
Bloom-Davis Desmond Niall Laurence	Pump Court Chambers, London	0171 353 0711
	Pump Court Chambers, Winchester	01962 868161
Booth Alan James	Deans Court Chambers, Manchester	0161 834 4097
	Deans Court Chambers, Preston	01772 555163
Boydell Edward Patrick Stirrup	Pump Court Chambers, London	0171 353 0711
	Pump Court Chambers, Winchester	01962 868161
Bradley Miss Clodagh Maria	3 Serjeants' Inn, London	0171 353 5537
Brahams Mrs Diana Joyce	Old Square Chambers, London	0171 269 0300
	Old Square Chambers, Bristol	0117 927 7111
Braithwaite William Thomas Scatchard	• Two Crown Office Row, London	0171 797 8100
	• Exchange Chambers, Liverpool	0151 236 7747
Breen Carlo Enrico	Chambers of John Hand QC, Manchester	0161 955 9000
Brennan Daniel Joseph	39 Essex Street, London	0171 832 1111
	18 St John Street, Manchester	0161 278 1800
Briden Timothy John	• 8 Stone Buildings, London	0171 831 9881
Bright Christopher John	3 Fountain Court, Birmingham	0121 236 5854
Brilliant Simon Howard	Lamb Chambers, London	0171 797 8300
Brown Geoffrey Barlow	39 Essex Street, London	0171 832 1111
Brown (Geoffrey) Charles	39 Essex Street, London	0171 832 1111
Browne James William	Goldsworth Chambers, London	0171 405 7117
Brunner Adrian John Nelson	Stanbrook & Henderson, London	0171 353 0101
	2 Harcourt Buildings, London	0171 583 9020
Brunton Sean Alexander McKay	Pump Court Chambers, London	0171 353 0711
	Pump Court Chambers, Winchester	01962 868161
Bull (Donald) Roger	One Essex Court, London	0171 936 3030
Burns Peter Richard	Deans Court Chambers, Manchester	0161 834 4097
Butler Philip Andrew	Goldsmith Chambers, London	0171 353 6802/3/4/5
	Deans Court Chambers, Manchester	0161 834 4097
	Deans Court Chambers, Preston	01772 555163
Cameron Miss Barbara Alexander	Stanbrook & Henderson, London	0171 353 0101
	2 Harcourt Buildings, London	0171 583 9020
Candlin James Richard	Chambers of Geoffrey Hawker, London	0171 583 8899
Carlile Alexander Charles	9-12 Bell Yard, London	0171 400 1800
	Sedan House, Chester	01244 320480/348282
Carling Christopher James	Old Square Chambers, London	0171 269 0300
	Old Square Chambers, Bristol	0117 927 7111
Cartwright Richard John	Queen Elizabeth Building, London	0171 353 7181 (12 lines)
Cash Miss Joanne Catherine	Farrar's Building, London	0171 583 9241
Cawley Neil Robert Loudoun	55 Temple Chambers, London	0171 353 7400
	Milton Keynes Chambers, Milton Keynes	01908 217857

       • Expanded entry in Part D

Cherry John Mitchell	• 8 Stone Buildings, London	0171 831 9881
Christie-Brown Miss Sarah Louise	4 Paper Buildings, London	0171 353 3366/583 7155
Chudleigh Miss Louise Katrina	Old Square Chambers, London	0171 269 0300
	Old Square Chambers, Bristol	0117 927 7111
Clarke Miss Alison Lee	No 1 Serjeants' Inn, London	0171 415 6666
Clarke George Robert Ivan	Chambers of Geoffrey Hawker, London	0171 583 8899
Clarke Jonathan Christopher St John	Old Square Chambers, London	0171 269 0300
	Old Square Chambers, Bristol	0117 927 7111
Clegg Sebastian James Barwick	Deans Court Chambers, Manchester	0161 834 4097
Clover (Thomas) Anthony	New Court Chambers, London	0171 831 9500
Collett Ivor William	No 1 Serjeants' Inn, London	0171 415 6666
Collins John Morris	11 King's Bench Walk, London	0171 353 3337/8
	9 Woodhouse Square, Leeds	0113 245 1986
Collinson Miss Alicia Hester	Harcourt Chambers, London	0171 353 6961/7
	Harcourt Chambers, Oxford	01865 791559
Conlin Geoffrey David	3 Serjeants' Inn, London	0171 353 5537
Cooper Roger Bernard	Trinity Chambers, Newcastle upon Tyne	0191 232 1927
Cotter Barry Paul	Old Square Chambers, London	0171 269 0300
	Old Square Chambers, Bristol	0117 927 7111
Coulter Barry John	One Essex Court, London	0171 936 3030
Cowan Peter Sherwood McCrea	Oriel Chambers, Liverpool	0151 236 7191
Cross Mrs Joanna	9 Woodhouse Square, Leeds	0113 245 1986
Crowley John Desmond	Two Crown Office Row, London	0171 797 8100
Curwen Michael Jonathan	Chambers of Kieran Coonan QC, London	0171 583 6013/2510
Dallas Andrew Thomas Alastair	Chambers of Andrew Campbell QC, Leeds	0113 245 5438
Davies Richard Llewellyn	39 Essex Street, London	0171 832 1111
Davis Andrew Paul	Two Crown Office Row, London	0171 797 8100
Davis William Easthope	St Philip's Chambers, Birmingham	0121 246 7000
de Jehan David	St Paul's House, Leeds	0113 245 5866
Dean Paul Benjamin	5 Bell Yard, London	0171 333 8811
DeCamp Miss Jane Louise	Two Crown Office Row, London	0171 797 8100
Dixon Ian Frederick	Cathedral Chambers, Newcastle upon Tyne	0191 232 1311
Dixon John Watts	Harcourt Chambers, London	0171 353 6961/7
	Harcourt Chambers, Oxford	01865 791559
Donovan Joel	New Court Chambers, London	0171 831 9500
Dowse John	Chambers of Lord Goodhart QC, London	0171 405 5577
	Chambers of John Hand QC, Manchester	0161 955 9000
Eastman Roger	Stanbrook & Henderson, London	0171 353 0101
	2 Harcourt Buildings, London	0171 583 9020
Eccles Hugh William Patrick	Harcourt Chambers, London	0171 353 6961/7
	Harcourt Chambers, Oxford	01865 791559
Edwards Anthony Howard	Oriel Chambers, Liverpool	0151 236 7191
Ekins Charles Wareing		
Ewins Miss Catherine Jane	4 Paper Buildings, London	0171 353 3366/583 7155
Exall Gordon David	Chambers of Andrew Campbell QC, Leeds	0113 245 5438
Eyre Giles Stephen	2 Gray's Inn Square Chambers, London	0171 242 0328/405 1317
Faulks Edward Peter Lawless	No 1 Serjeants' Inn, London	0171 415 6666
Finlay Darren	Sovereign Chambers, Leeds	0113 245 1841/2/3
Fisher David	5 Bell Yard, London	0171 333 8811
Ford Gerard James	Baker Street Chambers, Middlesbrough	01642 873873
Formby Ms Emily Jane	Hardwicke Building, London	0171 242 2523
Forster Brian Clive	Trinity Chambers, Newcastle upon Tyne	0191 232 1927
Foster Charles Andrew	• Chambers of Kieran Coonan QC, London	0171 583 6013/2510
Foster Francis Alexander	St Paul's House, Leeds	0113 245 5866
Franklin Stephen Hall	5 Paper Buildings, London	0171 583 6117
	Fenners Chambers, Cambridge	01223 368761
Gabb Charles Henry Escott	Pump Court Chambers, London	0171 353 0711
	Pump Court Chambers, Winchester	01962 868161
Gadney George Munro	Two Crown Office Row, London	0171 797 8100
Gallagher John David Edmund	Goldsmith Building, London	0171 353 7881

B

• Expanded entry in Part D

Gibson Charles Anthony Warneford	2 Harcourt Buildings, London	0171 583 9020
Gilmour Nigel Benjamin Douglas	Peel House Chambers, Liverpool	0151 236 4321
Gilroy Paul	Farrar's Building, London	0171 583 9241
	Chambers of John Hand QC, Manchester	0161 955 9000
Godfrey Jonathan Saul	St Paul's House, Leeds	0113 245 5866
Goff Anthony Thomas	25–27 Castle Street, Liverpool	0151 227 5661/5666/236 5072
Goose Julian Nicholas	Chambers of Andrew Campbell QC, Leeds	0113 245 5438
Gorna Miss Anne Christina	4 Paper Buildings, London	0171 353 3366/583 7155
	Cathedral Chambers (Jan Wood Independent Barristers' Clerk), Exeter	01392 210900
Gough Miss Katherine Mary	Lamb Chambers, London	0171 797 8300
Grace John Oliver Bowman	3 Serjeants' Inn, London	0171 353 5537
Grace Jonathan Robert	Deans Court Chambers, Manchester	0161 834 4097
	Deans Court Chambers, Preston	01772 555163
Grayson Edward	• 9–12 Bell Yard, London	0171 400 1800
Greenbourne John Hugo	Two Crown Office Row, London	0171 797 8100
Gregory Richard Hamilton	Harcourt Chambers, London	0171 353 6961/7
Griffiths (John) Peter (Gwynne)	30 Park Place, Cardiff	01222 398421
Grodzinski Samuel Marc	39 Essex Street, London	0171 832 1111
Grundy Nigel Lawrence John	Chambers of John Hand QC, Manchester	0161 955 9000
Gulliver Miss Alison Louise	• 4 Paper Buildings, London	0171 353 3366/583 7155
Gumbel Miss Elizabeth Anne	199 Strand, London	0171 379 9779
Hall David Percy	9 Woodhouse Square, Leeds	0113 245 1986
Hamer Michael Howard Kenneth	2 Harcourt Buildings, London	0171 583 9020
	Westgate Chambers, Lewes	01273 480 510
Hamilton Graeme Montagu	Two Crown Office Row, London	0171 797 8100
Hand John Lester	Old Square Chambers, London	0171 269 0300
	Old Square Chambers, Bristol	0117 927 7111
	Chambers of John Hand QC, Manchester	0161 955 9000
Hargrove Jeremy John Loveday	Trinity Chambers, Newcastle upon Tyne	0191 232 1927
Harpwood Mrs Vivienne Margaret	30 Park Place, Cardiff	01222 398421
Harrap Giles Thresher	• Pump Court Chambers, London	0171 353 0711
	• Pump Court Chambers, Winchester	01962 868161
Harrison John Foster	St Paul's House, Leeds	0113 245 5866
Harrison Michael Thomas	199 Strand, London	0171 379 9779
Harvey Jonathan Robert William	2 Harcourt Buildings, London	0171 583 9020
Harvey Michael Llewellyn Tucker	Two Crown Office Row, London	0171 797 8100
Harwood-Stevenson John Francis Richard	9–12 Bell Yard, London	0171 400 1800
	East Anglian Chambers, Norwich	01603 617351
Haslam Andrew Peter	Sovereign Chambers, Leeds	0113 245 1841/2/3
Haven Kevin	2 Gray's Inn Square Chambers, London	0171 242 0328/405 1317
Hayes John Allan	Chambers of Andrew Campbell QC, Leeds	0113 245 5438
Henderson Roger Anthony	Stanbrook & Henderson, London	0171 353 0101
	2 Harcourt Buildings, London	0171 583 9020
Hendy John Giles	Old Square Chambers, London	0171 269 0300
	Old Square Chambers, Bristol	0117 927 7111
Herbert Mrs Rebecca Mary	2 New Street, Leicester	0116 262 5906
Heywood Michael Edmundson	Chambers of Lord Goodhart QC, London	0171 405 5577
	Cobden House Chambers, Manchester	0161 833 6000/6001
Higgins Anthony Paul	Goldsmith Building, London	0171 353 7881
Hill Nicholas Mark	Pump Court Chambers, London	0171 353 0711
	Pump Court Chambers, Winchester	01962 868161
Hill Robert Douglas	Pump Court Chambers, London	0171 353 0711
	Pump Court Chambers, Winchester	01962 868161
Hinchliffe Philip Nicholas	Chambers of John Hand QC, Manchester	0161 955 9000
Hodgson Miss Susan Ann	Two Crown Office Row, London	0171 797 8100
Hogg The Rt Hon Douglas Martin	4 Paper Buildings, London	0171 353 3366/583 7155
	37 Park Square, Leeds	0113 243 9422
Holdsworth James Arthur	Two Crown Office Row, London	0171 797 8100
Hollingworth Peter James Michael	22 Albion Place, Northampton	01604 636271
Hollow Paul John	Fenners Chambers, Cambridge	01223 368761

• Expanded entry in Part D

	Fenners Chambers, Peterborough	01733 562030
Holwill Derek Paul Winsor	4 Paper Buildings, London	0171 353 3366/583 7155
Horlock Timothy John	Chambers of John Hand QC, Manchester	0161 955 9000
Howard Anthony John	Chambers of John Hand QC, Manchester	0161 955 9000
Howard Charles Anthony Frederick	New Court Chambers, London	0171 831 9500
Howard-Jones Miss Sarah Rachel	8 Stone Buildings, London	0171 831 9881
Howarth Simon Stuart	Two Crown Office Row, London	0171 797 8100
Hull Leslie David	Chambers of John Hand QC, Manchester	0161 955 9000
Irving Miss Gillian	Chambers of John Hand QC, Manchester	0161 955 9000
Jackson Anthony Warren	3 Serjeants' Inn, London	0171 353 5537
Jackson Matthew David Everard	4 Paper Buildings, London	0171 353 3366/583 7155
Jackson Simon Malcolm Dermot	Park Court Chambers, Leeds	0113 243 3277
Jenkala Adrian Aleksander	11 Bolt Court, London	0171 353 2300
	Redhill Chambers, Redhill	01737 780781
Jenkins Dr Janet Caroline	Chambers of Kieran Coonan QC, London	0171 583 6013/2510
Jones Miss (Catherine) Charlotte	5 Bell Yard, London	0171 333 8811
Jones Miss Rhiannon	Lamb Chambers, London	0171 797 8300
Jones Rhys Charles Mansel	33 Bedford Row, London	0171 242 6476
Katrak Cyrus Pesi	Gough Square Chambers, London	0171 353 0924
Kealey Simon Thomas	Chambers of Andrew Campbell QC, Leeds	0113 245 5438
Kelly Geoffrey Robert	Pump Court Chambers, London	0171 353 0711
	Pump Court Chambers, Winchester	01962 868161
Kelly Matthias John	Old Square Chambers, London	0171 269 0300
	Old Square Chambers, Bristol	0117 927 7111
Kennedy Christopher Laurence Paul	Chambers of John Hand QC, Manchester	0161 955 9000
Kent Michael Harcourt	Two Crown Office Row, London	0171 797 8100
Khokhar Mushtaq Ahmed	Sovereign Chambers, Leeds	0113 245 1841/2/3
Kimbell John Ashley	5 Bell Yard, London	0171 333 8811
Knott Malcolm Stephen	New Court Chambers, London	0171 831 9500
Lambert Miss Sarah Katrina	1 Crown Office Row, London	0171 797 7500
Leech Brian Walter Thomas	No 1 Serjeants' Inn, London	0171 415 6666
Lehain Philip Peter	199 Strand, London	0171 379 9779
Levene Simon	199 Strand, London	0171 379 9779
Lewis Andrew William	Sovereign Chambers, Leeds	0113 245 1841/2/3
Ley (Nigel) Spencer	Farrar's Building, London	0171 583 9241
Lindsay Crawford Callum Douglas	No 1 Serjeants' Inn, London	0171 415 6666
Little Ian	Chambers of John Hand QC, Manchester	0161 955 9000
Livingstone Simon John	11 Bolt Court, London	0171 353 2300
	Redhill Chambers, Redhill	01737 780781
Lochrane Damien Horatio Ross	Pump Court Chambers, London	0171 353 0711
	Pump Court Chambers, Winchester	01962 868161
Logan Miss Maura	St John's Chambers, Hale Barns	0161 980 7379
Lynagh Richard Dudley	Two Crown Office Row, London	0171 797 8100
Lynch Terry John	22 Albion Place, Northampton	01604 636271
Macpherson Angus John	5 Bell Yard, London	0171 333 8811
Makey Christopher Douglas	Old Square Chambers, London	0171 269 0300
	Old Square Chambers, Bristol	0117 927 7111
Manasse Mrs Anne Katherine	Cathedral Chambers, Newcastle upon Tyne	0191 232 1311
Mangat Dr Tejina Kiran	New Court Chambers, London	0171 831 9500
Marris Miss Sarah Selena Rixar	No 1 Serjeants' Inn, London	0171 415 6666
Marshall Philip Derek	Farrar's Building, London	0171 583 9241
	Iscoed Chambers, Swansea	01792 652988/9/330
Mathews Deni	8 Fountain Court, Birmingham	0121 236 5514
Matthews Dennis Roland	5 Bell Yard, London	0171 333 8811
Maudslay Miss Diana Elizabeth		
May Miss Juliet Mary	3 Verulam Buildings, London	0171 831 8441
McCaul Colin Brownlie	39 Essex Street, London	0171 832 1111
McCluggage Brian Thomas	Chambers of John Hand QC, Manchester	0161 955 9000
McCredie Miss Fionnuala Mary Constance	3 Serjeants' Inn, London	0171 353 5537
McGregor Harvey	4 Paper Buildings, London	0171 353 3366/583 7155
McIvor Ian Walker	334 Deansgate Chambers, Manchester	0161 834 3767

B

McKenna Miss Anna Louise	Queen Elizabeth Building, London	0171 353 7181 (12 lines)
McKeon James Patrick	Peel House Chambers, Liverpool	0151 236 4321
McMinn Miss Valerie Kathleen	Baker Street Chambers, Middlesbrough	01642 873873
McParland Michael Joseph	New Court Chambers, London	0171 831 9500
Meakin Timothy William	Fenners Chambers, Cambridge	01223 368761
	Fenners Chambers, Peterborough	01733 562030
Melville Richard David	39 Essex Street, London	0171 832 1111
Menzies Richard Mark	8 Stone Buildings, London	0171 831 9881
Michael Simon Laurence	• Bedford Chambers, Bedford	0870 733 7333
Mishcon Miss Jane Malca	4 Paper Buildings, London	0171 353 3366/583 7155
Moat Frank Robert	Pump Court Chambers, London	0171 353 0711
	Pump Court Chambers, Winchester	01962 868161
Mondair Rashpal Singh	Claremont Chambers, Wolverhampton	01902 426222
Moon Philip Charles Angus	3 Serjeants' Inn, London	0171 353 5537
Morris-Coole Christopher	Goldsmith Building, London	0171 353 7881
Moses Miss Rebecca	Barristers' Common Law Chambers, London	0171 375 3012
	Lion Court, London	0171 404 6565
Mulcahy Miss Leigh-Ann Maria	Two Crown Office Row, London	0171 797 8100
Murray Ashley Charles	Oriel Chambers, Liverpool	0151 236 7191
Newman Austin Eric	9 Woodhouse Square, Leeds	0113 245 1986
Noble Andrew	Eldon Chambers, London	0171 353 4636
	Merchant Chambers, Manchester	0161 839 7070
Norie-Miller Jeffrey Reginald	55 Temple Chambers, London	0171 353 7400
O'Connor Andrew McDougal	Two Crown Office Row, London	0171 797 8100
Okoye Miss Joy Nwamala	Chambers of Joy Okoye, London	0171 405 7011
Ong Miss Grace Yu Mae	One Essex Court, London	0171 936 3030
Ough Dr Richard Norman	• Hardwicke Building, London	0171 242 2523
Outhwaite Mrs Wendy-Jane Tivnan	Stanbrook & Henderson, London	0171 353 0101
	2 Harcourt Buildings, London	0171 583 9020
Palmer James Savill	2 Harcourt Buildings, London	0171 583 9020
Paneth Miss Sarah Ruth	No 1 Serjeants' Inn, London	0171 415 6666
Parker John	2 Mitre Court Buildings, London	0171 353 1353
Perks Richard Howard	St Philip's Chambers, Birmingham	0121 246 7000
Pershad Rohan	Two Crown Office Row, London	0171 797 8100
Pickford Anthony James	Prince Henry's Chambers, London	0171 353 1183/1190
Picton Julian Mark	4 Paper Buildings, London	0171 353 3366/583 7155
Pinder Miss Mary Elizabeth	No 1 Serjeants' Inn, London	0171 415 6666
Pittaway David Michael	No 1 Serjeants' Inn, London	0171 415 6666
Pollock Dr Evelyn Marian Margaret	5 Essex Court, London	0171 410 2000
Pooles Michael Philip Holmes	4 Paper Buildings, London	0171 353 3366/583 7155
Portnoy Leslie Reuben	Chambers of John Hand QC, Manchester	0161 955 9000
Powell Miss Debra Ann	3 Serjeants' Inn, London	0171 353 5537
Pratt Allan Duncan	New Court Chambers, London	0171 831 9500
Prynne Andrew Geoffrey Lockyer	Stanbrook & Henderson, London	0171 353 0101
	2 Harcourt Buildings, London	0171 583 9020
Pulman George Frederick	• Hardwicke Building, London	0171 242 2523
	• Stour Chambers, Canterbury	01227 764899
Purchas Christopher Patrick Brooks	Two Crown Office Row, London	0171 797 8100
Rahman Muhammad Altafur	Barristers' Common Law Chambers, London	0171 375 3012
Rahman Ms Sadeqa Shaheen	1 Crown Office Row, London	0171 797 7500
Rankin William Peter	Oriel Chambers, Liverpool	0151 236 7191
Rea Miss Karen Marie-Jeanne	No 1 Serjeants' Inn, London	0171 415 6666
Readhead Simon John Howard	No 1 Serjeants' Inn, London	0171 415 6666
Rigby Terence	Chambers of John Hand QC, Manchester	0161 955 9000
Rigney Andrew James	Two Crown Office Row, London	0171 797 8100
Ritchie Andrew George	9 Gough Square, London	0171 353 5371
Ritchie Miss Jean Harris	4 Paper Buildings, London	0171 353 3366/583 7155
Rivalland Marc-Edouard	No 1 Serjeants' Inn, London	0171 415 6666
Robertson Ms Alice Michelle	Chambers of Kieran Coonan QC, London	0171 583 6013/2510
Robertson Andrew James	11 King's Bench Walk, London	0171 353 3337/8
	11 King's Bench Walk, Leeds	0113 2971 200
Rogers Paul John	1 Crown Office Row, London	0171 797 7500
	Crown Office Row Chambers, Brighton	01273 625625
Room Stewart	8 Stone Buildings, London	0171 831 9881
Ross John Graffin	No 1 Serjeants' Inn, London	0171 415 6666

• Expanded entry in Part D

Russell Robert John Finlay	5 Bell Yard, London	0171 333 8811
Ryan David Patrick	Chambers of Geoffrey Hawker, London	0171 583 8899
Sadd Patrick James Thomas	199 Strand, London	0171 379 9779
Sampson Graeme William	Chambers of Geoffrey Hawker, London	0171 583 8899
Samuels Leslie John	Pump Court Chambers, London	0171 353 0711
	Pump Court Chambers, Winchester	01962 868161
Sarony Neville Leslie		
Saunt Thomas William Gatty	Two Crown Office Row, London	0171 797 8100
Saxton Miss Nicola Helen	St Paul's House, Leeds	0113 245 5866
Schooling Simon John	Chambers of Harjit Singh, London	0171 353 1356
Scutt David Robert	11 Bolt Court, London	0171 353 2300
	Redhill Chambers, Redhill	01737 780781
Shay Stephen Everett	One King's Bench Walk, London	0171 936 1500
Shorrock John Michael	Peel Court Chambers, Manchester	0161 832 3791
Silvester Bruce Ross	Lamb Chambers, London	0171 797 8300
Smith Warwick Timothy Cresswell	• Deans Court Chambers, Manchester	0161 834 4097
	• Deans Court Chambers, Preston	01772 555163
Snowden John Stevenson	Two Crown Office Row, London	0171 797 8100
Somerset-Jones Miss Felicity	Oriel Chambers, Liverpool	0151 236 7191
Soole Michael Alexander	5 Bell Yard, London	0171 333 8811
Spain Timothy Harrisson	Trinity Chambers, Newcastle upon Tyne	0191 232 1927
Spencer James	11 King's Bench Walk, London	0171 353 3337/8
	11 King's Bench Walk, Leeds	0113 2971 200
Spencer Martin Benedict	4 Paper Buildings, London	0171 353 3366/583 7155
Staite Miss Sara Elizabeth	Stanbrook & Henderson, London	0171 353 0101
	2 Harcourt Buildings, London	0171 583 9020
Starks Nicholas Ernshaw	8 Fountain Court, Birmingham	0121 236 5514
Stead Miss Kate Rebecca	Barristers' Common Law Chambers, London	0171 375 3012
Stemmer-Baldwin Marcus Stephen	8 Stone Buildings, London	0171 831 9881
Stern Dr Kristina Anne	39 Essex Street, London	0171 832 1111
Stevenson John Melford	Two Crown Office Row, London	0171 797 8100
Stewart Mark Courtney	College Chambers, Southampton	01703 230338
Stewart Richard Paul	New Court Chambers, London	0171 831 9500
Stockdale David Andrew	9 Bedford Row, London	0171 242 3555
	Deans Court Chambers, Manchester	0161 834 4097
	Deans Court Chambers, Preston	01772 555163
Storey Jeremy Brian	4 Pump Court, London	0171 353 2656/9
Swan Ian Christopher	Two Crown Office Row, London	0171 797 8100
Taylor Miss Deborah Frances	Two Crown Office Row, London	0171 797 8100
Taylor Michael Richard	Park Court Chambers, Leeds	0113 243 3277
Taylor Simon Wheldon	• Cloisters, London	0171 827 4000
Temple Anthony Dominic	4 Pump Court, London	0171 353 2656/9
Tillett Michael Burn	39 Essex Street, London	0171 832 1111
Trotman Timothy Oliver	Deans Court Chambers, Manchester	0161 834 4097
	Deans Court Chambers, Preston	01772 555163
Tucker David William	Two Crown Office Row, London	0171 797 8100
Valks Michael	King's Chambers, Eastbourne	01323 416053
Waddington Nigel William James	8 Stone Buildings, London	0171 831 9881
Wadsworth James Patrick	4 Paper Buildings, London	0171 353 3366/583 7155
Wakefield Miss Anne Prudence	3 Verulam Buildings, London	0171 831 8441
Waley Eric Richard Thomas	Assize Court Chambers, Bristol	0117 926 4587
Walker Miss Jane	Chambers of John Hand QC, Manchester	0161 955 9000
Ward Ms Orla Mary	3 Serjeants' Inn, London	0171 353 5537
Warrender Miss Nichola Mary	New Court Chambers, London	0171 831 9500
Waters Julian William Penrose	No 1 Serjeants' Inn, London	0171 415 6666
Webb Robert Stopford	• 5 Bell Yard, London	0171 333 8811
Weddle Steven Edgar	Hardwicke Building, London	0171 242 2523
Welchman Charles Stuart	199 Strand, London	0171 379 9779
West Lawrence Joseph	Stanbrook & Henderson, London	0171 353 0101
	2 Harcourt Buildings, London	0171 583 9020
Weston Clive Aubrey Richard	Two Crown Office Row, London	0171 797 8100
White Peter-John Spencer	Pembroke House, Leatherhead	01372 376160/376493
Whitfield Adrian	3 Serjeants' Inn, London	0171 353 5537
Wignall Edward Gordon	• 1 Dr Johnson's Buildings, London	0171 353 9328
	• Dr Johnson's Chambers, Reading	01189 254221
Wilby David Christopher	• 199 Strand, London	0171 379 9779
	• Park Lane Chambers, Leeds	0113 228 5000

B

• Expanded entry in Part D

Wilkinson Nigel Vivian Marshall	Two Crown Office Row, London	0171 797 8100
Willer Robert Michael	Hardwicke Building, London	0171 242 2523
Williams Hugh David Haydn	St Philip's Chambers, Birmingham	0121 246 7000
Williams The Hon John Melville	• Old Square Chambers, London	0171 269 0300
	• Old Square Chambers, Bristol	0117 927 7111
Wilson Peter Julian		
Wood Simon Edward	Plowden Buildings, London	0171 583 0808
	Trinity Chambers, Newcastle upon Tyne	0191 232 1927
Woolf Eliot Charles Anthony	199 Strand, London	0171 379 9779
Wright Gerard Henry	25-27 Castle Street, Liverpool	0151 227 5661/5666/236 5072
Wright Norman Alfred	Oriel Chambers, Liverpool	0151 236 7191
Yell Nicholas Anthony	No 1 Serjeants' Inn, London	0171 415 6666
Yelton Michael Paul	Fenners Chambers, Cambridge	01223 368761
	Fenners Chambers, Peterborough	01733 562030

MENTAL HEALTH

Adejumo Mrs Hilda Ekpo	• Temple Chambers, London	0171 583 1001 (2 lines)
Al'Hassan Khadim	Equity Chambers, Birmingham	0121 233 2100
Beasley-Murray Mrs Caroline Wynne	Fenners Chambers, Cambridge	01223 368761
	Fenners Chambers, Peterborough	01733 562030
Boyd Phillip Joseph George	Lincoln House Chambers, Manchester	0161 832 5701
Brahams Mrs Diana Joyce	Old Square Chambers, London	0171 269 0300
	Old Square Chambers, Bristol	0117 927 7111
Brook Ian Stuart	Hardwicke Building, London	0171 242 2523
Campbell Miss Alexis Anne	Hardwicke Building, London	0171 242 2523
Candlin James Richard	Chambers of Geoffrey Hawker, London	0171 583 8899
Crossley Simon Justin	9 Woodhouse Square, Leeds	0113 245 1986
Curwen Michael Jonathan	Chambers of Kieran Coonan QC, London	0171 583 6013/2510
Dean Paul Benjamin	5 Bell Yard, London	0171 333 8811
Downham Miss Gillian Celia	Rougemont Chambers, Exeter	01392 410471
Fitzgerald Edward Hamilton	Doughty Street Chambers, London	0171 404 1313
Forster Ms Sarah Judith	14 Gray's Inn Square, London	0171 242 0858
	Westgate Chambers, Lewes	01273 480 510
Foster Francis Alexander	St Paul's House, Leeds	0113 245 5866
Godfrey Jonathan Saul	St Paul's House, Leeds	0113 245 5866
Gordon Miss Catherine Anne	140 Cholmeley Road, Reading	01734 665174
Gordon Richard John Francis	39 Essex Street, London	0171 832 1111
Grace John Oliver Bowman	3 Serjeants' Inn, London	0171 353 5537
Grey Miss Eleanor Mary Grace	39 Essex Street, London	0171 832 1111
Harrison John Foster	St Paul's House, Leeds	0113 245 5866
Hillier Andrew Charles	5 Bell Yard, London	0171 333 8811
Irving Miss Gillian	Chambers of John Hand QC, Manchester	0161 955 9000
Jackson Anthony Warren	3 Serjeants' Inn, London	0171 353 5537
Jackson Dirik George Allan	• Chambers of Mr Peter Crampin QC, London	0171 831 0081
King Miss Samantha Leonie	14 Gray's Inn Square, London	0171 242 0858
Kushner Miss Lindsey Joy	14 Gray's Inn Square, London	0171 242 0858
	28 St John Street, Manchester	0161 834 8418
Lieven Ms Nathalie Marie Daniella	4 Breams Buildings, London	0171 353 5835/430 1221
McFarlane Andrew Ewart	One King's Bench Walk, London	0171 936 1500
	Priory Chambers, Birmingham	0121 236 3882/1375
McMinn Miss Valerie Kathleen	Baker Street Chambers, Middlesbrough	01642 873873
Moses Miss Rebecca	Barristers' Common Law Chambers, London	0171 375 3012
	Lion Court, London	0171 404 6565
Moss Peter Jonathan	9-12 Bell Yard, London	0171 400 1800
Ofori George Edward	Chancery Chambers, London	0171 405 6879
	ACHMA Chambers, London	0171 639 7817
Okoye Miss Joy Nwamala	Chambers of Joy Okoye, London	0171 405 7011
Oliver Michael Richard	Hardwicke Building, London	0171 242 2523
Powell Miss Debra Ann	3 Serjeants' Inn, London	0171 353 5537
Rahman Ms Sadeqa Shaheen	1 Crown Office Row, London	0171 797 7500
Richards Miss Jennifer	39 Essex Street, London	0171 832 1111
Ritchie Miss Jean Harris	4 Paper Buildings, London	0171 353 3366/583 7155
Sharland Andrew John	4-5 Gray's Inn Square, London	0171 404 5252
Sidhu-Brar Nisharn Singh	6 Gray's Inn Square, London	0171 242 1052
Singh Balbir	• Equity Chambers, Birmingham	0121 233 2100

         • Expanded entry in Part D

Spain Timothy Harrisson	Trinity Chambers, Newcastle upon Tyne	0191 232 1927
Taylor Simon Wheldon	• Cloisters, London	0171 827 4000
Thorne Timothy Peter	33 Bedford Row, London	0171 242 6476
Vavrecka David Paul Frank	14 Gray's Inn Square, London	0171 242 0858
Wakeham Philip John Le Messurier	Hardwicke Building, London	0171 242 2523
Waley Eric Richard Thomas	Assize Court Chambers, Bristol	0117 926 4587
Wedderspoon Miss Rachel Leone	Chambers of John Hand QC, Manchester	0161 955 9000
Whittam Ms Samantha Abigail	14 Gray's Inn Square, London	0171 242 0858
Wyatt Guy Peter James	Earl Street Chambers, Maidstone	01622 671222

MINING ACCIDENTS

Spencer James	11 King's Bench Walk, London	0171 353 3337/8
	11 King's Bench Walk, Leeds	0113 2971 200

MINING ACCIDENTS/DISEASES

Robertson Andrew James	11 King's Bench Walk, London	0171 353 3337/8
	11 King's Bench Walk, Leeds	0113 2971 200

MINING AND MINERAL

Davidson Edward Alan	• 11 Old Square, London	0171 430 0341

MORTGAGE LAW

Ley (Nigel) Spencer	Farrar's Building, London	0171 583 9241

MORTGAGES & BORROWERS

Cawley Neil Robert Loudoun	55 Temple Chambers, London	0171 353 7400
	Milton Keynes Chambers, Milton Keynes	01908 217857

MOTOR VEHICLES/RACING CARS

Spollon Guy Merton	St Philip's Chambers, Birmingham	0121 246 7000

NATIONAL INSURANCE AND SOCIAL SECURITY

Harris David Raymond	Prince Henry's Chambers, London	0171 353 1183/1190

NEW YORK TRUSTS & ESTATES

Sagar (Edward) Leigh	12 New Square, London	0171 419 1212
	Sovereign Chambers, Leeds	0113 245 1841/2/3
	Newport Chambers, Newport	01633 267403/255855

NOISE INDUCED HEARING LOSS

Collinson Miss Alicia Hester	Harcourt Chambers, London	0171 353 6961/7
	Harcourt Chambers, Oxford	01865 791559

OCCUPATIONAL DISEASE

Cooper Alan George	39 Essex Street, London	0171 832 1111

PARLIAMENTARY

Alesbury Alun	2 Mitre Court Buildings, London	0171 583 1380
Anderson Anthony John	2 Mitre Court Buildings, London	0171 583 1380
Barnes (David) Michael (William)	4 Breams Buildings, London	0171 353 5835/430 1221
Bartlett George Robert	2 Mitre Court Buildings, London	0171 583 1380
Boyle Christopher Alexander David	2 Mitre Court Buildings, London	0171 583 1380
Cameron Neil St Clair	1 Serjeants' Inn, London	0171 583 1355
Cameron Miss Sheila Morag Clark	2 Harcourt Buildings, London	0171 353 8415
Davies Miss Louise	12 New Square, London	0171 419 1212
Dilhorne The Rt Hon Viscount	4 Breams Buildings, London	0171 353 5835/430 1221
Drabble Richard John Bloor	4 Breams Buildings, London	0171 353 5835/430 1221
Edwards Philip Douglas	2 Harcourt Buildings, London	0171 353 8415
FitzGerald Michael Frederick Clive	2 Mitre Court Buildings, London	0171 583 1380
Fookes Robert Lawrence	2 Mitre Court Buildings, London	0171 583 1380
Forsdick David John	4 Breams Buildings, London	0171 353 5835/430 1221
Hargreaves Miss Sara Jane	12 New Square, London	0171 419 1212

	Sovereign Chambers, Leeds	0113 245 1841/2/3
Harwood Richard John	1 Serjeants' Inn, London	0171 583 1355
Henderson Roger Anthony	Stanbrook & Henderson, London	0171 353 0101
	2 Harcourt Buildings, London	0171 583 9020
Hogg The Rt Hon Douglas Martin	4 Paper Buildings, London	0171 353 3366/583 7155
	37 Park Square, Leeds	0113 243 9422
Horton Matthew Bethell	2 Mitre Court Buildings, London	0171 583 1380
Howell John	4 Breams Buildings, London	0171 353 5835/430 1221
Huskinson George Nicholas Nevil	4-5 Gray's Inn Square, London	0171 404 5252
Jones Gregory Percy	• 2 Harcourt Buildings, London	0171 353 8415
King Neil Gerald Alexander	2 Mitre Court Buildings, London	0171 583 1380
Lewis Robert		
Lieven Ms Nathalie Marie Daniella	4 Breams Buildings, London	0171 353 5835/430 1221
Lockhart-Mummery Christopher John	4 Breams Buildings, London	0171 353 5835/430 1221
Macleod Nigel Ronald Buchanan	4 Breams Buildings, London	0171 353 5835/430 1221
	40 King Street, Manchester	0161 832 9082
Macpherson The Hon Mary Stewart	2 Mitre Court Buildings, London	0171 583 1380
McManus Jonathan Richard	4-5 Gray's Inn Square, London	0171 404 5252
Moriarty Gerald Evelyn	2 Mitre Court Buildings, London	0171 583 1380
Newcombe Andrew Bennett	• 2 Harcourt Buildings, London	0171 353 8415
Purchas Robin Michael	• 2 Harcourt Buildings, London	0171 353 8415
Read Lionel Frank	1 Serjeants' Inn, London	0171 583 1355
Roots Guy Robert Godfrey	2 Mitre Court Buildings, London	0171 583 1380
Stone Gregory	• 4-5 Gray's Inn Square, London	0171 404 5252
Thomas Miss Megan Moira	1 Serjeants' Inn, London	0171 583 1355
Village Peter Malcolm	• 4-5 Gray's Inn Square, London	0171 404 5252
Whybrow Christopher John	1 Serjeants' Inn, London	0171 583 1355
Widdicombe David Graham	2 Mitre Court Buildings, London	0171 583 1380
Woolley David Rorie	• 1 Serjeants' Inn, London	0171 583 1355

PARTNERSHIPS

Adamyk Simon Charles	12 New Square, London	0171 419 1212
Airey Simon Andrew	11 Bolt Court, London	0171 353 2300
	Redhill Chambers, Redhill	01737 780781
Al'Hassan Khadim	Equity Chambers, Birmingham	0121 233 2100
Amin Miss Farah	7 New Square, London	0171 430 1660
Asplin Miss Sarah Jane	• 3 Stone Buildings, London	0171 242 4937/405 8358
Baldwin John Grant	Oriel Chambers, Liverpool	0151 236 7191
Banks Roderick Charles I'Anson	• 48 Bedford Row, London	0171 430 2005
Barber Miss Sally	5 Stone Buildings, London	0171 242 6201
Barker James Sebastian	Enterprise Chambers, London	0171 405 9471
	Enterprise Chambers, Leeds	0113 246 0391
	Enterprise Chambers, Newcastle upon Tyne	0191 222 3344
Barker Simon George Harry	• 13 Old Square, London	0171 404 4800
Barstow Stephen Royden	Harcourt Chambers, London	0171 353 6961/7
	Harcourt Chambers, Oxford	01865 791559
Beal Kieron Conrad	4 Paper Buildings, London	0171 353 3366/583 7155
Beaumont Marc Clifford	• Pump Court Chambers, London	0171 353 0711
	• Harrow-on-the-Hill Chambers, Harrow on the Hill	0181 423 7444
	• Pump Court Chambers, Winchester	01962 868161
	• Windsor Barristers' Chambers, Windsor	01753 648 899
Berkley Michael Stuart	Rougemont Chambers, Exeter	01392 410471
Best Stanley Philip	Bracton Chambers, London	0171 242 4248
	Westgate Chambers, Lewes	01273 480 510
	Barnstaple Chambers, Winkleigh	0183 783763
Bhaloo Miss Zia Kurban	Enterprise Chambers, London	0171 405 9471
	Enterprise Chambers, Leeds	0113 246 0391
	Enterprise Chambers, Newcastle upon Tyne	0191 222 3344
Bird Nigel David	Chambers of John Hand QC, Manchester	0161 955 9000
Birtles William	Old Square Chambers, London	0171 269 0300
	Old Square Chambers, Bristol	0117 927 7111
Blackett-Ord Mark	• 5 Stone Buildings, London	0171 242 6201
Burton Michael John	Littleton Chambers, London	0171 797 8600
Carey Jeremy Reynolds Patrick	Lamb Chambers, London	0171 797 8300
Cawley Neil Robert Loudoun	55 Temple Chambers, London	0171 353 7400

B178

B

	Milton Keynes Chambers, Milton Keynes	01908 217857
Cawson Mark	• 12 New Square, London	0171 419 1212
	• St James's Chambers, Manchester	0161 834 7000
	• Park Lane Chambers, Leeds	0113 228 5000
Charman Andrew Julian	St Philip's Chambers, Birmingham	0121 246 7000
Chivers (Tom) David	Erskine Chambers, London	0171 242 5532
Clarke Miss Anna Victoria	5 Stone Buildings, London	0171 242 6201
Clarke Ian James	Hardwicke Building, London	0171 242 2523
Clegg Sebastian James Barwick	Deans Court Chambers, Manchester	0161 834 4097
Corbett James Patrick	St Philip's Chambers, Birmingham	0121 246 7000
Cranfield Peter Anthony	3 Verulam Buildings, London	0171 831 8441
Crawford Grant	11 Old Square, London	0171 430 0341
Creaner Paul Anthony	15 Winckley Square, Preston	01772 252 828
Cunningham Mark James	13 Old Square, London	0171 404 4800
Darbyshire William Robert	Chambers of John Hand QC, Manchester	0161 955 9000
Davidson Edward Alan	• 11 Old Square, London	0171 430 0341
de Jehan David	St Paul's House, Leeds	0113 245 5866
de Lacy Richard Michael	3 Verulam Buildings, London	0171 831 8441
Dean Brian John Anthony	St Philip's Chambers, Birmingham	0121 246 7000
Dodge Peter Clive	11 Old Square, London	0171 430 0341
Dougherty Nigel Peter	Erskine Chambers, London	0171 242 5532
Dowse John	Chambers of Lord Goodhart QC, London	0171 405 5577
	Chambers of John Hand QC, Manchester	0161 955 9000
Doyle Louis George	Chambers of Andrew Campbell QC, Leeds	0113 245 5438
Elleray Anthony John	• 12 New Square, London	0171 419 1212
	• St James's Chambers, Manchester	0161 834 7000
	• Park Lane Chambers, Leeds	0113 228 5000
Fawls Richard Granville	5 Stone Buildings, London	0171 242 6201
Foster Francis Alexander	St Paul's House, Leeds	0113 245 5866
Francis Edward Gerald Francis	Enterprise Chambers, London	0171 405 9471
	Enterprise Chambers, Leeds	0113 246 0391
	Enterprise Chambers, Newcastle upon Tyne	0191 222 3344
Freedman Sampson Clive	3 Verulam Buildings, London	0171 831 8441
French Richard Anthony Lister	Rougemont Chambers, Exeter	01392 410471
Garcia-Miller Miss Laura	Enterprise Chambers, London	0171 405 9471
	Enterprise Chambers, Leeds	0113 246 0391
	Enterprise Chambers, Newcastle upon Tyne	0191 222 3344
Gerald Nigel Mortimer	Enterprise Chambers, London	0171 405 9471
	Enterprise Chambers, Leeds	0113 246 0391
	Enterprise Chambers, Newcastle upon Tyne	0191 222 3344
Gilbert Ms Julia Jane	Trinity Chambers, Newcastle upon Tyne	0191 232 1927
Gillyon Philip Jeffrey	Erskine Chambers, London	0171 242 5532
Goodhart Lord	Chambers of Lord Goodhart QC, London	0171 405 5577
Graham Thomas Patrick Henry	Lamb Chambers, London	0171 797 8300
Grantham Andrew Timothy	• Deans Court Chambers, Manchester	0161 834 4097
	• Deans Court Chambers, Preston	01772 555163
Gregory John Raymond	Deans Court Chambers, Manchester	0161 834 4097
	Deans Court Chambers, Preston	01772 555163
Griffiths Peter Robert	4 Stone Buildings, London	0171 242 5524
Hall Taylor Alexander Edward	11 Old Square, London	0171 430 0341
Halpern David Anthony	Enterprise Chambers, London	0171 405 9471
	Enterprise Chambers, Leeds	0113 246 0391
	Enterprise Chambers, Newcastle upon Tyne	0191 222 3344
Hansen William Joseph	5 Bell Yard, London	0171 333 8811
Hantusch Robert Anthony	• 3 Stone Buildings, London	0171 242 4937/405 8358
Harbottle Gwilym Thomas	5 New Square, London	0171 404 0404
Hardwick Matthew Richard	Enterprise Chambers, London	0171 405 9471
	Enterprise Chambers, Leeds	0113 246 0391
	Enterprise Chambers, Newcastle upon Tyne	0191 222 3344
Hargreaves Miss Sara Jane	12 New Square, London	0171 419 1212

• Expanded entry in Part D

	Sovereign Chambers, Leeds	0113 245 1841/2/3
Harrison John Foster	St Paul's House, Leeds	0113 245 5866
Harrod Henry Mark	5 Stone Buildings, London	0171 242 6201
Hill Robert Douglas	Pump Court Chambers, London	0171 353 0711
	Pump Court Chambers, Winchester	01962 868161
Holland Charles Christopher	Trinity Chambers, Newcastle upon Tyne	0191 232 1927
Holmes Justin Francis	Chambers of Lord Goodhart QC, London	0171 405 5577
Horspool Anthony Bernard Graeme	Hardwicke Building, London	0171 242 2523
Ife Miss Linden Elizabeth	Enterprise Chambers, London	0171 405 9471
	Enterprise Chambers, Leeds	0113 246 0391
	Enterprise Chambers, Newcastle upon Tyne	0191 222 3344
Jackson Dirik George Allan	• Chambers of Mr Peter Crampin QC, London	0171 831 0081
Jackson Nicholas David Kingsley	The Chambers of Adrian Lyon, Liverpool	0151 236 4421/8240/6757
James Michael Frank	Enterprise Chambers, London	0171 405 9471
	Enterprise Chambers, Leeds	0113 246 0391
	Enterprise Chambers, Newcastle upon Tyne	0191 222 3344
Jarvis John Manners	3 Verulam Buildings, London	0171 831 8441
Jefferies Thomas Robert	Chambers of Lord Goodhart QC, London	0171 405 5577
Jenkala Adrian Aleksander	11 Bolt Court, London	0171 353 2300
	Redhill Chambers, Redhill	01737 780781
Jennings Timothy Robin Finnegan	Enterprise Chambers, London	0171 405 9471
	Enterprise Chambers, Leeds	0113 246 0391
	Enterprise Chambers, Newcastle upon Tyne	0191 222 3344
Johnson Michael Sloan	Chambers of John Hand QC, Manchester	0161 955 9000
Jory Robert John Hugh	Enterprise Chambers, London	0171 405 9471
	Enterprise Chambers, Leeds	0113 246 0391
	Enterprise Chambers, Newcastle upon Tyne	0191 222 3344
Kimbell John Ashley	5 Bell Yard, London	0171 333 8811
Kosmin Leslie Gordon	Erskine Chambers, London	0171 242 5532
Kremen Philip Michael	Hardwicke Building, London	0171 242 2523
Lamont Miss Camilla Rose	Chambers of Lord Goodhart QC, London	0171 405 5577
Landes Miss Anna-Rose	St Philip's Chambers, Birmingham	0121 246 7000
Laughton Samuel Dennis	17 Old Buildings, London	0171 405 9653
Leeming Ian	Lamb Chambers, London	0171 797 8300
	Chambers of John Hand QC, Manchester	0161 955 9000
Levy Benjamin Keith	Enterprise Chambers, London	0171 405 9471
	Enterprise Chambers, Leeds	0113 246 0391
	Enterprise Chambers, Newcastle upon Tyne	0191 222 3344
Levy Robert Stuart	9 Stone Buildings, London	0171 404 5055
	Assize Court Chambers, Bristol	0117 926 4587
Lowenstein Paul David	Littleton Chambers, London	0171 797 8600
Mabb David Michael	Erskine Chambers, London	0171 242 5532
Mann George Anthony	Enterprise Chambers, London	0171 405 9471
	Enterprise Chambers, Leeds	0113 246 0391
	Enterprise Chambers, Newcastle upon Tyne	0191 222 3344
Mauger Miss Claire Shanti Andrea	Enterprise Chambers, London	0171 405 9471
McAllister Miss Elizabeth Ann	Enterprise Chambers, London	0171 405 9471
	Enterprise Chambers, Leeds	0113 246 0391
	Enterprise Chambers, Newcastle upon Tyne	0191 222 3344
McCarthy William	New Bailey Chambers, Preston	01772 258 087
McKinnell Miss Soraya Jane	Enterprise Chambers, London	0171 405 9471
	Enterprise Chambers, Leeds	0113 246 0391
	Enterprise Chambers, Newcastle upon Tyne	0191 222 3344
McQuail Ms Katherine Emma	11 Old Square, London	0171 430 0341
Mendoza Neil David Pereira	Hardwicke Building, London	0171 242 2523
Milligan Iain Anstruther	20 Essex Street, London	0171 583 9294

• Expanded entry in Part D

Mills Simon Thomas	One Essex Court, London	0171 936 3030
Morgan Charles James Arthur	Enterprise Chambers, London	0171 405 9471
	Enterprise Chambers, Leeds	0113 246 0391
	Enterprise Chambers, Newcastle upon Tyne	0191 222 3344
Mullis Anthony Roger	Chambers of Lord Goodhart QC, London	0171 405 5577
Nebhrajani Miss Mel	9 Stone Buildings, London	0171 404 5055
Neville Stephen John	Gough Square Chambers, London	0171 353 0924
Newman Miss Catherine Mary	• 13 Old Square, London	0171 404 4800
Nicholls John Peter	13 Old Square, London	0171 404 4800
Noble Andrew	Eldon Chambers, London	0171 353 4636
	Merchant Chambers, Manchester	0161 839 7070
Norbury Luke Edward	17 Old Buildings, London	0171 405 9653
Norris Alastair Hubert	• 5 Stone Buildings, London	0171 242 6201
	• Southernhay Chambers, Exeter	01392 255777
Ohrenstein Dov	Chambers of Lord Goodhart QC, London	0171 405 5577
Ovey Miss Elizabeth Helen	11 Old Square, London	0171 430 0341
Peacock Ian Christopher	12 New Square, London	0171 419 1212
	Sovereign Chambers, Leeds	0113 245 1841/2/3
Peacocke Mrs Teresa Anne Rosen	Enterprise Chambers, London	0171 405 9471
	Enterprise Chambers, Leeds	0113 246 0391
	Enterprise Chambers, Newcastle upon Tyne	0191 222 3344
Picarda Hubert Alistair Paul	Chambers of Lord Goodhart QC, London	0171 405 5577
Pickering James Patrick	Enterprise Chambers, London	0171 405 9471
	Enterprise Chambers, Leeds	0113 246 0391
	Enterprise Chambers, Newcastle upon Tyne	0191 222 3344
Pimentel Carlos de Serpa Alberto Legg	3 Stone Buildings, London	0171 242 4937/405 8358
Potts James Rupert	Erskine Chambers, London	0171 242 5532
Potts Robin	Erskine Chambers, London	0171 242 5532
Prentice Professor Daniel David	Erskine Chambers, London	0171 242 5532
Pryke Stuart	Trinity Chambers, Newcastle upon Tyne	0191 232 1927
Rahman Muhammad Altafur	Barristers' Common Law Chambers, London	0171 375 3012
Randall John Yeoman	7 Stone Buildings, London	0171 405 3886/242 3546
	St Philip's Chambers, Birmingham	0121 246 7000
Richards David Anthony Stewart	Erskine Chambers, London	0171 242 5532
Roberts Miss Catherine Ann	Erskine Chambers, London	0171 242 5532
Robson John Malcolm	2 Gray's Inn Square Chambers, London	0171 242 0328/405 1317
	Assize Court Chambers, Bristol	0117 926 4587
Ross Martyn John Greaves	• 5 New Square, London	0171 404 0404
	• Octagon House, Norwich	01603 623186
Rowell David Stewart	Chambers of Lord Goodhart QC, London	0171 405 5577
Rule Jonathan Daniel	Merchant Chambers, Manchester	0161 839 7070
Ryan David Patrick	Chambers of Geoffrey Hawker, London	0171 583 8899
Sampson Graeme William	Chambers of Geoffrey Hawker, London	0171 583 8899
Selway Dr Katherine Emma	11 Old Square, London	0171 430 0341
Shah Bajul Amratlal Somchand	Twenty-Four Old Buildings, London	0171 404 0946
Singh Balbir	• Equity Chambers, Birmingham	0121 233 2100
Sisley Timothy Julian Crispin	9 Stone Buildings, London	0171 404 5055
	Westgate Chambers, Lewes	01273 480 510
Snowden Richard Andrew	Erskine Chambers, London	0171 242 5532
Staddon Miss Claire Ann	12 New Square, London	0171 419 1212
	Sovereign Chambers, Leeds	0113 245 1841/2/3
Stevens-Hoare Miss Michelle	• Hardwicke Building, London	0171 242 2523
Stewart Alexander Joseph	5 New Square, London	0171 404 0404
Stewart Nicholas John Cameron	Hardwicke Building, London	0171 242 2523
Stokes Miss Mary Elizabeth	Erskine Chambers, London	0171 242 5532
Sugar Simon Gareth	5 New Square, London	0171 404 0404
Sunnucks James Horace George	• 5 New Square, London	0171 404 0404
	• Octagon House, Norwich	01603 623186
Sutcliffe Andrew Harold Wentworth	3 Verulam Buildings, London	0171 831 8441

• Expanded entry in Part D

Tedd Rex Hilary	• St Philip's Chambers, Birmingham	0121 246 7000
	• 22 Albion Place, Northampton	01604 636271
Thompson Andrew Richard	Erskine Chambers, London	0171 242 5532
Thompson Steven Lim	Twenty-Four Old Buildings, London	0171 404 0946
Thornton Andrew James	Erskine Chambers, London	0171 242 5532
Tipples Miss Amanda Jane	13 Old Square, London	0171 404 4800
Trace Anthony John	• 13 Old Square, London	0171 404 4800
Vane The Hon Christopher John Fletcher	Trinity Chambers, Newcastle upon Tyne	0191 232 1927
West Mark	• 11 Old Square, London	0171 430 0341
Williamson Miss Bridget Susan	Enterprise Chambers, London	0171 405 9471
	Enterprise Chambers, Leeds	0113 246 0391
	Enterprise Chambers, Newcastle upon Tyne	0191 222 3344
Wright Robert Anthony Kent	Erskine Chambers, London	0171 242 5532
Zelin Geoffrey Andrew	Enterprise Chambers, London	0171 405 9471
	Enterprise Chambers, Leeds	0113 246 0391
	Enterprise Chambers, Newcastle upon Tyne	0191 222 3344

PASSING OFF

Hodgson Richard Andrew	New Court, London	0171 797 8999
Norris Andrew James Steedsman	5 New Square, London	0171 404 0404

PATENTS

Colley Dr Peter McLean	• 19 Old Buildings, London	0171 405 2001
Driscoll Miss Lynn	Sovereign Chambers, Leeds	0113 245 1841/2/3
	Lancaster Buildings, Manchester	0161 661 4444
Fitzgerald John Vincent	New Court, London	0171 797 8999
Harvey Miss Jayne Denise	Goldsworth Chambers, London	0171 405 7117
Henderson Roger Anthony	Stanbrook & Henderson, London	0171 353 0101
	2 Harcourt Buildings, London	0171 583 9020
Hicks Michael Charles	• 19 Old Buildings, London	0171 405 2001
Hodgson Richard Andrew	New Court, London	0171 797 8999
Holman Miss Tamsin Perdita	19 Old Buildings, London	0171 405 2001
Kime Matthew Jonathan	• New Court, London	0171 797 8999
	• Cobden House Chambers, Manchester	0161 833 6000/6001
Norris Andrew James Steedsman	5 New Square, London	0171 404 0404
Ogunbiyi Oluwole Afolabi	Horizon Chambers, London	0171 242 2440
Pickford Anthony James	Prince Henry's Chambers, London	0171 353 1183/1190
Puckrin Cedric Eldred	19 Old Buildings, London	0171 405 2001
Reid Brian Christopher	19 Old Buildings, London	0171 405 2001
Shipley Norman Graham	• 19 Old Buildings, London	0171 405 2001
Silverleaf Michael	• 11 South Square, London	0171 405 1222
Sullivan Rory Myles	19 Old Buildings, London	0171 405 2001
Wilson Alastair James Drysdale	• 19 Old Buildings, London	0171 405 2001

PENSIONS

Angus Miss Tracey Anne	5 Stone Buildings, London	0171 242 6201
Asplin Miss Sarah Jane	• 3 Stone Buildings, London	0171 242 4937/405 8358
Burroughs Nigel Alfred	11 Old Square, London	0171 430 0341
Campbell Miss Alexis Anne	Hardwicke Building, London	0171 242 2523
Cawley Neil Robert Loudoun	55 Temple Chambers, London	0171 353 7400
	Milton Keynes Chambers, Milton Keynes	01908 217857
Clarke Miss Anna Victoria	5 Stone Buildings, London	0171 242 6201
Cranfield Peter Anthony	3 Verulam Buildings, London	0171 831 8441
Deacock Adam Jason	Chambers of Lord Goodhart QC, London	0171 405 5577
Dodge Peter Clive	11 Old Square, London	0171 430 0341
Dowse John	Chambers of Lord Goodhart QC, London	0171 405 5577
	Chambers of John Hand QC, Manchester	0161 955 9000
Doyle Louis George	Chambers of Andrew Campbell QC, Leeds	0113 245 5438
Fricker Mrs Marilyn Ann	Farrar's Building, London	0171 583 9241
	Sovereign Chambers, Leeds	0113 245 1841/2/3
Gibaud Miss Catherine Alison Annetta	3 Verulam Buildings, London	0171 831 8441

                         • Expanded entry in Part D

Gilbertson Mrs Helen Alison	Sackville Chambers, Norwich	01603 613516
Goodhart Lord	Chambers of Lord Goodhart QC, London	0171 405 5577
Hall Taylor Alexander Edward	11 Old Square, London	0171 430 0341
Halpern David Anthony	Enterprise Chambers, London	0171 405 9471
	Enterprise Chambers, Leeds	0113 246 0391
	Enterprise Chambers, Newcastle upon Tyne	0191 222 3344
Hayes Miss Josephine Mary	Chambers of Lord Goodhart QC, London	0171 405 5577
Henderson Launcelot Dinadan James	• 5 Stone Buildings, London	0171 242 6201
Herbert Mark Jeremy	• 5 Stone Buildings, London	0171 242 6201
Hill Raymond	Monckton Chambers, London	0171 405 7211
Humberstone Mrs Pearl Edith	Verulam Chambers, London	0171 813 2400
Jackson Dirik George Allan	• Chambers of Mr Peter Crampin QC, London	0171 831 0081
Jones Geraint Martyn	Fenners Chambers, Cambridge	01223 368761
	Fenners Chambers, Peterborough	01733 562030
Lamont Miss Camilla Rose	Chambers of Lord Goodhart QC, London	0171 405 5577
Legge Henry	5 Stone Buildings, London	0171 242 6201
Mann George Anthony	Enterprise Chambers, London	0171 405 9471
	Enterprise Chambers, Leeds	0113 246 0391
	Enterprise Chambers, Newcastle upon Tyne	0191 222 3344
Marten Richard Hedley Westwood	Chambers of Lord Goodhart QC, London	0171 405 5577
McQuail Ms Katherine Emma	11 Old Square, London	0171 430 0341
Norris Alastair Hubert	• 5 Stone Buildings, London	0171 242 6201
	• Southernhay Chambers, Exeter	01392 255777
Oakley Tony	• 11 Old Square, London	0171 430 0341
Ovey Miss Elizabeth Helen	11 Old Square, London	0171 430 0341
Paines Nicholas Paul Billot	Monckton Chambers, London	0171 405 7211
Pryke Stuart	Trinity Chambers, Newcastle upon Tyne	0191 232 1927
Rees David Benjamin	5 Stone Buildings, London	0171 242 6201
Rich Miss Ann Barbara	5 Stone Buildings, London	0171 242 6201
Robinson Richard John	2 Gray's Inn Square Chambers, London	0171 242 0328/405 1317
Ross Martyn John Greaves	• 5 New Square, London	0171 404 0404
	• Octagon House, Norwich	01603 623186
Simmonds Andrew John	5 Stone Buildings, London	0171 242 6201
Stagg Paul Andrew	No 1 Serjeants' Inn, London	0171 415 6666
Thomas Stephen Edward Owen	St Philip's Chambers, Birmingham	0121 246 7000
Tidmarsh Christopher Ralph Francis	5 Stone Buildings, London	0171 242 6201
Walker Andrew Greenfield	Chambers of Lord Goodhart QC, London	0171 405 5577
Wallington Peter Thomas	11 King's Bench Walk, London	0171 632 8500
Warnock-Smith Mrs Shan	5 Stone Buildings, London	0171 242 6201
Zelin Geoffrey Andrew	Enterprise Chambers, London	0171 405 9471
	Enterprise Chambers, Leeds	0113 246 0391
	Enterprise Chambers, Newcastle upon Tyne	0191 222 3344

PERSONAL INJURY

Abbott Francis Arthur	Pump Court Chambers, London	0171 353 0711
	Pump Court Chambers, Winchester	01962 868161
Ahmed Farooq Tahir	8 King Street Chambers, Manchester	0161 834 9560
Al'Hassan Khadim	Equity Chambers, Birmingham	0121 233 2100
Alexander Ian Douglas Gavin	11 Bolt Court, London	0171 353 2300
	Redhill Chambers, Redhill	01737 780781
Alldis Christopher John	Peel House Chambers, Liverpool	0151 236 4321
Alliott George Beckles	2 Harcourt Buildings, London	0171 583 9020
Alomo Richard Olusoji	14 Gray's Inn Square, London	0171 242 0858
Althaus Antony Justin	No 1 Serjeants' Inn, London	0171 415 6666
Ames Geoffrey Alan	29 Bedford Row Chambers, London	0171 831 2626
Andrews Peter John	• 199 Strand, London	0171 379 9779
	• 3 Fountain Court, Birmingham	0121 236 5854
Anthony Michael Guy	Two Crown Office Row, London	0171 797 8100
Archer John Francis Ashweek	Two Crown Office Row, London	0171 797 8100
Ashley Mark Robert	Tindal Chambers, Chelmsford	01245 267742

	Tindal Chambers, St Albans	01727 843383
Ashworth Piers	Stanbrook & Henderson, London	0171 353 0101
	2 Harcourt Buildings, London	0171 583 9020
	Priory Chambers, Birmingham	0121 236 3882/1375
Aslett Pepin Charles Maguire	22 Albion Place, Northampton	01604 636271
Asteris Peter David	Eighteen Carlton Crescent, Southampton	01703 639001
Attala Jean Etienne	Cathedral Chambers, Newcastle upon Tyne	0191 232 1311
Aylen Walter Stafford	Hardwicke Building, London	0171 242 2523
Baker Ms Rachel Mary Theresa	Hardwicke Building, London	0171 242 2523
Baldwin John Grant	Oriel Chambers, Liverpool	0151 236 7191
Ball Steven James	Earl Street Chambers, Maidstone	01622 671222
Barlow Miss Sarah Helen	St Paul's House, Leeds	0113 245 5866
Barnett Andrew John	Pump Court Chambers, London	0171 353 0711
	Pump Court Chambers, Winchester	01962 868161
Barstow Stephen Royden	Harcourt Chambers, London	0171 353 6961/7
	Harcourt Chambers, Oxford	01865 791559
Bates Alexander Andrew	St Paul's House, Leeds	0113 245 5866
Battcock Benjamin George	Stanbrook & Henderson, London	0171 353 0101
	2 Harcourt Buildings, London	0171 583 9020
Beal Kieron Conrad	4 Paper Buildings, London	0171 353 3366/583 7155
Beaumont Marc Clifford	• Pump Court Chambers, London	0171 353 0711
	• Harrow-on-the-Hill Chambers, Harrow on the Hill	0181 423 7444
	• Pump Court Chambers, Winchester	01962 868161
	• Windsor Barristers' Chambers, Windsor	01753 648 899
Bedeau Stephen	Sovereign Chambers, Leeds	0113 245 1841/2/3
	Lancaster Buildings, Manchester	0161 661 4444
Beech Ms Jacqueline Elaine	199 Strand, London	0171 379 9779
	York Chambers, York	01904 620 048
Beer Jason Barrington	5 Essex Court, London	0171 410 2000
Belbin Miss Heather Patricia	Oriel Chambers, Liverpool	0151 236 7191
Bendall Richard Giles	33 Bedford Row, London	0171 242 6476
Bennett John Martyn	• Peel House Chambers, Liverpool	0151 236 4321
Benson Julian Christopher Woodburn	One Essex Court, London	0171 936 3030
Bentwood Richard	Chambers of Geoffrey Hawker, London	0171 583 8899
Bergin Timothy William	Sussex Chambers, Brighton	01273 607953
Bhattacharyya Ardhendu	1 Gray's Inn Square, London	0171 405 8946
	11 St Bernards Road, Slough	01753 553806/817989
Bishop Edward James	No 1 Serjeants' Inn, London	0171 415 6666
Blakesley Patrick James	Two Crown Office Row, London	0171 797 8100
Block Neil Selwyn	39 Essex Street, London	0171 832 1111
Bloom-Davis Desmond Niall Laurence	Pump Court Chambers, London	0171 353 0711
	Pump Court Chambers, Winchester	01962 868161
Boney Guy Thomas Knowles	Pump Court Chambers, London	0171 353 0711
	Harrow-on-the-Hill Chambers, Harrow on the Hill	0181 423 7444
	Pump Court Chambers, Winchester	01962 868161
Boora Jinder Singh	Regent Chambers, Stoke-on-Trent	01782 286666
Booth Alan James	Deans Court Chambers, Manchester	0161 834 4097
	Deans Court Chambers, Preston	01772 555163
Boothroyd Miss Susan Elizabeth	Westgate Chambers, Newcastle upon Tyne	0191 261 4407/232 9785
Boydell Edward Patrick Stirrup	Pump Court Chambers, London	0171 353 0711
	Pump Court Chambers, Winchester	01962 868161
Boyle David Stuart	Deans Court Chambers, Manchester	0161 834 4097
Boyle Gerard James	No 1 Serjeants' Inn, London	0171 415 6666
Bradley Miss Clodagh Maria	3 Serjeants' Inn, London	0171 353 5537
Bradley Richard	Oriel Chambers, Liverpool	0151 236 7191
Brahams Mrs Diana Joyce	Old Square Chambers, London	0171 269 0300
	Old Square Chambers, Bristol	0117 927 7111
Braithwaite William Thomas Scatchard	• Two Crown Office Row, London	0171 797 8100
	• Exchange Chambers, Liverpool	0151 236 7747
Brant Paul David	Oriel Chambers, Liverpool	0151 236 7191
Brasse Miss Gillian Denise	14 Gray's Inn Square, London	0171 242 0858
Brazil Dominic Thomas George	14 Gray's Inn Square, London	0171 242 0858

• Expanded entry in Part D

Breen Carlo Enrico	Chambers of John Hand QC, Manchester	0161 955 9000
Brennan Daniel Joseph	39 Essex Street, London	0171 832 1111
	18 St John Street, Manchester	0161 278 1800
Briden Timothy John	• 8 Stone Buildings, London	0171 831 9881
Bright Christopher John	3 Fountain Court, Birmingham	0121 236 5854
Brilliant Simon Howard	Lamb Chambers, London	0171 797 8300
Brotherton John Paul	New Court Chambers, Birmingham	0121 693 6656
Brown (Geoffrey) Charles	39 Essex Street, London	0171 832 1111
Brown Miss Joanne	2 Gray's Inn Square Chambers, London	0171 242 0328/405 1317
Browne James William	Goldsworth Chambers, London	0171 405 7117
Brunner Adrian John Nelson	Stanbrook & Henderson, London	0171 353 0101
	2 Harcourt Buildings, London	0171 583 9020
Brunton Sean Alexander McKay	Pump Court Chambers, London	0171 353 0711
	Pump Court Chambers, Winchester	01962 868161
Bull (Donald) Roger	One Essex Court, London	0171 936 3030
Burles David John	Goldsmith Building, London	0171 353 7881
Burns Peter Richard	Deans Court Chambers, Manchester	0161 834 4097
Bush Keith	30 Park Place, Cardiff	01222 398421
Butler Philip Andrew	Goldsmith Chambers, London	0171 353 6802/3/4/5
	Deans Court Chambers, Manchester	0161 834 4097
	Deans Court Chambers, Preston	01772 555163
Cameron Miss Barbara Alexander	Stanbrook & Henderson, London	0171 353 0101
	2 Harcourt Buildings, London	0171 583 9020
Campbell Oliver Edward Wilhelm	2 Harcourt Buildings, London	0171 583 9020
Candlin James Richard	Chambers of Geoffrey Hawker, London	0171 583 8899
Capon Philip Christopher William	St Philip's Chambers, Birmingham	0121 246 7000
Carlile Alexander Charles	9-12 Bell Yard, London	0171 400 1800
	Sedan House, Chester	01244 320480/348282
Carling Christopher James	Old Square Chambers, London	0171 269 0300
	Old Square Chambers, Bristol	0117 927 7111
Carter Miss Lesley Ann	25-27 Castle Street, Liverpool	0151 227 5661/5666/236 5072
Cartwright Richard John	Queen Elizabeth Building, London	0171 353 7181 (12 lines)
Carville Owen Brendan Neville	25-27 Castle Street, Liverpool	0151 227 5661/5666/236 5072
Cave Jeremy Stephen	1 Crown Office Row, London	0171 797 7500
	Crown Office Row Chambers, Brighton	01273 625625
Cawley Neil Robert Loudoun	55 Temple Chambers, London	0171 353 7400
	Milton Keynes Chambers, Milton Keynes	01908 217857
Chalmers Miss Suzanne Frances	Two Crown Office Row, London	0171 797 8100
Charles Ms Deborah Ann	6 Pump Court, London	0171 797 8400
Cherry John Mitchell	• 8 Stone Buildings, London	0171 831 9881
Christie-Brown Miss Sarah Louise	4 Paper Buildings, London	0171 353 3366/583 7155
Chudleigh Miss Louise Katrina	Old Square Chambers, London	0171 269 0300
	Old Square Chambers, Bristol	0117 927 7111
Clark Christopher Harvey	Pump Court Chambers, London	0171 353 0711
	Westgate Chambers, Lewes	01273 480 510
	Pump Court Chambers, Winchester	01962 868161
Clarke Miss Alison Lee	No 1 Serjeants' Inn, London	0171 415 6666
Clarke George Robert Ivan	Chambers of Geoffrey Hawker, London	0171 583 8899
Clarke Jonathan Christopher St John	Old Square Chambers, London	0171 269 0300
	Old Square Chambers, Bristol	0117 927 7111
Clegg Sebastian James Barwick	Deans Court Chambers, Manchester	0161 834 4097
Collett Ivor William	No 1 Serjeants' Inn, London	0171 415 6666
Collins John Morris	11 King's Bench Walk, London	0171 353 3337/8
	9 Woodhouse Square, Leeds	0113 245 1986
Collinson Miss Alicia Hester	Harcourt Chambers, London	0171 353 6961/7
	Harcourt Chambers, Oxford	01865 791559
Conlin Geoffrey David	3 Serjeants' Inn, London	0171 353 5537
Cooper Alan George	39 Essex Street, London	0171 832 1111
Cooper Roger Bernard	Trinity Chambers, Newcastle upon Tyne	0191 232 1927
Cory-Wright Charles Alexander	39 Essex Street, London	0171 832 1111
Cotter Barry Paul	Old Square Chambers, London	0171 269 0300
	Old Square Chambers, Bristol	0117 927 7111
Cotter Miss Sara Elizabeth	• Higher Combe, Minehead	01643 862722
Cottrell Matthew Robert	Oriel Chambers, Liverpool	0151 236 7191
Coulter Barry John	One Essex Court, London	0171 936 3030

• Expanded entry in Part D

B

Cowan Peter Sherwood McCrea	Oriel Chambers, Liverpool	0151 236 7191
Cowen Miss Sally Emma	Chambers of Geoffrey Hawker, London	0171 583 8899
Cox Bryan Richard	9 Woodhouse Square, Leeds	0113 245 1986
Crane Miss Suzanne Denise	New Court Chambers, Birmingham	0121 693 6656
Crookes Miss Alison Naomi		
Cross Mrs Joanna	9 Woodhouse Square, Leeds	0113 245 1986
Crossley Simon Justin	9 Woodhouse Square, Leeds	0113 245 1986
Crosthwaite Graham Andrew	One King's Bench Walk, London	0171 936 1500
Crowley John Desmond	Two Crown Office Row, London	0171 797 8100
Crowson Howard Keith	St Paul's House, Leeds	0113 245 5866
Curtis Michael Alexander	Two Crown Office Row, London	0171 797 8100
Curwen Michael Jonathan	Chambers of Kieran Coonan QC, London	0171 583 6013/2510
Dallas Andrew Thomas Alastair	Chambers of Andrew Campbell QC, Leeds	0113 245 5438
Davidson Nicholas Ranking	4 Paper Buildings, London	0171 353 3366/583 7155
Davies Andrew	Angel Chambers, Swansea	01792 464623/464648
Davies Richard Llewellyn	39 Essex Street, London	0171 832 1111
Davis William Easthope	St Philip's Chambers, Birmingham	0121 246 7000
Dawes Gordon Stephen Knight	Goldsmith Building, London	0171 353 7881
Dawson James Robert	Oriel Chambers, Liverpool	0151 236 7191
de Jehan David	St Paul's House, Leeds	0113 245 5866
de Voghelaere Parr Adam Stephen	2 Mitre Court Buildings, London	0171 583 1380
Dean Paul Benjamin	5 Bell Yard, London	0171 333 8811
DeCamp Miss Jane Louise	Two Crown Office Row, London	0171 797 8100
Dedezade Taner	Tindal Chambers, Chelmsford	01245 267742
Denney Stuart Henry Macdonald	Deans Court Chambers, Manchester	0161 834 4097
	Deans Court Chambers, Preston	01772 555163
Dixon David Steven	Sovereign Chambers, Leeds	0113 245 1841/2/3
Dixon Ian Frederick	Cathedral Chambers, Newcastle upon Tyne	0191 232 1311
Dixon John Watts	Harcourt Chambers, London	0171 353 6961/7
	Harcourt Chambers, Oxford	01865 791559
Doggart Piers Graham	• King's Chambers, Eastbourne	01323 416053
Doherty Bernard James	39 Essex Street, London	0171 832 1111
Donovan Joel	New Court Chambers, London	0171 831 9500
Dowokpor Jonathan Kukasi	Tollgate Mews Chambers, London	0171 511 1838
Doyle Peter John	9-12 Bell Yard, London	0171 400 1800
Du Cann Christian Dillon Lott	39 Essex Street, London	0171 832 1111
Dubbery Mark Edward	Pump Court Chambers, London	0171 353 0711
Eastman Roger	Stanbrook & Henderson, London	0171 353 0101
	2 Harcourt Buildings, London	0171 583 9020
Eccles Hugh William Patrick	Harcourt Chambers, London	0171 353 6961/7
	Harcourt Chambers, Oxford	01865 791559
Edwards Anthony Howard	Oriel Chambers, Liverpool	0151 236 7191
Egan Eugene Christopher	30 Park Place, Cardiff	01222 398421
Ekins Charles Wareing		
Emanuel Mark Pering Wolff	14 Gray's Inn Square, London	0171 242 0858
Evans Lee John	Farrar's Building, London	0171 583 9241
Evans Miss Lisa Claire	St Philip's Chambers, Birmingham	0121 246 7000
Evans Thomas Gareth	Rougemont Chambers, Exeter	01392 410471
Evans-Tovey Jason Robert	Two Crown Office Row, London	0171 797 8100
Ewins Miss Catherine Jane	4 Paper Buildings, London	0171 353 3366/583 7155
Exall Gordon David	Chambers of Andrew Campbell QC, Leeds	0113 245 5438
Eyre Giles Stephen	2 Gray's Inn Square Chambers, London	0171 242 0328/405 1317
Falk Miss Josephine Ruth Ann	12 Old Square, London	0171 404 0875
Fane Miss Angela Elizabeth	Goldsmith Building, London	0171 353 7881
Farmer Pryce Michael	1 Dr Johnson's Buildings, London	0171 353 9328
	Goldsmith Building, London	0171 353 7881
	Sedan House, Chester	01244 320480/348282
Farquharson Miss Jane Caroline	One Essex Court, London	0171 936 3030
Faulks Edward Peter Lawless	No 1 Serjeants' Inn, London	0171 415 6666
Fenston Miss Felicia Donovan	Stanbrook & Henderson, London	0171 353 0101
	2 Harcourt Buildings, London	0171 583 9020
Ferguson Mrs Katharine Ann	Fenners Chambers, Cambridge	01223 368761
	Fenners Chambers, Peterborough	01733 562030
Finlay Darren	Sovereign Chambers, Leeds	0113 245 1841/2/3
Fletcher Marcus Alexander	One King's Bench Walk, London	0171 936 1500
Forbes Peter George	6 Pump Court, London	0171 797 8400

• Expanded entry in Part D

	6-8 Mill Street, Maidstone	01622 688 094
Ford Gerard James	Baker Street Chambers, Middlesbrough	01642 873873
Formby Ms Emily Jane	Hardwicke Building, London	0171 242 2523
Forster Brian Clive	Trinity Chambers, Newcastle upon Tyne	0191 232 1927
Foster Charles Andrew	• Chambers of Kieran Coonan QC, London	0171 583 6013/2510
Foster Francis Alexander	St Paul's House, Leeds	0113 245 5866
Fox Miss Anna Katherine Helen	Oriel Chambers, Liverpool	0151 236 7191
Foxwell George (Augustus)	Fenners Chambers, Cambridge	01223 368761
	Fenners Chambers, Peterborough	01733 562030
Franck Richard David William	Equity Chambers, Birmingham	0121 233 2100
Franklin Stephen Hall	5 Paper Buildings, London	0171 583 6117
	Fenners Chambers, Cambridge	01223 368761
French Richard Anthony Lister	Rougemont Chambers, Exeter	01392 410471
Friel John Anthony	Goldsmith Building, London	0171 353 7881
	Southsea Chambers, Portsmouth	01705 291261
Frodsham Alexander Miles	Oriel Chambers, Liverpool	0151 236 7191
Gabb Charles Henry Escott	Pump Court Chambers, London	0171 353 0711
	Pump Court Chambers, Winchester	01962 868161
Gadney George Munro	Two Crown Office Row, London	0171 797 8100
Gallagher John David Edmund	Goldsmith Building, London	0171 353 7881
Garside Charles Roger	Chambers of John Hand QC, Manchester	0161 955 9000
Gatty Daniel Simon	New Court Chambers, London	0171 831 9500
Gibson Charles Anthony Warneford	2 Harcourt Buildings, London	0171 583 9020
Gilbertson Mrs Helen Alison	Sackville Chambers, Norwich	01603 613516
Gilmour Nigel Benjamin Douglas	Peel House Chambers, Liverpool	0151 236 4321
Gilroy Paul	Farrar's Building, London	0171 583 9241
	Chambers of John Hand QC, Manchester	0161 955 9000
Gittins Timothy James	Trinity Chambers, Newcastle upon Tyne	0191 232 1927
Glasgow Edwin John	39 Essex Street, London	0171 832 1111
Godfrey Jonathan Saul	St Paul's House, Leeds	0113 245 5866
Godfrey Miss Louise Sarah	14 Gray's Inn Square, London	0171 242 0858
	Park Court Chambers, Leeds	0113 243 3277
Goff Anthony Thomas	25-27 Castle Street, Liverpool	0151 227 5661/5666/236 5072
Goose Julian Nicholas	Chambers of Andrew Campbell QC, Leeds	0113 245 5438
Gore-Andrews Gavin Angus Russell	Stanbrook & Henderson, London	0171 353 0101
	2 Harcourt Buildings, London	0171 583 9020
Gorna Miss Anne Christina	4 Paper Buildings, London	0171 353 3366/583 7155
	Cathedral Chambers (Jan Wood Independent Barristers' Clerk), Exeter	01392 210900
Gough Miss Katherine Mary	Lamb Chambers, London	0171 797 8300
Gower Miss Helen Clare	Old Square Chambers, London	0171 269 0300
	Old Square Chambers, Bristol	0117 927 7111
Grace John Oliver Bowman	3 Serjeants' Inn, London	0171 353 5537
Grace Jonathan Robert	Deans Court Chambers, Manchester	0161 834 4097
	Deans Court Chambers, Preston	01772 555163
Grayson Edward	• 9-12 Bell Yard, London	0171 400 1800
Green Patrick Curtis	Stanbrook & Henderson, London	0171 353 0101
	2 Harcourt Buildings, London	0171 583 9020
Greenan Miss Sarah Octavia	• 9 Woodhouse Square, Leeds	0113 245 1986
Greenbourne John Hugo	Two Crown Office Row, London	0171 797 8100
Gregory Richard Hamilton	Harcourt Chambers, London	0171 353 6961/7
Griffiths (John) Peter (Gwynne)	30 Park Place, Cardiff	01222 398421
Grodzinski Samuel Marc	39 Essex Street, London	0171 832 1111
Gruffydd John	Oriel Chambers, Liverpool	0151 236 7191
Grundy Nicholas John	One Essex Court, London	0171 936 3030
Grundy Nigel Lawrence John	Chambers of John Hand QC, Manchester	0161 955 9000
Guggenheim Miss Anna Maeve	Two Crown Office Row, London	0171 797 8100
Guirguis Miss Sheren	White Friars Chambers, Chester	01244 323070
Gulliver Miss Alison Louise	• 4 Paper Buildings, London	0171 353 3366/583 7155
Gumbel Miss Elizabeth Anne	199 Strand, London	0171 379 9779
Gunther Miss Elizabeth Ann	Pump Court Chambers, London	0171 353 0711
	Pump Court Chambers, Winchester	01962 868161
Hall David Percy	9 Woodhouse Square, Leeds	0113 245 1986

B

Hall-Smith Martin Clive William	Goldsmith Building, London	0171 353 7881
Halpin Thomas Gavin	Earl Street Chambers, Maidstone	01622 671222
Hamer Michael Howard Kenneth	2 Harcourt Buildings, London	0171 583 9020
	Westgate Chambers, Lewes	01273 480 510
Hamilton Graeme Montagu	Two Crown Office Row, London	0171 797 8100
Hammerton Miss Veronica Lesley	No 1 Serjeants' Inn, London	0171 415 6666
Hand John Lester	Old Square Chambers, London	0171 269 0300
	Old Square Chambers, Bristol	0117 927 7111
	Chambers of John Hand QC, Manchester	0161 955 9000
Hargrove Jeremy John Loveday	Trinity Chambers, Newcastle upon Tyne	0191 232 1927
Harpwood Mrs Vivienne Margaret	30 Park Place, Cardiff	01222 398421
Harrap Giles Thresher	• Pump Court Chambers, London	0171 353 0711
	• Pump Court Chambers, Winchester	01962 868161
Harrison Ms Averil	2 Harcourt Buildings, London	0171 583 9020
Harrison John Foster	St Paul's House, Leeds	0113 245 5866
Harrison Michael Thomas	199 Strand, London	0171 379 9779
Harrison Robert John Mackintosh	30 Park Place, Cardiff	01222 398421
Harvey Miss Jayne Denise	Goldsworth Chambers, London	0171 405 7117
Harvey Jonathan Robert William	2 Harcourt Buildings, London	0171 583 9020
Harvey Michael Llewellyn Tucker	Two Crown Office Row, London	0171 797 8100
Harwood-Stevenson John Francis Richard	9-12 Bell Yard, London	0171 400 1800
	East Anglian Chambers, Norwich	01603 617351
Haslam Andrew Peter	Sovereign Chambers, Leeds	0113 245 1841/2/3
Haven Kevin	2 Gray's Inn Square Chambers, London	0171 242 0328/405 1317
Hawkesworth (Walter) Gareth	5 Paper Buildings, London	0171 583 6117
	Fenners Chambers, Cambridge	01223 368761
	Fenners Chambers, Peterborough	01733 562030
Hay Ms Deborah Jane	Goldsmith Building, London	0171 353 7881
Hay Robin William Patrick Hamilton	Goldsmith Building, London	0171 353 7881
Hayes John Allan	Chambers of Andrew Campbell QC, Leeds	0113 245 5438
Heap Gerard Miles	Sovereign Chambers, Leeds	0113 245 1841/2/3
Henderson Lawrence Mark	11 Bolt Court, London	0171 353 2300
	Redhill Chambers, Redhill	01737 780781
Henderson Roger Anthony	Stanbrook & Henderson, London	0171 353 0101
	2 Harcourt Buildings, London	0171 583 9020
Hendy John Giles	Old Square Chambers, London	0171 269 0300
	Old Square Chambers, Bristol	0117 927 7111
Henley Mark Robert Daniel	9 Woodhouse Square, Leeds	0113 245 1986
Herbert Mrs Rebecca Mary	2 New Street, Leicester	0116 262 5906
Heywood Michael Edmundson	Chambers of Lord Goodhart QC, London	0171 405 5577
	Cobden House Chambers, Manchester	0161 833 6000/6001
Higgins Anthony Paul	Goldsmith Building, London	0171 353 7881
Hilder Miss Carolyn Hayley-Jane	3 Fountain Court, Birmingham	0121 236 5854
Hill Nicholas Mark	Pump Court Chambers, London	0171 353 0711
	Pump Court Chambers, Winchester	01962 868161
Hill Robert Douglas	Pump Court Chambers, London	0171 353 0711
	Pump Court Chambers, Winchester	01962 868161
Hinchliffe Philip Nicholas	Chambers of John Hand QC, Manchester	0161 955 9000
Hodgkinson Tristram Patrick	• 5 Pump Court, London	0171 353 2532
Hodgson Miss Susan Ann	Two Crown Office Row, London	0171 797 8100
Hogg The Rt Hon Douglas Martin	4 Paper Buildings, London	0171 353 3366/583 7155
	37 Park Square, Leeds	0113 243 9422
Hogg Miss Katharine Elizabeth	1 Crown Office Row, London	0171 797 7500
Holdsworth James Arthur	Two Crown Office Row, London	0171 797 8100
Hollingworth Peter James Michael	22 Albion Place, Northampton	01604 636271
Hollow Paul John	Fenners Chambers, Cambridge	01223 368761
	Fenners Chambers, Peterborough	01733 562030
Holroyd John James	• 9 Woodhouse Square, Leeds	0113 245 1986
Holwill Derek Paul Winsor	4 Paper Buildings, London	0171 353 3366/583 7155
Horlock Timothy John	Chambers of John Hand QC, Manchester	0161 955 9000
Horton Miss Caroline Ann	Fenners Chambers, Cambridge	01223 368761
	Fenners Chambers, Peterborough	01733 562030
Horwood Miss Anya Louise	25-27 Castle Street, Liverpool	0151 227 5661/5666/236 5072
House James Michael	2 New Street, Leicester	0116 262 5906

• Expanded entry in Part D

Howard Anthony John	Chambers of John Hand QC, Manchester	0161 955 9000
Howard Charles Anthony Frederick	New Court Chambers, London	0171 831 9500
Howard-Jones Miss Sarah Rachel	8 Stone Buildings, London	0171 831 9881
Howarth Simon Stuart	Two Crown Office Row, London	0171 797 8100
Hughes Miss Mary Josephine	Chambers of Lord Goodhart QC, London	0171 405 5577
Hull Leslie David	Chambers of John Hand QC, Manchester	0161 955 9000
Hunter William Quigley	No 1 Serjeants' Inn, London	0171 415 6666
Iqbal Abdul Shaffaq	Chambers of Andrew Campbell QC, Leeds	0113 245 5438
Irving Miss Gillian	Chambers of John Hand QC, Manchester	0161 955 9000
Islam-Choudhury Mugni	11 Bolt Court, London	0171 353 2300
Jackson Anthony Warren	3 Serjeants' Inn, London	0171 353 5537
Jackson Matthew David Everard	4 Paper Buildings, London	0171 353 3366/583 7155
Jackson Simon Malcolm Dermot	Park Court Chambers, Leeds	0113 243 3277
James Roderick Morrice	23 Essex Street, London	0171 413 0353
James Simon John	Chambers of John Hand QC, Manchester	0161 955 9000
Jayanathan Miss Shamini	30 Park Place, Cardiff	01222 398421
Jenkala Adrian Aleksander	11 Bolt Court, London	0171 353 2300
	Redhill Chambers, Redhill	01737 780781
Jenkins Dr Janet Caroline	Chambers of Kieran Coonan QC, London	0171 583 6013/2510
John Peter Charles	One Essex Court, London	0171 936 3030
John Stephen Alun	9-12 Bell Yard, London	0171 400 1800
Jones Miss (Catherine) Charlotte	5 Bell Yard, London	0171 333 8811
Jones Miss Rhiannon	Lamb Chambers, London	0171 797 8300
Jones Rhys Charles Mansel	33 Bedford Row, London	0171 242 6476
Katrak Cyrus Pesi	Gough Square Chambers, London	0171 353 0924
Kealey Simon Thomas	Chambers of Andrew Campbell QC, Leeds	0113 245 5438
Kelly Geoffrey Robert	Pump Court Chambers, London	0171 353 0711
	Pump Court Chambers, Winchester	01962 868161
Kelly Miss Geraldine Therese		
Kelly Matthias John	Old Square Chambers, London	0171 269 0300
	Old Square Chambers, Bristol	0117 927 7111
Kennedy Christopher Laurence Paul	Chambers of John Hand QC, Manchester	0161 955 9000
Kent Miss Georgina	5 Essex Court, London	0171 410 2000
Kent Michael Harcourt	Two Crown Office Row, London	0171 797 8100
Kenward Timothy David Nelson	25-27 Castle Street, Liverpool	0151 227 5661/5666/236 5072
Khan Avicenna Alkindi Cornelius	55 Temple Chambers, London	0171 353 7400
Khan Saadallah Frans Hassan	55 Temple Chambers, London	0171 353 7400
Khokhar Mushtaq Ahmed	Sovereign Chambers, Leeds	0113 245 1841/2/3
Kimbell John Ashley	5 Bell Yard, London	0171 333 8811
Kinch Christopher Anthony	23 Essex Street, London	0171 413 0353
King Peter Duncan	5 Pump Court, London	0171 353 2532
	Fenners Chambers, Cambridge	01223 368761
Kinnier Andrew John	2 Harcourt Buildings, London	0171 583 9020
Knott Malcolm Stephen	New Court Chambers, London	0171 831 9500
Kolodynski Stefan Richard	New Court Chambers, Birmingham	0121 693 6656
Lambert Miss Sarah Katrina	1 Crown Office Row, London	0171 797 7500
Lander Charles Gideon	25-27 Castle Street, Liverpool	0151 227 5661/5666/236 5072
Law John Edward	33 Bedford Row, London	0171 242 6476
Lawrence Miss Rachel Camilla	One Essex Court, London	0171 936 3030
Lawson Daniel George	Goldsmith Building, London	0171 353 7881
Leech Brian Walter Thomas	No 1 Serjeants' Inn, London	0171 415 6666
Lees Andrew James	St Paul's House, Leeds	0113 245 5866
Lehain Philip Peter	199 Strand, London	0171 379 9779
Leigh-Morgan (David) Paul	Fenners Chambers, Cambridge	01223 368761
	Fenners Chambers, Peterborough	01733 562030
Leonard Charles Robert Weston	Goldsmith Building, London	0171 353 7881
Levene Simon	199 Strand, London	0171 379 9779
Lewer Michael Edward	Farrar's Building, London	0171 583 9241
Lewis Andrew William	Sovereign Chambers, Leeds	0113 245 1841/2/3
Lewis Jeffrey Allan	9 Woodhouse Square, Leeds	0113 245 1986
Ley (Nigel) Spencer	Farrar's Building, London	0171 583 9241
Lindsay Crawford Callum Douglas	No 1 Serjeants' Inn, London	0171 415 6666
Linstead Peter James	11 Bolt Court, London	0171 353 2300

Little Ian	Chambers of John Hand QC, Manchester	0161 955 9000
Livingstone Simon John	11 Bolt Court, London	0171 353 2300
	Redhill Chambers, Redhill	01737 780781
Lobo Matthew Joseph Edwin	Fenners Chambers, Cambridge	01223 368761
	Fenners Chambers, Peterborough	01733 562030
Lochrane Damien Horatio Ross	Pump Court Chambers, London	0171 353 0711
	Pump Court Chambers, Winchester	01962 868161
Lodge John Robert	Park Court Chambers, Leeds	0113 243 3277
Loftus Miss Teresa Anne Martine	25-27 Castle Street, Liverpool	0151 227 5661/5666/236 5072
Logan Miss Maura	St John's Chambers, Hale Barns	0161 980 7379
Lumley Nicholas James Henry	Sovereign Chambers, Leeds	0113 245 1841/2/3
Lynagh Richard Dudley	Two Crown Office Row, London	0171 797 8100
Lynch Terry John	22 Albion Place, Northampton	01604 636271
Lyon Stephen John	14 Gray's Inn Square, London	0171 242 0858
	Westgate Chambers, Lewes	01273 480 510
Machell Raymond Donatus	2 Pump Court, London	0171 353 5597
	Deans Court Chambers, Manchester	0161 834 4097
Mackay Colin Crichton	39 Essex Street, London	0171 832 1111
Macpherson Angus John	5 Bell Yard, London	0171 333 8811
Maitland Jones Mark Griffith	Goldsmith Building, London	0171 353 7881
Maitland Marc Claude	11 Old Square, London	0171 242 5022
Makey Christopher Douglas	Old Square Chambers, London	0171 269 0300
	Old Square Chambers, Bristol	0117 927 7111
Malecka Dr Mary Margaret	Goldsworth Chambers, London	0171 405 7117
Manasse Mrs Anne Katherine	Cathedral Chambers, Newcastle upon Tyne	0191 232 1311
Mandel Richard	11 Bolt Court, London	0171 353 2300
	Redhill Chambers, Redhill	01737 780781
Mangat Dr Tejina Kiran	New Court Chambers, London	0171 831 9500
Marks Jonathan Clive	4 Pump Court, London	0171 353 2656/9
Marris Miss Sarah Selena Rixar	No 1 Serjeants' Inn, London	0171 415 6666
Marshall Philip Derek	Farrar's Building, London	0171 583 9241
	Iscoed Chambers, Swansea	01792 652988/9/330
Martin David John	Cathedral Chambers, Newcastle upon Tyne	0191 232 1311
Martineau Henry Ralph Adeane	Goldsmith Building, London	0171 353 7881
Mathews Deni	8 Fountain Court, Birmingham	0121 236 5514
Matthews Dennis Roland	5 Bell Yard, London	0171 333 8811
Maudslay Miss Diana Elizabeth		
Maxwell-Scott James Herbert	Two Crown Office Row, London	0171 797 8100
Mayhew Jerome Patrick Burke	Goldsmith Building, London	0171 353 7881
McCahey Miss Catherine Anne Mary	St Philip's Chambers, Birmingham	0121 246 7000
McCann Simon Howard	Deans Court Chambers, Manchester	0161 834 4097
McCarthy William	New Bailey Chambers, Preston	01772 258 087
McCaul Colin Brownlie	39 Essex Street, London	0171 832 1111
McCluggage Brian Thomas	Chambers of John Hand QC, Manchester	0161 955 9000
McGahey Miss Elizabeth Clare	30 Park Place, Cardiff	01222 398421
McGrath Miss Elizabeth Ann	St Philip's Chambers, Birmingham	0121 246 7000
McGregor Harvey	4 Paper Buildings, London	0171 353 3366/583 7155
McIvor Ian Walker	334 Deansgate Chambers, Manchester	0161 834 3767
McKay Christopher Alexander	Angel Chambers, Swansea	01792 464623/464648
McKenna Miss Anna Louise	Queen Elizabeth Building, London	0171 353 7181 (12 lines)
McKeon James Patrick	Peel House Chambers, Liverpool	0151 236 4321
McLachlan David Robert		
McMinn Miss Valerie Kathleen	Baker Street Chambers, Middlesbrough	01642 873873
McParland Michael Joseph	New Court Chambers, London	0171 831 9500
Meakin Timothy William	Fenners Chambers, Cambridge	01223 368761
	Fenners Chambers, Peterborough	01733 562030
Melville Richard David	39 Essex Street, London	0171 832 1111
Menzies Richard Mark	8 Stone Buildings, London	0171 831 9881
Michael Simon Laurence	• Bedford Chambers, Bedford	0870 733 7333
Middleton Miss Georgina Claire	New Court Chambers, London	0171 831 9500
Mitchell Miss Juliana Marie	2 Harcourt Buildings, London	0171 583 9020
Moat Frank Robert	Pump Court Chambers, London	0171 353 0711
	Pump Court Chambers, Winchester	01962 868161
Mondair Rashpal Singh	Claremont Chambers, Wolverhampton	01902 426222
Moore James Anthony	2 Gray's Inn Square Chambers, London	0171 242 0328/405 1317
Moores Timothy Kieron	17 Carlton Crescent, Southampton	01703 320320

Moorman Miss Lucinda Claire	Farrar's Building, London	0171 583 9241
Morris Miss Brenda Alison	14 Gray's Inn Square, London	0171 242 0858
Morris-Coole Christopher	Goldsmith Building, London	0171 353 7881
Moses Miss Rebecca	Barristers' Common Law Chambers, London	0171 375 3012
	Lion Court, London	0171 404 6565
Moulson Peter Charles Edward	Chambers of Andrew Campbell QC, Leeds	0113 245 5438
Mulcahy Miss Leigh-Ann Maria	Two Crown Office Row, London	0171 797 8100
Muller Franz Joseph	11 King's Bench Walk, London	0171 353 3337/8
	11 King's Bench Walk, Leeds	0113 2971 200
Murray Ashley Charles	Oriel Chambers, Liverpool	0151 236 7191
Myatt Charles Edward	Fenners Chambers, Cambridge	01223 368761
	Fenners Chambers, Peterborough	01733 562030
Nesbitt Timothy John Robert	199 Strand, London	0171 379 9779
Newman Austin Eric	9 Woodhouse Square, Leeds	0113 245 1986
Newton Miss Claire Elaine Maria Bailey	Goldsmith Building, London	0171 353 7881
Nicholls Peter John	5 Pump Court, London	0171 353 2532
Noble Roderick Grant	39 Essex Street, London	0171 832 1111
Nolan Damian Francis	25–27 Castle Street, Liverpool	0151 227 5661/5666/236 5072
Norie-Miller Jeffrey Reginald	55 Temple Chambers, London	0171 353 7400
Norman Christopher John George	No 1 Serjeants' Inn, London	0171 415 6666
Norris Paul Howard	One Essex Court, London	0171 936 3030
O'Connor Andrew McDougal	Two Crown Office Row, London	0171 797 8100
Okoye Miss Joy Nwamala	Chambers of Joy Okoye, London	0171 405 7011
Ong Miss Grace Yu Mae	One Essex Court, London	0171 936 3030
Ough Dr Richard Norman	• Hardwicke Building, London	0171 242 2523
Outhwaite Mrs Wendy-Jane Tivnan	Stanbrook & Henderson, London	0171 353 0101
	2 Harcourt Buildings, London	0171 583 9020
Overs Ms Estelle Fae	New Court Chambers, London	0171 831 9500
Pack Miss Melissa Elizabeth Jane	Farrar's Building, London	0171 583 9241
Palmer James Savill	2 Harcourt Buildings, London	0171 583 9020
Palmer Patrick John Steven	Sovereign Chambers, Leeds	0113 245 1841/2/3
Paneth Miss Sarah Ruth	No 1 Serjeants' Inn, London	0171 415 6666
Parker John	2 Mitre Court Buildings, London	0171 353 1353
Parr John Edward	8 King Street Chambers, Manchester	0161 834 9560
Pawson Robert Edward Cruickshank	Pump Court Chambers, London	0171 353 0711
	Pump Court Chambers, Winchester	01962 868161
Pearson Thomas Adam Spenser	Pump Court Chambers, London	0171 353 0711
	Pump Court Chambers, Winchester	01962 868161
Peirson Oliver James	Pump Court Chambers, London	0171 353 0711
	Pump Court Chambers, Winchester	01962 868161
Pelling Richard Alexander	New Court Chambers, London	0171 831 9500
Pema Anesh Bhumin Laloo	9 Woodhouse Square, Leeds	0113 245 1986
Pershad Rohan	Two Crown Office Row, London	0171 797 8100
Phillips Andrew Charles	Two Crown Office Row, London	0171 797 8100
Pinder Miss Mary Elizabeth	No 1 Serjeants' Inn, London	0171 415 6666
Pittaway David Michael	No 1 Serjeants' Inn, London	0171 415 6666
Pitter Jason Karl	Park Court Chambers, Leeds	0113 243 3277
Playford Jonathan Richard	2 Harcourt Buildings, London	0171 583 9020
Pollock Dr Evelyn Marian Margaret	5 Essex Court, London	0171 410 2000
Pooles Michael Philip Holmes	4 Paper Buildings, London	0171 353 3366/583 7155
Popat Prashant	Stanbrook & Henderson, London	0171 353 0101
	2 Harcourt Buildings, London	0171 583 9020
Portnoy Leslie Reuben	Chambers of John Hand QC, Manchester	0161 955 9000
Pratt Allan Duncan	New Court Chambers, London	0171 831 9500
Priestley Ms Rebecca Janet	2 Gray's Inn Square Chambers, London	0171 242 0328/405 1317
Prynne Andrew Geoffrey Lockyer	Stanbrook & Henderson, London	0171 353 0101
	2 Harcourt Buildings, London	0171 583 9020
Pugh Michael Charles	Old Square Chambers, London	0171 269 0300
	Old Square Chambers, Bristol	0117 927 7111
Pulman George Frederick	• Hardwicke Building, London	0171 242 2523
	• Stour Chambers, Canterbury	01227 764899
Purchas Christopher Patrick Brooks	Two Crown Office Row, London	0171 797 8100
Quinlan Christopher John	30 Park Place, Cardiff	01222 398421
Rahman Ms Sadeqa Shaheen	1 Crown Office Row, London	0171 797 7500
Rai Amarjit Singh	St Philip's Chambers, Birmingham	0121 246 7000
Rankin William Peter	Oriel Chambers, Liverpool	0151 236 7191
Rawlings Clive Patrick	Goldsmith Building, London	0171 353 7881

• Expanded entry in Part D

Rea Miss Karen Marie-Jeanne	No 1 Serjeants' Inn, London	0171 415 6666
Readhead Simon John Howard	No 1 Serjeants' Inn, London	0171 415 6666
Richards Miss Jennifer	39 Essex Street, London	0171 832 1111
Richardson Garth Douglas Anthony	3 Paper Buildings, London	0171 583 8055
	20 Lorne Park Road, Bournemouth	01202 292102
	4 St Peter Street, Winchester	01962 868 884
Rigby Terence	Chambers of John Hand QC, Manchester	0161 955 9000
Rigney Andrew James	Two Crown Office Row, London	0171 797 8100
Riley-Smith Tobias Augustine William	2 Harcourt Buildings, London	0171 583 9020
Ritchie Andrew George	9 Gough Square, London	0171 353 5371
Ritchie Miss Jean Harris	4 Paper Buildings, London	0171 353 3366/583 7155
Rivalland Marc-Edouard	No 1 Serjeants' Inn, London	0171 415 6666
Robb Adam Duncan	39 Essex Street, London	0171 832 1111
Robertson Ms Alice Michelle	Chambers of Kieran Coonan QC, London	0171 583 6013/2510
Robertson Andrew James	11 King's Bench Walk, London	0171 353 3337/8
	11 King's Bench Walk, Leeds	0113 2971 200
Rodgers Miss Doris June	Harcourt Chambers, London	0171 353 6961/7
	Harcourt Chambers, Oxford	01865 791559
Roe Thomas Idris	Goldsmith Building, London	0171 353 7881
Rogers Ian Paul	1 Crown Office Row, London	0171 583 9292
Rogers Paul John	1 Crown Office Row, London	0171 797 7500
	Crown Office Row Chambers, Brighton	01273 625625
Room Stewart	8 Stone Buildings, London	0171 831 9881
Ross John Graffin	No 1 Serjeants' Inn, London	0171 415 6666
Rowlands Ms Catherine Janet	Victoria Chambers, Birmingham	0121 236 9900
Russell Robert John Finlay	5 Bell Yard, London	0171 333 8811
Ryan David Patrick	Chambers of Geoffrey Hawker, London	0171 583 8899
Sadd Patrick James Thomas	199 Strand, London	0171 379 9779
Sadiq Tariq Mahmood	Chambers of John Hand QC, Manchester	0161 955 9000
Sampson Graeme William	Chambers of Geoffrey Hawker, London	0171 583 8899
Samuel Glyn Ross	St Philip's Chambers, Birmingham	0121 246 7000
Samuels Leslie John	Pump Court Chambers, London	0171 353 0711
	Pump Court Chambers, Winchester	01962 868161
Sander Andrew Thomas	Goldsmith Building, London	0171 353 7881
	Oriel Chambers, Liverpool	0151 236 7191
Sarony Neville Leslie		
Saunt Thomas William Gatty	Two Crown Office Row, London	0171 797 8100
Schooling Simon John	Chambers of Harjit Singh, London	0171 353 1356
Scott-Phillips Alexander James	Earl Street Chambers, Maidstone	01622 671222
Scutt David Robert	11 Bolt Court, London	0171 353 2300
	Redhill Chambers, Redhill	01737 780781
Sefton Mark Thomas Dunblane	199 Strand, London	0171 379 9779
Segal Oliver Leon	Old Square Chambers, London	0171 269 0300
	Old Square Chambers, Bristol	0117 927 7111
Seligman Matthew Thomas Arthur	39 Essex Street, London	0171 832 1111
Semple Andrew Blair	Sovereign Chambers, Leeds	0113 245 1841/2/3
Shay Stephen Everett	One King's Bench Walk, London	0171 936 1500
Sheehan Malcolm Peter	Stanbrook & Henderson, London	0171 353 0101
	2 Harcourt Buildings, London	0171 583 9020
Sheridan Norman Patrick	• 11 Bolt Court, London	0171 353 2300
	• Redhill Chambers, Redhill	01737 780781
Shorrock John Michael	Peel Court Chambers, Manchester	0161 832 3791
Silvester Bruce Ross	Lamb Chambers, London	0171 797 8300
Sinclair-Morris Charles Robert	9 Woodhouse Square, Leeds	0113 245 1986
Singh Balbir	• Equity Chambers, Birmingham	0121 233 2100
Sleeman Miss Rachel Sarah Elizabeth	One Essex Court, London	0171 936 3030
Smith Matthew Robert	Sovereign Chambers, Leeds	0113 245 1841/2/3
Smith Warwick Timothy Cresswell	• Deans Court Chambers, Manchester	0161 834 4097
	• Deans Court Chambers, Preston	01772 555163
Snowden John Stevenson	Two Crown Office Row, London	0171 797 8100
Somerset-Jones Miss Felicity	Oriel Chambers, Liverpool	0151 236 7191
Spain Timothy Harrisson	Trinity Chambers, Newcastle upon Tyne	0191 232 1927
Sparks Kevin Laurence	Earl Street Chambers, Maidstone	01622 671222
Spencer James	11 King's Bench Walk, London	0171 353 3337/8

• Expanded entry in Part D

	11 King's Bench Walk, Leeds	0113 2971 200
Spencer Martin Benedict	4 Paper Buildings, London	0171 353 3366/583 7155
Spollon Guy Merton	St Philip's Chambers, Birmingham	0121 246 7000
St Louis Brian Lloyd	Hardwicke Building, London	0171 242 2523
Staite Miss Sara Elizabeth	Stanbrook & Henderson, London	0171 353 0101
	2 Harcourt Buildings, London	0171 583 9020
Stanislas Paul Junior	Somersett Chambers, London	0171 404 6701
Starcevic Petar	St Philip's Chambers, Birmingham	0121 246 7000
Starks Nicholas Ernshaw	8 Fountain Court, Birmingham	0121 236 5514
Stead Miss Kate Rebecca	Barristers' Common Law Chambers, London	0171 375 3012
Stemmer-Baldwin Marcus Stephen	8 Stone Buildings, London	0171 831 9881
Stern Dr Kristina Anne	39 Essex Street, London	0171 832 1111
Stevenson John Melford	Two Crown Office Row, London	0171 797 8100
Stewart Mark Courtney	College Chambers, Southampton	01703 230338
Stewart Richard Paul	New Court Chambers, London	0171 831 9500
Stockdale David Andrew	9 Bedford Row, London	0171 242 3555
	Deans Court Chambers, Manchester	0161 834 4097
	Deans Court Chambers, Preston	01772 555163
Storey Jeremy Brian	4 Pump Court, London	0171 353 2656/9
Studd Miss Anne Elizabeth	5 Essex Court, London	0171 410 2000
Sutton Richard William Wallace	Chambers of Andrew Campbell QC, Leeds	0113 245 5438
Swan Ian Christopher	Two Crown Office Row, London	0171 797 8100
Tattersall Simon Mark Rogers	Fenners Chambers, Cambridge	01223 368761
	Fenners Chambers, Peterborough	01733 562030
Taylor Miss Deborah Frances	Two Crown Office Row, London	0171 797 8100
Taylor Michael Richard	Park Court Chambers, Leeds	0113 243 3277
Taylor Simon Wheldon	• Cloisters, London	0171 827 4000
Tedd Rex Hilary	• St Philip's Chambers, Birmingham	0121 246 7000
	• 22 Albion Place, Northampton	01604 636271
Temple Anthony Dominic	4 Pump Court, London	0171 353 2656/9
Ter Haar Roger Eduard Lound	Two Crown Office Row, London	0171 797 8100
Thompson Jonathan Richard	8 King Street Chambers, Manchester	0161 834 9560
Ticciati Oliver	4 Pump Court, London	0171 353 2656/9
Tillett Michael Burn	39 Essex Street, London	0171 832 1111
Tobin Daniel Alphonsus Joseph	Chambers of Geoffrey Hawker, London	0171 583 8899
Treasure Francis Seton	199 Strand, London	0171 379 9779
Trotman Timothy Oliver	Deans Court Chambers, Manchester	0161 834 4097
	Deans Court Chambers, Preston	01772 555163
Tucker David William	Two Crown Office Row, London	0171 797 8100
Tucker Miss Katherine Jane Greening	St Philip's Chambers, Birmingham	0121 246 7000
Tyack David Guy	St Philip's Chambers, Birmingham	0121 246 7000
Valks Michael	King's Chambers, Eastbourne	01323 416053
Vaughan-Neil Miss Catherine Mary Bernardine	5 Bell Yard, London	0171 333 8811
Vincent Miss Ruth Carolyn	Colleton Chambers, Exeter	01392 274898
Vine Aidan James Wilson	Harcourt Chambers, London	0171 353 6961/7
	Harcourt Chambers, Oxford	01865 791559
Waddington Nigel William James	8 Stone Buildings, London	0171 831 9881
Wadsworth James Patrick	4 Paper Buildings, London	0171 353 3366/583 7155
Waley Eric Richard Thomas	Assize Court Chambers, Bristol	0117 926 4587
Walker Miss Jane	Chambers of John Hand QC, Manchester	0161 955 9000
Ward Ms Orla Mary	3 Serjeants' Inn, London	0171 353 5537
Ward Timothy Justin	39 Essex Street, London	0171 832 1111
Warnock Andrew Ronald	No 1 Serjeants' Inn, London	0171 415 6666
Warrender Miss Nichola Mary	New Court Chambers, London	0171 831 9500
Waters Julian William Penrose	No 1 Serjeants' Inn, London	0171 415 6666
Watson Mark	6 Pump Court, London	0171 797 8400
	6-8 Mill Street, Maidstone	01622 688 094
Webb Geraint Timothy	2 Harcourt Buildings, London	0171 583 9020
Webb Robert Stopford	• 5 Bell Yard, London	0171 333 8811
Wedderspoon Miss Rachel Leone	Chambers of John Hand QC, Manchester	0161 955 9000
Weddle Steven Edgar	Hardwicke Building, London	0171 242 2523
Welchman Charles Stuart	199 Strand, London	0171 379 9779
West Lawrence Joseph	Stanbrook & Henderson, London	0171 353 0101
	2 Harcourt Buildings, London	0171 583 9020
Weston Clive Aubrey Richard	Two Crown Office Row, London	0171 797 8100

Whitcombe Mark David	Old Square Chambers, London	0171 269 0300
	Old Square Chambers, Bristol	0117 927 7111
White Darren Paul	Cathedral Chambers (Jan Wood Independent Barristers' Clerk), Exeter	01392 210900
White Peter-John Spencer	Pembroke House, Leatherhead	01372 376160/376493
Whiteley Miss Miranda Blyth	4 Field Court, London	0171 440 6900
Whitfield Adrian	3 Serjeants' Inn, London	0171 353 5537
Wightwick (William) Iain	Assize Court Chambers, Bristol	0117 926 4587
Wignall Edward Gordon	• 1 Dr Johnson's Buildings, London	0171 353 9328
	• Dr Johnson's Chambers, Reading	01189 254221
Wilby David Christopher	• 199 Strand, London	0171 379 9779
	• Park Lane Chambers, Leeds	0113 228 5000
Wilcox Nicholas Hugh	5 Essex Court, London	0171 410 2000
Wilkinson Nigel Vivian Marshall	Two Crown Office Row, London	0171 797 8100
Willer Robert Michael	Hardwicke Building, London	0171 242 2523
Williams A John	• 13 King's Bench Walk, London	0171 353 7204
	• King's Bench Chambers, Oxford	01865 311066
Williams Hugh David Haydn	St Philip's Chambers, Birmingham	0121 246 7000
Williams John Griffith	Goldsmith Building, London	0171 353 7881
	33 Park Place, Cardiff	01222 233313
Williams The Hon John Melville	• Old Square Chambers, London	0171 269 0300
	• Old Square Chambers, Bristol	0117 927 7111
Williams Thomas Ellis	30 Park Place, Cardiff	01222 398421
Wilson Andrew Robert	9 Woodhouse Square, Leeds	0113 245 1986
Wilson Peter Julian		
Wilton Simon Daniel	4 Paper Buildings, London	0171 353 3366/583 7155
Wood Richard Michael	Sackville Chambers, Norwich	01603 613516
Wood Simon Edward	Plowden Buildings, London	0171 583 0808
	Trinity Chambers, Newcastle upon Tyne	0191 232 1927
Wood Simon Richard Henry	Lamb Chambers, London	0171 797 8300
Woods Jonathan	Two Crown Office Row, London	0171 797 8100
Woodward Nicholas Frederick	White Friars Chambers, Chester	01244 323070
Woolf Eliot Charles Anthony	199 Strand, London	0171 379 9779
Wordsworth Mrs Philippa Lindsey	Chambers of Andrew Campbell QC, Leeds	0113 245 5438
Worrall John Raymond Guy	Chambers of Andrew Campbell QC, Leeds	0113 245 5438
Worsley Daniel	Stanbrook & Henderson, London	0171 353 0101
	2 Harcourt Buildings, London	0171 583 9020
Worster David James Stewart	St Philip's Chambers, Birmingham	0121 246 7000
Wright Miss Clare Elizabeth	6 Pump Court, London	0171 797 8400
Wright Gerard Henry	25–27 Castle Street, Liverpool	0151 227 5661/5666/236 5072
Wright Norman Alfred	Oriel Chambers, Liverpool	0151 236 7191
Yell Nicholas Anthony	No 1 Serjeants' Inn, London	0171 415 6666
Yelton Michael Paul	Fenners Chambers, Cambridge	01223 368761
	Fenners Chambers, Peterborough	01733 562030
Yeung Stuart Roy	22 Albion Place, Northampton	01604 636271
Zornoza Miss Isabella	Stanbrook & Henderson, London	0171 353 0101
	2 Harcourt Buildings, London	0171 583 9020

PHARMACY

Fisher Jonathan Simon	• 18 Red Lion Court, London	0171 520 6000
	• Thornwood House, Chelmsford	01245 280880

PLANNING

Alesbury Alun	2 Mitre Court Buildings, London	0171 583 1380
Anderson Anthony John	2 Mitre Court Buildings, London	0171 583 1380
Atherton Ian David	Enterprise Chambers, London	0171 405 9471
	Enterprise Chambers, Leeds	0113 246 0391
	Enterprise Chambers, Newcastle upon Tyne	0191 222 3344
Bailey Mark Henry Arthur	• 6 Pump Court, London	0171 797 8400
	• 6-8 Mill Street, Maidstone	01622 688 094
Barnes (David) Michael (William)	4 Breams Buildings, London	0171 353 5835/430 1221
Bartlett George Robert	2 Mitre Court Buildings, London	0171 583 1380
Beard Mark Christopher	6 Pump Court, London	0171 797 8400
Bhattacharyya Ardhendu	1 Gray's Inn Square, London	0171 405 8946
	11 St Bernards Road, Slough	01753 553806/817989

• Expanded entry in Part D

Bird Nigel David	Chambers of John Hand QC, Manchester	0161 955 9000
Birtles William	Old Square Chambers, London	0171 269 0300
	Old Square Chambers, Bristol	0117 927 7111
Boyle Christopher Alexander David	2 Mitre Court Buildings, London	0171 583 1380
Burton Nicholas Anthony	2 Mitre Court Buildings, London	0171 583 1380
Calvert Peter Charles	Goldsmith Building, London	0171 353 7881
Cameron Neil St Clair	1 Serjeants' Inn, London	0171 583 1355
Cameron Miss Sheila Morag Clark	2 Harcourt Buildings, London	0171 353 8415
Carlile Alexander Charles	9-12 Bell Yard, London	0171 400 1800
	Sedan House, Chester	01244 320480/348282
Caws Eian Richard Edwin	4 Breams Buildings, London	0171 353 5835/430 1221
Clay Jonathan Roger	11 Bolt Court, London	0171 353 2300
	Redhill Chambers, Redhill	01737 780781
Collett Gavin Charles	Rougemont Chambers, Exeter	01392 410471
	Cathedral Chambers (Jan Wood Independent Barristers' Clerk), Exeter	01392 210900
Colquhoun Miss Celina Daphne Marion	11 Bolt Court, London	0171 353 2300
	Redhill Chambers, Redhill	01737 780781
Dowse John	Chambers of Lord Goodhart QC, London	0171 405 5577
	Chambers of John Hand QC, Manchester	0161 955 9000
Drabble Richard John Bloor	4 Breams Buildings, London	0171 353 5835/430 1221
Driscoll Miss Lynn	Sovereign Chambers, Leeds	0113 245 1841/2/3
	Lancaster Buildings, Manchester	0161 661 4444
Druce Michael James	2 Mitre Court Buildings, London	0171 583 1380
Duffy Michael	Cathedral Chambers, Ely, Ely	01353 666775
Edwards Philip Douglas	2 Harcourt Buildings, London	0171 353 8415
Elvin David John	4 Breams Buildings, London	0171 353 5835/430 1221
Farmer Pryce Michael	1 Dr Johnson's Buildings, London	0171 353 9328
	Goldsmith Building, London	0171 353 7881
	Sedan House, Chester	01244 320480/348282
Finlay Darren	Sovereign Chambers, Leeds	0113 245 1841/2/3
FitzGerald Michael Frederick Clive	2 Mitre Court Buildings, London	0171 583 1380
Fookes Robert Lawrence	2 Mitre Court Buildings, London	0171 583 1380
Forsdick David John	4 Breams Buildings, London	0171 353 5835/430 1221
Furber (Robert) John	4 Breams Buildings, London	0171 353 5835/430 1221
Gore Andrew Roger	Fenners Chambers, Cambridge	01223 368761
	Fenners Chambers, Peterborough	01733 562030
Greaves John	9-12 Bell Yard, London	0171 400 1800
Gullick Stephen John	Sovereign Chambers, Leeds	0113 245 1841/2/3
Hands David Richard Granville	4 Breams Buildings, London	0171 353 5835/430 1221
	40 King Street, Manchester	0161 832 9082
Hansen William Joseph	5 Bell Yard, London	0171 333 8811
Harper Joseph Charles	4 Breams Buildings, London	0171 353 5835/430 1221
Harrison Peter John	6 Pump Court, London	0171 797 8400
	6-8 Mill Street, Maidstone	01622 688 094
Harwood Richard John	1 Serjeants' Inn, London	0171 583 1355
Heap Gerard Miles	Sovereign Chambers, Leeds	0113 245 1841/2/3
Heywood Michael Edmundson	Chambers of Lord Goodhart QC, London	0171 405 5577
	Cobden House Chambers, Manchester	0161 833 6000/6001
Hill Nicholas Mark	Pump Court Chambers, London	0171 353 0711
	Pump Court Chambers, Winchester	01962 868161
Holgate David John	4 Breams Buildings, London	0171 353 5835/430 1221
Holroyd John James	• 9 Woodhouse Square, Leeds	0113 245 1986
Horton Matthew Bethell	2 Mitre Court Buildings, London	0171 583 1380
Howell John	4 Breams Buildings, London	0171 353 5835/430 1221
Huskinson George Nicholas Nevil	4-5 Gray's Inn Square, London	0171 404 5252
Jefferies Thomas Robert	Chambers of Lord Goodhart QC, London	0171 405 5577
Johnson Michael Sloan	Chambers of John Hand QC, Manchester	0161 955 9000
Jones Geraint Martyn	Fenners Chambers, Cambridge	01223 368761
	Fenners Chambers, Peterborough	01733 562030
Karas Jonathan Marcus	4 Breams Buildings, London	0171 353 5835/430 1221
Katkowski Christopher Andrew Mark	4 Breams Buildings, London	0171 353 5835/430 1221
Keen Graeme	4 Breams Buildings, London	0171 353 5835/430 1221
King Neil Gerald Alexander	2 Mitre Court Buildings, London	0171 583 1380

B

Kingsland Rt Hon Lord	4 Breams Buildings, London	0171 353 5835/430 1221
Langham Richard Geoffrey	1 Serjeants' Inn, London	0171 583 1355
Lawson Rogers George Stuart	23 Essex Street, London	0171 413 0353
Leeming Ian	Lamb Chambers, London	0171 797 8300
	Chambers of John Hand QC, Manchester	0161 955 9000
Lewis Robert		
Lewsley Christopher Stanton	4 Breams Buildings, London	0171 353 5835/430 1221
Lieven Ms Nathalie Marie Daniella	4 Breams Buildings, London	0171 353 5835/430 1221
Litton John Letablere	4 Breams Buildings, London	0171 353 5835/430 1221
Lockhart-Mummery Christopher John	4 Breams Buildings, London	0171 353 5835/430 1221
Macleod Nigel Ronald Buchanan	4 Breams Buildings, London	0171 353 5835/430 1221
	40 King Street, Manchester	0161 832 9082
Macpherson The Hon Mary Stewart	2 Mitre Court Buildings, London	0171 583 1380
Male John Martin	4 Breams Buildings, London	0171 353 5835/430 1221
Mandel Richard	11 Bolt Court, London	0171 353 2300
	Redhill Chambers, Redhill	01737 780781
Marshall Philip Derek	Farrar's Building, London	0171 583 9241
	Iscoed Chambers, Swansea	01792 652988/9/330
Marson Geoffrey Charles	Sovereign Chambers, Leeds	0113 245 1841/2/3
Mathews Deni	8 Fountain Court, Birmingham	0121 236 5514
Mathias Miss Anna	11 Bolt Court, London	0171 353 2300
Maudslay Miss Diana Elizabeth		
Maurici James Patrick	4 Breams Buildings, London	0171 353 5835/430 1221
McCracken Robert Henry Joy	• 2 Harcourt Buildings, London	0171 353 8415
McHugh Miss Karen	4 Breams Buildings, London	0171 353 5835/430 1221
Moore Professor Victor William Edward	2 Mitre Court Buildings, London	0171 583 1380
Moriarty Gerald Evelyn	2 Mitre Court Buildings, London	0171 583 1380
Morshead Timothy Francis	4 Breams Buildings, London	0171 353 5835/430 1221
Mould Timothy James	4 Breams Buildings, London	0171 353 5835/430 1221
Murch Stephen James	• 11 Bolt Court, London	0171 353 2300
Ouseley Duncan Brian Walter	4-5 Gray's Inn Square, London	0171 404 5252
Pearson Thomas Adam Spenser	Pump Court Chambers, London	0171 353 0711
	Pump Court Chambers, Winchester	01962 868161
Purchas Robin Michael	• 2 Harcourt Buildings, London	0171 353 8415
Richards David Wyn	Iscoed Chambers, Swansea	01792 652988/9/330
Robinson Miss Alice	4 Breams Buildings, London	0171 353 5835/430 1221
Roots Guy Robert Godfrey	2 Mitre Court Buildings, London	0171 583 1380
Sampson Graeme William	Chambers of Geoffrey Hawker, London	0171 583 8899
Silsoe The Lord	2 Mitre Court Buildings, London	0171 583 1380
Simpson Edwin John Fletcher	12 New Square, London	0171 419 1212
Sisley Timothy Julian Crispin	9 Stone Buildings, London	0171 404 5055
	Westgate Chambers, Lewes	01273 480 510
Smith David Anthony	4 Breams Buildings, London	0171 353 5835/430 1221
Straker Timothy Derrick	• 2-3 Gray's Inn Square, London	0171 242 4986
Sunnucks James Horace George	• 5 New Square, London	0171 404 0404
	• Octagon House, Norwich	01603 623186
Taylor Reuben Mallinson	2 Mitre Court Buildings, London	0171 583 1380
Thomas Miss Megan Moira	1 Serjeants' Inn, London	0171 583 1355
Village Peter Malcolm	• 4-5 Gray's Inn Square, London	0171 404 5252
Vine Aidan James Wilson	Harcourt Chambers, London	0171 353 6961/7
	Harcourt Chambers, Oxford	01865 791559
Warren Rupert Miles	2 Mitre Court Buildings, London	0171 583 1380
Whybrow Christopher John	1 Serjeants' Inn, London	0171 583 1355
Widdicombe David Graham	2 Mitre Court Buildings, London	0171 583 1380
Williams Miss Anne Margaret	4 Breams Buildings, London	0171 353 5835/430 1221
	37 Park Square, Leeds	0113 243 9422
Woolley David Rorie	• 1 Serjeants' Inn, London	0171 583 1355

POLICE ACTIONS

Parr John Edward	8 King Street Chambers, Manchester	0161 834 9560

POLICE ACTIONS AND JURY TRIALS

Challinor Robert Michael	St Philip's Chambers, Birmingham	0121 246 7000

POLICE CIVIL JURY ACTIONS

Kent Miss Georgina	5 Essex Court, London	0171 410 2000

• Expanded entry in Part D

POLICE DISCIPLINE

Beer Jason Barrington	5 Essex Court, London	0171 410 2000
Merz Richard James	9–12 Bell Yard, London	0171 400 1800

POLICE LAW

Byers The Hon Charles William	23 Essex Street, London	0171 413 0353
Byrne Garrett Thomas	23 Essex Street, London	0171 413 0353
Jackson Anthony Warren	3 Serjeants' Inn, London	0171 353 5537
James Roderick Morrice	23 Essex Street, London	0171 413 0353
Janner Daniel Joseph Mitchell	23 Essex Street, London	0171 413 0353
Miskin Charles James Monckton	23 Essex Street, London	0171 413 0353
Pardoe Rupert Adam Corin	23 Essex Street, London	0171 413 0353
Powell Miss Debra Ann	3 Serjeants' Inn, London	0171 353 5537
Price Albert John	23 Essex Street, London	0171 413 0353
Wood Michael Mure	23 Essex Street, London	0171 413 0353

POLICE LAW (CIVIL)

Austin-Smith Michael Gerard	23 Essex Street, London	0171 413 0353

PRIVATE CLIENT

Purdie Robert Anthony James	28 Western Road, Oxford	01865 204911

PRIVATE INTERNATIONAL

Adamyk Simon Charles	12 New Square, London	0171 419 1212
Akka Lawrence Mark	20 Essex Street, London	0171 583 9294
Ambrose Miss Clare Mary Geneste	20 Essex Street, London	0171 583 9294
Beal Kieron Conrad	4 Paper Buildings, London	0171 353 3366/583 7155
Blair William James Lynton	3 Verulam Buildings, London	0171 831 8441
Brownbill David John	Gray's Inn Square, London	0171 242 3529
Brunner Adrian John Nelson	Stanbrook & Henderson, London	0171 353 0101
	2 Harcourt Buildings, London	0171 583 9020
Burton Michael John	Littleton Chambers, London	0171 797 8600
Coburn Michael Jeremy Patrick	20 Essex Street, London	0171 583 9294
Collett Michael John	20 Essex Street, London	0171 583 9294
Connerty Anthony Robin	Lamb Chambers, London	0171 797 8300
Conroy Miss Marian	3 Stone Buildings, London	0171 242 4937/405 8358
Creaner Paul Anthony	15 Winckley Square, Preston	01772 252 828
Edwards-Stuart Antony James Cobham	Two Crown Office Row, London	0171 797 8100
Fawls Richard Granville	5 Stone Buildings, London	0171 242 6201
Freedman Sampson Clive	3 Verulam Buildings, London	0171 831 8441
Grantham Andrew Timothy	• Deans Court Chambers, Manchester	0161 834 4097
	• Deans Court Chambers, Preston	01772 555163
Gun Cuninghame Julian Arthur	• Gough Square Chambers, London	0171 353 0924
Hamblen Nicholas Archibald	20 Essex Street, London	0171 583 9294
Harvey Michael Llewellyn Tucker	Two Crown Office Row, London	0171 797 8100
Haynes Miss Rebecca	Monckton Chambers, London	0171 405 7211
Hoyal Ms Jane	• 1 Pump Court, London	0171 583 2012/353 4341
Jarvis John Manners	3 Verulam Buildings, London	0171 831 8441
Jenkala Adrian Aleksander	11 Bolt Court, London	0171 353 2300
	Redhill Chambers, Redhill	01737 780781
Kime Matthew Jonathan	• New Court, London	0171 797 8999
	• Cobden House Chambers, Manchester	0161 833 6000/6001
Kolodziej Andrzej Jozef	• Littman Chambers, London	0171 404 4866
Lasok Karol Paul Edward	Monckton Chambers, London	0171 405 7211
Lawson Robert John	5 Bell Yard, London	0171 333 8811
Lazarus Michael Steven	1 Crown Office Row, London	0171 583 9292
Le Poidevin Nicholas Peter	12 New Square, London	0171 419 1212
	Sovereign Chambers, Leeds	0113 245 1841/2/3
Lewis Robert		
Lowenstein Paul David	Littleton Chambers, London	0171 797 8600
Malek Ali	3 Verulam Buildings, London	0171 831 8441
Masters Miss Sara Alayna	20 Essex Street, London	0171 583 9294
Mathew Miss Nergis-Anne	2 Gray's Inn Square Chambers, London	0171 242 0328/405 1317
McGregor Harvey	4 Paper Buildings, London	0171 353 3366/583 7155
McParland Michael Joseph	New Court Chambers, London	0171 831 9500
Meeson Nigel Keith	4 Field Court, London	0171 440 6900
Milligan Iain Anstruther	20 Essex Street, London	0171 583 9294

Morgan Richard Hugo Lyndon	13 Old Square, London	0171 404 4800
Newman Austin Eric	9 Woodhouse Square, Leeds	0113 245 1986
Owen David Christopher	20 Essex Street, London	0171 583 9294
Paines Nicholas Paul Billot	Monckton Chambers, London	0171 405 7211
Parker Kenneth Blades	Monckton Chambers, London	0171 405 7211
Peglow Dr Michael Alfred Herman	Chambers of Geoffrey Hawker, London	0171 583 8899
Pope David James	3 Verulam Buildings, London	0171 831 8441
Rahman Muhammad Altafur	Barristers' Common Law Chambers, London	0171 375 3012
Reed Philip James William	5 Bell Yard, London	0171 333 8811
Roth Peter Marcel	Monckton Chambers, London	0171 405 7211
Sagar (Edward) Leigh	12 New Square, London	0171 419 1212
	Sovereign Chambers, Leeds	0113 245 1841/2/3
	Newport Chambers, Newport	01633 267403/255855
Salter Richard Stanley	3 Verulam Buildings, London	0171 831 8441
Saunders Nicholas Joseph	4 Field Court, London	0171 440 6900
Selvaratnam Miss Vasanti Emily Indrani	4 Field Court, London	0171 440 6900
Shepherd Philip Alexander	• 5 Bell Yard, London	0171 333 8811
Sheridan Maurice Bernard Gerard	• 3 Verulam Buildings, London	0171 831 8441
Southwell Richard Charles	One Hare Court, London	0171 353 3171
Spearman Richard	5 Raymond Buildings, London	0171 242 2902
Stewart Alexander Joseph	5 New Square, London	0171 404 0404
Stewart Nicholas John Cameron	Hardwicke Building, London	0171 242 2523
Tucker David William	Two Crown Office Row, London	0171 797 8100
Vajda Christopher Stephen	Monckton Chambers, London	0171 405 7211
Vaughan-Neil Miss Catherine Mary Bernardine	5 Bell Yard, London	0171 333 8811
Waley Eric Richard Thomas	Assize Court Chambers, Bristol	0117 926 4587
Wheeler Miss Marina Claire	Stanbrook & Henderson, London	0171 353 0101
	2 Harcourt Buildings, London	0171 583 9020
Whiteley Miss Miranda Blyth	4 Field Court, London	0171 440 6900
Williams The Hon John Melville	• Old Square Chambers, London	0171 269 0300
	• Old Square Chambers, Bristol	0117 927 7111

PROBATE AND ADMINISTRATION

Adamyk Simon Charles	12 New Square, London	0171 419 1212
Angus Miss Tracey Anne	5 Stone Buildings, London	0171 242 6201
Arnfield Robert John	17 Old Buildings, London	0171 405 9653
Asplin Miss Sarah Jane	• 3 Stone Buildings, London	0171 242 4937/405 8358
Barker James Sebastian	Enterprise Chambers, London	0171 405 9471
	Enterprise Chambers, Leeds	0113 246 0391
	Enterprise Chambers, Newcastle upon Tyne	0191 222 3344
Blackett-Ord Mark	• 5 Stone Buildings, London	0171 242 6201
Brownbill David John	Gray's Inn Square, London	0171 242 3529
Cameron Miss Barbara Alexander	Stanbrook & Henderson, London	0171 353 0101
	2 Harcourt Buildings, London	0171 583 9020
Charman Andrew Julian	St Philip's Chambers, Birmingham	0121 246 7000
Clarke Miss Anna Victoria	5 Stone Buildings, London	0171 242 6201
Clarke Peter John	Harcourt Chambers, London	0171 353 6961/7
	St Philip's Chambers, Birmingham	0121 246 7000
	Harcourt Chambers, Oxford	01865 791559
Clegg Sebastian James Barwick	Deans Court Chambers, Manchester	0161 834 4097
Collins John Morris	11 King's Bench Walk, London	0171 353 3337/8
	9 Woodhouse Square, Leeds	0113 245 1986
Conroy Miss Marian	3 Stone Buildings, London	0171 242 4937/405 8358
Craig Kenneth Allen	Hardwicke Building, London	0171 242 2523
Crail Miss (Elspeth) Ross	12 New Square, London	0171 419 1212
	Sovereign Chambers, Leeds	0113 245 1841/2/3
Crawford Grant	11 Old Square, London	0171 430 0341
Creaner Paul Anthony	15 Winckley Square, Preston	01772 252 828
Crosthwaite Graham Andrew	One King's Bench Walk, London	0171 936 1500
Cunningham Mark James	13 Old Square, London	0171 404 4800
Deacock Adam Jason	Chambers of Lord Goodhart QC, London	0171 405 5577
Dodge Peter Clive	11 Old Square, London	0171 430 0341
Fawls Richard Granville	5 Stone Buildings, London	0171 242 6201
Francis Edward Gerald Francis	Enterprise Chambers, London	0171 405 9471
	Enterprise Chambers, Leeds	0113 246 0391

• Expanded entry in Part D

	Enterprise Chambers, Newcastle upon Tyne	0191 222 3344
Garcia-Miller Miss Laura	Enterprise Chambers, London	0171 405 9471
	Enterprise Chambers, Leeds	0113 246 0391
	Enterprise Chambers, Newcastle upon Tyne	0191 222 3344
Garnett Kevin Mitchell	5 New Square, London	0171 404 0404
Gore Andrew Roger	Fenners Chambers, Cambridge	01223 368761
	Fenners Chambers, Peterborough	01733 562030
Gregory John Raymond	Deans Court Chambers, Manchester	0161 834 4097
	Deans Court Chambers, Preston	01772 555163
Hall Taylor Alexander Edward	11 Old Square, London	0171 430 0341
Halpern David Anthony	Enterprise Chambers, London	0171 405 9471
	Enterprise Chambers, Leeds	0113 246 0391
	Enterprise Chambers, Newcastle upon Tyne	0191 222 3344
Harbottle Gwilym Thomas	5 New Square, London	0171 404 0404
Hardwick Matthew Richard	Enterprise Chambers, London	0171 405 9471
	Enterprise Chambers, Leeds	0113 246 0391
	Enterprise Chambers, Newcastle upon Tyne	0191 222 3344
Hargreaves Miss Sara Jane	12 New Square, London	0171 419 1212
	Sovereign Chambers, Leeds	0113 245 1841/2/3
Harrod Henry Mark	5 Stone Buildings, London	0171 242 6201
Hayes Miss Josephine Mary	Chambers of Lord Goodhart QC, London	0171 405 5577
Herbert Mark Jeremy	• 5 Stone Buildings, London	0171 242 6201
Hess Edward John Watkin	Harcourt Chambers, London	0171 353 6961/7
	Harcourt Chambers, Oxford	01865 791559
Heywood Michael Edmundson	Chambers of Lord Goodhart QC, London	0171 405 5577
	Cobden House Chambers, Manchester	0161 833 6000/6001
Holmes Justin Francis	Chambers of Lord Goodhart QC, London	0171 405 5577
Hughes Miss Mary Josephine	Chambers of Lord Goodhart QC, London	0171 405 5577
Hunter William Quigley	No 1 Serjeants' Inn, London	0171 415 6666
Ife Miss Linden Elizabeth	Enterprise Chambers, London	0171 405 9471
	Enterprise Chambers, Leeds	0113 246 0391
	Enterprise Chambers, Newcastle upon Tyne	0191 222 3344
Iwi Quintin Joseph	Stanbrook & Henderson, London	0171 353 0101
	2 Harcourt Buildings, London	0171 583 9020
Jackson Dirik George Allan	• Chambers of Mr Peter Crampin QC, London	0171 831 0081
James Michael Frank	Enterprise Chambers, London	0171 405 9471
	Enterprise Chambers, Leeds	0113 246 0391
	Enterprise Chambers, Newcastle upon Tyne	0191 222 3344
Jefferies Thomas Robert	Chambers of Lord Goodhart QC, London	0171 405 5577
Jennings Timothy Robin Finnegan	Enterprise Chambers, London	0171 405 9471
	Enterprise Chambers, Leeds	0113 246 0391
	Enterprise Chambers, Newcastle upon Tyne	0191 222 3344
John Peter Charles	One Essex Court, London	0171 936 3030
Johnson Michael Sloan	Chambers of John Hand QC, Manchester	0161 955 9000
Jory Robert John Hugh	Enterprise Chambers, London	0171 405 9471
	Enterprise Chambers, Leeds	0113 246 0391
	Enterprise Chambers, Newcastle upon Tyne	0191 222 3344
Lamont Miss Camilla Rose	Chambers of Lord Goodhart QC, London	0171 405 5577
Laughton Samuel Dennis	17 Old Buildings, London	0171 405 9653
Le Poidevin Nicholas Peter	12 New Square, London	0171 419 1212
	Sovereign Chambers, Leeds	0113 245 1841/2/3
Legge Henry	5 Stone Buildings, London	0171 242 6201
Levy Benjamin Keith	Enterprise Chambers, London	0171 405 9471
	Enterprise Chambers, Leeds	0113 246 0391
	Enterprise Chambers, Newcastle upon Tyne	0191 222 3344

Levy Robert Stuart	9 Stone Buildings, London	0171 404 5055
	Assize Court Chambers, Bristol	0117 926 4587
Mann George Anthony	Enterprise Chambers, London	0171 405 9471
	Enterprise Chambers, Leeds	0113 246 0391
	Enterprise Chambers, Newcastle upon Tyne	0191 222 3344
Marten Richard Hedley Westwood	Chambers of Lord Goodhart QC, London	0171 405 5577
Mauger Miss Claire Shanti Andrea	Enterprise Chambers, London	0171 405 9471
McAllister Miss Elizabeth Ann	Enterprise Chambers, London	0171 405 9471
	Enterprise Chambers, Leeds	0113 246 0391
	Enterprise Chambers, Newcastle upon Tyne	0191 222 3344
McCarthy William	New Bailey Chambers, Preston	01772 258 087
McKinnell Miss Soraya Jane	Enterprise Chambers, London	0171 405 9471
	Enterprise Chambers, Leeds	0113 246 0391
	Enterprise Chambers, Newcastle upon Tyne	0191 222 3344
McQuail Ms Katherine Emma	11 Old Square, London	0171 430 0341
Morgan Charles James Arthur	Enterprise Chambers, London	0171 405 9471
	Enterprise Chambers, Leeds	0113 246 0391
	Enterprise Chambers, Newcastle upon Tyne	0191 222 3344
Mullis Anthony Roger	Chambers of Lord Goodhart QC, London	0171 405 5577
Nebhrajani Miss Mel	9 Stone Buildings, London	0171 404 5055
Newman Miss Catherine Mary	• 13 Old Square, London	0171 404 4800
Nicol-Gent William Philip Trahair	King's Chambers, Eastbourne	01323 416053
Norris Alastair Hubert	• 5 Stone Buildings, London	0171 242 6201
	• Southernhay Chambers, Exeter	01392 255777
Norris Paul Howard	One Essex Court, London	0171 936 3030
Nurse Gordon Bramwell William	11 Old Square, London	0171 430 0341
O'Sullivan Michael Morton	5 Stone Buildings, London	0171 242 6201
Oakley Tony	• 11 Old Square, London	0171 430 0341
Ohrenstein Dov	Chambers of Lord Goodhart QC, London	0171 405 5577
Ovey Miss Elizabeth Helen	11 Old Square, London	0171 430 0341
Parry David Julian Thomas	Chambers of Lord Goodhart QC, London	0171 405 5577
Peacocke Mrs Teresa Anne Rosen	Enterprise Chambers, London	0171 405 9471
	Enterprise Chambers, Leeds	0113 246 0391
	Enterprise Chambers, Newcastle upon Tyne	0191 222 3344
Pilkington Mrs Mavis Patricia	9 Woodhouse Square, Leeds	0113 245 1986
Pimentel Carlos de Serpa Alberto Legg	3 Stone Buildings, London	0171 242 4937/405 8358
Pryke Stuart	Trinity Chambers, Newcastle upon Tyne	0191 232 1927
Purdie Robert Anthony James	28 Western Road, Oxford	01865 204911
Quint Mrs Joan Francesca Rae	11 Old Square, London	0171 242 5022
Reed Miss Penelope Jane	9 Stone Buildings, London	0171 404 5055
Rees David Benjamin	5 Stone Buildings, London	0171 242 6201
Rich Miss Ann Barbara	5 Stone Buildings, London	0171 242 6201
Richardson Miss Sarah Jane	Enterprise Chambers, London	0171 405 9471
	Enterprise Chambers, Leeds	0113 246 0391
	Enterprise Chambers, Newcastle upon Tyne	0191 222 3344
Robson John Malcolm	2 Gray's Inn Square Chambers, London	0171 242 0328/405 1317
	Assize Court Chambers, Bristol	0117 926 4587
Ross Martyn John Greaves	• 5 New Square, London	0171 404 0404
	• Octagon House, Norwich	01603 623186
Rowell David Stewart	Chambers of Lord Goodhart QC, London	0171 405 5577
Sagar (Edward) Leigh	12 New Square, London	0171 419 1212
	Sovereign Chambers, Leeds	0113 245 1841/2/3
	Newport Chambers, Newport	01633 267403/255855
Selway Dr Katherine Emma	11 Old Square, London	0171 430 0341
Shah Bajul Amratlal Somchand	Twenty-Four Old Buildings, London	0171 404 0946
Simmonds Andrew John	5 Stone Buildings, London	0171 242 6201
Smart Miss Jacqueline Anne	Trinity Chambers, Newcastle upon Tyne	0191 232 1927

• Expanded entry in Part D

Sugar Simon Gareth	5 New Square, London	0171 404 0404
Sunnucks James Horace George	• 5 New Square, London	0171 404 0404
	• Octagon House, Norwich	01603 623186
Tidmarsh Christopher Ralph Francis	5 Stone Buildings, London	0171 242 6201
Trace Anthony John	• 13 Old Square, London	0171 404 4800
Vane The Hon Christopher John Fletcher	Trinity Chambers, Newcastle upon Tyne	0191 232 1927
Walker Andrew Greenfield	Chambers of Lord Goodhart QC, London	0171 405 5577
Warnock-Smith Mrs Shan	5 Stone Buildings, London	0171 242 6201
Weatherill Bernard Richard	Chambers of Lord Goodhart QC, London	0171 405 5577
West Mark	• 11 Old Square, London	0171 430 0341
Whitehouse Christopher John	Gray's Inn Square, London	0171 242 3529
Williamson Miss Bridget Susan	Enterprise Chambers, London	0171 405 9471
	Enterprise Chambers, Leeds	0113 246 0391
	Enterprise Chambers, Newcastle upon Tyne	0191 222 3344
Yelton Michael Paul	Fenners Chambers, Cambridge	01223 368761
	Fenners Chambers, Peterborough	01733 562030

PRODUCT LIABILITY

Ashworth Piers	Stanbrook & Henderson, London	0171 353 0101
	2 Harcourt Buildings, London	0171 583 9020
	Priory Chambers, Birmingham	0121 236 3882/1375
Brahams Mrs Diana Joyce	Old Square Chambers, London	0171 269 0300
	Old Square Chambers, Bristol	0117 927 7111
Campbell Oliver Edward Wilhelm	2 Harcourt Buildings, London	0171 583 9020
Eastman Roger	Stanbrook & Henderson, London	0171 353 0101
	2 Harcourt Buildings, London	0171 583 9020
Gibson Charles Anthony Warneford	2 Harcourt Buildings, London	0171 583 9020
Harvey Jonathan Robert William	2 Harcourt Buildings, London	0171 583 9020
Playford Jonathan Richard	2 Harcourt Buildings, London	0171 583 9020
Popat Prashant	Stanbrook & Henderson, London	0171 353 0101
	2 Harcourt Buildings, London	0171 583 9020
Powles Stephen Robert	Stanbrook & Henderson, London	0171 353 0101
	2 Harcourt Buildings, London	0171 583 9020
Pratt Allan Duncan	New Court Chambers, London	0171 831 9500
Prynne Andrew Geoffrey Lockyer	Stanbrook & Henderson, London	0171 353 0101
	2 Harcourt Buildings, London	0171 583 9020
Riley-Smith Tobias Augustine William	2 Harcourt Buildings, London	0171 583 9020
Sarony Neville Leslie		
Weitzman Thomas Edward Benjamin	3 Verulam Buildings, London	0171 831 8441
Williams The Hon John Melville	• Old Square Chambers, London	0171 269 0300
	• Old Square Chambers, Bristol	0117 927 7111

PROFESSIONAL AND REGULATORY DISCIPLINARY

Hill (Eliot) Michael	23 Essex Street, London	0171 413 0353
Purnell Nicholas Robert	23 Essex Street, London	0171 413 0353

PROFESSIONAL NEGLIGENCE

Abbott Francis Arthur	Pump Court Chambers, London	0171 353 0711
	Pump Court Chambers, Winchester	01962 868161
Acton Davis Jonathan James	4 Pump Court, London	0171 353 2656/9
Adamyk Simon Charles	12 New Square, London	0171 419 1212
Airey Simon Andrew	11 Bolt Court, London	0171 353 2300
	Redhill Chambers, Redhill	01737 780781
Akenhead Robert	Atkin Chambers, London	0171 404 0102
Al'Hassan Khadim	Equity Chambers, Birmingham	0121 233 2100
Aldridge James Hugh	13 Old Square, London	0171 404 4800
Alexander Ian Douglas Gavin	11 Bolt Court, London	0171 353 2300
	Redhill Chambers, Redhill	01737 780781
Alldis Christopher John	Peel House Chambers, Liverpool	0151 236 4321
Alliott George Beckles	2 Harcourt Buildings, London	0171 583 9020
Althaus Antony Justin	No 1 Serjeants' Inn, London	0171 415 6666
Ambrose Miss Clare Mary Geneste	20 Essex Street, London	0171 583 9294
Ames Geoffrey Alan	29 Bedford Row Chambers, London	0171 831 2626
Amin Miss Farah	7 New Square, London	0171 430 1660
Angus Miss Tracey Anne	5 Stone Buildings, London	0171 242 6201
Anthony Michael Guy	Two Crown Office Row, London	0171 797 8100

Archer John Francis Ashweek | Two Crown Office Row, London | 0171 797 8100

Archer John Francis Ashweek	Two Crown Office Row, London	0171 797 8100
Ashworth Piers	Stanbrook & Henderson, London	0171 353 0101
	2 Harcourt Buildings, London	0171 583 9020
	Priory Chambers, Birmingham	0121 236 3882/1375
Aslett Pepin Charles Maguire	22 Albion Place, Northampton	01604 636271
Asplin Miss Sarah Jane	• 3 Stone Buildings, London	0171 242 4937/405 8358
Atherton Ian David	Enterprise Chambers, London	0171 405 9471
	Enterprise Chambers, Leeds	0113 246 0391
	Enterprise Chambers, Newcastle upon Tyne	0191 222 3344
Aylen Walter Stafford	Hardwicke Building, London	0171 242 2523
Ayres Andrew John William	13 Old Square, London	0171 404 4800
Baatz Nicholas Stephen	Atkin Chambers, London	0171 404 0102
Bailey Edward Henry	5 Bell Yard, London	0171 333 8811
Baker Miss Anne Jacqueline	Enterprise Chambers, London	0171 405 9471
	Enterprise Chambers, Leeds	0113 246 0391
	Enterprise Chambers, Newcastle upon Tyne	0191 222 3344
Baldwin John Grant	Oriel Chambers, Liverpool	0151 236 7191
Barber Miss Sally	5 Stone Buildings, London	0171 242 6201
Barker James Sebastian	Enterprise Chambers, London	0171 405 9471
	Enterprise Chambers, Leeds	0113 246 0391
	Enterprise Chambers, Newcastle upon Tyne	0191 222 3344
Barker Simon George Harry	• 13 Old Square, London	0171 404 4800
Barstow Stephen Royden	Harcourt Chambers, London	0171 353 6961/7
	Harcourt Chambers, Oxford	01865 791559
Barwise Miss Stephanie Nicola	Atkin Chambers, London	0171 404 0102
Baxter Gerald Pearson	25-27 Castle Street, Liverpool	0151 227 5661/5666/236 5072
Beal Kieron Conrad	4 Paper Buildings, London	0171 353 3366/583 7155
Beaumont Marc Clifford	• Pump Court Chambers, London	0171 353 0711
	• Harrow-on-the-Hill Chambers, Harrow on the Hill	0181 423 7444
	• Pump Court Chambers, Winchester	01962 868161
	• Windsor Barristers' Chambers, Windsor	01753 648 899
Beer Jason Barrington	5 Essex Court, London	0171 410 2000
Bellamy Jonathan Mark	39 Essex Street, London	0171 832 1111
Beltrami Adrian Joseph	3 Verulam Buildings, London	0171 831 8441
Bendall Richard Giles	33 Bedford Row, London	0171 242 6476
Bennett Gordon Irvine	5 Bell Yard, London	0171 333 8811
Bennett John Martyn	• Peel House Chambers, Liverpool	0151 236 4321
Benson Julian Christopher Woodburn	One Essex Court, London	0171 936 3030
Bergin Terence Edward	New Court Chambers, London	0171 831 9500
Berkley Michael Stuart	Rougemont Chambers, Exeter	01392 410471
Berragan (Howard) Neil	Merchant Chambers, Manchester	0161 839 7070
Best Stanley Philip	Bracton Chambers, London	0171 242 4248
	Westgate Chambers, Lewes	01273 480 510
	Barnstaple Chambers, Winkleigh	0183 783763
Bhaloo Miss Zia Kurban	Enterprise Chambers, London	0171 405 9471
	Enterprise Chambers, Leeds	0113 246 0391
	Enterprise Chambers, Newcastle upon Tyne	0191 222 3344
Bhattacharyya Ardhendu	1 Gray's Inn Square, London	0171 405 8946
	11 St Bernards Road, Slough	01753 553806/817989
Bickford-Smith Stephen William	4 Breams Buildings, London	0171 353 5835/430 1221
Birtles William	Old Square Chambers, London	0171 269 0300
	Old Square Chambers, Bristol	0117 927 7111
Birts Peter William	• Farrar's Building, London	0171 583 9241
Bishop Edward James	No 1 Serjeants' Inn, London	0171 415 6666
Blackburn John	Atkin Chambers, London	0171 404 0102
Blackett-Ord Mark	• 5 Stone Buildings, London	0171 242 6201
Blakesley Patrick James	Two Crown Office Row, London	0171 797 8100
Block Neil Selwyn	39 Essex Street, London	0171 832 1111
Bloom-Davis Desmond Niall Laurence	Pump Court Chambers, London	0171 353 0711
	Pump Court Chambers, Winchester	01962 868161
Bompas Anthony George	4 Stone Buildings, London	0171 242 5524
Booth Alan James	Deans Court Chambers, Manchester	0161 834 4097
	Deans Court Chambers, Preston	01772 555163
Boswell Miss Lindsay Alice	4 Pump Court, London	0171 353 2656/9
Bourne Robert	• 4 Field Court, London	0171 440 6900

       • Expanded entry in Part D

Bowdery Martin	Atkin Chambers, London	0171 404 0102
Boydell Edward Patrick Stirrup	Pump Court Chambers, London	0171 353 0711
	Pump Court Chambers, Winchester	01962 868161
Boyle David Stuart	Deans Court Chambers, Manchester	0161 834 4097
Boyle Gerard James	No 1 Serjeants' Inn, London	0171 415 6666
Bradley Richard	Oriel Chambers, Liverpool	0151 236 7191
Brahams Mrs Diana Joyce	Old Square Chambers, London	0171 269 0300
	Old Square Chambers, Bristol	0117 927 7111
Brannigan Peter John Sean	One Essex Court, London	0171 936 3030
Breen Carlo Enrico	Chambers of John Hand QC, Manchester	0161 955 9000
Brent Richard	3 Verulam Buildings, London	0171 831 8441
Brett Matthew Christopher Anthony	Harcourt Chambers, London	0171 353 6961/7
	Harcourt Chambers, Oxford	01865 791559
Briden Timothy John	• 8 Stone Buildings, London	0171 831 9881
Brilliant Simon Howard	Lamb Chambers, London	0171 797 8300
Brodie (James) Bruce	39 Essex Street, London	0171 832 1111
Brown Geoffrey Barlow	39 Essex Street, London	0171 832 1111
Browne James William	Goldsworth Chambers, London	0171 405 7117
Browne Miss Julie Rebecca	Goldsmith Building, London	0171 353 7881
Brunner Adrian John Nelson	Stanbrook & Henderson, London	0171 353 0101
	2 Harcourt Buildings, London	0171 583 9020
Brunton Sean Alexander McKay	Pump Court Chambers, London	0171 353 0711
	Pump Court Chambers, Winchester	01962 868161
Budden Miss Caroline Rachel	One King's Bench Walk, London	0171 936 1500
Bull (Donald) Roger	One Essex Court, London	0171 936 3030
Burles David John	Goldsmith Building, London	0171 353 7881
Burns Peter Richard	Deans Court Chambers, Manchester	0161 834 4097
Burr Andrew Charles	Atkin Chambers, London	0171 404 0102
Burton Michael John	Littleton Chambers, London	0171 797 8600
Bush Keith	30 Park Place, Cardiff	01222 398421
Butler Philip Andrew	Goldsmith Chambers, London	0171 353 6802/3/4/5
	Deans Court Chambers, Manchester	0161 834 4097
	Deans Court Chambers, Preston	01772 555163
Butt Miss Romasa	Goldsworth Chambers, London	0171 405 7117
Calvert Peter Charles	Goldsmith Building, London	0171 353 7881
Cameron Miss Barbara Alexander	Stanbrook & Henderson, London	0171 353 0101
	2 Harcourt Buildings, London	0171 583 9020
Cameron Neil Alexander	Wilberforce Chambers, Hull	01482 323 264
Candlin James Richard	Chambers of Geoffrey Hawker, London	0171 583 8899
Cape Robert Paul	Milburn House Chambers, Newcastle upon Tyne	0191 230 5511
Carey Jeremy Reynolds Patrick	Lamb Chambers, London	0171 797 8300
Carling Christopher James	Old Square Chambers, London	0171 269 0300
	Old Square Chambers, Bristol	0117 927 7111
Carrodus Miss Gail Caroline	New Court Chambers, London	0171 831 9500
Cartwright Richard John	Queen Elizabeth Building, London	0171 353 7181 (12 lines)
Cash Miss Joanne Catherine	Farrar's Building, London	0171 583 9241
Catchpole Stuart Paul	39 Essex Street, London	0171 832 1111
Cawley Neil Robert Loudoun	55 Temple Chambers, London	0171 353 7400
	Milton Keynes Chambers, Milton Keynes	01908 217857
Caws Eian Richard Edwin	4 Breams Buildings, London	0171 353 5835/430 1221
Cawson Mark	• 12 New Square, London	0171 419 1212
	• St James's Chambers, Manchester	0161 834 7000
	• Park Lane Chambers, Leeds	0113 228 5000
Chalmers Miss Suzanne Frances	Two Crown Office Row, London	0171 797 8100
Charlwood Spike Llewellyn	4 Paper Buildings, London	0171 353 3366/583 7155
Charman Andrew Julian	St Philip's Chambers, Birmingham	0121 246 7000
Cherry John Mitchell	• 8 Stone Buildings, London	0171 831 9881
Cherryman John Richard	4 Breams Buildings, London	0171 353 5835/430 1221
Cheyne Miss Phyllida Alison	4 Pump Court, London	0171 353 2656/9
Choudhury Akhlaq	11 King's Bench Walk, London	0171 632 8500
Christie-Brown Miss Sarah Louise	4 Paper Buildings, London	0171 353 3366/583 7155
Clarke Miss Alison Lee	No 1 Serjeants' Inn, London	0171 415 6666
Clarke Miss Anna Victoria	5 Stone Buildings, London	0171 242 6201
Clarke George Robert Ivan	Chambers of Geoffrey Hawker, London	0171 583 8899
Clarke Jonathan Christopher St John	Old Square Chambers, London	0171 269 0300
	Old Square Chambers, Bristol	0117 927 7111
Clay Robert Charles	Atkin Chambers, London	0171 404 0102

• Expanded entry in Part D

Clegg Sebastian James Barwick	Deans Court Chambers, Manchester	0161 834 4097
Clover (Thomas) Anthony	New Court Chambers, London	0171 831 9500
Coburn Michael Jeremy Patrick	20 Essex Street, London	0171 583 9294
Collaco Moraes Francis Thomas	• 2 Gray's Inn Square Chambers, London	0171 242 0328/405 1317
Collard Michael David	5 Pump Court, London	0171 353 2532
Collett Ivor William	No 1 Serjeants' Inn, London	0171 415 6666
Collins John Morris	11 King's Bench Walk, London	0171 353 3337/8
	9 Woodhouse Square, Leeds	0113 245 1986
Collinson Miss Alicia Hester	Harcourt Chambers, London	0171 353 6961/7
	Harcourt Chambers, Oxford	01865 791559
Conlin Geoffrey David	3 Serjeants' Inn, London	0171 353 5537
Connerty Anthony Robin	Lamb Chambers, London	0171 797 8300
Cooper Adrian Edgar Mark	Stanbrook & Henderson, London	0171 353 0101
	2 Harcourt Buildings, London	0171 583 9020
Corbett James Patrick	St Philip's Chambers, Birmingham	0121 246 7000
Cory-Wright Charles Alexander	39 Essex Street, London	0171 832 1111
Cotter Miss Sara Elizabeth	• Higher Combe, Minehead	01643 862722
Cottrell Matthew Robert	Oriel Chambers, Liverpool	0151 236 7191
Coulter Barry John	One Essex Court, London	0171 936 3030
Cowan Peter Sherwood McCrea	Oriel Chambers, Liverpool	0151 236 7191
Cowen Miss Sally Emma	Chambers of Geoffrey Hawker, London	0171 583 8899
Craig Kenneth Allen	Hardwicke Building, London	0171 242 2523
Crail Miss (Elspeth) Ross	12 New Square, London	0171 419 1212
	Sovereign Chambers, Leeds	0113 245 1841/2/3
Cranfield Peter Anthony	3 Verulam Buildings, London	0171 831 8441
Crawford Grant	11 Old Square, London	0171 430 0341
Creaner Paul Anthony	15 Winckley Square, Preston	01772 252 828
Cross James Edward Michael	4 Pump Court, London	0171 353 2656/9
Cross (Joseph) Edward	2 Gray's Inn Square Chambers, London	0171 242 0328/405 1317
Crossley Simon Justin	9 Woodhouse Square, Leeds	0113 245 1986
Crowley John Desmond	Two Crown Office Row, London	0171 797 8100
Curtis Michael Alexander	Two Crown Office Row, London	0171 797 8100
Daiches Michael Salis	• 22 Old Buildings, London	0171 831 0222
Davidson Edward Alan	• 11 Old Square, London	0171 430 0341
Davidson Nicholas Ranking	4 Paper Buildings, London	0171 353 3366/583 7155
Davies Andrew Christopher	New Court Chambers, London	0171 831 9500
Davies Miss Louise	12 New Square, London	0171 419 1212
Davies Stephen Richard	8 King Street Chambers, Manchester	0161 834 9560
Davies-Jones Jonathan	3 Verulam Buildings, London	0171 831 8441
Davis Andrew Paul	Two Crown Office Row, London	0171 797 8100
de Jehan David	St Paul's House, Leeds	0113 245 5866
de Lacy Richard Michael	3 Verulam Buildings, London	0171 831 8441
Deacock Adam Jason	Chambers of Lord Goodhart QC, London	0171 405 5577
Dean Paul Benjamin	5 Bell Yard, London	0171 333 8811
DeCamp Miss Jane Louise	Two Crown Office Row, London	0171 797 8100
Dennison Stephen Randell	Atkin Chambers, London	0171 404 0102
Dennys Nicholas Charles Jonathan	Atkin Chambers, London	0171 404 0102
Dilhorne The Rt Hon Viscount	4 Breams Buildings, London	0171 353 5835/430 1221
Dodge Peter Clive	11 Old Square, London	0171 430 0341
Doerries Miss Chantal-Aimee Renee Aemelia Annemarie	Atkin Chambers, London	0171 404 0102
Doggart Piers Graham	• King's Chambers, Eastbourne	01323 416053
Donovan Joel	New Court Chambers, London	0171 831 9500
Dougherty Nigel Peter	Erskine Chambers, London	0171 242 5532
Dowse John	Chambers of Lord Goodhart QC, London	0171 405 5577
	Chambers of John Hand QC, Manchester	0161 955 9000
Doyle Louis George	Chambers of Andrew Campbell QC, Leeds	0113 245 5438
Dubbery Mark Edward	Pump Court Chambers, London	0171 353 0711
Dumaresq Ms Delia Jane	Atkin Chambers, London	0171 404 0102
Dyer Nigel Ingram John	1 Mitre Court Buildings, London	0171 797 7070
Eastman Roger	Stanbrook & Henderson, London	0171 353 0101
	2 Harcourt Buildings, London	0171 583 9020
Edwards Anthony Howard	Oriel Chambers, Liverpool	0151 236 7191
Edwards-Stuart Antony James Cobham	Two Crown Office Row, London	0171 797 8100

     • Expanded entry in Part D

Elleray Anthony John	• 12 New Square, London	0171 419 1212
	• St James's Chambers, Manchester	0161 834 7000
	• Park Lane Chambers, Leeds	0113 228 5000
Elliott Nicholas Blethyn	3 Verulam Buildings, London	0171 831 8441
Elvidge John Allan	1 Mitre Court Buildings, London	0171 797 7070
Elvin David John	4 Breams Buildings, London	0171 353 5835/430 1221
Evans James Frederick Meurig	3 Verulam Buildings, London	0171 831 8441
Evans Lee John	Farrar's Building, London	0171 583 9241
Evans-Gordon Mrs Jane-Anne Mary	12 New Square, London	0171 419 1212
Evans-Tovey Jason Robert	Two Crown Office Row, London	0171 797 8100
Everall Mark Andrew	1 Mitre Court Buildings, London	0171 797 7070
Ewins Miss Catherine Jane	4 Paper Buildings, London	0171 353 3366/583 7155
Exall Gordon David	Chambers of Andrew Campbell QC, Leeds	0113 245 5438
Faulks Edward Peter Lawless	No 1 Serjeants' Inn, London	0171 415 6666
Fawls Richard Granville	5 Stone Buildings, London	0171 242 6201
Field Richard Alan	11 King's Bench Walk, London	0171 632 8500
Fisher David	5 Bell Yard, London	0171 333 8811
Flenley William David Wingate	4 Paper Buildings, London	0171 353 3366/583 7155
Ford Gerard James	Baker Street Chambers, Middlesbrough	01642 873873
Foster Charles Andrew	• Chambers of Kieran Coonan QC, London	0171 583 6013/2510
Foster Francis Alexander	St Paul's House, Leeds	0113 245 5866
Franklin Miss Kim	• Lamb Chambers, London	0171 797 8300
Franklin Stephen Hall	5 Paper Buildings, London	0171 583 6117
	Fenners Chambers, Cambridge	01223 368761
Fraser Peter Donald	Atkin Chambers, London	0171 404 0102
Freedman Sampson Clive	3 Verulam Buildings, London	0171 831 8441
Friedman David Peter	4 Pump Court, London	0171 353 2656/9
Friel John Anthony	Goldsmith Building, London	0171 353 7881
	Southsea Chambers, Portsmouth	01705 291261
Furber (Robert) John	4 Breams Buildings, London	0171 353 5835/430 1221
Gadney George Munro	Two Crown Office Row, London	0171 797 8100
Gallagher John David Edmund	Goldsmith Building, London	0171 353 7881
Garcia-Miller Miss Laura	Enterprise Chambers, London	0171 405 9471
	Enterprise Chambers, Leeds	0113 246 0391
	Enterprise Chambers, Newcastle upon Tyne	0191 222 3344
Gatty Daniel Simon	New Court Chambers, London	0171 831 9500
Geering Ian Walter	3 Verulam Buildings, London	0171 831 8441
Gerald Nigel Mortimer	Enterprise Chambers, London	0171 405 9471
	Enterprise Chambers, Leeds	0113 246 0391
	Enterprise Chambers, Newcastle upon Tyne	0191 222 3344
Gibaud Miss Catherine Alison Annetta	3 Verulam Buildings, London	0171 831 8441
Gibson Charles Anthony Warneford	2 Harcourt Buildings, London	0171 583 9020
Giffin Nigel Dyson	11 King's Bench Walk, London	0171 632 8500
Gilbert Ms Julia Jane	Trinity Chambers, Newcastle upon Tyne	0191 232 1927
Gilchrist David Somerled	Chambers of John Hand QC, Manchester	0161 955 9000
Gilmour Nigel Benjamin Douglas	Peel House Chambers, Liverpool	0151 236 4321
Goddard Andrew Stephen	Atkin Chambers, London	0171 404 0102
Godfrey Jonathan Saul	St Paul's House, Leeds	0113 245 5866
Godwin William George Henry	Atkin Chambers, London	0171 404 0102
Goff Anthony Thomas	25-27 Castle Street, Liverpool	0151 227 5661/5666/236 5072
Goodhart Lord	Chambers of Lord Goodhart QC, London	0171 405 5577
Goodman Andrew David	199 Strand, London	0171 379 9779
Goose Julian Nicholas	Chambers of Andrew Campbell QC, Leeds	0113 245 5438
Gore Andrew Roger	Fenners Chambers, Cambridge	01223 368761
	Fenners Chambers, Peterborough	01733 562030
Gore-Andrews Gavin Angus Russell	Stanbrook & Henderson, London	0171 353 0101
	2 Harcourt Buildings, London	0171 583 9020
Gorna Miss Anne Christina	4 Paper Buildings, London	0171 353 3366/583 7155
	Cathedral Chambers (Jan Wood Independent Barristers' Clerk), Exeter	01392 210900
Gough Miss Karen Louise	Arbitration Chambers, London	0171 267 2137

	West Lodge Farm, Meopham	01474 812280
Grace John Oliver Bowman	3 Serjeants' Inn, London	0171 353 5537
Grace Jonathan Robert	Deans Court Chambers, Manchester	0161 834 4097
	Deans Court Chambers, Preston	01772 555163
Grant Thomas Paul Wentworth	New Court Chambers, London	0171 831 9500
Grantham Andrew Timothy	• Deans Court Chambers, Manchester	0161 834 4097
	• Deans Court Chambers, Preston	01772 555163
Gray Richard Paul	39 Essex Street, London	0171 832 1111
Greenan Miss Sarah Octavia	• 9 Woodhouse Square, Leeds	0113 245 1986
Greenbourne John Hugo	Two Crown Office Row, London	0171 797 8100
Gregory John Raymond	Deans Court Chambers, Manchester	0161 834 4097
	Deans Court Chambers, Preston	01772 555163
Gregory Richard Hamilton	Harcourt Chambers, London	0171 353 6961/7
Griffiths (John) Peter (Gwynne)	30 Park Place, Cardiff	01222 398421
Griffiths Peter Robert	4 Stone Buildings, London	0171 242 5524
Grodzinski Samuel Marc	39 Essex Street, London	0171 832 1111
Groves Hugo Gerard	Enterprise Chambers, London	0171 405 9471
	Enterprise Chambers, Leeds	0113 246 0391
	Enterprise Chambers, Newcastle upon Tyne	0191 222 3344
Gruffydd John	Oriel Chambers, Liverpool	0151 236 7191
Guggenheim Miss Anna Maeve	Two Crown Office Row, London	0171 797 8100
Gulliver Miss Alison Louise	• 4 Paper Buildings, London	0171 353 3366/583 7155
Gun Cuninghame Julian Arthur	• Gough Square Chambers, London	0171 353 0924
Gunning Alexander Rupert	4 Pump Court, London	0171 353 2656/9
Hall Mrs Melanie Ruth	Monckton Chambers, London	0171 405 7211
Hall-Smith Martin Clive William	Goldsmith Building, London	0171 353 7881
Halpern David Anthony	Enterprise Chambers, London	0171 405 9471
	Enterprise Chambers, Leeds	0113 246 0391
	Enterprise Chambers, Newcastle upon Tyne	0191 222 3344
Hamer Michael Howard Kenneth	2 Harcourt Buildings, London	0171 583 9020
	Westgate Chambers, Lewes	01273 480 510
Hamilton Graeme Montagu	Two Crown Office Row, London	0171 797 8100
Hamilton Peter Bernard	4 Pump Court, London	0171 353 2656/9
Hammerton Alastair Rolf	No 1 Serjeants' Inn, London	0171 415 6666
Hammerton Miss Veronica Lesley	No 1 Serjeants' Inn, London	0171 415 6666
Hand John Lester	Old Square Chambers, London	0171 269 0300
	Old Square Chambers, Bristol	0117 927 7111
	Chambers of John Hand QC, Manchester	0161 955 9000
Hansen William Joseph	5 Bell Yard, London	0171 333 8811
Hantusch Robert Anthony	• 3 Stone Buildings, London	0171 242 4937/405 8358
Harbottle Gwilym Thomas	5 New Square, London	0171 404 0404
Hargreaves Miss Sara Jane	12 New Square, London	0171 419 1212
	Sovereign Chambers, Leeds	0113 245 1841/2/3
Harper Joseph Charles	4 Breams Buildings, London	0171 353 5835/430 1221
Harrap Giles Thresher	• Pump Court Chambers, London	0171 353 0711
	• Pump Court Chambers, Winchester	01962 868161
Harris Paul Best	Monckton Chambers, London	0171 405 7211
Harrison John Foster	St Paul's House, Leeds	0113 245 5866
Harrison Michael Thomas	199 Strand, London	0171 379 9779
Harvey Jonathan Robert William	2 Harcourt Buildings, London	0171 583 9020
Harvey Michael Llewellyn Tucker	Two Crown Office Row, London	0171 797 8100
Harwood-Stevenson John Francis Richard	9-12 Bell Yard, London	0171 400 1800
	East Anglian Chambers, Norwich	01603 617351
Haven Kevin	2 Gray's Inn Square Chambers, London	0171 242 0328/405 1317
Hay Ms Deborah Jane	Goldsmith Building, London	0171 353 7881
Hay Robin William Patrick Hamilton	Goldsmith Building, London	0171 353 7881
Hayes Miss Josephine Mary	Chambers of Lord Goodhart QC, London	0171 405 5577
Healy Miss Alexandra	9-12 Bell Yard, London	0171 400 1800
Henderson Roger Anthony	Stanbrook & Henderson, London	0171 353 0101
	2 Harcourt Buildings, London	0171 583 9020
Herbert Mrs Rebecca Mary	2 New Street, Leicester	0116 262 5906
Heywood Michael Edmundson	Chambers of Lord Goodhart QC, London	0171 405 5577
	Cobden House Chambers, Manchester	0161 833 6000/6001
Higgins Anthony Paul	Goldsmith Building, London	0171 353 7881
Hill Nicholas Mark	Pump Court Chambers, London	0171 353 0711

• Expanded entry in Part D

Hinchliffe Philip Nicholas	Pump Court Chambers, Winchester	01962 868161
	Chambers of John Hand QC, Manchester	0161 955 9000
Hodgkinson Tristram Patrick	• 5 Pump Court, London	0171 353 2532
Hodgson Miss Susan Ann	Two Crown Office Row, London	0171 797 8100
Hogg The Rt Hon Douglas Martin	4 Paper Buildings, London	0171 353 3366/583 7155
	37 Park Square, Leeds	0113 243 9422
Holdsworth James Arthur	Two Crown Office Row, London	0171 797 8100
Holgate David John	4 Breams Buildings, London	0171 353 5835/430 1221
Holland Charles Christopher	Trinity Chambers, Newcastle upon Tyne	0191 232 1927
Holland David Moore	29 Bedford Row Chambers, London	0171 831 2626
Hollingworth Peter James Michael	22 Albion Place, Northampton	01604 636271
Holmes Justin Francis	Chambers of Lord Goodhart QC, London	0171 405 5577
Holroyd John James	• 9 Woodhouse Square, Leeds	0113 245 1986
Holwill Derek Paul Winsor	4 Paper Buildings, London	0171 353 3366/583 7155
Horlock Timothy John	Chambers of John Hand QC, Manchester	0161 955 9000
Horspool Anthony Bernard Graeme	Hardwicke Building, London	0171 242 2523
Horton Matthew Bethell	2 Mitre Court Buildings, London	0171 583 1380
Howard Charles Anthony Frederick	New Court Chambers, London	0171 831 9500
Howarth Simon Stuart	Two Crown Office Row, London	0171 797 8100
Howells James Richard	Atkin Chambers, London	0171 404 0102
Hughes Miss Mary Josephine	Chambers of Lord Goodhart QC, London	0171 405 5577
Hunter William Quigley	No 1 Serjeants' Inn, London	0171 415 6666
Hurst Brian	17 Bedford Row, London	0171 831 7314
Huskinson George Nicholas Nevil	4-5 Gray's Inn Square, London	0171 404 5252
Hutton Miss Caroline	Enterprise Chambers, London	0171 405 9471
	Enterprise Chambers, Leeds	0113 246 0391
	Enterprise Chambers, Newcastle upon Tyne	0191 222 3344
Ife Miss Linden Elizabeth	Enterprise Chambers, London	0171 405 9471
	Enterprise Chambers, Leeds	0113 246 0391
	Enterprise Chambers, Newcastle upon Tyne	0191 222 3344
Iqbal Abdul Shaffaq	Chambers of Andrew Campbell QC, Leeds	0113 245 5438
Iwi Quintin Joseph	Stanbrook & Henderson, London	0171 353 0101
	2 Harcourt Buildings, London	0171 583 9020
Jack Adrian Laurence Robert	Enterprise Chambers, London	0171 405 9471
Jackson Dirik George Allan	• Chambers of Mr Peter Crampin QC, London	0171 831 0081
Jackson Hugh Woodward	Hardwicke Building, London	0171 242 2523
Jackson Matthew David Everard	4 Paper Buildings, London	0171 353 3366/583 7155
Jackson Simon Malcolm Dermot	Park Court Chambers, Leeds	0113 243 3277
James Michael Frank	Enterprise Chambers, London	0171 405 9471
	Enterprise Chambers, Leeds	0113 246 0391
	Enterprise Chambers, Newcastle upon Tyne	0191 222 3344
Jarvis John Manners	3 Verulam Buildings, London	0171 831 8441
Jefferies Thomas Robert	Chambers of Lord Goodhart QC, London	0171 405 5577
Jenkala Adrian Aleksander	11 Bolt Court, London	0171 353 2300
	Redhill Chambers, Redhill	01737 780781
Jess Digby Charles	• 8 King Street Chambers, Manchester	0161 834 9560
John Stephen Alun	9-12 Bell Yard, London	0171 400 1800
Johnson Michael Sloan	Chambers of John Hand QC, Manchester	0161 955 9000
Jones Miss (Catherine) Charlotte	5 Bell Yard, London	0171 333 8811
Jones Geraint Martyn	Fenners Chambers, Cambridge	01223 368761
	Fenners Chambers, Peterborough	01733 562030
Jones Rhys Charles Mansel	33 Bedford Row, London	0171 242 6476
Jones Stephen Hugh	• Farrar's Building, London	0171 583 9241
Jordan Andrew	Stanbrook & Henderson, London	0171 353 0101
	2 Harcourt Buildings, London	0171 583 9020
Jory Robert John Hugh	Enterprise Chambers, London	0171 405 9471
	Enterprise Chambers, Leeds	0113 246 0391
	Enterprise Chambers, Newcastle upon Tyne	0191 222 3344
Karas Jonathan Marcus	4 Breams Buildings, London	0171 353 5835/430 1221

• Expanded entry in Part D

Kavanagh Giles Wilfred Conor	• 5 Bell Yard, London	0171 333 8811
Kay Michael Jack David	3 Verulam Buildings, London	0171 831 8441
	Park Lane Chambers, Leeds	0113 228 5000
Kealey Simon Thomas	Chambers of Andrew Campbell QC, Leeds	0113 245 5438
Kearl Guy Alexander	St Paul's House, Leeds	0113 245 5866
Kelly Geoffrey Robert	Pump Court Chambers, London	0171 353 0711
	Pump Court Chambers, Winchester	01962 868161
Kent Miss Georgina	5 Essex Court, London	0171 410 2000
Kent Michael Harcourt	Two Crown Office Row, London	0171 797 8100
Kerr Tim Julian	4-5 Gray's Inn Square, London	0171 404 5252
Kimbell John Ashley	5 Bell Yard, London	0171 333 8811
Kinnier Andrew John	2 Harcourt Buildings, London	0171 583 9020
Kirby Peter John	• Hardwicke Building, London	0171 242 2523
Knight Brian Joseph	Atkin Chambers, London	0171 404 0102
Knott Malcolm Stephen	New Court Chambers, London	0171 831 9500
Kolodynski Stefan Richard	New Court Chambers, Birmingham	0121 693 6656
Kolodziej Andrzej Jozef	• Littman Chambers, London	0171 404 4866
Kremen Philip Michael	Hardwicke Building, London	0171 242 2523
Lambert Miss Sarah Katrina	1 Crown Office Row, London	0171 797 7500
Lamont Miss Camilla Rose	Chambers of Lord Goodhart QC, London	0171 405 5577
Laughton Samuel Dennis	17 Old Buildings, London	0171 405 9653
Lawrence The Hon Patrick John Tristram	4 Paper Buildings, London	0171 353 3366/583 7155
Lawson Edmund James	9-12 Bell Yard, London	0171 400 1800
Lazarus Michael Steven	1 Crown Office Row, London	0171 583 9292
Le Poidevin Nicholas Peter	12 New Square, London	0171 419 1212
	Sovereign Chambers, Leeds	0113 245 1841/2/3
Leech Brian Walter Thomas	No 1 Serjeants' Inn, London	0171 415 6666
Leeming Ian	Lamb Chambers, London	0171 797 8300
	Chambers of John Hand QC, Manchester	0161 955 9000
Lees Andrew James	St Paul's House, Leeds	0113 245 5866
Legge Henry	5 Stone Buildings, London	0171 242 6201
Lehain Philip Peter	199 Strand, London	0171 379 9779
Lennard Stephen Charles	Hardwicke Building, London	0171 242 2523
Leonard Charles Robert Weston	Goldsmith Building, London	0171 353 7881
Levy Benjamin Keith	Enterprise Chambers, London	0171 405 9471
	Enterprise Chambers, Leeds	0113 246 0391
	Enterprise Chambers, Newcastle upon Tyne	0191 222 3344
Levy Robert Stuart	9 Stone Buildings, London	0171 404 5055
	Assize Court Chambers, Bristol	0117 926 4587
Lewer Michael Edward	Farrar's Building, London	0171 583 9241
Lewis Andrew William	Sovereign Chambers, Leeds	0113 245 1841/2/3
Lewis Miss Caroline Susannah	3 Verulam Buildings, London	0171 831 8441
Lewis Jeffrey Allan	9 Woodhouse Square, Leeds	0113 245 1986
Ley (Nigel) Spencer	Farrar's Building, London	0171 583 9241
Lindsay Crawford Callum Douglas	No 1 Serjeants' Inn, London	0171 415 6666
Litton John Letablere	4 Breams Buildings, London	0171 353 5835/430 1221
Livingstone Simon John	11 Bolt Court, London	0171 353 2300
	Redhill Chambers, Redhill	01737 780781
Lochrane Damien Horatio Ross	Pump Court Chambers, London	0171 353 0711
	Pump Court Chambers, Winchester	01962 868161
Lofthouse Simon Timothy	Atkin Chambers, London	0171 404 0102
Logan Miss Maura	St John's Chambers, Hale Barns	0161 980 7379
Lonsdale Miss Marion Mary	Chambers of Geoffrey Hawker, London	0171 583 8899
Lowenstein Paul David	Littleton Chambers, London	0171 797 8600
Lynagh Richard Dudley	Two Crown Office Row, London	0171 797 8100
Lynch Terry John	22 Albion Place, Northampton	01604 636271
Lyne Mark Hilary	One Essex Court, London	0171 936 3030
Machell Raymond Donatus	2 Pump Court, London	0171 353 5597
	Deans Court Chambers, Manchester	0161 834 4097
Macnab Alexander Andrew	Monckton Chambers, London	0171 405 7211
Macpherson Angus John	5 Bell Yard, London	0171 333 8811
Makey Christopher Douglas	Old Square Chambers, London	0171 269 0300
	Old Square Chambers, Bristol	0117 927 7111
Male John Martin	4 Breams Buildings, London	0171 353 5835/430 1221
Malecka Dr Mary Margaret	Goldsworth Chambers, London	0171 405 7117
Malek Ali	3 Verulam Buildings, London	0171 831 8441

• Expanded entry in Part D

Males Stephen Martin	20 Essex Street, London	0171 583 9294
Mandel Richard	11 Bolt Court, London	0171 353 2300
	Redhill Chambers, Redhill	01737 780781
Mann George Anthony	Enterprise Chambers, London	0171 405 9471
	Enterprise Chambers, Leeds	0113 246 0391
	Enterprise Chambers, Newcastle upon Tyne	0191 222 3344
Mantle Peter John	Monckton Chambers, London	0171 405 7211
Manzoni Charles Peter	39 Essex Street, London	0171 832 1111
Marks Jonathan Clive	4 Pump Court, London	0171 353 2656/9
Marks Jonathan Harold	3 Verulam Buildings, London	0171 831 8441
Marris Miss Sarah Selena Rixar	No 1 Serjeants' Inn, London	0171 415 6666
Marten Richard Hedley Westwood	Chambers of Lord Goodhart QC, London	0171 405 5577
Martineau Henry Ralph Adeane	Goldsmith Building, London	0171 353 7881
Masters Miss Sara Alayna	20 Essex Street, London	0171 583 9294
Matthews Dennis Roland	5 Bell Yard, London	0171 333 8811
Mauleverer Peter Bruce	4 Pump Court, London	0171 353 2656/9
Maxwell David	Claremont Chambers, Wolverhampton	01902 426222
Maxwell Miss Karen Laetitia	20 Essex Street, London	0171 583 9294
Maxwell-Scott James Herbert	Two Crown Office Row, London	0171 797 8100
May Miss Juliet Mary	3 Verulam Buildings, London	0171 831 8441
McAllister Miss Elizabeth Ann	Enterprise Chambers, London	0171 405 9471
	Enterprise Chambers, Leeds	0113 246 0391
	Enterprise Chambers, Newcastle upon Tyne	0191 222 3344
McCall Duncan James	4 Pump Court, London	0171 353 2656/9
McCredie Miss Fionnuala Mary Constance	3 Serjeants' Inn, London	0171 353 5537
McGregor Harvey	4 Paper Buildings, London	0171 353 3366/583 7155
McIvor Ian Walker	334 Deansgate Chambers, Manchester	0161 834 3767
McKenna Miss Anna Louise	Queen Elizabeth Building, London	0171 353 7181 (12 lines)
McKeon James Patrick	Peel House Chambers, Liverpool	0151 236 4321
McKinnell Miss Soraya Jane	Enterprise Chambers, London	0171 405 9471
	Enterprise Chambers, Leeds	0113 246 0391
	Enterprise Chambers, Newcastle upon Tyne	0191 222 3344
McManus Jonathan Richard	4-5 Gray's Inn Square, London	0171 404 5252
McMullan Manus Anthony	Atkin Chambers, London	0171 404 0102
McQuail Ms Katherine Emma	11 Old Square, London	0171 430 0341
McQuater Ewan Alan	3 Verulam Buildings, London	0171 831 8441
Meeson Nigel Keith	4 Field Court, London	0171 440 6900
Mendoza Neil David Pereira	Hardwicke Building, London	0171 242 2523
Merriman Nicholas Flavelle	3 Verulam Buildings, London	0171 831 8441
Middleton Miss Georgina Claire	New Court Chambers, London	0171 831 9500
Milligan Iain Anstruther	20 Essex Street, London	0171 583 9294
Milne Michael	Chambers of Geoffrey Hawker, London	0171 583 8899
	Resolution Chambers, Malvern	01684 561279
Mishcon Miss Jane Malca	4 Paper Buildings, London	0171 353 3366/583 7155
Mitchell Gregory Charles Mathew	3 Verulam Buildings, London	0171 831 8441
Morgan Charles James Arthur	Enterprise Chambers, London	0171 405 9471
	Enterprise Chambers, Leeds	0113 246 0391
	Enterprise Chambers, Newcastle upon Tyne	0191 222 3344
Morgan Jeremy	Chambers of Kieran Coonan QC, London	0171 583 6013/2510
Morgan Richard Hugo Lyndon	13 Old Square, London	0171 404 4800
Moses Miss Rebecca	Barristers' Common Law Chambers, London	0171 375 3012
	Lion Court, London	0171 404 6565
Mould Timothy James	4 Breams Buildings, London	0171 353 5835/430 1221
Mulcahy Miss Leigh-Ann Maria	Two Crown Office Row, London	0171 797 8100
Mullis Anthony Roger	Chambers of Lord Goodhart QC, London	0171 405 5577
Munro Kenneth Stuart	5 Bell Yard, London	0171 333 8811
Murray Ashley Charles	Oriel Chambers, Liverpool	0151 236 7191
Nash Jonathan Scott	3 Verulam Buildings, London	0171 831 8441
Nebhrajani Miss Mel	9 Stone Buildings, London	0171 404 5055
Neish Andrew Graham	4 Pump Court, London	0171 353 2656/9
Nesbitt Timothy John Robert	199 Strand, London	0171 379 9779
Neville Stephen John	Gough Square Chambers, London	0171 353 0924

B

Newman Miss Catherine Mary	• 13 Old Square, London	0171 404 4800
Newman Ms Ingrid	Hardwicke Building, London	0171 242 2523
Nicholls John Peter	13 Old Square, London	0171 404 4800
Nicholls Peter John	5 Pump Court, London	0171 353 2532
Nicholson Jeremy Mark	4 Pump Court, London	0171 353 2656/9
Nicol-Gent William Philip Trahair	King's Chambers, Eastbourne	01323 416053
Noble Andrew	Eldon Chambers, London	0171 353 4636
	Merchant Chambers, Manchester	0161 839 7070
Noble Roderick Grant	39 Essex Street, London	0171 832 1111
Norbury Luke Edward	17 Old Buildings, London	0171 405 9653
Norie-Miller Jeffrey Reginald	55 Temple Chambers, London	0171 353 7400
Norman Christopher John George	No 1 Serjeants' Inn, London	0171 415 6666
Norris Alastair Hubert	• 5 Stone Buildings, London	0171 242 6201
	• Southernhay Chambers, Exeter	01392 255777
Nurse Gordon Bramwell William	11 Old Square, London	0171 430 0341
O'Connor Andrew McDougal	Two Crown Office Row, London	0171 797 8100
O'Sullivan Bernard Anthony	Stanbrook & Henderson, London	0171 353 0101
	2 Harcourt Buildings, London	0171 583 9020
O'Sullivan Michael Morton	5 Stone Buildings, London	0171 242 6201
Odgers John Arthur	3 Verulam Buildings, London	0171 831 8441
Ohrenstein Dov	Chambers of Lord Goodhart QC, London	0171 405 5577
Onslow Andrew George	3 Verulam Buildings, London	0171 831 8441
Ornsby Miss Suzanne Doreen	• 2 Harcourt Buildings, London	0171 353 8415
Ough Dr Richard Norman	• Hardwicke Building, London	0171 242 2523
Overs Ms Estelle Fae	New Court Chambers, London	0171 831 9500
Ovey Miss Elizabeth Helen	11 Old Square, London	0171 430 0341
Padfield Ms Alison Mary	One Hare Court, London	0171 353 3171
Palmer James Savill	2 Harcourt Buildings, London	0171 583 9020
Paneth Miss Sarah Ruth	No 1 Serjeants' Inn, London	0171 415 6666
Parker John	2 Mitre Court Buildings, London	0171 353 1353
Parkin Miss Fiona Jane	Atkin Chambers, London	0171 404 0102
Parkin Jonathan	• Chambers of John Hand QC, Manchester	0161 955 9000
Parry David Julian Thomas	Chambers of Lord Goodhart QC, London	0171 405 5577
Patchett-Joyce Michael Thurston	Monckton Chambers, London	0171 405 7211
Patten Benedict Joseph	Two Crown Office Row, London	0171 797 8100
Patterson Stewart	• Pump Court Chambers, London	0171 353 0711
	• Pump Court Chambers, Winchester	01962 868161
Peacock Ian Christopher	12 New Square, London	0171 419 1212
	Sovereign Chambers, Leeds	0113 245 1841/2/3
Peacock Nicholas Christopher	13 Old Square, London	0171 404 4800
Peacocke Mrs Teresa Anne Rosen	Enterprise Chambers, London	0171 405 9471
	Enterprise Chambers, Leeds	0113 246 0391
	Enterprise Chambers, Newcastle upon Tyne	0191 222 3344
Peglow Dr Michael Alfred Herman	Chambers of Geoffrey Hawker, London	0171 583 8899
Pelling (Philip) Mark	Monckton Chambers, London	0171 405 7211
Pelling Richard Alexander	New Court Chambers, London	0171 831 9500
Perks Richard Howard	St Philip's Chambers, Birmingham	0121 246 7000
Pershad Rohan	Two Crown Office Row, London	0171 797 8100
Phillips Andrew Charles	Two Crown Office Row, London	0171 797 8100
Phillips David John	199 Strand, London	0171 379 9779
	30 Park Place, Cardiff	01222 398421
Phillips Jonathan Mark	3 Verulam Buildings, London	0171 831 8441
Phillips Rory Andrew Livingstone	3 Verulam Buildings, London	0171 831 8441
Phillips Stephen Edmund	3 Verulam Buildings, London	0171 831 8441
Picarda Hubert Alistair Paul	Chambers of Lord Goodhart QC, London	0171 405 5577
Pickering James Patrick	Enterprise Chambers, London	0171 405 9471
	Enterprise Chambers, Leeds	0113 246 0391
	Enterprise Chambers, Newcastle upon Tyne	0191 222 3344
Picton Julian Mark	4 Paper Buildings, London	0171 353 3366/583 7155
Pinder Miss Mary Elizabeth	No 1 Serjeants' Inn, London	0171 415 6666
Pittaway David Michael	No 1 Serjeants' Inn, London	0171 415 6666
Planterose Rowan Michael	Littman Chambers, London	0171 404 4866
Pollock Dr Evelyn Marian Margaret	5 Essex Court, London	0171 410 2000
Pooles Michael Philip Holmes	4 Paper Buildings, London	0171 353 3366/583 7155
Pope David James	3 Verulam Buildings, London	0171 831 8441

• Expanded entry in Part D

Potter Miss Louise	1 Mitre Court Buildings, London	0171 797 7070
Powles Stephen Robert	Stanbrook & Henderson, London	0171 353 0101
	2 Harcourt Buildings, London	0171 583 9020
Pratt Allan Duncan	New Court Chambers, London	0171 831 9500
Pryke Stuart	Trinity Chambers, Newcastle upon Tyne	0191 232 1927
Pulman George Frederick	• Hardwicke Building, London	0171 242 2523
	• Stour Chambers, Canterbury	01227 764899
Purchas Christopher Patrick Brooks	Two Crown Office Row, London	0171 797 8100
Purchas Robin Michael	• 2 Harcourt Buildings, London	0171 353 8415
Radevsky Anthony Eric	• 5 Bell Yard, London	0171 333 8811
Raeside Mark Andrew	Atkin Chambers, London	0171 404 0102
Rahman Ms Sadeqa Shaheen	1 Crown Office Row, London	0171 797 7500
Randall John Yeoman	7 Stone Buildings, London	0171 405 3886/242 3546
	St Philip's Chambers, Birmingham	0121 246 7000
Rankin William Peter	Oriel Chambers, Liverpool	0151 236 7191
Rawley Miss Dominique Jane	Atkin Chambers, London	0171 404 0102
Rea Miss Karen Marie-Jeanne	No 1 Serjeants' Inn, London	0171 415 6666
Readhead Simon John Howard	No 1 Serjeants' Inn, London	0171 415 6666
Reed Philip James William	5 Bell Yard, London	0171 333 8811
Rees David Benjamin	5 Stone Buildings, London	0171 242 6201
Reese Colin Edward	Atkin Chambers, London	0171 404 0102
Reeve Matthew Francis	5 Bell Yard, London	0171 333 8811
Reynold Frederic	New Court Chambers, London	0171 831 9500
Rich Miss Ann Barbara	5 Stone Buildings, London	0171 242 6201
Richards Miss Jennifer	39 Essex Street, London	0171 832 1111
Richardson Miss Sarah Jane	Enterprise Chambers, London	0171 405 9471
	Enterprise Chambers, Leeds	0113 246 0391
	Enterprise Chambers, Newcastle upon Tyne	0191 222 3344
Rigby Terence	Chambers of John Hand QC, Manchester	0161 955 9000
Rigney Andrew James	Two Crown Office Row, London	0171 797 8100
Ritchie Andrew George	9 Gough Square, London	0171 353 5371
Rivalland Marc-Edouard	No 1 Serjeants' Inn, London	0171 415 6666
Robb Adam Duncan	39 Essex Street, London	0171 832 1111
Robertson Andrew James	11 King's Bench Walk, London	0171 353 3337/8
	11 King's Bench Walk, Leeds	0113 2971 200
Robinson Miss Alice	4 Breams Buildings, London	0171 353 5835/430 1221
Robinson Richard John	2 Gray's Inn Square Chambers, London	0171 242 0328/405 1317
Robson John Malcolm	2 Gray's Inn Square Chambers, London	0171 242 0328/405 1317
	Assize Court Chambers, Bristol	0117 926 4587
Roe Thomas Idris	Goldsmith Building, London	0171 353 7881
Rogers Ian Paul	1 Crown Office Row, London	0171 583 9292
Room Stewart	8 Stone Buildings, London	0171 831 9881
Ross John Graffin	No 1 Serjeants' Inn, London	0171 415 6666
Ross Martyn John Greaves	• 5 New Square, London	0171 404 0404
	• Octagon House, Norwich	01603 623186
Roth Peter Marcel	Monckton Chambers, London	0171 405 7211
Routley Patrick	Goldsmith Building, London	0171 353 7881
Royce Darryl Fraser	Atkin Chambers, London	0171 404 0102
Rumney Conrad William Arthur	St Philip's Chambers, Birmingham	0121 246 7000
Russell Miss Christina Martha	9-12 Bell Yard, London	0171 400 1800
Russell Christopher Garnet	12 New Square, London	0171 419 1212
	Sovereign Chambers, Leeds	0113 245 1841/2/3
Russell Robert John Finlay	5 Bell Yard, London	0171 333 8811
Russen Jonathan Huw Sinclair	13 Old Square, London	0171 404 4800
Ryan David Patrick	Chambers of Geoffrey Hawker, London	0171 583 8899
Sadd Patrick James Thomas	199 Strand, London	0171 379 9779
Sadiq Tariq Mahmood	Chambers of John Hand QC, Manchester	0161 955 9000
Salter Richard Stanley	3 Verulam Buildings, London	0171 831 8441
Sampson Graeme William	Chambers of Geoffrey Hawker, London	0171 583 8899
Samuels Leslie John	Pump Court Chambers, London	0171 353 0711
	Pump Court Chambers, Winchester	01962 868161
Sander Andrew Thomas	Goldsmith Building, London	0171 353 7881
	Oriel Chambers, Liverpool	0151 236 7191
Sarony Neville Leslie		

B

Saunt Thomas William Gatty	Two Crown Office Row, London	0171 797 8100
Scarratt Richard John	One Garden Court Family Law Chambers, London	0171 797 7900
Schaw-Miller Stephen Grant	5 Bell Yard, London	0171 333 8811
Schooling Simon John	Chambers of Harjit Singh, London	0171 353 1356
Scutt David Robert	11 Bolt Court, London	0171 353 2300
	Redhill Chambers, Redhill	01737 780781
Seal Julius Damien	189 Randolph Avenue, London	0171 624 9139
	3 Temple Gardens, London	0171 353 0832
Seifert Miss Anne Miriam	4 Breams Buildings, London	0171 353 5835/430 1221
Seymour Richard William	Monckton Chambers, London	0171 405 7211
Shah Bajul Amratlal Somchand	Twenty-Four Old Buildings, London	0171 404 0946
Shaikh Eur.Ing. (Jaikumar) Christopher (Samuel	Avondale Chambers, London	0181 445 9984
	Equity Chambers, Birmingham	0121 233 2100
Shay Stephen Everett	One King's Bench Walk, London	0171 936 1500
Sheehan Malcolm Peter	Stanbrook & Henderson, London	0171 353 0101
	2 Harcourt Buildings, London	0171 583 9020
Shorrock John Michael	Peel Court Chambers, Manchester	0161 832 3791
Silvester Bruce Ross	Lamb Chambers, London	0171 797 8300
Simmonds Andrew John	5 Stone Buildings, London	0171 242 6201
Simpson Mark Taylor	4 Paper Buildings, London	0171 353 3366/583 7155
Sisley Timothy Julian Crispin	9 Stone Buildings, London	0171 404 5055
	Westgate Chambers, Lewes	01273 480 510
Sleeman Miss Rachel Sarah Elizabeth	One Essex Court, London	0171 936 3030
Sliwinski Robert Andrew	Chambers of Geoffrey Hawker, London	0171 583 8899
Smart Miss Jacqueline Anne	Trinity Chambers, Newcastle upon Tyne	0191 232 1927
Smith Ms Katherine Emma	Monckton Chambers, London	0171 405 7211
Smith Warwick Timothy Cresswell	• Deans Court Chambers, Manchester	0161 834 4097
	• Deans Court Chambers, Preston	01772 555163
Snowden John Stevenson	Two Crown Office Row, London	0171 797 8100
Somerset Jones Eric	Goldsmith Building, London	0171 353 7881
Soole Michael Alexander	5 Bell Yard, London	0171 333 8811
Southwell Richard Charles	One Hare Court, London	0171 353 3171
Spain Timothy Harrisson	Trinity Chambers, Newcastle upon Tyne	0191 232 1927
Spearman Richard	5 Raymond Buildings, London	0171 242 2902
Spencer James	11 King's Bench Walk, London	0171 353 3337/8
	11 King's Bench Walk, Leeds	0113 2971 200
Spencer Martin Benedict	4 Paper Buildings, London	0171 353 3366/583 7155
Spon-Smith Robin Witterick	1 Mitre Court Buildings, London	0171 797 7070
Staddon Miss Claire Ann	12 New Square, London	0171 419 1212
	Sovereign Chambers, Leeds	0113 245 1841/2/3
Stagg Paul Andrew	No 1 Serjeants' Inn, London	0171 415 6666
Starks Nicholas Ernshaw	8 Fountain Court, Birmingham	0121 236 5514
Steinert Jonathan	New Court Chambers, London	0171 831 9500
Stevens-Hoare Miss Michelle	• Hardwicke Building, London	0171 242 2523
Stevenson John Melford	Two Crown Office Row, London	0171 797 8100
Stewart Mark Courtney	College Chambers, Southampton	01703 230338
Stewart Nicholas John Cameron	Hardwicke Building, London	0171 242 2523
Stockdale David Andrew	9 Bedford Row, London	0171 242 3555
	Deans Court Chambers, Manchester	0161 834 4097
	Deans Court Chambers, Preston	01772 555163
Storey Jeremy Brian	4 Pump Court, London	0171 353 2656/9
Streatfeild-James David Stewart	Atkin Chambers, London	0171 404 0102
Sugar Simon Gareth	5 New Square, London	0171 404 0404
Susman Peter Joseph	New Court Chambers, London	0171 831 9500
Sutcliffe Andrew Harold Wentworth	3 Verulam Buildings, London	0171 831 8441
Swan Ian Christopher	Two Crown Office Row, London	0171 797 8100
Symons Christopher John Maurice	3 Verulam Buildings, London	0171 831 8441
Taelor Start Miss Angharad Jocelyn	3 Verulam Buildings, London	0171 831 8441
Taggart Nicholas	4 Breams Buildings, London	0171 353 5835/430 1221
Taylor Miss Deborah Frances	Two Crown Office Row, London	0171 797 8100
Taylor Michael Richard	Park Court Chambers, Leeds	0113 243 3277
Taylor Simon Wheldon	• Cloisters, London	0171 827 4000
Tedd Rex Hilary	• St Philip's Chambers, Birmingham	0121 246 7000
	• 22 Albion Place, Northampton	01604 636271
Temple Anthony Dominic	4 Pump Court, London	0171 353 2656/9
Ter Haar Roger Eduard Lound	Two Crown Office Row, London	0171 797 8100

• Expanded entry in Part D

Ticciati Oliver	4 Pump Court, London	0171 353 2656/9
Tidmarsh Christopher Ralph Francis	5 Stone Buildings, London	0171 242 6201
Tipples Miss Amanda Jane	13 Old Square, London	0171 404 4800
Tolaney Miss Sonia	3 Verulam Buildings, London	0171 831 8441
Tomlinson Hugh Richard Edward	New Court Chambers, London	0171 831 9500
Townend James Barrie Stanley	One King's Bench Walk, London	0171 936 1500
Tozzi Nigel Kenneth	4 Pump Court, London	0171 353 2656/9
Trace Anthony John	• 13 Old Square, London	0171 404 4800
Travers Hugh	Pump Court Chambers, London	0171 353 0711
	Pump Court Chambers, Winchester	01962 868161
Treasure Francis Seton	199 Strand, London	0171 379 9779
Trotman Timothy Oliver	Deans Court Chambers, Manchester	0161 834 4097
	Deans Court Chambers, Preston	01772 555163
Trowell Stephen Mark	1 Mitre Court Buildings, London	0171 797 7070
Tucker David William	Two Crown Office Row, London	0171 797 8100
Turner James	One King's Bench Walk, London	0171 936 1500
Turner Miss Janet Mary	3 Verulam Buildings, London	0171 831 8441
Twigger Andrew Mark	3 Stone Buildings, London	0171 242 4937/405 8358
Tyack David Guy	St Philip's Chambers, Birmingham	0121 246 7000
Valentine Donald Graham	Atkin Chambers, London	0171 404 0102
Vaughan-Neil Miss Catherine Mary Bernardine	5 Bell Yard, London	0171 333 8811
Vine Aidan James Wilson	Harcourt Chambers, London	0171 353 6961/7
	Harcourt Chambers, Oxford	01865 791559
Wadsworth James Patrick	4 Paper Buildings, London	0171 353 3366/583 7155
Walker Andrew Greenfield	Chambers of Lord Goodhart QC, London	0171 405 5577
Walker Steven John	Atkin Chambers, London	0171 404 0102
Wallace Ian Norman Duncan	Atkin Chambers, London	0171 404 0102
Ward Ms Orla Mary	3 Serjeants' Inn, London	0171 353 5537
Ward Miss Siobhan Marie Lucia	11 King's Bench Walk, London	0171 632 8500
Wardell John David Meredith	New Court Chambers, London	0171 831 9500
Warnock Andrew Ronald	No 1 Serjeants' Inn, London	0171 415 6666
Warnock-Smith Mrs Shan	5 Stone Buildings, London	0171 242 6201
Warshaw Justin Alexander Edward	1 Mitre Court Buildings, London	0171 797 7070
Waters Julian William Penrose	No 1 Serjeants' Inn, London	0171 415 6666
Waters Malcolm Ian	• 11 Old Square, London	0171 430 0341
Weatherill Bernard Richard	Chambers of Lord Goodhart QC, London	0171 405 5577
Webb Geraint Timothy	2 Harcourt Buildings, London	0171 583 9020
Webb Robert Stopford	• 5 Bell Yard, London	0171 333 8811
Weitzman Thomas Edward Benjamin	3 Verulam Buildings, London	0171 831 8441
Welchman Charles Stuart	199 Strand, London	0171 379 9779
West Lawrence Joseph	Stanbrook & Henderson, London	0171 353 0101
	2 Harcourt Buildings, London	0171 583 9020
West Mark	• 11 Old Square, London	0171 430 0341
Weston Clive Aubrey Richard	Two Crown Office Row, London	0171 797 8100
Whitaker Steven Dixon	199 Strand, London	0171 379 9779
	All Saints Chambers, Bristol	0117 921 1966
White Andrew	Atkin Chambers, London	0171 404 0102
White Darren Paul	Cathedral Chambers (Jan Wood Independent Barristers' Clerk), Exeter	01392 210900
White Peter-John Spencer	Pembroke House, Leatherhead	01372 376160/376493
Whiteley Miss Miranda Blyth	4 Field Court, London	0171 440 6900
Whitfield Adrian	3 Serjeants' Inn, London	0171 353 5537
Wightwick (William) Iain	Assize Court Chambers, Bristol	0117 926 4587
Wilby David Christopher	• 199 Strand, London	0171 379 9779
	• Park Lane Chambers, Leeds	0113 228 5000
Wilcox Nicholas Hugh	5 Essex Court, London	0171 410 2000
Wilken Sean David Henry	39 Essex Street, London	0171 832 1111
Wilkinson Nigel Vivian Marshall	Two Crown Office Row, London	0171 797 8100
Willer Robert Michael	Hardwicke Building, London	0171 242 2523
Williams A John	• 13 King's Bench Walk, London	0171 353 7204
	• King's Bench Chambers, Oxford	01865 311066
Williams John Griffith	Goldsmith Building, London	0171 353 7881
	33 Park Place, Cardiff	01222 233313
Williams The Hon John Melville	• Old Square Chambers, London	0171 269 0300
	• Old Square Chambers, Bristol	0117 927 7111
Williamson Miss Bridget Susan	Enterprise Chambers, London	0171 405 9471
	Enterprise Chambers, Leeds	0113 246 0391

B

B

	Enterprise Chambers, Newcastle upon Tyne	0191 222 3344
Wilmot-Smith Richard James Crosbie	39 Essex Street, London	0171 832 1111
Wilson Ian Robert	3 Verulam Buildings, London	0171 831 8441
Wilton Simon Daniel	4 Paper Buildings, London	0171 353 3366/583 7155
Wolfson David	3 Verulam Buildings, London	0171 831 8441
Wonnacott Mark Andrew	199 Strand, London	0171 379 9779
Wood Richard Michael	Sackville Chambers, Norwich	01603 613516
Wood Simon Richard Henry	Lamb Chambers, London	0171 797 8300
Woods Jonathan	Two Crown Office Row, London	0171 797 8100
Woodwark Ms Jane Elizabeth	Milburn House Chambers, Newcastle upon Tyne	0191 230 5511
Woolf Eliot Charles Anthony	199 Strand, London	0171 379 9779
Woolf Steven Jeremy	Hardwicke Building, London	0171 242 2523
Worsley Daniel	Stanbrook & Henderson, London	0171 353 0101
	2 Harcourt Buildings, London	0171 583 9020
Worster David James Stewart	St Philip's Chambers, Birmingham	0121 246 7000
Wright Colin John	4 Field Court, London	0171 440 6900
Wright Frederick George Ian	• 3 Serjeants' Inn, London	0171 353 5537
Wright Gerard Henry	25-27 Castle Street, Liverpool	0151 227 5661/5666/236 5072
Wright Norman Alfred	Oriel Chambers, Liverpool	0151 236 7191
Wright Ms Sadie	Goldsmith Building, London	0171 353 7881
Yates Nicholas Gilmore	1 Mitre Court Buildings, London	0171 797 7070
Yell Nicholas Anthony	No 1 Serjeants' Inn, London	0171 415 6666
Zelin Geoffrey Andrew	Enterprise Chambers, London	0171 405 9471
	Enterprise Chambers, Leeds	0113 246 0391
	Enterprise Chambers, Newcastle upon Tyne	0191 222 3344

PUBLIC AND PRIVATE INQUIRIES

Hand John Lester	Old Square Chambers, London	0171 269 0300
	Old Square Chambers, Bristol	0117 927 7111
	Chambers of John Hand QC, Manchester	0161 955 9000

PUBLIC INTERNATIONAL

Birnbaum Michael Ian	9-12 Bell Yard, London	0171 400 1800
	New Court Chambers, Birmingham	0121 693 6656
Cameron Jonathan James O'Grady	3 Verulam Buildings, London	0171 831 8441
Choudhury Akhlaq	11 King's Bench Walk, London	0171 632 8500
Dashwood Professor Arthur Alan	Stanbrook & Henderson, London	0171 353 0101
	2 Harcourt Buildings, London	0171 583 9020
Elvidge John Allan	1 Mitre Court Buildings, London	0171 797 7070
Haynes Miss Rebecca	Monckton Chambers, London	0171 405 7211
Jarvis John Manners	3 Verulam Buildings, London	0171 831 8441
Jenkala Adrian Aleksander	11 Bolt Court, London	0171 353 2300
	Redhill Chambers, Redhill	01737 780781
Kingsland Rt Hon Lord	4 Breams Buildings, London	0171 353 5835/430 1221
Lasok Karol Paul Edward	Monckton Chambers, London	0171 405 7211
Maurici James Patrick	4 Breams Buildings, London	0171 353 5835/430 1221
Newman Austin Eric	9 Woodhouse Square, Leeds	0113 245 1986
Paines Nicholas Paul Billot	Monckton Chambers, London	0171 405 7211
Parker Kenneth Blades	Monckton Chambers, London	0171 405 7211
Roth Peter Marcel	Monckton Chambers, London	0171 405 7211
Salter Richard Stanley	3 Verulam Buildings, London	0171 831 8441
Sands Mr Philippe Joseph	3 Verulam Buildings, London	0171 831 8441
Vajda Christopher Stephen	Monckton Chambers, London	0171 405 7211
Watts Sir Arthur Desmond	20 Essex Street, London	0171 583 9294

PUBLIC LAW

Newbury Richard Lennox	Sovereign Chambers, Leeds	0113 245 1841/2/3
Reynold Frederic	New Court Chambers, London	0171 831 9500

RADIATION INDUCED INJURIES

Pulman George Frederick	• Hardwicke Building, London	0171 242 2523
	• Stour Chambers, Canterbury	01227 764899

• Expanded entry in Part D

RATING

Alesbury Alun	2 Mitre Court Buildings, London	0171 583 1380
Anderson Anthony John	2 Mitre Court Buildings, London	0171 583 1380
Bartlett George Robert	2 Mitre Court Buildings, London	0171 583 1380
Boyle Christopher Alexander David	2 Mitre Court Buildings, London	0171 583 1380
Burton Nicholas Anthony	2 Mitre Court Buildings, London	0171 583 1380
Druce Michael James	2 Mitre Court Buildings, London	0171 583 1380
FitzGerald Michael Frederick Clive	2 Mitre Court Buildings, London	0171 583 1380
Fookes Robert Lawrence	2 Mitre Court Buildings, London	0171 583 1380
Glover Richard Michael	2 Mitre Court Buildings, London	0171 583 1380
Holgate David John	4 Breams Buildings, London	0171 353 5835/430 1221
Horton Matthew Bethell	2 Mitre Court Buildings, London	0171 583 1380
King Neil Gerald Alexander	2 Mitre Court Buildings, London	0171 583 1380
Macpherson The Hon Mary Stewart	2 Mitre Court Buildings, London	0171 583 1380
Moriarty Gerald Evelyn	2 Mitre Court Buildings, London	0171 583 1380
Mould Timothy James	4 Breams Buildings, London	0171 353 5835/430 1221
Roots Guy Robert Godfrey	2 Mitre Court Buildings, London	0171 583 1380
Silsoe The Lord	2 Mitre Court Buildings, London	0171 583 1380
Taylor Reuben Mallinson	2 Mitre Court Buildings, London	0171 583 1380
Warren Rupert Miles	2 Mitre Court Buildings, London	0171 583 1380
Widdicombe David Graham	2 Mitre Court Buildings, London	0171 583 1380

RATING/COUNCIL TAX

Sawyer John Frederick

REAL PROPERTY

Farmer Pryce Michael	1 Dr Johnson's Buildings, London	0171 353 9328
	Goldsmith Building, London	0171 353 7881
	Sedan House, Chester	01244 320480/348282

REGULATION OF NEW DRUG APPROVALS

Pickford Anthony James	Prince Henry's Chambers, London	0171 353 1183/1190

REGULATORY WORK

Cutts Miss Johannah	23 Essex Street, London	0171 413 0353
Glynn Miss Joanna Elizabeth	23 Essex Street, London	0171 413 0353
Hurst Andrew Robert	23 Essex Street, London	0171 413 0353

RESTITUTION

West Mark	• 11 Old Square, London	0171 430 0341

ROAD INQUIRIES

Calvert Peter Charles	Goldsmith Building, London	0171 353 7881

ROAD TRAFFIC

Maitland Marc Claude	11 Old Square, London	0171 242 5022

ROAD TRAFFIC AND PARKING

Thorne Timothy Peter	33 Bedford Row, London	0171 242 6476

SALE AND CARRIAGE OF GOODS

Airey Simon Andrew	11 Bolt Court, London	0171 353 2300
	Redhill Chambers, Redhill	01737 780781
Akka Lawrence Mark	20 Essex Street, London	0171 583 9294
Alexander Ian Douglas Gavin	11 Bolt Court, London	0171 353 2300
	Redhill Chambers, Redhill	01737 780781
Althaus Antony Justin	No 1 Serjeants' Inn, London	0171 415 6666
Ambrose Miss Clare Mary Geneste	20 Essex Street, London	0171 583 9294
Amin Miss Farah	7 New Square, London	0171 430 1660
Aslett Pepin Charles Maguire	22 Albion Place, Northampton	01604 636271
Baldwin John Grant	Oriel Chambers, Liverpool	0151 236 7191
Benson Julian Christopher Woodburn	One Essex Court, London	0171 936 3030
Berragan (Howard) Neil	Merchant Chambers, Manchester	0161 839 7070
Bird Nigel David	Chambers of John Hand QC, Manchester	0161 955 9000
Blakesley Patrick James	Two Crown Office Row, London	0171 797 8100

• Expanded entry in Part D

Boyle Gerard James	No 1 Serjeants' Inn, London	0171 415 6666
Brant Paul David	Oriel Chambers, Liverpool	0151 236 7191
Brook Ian Stuart	Hardwicke Building, London	0171 242 2523
Browne Miss Julie Rebecca	Goldsmith Building, London	0171 353 7881
Burns Peter Richard	Deans Court Chambers, Manchester	0161 834 4097
Carey Jeremy Reynolds Patrick	Lamb Chambers, London	0171 797 8300
Carrodus Miss Gail Caroline	New Court Chambers, London	0171 831 9500
Clegg Sebastian James Barwick	Deans Court Chambers, Manchester	0161 834 4097
Coburn Michael Jeremy Patrick	20 Essex Street, London	0171 583 9294
Collett Michael John	20 Essex Street, London	0171 583 9294
Connerty Anthony Robin	Lamb Chambers, London	0171 797 8300
Corbett James Patrick	St Philip's Chambers, Birmingham	0121 246 7000
Curtis Michael Alexander	Two Crown Office Row, London	0171 797 8100
Davies Stephen Richard	8 King Street Chambers, Manchester	0161 834 9560
Davies-Jones Jonathan	3 Verulam Buildings, London	0171 831 8441
Dawson James Robert	Oriel Chambers, Liverpool	0151 236 7191
de Voghelaere Parr Adam Stephen	2 Mitre Court Buildings, London	0171 583 1380
Dodd Christopher John Nicholas	9 Woodhouse Square, Leeds	0113 245 1986
Doherty Bernard James	39 Essex Street, London	0171 832 1111
Doyle Louis George	Chambers of Andrew Campbell QC, Leeds	0113 245 5438
Eastman Roger	Stanbrook & Henderson, London	0171 353 0101
	2 Harcourt Buildings, London	0171 583 9020
Edey Philip David	20 Essex Street, London	0171 583 9294
Edwards Anthony Howard	Oriel Chambers, Liverpool	0151 236 7191
Edwards-Stuart Antony James Cobham	Two Crown Office Row, London	0171 797 8100
Evans James Frederick Meurig	3 Verulam Buildings, London	0171 831 8441
Ferguson Mrs Katharine Ann	Fenners Chambers, Cambridge	01223 368761
	Fenners Chambers, Peterborough	01733 562030
Ford Gerard James	Baker Street Chambers, Middlesbrough	01642 873873
Franklin Stephen Hall	5 Paper Buildings, London	0171 583 6117
	Fenners Chambers, Cambridge	01223 368761
Freedman Sampson Clive	3 Verulam Buildings, London	0171 831 8441
French Richard Anthony Lister	Rougemont Chambers, Exeter	01392 410471
Gadney George Munro	Two Crown Office Row, London	0171 797 8100
Goodbody Peter James	• Oriel Chambers, Liverpool	0151 236 7191
Grant Thomas Paul Wentworth	New Court Chambers, London	0171 831 9500
Grantham Andrew Timothy	• Deans Court Chambers, Manchester	0161 834 4097
	• Deans Court Chambers, Preston	01772 555163
Greenbourne John Hugo	Two Crown Office Row, London	0171 797 8100
Grodzinski Samuel Marc	39 Essex Street, London	0171 832 1111
Gun Cuninghame Julian Arthur	• Gough Square Chambers, London	0171 353 0924
Gunning Alexander Rupert	4 Pump Court, London	0171 353 2656/9
Hamblen Nicholas Archibald	20 Essex Street, London	0171 583 9294
Hanson Timothy Vincent Richard	St Philip's Chambers, Birmingham	0121 246 7000
Hantusch Robert Anthony	• 3 Stone Buildings, London	0171 242 4937/405 8358
Harvey Michael Llewellyn Tucker	Two Crown Office Row, London	0171 797 8100
Hayward Peter Michael	The Outer Temple, Room 26, London	0171 353 4647
Henderson Lawrence Mark	11 Bolt Court, London	0171 353 2300
	Redhill Chambers, Redhill	01737 780781
Holland Charles Christopher	Trinity Chambers, Newcastle upon Tyne	0191 232 1927
Hollingworth Peter James Michael	22 Albion Place, Northampton	01604 636271
Howarth Simon Stuart	Two Crown Office Row, London	0171 797 8100
Jarvis John Manners	3 Verulam Buildings, London	0171 831 8441
Jenkala Adrian Aleksander	11 Bolt Court, London	0171 353 2300
	Redhill Chambers, Redhill	01737 780781
Kimbell John Ashley	5 Bell Yard, London	0171 333 8811
Kolodziej Andrzej Jozef	• Littman Chambers, London	0171 404 4866
Kremen Philip Michael	Hardwicke Building, London	0171 242 2523
Legh-Jones Piers Nicholas	• 20 Essex Street, London	0171 583 9294
Lowenstein Paul David	Littleton Chambers, London	0171 797 8600
Lynch Terry John	22 Albion Place, Northampton	01604 636271
Macpherson Angus John	5 Bell Yard, London	0171 333 8811
Malek Ali	3 Verulam Buildings, London	0171 831 8441
Males Stephen Martin	20 Essex Street, London	0171 583 9294
Mandel Richard	11 Bolt Court, London	0171 353 2300
	Redhill Chambers, Redhill	01737 780781
Masters Miss Sara Alayna	20 Essex Street, London	0171 583 9294
Maxwell Miss Karen Laetitia	20 Essex Street, London	0171 583 9294

       • Expanded entry in Part D

McGregor Harvey	4 Paper Buildings, London	0171 353 3366/583 7155
Meakin Timothy William	Fenners Chambers, Cambridge	01223 368761
	Fenners Chambers, Peterborough	01733 562030
Meeson Nigel Keith	4 Field Court, London	0171 440 6900
Milligan Iain Anstruther	20 Essex Street, London	0171 583 9294
Mills Simon Thomas	One Essex Court, London	0171 936 3030
Morgan Richard Hugo Lyndon	13 Old Square, London	0171 404 4800
Murray Ashley Charles	Oriel Chambers, Liverpool	0151 236 7191
Naylor Jonathan Peter	King's Chambers, Eastbourne	01323 416053
Neville Stephen John	Gough Square Chambers, London	0171 353 0924
Nicholls Paul Richard	11 King's Bench Walk, London	0171 632 8500
Norris Paul Howard	One Essex Court, London	0171 936 3030
Odgers John Arthur	3 Verulam Buildings, London	0171 831 8441
Owen David Christopher	20 Essex Street, London	0171 583 9294
Patchett-Joyce Michael Thurston	Monckton Chambers, London	0171 405 7211
Peirson Oliver James	Pump Court Chambers, London	0171 353 0711
	Pump Court Chambers, Winchester	01962 868161
Pelling (Philip) Mark	Monckton Chambers, London	0171 405 7211
Pelling Richard Alexander	New Court Chambers, London	0171 831 9500
Peretz George Michael John		
Pershad Rohan	Two Crown Office Row, London	0171 797 8100
Phillips Andrew Charles	Two Crown Office Row, London	0171 797 8100
Pittaway David Michael	No 1 Serjeants' Inn, London	0171 415 6666
Pope David James	3 Verulam Buildings, London	0171 831 8441
Reed Philip James William	5 Bell Yard, London	0171 333 8811
Reeve Matthew Francis	5 Bell Yard, London	0171 333 8811
Rigney Andrew James	Two Crown Office Row, London	0171 797 8100
Robb Adam Duncan	39 Essex Street, London	0171 832 1111
Robson John Malcolm	2 Gray's Inn Square Chambers, London	0171 242 0328/405 1317
	Assize Court Chambers, Bristol	0117 926 4587
Rogers Ian Paul	1 Crown Office Row, London	0171 583 9292
Rowlands Ms Catherine Janet	Victoria Chambers, Birmingham	0121 236 9900
Russell Robert John Finlay	5 Bell Yard, London	0171 333 8811
Ryan David Patrick	Chambers of Geoffrey Hawker, London	0171 583 8899
Sadiq Tariq Mahmood	Chambers of John Hand QC, Manchester	0161 955 9000
Salter Richard Stanley	3 Verulam Buildings, London	0171 831 8441
Sampson Graeme William	Chambers of Geoffrey Hawker, London	0171 583 8899
Saunders Nicholas Joseph	4 Field Court, London	0171 440 6900
Scutt David Robert	11 Bolt Court, London	0171 353 2300
	Redhill Chambers, Redhill	01737 780781
Selvaratnam Miss Vasanti Emily Indrani	4 Field Court, London	0171 440 6900
Seymour Richard William	Monckton Chambers, London	0171 405 7211
Shepherd Philip Alexander	• 5 Bell Yard, London	0171 333 8811
Smith Miss Julia Mair Wheldon	Gough Square Chambers, London	0171 353 0924
Smith Warwick Timothy Cresswell	• Deans Court Chambers, Manchester	0161 834 4097
	• Deans Court Chambers, Preston	01772 555163
Snowden John Stevenson	Two Crown Office Row, London	0171 797 8100
Somerset-Jones Miss Felicity	Oriel Chambers, Liverpool	0151 236 7191
Spearman Richard	5 Raymond Buildings, London	0171 242 2902
Starks Nicholas Ernshaw	8 Fountain Court, Birmingham	0121 236 5514
Stern Dr Kristina Anne	39 Essex Street, London	0171 832 1111
Stewart Alexander Joseph	5 New Square, London	0171 404 0404
Stewart Mark Courtney	College Chambers, Southampton	01703 230338
Susman Peter Joseph	New Court Chambers, London	0171 831 9500
Swan Ian Christopher	Two Crown Office Row, London	0171 797 8100
Tobin Daniel Alphonsus Joseph	Chambers of Geoffrey Hawker, London	0171 583 8899
Trotman Timothy Oliver	Deans Court Chambers, Manchester	0161 834 4097
	Deans Court Chambers, Preston	01772 555163
Tucker David William	Two Crown Office Row, London	0171 797 8100
Turner Miss Janet Mary	3 Verulam Buildings, London	0171 831 8441
Tyack David Guy	St Philip's Chambers, Birmingham	0121 246 7000
Vaughan-Neil Miss Catherine Mary Bernardine	5 Bell Yard, London	0171 333 8811
Vine Aidan James Wilson	Harcourt Chambers, London	0171 353 6961/7
	Harcourt Chambers, Oxford	01865 791559
Ward Miss Siobhan Marie Lucia	11 King's Bench Walk, London	0171 632 8500

B

• Expanded entry in Part D

Wardell John David Meredith	New Court Chambers, London	0171 831 9500
Webb Robert Stopford	• 5 Bell Yard, London	0171 333 8811
Weston Clive Aubrey Richard	Two Crown Office Row, London	0171 797 8100
Whiteley Miss Miranda Blyth	4 Field Court, London	0171 440 6900
Wolfson David	3 Verulam Buildings, London	0171 831 8441
Wright Colin John	4 Field Court, London	0171 440 6900

SCIENTIFIC AND TECHNICAL DISPUTES

Colley Dr Peter McLean	• 19 Old Buildings, London	0171 405 2001

SHARE OPTIONS

Arden Peter Leonard	Enterprise Chambers, London	0171 405 9471
	Enterprise Chambers, Leeds	0113 246 0391
	Enterprise Chambers, Newcastle upon Tyne	0191 222 3344
Dougherty Nigel Peter	Erskine Chambers, London	0171 242 5532
Griffiths Peter Robert	4 Stone Buildings, London	0171 242 5524
Groves Hugo Gerard	Enterprise Chambers, London	0171 405 9471
	Enterprise Chambers, Leeds	0113 246 0391
	Enterprise Chambers, Newcastle upon Tyne	0191 222 3344
Jarvis John Manners	3 Verulam Buildings, London	0171 831 8441
Jory Robert John Hugh	Enterprise Chambers, London	0171 405 9471
	Enterprise Chambers, Leeds	0113 246 0391
	Enterprise Chambers, Newcastle upon Tyne	0191 222 3344
Marquand Charles Nicholas Hilary	Chambers of Lord Goodhart QC, London	0171 405 5577
Milligan Iain Anstruther	20 Essex Street, London	0171 583 9294
Stewart Alexander Joseph	5 New Square, London	0171 404 0404
Sykes (James) Richard	Erskine Chambers, London	0171 242 5532
Zelin Geoffrey Andrew	Enterprise Chambers, London	0171 405 9471
	Enterprise Chambers, Leeds	0113 246 0391
	Enterprise Chambers, Newcastle upon Tyne	0191 222 3344

SHIPPING, ADMIRALTY

Akka Lawrence Mark	20 Essex Street, London	0171 583 9294
Ambrose Miss Clare Mary Geneste	20 Essex Street, London	0171 583 9294
Charkham Graham Harold	20 Essex Street, London	0171 583 9294
Coburn Michael Jeremy Patrick	20 Essex Street, London	0171 583 9294
Collett Michael John	20 Essex Street, London	0171 583 9294
Edey Philip David	20 Essex Street, London	0171 583 9294
Hamblen Nicholas Archibald	20 Essex Street, London	0171 583 9294
Haven Kevin	2 Gray's Inn Square Chambers, London	0171 242 0328/405 1317
James Michael Frank	Enterprise Chambers, London	0171 405 9471
	Enterprise Chambers, Leeds	0113 246 0391
	Enterprise Chambers, Newcastle upon Tyne	0191 222 3344
Legh-Jones Piers Nicholas	• 20 Essex Street, London	0171 583 9294
Males Stephen Martin	20 Essex Street, London	0171 583 9294
Masters Miss Sara Alayna	20 Essex Street, London	0171 583 9294
Mawrey Richard Brooks	Stanbrook & Henderson, London	0171 353 0101
	2 Harcourt Buildings, London	0171 583 9020
Maxwell Miss Karen Laetitia	20 Essex Street, London	0171 583 9294
Meeson Nigel Keith	4 Field Court, London	0171 440 6900
Milligan Iain Anstruther	20 Essex Street, London	0171 583 9294
Owen David Christopher	20 Essex Street, London	0171 583 9294
Saunders Nicholas Joseph	4 Field Court, London	0171 440 6900
Selvaratnam Miss Vasanti Emily Indrani	4 Field Court, London	0171 440 6900
Whiteley Miss Miranda Blyth	4 Field Court, London	0171 440 6900
Wright Colin John	4 Field Court, London	0171 440 6900

SOCIAL SECURITY

Boyd Phillip Joseph George	Lincoln House Chambers, Manchester	0161 832 5701
Drabble Richard John Bloor	4 Breams Buildings, London	0171 353 5835/430 1221
Forsdick David John	4 Breams Buildings, London	0171 353 5835/430 1221
Lieven Ms Nathalie Marie Daniella	4 Breams Buildings, London	0171 353 5835/430 1221

        • Expanded entry in Part D

Sutherland Williams Mark   4 King's Bench Walk, London   0171 822 8822
King's Bench Chambers,   01202 250025
Bournemouth

SPORTS

Akiwumi Anthony Sebastian Akitayo	Pump Court Chambers, London	0171 353 0711
	Pump Court Chambers, Winchester	01962 868161
Anderson Rupert John	Monckton Chambers, London	0171 405 7211
Baxter Gerald Pearson	25-27 Castle Street, Liverpool	0151 227 5661/5666/236 5072
Beard Daniel Matthew	Monckton Chambers, London	0171 405 7211
Bellamy Jonathan Mark	39 Essex Street, London	0171 832 1111
Bergin Terence Edward	New Court Chambers, London	0171 831 9500
Block Neil Selwyn	39 Essex Street, London	0171 832 1111
Burles David John	Goldsmith Building, London	0171 353 7881
Burton Michael John	Littleton Chambers, London	0171 797 8600
Carling Christopher James	Old Square Chambers, London	0171 269 0300
	Old Square Chambers, Bristol	0117 927 7111
Cash Miss Joanne Catherine	Farrar's Building, London	0171 583 9241
Chudleigh Miss Louise Katrina	Old Square Chambers, London	0171 269 0300
	Old Square Chambers, Bristol	0117 927 7111
Craig Kenneth Allen	Hardwicke Building, London	0171 242 2523
Davies Miss Penny May	Chambers of Harjit Singh, London	0171 353 1356
Davies Richard Llewellyn	39 Essex Street, London	0171 832 1111
de Jehan David	St Paul's House, Leeds	0113 245 5866
Donovan Joel	New Court Chambers, London	0171 831 9500
Driscoll Miss Lynn	Sovereign Chambers, Leeds	0113 245 1841/2/3
	Lancaster Buildings, Manchester	0161 661 4444
Du Cann Christian Dillon Lott	39 Essex Street, London	0171 832 1111
Duffy Michael	Cathedral Chambers, Ely, Ely	01353 666775
Fowler Richard Nicholas	Monckton Chambers, London	0171 405 7211
Gallagher John David Edmund	Goldsmith Building, London	0171 353 7881
Gillibrand Philip Martin Mangnall	Pump Court Chambers, London	0171 353 0711
	Pump Court Chambers, Winchester	01962 868161
Glasgow Edwin John	39 Essex Street, London	0171 832 1111
Goudie James	• 11 King's Bench Walk, London	0171 632 8500
Grayson Edward	• 9-12 Bell Yard, London	0171 400 1800
Griffiths (John) Peter (Gwynne)	30 Park Place, Cardiff	01222 398421
Harris Paul Best	Monckton Chambers, London	0171 405 7211
Haynes Miss Rebecca	Monckton Chambers, London	0171 405 7211
Henderson Lawrence Mark	11 Bolt Court, London	0171 353 2300
	Redhill Chambers, Redhill	01737 780781
Hill Raymond	Monckton Chambers, London	0171 405 7211
Holdsworth James Arthur	Two Crown Office Row, London	0171 797 8100
Kearl Guy Alexander	St Paul's House, Leeds	0113 245 5866
Kerr Tim Julian	4-5 Gray's Inn Square, London	0171 404 5252
Lasok Karol Paul Edward	Monckton Chambers, London	0171 405 7211
Lawrence The Hon Patrick John Tristram	4 Paper Buildings, London	0171 353 3366/583 7155
Lehain Philip Peter	199 Strand, London	0171 379 9779
Lennard Stephen Charles	Hardwicke Building, London	0171 242 2523
Mackay Colin Crichton	39 Essex Street, London	0171 832 1111
Makey Christopher Douglas	Old Square Chambers, London	0171 269 0300
	Old Square Chambers, Bristol	0117 927 7111
McIvor Ian Walker	334 Deansgate Chambers, Manchester	0161 834 3767
McParland Michael Joseph	New Court Chambers, London	0171 831 9500
Middleton Miss Georgina Claire	New Court Chambers, London	0171 831 9500
Moorman Miss Lucinda Claire	Farrar's Building, London	0171 583 9241
Nelson Vincent Leonard	39 Essex Street, London	0171 832 1111
Nicholls John Peter	13 Old Square, London	0171 404 4800
Nurse Gordon Bramwell William	11 Old Square, London	0171 430 0341
Oke Olanrewaju Oladipupo	Kingsway Chambers, London	07000 653529
Parker Kenneth Blades	Monckton Chambers, London	0171 405 7211
Patterson Stewart	• Pump Court Chambers, London	0171 353 0711
	• Pump Court Chambers, Winchester	01962 868161
Pershad Rohan	Two Crown Office Row, London	0171 797 8100
Peters Nigel Melvin	18 Red Lion Court, London	0171 520 6000
	Thornwood House, Chelmsford	01245 280880
Phillips Stephen Edmund	3 Verulam Buildings, London	0171 831 8441
Rawlings Clive Patrick	Goldsmith Building, London	0171 353 7881
Sampson Graeme William	Chambers of Geoffrey Hawker, London	0171 583 8899
Segal Oliver Leon	Old Square Chambers, London	0171 269 0300

• Expanded entry in Part D

	Old Square Chambers, Bristol	0117 927 7111
Singh Balbir	• Equity Chambers, Birmingham	0121 233 2100
Spearman Richard	5 Raymond Buildings, London	0171 242 2902
Stewart Nicholas John Cameron	Hardwicke Building, London	0171 242 2523
Sugar Simon Gareth	5 New Square, London	0171 404 0404
Supperstone Michael Alan	11 King's Bench Walk, London	0171 632 8500
Thompson Rhodri William Ralph	Monckton Chambers, London	0171 405 7211
Tomlinson Hugh Richard Edward	New Court Chambers, London	0171 831 9500
Trace Anthony John	• 13 Old Square, London	0171 404 4800
Tucker David William	Two Crown Office Row, London	0171 797 8100
Turner Jonathan Richard	Monckton Chambers, London	0171 405 7211
Vajda Christopher Stephen	Monckton Chambers, London	0171 405 7211
Wardell John David Meredith	New Court Chambers, London	0171 831 9500
Weddle Steven Edgar	Hardwicke Building, London	0171 242 2523
Whitcombe Mark David	Old Square Chambers, London	0171 269 0300
	Old Square Chambers, Bristol	0117 927 7111

SPORTS - MOTOR RACING LAW

Gillibrand Philip Martin Mangnall	Pump Court Chambers, London	0171 353 0711
	Pump Court Chambers, Winchester	01962 868161

SPORTS MEDICINE

Grayson Edward	• 9-12 Bell Yard, London	0171 400 1800

STATUTORY NUISANCE

Williams A John	• 13 King's Bench Walk, London	0171 353 7204
	• King's Bench Chambers, Oxford	01865 311066

TAX - CAPITAL AND INCOME

Akin Barrie Simon	Gray's Inn Tax Chambers, London	0171 242 2642
Angus Miss Tracey Anne	5 Stone Buildings, London	0171 242 6201
Arnfield Robert John	17 Old Buildings, London	0171 405 9653
Baker Philip Woolf	Gray's Inn Tax Chambers, London	0171 242 2642
Birch Roger Allen	12 New Square, London	0171 419 1212
	Sovereign Chambers, Leeds	0113 245 1841/2/3
	Lancaster Buildings, Manchester	0161 661 4444
Bramwell Richard Mervyn	3 Temple Gardens Tax Chambers, London	0171 353 7884
Brownbill David John	Gray's Inn Square, London	0171 242 3529
Butt Miss Romasa	Goldsworth Chambers, London	0171 405 7117
Conroy Miss Marian	3 Stone Buildings, London	0171 242 4937/405 8358
Crawford Grant	11 Old Square, London	0171 430 0341
Cullen Mrs Felicity Ann	Gray's Inn Tax Chambers, London	0171 242 2642
Dilhorne The Rt Hon Viscount	4 Breams Buildings, London	0171 353 5835/430 1221
Fernandes John Piedade Amaranto Lorencio	• Arcadia Chambers, London	0171 938 1285
Ferrier Ian Gilbert Straton	Gray's Inn Square, London	0171 242 3529
Flesch Michael Charles	Gray's Inn Tax Chambers, London	0171 242 2642
Goldberg David Gerard	Gray's Inn Tax Chambers, London	0171 242 2642
Goodhart Lord	Chambers of Lord Goodhart QC, London	0171 405 5577
Goy David John Lister	Gray's Inn Tax Chambers, London	0171 242 2642
Grundy James Milton	Gray's Inn Tax Chambers, London	0171 242 2642
Harris David Raymond	Prince Henry's Chambers, London	0171 353 1183/1190
Henderson Launcelot Dinadan James	• 5 Stone Buildings, London	0171 242 6201
Herbert Mark Jeremy	• 5 Stone Buildings, London	0171 242 6201
Johnson Michael Sloan	Chambers of John Hand QC, Manchester	0161 955 9000
Legge Henry	5 Stone Buildings, London	0171 242 6201
Lonsdale Miss Marion Mary	Chambers of Geoffrey Hawker, London	0171 583 8899
McDonnell Conrad Mortimer	Gray's Inn Tax Chambers, London	0171 242 2642
McKay Hugh Joseph Peter	Gray's Inn Tax Chambers, London	0171 242 2642
Nathan Miss Aparna	Gray's Inn Tax Chambers, London	0171 242 2642
Oakley Tony	• 11 Old Square, London	0171 430 0341
Parry David Julian Thomas	Chambers of Lord Goodhart QC, London	0171 405 5577
Pilkington Mrs Mavis Patricia	9 Woodhouse Square, Leeds	0113 245 1986
Reed Miss Penelope Jane	9 Stone Buildings, London	0171 404 5055

     • Expanded entry in Part D

Rees David Benjamin	5 Stone Buildings, London	0171 242 6201
Rowell David Stewart	Chambers of Lord Goodhart QC, London	0171 405 5577
Schwarz Jonathan Simon		
Shaw Miss Nicola Jane		
Sherry Michael Gabriel	• 3 Temple Gardens Tax Chambers, London	0171 353 7884
	• Peel Court Chambers, Manchester	0161 832 3791
Soares Patrick Claude	Gray's Inn Square, London	0171 242 3529
Southern Professor David Boardman	• 3 Temple Gardens Tax Chambers, London	0171 353 7884
Sunnucks James Horace George	• 5 New Square, London	0171 404 0404
	• Octagon House, Norwich	01603 623186
Tedd Rex Hilary	• St Philip's Chambers, Birmingham	0121 246 7000
	• 22 Albion Place, Northampton	01604 636271
Thomas Nigel Matthew	13 Old Square, London	0171 404 4800
Tidmarsh Christopher Ralph Francis	5 Stone Buildings, London	0171 242 6201
Walters John Latimer	Gray's Inn Tax Chambers, London	0171 242 2642
Warnock-Smith Mrs Shan	5 Stone Buildings, London	0171 242 6201
Way Patrick Edward	Gray's Inn Square, London	0171 242 3529
Whitehouse Christopher John	Gray's Inn Square, London	0171 242 3529
Whiteman Peter George	Queen Elizabeth Building, London	0171 583 5766
Woolley David Rorie	• 1 Serjeants' Inn, London	0171 583 1355

TAX · CORPORATE

Akin Barrie Simon	Gray's Inn Tax Chambers, London	0171 242 2642
Baker Philip Woolf	Gray's Inn Tax Chambers, London	0171 242 2642
Birch Roger Allen	12 New Square, London	0171 419 1212
	Sovereign Chambers, Leeds	0113 245 1841/2/3
	Lancaster Buildings, Manchester	0161 661 4444
Bramwell Richard Mervyn	3 Temple Gardens Tax Chambers, London	0171 353 7884
Brownbill David John	Gray's Inn Square, London	0171 242 3529
Butt Miss Romasa	Goldsworth Chambers, London	0171 405 7117
Cullen Mrs Felicity Ann	Gray's Inn Tax Chambers, London	0171 242 2642
Dilhorne The Rt Hon Viscount	4 Breams Buildings, London	0171 353 5835/430 1221
Fernandes John Piedade Amaranto Lorencio	• Arcadia Chambers, London	0171 938 1285
Ferrier Ian Gilbert Straton	Gray's Inn Square, London	0171 242 3529
Flesch Michael Charles	Gray's Inn Tax Chambers, London	0171 242 2642
Goldberg David Gerard	Gray's Inn Tax Chambers, London	0171 242 2642
Goy David John Lister	Gray's Inn Tax Chambers, London	0171 242 2642
Grundy James Milton	Gray's Inn Tax Chambers, London	0171 242 2642
Harris David Raymond	Prince Henry's Chambers, London	0171 353 1183/1190
Henderson Launcelot Dinadan James	• 5 Stone Buildings, London	0171 242 6201
McCutcheon Barry Duff	Gray's Inn Square, London	0171 242 3529
McDonnell Conrad Mortimer	Gray's Inn Tax Chambers, London	0171 242 2642
McKay Hugh Joseph Peter	Gray's Inn Tax Chambers, London	0171 242 2642
Nathan Miss Aparna	Gray's Inn Tax Chambers, London	0171 242 2642
Schwarz Jonathan Simon		
Shaw Miss Nicola Jane		
Sherry Michael Gabriel	• 3 Temple Gardens Tax Chambers, London	0171 353 7884
	• Peel Court Chambers, Manchester	0161 832 3791
Soares Patrick Claude	Gray's Inn Square, London	0171 242 3529
Southern Professor David Boardman	• 3 Temple Gardens Tax Chambers, London	0171 353 7884
Tedd Rex Hilary	• St Philip's Chambers, Birmingham	0121 246 7000
	• 22 Albion Place, Northampton	01604 636271
Walters John Latimer	Gray's Inn Tax Chambers, London	0171 242 2642
Way Patrick Edward	Gray's Inn Square, London	0171 242 3529
Whitehouse Christopher John	Gray's Inn Square, London	0171 242 3529
Whiteman Peter George	Queen Elizabeth Building, London	0171 583 5766
Woolley David Rorie	• 1 Serjeants' Inn, London	0171 583 1355

TAXATION OF COSTS

Birts Peter William	• Farrar's Building, London	0171 583 9241
Morgan Richard Hugo Lyndon	13 Old Square, London	0171 404 4800

• Expanded entry in Part D

TELECOMMUNICATIONS

Akenhead Robert	Atkin Chambers, London	0171 404 0102
Baatz Nicholas Stephen	Atkin Chambers, London	0171 404 0102
Bartlett George Robert	2 Mitre Court Buildings, London	0171 583 1380
Barwise Miss Stephanie Nicola	Atkin Chambers, London	0171 404 0102
Blackburn John	Atkin Chambers, London	0171 404 0102
Bourne Charles Gregory	Stanbrook & Henderson, London	0171 353 0101
	2 Harcourt Buildings, London	0171 583 9020
Bowdery Martin	Atkin Chambers, London	0171 404 0102
Burr Andrew Charles	Atkin Chambers, London	0171 404 0102
Clay Robert Charles	Atkin Chambers, London	0171 404 0102
Dashwood Professor Arthur Alan	Stanbrook & Henderson, London	0171 353 0101
	2 Harcourt Buildings, London	0171 583 9020
Dennison Stephen Randell	Atkin Chambers, London	0171 404 0102
Dennys Nicholas Charles Jonathan	Atkin Chambers, London	0171 404 0102
Doerries Miss Chantal-Aimee Renee Aemelia Annemarie	Atkin Chambers, London	0171 404 0102
Dumaresq Ms Delia Jane	Atkin Chambers, London	0171 404 0102
Fenston Miss Felicia Donovan	Stanbrook & Henderson, London	0171 353 0101
	2 Harcourt Buildings, London	0171 583 9020
Fitzgerald John Vincent	New Court, London	0171 797 8999
Fowler Richard Nicholas	Monckton Chambers, London	0171 405 7211
Fraser Peter Donald	Atkin Chambers, London	0171 404 0102
Goddard Andrew Stephen	Atkin Chambers, London	0171 404 0102
Godwin William George Henry	Atkin Chambers, London	0171 404 0102
Henderson Roger Anthony	Stanbrook & Henderson, London	0171 353 0101
	2 Harcourt Buildings, London	0171 583 9020
Hodgson Richard Andrew	New Court, London	0171 797 8999
Howells James Richard	Atkin Chambers, London	0171 404 0102
Kime Matthew Jonathan	• New Court, London	0171 797 8999
	• Cobden House Chambers, Manchester	0161 833 6000/6001
Knight Brian Joseph	Atkin Chambers, London	0171 404 0102
Lasok Karol Paul Edward	Monckton Chambers, London	0171 405 7211
Lofthouse Simon Timothy	Atkin Chambers, London	0171 404 0102
Macpherson The Hon Mary Stewart	2 Mitre Court Buildings, London	0171 583 1380
McCall Duncan James	4 Pump Court, London	0171 353 2656/9
McCutcheon Barry Duff	Gray's Inn Square, London	0171 242 3529
McMullan Manus Anthony	Atkin Chambers, London	0171 404 0102
Nicholls John Peter	13 Old Square, London	0171 404 4800
Parkin Miss Fiona Jane	Atkin Chambers, London	0171 404 0102
Raeside Mark Andrew	Atkin Chambers, London	0171 404 0102
Rawley Miss Dominique Jane	Atkin Chambers, London	0171 404 0102
Reese Colin Edward	Atkin Chambers, London	0171 404 0102
Robertson Aidan Malcolm David	Monckton Chambers, London	0171 405 7211
Royce Darryl Fraser	Atkin Chambers, London	0171 404 0102
Streatfeild-James David Stewart	Atkin Chambers, London	0171 404 0102
Turner Jonathan Richard	Monckton Chambers, London	0171 405 7211
Valentine Donald Graham	Atkin Chambers, London	0171 404 0102
Walker Steven John	Atkin Chambers, London	0171 404 0102
Wallace Ian Norman Duncan	Atkin Chambers, London	0171 404 0102
White Andrew	Atkin Chambers, London	0171 404 0102
Wilson Alastair James Drysdale	• 19 Old Buildings, London	0171 405 2001

TOWN AND COUNTRY PLANNING

Alesbury Alun	2 Mitre Court Buildings, London	0171 583 1380
Anderson Anthony John	2 Mitre Court Buildings, London	0171 583 1380
Bailey Mark Henry Arthur	• 6 Pump Court, London	0171 797 8400
	• 6-8 Mill Street, Maidstone	01622 688 094
Barnes (David) Michael (William)	4 Breams Buildings, London	0171 353 5835/430 1221
Bartlett George Robert	2 Mitre Court Buildings, London	0171 583 1380
Beard Mark Christopher	6 Pump Court, London	0171 797 8400
Bhattacharyya Ardhendu	1 Gray's Inn Square, London	0171 405 8946
	11 St Bernards Road, Slough	01753 553806/817989
Birtles William	Old Square Chambers, London	0171 269 0300
	Old Square Chambers, Bristol	0117 927 7111
Boyle Christopher Alexander David	2 Mitre Court Buildings, London	0171 583 1380
Burton Nicholas Anthony	2 Mitre Court Buildings, London	0171 583 1380
Bush Keith	30 Park Place, Cardiff	01222 398421
Cameron Neil Alexander	Wilberforce Chambers, Hull	01482 323 264
Cameron Neil St Clair	1 Serjeants' Inn, London	0171 583 1355
Cameron Miss Sheila Morag Clark	2 Harcourt Buildings, London	0171 353 8415

Caws Eian Richard Edwin	4 Breams Buildings, London	0171 353 5835/430 1221
Clarke George Robert Ivan	Chambers of Geoffrey Hawker, London	0171 583 8899
Clay Jonathan Roger	11 Bolt Court, London	0171 353 2300
	Redhill Chambers, Redhill	01737 780781
Collett Gavin Charles	Rougemont Chambers, Exeter	01392 410471
	Cathedral Chambers (Jan Wood Independent Barristers' Clerk), Exeter	01392 210900
Colquhoun Miss Celina Daphne Marion	11 Bolt Court, London	0171 353 2300
	Redhill Chambers, Redhill	01737 780781
de Voghelaere Parr Adam Stephen	2 Mitre Court Buildings, London	0171 583 1380
Dineen Michael Laurence	Pump Court Chambers, London	0171 353 0711
	All Saints Chambers, Bristol	0117 921 1966
	Pump Court Chambers, Winchester	01962 868161
Doerries Miss Chantal-Aimee Renee Aemelia Annemarie	Atkin Chambers, London	0171 404 0102
Drabble Richard John Bloor	4 Breams Buildings, London	0171 353 5835/430 1221
Druce Michael James	2 Mitre Court Buildings, London	0171 583 1380
Duffy Michael	Cathedral Chambers, Ely, Ely	01353 666775
Edwards Philip Douglas	2 Harcourt Buildings, London	0171 353 8415
Elvin David John	4 Breams Buildings, London	0171 353 5835/430 1221
FitzGerald Michael Frederick Clive	2 Mitre Court Buildings, London	0171 583 1380
Fookes Robert Lawrence	2 Mitre Court Buildings, London	0171 583 1380
Forsdick David John	4 Breams Buildings, London	0171 353 5835/430 1221
Franklin Stephen Hall	5 Paper Buildings, London	0171 583 6117
	Fenners Chambers, Cambridge	01223 368761
Furber (Robert) John	4 Breams Buildings, London	0171 353 5835/430 1221
Gore Andrew Roger	Fenners Chambers, Cambridge	01223 368761
	Fenners Chambers, Peterborough	01733 562030
Greaves John	9-12 Bell Yard, London	0171 400 1800
Hands David Richard Granville	4 Breams Buildings, London	0171 353 5835/430 1221
	40 King Street, Manchester	0161 832 9082
Harper Joseph Charles	4 Breams Buildings, London	0171 353 5835/430 1221
Harrison Peter John	6 Pump Court, London	0171 797 8400
	6-8 Mill Street, Maidstone	01622 688 094
Harwood Richard John	1 Serjeants' Inn, London	0171 583 1355
Heap Gerard Miles	Sovereign Chambers, Leeds	0113 245 1841/2/3
Hill Nicholas Mark	Pump Court Chambers, London	0171 353 0711
	Pump Court Chambers, Winchester	01962 868161
Hockman Stephen Alexander	• 6 Pump Court, London	0171 797 8400
	• 6-8 Mill Street, Maidstone	01622 688 094
Holgate David John	4 Breams Buildings, London	0171 353 5835/430 1221
Holroyd John James	• 9 Woodhouse Square, Leeds	0113 245 1986
Horton Matthew Bethell	2 Mitre Court Buildings, London	0171 583 1380
Howell John	4 Breams Buildings, London	0171 353 5835/430 1221
Howells James Richard	Atkin Chambers, London	0171 404 0102
Huskinson George Nicholas Nevil	4-5 Gray's Inn Square, London	0171 404 5252
Jackson Nicholas David Kingsley	The Chambers of Adrian Lyon, Liverpool	0151 236 4421/8240/6757
Jones Geraint Martyn	Fenners Chambers, Cambridge	01223 368761
	Fenners Chambers, Peterborough	01733 562030
Jones Gregory Percy	• 2 Harcourt Buildings, London	0171 353 8415
Jones Timothy Arthur	• Arden Chambers, London	0171 242 4244
	• St Philip's Chambers, Birmingham	0121 246 7000
Karas Jonathan Marcus	4 Breams Buildings, London	0171 353 5835/430 1221
Katkowski Christopher Andrew Mark	4 Breams Buildings, London	0171 353 5835/430 1221
Kavanagh Giles Wilfred Conor	• 5 Bell Yard, London	0171 333 8811
Keen Graeme	4 Breams Buildings, London	0171 353 5835/430 1221
King Neil Gerald Alexander	2 Mitre Court Buildings, London	0171 583 1380
Kingsland Rt Hon Lord	4 Breams Buildings, London	0171 353 5835/430 1221
Knight Brian Joseph	Atkin Chambers, London	0171 404 0102
Kremen Philip Michael	Hardwicke Building, London	0171 242 2523
Langham Richard Geoffrey	1 Serjeants' Inn, London	0171 583 1355
Lawson Rogers George Stuart	23 Essex Street, London	0171 413 0353
Lewis Robert		
Lewsley Christopher Stanton	4 Breams Buildings, London	0171 353 5835/430 1221
Lieven Ms Nathalie Marie Daniella	4 Breams Buildings, London	0171 353 5835/430 1221
Litton John Letablere	4 Breams Buildings, London	0171 353 5835/430 1221
Lockhart-Mummery Christopher John	4 Breams Buildings, London	0171 353 5835/430 1221

Lyness Scott Edward	1 Serjeants' Inn, London	0171 583 1355
Macleod Nigel Ronald Buchanan	4 Breams Buildings, London	0171 353 5835/430 1221
	40 King Street, Manchester	0161 832 9082
Male John Martin	4 Breams Buildings, London	0171 353 5835/430 1221
Mandel Richard	11 Bolt Court, London	0171 353 2300
	Redhill Chambers, Redhill	01737 780781
Marshall Philip Derek	Farrar's Building, London	0171 583 9241
	Iscoed Chambers, Swansea	01792 652988/9/330
Mathias Miss Anna	11 Bolt Court, London	0171 353 2300
Maurici James Patrick	4 Breams Buildings, London	0171 353 5835/430 1221
McCracken Robert Henry Joy	• 2 Harcourt Buildings, London	0171 353 8415
McHugh Miss Karen	4 Breams Buildings, London	0171 353 5835/430 1221
McMullan Manus Anthony	Atkin Chambers, London	0171 404 0102
McParland Michael Joseph	New Court Chambers, London	0171 831 9500
Moore Professor Victor William Edward	2 Mitre Court Buildings, London	0171 583 1380
Moriarty Gerald Evelyn	2 Mitre Court Buildings, London	0171 583 1380
Morshead Timothy Francis	4 Breams Buildings, London	0171 353 5835/430 1221
Mould Timothy James	4 Breams Buildings, London	0171 353 5835/430 1221
Murch Stephen James	• 11 Bolt Court, London	0171 353 2300
Newcombe Andrew Bennett	• 2 Harcourt Buildings, London	0171 353 8415
Ornsby Miss Suzanne Doreen	• 2 Harcourt Buildings, London	0171 353 8415
Ouseley Duncan Brian Walter	4-5 Gray's Inn Square, London	0171 404 5252
Parkin Miss Fiona Jane	Atkin Chambers, London	0171 404 0102
Perks Richard Howard	St Philip's Chambers, Birmingham	0121 246 7000
Purchas Robin Michael	• 2 Harcourt Buildings, London	0171 353 8415
Randall John Yeoman	7 Stone Buildings, London	0171 405 3886/242 3546
	St Philip's Chambers, Birmingham	0121 246 7000
Randle Simon Patrick	11 Bolt Court, London	0171 353 2300
	Redhill Chambers, Redhill	01737 780781
Read Lionel Frank	1 Serjeants' Inn, London	0171 583 1355
Richards David Wyn	Iscoed Chambers, Swansea	01792 652988/9/330
Robinson Miss Alice	4 Breams Buildings, London	0171 353 5835/430 1221
Roots Guy Robert Godfrey	2 Mitre Court Buildings, London	0171 583 1380
Rumney Conrad William Arthur	St Philip's Chambers, Birmingham	0121 246 7000
Sampson Graeme William	Chambers of Geoffrey Hawker, London	0171 583 8899
Silsoe The Lord	2 Mitre Court Buildings, London	0171 583 1380
Simpson Edwin John Fletcher	12 New Square, London	0171 419 1212
Smith David Anthony	4 Breams Buildings, London	0171 353 5835/430 1221
Stone Gregory	• 4-5 Gray's Inn Square, London	0171 404 5252
Straker Timothy Derrick	• 2-3 Gray's Inn Square, London	0171 242 4986
Sunnucks James Horace George	• 5 New Square, London	0171 404 0404
	• Octagon House, Norwich	01603 623186
Symons Christopher John Maurice	3 Verulam Buildings, London	0171 831 8441
Taylor Reuben Mallinson	2 Mitre Court Buildings, London	0171 583 1380
Tedd Rex Hilary	• St Philip's Chambers, Birmingham	0121 246 7000
	• 22 Albion Place, Northampton	01604 636271
Thomas Miss Megan Moira	1 Serjeants' Inn, London	0171 583 1355
Tobin Daniel Alphonsus Joseph	Chambers of Geoffrey Hawker, London	0171 583 8899
Village Peter Malcolm	• 4-5 Gray's Inn Square, London	0171 404 5252
Walker Steven John	Atkin Chambers, London	0171 404 0102
Warren Rupert Miles	2 Mitre Court Buildings, London	0171 583 1380
Whybrow Christopher John	1 Serjeants' Inn, London	0171 583 1355
Widdicombe David Graham	2 Mitre Court Buildings, London	0171 583 1380
Williams Miss Anne Margaret	4 Breams Buildings, London	0171 353 5835/430 1221
	37 Park Square, Leeds	0113 243 9422
Woolley David Rorie	• 1 Serjeants' Inn, London	0171 583 1355

TRADEMARKS

Anderson Rupert John	Monckton Chambers, London	0171 405 7211
Clark Ms Julia Elisabeth	5 New Square, London	0171 404 0404
Colley Dr Peter McLean	• 19 Old Buildings, London	0171 405 2001
de Jehan David	St Paul's House, Leeds	0113 245 5866
Driscoll Miss Lynn	Sovereign Chambers, Leeds	0113 245 1841/2/3
	Lancaster Buildings, Manchester	0161 661 4444
Fitzgerald John Vincent	New Court, London	0171 797 8999
Garnett Kevin Mitchell	5 New Square, London	0171 404 0404
Henderson Roger Anthony	Stanbrook & Henderson, London	0171 353 0101
	2 Harcourt Buildings, London	0171 583 9020
Hicks Michael Charles	• 19 Old Buildings, London	0171 405 2001

• Expanded entry in Part D

Hodgson Richard Andrew	New Court, London	0171 797 8999
Holman Miss Tamsin Perdita	19 Old Buildings, London	0171 405 2001
Kime Matthew Jonathan	• New Court, London	0171 797 8999
	• Cobden House Chambers, Manchester	0161 833 6000/6001
Mason Ian Douglas	11 Bolt Court, London	0171 353 2300
	Redhill Chambers, Redhill	01737 780781
Norris Andrew James Steedsman	5 New Square, London	0171 404 0404
Pickford Anthony James	Prince Henry's Chambers, London	0171 353 1183/1190
Puckrin Cedric Eldred	19 Old Buildings, London	0171 405 2001
Reid Brian Christopher	19 Old Buildings, London	0171 405 2001
Robertson Aidan Malcolm David	Monckton Chambers, London	0171 405 7211
Shipley Norman Graham	• 19 Old Buildings, London	0171 405 2001
Sullivan Rory Myles	19 Old Buildings, London	0171 405 2001
Wilson Alastair James Drysdale	• 19 Old Buildings, London	0171 405 2001

TRADING STANDARDS

Hamilton Jaime Richard	Chambers of John Hand QC, Manchester	0161 955 9000
Leeming Michael Peter George	Chambers of John Hand QC, Manchester	0161 955 9000
Wedderspoon Miss Rachel Leone	Chambers of John Hand QC, Manchester	0161 955 9000

TRAIN AND COACH CRASHES/CORPORATE MANSLAUGHTER

Forlin Gerard Emlyn	Phoenix Chambers, London	0171 404 7888

TRANSPORT LAW

Beech Ms Jacqueline Elaine	199 Strand, London	0171 379 9779
	York Chambers, York	01904 620 048

TRANSPORT LICENSING

Sadd Patrick James Thomas	199 Strand, London	0171 379 9779

TRAVEL

Middleton Miss Georgina Claire	New Court Chambers, London	0171 831 9500
Overs Ms Estelle Fae	New Court Chambers, London	0171 831 9500
Pelling Richard Alexander	New Court Chambers, London	0171 831 9500
Tomlinson Hugh Richard Edward	New Court Chambers, London	0171 831 9500
Wardell John David Meredith	New Court Chambers, London	0171 831 9500

TRIBUNALS

Chawla Mukul	9-12 Bell Yard, London	0171 400 1800
Jory Richard Norman	9-12 Bell Yard, London	0171 400 1800

TRIBUNALS/INQUIRIES

Taylor Simon Wheldon	• Cloisters, London	0171 827 4000

TRUSTS

Davidson Edward Alan	• 11 Old Square, London	0171 430 0341

UNIT TRUSTS

Marquand Charles Nicholas Hilary	Chambers of Lord Goodhart QC, London	0171 405 5577
Sykes (James) Richard	Erskine Chambers, London	0171 242 5532

UTILITIES

Fowler Richard Nicholas	Monckton Chambers, London	0171 405 7211
Turner Jonathan Richard	Monckton Chambers, London	0171 405 7211

VAT

Gresty Miss Denise Lynn	Sovereign Chambers, Leeds	0113 245 1841/2/3
Jack Miss Katrina Mabel	Prince Henry's Chambers, London	0171 353 1183/1190
Kent Michael Harcourt	Two Crown Office Row, London	0171 797 8100
Lonsdale Miss Marion Mary	Chambers of Geoffrey Hawker, London	0171 583 8899

• Expanded entry in Part D

:hwarz Jonathan Simon
ɔnerry Michael Gabriel

| | • 3 Temple Gardens Tax Chambers, London | 0171 353 7884 |
| | • Peel Court Chambers, Manchester | 0161 832 3791 |

VAT AND CUSTOMS & EXCISE

Anderson Rupert John	Monckton Chambers, London	0171 405 7211
Foster Miss Alison Lee Caroline	39 Essex Street, London	0171 832 1111
Hall Mrs Melanie Ruth	Monckton Chambers, London	0171 405 7211
Harris Paul Best	Monckton Chambers, London	0171 405 7211
Hill Raymond	Monckton Chambers, London	0171 405 7211
Lasok Karol Paul Edward	Monckton Chambers, London	0171 405 7211
Macnab Alexander Andrew	Monckton Chambers, London	0171 405 7211
Mantle Peter John	Monckton Chambers, London	0171 405 7211
Paines Nicholas Paul Billot	Monckton Chambers, London	0171 405 7211
Parker Kenneth Blades	Monckton Chambers, London	0171 405 7211
Peretz George Michael John		
Pleming Nigel Peter	39 Essex Street, London	0171 832 1111
Robertson Aidan Malcolm David	Monckton Chambers, London	0171 405 7211
Smith Ms Katherine Emma	Monckton Chambers, London	0171 405 7211
Vajda Christopher Stephen	Monckton Chambers, London	0171 405 7211

VETERINARY PRACTICE

Gilmour Nigel Benjamin Douglas	Peel House Chambers, Liverpool	0151 236 4321

WARRANTY CLAIMS

Barker Simon George Harry	• 13 Old Square, London	0171 404 4800

WASTE MANAGEMENT

Sheridan Maurice Bernard Gerard	• 3 Verulam Buildings, London	0171 831 8441

WATER

Holroyd John James	• 9 Woodhouse Square, Leeds	0113 245 1986

WATER/UTILITIES

Baldwin John Grant	Oriel Chambers, Liverpool	0151 236 7191

WEST INDIES LAW

Al'Hassan Khadim	Equity Chambers, Birmingham	0121 233 2100

WILLS AND TRUSTS

Sunnucks James Horace George	• 5 New Square, London	0171 404 0404
	• Octagon House, Norwich	01603 623186

• Expanded entry in Part D

WILSON ASSOCIATES

INTERNATIONAL LAWYERS

9 avenue Guillaume   Tel: +352 25 27 40
Luxembourg L-1651   Fax: +352 25 27 41

A law firm with lawyers qualified in various jurisdictions who
specialize in European law, international corporate law with
an emphasis on international taxation, insurance law,
investment funds, finance, trusts and related fields. In addition
we disseminate juridicial information concerning Luxembourg.

Please address all enquiries in the first instance to
Graham J Wilson (Barrister).

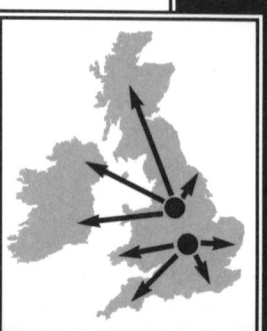

Chambers by Location

This section lists chambers in England and Wales by the town or city in which they are located. The town/city names are in alphabetical order and under those main headings chambers are listed alphabetically, thus 7 King's Bench Walk would be listed before 4 Pump Court under London.

Information for each set of chambers includes full contact details with names of clerks and Head of Chambers (where provided). Chambers also provided information on their list of practising barristers including indications as to whether members are Recorders, Assistant Recorders, or Door Tenants (see below). Some chambers have opted to include additional information about themselves in this part of the Directory such as the date chambers was established, opening times, chambers' facilities, languages spoken, details regarding fees and a list of the types of work undertaken, including where supplied the number of counsel practising in each area. Please note that details of the types of work undertaken by those chambers which have chosen not to include this information in Part C may be found in *Part A Types of Work by Chambers*.

Note: For those chambers listed in the 1999 edition, information has been supplied by chambers in the first instance and supplemented with Bar Council information where necessary.

The following symbols indicate that barristers are:

† Recorders
‡ Assistant Recorders
* Door Tenants

C

PRIMROSE CHAMBERS

5 Primrose Way, Alperton, Middlesex
HA0 1DS
0181 998 1806

Chambers of Mr B P Sharma

CHAMBERS OF PAUL HOGBEN

199 Kingsworth Road, Ashford, Kent
TN23 6NB
01233 645805
Fax: 01233 645805

Chambers of Mr P R Hogben

PULTENEY CHAMBER

14 Johnstone Street, Bath, Somerset BA2 4DH
01225 465667
Fax: 01225 465667

Chambers of Miss L J Adams

BEDFORD CHAMBERS

The Clock House, 2 Bedford Street, Ampthill,
Bedford, Bedfordshire MK45 2NB
0870 733 7333
Fax: 0870 733 7331; DX 36901 Ampthill
E-mail: simon_michael@pilawyer.demon.co.uk

Chambers of Simon Michael
Clerk: Elaine Duncan

Michael, Simon 1978

GRANARY CHAMBERS

4 Glenleigh Park Road, Bexhill-on-Sea, East
Sussex TN39 4EH
01424 733008
Fax: 01424 733008

Chambers of Mr T G Restell

COLERIDGE CHAMBERS

Citadel, 190 Corporation Street, Birmingham
B4 6QD
0121 233 3303
Fax: 0121 236 6966; DX 23503 Birmingham 3

Chambers of Mr S D Brand

COMMONWEALTH CHAMBERS

354 Moseley Road, Birmingham B12 9AZ
0121 446 5732

Chambers of Mr M A Rashid

EQUITY CHAMBERS

153A Corporation Street, Birmingham, West
Midlands B4 6PH
0121 233 2100
Fax: 0121 233 2102; DX 23531 Birmingham 3
Out of hours telephone: 01543 677321

Chambers of Mohammed Latif
Clerks: Andrew Mowbray Trotter, Patricia
Anne Walker

Latif, Mohammed 1985	**Sharma**, Pavan 1993
Shaikh, Christopher 1980*	**Franck**, Richard 1993
Singh, Balbir 1984	**Bell**, Gary 1989
Suggett, Iain 1989	**Al'Hassan**, Khadim 1993
Sandhu, Sunit 1990	**Knowles**, Mark 1989
Scott-Jones, Alison 1991	**Mahon**, Brian 1996

Chambers established: 1996
Opening times: 8.30 am-6.30 pm

**Types of work (and number of counsel
practising in that area if supplied)**
Administrative · Bankruptcy · Care proceedings
· Chancery (general) · Charities · Civil liberties
· Commercial · Commercial litigation
· Common law (general) · Company and
commercial · Construction · Consumer Law
· Copyright · Crime · Crime - corporate fraud
· Discrimination · Education · Employment
· Entertainment · Equity, wills and trusts
· Family · Foreign law · Housing · Immigration
· Information technology · Insolvency
· Insurance · Intellectual property
· International trade · Landlord and tenant
· Licensing · Local government · Medical
negligence · Mental health · Partnerships
· Patents · Personal injury · Planning
· Professional negligence · Sale and carriage of
goods · Sports · Town and country planning
· Trademarks

C

Chambers' facilities
Conference rooms, Video conferences, Disks accepted, Disabled access

Languages spoken
Afrikaans, Arabic, Bengali, French, German, Gujarati, Hindi, Punjabi, Swahili, Urdu

Fees policy
Up to five years call £60-90, Five to ten years call £85-110, Ten years call £125-250. Chambers adopts a flexible approach to fees. We aim to provide value for money, with complete transparency. Fees can be time-costed or if preferred a global amount agreed. We will provide detailed estimates upon request.

1 FOUNTAIN COURT

Steelhouse Lane, Birmingham, West Midlands B4 6DR
0121 236 5721
Fax: 0121 236 3639; DX 16077 Birmingham

Chambers of D Crigman QC
Clerk: C T Hayfield

Crigman, David QC 1969†	Williams, Neal 1984
Morse, Malcolm 1967	Ward, Simon 1986
Hodgkinson, John 1968	Salmon, Jonathan 1987
Dudley, Michael 1972‡	Thompson, Blondelle 1987
Griffith-Jones, Richard 1974†	Buxton, Sarah 1988
	Farrer, Paul 1988
Busby, Thomas 1975	Atkins, Richard 1989
Millington, Christopher 1976‡	Puzey, James 1990
	Thornett, Gary 1991
Harrison-Hall, Giles 1977	Considine, Paul 1992
Nicholls, Christopher 1978	Johnston, Anthony 1993
Conry, Michael 1979	Smith, Nicholas 1994
Inman, Melbourne QC 1979‡	Williams, Thomas 1995
Eyre, Stephen 1981	Baker, Stuart 1995
Dillon, Thomas 1983	Phillips, Simon 1996
Evans, John 1983	Smith, Andrew 1997

See the *Index of Languages Spoken* **in Part G to locate a chambers where a particular language is spoken, or find an individual who speaks a particular language.**

---

3 FOUNTAIN COURT

Steelhouse Lane, Birmingham, West Midlands B4 6DR
0121 236 5854
Fax: 0121 236 7008; DX 16079 Birmingham 4

Chambers of C M Treacy QC
Clerks: Jonathan Maskew (Senior Clerk), Justin Luckman, Carl Streeting, Alex Brown; Administrator: Jackie McNab

Treacy, Colman QC 1971†	Anderson, Mark 1983
Palmer, Anthony QC 1962†	Bright, Christopher 1985
Andrews, Peter QC 1970†	Wall, Daryl 1985
McConville, Donald 1963	Jackson, Andrew 1986
Calderwood, Patricia 1964	Laird, Francis 1986
Jones, David 1967†	Mason, David 1986
Faber, Trevor 1970†	Duck, Michael 1988
Chavasse, Anne 1971	Wallace, Andrew 1988
Arnold, Peter 1972	Keeling, Adrian 1990
Juckes, Robert 1974†	Hilder, Carolyn 1991
Challinor, Michael 1974†	Bailey, Steven 1992
Parker, Philip 1976‡	Barnes, Matthew 1992
Thomas, Sybil 1976‡	Lattimer, Justine 1992
Mackintosh, Colin 1976	Kubik, Heidi 1993
Darby, Patrick 1978	Montgomery, Kristina 1993
Burrows, Michael 1979	Harvey, Simon 1994
Warner, Anthony 1979	Jones, Jonathan 1994
Linnemann, Bernard 1980	Leader, Tim 1994
Engel, Anthony 1965	Butterfield, John 1995
Travers, David 1981	Chatterjee, Adreeja 1997

Chambers established: 1913
Opening times: 8.30 am-6 pm

Types of work (and number of counsel practising in that area if supplied)
Banking 3 · Bankruptcy 3 · Care proceedings 8 · Chancery (general) 3 · Chancery land law 3 · Commercial litigation 6 · Common law (general) 12 · Company and commercial 6 · Crime 20 · Crime - corporate fraud 9 · Education 3 · Employment 5 · Environment 6 · Equity, wills and trusts 6 · Family 8 · Family provision 8 · Information technology 2 · Insolvency 6 · Intellectual property 3 · Landlord and tenant 4 · Licensing 3 · Local government 3 · Medical negligence 6 · Partnerships 3 · Personal injury 12 · Professional negligence 6 · Sale and carriage of goods 8 · Town and country planning 4

Chambers' facilities
Conference rooms, Disabled access

Languages spoken
French, German

† Recorder ‡ Assistant Recorder * Door Tenant

Fees policy

Fees will be negotiated with the clerk depending on the case but as a general guide: under three years call £50-75 per hour, three to five years call £50-100 per hour, five to ten years £70-125 per hour. Fees are negotiable with the clerk on a case by case basis.

4 FOUNTAIN COURT

Steelhouse Lane, Birmingham B4 6DR
0121 236 3476
Fax: 0121 200 1214; DX 16074 Birmingham

Chambers of Mr R M Wakerley QC

5 FOUNTAIN COURT

FOUNTAIN 5 COURT

B I R M I N G H A M

Steelhouse Lane, Birmingham, West Midlands B4 6DR
0121 606 0500
Fax: 0121 606 1501; DX 16075 Birmingham
Out of hours telephone: 0374 298047

Chambers of Mr Anthony Barker QC, Mr Gareth Evans QC (Deputy Head)
Clerks: Tony McDaid (Practice Director), Sandra Astbury (PA); Practice managers: Gary Bryant, Patrick Hawkins, Matthew Lane (Senior Practice Managers)

Barker, Anthony QC *1966†*
Wolton, Harry QC *1969†*
Stembridge, David QC *1955†*
Kingston, Martin QC *1972†*
Linehan, Stephen QC *1970†*
Evans, Gareth QC *1973†*
Oliver-Jones, Stephen QC *1970†*
Wood, William QC *1970†*
Budgen, Nicholas *1962*
West, John *1965*
Whitaker, Stephen *1970*
Elsom, Michael *1972‡*
Eades, Mark *1974†*
Cahill, Jeremy *1975*
Giles, Roger *1976*
Bealby, Walter *1976*
Smallwood, Anne *1977*
Rowland, Robin *1977*
James, Christopher *1977*
Iles, David *1977*
O'Donovan, Kevin *1978*
Bleasdale, Paul *1978†*
Lewis, Ralph *1978‡*
Bush, Rosalind *1978*
Draycott, Jean *1980*
Newman, Timothy *1981*
Brown, Stephanie *1982*
Thompson, Neil *1982*
Stephens, Michael *1983*
McGrath, Andrew *1983*
Hunjan, Satinder *1984*
Stockill, David *1985*
Lee, Richard *1993*
Moat, Richard *1985*
Dove, Ian *1986*
Meyer, Lorna *1986*
Thorogood, Bernard *1986*
Heywood, Mark *1986*

Drew, Simon *1987*
Craig, Aubrey *1987*
Oyebanji, Adam *1987*
Hickey, Eugene *1988*
Baker, Caroline *1988*
Chadwick, Joanna *1988*
Williams, Sara *1989*
Duthie, Malcolm *1989*
Liddiard, Martin *1989*
Bedford, Becket *1989*
Anning, Michael *1990*
McDonald, Melanie *1990*
Wynne, Ashley *1990*
Bennett, Mary *1990*
Dooley, Allan *1991†*
Radburn, Mark *1991*
Friel, Michele *1991*
Jones, Jennifer *1991*
Wilson, Marion *1991*
O'Brien-Quinn, Hugh *1992*
Park, David *1992*
Goatley, Peter *1992*
Xydias, Nicholas *1992*
Wilkinson, Marc *1992*
Preston, Nicola *1992*
Richards, Hugh *1992*
Hitching, Isabel *1992*
Down, Jonathan *1993*
Taylor, David *1993*
Khalique, Nageena *1994*
Price, Rachael *1994*
Smallwood, Robert *1994*
Cotter, Rachel *1994*
Duffy, Joanne *1994*
Diamond, Anna *1995*
Mitchell, David *1995*
Gilchrist, Naomi *1996*
Taylor, Matthew *1996*
Wright, Jeremy *1996*
Hogan, Emma *1996*

Opening times: 8 am-6.30 pm

Types of work (and number of counsel practising in that area if supplied)
Administrative · Agriculture · Arbitration · Asset finance · Banking · Bankruptcy · Care proceedings · Chancery (general) · Chancery land law · Civil liberties · Commercial · Commercial litigation · Commercial property · Common land · Common law (general) · Company and commercial · Competition · Construction · Consumer Law · Conveyancing · Copyright · Corporate finance · Courts martial · Crime · Crime - corporate fraud · Defamation · Discrimination · EC and competition law · Education · Employment · Entertainment · Environment · Equity, wills and trusts · Family · Family provision · Financial services · Foreign law · Franchising · Housing · Immigration · Information

† Recorder ‡ Assistant Recorder * Door Tenant

technology · Insolvency · Insurance
· Insurance/reinsurance · Intellectual property
· International trade · Landlord and tenant
· Licensing · Local government · Medical
negligence · Mental health · Partnerships
· Patents · Pensions · Personal injury · Planning
· Probate and administration · Professional
negligence · Sale and carriage of goods · Share
options · Sports · Tax - capital and income
· Tax - corporate · Town and country planning
· Trademarks · Unit trusts

Chambers' facilities
Conference rooms, Video conferences, Disks
accepted, Disabled access, Seminar suite

Languages spoken
French, German, Spanish

Additional information

5 Fountain Court, Birmingham is the largest set
of barristers' chambers in the UK, with 78
members including eight Queen's Counsel.
Within chambers we have six specialist practice
groups, each with its own membership, group
identity and head of group, co-ordinated under
one administration team. Video conferencing
and arbitration facilities are available within
chambers, which is also committed to
alternative dispute resolution.
Crime and licensing
The criminal group covers a broad area of
criminal, licensing and administrative law,
ranging from appearances before magistrates'
courts and Crown Courts in England and Wales,
to the specific demands of disciplinary,
regulatory and appellate tribunals and to
offering specialist skills in defence and
prosecution cases involving complex fraud.
Planning
The town and country planning group has
expanded from its Midlands base to its present
nationwide client base which includes local
planning, mineral and highway authorities,
airport authorities, employed solicitors and
barristers, planning consultancies, government
agencies, foreign lawyers and governments in
respect of overseas work. Chambers is
instructed directly by members of The Royal
Institution of Chartered Surveyors, The Royal
Institute of British Architects and the Architects
Registration Council of the UK.
**Personal injury and medical negligence
(including disaster injuries)**
Members undertake litigation on behalf of
plaintiffs and defendants and have extensive
experience of asbestos-related injury, repetitive
strain injury, industrial deafness, occupational
asthma and respiratory disease, occupational
cancer, dermatitis, vibration white finger as well

as industrial accident claims, tetraplegic and
paraplegic claims and those involving brain
damage, major spinal injury and other injuries of
the utmost severity. Counsel are also
experienced in health and safety at work and
medical negligence litigation on behalf of both
plaintiffs and defendants.
Family
Counsel have considerable experience in
financial provision on divorce, matrimonial
finance, custody and access, co-habitation,
family provision on death, adoption and
wardship, property disputes between
unmarried couples and registered homes
tribunals.
Commercial and Chancery
Eighteen specialist counsel, virtually all
commercial and Chancery work, contentious
and non-contentious, including: general
commercial litigation, real and personal
property, probate, trusts, tax, banking,
intellectual property, competition, EU, US
commercial, competition and intellectual
property law, emergency interlocutory
applications, drafting applications and settling
affidavits, advice upon enforcement and
strategy, non-contentious drafting and
consultative work.
Employment
Counsel specialise in matters involving
redundancy, harrassment, disablement and
industrial injury, restraint of trade and safety of
confidential information and wrongful and
unfair dismissal, representing both employers
and employees before tribunals and courts.

6 FOUNTAIN COURT

Steelhouse Lane, Birmingham, West
Midlands B4 6DR
0121 233 3282
Fax: 0121 236 3600; DX 16076 Birmingham
Clerk: M Harris

Smith, Roger QC *1972*†
Hutt, Michael *1968*
Mason, John *1971*
Bown, Philip *1974*
Desmond, Denis *1974*
Quirke, James *1974*
Seddon, Dorothy *1974*
Gregory, Philip *1975*‡
Rickarby, William *1975*
Lowe, Anthony *1976*
Pitt-Lewis, Janet *1976*
Tucker, Andrew *1977*
Pittaway, Amanda *1980*
Somerville, Bryce *1980*
Davis, Jonathan *1983*
Cooke, Peter *1985*

Khangure, Avtar *1985*
Stenhouse, John *1986*
Tarbitt, Nicholas *1988*
Attwood, John *1989*
Davis, Simon *1990*
Price, Robert *1990*
Cadwaladr, Stephen *1992*
Shakoor, Tariq *1992*
Egan, Caroline *1993*
Marklew, Lee *1993*
Watson, David *1994*
Dunstan, James *1995*
Bushell, Terence *1982*
Swinnerton, David *1995*
Walker, Jane *1974**

8 FOUNTAIN COURT

Steelhouse Lane, Birmingham, West
Midlands B4 6DR
0121 236 5514
Fax: 0121 236 8225; DX 16078 Birmingham
E-mail: clerks@no8chambers.co.uk
Out of hours telephone: Emergency no: 01426
129889

Chambers of Ian Strongman TD
*Clerks: Christina Maloney, Rosemarie
Maloney*

Strongman, Ian *1981*
Vaughan, Keith *1968*
Pirotta, Monica *1976*
White, Amanda *1976*
Perkins, Jonathan *1980*
Hickman, Derek *1982*
Murray, Stephen *1986*
Hickman, Sally *1987*
Starks, Nicholas *1989*
Hartley, Antony *1991*

Cowley, Robert *1992*
Sparrow, Julie *1992*
Mahmood, Abid *1992*
Dutta, Nandini *1993*
Ace, Richard *1993*
Clarke, Timothy *1992*
Mathews, Deni *1996*
Archer of Sandwell, Lord
  QC *1952**
Jones, Richard *1979**

Chambers established: 1974
Opening times: 8.30 am-6 pm

**Types of work (and number of counsel
practising in that area if supplied)**
Arbitration 1 · Bankruptcy 2 · Care
proceedings 6 · Chancery (general) 1
· Chancery land law 1 · Civil liberties 1
· Commercial litigation 2 · Commercial
property 1 · Common law (general) 11
· Company and commercial 3 · Construction 2
· Conveyancing 1 · Crime 8 · Discrimination 1
· Employment 3 · Equity, wills and trusts 3
· Family 12 · Family provision 11 · Film, cable,
TV 1 · Housing 1 · Immigration 2 · Insolvency
1 · Insurance 1 · Landlord and tenant 3
· Medical negligence 3 · Mental health 2
· Partnerships 3 · Personal injury 9 · Probate
and administration 2 · Professional negligence
4 · Sale and carriage of goods 2 · Sports 1
· Town and country planning 1

Chambers' facilities
Conference rooms, E-mail

Fees policy
Chambers offer very competitive rates, negotiated by experienced and efficient clerks of 25 years' standing.

NEW COURT CHAMBERS

168 Corporation Street, Suite 200, Gazette Building, Birmingham, West Midlands B4 6TZ
0121 693 6656
Fax: 0121 693 6657; DX 23533 Birmingham 3

Chambers of Christopher Morris
Clerk: Paul McNab; Administrator: Gillian Petrie

Morris, Christopher *1977*	**Russell**, Jennifer *1990*
Birnbaum, Michael QC *1969**	**Reid**, Howard *1991*
	Sidhu-Brar, Sean *1991*
de Mello, Rembert *1983**	**Kalsi**, Maninder *1992*
Twana, Ekwall *1988*	**Kolodynski**, Stefan *1993*
Kenning, Thomas *1989*	**Ashton**, Raglan *1994*
Billingham, Rex *1990*	**Brotherton**, John *1994*
Dhaliwal, Davinder *1990*	**Crane**, Suzanne *1995*
Nduka-Eze, Chuck *1990**	

PRIORY CHAMBERS

2 Fountain Court, Steelhouse Lane, Birmingham B4 6DR
0121 236 3882/1375
Fax: 0121 233 3205; DX 16071 Birmingham

Chambers of Mrs P A Deeley

ROWCHESTER CHAMBERS

4 Rowchester Court, Whittall Street, Birmingham B4 6DH
0121 233 2327/2361951
Fax: 0121 236 7645; DX 16080 Birmingham

Chambers of Mr W A Harris

85 SPRINGFIELD ROAD

King's Heath, Birmingham B14 7DU
0121 444 2818
Fax: 0121 247 6935; DX 10795 MOSELEY 1

Chambers of Mr A S J Bean

ST IVE'S CHAMBERS

9 Fountain Ct, Birmingham B4 6DR
0121 236 0863/0929
Fax: 0121 236 6961; DX 16072 Birmingham

Chambers of Mr E P Coke

ST PHILIP'S CHAMBERS

Fountain Court, Steelhouse Lane, Birmingham, West Midlands B4 6DR
0121 246 7000
Fax: 0121 246 7001; DX 16073 Birmingham

Chambers of Rex Tedd QC, Deputies: Mrs Patricia Deeley and Mr John Randall QC
Clerks: David Partridge, Matthew Fleming, Richard Fowler, Su Gilbert, Charles Jones, Marguerite Lawrence;
Practice managers: Robin Butchard, Clive Witcomb; Administrator: Linda Taylor

---

Tedd, Rex QC *1970*†
Deeley, Patricia *1970*†
Randall, John QC *1978*‡
Rogers, John QC *1963*†
Stokes, Michael QC *1971*†
McCahill, Patrick QC *1975*†
Davis, William QC *1975*†
Newbold, Ronald *1965*
Garrett, Michael *1967*
Healy, Brian *1967*
Price, John *1969*†
Clarke, Peter *1970*
Readings, Douglas *1972*‡
Cliff, Graham *1973*
Corbett, James *1975*‡
Jones, Timothy *1975*
Spollon, Guy *1976*
Perks, Richard *1977*
Pusey, William *1977*
Cooper, Morris *1979*
Burbidge, James *1979*
Thomas, Stephen *1980*
Dyer, Roger *1980*
Worster, David *1980*
Shoker, Makhan *1981*
Hershman, David *1981*
Campbell, Stephen *1982*
Hegarty, Kevin *1982*
Messling, Lawrence *1983*
Edwards, John *1983*
Haynes, Peter *1983*
Starcevic, Petar *1983*
McCartney, Peter *1983*
Rochford, Thomas *1984*
Powis, Samantha *1985*
Adams, Christopher *1986*
Cartwright, Nicolas *1986*
Landes, Anna-Rose *1986*
Walters, Gareth *1986*
Findlay, Lorna *1987*
Ashworth, Lance *1987*
McGrath, Elizabeth *1987*
Smail, Alastair *1987*

Rumney, Conrad *1988*
Watts, Lawrence *1988*
Cook, Alison *1989*
Cox, Ailsa *1989*
Hanson, Timothy *1989*
Pepperall, Edward *1989*
Rai, Amarjit *1989*
Beever, Edmund *1990*
Capon, Philip *1990*
Meachin, Vanessa *1990*
Lockhart, Andrew *1991*
Evans, Lisa *1991*
George, Sarah *1991*
Lewis, Robin *1991*
Samuel, Glynn *1975*
Starkie, Claire *1991*
Williams, Hugh *1992*
de Waal, John *1992*
Le Cornu, Philip *1992*
Moseley, Julie *1992*
Tucker, Katherine *1993*
Verduyn, Anthony *1993*
Owens, Jane *1994*
Charman, Andrew *1994*
Rampersad, Devan *1994*
Walker, Elizabeth *1994*
Burden, Angus *1994*
Carter, Rosalyn *1994*
Tyack, David *1994*
Dean, Brian *1994*
Fryer, Anthony *1995*
MacDonald, Alistair *1995*
McCahey, Catherine *1996*
Morgan, James *1996*
Cunningham, Claire *1996*
McCabe, Louise *1996*
Wilson, Martin QC *1963**
Hotten, Christopher QC
   1972*
McFarlane, Andrew QC
   1977*
Lock, David MP *1985**

Chambers established: 1998
Opening times: 8 am-6 pm

Types of work (and number of counsel practising in that area if supplied)
Administrative 6 · Arbitration 2 · Aviation 2 · Banking 4 · Bankruptcy 13 · Care proceedings 21 · Chancery (general) 18 · Chancery land law 5 · Charities 1 · Commercial litigation 23 · Commercial property 4 · Common law (general) 28 · Company and commercial 17 · Construction 7 · Consumer Law 5 · Conveyancing 2 · Courts martial 2 · Crime 41 · Crime - corporate fraud 16 · Discrimination 5 · EC and competition law 1 · Education 2 · Employment 14 · Entertainment 1 · Environment 8 · Equity,

wills and trusts 6 · Family 26 · Family provision 18 · Film, cable, TV 1 · Franchising 2 · Housing 8 · Immigration 2 · Insolvency 17 · Insurance 15 · Landlord and tenant 11 · Licensing 12 · Local government 9 · Medical negligence 30 · Partnerships 11 · Pensions 1 · Personal injury 30 · Planning 6 · Probate and administration 5 · Professional negligence 26 · Sale and carriage of goods 11 · Tax - capital and income 1 · Tax - corporate 1 · Town and country planning 10

Chambers' facilities
Conference rooms, Disks accepted

Languages spoken
French, German, Italian, Punjabi, Spanish, Welsh

Additional information

The Chambers: St Philip's Chambers was formed on 1st June 1998 and results from the merger of Priory Chambers and No 7 Fountain Court. St Philip's is one of the UK's most broadly based set of chambers with considerable strength and depth.

Work undertaken: Counsel act in a very wide range of cases and it is this diversity of specialisms that gives St Philip's Chambers particular strength and versatility. It has five practice groups, these being:

Chancery and Commercial
Criminal
Personal Injury and Medical Negligence
Family Law
Property, Planning and Public Law

St Philip's Chambers also has expertise in a wide range of subjects including Employment, Licensing and General Common Law.

The combined premises at Fountain Court have been extensively refurbished to provide purpose-built conference rooms and arbitration facilities. These are complemented by extensive IT facilities. St Philip's provides a friendly service of the highest quality, and to this end our practice managers and their team will always be pleased to assist with detailed information on the specialisations and availability of individual members of Chambers.

VICTORIA CHAMBERS

3rd Floor, 177 Corporation Street,
Birmingham B4 6RG
0121 236 9900
Fax: 0121 233 0675; DX 23520 Birmingham

Chambers of Mr D E Pearson

KING'S BENCH CHAMBERS

175 Holdenhurst Road, Bournemouth, Dorset
BH8 8DQ
01202 250025
Fax: 01202 250026; DX 7617 Bournemouth

Chambers of William Andreae-Jones QC, Kenneth Cameron
Clerk: Alan Conner (Senior Clerk)

Also at: 4 Kings Bench Walk, Temple EC4Y 7DL

Andreae-Jones, William QC 1965	**Matthews,** Ann 1994
Cameron, Kenneth 1969	**Hepher,** Paul 1994
Van Hagen, Christopher 1980	**Jenkins,** Rowan 1994
Shale, Justin 1982	**Wilson,** James 1995
Hine, Roderick 1985	**Florida-James,** Mark 1995
Kessler, Mark 1988	**Sutherland-Williams,** Mark 1995
Greenfield, Peter 1989	**Kennedy,** Beresford 1995
Becker, Timothy 1992	**Ward-Prowse,** John 1997

Crime Desktop CD-ROM

Never before has criminal law research been so efficient. With Crime Desktop, you have quick and easy access to:

Archbold – *the leading authority on criminal law, practice and procedure*

Criminal Law Review *(since 1967) – the latest case law and legislative developments, plus analysis of current issues and changes in the law*

Criminal Appeal Reports *(since 1967) – extensive coverage of all major criminal appeal cases.*

Put time on your side, phone Sweet & Maxwell on 0171 449 1111 for more information or a free demonstration

---

20 LORNE PARK ROAD

Bournemouth, Dorset BH1 1JN
01202 292102
Fax: 01202 298498; DX 7612 Bournemouth

Chambers of M P Parroy QC
Clerks: Stephen Clark (Senior Clerk), Debbie Smyth, Simon Coady

Annexe of: 3 Paper Buildings, 1st Floor, Temple, London EC4Y 7EU
Tel: 0171 583 8055
Fax: 0171 353 6271 (2 lines)

Parroy, Michael QC 1969	**Branigan,** Kate 1984
Harris, David QC 1969†	**O'Hara,** Sarah 1984
Hughes, Peter QC 1971	**Chamberlain,** Francis 1985
Jones, Stewart QC 1972†	**Sanderson,** David 1985
Aspinall, John QC 1971	**Bailey,** Russell 1985
Hebron, Harold 1960	**Parker,** Christopher 1986
Parrish, Samuel 1962	**Hudson,** Elisabeth 1987
Trevethan, Susan 1967	**Letman,** Paul 1987
Haynes, John 1968	**Rowland,** Nicholas 1988
Swinstead, David 1970	**Kelly,** Patricia 1988
Hope, Derwin 1970†	**Woolgar,** Dermot 1988
Norman, Michael 1971†	**Hester,** Paul 1989
Ward, Anthony 1971	**Opperman,** Guy 1989
Curran, Leo 1972	**Bradbury,** Timothy 1989
Jennings, Peter 1972	**Kilpatrick,** Jean 1990
Coleman, Anthony 1973	**Buckley-Clarke,** Amanda 1991
Stephenson, Ben 1973	**Ross,** Iain 1991
Litchfield, Linda 1974	**Steenson,** David 1991
Bartlett, David 1975†	**Sweeney,** Christian 1992
Richardson, Garth 1975	**Kelly,** Marie 1992
Tyson, Richard 1975‡	**Kirkpatrick,** Krystyna 1992
Henry, Peter 1977	**Weir,** Robert 1992
Mitchell, Nigel 1978	**Fitzharris,** Ginnette 1993
Seed, Nigel 1978‡	**Earle,** Judy 1994
Kent, Peter 1978	**Geraghty,** Sarah 1994
Partridge, Ian 1979	**Reid,** David 1994
Grey, Robert 1979	**Williams,** Ben 1994
Leviseur, Nicholas 1979	**Hughes,** Melanie 1995
Coombes, Timothy 1980	**McIlroy,** David 1995
Cairnes, Paul 1980	**Strachan,** Elaine 1995
Edge, Ian 1981	**Case,** Richard 1996
Strutt, Martin 1981	**Gourley,** Claire 1996
Lickley, Nigel 1983	**Wood,** Graham 1979‡*
Lomas, Mark 1983	**Ball,** Sally 1989*
Maccabe, Irvine 1983	

Crime Desktop CD-ROM

Containing the three most important titles in criminal law: Archbold, Criminal Law Review and Criminal Appeal Reports, this is the most efficient criminal law research tool you can own.

Put time on your side, phone Sweet & Maxwell on 0171 449 1111 for more information or a free demonstration

---

BROADWAY HOUSE CHAMBERS

9 Bank Street, Bradford BD1 1TW
01274 722560
Fax: 01274 370708; DX 11746 Bradford

Chambers of S Levine
Clerk: N Appleyard

Levine, Sydney *1952*	**Askins**, Nicholas *1989*
Mitchell, David *1972*†	**Wilson**, Paul *1989*
Wood, Martin *1973*	**Drake**, Sophie *1990*
Topham, John *1970*	**Fletton**, Mark *1991*
Thomas, Roger *1976*†	**Wood**, Stephen *1991*
Newbon, Ian *1977*	**Khan**, Tahir *1986*
Hyland, Graham QC *1978*†	**Crosland**, Ben *1993*
Kelly, David *1980*	**Hendron**, Gerald *1992*
Shelton, Gordon *1981*	**Colborne**, Michelle *1993*
Gibson, Jonathan *1982*	**Nelson**, Julia *1993*
Walker, Brian *1985*	**Jamil**, Aisha *1995*
Jones, David *1985*	**Chaplain**, Jayne *1995*
Brook, Paul *1986*	**Peers**, Nicola *1996*
Birkby, Peter *1987*	**Morland**, Camille *1996*
Howard, Ian *1987*	**Cannan**, Jonathan *1989**

THETFORD LODGE FARM

Santon Downham, Brandon, Suffolk
IP27 0TU
01842 813132

Chambers of J H Barnett
Clerk: J H Barnett

Barnett, John *1981*

CHAMBERS OF LESLEY MITCHELL

Stapleton Lodge, 71 Hamilton Road,
Brentford, Middlesex TW8 0QJ
0181 568 2164
Fax: 0181 560 2798

Chambers of Ms L Mitchell

See the *Index of Languages Spoken* **in Part G to locate a chambers where a particular language is spoken, or find an individual who speaks a particular language.**

CROWN OFFICE ROW CHAMBERS

Blenheim House, 120 Church Street,
Brighton, Sussex BN1 1WH
01273 625625
Fax: 01273 698888; DX 36670 Brighton 2

Chambers of R J Seabrook QC
Clerks: Alan G Smith, Jenny Lewis

Seabrook, Robert QC *1964*†	**Garnham**, Neil *1982*
Owen, Robert QC *1968*†	**Waddicor**, Janet *1985*
Matheson, Duncan QC *1965*†	**Ross**, Jacqueline *1985*
Badenoch, James QC *1968*†	**Gimlette**, John *1986*
	Smith, Adam *1987*
Miller, Stephen QC *1971*†	**Burgin**, Timothy *1987*
Coghlan, Terence QC *1968*†	**Grant**, Kim *1988*
Havers, Philip QC *1974*†	**Rogers**, Paul *1989*
Chambers, Gregory *1973*	**Bishop**, Keeley *1990*
Smyth, Christopher *1972*‡	**Downs**, Martin *1990*
Niblett, Anthony *1976*‡	**Cave**, Jeremy *1992*
Bowron, Margaret *1978*†	**Bugg**, Ian *1992*
Balcombe, David *1980*	**Whipple**, Philippa *1994*
King-Smith, James *1980*	**Colin**, Giles *1994*
Hart, David *1982*	**Sinnatt**, Simon *1993*
	Smith, Sally-Ann *1996*

Types of work (and number of counsel practising in that area if supplied)
Bankruptcy 2 · Care proceedings 30 · Common law (general) 30 · Construction 4 · Crime 18 · Crime - corporate fraud 6 · Employment 3 · Family 14 · Family provision 14 · Insolvency 2 · Landlord and tenant 8 · Licensing 3 · Medical negligence 30 · Personal injury 30 · Professional negligence 30 · Sale and carriage of goods 20

Chambers' facilities
Conference rooms, Disks accepted

Languages spoken
French, Italian, Spanish

Additional information

This set has been established in Brighton for some 20 years and has maintained strong London connections for nearly half a century.

Members of chambers undertake all types of general common law work – civil, criminal and family. Particular expertise can be offered in the following areas: professional negligence, personal injury, landlord and tenant, building, employment, licensing, and planning. Other areas include fraud, drug trafficking, matrimonial finance and childcare.

The Brighton county and magistrates courts are

a few minutes' walk away. Conference facilities are excellent.

Chambers is administered with the benefit of modern computer technology and there are direct telephone and computer links to 1 Crown Office Row, Temple.

A brochure is available on request.

CHAMBERS OF ELIZABETH STEVENTON

50 Firle Road, Brighton, Sussex BN2 2YH
01273 670394
Fax: 01273 670394

Chambers of Mrs E A Steventon

SUSSEX CHAMBERS

9 Old Steine, Brighton BN1 1FJ
01273 607953
Fax: 01273 571839; DX 2724 Brighton 1

Chambers of Mr P M Ashwell

ALBION CHAMBERS

Broad Street, Bristol BS1 1DR
0117 9272144
Fax: 0117 9262569; DX 7822 Bristol

Chambers of Mr J C T Barton QC

ALL SAINTS CHAMBERS

9/11 Broad Street, Bristol BS1 2HP
0117 921 1966
Fax: 0117 927 6493; DX 7870 Bristol

Chambers of Mr T A Jenkins QC

The Supreme Court Practice 1999

- *the most authoritative title on Civil Court Practice and Procedure*

- *available in book and CD-ROM formats*

Phone Sweet & Maxwell on 0171 449 1111 to order your copy

ASSIZE COURT CHAMBERS

14 Small Street, Bristol BS1 1DE
0117 926 4587
Fax: 0117 922 6835; DX 78134 Bristol

Chambers of J S Isherwood
Clerks: Peter Nixon (Senior Clerk), Judith Taylor (Junior Clerk)

Owen-Thomas, David QC 1952†*	Hudson, Elisabeth 1987*
	Sproston-Matthews, Lynne 1987
Tackaberry, John QC 1967*	
Vere-Hodge, Michael QC 1970†*	Warren, Philip 1988*
	Austins, Christopher 1988
Isherwood, John 1978	Levy, Robert 1988
Wood, Graeme 1968	Ralph, Caroline 1990
Wyatt, Jonathan 1973	Smith, Nicholas 1990
Robson, John 1974*	Langlois, Peter 1991
Waley, Eric 1976	Halliwell, Toby 1992
Thomas, Nigel 1976*	Stanniland, Jonathan 1993
Ferguson, Christopher 1979	Dawson, Judy 1993
Evans, Timothy 1982	Hufford, Victoria 1994
Curwen, David 1982	Marven, Robert 1994
Qureshi, Shamim 1982	Dawar, Archna 1996
Howells, Julian 1985	Currie, Fergus 1997
Wightwick, Iain 1985	

CASTLE CHAMBERS

Court House, Taylor's Yard, Broad Street, Bristol BS1 2EY
0117 934 9833
Fax: 0117 934 9844

Chambers of Miss A C Gorna

THE CLOVE HITCH

High Street, Iron Acton, Bristol BS17 1UG
01454 228243

Chambers of Mr H W Aplin

FREDERICK PLACE CHAMBERS

9 Frederick Place, Clifton, Bristol BS8 1AS
0117 9738667
Fax: 0117 9738667

Chambers of Mr R H Spicer

Use the *Types of Work* **listings in Parts A and B to locate chambers and individual barristers who specialise in particular areas of work.**

GUILDHALL CHAMBERS

23 Broad Street, Bristol BS1 2HG
0117 9273366
Fax: 0117 9298941; DX 7823 Bristol

Chambers of Mr R J Royce QC

OLD SQUARE CHAMBERS

*Hanover House, 47 Corn Street, Bristol
BS1 1HT*
0117 927 7111
Fax: 0117 927 3478; DX 78229 Bristol
Out of hours telephone: 0973 330793

Chambers of Hon John Melville Williams QC
*Clerks: John Taylor, William Meade, Andrew
York, Robert Bocock, Bill Rice, Casta Albon;
Administrator: Brenda Brown; Bristol
Administrator: Sarah Hassall*

Annexe of: Old Square Chambers, 1 Verulam
Buildings, Gray's Inn, London WC1R 5LQ
Tel: 0171 269 0300
Fax: 0171 405 1387

Williams, The Hon John QC *1955†*	**McNeill,** Jane *1982*
Hendy, John QC *1972*	**Cotter,** Barry *1985*
Hand, John QC *1972†*	**Chudleigh,** Louise *1987*
Wedderburn of Charlton, Lord QC *1953*	**Omambala,** Ijeoma *1989*
McMullen, Jeremy QC *1971‡*	**Eady,** Jennifer *1989*
Truscott, Ian (QC Scot) *1995*	**Mead,** Philip *1989*
Lewis, Charles *1963*	**Brown,** Damian *1989*
Carling, Christopher *1969*	**Clarke,** Jonathan *1990*
Birtles, William *1970†*	**Gill,** Tess *1990*
Brahams, Diana *1972*	**Walker,** Christopher *1990*
Bates, John *1973*	**Booth,** Nicholas *1991*
Cooksley, Nigel *1975*	**Moor,** Sarah *1991*
Makey, Christopher *1975*	**Scott,** Ian *1991*
Pugh, Charles *1975*	**Segal,** Oliver *1992*
Kelly, Matthias *1979*	**Gower,** Helen *1992*
Kempster, Toby *1980*	**Lewis,** Prof Roy *1992*
Rose, Paul *1981*	**Whitcombe,** Mark *1994*
	Melville, Elizabeth *1994*
	Tether, Melanie *1995*
	Smith, Emma *1995*
	Pirani, Rohan *1995*

ST JOHN'S CHAMBERS

Small Street, Bristol BS1 1DW
0117 921 3456/929 8514
Fax: 0117 929 4821; DX 78138 Bristol
E-mail: clerks@stjohns.uk.com
Other comms: Video Conference Number:
0117 922 1586

Chambers of R L Denyer QC
*Clerks: Richard Hyde, Maureen Rowe,
Annette Moles*

Denyer, Roderick QC *1970†*	**Corston,** Jean *1991*
Hamilton, Nigel QC *1965*	**Ironside,** Julian *1985*
Kaye, Roger QC *1970†*	**Levy,** Neil *1986*
Grumbar, Paul *1974*	**Adams,** Guy *1989*
Sharp, Christopher *1975*	**Evans,** Susan *1989*
Bullock, Ian *1975*	**Hopkins,** Andrea *1992*
Marston, Nicholas *1975‡*	**Sharples,** John *1992*
Grice, Timothy *1975*	**Martin,** Dianne *1992*
Horton, Mark *1976*	**Light,** Prof Roy *1992*
Blackmore, John *1983*	**Bateman,** Christine *1992*
Longman, Michael *1978*	**Burgess,** Edward *1993*
Stead, Richard *1979‡*	**Skellorn,** Kathryn *1993*
Duval, Robert *1979*	**Maunder,** David *1993*
Dixon, Ralph *1980*	**McLaughlin,** Andrew *1993*
Jacklin, Susan *1980‡*	**Humphreys,** Jacqueline *1994*
Auld, Charles *1980*	**Walker,** Bruce *1994*
Wadsley, Peter *1984*	**Doig,** Gavin *1995*
Dixey, Ian *1984*	**Lebasci,** Jetsun *1995*
Bromilow, Richard *1977‡*	**Dickinson,** John *1995*
Blohm, Leslie *1982*	**Evans,** Judi *1996*
Hunter, Susan *1985*	**Goodman,** Simon *1996*
Edwards, Glyn *1987*	**Lowe,** Prof Nigel *1972**
Morgan, Simon *1988*	**Das,** Kamala *1975**
O'Neill, Louise *1989*	

THEATRE HOUSE

Percival Road, Clifton, Bristol BS8 3LE
0117 974 1553
Fax: 0117 974 1554

Chambers of Mr P Chadd QC

29 GWILLIAM STREET

Bristol BS3 4LT
0117 966 8997

Chambers of T Thornhill
Clerk: Self

Thornhill, Teresa *1986*

---

† Recorder   ‡ Assistant Recorder   * Door Tenant

Regency Chambers is a general common law chambers offering a broad based expertise in all areas of civil, family and criminal law.

In particular, members of chambers can provide a comprehensive service in the following areas:

Civil — personal injury and medical negligence, professional negligence, employment, licensing, landlord & tenant, personal and real property, contract, commercial litigation, consumer credit and planning;

Family — ancillary relief, public and private law, children act applications;

Crime — defence and prosecution work is undertaken.

A brochure is available on request.

Please also see entry.

Regency Chambers is located in the city centre of Peterborough and Cambridge. Conference facilities are available in both locations. In addition, conferences can easily be arranged at Solicitors' offices. Chambers' work is concentrated in East Anglia but members regularly travel to London and the Midlands.

Chambers has a fresh outlook and a continuing policy of expansion to meet increasing demand. Our aims are to provide a friendly and efficient service, relying on its members' range and depth of expertise. A full and frank appraisal of individuals may be obtained from the Senior Clerk. Chambers operates a flexible and practical approach to fees. The Senior Clerk will be happy to discuss a fee and provide guidance to suit each client and each piece of work, including conditional fees, where appropriate.

VERITAS CHAMBERS

33 Corn Street, Bristol BS1 1HT
0117 930 8802
Fax: 0117 922 1320; DX 133602 Bristol 1

Chambers of Mr N C Sweeney

HERONS REST

Parkham Lane, Brixham, Devon TQ5 9JR
01803 882293
Fax: 01803 852168

Chambers of Mr M A Furminger

BROMLEY CHAMBERS

39 Durham Road, Bromley, Kent BR2 OSN
0181 325 0863
Fax: 0181 325 1431; DX 40604 Beckenham

Chambers of E Georghiades

Georghiades, Ellikos *1975*

27 ROSE GROVE

Bury, Greater Manchester BL8 2UJ
0161 763 4739
Fax: 0161 763 4739

Chambers of Mr F A Chaudhry

FENNERS CHAMBERS

3 Madingley Road, Cambridge CB3 0EE
01223 368761
Fax: 01223 313007; DX 5809 Cambridge 1

Chambers of Lindsay Davies
Clerks: Mark Springham, Louis Rankin, Ian Spencer; Administrator: Jane Longhurst

Also at: Fenners Chambers, 8-12 Priestgate, Peterborough PE1 1JA
Tel: 01733 562030

Davies, Lindsay *1975‡*
Wheeler, Kenneth *1956**
Stokes, David QC *1968†**
King, Peter *1970*
Sells, Oliver QC *1972†**
Yelton, Michael *1972†*
Hawkesworth, Gareth *1972†*
Jones, Geraint *1972*
Gore, Andrew *1973*
Franklin, Stephen *1974*
Espley, Susan *1976*
Pointon, Caroline *1976*
Heald, Oliver *1977*
Tattersall, Simon *1977*
Leigh-Morgan, Paul *1978*
Brown, T C E *1980*
Hollow, Paul *1981*
Bridge, Stuart *1981*

Collier, Martin *1982*
Gordon-Saker, Liza *1982*
Hughes, Meryl *1987*
Litherland, Rebecca *1987*
Foxwell, George *1987*
Wilson, Alasdair *1988*
Beasley-Murray, Caroline *1988*
Pithers, Clive *1989*
Meakin, Timothy *1989*
Taylor, Andrew *1989*
Clark, Hazel *1990*
Wilson, James *1991*
Horton, Caroline *1993*
Myatt, Charles *1993*
Josling, William *1995*
Ferguson, Katharine *1995*
Lobo, Matthew *1995*

Chambers established: 1973
Opening times: 8.45 am-6.30 pm

Types of work (and number of counsel practising in that area if supplied)
Administrative 3 · Agriculture 3 · Arbitration 3 · Bankruptcy 6 · Care proceedings 14 · Chancery (general) 5 · Chancery land law 6 · Commercial litigation 8 · Commercial property 7 · Common land 4 · Common law (general) 32 · Company and commercial 5 · Construction 3 · Consumer Law 5 · Conveyancing 6 · Courts martial 12 · Crime 14 · Crime - corporate fraud 5 · Discrimination 2 · Employment 7 · Environment 5 · Equity, wills and trusts 5 · Family 22 · Family provision 10 · Financial services 5 · Housing 7 · Insolvency 7 · Landlord and tenant 8 · Licensing 6 · Local government 5 · Medical negligence 7 · Partnerships 5 · Pensions 2 · Personal injury 16 · Probate and administration 4 · Professional negligence 7 · Sale and carriage of goods 9 · Town and country planning 4

Chambers' facilities
Conference rooms, Video conferences, Disks accepted, Disabled access, E-mail, On site car park

Languages spoken
French, German

Fees policy
Chambers will agree global or hourly rates as solicitors may prefer. We are happy to peruse papers without obligation so that a fair fee may be agreed.

7 NORWICH STREET

Cambridge CB2 1ND
07000 226584
Fax: 01223 562362

Chambers of Mr A D R Colvin

REGENCY CHAMBERS

Sheraton House, Castle Park, Cambridge CB3 0AX
01223 301517
Fax: 01223 359267; DX 12349 Peterborough 1

Chambers of R P Croxon QC
Clerk: Paul Wright

Also at: Peterborough - principal office

Croxon, Raymond QC *1960*
Martignetti, Ian *1990*
Tettenborn, Andrew *1988*
Thind, Anita *1988*
Elliott, Margot *1989*
Buckle, Jonathan *1990*

Ellis, Christopher *1991*
Bennet, Pauline *1991*
Fender, Carl *1994*
Akerman, Kate *1994*
Roberts, Sir Samuel Bt *1972*
Leigh, Kevin *1986**

BECKET CHAMBERS

17 New Dover Road, Canterbury, Kent CT1 3AS
01227 786331
Fax: 01227 786329; DX 5330 Canterbury

Chambers of Mr P Newton

STOUR CHAMBERS

Barton Mill House, Barton Mill Road, Canterbury, Kent CT1 1BP
01227 764899
Fax: 01227 764941; DX 5342 Canterbury
E-mail: clerks@stourchambers.co.uk
URL: http://www.stourchambers.co.uk

Chambers of R L Warne
Clerk: Neil Terry

Warne, Roy *1979*
Pulman, George QC *1971†**
Kirwan, Helen *1983*
Cox, Sita *1987*
Johnson, Simon *1987*

Batey, Michael *1989*
Buckley, Gerardine *1991*
Mehendale, Neelima *1993*
Clegg, Adam *1994*

C

9 PARK PLACE

9 & 10 Park Place, Cardiff CF1 3DP
01222 382731
Fax: 01222 222542; DX 50751 Cardiff 2
Out of hours telephone: 01222 382731

Chambers of I Murphy QC
Clerk: James Williams

Rees, Phillip *1965**	**Williams**, Karl *1982*
Lewis, Kynric QC *1954**	**MacDonald**, Janet *1984*
Elias, Gerard QC *1968**	**Ferrier**, Susan *1985*
Roddick, Winston QC	**Lewis**, Owen *1985*
1968†*	**Brooks**, Peter *1986*
Llewellyn-Jones,	**Keyser**, Andrew *1986*
Christopher QC *1965†**	**Abbott**, Helen *1988**
Murphy, Ian QC *1972*	**Jones**, Sarah *1989*
Thomas, Roger QC *1969*	**Donoghue**, Steven *1992*
Davies, Leighton QC *1975**	**Jones**, Brian *1992*
Kelly, Martyn *1972*	**McGlyne**, John *1993*
Francis, Richard *1974*	**Wallace**, Hugh *1993*
Taylor, Gregory *1974*	**Elias**, David *1994*
Essex-Williams, David *1975*	**Gibbon**, Juliet *1994*
Twomlow, Richard *1976‡*	**Hughes**, Gwydion *1994*
Cooke, Nicholas QC *1977‡*	**Thomas**, Owen *1994*
Thomas, Keith *1977‡*	**George**, Gareth *1977**
Davies, Philip *1978*	**Jones**, Geraint *1976*
Morris, Ieuan *1979*	**Lewis**, Marian *1977*
Parry, Isabel *1979‡*	**Hopkins**, Paul *1989*
Jarman, Milwyn *1980*	**Reed**, Julian *1991*

---

30 PARK PLACE

Park Place
30
Plas-y-Parc

Cardiff/Caerdydd.
CF1 3BA

Cardiff CF1 3BA
01222 398421
Fax: 01222 398725; DX 50756 Cardiff 2
E-mail: 100757.1456@compuserve.com

Chambers of P B Richards
Clerks: Huw Davies, Phillip Griffiths,
Catherine Spencer

Richards, Philip *1969‡*	**Harrison**, Robert *1988*
Bishop, Malcolm QC *1968*	**Coombes Davies**, Mair *1988*
Jenkins, John QC *1970†*	**Austin**, Jonathan *1991*
Griffiths, Peter QC *1970†*	**Sahota**, Sukhjinder *1992*
Venmore, John *1971*	**John**, Catrin *1992*
Curran, Patrick QC *1972†**	**Baker**, Harry *1992*
Hopkins, Stephen *1973†*	**Quinlan**, Christopher *1992*
Green, Andrew *1974*	**Hermer**, Richard *1993**
Morgan, David Wynn *1976†*	**Crowther**, Tom *1993*
Crowley, Jane QC *1976†*	**Egan**, Eugene *1993*
Hartley-Davies, Paul *1977*	**McGahey**, Elizabeth *1994*
Bush, Keith *1977†*	**Hughes**, Hywel *1995*
Lewis, Marian *1977*	**Jones**, Andrew *1996*
Tillyard, James *1978*	**Williams**, Thomas *1996*
Davies, Huw *1978‡*	**Jayanathan**, Shamini *1996*
Furness, Jonathan *1979*	**Pitchford**, Christopher QC
Murphy, Peter *1980‡*	*1969**
Williams, Lloyd *1981*	**Harrington**, Patrick QC
Lewis, Paul *1981*	*1973**
Allen, Mark *1981*	**Phillips**, David QC *1976**
Mifflin, Helen *1982*	**Picken**, Simon *1989**
Rees, Ieuan *1982*	**Harpwood**, Vivienne *1969*
Williams, Rhodri *1987*	

See the *Index of Languages Spoken* **in Part G to locate a chambers where a particular language is spoken, or find an individual who speaks a particular language.**

32 PARK PLACE

Cardiff CF1 3BA
01222 397364
Fax: 01222 238423; DX 50769 Cardiff 2

Chambers of David Aubrey QC
Clerks: David Brinning, Craig Mansfield

Aubrey, David QC‡	**Rowley**, Lesley *1988*
Williams, Christopher *1972*	**Jenkins**, D Morgan *1990*
Evans, Jane *1971*	**Jonathan-Jones**, Gareth
Christie, Ronald *1974*	*1991*
Davies, John *1975*	**Kember**, Richard *1993*
Jones, Guy *1975*	**Webster**, David *1993*
Harris, David *1979*	**Lewis**, Raymond *1994*†
Price, Wayne *1982*	**Edwards**, Helen *1995*
Griffiths, Roger *1983*	**Sprunks**, James *1995*
Morgan, Lynne *1984*	**Thomas**, David *1975*
Evans, Huw *1985*	**Thomas**, Stephen *1993*
Jeary, Stephen *1987*	**Ingham**, R Lee *1994*
Smith, Ruth *1987*	

33 PARK PLACE

Cardiff CF1 3BA
01222 233313
Fax: 01222 228294; DX 50755 Cardiff

Chambers of Wyn Williams QC
Clerks: Graham Barrett, Stephen Price, Sandra Williams

Williams, Wyn QC *1974*†	**Harris**, Nicola *1992*
Griffith Williams, John QC	**Higginson**, Lucy *1992*
1968†*	**Jones**, Gareth *1992*
Pugh, Vernon QC *1969*†*	**Griffiths**, Michael *1993*
Rees, John QC *1972*‡	**Hardy**, David *1993*
Price, Gerald QC†	**Osborne**, Nigel *1993*
Davies, Peter *1996*	**Williams**, Daniel *1993*
Cook, Charles *1966*†	**Rees**, Caroline *1994*
Jenkins, Philip *1970*	**Parry Evans**, Mary *1953*†
Davies, Colin *1973*	**Howells**, Cenydd *1964*†*
Bidder, Neil *1976*‡	**Garfield**, Roger *1965*
Bull, Gregory *1976*‡	**Jones**, Richard *1969*
Walters, Jill *1979*	**Jones**, Nicholas *1970*‡
Evans, Timothy *1984*	**Parsley**, Charles *1973**
Walters, Jonathan *1984*	**Price-Lewis**, Rhodri *1975**
Huckle, Theodore *1985*	**Treharne**, Jennet *1975*
Walters, Graham *1986*	**Harris**, Russell *1986**
Jones, Nicholas David *1987*	**Arentsen**, Andrew *1995*
Bennett, Ieuan *1989*	**Jenkins**, Jeremy *1984*
O'Leary, Robert *1990*	**Rees**, Christopher *1996*
Brace, Michael *1991*	**Taylor**, Rhys *1996*
Morris, Shan *1991*	

Opening times: 8.30 am-6.15 pm

Types of work (and number of counsel practising in that area if supplied)
Arbitration · Care proceedings · Chancery (general) · Chancery land law · Commercial litigation · Commercial property · Common law (general) · Company and commercial · Construction · Crime · Crime - corporate fraud · Employment · Environment · Equity, wills and trusts · Family · Family provision · Housing · Insolvency · Insurance · Landlord and tenant · Licensing · Local government · Medical negligence · Partnerships · Personal injury · Private international · Probate and administration · Professional negligence · Town and country planning

Chambers' facilities
Video conferences, Disks accepted

Languages spoken
Welsh

Additional information

33 Park Place offers a comprehensive service in the traditional areas of work undertaken by an established provincial set of chambers, namely crime, general common law and family.

Additionally, however, individuals and groups within chambers have particular specialisations which are in the fields of Chancery, company, construction, employment, local government, personal injury (including medical negligence) and town and country planning.

The work undertaken by chambers covers the whole of Wales and work is also undertaken in the West Midlands and the West Country.

A number of members of chambers operate direct access to recognised professional bodies.

CARMARTHEN CHAMBERS

30 Spilman Street, Carmarthen, Dyfed SA31 1LQ
01267 234410
Fax: 01267 223397

Chambers of Mr R S Griffiths

146 CARSHALTON PARK ROAD

Carshalton, Surrey SM5 3SG
0181 773 0531
Fax: 0181 773 0531

Chambers of Mr B S Mustafa

THE RALEK

66 Carshalton Park Road, Carshalton, Surrey
SM5 3SS
0181 669 1777
Fax: 0181 669 1777

Chambers of Mr R K Tay

THORNWOOD HOUSE

102 New London Road, Chelmsford, Essex
CM2 0RG
01245 280880
Fax: 01245 280882; DX 89706 Chelmsford 2

Chambers of Mr D J Cocks QC

TINDAL CHAMBERS

3/5 New Street, Chelmsford, Essex CM1 1NT
01245 267742
Fax: 01245 359766; DX 3358 Chelmsford

Chambers of Mr G J Nixon-Moss

TRINITY CHAMBERS

140 New London Road, Chelmsford, Essex
CM2 0AW
01245 605040
Fax: 01245 605041; DX 89725 Chelmsford 2

Chambers of Mr R W J Howard

CHAMBERS OF CHRISTOPHER J MORRISON

5 Gladeside, Chessington, Surrey KT9 2JQ

Chambers of Mr C J Morrison

40 KING STREET

Chester CH1 2AH
01244 323886
Fax: 01244 347732; DX 22154 Chester

Chambers of R P Hughes
Clerks: Robert King, Angela Malcolmson, Gareth Stickels

Hughes, Robert 1971†	Billington, Moira 1988
Hughes, Peter QC 1971	Swallow, Jodie 1989
Hughes, Merfyn QC 1971	Sammon, Sarah 1991
Case, Janet 1975	Drummond, Bruce 1992
Teague, Edward 1977	Dunford, Matthew 1992
Trevor-Jones, Robert 1977	Jebb, Andrew 1993
Lever, John 1978	Jesudason, Christine 1993
O'Leary, Catherine 1979	O'Toole, Anthony 1993
Le Brocq, Mark 1982	Abberton, David 1994
Ganner, Joseph 1983	Hewitt, Alexandra 1995
Leigh, Sarah 1983	Parry, Desmond 1995
Bould, Duncan 1984	Price, Anna 1996
Mason, Nicholas 1984	Anderson, Brendan 1985*

SEDAN HOUSE

Stanley Place, Chester CH1 2LU
01244 320480/348282
Fax: 01244 342336; DX 19984 Chester

Chambers of M Lewis-Jones
Clerk: Gavin James Reeves

Lewis-Jones, Meirion 1971	Everett, Steven 1989
Thomas of Gresford, Lord QC 1967	Thomas, Andrew 1989
	Hornby, Robert 1990
Carlile, Alex QC 1970	Edwards, Owen 1992
Farmer, Michael QC 1972†	Lloyd, Gaynor 1992
Little, Geoffrey 1973‡	Williams, John 1992
Spencer, Robin 1978‡	Knowles, Linda 1993
Jones, I W L 1979	Roberts, Huw 1993
Chambers, Michael 1980‡	Stanton, Carolyn 1993
Moss, Peter 1980	Mullan, Richard 1994
Rowlands, Rhys 1986	Clarke, Andrew 1996

WHITE FRIARS CHAMBERS

21 White Friars, Chester CH1 1NZ
01244 323070
Fax: 01244 342930; DX 19979 Chester
Out of hours telephone: 0973 766550

Chambers of John Hedgecoe
Clerks: Robin Whinnett (Senior Clerk), Mark Robinson

Hedgecoe, John *1972*	**Roberts**, Mark *1991*
Jamieson, Anthony *1974*	**Shield**, Deborah *1991*
Woodward, Nicholas *1975‡*	**Green**, Andrew *1992*
Garside, David *1982*	**Unsworth**, Ian *1992*
Shaw, Richard *1984*	**Pates**, Richard *1993*
Lloyd, Julian *1985*	**Wilson**, Myles *1993*
Mills, Simon *1986*	**Connor**, Mark *1994*
Oates, John *1987*	**Shenton**, Rachel *1993*
Britcliffe, Anne *1989*	**Guirguis**, Sheren *1996*
Potter, David *1990*	

26 MORLEY AVENUE

Ashgate, Chesterfield S40 4DA
01246 234790

Chambers of N R Grainger

Grainger, Norman *1973*

CHICHESTER CHAMBERS

12 North Pallant, Chichester, West Sussex PO19 1TQ
01243 784538
Fax: 01243 780861; DX 30303 Chichester
Out of hours telephone: 0836 600508

Chambers of Michael Beckman QC, Charles Taylor (Executive Head)
Clerk: Jonathan Kay

Also at: Ground Floor Chambers, 11 Stone Buildings, London WC2A 3TG
Tel: 0171 831 6381
Fax: 0171 831 2575

Beckman, Michael QC *1954*	**Regan**, David *1994*
Taylor, Charles *1974*	**Mogridge**, Fraser *1995*
Davis, Lucinda *1981*	**Whitehead**, Darron *1995*
Rowlinson, Wendy *1981*	**Cherrill**, Beverley *1996*
Darton, Clifford *1988*	**Cousins**, Edward *1971**
Morgan, Colin *1989*	**Salter**, Adrian *1973**
Loosemore, Mary *1992*	**Deacon**, Robert *1976**
Emerson, William *1992*	**Giret**, Jane *1981**
Burgess, Emma *1995*	**Dight**, Marc *1984**
Magee, Rosein *1994*	

2 SOUTH AVENUE

Cleverley, Lancashire BFY5 1JY

Chambers of Mr R A Burgess

See the *Index of Languages Spoken* **in Part G to locate a chambers where a particular language is spoken, or find an individual who speaks a particular language.**

C

EAST ANGLIAN CHAMBERS

52 North Hill, Colchester, Essex CO1 1PY
01206 572756
Fax: 01206 562447; DX 3611 Colchester
Out of hours telephone: 0585 505333

Chambers of Roderick Newton
Clerk: Fraser McLaren; Administrator: Carol Bull

Also at: 5 Museum Street, Ipswich, Suffolk IP1 1HQ;
57 London Street, Norwich, Norfolk NR2 1HL

Akast, John *1968*	Mandil-Wade, Rosalyne *1988*
Wardlow, John *1971*†	
Pearce, Marcus *1972*	Richards, David *1989*
Wain, Peter *1972*	Greaves, Ann *1989*
Marsden, Andrew *1975*‡	Greenwood, John *1990*
Bryant, Caroline *1976*	Jackson, Andrew *1990*
Levett, Martyn *1978*	Bell, Marika *1991*
McLoughlin, Timothy *1978*	Bundell, Katharine *1991*
Miller, Celia *1978*	Smith, Raymond *1991*
Pugh, David *1978*	Barratt, Dominic *1992*
Hamey, John *1979*	Parry-Jones, Carole *1992*
Sinclair, Graham *1979*	Rippon, Amanda *1993*
Kefford, Anthony *1980*	Walsh, Patricia *1993*
Brooke-Smith, John *1981*	Hanlon, Jacqueline *1994*
Newton, Roderick *1982*‡	Phelps, Mark *1994*
Parnell, Graham *1982*	Walter, Francesca *1994*
Redmayne, Simon *1982*	Kelly, Richard *1994*
Davies, Jane *1983*	de Mounteney, Jonathan *1994*
Lane, Michael *1983*	
Vass, Hugh *1983*	Wheetman, Alan *1995*
Cox, Lindsay *1984*	Freeman, Sally *1995*
Shadarevian, Paul *1984*	Moore, Katharine *1995*
Bettle, Janet *1985*	Leigh, Samantha *1995*
Dyble, Steven *1986*	Wilson, David *1996*
Bate, Anthony *1987*	Morgans, John *1996*
Degel, Rebecca *1987*	Baruah, Fiona *1996*
Elcombe, Nicholas *1987*	Durr, Jude *1995*

ADVOLEX CHAMBERS

70 Coulsdon Road, Coulsdon, Surrey CR5 2LB
0181 763 2345
Fax: 0181 763 2345

Chambers of Geoffrey Leech
Clerk: Self

Leech, Geoffrey *1992*

26 SHAFTESBURY ROAD

Earlsdon, Coventry, Warwickshire CV5 6FN
01203 677337
Fax: 01203 677337

Chambers of Dr B A Brobbey

SPON CHAMBERS

13 Spon Street, Coventry, Warwickshire CV1 3BA
01203 632977
Fax: 01203 632108; DX 11257 Coventry

Chambers of Mr A Sharpe

BRENTWOOD CHAMBERS

Denton, North Yorkshire LS29 OHE
01943 817230
Fax: 01943 817230

Chambers of Miss S I Bedell-Pearce

DEVIZES CHAMBERS

11 High Street, Potterne, Devizes, Wiltshire SN10 5PY
01380 724896

Chambers of Mr P F T L Codner

3 AISBY DRIVE

Rossington, Doncaster DN11 0YY
01302 866495

Chambers of Mr W A P O'Reilly

3 ATHOL STREET

Douglas, Isle of Man
01624 897 420
Fax: 01624 897 420

Chambers of Mr J A Nutter

The Supreme Court Practice 1999

- *the most authoritative title on Civil Court Practice and Procedure*
- *available in book and CD-ROM formats*

Phone Sweet & Maxwell on 0171 449 1111 to order your copy

DURHAM BARRISTERS' CHAMBERS

27 Old Elvet, Durham City DH1 3HN
0191 386 9199
Fax: 0191 384 6020; DX 60229 Durham 1
Out of hours telephone: 01913 869199

Chambers of C L Roy-Toole
Clerk: Iain Johnston Dip Law

Roy-Toole, Christopher *1990*   **Feather,** Janet *1990*
Morrison, Christopher *1986*   **Towers,** Martin *1996*
Powell, Jonathan *1984*   **MacFaul,** Donald *1998*
McEwan, Vera *1979*

EASTBOURNE CHAMBERS

*15 Hyde Gardens, Eastbourne, East Sussex
BN21 4PR*
01323 642102/416466
Fax: 01323 641402; DX 6925 Eastbourne

Chambers of Mr A W Khan

KING'S CHAMBERS

*5a Gildredge Road, Eastbourne, East Sussex
BN21 4RB*
01323 416053
Fax: 01323 416110; DX 6931 Eastbourne

Chambers of P G Doggart
Administrator: Sharon Longhurst

Doggart, Piers *1991*   **Valks,** Michael *1994*
Nicol-Gent, Philip *1991*   **Naylor,** Jonathan *1995*
Russell, Alison *1993*   **Hall-Jones,** Stephen *1973**

CLAVENES CHAMBERS

46 Stag Lane, Edgware, Middlesex HA8 5JY
0181 931 2648
Fax: 0181 931 2648

Chambers of Mr J E Bankole-Jones

CATHEDRAL CHAMBERS, ELY

P O Box 24, Ely, Cambridgeshire CB6 1SL
01353 666775
Fax: 01353 666776; DX 41010 Ely
Other comms: Mobile: 0385 733920

Chambers of Mr Michael Duffy
Clerk: Michael Duffy; Administrator: H S Duffy Esq

Duffy, Michael *1992*

ENFIELD CHAMBERS

*1st Floor, Refuge House, 9-10 River Front,
Enfield, Middlesex EN2 3SZ*
0181 364 5627
Fax: 0181 364 5973; DX 90638 Enfield 1
E-mail: Enfieldchambers@compuserve.com
Out of hours telephone: 0468 498763

Chambers of Mr Adrian Hall
Clerks: Kevin Tarrent, Mr Chris Singleton

Hall, Adrian *1989*   **Monaghan,** Susan *1995*
McCartney, Joanne *1990*   **Gibbs,** Lisa *1995*
Gillespie, James *1991*   **Langdale,** Adrian *1996*
Spencer, Margaret *1992*   **Miller,** Simon *1996*
Taylor, Maureen *1993*   **Mukherjee,** Tablu *1996*
Cafferkey, Annette *1994*

C

CATHEDRAL CHAMBERS (JAN WOOD INDEPENDENT BARRISTERS' CLERK)

15 Castle Street, Exeter, Devon EX4 3PT
01392 210900
Fax: 01392 210901; DX 122699 Exeter
E-mail: cathedral.chambers@eclipse.co.uk
Out of hours telephone: 01392 204259
Clerk: Jan Wood

Gorna, Christina *1960*	**Moore**, Jennifer *1992*
Leckie, James *1964*	**Ives**, Annie *1994*
Wood, Richard *1975*	**White**, Darren *1996*
Hayward, James *1985*	**Hogg**, The Rt Hon Douglas
Vaughan-Williams,	QC MP *1968**
Laurence *1988*	

Chambers established: 1997
Opening times: 8.30 am-6 pm

Types of work (and number of counsel practising in that area if supplied)
Administrative · Agriculture · Arbitration
· Aviation · Banking · Care proceedings
· Chancery (general) · Commercial
· Commercial litigation · Commercial property
· Commodities · Common law (general)
· Company and commercial · Construction
· Consumer Law · Crime · Employment · Family
· Family provision · Immigration · Insolvency
· Insurance/reinsurance · Landlord and tenant
· Licensing · Local government · Medical
negligence · Partnerships · Personal injury
· Planning · Professional negligence · Sale and
carriage of goods · Shipping, admiralty · Tax -
capital and income · Tax - corporate
· Timeshare · Town and country planning

Chambers' facilities
Conference rooms, Disks accepted

Languages spoken
French, German, Italian

Fees policy
A flexible and open approach is adopted to fees
and all areas of administration. Fees are charged
either on a time-costed or inclusive 'global'
basis. Estimates can be provided or limits agreed
prior to work being undertaken.

The Bar Directory is also available on the
Internet at the following address:

http://www.smlawpub-holborn.co.uk/bar

COLLETON CHAMBERS

Colleton Crescent, Exeter, Devon EX2 4DG
01392 274898
Fax: 01392 412368; DX 8330 Exeter

Chambers of R M J Meeke
Clerk: Philip Alden

Annexe: Colleton Chambers, 22 The Crescent,
Taunton, Somerset TA1 4EB
Tel: 01823 324252
Fax: 01823 327489

Meeke, Martin *1973*‡	**Horton**, Mark *1981*
Chadd, Paul QC *1952**	**Whitehall**, Mark *1983*
Merrett, Richard *1959*	**Holder**, Terence *1984*
Lowry, Stephen *1960*	**Ashman**, Peter *1985*
Rains, Richard *1963*	**Farquharson**, Jonathan
Brabin, Michael *1976*	*1988*
Puttick, Anthony *1971*	**Barlow**, Melissa *1991*
Crabb, Richard *1975*	**Drinkwater**, Philip *1995*
Steele, David *1975*	**Vincent**, Ruth *1995*
Mackenzie, Julie *1978*	

ROUGEMONT CHAMBERS

15 Barnfield Road, Exeter, Devon EX1 1RR
01392 410471
Fax: 01392 410401; DX 8396 Exeter 1
E-mail: rougemont.chambers@eclipse.co.uk
Out of hours telephone: 01647 61302 (Clerk)

Chambers of Michael Berkley
Clerk: David Parker

Berkley, Michael *1989*	**Evans**, T Gareth *1996*
Collett, Gavin *1993*	**Crookes**, Alison N *1996*
Downham, Gillian *1993*	**Owen**, Alex *1996*
French, Richard *1995*	**Richardson**, Garth *1975**

Use the *Types of Work* listings in Parts A
and B to locate chambers and individual
barristers who specialise in particular areas
of work.

---

† Recorder ‡ Assistant Recorder * Door Tenant

SOUTHERNHAY CHAMBERS

33 Southernhay East, Exeter, Devon
EX1 1NX
01392 255777
Fax: 01392 412021; DX 8353 Exeter
E-mail: southernhay.chambers@lineone.net
Out of hours telephone: 01626 888121

Chambers of D I H Tyzack
Clerks: J Daniell, A Choules

Tyzack, David *1970‡*	**Naish**, Christopher *1980*
Posnansky, Jeremy QC *1972‡**	**Campbell**, Susan *1986*
	Berry, Nicholas *1988*
Norris, Alastair QC *1973**	**Ahmed**, Jacqueline *1988*
Meredith, George *1969*	**Ogle**, Rebecca *1989*
Alford, Robert *1970*	**Foster**, Juliet *1989*
Lewis, Hugh *1970*	**Crawforth**, Emma *1992*
Templeman, Michael *1973*	**Hassall**, James *1995*
Le Grice, Valentine *1977**	

WALNUT HOUSE

63 St David's Hill, Exeter, Devon EX4 4DW
01392 279751
Fax: 01392 412080; DX 115582 Exeter, St
Davids
E-mail: 106627.2451@compuserve.com
Out of hours telephone: 0467 790471

Chambers of Francis Gilbert QC
Clerk: Chris Doe (Senior Clerk)

Gilbert, Francis QC *1970†*	**Treneer**, Mark *1987*
Dunkels, Paul QC *1972†*	**Eaton Hart**, Andrew *1989*
Burkett, Francis *1969*	**Ingham**, Elizabeth *1989*
Barnes, Jonathan *1970†*	**MacRae**, Robert *1990*
Mercer, Geoffrey *1975‡*	**Oldland**, Andrew *1990*
Chubb, Andrew *1975†*	**Lyon**, Shane *1976*
Leadbetter, Iain *1975*	**McCarthy**, Mary *1994*
Searle, Corinne *1982*	**Evans**, David *1996*
Edmunds, Martin *1983*	**Vaitilingam**, Adam *1987*
Munro, Sarah *1984‡*	
Melville-Shreeve, Michael *1986*	

1 APPLETON ROAD

Catisfield, Fareham, Hampshire PO15 5QH
01329 847711
Fax: 01329 847706

Chambers of Mr E B P de Vries

HARBOUR COURT CHAMBERS

11 William Price Gardens, Fareham,
Hampshire PO16 7PD
01329 827828
Fax: 01329 829282; DX 40835 Fareham

Chambers of Mr P G S Renfree

GUILDFORD CHAMBERS

Stoke House, Leapale Lane, Guildford, Surrey
GU1 4LY
01483 539131
Fax: 01483 300542; DX 97863 Guildford 5
E-mail: guildford.barristers@btinternet.com

Chambers of S J P Widdup
Clerks: Richard Moore (Senior Clerk), Pippa
Sherriff (Assistant Clerk)

Widdup, Stanley Jeffrey *1973‡*	**Smallwood**, Laura *1987*
	Blatch, Francesca *1987*
Matthews, Suzan QC *1974†*	**Wilcox**, Jerome *1988*
Shapiro, Selwyn *1979*	**Coates**, George *1990*
Oliver, Simon *1981*	**Watson-Hopkinson**,
Davies, Jonathan N *1981*	Ghislaine *1991*
Shrimpton, Claire *1983*	**Button**, Richard *1993*
Pascall, Matthew *1984*	**Sellers**, Robin *1994*
Clements, Paula *1985*	**Hatcher**, Nichola *1995*
Haywood, Janet *1985*	**Page**, Jonathan *1996*

Chambers established: 1976

**Types of work (and number of counsel
practising in that area if supplied)**
Arbitration · Bankruptcy · Care proceedings
· Chancery (general) · Chancery land law
· Commercial · Common law (general)
· Competition · Courts martial · Crime · Crime -
corporate fraud · EC and competition law
· Education · Employment · Family · Family
provision · Housing · Landlord and tenant
· Licensing · Local government · Medical
negligence · Mental health · Personal injury
· Professional negligence · Town and country
planning

C

Chambers' facilities
Conference rooms, Video conferences, Disks accepted

Languages spoken
French

ST JOHN'S CHAMBERS

One High Elm Drive, Hale Barns, Cheshire WA15 0JD
0161 980 7379
Fax: 0161 980 7379

Chambers of Miss M Logan

10 KINGSFIELD AVENUE

Harrow, Middlesex HA2 6AH
0181 427 8709/081 248 4943
Fax: 0181 427 8709

Chambers of Mr N Alsolaimani

WESTGATE CHAMBERS

16-17 Wellington Square, Hastings, East Sussex TN34 1PB
01424 432105
Fax: 01424 717850; DX 7062 Hastings

Chambers of Mr J J Collins

HELIONS CHAMBERS

Pilgrims' Waye, Camps Road, Helions Bumpstead, Haverhill, Suffolk CB9 7AS
01440 730523
Fax: 01440 730523
E-mail: helionslaw@aol.com
Out of hours telephone: 01440 730523

Chambers of M H M Hely
Clerk: Ms S F Norgate

Hely, Michael *1975*

23 HARRIES ROAD

Hayes, Middlesex UB4 9DD
0181 841 8236

Chambers of Mr B Esprit

BERKELEY CHAMBERS

52 High Street, Henley-in-Arden, Warwickshire B95 5AN
01564 795546
Fax: 01564 795549

Chambers of A T Smith QC
Clerk: Mrs Julia Meehan

Smith, Anthony QC *1958†*	**Sharif,** Nadia *1985*
Neville-Clarke, Sebastian *1973*	

HICKSTEAD COTTAGE

Brighton Road, Hickstead, West Sussex RH17 5NU
01444 881182

Chambers of Mr N J Perry

A K CHAMBERS

19 Headlands Drive, Hessle, Hull, East Yorkshire HU13 0JP
01482 641180
Fax: 01482 642275

Chambers of Mr A Khan

WILBERFORCE CHAMBERS

7 Bishop Lane, Hull HU1 1PA
01482 323 264
Fax: 01482 325 533; DX 11940 Hull
E-mail: clerks@hullbar.demon.co.uk
URL: http://www.hullbar.demon.co.uk

Chambers of J B Gateshill
Clerks: John M Kennedy, Frances Sheard

Gateshill, Bernard *1972‡*	**Bury,** Mark *1986*
Cole, Lorna *1950*	**Shaw,** Elizabeth *1986*
Bevan, Hugh *1959**	**Wray,** Nigel *1986*
Stevenson, Robert *1972*	**Comaish,** Andrew *1989*
Miller, Paul *1974‡*	**Murray,** Anil *1989*
Genney, Paul *1976*	**Golder-Welby,** Andrew *1992*
Hands, Jane *1978*	**Woolfall,** Richard *1992*
Cameron, Neil *1984*	**Trimmer,** Carol *1993*
Godfrey, John *1985*	**Hirst,** Simon *1993*
Sampson, James *1985*	**Thackray,** John *1994*
Tremberg, David *1985*	**Bryan,** Jayne *1994*

† Recorder ‡ Assistant Recorder * Door Tenant

54 ANNE WAY

Ilford, Essex IG6 2RL
0181 501 4311
Fax: 0181 501 4311

Chambers of Mrs M Mbatha

EAST ANGLIAN CHAMBERS

Gresham House, 5 Museum Street, Ipswich,
Suffolk IP1 1HQ
01473 214 481
Fax: 01473 231 388; DX 3227 Ipswich

Chambers of Roderick Newton
Clerk: Peter Hall; Administrator: Carol Bull

Also at: 52 North Hill, Colchester, Essex CO1 1PY;
57 London Street, Norwich, Norfolk NR2 1HL

Akast, John *1968*	**Elcombe,** Nicholas *1987*
Wardlow, John *1971*†	**Mandil-Wade,** Rosalyne *1988*
Pearce, Marcus *1972*	
Wain, Peter *1972*	**Greaves,** Ann *1989*
Marsden, Andrew *1975*‡	**Greenwood,** John *1990*
Bryant, Caroline *1976*	**Jackson,** Andrew *1990*
Levett, Martyn *1978*	**Bell,** Marika *1991*
McLoughlin, Timothy *1978*	**Bundell,** Katharine *1991*
Miller, Celia *1978*	**Smith,** Raymond *1991*
Pugh, David *1978*	**Barratt,** Dominic *1992*
Hamey, John *1979*	**Parry-Jones,** Carole *1992*
Sinclair, Graham *1979*	**Rippon,** Amanda *1993*
Kefford, Anthony *1980*	**Walsh,** Patricia *1993*
Brooke-Smith, John *1981*	**Hanlon,** Jacqueline *1994*
Newton, Roderick *1982*	**Phelps,** Mark *1994*
Parnell, Graham *1982*	**Walter,** Francesca *1994*
Redmayne, Simon *1982*	**Kelly,** Richard *1994*
Davies, Jane *1983*	**de Mounteney,** Jonathan *1994*
Lane, Michael *1983*	
Vass, Hugh *1983*	**Wheetman,** Alan *1995*
Cox, Lindsay *1984*	**Freeman,** Sally *1995*
Shadarevian, Paul *1984*	**Durr,** Jude *1995*
Richards, David *1989*	**Moore,** Katharine *1995*
Bettle, Janet *1985*	**Leigh,** Samantha *1995*
Dyble, Steven *1986*	**Wilson,** David *1996*
Bate, Anthony *1987*	**Baruah,** Fiona *1996*
Degel, Rebecca *1987*	**Morgans,** John *1996*

66 WORTHINGTON ROAD

Surbiton, Kingston, Surrey KT6

Chambers of Mr O G Hinds

21 CRAVEN ROAD

Kingston-Upon-Thames, Surrey KT2 6LW
0181 974 6799
Fax: 0181 287 5466

Chambers of Mr K Prasad

WESTLEIGH CHAMBERS

Westleigh Wiltown, Curry Rivel, Langport,
Somerset TA10 OJE
01458 251261
Fax: 01458 251261

Chambers of Mr J H L Leckie

PEMBROKE HOUSE

18 The Crescent, Leatherhead, Surrey
KT22 8EE
01372 376160/376493
Fax: 01372 376188; DX 7301 Leatherhead 1
Out of hours telephone: 01372 376493

Chambers of P J White, T White
Clerks: P J White, T White

White, Peter-John *1977*	**White,** Tanya *1983*

CHAMBERS OF ANDREW CAMPBELL QC

10 Park Square, Leeds LS1 2LH
0113 245 5438
Fax: 0113 242 3515; DX 26412 Leeds
E-mail: chambers@bandit.legend.co.uk
Out of hours telephone: 07000 781576

Chambers of A N Campbell QC
Clerks: Mr Craig Place (Senior Clerk), Miss Sarah Farnill (Second Clerk); Practice Director: Victoria Thompson LLB

Campbell, Andrew QC *1972*†	**Worrall,** John *1984*
	Hickey, Simon *1985*
Munkman, John *1948*	**Kealey,** Simon *1991*
Kealy, Charles *1965*†	**Exall,** Gordon *1991*
Sutton, Richard *1968*	**Moulson,** Peter *1991*
Woolman, Andrew *1973*†	**Heaton,** Clive *1992*
Bradshaw, David *1975*†	**Hayes,** John *1992*
Rudland, Martin *1977*†	**Bindloss,** Edward *1993*
Dallas, Andrew *1978*‡	**Iqbal,** Abdul *1994*
Davies, Felicity *1980*	**Wordsworth,** Philippa *1995*
Clappison, William *1981*	**Doyle,** Louis *1996*
Goose, Julian *1984*	**Kelly,** Geraldine *1996*

C

---

† Recorder ‡ Assistant Recorder * Door Tenant

CHANCERY HOUSE CHAMBERS

7 Lisbon Square, Leeds LS1 4LY
0113 244 6691
Fax: 0113 244 6766; DX 26421 Leeds
E-mail: Chanceryhouse@btinternet.com
Out of hours telephone: 0370 624448

Chambers of James H Allen QC
Clerk: Colin Hedley

Allen, James QC *1973*†	**Partington**, David *1987*
Dent, Adrian *1974*	**Howd**, Stephen *1989*
Emm, Roger *1977*	**Williamson**, Melanie *1990*
Walker, Patrick *1979*	**Klein**, Jonathan *1992*
Carpenter, Richard *1981*	**Pipe**, Gregory *1995*
Walker, Mark *1986*	**Linklater**, Lisa *1995*
Morris, Paul *1986*	

Chambers established: 1996
Opening times: 8 am-6 pm (weekdays)

Types of work (and number of counsel practising in that area if supplied)
Agriculture 2 · Banking 3 · Bankruptcy 3 · Chancery (general) 4 · Chancery land law 4 · Commercial litigation 7 · Commercial property 4 · Common law (general) 9 · Company and commercial 4 · Construction 3 · Copyright 2 · Corporate finance 3 · EC and competition law 1 · Education 3 · Employment 3 · Equity, wills and trusts 3 · Insolvency 3 · Insurance 3 · Intellectual property 2 · International trade 3 · Landlord and tenant 4 · Medical negligence 3 · Partnerships 4 · Personal injury 4 · Professional negligence 4 · Sale and carriage of goods 4 · Trademarks 1

Chambers' facilities
Conference rooms, Disks accepted, Disabled access, E-mail

Languages spoken
Dutch, French, German

Fees policy
Chambers adopts a flexible and open approach to fees and indeed, all areas of administration. Fees are charged either on a time-costed or inclusive 'global' basis. In appropriate cases estimates can be provided or limits agreed prior to work being undertaken.

ENTERPRISE CHAMBERS

38 Park Square, Leeds LS1 2PA
0113 246 0391
Fax: 0113 242 4802; DX 26448 Leeds Park Square

Chambers of Anthony Mann QC
Clerks: Joanne Glew, Barry Clayton

Mann, Anthony QC *1974*	**Barker**, James *1984*
Levy, Benjamin *1956*	**Jack**, Adrian *1986*
Jennings, Timothy *1962*	**Groves**, Hugo *1980*
Halpern, David *1978*	**Atherton**, Ian *1988*
Morgan, Charles *1978*	**Henry**, Alastair *1998*
Hutton, Caroline *1979*	**Garcia-Miller**, Laura *1989*
James, Michael *1976*	**Bhaloo**, Zia *1990*
Rosen Peacocke, Teresa *1982*	**Pickering**, James *1991*
	McKinnell, Soraya *1991*
Ife, Linden *1982*	**Jory**, Hugh *1992*
McAllister, Ann *1982*	**Williamson**, Bridget *1993*
Arden, Peter *1983*	**Richardson**, Sarah *1993*
Zelin, Geoffrey *1984*	**Hardwick**, Matthew *1994*
Baker, Jacqueline *1985*	**Francis**, Edward *1995*
Gerald, Nigel *1985*	**Mauger**, Shanti *1996*

See the *Index of Languages Spoken* **in Part G** to locate a chambers where a particular language is spoken, or find an individual who speaks a particular language.

11 KING'S BENCH WALK

*3 Park Court, Park Cross Street, Leeds
LS1 2QH*
0113 2971 200
Fax: 0113 2971 201; DX 26433 Leeds, Park
Square
Out of hours telephone: 01423 359252

Chambers of F J Muller QC
Clerks: A T Blaney, A P Dunstone

Annexe of: 11 King's Bench Walk, 1st Floor,
Temple, London EC4Y 7EQ
Tel: 0171 353 3337/8
Fax: 0171 583 2190

Muller, Franz QC *1961*†	**Swain**, Fiona *1983*
Spencer, James QC *1975*†	**Reeds**, Graham *1984*
Robertson, Andrew QC *1975*†	**Cooper**, John *1985*
Radcliffe, Francis *1962*	**Mallett**, Simon *1986*
Caswell, Matthew *1968*	**Waterman**, Adrian *1988*
Barlow, Richard *1970*	**Brooke**, David *1990*
Campbell, Nicholas *1978*	**Toone**, Robert *1993*
Richardson, Jeremy *1980*	**Skelt**, Ian *1994*
Attwooll, Christopher *1980*	**Antrobus**, Simon *1995*
Wynn, Toby *1982*	**Margree**, Sarah *1996*
Caswell, Rebecca *1983*	**Dempster**, Tina *1997*

8 KING'S BENCH WALK NORTH

1 Park Square East, Leeds LS1 2NE
0113 2439797
Fax: 0113 2457215; DX 713111 Leeds Park
Square

Chambers of Mr L G Woodley QC

**Take your law library home with you …
CLI on CD-ROM and Internet**

An easily searchable source of reference to:

* *cases*

* *statutes*

* *Statutory Instruments*

* *articles from legal and financial journals*

* *Grey Paper*

* *official publications*

* *press comment*

*For more information or a free
demonstration, phone Sweet & Maxwell
on 0171 449 1111*

MERCURY CHAMBERS

MERCURY
CHAMBERS

*Mercury House, 33-35 Clarendon Road, Leeds
LS2 9NZ*
0113 234 2265
Fax: 0113 244 4243; DX 713115 Leeds
E-mail: cdexter@mercurychambers.co.uk

Chambers of Mr Benjamin Nolan QC
Clerk: Miss Carole Dexter

Nolan, Benjamin QC *1971*†	**Cohen**, Raphael *1981*
Horowitz, Michael QC *1968*†*	**Stiles**, John *1986*
	Baltaian, Anna *1995*
Upward, Patrick QC *1972*‡*	**Serr**, Ashley *1996*
Isaacs, Paul *1974*†	

Chambers established: 1998
Opening times: 8.30 am-6 pm Mon-Fri

**Types of work (and number of counsel
practising in that area if supplied)**
Chancery (general) · Commercial · Commercial
litigation · Commercial property · Company
and commercial · Employment · Family
provision · Insolvency · Personal injury
· Professional negligence

Chambers' facilities
Conference rooms, Video conferences, Disks
accepted, Disabled access, Lecture theatre

Fees policy
Fees discussed in confidence with clerk to
Chambers

The Supreme Court Practice 1999

* *the most authoritative title on Civil Court
  Practice and Procedure*

* *available in book and CD-ROM formats*

*Phone Sweet & Maxwell on 0171 449 1111
to order your copy*

NO. 6

Barristers Chambers, 6 Park Square, Leeds
LS1 2LW
0113 245 9763
Fax: 0113 242 4395; DX 26402 Leeds, Park
Square
E-mail: chambers@no6.co.uk
URL: http://www.no6.co.uk

Chambers of Shaun Spencer QC

*Clerks: Andrea Nettleton, Kate Birkbeck,
Richard Sadler; Practice Director: Tim Collins*

Spencer, Shaun QC *1968†*	**Gargan,** Mark *1983*
Lyons, Edward QC *1952†*	**Hill-Baker,** Jeremy *1983*
Williamson, Stephen QC *1964†*	**Morris,** Sean *1983*
	Frieze, Robin *1985*
Lawler, Simon QC *1971*	**Capstick,** Timothy *1986*
Goss, James QC *1975†*	**Clews,** Richard *1986*
Kershaw, Jennifer QC *1974‡*	**Troy,** Jill *1986*
	Clark, Neil *1987*
Hitchen, John *1961†*	**Reeds,** Madeleine *1988*
Winteler, John *1969*	**Smales,** Suzanne *1990*
Lakin, Gordon *1972*	**Mansell,** Richard *1991*
Clayson, Timothy *1974†*	**Mitchell,** Andrew *1991*
Shipley, Jane *1974†*	**Gioserano,** Richard *1992*
Jameson, Rodney *1976‡*	**Caswell,** Benjamin *1993*
Rose, David *1977*	**Hill,** Nicholas *1993*
Hamilton, Eleanor *1979‡*	**Valli,** Yunus *1994*
Stead, Timothy *1979*	**Wilson,** Adam *1994*
Smith, Michael *1980*	

Chambers established: 1892

Types of work (and number of counsel practising in that area if supplied)
Agriculture 1 · Care proceedings 7 · Chancery (general) 3 · Chancery land law 3 · Commercial litigation 4 · Crime 24 · Crime - corporate fraud 4 · Employment 5 · Environment 1 · Equity, wills and trusts 3 · Family 8 · Family provision 6 · Insolvency 3 · Landlord and tenant 3 · Medical negligence 3 · Partnerships 5 · Personal injury 14 · Probate and administration 4 · Professional negligence 3

Chambers' facilities
Conference rooms, Disks accepted, E-mail

Languages spoken
French, Hindi, Italian, Urdu

Fees policy
Rates available on request.

PARK COURT CHAMBERS

16 Park Place, Leeds LS1 1SJ
0113 243 3277
Fax: 0113 242 1285; DX 26401 Leeds, Park
Square

Chambers of Mr J S H Stewart QC, Mr R S Smith QC
Clerk: Roy Kemp

Steer, Wilfred QC *1950*	**Taylor,** Michael *1980*
Chadwin, James QC *1958*	**Jackson,** Simon *1982*
Stewart, James QC *1966†*	**MacDonald,** Alistair *1983‡*
Smith, Robert QC *1971†*	**Wigin,** Caroline *1984*
Harrison, Michael QC *1969†*	**Phillips,** Simon *1985*
Swift, Malcolm QC *1970†*	**Beattie,** Sharon *1986*
Lodge, Anton QC *1966†*	**Myerson,** Simon *1986*
Worsley, Paul QC *1970†*	**Bashir,** Nadim *1988*
Godfrey, Louise QC *1972†*	**Turner,** Taryn *1990*
Bourne-Arton, Simon QC *1975†*	**Thompson,** Andrew *1989*
	Davies, Maria *1988*
Hatton, David QC *1976†*	**Patel,** Elyas *1991*
Prosser, Henry *1969†*	**Tucker,** Ashley *1990*
Hirst, Tim *1970†*	**Wilson,** Scott *1993*
Hartley, Timothy *1970*	**Greaney,** Paul *1993*
Addleman, Andrea *1977*	**Johnson,** Nicholas *1994*
Bayliss, Thomas *1977‡*	**Kent,** Jenny *1993*
Devlin, Jonathan *1978*	**Pitter,** Jason *1994*
Robinson, Adrian *1981*	**Gray,** Gilbert QC *1953**
Lodge, John *1980*	**Dodson,** Joanna QC *1970**

Types of work (and number of counsel practising in that area if supplied)
Company and commercial 6 · Crime 34 · Family 8 · Landlord and tenant 6 · Licensing 4 · Personal injury 31

Chambers' facilities
Conference rooms, Disks accepted, Disabled access

Languages spoken
French, German, Hindi, Urdu

Additional information

Park Court Chambers is one of the largest sets of chambers outside London, having 11 silks and 26 juniors. It is a long-established but modern and expanding set based in the thriving commercial centre of Leeds. It offers a wide range of services. Specialist areas of practice include crime, corporate fraud, personal injury, general commercial, family, landlord and tenant and licensing.

PARK LANE CHAMBERS

19 Westgate, Leeds LS1 2RU
0113 228 5000
Fax: 0113 228 1500; DX 26404 Leeds, Park Square

Chambers of Mr Martin Bethel QC
Clerks: Mr John Payne, Mr Andy Gray, Mr Jason Middlewood; Administrator: Mrs Dawn Bell (Fees)

Bethel, Martin QC *1965†*	**Hanbury**, William *1985*
Brown, Stuart QC *1974†*	**Thorp**, Simon *1988*
Storey, Christopher QC *1979‡*	**Fielding**, Joanne *1989*
	Copnall, Richard *1990*
Wilby, David QC *1974*	**Nazir**, Kaiser *1991*
Dalziel, Alaric *1967†*	**Axon**, Andrew *1992*
Elgot, Howard *1974*	**Korn**, Adam *1992*
Finnerty, Angela *1976‡*	**Murphy**, James *1993*
Cahill, Sally *1978*	**Furness**, Corin *1994*
O'Hare, Elizabeth *1980*	**Turner**, Steven *1993*
Sigsworth, George *1977*	**Whittaker**, Dornier *1994*
Armitage, Lindy *1985*	**Anning**, Sara *1995*
Zucker, David *1986*	**Friday**, Stephen *1996*

The UK College of Family Mediators Directory & Handbook 1998/99

- *provides expert commentary on family mediation training and professional development and includes contributions by leading family mediation professionals*

- *lists over 100 family mediation groups/services and over 950 individual family mediators by region and alphabetically*

- *gives details of all members and associates of the UK College of Family Mediators*

- *includes the UK College of Family Mediators Standards and Code of Practice*

- *gives details of all the family mediation bodies which make up the UK College of Family Mediators*

For more information call Sweet & Maxwell on 0171 449 1111

THE CHAMBERS OF PHILIP RAYNOR QC

5 Park Place, Leeds LS1 2RU
0113 242 1123
Fax: 0113 242 1124; DX 713113 Leeds Park Square

Chambers of Philip Raynor QC
Clerks: William Brown, Colin Griffin, Michael Stubbs; Administrator: Gina Pinkerton

Also at: The Chambers of Philip Raynor QC, 40 King Street, Manchester M2 6BA
Tel: 0161 832 9082
Fax: 0161 835 2139

Raynor, Philip QC *1973†*	**Crean**, Anthony *1987*
Macleod, Nigel QC *1961†*	**Dunn**, Katherine *1987*
Hoggett, John QC *1969†*	**Ashworth**, Fiona *1988*
Tackaberry, John QC *1967†*	**Stockley**, Ruth *1988*
Gilbart, Andrew QC *1972†*	**Pritchett**, Stephen *1989*
Smith, Peter QC *1975†*	**Anderson**, Lesley *1989*
Farley, Roger QC *1974†*	**Campbell**, John *1990*
Sauvain, Stephen QC *1977*	**Singer**, Andrew *1990*
Patterson, Frances QC *1977‡*	**Tucker**, Paul *1990*
	Smith, Matthew *1991*
Owen, Eric *1969*	**Carter**, Martin *1992*
Jackson, John *1970*	**Harrison**, Sally *1992*
Halliday, Harold *1972*	**Horne**, Wilson *1992*
Pass, Geoffrey *1975*	**Powis**, Lucy *1992*
Evans, Alan *1978*	**Johnson**, Amanda *1992*
Khan, Shokat *1979*	**Ghosh**, Julian *1993*
Booth, Michael *1981*	**Harper**, Mark *1993*
Fraser, Vincent *1981*	**Lander**, Richard *1993*
Manley, David *1981*	**Pritchard**, Sarah *1993*
Barrett, John *1982*	**Latimer**, Andrew *1995*
Chaisty, Paul *1982*	**Berridge**, Elizabeth *1996*
Gal, Sonia *1982‡*	**Farrow**, Adrian *1997*
Braslavsky, Nicholas *1983*	**Nowell**, Katie *1996*
Halliwell, Mark *1985*	

The Bar Directory **is also available on the Internet at the following address:**

http://www.smlawpub-holborn.co.uk/bar

C

† Recorder ‡ Assistant Recorder * Door Tenant

30 PARK SQUARE

Leeds LS1 2PF
0113 243 6388
Fax: 0113 242 3510; DX 26411 Leeds

Chambers of J W Mellor
Clerk: Jennifer Thompson

Mellor, John 1953	**Pearson**, Michael 1984
Collier, Peter QC 1970†	**Granville-Fall**, Anthony 1990
Black, Jill QC 1976‡	**Hargan**, James 1990
Kershaw, Andrew 1975	**Cole**, Robert 1991
McGonigal, David 1982	**Frith**, Nicholas 1992
Haigh, Martin 1970	**Teeman**, Miriam 1993
Haring, Simon 1982	**White**, Timothy 1993
Rodger, Mark 1983	**Shiels**, Ian 1992
Hallam, Louise 1984	**Barker**, Nicholas 1994
Buckingham, Kate 1986	**Auckland**, Elizabeth 1995
Hill, Louise 1988	**Gilmore**, Ian 1996
Burn, Colin 1985	**Tyler**, William 1996

Chambers established: 1984
Opening times: 8.30 am-6 pm

Types of work (and number of counsel practising in that area if supplied)
Administrative 1 · Care proceedings 16 · Common law (general) 11 · Courts martial 2 · Crime 21 · Crime - corporate fraud 4 · Ecclesiastical 1 · Employment 4 · Family 16 · Family provision 8 · Licensing 3 · Local government 1 · Personal injury 11

Chambers' facilities
Conference rooms, Disks accepted

Languages spoken
French, German, Icelandic, Japanese

Fees policy
Chambers operates a flexible and open policy towards the negotiation of fees.

37 PARK SQUARE

Leeds LS1 2NY
0113 243 9422
Fax: 0113 242 4229; DX 26405 Leeds

Chambers of J T Sleightholme, R E Ferm
Clerk: Mrs Ann Fothergill

Ferm, Rodney 1972	**Tighe**, Dawn 1989
Sleightholme, John 1982	**Kelbrick**, Anthony 1992
Hogg, The Rt Hon Douglas QC MP 1968	**Cains**, Linda 1990
	Crossley, Steven 1992
Graham, John 1955	**Ford**, Caroline 1993
Wootliff, Barbara 1956	**Hill**, Piers 1987
Dunning, John 1973	**Gore**, Mark 1994
Glover, Stephen 1978	**Taylor**, David 1995
Kirtley, Paul 1982	**Holroyd**, Joanne 1994
Fleming, Paul 1983	**Lee**, Taryn 1992
Apfel, Freddy 1986	**Roberts**, Stuart 1994
Lindsay, Jeremy 1986	**MacAdam**, Jason 1990
Ginsburg, Amanda 1985	**Burdon**, Michael 1993

Types of work (and number of counsel practising in that area if supplied)
Agriculture · Arbitration · Care proceedings · Common law (general) · Courts martial · Crime · Employment · Family · Family provision · Landlord and tenant · Licensing · Medical negligence · Mental health · Partnerships · Personal injury · Professional negligence · Town and country planning

Chambers' facilities
Conference rooms, Video conferences, Disks accepted

Languages spoken
French, German, Hebrew

39 PARK SQUARE

Leeds LS1 2NU
0113 2456633
Fax: 0113 2421567; DX 26407 Leeds

Chambers of Mr T M A Bubb

SOVEREIGN CHAMBERS

SOVEREIGN
C H A M B E R S

25 Park Square, Leeds LS1 2PW
0113 245 1841/2/3
Fax: 0113 242 0194; DX 26408 Leeds Park
Sqare
E-mail: sovereignchambers@btinternet.com
URL: http://www.sovereignchambers.co.uk
Out of hours telephone: Home phone: 01977
620780 Mobile: 07775 615580

Chambers of G C Marson QC
Practice manager: S Paul Slater (Practice and Finance Manager); Administrator: Chris Dixon

Also at: 12 New Square, Lincoln's Inn, London
WC2A 3SW
Tel: 0171 419 1212
Fax: 0171 419 1313

Marson, Geoffrey QC *1975†*	**Keeley**, James *1993*
Muir, John *1969†*	**Wilson**, Peter *1995*
Newbury, Richard *1976*	**Maudslay**, Diana *1997*
Palmer, Patrick *1978‡*	**Mowbray**, John QC *1953**
Ekins, Charles *1980‡*	**Macdonald**, John QC *1955**
Khokhar, Mushtaq *1982‡*	**Purle**, Charles QC *1970**
Garth, Steven *1983*	**Laurence**, George QC
Gordon, David *1984*	*1972‡**
Fricker, Marilyn *1969*	**Tucker**, Lynton *1971**
Driscoll, Lynn *1981*	**Braham**, Colin *1971**
Heap, Gerard *1985*	**Russell**, Christopher *1971**
Lewis, Andrew *1985*	**Le Poidevin**, Nicholas *1975**
McKone, Mark *1988*	**Barber**, Stuart *1979**
Bedeau, Stephen *1980*	**Hargreaves**, Sara *1979**
Gresty, Denise *1990*	**Bridge**, Jane *1981**
Haslam, Andrew *1991*	**McCabe**, Margaret *1981**
Birch, Roger *1979**	**Smith**, Stephen *1983**
Dixon, David *1992*	**Sagar**, Leigh *1983**
Lumley, Nicholas *1992*	**Staddon**, Claire *1985**
Rigby, Charity *1993*	**Crail**, Ross *1986**
Semple, Andrew *1993*	**Peacock**, Ian *1990**
Pye, Jayne *1995*	**Evans-Gordon**, Jane *1992**
Finlay, Darren *1994*	**Terras**, Nicholas *1993**
Smith, Matthew *1996*	**Davies**, Louise *1995**
Dunn, Christopher *1996*	

Types of work (and number of counsel practising in that area if supplied)
Arbitration · Banking · Care proceedings · Chancery (general) · Civil liberties · Commercial litigation 11 · Company and commercial · Competition · Construction · Copyright · Crime 19 · Crime - corporate fraud 8 · Discrimination · EC and competition law · Employment 6 · Environment 2 · Family 9 · Family provision · Housing · Immigration · Insolvency · Intellectual property 1 · Landlord and tenant · Licensing · Local government · Medical negligence · Partnerships · Patents · Pensions · Personal injury 14 · Planning 5 · Professional negligence · Sports · Tax - corporate · Town and country planning · Trademarks

Chambers' facilities
Conference rooms, Disks accepted

Languages spoken
Czech, French, German, Greek, Hindi, Italian, Punjabi, Urdu

Fees policy
Please refer to Practice and Finance Manager. (Can be charged on a time-costed or inclusive 'global' basis.)

Additional information

Teams of Members have developed considerable expertise forming specialist groups which among others include family/matrimonial, crime, (both Prosecution and Defence), commercial/Chancery, intellectual property, environmental/planning, employment, personal injury, fraud.

The new trading name and logo mark the profound changes and restructuring that Chambers has recently undertaken and represents a new approach, a new structure and a new strategy.

Reorganising the traditional clerking arrangements combined with the recent implementation of the very latest computer technology, Chambers feels well placed to continue its policy of expansion and to maintain its position as one of the leading sets in the rapidly expanding commercial city of Leeds.

Use the *Types of Work* **listings in Parts A and B to locate chambers and individual barristers who specialise in particular areas of work.**

C

---

† Recorder ‡ Assistant Recorder * Door Tenant

ST PAUL'S HOUSE

*5th Floor, 23 Park Square South, Leeds
LS1 2ND*
0113 245 5866
Fax: 0113 245 5807; DX 26410 Leeds, Park
Square
Out of hours telephone: 0113 250 9857
(Senior Clerk)

Chambers of Nigel Sangster QC
*Clerk: Catherine J Grimshaw;
Administrator: Vine Pemberton Joss*

Sangster, Nigel QC *1976‡*	Stubbs, Andrew *1988*
Newcombe, Timothy *1972*	Batty, Christopher *1989*
Benson, Peter *1975†*	Foster, Francis *1990*
Harvey, Colin *1975*	Godfrey, Jonathan *1990*
Barnett, Jeremy *1980*	Sandiford, Jonathan *1992*
Standfast, Philip *1980*	Saxton, Nicola *1992*
Rose, Jonathan *1981*	Barlow, Sarah *1993*
Kearl, Guy *1982*	Bassra, Sukhbir *1993*
Lees, Andrew *1984*	Bates, Alexander *1994*
Hunt, Alison *1986*	Harrison, John *1994*
Dix-Dyer, Fiona *1986*	Watson, Kirstie *1994*
Crowson, Howard *1987*	Edwards, Nigel *1995*
Bickler, Simon *1988*	Duffy, Derek *1997*
de Jehan, David *1988*	Gordon-Dean, Natasha *1997*

Chambers established: 1982
Opening times: 8.30 am-6 pm

Types of work (and number of counsel practising in that area if supplied)
Care proceedings 7 · Chancery (general) 6
· Common law (general) 15 · Company and
commercial 9 · Courts martial 1 · Crime 15
· Crime - corporate fraud 6 · Employment 6
· Family 7 · Family provision 7 · Insolvency 8
· Landlord and tenant 8 · Medical negligence 9
· Mental health 9 · Personal injury 15
· Professional negligence 10

Chambers' facilities
Conference rooms, Disks accepted

Languages spoken
French, Hindi, Italian, Urdu

Fees policy
Chambers undertakes all types of legal aid work.
Private fees are negotiated with the clerk
depending on the case and the experience of
counsel instructed.

Additional information

Additional Information

Nigel Sangster QC is elected Member of the
Bar Council and sits on the Legal Aid/Fees
Committee. He also sits as an Assistant
Recorder.

Peter Benson sits as a Recorder.

Jeremy Barnett and Chris Batty are North
Eastern Circuit representatives of the Criminal
Bar Association.

Several members of chambers belong to the
Family Bar Association or the Criminal Bar
Association.

9 WOODHOUSE SQUARE

9 Woodhouse Square, Leeds LS3 1AD
0113 245 1986
Fax: 0113 244 8623; DX 26406 Leeds

Chambers of John M Collins
*Clerks: Samantha Ashford, Helen Dring; Fees
Administrator: Erica Newby*

Collins, John *1956†**	Newman, Austin *1987*
Saleem, Sarwar *1960*	Bickerdike, Roger *1986*
Sinclair-Morris, Charles *1966*	Hodgson, Jane *1989*
	Holroyd, John *1989*
Lumley, Gerald *1972*	Pilkington, Mavis *1990*
Jack, Simon *1974†*	Lunt, Steven *1991*
Thornton, Rebecca *1976*	Cross, Joanna *1992*
Lewis, Jeffrey *1978†*	McAllister, Eimear *1992*
Cox, Bryan *1979*	Crossley, Justin *1993*
Hall, David *1980*	Pema, Anesh *1994*
Hendry, Helen *1983*	Henley, Mark *1994*
Dodd, Christopher *1984*	Wilson, Andrew *1995*
Greenan, Sarah *1987*	Humpage, Heather *1996*

         † Recorder ‡ Assistant Recorder * Door Tenant

Chambers established: 1928
Opening times: 8.30 am-6 pm (Monday to Friday)

Types of work (and number of counsel practising in that area if supplied)

Administrative 1 · Ancillary relief · Arbitration 1 · Aviation 1 · Bankruptcy 1 · Care proceedings 7 · Chancery (general) 1 · Chancery land law 2 · Charities 1 · Civil liberties 3 · Commercial litigation 4 · Common land 2 · Common law (general) 5 · Construction 1 · Crime 12 · Employment 4 · Environment 1 · Equity, wills and trusts 2 · Family 11 · Family provision 5 · Housing 8 · Immigration 1 · Landlord and tenant 7 · Licensing 1 · Medical negligence 4 · Mental health 1 · Personal injury 13 · Planning 1 · Private international 1 · Probate and administration 2 · Professional negligence 5 · Public international 1 · Sale and carriage of goods 1 · Tax - capital and income 1 · Town and country planning 1

Chambers' facilities

Conference rooms, Disks accepted, Disabled access

Languages spoken

French, German, Spanish, Urdu

Fees policy

Up to five years call £25-75, Five to ten years call £60-85, Ten years call £75-125. Fees should be negotiated with the clerks depending upon the complexity of the case, together with the expertise of counsel. Financial limits can be agreed before work is undertaken and an estimate of fees provided if required.

65-67 KING STREET

Leicester LE1 6RP
0116 2547710
Fax: 0116 2470145; DX 10873 Leicester

Chambers of Mr W S Bach

MELBURY HOUSE

55 Manor Road, Oadby, Leicester LE2 2LL
0116 2711848

Chambers of Mr M T Khan

2 NEW STREET

2 NEW STREET is a long-established set of chambers on the Midland and Oxford Circuit covering all aspects of civil, matrimonial and criminal law.

Individual members have areas of practice in which they have special expertise including: commercial law, land law, Chancery work, landlord and tenant, planning, employment law, licensing, immigration, EC law, crime (both defence and prosecution), and family law (including divorce, ancillary relief, children's cases etc). Local authority work is undertaken, including tribunals, enquiries and PII disclosure cases.

Chambers brochure is available upon request and clerks will be happy to assist with any enquiry.

C

2 NEW STREET

Leicester LE1 5NA
0116 262 5906
Fax: 0116 251 2023; DX 10849 Leics 1
Out of hours telephone: 0589 248677

Chambers of Mr Paul Spencer
Clerk: Miss Carey Hutt

Spencer, Paul *1965*	McCandless, Paul *1991*
Clark, Timothy *1974‡*	Gibbs, Philip *1991*
Wyatt, Mark *1976*	Peet, Andrew *1991*
Brown, Robert *1979*	Herbert, David *1992*
Gasztowicz, Steven *1981*	Herbert, Rebecca *1993*
Scott, Alexandra *1983*	Burden, Emma *1994*
Barr, Edward *1983*	Gerry, Felicity *1994*
Barnett, Sally *1987*	Allingham-Nicholson,
Birk, Dewinder *1988*	Elizabeth *1995*
Allen, David *1975*	House, James *1995*
Iyer, Sunil *1988*	Davies, Carol *1995*
Neal, Alan *1975*	Chapman, Vivian *1970†**
Monk, David *1991*	

NEW WALK CHAMBERS

27 New Walk, Leicester LE1 6TE
0116 2559144
Fax: 0116 2559084; DX 10872 Leicester 1

Chambers of Mr J Snell

4 OVERDALE ROAD

Knighton, Leicester LE2 3YH
0116 2883930
Fax: 0116 2883930

Chambers of Mr M J P Conlon

21 PORTLAND ROAD

Clarendon Park, Leicester LE2 3AB
0116 2706235
Fax: 0116 2705532

Chambers of Mr J Whitmore

7 WESTMEATH AVENUE

Evington, Leicester LE5 6SS
0116 2412003

Chambers of Mr J T Nisbett

WESTGATE CHAMBERS

144 High Street, Lewes, East Sussex BN7 1XT
01273 480510
Fax: 01273 483179; DX 50250 Lewes 2

Chambers of Mr J J Collins

25-27 CASTLE STREET

25-27 Castle Street, 1st Floor, Liverpool,
Merseyside L2 4TA
0151 227 5661/5666/236 5072
Fax: 0151 236 4054; DX 14224 Liverpool
Out of hours telephone: 0151 201 2516

Chambers of S V Riordan QC
Clerk: Joanne Stapley (Senior Clerk)

Riordan, Stephen QC *1972†*	Haygarth, Edmund *1988*
Wright, Gerard QC *1954*	Smith, Jason *1989*
Baxter, Gerald *1971*	Carter, Lesley *1990*
Badley, Pamela *1974†*	Harris, Ian *1990*
Biddle, Neville *1974‡*	Driver, Simon *1991*
Barraclough, Anthony *1978*	Horwood, Anya *1991*
Goff, Anthony *1978*	Power, Nigel *1992*
Carville, Brendan *1980*	Lander, Charles *1993*
Owen, David *1981*	Nolan, Damian *1994*
Lloyd, Wendy-Jane *1983*	Loftus, Teresa *1995*
Lennon, Desmond *1986*	McLachlan, David *1997*
Johnson, Nicholas *1987*	Grant, Kenneth *1998*
Kenward, Tim *1987*	

19 CASTLE STREET CHAMBERS

Liverpool, Merseyside L2 4SX
0151 236 9402
Fax: 0151 231 1296; DX 14193 Liverpool
E-mail: Fa45@rapid.co.uk
Out of hours telephone: 0151 220 1521

Chambers of Vincent Deane
Clerks: Jennie Connor, Damien Breingan

Deane, Vincent *1976*	Woosey, Jane *1993*
Hope, Nadine *1988*	Frieze, Daniel *1994*
Flood, Diarmuid *1989*	Burke, Brendan *1995*
Sinker, Andrew *1991*	Gow, Henry *1995*
Mairs, Robin *1992*	Cooksammy, Natalie *1995*
Ackerley, David *1992*	Morris, Ben *1996*
Polglase, David *1993*	

The Bar Directory **is also available on the Internet at the following address:**

http://www.smlawpub-holborn.co.uk/bar

† Recorder ‡ Assistant Recorder * Door Tenant

CHAVASSE COURT CHAMBERS

2nd Floor, Chavasse Court, 24 Lord Street,
Liverpool, Merseyside L2 1TA
0151 707 1191
Fax: 0151 707 1189; DX 14223 Liverpool

Chambers of Miss Theresa Pepper
Clerks: Colin Cubley (Senior Clerk), Sandra
McConnell (Civil Clerk)

Pepper, Theresa 1973‡	**Bagley**, Michael 1984
Carus, Anthony 1938	**Knifton**, David 1986
Mattison, Andrew 1963	**Abrahamson**, Judith 1988*
Limont, William 1964	**Williams**, David 1990‡
Pickavance, Graham 1973	**Watson**, Tom 1990
Cliff, Elizabeth 1975	**Crallan**, Richard 1990
McDermott, John 1976	**Greenwood**, Celestine 1991
Simms, Alan 1976	**Sherman**, Susan 1993
Bennett, David 1977	**Carroll**, Jonathan 1994*
Rose, Anthony 1978	**Mintz**, Simon 1996
Forsyth, Julie 1983	**Povoas**, Simon 1996
O'Donohoe, Anthony 1983	**Biswas**, Nisha 1996

THE CORN EXCHANGE CHAMBERS

5th Floor, Fenwick Street, Liverpool,
Merseyside L2 7QS
0151 227 1081/5009
Fax: 0151 236 1120; DX 14221 Liverpool

Chambers of David Steer QC, I S Goldrein QC
Clerks: Alex Keith, Rachel Kehoe;
Practice manager: Alex Keith

Steer, David QC 1974†	**O'Neill**, Philip 1983
Goldrein, Iain QC 1975‡	**McGuire**, Donal 1983
Aubrey, David QC 1974†	**Killeen**, Simon 1984
Bellis, Gordon 1972	**Khan**, Jamil 1986
Pickavance, Michael 1974	**Davies**, Peter 1986
de Haas, Margaret QC	**Reaney**, Janet 1987
1977‡	**Parker**, Steven 1987
Gilchrist, Nicholas 1975†	**Sutton**, Keith 1988
Brown, Mark 1975‡	**Bispham**, Christine 1991
Abelson, Michael 1976‡	**Parry-Jones**, Trevor 1992
Grice, Kevin 1977‡	**Jordan**, Fiona 1991
Pratt, Richard 1980‡	**Altham**, Rob 1993
Flewitt, Neil 1981	**Jones**, Elaine 1984
Riding, Henry 1981	**Baker**, Clive 1995
Lazarus, Grant 1981	**Mitchell**, Tom 1995
Loveridge, Andrew 1983	**Clare**, Stuart 1997

Opening times: 9 am-6.30 pm

Types of work (and number of counsel practising in that area if supplied)
Admiralty 1 · Care proceedings 10 · Civil liberties 2 · Commercial litigation 7 · Common law (general) 31 · Construction 5 · Crime 28 · Crime - corporate fraud 28 · Defamation 5 · Discrimination 5 · Employment 5 · Environment 3 · Family 15 · Family provision 15 · Housing 3 · Landlord and tenant 3 · Licensing 7 · Medical negligence 8 · Mental health 3 · Partnerships 4 · Personal injury 18 · Professional negligence 10 · Sale and carriage of goods 10 · Shipping, admiralty 1 · Sports 1

Chambers' facilities
Conference rooms, Video conferences, Disabled access

Additional information

Areas of practice

These chambers have their work-base in the North but with established contacts in Cheshire and North Wales. The size of chambers has enabled a broad basis of specialisations to be developed especially in the following fields: crime, family law, personal injuries (including catastrophic injuries and multi-party actions), professional negligence (in particular medical, legal and surveyors'), all forms of local government work and general common law work.

Specialists are also available in the following fields: employment, mental health, commercial work, licensing, housing and general landlord and tenant law. Major claims handling: Ian S Goldrein and Margaret R de Haas (authors and editors of the *Butterworths Personal Injury Litigation Service*) operate the Corn Exchange Chambers major claims handling unit.

DERBY SQUARE CHAMBERS

Merchants Court, Derby Square, Liverpool
L2 1TS
0151 709 4222
Fax: 0151 708 6311; DX 14213 L'pool 1

Chambers of Mr J S Newton

See the *Index of Languages Spoken* **in Part G to locate a chambers where a particular language is spoken, or find an individual who speaks a particular language.**

EXCHANGE CHAMBERS

Pearl Assurance House, Derby Square, Liverpool, Merseyside L2 9XX
0151 236 7747
Fax: 0151 236 3433; DX 14207 Liverpool
E-mail: exchangechambers@btinternet.com
Out of hours telephone: 017048 77272

Chambers of William Waldron QC
Clerks: Roy Finney, Barbara Jones;
Practice manager: Tom Handley

Waldron, William QC 1970†	**Clark**, Paul 1994
Turner, David QC 1971†*	**Jones**, Gerald 1995
Braithwaite, William QC 1970†	**Berkson**, Simon 1986
	James, Alun 1986
Globe, Henry QC 1972†	**Waldron**, William 1986
Morrow, Graham QC 1974‡	**McCarroll**, John 1988
Holroyde, Timothy QC 1977‡	**Cummings**, Brian 1988
	Mulrooney, Mark 1988
Jones, Edward QC 1975‡	**Clark**, Rebecca 1989
Smith, Peter 1954	**Howells**, Catherine 1989
Nance, Francis 1970	**Wood**, Michael 1989
Cornwall, Christopher 1975†	**Stables**, Christopher 1990
Earlam, Simon 1975‡	**Case**, Julie 1990
Lamb, Eric 1975	**Philpotts**, John 1990
Rae, James 1976	**Yip**, Amanda 1991
Martin, Gerard 1978‡	**Casement**, David 1992
Fordham, Judith 1991	**Evans**, Paul 1992
Cole, Gordon 1979	**Dudley**, Robert 1993
Griffiths, Tania 1982	**Kenny**, Charlotte 1993
Hillman, Roger 1983	**Fox**, Simon 1994
Cadwallader, Neil 1984	**Pennifer**, Kelly 1994
Gregory, Karen 1985	**Silverbeck**, Rachel 1996
Talbot, Dennis 1985	

Opening times: 8 am-7 pm

Types of work (and number of counsel practising in that area if supplied)
Administrative · Asset finance · Banking · Bankruptcy · Care proceedings · Chancery (general) · Chancery land law · Charities · Commercial · Commercial litigation · Commercial property · Common land · Common law (general) · Company and commercial · Conveyancing · Corporate finance · Crime · Crime - corporate fraud · Employment · Environment · Equity, wills and trusts · Family · Family provision · Housing · Insolvency · Insurance · Insurance/reinsurance · International trade · Landlord and tenant · Licensing · Local government · Medical negligence · Mental health · Partnerships · Pensions · Personal injury · Planning · Probate and administration · Professional negligence · Sale and carriage of goods · Share options · Shipping, admiralty · Tax - capital and income · Tax - corporate · Town and country planning

Chambers' facilities
Conference rooms, Disks accepted, Disabled access, E-mail

Languages spoken
French, Welsh

Fees policy
Chambers adopts a flexible and open approach to fees. Estimates can be provided prior to work being undertaken. Fees are charged on an agreed hourly rate or inclusive global basis. Please feel free to discuss this with the clerks.

FIRST NATIONAL CHAMBERS

2nd Floor, 24 Fenwick Street, Liverpool, Merseyside L2 7NE
0151 236 2098
Fax: 0151 255 0484; DX 14167 Liverpool 1
Clerk: Mark Bloor

Barnes, Ashley 1990	**Iro**, Augustine 1995
Beeson, Nigel 1983	**Mills**, Stuart 1992
Gatenby, James 1994	**O'Halloran**, Jill 1994
Gray, Mark 1996	**Simpson**, Paul 1980
Holt, Margaret 1978	

† Recorder ‡ Assistant Recorder * Door Tenant

INDIA BUILDINGS CHAMBERS

India Buildings, Water Street, Liverpool,
Merseyside L2 0XG
0151 243 6000
Fax: 0151 243 6040; DX 14227 Liverpool

Chambers of D M Harris QC
Clerks: Robert Moss (Senior Clerk/Practice
Manager), Helen Southworth, Gail Curran,
Alastair Webster, Neil McHugh

Harris, David QC *1969*†	**Sanders,** Damian *1988*
Briggs, John *1953*	**Holder,** Simon *1989*
Wolff, Michael *1964*	**Andrews,** Rachel *1989*
Atherton, Robert *1970*‡	**Browne,** Louis *1988*
Byrne, Michael *1971*†	**Chaudhry,** Zia *1991*
Herman, Raymond *1972*†	**Taylor,** Jonathan *1991*
Brittain, Richard *1971*†	**Pratt,** Patricia *1991*
Bedford, Stephen *1974*‡	**Swift,** Steven *1991*
Lowe, Geoffrey *1975*	**Butler,** Jonathan *1992*
Roddy, Maureen *1977*†	**Gibson,** John *1993*
Duggan, James *1978*†	**Jones,** Ben *1993*
Wood, Graham *1979*‡*	**Flood,** David *1993*
Owen, Gail *1980*	**Harrison,** Leona *1993*
Jones, Gareth *1984*	**Mann,** Sara *1994*
Kennedy, Michael *1985*	**Scholes,** Michael *1996*
Wall, Jacqueline *1986*	**Dixon,** John *1995*
France-Hayhurst, Jean *1972*	**Chukwuemeka,** John *1994*
Davey, Charles *1989*	

JOHN PUGH'S CHAMBERS

3rd Floor 14 Castle Street, Liverpool L2 0NE
0151 236 5415
Fax: 0151 227 5468; DX 14182 Liverpool 1

Chambers of Mr J B Pugh

**The *new* Supreme Court Practice 1999
(The White Book)**

* the most authoritative guide to Civil
  Court Practice and Procedure

* whatever the case, whatever the court

* updates following implementation of the
  Woolf Reforms

The new Supreme Court Practice *is also
available on CD-ROM using Folio Views™
technology. With this intuitive software, you
will find your way around* The White Book
*with ease, enhancing your research by leaps
and bounds.*

*Phone Sweet & Maxwell on 0171 449 1111
to order your copy*

THE CHAMBERS OF ADRIAN LYON

CASTLE XIV STREET

14 Castle Street, Liverpool, Merseyside
L2 0NE
0151 236 4421/8240/6757
Fax: 0151 236 1559/ 227 3005; DX 14176
Liverpool 1
E-mail: chambers14@aol.com

Chambers of Adrian Lyon
Clerks: Stuart Jones & David Blunsden
(Common Law), Gary Quinn & Neil Grisdale
(Chancery)

Lyon, Adrian *1975*‡	**Lund,** Celia *1988*
Edis, Andrew QC *1980*‡*	**Sharpe,** Malcolm *1989*
Goldrein, Eric *1961*	**Golinski,** Robert *1990*
Riddle, Nicholas *1970*	**Sellers,** Graham *1990*
Orr, Nicholas *1970*	**Watson,** David *1990*
Haselhurst, Ian *1976*	**Johnson,** Christine *1991*
Warnock, Robert *1977*‡	**Hall,** Richard *1991*
Eaton, Thomas *1976*	**Jackson,** Nicholas *1992*
Benson, John *1978*	**Grace,** Timothy *1993*
Ginniff, Nigel *1978*	**Whyte,** Anne *1993*
Dennis, David *1979*	**Green,** David *1993*
Sellars, Michael *1980*	**Davey,** Michelle *1993*
Gibson, Arthur *1980*	**Banks,** Rachael *1993*
Johnson, Ian *1982*	**Williams,** Andrew *1994*
Corless, John *1984*	**Banks,** F Andrew *1995*
Woolfenden, Ivan *1985*	**Grundy,** Liam *1995*
Ryan, Nicholas *1984*	**Prior,** Charles *1995*
Booth, Simon *1985*	**Horne,** Kenderik *1996*
Driver, Stuart *1988*	**Rawcliffe,** Mark *1996*
Gorton, Simon *1988*	

Opening times: 8.45 am-6.30 pm

**Types of work (and number of counsel
practising in that area if supplied)**
Agriculture 8 · Arbitration 2 · Banking 6
· Bankruptcy 12 · Care proceedings 9
· Chancery (general) 12 · Chancery land law
12 · Civil liberties 2 · Commercial litigation 8
· Commercial property 8 · Common land 8
· Company and commercial 8 · Conveyancing
12 · Copyright 2 · Courts martial 1 · Crime 11
· Crime - corporate fraud 6 · Defamation 1
· Discrimination 3 · Ecclesiastical 1 · Education
1 · Employment 7 · Equity, wills and trusts 12
· Family 10 · Family provision 12 · Housing 5

· Immigration 1 · Insolvency 12 · Insurance 5
· Intellectual property 4 · Landlord and tenant
12 · Licensing 5 · Medical negligence 8
· Mental health 2 · Partnerships 12 · Pensions 2
· Personal injury 12 · Probate and
administration 12 · Professional negligence 8
· Sale and carriage of goods 4 · Tax - capital
and income 2 · Tax - corporate 2 · Town and
country planning 2

Chambers' facilities
Conference rooms, Disks accepted, E-mail,
Lexis terminal

Languages spoken
French, German, Italian

· Common law (general) · Company and
commercial · Construction · Consumer Law
· Crime · Crime - corporate fraud
· Employment · Family · Family provision
· Insolvency · Landlord and tenant · Licensing
· Medical negligence · Mental health · Pensions
· Personal injury · Professional negligence
· Sale and carriage of goods

Chambers' facilities
Conference rooms, Video conferences, Disks
accepted, Disabled access

Languages spoken
French, German, Greek, Russian

MARTINS BUILDING

Water Street, Liverpool, Merseyside L2 3SP
0151 236 5818/4919
Fax: 0151 236 2800; DX 14232 Liverpool
Out of hours telephone: 01695 424369

Chambers of R A Fordham QC, D J Boulton
*Clerks: John Kilgallon, Nick Roberts, Denise
Sheen, Carolyn O'Connor*

Fordham, Robert QC 1967†
Boulton, David 1970†
Geey, David 1970†
Cowan, Jack 1971
Kerr, David 1971†
McDonald, Andrew 1971
Compton-Rickett, Mary 1972
Georges, Antonis 1972
Halligan, Rodney 1972
Davies, Michael 1979
Menary, Andrew 1982
Chatterton, Mark 1983
McGuire, Deirdre 1983
Reade, Kevin 1983
Knapp, Stephen 1986

Kidd, Peter 1987
Lawrence, Nigel 1988
Downie, Andrew 1990
Symms, Kathryn 1990
Grover, Tim 1991
Dale, Jonathan 1991
Romain, Charan 1991
Seed, Stephen 1991
Shaw, Nicola 1992
Edwards, David 1994
Wrenn, Helen 1994
Carney, Andrew 1995
Greenfield, Jeremy 1995
Dutchman-Smith, Malcolm 1995
Hoare, Gregory 1992

Types of work (and number of counsel practising in that area if supplied)
Administrative · Care proceedings · Civil
liberties · Commercial · Commercial property

ORIEL CHAMBERS

*14 Water Street, Liverpool, Merseyside
L2 8TD*
0151 236 7191
Fax: 0151 227 5909; DX 14106 Liverpool
E-mail: oriel_chambers@link.org
Other comms: Lix: Liv 001

Chambers of A T Sander
Clerk: John Laking

Sander, Andrew†
Joynes, Bryan 1957
Edwards, Anthony 1972†
Rankin, William 1972
Murray, Ashley 1974‡
Wright, Norman 1974‡
Bradley, Richard 1978
Cowan, Peter 1980
Fogarty, Peter 1982
Bundred, Gillian 1982
Evans, Suzanne 1985
Thomas, Gareth MP 1977
Fox, Anna 1986

Goodbody, Peter 1986
Nicholls, Jane 1989
Baldwin, John 1990
Gruffydd, John 1992
Belbin, Heather 1992
Brant, Paul 1993
Brandon, Helen 1993
Dawson, James 1994
Somerset-Jones, Felicity 1994
Cottrell, Matthew 1996
Frodsham, Alexander 1996
Sawyer, John 1978

Chambers established: 1965
Opening times: 8.45 am-6.30 pm

Types of work (and number of counsel practising in that area if supplied)
Asset finance 1 · Bankruptcy 1 · Care
proceedings 8 · Commercial 3 · Commercial

litigation 10 · Common law (general) 19 · Consumer Law 6 · Crime 5 · Crime - corporate fraud 2 · Employment 11 · Environment 5 · Factoring · Family 11 · Family provision 10 · Housing 2 · Information technology 1 · Insolvency 1 · Landlord and tenant 5 · Licensing 1 · Medical negligence 5 · Partnerships 1 · Personal injury 16 · Professional negligence 10 · Sale and carriage of goods 7

Chambers' facilities
Conference rooms, Disks accepted, E-mail

Languages spoken
Dutch, French

PEEL HOUSE CHAMBERS

PEEL HOUSE CHAMBERS

Ground Floor, Peel House, 5-7 Harrington Street, Liverpool, Merseyside L2 9QA
0151 236 4321
Fax: 0151 236 3332; DX 14225 Liverpool
Out of hours telephone: 0151 652 0669

Chambers of N B D Gilmour QC
Clerks: Michael R Gray, Andrew Heap, Mark Shannon, Denise Larkin, Athene Moreton (Fees Clerk)

Gilmour, Nigel QC *1970†*	**Christie,** Simon *1988*
Noble, Arthur *1965†*	**Hickland,** Margaret *1988*
Bennett, Martyn *1969*	**Gould,** Deborah *1990*
Alldis, Christopher *1970†*	**Lewthwaite,** Joanne *1990*
Hall, Philip *1973*	**Becker,** Paul *1990*
Feeny, Charles *1977‡*	**Sellers,** Alan *1991*
Lloyd, Heather *1979*	**Rahman,** Yaqub *1991*
Somerville, Thomas *1979*	**McNeill,** Fiona *1992*
Gibson, Titus *1981*	**Foster,** Peter *1992*
Gregory, Peter *1982*	**Mates,** Rory *1993*
McKeon, James *1982*	**Rankin,** William *1994*
Price Rowlands, Gwynn *1985*	**Kemp,** Stephen *1995*
	Hughes, Rachel *1995*
Connolly, Michael *1985*	**Clarke,** Susan *1996*
Breheny, Mark *1986*	

Chambers established: 1920
Opening times: 8.45 am-6.30 pm

Types of work (and number of counsel practising in that area if supplied)
Care proceedings 6 · Common law (general) 22 · Crime 12 · Discrimination 2 · Employment 4 · Family 6 · Family provision 6 · Licensing 1 · Medical negligence 6 · Personal injury 10 · Professional negligence 2 · Town and country planning 1

Chambers' facilities
Conference rooms, Disks accepted, Disabled access

Languages spoken
Spanish, Welsh

Fees policy
Fees will be negotiated with the clerk. Level of fees depends on seniority of counsel, complexity of case and urgency.

Additional information

Peel House Chambers is a long-established general common law set dealing with all aspects of the laws of tort, contract, crime and family.

Civil litigation: particular expertise is claimed in medical negligence, solicitors' negligence, industrial injuries.

Crime: practitioners of all levels of experience are available and particular expertise is claimed in sexual offences and fraud.

Family: all types of family work are handled including care proceedings, injunctions, wardship and ancillary relief.

WESTMINSTER CHAMBERS

3 Crosshall Street, Liverpool L1 6DQ
0151 236 4774
Fax: 0151 236 4774

Chambers of Miss L Brown

C

ACHMA CHAMBERS

*44 Yarnfield Square, Clayton Road, London
SE15 5JD*
0171 639 7817
Fax: 0171 635 9098
Out of hours telephone: 0958 301089

Chambers of George Edward Ofori
*Clerk: Lucy Akua Ofori; Administrator: Lucy
Akua Ofori*

Ofori, George *1982*

ACRE LANE NEIGHBOURHOOD CHAMBERS

30A Acre Lane, London SW2 5SG
0171 274 4400
Fax: 0171 274 4333

Chambers of Ms N Sultan

CHAMBERS OF IBRAHIM ADDOO

*Bloxworth Villa, 38 Delafield Road, Charlton,
London SE7 7NP*
0181 244 3555
Fax: 0181 858 9239

Chambers of Mr I N K Addoo

ALBAN CHAMBERS

Alban Chambers

27 Old Gloucester Street, London WC1N 3XX
0171 419 5051
Fax: 0181 858 3533; DX 35209 Greenwich 2
E-mail: wpmd@clara.net
Out of hours telephone: 0385 564775

Chambers of Mrs W P M Datta

ALBANY CHAMBERS

*91 Kentish Town Road, Camden, London
NW1 8NY*
0171 485 5736/38
Fax: 0171 485 6752; DX 46451 Kentish Town
E-mail: albanychambers@usanet
URL: http://www.eyerhyme.demon.co.uk/
albany/
Out of hours telephone: 0171 435 8533

Chambers of P A Lawrence

Lawrence, Pamela *1975*	**Kavanagh**, Jennifer *1993*
Davies, Harold *1978*	**Almeyda**, Genevieve *1994*
Omideyi, Christina *1987*	**Martin**, Philip *1995*
Martins, Yetunde *1989*	**Goldsbrough**, Felicity *1997*
Babajide, Ibukun *1990*	

CHAMBERS OF JAMES APEA

11 Helix Road, London SW2 2JR
0181 244 5545

Chambers of Mr J B Apea

ARBITRATION CHAMBERS

22 Willes Road, London NW5 3DS
0171 267 2137
Fax: 0171 482 1018; DX 46454 Kentish Town
E-mail: jatqc@atack.demon.co.uk

Chambers of J A Tackaberry QC
Clerk: Pearl O'Brien

Tackaberry, John QC *1967*†   **Morris**, Derrick *1983*
Gough, Karen *1983*

**Types of work (and number of counsel
practising in that area if supplied)**
Arbitration 6 · Construction

Additional information

John Tackaberry: During his career at the Bar,
Mr Tackaberry has undertaken a wide range of
work. In more recent years as an advocate he
has had a substantial degree of experience in
building and civil engineering work.

As well as work in the UK, counsel has a great
deal of expertise in international disputes
throughout Europe, the USA, the West Indies,
Africa, Hong Kong, Singapore, Malaysia, and,
more recently, India and South America.
He is spending an increasing amount of time as
arbitrator both within the UK and overseas. In
this context Mr Tackaberry was the first QC to
appear on the list of all three of the following

organisations: the Institute of Civil Engineers; the Royal Institute of British Architects; and the Chartered Institute of Arbitrators.

He is also a member of, and/or on the arbitration panels of, the American Arbitration Association, the Los Angeles Center for Commercial Arbitration, the Chartered Institute of Arbitrators (past chairman), the Society of Construction Law (past president), the Indian Council of Arbitrators and its panel of international arbitrators, the Association of Arbitrators in South Africa, the Singapore International Arbitration Council, the Hong Kong Centre for International Arbitration, Mauritius Chamber of Commerce and Industry and the Institute for Transnational Arbitration and the Advisory Board thereof of the South Western Legal Foundation Texas.

Mr Tackaberry is a member, or has been admitted *ad hoc*, to the Bars of California, Ireland, Hong Kong, Malaysia, and New South Wales, and is heavily involved in ICC arbitrations.

He has written and contributed to many books and conferences over the years.

Mr Tackaberry is also associated with the following chambers:
Assize Court Chambers, Small Street, Bristol BS1 1DE (telephone: 01272 264587); Chambers of Philip Raynor QC, 40 King Street, Manchester M2 6BA (telephone: 0161 832 9082).

Derrick Morris: Prior to being called to the Bar, Mr Morris had a comprehensive career in the building and civil engineering industries. Since his call to the Bar he has had substantial experience as an advocate in building and civil engineering particularly in the field of arbitrations. A great deal of Mr Morris's experience has been gained in arbitration work in South East Asia and the Far East as well as in England and Wales.

Mr Morris has written and contributed articles and papers to a number of journals and conferences - particularly on legal matters in the construction and engineering field in South East Asia and the Far East.

Both members undertake direct professional access work. A full CV and a copy of terms of engagement are available.

ARCADIA CHAMBERS

P O Box 16674, 18 Kensington Court, London W8 5DW
0171 938 1285
Fax: 0171 938 1285

Chambers of Mr J P A L Fernandes

C

ARDEN CHAMBERS

27 John Street, London WC1N 2BL
0171 242 4244
Fax: 0717 242 3224; DX 29 London, Chancery
Lane
URL: http://www.arden-chambers.lawco.uk/
arden chambers

Chambers of A P R Arden QC
Clerk: Barry Landa (Senior Clerk)

Arden, Andrew QC *1974*	**Henderson,** Josephine *1990*
Carter, David *1971*	**Jenrick,** Kate *1990*
Jones, Timothy *1975*	**Kilpatrick,** Alyson *1991*
Hayton, Linda *1975*	**Dymond,** Andrew *1991*
O'Mahony, Declan *1980*	**Bretherton,** Kerry *1992*

**Types of work (and number of counsel
practising in that area if supplied)**
Administrative 3 · EC and competition law 1
· Environment 10 · Housing 16 · Landlord and
tenant 16 · Local government 5 · Town and
country planning 1

Chambers' facilities
Disks accepted

Languages spoken
French

Fees policy
Fees will be negotiated with the clerk
depending on the case. The range of fees is
available in writing from the clerks.

ARDEN

CHAMBERS

These specialist chambers were established to provide a centre for practice
which both reflected the series of works edited or written by members (see
below) and promoted their corresponding expertise and experience. For up to
date information on members, publications and articles, visit our web site at
http://www.arden-chambers.law.co.uk/arden-chambers.

Litigation and advisory work are undertaken for a wide range of clients, in the
public and private sectors. All members accept instructions on the basis of direct
professional access. Andrew Arden QC has also conducted 5 local government
inquiries/reviews.

Members of chambers have either written, edited or collaborated in:
Encyclopaedia of Housing Law; *Housing Law Reports*; Arden & Hunter's *Local
Government Finance, Law and Practice*; Arden & Partington's *Housing Law*;
Arden's *Manual of Housing Law*; *Housing Law – Cases, Materials and
Commentary*; *Homeless and Allocation*; *Quiet Enjoyment*; *vol 3* Megarry's *The
Rent Acts (11th ed)*, *Assured Tenancies*; Arden's *Housing Library*; *Judicial
Review Proceedings*; *Housing Law: Pleadings in Practice*; Atkin's *Court Forms*;
Bibliography of Social Security Law; *Claim in Time*; Current Law.

Partington, Prof Martin *1984*	**Moore,** Arthur *1992*
Baker, Christopher *1984*	**Halloran,** Celidh *1992*
Balogh, Christopher *1984*	**Collins,** Scott *1994*
Hunter, Caroline *1985*	**Preston,** Dominic *1995*
Manning, Jonathan *1989*	**Challen,** Lydia *1995*
Colville, Iain *1989*	**Pengelly,** Sarah *1996*
Okoya, William *1989*	**McGrath,** Siobhan *1982*
Kilcoyne, Desmond *1990*	**Saunders,** Emma *1994**

Chambers established: 1993
Opening times: 9 am-6 pm

CHAMBERS OF DR MICHAEL ARNHEIM

*101 Queen Alexandra Mansions, Judd Street,
London WC1H 9DP*
0171 833 5093
Fax: 0171 916 0962; DX 330 London,
Chancery Lane

Chambers of Dr M T W Arnheim

Arnheim, Dr Michael *1988*

† Recorder ‡ Assistant Recorder * Door Tenant

ATKIN CHAMBERS

ATKIN CHAMBERS
Barristers

1 Atkin Building, Gray's Inn, London
WC1R 5AT
0171 404 0102
Fax: 0171 405 7456; DX LDE Box 1033
E-mail: clerks@atkin-chambers.co.uk
Other comms: LON 075

Chambers of Mr J Blackburn QC
Clerks: S Goldsmith, D Barnes

Wallace, Ian QC *1948*	Goddard, Andrew *1985*
Knight, Brian QC *1964*†	Streatfeild-James, David
Blackburn, John QC *1969*	*1986*
Reese, Colin QC *1973*†	Godwin, William *1986*
Akenhead, Robert QC	Barwise, Stephanie *1988*
1972†	Lofthouse, Simon *1988*
Dennys, Nicholas QC *1975*‡	Clay, Robert *1989*
White, Andrew QC *1980*	Fraser, Peter *1989*
Valentine, Donald *1956*	Rawley, Dominique *1991*
Royce, Darryl *1976*	Doerries, Chantal-Aimee
Baatz, Nicholas QC *1978*	*1992*
Bowdery, Martin *1980*	Parkin, Fiona *1993*
Burr, Andrew *1981*	Walker, Steven *1993*
Raeside, Mark *1982*	McMullan, Manus *1994*
Dumaresq, Delia *1984*	Howells, James *1995*
Dennison, Stephen *1985*	Lane, Patrick *1997**

AVONDALE CHAMBERS

2 Avondale Avenue, London N12 8EJ
0181 445 9984

Chambers of Eur Ing Christopher Shaikh
Clerk: J C S Shaikh

Shaikh, Christopher *1980*

BARCLAY CHAMBERS

2a Barclay Road, Leytonstone, London
E11 3DG
0181 558 2289/925 0688
Fax: 0181 558 2289

Chambers of Mr A S Qureshi

17A BARCLAY ROAD

Walthamstow, London E17 9JH
0181 521 3112
Fax: 0181 521 3112

Chambers of Mr D J Newberry

BARNARD'S INN CHAMBERS

Halton House, 20–23 Holborn, London
EC1N 2JD
0171 242 8508
Fax: 0171 404 3139; DX 336 London,
Chancery Lane
E-mail: clerks@barnards-inn-chambers.co.uk

Chambers of Timothy Bowles
Clerks: Andrew Flanagan, Toby Eales

Bowles, Timothy *1973*	Martin, Jill *1993*
Bryant, John *1976*	Potter, Harry *1993*
Korn, Anthony *1978*	Cowen, Timothy *1993*
Blackford, Simon *1979*	Elliott, Jason *1993*
Bott, Charles *1979*	Thomson, David *1994*
Saggerson, Alan *1981*	Chapman, Michael *1994*
Dutton, Timothy *1986*	Chapman, Matthew *1994*
Moore, Craig *1989*	Bredemear, Zachary *1996*
Sullivan, Scott *1991*	

C

See the *Index of Languages Spoken* **in Part G to locate a chambers where a particular language is spoken, or find an individual who speaks a particular language.**

BARRISTERS' COMMON LAW CHAMBERS

57 Whitechapel Road, Aldgate East, London E1 1DU
0171 375 3012
Fax: 0171 375 3068
E-mail: barristers@hotmail:com

Chambers of Muhammad Altafur Rahman
Clerks: Ms Hafsa Rahman Khan, Ms Sarah Rahman Hussain

Rahman, Muhammad *1970*	**Stead**, Kate *1996*
Rahman, Mian *1972*	**Moses**, Rebecca *1996*

9 BEDFORD ROW

London WC1R 4AZ
0171 242 3555
Fax: 0171 242 2511; DX 347 London
E-mail: clerks@9br.co.uk
Out of hours telephone: Answering machine gives emergency number

Chambers of John Goldring QC
Clerks: Chris Owen (Senior Clerk), Perry Allen (Senior Civil Clerk), Wayne King (Senior Criminal Clerk); Administrator: Don Seligmann

Goldring, John QC *1969†*	**Coen**, Yvonne *1982‡*
Coward, Stephen QC *1964†*	**Dean**, Nicholas *1982*
Farrer, David QC *1967†*	**Sweeting**, Derek *1983*
Barnes, Timothy QC *1968†*	**Mooncey**, Ebraham *1983*
Baker, Nigel QC *1969†*	**Reed**, Susan *1984*
Latham, Richard QC *1971†*	**Baker**, Maureen *1984*
Hotten, Christopher QC *1972†*	**Connolly**, Barbara *1986*
Coker, William QC *1973†*	**Varty**, Louise *1986*
Rumfitt, Nigel QC *1974†*	**King**, Simon *1987*
Wide, Charles QC *1974†*	**Matthew**, David *1987*
Shears, Philip QC *1972†*	**Mayo**, Rupert *1987*
Thompson, Collingwood QC *1975†*	**Baker**, Stephen *1989*
Maskrey, Simeon QC *1977†*	**Roche**, Brendan *1989*
Butler, Joan QC *1977†*	**Langdale**, Rachel *1990*
Pawlak, Witold *1970†*	**McGahey**, Cathryn *1990*
Christie, David *1973*	**Ford**, Steven *1992*
Head, Philip *1976‡*	**Dakyns**, Isabel *1992*
Matthews, Julian *1979*	**Weitzman**, Adam *1993*
Wheatley, Simon *1979*	**Marshall**, Vanessa *1994*
Godsmark, Nigel *1979*	**Jowitt**, Matthew *1994*
Pendlebury, Jeremy *1980*	**Rawat**, Bilal *1995*
Pini, John *1981*	**Redgrave**, William *1995*
Spencer, Timothy *1982*	**Nashashibi**, Anwar *1995*
Thirlwall, Kate *1982‡*	**Johnson**, Susannah *1996*
	Thomas, Simon *1995*

17 BEDFORD ROW

London WC1R 4EB
0171 831 7314
Fax: 0171 831 0061; DX 370 London, Chancery Lane
E-mail: IBoard7314@AOL.com
Other comms: Mobile: 0831 234861
Out of hours telephone: 01494 676504

Chambers of Allan Levy QC
Clerk: Ian D Boardman

Levy, Allan QC *1969†*	**Hurst**, Brian *1983*
Gettleson, Michael *1952*	**Southall**, Richard *1983*
Jennings, Nigel *1967*	**Critchley**, John *1985*
Gill, Jane *1973*	**Croally**, Miles *1987*
McLinden, John (QC, NZ) *1991*	**Date**, Julian *1988*
	Raffray, Frederic *1991*
Sharpe, Dennis *1976*	**Lo**, Bernard *1991*
Huyton, Brian *1977*	**McAlinden**, Barry *1993*
Russell, Martin *1977*	**Michalos**, Christina *1994*
Belson, Jane *1978*	**Maryan-Green**, Neville *1963**
Callaway, Anthony *1978*	
Reza, Hashim *1981*	**Chapman**, James *1987**

33 BEDFORD ROW

London WC1R 4JH
0171 242 6476
Fax: 0171 831 6065; DX 75 London, Chancery Lane

Chambers of David Barnard
Clerks: Michael Lieberman, Richard Cunningham; Administrator: M J Lieberman

Barnard, David *1967†*	**Thorne**, Timothy *1987*
Kogan, Barry *1973‡*	**Lonsdale**, David *1988*
May, Nigel *1974‡*	**Oxlade**, Joanne *1988*
Zeidman, Martyn QC *1974‡*	**Soor**, Smair *1988*
Whippman, Constance *1978*	**Sinclair**, Jean-Paul *1989*
Bendall, Richard *1979*	**Jones**, Rhys *1990*
Stanton, David *1979*	**Clarke**, Joanne *1993*
Webber, Gary *1979*	**Cleeve**, Thomas *1993*
Carrow, Robert *1981**	**Pullen**, Timothy *1993*
Galberg, Marc *1982*	**Boyd**, Tom *1995*
Gray, Peter *1983**	**Armstrong**, Stuart *1995*
Burke, Michael *1985*	**Law**, John *1996*
Castle, Susan *1986*	**Hanlon**, Keith *1979**
Fitzgibbon, Francis *1986*	**Houghton**, Mark *1980**
Spratt, Christopher *1986*	**Leader**, Sheldon *1980**

> Use the *Types of Work* listings in Parts A and B to locate chambers and individual barristers who specialise in particular areas of work.

† Recorder ‡ Assistant Recorder * Door Tenant

CHAMBERS OF JAMES HUNT QC

Formerly 1 King's Bench Walk

36 Bedford Row, London WC1R 4JH
0171 421 8000
Fax: 0171 421 8080; DX 360 London,
Chancery Lane
E-mail: 36bedfordrow@link.org
URL: http://www.36bedfordrow.co.uk
Other comms: Link: 36bedfordrow

Chambers of J Hunt QC

*Clerks: Martin Poulter (Senior Clerk),
Graeme Logan (Silks Clerk), Joanne
Pickersgill (Criminal Clerk), Richard Cade
(Civil and Family Clerk), Everton
Wedderburn (Civil and Family Clerk), Lynne
Edmond (Senior Fees Clerk);
Practice manager: Peter Bennett FCCA MCIM;
Administrator: Louise Smith*

Also at: 24 Albion Place, Northampton NN1
1UD
Tel: 01604 602333
Fax: 01604 601600;
104 New Walk, Leicester LE1 7EA
Tel: 0116 2492020
Fax: 0116 2550885

**The Law Society's Directory of Expert
Witnesses 1999**

- *lists over 3,500 expert witnesses*

- *all entrants agree to comply with The Law
  Society's Code of Practice and provide two
  professional references*

- *contains information on choosing and
  instructing an expert witness*

- *includes 1,700+ specialists in areas of
  expertise*

- *provides an alphabetical index to assist in
  finding detailed terms*

- *also available on CD-ROM*

*For more information call Sweet & Maxwell on
0171 449 1111*

Hunt, James QC *1968*†
Escott-Cox, Brian QC *1954*
Bowley, Martin QC *1962*
Pert, Michael QC *1970*†
Raggatt, Timothy QC *1972*†
Stokes, Michael QC *1971*†
Oldham, Frances QC *1977*†
Benson, Richard QC *1974*†
Swindells, Heather QC *1974*†
Urquhart, Andrew *1963*
Waine, Stephen *1969*†
Altaras, David *1969*
Metcalf, Christopher *1972*†
Lee, David *1973*
de Burgos, Jamie *1973*
Fowler, Michael *1974*‡
Solomons, Geoffrey *1974*
Greaves, Michael *1976*
Mainds, Allan *1977*†
Lewis, Charles *1977*
Neaves, Andrew *1977*
Morrison, Howard OBE *1977*†
Farrell, David *1978*‡
Gargan, Catherine *1978*
Beddoe, Martin *1979*
Kushner, Martine *1980*
Donnellan, Christopher *1981*
Tayton, Lynn *1981*

Farrell, Edmund *1981*
Weekes, Anesta *1981*
Wilson, Richard *1981*
Akman, Mercy *1982*
Plunkett, Christopher *1983*
Harbage, William *1983*
Bull, Simon *1984*
Ecob, Joanne *1985*
Underwood, Robert *1986*
Malik, Amjad *1987*
Pryce, Gregory *1988*
Aspden, Gordon *1988*
Howarth, Andrew *1988*
Johnson, Amanda *1990*
Gibson, John *1991*
Lowe, Matthew *1991*
Alford, Stuart *1992*
Gaunt, Sarah *1992*
Dean, Rosa *1993*
Lloyd-Jones, John *1993*
Johnston, Karen *1994*
Jupp, Jeffrey *1994*
Bojarski, Andrzej *1995*
Kirk, Jonathan *1995*
Ferguson, Niall *1996*
Skilbeck, Rupert *1996*
Joyce, Peter QC *1968*†*
Treacy, Colman QC *1971*†*
Ingham, Elizabeth *1989**

Chambers established: 1890
Opening times: 8.30 am-6.30 pm

Types of work (and number of counsel practising in that area if supplied)

Administrative 3 · Agriculture 2 · Bankruptcy 2
· Care proceedings 20 · Commercial 14
· Commercial property 2 · Common land 1
· Common law (general) 10 · Courts martial 1
· Crime 41 · Crime - corporate fraud 17
· Discrimination 2 · Employment 8
· Environment 2 · Family 20 · Family provision
20 · Foreign law 1 · Housing 2 · Landlord and
tenant 6 · Licensing 1 · Local government 2
· Medical negligence 14 · Mental health 1
· Personal injury 25 · Professional negligence
14 · Sports 1 · Town and country planning 3

Chambers' facilities

Conference rooms, Video conferences, Disks
accepted, Disabled access, E-mail, Also at
Northampton and Leicester Annexe, ISO 9002
quality accredited chambers, www site at http:/
/www.36bedfordrow.co.uk, conditional fees,
Direct Professional Access

Languages spoken

French, German, Polish, Punjabi, Serbo-Croat,
Spanish, Urdu

---

† Recorder ‡ Assistant Recorder * Door Tenant

Fees policy

We are a large set with low overheads which allows good barristers to be charged at competitive rates. Fee rates are available to clients.

Additional information

Chambers of James Hunt QC

Chambers is a progressive, London based, Midland and Oxford Circuit set, founded 1890.

Fifty five members including nine Silks operate within three specialist teams: **crime, civil and commercial and family**. Among these are 13 Recorders or Assistant Recorders. James Hunt QC was elected Leader of the Circuit in 1996.

A full list of our specialities is given above. We have a brochure for chambers generally, for each team and for our commercial and fraud expertise. All of these are available on request and are available, together with a short CV for every Barrister, on our world wide web site.

Each team has the strength and depth to handle cases of the utmost complexity or sensitivity. Recent cases include Matrix Churchill, the Herald of Free Enterprise, Ruth Neave murder trial and the Twyford Down M3 motorway planning inquiry. Teams follow published standards, including maximum response times, for briefs and other communications.

Annexes in Northampton and Leicester are fully staffed, have computer links to chambers and have good video conferencing facilities, offered at no charge to clients.

Through our compliance with the Bar Practice Management Standard and Equality Code we are the **only chambers to have been awarded ISO 9002 quality accreditation**. We see this as indicative of our commitment to a modern approach, which treats instructing solicitors as valued clients.

48 BEDFORD ROW

London WC1R 4LR
0171 430 2005
Fax: 0171 831 4885; DX 284 London
Out of hours telephone: 0181 857 5418

Chambers of Roderick l'Anson Banks
Practice manager: Mrs K E Pangratis

l'Anson Banks, Roderick
  1974

---

29 BEDFORD ROW CHAMBERS

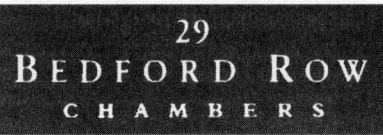

Bedford Row, London WC1R 4HE
0171 831 2626
Fax: 0171 831 0626; DX 1044 London

Chambers of Peter Ralls QC
Clerk: Robert Segal

Ralls, Peter QC *1972*	**Francis,** Nicholas *1981*
Stone, Evan QC *1954*‡	**Hussey,** Ann *1981*
Ullstein, Augustus QC *1970*‡	**Wilson,** John *1981*
Scott, Timothy QC *1975*‡	**Storey,** Paul *1982*
Hossain, Ajmalul QC *1976*	**Stone,** Lucy *1983*
Zieger, John *1962*	**Bowen,** Nicholas *1984*
Duckworth, Peter *1971*	**Walker,** Timothy *1984*
Renton, Clare *1972*	**Holland,** David *1986*
Shaw, Howard *1973*	**Reynolds,** Stephen *1987*
Upex, Robert *1973*	**Butler,** Rupert *1988*
Tonna, John *1974*	**Tettenborn,** Andrew *1988**
Warwick, Mark *1974*	**Chapman,** Nicholas *1990*
Atkins, Charles *1975*	**Peel,** Robert *1990*
Cayford, Philip *1975*	**Gray,** Nichola *1991*
Sanders, Neil *1975*	**Barlow,** Craig *1992*
Ames, Geoffrey *1976*	**Hornett,** Stuart *1992*
Boyd, Stephen *1977*	**Southgate,** Jonathan *1992*
Gill, Simon *1977*	**Domenge,** Victoria *1993*
Edwards, Simon *1978*	**Molyneux,** Brent *1994*
Ferris, Jonathan *1979*‡	**Kynoch,** Duncan *1994*
Keane, Michael *1979*	**Tse,** Nicholas *1995*
Bangay, Deborah *1981*	**Allen,** Nicholas *1995*
	Mitchell, Peter *1996*

Chambers established: 1965
Opening times: 8.30 am-6.30 pm

Types of work (and number of counsel practising in that area if supplied)
Administrative 2 · Arbitration 3 · Bankruptcy 6 · Care proceedings 8 · Chancery (general) 7 · Chancery land law 7 · Civil liberties 2 · Commercial litigation 5 · Commercial property 4 · Common land 10 · Common law (general) 39 · Company and commercial 8 · Construction 2 · Conveyancing 4 · Crime 1 · Discrimination 6 · EC and competition law 3 · Education 1 · Employment 6 · Entertainment 1 · Environment 3 · Equity, wills and trusts 5 · Family 28 · Family provision 19 · Film, cable, TV 1 · Financial services 2 · Franchising 3 · Housing 5 · Immigration 3 · Insolvency 6 · Intellectual property 3 · Landlord and tenant 15 · Licensing 3 · Local government 3 · Medical negligence 5 · Mental health 1 · Partnerships 4 · Personal injury 14 · Probate and administration 5 · Professional negligence 10 · Sale and carriage of goods 6 · Town and country planning 5

Chambers' facilities
Conference rooms, Disks accepted

Languages spoken
French, German, Hebrew, Spanish, Urdu

Additional information

The work of chambers covers numerous aspects of UK civil law. Areas of specialist practice include commercial, family, professional negligence, property, personal injury, insolvency, and consumer credit.

Members of all different calls have their own individual specialist preferences within the above fields and the senior clerk is available to advise solicitors. Members practise in all forums, including tribunals and arbitrations. All forms of advisory and court work are undertaken from preparation of pleadings to interlocutory matters and trial.

Some members publish regularly, while others conduct lectures and seminars as part of the Law Society continuing education programme. Several members are retained to advise national newspapers and magazines on defamation and contempt of court.

5 BELL YARD

BELL **5** YARD

London WC2A 2JR
0171 333 8811
Fax: 0171 333 8831; DX 400 Chancery Lane,
WC2

Chambers of Robert Webb QC
Clerks: Kevin Moore, Adrian Hawes

Webb, Robert QC 1971†	**Kavanagh**, Giles 1984
Mathew, Robin QC 1974	**Fisher**, David 1985
Bailey, Edward 1970†	**Reed**, Philip 1985
Hillier, Andrew 1972	**Ng**, Ray 1987
Matthews, Dennis 1973	**Reeve**, Matthew 1987
Munro, Kenneth 1973	**Schaw-Miller**, Stephen 1988
Bennett, Gordon 1974	**Lawson**, Robert 1989
Shepherd, Philip 1975‡	**Brown**, Hannah 1992
Macpherson, Angus 1977	**Hansen**, William 1992
Soole, Michael 1977‡	**Russell**, John 1993
Radevsky, Anthony 1978	**Vaughan-Neil**, Kate 1994
Lydiard, Andrew 1980	**Kimbell**, John 1995
Dean, Paul 1982	**Gardiner**, Richard 1969*
Jones, Charlotte 1982	**Selwyn-Sharpe**, Richard
Sullivan, Michael 1983	1985*

Opening times: 8.30 am-6.30 pm

Types of work (and number of counsel practising in that area if supplied)
Administrative · Aviation · Banking
· Bankruptcy · Chancery (general)
· Commercial · Commercial litigation
· Commercial property · Common law
(general) · Competition · Construction
· Consumer Law · Copyright · Corporate
finance · Discrimination · EC and competition
law · Employment · Entertainment · Financial
services · Insolvency · Insurance · Insurance/
reinsurance · Landlord and tenant · Local
government · Medical negligence · Mental
health · Partnerships · Pensions · Personal
injury · Planning · Professional negligence
· Sale and carriage of goods · Share options
· Shipping, admiralty · Tax - capital and
income · Tax - corporate · Town and country
planning

Chambers' facilities
Conference rooms, Disks accepted

Languages spoken
French, German, Italian

Fees policy
We do not have a formal band of fees. We aim to
be as flexible as possible and are happy to
supply estimates and fix fees in advance.

Additional information

Types of work undertaken
Members of 5 Bell Yard practise in most areas of
civil and commercial law. In particular,
expertise is offered by individual members in
one or more of the following:

Aviation law
Liability - passenger and cargo, leasing,
regulatory - CAA and European, insurance.

Commercial law
Banking, carriage of goods, commercial
contracts, company and insolvency, insurance
and reinsurance, taxation.

Civil law
Building and engineering, landlord and tenant,
personal injury, professional and medical
negligence, product and environmental liability,
and mass disasters.

Public and employment law
Judicial review, mental health, National Health
Service, pharmaceutical, coroners, town and
country planning, individual and collective
employment, trade union, disciplinary
tribunals, and public inquiries.

9-12 BELL YARD

London WC2A 2LF
0171 400 1800
Fax: 0171 404 1405; DX 390 London
Out of hours telephone: 01702 200858

Chambers of D Anthony Evans QC
Clerk: Gary Reed (Senior Clerk)

Evans, Anthony QC *1965†*	**Moss,** Peter *1976*
Lawson, Edmund QC *1971*	**Spencer,** Timothy *1976*
Carlile, Alex QC *1970†*	**Hadrill,** Keith *1977*
Birnbaum, Michael QC *1969†*	**Orsulik,** Michael *1978*
	Chan, Dianne *1979*
Carter-Manning, Jeremy QC *1975†*	**Williams,** John *1979*
	McGuinness, John *1980*
Curran, Patrick QC *1972†*	**Egan,** Michael *1981*
Woodley, Sonia QC *1968†*	**Enright,** Sean *1982*
Rouch, Peter QC *1972†*	**Chawla,** Mukul *1983*
Kerrigan, Herbert QC (Scot) *1990*	**Laing,** Christine *1984*
	Khamisa, Mohammed *1985*
Grayson, Edward *1948*	**McAtasney,** Philippa *1985*
Caton, Peter *1963*	**Bryant-Heron,** Mark *1986*
Cherrill, Richard *1967*	**Elliott,** Tracey *1986*
Field, Martin *1966†*	**Hughes,** William *1989*
Merz, Richard *1972*	**Chaplin,** Adrian *1990*
Barker, Alison *1973*	**Healy,** Alexandra *1992*
Greaves, John *1973*	**Seymour,** Mark *1992*
Heaton-Armstrong, Anthony *1973*	**Jory,** Richard *1993*
	Reeve, Suzanne *1993*
Owen, Tudor *1974†*	**Tatford,** Warwick *1993*
Cranbrook, Alexander *1975*	**Kinnear,** Jonathan *1994*
Doyle, Peter *1975*	**Russell,** Christina *1994*
John, Stephen *1975*	**Davey,** Tina *1993*
Harwood-Stevenson, John *1975*	**Gavron,** Jessica *1995*
	Denton, Michelle *1996*
Katz, Philip *1976*	**Griffin,** Neil *1996*

Opening times: 8 am-6.30 pm

Types of work (and number of counsel practising in that area if supplied)
Administrative 10 · Chancery (general) 10 · Commercial litigation 10 · Common law (general) 27 · Courts martial 1 · Crime 49 · Crime - corporate fraud 25 · Licensing 17 · Local government 32 · Personal injury 20 · Professional negligence 10 · Sports 1

Chambers' facilities
Conference rooms, Video conferences, Disks accepted, Disabled access, Chambers is fully computerised

Languages spoken
French, German, Hindi, Italian, Russian, Spanish, Urdu

Fees policy
Further information, including fees rates, can be obtained from the clerks.

Additional information

A long-established set of chambers which until 1995 practised from 4 Paper Buildings in the Temple.

A criminal and common law chambers offering a broad-based expertise (both in terms of advocacy and advisory work) in all fields of criminal and civil law.

Civil litigation: All general civil litigation work including: banking, building, children, Chancery, company, consumer credit, contract, employment, insurance, landlord and tenant, partnership, personal injury, professional negligence, and sports law.

Criminal litigation: Defence and prosecution work undertaken at all levels. Many members specialise in fraud and financial services work.

Other areas of practice: Arbitration, comparative law, criminal injuries compensation, inquests, judicial review, licensing, local government, planning, professional disciplinary and self-regulatory tribunals and public inquiries.

Clientele: Professional clients include solicitors and accountants, City institutions, the Police Federation and its members, local authorities, retailers, and a varied private clientele.

Recruitment and training: Tenancy applications to D Anthony Evans QC. On average, there are six pupillages in chambers at any one time. Pupillage applications are only accepted if made through PACH. Further inquiries can be made to William Hughes.

The Bar Directory **is also available on the Internet at the following address:**
http://www.smlawpub-holborn.co.uk/bar

BELL YARD CHAMBERS

116-118 Chancery Lane, London WC2A 1PP
0171 306 9292
Fax: 0171 404 5143; DX 0075 London,
Chancery Lane
Out of hours telephone: 0181 290 5129
Clerks: Mrs Karen Bardens, Mr Paul Harding

Lethbridge, Nemone 1956	Bell, Dominic 1992
Lee, John 1960	Campbell, David 1992
Kerner, Angela 1965	Wright, Trevor 1992
de Moller, Andre 1965*	Carter, Charlotte-Emma
Brigden, Anthony 1967†	1992
Gibson-Lee, David 1970	Richardson, Paul 1993
Sutton, Philip 1971	Robinson, Daniel 1993
Mitchell, Brenton 1973	West, Stephanie 1993
Roebuck, Roy 1974	Stirling, Christopher 1993
Guy-Davies, Judith 1976	Ashley, Mark 1993*
Webb, Lorraine 1980*	Peel, Stuart 1994
Moore, David 1983*	Sheehan, Anne-Marie 1994
Taylor, Ross 1984*	Nixon-Moss, Gareth 1994*
Carter, Lesley 1986*	Compton, Allan 1994*
Anders, Jonathan 1990	Hartley, Robert 1995
Beard, David 1990	Reilly, Daniel 1995*
Simpson, James 1990	Siva, Kannan 1996
Sims, Paul 1990	Pickersgill, David 1996
Twomey, Mark 1990	Kelleher, Keith 1987*
Salmon, Louise 1991	Booth, Roger 1966*
Bekoe-Tabiri, Christian 1992	

BELMARSH CHAMBERS

20 Warland Road, London SE18 2EU
0181 316 7322

Chambers of Miss V C Cameron

4 BINGHAM PLACE

London W1M 3FF
0171 486 5347/071 487 5910
Fax: 0171 224 6057

Chambers of Mr S M Bhanji

BLACKSTONE CHAMBERS (FORMERLY KNOWN AS 2 HARE COURT)

Blackstone House, Temple, London EC4
0171 583 1770
Fax: 0171 583 9269; DX 281 London
E-mail: 2_Hare_Court@link.org
Other comms: Mobile: 0410 023044

Chambers of Presiley Baxendale QC, Charles Flint QC
Clerks: Martin Smith, Gary Oliver;
Practice manager: Julia Hornor

Ross-Munro, Colin QC 1951	Lang, Beverley 1978
Brodie, Stanley QC 1954	Beazley, Thomas 1979
Lester of Herne Hill, Lord QC 1963	Mill, Ian 1981
	Goulding, Paul 1984
Sinclair, Ian QC 1952	Carss-Frisk, Monica 1985
Brownlie, Ian QC 1958	Lewis, Adam 1985
Donaldson, David QC 1968†	Peto, Anthony 1985
	Anderson, Robert 1986
Englehart, Robert QC 1969†	Clarke, Gerard 1986
Hunt, David QC 1969†	Shaw, Mark 1987
Dohmann, Barbara QC 1971†	Green, Andrew 1988
	Howe, Robert 1988
Pugh, Andrew QC 1961†	Briggs, Adrian 1989
Forrester, Ian (QC Scot)	Rose, Dinah 1989
Goode, Roy QC 1988	Fordham, Michael 1990
Mendelson, Maurice QC 1965	Saini, Pushpinder 1991
	Croxford, Thomas 1992
Harvie, Jonathan QC 1973‡	Herberg, Javan 1992
Baxendale, Presiley QC 1974	Hunter, Andrew 1993
	Pollard, Joanna 1993
Pannick, David QC 1979†	Collier, Jane 1994
Jowell, Jeffrey QC 1965	Dixon, Emma 1994
Nathan, Stephen QC 1969‡	White, Gemma 1994
Flint, Charles QC 1975	de la Mare, Thomas 1995
Hepple, Bob QC 1966	Mulcahy, Jane 1995
Levy, Gerald 1964	Weisselberg, Tom 1995
Oliver, Dawn 1965	Ellins, Julia 1994
Sutton, Alastair 1972	Fitzmaurice, Maurice 1969*
Page, Hugo 1977	Morse, Christopher 1972*
Beale, Judith 1978	

Opening times: 8.15 am-7 pm; out of hours contact always available.

Types of work (and number of counsel practising in that area if supplied)
Administrative · Arbitration · Banking · Chancery (general) · Civil liberties · Commercial · Commodities · Company and commercial · Competition · Copyright · Corporate finance · Crime - corporate fraud · Defamation · Discrimination · EC and competition law · Employment · Energy · Entertainment · Environment · Film, cable, TV · Financial services · Foreign law · Immigration

· Insurance · Insurance/reinsurance
· Intellectual property · International trade
· Partnerships · Private international
· Professional negligence · Public international
· Sale and carriage of goods · Sports

Chambers' facilities
Conference rooms, Disks accepted, Disabled access, E-mail

Languages spoken
Dutch, Finnish, French, German, Hindi, Italian, Japanese, Norwegian, Portuguese, Russian, Spanish, Swedish, Urdu

Additional information

The reputation of Blackstone Chambers (formerly 2 Hare Court) is founded on its special mix of commercial and public law work.

Commercial work covers a wide range of general contract and business law including international trade, banking, insurance, shipping, conflict of laws, financial services, media and entertainment, intellectual property and professional negligence. Members of chambers appear regularly in all divisions of the High Court. Instructions are undertaken in arbitrations, both domestic and international, and in proceedings before different types of tribunals. Blackstone Chambers has a strong specialist practice, experienced in advising and litigating on public international law disputes.

The public law work undertaken by chambers covers judicial review work both for and against public bodies arising from decisions in many and varied areas. Such areas include freedom of expression, immigration, education, social security, housing, planning, and local government.

A team of employment law specialists offers advice and representation in all relevant tribunals and the High Court covering all aspects of employment law, including sex, race and disability discrimination.

Members appear not only in the English courts but also before the European Court of Justice, the European Court of Human Rights and in other Commonwealth jurisdictions.

Within these broad categories individual members of chambers offer advice and representation over a wide range of commercial and public law topics. Reference should be made to the clerks for further details.

11 BOLT COURT

London EC4A 3DQ
0171 353 2300
Fax: 0171 353 1878; DX 0022 London, Chancery Lane
E-mail: boltct11@aol.com
Out of hours telephone: 01403 891469

Chambers of R Mandel
Clerks: John Bowker, John Harwood;
Practice manager: (Redhill Chambers) Jan
Rogers

Also at: Redhill Chambers, Seloduct House, 30 Station Road RH1 1NF
Tel: 01737 780781
Fax: 01737 761760

Mandel, Richard *1972*	Livingstone, Simon *1990*
Alexander, Ian QC *1964*†	Colquhoun, Celina *1990*
Lane, David QC *1968*†	Sheridan, Norman *1990*
Mason, Ian *1978*	Gordon, Mark *1990*
Lewis, Robert *1996*	Murch, Stephen *1991*
Randle, Simon *1982*	Benner, Lucinda *1992*
Jenkala, Adrian *1984*	Carron, Richard *1992*
Manson, Juliann *1985*	Rudd, Matthew *1994*
Scutt, David *1989*	Mathias, Anna *1994*
Airey, Simon *1989*	Linstead, Peter *1994*
Bacon, Jonathan *1989*	Islam-Choudhury, Mugni *1996*
Matthews, Alison *1989*	Porter, Sarah *1996*
Clay, Jonathan *1990*	

BOND STREET CHAMBERS

Standbrook House 2-5 Old Bond Street, Mayfair, London W1X 3TB
01932 342951
Fax: 01932 336176

Chambers of Mr R T F Turrall-Clarke

23 BRACKEN GARDENS

Barnes, London SW13 9HW
0181 748 4924
Fax: 0181 741 4814

Chambers of Mr A T Nicolson

C

† Recorder ‡ Assistant Recorder * Door Tenant

BRACTON CHAMBERS

95a Chancery Lane, London WC2A 1DT
0171 242 4248
Fax: 0171 242 4232; DX 416 LDE
Other comms: Mobile: 0421 866858
Out of hours telephone: 0421 866858

Chambers of Ian McCulloch
Clerks: Ian Hogg (Senior Clerk), John Crimmins (Junior Clerk), David Hogg (Junior Clerk)

McCulloch, Ian *1951*	Campbell Brown, Louise *1993*
Keane, Desmond QC *1964*	
Ghorpade, Bhasker *1973**	Webb, Stanley *1993*
Bailey, Thomas *1984*	Dedezade, Sibel *1994*
Harries, Raymond *1988*	Macpherson, Duncan *1994*
Lamacraft, Ian *1989*	McHugh, David *1994*
Best, Stanley P *1989*	Chesner, Howard *1995*
Shuman, Karen *1991*	Sheppard, Timothy *1995*
Brockley, Nigel *1992*	Paget, Michael *1995*
Bensted, Rebecca *1993*	

Chambers established: 1993
Opening times: 8.30 am-6.00 pm

Types of work (and number of counsel practising in that area if supplied)
Arbitration · Banking · Bankruptcy · Chancery (general) · Chancery land law · Charities · Commercial · Commercial litigation · Commercial property · Common law (general) · Company and commercial · Crime - corporate fraud · Employment · Equity, wills and trusts · Family · Family provision · Financial services · Immigration · Insolvency · Insurance · Landlord and tenant · Licensing · Local government · Personal injury · Planning · Professional negligence · Tax - capital and income · Tax - corporate

Chambers' facilities
Disks accepted

Languages spoken
French, German, Spanish

Fees policy
To be negotiated with the clerk.

4 BREAMS BUILDINGS

London EC4A 1AQ
0171 353 5835/430 1221
Fax: 0171 430 1677; DX 1042 London
URL: http://www.4breamsbuildings.law.co.uk

Chambers of C J Lockhart-Mummery QC
Clerks: S Graham, J Fullilove

Lockhart-Mummery, Christopher QC *1971*	Male, John *1976*
	Dilhorne, The Rt Hon Viscount *1979*
Cherryman, John QC *1955*†	
Macleod, Nigel QC *1961*†	Smith, David *1980*
Barnes, Michael QC *1965*	Williams, Anne *1980*
Hands, David QC *1965*	Barrett, John *1982**
Kingsland, Lord QC *1972*	Katkowski, Christopher *1982*
Gilbart, Andrew QC *1972*†*	Elvin, David *1983*
Harper, Joseph QC *1970*	Robinson, Alice *1983*
Furber, John QC *1973*	Karas, Jonathan *1986*
Howell, John QC *1979*	Mould, Timothy *1987*
Drabble, Richard QC *1975*	Lieven, Nathalie *1989*
Holgate, David QC *1978*	Litton, John *1989*
Sydenham, Colin *1963*	Taggart, Nicholas *1991*
Owen, Eric *1969**	McHugh, Karen *1992*
Bickford-Smith, Stephen *1972*	Forsdick, David *1993*
	Morshead, Timothy *1995*
Caws, Eian *1974*	Keen, Graeme *1995*
Bailey-King, Robert *1975*	Maurici, James *1996*
Seifert, Anne *1975*	Oakes, Alison *1996*
Lewsley, Christopher *1976*	

Chambers established: 1945
Opening times: 9 am-6.15 pm

Types of work (and number of counsel practising in that area if supplied)
Administrative 28 · Agriculture 10 · Arbitration 4 · Chancery (general) 2 · Chancery land law 15 · Charities 1 · Commercial property 20 · Common land 7 · Construction 1 · Conveyancing 2 · EC and competition law 2 · Ecclesiastical 1 · Education 4 · Employment 3 · Energy 6 · Environment 32 · Equity, wills and trusts 1 · Housing 8 · Immigration 2 · Landlord and tenant 24 · Local government 33 · Parliamentary 20 · Partnerships 1 · Professional negligence 8 · Tax - capital and income 1 · Tax - corporate 1 · Town and country planning 33

Chambers' facilities
Conference rooms, Disks accepted, Disabled access, Air conditioning

Languages spoken
French

Additional information

This is a long-established chambers which formerly practised at 2 Paper Buildings. It provides experience and expertise in advocacy, drafting and advisory work, and specialised fields include public and property law, all aspects of local government law, planning, judicial review and landlord and tenant.

Members act for a wide range of clients including individuals (some of whom may be legally aided), companies, local authorities and government agencies. It also accepts direct instructions from other professions in accordance with the Bar Council direct professional access arrangements. In addition, special expertise in taxation, social security law and European law is available within chambers.

Being a new building, facilities have been tailored to the precise requirements of chambers' practice. It provides four fully-equipped conference rooms, air conditioning, and computer network links enabling the facility for rapid drafting and finalisation of documents. For further information contact the clerks.

Published works include:
Hill's Law of Town & Country Planning (4th edn)
Town Planning Law Handbook & Casebook
Atkins Court Forms: Town & Country Planning
Halsbury's Laws: Town & Country Planning (edited entirely within chambers)
Hill & Redman's Law of Landlord & Tenant
Halsbury's Laws: Landlord & Tenant
Encyclopaedia of Rating & Local Taxation
Atkins Court Forms: Rating & Local Taxation
Corfield & Carnwath's Compulsory Acquisition & Compensation
Unlawful Interference with Land
Emdens Building Contracts & Practice
Halsbury's Laws: European Communities
Halsbury's Laws: Compulsory Purchase
Party Walls: The New Law

1 BRICK COURT

1st Floor, Temple, London EC4Y 9BY
0171 353 8845
Fax: 0171 583 9144; DX 468 London
E-mail: clerks@1brickcourt.co.uk

Chambers of R L C Hartley QC
Clerks: J Woodcock, D Mace, E Billimore

Hartley, Richard QC *1956*	Starte, Harvey *1985*
Rampton, Richard QC *1965*	Barca, Manuel *1986*
Shaw, Geoffrey QC *1968*	Atkinson, Timothy *1988*
Shields, Thomas QC *1973*	Elliott, Rupert *1988*
Caldecott, Andrew QC *1975*	Phillips, Jane *1989*
Garnier, Edward QC *1976*	Addy, Caroline *1991*
Boggis-Rolfe, Harry *1969*	Hinchliff, Benjamin *1992*
Moloney, Patrick QC *1976*	Crown, Giles *1993*
Sharp, Victoria *1979*	Evans, Catrin *1994*
Suttle, Stephen *1980*	Skinner, Lorna *1997*

4 BRICK COURT

Temple, London EC4Y 9AD
0171 797 8910
Fax: 0171 797 8929; DX 491 London

Chambers of D C Medhurst
Clerk: Michael Corrigan

Medhurst, David *1969*	Archer, Deborah *1989*
Lyons, Edward QC *1952†*	Ishmael, Colin *1989*
Chatterjee, Mira *1973*	Sheppard, Abigail *1990*
Burgess, David *1975*	Storey-Rea, Alexa *1990*
Colover, Robert *1975*	Wentworth, Annabel *1990*
Easterman, Nicholas *1975*	Knapp, Edward *1992*
Hildyard, Marianna *1977*	Simon, Michael *1992*
Mitchell, Janet *1978*	Knowles, Gwynneth *1993*
Haynes, Michael *1979*	Peter, Levi *1993*
Quinn, Susan *1983*	Sumeray, Caroline *1993*
St Clair-Gainer, Richard *1983*	Gallagher, Stanley *1994*
Roberts, Marc *1984*	Piyadasa, Sue *1994*
Lynch, Peter *1985*	Perks, Jolyon *1994*
Bell, Anthony *1985*	Pritchard, Teresa *1994*
Molyneux, Simon *1986*	Morton, Rachael *1995*
Long, Tobias *1988*	Morris, Sarah *1996*
Mylonas-Widdall, Michael *1988*	Burton, Mervyn *1973**
	Cripps, Beverly *1988**

Opening times: 8.30 am-6.30 pm

Types of work (and number of counsel practising in that area if supplied)
Common law (general) 9 · Crime 21 · EC and competition law 2 · Extradition 2 · Family 14 · Immigration 3 · Landlord and tenant 6 · Licensing 3 · Medical negligence 2 · Personal injury 4 · Planning 4

---

† Recorder ‡ Assistant Recorder * Door Tenant

Chambers' facilities
Conference rooms, Video conferences

Languages spoken
French, Greek, Hebrew, Hindi, Italian, Mandarin, Russian, Spanish

Fees policy
Please refer to clerks.

4 BRICK COURT

Ground Floor, Temple, London EC4Y 9AD
0171 797 7766
Fax: 0171 797 7700; DX 404 London
E-mail: chambers@4brick.co.uk
Out of hours telephone: 0973 620618

Chambers of A M N Shaw QC
Clerks: Paul Sampson, George Mo, Danny Norman, Samantha Gibbs;
Administrator: Gloria Zimmerman; Fees Clerk: Chamira Athauda; Office Junior: Christopher Halls

Shaw, Antony QC *1975*	Evans, William *1988*
Prais, Edgar (QC Scot) *1990*	Magarian, Michael *1988*
Reilly, Laxmi *1972*	Mullins, Mark *1988*
Drew, Jane *1976*	Belgrave, Susan *1989*
Boyd, David *1977*	Mostyn, Piers *1989*
Nicholes, Catherine *1977*	Orchover, Frances *1989*
Sen, Aditya *1977*	Baker, Michael *1990*
Taylor, Adrian *1977*	Conning, Michael *1990*
Wadling, Anthony *1977*	Morris, Fenella *1990*
Mayer, Vera *1978*	Parker, Anthea *1990*
Seaward, Martin *1978*	Rowlands, Peter *1990*
Cover, Martha *1979*	Short, Andrew *1990*
Lewis, Melanie *1980*	Brown, Jillian *1991*
Spratling, Anne *1980*	Curtis, Helen *1992*
Cohen, Andrew *1982*	Krish, Julia *1992*
Gill, Meena *1982*	Horton, Michael *1993*
Jones, Roderick *1983*	Thacker, Rajeev *1993*
Briscoe, Constance *1983*	Casey, Dermot *1994*
Burton, Charles *1983*	Trowler, Rebecca *1995*
Gibberd, Anne *1985*	Allen, Andrew *1995*
O'Brien, Nicholas *1985*	Cull, Lesley-Anne *1995*
Lyons, John *1986*	Fitzpatrick, Jerry *1996*
O'Dempsey, Declan *1987*	Elliott, Sarah *1996*

Chambers established: 1975
Opening times: 8.30 am-6.30 pm

Types of work (and number of counsel practising in that area if supplied)
Administrative 10 · Care proceedings 15 · Chancery (general) 2 · Civil liberties 6 · Common land 9 · Common law (general) 12 · Crime 15 · Crime - corporate fraud 5 · Discrimination 9 · EC and competition law 1 · Education 2 · Employment 8 · Environment 3

· European law · Family 15 · Family provision 15 · Housing 9 · Immigration 5 · Landlord and tenant 7 · Licensing 3 · Local government 4 · Medical negligence 2 · Mental health 5 · Personal injury 1 · Probate and administration 3 · Professional negligence 4

Chambers' facilities
Conference rooms, Disks accepted, Disabled access, E-mail

Languages spoken
French, German, Hebrew, Hindi, Italian, Malay, Spanish, Urdu

4 BRICK COURT, CHAMBERS OF ANNE RAFFERTY QC

BRICK | COURT

1st Floor, Temple, London EC4Y 9AD
0171 583 8455
Fax: 0171 353 1699; DX 453 London, Chancery Lane

Chambers of Anne J Rafferty QC
Clerk: Michael Eves

Rafferty, Anne QC *1973†*	French, Louis *1979*
Self, Michael QC *1951*	Kennedy, Matthew *1981*
Berry, Anthony QC *1976‡*	Markson, Jonathan *1980*
Colton, Mary *1955†*	Rouse, Justin *1982*
May, Patricia *1965†*	Speak, Michael *1983*
Germain, Richard *1968*	Henderson, James *1984*
Carne, Roger *1969*	Lakha, Abbas *1984*
Lockyer, Jane *1970*	Monro-Davies, Tiffany *1984*
Chinn, Antony *1972‡*	Whittaker, David *1986*
Williams, David *1972*	Young, David *1986*
Bright, Andrew *1973*	Cammegh, John *1987*
Sheridan, Shane *1973*	D'Arcy, Louise *1988*
Mirwitch, Jane *1974*	Stirling, Simon *1989*
Williams, Owen *1974*	Smart, Roger *1989*
Testar, Peter *1974*	Wicks, Iain *1990*
Zeitlin, Derek *1974*	Akinsanya, Jonathan *1993*
Pitts, Anthony *1975‡*	Mackeson, Antoinette *1993*
Jones, Nicholas *1975†*	Arora, Anita *1994*
Fortune, Robert *1976*	Rappo, Patrick *1995*
Carey-Hughes, Richard *1977‡*	Cohen, Samantha *1995*
	Maher, Michael *1995*
Traversi, John *1977*	Hughes, Ignatius *1986**
Marsh, Elizabeth *1979*	

† Recorder ‡ Assistant Recorder * Door Tenant

Opening times: 8.30 am-7 pm

Types of work (and number of counsel practising in that area if supplied)
Courts martial · Crime · Crime - corporate fraud

Chambers' facilities
Conference rooms

Languages spoken
French, Hindi, Italian, Spanish, Welsh

Additional information

This is a large set of chambers with 40 members which undertakes all aspects of criminal law in courts ranging from the magistrates and crown courts through to the Court of Appeal (Criminal Division), the House of Lords and the Privy Council. The set undertakes a well-balanced mixture of prosecution and defence cases which encompasses all areas of criminal work, including serious fraud matters. In addition, members regularly undertake a wide range of work in courts martial, police disciplinary hearings and licensing applications.

As the turn of the century approaches chambers is in a position to deal with the changes imposed on the Criminal Bar. Our Head of Chambers, the former Chairman of the Criminal Bar Association, and other members serving on that and other committees are instrumental in protecting the interests of the Bar and those we represent.

Also at: 36 Avenue D'Augerham, B 1040
Brussels
Tel: 00322 230 3161
Fax: 00322 230 03347

Clarke, Christopher QC 1969†	Otton-Goulder, Catharine 1983
Lyell, Sir Nicholas QC 1965	Brealey, Mark 1984
Owen, Philip QC 1949	Anderson, David 1985
Kentridge, Sydney QC 1977	Swainston, Michael 1985
Vaughan, David 1963†	Randolph, Fergus 1985
Chambers, Nicholas QC 1966†	Quigley, Conor 1985
	Garland, David 1986
Aikens, Richard QC 1973†	Green, Nicholas QC 1986
Sumption, Jonathan QC 1975†	Calver, Neil 1987
	Slade, Richard 1987
Heilbron, Hilary QC 1971	Matovu, Harry 1988
Forwood, Nicholas QC 1970*	Kinsky, Cyril 1988
	Wright, Paul 1990
Cran, Mark QC 1973	Lee, Sarah 1990
Hirst, Jonathan QC 1975	Davies, Helen 1991
Barling, Gerald QC 1972†*	Adam, Tom 1991
Simon, Peregrine QC 1973‡	Hoskins, Mark 1991
Charlton, Timothy QC 1974	Roxburgh, Alan 1992
Hapgood, Mark QC 1979	Stratford, Jemima 1993
Howard, Mark QC 1980	Haydon, Alec 1993
Ruttle, Stephen QC 1976	Bools, Michael 1991
Popplewell, Andrew QC 1981	Masefield, Roger 1994
	Salzedo, Simon 1995
Leggatt, George QC 1983	Thomas, Andrew 1996
Irvin, Peter 1972	Griffiths, John QC 1956*
Brunner, Peter 1971	Jolowicz, John QC 1952*
Lloyd Jones, David 1975†	MacRory, Richard 1974*
Hollander, Charles 1978	Muchlinski, Peter 1981*
Flynn, James 1978	Reed, Robert 1991*
Walker, Paul 1979	Cooke, Lord 1954*
Wood, William QC 1980	Ma, Geoffrey 1978*
Lord, Richard 1981	Wyatt, Derrick QC 1972*

The Law Society's Directory of Expert Witnesses 1999

- lists over 3,500 expert witnesses
- all entrants agree to comply with The Law Society's Code of Practice and provide two professional references
- contains information on choosing and instructing an expert witness
- includes 1,700+ specialists in areas of expertise
- provides an alphabetical index to assist in finding detailed terms
- also available on CD-ROM

For more information call Sweet & Maxwell on 0171 449 1111

BRIDEWELL CHAMBERS

2 Bridewell Place, London EC4V 6AP
0171 797 8800
Fax: 0171 797 8801; DX 383 London,
Chancery Lane
E-mail: clerks@bridewell.law.co.uk
URL: http://www.bridewell.law.co.uk
Out of hours telephone: 0973 680015/0402 437436

Chambers of C W Challenger
Clerk: Norman Brooks (Senior)

Challenger, Colin 1970	Williams, Vincent 1985
Boothby, Joseph 1972†	Walsh, Simon 1987
Pringle, Gordon 1973	Roberts, Patricia 1987
Oliver, Juliet 1974	Atherton, Sally 1887
Willard, Neville 1976	Graffius, Mark 1990
James, Ernest 1977	Michell, Paul 1991
Knight, Adrienne 1981	Rothwell, Carolyn 1991
Gray, Peter 1984	Walmsley, Alan 1991
Clemens, Adam 1985	Cummins, Brian 1992
Doyle, James 1985	Sefton-Smith, Lloyd 1993
Enoch, Dafydd 1985	Slaughter, Andrew 1993
Josse, David 1985	Walker, Paul 1993
Lawrie, Ian 1985	Scotland, Maria 1995

BRITTON STREET CHAMBERS

20 Britton Street, 1st Floor, London EC1M 5NQ
0171 608 3765
Fax: 0171 608 3746; DX 53329 Clerkenwell

Chambers of M T Gederon
Clerk: Ms R M Phillips

Gederon, Marvin 1979	Desouza, Esperanza 1994
Aslangul, Michel 1978	Lanlehin, Olajide 1994
Ramdeen, Kamala 1978	Hallowes, Rupert 1995
Lovell, Jeanette 1976	Savage, Ayisha 1995
Napal, Raj 1981	Carrington, Dominic 1996
Wallace, Shaun 1984	Bhadresa, Irene 1987*
Sheikh, Amjad 1988	Pepper, Dr William 1991*
Atunwa, Razak 1994	Horsington, Simon 1978*

517 BUNYAN COURT

Barbican, London EC2Y 8DH
0171 638 5076

Chambers of Mr R H Temblett

---

† Recorder ‡ Assistant Recorder * Door Tenant

CAMBERWELL CHAMBERS

66 Grove Park, Camberwell, London SE5 8LF
0171 274 0830
Fax: 0171 274 0830

Chambers of Mr K Gledhill

16A CAMPDEN HILL COURT

Campden Hill Road, London W8 7HS
0171 937 3492

Chambers of Mr J W Rae

CHANCERY CHAMBERS

1st Floor Offices, 70/72 Chancery Lane,
London WC2A 1AB
0171 405 6879/6870
Fax: 0171 430 0502

Chambers of Mr L A I St Ville

74 CHANCERY LANE

First Floor, London WC2A 1AA
0171 430 0667
Fax: 0171 430 1358

Chambers of Mr E M Yakubu

95A CHANCERY LANE

London WC2A 1DT
0171 405 3101
Fax: 0171 405 3112

Chambers of Mrs M Sparrow

FLAT 4, CHURSTON MANSIONS

Churston Mansions, 176 Gray's Inn Road,
London WC1R 4DB
0171 837 1596

Chambers of Miss L E Webb

CLAPHAM CHAMBERS

21-25 Bedford Road, Clapham North, London
SW4 7SH
0171 978 8482/642 5777
Fax: 0171 642 5777; DX 53263 CLAPHAM
COMMON

Chambers of Mrs B N Hamid

CLOISTERS

1 Pump Court, Temple, London EC4Y 7AA
0171 827 4000
Fax: 0171 827 4100; DX 452 London,
Chancery Lane
E-mail: clerks@cloisters.com

Chambers of Laura Cox QC
Clerks: Michael Martin, Glenn Hudson, Julian
Bassett, Rod McGurk, Alberta Sharpe

Cox, Laura QC *1975*†	**Hendy**, Pauline *1985*
Platts-Mills, John QC *1932*	**Bradley**, Anthony *1989*
Worrall, Anna QC *1959*†	**Hitchcock**, Patricia *1988*
Newman, Alan QC *1968*	**Epstein**, Paul *1988*
Lawson, Elizabeth QC *1969*	**Spencer**, Paul *1988*
Solley, Stephen QC *1969*	**Kibling**, Thomas *1990*
Kershen, Lawrence QC *1967*	**Power**, Lewis *1990*
Davidson, Arthur QC *1953*	**Galbraith-Marten**, Jason
Langstaff, Brian QC *1971*†	*1991*
Allen, Robin QC *1974*	**Quinn**, Christopher *1992*
McCarthy, Roger QC *1975*	**Ryder**, Matthew *1992*
Price, Roderick *1971*	**Shaw**, Peter *1992*
Montrose, Stuart *1972*	**Glyn**, Caspar *1992*
Crystal, Jonathan *1972*	**D'Cruz**, Rufus *1993*
Guest, Peter *1975*	**Sidhu**, Navjot *1993*
Culver, Thomas *1976*†	**Brooks**, Louise *1994*
Engleman, Philip *1979*	**Crasnow**, Rachel *1994*
Algazy, Jacques *1980*	**Robertson**, Sally *1995*
Buchan, Andrew *1981*	**Laddie**, James *1995*
Turner, Michael *1981*	**Burnham**, Ulele *1997*
White, Antony *1983*	**Thomas**, David QC *1992**
Horgan, Timothy *1982*	**Pimm**, Peter *1991**
Lynch, Jerome *1983*	**Whitmore**, John *1976**
Taylor, Dr Simon *1984*	**Majid**, Amir *1980**

21 COLLESS ROAD

Seven Sisters, London N15 4NR
0181 365 1706

Chambers of Mr B Press

THE COURTS

8 Abbotsleigh Road, Streatham, London
SW16 1SP
0181 769 6243
Fax: 0181 769 0448

Chambers of Mr R S Sukul

CHAMBERS OF MR PETER CRAMPIN QC

11 New Square, Lincoln's Inn, London
WC2A 3QB
0171 831 0081
Fax: 0171 405 2560; DX 319
E-mail: 11newsquare.co.uk
Other comms: Lix: Lon 068

Chambers of Peter Crampin QC
Clerks: M J Gibbs (Senior Clerk), G Ventura
(Assistant Senior Clerk)

Crampin, Peter QC 1976†	Pearce, Robert 1977
Proudman, Sonia QC 1972	Francis, Andrew 1977
Craven, Jock 1961	Dumont, Thomas 1979
Shillingford, Miles 1964	Craig, Alistair 1983
Horne, Roger 1967	Cooper, Gilead 1983
Jackson, Dirik 1969†	Staunton, Ulick 1984
Castle, Peter 1970	Feltham, Piers 1985
Lloyd, Stephen 1971	Smith, Howard 1986
Gibson, Jill 1972	Bleasdale, Marie-Claire 1993
Jefferis, Michael 1976	Margolin, Daniel 1995
Studer, Mark 1976	

Opening times: 8.45 am-6.30 pm

Types of work (and number of counsel practising in that area if supplied)
Arbitration · Banking · Bankruptcy · Chancery (general) · Chancery land law · Charities · Commercial · Commercial litigation · Commercial property · Common land · Company and commercial · Conveyancing · Court of Protection · Environment · Equity, wills and trusts · Family provision · Housing · Insolvency · Insurance/reinsurance · Landlord and tenant · Local government · Mines and minerals · Partnerships · Pensions · Planning · Probate and administration · Professional negligence · Rights of light · Sale and carriage of goods · Tax - capital and income · Town and country planning

Chambers' facilities
Conference rooms, Disks accepted

Languages spoken
French, German, Italian

CROMWELL-AYEH-KUMI CHAMBERS

1st Floor Suite, 119 Cricklewood Broadway,
London NW2 3JG
0181 450 6620
Fax: 0181 450 6620; DX 35364 Cricklewood

Chambers of Mr I J Kumi

1 CROWN OFFICE ROW

Ground Floor, Temple, London EC4Y 7HH
0171 797 7500
Fax: 0171 797 7550; DX 1020 London,
Chancery Lane

Chambers of Robert J Seabrook QC
Clerks: Alan G Smith (Senior Clerk), Matthew Phipps

Seabrook, Robert QC 1964†	Forde, Martin 1984
Owen, Robert QC 1968†	Edis, William 1985
Matheson, Duncan QC 1965†	Waddicor, Janet 1985
	Freeman, Keith 1985
Vallance, Philip QC 1968	Gimlette, John 1986
Badenoch, James QC 1968†	Evans, David 1988
	Grant, Kim 1988
Miller, Stephen QC 1971†	Rogers, Paul 1989
Foskett, David QC 1972†	McCullough, Angus 1990
Coghlan, Terence QC 1968†	Bishop, Keeley 1990
Mansfield, Guy QC 1972†	Whitting, John 1991
Havers, Philip QC 1974†	Downs, Martin 1990
Smith, Sally QC 1977	Cave, Jeremy 1992
Chambers, Gregory 1973	Booth, Richard 1993
Smyth, Christopher 1972†	Whipple, Philippa 1994
Niblett, Anthony 1976‡	Chawatama, Sydney 1994
Bowron, Margaret 1978†	Lambert, Sarah 1994
Rees, Paul 1980	Thomas, William 1995
Balcombe, David 1980	Hyam, Jeremy 1995
King-Smith, James 1980	Hogg, Katharine 1996
Hart, David 1982	Collins, Ben 1996
Garnham, Neil 1982	Rahman, Shaheen 1996

Types of work (and number of counsel practising in that area if supplied)
Administrative 9 · Common law (general) 42 · Construction 10 · Crime 23 · Crime-corporate fraud 8 · Environment 10 · Family 18 · Family provision 18 · Insurance 40 · Insurance/reinsurance 42 · Landlord and tenant 12 · Medical negligence 42 · Personal injury 42 · Professional negligence 42 · Sale and carriage of goods 42 · Town and country planning 9

Chambers' facilities
Conference rooms, Disks accepted

Languages spoken
French, Spanish

Additional information

Chambers' history dates from 1925 when it was established in Fig Tree Court. Following the Second World War, the set moved to Crown Office Row.

This is a common law set now predominantly undertaking civil work with a strong emphasis on all areas of professional negligence work especially medical negligence. Chambers also offers particular expertise in the fields of commercial contract work, personal injury, administrative law, matrimonial finance, environmental pollution, building law and insurance law.

Advocacy is complemented by advisory work. By virtue of its size - 42 barristers of whom 11 are QCs - and the nature of individuals' practices, chambers can offer considerable expertise in specialist areas of the common law.

Chambers insists on the highest professional standards and has a long tradition of providing a thorough training in pupillage, being one of the first sets to organise structured tuition and funding for pupils. As a result, chambers has always been able to select new tenants from among the very ablest candidates.

**Take your law library home with you ...
CLI on CD-ROM and Internet**

An easily searchable source of reference to:

- *cases*

- *statutes*

- *Statutory Instruments*

- *articles from legal and financial journals*

- *Grey Paper*

- *official publications*

- *press comment*

For more information or a free demonstration, phone Sweet & Maxwell on 0171 449 1111

---

1 CROWN OFFICE ROW

2nd Floor, Temple, London EC4Y 7HH
0171 797 7111
Fax: 0171 797 7120; DX 226 London,
Chancery Lane

Chambers of Richard Ferguson QC
Clerk: John Phipps

Ferguson, Richard QC 1972	Canavan, Sandy 1987
Purnell, Paul QC 1962†	Clark, Peter 1988
Henriques, Richard QC 1967†	Montgomery, James 1989
	Henley, Christopher 1989
Feinberg, Peter QC 1972†	Beck, James 1989
Leslie, Stephen QC 1971	Sherry, Eamonn 1990
O'Connor, Patrick QC 1970	Squirrell, Benjamin 1990
Goldstone, Clement QC 1971†	Modgil, Sangita 1990
	Binder, Peter 1991
Farley, Roger QC 1974†	Orchard, Anthony 1991
Lassman, Lionel 1955	Kincade, Julie-Anne 1991
Greenwood, Alan 1970†	England, William 1991
Martin-Sperry, David 1971	Ventham, Anthony 1991
Grunwald, Henry 1972	Tayo, Ann 1991
Cousens, Michael 1973	Gruchy, Simon 1993
Winberg, Stephen 1974	Doran, Gerard 1993
Lambert, Nigel 1974†	McGrath, David 1993
McGrail, Peter 1977	Sweet, Louise 1994
Shields, Sonja 1977	Bell, Alphege 1995
Turton, Andrew 1977	Watts, Martin 1995
Hunter, Mack 1979	Slee, Jacqueline 1995
Hislop, David 1989	Wootton, Victoria 1995
Gillard, Isabelle 1980	Haeems, David 1996
Dass, Preston 1983	
Ward-Jackson, Charles 1985	

Chambers established: 1984
Opening times: 8.30 am-6.30 pm

Types of work (and number of counsel practising in that area if supplied)
Civil liberties 5 · Crime 42 · Crime - corporate fraud 15 · Defamation · Entertainment 2 · Extradition 8 · Licensing 20 · Personal injury 4 · Sports 8

Chambers' facilities
Conference rooms, Disks accepted, Disabled access

Languages spoken
Dutch, French, German, Hebrew, Italian, Portuguese, Spanish

C

---

1 CROWN OFFICE ROW

3rd Floor, Temple, London EC4Y 7HH
0171 583 9292
Fax: 0171 353 9292; DX 212 London,
Chancery Lane
E-mail: onecor@link.org
Out of hours telephone: 0956 498217

Chambers of Mark Strachan QC
Clerks: James Donovan, Michael Couser,
Russell Patterson, David Thomas;
Administrator: Michael Oliver

Strachan, Mark QC *1969*†	**Lazarus**, Michael *1987*
Le Quesne, Sir Godfray QC	**Dean**, Peter *1987*
1947	**O'Neill**, Joseph *1987*
Guthrie, James QC *1975*‡	**Stevens**, Howard *1990*
Jones, Richard QC *1972*	**Boadita-Cormican**, Aedeen
Irvine, Michael *1964*	*1990*
McLeod, Iain *1969*†	**Marshall**, Paul *1991*
Neville-Clarke, Sebastian	**Casey**, Aidan *1992*
1973	**Aslam**, Farzana *1993*
Walker, Terence *1973*	**Dignum**, Marcus *1994*
Hewitson, William *1975*	**Cooper-Rousseau**, Bertha
Young, Andrew *1977*	*1993**
Janusz, Pierre *1979*	**Rogers**, Ian *1995*
Knox, Peter *1983*	**Kumar**, Umesh *1995*
Dingemans, James *1987*	

TWO CROWN OFFICE ROW

**TWO CROWN
OFFICE ROW**

Ground Floor, London EC4Y 7HJ
0171 797 8100
Fax: 0171 797 8101; DX 344 London,
Chancery Lane
E-mail: mail@2cor.co.uk, or to individual
barristers at: [barrister's surname]@2cor.co.uk
URL: http://www.2cor.co.uk
Other comms: Lix: Lon 144

Chambers of Graeme Hamilton QC
Clerks: David Newcomb, Nick Hamilton, Jon
Miller, Greg Frewin; Administration: Yvonne
Probert, Accounts: Sandra Gidaree

Hamilton, Graeme QC	**Guggenheim**, Anna *1982*
1959†	**Curtis**, Michael *1982*
Archer, John QC *1950*†	**Taylor**, Deborah *1983*
Crowley, John QC *1962*†	**Swan**, Ian *1985*
Harvey, Michael QC *1966*†	**Patten**, Ben *1986*
Purchas, Christopher QC	**DeCamp**, Jane *1987*
1966†	**Snowden**, Steven *1989*
Wilkinson, Nigel QC *1972*†	**Hodgson**, Susan *1989*
Edwards-Stuart, Antony QC	**Evans-Tovey**, Jason *1990*
1976‡	**Howarth**, Simon *1991*
ter Haar, Roger QC *1974*	**Pershad**, Rohan *1991*
Lynagh, Richard QC *1975*	**Rigney**, Andrew *1992*
Kent, Michael QC *1975*	**Blakesley**, Patrick *1993*
Woods, Jonathan *1965*†	**Mulcahy**, Leigh-Ann *1993*
Tucker, David *1973*‡	**Weston**, Clive *1993*
Gadney, George *1974*	**Maxwell-Scott**, James *1995*
Saunt, Thomas *1974*	**Stokell**, Robert *1995*
Stevenson, John *1975*	**Chalmers**, Suzanne *1995*
Holdsworth, James *1977*	**O'Connor**, Andrew *1996*
Greenbourne, John *1978*	**Davis**, Andrew *1996*
Phillips, Andrew *1978*	

Chambers established: 1940s
Opening times: 8 am-7.30 pm

Types of work (and number of counsel practising in that area if supplied)
Commercial litigation · Common law (general)
· Construction · Insurance · Insurance/
reinsurance · Medical negligence · Personal
injury · Professional negligence · Sale and
carriage of goods

Chambers' facilities
Conference rooms, Disks accepted, Disabled access, E-mail

Languages spoken
French, Italian

Fees policy
Up to five years call £35-100 per hour. Five to ten years call £75-150 per hour. Over ten years call £100-350 per hour. Hourly rates are intended as a guide and will vary according to the nature and complexity of the work involved. The senior clerk is always happy to discuss rates for particular cases and suggest counsel who can undertake the work at a range of fee rates.

CRYSTAL CHAMBERS

25A Cintra Park, London SE19 2LH
0181 402 5801
Fax: 0181 289 8401

Chambers of Mr A Padman

66 DAUBENEY ROAD

London E5 0EF
0181 985 3030
Fax: 0181 985 3030

Chambers of Mrs E A A Joseph

CHAMBERS OF TIMOTHY DEAL

First Floor, 5 Eastbrook Road, Blackheath, London SE3 8BP
0181 856 8738
Fax: 0181 856 3888

Chambers of Mr T J Deal

See the *Index of Languages Spoken* in **Part G** to locate a chambers where a particular language is spoken, or find an individual who speaks a particular language.

DEVEREUX CHAMBERS

DEVEREUX CHAMBERS

Devereux Court, London WC2R 3JJ
0171 353 7534
Fax: 0171 353 1724; DX 349 London, Chancery Lane
E-mail: elton@devchambers.co.uk
URL: http://www.devchambers.co.uk
Out of hours telephone: 0171 353 7534

Chambers of Jeffrey Burke QC
Clerk: Elton Maryon (Senior Clerk); Practice managers: Clifford Holland, Nicholas Wise; Practice Development Manager: Angela Griffiths

Burke, Jeffrey QC *1964*†	**Bard**, Nicholas *1979*
Weitzman, Peter QC *1952*†	**Brennan**, Timothy *1981*‡
Cotton, Diana QC *1964*†	**Killalea**, Stephen *1981*
Pardoe, Alan QC *1971*†	**Read**, Graham *1981*
Edelman, Colin QC *1977*†	**Wynter**, Colin *1984*
Glancy, Robert QC *1972*‡	**Carr**, Bruce *1986*
Bean, David QC *1976*†	**Simler**, Ingrid *1987*
Lemon, Roy *1970*	**Heal**, Joanna *1988*
Wulwik, Peter *1972*‡	**Thornton**, Philip *1988*
Smith, Prof Ian *1972*	**Tayler**, James *1989*
Rabie, Gerald *1973*	**Randall**, Nicholas *1990*
Goddard, Christopher *1973*	**Bryant**, Keith *1991*
Lee, Ian *1973*	**Harrison**, Richard *1991*
Andrew, Elizabeth *1974*‡	**Joffe**, Natasha *1992*
Greening, Richard *1975*	**Burns**, Andrew *1993*
Griffith-Jones, David *1975*†	**Edwards**, Peter *1992*
Clayton, Richard *1977*	**Basu**, Dijen *1994*
Downing, Ruth *1978*	**Haitink**, Patricia *1995*

Chambers established: 1948
Opening times: 8.30 am-6.30 pm (24-hr answering service available)

Types of work (and number of counsel practising in that area if supplied)
Administrative · Arbitration · Civil liberties · Commercial litigation · Commercial property · Construction · Consumer Law · Crime · Crime - corporate fraud · Defamation · Discrimination · Education · Employment · Environment · Housing · Information technology · Insurance · Insurance/reinsurance · Landlord and tenant · Local government · Medical negligence · Mental health · Pensions · Personal injury

· Professional negligence · Sports · Tax - capital and income · Telecommunications

Chambers' facilities
Conference rooms, Video conferences, Disks accepted, Disabled access, Law Society accredited seminar programme

Languages spoken
French, German

Fees policy
Devereux Chambers aims to offer competitive rates which the senior clerk will be happy to discuss.

Estimates of fees will be given on request.

Additional information

Devereux Chambers - Chambers of Jeffrey Burke QC
Devereux Chambers offers a comprehensive inter-disciplinary service to its clients. Areas of special expertise include administrative and local government law, commercial litigation, employment law, insurance and reinsurance, professional negligence, personal injury and medical negligence.

Chambers has a wide client base ranging from public companies, underwriters and brokers to local authorities, government departments, trades unions and individual litigants.

All Members of Chambers are advocates making regular appearances before Judges, Tribunals and Arbitrators.

A number of senior Members of Chambers serve as Deputy High Court Judges, Recorders and Assistant Recorders. Members of Chambers sit on the Criminal Injuries Compensation Board, Criminal Injuries Compensation Appeals Panel and Mental Health Independent Review Tribunal and also chair Tribunals and Inquiries.

The junior Members of Chambers include the Junior Counsel to the Inland Revenue and members of the Supplementary Panel of Treasury Counsel, Common Law. Members of Chambers play a prominent role in the Bar's professional bodies and associations and Chambers includes members of the Bar Council and its Professional Conduct Committee and other Bar Council committees.

Chambers also includes founders, committee members and members of COMBAR, the London Common Law and Commercial Bar Association, the Employment Law Bar Association, the Personal Injuries Bar Association, the Association of Personal Injuries Lawyers, the Industrial Law Society, the British Association for Sport and Law, the Revenue Bar Association, the London Maritime Association and CENTREBAR.

Members of Chambers regularly appear in leading cases and have written or co-written prominent text and practitioners books in their specialist fields.

Three Members of Chambers: Professor Ian Smith, Christopher Goddard and Nicholas Randall co-wrote *Health and Safety the New Legal Framework* published by Butterworths. Ian Smith also co-wrote *Smith and Wood on Industrial Law* and is the author of the Employment Law and Social Security titles in Halsbury's Laws. He and Nicholas Randall are editors of *Harvey on Industrial Relations and Employment Law*.

David Bean is the author of *Injunctions* published by FT Law & Tax, co-author of *Injunctions and Undertakings* (Jordans) and editor of *Law Reform for All* (Blackstones). Richard Clayton is the author of *Practice and Procedure in Industrial Tribunals* (LAG 1986) and co-author of *Civil Actions against the Police* (Sweet and Maxwell 2nd edn 1992), *Judicial Review Procedure* (Wiley 2nd edition 1997) and, in preparation, co-author of *The Bill of Rights in English Law* (Oxford University Press), *Judicial Review of Local Government Decisions* (Wiley) and *Commercial Judicial Review* (Wiley).

David Griffith-Jones is the author of *Law and the Business of Sport* (Butterworths).

Bruce Carr is a contributing author to FT Law & Tax, *The Litigation Practice* ('Emergency Procedures'). Ingrid Simler is a contributing author to Tolley's *Employment Law* (1994).

James Tayler is a contributor to *Dix on Employment Law* (Butterworths) and Nicholas Randall is the author of the Pensions title in Halsbury's Laws.

Members of Chambers also write for legal publications and give lectures and seminars both externally and as part of Chambers own continuing education programme which is fully accredited by the Law Society.

Great emphasis is placed on the calibre of pupils recruited to ensure that the high standards are maintained and generous pupillage awards are offered.

Additional Specialisms:

Civil liberties and human rights · Community Care · Consumer and business credit · Contempt · Electoral and Parliamentary Law · Europe · Family · Health and Safety · Industrial injury and disease · Judicial review · Mortgage and guarantee litigation · Police complaints · Product liability · Property · Public interest immunity · Revenue · Tribunals and Inquiries · VAT/customs and excise.

The UK College of Family Mediators Directory & Handbook 1998/99

- *provides expert commentary on family mediation training and professional development and includes contributions by leading family mediation professionals*

- *lists over 100 family mediation groups/services and over 950 individual family mediators by region and alphabetically*

- *gives details of all members and associates of the UK College of Family Mediators*

- *includes the UK College of Family Mediators Standards and Code of Practice*

- *gives details of all the family mediation bodies which make up the UK College of Family Mediators*

For more information call Sweet & Maxwell on 0171 449 1111

DOUGHTY STREET CHAMBERS

11 Doughty Street, London WC1N 2PG
0171 404 1313
Fax: 0171 404 2283/4; DX 223 London, Chancery Lane
E-mail: doughty_street@compuserve.com
Other comms: Lix: Lon 039; Link: (Individual users)
Out of hours telephone: 0171 404 1313 (24 hours with emergency no's)

Chambers of Geoffrey Robertson QC, Peter Thornton QC (Deputy)
Clerks: Michelle Simpson, Justin Hebbs, Richard Bayliss, Paul Friend, Kelly Wild, Melanie Stephenson;
Practice manager: Christine Kings;
Administrator: Steffan Roberts

Robertson, Geoffrey QC 1973‡	**Metzer**, Anthony 1987
Blom-Cooper, Louis QC 1952	**Starmer**, Keir 1987
	Hatfield, Sally 1988
Maxwell, Richard QC 1968†	**Oppenheim**, Robin 1988
Thornton, Peter QC 1969‡	**Strange**, Michelle 1989
Kennedy, Helena QC 1972	**Maidment**, Kieran 1989
Sallon, Christopher QC 1973†	**Taylor**, Paul 1989
	Barton, Hugh 1989
Fitzgerald, Edward QC 1978	**Brooks**, Paul 1989
Irwin, Stephen QC 1976	**Kadri**, Sadakat 1989
Nicol, Andrew QC 1978‡	**Hall**, Andrew 1991
Walker-Smith, Jonah 1963‡	**Kaufmann**, Phillippa 1991
Thorold, Oliver 1971	**Whitaker**, Quincy 1991
Panford, Frank 1972	**Ford**, Michael 1992
Rees, Edward QC 1973	**Wise**, Ian 1992
Allfrey, Richard 1974	**Hermer**, Richard 1993
Grieve, Michael QC 1975‡	**Brown**, Althea 1995
Wood, James 1975‡	**Glasson**, Jonathan 1996
Paul, Nicholas 1980	**Hudson**, Anthony 1996
Millar, Gavin 1981	**Mahomed**, Ismail SC 1984*
Markus, Kate 1981	**Ollivry**, Guy QC 1957*
Forshall, Isabella 1982	**Ramsahoye**, Fenton SC 1953*
Bogan, Paul 1983	**Hardiman**, Adrian SC 1988*
Owen, Timothy 1983	**Boyle**, Kevin 1992*
Bentley, David 1984	**Fulbrook**, Julian 1977*
Westgate, Martin 1985	**Booker**, Christine 1978*
Williams, Heather 1985	**Van Bueren**, Geraldine 1979*
Emmerson, Ben 1986	**Peay**, Jill 1991*
Evans, Jill 1986	**Cooper**, Jonathan 1992*
Weereratne, Aswini 1986	

Chambers established: 1990
Opening times: 8.30 am-6.30 pm

Types of work (and number of counsel practising in that area if supplied)
Administrative 29 · Civil liberties 46 · Common law (general) 31 · Copyright 4 · Crime 29 · Crime - corporate fraud 22 · Defamation 11 · Discrimination 11 · Education 8

· Employment 13 · Environment 6 · Film, cable, TV 10 · Housing 12 · Immigration 6 · Intellectual property 3 · Landlord and tenant 12 · Local government 8 · Medical negligence 12 · Mental health 10 · Personal injury 12 · Professional negligence 10

Chambers' facilities
Conference rooms, Disks accepted, Disabled access, E-mail

Languages spoken
British Sign Language, Czech, French, German, Greek, Hebrew, Italian, Spanish

Fees policy
Up to five years call £50–80, Five to ten years call £70–100. Ten to fifteen years call £100–130 per hour. Fifteen to twenty years call £130-160 per hour. Silks £200-500 per hour.

The clerks will be pleased to discuss fees appropriate to your case within these general fee bands, arrangements for volume work, and subsidised/pro bono work. Fee notes will itemise work done and time spent.

Additional information

Chambers offers a wide range of experience and specialisations, notably in the advocacy of civil liberties and human rights. Counsel are engaged in crown court trials of all kinds, judicial review proceedings, and actions in the High Court and the county courts. They appear regularly at inquests and a variety of tribunals. Many have taken leading cases to the European Court of Human Rights.

Individual practitioners specialise in criminal law, media law and defamation, public and administrative law, prisoners' rights and cases involving issues of mental health, discrimination, immigration, employment and housing, personal injury and medical negligence. Members of chambers have written or contributed to numerous books and publications in their specialist areas.

The emphasis in chambers is on customer care and a friendly but professional service. Our offices have been recently expanded and refurbished providing dedicated reception and conference rooms with disability access and two fully equipped libraries. Doughty Street Chambers was awarded Barristers Chambers of the Year in 1995 and 1996 by *The Lawyer* and shortlisted for the Law Firm Management Award in 1997.

Details of specialist teams are available on request.

1 DR JOHNSON'S BUILDINGS

Ground Floor, Temple, London EC4Y 7AX
0171 353 9328
Fax: 0171 353 4410; DX 297 London, Chancery Lane

Chambers of Lord Thomas OBE QC
Clerks: J Francis, T McBennett

Annexe: Dr Johnson's Chambers, The Atrium Court, Apex Plaza, Reading, Berkshire RG1 1AX
Tel: 01189 254221
Fax: 01189 560380

Thomas of Gresford, Lord QC *1967†*	**Habboo,** Camille *1987*
	Mailer, Clifford *1987*
Digney, Peter *1968†*	**Wignall,** Gordon *1987*
Britton, Robert *1973†*	**Brodie,** Graham *1989*
Sabido, John *1976*	**Gill,** Pamilla *1989*
Granville, Alexander *1978*	**Kane,** Adam *1993*
Oldland, Jennifer *1978*	**Pollock,** Hilary *1993*
Clark, Dingle *1981*	**Hickman,** Claire *1994*
Hamblin, Nicholas *1981*	**Levinson,** Justin *1994*
Wernham, Stewart *1984*	**Mackie,** Jeannie *1995*
Anderson, Brendan *1985*	**Nott,** Emma *1995*
McIlwain, Sylvester *1985*	**Jay,** Elizabeth *1996*

† Recorder ‡ Assistant Recorder * Door Tenant

3 DR JOHNSON'S BUILDINGS

THREE DR JOHNSON'S BUILDINGS

Ground Floor, London EC4Y 7BA
0171 353 4854
Fax: 0171 583 8784; DX 1009 London,
Chancery Lane

Chambers of J A Hodgson
Clerk: J E Hubbard

Hodgson, John *1963*	**Toch**, Joanna *1988*
Vain, Richard *1970*	**Chisholm**, Malcolm *1989*
Hay, Malcolm *1972*	**Heppenstall**, Claire *1990*
Houston, Russell *1973*	**Hellens**, Matthew *1992*
Harris, Annmarie *1975*	**Peacock**, Lisa *1992*
Sheldrake, Christine *1977*	**Abey**, Mahie *1993*
King, Barbara *1980*	**Erwood**, Heather *1993*
Hames, Christopher *1987*	**Carter**, Holly *1993*
Hasan, Ayesha *1987*	**Redford**, Jessica *1994*
Daniels, Nicholas *1988*	**Williams**, Jason *1995*
Gillman, Rachel *1988*	**Barnes**, Luke *1996*
Moore, Finola *1988*	**Collins**, Ken *1996*

Chambers established: 1946
Opening times: 8.45 am-6.15 pm

Types of work (and number of counsel practising in that area if supplied)
Care proceedings 22 · Common law (general) 18 · Crime 6 · Family 23 · Family provision 23 · Housing 10 · Landlord and tenant 14

Languages spoken
French, Urdu

Additional information

This set of chambers was established 50 years ago at this address. Throughout its history most of the members of chambers have specialised in family law and that continues to be the case today. The building has recently been renovated and refurbished. We have taken on extra accommodation at this address and we are now the only set of chambers at No 3. In answer to the question 'What do you particularly value about the service you obtain from Chambers?' contained in a questionnaire sent recently to our regular instructing solicitors, the most popular answers were 'friendliness' and 'efficiency'.

Although nearly all members specialise in family work there are individuals who practise in other areas such as real property, landlord and tenant, common law and crime.

DR JOHNSON'S CHAMBERS

Two Dr Johnson's Buildings, Temple, London EC4Y 7AY
0171 353 4716
Fax: 0171 334 0242; DX 429 London,
Chancery Lane

Chambers of David J Batcup
Clerks: Patrick Duane (Senior Clerk), Kevin Crawley, Ashley Baum, Claire Wright, Chris Blake; Administrator: Nick Pickels

Batcup, David *1974‡*	**Rose**, Jonathan *1986*
Bishop, Malcolm QC *1968*	**Ross**, Gordon *1986*
Bayliss, Alan *1966†*	**Taylor**, David *1986*
Gould, Dennis *1969*	**Buck**, John *1987*
Fogg, Anthony *1970*	**Hamilton-Shield**, Anna-Maria *1989*
Davies, Graham *1971*	
Bruce, Richard *1974*	**Hawes**, Neil *1989*
Wurtzel, David *1974*	**Fraser**, Alan *1990*
Higginson, Peter *1975*	**Hastings**, Frances *1990*
Sherman, Robert *1977*	**Lavers**, Michael *1990*
Wheatly, Ian *1977*	**Wade**, Clare *1990*
Armstrong, Grant *1978*	**Williams**, David *1990*
Mejzner, Stephen *1978*	**Deignan**, Mary-Teresa *1991*
Davey, Roger *1978*	**Phillips**, Paul *1991*
Williams, Susan *1978*	**Robinson**, Claire *1991*
Paltenghi, Mark *1979*	**Benzynie**, Robert *1992*
Barnes, David *1981*	**Edwards**, Jennifer *1992*
Rhodes, Nicholas *1981*	**Hale**, Charles *1992*
Stork, Brian *1981*	**Flanagan**, Julia *1993*
Tomassi, Mark *1981*	**Grey**, Siobhan *1994*
Oon, Pamela *1982*	**McCalla**, Tarquin *1994*
Buxton, Thomas *1983*	**Raudnitz**, Paul *1994*
Belger, Tyrone *1984*	**Jones**, Daniel *1994*
Tetlow, Bernard *1984*	**Goudie**, Martin *1996*
Marsh, Carolyn *1985*	**Morgan**, Adam *1996*
Davies, Graham *1986*	

Opening times: 8.30 am-6.30 pm

C

Types of work (and number of counsel practising in that area if supplied)
Aviation 1 · Chancery (general) 1 · Chancery land law 2 · Common law (general) 12 · Courts martial 1 · Crime 42 · Employment 2 · Family 15 · Family provision 5 · Inquests 1 · Insolvency 1 · Landlord and tenant 4 · Local government 2 · Malicious prosecution 8 · Medical negligence 2 · Personal injury 13 · Professional negligence 3 · Sale and carriage of goods 1

Chambers' facilities
Conference rooms, Video conferences, Disks accepted

Languages spoken
French, Spanish, Welsh

2 EASTWOOD ROAD

South Woodford, London E18 1BW
0181 491 0980
Fax: 0181 491 0980

Chambers of Mr R A Smith

43 EGLANTINE ROAD

London SW18 2DE
0181 874 3469

Chambers of Miss J S Walker

ELDON CHAMBERS

Fourth Floor, 30/32 Fleet Street, London EC4Y 1AA
0171 353 4636
Fax: 0171 353 4637

Chambers of Mr M J Burr

197 ELLESMERE ROAD

London NW10 1LG
0181 208 1663
Fax: 0181 208 1663

Chambers of Mr G M G Haque

> Use the *Types of Work* listings in Parts A and B to locate chambers and individual barristers who specialise in particular areas of work.

ENTERPRISE CHAMBERS

9 Old Square, Lincoln's Inn, London WC2A 3SR
0171 405 9471
Fax: 0171 242 1447; DX LDE 301

Chambers of Anthony Mann QC
Clerks: Barry Clayton, Tony Armstrong, Dennis Peck

Also at: 38 Park Square, Leeds LS1 2PA; 65 Quayside, Newcastle upon Tyne NE1 3DS

Mann, Anthony QC *1974*	**Barker,** James *1984*
Levy, Benjamin *1956*	**Jack,** Adrian *1986*
Jennings, Timothy *1962*	**Groves,** Hugo *1980*
Halpern, David *1978*	**Atherton,** Ian *1988*
Morgan, Charles *1978*	**Henry,** Alastair *1998*
Hutton, Caroline *1979*	**Garcia-Miller,** Laura *1989*
James, Michael *1976*	**Bhaloo,** Zia *1990*
Rosen Peacocke, Teresa *1982*	**Pickering,** James *1991*
	McKinnell, Soraya *1991*
Ife, Linden *1982*	**Jory,** Hugh *1992*
McAllister, Ann *1982*	**Williamson,** Bridget *1993*
Arden, Peter *1983*	**Richardson,** Sarah *1993*
Zelin, Geoffrey *1984*	**Hardwick,** Matthew *1994*
Baker, Jacqueline *1985*	**Francis,** Edward *1995*
Gerald, Nigel *1985*	**Mauger,** Shanti *1996*

Chambers established: 1964
Opening times: 8.45 am-7 pm

Types of work (and number of counsel practising in that area if supplied)
Arbitration 6 · Banking 15 · Bankruptcy 27 · Chancery (general) 28 · Charities 4 · Commercial litigation 28 · Commercial property 25 · Company and commercial 28 · Conveyancing 20 · Employment 2 · Equity, wills and trusts 14 · Housing 20 · Insolvency 27 · Landlord and tenant 27 · Partnerships 18 · Probate and administration 14 · Professional negligence 20

Chambers' facilities
Disks accepted, Conference rooms and out of hours contact

† Recorder ‡ Assistant Recorder * Door Tenant

Languages spoken
French, German, Italian, Portuguese, Spanish

Fees policy
Fees are negotiated with the clerk depending on the case, but as a general guide, charge out rates are as follows: Up to five years call £300-750 per day, six to ten years call £600-900 per day, over ten years call £800-1500 per day, QC £1500-2250 per day. The chambers was the *first* set to publish charge out rates for all members and we are happy to provide estimates of fees before any work starts.

EQUITY BARRISTERS' CHAMBERS

EQUITY
BARRISTERS'
CHAMBERS

50 Claude Road, London E10 6ND
0181 558 8336
Fax: 0181 558 6757
E-mail: equitylawyer@equitybar.co.uk
URL: http://www.equitybar.co.uk
Out of hours telephone: 0181 558 8336

Chambers of Dr R K Glah
Clerks: Richard Glah, Mrs Sierra Ahiafor (Practice Manager)

Glah, Dr Robert *1971*

ERSKINE CHAMBERS

30 Lincoln's Inn Fields, Lincoln's Inn, London WC2A 3PF
0171 242 5532
Fax: 0171 831 0125; DX 308 London
E-mail: Clerks@Erskine-Chambers.law.co.uk
Other comms: Lix: Lon 033
Out of hours telephone: Emergency no's available on Answerphone via main no.

Chambers of Richard Sykes QC
Clerk: Mike Hannibal; Administrator: Lucy Paterson

Sykes, Richard QC *1958*	**Bryant,** Ceri *1984*
Wright, Robert QC *1949*	**Snowden,** Richard *1986*
Stubbs, William QC *1957*	**Roberts,** Catherine *1986*
Stockdale, Sir Thomas *1966*	**Gillyon,** Philip *1988*
Potts, Robin QC *1968*	**Stokes,** Mary *1989*
Richards, David QC *1974*	**Thompson,** Andrew *1991*
Cone, John *1975*	**Prentice,** Prof Daniel *1982*
Kosmin, Leslie QC *1976*	**Dougherty,** Nigel *1993*
Todd, Michael QC *1977*	**Kuschke,** Leon *1993*
Mabb, David *1979*	**Potts,** James *1994*
Moore, Martin *1982*	**Thornton,** Andrew *1994*
Chivers, David *1983*	

Opening times: 8.30 am-7 pm

Types of work (and number of counsel practising in that area if supplied)
Banking · Company and commercial · Corporate finance · Financial services · Insolvency · Partnerships · Professional negligence · Share options · Unit trusts

Chambers' facilities
Conference rooms, Disks accepted, Disabled access, E-mail

---

† Recorder ‡ Assistant Recorder * Door Tenant

ONE ESSEX COURT

Ground Floor, Temple, London EC4Y 9AR
0171 583 2000
Fax: 0171 583 0118; DX 430 London
E-mail: clerks@oneessexcourt.co.uk
URL: http://www.oneessexcourt.co.uk

Chambers of A S Grabiner QC
Clerks: Robert Ralphs, Paul Shrubsall

Grabiner, Anthony QC 1968†	**Grainger**, Ian *1978*
Butler, Gerald QC *1955*	**Auld**, Stephen *1979*
Burnton, Stanley QC 1965‡	**Davies**, Rhodri *1979*
Aaronson, Graham QC *1966*	**Griffiths**, Alan *1981*
Carr, Christopher QC *1968*	**Reffin**, Clare *1981*
Strauss, Nicholas QC 1965‡	**Gillis**, Richard *1982*
Thomas, Roydon QC 1960†	**Lenon**, Andrew *1982*
Leaver, Peter QC 1967‡	**McCaughran**, John *1982*
Glick, Ian QC *1970*	**MacLean**, Kenneth *1985*
Gloster, Elizabeth QC 1971†	**Graham**, Charles *1986*
Hobbs, Geoffrey QC *1977*	**de Garr Robinson**, Anthony *1987*
Barnes, Mark QC *1974*	**Rabinowitz**, Laurence *1987*
Gee, Steven QC *1975*	**Choo Choy**, Alain *1991*
MacGregor, Alastair QC *1974*	**Hage**, Joseph *1991*
Sharpe, Thomas QC *1976*	**Kitchener**, Neil *1991*
Mowschenson, Terence QC *1977*	**Rollason**, Michael *1992*
	Cavender, David *1993*
Gruder, Jeffrey QC *1977*	**Grierson**, Jacob *1993*
Ivory, Thomas QC *1978*	**Himsworth**, Emma *1993*
Bloch, Michael QC *1979*	**O'Sullivan**, Zoë *1993*
Onions, Jeffery QC *1981*	**Toledano**, Daniel *1993*
Redfern, Alan *1995*	**Lake**, Lisa *1994*
Behar, Richard 1965†	**Halkerston**, Graeme *1994*
FitzGerald, Susanna *1973*	**Nourse**, Edmund *1994*
Conlon, Michael *1974*	**Hossain**, Sa'ad *1995*
Gammie, Malcolm *1997*	**Jowell**, Daniel *1995*
Malone, Michael *1975*	**Bingham**, Camilla *1996*
	Roberts, Philip *1996*

Chambers established: 1966
Opening times: 8 am-10 pm

Types of work (and number of counsel practising in that area if supplied)
Administrative 4 · Arbitration 13 · Asset finance 10 · Banking 20 · Bankruptcy 15 · Commercial litigation 41 · Company and commercial 30 · Competition 3 · Copyright 4 · Corporate finance 12 · EC and competition law 3 · Energy 20 · Financial services 20 · Franchising 1 · Insolvency 20 · Insurance 20 · Insurance/reinsurance 20 · Intellectual property 4 · Licensing 1 · Partnerships 10 · Professional negligence 20 · Share options 10 · Shipping, admiralty 5 · Tax - corporate 3 · Telecommunications 3 · Trademarks 4

Chambers' facilities
Disks accepted, E-mail

Languages spoken
Arabic, French, German, Hebrew, Italian, Spanish

Fees policy
Fees will be negotiated with the clerk depending on the case but as a general guide: Advisory work at One Essex Court is in most cases time costed. Charge rates range, in the main, from £20 to £200 per hour for junior counsel and from £240 per hour upwards for Queen's Counsel. If requested, charge rates and times spent will be shown on fee notes. In appropriate cases charge rates can be negotiated prior to the commencement of work. Currently hourly charge rates for individuals or groups of individuals will be faxed on request.

Additional information

One Essex Court is among the largest sets of commercial barristers' chambers in Great Britain. It occupies 1, 2, and 3 Essex Court, a site which has historically been synonymous with commercial law. The range of work carried out embraces almost every aspect of domestic and international commerce and finance.

Kime's International Law Directory 1999

- *established guide to the international legal community*
- *reliable and relevant information on over 600 law firms and chambers*
- *entries can be found by types of work undertaken and location*
- *the only law directory to provide editorial on every jurisdiction's legal system and enforcement of judgements*
- *now on the Internet at http://www.smlawpub-holborn.co.uk/kimes*

For more information call Sweet & Maxwell on 0171 449 1111

ONE ESSEX COURT

ONE ESSEX COURT

—◆—

Temple, London EC4Y 9AR
0171 936 3030
Fax: 0171 583 1606; DX 371 London
E-mail: one.essex_court@virgin.net

Chambers of Sir Ivan Lawrence QC
*Clerks: Christopher J Doe (Senior Clerk),
Sarah Willcox*

Norris, Paul 1963†	**Benson**, Julian 1991
Lawrence, Ivan QC 1962†	**Lawrence**, Rachel 1992
Mullen, Patrick 1967	**Farquharson**, Jane 1993
Bull, Roger 1974	**Grundy**, Nicholas 1993
Lyne, Mark 1981	**Brannigan**, Sean 1994
Joss, Norman 1982	**Mills**, Simon 1994
Coulter, Barry 1985	**Sleeman**, Rachel 1996
Ong, Grace 1985	**Mew**, Graeme 1982*
John, Peter 1989	

Chambers established: 1947
Opening times: 8 am-6.30 pm

Types of work (and number of counsel practising in that area if supplied)
Administrative 2 · Arbitration 4 · Bankruptcy 1 · Care proceedings 7 · Chancery (general) 2 · Chancery land law 2 · Civil liberties 4 · Commercial 10 · Commercial litigation 5 · Commercial property 3 · Common land 1 · Common law (general) 15 · Company and commercial 10 · Construction 3 · Crime 10 · Crime - corporate fraud 4 · Defamation 2 · Employment 7 · Equity, wills and trusts 2 · Family 7 · Family provision 4 · Financial services 2 · Housing 5 · Immigration 4 · Insurance 2 · Landlord and tenant 5 · Licensing 3 · Local government 5 · Medical negligence 5 · Probate and administration 3 · Professional negligence 5 · Sale and carriage of goods 5

Chambers' facilities
Conference rooms, Disks accepted, E-mail

Languages spoken
Cantonese, French

Fees policy
Up to five years call £50-90, Five to ten y call £60-100, Ten years call £80-120. Fees be negotiated with the clerk depending on the case but as a general guide: fees are negotiated by our clerks on basis of call, time engaged, turnaround time or urgency, complexity and importance to the client. Certain areas of law are covered by standard fees.

4 ESSEX COURT

Temple, London EC4Y 9AJ
0171 797 7970
Fax: 0171 353 0998; DX 292 Chancery Lane
E-mail: clerks@4essexcourt.law.co.uk

Chambers of Nigel Teare QC
Clerk: Gordon Armstrong

Teare, Nigel QC 1974†	**Nolan**, Michael 1981
Howard, M N QC 1971†	**Smith**, Marion 1981
Bucknall, Belinda QC 1974†	**Rainey**, Simon 1982
Macdonald, Charles QC 1972‡	**Kverndal**, Simon 1982
	Jacobs, Nigel 1983
Russell, Jeremy QC 1975	**Parsons**, Luke 1985
Brenton, Timothy QC 1981	**Croall**, Simon 1986
de Cotta, John 1955	**Cooper**, Nigel 1987
Economou, George 1965	**Melwani**, Poonam 1989
Gault, Simon 1970†	**Turner**, James M 1990
Kinley, Geoffrey 1970	**Thomas**, Robert 1992
Caldin, Giles 1974	**Phillips**, Nevil 1992
Sussex, Charles 1982	**Macey-Dare**, Thomas 1994
Haddon-Cave, Charles 1978	**Chambers**, Jonathan 1996
Griffin, Paul 1979	**Buckingham**, Stewart 1996

Opening times: 8 am-7 pm

Types of work (and number of counsel practising in that area if supplied)
Admiralty 20 · Arbitration 24 · Aviation 5 · Banking 5 · Commercial litigation 24 · Commodities 4 · Construction 6 · EC and competition law 4 · Employment 3 · Entertainment 3 · Environment 9 · Insurance 24 · Insurance/reinsurance 24 · International trade 24 · Personal injury 3 · Private international 24 · Professional negligence 4 · Sale and carriage of goods 24 · Shipping, admiralty 22

Chambers' facilities
Conference rooms, Disks accepted, Arbitration room

Languages spoken
Dutch, French, German, Greek, Italian, Portuguese, Spanish

---

† Recorder ‡ Assistant Recorder * Door Tenant

Fees policy

Fees charged are generally tied to the time spent on (or allocated to) each item of work. There is, however, a wide measure of flexibility in the arrangements that will be agreed.

Additional information

Types of work undertaken: Most of the work at 4 Essex Court is for international clients and/or involves international commercial law. Individual members will act as advocates, legal advisers, arbitrators, and expert witnesses. They will also draft and prepare commercial contracts and other instruments. Many of the barristers have membership of overseas Bars including America (NY), Hong Kong, New South Wales, Spain, Greece and Cyprus.

Several members are authors or editors of or contributors to a wide variety of publications. For further information contact Gordon Armstrong.

The main telephone number provides an alternative service for out-of-hours emergencies.

International Arbitration Law Review

Editorial Board includes:

Alan Redfern	Neil Kaplan
Toby Landau	David Rivkin
Dr Julian Lew	Martin Hunter
Nigel Rawding	Matthieu de Boisseson

The new International Arbitration Law Review *brings together for the first time all the requirements of an arbitration practitioner.*

- *up-to-the-minute news on legislation and decisions*

- *expert commentary on worldwide trends and issues from a panel of top arbitration specialists*

- *detailed case summaries and analysis of the cases making the headlines*

- *covers all major jurisdictions worldwide*

To order a subscription or a free sample copy call Sweet & Maxwell on 0171 449 1111

---

5 ESSEX COURT

1st Floor, Temple, London EC4Y 9AN
0171 410 2000
Fax: 0171 410 2010; DX 1048 Chancery Lane
Out of hours telephone: 0370 533599

Chambers of J Gompertz QC
Clerks: Michael Dean, Mark Waller, Rachel Shepherd

Gompertz, Jeremy QC 1962†	**Farrimond,** Stephanie 1987
Roberts, Mervyn 1963†	**Walbank,** David 1987
Catterson, Marie 1972†	**Studd,** Anne 1988
Moss, Christopher QC 1972†	**Kerr,** Christopher 1988
Ainley, Nicholas 1973‡	**Kent,** Georgina 1989
Bassett, John 1975	**Powell,** Giles 1990
Freeland, Simon 1978	**Hayhow,** Lyn 1990
Spink, Peter 1979	**Buckingham,** Sarah 1991
Wilcox, Nicholas 1977	**Pollock,** Dr Evelyn 1991
Pounder, Gerard 1980	**Beer,** Jason 1992
Apthorp, Charles 1983	**Leek,** Samantha 1993
Butcher, John 1984	**Johnson,** Jeremy 1994
Barton, Fiona 1986	**Virdi,** Prabjhot 1995
Davenport, Simon 1987	**Rose,** Stephen 1995
Waters, Andrew 1987	**Ahmad,** Nadeem 1996
	McLean, Mandy 1996

The *new* Supreme Court Practice 1999 (The White Book)

- *the most authoritative guide to Civil Court Practice and Procedure*

- *whatever the case, whatever the court*

- *updates following implementation of the Woolf Reforms*

The new Supreme Court Practice *is also available on CD-ROM using Folio Views™ technology. With this intuitive software, you will find your way around* The White Book *with ease, enhancing your research by leaps and bounds.*

Phone Sweet & Maxwell on 0171 449 1111 to order your copy

ESSEX COURT CHAMBERS

24 Lincoln's Inn Fields, London WC2A 3ED
0171 813 8000
Fax: 0171 813 8080; DX 320 London,
Chancery Lane
E-mail: clerksroom@essexcourt-chambers.co.uk
URL: http://www.essexcourt-chambers.co.uk

Chambers of Gordon Pollock QC
*Clerks: David Grief, Joe Ferrigno, Nigel Jones,
Sam Biggerstaff, Mathew Kesby, Ben Perry,
Tim Rycroft; Office Manager: Jo Morris*

Pollock, Gordon QC *1968*	**Smouha**, Joe *1986*
Thomas, Michael QC *1955*	**Watson**, Philippa *1988*
Hunter, Ian QC *1967*†	**Mercer**, Hugh *1985*
Boyd, Stewart QC *1967*†	**Griffiths**, Martin *1986*
Veeder, VV QC *1971*‡	**Troy-Davies**, Karen *1981*
Collins, Michael QC *1971*†	**Lockey**, John *1987*
Siberry, Richard QC *1974*‡	**Bryan**, Simon *1988*
Gilman, Jonathan QC *1965*	**Foxton**, David *1989*
Eder, Bernard QC *1975*‡	**Shaw**, Malcolm *1988*
Cordara, Roderick QC *1975*	**Cockerill**, Sara *1990*
Crookenden, Simon QC *1975*‡	**Snider**, John *1982*
	Flynn, James *1991*
Hochhauser, Andrew QC *1977*	**Dye**, Brian *1991*
	Eaton, Nigel *1991*
Duffy, Peter QC *1978*	**Blanchard**, Claire *1992*
Dicks, Anthony *1961*	**Cargill-Thompson**, Perdita *1993*
Beatson, Jack QC *1973*†	
Jacobs, Richard QC *1979*	**Lowe**, Vaughan *1993*
Greenwood, Christopher *1978*	**Landau**, Toby *1993*
	Stanley, Paul *1993*
Mildon, David *1980*	**Hunter**, Martin *1994*
Lyon, Victor *1980*	**Hopkins**, Philippa *1994*
Smith, Mark *1981*	**McGrath**, Paul *1994*
Andrews, Geraldine *1981*	**Collins**, James *1995*
Dunning, Graham *1982*	**Houseman**, Stephen *1995*
Templeman, Mark *1981*	**Key**, Paul *1997*
Prevezer, Sue *1983*	**Scorey**, David *1997*
Berry, Steven *1984*	**Wordsworth**, Sam *1997*
Joseph, David *1984*	**Pillow**, Nathan *1997*
Millett, Richard *1985*	**O'Reilly**, James *1983**
Davies, Huw *1985*	**Lau**, Martin *1996**

Chambers established: 1961
Opening times: 7.45 am-7 pm

Types of work (and number of counsel practising in that area if supplied)
Administrative · Admiralty · Agriculture
· Arbitration · Aviation · Banking · Bankruptcy
· Civil liberties · Commercial litigation
· Commodities · Company and commercial
· Competition · Construction · Corporate
finance · Discrimination · EC and competition
law · Employment · Energy · Entertainment
· Environment · Film, cable, TV · Financial
services · Foreign law · Franchising
· Immigration · Information technology
· Insolvency · Insurance · Insurance/
reinsurance · Intellectual property
· International trade · Partnerships · Private
international · Professional negligence · Public
international · Sale and carriage of goods
· Share options · Shipping, admiralty · South
Asian law · Sports · Telecommunications

Chambers' facilities
Conference rooms, Video conferences, Disks
accepted, Disabled access, E-mail, Website

Languages spoken
Chinese, French, German, Italian, Spanish

Additional information

A full-service commercial set, acting for clients
ranging from major institutions and multinational corporations to private companies and
individuals. Members advise across the whole
spectrum of international, commercial and
European law, and act as advocates in litigation
and commercial arbitration worldwide.

The set: Essex Court Chambers, called Four
Essex Court until its relocation to Lincoln's Inn
Fields in 1994, was formed as a separate
chambers in 1961, when the set at Three Essex
Court split into two sets. The founding
members of Four Essex Court were Michael
Kerr (later Lord Justice Kerr), Robert
MacCrindle, Michael Mustill (later Lord Mustill),
Anthony Evans (later Lord Justice Evans), and
Anthony Diamond (later Judge Diamond).
Chambers grew rapidly in the late 1960s and
1970s, developing a reputation as one of the
leading sets of commercial barristers in England,
during which time Mark Saville (later Lord
Saville), Johan Steyn (later Lord Steyn), Anthony
Colman (later Mr Justice Colman) and John
Thomas (later Mr Justice Thomas) joined.

Types of work undertaken: The work of
chambers covers the entire range of
international and commercial litigation and
arbitration. The fields of work for which
chambers is best known are: Administrative Law
and Judicial Review, Agriculture and Farming,
Arbitration, Aviation, Banking, Chinese Law,
Company Law and Insolvency, Conflict of Laws,
Construction and Engineering, Commodity
Transactions, Computer Law, Employment Law,
Energy and Utilities Law, Entertainment and
Sports Law, Environmental Law, European Law,
Financial Services, Human Rights, Injunctions
and Arrests, Insurance and Reinsurance,
International Commerical Fraud, International
Trade and Transport, Professional Negligence,
Public International Law, Public Law, Sale of
Goods and Product Liability, Shipping, South

C

Asian Law, VAT and Excise. Also members act as arbitrators and mediators in domestic and international disputes when invited to do so by the parties concerned, or by the person or body named in the contract.

Several members have written or co-operated on legal works. These include: *Arnould on Marine Insurance* (co-editor: Jonathan Gilman QC); *Mustill & Boyd on Commercial Arbitration* (co-author: Stewart Boyd QC); *Scrutton on Charterparties* (co-editors: Stewart Boyd QC and David Foxton); *Chitty on Contracts* (co-editor: Jack Beatson); *International Law* (Professor Malcolm Shaw); *The Law of Guarantees* (Geraldine Andrews and Richard Millett) and *International Commercial Arbitration* (co-author: Martin Hunter); *The Law of the Sea* co-author: Vaughan Lowe), *Commercial Debt in Europe: Recovery and Remedies* (Hugh Mercer); *Cross Border litigation within ASEAN: The Prospects for Harmonization of Civil and Commercialisation Litigation*, by Kluwer Law Intl (1997); *Various legal complexities of syndicated loans* (Malek & Ong).

The international nature of chambers' practice is underlined by the fact that French, German, Italian, Spanish and Chinese are spoken within chambers. Members have appeared as advocates in the European Commission, European Court of Justice, and European Court of Human Rights; in the Courts of jurisdictions including Hong Kong, Malaysia, Australia, Belfast, Dublin, Gibraltar, St Vincent, Brunei, Kenya and the Cayman Islands; and in arbitrations in places such as Paris, Geneva, Singapore, New Orleans and Beijing.

ESSEX HOUSE CHAMBERS

Essex House, 375-377 Stratford High Street, Stratford, London E15 4QZ
0181 536 1077

Chambers of Mr Y N K S Serugo-Lugo

20 ESSEX STREET

20 Essex Street

20 Essex Street, London WC2R 3AL
0171 583 9294
Fax: 0171 583 1341; DX 0009 London, Chancery Lane
E-mail: clerks@20essexst.com
URL: http://www.20essexst.com

Chambers of D B Johnson QC
Clerks: Neil Palmer, Brian Lee

Johnson, David QC *1967†*	Morris, Stephen *1981‡*
Rokison, Kenneth QC *1961*	Hancock, Christopher *1983*
Lauterpacht, Sir Elihu QC *1950*	Owen, David *1983*
	Matthews, Duncan *1986*
Watts, Sir Arthur QC *1957*	Baker, Andrew *1988*
Pickering, Murray QC *1963†*	Bethlehem, Daniel *1988*
Legh-Jones, Nicholas QC *1968*	Clark, Geraldine *1988*
	Coburn, Michael *1990*
Plender, Richard QC *1972†*	Akka, Lawrence *1991*
Milligan, Iain QC *1973*	Morpuss, Guy *1991*
Glennie, Angus QC *1974*	Ambrose, Clare *1992*
Gross, Peter QC *1977†*	Maxwell, Karen *1992*
Havelock-Allan, Mark QC *1974‡*	Charkham, Graham *1993*
	Masters, Sara *1993*
Young, Timothy QC *1977*	Edey, Philip *1994*
Hamblen, Nicholas QC *1981*	Kimmins, Charles *1994*
Cooke, Julian *1965*	Collett, Michael *1995*
Wood, Richard *1975*	Ashcroft, Michael *1997*
Birch, Elizabeth *1978*	Collier, John *1961**
Males, Stephen QC *1978*	Allott, Philip *1960**
Tselentis, Michael SC *1995*	Procter, Diana *1973**
Broadbent, Edmund *1980*	

Types of work (and number of counsel practising in that area if supplied)
Administrative · Admiralty · Arbitration · Aviation · Banking · Civil liberties · Commercial litigation · Commodities · Competition · EC and competition law · Energy · Environment · Financial services · Human rights · Immigration · Insurance · Insurance/reinsurance · Intellectual property · International trade · Private international · Professional negligence · Public international · Sale and carriage of goods · Shipping, admiralty

† Recorder ‡ Assistant Recorder * Door Tenant

Chambers' facilities
Conference rooms, Disks accepted

Languages spoken
French, German, Italian, Spanish

23 ESSEX STREET

35 ESSEX STREET

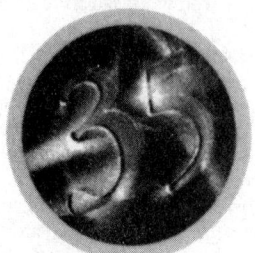

23 ESSEX STREET LONDON WC2R 3AS

London WC2R 3AS
0171 413 0353
Fax: 0171 413 0374; DX LDE 148 Chancery
Lane
E-mail: clerks@essexstreet23.demon.co.uk
Out of hours telephone: on answerphone

Chambers of M H Lawson QC
Clerk: David Burt (Chambers Manager);
Practice manager: Nicholas Hopgood

Lawson, Michael QC *1969†*	Carnes, Andrew *1984*
Hill, Michael QC *1958*	Kent, Alan *1986*
Purnell, Nicholas QC *1968†*	Cutts, Johannah *1986*
Hallett, Heather QC *1972†*	Cranston-Morris, Wayne
Austin-Smith, Michael QC	*1986*
1969†	Byrne, Garrett *1986*
Edwards, Susan QC *1972†*	Ozin, Paul *1987*
Lawson Rogers, Stuart QC	Norton, Heather *1988*
1969†	Morley, Iain *1988*
Miskin, Charles QC *1975‡*	Carter, William *1989*
Byers, Charles *1973†*	Hotten, Keith *1990*
Richardson, James *1975*	Ascherson, Isobel *1991*
Wood, Michael *1976‡*	Medland, Simon *1991*
Finucane, Brendan *1976*	Acheson, Ian *1992*
Kinch, Christopher *1976‡*	Fenhalls, Mark *1992*
Davis, Simon *1978‡*	Hurst, Andrew *1992*
James, Roderick *1979*	Milne, Richard *1992*
Causer, John *1979*	Horlick, Fiona *1992*
Janner, Daniel *1980*	Marshall, Eloise *1994*
Russell Flint, Simon *1980‡*	Swain, Hannah *1994*
Price, John *1982*	Stilgoe, Rufus *1994*
Del Fabbro, Oscar *1982*	Durran, Alexia *1995*
Cooke, Graham *1983*	Strickland, Clare *1995*
Glynn, Joanna *1983‡*	May, Alan *1995*
Claxton, Elroy *1983‡*	Goldsworthy, Ian QC *1968**
Pardoe, Rupert *1984*	Jones, Alison *1988**

Temple, London WC2R 3AR
0171 353 6381
Fax: 0171 583 1786; DX 351 London
Other comms: Link: 35 Essex Street

Chambers of Nigel Inglis-Jones QC
Clerk: Derek Jenkins

Inglis-Jones, Nigel QC	Climie, Stephen *1982*
1959†	Westcott, David *1982*
Rawley, Alan QC *1958†*	Kemp, Christopher *1984*
Calcutt, David QC *1955*	Spink, Andrew *1985*
Lasok, Dominik QC *1954**	Trusted, Harry *1985*
Wilson-Smith, Christopher	McCormick, Alison *1988*
QC *1965†*	Freeborn, Susan *1989*
Mott, Philip QC *1970†*	Hitchcock, Richard *1989*
Sullivan, Linda QC *1973†*	Hand, Jonathan *1990*
Gibbons, Jeremy QC	Leeper, Thomas *1991*
1973†*	Tavares, Nathan *1992*
Lissack, Richard QC *1978‡*	Malden, Grace *1993*
Rains, Richard *1963**	Phillips, Matthew *1993*
Jenkins, Hywel *1974*	Stallworthy, Nicolas *1993*
Stephens, John *1975*	Willmot, Rachel *1994*
Mawhinney, Richard *1977*	Temmink, Robert-Jan *1996*
Coley, William *1980*	Vines, Clare *1997*
Tolson, Robin *1980*	Skelton, Peter *1997*

Opening times: 9 am-6 pm

**Types of work (and number of counsel
practising in that area if supplied)**
Arbitration 2 · Care proceedings 6
· Commercial litigation 2 · Common law
(general) 20 · Construction 2 · Copyright 2
· Crime 5 · Crime - corporate fraud 7
· Employment 6 · Family 4 · Information
technology 2 · Intellectual property 2
· Landlord and tenant 6 · Local government 6
· Medical negligence 10 · Pensions 5 · Personal
injury 20 · Professional negligence 20 · Sale
and carriage of goods 20

Chambers' facilities
Conference rooms, Disks accepted, Disabled
access, E-mail, Disabled toilets

Languages spoken
French, German, Italian, Polish

Fees policy
Up to five years call £25-75, Five to ten years call £75-125, Ten years call £100-150

Additional information

Types of work undertaken
35 Essex Street is primarily a commercial and common law set of chambers. It offers clients experienced representation and advice covering a wide range of legal work and the aim is to provide these services in an accessible manner at both a general and a specialist level.

The past decade has seen a shift in emphasis in the types of work undertaken. Historically, a large proportion of work was carried out on the Western Circuit and emphasis was placed on advocacy and the ability to deal with varied general common law work. Today, much of the work undertaken by chambers is based in and around central London and is of a commercial and, in particular, City-based nature. It now involves considerable specialist expertise which is able to be provided at all levels.

However, the importance that was traditionally attached to the art of advocacy and the provision of a general service has not been lost but combined with the ability to provide a real range of specialisations. As such, many members are also active in areas of law outside the fields in which they have particular expertise.

Various members serve on the committees of the Bar Council and the Inns of Court. One is a former chairman of the Bar Council and is the chairman of the Takeover Panel.

Six members of chambers are Recorders of the Crown Court.

Additional specialisations: The areas of practice in which individual members have particular expertise and experience are as follows: commercial fraud, company and commercial contract, European and international law, intellectual property, landlord and tenant, local government law, medical negligence, occupational pension schemes and trusts, personal injury, professional negligence, property law, and sale and carriage of goods. A brochure is available on request.

39 ESSEX STREET

London WC2R 3AT
0171 832 1111
Fax: 0171 353 3978; DX 298 London, Chancery Lane
E-mail: clerks@39essex.co.uk
Out of hours telephone: 01730 263 631/01634 262 332

Chambers of Edwin Glasgow QC
Clerks: Nigel Connor, Michael Phipps (Assistant), David Smith (Assistant), Sandie Smith (Assistant), Stuart Ritchie (Assistant); Administrator: Susan Rice

Glasgow, Edwin QC 1969	Cory-Wright, Charles 1984
Mackay, Colin QC 1967†	Foster, Alison 1984
Goldblatt, Simon QC 1953	Bellamy, Jonathan 1986
Brennan, Daniel QC 1967†	Catchpole, Stuart 1987
Gray, Richard QC 1970	Bradley, David 1987
Pleming, Nigel QC 1971	Manzoni, Charles 1988
Gordon, Richard QC 1972	Kovats, Steven 1989
Davies, Richard QC 1973	Grey, Eleanor 1990
Wilmot-Smith, Richard QC 1978	Doherty, Bernard 1990
	Nelson, Vincent 1980
Tillett, Michael QC 1965†	Richards, Jennifer 1991
Jay, Robert QC 1981	Wilken, Sean 1991
Cooper, Alan 1969	Brodie, Bruce 1993
Melville, David 1975	Maclean, Alan 1993
Brown, Charles 1976	Seligman, Matthew 1994
Noble, Roderick 1977	Ward, Timothy 1994
McCaul, Colin 1978	Robb, Adam 1995
Block, Neil 1980	Grodzinski, Samuel 1996
Brown, Geoffrey 1981	Patel, Parishil 1996
Du Cann, Christian 1982	Stern, Kristina 1996

Chambers established: 1796
Opening times: 8 am-7 pm

Types of work (and number of counsel practising in that area if supplied)
Administrative · Arbitration · Civil liberties · Commercial litigation · Common law (general) · Construction · Discrimination · EC and competition law · Education · Employment · Energy · Entertainment · Environment · Film, cable, TV · Immigration · Insurance · Insurance/reinsurance · Local government · Medical negligence · Mental

† Recorder ‡ Assistant Recorder * Door Tenant

health · Personal injury · Professional negligence · Sale and carriage of goods · Sports · VAT and Customs & Excise

Chambers' facilities
Conference rooms, Video conferences, Disks accepted, E-mail

Languages spoken
French, German, Spanish

Additional information

39 Essex Street is a long-established set whose barristers have widespread expertise and experience in almost every aspect of commercial, public and common law. Chambers has a particularly strong reputation in the fields of judicial review, accident litigation and inquiries, construction, commercial law and professional negligence.

Within these broad catagories, individual members of chambers offer specialist advice and representation over a wide range of subjects including:

Commercial: insurance and reinsurance, oil and gas law, media and entertainment, sports law, insolvency and company law.

Personal Injury: multi-plaintiff group actions, disaster litigation and injuries of maximum severity.

Public: all aspects of judicial review for both applicants and respondents. Areas of expertise include commercial; local authorities and other public bodies; environmental law; health trusts; education; civil liberties and human rights; community care; mental health; housing and immigration.

Construction and Engineering

Professional Indemnity: act both for and against solicitors and barristers, doctors and other medical practitioners, surveyors, architects, engineers, accountants, insurers and insurance brokers and other professionals.

Members of chambers appear regularly in all divisions of the High Court, Industrial and VAT tribunals, public inquiries and international and domestic arbitrations. They also appear before the European Court of Justice and accept instructions from other jurisdictions such as Hong Kong and Singapore. Members undertake pro bono work and act for public interest organisations.

The clerks are knowledgeable and frank in their appraisal of a barrister's suitability and availability for a particular matter. A brochure describing the services offered is available on request.

39 Essex Street is accredited by The Law Society as a CPD course provider.

CHAMBERS OF GEOFFREY HAWKER

46 Essex Street, London WC2R 3GH
0171 583 8899
Fax: 0171 583 8800; DX 1014 London, Chancery Lane
Other comms: Mobile: 0850 828177

Chambers of G F Hawker TD
Clerks: Stephen English (Senior Clerk), Gawin Cole (Junior Clerk), Elizabeth Wolfe (Fees Clerk)

Hawker, Geoffrey 1970	Sliwinski, Robert 1990
Sofer, Jonathan 1942	Candlin, James 1991
Bridges-Adams, John 1958	Keogh, Richard 1991
Storr, Philip 1990*	Chapman, Peter 1991
Clarke, Ivan 1973	Marks, Medina 1992*
Goh, Allan 1984	Copeland, Andrew 1992
Lonsdale, Marion 1984	Walshe, Annie 1993
Turner, Alan 1984	Bagnell, Matthew 1993
Ryan, David 1985	Peglow, Michael 1993
Milne, Michael 1987*	Volz, Karl 1993
Toussaint, Deborah 1988	Hughes, Mary 1994
Mitropoulos, Georgia 1989	Tobin, Daniel 1994
Cheah, Albert 1989	Cowen, Sally 1995
Aeberli, Peter 1990†	Bentwood, Richard 1994

EUROLAWYER CHAMBERS

PO Box 3621, London N7 0BQ
0171 607 0075
Fax: 0171 607 2081

Chambers of Mr O G Ernstzen

C

See the *Index of Languages Spoken* in Part G to locate a chambers where a particular language is spoken, or find an individual who speaks a particular language.

---

† Recorder ‡ Assistant Recorder * Door Tenant

FALCON CHAMBERS

Falcon Chambers

Falcon Court, London EC4Y 1AA
0171 353 2484
Fax: 0171 353 1261; DX 408 London

Chambers of Jonathan Gaunt QC, Kim Lewison QC
Clerks: Mark Clewley, Steven Francis;
Administrator: Tarlika Patel

Wood, Derek QC CBE 1964†	**Fetherstonhaugh**, Guy 1983
Gaunt, Jonathan QC 1972	**Rodger**, Martin 1986
Lewison, Kim QC 1975†	**Fancourt**, Timothy 1987
Morgan, Paul QC 1975	**Denyer-Green**, Barry 1972
Reynolds, Kirk QC 1974	**Jourdan**, Stephen 1989
Brock, Jonathan QC 1977‡	**Cowen**, Gary 1990
Dowding, Nicholas QC 1979	**Small**, Jonathan 1990
Prince, Edwin 1955	**Bignell**, Janet 1992
de la Piquerie, Paul 1966†	**Dray**, Martin 1992
Moss, Joanne 1976	**Shea**, Caroline 1994
Cole, Edward 1980	**Tanney**, Anthony 1994
Clark, Wayne 1982	**Taskis**, Catherine 1995
	Windsor, Emily 1995

FARRAR'S BUILDING

Temple, London EC4Y 7BD
0171 583 9241
Fax: 0171 583 0090; DX 406 London, Chancery Lane
E-mail: chambers@farrarsbuilding.co.uk
Out of hours telephone: Home: 01245 601710,
Mobile: 0468 366558

Chambers of Gerard Elias QC
Clerk: Alan Kilbey (Senior Clerk)

Elias, Gerard QC 1968†	**Watt-Pringle**, Jonathan 1987
Lewer, Michael QC 1958†	**Wicks**, David 1989
Williams, John QC 1964†	**Todd**, Alan 1990
Pitchford, Christopher QC 1969†	**Hobhouse**, Helen 1990
Day, Douglas QC 1967†	**Moorman**, Lucinda 1992
Birts, Peter QC 1968†	**Cash**, Joanne 1994
Nice, Geoffrey QC 1971†	**Pack**, Melissa 1995
Harrington, Patrick QC 1973†	**Allen**, Darryl 1995
Davies, Leighton QC 1975†	**Evans**, Lee 1996
Jeffreys, Alan QC 1970†	**Garfield**, Roger 1965*
Norris, William QC 1974	**Thomas**, Roger QC 1969*
Dutton, Timothy QC 1979‡	**Rees**, Phillip 1965*
Southwell, Edward 1970†	**Fricker**, Marilyn 1969*
Webb, Anthony 1970†	**Jones**, Richard 1969*
Nussey, Richard 1971	**Singh**, Rameswar 1969*
Seys Llewellyn, Anthony 1972†	**McLaughlin**, Richard 1974*
Rubin, Stephen 1977	**Murphy**, Ian QC 1972*
Treverton-Jones, Gregory 1977‡	**Jenkins**, James 1974‡*
Jones, Stephen 1978	**Marshall**, Philip 1975‡*
McDermott, Thomas 1980	**Brabin**, Michael 1976*
Browne, Simon 1982	**Jones**, Geraint 1976*
Ayling, Tracy 1983	**Morgan**, David Wynn 1976†*
Matovu, Daniel 1985	**Lewis**, Marian 1977*
Ley, Spencer 1985	**Vosper**, Christopher 1977‡*
Peebles, Andrew 1987	**Davies**, Huw 1978‡*
	Thomas, Paul 1979*
	Barnett, Jeremy 1980*
	Gilroy, Paul 1985*

Types of work (and number of counsel practising in that area if supplied)
Administrative · Agriculture · Chancery (general) · Civil liberties · Commercial litigation · Common law (general) · Construction · Courts martial · Crime · Defamation · Employment · Landlord and tenant · Medical negligence · Personal injury · Professional negligence · Sale and carriage of goods · Sports · Taxation and costs

Chambers' facilities
Conference rooms, Disks accepted, Disabled access

Languages spoken
French, Italian, Welsh

Fees policy

Up to five years call £50-75, Five to ten years call £65-100, Ten years call £85-250. Fees are assessed to take account of a number of factors and are not charged purely on an hourly rate basis. The Senior Clerk Alan Kilbey is happy to give an indication as to the likely fee range on inquiry.

Additional information

This is a large and long-established chambers consisting of 12 QCs and 22 other members. The set concentrates on all types of general and common law with a high proportion of commercial, insurance, landlord and tenant, personal injury, employment, professional negligence, medical negligence and heavy criminal work.

The chambers also offers specialists in the following areas: defamation, judicial review, sports, civil rights of prisoners, trespass and rights of way, planning, agricultural holdings (including milk quotas), countryside law and taxation and costs.

The set has strong links with the South Eastern, and Wales and Chester circuits, while conducting the majority of its work in London.

Chambers has been refurbished to a very high standard, offering conference rooms and facilities for disabled clients and a fully computerised network system.

Farrar's Building also offers arbitration services and an arbitration room is available for hire.

For further information, please contact the Senior Clerk/Practice Manager.

Kime's International Law Directory 1999

- established guide to the international legal community

- reliable and relevant information on over 600 law firms and chambers

- entries can be found by types of work undertaken and location

- the only law directory to provide editorial on every jurisdiction's legal system and enforcement of judgements

- now on the Internet at http://www.smlawpub-holborn.co.uk/kimes

For more information call Sweet & Maxwell on 0171 449 1111

CHAMBERS OF NORMAN PALMER

2 Field Court, Gray's Inn, London WC1R 5BB
0171 405 6114
Fax: 0171 831 6112; DX 457 London, Chancery Lane
E-mail: fieldct2@netcomuk.co.uk.

Chambers of Norman E Palmer, Ashley Underwood (Deputy)
Clerk: Michael Clark

Palmer, Norman 1973	Swirsky, Joshua 1987
Bowring, William 1974	Lewis, Eleri 1989
Jones, Kay 1974	Rutledge, Kelvin 1989
Littman, Jeffrey 1974	Youll, Joanna 1989
Walter, Philip 1975	Champion, Rowena 1990
Underwood, Ashley 1976	Deighton, Richard 1990
Harrop-Griffiths, Hilton 1978	Fox, Ian 1990
Bennington, Jane 1981	Giovannetti, Lisa 1990
Evans, Franklin 1981	Howling, Rex 1991
Theis, Lucy 1982‡	Nicholson, Michael 1993
McGuire, Bryan 1983	Tyson, Thomas 1995
Carlisle, Timothy 1984	Godfrey, Emma 1995
Presland, Frederick 1985	Davis, Adrian 1996
Stevenson-Watt, Neville 1985	

Chambers established: 1976
Opening times: 8.30 am-6.30 pm

Types of work (and number of counsel practising in that area if supplied)

Administrative 5 · Asset finance 9 · Banking 5 · Bankruptcy 5 · Care proceedings 11 · Chancery (general) 6 · Chancery land law 4 · Charities 2 · Civil liberties 6 · Commercial litigation 4 · Commercial property 4 · Common land 4 · Common law (general) 10 · Company and commercial 6 · Construction 6 · Conveyancing 3 · Copyright 2 · Corporate finance 6 · Defamation 4 · Discrimination 5 · Education 2 · Employment 7 · Entertainment 2 · Equity, wills and trusts 2 · Family 12 · Family provision 10 · Financial services 5 · Foreign law 2 · Housing 6 · Immigration 4 · Insolvency 6 · Insurance 2 · Insurance/reinsurance 2 · International trade 2 · Landlord and tenant 2 · Licensing 3 · Local government 2 · Medical negligence 5 · Mental health 2 · Partnerships 3 · Personal injury 5 · Private international 2 · Probate and administration 2 · Professional negligence 7 · Public international 1 · Sale and carriage of goods 4 · Share options · Town and country planning 2

Chambers' facilities

Conference rooms, Disks accepted, E-mail

Languages spoken
Chinese, French, German, Hebrew, Italian, Mandarin, Russian, Serbo-Croat, Spanish, Welsh

Fees policy
Speak to clerks.

4 FIELD COURT

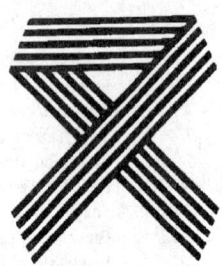

Gray's Inn, London WC1R 5EA
0171 440 6900
Fax: 0171 242 0197; DX LDE 483
E-mail: chambers@4fieldcourt.co.uk

Chambers of Geoffrey Brice QC
Clerks: Christopher James (Senior Clerk), Paul Coveney, Venetia Jeffcock, Jean-Pierre Schultz

Brice, Geoffrey QC 1960†	Green, Yvonne 1982
Rankin, Andrew QC 1950†	Selvaratnam, Vasanti 1983
Stone, Richard QC 1952	Sutton, Mark 1982
Reeder, John QC 1971	Turner, Jonathan D C 1982
Kay, Jervis QC 1972	Whiteley, Miranda 1985
Persey, Lionel QC 1981	Goldstone, David 1986
Blackburn, Elizabeth QC 1978	Wright, Colin 1987
	Saunders, Nicholas 1989
Myers, Allan (QC Aus) 1988	Smith, Christopher 1989
Miller, Sarah 1971	Wilson, Stephen 1990
Lloyd, Lloyd 1973	Davey, Michael 1990
Green, Alison 1974	Hill, Timothy 1990
Thom, James 1974	Ghaffar, Arshad 1991
Speller, Bruce 1976	Dugdale, Nicholas 1992
Whitehouse-Vaux, William 1977	Taylor, Julian 1994
	Davies, Charles 1995
Bourne, Robert 1978	Heal, Madeleine 1996
Romney, Daphne 1979	O'Shea, Eion 1996
Meeson, Nigel 1982	

Types of work (and number of counsel practising in that area if supplied)
Admiralty 20 · Arbitration 33 · Aviation 4 · Banking 10 · Bankruptcy 5 · Commercial 33 · Commercial property 5 · Company and commercial 8 · Competition 3 · Construction 10 · Copyright 2 · Defamation 1 · Discrimination 6 · EC and competition law 3 · Employment 8 · Entertainment 2 · Environment 10 · Film, cable, TV 1 · Financial services 5 · Housing 5 · Information technology 2 · Insolvency 4 · Insurance 33 · Insurance/reinsurance 25 · Intellectual property 2 · International trade 20 · Landlord and tenant 8 · Licensing 1 · Local government 6 · Medical negligence 2 · Partnerships 1 · Personal injury 10 · Professional negligence 12 · Sale and carriage of goods 32 · Shipping, admiralty 20 · Sports 4 · Tax - corporate 1 · Trademarks 2

Chambers' facilities
Conference rooms, Disks accepted, E-mail

Languages spoken
French, German, Italian, Urdu

Additional information

Established in the 1920's, 4 Field Court is a commercial set. Barristers at 4 Field Court offer advocacy and advisory expertise and experience in many aspects of commercial, chancery/commercial and civil law.

Members appear before all courts and tribunals in England and Wales, as well as in the European Court and range of overseas courts and tribunals. Members of Chambers also act as arbitrators, as mediators in Alternative Dispute Resolution and as expert witnesses.

The breadth of expertise and experience within Chambers is such that Members are able to deal with a very wide range of civil litigation and other matters.

Principal areas of practice include: Shipping and Maritime law; Commercial Contracts; Insurance and Reinsurance; Banking and Financial Services; Road, Rail and Air law; Professional Negligence; Employment Law; Property Law; Intellectual Property; EC, Free Trade and Competition; Public, Administrative and Local Government; Licensing.

Barristers at 4 Field Court are members of the Bars of Antigua, California, Gibraltar, New South Wales, New York, New Zealand, Papua New Guinea, St Vincent and the Grenadines and Victoria.

Some members are contributors to various works: Geoffrey Brice, author of *The Maritime Law of Salvage* and contributor to *Lloyd's Maritime Law Quarterly*, as are Elizabeth Blackburn, Nigel Meeson; Allan Myers, editor *Australian Taxation Review*; Jervis Kay, editor *Atkin's Court Forms (Admiralty)*; James Thom, co-editor *Handbook of Dilapidations*; Alison Green, editorial adviser *Insurance Contract*

Law (Kluwer) and EC editor *Current Law*; Robert Bourne has edited the Admiralty section of the *County Court Practice*; Nigel Meeson, author of *Practice and Procedure of the Admiralty Court, Ship and Aircraft Mortgages, Admiralty Jurisdiction and Practice* and contributor to *Ship Sale and Purchase* (2nd edition); Daphne Romney is a libel reader for the *Observer*. Jonathan D C Turner, co-author of *Vaughan's Law of the EC* and *Halsbury's Laws* (on EC competition law), *Countdown to 2000 - A Guide to the Legal Issues, Melville's Forms and Agreements on Intellectual Property and International Licensing*, co-editor *European Patent Office Reports*.

Direct professional access work and matters relating to the Overseas Practice Rules are accepted. A brochure is available.

FIELD COURT CHAMBERS

2nd Floor, 3 Field Court, Gray's Inn, London WC1R 4EP
0171 404 7474
Fax: 0171 404 7475; DX 136 Chancery Lane

Chambers of Miss M D Spencer

FLEET CHAMBERS

Mitre House, 44-46 Fleet Street, London EC4Y 1BN
0171 936 3707
Fax: 0171 936 3708; DX 274 CHANCERY LANE

Chambers of Mr J D C Cartwright

FOREST HOUSE CHAMBERS

15 Granville Road, Walthamstow, London E17 9BS
0181 925 2240
Fax: 0181 556 6125

Chambers of Mr H D Singer

The Supreme Court Practice 1999

- *the most authoritative title on Civil Court Practice and Procedure*

- *available in book and CD-ROM formats*

Phone Sweet & Maxwell on 0171 449 1111 to order your copy

FOUNTAIN COURT

Fountain Court
CHAMBERS

Temple, London EC4Y 9DH
0171 583 3335
Fax: 0171 353 0329/1794; DX 5 London, Chancery Lane
E-mail: chambers@fountaincourt.co.uk
Out of hours telephone: 0831 465 305

Chambers of P D J Scott QC
Clerks: Ric Martin (Chambers Director), Mark Watson (Head of Clerking), Michael Couling, Vince Plant, Danny Wilkinson, Rob Smith; Administrator: Prue Woodbridge

Dehn, Conrad QC *1952*†	**Shanks,** Murray *1984*
Bathurst, Christopher QC *1959*	**Philipps,** Guy *1986*
	Moriarty, Stephen *1986*
Scott, Peter QC *1960*	**Orr,** Craig *1986*
Boswood, Anthony QC *1970*	**Green,** Michael *1987*
Goldsmith, Peter QC *1972*†	**Howe,** Timothy *1987*
Philipson, Trevor QC *1972*	**Thanki,** Bankim *1988*
Lerego, Michael QC *1972*	**Robertson,** Patricia *1988*
Smith, Andrew QC *1974*†	**Chapman,** Jeffrey *1989*
Falconer of Thoroton, Lord QC *1974*†	**Napier,** Brian *1990*
	Dale, Derrick *1990*
Brindle, Michael QC *1975*	**Shah,** Akhil *1990*
Crane, Michael QC *1975*	**Smith,** Marcus *1991*
Underhill, Nicholas QC *1976*†	**Gott,** Paul *1991*
	Buehrlen, Veronique *1991*
Stadlen, Nicholas QC *1976*‡	**Mitchell,** Andrew *1992*
Wormington, Timothy *1977*	**Handyside,** Richard *1993*
Railton, David QC *1979*	**Taylor,** John *1993*
Doctor, Brian *1991*	**Coleman,** Richard *1994*
Keene, Gillian *1980*	**Butters,** James *1994*
McLaren, Michael *1981*	**Tolley,** Adam *1994*
Browne-Wilkinson, Simon QC *1981*	**Merrett,** Louise *1995*
	Hamilton, Philippa *1996*
Brook Smith, Philip *1982*	**Carter,** Peter QC *1947**
Cox, Raymond *1982*	**Hooley,** Richard *1984**
Waksman, David *1982*	**Sinan,** Izzet *1981**
Martino, Anthony *1982*	**Li,** Gladys *1971**
Keith, Thomas *1983*	

Chambers established: 1939
Opening times: 8 am-9 pm (Monday to Friday), 8 am-1 pm (Saturday)

C

Types of work (and number of counsel practising in that area if supplied)

Administrative · Arbitration · Aviation · Banking · Chancery (general) · Commercial litigation · Common law (general) · Company and commercial · Construction · Copyright · Defamation · Discrimination · Employment · Energy · Entertainment · Film, cable, TV · Financial services · Information technology · Insolvency · Insurance · Insurance/ reinsurance · Intellectual property · International trade · Medical negligence · Parliamentary · Partnerships · Personal injury · Private international · Professional negligence · Sale and carriage of goods · Share options · Shipping, admiralty · Sports · Tax - capital and income · Telecommunications · Trademarks

Chambers' facilities

Conference rooms, Disks accepted, Catering for conferences, including light lunches, E-mail

Languages spoken

Afrikaans, French, German, Greek, Italian, Russian

FRANCIS TAYLOR BUILDING

Ground Floor, Temple, London EC4Y 7BY
0171 353 7768/2711
Fax: 0171 353 0659; DX 441 London, Chancery Lane

Chambers of N P Valios QC

Clerk: David Green; Administrator: Janet P Clark

Valios, Nicholas QC *1964*†	**Ingram**, Jonathan *1984*
Lewis, Peter *1964*	**McFarlane**, Alastair *1985*
Cartwright, John *1964*	**Giret**, Joseph *1985*
Rylance, John *1968*†	**Bermingham**, Gerald *1985*
Mason, James *1969*	**Lewis**, Andrew *1986*
Lodge, Graham *1971*	**Braithwaite**, Garfield *1987*
Lewis, Edward *1972*	**Morgan**, Sarah *1988*
Piercy, Mark *1976*	**English**, Caroline *1989*
Cunningham, Graham *1976*	**Shaw**, Jenny *1990*
Parker, Wendy *1978*	**Ancliffe**, Shiva *1991*
Mayall, David *1979*	**Watson**, Isabelle *1991*
Cheves, Simon *1980*	**Taylor**, Simon *1993*
Bazley, Janet *1980*	**Vaughan**, Kieran *1993*
Tapson, Lesley *1982*	**McCourt**, Christopher *1993*
Brown, Roy *1983*	**McLoughlin**, Ian *1993*
Rimmer, Anthony *1983*	**Kerr**, Derek *1994*
Jones, Richard *1984*	**Stone**, Sally *1994*
Scobie, James *1984*	

2ND FLOOR, FRANCIS TAYLOR BUILDING

SECOND FLOOR

FRANCIS TAYLOR BUILDING

barristers chambers
2nd Floor, Francis Taylor Building, Temple, London EC4Y 7BY
0171 353 9942
Fax: 0171 353 9924; DX 211 London, Chancery Lane

Chambers of D A Pears

Clerks: Kathryn Thornton, Ryan Bartlett, Susan Yacoub

Williamson, Stephen QC *1964*†	**Matthews-Stroud**, Jacqueline *1984*
Merrylees, Gavin *1964*	**Dixon**, Philip *1986*
Naish, Dennis *1966*	**Buckpitt**, Michael *1988*
Conrath, Philip *1972*	**Roberts**, Clare *1988*
Matthews, Phillip *1974*†	**Wilson**, Gerald *1989*
Mallison, Kate *1974*	**Rainey**, Philip *1990*
Pears, Derrick *1975*	**Chirimuuta**, Gilbert *1990*
Staddon, Paul *1976*	**Barraclough**, Nicholas *1990*
Cakebread, Stuart *1978*	**Brimelow**, Kirsty *1991*
Dencer, Mark *1978*	**Heath**, Stephen *1992*
Boyd, Kerstin *1979*	**Jones**, Howard *1992*
Manners, Henrietta *1981*	**MacLaren**, Catriona *1993*
Holland, William *1982*	**Butler**, Andrew *1993*
Reid, Sebastian *1982*	**Aleeson**, Warwick *1994*
Clarke, Kevin *1983*	**Bastin**, Alexander *1995*
Carpenter, Jane *1984*	**Bowker**, Robert *1995*

Opening times: 8.45 am-6.30 pm

Types of work (and number of counsel practising in that area if supplied)

Banking · Bankruptcy · Care proceedings · Chancery (general) · Chancery land law · Commercial property · Common law (general) · Company and commercial · Consumer Law · Crime · Employment · Equity, wills and trusts · Family · Family provision · Housing · Immigration · Insolvency · Landlord and tenant · Licensing · Medical negligence · Partnerships · Personal injury · Probate and administration · Professional negligence · Sale and carriage of goods · Town and country planning

Chambers' facilities

Conference rooms, Disks accepted

Languages spoken
French

Fees policy
Fees vary according to case, client and counsel:
refer for details to clerks.

FRANCIS TAYLOR BLDG

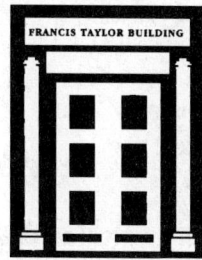

3rd Floor, Temple, London EC4Y 7BY
0171 797 7250
Fax: 0171 797 7299; DX 46 London

Chambers of Mr J D C Guy

**The UK College of Family Mediators
Directory & Handbook 1998/99**

- *provides expert commentary on family
  mediation training and professional
  development and includes contributions
  by leading family mediation professionals*

- *lists over 100 family mediation
  groups/services and over 950 individual
  family mediators by region and
  alphabetically*

- *gives details of all members and
  associates of the UK College of Family
  Mediators*

- *includes the UK College of Family
  Mediators Standards and Code of Practice*

- *gives details of all the family mediation
  bodies which make up the UK College of
  Family Mediators*

*For more information call Sweet & Maxwell
on 0171 449 1111*

FURNIVAL CHAMBERS

32 Furnival Street, London EC4A 1JQ
0171 405 3232
Fax: 0171 405 3322; DX 72 London, Chancery
Lane
E-mail: clerks@furnivallaw.co.uk
URL: http://www.furnivallaw.co.uk

Chambers of Andrew Mitchell
Clerks: John Gutteridge, Paul Richardson

Mitchell, Andrew QC *1976‡*	**Talbot**, Kennedy *1984*
Blunt, Oliver QC *1974†*	**Blore**, Carolyn *1985*
O'Neill, Sally QC *1976*	**Sherrard**, Charles *1986*
Griffiths, Hugh *1972*	**Romans**, Philip *1982*
Baur, Christopher *1972*	**Gregory**, Barry *1987*
Connor, Gino *1974*	**Lees**, Patricia *1988*
Matthews, Lisa *1974*	**Gerasimidis**, Nicolas *1988*
Latham, Michael *1975*	**Earnshaw**, Stephen *1990*
Clompus, Joel *1976*	**Hurtley**, Diane *1990*
Henson, Graham *1976*	**Forster**, Timothy *1990*
Holt, Stephen *1978*	**Woolls**, Tanya *1991*
Coughlin, Vincent *1980*	**Patel**, Sandip *1991*
Sheridan, Francis *1980*	**de Costa**, Leon *1992*
Mytton, Paul *1982*	**Henley**, Andrew *1992*
Whittam, Richard *1983*	**Panayioti**, Lefi *1992*
Merrick, Nicola *1983*	**Giuliani**, Mark *1993*
Swain, Jon *1983*	**Pearce**, Ivan *1994*
Caddle, Sherrie *1983*	**McEvilly**, Gerard *1994*
Headlam, Roy *1983*	**Winship**, Julian *1995*
Dootson, Iain *1984*	**Cockings**, Giles *1996*
Carmichael, John *1984*	

Chambers established: 1985
Opening times: 8.15 am-6.45 pm

**Types of work (and number of counsel
practising in that area if supplied)**
Confiscation 6 · Copyright 4 · Courts martial 4
· Crime 41 · Crime - corporate fraud 6

Chambers' facilities
Conference rooms, Disks accepted, Disabled
access, E-mail

Languages spoken
French, German, Greek, Italian, Portuguese,
Serbo-Croat, Spanish

C

Additional information

Established in 1985, Furnival Chambers offers expertise in all areas of criminal law. Chambers' practice ranges from the most complex and involved commercial fraud to minor driving cases. Expertise is available for matters of fraud, sexual offences including rape and child abuse, Customs and Excise offences, drugs-related cases and crimes of violence including murder and terrorism. In addition chambers has a specialist team that deals with criminal confiscation proceedings in the Crown, High Court and Court of Appeal. The team offers a comprehensive range of services in this field including drafting of all relevant documentation and representation.

Furnival Chambers recognises that urgent advice is often required and so informal telephone contact from solicitors and professional clients is welcomed.

ONE GARDEN COURT FAMILY LAW CHAMBERS

Temple, London EC4Y 9BJ
0171 797 7900
Fax: 0171 797 7929; DX 1034 London, Chancery Lane

Chambers of Eleanor F Platt QC, Alison Ball QC
Clerks: Howard Rayner (Senior Clerk), Dennis Davies (Fees Clerk), Chris Ferrison, Paul Harris, James Mitchell (Junior Clerks); Chief Executive: Nicholas Martin

Annexe of: Brentwood Chambers, Denton, North Yorkshire LS29 OHE
Tel: 01943 817230
Fax: 01943 817230

Platt, Eleanor QC *1960*†	**Rippon,** Paul *1985*
Ball, Alison QC *1972*‡	**Walker,** Susannah *1985*
Peddie, Ian QC *1971*†	**Cobb,** Stephen *1985*
Solomons, Ellen *1964*	**Stocker,** John *1985*
Willbourne, Caroline *1970*	**Cleave,** Gillian *1988*
Mitchell, John *1972*	**Crawley,** Gary *1988*
Coleman, Bruce *1972*	**Inglis,** Alan *1989*
Beckhough, Jennifer *1973*	**Bagchi,** Andrew *1989*
Nathan, Peter *1973*	**Liebrecht,** Michael *1989*
Shenton, Suzanne *1973*	**Jenkins,** Catherine *1990*
Szwed, Elizabeth *1974*	**Rozhan,** Ariff *1990*
Crowley, Jane QC *1976*†	**O'Flaherty,** Nora *1991*
Horrocks, Peter *1977*	**Robbins,** Ian *1991*
Bedell-Pearce, Sheron *1978*	**Geddes,** Joanna *1992*
O'Dwyer, Martin *1978*	**Norton,** Andrew *1992*
Wicherek, Ann *1978*	**Budaly,** Susan *1994*
Scarratt, Richard *1979*	**Hudson,** Emma *1995*
Rowe, Judith *1979*	**Chandler,** Alexander *1995*
Halkyard, Kay *1980*	**Fox,** Nicola *1996*
Lachkovic, Veronica *1982*	**Amaouche,** Sassa-Ann *1996*
Hely-Hutchinson, Caroline *1983*	

---

† Recorder ‡ Assistant Recorder * Door Tenant

2 GARDEN COURT

CHAMBERS

Middle Temple, London EC4Y 9BL
0171 353 1633
Fax: 0171 353 4621; DX 34 London, Chancery Lane
E-mail: barristers@2gardenct.law.co.uk

Chambers of Ian Macdonald QC, Owen Davies
Clerk: Colin Cook MBA; Administrator: Judy Ware

Macdonald, Ian QC *1963*	**Prevatt**, Beatrice *1985*
Davies, Owen *1973*	**McKeone**, Mary *1986*
Blake, Nicholas QC *1974*	**Meusz**, Amanda *1986*
House, Michael *1972*	**Scannell**, Richard *1986*
Munyard, Terry *1972*	**Veats**, Elizabeth *1986*
Russell, Marguerite *1972*	**Dias**, Dexter *1988*
Watkinson, David *1972*	**Eissa**, Adrian *1988*
George, Mark *1976*	**Thomas**, Leslie *1988*
Blaxland, Henry *1978*	**Khan**, Judy *1989*
de Kauwe, Lalith *1978*	**Grief**, Alison *1990*
Macdonald, Kenneth QC *1978*	**Hutchinson**, Colin *1990*
	Jones, Maggie *1990*
Peart, Icah *1978‡*	**Chahall**, Jasbinder *1991*
Webber, Frances *1978*	**Genn**, Yvette *1991*
Fransman, Laurens *1979*	**Harris**, Joanne *1991*
Griffiths, Courtenay QC *1980*	**Holbrook**, Jon *1991*
	Simblet, Stephen *1991*
Luba, Jan *1980*	**Harrison**, Stephanie *1991*
Graves, Celia *1981*	**Easty**, Valerie *1992*
Jessup, Anne *1981*	**Edie**, Alastair *1992*
Cudby, Markanza *1983*	**Weatherby**, Pete *1992*
Farrell, Simon *1983*	**Husain**, Raza *1993*
Hall, Michael *1983*	**Littlewood**, Robert *1993*
Jennings, Anthony *1983*	**Menon**, Rajiv *1993*
Rahal, Ravinder *1983*	**Davies**, Liz *1994*
Cottle, Stephen *1984*	**Seddon**, Duran *1994*
Harford-Bell, Nerida *1984*	**Cragg**, Stephen *1996*
Gold, Debra *1985*	**Friedman**, Daniel *1996*

Chambers established: 1974
Opening times: 8.45 am-6.15 pm

Types of work (and number of counsel practising in that area if supplied)
Administrative 25 · Care proceedings 10 · Civil liberties 19 · Crime 24 · Crime - corporate fraud 4 · Discrimination 4 · EC and competition law 3 · Education 4 · Employment 4 · Environment 2 · Family 10 · Family provision 10 · Foreign law 2 · Housing 11 · Immigration 10 · Information technology 2 · Landlord and tenant 10 · Local government 3 · Medical negligence 4 · Mental health 3 · Personal injury 5 · Professional negligence 3

Chambers' facilities
Conference rooms, Disks accepted, E-mail

Languages spoken
Afrikaans, Dutch, French, German, Hindi, Punjabi, Sinhala, Spanish, Urdu

Fees policy
Open to discussion with clients.

Additional information

Since its inception 24 years ago this set of chambers has grown to make it one of the largest in the Temple. In the areas in which members specialise, a complete range of services can be provided, with professional and efficient back-up from the clerks and other supporting staff. The reputation of chambers rests on its high-profile public law cases, its criminal defence work and its immigration, family and housing law practices. The commitment of chambers to fostering a multi-disciplinary set has enabled it to benefit from cross-fertilisation of ideas between colleagues.

This is of particular benefit for some of the more unusual cases undertaken, but helps all practitioners to remain fresh, innovative and enthusiastic about their work. Recently the civil team has been strengthened in order to fill a gap in demand for such work as civil actions against public authorities, cases for employees and personal injury work.

The atmosphere in chambers and its client care are friendly and informal. The facilities are second to none and up-to-date; the premises have been refurbished inside and out and the latest technology is fully utilised by the administration and counsel. The demands of looking after the library have led to the employment of a librarian. The recent appointment of an administrator enables our clerks to concentrate exclusively on client care and the clerks' room is being reorganised to provide teams of clerks dedicated to the specialised areas of work.

C

---

† Recorder ‡ Assistant Recorder * Door Tenant

THE GARDEN HOUSE

14 New Square, Lincoln's Inn, London
WC2A 3SH
0171 404 6150
Fax: 0171 404 7395; DX 227 Chancery Lane

Chambers of Miss J M A Maxwell

1 GARFIELD ROAD

Battersea, London SW11 5PL
0171 228 1137
Fax: 0171 228 1137

Chambers of Mr F Shah

243A GOLDHURST TERRACE

2nd Floor, London NW6 3EP
0171 625 8455
Fax: 0171 625 4846

Chambers of Mr Y Bassa

The UK College of Family Mediators
Directory & Handbook 1998/99

- *provides expert commentary on family mediation training and professional development and includes contributions by leading family mediation professionals*

- *lists over 100 family mediation groups/services and over 950 individual family mediators by region and alphabetically*

- *gives details of all members and associates of the UK College of Family Mediators*

- *includes the UK College of Family Mediators Standards and Code of Practice*

- *gives details of all the family mediation bodies which make up the UK College of Family Mediators*

For more information call Sweet & Maxwell on 0171 449 1111

GOLDSMITH BUILDING

GOLDSMITH BUILDING

1st Floor, Temple, London EC4Y 7BL
0171 353 7881
Fax: 0171 353 5319; DX 435 London
E-mail: clerks@goldsmith-building.law.co.uk

Chambers of John Griffith Williams QC
Clerks: Edith A Robertson (Senior Clerk), Danny O'Brien (First Junior Clerk)

Griffith Williams, John QC 1968†	**Maitland Jones**, Mark 1986
	Dawes, Gordon 1989
Maguire, Michael QC 1949	**Burles**, David 1984
Somerset Jones, Eric QC 1952†	**Browne**, Julie 1989
	Hay, Deborah 1991
Llewellyn-Jones, Christopher QC 1965†	**Newton**, Claire 1992
	Lawson, Daniel 1994
Hughes, Merfyn QC 1971†	**Wright**, Sadie 1994
Farmer, Michael QC 1972†	**Rawlings**, Clive 1994
Hay, Robin 1964†	**Roe**, Thomas 1995
Martineau, Henry 1966†	**Mayhew**, Jerome 1995
Hall-Smith, Martin 1972	**Fane**, Angela 1992
Morris-Coole, Christopher 1974†	**Williams**, Wyn QC 1974†*
	Price, Gerald QC†*
Gallagher, John 1974‡	**Aubrey**, David QC*
Friel, John 1974	**Jones**, Nicholas 1970*
Calvert, Charles 1975	**Sander**, Andrew†*
Leonard, Robert 1976	**Parsley**, Charles 1973*
Routley, Patrick 1979	**Ryan**, Thomas*
Higgins, Anthony 1978	

Opening times: 8.45 am-6.30 pm

Types of work (and number of counsel practising in that area if supplied)
Administrative 5 · Admiralty 1 · Arbitration 6 · Bankruptcy 4 · Care proceedings 7 · Chancery (general) 5 · Chancery land law 2 · Civil liberties 1 · Commercial litigation 15 · Commercial property 6 · Common land 6 · Common law (general) 20 · Company and commercial 6 · Courts martial 2 · Crime 12 · Crime - corporate fraud 8 · Defamation 2 · Discrimination 1 · Education 4 · Employment 9 · Environment 2 · Family 11 · Family provision 11 · Housing 3 · Immigration 2 · Insolvency 4 · Insurance 4 · Landlord and tenant 14 · Licensing 5 · Local government 5 · Medical negligence 6 · Mental health 4

· Partnerships 5 · Personal injury 18 · Planning 3 · Professional negligence 17 · Shipping, admiralty 2 · Sports 3

Chambers' facilities
Conference rooms, Disks accepted, E-mail, Link, Internet

Languages spoken
French, Welsh

Additional information

Goldsmith Building is an established set of chambers with members at all levels of seniority. Chambers is able to provide individuals or teams of Counsel to undertake a wide variety of litigation, arbitration and advisory work. The traditional strength of chambers has been its high standard of advocacy. Chambers' work is centred on London and the South Eastern Circuit, with strong senior connections on the Wales and Chester and Northern Circuits. We provide an efficient, flexible and comprehensive legal service with established specialist practice groups.

Chambers has eight Practice Groups, namely, Personal Injury, Professional Negligence, Crime, Family, Business Law, Landlord and Tenant, Public and Administrative Law and Employment. These groups form the core of the infrastructure of chambers. The groups meet on a regular basis and continuing education is one of their objectives. In addition to the practice groups, chambers also has specialists in the areas of environmental law, insolvency, and commercial fraud.

Goldsmith Building has developed a programme to provide seminars on a range of legal topics, and as authorised providers of continuing education by the Law Society, all seminars carry a CPD rating. Chambers publishes a range of newsletters, which contain news and information about chambers and comments on current developments in the law.

Chambers has an experienced clerking team and the clerks are always ready to advise on suitable counsel and fee levels along with liaising with courts on the listing of cases. Members of chambers and the clerks are aware of the needs of clients and strive to give the highest quality of service. A Chambers Charter has been adopted which details the level of service you can expect when you instruct a member of chambers or deal with the clerks. More specific information, fee levels, chambers brochures and other chambers publications are available from the clerks.

GOLDSMITH CHAMBERS

Ground Floor, Goldsmith Building, Temple, London EC4Y 7BL
0171 353 6802/3/4/5
Fax: 0171 583 5255/427 6847; DX 376 London, Chancery Lane
E-mail: celiamonksfield@btinternet.com

Chambers of Philip Sapsford QC
Clerk: Celia Monksfield

Sapsford, Philip QC 1974‡	Hynes, Paul 1987
Hall, Jonathan D QC 1975†*	Smith, David 1988
Morrish, Peter 1962	Evans, Charles 1988
Torrance, Hugh 1956	Williams, Richard 1988
Meikle, Robert 1970	Calway, Mark 1989
Harkus, George 1975	James, Grahame 1989
Leigh, Edward 1977	Singh, Gurdial 1989
Barnett, Diane 1978	Fitzgibbon, Neil 1989
Burrow, John 1980	Hargreaves, Ben 1989
Woodall, Peter 1983	Katan, Jonathan 1990
Hulme, John 1983	Moss, Norman 1990
O'Leary, Michele 1983	George, Michael 1990
Whelan, Roma 1984	McLevy, Tracey 1993
Norris, James 1984	Brennan, Christopher 1995
Dabbs, David 1984	Allen, Douglas 1995
Morris, Michael 1984	Foster, Julien 1995
Wehrle, Jacqueline 1984	Cadman, David 1996
Buswell, Richard 1985	Fish, David QC 1973*
Munonyedi, Ifey 1985	Jakens, Claire 1988*
Szerard, Andrei 1986	Devitt, Stephen 1994*
Day, Dorian 1987	

C

GOLDSWORTH CHAMBERS

11 Gray's Inn Square, First Floor, London WC1R 5JD
0171 405 7117
Fax: 0171 831 8308; DX 1057 Chancery Lane
Out of hours telephone: 0421 868 653
Clerk: tba (Correspondence to: Management Committee)

Kwiatkowski, Feliks *1977*	**Gray**, Kären *1995*
Butt, Romasa *1985*	**Gandhi**, Paulene *1995*
Marks, Peter *1987*	**Pimm**, Geoffrey *1952**
Middleton, Sean *1991*	**Goldsworth**, John *1965**
Harvey, Jayne *1992*	**Whitworth**, Peter *1946**
Malecka, Dr Mary *1994*	**Scrantom**, Timothy *1995**
Ogun, Kemi *1994*	

9 GOUGH SQUARE

GOUGH
SQUARE

London EC4A 3DE
0171 353 5371
Fax: 0171 353 1344; DX 439 London, Chancery Lane

Chambers of Jeremy Roberts QC
Practice Director: Joanna Poulton

Roberts, Jeremy QC *1965†*	**Naik**, Gaurang *1985*
Rogers, John QC *1963†*	**Levy**, Jacob *1986*
Brent, Michael QC *1961†*	**Loades**, Jonathan *1986*
Upward, Patrick QC *1972‡*	**Verdan**, Alexander *1987*
Burrell, Gary QC *1977†*	**Buckett**, Edwin *1988*
Foy, John *1969*	**Wheeler**, Andrew *1988*
Reddihough, John *1969†*	**Hales**, Sally-Ann *1988*
Baillie, Andrew *1970†*	**Glynn**, Stephen *1990*
Gerrey, David *1975†*	**Sinclair**, Jane *1990*
Joyce, Michael *1976*	**Jones**, Philip *1990*
Davies, Trevor *1978*	**Padley**, Clare *1991*
Ferguson, Frederick *1978*	**Tughan**, John *1991*
Aldous, Grahame *1979*	**Crowther**, Jeremy *1991*
Macleod, Duncan *1980*	**Downey**, Aileen *1991*
Wilson, Christopher *1980*	**Ashmole**, Timothy *1993*
Hillier, Nicolas *1982*	**Begley**, Laura *1993*
Hiorns, Roger *1983*	**Neilson**, Louise *1994*
Carr, Simon *1984*	**Stephenson**, Christopher *1994*
Ritchie, Andrew *1985*	

Chambers established: 1940
Opening times: 8 am-6.30 pm

Types of work (and number of counsel practising in that area if supplied)
Admiralty 1 · Care proceedings 9 · Commercial litigation 4 · Commercial property 4 · Common law (general) 30 · Company and commercial 4 · Crime 15 · Crime - corporate fraud 8 · Family 9 · Family provision 9 · Landlord and tenant 5 · Medical negligence 10 · Personal injury 25

Chambers' facilities
Conference rooms, Disks accepted, Disabled access

Languages spoken
French, German, Hebrew

Additional information

The chambers: We are a long-established general common law set specialising in particular in personal injury, medical and professional negligence, serious fraud and family work.

We are noted for our friendly yet commercial approach which we believe enhances our ability to provide realistic advice to our clients. Focused along the lines of specialist teams, we draw upon the considerable depth of knowledge and expertise held in chambers through regular team meetings.

Our facilities are modern and up-to-date, including disabled facilities, large dedicated conference rooms and full computerisation. We are professionally managed by a qualified Practice Director who is happy to discuss any aspects of our service and in particular to recommend suitable counsel. A brochure is available on request.

Work undertaken:
Personal injury: We can offer experts in complex multi-party actions, industrial diseases, RSI, deafness, lifting, marine accidents, etc, representing either plaintiffs or defendants. Special payment terms are negotiable for union or insurance-backed claims. All members of chambers have agreed to accept conditional fee work and where appropriate single agreements covering individual firms can be negotiated.

Medical negligence: We can offer true experts who are renowned for being sensitive to the issues in these cases yet are tenacious advocates and negotiators. Our experience for both plaintiffs and defendants includes brain injuries, birth defects, failed sterilisations, surgical and non-surgical maltreatment.

Professional negligence: Members of our professional negligence team regularly advise on and appear in cases involving all aspects of professional negligence, but in particular actions involving solicitors, accountants, insurance brokers and surveyors.

Serious fraud: Chambers has some of the country's leading fraud practitioners. More than 12 members of chambers regularly prosecute for the SFO and for CPS HQ, as well as defending some of the most complex fraud cases such as Blue Arrow and Nissan. We can provide experts on advance fee frauds, city frauds, pension frauds, etc.

General crime: The crime team has established an enviable reputation in both prosecuting and defending general crime on the M and O Circuit, in particular at Northampton, Luton, St Albans, Aylesbury and Birmingham Crown Courts. In addition, members of chambers regularly appear in the major London Crown Courts.

Family: A full range of family work is undertaken. We have particular expertise in local authority child care work and regularly appear in the High Courts on contested family matters.

Other work: Chambers also has smaller specialist groups working in such areas as landlord and tenant, insurance, contract, civil actions against police, employment, judicial review and inheritance.

GOUGH SQUARE CHAMBERS

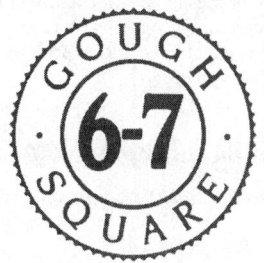

6-7 Gough Square, London EC4A 3DE
0171 353 0924
Fax: 0171 353 2221; DX 476 London
E-mail: gsc@goughsq.co.uk
URL: http://www.goughsq.co.uk
Out of hours telephone: 0860 219162

Chambers of Fred Philpott
Clerks: Bob Weekes (Senior Clerk), Paul Messenger; Chambers' Administrator: Elizabeth Owen-Ward

Philpott, Fred *1974*	**Smith,** Julia *1988*
Sayer, Peter *1975*	**Gun Cuninghame,** Julian *1989*
Andrews, Claire *1979*	
Hibbert, William *1979*	**Katrak,** Cyrus *1991*
Stancombe, Barry *1983*	**Vines,** Anthony *1993*
Goulding, Jonathan *1984*	**Cogswell,** Frederica *1995*
Neville, Stephen *1986*	**MacDonald,** Iain *1996*

Chambers established: 1986
Opening times: 8.30 am-6.15 pm

Types of work (and number of counsel practising in that area if supplied)
Administrative · Banking 4 · Bankruptcy 4 · Chancery land law 4 · Commercial litigation 4 · Company and commercial 4 · Consumer Law 10 · Crime - corporate fraud 7 · Employment · Entertainment · Financial services · Food 5 · Insolvency 4 · Landlord and tenant 5 · Medical negligence · Partnerships · Personal injury · Private international · Professional negligence · Sale and carriage of goods 4

Chambers' facilities
Conference rooms, Disks accepted, Disabled access, E-mail

Languages spoken
French

C

Fees policy
The senior clerk will be pleased to provide an indication of fees in advance and will negotiate the fees depending upon each case. A flexible approach is maintained and, if preferred, hourly rates can be agreed.

34 GRAHAM ROAD

Wood Green, London N15 3NL
0181 889 7671
Fax: 0181 889 7671

Chambers of Mr P S Hall

GRAY'S INN CHAMBERS

1st Floor, Gray's Inn Chambers, Gray's Inn, London WC1R 5JA
0171 831 5344
Fax: 0171 242 7799; DX 182 London, Chancery Lane
E-mail: s.mcblain@btinternet.com
Out of hours telephone: 0973 132347
Clerks: Spencer McBlain (01245 280 213) (Senior Clerk), James Parker (0181 949 0786)

White, Geoffrey 1985*	Akinsanya, Stephen 1993
Rattigan, Paul 1991	Kashmiri, Sophia 1994
O'Sullivan, Michael 1991*	Owen, Helen 1994
Gubbay, Jeffrey 1992	Millard, Martin 1995
Counihan, Caroline 1994*	Rahman, Sami 1996
Bergenthal, Ronnie 1993	Myers, Keith 1996
Burnett, Iain 1993	Selby, Lawrence 1997

Types of work (and number of counsel practising in that area if supplied)
Administrative · Arbitration · Care proceedings · Chancery (general) · Civil liberties · Common law (general) · Courts martial · Crime · Crime - corporate fraud · Discrimination · Employment · Family · Housing · Immigration · Landlord and tenant · Licensing · Medical negligence · Mental health · Personal injury · Professional negligence

Chambers' facilities
Conference rooms, Disks accepted

Languages spoken
French, German, Hebrew, Hindi, Italian, Punjabi, Spanish, Urdu, Yoruba

GRAY'S INN CHAMBERS

Gray's Inn, London WC1R 5JA
0171 404 1111
Fax: 0171 430 1522/1050; DX 0074 London, Chancery Lane

Chambers of Brian P Jubb
Clerk: Paul Clinnick

Jubb, Brian 1971	Dashwood, Robert 1984
Rodger, Caroline 1968	Perkins, Alistair 1986
Brann, Elisabeth 1970	Cox, Nigel 1986
Clough, Richard 1971	Lewis, Ian 1989
Higson-Smith, Gillian 1973	Seymour, Judit 1990
Malcolm, Rozanna 1974	Clarke, Joanna 1993
Houston, David 1976	Gray, Justin 1993
Haywood, Janette 1977	Ahmed, Amina 1995
Redgrave, Diane 1977	Metaxa, William 1995
Harding, Cherry 1978	Bayati, Charlotte 1995
Wingert, Rachel 1980	Fletcher-Cooke, Sir Charles
Marks, Gillian 1981	QC 1938*
MacGregor, Heather 1982	Hinchcliffe, Doreen 1953*
Mott, Geoffrey 1982	Oliver, Lindsey 1977*
Cowen, Jonathan 1983	den Brinker, Melanie 1984*
Compton, Timothy 1984	Freeman, Marilyn 1986*
Nazareth, Melanie 1984	Stonor, Nicholas 1993*
Weiniger, Noah 1984	

Chambers established: 1989
Opening times: 8.30 am-6.15 pm

Types of work (and number of counsel practising in that area if supplied)
Administrative 6 · Agriculture · Bankruptcy · Care proceedings 21 · Chancery land law · Common law (general) 6 · Courts martial · Crime · Education · Family 19 · Family provision 5 · Housing · Immigration 3 · Landlord and tenant 3 · Licensing · Local government 2 · Partnerships · Personal injury · Professional negligence

Chambers' facilities
Conference rooms, Disks accepted

Languages spoken
Arabic, French, Hebrew

Fees policy
Each case is considered individually, taking into account its complexity, the issues involved, the consequences of any litigation and the seniority of the member involved.

Additional information

Gray's Inn Chambers is committed to providing the highest standard of advice and advocacy over an extensive range of legal and practical issues. Chambers specialise in all aspects of family law including adoption (UK and foreign), international child abduction, Children Act proceedings (public and private), divorce, matrimonial finance and inheritance. Chambers is also well established in the fields of administrative law and immigration. Chancery, commercial and general common law work is also undertaken, including landlord and tenant, housing, personal injury, professional and medical negligence, building, licensing, tribunals and crime. Several members of chambers have written books and regularly contribute academic papers within their areas of practice.

1 GRAY'S INN SQUARE, CHAMBERS OF THE BARONESS SCOTLAND OF ASTHAL QC

1 Gray's Inn Square, London WC1R 5AG
0171 405 3000
Fax: 0171 405 9942; DX 238 London, Chancery Lane
E-mail: clerks@onegrays.demon.co.uk
Other comms: Mobile: Senior Clerk–0468 121113, Clerks–0836 655633
Out of hours telephone: 0468 121113/0836 655633

Chambers of The Baroness Scotland of Asthal QC
Clerks: Steven Ashton (Senior Clerk), Mark Venables, Matthew Laffan;
Administrators: Michelle Cross, Deborah Hayns

Scotland, Patricia QC *1977*†	Klein, Leonora *1989*
Downing, John *1958*	Murray, Carole *1989*
Waylen, Barnaby *1968*†	Rodham, Susan *1989*
Beckhough, Nigel *1976*	Gupta, Teertha *1990*
Main Thompson, Dermot *1977*	Seitler, Deborah *1991*
	Morgan, Helen *1993*
Gold, Jeremy *1977*	O'Donovan, John *1993*
Newman, Philip *1977*	Fisher, Sandra *1993*
Hoyle, Mark *1978*	Wilshire, Simon *1994*
Hingston, Tessa *1978*	Evans, Clare *1995*
Frank, Ivor *1979*	Alexander, Dominic *1995*
Setright, Henry *1979*	Archer, Christopher *1996*
Firth-Butterfield, Kay *1980*	Matthewson, Scott *1996*
Lillington, Simon *1980*	Stanger, Nina *1965**
Cox, Kharin *1982*	King, Michael *1971**
Jenkins, Kim *1982*	Kennedy, Ian *1974**
D'Arcy, Leo *1983*	Harris, Paul *1976**
Hughes, Gareth *1985*	Schwarzschild, Maimon *1987**
Myers, Simon *1987*	
Davey, Kate *1988*	Cleave, Barbara *1989**
Meredith, Christopher *1988*	Chatterjee, Charles *1992**

Chambers established: 1979
Opening times: 8.30 am-6.30 pm

Types of work (and number of counsel practising in that area if supplied)
Arbitration 3 · Banking 2 · Care proceedings 11 · Crime 16 · Crime - corporate fraud 3

---

† Recorder ‡ Assistant Recorder * Door Tenant

· Entertainment 2 · Environment 3 · Family 13
· Foreign law 3 · Immigration 2 · International
trade 4 · Landlord and tenant 4 · Licensing 5
· Local government 3 · Medical negligence 2
· Mental health 2 · Sale and carriage of goods 5
· Shipping, admiralty 3

Chambers' facilities
Conference rooms, E-mail

Languages spoken
Arabic, Bengali, French, German, Hebrew,
Italian, Mandarin, Spanish

Fees policy
Fees will be negotiated by the clerk according to
the individual details of each case. We are happy
to negotiate fixed hourly rates and/or standard
fees for particular case types.

Additional information

Number One Gray's Inn Square was established
in 1979 and offers practitioners expert in:

Family and Matrimonial: All aspects of family
and matrimonial work including injunctions,
divorce and nullity, ancillary relief, international
children's cases including: international child
adbuction, child abuse, wardship, residence
and contact, adoption and care proceedings.

Criminal: Criminal law at all levels, but
especially serious crime including all offences of
violence, sexual offences, robbery, burglary,
theft and drug offences. White-collar crime
including mortgage, copyright and insurance
frauds.

Civil and Commercial: All types of civil work,
including contract, negligence, international
trade, arbitration, private international law,
insurance, shipping, commodities, enforcement
of judgments, state immunity, general
commercial, commercial Chancery,
interlocutory injunctions (especially Marevas
and Anton Pillers), entertainment law,
professional negligence, personal injury,
housing, landlord and tenant, medical
negligence, immigration, licensing, Official
Referee's business, planning law and
professional disciplinary work.

**Judicial Review, Public and Private
Inquiries:** Child abuse, mental health, housing,
local authorities and professional conduct.

Foreign Laws: Advice is offered on Arab and
Islamic law, and on the law of the People's
Republic of China. These specialists are
available to act as expert witnesses. Door

tenants practise in Australia, USA and Hong
Kong.

Publications include *The Law of International
Trade* (Hoyle); *Mareva Injunctions and
Related Orders* (Hoyle); *The Mixed Courts of
Egypt* (Hoyle); *Ridley on Carriage of Goods*
(D'Arcy); Schmitthoff's *Export Trade* (10th
edn) (D'Arcy, Cleave & Murray).

Judicial appointments include a Deputy High
Court Judge, a Recorder and an Immigration
Adjudicator.

1 GRAY'S INN SQUARE

Ground Floor, London WC1R 5AA
0171 405 8946
Fax: 0171 405 1617; DX 1013 London

Chambers of C W Teper
Practice manager: Jacqueline Chase

Also at: 10 Gray's Inn Square

Teper, Carl *1980*	**Braganza**, Nicola *1992*
Money, Ernle *1958*	**Jegarajah**, Shivani *1993*
Weisman, Malcolm *1961†*	**Cox**, Buster *1993*
Cruickshank, Cynthia *1968*	**Nassar**, Victoria *1994*
Tan, Cheng Sioh *1970*	**Walker**, James *1994*
Johnson, Alan *1971*	**Wayne**, Nicholas *1994*
Curwen, David *1982**	**Rhodes**, Colin *1994*
Gelbart, Geoffrey *1982*	**Ali**, Zafar *1994*
King, John *1983*	**McElroy**, Joanne *1995*
Agbaje, Edward *1984*	**Lucas**, Phillip *1995*
Simons, Angela *1985*	**Hargan**, Carl *1995*
Quinn, Joseph *1987*	**Brown**, Grace *1995*
Williams, Chris *1988*	**Lawson**, Matthew *1995*
Alder, Claire *1988*	**Cole-Wilson**, Lois *1995*
Berry, Nicholas *1988*	**Winter**, Melanie *1996*
Coates, John *1988*	**Kay**, Nicola *1996*
Bromfield, Colin *1988*	**Lennon**, Jonathan *1997*
Morris, Deborah *1989*	**Grounds**, Christopher *1977**
Kayne, Adrian *1989*	**Rufus-Isaacs**, Lord
Dias, Asoka *1989*	Alexander *1982**
Charalambous, Dino *1990*	**Dehn**, Guy *1982**
Greene, Richard *1990**	**Watson**, Andrew *1982**
Fitzpatrick, Edward *1990*	**Mensah**, Barbara *1984**
Shaw, Noel *1991*	**Clarke**, Jeffrey *1985**
Salter, Sibby *1991*	**Samwell-Smith**, Rosemary
Maryniak, Andrew *1991**	*1986**
Attridge, Steven *1991*	**Spencer**, John *1988**
Gloag, Angus *1992*	**Langley**, Caroline *1989**
Tippett, Giles *1992*	**Bhattacharyya**, Ardhendu
Wetton, Paul *1992*	*1974**

Chambers established: 1971
Opening times: 8.30 am-6.30 pm

† Recorder ‡ Assistant Recorder * Door Tenant

Types of work (and number of counsel practising in that area if supplied)

Care proceedings 4 · Chancery (general) 2 · Civil actions against the police 3 · Common law (general) 22 · Crime 33 · Crime - corporate fraud 5 · Discrimination 8 · Ecclesiastical 1 · Employment 7 · Family 8 · Family provision 6 · Housing 2 · Immigration 8 · Insolvency 3 · Landlord and tenant 8 · Licensing 4 · Medical negligence 1 · Mental health 3 · Parliamentary 1 · Personal injury 9 · Professional negligence 5 · Sale and carriage of goods 2

Chambers' facilities

Video conferences, Disks accepted, Disabled access, E-mail

Languages spoken

Afrikaans, Arabic, French, German, Greek, Hindi, Hokkein, Italian, Krio, Malay, Punjabi, Spanish, Swahili, Urdu

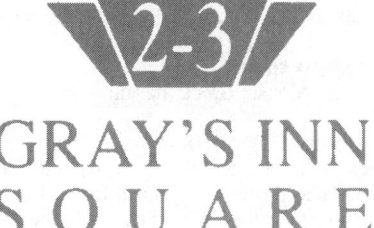

2-3 GRAY'S INN SQUARE

GRAY'S INN SQUARE

2-3 Gray's Inn Square, Gray's Inn, London WC1R 5JH
0171 242 4986
Fax: 0171 405 1166; DX 316 London, Chancery Lane
E-mail: chambers@2-3graysinnsquare.co.uk

Chambers of Anthony F B Scrivener QC
Clerks: Martin Hart, Stuart Pullum

Scrivener, Anthony QC 1958†	Albutt, Ian 1981
	Gasztowicz, Steven 1981
Eyre, Sir Graham QC 1954†	Cook, Mary 1982
Spence, Malcolm QC 1958†	Ellis, Morag 1984
Ground, Patrick QC 1960	Findlay, James 1984
Cochrane, Christopher QC 1965†	Astaniotis, Katerine 1985
	Bedford, Michael 1985
Porten, Anthony QC 1969†	Kolvin, Philip 1985
Dinkin, Anthony QC 1968†	Bird, Simon 1987
Pugh, Vernon QC 1969†	Bhose, Ranjit 1989
Wolton, Harry QC 1969†	Carrington, Gillian 1990
Lowe, Mark QC 1972	Green, Robin 1992
Straker, Timothy QC 1977‡	Murray, Harriet 1992
Haines, John 1967†	Miller, Peter 1993
Rundell, Richard 1971†	Ponter, Ian 1993
Stephenson, Geoffrey 1971	Coppel, Philip 1994
Lamming, David 1972	Cosgrove, Thomas 1994
Trevelyan-Thomas, Adrian 1974	Ground, Richard 1994
	Beglan, Wayne 1996
Nardecchia, Nicholas 1974	Lintott, David 1996
Davey, Tobias 1977	Easton, Jonathan 1996
Stoker, Graham 1977	

Chambers established: Before 1914
Opening times: 8 am-7 pm

Types of work (and number of counsel practising in that area if supplied)

Administrative 27 · Arbitration 5 · Bankruptcy 3 · Care proceedings 3 · Commercial litigation 12 · Common law (general) 9 · Construction 7 · Crime 9 · Discrimination 6 · Employment 12 · Environment 15 · Information technology 2 · Landlord and tenant 11 · Licensing 5 · Local government 38 · Partnerships 2 · Personal injury 6 · Planning 38 · Professional negligence 8 · Sale and carriage of goods 7 · Town and country planning 38

C

Chambers' facilities
Conference rooms, Video conferences, Disks accepted, Disabled access, Direct-dial telephone, Voice-mail, Individual e-mail boxes

Languages spoken
French, German, Greek, Italian

Fees policy
Fees will be negotiated with the clerks depending on the case and the seniority and experience of the selected counsel. The clerks will always strive to accommodate the particular requirements of each client, and flexible terms, including all-in fees, fixed rates and bulk billing can be arranged.

Additional information

The Chambers

2-3 Gray's Inn Square is a long-established set of Chambers. It provides a comprehensive, in-depth service in all areas relating to local government and planning, including common law actions involving government agencies.

Specialisms covered by various members of Chambers:

1. Planning, including all types of planning and highway inquiries.

2. Administrative law, including judicial review applications and tribunal hearings.

3. Environmental and public health law, including EPA hearings, waste and pollution control, and statutory nuisances.

4. Other local government matters, including public health, compulsory purchase, highways, local government finance, housing law and rating.

5. Prosecuting and defending local government prosecutions, including breach of planning/listed building control, EPA enforcement, and offences relating to pollution, trade descriptions, weights and measures, food safety and building regulations.

6. Contractual claims and tortious disputes involving governmental bodies, including building and computing claims and arbitrations, and sale of goods/services contracts.

7. Employment law including unfair and wrongful dismissal claims, discrimination claims and professional disciplinary hearings (doctors, dentists *etc*).

8. Landlord and tenant law, particularly leases under the *Housing Act 1985* and restraint of unneighbourly conduct.

9. Personal injury actions.

10. Privy Council appeals.

Counsel are available at all levels of experience. Junior tenants are available at short notice for all magistrates' court, county court and tribunal hearings, as well as for procedural applications. Members of Chambers work in all parts of England and Wales. Various members of Chambers also practise or are admitted in other jurisdictions.

Work will be provided on diskette or to an e-mail address where requested. Chambers can provide documents in most word-processing formats.

Further details about Chambers and its members are set out in its brochure: the clerks will send a copy on request.

2 GRAY'S INN SQUARE CHAMBERS

Gray's Inn Square, London WC1R 5AA
0171 242 0328/405 1317
Fax: 0171 405 3082; DX 43 London, Chancery
Lane
E-mail: clerks@2gis.co.uk
URL: http://www.2gis.co.uk

Chambers of Giles Eyre
Clerks: Bill Harris (Senior Clerk), Sue Reding, Emma Wallace; Practice manager: Paul Simpson

Eyre, Giles *1974*	King, Fawzia *1985*
Leighton, Peter *1966*	Collaco Moraes, Francis
Knight, Keith *1969*	*1985*
Robson, John *1974*	Bhakar, Surinder *1986*
Cross, Edward *1975*	Dixon, Sorrel *1987*
Robinson, Richard *1977*	Baldock, Susan *1988*
Fortune, Peter *1978*	Roberts, Adrian *1988*
McConnell, Christopher	Whalan, Mark *1988*
1979	Priestley, Rebecca *1989*
Hughes, David *1980*	Woods, Terence *1989*
Mathew, Nergis-Anne *1981*	Brown, Joanne *1990*
Dulovic, Milan *1982*	Rivers, Andrea *1990*
Rayson, Jane *1982*	Watkins, Myles *1990*
Haven, Kevin *1982*	Rice, Christopher *1991*
Church, John *1984*	Arney, James *1992*
Marks, Jacqueline *1984*	Drayton, Henry *1993*
Moore, Anthony *1984*	Barnett, Daniel *1993*
Posner, Gabrielle *1984*	Parr, Judith *1994*

See the *Index of Languages Spoken* **in Part G to locate a chambers where a particular language is spoken, or find an individual who speaks a particular language.**

3 GRAY'S INN SQUARE

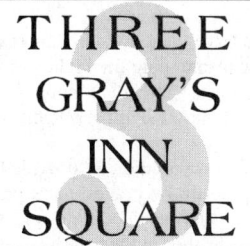

Ground Floor, London WC1R 5AH
0171 520 5600
Fax: 0171 520 5607; DX 1043 London,
Chancery Lane
E-mail: gis3@btinternet.com
Out of hours telephone: 0410 354598

Chambers of Rock Tansey QC
Clerks: Graham Islin, Guy Williams, Marc King

Tansey, Rock QC *1966*†	Keleher, Paul *1980*
Perry, John QC *1975*†	Mendelle, Paul *1981*
Radford, Nadine QC *1974*†	Barrett, Penelope *1982*
Kay, Steven QC *1977*‡	Dein, Jeremy *1982*
Carter-Stephenson, George	Pentol, Simon *1982*
1975	Maley, Bill *1982*
Taylor, William QC (Scot)	Redhead, Leroy *1982*
QC *1990*	Jobling, Ian *1982*
Hooper, David *1971*	Kaul, Kaly *1983*
Allan, Colin *1971*	Hammond, Karen *1985*
Farrington, David *1972*	Wells, Colin *1987*
Jaffa, Ronald *1974*	Levitt, Alison *1988*
Keany, Brendan *1974*	Harris, Sarah *1989*
Mitchell, Jonathan *1974*	Valley, Helen *1990*
Statman, Philip *1975*‡	Piercy, Arlette *1990*
Gledhill, Michael *1976*‡	Akuwudike, Emma *1991*
Fortson, Rudi *1976*	De Bertodano, Sylvia *1993*
Ellis, Diana *1978*‡	Furlong, Richard *1994*
Offenbach, Roger *1978*	Byrnes, Aisling *1994*
Beyts, Chester *1978*	Smith, Tyrone *1994*
Anthony, Robert *1979*	Caldwell, Peter *1995*

Chambers established: 1975

**Types of work (and number of counsel
practising in that area if supplied)**
Crime 43 · Crime - corporate fraud 43

Chambers' facilities
Conference rooms, Video conferences, Disks
accepted, E-mail, Voice-mail for all Members of
Chambers

Additional information

Chambers

C

---

† Recorder ‡ Assistant Recorder * Door Tenant

3 Gray's Inn Square is a specialist Criminal Defence Set which aims to ensure that everyone has equal access to the best representation.

Chambers has earned a reputation as a leader in its field by maintaining the highest standards of professionalism, integrity, commitment and both accessibility and approachability.

First-class representation is provided at every level of seniority by practitioners who appear regularly in 'high profile cases' and who offer experience in the conduct of all categories of criminal case including European Human Rights, International Criminal Tribunal, (International) Terrorism and War Crimes, Murder, Serious Fraud, Organised Crime, International Drugs Trafficking/allied Money Laundering and offences of Extreme/Sexual Violence.

Within this framework there is a positive commitment to legally-aided clients and where appropriate, pro bono work is undertaken.

Particular expertise is provided in all aspects of Appellate Work, including Judicial Review and Privy Council. Further, there is experience in the conduct of Civil Cases, especially Actions against the Police and allied issues and Mental Health Review Tribunals.

In recent years Chambers has presented lectures to solicitors and practitioners generally, concerning the effect of significant changes in Criminal Legislation. Some members have also lectured nationally and internationally to and on behalf of Legal/Human Rights organisations on Drug Trafficking and International War Crimes.

Publications
Rudi Forston: *Law on the Misuse of Drugs*; Sweet & Maxwell Practical Research Papers - Crime:
(a) *Pre-Trial Disclosure* - Rock Tansey QC and Paul Keleher
(b) *Identification by Police Officers* - Ronald Jaffa
(c) *Pre-Trial Disclosure* - Colin Well.

Foreign connections
Rock Tansey QC and Steven Kay QC have founded the European Criminal Bar Association in order to advance issues of mutual concern for European Criminal Defence Lawyers.

Rock Tansey QC is the First Chairman of the ECBA and organised its inaugural conference at the European Commission for Human Rights, Strasbourg.

Steven Kay QC, Defence Counsel in the first International Criminal Tribunal for the former Yugoslavia, undertakes European Human Rights cases.

John Perry QC also practises in Bermuda and is a member of the West Indian Bar.

4-5 GRAY'S INN SQUARE

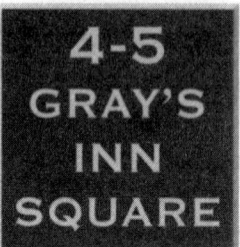

Ground Floor, Gray's Inn, London
WC1R 5AY
0171 404 5252
Fax: 0171 242 7803; DX 1029 London
E-mail: chambers@4-5graysinnsquare.co.uk

Chambers of Miss Elizabeth Appleby QC, The Hon Michael J Beloff QC
Clerks: Michael Kaplan, Mark Regan; Administrator: Barbara Morris; Chambers Director: Anthony Wells, Chambers Operations Manager: Miriam Don

Appleby, Elizabeth QC 1965†	**Oldham,** Jane 1985
	Stinchcombe, Paul 1985
Beloff, Michael QC 1967†	**Aaron,** Sam 1986
Wade, William QC 1946	**Humphreys,** Richard 1986
Flather, Gary QC 1962†	**Sharma,** Kishore 1986
Mole, David QC 1970†	**Lewis,** Clive 1987
Ash, Brian QC 1975	**Ramsden,** James 1987
Isaacs, Stuart QC 1975‡	**Hill,** Thomas 1988
Ouseley, Duncan QC 1973†	**Singh,** Rabinder 1989
Fox, Hazel QC 1950	**Linden,** Thomas 1989
Griffiths, Robert QC 1974	**Moore,** Sarah 1990
Newberry, Clive QC 1978	**Brown,** Paul 1991
Steel, John QC 1978	**Mountfield,** Helen 1991
Stone, Gregory QC 1976	**Tabachnik,** Andrew 1991
Booth, Cherie QC 1976‡	**Hunt,** Murray 1992
Spearman, Richard QC 1977	**Wolfe,** David 1992
Campbell, Robin 1967	**Fraser-Urquhart,** Andrew 1993
Huskinson, Nicholas 1971‡	
Chichester, Julian 1977	**Barav,** Amihud 1993
Hobson, John 1980	**Steyn,** Karen 1995
Corner, Timothy 1981	**Demetriou,** Marie-Eleni 1995
McManus, Richard 1982	**Davies,** Sarah-Jane 1996
Kerr, Tim 1983	**Moffett,** Jonathan 1996
Malek, Hodge 1983	**Sharland,** Andrew 1996
Village, Peter 1983	**Strachan,** James 1996
Havey, Peter 1984	

† Recorder ‡ Assistant Recorder * Door Tenant

Chambers established: 1936
Opening times: 8 am-7 pm

Types of work (and number of counsel practising in that area if supplied)

Administrative 25 · Arbitration 6 · Aviation 6 · Banking 5 · Civil liberties 6 · Commercial 20 · Competition 2 · Crime - corporate fraud 3 · Defamation 4 · Discrimination 16 · EC and competition law 10 · Education 15 · Employment 19 · Environment 25 · Housing 26 · Immigration 5 · Insurance 6 · Insurance/reinsurance 20 · Landlord and tenant 3 · Local government 33 · Parliamentary 10 · Professional negligence 3 · Public international 2 · Shipping, admiralty 2 · Sports 4 · Telecommunications 2 · Town and country planning 25

Chambers' facilities

Conference rooms, Disks accepted, E-mail, Facilities for the disabled

Languages spoken

French, German, Greek, Spanish

Fees policy

Clerk will quote fees on request.

Additional information

Chambers offers a wide range of advisory and advocacy services, in particular in the areas of public, environmental, commercial, and EC law. Silks and juniors are available in all areas of judicial review, of local government, town planning, banking, insurance, and international trade. Individual members are specialists in employment, landlord and tenant, air, parliamentary, discrimination, human rights, immigration, education, rating, housing, extradition, professional negligence, compensation, compulsory purchase, libel, tax, and commercial fraud law.

Members of chambers apply their skill and expertise acquired in one speciality to other fields; in particular at the boundaries of public, EC, and commercial law.

Barristers appear in all domestic courts and public inquiries, the Privy Council, the European Court of Justice and the European Court of Human Rights, arbitration, tribunals, and in other courts worldwide. Members have, between them, appeared in thousands of reported cases and include deputy High Court judges, recorders of the crown court, past and present officers of specialist bar associations, holders of Treasury appointments, DTI inspectors, members of international tribunals and commissions, ICC arbitrators, counsel to major public inquiries, and keynote speakers at domestic and international law conferences.

Michael Beloff QC is President of Trinity College, Oxford.

Several members of chambers are authors and editors of legal textbooks and commentaries.

Michael Beloff QC is the author of *The Sex Discrimination Act* (Butterworths, 1976); *Halsbury's Laws* (4th edn) Vol 45 *Time*; a contributor to *Public Law, Current Legal Problems* and *The Modern Law Review*; and contributing editor to *Judicial Review* (Butterworths).

Professor Sir William Wade QC is the author of *Wade on Administrative Law* (7th edn).

Stuart Isaacs QC is the author of *EEC Banking Law* (Lloyd's of London Press, 1985 and 1990); and *Banking and the Competition Law of the EEC* (Lloyd's of London Press, 1978); and consultant editor of Butterworths' *EEC Case Citator*.

Sam Aaron SC is the consultant editor of *S African Company Law Journal* and *S African Insurance Law Journal*; and a contributor to the *S African Journal on International Commercial Arbitration*.

Robin Campbell is the former joint editor of *Lumley's Public Health*.

Nicholas Huskinson is the former assistant editor of *Woodfall's Landlord and Tenant* (28th edn).

Richard McManus and Peter Havey are contributors to *Paget's Law of Banking* (Butterworths, 10th edn) and Peter Havey is a contributor to the *Journal of International Banking Law* (ESC Publications).

Chambers has produced a book *Education and The Courts* (Sweet & Maxwell, 1998) written by Richard McManus, with contributions by Cherie Booth QC, Clive Lewis, Murray Hunt and Sarah-Jane Davies.

Hodge Malek is the co-author of *Discovery* (Sweet & Maxwell, 1992).

Richard Humphreys, Rabinder Singh and Murray Hunt have been co-editors of *Crown Office Digest*. Rabinder Singh is a contributor to *Public Law* and *Family Law*. He is the author of

The Future of Human Rights in the United Kingdom (Hart Publishing, 1997).

Clive Lewis is the author of *Judicial Remedies in Public Law* (Sweet & Maxwell, 1992), *Remedies and the Enforcement of EC Law* (Sweet & Maxwell, 1995) and a contributor to the *Cambridge Law Journal* and *Public Law*.

Sarah Moore is a contributor to the *Public Law* and Butterworths' *EEC Case Citator* and co-editor of the *European Law Monitor*. She was until 1996 law clerk to Judge Bellamy at the European Court.

Helen Mountfield is a contributor to *Commercial Lawyer* and she, together with Murray Hunt, is joint editor of *European Human Rights Law Review*. Murray Hunt is the Author of *Using Human Rights Law in English Courts* (Hart Publishing, 1997).

Associate tenants include academics of international reputation, among them Sir David Williams QC and Professor G Treitel QC and lawyers from France, Belgium, Australia, Singapore and Bermuda. Dr Ami Barav Professor at the University of Oxford is an associate tenant and will practise from chambers in European Community law.

Chambers formed an academic panel of distinguished legal scholars in 1991 that provides a unique research facility and maintains the chambers' close links with the academic community.

Chambers has established formal links with the Public Law Project and Liberty in 1994 to provide pro bono services to both organisations. Areas of expertise of individual members are included in chambers' brochure.

6 GRAY'S INN SQUARE

Gray's Inn, London WC1R 5AZ
0171 242 1052
Fax: 0171 405 4934; DX 224 London,
Chancery Lane
Out of hours telephone: 0171 242 1052

Chambers of M L Boardman
Clerks: Russell Kinsley, Matthew Corrigan

Boardman, Michael 1979	Cleaver, Wayne 1986
Owen-Thomas, David QC 1952†	Lobbenberg, Nicholas 1987
	Minihan, Sean 1988
Chadwin, James QC 1958†	Van Stone, Grant 1988
Swift, Malcolm QC 1970†	O'Connor, Maureen 1988
Yajnik, Ram 1965	Bickerstaff, Jane 1989
Addezio, Mario 1971	Hunter, Win 1990
Gordon, Ashley 1973	Smith, Helen 1990
Landsbury, Alan 1975	McKay, Annmarie 1992
Trimmer, Stuart 1977	McAulay, Mark 1993
Heimler, George 1978	Alderson, Pippa 1993
Barker, John 1982	Spiro, Dafna 1994
Kopieczek, Louis 1983	Crook, Adam 1994
Evans, Ann 1983	Harries, Mark 1995
Misner, Philip 1984	Evans, Philip 1995
Price, Tom 1985	

GRAY'S INN SQUARE

8 Gray's Inn Square, Gray's Inn, London WC1R 5AZ
0171 242 3529
Fax: 0171 404 0395; DX 411 London,
Chancery Lane

Chambers of Patrick C Soares
Clerks: Mrs Marie Burke, Miss Jane Fullbrook

Soares, Patrick 1983	Ferrier, Ian 1976
McCutcheon, Barry 1975	Davies, The Rt Hon Denzil 1965
Brownbill, David 1989	
Way, Patrick 1994	
Whitehouse, Christopher 1997	

---

† Recorder ‡ Assistant Recorder * Door Tenant

10 · 11 GRAY'S INN SQUARE

2nd Floor, 10-11 Gray's Inn Square, Gray's Inn, London WC1R 5JD
0171 405 2576
Fax: 0171 831 2430; DX 484 London, Chancery Lane
Other comms: Mobile: 0831 868383; Message Pager: 0181 884 3344
Out of hours telephone: 01428 644863/0802 217096/0831 868383

Chambers of A B R Masters
Clerk: Richard Loasby

Masters, Alan *1979*	**Pardoe,** Matthew *1992*
McCreath, Jean *1978*	**Solari,** Yolanda *1992*
Donnelly, John *1983*	**Morel,** Peter *1993*
Black, Harriette *1986*	**Marriage,** Henrietta *1993*
Boulter, Terence *1986*	**Field,** Stephen *1993*
Magill, Ciaran *1988*	**Painter,** Ian *1993*
Trevis, Robert *1990*	**Baruah,** Rima *1994*
Muller, Mark *1991*	**Moore,** Alison *1994*
Ivers, Michael *1991*	**Thorne,** Katie *1994*
Eldergill, Edmund *1991*	**Davidson,** Tom *1973**
Dixon, Anne *1991*	**Mitchell,** Sally *1990**
McCrimmon, Kate *1991*	**Simpson,** Graeme *1994**

14 GRAY'S INN SQUARE

Gray's Inn, London WC1R 5JP
0171 242 0858
Fax: 0171 242 5434; DX 399 London
E-mail: 100712.2134@compuserve.com

Chambers of J Dodson QC
Clerk: Stephen Lavell

Dodson, Joanna QC *1970*	**Emanuel,** Mark *1985*
Godfrey, Louise QC *1972†*	**Warner,** Pamela *1985*
Kushner, Lindsey QC *1974†*	**Sutton,** Karoline *1986*
Dangor, Patricia *1970†*	**Corbett,** Michelle *1987*
Hall, Joanna *1973*	**Lyon,** Stephen *1987*
McNab, Mhairi *1974*	**Brown,** Rebecca *1989*
Forster, Sarah *1976*	**Jarman,** Mark *1989*
Slomnicka, Barbara *1976*	**King,** Samantha *1990*
Turner, David GP *1976‡*	**Alomo,** Richard *1990*
Brasse, Gillian *1977*	**Bedingfield,** David *1991*
Morris, Brenda *1978*	**Vavrecka,** David *1992*
Hudson, Kathryn *1981*	**De Zonie,** Jane *1993*
McLaughlin, Karen *1982*	**Brazil,** Dominic *1995*
Reid, Caroline *1982*	**Whittam,** Samantha *1995*
Ford, Monica *1984*	

GRAY'S INN TAX CHAMBERS

3rd Floor, Gray's Inn Chambers, Gray's Inn, London WC1R 5JA
0171 242 2642
Fax: 0171 831 9017/405 4078; DX 352 London, Chancery Lane
E-mail: clerks@taxbar.com
URL: http://www.taxbar.com
Out of hours telephone: 0956 144042

Chambers of J M Grundy
Clerk: Chris Broom (Senior Clerk)

Grundy, Milton *1954*	**McKay,** Hugh *1990*
Flesch, Michael QC *1963*	**Nathan,** Aparna *1994*
Goldberg, David QC *1971*	**McDonnell,** Conrad *1994*
Goy, David QC *1973*	**Akin,** Barrie *1976*
Walters, John QC *1977*	**Shaw,** Nicola *1995*
Cullen, Felicity *1985*	**Wilson,** Graham *1975**
Baker, Philip *1979*	**Swersky,** Abe *1996**

100E GREAT PORTLAND STREET

London W1N 5PD
0171 636 6323
Fax: 0171 436 3544; DX 94252 Marylebone
Other comms: Mobile: 0410 077566
Out of hours telephone: 0171 636 6323

Chambers of Robert Banks
Practice manager: Shane McMechan

Banks, Robert *1978*

CHAMBERS OF HELEN GRINDROD QC

95A
CHANCERY LANE

*1st Floor, 95a Chancery Lane, London
WC2A 2JG*
0171 404 4777
Fax: 0171 404 8777; DX 425 London,
Chancery Lane

Chambers of H M Grindrod QC
Clerks: Mark Auger, Reg Harris

Grindrod, Helen QC *1966*	O'Higgins, John *1990*
Rowling, Fiona *1980*	Adkin, Tana *1992*
Blake, Richard *1982*	Keigan, Linda *1992*
Johnston, Christopher *1983*	Fuad, Kerim *1992*
Manley, Lesley *1983*	Gatley, Mark *1993*
Gedge, Simon *1984*	Maylin, Kerry *1994*
Brain, Pamela *1985*	Walker, Andrew *1994*
Smullen, Marion *1985*	

CHAMBERS OF BEVERLEY GUTTERIDGE

*36 Dunmore Road, Wimbledon, London
SW20 8TN*
0181 947 0717

Chambers of Miss B J Gutteridge

1 HARCOURT BUILDINGS

Temple, London EC4Y 9DA
0171 353 9421/0375
Fax: 0171 353 4170; DX 417 London,
Chancery Lane
Out of hours telephone: Emergency 24-hour
mobile: 0973 675 426

Chambers of Simon Buckhaven
*Clerks: William Lavell, Gary Norton, Theresa
Burke, Keith Sharman, Victoria Leone;
Practice Development Manager: Natalie
Jones*

Buckhaven, Simon *1970*	Foinette, Ian *1986*
Walker, Raymond QC *1966†*	Knight, Caroline *1985*
Cripps, Seddon *1965†*	Rupasinha, Sunil *1983*
Bartlett, Roger *1968*	Bird, Andrew *1987*
Glossop, Willliam *1969*	Munir, Edward *1956*
Gratwicke, Charles *1974‡*	Connolly, Dominic *1989*
Ross, David *1974*	Ellis, Sarah *1989*
Hungerford, Guy *1971*	Dunlop, Hamish *1991*
Bennett, Charles *1972*	Hewitt, David *1991*
Van Der Bijl, Nigel *1973†*	McLaren, Nicola *1991*
Harris, James *1975*	Lundie, Christopher *1991*
Griffith, Martin *1977*	Eilledge, Amanda *1991*
Beecroft, Robert *1977*	Goldring, Jenny *1993*
Coggins, Jonathan *1980*	Galway-Cooper, Philip *1993*
Devlin, Bernard *1980*	Baum, Victoria *1993*
Sampson, Graeme *1981*	Valder, Paul *1994*
Richards, David *1981*	Mullins, Mark *1995*
May, Christopher *1983*	Blakemore, Jessica *1995*
Prosser, Anthony *1985*	Webster, Robert *1979**

Chambers established: 1950
Opening times: 9 am-6 pm

**Types of work (and number of counsel
practising in that area if supplied)**
Banking 7 · Bankruptcy 3 · Care proceedings 2
· Chancery (general) 7 · Chancery land law 7
· Commercial litigation 7 · Commercial
property 4 · Common law (general) 30
· Company and commercial 5 · Construction 4
· Crime 21 · Crime - corporate fraud 15 · EC
and competition law 2 · Employment 5
· Environment 5 · Equity, wills and trusts 5
· Family 3 · Family provision 3 · Financial
services 3 · Housing 5 · Immigration 2
· Insolvency 3 · Insurance 5 · Landlord and
tenant 5 · Licensing 4 · Local government 8
· Medical negligence 10 · Partnerships 3
· Personal injury 15 · Probate and
administration 5 · Professional negligence 10
· Sale and carriage of goods 10

Chambers' facilities
Conference rooms, Disks accepted, Disabled
access

† Recorder ‡ Assistant Recorder * Door Tenant

Languages spoken
French, German, Spanish

Additional information

This is a common law set of chambers, in which members appear before a wide range of courts and tribunals, and advise on questions in most areas of the law. Civil and criminal work is undertaken at all levels. Some members tend to specialise in particular fields.

On the civil side, members undertake work in all divisions of the High Court and in the county courts. They appear in commercial arbitrations and building disputes. The work includes contract, negligence (including professional negligence), personal property, and land law (including easements and boundary disputes). Family Division work undertaken includes matrimonial finance, wardship and other child cases. A particular area recently emphasised is that of interests in land and trusts for sale, and the rights of banks under mortgages: Simon Buckhaven and Bernard Devlin represented the successful wife in *Barclays Bank v O' Brien* in the House of Lords.

The criminal work undertaken involves all kinds of crime including fraud, drugs, health and safety at work, and proceedings before disiplinary tribunals. All criminal practitioners both prosecute and defend. Some are on the approved lists for HM Customs and Excise, the Department of Social Security, the Health and Safety Executive and the Department of Trade and Industry. Some prosecute on behalf of local authorities. Raymond Walker QC represented the Appellant in *R v Associated Octel Ltd.*

In addition to the general work undertaken, particular members can offer individual specialisations in a number of areas.

Direct professional access work is accepted. Documents and pleadings can be produced on disk if required.

In view of the wide area of litigation undertaken by chambers, members tend to specialise in different fields. The clerks are available to offer advice. A brochure is available on request.

> Use the *Types of Work* listings in Parts A and B to locate chambers and individual barristers who specialise in particular areas of work.

2 HARCOURT BUILDINGS

Ground Floor, Temple, London EC4Y 9DB
0171 583 9020
Fax: 0171 583 2686; DX 1039 London
E-mail: clerks@harcourt.co.uk

Chambers of Roger Henderson QC
Clerks: John White, Simon Boutwood;
Chambers Development Manager: Martin Dyke

Henderson, Roger QC 1964†	**Palmer,** James 1983
Ashworth, Piers QC 1956†	**Gibson,** Charles 1984
Playford, Jonathan QC 1962†	**Alliott,** George 1981
Mawrey, Richard QC 1964†	**Griffiths,** Conrad 1986
Brunner, Adrian QC 1968†	**Battcock,** Benjamin 1987
Powles, Stephen QC 1972†	**Wheeler,** Marina 1987
Prynne, Andrew QC 1975	**Outhwaite,** Wendy-Jane 1990
Iwi, Quintin 1956	**Harrison,** Averil 1990
Dashwood, Prof Alan 1969	**Green,** Patrick 1990
Cooper, Adrian 1970‡	**Bourne,** Charles 1991
Worsley, Daniel 1971†	**Popat,** Prashant 1992
O'Sullivan, Bernard 1971	**Campbell,** Oliver 1992
Gore-Andrews, Gavin 1972	**Zornoza,** Isabella 1993
Jordan, Andrew 1973	**Sheehan,** Malcolm 1993
Harvey, Jonathan 1974	**Fenston,** Felicia 1994
Hamer, Kenneth 1975‡	**Webb,** Geraint 1995
West, Lawrence 1979‡	**Riley-Smith,** Toby 1995
Eastman, Roger 1978	**Mitchell,** Julianna 1994
Staite, Sara 1979‡	**Kinnier,** Andrew 1996
Cameron, Barbara 1979	**Schoneveld,** Frank 1992*
	Ashworth, Lance 1987*

Chambers established: 1954

Types of work (and number of counsel practising in that area if supplied)
Administrative 7 · Arbitration 4 · Asset finance 8 · Care proceedings 11 · Chancery (general) 6 · Commercial litigation 25 · Common law (general) 34 · Company and commercial 5 · Competition 8 · Construction 17 · Consumer Law 7 · Copyright 3 · Courts martial 3 · Crime 7 · Crime - corporate fraud 7 · Ecclesiastical 1 · Education 1 · Employment 20 · Environment 7 · Equity, wills and trusts 5 · Family 11 · Family provision 11 · Financial services 8 · Franchising 2 · Housing 14 · Information

C

† Recorder ‡ Assistant Recorder * Door Tenant

technology 5 · Insurance 25 · Insurance/
reinsurance 25 · Intellectual property 3
· International trade 4 · Landlord and tenant 14
· Local government 10 · Medical negligence 20
· Parliamentary 3 · Partnerships 8 · Patents 3
· Personal injury 34 · Probate and
administration 3 · Professional negligence 34
· Sale and carriage of goods 20 · Sports 5 · Tax
- capital and income 1 · Tax - corporate 1
· Telecommunications 4

Chambers' facilities
Conference rooms, Disks accepted, E-mail

Languages spoken
French, Italian, Japanese, Spanish

Fees policy
Fees are negotiated with the clerk: our aim is
that fees will be reasonable and competitive,
depending on the importance and nature of the
work, the expertise and seniority of Counsel.

Additional information

The work of chambers covers all aspects of
commercial and common law. Areas covered
include: contract and business law; insurance
work; product liability and multi-plaintiff
litigation; personal injury and fatal accident
claims and work-related illness; sports law;
professional negligence (medical, building,
valuers, architects, surveyors, solicitors and
accountants); financial services (hire purchase
and consumer credit); food law; administrative
and public law; judicial review, local authorities
- finance and contracts; computer-related law;
property litigation (including landlord and
tenant, housing and real property);
environmental law; railway law; disaster
litigation; family; probate and family
inheritance; and European law (see Stanbrook &
Henderson).

Within these broad sectors, chambers has many
areas of specific expertise and experience.
Chambers is one of the leading sets in the field
of personal injury and fatal accident claims,
acting not only in litigation from the one-off
accident but also in the field of work-related
illness such as industrial deafness and repetitive
strain injury.

In product liability and multi-plaintiff litigation,
chambers has been involved in most of the
major cases in a field which has seen a vast
increase in activity in the past two decades. This
is especially true of multi-plaintiff cases where
generic drugs are claimed to have caused long-
term physical or psychological illnesses.

In the field of medical negligence, chambers
handles a considerable amount of litigation
involving allegations of negligence in all areas of
the medical, nursing and dental professions.

In family and inheritance law, chambers has
substantial experience in areas including
matrimonial finance; property; trusts; disputes
concerning children; the Children Act 1989;
adoption; and probate.

In land law, chambers' work includes
residential tenancies and occupancies; business
tenancies; agricultural holdings; title to land;
neighbour disputes; contracts for the sale of
land; mortgages; restrictive covenants;
easements; profits, and nuisance.

In the area of environmental law, chambers is
especially well placed, members having had
experience in major environmental matters of
all descriptions, and is able to draw upon its EC
connection with Stanbrook & Henderson.

Chambers has further specific experience in the
following areas: markets and fairs, railway law
and disaster inquiries. Chambers acts for a large
number of local authorities both in litigation and
non-litigation areas, particularly in all aspects of
finance, competitive tendering, local authority
contracts and transport.

       † Recorder ‡ Assistant Recorder * Door Tenant

2 HARCOURT BUILDINGS

1st Floor, Temple, London EC4Y 9DB
0171 353 2112/2817
Fax: 0171 353 8339; DX 489 London,
Chancery Lane

Chambers of N Mylne QC
Clerk: Michael Watts

Mylne, Nigel QC *1963†*	Darling, Ian *1985*
Harman, Robert QC *1954†*	Gibbs, Patrick *1986*
Atkinson, Nicholas QC *1971†*	Whittle-Martin, Lucia *1985*
	Rees, Jonathan *1987*
Cooper, Peter QC *1974†*	Clement, Peter *1988*
Bevan, John QC *1970†*	Churchill, Marina *1989*
Williams, John *1973*	Cobbs, Laura *1989*
Smyth, Stephen *1974*	Hamblin, Stewart *1990*
Clayton, Stephen *1975*	Fitzgerald, Toby *1993*
Loraine-Smith, Nicholas *1977*	Coombe, Peter *1993*
	Wilkins, Thomas *1993*
Shorrock, Philip *1978*	Wilding, Lisa *1993*
Adlard, William *1978*	Dawes, James *1993**
Leach, Robin *1979*	Halkerston, Sally *1994**
Gadsden, Mark *1980*	Farmer, Matthew *1987*
Jafferjee, Aftab *1980*	Thompson, Sally *1994*
Probert-Wood, Timothy *1982*	Kelleher, Benedict *1994*
	Emlyn Jones, William *1996*
Willis, Rhyddian *1984*	

2 HARCOURT BUILDINGS

Temple, London EC4Y 9DB
0171 353 8415
Fax: 0171 353 7622; DX 402 London
E-mail: clerks@twoharcourtbldgs.demon.co.uk

Chambers of Gerard Ryan QC
Clerks: Allen Collier (Senior Clerk), Paul Munday (First Junior Clerk), Andrew Briton (Second Junior Clerk)

Ryan, Gerard QC *1955†*	Comyn, Timothy *1980*
Cameron, Sheila QC *1957†*	Tait, Andrew *1981*
Purchas, Robin QC *1968†*	Howell Williams, Craig *1983*
Phillips, Richard QC *1970*	Ornsby, Suzanne *1986*
George, Charles QC *1974†*	Lewis, Meyric *1986*
Lindblom, Keith QC *1980*	Newcombe, Andrew *1987*
Beaumont, Christopher *1950†*	Mynors, Charles *1988*
	Jones, Gregory *1991*
McCracken, Robert *1973*	Edwards, Douglas *1992*
Petchey, Philip *1976*	Burrows, Euan *1995*
Milner, Jonathan *1977*	Clayton, Joanna *1995*
Kelly, Andrew *1978*	Pereira, James *1996*

Types of work (and number of counsel practising in that area if supplied)
Administrative · Agriculture · Common land · Compulsory purchase · EC law · Ecclesiastical · Education · Energy · Environment · Housing · Landlord and tenant · Licensing · Local government · Parliamentary · Planning

Languages spoken
French, German

Additional information

The Chambers: A specialist chambers for more than half a century with particular expertise in planning, environmental, property and administrative law. Disabled conference facilities are available by prior arrangement. Members accept Direct Professional Access from the approved professions. A chambers brochure is available on request.

All members of chambers belong to the Planning and Environment Bar Association of which Douglas Edwards is Secretary. Members of chambers also belong to the Administrative Law Bar Association, the Education Law Society, the Bar European Group, the Association for Regulated Procurement, the United Kingdom Environmental Law Association, JUSTICE, the Ecclesiastical Law Society and the Parliamentary Bar.

Two members of chambers are Deputy High Court Judges, five are Recorders of the Crown Court and three are Diocesan Chancellors. Craig Howell Williams and Meyric Lewis are members of the Supplementary Panel of Junior Counsel to the Crown. Gerard Ryan QC chaired the Tribunal of Inquiry into the gas explosion at Loscoe, Derbyshire. Charles George QC conducted the Independent Inquiry into Planning Decisions in the London Borough of Brent. Robert McCracken was Chairman of the United Kingdom Environmental Law Association. Christopher Beaumont is a Chairman of the Agricultural Land Tribunal. Sheila Cameron QC is Vicar General of the Province of Canterbury and was a Parliamentary Boundary Commissioner for England. Richard Phillips QC is an assistant Parliamentary Commissioner for England.

Publications include: *Education Case Reports* (editor-in-chief), *Journal of Planning and Environment Law* (editorial board), *Planning Appeal Decisions* (joint editor), *Planning and Environmental Law Bulletin* (joint editor), *Journal of Architectural Conservation* (editorial board). Charles Mynors is the author of *Planning Applications and Appeals* (1987), *Planning Control and the Display of Advertisements* (1992) and *Listed Buildings and Conservation Areas*.

Work undertaken:

Main Areas of Work: planning, environmental, compulsory purchase, administrative, local government finance, public procurement, parliamentary, transport and works, energy, utilities, education, highways, licensing, housing, human rights (European Convention) and European Community law.

Additional Areas: ecclesiastical law, landlord and tenant, the law of commons and that relating to easements, agricultural tenancies, rating and restrictive covenants.

Foreign Connections: Chambers includes members called to the Dublin and Northern Ireland Bars.

Former Members of Chambers include: Roy Vandermeer QC, currently inspector at the Terminal Five inquiry; Peter Boydell QC, Leader of the Parliamentary Bar and first Chairman of what is now the Planning and Environment Bar Association; Michael Harrison QC, now Mr Justice Harrison, Michael Mann QC, later Lord Justice Mann and Sir John Drinkwater QC.

International Arbitration Law Review

Editorial Board includes:

Alan Redfern	Neil Kaplan
Toby Landau	David Rivkin
Dr Julian Lew	Martin Hunter
Nigel Rawding	Matthieu de Boisseson

The new International Arbitration Law Review *brings together for the first time all the requirements of an arbitration practitioner.*

- *up-to-the-minute news on legislation and decisions*

- *expert commentary on worldwide trends and issues from a panel of top arbitration specialists*

- *detailed case summaries and analysis of the cases making the headlines*

- *covers all major jurisdictions worldwide*

To order a subscription or a free sample copy call Sweet & Maxwell on 0171 449 1111

HARCOURT CHAMBERS

HARCOURT CHAMBERS

2 Harcourt Buildings, Temple, London EC4Y 9DB
0171 353 6961/7
Fax: 0171 353 6968; DX 373 London, Chancery Lane

Chambers of Patrick Eccles QC
Clerks: Brian Wheeler, Timothy Wheeler, Judith Partington

Also at: Harcourt Chambers, Churchill House, 3 St Aldate's Courtyard, 38 St Aldate's, Oxford OX1 1BN 01865 791 559 01865 791 585, DX 96453 Oxford 4

Eccles, Patrick QC *1968†*	**Blackwood**, Clive *1986*
Evans, Roger *1970*	**Brett**, Matthew *1987*
Rodgers, June *1971†*	**Miles**, Edward *1989*
Sefi, Benedict *1972*	**Clarke**, Peter *1970**
Arthur, Gavyn *1975*	**De Sousa Turner**, Camilla *1989*
Dixon, John *1975*	
Lever, Bernard *1975†**	**Pressdee**, Piers *1991*
Barstow, Stephen *1976*	**Granshaw**, Sara *1991*
Baker, Jonathan *1978*	**Max**, Sally *1991*
Collinson, Alicia *1982*	**Auld**, Catherine *1992*
Frazer, Christopher *1983*	**Vater**, John *1995*
Judd, Frances *1984*	**Goodwin**, Nicholas *1995*
Hess, Edward *1985*	**Vine**, Aidan *1995*

Chambers established: Mid 19th century
Opening times: 24 Hrs on 0973 316959

Types of work (and number of counsel practising in that area if supplied)
Administrative 4 · Care proceedings 17 · Chancery land law 8 · Commercial 8 · Company and commercial 8 · Crime 3 · Ecclesiastical 1 · Education 4 · Employment 16 · Equity, wills and trusts 8 · Family 17 · Family provision 17 · Local government 4 · Medical negligence 9 · Personal injury 9 · Professional negligence 13 · Town and country planning 8

Chambers' facilities
Conference rooms, Disks accepted, Annexe and conference rooms in Oxford

Languages spoken
French, German

HARDWICKE BUILDING

New Square, Lincoln's Inn, London
WC2A 3SB
0171 242 2523
Fax: 0171 691 1234; DX 393 London
E-mail: clerks@hardwicke.co.uk
URL: http://www.hardwicke.co.uk

Chambers of Walter Aylen QC
Clerks: Kevin Mitchell, Greg Piner, Gary
Brown, Lloyd Smith, Jason Housden

The UK College of Family Mediators
Directory & Handbook 1998/99

- *provides expert commentary on family mediation training and professional development and includes contributions by leading family mediation professionals*

- *lists over 100 family mediation groups/services and over 950 individual family mediators by region and alphabetically*

- *gives details of all members and associates of the UK College of Family Mediators*

- *includes the UK College of Family Mediators Standards and Code of Practice*

- *gives details of all the family mediation bodies which make up the UK College of Family Mediators*

For more information call Sweet & Maxwell on 0171 449 1111

Aylen, Walter QC *1962*†
Stewart, Nicholas QC *1971*†
Pulman, George QC *1971*†
Tager, Romie QC *1970*†
Raynor, Philip QC *1973*†
Smith, Zoe *1970*†
Willer, Robert *1970*
Hopmeier, Michael *1974*†
Craig, Kenneth *1975*
Kremen, Philip *1975*
Jones, Nigel *1976*
Lennard, Stephen *1976*
Warner, Stephen *1976*
Landaw, John *1976*
Vine, James *1977*
Weddle, Steven *1977*
Oliver, Michael *1977*
Wakeham, Philip *1978*
Baker, Nicholas *1980*
Field, Rory *1980*
Matthias, David *1980*
Ramsahoye, Indira *1980*
Aaronberg, David *1981*
Jackson, Hugh *1981*
Smith, Alan *1981*
Mendoza, Neil *1982*
Flahive, Daniel *1982*
Bojczuk, William *1983*
Brook, Ian *1983*
Banks, Timothy *1983*
Forlin, Gerard *1984*
Greenan, John *1984*
Taylor, Debbie *1984*
Briefel, Charles *1984*
MacDonald, Lindsey *1985*
Ough, Richard *1985*
King, Karl *1985*
Webster, Justin *1985*
Palfrey, Monty *1985*
Whitfield, Jonathan *1985*

Stevens-Hoare, Michelle *1986*
Nicholson Pratt, Tom *1986*
Mulholland, James *1986*
Lloyd, Francis *1987*
Spooner, Judith *1987*
Reed, Paul *1988*
Kirby, Peter *1989*
Mulligan, Ann *1989*
Woolf, Steven *1989*
Hallissey, Caroline *1990*
Campbell, Alexis *1990*
Benbow, Sara *1990*
Baker, Rachel *1990*
Ryan, Eithne *1990*
Clarke, Ian *1990*
Argyropoulos, Kyriakos *1991*
McCartney, Kevin *1991*
Horspool, Tony *1991*
Newman, Ingrid *1992*
Nugent, Colm *1992*
Bates, Richard *1992*
Preston, David *1993*
Jarzabkowski, Julia *1993*
Formby, Emily *1993*
Amiraftabi, Roshi *1993*
Chaudhry, Sabuhi *1993*
Langridge, Niki *1993*
St Louis, Brian *1994*
Clargo, John *1994*
Goold, Alexander *1994*
Leckie, David *1994*
Heer, Deanna *1994*
Freeston, Lynn *1996*
Mosteshar, Sa'id *1975**
Treharne, Jennet *1975**
Joelson, Stephen *1980**
Gray, Pauline *1980**

Opening times: 8.30 am-6.30 pm

Types of work (and number of counsel practising in that area if supplied)
Administrative · Arbitration · Banking · Bankruptcy · Care proceedings · Chancery (general) · Commercial · Common law (general) · Company and commercial · Construction · Contract · Conveyancing · Crime · Crime - corporate fraud · Defamation · Employment · Energy · Entertainment · Equity, wills and trusts · Family · Financial services · Housing · Insolvency · Insurance · Intellectual property · Landlord and tenant · Licensing · Medical negligence · Partnerships · Personal injury · Planning · Private international · Probate and administration · Professional negligence · Public international · Sale and carriage of goods · Sports · Telecommunications

---

† Recorder ‡ Assistant Recorder * Door Tenant

Languages spoken

Farsi, French, German, Greek, Hindi, Italian, Portuguese, Russian, Spanish, Urdu

Additional information

Hardwicke Building
(Chambers of Walter Aylen QC)

This large set has 73 members and practises mainly civil and commercial law, crime and family law. Notable specialisms include professional negligence, landlord and tenant and international child abduction.

The set: Hardwicke Building is a modern progressive set with a strong business culture. It is committed to providing a specialist, high quality service to all its solicitors.

Members act for corporate and non-corporate clients as well as local authorities, government agencies and other professionals with direct access to the bar.

Walter Aylen QC became head of chambers in 1991. As a result of its continued expansion, its premises became too small and chambers moved into its current modern premises in August 1996.

Membership of chambers is regulated to suit the changing demands of the legal marketplace so that appropriately qualified specialist counsel are available for all classes of cases, at all levels, including publicly funded litigation and conditional fee work. Developments in the past year include the recruitment of Daniel Flahive, James Mulholland and Gerard Forlin to strengthen the specialist criminal group in chambers.

Technology has an important role in chambers as a whole and it has this year appointed an IT Manager. Tenants practise individually and in groups using the latest networked computer technology from research and conference facilities. As part of its technology development, chambers is installing video conferencing facilities to improve its communication with clients, both in the UK and overseas.

Type of work undertaken: The main groups in chambers are civil, crime and family. Within the civil group, which undertakes a broad spectrum of commercial work, there are also a number of specialist teams covering professional negligence, landlord and tenant, personal injury and medical negligence. Hardwicke Building is one of the foremost sets in the area of professional negligence and has represented

clients in many leading cases, both at first instance and in the Court of Appeal. Both the civil and family groups are able to provide arbitration and mediation facilities as well as trained arbitrators and mediators.

The criminal group is 31-strong and carries out the entire range of both defence and prosecution work (including CPS, SFO, FIG and Customs and Excise). Some members of the group have particular specialisation in the conduct of cases of serious fraud.

The family team of 15 members undertakes all aspects of family and matrimonial work and is especially strong in the field of financial and international child abduction.

Chambers has a strong commitment to providing a range of specialist barristers whose individual skills appropriately reflect the demands of specialist solicitors. It is anticipated that chambers will continue to grow to meet the increasing demand for its specialist skills.

Clerks: Greg Piner, Kevin Mitchell, Gary Brown, Lloyd Smith.

† Recorder ‡ Assistant Recorder * Door Tenant

1 HARE COURT

Ground Floor, Temple, London EC4Y 7BE
0171 353 3982/5324
Fax: 0171 353 0667; DX 444 London,
Chancery Lane

Chambers of Stephen Kramer QC
Clerks: Deryk Butler, Ian Fitzgerald;
Administrator: Stephen Wall

Kramer, Stephen QC *1970†*	**Howes,** Sally *1983*
Green, Sir Allan QC *1959*	**Bennett Jenkins,** Sallie
Worsley, Paul QC *1970†**	*1984*
Heslop, Martin QC *1972†*	**Dawson,** James *1984*
Salmon, Charles QC *1972†*	**Holland,** Michael *1984*
Warner, Brian *1969‡*	**Barnes,** Shani *1986*
Coleman, Nicholas *1970†*	**O'Neill,** Brian *1987*
Samuel, Jacqueline *1971*	**Kelly,** Brendan *1988*
Jones, John *1972†*	**Logsdon,** Michael *1988*
Waters, David *1973†*	**Millett,** Kenneth *1988*
Kamill, Louise *1974†*	**Cheema,** Parmjit *1989*
Dodgson, Paul *1975†*	**Hehir,** Christopher *1990*
Pownall, Orlando *1975*	**Lewis,** Alex *1990*
Radcliffe, Andrew *1975‡*	**Bex,** Kate *1992*
Hicks, Martin *1977*	**Ferguson,** Craig *1992*
Benson, Jeremy *1978†*	**Grahame,** Nina *1993*
Lloyd-Eley, Andrew *1979*	**Foulkes,** Christopher *1994*
Colman, Andrew *1980*	**Johnson,** Matthew *1995*
Leist, Ian *1981*	**Glasgow,** Oliver *1995*
Howker, David *1982‡*	**Karmy-Jones,** Riel *1995*
Laidlaw, Jonathan *1982‡*	

Opening times: 8.30 am-6.30 pm

Types of work (and number of counsel practising in that area if supplied)
Courts martial 40 · Crime 40 · Crime -
corporate fraud 40 · Licensing 40 · Personal
injury 1 · Professional negligence 1

Chambers' facilities
Conference rooms

Languages spoken
French, Hindi, Spanish, Urdu

Additional information

Chambers is a leading set specialising in
criminal law. We prosecute and defend at all
levels, in London and throughout England and
Wales.

In recent years, chambers has increasingly
specialised in commercial fraud and corruption
cases.

We also offer expertise in related fields
including extradition, courts martial, coroners'
inquests, immigration, food and drugs and trade
descriptions.

A brochure is available on request.

ONE HARE COURT

ONE HARE COURT

1st Floor, Temple, London EC4Y 7BE
0171 353 3171
Fax: 0171 583 9127; DX 0065 London,
Chancery Lane
E-mail: admin-oneharecourt@btinternet.com

Chambers of Lord Neill of Bladen QC, Richard Southwell QC
Clerks: Barry Ellis, Paul Ballard

Neill of Bladen, Lord QC	**Dowley,** Dominic *1983*
1951	**Eadie,** James *1984*
Southwell, Richard QC	**Lavender,** Nicholas *1989*
1959†	**Moran,** Andrew *1989*
Page, Howard QC *1967*	**Qureshi,** Khawar *1990*
Bratza, Nicolas QC *1969†*	**Padfield,** Alison *1992*
Padfield, Nicholas QC	**Adkin,** Jonathan W *1997*
1972†	**de Lupis Frankopan,** Prof
Ballantyne, William *1977*	Ingrid *1977**
Smith, Paul *1978*	

Opening times: 8.30 am-6.30 pm

Types of work (and number of counsel practising in that area if supplied)
Administrative · Arbitration · Asset finance
· Banking · Bankruptcy · Chancery (general)
· Civil liberties · Commercial · Commodities
· Common law (general) · Company and

---

† Recorder ‡ Assistant Recorder * Door Tenant

commercial · Competition · Construction
· Corporate finance · Crime - corporate fraud
· Discrimination · EC and competition law
· Education · Energy · Entertainment
· Environment · Film, cable, TV · Financial
services · Foreign law · Franchising
· Immigration · Information technology
· Insolvency · Insurance · Insurance/
reinsurance · Intellectual property
· International trade · Landlord and tenant
· Local government · Parliamentary
· Partnerships · Patents · Private international
· Professional negligence · Public international
· Sale and carriage of goods · Share options

Chambers' facilities
Video conferences, Disks accepted, E-mail

Languages spoken
Arabic, French

Fees policy
Fees are available on enquiry to the clerks.

Additional information

Types of work undertaken: One Hare Court
is a long-established, small set of chambers
which specialises in commercial and
international work and other related fields of
litigation, arbitration and legal advice.

Litigation work is undertaken in the High Court
(with the emphasis on Commercial Court
litigation) and in international and domestic
arbitrations. Junior members also undertake
work in the county courts and in tribunals.

Individual practices vary from one member to
another; however, together they cover the
following areas of law: commercial contracts,
international trade and carriage of goods,
commodities, sale of goods, insurance and
reinsurance, banking and negotiable
instruments, commercial aspects of company
and insolvency law, commercial fraud claims,
intellectual property, public international law,
constitutional law and administrative law. Also
undertaken are arbitration, both international
and domestic, construction and engineering,
private international law, competition,
regulation of trade, insurance and financial
markets, financial services, European
Community law, professional negligence,
professional regulatory and disciplinary
proceedings, and Privy Council appeals.

A high proportion of chambers' work originates
from overseas and, subject to admission to local
Bars, instructions are accepted to appear in the

courts of Hong Kong, Singapore, Malaysia,
Caribbean and other foreign jurisdictions.

Arbitration: Members of chambers are highly
experienced in the field of arbitration,
(international commercial and construction:
ICC, LCIA, Lloyd's, UNCITRAL, amongst
others).

Chambers is a founder member of the London
Court of International Arbitration and is a
member of the Commercial Bar Association
(COMBAR).

All members of chambers accept instructions
under the direct professional access
arrangements.

Additional specialisations: Arab Laws (Prof
Ballantyne, formerly solicitor 1949);
Scandinavian and environmental law (Prof De
Lupis Frankopan).
Richard Southwell QC and Nicholas Padfield QC
are members of the Executive Committee of
COMBAR.
Richard Southwell QC (who sits as a Deputy
High Court Judge) is President and Howard Page
QC is Deputy President of Lloyd's Appeal
Tribunal. Nicolas Bratza QC is a member of the
European Commission of Human Rights.

Former Members: Sir Henry Fisher, President
of Wolfson College, Oxford 1975-85, Arbitrator;
Lord Slynn of Hadley, Lord of Appeal in
Ordinary (former Judge of the Court of Justice
of the European Communities); Sir Roger
Parker, former Lord Justice of Appeal,
Arbitrator; Sir Mark Waller, a Lord Justice of the
High Court; HH Judge Raymond Jack QC,
Circuit Mercantile Judge of the Bristol
Mercantile Court.

† Recorder ‡ Assistant Recorder * Door Tenant

3 HARE COURT

HARE COURT

1st Floor, Temple, London EC4Y 7BJ
0171 353 7561
Fax: 0171 353 7741; DX 17 London, Chancery
Lane
Out of hours telephone: 0956 243560/0181
886 4772

Chambers of William Clegg QC
Clerk: John Grimmer

Clegg, William QC *1972†*	**Lodder**, Peter *1981*
Morris, The Rt Hon John QC	**Mitchell**, Keith *1981*
1954†	**Sturman**, James *1982*
Lewis, Michael QC *1956†*	**McIvor**, Jane *1983*
Godfrey, Howard QC *1970†*	**King**, Gelaga *1985*
Munday, Andrew QC *1973‡*	**Kendal**, Timothy *1985*
Jenkins, Alun QC *1972**	**Milliken-Smith**, Mark *1986*
Griffiths, Peter QC *1970**	**Campbell-Clyne**, Christopher
Lithman, Nigel QC *1976‡*	*1988*
Flach, Robert *1950*	**Matthews**, Richard *1989*
Conway, Charles *1969*	**Ashley-Norman**, Jonathan
Champion, Deborah *1970†*	*1989*
Ingram, Nigel *1972*	**Derbyshire**, Thomas *1989*
Halsey, Mark *1974*	**Rush**, Craig *1989*
Neill, Robert *1975*	**Ageros**, James *1990*
Williams, Andrew *1975*	**Agnew**, Christine *1992*
Barnes, Margaret *1976*	**Charbit**, Valerie *1992*
Caudle, John *1976*	**Budworth**, Adam *1992*
Abell, Anthony *1977*	**Epstein**, Michael *1992*
Hackett, Philip *1978*	**Hurlock**, John *1993*
Dodd, John *1979*	**Pople**, Alison *1993*
Levy, Michael *1979*	**Henson**, Christine *1994*
Livingston, Richard *1980*	**Trott**, Ronald *1956**
McGowan, Maura *1980‡*	**Dodd**, Margaret *1979**
Altman, Brian *1981*	

Opening times: 8 am-7 pm

Types of work (and number of counsel practising in that area if supplied)
Administrative · Courts martial · Crime · Crime
- corporate fraud · Foreign law · Insolvency
· Licensing · Local government · Sports

Languages spoken
Dutch, French, German, Hebrew, Italian, Krio
(Sierra Leone), Serbo-Croat, Welsh

Additional information

3 Hare Court is a leading set of specialist
criminal practitioners, at the forefront of
defence and prosecution work in the South East
and throughout the country.

The seven Silks and body of active juniors
spread across the call range are well respected
and frequently involved in high-profile cases.

Fraud remains an important part of chambers
practice, embracing corporate, financial
services, insolvency, DTI, revenue and VAT.

Some members of chambers specialise in
Divisional and Appellate Court proceedings and
undertake regulatory and supervisory bodies
tribunal advocacy. Immigration work is also
undertaken.

All aspects of pre-trial advice and representation
are competently provided and the chambers is
able to offer a 24-hour clerking service for
emergencies and overnight cases.

CHAMBERS OF HARJIT SINGH

*2 Middle Temple Lane, Ground Floor,
London EC4Y 9AA*
0171 353 1356
Fax: 0171 583 4928; DX LDE 0072 Chancery
Lane

Chambers of Mr Harjit Singh
Clerk: Mr Matthew Jones

Singh, Harjit *1956*	**Miszkiel**, Ursula *1994*
Lakha, Murtaza *1961*	**Leslie**, Nigel *1994*
O'Brien, John *1976*	**Fripp**, Eric *1994*
Calder, Renée *1978*	**Noble**, Antonia *1995*
Bulloch, Anne *1989*	**Davies**, Penny *1995*
Dogra, Tanyia *1994*	**Schooling**, Simon *1995*

† Recorder ‡ Assistant Recorder * Door Tenant

HARROW-ON-THE-HILL CHAMBERS

60 High Street, Harrow on the Hill, Middlesex HA1 3LL
0181 423 7444
Fax: 0181 423 7368; DX 130112 Slough 6

Chambers of M C Beaumont
Chambers Manager: Michele Acton

Also at: Windsor Barristers' Chambers
Tel: 01753 648899
Fax: 01753 648877

Boney, Guy QC *1968*†*	**Bearman,** Justin *1992*
Clark, Christopher QC *1969*†*	**Whitley,** Jonathan *1993*
	Green, Victoria *1994*
Beaumont, Marc *1985*	**Nugent,** Peter *1994*
Hill, Andrew *1982**	**Simpson,** Graeme *1994*
Kimsey, Mark *1990*	**Gopinathan,** Anu *1994*
Bergin, Terence *1985**	**Shetty,** Rajeev *1996*
Swift, Antony *1984*	**Wilkins,** Andrew *1995*
Bridges, Dr Paul *1984**	**Sheikh,** Khalid *1993*
Dowden, Andrew *1991*	

Chambers established: 1990
Opening times: 8 am-6 pm

Types of work (and number of counsel practising in that area if supplied)
Administrative · Agriculture · Banking · Bankruptcy · Care proceedings · Chancery (general) · Chancery land law · Civil liberties · Commercial · Commercial litigation · Commercial property · Common land · Common law (general) · Company and commercial · Competition · Construction · Consumer Law · Conveyancing · Crime · Crime - corporate fraud · Defamation · Discrimination · Education · Employment · Equity, wills and trusts · Family · Family provision · Financial services · Franchising · Housing · Immigration · Insolvency · Insurance · Landlord and tenant · Local government · Medical negligence · Partnerships · Personal injury · Planning · Probate and administration · Professional negligence · Sale and carriage of goods · Sports · Town and country planning

Chambers' facilities
Conference rooms, Disks accepted

Languages spoken
French

Fees policy
Our fees are designed to be competitive, whilst reflecting the complexity and importance of the case and the seniority of counsel. Specific requests for information should be made to the chambers manager.

10 HIGHLEVER ROAD

North Kensington, London W10 6PS
0181 969 8514
Fax: 0181 969 8514

Chambers of Mr M A Sayeed

HOLBORN CHAMBERS

6 Gate Street, Lincoln's Inn Fields, London WC2A 3HP
0171 242 6060
Fax: 0171 242 2777; DX 159 London

Chambers of Mr S S Stevens

HORIZON CHAMBERS

95a Chancery Lane, London WC2A 1DT
0171 242 2440
Fax: 0171 242 2443; DX 275 LDE

INTERNATIONAL LAW CHAMBERS

ILC House 77/79 Chepstow Road, Bayswater, London W2 5QR
0171 221 5684/5/4840
Fax: 0171 221 5685 Gps12&3

Chambers of Mr S D El-Falahi

See the *Index of Languages Spoken* **in Part G to locate a chambers where a particular language is spoken, or find an individual who speaks a particular language.**

JOHN STREET CHAMBERS

2 John Street, London WC1N 2HJ
0171 242 1911
Fax: 0171 242 2515; DX 1000 London,
Chancery Lane
E-mail: john.street_chambers@virgin.net.uk

Chambers of Mr Jean-Gilles Raymond
Clerks: Danny Currie, Sheila Doyle

Raymond, Jean-Gilles *1982*	**Oji**, Atim *1992*
Bignall, Paula *1988*	**Richards**, Joanne *1992*
Hopewell, Gregory *1992*	**Foster**, Margaret *1993*
Cheltenham, Jacqueline *1992*	**Heller**, Anne *1995*
	Weir, Olivia *1995*
Labelle, Jean-Marie *1992*	**Gladwell**, Simon M *1996*

Chambers established: 1997
Opening times: 8.30 am-6.30 pm

Types of work (and number of counsel practising in that area if supplied)
Administrative 2 · Care proceedings 3 · Common law (general) 10 · Crime 8 · Crime - corporate fraud 2 · Defamation 1 · Family 8 · Foreign law 2 · Housing 5 · Immigration 6 · International trade 1 · Landlord and tenant 6 · Licensing 3 · Medical negligence 2 · Mental health 1 · Personal injury 5 · Probate and administration 2 · Professional negligence 4

Chambers' facilities
Conference rooms, Disks accepted

Languages spoken
French

Fees policy
Up to five years call £50–75, Five to ten years call £75–125, Ten years call £75–150. Chambers has a supple and flexible approach based on the approximations provided by the bands of fees and a sober assessment of each case.

JUSTICE COURT CHAMBERS

75 Kendal Road, Willesden Green, London NW10 1JE
0181 830 7786
Fax: 0181 830 7787
Out of hours telephone: 0973 617277

Chambers of Mr F A Siddiqi
Clerks: Mr M Ammar, Ms A Butt

Siddiqi, Faizul *1990*

KEATING CHAMBERS

10 Essex Street, London WC2R 3AA
0171 544 2600
Fax: 0171 240 7722; DX 1045 London

Chambers of Richard Fernyhough QC
Clerk: Barry Bridgman

Fernyhough, Richard QC *1970†*	**Darling**, Paul *1983*
	O'Farrell, Finola *1983*
Uff, John QC *1970‡*	**Williamson**, Adrian *1983*
Collins, Martin QC *1952*	**Nissen**, Alexander *1985*
Thomas, Christopher QC *1973‡*	**Bowsher**, Michael *1985*
	Jefford, Nerys *1986*
Marrin, John QC *1974†*	**Randall**, Louise *1988*
Furst, Stephen QC *1975‡*	**Evans**, Robert *1989*
Elliott, Timothy QC *1975*	**Hannaford**, Sarah *1989*
Ramsey, Vivian QC *1979*	**Hargreaves**, Simon *1991*
Gaitskell, Robert QC *1978‡*	**Harding**, Richard *1992*
Boulding, Philip QC *1979*	**Lemon**, Jane *1993*
Steynor, Alan *1975†*	**Stansfield**, Piers *1993*
Jackson, Rosemary *1981*	**Lee**, Jonathan *1993*
Taverner, Marcus *1981*	**Hughes**, Simon *1995*
Coulson, Peter *1982*	**Jinadu**, Abdul-Lateef *1995*
Pennicott, Ian *1982*	**Jobanputra**, Sandip *1996*

Opening times: 8 am-6.45 pm

Types of work (and number of counsel practising in that area if supplied)
Arbitration 32 · Commercial litigation 32 · Construction 32 · EC and competition law 3 · Information technology · Insurance/reinsurance · Landlord and tenant 3 · Local government

Chambers' facilities
Conference rooms, Disks accepted, E-mail

Languages spoken
Arabic, French, German, Spanish

Fees policy
Estimates for members of chambers are available on request from the Senior Clerk or his assistants.

Additional information

This set specialises in building and all kinds of engineering matters in the UK and abroad, acting for employers, contractors, sub-contractors and consultants. These specialisations include contractual claims, development contracts, claims in respect of defective buildings and structures and the professional negligence of architects, surveyors, valuers, engineers and other consultants concerned with building and engineering matters. Other areas include local authority work (including building control work), environmental law and EC law (in particular, public procurement).

Members of chambers also undertake work relating to information technology, commercial and insurance contracts, performance bonds and warranties and Mareva and other types of injunction. Some members also practise in landlord and tenant, planning, other property-related matters and competition law.

Members of chambers act and advise in litigation, arbitration, adjudication and all forms of ADR. Their work abroad includes ICC and FIDIC arbitrations and other arbitral work, particularly in Paris, Hong Kong, Singapore and the Middle East. Senior members act as arbitrators, legal assessors, adjudicators, mediators and conciliators in the UK and internationally.

ONE KING'S BENCH WALK

ONE KING'S BENCH WALK

Temple, London EC4Y 7DB
0171 936 1500
Fax: 0171 936 1590; DX LDE 20 (Delivery Only)
E-mail: ddear@1kbw.co.uk
URL: http://www.1kbw.co.uk
Out of hours telephone: 0831 339391

Chambers of J B S Townend QC
Clerks: David Dear, Nicola Cade, Tim Madden, David McDonald, Christopher Tuley; Practice manager: Elise Newman; Administrators: Jud Lisette, Paul Rudd

Also at: Kings Bench Chambers, 174 High Street, Lewes, East Sussex BN7 1YE
Tel: 01273 402600
Fax: 01273 402609

Townend, James QC *1962*†	**Kirk**, Anthony *1981*
Hacking, Anthony QC *1965*†	**Maidment**, Susan *1968*‡
Hayward-Smith, Rodger QC *1967*†	**Woodbridge**, Julian *1981*
	Pocock, Christopher *1984*
Singleton, Barry QC *1968*	**Shay**, Stephen *1984*
Parker, Judith QC *1973*‡	**Eaton**, Deborah *1985*
Pratt, Camden QC *1970*†	**O'Connor**, Sarah *1986*
Scriven, Pamela QC *1970*‡	**Cellan-Jones**, Deiniol *1988*
Anelay, Richard QC *1970*†	**Marshall**, Philip *1989*
Wood, Roderic QC *1974*‡	**Selman**, Elizabeth *1989*
Bellamy, Stephen QC *1974*†	**Barton**, Richard *1990*
Gale, Michael QC *1957*	**Fletcher**, Marcus *1990*
Turner, James QC *1976*	**Gibson**, Caroline *1990*
McFarlane, Andrew QC *1977*‡	**Grice**, Joanna *1991*
	James, Rebecca *1992*
Newton, Clive *1968*	**Harrison**, Richard *1993*
Warren, Michael *1971*	**Roberts**, James *1993*
McDowall, Andrew *1972*†	**Cook**, Ian *1994*
Kemp, Charles *1973*†	**Mulholland**, Shona *1994*
Reddish, John *1973*	**Crosthwaite**, Graham *1995*
Tanzer, John *1975*‡	**Jay**, Adam *1995*
Rennie, David *1976*‡	**Rayment**, Benedick *1996*
Budden, Caroline *1977*‡	**Esprit**, Shaun *1996*
Lister, Caroline *1980*	

Chambers established: 1962
Opening times: 8.30 am-7 pm

---

       † Recorder ‡ Assistant Recorder * Door Tenant

Types of work (and number of counsel practising in that area if supplied)
Administrative · Common law (general) · Courts martial · Crime · Crime - corporate fraud · Education · Environment · Family · Family provision · Immigration · Local government · Medical negligence · Mental health · Parliamentary · Personal injury · Professional negligence · Sports

Chambers' facilities
Conference rooms, Disks accepted, Disabled access, E-mail, Telephone conferences

Languages spoken
French, German, Hebrew, Portuguese, Spanish

2 KING'S BENCH WALK

Ground Floor, Temple, London EC4Y 7DE
0171 353 1746
Fax: 0171 583 2051; DX 1032 London

Chambers of Mr A M Donne QC

The UK College of Family Mediators Directory & Handbook 1998/99

- *provides expert commentary on family mediation training and professional development and includes contributions by leading family mediation professionals*

- *lists over 100 family mediation groups/services and over 950 individual family mediators by region and alphabetically*

- *gives details of all members and associates of the UK College of Family Mediators*

- *includes the UK College of Family Mediators Standards and Code of Practice*

- *gives details of all the family mediation bodies which make up the UK College of Family Mediators*

For more information call Sweet & Maxwell on 0171 449 1111

---

4 KING'S BENCH WALK

Ground/1st Floor, Temple, London EC4Y 7DL
0171 822 8822
Fax: 0171 822 8844; DX 422 London, Chancery Lane
E-mail: 4kbw@barristersatlaw.com
URL: http://www.barristersatlaw.com

Chambers of Chamber of Robert Rhodes QC
Clerk: Ian Lee

Also at: King's Bench Chambers, 175 Holdenhurst Road, Bournemouth, Dorset BN8 8DQ
Tel: 01202 250025
Fax: 01202 250026

Rhodes, Robert QC *1968*†	**Harounoff**, David *1984*
Heppel, Peter QC *1970*†	**Hurst**, Martin *1985*
Toogood, John *1957*	**Jarman**, Samuel *1989*
Evans, Keith *1962*	**Stern**, David *1989*
Cameron, Kenneth *1969*	**Huston**, Graham *1991*
Rees, William *1973*	**Bowen**, Paul *1993*
Cattle, David *1975*	**Maxwell**, Adrian *1993*
Anderson, Clive *1976*	**Dunn**, Katherine *1993*
Davis, Greville *1976*	**Crossfield**, Anne *1993*
Howard, Margaret *1977*	**Edhem**, Emma *1993*
Hulme, Graham *1977*	**Hood**, Nigel *1993*
Stuart, Bruce *1977*	**Shaw**, Peter *1995*
Van Hagen, Christopher *1980*	**Mishcon**, Oliver *1993*
	Yazawa, Yutaka *1994*
Gordon-Saker, Andrew *1981*	**Murphy**, Nicola *1995*
Watts, Alison *1981*	**Nelson**, Michael *1992*
Shale, Justin *1982*	**Aiken**, Kimberley *1995*
Stafford-Michael, Simon *1982*	**Farmer**, Kimberly *1997*
	Power, Lawrence *1995*

Opening times: 8.45 am-6.30 pm

Types of work (and number of counsel practising in that area if supplied)
Banking 5 · Bankruptcy 6 · Care proceedings 4 · Chancery (general) 4 · Civil liberties 2 · Commercial litigation 14 · Common law (general) 20 · Company and commercial 16 · Corporate finance 4 · Courts martial 2 · Crime 20 · Crime - corporate fraud 14 · EC and competition law 2 · Employment 2 · Environment 8 · Family 4 · Family provision 4

· Financial services 10 · Housing 2 · Immigration 1 · Insolvency 6 · Insurance 10 · Insurance/reinsurance 10 · International trade 10 · Landlord and tenant 8 · Licensing 10 · Medical negligence 8 · Personal injury 14 · Private international 8 · Professional negligence 10 · Shipping, admiralty 2

Chambers' facilities
Conference rooms

Languages spoken
French, German, Japanese, Spanish, Turkish

Fees policy
Information on individual areas of practice, fees and hourly charging rates is available from the Senior Clerk.

Additional information

A long-established common law set providing a complete advisory service across a wide range of work.

Principal areas of practice: crime (defence), commercial fraud (criminal and civil), personal injury (including disaster litigation), professional negligence (principally doctors, lawyers, surveyors and accountants), matrimonial and family, contract and commercial (including sale of goods).

Other areas of practice: landlord and tenant and property disputes, partnerships, engineering and building contracts, insolvency, employment, insurance and reinsurance, product liability.

Particular emphasis is placed on advocacy skills. Some members of chambers regularly appear as leading juniors.

Members of chambers are willing to travel to all parts of the country and overseas for hearings and conferences and are available to advise upon and appear in urgent applications at short notice. Chambers is equipped with the latest computer technology to aid efficient administration.

The Supreme Court Practice 1999

- *the most authoritative title on Civil Court Practice and Procedure*
- *available in book and CD-ROM formats*

Phone Sweet & Maxwell on 0171 449 1111 to order your copy

Chambers of N F B Jarman QC
Clerks: Lee Cook, Philip Burnell

Jarman QC, Nicholas QC 1965†	Williams, Rhodri 1987*
	Morgan, Adrienne 1988
Hillman, Basil 1968	Jacobs, Claire 1989
Spencer Bernard, Robert 1969†	Juss, Satvinder 1989
	Metcalf, John 1990
Cousins, Christopher 1969	Higgins, Kevin 1990
Harvey, John 1973†	Wakerley, Paul 1990
Denniss, John 1974	Mather, Kate 1990
Pooley, Moira 1974	Murphy, Cressida 1991
Pearl, David A 1977	Skelley, Michael 1991
Evans, Barnaby 1978	Preston, Kim 1991
Riley, John 1983	McCreath, Fiona 1991
Arkhurst, Reginald 1984	Curtis-Raleigh, Giles 1992
Alt, Jane 1984	Rees, Hefin 1992
Goddard, Philip 1985	Davis, Brendan 1994
Nightingale, Peter 1986	Maguire, Benn 1994
Gumpert, Benjamin 1987	Drane, Amanda 1996
Granville Stafford, Andrew 1987	

International Arbitration Law Review

Editorial Board includes:

Alan Redfern	Neil Kaplan
Toby Landau	David Rivkin
Dr Julian Lew	Martin Hunter
Nigel Rawding	Matthieu de Boisseson

The new International Arbitration Law Review *brings together for the first time all the requirements of an arbitration practitioner.*

- *up-to-the-minute news on legislation and decisions*

- *expert commentary on worldwide trends and issues from a panel of top arbitration specialists*

- *detailed case summaries and analysis of the cases making the headlines*

- *covers all major jurisdictions worldwide*

To order a subscription or a free sample copy call Sweet & Maxwell on 0171 449 1111

---

        † Recorder ‡ Assistant Recorder * Door Tenant

6 KING'S BENCH WALK

Ground Floor, Temple, London EC4Y 7DR
0171 583 0410
Fax: 0171 353 8791; DX 26 London, Chancery
Lane

Chambers of M D L Worsley QC
Clerk: David Garstang

Worsley, Michael QC *1955*	**Perry,** David *1980*
Curnow, Ann QC *1957*†	**Ryder,** John *1980*‡
Mallalieu, Ann QC *1970*	**Hilliard,** Nicholas *1981*
Amlot, Roy QC *1963*	**Wass,** Sasha *1981*‡
Curtis, James QC *1970*†	**Bowyer,** Martin *1984*
Lovell-Pank, Dorian QC	**Brierley,** Andrew *1984*
1971†	**Denison,** Simon *1984*
Temple, Victor QC *1971*†	**Armstrong,** Dean *1985*
Korner, Joanna QC *1974*†	**Broadbent,** Emma *1986*
Houlder, Bruce QC *1969*†	**Cray,** Timothy *1989*
Spens, David QC *1973*†	**Grieves-Smith,** Peter *1989*
Fisher, David QC *1973*†	**Oldland,** Andrew *1990***
Joseph, Wendy QC *1975*‡	**Ray-Crosby,** Irena *1990*
Turner, David QC *1971*†*	**Laws,** Simon *1991*
Turner, Jonathan *1974*‡	**Dunn-Shaw,** Jason *1992*
Vagg, Howard *1974*‡	**Penny,** Duncan *1992*
Sweeney, Nigel *1976*†	**Darlow,** Annabel *1993*
Dennis, Mark *1977*‡	**Whitehouse,** Sarah *1993*
Jessel, Philippa *1978*	**Atkinson,** Duncan *1995*
Leonard, Anthony *1978*‡	**Pilling,** Annabel *1995*
Moore, Marks *1979*‡	

Opening times: 8.30 am-7 pm

Types of work (and number of counsel practising in that area if supplied)
Crime 38 · Crime - corporate fraud 38

Chambers' facilities
Conference rooms, Video conferences, Disks
accepted

Languages spoken
French, German, Italian, Spanish

Additional information

The chambers of Michael Worsley QC at 6
King's Bench Walk is recognised as one of the
leading sets in the field of criminal law with
strength at all levels of seniority. There are at
present 38 members including 12 QCs and four
Treasury Counsel.

Chambers' practice covers all aspects of
criminal law and members specialise in
advocacy in the higher courts in both defence
and prosecution work. Senior members have
participated in many of the major criminal trials
in recent years.

In particular, members of chambers defend and
prosecute in a large number of commercial
crime, fraud and regulatory cases. All aspects of
work in the field of financial services are
undertaken.

Individual members also appear in libel,
licensing, extradition and trade description
cases; before coroners' courts, inquiries,
disciplinary and industrial tribunals; and
undertake work involving human rights.

6 KING'S BENCH WALK

Temple, London EC4Y 7DR
0171 353 4931/583 0695
Fax: 0171 353 1726; DX 471 London,
Chancery Lane

Chambers of S Kadri QC
*Clerks: Gary Jeffery, Ms Janet McGlasson,
Philip Bampfylde*

Kadri, Sibghatullah QC *1969*	**Cogan,** Michael *1986*
Rafique, Tariq *1961*	**Howat,** Robin *1986*
Yazdani, Ghulam *1963*	**Clarke,** Helen *1988*
Geldart, William *1975*	**Driver,** Emily *1988*
Bowen, James *1979*	**Giz,** Alev *1988*
Carrott, Sylvester *1980*	**Taylor,** Martin *1988*
Grewal, Harjit *1980*	**Panesar,** Manjit *1989*
Gallivan, Terence *1981*	**Tagliavini,** Lorna *1989*
Gill, Manjit *1982*	**Neathey,** Rona *1990*
Pearce, Linda *1982*	**Wan Daud,** Malek *1991*
Gumbiti-Zimuto, Andrew	**Knafler,** Stephen *1993*
1983	**Najand,** Maryam *1993*
de Mello, Rembert *1983*	**Taghavi,** Shahram *1994*

C

---

† Recorder ‡ Assistant Recorder * Door Tenant

S TOMLINSON QC

7 King's Bench Walk, Temple, London
EC4Y 7DS
0171 583 0404
Fax: 0171 583 0950/0171 353 2455; DX LDE
239
Other comms: Lix: Lon 084
Out of hours telephone: 0831 394225

Chambers of Stephen Tomlinson QC
Clerks: Linda Stinton, Bernie Hyatt, Greg
Leyden; Administrator: Sue Luxford

Tomlinson, Stephen QC 1974†	Butcher, Christopher 1986
Hamilton, Adrian QC 1949	Kenny, Stephen 1987
Willmer, John QC 1955	Southern, Richard 1987
Cooke, Jeremy QC 1976‡	Bright, Robert 1987
Saloman, Timothy QC 1975‡	Geary, Gavin 1989
Reynolds, Prof Francis QC 1960	Bailey, David 1989
	Edwards, David 1989
	Allen, David 1990
Kealey, Gavin QC 1977	Picken, Simon 1989
Flaux, Julian QC 1978	Wales, Andrew 1992
Gaisman, Jonathan QC 1979	Healy, Siobán 1993
Kendrick, Dominic QC 1981	Phillips, Stephen 1993
Stewart-Richardson, Alastair 1952	Sabben-Clare, Rebecca 1993
Priday, Charles 1982	Khurshid, Jawdat 1994
Schaff, Alistair 1983	Waller, Richard 1994
Fenton, Adam 1984	Williams, Leigh 1996
Dias, Julia 1982	Kenefick, Timothy 1996
Hofmeyr, Stephen 1982	Bignall, John 1996

The Law Society's Directory of Expert Witnesses 1999

- *lists over 3,500 expert witnesses*

- *all entrants agree to comply with The Law Society's Code of Practice and provide two professional references*

- *contains information on choosing and instructing an expert witness*

- *includes 1,700+ specialists in areas of expertise*

- *provides an alphabetical index to assist in finding detailed terms*

- *also available on CD-ROM*

For more information call Sweet & Maxwell on 0171 449 1111

---

8 KING'S BENCH WALK

Temple, London EC4Y 7DU
0171 797 8888
Fax: 0171 797 8880/8854; DX 195 London,
Chancery Lane
Other comms: Mobiles: 07771 845605 (Marc
Foss) 07771 845606 (Del Edgeler) 07771
845607 (Tony Burton) 07771 845608 (Scott
Haley)

Chambers of L G Woodley QC
Clerks: Marc Foss, Del Edgeler, Tony Burton,
Scott Haley; Accountant: St Hilliare Bastien

Also at: 1 Park Square East, Leeds LS1 2NE
Tel: 0113 243 9797
Fax: 0113 245 7215

Woodley, Leonard QC 1963†	Fraser, Nigel 1986
	Ladak, Tahera 1986
Croxon, Raymond QC 1960	Gatto, Nicola 1987
Hart-Leverton, Colin QC 1957	Kitchen, Simon 1988
	Boateng, Paul 1989
Gifford, Lord Anthony QC 1962	Read, Simon 1989
	Tizzano, Franco 1989
Paulusz, Jan 1957†	Huda, Abida 1989
Allum, Desmond SC 1962	Mann, Jonathan 1989
Gibbs, Jocelyn 1972	Taylor-Camara, Alex 1989
Rubery, Philip 1973	Murray-Smith, James 1990
Shepherd, Nigel 1973	George, Susan 1990
Gassman, Caroline 1974	Harrill, Jayne 1990
Daniells-Smith, Roger 1974	Henderson, Ian 1990
Yearwood, Jeffrey 1975‡	Tehrani, Christopher 1990
Bart, Delano 1977	Sapnara, Khatun 1990
Jones, Martin Wynne 1977	Ryan, Timothy 1991
Keogh, Andrew 1978	Breese-Laughran, Delphine 1991
Williams, Alan 1978	
Collins, Robert 1978	Evans, Stephen 1992
Howe, Carole 1984	Bazini, Danny 1994
Rose, Pamela 1980	Igori, Kingsly 1993
Hodgson, Martin 1980	Gannon, Kevin 1993
Munro, Sanderson 1981	Taylor, Steven 1992
Salter, Charles 1981	Williams, Paul 1994
Fessal, Ignatius 1981	Ivens, Jemma 1994
Barnett, Adrienne 1981	Ryan, William 1994
MacKinnon, Tom 1982	Jones, David 1994
Hill, Andrew 1982	Munday, Anne 1994
Dunn, Alex 1985	McCarthy, Martin 1994
Williams, Nicola 1985	Gordon, Clare 1995

Opening times: 9 am-6.30 pm

Types of work (and number of counsel practising in that area if supplied)
Administrative · Care proceedings · Chancery
(general) · Civil liberties · Common law
(general) · Courts martial · Crime · Crime -
corporate fraud · Discrimination · Education
· Employment · Environment · Family · Family
provision · Housing · Immigration · Insurance

· Insurance/reinsurance · Landlord and tenant · Licensing · Local government · Medical negligence · Mental health · Personal injury · Professional negligence

Chambers' facilities
Conference rooms, Disks accepted, E-mail

Languages spoken
French, German, Greek, Hindi, Italian, Urdu

9 KING'S BENCH WALK

Ground Floor, Temple, London EC4Y 7DX
0171 353 7202/3909
Fax: 0171 583 2030; DX 472 London, Chancery Lane

Chambers of F Ashe Lincoln QC
Clerks: Gary Morgan (Senior Clerk), Gary Nichols, Alexis McBlain (Junior Clerks)

Lincoln, Ashe QC *1929†*	**Miah,** Zacharias *1990*
Popat, Surendra *1969‡*	**Sheffi,** Bosmath *1991*
Gribble, Peter *1972*	**St John Howe,** Peter *1992*
Marsh, Peter *1975*	**Obuka,** Obijuo *1993*
Stones, Keith *1975*	**Pavlou,** Paul *1993*
Deschampsneufs, Alice *1976*	**Jacobs,** Christopher *1994*
	Sneller, Elaine *1994*
Greenslade, Henry *1982*	**Ladmore,** Richard *1995*
Sultan, Amir *1983*	**Murphy,** Michael *1992*
Delamere, Isabel *1985*	**Lowry,** Anne-Marie *1995*
McGivern, William *1987*	**Burgher,** Benjamin *1995*
Trigg, Miles *1987*	**Bankole-Jones,** Gwen *1991*
Brown, Susan *1989*	**Villarosa,** Annunziata *1995*

Chambers established: 1910
Opening times: 9 am-6 pm

Types of work (and number of counsel practising in that area if supplied)
Administrative 1 · Bankruptcy 2 · Care proceedings 5 · Chancery (general) 4 · Charities 1 · Commercial litigation 5 · Commercial property 3 · Common law (general) 14 · Company and commercial 5 · Construction 2 · Conveyancing 2 · Copyright 2 · Courts martial 1 · Crime 16 · Crime - corporate fraud 4 · Defamation 2

· Employment 6 · Equity, wills and trusts 2 · Family 11 · Family provision 8 · Housing 4 · Immigration 5 · Insolvency 5 · Intellectual property 2 · Landlord and tenant 4 · Licensing 6 · Medical negligence 3 · Mental health 1 · Patents 1 · Personal injury 8 · Probate and administration 2 · Professional negligence 8 · Sale and carriage of goods 2 · Trademarks 1

Chambers' facilities
Conference rooms, Video conferences, Disks accepted, E-mail

Languages spoken
Bengali, French, German, Greek, Gujarati, Hebrew, Hindi, Italian, Punjabi, Swahili, Urdu

Fees policy
To be negotiated with the Senior Clerk.

THE CHAMBERS OF MR ALI MOHAMMAD AZHAR

9 King's Bench Walk (Lower Ground South), Temple, London EC4Y 7DX
0171 353 9564 (4 lines)
Fax: 0171 353 7943; DX 118 London, Chancery Lane
E-mail: jvlee@btinternet.com

Chambers of A M Azhar
Clerk: Mr J V Lee; Practice manager: Mr J V Lee; Administrator: Mr Azhar

Azhar, Ali *1962*	**Bhardwaj,** Sunita *1992*
Khan, Mohamed *1969*	**Simpson,** David *1992*
Offoh, Johnson *1972*	**Kodagoda,** Fritz *1993*
Nusrat, Mahmood *1977*	**Azhar,** Shabeena *1995*
Chowdhary, Islamuddin *1982*	**Adewale,** Remi *1995*
	Beresford-Evans, Cerys *1995*
Slevin, Frank *1985*	
Blackford, Robert *1988*	**Al-Ani,** Abdul-Haq *1996*
Navaratne, Francis *1990*	**Gerrard,** Lee *1996*
Al-Rashid, Mahmud *1991*	**Siddique,** Bilal *1996*

C

† Recorder ‡ Assistant Recorder * Door Tenant

10 KING'S BENCH WALK

10 KING'S BENCH WALK

Ground Floor, Temple, London EC4Y 7EB
0171 353 7742
Fax: 0171 583 0579; DX 24 London
E-mail: 10kbw@lineone.net

Chambers of Claudius John Algar
Clerks: Lee Kyprian, Alan Curtis

Algar, Claudius *1972*	Robins, Alison *1987*
Hare, Rosina QC *1956†*	Devoy-Williams, David *1989*
Hart, Colin *1966*	Cheshire, Anthony *1992*
Urquhart, Doris *1967*	McShane, Anne *1992*
Vaudin, Charles *1971*	Serle, Diana *1992*
Tapping, Susan *1975‡*	Harris, Michael *1993*
Boston, Janet *1976*	Hurworth, Jillian *1993*
Christensen, Carlton *1977*	Swainson, Richard *1994*
Pearce, Reid *1979*	Harding, Patricia *1994*
Hedworth, Leonard *1979*	Martin, Jonathan *1994*
Miscampbell, Bernadette *1980*	O'Callaghan, Declan *1995*
	Galpin, Diana *1995*
Lanigan, William *1980*	Butler, Simon *1996*
Powell, Dean *1982*	Bui, Victoria *1996*
Gibbons, Orlando *1982*	McNally, John *1996*
Evans, Andrew *1984*	Back, Patrick QC *1940†**
Talacchi, Carlo *1986*	

10 KING'S BENCH WALK

1st Floor, Temple, London EC4Y 7EB
0171 353 2501
Fax: 0171 353 0658; DX 294 London

Chambers of Mr R Thwaites QC

> **See the** *Index of Languages Spoken* **in Part G to locate a chambers where a particular language is spoken, or find an individual who speaks a particular language.**

11 KING'S BENCH WALK

Temple, London EC4Y 7EQ
0171 632 8500
Fax: 0171 583 9123/3690; DX LDE 368
E-mail: clerksroom@11-kbw.law.co.uk
URL: http://www.11-kbw.law.co.uk
Out of hours telephone: 0181 658 1034
(Philip Monham)

Chambers of Eldred Tabachnik QC, James Goudie QC
Clerks: Philip Monham, Nicholas Hill, Lucy Barbet, Stephen Penson

Tabachnik, Eldred QC *1970‡*	Giffin, Nigel *1986*
	Wallington, Peter *1987*
Goudie, James QC *1970†*	Pitt-Payne, Timothy *1989*
Field, Richard QC *1977‡*	Swift, Jonathan *1989*
Elias, Patrick QC *1973‡*	Oldham, Peter *1990*
Supperstone, Michael QC *1973†*	Jones, Sean *1991*
	Sheldon, Clive *1991*
Slade, Elizabeth QC *1972‡*	Choudhury, Akhlaq *1992*
McGregor, Alistair QC *1974*	Nicholls, Paul *1992*
Jeans, Christopher QC *1980*	Stilitz, Daniel *1992*
Sales, Philip *1985*	Coppel, Jason *1994*
Laing, Elisabeth *1980*	Porter, Nigel *1994*
Lynch, Adrian *1983*	Ivimy, Cecilia *1995*
Ward, Siobhan *1984*	Restrick, Thomas *1995*
Cavanagh, John *1985*	Leiper, Richard *1996*
Bear, Charles *1986*	Wilson, Julian *1997*

Chambers established: 1981
Opening times: 8 am-7 pm

Types of work (and number of counsel practising in that area if supplied)
Administrative 21 · Bankruptcy 5 · Civil liberties 12 · Commercial litigation 19 · Defamation 2 · Discrimination 24 · EC and competition law 8 · Education 13 · Employment 28 · Entertainment 3 · Environment 6 · Housing 5 · Immigration 3 · Insurance/reinsurance 6 · Intellectual property 3 · International trade 8 · Local government 21 · Private international 7 · Professional negligence 10 · Public international 8 · Sale and carriage of goods 14 · Share options 7 · Shipping, admiralty 3 · Town and country planning 2

† Recorder ‡ Assistant Recorder * Door Tenant

Chambers' facilities
Conference rooms, Disks accepted, E-mail

Languages spoken
French, Italian, Spanish

Additional information

11 King's Bench Walk is a set of chambers which has always undertaken a special mix of work in the fields of Commercial law, Public law, and Employment law. Recent years have seen a steady expansion in numbers within chambers and there are now eight silks and 22 juniors. The commercial work undertaken both in the UK and overseas includes: insurance and reinsurance; banking: especially letters of credit, performance bonds, and bankers' securities; arbitration; carriage of goods; Stock Exchange transactions; mergers and acquisitions; financial services; Competition law; commodities and futures; Corporation law; professional malpractice especially accountants' negligence; intellectual property; and entertainment industry agreements. The Public law work undertaken by chambers covers judicial review, tribunals, inquiries and advisory work both for and against public bodies arising from decisions in many and varied areas including: education; Environmental law; commercial and financial regulation; local authority finance and powers; competitive tendering and public authority contracts; elections; and housing. The Employment law covered includes: industrial disputes and Trade Union law; pensions, share options, and bonus schemes; restrictive covenants and breach of confidence; wrongful and unfair dismissal; transfers of undertakings; EC Employment law; sex and race discrimination and equal pay. Several members have written or collaborated on legal works which include: *Harvey on Industrial Relations and Employment Law* (editor Patrick Elias QC), *Tolley's Employment Handbook* (Elizabeth Slade QC and other members of chambers), *Butterworths' Employment Law Handbook* (editor Peter Wallington), *Halsbury's Laws of England: Administrative Law* (Michael Supperstone QC, John Cavanagh, Nigel Giffin and Philip Sales), *Immigration: The Law and Practice* (Michael Supperstone QC), and *Supperstone and Goudie: Judicial Review* (including contributions from Patrick Elias QC, Peter Wallington, Jonathan Swift and Timothy Pitt-Payne). Chambers' brochure is available on request.

11 KING'S BENCH WALK

1st Floor, Temple, London EC4Y 7EQ
0171 353 3337/8
Fax: 0171 583 2190; DX LDE 389 Chancery Lane

Chambers of F J Muller QC
Clerks: A T Blaney (London), A Dunstone (Leeds)

Annexe: 11 King's Bench Walk, 3 Park Court, Park Cross Street, Leeds LS1 2QH
Tel: 0113 2971 200
Fax: 0113 2971 201

Muller, Franz QC *1961*†	Campbell, Nicholas *1978*
Robson, David QC *1965*†	Richardson, Jeremy *1980*
Spencer, James QC *1975*†	Attwooll, Christopher *1980*
Lawler, Simon QC *1971**	Wynn, Toby *1982*
Cosgrove, Patrick QC *1976**	Caswell, Rebecca *1983*
Batty, Paul QC *1975*†	Swain, Fiona *1983*
Robertson, Andrew QC *1975*†	Reeds, Graham *1984*
	Cooper, John *1985*
Richardson, Henry *1951*†	Mallett, Simon *1986*
Graham, John *1955*	Waterman, Adrian *1988*
Collins, John *1956*†*	Brooke, David *1990*
Radcliffe, Francis *1962*	Toone, Robert *1993*
Caswell, Matthew *1968*	Skelt, Ian *1994*
Barlow, Richard *1970*	Antrobus, Simon *1995*
Winch, John *1973**	Margree, Sarah *1996*
Adams, James *1978**	

The Supreme Court Practice 1999
* the most authoritative title on Civil Court Practice and Procedure
* available in book and CD-ROM formats
Phone Sweet & Maxwell on 0171 449 1111 to order your copy

12 KING'S BENCH WALK

Temple, London EC4Y 7EL
0171 583 0811
Fax: 0171 583 7228; DX 1037 London
E-mail: chambers@12kbw.co.uk
Out of hours telephone: 0468 200252/0378 192289

Chambers of R J Walker QC
Clerks: Tony Day, John Cooper;
Practice manager: Lisa Pavlovsky

Walker, Ronald QC 1962†	**Hill-Smith**, Alexander 1978
Whitby, Charles QC 1952†	**Featherby**, William 1978
Stow, Timothy QC 1965†	**Rodway**, Susan 1981
Goldstaub, Anthony QC 1972	**Howard**, Jonathan 1983
	Russell, Paul 1984
Speaight, Anthony QC 1973	**Lewers**, Nigel 1986
Methuen, Richard QC 1972	**Newbery**, Freya 1986
Goldrein, Iain QC 1975‡	**Pickering**, Andrew 1987
de Haas, Margaret QC 1977‡	**Hamill**, Hugh 1988
	Vineall, Nicholas 1988
Burton, Frank QC 1982	**Chambers**, Adam 1989
Grobel, Peter 1967†	**Brown**, Catherine 1990
Dedman, Peter 1968†	**Chandler**, Kate 1990
Spencer-Lewis, Neville 1970	**Evans**, Caroline 1991
Hooper, Toby 1973‡	**Moran**, Vincent 1991
King, John 1973	**Audland**, William 1992
Hogarth, Andrew 1974	**Vincent**, Patrick 1992
Gallagher, Brian 1975	**Kendall**, Joel 1993
Heathcote Williams, Nicholas 1976	**Viney**, Richard 1994
	D'Souza, Carolyn 1994
Worthington, Stephen 1976	**Ginn**, Michael 1994
Crawford, Lincoln 1977†	**Peck**, Catherine 1995
Gore, Allan 1977	**Petts**, Timothy 1996

Types of work (and number of counsel practising in that area if supplied)
Arbitration 7 · Banking 4 · Commercial litigation 12 · Construction 18 · Employment 12 · Environment 4 · Housing 6 · Insurance 20 · Insurance/reinsurance 16 · Landlord and tenant 13 · Medical negligence 19 · Personal injury 38 · Professional negligence 34 · Sale and carriage of goods 10

Chambers' facilities
Conference rooms, Disks accepted, E-mail

Languages spoken
French, Italian, Portuguese, Spanish

Fees policy
Chambers is always willing to negotiate fees on a basis suitable to the client.

Additional information
This established civil and commercial set of chambers has specialist groups of barristers with particular expertise in the fields of Construction and Employment law. Chambers has a progressive outlook: it has modern staffing arrangements and is equipped with the latest computerisation, thus ensuring that the work is dealt with quickly and efficiently with the needs of each individual client in mind.

Commercial (including banking, credit transactions and accountants' negligence). **Construction** (including all standard form building and engineering contracts, computer law and architects', engineers' and surveyors' negligence). **Employment** (including race relations and equal opportunities). **Insurance and Reinsurance** (including drafting and constructing policies, material damage claims, employers' and public liability claims). **Personal Injury and Medical Negligence** (including industrial disease claims and disaster inquiries). **Professional Negligence** (all aspects of this work including the above-mentioned and solicitors' and barristers' negligence). **Property law** (in particular, landlord and tenant and housing). **Public law** (including judicial review, local government and Environmental law).

Publications:
Members of chambers have written, edited or contributed to a significant number of publications, including: Walker & Walker: *The English Legal System*; Bullen & Leake & Jacob's *Precedents of Pleadings; Master and Servant*, in *Halsbury's Laws of England*, 3rd edition; *Atkins Court Forms*, 2nd edition; *Law of Defective Premises; Architects' Journal Legal Handbook; Construction Disputes: Liability and the Expert Witness* ; Odgers: *Pleadings and Practice; Consumer Credit Law and Practice; Medical Negligence: Case law; Architect's Legal Handbook; Butterworths Personal Injury Litigation Service; Commercial Litigation: Pre-emptive Remedies; Personal Injury Litigation Law; Cordery on Solicitors.*

Chambers' brochure is available on request.

† Recorder ‡ Assistant Recorder * Door Tenant

13 KING'S BENCH WALK

Temple, London EC4Y 7EN
0171 353 7204
Fax: 0171 583 0252; DX LDE 359
E-mail: clerks@13kbw.law.co.uk
Other comms: Lix: Lon 066

Chambers of Graeme Williams QC
Clerks: Stephen Buckingham, Kevin Kelly;
Administrator: Penny McFall

Annexe: King's Bench Chambers, 32
Beaumont Street, Oxford OX1 2NP
Tel: 01865 311066
Fax: 01865 311077

Williams, Graeme QC *1959†*	**Glennie**, Andrew *1982*
Baughan, Julian QC *1967†*	**Williams**, A *1983*
Ellis, Roger QC *1962*	**Coode**, Jonathan *1984*
Ashton, David *1962*	**Vickery**, Neil *1985*
Dawson, Alexander *1969†*	**Moore**, Neil *1986*
McGeorge, Anthony *1969*	**Gibbons**, Sarah *1987*
Lamb, Robert *1973*	**Blake**, Arthur *1988*
Richardson, David *1973†*	**Cramsie**, Sinclair *1988*
Gibbons, James *1974*	**Quirke**, Gerard *1988*
Goodwin, Deirdre *1974*	**Hay**, Fiona *1989*
Hughes, Simon *1974*	**Pote**, Andrew *1983**
Grant, David *1975‡*	**Higgins**, Adrian *1990*
Reid, Paul *1975*	**Walters**, Edmund *1991*
Tracy Forster, Jane *1975*	**Wenlock**, Heather *1991*
Bright, David *1976†*	**Walters**, Vivian *1991*
Draycott, Simon *1977‡*	**Majumdar**, Shantanu *1992*
Lambie, Donald *1978*	**Panesar**, Deshpal *1993*
Brough, Alasdair *1979*	**Chan**, Susan *1994*
Daly, Nigel *1979*	**Mitchell**, Paul *1994*
Syfret, Nicholas *1979*	

Chambers established: 1971
Opening times: 8.30 am-6.30 pm

Types of work (and number of counsel practising in that area if supplied)
Administrative 2 · Arbitration 2 · Banking 2
· Bankruptcy 7 · Care proceedings 4
· Chancery (general) 5 · Chancery land law 3
· Civil liberties 2 · Club law 2 · Commercial
litigation 4 · Common law (general) 18
· Company and commercial 6 · Construction 6
· Consumer Law 5 · Conveyancing 2
· Copyright 2 · Crime 15 · Crime - corporate
fraud 4 · Defamation 1 · Employment 14
· Family 6 · Family provision 6 · Financial
services 2 · Housing 2 · Immigration 2
· Insolvency 8 · Insurance 3 · Intellectual
property 2 · Landlord and tenant 7 · Licensing
3 · Medical negligence 6 · Mental health 2
· Partnerships 2 · Personal injury 14 · Private
international 4 · Professional negligence 8
· Sale and carriage of goods 11

Languages spoken
Cantonese, French, Italian, Portuguese

Fees policy
Up to five years call £35-75 per hour. Five to ten
years call £50-125 per hour. Over ten years call
£75-250 per hour. Fees are charged on an hourly
basis, by reference to the complexity and value
of the matter and the seniority of counsel. The
senior clerks will be pleased to discuss the level
of fees in advance of work commencing on any
matter.

CHAMBERS OF LORD CAMPBELL OF ALLOWAY QC

2 King's Bench Walk Chambers, Temple,
London EC4Y 7DE
0171 353 9276
Fax: 0171 353 9949; DX 477 London,
Chancery Lane

Chambers of George Papageorgis
Clerk: Brenda Anderson (Senior Clerk)

Campbell of Alloway, Lord QC *1939*	**Davies**, Sarah *1984*
Papageorgis, George *1981*	**Kapur**, Deepak *1984*
Rueff, Philip *1969†*	**Livesey**, Simon *1987*
Dalgleish, Anthony *1971*	**Perian**, Steven *1987*
Evans, Alun *1971*	**Alban-Lloyd**, Nan *1988*
Wong, Rene *1973*	**Gokhool**, Vishnu *1978*
Colegate-Stone, Jefferson *1975*	**Meadowcroft**, Gregory *1990*
Slack, Ian *1974*	**Lorenzo**, Claudia *1991*
Mendes Da Costa, David *1976*	**Kennedy**, Brian *1992*
Gifford, Robert *1977*	**Callman**, Tanya *1993*
Lloyd, Patricia *1979*	**Katyar**, Arun *1993*
Gaylord, Sheila *1983*	**Sandeman**, David *1993*
Levy, Anthony *1983*	**Freeman**, Lee *1994*
Lynn, Jeremy *1983*	**Johnson**, Janice *1994*
	Dean, Abigail *1995*
	Wilson, Lachlan *1996*

Chambers established: 1960
Opening times: 8.30 am-6.30 pm

C

Types of work (and number of counsel practising in that area if supplied)

Administrative · Arbitration · Aviation · Banking · Bankruptcy · Care proceedings · Commercial · Common law (general) · Defamation · Education · Employment · Family · Housing · Immigration · Landlord and tenant · Licensing · Local government · Personal injury · Professional negligence · Shipping, admiralty · Sports

Chambers' facilities

Conference rooms, Disks accepted

Languages spoken

Greek

Additional information

King's Bench Walk Chambers

These Chambers are located on the first and second floors of one of the oldest buildings in the Temple.

A wide range of work is undertaken in the field of General Common Law as well as Criminal Law, Family Law, Administrative Law, work before Tribunals in Education Law, Employment Law, and Human Rights.

Constant review is kept on the changing needs of solicitors and the public, while at the same time the Bar's traditional values are maintained and fostered by members who present a welcoming attitude to lay and professional clients.

KING'S CHAMBERS

49a Broadway, Stratford, London E15 4BW
Fax: 0181 368 8130; DX 5400 STRATFORD

Chambers of Mr V C S Gokhool

KINGSWAY CHAMBERS

88 Kingsway, London WC2B 6AA
07000 653529
Fax: 07000 781115; DX 205 London, Chancery Lane
E-mail: lanreoke@lineone.net
Out of hours telephone: 0973 145448

Chambers of Mr Lanre Oke
Clerk: Mr Lanre Oke

Oke, Olanrewaju *1979*   Sharma, Rakhee *1995*

LAMB BUILDING

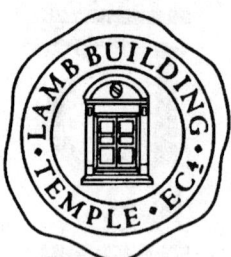

Ground Floor, Temple, London EC4Y 7AS
0171 797 7788
Fax: 0171 353 0535; DX 1038 London, Chancery Lane
E-mail: lamb.building@link.org
Out of hours telephone: 0421 339232

Chambers of Ami Feder
Clerks: Gary Goodger, David Corne, Paul Hammond, Sarah Fowler, Simon Bewsey

Also at: 3 Temple Gardens

Feder, Ami *1965*	Roberts, Richard *1983*
Wheeler, Kenneth *1956*	Sawhney, Debbie *1987*
Mullally, Maureen *1957*	Cotterill, Susan *1988*
Krolick, Ivan *1966*	Richmond, Bernard *1988*
Edlin, David *1971*	Terry, Jane *1988*
Fox, John *1973*	Haughty, Jeremy *1989*
Edie, Anthony *1974*	Brounger, David *1990*
Gordon, Jeremy *1974*	Hindle, Frances *1990*
Waters, John *1974*	Crampin, Paul *1992*
Barton, Alan *1975*	Geser, Anita *1992*
Hilliard, Spenser *1975*	Kearney, Seamus *1992*
Perry, Jacqueline *1975*	Weinstein, Lindsay *1992*
Hartman, Michael *1975*	Rothwell, Joanne *1993*
Hodes, Angela *1979*	Cole, Martin *1994*
Phillips, Michael *1980*	Dykers, Joy *1995*
Cook, David *1982*	Bitmead, Paul *1996*
Fielden, Christa *1982*	

Opening times: 8.30 am-6.30 pm

Types of work (and number of counsel practising in that area if supplied)

Arbitration · Banking · Bankruptcy · Care proceedings · Chancery (general) · Chancery land law · Commercial · Common law (general) · Company and commercial · Construction · Courts martial · Crime · Crime - corporate fraud · Employment · Equity, wills and trusts · Family · Family provision · Foreign law · Housing · Immigration · Insolvency · Landlord and tenant · Licensing · Local government · Medical negligence · Mental health · Partnerships · Probate and administration · Professional negligence · Sale and carriage of goods · Town and country planning

Chambers' facilities
Conference rooms, Video conferences, Disks accepted, Disabled access, E-mail

Languages spoken
Dutch, French, German, Hebrew, Italian, Spanish

Fees policy
Upon request, fees will be negotiated with the clerk depending on the case.

LAMB CHAMBERS

• L A M B   C H A M B E R S •

Lamb Building, Elm Court, Temple, London EC4Y 7AS
0171 797 8300
Fax: 0171 797 8308; DX 418 London
E-mail: lambchambers@link.org

Chambers of Jonathan R Cole
Clerk: John Kelly; Administrator: Linda Spanner

Cole, Jonathan 1964†	**Thoresby**, Robert 1978
Priest, Julian QC 1954	**Silvester**, Bruce 1983
Burke-Gaffney, Michael QC 1959	**Mendoza**, Colin 1983
Leeming, Ian QC 1970†	**Emerson**, Paul 1984
Gardner, Christopher QC 1968†	**Franklin**, Kim 1984
	Graham, Thomas 1985
Sterling, John 1953	**Samuel**, Gerwyn 1986
Anderson, Donald MP 1969	**Rolfe**, Patrick 1987
McNeile, Anthony 1970	**Wood**, Simon 1987
West, Mark 1973‡	**Stuart**, James 1990
di Mambro, David 1973	**Walden-Smith**, Karen 1990
Carey, Jeremy 1974‡	**Gough**, Katherine 1990
Connerty, Anthony 1974	**Haggerty**, Elizabeth 1994
Shaw, Stephen 1975	**Jones**, Rhiannon 1993
Farber, Martin 1976	**Hayes**, Richard 1995
Brilliant, Simon 1976	**Frith**, Timothy 1996

8 LAMBERT JONES MEWS

Barbican, London EC2Y 8DP
0171 638 8804

Chambers of Mr M C B West QC

29A LAMBS CONDUIT STREET

Holborn, London WC1N 3NG
0171 831 9907
Fax: 0171 831 9907

Chambers of Mr J M Taylor

21 LAUDERDALE TOWER

Barbican, London EC2Y 8BY
0171 920 9308
Fax: 0171 628 8124

Chambers of Mr E J Wollner

LEONE CHAMBERS

72 Evelyn Avenue, Kingsbury, London NW9 OJH
0181 931 1712
Fax: 0181 200 4020

Chambers of Mr D E J George

CHAMBERS OF NIGEL LEY

Second Floor, South Gray's Inn Chambers, Gray's Inn, London WC1R 5JA
0171 831 7888
Fax: 0171 831 7227

Chambers of Mr N J Ley

LIBRARY CHAMBERS

First Floor, Gray's Inn Chambers, Gray's Inn, London WC1R 5JA
0171 404 6500
Fax: 0171 404 6394; DX 78 Chancery Lane
*Clerks: Laurie Gallogly, Sean Phelan;
Practice manager: Peter Hoskins; Managed by: Mayfax Limited*

Lowther, Samantha *1995*	**Ronksley,** Andrew *1995*
Sillis, Louise *1994*	**Allen,** Frances *1995*
Smith, Lisa *1994*	**Chipperfield,** Jeremy *1995*
Mutch, Alison *1995*	**Bustani,** Navaz *1995*
Craven, Richard *1995*	**Momtaz,** Sam *1995*
Miller, Hayley *1995*	**Pidcock,** Steven *1996*

LION COURT

Chancery House, 53-64 Chancery Lane, London WC2A 1SJ
0171 404 6565
Fax: 0171 404 6659; DX 98 London, Chancery Lane

Chambers of S N Jacobs
Practice manager: Kim Brown

Jacobs, Steven *1974*	**Newberry,** David *1990*
Taylor, Neil QC *1949†*	**Honey,** John *1990*
Boyd, Gerard *1967*	**Bailey,** Stephen *1991*
Kaye, Laraine *1971*	**McCullough,** Louise *1991*
Cooksley, Subhashini *1975*	**Mendel,** Philippa *1992*
Nicholas, Georgina *1983*	**Kaffel,** Paul *1993*
Hosking, Steve *1988*	**Myerson,** Victoria *1995*
Brinkworth, Paul *1990*	**Krikler,** Alex *1995*

See the *Index of Languages Spoken* **in Part G to locate a chambers where a particular language is spoken, or find an individual who speaks a particular language.**

LITTLETON CHAMBERS

3 King's Bench Walk North, Temple, London EC4Y 7HR
0171 797 8600
Fax: 0171 797 8699; DX 1047 London, Chancery Lane
E-mail: littletonchambers@compuserve.com
Other comms: Link: Chambers & Barristers; Lix: Lon 052
Out of hours telephone: Answerphone or David Douglas: 01525 876495, Deborah Anderson: 0171 701 0576

Chambers of M J Burton QC
Clerks: David Douglas (Chief Executive), Deborah Anderson, Alistair Coyne, Tim Tarring, Tony Shaddock (Fees Clerk), Nita Johnston (Accounts Receivable Manager)

Burton, Michael QC *1970†*	**Sendall,** Antony *1984*
Kallipetis, Michel QC *1968†*	**Gatt,** Ian *1985*
Serota, Daniel QC *1969†*	**Duggan,** Michael *1984*
Mayes, Ian QC *1974*	**Trepte,** Peter *1987*
Price, Richard QC OBE *1969*	**Lowenstein,** Paul *1988*
Freedman, Clive QC *1978‡*	**Downey,** Raoul *1988*
Clarke, Andrew QC *1980*	**Barklem,** Martyn *1989*
Bowers, John QC *1979*	**Samek,** Charles *1989*
Manning, Colin *1970*	**Bacon,** Jeffrey *1989*
Perkoff, Richard *1971*	**Lewis,** Jeremy *1992*
Bartle, Philip *1976*	**Ellenbogen,** Naomi *1992*
Lomas, Mark *1977*	**Tatton-Brown,** Daniel *1994*
Higginson, Timothy *1977*	**Bather,** Victoria *1995*
Harry Thomas, Caroline *1981*	**Ritchie,** Stuart *1995*
Davies, John *1981*	**Davis,** Carol *1996*
Bothroyd, Shirley *1982*	**Harris,** Donald *1958**
Bloch, Selwyn *1982*	**MacCormick,** Prof Neil *1971**

Chambers established: 1954
Opening times: 8.30am-9 pm

Types of work (and number of counsel practising in that area if supplied)
ADR 11 · Arbitration 8 · Banking 7 · Bankruptcy 10 · Care proceedings 2 · Chancery (general) 11 · Commercial litigation 31 · Common law (general) 31 · Company and commercial 10 · Competition 8 · Construction 12 · Copyright 12 · Crime - corporate fraud 6

· Defamation 8 · Discrimination 25 · EC and competition law 6 · Education 20 · Employment 25 · Entertainment 30 · Family 2 · Film, cable, TV 10 · Financial services 10 · Information technology 7 · Insolvency 10 · Insurance 7 · Intellectual property 15 · International trade 5 · Landlord and tenant 3 · Medical negligence 5 · Parliamentary 2 · Partnerships 6 · Personal injury 5 · Professional negligence 27 · Sale and carriage of goods 8 · Share options 2 · Sports 8 · Trademarks 10

Chambers' facilities
Conference rooms, Disks accepted, Disabled access, E-mail, Pre-meeting room, Out of hours contacts, Access to video conferences, Arbitration rooms, Lectures

Languages spoken
French, German, Greek, Hebrew, Italian, Mandarin

Fees policy
We have a flexible approach to fees and a dedicated fees negotiator who will be happy to provide quotations and discuss fees for individual cases.

Additional information

Littleton Chambers is a broad commercial set, able and determined to solve problems speedily and to offer a complete service in the commercial field. We aim to respond quickly and efficiently to instructions and in particular to the need for injunctive or other interlocutory relief.

As barristers we feel our special role and expertise is in advocacy, litigation strategy and aiming for the resolution of disputes by the most effective means possible.

Specialities of individual members of chambers include: Employment and Industrial Relations law, Intellectual Property and Entertainment, Banking and Insolvency, Commercial Crime and Tax Fraud, Professional Negligence, Defamation, Building and Construction law and Official Referees' Business and Public law and ADR (numerous members CEDR accredited).

Chambers recognises the requirement to provide a comprehensive and efficient service to both solicitors and lay clients. Barristers are organised into teams, covering all ranges of experience, in the main areas of specialism. Members have embraced new technology, in addition to word processing ability, an extensive use of electronic mail through Link

and Internet is undertaken, disk exchange operated and video conferencing arranged.

Clerical support is provided through experienced staff structured into specialist functional units. Members of the team are happy to provide guidance and assistance and welcome all inquiries.

LITTMAN CHAMBERS

LITTMAN CHAMBERS
BARRISTERS

12
GRAY'S INN SQUARE

GRAY'S INN
LONDON WC1R 5JP
TEL: (+44) 0171 404 4866
FAX: (+44) 0171 404 4812

12 Gray's Inn Square, Gray's Inn, London WC1R 5JP
0171 404 4866
Fax: 0171 404 4812; DX 0055 London, Chancery Lane
E-mail: admin@littmanchambers.com
Out of hours telephone: 01992 421630

Chambers of Mark Littman QC
Clerks: Lee Cutler (Senior Clerk), Stephen Lawrence; Administrator: Karen Raymond

Littman, Mark QC *1947*	**Allan**, Monique *1986*
Lewis, Philip *1958**	**Naidoo**, Seán *1990*
Stimpson, Michael *1969*	**Gibson**, Martin *1990*
Finnis, John *1970**	**Higgins**, Rupert *1991*
Kirk, Robert *1972*	**McCarthy**, Niamh *1991*
McClure, Brian *1976*	**Anderson**, Julie *1993*
Planterose, Rowan *1978*	**Falkowski**, Damian *1994*
Kolodziej, Andrzej *1978*	**Hickey**, Alexander *1995*
Tecks, Jonathan *1978*	**Roberts**, James *1996*
Hewson, Barbara *1985*	

Chambers established: 1980
Opening times: 8.30 am-6.30 pm

Types of work (and number of counsel practising in that area if supplied)
Administrative · Arbitration · Banking · Bankruptcy · Chancery (general) · Chancery land law · Commercial litigation · Commercial property · Company and commercial · Competition · Construction · Conveyancing · Discrimination · EC and competition law · Employment · Energy · Environment · Equity, wills and trusts · Immigration · Information technology · Insolvency · Insurance · International trade · Landlord and tenant

· Partnerships · Private international · Probate and administration · Professional negligence · Sale and carriage of goods · Shipping, admiralty · Telecommunications · Town and country planning

Chambers' facilities
Conference rooms, Disks accepted, E-mail

Languages spoken
Afrikaans, Dutch, French, German, Polish, Russian, Spanish

Fees policy
The clerks will be pleased to provide information on the fees by reference to hourly rates. In many cases all-inclusive fees may be fixed in advance. A fee scale showing hourly rates is available upon request.

114 LIVERPOOL ROAD

Islington, London N1 0RE
0171 226 9863
Fax: 0171 704 1111

Chambers of Mr M Eldridge

235 LONDON ROAD

Twickenham, London TW1 1ES
0181 892 5947
Fax: 0181 892 5947

Chambers of Mr L S Munasinghe

LUTON BEDFORD CHAMBERS

C/O Mr Alex Reid, 92 Holly Park Road, Friern Barnet, London N11 3HB
0181 361 9024/0181 444 6337

Chambers of Miss M A Gee

5 MARNEY ROAD

Battersea, London SW11 1ES
0171 978 4492
Fax: 0181 679 5037

The Bar Directory **is also available on the Internet at the following address:**

http://www.smlawpub-holborn.co.uk/bar

Middle Temple Lane

Temple, London EC4Y 9AA
0171 583 0659 (12 lines)
Fax: 0171 353 0652; DX 464 London, Chancery Lane
Other comms: Mobile: 0976 281902
Out of hours telephone: 01708 641671

Chambers of Colin Edward Dines, Andrew H Trollope QC
Clerks: John Pyne (Senior Clerk), Clifford Strong, Richard Vile, Richard Willicombe, Jake Outhwaite; Administrator: Stanley Mott

Dines, Colin *1970*†	**Lucas,** Noel *1979*
Trollope, Andrew QC *1971*†	**Amor,** Christopher *1984*
Backhouse, Roger QC *1965**	**Gluckstein,** Emma *1985*
	Mayo, Simon *1985*
Ashby, David *1963*	**Rainsford,** Mark *1985*
Gardiner, Nicholas *1967*	**Marshall,** Andrew *1986*
Docking, Tony *1969*	**Butcher,** Richard *1985*
Arran, Graham *1969*†	**Strachan,** Barbara *1986*
Browne, Godfree *1971*	**Lachkovic,** James *1987*
Davies, Jonathan *1971*†	**Bowyer,** Harry *1989*
Argyle, Brian *1972*‡	**Korda,** Anthony *1988*
Campbell, Andrew *1972*	**Newton,** Andrew *1989*
Hooper, Gopal *1973*‡	**Chaudhuri,** Avirup *1990*
King, Philip *1974*	**Bright,** Rachel *1991*
Reece, Brian *1974*	**Beynon,** Richard *1990*
Plumstead, John *1975*	**Murphy,** Philomena *1992*
Borrelli, Michael *1977*	**Wong,** Natasha *1993*
Copeman, Ian *1977*	**Jones,** Robert *1993*
Eaton, Bernard *1978*	

Chambers established: 1976
Opening times: 8.45 am-6 pm

Types of work (and number of counsel practising in that area if supplied)
Crime 36 · Crime - corporate fraud 20 · Immigration 3 · Licensing 3 · Medical negligence 2 · Personal injury 2

Languages spoken
French, German

---

† Recorder ‡ Assistant Recorder * Door Tenant

2 MIDDLE TEMPLE LANE

3rd Floor, Temple, London EC4Y 9AA
0171 583 4540
Fax: 0171 583 9178

Chambers of Mr S P Dhama

1A MIDDLE TEMPLE LANE

Ground Floor, Temple, London EC4Y 9AA
0171 353 8815
Fax: 0171 353 8815; DX 200650 Cheam

Chambers of Mrs J S Wallace

10 MILLFIELDS ROAD

London E5 OSB
0181 986 8059
Fax: 0181 986 8059

Chambers of Mr M A Syed

**The UK College of Family Mediators
Directory & Handbook 1998/99**

- *provides expert commentary on family mediation training and professional development and includes contributions by leading family mediation professionals*

- *lists over 100 family mediation groups/services and over 950 individual family mediators by region and alphabetically*

- *gives details of all members and associates of the UK College of Family Mediators*

- *includes the UK College of Family Mediators Standards and Code of Practice*

- *gives details of all the family mediation bodies which make up the UK College of Family Mediators*

For more information call Sweet & Maxwell on 0171 449 1111

---

1 MITRE COURT BUILDINGS

Temple, London EC4Y 7BS
0171 797 7070
Fax: 0171 797 7435; DX 342 Chancery Lane

Chambers of Bruce Blair QC
Clerks: Richard Beams, Steven McCrone

Blair, Bruce QC *1969*†	**Platts,** Rachel *1989*
Horowitz, Michael QC *1968*†	**Todd,** Elisabeth *1990*
Posnansky, Jeremy QC *1972*‡	**Bishop,** Timothy *1991*
	Kingscote, Geoffrey *1993*
Hughes, Judith QC *1974*†	**Potter,** Louise *1993*
Everall, Mark QC *1975*†	**Trowell,** Stephen *1995*
Pointer, Martin QC *1976*	**Warshaw,** Justin *1995*
Mostyn, Nicholas QC *1980*‡	**Yates,** Nicholas *1996*
Elvidge, John *1968*†	**Rodway,** Gilbert (QC Hong
Spon-Smith, Robin *1976*†	Kong) *1962**
Le Grice, Valentine *1977*	**Leong,** Jacqueline (QC Hong
Pope, Heather *1977*	Kong) *1970**
Carden, Nicholas *1981*	**Ryder,** Ernest QC *1981**
Murfitt, Catriona *1981*‡	**Williams,** Leon *1943**
Smith, Gavin *1981*	**Tyzack,** David *1970**
Dyer, Nigel *1982*	**Dodds,** Stephen *1976**
Moor, Philip *1982*	**Swift,** Jonathan *1977**
Todd, Charles *1983*	**Bradley,** Sally *1978**
Wood, Christopher *1986*	**Hershman,** David *1981**
Cusworth, Nicholas *1986*	**Hodgkin,** Harry *1983**
Davidson, Katharine *1987*	**Irving,** Gillian *1984**
Todd, Richard *1988*	**Smithburn,** Prof Eric *1989**

Chambers established: 1939
Opening times: 9 am-7 pm

Types of work (and number of counsel practising in that area if supplied)
Care proceedings 29 · Family 29 · Family provision 29 · Professional negligence 3

Chambers' facilities
Disks accepted, E-mail

Languages spoken
French

Additional information

1 Mitre Court Buildings is the longest established Chambers practising exclusively in

the area of family law. Chambers offers advocacy, advisory and drafting expertise over the entire range of family and matrimonial law, whether child or finance oriented, and undertakes work at all levels of court. Together with its service to privately paying clients, 1 Mitre Court Buildings has a strong commitment to and involvement in legally aided family work. Chambers is regularly instructed by the Official Solicitor and local authorities as well as on behalf of individual clients.

All members of 1 Mitre Court Buildings belong to the Family Law Bar Association. They have been involved in a large number of the leading financial cases listed in *At A Glance* and in many of the important cases concerning children. Members of Chambers are well used to handling cases with an international element and several are Fellows of the International Academy of Matrimonial Lawyers. A number of members of Chambers speak French or German.

One former and two current members of 1 Mitre Court Buildings are editors of *Rayden & Jackson on Divorce and Family Matters*, the leading textbook. Other members of Chambers have also published books or articles on family law topics. *At A Glance: Essential Court Tables for Ancillary Relief*, published by the Family Law Bar Association, is edited largely by members of 1 Mitre Court Buildings. Nicholas Mostyn QC has devised the *Child's PAY* computer software for calculating child support maintenance assessments and, with Mr Justice Singer, has recently produced *Capitalise*, a program for calculating *Duxbury* payments.

Members of Chambers are regular speakers at conferences and seminars on family law subjects.

Of the current Supreme Court judiciary, Lady Justice Butler-Sloss and Lord Justice Thorpe are former members of Chambers, as are Mr Justice Singer, Mr Justice Wall and Mrs Justice Hogg.

2 MITRE COURT BUILDINGS

2 Mitre Court Buildings
Barristers' Chambers

1st Floor, Temple, London EC4Y 7BX
0171 353 1353
Fax: 0171 353 8188; DX 0023 London,
Chancery Lane

Chambers of Roger Gray
Clerks: John H Markham (Senior Clerk), Miss Julie Kempston

Pearson, Michael *1952*	**Evans**, Delyth *1991*
O'Donoghue, Florence *1959*	**Clover**, Sarah *1993*
Parker, John *1975*	**Shaw**, Michael *1994*
Forward, Barry *1981*	**McCormack**, Philip *1994*
Gray, Roger *1984*	**Parker**, Timothy *1995*
O'Toole, Simon *1984*	**Hunt**, Peter *1964**
Holmes-Milner, James *1989*	**Throp**, Alison *1992**

2 MITRE COURT BUILDINGS

2MCB

2nd Floor, Temple, London EC4Y 7BX
0171 583 1380
Fax: 0171 353 7772; DX LDE 0032
Out of hours telephone: 01372 466348

Chambers of M F C FitzGerald QC
Clerk: Robert Woods

FitzGerald, Michael QC *1961*	Fookes, Robert *1975*
Widdicombe, David QC *1950*	Burton, Nicholas *1979*
Silsoe, Lord QC *1951*	King, Neil *1980*
Moriarty, Gerald QC *1951†*	Humphries, Michael *1982*
Anderson, Anthony QC *1964†*	Glover, Richard *1984*
Taylor, John QC *1958*	Macpherson, Mary *1984*
Bartlett, George QC *1966†*	Druce, Michael *1988*
Horton, Matthew QC *1969*	Taylor, Reuben *1990*
Roots, Guy QC *1969‡*	Moore, Victor *1992*
Alesbury, Alun *1974*	Boyle, Christopher *1994*
	Warren, Rupert *1994*

MITRE COURT CHAMBERS

3rd Floor, Mitre Court, Temple, London EC4Y 7BP
0171 353 9394
Fax: 0171 353 1488; DX 449 London, Chancery Lane
Out of hours telephone: 0171 353 9394

Chambers of John M Burton
Clerk: William Ingleton;
Practice manager: Alistair Adams

Burton, John *1979*	Bretherick, Diana *1989*
Shier, Francis *1952*	Forsyth, Andrew *1989*
Ford, David *1972*	Blake, Christopher *1990*
Frost, Gillian *1979*	Hackman, Carl *1990*
Hofford, Peter *1979*	Brown, Philip *1991*
O'Toole, Bartholomew *1980*	Goring, Julia *1991*
Laban, Alexander *1981*	Otwal, Mukhtiar *1991*
Turner, Roger *1982*	Bolton, Lucy *1994*
Wise, Leslie *1985*	Glass, Adam *1994*
Briegel, Pieter *1986*	Newell, Charlotte *1994*
Bridge, Ian *1988*	Thorowgood, Max *1995*
Mercer, Neil *1988*	

Opening times: 7.30 am-6.30 pm

Types of work (and number of counsel practising in that area if supplied)
Bankruptcy · Care proceedings · Chancery (general) · Chancery land law · Commercial · Commercial property · Commodities · Common land · Common law (general) · Company and commercial · Construction · Consumer Law · Copyright · Crime · Crime - corporate fraud · Discrimination · Ecclesiastical · Employment · Equity, wills and trusts · Family · Family provision · Financial services · Housing · Immigration · Information technology · Insolvency · Insurance · Insurance/reinsurance · Landlord and tenant · Licensing · Local government · Medical negligence · Mental health · Partnerships · Personal injury · Probate and administration · Professional negligence · Sale and carriage of goods · Sports · Telecommunications · Town and country planning

Chambers' facilities
Conference rooms, Disks accepted, Conferences out of Chambers

Languages spoken
Bengali, French, German, Serbo-Croat, Spanish

Fees policy
Up to five years call £50-90, Five to ten years call £90-130, Ten years call £130-200. Fees within those rates depend upon time engaged, urgency of instructions and complexity. We also accept conditional fees.

C

MITRE HOUSE CHAMBERS

MITRE HOUSE CHAMBERS

Mitre House, 44 Fleet Street, London EC4Y 1BN
0171 583 8233
Fax: 0171 583 2692; DX 0005 London
Out of hours telephone: 0956 316 404

Chambers of F P Gilbert
Clerk: Osman Avdji; Administrator: Frances Shaw

Barry, Joseph *1987*	**McCarthy,** Damian *1994*
Bond, Jackie *1994*	**McCrindell,** James *1993*
Chand, Ragveer *1994*	**McVay,** Bridget *1990*
Cooray, Upali *1974*	**Osman,** Osman *1995*
Dent, Sally *1989*	**Osman,** Sona *1986*
Gilbert, Francis *1980*	**Payne,** Tracey *1991*
Gilling, Denise *1992*	**Phelan,** Margaret *1993*
Glanville, Susan *1991*	**Pontac,** Sandra *1981*
Henderson, Mark *1994*	**Raffell,** Andrew *1983*
Henry, Jennifer *1990*	**Rogers,** Donald *1991*
Heraghty, David *1995*	**Steadman,** Russell *1995*
Holloway, Sharon *1994*	**Teggin,** Victoria *1990*
Illingworth, Stephen *1993*	**Toms,** Nicholas *1996*
Kirby, Ruth *1994*	**Walker,** Stuart *1990*
Lawrenson, Mary *1994*	**Flockton,** Seanie *1977**
Lygo, Carl *1991*	**Gingell,** Melanie *1988**

Chambers established: 1984
Opening times: 8.45 am-6.30 pm

Types of work (and number of counsel practising in that area if supplied)
Administrative 6 · Care proceedings 11 · Chancery (general) 1 · Chancery land law 1 · Charities 1 · Civil liberties 12 · Common law (general) 7 · Construction 1 · Courts martial 2 · Crime 18 · Crime - corporate fraud 6 · Discrimination 4 · EC and competition law 1 · Education 1 · Employment 12 · Environment 2 · Equity, wills and trusts 1 · Family 12 · Family provision 7 · Foreign law 1 · Housing 7 · Immigration 7 · Landlord and tenant 6 · Licensing 3 · Local government 2 · Medical negligence 2 · Mental health 3 · Pensions 2 · Personal injury 10 · Professional disciplinary matters (sols) - CICB · Professional negligence 1

Chambers' facilities
Conference rooms, Video facilities

Languages spoken
French, German, Hindi, Italian, Punjabi, Sinhala, Spanish, Turkish

Fees policy
Please refer to the clerks.

Additional information

Mitre House is well established as a busy, progressive set with efficient clerking. The main areas of work are criminal defence, family law and civil litigation, which is continuing to expand with a particular emphasis on civil liberties, civil actions against the police, immigration, personal injury, employment, housing and judicial review. A full prospectus of work undertaken by individual tenants is available on request. From the beginning Mitre House has undertaken work free of charge or at a reduced rate in appropriate cases, particularly before tribunals for which legal aid is not available. Chambers provides an informed and reliable service to our professional clients.

MONCKTON CHAMBERS

MONCKTON CHAMBERS
4 RAYMOND BUILDINGS

4 Raymond Buildings, Gray's Inn, London WC1R 5BP
0171 405 7211
Fax: 0171 405 2084; DX 257 London
E-mail: chambers@monckton.co.uk

Chambers of Richard Fowler QC
Clerk: Graham Lister; Practice manager: Milly Ayliffe

Fowler, Richard QC *1969*	**Thompson,** Rhodri *1989*
Seymour, Richard QC *1972*†	**Skilbeck,** Jennifer *1991*
	Hill, Raymond *1992*
Parker, Kenneth QC *1975*	**Simor,** Jessica *1992*
Lasok, Paul QC *1977*	**Harris,** Paul *1994*
Roth, Peter QC *1976*	**Haynes,** Rebecca *1994*
Paines, Nicholas QC *1978*	**Robertson,** Aidan *1995*
Vajda, Christopher QC *1979*	**Smith,** Kassie *1995*
Pelling, Mark *1979*	**Beard,** Daniel *1996*
Anderson, Rupert *1981*	**Peretz,** George *1990*
Patchett-Joyce, Michael *1981*	**Kemp,** David QC *1948**
Hall, Melanie *1982*	**Forde,** Michael SC *1987**
Macnab, Andrew *1986*	**Roberts,** Julian (Rechtsanwelt) *1987**
Turner, Jonathan *1988*	**Matsushima,** Masumi *1990**
Mantle, Peter *1989*	

Chambers established: 1940
Opening times: 8.30 am-6.30 pm

Types of work (and number of counsel practising in that area if supplied)
Administrative 18 · Agriculture 12 · Arbitration 5 · Aviation 1 · Banking 3 · Civil liberties 3 · Commercial 7 · Commercial litigation 16 · Company and commercial 3 · Competition 20 · Construction 8 · Consumer Law 5 · Copyright 3 · Crime - corporate fraud 2 · EC and competition law 19 · Employment 9 · Environment 6 · Film, cable, TV 4 · Immigration 2 · Insolvency 3 · Insurance/reinsurance 1 · Intellectual property 1 · International trade 2 · Pensions 2 · Private international 6 · Professional negligence 9 · Public international 6 · Sale and carriage of goods 4 · Sports 11 · Telecommunications 3 · Trademarks 2 · VAT and Customs & Excise 13

Chambers' facilities
Conference rooms, Disks accepted, E-mail

Languages spoken
Dutch, French, German, Japanese

Fees policy
Fees will be negotiated with the clerk depending on the case, but as a general guide: Chambers' fees are charged on an hourly rate basis agreed in advance. Hourly rates for each member of Chambers are available upon request.

MOTTINGHAM BARRISTER'S CHAMBERS

43 West Park, London SE9 4RZ
0181 857 5565
Fax: 0181 857 5565

Chambers of Mr C A Deve

CHAMBERS OF DR JAMAL NASIR

1st Floor, 2 Stone Buildings, Lincoln's Inn, London WC2A 3RH
0171 405 3818/9
Fax: 0171 831 1971

Chambers of J J Nasir
Clerk: Mrs A Bianchet

Nasir, Jamal *1948*

C

---

† Recorder ‡ Assistant Recorder * Door Tenant

NEW COURT

NEW COURT

Temple, London EC4Y 9BE
0171 583 5123
Fax: 0171 353 3383; DX 0018 London

Chambers of Christian V Bevington
Clerks: Paul Bloomfield, Paul Leahy, Adam Burton, James Stammers

Bevington, Christian 1961†	Hyams, Oliver 1989
Gilmartin, John 1972	Lamb, John 1990
Stanford Gordon, John 1970	Laming, Norma 1990
	Soffa, Helen 1990
Randolph, Paul 1971	Humphreys, Jane 1990
Cala, Guiseppe 1971	Krish, Doushka 1991
Arnold, Robert 1974	Charlton, Judith 1991
Kumalo, Dabi 1974	Todman, Deborah 1991
Kingsley, Richard 1977	Levy, Juliette 1992
Harrison, Michael 1979	Hasslacher, James 1993
Shackleford, Susan 1980	Taylor, Nigel 1993
Jenkins, Alun 1981	Bain, Giles 1993
Dickens, Andrew 1983	Powell, Robin 1993
Whitehouse, Stuart 1987	Murray, Judith 1994
Courtney, Ann 1987	Ferris, Caitlin 1996
Maynard, Christopher 1988	Garrood, Jeremy 1996
Nichols, Stuart 1989	Poole, Christopher 1996
Livingstone, Douglas 1989	

Chambers established: 1981
Opening times: 8.30 am-6.30 pm

Types of work (and number of counsel practising in that area if supplied)
Banking 1 · Bankruptcy 1 · Care proceedings 9 · Chancery (general) 5 · Common law (general) 1 · Crime 13 · Crime - corporate fraud 13 · Employment 5 · Family 12 · Family provision 10 · Foreign law 1 · Housing 5 · Insolvency 1 · Landlord and tenant 6 · Licensing 2 · Medical negligence 6 · Mental health 2 · Personal injury 8 · Probate and administration 2 · Professional negligence 5

Chambers' facilities
Conference rooms, Video conferences

Languages spoken
French, German, Italian, Russian

Fees policy
Fees will be negotiated with clerk depending on the case, seniority of counsel and nature of work involved.

NEW COURT

1st Floor, Temple, London EC4Y 9BE
0171 797 8999
Fax: 0171 583 5885; DX 420 London, Chancery Lane
Out of hours telephone: 0181 856 1077

Chambers of John V Fitzgerald
Clerk: Simon Coomber

Fitzgerald, John 1971	Kime, Matthew 1988
Firth, Alison 1980	Coulthard, Alan 1987
Hodgson, Richard 1980	

Chambers established: Before 1900

Types of work (and number of counsel practising in that area if supplied)
Commercial 5 · Copyright 5 · Defamation 4 · Entertainment 5 · Film, cable, TV 5 · Franchising 5 · Information technology 5 · Intellectual property 5 · International trade 4 · Patents 5 · Telecommunications 5 · Trademarks 5

Chambers' facilities
Disks accepted

Languages spoken
French

Fees policy
Chambers has a friendly approach to all its clients and flexibility is the key to fee negotiation.

† Recorder ‡ Assistant Recorder * Door Tenant

NEW COURT CHAMBERS

5 Verulam Buildings, Gray's Inn, London
WC1R 5LY
0171 831 9500
Fax: 0171 269 5700; DX 363 London,
Chancery Lane
E-mail: mail@newcourtchambers.com
URL: http://www.newcourtchambers.com

Chambers of George Carman QC
Clerks: Bill Conner (Senior Clerk), Paul Read,
Kathryn Jolly, Andrew Burrows, David
Poyser

Carman, George QC *1953*	**Bergin**, Terence *1985*
Reynold, Frederic QC *1960*	**Steinert**, Jonathan *1986*
Susman, Peter QC *1966†*	**Davies**, Andrew *1988*
Sarony, Neville (QC Hong	**Middleton**, Georgina *1989*
Kong) *1964*	**Mangat**, Dr Tejina *1990*
Knott, Malcolm *1968†*	**Gatty**, Daniel *1990*
Clover, Anthony *1971†*	**Donovan**, Joel *1991*
Pratt, Duncan *1971*	**Wagstaffe**, Christopher *1992*
Brompton, Michael *1973*	**Korn**, Adam *1992*
Howard, Charles *1975*	**Grant**, Thomas *1993*
Stewart, Paul *1975*	**Overs**, Estelle *1994*
Carrodus, Gail *1978*	**Pelling**, Alexander *1995*
Wardell, John *1979*	**Warrender**, Nichola *1995*
McParland, Michael *1983*	**Pliener**, David *1996*
Tomlinson, Hugh *1983*	

Chambers established: 1981
Opening times: 8.30 am-6.30 pm (Monday to
Friday)

Types of work (and number of counsel practising in that area if supplied)
Care proceedings · Civil liberties · Commercial
· Commercial property · Common law
(general) · Defamation · Discrimination
· Employment · Family · Family provision
· Information technology · Landlord and tenant
· Medical negligence · Personal injury · Probate
and administration · Professional negligence
· Sports · Travel

Chambers' facilities
Conference rooms, Video conferences, Disks
accepted, Disabled access, E-mail, Accredited by
the Law Society as an authorised external
course provider

Languages spoken
French, German, Hebrew, Hindi, Nepali

1 NEW SQUARE

Ground Floor, Lincoln's Inn, London
WC2A 3SA
0171 405 0884/5/6/7
Fax: 0171 831 6109; DX 295 London,
Chancery Lane
E-mail: 1newsquare@compuserve.com

Chambers of Eben W Hamilton QC
Clerks: Warren Lee (0193 2828546), Haydn
Powell (0181 301 6546), Justin Brown
(0181 347 9690)

Hamilton, Eben QC *1962*	**Jones**, Clive *1981*
McDonnell, John QC *1968‡*	**Eaton Turner**, David *1984*
Munby, James QC *1971*	**Corbett**, Sandra *1988*
Stewart Smith, Rodney	**Wilkins**, Colette *1989*
1964†	**Van Tonder**, Gerard *1990*
Kennedy, Michael *1967*	**Hubbard**, Mark *1991*
Chapple, Malcolm *1975*	**Eidinow**, John *1992*
Semken, Christopher *1977*	**Prentis**, Sebastian *1996*
Roberts, Michael *1978*	**Warner**, David *1996*
Hollington, Robin *1979*	

Opening times: 8.30 am-6.30 pm

Types of work (and number of counsel practising in that area if supplied)
Arbitration 10 · Banking 10 · Bankruptcy 15
· Chancery (general) 19 · Chancery land law
19 · Charities 3 · Commercial property 15
· Common land 10 · Common law (general) 10
· Company and commercial 15 · Competition 2
· Conveyancing 15 · Corporate finance 8
· Employment 2 · Entertainment 5 · Equity,
wills and trusts 15 · Family 1 · Housing 1
· Insolvency 15 · Insurance/reinsurance 5
· Intellectual property 2 · Landlord and tenant
19 · Local government 2 · Partnerships 19

· Pensions 2 · Personal injury 1 · Probate and administration 19 · Professional negligence 19 · Share options 15 · Sports 5

Chambers' facilities
Conference rooms, Disks accepted, E-mail

Languages spoken
French

3 NEW SQUARE

Lincoln's Inn, London WC2A 3RS
0171 405 1111
Fax: 0171 405 7800; DX 454 London, Chancery Lane
Out of hours telephone: 01582 765502

Chambers of D E M Young QC
Clerk: Ian Bowie

Young, David QC *1966†*	McFarland, Denise *1987*
Watson, Antony QC *1968*	Birss, Colin *1990*
Thorley, Simon QC *1972*	Turner, Justin *1992*
Miller, Richard QC *1976*	Campbell, Douglas *1993*
Burkill, Guy *1981*	Mitcheson, Thomas *1996*
Waugh, Andrew QC *1982*	

Chambers established: 1940
Opening times: 8.45 am-7.30 pm

Types of work (and number of counsel practising in that area if supplied)
Arbitration 10 · Copyright 11 · Entertainment 10 · Environment 1 · Film, cable, TV 7 · Franchising 4 · Information technology 4 · Intellectual property 11 · Licensing 4 · Patents 11 · Professional negligence 3 · Sale and carriage of goods 7 · Telecommunications 10 · Trademarks 11

Chambers' facilities
Conference rooms, Disks accepted, E-mail

Languages spoken
Japanese

Crime Desktop CD-ROM

Containing the three most important titles in criminal law: Archbold, Criminal Law Review *and* Criminal Appeal Reports, *this is the most efficient criminal law research tool you can own.*

Put time on your side, phone Sweet & Maxwell on 0171 449 1111 for more information or a free demonstration

---

CHAMBERS OF LORD GOODHART QC

3 New Square, Lincoln's Inn, London WC2A 3RS
0171 405 5577
Fax: 0171 404 5032; DX 384 London, Chancery Lane
E-mail: law@threenewsquare.demon.co.uk
Out of hours telephone: 04325 106926

Chambers of Lord Goodhart QC
Clerks: Richard A Bayliss, Alister Williams, David Bingham

Goodhart, Lord QC *1957*	Jefferies, Thomas *1981*
Picarda, Hubert QC *1962*	Mullis, Roger *1987*
Marten, Hedley *1966*	Marquand, Charles *1987*
Rowell, David *1972*	Deacock, Adam *1991*
Parry, David *1972†*	Holmes, Justin *1994*
Weatherill, Bernard QC *1974*	Hughes, Mary *1995*
Walker, Andrew *1975*	Ohrenstein, Dov *1995*
Heywood, Michael *1975*	Lamont, Camilla *1995*
Hayes, Josephine *1980*	Dowse, John *1973**

5 NEW SQUARE

1st Floor, Lincoln's Inn, London WC2A 3RJ
0171 404 0404
Fax: 0171 831 6016; DX 272 London
E-mail: Chambers@
FiveNewSquare.CityScape.co.uk
URL: http://www.cityscape.co.uk/users/fk40
Other comms: Pager: 01426 109206

Chambers of Jonathan Rayner James QC
Clerks: Ian Duggan, Clive Nicholls

Rayner James, Jonathan QC *1971‡*	Dickens, Paul *1978*
	Michaels, Amanda *1981*
Garnett, Kevin QC *1975‡*	Clark, Julia *1984*
Sunnucks, James *1950*	Caddick, Nicholas *1986*
Scamell, Ernest *1949*	Harbottle, Gwilym *1987*
Sinclair, Sir Patrick *1961*	Sugar, Simon *1990*
Ross Martyn, John *1969†*	Norris, Andrew *1995*
Stewart, Alexander *1975*	Abbott, Alistair *1996*
Bragiel, Edward *1977*	

3 New Square

3 New Square is a modern commercial chancery set committed to a vigorous tradition of excellence. Advocacy, advice and drafting are available in all areas, with efficient administration.

Work undertaken:

Commercial: banking, credit and security, competition, contracts, consumer credit, economic torts, finance, franchising, fraud, forgery & misrepresentation, guarantees, partnerships, title retention, restitution and tracing.

Company: Companies Court, capital, charges, directors' disqualification, directors' duties, liquidation, receiverships, securities, shareholder disputes.

European law: all aspects relating to other work undertaken.

Financial services: City regulation; tribunals; derivative instruments.

Insolvency: corporate and personal, including international.

Judicial review

Professional negligence: legal, financial, surveyors & valuers.

Pension Schemes: all aspects of occupational and personal pensions schemes; fraud and insolvency.

Property: commercial, agricultural and residential: constructive trusts, conveyancing, easements, highways, landlord and tenant, Lands Tribunal, licences, mortgages and securities, property-related torts, restrictive convenants.

Traditional Chancery: Charities, Court of Protection, equitable remedies, fiduciary duties, probate, tax & tax planning (including VAT), trusts & settlements, wills.

Publications:

Sir William Goodhart QC is co-author (with Prof. Gareth Jones QC) of *Specific Performance*, and of sections on *Corporations* and *Specific Performance* in *Halsbury's Laws*.

Hubert Picarda QC is the author of *The Law and Practice Relating to Charities* and *The Law Relating to Receivers Managers and Administrators*.

Direct professional access (inc overseas). Brochure available.
Fees negotiated with clerk, fixed or hourly basis.

C

Lincoln's Inn, London WC2A 3QS
0171 430 1660
Fax: 0171 430 1531; DX 106 CHANCERY LANE

Chambers of Mr N J Storey

See the *Index of Languages Spoken* in **Part G** to locate a chambers where a particular language is spoken, or find an individual who speaks a particular language.

8 NEW SQUARE

8
NEW SQUARE

LINCOLN'S INN

Lincoln's Inn, London WC2A 3QP
0171 405 4321
Fax: 0171 405 9955; DX 379 London,
Chancery Lane
Other comms: Pager: 0459 115439 (24 hours)

Chambers of M Fysh QC SC
*Clerks: John F Call (Senior Clerk), Tony
Liddon (Deputy Senior Clerk), Sue Harding
(Principal Clerk)*

Fysh, Michael SC *1965*	**Alexander**, Daniel *1988*
Prescott, Peter QC *1970*	**Meade**, Richard *1991*
Baldwin, John QC *1977*	**Onslow**, Robert *1991*
Kitchin, David QC *1977*	**Tappin**, Michael *1991*
Platts-Mills, Mark QC *1974*	**Speck**, Adrian *1993*
Howe, Martin QC *1978*	**St Ville**, James *1995*
Vitoria, Mary QC *1975*	**May**, Charlotte *1995*
Hamer, George *1974*	**Moody-Stuart**, Thomas *1995*
Clark, Fiona *1982*	**Lane**, Lindsay *1996*
Mellor, James *1986*	

Chambers established: Over 80 years
Opening times: 8.30 am-7 pm

Types of work (and number of counsel practising in that area if supplied)
Competition 20 · Copyright 20 · EC and
competition law 20 · Entertainment 20 · Film,
cable, TV 20 · Information technology 20
· Intellectual property 20 · Patents 20
· Telecommunications 20 · Trademarks 20

Chambers' facilities
E-mail, Conference room

Languages spoken
French, German, Spanish

Additional information

8 New Square is one of the largest sets in the UK
specialising in intellectual property and related
fields of law. Members of chambers have a very
wide range of legal, technical and strategic
expertise covering every aspect of intellectual
property and a wide variety of other cases,
especially those where technical knowledge is
of importance. Cases undertaken by members
cover four principal areas:

Intellectual property
Work includes patents, trade and service marks,
copyright (industrial and artistic), registered
and unregistered designs, passing-off,
counterfeiting and trade libel, confidential
information and trade secrets, technology
transfer and licensing, plant breeders' rights,
merchandising, and franchising.

High technology and information technology
This covers biotechnology, data protection and
privacy, technical commercial disputes,
pharmaceutical regulation and licensing,
computers and electronic engineering,
environmental regulation, and public inquiries.

Media and entertainment
Work undertaken includes performers' rights,
television (including cable and satellite),
broadcasting, film, literary, musical and artistic
copyright litigation, publishing and
entertainment contracts and disputes,
advertising and marketing.

Competition and EC law
This includes restraint of trade, restrictive trade
practices, trade descriptions, competition
aspects of intellectual property, EC competition
law, and free movement of goods and services.

Several members of chambers are editors of, or
contributors to, the leading books and
encyclopedias on intellectual property, EC law,
and related subjects. All members belong to the
Patent Bar Association and Chancery Bar
Association.

Chambers is open from 8.30 am to 7.00 pm
Mondays to Fridays but arrangements can be
made for conferences and other services
outside these hours. Draft documents can be
made available on computer disk by
arrangement.

Our clerks, John Call, Tony Liddon and Sue
Harding have each been with chambers over 20
years. They have considerable experience and
excellent links with the court administration.
They will be happy to assist you in choice of
counsel.

Former members of chambers include Mr
Justice Jacob and Mr Justice Laddie. Professor
William Cornish (Cambridge University) is
among the door tenants.

CHAMBERS OF JOHN GARDINER QC

*11 New Square, Lincoln's Inn, London
WC2A 3QB*
0171 242 4017
Fax: 0171 831 2391; DX 315 London,
Chancery Lane
E-mail: taxlaw@11newsquare.com
URL: http://www.11newsquare.com

Chambers of J R Gardiner QC
Clerk: John Moore (Senior Clerk)

Gardiner, John QC *1968*	**Maugham,** Jolyon *1997*
Trevett, Peter QC *1971*	**Rees,** The Rt Hon Lord Peter
Peacock, Jonathan *1987*	QC *1953*
Fitzpatrick, Francis *1990*	**Pinson,** Barry QC *1949**
Lyster, Grania *1992*	

International Arbitration Law Review

Editorial Board includes:

Alan Redfern	*Neil Kaplan*
Toby Landau	*David Rivkin*
Dr Julian Lew	*Martin Hunter*
Nigel Rawding	*Matthieu de Boisseson*

The new International Arbitration Law Review
*brings together for the first time all the
requirements of an arbitration practitioner.*

- *up-to-the-minute news on legislation and
  decisions*

- *expert commentary on worldwide trends
  and issues from a panel of top arbitration
  specialists*

- *detailed case summaries and analysis of
  the cases making the headlines*

- *covers all major jurisdictions worldwide*

*To order a subscription or a free sample copy
call Sweet & Maxwell on 0171 449 1111*

---

12 NEW SQUARE

Lincoln's Inn, London WC2A 3SW
0171 419 1212
Fax: 0171 419 1313; DX 366 London,
Chancery Lane
E-mail: 12newsquare@compuserve.com
Other comms: Lix: Lon 057
Out of hours telephone: 01621 816904

Chambers of W John Mowbray QC
Clerk: Clive Petchey

Annexe: Newport Chambers, 12 Clytha Park
Road, Newport, Gwent NP9 47L
Tel: 01633 267403/255855
Fax: 01633 253441

Annexe: Octagon House, 19 Colegate,
Norwich, Norfolk NR3 1AT
Tel: 01603 623186
Fax: 01603 760519

Also at: Sovereign Chambers, 25 Park Square,
Leeds LS1 2PW
Tel: 0113 245 8141
Fax: 0113 242 0194

Mowbray, John QC *1953*	**Crail,** Ross *1986*
Macdonald, John QC *1955*	**Peacock,** Ian *1990*
Purle, Charles QC *1970*	**Adamyk,** Simon *1991*
Laurence, George QC	**Evans-Gordon,** Jane *1992*
1972‡	**Terras,** Nicholas *1993*
Tucker, Lynton *1971*	**Davies,** Louise *1995*
Braham, Colin *1971*	**Simpson,** Edwin *1990*
Russell, Christopher *1971*	**Buckley,** Richard *1969*
Le Poidevin, Nicholas *1975*	**Elleray,** Anthony QC *1977‡**
Barber, Stuart *1979*	**Muir,** John *1969†**
Hargreaves, Sara *1979*	**Sterling,** Robert *1970**
Smith, Stephen *1983*	**Birch,** Roger *1979**
Sagar, Leigh *1983*	**Cawson,** Mark *1982**
Staddon, Claire *1985*	

Opening times: 8.30 am-7 pm

**Types of work (and number of counsel
practising in that area if supplied)**
Administrative 4 · Arbitration 20 · Banking 8
· Bankruptcy 10 · Chancery (general) 21
· Chancery land law 17 · Charities 3 · Civil
liberties 2 · Commercial litigation 16
· Commercial property 15 · Common land 4
· Company and commercial 21 · Conveyancing
6 · Corporate finance 4 - corporate
fraud 8 · Entertainment 6 · Environment 4
· Equity, wills and trusts 6 · Family provision 5
· Financial services 7 · Foreign law 10
· Information technology 2 · Insolvency 12
· Insurance 6 · Insurance/reinsurance 6
· Intellectual property 2 · International trade 9
· Landlord and tenant 14 · Local government 5

---

† Recorder ‡ Assistant Recorder * Door Tenant

· Medical negligence 4 · Mental health 2 · Parliamentary 3 · Partnerships 8 · Pensions 4 · Private international 7 · Probate and administration 5 · Professional negligence 15 · Public international 3 · Sale and carriage of goods 6 · Sports 4 · Tax - capital and income 2 · Tax - corporate 3 · Town and country planning 7 · Unit trusts 2

Chambers' facilities
Conference rooms, Disks accepted, E-mail

Languages spoken
French, German

Fees policy
Before any work is undertaken, the clerks will if requested give an estimate of the fee for a particular set of papers and of how long the work is likely to take.

Additional information

12 New Square undertakes litigation and advisory work; both in the UK and internationally, including direct professional access and legal aid work. The set acts for corporate clients, local authorities and individuals.

The work of chambers centres on company, commercial and property litigation and includes arbitration, personal and corporate insolvency, civil aspects of commercial fraud, intellectual property, landlord and tenant, building societies and mortgages, Mareva Injunctions and Anton Piller Orders, partnership disputes, trusts, equity, pension schemes and capital taxation and professional negligence, including public/administrative law aspects of these areas. Such work covers judicial review of actions by central and local government, constitutional law, human rights, environmental law, highways, Public Inquiries and the promotion of, or petitioning against, private bills in Parliament.

The practice is international, with members having advised, conferred or negotiated in New York, Washington, Detroit, Toronto, Santo Domingo, Berlin and Geneva. In human rights cases, members have represented Soviet dissidents, the people of Ocean Island, Canadian Indians and the Illois who were removed from Diego Garcia to make way for a US base. Members have appeared in courts in the Bahamas, Antigua, Zurich, the Cayman Islands, Hong Kong, British Virgin Islands, and before the European Court of Human Rights at Strasbourg. John Mowbray QC is a member of the Bahamian Bar and he has also been called to

the Eastern Caribbean Bar as have John Macdonald QC, Charles Purle QC, Stephen Smith and Nicholas Terras. Mr Le Poidevin is a member of the Isle of Man Bar. In London the set has worked with lawyers from all parts of the world.

John Mowbray QC, Lynton Tucker, Nicholas Le Poidevin and Edwin Simpson are currently preparing the 17th edition of *Lewin on Trusts*. George Laurence QC and Edwin Simpson are on the editorial board of *Rights of Way Law Review*.

12 New Square chambers aims to provide a speedy and efficient service. A brochure, which includes a variety of reported cases in many different fields, is available on request or via our website: http://ourworld.compuserve.com/homepages/12newsquare. For further information please contact the Senior Clerk.

NORTH LONDON CHAMBERS

14 Keyes Road, London NW2 3XA
0181 208 4651
Fax: 0181 208 2075

Chambers of Mr T D Putnam

NORTHEASTERN LAW CHAMBERS

The Chocolate Factory, B305 Clarendon Road / Western Road, Wood Green, London N22 6UN
0181 881 3890
Fax: 0181 881 0274

Chambers of Mrs T E Osborne-Halsey

ODOGOR CHAMBERS

14 Cairns Road, Battersea, London SW11 1ES

Chambers of Mr N D A Ezechie

† Recorder ‡ Assistant Recorder * Door Tenant

CHAMBERS OF JOY OKOYE

Suite 1, 2nd Floor, Grays Inn Chambers,
Grays Inn, London WC1R 5JA
0171 405 7011
Fax: 0171 405 7012; DX 442 LDE Chancery
Lane
Out of hours telephone: 0181 262 0932

Chambers of Joy Okoye

Okoye, Joy *1981*	**Treip,** Michael *1995*
Kumar, Mousumi *1992*	**Woodward,** Jeremy *1996*
Reid-Chalmers, Emma *1996*	**Gray,** Howard *1980**

17 OLD BLDGS

Ground Floor, Lincoln's Inn, London
WC2A 3UP
0171 405 9653
Fax: 0171 404 8089; DX 300 London

Chambers of Mr G W Jaques

19 OLD BUILDINGS

Lincoln's Inn, London WC2A 3UP
0171 405 2001
Fax: 0171 405 0001; DX 397 London,
Chancery Lane
E-mail: clerks@oldbuildingsip.com
URL: http://www.oldbuildingsip.com

Chambers of A J D Wilson QC
Clerk: Barbara Harris

Wilson, Alastair QC *1968*†	**Colley,** Peter *1989*
Reid, Brian *1971*	**Puckrin,** Cedric *1990*
Shipley, Graham *1973*	**Sullivan,** Rory *1992*
Hicks, Michael *1976*	**Holman,** Tamsin *1995*

19 Old Buildings

One of the few dedicated intellectual property sets, all tenants are members of the Intellectual Property Bar Association and most have degrees or higher level qualifications in scientific, computing or mathematical disciplines. The work of Chambers covers every aspect of advice and litigation relating to the following:

Intellectual Property – patents, copyright, designs, moral rights, trade marks, passing off, confidential information;

Science and Technology – cases with scientific or technical issues, including contractual disputes, inquiries, applications for licences or registrations, and other litigation;

Computers and Information Technology – including data protection and internet disputes;

Entertainment and Media – publishing, public performance, film and recording rights, broadcasting, cable and satellite distribution, rights of performers, and merchandising;

EU Competition and Free Trade – particularly relating to intellectual property, research and development, employment contracts, franchising and distribution and restraint of trade.

Members of Chambers appear before a wide variety of Courts, the Patent Office and Trade Mark Registry, and other tribunals in London and elsewhere in the UK. Some tenants also have experience in the European Patent Office and the European Court of Justice.

Publications include *European Patent Office Reports, Melville on Forms and Licensing* and *A Practical Guide to Patent Law* amongst many others.

22 OLD BUILDINGS

Lincoln's Inn, London WC2A 3UJ
0171 831 0222
Fax: 0171 831 2239; DX 201 LDE

Chambers of Mr B A Hytner QC
*Clerks: Alan Brewer (London), Peter Collison
(Manchester)*

Also at: All the silks are based at 25 Byrom
Street, Manchester and all the juniors at 22
Old Buildings, Lincoln's Inn

Hytner, Benet QC *1952*	**Chapman**, Simon *1988*
Price, John QC *1961*	**Feehan**, Frank *1988*
Wingate-Saul, Giles QC *1967*	**Taylor**, Gemma *1988*
	Coster, Ronald *1989*
Leveson, Brian QC *1970*	**Jerman**, Anthony *1989*
Scholes, Rodney QC *1968*	**Arnot**, Lee *1990*
King, Timothy QC *1973*	**Furniss**, Richard *1991*
Tattersall, Geoffrey QC *1970*	**Lazarus**, Mary *1991*
Swift, Caroline QC *1977*	**Lonergan**, Paul *1991*
Moran, Andrew QC *1976*	**Romer**, Emma *1992*
Allan, David QC *1974*	**Hyde**, Marcia *1992*
Black, Michael QC *1978*	**Oudkerk**, Daniel *1992*
Stewart, Stephen QC *1975*	**Horan**, John *1993*
Hamlin, Patrick *1970†*	**Hutchings**, Matthew *1993*
Batchelor, Mark *1971*	**Rogers**, Philip *1994*
Cooper, Susan *1976*	**Kewley**, Sarah *1994*
Daiches, Michael *1977*	**Hawkes**, Naomi *1994*
Ralphs, Anne *1977‡*	**Nuvoloni**, Stefano *1994*
Utley, Charles *1979*	**Woodward-Carlton**, Damian *1995*
Hill, Jane *1980*	
Lederman, Howard *1982*	**Thomas**, Anna *1995*
Azim, Rehna *1984*	**Withington**, Angus *1995*
Bennett, Jonathan *1985*	**Pitchers**, Henry *1996*
Sahonte, Rajinder *1986*	**Compton**, Gareth *1997*
Cook, Tina *1988*	

Opening times: 8.30 am-6.30 pm

Types of work (and number of counsel practising in that area if supplied)
Administrative 10 · Bankruptcy 8 · Care
proceedings 25 · Chancery (general) 10
· Chancery land law 5 · Commercial 14
· Common law (general) 23 · Company and
commercial 8 · Construction 5 · Conveyancing
4 · Education 6 · Employment 10
· Environment 8 · Family 20 · Family provision
20 · Housing 10 · Insolvency 8 · Insurance 5
· Landlord and tenant 15 · Licensing 8 · Local
government 10 · Medical negligence 7 · Mental
health 4 · Partnerships 6 · Personal injury 24
· Professional negligence 22 · Sale and carriage
of goods 15 · Town and country planning 6

Chambers' facilities
Conference rooms, Disks accepted, Disabled
access

Languages spoken
French, Italian

TWENTY-FOUR OLD BUILDINGS

*Ground Floor, Lincoln's Inn, London
WC2A 3UJ*
0171 404 0946
Fax: 0171 405 1360; DX 307 London
E-mail: clerks@24oldbuildings.law.co.uk
URL: http://www.24oldbuildings.law.co.uk
Other comms: Lix: Lon 073; Link: Jeremy
Hopkins
Out of hours telephone: 0374 240 112

Chambers of C A Brodie QC
Clerk: Nicholas Luckman

Brodie, Colin QC *1954*	**Weaver**, Elizabeth *1982*
Mann, Martin QC *1968†*	**Moverley Smith**, Stephen *1985*
Steinfeld, Alan QC *1968*	
Kaye, Roger QC *1970†*	**Galley**, Helen *1987*
Cohen, Lawrence QC *1974‡*	**Francis**, Adrian *1988*
Baxendale, Thomas *1962‡*	**Harington**, Amanda *1989*
King, Michael *1971*	**Talbot Rice**, Elspeth *1990*
Teverson, Paul *1976*	**Cherryman**, Nicholas *1991*
Davies, John *1977*	**Young**, Christopher *1988*
Ritchie, Richard *1978*	**Stanley**, Clare *1994*
Tregear, Francis *1980*	**Adair**, Stuart *1995*
Gadd, Michael *1981*	**Shah**, Bajul *1996*
Gerrans, Daniel *1981*	**Thompson**, Steven *1996*

Opening times: 8 am-7 pm

Types of work (and number of counsel practising in that area if supplied)
Banking 3 · Bankruptcy 24 · Chancery
(general) 25 · Chancery land law 25
· Commercial 24 · Commercial litigation 24
· Commercial property 24 · Common land 3
· Company and commercial 24 · Conveyancing
3 · Ecclesiastical 1 · Entertainment 5 · Equity,
wills and trusts 12 · Family 5 · Family
provision 5 · Financial services 7 · Insolvency
24 · Landlord and tenant 24 · Partnerships 25
· Pensions 5 · Probate and administration 10
· Professional negligence 23 · Share options 1
· Town and country planning 1

Chambers' facilities
Conference rooms, Disks accepted, E-mail, Link, Lix

Languages spoken
French, Spanish

Fees policy
Under three years call £35-100, three to five years call £100-125, five to ten years call £125-175. Chambers adopts a flexible and open approach to fees and all areas of administration. Fees are charged either on a time-costed or inclusive 'global' basis. Estimates can be provided or limits agreed prior to work being undertaken.

Additional information

24 Old Buildings is an established chambers, specialising in advising on and conducting litigation across a broad range of commercial and Chancery work. Members of chambers are instructed by large and small firms both in London and the provinces, acting for a wide range of clients from major financial institutions to legally-aided individuals.

Members include Martin Mann QC, Alan Steinfeld QC and Roger Kaye QC, who sit as Deputy Judges in the Chancery Division of the High Court. Richard Ritchie is Standing Counsel to the Department of Trade and Industry (Insolvency) and Junior Counsel to the Crown (Chancery). Stephen Moverley Smith is Junior Counsel to the Crown (Chancery).

Members appear in the civil courts (particularly the High Court Chancery and Queen's Bench Divisions – including Commercial Court and Official Referees – and county courts throughout the UK), tribunals (including Insolvency Practitioners and the Institute of Chartered Accountants) and overseas courts (including the Cayman Islands, the British Virgin Islands, Bermuda, Hong Kong, Singapore and the Turks and Caicos). Chambers has connections in New York, Geneva, Rome and Milan.

24 OLD BUILDINGS

1st Floor, Lincoln's Inn, London WC2A 3UJ
0171 242 2744
Fax: 0171 831 8095; DX 386 London

Chambers of G R Bretten QC
Clerk: Anthony Hall

Bretten, George QC *1965*	**Lyons,** Timothy *1980*
Venables, Robert QC *1973*	**Kessler,** James *1984*
Brandon, Stephen QC *1978*	**Ghosh,** Julian *1993*
Argles, Guy *1965*	**Hardy,** Amanda *1993*
Sokol, Christopher *1975*	

9 OLD SQUARE

9 OLD SQUARE

Ground Floor, Lincoln's Inn, London WC2A 3SR
0171 405 4682
Fax: 0171 831 7107; DX 305 London, Chancery Lane
E-mail: chambers@9oldsquare.co.uk
Other comms: Lix: Lon 069
Out of hours telephone: 0831 296871/01474 357503

Chambers of Robert Reid QC
Clerk: Christopher McSweeney (Senior Clerk)

Reid, Robert QC *1965*†	**Johnson,** Edwin *1987*
Driscoll, Michael QC *1970*	**Leech,** Thomas *1988*
Patten, Nicholas QC *1974*	**Holland,** Katharine *1989*
Jackson, Judith QC *1975*	**Stoner,** Christopher *1991*
Berry, Simon QC *1977*	**Walker,** Andrew *1991*
Hodge, David QC *1979*	**Burrell,** Simon *1988*
Hochberg, Daniel *1982*	**Pryor,** Michael *1992*
Dagnall, John *1983*	**Johns,** Alan *1994*
McGhee, John *1984*	**Tozer,** Stephanie *1996*
Harry, Timothy *1983*	**Norris,** William V W *1997*

Opening times: 8.30 am-6.30 pm

Types of work (and number of counsel practising in that area if supplied)
Administrative · Agriculture · Arbitration · Banking · Bankruptcy · Chancery (general) · Chancery land law · Charities · Commercial property · Common land · Company and

---

commercial · Conveyancing · Energy · Environment · Equity, wills and trusts · Family provision · Financial services · Insolvency · Landlord and tenant · Local government · Parliamentary · Partnerships · Probate and administration · Professional negligence · Sports · Tax - capital and income

Languages spoken
French, German, Spanish

Additional information

9 Old Square is a modern set of Chancery chambers specialising in a wide range of commercial and property litigation. All members of chambers have expertise in real property, professional negligence, landlord and tenant and securities. Other areas of expertise include banking, insolvency, company and partnership disputes, trusts, judicial review and local government, sports law, minerals and mining.

Members of chambers accept direct instructions from recognised professional clients and carry out Legal Aid work, and they appear in courts, tribunals and arbitrations in the UK and overseas.

Further details and a brochure can be obtained from the Senior Clerk.

THE CHAMBERS OF LEOLIN PRICE CBE, QC

10 OLD SQUARE

10 Old Square, Lincoln's Inn, London WC2A 3SU
0171 405 0758/242 5002
Fax: 0171 831 8237/9188; DX 306 London, Chancery Lane

Chambers of A L Price CBE QC
Clerk: Keith Plowman

Price, Leolin QC CBE *1949*	**Rhys,** Owen *1976*
Bonney, James QC *1975*	**Thomas,** Geraint *1976**
Mello, Michael J (QC Bermuda) *1972**	**Taube,** Simon *1980*
	De La Rosa, Andrew *1981*
Rossdale, Philip *1948*	**Michell,** Michael *1984*
Ainger, David *1961*	**Stafford,** Dr Paul *1987*
Mark, Michael *1964*	**Partington,** David *1987**
Barlow, Francis *1965*	**Meadway,** Susannah *1988*
Ritchie, David *1970*	**Rajah,** Eason *1989*
Burton, Frances *1970**	**D'Cruz,** Rupert *1989*
Hill, Gregory *1972*	**Callman,** Jeremy *1991*
Wallington, Richard *1972*	**Gavaghan,** Jonathan *1992*
Newsom, George *1973*	**Laughton,** Samuel *1993*
Lloyd-Davies, Andrew *1973*	**Farrelly,** Kevin *1993*
Arbuthnot, The Rt Hon James MP *1975**	**Waterworth,** Michael *1994*
	Norbury, Luke *1995*
Price, Jeffrey *1975**	**Harries,** Nicholas *1995*
Schmitz, David *1976*	**Arnfield,** Robert *1996*

11 OLD SQUARE

Ground Floor, Lincoln's Inn, London
WC2A 3TS
0171 242 5022
Fax: 0171 404 0445; DX 164 London,
Chancery Lane
Out of hours telephone: 0181 462 1917

Chambers of Simeon Thrower
Clerk: Christopher Watts

Thrower, Simeon *1973*	**Maitland**, Marc *1988*
Quint, Francesca *1970*	**Lloyd**, John *1985*
Cutting, Christopher *1973*	**Gray**, Jennifer *1992*
Mydeen, Kalandar *1973*	**Buttimore**, Gabriel *1993*
Wellesley-Cole, Patrice *1975*	**Kaler**, Manjeet *1993*
Apsion, Robert *1977*	**Ball**, Steven *1995*
Sinclair, Malcolm *1978*	
Macleod-James, Nicholas *1986*	

11 OLD SQUARE

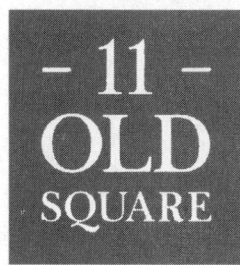

Ground Floor, Lincoln's Inn, London
WC2A 3TS
0171 430 0341
Fax: 0171 831 2469; DX 1031 London
E-mail: clerks@11oldsquare.co.uk
Other comms: Lix: Lon 042

Chambers of Grant Crawford & Jonathan Simpkiss
Clerks: K Nagle, A Downey

Ellis, Carol QC *1951*	**Thomas**, Siân *1981*
Davidson, Edward QC *1966*	**Campbell**, Glenn *1985*
Nurse, Gordon *1973*	**West**, Mark *1987*
Crawford, Grant *1974*	**McQuail**, Katherine *1989*
Simpkiss, Jonathan *1975*	**Burroughs**, Nigel *1991*
Smith, Peter QC *1975*	**Dodge**, Peter *1992*
Harrison, Reziya *1975*	**Oakley**, Tony *1994*
Acton, Stephen *1977*	**Davey**, Benjamin *1994*
Waters, Malcolm QC *1977*	**Sandells**, Nicole *1994*
Ovey, Elizabeth *1978*	**Selway**, Kate *1995*
Rowley, Keith *1979*	**Hall Taylor**, Alex *1996*

Opening times: 9 am-6.30 pm

Types of work (and number of counsel practising in that area if supplied)

Agriculture 1 · American law 1 · Arbitration 2 · Bahamas law 1 · Banking 7 · Bankruptcy 7 · Chancery (general) 21 · Chancery land law 21 · Charities 9 · Commercial 6 · Commercial property 14 · Common law (general) 6 · Company and commercial 8 · Conveyancing 13 · Copyright 1 · Ecclesiastical 1 · Equity, wills and trusts 16 · Family provision 13 · Financial services 1 · Housing 2 · Insolvency 10 · Intellectual property 1 · Landlord and tenant 16 · Mining and mineral 1 · Partnerships 11 · Pensions 6 · Probate and administration 14 · Professional negligence 13 · Tax - capital and income 2 · Trademarks 1

Chambers' facilities
Disks accepted

Languages spoken
French, Spanish

Additional information

Chambers covers a wide range of Chancery, company and commercial work, with an emphasis towards advice and litigation in both the Chancery and Queen's Bench Divisions. Junior members of chambers also appear frequently in the county court. Chambers' work includes:

Real property and the sale of land
Mortgages; landlord and tenant (including rent reviews, agricultural tenancies and leasehold enfranchisement); easements; nuisance and other property-related torts; covenants and licences affecting land.

Commercial work
Contracts (including sale of goods); economic torts; restraint of trade; abuse of confidence; copyright; passing-off; equitable doctrines and remedies including tracing, resulting and constructive trusts, Mareva and Anton Piller orders and other injunctions; banking; securities and guarantees; insurance; mortgage and other financial or security-related frauds.

Company law and insolvency
Shareholder and other company disputes; corporate insolvency including administration, receivership, and liquidation; partnership; and bankruptcy.

Professional negligence
Involving solicitors, barristers, accountants, surveyors, financial advisers and intermediaries, and others.

Trusts, charities and administration of estates

Creation, administration, and variation of trusts; wills and probate; family provision.

Members of chambers also undertake work involving building societies including their constitution and powers, relations with members and third parties, mergers, takeovers, and conversion and standard form documentation; financial services; capital taxation; pension schemes; judicial review; and interest rate swaps.

Jonathan Simpkiss and Reziya Harrison are Fellows of the Chartered Institute of Arbitrators. All members of chambers accept instructions under the direct professional access arrangements.

Malcolm Waters, Elizabeth Ovey and Kate Selway are the editors of *Wurtzburg & Mills on Building Society Law*. Malcolm Waters and Elizabeth Ovey wrote the commentary to the Building Societies Act 1986 in *Current Law Statutes*.

Publications:

Mark West
Chapter 4, *Swaps and Local Authorities: A Mistake?* Mark West and Catherine Newman QC in: *Swaps and Off-Exchange Derivatives Trading: Law and Regulation,* Editors: Eric Bettelheim, Helen Parry and William Rees, FT Law & Tax (1996).

Reziya Harrison FCI (Arb)
Good Faith in Sales, Sweet & Maxwell (1997).

12 OLD SQUARE

1st Floor, Lincoln's Inn, London WC2A 3TX
0171 404 0875
Fax: 0171 404 3877; DX 130 London

Chambers of Miss C Boaitey

See the *Index of Languages Spoken* in Part G to locate a chambers where a particular language is spoken, or find an individual who speaks a particular language.

13 OLD SQUARE

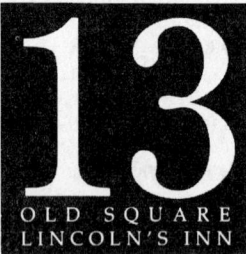

Lincoln's Inn, London WC2A 3UA
0171 404 4800
Fax: 0171 405 4267; DX 326 London
Out of hours telephone: 01992 441374/ 445142

Chambers of Michael Lyndon-Stanford QC
Clerk: John C Moore

Lyndon-Stanford, Michael QC 1962	Girolami, Paul 1983
McCall, Christopher QC 1966	Collings, Matthew 1985
Oliver, David QC 1972	Nicholls, John 1986
Williamson, Hazel QC 1972†	Walton, Carolyn 1980
McCombe, Richard QC 1975†	Russen, Jonathan 1986
Thomas, Nigel 1976	Morgan, Richard 1988
Pymont, Christopher QC 1979	Peacock, Nicholas 1989
Newman, Catherine QC 1979‡	Banner, Gregory 1989
Evans, Timothy 1979	Tipples, Amanda 1991
Barker, Simon 1979‡	Gibbon, Michael 1993
Cunningham, Mark 1980	Stubbs, Rebecca 1994
Trace, Anthony QC 1981	Aldridge, James 1994
	Ayres, Andrew 1996
	Swerling, Robert 1996
	Dias, Reginald 1945*
	Christie, Richard 1949*
	Lipstein, Kurt 1950*
	Shankardass, Vijay 1972*

Chambers established: 1890
Opening times: 8.30 am-6.45 pm

Types of work (and number of counsel practising in that area if supplied)
Arbitration · Banking · Bankruptcy · Chancery (general) · Chancery land law · Charities · Commercial · Commercial property · Company and commercial · Competition · Conveyancing · Copyright · EC and competition law · Equity, wills and trusts · Family provision · Financial services · Insolvency · Insurance · Insurance/ reinsurance · Intellectual property · Landlord and tenant · Media law · Mental health · Partnerships · Pensions · Private international · Probate and administration · Professional negligence · Sports · Tax - capital and income · Tax - corporate · Telecommunications

Chambers' facilities
Conference rooms, Disks accepted

Languages spoken
Dutch, French, German, Hindi, Italian, Russian, Welsh

Fees policy
We have a flexible and competitive approach as regards fees and the clerks are entirely happy to quote and agree fees prior to the commencement of work.

Additional information

This is a long-established set and believes it has maintained its position amongst the best of Chancery litigators, providing high quality, well-researched advice and excellent advocacy skills across a broad range of legal expertise. The vast majority of work involves litigation, actual or potential. Urgent cases are dealt with at short notice and matters requiring expertise in a number of different specialist areas are also routinely handled.

Types of work undertaken:
Company law: work includes shareholders' rights, breach of fiduciary duty, corporate insolvency, financial regulation, monopolies and mergers. Members also appear in applications under the Company Directors Disqualification Act and before the tribunals which regulate the provision of financial and insolvency services.
Commercial law: work includes judicial review, commercial contracts, banking, guarantees and securities, insurance, consumer credit, restraint of trade, partnership, personal insolvency/bankruptcy and pre-trial remedies (urgent or otherwise).
Property: work includes landlord and tenant, vendor and purchaser, conveyancing, mortgages and securities on land, easements and covenants, boundaries, trespass and nuisance.
Professional negligence: work includes claims against solicitors, barristers, accountants, actuaries, surveyors, valuers and architects in a company, property or commercial context.
Trusts and related areas: work includes wills and probate, administration of estates, family provision, charities, building and friendly societies, trusts, unincorporated associations and revenue/tax.
Intellectual property: work includes copyright, performers' rights, design rights, moral rights, trademarks, passing off, breach of confidence, music, publishing, television and film industry work.
In addition to the above main areas, practitioners have experience in diverse specialist fields including private international law, competition law, highways, markets and commons, telecommunications, matrimonial finance and property, mental health, pensions and superannuations and lotteries. Many of Chambers' clients come from the corporate business community, but individual clients are equally welcome and legal aid matters are regularly undertaken.

On top of their work in London, members of Chambers appear in court and give advice throughout the UK and abroad. QCs in Chambers have appeared in courts in Hong Kong, Bermuda, the Cayman Islands and elsewhere. Several members are called to the bars of Isle of Man, Singapore and Hong Kong. David Oliver has a License Spéciale en Droit Européen (Brussels). Hazel Williamson is a fellow of the Chartered Institute of Arbitrators. Richard McCombe is the present Attorney-General to the Duchy of Lancaster. Mark Cunningham and Paul Girolami are junior counsel to the Crown, Chancery.

---

† Recorder ‡ Assistant Recorder * Door Tenant

OLD SQUARE CHAMBERS

*1 Verulam Buildings, Gray's Inn, London
WC1R 5LQ*
0171 269 0300
Fax: 0171 405 1387; DX 1046 London
Out of hours telephone: 0973 330793

Chambers of The Hon J M Williams QC
*Clerks: John Taylor, William Meade, Andrew
York, Robert Bocock, Bill Rice, Casta Albon;
Administrator: Brenda Brown*

Annexe: Old Square Chambers, Hanover
House, 47 Corn Street, Bristol BS1 1HT
Tel: 0117 927 7111
Fax: 0117 927 3478

Williams, The Hon John QC 1955†	**McNeill,** Jane *1982*
Hendy, John QC *1972*	**Cotter,** Barry *1985*
Hand, John QC *1972*†	**Chudleigh,** Louise *1987*
Wedderburn of Charlton, Lord QC *1953*	**Omambala,** Ijeoma *1989*
McMullen, Jeremy QC 1971†	**Eady,** Jennifer *1989*
Truscott, Ian (QC Scot) 1995	**Mead,** Philip *1989*
Lewis, Charles *1963*	**Brown,** Damian *1989*
Carling, Christopher *1969*	**Clarke,** Jonathan *1990*
Birtles, William *1970*†	**Gill,** Tess *1990*
Brahams, Diana *1972*	**Walker,** Christopher *1990*
Bates, John *1973*	**Booth,** Nicholas *1991*
Cooksley, Nigel *1975*	**Moor,** Sarah *1991*
Makey, Christopher *1975*	**Scott,** Ian *1991*
Pugh, Charles *1975*	**Segal,** Oliver *1992*
Kelly, Matthias *1979*	**Gower,** Helen *1992*
Kempster, Toby *1980*	**Lewis,** Prof Roy *1992*
Rose, Paul *1981*	**Whitcombe,** Mark *1994*
	Melville, Elizabeth *1994*
	Tether, Melanie *1995*
	Smith, Emma *1995*
	Pirani, Rohan *1995*

Opening times: 8.30 am-7 pm

Types of work (and number of counsel practising in that area if supplied)
Administrative · Arbitration · Chancery (general) · Civil liberties · Commercial litigation · Construction · Discrimination · EC and competition law · Education · Employment · Environment · Medical negligence · Personal injury · Product liability · Professional negligence · Sale and carriage of goods · Sports

Chambers' facilities
Conference rooms

Languages spoken
French, Italian, Spanish

Fees policy
Scale fees generally adopted for personal injury pleadings and advice depending on seniority of counsel. Conditional fee agreements are entered into. Flexible and practical approach taken to charging of fees on all cases. Some pro bono work undertaken. Clients' means are always considered. For work in Bristol and the southwest fees calculated on basis of travel and cost from Bristol and not London.

Additional information

Types of work undertaken

Employment Law Chambers boasts several of the UK's leading specialists in this field. Cases involve all aspects of individual and collective employment law including interpretation of EU directives.

The full range of **Personal Injury** work is covered including health and safety. We have particular expertise in disaster litigation and complex multi-party actions. Recent matters handled have included the VWF litigation. Members of chambers have acted as consultants to the EC on the implementation of European health and safety directives in the UK.

Environmental work includes major toxic tort litigation, work for regulatory bodies and a wide variety of prosecutions for statutory nuisance.

The **Product Liability** special interest group has advised a large number of companies, local authorities, individuals and specialist associations with regard to virtually all aspects of civil and criminal liability in respect of defective and unsafe products.

Sports Law is another area of expertise in which members of chambers have represented various clubs as well as individual sports people.

Seminars are provided in both London and Bristol, (Law Society accredited for CPD). Members regularly feature at professionally organised conferences and many are respected authors in their area of specialisation. Brochure available on request.

THE OUTER TEMPLE

*Room 26, 222/225 Strand, London
WC2R 1BQ*
0171 353 4647
Fax: 0171 353 4655

Chambers of Mr P M Hayward

     † Recorder ‡ Assistant Recorder * Door Tenant

90 OVERSTRAND MANSIONS

Prince of Wales Drive, London SW11 4EU
0171 622 7415
Fax: 0171 622 6929

Chambers of Mr D Hood

ONE PAPER BUILDINGS

Ground Floor, Temple, London EC4Y 7EP
0171 583 7355
Fax: 0171 353 2144; DX 80 London, Chancery Lane
E-mail: clerks@1pb.co.uk
Other comms: Voice Mail: 0171 583 1004, Lix: Lon 070
Out of hours telephone: 01689 829362 Julian Campbell Home No.

Chambers of John Slater QC, Michael Spencer QC
Clerks: Julian Campbell, Mark Walter; Administrator: Lea Hudson

Slater, John QC *1969†*	**Catford**, Gordon *1980*
Spencer, Michael QC *1970†*	**Field**, Julian *1980*
Bartlett, Andrew QC *1974*	**Davies**, Jane *1981*
Brown, Simon QC *1976*	**Coles**, Steven *1983*
Powers, Michael QC *1979*	**Ferris**, Shaun *1985*
Stevenson, William QC *1968†*	**Medd**, James *1985*
	Platt, David *1987*
Hone, Richard QC *1970†*	**Egan**, Marion *1988*
Berkin, Martyn *1966*	**Vandyck**, William *1988*
Bickford-Smith, Margaret *1973†*	**Power**, Erica *1990*
	Newman, Benedict *1991*
Nixon, Colin *1973*	**Gee**, Toby *1992*
Davies, Nicholas *1975*	**Antelme**, Alexander *1993*
Powles, John *1975*	**Branthwaite**, Margaret *1993*
Waite, Jonathan *1978*	**Toogood**, Claire *1995*

---

1 PAPER BUILDINGS

1st Floor, Temple, London EC4Y 7EP
0171 353 3728/4953
Fax: 0171 353 2911; DX 332 London, Chancery Lane

Chambers of R N Titheridge QC
Clerks: N Witchell, M Cornell

Titheridge, Roger QC *1954†*	**Seely**, Jonathan *1987*
Hubbard, Michael QC *1972†*	**Norman**, Mark *1989*
Leigh, Christopher QC *1967†*	**Burke-Gaffney**, Rupert *1988*
	Jewell, Matthew *1989*
Malcolm, Alastair QC *1971†*	**Thomas**, Charles *1990*
Bullen, James *1966†*	**Johnston**, Anne-Marie *1990*
Harrison, Roger *1970‡*	**McCarraher**, Colin *1990*
Buckley, Bernard *1970*	**Ferguson**, Stephen *1991*
Farmer, John *1970*	**Curtis**, Nicole *1992*
Davies, Anthony *1971†*	**Small**, Penelope *1992*
Kellett, Charles *1971*	**O'Donnell**, Duncan *1992*
Privett, Frank *1976‡*	**Bryan**, Robert *1992*
Spence, Stephen *1983*	**Hickling**, Sally *1993*
Swan, Timothy *1983*	**Topliss**, Megan *1994*
Khalil, Karim *1984*	**Rafferty**, Angela *1995*
Lamb, Maria-Jane *1984*	**Ahmad**, Zubair *1995*
Morgan, Christopher *1987*	**Ashworth**, William *1996*
Edwards, Simon *1987*	**Shaw**, Barnaby *1996*

2 PAPER BUILDINGS

Temple, London EC4Y 7ET
0171 353 0933
Fax: 0171 353 0937; DX 286 London, Chancery Lane

Chambers of S F Hadley
Clerk: Lynn Pilkington

Hadley, Steven *1987*	**Tedore**, Amanda *1992*
Adonis, George *1973*	**McNiff**, Matthew *1992*
Sheikh, Irshad *1983*	**Baker**, William *1992*
Baylis, Christopher *1986**	**Clark**, Timothy *1993*
Etherton, Gillian *1988*	**Hart**, Jenny *1993*
McCann, Catryn *1988*	**D'Souza**, Dominic *1993*
Lindop, Sarah *1989*	**Whaites**, Louise *1994*
Le Foe, Sarah *1989*	**McDonagh**, Matthew *1994*
Rhodes, Karen *1990*	**Baughan**, Andrew *1994*
Cornwall, Virginia *1990*	**Connell**, Edward *1996*
Thompson, Andrew *1991*	

Opening times: 8.30 am-6.30 pm

Types of work (and number of counsel practising in that area if supplied)
Care proceedings 6 · Civil liberties 4 · Common law (general) 8 · Crime 19 · Employment 4 · Family 6 · Family provision 6 · Housing 4 · Immigration 1 · Landlord and tenant 4 · Licensing 6 · Personal injury 6

C

---

† Recorder ‡ Assistant Recorder * Door Tenant

Chambers' facilities
Conference rooms, Disks accepted

Languages spoken
Cantonese, French, Greek, Italian

2 PAPER BUILDINGS

1st Floor, Temple, London EC4Y 7ET
0171 936 2611 (10 lines)
Fax: 0171 583 3423; DX LDE 494
E-mail: clerks@2pbbarristers.co.uk
URL: http://www.2pbbarristers.co.uk
Out of hours telephone: 0860 416061

Chambers of Desmond de Silva QC
Clerks: Robin Driscoll (Senior Clerk), Stephen Ball, John Gillespie, Marc Jennings (Fees Clerk); Administrator: Marc Jennings

de Silva, Desmond QC *1964*	**Pasiuk**, Janina *1983*
Richard, Lord QC *1955*	**Brock**, David *1984*
Salts, Nigel QC *1961*	**Ward**, Simon *1984*
de Silva, Harendra QC *1970†*	**Karu**, Lee *1985*
	Femi-Ola, John *1985*
Kothari, Vasant *1960*	**Chandran**, Aruna *1985*
Zorbas, Panos *1964*	**McCoy**, Gerard *1986*
Martin, Peter *1969*	**Berrick**, Steven *1986*
Lewis, Raymond *1971*	**Baxter**, Sharon *1987*
Pearse Wheatley, Robin *1971†*	**Folkes**, Sandra *1989*
	Lambis, Marios *1989*
Ponsonby, Lady *1971*	**Benson**, Charles *1990*
Corrigan, Peter *1972*	**Martin**, Zoe *1990*
Hoon, Notu *1975*	**Hill**, Catherine *1991*
Johnson, Roderick *1975*	**Duff**, Morag *1991*
O'Donovan, Paul *1975*	**Samat**, Daren *1992*
Sutton-Mattocks, Chris *1975†*	**Henderson**, Fiona *1993*
	Mylvaganam, Paul *1993*
Strachan, Chris *1971*	**Brassington**, Stephen *1994*
Hayes, Jerry *1977*	**Kearney**, John *1994*
Cahill, Patrick *1979*	**Panayi**, Pavlos *1995*
Hollis, Kim *1979*	**Tilbury**, James *1996*
Massih, Michel *1979*	**Summers**, Mark *1996*
Campbell, Colin *1979*	

Opening times: 8.30 am-6.30 pm

Types of work (and number of counsel practising in that area if supplied)
Civil liberties · Common law (general) · Courts martial · Crime · Crime - corporate fraud · Family · Foreign law · Housing · Immigration · Landlord and tenant · Licensing · Sports

Chambers' facilities
Large conference rooms

Languages spoken
Arabic, French, German, Greek, Gujarati, Hindi, Italian, Marathi, Polish, Punjabi, Spanish

Fees policy
Please contact the clerks who will be happy to discuss fees.

Additional information

2 Paper Buildings is one of the longest established sets in the Temple, with a continuous clerking tradition.

Chambers is a specialist Criminal Defence set practising principally in white-collar fraud, terrorist cases, major drugs and sexual abuse cases. Chambers also has a strong history of civil liberties work which includes appeals to the Privy Council, immigration and civil actions against the Police. Some members prosecute in high profile cases requiring expert representation. An example being Desmond de Silva QC's involvement in the prosecution of the Newall case in Gibraltar which was one of the most high profile murder cases of the decade.

Individual members of Chambers also practise in the fields of family and civil law.

Chambers has a very long standing Commonwealth connection acting in appeals to the Privy Council. The international flavour of Chambers is reflected in its diverse membership.

2 Paper Buildings has a reputation of excellence in the Criminal Defence field both in this country and abroad.

The current Head of Chambers has saved the lives of no less than 35 persons either in the Privy Council, in trials, or in appeals in Commonwealth countries. Desmond de Silva QC has probably saved more persons on capital cases than any other member of the Bar currently practising in England and Wales.

2 PAPER BUILDINGS, BASEMENT NORTH

PAPER BUILDINGS

Temple, London EC4Y 7ET
0171 936 2613
Fax: 0171 353 9439; DX 210 London,
Chancery Lane

Chambers of R C Griffiths
Clerks: Joanne Thomas (Senior Clerk), Marc Newson (Junior Clerk)

Griffiths, Robin *1970*	**Stone**, Joseph *1989*
Hayden, Richard *1964*	**Comfort**, Polly-Anne *1988*
Gee, Peta *1973**	**Talbot-Bagnall**, John *1988*
Love, Mark *1979*	**Dent**, Kevin *1991*
Wyeth, Mark *1983*	**Tolkien**, Simon *1994*
Ogden, Eric *1983*	**Pathak**, Pankaj *1992*
Fisher-Gordon, Wendy *1983*	**James**, Rachael *1992*
Purdy, Quentin *1983*	**Dempster**, Jennifer *1993*
Petersen, Neil *1983*	**Syed**, Maryam *1993*
Rector, Penelope *1980*	**Whysall**, Caroline *1993*
Dennison, James *1986*	**Baker**, Fay *1994*
Stern, Mark *1988*	**Crosfill**, John *1995*
Briggs-Watson, Sandra *1985*	**Dahlsen**, Peter *1996*
	Hancox, Sally *1996*
Sapsard, Jamal *1987*	

3 PAPER BUILDINGS

Ground Floor, Temple, London EC4Y 7EU
0171 797 7000
Fax: 0171 797 7100; DX 0071 London
E-mail: clerks@3pb.co.uk
Out of hours telephone: 0956 285608

Chambers of I E Jacob
Clerk: M Curness; Practice manager: M Stannard

Jacob, Isaac *1963†*	**Foley**, Sheila *1988*
Owen, Gerald QC *1949†*	**Killen**, Geoffrey *1990*
Bresler, Fenton *1951*	**Piper**, Angus *1991*
Solomon, Susan *1967*	**Bingham**, Anthony *1992*
Aylwin, Christopher *1970*	**Bruce**, Andrew *1992*
Denehan, Edward *1981*	**Wood**, Lana *1993*
Marshall, David *1981*	**Elgot**, Howard *1974**
McMaster, Peter *1981*	**Lewis**, Jonathan *1996*
Young, Martin *1984*	**Hanham**, James *1996*

Chambers established: 1970
Opening times: 8.30 am-6.30 pm

Types of work (and number of counsel practising in that area if supplied)
Arbitration 2 · Banking 4 · Bankruptcy 4 · Commercial litigation 8 · Commercial property 4 · Company and commercial 6 · Construction 4 · Conveyancing 2 · Employment 5 · Family 1 · Family provision 1 · Financial services 4 · Information technology 3 · Insolvency 4 · Insurance 4 · Intellectual property 2 · Landlord and tenant 7 · Medical negligence 3 · Partnerships 3 · Patents 1 · Pensions 3 · Personal injury 6 · Professional negligence 10 · Sale and carriage of goods 6 · Town and country planning 1

Chambers' facilities
Conference rooms, Disks accepted

Languages spoken
French, German

Additional information

The work of chambers covers company and commercial, building and engineering, landlord and tenant, real property, professional negligence and personal injury.

Chambers' commercial work covers those areas of the law particularly relevant to contemporary business and commerce, including company law, banking and bills of exchange, carriage of goods, sale of goods, insurance, intellectual property, financial services, partnerships, employment and insolvency.

Chambers' building and engineering work includes litigation and arbitration (both UK and international) and the drafting of contracts.

Members deal with commercial, residential and agricultural leases, rent reviews and leasehold enfranchisement. Draft leases are prepared and the contentious and non-contentious aspects of the sale of property and mortgages are also covered.

All types of professional negligence work are undertaken.

Members of chambers deal regularly with pre-emptive remedies. Using modern technology the set is able to draft and obtain Mareva and Anton Piller orders efficiently and at short notice.

Individual members of chambers also undertake work in the following fields: planning and local government, licensing, judicial review, information technology and data protection, entertainment law, human rights, competition law and matrimonial finance.

Isaac Jacob is a member of the California and Arizona Federal Bars. Isaac Jacob and Tony Bingham are Fellows of the Chartered Institute of Arbitrators. Tony Bingham is a member of the City Disputes Panel. David Marshall is a member of the Society for Computers and Law.

3 PAPER BUILDINGS

1st Floor, Temple, London EC4Y 7EU
0171 583 8055
Fax: 0171 353 6271 (2 lines); DX 1024
London, Chancery Lane
E-mail: london@3paper.com

Chambers of M P Parroy QC
Clerks: J C Charlick (Chief Clerk), Alan Odiam (Senior Clerk), David Phillips, Danny Carroll, William Parmenter, Paul Queenan (Fees/Admin), Helen Binks (Bursar)

Annexe: 1 Alfred Street, High Street, Oxford OX1 4EH
Tel: 01865 793736
Fax: 01865 790760

Annexe: 20 Lorne Park Road, Bournemouth, Dorset BH1 1JN
Tel: 01202 292102
Fax: 01202 298498

Annexe: 4 St Peter Street, Winchester SO23 8BW
Tel: 01962 868 884
Fax: 01962 868 644

> **Use the** *Types of Work* **listings in Parts A and B to locate chambers and individual barristers who specialise in particular areas of work.**

Parroy, Michael QC *1969*	**Branigan**, Kate *1984*
Harris, David QC *1969†*	**O'Hara**, Sarah *1984*
Hughes, Peter QC *1971*	**Chamberlain**, Francis *1985*
Jones, Stewart QC *1972†*	**Sanderson**, David *1985*
Aspinall, John QC *1971*	**Bailey**, Russell *1985*
Hebron, Harold *1960*	**Parker**, Christopher *1986*
Parrish, Samuel *1962*	**Hudson**, Elisabeth *1987*
Trevethan, Susan *1967*	**Letman**, Paul *1987*
Haynes, John *1968*	**Rowland**, Nicholas *1988*
Swinstead, David *1970*	**Kelly**, Patricia *1988*
Hope, Derwin *1970†*	**Woolgar**, Dermot *1988*
Norman, Michael *1971†*	**Hester**, Paul *1989*
Ward, Anthony *1971*	**Opperman**, Guy *1989*
Curran, Leo *1972*	**Bradbury**, Timothy *1989*
Jennings, Peter *1972*	**Kilpatrick**, Jean *1990*
Coleman, Anthony *1973*	**Buckley-Clarke**, Amanda *1991*
Stephenson, Ben *1973*	
Litchfield, Linda *1974*	**Ross**, Iain *1991*
Bartlett, David *1975†*	**Steenson**, David *1991*
Richardson, Garth *1975*	**Sweeney**, Christian *1992*
Tyson, Richard *1975‡*	**Kelly**, Marie *1992*
Henry, Peter *1977*	**Kirkpatrick**, Krystyna *1992*
Mitchell, Nigel *1978*	**Weir**, Robert *1992*
Seed, Nigel *1978‡*	**Fitzharris**, Ginnette *1993*
Kent, Peter *1978*	**Earle**, Judy *1994*
Partridge, Ian *1979*	**Geraghty**, Sarah *1994*
Grey, Robert *1979*	**Reid**, David *1994*
Leviseur, Nicholas *1979*	**Williams**, Ben *1994*
Coombes, Timothy *1980*	**Hughes**, Melanie *1995*
Cairnes, Paul *1980*	**McIlroy**, David *1995*
Edge, Ian *1981*	**Strachan**, Elaine *1995*
Strutt, Martin *1981*	**Case**, Richard *1996*
Lickley, Nigel *1983*	**Gourley**, Claire *1996*
Lomas, Mark *1983*	**Wood**, Graham *1979‡**
Maccabe, Irvine *1983*	**Ball**, Sally *1989**

Chambers established: 1892
Opening times: 8.30 am-6.15 pm

Types of work (and number of counsel practising in that area if supplied)
Care proceedings · Chancery (general) · Commercial litigation · Common law (general) · Company and commercial · Competition · Construction · Courts martial · Crime · EC and competition law · Ecclesiastical · Employment · Family · Foreign law · Landlord and tenant · Licensing · Medical negligence · Personal injury · Private international · Professional negligence · Sale and carriage of goods · Town and country planning

Chambers' facilities
Conference rooms, Video conferences, Disks accepted, E-mail

Languages spoken
Arabic, French, German, Greek, Spanish

† Recorder ‡ Assistant Recorder * Door Tenant

Additional information

This is a large and well-established set of chambers with annexes in Bournemouth, Oxford and Winchester and a strong Western Circuit connection. The aim is to provide a comprehensive advocacy and advisory service to clients, both in London and at the annexes. The size enables groups of tenants to specialise in a wide variety of work. Accordingly, all types of common law work are undertaken, including contract/commercial, personal injury, professional negligence, employment and building. The specialist criminal practitioners undertake all types of criminal work, including corporate misfeasance, health and safety, and Privy Council appeals. The specialist family practitioners undertake all types of family work, including wardship, financial provision and inheritance. The specialist Chancery group undertake landlord and tenant, real property, planning, insolvency, company, passing-off, partnership, probate, ecclesiastical law, judicial review and EC law.

3 PAPER BLDGS

2nd Floor, Temple, London EC4Y 7EU
0171 353 6208
Fax: 0171 353 5435; DX 337 London

Chambers of Mr S N Parrish

The Law Society's Directory of Expert Witnesses 1999

- *lists over 3,500 expert witnesses*

- *all entrants agree to comply with The Law Society's Code of Practice and provide two professional references*

- *contains information on choosing and instructing an expert witness*

- *includes 1,700+ specialists in areas of expertise*

- *provides an alphabetical index to assist in finding detailed terms*

- *also available on CD-ROM*

For more information call Sweet & Maxwell on 0171 449 1111

---

4 PAPER BUILDINGS

4 Paper Buildings

Ground Floor, Temple, London EC4Y 7EX
0171 353 3366/583 7155
Fax: 0171 353 5778; DX 1036 London, Chancery Lane
E-mail: clerks@4paperbuildings.com
URL: http://www.4paperbuildings.com
Out of hours telephone: 01277 264828

Chambers of Harvey McGregor QC
Clerks: Stephen Smith (Senior Clerk), Michael Kilbey

McGregor, Harvey QC *1955*	Spencer, Martin *1979*
Wadsworth, James QC *1963†*	Sharpston, Eleanor *1980*
	Holwill, Derek *1982*
Burnett, Harold QC *1962†*	Lawrence, Patrick *1985*
Marshall-Andrews, Robert QC MP *1967†*	Jackson, Matthew *1986*
	Bacon, Francis *1988*
Hogg, The Rt Hon Douglas QC MP *1968*	Flenley, William *1988*
	Picton, Julian *1988*
Ritchie, Jean QC *1970†*	Price, Clare *1988*
Davidson, Nicholas QC *1974*	Gulliver, Alison *1989*
Goddard, Keith QC *1959†**	Simpson, Mark *1992*
Gorna, Christina *1960*	Moser, Philip *1992*
Keane, Michael *1963†*	Reid, Graham *1993*
De Freitas, Anthony *1971‡*	Wilton, Simon *1993*
West-Knights, Laurence *1977‡*	Christie-Brown, Sarah *1994*
	Charlwood, Spike *1994*
Pooles, Michael *1978*	Beal, Kieron *1995*
Mishcon, Jane *1979*	Ewins, Catherine *1995*

Opening times: 8 am-6 pm

Types of work (and number of counsel practising in that area if supplied)

Agriculture 1 · Commercial litigation 3 · Commercial property 6 · Construction 14 · Crime - corporate fraud 2 · EC and competition law 1 · Employment 2 · Entertainment 2 · Housing 5 · Information technology 3 · Insolvency 3 · Insurance 4 · Intellectual property 1 · Landlord and tenant 5 · Medical negligence 13 · Partnerships 2 · Personal injury 14 · Professional negligence 23 · Sports 1

C

---

† Recorder ‡ Assistant Recorder * Door Tenant

Chambers' facilities
Conference rooms, Video conferences, Disks accepted, E-mail

Languages spoken
Danish, Dutch, French, German, Italian, Portuguese, Russian, Spanish

Fees policy
Please refer to the Senior Clerk. The Senior Clerk is alive to the need to agree competitive fees, and is pleased to discuss fees in advance of barristers being instructed. Work is accepted by direct professional access and pursuant to conditional fees, by agreement.

Additional information

Types of work undertaken

This is one of the specialist sets of chambers in the areas of professional negligence and medical negligence. Members of chambers act for both plaintiffs and defendants. In the field of professional negligence, they appear in cases concerning all the various professions particularly solicitors, accountants, surveyors and insurance brokers, and in the area of medical negligence represent patients, the NHSLA, NHS Trusts, and individual doctors, midwives and nurses. Chambers has a long tradition of expertise in the personal injury field, the Head of Chambers, Harvey McGregor QC, having acted in a number of the leading cases in this area and being the author of *McGregor on Damages.*

Additional Specialisations

Chambers also has considerable expertise in European law, computer law, agriculture law, commercial fraud, urgent interlocutory relief, building and construction and judicial review.

Service to clients

Chambers aims to provide a flexible, practical and commercial approach to litigation which is driven by the needs and convenience of our clients. The set is happy to provide written work on disk or by E-mail and is willing to give advice (both within the UK and abroad) via the Bar Council's video-conference link.

The *Bar Directory* **is also available on the Internet at the following address:**

http://www.smlawpub-holborn.co.uk/bar

4 PAPER BUILDINGS

PAPER BUILDINGS

1st Floor, Temple, London EC4Y 7EX
0171 583 0816
Fax: 0171 353 4979; DX LDE: 1035 London, Chancery Lane
E-mail: clerks@4paperbuildings.co.uk
Out of hours telephone: 01708 379332

Chambers of Lionel Swift QC
Clerks: Michael Reeves, Mike Lay; Chambers Manager: Kay May

Swift, Lionel QC *1959*	**Stern,** Michael *1983*
Murdoch, Gordon QC *1970†*	**Reade,** David *1983*
Pauffley, Anna QC *1979†*	**Johnstone,** Mark *1984*
Cohen, Jonathan QC *1974†*	**Coleman,** Elizabeth *1985*
Turcan, Henry *1965†*	**Wood,** Catherine *1985*
Smith, Roge *1968*	**Rosenblatt,** Jeremy *1985*
Barrington-Smyth, Amanda *1972*	**Neaman,** Sam *1988*
	Mills, Barbara *1990*
Ridd, Ian *1975*	**Cope,** Christopher *1990*
Barda, Robin *1975*	**Brereton,** Joy *1990*
Sternberg, Michael *1975*	**Mansfield,** Gavin *1992*
Jackson, Peter *1978‡*	**Larizadeh,** Cyrus *1992*
Coney, Christopher *1979*	**Ageros,** Justin *1993*
Scott-Manderson, Marcus *1980*	**Lowe,** Sarah *1995*
	Schofield, Alexander *1997*
Joseph, Charles *1980*	

Chambers established: 1946
Opening times: 8.30 am-6.30 pm

Types of work (and number of counsel practising in that area if supplied)
Arbitration 2 · Banking 4 · Bankruptcy 1 · Chancery (general) 1 · Chancery land law 1 · Commercial 9 · Commercial property 1 · Company and commercial 2 · Construction 5 · Consumer Law 1 · Discrimination 3 · Employment 5 · Family 22 · Family provision 9 · Foreign law 1 · Immigration 3 · Insolvency 1 · Landlord and tenant 8 · Medical negligence 8 · Mental health 1 · Partnerships 8 · Professional negligence 9 · Sale and carriage of goods 9

Chambers' facilities
Disks accepted, E-mail

                             † Recorder ‡ Assistant Recorder * Door Tenant

Languages spoken
French, German, Hebrew, Spanish

Fees policy
Quotation available from clerks upon request.

5 PAPER BLDGS

*Lower Ground Floor, Temple, London
EC4Y 7HB*
0171 353 5638
Fax: 0171 353 6166; DX 367 London

Chambers of Mr B J Higgs QC

5 PAPER BUILDINGS

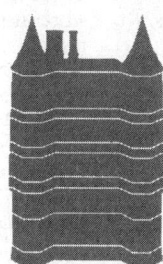

Ground Floor, Temple, London EC4Y 7HB
0171 583 9275
Fax: 0171 583 1926; DX 415 London,
Chancery Lane
E-mail: 5paper@link.org

Chambers of A D P J M Bueno QC
Clerk: Alan Stammers

Bueno, Antonio QC 1964†	Wright, Ian 1983
Percival, Sir Ian QC 1948†	Brownlow, Ann 1984
Nicol, Angus 1963†	Jacobson, Lawrence 1985
Walsh, Steven 1965	Devonshire, Simon 1988
Denman, Robert 1970	Rich, Jonathan 1989
Platford, Graham 1970	Gill, Satinder 1991
Wood, Nicholas 1970†	Stallebrass, Paul 1991
Broatch, Donald 1971	Evans, Richard 1993
Percival, Robert 1971	Rushton, Nicola 1993
King, Richard 1978	Adjei, Cyril 1995
Iles, Adrian 1980	Reichert, Klaus 1996
Infield, Paul 1980	

Opening times: 8 am-6.30 pm

**Types of work (and number of counsel
practising in that area if supplied)**
Administrative · Banking · Bankruptcy
· Commercial litigation · Company and
commercial · Competition · Construction · EC
and competition law · Equity, wills and trusts
· Family · Family provision · Financial services

· Foreign law · Immigration · Insolvency
· International trade · Landlord and tenant
· Medical negligence · Personal injury · Private
international · Probate and administration
· Professional negligence · Sale and carriage of
goods · Tax - capital and income

Chambers' facilities
Video conferences, Disks accepted

Languages spoken
French, Italian, Punjabi, Spanish

Fees policy
On application to the senior clerk.

5 PAPER BUILDINGS

1st Floor, Temple, London EC4Y 7HB
0171 583 6117
Fax: 0171 353 0075; DX 365 London,
Chancery Lane
E-mail: clerks@5-paperbuildings.law.co.uk

Chambers of J C Mathew QC
Clerk: Stuart Bryant (Senior Clerk)

Mathew, John QC 1949	Pinto, Amanda 1983
Tabor, James QC 1974*	Bennett, Miles 1986
Corkery, Michael QC 1949	Groome, David 1987
Cassel, Timothy QC 1965	O'Sullivan, Robert 1988
Stokes, David QC 1968†	Christopher, Julian 1988
Carey, Godfrey QC 1969†	Evans, Martin 1989
Caplan, Jonathan QC 1973†	Dhir, Anuja 1989
Singh, Kuldip QC 1975	Griffin, Lynn 1991
Sells, Oliver QC 1972†	Cole, Justin 1992
Hughes, Stanley 1971	Griffin, Nicholas 1992
Jenkins, Edward 1977	Mpanga, David 1993
Wade, Ian 1977	Deacon, Emma 1993
Trembath, Graham 1978	Allen, Tom 1994
Fooks, Nicholas 1978	Hick, Michael 1995
Mehigan, Simon 1980	Bailin, Alex 1995
Judge, Charles 1981	Barton, Charles QC 1969*
Aston, Maurice 1982	Hawkesworth, Gareth 1972*
Moore, Miranda 1983	Franklin, Stephen 1974*

The Supreme Court Practice 1999

• *the most authoritative title on Civil Court
Practice and Procedure*

• *available in book and CD-ROM formats*

*Phone Sweet & Maxwell on 0171 449 1111
to order your copy*

PEPYS' CHAMBERS

17 Fleet Street, London EC4Y 1AA
0171 936 2710
Fax: 0171 936 2501; DX 463 London,
Chancery Lane
Out of hours telephone: 0171 936 2710

Chambers of Terence de Lury
Clerk: Wanda Bogucka

de Lury, Terence *1985*	**Ferguson**, Christopher
Keane, Desmond QC *1964*	*1979**
Joseph, Clifford *1975*	**Skinner**, Conor *1979**
de Speville, Patrice *1978**	**Brown**, James *1989*
Pawlowski, Mark *1978**	**Morton**, Gary *1993*

PHOENIX CHAMBERS

*First Floor, Gray's Inn Chambers, Gray's Inn,
London WC1R 5JA*
0171 404 7888
Fax: 0171 404 7897; DX 78 London, Chancery
Lane

Chambers of The Hon B M D Pitt
*Clerks: Laurie Gallogly, Sean Phelan, Mark
Jordan; Practice Managers: Mayfax Ltd*

Pitt, Bruce *1970**	**Vincent**, Claire *1993*
Bradley, Denis *1965*	**Zahed**, Yasreeb *1993*
Campbell, Donald *1976*	**Payne**, Brian *1993*
Forlin, Gerard *1984*	**Shah**, Sheena *1993*
Fama, Gudrun *1991*	**Roberts**, Adrian *1993*
Boumphrey, John *1992*	**Kendal**, Mark *1994*
Cavender, Simon *1992*	**Kirby**, James *1994*
Cole, Vanessa *1992*	**McAteer**, Shanda *1994*
Reiff-Musgrove, Kaja *1992*	**Reed**, Jason *1994*
Blackmore, Sarah *1993*	**Choudhury**, Fareha *1995*
Coy, Michael *1993*	**Bsis**, Ibtihal *1995*
Hussein, Timur *1993*	**Mitchell**, Ian *1995*

Use the *Types of Work* listings in Parts A
and B to locate chambers and individual
barristers who specialise in particular areas
of work.

PLOWDEN BUILDINGS

Temple, London EC4Y 9BU
0171 583 0808
Fax: 0171 583 5106; DX 020 London,
Chancery Lane
E-mail: bar@plowdenbuildings.co.uk

Chambers of William Lowe QC
*Clerk: Paul Hurst; Practice manager: Anthony
Long*

Lowe, William QC *1972†*	**Quigley**, Camilla *1988*
Cooper, Arnold *969*	**Brook**, David *1988*
McIntyre, Bruce *1969†*	**Dines**, Sarah *1988*
Buckhaven, Charlotte *1969*	**James**, Michael *1989*
Hindmarsh, Elizabeth *1974*	**Haukeland**, Martin *1989*
Trotter, David *1975*	**de Rohan**, Jonathan *1989*
Craven, Richard *1976*	**Cox**, Kerry *1990*
Sandford, Simon *1979*	**Watson-Gandy**, Mark *1990*
Azam, Javad *1981*	**Henderson**, Sophie *1990*
Shrimpton, R James *1981*	**Anthony**, Christina *1990*
Holdham, Susan *1983*	**Gaston**, Graeme *1991*
Dacey, Mark *1985*	**Lindsay**, Claire *1991*
Holmes, Jonathan *1985*	**Freeman**, Peter *1992*
McNulty, Lawrence *1985*	**Lamb**, Jeffrey *1992*
West, Ian *1985*	**Cox**, Simon *1992*
Foster, Catherine *1986*	**Farbey**, Judith *1992*
Bailey, Michael *1986*	**Walsh**, John *1993*
Moore-Graham, Fiona *1986*	**Bajwa**, Ali *1993*
Collings, Andrew *1987*	**Potter**, Anthony *1994*
Lyons, David *1987*	**Cade**, Diane *1994*
Dyer, Simon *1987*	**MacKenzie**, Anna *1994*
Gordon, Kate *1988*	**Speirs**, Alistair *1995*
Morton, Peter *1988*	**Clarke**, Jamie *1995*
Jones, Lawrence *1988*	**Broome**, Edward *1996*
Orton, Paul *1988*	

    † Recorder ‡ Assistant Recorder * Door Tenant

CHAMBERS OF JOHN L POWELL QC

2nd Floor, 2 Crown Office Row, Temple,
London EC4Y 7HJ
0171 797 8000
Fax: 0171 797 8001; DX 1041 London,
Chancery Lane
Out of hours telephone: 01621 893536,
Mobile: 0370 277977

Chambers of J L Powell QC
Clerk: Annie Hopkins;
Practice manager: Lizzy Wiseman

Powell, John QC 1974‡	**Parker,** Paul 1986
Jackson, Rupert QC 1972†	**Stewart,** Roger 1986
Livesey, Bernard QC 1969†	**Carr,** Sue 1987
Fenwick, Justin QC 1980‡	**Evans,** Hugh 1987
Brooke, Michael QC 1968‡	**Asif,** Jalil 1988
Gibson, Christopher QC 1976	**Sinclair,** Fiona 1989
	Brown, Nicholas 1989
Hughes, Iain QC 1974	**Nicol,** Andrew 1991
Critchlow, Christopher 1973†	**Hubble,** Benedict 1992
	Phipps, Charles 1992
Lomnicka, Prof Eva 1974	**Sutherland,** Paul 1992
Russen, Simon 1976	**McPherson,** Graeme 1993
Douthwaite, Charles 1977	**Bijlani,** Aisha 1993
Tyrell, Glen 1977	**Shaldon,** Nicola 1994
Hamilton, Gavin 1979	**Goldberg,** Charlotte 1995
Stafford, Andrew 1980	**Smith,** Jamie 1995
Kaplan, Barbara 1980	**Millar,** Alison 1995
Monty, Simon 1982	**Day,** Anneliese 1996
Fodder, Martin 1983	**Elkington,** Ben 1996
Cannon, Mark 1985	**Gilmore,** Seánin 1996
Holtum, Ian 1985	

Chambers established: 1940
Opening times: 8.30 am-7 pm

Types of work (and number of counsel practising in that area if supplied)
Administrative 10 · Arbitration 10 · Banking 1 · Chancery (general) 5 · Commercial litigation 25 · Common law (general) 36 · Company and commercial 4 · Construction 28 · Discrimination 5 · Education 3 · Employment 10 · Environment 10 · Financial services 3 · Insolvency 3 · Insurance 11 · Insurance/reinsurance 11 · Landlord and tenant 6 · Medical negligence 15 · Partnerships 5 · Personal injury 15 · Private international 3 · Professional negligence 39 · Sale and carriage of goods 5 · Town and country planning 3 · Unit trusts 2

Chambers' facilities
Disks accepted, Disabled access, E-mail

Languages spoken
French, German, Hindi, Spanish, Welsh

Additional information

A long-established chambers, we are best known for our expertise as advocates and advisers in the field of professional negligence and related areas. While individual practices vary, we cover a broad range of other commercial and civil work.

Our expertise in the field of professional liability extends to accountants, auditors and financial advisers, barristers and solicitors, construction professionals, doctors, insurance intermediaries, surveyors and valuers, as well as other consultants and advisers. Some individuals concentrate on some professions more than others. Members who specialise in medical negligence also conduct pharmaceutical and personal injury claims. Seven members of chambers contribute to the leading text *Jackson & Powell on Professional Negligence.* Recently published is *Lawyers' Liabilities* by Hugh Evans.

The commercial work of chambers covers a wide range of contract disputes, especially in insurance and reinsurance, financial services, regulatory, privatisation, sale of goods and other commercial contexts. Construction, engineering and environmental claims feature large in the practices of many members. Other civil work includes employment, education and local government, judicial review and public law, the law of confidence, as well as EC law and private international law relating to principal areas of work. We have considerable experience in group litigation in commercial fraud, financial services, disaster, pharmaceutical, medical and other contexts.

As well as regularly appearing in the High Court and appellate courts, we also appear in arbitrations, industrial, disciplinary and other tribunals.

We seek to provide an efficient and friendly service to all our clients. We are instructed by professional clients from all over the UK as well as from London and overseas. Our Senior Clerk

---

† Recorder ‡ Assistant Recorder * Door Tenant

can be contacted out of hours on 01621 893536, Mobile: 0370 277977.

Further specialisations Securities regulation (UK, EC and international) and collective investment schemes (John Powell QC and Professor Lomnicka, who edit the *Encyclopedia of Financial Services)*. Consumer credit (Professor Lomnicka who edits the *Encyclopedia of Consumer Credit Law*). Michael Brooke QC is also a practising advocate at the Paris Bar.

We seek to retain and develop our reputation by publication and lectures. In addition to those mentioned above, other major publications by members of chambers include *Confidentiality* by Charles Phipps (with Toulson J) and *The Law of Banking* by Professor Lomnicka (with Professor Ellinger).

PRINCE HENRY'S CHAMBERS

17 Fleet Street, London EC4Y 1AA
0171 353 1183/1190
Fax: 0171 353 1204

Chambers of David R Harris

Harris, David 1973	Jack, Katrina 1978
Pickford, Anthony 1951	

The *new* Supreme Court Practice 1999 (The White Book)

- *the most authoritative guide to Civil Court Practice and Procedure*

- *whatever the case, whatever the court*

- *updates following implementation of the Woolf Reforms*

The new Supreme Court Practice *is also available on CD-ROM using Folio Views™ technology. With this intuitive software, you will find your way around* The White Book *with ease, enhancing your research by leaps and bounds.*

Phone Sweet & Maxwell on 0171 449 1111 to order your copy

1 PUMP COURT

Temple, London EC4Y 7AB
0171 583 2012/353 4341
Fax: 0171 353 4944; DX LDE 109
E-mail: (name) @1pumpcourt.co.uk
URL: http://www.1pumpcourt.co.uk
Other comms: Lix: Lon 217
Out of hours telephone: 0374 238444

Chambers of Jane Hoyal and Robert Latham
Clerks: Ian Burrow (Senior Clerk), Mycal Thomas (Assistant Clerk), Danny Wallis (Assistant Clerk), Martin Cornwell (Fees Clerk), Gary Carney (Junior Clerk); Receptionist: Deborah Coles

Adams, Lindsay 1987	**Killeen**, Robert 1995
Atreya, Navita 1994	**Kothari**, Sima 1992
Bevan, Stephen 1986	**Latham**, Robert 1976
Bloom, Tracey 1984	**Lecointe**, Elpha 1988
Boswell, Jenny 1982	**Montague**, Susan 1981
Bradley, Sally 1989	**More O'Ferrall**, Geraldine
Bryan, Deborah 1987	1983
Bullock, Neil 1989	**Nabi**, Zia 1991
Carne, Rosalind 1986	**Polson**, Alistair 1989
Chesters, Colette 1996	**Reeder**, Stephen 1991
Collier, Patricia 1983	**Russell**, Alison 1983
Delaney, Mary 1984	**Sharpe**, Martin 1989
Farnon, Patricia 1986	**Stein**, Sam 1988
Frances, Jill 1992	**Teji**, Usha 1981
Friedman, Charlotte 1982	**Warren**, Lynnette 1987
Ghose, Katie 1996	**Willers**, Marc 1987
Harris, Bethan 1990	**Wright**, Stewart 1993
Higham, Paul 1982	**McKeon**, Caroline 1983
Hilken, Alice 1994	**Hammerton**, Gillian 1973
Hodson, Peter 1994	**Connolly**, James 1985*
Hoyal, Jane 1976	**Sprack**, John 1984*
Isles, Mary 1984	**Sunkin**, Maurice 1975*
Jefferies, Andrew 1990	**Wallace**, Ann 1979*
Keegan, Leslie 1989	**Bradley**, Phillip 1993*
Khanzada, Najma 1992	

Chambers established: 1978

Types of work (and number of counsel practising in that area if supplied)
Administrative · Care proceedings · Chancery (general) · Chancery land law · Civil liberties · Common law (general) · Crime · Crime -

corporate fraud · Discrimination · Education · Employment · Environment · Equity, wills and trusts · Family · Family provision · Housing · Immigration · Landlord and tenant · Licensing · Local government · Medical negligence · Mental health · Personal injury · Professional negligence

Chambers' facilities
Conference rooms, Disks accepted

Languages spoken
Dutch, French, German, Gujarati, Hindi, Punjabi, Spanish, Urdu

Additional information

1 PUMP COURT is a radical and progressive set of chambers providing a specialist service to legally-aided and private clients, and which seeks to secure equality of access to justice. Chambers undertakes work at all levels, and members practise in the following specialist groups: crime, family, housing and civil.

Criminal practitioners practise in criminal defence and civil actions against the police. Family practitioners provide a progressive, multi-disciplinary and socially-responsible approach to family legal services in all areas of national and international law. Housing work concentrates on problems faced by tenants and the homeless. The civil group specialises in social security, employment, immigration, mental health, personal injury and medical negligence. Judicial review is an important and expanding area of work within chambers.

Chambers works closely with Law Centres and other agencies addressing unmet legal needs. Members are prominent in legal pressure groups and voluntary organisations, seeking to reform and improve the provision of legal services and access to justice. **1 PUMP COURT** seeks to ensure equality of opportunity both in the work we undertake and in the structures within chambers. Chambers has a strong commitment to its equal opportunities policy, ensuring we reflect the community we serve.

Crime Desktop CD-ROM

Containing the three most important titles in criminal law: Archbold, Criminal Law Review *and* Criminal Appeal Reports, *this is the most efficient criminal law research tool you can own.*

Put time on your side, phone Sweet & Maxwell on 0171 449 1111 for more information or a free demonstration

2 PUMP COURT

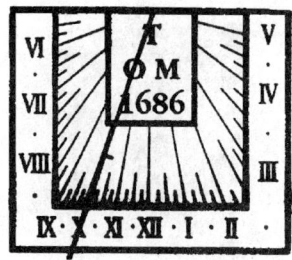

1st Floor, Temple, London EC4Y 7AH
0171 353 5597
Fax: 0171 583 2122; DX 290 London, Chancery Lane
Out of hours telephone: 01708 732138

Chambers of P F Singer QC
Clerk: John Arter

Singer, Philip QC *1964*†	**O'Brien,** Haylee *1984*
Grenfell, Gibson QC *1969*†	**Williams,** Simon *1984*
Giovene, Laurence *1962*†	**Christie,** Richard *1986*
Sharp, Alastair *1968*†	**Lickert,** Martin *1986*
Lyons, Graham *1972*	**Agbamu,** Alexander *1988*
Russell, Jeremy *1973*	**Knapp,** Sophie *1990*
Mallender, Paul *1974*	**Thompson,** Polly *1990*
Allston, Anthony *1975*	**Aliker,** Philip *1990*
Caun, Lawrence *1977*	**Hunter,** John *1991*
Renouf, Gerard *1977*	**Paxton,** Christopher *1991*
Barrett, Robert *1978*	**Dugdale,** Jeremy *1992*
Fleischmann, Laureen *1978*	**Cronshaw,** Michael *1993*
Pigot, Diana *1978*	**Garrido,** Damian *1993*
Dooley, Christine *1980*	**Sugarman,** Jason *1995*
Waddington, James *1983*	**Tarr,** Beverly *1995*
Davey, Helen *1984*	

Crime Desktop CD-ROM

Never before has criminal law research been so efficient. With Crime Desktop, *you have quick and easy access to:*

Archbold *– the leading authority on criminal law, practice and procedure*

Criminal Law Review *(since 1967) – the latest case law and legislative developments, plus analysis of current issues and changes in the law*

Criminal Appeal Reports *(since 1967) – extensive coverage of all major criminal appeal cases.*

Put time on your side, phone Sweet & Maxwell on 0171 449 1111 for more information or a free demonstration

C

PUMP COURT CHAMBERS

*Upper Ground Floor, 3 Pump Court, London
EC4Y 7AJ*
0171 353 0711
Fax: 0171 353 3319; DX 362 London,
Chancery Lane
URL: http://www.3pumpcourt.com

Chambers of Guy Boney QC
*Clerks: David Barber, Danny Fantham;
Administrator: Sally Woolley*

Also at: 31 Southgate Street, Winchester SO23
9EE
Tel: 01962 868161
Fax: 01962 867645;
5 Temple Chambers, Swindon SN1 1SQ
Tel: 01793 539899
Fax: 01793 539866

Boney, Guy QC *1968*†
Pascoe, Nigel QC *1966*†
Clark, Christopher QC *1969*†
Garlick, Paul QC *1974*†
Still, Geoffrey *1966*†
Patterson, Stewart *1967*‡
Pearson, Adam *1969*
Moat, Frank *1970*†
Harrap, Giles *1971*†
Abbott, Frank *1972*†
Montgomery, Michael *1972*
Parry, Charles *1973*
Butt, Michael *1974*
Ker-Reid, John *1974*
Gabb, Charles *1975*
Gillibrand, Phillip *1975*
Barnett, Andrew *1977*†
Dineen, Michael *1977*
Miller, Jane *1979*‡
O'Flynn, Timothy *1979*
Hill, Robert *1980*
Allardice, Miranda *1982*
Lochrane, Damien *1983*
Nsugbe, Oba *1985*
Scott, Matthew *1985*
Bloom-Davis, Desmond *1986*

Hill, Mark *1987*
Howard, Graham *1987*
Travers, Hugh *1988*
Waddington, Anne *1988*
Warren, Philip *1988*
Akiwumi, Anthony *1989*
Boydell, Edward *1989*
Gau, Justin *1989*
Samuels, Leslie *1989*
Brunton, Sean *1990*
Khan, Helen *1990*
Howe, Penny *1991*
Kelly, Geoffrey *1992*
Newton-Price, James *1992*
Poyer-Sleeman, Patricia *1992*
Gunther, Elizabeth *1993*
Peirson, Oliver *1993*
Fields, Helen *1993*
Blackburn, Luke *1993*
Ashley, Mark *1993*
Pawson, Robert *1994*
Dubbery, Mark *1996*
Beaumont, Marc *1985**

Opening times: 8.30 am-6.15 pm

**Types of work (and number of counsel
practising in that area if supplied)**
Administrative 5 · Bankruptcy 4 · Care
proceedings 12 · Common law (general) 48
· Construction 3 · Courts martial 7 · Crime 24
· Crime - corporate fraud 9 · Ecclesiastical 2
· Employment 6 · Environment 1 · Family 18
· Family provision 13 · Foreign law 2
· Immigration 1 · Insolvency 3 · Landlord and
tenant 4 · Medical negligence 5 · Partnerships
5 · Personal injury 21 · Planning 3
· Professional negligence 5 · Town and
country planning 3

Chambers' facilities
Conference rooms

Languages spoken
French, German

Additional information

The Chambers We are a long-established and
forward looking set whose main areas of
practice are Family, Crime and General
Common Law.

Work undertaken Members of Chambers
practise in specialist teams and their areas of
particular specialisation include Professional
and Medical Negligence; Personal Injury;
Matrimonial; Inheritance Act; Criminal Law
(including Customs and Excise, Serious Fraud,
Courts Martial, Animal Litigation); Construction
Law; Ecclesiastical law; Environment law;
Extradition and Judicial Review; Nigerian Law.

Additional areas of work Boundary disputes;
Contracts; Discipline Tribunals; Employment
law; Immigration law; Insolvency; Planning;
Road Traffic.

Publications Mr Mark Hill is the author of *Hill
on Ecclesiastical Law.*

Mr Nigel Pascoe QC is the Leader of the Western
Circuit.
Mr Michael Montgomery is Standing Counsel to
the DTI (SE Circuit).
Mr Oba Nsugbe is a barrister and solicitor of the
Supreme Court of Nigeria with direct access to
chambers in Lagos.
Dr Gerhard Dannerman is a member of the
German Bar.

† Recorder ‡ Assistant Recorder * Door Tenant

4 PUMP COURT

Temple, London EC4Y 7AN
0171 353 2656/9
Fax: 0171 583 2036; DX 303 London
E-mail: 4_pump_court@compuserve.com

Chambers of Bruce Mauleverer QC
*Clerks: Carolyn McCombe, Simon Slattery,
Carl Wall, Stewart Gibbs*

Mauleverer, Bruce QC 1969†	**Charlton,** Alexander 1983
Temple, Anthony QC 1968†	**Sears,** David 1984
Friedman, David QC 1968‡	**Hughes,** Adrian 1984
Blunt, David QC 1967†	**Cross,** James 1985
Moger, Christopher QC 1972†	**McCall,** Duncan 1988
Storey, Jeremy QC 1974†	**Christie,** Aidan 1988
Marks, Jonathan QC 1975	**Neish,** Andrew 1988
Acton Davis, Jonathan QC 1977‡	**Houghton,** Kirsten 1989
Rowland, John QC 1979	**Rowlands,** Marc 1990
Douglas, Michael QC 1974	**McCahill,** Dominic 1991
Boswell, Lindsay QC 1982	**Cheyne,** Phyllida 1992
Marsh, Laurence 1975	**Henderson,** Simon 1993
Dyer, Allen 1976	**Davie,** Michael 1993
Nicholson, Jeremy 1977	**Gunning,** Alexander 1994
Ticciati, Oliver 1979	**Ansell,** Rachel 1995
Tozzi, Nigel 1980	**Packman,** Claire 1996
Fletcher, Andrew 1980	**Aird,** Richard 1976*
Hamilton, Peter 1968	**Ackner,** The Hon Claudia 1977*
	Coleman, Russell 1986
	Potter, Alison 1987*

Chambers established: 1954
Opening times: 8.30 am-7 pm

Types of work (and number of counsel practising in that area if supplied)
Arbitration 21 · Aviation 3 · Banking 10 · Commercial 34 · Common law (general) 23 · Construction 21 · Employment 9 · Entertainment 2 · Environment 1 · Family provision 2 · Financial services 1 · Information technology 6 · Insurance 34 · Insurance/reinsurance 10 · Licensing 8 · Medical negligence 10 · Personal injury 15 · Professional negligence 34 · Sale and carriage of goods 10 · Sports 2

Chambers' facilities
Conference rooms, Disks accepted, E-mail

Languages spoken
French, German, Italian, Spanish

Fees policy
The clerks are happy to discuss hourly rates or provide estimates for brief fees. Realistic rates are charged at all levels. We are anxious that our clients understand the rationale behind fees charged and are satisfied with the value of work done.

Additional information

Commercial Work

Insurance and reinsurance, including litigation and arbitration, disciplinary hearings and regulatory control; contracts, including sale of goods; restraint of trade; passing off; banking; financial services; Mareva and Anton Piller orders and other injunctive relief.

Construction and Civil Engineering

National and international arbitration and litigation, acting for employers, contractors and sub-contractors and professional advisors.

Professional Negligence

Representing plaintiffs and insurers and involving doctors and other medical professionals, solicitors and barristers, accountants, valuers and surveyors, insurance brokers and other professional advisors.

Information Technology and Telecommunications

Expertise primarily concerns disputes of a contractual nature, involving a detailed understanding of the technical aspects of computer systems, their implementation and application.

Licensing, Gaming and Lotteries

All aspects of gaming law, especially casino gaming and lotteries acting both for the regulator of the gaming industry and many of its major operators.

Other Fields

General common law including personal injury, landlord and tenant, and matrimonial finance.

Arbitration

Lord Ackner, Lord Jauncey and James Fox-Andrews QC are full-time arbitrators while other members of chambers, at different levels of seniority, also sit as arbitrators.

Direct Professional Access

DPA is welcomed by all members of chambers.

5 PUMP COURT

Ground Floor, Temple, London EC4Y 7AP
0171 353 2532
Fax: 0171 353 5321; DX 497 London, Chancery Lane
E-mail: fivepump@netcomuk.co.uk
Out of hours telephone: 0976 368031

Chambers of R V Bryan
Clerks: Tim Markham (Senior Clerk), Jayne Goodrham

Bryan, Rex 1971†	**Hasan**, Tazeen 1988
Primost, Norman 1954	**Gooch**, Sebastian 1989
Hunter, Anthony 1962	**Schiffer**, Corinna 1989
Hopkins, Simeon 1968	**O'Sullivan**, Derek 1990
Dow, Kenneth 1970	**Walker**, Allister 1990
Christodoulou, Helen 1972	**Humphreys**, Jane 1990
Evison, John 1974	**Nicholls**, Jack 1991
Keith, Alistair 1974	**Ross**, Anthony 1991
Cartwright, Crispian 1976‡	**Ellis-Jones**, Stephen 1992
Chaize, Tristan 1977	**Say**, Bradley 1993
Charlton, Hugo 1978	**Marley**, Sarah 1995
Campbell, Graham 1979	**Smith**, Emma 1995
Ratcliffe, Anne 1981	**Elfield**, Laura 1996
Hodgkinson, Tristram 1982	**King**, Peter 1970*
Morris, Christina 1983	**Snell**, John 1973*
Collard, Michael 1986	**Spencer**, Hannah 1993*
James, Mark 1987	

Chambers established: 1870
Opening times: 8.30 am-7 pm

Types of work (and number of counsel practising in that area if supplied)
Administrative 3 · Arbitration 3 · Bankruptcy 2 · Care proceedings 8 · Chancery (general) 3 · Chancery land law 2 · Commercial 3 · Commercial property 2 · Common law (general) 10 · Company and commercial 2 · Construction 5 · Crime 13 · EC and competition law 1 · Employment 4 · Environment 2 · Family 9 · Family provision 7 · Housing 4 · Insolvency 3 · Insurance 2 · Landlord and tenant 5 · Licensing 5 · Medical negligence 2 · Personal injury 9 · Probate and administration 1 · Professional negligence 4 · Sale and carriage of goods 2 · Town and country planning 1

Chambers' facilities
Conference rooms, Disks accepted, E-mail, Free parking by arrangement, Video playback facilities

Languages spoken
French, German, Greek, Hindi, Italian, Urdu

Fees policy
No set rates for paperwork, although fees can be agreed in advance on sight of the papers, or guidance given as to appropriate hourly rates.

Additional information

Types of work undertaken
Five Pump Court Chambers is a long-established common law set with three specialist practice groups focusing on civil, criminal and family law. Conditional fee and DPA work is undertaken. Chambers has dedicated conference rooms with video facilities, and free parking is available. Conferences can be arranged out of London.

Principal areas of practice
Civil: Landlord and tenant, building, contract/commercial, professional negligence, personal injury, partnership, trusts, judical review, employment, arbitration, consumer credit and licensing.
Criminal: Fraud, sexual offences, DTI, serious violence, car ringing and importation of drugs.
Family: Financial provision and children.

CHAMBERS OF KIERAN COONAN QC

6 Pump Court, Ground Floor & Lower Ground Floor, London EC4Y 7AR
0171 583 6013/2510
Fax: 0171 353 0464; DX 409 London, Chancery Lane

Chambers of K B Coonan QC
Clerks: Adrian Barrow, Stephen Somerville

Coonan, Kieran QC 1971†	**Gordon**, John 1989
Davies, John 1955	**Kennedy**, Andrew 1989
Curwen, Michael 1966†	**Morgan**, Jeremy 1989
Williams, Jon 1970	**Garrett**, Annalissa 1991
Morris, David 1976	**Lacey**, Roisin 1991
Goodrich, Siobhan 1980	**Hutton**, Alexander 1992
Power, Richard 1983	**Peacock**, Nicholas 1992
Hockton, Andrew 1984	**Gollop**, Katharine 1993
Jenkins, Alan 1984	**Jenkins**, Janet 1994
Burden, Susan 1985	**Brown**, Emma 1995
Foster, Charles 1988	**Robertson**, Alice 1996
Lambert, Christina 1988	**Craven**, Richard 1976*
Post, Andrew 1988	

† Recorder ‡ Assistant Recorder * Door Tenant

Opening times: 8.45 am-6.30 pm

Types of work (and number of counsel practising in that area if supplied)
Care proceedings 4 · Common law (general) 20 · Crime - corporate fraud 10 · Employment 4 · Family 4 · Family provision 3 · Housing 5 · Landlord and tenant 4 · Medical negligence 24 · Mental health 10 · Personal injury 20 · Professional negligence 10

Chambers' facilities
Conference rooms, Disabled access, Video conferences by arrangement

Fees policy
Fees are negotiated with the clerks who adopt a realistic charging policy.

Additional information

These Chambers have enjoyed a reputation over the past 25 years for providing specialist advice and advocacy on behalf of Plaintiffs and Defendants in the field of Healthcare Law.

Most members of Chambers specialise in the major areas of medical and dental negligence, mental health law and the professional conduct regulation of care professionals.

The work of Chambers is undertaken before Inquests, Inquiries (both public and private) and before various Judicial/Administrative Tribunals. Individual members of Chambers also undertake criminal cases which frequently incorporate medico-legal issues.

Personal injury and professional negligence work (particularly affecting solicitors), housing, family, and employment law, are strongly represented. A small group practises in the specialist area of the law relating to Costs.

Many of the leading cases in these fields have featured members of this set.

Some members of Chambers have practised formerly in the professions of solicitor, medical practitioner and veterinary surgeon.

---

6 PUMP COURT

1st Floor, Temple, London EC4Y 7AR
0171 797 8400
Fax: 0171 797 8401; DX 293 London, Chancery Lane
E-mail: sa_hockman_qc@link.org

Chambers of Stephen Hockman QC
Clerk: Richard Constable (Senior Clerk)

Also at: 6-8 Mill Street, Maidstone, Kent ME15 6XH
Tel: 01622 688094/95
Fax: 01622 688096

Hockman, Stephen QC 1970†	**Forbes,** Peter 1990
	Saxby, Oliver 1992
Goymer, Andrew 1970†	**Chamberlayne,** Patrick 1992
Williams, Adèle 1972†	**Butler,** Judith 1993
Harington, Michael 1974†	**Mee,** Paul 1992
Barraclough, Richard 1980	**Watson,** Mark 1994
Baldock, Nicholas 1983	**Grant,** Edward 1994
Bailey, Mark 1984	**Ellin,** Nina 1994
Topping, Caroline 1984	**Wright,** Clare 1995
Walden-Smith, David 1985	**Beard,** Mark 1996
Gower, Peter 1985	**Charles,** Deborah 1996
Harrison, Peter 1987	

PUMP COURT TAX CHAMBERS

16 Bedford Row, London WC1R 4EB
0171 414 8080
Fax: 0171 414 8099; DX 312 London

Chambers of A R Thornhill QC
Clerks: Graham Kettle, Geraldine O'Sullivan

Thornhill, Andrew QC 1969	**Prosser,** Kevin QC 1982
Milne, David QC 1970	**Goodfellow,** Giles 1983
Allcock, Stephen QC 1975	**Ewart,** David 1987
Richards, Ian 1971	**Woolf,** Jeremy 1986
Matthews, Janek 1972	**Hitchmough,** Andrew 1991
Tallon, John 1975	**Shipwright,** Adrian 1993
Massey, William QC 1977	**Baldry,** Rupert 1987
Thomas, Roger 1979	**Wilson,** Elizabeth 1995

See the *Index of Languages Spoken* **in Part G to locate a chambers where a particular language is spoken, or find an individual who speaks a particular language.**

The Supreme Court Practice 1999

- *the most authoritative title on Civil Court Practice and Procedure*

- *available in book and CD-ROM formats*

Phone Sweet & Maxwell on 0171 449 1111 to order your copy

---

† Recorder ‡ Assistant Recorder * Door Tenant

QUEEN ELIZABETH BUILDING

G r o u n d   F l o o r

Ground Floor, Temple, London EC4Y 9BS
0171 353 7181 (12 lines)
Fax: 0171 353 3929; DX 340 LDE

Chambers of Lindsay Burn
Clerk: Michael A Price; Administrator: Brian Warmington

Burn, Lindsay 1972‡	**Bhatia,** Divya 1986
Guy, Richard 1970	**Munro,** Fiona 1986
Farror, Shelagh 1970	**Price,** Debora 1987
Miskin, Claire 1970†	**Holt,** Karen 1987
Stage, Peter 1971	**Probyn,** Jane 1988
Lowen, Jonathan 1972†	**Philcox,** Barbara 1988
Prideaux-Brune, Peter 1972	**Purkiss,** Kate 1988
Pavry, James 1974	**Driscoll,** Jennifer 1989
Salvesen, Keith 1974	**Adebayo,** Ibitayo 1989
Wild, Simon 1977	**Henderson,** Lawrence 1990
Jeremy, David 1977	**Fry,** Neil 1992
Harris, Laura 1977	**Jackson,** Stephanie 1992
Walsh, Peter 1978	**Field,** Amanda-Jane 1992
Hornsby, Walton 1980	**Weeks,** Janet 1993
Blower, Graham 1980	**McKenna,** Anna 1994
Simpson, Nicola 1982	**Cartwright,** Richard 1994
Digby, Charles 1982	**Browne,** Gerald 1995
Haycroft, Anthony 1982	**Fine,** Suzanne 1976*
Gibb, Fiona 1983	**Gore,** Susan 1993
Atkinson, Carol 1985	**Easton,** Alison 1994
St John-Stevens, Philip 1985	**Aiolfi,** Laurence 1996
Devlin, Tim 1985	**Thompson,** Marcus 1996
	Gardiner, Emma 1995

Chambers established: 1976
Opening times: 8.15 am-7 pm

Types of work (and number of counsel practising in that area if supplied)
Common law (general) 8 · Crime 21 · Crime - corporate fraud 8 · Education 4 · Family 14 · Licensing 3

Chambers' facilities
Conference rooms, Video conferences, Disks accepted, Disabled access

Languages spoken
French, Hindi, Spanish

QUEEN ELIZABETH BUILDING

Hollis Whiteman Chambers, Temple, London EC4Y 9BS
0171 583 5766
Fax: 0171 353 0339; DX 482 London, Chancery Lane
E-mail: hollis.whiteman@btinternet.com
Out of hours telephone: Duty Clerk 24 hour 07970 439915

Chambers of David Jeffreys QC, Peter Whiteman QC
Clerk: Michael J Greenaway;
Administrator: Sarah Finlayson

Jeffreys, David QC 1958†	**Donne,** Jeremy 1978
Whiteman, Peter QC 1967†	**Kelsey-Fry,** John 1978
Carlisle of Bucklow, Lord QC 1954†	**Ellison,** Mark 1979
Grey, Robin QC 1957†	**Finnigan,** Peter 1978
Suckling, Alan QC 1963†	**Wood,** Nick 1980
Glass, Anthony QC 1965†	**Rees,** Gareth 1981
Robinson, Vivian QC 1967†	**Kark,** Thomas 1982
Hilton, John QC 1964†	**Stern,** Ian 1983
Barker, Brian QC 1969†	**Brown,** Edward 1983
Bevan, Julian QC 1962	**Sullivan,** Jane 1984
Evans, David QC 1972†	**Bennetts,** Philip 1986
Langdale, Timothy QC 1966†	**Sparks,** Jocelyn 1987
Bate, David QC 1969†	**Larkin,** Sean 1987
Poulet, Rebecca QC 1975†	**Plaschkes,** Sarah 1988
Kyte, Peter QC 1970†	**Henry,** Edward 1988
Calvert-Smith, David QC 1969†	**Winter,** Ian 1988
Clarke, Peter QC 1973†	**Johnson,** Zoe 1990
Wilcken, Anthony 1966†	**Lowry,** Emma 1991
Longden, Anthony 1967	**Barnfather,** Lydia 1992
Mitchell, Christopher 1968†	**Coward,** Victoria 1992
Stewart, Neill 1973†	**Wastie,** William 1993
Strudwick, Linda 1973	**Warne,** Peter 1993
Paton, Ian 1975	**Ramasamy,** Selvaraju 1992
Boyce, William 1976†	**Darbishire,** Adrian 1993
Horwell, Richard 1976	**Summers,** Benjamin 1994
	Saffian, Leah 1992
	Aldred, Mark 1996

Opening times: 8.30 am-7 pm

Types of work (and number of counsel practising in that area if supplied)
Courts martial 51 · Crime 51 · Crime - corporate fraud 51 · Financial services 51 · Judicial review 51 · Licensing 51 · Tax - capital and income 1 · Tax - corporate 1

Chambers' facilities
Conference rooms, Disks accepted, Disabled access

Languages spoken
French, German, Greek, Italian, Russian, Spanish

Fees policy
Fees will be negotiated with the clerk.

Additional information

Hollis Whiteman Chambers (QEB) is a long-established specialist criminal set. We provide advocacy and advice of the highest quality. We are dedicated to giving an effective service whenever needed, and at short notice.

Our 52 members have expertise at all levels of seniority: 17 QCs and four Treasury Counsel are matched with a strong middle order and 20 tenants of less than 15 years' call. Twenty tenants sit as Recorders in the Crown Court.

We defend and prosecute from the Magistrates' Court to the House of Lords. Members of chambers are regularly involved in complex, high profile and grave cases. There is also daily representation in courts of all levels, at every stage of proceedings.

In addition to 'pure crime', we specialise in Judicial Review, Food Law, Health and Safety Act and Trading Standards cases, Licensing and Extradition. Members of chambers also appear in other tribunals including: Public Inquiries, the General Medical Council, the General Optical Council, Courts Martial and Police Disciplinary Proceedings.

Peter Whiteman QC, a Deputy High Court Judge, provides specialist revenue advice, particularly on corporate and international tax law, and representation at both national and international levels.

QUEEN ELIZABETH BLDG

2nd Floor, Temple, London EC4Y 9BS
0171 797 7837
Fax: 0171 353 5422; DX 339 LONDON
CHANCERY LANE

Chambers of Mr I G F Karsten QC

189 RANDOLPH AVENUE

London W9 1DJ
0171 624 9139
Fax: 0171 624 9139

Chambers of Mr J D Seal

1 RAYMOND BUILDINGS

Gray's Inn, London WC1R 5BH
0171 430 1234
Fax: 0171 430 1004; DX 16 London, Chancery Lane
E-mail: chambers@ipbar1rb.com;
clerks@ipbar1rb.com

Chambers of Christopher Morcom QC
Clerk: Geoffrey C B Maw

Morcom, Christopher QC *1963*	**Tritton,** Guy *1987*
	Jones, Jessica *1991*
Micklethwait, David *1970*	**Edenborough,** Michael *1992*
Wyand, Roger QC *1973‡*	**Roughton,** Ashley *1992*
Chapple, Malcolm *1975*	**Graham,** James *1994*
Ashton, Arthur *1988*	**Turner,** Amedee QC *1954**
Farmery, Peter *1979*	**Zornoza,** Philip *1983**
Adams, John *1984*	**Kay,** David *1979**
Diamond, Paul *1985*	

Types of work (and number of counsel practising in that area if supplied)
Commercial 12 · Competition 12 · Copyright 12 · Design 12 · EC and competition law 12 · Entertainment 12 · Franchising 12 · Information technology 12 · Intellectual property 12 · Patents 12 · Trademarks 12

Chambers' facilities
Conference rooms, Video conferences, Disks accepted

Languages spoken
French, German, Spanish

C

---

3 RAYMOND BUILDINGS

Gray's Inn, London WC1R 5BH
0171 831 3833
Fax: 0171 242 4221; DX 237 London,
Chancery Lane
E-mail: chambers@threeraymond.demon.co.uk

Chambers of Clive Nicholls QC
Clerk: Ian Collins

Nicholls, Clive QC *1957†*	**Harris**, Mark *1980*
Nicholls, Colin QC *1957†*	**Hines**, James *1982*
Gray, Gilbert QC *1953†*	**Rankin**, James *1983*
Beckett, Richard QC *1965*	**Humphryes**, Jane *1983*
Nutting, John QC *1968†*	**Saunders**, Neil *1983*
Batten, Stephen QC *1968†*	**Walsh**, Stephen *1983*
Jones, Alun QC *1972†*	**Aylett**, Crispin *1985*
Whitehouse, David QC *1969†*	**Cameron**, Alexander *1986*
	Malcolm, Helen *1986*
Price, Nicholas QC *1968†*	**Lewis**, James *1987*
Sherborne, Montague QC *1960*	**Hardy**, John *1988*
	Keith, Hugo *1989*
Evans, Francis QC *1977†*	**Davies**, Hugh *1990*
Montgomery, Clare QC *1980*	**Lloyd-Jacob**, Campaspe *1990*
Pitt, Colin *1968*	**Bromley-Martin**, Tania *1983*
Blair-Gould, John *1970†*	**Wormald**, Richard *1993*
Muir, Andrew *1975*	**Williamson**, Alisdair *1994*
Gouriet, Gerald *1974**	**Knowles**, Julian *1994*
De Haan, Kevin *1976*	**Naqshbandi**, Saba *1996*
Atchley, Richard *1977*	
Bromley-Martin, Michael *1979*	

**Types of work (and number of counsel
practising in that area if supplied)**
Administrative 10 · Civil liberties · Common
law (general) · Courts martial · Crime 34
· Crime - corporate fraud 12 · Environment 10
· Licensing 12

Chambers' facilities
Conference rooms, Disks accepted, Disabled
access, E-mail

Languages spoken
Arabic, Dutch, French, German, Italian

See the *Index of Languages Spoken* **in Part G
to locate a chambers where a particular language is spoken, or find an individual who
speaks a particular language.**

---

5 RAYMOND BUILDINGS

1st Floor, Gray's Inn, London WC1R 5BP
0171 242 2902
Fax: 0171 831 2686; DX 1054 London
URL: http://www.media-ent-law.co.uk

Chambers of P H Milmo QC
Clerk: Kim Janes

Milmo, Patrick QC *1962*	**Monson**, Andrew *1983*
Gray, Charles QC *1966†*	**Rogers**, Heather *1983*
Bishop, Gordon *1968*	**Marzec**, Alexandra *1990*
Tugendhat, Michael QC *1969†*	**Sherborne**, David *1992*
	Rushbrooke, Justin *1992*
Browne, Desmond QC *1969†*	**Nicklin**, Matthew *1993*
	Busuttil, Godwin *1994*
Page, Adrienne *1974‡*	**Wolanski**, Adam *1995*
Price, James QC *1974*	**Bennett**, William *1994*
Parkes, Richard *1977*	**Dean**, Jacob *1995*
Warby, Mark *1981*	**Coppola**, Anna *1996*
Bate, Stephen *1981*	

Chambers established: 1932
Opening times: 8.30 am-6.30 pm

**Types of work (and number of counsel
practising in that area if supplied)**
Commercial litigation 3 · Copyright 8
· Defamation 16 · Entertainment 5 · Film,
cable, TV 1 · Information technology 1
· Insurance/reinsurance 3 · Intellectual
property 8 · International trade 3 · Professional
negligence 2 · Sale and carriage of goods 3
· Sports 5 · Telecommunications 1

Languages spoken
French, German, Italian, Polish

Fees policy
Please refer to clerks.

---

18 RED LION COURT

(off Fleet Street), London EC4A 3EB
0171 520 6000
Fax: 0171 520 6248/49; DX LDE 478

Chambers of Anthony Arlidge QC
Clerks: Ken Darvill, Mark Bennett

Also at: Thornwood House, 102 New London
Road, Chelmsford, Essex CM2 0RG
Tel: 01245 280880
Fax: 01245 280882
DX:89706 Chelmsford 2

Spencer, Sir Derek QC MP 1961†	**Kovalevsky,** Richard *1983*
	Lucraft, Mark *1984*
Arlidge, Anthony QC *1962*†	**Morris,** Angela *1984*
Cocks, David QC *1961*†	**Overbury,** Rupert *1984*
Stewart, James QC *1966*†	**Marshall,** David *1985*
Green, Henry QC *1962*†	**Morris,** Brendan *1985*
Lederman, David QC *1966*†	**Spence,** Simon *1985*
Parkins, Graham QC *1972*†	**Boyle,** Robert *1985*
Stern, Linda QC *1971*†	**du Preez,** Robin *1985*
Rook, Peter QC *1973*†	**Bewsey,** Jane *1986*
Sutton, Richard QC *1969*†	**Hill,** Max *1987*
Ball, Christopher QC *1972*†	**Collery,** Shane *1988*
Carter, Peter QC *1974*	**Williams,** David Huw *1988*
Horwood-Smart, Rosamund QC *1974*†	**Anderson,** John *1989*
	Hill, Candida *1990*
Peters, Nigel QC *1976*‡	**Lawson,** Sara *1990*
Black, John QC *1975*	**Holborn,** David *1991*
Lynch, Patricia QC *1979*‡	**Hammond,** Sean *1991*
Etherington, David QC *1979*‡	**Clare,** Allison *1992*
	Gowen, Matthew *1992*
Dobbs, Linda QC *1981*	**Hardy,** Paul *1992*
Radcliffe, David *1966*†	**Forster,** Thomas *1993*
Johnston, Carey *1977*	**Jameson,** Barnaby *1993*
Green, David *1979*‡	**Mortimore,** Claudia *1994*
Harvey, Stephen *1979*	**Nelson,** Michelle *1994*
Fenn, Peter *1979*	**Hall,** Jacqueline *1994*
Fisher, Jonathan *1980*	**Wiseman,** Adam *1994*
Milne, Alexander *1981*	**Webster,** Elizabeth *1995*
Sheff, Janine *1983*	**Jones,** Gillian *1996*

Chambers established: 1946
Opening times: 8.30 am-6.30 pm

Types of work (and number of counsel practising in that area if supplied)
Crime · Crime - corporate fraud

Chambers' facilities
Conference rooms

Additional information

The set has always specialised in criminal work, both prosecuting and defending. There is particular expertise in commercial fraud, Customs and Inland Revenue work and in money laundering. A number of members of chambers act frequently in sex, child abuse and pornography cases. Others have considerable expertise in domestic disciplinary tribunals particularly those connected with financial services and medicine. There is also expertise in judicial review and Human Rights cases. Individual members practise in general common law work (particularly personal injury, family work and aviation and also in licensing and environmental law). Pro Bono work is done in the Privy Council and the FRU unit.

20 RICHMOND WAY

1st Floor, London W12 8LY
0181 749 2004
Fax: 0181 740 1192

Chambers of Dr J A Roberts QC D.C.L.

RIDGEWAY CHAMBERS

6 The Ridgeway, Golders Green, London NW11 8TB
0181 455 2939
Fax: 0181 905 5104
E-mail: 101337.1722@compuserve.com

Chambers of C D H Wolchover
Clerk: Self

Wolchover, David *1971*

ROEHAMPTON CHAMBERS

30 Stoughton Close, Roehampton, London SW15 4LS
0181 788 1238
Fax: 0181 788 1238

Chambers of Mr P G Proghoulis

C

ROSEMONT CHAMBERS

26 Rosemont Court, Rosemont Road, London W3 9LS
0181 992 1100
Fax: 0181 992 1100

Chambers of Mr M Byrd

NO 1 SERJEANTS' INN

Fleet Street, Temple, London EC4Y 1LL
0171 415 6666
Fax: 0171 583 2033; DX 364 London
E-mail: no1serjeantsinn@btinternet.com
Out of hours telephone: 0171 415 6666

Chambers of Edward Faulks QC
Clerks: Clark Chessis, Ann Winders;
Practice manager: Rosemary Thorpe;
Administrator: Jenny Fensham

Faulks, Edward QC *1973‡*	**Yell**, Nicholas *1979*
Wilson, Martin QC *1963†*	**Norman**, John *1979*
Lindsay, Crawford QC *1961†*	**Hammerton**, Alastair *1983*
Redgrave, Adrian QC *1968†*	**Bishop**, Edward *1985*
Browne, Nicholas QC *1971†*	**Paneth**, Sarah *1985*
Andreae-Jones, William QC *1965†**	**Waters**, Julian *1986*
	Rivalland, Marc *1987*
Foster, Jonathan QC *1970†**	**Althaus**, Justin *1988*
Leech, Brian *1967†*	**Pinder**, Mary *1989*
Ross, John *1971†*	**Marris**, Selena *1991*
Hunter, William *1972*	**Boyle**, Gerard *1992*
Baldry, Antony MP *1975*	**Warnock**, Andrew *1993*
Hammerton, Veronica *1977‡*	**Clarke**, Alison *1994*
Pittaway, David *1977*	**Stagg**, Paul *1994*
Readhead, Simon *1979‡*	**Collett**, Ivor *1995*

The Law Society's Directory of Expert Witnesses 1999

- *lists over 3,500 expert witnesses*

- *all entrants agree to comply with The Law Society's Code of Practice and provide two professional references*

- *contains information on choosing and instructing an expert witness*

- *includes 1,700+ specialists in areas of expertise*

- *provides an alphabetical index to assist in finding detailed terms*

- *also available on CD-ROM*

For more information call Sweet & Maxwell on 0171 449 1111

---

1 SERJEANTS' INN

4th Floor, Temple, London EC4Y 1NH
0171 583 1355
Fax: 0171 583 1672; DX 440 LDE
E-mail: serjeants.inn@virgin.net
Out of hours telephone: 01622 735837

Chambers of Lionel Read QC
Clerks: William King, Geoffrey Carr

Read, Lionel QC *1954†*	**Cameron**, Neil *1982*
Woolley, David QC *1962*	**Morgan**, Stephen *1983*
Rumbelow, Anthony QC *1967†*	**Langham**, Richard *1986*
	Harris, Russell *1986*
Clarkson, Patrick QC *1972‡*	**Thomas**, Megan *1987*
Whybrow, Christopher QC *1965*	**Martin QC (Scot)**, Roy *1990*
	Upton, William *1990*
Hicks, William QC *1975*	**White**, Sasha *1991*
Wood, Martin *1972*	**Douglas White**, Robert *1993*
Price-Lewis, Rhodri *1975‡*	**Harwood**, Richard *1993*
Pugh-Smith, John *1977*	**Edwards**, Martin *1995*
Pickles, Simon *1978*	**Reed**, Matthew *1995*
Dagg, John *1980*	**Lyness**, Scott *1996*

International Arbitration Law Review

Editorial Board includes:

Alan Redfern	*Neil Kaplan*
Toby Landau	*David Rivkin*
Dr Julian Lew	*Martin Hunter*
Nigel Rawding	*Matthieu de Boisseson*

The new International Arbitration Law Review *brings together for the first time all the requirements of an arbitration practitioner.*

- *up-to-the-minute news on legislation and decisions*

- *expert commentary on worldwide trends and issues from a panel of top arbitration specialists*

- *detailed case summaries and analysis of the cases making the headlines*

- *covers all major jurisdictions worldwide*

To order a subscription or a free sample copy call Sweet & Maxwell on 0171 449 1111

3 SERJEANTS' INN

THREE SERJEANTS' INN

London EC4Y 1BQ
0171 353 5537
Fax: 0171 353 0425; DX 421 London,
Chancery Lane
E-mail: available upon request
Out of hours telephone: 0385 736 6844

Chambers of P A Naughton QC
Clerks: Nick Salt, Lee Johnson, Tracy Barker;
Administrator: Helen Ensor

Naughton, Philip QC *1970*	Moon, Angus *1986*
Whitfield, Adrian QC *1964†*	Wright, Ian *1989*
Francis, Robert QC *1973‡*	Beggs, John *1989*
Davies, Nicola QC *1976‡*	Holl-Allen, Jonathan *1990*
Grace, John QC *1973*	Johnston, Christopher *1990*
Gaisford, Philip *1969*	Horne, Michael *1992*
Fortune, Malcolm *1972†*	McCredie, Fionnuala *1992*
Conlin, Geoffrey *1973†*	Partridge, Richard *1994*
Lloyd, Huw *1975*	Ley-Morgan, Mark *1994*
Cottle, Tony *1978*	Jackson, Anthony *1995*
Watson, James *1979*	Powell, Debra *1995*
Burns, Sue *1979*	Thomas, George *1995*
Grubb, Andrew *1980*	Bradley, Clodagh *1996*
Neale, Fiona *1981*	Ward, Orla *1996*
O'Rourke, Mary *1981*	Davidson, Ranald *1996*
Hugh-Jones, George *1983*	Lim, Malcolm *1989*
Hopkins, Adrian *1984*	

Chambers established: 1973
Opening times: 8.30 am-6.30 pm

Types of work (and number of counsel practising in that area if supplied)
Arbitration 6 · Civil actions against the police
10 · Commercial litigation 9 · Common law
(general) 28 · Construction 11 · Crime 5
· Defamation 2 · Employment 19
· Environment 10 · Medical negligence 25
· Mental health 21 · Personal injury 24
· Professional negligence 28 · Sale and carriage
of goods 10

Chambers' facilities
Conference rooms, Disks accepted, Disabled
access by arrangement, Limited car parking may
be available by arrangement

Languages spoken
French, German

Additional information

Medical Law and professional discipline
The largest field of specialisation in Chambers.
Tenants have appeared for plaintiffs and
defendants in many of the most important
medical negligence, mental health and medical
ethics cases. Tenants regularly appear in
disciplinary tribunals including the GMC, GDC
and in major public inquiries. Tenants also
appear in major criminal trials concerning
medical practice and inquests.
Construction and Engineering Law
Tenants act in national and international
arbitration and litigation concerning standard
form and special contracts relating to building,
and engineering works for employers, including
governments, contractors, subcontractors and
professionals.
Commercial Contracts
Particularly disputes concerning contracts for
the design manufacture and leasing of plant and
equipment.
Professional Negligence
All medical, architects, surveyors, engineers,
lawyers, accountants, valuers, etc.
Employment Law
Tenants act in unfair and wrongful dismissal
cases and race and sex discrimination claims.
Civil actions involving the police
Tenants act for over 15 constabularies,
principally in malicious prosecution cases.
Crime
Prosecution and defence work is undertaken.
Tenants have recognised experience in
environmental and medical cases.
ADR
Chambers is a member of CEDR; tenants include
accredited mediators.
Other Fields
General common law, personal injury, landlord
and tenant, defamation and environmental law.

SERLE COURT CHAMBERS

*Thirteen Old Square, Lincoln's Inn, London
WC2A 3UA*
0171 242 6105
Fax: 0171 405 4004; DX LDE 1025
E-mail: clerks@serlecourt.co.uk
URL: http://www.serlecourt.co.uk

Chambers of Charles Sparrow QC DL
*Clerks: T R Buck, S A Whitaker; Chief
Executive: Helena Miles*

Sparrow, Charles QC *1950*	**Jones**, Philip *1985*
Talbot, Patrick QC *1969‡*	**Marshall**, Philip *1987*
Boyle, Alan QC *1972*	**Harrison**, Nicholas *1988*
Briggs, Michael QC *1978*	**Lucas**, Bridget *1989*
Farrow, Kenneth *1966†*	**Hoffmann**, Clare *1990*
Asprey, Nicholas *1969*	**Johnston**, Jill *1990*
Whittaker, John *1969*	**Close**, Douglas *1991*
Hinks, Frank *1973*	**Purkis**, Kathryn *1991*
Joffe, Victor *1975*	**Blayney**, David *1992*
Rogers, Beverly-Ann *1978*	**Machell**, John *1993*
Henderson, William *1978*	**Drake**, David *1994*
Behrens, James *1979*	**Higgo**, Justin *1995*
Hoser, Philip *1982*	**Lightman**, Daniel *1995*
Jones, Elizabeth *1984*	**Norbury**, Hugh *1995*
Walford, Richard *1984*	**Collingwood**, Timothy *1996*

Opening times: 8.30 am-7 pm

Types of work (and number of counsel practising in that area if supplied)
Chancery (general) · Chancery land law
· Commercial litigation · Commercial property
· Company and commercial · Equity, wills and
trusts · Insolvency · Landlord and tenant
· Partnerships · Professional negligence

Chambers' facilities
Disks accepted, E-mail

Languages spoken
French, German, Hebrew

Additional information

Serle Court Chambers is a leading set of
chambers in Lincoln's Inn which provides
effective litigation and practical creative advice
across a broad range of work in the chancery
and commercial fields.

In addition to the specialisations listed above, in
each of which Serle Court Chambers can
provide a full team of barristers at all levels of
seniority, individual members of chambers also
have significant expertise in media and
entertainment, sports law, intellectual property
(especially passing-off and confidential
information), computer law, charities, common
land, probate and Parliamentary work.

Chambers has a comprehensive library of texts
and materials and subscribes to the most up-to-
date electronic research facilities, including
ELR, WLR, Lexis and Badger.

Members of Chambers accept instructions to
appear in any court or tribunal in England and
Wales, and in arbitrations; they also frequently
advise and appear in matters arising in overseas
jurisdictions. Direct professional access is
accepted. Work can be undertaken, and advice
given, at short notice and out of office hours;
outside office hours please telephone Terry
Buck on 01268 743324 or Steven Whitaker on
01708 556884.

Fees are based on a number of considerations,
including time commitment, degree of
responsibility and complexity. They may be
charged on an hourly or inclusive basis, and the
Senior Clerks, who each have over 20 years'
clerking experience, will be glad to discuss a fee
and provide information as to its composition
before work is undertaken.

20 SEWARDSTONE GARDENS

Chingford, London E4 7QE
0181 524 3054

Chambers of Mr A Amihere

SOMERSETT CHAMBERS

52 Bedford Row, London WC1R 4LR
0171 404 6701
Fax: 0171 404 6702; DX 44 LDE

The Bar Directory **is also available on the
Internet at the following address:**

http://www.smlawpub-holborn.co.uk/bar

3-4 SOUTH SQUARE

Gray's Inn, London WC1R 5HP
0171 696 9900
Fax: 0171 696 9911; DX 338 London,
Chancery Lane
E-mail: clerks@southsquare.com
URL: http://www.southsquare.com

Chambers of Michael Crystal QC
Clerks: Jason Pithers, Michael Killick, Jim Costa; Administrator: Lynne Isaacs

Crystal, Michael QC *1970*	**Alexander**, David *1987*
Hunter, Muir QC *1938*	**Zacaroli**, Antony *1987*
Brougham, Christopher QC *1969*	**Arnold**, Mark *1988*
	Hilliard, Lexa *1987*
Moss, Gabriel QC *1974*	**Atherton**, Stephen *1989*
Mortimore, Simon QC *1972*	**Bristoll**, Sandra *1989*
Higham, John QC *1976‡*	**Goodison**, Adam *1990*
Simmons, Marion QC *1970‡*	**Stonefrost**, Hilary *1991*
Adkins, Richard QC *1982*	**Tamlyn**, Lloyd *1991*
Sheldon, Richard QC *1979*	**Davis**, Glen *1992*
Hacker, Richard QC *1977*	**Gledhill**, Andreas *1992*
Cohen, Clive *1989*	**Oditah**, Fidelis *1992*
Briggs, John *1973*	**Ismail**, Roxanne *1993*
Marks, David *1974*	**Isaacs**, Barry *1994*
Pascoe, Martin *1977*	**Valentin**, Ben *1995*
Knowles, Robin *1982*	**Toube**, Felicity *1995*
Trower, William *1983*	**Goldring**, Jeremy *1996*
Phillips, Mark *1984*	**Knights**, Samantha *1996*
Dicker, Robin *1986*	**Frazer**, Lucy *1996*

Opening times: 8 am-7 pm. Evening reception manned until 8.15 pm

Types of work (and number of counsel practising in that area if supplied)
Arbitration · Asset finance · Banking · Bankruptcy · Chancery (general) · Commercial litigation · Commercial property · Commodities · Common law (general) · Company and commercial · Corporate finance · Financial services · Insolvency · Insurance · Insurance/reinsurance · International trade · Partnerships · Pensions · Professional negligence · Sale and carriage of goods · Share options · Tax - corporate

Chambers' facilities
Conference rooms, Disks accepted, E-mail

Languages spoken
French, German, Italian, Mandarin, Spanish

Fees policy
Details will be provided on request.

Additional information

3-4 South Square practise primarily in business, financial and commercial law and have a well-known expertise in insolvency law. Chambers' practice regularly covers the following subjects: corporate, international and personal insolvency, including receivership, administration, liquidation, arrangements with creditors and bankruptcy; banking and finance; company law, including mergers and acquisitions, shareholders' and directors' disputes and partnership disputes; financial services.

Within chambers individual members also practise in a variety of other areas, including civil aspects of commercial fraud; insurance and reinsurance; international trade; sale of goods, commercial and business agreements; professional negligence and disciplinary proceedings; tracing remedies; pre-trial remedies; enforcement of domestic and foreign judgments; obtaining evidence for foreign proceedings.

Members of chambers adopt a commercial and businesslike approach to their practices and are capable of reacting swiftly (individually or as members of a team) to urgent problems as the need may arise and are accustomed to dealing with matters at all levels of complexity, often at very short notice. Members are ready to appear as advocates and to advise outside London and are in a position to accept instructions direct from overseas lawyers and from other professional bodies such as accountants and architects. The overall aim of chambers is to provide an effective professional service to clients as promptly and efficiently as possible.

11 SOUTH SQUARE

11
SOUTH
SQUARE

2nd Floor, Gray's Inn, London WC1R 5EU
0171 405 1222
Fax: 0171 242 4282; DX 433 Chancery Lane

Chambers of C D Floyd QC
Clerks: Rochelle Haring, Martyn Nicholls

Floyd, Christopher QC 1975‡	**Arnold**, Richard 1985
Whittle, Christopher 1975	**Lawrence**, Heather 1990
Silverleaf, Michael QC 1980	**Vanhegan**, Mark 1990
Carr, Henry QC 1982	**Reid**, Jacqueline 1992
Hacon, Richard 1979	**Acland**, Piers 1993
Purvis, Iain 1986	**Cuddigan**, Hugo 1995

Chambers established: 1925
Opening times: 9 am-6 pm

Types of work (and number of counsel practising in that area if supplied)
Copyright 12 · Information technology 12 · Intellectual property 12 · Patents 12 · Trademarks 12

Chambers' facilities
Conference rooms, Disks accepted, E-mail

Languages spoken
French, German

Kime's International Law Directory 1999

- *established guide to the international legal community*
- *reliable and relevant information on over 600 law firms and chambers*
- *entries can be found by types of work undertaken and location*
- *the only law directory to provide editorial on every jurisdiction's legal system and enforcement of judgements*
- *now on the Internet at http://www.smlawpub-holborn.co.uk/kimes*

For more information call Sweet & Maxwell on 0171 449 1111

STANBROOK & HENDERSON

STANBROOK & HENDERSON
BARRISTERS

2 Harcourt Buildings, Ground Floor, Temple, London EC4Y 9DB
0171 353 0101
Fax: 0171 583 2686; DX 1039 London, Chancery Lane
E-mail: clerks@harcourt.co.uk

Chambers of C S G Stanbrook QC OBE and R H Henderson QC
Clerks: John White (Chief Clerk), Simon Boutwood; Chambers Development Manager: Martin Dyke

Stanbrook, Clive QC 1972	**Ratliff**, John 1980
Bentley, Philip QC 1970	**Holland**, Debra 1996

Chambers established: 1991

Types of work (and number of counsel practising in that area if supplied)
Administrative 7 · Arbitration 4 · Asset finance 8 · Banking 4 · Care proceedings 11 · Chancery (general) 6 · Commercial litigation 25 · Common law (general) 34 · Company and commercial 5 · Competition 8 · Construction 17 · Consumer Law 9 · Copyright 3 · Courts martial 3 · Crime 7 · Crime - corporate fraud 7 · Ecclesiastical 1 · Employment 20 · Environment 7 · Equity, wills and trusts 5 · Family 11 · Family provision 11 · Financial services 8 · Franchising 2 · Housing 14 · Information technology 5 · Insurance 25 · Insurance/reinsurance 25 · Intellectual property 3 · International trade 4 · Landlord and tenant 14 · Local government 10 · Medical negligence 20 · Parliamentary 3 · Partnerships 8 · Patents 3 · Personal injury 34 · Probate and administration 3 · Professional negligence 34 · Sale and carriage of goods 20 · Sports 5 · Tax - capital and income 1 · Tax - corporate 1 · Telecommunications 4

Chambers' facilities
Conference rooms, Disks accepted, E-mail

Languages spoken
French, Italian, Japanese, Portuguese, Spanish

Fees policy

Fees will be negotiated with the clerk. Our aim is that fees will be reasonable and competitive, depending on the importance and nature of the work, the expertise and seniority of Counsel.

Additional information

Stanbrook and Henderson is an association between the chambers of Roger Henderson QC at 2 Harcourt Buildings (see entry earlier in this section) and the members of the European law firm of Stanbrook and Hooper in Brussels who are also members of the English bar.

The work undertaken reflects chambers' wide knowledge of EU institutions and the way in which they work - knowledge which is essential for anyone affected by EU actions or legislation. The Brussels-based barristers of Stanbrook & Henderson have a close link with daily developments in the European Commission, the Council and the Parliament Secretariat, meaning chambers can offer a complete legal monitoring and information service.

In business law, chambers undertakes advisory, drafting and litigation work in a wide range of areas, including environmental law; financial services; insurance, including drafting and interpreting policies and advice on the structure of the market; offshore investment funds; credit, including consumer credit and leasing; product liability; food law; sports law; and general EU regulatory policy, including market representations to the EU institutions in Brussels.

In the corporate sphere, chambers provides specialist advisory and drafting expertise as well as advocacy at administrative level, from UK industrial tribunals to the Competition Directorate of the European Commission in Brussels, as well as at judicial level, both in the UK and in the European courts in Luxembourg.

The specialist areas covered include company law (including EU developments and freedom of establishment); joint ventures (including EU competition aspects); merger control (UK and EU); competition law (UK and EU); employment law (including EU rules on the free movement of works and health and safety at work); distribution agreements (including the EU competition aspects); EU rules on freedom to provide services, free movement of goods and non-discrimination in fiscal and other matters; and intellectual property.

In public sector law, chambers advises local authorities in particular on local government finance, fiduciary duties and compulsory competition tendering, combining such advice with an EU point of view. In private law, chambers provides a similarly comprehensive service, for example, in immigration and rights of free movement.

STAPLE INN CHAMBERS

1st Floor, 9 Staple Inn, Holborn Bars, London WC1V 7QH
0171 242 5240
Fax: 0171 405 9495; DX 132 London, Chancery Lane
E-mail: clerks@staple-inn.org

Chambers of V M Ramsden
Clerks: Stuart Davis, Yvonne Simmons, Brian Monument

Ramsden, Veronica *1979*	**Panagiotopoulou,** Tania *1994*
Limbrey, Bernard *1980*	
Tresman, Lewis *1980*	**Sheikh,** Raana *1977*
Aslam, Qazi *1983*	**Llewellyn,** Charles *1978*
Codner, Peter *1983**	**Fordham,** Allison *1990*
Masniuk, Peter *1983*	**Panagiotopoulou,** Sophie *1995*
Trumpington, John *1985*	
Nicol, Nicholas *1986*	**Feldman,** Matthew *1995*
Brooks, Alison *1989*	**Briand,** Pauline *1996*
McCormack, Alan *1990*	**Tyler,** Tom *1996*
Brown, Andrea *1991*	**Corry,** Carol *1981*
Vakil, Jimmy *1993*	**Jones,** Paul *1981*
Falk, Charles *1994*	**Mullee,** Brendan *1996*
McManus, Rebecca *1994*	**Brissett,** Nicola *1995*

† Recorder ‡ Assistant Recorder * Door Tenant

3 STONE BUILDINGS

Ground Floor, Lincoln's Inn, London
WC2A 3XL
0171 242 4937/405 8358
Fax: 0171 405 3896; DX 317 London

Chambers of G C Vos QC
Clerk: Andrew Palmer

Vos, Geoffrey QC *1977*	**Asplin**, Sarah *1984*
Bannister, Edward QC *1974*	**Girling**, Sarah *1986*
Stanford, David *1951*	**Lord**, David *1987*
Topham, Geoffrey *1964*	**Pimentel**, Carlos *1990*
Cosedge, Andrew *1972*	**Kayani**, Asaf *1991*
Tunkel, Alan *1976*	**Lacey**, Sarah *1991*
da Silva, David *1978*	**Conroy**, Marian *1991*
Mason, Alexandra *1981*	**Twigger**, Andrew *1994*
Hantusch, Robert *1982*	**Moeran**, Fenner *1996*

Chambers established: 1938
Opening times: 8.30 am-6.30 pm

Types of work (and number of counsel practising in that area if supplied)
Banking · Bankruptcy · Chancery (general) · Chancery land law · Charities · Commercial litigation · Commercial property · Company and commercial · Conveyancing · Copyright · Entertainment · Equity, wills and trusts · Family provision · Film, cable, TV · Financial services · Insolvency · Insurance · Insurance/reinsurance · Landlord and tenant · Partnerships · Pensions · Private international · Probate and administration · Professional negligence · Sports · Tax - capital and income · Tax - corporate

Languages spoken
French, Portuguese, Spanish

Additional information

Types of work undertaken: 3 Stone Buildings is a long-established and expanding Chancery set with a considerable breadth of experience. Individual attention is combined with professional efficiency. The chambers has experienced practitioners in most areas of financial litigation and advisory work.

Litigation: The chambers has experienced practitioners in financial and property litigation and advice with particular emphasis being placed on company and commercial litigation.

Advisory: Chambers has particular expertise in revenue law and tax planning, pensions, trusts and property, insolvency, and partnership matters. As a result all aspects of families' financial and property affairs (including their trusts, companies and partnerships, the succession thereto and the tax thereon) can be dealt with in a unified manner.

Drafting: The drafting of conveyancing and commercial documentation and settlements is extensively undertaken by members of chambers.

Additional specialisations: In addition to the above, chambers has expertise in the following fields of practice: administration of estates, agricultural holdings, arbitration, banking, bankruptcy, building disputes, charities, commercial contracts, companies, conveyancing, copyright and intellectual property, corporate insolvency, Court of Protection, financial services, insurance, landlord and tenant, mortgages and securities, pensions and share schemes, professional negligence, real property, sale of goods, shipping, Stock Exchange work, taxation and tax planning, trusts, and wills and probate.

Instructions may be taken in writing, by fax, or in conference. The Senior Clerk is always willing to discuss any queries concerning choice of, and instructions to, counsel, including particular expertise, availability, and level of fees.

Direct access instructions are accepted from members of all recognised professional bodies in accordance with the guidance notes issued by the General Council of the Bar. Direct instructions are also accepted from overseas lawyers.

The chambers has founder membership of CEDR (alternative dispute resolution).

> Use the *Types of Work* listings in Parts A and B to locate chambers and individual barristers who specialise in particular areas of work.

4 STONE BUILDINGS

Ground Floor, Lincoln's Inn, London
WC2A 3XT
0171 242 5524
Fax: 0171 831 7907; DX 385 London
E-mail: d.goddard@4stonebuildings.law.co.uk
Out of hours telephone: 01277 229180 or
0860 452552 (Senior Clerk)

Chambers of Philip Heslop QC
Clerk: David Goddard

Heslop, Philip QC *1970*	Harman, Sarah *1987*
Curry, Peter QC *1953*	Harrison, Christopher *1988*
Bompas, A G QC *1975*	Brettler, Jonathan *1988*
Hildyard, Robert QC *1977*	Greenwood, Paul *1991*
Brisby, John QC *1978*	Clutterbuck, Andrew *1992*
Hunt, Stephen *1968*	Cox, Nicholas *1992*
Griffiths, Peter *1977*	Hill, Richard *1993*
Crow, Jonathan *1981*	Fraser, Orlando *1994*
Scott, John *1982*	Markham, Anna *1996*
Davis-White, Malcolm *1984*	Boeddinghaus, Hermann
Miles, Robert *1987*	*1996*
Nicholson, Rosalind *1987*	

The UK College of Family Mediators
Directory & Handbook 1998/99

- *provides expert commentary on family mediation training and professional development and includes contributions by leading family mediation professionals*

- *lists over 100 family mediation groups/services and over 950 individual family mediators by region and alphabetically*

- *gives details of all members and associates of the UK College of Family Mediators*

- *includes the UK College of Family Mediators Standards and Code of Practice*

- *gives details of all the family mediation bodies which make up the UK College of Family Mediators*

For more information call Sweet & Maxwell on 0171 449 1111

---

5 STONE BUILDINGS

Lincoln's Inn, London WC2A 3XT
0171 242 6201
Fax: 0171 831 8102; DX 304 London,
Chancery Lane
E-mail: clerks@5-stonebuildings.law.co.uk
Out of hours telephone: 0181 995 9904

Chambers of Henry M Harrod
Clerks: David T Butler, Paul Jennings

Harrod, Henry *1963†*	Angus, Tracey *1991*
Warnock-Smith, Shan *1971*	Legge, Henry *1993*
Norris, Alastair QC *1973‡*	Rees, David *1994*
Fawls, Richard *1973*	Clarke, Anna *1994*
Herbert, Mark QC *1974*	Sartin, Leon *1997*
Blackett-Ord, Mark *1974*	Templeman, Michael *1973**
Farber, Martin *1976*	Hayton, David *1968**
Henderson, Launcelot QC	Orr, Nicholas *1970**
1977	Dennis, David *1979**
Simmonds, Andrew *1980*	Johnson, Ian *1982**
Tidmarsh, Christopher *1985*	Cadwallader, Neil *1984**
O'Sullivan, Michael *1986*	Morris, Paul *1986**
Rolfe, Patrick *1987*	Lund, Celia *1988**
Rich, Barbara *1990*	Pritchett, Stephen *1989**
Walden-Smith, Karen *1990*	

Opening times: 8.45 am-6.15 pm

Types of work (and number of counsel practising in that area if supplied)
Arbitration 1 · Banking 12 · Bankruptcy 8
· Chancery (general) 18 · Chancery land law
18 · Charities 6 · Commercial litigation 10
· Commercial property 15 · Common land 8
· Conveyancing 18 · Equity, wills and trusts 18
· Family provision 18 · Financial services 6
· Insolvency 8 · Landlord and tenant 15
· Mental health 7 · Partnerships 12 · Pensions 6
· Probate and administration 18 · Professional
negligence 12 · Tax - capital and income 5

Chambers' facilities
Conference rooms, Disks accepted, Disks provided, E-mail

Languages spoken
French, Italian, Spanish

---

† Recorder ‡ Assistant Recorder * Door Tenant

Fees policy

Fees will be negotiated with the clerk. We are happy to give estimates. Our aim is to be competitive.

Additional information

We are a Chancery set offering specialist expertise in the fields of property litigation, professional negligence and occupational pensions. Two former members are now in the Court of Appeal and a third has recently been appointed to the Chancery bench. Members have been involved in the Polly Peck and Maxwell litigation and a number of the leading cases on tax avoidance, undue influence, right to buy, ethical investment, pension surplus, duties of pension trustees. All members are well versed in trusts, wills, administration of estates, land law and conveyancing. A number of members specialise in private client and estate planning and partnership. Commercial litigation and insolvency work is also undertaken. Our aim is to provide an efficient modern service of the highest standard.

7 STONE BUILDINGS

7 STONE BUILDINGS

Ground Floor, Lincoln's Inn, London
WC2A 3SZ
0171 405 3886/242 3546
Fax: 0171 242 8502; DX 335 London
E-mail: chaldous@vossnet.co.uk

Chambers of C Aldous QC

Clerks: T Marsh, M Newton;
Practice manager: Shona Kelly

Aldous, Charles QC *1967*	**Clifford**, James *1984*
Nield, Michael *1969*	**Stewart**, Lindsey *1983*
Unwin, David QC *1971*	**Cullen**, Edmund *1990*
Davis, Nigel QC *1975‡*	**Carswell**, Patricia *1993*
Walton, Alastair *1977*	**Bannister**, Thomas *1993*
Randall, John QC *1978**	**Westwood**, Andrew *1994*
Newey, Guy *1982*	**Atkins**, Siward *1995*
Parker, Christopher *1984*	

Chambers established: 1870
Opening times: 8.30 am-6.45 pm

Types of work (and number of counsel practising in that area if supplied)

Arbitration · Banking · Bankruptcy · Chancery (general) · Chancery land law · Charities · Commercial litigation · Commercial property · Common land · Company and commercial · Corporate finance · Energy · Entertainment · Equity, wills and trusts · Financial services · Insolvency · Intellectual property · Landlord and tenant · Partnerships · Pensions · Private international · Professional negligence

Chambers' facilities

Disks accepted, E-mail

Languages spoken

Spanish

Fees policy

Fees will be negotiated with the clerk depending on the case.

Additional information

The work undertaken by members covers all aspects of Chancery and commercial practice other than shipping.

Principal specialisations include commercial law and contracts; company law and partnership; corporate and personal insolvency; credit and security; entertainment law; equitable remedies; financial services and regulation; fraud; insurance; landlord and tenant; passing-off, confidential information, and copyright; pensions; pre-trial remedies; professional negligence; real property; trusts, settlements, and capital taxation; and wills, probate, and the administration of estates.

Other specialist areas, such as European Community law, administrative law, and private international law, are undertaken in the context of these areas of practice.

See the *Index of Languages Spoken* in **Part G** to locate a chambers where a particular language is spoken, or find an individual who speaks a particular language.

7 STONE BUILDINGS

1st Floor, Lincoln's Inn, London WC2A 3SZ
0171 242 0961
Fax: 0171 405 7028; DX 1007 London

Chambers of J M Bishop
Clerks: Miss Trace Grant, Miss Rita Vella,
Miss Louisa Arthur, Miss Georgina Sellen

Bishop, John *1970*	**Lakha**, Shabbir *1989*
Ashmore, Terence *1961*	**Swirsky**, Adam *1989*
Martin, Gay *1970*	**Goldman**, Linda *1990*
Conway, Robert *1974*	**Tod**, Jonathan *1990*
Lynch, Julian *1976*	**Chadwick**, Charles *1992*
Temple-Bone, Gillian *1978*	**Burrington**, Richard *1993*
Birks, Simon *1981*	**Gerrish**, Simon *1993*
Williams, Cheryl *1982*	**Le Quesne**, Catherine *1993*
Cooper, John *1983*	**Casey**, Noel *1995*
Pyle, Susan *1985*	**Ellis**, Jonathan *1995*
Owens, Matthew *1988*	**Simkin**, Iain *1995*
Cave, Patricia *1989*	**Badenoch**, Tony *1996*

8 STONE BUILDINGS

Lincoln's Inn, London WC2A 3TA
0171 831 9881
Fax: 0171 831 9392; DX 216 Chancery Lane
Out of hours telephone: 0181 894 1416,
Mobile 0802 411348

Chambers of John Cherry QC, Timothy Briden
Clerks: Alan Luff (Senior Clerk), Paul Eeles
(Junior Clerk)

Cherry, John QC *1961*†	**Menzies**, Richard *1993*
Briden, Timothy *1976*	**Baldwin**, Marcus *1994*
Room, Stewart *1991*	**Howard-Jones**, Sarah *1994*
Waddington, Nigel *1992*	

9 STONE BUILDINGS

9 STONE BUILDINGS

Lincoln's Inn, London WC2A 3NN
0171 404 5055
Fax: 0171 405 1551; DX 314 London,
Chancery Lane
E-mail: 9stoneb@compuserve.com

Chambers of Michael Ashe QC
Clerk: Alan Austin

Ashe, Michael QC (QC N Ireland) *1971*‡	**Smart**, John *1989*
Iwi, David *1961*	**Flower**, Philip *1979*
Howells, Cenydd *1964*†	**Pines-Richman**, Helene *1992*
Chapman, Vivian *1970*†	**Nebhrajani**, Mel *1994*
Cant, Christopher *1973*	**Bromilow**, Daniel *1996*
Reed, Penelope *1983*	**Ruffin**, William *1972**
Taylor, Araba *1985*	**Clayton**, Peter *1977**
Counsell, Lynne *1986*	**Critelli**, Nicholas *1991**
Levy, Robert *1988*	**Wood**, Graeme *1968**
Sisley, Timothy *1989*	

Chambers established: 1900
Opening times: 8.45 am-6.30 pm

Types of work (and number of counsel practising in that area if supplied)
Agriculture 3 · Arbitration 5 · Banking 3
· Bankruptcy 12 · Chancery (general) 15
· Chancery land law 15 · Charities 6
· Commercial litigation 10 · Commercial
property 16 · Commodities 2 · Common land 3
· Company and commercial 15 · Conveyancing
15 · Copyright 2 · Corporate finance 3 · Crime
- corporate fraud 4 · Discrimination 1 · EC and
competition law 2 · Employment 3
· Entertainment 2 · Equity, wills and trusts 16
· Family provision 15 · Film, cable, TV 1
· Financial services 5 · Foreign law 4 · Housing
5 · Information technology 2 · Insolvency 14
· Insurance 2 · Insurance/reinsurance 2
· Intellectual property 2 · International trade 2
· Landlord and tenant 14 · Medical negligence
2 · Partnerships 15 · Pensions 2 · Personal
injury 2 · Private international 4 · Probate and
administration 15 · Professional negligence 15
· Share options 2 · Tax - capital and income 5
· Tax - corporate 5 · Town and country
planning 2

---

† Recorder ‡ Assistant Recorder * Door Tenant

Chambers' facilities
Conference rooms, Disks accepted, E-mail

Languages spoken
French, Welsh

Fees policy
There is no fixed fee policy to enable all clients access to members of chambers irrespective of the financial worth of the lay client. The senior clerk would be delighted to discuss fee levels as and when required.

11 STONE BUILDINGS

Lincoln's Inn, London WC2A 3TG
+44 (0)171 831 6381
Fax: +44 (0)171 831 2575; DX 1022 London
E-mail: clerks@11StoneBuildings.law.co.uk
URL: http://www.11StoneBuildings.law.co.uk
Out of hours telephone: Chris Berry: +44 (0)181 946 9139 (Mobile: 0836 566251)
Gareth Davies: +44 (0)181 542 1211(Mobile: 0467 443519)

Chambers of M D Beckman QC
Clerks: Christopher Berry (Senior Clerk), Gareth Davies, Caron Levy, Will Sheldon (Listing), Nicholas Ozga (Communications and Client Care)

Beckman, Michael QC *1954*	Shekerdemian, Marcia *1987*
Sheridan, Peter QC *1955*	Holbech, Charles *1988*
Rosen, Murray QC *1976*	Penny, Tim *1988*
Cousins, Edward *1971*	Barber, Sally *1988*
Cohen, Edward *1972*	Kennedy-McGregor, Marilyn *1989*
Bishop, Alan *1973*	
Salter, Adrian *1973*	Middleburgh, Jonathan *1990*
McCue, Donald *1974*	Meyer, Birgitta *1992*
Phillips, John *1975**	Macdonald, Shelia *1993*
Meares, Nigel *1975*	Wilkins, Christopher *1993*
Deacon, Robert *1976*	Mallin, Max *1993*
Arkush, Jonathan *1977*	Barnard, James *1993*
Giret, Jane *1981*	Parfitt, Nicholas *1993*
Ross, Sidney *1983*	Lopian, Jonathan *1994*
Higgs, Roland *1984*	Daly, Denis *1995*
Dight, Marc *1984*	Boardman, Christopher *1995*
Gourgey, Alan *1984*	Weekes, Tom *1995*
Kyriakides, Tina *1984*	Riley, Jamie *1995*
Agnello, Raquel *1986*	

---

199 STRAND

London WC2R 1DR
0171 379 9779
Fax: 0171 379 9481; DX 322 London, Chancery Lane
E-mail: chambers@199strand.co.uk
URL: http://www.one99strand.demon.co.uk
Other comms: Link: Martin Griffiths
Out of hours telephone: 01233 756691

Chambers of Peter Andrews QC
Clerk: Martin Griffiths

Stewart, Robin QC *1963†*	Sadd, Patrick *1984*
Hawkesworth, Simon QC *1967†*	Hutchings, Martin *1986*
	Harrison, Philomena *1985*
Andrews, Peter QC *1970†*	Harrison, Michael *1986*
de Wilde, Robin QC *1971‡*	Aldridge, James *1987*
Phillips, David QC *1976‡*	Charles, Henry *1987*
Wilby, David QC *1974*	Serlin, Richard *1987*
May, Kieran *1971*	Witcomb, Henry *1989*
Stitcher, Malcolm *1971*	Wonnacott, Mark *1989*
Green, Alan *1973*	Garner, Sophie *1990*
Walmsley, Keith *1973*	Nesbitt, Timothy *1991*
Whitaker, Stephen *1970*	Vickers, Rachel *1992*
Gumbel, Elizabeth *1974*	Spears, Portia *1992*
Levene, Simon *1977‡*	Woolf, Eliot *1993*
Tudor-Evans, Quintin *1977*	Isaac, Nicholas *1993*
Goodman, Andrew *1978*	Davies, Louise *1995*
Lehain, Philip *1978*	Sefton, Mark *1996*
Treasure, Francis *1980*	Guest, Stephen *1980**
Beech, Jacqueline *1981*	Melton, Christopher *1982**
Hough, Christopher *1981*	Coleman, Clive *1986**
Kurrein, Martin *1981*	Northrop, Keith *1989**

Opening times: 8.30 am-6.30 pm

Types of work (and number of counsel practising in that area if supplied)
Chancery land law · Commercial litigation · Common law (general) · Consumer Law · Employment · Environment · Franchising · Housing · Information technology · Insolvency · Insurance · Intellectual property · Landlord and tenant · Medical negligence · Partnerships · Personal injury · Professional negligence · Sale and carriage of goods · Sports

† Recorder ‡ Assistant Recorder * Door Tenant

Chambers' facilities
Conference rooms, Video conferences, Disks accepted, Disabled access, Conditional fee work and Direct Professional Access accepted

Languages spoken
French, German, Hebrew, Japanese, Mandarin

Additional information

Areas of work
Personal Injury
Employers', public and occupiers' liability, road traffic accidents, occupational diseases, health and safety, product liability, disaster litigation.

Medical Negligence
Negligence of doctors, dentists and nurses. Inquests. Hospital inquiries. Criminal cases in respect of medical malpractice. Disciplinary proceedings.

Property
Conveyancing, boundary disputes, commercial development of land and mortgages.

Landlord and Tenant
Housing, residential and commercial leases, rent reviews, dilapidation, agricultural tenancies.

Professional Indemnity
Negligence claims for and against lawyers, architects, engineers, surveyors, valuers, accountants, financial intermediaries and insurance brokers. Proceedings before professional and other regulatory bodies.

Commercial
Contract, sale of goods, carriage of goods, insolvency, partnership, insurance, consumer credit, company law, competition law, computers and information technology, passing-off, restraint of trade, copyright, utilities, financial services, fraud, franchising, building disputes.

Employment
Wrongful and unfair dismissal, protection of confidential information, restrictive covenants, sex and race discrimination, transfer of undertakings. Disciplinary proceedings before professional and regulatory bodies.

Transport
Operators' licensing and construction and use, in the road haulage and coach industries.

SWAN HOUSE

P.O.Box 8749, London W13 9WQ
0181 998 3035
Fax: 0181 998 3055; DX 5132 EALING

Chambers of Mr G B Purves

16 TATNELL ROAD

Forest Hill, London SE23 1JY
0181 699 3818
Fax: 0181 299 2844

Chambers of Mr N R Parchment

TEMPLE CHAMBERS

Rooms 111/112, 3/7 Temple Avenue, London EC4Y 0HP
0171 583 1001 (2 lines)
Fax: 0171 583 2112

Chambers of Mrs H E Adejumo

199B TEMPLE CHAMBERS

3-7 Temple Avenue, London EC4Y 0DB
0171 583 8008
Fax: 0171 583 8007; DX 150 Chancery Lane

Chambers of Miss S E Dobbyn

55 TEMPLE CHAMBERS

Temple Avenue, London EC4Y 0HP
0171 353 7400
Fax: 0171 353 7100; DX 260 CHANCERY LANE

Chambers of Mr C E Moll

C

Crime Desktop CD-ROM

Containing the three most important titles in criminal law: Archbold, Criminal Law Review *and* Criminal Appeal Reports, *this is the most efficient criminal law research tool you can own.*

Put time on your side, phone Sweet & Maxwell on 0171 449 1111 for more information or a free demonstration

169 TEMPLE CHAMBERS

Temple Avenue, London EC4Y 0DA
0171 583 7644
Fax: 0171 353 8554; DX 348 London,
Chancery Lane

Chambers of E M Ashfield
Practice manager: Mrs Sylvia Tucker

Ashfield, Evan *1980*	**Bullock**, Andrew *1992*
Corben, Paul *1979*	**Roach**, Susan *1993*
Scott, Charles *1980*	**Noordeen**, Samiya *1994*
Sime, Stuart *1983*	**Peyton**, Daniel *1995*
Poplawski, Roman *1989*	**Hill**, Peregrine *1995*
Stanton, Nicholas *1991*	**McMorrow**, Patrick *1996*

TEMPLE FIELDS

Hamilton House, 1 Temple Avenue, London EC4Y 0HA
0171 353 4212
Fax: 0171 353 6556; DX 129 LONDON
CHANCERY LANE

Chambers of Mrs C L Churchill

International Arbitration Law Review

Editorial Board includes:

Alan Redfern	Neil Kaplan
Toby Landau	David Rivkin
Dr Julian Lew	Martin Hunter
Nigel Rawding	Matthieu de Boisseson

The new International Arbitration Law Review *brings together for the first time all the requirements of an arbitration practitioner.*

- *up-to-the-minute news on legislation and decisions*

- *expert commentary on worldwide trends and issues from a panel of top arbitration specialists*

- *detailed case summaries and analysis of the cases making the headlines*

- *covers all major jurisdictions worldwide*

To order a subscription or a free sample copy call Sweet & Maxwell on 0171 449 1111

1 TEMPLE GARDENS

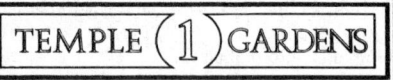

1st Floor, Temple, London EC4Y 9BB
0171 353 0407/583 1315
Fax: 0171 353 3969; DX 382 London
E-mail: clerks@1templegardens.co.uk

Chambers of H B H Carlisle QC
Clerks: Dean Norton (Senior Clerk), Nancy Fernée (First Junior Clerk); Administrator: Gaye Spencer-King

Carlisle, Hugh QC *1961*†	**Llewelyn**, Jane *1989*
Mayhew of Twysden, Lord QC *1955*	**Astor**, Philip *1989*
	Morton, Keith *1990*
Miscampbell, Norman QC *1952*†	**Laughland**, James *1991*
	Ciumei, Charles *1991*
Sankey, Guy QC *1966*†	**Curtis**, Charles *1992*
Bate-Williams, John *1976*	**Wilkinson**, Richard *1992*
Ashford-Thom, Ian *1977*	**Bacon**, Nicholas *1992*
Burnett, Ian QC *1980*	**Grant**, Marcus *1993*
Hoskins, William *1980*	**Barr**, David *1993*
Grieve, Dominic *1980*	**Issa**, Alexandra *1993*
Bishop, Mark *1981*	**Glassbrook**, Alexander *1995*
Hewitt, Alison *1984*	**Moss**, Nicholas *1995*
Tam, Robin *1986*	**Kevan**, Timothy *1996*
Kilcoyne, Paul *1985*	**Smyth**, Julia *1996*
Bell, James *1987*	**Hobbs**, Emma-Jane *1996*
Brown, Simon *1988*	

Chambers established: 1954
Opening times: 8.30 am-6.30 pm

Types of work (and number of counsel practising in that area if supplied)
Administrative · Common law (general) · Crime · Crime - corporate fraud · Employment · Health and safety · Immigration · Insurance · Landlord and tenant · Medical negligence · Mental health · Personal injury · Professional negligence · Sale and carriage of goods

Chambers' facilities
Conference rooms, E-mail

Languages spoken
French, German, Spanish

Fees policy
Refer to the Senior Clerk. Estimate of fees and conditional fees available.

Additional information

1 Temple Gardens is a long-established common law set committed to providing a professional, efficient and friendly service to all our clients.

The work of chambers covers most aspects of civil common law particularly personal injury, professional and medical negligence, employment law, public and administrative law and judicial review, general commercial work, public and judicial inquiries and inquests.

Individual members provide specialist services in health and safety litigation, immigration, costs and taxation reviews, landlord and tenant, and criminal law including VAT and corporate fraud.

The clerking team is happy to provide guidance on any matter and prides itself on its open and friendly approach. A brochure is available on request.

The UK College of Family Mediators Directory & Handbook 1998/99

- *provides expert commentary on family mediation training and professional development and includes contributions by leading family mediation professionals*

- *lists over 100 family mediation groups/services and over 950 individual family mediators by region and alphabetically*

- *gives details of all members and associates of the UK College of Family Mediators*

- *includes the UK College of Family Mediators Standards and Code of Practice*

- *gives details of all the family mediation bodies which make up the UK College of Family Mediators*

For more information call Sweet & Maxwell on 0171 449 1111

---

2 TEMPLE GARDENS

Temple, London EC4Y 9AY
0171 583 6041
Fax: 0171 583 2094; DX 134 London, Chancery Lane

Chambers of J P M Phillips QC
Clerk: Christopher Willans

Phillips, Jeremy QC *1964*	**Russell**, Christopher *1982*
Crowther, William QC *1963*†	**Thomas**, David *1982*
Preston, Timothy QC *1964*†	**Vaughan-Jones**, Sarah *1983*
O'Brien, Dermod QC *1962*†	**Eklund**, Graham *1984*
Twigg, Patrick QC *1967*†	**Porter**, Martin *1986*
de Navarro, Michael QC *1968*†	**Rabey**, Catherine *1987*
	Gray, Jennifer *1988*
Moxon Browne, Robert QC *1969*†	**Miller**, Andrew *1989*
	Moody, Neil *1989*
Collender, Andrew QC *1969*†	**Crowley**, Daniel *1990*
	Martin, Bradley *1990*
Lamb, Timothy QC *1974*‡	**Otty**, Timothy *1990*
Layton, Alexander QC *1976*‡	**Downes**, Paul *1991*
	Snell, John *1991*
Browne, Benjamin QC *1976*‡	**Lord**, Timothy *1992*
	Kinsler, Marie *1992*
de Lotbiniere, Henry *1968*	**Reece**, Rupert *1992*
Foster, Rosalind *1969*†	**Turner**, David *1992*
Hetherington, Roger *1973*‡	**Brown**, Clare *1993*
Pearce-Higgins, Daniel QC *1973*‡	**Gardiner**, Bruce *1994*
	Green, Dore *1994*
Palmer, Howard *1977*	**Mort**, Justin *1994*
Stuart-Smith, Jeremy QC *1978*‡	**Wyles**, Lucy *1994*
	Goolamali, Nina *1995*
Archer, Stephen *1979*	**Constable**, Adam *1995*
Anyadike-Danes, Monya *1980*	**Hext**, Neil *1995*
	Harris, Roger *1996*
McDonald, John *1981*	

Chambers established: 1945
Opening times: 7.30 am-7.30 pm

Types of work (and number of counsel practising in that area if supplied)
Arbitration 10 · Aviation 4 · Banking 4 · Bankruptcy 3 · Chancery (general) 6 · Civil liberties 3 · Commercial litigation 27 · Commercial property 6 · Common law (general) 47 · Company and commercial 10 · Construction 15 · EC and competition law 4 · Employment 4 · Environment · Financial services 4 · Information technology 3 · Insolvency 4 · Insurance 15 · Insurance/reinsurance 15 · Landlord and tenant 5 · Medical negligence 39 · Personal injury · Professional negligence 36 · Sale and carriage of goods 7

Chambers' facilities
Conference rooms, Disks accepted, Disabled access, E-mail

---

† Recorder ‡ Assistant Recorder * Door Tenant

Languages spoken
French, German, Italian, Spanish

3 TEMPLE GARDENS

TEMPLE
GARDENS

*Lower Ground Floor, Temple, London
EC4Y 9AU*
0171 353 3102/5/9297
Fax: 0171 353 0960; DX 485 London,
Chancery Lane

Chambers of John J Coffey QC
*Clerks: Kevin Aldridge (Senior Clerk), Hadyn
Robson (First Junior Clerk)*

Coffey, John QC *1970*†	**Reynolds**, Stella *1983*
Pegden, Jeffrey QC *1973*†	**Lahiffe**, Martin *1984*
Birch, William *1972*	**Geekie**, Charles *1985*
Ader, Peter *1973*†	**Popert**, Catherine *1987*
Scholz, Karl *1973*	**Aina**, Benjamin *1987*
Crabtree, Richard *1974*	**Krikler**, Susan *1988*
Reed, Piers *1974*	**Bleaney**, Nicholas *1988*
Gilbert, Jayne *1976*	**McKeever**, Frances *1988*
Whittaker, Robert *1977*	**Rutherford**, Martin *1990*
Campbell-Tiech, Andrew *1978*	**Pearson**, Carolyn *1990*
Cotcher, Ann *1979*	**Firth**, Clemency *1992*
Saunders, William *1980*	**Emir**, Astra *1992*
Connolly, Simon *1981*	**Nuttall**, Evan *1993*
Smith, Simon *1981*	**Corsellis**, Nicholas *1993*
Smith, Alisdair *1981*	**Williams**, Alexander *1995*
Halsall, Louise *1982*	**Patterson**, Gareth *1995*
Connolly, Deirdre *1982*	**Hamilton**, Amanda *1995*

Chambers established: 1969
Opening times: 8.30 am-6.30 pm

Types of work (and number of counsel practising in that area if supplied)
Care proceedings 6 · Chancery (general) 2
· Common law (general) 7 · Courts martial 2
· Crime 31 · Crime - corporate fraud 10
· Education 1 · Employment 2 · Environment 3
· Family 10 · Family provision 10 · Housing 2
· Licensing 6 · Local government 15 · Mental
health 5 · Personal injury 5 · Town and
country planning 1

Chambers' facilities
Conference rooms, Video conferences, Disks
accepted

Languages spoken
French, German

Additional information

Chambers is a well-established set specialising
particularly in all areas of criminal law.
Individual members also provide a similar
service in family law, and in many areas of
common law.

Chambers has a number of criminal
practitioners at all levels of seniority. They
advise upon and appear in proceedings in all
magistrates' courts, the crown court, the
Queen's Bench Divisional Court and the House
of Lords. Experience extends to all preparation
and conduct of both defence and prosecution
work. In particular, members defend and
prosecute in a large number of commercial
crime and fraud cases.

Judicial Review and disiplinary tribunal work
are a speciality of a number of tenants.

The matrimonial practitioners are available to
advise and handle work in all areas of family law,
including substantial matrimonial property and
inheritance cases, residence and contact,
childcare, abduction, adoption and wardship.
A number of tenants practise in road transport
law.

Chambers is frequently instructed by local
authorities in respect of a wide range of matters
including health and safety, trading standards
and planning.

The administration of chambers is the
responsibility of Kevin Aldridge, the Senior
Clerk, and his colleagues. They will be pleased
to discuss particular requirements and offer
guidance on the suitability and availability of
individual members of chambers in any given
area of practice. A brochure is available on
request.

Training and pupillage are dealt with by
Nicholas Corsellis. A pupillage application form
is available.

3 TEMPLE GARDENS

2nd Floor, Temple, London EC4Y 9AU
0171 583 1155
Fax: 0171 353 5446; DX 0064 London

Chambers of Mr J J Goldberg QC

3 TEMPLE GARDENS

3rd Floor, Temple, London EC4Y 9AU
0171 353 0832
Fax: 0171 353 4929; DX 427 London

Chambers of Mr D C Gordon

3 TEMPLE GARDENS

3rd Floor, Temple, London EC4Y 9AU
0171 583 0010
Fax: 0171 353 3361; DX 0073 London

Chambers of Mr D J F Wright

3 TEMPLE GARDENS (NORTH)

Fifth Floor, Temple, London EC4Y 9AU
0171 353 0853/4/7222
Fax: 0171 583 2823; DX 0008 London,
Chancery Lane
E-mail: 100106.1577@compuserve.com

Chambers of W J E Forster-Jones
Clerk: Brian Peters

Forster-Jones, Wilfred *1976*	**Thompson**, Glenna *1993*
Roberts, Dominic *1977*	**Sharma**, Suman *1994*
Macaulay, Donora *1982*	**Fell**, Alistair *1994*
Metzger, Kevin *1984*	**Palmer**, Nathan *1994*
Aderemi, Adedamola *1992*	**Lams**, Barnabas *1995*
Kivdeh, Shahrokh-Sean *1992*	**Stevens**, Nina *1994*
Owusu-Yianoma, David *1992*	

> See the *Index of Languages Spoken* in Part G to locate a chambers where a particular language is spoken, or find an individual who speaks a particular language.

3 TEMPLE GARDENS TAX CHAMBERS

1st Floor, Temple, London EC4Y 9AU
0171 353 7884
Fax: 0171 583 2044

Chambers of D G H Braham QC
Clerks: F L Skelton, Anne de Rose

Braham, David QC *1957*	**James**, Alun *1986*
Bramwell, Richard QC *1967*	**McNicholas**, Eamon *1994*
Dick, John *1974*	**Southern**, David *1982*
Sherry, Michael *1978*	**Schwarz**, Jonathan *1998*

THE THAMES CHAMBERS

Wickham House, 10 Cleveland Way, London E1 4TR
0171 790 7377
Fax: 0171 790 2616

Chambers of Mr E A Oteng

THOMAS MORE CHAMBERS

More House, 51-2 Carey Street, Lincoln's Inn, London WC2A 2JB
0171 404 7000
Fax: 0171 831 4606; DX 90 London, Chancery Lane
Clerks: Christopher Hallett (Senior Clerk), Stuart Sellen, Steven Parr

Noble, Philip *1978*	**Gottlieb**, David *1988*
Garnett, Susan *1973*	**Aylott**, Colin *1989*
Macdonald, Jeanie *1979*	**Wells**, Nicholas *1990*
Ray, Jonathan *1980*	**Farmer**, Sarah *1991*
Cox, Geoffrey *1982*	**Egan**, Manus *1991*
Davison, Richard *1982*	**Cross**, Richard *1993*
Dias, Sappho *1982*	**Sherratt**, Matthew *1994*
Snelson, Anthony *1982*	**Cooper**, Sarah Lucy *1993*
Egan, Fiona *1987*	**MacLaren**, Alexander *1997*

Chambers established: 1992
Opening times: 9am-6pm (24-hr answering service available).

Types of work (and number of counsel practising in that area if supplied)
Bankruptcy · Care proceedings · Civil liberties · Commercial · Common law (general) · Company and commercial · Consumer Law · Contract · Courts martial · Crime · Crime - corporate fraud · Defamation · Discrimination · Employment · European Union · Family · Family provision · Financial services · Fraud · Housing · Human rights · Immigration · Insolvency · Judicial review · Landlord and tenant · Licensing · Medical negligence · Partnerships · Personal injury · Planning · Privy Council Appeals · Professional negligence · Sale and carriage of goods · Town and country planning · Trading standards

Chambers' facilities
Conference rooms, Video conferences, Disks accepted

Languages spoken
French, Spanish, Urdu

TOLLGATE MEWS CHAMBERS

113 Tollgate Road, Tollgate Mews, North Beckton, London E6 4JY
0171 511 1838
Fax: 0171 511 1838

Chambers of Mr J K Dowokpor

The *new* Supreme Court Practice 1999 (The White Book)

- *the most authoritative guide to Civil Court Practice and Procedure*

- *whatever the case, whatever the court*

- *updates following implementation of the Woolf Reforms*

The new Supreme Court Practice is also available on CD-ROM using Folio Views™ technology. With this intuitive software, you will find your way around The White Book with ease, enhancing your research by leaps and bounds.

Phone Sweet & Maxwell on 0171 449 1111 to order your copy

---

14 TOOKS COURT

Cursitor Street, London EC4A 1LB
0171 405 8828
Fax: 0171 405 6680; DX 68 London, Chancery Lane
E-mail: clerks@tooks.law.co.uk
Other comms: Mobile: 0850 823676/Pager: 0941 119610

Chambers of M Mansfield QC
Clerks: C Thomas, M Parker, M Hughton, K Jackson, L Wakeling (Fees Clerk); Administrator: Sandra Watson

Mansfield, Michael QC 1967	Wilcock, Peter 1988
Fulford, Adrian QC 1978‡	Boye-Anawoma, Margo 1989
Alexander, Edmond 1961	
Reilly, John 1972	Monaghan, Karon 1989
Baird, Vera 1975	Bowen, Stephen 1990
Belford, Dora 1977	Chapman, Rebecca 1990
Roche, Patrick 1977	Hawley, Carol 1990
Yeboah, Yaa 1977*	Maguire, Sarah 1990
Kamlish, Stephen 1979	Soorjoo, Martin 1990
Plange, Janet 1981	Daniel, Leon 1992
Hyde, Christiana 1982	Munroe, Allison 1992
Mylvaganam, Tanoo 1983	Drew, Sandhya 1993
Thornberry, Emily 1983	Moloney, Timothy 1993
Bennathan, Joel 1985	Dubicka, Elizabeth 1994
Delahunty, Johanne 1986	Graham, Sandra 1982*
Shamash, Anne 1986	Woodcraft, Elizabeth 1980
Topolski, Michael 1986	Guthrie, Mark 1984
Dick, Julia 1988	Herbert, Peter 1982
Huseyin, Martin 1988	Jordash, Wayne 1995

Chambers established: 1984
Opening times: 8.30 am-6.30 pm

Types of work (and number of counsel practising in that area if supplied)
Administrative 16 · Care proceedings 12 · Civil liberties 23 · Common law (general) 5 · Crime 23 · Defamation 3 · Discrimination 9 · Education 3 · Employment 6 · Family 12 · Housing 4 · Immigration 9 · Landlord and tenant 5 · Medical negligence 8 · Mental health 9 · Personal injury 12 · Prison law · Professional negligence 7 · Public inquiries/inquests 23

Chambers' facilities
Video conferences, Disks accepted, Disabled access

Languages spoken
French, German, Italian, Spanish, Turkish, Urdu

Additional information
Tooks Court was founded in 1984. Since then the set has demonstrated a strong and

       † Recorder ‡ Assistant Recorder * Door Tenant

consistent commitment to providing the highest professional standards for both solicitors and lay clients. Chambers offers a broad range of civil and criminal work.

Chambers has a reputation for high-profile criminal defence work and has particular expertise in dealing with public order offences and Irish cases. However, the range of practice encompasses the full spectrum of criminal offences from murder to gross indecency, and fraud to shoplifting.

14 Tooks Court offers specialists in civil matters including family, employment, and discrimination cases, and has particular expertise in dealing with actions involving the police.

Individual members also specialise in various areas of law including family, employment, discrimination, immigration, landlord and tenant, personal injury, civil actions against the police, mental health, and administrative law and judicial review.

TOWER HAMLETS BARRISTERS CHAMBERS

First Floor, 45 Brick Lane, London E1 6PU
0171 247 9825
Fax: 0171 247 9825

TOWER HAMLETS BARRISTERS CHAMBERS

37B Princelet Street, London E1 5LP
0171 377 8090
Fax: 0171 377 6322

Kime's International Law Directory 1999

- *established guide to the international legal community*

- *reliable and relevant information on over 600 law firms and chambers*

- *entries can be found by types of work undertaken and location*

- *the only law directory to provide editorial on every jurisdiction's legal system and enforcement of judgements*

- *now on the Internet at http://www.smlawpub-holborn.co.uk/kimes*

For more information call Sweet & Maxwell on 0171 449 1111

TRAFALGAR CHAMBERS

53 Fleet Street, London EC4Y 1BE
0171 583 5858
Fax: 0171 353 5302; DX 89 London
E-mail: TrafalgarChambers@easynet.co.uk
Out of hours telephone: 0850 550 510/0421 414 894

Chambers of Christopher Cleverly
Clerk: Michael Sweeney

Cleverly, Christopher *1990*	**McLaughlin**, Elaine *1993*
Littlewood, Rebecca *1988*	**Gersch**, Adam *1993*
Rogerson, Andrew *1981*	**Hope**, Heather *1993*
Rubens, Jacqueline *1989*	**Haleema**, Safina *1993*
Marshall, Peter *1991*	**Waritay**, Samuel *1993*
Umezuruike, Chima *1991*	**Harris**, Glenn *1994*
Grant-Garwood, Joshua *1992*	**Jones**, Lesley *1995*
Ruffell, Mark *1992*	**Kelly**, Siobhan *1995*
Duddridge, Robert *1992*	**Healey**, Susan *1995*
Morris, Antonia *1993*	**Ffitch**, Nigel *1996*

CHAMBERS OF MOHAMMED HASHMOT ULLAH

72 Brick Lane, London E1 6RL
0171 377 0119
Fax: 0171 247 6648
Out of hours telephone: 0181 342 8573

Chambers of Mohammed Hashmot Ullah
Clerks: Irma La Rose, Lynn Fawcett

Ullah, Mohammed *1989*

45 ULLSWATER CRESCENT

Kingston Vale, London SW15 3RG
0181 546 9284

Chambers of Mr M N Islam

C

The Supreme Court Practice 1999

- *the most authoritative title on Civil Court Practice and Procedure*

- *available in book and CD-ROM formats*

Phone Sweet & Maxwell on 0171 449 1111 to order your copy

---

3 VERULAM BUILDINGS

London WC1R 5NT
0171 831 8441
Fax: 0171 831 8479; DX 331 London
E-mail: clerks@3verulam.co.uk
URL: http://www.3verulam.co.uk

Chambers of R N Thomas QC
Practice manager: Roger Merry-Price

Thomas, Neville QC *1962*	McQuater, Ewan *1985*
Merriman, Nicholas QC	Sands, Philippe *1985*
1969†	Nash, Jonathan *1986*
Jarvis, John QC *1970*†	Cameron, James *1987*
Symons, Christopher QC	Lewis, Caroline *1988*
1972†	May, Juliet *1988*
Geering, Ian QC *1974*†	Start, Angharad *1988*
Blair, William QC *1972*‡	Beltrami, Adrian *1989*
Elliott, Nicholas QC *1972*	Green, Amanda *1990*
Salter, Richard QC *1975*‡	Hockaday, Annie *1990*
Turner, Janet QC *1979*	Odgers, John *1990*
Malek, Ali QC *1980*‡	Phillips, Jonathan *1991*
Mitchell, Gregory QC *1979*	Evans, James *1991*
Wakefield, Anne *1968*†	Wolfson, David *1992*
Freedman, Clive *1975*	Marks, Jonathan *1992*
Cranston, Ross *1976*†	Quest, David *1993*
de Lacy, Richard *1976*	Edwards, Richard *1993*
Kay, Michael *1981*	Davies-Jones, Jonathan
Cranfield, Peter *1982*	*1994*
Onslow, Andrew *1982*	Pope, David *1995*
Sutcliffe, Andrew *1983*	Brent, Richard *1995*
Phillips, Stephen *1984*	Tolaney, Sonia *1995*
Phillips, Rory *1984*	Wilson, Ian *1995*
Sheridan, Maurice *1984*	Baylis, Natalie *1996*
Weitzman, Thomas *1984*	Gibaud, Catherine *1996*

Chambers established: 1910
Opening times: 8 am-8 pm

Types of work (and number of counsel practising in that area if supplied)
Administrative 3 · Agriculture 2 · Arbitration 14 · Banking 37 · Commercial litigation 35 · Commercial property 1 · Commodities 2 · Common law (general) 4 · Company and commercial 21 · Construction 3 · EC and competition law 7 · Employment 7 · Entertainment 13 · Environment 4 · Financial services 12 · Information technology 3 · Insolvency 22 · Insurance 11 · Insurance/reinsurance 9 · Intellectual property 6 · International trade 10 · Landlord and tenant 2 · Medical negligence 1 · Partnerships 4 · Pensions 2 · Private international 5 · Professional negligence 37 · Public international 6 · Sale and carriage of goods 20 · Shipping, admiralty 2

Chambers' facilities
Conference rooms, Disks accepted, Disabled access, E-mail

Languages spoken
French, German, Hebrew, Italian, Portuguese, Russian, Spanish

Fees policy
Up to five years call £40-100, Five to ten years call £100-150, Ten years call plus £150-200. QC £200-350 per hour.

Additional information

Members of Chambers deal with a wide range of commercial work. They are all specialist advocates. As well as representing clients in court, in arbitrations and before tribunals, they undertake advisory work, settle pleadings and draft contracts and other documentation to meet the needs of their clients.

Members of Chambers are recognised as specialists in the fields of commercial law, banking, insurance and reinsurance, professional negligence, media and entertainment, public international and environmental law. In addition, 3 Verulam Buildings has recognised specialists in many other areas of law.

This diversity enables 3 Verulam Buildings to offer advice and representation to clients in the huge variety of business contexts in which legal issues arise. It also provides clients with the opportunity to seek specialised assistance on different legal aspects of the same problem.

VERULAM CHAMBERS

Peer House, 8-14 Verulam Street, Gray's Inn, London WC1X 8LZ
0171 813 2400
Fax: 0171 405 3870; DX 436 London, Chancery Lane
Out of hours telephone: 0467 762515

Chambers of J M Edwards QC CBE
Clerk: Trevor Austin (01268 711007 Mobile: 0467 762515)

Edwards, John QC *1949*	**da Costa**, Elissa *1990*
Wheatley, Derek QC *1951**	**Rifat**, Maurice *1990*
Payton, Clifford *1972*	**Khan**, Karimulla *1990*
Dethridge, David *1975*	**Williamson**, Tessa *1990**
Sofaer, Moira *1975*	**Jago**, Ann *1991*
Putnam, Thomas *1976*	**Siddle**, Trevor *1991*
Putnam, Sheelagh *1976**	**Passmore**, John *1992*
Mullen, Peter *1977*	**Goodwin**, Katherine *1993*
d'Aigremont, Gilles *1978*	**O'Connor**, Gerard *1993*
Ernstzen, Olav *1981**	**Simpson**, Jonathan *1993*
Lawe, Susan *1982*	**Smart**, Julia *1993*
Webber, Dominic *1985*	**Smith**, Leonorah *1994*
Mehta, Sailesh *1986*	**Fowler**, Tracey *1994*
Moore, Joan *1986*	**Quinn**, Victoria *1995*
Humberstone, Pearl *1987*	**Themis**, Sam *1995*
McIntosh, Jacqueline *1987*	**Welch**, Brett *1996*
White, Joanne *1987*	**Leckie**, James *1964**
Sowerby, Matthew *1987*	**Lewis**, Cherry *1973**
Giles, David *1988*	**Hawkins**, Nicholas *1979**
Gifford, Cynthia *1988*	**Fitzpatrick**, Edward *1985*

WARWICK HOUSE CHAMBERS

8 Warwick Court, Gray's Inn, London WC1R 5DJ
0171 430 2323
Fax: 0171 430 9171; DX 1001 London, Chancery Lane

Chambers of Mrs C Drew, Mr C T Drew
Clerk: Christopher Dear;
Practice manager: Neil Calver

Drew, Christopher *1969*	**Moser**, Philip *1992*
Drew, Cheryl *1972*	**Moore**, Roderick *1993*
Wickremeratne, Upali *1962*	**Lal**, Sanjay *1993*
Mackintosh, Andrew *1990*	**Papazian**, Cliona *1994*
Patel, Jayaben *1990*	**Sternberg**, Lesli *1994*
Rowe, Deborah *1990*	**Mansfield**, Eleanor *1995*
Kennedy, Paul *1991*	**Bagral**, Ravinder *1996*
Haidemenos, Stavros *1992*	**Wilson**, Jonathan *1995*

243 WESTBOURNE GROVE

London W11 2SE
0171 229 3819
Fax: 0171 229 3819

Chambers of Miss C A Holder

WILBERFORCE CHAMBERS

8 New Square, Lincoln's Inn, London WC2A 3QP
0171 306 0102
Fax: 0171 306 0095; DX 311 London
E-mail: chambers@wilberforce.co.uk

Chambers of Edward Nugee QC
Clerk: Declan Redmond (Senior Clerk); Chambers Director: Suzanne Cosgrave

Nugee, Edward QC *1955*	**Furness**, Michael *1982*
Sher, Jules QC *1968*	**Tennet**, Michael *1985*
Lowe, David QC *1965*	**Seitler**, Jonathan *1985*
Etherton, Terence QC *1974*	**Lowe**, Thomas *1985*
Martin, John QC *1972*	**Ayliffe**, James *1987*
Warren, Nicholas QC *1972*	**Bryant**, Judith *1987*
Croxford, Ian QC *1976*	**Smith**, Joanna *1990*
Ham, Robert QC *1973*	**Wicks**, Joanne *1990*
Green, Brian QC *1980*	**Newman**, Paul *1991*
Nugee, Christopher QC *1983*	**Fadipe**, Gabriel *1991*
Taussig, Anthony *1966*	**Furze**, Caroline *1992*
Child, John *1966*	**Evans**, Jonathan *1994*
Turnbull, Charles *1975*	**Campbell**, Emily *1995*
Seymour, Thomas *1975*	**Reed**, Rupert *1996*
Hughes, Gabriel *1978*	

Opening times: 8.45 am-6.30 pm

Types of work (and number of counsel practising in that area if supplied)
Banking · Chancery (general) · Chancery land law · Charities · Commercial · Commercial litigation · Commercial property · Company and commercial · Equity, wills and trusts · Financial services · Landlord and tenant · Pensions · Probate and administration · Professional negligence

C

Chambers' facilities
Conference rooms, Disks accepted, E-mail

Languages spoken
French, German

Additional information

Chambers' work: Litigation advice and drafting in all areas of modern Chancery practice. The main categories are listed below, but are not intended to be exhaustive, please contact Declan Redmond, Senior Clerk, or Suzanne Cosgrave, Chambers Director, for more information and a brochure.

Commercial: Commercial and other contract, banking and securities, financial services, Lloyd's litigation, economic torts, breach of confidence, oil and gas law, sports law and white-collar crime.

Company: Shareholders' disputes, directors' disqualification proceedings, mergers and acquisitions, corporate insolvency, partnerships and joint ventures.

Employment: Wrongful dismissal and all forms of discrimination.

Equitable remedies: Injunctions, breach of fiduciary duties, tracing.

Local Government and administrative law

Pensions: All aspects of occupational and personal pension schemes.

Professional negligence: Accountants, actuaries, auditors, barristers, solicitors, surveyors, trustees and others.

Property: All matters relating to land, commercial property transactions, landlord and tenant, property finance negligence and fraud, mortgages and other securities, nuisance and trespass, commons, highways, school sites, heritage property and church property.

Trusts: Trusts, settlements, wills, charities, estate planning and associated tax advice.

The Chambers: A prominent commercial Chancery set, Wilberforce Chambers has a committed and direct approach which combines imagination and intellectual rigour to provide expert legal analysis, practical advice and effective conduct of litigation over an exceptionally wide range of work. Chambers has introduced a new staffing structure to ensure that it follows best practice in its business operations, and makes extensive use of the new information technology tools now available to aid legal research and communication with all its clients.

Members of chambers belong to the Chancery Bar Association, the Commercial Bar Association, the Association of Pension Lawyers the Revenue Bar Association and STEP.

Members also sit as Deputy High Court judges, Recorders and as First Standing Junior Counsel in Chancery matters.
A brochure is available on request.

39 WINDSOR ROAD

London N3 3SN
0181 349 9194
Fax: 0181 346 8506
E-mail: lindacohen@cobeck.clara.net

Chambers of Linda Cohen
Clerk: F Beckett

Cohen, Linda *1985*

WYNNE CHAMBERS

1 Wynne Road, London SW9 0BB
0171 737 7266
Fax: 0171 737 7267

Chambers of Mr M H A Thomson

2 GOLDINGHAM AVENUE

Loughton, Essex IG10 2JF
0181 502 4247

Chambers of Mrs F L Bolton

BERESFORD CHAMBERS

21 King Street, Luton, Bedfordshire LU1 2DW
01582 429111
Fax: 01582 410555; DX 5966 Luton 1

Chambers of Mr D R Abbott

LAW CHAMBERS

2nd Floor, 5 Cardiff Road, Luton,
Bedfordshire LU1 1PP
01582 431352 or 0958 674785

Chambers of Mr S H Mahmood

EARL STREET CHAMBERS

47 Earl Street, Maidstone, Kent ME14 1PD
01622 671222
Fax: 01622 671776; DX 4844 Maidstone 1
E-mail: gunner-sparks@msn.com
Out of hours telephone: 0831 325122

Chambers of Kevin Sparks
Clerks: Mary Gunner (Senior Clerk), Clare Cheeseman (Junior Clerk)

Sparks, Kevin *1983*	**Halpin,** Thomas *1994*
Clarke, Michelle *1988*	**Greene,** Paul *1994*
Scott-Phillips, Alexander *1995*	**Nathan,** Philip *1996*
Wyatt, Guy *1981*	**Ball,** Steven J *1996*

MAIDSTONE CHAMBERS

MAIDSTONE CHAMBERS

Broughton House, 33 Earl Street, Maidstone, Kent ME14 1PF
01622 688592
Fax: 01622 683305; DX 51982 Maidstone 2
Out of hours telephone: 0467 351682

Chambers of Alison Ginn and Richard Travers
Clerks: Robert Davis (Senior Clerk), James Shaw (1st Junior)

Ginn, Alison *1980*	**Fawcett,** Michelle *1993*
Travers, Richard *1985*	**Clarke,** Malcolm *1994*
Le Prevost, Aviva *1990*	**Burns,** Rosemary *1978*
Pottinger, Gavin *1991*	**Stern,** Thomas *1995*
Jacobson, Mary *1992*	**Sinclair,** Philip *1995*
Dubarry, Adele *1993*	**Bowers,** Rupert *1995*

Types of work (and number of counsel practising in that area if supplied)
Care proceedings 3 · Common law (general) 11 · Courts martial 4 · Crime 10 · Employment 6 · Environment 2 · Family 6 · Family provision 3 · Immigration 3 · Landlord and tenant 2 · Licensing 3 · Medical negligence 2 · Personal injury 5 · Professional negligence 5 · Town and country planning 2

Chambers' facilities
Conference rooms, Disks accepted

Languages spoken
French, Italian

6-8 MILL STREET

Maidstone, Kent ME15 6XH
01622 688094
Fax: 01622 688096

Chambers of Mr S A Hockman QC

RESOLUTION CHAMBERS

Oak Lodge, 55 Poolbrook Road, Malvern, Worcestershire WR14 3JN
01684 561279
Fax: 01684 561279; DX 17617 Malvern
Out of hours telephone: 0468 070111

Chambers of Michael Milne
Clerk: Penny Milne

Milne, Michael *1987*

BYROM STREET CHAMBERS

25 Byrom Street, Manchester M3 4PF
0161 829 2100
Fax: 0161 829 2101; DX 718156 Manchester 3
E-mail: Byromst25@aol.com

Chambers of B A Hytner QC
Clerk: Peter Collison

Also at: 22 Old Buildings, Lincoln's Inn, London WC2A 3UJ
Tel: 0171 831 0222
Fax: 0181 831 2239

Hytner, Benet QC *1952*	**Tattersall,** Geoffrey QC *1970*†
Price, John QC *1961*†	
Wingate-Saul, Giles QC *1967*†	**Swift,** Caroline QC *1977*†
	Moran, Andrew QC *1976*†
Leveson, Brian QC *1970*†	**Allan,** David QC *1974*†
Scholes, Rodney QC *1968*†	**Black,** Michael QC *1978*‡
King, Timothy QC *1973*†	**Stewart,** Stephen QC *1975*‡

Opening times: 8.30 am-7 pm

Types of work (and number of counsel practising in that area if supplied)
Arbitration · Banking · Commercial · Common law (general) · Construction · Crime · Insurance · Intellectual property · International Trade · Medical negligence · Personal injury · Professional negligence · Shipping

---

† Recorder ‡ Assistant Recorder * Door Tenant

Chambers' facilities
Conference rooms, Disks accepted, Disabled access

Additional information

Byrom Street Chambers consists of twelve Queen's Counsel who practise in Manchester at 25 Byrom Street and from Chambers at 22 Old Buildings, Lincoln's Inn. Manchester Chambers are exclusively dedicated to the work of Leading Counsel. The set was founded in the early 1950's. Each member offers advice and advocacy in the fields of law in which he or she practises. These include:

· Administrative Law and Judicial Review, Local Government and Public Inquiries;
· Commercial Law and in particular Banking, Financial Services, Intellectual Property and Sale of Goods;
· Company Law;
· Crime, with an emphasis on Homicide, Sexual Offences, Commercial Fraud and Conspiracy;
· Computers and Information Technology;
· Construction, Building and Engineering and associated matters of Procurement, Insurance, Funding and Professional Liabilities;
· Domestic and International Commercial Arbitration and ADR;
· Environmental Law;
· General Common Law;
· Insurance and Reinsurance;
· Personal Injury Claims, especially Disaster Litigation, Severe and Permanent Disablement, Industrial Diseases and Class Actions;
· Product Liability;
· Professional Negligence including that of Doctors, Lawyers, Architects, Engineers, Surveyors, Accountants and Financial Intermediaries;
· Shipping and International Trade;
· Sports Law;
· Tribunals and Inquiries.

Members of Chambers accept references as Arbitrators, Mediators, Adjudicators and Legal Assessors.

All Silks hold, or have held, part-time judicial office. Mr Wingate-Saul and Mr Leveson sit as Deputy High Court Judges, Mr Tattersall sits as Judge of Appeal in the Isle of Man, having succeeded Mr Hytner who was Judge of Appeal from 1980 to 1997, and who sat as a Deputy High Court Judge from 1974 to 1997 and as a Recorder from 1971 to 1996.

Former members of Chambers include the Right Honourable Sir Patrick Russell (formerly Lord Justice, who is now available through Chambers for arbitration cases), Lord Justice Rose, Mrs Justice Smith, the Senior Mercantile Judge of the Northern Circuit, Judge Michael Kershaw QC, and the Recorder of Liverpool His Honour Judge David Clarke QC. Mr Hytner was the elected Leader of the Northern Circuit from 1984 to 1988, as was Sir Patrick Russell from 1979 to 1980.

Further information regarding individual expertise and fee structure can be obtained from the senior clerk, Peter Collison.

CENTRAL CHAMBERS

CENTRAL CHAMBERS

Greg's Buildings, 1 Booth Street, Manchester M2 4DU
0161 833 1774
Fax: 0161 835 1405; DX 14467 Manchester 2
Other comms: Emergency Number: 0973 744906 (24 hours)
Clerks: Jayne Lever, Neil Vickers

Khan, Fauz *1988*	**Qazi,** M Ayaz *1993*
Massey, Stella *1990*	**Ward,** Peter *1996*
Grace, Tonia *1992*	**Sastry,** Bob *1996*
Ismail, Nazmun Nisha *1992*	**Collins,** James *1997*

Chambers established: 1996 (formerly known as Garden Court North)
Opening times: 8.45 am-6.15 pm

Types of work (and number of counsel practising in that area if supplied)
Administrative · Care proceedings · Civil liberties · Crime · Crime - corporate fraud · Discrimination · Education · Employment · Family · Family provision · Housing · Immigration · Judicial review · Landlord and tenant · Medical negligence · Mental health · Personal injury · Prisoners rights · Professional negligence

Chambers' facilities
Conference rooms, Disks accepted

Languages spoken
French, German, Gujarati, Hebrew, Hindi, Punjabi, Urdu

COBDEN HOUSE CHAMBERS

19 Quay Street, Manchester M3 3HN
0161 833 6000/6001
Fax: 0161 833 6001; DX 14327 Manchester 3
E-mail: clerks@cobden.co.uk
URL: http://www.cobden.co.uk

Chambers of Howard Baisden, Peter Keenan
Clerks: Mr Trevor Doyle (Senior Clerk/ Practice Manager), David Hewitt (Assistant Clerk), Scott Baldwin (Assistant Clerk), Daniel Monaghan (Assistant Clerk); Administrator: Mrs Jackie Morton

Baisden, Howard *1972*	**Littler**, Martin *1989*
Keenan, Peter *1962*	**Harrison**, Sarah *1989*
Watkins, Peter *1952*	**Gregg**, William *1990*
Narayan, Harry *1970†*	**Kelly**, Sean *1990*
Broadley, John *1973*	**Cheetham**, Julia *1990*
Machin, Charles *1973*	**Willems**, Marc *1990*
Fieldhouse, Nigel *1976*	**Dalal**, Rajen *1991*
Neale, Stuart *1976*	**Smith**, Jonathan *1991*
Goldwater, Michael *1977*	**Woodward**, Alison *1992*
Oughton, Richard *1978*	**Riddell**, David *1993*
Fallows, Mary *1981*	**Gee**, Richard *1993*
Uff, David *1981*	**Hilsdon**, James *1993*
Green, Colin *1982*	**Nichol**, Simon *1994*
Webster, Leonard *1984*	**Gilmour**, Susan *1994*
Blackwell, Louise *1985*	**Orr**, Julian *1995*
Metcalfe, Ian *1985*	**Oakes**, Christopher *1996*
Hartley, Richard *1985*	**Manley**, Hilary *1996*
Monaghan, Mark *1987*	**Callery**, Martin *1997*
Woodward, Joanne *1989*	**Heywood**, Michael *1975**
Kitching, Robin *1989*	**Hymanson**, Deanna *1988**
Willitts, Timothy *1989*	**Kime**, Matthew *1988**

Types of work (and number of counsel practising in that area if supplied)
Administrative 1 · Agriculture 1 · Arbitration 1 · Banking 2 · Bankruptcy 2 · Care proceedings 5 · Chancery (general) 11 · Chancery land law 6 · Charities 2 · Commercial 8 · Commercial litigation 2 · Commercial property 5 · Common land 1 · Common law (general) 9 · Company and commercial 6 · Competition 1 · Consumer Law 2 · Conveyancing 7 · Copyright 1 · Courts martial 1 · Crime 16 · Crime - corporate fraud 4 · Defamation 3 · Employment 3 · Environment 2 · Equity, wills and trusts 7 · Family 6 · Family provision 12 · Housing 4 · Information technology 2 · Insolvency 5 · Intellectual property 2 · Landlord and tenant 7 · Licensing 3 · Medical negligence 5 · Partnerships 5 · Patents 1 · Pensions 1 · Personal injury 11 · Planning 1 · Probate and administration 6 · Professional negligence 9 · Sale and carriage of goods 2 · Tax - capital and income 1 · Trademarks 1

Chambers' facilities
Conference rooms, Disks accepted, Disabled access, Facilities for seminars and arbitrations.

Languages spoken
French

Additional information
Cobden House Chambers is comprised of the members of the former Hollins and Bridge Street Chambers and occupies the recently renovated premises of the old Manchester County Court. Chambers is able to offer a wide range of expertise by means of specialist departments. In addition, Chambers provides a fast and efficient service and a timetable for the completion of instructions can be given on delivery. A new brochure is available on request.

DEANS COURT CHAMBERS

Cumberland House, Crown Square,
Manchester M3 3HA
0161 834 4097
Fax: 0161 834 4805; DX 718155 Manchester 3
E-mail: deanscourt@compuserve.com
Out of hours telephone: 0860 159488/0802
882318

Chambers of H K Goddard QC
Clerk: Mrs Terry Creathorn

Annexe: Deans Court Chambers, 41-43 Market
Place, Preston, Lancashire PR1 1AH
Tel: 01772 555163
Fax: 01772 555941

Goddard, Keith QC *1959†*	**Denney**, Stuart *1982*
Henriques, Richard QC	**Trotman**, Timothy *1983*
1967†	**Smith**, Timothy *1982*
Grime, Stephen QC *1970†*	**Davies**, Russell *1983*
Machell, Raymond QC	**Bancroft**, Louise *1985*
1973†	**Heaton**, Frances *1985*
Stockdale, David QC *1975†*	**Humphries**, Paul *1986*
Fish, David QC *1973†*	**Brody**, Karen *1986*
Turner, Mark QC *1981‡*	**Hudson**, Christopher *1987*
Talbot, Kevin *1970†*	**Grace**, Jonathan *1989*
Duncan, John *1971*	**Grimshaw**, Nicholas *1988*
Bromley-Davenport, John	**Morgan**, Edward *1989*
1972†	**Grantham**, Andrew *1991*
Gregory, John *1972*	**Andrew**, Seamus *1991*
Atherton, Peter *1975‡*	**Ironfield**, Janet *1992*
Booth, Alan *1978‡*	**Burns**, Peter *1993*
Trippier, Ruth *1978*	**Savill**, Mark *1993*
Butler, Philip *1979*	**Clegg**, Sebastian *1994*
Sephton, Craig *1981*	**Boyle**, David *1996*
Field, Patrick *1981*	**McCann**, Simon *1996*

334 DEANSGATE

Manchester M3 4LY
0161 834 3767
Fax: 0161 839 6868

Chambers of Mr I W McIvor

> **See the** *Index of Languages Spoken* **in Part G**
> **to locate a chambers where a particular lan-**
> **guage is spoken, or find an individual who**
> **speaks a particular language.**

CHAMBERS OF JOHN HAND QC

9 St John Street, Manchester M3 4DN
0161 955 9000
Fax: 0161 955 9001/9004; DX 14326
Manchester
E-mail: ninesjs@gconnect.com

Chambers of J L Hand QC
Clerks: Graham Rogers, Graham Livesey,
Tony Morrissey, Paul Morecroft;
Administrator: J Eagle

Hand, John QC *1972†*	**Leeming**, Michael *1983*
Leeming, Ian QC *1970†*	**Irving**, Gillian *1984*
Carus, Roderick QC *1971†*	**Johnson**, Steven *1984*
Garside, Charles QC *1971†*	**Gilroy**, Paul *1985*
Horlock, Timothy QC *1981‡*	**Walker**, Jane *1987*
Portnoy, Leslie *1961†*	**Breen**, Carlo *1987*
Knight, Christopher *1966*	**Gilchrist**, David *1987*
Rigby, Terence *1971†*	**James**, Simon *1988*
Johnson, Michael *1971‡*	**Friesner**, David *1988*
Hull, Leslie *1972†*	**Little**, Ian *1989*
Riley, Christine *1974*	**Kennedy**, Christopher *1989*
Dowse, John *1973†*	**Bird**, Nigel *1991*
Cadwallader, Peter *1973*	**Howard**, Anthony *1992*
Temple, Simon *1977*	**Spencer**, Hannah *1993*
Parkin, Jonathan *1978*	**Wedderspoon**, Rachel *1993*
Murray, Michael *1979*	**Hamilton**, Jaime *1993*
Hinchliffe, Nicholas *1980*	**Sadiq**, Tariq *1993*
Clarke, Nicholas *1981*	**Darbyshire**, Robert *1995*
Grundy, Nigel *1983*	**McCluggage**, Brian *1995*

Chambers established: 1860
Opening times: 8.45 am-6.15 pm

**Types of work (and number of counsel
practising in that area if supplied)**
Agriculture 2 · Arbitration 2 · Asset finance 2
· Banking 6 · Bankruptcy 6 · Care proceedings
5 · Chancery (general) 7 · Chancery land law 7
· Charities 2 · Civil liberties 2 · Commercial
litigation 10 · Commercial property 6
· Common law (general) 22 · Company and
commercial 10 · Construction 6
· Conveyancing 6 · Copyright 4 · Corporate
finance 4 · Crime 12 · Crime - corporate fraud
7 · Defamation 2 · Discrimination 2
· Ecclesiastical 1 · Employment 12
· Environment 4 · Family 8 · Family provision 8
· Financial services 2 · Housing 4 · Immigration
1 · Insolvency 8 · Insurance 6 · Insurance/
reinsurance 4 · Intellectual property 4
· Landlord and tenant 8 · Licensing 2 · Local
government 3 · Medical negligence 8 · Mental
health 1 · Partnerships 8 · Patents 2 · Pensions
4 · Personal injury 17 · Probate and
administration 6 · Professional negligence 8
· Sale and carriage of goods 10 · Share options
2 · Tax - capital and income 1 · Tax -

† Recorder ‡ Assistant Recorder * Door Tenant

corporate 1 · Telecommunications 2 · Town and country planning 4

Chambers' facilities
Disks accepted, Disabled access, E-mail, Specialist brochures

Languages spoken
French, German, Hebrew, Italian, Punjabi, Spanish, Urdu

KENWORTHY'S CHAMBERS

83 Bridge Street, Manchester M3 2RF
0161 832 4036
Fax: 0161 832 0370; DX 718200 Manchester 3

Chambers of Francis Burns
Clerks: Joan Walter, Sarah Wright;
Administrator: David Wright

Burns, Francis *1971*	**Preston**, Darren *1991*
Heap, Walter *1963*	**Bassano**, Alaric *1993*
Pritchard, Rodney *1964*	**Usher**, Neil *1993*
Grennan, Barry *1977*	**Korol**, Kathryn *1996*
Lambert, Deborah *1977*	**Marrs**, Andrew *1995*
Cassidy, Patrick *1982*	**Littler**, Richard *1994*
Patel, Gita *1988*	**Smith**, Mark *1997*
Frith, Heather *1989*	

---

40 KING STREET

Manchester M2 6BA
0161 832 9082
Fax: 0161 835 2139; DX 718188 Manchester
E-mail: Kingst40@aol.com

Chambers of Philip Raynor QC
Clerks: William Brown, Colin Griffin, Michael Stubbs; Administrator: Gina Pinkerton

Raynor, Philip QC *1973*†	**Crean**, Anthony *1987*
Macleod, Nigel QC *1961*†	**Dunn**, Katherine *1987*
Hoggett, John QC *1969*†	**Hilton**, Simon *1987*
Tackaberry, John QC *1967*†	**Ashworth**, Fiona *1988*
Gilbart, Andrew QC *1972*†	**Stockley**, Ruth *1988*
Smith, Peter QC *1975*†	**Pritchett**, Stephen *1989*
Farley, Roger QC *1974*†	**Anderson**, Lesley *1989*
Sauvain, Stephen QC *1977*	**Campbell**, John *1990*
Patterson, Frances QC *1977*‡	**Singer**, Andrew *1990*
	Tucker, Paul *1990*
Owen, Eric *1969*	**Smith**, Matthew *1991*
Jackson, John *1970*	**Carter**, Martin *1992*
Halliday, Harold *1972*	**Harrison**, Sally *1992*
Pass, Geoffrey *1975*	**Horne**, Wilson *1992*
Evans, Alan *1978*	**Powis**, Lucy *1992*
Khan, Shokat *1979*	**Johnson**, Amanda *1992*
Booth, Michael *1981*	**Ghosh**, Julian *1993*
Fraser, Vincent *1981*	**Harper**, Mark *1993*
Manley, David *1981*	**Lander**, Richard *1993*
Barrett, John *1982*	**Pritchard**, Sarah *1993*
Chaisty, Paul *1982*	**Latimer**, Andrew *1995*
Gal, Sonia *1982*‡	**Berridge**, Elizabeth *1996*
Braslavsky, Nicholas *1983*	**Farrow**, Adrian *1997*
Halliwell, Mark *1985*	**Nowell**, Katie *1996*

Chambers established: 1946
Opening times: 8.30 am-7 pm

Types of work (and number of counsel practising in that area if supplied)
Administrative · Arbitration · Banking · Bankruptcy · Care proceedings · Chancery (general) · Chancery land law · Charities · Commercial · Commercial litigation · Common law (general) · Company and commercial · Construction · Consumer Law · Conveyancing · Copyright · Corporate finance · Crime · Crime - corporate fraud · Defamation · Discrimination · EC and

---

† Recorder ‡ Assistant Recorder * Door Tenant

competition law · Education · Employment · Environment · Equity, wills and trusts · Family · Family provision · Financial services · Housing · Immigration · Information technology · Insolvency · Insurance · Intellectual property · Landlord and tenant · Licensing · Local government · Medical negligence · Parliamentary · Partnerships · Pensions · Personal injury · Probate and administration · Professional negligence · Sale and carriage of goods · Tax - capital and income · Tax - corporate · Town and country planning

Chambers' facilities
Conference rooms, Disks accepted, E-mail, Link

Languages spoken
French, German, Norwegian, Urdu

Additional information

A wide range of specialist advisory and advocacy services, mainly: town and country planning, local government law and finance, administrative law, compulsory purchase and comprehension, highways law, environmental protection, and public health; commercial Chancery litigation, law of landlord and tenant, law of trusts, partnerships, intellectual property, and insolvency (corporate and individual); banking, wills and intestacy, civil liability, personal injury, professional liability, employment law, industrial law, and building disputes; consumer credit, sale of goods, family and matrimonial law, hire and purchase, licensing, and criminal law.

Members appear not only before the established courts, including Crown Office work, but also in front of a wide range of specialist tribunals which include the Lands Tribunal, planning, highway, compulsory purchase and other departmental inquiries, professional and disciplinary hearings, industrial tribunals and the data protection tribunal.

Additional specialisations: It is well recognised by chambers that clients often need advice on matters where specialist disciplines overlap and it is therefore able to provide a multi-disciplinary approach where this is necessary. Chambers has a heavy emphasis on planning and local government work. There is also a thriving Chancery and commercial section.

In addition, the following areas are also undertaken: judicial review, Parliamentary work, market law, crime, rating, immigration, data protection, trading standards, housing, and

markets and fairs. All members accept instructions under the direct professional access arrangements.

Publications: Members have contributed to numerous publications relating to their specialist fields.

Arbitrator: Sir Iain Glidewell

8 KING STREET CHAMBERS

8 King Street, Manchester M2 6AQ
0161 834 9560
Fax: 0161 834 2733 Gps 2&3; DX 14354 Manchester 1; ISDN: 0161 835 1402 X2

Chambers of Keith Armitage QC
Clerks: Peter Whitman, David Lea;
Practice manager: Peter Whitman

Armitage, K QC *1970*†	**Thompson,** Jonathan *1990*
Rowe, John QC *1960*†	**Wood,** Ian *1990*
Ryder, Ernest QC *1981*‡	**Hodgson,** Timothy *1991*
Rylands, Elizabeth *1973*‡	**Scorah,** Christopher *1991*
Eccles, David *1976*	**Connolly,** Joanne *1992*
Terry, Jeffrey *1976*	**Edge,** Timothy *1992*
McDermott, Gerard *1978*‡	**Naylor,** Kevin *1992*
Jess, Digby *1978*	**Barry,** Kirsten *1993*
Holmes, Philip *1980*	**Boyd,** James *1994*
Main, Peter *1981*	**Sandiford,** David *1995*
Foudy, Kim *1982*	**Collins,** Martin QC *1952**
Ahmed, Farooq *1983*	**Forwood,** Nicholas QC
Davies, Stephen *1985*	*1970**
Worrall, Shirley *1987*	**Worrall,** Anna QC *1959*†*
Forte, Mark *1989*	**Barling,** Gerald QC *1972*†*
Parr, John *1989*	**Prosser,** Kevin QC *1982**
Smith, Michael *1989*	

Chambers established: 1936
Opening times: 8.30 am-6.30 pm

Types of work (and number of counsel practising in that area if supplied)
Administrative 3 · Arbitration 4 · Banking 4 · Care proceedings 5 · Chancery (general) 2 · Chancery land law 4 · Commercial 8 · Common law (general) 20 · Company and commercial 8 · Competition 2 · Construction 4

· Courts martial 1 · Crime 5 · Crime - corporate fraud 2 · Discrimination 4 · EC and competition law 1 · Education 2 · Employment 4 · Environment 1 · Family 8 · Family provision 5 · Financial services 2 · Franchising 2 · Housing 5 · Insolvency 2 · Insurance 4 · Insurance/reinsurance 4 · Intellectual property 2 · Landlord and tenant 4 · Licensing 3 · Local government 4 · Medical negligence 9 · Mental health 1 · Partnerships 4 · Pensions 4 · Personal injury 17 · Probate and administration 1 · Professional negligence 9 · Sale and carriage of goods 2 · Share options 3

Chambers' facilities

Conference rooms, Video conferences, Disks accepted, Disabled access, E-mail, Website at 8kingstreet.co.uk

Additional information

Established over 50 years ago we are one of the leading Civil and Commercial Chambers outside London. Our strong generalist tradition is complemented by the experience of many of our members in specialist areas of work.

Areas of particular expertise:

· Commercial contract and building contact work
· Personal injury
· Professional negligence, building and medical negligence
· Insurance law
· All aspects of family and children law
· Employment law
· General commercial litigation

In addition, some members have considerable experience in company and related work, together with insolvency litigation. Two members are Fellows of the Institute of Arbitrators and another is admitted to the New York State Bar.

These chambers have the benefit of a video conferencing link, which gives direct access to other such facilities throughout the UK and abroad (including the Bar Council Offices in London).

The Bar Directory **is also available on the Internet at the following address:**

http://www.smlawpub-holborn.co.uk/bar

---

58 KING STREET CHAMBERS

1st Floor, Kingsgate House, 51–53 South King Street, Manchester M2 6DE
0161 831 7477
Fax: 0161 832 5645; DX 710297 Manchester 3

Chambers of Miss B A Lunt
Clerk: Fredric Greene

Lunt, Beverly *1977*	Fitzpatrick, Thomas *1988*
O'Shea, John *1983*	Holloran, Fiona *1989*
Dickinson, Jonathan *1986*	Matuk, Helen *1990*
Staunton, William *1986*	Carter, Richard *1990*
McMeekin, Ian *1987*	Swiffen, Guy *1991*
Dodd, Sara *1987*	Brady, Michael *1992*
Batra, Bunty *1988*	Treble, Paul *1994*
Rankin, Ciaran *1988*	Houghton, Lisa *1994*
Singh-Hayer, Bansa *1988*	Acton, Jayne *1996*

LANCASTER BUILDING CHAMBERS

77 Deansgate, Manchester M3 2BW
0161 661 4444
Fax: 0161 661 4445; DX 14488 Manchester 2

Chambers of Mr J Lambert

The UK College of Family Mediators Directory & Handbook 1998/99

• *provides expert commentary on family mediation training and professional development and includes contributions by leading family mediation professionals*

• *lists over 100 family mediation groups/services and over 950 individual family mediators by region and alphabetically*

• *gives details of all members and associates of the UK College of Family Mediators*

• *includes the UK College of Family Mediators Standards and Code of Practice*

• *gives details of all the family mediation bodies which make up the UK College of Family Mediators*

For more information call Sweet & Maxwell on 0171 449 1111

C

---

† Recorder ‡ Assistant Recorder * Door Tenant

LINCOLN HOUSE CHAMBERS

LINCOLN HOUSE CHAMBERS

5th Floor, Lincoln House, 1 Brazennose
Street, Manchester M2 5EL
0161 832 5701
Fax: 0161 832 0839; DX 14338 Manchester 1
E-mail: LincolnHouseChambers@link.org
Out of hours telephone: 0411 675887

Chambers of M Hussain QC
*Clerks: Andrew Weaver (Senior Clerk, Direct
Line: 0161 819 2506), Nick Buckley, Gary
Douglas, Pauline Holden, Mandy Hyde*

Hussain, Mukhtar QC *1971*†	**Nicholls**, Elizabeth *1984*
Webster, Alistair QC *1976*†	**Bloomer**, Charles *1985*
Gozem, Gaias QC *1972*†	**Watson**, Denis *1985*
Sumner, David *1963*†	**Goddard**, Suzanne *1986*
Gregory, James *1970*	**Baxter**, Bernadette *1987*
Platts, Robert *1973*†	**Wolstenholme**, Alan *1989*
Reid, Paul *1973*†	**Bowley**, Ivan *1990*
Conrad, Alan *1976*†	**Donnelly**, Kevin *1991*
Pickup, James *1976*†	**Simons**, Richard *1991*
Lasker, Jeremy *1976*	**Boyd**, Joe *1993*
Nuttall, Andrew *1978*	**Blackwell**, Katherine *1992*
Curran, Philip *1979*	**Roberts**, Lisa *1993*
Elias, Robert *1979*	**Tucker**, Nicholas *1993*
Tait, Campbell *1979*‡	**Holland**, Ricky *1994*
Wright, Peter *1981*	**Nawaz**, Mohammed *1995*
Davies, Hugh *1982*	**Priestley**, Roderick *1996*

LLOYDS HOUSE CHAMBERS

3rd Floor, 18 Lloyds House, Lloyd Street,
Manchester M2 5WA
0161 839 3371
Fax: 0161 832 3371; DX 14388 Manchester 1

Chambers of P R Marshall
Clerk: Hilary Smith

Marshall, Paul *1982*	**Jarvis**, Oliver *1992*
Backhouse, Roger QC *1965**	**Chapman**, Rennick *1997*
	McLusky, Nigel *1960**
Riza, Alper QC *1973*‡*	**McCulloch**, Ian *1951**
Leon, Marc *1988*	**Khan**, Ashraf *1960**
Csoka, Simon *1991*	**Harvey**, Colin *1975**

CHAMBERS OF IAN MACDONALD QC

Chambers of Ian Macdonald QC

Waldorf House, 2nd Floor, 5 Cooper Street,
Manchester M2 2FW
0161 236 1840
Fax: 0161 236 0929; DX 715637 Manchester 2
Out of hours telephone: 07970 721337

Chambers of Ian Macdonald QC
*Clerks: David Skinner (Senior Clerk), Rachel
Jones (Junior Clerk)*

Macdonald, Ian QC *1963*	**Martin**, John *1977*
Barlow, Mark *1992*	**Plimmer**, Melanie *1996*
Edusei, Francis *1989*	**Robinson**, Simon *1991*
Firth, Georgina *1995*	**Weatherby**, Pete *1992*
Fullwood, Adam *1996*	**Weston**, Amanda *1995*
Kaur, Rani *1993*	

MANCHESTER HOUSE CHAMBERS

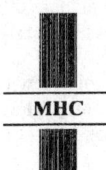

MHC

Manchester House Chambers

18-22 Bridge Street, Manchester M3 3BZ
0161 834 7007
Fax: 0161 834 3462; DX 718153 Manchester 3

Chambers of J D S Wishart
Clerks: Teresa Thiele, Susan Mercer

Also at: St Ignations Square, Preston,
Lancashire PR1 1TT

Wishart, John *1974*	**Brogan**, Michael *1990*
Kirsten, Adrian *1962*	**Mawdsley**, Matthew *1991*
Stuttard, Arthur *1967*	**Sechiari**, Helen *1991*
McKee, Hugh *1983*	**Sabry**, Karim *1992*
McKenna, Brian *1983*	**Bailey**, Graham *1993*
Jackson, Wayne *1984*	**Judge**, Lisa *1993*
Sheridan, Paul *1984*	**Clark**, Andrew *1994*
Fireman, Mark *1986*	**Reynolds**, Gary *1994*
Brennand, Timothy *1987*	**Jones**, Brian *1994*
Vaughan, Simon *1989*	**Woods**, Rachael *1992*

MERCHANT CHAMBERS

MERCHANT CHAMBERS

1 North Parade, Parsonage Gardens,
Manchester M3 2NH
0161 839 7070
Fax: 0161 839 7111; DX 14319 Manchester 1

Chambers of David Berkley
Clerk: Alastair Campbell

Berkley, David *1979*	**Rule**, Jonathan *1993*
Berragan, Neil *1982*	**Feetham**, Daniel *1994*
Cogley, Stephen *1984*	**Brochwicz-Lewinski**, Stefan
Fisher, Catherine *1990*	*1995*
Noble, Andrew *1992*	

**Types of work (and number of counsel
practising in that area if supplied)**
Banking · Bankruptcy · Chancery (general)
· Chancery land law · Commercial
· Commercial property · Company and
commercial · Construction · Copyright
· Corporate finance · Employment · Equity,
wills and trusts · Financial services
· Franchising · Housing · Insolvency · Insurance
· Insurance/reinsurance · Intellectual property
· Landlord and tenant · Medical negligence
· Partnerships · Professional negligence · Sale
and carriage of goods · Share options

Chambers' facilities
Conference rooms, Disks accepted

Languages spoken
French, Hebrew, Polish, Spanish

OLD COLONY HOUSE

6 South King Street, Manchester M2 6DQ
0161 834 4364
Fax: 0161 832 9149; DX 718160 Manchester

Chambers of P McDonald
Clerk: L F Dooley

McDonald, Paul *1975*	**Williamson**, Patrick *1989*
Booth, Roger *1966*	**Toal**, David *1990*
Klonin, Susan *1970*	**Cohen**, Joseph *1992*
Brown, Roger *1976*	**Rodikis**, Joanna *1993*
Longworth, Antony *1978*	**Storrie**, Timothy *1993*
Parkinson, Frederick *1981*	**Lemmy**, Michael *1994*
Maxwell, John *1985*	**Higgins**, Paul *1996*
Landale, Tina *1988*	**Holland**, Charlotte *1996*
Duke, Stuart *1989*	

PALL MALL CHAMBERS

Executive House, 40A Young Street,
Manchester M3 3FT
0161 832 3373/4
Fax: 0161 832 4399; DX 20821 Wilmslow

Chambers of Mr P L Crichton-Gold

PARSONAGE CHAMBERS

5th Floor, 3 The Parsonage, Manchester
M3 2HW
0161 833 1996
Fax: 0161 832 5027

Chambers of Mr M J Holt

C

PEEL COURT CHAMBERS

45 Hardman Street, Manchester M3 3PL
0161 832 3791
Fax: 0161 835 3054; DX 14320 Manchester
Out of hours telephone: 0961 998689

Chambers of J M Shorrock QC
Clerks: Mr Shell Edmonds, Mr David Haley

Shorrock, Michael QC 1966†	Pearce, Richard 1985
Morris, Anthony QC 1970†	Grout-Smith, Jeremy 1986
Openshaw, Peter QC 1970†	Taylor, Julian 1986
Bentham, Howard QC 1970†	Fryman, Neil 1989
Simmonds, Nicholas 1969	Knowles, Graham 1990
Richardson, Paul 1972	Smith, Rachel 1990
Meadowcroft, Stephen 1973	Walsh, Martin 1990
Russell, Anthony 1974	Baker, William 1991
Marks, Richard 1975†	Ainsworth, Mark 1992
Lever, Bernard 1975†	Blackshaw, Henry 1993
O'Byrne, Andrew 1978	Orme, Richard 1993
Brereton, Fiorella 1979	Evans, Claire 1994
Wallace, Adrian 1979	Lloyd-Smith, Rebecca 1994
Long, Andrew 1981	Morris, June 1995
Melton, Christopher 1982	McBride, Gavin 1996
Pickup, David 1984	Mazzag, Anthony 1996
	Green, Alan 1973*
	Sherry, Michael 1978*

QUEEN'S CHAMBERS

5 John Dalton Street, Manchester M2 6ET
0161 834 6875/4738
Fax: 0161 834 8557; DX 718182 Manchester 3

Chambers of Mark Lamberty
Clerk: Terence Mylchreest (Senior Clerk)

Annexe: 4 Camden Place, Preston, Lancashire
PR1 3JL
Tel: 01772 828300
Fax: 01772 825380

Lamberty, Mark 1970	Thompson, Patrick 1990
Bailey, John 1966	Godfrey, Christopher 1993
Stalker, Monica 1967	Hayton, Michael 1993
Green, Roger 1972	Brown, Charles 1982
Buckley, Peter 1972	Rothery, Peter 1994
Shannon, Eric 1974	Courtney, Nicholas 1990
Ryder, Timothy 1977	McCullough, Judith 1991
Bradshaw, Howard 1977	Potts, Warren 1995
Holmes, Paul 1979	Prudhoe, Timothy 1994
Mercer, David 1980	Horgan, Peter 1993
Osman, Robert 1974	Pearson, Wendy 1996
Hennell, Gordon 1982	Wood, Sir John 1950*
Barker, Steven 1983	Laing, Paula 1991*
Grocott, Susan 1986	Paonessa, Laura 1993*
Hobson, Heather 1987	

Chambers established: 1879
Opening times: 8.30 am-6.30 pm

Types of work (and number of counsel practising in that area if supplied)
Care proceedings 5 · Chancery (general) · Commercial · Common law (general) 10 · Company and commercial 2 · Consumer Law · Crime 16 · Defamation 2 · Discrimination 4 · Employment 4 · Family 6 · Family provision 6 · Insolvency 3 · Intellectual property 1 · Landlord and tenant 4 · Licensing 1 · Medical negligence 5 · Partnerships · Personal injury 10 · Professional negligence 5 · Sale and carriage of goods 6 · Town and country planning 2

Chambers' facilities
Annexe in Preston available for conferences

Languages spoken
French

ST JAMES'S CHAMBERS

ST. JAMES'S CHAMBERS

68 Quay Street, Manchester M3 3EJ
0161 834 7000
Fax: 0161 834 2341; DX 14350 Manchester 1
E-mail: 106241.2625@compuserve.com
Out of hours telephone: 0161 643 2630

Chambers of R A Sterling
Clerk: Stephen Diggles

Sterling, Robert 1970	Wheeldon, Sarah 1990
Elleray, Anthony QC 1977‡	Tankel, Ruth 1990
Wood, Percy 1960	Cook, Christopher 1990
Mundy, Robert 1966	Maynard-Connor, Giles 1992
Searle, Barrie 1975	
Porter, David 1980	Wills, Janice 1991
Lyons, Timothy 1980	Hurd, James 1994
Cawson, Mark 1982	Calvert, David 1995
Mulholland, Michael 1976	Fryer-Spedding, James 1994
Binns, David 1983	
Foster, Ian 1988	Rubin, Anthony 1960*
Wilson-Barnes, Lucy 1989	Jaconelli, Joseph 1972*
Cannan, Jonathan 1989	

Chambers established: 1800
Opening times: 7.30 am-6.30 pm

† Recorder ‡ Assistant Recorder * Door Tenant

Types of work (and number of counsel practising in that area if supplied)
Administrative 2 · Agriculture 5 · Arbitration 3 · Aviation 1 · Banking 6 · Bankruptcy 10 · Care proceedings 8 · Chancery (general) 12 · Chancery land law 10 · Charities 10 · Civil liberties 1 · Commercial 14 · Commercial property 8 · Common land 5 · Common law (general) 13 · Company and commercial 15 · Construction 2 · Consumer Law 3 · Conveyancing 3 · Copyright 5 · Crime 7 · Crime - corporate fraud 2 · Defamation 2 · Discrimination 3 · Education 2 · Employment 3 · Environment 1 · Equity, wills and trusts 12 · Family 11 · Family provision 11 · Financial services 5 · Franchising 1 · Housing 1 · Information technology 1 · Insolvency 10 · Insurance 4 · Intellectual property 4 · Landlord and tenant 10 · Licensing 2 · Medical negligence 6 · Mental health 1 · Partnerships 13 · Patents 1 · Pensions 2 · Personal injury 9 · Probate and administration 7 · Professional negligence 15 · Sale and carriage of goods 7 · Share options 2 · Tax - capital and income 2 · Tax - corporate 2 · Telecommunications 1 · Trademarks 2

Chambers' facilities
Conference rooms, Disks accepted, E-mail

Languages spoken
French, German, Russian, Spanish

The Law Society's Directory of Expert Witnesses 1999

- *lists over 3,500 expert witnesses*

- *all entrants agree to comply with The Law Society's Code of Practice and provide two professional references*

- *contains information on choosing and instructing an expert witness*

- *includes 1,700+ specialists in areas of expertise*

- *provides an alphabetical index to assist in finding detailed terms*

- *also available on CD-ROM*

For more information call Sweet & Maxwell on 0171 449 1111

---

18 ST JOHN STREET

Manchester M3 4EA
0161 278 1800
Fax: 0161 835 2051; DX 728854 Manchester 4

Chambers of R C Klevan QC
Clerk: Michael Farrell (Senior Clerk); Administrator: Jo Kelly

Klevan, Rodney QC *1966*†	Fewtrell, Nicholas *1977*
Carlisle of Bucklow, Lord QC *1954*†*	Laprell, Mark *1979*‡
	Heaton, David *1983*
Grindrod, Helen QC *1966**	Vardon, Richard *1985*
Brennan, Daniel QC *1967*†*	Williams, Brian *1986*
Foster, Jonathan QC *1970*†	Brown, Mandy *1987*
Birkett, Peter QC *1972*†	Sasse, Toby *1988*
Steiger, Martin QC *1969*†	Birtles, Samantha *1989*
Edis, Andrew QC *1980*‡	Poole, Nigel *1989*
Blake, Andrew *1971*†	Tythcott, Elisabeth *1989*
Forrest, Alastair *1972*†	Simpson, Raquel *1990*
Hedgeland, Roger *1972*‡	Benson, Mark *1992*
Caldwell, Jennifer *1973*	Booth, Joy *1992*
Dockery, Paul *1973*	Harrison, Susan *1993*
O'Brien, Paul *1974*‡	Broadhurst, Simon *1994*
Wigglesworth, Raymond *1974*†	Garvin, Michael *1994*
	Williams, Sarah *1995*
Diamond, Christopher *1975*	Kilvington, Simon *1995*
Stout, Roger *1976*	Brody, Saul *1996*
McEwan, Malcolm *1976*	Moore, Andrew *1996*

24A ST JOHN STREET

Manchester M3 4DF
0161 833 9628
Fax: 0161 834 0243; DX 710301 Manchester 3

Chambers of P V Chambers
Clerks: Lynn Wallwork, Mark Latham

Chambers, Paul *1973*	Crabtree, Simon *1988*
McNeill, John *1974*	Wilson, John *1988*
Coppel, Yvonne *1976*‡	Partington, Lisa *1989*
McClure, John *1975*	Lavery, Michael *1990*
Dennett, Angelina *1980*	Simpson, Alexandra *1989*
Bruce, David *1982*	Rhind, Mark *1989*
Campbell, Graham *1982*	Holt, Abigail *1993*
Harrison, Peter *1983*	Barr, Finola *1994*
Khawar, Aftab *1983*	Sutton, Ruth *1994*
Harrison, J Keith *1983*	Eyers, Anthony *1994*
Chaplin, John *1986*	Douglas, Stephen *1994*
Gray, Richard *1986*	Lawson, Andrew *1995*
Davitt, Paula *1988*	Smith, Andrew *1996*
Smith, Peter *1988*	

---

† Recorder ‡ Assistant Recorder * Door Tenant

28 ST JOHN STREET

28.

St. John
Street

Manchester M3 4DJ
0161 834 8418
Fax: 0161 835 3929; DX 728861 Manchester 4
E-mail: clerk@28stjohnst.co.uk

Chambers of Anthony Rumbelow
Clerks: Jack Pickles, Christopher Ronan;
Practice manager: Bridget Knight

Rumbelow, Anthony QC 1967†	Hunter, Winston 1985
Gee, Anthony QC 1972†	Vickers, Guy 1986
Chruszcz, Charles QC 1973†	Rowley, James 1987
	Clayton, Nigel 1987
	Hayden, Anthony 1987
Kushner, Lindsey QC 1974†	Humphries, David 1988
Redfern, Michael QC 1970‡	Eastwood, Charles 1988
Goldstone, Clement QC 1971†	Samuels, Jeffrey 1988
	Grundy, Clare 1989
Freedman, Clive QC 1978	Ross, Sally-Ann 1990
Cattan, Philip 1970†	Taylor, Paul 1985
Humphry, Richard 1972	Rawlinson, Michael 1991
Lowcock, Andrew 1973†	Wright, Alastair 1991
Goode, Rowena 1974†	Kloss, Diana 1986
Phillips, John 1976†	Norton, Richard 1992
Wallwork, Bernard 1976‡	Case, Magdalen 1992
Rothwell, Stephen 1977	Tyrrell, Richard 1993
Platts, Graham 1978	Mathieson, Guy 1993
Grundy, Philip 1980‡	Kloss, Alexander 1993
Jones, John 1981	Gumbs, Annette 1994
Singleton, Sarah 1983	Crilley, Darrel 1996

Chambers established: 1930
Opening times: 8 am-6 pm

Types of work (and number of counsel practising in that area if supplied)
Care proceedings 17 · Chancery (general) 2 · Common law (general) 25 · Company and commercial 15 · Conveyancing 1 · Crime 26 · Crime - corporate fraud 10 · EC and competition law 1 · Employment 9 · Environment 4 · Family 17 · Family provision 17 · Landlord and tenant 7 · Licensing 4 · Medical negligence 21 · Pensions 1 · Personal injury 25 · Private international 1 · Professional negligence 21 · Tax - capital and income 1 · Town and country planning 2

Chambers' facilities
Conference rooms, Video conferences, Disks accepted, Disabled access

Languages spoken
French, Spanish

Fees policy
Details of fees and/or hourly rates will be provided upon inquiry and will vary depending upon the seniority of counsel.

ST JOHN'S CHAMBERS

2 St John's Street, Manchester M3 4DT
0161 832 1633
Fax: 0161 834 3048

Chambers of Ms L M Cox QC

YOUNG STREET CHAMBERS

38 Young Street, Manchester M3 3FT
0161 833 0489
Fax: 0161 835 3938; DX 25583 Manchester 5
E-mail: clerks@young-st-chambers.com
URL: http://www.clerks@young-st-chambers.com
Out of hours telephone: 0161 834 6588

Chambers of Miss Lesley Newton
Clerks: Mr Peter Wright (Senior Clerk), Mr Nicholas Geary (Criminal Clerk), Miss Fiona McKay (Civil and Family Clerk), Krissy Juttla (Junior Clerk), Denise Nield (Fees Clerk)

Newton, Lesley 1977‡	Fox, Andrew 1990
Limb, Christopher 1975	Ford, Mark 1991
Elliott, Christopher 1974	Blakey, Michael 1989
Jay, Grenville 1975	McIvor, Helen 1992
Andrews, Philip 1977	Rouse, Philip 1993
Hernandez, David 1976‡	Warnock, Ceri 1993
Coveney, Christopher 1976	Myers, Benjamin 1994
Huffer, Ian 1979	Rowley, Karl 1994
Nadim, Ahmed 1982	Manasse, Paul 1995
Greene, Maurice 1982	Bland, Carolyn 1995
Stansby, Alexandra 1985	Delaney, Rory 1996
Healing, Yvonne 1987	Tyler, Paula 1997
Lawton, Paul 1987	Hesford, Stephen 1981*

OXDALE

2 Hoby Road, Ragdale, Melton Mowbray, Leics LE14 3PE
01664 434787

Chambers of Miss K H Brown

WEST LODGE FARM

Wrotham Road, Meopham, Kent DA13 0QG
01474 812280
Fax: 01474 814759; DX 51254 Longfield
Out of hours telephone: 01474 812280

Chambers of Karen Gough
Administrator: K J Douglas

Also at: Arbitration Chambers, 22 Willes Road,
London NW5 3DS

Gough, Karen *1983*

BAKER STREET CHAMBERS

BAKER STREET

C   H   A   M   B   E   R   S

*9 Baker Street, Middlesbrough, Cleveland
TS1 2LF*
01642 873873
Fax: 01642 873877; DX 60591 Middlesbrough

Chambers of Mr Gerard Ford
Clerks: Rachel Grimwood, Barbara Hudson

Ford, Gerard *1986*	**McMinn,** Valerie *1990*
Constable, John *1972*	**Bradshaw,** Ian *1992*
Dodds, Shaun *1990*	**Robson,** Nicholas *1994*
Newcombe, Paul *1991*	**Dryden,** Shaun *1994*
Sabiston, Peter *1992*	**Fagan,** Catherine *1993*
Gillette, John *1990*	**Crean,** Mary *1996*
Constantine, Stephen *1992*	

CLEVELAND CHAMBERS

*63-65 Borough Road, Middlesbrough,
Cleveland TS1 3AA*
01642 226036
Fax: 01642 245987; DX 60549 Middlesbrough

Chambers of Mr G B Stewart

FOUNTAIN CHAMBERS

*Cleveland Business Centre, 1 Watson Street,
Middlesbrough, Cleveland TS1 2RQ*
01642 217037
Fax: 01642 232275; DX 711700
Middlesbrough 11

Chambers of Peter J B Armstrong
Clerk: Robert F Minns

Armstrong, Peter *1974†*	**Gilbert,** Robert *1986*
Davey, Geoffrey *1954†*	**Perry,** Amanda *1987*
Denny, Robin *1969*	**Burke,** Patricia *1990*
Miller, Keith *1973†*	**Crouch,** Andrew *1990*
Merritt, Richard *1981*	**Waugh,** Jane *1992*
Pinkney, Giles *1978**	**Finlay,** Andrew *1993*
Roberts, Timothy *1978†*	**Trousdale,** Malcolm *1993*
Ashurst, Stephen *1979‡*	**Wadoodi,** Aisha *1994*
Sherwin, Deborah *1979‡*	**Bennett,** Richard *1996*
Hunt, Roderick *1981*	**Turton,** Robin *1996*
Hill, James *1984*	

**Types of work (and number of counsel
practising in that area if supplied)**
Administrative · Agriculture 3 · Care
proceedings 8 · Chancery (general) 8
· Chancery land law 2 · Commercial litigation
6 · Commercial property 3 · Common law
(general) 10 · Company and commercial 2
· Construction 4 · Conveyancing · Courts
martial 4 · Crime · Crime - corporate fraud 6
· Employment 4 · Environment 3 · Equity, wills
and trusts 3 · Family 9 · Family provision
· Housing 2 · Insolvency 2 · Landlord and
tenant 2 · Licensing 5 · Local government 5
· Medical negligence 6 · Personal injury 6
· Professional negligence 2 · Sale and carriage
of goods · Town and country planning 1

Chambers' facilities
Conference rooms, Video conferences,
Disabled access

Languages spoken
Urdu

Additional information

Established in 1969 with two members in Baker
Street, Middlesbrough, Fountain Chambers has
expanded steadily and now offers a
comprehensive advocacy and advising service
throughout the North Eastern Circuit.

Chambers operates from modern
accommodation adjoining Teeside Combined
Courts, with a substantial library, conference
rooms and facilities for disabled clients. Video
conferences or conferences outside chambers
can be arranged whenever more convenient.

Fountain Chambers has established a strong reputation not only in general common law, personal injury, family and criminal work but also in specialist areas, such as local government, planning and disciplinary proceedings, not often available in provincial chambers. Our clerks will be pleased to advise on practitioners suited for particular cases. Some members offer direct professional access.

Six members of Fountain Chambers sit as Recorders, Assistant Recorders and Chairmen of Tribunals.

YORK HOUSE

Borough Road, Middlesbrough, Cleveland TS1 2HJ
01642 213000
Fax: 01642 213003; DX 60524 Middlesbrough

Chambers of S Lightwing
Clerk: Pam Haw

Lightwing, Stuart *1972*	Hall, Derek *1994*
Swinhoe, Luke *1987*	Richards, Janine *1995*

MILTON KEYNES CHAMBERS

27 Broad Street, Milton Keynes, N Buckinghamshire MK16 0AN
01908 217857
Fax: 01908 217857
E-mail: Neil_Cawley@compuserve.com
URL: http://ourworld.compuserve.com/homepages/Neil_Cawley
Other comms: E-Dx: neil_rl_cawley@link.org
Out of hours telephone: 01908 217857

Chambers of Mr Neil Cawley
Clerks: Joanne Haigh, Donna Parham

Also at: 55 Temple Chambers, Temple Avenue, London EC4Y 0HP
Tel: 0171 353 7400
Fax: 0171 353 7100

Cawley, Neil *1992*

HIGHER COMBE

Hawkcombe, Porlock, Minehead, Somerset TA24 8LP
01643 862722
Fax: 01643 862871; DX 17405 Minehead

Chambers of Miss S E Cotter

39 PARK AVENUE

Mitcham, Surrey CR4 2ER
0181 648 1684
Fax: 0181 715 6615

Chambers of Mr M A Syed

LAVENHAM CHAMBERS

Rookery Farm, Near Lavenham, Suffolk CO10 0BJ
01787 248247
Fax: 01787 247846

Chambers of Miss S A Gratwicke

CHAMBERS OF RICHARD BLOOMFIELD

2 Lansdowne Place, Gosforth, Newcastle Upon Tyne NE3 1HR
0191 285 4664
Fax: 0191 285 6377; DX 60362 GOSFORTH

Chambers of Mr R W Bloomfield

BROAD CHARE

33 Broad Chare, Newcastle upon Tyne NE1 3DQ
0191 232 0541
Fax: 0191 261 0043; DX 61001 Newcastle

Chambers of E A Elliot
Clerk: Brian Bell

Chadwin, James QC *1958†*	McKenzie, Lesley *1983*
Cosgrove, Patrick QC *1976†*	Moulder, Pauline *1983*
Batty, Paul QC *1975†*	O'Sullivan, John *1984*
Harper, James *1957*	Richardson, Anne *1986*
Such, Frederick *1960†*	Rowlands, David *1988*
Harte, David *1967*	Styles, Mark *1988*
Duff, Euan *1973*	Gumsley, Carl *1989*
Harmer, Christine *1973*	Brown, James *1990*
Hewitt, Timothy *1973†*	Temple, Michelle *1992*
Mitchell, Ronald *1973†*	Anderson, Stanley *1993*
Elliott, Eric *1974†*	Lugg, Elizabeth *1994*
Bolton, Beatrice *1975‡*	Lowe, William QC *1972†**
Hawks, Anthony *1975*	Craven, Richard *1976**
Horner, Robin *1975*	Bradley, Sally *1978**
Moir, Judith *1978†*	Elsey, Roger *1977*
Dorman-O'Gowan, Christopher *1979*	Clemitson, Julie *1991*
Armstrong, Kester *1982*	Smith, Eleanor *1992*
Kennerley, Ian *1983*	Robinson, Sara *1994*

Opening times: 9 am-5.30 pm

† Recorder ‡ Assistant Recorder * Door Tenant

Types of work (and number of counsel practising in that area if supplied)
Arbitration 1 · Bankruptcy 5 · Care proceedings 12 · Chancery (general) 5 · Chancery land law 5 · Common law (general) 13 · Copyright 1 · Courts martial 1 · Crime 17 · Defamation 1 · Ecclesiastical 1 · Employment 4 · Environment 1 · Equity, wills and trusts 5 · Family 12 · Family provision 12 · Insolvency 5 · Landlord and tenant 5 · Licensing 7 · Medical negligence 5 · Personal injury 7 · Sale and carriage of goods 2

Chambers' facilities
Conference rooms

CATHEDRAL CHAMBERS

Milburn House, Dean Street, Newcastle upon Tyne NE1 1LE
0191 232 1311
Fax: 0191 232 1422; DX 61277 Newcastle 1
Clerk: Kelly Forster

Addison, Neil *1976*	**Attala,** Etienne *1994*
Dixon, Ian *1982*	**Manasse,** Anne *1994*
Brown, David *1993*	**Martin,** David *1994*

International Arbitration Law Review

Editorial Board includes:

Alan Redfern	*Neil Kaplan*
Toby Landau	*David Rivkin*
Dr Julian Lew	*Martin Hunter*
Nigel Rawding	*Matthieu de Boisseson*

The new International Arbitration Law Review *brings together for the first time all the requirements of an arbitration practitioner.*

- *up-to-the-minute news on legislation and decisions*

- *expert commentary on worldwide trends and issues from a panel of top arbitration specialists*

- *detailed case summaries and analysis of the cases making the headlines*

- *covers all major jurisdictions worldwide*

To order a subscription or a free sample copy call Sweet & Maxwell on 0171 449 1111

ENTERPRISE CHAMBERS

65 Quayside, Newcastle upon Tyne NE1 3DS
0191 222 3344
Fax: 0191 222 3340; DX 61134 Newcastle upon Tyne 1

Chambers of Mr G A Mann QC
Clerks: Barry Clayton, Tony Armstrong, Dennis Peck; Newcastle Receptionists: Elaine Brown and Emma Sutherland

Mann, Anthony QC *1974*	**Barker,** James *1984*
Levy, Benjamin *1956*	**Jack,** Adrian *1986*
Jennings, Timothy *1962*	**Groves,** Hugo *1980*
Halpern, David *1978*	**Atherton,** Ian *1988*
Morgan, Charles *1978*	**Henry,** Alastair *1998*
Hutton, Caroline *1979*	**Garcia-Miller,** Laura *1989*
James, Michael *1976*	**Bhaloo,** Zia *1990*
Rosen Peacocke, Teresa *1982*	**Pickering,** James *1991*
	McKinnell, Soraya *1991*
Ife, Linden *1982*	**Jory,** Hugh *1992*
McAllister, Ann *1982*	**Williamson,** Bridget *1993*
Arden, Peter *1983*	**Richardson,** Sarah *1993*
Zelin, Geoffrey *1984*	**Hardwick,** Matthew *1994*
Baker, Jacqueline *1985*	**Francis,** Edward *1995*
Gerald, Nigel *1985*	**Mauger,** Shanti *1996*

MILBURN HOUSE CHAMBERS

'A' Floor, Milburn House, Dean Street, Newcastle upon Tyne NE1 1LE
0191 230 5511
Fax: 0191 230 5544; DX 716640 Newcastle 20
E-mail: milburnhousechambers@btinternet.com
URL: btinternet.com/~milburnhousechambers/mhc.htm

Chambers of Paul Cape
Clerk: Dorothy Toase

Cape, Paul *1990*	**Woodwark,** Jane *1995*

NEW COURT CHAMBERS

3 Broad Chare, Newcastle upon Tyne
NE1 3DQ
0191 232 1980
Fax: 0191 232 3730; DX 61012 Newcastle

Chambers of D E H Robson QC
Clerk: F Hughes; Practice manager: B Dickson

Robson, David QC *1965*†	**Walsh**, Peter *1982*
Thorn, Roger QC *1970*‡	**Moreland**, Penelope *1986*
Moore, Roger *1969*	**Richardson**, Paul *1986*
Parkin, Timothy *1971*	**Burns**, Alexander *1988*
Gatland, Glenn *1972*	**Menon**, Harigovind *1989*
Evans, John *1973*‡	**Taylor**, Susan *1987*
Hodson, Michael *1977*	**Cartmell**, Nicholas *1990*
Adams, James *1978**	**Aitken**, John *1984*
Graham, Ian *1978*	**Brodrick**, William *1991*
Callan, David *1979*	**Smith**, Julian *1991*
Cross, Geoffrey *1981*	**Carr**, Jonathan *1990*
Prince, Christopher *1981*	**Adkin**, James *1992*
Freedman, Jeremy *1982*	**Atkinson**, Elizabeth *1994*
Kramer, Philip *1982*	**Choudhury**, Nafeesa *1990*
Schofield, Peter *1982*	**Moran**, Thomas *1996*
Patton, Robin *1983*	**Wadge**, Richard *1997*
Woodcock, Robert *1978*	**Sweeting**, Margaret *1996*

Types of work (and number of counsel practising in that area if supplied)
Administrative 2 · Arbitration 5 · Aviation 1 · Bankruptcy 5 · Care proceedings 7 · Commercial litigation 3 · Courts martial 1 · Crime 22 · Ecclesiastical 1 · Employment 2 · Equity, wills and trusts 2 · Family 5 · Family provision 5 · Immigration 1 · Insolvency 6 · Landlord and tenant 4 · Licensing 4 · Medical negligence 4 · Personal injury 8 · Professional negligence 5

Chambers' facilities
Conference rooms, Disabled access

Languages spoken
French, German, Italian, Spanish

Additional information

Members of New Court Chambers offer expertise in a wide variety of fields of practice.

Principal specialisations are: commercial law including company law, contractual disputes and credit and securities; criminal law (civilian courts and courts martial); family law dealing with all areas from child custody and care disputes to financial claims in divorce and against estates; corporate and personal insolvency; personal injury (injuries at work, on the road and in the procedure to be adopted when pursuing this type of litigation); professional negligence work is undertaken against the medical profession, engineers, architects and surveyors, as well as against the legal profession itself. All aspects of landlord and tenant work are dealt with as is arbitration law, aviation law, Official Referees' business, revenue law and wills and probate.

Individual members also have experience in other areas of law and Frank Hughes will be happy to advise solicitors on the selection of appropriate counsel.

PLOWDEN BUILDINGS

1 Jesmond Dene Terrace, Newcastle upon Tyne NE2 2ET
0191 281 2096

Chambers of Mr G W Lowe QC

The UK College of Family Mediators Directory & Handbook 1998/99

- *provides expert commentary on family mediation training and professional development and includes contributions by leading family mediation professionals*

- *lists over 100 family mediation groups/services and over 950 individual family mediators by region and alphabetically*

- *gives details of all members and associates of the UK College of Family Mediators*

- *includes the UK College of Family Mediators Standards and Code of Practice*

- *gives details of all the family mediation bodies which make up the UK College of Family Mediators*

For more information call Sweet & Maxwell on 0171 449 1111

---

† Recorder ‡ Assistant Recorder * Door Tenant

TRINITY CHAMBERS

9-12 Trinity Chare, Quayside, Newcastle upon Tyne NE1 3DF
0191 232 1927
Fax: 0191 232 7975; DX 61185 Newcastle

Chambers of J T Milford QC
Clerks: C Hands (Senior Clerk), Philip Alexanders (Criminal Clerk), Andrea Goodwin (Civil Clerk), Christopher Swann (Civil Clerk)

Milford, John QC *1969†*	**Hudson**, Rachel *1985*
Hedworth, Alan QC *1975†*	**McCrae**, Fiona *1986*
Kelly, Charles *1965*	**Goodwin**, Caroline *1988*
Duffield, Stephen *1969†*	**Routledge**, Shaun *1988*
Hargrove, Jeremy *1970*	**Cooper**, Roger *1989*
Knox, Christopher *1974†*	**Gittins**, Timothy *1990*
Lowe, John *1976*	**Oliver**, Crispin *1990*
Vane, Christopher *1976*	**Adams**, Robert *1993*
Forster, Brian *1977†*	**Ditchfield**, Anthony *1993*
Smith, Duncan *1979‡*	**Stonor**, Nicholas *1993**
Wilkinson, Michael *1979*	**Scott Bell**, Rosalind *1993*
Sloan, Paul *1981*	**Gilbert**, Julia *1994*
Smart, Jacqueline *1981*	**Pryke**, Stuart *1994*
Wood, Simon *1981*	**Holland**, Charles *1994*
Richardson, James *1982*	**Woolrich**, Sarah *1994*
Spain, Timothy *1983*	**Caulfield**, Paul *1996*

Opening times: 8.30 am-6 pm

Types of work (and number of counsel practising in that area if supplied)
Admiralty 1 · Arbitration 5 · Banking 6 · Bankruptcy 6 · Care proceedings 7 · Chancery (general) 4 · Chancery land law 4 · Charities 1 · Commercial litigation 10 · Common land 1 · Common law (general) 17 · Company and commercial 5 · Construction 5 · Conveyancing 3 · Crime 16 · Employment 4 · Equity, wills and trusts 4 · Family 9 · Family provision 9 · Housing 6 · Insolvency 6 · Insurance 6 · Landlord and tenant 8 · Licensing 4 · Local government 1 · Medical negligence 4 · Partnerships 8 · Personal injury 10 · Probate and administration 4 · Professional negligence 6 · Sale and carriage of goods 6 · Town and country planning 1

Chambers' facilities
Conference rooms, Disks accepted, Disabled access

Fees policy
Up to five years call £50-85, Five to ten years call £75-120, Ten years call £120+. QC £200-250.

WESTGATE CHAMBERS

67a Westgate Road, Newcastle upon Tyne NE1 1SG
0191 261 4407/232 9785
Fax: 0191 222 1845; DX 61044 Newcastle

Chambers of I J Dawson
Clerks: Shaun Murtagh, Lynn Davis; Administrator: Stan Zych

Dawson, Ian *1971*	**Davis**, Anthony *1986*
Braithwaite, Antony *1971*	**Walling**, Philip *1986*
Rich, Charles *1972*	**Mallett**, Sarah *1988*
Pinkney, Giles *1978**	**O'Brien**, Joseph *1989*
Hunter, Geoffrey *1979*	**Boothroyd**, Susan *1990*
Finch, Thomas *1981*	**Jarron**, Stephanie *1990*
Mark, Brian *1981*	**Middleton**, Claire *1991*
Mason, David *1984*	**Hare**, William *1994*
Selwyn-Sharpe, Richard *1985*	**Peacock**, Nicholas *1996*

NEWPORT CHAMBERS

12 Clytha Park Road, Newport, Gwent NP9 47L
01633 267403/255855
Fax: 01633 253441; DX 33208 Newport

Chambers of Mr H L A Roberts

22 ALBION PLACE

Northampton NN1 1UD
01604 636271
Fax: 01604 232931; DX 12464 Northampton
Out of hours telephone: 0973 922124

Chambers of P Hollingworth
Clerks: Victoria Clent, Angela Kilsby

Hollingworth, Peter *1993*
Tedd, Rex QC *1970**
Crouch, Stephen *1982*
Ashton, Roy *1954†*
Savvides, Maria *1986*
Willis, Elizabeth *1986*
Sutton, Clive *1987*
Deegan, Lawrence *1989*
Lynch, Terry *1989*
Yeung, Stuart *1989*
Burns, Terence *1990*

Ellis, Michael *1993*
Holloway, Richard *1993*
Abbott, Mary *1994*
Whittaker, Ian *1994*
Smith, Nicola *1994*
Williams, Barbara *1995*
Willans, David *1995*
Gow, Ben *1994*
Downs, Simon *1996*
Aslett, Pepin *1996*

CHAMBERS OF KAREN R BOYES

*P.O.Box 458, Brixworth, Northampton
NN6 9ZT*
01604 882942
Fax: 01604 882942; DX 16052
Kingsthorpe(N'ton)

Chambers of Mrs K R Boyes

CHARTLANDS CHAMBERS

3 St Giles Terrace, Northampton NN1 2BN
01604 603322
Fax: 01604 603388; DX 12408 Northampton 1
Out of hours telephone: 01536 521859

Chambers of J E Page
Clerk: Andrew Davies

Page, Jane *1982*
Van Besouw, Eufron *1988*
Tapper, Paul *1991*
Pinkham, Joy *1993*

Slade Jones, Robin *1993*
Knight, Christopher *1994*
Robinson, Matthew *1994*
MacKillop, Norman *1994*

WESTGATE CHAMBERS

*4 Copse Close, Northwood, Middlesex
HA6 2XG*
01923 823671
Fax: 01923 821890

Chambers of Mr H B Hargrave

EAST ANGLIAN CHAMBERS

57 London Street, Norwich, Norfolk NR2 1HL
01603 617351
Fax: 01603 633589; DX 5213 Norwich
Out of hours telephone: 0585 100461

Chambers of Roderick Newton
*Clerk: Stephen Collis (Senior Clerk);
Administrator: Carol Bull*

Also at: 52 North Hill, Essex, CO1 1PY and 5
Museum Street, Ipswich, IP1 1HQ

Akast, John *1968*
Wardlow, John *1971†*
Pearce, Marcus *1972*
Wain, Peter *1972*
Marsden, Andrew *1975‡*
Bryant, Caroline *1976*
Levett, Martyn *1978*
McLoughlin, Timothy *1978*
Miller, Celia *1978*
Pugh, David *1978*
Hamey, John *1979*
Sinclair, Graham *1979*
Kefford, Anthony *1980*
Brooke-Smith, John *1981*
Newton, Roderick *1982‡*
Parnell, Graham *1982*
Redmayne, Simon *1982*
Davies, Jane *1983*
Lane, Michael *1983*
Vass, Hugh *1983*
Shadarevian, Paul *1984*
Cox, Lindsay *1984*
Bettle, Janet *1985*
Dyble, Steven *1986*
Bate, Anthony *1987*
Degel, Rebecca *1987*
Elcombe, Nicholas *1987*

Mandil-Wade, Rosalyne *1988*
Richards, David *1989*
Greaves, Ann *1989*
Greenwood, John *1990*
Jackson, Andrew *1990*
Bell, Marika *1991*
Bundell, Katharine *1991*
Smith, Raymond *1991*
Barratt, Dominic *1992*
Parry-Jones, Carole *1992*
Rippon, Amanda *1993*
Walsh, Patricia *1993*
Hanlon, Jacqueline *1994*
Phelps, Mark *1994*
Walter, Francesca *1994*
Kelly, Richard *1994*
de Mounteney, Jonathan *1994*
Wheetman, Alan *1995*
Moore, Katharine *1995*
Freeman, Sally *1995*
Leigh, Samantha *1995*
Durr, Jude *1995*
Wilson, David *1996*
Baruah, Fiona *1996*
Morgans, John *1996*

The Supreme Court Practice 1999

* *the most authoritative title on Civil Court Practice and Procedure*
* *available in book and CD-ROM formats*

Phone Sweet & Maxwell on 0171 449 1111 to order your copy

† Recorder ‡ Assistant Recorder * Door Tenant

OCTAGON HOUSE

19 Colegate, Norwich, Norfolk NR3 1AT
01603 623186
Fax: 01603 760519; DX 5249 Norwich 1
E-mail: octagon@netmatters.co.uk

Chambers of A G N Lindqvist, G R Ayers
Clerk: Corinne Ashton;
Administrator: Stephen Unsworth

Annexe of: 12 New Square, Lincoln's Inn,
London WC2A 3SW
Tel: 0171 419 1212
Fax: 0171 419 1313

Lindqvist, Andrew *1968*	**Fletcher**, Christopher *1984*
Ayers, Guy *1979*	**Khalil**, Karim *1984**
Sunnucks, James *1950**	**Aldous**, Robert *1985*
Ross Martyn, John *1969†**	**Caddick**, Nicholas *1986**
Farmer, John *1970**	**Potts**, Richard *1991*
Harrison, Roger *1970**	**Gowen**, Matthew *1992*
Kellett, Charles *1971**	**Oliver**, Andrew *1993*
Townshend, Timothy *1972*	**Prinn**, Helen *1993*
James, Ian *1981*	**Barber**, Stuart *1979**
Richards, Jeremy *1981‡*	**Clare**, Michael *1986*
Butterworth, Paul *1982*	

SACKVILLE CHAMBERS

Sackville Place, 44–48 Magdalen Street,
Norwich, Norfolk NR3 1JU
01603 613516
Fax: 01603 620799
Out of hours telephone: 0961 868981

Chambers of S Ridley
Clerk: Richard Nunn

Ridley, Stephen *1977*	**Mantell-Sayer**, Peter *1992*
Gilbertson, Helen *1993*	**Wood**, Richard *1995*

> **Use the *Types of Work* listings in Parts A and B to locate chambers and individual barristers who specialise in particular areas of work.**

70 CHARLECOTE DRIVE

Wollaton, Nottingham NG8 2SB
0115 928 8901
Fax: 0115 928 8901

Chambers of Mrs U R Sood

NO. 1 HIGH PAVEMENT CHAMBERS

Nottingham NG1 1HF
0115 941 8218
Fax: 0115 941 8240; DX 10168 Nottingham

Chambers of J B Milmo QC
Clerks: David Duric, Nigel Wragg

Milmo, John QC *1966**	**Campbell-Moffat**, Audrey *1987*
Joyce, Peter QC *1968†*	
Warren, John QC *1968†*	**Eley**, Jonathan *1987*
Walmsley, Peter *1964*	**Evans**, Michael *1988*
Pearce, Frederick *1975‡*	**Stockwell**, Clive *1988*
Rafferty, Stuart *1975*	**Geeson**, Christopher *1989*
Wigoder, Lewis *1977*	**Thatcher**, Richard *1989*
Burgess, John *1978‡*	**Auty**, Michael *1990*
Napthine, Guy *1979*	**Easteal**, Andrew *1990*
Mann, Paul *1980*	**McNamara**, James *1990*
Dickinson, Gregory *1981‡*	**Mukherjee**, Avik *1990*
Elwick, Bryan *1981*	**Munro**, Sarah *1990*
Smith, Shaun *1981*	**Hargreaves**, Katie *1991*
Bhatia, Balraj *1982*	**King**, Paul *1992*
Palmer, Timothy *1982*	**Pritchard**, Dawn *1992*
Ballentyne, Errol *1983*	**Coupland**, Steven *1993*
Napthine, Godfrey *1983*	**Gosnell**, Steven *1995*
Shant, Nirmal *1984*	**Ahya**, Sonal *1995*

C

---

† Recorder ‡ Assistant Recorder * Door Tenant

KING CHARLES HOUSE

Standard Hill, Nottingham NG1 6FX
0115 941 8851
Fax: 0115 941 4169; DX 10042 Nottingham
E-mail: clerks@kch.co.uk

Chambers of W Everard
Clerks: Geoff Rotherham, Russell Hobbs

Everard, William 1973‡
O'Connell, Michael 1966
Dumbill, Eric 1971
Fitzpatrick, Ross 1972
Stobart, John 1974
Bridge, Rowena 1975
Howlett, James 1980
Buchanan, Vivien 1981
Lowne, Stephen 1981
Toombs, Richard 1983
Dhadli, Perminder 1984
Cranny, Amanda 1984
Gallagher, Patrick 1984
Salmon, Kevin 1984
Bradley, Caroline 1985
Zaman, Mohammed 1985
Cranmer-Brown, Michael 1986
Van Der Zwart, Mark 1988
Way, Ian 1988
Dee, Jonathon 1989
Munt, Alastair 1989
Jackson, Adrian 1990
McNeilis, Sharron 1990
Jones, Richard 1991
Morris, Jane 1991
Janes, Jeremy 1992
Leonard, Edna 1992
Straw, Jonathan 1992
Grimshaw, Elizabeth 1993
Warburton, Julie 1993
Kirwin, Tracey 1995
Wylie, Neil 1996
Hale, Grace 1998

ROPEWALK CHAMBERS

24 The Ropewalk, Nottingham NG1 5EF
0115 947 2581
Fax: 0115 947 6532; DX 10060 Nottingham 17
E-mail: clerk@ropewalk.co.uk
URL: http://www.ropewalk.co.uk

Chambers of R Maxwell QC
Clerk: David Austin

Maxwell, Richard QC 1968†
Woodward, William QC 1964†
Goldstaub, Anthony QC 1972‡
McLaren, Ian QC 1962†
Owen, Robert QC 1977‡
Payne, Richard 1964
Jarand, Godfrey 1965
Machin, Graham 1965
Burns, Richard 1967†
Swain, Richard 1969‡
Berrisford, Anthony 1972
Herbert, Douglas 1973‡
Bridge, Prof Michael 1975*
Beresford, Stephen 1976
Gash, Simon 1977
Hampton, Alison 1977‡
Beard, Simon 1980
Adams, Jayne 1982
Coe, Rosalind 1983
Din, Soofi 1984
Nolan, Dominic 1985
Clark, Bryony 1985
Prestwich, Andrew 1986
Limb, Patrick 1987
Seabrook, Richard 1987
Turton, Philip 1989
Stewart, Toby 1989
Boora, Jinder 1990
Mitchell, Jonathan 1992
Cox, Jason 1992
Davies, Deborah 1993
Hodgson, Elizabeth 1993
Mulvein, Helen 1993
Gregory, Richard 1993
McCowan, Hester 1995

ST MARY'S CHAMBERS

50 High Pavement, Nottingham NG1 1HW
0115 950 3503
Fax: 0115 958 3060; DX 10036 Nottingham
E-mail: clerks@smc.law.co.uk

Chambers of Colin Anderson
Clerk: D J Wilson

Anderson, Colin 1973
Hamilton, Andrew 1970‡
Jose, Calder 1971‡
Butler, Christopher 1972‡
Lloyd-Davies, Andrew 1973
Philo, Noel 1975
Rhys, Owen 1976
Page, Nigel 1976
Smart, David 1977
Lea, Jeremy 1978
Watson, Hilary 1979
Rogers, Mark 1980
Hodges, Victoria 1980
Reynolds, Adrian 1982
Hedley, Richard 1983
Michell, Michael 1984
Farquhar, Stuart 1985
Hale, Sean 1988
Egbuna, Robert 1988
Gilead, Beryl 1989
Casey, Mairin 1989
Mulrennan, Maria 1990
Hett, James 1991
Lody, Stuart 1991
Claxton, Judith 1991
McNamara, Andrew 1992
Macfarlane, Alison 1993
Wainwright, Patrick 1994
Soubry, Anna 1995
Eckersley, Simon 1995
Knight, Sarah 1996
Rowley, Rachel 1997

MERRIEMORE COTTAGE

Sawbridge, Nr Rugby, Warwickshire CV23 8BB
01788 891832
Fax: 01788 891832; DX 29403 Rugby

Chambers of Mrs K Hayter

1 ALFRED STREET

High Street, Oxford OX1 4EH
01865 793736
Fax: 01865 790760; DX 4302 Oxford

Chambers of M P Parroy QC
Clerks: Russell Porter, David Snook

Annexe of: 3 Paper Buildings, 1st Floor,
Temple, London EC4Y 7EU
Tel: 0171 583 8055
Fax: 0171 353 6271 (2 lines)

Parroy, Michael QC *1969*	**Branigan**, Kate *1984*
Harris, David QC *1969*†	**O'Hara**, Sarah *1984*
Hughes, Peter QC *1971*	**Chamberlain**, Francis *1985*
Jones, Stewart QC *1972*†	**Sanderson**, David *1985*
Aspinall, John QC *1971*	**Bailey**, Russell *1985*
Hebron, Harold *1960*	**Parker**, Christopher *1986*
Parrish, Samuel *1962*	**Hudson**, Elisabeth *1987*
Trevethan, Susan *1967*	**Letman**, Paul *1987*
Haynes, John *1968*	**Rowland**, Nicholas *1988*
Swinstead, David *1970*	**Kelly**, Patricia *1988*
Hope, Derwin *1970*†	**Woolgar**, Dermot *1988*
Norman, Michael *1971*†	**Hester**, Paul *1989*
Ward, Anthony *1971*	**Opperman**, Guy *1989*
Curran, Leo *1972*	**Bradbury**, Timothy *1989*
Jennings, Peter *1972*	**Kilpatrick**, Jean *1990*
Coleman, Anthony *1973*	**Buckley-Clarke**, Amanda
Stephenson, Ben *1973*	*1991*
Litchfield, Linda *1974*	**Ross**, Iain *1991*
Bartlett, David *1975*†	**Steenson**, David *1991*
Richardson, Garth *1975*	**Sweeney**, Christian *1992*
Tyson, Richard *1975*‡	**Kelly**, Marie *1992*
Henry, Peter *1977*	**Kirkpatrick**, Krystyna *1992*
Mitchell, Nigel *1978*	**Weir**, Robert *1992*
Seed, Nigel *1978*‡	**Fitzharris**, Ginnette *1993*
Kent, Peter *1978*	**Earle**, Judy *1994*
Partridge, Ian *1979*	**Geraghty**, Sarah *1994*
Grey, Robert *1979*	**Reid**, David *1994*
Leviseur, Nicholas *1979*	**Williams**, Ben *1994*
Coombes, Timothy *1980*	**Hughes**, Melanie *1995*
Cairnes, Paul *1980*	**McIlroy**, David *1995*
Edge, Ian *1981*	**Strachan**, Elaine *1995*
Strutt, Martin *1981*	**Case**, Richard *1996*
Lickley, Nigel *1983*	**Gourley**, Claire *1996*
Lomas, Mark *1983*	**Wood**, Graham *1979*‡*
Maccabe, Irvine *1983*	**Ball**, Sally *1989**

EASTERN CHAMBERS

*Badgers Bottom, Dysons Wood Lane, Tokers
Green, Oxford RG4 9EY*
0118 972 3722
Fax: 0118 972 1190

Chambers of Miss H M McGregor

HARCOURT CHAMBERS

*Churchill House, 3 St Aldate's Courtyard, St
Aldate's, Oxford OX1 1BN*
01865 791559
Fax: 01865 791585; DX 96453 Oxford 4

Chambers of Mr H W P Eccles QC

KING'S BENCH CHAMBERS

32 Beaumont Street, Oxford OX1 2NP
01865 311066
Fax: 01865 311077; DX 4318 Oxford
E-mail: clerks@kbc-oxford.law.co.uk
Other comms: Lix: Oxf 003

Chambers of Graeme Williams QC
*Clerks: Stephen Buckingham, Kevin Kelly;
Administrator: Penny McFall*

Annexe of: 13 King's Bench Walk, Temple,
London EC4Y 7EN
Tel: 0171 353 7204
Fax: 0171 583 0252

Williams, Graeme QC *1959*†	**Glennie**, Andrew *1982*
Baughan, Julian QC *1967*†	**Williams**, A *1983*
Ellis, Roger QC *1962*	**Coode**, Jonathan *1984*
Ashton, David *1962*	**Vickery**, Neil *1985*
Dawson, Alexander *1969*†	**Moore**, Neil *1986*
McGeorge, Anthony *1969*	**Gibbons**, Sarah *1987*
Lamb, Robert *1973*	**Blake**, Arthur *1988*
Richardson, David *1973*†	**Cramsie**, Sinclair *1988*
Gibbons, James *1974*	**Quirke**, Gerard *1988*
Goodwin, Deirdre *1974*	**Hay**, Fiona *1989*
Hughes, Simon *1974*	**Pote**, Andrew *1983*
Grant, David *1975*‡	**Higgins**, Adrian *1990*
Reid, Paul *1975*	**Walters**, Edmund *1991*
Tracy Forster, Jane *1975*	**Wenlock**, Heather *1991*
Bright, David *1976*†	**Walters**, Vivian *1991*
Draycott, Simon *1977*‡	**Majumdar**, Shantanu *1992*
Lambie, Donald *1978*	**Panesar**, Deshpal *1993*
Brough, Alasdair *1979*	**Chan**, Susan *1994*
Daly, Nigel *1979*	**Mitchell**, Paul *1994*
Syfret, Nicholas *1979*	

Chambers established: 1971
Opening times: 8 am-6 pm

---

† Recorder ‡ Assistant Recorder * Door Tenant

Types of work (and number of counsel practising in that area if supplied)

Administrative 2 · Arbitration 2 · Banking 2 · Bankruptcy 7 · Care proceedings 4 · Chancery (general) 5 · Chancery land law 3 · Civil liberties 2 · Club law 2 · Commercial litigation 4 · Common law (general) 18 · Company and commercial 6 · Construction 6 · Consumer Law 5 · Conveyancing 2 · Copyright 2 · Crime 15 · Crime - corporate fraud 4 · Defamation 1 · Employment 14 · Family 6 · Family provision 6 · Financial services 2 · Housing 2 · Immigration 2 · Insolvency 8 · Insurance 3 · Intellectual property 2 · Landlord and tenant 7 · Licensing 3 · Medical negligence 6 · Mental health 2 · Partnerships 2 · Personal injury 14 · Private international 4 · Professional negligence 8 · Sale and carriage of goods 11

Languages spoken
Cantonese, French, Italian, Portuguese

Fees policy
Up to five years call £35-75, Five to ten years call £50-125, Ten years call £75-250. Fees are charged on an hourly basis, by reference to the complexity and value of the matter, and the seniority of counsel. The senior clerks will be pleased to discuss the level of fees in advance of work commencing on any matter.

28 WESTERN ROAD

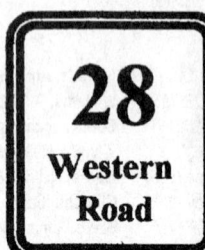

Oxford OX1 4LG
01865 204911
Fax: 01865 721692
Out of hours telephone: 01865 204911

Chambers of R A J Purdie
Practice manager: Elisabeth Calman

Purdie, Robert *1979*

PERIVALE CHAMBERS

15 Colwyn Avenue, Perivale, Middlesex UB6 8JY
0181 998 1935/081 248 0246
Fax: 0181 998 1935

Chambers of Mr S Ahmed

2 SALVIA GARDENS

Perivale, Middlesex UB6 7PG
0181 997 9905
Fax: 0181 997 9905

Chambers of Mr Y U R K Suri

FENNERS CHAMBERS

8-12 Priestgate, Peterborough PE1 1JA
01733 562030
Fax: 01733 343660; DX 12314 Peterborough 1

Chambers of Lindsay Davies
Clerks: Mark Springham, Louis Rankin, Ian Spencer; Administrator: Jane Longhurst

Also at: Fenners Chambers, 3 Madingley Road, Cambridge CB3 0EE
Tel: 01223 368761

Davies, Lindsay *1975‡*	Gordon-Saker, Liza *1982*
Wheeler, Kenneth *1956**	Hughes, Meryl *1987*
King, Peter *1970*	Litherland, Rebecca *1987*
Yelton, Michael *1972†*	Foxwell, George *1987*
Hawkesworth, Gareth *1972†*	Wilson, Alasdair *1988*
Jones, Geraint *1972*	Beasley-Murray, Caroline *1988*
Gore, Andrew *1973*	
Franklin, Stephen *1974*	Pithers, Clive *1989*
Espley, Susan *1976*	Meakin, Timothy *1989*
Pointon, Caroline *1976*	Taylor, Andrew *1989*
Heald, Oliver *1977*	Clark, Hazel *1990*
Tattersall, Simon *1977*	Wilson, James *1991*
Leigh-Morgan, Paul *1978*	Horton, Caroline *1993*
Brown, T C E *1980*	Myatt, Charles *1993*
Hollow, Paul *1981*	Ferguson, Katharine *1995*
Bridge, Stuart *1981*	Josling, William *1995*
Collier, Martin *1982*	Lobo, Matthew *1995*

See the *Index of Languages Spoken* **in Part G to locate a chambers where a particular language is spoken, or find an individual who speaks a particular language.**

REGENCY CHAMBERS
B A R R I S T E R S

Regency Chambers is a general common law chambers offering a broad based expertise in all areas of civil, family and criminal law.

In particular, members of chambers can provide a comprehensive service in the following areas:

Civil — personal injury and medical negligence, professional negligence, employment, licensing, landlord & tenant, personal and real property, contract, commercial litigation, consumer credit and planning;

Family — ancillary relief, public and private law, children act applications;

Crime — defence and prosecution work is undertaken.

A brochure is available on request.

Please also see entry.

Regency Chambers is located in the city centre of Peterborough and Cambridge. Conference facilities are available in both locations. In addition, conferences can easily be arranged at Solicitors' offices. Chambers' work is concentrated in East Anglia but members regularly travel to London and the Midlands.

Chambers has a fresh outlook and a continuing policy of expansion to meet increasing demand. Our aims are to provide a friendly and efficient service, relying on its members' range and depth of expertise. A full and frank appraisal of individuals may be obtained from the Senior Clerk. Chambers operates a flexible and practical approach to fees. The Senior Clerk will be happy to discuss a fee and provide guidance to suit each client and each piece of work, including conditional fees, where appropriate.

REGENCY CHAMBERS

Cathedral Square, Peterborough PE1 1XW
01733 315215
Fax: 01733 315851; DX 12349 Peterborough 1

Chambers of Raymond Croxon QC
Clerk: Paul Wright (Senior Clerk)

Also at: Cambridge

Croxon, Raymond QC *1960*	**Ellis**, Christopher *1991*
Martignetti, Ian *1990*	**Bennet**, Pauline *1991*
Tettenborn, Andrew *1988*	**Fender**, Carl *1994*
Thind, Anita *1988*	**Akerman**, Kate *1994*
Elliott, Margot *1989*	**Roberts**, Sir Samuel Bt *1972*
Buckle, Jonathan *1990*	**Leigh**, Kevin *1986**

19 CHESTNUT DRIVE

Pinner, Middlesex HA5 1LX
0181 866 7603/933 2382
Fax: 0181 866 7603

Chambers of Mr K A Quddus

DEVON CHAMBERS

3 St Andrew Street, Plymouth, Devon PL1 2AH
01752 661659
Fax: 01752 601346; DX 8290 Plymouth 2

Chambers of R A Hough
Clerk: Mr Peter Kerslake

Hough, Richard *1979*	**Taylor**, Rupert *1990*
Bush, John *1964*	**Welsh**, James *1994*
Down, Susan *1984*	**Bailey**, Elizabeth *1995*
Telford, Peter *1985*	**Mann**, Daya *1995*
Taylor, Ian *1986*	**Hinton**, Neil *1997*
Linford, Robert *1987*	

KING'S BENCH CHAMBERS

115 North Hill, Plymouth PL4 8JY
01752 221551
Fax: 01752 664379; DX 8237 Plymouth

Chambers of Mr A M Donne QC

C

TWIN FIRS

P.O.Box 32, Talygarn, Pontyclun, South Wales CF72 9BY
01443 229850
Fax: 01443 222252

Chambers of Mr R N J Everest

WINDSOR CHAMBERS

2 Penuel Lane, Pontypridd, Mid Glamorgan, South Wales CF37 4UF
01443 402067
Fax: 01443 491399

Chambers of Miss M J M Withers

EATON HOUSE

1st Floor, 4 Eaton Road, Branksome Park, Poole, Dorset BH13 6DG
01202 766301/768068

Chambers of Mr R J Massey

GUILDHALL CHAMBERS PORTSMOUTH

Prudential Buildings, 16 Guildhall Walk, Portsmouth, Hampshire PO1 2DE
01705 752400
Fax: 01705 753100; DX 2225 Portsmouth 1

Chambers of Mr E B P de Vries

HAMPSHIRE CHAMBERS

Malton House, 24 Hampshire Terrace, Portsmouth, Hampshire PO1 2QF
01705 826636
Fax: 01705 297101; DX 2270 Portsmouth

Chambers of Dr P M McCormick
Clerks: Miss Joanne Gutteridge, Mrs Julie Morgan (Assistant Clerk)

McCormick, Paul *1983*

The Bar Directory **is also available on the Internet at the following address:**
http://www.smlawpub-holborn.co.uk/bar

PORTSMOUTH BARRISTERS' CHAMBERS

Victory House, 7 Bellevue Terrace, Portsmouth, Hampshire PO5 3AT
01705 831292
Fax: 01705 291262; DX 2239 Portsmouth
E-mail: clerks@portsmouthbar.com
Out of hours telephone: 01705 553783

Chambers of A J Parsons
Clerk: Jackie Morrison

Parsons, Andrew *1985*	Booth, Martyn *1996*
Brookes, Lincoln *1992*	Warren, Sasha *1996*
Concannon, Timothy *1993*	Russell, Guy *1985**
McGrath, Simon *1995*	

Chambers established: 1990

Types of work (and number of counsel practising in that area if supplied)
Banking 1 · Bankruptcy 2 · Chancery (general) 2 · Chancery land law 2 · Commercial litigation 3 · Common law (general) 6 · Company and commercial 2 · Construction 1 · Crime 3 · Employment 3 · Equity, wills and trusts 2 · Family 6 · Family provision 6 · Financial services 1 · Insolvency 2 · Insurance 1 · Intellectual property 2 · Landlord and tenant 4 · Medical negligence 2 · Partnerships 4 · Pensions 1 · Personal injury 6 · Professional negligence 2 · Sale and carriage of goods 4 · Shipping, admiralty 1

Chambers' facilities
Conference rooms, Disks accepted, Conferences regularly undertaken in the late evening and at weekends

Languages spoken
French, German

Fees policy

Fees will be negotiated with the clerk depending on the case, but as a general guide: under three years call up to £90 per hour, three to five years call up to £150 per hour, five to ten years up to £200 per hour. All fees are negotiable with the clerk to chambers. By prior arrangement work may be sent to us without obligation to be considered by a member of chambers and if no fee can be agreed returned without charge.

SOUTHSEA CHAMBERS

PO Box 148, Southsea, Portsmouth, Hampshire PO5 2TU
01705 291261
Fax: 01705 753152; DX 2266 Portsmouth

Chambers of Mr G H Garner

4 CAMDEN PLACE

Preston, Lancashire PR1 3JL
01772 828300
Fax: 01772 825380; DX 17156 Preston 1

Chambers of Mark Lamberty
Clerk: Terence Mylchreest

Annexe of: Queen's Chambers, 5 John Dalton Street, Manchester M2 6ET
Tel: 0161 834 6875/4738
Fax: 0161 834 8557

Lamberty, Mark *1970*	Hobson, Heather *1987*
Bailey, John *1966*	Thompson, Patrick *1990*
Stalker, Monica *1967*	Godfrey, Christopher *1993*
Buckley, Peter *1972*	Hayton, Michael *1993*
Green, Roger *1972*	Brown, Charles *1982*
Osman, Robert *1974*	Rothery, Peter *1994*
Shannon, Eric *1974*	Courtney, Nicholas *1990*
Bradshaw, Howard *1977*	McCullough, Judith *1991*
Ryder, Timothy *1977*	Prudhoe, Timothy *1994*
Holmes, Paul *1979*	Potts, Warren *1995*
Mercer, David *1980*	Horgan, Peter *1993*
Hennell, Gordon *1982*	Pearson, Wendy *1996*
Barker, Steven *1983*	Wood, Sir John *1950**
Grocott, Susan *1986*	Laing, Paula *1991**

DEANS COURT CHAMBERS

41-43 Market Place, Preston, Lancashire PR1 1AH
01772 555163
Fax: 01772 555941; DX 713129 Preston 11
E-mail: deanscourt@compuserve.com
Out of hours telephone: 0860 159488/0802 882318

Chambers of H K Goddard QC
Clerk: Mrs Terry Creathorn

Annexe of: Deans Court Chambers, Cumberland House, Crown Square, Manchester M3 3HA
Tel: 0161 834 4097
Fax: 0161 834 4805

Goddard, Keith QC *1959†*	Denney, Stuart *1982*
Henriques, Richard QC *1967†*	Smith, Timothy *1982*
	Trotman, Timothy *1983*
Grime, Stephen QC *1970†*	Davies, Russell *1983*
Machell, Raymond QC *1973†*	Bancroft, Louise *1985*
	Heaton, Frances *1985*
Stockdale, David QC *1975†*	Humphries, Paul *1986*
Fish, David QC *1973†*	Brody, Karen *1986*
Talbot, Kevin *1970†*	Hudson, Christopher *1987*
Duncan, John *1971*	Grace, Jonathan *1989*
Bromley-Davenport, John *1972†*	Grimshaw, Nicholas *1988*
	Morgan, Edward *1989*
Gregory, John *1972*	Grantham, Andrew *1991*
Atherton, Peter *1975‡*	Andrew, Seamus *1991*
Booth, Alan *1978‡*	Ironfield, Janet *1992*
Trippier, Ruth *1978*	Burns, Peter *1993*
Butler, Philip *1979*	Savill, Mark *1993*
Turner, Mark QC *1981‡*	Clegg, Sebastian *1994*
Sephton, Craig *1981*	Boyle, David *1996*
Field, Patrick *1981*	McCann, Simon *1996*

NEW BAILEY CHAMBERS

10 Lawson Street, Preston, Lancashire PR1 2QT
01772 258 087
Fax: 01772 880 100; DX 710050 Preston 10

Chambers of Miss Patricia Bailey
Clerks: Savannah Biswas, John Stewart

Bailey, Patricia *1969*	Alty, Andrew *1992*
Thomas, Keith *1969*	McGinty, Robert *1994*
Wood, Graeme *1968**	Watson, Sharon *1994*
Robertson, James *1991**	Lowson, Norman *1989*
Wright, Yasmin *1990*	Smith, Robert *1995*
Musaheb, Kevin *1990*	Whitehurst, Ian *1994*
Dacre, Ian *1991*	McCarthy, William *1996*
Dable, Jeremy *1987*	Mustakim, Abdul *1997*

C

---

† Recorder ‡ Assistant Recorder * Door Tenant

15 WINCKLEY SQUARE

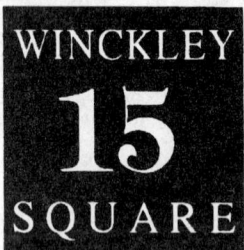

Preston, Lancashire PR1 3JJ
01772 252 828
Fax: 01772 258 520; DX 17110 Preston 1
E-mail: clerks@winckleysq.demon.co.uk
URL: http://www.winckley.sq.demon.co.uk

Chambers of R S Dodds
*Clerks: Michael Jones, Nicholas Haley;
Practice manager: John Schofield*

Dodds, Stephen *1976*	Anderson, Peter *1988*
Bonney, James QC *1975**	Henry, Bruce *1988*
Baldwin, Roger *1969*	Johnson, Kathryn *1989*
Newell, Simon *1973*	Bowcock, Samantha *1990*
Watson, Barbara *1973*	Burrows, Simon *1990*
Crawford, Robert *1976*	Creaner, Paul *1990*
Kennedy, Nicholas *1977*	Harvey, Louise *1991*
Haworth, Richard *1978*	Mitchell, Marie *1991*
White, Timothy *1978*	Cornah, Emma *1992*
Williams, Glyn *1981*	Livesey, Fraser *1992*
Cross, Jane *1982*	Taylor, Julie *1992*
Cross, Anthony *1982*	Whyatt, Michael *1992*
Hart, Paul *1982*	Buchan, Jonathan *1994*
Kenny, David *1982*	Hackett, Martin *1995*
Hague, Paul *1983*	Blakey, Lee *1995*
Woodward, John *1984*	Davis, Paul *1996*
Hunt, Richard *1985*	Dyer, Jacob *1995*
Stuart, Mark *1985*	Gillott, Paul *1996*
Bennett, Richard *1986*	

140 CHOLMELEY ROAD

Reading, Berkshire RG1 3LR
01189 676318
Fax: 01189 814138; DX 4078 Reading 1

Chambers of Miss C A Gordon

DR JOHNSON'S CHAMBERS

The Atrium Court, Apex Plaza, Reading, Berkshire RG1 1AX
01189 254221
Fax: 01189 560380; DX 117880 Reading, Apex Plaza

Chambers of Lord Thomas of Gresford OBE QC
Clerk: John Francis

Annexe of: 1 Dr Johnson's Buildings, Ground Floor, Temple, London EC4Y 7AX
Tel: 0171 353 9328
Fax: 0171 353 4410

Thomas of Gresford, Lord QC *1967*	Anderson, Brendan *1985*
	McIlwain, Sylvester *1985*
Digney, Peter *1968*	Rowlands, Rhys *1986*
Lewis-Jones, Meirion *1971**	Habboo, Camille *1987*
Britton, Robert *1973†*	Mailer, Clifford *1987*
Little, Geoffrey *1973‡**	Wignall, Gordon *1987*
Sabido, John *1976*	Gill, Pamilla *1989*
Dean, James *1977*	Levinson, Justin *1994*
Granville, Alexander *1978*	Mackie, Jeannie *1995*
Oldland, Jennifer *1978*	Brodie, Graham *1989*
Spencer, Robin *1978‡**	Donnabella, Rosemary *1991*
Chambers, Michael *1980*	Shipman, Anthony *1992*
Clark, Dingle *1981*	Pollock, Hilary *1993*
Newdick, Christopher *1983*	Hickman, Claire *1994*
Wernham, Stewart *1984*	Kane, Adam *1993*

10 LAUNCESTON AVENUE

Caversham Park Village, Reading, Berkshire RG4 6SW
01189 479548
Fax: 01189 479548

Chambers of Mr J S Price

WESSEX CHAMBERS

Wessex

48 Queens Road, Reading, Berkshire
RG1 4BD
0118 956 8856
Fax: 0118 956 8857; DX 4012 Reading 1
E-mail: wessexchambers@compuserve.com
Out of hours telephone: as above
Clerk: Martin Davies

Khan, William *1971*	**McDevitt,** Colin *1995*
Smithers, Dr Roger *1990*	**Drake,** Rachel *1995*
Omar, Robina *1991*	**Ireland,** Penny *1996*
Joshi, Pramod *1992*	**Turtle,** Alister *1994**
Duncan, Nikki *1994*	**Glanville,** Susan *1991**

REDHILL CHAMBERS

Seloduct House, 30 Station Road, Redhill,
Surrey RH1 1NF
01737 780781
Fax: 01737 761760; DX 100203 Redhill
Out of hours telephone: 0181 668 1234

Chambers of R Mandel
*Clerk: John Bowker; Practice manager: Jan
Rogers*

Also at: 11 Bolt Court, Fleet Street, London
EC4A 3DQ
Tel: 0171 353 2300
Fax: 0171 353 1878

Mandel, Richard *1972*	**Livingstone,** Simon *1990*
Alexander, Ian QC *1964†*	**Colquhoun,** Celina *1990*
Lane, David QC *1968†*	**Sheridan,** Norman *1990*
Mason, Ian *1978*	**Gordon,** Mark *1990*
Lewis, Robert *1996*	**Murch,** Stephen *1991*
Randle, Simon *1982*	**Benner,** Lucinda *1992*
Jenkala, Adrian *1984*	**Carron,** Richard *1992*
Manson, Juliann *1985*	**Rudd,** Matthew *1994*
Scutt, David *1989*	**Mathias,** Anna *1994*
Airey, Simon *1989*	**Linstead,** Peter *1994*
Bacon, Jonathan *1989*	**Islam-Choudhury,** Mugni
Matthews, Alison *1989*	*1996*
Clay, Jonathan *1990*	**Porter,** Sarah *1996*

7 WILTON ROAD

Redhill, Surrey RH1 6QR
01737 760264
Fax: 01737 778769

Chambers of Mr W E P McIlroy

12 PAXTON CLOSE

Kew Gardens, Richmond, Surrey TW9 2AW
0181 940 5895
Fax: 0181 255 4170; DX 200117 Richmond

Chambers of Mr R H Bruce

RICHMOND GREEN CHAMBERS

Greyhound House, 23-24 George Street,
Richmond-upon-Thames, Surrey TW9 1HY
0181 940 1841
Fax: 0181 948 5885; DX 100263 Richmond 2
Out of hours telephone: 0181 948 4801

Chambers of P B Taylor MBE
Practice manager: E Robson

Baker, Andrew *1990*	**Rathbone,** Brian *1960*
Taylor, Phillip *1991*	

CHAMBERS OF DEREK WILLMOTT

8 Links Crescent, St Marys Bay, Romney
Marsh, Kent TN29 0RS
01303 87 3899
Fax: 01303 87 3899

Chambers of Mr W D I Willmott

CHAMBERS OF MELANIE DEN BRINKER

West House Town Row, Rotherfield, East
Sussex TN6 3QU
01892 783505
Fax: 01892 783505

Chambers of Miss M J M den Brinker

3 & 4 FARNHAM HALL

Farnham, Saxmundham, Suffolk IP17 1LB
01728 602758
Fax: 01728 602758

Chambers of Mr M C B West QC

---

23 WARHAM ROAD

Otford, Sevenoaks, Kent TN14 5PF
01959 522325
Fax: 01959 522325

Chambers of Mr D G Cracknell

BANK HOUSE CHAMBERS

Old Bank House, Hartshead, Sheffield S1 2EL
0114 275 1223
Fax: 0114 276 8439; DX 10522 Sheffield

Chambers of J D D Hall QC
Clerks: Mrs Deborah Chilton, Mrs Nicola Cooke

Hall, Jonathan D QC *1975*†	Goddard, Katherine *1987*
Battersby, Graham *1964*	Hawkins, David *1991*
Nimmo, Adrian *1971*	Pimm, Peter *1991**
England, George *1972*	Smith, Andrew *1991*
Smith, Robert *1974*	Walker, Fiona *1992*
Cranfield, Tony *1975*	Upson, Michael *1993*
Baird, James *1977*	Webb, Robert *1993*
Mason, David *1979*	Cole, Justine *1994*
Kelson, Peter *1981*‡	Batiste, Simon *1995*
Hillis, John *1982*	Hill, Jason *1995*
Cook, Lesley *1984*	West, Ian *1996*
Sheldon, Richard *1984*	Sapsford, Philip QC *1974**

62 CORTWORTH ROAD

Ecclesall, Sheffield S11 9LP
0114 236 0988
Fax: 0114 236 0988

Chambers of Mr J G Stevenson

19 FIGTREE LANE

Sheffield S1 2DJ
0114 2759708/2738380
Fax: 0114 2724915; DX 10629 Sheffield 1

Chambers of Mr D Gothorp

See the *Index of Languages Spoken* in **Part G** to locate a chambers where a particular language is spoken, or find an individual who speaks a particular language.

PARADISE SQUARE CHAMBERS

26 Paradise Square, Sheffield S1 2DE
0114 273 8951
Fax: 0114 276 0848; DX 10565 Sheffield
Other comms: Emergency Number: 0850 755440

Chambers of Roger Keen QC
Clerk: Timothy Booth

Keen, Roger QC *1976*†	O'Reilly, Michael *1988*
Murphy, Michael QC *1973*†	Groom, Ian *1990*
Burrell, Gary QC *1977*†	Rosario, Desmond *1990*
Walker, Annabel QC *1976*†	Edwards, Mererid *1991*
Hargan, Martin *1964*	Savage, Timothy *1991*
Phillips, Bernard *1970*†	McLauchlan, Ian *1992*
Neale, Nicholas *1972*	Syed, Gulzar *1983*
Bingham, Philip *1975*	Harrison, Rachael *1993*
Watson, Paul *1978*‡	Hughes, Dermot *1993*
Baker, Jeremy *1979*‡	Nijabat, Sharma *1993*
Robinson, Graham *1981*	Walker-Kane, Jonathan *1994*
Slater, Michael *1983*	Rhys, Megan *1994*
Wright, Sarah *1984*	Stables, Gordon *1995*
Coles, Michael *1986*	Kelly, Siobhan *1995*
Hatton, Andrew *1987*	McMillan, Carol *1996*
Crosbie, Susan *1988*	

ABBEY CHAMBERS

PO Box 47, 47 Ashurst Drive, Shepperton, Middlesex TW17 0LD
01932 560913
Fax: 01932 567764

Chambers of Arthur R A James
Administrator: Mrs Ann Woodhead

James, Arthur *1975*	Aslangul, Michel *1978*
Marsh, Peter *1975*	

11 ST BERNARDS ROAD

Slough, Berkshire SL3 7NT
01753 553806/817989
Fax: 01753 553806

Chambers of A Bhattacharyya
Clerk: S P Chadha

Bhattacharyya, Ardhendu
1974

GREENWAY

Sonning Lane, Sonning-on-Thames, Berkshire RG4 6ST
0118 969 2484
Fax: 0118 969 2484
Out of hours telephone: 0118 969 2484

Chambers of Jack A Denbin

Denbin, Jack *1973*

17 CARLTON CRESCENT

Southampton, Hampshire SO15 2XR
01703 320320
Fax: 01703 320321; DX 96875 Southampton 10
E-mail: km@bar-17cc.demon.co.uk

Chambers of J S Gibbons QC
Clerks: Gregory Townsend, Mark Harrison; Administrator: Sue Benoke

Gibbons, Jeremy QC *1973†*	**Morgan**, Dylan *1986*
Sullivan, Linda QC *1973†**	**Moores**, Timothy *1987*
Fulthorpe, Jonathan *1970*	**Doughty**, Peter *1988*
Towler, Peter *1974†*	**Holland**, Roberta *1989*
Kolanko, Michael *1975*	**Griffiths**, Hayley *1990*
Webster, William *1975*	**Hiddleston**, Adam *1990*
Haggan, Nicholas *1977*	**Ward**, Trevor *1991*
Merry, Hugh *1979*	**Burrett**, Catherine *1992*
Gibney, Malcolm *1981*	**Tucker**, Nicholas *1993*
Howard, Timothy *1981*	**Ferrari**, Sarah *1993*
Pine-Coffin, Margaret *1981*	**Hussain**, Frida *1995*
Glen, Philip *1983*	**Savill**, Peter *1995*
Forster, Michael *1984*	**Burns**, Jeremy *1996*
Grant, Gary *1985*	

Chambers established: 1976
Opening times: 9 am-6 pm

Types of work (and number of counsel practising in that area if supplied)
Arbitration 1 · Care proceedings 8 · Chancery (general) 1 · Chancery land law 3 · Common land 3 · Common law (general) 10 · Conveyancing 1 · Crime 8 · Crime - corporate fraud 3 · Education 1 · Employment 6 · Environment 2 · Family 8 · Family provision 8 · Housing 2 · Landlord and tenant 4 · Local government 8 · Medical negligence 2 · Partnerships 1 · Personal injury 7 · Probate and administration 1 · Professional negligence 2 · Town and country planning 6

Chambers' facilities
Conference rooms, Disks accepted, E-mail

Languages spoken
French, Italian

Fees policy
Up to five years call £30-60, Five to ten years call £50-75, Ten years call £65-125. Our policy is to set our fee levels to reflect the work necessarily done, whilst acknowledging the requirements and abilities of our clients to pay. Therefore please approach the clerks to discuss fixed fees tailored to your case.

COLLEGE CHAMBERS

19 Carlton Crescent, Southampton, Hampshire SO15 2ET
01703 230338
Fax: 01703 230376; DX 38533 Soton 3

Chambers of R W Belben
Clerk: Wayne Effeny

Belben, Robin *1969†*	**Breslin**, Catherine *1990*
Pain, Kenneth *1969*	**Self**, Gary *1991*
Swift, Jonathan *1977‡*	**Kinghorn**, Andrew *1991*
Sabine, John *1979*	**Nother**, Daniel *1994*
Marshall, Derek *1980*	**Grundy**, Arabella *1995*
Taylor, Douglas *1981*	**Lorie**, Andrew *1996*
Stewart, Mark *1989*	**Uppal**, Baljinder *1996*
Hand, Anthony *1989*	**Compton**, Timothy *1984**
Habel, Jessica *1991*	**Moore**, Roderick *1993**

Chambers established: 1989
Opening times: 8.45 am-6 pm

Types of work (and number of counsel practising in that area if supplied)
Care proceedings 8 · Chancery (general) 2 · Common law (general) 13 · Company and commercial 2 · Crime 3 · Employment 3 · Environment 1 · Family 11 · Insolvency 3 · Landlord and tenant 7 · Licensing 1 · Medical negligence 4 · Mental health 1 · Personal injury 13 · Professional negligence 4 · Town and country planning 1

Chambers' facilities
Conference rooms

Languages spoken
French

Fees policy
Up to five years call £30-50, Five to ten years call £50-85, Ten years call £75-125. Solicitors are always welcome to discuss fees on any specialisms with the clerk.

EIGHTEEN CARLTON CRESCENT

Southampton, Hampshire SO15 2XR
01703 639001
Fax: 01703 339625; DX 96877 Southampton
Out of hours telephone: 01703 639001

Chambers of J A H Haig-Haddow
Clerks: Paul Cooke, Lynda Knight

Haig-Haddow, Alastair *1972*	**Houston**, Andrew *1989*
Massey, Andrew *1969*	**Malik**, Omar *1990*
Ailes, Ashley *1975*	**Munks**, Christine *1991*
Fawcett, Gary *1975*	**Robins**, Imogen *1991*
Wylie, Keith *1976*	**Glenser**, Peter *1993*
Cochand, Charles *1978*	**Carter**, Sally *1994*
Robertson, Angus *1978*	**Thom**, Michael *1994*
Egleton, Richard *1981*	**Hall**, Richard *1995*
Blount, Martin *1982*	**Case**, Toby *1996*
Wing, Christopher *1985*	**Asteris**, Peter *1996*
Manuel, Elizabeth *1987*	

Chambers established: 1948
Opening times: 9 am-6 pm (24-hour service)

Types of work (and number of counsel practising in that area if supplied)
Arbitration 4 · Bankruptcy 4 · Care proceedings 12 · Chancery (general) 3 · Common law (general) 14 · Company and commercial 4 · Courts martial 4 · Crime 15 · Employment 2 · Family 17 · Family provision 10 · Information technology 2 · Insolvency 2 · Intellectual property 2 · Landlord and tenant 4 · Licensing 2 · Medical negligence 4 · Partnerships 2 · Pensions 4 · Personal injury 10 · Probate and administration 2 · Professional negligence 2 · Sale and carriage of goods 2 · Town and country planning 1

Chambers' facilities
Conference rooms, Video conferences, Law Society accredited seminars plus use of large seminar room

Languages spoken
French, German

Fees policy
Fees will be negotiated with the clerks who openly encourage any discussions in this regard on a flexible, professional basis.

FYFIELD CHAMBERS

Field Cottage, Fyfield, Southrop, Gloucestershire GL7 3NT
01367 850304
Fax: 01367 850304

Chambers of Mr B Sinclair

NEW CHAMBERS

3 Sadleir Road, St Albans, Hertfordshire AL1 2BL
0966 212126
Fax: 01727 841755; DX 6183 St Albans 1

Chambers of Mr K G Aylett

TINDAL CHAMBERS

3 Waxhouse Gate, St Albans, Herts AL5 4DU
01727 843383
DX 6116 St Albans 1

Chambers of Mr A T C Nicholson

"RYDAL MOUNT"

164 Heaton Moor Road, Heaton Moor, Stockport, Cheshire SK4 4HS
0161 432 8875
Fax: 0161 432 8875

Chambers of Mr C W S Shelton-Agar

REGENT CHAMBERS

REGENT CHAMBERS

29 Regent Road, Hanley, Stoke-on-Trent
ST1 3BT
01782 286666
Fax: 01782 201866; DX 20720 Hanley
E-mail: regent@ftech.co.uk
Out of hours telephone: 0973 906743

Chambers of Barry Cliff
Clerks: Lisa Kemp, Sarah L Chadwick

Rank, Peter 1976	**Johnson**, John 1993
Brown, Frederick 1983	**Cliff**, Paul 1992
Cliff, Barry 1988	**Moore**, Kirstie 1994
Robinson, David 1992	**O'Hagan**, Sophia 1996

61 ELM GROVE

Sutton, Surrey SM1 4EX
0181 643 9714
Fax: 0181 643 9714

Chambers of Miss V T Dsane

ANGEL CHAMBERS

94 Walter Road, Swansea, West Glamorgan
SA1 5QA
01792 464623/464648
Fax: 01792 648501; DX 39566 Swansea
Out of hours telephone: 0410 180974

Chambers of Thomas Glanville-Jones
Clerks: Crispin Cormack, Steven Welsh,
Elizabeth Bennett

Jones, Thomas 1956†	**Davies**, Andrew 1992
Cronin, William 1971	**Harris**, Elizabeth 1992
McKay, Christopher 1976	**Thomas**, Dyfed 1992
Thomas, Nigel 1976*	**Parry**, Richard 1993
Walters, Geraint 1981	**Foulser**, Jane 1994
Clee, Christopher 1983	**Vosper**, Christopher 1977‡
McCann, Colleen 1988	**James**, Sharon 1995
Davies, Emily 1989	**Blake**, David 1992
Harris-Jenkins, Philip 1990	**Davis**, Jim 1997

CHAMBERS OF DAVINA GAMMON

Ground Floor, 103 Walter Road, Swansea
SA1 5QS
01792 480770
Fax: 01792 480547; DX 52982 SWANSEA 1

Chambers of Mrs D A Gammon

GOWER CHAMBERS

57 Walter Road, Swansea, West Glamorgan
SA1 5PZ
01792 644466
Fax: 01792 644321; DX 52956 Swansea
E-mail: clerk@gowerchambers.co.uk

Chambers of B M Thomas
Clerks: David Houston, Paul Rees

Thomas, Bryan 1978	**Vallack**, Julie 1993
Clemes, Andrew 1984	**Pulling**, Dean 1993
Clarke, Jeffrey 1985	**Maddox**, Peter 1994
David, Andrew 1986	**Parry**, Sian 1994
Barnett, Joanne 1989	**Jones**, Michael 1995
Jones, Carwyn 1989	**Powell**, Nicola 1996
Wood, Joanna 1989	**McConnochie**, Dr Kathryn
Boothroyd, Alec 1991	1997

ISCOED CHAMBERS

86 St Helen's Road, Swansea, West
Glamorgan SA1 4BQ
01792 652988/9/330
Fax: 01792 458089; DX 39554 Swansea

Chambers of Trefor Davies
Clerks: W J Rainbird, Jeff Evans, Kris Thorne;
Practice manager: Sheila Budge

Davies, Trefor 1972	**Rees**, Huw 1983
Griffiths, Lawrence 1957	**Spackman**, Mark 1986
Thomas, Kenneth 1966	**Henke**, Ruth 1987
Richards, Wyn 1968†	**Hipkin**, John 1989
Rouch, Peter QC 1972*	**Harris**, David 1990
Griffiths, Patrick 1972	**Buckland**, Robert 1991
Phillips, Frank 1972	**Heyworth**, Catherine 1991
Riordan, Kevin 1972	**Hughes**, Kate 1992
Jenkins, James 1974‡	**Peters**, William 1992
Marshall, Philip 1975‡	**Wright**, Ian 1994
Thomas, Paul 1979	**Davies**, Iwan 1995
Craven, Robert 1979	**Gow**, Elizabeth 1995
Rees, Stephen 1979	**Hayes**, Timothy 1996
Evans, Elwen 1980	**Rees**, Matthew 1996
Jones, Francis 1980	
Sandbrook-Hughes, Stewert 1980	

C

---

† Recorder ‡ Assistant Recorder * Door Tenant

PENDRAGON CHAMBERS

124 Walter Road, Swansea, West Glamorgan
SA1 5RG
01792 411188
Fax: 01792 411189; DX 39572 Swansea 1

Chambers of N Wayne Beard
Clerk: Gwyn Davies

Beard, N Wayne *1991*	**Rudman**, Sara *1992*
Keane, Desmond QC *1964*	**Jones**, Catherine A *1992*
Edwards, Jonathan *1981*	**Thomas**, Gareth *1993*
Davies, Huw *1982*	**Mann**, Rebecca *1995*
Thomas, Philip *1982*	**Anderson**, Donald MP *1969**
Brooks, John *1990*	**Bourne**, Prof Nicholas *1976*

NESTON HOME CHAMBERS

42 Greenhill, Neston, Corsham, Wiltshire
SN13 9SQ
01225 811909
Fax: 01225 811909
Out of hours telephone: 01225 811909

Chambers of Mrs Jetta Doig
Clerk: J R Doig

Doig, Jeanetta *1988*

International Arbitration Law Review

Editorial Board includes:

Alan Redfern	*Neil Kaplan*
Toby Landau	*David Rivkin*
Dr Julian Lew	*Martin Hunter*
Nigel Rawding	*Matthieu de Boisseson*

The new International Arbitration Law Review *brings together for the first time all the requirements of an arbitration practitioner.*

* *up-to-the-minute news on legislation and decisions*

* *expert commentary on worldwide trends and issues from a panel of top arbitration specialists*

* *detailed case summaries and analysis of the cases making the headlines*

* *covers all major jurisdictions worldwide*

To order a subscription or a free sample copy call Sweet & Maxwell on 0171 449 1111

PUMP COURT CHAMBERS

1st Floor, 5 Temple Chambers, Temple Street,
Swindon, Wiltshire SN1 1SQ
01793 539899
Fax: 01793 539866; DX 38639 Swindon 2
URL: http://www.3pumpcourt.com

Chambers of Guy Boney QC
Clerk: Dorothy Hewitt

Also at: 3 Pump Court, Upper Ground Floor,
London EC4Y 7AJ
Tel: 0171 353 0711
Fax: 0171 353 3319;
31 Southgate Street, Winchester SO23 9EE
Tel: 01962 868161
Fax: 01962 867645

Boney, Guy QC *1968*	**Hill**, Mark *1987*
Pascoe, Nigel QC *1966*	**Howard**, Graham *1987*
Clark, Christopher QC *1969*	**Travers**, Hugh *1988*
Garlick, Paul QC *1974*	**Waddington**, Anne *1988*
Still, Geoffrey *1966*	**Warren**, Philip *1988*
Patterson, Stewart *1967‡*	**Akiwumi**, Anthony *1989*
Pearson, Adam *1969*	**Samuels**, Leslie *1989*
Moat, Frank *1970*	**Boydell**, Edward *1989*
Harrap, Giles *1971*	**Gau**, Justin *1989*
Abbott, Frank *1972*	**Brunton**, Sean *1990*
Montgomery, Michael *1972*	**Khan**, Helen *1990*
Parry, Charles *1973*	**Howe**, Penny *1991*
Butt, Michael *1974*	**Kelly**, Geoffrey *1992*
Ker-Reid, John *1974*	**Newton-Price**, James *1992*
Gabb, Charles *1975*	**Poyer-Sleeman**, Patricia *1992*
Gillibrand, Phillip *1975*	
Barnett, Andrew *1977*	**Gunther**, Elizabeth *1993*
Dineen, Michael *1977*	**Peirson**, Oliver *1993*
Miller, Jane *1979‡*	**Fields**, Helen *1993*
O'Flynn, Timothy *1979*	**Blackburn**, Luke *1993*
Hill, Robert *1980*	**Pawson**, Robert *1994*
Allardice, Miranda *1982*	**Ashley**, Mark *1993*
Lochrane, Damien *1983*	**Dubbery**, Mark *1996*
Nsugbe, Oba *1985*	**Beaumont**, Marc *1985**
Scott, Matthew *1985*	
Bloom-Davis, Desmond *1986*	

Crime Desktop CD-ROM

Containing the three most important titles in criminal law: Archbold, Criminal Law Review *and* Criminal Appeal Reports, *this is the most efficient criminal law research tool you can own.*

Put time on your side, phone Sweet & Maxwell on 0171 449 1111 for more information or a free demonstration

COLLETON CHAMBERS

22 The Crescent, Taunton, Somerset TA1 4EB
01823 324252
Fax: 01823 327489; DX 96100 Taunton 1

Chambers of R M J Meeke
Clerk: Philip Alden

Annexe of: Colleton Chambers, Colleton
Crescent, Exeter, Devon EX2 4DG
Tel: 01392 274898
Fax: 01392 412368

Meeke, Martin *1973‡*	**Horton**, Mark *1981*
Chadd, Paul QC *1952**	**Whitehall**, Mark *1983*
Merrett, Richard *1959*	**Holder**, Terence *1984*
Lowry, Stephen *1960*	**Ashman**, Peter *1985*
Rains, Richard *1963*	**Farquharson**, Jonathan
Brabin, Michael *1976*	*1988*
Puttick, Anthony *1971*	**Barlow**, Melissa *1991*
Crabb, Richard *1975*	**Drinkwater**, Philip *1995*
Steele, David *1975*	**Vincent**, Ruth *1995*
Mackenzie, Julie *1978*	

SOUTH WESTERN CHAMBERS

Melville House, 12 Middle Street, Taunton,
Somerset TA1 1SH
01823 331919
Fax: 01823 330553; DX 32146 Taunton

Chambers of Mr H B G Lett

GODOLPHIN CHAMBERS

50 Castle Street, Truro, Cornwall TR1 3AF
01872 276312
Fax: 01872 271920; DX 81233 Truro

Chambers of B P van den Berg
Clerks: Julian Coia TD, BA, MIMgt (Senior
Clerk), Andrea Hellings (1st Junior)

van den Berg, Barrie *1978*	**Taylor**, Jonathan *1987*
Guy, Richard *1970*	**Smith**, Abigail *1989*
Wallace, Ann *1979*	**Taurah**, Sheila *1991*
Perry, Christopher *1980*	**Holland**, Anne *1994*
Elliott, Colin *1987*	**Richards**, Jonathan *1995*
Beechey, Hilary *1987*	

CHAMBERS OF STEWART DUNN

93 Millview Drive, Tynemouth, North Shields
NE30 2QJ
0191 258 0520
Fax: 0191 258 0520

Chambers of Mr S W Dunn

136B VINE LANE

Hillingdon, Uxbridge, Middlesex UB10 0BQ
01895 270221

Chambers of Mr G R Haines

9 FOUNTAINS WAY

Pinders Heath, Wakefield, West Yorkshire
WF1 4TQ
01924 378631
Fax: 01924 378631

Chambers of Mr P Martin

WATFORD CHAMBERS

74 Mildred Avenue, Watford, Hertfordshire
WD1 7DX
01923 220553
Fax: 01923 222618; DX 42551 Bushey

Chambers of Mrs A Henthorn

MIDDLESEX CHAMBERS

Suite 3 & 4, Stanley House, Stanley Avenue,
Wembley, Middlesex HA0 4SB
0181 902 1499
Fax: 0181 902 1509

52 WEMBLEY PARK DRIVE

Wembley, Middlesex HA9 8HB
0181 902 5629
Fax: 0181 902 5629

Chambers of Mr I S Kulatilake

CRAYSHOTT HOUSE

Woodlands Road, West Byfleet, Surrey
KT14 6JW
01932 342951
Fax: 01932 336176

Chambers of Mr R T F Turrall-Clarke

10 WINTERBOURNE GROVE

Weybridge, Surrey KT13 0PP
0181 941 3939
Fax: 0181 941 3939

Chambers of Mr M C Wyatt

C

CHAMBERS OF JOSEPH DALBY

First Floor, No 28 St Stephens Road,
Winchester SO22 6DE
01962 886555
Fax: 01962 886222

Chambers of Mr J F Dalby

PUMP COURT CHAMBERS

31 Southgate Street, Winchester SO23 9EE
01962 868161
Fax: 01962 867645; DX 2514 Winchester
URL: http://www.3pumpcourt.com

Chambers of Guy Boney QC
Clerks: D Barber, Tony George;
Administrator: Sally Woolley

Also at: 3 Pump Court, Upper Ground Floor,
London EC4Y 7AJ
Tel: 0171 353 0711
Fax: 0171 353 3319;
5 Temple Chambers, Swindon SN1 1SQ
Tel: 01793 539899
Fax: 01793 539866

Boney, Guy QC *1968*†	**Hill**, Mark *1987*
Pascoe, Nigel QC *1966*†	**Howard**, Graham *1987*
Clark, Christopher QC *1969*†	**Travers**, Hugh *1988*
Garlick, Paul QC *1974*†	**Waddington**, Anne *1988*
Still, Geoffrey *1966*†	**Warren**, Philip *1988*
Patterson, Stewart *1967*‡	**Akiwumi**, Anthony *1989*
Pearson, Adam *1969*	**Samuels**, Leslie *1989*
Moat, Frank *1970*†	**Boydell**, Edward *1989*
Harrap, Giles *1971*†	**Gau**, Justin *1989*
Abbott, Frank *1972*†	**Brunton**, Sean *1990*
Montgomery, Michael *1972*	**Khan**, Helen *1990*
Parry, Charles *1973*	**Howe**, Penny *1991*
Butt, Michael *1974*	**Kelly**, Geoffrey *1992*
Ker-Reid, John *1974*	**Newton-Price**, James *1992*
Gabb, Charles *1975*	**Poyer-Sleeman**, Patricia
Gillibrand, Phillip *1975*	*1992*
Barnett, Andrew *1977*†	**Gunther**, Elizabeth *1993*
Dineen, Michael *1977*	**Peirson**, Oliver *1993*
Miller, Jane *1979*‡	**Fields**, Helen *1993*
O'Flynn, Timothy *1979*	**Blackburn**, Luke *1993*
Hill, Robert *1980*	**Ashley**, Mark *1993*
Allardice, Miranda *1982*	**Pawson**, Robert *1994*
Lochrane, Damien *1983*	**Dubbery**, Mark *1996*
Nsugbe, Oba *1985*	**Beaumont**, Marc *1985**
Scott, Matthew *1985*	
Bloom-Davis, Desmond *1986*	

4 ST PETER STREET

Winchester SO23 8BW
01962 868 884
Fax: 01962 868 644; DX 2507 Winchester

Chambers of M P Parroy QC
Clerks: Stuart Pringle (Senior Clerk), Lee Giles, Robert Leonard, John Wanless

Annexe of: 3 Paper Buildings, 1st Floor, Temple, London EC4Y 7EU
Tel: 0171 583 8055
Fax: 0171 353 6271 (2 lines)

Parroy, Michael QC *1969*	**Branigan,** Kate *1984*
Harris, David QC *1969†*	**O'Hara,** Sarah *1984*
Hughes, Peter QC *1971*	**Chamberlain,** Francis *1985*
Jones, Stewart QC *1972†*	**Sanderson,** David *1985*
Aspinall, John QC *1971*	**Bailey,** Russell *1985*
Hebron, Harold *1960*	**Parker,** Christopher *1986*
Parrish, Samuel *1962*	**Hudson,** Elisabeth *1987*
Trevethan, Susan *1967*	**Letman,** Paul *1987*
Haynes, John *1968*	**Rowland,** Nicholas *1988*
Swinstead, David *1970*	**Kelly,** Patricia *1988*
Hope, Derwin *1970†*	**Woolgar,** Dermot *1988*
Norman, Michael *1971†*	**Hester,** Paul *1989*
Ward, Anthony *1971*	**Opperman,** Guy *1989*
Curran, Leo *1972*	**Bradbury,** Timothy *1989*
Jennings, Peter *1972*	**Kilpatrick,** Jean *1990*
Coleman, Anthony *1973*	**Buckley-Clarke,** Amanda *1991*
Stephenson, Ben *1973*	
Litchfield, Linda *1974*	**Ross,** Iain *1991*
Bartlett, David *1975†*	**Steenson,** David *1991*
Richardson, Garth *1975*	**Sweeney,** Christian *1992*
Tyson, Richard *1975‡*	**Kelly,** Marie *1992*
Henry, Peter *1977*	**Kirkpatrick,** Krystyna *1992*
Mitchell, Nigel *1978*	**Weir,** Robert *1992*
Seed, Nigel *1978‡*	**Fitzharris,** Ginnette *1993*
Kent, Peter *1978*	**Earle,** Judy *1994*
Partridge, Ian *1979*	**Geraghty,** Sarah *1994*
Grey, Robert *1979*	**Reid,** David *1994*
Leviseur, Nicholas *1979*	**Williams,** Ben *1994*
Coombes, Timothy *1980*	**Hughes,** Melanie *1995*
Cairnes, Paul *1980*	**McIlroy,** David *1995*
Edge, Ian *1981*	**Strachan,** Elaine *1995*
Strutt, Martin *1981*	**Case,** Richard *1996*
Lickley, Nigel *1983*	**Gourley,** Claire *1996*
Lomas, Mark *1983*	**Wood,** Graham *1979‡**
Maccabe, Irvine *1983*	**Ball,** Sally *1989**

WINDSOR BARRISTERS' CHAMBERS

Windsor
01753 648899
DX 130112 Slough 6

Chambers of Mr M C Beaumont

Also at: Harrow-on-the-Hill Chambers, 60 High Street, Harrow-on-the-Hill, Middlesex HA1 3LL
Tel: 0181 423 7444
Fax: 0181 423 7368

BARNSTAPLE CHAMBERS

c/o Glebe Cottage, Broadwoodkelly, Winkleigh, Devon EX19 8ED
0183 783763
Fax: 0183 783763
Other comms: Pager 01426 162407

Chambers of Stanley Best
Clerk: Self

Best, Stanley P *1989*

MENDHIR CHAMBERS

38 Priest Avenue, Wokingham, Berkshire RG40 2LX
0118 9771274
Fax: 0118 9627132; DX 6411 MAIDENHEAD

Chambers of Mrs M Mendhir

1 ARGYLE ROAD

Wolverhampton WV2 4NY
01902 561047
Fax: 01902 561047

Chambers of Mr A S Garcha

See the *Index of Languages Spoken* in **Part G** to locate a chambers where a particular language is spoken, or find an individual who speaks a particular language.

The Supreme Court Practice 1999

- *the most authoritative title on Civil Court Practice and Procedure*
- *available in book and CD-ROM formats*

Phone Sweet & Maxwell on 0171 449 1111 to order your copy

---

† Recorder ‡ Assistant Recorder * Door Tenant

CLAREMONT CHAMBERS

26 Waterloo Road, Wolverhampton WV1 4BL
01902 426222
Fax: 01902 426333; DX 722200
Wolverhampton 15
Out of hours telephone: 0976 805643

Chambers of Ian McCulloch
Clerk: Meriel Acton

McCulloch, Ian *1951*	**Maxwell**, David *1994*
Keane, Desmond QC *1964*	**Brown**, Jain *1994*
Khan, Asif *1983*	**Thorndike**, Tony *1994*
Gidney, Jonathan *1991*	**Fairburn**, George *1995*
Garside, Mark *1993*	**Mondair**, Rashpal *1995*
Hobbs, Naomi *1993*	**Harding**, Fiona *1993**
Tonge, Ruth *1993*	

CLOCK CHAMBERS

*78 Darlington Street, Wolverhampton
WV1 4LY*
01902 313444
Fax: 01902 21110; DX 10423 Wolverhampton
1

1 WENSLEY AVENUE

Woodford Green, Essex IG8 9HE
0181 505 9259

Chambers of Mr S Huda

ST GEORGE'S CHAMBERS

32/33 Foregate Street, Worcester WR1 1EE
0345 413635
Fax: 01905 611601

Chambers of Mr I D Whitney

YORK CHAMBERS

14 Toft Green, York YO1 6JT
01904 620 048
Fax: 01904 610 056; DX 65517 York 7
E-mail: yorkchambers.co.uk

Chambers of Simon Hawkesworth QC
Clerk: Kevin Beaumont

Hawkesworth, Simon QC *1967*†	**Terry**, Robert *1986*
	Lee, Rosslyn *1987*
Marron, Aidan QC *1973*†	**Price**, Nicholas *1987*
Gripton, David *1969*	**Lamb**, David *1987*
Grenyer, Mark *1969*	**Makepeace**, Peter *1988*
Bowerman, Michael *1970*‡	**Elvidge**, John *1988*
Priest, John *1973*	**Norman**, Charity *1988*
Lindsay, Martin *1977*	**Cordey**, Daniel *1990*
O'Neill, Michael *1979*	**Todd**, Martin *1991*
Twist, Stephen *1979*	**Robinson**, James *1992*
Williams, Christopher *1981*	**Scott**, Richard *1992*
Matthews, Gillian *1985*	**Edwards**, Daniel *1993*
Crayton, Philip *1985*	**Campbell**, Diane *1995*
Proops, Helen *1986*	**Randhawa**, Ravinder *1995*
Johnson, Peter *1986*	**Legard**, Edward *1996*

**Types of work (and number of counsel
practising in that area if supplied)**
Care proceedings 14 · Commercial litigation 6
· Common land 1 · Company and commercial
1 · Courts martial 3 · Crime 18 · Education 2
· Employment 5 · Environment 1 · Equity, wills
and trusts 1 · Family provision 12
· Immigration 3 · Landlord and tenant 5
· Licensing 3 · Medical negligence 11 · Mental
health 3 · Personal injury 21 · Professional
negligence 9 · Sale and carriage of goods 4
· Town and country planning

Chambers' facilities
Conference rooms, Video conferences, Disks
accepted, Disabled access, E-mail

Languages spoken
French, German, Punjabi

Soon you'll be able to beat the clock?

With **Crime Desktop**, time will be on *your* side

Never have three such titles been put together in a single, easy to use research tool. You can search individual titles, or all three in one go. And there's no need to go traipsing off to the library to look up past volumes, since both the **Criminal Law Review** and **Criminal Appeal Reports** are reproduced from 1967 onwards.

If you would like a demonstration, or would like to take **Crime Desktop** on a no-obligation 28 days' trial, call **0171 449 1111**.

SWEET & MAXWELL

connections

Individual Barristers

D

Individual Barristers in Private Practice

This section lists barristers in private practice. Individuals are listed alphabetically by surname and details include the chambers at which they practise, date of call to the Bar, Inn of Court and academic qualifications.

Some individuals have opted to include additional information about themselves in this part of the Directory such as qualifications, membership of foreign bars, other professional experience, languages spoken, publications, reported cases and a list of the types of work undertaken. Please note that details of the types of work undertaken by individual barristers who have chosen not to include this information in Part D may be found in *Part B Types of Work by Individual Barristers*.

Note: The General Council of the Bar information on individual barristers in private practice dates up to 19 March 1998. Sweet & Maxwell accepted bronze entries up to 15 April 1998, and silver and gold entries up to 30 April 1998. In some instances the information in this section may have been superseded by information provided by chambers after this date. Any changes made by chambers after this date will not be reflected in this section.

D

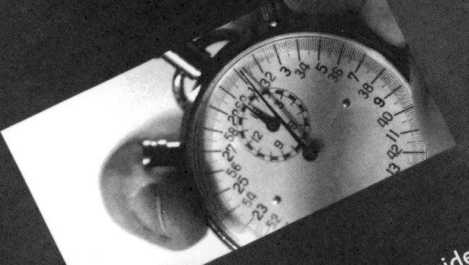

AARON SAMUEL

4-5 Gray's Inn Square
Ground Floor, Gray's Inn, London WC1R 5AY,
Telephone: 0171 404 5252
E-mail: chambers@4-5graysinnsquare.co.uk
Call date: July 1986, Gray's Inn
Qualifications: [BA, LLB (Cape Town), BA
(Hons)(S.Africa), FCI Arb.]

AARONBERG DAVID JEFFREY

Hardwicke Building
New Square, Lincoln's Inn, London
WC2A 3SB, Telephone: 0171 242 2523
E-mail: clerks@hardwicke.co.uk
Call date: July 1981, Inner Temple
Qualifications: [BA]

AARONSON GRAHAM RAPHAEL
QC (1982)

1 Essex Court
Ground Floor, Temple, London EC4Y 9AR,
Telephone: 0171 583 2000
E-mail: clerks@oneessexcourt.co.uk
Call date: Nov 1966, Middle Temple
Qualifications: [MA (Cantab)]

ABBERTON DAVID EDWARD

40 King Street
Chester CH1 2AH, Telephone: 01244 323886
Call date: Nov 1994, Middle Temple
Qualifications: [BA (Hons)]

ABBOTT ALISTAIR JAMES HUGH

5 New Square
1st Floor, Lincoln's Inn, London WC2A 3RJ,
Telephone: 0171 404 0404
E-mail: Chambers@FiveNewSquare.CityScape.co.uk
Call date: Nov 1996, Middle Temple
Qualifications: [BA (Hons) (Cantab)]

ABBOTT DAVID ROBERT

Beresford Chambers
21 King Street, Luton, Bedfordshire LU1 2DW,
Telephone: 01582 429111
E-mail: info@it-law.com
Call date: July 1987, Lincoln's Inn
Qualifications: [LLB MSc DPA DMS Dip, Ed.]

ABBOTT FRANCIS ARTHUR

Pump Court Chambers
Upper Ground Floor 3 Pump Court, Temple,
London EC4Y 7AJ, Telephone: 0171 353 0711
Pump Court Chambers
31 Southgate Street, Winchester SO23 8EE,
Telephone: 01962 868161
Call date: Nov 1972, Lincoln's Inn
Recorder
Qualifications: [BA (Nott'm)]

ABBOTT MRS MARY MACCONNACHIE

22 Albion Place
Northampton NN1 1UD,
Telephone: 01604 36271
Call date: Oct 1994, Gray's Inn
Qualifications: [BA]

ABEBRESE OWUSU EMANUEL

12 Old Square
1st Floor, Lincoln's Inn, London WC2A 3TX,
Telephone: 0171 404 0875
Call date: Sept 1985, Inner Temple
Qualifications: [BA (Hons), LLM]

ABELL ANTHONY ROGER

3 Hare Court
1st Floor, Temple, London EC4Y 7BJ,
Telephone: 0171 353 7561
Call date: July 1977, Gray's Inn
Qualifications: [LLB (Lond)]

ABELSON MICHAEL ANDREW

The Corn Exchange
5th Floor Fenwick Street, Liverpool L2 7QS,
Telephone: 0151 227 1081/5009
Call date: July 1976, Middle Temple
Assistant Recorder
Qualifications: [LLB (Hons)(Lond)]

ABEY MAHIE

3 Dr Johnson's Bldgs
Ground Floor, Temple, London EC4Y 7BA,
Telephone: 0171 353 4854
Call date: Oct 1993, Gray's Inn
Qualifications: [BA (Cantab)]

D

ABRAHAMSON MISS JUDITH SHARON

Chavasse Court Chambers
2nd Floor Chavasse Court, 24 Lord Street,
Liverpool L2 1TA, Telephone: 0151 707 1191
Door Tenant
Call date: Nov 1988, Gray's Inn
Qualifications: [LLB (L'Pool)]

ACE RICHARD WILLIAM

8 Fountain Court
Steelhouse Lane, Birmingham B4 6DR,
Telephone: 0121 236 5514/5
E-mail: clerks@no8chambers.co.uk
Call date: Oct 1993, Lincoln's Inn
Qualifications: [BSc (Hons)(Reading), Dip in Law (Lond)]

ACHESON ROBERT IAN

23 Essex Street
London WC2R 3AS,
Telephone: 0171 413 0353/353 3533
E-mail: clerks@essexstreet23.demon.co.uk
Call date: Feb 1992, Gray's Inn
Qualifications: [BA (Oxon)]

ACKERLEY DAVID ALBERT

Victoria Chambers
19 Castle Street, Liverpool L2 4SX,
Telephone: 0151 236 9402
E-mail: Fa45@rapid.co.uk
Call date: Nov 1992, Inner Temple
Qualifications: [LLB]

ACKNER THE HON CLAUDIA MADELEINE

4 Pump Court
Temple, London EC4Y 7AN,
Telephone: 0171 353 2656/9
E-mail: 4_pump_court@compuserve.com
Door Tenant
Call date: July 1977, Middle Temple
Qualifications: [BA (Cantab)]

ACLAND DR PIERS DYKE

11 South Square
2nd Floor, Gray's Inn, London WC1R 5EU,
Telephone: 0171 405 1222
Call date: Nov 1993, Lincoln's Inn
Qualifications: [BSc (Hons), PhD (Lond)]

ACTON MISS JAYNE

58 King Street Chambers
1st Floor, Kingsgate House 51-53 South King Street, Manchester M2 6DE,
Telephone: 0161 831 7477
Call date: Mar 1996, Lincoln's Inn
Qualifications: [LLB (Hons) (Sheff)]

ACTON STEPHEN NEIL

11 Old Square
Ground Floor, Lincoln's Inn, London
WC2A 3TS, Telephone: 0171 430 0341
E-mail: clerks@11oldsquare.co.uk
Call date: July 1977, Inner Temple
Qualifications: [MA (Cantab)]

ACTON DAVIS JONATHAN JAMES QC (1996)

4 Pump Court
Temple, London EC4Y 7AN,
Telephone: 0171 353 2656/9
E-mail: 4_pump_court@compuserve.com
Call date: July 1977, Inner Temple
Assistant Recorder
Qualifications: [LLB (Lond)]

ADAIR STUART ANTHONY

24 Old Bldgs
Ground Floor, Lincoln's Inn, London
WC2A 3UJ, Telephone: 0171 404 0946
E-mail: clerks@24oldbuildings.law.co.uk
Call date: Oct 1995, Inner Temple
Qualifications: [LLB (Exon)]

ADAM THOMAS NOBLE

Brick Court Chambers
15/19 Devereux Court, London WC2R 3JJ,
Telephone: 0171 583 0777
E-mail: (surname)@brickcourt.demon.co.uk
Call date: Nov 1991, Inner Temple
Qualifications: [MA (Cantab)]

ADAMS CHRISTOPHER ALAN

Priory Chambers
2 Fountain Court, Steelhouse Lane,
Birmingham B4 6DR,
Telephone: 0121 236 3882/1375
Call date: July 1986, Lincoln's Inn
Qualifications: [LLB (Lond)]

ADAMS DEREK ADAMA

2 Middle Temple Lane
3rd Floor, Temple, London EC4Y 9AA,
Telephone: 0171 583 4540
Door Tenant
Call date: Nov 1988, Middle Temple
Qualifications: [BA, Dip Law, LLM (LSE)]

ADAMS GUY LAIRD

St John's Chambers
Small Street, Bristol BS1 1DW,
Telephone: 0117 9213456/298514
E-mail: clerks@stjohns.uk.com
Call date: July 1989, Middle Temple
Qualifications: [MA (Cantab)]

ADAMS JAMES ROBERT

New Court Chambers
3 Broad Chare, Newcastle Upon Tyne
NE1 3DQ, Telephone: 0191 232 1980
Door Tenant
11 King's Bench Walk
1st Floor, Temple, London EC4Y 7EQ,
Telephone: 0171 353 3337
Door Tenant
Call date: July 1978, Gray's Inn
Qualifications: [LLB (Newc)]

ADAMS MISS JAYNE MARGARET

24 The Ropewalk
Nottingham NG1 5EF,
Telephone: 0115 9472581
E-mail: clerk@ropewalk.co.uk
Call date: July 1982, Gray's Inn
Qualifications: [LLB]

ADAMS JOHN NORMAN

One Raymond Buildings
Gray's Inn, London WC1R 5BH,
Telephone: 0171 430 1234
E-mail: chambers@ipbar1rb.com;
clerks@ipbar1rb.com
Call date: Nov 1984, Inner Temple
Qualifications: [LLB (Dunelm) MIEX, ACIPA]

ADAMS MS LINDSAY EVELINE

1 Pump Court
Lower Ground Floor, Temple, London
EC4Y 7AB, Telephone: 0171 583 2012/
353 4341
E-mail: (name) @1pumpcourt.co.uk
Call date: Nov 1987, Middle Temple
Qualifications: [LLB(Hons)]

ADAMS MISS LORRAINE JOAN

Pulteney Chamber
14 Johnstone Street, Bath, Somerset BA2 4DH,
Telephone: 01225 465667
Call date: Oct 1992, Inner Temple
Qualifications: [LLB]

ADAMS ROBERT GEORGE SETON

Trinity Chambers
9-12 Trinity Chare, Quayside, Newcastle Upon
Tyne NE1 3DF, Telephone: 0191 232 1927
Call date: Oct 1993, Inner Temple
Qualifications: [MA (Cantab)]

ADAMSON MISS LILIAS LOUISA

Becket Chambers
17 New Dover Road, Canterbury, Kent
CT1 3AS, Telephone: 01227 786331
Call date: Nov 1994, Gray's Inn
Qualifications: [BA (Hons) (Keele)]

ADAMYK SIMON CHARLES

12 New Square
Ground Floor, Lincoln's Inn, London
WC2A 3SW, Telephone: 0171 419 1212
E-mail: 12newsquare@compuserve.com
Call date: Nov 1991, Lincoln's Inn
Qualifications: [BA (Hons) (Camb), LLM
(Harvard)]

ADDEZIO MARIO

6 Gray's Inn Square
Ground Floor, Gray's Inn, London WC1R 5AZ,
Telephone: 0171 242 1052
Call date: July 1971, Lincoln's Inn
Qualifications: [LLB (Lond)]

D

ADDISON MISS FIONA ROSALINDA

Goldsworth Chambers
1st Floor 10-11 Gray's Inn Square, London
WC1R 5JD, Telephone: 0171 405 7117
Call date: July 1993, Inner Temple
Qualifications: [BSc (Econ), Dip Econ, MA]

ADDISON KENNETH PAUL

3 Temple Gardens
2nd Floor, Temple, London EC4Y 9AU,
Telephone: 0171 583 1155
Call date: July 1988, Middle Temple
Qualifications: [LLB (Hons)]

ADDISON NEIL PATRICK

Cathedral Chambers
Milburn House Dean Street, Newcastle Upon
Tyne NE1 1LE, Telephone: 0191 232 1311
Call date: Nov 1976, Gray's Inn
Qualifications: [BA]

ADDLEMAN MISS ANDREA MICHELE

Park Court Chambers
40 Park Cross Street, Leeds LS1 2QH,
Telephone: 0113 2433277
Call date: July 1977, Middle Temple

ADDOO IBRAHIM NEE KWAMINA-ASHONG

Chambers of Ibrahim Addoo
Bloxworth Villa 38 Delafield Road, Charlton,
London SE7 7NP, Telephone: 0181 244 3555
Call date: Nov 1980, Middle Temple
Qualifications: [RMN, SRN Dip (Lond), Dip
Nursing (Lond)]

ADDY MISS CAROLINE KORDAI

1 Brick Court
1st Floor, Temple, London EC4Y 9BY,
Telephone: 0171 353 8845
E-mail: clerks@1brickcourt.co.uk
Call date: Nov 1991, Inner Temple
Qualifications: [LLB (Euro)(Exon)]

ADEBAYO IBITAYO ALADE

Queen Elizabeth Bldg
Ground Floor, Temple, London EC4Y 9BS,
Telephone: 0171 353 7181 (12 Lines)
Call date: Nov 1989, Inner Temple

Qualifications: [BA (Hons)(Bris), DP in Law
(Bris)]

ADEBIYI SAMUEL DUROJAIYE

Leone Chambers
72 Evelyn Avenue, Kingsbury, London
NW9 OJH, Telephone: 0181 931 1712
Call date: June 1953, Middle Temple

ADEJUMO MRS HILDA EKPO

Temple Chambers
Rooms 111/112 3/7 Temple Avenue, London
EC4Y 0HP,
Telephone: 0171 583 1001 (2 lines)
Call date: Nov 1989, Lincoln's Inn
Qualifications: [BSc (Nigeria), LLB (Hons)
(Lond), LLM, BL (Lond), LLM (Lond)]

Fax: 0171 583 2112;
Out of hours telephone: 0956 610 205;
DX: 355 Chancery Lane; Other comms: E-mail
hadejum@aol.com

Types of work: African customary law; Chancery
(general); Company and commercial;
Employment; Family; Housing; Immigration;
Intellectual property; Judicial review; Landlord
and tenant; Mental health

Awards and memberships: Housing Law
Practitioners Association (HLPA); Vice-Chair,
Nigerian Legal Practitioners, UK; Member,
British Association of Women Entrepreneurs;
Friend, Institute of Advanced Legal Studies,
Russell Square, London

Other professional experience: Two years'
experience as a member of Board of Governors
of one of the Harrow colleges

Languages spoken: French, Ibo, Yoruba

ADENEKAN LATIFF AREMU

Chancery Chambers
1st Floor Offices 70/72 Chancery Lane,
London WC2A 1AB,
Telephone: 0171 405 6879/6870
Call date: Nov 1970, Inner Temple
Qualifications: [LLB (Lond)]

ADER PETER CHARLES

3 Temple Gardens
Lower Ground Floor, Temple, London
EC4Y 9AU, Telephone: 0171 353 3102/5/9297
Call date: July 1973, Middle Temple
Recorder
Qualifications: [LLB (Hons)(So'ton)]

ADEREMI ADEDAMOLA OLASUPO

3 Temple Gardens (North)
Fifth Floor, Temple, London EC4Y 9AU,
Telephone: 0171 353 0853/4/7222
E-mail: 100106.1577@compuserve.com
Call date: Feb 1992, Inner Temple
Qualifications: [LLB (Nigeria), LLM (Nigeria)]

ADEWALE REMI ADETOKUNBO SANNI

9 King's Bench Walk
Basement, Temple, London EC4Y 7DX,
Telephone: 0171 353 9564
E-mail: jvlee@btinternet.com
Call date: Oct 1995, Middle Temple
Qualifications: [LLB(Hons), LLM (Lond)]

ADJEI CYRIL JOHN

5 Paper Bldgs
Ground Floor, Temple, London EC4Y 7HB,
Telephone: 0171 583 9275/583 4555
E-mail: 5paper@link.org
Call date: Oct 1995, Inner Temple
Qualifications: [LLB (Lond), LLM (Cantab), LLD
(EUI,Florence)]

ADKIN JAMES SIMON

New Court Chambers
3 Broad Chare, Newcastle Upon Tyne
NE1 3DQ, Telephone: 0191 232 1980
Call date: Oct 1992, Lincoln's Inn
Qualifications: [LLB(Hons)(Newc)]

ADKIN MS TANA MARIE THERESE

Chambers of Helen Grindrod QC
1st Floor 95a Chancery Lane, London
WC2A 2JG, Telephone: 0171 404 4777
Call date: Nov 1992, Inner Temple
Qualifications: [BA (Hons)(Leic), Dip in Law
(City)]

ADKINS RICHARD DAVID QC (1995)

3/4 South Square
Gray's Inn, London WC1R 5HP,
Telephone: 0171 696 9900
E-mail: clerks@southsquare.com
Call date: July 1982, Middle Temple
Qualifications: [MA (Oxon)]

ADLARD WILLIAM BRICE

2 Harcourt Bldgs
1st Floor, Temple, London EC4Y 9DB,
Telephone: 0171 353 2112/2817
Call date: July 1978, Middle Temple

ADLINGTON NICHOLAS DAVID

2 New Street
Leicester LE1 5NA, Telephone: 0116 2625906
Call date: July 1988, Inner Temple
Qualifications: [LLB]

ADONIS GEORGIOS

2 Paper Buildings
Basement, Temple, London EC4Y 7ET,
Telephone: 0171 353 0933
Call date: July 1973, Lincoln's Inn

AEBERLI PETER DOLPH

46/48 Essex Street
London WC2R 3GH,
Telephone: 0171 583 8899
Call date: Nov 1990, Middle Temple
Recorder
Qualifications: [MA (Edin) BA (Oxon), Dip
Arch, R.I.B.A., A.R.I.A.S FCIArb]

AGBAJE EDWARD PAUL ABAYOMI

1 Gray's Inn Square
Ground Floor, London WC1R 5AA,
Telephone: 0171 405 8946/7/8
Call date: Nov 1984, Middle Temple
Qualifications: [BA(Exon)]

AGBAMU ALEXANDER ONAKOMEME

2 Pump Court
1st Floor, Temple, London EC4Y 7AH,
Telephone: 0171 353 5597
Call date: Nov 1988, Lincoln's Inn
Qualifications: [LLB Hons (B'ham)]

D

AGEROS DAVID KEITH JUSTIN

4 Paper Bldgs
2nd Floor, Temple, London EC4Y 7EX,
Telephone: 0171 583 0816/071 353 1131
E-mail: clerks@4paperbuildings.co.uk
Call date: Nov 1993, Inner Temple
Qualifications: [BA (Hons)(Cantab), Dip Law
(City)]

AGEROS JAMES HUGH PAUL

3 Hare Court
1st Floor, Temple, London EC4Y 7BJ,
Telephone: 0171 353 7561
Call date: May 1990, Inner Temple
Qualifications: [B.A. (So'ton), Dip Law]

AGHA SIZA

10 King's Bench Walk
1st Floor, Temple, London EC4Y 7EB,
Telephone: 0171 353 2501
Call date: Feb 1994, Lincoln's Inn
Qualifications: [LLB (Hons, Wales)]

AGNELLO MISS RAQUEL

11 Stone Bldgs
Ground Floor, Lincoln's Inn, London
WC2A 3TG, Telephone: 0171 831 6381
E-mail: clerks@11StoneBuildings.law.co.uk
Call date: Nov 1986, Inner Temple
Qualifications: [BA (Sussex) Dip, D'Etudes
Juridiques, Francaises, ACI Arb, Strasbourg,
ACI Arb]

AGNEW MISS CHRISTINE

3 Hare Court
1st Floor, Temple, London EC4Y 7BJ,
Telephone: 0171 353 7561
Call date: Nov 1992, Inner Temple
Qualifications: [LLB]

AGYEMAN BERNARD OSEI

2 Gray's Inn Square Chambers
2nd Floor, Gray's Inn, London WC1R 5AA,
Telephone: 0171 242 0328/071 405 1317
E-mail: clerks@2gis.co.uk
Call date: July 1972, Middle Temple
Qualifications: [BA]

AHMAD NADEEM

5 Essex Court
1st Floor, Temple, London EC4Y 9AH,
Telephone: 0171 410 2000
Call date: Oct 1996, Gray's Inn
Qualifications: [BA]

AHMAD MISS SIRAT

Chancery Chambers
1st Floor Offices 70/72 Chancery Lane,
London WC2A 1AB,
Telephone: 0171 405 6879/6870
Call date: Feb 1988, Lincoln's Inn
Qualifications: [LLB (Hons)]

AHMAD ZUBAIR

1 Paper Bldgs
1st Floor, Temple, London EC4Y 7EP,
Telephone: 0171 353 3728/4953
Call date: Oct 1995, Lincoln's Inn
Qualifications: [LLB (Hons)(Lond)]

AHMED MISS AMINA

Gray's Inn Chambers
5th Floor, Gray's Inn, London WC1R 5JA,
Telephone: 0171 404 1111
Call date: Feb 1995, Middle Temple
Qualifications: [BSc (Hons)(Lond), CPE (Lond)]

AHMED FAROOQ TAHIR

8 King Street
Manchester M2 6AQ,
Telephone: 0161 834 9560
Call date: Nov 1983, Inner Temple
Qualifications: [LLB (Hons) (Lond)]

AHMED MISS JACQUELINE MICHELLE

Southernhay Chambers
33 Southernhay East, Exeter EX1 1NX,
Telephone: 01392 255777
E-mail: southernhay.chambers@lineone.net
Call date: July 1988, Inner Temple
Qualifications: [LLB (City)]

AHMED MOBIN UDDIN

Tower Hamlets Barristers Chambers
First Floor 45 Brick Lane, London E1 6PU,
Telephone: 0171 247 9825
Call date: Nov 1969, Lincoln's Inn
Qualifications: [B.Com (Dhaka)]

AHMED SALEEM

Perivale Chambers
15 Colwyn Avenue, Perivale, Middlesex
UB6 8JY, Telephone: 0181 998 1935/
081 248 0246
Call date: Feb 1971, Inner Temple
Qualifications: [BA]

AHYA MISS SONAL

1 High Pavement
Nottingham NG1 1HF,
Telephone: 0115 9418218
Call date: Nov 1995, Lincoln's Inn
Qualifications: [LLB (Hons)(Leic)]

AIKEN MRS GILLIAN MARJORIE

2 Middle Temple Lane
3rd Floor, Temple, London EC4Y 9AA,
Telephone: 0171 583 4540
Call date: July 1993, Inner Temple
Qualifications: [BPharm, LLB (Lond), M R
Pharms, LLM (Lond)]

AIKENS RICHARD JOHN PEARSON QC (1986)

Brick Court Chambers
15/19 Devereux Court, London WC2R 3JJ,
Telephone: 0171 583 0777
E-mail: (surname)@brickcourt.demon.co.uk
Call date: July 1973, Middle Temple
Recorder
Qualifications: [MA (Cantab)]

AILES JOHN ASHLEY

Eighteen Carlton Crescent
Southampton SO15 2XR,
Telephone: 01703 639001
Call date: July 1975, Middle Temple
Qualifications: [BA M.Phil]

AINA BENJAMIN ADEJOWON OLUFEMI

3 Temple Gardens
Lower Ground Floor, Temple, London
EC4Y 9AU, Telephone: 0171 353 3102/5/9297
Call date: July 1987, Lincoln's Inn
Qualifications: [LLB LLM (London)]

AINGER WILLIAM DAWSON

10 Old Square
Ground Floor, Lincoln's Inn, London
WC2A 3SU, Telephone: 0171 405 0758
Call date: June 1961, Lincoln's Inn
Qualifications: [MA (Oxon)]

AINLEY NICHOLAS JOHN

5 Essex Court
1st Floor, Temple, London EC4Y 9AH,
Telephone: 0171 410 2000
Call date: July 1973, Lincoln's Inn
Assistant Recorder

AINSWORTH MARK JUSTIN SIMON

Peel Court Chambers
45 Hardman Street, Manchester M3 3HA,
Telephone: 0161 832 3791
Call date: Oct 1992, Lincoln's Inn
Qualifications: [BA(Hons)(L'pool), Dip Law]

AIOLFI LAURENCE

Queen Elizabeth Bldg
Ground Floor, Temple, London EC4Y 9BS,
Telephone: 0171 353 7181 (12 Lines)
Call date: Oct 1996, Inner Temple
Qualifications: [LLB (Bris)]

AIRD RICHARD ERSKINE

4 Pump Court
Temple, London EC4Y 7AN,
Telephone: 0171 353 2656/9
E-mail: 4_pump_court@compuserve.com
Door Tenant
Lancaster Building Chambers
77 Deansgate, Manchester M3 2BW,
Telephone: 0161 661 4444
E-mail: sandra@lbnipc.com
Door Tenant
Call date: Nov 1976, Inner Temple
Qualifications: [LLB]

AIREY SIMON ANDREW

11 Bolt Court
London EC4A 3DQ,
Telephone: 0171 353 2300
E-mail: boltct11@aol.com
Redhill Chambers
Seloduct House 30 Station Road, Redhill
RH1 1NK, Telephone: 01737 780781
Call date: Nov 1989, Inner Temple
Qualifications: [LLB (Sheff)]

AITKEN JOHN RUSSELL

New Court Chambers
3 Broad Chare, Newcastle Upon Tyne
NE1 3DQ, Telephone: 0191 232 1980
Call date: July 1984, Gray's Inn
Qualifications: [BA]

AKAST JOHN FRANCIS

East Anglian Chambers
Gresham House 5 Museum Street, Ipswich
IP1 1HQ, Telephone: 01473 214481
East Anglian Chambers
Sanders House 52 North Hill, Colchester
CO1 1PY, Telephone: 01206 572756
East Anglian Chambers
57 London Street, Norwich NR2 1HL,
Telephone: 01603 617351
Call date: Nov 1968, Inner Temple
Qualifications: [LLB]

AKENHEAD ROBERT QC (1989)

1 Atkin Building
Gray's Inn, London WC1R 5AT,
Telephone: 0171 404 0102
E-mail: clerks@atkin-chambers.co.uk
Call date: July 1972, Inner Temple
Recorder
Qualifications: [LLB]

AKERMAN MISS KATE LOUISE

Regency Chambers
18 Cowgate, Peterborough PE1 1NA,
Telephone: 01733 315215
Regency Chambers
Sheraton House, Castle Park, Cambridge
CB3 0AX, Telephone: 01223 301517
Call date: Oct 1994, Middle Temple
Qualifications: [LLB (Hons)(Lond)]

AKIN BARRIE SIMON

Gray's Inn Chambers
3rd Floor, Gray's Inn, London WC1R 5JA,
Telephone: 0171 242 2642
E-mail: clerks@taxbar.com
Call date: July 1976, Middle Temple
Qualifications: [LLB, FCA]

AKINJIDE RICHARD

10 King's Bench Walk
1st Floor, Temple, London EC4Y 7EB,
Telephone: 0171 353 2501
Call date: Feb 1956, Inner Temple
Qualifications: [LLB (London), FCIArb]

AKINSANYA JONATHAN

4 Brick Court
1st Floor, Temple, London EC4Y 9AD,
Telephone: 0171 583 8455
Call date: Nov 1993, Inner Temple
Qualifications: [LLB (South Bank)]

AKIWUMI ANTHONY SEBASTIAN AKITAYO

Pump Court Chambers
Upper Ground Floor 3 Pump Court, Temple,
London EC4Y 7AJ, Telephone: 0171 353 0711
Pump Court Chambers
31 Southgate Street, Winchester SO23 8EE,
Telephone: 01962 868161
Call date: July 1989, Inner Temple
Qualifications: [BA (Kent)]

AKKA LAWRENCE MARK

20 Essex Street
London WC2R 3AL,
Telephone: 0171 583 9294
E-mail: clerks@20essexst.com
Call date: Oct 1991, Lincoln's Inn
Qualifications: [BA (Hons) (Oxon)]

AKMAN MISS MERCY LOUISE

36 Bedford Row
London WC1R 4JH,
Telephone: 0171 421 8000
E-mail: 36bedfordrow@link.org
Call date: Nov 1982, Gray's Inn
Qualifications: [LLB (Hons) (Wales)]

AKRAM UMER

Perivale Chambers
15 Colwyn Avenue, Perivale, Middlesex
UB6 8JY, Telephone: 0181 998 1935/
081 248 0246
Call date: Mar 1997, Lincoln's Inn
Qualifications: [LLB (Hons)]

AKUSU-OSSAI MRS AUGUSTA OVO

Chancery Chambers
1st Floor Offices 70/72 Chancery Lane,
London WC2A 1AB,
Telephone: 0171 405 6879/6870
Call date: Oct 1993, Lincoln's Inn
Qualifications: [LLB (Hons)(Bucks)]

AKUWUDIKE MISS EMMA CHIAWUOTU

3 Gray's Inn Square
Ground Floor, London WC1R 5AH,
Telephone: 0171 520 5600
E-mail: gis3@btinternet.com
Call date: Nov 1992, Inner Temple
Qualifications: [LLB (Hons)]

AKWAGYIRAM SAMUEL MANTEAW

12 Old Square
1st Floor, Lincoln's Inn, London WC2A 3TX,
Telephone: 0171 404 0875
Call date: Nov 1985, Inner Temple
Qualifications: [BA (Hons)]

AL'HASSAN KHADIM

Equity Chambers
Suite 110, Gazette Buildings 168 Corporation
Street, Birmingham B4 6TS,
Telephone: 0121 233 2100
Call date: Nov 1993, Inner Temple
Qualifications: [LLB (Leic)]

AL-ANI DR ABDUL-HAQ

9 King's Bench Walk
Basement, Temple, London EC4Y 7DX,
Telephone: 0171 353 9564
E-mail: jvlee@btinternet.com
Call date: Oct 1996, Inner Temple
Qualifications: [BSc (Baghdad), MSc, PhD
(Lond), MSc (Middx), CPE (Lond)]

AL-QASIM DR ANIS

2 Paper Bldgs
1st Floor, Temple, London EC4Y 7ET,
Telephone: 0171 936 2611 (10 Lines)
E-mail: clerks@2pbbarristers.co.uk
Call date: Jan 1950, Lincoln's Inn
Qualifications: [LLB, LLM, PhD (Lond), Dip Oil
& Gas Law, (Dallas)]

AL-RASHID MAHMUD

9 King's Bench Walk
Basement, Temple, London EC4Y 7DX,
Telephone: 0171 353 9564
E-mail: jvlee@btinternet.com
Call date: Oct 1991, Gray's Inn
Qualifications: [LLB (Leics)]

AL-YUNUSI ABDULLAH MUHAMMAD

Harrow on the Hill Chambers
60 High Street, Harrow on the Hill, Middlesex
HA1 3LL, Telephone: 0181 423 7444
Call date: Nov 1994, Inner Temple
Qualifications: [BSc (Wales), CPE
(Wolverhampton)]

ALBAN-LLOYD MRS NAN

2 King's Bench Walk
1st Floor, Temple, London EC4Y 7DE,
Telephone: 0171 353 9276
Call date: Nov 1988, Inner Temple
Qualifications: [BFA (Boston), LLB (Hons)]

ALBUTT IAN LESLIE

2-3 Gray's Inn Square
Gray's Inn, London WC1R 5JH,
Telephone: 0171 242 4986
E-mail: chambers@2-3graysinnsquare.co.uk
Call date: July 1981, Gray's Inn

ALDER MRS CLAIRE

1 Gray's Inn Square
Ground Floor, London WC1R 5AA,
Telephone: 0171 405 8946/7/8
Call date: July 1988, Inner Temple
Qualifications: [LLB (LSE)]

D

ALDERSON MISS PHILIPPA ELIZABETH LOVEDAY

6 Gray's Inn Square
Ground Floor, Gray's Inn, London WC1R 5AZ,
Telephone: 0171 242 1052
Call date: Nov 1993, Middle Temple
Qualifications: [BA (Hons)(Dunelm)]

ALDOUS CHARLES QC (1985)

7 Stone Bldgs
Ground Floor, Lincoln's Inn, London
WC2A 3SZ, Telephone: 0171 405 3886/
242 3546
E-mail: chaldous@vossnet.co.uk
Call date: Feb 1967, Inner Temple
Qualifications: [LLB (Lond)]

ALDOUS GRAHAME LINLEY

9 Gough Square
London EC4A 3DE, Telephone: 0171 353 5371
Call date: July 1979, Inner Temple
Qualifications: [LLB (Exon)]

ALDOUS ROBERT JOHN

Octagon House
19 Colegate, Norwich NR3 1AT,
Telephone: 01603 623186
E-mail: octagon@netmatters.co.uk
Call date: July 1985, Inner Temple
Qualifications: [BA (Cantab)]

ALDRED BRIAN PETER

Westgate Chambers
144 High Street, Lewes, East Sussex BN7 1XT,
Telephone: 01273 480510
Call date: Nov 1994, Inner Temple
Qualifications: [LLB (Kent)]

ALDRED MARK STEVEN

Hollis Whiteman Chambers
3rd/4th Floor Queen Elizabeth Bldg, Temple,
London EC4Y 9BS, Telephone: 0171 583 5766
E-mail: hollis.whiteman@btinternet.com
Call date: Mar 1996, Middle Temple
Qualifications: [LLB (Hons)]

ALDRIDGE JAMES HUGH

13 Old Square
Ground Floor, Lincoln's Inn, London
WC2A 3UA, Telephone: 0171 404 4800
Call date: Oct 1994, Lincoln's Inn
Qualifications: [BA (Hons)]

ALDRIDGE JAMES WILLIAM

199 Strand
London WC2R 1DR,
Telephone: 0171 379 9779
E-mail: chambers@199strand.co.uk
Call date: July 1987, Inner Temple
Qualifications: [BA (Lond),Dip Law]

ALEESON WARWICK LAN GRIEG

Francis Taylor Bldg
2nd Floor, Temple, London EC4Y 7BY,
Telephone: 0171 353 9942/3157
Call date: Nov 1994, Gray's Inn
Qualifications: [LLB (Hons)(Wales)]

ALESBURY ALUN

2 Mitre Ct Bldgs
2nd Floor, Temple, London EC4Y 7BX,
Telephone: 0171 583 1380
Call date: July 1974, Inner Temple
Qualifications: [MA (Cantab)]

ALEXANDER DANIEL SAKYI

8 New Square
Lincoln's Inn, London WC2A 3QP,
Telephone: 0171 405 4321
Call date: July 1988, Middle Temple
Qualifications: [BA (Hons) (Oxon), LLM
(Harvard), Dip Law]

ALEXANDER DAVID ROBERT JAMES

3/4 South Square
Gray's Inn, London WC1R 5HP,
Telephone: 0171 696 9900
E-mail: clerks@southsquare.com
Call date: Nov 1987, Middle Temple
Qualifications: [MA (Cantab)]

ALEXANDER EDMOND MICHAEL

14 Tooks Court
Cursitor St, London EC4A 1LB,
Telephone: 0171 405 8828
E-mail: clerks @tooks.law.co.uk
Call date: June 1961, Gray's Inn
Qualifications: [BA (Hons)]

ALEXANDER IAN DOUGLAS GAVIN QC (1989)

11 Bolt Court
London EC4A 3DQ,
Telephone: 0171 353 2300
E-mail: boltct11@aol.com
Redhill Chambers
Seloduct House 30 Station Road, Redhill
RH1 1NK, Telephone: 01737 780781
Call date: June 1964, Lincoln's Inn
Recorder
Qualifications: [LLB (Lond)]

ALEXANDER ROBERT DOMINIC

1 Gray's Inn Square
1st Floor, London WC1R 5AG,
Telephone: 0171 405 3000
E-mail: clerks@onegrays.demon.co.uk
Call date: Nov 1995, Middle Temple
Qualifications: [BA (Hons)(Bris)]

ALFORD ROBERT JOHN

Southernhay Chambers
33 Southernhay East, Exeter EX1 1NX,
Telephone: 01392 255777
E-mail: southernhay.chambers@lineone.net
Call date: Nov 1970, Gray's Inn
Qualifications: [LLB (Sheff)]

ALFORD STUART ROBERT

36 Bedford Row
London WC1R 4JH,
Telephone: 0171 421 8000
E-mail: 36bedfordrow@link.org
Call date: Oct 1992, Middle Temple
Qualifications: [B.Sc (Hons, Reading)]

ALGAR CLAUDIUS JOHN

10 King's Bench Walk
Ground Floor, Temple, London EC4Y 7EB,
Telephone: 0171 353 7742
E-mail: 10kbw@lineone.net
Call date: Nov 1972, Inner Temple

ALGAZY JACQUES MAX

Cloisters
1st Floor, Temple, London EC4Y 7AA,
Telephone: 0171 827 4000
E-mail: clerks@cloisters.com
Call date: Nov 1980, Gray's Inn
Qualifications: [LLB (Reading), D.E.S.Eu]

ALI RAYMOND AZEEZ

Middlesex Chambers
Suite 3 & 4 Stanley House Stanley Avenue,
Wembley, Middlesex HA0 4SB,
Telephone: 0181 902 1499
Call date: May 1995, Gray's Inn
Qualifications: [LLB, LLM (Lond), LEC
(Trinidad)]

ALIKER PHILIP BLISS

2 Pump Court
1st Floor, Temple, London EC4Y 7AH,
Telephone: 0171 353 5597
Call date: Oct 1990, Inner Temple
Qualifications: [BA (Vanderbilt), LLB (Leeds)]

ALLAN CHRISTOPHER DAVID QC (1995)

22 Old Bldgs
Lincoln's Inn, London WC2A 3UJ,
Telephone: 0171 831 0222
25 Byrom Street
Manchester M3 4PF,
Telephone: 0161 829 2100
E-mail: Byromst25@aol.com
Call date: July 1974, Gray's Inn
Recorder
Qualifications: [LLB]

ALLAN COLIN STEWART

3 Gray's Inn Square
Ground Floor, London WC1R 5AH,
Telephone: 0171 520 5600
E-mail: gis3@btinternet.com
Call date: July 1971, Inner Temple

ALLAN MISS MONIQUE ANNE FORTUNE

Littman Chambers
12 Gray's Inn Square, London WC1R 5JP,
Telephone: 0171 404 4866
E-mail: admin@littmanchambers.com
Call date: Nov 1986, Inner Temple
Qualifications: [BA (Bristol) Dip Law]

ALLARDICE MISS MIRANDA JANE

Pump Court Chambers
Upper Ground Floor 3 Pump Court, Temple,
London EC4Y 7AJ, Telephone: 0171 353 0711
Pump Court Chambers
31 Southgate Street, Winchester SO23 8EE,
Telephone: 01962 868161
Call date: July 1982, Lincoln's Inn
Qualifications: [BA (Oxon)]

ALLCOCK STEPHEN JAMES QC (1993)

Pump Court Tax Chambers
16 Bedford Row, London WC1R 4EB,
Telephone: 0171 414 8080
Call date: July 1975, Gray's Inn
Qualifications: [BA (Cantab)]

ALLDIS CHRISTOPHER JOHN

Peel House Chambers
Ground Floor, Peel House 5 Harrington Street,
Liverpool L2 9QA, Telephone: 0151 236 4321
Call date: Nov 1970, Gray's Inn
Recorder
Qualifications: [MA, LLB (Cantab)]

ALLEN DARRYL JOHN

Farrar's Building
Temple, London EC4Y 7BD,
Telephone: 0171 583 9241
E-mail: chambers@farrarsbuilding.co.uk
Call date: Oct 1995, Lincoln's Inn
Qualifications: [LLB (Hons)(Leeds)]

ALLEN DAVID KENNETH

2 New Street
Leicester LE1 5NA, Telephone: 0116 2625906
Call date: July 1975, Middle Temple
Qualifications: [MA, BA (Hons),LLM]

ALLEN DOUGLAS STEPHEN

Goldsmith Chambers
Ground Floor Goldsmith Building, Temple,
London EC4Y 7BL,
Telephone: 0171 353 6802/3/4/5
E-mail: celiamonksfield@btinternet.com
Call date: Oct 1995, Lincoln's Inn
Qualifications: [BA (Hons)(B'ham)]

ALLEN MS FRANCES

Library Chambers
Gray's Inn Chambers, Gray's Inn, London
WC1R 5JA, Telephone: 0171 404 6500
Call date: Oct 1995, Inner Temple
Qualifications: [BSc (Lond), CPE (City)]

ALLEN JAMES HENDRICUSS QC (1995)

Chancery House Chambers
7 Lisbon Square, Leeds LS1 4LY,
Telephone: 0113 244 6691
E-mail: Chanceryhouse@btinternet.com
Call date: Nov 1973, Gray's Inn
Recorder
Qualifications: [BA Law]

ALLEN MARK GRAHAM

30 Park Place
Cardiff CF1 3BA, Telephone: 01222 398421
E-mail: 100757.1456@compuserve.com
Call date: July 1981, Middle Temple
Qualifications: [LLB (Cardiff)]

ALLEN MICHAEL DAVID PRIOR

7 King's Bench Walk
Ground Floor, Temple, London EC4Y 7DS,
Telephone: 0171 583 0404
Call date: Oct 1990, Gray's Inn
Qualifications: [BSc, LLB, FRICS, ACIArb]

ALLEN NICHOLAS PAUL

29 Bedford Row Chambers
London WC1R 4HE,
Telephone: 0171 831 2626
Call date: Oct 1995, Middle Temple
Qualifications: [BA (Hons), LLM]

ALLEN ROBIN GEOFFREY BRUERE QC (1995)

Cloisters
1st Floor, Temple, London EC4Y 7AA,
Telephone: 0171 827 4000
E-mail: clerks@cloisters.com
Call date: Nov 1974, Middle Temple
Qualifications: [BA (Oxon)]

ALLEN MISS SYLVIA DELORES

Somersett Chambers
52 Bedford Row, London WC1R 4LR,
Telephone: 0171 404 6701
E-mail: Somersettchambers@cocoon.co.uk
Call date: July 1983, Gray's Inn
Qualifications: [LLB (Lond)]

ALLEN THOMAS MICHAEL CHARD

5 Paper Bldgs
1st Floor, Temple, London EC4Y 7HB,
Telephone: 0171 583 6117
E-mail: clerks@5-paperbuildings.law.co.uk
Call date: Feb 1994, Middle Temple
Qualifications: [BA (Hons)(Durham), Dip in
Law (City)]

ALLEN WILLIAM ANDREW

4 Brick Court
Ground Floor, Temple, London EC4Y 9AD,
Telephone: 0171 797 7766
E-mail: chambers@4brick.co.uk
Call date: Oct 1995, Inner Temple
Qualifications: [BA (Cantab), LLM (Lond)]

ALLFREY RICHARD FORBES

Doughty Street Chambers
11 Doughty Street, London WC1N 2PG,
Telephone: 0171 404 1313
E-mail: doughty_street@compuserve.com
Call date: July 1974, Middle Temple
Qualifications: [LLB (Lond)]

ALLINGHAM-NICHOLSON MISS ELIZABETH SARAH

2 New Street
Leicester LE1 5NA, Telephone: 0116 2625906
Call date: Oct 1995, Lincoln's Inn
Qualifications: [LLB (Hons)(Lond), BA
(Toronto)]

ALLIOTT GEORGE BECKLES

2 Harcourt Bldgs
Ground Floor/Left, Temple, London
EC4Y 9DB, Telephone: 0171 583 9020
E-mail: clerks@harcourt.co.uk
Call date: July 1981, Inner Temple
Qualifications: [LLB Warwick]

ALLOTT PHILIP JAMES

20 Essex Street
London WC2R 3AL,
Telephone: 0171 583 9294
E-mail: clerks@20essexst.com
Door Tenant
Call date: Feb 1960, Gray's Inn
Qualifications: [BA, LLB (Cantab)]

ALLOWAY TOR HUGH

3 Temple Gardens
3rd Floor, Temple, London EC4Y 9AU,
Telephone: 0171 583 0010
Call date: July 1985, Lincoln's Inn
Qualifications: [BSc BA ACII]

ALLSTON ANTHONY STANLEY

2 Pump Court
1st Floor, Temple, London EC4Y 7AH,
Telephone: 0171 353 5597
Call date: July 1975, Gray's Inn
Qualifications: [BA]

ALLUM DESMOND ERIC QUINTIN

8 King's Bench Walk
2nd Floor, Temple, London EC4Y 7DU,
Telephone: 0171 797 8888
8 King's Bench Walk North
1 Park Square East, Leeds LS1 2NE,
Telephone: 0113 2439797
Call date: July 1962, Middle Temple

ALMEYDA MISS GENEVIEVE MARGARET MARY

Albany Chambers
91 Kentish Town Road, London NW1 8NY,
Telephone: 0171 485 5736/5758
E-mail: albanychambers@usanet
Call date: Nov 1994, Inner Temple
Qualifications: [LLB (Hons)(Lon), LLM]

D

ALOMO RICHARD OLUSOJI

14 Gray's Inn Square
Gray's Inn, London WC1R 5JP,
Telephone: 0171 242 0858
E-mail: 100712.2134@compuserve.com
Call date: Nov 1990, Inner Temple
Qualifications: [LLB (Lond)]

ALSOLAIMANI NASIRUDDIN

10 Kingsfield Avenue
Harrow, Middlesex HA2 6AH,
Telephone: 0181 427 8709/081 248 4943
Call date: Nov 1971, Lincoln's Inn
Qualifications: [BA]

ALT MRS ELIZABETH JANE

4 King's Bench Walk
2nd Floor, Temple, London EC4Y 7DL,
Telephone: 0171 353 3581
Call date: July 1984, Lincoln's Inn
Qualifications: [LLB (Hull)]

ALTARAS DAVID MAURICE

36 Bedford Row
London WC1R 4JH,
Telephone: 0171 421 8000
E-mail: 36bedfordrow@link.org
Call date: Nov 1969, Lincoln's Inn
Qualifications: [BA MA TCD, Dip Crim
(Cantab), ACIArb]

ALTHAM JOHN ROBERT CARR

The Corn Exchange
5th Floor Fenwick Street, Liverpool L2 7QS,
Telephone: 0151 227 1081/5009
Call date: Nov 1993, Gray's Inn
Qualifications: [BA]

ALTHAUS ANTONY JUSTIN

1 Serjeants' Inn
5th Floor Fleet Street, Temple, London
EC4Y 1LL, Telephone: 0171 415 6666
E-mail: no1serjeantsinn@btinternet.com
Call date: July 1988, Inner Temple
Qualifications: [BA (Oxon), Dip Law (City)]

ALTMAN BRIAN

3 Hare Court
1st Floor, Temple, London EC4Y 7BJ,
Telephone: 0171 353 7561
Call date: July 1981, Middle Temple
Qualifications: [LLB (Lond) Dip Eur, Int
(Amsterdam)]

ALTON MISS ELISABETH

St James's Chambers
68 Quay Street, Manchester M3 3EJ,
Telephone: 0161 834 7000
E-mail: 106241.2625@compuserve.com
Call date: Oct 1990, Middle Temple
Qualifications: [LLB (Nott'm)]

ALTY ANDREW STEPHEN JOHN

New Bailey Chambers
10 Lawson Street, Preston PR1 2QT,
Telephone: 01772 258087
Call date: Feb 1992, Inner Temple
Qualifications: [LLB (Hons)]

AMAKYE MISS GRACE TINA

3 Temple Gardens
2nd Floor, Temple, London EC4Y 9AU,
Telephone: 0171 583 1155
Call date: Nov 1983, Gray's Inn
Qualifications: [LLB (Lond)]

AMAOUCHE MISS SASSA-ANN

One Garden Court
Ground Floor, Temple, London EC4Y 9BJ,
Telephone: 0171 797 7900
Call date: Oct 1996, Inner Temple
Qualifications: [LLB (Lond)]

AMBROSE MISS CLARE MARY GENESTE

20 Essex Street
London WC2R 3AL,
Telephone: 0171 583 9294
E-mail: clerks@20essexst.com
Call date: Nov 1992, Gray's Inn
Qualifications: [BA (Oxon), LLM (Cantab)]

AMBROSE EUAN JAMES

Guildhall Chambers
23 Broad Street, Bristol BS1 2HG,
Telephone: 0117 9273366
Call date: Nov 1992, Middle Temple
Qualifications: [BA (Hons), MA (Hons)]

AMES GEOFFREY ALAN

29 Bedford Row Chambers
London WC1R 4HE,
Telephone: 0171 831 2626
Call date: July 1976, Lincoln's Inn
Qualifications: [BSc]

AMIHERE ANWOBO

20 Sewardstone Gardens
Chingford, London E4 7QE,
Telephone: 0181 524 3054
Call date: Nov 1970, Middle Temple
Qualifications: [LLB (Lond), ACCS]

AMIN MISS FARAH

7 New Square
Lincoln's Inn, London WC2A 3QS,
Telephone: 0171 430 1660
Call date: July 1991, Lincoln's Inn
Qualifications: [LLB (Hons) (Lond)]

AMIRAFTABI MISS ROSHANAK

Hardwicke Building
New Square, Lincoln's Inn, London
WC2A 3SB, Telephone: 0171 242 2523
E-mail: clerks@hardwicke.co.uk
Call date: Feb 1993, Gray's Inn
Qualifications: [BA]

AMIS CHRISTOPHER JOCELYN

2 King's Bench Walk
Ground Floor, Temple, London EC4Y 7DE,
Telephone: 0171 353 1746
E-mail: 2kbw@atlas.co.uk
King's Bench Chambers
115 North Hill, Plymouth PL4 8JY,
Telephone: 01752 221551
Call date: Nov 1991, Gray's Inn
Qualifications: [LLB (Lond)]

AMLOT ROY DOUGLAS QC (1989)

6 King's Bench Walk
Ground Floor, Temple, London EC4Y 7DR,
Telephone: 0171 583 0410
Call date: Nov 1963, Lincoln's Inn

AMOR CHRISTOPHER LEWIS

1 Middle Temple Lane
Temple, London EC4Y 1LT,
Telephone: 0171 583 0659 (12 Lines)
Call date: May 1984, Gray's Inn
Qualifications: [MA (Oxon)]

AMOS TIMOTHY ROBERT

Queen Elizabeth Bldg
2nd Floor, Temple, London EC4Y 9BS,
Telephone: 0171 797 7837
Call date: July 1987, Lincoln's Inn
Qualifications: [MA (Oxon) Dip Law]

ANCLIFFE MRS SHIVA EDWINA

Francis Taylor Bldg
Ground Floor, Temple, London EC4Y 7BY,
Telephone: 0171 353 7768/7769/2711
Call date: Nov 1991, Lincoln's Inn
Qualifications: [LLB (Hons)]

ANDENAS DR MADS

Brick Court Chambers
15/19 Devereux Court, London WC2R 3JJ,
Telephone: 0171 583 0777
E-mail: (surname)@brickcourt.demon.co.uk
Call date: July 1997, Middle Temple
Qualifications: [PhD (Cantab)]

ANDERS JONATHAN JAMES

Bell Yard Chambers
116/118 Chancery Lane, London WC2A 1PP,
Telephone: 0171 306 9292
Call date: Feb 1990, Inner Temple
Qualifications: [LLB]

ANDERSON ANTHONY JOHN QC (1982)

2 Mitre Ct Bldgs
2nd Floor, Temple, London EC4Y 7BX,
Telephone: 0171 583 1380
Call date: Feb 1964, Inner Temple
Recorder
Qualifications: [MA (Oxon)]

D

ANDERSON BRENDAN JOSEPH

1 Dr Johnson's Bldgs
Ground Floor, Temple, London EC4Y 7AX,
Telephone: 0171 353 9328
40 King Street
Chester CH1 2AH, Telephone: 01244 323886
Door Tenant
Call date: July 1985, Gray's Inn
Qualifications: [LLB (Leeds)]

ANDERSON CLIVE STUART

4 King's Bench Walk
Ground/First Floor, Temple, London
EC4Y 7DL, Telephone: 0171 822 8822
E-mail: 4kbw@barristersatlaw.com
Call date: Nov 1976, Middle Temple
Qualifications: [BA (Cantab)]

ANDERSON COLIN JAMES DOUGLAS

St Mary's Chambers
50 High Pavement, Lace Market, Nottingham
NG1 1HW, Telephone: 0115 9503503
E-mail: clerks@smc.law.co.uk
Call date: Nov 1973, Gray's Inn
Qualifications: [MA (Cantab)]

ANDERSON DAVID WILLIAM KINLOCH

Brick Court Chambers
15/19 Devereux Court, London WC2R 3JJ,
Telephone: 0171 583 0777
E-mail: (surname)@brickcourt.demon.co.uk
Call date: July 1985, Middle Temple
Qualifications: [MA (Oxon), BA (Cantab)]

ANDERSON DONALD

Lamb Chambers
Lamb Building, Temple, London EC4Y 7AS,
Telephone: 0171 797 8300
E-mail: lambchambers@link.org
Pendragon Chambers
124 Walter Road, Swansea SA1 5RG,
Telephone: 01792 411188
Door Tenant
Call date: July 1969, Inner Temple
Qualifications: [BA (Wales)]

ANDERSON JOHN ADRIAN

18 Red Lion Court
(Off Fleet Street), London EC4A 3EB,
Telephone: 0171 520 6000
Thornwood House
102 New London Road, Chelmsford, Essex
CM2 0RG, Telephone: 01245 280880
Call date: July 1989, Middle Temple

ANDERSON MISS JULIE

Littman Chambers
12 Gray's Inn Square, London WC1R 5JP,
Telephone: 0171 404 4866
E-mail: admin@littmanchambers.com
Call date: Nov 1993, Gray's Inn
Qualifications: [BA (Hons) (Oxon), Dip Law]

ANDERSON MS LESLEY JANE

40 King Street
Manchester M2 6BA,
Telephone: 0161 832 9082
E-mail: Kingst40@aol.com
Call date: Nov 1989, Middle Temple
Qualifications: [LLB (Manc)]

ANDERSON MARK ROGER

3 Fountain Court
Steelhouse Lane, Birmingham B4 6DR,
Telephone: 0121 236 5854
Call date: July 1983, Middle Temple
Qualifications: [BA (Oxon)]

ANDERSON PETER JOHN

15 Winckley Square
Preston PR1 3JJ, Telephone: 01772 252828
E-mail: clerks@winckleysq.demon.co.uk
Call date: July 1988, Inner Temple
Qualifications: [LLB]

ANDERSON ROBERT EDWARD

2 Hare Court
Ground Floor, Temple, London EC4Y 7BH,
Telephone: 0171 583 1770
E-mail: 2_Hare_Court@link.org
Call date: Nov 1986, Middle Temple
Qualifications: [BA(Cantab)]

ANDERSON RUPERT JOHN

Monckton Chambers
4 Raymond Buildings, Gray's Inn, London
WC1R 5BP, Telephone: 0171 405 7211
E-mail: chambers@monckton.co.uk
Call date: July 1981, Inner Temple
Qualifications: [MA (Cantab)]

ANDERSON STANLEY

Broad Chare
33 Broad Chare, Newcastle Upon Tyne
NE1 3DQ, Telephone: 0191 232 0541
Call date: Oct 1993, Lincoln's Inn
Qualifications: [LLB (Hons)(Newc)]

ANDREAE-JONES WILLIAM PEARCE QC (1984)

Coleridge Chambers
Citadel 190 Corporation Street, Birmingham
B4 6QD, Telephone: 0121 233 3303
1 Serjeants' Inn
5th Floor Fleet Street, Temple, London
EC4Y 1LL, Telephone: 0171 415 6666
E-mail: no1serjeantsinn@btinternet.com
Door Tenant
Call date: Nov 1965, Inner Temple
Recorder
Qualifications: [BA (Cantab)]

ANDREW MISS ELIZABETH HONORA

Devereux Chambers
Devereux Court, London WC2R 3JJ,
Telephone: 0171 353 7534
E-mail: elton@devchambers.co.uk
Call date: Nov 1974, Middle Temple
Assistant Recorder
Qualifications: [LLB (Lond)]

ANDREW SEAMUS RONALD

Deans Court Chambers
Cumberland House Crown Square, Manchester
M3 3HA, Telephone: 0161 834 4097
E-mail: deanscourt@compuserve.com
Call date: Feb 1991, Gray's Inn
Qualifications: [LLB (Lond), LLM (Lond)]

ANDREWS MISS CLAIRE MARGUERITE

Gough Square Chambers
6-7 Gough Square, London EC4A 3DE,
Telephone: 0171 353 0924
E-mail: gsc@goughsq.co.uk
Call date: Nov 1979, Gray's Inn
Qualifications: [LLB (Manch)]

ANDREWS MISS GERALDINE MARY

Essex Court Chambers
24 Lincoln's Inn Fields, London WC2A 3ED,
Telephone: 0171 813 8000
E-mail: clerksroom@essexcourt-chambers.co.uk
Call date: Nov 1981, Gray's Inn
Qualifications: [LLB, LLM, AKC (Lond)]

ANDREWS MISS JANE RACHEL

India Buildings Chambers
Water Street, Liverpool L2 OXG,
Telephone: 0151 243 6000
Call date: Nov 1989, Inner Temple
Qualifications: [LLB (Dub)]

ANDREWS PETER JOHN QC (1991)

199 Strand
London WC2R 1DR,
Telephone: 0171 379 9779
E-mail: chambers@199strand.co.uk
3 Fountain Court
Steelhouse Lane, Birmingham, West Midlands
B4 6DR, Telephone: 0121 236 5854
Call date: July 1970, Lincoln's Inn
Recorder
Qualifications: [LLB (Bris), D Crim (Cantab)]

Fax: 0171 379 9481;
Out of hours telephone: 01233 756691;
DX: 322 London, Chancery Lane;
Other comms: E-mail
pjandrews@199strand.co.uk

Types of work: Medical negligence; Personal injury

Circuit: Midland and Oxford

Awards and memberships: Professional Negligence Bar Association; Personal Injury Bar Association; AVMA

D

Publications: *Catastrophic Injuries: A Practical Guide to Compensation*, 1997; *Quantum of Damages: Kemp & Kemp* (contributor to 'Structured Settlements'), 1998; *Personal Injury Handbook* (contributor), 1997

Reported cases: *Smoldon v Nolan*, [1997] P1QR P133, 1996. Personal injury - spinally injured rugby player - referee's liability.
Mansfield v Weetabix, [1997] PIQR P526, 1997. Negligence - hypoglycaemia as defence to negligent driving.
Hill v West Lancashire Health Authority, [1997] MLR 196, 1997. Medical negligence - cerebral palsy - partial prolonged hypoxia.
Chaplain v Scout Association, [1997] JPIL 207, 1996. Climbing accident - negligence - new cause of action.
Oksvzoglv v Kay, [1998] TLR 26 February, 1998. Medical negligence - service of medical report - costs.

ANDREWS PHILIP BRYAN

38 Young Street
Manchester M3 3FT,
Telephone: 0161 833 0489
E-mail: clerks@young-st-chambers.com
Call date: Feb 1977, Inner Temple
Qualifications: [LLB (Hons)]

ANDREWS SAMUEL JAMES

19 Figtree Lane
Sheffield S1 2DJ, Telephone: 0114 2759708/2738380
Call date: Nov 1991, Gray's Inn
Qualifications: [LLB (Sheff)]

ANELAY RICHARD ALFRED QC (1993)

1 King's Bench Walk
2nd Floor, Temple, London EC4Y 7DB,
Telephone: 0171 936 1500
E-mail: ddear@1kbw.co.uk
Call date: July 1970, Middle Temple
Recorder
Qualifications: [BA (Bristol)]

ANGAMMANA GAMINI BERTRAM

2 Middle Temple Lane
3rd Floor, Temple, London EC4Y 9AA,
Telephone: 0171 583 4540
Door Tenant
Call date: Nov 1983, Lincoln's Inn
Qualifications: [LLB (Lond)]

ANGUS MISS TRACEY ANNE

5 Stone Buildings
Lincoln's Inn, London WC2A 3XT,
Telephone: 0171 242 6201
E-mail: clerks@5-stonebuildings.law.co.uk
Call date: Nov 1991, Inner Temple
Qualifications: [MA (Edin), Dip Law]

ANIM-ADDO PATRICK KWESI

Horizon Chambers
95a Chancery Lane, London WC2A 1DT,
Telephone: 0171 242 2440
Call date: Nov 1974, Lincoln's Inn
Qualifications: [BA]

ANNING MICHAEL

5 Fountain Court
Steelhouse Lane, Birmingham B4 6DR,
Telephone: 0121 606 0500
Call date: Nov 1990, Inner Temple
Qualifications: [BA (Dunelm), LLB (Lond)]

ANNING MISS SARA ELIZABETH

Park Lane Chambers
19 Westgate, Leeds LS1 2RD,
Telephone: 0113 2285000
Call date: Oct 1995, Inner Temple
Qualifications: [BA (Newc), CPE (Huddersfield)]

ANSELL MISS RACHEL LOUISE

4 Pump Court
Temple, London EC4Y 7AN,
Telephone: 0171 353 2656/9
E-mail: 4_pump_court@compuserve.com
Call date: Oct 1995, Middle Temple
Qualifications: [BA (Hons)]

ANTELME ALEXANDER JOHN

1 Paper Bldgs
Ground Floor, Temple, London EC4Y 7EP,
Telephone: 0171 583 7355
E-mail: clerks@1pb.co.uk
Call date: Oct 1993, Gray's Inn
Qualifications: [MA (Hons)(Oxon)]

ANTHONY MISS CHRISTINA

3 Paper Bldgs
2nd Floor, Temple, London EC4Y 7EU,
Telephone: 0171 353 6208
Call date: Nov 1990, Lincoln's Inn
Qualifications: [LLB (Hons)]

ANTHONY MICHAEL GUY

2 Crown Office Row
Ground Floor, Temple, London EC4Y 7HJ,
Telephone: 0171 797 8100
E-mail: mail@2cor.co.uk, or to individual
barristers at: [barrister's surname]@2cor.co.uk
Call date: July 1972, Middle Temple
Qualifications: [MA (Oxon)]

ANTHONY PETER FRANCIS

St Ive's Chambers
9 Fountain Ct, Birmingham B4 6DR,
Telephone: 0121 236 0863/0929
Call date: July 1981, Gray's Inn
Qualifications: [LLB (Warw)]

ANTHONY ROBERT JEFFREY BONNELL

3 Gray's Inn Square
Ground Floor, London WC1R 5AH,
Telephone: 0171 520 5600
E-mail: gis3@btinternet.com
Call date: Nov 1979, Gray's Inn
Qualifications: [LLB (Lond)]

ANTROBUS SIMON JAMES

11 King's Bench Walk
1st Floor, Temple, London EC4Y 7EQ,
Telephone: 0171 353 3337
3 Park Court
Leeds LS1 2QH, Telephone: 0113 297 1200
Call date: Oct 1995, Inner Temple
Qualifications: [LLB (Sheff)]

ANUCHA DOMINIC UKA

Essex House Chambers
Essex House 375-377 Stratford High Street,
Stratford, London E15 4QZ,
Telephone: 0181 536 1077
Call date: May 1987, Gray's Inn
Qualifications: [MA, LLB]

ANYADIKE-DANES MRS MONYA NNENNA MARY

2 Temple Gardens
Temple, London EC4Y 9AY,
Telephone: 0171 583 6041 (12 Lines)
Call date: July 1980, Gray's Inn
Qualifications: [BA (Bris) M.Phil, (Cantab)]

APEA JAMES BENJAMIN

Chambers of James Apea
11 Helix Road, London SW2 2JR,
Telephone: 0181 244 5545
Call date: Nov 1971, Lincoln's Inn
Qualifications: [BA [Lond]]

APFEL FREDDY

37 Park Square
Leeds LS1 2NY, Telephone: 0113 2439422
Call date: July 1986, Middle Temple
Qualifications: [LLB, LLM]

APLIN HOWARD WESTON

The Clove Hitch
High Street, Iron Acton, Bristol BS17 1UG,
Telephone: 01454 228243
Call date: Nov 1955, Inner Temple
Qualifications: [MA]

APPLEBY MISS ELIZABETH QC (1979)

4-5 Gray's Inn Square
Ground Floor, Gray's Inn, London WC1R 5AY,
Telephone: 0171 404 5252
E-mail: chambers@4-5graysinnsquare.co.uk
Call date: July 1965, Gray's Inn
Recorder
Qualifications: [LLB (Hons)]

APSION ROBERT GORDON LENNOX O'REILLY

11 Old Square
Ground Floor, Lincoln's Inn, London
WC2A 3TS, Telephone: 0171 242 5022/
405 1074
Call date: July 1977, Lincoln's Inn
Qualifications: [MBA (Penn)]

D

APTHORP GEORGE CHARLES

5 Essex Court
1st Floor, Temple, London EC4Y 9AH,
Telephone: 0171 410 2000
Call date: Feb 1983, Inner Temple
Qualifications: [BA]

ARCHER MISS DEBORAH ELIZABETH

4 Brick Court
Temple, London EC4Y 9AD,
Telephone: 0171 797 8910
Call date: Nov 1989, Inner Temple
Qualifications: [LLB]

ARCHER JAMES CHRISTOPHER

1 Gray's Inn Square
1st Floor, London WC1R 5AG,
Telephone: 0171 405 3000
E-mail: clerks@onegrays.demon.co.uk
Call date: Nov 1996, Gray's Inn
Qualifications: [LLB (Leeds)]

ARCHER JOHN FRANCIS ASHWEEK QC (1975)

2 Crown Office Row
Ground Floor, Temple, London EC4Y 7HJ,
Telephone: 0171 797 8100
E-mail: mail@2cor.co.uk, or to individual
barristers at: [barrister's surname]@2cor.co.uk
Call date: June 1950, Inner Temple
Recorder
Qualifications: [BA (Oxon)]

ARCHER STEPHEN KENDRAY

2 Temple Gardens
Temple, London EC4Y 9AY,
Telephone: 0171 583 6041 (12 Lines)
Call date: Nov 1979, Inner Temple
Qualifications: [MA (Oxon)]

ARCHER OF SANDWELL THE RT HON QC (1971)

29 Bedford Row Chambers
London WC1R 4HE,
Telephone: 0171 831 2626
8 Fountain Court
Steelhouse Lane, Birmingham B4 6DR,
Telephone: 0121 236 5514/5
E-mail: clerks@no8chambers.co.uk
Door Tenant
Call date: Feb 1952, Gray's Inn
Qualifications: [BA, LLM]

ARDEN ANDREW PAUL RUSSEL QC (1991)

Arden Chambers
27 John Street, London WC1N 2BL,
Telephone: 0171 242 4244
Call date: Feb 1974, Gray's Inn
Qualifications: [LLB (Lond)]

ARDEN PETER LEONARD

Enterprise Chambers
9 Old Square, Lincoln's Inn, London
WC2A 3SR, Telephone: 0171 405 9471
Enterprise Chambers
38 Park Square, Leeds LS1 2PA,
Telephone: 01132 460391
Enterprise Chambers
65 Quayside, Newcastle upon Tyne NE1 3DS,
Telephone: 0191 222 3344
Call date: July 1983, Gray's Inn
Qualifications: [LLB (Lond), LLB, (Cantab)]

ARENTSEN ANDREW NICHOLAS

33 Park Place
Cardiff CF1 3BA, Telephone: 01222 233313
Call date: Oct 1995, Gray's Inn
Qualifications: [BA (Cantab)]

ARGLES (GUY) ROBERT AINSWORTH

24 Old Bldgs
First Floor, Lincoln's Inn, London WC2A 3UJ,
Telephone: 0171 242 2744
Call date: Nov 1965, Middle Temple
Qualifications: [BA (Oxon)]

ARGYLE BRIAN JOHN

1 Middle Temple Lane
Temple, London EC4Y 1LT,
Telephone: 0171 583 0659 (12 Lines)
Call date: July 1972, Gray's Inn
Assistant Recorder

ARGYROPOULOS KYRIAKOS

Hardwicke Building
New Square, Lincoln's Inn, London
WC2A 3SB, Telephone: 0171 242 2523
E-mail: clerks@hardwicke.co.uk
Call date: Nov 1991, Inner Temple
Qualifications: [BA (York), Dip Law]

ARKHURST REGINALD LEON

4 King's Bench Walk
2nd Floor, Temple, London EC4Y 7DL,
Telephone: 0171 353 3581
Call date: July 1984, Middle Temple
Qualifications: [BA (Hons)(Newcastle)]

ARKUSH JONATHAN HARRY SAMUEL

11 Stone Bldgs
Ground Floor, Lincoln's Inn, London
WC2A 3TG, Telephone: 0171 831 6381
E-mail: clerks@11StoneBuildings.law.co.uk
The Corn Exchange
5th Floor Fenwick Street, Liverpool L2 7QS,
Telephone: 0151 227 1081/5009
Call date: Nov 1977, Middle Temple
Qualifications: [MA (Oxon)]

ARLIDGE ANTHONY JOHN QC (1981)

18 Red Lion Court
(Off Fleet Street), London EC4A 3EB,
Telephone: 0171 520 6000
Thornwood House
102 New London Road, Chelmsford, Essex
CM2 0RG, Telephone: 01245 280880
Call date: Feb 1962, Middle Temple
Recorder
Qualifications: [MA (Cantab)]

ARMITAGE ERNEST KEITH QC (1994)

8 King Street
Manchester M2 6AQ,
Telephone: 0161 834 9560
Call date: Nov 1970, Middle Temple
Recorder
Qualifications: [LLB (Hons) (L'pool)]

ARMITAGE MRS LINDY ELIZABETH

Park Lane Chambers
19 Westgate, Leeds LS1 2RD,
Telephone: 0113 2285000
Call date: July 1985, Lincoln's Inn
Qualifications: [LLB (Hons)(Leeds)]

ARMOUR MISS ALISON JANE

1 Gray's Inn Square
Ground Floor, London WC1R 5AA,
Telephone: 0171 405 8946/7/8
Call date: July 1979, Lincoln's Inn
Qualifications: [MA (Business Law), BA
(Hons)(Newc)]

ARMSTRONG DEAN PAUL

6 King's Bench Walk
Ground Floor, Temple, London EC4Y 7DR,
Telephone: 0171 583 0410
Call date: July 1985, Gray's Inn
Qualifications: [MA (Cantab)]

ARMSTRONG GRANT BRUCE

2 Dr Johnson's Building
Temple, London EC4Y 7AY,
Telephone: 0171 353 4716
Call date: July 1978, Lincoln's Inn
Qualifications: [LLB (Lond)]

ARMSTRONG KESTER IDRIS SCOBELL

Broad Chare
33 Broad Chare, Newcastle Upon Tyne
NE1 3DQ, Telephone: 0191 232 0541
Call date: Nov 1982, Inner Temple
Qualifications: [BA (York)]

ARMSTRONG PETER JOHN BOWDEN

Fountain Chambers
Cleveland Business Centre 1 Watson Street,
Middlesbrough TS1 2RQ,
Telephone: 01642 217037
Call date: Nov 1974, Middle Temple
Recorder
Qualifications: [MA (Cantab)]

D

D

ARMSTRONG STUART DAVID

33 Bedford Row
London WC1R 4JH,
Telephone: 0171 242 6476
Call date: Oct 1995, Gray's Inn
Qualifications: [LLM, LLB]

ARNEY JAMES EDWARD

2 Gray's Inn Square Chambers
2nd Floor, Gray's Inn, London WC1R 5AA,
Telephone: 0171 242 0328/071 405 1317
E-mail: clerks@2gis.co.uk
Call date: Oct 1992, Lincoln's Inn
Qualifications: [LLB(Hons)]

ARNFIELD ROBERT JOHN

17 Old Bldgs
Ground Floor, Lincoln's Inn, London
WC2A 3UP, Telephone: 0171 405 9653
Call date: Oct 1996, Inner Temple
Qualifications: [BA (Oxon), CPE]

ARNHEIM DR MICHAEL THOMAS WALTER

Chambers of Dr Michael Arnheim
101 Queen Alexandra Mansions Judd Street,
London WC1H 9DP,
Telephone: 0171 833 5093
Call date: July 1988, Lincoln's Inn
Qualifications: [MA,BA(Witwatersrand), LLB
(Hons) (Lond), PhD (Cantab)]

ARNOLD MARK GRAHAM

3/4 South Square
Gray's Inn, London WC1R 5HP,
Telephone: 0171 696 9900
E-mail: clerks@southsquare.com
Call date: July 1988, Middle Temple
Qualifications: [MA (Hons) (Cantab)]

ARNOLD PETER MATTHEW MILLER

3 Fountain Court
Steelhouse Lane, Birmingham B4 6DR,
Telephone: 0121 236 5854
Call date: July 1972, Lincoln's Inn
Qualifications: [LLB]

ARNOLD RICHARD DAVID

11 South Square
2nd Floor, Gray's Inn, London WC1R 5EU,
Telephone: 0171 405 1222
Call date: July 1985, Middle Temple
Qualifications: [MA (Oxon) Dip Law, (PCL)]

ARNOLD ROBERT CHARLES

New Court
Temple, London EC4Y 9BE,
Telephone: 0171 583 5123/0171 583 0510
Call date: Nov 1974, Middle Temple
Qualifications: [LLB (Edin), LLM (UCL,London),
(IMM.PRd.SpR Urrin, Bonn)]

ARNOT LEE ALEXANDER

22 Old Bldgs
Lincoln's Inn, London WC2A 3UJ,
Telephone: 0171 831 0222
Call date: Oct 1990, Lincoln's Inn
Qualifications: [BA (Cantab)]

ARORA MISS ANITA

4 Brick Court
1st Floor, Temple, London EC4Y 9AD,
Telephone: 0171 583 8455
Call date: Oct 1994, Lincoln's Inn
Qualifications: [LLB (Hons)(Coventry)]

ARRAN GRAHAM KENT

1 Middle Temple Lane
Temple, London EC4Y 1LT,
Telephone: 0171 583 0659 (12 Lines)
Call date: Nov 1969, Lincoln's Inn
Recorder
Qualifications: [LLB]

ARTHUR GAVYN FARR

2 Harcourt Bldgs
1st Floor, Temple, London EC4Y 9DB,
Telephone: 0171 353 6961/7
Harcourt Chambers
Churchill House 3 St Aldate's Courtyard, St
Aldate's, Oxford OX1 1BN,
Telephone: 01865 791559
Call date: Nov 1975, Middle Temple
Qualifications: [MA (Oxon), Jurisprudence]

ASAD MISS SABEENA

Chambers of Raana Sheikh
Gray's Inn Chambers, Gray's Inn, London
WC1R, Telephone: 0171 831 5344
E-mail: s.mcblain@btinternet.com
Call date: July 1989, Middle Temple
Qualifications: [LLB (Lond)]

ASCHERSON MISS ISOBEL RUTH

23 Essex Street
London WC2R 3AS,
Telephone: 0171 413 0353/353 3533
E-mail: clerks@essexstreet23.demon.co.uk
Call date: Feb 1991, Gray's Inn
Qualifications: [LLB (Lond)]

ASH BRIAN MAXWELL QC (1990)

4-5 Gray's Inn Square
Ground Floor, Gray's Inn, London WC1R 5AY,
Telephone: 0171 404 5252
E-mail: chambers@4-5graysinnsquare.co.uk
Call date: Nov 1975, Gray's Inn
Qualifications: [BA (Oxon)]

ASHBY DAVID GLYNN

1 Middle Temple Lane
Temple, London EC4Y 1LT,
Telephone: 0171 583 0659 (12 Lines)
Call date: July 1963, Gray's Inn
Qualifications: [LLB]

ASHCROFT MICHAEL JAMES

20 Essex Street
London WC2R 3AL,
Telephone: 0171 583 9294
E-mail: clerks@20essexst.com
Call date: Mar 1997, Gray's Inn
Qualifications: [BA, BCL (Ocon)]

ASHE THOMAS MICHAEL QC (1994)

11 Stone Bldgs
1st Floor, Lincoln's Inn, London WC2A 3TG,
Telephone: 0171 404 5055
E-mail: 9stoneb@compuserve.com
Westgate Chambers
144 High Street, Lewes, East Sussex BN7 1XT,
Telephone: 01273 480510
Call date: July 1971, Middle Temple
Assistant Recorder

ASHER MS JUDITH

21 Colless Road
Seven Sisters, London N15 4NR,
Telephone: 0181 365 1706
Call date: June 1958, Gray's Inn

ASHFIELD EVAN MORGAN

169 Temple Chambers
Temple Avenue, London EC4Y 0DA,
Telephone: 0171 583 7644
Call date: July 1980, Lincoln's Inn
Qualifications: [LLB (Lond)]

ASHFORD-THOM IAN

1 Temple Gardens
1st Floor, Temple, London EC4Y 9BB,
Telephone: 0171 353 0407/583 1315
E-mail: clerks@1templegardens.co.uk
Call date: July 1977, Gray's Inn
Qualifications: [LL.B (Exeter)]

ASHLEY MARK ROBERT

Tindal Chambers
3/5 New Street, Chelmsford, Essex CM1 1NT,
Telephone: 01245 267742
Tindal Chambers
3 Waxhouse Gate, St Albans, Herts AL5 4DU,
Telephone: 01727 843383
Call date: Nov 1993, Lincoln's Inn
Qualifications: [LLB (Hons)]

ASHLEY-NORMAN JONATHAN CHARLES

3 Hare Court
1st Floor, Temple, London EC4Y 7BJ,
Telephone: 0171 353 7561
Call date: July 1989, Middle Temple
Qualifications: [LLB (Exon)]

ASHMAN PETER MICHAEL

Colleton Chambers
Colleton Crescent, Exeter, Devon EX2 4DG,
Telephone: 01392 74898/9
22 Old Bldgs
Lincoln's Inn, London WC2A 3UJ,
Telephone: 0171 831 0222
Call date: July 1985, Inner Temple
Qualifications: [LLB (Exon), LLM (Inter Business, Legal Studies),]

D

D

ASHMOLE TIMOTHY MICHAEL

9 Gough Square
London EC4A 3DE, Telephone: 0171 353 5371
Call date: Oct 1992, Inner Temple
Qualifications: [LLB (E.Ang)]

ASHMORE (TERENCE) GODFREY

7 Stone Bldgs
1st Floor, Lincoln's Inn, London WC2A 3SZ,
Telephone: 0171 242 0961
Call date: Nov 1961, Gray's Inn

ASHTON ARTHUR HENRY

One Raymond Buildings
Gray's Inn, London WC1R 5BH,
Telephone: 0171 430 1234
E-mail: chambers@ipbar1rb.com;
clerks@ipbar1rb.com
Call date: July 1988, Inner Temple
Qualifications: [BA, LLB (Rhodes)]

ASHTON DAVID SAMBROOK

13 King's Bench Walk
1st Floor, Temple, London EC4Y 7EN,
Telephone: 0171 353 7204
E-mail: clerks@13kbw.law.co.uk
King's Bench Chambers
32 Beaumont Street, Oxford OX1 2NP,
Telephone: 01865 311066
E-mail: clerks@kbc-oxford.law.co.uk
Call date: July 1962, Gray's Inn
Qualifications: [MA (Oxon)]

ASHTON RAGLAN HALLEY

New Court Chambers
Suite 200 Gazette Building, 168 Corporation
Street, Birmingham B4 6TZ,
Telephone: 0121 693 6656
Call date: Oct 1994, Lincoln's Inn
Qualifications: [LLB (Hons)(Lond)]

ASHURST STEPHEN JOHN

Fountain Chambers
Cleveland Business Centre 1 Watson Street,
Middlesbrough TS1 2RQ,
Telephone: 01642 217037
9 Woodhouse Square
Leeds LS3 1AD, Telephone: 0113 2451986
Call date: July 1979, Inner Temple
Assistant Recorder
Qualifications: [LLB (Newc)]

ASHWELL PAUL MARTYN

Sussex Chambers
9 Old Steine, Brighton BN1 1FJ,
Telephone: 01273 607953
Call date: July 1977, Inner Temple
Qualifications: [BA]

ASHWORTH MISS FIONA KATHERINE ANNE

40 King Street
Manchester M2 6BA,
Telephone: 0161 832 9082
E-mail: Kingst40@aol.com
Call date: July 1988, Lincoln's Inn
Qualifications: [LLB (Hons)(Leeds)]

ASHWORTH LANCE DOMINIC PIERS

Priory Chambers
2 Fountain Court, Steelhouse Lane,
Birmingham B4 6DR,
Telephone: 0121 236 3882/1375
2 Harcourt Bldgs
Ground Floor/Left, Temple, London
EC4Y 9DB, Telephone: 0171 583 9020
E-mail: clerks@harcourt.co.uk
Door Tenant
Call date: Nov 1987, Middle Temple
Qualifications: [MA (Cantab)]

ASHWORTH PIERS QC (1973)

2 Harcourt Bldgs
Ground Floor/Left, Temple, London
EC4Y 9DB, Telephone: 0171 583 9020
E-mail: clerks@harcourt.co.uk
Priory Chambers
2 Fountain Court, Steelhouse Lane,
Birmingham B4 6DR,
Telephone: 0121 236 3882/1375
Door Tenant
Stanbrook & Henderson
2 Harcourt Bldgs 2nd Floor, Temple, London
EC4Y 9DB, Telephone: 0171 353 0101
E-mail: clerks@harcourt.co.uk
Call date: Feb 1956, Middle Temple
Recorder
Qualifications: [MA (Cantab)]

ASPLIN

ASHWORTH WILLIAM RUPERT EVERARD

1 Paper Bldgs
1st Floor, Temple, London EC4Y 7EP,
Telephone: 0171 353 3728/4953
Call date: Nov 1996, Inner Temple
Qualifications: [BA (Cantab)]

ASIF MOHAMMED JALIL AHKTER

2 Crown Office Row
2nd Floor, Temple, London EC4Y 7HJ,
Telephone: 0171 797 8000
Call date: Nov 1988, Lincoln's Inn
Qualifications: [MA (Cantab)]

ASKHAM NIGEL HEAL

South Western Chambers
Melville House 12 Middle Street, Taunton,
Somerset TA1 1SH, Telephone: 01823 331919
Call date: Feb 1973, Inner Temple
Qualifications: [LLB]

ASKINS NICHOLAS PETER

Broadway House Chambers
Broadway House 9 Bank Street, Bradford,
West Yorkshire BD1 1TW,
Telephone: 01274 722560
Call date: Nov 1989, Gray's Inn
Qualifications: [LLB [Lond]]

ASLAM MS FARZANA ANN

1 Crown Office Row
3rd Floor, Temple, London EC4Y 7HH,
Telephone: 0171 583 9292
E-mail: onecor@link.org
Call date: Oct 1993, Middle Temple
Qualifications: [LLB (Hons), BCL]

ASLAM QAZI MAHMUD

Staple Inn Chambers
1st Floor 9 Staple Inn, Holborn, London
WC1V 7QH, Telephone: 0171 242 5240
E-mail: clerks@staple-inn.org
Call date: Nov 1983, Gray's Inn
Qualifications: [BA (Hons) (Leics)]

ASLANGUL MICHEL JOSEPH LEON

20 Britton Street
1st Floor, London EC1M 5NQ,
Telephone: 0171 608 3765
Abbey Chambers
PO Box 47 47 Ashurst Drive, Shepperton,
Middlesex TW17 0LD,
Telephone: 01932 560913
Call date: Nov 1978, Middle Temple
Qualifications: [MA (Business Law), BA (Hons)]

ASLETT PEPIN CHARLES MAGUIRE

22 Albion Place
Northampton NN1 1UD,
Telephone: 01604 36271
Call date: Nov 1996, Lincoln's Inn
Qualifications: [LLB (Hons)(Bucks)]

ASPDEN GORDON JAMES

36 Bedford Row
London WC1R 4JH,
Telephone: 0171 421 8000
E-mail: 36bedfordrow@link.org
Call date: Nov 1988, Gray's Inn
Qualifications: [LLB (Hull)]

ASPINALL JOHN MICHAEL QC (1995)

3 Paper Bldgs
1st Floor, Temple, London EC4Y 7EU,
Telephone: 0171 583 8055
E-mail: london@3paper.com
20 Lorne Park Road
Bournemouth BH1 1JN,
Telephone: 01202 292102 (5 Lines)
1 Alfred Street
High Street, Oxford OX1 4EH,
Telephone: 01865 793736
Call date: Nov 1971, Inner Temple
Qualifications: [LLB]

ASPLIN MISS SARAH JANE

3 Stone Buildings
Ground Floor, Lincoln's Inn, London
WC2A 3XL, Telephone: 0171 242 4937/
405 8358
Call date: July 1984, Gray's Inn
Qualifications: [MA(Cantab), BCL(Oxon)]

Fax: 0171 405 3896;
Out of hours telephone: 0171 242 4937;
DX: London 317

D

Types of work: Chancery (general); Chancery land law; Charities; Equity, wills and trusts; Family provision; Partnerships; Pensions; Probate and administration; Professional negligence

Awards and memberships: Association Pension Lawyers; Chancery Bar Association; Revenue Bar Association; Ecclesiastical Law Society; Association of Women Barristers

Reported cases: *Imperial Group Pension Trust Ltd v Imperial Tobacco Ltd*, [1991] I WLR 589, 1990. Major pensions case concerning duties of principal employer.
British Coal Corp v British Coal Staff Superannuation Scheme Ltd, [1994] OPLR 51, 1993. Major pensions case concerning use of surplus and return of monies to company.
Hillsdown Holdings Plc v Pensions Ombudsman, [1996] PLR 427, 1996. Major pensions case concerning merger of schemes and return of surplus to company.

Principal Areas of Practice
Pensions litigation, advice and drafting, acts for principal employers, trustees, liquidators and receivers and beneficiaries on questions arising in relation to surplus, construction of rules, winding up, merger, general administration and misappropriation of assets from pension schemes. Also advises actuaries and pensions administrators in relation to professional negligence claims and in relation to all aspects of complaints to and appeals from the Pensions Ombudsman.

ASPREY NICHOLAS

13 Old Square
1st Floor, Lincoln's Inn, London WC2A 3UA,
Telephone: 0171 242 6105
E-mail: clerks@serlecourt.co.uk
Call date: July 1969, Inner Temple
Qualifications: [LLB (Edin)]

ASTANIOTIS MISS KATERINE MARGARET

2-3 Gray's Inn Square
Gray's Inn, London WC1R 5JH,
Telephone: 0171 242 4986
E-mail: chambers@2-3graysinnsquare.co.uk
Call date: July 1985, Gray's Inn
Qualifications: [LLB (Bristol)]

ASTBURY MRS JOANNE

Park Lane Chambers
19 Westgate, Leeds LS1 2RD,
Telephone: 0113 2285000
Call date: July 1989, Lincoln's Inn
Qualifications: [LLB (Nott'm)]

ASTERIS PETER DAVID

Eighteen Carlton Crescent
Southampton SO15 2XR,
Telephone: 01703 639001
Call date: Oct 1996, Lincoln's Inn
Qualifications: [LLB (Hons)(Leic)]

ASTON MAURICE CHARLES

5 Paper Bldgs
1st Floor, Temple, London EC4Y 7HB,
Telephone: 0171 583 6117
E-mail: clerks@5-paperbuildings.law.co.uk
Call date: July 1982, Inner Temple
Qualifications: [LLB (Soton)]

ASTOR PHILIP DOUGLAS PAUL

1 Temple Gardens
1st Floor, Temple, London EC4Y 9BB,
Telephone: 0171 353 0407/583 1315
E-mail: clerks@1templegardens.co.uk
Call date: Nov 1989, Inner Temple
Qualifications: [MA (Oxon), Dip Law (City)]

ATCHLEY RICHARD WALDEGRAVE

3 Raymond Buildings
Gray's Inn, London WC1R 5BH,
Telephone: 0171 831 3833
E-mail: chambers@threeraymond.demon.co.uk
Call date: Nov 1977, Middle Temple

ATHERTON IAN DAVID

Enterprise Chambers
9 Old Square, Lincoln's Inn, London
WC2A 3SR, Telephone: 0171 405 9471
Enterprise Chambers
65 Quayside, Newcastle upon Tyne NE1 3DS,
Telephone: 0191 222 3344
Enterprise Chambers
38 Park Square, Leeds LS1 2PA,
Telephone: 01132 460391
Call date: July 1988, Inner Temple
Qualifications: [BSc LLB, ARICS, ACIArb]

ATHERTON PETER

Deans Court Chambers
Cumberland House Crown Square, Manchester
M3 3HA, Telephone: 0161 834 4097
E-mail: deanscourt@compuserve.com
Deans Court Chambers
41-43 Market Place, Preston PR1 1AH,
Telephone: 01772 555163
E-mail: deanscourt@compuserve.com
Call date: July 1975, Gray's Inn
Assistant Recorder
Qualifications: [LLB (Hons) (B'ham)]

ATHERTON ROBERT KENNETH

India Buildings Chambers
Water Street, Liverpool L2 OXG,
Telephone: 0151 243 6000
Call date: July 1970, Gray's Inn
Assistant Recorder
Qualifications: [LLB]

ATHERTON MISS SALLY

Bridewell Chambers
2 Bridewell Place, London EC4V 6AP,
Telephone: 0171 797 8800
E-mail: clerks@bridewell.law.co.uk
Call date: July 1987, Middle Temple
Qualifications: [LLB (Man)]

ATHERTON STEPHEN NICHOLAS

3/4 South Square
Gray's Inn, London WC1R 5HP,
Telephone: 0171 696 9900
E-mail: clerks@southsquare.com
Call date: July 1989, Middle Temple
Qualifications: [LLB (Lancs), LLM (Cantab)]

ATHERTON-HAM JAMES WEST

Newport Chambers
12 Clytha Park Road, Newport, Gwent
NP9 47L, Telephone: 01633 267403/255855
Call date: Oct 1994, Lincoln's Inn
Qualifications: [LLB (Hons)(Glamorg)]

ATKINS CHARLES EDWARD SPENCER

29 Bedford Row Chambers
London WC1R 4HE,
Telephone: 0171 831 2626
Call date: July 1975, Inner Temple
Qualifications: [MA (Cantab)]

ATKINS RICHARD PAUL

1 Fountain Court
Steelhouse Lane, Birmingham B4 6DR,
Telephone: 0121 236 5721
Call date: July 1989, Gray's Inn
Qualifications: [BA (Oxon)]

ATKINS WILLIAM SIWARD

7 Stone Bldgs
Ground Floor, Lincoln's Inn, London
WC2A 3SZ, Telephone: 0171 405 3886/
242 3546
E-mail: chaldous@vossnet.co.uk
Call date: Oct 1995, Inner Temple
Qualifications: [MA (Edinburgh), CPE (City)]

ATKINSON MISS CAROL LESLEY

Queen Elizabeth Bldg
Ground Floor, Temple, London EC4Y 9BS,
Telephone: 0171 353 7181 (12 Lines)
Call date: July 1985, Gray's Inn
Qualifications: [LLB (Lancaster)]

ATKINSON MISS ELIZABETH JAYNE

New Court Chambers
3 Broad Chare, Newcastle Upon Tyne
NE1 3DQ, Telephone: 0191 232 1980
Call date: Oct 1994, Lincoln's Inn
Qualifications: [LLB (Hons)(Leeds), BCL]

ATKINSON NICHOLAS JEREMY QC (1991)

2 Harcourt Bldgs
1st Floor, Temple, London EC4Y 9DB,
Telephone: 0171 353 2112/2817
Call date: Nov 1971, Inner Temple
Recorder

ATKINSON PAUL CHRISTOPHER

New Walk Chambers
27 New Walk, Leicester LE1 6TE,
Telephone: 0116 2559144
Call date: July 1978, Lincoln's Inn
Qualifications: [MA (Oxon)]

D

D

ATKINSON RICHARD DUNCAN

6 King's Bench Walk
Ground Floor, Temple, London EC4Y 7DR,
Telephone: 0171 583 0410
Call date: Oct 1995, Gray's Inn
Qualifications: [LLB (Bris)]

ATKINSON TIMOTHY GEORGE BRYANT

1 Brick Court
1st Floor, Temple, London EC4Y 9BY,
Telephone: 0171 353 8845
E-mail: clerks@1brickcourt.co.uk
Call date: July 1988, Inner Temple
Qualifications: [BA (Oxon), Dip Law (City)]

ATREYA MS NAVITA

1 Pump Court
Lower Ground Floor, Temple, London
EC4Y 7AB, Telephone: 0171 583 2012/
353 4341
E-mail: (name) @1pumpcourt.co.uk
Call date: Oct 1994, Lincoln's Inn
Qualifications: [BSc (Hons)(Lond)]

ATTALA JEAN ETIENNE

Cathedral Chambers
Milburn House Dean Street, Newcastle Upon
Tyne NE1 1LE, Telephone: 0191 232 1311
Call date: May 1994, Gray's Inn
Qualifications: [LLB]

ATTRIDGE STEVEN JEFFREY

1 Gray's Inn Square
Ground Floor, London WC1R 5AA,
Telephone: 0171 405 8946/7/8
Call date: Nov 1991, Inner Temple
Qualifications: [LLB]

ATTWOOD JOHN JULIAN

6 Fountain Court
Steelhouse Lane, Birmingham B4 6DR,
Telephone: 0121 233 3282
Call date: Nov 1989, Gray's Inn
Qualifications: [LLB (B'ham)]

ATTWOOLL CHRISTOPHER BENJAMIN

11 King's Bench Walk
1st Floor, Temple, London EC4Y 7EQ,
Telephone: 0171 353 3337
3 Park Court
Leeds LS1 2QH, Telephone: 0113 297 1200
Call date: July 1980, Middle Temple
Qualifications: [BA (Keele)]

ATUNWA RAZAK OLATUNDE

20 Britton Street
1st Floor, London EC1M 5NQ,
Telephone: 0171 608 3765
Call date: Oct 1994, Inner Temple
Qualifications: [LLB (Lond), LLM (Lond)]

AUBREY DAVID JOHN MORGAN QC (1996)

32 Park Place
Cardiff CF1 3BA, Telephone: 01222 397364
Call date: July 1976, Middle Temple
Assistant Recorder
Qualifications: [LLB (Wales)]

AUBREY DAVID STUART

The Corn Exchange
5th Floor Fenwick Street, Liverpool L2 7QS,
Telephone: 0151 227 1081/5009
Call date: July 1974, Gray's Inn
Recorder
Qualifications: [LLB (Hons)]

AUCKLAND MISS ELIZABETH RACHEL

30 Park Square
Leeds LS1 2PF, Telephone: 0113 2436388
Call date: Oct 1995, Lincoln's Inn
Qualifications: [MA (Cantab)]

AUDLAND WILLIAM GRANT

12 King's Bench Walk
Temple, London EC4Y 7EL,
Telephone: 0171 583 0811
E-mail: chambers@12kbw.co.uk
Call date: Nov 1992, Gray's Inn
Qualifications: [BA (Hons)(Oxon), Dip Law]

AULD MISS CATHERINE ROHAN

2 Harcourt Bldgs
1st Floor, Temple, London EC4Y 9DB,
Telephone: 0171 353 6961/7
Harcourt Chambers
Churchill House 3 St Aldate's Courtyard, St
Aldate's, Oxford OX1 1BN,
Telephone: 01865 791559
Call date: Nov 1992, Gray's Inn
Qualifications: [MA (Hons)(Cantab)]

AULD CHARLES JOHN DENHAM

St John's Chambers
Small Street, Bristol BS1 1DW,
Telephone: 0117 9213456/298514
E-mail: clerks@stjohns.uk.com
Call date: July 1980, Middle Temple
Qualifications: [BA (Dunelm)]

AULD STEPHEN ROBERT

1 Essex Court
Ground Floor, Temple, London EC4Y 9AR,
Telephone: 0171 583 2000
E-mail: clerks@oneessexcourt.co.uk
Call date: July 1979, Gray's Inn
Qualifications: [BA (Cantab)]

AUSTIN JONATHAN EDWARD NEWNS

30 Park Place
Cardiff CF1 3BA, Telephone: 01222 398421
E-mail: 100757.1456@compuserve.com
Call date: Oct 1991, Middle Temple
Qualifications: [BA (Hons), LLB (Hons)]

AUSTIN-SMITH MICHAEL GERARD QC (1990)

23 Essex Street
London WC2R 3AS,
Telephone: 0171 413 0353/353 3533
E-mail: clerks@essexstreet23.demon.co.uk
Call date: July 1969, Inner Temple
Recorder
Qualifications: [LLB (Exeter)]

AUSTINS CHRISTOPHER JOHN

Assize Court Chambers
14 Small Street, Bristol BS1 1DE,
Telephone: 0117 9264587
Call date: July 1988, Gray's Inn
Qualifications: [LLB (Hons)]

AUTY MICHAEL ROY

1 High Pavement
Nottingham NG1 1HF,
Telephone: 0115 9418218
Call date: Nov 1990, Inner Temple
Qualifications: [BA]

AXON ANDREW ELIOT

Park Lane Chambers
19 Westgate, Leeds LS1 2RD,
Telephone: 0113 2285000
Call date: Oct 1992, Middle Temple
Qualifications: [BA (Hons)]

AYERS GUY RUSSELL

Octagon House
19 Colegate, Norwich NR3 1AT,
Telephone: 01603 623186
E-mail: octagon@netmatters.co.uk
1 Paper Bldgs
1st Floor, Temple, London EC4Y 7EP,
Telephone: 0171 353 3728/4953
Call date: July 1979, Inner Temple
Qualifications: [LLB (Soton)]

AYLEN WALTER STAFFORD QC (1983)

Hardwicke Building
New Square, Lincoln's Inn, London
WC2A 3SB, Telephone: 0171 242 2523
E-mail: clerks@hardwicke.co.uk
Call date: Feb 1962, Middle Temple
Recorder
Qualifications: [MA, BCL, ACIArb]

AYLETT CRISPIN DAVID WILLIAM

3 Raymond Buildings
Gray's Inn, London WC1R 5BH,
Telephone: 0171 831 3833
E-mail: chambers@threeraymond.demon.co.uk
Call date: July 1985, Inner Temple
Qualifications: [BA (Hons)(Bris), Dip Law]

AYLETT KENNETH GEORGE

New Chambers
3 Sadleir Road, St Albans, Hertfordshire
AL1 2BL, Telephone: 0966 212126
Call date: July 1972, Inner Temple
Qualifications: [BA,BL]

AYLIFFE JAMES JUSTIN BARNETT

Wilberforce Chambers
8 New Square, Lincoln's Inn, London
WC2A 3QP, Telephone: 0171 306 0102
E-mail: chambers@wilberforce.co.uk
Call date: Nov 1987, Lincoln's Inn
Qualifications: [BA (Oxon), Dip Law (City)]

AYLING MISS TRACY JANE

Farrar's Building
Temple, London EC4Y 7BD,
Telephone: 0171 583 9241
E-mail: chambers@farrarsbuilding.co.uk
Call date: July 1983, Inner Temple
Qualifications: [BA (Hons) (Dunelm)]

AYLOTT COLIN CHRISTOPHER

Thomas More Chambers
52 Carey Street, Lincoln's Inn, London
WC2A 2JB, Telephone: 0171 404 7000
Call date: Nov 1989, Inner Temple
Qualifications: [LLB (B'ham)]

AYLWIN CHRISTOPHER GRANVILLE ANGUS

3 Paper Bldgs
Ground Floor, Temple, London EC4Y 7EU,
Telephone: 0171 797 7000
E-mail: clerks@3pb.co.uk
Call date: Nov 1970, Inner Temple
Qualifications: [MA (Cantab)]

AYRES ANDREW JOHN WILLIAM

13 Old Square
Ground Floor, Lincoln's Inn, London
WC2A 3UA, Telephone: 0171 404 4800
Call date: Oct 1996, Gray's Inn
Qualifications: [BA (Oxon)]

AYUB MISS SALIHA

Holborn Chambers
6 Gate Street, Lincoln's Inn Fields, London
WC2A 3HP, Telephone: 0171 242 6060
Call date: Nov 1992, Lincoln's Inn

AZAM JAVAID

3 Paper Bldgs
2nd Floor, Temple, London EC4Y 7EU,
Telephone: 0171 353 6208
Call date: July 1981, Gray's Inn
Qualifications: [BA (Hons)]

AZHAR ALI MOHAMMAD

9 King's Bench Walk
Basement, Temple, London EC4Y 7DX,
Telephone: 0171 353 9564
E-mail: jvlee@btinternet.com
Call date: July 1962, Gray's Inn
Qualifications: [MA]

AZHAR MISS SHABEENA

9 King's Bench Walk
Basement, Temple, London EC4Y 7DX,
Telephone: 0171 353 9564
E-mail: jvlee@btinternet.com
Call date: Nov 1995, Inner Temple
Qualifications: [BA, CPE (Sussex)]

AZIM MISS TABSUM REHNA

St Ive's Chambers
9 Fountain Ct, Birmingham B4 6DR,
Telephone: 0121 236 0863/0929
Call date: July 1984, Middle Temple
Qualifications: [LLB]

BAATZ NICHOLAS STEPHEN

1 Atkin Building
Gray's Inn, London WC1R 5AT,
Telephone: 0171 404 0102
E-mail: clerks@atkin-chambers.co.uk
Call date: Nov 1978, Gray's Inn
Qualifications: [MA, BCL (Oxon)]

BABAJIDE IBUKUNOLU ALAO OLATOKUNBO O

Albany Chambers
91 Kentish Town Road, London NW1 8NY,
Telephone: 0171 485 5736/5758
E-mail: albanychambers@usanet
Call date: July 1990, Lincoln's Inn
Qualifications: [LLB (Ife), LLM (Ife)]

BACH WILLIAM STEPHEN

65-67 King Street
Leicester LE1 6RP, Telephone: 0116 2547710
Call date: July 1972, Middle Temple
Qualifications: [BA (Oxon)]

BACK PATRICK QC (1970)

10 King's Bench Walk
Ground Floor, Temple, London EC4Y 7EB,
Telephone: 0171 353 7742
E-mail: 10kbw@lineone.net
Door Tenant
Call date: Jan 1940, Gray's Inn
Recorder
Qualifications: [BA (Cantab)]

BACKHOUSE ROGER BAINBRIDGE QC (1984)

1 Middle Temple Lane
Temple, London EC4Y 1LT,
Telephone: 0171 583 0659 (12 Lines)
Door Tenant
Lloyds House Chambers
3rd Floor 18 Lloyds House, Lloyd Street,
Manchester M2 5WA,
Telephone: 0161 839 3371
Door Tenant
Call date: July 1965, Middle Temple
Qualifications: [MA (Cantab)]

BACON FRANCIS MICHAEL

4 Paper Bldgs
Ground Floor, Temple, London EC4Y 7EX,
Telephone: 0171 353 3366/583 7155
E-mail: clerks@4paperbuildings.com
Call date: July 1988, Gray's Inn
Qualifications: [BA (Keele), MSc
(Loughborough)]

BACON JEFFREY DAVID

Littleton Chambers
3 King's Bench Walk North, Temple, London
EC4Y 7HR, Telephone: 0171 797 8600
E-mail: littletonchambers@compuserve.com
Call date: Nov 1989, Middle Temple
Qualifications: [BA Hons (Sussex), Dip EEC
(Brussels)]

BACON JONATHAN FRANCIS

11 Bolt Court
London EC4A 3DQ,
Telephone: 0171 353 2300
E-mail: boltct11@aol.com
Redhill Chambers
Seloduct House 30 Station Road, Redhill
RH1 1NK, Telephone: 01737 780781
Call date: July 1989, Inner Temple
Qualifications: [LLB,BCL (Oxon)]

BACON NICHOLAS MICHAEL

1 Temple Gardens
1st Floor, Temple, London EC4Y 9BB,
Telephone: 0171 353 0407/583 1315
E-mail: clerks@1templegardens.co.uk
Call date: Oct 1992, Inner Temple
Qualifications: [LLB (Essex)(Hons)]

BADENOCH (IAN) JAMES FORSTER QC (1989)

1 Crown Office Row
Ground Floor, Temple, London EC4Y 7HH,
Telephone: 0171 797 7500
Crown Office Row Chambers
Blenheim House 120 Church Street, Brighton,
Sussex BN1 1WH, Telephone: 01273 625625
Call date: Nov 1968, Lincoln's Inn
Recorder
Qualifications: [MA (Oxon)]

BADENOCH TONY DAVID

7 Stone Bldgs
1st Floor, Lincoln's Inn, London WC2A 3SZ,
Telephone: 0171 242 0961
Call date: Nov 1996, Middle Temple
Qualifications: [BSc (Hons), Dip Law]

BADLEY MISS PAMELA HILARY

25-27 Castle Street
1st Floor, Liverpool L2 4TA,
Telephone: 0151 227 5661/051 236 5072
Call date: Nov 1974, Lincoln's Inn
Recorder
Qualifications: [LLB (Warw), LLM]

D

D

BAGCHI ANDREW KUMAR

One Garden Court
Ground Floor, Temple, London EC4Y 9BJ,
Telephone: 0171 797 7900
Call date: July 1989, Middle Temple
Qualifications: [LLB (Lond)]

BAGLEY MICHAEL WALLACE WELSBY

Chavasse Court Chambers
2nd Floor Chavasse Court, 24 Lord Street,
Liverpool L2 1TA, Telephone: 0151 707 1191
Call date: Nov 1984, Gray's Inn
Qualifications: [BSc (Bristol)]

BAGNALL MATTHEW PHILIP COOPER

46/48 Essex Street
London WC2R 3GH,
Telephone: 0171 583 8899
Call date: Oct 1993, Middle Temple
Qualifications: [LLB (Hons)]

BAILEY ANTHONY REGINALD

2 King's Bench Walk
Ground Floor, Temple, London EC4Y 7DE,
Telephone: 0171 353 1746
E-mail: 2kbw@atlas.co.uk
King's Bench Chambers
115 North Hill, Plymouth PL4 8JY,
Telephone: 01752 221551
Call date: Nov 1972, Inner Temple

BAILEY CHARLES ANDREW STUART

Trinity Chambers
140 New London Road, Chelmsford, Essex
CM2 0AW, Telephone: 01245 605040
Call date: Oct 1993, Lincoln's Inn
Qualifications: [BA (Hons), LLB (Lond)]

BAILEY DAVID JOHN

7 King's Bench Walk
Ground Floor, Temple, London EC4Y 7DS,
Telephone: 0171 583 0404
Call date: July 1989, Gray's Inn
Qualifications: [BA (Oxon), LLM (UCLA)]

BAILEY EDWARD GRENFELL

2 King's Bench Walk
Ground Floor, Temple, London EC4Y 7DE,
Telephone: 0171 353 1746
E-mail: 2kbw@atlas.co.uk
King's Bench Chambers
115 North Hill, Plymouth PL4 8JY,
Telephone: 01752 221551
Call date: July 1990, Gray's Inn
Qualifications: [MA (Edin), Dip Law (City)]

BAILEY EDWARD HENRY

5 Bell Yard
London WC2A 2JR, Telephone: 0171 333 8811
Call date: Nov 1970, Middle Temple
Recorder
Qualifications: [MA, LLB (Cantab)]

BAILEY MRS ELIZABETH

Devon Chambers
3 St Andrew Street, Plymouth PL1 2AH,
Telephone: 01752 661659
Call date: Oct 1995, Middle Temple
Qualifications: [LLB (Hons)]

BAILEY GRAHAM ROBERT

Manchester House Chambers
18-22 Bridge Street, Manchester M3 3BZ,
Telephone: 0161 834 7007
Call date: Feb 1993, Inner Temple
Qualifications: [LLB (Brunel) (Hons)]

BAILEY JOHN CHARLES WILLIAMS

Queen's Chambers
5 John Dalton Street, Manchester M2 6ET,
Telephone: 0161 834 6875/4738
4 Camden Place
Preston PR1 3JL, Telephone: 01772 828300
Call date: Nov 1966, Gray's Inn
Qualifications: [MA (Oxon)]

BAILEY MARK HENRY ARTHUR

6 Pump Court
1st Floor, Temple, London EC4Y 7AR,
Telephone: 0171 797 8400
E-mail: sa_hockman_qc@link.org
6-8 Mill Street
6-8 Mill Street, Maidstone, Kent ME15 6XH,
Telephone: 01622 688 094
Call date: July 1984, Inner Temple

Qualifications: [MA (Oxon)]

Fax: 0171 797 8401; DX: 293 London, Chancery Lane; Other comms: 0836 690058

Types of work: Administrative; Environment; Local government; Planning; Town and country planning

Circuit: South Eastern

Reported cases: *Empress Cars (Abertillery) Ltd v Environment Agency*, [1998] 2 WLR 350, 1997. Leading House of Lords case on liability for water pollution under Water Resources Act 1991.
R v NRA ex parte Moreton, [1996] Env LR, 1995. Judicial review of powers to grant discharge consents into bathing waters.
Bowden v South West Water and Others, [1998] Env LR, 1997. Leading case on environmental damage and liability for breach of statutory duty and European law.

Practice

Specialist in environmental law and pollution prevention and control. Clients include the major water plcs, oil companies and manufacturing industry, the Environment Agency and environmental interest groups such as the Anglers' Conservation Association and the Salmon and Trout Association. Expertise and extensive experience in public inquiries and hearings under the Water Resources Act 1991, Planning Acts etc, statutory appeals and Judicial Review.

Present instructions include the conduct of the prosecution by the Environment Agency of Milford Haven Port Authority arising out of the *Sea Empress* disaster, and advising a major oil company upon IPC compliance at a substantial refinery installation. DPA work accepted from those approved.

BAILEY MICHAEL ROBERT

3 Paper Bldgs
2nd Floor, Temple, London EC4Y 7EU,
Telephone: 0171 353 6208
Call date: Nov 1986, Gray's Inn
Qualifications: [BA (Essex), LLM]

BAILEY MISS PATRICIA LUCY

New Bailey Chambers
10 Lawson Street, Preston PR1 2QT,
Telephone: 01772 258087
Call date: Nov 1969, Middle Temple
Qualifications: [LLB]

BAILEY MISS ROSANA HENRIETTA

Eldon Chambers
Fourth Floor 30/32 Fleet Street, London
EC4Y 1AA, Telephone: 0171 353 4636
Call date: Oct 1994, Gray's Inn
Qualifications: [LLB]

BAILEY RUSSELL STUART

3 Paper Bldgs
1st Floor, Temple, London EC4Y 7EU,
Telephone: 0171 583 8055
E-mail: london@3paper.com
20 Lorne Park Road
Bournemouth BH1 1JN,
Telephone: 01202 292102 (5 Lines)
4 St Peter Street
Winchester SO23 8OW,
Telephone: 01962 868884
Call date: Nov 1985, Inner Temple
Qualifications: [LLB (Lond)]

BAILEY STEPHEN JOHN

Lion Court
Chancery House 53-64 Chancery Lane, London
WC2A 1SJ, Telephone: 0171 404 6565
Call date: July 1991, Gray's Inn
Qualifications: [LLB]

BAILEY STEVEN WILLIAM

3 Fountain Court
Steelhouse Lane, Birmingham B4 6DR,
Telephone: 0121 236 5854
Call date: Oct 1992, Middle Temple
Qualifications: [BA (Hons Oxford), M.Phil (Cambridge)]

BAILEY THOMAS IAIN

Bracton Chambers
95a Chancery Lane, London WC2A 1DT,
Telephone: 0171 242 4248
Call date: July 1984, Gray's Inn
Qualifications: [BA (Oxon)]

BAILEY-KING ROBERT WYNTER

4 Breams Buildings
London EC4A 1AQ,
Telephone: 0171 353 5835/430 1221
Call date: July 1975, Inner Temple
Qualifications: [MA (Cantab)]

BAILIN ALEXANDER

5 Paper Bldgs
1st Floor, Temple, London EC4Y 7HB,
Telephone: 0171 583 6117
E-mail: clerks@5-paperbuildings.law.co.uk
Call date: Nov 1995, Lincoln's Inn
Qualifications: [MA (Hons)]

BAILLIE ANDREW BRUCE

9 Gough Square
London EC4A 3DE, Telephone: 0171 353 5371
Call date: Nov 1970, Inner Temple
Recorder
Qualifications: [BA]

BAIN GILES DAVID

New Court
Temple, London EC4Y 9BE,
Telephone: 0171 583 5123/0171 583 0510
Call date: Nov 1993, Lincoln's Inn
Qualifications: [LLB (Hons, Hull)]

BAIRD JAMES STEVENSON

Bank House Chambers
Old Bank House, Hartshead, Sheffield S1 2EL,
Telephone: 0114 2751223
Call date: Nov 1977, Middle Temple
Qualifications: [LLB]

BAIRD MRS VERA

14 Tooks Court
Cursitor St, London EC4A 1LB,
Telephone: 0171 405 8828
E-mail: clerks @tooks.law.co.uk
Call date: Nov 1975, Gray's Inn
Qualifications: [LLB, LARTPI, BA]

BAISDEN HOWARD RALPH

Cobden House Chambers
19 Quay Street, Manchester M3 3HN,
Telephone: 0161 833 6000
E-mail: clerks@cobden.co.uk
Call date: July 1972, Middle Temple
Qualifications: [LLM]

BAJWA ALI NASEEM

3 Paper Bldgs
2nd Floor, Temple, London EC4Y 7EU,
Telephone: 0171 353 6208
Call date: Nov 1993, Gray's Inn
Qualifications: [LLB]

BAKER ANDREW JAMES

7 New Square
Lincoln's Inn, London WC2A 3QS,
Telephone: 0171 430 1660
Richmond Green Chambers
Greyhound House 23-24 George Street,
Richmond-upon-Thames, Surrey TW9 1HY,
Telephone: 0181 940 1841
Call date: Oct 1990, Middle Temple
Qualifications: [BSc, Dip Law (City), MRPharmS]

BAKER ANDREW WILLIAM

20 Essex Street
London WC2R 3AL,
Telephone: 0171 583 9294
E-mail: clerks@20essexst.com
Call date: July 1988, Lincoln's Inn
Qualifications: [BA (Hons) (Oxon), Dip Law (City)]

BAKER MISS ANNE JACQUELINE

Enterprise Chambers
9 Old Square, Lincoln's Inn, London
WC2A 3SR, Telephone: 0171 405 9471
Enterprise Chambers
38 Park Square, Leeds LS1 2PA,
Telephone: 01132 460391
Enterprise Chambers
65 Quayside, Newcastle upon Tyne NE1 3DS,
Telephone: 0191 222 3344
Call date: Nov 1985, Gray's Inn
Qualifications: [BA (Oxon)]

BAKER CHRISTOPHER FRANCIS JOHN

Arden Chambers
27 John Street, London WC1N 2BL,
Telephone: 0171 242 4244
Call date: July 1984, Middle Temple
Qualifications: [MA (Cantab), LLM (Lond)]

BAKER CHRISTOPHER MICHAEL

Cleveland Chambers
63-65 Borough Road, Middlesbrough,
Cleveland TS1 3AA, Telephone: 01642 226036
Call date: Oct 1994, Middle Temple
Qualifications: [LLB (Hons)(Manc)]

BAKER CLIVE ADRIAN

The Corn Exchange
5th Floor Fenwick Street, Liverpool L2 7QS,
Telephone: 0151 227 1081/5009
Call date: Oct 1995, Gray's Inn
Qualifications: [LLB]

BAKER MS FAY ELIZABETH

2 Paper Bldgs
Temple, London EC4Y 7ET,
Telephone: 0171 936 2613
Call date: Nov 1994, Gray's Inn
Qualifications: [LLB (Wales)]

BAKER HAROLD WILLIAM

30 Park Place
Cardiff CF1 3BA, Telephone: 01222 398421
E-mail: 100757.1456@compuserve.com
Call date: Nov 1992, Middle Temple
Qualifications: [LLB (Hons)]

BAKER JEREMY RUSSELL

Paradise Square Chambers
26 Paradise Square, Sheffield S1 2DE,
Telephone: 0114 2738951
Call date: July 1979, Middle Temple
Assistant Recorder
Qualifications: [LLB (Hull)]

BAKER JONATHAN LESLIE

2 Harcourt Bldgs
1st Floor, Temple, London EC4Y 9DB,
Telephone: 0171 353 6961/7
Harcourt Chambers
Churchill House 3 St Aldate's Courtyard, St
Aldate's, Oxford OX1 1BN,
Telephone: 01865 791559
Call date: July 1978, Middle Temple
Qualifications: [MA (Cantab)]

BAKER MISS MAUREEN ANNE

9 Bedford Row
London WC1R 4AZ,
Telephone: 0171 242 3555
E-mail: clerks@9br.co.uk
Call date: July 1984, Gray's Inn
Qualifications: [BA]

BAKER MICHAEL JAMES BARRINGTON

4 Brick Court
Ground Floor, Temple, London EC4Y 9AD,
Telephone: 0171 797 7766
E-mail: chambers@4brick.co.uk
Call date: Nov 1990, Gray's Inn
Qualifications: [BA (Cantab)]

BAKER NICHOLAS MICHAEL BRIDGMAN

Hardwicke Building
New Square, Lincoln's Inn, London
WC2A 3SB, Telephone: 0171 242 2523
E-mail: clerks@hardwicke.co.uk
Call date: July 1980, Gray's Inn
Qualifications: [BA (Oxon)]

BAKER NIGEL ROBERT JAMES QC (1988)

9 Bedford Row
London WC1R 4AZ,
Telephone: 0171 242 3555
E-mail: clerks@9br.co.uk
Call date: Nov 1969, Middle Temple
Recorder
Qualifications: [BA (Soton), LLM, (Cantab)]

D

BAKER PHILIP WOOLF

Gray's Inn Chambers
3rd Floor, Gray's Inn, London WC1R 5JA,
Telephone: 0171 242 2642
E-mail: clerks@taxbar.com
Call date: July 1979, Gray's Inn
Qualifications: [BA (Cantab), BCL (Oxon), LLM
(Lond) PhD, MBA]

BAKER MS RACHEL MARY THERESA

Hardwicke Building
New Square, Lincoln's Inn, London
WC2A 3SB, Telephone: 0171 242 2523
E-mail: clerks@hardwicke.co.uk
Call date: Nov 1990, Gray's Inn
Qualifications: [BSc (Lond)]

BAKER ROBERT EDWARD NICOLAS

2 King's Bench Walk
1st Floor, Temple, London EC4Y 7DE,
Telephone: 0171 353 9276
Call date: Nov 1977, Middle Temple

BAKER STEPHEN GEORGE

40 King Street
Manchester M2 6BA,
Telephone: 0161 832 9082
E-mail: Kingst40@aol.com
Call date: Feb 1994, Middle Temple
Qualifications: [BA (Hons)(York)]

BAKER MR STEPHEN MARK

9 Bedford Row
London WC1R 4AZ,
Telephone: 0171 242 3555
E-mail: clerks@9br.co.uk
Call date: July 1989, Middle Temple
Qualifications: [LLB (Manch), LLM (Cantab)]

BAKER STUART CHRISTOPHER

1 Fountain Court
Steelhouse Lane, Birmingham B4 6DR,
Telephone: 0121 236 5721
Call date: Oct 1995, Middle Temple
Qualifications: [LLB (Hons) (Manch)]

BAKER WILLIAM ARTHUR

Peel Court Chambers
45 Hardman Street, Manchester M3 3HA,
Telephone: 0161 832 3791
Call date: Oct 1991, Middle Temple
Qualifications: [LLB Hons (Lancaster)]

BAKER WILLIAM DAVID

2 Paper Buildings
Basement, Temple, London EC4Y 7ET,
Telephone: 0171 353 0933
Call date: Oct 1992, Inner Temple
Qualifications: [LLB]

BALCOMBE DAVID JULIAN

1 Crown Office Row
Ground Floor, Temple, London EC4Y 7HH,
Telephone: 0171 797 7500
Crown Office Row Chambers
Blenheim House 120 Church Street, Brighton,
Sussex BN1 1WH, Telephone: 01273 625625
Call date: Nov 1980, Lincoln's Inn
Qualifications: [BA (Kent)]

BALDOCK NICHOLAS JOHN

6 Pump Court
1st Floor, Temple, London EC4Y 7AR,
Telephone: 0171 797 8400
E-mail: sa_hockman_qc@link.org
6-8 Mill Street
Maidstone, Kent ME15 6XH,
Telephone: 01622 688094
Call date: Nov 1983, Lincoln's Inn
Qualifications: [MA (Cantab)]

BALDOCK MISS SUSAN ANNE

2 Gray's Inn Square Chambers
2nd Floor, Gray's Inn, London WC1R 5AA,
Telephone: 0171 242 0328/071 405 1317
E-mail: clerks@2gis.co.uk
Call date: July 1988, Lincoln's Inn
Qualifications: [BA (Hons) (Sussex), Dip Law
(city)]

BALDRY ANTONY BRIAN

1 Serjeants' Inn
5th Floor Fleet Street, Temple, London
EC4Y 1LL, Telephone: 0171 415 6666
E-mail: no1serjeantsinn@btinternet.com
Call date: Nov 1975, Middle Temple
Qualifications: [BA, LLB (Sussex)]

BALDRY RUPERT PATRICK CRAIG

Pump Court Tax Chambers
16 Bedford Row, London WC1R 4EB,
Telephone: 0171 414 8080
Call date: Feb 1987, Middle Temple
Qualifications: [BA (Lond) Dip Law, (City)]

BALDWIN JOHN GRANT

Oriel Chambers
14 Water Street, Liverpool L2 8TD,
Telephone: 0151 236 7191
E-mail: oriel_chambers@link.org
Call date: Oct 1990, Gray's Inn
Qualifications: [MA (Cantab)]

BALDWIN JOHN PAUL QC (1991)

8 New Square
Lincoln's Inn, London WC2A 3QP,
Telephone: 0171 405 4321
Call date: July 1977, Gray's Inn
Qualifications: [BSc, DPhil (Oxon)]

BALDWIN ROGER MILES

15 Winckley Square
Preston PR1 3JJ, Telephone: 01772 252828
E-mail: clerks@winckleysq.demon.co.uk
Call date: July 1969, Gray's Inn
Qualifications: [LLB]

BALL MISS ALISON QC (1995)

One Garden Court
Ground Floor, Temple, London EC4Y 9BJ,
Telephone: 0171 797 7900
Call date: Nov 1972, Middle Temple
Assistant Recorder
Qualifications: [LLB (Lond)]

BALL CHRISTOPHER GEOFFREY QC (1993)

18 Red Lion Court
(Off Fleet Street), London EC4A 3EB,
Telephone: 0171 520 6000
Thornwood House
102 New London Road, Chelmsford, Essex
CM2 0RG, Telephone: 01245 280880
Call date: July 1972, Middle Temple
Recorder
Qualifications: [LLB]

BALL STEVEN

11 Old Square
Ground Floor, Lincoln's Inn, London
WC2A 3TS, Telephone: 0171 242 5022/
405 1074
Call date: Oct 1995, Inner Temple
Qualifications: [BSc (Reading), LLB (Herts)]

BALL STEVEN JAMES

Earl Street Chambers
47 Earl Street, Maidstone, Kent ME14 1PD,
Telephone: 01622 671222
E-mail: gunner-sparks@msn.com
Call date: Oct 1996, Inner Temple
Qualifications: [LLB (Hull)]

BALLANTINE DYKES THOMAS LAMPLUGH

Southsea Chambers
PO Box 148, Southsea, Portsmouth,
Hampshire PO5 2TU,
Telephone: 01705 291261
Call date: Oct 1991, Middle Temple
Qualifications: [BSc (Elect Eng), Dip Law, Cert
Ed]

BALLANTYNE PROFESSOR WILLIAM MORRIS

One Hare Court
1st Floor, Temple, London EC4Y 7BE,
Telephone: 0171 353 3171
E-mail: admin-oneharecourt@btinternet.com
Call date: Nov 1977, Inner Temple
Qualifications: [MA (Cantab)]

BALLENTYNE ERROL STANLEY

1 High Pavement
Nottingham NG1 1HF,
Telephone: 0115 9418218
Call date: Nov 1983, Gray's Inn
Qualifications: [BA]

BALOGH CHRISTOPHER THOMAS

Arden Chambers
27 John Street, London WC1N 2BL,
Telephone: 0171 242 4244
Call date: Nov 1984, Middle Temple
Qualifications: [MA (Cantab), MSc (Econ), Dip
in, Law]

D

D

BALYSZ MARK ALEXANDER

Holborn Chambers
6 Gate Street, Lincoln's Inn Fields, London
WC2A 3HP, Telephone: 0171 242 6060
Call date: Nov 1995, Gray's Inn
Qualifications: [LLB]

BAMFORD CHRISTOPHER DAVID

Francis Taylor Bldg
3rd Floor, Temple, London EC4Y 7BY,
Telephone: 0171 797 7250
Call date: Nov 1987, Inner Temple
Qualifications: [LLB (Hons)(Hull)]

BAMFORD JEREMY RICHARD

Guildhall Chambers
23 Broad Street, Bristol BS1 2HG,
Telephone: 0117 9273366
Call date: Nov 1989, Lincoln's Inn
Qualifications: [BA (Oxon)]

BAMFORD RONALD GLEN

Guildford Chambers
Stoke House Leapale Lane, Guildford, Surrey
GU1 4LY, Telephone: 01483 539131
E-mail: guildford.barristers@btinternet.com
Call date: Nov 1972, Lincoln's Inn

BANCROFT MISS ANNA LOUISE

Deans Court Chambers
Cumberland House Crown Square, Manchester
M3 3HA, Telephone: 0161 834 4097
E-mail: deanscourt@compuserve.com
Deans Court Chambers
41-43 Market Place, Preston PR1 1AH,
Telephone: 01772 555163
E-mail: deanscourt@compuserve.com
Call date: July 1985, Inner Temple
Qualifications: [MA (Oxon)]

BANERJEE BALADEB

Chancery Chambers
1st Floor Offices 70/72 Chancery Lane,
London WC2A 1AB,
Telephone: 0171 405 6879/6870
Call date: July 1970, Middle Temple
Qualifications: [MA, LLB]

BANGAY MISS DEBORAH JOANNA JANET

29 Bedford Row Chambers
London WC1R 4HE,
Telephone: 0171 831 2626
Call date: Feb 1981, Gray's Inn
Qualifications: [LLB (Exon)]

BANKOLE-JONES JOHN EDWARD

Clavenes Chambers
46 Stag Lane, Edgware, Middlesex HA8 5JY,
Telephone: 0181 931 2648
Call date: Oct 1963, Middle Temple

BANKS FRANCIS ANDREW

Adrian Lyon's Chambers
14 Castle Street, Liverpool L2 0NE,
Telephone: 0151 236 4421/8240
E-mail: chambers14@aol.com
Call date: July 1995, Gray's Inn
Qualifications: [BA]

BANKS MISS RACHAEL EDA

Adrian Lyon's Chambers
14 Castle Street, Liverpool L2 0NE,
Telephone: 0151 236 4421/8240
E-mail: chambers14@aol.com
Call date: Nov 1993, Inner Temple
Qualifications: [LLB (Manch)]

BANKS ROBERT JAMES

100e Great Portland Street
London W1N 5PD, Telephone: 0171 636 6323
Call date: July 1978, Inner Temple
Qualifications: [BSc (Econ) Hons]

BANKS RODERICK CHARLES I'ANSON

48 Bedford Row
London WC1R 4LR,
Telephone: 0171 430 2005
Call date: July 1974, Lincoln's Inn
Qualifications: [LLB]

Fax: 0171 831 4885;
Out of hours telephone: 0181 857 5418;
DX: 284 London

Types of work: Limited partnerships;
Partnerships

Other professional qualifications: CEDR Accredited Mediator

Publications: *Lindley on Partnership*, 14th edn (Co-editor), 1979; *Lindley on Partnership*, 15th edn (Co-editor), 1984; *Lindley and Banks on Partnership*, 16th edn, 1990; *Lindley & Banks on Partnership*, 17th edn, 1995; *Encyclopedia of Professional Partnerships*, 1987

Practice

Specialises exclusively in partnership law, dealing primarily with problems affecting solicitors' partnerships and other professional firms (including doctors practising within the NHS). He has extensive experience in cases involving expulsions and compulsory retirements, 'lock-ins' and 'extractions', dissolutions, garden leave provisions and restrictive covenants. He has drafted numerous partnership agreements and related documentation and is frequently asked to devise novel solutions to specific problems. He also has a particular expertise in the field of limited partnerships and in the structuring of business ventures so as to avoid partnership status. He was closely involved in the development of the new form of limited liability partnership recently introduced into Jersey law. He is known for his 'hands on' approach to partnership disputes, yet advocates a subtle and, where possible, preventative approach in the embryonic stages. He has spoken at numerous seminars and conferences and written widely on partnership-related subjects, as well as appearing in training videos for Legal Network TV. He is a founder member of the Association of Partnership Practitioners, an Hon Associate of the British Veterinary Association and a Fellow of the Institute of Continuing Professional Development.

BANKS TIMOTHY JAMES

Hardwicke Building
New Square, Lincoln's Inn, London WC2A 3SB, Telephone: 0171 242 2523
E-mail: clerks@hardwicke.co.uk
Call date: Nov 1983, Inner Temple
Qualifications: [BA]

BANNER GREGORY STUART

13 Old Square
Ground Floor, Lincoln's Inn, London WC2A 3UA, Telephone: 0171 404 4800
Call date: July 1989, Gray's Inn
Qualifications: [MA (Cantab)]

BANNISTER EDWARD ALEXANDER QC (1991)

3 Stone Bldgs
Ground Floor, Lincoln's Inn, London WC2A 3XL, Telephone: 0171 242 4937/ 405 8358
Call date: July 1974, Lincoln's Inn
Qualifications: [BA (Oxon)]

BANNISTER THOMAS EDWARD JOHN

7 Stone Bldgs
Ground Floor, Lincoln's Inn, London WC2A 3SZ, Telephone: 0171 405 3886/ 242 3546
E-mail: chaldous@vossnet.co.uk
Call date: Nov 1993, Middle Temple
Qualifications: [BA (Hons)(Oxon), CPE]

BANNON MISS TAMMI ELIZABETH

The Corn Exchange
5th Floor Fenwick Street, Liverpool L2 7QS, Telephone: 0151 227 1081/5009
Call date: Nov 1994, Lincoln's Inn
Qualifications: [LLB (Hons)(Sheff)]

BARAV DR AMIHUD

4-5 Gray's Inn Square
Ground Floor, Gray's Inn, London WC1R 5AY, Telephone: 0171 404 5252
E-mail: chambers@4-5graysinnsquare.co.uk
Call date: Oct 1993, Gray's Inn
Qualifications: [MSc (Econ), LLM (Lond)]

BARBER MISS SALLY

5 Stone Buildings
Lincoln's Inn, London WC2A 3XT, Telephone: 0171 242 6201
E-mail: clerks@5-stonebuildings.law.co.uk
Call date: July 1988, Lincoln's Inn
Qualifications: [BA (Hons) (Cantab)]

BARBER STUART CECIL

12 New Square
Ground Floor, Lincoln's Inn, London
WC2A 3SW, Telephone: 0171 419 1212
E-mail: 12newsquare@compuserve.com
Octagon House
19 Colegate, Norwich NR3 1AT,
Telephone: 01603 623186
E-mail: octagon@netmatters.co.uk
Door Tenant
25 Park Square
Leeds LS1 2PW, Telephone: 0113 2451841/2/3
E-mail: sovereignchambers@btinternet.com
Door Tenant
Call date: July 1979, Middle Temple
Qualifications: [FCIS]

BARCA MANUEL DAVID

1 Brick Court
1st Floor, Temple, London EC4Y 9BY,
Telephone: 0171 353 8845
E-mail: clerks@1brickcourt.co.uk
Call date: Nov 1986, Lincoln's Inn
Qualifications: [MA (Cantab)]

BARCLAY PAUL ROBERT

Albion Chambers
Broad Street, Bristol BS1 1DR,
Telephone: 0117 9272144
Call date: July 1972, Middle Temple
Recorder
Qualifications: [MA (Cantab)]

BARD NICHOLAS JAMES

Devereux Chambers
Devereux Court, London WC2R 3JJ,
Telephone: 0171 353 7534
E-mail: elton@devchambers.co.uk
Call date: July 1979, Gray's Inn
Qualifications: [MA (Oxon)]

BARDA ROBIN JOHN BLACKMORE

4 Paper Bldgs
2nd Floor, Temple, London EC4Y 7EX,
Telephone: 0171 583 0816/071 353 1131
E-mail: clerks@4paperbuildings.co.uk
Call date: July 1975, Gray's Inn
Qualifications: [BA (Hons)(Oxon)]

BARKER MISS ALISON

9-12 Bell Yard
London WC2A 2LF,
Telephone: 0171 400 1800
Call date: July 1973, Middle Temple
Qualifications: [LLB (Hons)]

BARKER ANTHONY QC (1985)

5 Fountain Court
Steelhouse Lane, Birmingham B4 6DR,
Telephone: 0121 606 0500
1 Crown Office Row
Ground Floor, Temple, London EC4Y 7HH,
Telephone: 0171 797 7500
Call date: Nov 1966, Middle Temple
Recorder
Qualifications: [BA (Cantab)]

BARKER BRIAN JOHN QC (1990)

Hollis Whiteman Chambers
3rd/4th Floor Queen Elizabeth Bldg, Temple,
London EC4Y 9BS, Telephone: 0171 583 5766
E-mail: hollis.whiteman@btinternet.com
Call date: July 1969, Gray's Inn
Recorder
Qualifications: [LLB, MA]

BARKER DAVID QC (1976)

65-67 King Street
Leicester LE1 6RP, Telephone: 0116 2547710
Call date: July 1954, Inner Temple
Recorder
Qualifications: [LLB (Lond), LLM (Michigan)]

BARKER JAMES SEBASTIAN

Enterprise Chambers
9 Old Square, Lincoln's Inn, London
WC2A 3SR, Telephone: 0171 405 9471
Enterprise Chambers
38 Park Square, Leeds LS1 2PA,
Telephone: 01132 460391
Enterprise Chambers
65 Quayside, Newcastle upon Tyne NE1 3DS,
Telephone: 0191 222 3344
Call date: July 1984, Gray's Inn
Qualifications: [LLB (B'Ham)]

BARKER JOHN CHARLES

6 Gray's Inn Square
Ground Floor, Gray's Inn, London WC1R 5AZ,
Telephone: 0171 242 1052
Call date: July 1982, Middle Temple
Qualifications: [BA LLM (Lond)]

BARKER JOHN STEVEN ROY

Queen's Chambers
5 John Dalton Street, Manchester M2 6ET,
Telephone: 0161 834 6875/4738
4 Camden Place
Preston PR1 3JL, Telephone: 01772 828300
Call date: July 1983, Lincoln's Inn
Qualifications: [MA (Cantab), MA (Cornell)]

BARKER KERRY

Guildhall Chambers
23 Broad Street, Bristol BS1 2HG,
Telephone: 0117 9273366
Call date: July 1972, Gray's Inn
Qualifications: [LLB (Lond)]

BARKER NICHOLAS

30 Park Square
Leeds LS1 2PF, Telephone: 0113 2436388
Call date: Oct 1994, Gray's Inn
Qualifications: [BA]

BARKER SIMON GEORGE HARRY

13 Old Square
Lincoln's Inn, London WC2A 3UA,
Telephone: 0171 404 4800
Call date: July 1979, Lincoln's Inn
Assistant Recorder
Qualifications: [BA]

Fax: 0171 405 4267;
Out of hours telephone: 0171 405 6460;
DX: LDE 326

Types of work: Accountancy; Arbitration;
Banking; Bankruptcy; Commercial litigation;
Company and commercial; Construction;
Copyright; Corporate finance; Entertainment;
Family provision; Film, TV; Intellectual
property; Partnerships; Professional negligence;
Warranty claims

Other professional qualifications: FCA (Fellow of
the Institute of Chartered Accountants)

Circuit: South Eastern

Other professional experience: Assistant
Recorder since 1995

Reported cases: *Newsgroup Newspapers v ITP
Ltd*, [1993] RPC 173. Copyright Tribunal
reference concerning licences and fees for TV
and radio listings.
AIRC v Phonographic Performance Ltd, [1994]
RPC 181. Copyright Tribunal reference
concerning licences and fees for broadcasting
recorded music.
Re A Debtor No 87 of 1993 (No 1 and No 2),
(1996) BCC 74 and 80. Individual voluntary
arrangement, debtor's duty of disclosure and
challenge for material irregularity.
Neville v Wilson, [1997] Ch 144 and (1997) *The
Times*, 28 July. Implied and constructive trusts
of shares and effect of solicitors' agreement as to
costs on courts' discretion.
Coulthard v Neville Russell, (1998) BCLC 359.
Potential scope of auditors' and accountants'
duty of care to directors.

BARKLEM MARTYN STEPHEN

Littleton Chambers
3 King's Bench Walk North, Temple, London
EC4Y 7HR, Telephone: 0171 797 8600
E-mail: littletonchambers@compuserve.com
Call date: July 1989, Middle Temple
Qualifications: [LLB (Lond)]

BARKWORTH TERENCE CHARLES COTHERSTONE

6 Pump Court
Ground Floor, Temple, London EC4Y 7AR,
Telephone: 0171 583 6013/2510
Call date: May 1946, Lincoln's Inn
Qualifications: [BA (Oxon)]

BARLING GERALD EDWARD QC (1991)

Brick Court Chambers
15/19 Devereux Court, London WC2R 3JJ,
Telephone: 0171 583 0777
E-mail: (surname)@brickcourt.demon.co.uk
Door Tenant
8 King Street
Manchester M2 6AQ,
Telephone: 0161 834 9560
Door Tenant
Call date: Nov 1972, Middle Temple
Recorder
Qualifications: [MA (Oxon)]

D

BARLOW CRAIG MARTIN

29 Bedford Row Chambers
London WC1R 4HE,
Telephone: 0171 831 2626
Call date: Oct 1992, Gray's Inn
Qualifications: [LL.B]

BARLOW MARK DAVID

Chambers of Ian Macdonald QC
Waldorf House Cooper Street, Manchester
M2 2FW, Telephone: 0161 236 1840
Call date: Oct 1992, Middle Temple
Qualifications: [LL.B (Hons)]

BARLOW MISS MELISSA EMMA BENSON

Colleton Chambers
Colleton Crescent, Exeter, Devon EX2 4DG,
Telephone: 01392 74898/9
Call date: Oct 1991, Middle Temple
Qualifications: [BA (Hons) (Exon)]

BARLOW RICHARD FRANCIS DUDLEY

10 Old Square
Ground Floor, Lincoln's Inn, London
WC2A 3SU, Telephone: 0171 405 0758
Call date: Feb 1965, Inner Temple
Qualifications: [MA (Oxon)]

BARLOW RICHARD LEONARD

11 King's Bench Walk
1st Floor, Temple, London EC4Y 7EQ,
Telephone: 0171 353 3337
3 Park Court
Leeds LS1 2QH, Telephone: 0113 297 1200
Call date: July 1970, Middle Temple
Qualifications: [LLB (Lond)]

BARLOW MISS SARAH HELEN

St Paul's House
5th Floor 23 Park Square South, Leeds
LS1 2ND, Telephone: 0113 2455866
Call date: Oct 1993, Gray's Inn
Qualifications: [LLB (Hons)]

BARNARD DAVID NOWELL

33 Bedford Row
London WC1R 4JH,
Telephone: 0171 242 6476
Call date: July 1967, Gray's Inn
Recorder
Qualifications: [BA (Cantab)]

BARNARD JAMES PHILIP

11 Stone Bldgs
Ground Floor, Lincoln's Inn, London
WC2A 3TG, Telephone: 0171 831 6381
E-mail: clerks@11StoneBuildings.law.co.uk
Call date: Oct 1993, Middle Temple
Qualifications: [BA (Hons)(Bris), CPE (City)]

BARNES (DAVID) MICHAEL (WILLIAM) QC (1981)

4 Breams Buildings
London EC4A 1AQ,
Telephone: 0171 353 5835/430 1221
Call date: July 1965, Middle Temple
Qualifications: [BA (Oxon)]

BARNES ASHLEY JAMES

First National Building
2nd Floor 24 Fenwick Street, Liverpool
L2 7NE, Telephone: 0151 236 2098
Call date: Oct 1990, Inner Temple
Qualifications: [LLB]

BARNES DAVID JONATHAN

2 Dr Johnson's Building
Temple, London EC4Y 7AY,
Telephone: 0171 353 4716
Call date: Nov 1981, Gray's Inn
Qualifications: [BSc (Econ)]

BARNES HENRY JONATHAN

Walnut House
63 St. David's Hill, Exeter, Devon EX4 4DW,
Telephone: 01392 279751
E-mail: 106627.2451@compuserve.com
Call date: July 1970, Gray's Inn
Recorder
Qualifications: [LLB (So'ton)]

BARNES LUKE CLIVE

3 Dr Johnson's Bldgs
Ground Floor, Temple, London EC4Y 7BA,
Telephone: 0171 353 4854
Call date: Nov 1996, Gray's Inn
Qualifications: [BA (Oxon), MA (City), Dip Law]

BARNES MISS MARGARET SUSANNE

3 Hare Court
1st Floor, Temple, London EC4Y 7BJ,
Telephone: 0171 353 7561
Call date: July 1976, Gray's Inn
Qualifications: [B of Jurisprudence]

BARNES MARK RICHARD PURCELL QC (1992)

1 Essex Court
Ground Floor, Temple, London EC4Y 9AR,
Telephone: 0171 583 2000
E-mail: clerks@oneessexcourt.co.uk
Call date: July 1974, Lincoln's Inn
Qualifications: [MA (Oxon)]

BARNES MATTHEW JOHN CAMPBELL

3 Fountain Court
Steelhouse Lane, Birmingham B4 6DR,
Telephone: 0121 236 5854
Call date: July 1992, Middle Temple
Qualifications: [MA (Cantab)]

BARNES MISS SHANI ESTELLE

1 Hare Court
Ground Floor, Temple, London EC4Y 7BE,
Telephone: 0171 353 3982/5324
Call date: Nov 1986, Middle Temple
Qualifications: [BA, Dip Law (City)]

BARNES TIMOTHY PAUL QC (1986)

9 Bedford Row
London WC1R 4AZ,
Telephone: 0171 242 3555
E-mail: clerks@9br.co.uk
Call date: July 1968, Gray's Inn
Recorder
Qualifications: [MA (Cantab)]

BARNETT MISS ADRIENNE ELISE

8 King's Bench Walk
2nd Floor, Temple, London EC4Y 7DU,
Telephone: 0171 797 8888
8 King's Bench Walk North
1 Park Square East, Leeds LS1 2NE,
Telephone: 0113 2439797
Call date: July 1981, Middle Temple
Qualifications: [BA Cape Town]

BARNETT ANDREW JOHN

Pump Court Chambers
Upper Ground Floor 3 Pump Court, Temple,
London EC4Y 7AJ, Telephone: 0171 353 0711
Pump Court Chambers
31 Southgate Street, Winchester SO23 8EE,
Telephone: 01962 868161
Call date: Nov 1977, Gray's Inn
Recorder
Qualifications: [BA (Lond)]

BARNETT DANIEL ALEXANDER

2 Gray's Inn Square Chambers
2nd Floor, Gray's Inn, London WC1R 5AA,
Telephone: 0171 242 0328/071 405 1317
E-mail: clerks@2gis.co.uk
Call date: Oct 1993, Lincoln's Inn
Qualifications: [LLB (Hons)(Leeds)]

BARNETT MRS DIANE JUNE

Goldsmith Chambers
Ground Floor Goldsmith Building, Temple,
London EC4Y 7BL,
Telephone: 0171 353 6802/3/4/5
E-mail: celiamonksfield@btinternet.com
Call date: Nov 1978, Gray's Inn
Qualifications: [BA]

BARNETT JEREMY VICTOR

St Paul's House
5th Floor 23 Park Square South, Leeds
LS1 2ND, Telephone: 0113 2455866
Farrar's Building
Temple, London EC4Y 7BD,
Telephone: 0171 583 9241
E-mail: chambers@farrarsbuilding.co.uk
Door Tenant
Call date: July 1980, Gray's Inn
Qualifications: [LLB (L'pool)]

BARNETT MISS JOANNE KAREN

Gower Chambers
57 Walter Road, Swansea, West Glamorgan
SA1 5PZ, Telephone: 01792 644466
E-mail: clerk@gowerchambers.co.uk
3 Temple Gardens
3rd Floor, Temple, London EC4Y 9AU,
Telephone: 0171 583 0010
Call date: Nov 1989, Middle Temple
Qualifications: [LLB [Wales]]

BARNETT JOHN HASKINS

Thetford Lodge Farm
Santon Downham, Brandon, Suffolk IP27 OTU,
Telephone: 01842 813132
Call date: July 1981, Gray's Inn

BARNETT MISS SALLY LOUISE

2 New Street
Leicester LE1 5NA, Telephone: 0116 2625906
Call date: Nov 1987, Middle Temple
Qualifications: [LLB]

BARNFATHER MISS LYDIA HELEN

Hollis Whiteman Chambers
3rd/4th Floor Queen Elizabeth Bldg, Temple,
London EC4Y 9BS, Telephone: 0171 583 5766
E-mail: hollis.whiteman@btinternet.com
Call date: Oct 1992, Middle Temple
Qualifications: [BA (Hons)]

BARON MISS FLORENCE JACQUELINE QC (1995)

Queen Elizabeth Bldg
2nd Floor, Temple, London EC4Y 9BS,
Telephone: 0171 797 7837
Call date: Nov 1976, Middle Temple
Qualifications: [BA (Oxon)]

BARR CHARLES DAVID

1 Temple Gardens
1st Floor, Temple, London EC4Y 9BB,
Telephone: 0171 353 0407/583 1315
E-mail: clerks@1templegardens.co.uk
Call date: Nov 1993, Gray's Inn
Qualifications: [MA (Cantab)]

BARR EDWARD ROBERT

2 New Street
Leicester LE1 5NA, Telephone: 0116 2625906
Call date: Nov 1983, Inner Temple
Qualifications: [LLB]

BARR MISS FINOLA KATHERINE FRANKLAND

24a St John Street
Manchester M3 4DF,
Telephone: 0161 833 9628
Call date: Nov 1994, Gray's Inn
Qualifications: [LLB]

BARRACLOUGH ANTHONY ROGER

25-27 Castle Street
1st Floor, Liverpool L2 4TA,
Telephone: 0151 227 5661/051 236 5072
Call date: Nov 1978, Inner Temple
Qualifications: [BA (Dunelm)]

BARRACLOUGH NICHOLAS MAYLIN

Francis Taylor Bldg
2nd Floor, Temple, London EC4Y 7BY,
Telephone: 0171 353 9942/3157
Call date: Nov 1990, Inner Temple
Qualifications: [LLB (Hons)]

BARRACLOUGH RICHARD MICHAEL

6 Pump Court
1st Floor, Temple, London EC4Y 7AR,
Telephone: 0171 797 8400
E-mail: sa_hockman_qc@link.org
6-8 Mill Street
Maidstone, Kent ME15 6XH,
Telephone: 01622 688094
Call date: Nov 1980, Inner Temple
Qualifications: [MA (Oxon)]

BARRADELL RICHARD MARK

19 Figtree Lane
Sheffield S1 2DJ, Telephone: 0114 2759708/
2738380
Call date: Oct 1990, Inner Temple
Qualifications: [LLB]

D

BARRATT DOMINIC ANTHONY

East Anglian Chambers
Gresham House 5 Museum Street, Ipswich
IP1 1HQ, Telephone: 01473 214481
East Anglian Chambers
Sanders House 52 North Hill, Colchester
CO1 1PY, Telephone: 01206 572756
East Anglian Chambers
57 London Street, Norwich NR2 1HL,
Telephone: 01603 617351
Call date: Nov 1992, Gray's Inn
Qualifications: [BA (Hons)(Leeds)]

BARRATT ROBIN ALEXANDER QC (1989)

4-5 Gray's Inn Square
Ground Floor, Gray's Inn, London WC1R 5AY,
Telephone: 0171 404 5252
E-mail: chambers@4-5graysinnsquare.co.uk
Call date: Nov 1970, Middle Temple
Qualifications: [MA (Oxon)]

BARRETT MISS ELIZABETH ANNE MITFORD

Devereux Chambers
Devereux Court, London WC2R 3JJ,
Telephone: 0171 353 7534
E-mail: elton@devchambers.co.uk
Call date: Oct 1992, Lincoln's Inn
Qualifications: [BA(Hons, Cantab), Dip Law]

BARRETT JOHN MICHAEL PAUL GOWRAN

40 King Street
Manchester M2 6BA,
Telephone: 0161 832 9082
E-mail: Kingst40@aol.com
4 Breams Buildings
London EC4A 1AQ,
Telephone: 0171 353 5835/430 1221
Door Tenant
Call date: May 1982, Gray's Inn
Qualifications: [BA]

BARRETT MS PENELOPE JANE

3 Gray's Inn Square
Ground Floor, London WC1R 5AH,
Telephone: 0171 520 5600
E-mail: gis3@btinternet.com
Call date: July 1982, Middle Temple
Qualifications: [MA (Cantab)]

BARRETT ROBERT SCOTT

2 Pump Court
1st Floor, Temple, London EC4Y 7AH,
Telephone: 0171 353 5597
Call date: July 1978, Gray's Inn
Qualifications: [MA (Cantab)]

BARRIE PETER ANTHONY STANFIELD

Guildhall Chambers
23 Broad Street, Bristol BS1 2HG,
Telephone: 0117 9273366
Call date: Nov 1976, Middle Temple
Qualifications: [MA (Oxon)]

BARRINGTON-SMYTH MISS AMANDA ROWENA

4 Paper Bldgs
2nd Floor, Temple, London EC4Y 7EX,
Telephone: 0171 583 0816/071 353 1131
E-mail: clerks@4paperbuildings.co.uk
Call date: Nov 1972, Middle Temple
Qualifications: [LLB (Lond)]

BARRY JOSEPH MICHAEL

Mitre House Chambers
Mitre House 44 Fleet Street, London
EC4Y 1BN, Telephone: 0171 583 8233
Call date: Nov 1987, Lincoln's Inn
Qualifications: [BA (Hons)]

BARRY MISS KIRSTEN LESLEY

8 King Street
Manchester M2 6AQ,
Telephone: 0161 834 9560
Call date: Nov 1993, Lincoln's Inn
Qualifications: [LLB (Hons, Sheff)]

BARSTOW STEPHEN ROYDEN

2 Harcourt Bldgs
1st Floor, Temple, London EC4Y 9DB,
Telephone: 0171 353 6961/7
Harcourt Chambers
Churchill House 3 St Aldate's Courtyard, St
Aldate's, Oxford OX1 1BN,
Telephone: 01865 791559
Call date: July 1976, Gray's Inn
Qualifications: [MA (Cantab)]

D

BART DELANO FRANK

8 King's Bench Walk
2nd Floor, Temple, London EC4Y 7DU,
Telephone: 0171 797 8888
8 King's Bench Walk North
1 Park Square East, Leeds LS1 2NE,
Telephone: 0113 2439797
Call date: July 1977, Lincoln's Inn
Qualifications: [LLB (Lond)]

BARTLE PHILIP MARTYN

Littleton Chambers
3 King's Bench Walk North, Temple, London
EC4Y 7HR, Telephone: 0171 797 8600
E-mail: littletonchambers@compuserve.com
Call date: July 1976, Middle Temple
Qualifications: [MA, BCL (Oxon)]

BARTLETT ANDREW VINCENT BRAMWELL QC (1993)

1 Paper Bldgs
Ground Floor, Temple, London EC4Y 7EP,
Telephone: 0171 583 7355
E-mail: clerks@1pb.co.uk
Call date: July 1974, Middle Temple
Qualifications: [BA (Oxon), FCIArb]

BARTLETT DAVID ALAN

3 Paper Bldgs
1st Floor, Temple, London EC4Y 7EU,
Telephone: 0171 583 8055
E-mail: london@3paper.com
20 Lorne Park Road
Bournemouth BH1 1JN,
Telephone: 01202 292102 (5 Lines)
4 St Peter Street
Winchester SO23 8OW,
Telephone: 01962 868884
Call date: July 1975, Gray's Inn
Recorder
Qualifications: [BA (Oxon)]

BARTLETT GEORGE ROBERT QC (1986)

2 Mitre Ct Bldgs
2nd Floor, Temple, London EC4Y 7BX,
Telephone: 0171 583 1380
Call date: July 1966, Middle Temple
Recorder
Qualifications: [MA (Oxon)]

BARTLETT ROGER JAMES LAWRENCE

1 Harcourt Bldgs
2nd Floor, Temple, London EC4Y 9DA,
Telephone: 0171 353 9421/9151
Call date: July 1968, Middle Temple
Qualifications: [BA]

BARTON ALAN JOHN

Lamb Building
Ground Floor, Temple, London EC4Y 7AS,
Telephone: 0171 797 7788
E-mail: lamb.building@link.org
Call date: Nov 1975, Middle Temple
Qualifications: [LLB, LLM]

BARTON MISS FIONA

5 Essex Court
1st Floor, Temple, London EC4Y 9AH,
Telephone: 0171 410 2000
Call date: Nov 1986, Middle Temple
Qualifications: [LLB(Lond)]

BARTON HUGH GEOFFREY

Doughty Street Chambers
11 Doughty Street, London WC1N 2PG,
Telephone: 0171 404 1313
E-mail: doughty_street@compuserve.com
Call date: Nov 1989, Middle Temple
Qualifications: [BA (Hons), Dip in, Law]

BARTON JOHN CHARLES TOMLIN QC (1989)

Albion Chambers
Broad Street, Bristol BS1 1DR,
Telephone: 0117 9272144
Door Tenant
5 Paper Bldgs
1st Floor, Temple, London EC4Y 7HB,
Telephone: 0171 583 6117
E-mail: clerks@5-paperbuildings.law.co.uk
Door Tenant
Call date: Nov 1969, Middle Temple
Qualifications: [LLB]

BARTON RICHARD JAMES

1 King's Bench Walk
2nd Floor, Temple, London EC4Y 7DB,
Telephone: 0171 936 1500
E-mail: ddear@1kbw.co.uk
Call date: Oct 1990, Lincoln's Inn
Qualifications: [BA, BCL (Oxon)]

BARUAH MISS RIMA

Counsels' Chambers
2nd Floor 10-11 Gray's Inn Square, London
WC1R 5JD, Telephone: 0171 405 2576
Call date: Feb 1994, Inner Temple

BARWISE MISS STEPHANIE NICOLA

1 Atkin Building
Gray's Inn, London WC1R 5AT,
Telephone: 0171 404 0102
E-mail: clerks@atkin-chambers.co.uk
Call date: July 1988, Middle Temple
Qualifications: [MA, LLM (Cantab)]

BASHIR NADIM

Park Court Chambers
40 Park Cross Street, Leeds LS1 2QH,
Telephone: 0113 2433277
Call date: Nov 1988, Middle Temple
Qualifications: [LLB (Hons)]

BASSA YOUSEF

243A Goldhurst Terrace
2nd Floor, London NW6 3EP,
Telephone: 0171 625 8455
Call date: Nov 1989, Lincoln's Inn
Qualifications: [LLB (Essex)]

BASSANO ALARIC JULIAN

Kenworthy's Buildings
83 Bridge Street, Manchester M3 2RF,
Telephone: 0161 832 4036/834 6954
Call date: Nov 1993, Gray's Inn
Qualifications: [BA]

BASSETT JOHN STEWART BRITTEN

5 Essex Court
1st Floor, Temple, London EC4Y 9AH,
Telephone: 0171 410 2000
Call date: July 1975, Inner Temple
Qualifications: [LLB (Leeds)]

BASSIRI-DEZFOULI MISS SOROUR

Horizon Chambers
95a Chancery Lane, London WC2A 1DT,
Telephone: 0171 242 2440
Call date: Oct 1996, Lincoln's Inn
Qualifications: [LLB (Hons)(B'ham)]

BASSRA SUKHBIR SINGH

St Paul's House
5th Floor 23 Park Square South, Leeds
LS1 2ND, Telephone: 0113 2455866
Call date: May 1993, Middle Temple

BASTIN ALEXANDER CHARLES

Francis Taylor Bldg
2nd Floor, Temple, London EC4Y 7BY,
Telephone: 0171 353 9942/3157
Call date: Oct 1995, Middle Temple
Qualifications: [BA (Hons) (Reading), LLB
(Hons)]

BASU DR DIJENDRA BHUSHAN

Devereux Chambers
Devereux Court, London WC2R 3JJ,
Telephone: 0171 353 7534
E-mail: elton@devchambers.co.uk
Call date: Oct 1994, Lincoln's Inn
Qualifications: [MB, BS]

BATCHELOR MARK ALFRED LOWE

22 Old Bldgs
Lincoln's Inn, London WC2A 3UJ,
Telephone: 0171 831 0222
Call date: Nov 1971, Inner Temple

BATCUP DAVID JOHN

2 Dr Johnson's Building
Temple, London EC4Y 7AY,
Telephone: 0171 353 4716
Call date: July 1974, Gray's Inn
Assistant Recorder
Qualifications: [LLB (Lond)]

D

BATE ANTHONY JOHN

East Anglian Chambers
57 London Street, Norwich NR2 1HL,
Telephone: 01603 617351
East Anglian Chambers
Sanders House 52 North Hill, Colchester
CO1 1PY, Telephone: 01206 572756
East Anglian Chambers
Gresham House 5 Museum Street, Ipswich
IP1 1HQ, Telephone: 01473 214481
Call date: July 1987, Lincoln's Inn
Qualifications: [MA, Vet.MB (Cantab)]

BATE DAVID CHRISTOPHER QC (1994)

Hollis Whiteman Chambers
3rd/4th Floor Queen Elizabeth Bldg, Temple,
London EC4Y 9BS, Telephone: 0171 583 5766
E-mail: hollis.whiteman@btinternet.com
Call date: Feb 1969, Gray's Inn
Recorder
Qualifications: [LLB]

BATE STEPHEN ROBERT DE BRETEUIL

5 Raymond Buildings
1st Floor, Gray's Inn, London WC1R 5BP,
Telephone: 0171 242 2902
Call date: July 1981, Middle Temple
Qualifications: [MA (Cantab), Dip Law (City)]

BATE-WILLIAMS JOHN ROBERT ALEXANDER

1 Temple Gardens
1st Floor, Temple, London EC4Y 9BB,
Telephone: 0171 353 0407/583 1315
E-mail: clerks@1templegardens.co.uk
Call date: Nov 1976, Inner Temple
Qualifications: [LLB (Wales)]

BATEMAN MISS CHRISTINE JUNE

St John's Chambers
Small Street, Bristol BS1 1DW,
Telephone: 0117 9213456/298514
E-mail: clerks@stjohns.uk.com
Call date: Nov 1992, Lincoln's Inn
Qualifications: [LLB (Hons)(Nott'm)]

BATES (JONATHAN) PASCAL

3 Temple Gardens
2nd Floor, Temple, London EC4Y 9AU,
Telephone: 0171 583 1155
Call date: Nov 1994, Middle Temple
Qualifications: [BA (Hons)]

BATES ALEXANDER ANDREW

St Paul's House
5th Floor 23 Park Square South, Leeds
LS1 2ND, Telephone: 0113 2455866
Call date: Oct 1994, Gray's Inn
Qualifications: [BA (Hons) (Cantab)]

BATES JOHN HAYWARD

Old Square Chambers
1 Verulam Buildings, Gray's Inn, London
WC1R 5LQ, Telephone: 0171 831 0801
Old Square Chambers
Hanover House 47 Corn Street, Bristol
BS1 1HT, Telephone: 0117 9277111
Call date: July 1973, Middle Temple

BATES RICHARD GRAHAM

Hardwicke Building
New Square, Lincoln's Inn, London
WC2A 3SB, Telephone: 0171 242 2523
E-mail: clerks@hardwicke.co.uk
Call date: Oct 1992, Middle Temple
Qualifications: [BA (Hons, Dunelm), Common
Profesional, Examination]

BATEY DAVID MICHAEL

Stour Chambers
Barton Mill House Barton Mill Road,
Canterbury, Kent CT1 1BP,
Telephone: 01227 764899
E-mail: clerks@stourchambers.co.uk
Call date: July 1989, Gray's Inn
Qualifications: [BA (Keele)]

BATHER MISS VICTORIA MACLEAN

Littleton Chambers
3 King's Bench Walk North, Temple, London
EC4Y 7HR, Telephone: 0171 797 8600
E-mail: littletonchambers@compuserve.com
Call date: Oct 1995, Middle Temple
Qualifications: [BA (Hons)]

BATHURST THE HON CHRISTOPHER HILEY LUDLOW QC (1978)

Fountain Court
Temple, London EC4Y 9DH,
Telephone: 0171 583 3335
E-mail: chambers@fountaincourt.co.uk
Call date: Feb 1959, Gray's Inn

BATISTE SIMON ANTHONY

Bank House Chambers
Old Bank House, Hartshead, Sheffield S1 2EL,
Telephone: 0114 2751223
Call date: Oct 1995, Lincoln's Inn
Qualifications: [LLB (Hons)(Newc)]

BATRA BUNTY LALIT

58 King Street Chambers
1st Floor, Kingsgate House 51-53 South King
Street, Manchester M2 6DE,
Telephone: 0161 831 7477
Call date: Feb 1988, Gray's Inn
Qualifications: [LLB]

BATTCOCK BENJAMIN GEORGE

2 Harcourt Bldgs
Ground Floor/Left, Temple, London
EC4Y 9DB, Telephone: 0171 583 9020
E-mail: clerks@harcourt.co.uk
Stanbrook & Henderson
2 Harcourt Bldgs 2nd Floor, Temple, London
EC4Y 9DB, Telephone: 0171 353 0101
E-mail: clerks@harcourt.co.uk
Call date: July 1987, Middle Temple
Qualifications: [MA (Cantab)]

BATTEN STEPHEN DUVAL QC (1989)

3 Raymond Buildings
Gray's Inn, London WC1R 5BH,
Telephone: 0171 831 3833
E-mail: chambers@threeraymond.demon.co.uk
Call date: Nov 1968, Middle Temple
Recorder
Qualifications: [BA (Oxon)]

BATTERSBY PROF GRAHAM

Bank House Chambers
Old Bank House, Hartshead, Sheffield S1 2EL,
Telephone: 0114 2751223
Call date: June 1964, Lincoln's Inn
Qualifications: [BA]

BATTY CHRISTOPHER MICHAEL

St Paul's House
5th Floor 23 Park Square South, Leeds
LS1 2ND, Telephone: 0113 2455866
Call date: July 1989, Gray's Inn
Qualifications: [LLB (L'pool)]

BATTY PAUL DANIEL QC (1995)

Broad Chare
33 Broad Chare, Newcastle Upon Tyne
NE1 3DQ, Telephone: 0191 232 0541
11 King's Bench Walk
1st Floor, Temple, London EC4Y 7EQ,
Telephone: 0171 353 3337
Call date: July 1975, Lincoln's Inn
Recorder
Qualifications: [LLB]

BAUGHAN ANDREW ROBERT

2 Paper Buildings
Basement, Temple, London EC4Y 7ET,
Telephone: 0171 353 0933
Call date: Nov 1994, Middle Temple
Qualifications: [BA (Hons)(Lond), Dip Law]

BAUGHAN JULIAN JAMES QC (1990)

13 King's Bench Walk
1st Floor, Temple, London EC4Y 7EN,
Telephone: 0171 353 7204
E-mail: clerks@13kbw.law.co.uk
King's Bench Chambers
32 Beaumont Street, Oxford OX1 2NP,
Telephone: 01865 311066
E-mail: clerks@kbc-oxford.law.co.uk
Call date: Nov 1967, Inner Temple
Recorder
Qualifications: [BA (Oxon)]

BAUM MISS VICTORIA EMMA

1 Harcourt Bldgs
2nd Floor, Temple, London EC4Y 9DA,
Telephone: 0171 353 9421/9151
Call date: Oct 1993, Middle Temple
Qualifications: [BA (Hons) (Oxon)]

BAUR CHRISTOPHER THOMAS

Furnival Chambers
32 Furnival Street, London EC4A 1JQ,
Telephone: 0171 405 3232
E-mail: clerks@furnivallaw.co.uk
Call date: July 1972, Middle Temple

D

BAXENDALE MISS PRESILEY LAMORNA QC (1992)

2 Hare Court
Ground Floor, Temple, London EC4Y 7BH,
Telephone: 0171 583 1770
E-mail: 2_Hare_Court@link.org
Call date: July 1974, Lincoln's Inn
Qualifications: [MA (Oxon)]

BAXENDALE THOMAS DAWTREY

24 Old Bldgs
Ground Floor, Lincoln's Inn, London
WC2A 3UJ, Telephone: 0171 404 0946
E-mail: clerks@24oldbuildings.law.co.uk
Call date: July 1962, Inner Temple
Assistant Recorder

BAXTER MISS BERNADETTE

Lincoln House Chambers
5th Floor Lincoln House, 1 Brazennose Street,
Manchester M2 5EL,
Telephone: 0161 832 5701
E-mail: LincolnHouseChambers@link.org
Call date: July 1987, Middle Temple
Qualifications: [LLB (LSE)]

BAXTER GERALD PEARSON

25-27 Castle Street
1st Floor, Liverpool L2 4TA,
Telephone: 0151 227 5661/051 236 5072
Call date: July 1971, Lincoln's Inn
Qualifications: [LLB (Sheff), LLM]

BAXTER MRS SHARON YVONNE VERGETTE

2 Paper Bldgs
1st Floor, Temple, London EC4Y 7ET,
Telephone: 0171 936 2611 (10 Lines)
E-mail: clerks@2pbbarristers.co.uk
Call date: July 1987, Inner Temple
Qualifications: [LLB (Oxon)]

BAYATI MS CHARLOTTE ELIZABETH

Gray's Inn Chambers
5th Floor, Gray's Inn, London WC1R 5JA,
Telephone: 0171 404 1111
Call date: Nov 1995, Gray's Inn
Qualifications: [LLB]

BAYLIS CHRISTOPHER LLOYD GERSHWIN

2 Paper Buildings
Basement, Temple, London EC4Y 7ET,
Telephone: 0171 353 0933
Door Tenant
Call date: Nov 1986, Inner Temple
Qualifications: [BA (Hons), LLM, MTh, MBA
(Cantab), M.Phil, (Cantab)]

BAYLIS MS NATALIE JAYNE

3 Verulam Buildings
London WC1R 5NT,
Telephone: 0171 831 8441
E-mail: clerks@3verulam.co.uk
Call date: Oct 1996, Lincoln's Inn
Qualifications: [MA (Hons)(Edinburgh), Dip in
Law (City)]

BAYLISS RODERIC ALAN

2 Dr Johnson's Building
Temple, London EC4Y 7AY,
Telephone: 0171 353 4716
Call date: July 1966, Inner Temple
Recorder

BAYLISS THOMAS WILLIAM MAXWELL

Park Court Chambers
40 Park Cross Street, Leeds LS1 2QH,
Telephone: 0113 2433277
Call date: July 1977, Inner Temple
Assistant Recorder
Qualifications: [LLB (Hons)]

BAZINI DANIEL

8 King's Bench Walk
2nd Floor, Temple, London EC4Y 7DU,
Telephone: 0171 797 8888
8 King's Bench Walk North
1 Park Square East, Leeds LS1 2NE,
Telephone: 0113 2439797
Call date: Nov 1992, Gray's Inn
Qualifications: [BA (Econ), BA (Law)]

BAZLEY MISS JANET CLARE

Francis Taylor Bldg
Ground Floor, Temple, London EC4Y 7BY,
Telephone: 0171 353 7768/7769/2711
Call date: July 1980, Lincoln's Inn
Qualifications: [LLB (Lond)]

BEAL JASON PHILIP MARCUS

2 King's Bench Walk
Ground Floor, Temple, London EC4Y 7DE,
Telephone: 0171 353 1746
E-mail: 2kbw@atlas.co.uk
King's Bench Chambers
115 North Hill, Plymouth PL4 8JY,
Telephone: 01752 221551
Call date: Oct 1993, Gray's Inn
Qualifications: [BA]

BEAL KIERON CONRAD

4 Paper Bldgs
Ground Floor, Temple, London EC4Y 7EX,
Telephone: 0171 353 3366/583 7155
E-mail: clerks@4paperbuildings.com
Call date: Nov 1995, Inner Temple
Qualifications: [BA (Cantab), LLM (Harvard)]

BEALBY WALTER

5 Fountain Court
Steelhouse Lane, Birmingham B4 6DR,
Telephone: 0121 606 0500
Call date: July 1976, Middle Temple
Qualifications: [BA (Bristol)]

BEALE MISS JUDITH HELEN

2 Hare Court
Ground Floor, Temple, London EC4Y 7BH,
Telephone: 0171 583 1770
E-mail: 2_Hare_Court@link.org
Call date: July 1978, Inner Temple
Qualifications: [BA, M Phil(Lond)]

BEAN ALAN SIGMUND JOCELYN

85 Springfield Road
King's Heath, Birmingham B14 7DU,
Telephone: 0121 444 2818
E-mail: beanlaw.demon.co.uk
Call date: July 1990, Lincoln's Inn
Qualifications: [BA (Oxon), MA (Lond)]

BEAN DAVID MICHAEL QC (1997)

Devereux Chambers
Devereux Court, London WC2R 3JJ,
Telephone: 0171 353 7534
E-mail: elton@devchambers.co.uk
Call date: July 1976, Middle Temple
Recorder
Qualifications: [MA (Cantab) FCI Arb]

BEAR CHARLES

11 King's Bench Walk
Temple, London EC4Y 7EQ,
Telephone: 0171 632 8500
E-mail: clerksroom@11-kbw.law.co.uk
Call date: Nov 1986, Lincoln's Inn
Qualifications: [BA(Oxon)]

BEARD DANIEL MATTHEW

Monckton Chambers
4 Raymond Buildings, Gray's Inn, London
WC1R 5BP, Telephone: 0171 405 7211
E-mail: chambers@monckton.co.uk
Call date: Nov 1996, Middle Temple
Qualifications: [BA (Hons)(Cantab)]

BEARD DAVID JOHN

Bell Yard Chambers
116/118 Chancery Lane, London WC2A 1PP,
Telephone: 0171 306 9292
Call date: Oct 1990, Lincoln's Inn
Qualifications: [LLB]

BEARD MARK CHRISTOPHER

6 Pump Court
1st Floor, Temple, London EC4Y 7AR,
Telephone: 0171 797 8400
E-mail: sa_hockman_qc@link.org
Call date: Oct 1996, Gray's Inn

BEARD NEVILLE WAYNE

Pendragon Chambers
124 Walter Road, Swansea SA1 5RG,
Telephone: 01792 411188
Call date: Oct 1991, Gray's Inn
Qualifications: [MA (Oxon)]

BEARD SIMON

24 The Ropewalk
Nottingham NG1 5EF,
Telephone: 0115 9472581
E-mail: clerk@ropewalk.co.uk
Call date: Nov 1980, Gray's Inn
Qualifications: [BA (Oxon)]

BEARDSMORE DR VALERIE

2 Paper Bldgs
1st Floor, Temple, London EC4Y 7ET,
Telephone: 0171 936 2611 (10 Lines)
E-mail: clerks@2pbbarristers.co.uk
Call date: May 1990, Middle Temple
Qualifications: [B.A. (Wales), Ph.D. (Kent)]

BEARMAN JUSTIN IAN

Harrow on the Hill Chambers
60 High Street, Harrow on the Hill, Middlesex
HA1 3LL, Telephone: 0181 423 7444
Windsor Barristers' Chambers
Windsor, Telephone: 01753 648899
Call date: Nov 1992, Inner Temple
Qualifications: [LLB (Hull) (Hons)]

BEASLEY-MURRAY MRS CAROLINE WYNNE

Fenners Chambers
3 Madingley Road, Cambridge CB3 OEE,
Telephone: 01223 368761
Fenners Chambers
8-12 Priestgate, Peterborough PE1 1JA,
Telephone: 01733 62030
Call date: July 1988, Inner Temple
Qualifications: [MA (Cantab), CPE]

BEATSON PROFESSOR JACK

Essex Court Chambers
24 Lincoln's Inn Fields, London WC2A 3ED,
Telephone: 0171 813 8000
E-mail: clerksroom@essexcourt-chambers.co.uk
Call date: Feb 1972, Inner Temple
Recorder
Qualifications: [BA, BCL (Oxon), MA]

BEATTIE MISS ANN LOUISE

Derby Square Chambers
Merchants Court, Derby Square, Liverpool
L2 1TS, Telephone: 0151 709 4222
Call date: July 1989, Middle Temple
Qualifications: [BSc (Hons)(Dunelm), Dip Law (Hons)]

BEATTIE MISS SHARON MICHELLE

Park Court Chambers
40 Park Cross Street, Leeds LS1 2QH,
Telephone: 0113 2433277
Call date: Nov 1986, Inner Temple
Qualifications: [LLB (Hons)(Leeds)]

BEAUMONT CHRISTOPHER HUBERT

2 Harcourt Bldgs
2nd Floor, Temple, London EC4Y 9DB,
Telephone: 0171 353 8415
E-mail: clerks@twoharcourtbldgs.demon.co.uk
Call date: June 1950, Middle Temple
Recorder
Qualifications: [MA (Oxon)]

BEAUMONT MARC CLIFFORD

Harrow-on-the-Hill Chambers
60 High Street, Harrow on the Hill, Middlesex
HA1 3LL, Telephone: 0181 423 7444
Windsor Barristers' Chambers
Windsor, Berkshire,
Telephone: 01753 648 899
Pump Court Chambers
Upper Ground Floor, 3 Pump Court, London
EC4Y 7AJ, Telephone: 0171 353 0711
Door Tenant
Pump Court Chambers
31 Southgate Street, Winchester SO23 9EE,
Telephone: 01962 868161
Door Tenant
Call date: July 1985, Gray's Inn
Qualifications: [LLB (Manch)]

Fax: 0181 423 7368;
Out of hours telephone: 01753 648899;
DX: 130112 Slough 6

Types of work: Banking; Chancery land law;
Commercial litigation; Commercial property;
Common law (general); Company and
commercial; Competition; Consumer law;
Conveyancing; Education; Employment; Family;
Family provision; Franchising; Insurance;
Landlord and tenant; Local government;
Partnerships; Personal injury; Professional
negligence

Circuit: South Eastern

Awards and memberships: Head of Chambers;
Elected Member General Council of the Bar;
Committee Member South Eastern Circuit Bar
Mess; Committee Member London Common
Law and Commercial Bar Association;
Committee North London Bar Mess

Publications: *Effective Mortgage Enforcement*
(New Law Publishing), May 1998; Various
articles in legal journals and periodicals;
Lectures on Mortgage Law

Reported Cases

Doble v Haymills (1988) *The Times*, 5 July;
(1988) SJ 1063
Writ extension

Abbey National BS v Cann [1991] 1 AC 56, HL;
[1989] 2 FLR 265, CA
Overriding interests - subordination

Jones v Jones [1993] 2 FLR 377
Committal

S v W [1995] 1 FLR 862; (1994) *The Times*, 26
December
Action for damages for childhood sexual abuse
- s 11 Limitation Act 1980

Re Jayham Ltd [1995] 2 BCLC 455
Restoration to Companies Register - s 653
Companies Act 1985

First National Bank v Ann [1997] CCLR; CL
February; [1997] Hals, March; Encyc of
Consumer Credit
Limitation period for extortionate credit bargain
claim

Popat v Shonchhatra [1997] 3 All ER 799;
[1997] 1 WLR 1367
Division of post-dissolution partnership profits

Hurstanger Ltd v Ricketts [1997] CCLR; CL
September 1997; Encyc of Consumer Credit
Following *FNB v Ann* above, strike out -
limitation period for extortionate credit bargain
claim - issue estoppel - abuse of process

R v Rotherham MBC ex parte Clark and others
[1998] ELR 152, CA; (1997) *The Times*, 20
November, (Collins J); (1997) *The Times*, 4
December, CA
Education - judicial review of school admissions
policy based on catchment areas rather than
parental preference - s 411 Education Act 1996

Hill Samuel Personal Finance v Grundy 19
November 1997, CA; [1997] All ER (D); *Estates
Gazette*; to be reported in All ER 1998
Unless orders - *Hytec Information* criteria

Practice Details

In 1990, I established Harrow-on-the-Hill
Barristers' Chambers. Whilst at the time, this
was a novel and unorthodox idea, the set is now
firmly established, both within the London area
and across the country.

My practice is property orientated, embracing
mortgages, banking, conveyancing, professional
negligence and business and commercial
litigation. I have also developed an active
interest in education law. I have appeared in
leading cases in the property and education
fields. I try to bring to my work a fighting will to
win and a streak of originality.

BEAZLEY THOMAS ALAN GEORGE

2 Hare Court
Ground Floor, Temple, London EC4Y 7BH,
Telephone: 0171 583 1770
E-mail: 2_Hare_Court@link.org
Call date: July 1979, Middle Temple
Qualifications: [BA (Cantab), LLB]

BEBB GORDON MONTFORT

2 King's Bench Walk
Ground Floor, Temple, London EC4Y 7DE,
Telephone: 0171 353 1746
E-mail: 2kbw@atlas.co.uk
King's Bench Chambers
115 North Hill, Plymouth PL4 8JY,
Telephone: 01752 221551
Call date: Nov 1975, Middle Temple
Qualifications: [BA (Oxon)]

BECK JAMES HARRISON

1 Crown Office Row
2nd Floor, Temple, London EC4Y 7HH,
Telephone: 0171 797 7111
Call date: July 1989, Lincoln's Inn
Qualifications: [BSc, MSc (LSE)]

BECKER TIMOTHY GEORGE CHRISTIE

King's Bench Chambers
Wellington House 175 Holdenhurst Road,
Bournemouth, Dorset BH8 8DQ,
Telephone: 01202 250025
Call date: July 1992, Middle Temple
Qualifications: [BA (Hons) (Lond), Dip Law,
A.K.C.]

BECKETT RICHARD GERVASE QC (1988)

3 Raymond Buildings
Gray's Inn, London WC1R 5BH,
Telephone: 0171 831 3833
E-mail: chambers@threeraymond.demon.co.uk
Call date: Nov 1965, Middle Temple

D

BECKHOUGH MISS JENNIFER ANNE LINDSAY

One Garden Court
Ground Floor, Temple, London EC4Y 9BJ,
Telephone: 0171 797 7900
Call date: July 1973, Inner Temple
Qualifications: [LLB (Lond)]

BECKHOUGH NIGEL CHARLES LINDSAY

1 Gray's Inn Square
1st Floor, London WC1R 5AG,
Telephone: 0171 405 3000
E-mail: clerks@onegrays.demon.co.uk
Call date: Nov 1976, Middle Temple

BECKMAN MICHAEL DAVID QC (1976)

11 Stone Bldgs
Ground Floor, Lincoln's Inn, London
WC2A 3TG, Telephone: 0171 831 6381
E-mail: clerks@11StoneBuildings.law.co.uk
Chichester Chambers
12 North Pallant, Chichester, West Sussex
PO19 1TQ, Telephone: 01243 784538
Call date: May 1954, Lincoln's Inn
Qualifications: [LLB (Lond)]

BEDDOE MARTIN WILLIAM DENTON

36 Bedford Row
London WC1R 4JH,
Telephone: 0171 421 8000
E-mail: 36bedfordrow@link.org
Call date: Nov 1979, Gray's Inn
Qualifications: [MA (Cantab)]

BEDEAU STEPHEN

Lancaster Building Chambers
77 Deansgate, Manchester M3 2BW,
Telephone: 0161 661 4444
E-mail: sandra@lbnipc.com
Door Tenant
25 Park Square
Leeds LS1 2PW, Telephone: 0113 2451841/2/3
E-mail: sovereignchambers@btinternet.com
Call date: July 1980, Lincoln's Inn
Qualifications: [LLB (Hull)]

BEDELL-PEARCE MISS SHERON IRENE

Brentwood Chambers
Denton, North Yorkshire LS29 OHE,
Telephone: 01943 817230
One Garden Court
Ground Floor, Temple, London EC4Y 9BJ,
Telephone: 0171 797 7900
Call date: July 1978, Inner Temple
Qualifications: [LLB (Bris)]

BEDFORD BECKET NATHANIEL

Francis Taylor Bldg
3rd Floor, Temple, London EC4Y 7BY,
Telephone: 0171 797 7250
5 Fountain Court
Steelhouse Lane, Birmingham B4 6DR,
Telephone: 0121 606 0500
Call date: Nov 1989, Middle Temple
Qualifications: [LLB (Hons)(Cardiff), Deug 1
(Nantes)]

BEDFORD MICHAEL CHARLES ANTHONY

2-3 Gray's Inn Square
Gray's Inn, London WC1R 5JH,
Telephone: 0171 242 4986
E-mail: chambers@2-3graysinnsquare.co.uk
Call date: July 1985, Gray's Inn
Qualifications: [LLB (Lond)]

BEDFORD STEPHEN JOHN

India Buildings Chambers
Water Street, Liverpool L2 OXG,
Telephone: 0151 243 6000
Call date: July 1974, Gray's Inn
Assistant Recorder
Qualifications: [BA (Oxon)]

BEDINGFIELD DAVID HERBERT

14 Gray's Inn Square
Gray's Inn, London WC1R 5JP,
Telephone: 0171 242 0858
E-mail: 100712.2134@compuserve.com
Call date: Nov 1991, Gray's Inn
Qualifications: [BA (Florida State), Juris Doctor
(Emory)]

BEECH MS JACQUELINE ELAINE

199 Strand
London WC2R 1DR,
Telephone: 0171 379 9779
E-mail: chambers@199strand.co.uk
York Chambers
14 Toft Green, York YO1 1JT,
Telephone: 01904 620048
E-mail: yorkchambers.co.uk
Call date: Nov 1981, Middle Temple
Qualifications: [BA]

BEECHEY MISS HILARY JANE

Godolphin Chambers
50 Castle Street, Truro, Cornwall TR1 3AF,
Telephone: 01872 276312
Call date: Nov 1987, Middle Temple
Qualifications: [BA (Hons), Dip Law (City)]

BEECROFT ROBERT GEORGE

1 Harcourt Bldgs
2nd Floor, Temple, London EC4Y 9DA,
Telephone: 0171 353 9421/9151
Call date: Nov 1977, Gray's Inn
Qualifications: [LLB]

BEER JASON BARRINGTON

5 Essex Court
1st Floor, Temple, London EC4Y 9AH,
Telephone: 0171 410 2000
Call date: Oct 1992, Inner Temple
Qualifications: [LLB (Warw)]

BEESON NIGEL ADRIAN LAURENCE

First National Building
2nd Floor 24 Fenwick Street, Liverpool
L2 7NE, Telephone: 0151 236 2098
Call date: July 1983, Lincoln's Inn
Qualifications: [LLB (Hons)]

BEEVER EDMUND DAMIAN

Priory Chambers
2 Fountain Court, Steelhouse Lane,
Birmingham B4 6DR,
Telephone: 0121 236 3882/1375
Call date: Oct 1990, Lincoln's Inn
Qualifications: [BA (Oxon)]

BEGGS JOHN PETER

3 Serjeants Inn
London EC4Y 1BQ,
Telephone: 0171 353 5537
E-mail: available upon request
Call date: Nov 1989, Gray's Inn
Qualifications: [LLB (Brunel)]

BEGLAN WAYNE STUART

2-3 Gray's Inn Square
Gray's Inn, London WC1R 5JH,
Telephone: 0171 242 4986
E-mail: chambers@2-3graysinnsquare.co.uk
Call date: Oct 1996, Lincoln's Inn
Qualifications: [BA (Hons)(Keele)]

BEGLEY MISS LAURA ANNE

9 Gough Square
London EC4A 3DE, Telephone: 0171 353 5371
Call date: Nov 1993, Lincoln's Inn
Qualifications: [LLB (Hons, Leeds)]

BEHAR RICHARD VICTOR MONTAGUE EDWARD

1 Essex Court
Ground Floor, Temple, London EC4Y 9AR,
Telephone: 0171 583 2000
E-mail: clerks@oneessexcourt.co.uk
Call date: Nov 1965, Middle Temple
Recorder
Qualifications: [MA(Oxon)]

BEHRENS JAMES NICHOLAS EDWARD

13 Old Square
1st Floor, Lincoln's Inn, London WC2A 3UA,
Telephone: 0171 242 6105
E-mail: clerks@serlecourt.co.uk
Call date: July 1979, Middle Temple
Qualifications: [MA (Cantab)]

BEKOE SAMUEL YAW

Chancery Chambers
1st Floor Offices 70/72 Chancery Lane,
London WC2A 1AB,
Telephone: 0171 405 6879/6870
Call date: Nov 1980, Lincoln's Inn
Qualifications: [BA (Manch)]

BEKOE-TABIRI CHRISTIAN GOTTFRIED

Bell Yard Chambers
116/118 Chancery Lane, London WC2A 1PP,
Telephone: 0171 306 9292
Southsea Chambers
PO Box 148, Southsea, Portsmouth,
Hampshire PO5 2TU,
Telephone: 01705 291261
Call date: July 1992, Lincoln's Inn
Qualifications: [BA (Hons), BL]

BELBEN ROBIN WILLIAM

College Chambers
19 Carlton Cresent, Southampton, Hants
SO15 2ET, Telephone: 01703 230338
Call date: Nov 1969, Lincoln's Inn
Recorder
Qualifications: [LLB (Hons)(Lond)]

BELBIN MISS HEATHER PATRICIA

Oriel Chambers
14 Water Street, Liverpool L2 8TD,
Telephone: 0151 236 7191
E-mail: oriel_chambers@link.org
Call date: Oct 1992, Lincoln's Inn
Qualifications: [LLB(Hons)(Shef)]

BELFORD MISS DORA JOY

14 Tooks Court
Cursitor St, London EC4A 1LB,
Telephone: 0171 405 8828
E-mail: clerks @tooks.law.co.uk
Call date: July 1977, Middle Temple

BELGER TYRONE

2 Dr Johnson's Building
Temple, London EC4Y 7AY,
Telephone: 0171 353 4716
Call date: July 1984, Inner Temple
Qualifications: [LLB (Lond)]

BELGRAVE MISS SUSAN LORRAINE

4 Brick Court
Ground Floor, Temple, London EC4Y 9AD,
Telephone: 0171 797 7766
E-mail: chambers@4brick.co.uk
Call date: July 1989, Inner Temple
Qualifications: [BA, LLB, MSc (Econ),
Lic.Spec.En Droit, European (LLM)]

BELL ADRIAN JOHN

1 Serjeants' Inn
5th Floor Fleet Street, Temple, London
EC4Y 1LL, Telephone: 0171 415 6666
E-mail: no1serjeantsinn@btinternet.com
Call date: July 1976, Middle Temple

BELL ALPHEGE

1 Crown Office Row
2nd Floor, Temple, London EC4Y 7HH,
Telephone: 0171 797 7111
Call date: Oct 1995, Inner Temple
Qualifications: [BA (Oxon)]

BELL MISS ANNE MARGARET

Holborn Chambers
6 Gate Street, Lincoln's Inn Fields, London
WC2A 3HP, Telephone: 0171 242 6060
Middlesex Chambers
Suite 3 & 4 Stanley House Stanley Avenue,
Wembley, Middlesex HA0 4SB,
Telephone: 0181 902 1499
Call date: Nov 1975, Gray's Inn
Qualifications: [BA (Hons)]

BELL ANTHONY JOHN

2 Mitre Ct Bldgs
1st Floor, Temple, London EC4Y 7BX,
Telephone: 0171 353 1353
Call date: Nov 1985, Inner Temple
Qualifications: [BA (Hons)]

BELL DOMINIC MICHAEL ST. JOHN

Bell Yard Chambers
116/118 Chancery Lane, London WC2A 1PP,
Telephone: 0171 306 9292
Call date: Nov 1992, Inner Temple
Qualifications: [LLB (Lond)]

BELL GARY TERENCE

Equity Chambers
Suite 110, Gazette Buildings 168 Corporation
Street, Birmingham B4 6TS,
Telephone: 0121 233 2100
Call date: Feb 1989, Inner Temple
Qualifications: [LLB (Bris)]

BELL JAMES

1 Temple Gardens
1st Floor, Temple, London EC4Y 9BB,
Telephone: 0171 353 0407/583 1315
E-mail: clerks@1templegardens.co.uk
Call date: Nov 1987, Middle Temple
Qualifications: [LLB(Hons) Wales]

BELL MISS MARIKA PAMELA TRACEY

East Anglian Chambers
57 London Street, Norwich NR2 1HL,
Telephone: 01603 617351
East Anglian Chambers
Sanders House 52 North Hill, Colchester
CO1 1PY, Telephone: 01206 572756
East Anglian Chambers
Gresham House 5 Museum Street, Ipswich
IP1 1HQ, Telephone: 01473 214481
Call date: Nov 1991, Gray's Inn
Qualifications: [LLB (B'ham)]

BELLAMY JONATHAN MARK

39 Essex Street
London WC2R 3AT,
Telephone: 0171 583 1111
E-mail: clerks@39essex.co.uk
Call date: Nov 1986, Lincoln's Inn
Qualifications: [MA(Oxon)]

BELLAMY STEPHEN HOWARD QC (1996)

1 King's Bench Walk
2nd Floor, Temple, London EC4Y 7DB,
Telephone: 0171 936 1500
E-mail: ddear@1kbw.co.uk
Call date: Nov 1974, Lincoln's Inn
Recorder
Qualifications: [MA (Cantab), ACIArb]

BELLIS WILLIAM GORDON

The Corn Exchange
5th Floor Fenwick Street, Liverpool L2 7QS,
Telephone: 0151 227 1081/5009
Call date: July 1972, Inner Temple
Qualifications: [MA (Cantab)]

BELOFF THE HON MICHAEL JACOB QC (1981)

4-5 Gray's Inn Square
Ground Floor, Gray's Inn, London WC1R 5AY,
Telephone: 0171 404 5252
E-mail: chambers@4-5graysinnsquare.co.uk
Call date: Nov 1967, Gray's Inn
Recorder
Qualifications: [MA (Oxon)]

BELSON MISS JANE ELIZABETH

17 Bedford Row
London WC1R 4EB,
Telephone: 0171 831 7314
E-mail: IBoard7314@AOL.com
Call date: July 1978, Inner Temple
Qualifications: [BA (Oxon)]

BELTRAMI ADRIAN JOSEPH

3 Verulam Buildings
London WC1R 5NT,
Telephone: 0171 831 8441
E-mail: clerks@3verulam.co.uk
Call date: July 1989, Lincoln's Inn
Qualifications: [BA (Cantab), LLM (Harvard)]

BENBOW MISS SARA ELIZABETH

Hardwicke Building
New Square, Lincoln's Inn, London
WC2A 3SB, Telephone: 0171 242 2523
E-mail: clerks@hardwicke.co.uk
Call date: Nov 1990, Middle Temple
Qualifications: [LLB (Exon)]

BENDALL RICHARD GILES

33 Bedford Row
London WC1R 4JH,
Telephone: 0171 242 6476
Call date: July 1979, Lincoln's Inn
Qualifications: [LLB]

BENEDICT JOHN IDOWU

3 Temple Gardens
3rd Floor, Temple, London EC4Y 9AU,
Telephone: 0171 353 0832
Call date: July 1963, Middle Temple

D

BENNATHAN JOEL NATHAN

14 Tooks Court
Cursitor St, London EC4A 1LB,
Telephone: 0171 405 8828
E-mail: clerks @tooks.law.co.uk
Call date: Nov 1985, Middle Temple
Qualifications: [LLB(Lond)]

BENNER MISS LUCINDA DIANA KATE

11 Bolt Court
London EC4A 3DQ,
Telephone: 0171 353 2300
E-mail: boltct11@aol.com
Redhill Chambers
Seloduct House 30 Station Road, Redhill
RH1 1NK, Telephone: 01737 780781
Call date: Oct 1992, Middle Temple
Qualifications: [LL.B (Hons, Leeds)]

BENNET MS PAULINE AGNES

Regency Chambers
18 Cowgate, Peterborough PE1 1NA,
Telephone: 01733 315215
Regency Chambers
Sheraton House, Castle Park, Cambridge
CB3 0AX, Telephone: 01223 301517
Call date: Oct 1991, Lincoln's Inn
Qualifications: [BSc (Hons, Lond), BA (Lond)]

BENNETT CHARLES HENRY

1 Harcourt Bldgs
2nd Floor, Temple, London EC4Y 9DA,
Telephone: 0171 353 9421/9151
Call date: July 1972, Inner Temple
Qualifications: [BA (Oxon)]

BENNETT DAVID LAURENCE

Chavasse Court Chambers
2nd Floor Chavasse Court, 24 Lord Street,
Liverpool L2 1TA, Telephone: 0151 707 1191
Call date: Nov 1977, Middle Temple
Qualifications: [BA (Hons)]

BENNETT PROFESSOR GEOFFREY JOHN

Francis Taylor Bldg
3rd Floor, Temple, London EC4Y 7BY,
Telephone: 0171 797 7250
Call date: July 1975, Inner Temple
Qualifications: [BA (Cantab)]

BENNETT GORDON IRVINE

5 Bell Yard
London WC2A 2JR, Telephone: 0171 333 8811
Call date: Feb 1974, Gray's Inn
Qualifications: [LLB, LLM (Calif), Dip Int Law
(Cantab)]

BENNETT IEUAN GEREINT

33 Park Place
Cardiff CF1 3BA, Telephone: 01222 233313
Call date: July 1989, Middle Temple
Qualifications: [LLB (Wales), MA (Hull)]

BENNETT JOHN MARTYN

Peel House Chambers
Ground Floor, Peel House, 5-7 Harrington
Street, Liverpool, Merseyside L2 9QA,
Telephone: 0151 236 4321
Call date: July 1969, Gray's Inn
Qualifications: [LLB]

Fax: 01829 781524;
Out of hours telephone: 01829 781524

Types of work: Care proceedings; Common law
(general); Employment; Family; Family
provision; Medical negligence; Personal injury;
Professional negligence

Circuit: Northern

Awards and memberships: FLBA; Associate
Member of BALM

Other professional experience: Non-executive
Director of family manufacturing company

Publications: 'The Cost of the Clean Break' in
Family Law, 1989; 'The Mechanics of the Offer:
The Art of Settlement' in *Family Law*, 1990;
'Challenging Ancillary Relief Orders' in *Family
Law*, 1993

Reported cases: *Allen v Allen*, [1985] FLR 107,
1984. Whether court had jurisdiction to
entertain husband's appeal by notice of motion
against magistrates' refusal to remit arrears.
Simister v Simister (No 1 and No 2), [1987] 1
FLR 189 and [1987] 1 FLR 194, 1986.
Jurisdiction of court to entertain application for
periodical payments by husband against
himself.
F v Wirral MBC, [1991] 2 All ER 648, 1990.
Whether right of action in tort for interference
with parental rights.

Halford v Sharples, [1992] 3 All ER 624, 1992. Whether police complaints and disciplinary files protected from disclosure by reason of public interest immunity.
Vicary v Vicary, [1992] 2 FLR, 1991. Substantial assets - weight to be given to 'Duxbury' calculation - correct approach as to costs as a need.

BENNETT JONATHAN CHARLES LYDDON

22 Old Bldgs
Lincoln's Inn, London WC2A 3UJ,
Telephone: 0171 831 0222
Call date: July 1985, Gray's Inn
Qualifications: [MA (Cantab)]

BENNETT MISS MARY

Clock Chambers
78 Darlington Street, Wolverhampton
WV1 4LY, Telephone: 01902 313444
Call date: Oct 1990, Gray's Inn
Qualifications: [LLB]

BENNETT MILES ALEXANDER FORDHAM

5 Paper Bldgs
1st Floor, Temple, London EC4Y 7HB,
Telephone: 0171 583 6117
E-mail: clerks@5-paperbuildings.law.co.uk
Call date: Nov 1986, Inner Temple
Qualifications: [LLB(Hull)]

BENNETT RICHARD ANTHONY

Fountain Chambers
Cleveland Business Centre 1 Watson Street,
Middlesbrough TS1 2RQ,
Telephone: 01642 217037
Call date: Oct 1996, Inner Temple
Qualifications: [BSc, CPE]

BENNETT RICHARD JOHN

15 Winckley Square
Preston PR1 3JJ, Telephone: 01772 252828
E-mail: clerks@winckleysq.demon.co.uk
Call date: July 1986, Middle Temple
Qualifications: [LLB]

BENNETT WILLIAM

5 Raymond Buildings
1st Floor, Gray's Inn, London WC1R 5BP,
Telephone: 0171 242 2902
Call date: Oct 1994, Inner Temple
Qualifications: [BA (L'pool), CPE]

BENNETT JENKINS MISS SALLIE ANN

1 Hare Court
Ground Floor, Temple, London EC4Y 7BE,
Telephone: 0171 353 3982/5324
Call date: July 1984, Gray's Inn
Qualifications: [LLB (Lond)]

BENNETTS PHILIP JAMES

Hollis Whiteman Chambers
3rd/4th Floor Queen Elizabeth Bldg, Temple,
London EC4Y 9BS, Telephone: 0171 583 5766
E-mail: hollis.whiteman@btinternet.com
Call date: July 1986, Lincoln's Inn
Qualifications: [LLB (Brunel)]

BENNINGTON MS JANE SUSAN

2 Field Court
Gray's Inn, London WC1R 5BB,
Telephone: 0171 405 6114
E-mail: fieldct2@netcomuk.co.uk.
Call date: July 1981, Gray's Inn
Qualifications: [BA Hons]

BENSON CHARLES JEFFERIUS WOODBURN

2 Paper Bldgs
1st Floor, Temple, London EC4Y 7ET,
Telephone: 0171 936 2611 (10 Lines)
E-mail: clerks@2pbbarristers.co.uk
Call date: Feb 1990, Middle Temple
Qualifications: [MA LLM (Cantab), B.Admin (Hons)]

BENSON JAMES D'ARCY

Derby Square Chambers
Merchants Court, Derby Square, Liverpool
L2 1TS, Telephone: 0151 709 4222
Call date: Nov 1995, Gray's Inn
Qualifications: [BA]

BENSON JEREMY KEITH

1 Hare Court
Ground Floor, Temple, London EC4Y 7BE,
Telephone: 0171 353 3982/5324
Call date: July 1978, Middle Temple
Recorder
Qualifications: [BA]

BENSON JOHN TREVOR

Adrian Lyon's Chambers
14 Castle Street, Liverpool L2 0NE,
Telephone: 0151 236 4421/8240
E-mail: chambers14@aol.com
Call date: July 1978, Middle Temple
Qualifications: [LLB (Hons) (L'pool)]

BENSON JULIAN CHRISTOPHER WOODBURN

1 Essex Court
1st Floor, Temple, London EC4Y 9AR,
Telephone: 0171 936 3030
E-mail: one.essex_court@virgin.net
Call date: Nov 1991, Middle Temple
Qualifications: [BA Hons (Dunelm), BA Hons,LLM (Cantab)]

BENSON MARK GILPIN

18 St John Street
Manchester M3 4EA,
Telephone: 0161 278 1800
Call date: Oct 1992, Middle Temple
Qualifications: [BA (Hons, B'ham)]

BENSON PETER CHARLES

St Paul's House
5th Floor 23 Park Square South, Leeds
LS1 2ND, Telephone: 0113 2455866
Call date: July 1975, Middle Temple
Recorder
Qualifications: [BSc]

BENSON RICHARD ANTHONY QC (1995)

36 Bedford Row
London WC1R 4JH,
Telephone: 0171 421 8000
E-mail: 36bedfordrow@link.org
Call date: July 1974, Inner Temple
Recorder

BENSTED MISS REBECCA CLAIRE

Bracton Chambers
95a Chancery Lane, London WC2A 1DT,
Telephone: 0171 242 4248
Call date: Nov 1993, Gray's Inn
Qualifications: [MA (Cantab)]

BENTHAM HOWARD LOWNDS QC (1996)

Peel Court Chambers
45 Hardman Street, Manchester M3 3HA,
Telephone: 0161 832 3791
Call date: Nov 1970, Gray's Inn
Recorder
Qualifications: [LLB]

BENTLEY ANTHONY PHILIP QC (1991)

2 Harcourt Bldgs
Ground Floor/Left, Temple, London
EC4Y 9DB, Telephone: 0171 583 9020
E-mail: clerks@harcourt.co.uk
Stanbrook & Henderson
2 Harcourt Bldgs 2nd Floor, Temple, London
EC4Y 9DB, Telephone: 0171 353 0101
E-mail: clerks@harcourt.co.uk
Call date: Nov 1970, Lincoln's Inn

BENTLEY DAVID NEIL

Doughty Street Chambers
11 Doughty Street, London WC1N 2PG,
Telephone: 0171 404 1313
E-mail: doughty_street@compuserve.com
Call date: Feb 1984, Gray's Inn
Qualifications: [LLB (Lond)]

BENTWOOD RICHARD

46/48 Essex Street
London WC2R 3GH,
Telephone: 0171 583 8899
Call date: Nov 1994, Inner Temple
Qualifications: [LLB (Notts)]

BENZYNIE ROBERT JOSEPH

2 Dr Johnson's Building
Temple, London EC4Y 7AY,
Telephone: 0171 353 4716
Call date: Nov 1992, Gray's Inn
Qualifications: [LLB (Buckingham)]

BERESFORD COLIN THOMAS

4 Brick Court
Ground Floor, Temple, London EC4Y 9AD,
Telephone: 0171 797 7766
E-mail: chambers@4brick.co.uk
Call date: Feb 1979, Gray's Inn
Qualifications: [BA]

BERESFORD STEPHEN ROGER

24 The Ropewalk
Nottingham NG1 5EF,
Telephone: 0115 9472581
E-mail: clerk@ropewalk.co.uk
Call date: July 1976, Gray's Inn
Qualifications: [LLB (B'ham)]

BERESFORD-EVANS MISS CERYS

9 King's Bench Walk
Basement, Temple, London EC4Y 7DX,
Telephone: 0171 353 9564
E-mail: jvlee@btinternet.com
Call date: Nov 1995, Middle Temple
Qualifications: [LLB (Hons)]

BERGIN TERENCE EDWARD

New Court Chambers
5 Verulam Buildings, Gray's Inn, London
WC1R 5LY, Telephone: 0171 831 9500
E-mail: mail@newcourtchambers.com
Call date: Nov 1985, Inner Temple
Qualifications: [BA(Cantab)]

BERGIN TIMOTHY WILLIAM

Sussex Chambers
9 Old Steine, Brighton BN1 1FJ,
Telephone: 01273 607953
Call date: July 1987, Middle Temple
Qualifications: [LLB, M.Phil (Exon)]

BERKIN MARTYN DAVID MAURICE

1 Paper Bldgs
Ground Floor, Temple, London EC4Y 7EP,
Telephone: 0171 583 7355
E-mail: clerks@1pb.co.uk
Call date: July 1966, Inner Temple
Qualifications: [MA (Cantab)]

BERKLEY DAVID NAHUM

Merchant Chambers
1 North Parade, Parsonage Gardens,
Manchester M3 2NH,
Telephone: 0161 839 7070
Call date: May 1979, Middle Temple
Qualifications: [LLB (Manch)]

BERKLEY MICHAEL STUART

Rougemont Chambers
15 Barnfield Road, Exeter EX1 1RR,
Telephone: 01392 410471
E-mail: rougemont.chambers@eclipse.co.uk
Call date: July 1989, Middle Temple
Qualifications: [LLB (Hons)(Bus. Law)]

BERKSON SIMON NATHANIEL

Exchange Chambers
Pearl Assurance House Derby Square,
Liverpool L2 9XX, Telephone: 0151 236 7747/
0458
E-mail: exchangechambers@btinternet.com
Call date: July 1986, Gray's Inn
Qualifications: [LLB]

BERLIN BARRY ADRIAN

St Ive's Chambers
9 Fountain Ct, Birmingham B4 6DR,
Telephone: 0121 236 0863/0929
Call date: July 1981, Gray's Inn
Qualifications: [BSc (Brunel), MSc
Environmental, Health]

BERMINGHAM GERALD EDWARD

Francis Taylor Bldg
Ground Floor, Temple, London EC4Y 7BY,
Telephone: 0171 353 7768/7769/2711
Westgate Chambers
144 High Street, Lewes, East Sussex BN7 1XT,
Telephone: 01273 480510
Call date: Feb 1985, Gray's Inn
Qualifications: [LLB (Hons)(Sheff)]

BERRAGAN (HOWARD) NEIL

Merchant Chambers
1 North Parade, Parsonage Gardens,
Manchester M3 2NH,
Telephone: 0161 839 7070
Call date: July 1982, Gray's Inn
Qualifications: [BA (Oxon)]

D

BERRICK STEVEN ISAAC

2 Paper Bldgs
1st Floor, Temple, London EC4Y 7ET,
Telephone: 0171 936 2611 (10 Lines)
E-mail: clerks@2pbbarristers.co.uk
Call date: July 1986, Middle Temple
Qualifications: [BA London]

BERRIDGE MISS ELIZABETH ROSE

40 King Street
Manchester M2 6BA,
Telephone: 0161 832 9082
E-mail: Kingst40@aol.com
Call date: Nov 1996, Inner Temple
Qualifications: [BA (Cantab)]

BERRIMAN TREVOR ST JOHN

10 King's Bench Walk
1st Floor, Temple, London EC4Y 7EB,
Telephone: 0171 353 2501
Call date: Nov 1988, Inner Temple
Qualifications: [LLB (Hons)]

BERRISFORD ANTHONY EDWARD

24 The Ropewalk
Nottingham NG1 5EF,
Telephone: 0115 9472581
E-mail: clerk@ropewalk.co.uk
Call date: July 1972, Inner Temple

BERRY ANTHONY CHARLES QC (1994)

4 Brick Court
1st Floor, Temple, London EC4Y 9AD,
Telephone: 0171 583 8455
Call date: July 1976, Gray's Inn
Assistant Recorder
Qualifications: [BA (Oxon)]

BERRY MARTIN DAMIAN JOSEPH

Tindal Chambers
3/5 New Street, Chelmsford, Essex CM1 1NT,
Telephone: 01245 267742
Tindal Chambers
3 Waxhouse Gate, St Albans, Herts AL5 4DU,
Telephone: 01727 843383
Fleet Chambers
Mitre House 44-46 Fleet Street, London
EC4Y 1BN, Telephone: 0171 936 3707
Call date: Nov 1992, Lincoln's Inn
Qualifications: [BA (Hons)]

BERRY NICHOLAS MICHAEL

Southernhay Chambers
33 Southernhay East, Exeter EX1 1NX,
Telephone: 01392 255777
E-mail: southernhay.chambers@lineone.net
1 Gray's Inn Square
Ground Floor, London WC1R 5AA,
Telephone: 0171 405 8946/7/8
Call date: Nov 1988, Inner Temple
Qualifications: [BA (Hons)]

BERRY SIMON QC (1990)

9 Old Square
Ground Floor, Lincoln's Inn, London
WC2A 3SR, Telephone: 0171 405 4682
E-mail: chambers@9oldsquare.co.uk
Call date: July 1977, Middle Temple
Qualifications: [LLB]

BERRY STEVEN JOHN

Essex Court Chambers
24 Lincoln's Inn Fields, London WC2A 3ED,
Telephone: 0171 813 8000
E-mail: clerksroom@essexcourt-chambers.co.uk
Call date: Nov 1984, Middle Temple
Qualifications: [BA,BCL (Oxon)]

BEST STANLEY PHILIP

Chambers of Stanley Best
Glebe Cottage, Broadwoodkelly, Winkleigh,
Devon EX19 8ED, Telephone: 01837 83763
Westgate Chambers
144 High Street, Lewes, East Sussex BN7 1XT,
Telephone: 01273 480510
Bracton Chambers
95a Chancery Lane, London WC2A 1DT,
Telephone: 0171 242 4248
Call date: July 1989, Middle Temple

BETHEL MARTIN QC (1983)

Park Lane Chambers
19 Westgate, Leeds LS1 2RD,
Telephone: 0113 2285000
Call date: Nov 1965, Inner Temple
Recorder
Qualifications: [MA, LLM (Cantab)]

BETHLEHEM DANIEL LINCOLN

20 Essex Street
London WC2R 3AL,
Telephone: 0171 583 9294
E-mail: clerks@20essexst.com
Call date: Nov 1988, Middle Temple
Qualifications: [BA (Witwatersrand), LLB (Bris), LLM (Cantab)]

BETTLE MRS JANET ROSEMARY

East Anglian Chambers
Sanders House 52 North Hill, Colchester
CO1 1PY, Telephone: 01206 572756
East Anglian Chambers
57 London Street, Norwich NR2 1HL,
Telephone: 01603 617351
East Anglian Chambers
Gresham House 5 Museum Street, Ipswich
IP1 1HQ, Telephone: 01473 214481
Call date: July 1985, Inner Temple
Qualifications: [LLB (London)]

BEVAN EDWARD JULIAN QC (1991)

Hollis Whiteman Chambers
3rd/4th Floor Queen Elizabeth Bldg, Temple,
London EC4Y 9BS, Telephone: 0171 583 5766
E-mail: hollis.whiteman@btinternet.com
Call date: Nov 1962, Gray's Inn

BEVAN HUGH KEITH

Wilberforce Chambers
Bishop Lane, Hull HU1 1PA,
Telephone: 01482 323264
E-mail: clerks@hullbar.demon.co.uk
Door Tenant
Call date: June 1959, Middle Temple
Qualifications: [LLM]

BEVAN JOHN PENRY VAUGHAN QC (1997)

2 Harcourt Bldgs
1st Floor, Temple, London EC4Y 9DB,
Telephone: 0171 353 2112/2817
Call date: July 1970, Middle Temple
Recorder
Qualifications: [MA (Cantab)]

BEVAN STEPHEN THOMAS ROWLAND

1 Pump Court
Lower Ground Floor, Temple, London
EC4Y 7AB, Telephone: 0171 583 2012/
353 4341
E-mail: (name) @1pumpcourt.co.uk
Call date: Nov 1986, Inner Temple
Qualifications: [BA]

BEVINGTON MISS CHRISTIAN VERONICA

New Court
Temple, London EC4Y 9BE,
Telephone: 0171 583 5123/0171 583 0510
Call date: Nov 1961, Inner Temple
Recorder
Qualifications: [LL.B]

BEVITT MISS ANN

Francis Taylor Bldg
3rd Floor, Temple, London EC4Y 7BY,
Telephone: 0171 797 7250
Call date: Oct 1992, Gray's Inn
Qualifications: [BA (Hons)(Oxon)]

BEWSEY MISS JANE

18 Red Lion Court
(Off Fleet Street), London EC4A 3EB,
Telephone: 0171 520 6000
Thornwood House
102 New London Road, Chelmsford, Essex
CM2 0RG, Telephone: 01245 280880
Call date: July 1986, Inner Temple
Qualifications: [MA (Cantab)]

BEX MISS KATHARINE

1 Hare Court
Ground Floor, Temple, London EC4Y 7BE,
Telephone: 0171 353 3982/5324
Call date: Nov 1992, Inner Temple
Qualifications: [BA]

BEYNON RICHARD JOHN LLEWELLYN

1 Middle Temple Lane
Temple, London EC4Y 1LT,
Telephone: 0171 583 0659 (12 Lines)
Call date: Oct 1990, Inner Temple
Qualifications: [LLB]

D

BEYTS CHESTER ANDOE MICHAEL

3 Gray's Inn Square
Ground Floor, London WC1R 5AH,
Telephone: 0171 520 5600
E-mail: gis3@btinternet.com
Call date: Nov 1978, Inner Temple
Qualifications: [BA (Hons) (Lond)]

BEZZAM MISS JAYASHREE

2 Middle Temple Lane
3rd Floor, Temple, London EC4Y 9AA,
Telephone: 0171 583 4540
Call date: July 1997, Lincoln's Inn
Qualifications: [BSc (Andhra), BL, ML
(Madras)]

BHAKAR SURINDER SINGH

2 Gray's Inn Square Chambers
2nd Floor, Gray's Inn, London WC1R 5AA,
Telephone: 0171 242 0328/071 405 1317
E-mail: clerks@2gis.co.uk
Call date: Nov 1986, Gray's Inn
Qualifications: [LLB(Lon) LLM(Cantab)]

BHALLA BITU

3 Temple Gardens
3rd Floor, Temple, London EC4Y 9AU,
Telephone: 0171 353 0832
Call date: Nov 1978, Gray's Inn
Qualifications: [LLB, LLM, AKC (Lond), LLM
(USA)]

BHALOO MISS ZIA KURBAN

Enterprise Chambers
9 Old Square, Lincoln's Inn, London
WC2A 3SR, Telephone: 0171 405 9471
Enterprise Chambers
38 Park Square, Leeds LS1 2PA,
Telephone: 01132 460391
Enterprise Chambers
65 Quayside, Newcastle upon Tyne NE1 3DS,
Telephone: 0191 222 3344
Call date: Nov 1990, Middle Temple
Qualifications: [LLB (UCL), LLM (Lond)]

BHANJI SHIRAZ MUSA

4 Bingham Place
London W1M 3FF, Telephone: 0171 486 5347/
071 487 5910
Call date: July 1979, Gray's Inn
Qualifications: [BSc (Wales)]

BHARDWAJ MRS SUNITA

9 King's Bench Walk
Basement, Temple, London EC4Y 7DX,
Telephone: 0171 353 9564
E-mail: jvlee@btinternet.com
Call date: Nov 1992, Inner Temple
Qualifications: [LLB]

BHARDWAJ MISS UMA

12 Old Square
1st Floor, Lincoln's Inn, London WC2A 3TX,
Telephone: 0171 404 0875
Call date: Nov 1984, Middle Temple
Qualifications: [LLB (Lond)]

BHATIA BALRAJ SINGH

1 High Pavement
Nottingham NG1 1HF,
Telephone: 0115 9418218
Call date: Nov 1982, Inner Temple
Qualifications: [LLB]

BHATIA MISS DIVYA

Queen Elizabeth Bldg
Ground Floor, Temple, London EC4Y 9BS,
Telephone: 0171 353 7181 (12 Lines)
Call date: July 1986, Middle Temple
Qualifications: [MA (Oxon)]

BHATTACHARYYA ARDHENDU

11 St. Bernards Road
Slough, Berkshire SL3 7NT,
Telephone: 01753 553806/817988
1 Gray's Inn Square
Ground Floor, London WC1R 5AA,
Telephone: 0171 405 8946/7/8
Door Tenant
Call date: Nov 1974, Inner Temple
Qualifications: [BA, FBIM, FCIS, ACIArb, Dip
CL]

BHOSE RANJIT

2-3 Gray's Inn Square
Gray's Inn, London WC1R 5JH,
Telephone: 0171 242 4986
E-mail: chambers@2-3graysinnsquare.co.uk
Call date: Nov 1989, Gray's Inn
Qualifications: [BA [Oxon]]

BICKERDIKE ROGER JOHN

9 Woodhouse Square
Leeds LS3 1AD, Telephone: 0113 2451986
Call date: Nov 1986, Lincoln's Inn
Qualifications: [LLB (Notts)]

BICKERSTAFF MISS DEBORAH JANE

6 Gray's Inn Square
Ground Floor, Gray's Inn, London WC1R 5AZ,
Telephone: 0171 242 1052
Call date: Nov 1989, Inner Temple
Qualifications: [LLB]

BICKFORD-SMITH MRS MARGARET OSBORNE

1 Paper Bldgs
Ground Floor, Temple, London EC4Y 7EP,
Telephone: 0171 583 7355
E-mail: clerks@1pb.co.uk
Call date: July 1973, Inner Temple
Recorder
Qualifications: [BA (Oxon)]

BICKFORD-SMITH STEPHEN WILLIAM

4 Breams Buildings
London EC4A 1AQ,
Telephone: 0171 353 5835/430 1221
Call date: July 1972, Inner Temple
Qualifications: [BA (Oxon), FCIArb]

BICKLER SIMON LLOYD

St Paul's House
5th Floor 23 Park Square South, Leeds
LS1 2ND, Telephone: 0113 2455866
Call date: Nov 1988, Inner Temple
Qualifications: [BA (Hons)(Sheffield)]

BIDDER NEIL

33 Park Place
Cardiff CF1 3BA, Telephone: 01222 233313
Call date: July 1976, Lincoln's Inn
Assistant Recorder
Qualifications: [MA (Cantab), LLM]

BIDDLE NEVILLE LESLIE

25-27 Castle Street
1st Floor, Liverpool L2 4TA,
Telephone: 0151 227 5661/051 236 5072
Call date: Nov 1974, Gray's Inn
Assistant Recorder
Qualifications: [BSc (Econ)]

BIGNALL JOHN FRANCIS

7 King's Bench Walk
Ground Floor, Temple, London EC4Y 7DS,
Telephone: 0171 583 0404
Call date: Nov 1996, Lincoln's Inn
Qualifications: [BA (Hons)]

BIGNALL MISS PAULA-ANN

John Street Chambers
2 John Street, London WC1N 2HJ,
Telephone: 0171 242 1911
E-mail: john.street_chambers@virgin.net.uk
Call date: Nov 1988, Middle Temple
Qualifications: [LLB (Hons)(Manc)]

BIGNELL MISS JANET SUSAN

Falcon Chambers
Falcon Court, London EC4Y 1AA,
Telephone: 0171 353 2484/7
Call date: Oct 1992, Lincoln's Inn
Qualifications: [MA (Hons) (Cantab), BCL (Hons) (Oxon)]

BIJLANI DR AISHA

2 Crown Office Row
2nd Floor, Temple, London EC4Y 7HJ,
Telephone: 0171 797 8000
Call date: Oct 1993, Middle Temple
Qualifications: [MB, BS (Lond), CPE (City), Dip Law]

BILLINGHAM REX RICHARD

New Court Chambers
Suite 200 Gazette Building, 168 Corporation
Street, Birmingham B4 6TZ,
Telephone: 0121 693 6656
Call date: Oct 1990, Inner Temple
Qualifications: [BA (E Anglia), Dip Law]

D

D

BILLINGTON MISS MOIRA ANN

40 King Street
Chester CH1 2AH, Telephone: 01244 323886
Call date: May 1988, Middle Temple
Qualifications: [LLB(Hons) Manchester]

BINDER PETER HARDWICKE MALCOLM

4 Brick Court
Temple, London EC4Y 9AD,
Telephone: 0171 797 8910
Call date: Apr 1991, Middle Temple
Qualifications: [BA (Durham)]

BINDLOSS EDWARD CHRISTOPHER JAMES

10 Park Square
Leeds LS1 2LH, Telephone: 0113 2455438
E-mail: chambers@bandit.legend.co.uk
Call date: Nov 1993, Gray's Inn
Qualifications: [BA (York), Dip Law (City)]

BINGHAM ANTHONY WILLIAM

3 Paper Bldgs
Ground Floor, Temple, London EC4Y 7EU,
Telephone: 0171 797 7000
E-mail: clerks@3pb.co.uk
Call date: Nov 1992, Lincoln's Inn
Qualifications: [LLB (Hons) (Lond), FCIArb]

BINGHAM MISS CAMILLA

1 Essex Court
Ground Floor, Temple, London EC4Y 9AR,
Telephone: 0171 583 2000
E-mail: clerks@oneessexcourt.co.uk
Call date: Oct 1996, Inner Temple
Qualifications: [BA (Oxon), CPE (Lond)]

BINGHAM PHILIP JOHN

Paradise Square Chambers
26 Paradise Square, Sheffield S1 2DE,
Telephone: 0114 2738951
Call date: July 1975, Middle Temple
Qualifications: [LLB]

BINNS DAVID ANDREW

St James's Chambers
68 Quay Street, Manchester M3 3EJ,
Telephone: 0161 834 7000
E-mail: 106241.2625@compuserve.com
Call date: July 1983, Middle Temple
Qualifications: [LLB (Hons)(L'pool)]

BIRCH MISS ELIZABETH BLANCHE

20 Essex Street
London WC2R 3AL,
Telephone: 0171 583 9294
E-mail: clerks@20essexst.com
Call date: July 1978, Gray's Inn
Qualifications: [LLB (Lond)]

BIRCH ROGER ALLEN

Lancaster Building Chambers
77 Deansgate, Manchester M3 2BW,
Telephone: 0161 661 4444
E-mail: sandra@lbnipc.com
25 Park Square
Leeds LS1 2PW, Telephone: 0113 2451841/2/3
E-mail: sovereignchambers@btinternet.com
Door Tenant
12 New Square
Ground Floor, Lincoln's Inn, London
WC2A 3SW, Telephone: 0171 419 1212
E-mail: 12newsquare@compuserve.com
Door Tenant
Call date: Nov 1979, Gray's Inn
Qualifications: [BA (Cantab)]

BIRCH WILLIAM CHARLES JOSEPH G

3 Temple Gardens
Lower Ground Floor, Temple, London
EC4Y 9AU, Telephone: 0171 353 3102/5/9297
Call date: Feb 1972, Lincoln's Inn
Qualifications: [MA (Lond)]

BIRD ANDREW JAMES

1 Harcourt Bldgs
2nd Floor, Temple, London EC4Y 9DA,
Telephone: 0171 353 9421/9151
Call date: July 1987, Inner Temple
Qualifications: [MA (Cantab)]

BIRD NIGEL DAVID

9 St John Street
Manchester M3 4DN,
Telephone: 0161 955 9000
E-mail: ninesjs@gconnect.com
Call date: Nov 1991, Inner Temple
Qualifications: [BA (Cambs)]

BIRD SIMON CHRISTOPHER

2-3 Gray's Inn Square
Gray's Inn, London WC1R 5JH,
Telephone: 0171 242 4986
E-mail: chambers@2-3graysinnsquare.co.uk
Call date: July 1987, Middle Temple
Qualifications: [LLB (Reading)]

BIRK MISS DEWINDER

2 New Street
Leicester LE1 5NA, Telephone: 0116 2625906
Call date: July 1988, Lincoln's Inn
Qualifications: [LLB (Hons) (Essex)]

BIRKBY PETER DAVID

Broadway House Chambers
Broadway House 9 Bank Street, Bradford,
West Yorkshire BD1 1TW,
Telephone: 01274 722560
Call date: July 1987, Lincoln's Inn
Qualifications: [BA (Manc) Dip Law, City Univ,
Dip in Education, (Sheff)]

BIRKETT PETER VIDLER QC (1989)

18 St John Street
Manchester M3 4EA,
Telephone: 0161 278 1800
Old Square Chambers
1 Verulam Buildings, Gray's Inn, London
WC1R 5LQ, Telephone: 0171 831 0801
Call date: July 1972, Inner Temple
Recorder
Qualifications: [LLB]

BIRKS SIMON ALEXANDER

7 Stone Bldgs
1st Floor, Lincoln's Inn, London WC2A 3SZ,
Telephone: 0171 242 0961
Call date: May 1981, Middle Temple
Qualifications: [BA]

BIRNBAUM MICHAEL IAN QC (1992)

9-12 Bell Yard
London WC2A 2LF,
Telephone: 0171 400 1800
New Court Chambers
Suite 200 Gazette Building, 168 Corporation
Street, Birmingham B4 6TZ,
Telephone: 0121 693 6656
Door Tenant
Call date: Nov 1969, Middle Temple
Recorder
Qualifications: [BA (Oxon)]

BIRSS COLIN IAN

3 New Square
Lincoln's Inn, London WC2A 3RS,
Telephone: 0171 405 1111
Call date: Oct 1990, Middle Temple
Qualifications: [MA (Cantab)]

BIRTLES MISS SAMANTHA JANE

18 St John Street
Manchester M3 4EA,
Telephone: 0161 278 1800
Call date: July 1989, Lincoln's Inn
Qualifications: [LLB (B'ham)]

BIRTLES WILLIAM

Old Square Chambers
1 Verulam Buildings, Gray's Inn, London
WC1R 5LQ, Telephone: 0171 831 0801
Old Square Chambers
Hanover House 47 Corn Street, Bristol
BS1 1HT, Telephone: 0117 9277111
Call date: Nov 1970, Gray's Inn
Recorder
Qualifications: [LLM (Lond & Harv), AKC]

BIRTS PETER WILLIAM QC (1990)

Farrar's Building
Temple, London EC4Y 7BD,
Telephone: 0171 583 9241
E-mail: chambers@farrarsbuilding.co.uk
Call date: July 1968, Gray's Inn
Recorder
Qualifications: [MA (Cantab)]

Fax: 0171 583 0090;
Out of hours telephone: 0171 384 1602;
DX: 406 London

Types of work: Administrative; Common law
(general); Crime; Landlord and tenant; Local

D

government; Professional negligence; Taxation of costs

Other professional qualifications: QC Northern Ireland 1996

Circuit: South Eastern

Other professional experience: Member of Judicial Studies Board (and of Civil and Family Committee) 1991-6; Assistant Boundary Commissioner 1993-; Chairman Mental Health Review Tribunal 1994-; Lecturer to JSB seminars on housing law and costs 1989-; County Court Rule Committee 1990-6

Publications: *Trespass: Summary Procedure for Possession of Land*, 1987; *Remedies for Trespass*, 1990

Reported cases: *R v Secretary of State for Environment, ex parte Burrows and Simms*, [1991] 2 QB 354, 1989. Although conclusive that a right of way exists, the definitive map may be corrected by evidence showing an erroneous classification.
Associated British Ports v C H Bailey Plc, [1990] 2 AC 703, 1990. A landlord seeking leave to take forfeiture proceedings must prove a requirement of the 1938 Act to the civil standard.
Coldunell Ltd v Gallon, [1986] 1 QB 1184, 1985. A person exerting undue influence must be agent of third party against whom transaction is sought to be set aside.
Lord High Chancellor v Wright, [1993] 1 WLR 1561, 1993. In determining defence fees under criminal legal aid costs regulations, account can be taken of fees paid to prosecuting counsel.
Loveday v Renton (No 2), [1992] 3 All ER 184, 1991. Considerations governing assessment of solicitors' costs and counsels' brief and refresher fees in taxation of heavy civil actions.

BISHOP ALAN RICHARD

11 Stone Bldgs
Ground Floor, Lincoln's Inn, London WC2A 3TG, Telephone: 0171 831 6381
E-mail: clerks@11StoneBuildings.law.co.uk
Call date: July 1973, Middle Temple
Qualifications: [LLB (Lond), ACII]

BISHOP EDWARD JAMES

1 Serjeants' Inn
5th Floor Fleet Street, Temple, London EC4Y 1LL, Telephone: 0171 415 6666
E-mail: no1serjeantsinn@btinternet.com
Call date: Nov 1985, Middle Temple
Qualifications: [MA (Cantab), Dip Law]

BISHOP GORDON WILLIAM

5 Raymond Buildings
1st Floor, Gray's Inn, London WC1R 5BP, Telephone: 0171 242 2902
Call date: Nov 1968, Middle Temple
Qualifications: [MA (Cantab)]

BISHOP JOHN MICHAEL

7 Stone Bldgs
1st Floor, Lincoln's Inn, London WC2A 3SZ, Telephone: 0171 242 0961
Call date: Nov 1970, Middle Temple
Qualifications: [LLB (Lond)]

BISHOP MISS KEELEY SUSAN

1 Crown Office Row
Ground Floor, Temple, London EC4Y 7HH, Telephone: 0171 797 7500
Crown Office Row Chambers
Blenheim House 120 Church Street, Brighton, Sussex BN1 1WH, Telephone: 01273 625625
Call date: Oct 1990, Gray's Inn
Qualifications: [BSc, GIBIOL]

BISHOP MALCOLM LESLIE QC (1993)

2 Dr Johnson's Building
Temple, London EC4Y 7AY,
Telephone: 0171 353 4716
30 Park Place
Cardiff CF1 3BA, Telephone: 01222 398421
E-mail: 100757.1456@compuserve.com
Call date: July 1968, Inner Temple
Qualifications: [MA (Oxon)]

BISHOP MARK ANDREW

1 Temple Gardens
1st Floor, Temple, London EC4Y 9BB, Telephone: 0171 353 0407/583 1315
E-mail: clerks@1templegardens.co.uk
Call date: July 1981, Middle Temple
Qualifications: [MA (Cantab)]

BISHOP TIMOTHY HARPER PAUL

1 Mitre Ct Bldgs
Ground Floor, Temple, London EC4Y 7BS,
Telephone: 0171 797 7070
Call date: Nov 1991, Inner Temple
Qualifications: [MA (Hons)(Cantab)]

BISPHAM MISS CHRISTINE

The Corn Exchange
5th Floor Fenwick Street, Liverpool L2 7QS,
Telephone: 0151 227 1081/5009
Call date: Oct 1991, Lincoln's Inn
Qualifications: [LLB (Hons) (Leics)]

BLACK MISS HARRIETTE

Counsels' Chambers
2nd Floor 10-11 Gray's Inn Square, London
WC1R 5JD, Telephone: 0171 405 2576
Call date: Nov 1986, Lincoln's Inn
Qualifications: [LLB]

BLACK MRS JILL MARGARET QC (1994)

30 Park Square
Leeds LS1 2PF, Telephone: 0113 2436388
Call date: July 1976, Inner Temple
Assistant Recorder
Qualifications: [BA (Dunelm)]

BLACK JOHN ALEXANDER

18 Red Lion Court
(Off Fleet Street), London EC4A 3EB,
Telephone: 0171 520 6000
Thornwood House
102 New London Road, Chelmsford, Essex
CM2 0RG, Telephone: 01245 280880
Call date: July 1975, Inner Temple
Qualifications: [LLB Hons]

BLACK MICHAEL JONATHAN QC (1995)

22 Old Bldgs
Lincoln's Inn, London WC2A 3UJ,
Telephone: 0171 831 0222
25 Byrom Street
Manchester M3 4PF,
Telephone: 0161 829 2100
E-mail: Byromst25@aol.com
Call date: Feb 1978, Middle Temple
Assistant Recorder
Qualifications: [LLB (Lond), FCIArb]

BLACKBURN MRS ELIZABETH

4 Field Court
Gray's Inn, London WC1R 5EA,
Telephone: 0171 440 6900
E-mail: chambers@4fieldcourt.co.uk
Call date: July 1978, Middle Temple
Qualifications: [BA]

BLACKBURN JOHN QC (1984)

1 Atkin Building
Gray's Inn, London WC1R 5AT,
Telephone: 0171 404 0102
E-mail: clerks@atkin-chambers.co.uk
Call date: July 1969, Middle Temple
Qualifications: [BA (Oxon)]

BLACKBURN LUKE SEBASTIAN

7 New Square
Lincoln's Inn, London WC2A 3QS,
Telephone: 0171 430 1660
Call date: Nov 1993, Middle Temple
Qualifications: [MA (Cantab)]

BLACKETT-ORD MARK

5 Stone Buildings
Lincoln's Inn, London WC2A 3XT,
Telephone: 0171 242 6201
E-mail: clerks@5-stonebuildings.law.co.uk
Call date: July 1974, Lincoln's Inn
Qualifications: [MA (Oxon)]

Fax: 0171 831 8102; DX: 304 London,
Chancery Lane

Types of work: Chancery (general); Chancery
land law; Conveyancing; Equity, wills and trusts;
Family provision; Landlord and tenant;
Partnerships; Probate and administration;
Professional negligence

Publications: *Partnership*, 1997; *Partnership*
(4th edn title, *Halsbury's Laws of England*),
1981

Reported cases: *Polly Peck v Nadir*, [1992] *The
Times*, 30 July, 1992. Whether a Mareva
injunction will be granted against assets in a
jurisdiction where the injunction cannot be
enforced.
Re A Company No 007816 of 1994, [1996] 2
BCLC 685, CA, 1996. What is the meaning of the
statutory prohibition of unauthorised 'carrying
on insurance business'.

Webb v Webb, [1994] QB 696, ECJ and [1997] CA 8 July 1997, 1994 and 1997. Whether English courts may resolve the issue of a disputed gift of French land between English domiciliaries.

Orlando Investments v Grosvenor Estate, [1989] 43 EG 175, CA, 1989. Whether breaches of repair covenants in a lease will justify refusal by the landlord of licence to assign.

BLACKFORD ROBERT

9 King's Bench Walk
Basement, Temple, London EC4Y 7DX,
Telephone: 0171 353 9564
E-mail: jvlee@btinternet.com
Call date: Nov 1988, Inner Temple
Qualifications: [LLB (Hons) (Lond), FCIArb]

BLACKFORD SIMON JOHN

Barnard's Inn Chambers
6th Floor Halton House, 20-23 Holborn,
London EC1N 2JD, Telephone: 0171 242 8508
E-mail: clerks@barnards-inn-chambers.co.uk
Call date: July 1979, Middle Temple
Qualifications: [MA]

BLACKMORE JOHN HUGH

St John's Chambers
Small Street, Bristol BS1 1DW,
Telephone: 0117 9213456/298514
E-mail: clerks@stjohns.uk.com
Call date: May 1983, Inner Temple
Qualifications: [LLB (Lond)]

BLACKMORE MISS SARAH ELIZABETH

Phoenix Chambers
First Floor Gray's Inn Chambers, Gray's Inn,
London WC1R 5JA, Telephone: 0171 404 7888
Call date: Oct 1993, Inner Temple
Qualifications: [LLB]

BLACKSHAW HENRY WILLIAM RANDLE

Peel Court Chambers
45 Hardman Street, Manchester M3 3HA,
Telephone: 0161 832 3791
Call date: Oct 1993, Middle Temple
Qualifications: [BA (Hons)(Dunelm), CPE, Dip Law]

BLACKWELL MISS KATHERINE ELIZABETH

Lincoln House Chambers
5th Floor Lincoln House, 1 Brazennose Street,
Manchester M2 5EL,
Telephone: 0161 832 5701
E-mail: LincolnHouseChambers@link.org
Call date: Oct 1992, Lincoln's Inn
Qualifications: [LLB(Hons)(B'ham)]

BLACKWELL MISS LOUISE MARY

Cobden House Chambers
19 Quay Street, Manchester M3 3HN,
Telephone: 0161 833 6000
E-mail: clerks@cobden.co.uk
Call date: July 1985, Lincoln's Inn
Qualifications: [LLB (Hons) (Leeds)]

BLACKWOOD CLIVE DAVID

2 Harcourt Bldgs
1st Floor, Temple, London EC4Y 9DB,
Telephone: 0171 353 6961/7
Harcourt Chambers
Churchill House 3 St Aldate's Courtyard, St Aldate's, Oxford OX1 1BN,
Telephone: 01865 791559
Call date: Nov 1986, Inner Temple
Qualifications: [BA(Cantab)]

BLADON KENNETH NORMAN

St Ive's Chambers
9 Fountain Ct, Birmingham B4 6DR,
Telephone: 0121 236 0863/0929
Call date: July 1980, Gray's Inn
Qualifications: [LLB (Exon)]

BLAIR BRUCE GRAEME DONALD QC (1989)

1 Mitre Ct Bldgs
Ground Floor, Temple, London EC4Y 7BS,
Telephone: 0171 797 7070
Call date: July 1969, Middle Temple
Recorder
Qualifications: [MA (Cantab)]

BLAIR PETER MICHAEL

Guildhall Chambers
23 Broad Street, Bristol BS1 2HG,
Telephone: 0117 9273366
Call date: July 1983, Inner Temple
Qualifications: [MA (Oxon)]

BLAIR MISS RUTH MARY

2 King's Bench Walk
Ground Floor, Temple, London EC4Y 7DE,
Telephone: 0171 353 1746
E-mail: 2kbw@atlas.co.uk
King's Bench Chambers
115 North Hill, Plymouth PL4 8JY,
Telephone: 01752 221551
Call date: July 1987, Middle Temple
Qualifications: [LLB (Dunelm)]

BLAIR WILLIAM JAMES LYNTON QC (1994)

3 Verulam Buildings
London WC1R 5NT,
Telephone: 0171 831 8441
E-mail: clerks@3verulam.co.uk
Call date: July 1972, Lincoln's Inn
Assistant Recorder
Qualifications: [BA (Oxon)]

BLAIR-GOULD JOHN ANTHONY

3 Raymond Buildings
Gray's Inn, London WC1R 5BH,
Telephone: 0171 831 3833
E-mail: chambers@threeraymond.demon.co.uk
Call date: Apr 1970, Inner Temple
Recorder

BLAKE ANDREW NICHOLAS HUBERT

18 St John Street
Manchester M3 4EA,
Telephone: 0161 278 1800
Call date: Nov 1971, Inner Temple
Recorder
Qualifications: [MA (Oxon)]

BLAKE ARTHUR JOSEPH

13 King's Bench Walk
1st Floor, Temple, London EC4Y 7EN,
Telephone: 0171 353 7204
E-mail: clerks@13kbw.law.co.uk
King's Bench Chambers
32 Beaumont Street, Oxford OX1 2NP,
Telephone: 01865 311066
E-mail: clerks@kbc-oxford.law.co.uk
Call date: Feb 1988, Inner Temple
Qualifications: [LLB]

BLAKE CHRISTOPHER IAN

Mitre Court Chambers
3rd Floor, Temple, London EC4Y 7BP,
Telephone: 0171 353 9394
Call date: Nov 1990, Inner Temple
Qualifications: [LLB (Hons)]

BLAKE DAVID ANTHONY

Angel Chambers
94 Walter Road, Swansea SA1 5QA,
Telephone: 01792 6464623/6464648
Call date: Feb 1992, Lincoln's Inn
Qualifications: [BA (Hons) (Cantab)]

BLAKE NICHOLAS JOHN GORROD QC (1994)

2 Garden Court
1st Floor, Middle Temple, London EC4Y 9BL,
Telephone: 0171 353 1633
E-mail: barristers@2gardenct.law.co.uk
Call date: May 1974, Middle Temple
Qualifications: [BA (Cantab)]

BLAKE RICHARD ANDREW

Chambers of Helen Grindrod QC
1st Floor 95a Chancery Lane, London
WC2A 2JG, Telephone: 0171 404 4777
Call date: Nov 1982, Gray's Inn

BLAKEMORE MISS JESSICA MARY CASSANDRA

1 Harcourt Bldgs
2nd Floor, Temple, London EC4Y 9DA,
Telephone: 0171 353 9421/9151
Call date: Oct 1995, Inner Temple
Qualifications: [BA (Soton), CPE]

BLAKER GARY MARK

Francis Taylor Bldg
3rd Floor, Temple, London EC4Y 7BY,
Telephone: 0171 797 7250
Call date: Oct 1993, Middle Temple
Qualifications: [MA (Cantab)]

BLAKESLEY PATRICK JAMES

2 Crown Office Row
Ground Floor, Temple, London EC4Y 7HJ,
Telephone: 0171 797 8100
E-mail: mail@2cor.co.uk, or to individual
barristers at: [barrister's surname]@2cor.co.uk
Call date: Nov 1993, Inner Temple
Qualifications: [MA (Oxon), CPE (City)]

BLAKEY LEE

15 Winckley Square
Preston PR1 3JJ, Telephone: 01772 252828
E-mail: clerks@winckleysq.demon.co.uk
Call date: Oct 1995, Lincoln's Inn
Qualifications: [LLB (Hons)(Lanc)]

BLAKEY MICHAEL CHARLES

38 Young Street
Manchester M3 3FT,
Telephone: 0161 833 0489
E-mail: clerks@young-st-chambers.com
Call date: Nov 1989, Middle Temple
Qualifications: [LLB (Hons)]

BLANCHARD MISS CLAIRE

Essex Court Chambers
24 Lincoln's Inn Fields, London WC2A 3ED,
Telephone: 0171 813 8000
E-mail: clerksroom@essexcourt-chambers.co.uk
Call date: Oct 1992, Gray's Inn
Qualifications: [LLB (Hons)]

BLAND MISS CAROLYN

38 Young Street
Manchester M3 3FT,
Telephone: 0161 833 0489
E-mail: clerks@young-st-chambers.com
Call date: July 1995, Inner Temple
Qualifications: [LLB (Reading)]

BLAND PAUL HOWARD

Clock Chambers
78 Darlington Street, Wolverhampton
WV1 4LY, Telephone: 01902 313444
Call date: Nov 1972, Inner Temple
Qualifications: [BSc (Econ), LLB]

BLANTERN ROBERT IAN

Cleveland Chambers
63-65 Borough Road, Middlesbrough,
Cleveland TS1 3AA, Telephone: 01642 226036
Call date: Oct 1996, Middle Temple
Qualifications: [LLB (Hons)(Northum)]

BLATCH MISS FRANCESCA JANE

Guildford Chambers
Stoke House Leapale Lane, Guildford, Surrey
GU1 4LY, Telephone: 01483 539131
E-mail: guildford.barristers@btinternet.com
Call date: Nov 1987, Lincoln's Inn
Qualifications: [BA(Hons)]

BLAXLAND CHRISTOPHER HENRY

2 Garden Court
1st Floor, Middle Temple, London EC4Y 9BL,
Telephone: 0171 353 1633
E-mail: barristers@2gardenct.law.co.uk
Call date: Nov 1978, Middle Temple
Qualifications: [BA (York)]

BLAYNEY DAVID JAMES

13 Old Square
1st Floor, Lincoln's Inn, London WC2A 3UA,
Telephone: 0171 242 6105
E-mail: clerks@serlecourt.co.uk
Call date: Oct 1992, Lincoln's Inn
Qualifications: [BA(Hons)]

BLEANEY NICHOLAS SIMON

3 Temple Gardens
Lower Ground Floor, Temple, London
EC4Y 9AU, Telephone: 0171 353 3102/5/9297
Call date: Nov 1988, Lincoln's Inn
Qualifications: [LLB Hons (Nott'm)]

BLEASDALE MISS MARIE-CLAIRE

11 New Square
Ground Floor, Lincoln's Inn, London
WC2A 3QB, Telephone: 0171 831 0081
E-mail: 11newsquare.co.uk
Call date: Oct 1993, Lincoln's Inn
Qualifications: [MA (Cantab), Dip in, Law
(Westminster)]

BLEASDALE PAUL EDWARD

5 Fountain Court
Steelhouse Lane, Birmingham B4 6DR,
Telephone: 0121 606 0500
Call date: July 1978, Inner Temple
Recorder
Qualifications: [LLB (Lond)]

BLOCH MICHAEL GORDON

1 Essex Court
Ground Floor, Temple, London EC4Y 9AR,
Telephone: 0171 583 2000
E-mail: clerks@oneessexcourt.co.uk
Call date: July 1979, Lincoln's Inn
Qualifications: [MA (Cantab), M.Phil (UEA)]

BLOCH SELWYN IRVING

Littleton Chambers
3 King's Bench Walk North, Temple, London
EC4Y 7HR, Telephone: 0171 797 8600
E-mail: littletonchambers@compuserve.com
Call date: July 1982, Middle Temple
Qualifications: [BA, LLB]

BLOCK NEIL SELWYN

39 Essex Street
London WC2R 3AT,
Telephone: 0171 583 1111
E-mail: clerks@39essex.co.uk
Call date: July 1980, Gray's Inn
Qualifications: [BA (Hons), LLM (Exon)]

BLOHM LESLIE ADRIAN

St John's Chambers
Small Street, Bristol BS1 1DW,
Telephone: 0117 9213456/298514
E-mail: clerks@stjohns.uk.com
Call date: July 1982, Lincoln's Inn
Qualifications: [MA (Oxon)]

BLOOM DR MARGARET

7 New Square
Lincoln's Inn, London WC2A 3QS,
Telephone: 0171 430 1660
Call date: Oct 1994, Lincoln's Inn
Qualifications: [B.Med.Sci, BM, BS, MRCGP
(Notts), CPE (Notts)]

BLOOM MS TRACEY DORA

1 Pump Court
Lower Ground Floor, Temple, London
EC4Y 7AB, Telephone: 0171 583 2012/
353 4341
E-mail: (name) @1pumpcourt.co.uk
Call date: July 1984, Gray's Inn
Qualifications: [MA (Cantab)]

BLOOM-DAVIS DESMOND NIALL LAURENCE

Pump Court Chambers
Upper Ground Floor 3 Pump Court, Temple,
London EC4Y 7AJ, Telephone: 0171 353 0711
Pump Court Chambers
31 Southgate Street, Winchester SO23 8EE,
Telephone: 01962 868161
Call date: July 1986, Inner Temple
Qualifications: [BA (Lond)]

BLOOMER CHARLES HOWARD

Lincoln House Chambers
5th Floor Lincoln House, 1 Brazennose Street,
Manchester M2 5EL,
Telephone: 0161 832 5701
E-mail: LincolnHouseChambers@link.org
Call date: July 1985, Lincoln's Inn
Qualifications: [LLB (Nott'n)]

BLOOMFIELD RICHARD WILLIAM

Chambers of Richard Bloomfield
2 Lansdowne Place, Gosforth, Newcastle
Upon Tyne NE3 1HR,
Telephone: 0191 285 4664
Call date: July 1984, Gray's Inn
Qualifications: [BA (Hons)]

BLORE MISS CAROLYN ANNE

Furnival Chambers
32 Furnival Street, London EC4A 1JQ,
Telephone: 0171 405 3232
E-mail: clerks@furnivallaw.co.uk
Call date: July 1985, Gray's Inn
Qualifications: [LLB(Cardiff)]

BLOUNT MARTIN JOHN

Eighteen Carlton Crescent
Southampton SO15 2XR,
Telephone: 01703 639001
Call date: July 1982, Gray's Inn
Qualifications: [LL.B (Soton)]

D

D

BLOWER GRAHAM ROBERT

Queen Elizabeth Bldg
Ground Floor, Temple, London EC4Y 9BS,
Telephone: 0171 353 7181 (12 Lines)
Call date: Nov 1980, Gray's Inn
Qualifications: [BA (Leeds)]

BLUNT DAVID JOHN QC (1991)

4 Pump Court
Temple, London EC4Y 7AN,
Telephone: 0171 353 2656/9
E-mail: 4_pump_court@compuserve.com
Call date: Nov 1967, Middle Temple
Recorder
Qualifications: [MA (Cantab)]

BLUNT OLIVER SIMON PETER QC (1994)

Furnival Chambers
32 Furnival Street, London EC4A 1JQ,
Telephone: 0171 405 3232
E-mail: clerks@furnivallaw.co.uk
Call date: Nov 1974, Middle Temple
Recorder
Qualifications: [LLB]

BLYTH JOHN RODERICK MORRISON

Queen Elizabeth Bldg
2nd Floor, Temple, London EC4Y 9BS,
Telephone: 0171 797 7837
Call date: July 1981, Lincoln's Inn
Qualifications: [BA (Oxon)]

BOAITEY MISS CHARLOTTE

12 Old Square
1st Floor, Lincoln's Inn, London WC2A 3TX,
Telephone: 0171 404 0875
Call date: Nov 1976, Middle Temple
Qualifications: [LLB (Lond), Dip Soc Anthrop, (Oxon)]

BOARDMAN CHRISTOPHER LEIGH WILSON

11 Stone Bldgs
Ground Floor, Lincoln's Inn, London
WC2A 3TG, Telephone: 0171 831 6381
E-mail: clerks@11StoneBuildings.law.co.uk
Call date: Oct 1995, Lincoln's Inn
Qualifications: [LLB (Hons), LLM (Lond)]

BOARDMAN MICHAEL LEOPOLD

6 Gray's Inn Square
Ground Floor, Gray's Inn, London WC1R 5AZ,
Telephone: 0171 242 1052
Call date: July 1979, Middle Temple
Qualifications: [BA (Manch), LLB (Lond)]

BOATENG PAUL YAW

8 King's Bench Walk
2nd Floor, Temple, London EC4Y 7DU,
Telephone: 0171 797 8888
8 King's Bench Walk North
1 Park Square East, Leeds LS1 2NE,
Telephone: 0113 2439797
Call date: Nov 1989, Gray's Inn
Qualifications: [LLB (Bris)]

BODEY DAVID RODERIC LESSITER QC (1991)

Queen Elizabeth Bldg
2nd Floor, Temple, London EC4Y 9BS,
Telephone: 0171 797 7837
Assize Court Chambers
14 Small Street, Bristol BS1 1DE,
Telephone: 0117 9264587
Call date: July 1970, Middle Temple
Recorder
Qualifications: [LLB]

BOEDDINGHAUS HERMANN

4 Stone Bldgs
Ground Floor, Lincoln's Inn, London
WC2A 3XT, Telephone: 0171 242 5524
E-mail: d.goddard@4stonebuildings.law.co.uk
Call date: Nov 1996, Lincoln's Inn
Qualifications: [BSc(Hons)(Cape Town), BCL, MA (Oxon)]

BOGAN PAUL SIMON

Doughty Street Chambers
11 Doughty Street, London WC1N 2PG,
Telephone: 0171 404 1313
E-mail: doughty_street@compuserve.com
Call date: July 1983, Gray's Inn
Qualifications: [BA (Hons)]

BOGGIS-ROLFE HARRY MARK

1 Brick Court
1st Floor, Temple, London EC4Y 9BY,
Telephone: 0171 353 8845
E-mail: clerks@1brickcourt.co.uk
Call date: Nov 1969, Middle Temple
Qualifications: [MA (Cantab)]

BOGLE JAMES STEWART LOCKHART

Eldon Chambers
Fourth Floor 30/32 Fleet Street, London
EC4Y 1AA, Telephone: 0171 353 4636
Call date: Oct 1991, Middle Temple
Qualifications: [BA, Dip Law, ACIArb]

BOJARSKI ANDRZEJ LEONARD

36 Bedford Row
London WC1R 4JH,
Telephone: 0171 421 8000
E-mail: 36bedfordrow@link.org
Call date: Oct 1995, Gray's Inn
Qualifications: [LLB]

BOJCZUK WILLIAM JOHN

Hardwicke Building
New Square, Lincoln's Inn, London
WC2A 3SB, Telephone: 0171 242 2523
E-mail: clerks@hardwicke.co.uk
Call date: July 1983, Inner Temple
Qualifications: [LLB (Lond), MA]

BOLTON MISS BEATRICE MAUD

Broad Chare
33 Broad Chare, Newcastle Upon Tyne
NE1 3DQ, Telephone: 0191 232 0541
Call date: July 1975, Gray's Inn
Assistant Recorder
Qualifications: [LLB]

BOLTON MRS FRANCES LAWJUA

2 Goldingham Avenue
Loughton, Essex IG10 2JF,
Telephone: 0181 502 4247
Call date: July 1981, Middle Temple
Qualifications: [LLB (Hons)]

BOLTON MISS LUCY CAROLINE

Mitre Court Chambers
3rd Floor, Temple, London EC4Y 7BP,
Telephone: 0171 353 9394
Call date: Oct 1994, Lincoln's Inn
Qualifications: [BA (Hons)(Notts), Dip in Law
(City)]

BOLTON ROBERT JOHN

2 King's Bench Walk
Ground Floor, Temple, London EC4Y 7DE,
Telephone: 0171 353 1746
E-mail: 2kbw@atlas.co.uk
King's Bench Chambers
115 North Hill, Plymouth PL4 8JY,
Telephone: 01752 221551
Call date: July 1987, Gray's Inn
Qualifications: [B.A. (Manch)]

BOMPAS ANTHONY GEORGE QC (1994)

4 Stone Bldgs
Ground Floor, Lincoln's Inn, London
WC2A 3XT, Telephone: 0171 242 5524
E-mail: d.goddard@4stonebuildings.law.co.uk
Call date: July 1975, Middle Temple
Qualifications: [MA (Oxon)]

BOND MISS JACQUELINE KATHRYN

Mitre House Chambers
Mitre House 44 Fleet Street, London
EC4Y 1BN, Telephone: 0171 583 8233
Call date: Oct 1994, Middle Temple
Qualifications: [LLB (Hons)]

BOND MISS JOANNA MARY

22 Old Bldgs
Lincoln's Inn, London WC2A 3UJ,
Telephone: 0171 831 0222
Call date: Nov 1988, Gray's Inn
Qualifications: [LLB Hons (B'ham)]

BOND RICHARD IAN WINSOR

Coleridge Chambers
Citadel 190 Corporation Street, Birmingham
B4 6QD, Telephone: 0121 233 3303
Call date: July 1988, Middle Temple
Qualifications: [LLB (Hons) (Manch)]

D

D

BONEY GUY THOMAS KNOWLES QC (1990)

Pump Court Chambers
Upper Ground Floor 3 Pump Court, Temple,
London EC4Y 7AJ, Telephone: 0171 353 0711
Pump Court Chambers
31 Southgate Street, Winchester SO23 8EE,
Telephone: 01962 868161
Harrow on the Hill Chambers
60 High Street, Harrow on the Hill, Middlesex
HA1 3LL, Telephone: 0181 423 7444
Door Tenant
Call date: July 1968, Middle Temple
Recorder
Qualifications: [BA]

BONNEY JAMES WILLIAM QC (1995)

10 Old Square
Ground Floor, Lincoln's Inn, London
WC2A 3SU, Telephone: 0171 405 0758
15 Winckley Square
Preston PR1 3JJ, Telephone: 01772 252828
E-mail: clerks@winckleysq.demon.co.uk
Door Tenant
Call date: Nov 1975, Lincoln's Inn
Qualifications: [BCL,MA (Oxon)]

BOOKER MRS CHRISTINE MARGARET

Doughty Street Chambers
11 Doughty Street, London WC1N 2PG,
Telephone: 0171 404 1313
E-mail: doughty_street@compuserve.com
Door Tenant
Call date: Feb 1978, Middle Temple
Qualifications: [BA (Lond)]

BOOLS DR MICHAEL DAVID

Brick Court Chambers
15/19 Devereux Court, London WC2R 3JJ,
Telephone: 0171 583 0777
E-mail: (surname)@brickcourt.demon.co.uk
Call date: Oct 1991, Middle Temple
Qualifications: [LLB Hons (E.Anglia), D.Phil
(Oxon)]

BOORA JINDER SINGH

Regent Chambers
29 Regent Road, Hanley, Stoke On Trent
ST1 3BP, Telephone: 01782 286666
E-mail: regent@ftech.co.uk
Call date: Oct 1990, Gray's Inn
Qualifications: [LLB, LLM (Warw)]

BOOTH ALAN JAMES

Deans Court Chambers
Cumberland House Crown Square, Manchester
M3 3HA, Telephone: 0161 834 4097
E-mail: deanscourt@compuserve.com
Deans Court Chambers
41-43 Market Place, Preston PR1 1AH,
Telephone: 01772 555163
E-mail: deanscourt@compuserve.com
Call date: July 1978, Gray's Inn
Assistant Recorder
Qualifications: [MA (Cantab)]

BOOTH MISS CHERIE QC (1995)

4-5 Gray's Inn Square
Ground Floor, Gray's Inn, London WC1R 5AY,
Telephone: 0171 404 5252
E-mail: chambers@4-5graysinnsquare.co.uk
Call date: July 1976, Lincoln's Inn
Assistant Recorder
Qualifications: [LLB (Lond)]

BOOTH MARTYN PARKINSON

Portsmouth Barristers'Chambers
Victory House 7 Bellevue Terrace,
Portsmouth, Hampshire PO5 3AT,
Telephone: 01705 831292
E-mail: clerks@portsmouthbar.com
Call date: Oct 1996, Lincoln's Inn
Qualifications: [LLB (Hons)(Soton)]

BOOTH MICHAEL JOHN

40 King Street
Manchester M2 6BA,
Telephone: 0161 832 9082
E-mail: Kingst40@aol.com
Call date: Nov 1981, Lincoln's Inn
Qualifications: [MA (Cantab)]

BOOTH NICHOLAS JOHN

Old Square Chambers
1 Verulam Buildings, Gray's Inn, London
WC1R 5LQ, Telephone: 0171 831 0801
Old Square Chambers
Hanover House 47 Corn Street, Bristol
BS1 1HT, Telephone: 0117 9277111
Call date: July 1991, Middle Temple
Qualifications: [MA, BCL]

BOOTH RICHARD JOHN

1 Crown Office Row
Ground Floor, Temple, London EC4Y 7HH,
Telephone: 0171 797 7500
Call date: Oct 1993, Middle Temple
Qualifications: [MA (Hons)(Cantab), Lic Spec
Dr Eur, (Brussels)]

BOOTH ROGER GEORGE

Old Colony House
6 South King Street, Manchester M2 6DQ,
Telephone: 0161 834 4364
Bell Yard Chambers
116/118 Chancery Lane, London WC2A 1PP,
Telephone: 0171 306 9292
Door Tenant
Call date: Nov 1966, Gray's Inn
Qualifications: [LLB]

BOOTH SIMON MARK

Adrian Lyon's Chambers
14 Castle Street, Liverpool L2 0NE,
Telephone: 0151 236 4421/8240
E-mail: chambers14@aol.com
Call date: Nov 1985, Lincoln's Inn
Qualifications: [LLB (L'pool)]

BOOTH MISS SYLVIA JOY

18 St John Street
Manchester M3 4EA,
Telephone: 0161 278 1800
Call date: Oct 1992, Gray's Inn
Qualifications: [LLB (Sheff)]

BOOTHBY JOSEPH JOHN

Bridewell Chambers
2 Bridewell Place, London EC4V 6AP,
Telephone: 0171 797 8800
E-mail: clerks@bridewell.law.co.uk
Call date: July 1972, Middle Temple
Recorder
Qualifications: [BA (Lond)]

BOOTHROYD ALEC DOMINIC

Gower Chambers
57 Walter Road, Swansea, West Glamorgan
SA1 5PZ, Telephone: 01792 644466
E-mail: clerk@gowerchambers.co.uk
Call date: Nov 1991, Inner Temple
Qualifications: [LLB]

BOOTHROYD MISS SUSAN ELIZABETH

67a Westgate Road
Newcastle Upon Tyne NE1 1SQ,
Telephone: 0191 261 4407/2329785
Call date: Oct 1990, Lincoln's Inn
Qualifications: [LLB (Newc)]

BORRELLI MICHAEL FRANCIS ANTONY

1 Middle Temple Lane
Temple, London EC4Y 1LT,
Telephone: 0171 583 0659 (12 Lines)
Call date: Nov 1977, Middle Temple

BOSOMWORTH MICHAEL JOHN

39 Park Square
Leeds LS1 2NU, Telephone: 0113 2456633
Call date: July 1979, Middle Temple
Qualifications: [BA (Nottm)]

BOSTON MISS JANET SUSAN

10 King's Bench Walk
Ground Floor, Temple, London EC4Y 7EB,
Telephone: 0171 353 7742
E-mail: 10kbw@lineone.net
Call date: Nov 1976, Middle Temple
Qualifications: [LLB (Lond)]

BOSWELL MISS JENNIFER MARY

1 Pump Court
Lower Ground Floor, Temple, London
EC4Y 7AB, Telephone: 0171 583 2012/
353 4341
E-mail: (name) @1pumpcourt.co.uk
Call date: July 1982, Middle Temple
Qualifications: [BA Sussex]

BOSWELL MISS LINDSAY ALICE QC (1997)

4 Pump Court
Temple, London EC4Y 7AN,
Telephone: 0171 353 2656/9
E-mail: 4_pump_court@compuserve.com
Call date: July 1982, Gray's Inn
Qualifications: [BSc(London), Dip Law (City)]

D

BOSWOOD ANTHONY RICHARD
QC (1986)

Fountain Court
Temple, London EC4Y 9DH,
Telephone: 0171 583 3335
E-mail: chambers@fountaincourt.co.uk
Call date: Nov 1970, Middle Temple
Qualifications: [MA, BCL]

BOTHROYD MISS SHIRLEY ANN

Littleton Chambers
3 King's Bench Walk North, Temple, London
EC4Y 7HR, Telephone: 0171 797 8600
E-mail: littletonchambers@compuserve.com
Call date: July 1982, Middle Temple
Qualifications: [BA]

BOTT CHARLES ADRIAN

Barnard's Inn Chambers
6th Floor Halton House, 20-23 Holborn,
London EC1N 2JD, Telephone: 0171 242 8508
E-mail: clerks@barnards-inn-chambers.co.uk
Call date: Nov 1979, Gray's Inn
Qualifications: [MA (Cantab)]

BOULD DUNCAN JOHN

40 King Street
Chester CH1 2AH, Telephone: 01244 323886
Call date: July 1984, Gray's Inn
Qualifications: [BSc, LLB (Lond)]

BOULDING PHILIP VINCENT
QC (1996)

Keating Chambers
10 Essex Street, Outer Temple, London
WC2R 3AA, Telephone: 0171 544 2600
Call date: Nov 1979, Gray's Inn
Qualifications: [BA,M, LLB (Cantab)]

BOULTER TERENCE

Counsels' Chambers
2nd Floor 10-11 Gray's Inn Square, London
WC1R 5JD, Telephone: 0171 405 2576
Call date: July 1986, Lincoln's Inn
Qualifications: [BA(Hons)]

BOULTON DAVID JOHN

Martins Building
Water Street, Liverpool L2 3SP,
Telephone: 0151 236 5818/4919
Call date: July 1970, Middle Temple
Recorder
Qualifications: [LLB]

BOUMPHREY JOHN ROSS STAVELEY

Phoenix Chambers
First Floor Gray's Inn Chambers, Gray's Inn,
London WC1R 5JA, Telephone: 0171 404 7888
Library Chambers
Gray's Inn Chambers, Gray's Inn, London
WC1R 5JA, Telephone: 0171 404 6500
Call date: Nov 1992, Inner Temple
Qualifications: [BA (Hons)(Warw), Dip in Law]

BOURN COLIN JAMES

65-67 King Street
Leicester LE1 6RP, Telephone: 0116 2547710
Call date: Nov 1974, Middle Temple
Qualifications: [B.Sc. London]

BOURNE CHARLES GREGORY

2 Harcourt Bldgs
Ground Floor/Left, Temple, London
EC4Y 9DB, Telephone: 0171 583 9020
E-mail: clerks@harcourt.co.uk
Stanbrook & Henderson
2 Harcourt Bldgs 2nd Floor, Temple, London
EC4Y 9DB, Telephone: 0171 353 0101
E-mail: clerks@harcourt.co.uk
Call date: Oct 1991, Middle Temple
Qualifications: [MA Hons (Cantab), Dip Law
(PCL), Maitrise en Lettres, Modernes
(Sorbonne)]

BOURNE IAN MACLEAN

3 Temple Gardens
2nd Floor, Temple, London EC4Y 9AU,
Telephone: 0171 583 1155
Call date: July 1977, Inner Temple
Qualifications: [LLB Hons (Exon)]

BOURNE ROBERT

4 Field Court
Gray's Inn, London WC1R 5EA,
Telephone: 0171 440 6900
E-mail: chambers@4fieldcourt.co.uk
Call date: Nov 1978, Gray's Inn

Qualifications: [MA (Oxon)]

Fax: 0171 242 0197; DX: LDE 483

Types of work: Banking; Chancery land law; Commercial litigation; Commercial property; Consumer law; Landlord and tenant; Professional negligence

Circuit: South Eastern

Publications: *County Court Practice* (Editor 'Admiralty', 'Access to Neighbouring Land', 'Consumer Credit Act', and 'Deeds of Arrangement' sections), 1998

BOURNE-ARTON SIMON NICHOLAS QC (1994)

Park Court Chambers
40 Park Cross Street, Leeds LS1 2QH,
Telephone: 0113 2433277
Call date: Nov 1975, Inner Temple
Recorder
Qualifications: [LLB (Hons),]

BOWCOCK MISS SAMANTHA JANE

15 Winckley Square
Preston PR1 3JJ, Telephone: 01772 252828
E-mail: clerks@winckleysq.demon.co.uk
Call date: Oct 1990, Middle Temple
Qualifications: [LLB (Manch)]

BOWDERY MARTIN

1 Atkin Building
Gray's Inn, London WC1R 5AT,
Telephone: 0171 404 0102
E-mail: clerks@atkin-chambers.co.uk
Call date: July 1980, Inner Temple
Qualifications: [BA (Oxon)]

BOWEN JAMES FRANCIS

6 King's Bench Walk
Ground, Third & Fourth Floors, Temple,
London EC4Y 7DR,
Telephone: 0171 353 4931/583 0695
Call date: Nov 1979, Gray's Inn
Qualifications: [LLB (Exon)]

BOWEN NICHOLAS JAMES HUGH

29 Bedford Row Chambers
London WC1R 4HE,
Telephone: 0171 831 2626
Call date: Nov 1984, Gray's Inn
Qualifications: [BA (Sussex)]

BOWEN PAUL EDWARD

4 King's Bench Walk
Ground/First Floor, Temple, London
EC4Y 7DL, Telephone: 0171 822 8822
E-mail: 4kbw@barristersatlaw.com
Call date: Nov 1993, Inner Temple
Qualifications: [LLB (Exon)]

BOWEN STEPHEN

14 Tooks Court
Cursitor St, London EC4A 1LB,
Telephone: 0171 405 8828
E-mail: clerks @tooks.law.co.uk
Call date: Nov 1990, Middle Temple
Qualifications: [MA, LLM]

BOWERMAN MICHAEL JOHN

York Chambers
14 Toft Green, York YO1 1JT,
Telephone: 01904 620048
E-mail: yorkchambers.co.uk
Call date: July 1970, Inner Temple
Assistant Recorder
Qualifications: [MA (Oxon)]

BOWERS JOHN SIMON QC (1998)

Littleton Chambers
3 King's Bench Walk North, Temple, London
EC4Y 7HR, Telephone: 0171 797 8600
E-mail: littletonchambers@compuserve.com
Call date: Nov 1979, Middle Temple
Qualifications: [MA, BCL (Oxon)]

Fax: 0171 797 8699;
Out of hours telephone: 0181 458 1031;
DX: 1047 London, Chancery Lane;
Other comms: E-mail franksbower.com

Circuit: Midland and Oxford

Awards and memberships: Employment Law Bar Association; Administrative Law Bar Association; Employment Lawyers Association

Publications: *Transfer of Undertakings Encyclopaedia*, 1998; *Bowers on Employment Law* (4th edn), 1997; *Textbook on Employment Law* (5th edn), 1998; *Employment Tribunal Practice* (2nd edn), 1997; *Modern Law of Strikes*, 1988

Reported cases: *Chessington World of Adventures v Reed*, [1997] IRLR 550, 1997. Coverage of transsexuals by the Sex Discrimination Act.
Tracey v Crosville (Wales) Ltd, [1997] ICR 862, 1997. Whether deductions for contributory fault may be made from unfair dismissal compensation in the event of strikes.
Marley Tiles v Anderson, [1996] ICR 728, 1996. The test of reasonable practicability in late presentation of unfair dismissal applications.
R v Ministry of Defence ex parte Smith, [1996] ICR 740, 1995. Application for judicial review by four gay servicemen who were dismissed from the forces.
Baker v Kaye, [1997] IRLR 219, 1997. Duty of care of doctor carrying out pre-employment medical.

BOWERS RUPERT JOHN

55 Temple Chambers
Temple Avenue, London EC4Y 0HP,
Telephone: 0171 353 7400
Call date: Oct 1995, Gray's Inn
Qualifications: [BA]

BOWES MICHAEL ANTHONY

2 King's Bench Walk
Ground Floor, Temple, London EC4Y 7DE,
Telephone: 0171 353 1746
E-mail: 2kbw@atlas.co.uk
King's Bench Chambers
115 North Hill, Plymouth PL4 8JY,
Telephone: 01752 221551
Call date: July 1980, Middle Temple
Qualifications: [LLB (Manch)]

BOWKER ROBERT JAMES

Francis Taylor Bldg
2nd Floor, Temple, London EC4Y 7BY,
Telephone: 0171 353 9942/3157
Call date: Nov 1995, Lincoln's Inn
Qualifications: [BA (Hons)(So'ton)]

BOWLES TIMOTHY JOHN

Barnard's Inn Chambers
6th Floor Halton House, 20-23 Holborn,
London EC1N 2JD, Telephone: 0171 242 8508
E-mail: clerks@barnards-inn-chambers.co.uk
Call date: Nov 1973, Gray's Inn

BOWLEY IVAN RICHARD

Lincoln House Chambers
5th Floor Lincoln House, 1 Brazennose Street,
Manchester M2 5EL,
Telephone: 0161 832 5701
E-mail: LincolnHouseChambers@link.org
Call date: Nov 1990, Middle Temple
Qualifications: [Bsc (Newc), Dip Law (PCL)]

BOWLEY MARTIN RICHARD QC (1981)

36 Bedford Row
London WC1R 4JH,
Telephone: 0171 421 8000
E-mail: 36bedfordrow@link.org
Call date: Feb 1962, Inner Temple
Qualifications: [MA, BCL (Oxon)]

BOWN PHILIP CLIVE

6 Fountain Court
Steelhouse Lane, Birmingham B4 6DR,
Telephone: 0121 233 3282
Call date: Nov 1974, Middle Temple
Qualifications: [LLB, FCIArb]

BOWRING WILLIAM SCHUYLER BEAKBANE

2 Field Court
Gray's Inn, London WC1R 5BB,
Telephone: 0171 405 6114
E-mail: fieldct2@netcomuk.co.uk.
Call date: Nov 1974, Middle Temple
Qualifications: [BA (Kent)]

BOWRON MISS MARGARET RUTH

1 Crown Office Row
Ground Floor, Temple, London EC4Y 7HH,
Telephone: 0171 797 7500
Crown Office Row Chambers
Blenheim House 120 Church Street, Brighton,
Sussex BN1 1WH, Telephone: 01273 625625
Call date: Nov 1978, Inner Temple
Recorder
Qualifications: [LLB (Lond)]

BOWSHER MICHAEL FREDERICK THOMAS

Keating Chambers
10 Essex Street, Outer Temple, London
WC2R 3AA, Telephone: 0171 544 2600
Call date: Nov 1985, Middle Temple
Qualifications: [BA (Oxon), ACIArb]

BOWYER HENRY MARTIN MITFORD

1 Middle Temple Lane
Temple, London EC4Y 1LT,
Telephone: 0171 583 0659 (12 Lines)
Call date: Nov 1989, Inner Temple
Qualifications: [LLB (Buck)]

BOWYER MARTIN JOHN

6 King's Bench Walk
Ground Floor, Temple, London EC4Y 7DR,
Telephone: 0171 583 0410
Call date: Nov 1984, Inner Temple
Qualifications: [BA Hons (Cantab)]

BOYCE WILLIAM

Hollis Whiteman Chambers
3rd/4th Floor Queen Elizabeth Bldg, Temple,
London EC4Y 9BS, Telephone: 0171 583 5766
E-mail: hollis.whiteman@btinternet.com
Call date: July 1976, Gray's Inn
Recorder
Qualifications: [BA]

BOYD DAVID MARTIN

4 Brick Court
Ground Floor, Temple, London EC4Y 9AD,
Telephone: 0171 797 7766
E-mail: chambers@4brick.co.uk
Call date: Feb 1977, Middle Temple
Qualifications: [LLB (B'ham)]

BOYD GERARD DESMOND DWYER

Lion Court
Chancery House 53-64 Chancery Lane, London
WC2A 1SJ, Telephone: 0171 404 6565
Call date: July 1967, Middle Temple

BOYD JAMES ANDREW DONALDSON

8 King Street
Manchester M2 6AQ,
Telephone: 0161 834 9560
Call date: Nov 1994, Inner Temple
Qualifications: [LLB (Manc), LLM (U.S.A.)]

BOYD MISS KERSTIN MARGARET

Francis Taylor Bldg
2nd Floor, Temple, London EC4Y 7BY,
Telephone: 0171 353 9942/3157
Call date: July 1979, Gray's Inn
Qualifications: [BA (Cantab)]

BOYD PHILLIP JOSEPH GEORGE

Lincoln House Chambers
5th Floor Lincoln House, 1 Brazennose Street,
Manchester M2 5EL,
Telephone: 0161 832 5701
E-mail: LincolnHouseChambers@link.org
Call date: Nov 1993, Gray's Inn
Qualifications: [MA (Cantab)]

BOYD STEPHEN JAMES HARVEY

29 Bedford Row Chambers
London WC1R 4HE,
Telephone: 0171 831 2626
Call date: July 1977, Gray's Inn
Qualifications: [BSc]

BOYD STEWART CRAUFURD QC (1981)

Essex Court Chambers
24 Lincoln's Inn Fields, London WC2A 3ED,
Telephone: 0171 813 8000
E-mail: clerksroom@essexcourt-chambers.co.uk
Call date: July 1967, Middle Temple
Recorder
Qualifications: [MA (Cantab)]

BOYD THOMAS DIXON

33 Bedford Row
London WC1R 4JH,
Telephone: 0171 242 6476
Call date: Nov 1995, Inner Temple
Qualifications: [BA (Oxon), CPE]

D

BOYDELL EDWARD PATRICK STIRRUP

Pump Court Chambers
Upper Ground Floor 3 Pump Court, Temple,
London EC4Y 7AJ, Telephone: 0171 353 0711
Pump Court Chambers
31 Southgate Street, Winchester SO23 8EE,
Telephone: 01962 868161
Call date: Nov 1989, Middle Temple
Qualifications: [B.Ed Hons (Cantab)]

BOYE-ANAWOMA MISS MARGO CIARA

14 Tooks Court
Cursitor St, London EC4A 1LB,
Telephone: 0171 405 8828
E-mail: clerks @tooks.law.co.uk
Call date: Nov 1989, Inner Temple
Qualifications: [LLB]

BOYES MRS KAREN ROSALIE

Chambers of Karen R Boyes
P.O.Box 458, Brixworth, Northampton
NN6 9ZT, Telephone: 01604 882942
E-mail: karen_r_boyes@link.org
Call date: Oct 1991, Middle Temple
Qualifications: [LLB Hons (Newc)]

BOYLE ALAN GORDON QC (1991)

13 Old Square
1st Floor, Lincoln's Inn, London WC2A 3UA,
Telephone: 0171 242 6105
E-mail: clerks@serlecourt.co.uk
Call date: Nov 1972, Lincoln's Inn
Qualifications: [BA (Oxon)]

BOYLE CHRISTOPHER ALEXANDER DAVID

2 Mitre Ct Bldgs
2nd Floor, Temple, London EC4Y 7BX,
Telephone: 0171 583 1380
Call date: Nov 1994, Lincoln's Inn
Qualifications: [BA (Hons)]

BOYLE DAVID STUART

Deans Court Chambers
Cumberland House Crown Square, Manchester
M3 3HA, Telephone: 0161 834 4097
E-mail: deanscourt@compuserve.com
Call date: Mar 1996, Gray's Inn
Qualifications: [BA]

BOYLE GERARD JAMES

1 Serjeants' Inn
5th Floor Fleet Street, Temple, London
EC4Y 1LL, Telephone: 0171 415 6666
E-mail: no1serjeantsinn@btinternet.com
Call date: Nov 1992, Gray's Inn
Qualifications: [BA (Cantab)]

BOYLE ROBERT ALEXANDER

18 Red Lion Court
(Off Fleet Street), London EC4A 3EB,
Telephone: 0171 520 6000
Thornwood House
102 New London Road, Chelmsford, Essex
CM2 0RG, Telephone: 01245 280880
Call date: Nov 1985, Middle Temple
Qualifications: [BSc (Surrey)]

BRABIN MICHAEL EDWARD

Colleton Chambers
Colleton Crescent, Exeter, Devon EX2 4DG,
Telephone: 01392 74898/9
Farrar's Building
Temple, London EC4Y 7BD,
Telephone: 0171 583 9241
E-mail: chambers@farrarsbuilding.co.uk
Door Tenant
Call date: May 1976, Inner Temple

BRACE MICHAEL WESLEY

33 Park Place
Cardiff CF1 3BA, Telephone: 01222 233313
Call date: Apr 1991, Lincoln's Inn
Qualifications: [LLB (Hons)(Lond)]

BRADBERRY MISS REBECCA

South Western Chambers
Melville House 12 Middle Street, Taunton,
Somerset TA1 1SH, Telephone: 01823 331919
Call date: Oct 1996, Lincoln's Inn
Qualifications: [BA (Hons)(Warw), Dip in Law
(Exon)]

BRADBURY TIMOTHY BLACKBURN

3 Paper Bldgs
1st Floor, Temple, London EC4Y 7EU,
Telephone: 0171 583 8055
E-mail: london@3paper.com
20 Lorne Park Road
Bournemouth BH1 1JN,
Telephone: 01202 292102 (5 Lines)
4 St Peter Street
Winchester SO23 8OW,
Telephone: 01962 868884
Call date: July 1989, Inner Temple
Qualifications: [LLB (So'ton)]

BRADLEY ANTHONY WILFRED

Cloisters
1st Floor, Temple, London EC4Y 7AA,
Telephone: 0171 827 4000
E-mail: clerks@cloisters.com
Call date: Apr 1989, Inner Temple
Qualifications: [BA,MA,LLM (Cantab)]

BRADLEY MISS CAROLINE

King Charles House
Standard Hill, Nottingham NG1 6FX,
Telephone: 0115 9418851
E-mail: clerks@kch.co.uk
Call date: Nov 1985, Middle Temple
Qualifications: [BA (Hons)]

BRADLEY MISS CLODAGH MARIA

3 Serjeants Inn
London EC4Y 1BQ,
Telephone: 0171 353 5537
E-mail: available upon request
Call date: Oct 1996, Middle Temple
Qualifications: [BA (Hons)(Cantab)]

BRADLEY DENIS ARTHUR ROBERT

Library Chambers
Gray's Inn Chambers, Gray's Inn, London
WC1R 5JA, Telephone: 0171 404 6500
Phoenix Chambers
First Floor Gray's Inn Chambers, Gray's Inn,
London WC1R 5JA, Telephone: 0171 404 7888
Call date: Feb 1965, Gray's Inn

BRADLEY PHILLIP JAMES

1 Pump Court
Lower Ground Floor, Temple, London
EC4Y 7AB, Telephone: 0171 583 2012/
353 4341
E-mail: (name) @1pumpcourt.co.uk
Door Tenant
Call date: Nov 1993, Lincoln's Inn
Qualifications: [BA (Hons)]

BRADLEY RICHARD

Oriel Chambers
14 Water Street, Liverpool L2 8TD,
Telephone: 0151 236 7191
E-mail: oriel_chambers@link.org
Call date: July 1978, Middle Temple
Qualifications: [LLB]

BRADLEY MS SALLY CHRISTINA

1 Pump Court
Lower Ground Floor, Temple, London
EC4Y 7AB, Telephone: 0171 583 2012/
353 4341
E-mail: (name) @1pumpcourt.co.uk
Call date: Nov 1989, Inner Temple
Qualifications: [BA]

BRADLEY MS SALLY FRANCES

Broad Chare
33 Broad Chare, Newcastle Upon Tyne
NE1 3DQ, Telephone: 0191 232 0541
Door Tenant
1 Mitre Ct Bldgs
Ground Floor, Temple, London EC4Y 7BS,
Telephone: 0171 797 7070
Door Tenant
Call date: Nov 1978, Lincoln's Inn
Qualifications: [LLB]

BRADLY DAVID LAWRENCE

39 Essex Street
London WC2R 3AT,
Telephone: 0171 583 1111
E-mail: clerks@39essex.co.uk
Call date: July 1987, Middle Temple
Qualifications: [LLB (Lond)]

BRADSHAW DAVID LAWRENCE

10 Park Square
Leeds LS1 2LH, Telephone: 0113 2455438
E-mail: chambers@bandit.legend.co.uk
Call date: July 1975, Inner Temple
Recorder
Qualifications: [LLB]

BRADSHAW HOWARD SYDNEY

Queen's Chambers
5 John Dalton Street, Manchester M2 6ET,
Telephone: 0161 834 6875/4738
4 Camden Place
Preston PR1 3JL, Telephone: 01772 828300
Call date: July 1977, Middle Temple
Qualifications: [MA (Cantab)]

BRADSHAW IAN CHARLES

Baker Street Chambers
9 Baker Street, Middlesbrough TS1 2LF,
Telephone: 01642 873873
Call date: Oct 1992, Middle Temple
Qualifications: [LLB(Nott'm), LLM(Wales),
MA(Hull)]

BRADY MICHAEL ANTONY

58 King Street Chambers
1st Floor, Kingsgate House 51-53 South King
Street, Manchester M2 6DE,
Telephone: 0161 831 7477
Call date: Oct 1992, Gray's Inn
Qualifications: [LL.B (Hons)]

BRAGANZA MISS NICOLA JANICE

3 Temple Gardens (North)
Fifth Floor, Temple, London EC4Y 9AU,
Telephone: 0171 353 0853/4/7222
E-mail: 100106.1577@compuserve.com
Call date: Oct 1992, Middle Temple
Qualifications: [LL.B (Hons, Reading)]

BRAGIEL EDWARD BRONISLAW HENRYK

5 New Square
1st Floor, Lincoln's Inn, London WC2A 3RJ,
Telephone: 0171 404 0404
E-mail: Chambers@FiveNewSquare.CityScape.co.uk
Call date: July 1977, Middle Temple
Qualifications: [MA (Cantab)]

BRAHAM COLIN PHILIP LESLIE

12 New Square
Ground Floor, Lincoln's Inn, London
WC2A 3SW, Telephone: 0171 419 1212
E-mail: 12newsquare@compuserve.com
25 Park Square
Leeds LS1 2PW, Telephone: 0113 2451841/2/3
E-mail: sovereignchambers@btinternet.com
Door Tenant
Call date: Nov 1971, Middle Temple
Qualifications: [MA (Cantab), MSc (Lond)]

BRAHAM DAVID GERALD HENRY QC (1979)

3 Temple Gardens
1st Floor, Temple, London EC4Y 9AU,
Telephone: 0171 353 7884/5 8982/3
Call date: Feb 1957, Middle Temple
Qualifications: [BA (Cantab)]

BRAHAMS MRS DIANA JOYCE

Old Square Chambers
1 Verulam Buildings, Gray's Inn, London
WC1R 5LQ, Telephone: 0171 831 0801
Old Square Chambers
Hanover House 47 Corn Street, Bristol
BS1 1HT, Telephone: 0117 9277111
Call date: July 1972, Middle Temple

BRAIN MISS PAMELA FRANCIS

Chambers of Helen Grindrod QC
1st Floor 95a Chancery Lane, London
WC2A 2JG, Telephone: 0171 404 4777
Call date: Nov 1985, Inner Temple
Qualifications: [LLB (Lond)]

BRAITHWAITE CHARLES ANTONY ELLIOTT

67a Westgate Road
Newcastle Upon Tyne NE1 1SQ,
Telephone: 0191 261 4407/2329785
Call date: July 1971, Gray's Inn
Qualifications: [MA (Cantab)]

BRAITHWAITE GARFIELD ZIBEAN

Francis Taylor Bldg
Ground Floor, Temple, London EC4Y 7BY,
Telephone: 0171 353 7768/7769/2711
Call date: Feb 1987, Gray's Inn
Qualifications: [LLB (Lanc)]

BRAITHWAITE WILLIAM THOMAS SCATCHARD QC (1992)

Exchange Chambers
Pearl Assurance House, Derby Square,
Liverpool, Merseyside L2 9XX,
Telephone: 0151 236 7747
E-mail: exchangechambers@btinternet.com
Two Crown Office Row
Ground Floor, London EC4Y 7HJ,
Telephone: 0171 797 8100
E-mail: mail@2cor.co.uk, or to individual
barristers at: [barrister's surname]@2cor.co.uk
Call date: Nov 1970, Gray's Inn
Recorder
Qualifications: [LLB (L'pool)]

Fax: 0151 236 3433; DX: 14207 Liverpool;
Other comms: E-mail
billbraithwaite.qc@btinternet.com

Types of work: Medical negligence; Personal
injury

Circuit: Northern

Awards and memberships: European Brain
Injury Society; International Medical Society of
Paraplegia

Publications: Consultant Editor - *Kemp and
Kemp*; Joint Editor - *Medical Aspects of
Personal Injury Litigation*, 1997

Reported cases: *Knowles v Liverpool City
Council*, [1993] 1 WLR 1428, 1993. House of
Lords decision whether flagstone is equipment.

I practise exclusively in personal injury
litigation, almost all relating to injury to the
brain and spine, including medical negligence. I
am the Consultant Editor of *Kemp and Kemp
on The Quantum of Damages*, and a Joint
Editor of *Medical Aspects of Personal Injury
Litigation*, and a Contributor to *Brain Injury
and After*. I lecture in England and Europe on
these topics.

BRAMWELL RICHARD MERVYN QC (1989)

3 Temple Gardens
1st Floor, Temple, London EC4Y 9AU,
Telephone: 0171 353 7884/5 8982/3
Call date: July 1967, Middle Temple
Qualifications: [LLM]

BRANCH MISS ELIZABETH JAYNE

4 Fountain Court
Steelhouse Lane, Birmingham B4 6DR,
Telephone: 0121 236 3476
Call date: Oct 1992, Lincoln's Inn
Qualifications: [LLB(Hons)(Manch)]

BRAND MISS RACHEL RENNIE VIRGINIA ANN

Coleridge Chambers
Citadel 190 Corporation Street, Birmingham
B4 6QD, Telephone: 0121 233 3303
Call date: July 1981, Gray's Inn
Qualifications: [BA]

BRAND SIMON DAVID

Coleridge Chambers
Citadel 190 Corporation Street, Birmingham
B4 6QD, Telephone: 0121 233 3303
Call date: Nov 1973, Gray's Inn
Qualifications: [LLB (Lond)]

BRANDON DAVID STEPHEN QC (1996)

24 Old Bldgs
First Floor, Lincoln's Inn, London WC2A 3UJ,
Telephone: 0171 242 2744
Call date: July 1978, Gray's Inn
Qualifications: [BA (Nottm) LLM, (Keele)]

BRANDON MISS HELEN ELIZABETH

Oriel Chambers
14 Water Street, Liverpool L2 8TD,
Telephone: 0151 236 7191
E-mail: oriel_chambers@link.org
Call date: Oct 1993, Middle Temple
Qualifications: [LLB (Hons)(Lanc)]

BRANIGAN MISS KATE VICTORIA

3 Paper Bldgs
1st Floor, Temple, London EC4Y 7EU,
Telephone: 0171 583 8055
E-mail: london@3paper.com
4 St Peter Street
Winchester SO23 8OW,
Telephone: 01962 868884
20 Lorne Park Road
Bournemouth BH1 1JN,
Telephone: 01202 292102 (5 Lines)
Call date: July 1984, Inner Temple
Qualifications: [LLB (Soton)]

D

BRANN MISS ELIZABETH NINA

Gray's Inn Chambers
5th Floor, Gray's Inn, London WC1R 5JA,
Telephone: 0171 404 1111
6-8 Mill Street
Maidstone, Kent ME15 6XH,
Telephone: 01622 688094
Call date: July 1970, Middle Temple

BRANNIGAN PETER JOHN SEAN

1 Essex Court
1st Floor, Temple, London EC4Y 9AR,
Telephone: 0171 936 3030
E-mail: one.essex_court@virgin.net
Call date: Oct 1994, Gray's Inn
Qualifications: [BA]

BRANT PAUL DAVID

Oriel Chambers
14 Water Street, Liverpool L2 8TD,
Telephone: 0151 236 7191
E-mail: oriel_chambers@link.org
Call date: Oct 1993, Lincoln's Inn
Qualifications: [LLB (Hons)(L'pool)]

BRANTHWAITE DR MARGARET ANNIE

1 Paper Bldgs
Ground Floor, Temple, London EC4Y 7EP,
Telephone: 0171 583 7355
E-mail: clerks@1pb.co.uk
Call date: Oct 1993, Lincoln's Inn
Qualifications: [BA, MB Bchir, MD, FRCP, FFARCS]

BRASLAVSKY NICHOLAS JUSTIN

40 King Street
Manchester M2 6BA,
Telephone: 0161 832 9082
E-mail: Kingst40@aol.com
Call date: July 1983, Inner Temple
Qualifications: [LLB, M jur, PhD(B'ha]

BRASSE MISS GILLIAN DENISE

14 Gray's Inn Square
Gray's Inn, London WC1R 5JP,
Telephone: 0171 242 0858
E-mail: 100712.2134@compuserve.com
Call date: July 1977, Gray's Inn
Qualifications: [BA(L'pool)]

BRASSINGTON STEPHEN DAVID

2 Paper Bldgs
1st Floor, Temple, London EC4Y 7ET,
Telephone: 0171 936 2611 (10 Lines)
E-mail: clerks@2pbbarristers.co.uk
Call date: Nov 1994, Inner Temple
Qualifications: [BSc (Lond), CPE]

BRATZA NICOLAS DUSAN QC (1988)

One Hare Court
1st Floor, Temple, London EC4Y 7BE,
Telephone: 0171 353 3171
E-mail: admin-oneharecourt@btinternet.com
Call date: July 1969, Lincoln's Inn
Recorder
Qualifications: [MA (Oxon)]

BRAZIL DOMINIC THOMAS GEORGE

14 Gray's Inn Square
Gray's Inn, London WC1R 5JP,
Telephone: 0171 242 0858
E-mail: 100712.2134@compuserve.com
Call date: Nov 1995, Middle Temple
Qualifications: [BA (Hons)]

BREALEY MARK PHILIP

Brick Court Chambers
15/19 Devereux Court, London WC2R 3JJ,
Telephone: 0171 583 0777
E-mail: (surname)@brickcourt.demon.co.uk
Call date: July 1984, Middle Temple
Qualifications: [LLB, LLM, DEA]

BREDEMEAR ZACHARY CHARLES

Barnard's Inn Chambers
6th Floor Halton House, 20-23 Holborn,
London EC1N 2JD, Telephone: 0171 242 8508
E-mail: clerks@barnards-inn-chambers.co.uk
Call date: Oct 1996, Inner Temple
Qualifications: [LLB (Reading), LLM (Lond)]

BREEN CARLO ENRICO

9 St John Street
Manchester M3 4DN,
Telephone: 0161 955 9000
E-mail: ninesjs@gconnect.com
Call date: Nov 1987, Middle Temple
Qualifications: [LLB (Essex)]

BREESE-LAUGHRAN MS ELEANORE DELPHINE

8 King's Bench Walk
2nd Floor, Temple, London EC4Y 7DU,
Telephone: 0171 797 8888
8 King's Bench Walk North
1 Park Square East, Leeds LS1 2NE,
Telephone: 0113 2439797
Call date: Oct 1991, Lincoln's Inn
Qualifications: [MA (Hons) (Camb)]

BREHENY MARK PATRICK

Peel House Chambers
Ground Floor, Peel House 5 Harrington Street,
Liverpool L2 9QA, Telephone: 0151 236 4321
Call date: Nov 1986, Lincoln's Inn
Qualifications: [BA Law (Kent)]

BRENNAN CHRISTOPHER PATRICK

Goldsmith Chambers
Ground Floor Goldsmith Building, Temple,
London EC4Y 7BL,
Telephone: 0171 353 6802/3/4/5
E-mail: celiamonksfield@btinternet.com
Call date: Feb 1995, Gray's Inn
Qualifications: [LLB (Cardiff)]

BRENNAN DANIEL JOSEPH QC (1985)

39 Essex Street
London WC2R 3AT,
Telephone: 0171 583 1111
E-mail: clerks@39essex.co.uk
18 St John Street
Manchester M3 4EA,
Telephone: 0161 278 1800
Door Tenant
Call date: July 1967, Gray's Inn
Recorder
Qualifications: [LLB (Manch)]

BRENNAN MISS JANICE LESLEY

2 King's Bench Walk
Ground Floor, Temple, London EC4Y 7DE,
Telephone: 0171 353 1746
E-mail: 2kbw@atlas.co.uk
King's Bench Chambers
115 North Hill, Plymouth PL4 8JY,
Telephone: 01752 221551
Call date: July 1980, Middle Temple
Qualifications: [LLB (Lond)]

BRENNAN JOHN DAVID

4 Fountain Court
Steelhouse Lane, Birmingham B4 6DR,
Telephone: 0121 236 3476
Call date: Mar 1996, Lincoln's Inn
Qualifications: [BA (Hons)]

BRENNAN TIMOTHY ROGER

Devereux Chambers
Devereux Court, London WC2R 3JJ,
Telephone: 0171 353 7534
E-mail: elton@devchambers.co.uk
Call date: Nov 1981, Gray's Inn
Assistant Recorder
Qualifications: [BCL,MA (Oxon)]

BRENNAND TIMOTHY WILLIAM

Manchester House Chambers
18-22 Bridge Street, Manchester M3 3BZ,
Telephone: 0161 834 7007
Call date: Nov 1987, Gray's Inn
Qualifications: [LLB (Hons)]

BRENT MICHAEL LEON QC (1983)

9 Gough Square
London EC4A 3DE, Telephone: 0171 353 5371
Call date: May 1961, Gray's Inn
Recorder
Qualifications: [LLB (Manch)]

BRENT RICHARD

3 Verulam Buildings
London WC1R 5NT,
Telephone: 0171 831 8441
E-mail: clerks@3verulam.co.uk
Call date: July 1995, Middle Temple
Qualifications: [BA (Hons) (Cantab), D.Phil
(Oxon)]

BRENTON TIMOTHY DEANE

4 Essex Court
Temple, London EC4Y 9AJ,
Telephone: 0171 797 7970
E-mail: clerks@4essexcourt.law.co.uk
Call date: July 1981, Middle Temple
Qualifications: [LLB]

D

BRERETON MRS FIORELLA

Peel Court Chambers
45 Hardman Street, Manchester M3 3HA,
Telephone: 0161 832 3791
Call date: Nov 1979, Gray's Inn
Qualifications: [BA (Hons)]

BRERETON MISS JOY

4 Paper Bldgs
2nd Floor, Temple, London EC4Y 7EX,
Telephone: 0171 583 0816/071 353 1131
E-mail: clerks@4paperbuildings.co.uk
Call date: Nov 1990, Gray's Inn
Qualifications: [LLB (Cardiff), LLM (Bristol)]

BRESLER FENTON SHEA

3 Paper Bldgs
Ground Floor, Temple, London EC4Y 7EU,
Telephone: 0171 797 7000
E-mail: clerks@3pb.co.uk
Call date: June 1951, Middle Temple
Qualifications: [LLB (Lond)(Hons)]

BRESLIN MISS CATHERINE ELIZABETH

College Chambers
19 Carlton Cresent, Southampton, Hants
SO15 2ET, Telephone: 01703 230338
Call date: Nov 1990, Inner Temple
Qualifications: [LLB (Hons)(Lond)]

BRETHERICK MS DIANA

Mitre Court Chambers
3rd Floor, Temple, London EC4Y 7BP,
Telephone: 0171 353 9394
Call date: Nov 1989, Middle Temple
Qualifications: [BA (Hons), Dip Law]

BRETHERTON MS KERRY LOUISE

Arden Chambers
27 John Street, London WC1N 2BL,
Telephone: 0171 242 4244
Call date: Oct 1992, Lincoln's Inn
Qualifications: [BA(Hons)(B'ham), CPE(B'ham)]

BRETT MATTHEW CHRISTOPHER ANTHONY

2 Harcourt Bldgs
1st Floor, Temple, London EC4Y 9DB,
Telephone: 0171 353 6961/7
Harcourt Chambers
Churchill House 3 St Aldate's Courtyard, St
Aldate's, Oxford OX1 1BN,
Telephone: 01865 791559
Call date: Nov 1987, Middle Temple
Qualifications: [BA (Oxon)]

BRETTEN (GEORGE) REX QC (1980)

24 Old Bldgs
First Floor, Lincoln's Inn, London WC2A 3UJ,
Telephone: 0171 242 2744
Call date: May 1965, Lincoln's Inn
Qualifications: [MA, LLM (Cantab)]

BRETTLER JONATHAN SAMUEL

4 Stone Bldgs
Ground Floor, Lincoln's Inn, London
WC2A 3XT, Telephone: 0171 242 5524
E-mail: d.goddard@4stonebuildings.law.co.uk
Call date: July 1988, Middle Temple
Qualifications: [LLB (Hons) (LSE), BCL (Oxon)]

BRIAND MISS PAULINE MARY

Staple Inn Chambers
1st Floor 9 Staple Inn, Holborn, London
WC1V 7QH, Telephone: 0171 242 5240
E-mail: clerks@staple-inn.org
Call date: July 1996, Middle Temple
Qualifications: [LLB (Hons)(Staffs)]

BRICE GEOFFREY JAMES BARRINGTON GROV QC (1979)

4 Field Court
Gray's Inn, London WC1R 5EA,
Telephone: 0171 440 6900
E-mail: chambers@4fieldcourt.co.uk
Call date: July 1960, Middle Temple
Recorder
Qualifications: [LLB]

BRICKMAN MISS LAURA GILLIAN

10 King's Bench Walk
1st Floor, Temple, London EC4Y 7EB,
Telephone: 0171 353 2501
Call date: July 1976, Inner Temple

BRIDEN RICHARD JOHN

Goldsworth Chambers
1st Floor 10-11 Gray's Inn Square, London
WC1R 5JD, Telephone: 0171 405 7117
Call date: Nov 1982, Gray's Inn
Qualifications: [LLB (Hons) (E.Ang), FCIArb]

BRIDEN TIMOTHY JOHN

8 Stone Buildings
Lincoln's Inn, London WC2A 3TA,
Telephone: 0171 831 9881
Call date: July 1976, Inner Temple
Qualifications: [MA, LLB (Cantab)]

Fax: 0171 831 9342; DX: 216 London,
Chancery Lane

Types of work: Ecclesiastical; Insurance; Medical
negligence; Personal injury; Professional
negligence

Other professional qualifications: Chancellor of
the Diocese of Bath and Wells; Chancellor of
Diocese of Truro

Circuit: South Eastern

Publications: *Macmorran's Handbook for
Churchwardens and Parochial Church
Councillors*, 1997 edn; *Moore's Introduction to
English Canon Law* (3rd edn), 1992

Reported cases: *Re West Norwood Cemetery*,
[1994] Fam 210, 1994. Municipal cemetery -
consecrated part - unauthorised disturbance of
graves - powers of Consistory Court.
Re St Luke the Evangelist, Maidstone, [1995]
Fam 1, 1994. Reordering of interior of church -
whether adversely affecting character of
building - necessity for change.
Lightfoot v National Westminster Bank, [1996]
I WLR 583, 1995. County Court - practice -
automatic directions - striking out.
R v Board of Trustees of Science Museum,
[1993] I WLR 1171, 1993. Health and Safety -
bacteria in air conditioning system - whether
exposure of public a risk to health.

BRIDGE IAN CHARLES

Mitre Court Chambers
3rd Floor, Temple, London EC4Y 7BP,
Telephone: 0171 353 9394
Call date: Nov 1988, Inner Temple
Qualifications: [LLB (Hons) (Sheff)]

BRIDGE PROFESSOR MICHAEL GREENHALGH

24 The Ropewalk
Nottingham NG1 5EF,
Telephone: 0115 9472581
E-mail: clerk@ropewalk.co.uk
Door Tenant
Call date: Nov 1975, Middle Temple
Qualifications: [LLM]

BRIDGE MRS ROWENA

King Charles House
Standard Hill, Nottingham NG1 6FX,
Telephone: 0115 9418851
E-mail: clerks@kch.co.uk
Call date: Nov 1975, Middle Temple
Qualifications: [LLB (Lond), LLB,BCL (McGill)]

BRIDGE STUART NIGEL

Fenners Chambers
3 Madingley Road, Cambridge CB3 OEE,
Telephone: 01223 368761
Fenners Chambers
8-12 Priestgate, Peterborough PE1 1JA,
Telephone: 01733 62030
Call date: July 1981, Middle Temple
Qualifications: [MA (Cantab)]

BRIDGES-ADAMS JOHN NICHOLAS WILLIAM

2 Field Court
Gray's Inn, London WC1R 5BB,
Telephone: 0171 405 6114
E-mail: fieldct2@netcomuk.co.uk.
Call date: June 1958, Lincoln's Inn
Qualifications: [MA (Oxon), dip Ed, FCIArb]

BRIEFEL CHARLES JONATHAN

Hardwicke Building
New Square, Lincoln's Inn, London
WC2A 3SB, Telephone: 0171 242 2523
E-mail: clerks@hardwicke.co.uk
Call date: July 1984, Gray's Inn
Qualifications: [LLB (Manch)]

BRIEGEL PIETER DAVID ROY

Mitre Court Chambers
3rd Floor, Temple, London EC4Y 7BP,
Telephone: 0171 353 9394
Call date: Nov 1986, Middle Temple
Qualifications: [LLB (Lond) (Hons)]

D

BRIERLEY ANDREW DUNCAN

6 King's Bench Walk
Ground Floor, Temple, London EC4Y 7DR,
Telephone: 0171 583 0410
Call date: July 1984, Middle Temple
Qualifications: [BA]

BRIGDEN ANTHONY JOHN

Bell Yard Chambers
116/118 Chancery Lane, London WC2A 1PP,
Telephone: 0171 306 9292
Call date: July 1967, Inner Temple
Recorder
Qualifications: [LLB]

BRIGGS ADRIAN

2 Hare Court
Ground Floor, Temple, London EC4Y 7BH,
Telephone: 0171 583 1770
E-mail: 2_Hare_Court@link.org
Call date: Apr 1989, Middle Temple
Qualifications: [BCL, MA (Oxon)]

BRIGGS MISS JOANNE MARY ROBSON

Sussex Chambers
9 Old Steine, Brighton BN1 1FJ,
Telephone: 01273 607953
Call date: Oct 1993, Middle Temple
Qualifications: [M.Phil, CPE (Lond)]

BRIGGS JOHN

India Buildings Chambers
Water Street, Liverpool L2 OXG,
Telephone: 0151 243 6000
Call date: June 1953, Inner Temple
Qualifications: [BCL, MA]

BRIGGS JOHN BONAR

3/4 South Square
Gray's Inn, London WC1R 5HP,
Telephone: 0171 696 9900
E-mail: clerks@southsquare.com
Call date: July 1973, Gray's Inn
Qualifications: [LLB (Lond), Ex Du D d'u
(NANCY)]

BRIGGS MICHAEL TOWNLEY FEATHERSTONE QC (1994)

13 Old Square
1st Floor, Lincoln's Inn, London WC2A 3UA,
Telephone: 0171 242 6105
E-mail: clerks@serlecourt.co.uk
Call date: Nov 1978, Lincoln's Inn
Qualifications: [BA (Oxon)]

BRIGGS NICHOLAS NORMAN

All Saints Chambers
9/11 Broad Street, Bristol BS1 2HP,
Telephone: 0117 921 1966
Call date: Oct 1994, Lincoln's Inn
Qualifications: [Dip in Valuation &, Estate
Management, CPE (Bris)]

BRIGGS-WATSON MISS SANDRA MICHELLE

2 Paper Bldgs
Temple, London EC4Y 7ET,
Telephone: 0171 936 2613
Call date: Nov 1985, Middle Temple
Qualifications: [LLB (London)]

BRIGHT ANDREW JOHN

4 Brick Court
1st Floor, Temple, London EC4Y 9AD,
Telephone: 0171 583 8455
Call date: July 1973, Middle Temple
Qualifications: [LLB (Lond)]

BRIGHT CHRISTOPHER JOHN

3 Fountain Court
Steelhouse Lane, Birmingham B4 6DR,
Telephone: 0121 236 5854
Call date: Nov 1985, Gray's Inn
Qualifications: [BA (Dunelm)]

BRIGHT DAVID REGINALD

13 King's Bench Walk
1st Floor, Temple, London EC4Y 7EN,
Telephone: 0171 353 7204
E-mail: clerks@13kbw.law.co.uk
King's Bench Chambers
32 Beaumont Street, Oxford OX1 2NP,
Telephone: 01865 311066
E-mail: clerks@kbc-oxford.law.co.uk
Call date: July 1976, Lincoln's Inn
Recorder

BRIGHT MISS RACHEL ZELDA

1 Middle Temple Lane
Temple, London EC4Y 1LT,
Telephone: 0171 583 0659 (12 Lines)
Call date: Oct 1991, Lincoln's Inn
Qualifications: [LLB (Hons) (Manch)]

BRIGHT ROBERT GRAHAM

7 King's Bench Walk
Ground Floor, Temple, London EC4Y 7DS,
Telephone: 0171 583 0404
Call date: Nov 1987, Gray's Inn
Qualifications: [BA, BCL (Oxon)]

BRILLIANT SIMON HOWARD

Lamb Chambers
Lamb Building, Temple, London EC4Y 7AS,
Telephone: 0171 797 8300
E-mail: lambchambers@link.org
Call date: July 1976, Middle Temple
Qualifications: [LLB (Manch), BCL (Ox]

BRIMELOW MISS JANINE KIRSTY

Francis Taylor Bldg
2nd Floor, Temple, London EC4Y 7BY,
Telephone: 0171 353 9942/3157
Call date: Oct 1991, Gray's Inn
Qualifications: [LLB (Hons)]

BRINDLE MICHAEL JOHN QC (1992)

Fountain Court
Temple, London EC4Y 9DH,
Telephone: 0171 583 3335
E-mail: chambers@fountaincourt.co.uk
Call date: Nov 1975, Lincoln's Inn
Qualifications: [MA (Oxon)]

BRINKWORTH PAUL GREGORY

Lion Court
Chancery House 53-64 Chancery Lane, London
WC2A 1SJ, Telephone: 0171 404 6565
Call date: Oct 1990, Lincoln's Inn
Qualifications: [BA]

BRISBY JOHN CONSTANT SHANNON McBURNEY QC (1996)

4 Stone Bldgs
Ground Floor, Lincoln's Inn, London
WC2A 3XT, Telephone: 0171 242 5524
E-mail: d.goddard@4stonebuildings.law.co.uk
Call date: July 1978, Lincoln's Inn
Qualifications: [MA (Oxon)]

BRISCOE MISS CONSTANCE

4 Brick Court
Ground Floor, Temple, London EC4Y 9AD,
Telephone: 0171 797 7766
E-mail: chambers@4brick.co.uk
Call date: Nov 1983, Inner Temple
Qualifications: [LLB (Newcastle)]

BRISTOLL MISS SANDRA JAYNE

3/4 South Square
Gray's Inn, London WC1R 5HP,
Telephone: 0171 696 9900
E-mail: clerks@southsquare.com
Call date: July 1989, Middle Temple
Qualifications: [MA (Cantab)]

BRITCLIFFE MISS ANNE ELIZABETH

21 White Friars
Chester CH1 1NZ, Telephone: 01244 323070
Call date: Apr 1989, Gray's Inn
Qualifications: [LLB (Bristol)]

BRITTAIN MARC JOHN

10 King's Bench Walk
1st Floor, Temple, London EC4Y 7EB,
Telephone: 0171 353 2501
Call date: July 1983, Gray's Inn
Qualifications: [BA (Business Law)]

BRITTAIN RICHARD PAUL

India Buildings Chambers
Water Street, Liverpool L2 OXG,
Telephone: 0151 243 6000
Call date: Nov 1971, Inner Temple
Recorder
Qualifications: [MA, LLB]

BRITTON ROBERT ALEXANDER

1 Dr Johnson's Bldgs
Ground Floor, Temple, London EC4Y 7AX,
Telephone: 0171 353 9328
Dr Johnson's Chambers
The Atrium Court Apex Plaza, Reading
RG1 1AX, Telephone: 01734 254221
Call date: July 1973, Inner Temple
Recorder
Qualifications: [BA]

BROADBENT EDMUND JOHN

20 Essex Street
London WC2R 3AL,
Telephone: 0171 583 9294
E-mail: clerks@20essexst.com
Call date: July 1980, Gray's Inn
Qualifications: [MA, LLB (Cantab)]

BROADBENT MISS EMMA LOUISE

6 King's Bench Walk
Ground Floor, Temple, London EC4Y 7DR,
Telephone: 0171 583 0410
Call date: Nov 1986, Inner Temple
Qualifications: [BA (Lond), Dip Law (City)]

BROADHURST SIMON THOMAS

18 St John Street
Manchester M3 4EA,
Telephone: 0161 278 1800
Call date: Nov 1994, Inner Temple
Qualifications: [BA (Oxon), CPE]

BROADLEY JOHN

Cobden House Chambers
19 Quay Street, Manchester M3 3HN,
Telephone: 0161 833 6000
E-mail: clerks@cobden.co.uk
Call date: July 1973, Middle Temple
Qualifications: [LLB (Hons)]

BROATCH MICHAEL DONALD

5 Paper Bldgs
Ground Floor, Temple, London EC4Y 7HB,
Telephone: 0171 583 9275/583 4555
E-mail: 5paper@link.org
Call date: May 1971, Middle Temple
Qualifications: [LLB, LLM (Lond)]

BROBBEY DR BENJAMIN ASARE

26 Shaftesbury Road
Earlsdon, Coventry, Warwickshire CV5 6FN,
Telephone: 01203 677337
Call date: Nov 1968, Inner Temple
Qualifications: [LLB, LLM, PhD (Lond)]

BROCK DAVID JAMES

2 Paper Bldgs
1st Floor, Temple, London EC4Y 7ET,
Telephone: 0171 936 2611 (10 Lines)
E-mail: clerks@2pbbarristers.co.uk
Call date: Nov 1984, Middle Temple
Qualifications: [BHum (Lond)]

BROCK JONATHAN SIMON QC (1997)

Falcon Chambers
Falcon Court, London EC4Y 1AA,
Telephone: 0171 353 2484/7
Call date: July 1977, Lincoln's Inn
Assistant Recorder
Qualifications: [MA (Cantab), FCIArb]

BROCKLEY NIGEL SIMON

Bracton Chambers
95a Chancery Lane, London WC2A 1DT,
Telephone: 0171 242 4248
Call date: Nov 1992, Lincoln's Inn
Qualifications: [BA (Hons), CPE]

BRODIE (JAMES) BRUCE

39 Essex Street
London WC2R 3AT,
Telephone: 0171 583 1111
E-mail: clerks@39essex.co.uk
Call date: May 1993, Inner Temple
Qualifications: [BA (S.Africa), MA (Cantab)]

BRODIE COLIN ALEXANDER QC (1980)

24 Old Bldgs
Ground Floor, Lincoln's Inn, London
WC2A 3UJ, Telephone: 0171 404 0946
E-mail: clerks@24oldbuildings.law.co.uk
Call date: Feb 1954, Middle Temple

BRODIE GRAHAM PAUL

1 Dr Johnson's Bldgs
Ground Floor, Temple, London EC4Y 7AX,
Telephone: 0171 353 9328
Dr Johnson's Chambers
The Atrium Court Apex Plaza, Reading
RG1 1AX, Telephone: 01734 254221
Call date: July 1989, Middle Temple
Qualifications: [LLB (Lond)]

BRODIE STANLEY ERIC QC (1975)

2 Hare Court
Ground Floor, Temple, London EC4Y 7BH,
Telephone: 0171 583 1770
E-mail: 2_Hare_Court@link.org
Call date: Feb 1954, Inner Temple
Qualifications: [MA (Oxon)]

BRODRICK WILLIAM HENRY

New Court Chambers
3 Broad Chare, Newcastle Upon Tyne
NE1 3DQ, Telephone: 0191 232 1980
Call date: Oct 1991, Gray's Inn
Qualifications: [BA, M Th]

BRODY MISS KAREN RACHEL

Deans Court Chambers
Cumberland House Crown Square, Manchester
M3 3HA, Telephone: 0161 834 4097
E-mail: deanscourt@compuserve.com
Deans Court Chambers
41-43 Market Place, Preston PR1 1AH,
Telephone: 01772 555163
E-mail: deanscourt@compuserve.com
Call date: Nov 1986, Gray's Inn
Qualifications: [LLB (Notts)]

BRODY SAUL AMOS

18 St John Street
Manchester M3 4EA,
Telephone: 0161 278 1800
Call date: Oct 1996, Inner Temple
Qualifications: [LLB (Leeds)]

BROGAN MICHAEL SHAUN

Manchester House Chambers
18-22 Bridge Street, Manchester M3 3BZ,
Telephone: 0161 834 7007
Call date: Oct 1990, Inner Temple
Qualifications: [LLB (Hons)]

BROMFIELD COLIN HUGH

1 Gray's Inn Square
Ground Floor, London WC1R 5AA,
Telephone: 0171 405 8946/7/8
Call date: Nov 1988, Gray's Inn
Qualifications: [LLB (Hons)]

BROMILOW DANIEL JOHN

11 Stone Bldgs
1st Floor, Lincoln's Inn, London WC2A 3TG,
Telephone: 0171 404 5055
E-mail: 9stoneb@compuserve.com
Call date: Nov 1996, Gray's Inn
Qualifications: [BA (Cantab)]

BROMILOW RICHARD BRUCE DAVIES

St John's Chambers
Small Street, Bristol BS1 1DW,
Telephone: 0117 9213456/298514
E-mail: clerks@stjohns.uk.com
Call date: July 1977, Gray's Inn
Assistant Recorder
Qualifications: [LLB]

BROMLEY-DAVENPORT JOHN

Deans Court Chambers
Cumberland House Crown Square, Manchester
M3 3HA, Telephone: 0161 834 4097
E-mail: deanscourt@compuserve.com
Deans Court Chambers
41-43 Market Place, Preston PR1 1AH,
Telephone: 01772 555163
E-mail: deanscourt@compuserve.com
Call date: Feb 1972, Gray's Inn
Recorder

BROMLEY-MARTIN MICHAEL GRANVILLE

3 Raymond Buildings
Gray's Inn, London WC1R 5BH,
Telephone: 0171 831 3833
E-mail: chambers@threeraymond.demon.co.uk
Call date: Nov 1979, Gray's Inn
Qualifications: [BSc (Soton)]

D

BROMLEY-MARTIN MISS TANIA CATHERINE

3 Raymond Buildings
Gray's Inn, London WC1R 5BH,
Telephone: 0171 831 3833
E-mail: chambers@threeraymond.demon.co.uk
Call date: July 1983, Gray's Inn
Qualifications: [BA]

BROMPTON MICHAEL JOHN

New Court Chambers
5 Verulam Buildings, Gray's Inn, London
WC1R 5LY, Telephone: 0171 831 9500
E-mail: mail@newcourtchambers.com
Call date: Nov 1973, Middle Temple
Qualifications: [BA (Sussex)]

BROOK DAVID LESLIE

Plowden Bldgs
2nd Floor, Temple, London EC4Y 9BU,
Telephone: 0171 583 0808
E-mail: bar@plowdenbuildings.co.uk
Call date: July 1988, Inner Temple
Qualifications: [BA (Lond), Dip Law (City)]

BROOK IAN STUART

Hardwicke Building
New Square, Lincoln's Inn, London
WC2A 3SB, Telephone: 0171 242 2523
E-mail: clerks@hardwicke.co.uk
Call date: July 1983, Lincoln's Inn
Qualifications: [BA (Law)(Hons)]

BROOK PAUL ANTONY

Broadway House Chambers
Broadway House 9 Bank Street, Bradford,
West Yorkshire BD1 1TW,
Telephone: 01274 722560
Call date: Nov 1986, Inner Temple
Qualifications: [LLB (Leeds)]

BROOK SMITH PHILIP ANDREW

Fountain Court
Temple, London EC4Y 9DH,
Telephone: 0171 583 3335
E-mail: chambers@fountaincourt.co.uk
Call date: July 1982, Middle Temple
Qualifications: [BSc, MSc]

BROOKE DAVID MICHAEL GRAHAM

11 King's Bench Walk
1st Floor, Temple, London EC4Y 7EQ,
Telephone: 0171 353 3337
3 Park Court
Leeds LS1 2QH, Telephone: 0113 297 1200
Call date: Nov 1990, Inner Temple
Qualifications: [BA (Dunelm), Dip Law (City)]

BROOKE MICHAEL ECCLES MACKLIN QC (1994)

2 Crown Office Row
2nd Floor, Temple, London EC4Y 7HJ,
Telephone: 0171 797 8000
Call date: Nov 1968, Gray's Inn
Assistant Recorder
Qualifications: [LLB (Edin)]

BROOKE-SMITH JOHN

East Anglian Chambers
Sanders House 52 North Hill, Colchester
CO1 1PY, Telephone: 01206 572756
East Anglian Chambers
Gresham House 5 Museum Street, Ipswich
IP1 1HQ, Telephone: 01473 214481
East Anglian Chambers
57 London Street, Norwich NR2 1HL,
Telephone: 01603 617351
Call date: July 1981, Gray's Inn
Qualifications: [LLB (Exon)]

BROOKES LINCOLN PAUL

Portsmouth Barristers'Chambers
Victory House 7 Bellevue Terrace,
Portsmouth, Hampshire PO5 3AT,
Telephone: 01705 831292
E-mail: clerks@portsmouthbar.com
Call date: Nov 1992, Inner Temple
Qualifications: [LLB (Hons)(Lond)]

BROOKS MISS ALISON LOUISE

Staple Inn Chambers
1st Floor 9 Staple Inn, Holborn, London
WC1V 7QH, Telephone: 0171 242 5240
E-mail: clerks@staple-inn.org
Call date: July 1989, Inner Temple
Qualifications: [LLB (Hons)]

BROOKS JOHN DYLAN

Pendragon Chambers
124 Walter Road, Swansea SA1 5RG,
Telephone: 01792 411188
Call date: Feb 1990, Gray's Inn
Qualifications: [LLB (Wales)]

BROOKS MS LOUISE MARIA DIANA

Cloisters
1st Floor, Temple, London EC4Y 7AA,
Telephone: 0171 827 4000
E-mail: clerks@cloisters.com
Call date: Nov 1994, Middle Temple
Qualifications: [BA (Hons)]

BROOKS MR PAUL ANTHONY

Doughty Street Chambers
11 Doughty Street, London WC1N 2PG,
Telephone: 0171 404 1313
E-mail: doughty_street@compuserve.com
Call date: July 1989, Middle Temple
Qualifications: [LLB]

BROOKS PETER ANTHONY CHRISTOPHER

9 Park Place
Cardiff CF1 3DP, Telephone: 01222 382731
Call date: July 1986, Gray's Inn
Qualifications: [LLB (L'pool)]

BROOME CHARLES EDWARD

Plowden Bldgs
2nd Floor, Temple, London EC4Y 9BU,
Telephone: 0171 583 0808
E-mail: bar@plowdenbuildings.co.uk
Call date: Nov 1996, Inner Temple
Qualifications: [BA (Oxon)]

BROTHERTON JOHN PAUL

New Court Chambers
Suite 200 Gazette Building, 168 Corporation
Street, Birmingham B4 6TZ,
Telephone: 0121 693 6656
Call date: Nov 1994, Lincoln's Inn
Qualifications: [BA (Hons)(Leeds)]

BROUGH ALASDAIR MATHESON

13 King's Bench Walk
1st Floor, Temple, London EC4Y 7EN,
Telephone: 0171 353 7204
E-mail: clerks@13kbw.law.co.uk
King's Bench Chambers
32 Beaumont Street, Oxford OX1 2NP,
Telephone: 01865 311066
E-mail: clerks@kbc-oxford.law.co.uk
Call date: July 1979, Gray's Inn
Qualifications: [MA (Cantab)]

BROUGHAM CHRISTOPHER JOHN QC (1988)

3/4 South Square
Gray's Inn, London WC1R 5HP,
Telephone: 0171 696 9900
E-mail: clerks@southsquare.com
Call date: Nov 1969, Inner Temple
Qualifications: [BA (Oxon)]

BROUNGER DAVID WILLIAM JOHN

Lamb Building
Ground Floor, Temple, London EC4Y 7AS,
Telephone: 0171 797 7788
E-mail: lamb.building@link.org
Call date: Nov 1990, Inner Temple
Qualifications: [LLB]

BROWN (GEOFFREY) CHARLES

39 Essex Street
London WC2R 3AT,
Telephone: 0171 583 1111
E-mail: clerks@39essex.co.uk
Call date: July 1976, Middle Temple
Qualifications: [MA (Oxon)]

BROWN MISS ALTHEA SONIA

Doughty Street Chambers
11 Doughty Street, London WC1N 2PG,
Telephone: 0171 404 1313
E-mail: doughty_street@compuserve.com
Call date: Feb 1995, Lincoln's Inn
Qualifications: [LLB (Hons)(Leic)]

BROWN MISS ANDREA MARIE

Staple Inn Chambers
1st Floor 9 Staple Inn, Holborn, London
WC1V 7QH, Telephone: 0171 242 5240
E-mail: clerks@staple-inn.org
Call date: Nov 1991, Lincoln's Inn
Qualifications: [LLB (Hons)]

BROWN ANDREW CHARLES

Queen's Chambers
5 John Dalton Street, Manchester M2 6ET,
Telephone: 0161 834 6875/4738
4 Camden Place
Preston PR1 3JL, Telephone: 01772 828300
Call date: Nov 1982, Gray's Inn
Qualifications: [BSc (Lond) DipL.]

BROWN ANTHONY JAMES

Broad Chare
33 Broad Chare, Newcastle Upon Tyne
NE1 3DQ, Telephone: 0191 232 0541
Call date: Nov 1990, Lincoln's Inn
Qualifications: [LLB (Hons)]

BROWN MISS CATHERINE ROBERTA

12 King's Bench Walk
Temple, London EC4Y 7EL,
Telephone: 0171 583 0811
E-mail: chambers@12kbw.co.uk
Call date: Oct 1990, Middle Temple
Qualifications: [BCom (B'ham), Dip Law]

BROWN MISS CLARE VICTORIA

2 Temple Gardens
Temple, London EC4Y 9AY,
Telephone: 0171 583 6041 (12 Lines)
Call date: Oct 1993, Middle Temple
Qualifications: [BA (Hons)]

BROWN DAMIAN ROBERT

Old Square Chambers
1 Verulam Buildings, Gray's Inn, London
WC1R 5LQ, Telephone: 0171 269 0300
Old Square Chambers
Hanover House, 47 Corn Street, Bristol
BS1 1HT, Telephone: 0117 927 7111
Call date: Feb 1989, Inner Temple
Qualifications: [BA (Lond)]

Fax: 0171 405 1387; DX: 1046 London

Types of work: Discrimination; Employment

Awards and memberships: Industrial Law
Society; Employment Law Bar Association;
Employment Lawyers Association

Other professional experience: Lecturer in
International Labour Law, King's College,
London (current)

Publications: *Tolley's Employment Law*
(Contributor) Looseleaf 1994 (1st edn) 1997
(14th update); *Employment Tribunal Practice
and Procedure*, 1987, 1994, 1995; *Employment
Precedents and Company Policy Documents*,
1996

Reported cases: *Port of London Authority v
Payne*, [1994] ICR 555, 1994. Trade Union
activities, dismissal, international law, human
rights.
Kwik Save v Greaves, The Times, 1998.
Pregnancy, European law.
Burrell v Safeways, [1997] ICR 523, 1997.
Redundancy, meaning of.
Cornwall Care v Brightman, The Times, 1995.
TUPE, variation of contract.
RJB Mining v NUM, [1997] IRLR 621, 1997.
Industrial action, balloting, injunctions.
Wise v USDAW, [1996] IRLR 609, 1996. Ballots,
union rules, injunctions.

BROWN DAVID CHARLES

Cathedral Chambers
Milburn House Dean Street, Newcastle Upon
Tyne NE1 1LE, Telephone: 0191 232 1311
Southsea Chambers
PO Box 148, Southsea, Portsmouth,
Hampshire PO5 2TU,
Telephone: 01705 291261
Call date: Feb 1993, Middle Temple
Qualifications: [B.Sc (Hons)]

BROWN EDWARD FRANCIS TREVENEN

Hollis Whiteman Chambers
3rd/4th Floor Queen Elizabeth Bldg, Temple,
London EC4Y 9BS, Telephone: 0171 583 5766
E-mail: hollis.whiteman@btinternet.com
Call date: July 1983, Gray's Inn
Qualifications: [LLB (Bucks)]

BROWN MISS EMMA KATE

6 Pump Court
Ground Floor, Temple, London EC4Y 7AR,
Telephone: 0171 583 6013/2510
Call date: Oct 1995, Middle Temple
Qualifications: [BA (Hons)]

BROWN FREDERICK HUGH

Regent Chambers
29 Regent Road, Hanley, Stoke On Trent
ST1 3BP, Telephone: 01782 286666
E-mail: regent@ftech.co.uk
Call date: Nov 1983, Middle Temple
Qualifications: [BSc (Eng), BA, AMIMechE]

BROWN GEOFFREY BARLOW

39 Essex Street
London WC2R 3AT,
Telephone: 0171 583 1111
E-mail: clerks@39essex.co.uk
Call date: July 1981, Inner Temple
Qualifications: [MA (Cantab)]

BROWN MS GRACE

1 Gray's Inn Square
Ground Floor, London WC1R 5AA,
Telephone: 0171 405 8946/7/8
Call date: Oct 1995, Inner Temple
Qualifications: [BA (Hons)(Lond), CPE (City)]

BROWN MISS HANNAH BEATRICE

5 Bell Yard
London WC2A 2JR, Telephone: 0171 333 8811
Call date: Oct 1992, Inner Temple
Qualifications: [BA (Cambs)]

BROWN MISS JAIN RUSKIN

Claremont Chambers
26 Waterloo Road, Wolverhampton WV1 4BL,
Telephone: 01902 426222
Call date: Oct 1994, Lincoln's Inn
Qualifications: [BSc (Hons)]

BROWN JAMES PATRICK

Pepys' Chambers
17 Fleet Street, London EC4Y 1AA,
Telephone: 0171 936 2710
Call date: Nov 1989, Gray's Inn
Qualifications: [LLB]

BROWN MISS JILLIAN CLARE

4 Brick Court
Ground Floor, Temple, London EC4Y 9AD,
Telephone: 0171 797 7766
E-mail: chambers@4brick.co.uk
Call date: Nov 1991, Middle Temple
Qualifications: [BA Hons (Oxon)]

BROWN MISS JOANNE

2 Gray's Inn Square Chambers
2nd Floor, Gray's Inn, London WC1R 5AA,
Telephone: 0171 242 0328/071 405 1317
E-mail: clerks@2gis.co.uk
Call date: Nov 1990, Inner Temple
Qualifications: [LLB (Brunel)]

BROWN MISS KATHRYN HELEN

Oxdale
2 Hoby Road, Ragdale, Melton Mowbray, Leics
LE14 3PE, Telephone: 01664 434787
Call date: July 1980, Inner Temple
Qualifications: [LLB (Leic)]

BROWN LAURENCE FREDERICK MARK

The Corn Exchange
5th Floor Fenwick Street, Liverpool L2 7QS,
Telephone: 0151 227 1081/5009
Call date: July 1975, Inner Temple
Assistant Recorder
Qualifications: [BA (Dunelm)]

BROWN MISS LINDA

Westminster Chambers
3 Crosshall Street, Liverpool L1 6DQ,
Telephone: 0151 236 4774
Call date: Nov 1983, Middle Temple
Qualifications: [LLB (Lond), A.C.I.Arb]

BROWN MISS MANDY JOANNE

18 St John Street
Manchester M3 4EA,
Telephone: 0161 278 1800
Call date: Feb 1987, Middle Temple
Qualifications: [LLB(Lanc)]

BROWN NICHOLAS ROBERT DELANO

2 Crown Office Row
2nd Floor, Temple, London EC4Y 7HJ,
Telephone: 0171 797 8000
Call date: Nov 1989, Lincoln's Inn
Qualifications: [BA (Cantab)]

BROWN PAUL MARTIN

4-5 Gray's Inn Square
Ground Floor, Gray's Inn, London WC1R 5AY,
Telephone: 0171 404 5252
E-mail: chambers@4-5graysinnsquare.co.uk
Call date: Nov 1991, Inner Temple
Qualifications: [LLB (Cant), PhD (Cambs)]

BROWN PHILIP STEPHEN

Mitre Court Chambers
3rd Floor, Temple, London EC4Y 7BP,
Telephone: 0171 353 9394
Call date: Oct 1991, Lincoln's Inn
Qualifications: [LLB (Hons) (Leeds)]

BROWN MISS REBECCA JANE

14 Gray's Inn Square
Gray's Inn, London WC1R 5JP,
Telephone: 0171 242 0858
E-mail: 100712.2134@compuserve.com
Call date: July 1989, Inner Temple
Qualifications: [BA (York), Dip Law (City)]

BROWN ROBERT ALAN

2 New Street
Leicester LE1 5NA, Telephone: 0116 2625906
Call date: Nov 1979, Inner Temple
Qualifications: [LLB (Lond)]

BROWN ROBERT CHARLES WARREN

55 Temple Chambers
Temple Avenue, London EC4Y 0HP,
Telephone: 0171 353 7400
Call date: Nov 1992, Lincoln's Inn
Qualifications: [BSc (Lond), Dip in Law]

BROWN ROBERT LORIMER

Francis Taylor Bldg
Ground Floor, Temple, London EC4Y 7BY,
Telephone: 0171 353 7768/7769/2711
Call date: July 1983, Gray's Inn
Qualifications: [LLB (Leic)]

BROWN ROGER CHARLES ARTHUR

Old Colony House
6 South King Street, Manchester M2 6DQ,
Telephone: 0161 834 4364
Call date: Nov 1976, Inner Temple
Qualifications: [LLB]

BROWN SIMON GIDEON JONATHAN

1 Temple Gardens
1st Floor, Temple, London EC4Y 9BB,
Telephone: 0171 353 0407/583 1315
E-mail: clerks@1templegardens.co.uk
Call date: July 1988, Gray's Inn
Qualifications: [LLB (Lond)]

BROWN SIMON STALEY QC (1995)

1 Paper Bldgs
Ground Floor, Temple, London EC4Y 7EP,
Telephone: 0171 583 7355
E-mail: clerks@1pb.co.uk
Call date: July 1976, Inner Temple
Qualifications: [MA (Cantab)]

BROWN MISS STEPHANIE AMANDA

5 Fountain Court
Steelhouse Lane, Birmingham B4 6DR,
Telephone: 0121 606 0500
Call date: July 1982, Lincoln's Inn
Qualifications: [LLB (Exon)]

BROWN STUART CHRISTOPHER QC (1991)

Park Lane Chambers
19 Westgate, Leeds LS1 2RD,
Telephone: 0113 2285000
3 Serjeants Inn
London EC4Y 1BQ,
Telephone: 0171 353 5537
E-mail: available upon request
Call date: July 1974, Inner Temple
Recorder
Qualifications: [BA, BCL (Oxon)]

BROWN MISS SUSAN MARGARET

9 King's Bench Walk
Ground Floor, Temple, London EC4Y 7DX,
Telephone: 0171 353 7202/3909
Call date: July 1989, Lincoln's Inn
Qualifications: [BSc, LLB (Lond)]

D

BROWN THOMAS CHRISTOPHER ELLIS

Fenners Chambers
3 Madingley Road, Cambridge CB3 OEE,
Telephone: 01223 368761
Fenners Chambers
8-12 Priestgate, Peterborough PE1 1JA,
Telephone: 01733 62030
Call date: Nov 1980, Gray's Inn
Qualifications: [MA (Cantab)]

BROWNBILL DAVID JOHN

8 Gray's Inn Square
Gray's Inn, London WC1R 5AZ,
Telephone: 0171 242 3529
Call date: July 1989, Gray's Inn
Qualifications: [LLB [Nott'm]]

BROWNE BENJAMIN JAMES QC (1996)

2 Temple Gardens
Temple, London EC4Y 9AY,
Telephone: 0171 583 6041 (12 Lines)
Call date: July 1976, Inner Temple
Assistant Recorder
Qualifications: [MA (Oxon)]

BROWNE DESMOND JOHN MICHAEL QC (1990)

5 Raymond Buildings
1st Floor, Gray's Inn, London WC1R 5BP,
Telephone: 0171 242 2902
Call date: Nov 1969, Gray's Inn
Recorder
Qualifications: [BA (Oxon)]

BROWNE DR GERALD ROBERT

Queen Elizabeth Bldg
Ground Floor, Temple, London EC4Y 9BS,
Telephone: 0171 353 7181 (12 Lines)
Call date: Nov 1995, Inner Temple
Qualifications: [MBChB (B'ham)]

BROWNE HAROLD GODFREE RODAN

1 Middle Temple Lane
Temple, London EC4Y 1LT,
Telephone: 0171 583 0659 (12 Lines)
Call date: Nov 1971, Gray's Inn
Qualifications: [LLB (Lond)]

BROWNE JAMES NICHOLAS QC (1995)

1 Serjeants' Inn
5th Floor Fleet Street, Temple, London
EC4Y 1LL, Telephone: 0171 415 6666
E-mail: no1serjeantsinn@btinternet.com
Call date: July 1971, Inner Temple
Recorder
Qualifications: [LLB (L'pool)]

BROWNE JAMES WILLIAM

Goldsworth Chambers
1st Floor 10-11 Gray's Inn Square, London
WC1R 5JD, Telephone: 0171 405 7117
Call date: Oct 1994, Middle Temple
Qualifications: [BA (Hons)(B'ham), M.Litt
(Oxon), Dip in Law (City)]

BROWNE MISS JULIE REBECCA

Goldsmith Building
1st Floor, Temple, London EC4Y 7BL,
Telephone: 0171 353 7881
E-mail: clerks@goldsmith-building.law.co.uk
Call date: Nov 1989, Middle Temple
Qualifications: [LLB (Leic)]

BROWNE LOUIS BARTHOLOMEW ANTHONY

India Buildings Chambers
Water Street, Liverpool L2 OXG,
Telephone: 0151 243 6000
Call date: Nov 1988, Lincoln's Inn
Qualifications: [LLB (Hons), BCL (Oxon)]

BROWNE SIMON PETER BUCHANAN

Farrar's Building
Temple, London EC4Y 7BD,
Telephone: 0171 583 9241
E-mail: chambers@farrarsbuilding.co.uk
Call date: Nov 1982, Middle Temple
Qualifications: [LLB (Hons)]

BROWNE-WILKINSON SIMON

Fountain Court
Temple, London EC4Y 9DH,
Telephone: 0171 583 3335
E-mail: chambers@fountaincourt.co.uk
Call date: Nov 1981, Lincoln's Inn
Qualifications: [BA (Oxon)]

BROWNLIE IAN QC (1979)

2 Hare Court
Ground Floor, Temple, London EC4Y 7BH,
Telephone: 0171 583 1770
E-mail: 2_Hare_Court@link.org
Call date: Feb 1958, Gray's Inn
Qualifications: [BA,DPhil,DCL (Oxon), FBA]

BROWNLOW MISS ANN ELISABETH

5 Paper Bldgs
Ground Floor, Temple, London EC4Y 7HB,
Telephone: 0171 583 9275/583 4555
E-mail: 5paper@link.org
Call date: July 1984, Inner Temple
Qualifications: [MA (Oxon)]

BRUCE ANDREW JONATHAN

3 Paper Bldgs
Ground Floor, Temple, London EC4Y 7EU,
Telephone: 0171 797 7000
E-mail: clerks@3pb.co.uk
Call date: Oct 1992, Middle Temple
Qualifications: [MA (Oxon)]

BRUCE DAVID LIVINGSTONE

24a St John Street
Manchester M3 4DF,
Telephone: 0161 833 9628
Call date: July 1982, Middle Temple
Qualifications: [LLB (Lond)]

BRUCE RICHARD HENDERSON

2 Dr Johnson's Building
Temple, London EC4Y 7AY,
Telephone: 0171 353 4716
12 Paxton Close
Kew Gardens, Richmond, Surrey TW9 2AW,
Telephone: 0181 940 5895
Call date: July 1974, Gray's Inn
Qualifications: [LLB (Bris), FCIArb]

BRUDENELL THOMAS MERVYN

Queen Elizabeth Bldg
2nd Floor, Temple, London EC4Y 9BS,
Telephone: 0171 797 7837
Call date: Nov 1977, Inner Temple

BRUNNEN DAVID MARK

Derby Square Chambers
Merchants Court, Derby Square, Liverpool
L2 1TS, Telephone: 0151 709 4222
Call date: July 1976, Middle Temple
Assistant Recorder
Qualifications: [MA (Oxon)]

BRUNNER ADRIAN JOHN NELSON QC (1994)

2 Harcourt Bldgs
Ground Floor/Left, Temple, London
EC4Y 9DB, Telephone: 0171 583 9020
E-mail: clerks@harcourt.co.uk
Stanbrook & Henderson
2 Harcourt Bldgs 2nd Floor, Temple, London
EC4Y 9DB, Telephone: 0171 353 0101
E-mail: clerks@harcourt.co.uk
Call date: July 1968, Inner Temple
Recorder

BRUNNER PETER ROLAND

Brick Court Chambers
15/19 Devereux Court, London WC2R 3JJ,
Telephone: 0171 583 0777
E-mail: (surname)@brickcourt.demon.co.uk
Call date: July 1971, Middle Temple
Qualifications: [BA, LLB (Cantab)]

BRUNT PHILIP EDWIN

Rowchester Chambers
4 Rowchester Court Whittall Street,
Birmingham B4 6DH,
Telephone: 0121 233 2327/2361951
Call date: Nov 1991, Lincoln's Inn
Qualifications: [BSc (Econ) (Hons), Dip Law]

BRUNTON SEAN ALEXANDER MCKAY

Pump Court Chambers
Upper Ground Floor 3 Pump Court, Temple,
London EC4Y 7AJ, Telephone: 0171 353 0711
Pump Court Chambers
31 Southgate Street, Winchester SO23 8EE,
Telephone: 01962 868161
Call date: Oct 1990, Middle Temple
Qualifications: [BA (Cantab)]

BRYAN MISS CARMEL MARY

Holborn Chambers
6 Gate Street, Lincoln's Inn Fields, London
WC2A 3HP, Telephone: 0171 242 6060
Call date: Nov 1993, Middle Temple
Qualifications: [LLB (Hons)(Lond)]

BRYAN MS DEBORAH

1 Pump Court
Lower Ground Floor, Temple, London
EC4Y 7AB, Telephone: 0171 583 2012/
353 4341
E-mail: (name) @1pumpcourt.co.uk
Call date: July 1987, Lincoln's Inn
Qualifications: [LLB]

BRYAN MISS HELEN WEBSTER

11 Bolt Court
London EC4A 3DQ,
Telephone: 0171 353 2300
E-mail: boltct11@aol.com
Redhill Chambers
Seloduct House 30 Station Road, Redhill
RH1 1NK, Telephone: 01737 780781
Call date: July 1985, Inner Temple
Qualifications: [BA (Columbia)]

BRYAN MRS JAYNE MARIE

Wilberforce Chambers
Bishop Lane, Hull HU1 1PA,
Telephone: 01482 323264
E-mail: clerks@hullbar.demon.co.uk
Call date: Feb 1994, Gray's Inn
Qualifications: [LLB]

BRYAN REX VICTOR

5 Pump Court
Ground Floor, Temple, London EC4Y 7AP,
Telephone: 0171 353 2532
E-mail: fivepump@netcomuk.co.uk
Call date: Nov 1971, Lincoln's Inn
Recorder
Qualifications: [MA (Oxon)]

BRYAN ROBERT JOHN

1 Paper Bldgs
1st Floor, Temple, London EC4Y 7EP,
Telephone: 0171 353 3728/4953
Call date: Oct 1992, Middle Temple
Qualifications: [LL.B (Hons)]

BRYAN SIMON JAMES

Essex Court Chambers
24 Lincoln's Inn Fields, London WC2A 3ED,
Telephone: 0171 813 8000
E-mail: clerksroom@essexcourt-chambers.co.uk
Call date: July 1988, Lincoln's Inn
Qualifications: [MA (Hons) (Cantab)]

BRYANT MISS CAROLINE

East Anglian Chambers
Gresham House 5 Museum Street, Ipswich
IP1 1HQ, Telephone: 01473 214481
East Anglian Chambers
57 London Street, Norwich NR2 1HL,
Telephone: 01603 617351
East Anglian Chambers
Sanders House 52 North Hill, Colchester
CO1 1PY, Telephone: 01206 572756
Call date: July 1976, Middle Temple
Qualifications: [LLB]

BRYANT MISS CERI JANE

Erskine Chambers
30 Lincoln's Inn Fields, Lincoln's Inn, London
WC2A 3PF, Telephone: 0171 242 5532
E-mail: Clerks@Erskine-Chambers.law.co.uk
Call date: July 1984, Lincoln's Inn
Qualifications: [MA, LLM (Cantab)]

BRYANT JOHN MALCOLM CORNELIUS

Barnard's Inn Chambers
6th Floor Halton House, 20-23 Holborn,
London EC1N 2JD, Telephone: 0171 242 8508
E-mail: clerks@barnards-inn-chambers.co.uk
Call date: Nov 1976, Inner Temple
Qualifications: [MA (Cantab)]

BRYANT MISS JUDITH ANNE

Wilberforce Chambers
8 New Square, Lincoln's Inn, London
WC2A 3QP, Telephone: 0171 306 0102
E-mail: chambers@wilberforce.co.uk
Call date: July 1987, Lincoln's Inn
Qualifications: [BA, LLM (Cantab)]

D

BRYANT KEITH

Devereux Chambers
Devereux Court, London WC2R 3JJ,
Telephone: 0171 353 7534
E-mail: elton@devchambers.co.uk
Call date: Oct 1991, Middle Temple
Qualifications: [BA Hons (Cantab), CPE, MA
(Cantab), Dip.Com Sci (Cantab)]

BRYANT-HERON MARK NICHOLAS

9-12 Bell Yard
London WC2A 2LF,
Telephone: 0171 400 1800
Call date: Nov 1986, Middle Temple
Qualifications: [MA(Cantab)]

BSIS MISS IBTIHAL ISMAIL

Phoenix Chambers
First Floor Gray's Inn Chambers, Gray's Inn,
London WC1R 5JA, Telephone: 0171 404 7888
Call date: Feb 1995, Gray's Inn
Qualifications: [LLB]

BUBB TIMOTHY MICHAEL ANTHONY

39 Park Square
Leeds LS1 2NU, Telephone: 0113 2456633
Call date: July 1970, Gray's Inn
Assistant Recorder
Qualifications: [LLB]

BUCHAN ANDREW

Cloisters
1st Floor, Temple, London EC4Y 7AA,
Telephone: 0171 827 4000
E-mail: clerks@cloisters.com
Call date: July 1981, Gray's Inn
Qualifications: [LLB (Leeds)]

BUCHAN JONATHAN MAXFIELD

15 Winckley Square
Preston PR1 3JJ, Telephone: 01772 252828
E-mail: clerks@winckleysq.demon.co.uk
Call date: Oct 1994, Middle Temple
Qualifications: [MA (Cantab), CPE]

BUCHANAN GRAHAM JAMES

65-67 King Street
Leicester LE1 6RP, Telephone: 0116 2547710
Call date: July 1971, Inner Temple
Qualifications: [LLB]

BUCHANAN JAMES IAN CHARLES

3 Temple Gardens
2nd Floor, Temple, London EC4Y 9AU,
Telephone: 0171 583 1155
Call date: Nov 1993, Gray's Inn
Qualifications: [BA (Nott'm)]

BUCHANAN MISS VIVIEN JEAN

King Charles House
Standard Hill, Nottingham NG1 6FX,
Telephone: 0115 9418851
E-mail: clerks@kch.co.uk
Call date: July 1981, Inner Temple
Qualifications: [LLB (Hons) (Soton)]

BUCK DR ANDREW THEODORE

Eldon Chambers
Fourth Floor 30/32 Fleet Street, London
EC4Y 1AA, Telephone: 0171 353 4636
Call date: Nov 1992, Inner Temple
Qualifications: [Bsc, PhD (Lond), Msc (Aston),
LLB]

BUCK JOHN

2 Dr Johnson's Building
Temple, London EC4Y 7AY,
Telephone: 0171 353 4716
Call date: Nov 1987, Gray's Inn
Qualifications: [BA, MA (Hons) (Oxon), Dip
Law]

BUCKETT EDWIN GORDON

9 Gough Square
London EC4A 3DE, Telephone: 0171 353 5371
Call date: July 1988, Inner Temple
Qualifications: [LLB (Hull)]

BUCKHAVEN MRS CHARLOTTE VANDERLIP

Plowden Bldgs
2nd Floor, Temple, London EC4Y 9BU,
Telephone: 0171 583 0808
E-mail: bar@plowdenbuildings.co.uk
Call date: July 1969, Middle Temple
Qualifications: [MA (St Andrews)]

BUCKHAVEN SIMON

1 Harcourt Bldgs
2nd Floor, Temple, London EC4Y 9DA,
Telephone: 0171 353 9421/9151
Call date: July 1970, Gray's Inn

BUCKINGHAM MRS KATHLEEN ROSEMARY BERNADETTE

30 Park Square
Leeds LS1 2PF, Telephone: 0113 2436388
Call date: July 1986, Middle Temple
Qualifications: [BA (Hons) (Leeds), Dip Law
(City), PhD]

BUCKINGHAM MISS SARAH-JAYNE

5 Essex Court
1st Floor, Temple, London EC4Y 9AH,
Telephone: 0171 410 2000
Call date: Oct 1991, Inner Temple
Qualifications: [LLB (Hons)]

BUCKLAND ROBERT JAMES

Iscoed Chambers
86 St Helen's Road, Swansea SA1 4BQ,
Telephone: 01792 652988/9/330
Call date: Oct 1991, Inner Temple
Qualifications: [BA (Dunelm)]

BUCKLE JONATHAN

Regency Chambers
18 Cowgate, Peterborough PE1 1NA,
Telephone: 01733 315215
Regency Chambers
Sheraton House, Castle Park, Cambridge
CB3 0AX, Telephone: 01223 301517
Call date: Nov 1990, Lincoln's Inn
Qualifications: [BA (Hons), Dip Law]

BUCKLEY BERNARD CHRISTOPHER

1 Paper Bldgs
1st Floor, Temple, London EC4Y 7EP,
Telephone: 0171 353 3728/4953
Call date: Feb 1970, Gray's Inn
Qualifications: [LLB (Lond), LLM (Cantab)]

BUCKLEY CHRISTOPHER JOHN

First National Building
2nd Floor 24 Fenwick Street, Liverpool
L2 7NE, Telephone: 0151 236 2098
Call date: Mar 1997, Gray's Inn
Qualifications: [BA (L'pool)]

BUCKLEY MISS GERARDINE MARIA

Stour Chambers
Barton Mill House Barton Mill Road,
Canterbury, Kent CT1 1BP,
Telephone: 01227 764899
E-mail: clerks@stourchambers.co.uk
Call date: Nov 1991, Gray's Inn
Qualifications: [BA (Kent)]

BUCKLEY PETER EVERED

Queen's Chambers
5 John Dalton Street, Manchester M2 6ET,
Telephone: 0161 834 6875/4738
4 Camden Place
Preston PR1 3JL, Telephone: 01772 828300
Call date: July 1972, Gray's Inn
Qualifications: [BA (Oxon)]

BUCKLEY PROFESSOR RICHARD ANTHONY

12 New Square
Ground Floor, Lincoln's Inn, London
WC2A 3SW, Telephone: 0171 419 1212
E-mail: 12newsquare@compuserve.com
Call date: Nov 1969, Lincoln's Inn
Qualifications: [MA, DPhil (Oxon)]

BUCKLEY-CLARKE MRS AMANDA VICTORIA

3 Paper Bldgs
1st Floor, Temple, London EC4Y 7EU,
Telephone: 0171 583 8055
E-mail: london@3paper.com
20 Lorne Park Road
Bournemouth BH1 1JN,
Telephone: 01202 292102 (5 Lines)
4 St Peter Street
Winchester SO23 8OW,
Telephone: 01962 868884
Call date: Oct 1991, Lincoln's Inn
Qualifications: [BA (Oxon)]

D

BUCKNALL MISS BELINDA QC (1988)

4 Essex Court
Temple, London EC4Y 9AJ,
Telephone: 0171 797 7970
E-mail: clerks@4essexcourt.law.co.uk
Call date: Nov 1974, Middle Temple
Recorder
Qualifications: [MA (Oxon)]

BUCKPITT MICHAEL DAVID

Francis Taylor Bldg
2nd Floor, Temple, London EC4Y 7BY,
Telephone: 0171 353 9942/3157
Call date: Feb 1988, Gray's Inn
Qualifications: [LLB]

BUDALY MISS SUSAN

One Garden Court
Ground Floor, Temple, London EC4Y 9BJ,
Telephone: 0171 797 7900
Call date: Oct 1994, Middle Temple
Qualifications: [LLB (Hons)]

BUDDEN MISS CAROLINE RACHEL

1 King's Bench Walk
2nd Floor, Temple, London EC4Y 7DB,
Telephone: 0171 936 1500
E-mail: ddear@1kbw.co.uk
Call date: Nov 1977, Inner Temple
Assistant Recorder
Qualifications: [LLB (Bris)]

BUDGEN NICHOLAS WILLIAM

5 Fountain Court
Steelhouse Lane, Birmingham B4 6DR,
Telephone: 0121 606 0500
Call date: Nov 1962, Gray's Inn
Qualifications: [MA (Cantab)]

BUDWORTH ADAM JOHN DUTTON

3 Hare Court
1st Floor, Temple, London EC4Y 7BJ,
Telephone: 0171 353 7561
Call date: Nov 1992, Inner Temple
Qualifications: [BA (Lond), Dip in Law]

BUEHRLEN MISS VERONIQUE EIRA

Fountain Court
Temple, London EC4Y 9DH,
Telephone: 0171 583 3335
E-mail: chambers@fountaincourt.co.uk
Call date: Oct 1991, Middle Temple
Qualifications: [MA Hons, Dip Law]

BUENO ANTONIO DE PADUA JOSE MARIA QC (1989)

5 Paper Bldgs
Ground Floor, Temple, London EC4Y 7HB,
Telephone: 0171 583 9275/583 4555
E-mail: 5paper@link.org
Call date: June 1964, Middle Temple
Recorder

BUGG IAN STEPHEN

Crown Office Row Chambers
Blenheim House 120 Church Street, Brighton,
Sussex BN1 1WH, Telephone: 01273 625625
Call date: Oct 1992, Middle Temple
Qualifications: [LL.B (Hons)]

BULL (DONALD) ROGER

1 Essex Court
1st Floor, Temple, London EC4Y 9AR,
Telephone: 0171 936 3030
E-mail: one.essex_court@virgin.net
Call date: July 1974, Middle Temple
Qualifications: [LLB (Lond)]

BULL GREGORY

33 Park Place
Cardiff CF1 3BA, Telephone: 01222 233313
Call date: July 1976, Inner Temple
Assistant Recorder
Qualifications: [LLB (B'ham)]

BULL SIMON KEITH

36 Bedford Row
London WC1R 4JH,
Telephone: 0171 421 8000
E-mail: 36bedfordrow@link.org
Call date: Feb 1984, Gray's Inn
Qualifications: [BA (Cantab), LLM (Cantab)]

BULLEN JAMES EDWARD

1 Paper Bldgs
1st Floor, Temple, London EC4Y 7EP,
Telephone: 0171 353 3728/4953
Call date: July 1966, Gray's Inn
Recorder
Qualifications: [LLB (Lond)]

BULLOCH MS ANNE

3 Pump Court
2nd Floor, Temple, London EC4Y 7AJ,
Telephone: 0171 353 1356 (3 Lines)
Call date: Nov 1989, Gray's Inn
Qualifications: [MA (Hons) (Cantab)]

BULLOCK ANDREW JOHN

169 Temple Chambers
Temple Avenue, London EC4Y 0DA,
Telephone: 0171 583 7644
Call date: May 1992, Lincoln's Inn
Qualifications: [LLB (Hons) (Manch)]

BULLOCK DAVID NEIL

1 Pump Court
Lower Ground Floor, Temple, London
EC4Y 7AB, Telephone: 0171 583 2012/
353 4341
E-mail: (name) @1pumpcourt.co.uk
Call date: Nov 1989, Middle Temple
Qualifications: [BA]

BULLOCK IAN DAVID

St John's Chambers
Small Street, Bristol BS1 1DW,
Telephone: 0117 9213456/298514
E-mail: clerks@stjohns.uk.com
Call date: Nov 1975, Inner Temple
Qualifications: [LLB]

BULLOCK MRS SALLY

7 New Square
Lincoln's Inn, London WC2A 3QS,
Telephone: 0171 430 1660
Call date: Oct 1995, Middle Temple
Qualifications: [CPE]

BUNDELL MISS KATHARINE MICHELLE

East Anglian Chambers
Gresham House 5 Museum Street, Ipswich
IP1 1HQ, Telephone: 01473 214481
East Anglian Chambers
57 London Street, Norwich NR2 1HL,
Telephone: 01603 617351
East Anglian Chambers
Sanders House 52 North Hill, Colchester
CO1 1PY, Telephone: 01206 572756
Call date: Oct 1991, Middle Temple
Qualifications: [MA (Hons)(Cantab)]

BUNDRED MISS GILLIAN SARAH

Oriel Chambers
14 Water Street, Liverpool L2 8TD,
Telephone: 0151 236 7191
E-mail: oriel_chambers@link.org
Call date: July 1982, Gray's Inn
Qualifications: [LLB (Lond)]

BURBIDGE JAMES MICHAEL

7 Fountain Court
Steelhouse Lane, Birmingham B4 6DR,
Telephone: 0121 236 8531
Call date: Nov 1979, Lincoln's Inn
Qualifications: [LLB (Leic)]

BURDEN EDWARD ANGUS

Priory Chambers
2 Fountain Court, Steelhouse Lane,
Birmingham B4 6DR,
Telephone: 0121 236 3882/1375
Call date: Nov 1994, Lincoln's Inn
Qualifications: [BA (Hons)(Exon)]

BURDEN MISS EMMA LOUISE VERENA

2 New Street
Leicester LE1 5NA, Telephone: 0116 2625906
Call date: Oct 1994, Lincoln's Inn
Qualifications: [LLB (Hons)(Newc)]

BURDEN MISS SUSAN JANE

6 Pump Court
Ground Floor, Temple, London EC4Y 7AR,
Telephone: 0171 583 6013/2510
Call date: July 1985, Inner Temple
Qualifications: [BA (Oxon)]

D

BURDON MICHAEL STEWART

St Paul's House
5th Floor 23 Park Square South, Leeds
LS1 2ND, Telephone: 0113 2455866
Call date: Nov 1993, Lincoln's Inn
Qualifications: [LLB (Hons)(Leeds)]

BURGESS DAVID CLIFFORD

4 Brick Court
Temple, London EC4Y 9AD,
Telephone: 0171 797 8910
Call date: July 1975, Lincoln's Inn
Qualifications: [LLB (Hons)]

BURGESS EDWARD NORMAN

St John's Chambers
Small Street, Bristol BS1 1DW,
Telephone: 0117 9213456/298514
E-mail: clerks@stjohns.uk.com
Call date: Nov 1993, Inner Temple
Qualifications: [BA (Hons)(Oxon), MA (Bris),
CPE (Bris)]

BURGESS MISS EMMA VICTORIA

Chichester Chambers
12 North Pallant, Chichester, West Sussex
PO19 1TQ, Telephone: 01243 784538
Call date: Feb 1995, Middle Temple
Qualifications: [LLB (Hons)(Bris)]

BURGESS JOHN EDWARD RAMSEY

1 High Pavement
Nottingham NG1 1HF,
Telephone: 0115 9418218
Call date: July 1978, Middle Temple
Assistant Recorder
Qualifications: [LLB (Exon)]

BURGESS ROY ANTHONY

2 South Avenue
Cleverley, Lancashire BFY5 1JY
Call date: Nov 1970, Lincoln's Inn
Qualifications: [LLB (Bris) M Phil, (Lond)]

BURGHER BENJIMIN GEORGE

9 King's Bench Walk
Ground Floor, Temple, London EC4Y 7DX,
Telephone: 0171 353 7202/3909
Call date: Nov 1995, Gray's Inn
Qualifications: [LLB (Manc)]

BURGIN MS CATHERINE ANN

4 Essex Court
Temple, London EC4Y 9AJ,
Telephone: 0171 797 7970
E-mail: clerks@4essexcourt.law.co.uk
Call date: Oct 1990, Gray's Inn
Qualifications: [LLB (Lond)]

BURKE BRENDAN EDWARD

Victoria Chambers
19 Castle Street, Liverpool L2 4SX,
Telephone: 0151 236 9402
E-mail: Fa45@rapid.co.uk
Call date: Oct 1995, Inner Temple
Qualifications: [MA (Cantab), CPE
(Northumbria)]

BURKE JEFFREY PETER QC (1984)

Devereux Chambers
Devereux Court, London WC2R 3JJ,
Telephone: 0171 353 7534
E-mail: elton@devchambers.co.uk
5 Fountain Court
Steelhouse Lane, Birmingham B4 6DR,
Telephone: 0121 606 0500
Call date: June 1964, Inner Temple
Recorder
Qualifications: [MA (Oxon)]

BURKE MICHAEL JOHN

33 Bedford Row
London WC1R 4JH,
Telephone: 0171 242 6476
Call date: Nov 1985, Gray's Inn
Qualifications: [LLB (L'pool)]

BURKE MISS PATRICIA ANN

Fountain Chambers
Cleveland Business Centre 1 Watson Street,
Middlesbrough TS1 2RQ,
Telephone: 01642 217037
Call date: Oct 1990, Gray's Inn
Qualifications: [LLB (Newc)]

BURKE TREVOR MICHAEL

10 King's Bench Walk
1st Floor, Temple, London EC4Y 7EB,
Telephone: 0171 353 2501
Call date: July 1981, Middle Temple
Qualifications: [BA]

BURKE-GAFFNEY MICHAEL ANTHONY BOWES QC (1977)

Lamb Chambers
Lamb Building, Temple, London EC4Y 7AS,
Telephone: 0171 797 8300
E-mail: lambchambers@link.org
Call date: June 1959, Gray's Inn

BURKE-GAFFNEY RUPERT DAVID CHARLES JOHN

1 Paper Bldgs
1st Floor, Temple, London EC4Y 7EP,
Telephone: 0171 353 3728/4953
Call date: Nov 1988, Gray's Inn
Qualifications: [BSc (Lond)]

BURKETT FRANCIS MARTIN THOMAS

Walnut House
63 St. David's Hill, Exeter, Devon EX4 4DW,
Telephone: 01392 279751
E-mail: 106627.2451@compuserve.com
Call date: Nov 1969, Inner Temple
Qualifications: [LLB (Exon)]

BURKILL GUY ALEXANDER

3 New Square
Lincoln's Inn, London WC2A 3RS,
Telephone: 0171 405 1111
Call date: Feb 1981, Middle Temple
Qualifications: [MA (Cantab)]

BURLES DAVID JOHN

Goldsmith Building
1st Floor, Temple, London EC4Y 7BL,
Telephone: 0171 353 7881
E-mail: clerks@goldsmith-building.law.co.uk
Call date: Nov 1984, Middle Temple
Qualifications: [LLB (Bris)]

BURN COLIN RICHARD

30 Park Square
Leeds LS1 2PF, Telephone: 0113 2436388
Call date: Nov 1985, Middle Temple
Qualifications: [LLB (Hons)]

BURN LINDSAY STUART

Queen Elizabeth Bldg
Ground Floor, Temple, London EC4Y 9BS,
Telephone: 0171 353 7181 (12 Lines)
Call date: July 1972, Middle Temple
Assistant Recorder
Qualifications: [LLB]

BURNET MISS CRESSIDA JOHANNA

Bridewell Chambers
2 Bridewell Place, London EC4V 6AP,
Telephone: 0171 797 8800
E-mail: clerks@bridewell.law.co.uk
Call date: Nov 1989, Middle Temple
Qualifications: [LLB]

BURNETT HAROLD WALLACE QC (1982)

4 Paper Bldgs
Ground Floor, Temple, London EC4Y 7EX,
Telephone: 0171 353 3366/583 7155
E-mail: clerks@4paperbuildings.com
Call date: Feb 1962, Gray's Inn
Recorder
Qualifications: [BA (Oxon)]

BURNETT IAN DUNCAN

1 Temple Gardens
1st Floor, Temple, London EC4Y 9BB,
Telephone: 0171 353 0407/583 1315
E-mail: clerks@1templegardens.co.uk
Call date: Nov 1980, Middle Temple
Qualifications: [MA (Oxon)]

BURNHAM MISS ULELE IMOINDA

Cloisters
1st Floor, Temple, London EC4Y 7AA,
Telephone: 0171 827 4000
E-mail: clerks@cloisters.com
Call date: Mar 1997, Inner Temple
Qualifications: [BA (Sussex), MPhil (Cantab), CPE (Sussex)]

BURNS ALEXANDER LAURENCE

New Court Chambers
3 Broad Chare, Newcastle Upon Tyne
NE1 3DQ, Telephone: 0191 232 1980
Call date: July 1988, Inner Temple
Qualifications: [LLB (Sheffield)]

D

D

BURNS ANDREW PHILIP

Devereux Chambers
Devereux Court, London WC2R 3JJ,
Telephone: 0171 353 7534
E-mail: elton@devchambers.co.uk
Call date: Oct 1993, Middle Temple
Qualifications: [BA (Hons)(Cantab)]

BURNS FRANCIS JOSEPH

Kenworthy's Buildings
83 Bridge Street, Manchester M3 2RF,
Telephone: 0161 832 4036/834 6954
Call date: May 1971, Gray's Inn
Qualifications: [LLB]

BURNS JEREMY STUART

17 Carlton Crescent
Southampton SO15 2XR,
Telephone: 01703 320320
E-mail: km@bar-17cc.demon.co.uk
Call date: Nov 1996, Lincoln's Inn
Qualifications: [BA (Cape Town), LLB (Natal),
LLM (Cantab)]

BURNS PETER RICHARD

Deans Court Chambers
Cumberland House Crown Square, Manchester
M3 3HA, Telephone: 0161 834 4097
E-mail: deanscourt@compuserve.com
Call date: Oct 1993, Gray's Inn
Qualifications: [BA]

BURNS RICHARD HARCOURT

24 The Ropewalk
Nottingham NG1 5EF,
Telephone: 0115 9472581
E-mail: clerk@ropewalk.co.uk
Call date: Nov 1967, Middle Temple
Recorder
Qualifications: [LLB]

BURNS MRS ROSEMARY ANNE MACMAHON

Maidstone Chambers
33 Earl Street, Maidstone, Kent ME14 1PF,
Telephone: 01622 688592
Call date: Nov 1978, Inner Temple

BURNS SIMON HAMER

Albion Chambers
Broad Street, Bristol BS1 1DR,
Telephone: 0117 9272144
Call date: Oct 1992, Middle Temple
Qualifications: [LL.B (Hons)]

BURNS MISS SUSAN LINDA

3 Serjeants Inn
London EC4Y 1BQ,
Telephone: 0171 353 5537
E-mail: available upon request
Call date: July 1979, Gray's Inn
Qualifications: [LLB (L'pool)]

BURNS TERENCE

22 Albion Place
Northampton NN1 1UD,
Telephone: 01604 36271
Call date: Oct 1990, Middle Temple
Qualifications: [BA (Hons)]

BURNTON STANLEY JEFFREY QC (1982)

1 Essex Court
Ground Floor, Temple, London EC4Y 9AR,
Telephone: 0171 583 2000
E-mail: clerks@oneessexcourt.co.uk
Call date: Feb 1965, Middle Temple
Assistant Recorder
Qualifications: [MA (Oxon)]

BURR ANDREW CHARLES

1 Atkin Building
Gray's Inn, London WC1R 5AT,
Telephone: 0171 404 0102
E-mail: clerks@atkin-chambers.co.uk
Call date: Nov 1981, Inner Temple
Qualifications: [BA (Cantab), ACIArb]

BURR MARTIN JOHN

Eldon Chambers
Fourth Floor 30/32 Fleet Street, London
EC4Y 1AA, Telephone: 0171 353 4636
7 New Square
Lincoln's Inn, London WC2A 3QS,
Telephone: 0171 430 1660
Call date: July 1978, Middle Temple
Qualifications: [MA (Oxon), Dip Comp, Phil,
ACIArb, TEP]

BURRELL FRANCIS GARY QC (1996)

Paradise Square Chambers
26 Paradise Square, Sheffield S1 2DE,
Telephone: 0114 2738951
9 Gough Square
London EC4A 3DE, Telephone: 0171 353 5371
Call date: July 1977, Inner Temple
Recorder
Qualifications: [LLB]

BURRELL SIMON WILLIAM

9 Old Square
Ground Floor, Lincoln's Inn, London
WC2A 3SR, Telephone: 0171 405 4682
E-mail: chambers@9oldsquare.co.uk
Call date: July 1988, Inner Temple
Qualifications: [MA (Oxon)]

BURRETT MRS CATHERINE

17 Carlton Crescent
Southampton SO15 2XR,
Telephone: 01703 320320
E-mail: km@bar-17cc.demon.co.uk
Call date: Oct 1992, Middle Temple
Qualifications: [LL.B (Hons, Lond)]

BURRINGTON RICHARD JAMES HENRY

7 Stone Bldgs
1st Floor, Lincoln's Inn, London WC2A 3SZ,
Telephone: 0171 242 0961
Call date: Nov 1993, Inner Temple
Qualifications: [BA ((Hons)(So'ton)]

BURROUGHS NIGEL ALFRED

11 Old Square
Ground Floor, Lincoln's Inn, London
WC2A 3TS, Telephone: 0171 430 0341
E-mail: clerks@11oldsquare.co.uk
Call date: Apr 1991, Middle Temple
Qualifications: [BA (Hons)]

BURROW JOHN RICHARD

Goldsmith Chambers
Ground Floor Goldsmith Building, Temple,
London EC4Y 7BL,
Telephone: 0171 353 6802/3/4/5
E-mail: celiamonksfield@btinternet.com
Call date: July 1980, Middle Temple
Qualifications: [BA (Essex)]

BURROWES PATRICK CHARLES HENRY

Albion Chambers
Broad Street, Bristol BS1 1DR,
Telephone: 0117 9272144
Call date: Nov 1988, Inner Temple
Qualifications: [LLB (Bris)]

BURROWS EUAN MACLEAN

2 Harcourt Bldgs
2nd Floor, Temple, London EC4Y 9DB,
Telephone: 0171 353 8415
E-mail: clerks@twoharcourtbldgs.demon.co.uk
Call date: Nov 1995, Middle Temple
Qualifications: [MA (Hons) (Cantab)]

BURROWS MICHAEL PETER

3 Fountain Court
Steelhouse Lane, Birmingham B4 6DR,
Telephone: 0121 236 5854
Call date: Nov 1979, Inner Temple
Qualifications: [BA (Cantab)]

BURROWS SIMON PAUL

15 Winckley Square
Preston PR1 3JJ, Telephone: 01772 252828
E-mail: clerks@winckleysq.demon.co.uk
Call date: Nov 1990, Inner Temple
Qualifications: [BA (Dunelm), Dip Law (City)]

BURTON CHARLES DOMINIC PAUL

4 Brick Court
Ground Floor, Temple, London EC4Y 9AD,
Telephone: 0171 797 7766
E-mail: chambers@4brick.co.uk
Call date: Nov 1983, Inner Temple
Qualifications: [BA (Lond)]

BURTON MRS FRANCES ROSEMARY

10 Old Square
Ground Floor, Lincoln's Inn, London
WC2A 3SU, Telephone: 0171 405 0758
Door Tenant
Call date: Nov 1970, Middle Temple
Qualifications: [LLB (Lond), LLM (Leic)]

D

D

BURTON FRANK

12 King's Bench Walk
Temple, London EC4Y 7EL,
Telephone: 0171 583 0811
E-mail: chambers@12kbw.co.uk
Call date: July 1982, Gray's Inn
Qualifications: [BA (Kent), PhD (Lond)]

BURTON MISS JANICE ELAINE

Eldon Chambers
Fourth Floor 30/32 Fleet Street, London
EC4Y 1AA, Telephone: 0171 353 4636
Call date: July 1991, Lincoln's Inn
Qualifications: [LLB (Hons)]

BURTON JOHN MALCOLM

Mitre Court Chambers
3rd Floor, Temple, London EC4Y 7BP,
Telephone: 0171 353 9394
Call date: July 1979, Inner Temple
Qualifications: [LLB (Lond) (Hons)]

BURTON MERVYN JOHN

4 Brick Court
Temple, London EC4Y 9AD,
Telephone: 0171 797 8910
Door Tenant
Call date: July 1973, Middle Temple
Qualifications: [BA (Hons)]

BURTON MICHAEL JOHN QC (1984)

Littleton Chambers
3 King's Bench Walk North, Temple, London
EC4Y 7HR, Telephone: 0171 797 8600
E-mail: littletonchambers@compuserve.com
Call date: Nov 1970, Gray's Inn
Recorder
Qualifications: [MA (Oxon)]

BURTON NICHOLAS ANTHONY

2 Mitre Ct Bldgs
2nd Floor, Temple, London EC4Y 7BX,
Telephone: 0171 583 1380
Call date: Nov 1979, Gray's Inn
Qualifications: [BA (Cantab)]

BURWIN MRS HEATHER REES

2 King's Bench Walk
Ground Floor, Temple, London EC4Y 7DE,
Telephone: 0171 353 1746
E-mail: 2kbw@atlas.co.uk
King's Bench Chambers
115 North Hill, Plymouth PL4 8JY,
Telephone: 01752 221551
Call date: July 1983, Inner Temple
Qualifications: [LLB Exon]

BURY MARK

Wilberforce Chambers
Bishop Lane, Hull HU1 1PA,
Telephone: 01482 323264
E-mail: clerks@hullbar.demon.co.uk
Call date: July 1986, Inner Temple
Qualifications: [LLB (Hull)]

BUSBY THOMAS ANDREW

1 Fountain Court
Steelhouse Lane, Birmingham B4 6DR,
Telephone: 0121 236 5721
Call date: July 1975, Lincoln's Inn
Qualifications: [LLB (Lond)]

BUSFIELD MISS KATHLEEN NANCY

5 New Square
1st Floor, Lincoln's Inn, London WC2A 3RJ,
Telephone: 0171 404 0404
E-mail: Chambers@FiveNewSquare.CityScape.co.ul
Call date: Feb 1963, Gray's Inn
Qualifications: [ACIS]

BUSH JOHN ANTHONY

Devon Chambers
3 St Andrew Street, Plymouth PL1 2AH,
Telephone: 01752 661659
Call date: Feb 1964, Gray's Inn
Qualifications: [BA (Oxon)]

BUSH KEITH

30 Park Place
Cardiff CF1 3BA, Telephone: 01222 398421
E-mail: 100757.1456@compuserve.com
Call date: July 1977, Gray's Inn
Recorder
Qualifications: [BSc, LLM(Lond) MICE,]

BUSHELL TERENCE JOHN

6 Fountain Court
Steelhouse Lane, Birmingham B4 6DR,
Telephone: 0121 233 3282
Call date: July 1982, Middle Temple
Qualifications: [BA]

BUSUTTIL GODWIN JOHN ANTOINE

5 Raymond Buildings
1st Floor, Gray's Inn, London WC1R 5BP,
Telephone: 0171 242 2902
Call date: Oct 1994, Lincoln's Inn
Qualifications: [MA; MPhil (Cantab), Dip in
Law (City)]

BUSWELL RICHARD THOMAS

Goldsmith Chambers
Ground Floor Goldsmith Building, Temple,
London EC4Y 7BL,
Telephone: 0171 353 6802/3/4/5
E-mail: celiamonksfield@btinternet.com
Call date: July 1985, Middle Temple
Qualifications: [LLB Lond]

BUTCHER CHRISTOPHER JOHN

7 King's Bench Walk
Ground Floor, Temple, London EC4Y 7DS,
Telephone: 0171 583 0404
Call date: July 1986, Gray's Inn
Qualifications: [MA(Oxon) Dip Law]

BUTCHER JOHN MARCUS

5 Essex Court
1st Floor, Temple, London EC4Y 9AH,
Telephone: 0171 410 2000
Trinity Chambers
140 New London Road, Chelmsford, Essex
CM2 0AW, Telephone: 01245 605040
Call date: July 1984, Inner Temple
Qualifications: [Dip Law]

BUTCHER RICHARD

1 Middle Temple Lane
Temple, London EC4Y 1LT,
Telephone: 0171 583 0659 (12 Lines)
Call date: Nov 1985, Gray's Inn
Qualifications: [LLB (Cardiff)]

BUTLER ANDREW

Francis Taylor Bldg
2nd Floor, Temple, London EC4Y 7BY,
Telephone: 0171 353 9942/3157
Call date: Nov 1993, Middle Temple

BUTLER MISS AZEB MAGUEDA

Chancery Chambers
1st Floor Offices 70/72 Chancery Lane,
London WC2A 1AB,
Telephone: 0171 405 6879/6870
Call date: July 1966, Lincoln's Inn
Qualifications: [MA, LLB (Hons)]

BUTLER CHRISTOPHER MICHAEL

St Mary's Chambers
50 High Pavement, Lace Market, Nottingham
NG1 1HW, Telephone: 0115 9503503
E-mail: clerks@smc.law.co.uk
Devereux Chambers
Devereux Court, London WC2R 3JJ,
Telephone: 0171 353 7534
E-mail: elton@devchambers.co.uk
Call date: July 1972, Inner Temple
Assistant Recorder
Qualifications: [LLB (Lond)]

BUTLER GERALD QC (1975)

1 Essex Court
Ground Floor, Temple, London EC4Y 9AR,
Telephone: 0171 583 2000
E-mail: clerks@oneessexcourt.co.uk
Call date: Oct 1955, Middle Temple

BUTLER MISS JOAN

9 Bedford Row
London WC1R 4AZ,
Telephone: 0171 242 3555
E-mail: clerks@9br.co.uk
Call date: July 1977, Inner Temple
Recorder
Qualifications: [BA (Hons)]

BUTLER JONATHAN CHARLES

India Buildings Chambers
Water Street, Liverpool L2 OXG,
Telephone: 0151 243 6000
Call date: Oct 1992, Gray's Inn
Qualifications: [BA (Hons)(Lond), MA, MED]

BUTLER MISS JUDITH JANE SCOTT

6 Pump Court
1st Floor, Temple, London EC4Y 7AR,
Telephone: 0171 797 8400
E-mail: sa_hockman_qc@link.org
6-8 Mill Street
Maidstone, Kent ME15 6XH,
Telephone: 01622 688094
Call date: Oct 1993, Middle Temple
Qualifications: [BA (Hons)(Lond)]

BUTLER PHILIP ANDREW

Deans Court Chambers
Cumberland House Crown Square, Manchester
M3 3HA, Telephone: 0161 834 4097
E-mail: deanscourt@compuserve.com
Deans Court Chambers
41-43 Market Place, Preston PR1 1AH,
Telephone: 01772 555163
E-mail: deanscourt@compuserve.com
Goldsmith Chambers
Ground Floor Goldsmith Building, Temple,
London EC4Y 7BL,
Telephone: 0171 353 6802/3/4/5
E-mail: celiamonksfield@btinternet.com
Call date: July 1979, Middle Temple
Qualifications: [LLB, LLM (Manch)]

BUTLER RUPERT JAMES

29 Bedford Row Chambers
London WC1R 4HE,
Telephone: 0171 831 2626
Call date: July 1988, Middle Temple
Qualifications: [LLB (Hons) (Manch)]

BUTLER SIMON DAVID

10 King's Bench Walk
Ground Floor, Temple, London EC4Y 7EB,
Telephone: 0171 353 7742
E-mail: 10kbw@lineone.net
Call date: Oct 1996, Inner Temple
Qualifications: [LLB (Westminster)]

BUTT MISS ALIYA

Forest House Chambers
15 Granville Road, Walthamstow, London
E17 9BS, Telephone: 0181 925 2240
Call date: Oct 1994, Gray's Inn
Qualifications: [LLB]

BUTT MICHAEL ROBERT

Pump Court Chambers
Upper Ground Floor 3 Pump Court, Temple,
London EC4Y 7AJ, Telephone: 0171 353 0711
Pump Court Chambers
31 Southgate Street, Winchester SO23 8EE,
Telephone: 01962 868161
Call date: Nov 1974, Middle Temple
Qualifications: [LLB (Lond)]

BUTT MISS ROMASA

Goldsworth Chambers
1st Floor 10-11 Gray's Inn Square, London
WC1R 5JD, Telephone: 0171 405 7117
Call date: Nov 1985, Lincoln's Inn
Qualifications: [BA (Hons)]

BUTTERFIELD JOHN ARTHUR

3 Fountain Court
Steelhouse Lane, Birmingham B4 6DR,
Telephone: 0121 236 5854
Call date: Oct 1995, Lincoln's Inn
Qualifications: [LLB (Hons)(L'pool)]

BUTTERS JAMES SEBASTIAN

Fountain Court
Temple, London EC4Y 9DH,
Telephone: 0171 583 3335
E-mail: chambers@fountaincourt.co.uk
Call date: July 1994, Lincoln's Inn
Qualifications: [BA (Oxon), LLM (Florence),
LLM (Cantab)]

BUTTERWORTH MARTIN FRANK

Coleridge Chambers
Citadel 190 Corporation Street, Birmingham
B4 6QD, Telephone: 0121 233 3303
Call date: July 1985, Lincoln's Inn
Qualifications: [BA (Business Law)]

BUTTERWORTH PAUL ANTHONY

Octagon House
19 Colegate, Norwich NR3 1AT,
Telephone: 01603 623186
E-mail: octagon@netmatters.co.uk
Call date: July 1982, Middle Temple
Qualifications: [BA (Lond)]

D

BUTTIMORE GABRIEL

11 Old Square
Ground Floor, Lincoln's Inn, London
WC2A 3TS, Telephone: 0171 242 5022/
405 1074
Call date: Feb 1993, Gray's Inn
Qualifications: [LLB (Anglia)]

BUTTON RICHARD JAMES

Guildford Chambers
Stoke House Leapale Lane, Guildford, Surrey
GU1 4LY, Telephone: 01483 539131
E-mail: guildford.barristers@btinternet.com
Call date: Oct 1993, Gray's Inn
Qualifications: [LLB]

BUXTON MISS SARAH RUTH

1 Fountain Court
Steelhouse Lane, Birmingham B4 6DR,
Telephone: 0121 236 5721
Call date: July 1988, Inner Temple
Qualifications: [LLB (Sheffield)]

BUXTON THOMAS JUSTIN

2 Dr Johnson's Building
Temple, London EC4Y 7AY,
Telephone: 0171 353 4716
Call date: July 1983, Gray's Inn
Qualifications: [LLB (Nottm)]

BYERS THE HON CHARLES WILLIAM

23 Essex Street
London WC2R 3AS,
Telephone: 0171 413 0353/353 3533
E-mail: clerks@essexstreet23.demon.co.uk
Call date: Nov 1973, Gray's Inn
Recorder

BYRD MICHAEL

Rosemont Chambers
26 Rosemont Court Rosemont Road, London
W3 9LS, Telephone: 0181 992 1100
Call date: July 1952, Middle Temple
Qualifications: [MA (Oxon), LLB Hons (Lond)]

BYRNE GARRETT THOMAS

23 Essex Street
London WC2R 3AS,
Telephone: 0171 413 0353/353 3533
E-mail: clerks@essexstreet23.demon.co.uk
Call date: Nov 1986, Gray's Inn
Qualifications: [LLB]

BYRNE JAMES PATRICK

Derby Square Chambers
Merchants Court, Derby Square, Liverpool
L2 1TS, Telephone: 0151 709 4222
Call date: July 1983, Gray's Inn
Qualifications: [LLB (Hons L'Pool)]

BYRNE MICHAEL DAVID

India Buildings Chambers
Water Street, Liverpool L2 OXG,
Telephone: 0151 243 6000
Call date: July 1971, Gray's Inn
Recorder
Qualifications: [BA, LLB]

BYRNES MISS AISLING ALICE ELIZABETH

3 Gray's Inn Square
Ground Floor, London WC1R 5AH,
Telephone: 0171 520 5600
E-mail: gis3@btinternet.com
Call date: Oct 1994, Gray's Inn
Qualifications: [LLB]

CADDICK NICHOLAS DAVID

5 New Square
1st Floor, Lincoln's Inn, London WC2A 3RJ,
Telephone: 0171 404 0404
E-mail: Chambers@FiveNewSquare.CityScape.co.uk
Octagon House
19 Colegate, Norwich NR3 1AT,
Telephone: 01603 623186
E-mail: octagon@netmatters.co.uk
Door Tenant
Call date: Nov 1986, Middle Temple
Qualifications: [MA, BCL (Oxon)]

CADDLE MISS SHERRIE LORETTA

Furnival Chambers
32 Furnival Street, London EC4A 1JQ,
Telephone: 0171 405 3232
E-mail: clerks@furnivallaw.co.uk
Call date: Nov 1983, Lincoln's Inn
Qualifications: [BSc, Soc (Brunel)]

CADE MRS DIANA

3 Paper Bldgs
2nd Floor, Temple, London EC4Y 7EU,
Telephone: 0171 353 6208
Call date: Nov 1994, Inner Temple
Qualifications: [LLB (Anglia), LLM (Essex)]

CADIN DAVID MICHAEL

King's Bench Chambers
115 North Hill, Plymouth PL4 8JY,
Telephone: 01752 221551
2 King's Bench Walk
Ground Floor, Temple, London EC4Y 7DE,
Telephone: 0171 353 1746
E-mail: 2kbw@atlas.co.uk
Call date: Oct 1990, Middle Temple
Qualifications: [LLB (Exon)]

CADNEY PAUL DAVID

All Saints Chambers
9/11 Broad Street, Bristol BS1 2HP,
Telephone: 0117 921 1966
Call date: July 1984, Inner Temple
Qualifications: [BA (Bristol), Dip La]

CADWALADR STEPHEN KENNETH

6 Fountain Court
Steelhouse Lane, Birmingham B4 6DR,
Telephone: 0121 233 3282
Call date: July 1992, Middle Temple

CADWALLADER NEIL ANTHONY

Exchange Chambers
Pearl Assurance House Derby Square,
Liverpool L2 9XX, Telephone: 0151 236 7747/
0458
E-mail: exchangechambers@btinternet.com
5 Stone Buildings
Lincoln's Inn, London WC2A 3XT,
Telephone: 0171 242 6201
E-mail: clerks@5-stonebuildings.law.co.uk
Door Tenant
Call date: July 1984, Inner Temple
Qualifications: [MA (Cantab)]

CADWALLADER PETER

9 St John Street
Manchester M3 4DN,
Telephone: 0161 955 9000
E-mail: ninesjs@gconnect.com
Call date: July 1973, Gray's Inn
Qualifications: [LLB (Lond)]

CAFFERKEY MISS ANNETTE MARIE

Enfield Chambers
36-38 London Road, Enfield, Middlesex
EN2 6DT, Telephone: 0181 364 5627
E-mail: Enfieldchambers@compuserve.com
Call date: Nov 1994, Inner Temple
Qualifications: [LLB (Hons)]

CAHILL PATRICK JOHN

2 Paper Bldgs
1st Floor, Temple, London EC4Y 7ET,
Telephone: 0171 936 2611 (10 Lines)
E-mail: clerks@2pbbarristers.co.uk
Call date: July 1979, Lincoln's Inn
Qualifications: [BL (Dublin)]

CAHILL PAUL JEREMY

5 Fountain Court
Steelhouse Lane, Birmingham B4 6DR,
Telephone: 0121 606 0500
2 Mitre Ct Bldgs
2nd Floor, Temple, London EC4Y 7BX,
Telephone: 0171 583 1380
Call date: July 1975, Middle Temple
Qualifications: [LLB (L'pool)]

CAHILL MRS SALLY ELIZABETH MARY

Park Lane Chambers
19 Westgate, Leeds LS1 2RD,
Telephone: 0113 2285000
Call date: July 1978, Gray's Inn
Qualifications: [LLB (Leeds)]

CAINS MS LINDA HILARY

37 Park Square
Leeds LS1 2NY, Telephone: 0113 2439422
Call date: Oct 1990, Middle Temple
Qualifications: [BA (Leeds)]

CAIRNES SIMON PAUL STEVEN

3 Paper Bldgs
1st Floor, Temple, London EC4Y 7EU,
Telephone: 0171 583 8055
E-mail: london@3paper.com
20 Lorne Park Road
Bournemouth BH1 1JN,
Telephone: 01202 292102 (5 Lines)
4 St Peter Street
Winchester SO23 8OW,
Telephone: 01962 868884
Call date: Nov 1980, Gray's Inn
Qualifications: [LLB (Wales)]

CAKEBREAD STUART ALAN CHARLES

Francis Taylor Bldg
2nd Floor, Temple, London EC4Y 7BY,
Telephone: 0171 353 9942/3157
Call date: Nov 1978, Middle Temple
Qualifications: [BA (Exon)]

CALA DR GUISEPPE

New Court
Temple, London EC4Y 9BE,
Telephone: 0171 583 5123/0171 583 0510
Call date: Jan 1971, Inner Temple
Qualifications: [Doctor at Law]

CALCUTT SIR DAVID CHARLES QC (1972)

35 Essex Street
Temple, London WC2R 3AR,
Telephone: 0171 353 6381
Call date: June 1955, Middle Temple
Qualifications: [MA, LLB, MusB (Canta]

CALDECOTT ANDREW HILARY QC (1994)

1 Brick Court
1st Floor, Temple, London EC4Y 9BY,
Telephone: 0171 353 8845
E-mail: clerks@1brickcourt.co.uk
Call date: July 1975, Inner Temple
Qualifications: [BA (Oxon)]

CALDER MISS RENEE JOYCE

3 Pump Court
2nd Floor, Temple, London EC4Y 7AJ,
Telephone: 0171 353 1356 (3 Lines)
Call date: Nov 1978, Lincoln's Inn
Qualifications: [BA Hons (Leeds)]

CALDERWOOD MISS PATRICIA JAYNE

3 Fountain Court
Steelhouse Lane, Birmingham B4 6DR,
Telephone: 0121 236 5854
Call date: Apr 1964, Gray's Inn
Qualifications: [BA (Oxon)]

CALDIN PETER GILES

4 Essex Court
Temple, London EC4Y 9AJ,
Telephone: 0171 797 7970
E-mail: clerks@4essexcourt.law.co.uk
Call date: Nov 1974, Middle Temple
Qualifications: [LLB]

CALDWELL MRS JENNIFER JOAN

18 St John Street
Manchester M3 4EA,
Telephone: 0161 278 1800
Call date: Nov 1973, Middle Temple
Qualifications: [LLB (Manch)]

CALLAN DAVID ST CLAIR

New Court Chambers
3 Broad Chare, Newcastle Upon Tyne
NE1 3DQ, Telephone: 0191 232 1980
Call date: July 1979, Middle Temple
Qualifications: [MA]

CALLAWAY ANTHONY LEONARD

17 Bedford Row
London WC1R 4EB,
Telephone: 0171 831 7314
E-mail: IBoard7314@AOL.com
Call date: Nov 1978, Middle Temple
Qualifications: [BA (Hons), MA]

CALLERY MARTIN

Cobden House Chambers
19 Quay Street, Manchester M3 3HN,
Telephone: 0161 833 6000
E-mail: clerks@cobden.co.uk
Call date: Mar 1997, Middle Temple
Qualifications: [LLB (Hons)(Wales)]

CALLMAN JEREMY DAVID

10 Old Square
Ground Floor, Lincoln's Inn, London
WC2A 3SU, Telephone: 0171 405 0758
Call date: Oct 1991, Middle Temple
Qualifications: [MA (Hons) (Cantab)]

CALLMAN MISS TANYA SARA

2 King's Bench Walk
1st Floor, Temple, London EC4Y 7DE,
Telephone: 0171 353 9276
Call date: Oct 1993, Middle Temple
Qualifications: [BA (Hons)(Cantab)]

CALVER NEIL RICHARD

Brick Court Chambers
15/19 Devereux Court, London WC2R 3JJ,
Telephone: 0171 583 0777
E-mail: (surname)@brickcourt.demon.co.uk
Call date: Nov 1987, Gray's Inn
Qualifications: [MA (Cantab)]

CALVERT DAVID EDWARD

St James's Chambers
68 Quay Street, Manchester M3 3EJ,
Telephone: 0161 834 7000
E-mail: 106241.2625@compuserve.com
Call date: Nov 1995, Inner Temple
Qualifications: [BA (Oxon)]

CALVERT PETER CHARLES

Goldsmith Building
1st Floor, Temple, London EC4Y 7BL,
Telephone: 0171 353 7881
E-mail: clerks@goldsmith-building.law.co.uk
Call date: July 1975, Middle Temple
Qualifications: [BA]

CALVERT-SMITH DAVID QC (1997)

Hollis Whiteman Chambers
3rd/4th Floor Queen Elizabeth Bldg, Temple,
London EC4Y 9BS, Telephone: 0171 583 5766
E-mail: hollis.whiteman@btinternet.com
Call date: Nov 1969, Middle Temple
Recorder
Qualifications: [MA (Cantab)]

CALWAY MARK EDWARD

Goldsmith Chambers
Ground Floor Goldsmith Building, Temple,
London EC4Y 7BL,
Telephone: 0171 353 6802/3/4/5
E-mail: celiamonksfield@btinternet.com
Call date: Feb 1989, Inner Temple
Qualifications: [BA (Kent)]

CAMERON ALLAN ALEXANDER

3 Raymond Buildings
Gray's Inn, London WC1R 5BH,
Telephone: 0171 831 3833
E-mail: chambers@threeraymond.demon.co.uk
Call date: Nov 1986, Inner Temple
Qualifications: [LLB (Bris)]

CAMERON MISS BARBARA ALEXANDER

2 Harcourt Bldgs
Ground Floor/Left, Temple, London
EC4Y 9DB, Telephone: 0171 583 9020
E-mail: clerks@harcourt.co.uk
Stanbrook & Henderson
2 Harcourt Bldgs 2nd Floor, Temple, London
EC4Y 9DB, Telephone: 0171 353 0101
E-mail: clerks@harcourt.co.uk
Call date: Nov 1979, Lincoln's Inn
Qualifications: [MA (Cantab)]

CAMERON JONATHAN JAMES O'GRADY

3 Verulam Buildings
London WC1R 5NT,
Telephone: 0171 831 8441
E-mail: clerks@3verulam.co.uk
Call date: Nov 1987, Inner Temple
Qualifications: [LLB (Lond) LLM, (Cantab)]

CAMERON KENNETH ANGUS

4 King's Bench Walk
Ground/First Floor, Temple, London
EC4Y 7DL, Telephone: 0171 822 8822
E-mail: 4kbw@barristersatlaw.com
King's Bench Chambers
Wellington House 175 Holdenhurst Road,
Bournemouth, Dorset BH8 8DQ,
Telephone: 01202 250025
Call date: Nov 1969, Middle Temple
Qualifications: [BA (Cantab)]

CAMERON NEIL ALEXANDER

Wilberforce Chambers
Bishop Lane, Hull HU1 1PA,
Telephone: 01482 323264
E-mail: clerks@hullbar.demon.co.uk
Call date: July 1984, Gray's Inn
Qualifications: [LLB (Leics)]

CAMERON NEIL ST CLAIR

1 Serjeants' Inn
4th Floor, Temple, London EC4Y 1NH,
Telephone: 0171 583 1355
E-mail: serjeants.inn@virgin.net
Call date: July 1982, Gray's Inn
Qualifications: [BA (Dunelm)]

CAMERON MISS SHEILA MORAG CLARK QC (1983)

2 Harcourt Bldgs
2nd Floor, Temple, London EC4Y 9DB,
Telephone: 0171 353 8415
E-mail: clerks@twoharcourtbldgs.demon.co.uk
Call date: July 1957, Middle Temple
Recorder
Qualifications: [MA (Oxon)]

CAMERON MISS VIVECA CECILE

Belmarsh Chambers
20 Warland Road, London SE18 2EU,
Telephone: 0181 316 7322
E-mail: belmarsh@dircon.co.uk
Call date: Feb 1987, Middle Temple
Qualifications: [LLB]

CAMMEGH JOHN STEPHEN

4 Brick Court
1st Floor, Temple, London EC4Y 9AD,
Telephone: 0171 583 8455
Call date: Nov 1987, Inner Temple
Qualifications: [LLB (London)]

CAMPBELL MISS ALEXIS ANNE

Hardwicke Building
New Square, Lincoln's Inn, London
WC2A 3SB, Telephone: 0171 242 2523
E-mail: clerks@hardwicke.co.uk
Call date: Nov 1990, Inner Temple
Qualifications: [LLB (Leeds)]

CAMPBELL ANDREW BRUCE

1 Middle Temple Lane
Temple, London EC4Y 1LT,
Telephone: 0171 583 0659 (12 Lines)
Call date: July 1972, Inner Temple
Qualifications: [MA (Oxon)]

CAMPBELL ANDREW NEVILLE QC (1994)

10 Park Square
Leeds LS1 2LH, Telephone: 0113 2455438
E-mail: chambers@bandit.legend.co.uk
Call date: Nov 1972, Middle Temple
Recorder
Qualifications: [BA]

CAMPBELL COLIN WILLIAM

2 Paper Bldgs
1st Floor, Temple, London EC4Y 7ET,
Telephone: 0171 936 2611 (10 Lines)
E-mail: clerks@2pbbarristers.co.uk
Call date: July 1979, Gray's Inn
Qualifications: [BA(Hons) (Kent)]

CAMPBELL DAVID

Bell Yard Chambers
116/118 Chancery Lane, London WC2A 1PP,
Telephone: 0171 306 9292
Call date: Nov 1992, Inner Temple
Qualifications: [LLB (Sheff)]

CAMPBELL MISS DIANE EVA

York Chambers
14 Toft Green, York YO1 1JT,
Telephone: 01904 620048
E-mail: yorkchambers.co.uk
Call date: Oct 1995, Gray's Inn
Qualifications: [LLB]

CAMPBELL DONALD

Library Chambers
Gray's Inn Chambers, Gray's Inn, London
WC1R 5JA, Telephone: 0171 404 6500
Phoenix Chambers
First Floor Gray's Inn Chambers, Gray's Inn,
London WC1R 5JA, Telephone: 0171 404 7888
Call date: Nov 1976, Inner Temple

CAMPBELL DOUGLAS JAMES

3 New Square
Lincoln's Inn, London WC2A 3RS,
Telephone: 0171 405 1111
Call date: Oct 1993, Inner Temple
Qualifications: [MA (Oxon), Dip Law (City)]

CAMPBELL MISS EMILY CHARLOTTE

Wilberforce Chambers
8 New Square, Lincoln's Inn, London
WC2A 3QP, Telephone: 0171 306 0102
E-mail: chambers@wilberforce.co.uk
Call date: Nov 1995, Lincoln's Inn
Qualifications: [MA (Oxon), BCL]

CAMPBELL GLENN

11 Old Square
Ground Floor, Lincoln's Inn, London
WC2A 3TS, Telephone: 0171 430 0341
E-mail: clerks@11oldsquare.co.uk
Call date: July 1985, Lincoln's Inn
Qualifications: [LLB (Manchester)]

CAMPBELL GRAHAM JOHN

24a St John Street
Manchester M3 4DF,
Telephone: 0161 833 9628
Call date: Nov 1982, Middle Temple
Qualifications: [BA]

CAMPBELL JOHN DAVID

40 King Street
Manchester M2 6BA,
Telephone: 0161 832 9082
E-mail: Kingst40@aol.com
Call date: Nov 1990, Lincoln's Inn
Qualifications: [LLB (Edin)]

CAMPBELL NICHOLAS CHARLES WILSON

11 King's Bench Walk
1st Floor, Temple, London EC4Y 7EQ,
Telephone: 0171 353 3337
3 Park Court
Leeds LS1 2QH, Telephone: 0113 297 1200
Call date: July 1978, Inner Temple
Qualifications: [BA (Cantab)]

CAMPBELL OLIVER EDWARD WILHELM

2 Harcourt Bldgs
Ground Floor/Left, Temple, London
EC4Y 9DB, Telephone: 0171 583 9020
E-mail: clerks@harcourt.co.uk
Call date: Oct 1992, Middle Temple
Qualifications: [MA (Hons)]

CAMPBELL MS RHONA LYNN

4 Fountain Court
Steelhouse Lane, Birmingham B4 6DR,
Telephone: 0121 236 3476
Call date: Oct 1993, Inner Temple
Qualifications: [BA (Dunelm)]

CAMPBELL ROBIN ALEXANDER

4-5 Gray's Inn Square
Ground Floor, Gray's Inn, London WC1R 5AY,
Telephone: 0171 404 5252
E-mail: chambers@4-5graysinnsquare.co.uk
Call date: Apr 1967, Middle Temple
Qualifications: [MA (Oxon)]

CAMPBELL STAFFORD GRAHAM

5 Pump Court
Ground Floor, Temple, London EC4Y 7AP,
Telephone: 0171 353 2532
E-mail: fivepump@netcomuk.co.uk
Call date: July 1979, Gray's Inn
Qualifications: [LLB (Lond)]

CAMPBELL STEPHEN GORDON

Priory Chambers
2 Fountain Court, Steelhouse Lane,
Birmingham B4 6DR,
Telephone: 0121 236 3882/1375
Call date: July 1982, Middle Temple
Qualifications: [LLB (L'pool)]

CAMPBELL MISS SUSAN CLAIRE

Southernhay Chambers
33 Southernhay East, Exeter EX1 1NX,
Telephone: 01392 255777
E-mail: southernhay.chambers@lineone.net
Call date: Nov 1986, Middle Temple
Qualifications: [MA (Cantab)]

CAMPBELL OF ALLOWAY LORD QC (1965)

2 King's Bench Walk
1st Floor, Temple, London EC4Y 7DE,
Telephone: 0171 353 9276
Call date: May 1939, Inner Temple
Qualifications: [MA (Cantab)]

CAMPBELL-BROWN MISS ANNE LOUISE

Bracton Chambers
95a Chancery Lane, London WC2A 1DT,
Telephone: 0171 242 4248
Call date: Nov 1993, Middle Temple
Qualifications: [BA (Hons)(York), MA (Lond),
Dip in Law (City)]

CAMPBELL-CLYNE CHRISTOPHER FRANCIS GEORGE

3 Hare Court
1st Floor, Temple, London EC4Y 7BJ,
Telephone: 0171 353 7561
Call date: Nov 1988, Middle Temple
Qualifications: [LLB Hons]

CAMPBELL-MOFFAT MRS AUDREY PATRICIA

1 High Pavement
Nottingham NG1 1HF,
Telephone: 0115 9418218
Call date: July 1987, Middle Temple
Qualifications: [LLM (London), LLB (Reading)]

CAMPBELL-TIECH ANDREW

3 Temple Gardens
Lower Ground Floor, Temple, London
EC4Y 9AU, Telephone: 0171 353 3102/5/9297
Call date: July 1978, Inner Temple

CANAVAN MISS SHEELAGH MARY

1 Crown Office Row
2nd Floor, Temple, London EC4Y 7HH,
Telephone: 0171 797 7111
Call date: July 1987, Lincoln's Inn
Qualifications: [LLB (Hons) (Lond)]

CANDLIN JAMES RICHARD

46/48 Essex Street
London WC2R 3GH,
Telephone: 0171 583 8899
Call date: Oct 1991, Lincoln's Inn
Qualifications: [BSc (Hons), Dip Law]

CANNAN JONATHAN MICHAEL

St James's Chambers
68 Quay Street, Manchester M3 3EJ,
Telephone: 0161 834 7000
E-mail: 106241.2625@compuserve.com
Broadway House Chambers
Broadway House 9 Bank Street, Bradford,
West Yorkshire BD1 1TW,
Telephone: 01274 722560
Door Tenant
Call date: Nov 1989, Gray's Inn
Qualifications: [LLB (Lond), ACA, ATII]

CANNON MARK RENNISON NORRIS

2 Crown Office Row
2nd Floor, Temple, London EC4Y 7HJ,
Telephone: 0171 797 8000
Call date: July 1985, Middle Temple
Qualifications: [BA(Oxon)]

CANT CHRISTOPHER IAN

11 Stone Bldgs
1st Floor, Lincoln's Inn, London WC2A 3TG,
Telephone: 0171 404 5055
E-mail: 9stoneb@compuserve.com
Call date: July 1973, Lincoln's Inn
Qualifications: [MA (Cantab)]

CAPE ROBERT PAUL

Milburn House Chambers
"A" Floor Milburn House, Dean Street,
Newcastle Upon Tyne NE1 1LE,
Telephone: 0191 230 5511
E-mail: milburnhousechambers@btinternet.com
Call date: Oct 1990, Middle Temple
Qualifications: [LLB]

CAPLAN JONATHAN MICHAEL QC (1991)

5 Paper Bldgs
1st Floor, Temple, London EC4Y 7HB,
Telephone: 0171 583 6117
E-mail: clerks@5-paperbuildings.law.co.uk
Call date: July 1973, Gray's Inn
Recorder
Qualifications: [MA (Cantab)]

CAPLAN LEE RICHARD

20 Britton Street
1st Floor, London EC1M 5NQ,
Telephone: 0171 608 3765
Call date: Nov 1994, Middle Temple
Qualifications: [LLB (Hons)]

CAPON PHILIP CHRISTOPHER WILLIAM

7 Fountain Court
Steelhouse Lane, Birmingham B4 6DR,
Telephone: 0121 236 8531
Call date: Oct 1990, Inner Temple
Qualifications: [LLB (B'ham)]

CAPSTICK TIMOTHY

6 Park Square
Leeds LS1 2LW, Telephone: 0113 2459763
E-mail: chambers@no6.co.uk
Call date: July 1986, Gray's Inn
Qualifications: [BA]

CARDEN NICHOLAS

1 Mitre Ct Bldgs
Ground Floor, Temple, London EC4Y 7BS,
Telephone: 0171 797 7070
Call date: July 1981, Gray's Inn
Qualifications: [LLB (Lond)]

CAREY GODFREY MOHUN CECIL QC (1991)

5 Paper Bldgs
1st Floor, Temple, London EC4Y 7HB,
Telephone: 0171 583 6117
E-mail: clerks@5-paperbuildings.law.co.uk
Call date: July 1969, Inner Temple
Recorder

CAREY JEREMY REYNOLDS PATRICK

Lamb Chambers
Lamb Building, Temple, London EC4Y 7AS,
Telephone: 0171 797 8300
E-mail: lambchambers@link.org
Call date: July 1974, Inner Temple
Assistant Recorder
Qualifications: [MA (Cantab)]

CAREY-HUGHES RICHARD JOHN

4 Brick Court
1st Floor, Temple, London EC4Y 9AD,
Telephone: 0171 583 8455
Call date: July 1977, Gray's Inn
Assistant Recorder

CARGILL-THOMPSON MISS PERDITA

Essex Court Chambers
24 Lincoln's Inn Fields, London WC2A 3ED,
Telephone: 0171 813 8000
E-mail: clerksroom@essexcourt-chambers.co.uk
Call date: Feb 1993, Middle Temple
Qualifications: [BA (Hons)(Oxon), LLM (Lond)]

CARLILE ALEXANDER CHARLES QC (1984)

9-12 Bell Yard
London WC2A 2LF,
Telephone: 0171 400 1800
Sedan House
Stanley Place, Chester CH1 2LU,
Telephone: 01244 320480/348282
Call date: July 1970, Gray's Inn
Recorder
Qualifications: [LLB (AKC)]

CARLING CHRISTOPHER JAMES

Old Square Chambers
1 Verulam Buildings, Gray's Inn, London
WC1R 5LQ, Telephone: 0171 831 0801
Old Square Chambers
Hanover House 47 Corn Street, Bristol
BS1 1HT, Telephone: 0117 9277111
Call date: Nov 1969, Lincoln's Inn
Qualifications: [MA (Cantab)]

CARLISLE HUGH BERNARD HARWOOD QC (1978)

1 Temple Gardens
1st Floor, Temple, London EC4Y 9BB,
Telephone: 0171 353 0407/583 1315
E-mail: clerks@1templegardens.co.uk
Call date: Feb 1961, Middle Temple
Recorder
Qualifications: [MA (Cantab)]

CARLISLE TIMOTHY ST JOHN OGILVIE

2 Field Court
Gray's Inn, London WC1R 5BB,
Telephone: 0171 405 6114
E-mail: fieldct2@netcomuk.co.uk.
Call date: Nov 1984, Gray's Inn

CARLISLE OF BUCKLOW THE RT HON LORD QC (1971)

Hollis Whiteman Chambers
3rd/4th Floor Queen Elizabeth Bldg, Temple,
London EC4Y 9BS, Telephone: 0171 583 5766
E-mail: hollis.whiteman@btinternet.com
18 St John Street
Manchester M3 4EA,
Telephone: 0161 278 1800
Door Tenant
Call date: Feb 1954, Gray's Inn
Recorder
Qualifications: [LLB, MA (Cantab)]

CARMAN GEORGE ALFRED QC (1971)

New Court Chambers
5 Verulam Buildings, Gray's Inn, London
WC1R 5LY, Telephone: 0171 831 9500
E-mail: mail@newcourtchambers.com
Call date: June 1953, Lincoln's Inn
Qualifications: [BA (Oxon)]

CARMICHAEL JOHN

Furnival Chambers
32 Furnival Street, London EC4A 1JQ,
Telephone: 0171 405 3232
E-mail: clerks@furnivallaw.co.uk
Call date: July 1984, Inner Temple
Qualifications: [BA (Leeds) Dip Law, (City)]

CARNE ROGER ENYS

4 Brick Court
1st Floor, Temple, London EC4Y 9AD,
Telephone: 0171 583 8455
All Saints Chambers
9/11 Broad Street, Bristol BS1 2HP,
Telephone: 0117 921 1966
Call date: Nov 1969, Inner Temple
Qualifications: [LLB (Lond)]

CARNE MS ROSALIND PATRICIA

1 Pump Court
Lower Ground Floor, Temple, London
EC4Y 7AB, Telephone: 0171 583 2012/
353 4341
E-mail: (name) @1pumpcourt.co.uk
Call date: Nov 1986, Inner Temple
Qualifications: [BA (Oxon)]

D

CARNES ANDREW JAMES

23 Essex Street
London WC2R 3AS,
Telephone: 0171 413 0353/353 3533
E-mail: clerks@essexstreet23.demon.co.uk
Call date: July 1984, Lincoln's Inn
Qualifications: [LLB (Leics)]

CARNEY ANDREW PATRICK

Martins Building
Water Street, Liverpool L2 3SP,
Telephone: 0151 236 5818/4919
Call date: Oct 1995, Inner Temple
Qualifications: [BA (Durham), MSc (Lond)]

CARNEY MISS CAROLINE MARY

Hollis Whiteman Chambers
3rd/4th Floor Queen Elizabeth Bldg, Temple,
London EC4Y 9BS, Telephone: 0171 583 5766
E-mail: hollis.whiteman@btinternet.com
Call date: Nov 1980, Middle Temple
Qualifications: [BA (Belfast)]

CARPENTER MISS JANE PATRICIA ANNE

Francis Taylor Bldg
2nd Floor, Temple, London EC4Y 7BY,
Telephone: 0171 353 9942/3157
Call date: Nov 1984, Inner Temple
Qualifications: [BSc Hons]

CARR BRUCE CONRAD

Devereux Chambers
Devereux Court, London WC2R 3JJ,
Telephone: 0171 353 7534
E-mail: elton@devchambers.co.uk
Call date: Nov 1986, Inner Temple
Qualifications: [BSc(Econ)(Lond)]

CARR CHRISTOPHER QC (1983)

1 Essex Court
Ground Floor, Temple, London EC4Y 9AR,
Telephone: 0171 583 2000
E-mail: clerks@oneessexcourt.co.uk
Call date: Nov 1968, Lincoln's Inn
Qualifications: [LLB]

CARR HENRY JAMES

11 South Square
2nd Floor, Gray's Inn, London WC1R 5EU,
Telephone: 0171 405 1222
Call date: May 1982, Gray's Inn
Qualifications: [BA (Oxon) LLM, (British Columbia)]

CARR JONATHAN OLSON

New Court Chambers
3 Broad Chare, Newcastle Upon Tyne
NE1 3DQ, Telephone: 0191 232 1980
Call date: Nov 1990, Middle Temple
Qualifications: [LLB (Newc)]

CARR PETER

St Ive's Chambers
9 Fountain Ct, Birmingham B4 6DR,
Telephone: 0121 236 0863/0929
Call date: Nov 1976, Inner Temple
Qualifications: [LLB (Birm)]

CARR SIMON ANDREW

9 Gough Square
London EC4A 3DE, Telephone: 0171 353 5371
Call date: July 1984, Inner Temple
Qualifications: [LLB (Soton)]

CARR MISS SUE LASCELLES

2 Crown Office Row
2nd Floor, Temple, London EC4Y 7HJ,
Telephone: 0171 797 8000
Call date: July 1987, Inner Temple
Qualifications: [MA (Cantab)]

CARRINGTON MISS GILLIAN ELIZABETH

2-3 Gray's Inn Square
Gray's Inn, London WC1R 5JH,
Telephone: 0171 242 4986
E-mail: chambers@2-3graysinnsquare.co.uk
Call date: Nov 1990, Inner Temple
Qualifications: [BA (Oxon), Dip Law (City)]

CARRODUS MISS GAIL CAROLINE

New Court Chambers
5 Verulam Buildings, Gray's Inn, London
WC1R 5LY, Telephone: 0171 831 9500
E-mail: mail@newcourtchambers.com
Call date: Nov 1978, Gray's Inn
Qualifications: [BSc (L'pool)]

CARROLL JONATHAN NEIL

Cleveland Chambers
63-65 Borough Road, Middlesbrough,
Cleveland TS1 3AA, Telephone: 01642 226036
Chavasse Court Chambers
2nd Floor Chavasse Court, 24 Lord Street,
Liverpool L2 1TA, Telephone: 0151 707 1191
Door Tenant
Call date: Oct 1994, Gray's Inn
Qualifications: [BA, AKC]

CARRON RICHARD BYRON

11 Bolt Court
London EC4A 3DQ,
Telephone: 0171 353 2300
E-mail: boltct11@aol.com
Redhill Chambers
Seloduct House 30 Station Road, Redhill
RH1 1NK, Telephone: 01737 780781
Call date: Oct 1992, Middle Temple
Qualifications: [BA (Hons, Cantab)]

CARROTT SYLVESTER EMANUEL

6 King's Bench Walk
Ground, Third & Fourth Floors, Temple,
London EC4Y 7DR,
Telephone: 0171 353 4931/583 0695
Call date: July 1980, Gray's Inn
Qualifications: [LLB (Lond)]

CARSS-FRISK MISS MONICA GUNNEL CONSTANCE

2 Hare Court
Ground Floor, Temple, London EC4Y 7BH,
Telephone: 0171 583 1770
E-mail: 2_Hare_Court@link.org
Call date: July 1985, Gray's Inn
Qualifications: [LLB (Lond), BCL (Oxon)]

CARSWELL MISS PATRICIA LOUISE

7 Stone Bldgs
Ground Floor, Lincoln's Inn, London
WC2A 3SZ, Telephone: 0171 405 3886/
242 3546
E-mail: chaldous@vossnet.co.uk
Call date: Feb 1993, Middle Temple
Qualifications: [BA (Hons)(Oxon)]

CARTER MISS CHARLOTTE EMMA

Bell Yard Chambers
116/118 Chancery Lane, London WC2A 1PP,
Telephone: 0171 306 9292
Call date: Nov 1992, Gray's Inn
Qualifications: [LLB (Lond)]

CARTER DAVID JOHN

Arden Chambers
27 John Street, London WC1N 2BL,
Telephone: 0171 242 4244
Call date: Nov 1971, Gray's Inn
Qualifications: [LLB]

CARTER MISS HOLLY EUGENIE SOPHIA

3 Dr Johnson's Bldgs
Ground Floor, Temple, London EC4Y 7BA,
Telephone: 0171 353 4854
Call date: Oct 1993, Inner Temple
Qualifications: [BA (Manch), CPE]

CARTER MISS LESLEY ANN

25-27 Castle Street
1st Floor, Liverpool L2 4TA,
Telephone: 0151 227 5661/051 236 5072
Call date: Oct 1990, Gray's Inn
Qualifications: [BA (Sheff)]

CARTER MISS LESLEY ANNE

Tindal Chambers
3/5 New Street, Chelmsford, Essex CM1 1NT,
Telephone: 01245 267742
Tindal Chambers
3 Waxhouse Gate, St Albans, Herts AL5 4DU,
Telephone: 01727 843383
Call date: Nov 1986, Inner Temple
Qualifications: [BA]

D

CARTER MARTIN RICHARD

40 King Street
Manchester M2 6BA,
Telephone: 0161 832 9082
E-mail: Kingst40@aol.com
Call date: Nov 1992, Middle Temple
Qualifications: [BA (Hons)]

CARTER PETER QC (1995)

18 Red Lion Court
(Off Fleet Street), London EC4A 3EB,
Telephone: 0171 520 6000
Thornwood House
102 New London Road, Chelmsford, Essex
CM2 0RG, Telephone: 01245 280880
Call date: July 1974, Gray's Inn
Qualifications: [LLB (Lond)]

CARTER PETER BASIL QC (1990)

Fountain Court
Temple, London EC4Y 9DH,
Telephone: 0171 583 3335
E-mail: chambers@fountaincourt.co.uk
Door Tenant
Call date: June 1947, Middle Temple
Qualifications: [BCL; MA (Oxon)]

CARTER RICHARD CHARLES

58 King Street Chambers
1st Floor, Kingsgate House 51-53 South King
Street, Manchester M2 6DE,
Telephone: 0161 831 7477
Call date: Nov 1990, Inner Temple
Qualifications: [LLB (Hons)(Manc)]

CARTER MISS ROSALYN FRANCES

7 Fountain Court
Steelhouse Lane, Birmingham B4 6DR,
Telephone: 0121 236 8531
Call date: Nov 1994, Lincoln's Inn
Qualifications: [LLB (Hons)(Leeds)]

CARTER MISS SALLY CLAIRE

Eighteen Carlton Crescent
Southampton SO15 2XR,
Telephone: 01703 639001
Call date: Nov 1994, Inner Temple
Qualifications: [LLB (Soton)]

CARTER WILLIAM ANDREW

23 Essex Street
London WC2R 3AS,
Telephone: 0171 413 0353/353 3533
E-mail: clerks@essexstreet23.demon.co.uk
Call date: July 1989, Gray's Inn
Qualifications: [BA (Oxon)]

CARTER-MANNING JEREMY JAMES QC (1993)

9-12 Bell Yard
London WC2A 2LF,
Telephone: 0171 400 1800
Call date: Apr 1975, Middle Temple
Recorder

CARTER-STEPHENSON GEORGE ANTHONY

3 Gray's Inn Square
Ground Floor, London WC1R 5AH,
Telephone: 0171 520 5600
E-mail: gis3@btinternet.com
Call date: July 1975, Inner Temple
Qualifications: [LLB (Leeds)]

CARTMELL NICHOLAS JAMES

New Court Chambers
3 Broad Chare, Newcastle Upon Tyne
NE1 3DQ, Telephone: 0191 232 1980
Call date: Oct 1990, Inner Temple
Qualifications: [LLB (Hons)]

CARTWRIGHT DAVID CRISPIAN HIMLEY

5 Pump Court
Ground Floor, Temple, London EC4Y 7AP,
Telephone: 0171 353 2532
E-mail: fivepump@netcomuk.co.uk
Call date: Nov 1976, Middle Temple
Assistant Recorder
Qualifications: [MA (Oxon)]

CARTWRIGHT IVAN MATTHEW

Derby Square Chambers
Merchants Court, Derby Square, Liverpool
L2 1TS, Telephone: 0151 709 4222
Call date: Nov 1993, Gray's Inn
Qualifications: [LLB (Hons)]

CARTWRIGHT JAMES D'ARCY CAYLEY

Fleet Chambers
Mitre House 44-46 Fleet Street, London
EC4Y 1BN, Telephone: 0171 936 3707
Southsea Chambers
PO Box 148, Southsea, Portsmouth,
Hampshire PO5 2TU,
Telephone: 01705 291261
Call date: Feb 1968, Gray's Inn

CARTWRIGHT JOHN MARTIN

Francis Taylor Bldg
Ground Floor, Temple, London EC4Y 7BY,
Telephone: 0171 353 7768/7769/2711
Call date: June 1964, Gray's Inn

CARTWRIGHT NICHOLAS FREDERICK

7 Fountain Court
Steelhouse Lane, Birmingham B4 6DR,
Telephone: 0121 236 8531
Call date: July 1986, Middle Temple
Qualifications: [LLB (L'Pool)]

CARTWRIGHT RICHARD JOHN

Queen Elizabeth Bldg
Ground Floor, Temple, London EC4Y 9BS,
Telephone: 0171 353 7181 (12 Lines)
Call date: Nov 1994, Inner Temple
Qualifications: [BA (Hons)(Manch), FCA]

CARTWRIGHT MISS SUZANNE JANE

Holborn Chambers
6 Gate Street, Lincoln's Inn Fields, London
WC2A 3HP, Telephone: 0171 242 6060
Call date: Oct 1994, Lincoln's Inn
Qualifications: [BA (Hons)(Warw)]

CARUS ANTHONY

Chavasse Court Chambers
2nd Floor Chavasse Court, 24 Lord Street,
Liverpool L2 1TA, Telephone: 0151 707 1191
Call date: Jan 1938, Gray's Inn

CARUS RODERICK QC (1990)

9 St John Street
Manchester M3 4DN,
Telephone: 0161 955 9000
E-mail: ninesjs@gconnect.com
Call date: Nov 1971, Gray's Inn
Recorder
Qualifications: [BA (Oxon)]

CARVILLE OWEN BRENDAN NEVILLE

25-27 Castle Street
1st Floor, Liverpool L2 4TA,
Telephone: 0151 227 5661/051 236 5072
Call date: July 1980, Inner Temple
Qualifications: [BA]

CASE MRS JANET RUTH

40 King Street
Chester CH1 2AH, Telephone: 01244 323886
Call date: July 1975, Inner Temple
Qualifications: [LLB]

CASE MISS JULIE

Exchange Chambers
Pearl Assurance House Derby Square,
Liverpool L2 9XX, Telephone: 0151 236 7747/
0458
E-mail: exchangechambers@btinternet.com
Call date: Oct 1990, Middle Temple
Qualifications: [LLB (Leic)]

CASE MISS MAGDALEN MARY CLAIRE

28 St John Street
Manchester M3 4DJ,
Telephone: 0161 834 8418
E-mail: clerk@28stjohnst.co.uk
Call date: Oct 1992, Middle Temple
Qualifications: [MA (Oxon), Dip Law]

CASE RICHARD JOHN

3 Paper Bldgs
1st Floor, Temple, London EC4Y 7EU,
Telephone: 0171 583 8055
E-mail: london@3paper.com
4 St Peter Street
Winchester SO23 8OW,
Telephone: 01962 868884
Call date: Oct 1996, Middle Temple
Qualifications: [BA (Hons)(Cantab)]

D

CASE TOBY EDWARD JAMES

Eighteen Carlton Crescent
Southampton SO15 2XR,
Telephone: 01703 639001
Call date: Oct 1996, Inner Temple
Qualifications: [LLB (So'ton)]

CASEMENT DAVID JOHN

Exchange Chambers
Pearl Assurance House Derby Square,
Liverpool L2 9XX, Telephone: 0151 236 7747/
0458
E-mail: exchangechambers@btinternet.com
Call date: Oct 1992, Middle Temple
Qualifications: [BA (Hons, Oxon)]

CASEY AIDAN PATRICK

1 Crown Office Row
3rd Floor, Temple, London EC4Y 7HH,
Telephone: 0171 583 9292
E-mail: onecor@link.org
Call date: Nov 1992, Gray's Inn
Qualifications: [LLB]

CASEY DERMOT FINTAN

4 Brick Court
Ground Floor, Temple, London EC4Y 9AD,
Telephone: 0171 797 7766
E-mail: chambers@4brick.co.uk
Call date: Nov 1994, Middle Temple
Qualifications: [BA (Hons), M.Sc, C.Q.S.W, Dip
Law (City)]

CASEY MISS MAIRIN

St Mary's Chambers
50 High Pavement, Lace Market, Nottingham
NG1 1HW, Telephone: 0115 9503503
E-mail: clerks@smc.law.co.uk
Call date: Nov 1989, Inner Temple
Qualifications: [BA, LLB (Galway)]

CASEY NOEL

7 Stone Bldgs
1st Floor, Lincoln's Inn, London WC2A 3SZ,
Telephone: 0171 242 0961
Call date: Nov 1995, Lincoln's Inn
Qualifications: [BA (Hons)]

CASH MISS JOANNE CATHERINE

Farrar's Building
Temple, London EC4Y 7BD,
Telephone: 0171 583 9241
E-mail: chambers@farrarsbuilding.co.uk
Call date: Oct 1994, Gray's Inn
Qualifications: [BA (Oxon)]

CASSEL TIMOTHY FELIX HAROLD QC (1988)

5 Paper Bldgs
1st Floor, Temple, London EC4Y 7HB,
Telephone: 0171 583 6117
E-mail: clerks@5-paperbuildings.law.co.uk
Call date: July 1965, Lincoln's Inn

CASSIDY PATRICK STEPHEN

Kenworthy's Buildings
83 Bridge Street, Manchester M3 2RF,
Telephone: 0161 832 4036/834 6954
Call date: July 1982, Lincoln's Inn
Qualifications: [BA]

CASTLE PETER BOLTON

11 New Square
Ground Floor, Lincoln's Inn, London
WC2A 3QB, Telephone: 0171 831 0081
E-mail: 11newsquare.co.uk
Call date: July 1970, Middle Temple
Qualifications: [LLB (Lond)]

CASTLE MISS SUSAN ELIZABETH

33 Bedford Row
London WC1R 4JH,
Telephone: 0171 242 6476
Call date: July 1986, Middle Temple
Qualifications: [MA]

CASWELL BENJAMIN CECIL

6 Park Square
Leeds LS1 2LW, Telephone: 0113 2459763
E-mail: chambers@no6.co.uk
Call date: Oct 1993, Middle Temple
Qualifications: [BA (Hons)(Oxon), MA (Lond)]

CASWELL MATTHEW

11 King's Bench Walk
1st Floor, Temple, London EC4Y 7EQ,
Telephone: 0171 353 3337
3 Park Court
Leeds LS1 2QH, Telephone: 0113 297 1200
Call date: May 1968, Middle Temple
Qualifications: [MA]

CASWELL MISS REBECCA MARY

11 King's Bench Walk
1st Floor, Temple, London EC4Y 7EQ,
Telephone: 0171 353 3337
3 Park Court
Leeds LS1 2QH, Telephone: 0113 297 1200
Call date: July 1983, Middle Temple
Qualifications: [MA (Oxon)]

CATCHPOLE STUART PAUL

39 Essex Street
London WC2R 3AT,
Telephone: 0171 583 1111
E-mail: clerks@39essex.co.uk
Call date: July 1987, Inner Temple
Qualifications: [BA (Dunelm)]

CATFORD GORDON BAXTER

1 Paper Bldgs
Ground Floor, Temple, London EC4Y 7EP,
Telephone: 0171 583 7355
E-mail: clerks@1pb.co.uk
Call date: July 1980, Lincoln's Inn
Qualifications: [LLB (Lond)]

CATON PETER CHARLES DAVID

9-12 Bell Yard
London WC2A 2LF,
Telephone: 0171 400 1800
Call date: May 1963, Gray's Inn
Qualifications: [MA (Oxon)]

CATTAN PHILIP DAVID

28 St John Street
Manchester M3 4DJ,
Telephone: 0161 834 8418
E-mail: clerk@28stjohnst.co.uk
Call date: Nov 1970, Gray's Inn
Recorder
Qualifications: [LLB (Manch)]

CATTERSON MISS MARIE THERESE

5 Essex Court
1st Floor, Temple, London EC4Y 9AH,
Telephone: 0171 410 2000
Call date: Nov 1972, Gray's Inn
Recorder
Qualifications: [LLB (Lond)]

CATTLE DAVID JAMES

4 King's Bench Walk
Ground/First Floor, Temple, London
EC4Y 7DL, Telephone: 0171 822 8822
E-mail: 4kbw@barristersatlaw.com
Call date: July 1975, Middle Temple
Qualifications: [BA (Cantab)]

CAUDLE JOHN ARTHUR

3 Hare Court
1st Floor, Temple, London EC4Y 7BJ,
Telephone: 0171 353 7561
Call date: Nov 1976, Middle Temple
Qualifications: [LLB (Lond)]

CAULFIELD PAUL ANTHONY

Trinity Chambers
9-12 Trinity Chare, Quayside, Newcastle Upon
Tyne NE1 3DF, Telephone: 0191 232 1927
Call date: May 1996, Middle Temple
Qualifications: [LLB (Hons)]

CAUN LAWRENCE

2 Pump Court
1st Floor, Temple, London EC4Y 7AH,
Telephone: 0171 353 5597
Call date: Nov 1977, Lincoln's Inn
Qualifications: [MA (Oxon)]

CAUSER JOHN CHARLES

2 Paper Bldgs
1st Floor, Temple, London EC4Y 7ET,
Telephone: 0171 936 2611 (10 Lines)
E-mail: clerks@2pbbarristers.co.uk
Call date: July 1979, Inner Temple
Qualifications: [BA (Lond)]

CAVANAGH JOHN PATRICK

11 King's Bench Walk
Temple, London EC4Y 7EQ,
Telephone: 0171 632 8500
E-mail: clerksroom@11-kbw.law.co.uk
Call date: Nov 1985, Middle Temple
Qualifications: [MA (Oxon), LLM, (Cantab)]

CAVE JEREMY STEPHEN

1 Crown Office Row
Ground Floor, Temple, London EC4Y 7HH,
Telephone: 0171 797 7500
Crown Office Row Chambers
Blenheim House 120 Church Street, Brighton,
Sussex BN1 1WH, Telephone: 01273 625625
Call date: Nov 1992, Middle Temple
Qualifications: [LLB (Hons, Manch)]

CAVE MISS PATRICIA ANN

7 Stone Bldgs
1st Floor, Lincoln's Inn, London WC2A 3SZ,
Telephone: 0171 242 0961
Call date: Nov 1989, Middle Temple
Qualifications: [BA Hons [Manc], Dip in Law]

CAVENDER DAVID JOHN

1 Essex Court
Ground Floor, Temple, London EC4Y 9AR,
Telephone: 0171 583 2000
E-mail: clerks@oneessexcourt.co.uk
Call date: July 1993, Middle Temple
Qualifications: [LLB (Lond)]

CAVENDER SIMON JUSTIN

Phoenix Chambers
First Floor Gray's Inn Chambers, Gray's Inn,
London WC1R 5JA, Telephone: 0171 404 7888
Call date: Oct 1992, Middle Temple
Qualifications: [LL.B (Hons)(Exon)]

CAWLEY NEIL ROBERT LOUDOUN

55 Temple Chambers
Temple Avenue, London EC4Y 0HP,
Telephone: 0171 353 7400
Chambers of Neil Cawley
27 Broad Street, Newport Pagnell, Bucks
MK16 0AN, Telephone: 01908 217857
E-mail: Neil_Cawley@compuserve.com
Call date: Nov 1992, Inner Temple
Qualifications: [LLB (Buckingham)]

CAWS EIAN RICHARD EDWIN

4 Breams Buildings
London EC4A 1AQ,
Telephone: 0171 353 5835/430 1221
Call date: Nov 1974, Inner Temple
Qualifications: [BA (Oxon)]

CAWSON MARK

St James's Chambers
68 Quay Street, Manchester M3 3EJ,
Telephone: 0161 834 7000
E-mail: 106241.2625@compuserve.com
12 New Square
Lincoln's Inn, London WC2A 3SW,
Telephone: 0171 419 1212
E-mail: 12newsquare@compuserve.com
Door Tenant
Park Lane Chambers
19 Westgate, Leeds LS1 2RU,
Telephone: 0113 228 5000
Call date: July 1982, Lincoln's Inn
Qualifications: [LLB]

Fax: 0161 834 2341; DX: 14350 Manchester I;
Other comms: E-mail mcawson@aol.com;
Home fax: 01565 650410

Types of work: Bankruptcy; Chancery (general);
Company and commercial; Insolvency;
Partnerships; Professional negligence

Circuit: Northern

Awards and memberships: Junior Counsel to
Treasury (Charity Matters in Manchester);
Chancery Bar Association; Northern Chancery
Bar Association; Northern Circuit Commercial
Bar Association; Professional Negligence Bar
Association

Reported cases: *Fabric Sales v Eratex*, [1984] I
WLR 863, 1984. Issue as to which court has
jurisdiction to grant leave to sue a company in
compulsory liquidation.
Lloyds Bank Plc v Semmakie, [1993] I FLR 34,
1993. Issue as to effect of doctrine of *res
judicata* on order made in ancillary relief
proceedings.
Peck v Craighead, [1995] I BCLC 337, 1995.
Issue as to effect of individual voluntary
arrangement on secured creditor.
*Secretary of State for Trade and Industry v
Ashcroft*, [1998] Ch 71, 1997. Admissibility of
hearsay evidence in directors disqualification
proceedings.

Bararot Ltd v Epiette Ltd, [1998] 1 BCLC 283. Issue estoppel/*res judicata* in relation to proceedings previously brought by director of company.

CAYFORD PHILIP JOHN BERKELEY

29 Bedford Row Chambers
London WC1R 4HE,
Telephone: 0171 831 2626
Call date: July 1975, Middle Temple
Qualifications: [BA]

CELLAN-JONES DEINIOL JAMES

1 King's Bench Walk
2nd Floor, Temple, London EC4Y 7DB,
Telephone: 0171 936 1500
E-mail: ddear@1kbw.co.uk
Call date: Nov 1988, Middle Temple
Qualifications: [BA (Oxon)]

CHADD PAUL QC (1972)

Theatre House
Percival Road, Clifton, Bristol BS8 3LE,
Telephone: 0117 974 1553
Door Tenant
Colleton Chambers
Colleton Crescent, Exeter, Devon EX2 4DG,
Telephone: 01392 74898/9
Door Tenant
Call date: July 1952, Lincoln's Inn
Qualifications: [LLB]

CHADWICK CHARLES

7 Stone Bldgs
1st Floor, Lincoln's Inn, London WC2A 3SZ,
Telephone: 0171 242 0961
Call date: Nov 1992, Lincoln's Inn
Qualifications: [BSc (Pittsburgh), MBA, LLB
(Hons)(Lond)]

CHADWICK MISS JOANNA CERIDWEN

4 Fountain Court
Steelhouse Lane, Birmingham B4 6DR,
Telephone: 0121 236 3476
Call date: Nov 1988, Middle Temple
Qualifications: [LLB (Leeds)]

CHADWIN JAMES ARMSTRONG QC (1976)

Park Court Chambers
40 Park Cross Street, Leeds LS1 2QH,
Telephone: 0113 2433277
6 Gray's Inn Square
Ground Floor, Gray's Inn, London WC1R 5AZ,
Telephone: 0171 242 1052
Broad Chare
33 Broad Chare, Newcastle Upon Tyne
NE1 3DQ, Telephone: 0191 232 0541
Call date: Feb 1958, Gray's Inn
Recorder
Qualifications: [MA, LLB]

CHAHALL MISS JASBINDER PAL

2 Garden Court
1st Floor, Middle Temple, London EC4Y 9BL,
Telephone: 0171 353 1633
E-mail: barristers@2gardenct.law.co.uk
Call date: Nov 1991, Middle Temple
Qualifications: [BA Hons (Econ), LLM
(Nott'm), Dip Law]

CHAISTY PAUL

40 King Street
Manchester M2 6BA,
Telephone: 0161 832 9082
E-mail: Kingst40@aol.com
Call date: July 1982, Lincoln's Inn
Qualifications: [LLB (Notts), BCL (Oxon)]

CHAIZE TRISTAN PAUL

5 Pump Court
Ground Floor, Temple, London EC4Y 7AP,
Telephone: 0171 353 2532
E-mail: fivepump@netcomuk.co.uk
Call date: Nov 1977, Inner Temple

CHALLEN MISS LYDIA ANN

Arden Chambers
27 John Street, London WC1N 2BL,
Telephone: 0171 242 4244
Call date: Oct 1995, Gray's Inn
Qualifications: [BA (Hons)(Cantab), M.Jur
(Oxon)]

CHALLENGER COLIN WESTCOTT

Bridewell Chambers
2 Bridewell Place, London EC4V 6AP,
Telephone: 0171 797 8800
E-mail: clerks@bridewell.law.co.uk
Call date: Nov 1970, Inner Temple
Qualifications: [LLB (Lond), MBA, (Berkeley)]

CHALLINOR ROBERT MICHAEL

7 Fountain Court
Steelhouse Lane, Birmingham B4 6DR,
Telephone: 0121 236 8531
Call date: July 1974, Gray's Inn
Qualifications: [LLB]

CHALMERS GAVIN JAMES

Albion Chambers
Broad Street, Bristol BS1 1DR,
Telephone: 0117 9272144
Call date: July 1978, Inner Temple
Qualifications: [BA (Dunelm)]

CHALMERS MISS SUZANNE FRANCES

2 Crown Office Row
Ground Floor, Temple, London EC4Y 7HJ,
Telephone: 0171 797 8100
E-mail: mail@2cor.co.uk, or to individual
barristers at: [barrister's surname]@2cor.co.uk
Call date: Oct 1995, Gray's Inn
Qualifications: [BA]

CHAMBERLAIN FRANCIS GEORGE NEVILLE

3 Paper Bldgs
1st Floor, Temple, London EC4Y 7EU,
Telephone: 0171 583 8055
E-mail: london@3paper.com
4 St Peter Street
Winchester SO23 8OW,
Telephone: 01962 868884
Call date: July 1985, Lincoln's Inn
Qualifications: [LLB (Leeds)]

CHAMBERLAYNE PATRICK ALLIN GERRARD TANKERVI

6 Pump Court
1st Floor, Temple, London EC4Y 7AR,
Telephone: 0171 797 8400
E-mail: sa_hockman_qc@link.org
6-8 Mill Street
Maidstone, Kent ME15 6XH,
Telephone: 01622 688094
Call date: Nov 1992, Inner Temple
Qualifications: [BA (Hons)(Cantab), MA
(Cantab)]

CHAMBERS ADAM RUSHBY

12 King's Bench Walk
Temple, London EC4Y 7EL,
Telephone: 0171 583 0811
E-mail: chambers@12kbw.co.uk
Call date: July 1989, Middle Temple
Qualifications: [BA (Leeds), Dip Law]

CHAMBERS DOMINIC KERN

Brick Court Chambers
15/19 Devereux Court, London WC2R 3JJ,
Telephone: 0171 583 0777
E-mail: (surname)@brickcourt.demon.co.uk
Call date: Nov 1987, Gray's Inn
Qualifications: [LLB (Lond)]

CHAMBERS GREGORY JOHN ELLIS

1 Crown Office Row
Ground Floor, Temple, London EC4Y 7HH,
Telephone: 0171 797 7500
Crown Office Row Chambers
Blenheim House 120 Church Street, Brighton,
Sussex BN1 1WH, Telephone: 01273 625625
Call date: July 1973, Middle Temple
Qualifications: [MA (Dublin)]

CHAMBERS JONATHAN

4 Essex Court
Temple, London EC4Y 9AJ,
Telephone: 0171 797 7970
E-mail: clerks@4essexcourt.law.co.uk
Call date: Oct 1996, Inner Temple
Qualifications: [BA(Oxon), C.P.L.S., BCL
(Oxon)]

CHAMBERS MICHAEL LAURENCE

Sedan House
Stanley Place, Chester CH1 2LU,
Telephone: 01244 320480/348282
1 Dr Johnson's Bldgs
Ground Floor, Temple, London EC4Y 7AX,
Telephone: 0171 353 9328
Call date: July 1980, Lincoln's Inn
Assistant Recorder
Qualifications: [MA (Oxon)]

CHAMBERS NICHOLAS MORDAUNT QC (1985)

Brick Court Chambers
15/19 Devereux Court, London WC2R 3JJ,
Telephone: 0171 583 0777
E-mail: (surname)@brickcourt.demon.co.uk
Call date: July 1966, Gray's Inn
Recorder
Qualifications: [MA (Oxon)]

CHAMBERS PAUL VICTOR

24a St John Street
Manchester M3 4DF,
Telephone: 0161 833 9628
Call date: Nov 1973, Gray's Inn
Qualifications: [BA Hons]

CHAMPION MISS DEBORAH CURTIS

3 Hare Court
1st Floor, Temple, London EC4Y 7BJ,
Telephone: 0171 353 7561
Call date: July 1970, Gray's Inn
Recorder

CHAMPION MS ROWENA ELIZABETH

2 Field Court
Gray's Inn, London WC1R 5BB,
Telephone: 0171 405 6114
E-mail: fieldct2@netcomuk.co.uk.
Call date: Feb 1990, Middle Temple
Qualifications: [BSc]

CHAN MISS ABBERLAINE DIANNE PAO CHE

9-12 Bell Yard
London WC2A 2LF,
Telephone: 0171 400 1800
Call date: July 1979, Gray's Inn
Qualifications: [LLB (Bris)]

CHAN MISS SUSAN

13 King's Bench Walk
1st Floor, Temple, London EC4Y 7EN,
Telephone: 0171 353 7204
E-mail: clerks@13kbw.law.co.uk
King's Bench Chambers
32 Beaumont Street, Oxford OX1 2NP,
Telephone: 01865 311066
E-mail: clerks@kbc-oxford.law.co.uk
Call date: Oct 1994, Gray's Inn
Qualifications: [BA]

CHAND RAGVEER

Mitre House Chambers
Mitre House 44 Fleet Street, London
EC4Y 1BN, Telephone: 0171 583 8233
Call date: Nov 1994, Lincoln's Inn
Qualifications: [LLB (Hons)(Wolves)]

CHANDLER ALEXANDER CHARLES ROSS

One Garden Court
Ground Floor, Temple, London EC4Y 9BJ,
Telephone: 0171 797 7900
Call date: Oct 1995, Middle Temple
Qualifications: [MA (Oxon), Dip Law (City)]

CHANDLER MISS KATE

12 King's Bench Walk
Temple, London EC4Y 7EL,
Telephone: 0171 583 0811
E-mail: chambers@12kbw.co.uk
Call date: Oct 1990, Inner Temple
Qualifications: [LLB (Lond)]

CHAPLAIN MISS JAYNE LOUISE

Broadway House Chambers
Broadway House 9 Bank Street, Bradford,
West Yorkshire BD1 1TW,
Telephone: 01274 722560
Call date: Nov 1995, Middle Temple
Qualifications: [BA (Hons)(Cantab)]

CHAPLIN ADRIAN ROLAND

9-12 Bell Yard
London WC2A 2LF,
Telephone: 0171 400 1800
Call date: Oct 1990, Gray's Inn
Qualifications: [B.A (CANTAB)]

D

CHAPLIN JOHN LAWTON

24a St John Street
Manchester M3 4DF,
Telephone: 0161 833 9628
Call date: Nov 1986, Inner Temple
Qualifications: [BA (Exon)]

CHAPMAN JEFFREY PAUL

Fountain Court
Temple, London EC4Y 9DH,
Telephone: 0171 583 3335
E-mail: chambers@fountaincourt.co.uk
Call date: Nov 1989, Middle Temple
Qualifications: [BA Hons (Sussex), LLM (Cantab)]

CHAPMAN MATTHEW JAMES

Barnard's Inn Chambers
6th Floor Halton House, 20-23 Holborn,
London EC1N 2JD, Telephone: 0171 242 8508
E-mail: clerks@barnards-inn-chambers.co.uk
Call date: Oct 1994, Gray's Inn
Qualifications: [LLB, LLM]

CHAPMAN MICHAEL ANDREW

Barnard's Inn Chambers
6th Floor Halton House, 20-23 Holborn,
London EC1N 2JD, Telephone: 0171 242 8508
E-mail: clerks@barnards-inn-chambers.co.uk
Call date: Nov 1994, Middle Temple
Qualifications: [MA]

CHAPMAN NICHOLAS JOHN

29 Bedford Row Chambers
London WC1R 4HE,
Telephone: 0171 831 2626
Call date: Oct 1990, Inner Temple
Qualifications: [BSc (UCL), Dip Law (City)]

CHAPMAN MS REBECCA KATE

14 Tooks Court
Cursitor St, London EC4A 1LB,
Telephone: 0171 405 8828
E-mail: clerks @tooks.law.co.uk
Call date: Nov 1990, Inner Temple
Qualifications: [BA (York), Dip Law (PCL)]

CHAPMAN RENNICK ANDREW

Lloyds House Chambers
3rd Floor 18 Lloyds House, Lloyd Street,
Manchester M2 5WA,
Telephone: 0161 839 3371
Call date: Mar 1997, Middle Temple
Qualifications: [LLB (Hons)]

CHAPMAN SIMON CHARLES

22 Old Bldgs
Lincoln's Inn, London WC2A 3UJ,
Telephone: 0171 831 0222
Call date: July 1988, Inner Temple
Qualifications: [LLB (Bristol)]

CHAPMAN VIVIAN ROBERT

11 Stone Bldgs
1st Floor, Lincoln's Inn, London WC2A 3TG,
Telephone: 0171 404 5055
E-mail: 9stoneb@compuserve.com
2 New Street
Leicester LE1 5NA, Telephone: 0116 2625906
Door Tenant
Call date: July 1970, Middle Temple
Recorder
Qualifications: [MA LLM (Cantab)]

CHAPPLE JAMES MALCOLM DUNDAS

One Raymond Buildings
Gray's Inn, London WC1R 5BH,
Telephone: 0171 430 1234
E-mail: chambers@ipbar1rb.com;
clerks@ipbar1rb.com
Call date: Nov 1975, Gray's Inn
Qualifications: [BSc (Hons), FCIArb]

CHARALAMBOUS CONSTANDINO

1 Gray's Inn Square
Ground Floor, London WC1R 5AA,
Telephone: 0171 405 8946/7/8
Call date: Oct 1990, Middle Temple
Qualifications: [LLB]

CHARBIT MISS VALERIE JUDITH

3 Hare Court
1st Floor, Temple, London EC4Y 7BJ,
Telephone: 0171 353 7561
Call date: Oct 1992, Middle Temple
Qualifications: [LL.B (Hons, Sheff)]

CHARKHAM GRAHAM HAROLD

20 Essex Street
London WC2R 3AL,
Telephone: 0171 583 9294
E-mail: clerks@20essexst.com
Call date: May 1993, Inner Temple
Qualifications: [BSc (Bristol)]

CHARLES MS DEBORAH ANN

6 Pump Court
1st Floor, Temple, London EC4Y 7AR,
Telephone: 0171 797 8400
E-mail: sa_hockman_qc@link.org
Call date: Oct 1996, Lincoln's Inn
Qualifications: [BA (Hons)(Warw), CPE (Middx)]

CHARLES HENRY FREDERICK

199 Strand
London WC2R 1DR,
Telephone: 0171 379 9779
E-mail: chambers@199strand.co.uk
Call date: Nov 1987, Inner Temple
Qualifications: [LLB, LLM (Lond)]

CHARLTON ALEXANDER MURRAY

4 Pump Court
Temple, London EC4Y 7AN,
Telephone: 0171 353 2656/9
E-mail: 4_pump_court@compuserve.com
Call date: July 1983, Middle Temple
Qualifications: [MA (St Andrews), Dip Law (City)]

CHARLTON MISS JUDITH ANNE DOROTHY

New Court
Temple, London EC4Y 9BE,
Telephone: 0171 583 5123/0171 583 0510
Call date: Nov 1991, Inner Temple
Qualifications: [LLB (Lond)]

CHARLTON TIMOTHY ROGER QC (1993)

Brick Court Chambers
15/19 Devereux Court, London WC2R 3JJ,
Telephone: 0171 583 0777
E-mail: (surname)@brickcourt.demon.co.uk
Call date: Nov 1974, Inner Temple
Qualifications: [BA (Oxon)]

CHARLTON WILLIAM WINGATE HUGO

5 Pump Court
Ground Floor, Temple, London EC4Y 7AP,
Telephone: 0171 353 2532
E-mail: fivepump@netcomuk.co.uk
Call date: July 1978, Gray's Inn
Qualifications: [BA (York)]

CHARLWOOD SPIKE LLEWELLYN

4 Paper Bldgs
Ground Floor, Temple, London EC4Y 7EX,
Telephone: 0171 353 3366/583 7155
E-mail: clerks@4paperbuildings.com
Call date: Nov 1994, Inner Temple
Qualifications: [BA (Cantab)]

CHARMAN ANDREW JULIAN

7 Fountain Court
Steelhouse Lane, Birmingham B4 6DR,
Telephone: 0121 236 8531
Call date: Nov 1994, Lincoln's Inn
Qualifications: [MA]

CHATTERJEE DR CHARLES

1 Gray's Inn Square
1st Floor, London WC1R 5AG,
Telephone: 0171 405 3000
E-mail: clerks@onegrays.demon.co.uk
Door Tenant
Call date: Nov 1992, Inner Temple
Qualifications: [LLB, LLM, LLM, PhD]

CHATTERJEE MISS MIRA

4 Brick Court
Temple, London EC4Y 9AD,
Telephone: 0171 797 8910
Call date: Nov 1973, Middle Temple

CHATTERTON MARK

Martins Building
Water Street, Liverpool L2 3SP,
Telephone: 0151 236 5818/4919
Call date: July 1983, Gray's Inn
Qualifications: [LLB (L'Pool)]

CHAUDHRY FAROOQ AHMAD

27 Rose Grove
Bury, Greater Manchester BL8 2UJ,
Telephone: 0161 763 4739
Call date: July 1970, Lincoln's Inn

D

CHAUDHRY MISS SABUHI ASHFAQ

Hardwicke Building
New Square, Lincoln's Inn, London
WC2A 3SB, Telephone: 0171 242 2523
E-mail: clerks@hardwicke.co.uk
Call date: Oct 1993, Lincoln's Inn
Qualifications: [LLB (Hons)(Lond)]

CHAUDHRY ZIA UDDIN

India Buildings Chambers
Water Street, Liverpool L2 OXG,
Telephone: 0151 243 6000
Call date: Nov 1991, Inner Temple
Qualifications: [LLB (Hons)(Manch)]

CHAUDHURI AVIRUP

1 Middle Temple Lane
Temple, London EC4Y 1LT,
Telephone: 0171 583 0659 (12 Lines)
Call date: Feb 1990, Middle Temple
Qualifications: [LLB Hons [Lond]]

CHAUDHURI ROBIN GORA

New Walk Chambers
27 New Walk, Leicester LE1 6TE,
Telephone: 0116 2559144
Call date: Nov 1988, Lincoln's Inn
Qualifications: [BA Hons (Leics), Dip Law
(City)]

CHAVASSE MISS HILARY ANN

3 Fountain Court
Steelhouse Lane, Birmingham B4 6DR,
Telephone: 0121 236 5854
Call date: May 1971, Gray's Inn
Qualifications: [LLB (Bristol)]

CHAWATAMA SYDNEY

1 Crown Office Row
Ground Floor, Temple, London EC4Y 7HH,
Telephone: 0171 797 7500
Call date: Oct 1994, Middle Temple
Qualifications: [LLB (Hons)(Essex)]

CHAWLA MUKUL

9-12 Bell Yard
London WC2A 2LF,
Telephone: 0171 400 1800
Call date: July 1983, Gray's Inn
Qualifications: [LLB (Lond)]

CHEAH ALBERT SENG HEE

46/48 Essex Street
London WC2R 3GH,
Telephone: 0171 583 8899
Call date: Nov 1989, Inner Temple
Qualifications: [LLB (Hons) (UCL), LLM (LSE)]

CHEEMA MISS PARMJIT KAUR

1 Hare Court
Ground Floor, Temple, London EC4Y 7BE,
Telephone: 0171 353 3982/5324
Call date: July 1989, Gray's Inn
Qualifications: [LLB [Lond]]

CHEETHAM JAMES SIMON

10 King's Bench Walk
1st Floor, Temple, London EC4Y 7EB,
Telephone: 0171 353 2501
Call date: Oct 1991, Middle Temple
Qualifications: [MA]

CHEETHAM MISS JULIA ANN

Cobden House Chambers
19 Quay Street, Manchester M3 3HN,
Telephone: 0161 833 6000
E-mail: clerks@cobden.co.uk
Call date: Oct 1990, Lincoln's Inn
Qualifications: [LLB (Nott'm)]

CHELTENHAM MS JACQUELINE MIRANDA

John Street Chambers
2 John Street, London WC1N 2HJ,
Telephone: 0171 242 1911
E-mail: john.street_chambers@virgin.net.uk
Call date: Nov 1992, Middle Temple
Qualifications: [BA (Hons, Dunelm)]

CHERRILL MRS BEVERLEY SUSAN

Chichester Chambers
12 North Pallant, Chichester, West Sussex
PO19 1TQ, Telephone: 01243 784538
Call date: Oct 1996, Middle Temple
Qualifications: [BA (Hons)(Sussex)]

CHERRILL RICHARD

9-12 Bell Yard
London WC2A 2LF,
Telephone: 0171 400 1800
Call date: July 1965, Middle Temple
Qualifications: [MA (Cantab), LLB]

CHERRY JOHN MITCHELL QC (1988)

8 Stone Buildings
Lincoln's Inn, London WC2A 3TA,
Telephone: 0171 831 9881
Call date: Nov 1961, Gray's Inn
Recorder

Fax: 0171 831 9392;
Out of hours telephone: 0181 894 1416;
DX: 216 Chancery Lane; Other comms: Mobile
0802 411348

Types of work: Medical negligence; Personal
injury; Professional negligence

Circuit: South Eastern

Other professional experience: Recorder, CICB

CHERRYMAN JOHN RICHARD QC (1982)

4 Breams Buildings
London EC4A 1AQ,
Telephone: 0171 353 5835/430 1221
Call date: June 1955, Gray's Inn
Recorder
Qualifications: [LLB]

CHERRYMAN NICHOLAS CHARLES

24 Old Bldgs
Ground Floor, Lincoln's Inn, London
WC2A 3UJ, Telephone: 0171 404 0946
E-mail: clerks@24oldbuildings.law.co.uk
Call date: Nov 1991, Lincoln's Inn
Qualifications: [Ba (Hons)]

CHESHIRE ANTHONY PETER

10 King's Bench Walk
Ground Floor, Temple, London EC4Y 7EB,
Telephone: 0171 353 7742
E-mail: 10kbw@lineone.net
Call date: Oct 1992, Middle Temple
Qualifications: [BA (Oxon)]

CHESNER HOWARD MICHAEL

Bracton Chambers
95a Chancery Lane, London WC2A 1DT,
Telephone: 0171 242 4248
Call date: July 1995, Gray's Inn
Qualifications: [LLB (Lond), MBA]

CHESTERS MS COLETTE LOUISE

1 Pump Court
Lower Ground Floor, Temple, London
EC4Y 7AB, Telephone: 0171 583 2012/
353 4341
E-mail: (name) @1pumpcourt.co.uk
Call date: Mar 1996, Middle Temple
Qualifications: [LLB (Hons)]

CHEVES SIMON THOMSON

Francis Taylor Bldg
Ground Floor, Temple, London EC4Y 7BY,
Telephone: 0171 353 7768/7769/2711
Call date: July 1980, Inner Temple
Qualifications: [BA(Dunelm)]

CHEYNE MISS PHYLLIDA ALISON

4 Pump Court
Temple, London EC4Y 7AN,
Telephone: 0171 353 2656/9
E-mail: 4_pump_court@compuserve.com
Call date: Nov 1992, Inner Temple
Qualifications: [BA, MPhil (Cantab)]

CHHOTU JASVANT

189 Randolph Avenue
London W9 1DJ, Telephone: 0171 624 9139
Call date: July 1979, Gray's Inn
Qualifications: [BA (Hons)]

CHICHESTER JULIAN EDWARD MICHAEL

4-5 Gray's Inn Square
Ground Floor, Gray's Inn, London WC1R 5AY,
Telephone: 0171 404 5252
E-mail: chambers@4-5graysinnsquare.co.uk
Call date: Nov 1977, Inner Temple

CHILD JOHN FREDERICK

17 Old Bldgs
Ground Floor, Lincoln's Inn, London
WC2A 3UP, Telephone: 0171 405 9653
Call date: Nov 1966, Lincoln's Inn
Qualifications: [BA, LLM, Dip American Law]

CHINEGWUNDOH HAROLD EJIKE

Chancery Chambers
1st Floor Offices 70/72 Chancery Lane,
London WC2A 1AB,
Telephone: 0171 405 6879/6870
Call date: Oct 1994, Gray's Inn
Qualifications: [LLB]

CHINN ANTONY NIGEL CATON

4 Brick Court
1st Floor, Temple, London EC4Y 9AD,
Telephone: 0171 583 8455
Call date: Nov 1972, Middle Temple
Assistant Recorder

CHIPPECK STEPHEN

5 Paper Bldgs
Lower Ground Floor, Temple, London
EC4Y 7HB, Telephone: 0171 353 5638
E-mail: 107722,633@compuserve.com
Call date: July 1988, Lincoln's Inn
Qualifications: [LLB (Hons) (Leeds)]

CHIPPINDALL ADAM COURTENAY

Guildhall Chambers
23 Broad Street, Bristol BS1 2HG,
Telephone: 0117 9273366
Call date: Nov 1975, Gray's Inn
Assistant Recorder
Qualifications: [LLB (Soton)]

CHIRIMUUTA GILBERT MUSHORE

Francis Taylor Bldg
2nd Floor, Temple, London EC4Y 7BY,
Telephone: 0171 353 9942/3157
Call date: Nov 1990, Lincoln's Inn
Qualifications: [BL (Rhodesia), LLM (Lond)]

CHISHOLM MALCOLM DAVID

3 Dr Johnson's Bldgs
Ground Floor, Temple, London EC4Y 7BA,
Telephone: 0171 353 4854
Call date: Nov 1989, Inner Temple
Qualifications: [MA(Cantab)]

CHIVERS (TOM) DAVID

Erskine Chambers
30 Lincoln's Inn Fields, Lincoln's Inn, London
WC2A 3PF, Telephone: 0171 242 5532
E-mail: Clerks@Erskine-Chambers.law.co.uk
Call date: July 1983, Lincoln's Inn
Qualifications: [BA (Cantab)]

CHOO CHOY ALAIN

1 Essex Court
Ground Floor, Temple, London EC4Y 9AR,
Telephone: 0171 583 2000
E-mail: clerks@oneessexcourt.co.uk
Call date: Nov 1991, Inner Temple
Qualifications: [LLB (London)]

CHOUDHURY AKHLAQ

11 King's Bench Walk
Temple, London EC4Y 7EQ,
Telephone: 0171 632 8500
E-mail: clerksroom@11-kbw.law.co.uk
Call date: Oct 1992, Inner Temple
Qualifications: [BSc (Glasgow), LLB (Lond)]

CHOUDHURY MRS FAREHA ISLAM

Phoenix Chambers
First Floor Gray's Inn Chambers, Gray's Inn,
London WC1R 5JA, Telephone: 0171 404 7888
Call date: Nov 1995, Gray's Inn
Qualifications: [LLB (Sussex)]

CHOUDHURY MISS NAFEESA

New Court Chambers
3 Broad Chare, Newcastle Upon Tyne
NE1 3DQ, Telephone: 0191 232 1980
Call date: Nov 1990, Inner Temple
Qualifications: [LLB]

CHOWDHARY ISLAMUDDIN

9 King's Bench Walk
Basement, Temple, London EC4Y 7DX,
Telephone: 0171 353 9564
E-mail: jvlee@btinternet.com
Call date: July 1982, Lincoln's Inn
Qualifications: [BA, LLB (Punjab), LLM (Lond)]

CHRISTENSEN CARLTON

10 King's Bench Walk
Ground Floor, Temple, London EC4Y 7EB,
Telephone: 0171 353 7742
E-mail: 10kbw@lineone.net
Call date: July 1977, Middle Temple
Qualifications: [BSc, MSc, PhD (Manch]

CHRISTIE AIDAN PATRICK

4 Pump Court
Temple, London EC4Y 7AN,
Telephone: 0171 353 2656/9
E-mail: 4_pump_court@compuserve.com
Call date: July 1988, Middle Temple
Qualifications: [BA (Hons) (Oxon), MA (Hons) (Cantab)]

CHRISTIE DAVID HENDERSON

9 Bedford Row
London WC1R 4AZ,
Telephone: 0171 242 3555
E-mail: clerks@9br.co.uk
Call date: July 1973, Inner Temple
Qualifications: [BCom]

CHRISTIE RICHARD HAMISH

2 Pump Court
1st Floor, Temple, London EC4Y 7AH,
Telephone: 0171 353 5597
Call date: July 1986, Inner Temple
Qualifications: [LLB (Manch), ACA (Part)]

CHRISTIE RONALD DANIEL

32 Park Place
Cardiff CF1 3BA, Telephone: 01222 397364
Call date: July 1974, Lincoln's Inn
Qualifications: [LLB]

CHRISTIE SIMON PAUL WILLIAM

Peel House Chambers
Ground Floor, Peel House 5 Harrington Street,
Liverpool L2 9QA, Telephone: 0151 236 4321
Call date: Feb 1988, Middle Temple
Qualifications: [LLB (L'pool)]

CHRISTIE-BROWN MISS SARAH LOUISE

4 Paper Bldgs
Ground Floor, Temple, London EC4Y 7EX,
Telephone: 0171 353 3366/583 7155
E-mail: clerks@4paperbuildings.com
Call date: Oct 1994, Middle Temple
Qualifications: [BA (Hons)(Oxon), CPE (City)]

CHRISTODOULOU MISS HELEN JOAN

5 Pump Court
Ground Floor, Temple, London EC4Y 7AP,
Telephone: 0171 353 2532
E-mail: fivepump@netcomuk.co.uk
Call date: July 1972, Middle Temple
Qualifications: [LLB (Lond)]

CHRISTOPHER JULIAN MARK CARMICHAEL

5 Paper Bldgs
1st Floor, Temple, London EC4Y 7HB,
Telephone: 0171 583 6117
E-mail: clerks@5-paperbuildings.law.co.uk
Call date: Nov 1988, Gray's Inn
Qualifications: [BA (Hons)(Cantab)]

CHRUSZCZ CHARLES FRANCIS QC (1992)

28 St John Street
Manchester M3 4DJ,
Telephone: 0161 834 8418
E-mail: clerk@28stjohnst.co.uk
Call date: July 1973, Middle Temple
Recorder
Qualifications: [LLB]

D

CHUBB ANDREW VYVYAN

Walnut House
63 St. David's Hill, Exeter, Devon EX4 4DW,
Telephone: 01392 279751
E-mail: 106627.2451@compuserve.com
Call date: July 1975, Middle Temple
Recorder

CHUDLEIGH MISS LOUISE KATRINA

Old Square Chambers
1 Verulam Buildings, Gray's Inn, London
WC1R 5LQ, Telephone: 0171 831 0801
Old Square Chambers
Hanover House 47 Corn Street, Bristol
BS1 1HT, Telephone: 0117 9277111
Call date: July 1987, Lincoln's Inn
Qualifications: [BA Law (Kent)]

CHUKWUEMEKA JOHN OKECHUKWU

India Buildings Chambers
Water Street, Liverpool L2 OXG,
Telephone: 0151 243 6000
Call date: Nov 1994, Lincoln's Inn
Qualifications: [BSc (Hons)(Lond)]

CHURCH JOHN STEPHEN

2 Gray's Inn Square Chambers
2nd Floor, Gray's Inn, London WC1R 5AA,
Telephone: 0171 242 0328/071 405 1317
E-mail: clerks@2gis.co.uk
Call date: Nov 1984, Lincoln's Inn
Qualifications: [BA]

CHURCHILL MRS CAROL LENA

Temple Fields
Hamilton House 1 Temple Avenue, London
EC4Y 0HA, Telephone: 0171 353 4212
Call date: Nov 1979, Middle Temple
Qualifications: [BA (Hons)Kent), Maitre Du
Droit]

CHURCHILL MISS MARINA SPENCER

2 Harcourt Bldgs
1st Floor, Temple, London EC4Y 9DB,
Telephone: 0171 353 2112/2817
Call date: July 1989, Inner Temple
Qualifications: [LLB (Bucks)]

CIUMEI CHARLES GREGG

1 Temple Gardens
1st Floor, Temple, London EC4Y 9BB,
Telephone: 0171 353 0407/583 1315
E-mail: clerks@1templegardens.co.uk
Call date: Oct 1991, Middle Temple
Qualifications: [BA Hons (Oxon), Dip Law]

CLAPPISON WILLIAM JAMES

10 Park Square
Leeds LS1 2LH, Telephone: 0113 2455438
E-mail: chambers@bandit.legend.co.uk
Call date: Nov 1981, Gray's Inn
Qualifications: [BA (Oxon)]

CLARE MISS ALLISON JEAN

18 Red Lion Court
(Off Fleet Street), London EC4A 3EB,
Telephone: 0171 520 6000
Thornwood House
102 New London Road, Chelmsford, Essex
CM2 0RG, Telephone: 01245 280880
Call date: Oct 1992, Gray's Inn
Qualifications: [BA, BCL (Oxon)]

CLARE MICHAEL CHRISTOPHER

Octagon House
19 Colegate, Norwich NR3 1AT,
Telephone: 01603 623186
E-mail: octagon@netmatters.co.uk
1 Paper Bldgs
1st Floor, Temple, London EC4Y 7EP,
Telephone: 0171 353 3728/4953
Call date: Nov 1986, Gray's Inn
Qualifications: [LLB (E Anglia)]

CLARE REGINALD STUART

The Corn Exchange
5th Floor Fenwick Street, Liverpool L2 7QS,
Telephone: 0151 227 1081/5009
Call date: May 1997, Middle Temple

CLARGO JOHN PAUL

Hardwicke Building
New Square, Lincoln's Inn, London
WC2A 3SB, Telephone: 0171 242 2523
E-mail: clerks@hardwicke.co.uk
Call date: Oct 1994, Middle Temple
Qualifications: [BA (Hons)(Oxon), CPE]

CLARK ANDREW RICHARD

Manchester House Chambers
18-22 Bridge Street, Manchester M3 3BZ,
Telephone: 0161 834 7007
Call date: July 1994, Inner Temple
Qualifications: [MA (Oxon)]

CLARK MISS BRYONY JANE

24 The Ropewalk
Nottingham NG1 5EF,
Telephone: 0115 9472581
E-mail: clerk@ropewalk.co.uk
Call date: July 1985, Middle Temple
Qualifications: [LLB (Leeds)]

CLARK CHRISTOPHER HARVEY QC (1989)

Pump Court Chambers
Upper Ground Floor 3 Pump Court, Temple,
London EC4Y 7AJ, Telephone: 0171 353 0711
Pump Court Chambers
31 Southgate Street, Winchester SO23 8EE,
Telephone: 01962 868161
Westgate Chambers
144 High Street, Lewes, East Sussex BN7 1XT,
Telephone: 01273 480510
Call date: July 1969, Gray's Inn
Recorder
Qualifications: [MA (Cantab), Member of
Institute, of Arbitrators]

CLARK DINGLE

1 Dr Johnson's Bldgs
Ground Floor, Temple, London EC4Y 7AX,
Telephone: 0171 353 9328
Dr Johnson's Chambers
The Atrium Court Apex Plaza, Reading
RG1 1AX, Telephone: 01734 254221
Call date: July 1981, Middle Temple
Qualifications: [BSc (Soton)]

CLARK MISS FIONA JANE STEWART

8 New Square
Lincoln's Inn, London WC2A 3QP,
Telephone: 0171 405 4321
Call date: July 1982, Middle Temple
Qualifications: [MA (Cantab)]

CLARK MISS GERALDINE

20 Essex Street
London WC2R 3AL,
Telephone: 0171 583 9294
E-mail: clerks@20essexst.com
Call date: July 1988, Gray's Inn
Qualifications: [LLB (Hons), Dip Law]

CLARK GRAHAM JOHN LESLIE

4 Brick Court
Temple, London EC4Y 9AD,
Telephone: 0171 797 8910
Call date: July 1976, Middle Temple

CLARK MISS HAZEL ANNE

Fenners Chambers
3 Madingley Road, Cambridge CB3 OEE,
Telephone: 01223 368761
Fenners Chambers
8-12 Priestgate, Peterborough PE1 1JA,
Telephone: 01733 62030
Call date: Nov 1990, Middle Temple
Qualifications: [BA (Dunelm)]

CLARK MS JULIA ELISABETH

5 New Square
1st Floor, Lincoln's Inn, London WC2A 3RJ,
Telephone: 0171 404 0404
E-mail: Chambers@FiveNewSquare.CityScape.co.uk
Call date: July 1984, Gray's Inn
Qualifications: [MA (Oxon),MA (Lond)]

CLARK NEIL ANDREW

6 Park Square
Leeds LS1 2LW, Telephone: 0113 2459763
E-mail: chambers@no6.co.uk
Call date: July 1987, Inner Temple
Qualifications: [LLB (Leeds)]

CLARK PAUL ROBERT

Exchange Chambers
Pearl Assurance House Derby Square,
Liverpool L2 9XX, Telephone: 0151 236 7747/
0458
E-mail: exchangechambers@btinternet.com
Call date: May 1994, Middle Temple
Qualifications: [LLB (Hons)]

CLARK PETER LESTOR

1 Crown Office Row
2nd Floor, Temple, London EC4Y 7HH,
Telephone: 0171 797 7111
Call date: Nov 1988, Middle Temple
Qualifications: [BA (Oxon), Dip Law]

CLARK MISS REBECCA JANE

Exchange Chambers
Pearl Assurance House Derby Square,
Liverpool L2 9XX, Telephone: 0151 236 7747/
0458
E-mail: exchangechambers@btinternet.com
Call date: July 1989, Inner Temple
Qualifications: [LLB [Sheff]]

CLARK TIMOTHY ELWYN

2 Paper Buildings
Basement, Temple, London EC4Y 7ET,
Telephone: 0171 353 0933
Call date: Feb 1993, Inner Temple
Qualifications: [LLB (Hons, Bris)]

CLARK TIMOTHY NOEL

2 New Street
Leicester LE1 5NA, Telephone: 0116 2625906
Call date: July 1974, Middle Temple
Assistant Recorder
Qualifications: [BA]

CLARK MISS TONIA ANNE

Francis Taylor Bldg
Ground Floor, Temple, London EC4Y 7BY,
Telephone: 0171 353 7768/7769/2711
Call date: July 1986, Middle Temple
Qualifications: [BSc (Hons)(Aston)]

CLARK WAYNE VINCENT

Falcon Chambers
Falcon Court, London EC4Y 1AA,
Telephone: 0171 353 2484/7
Call date: July 1982, Middle Temple
Qualifications: [LLB (Lond), BCL, (Oxon)]

CLARKE MISS ALISON LEE

1 Serjeants' Inn
5th Floor Fleet Street, Temple, London
EC4Y 1LL, Telephone: 0171 415 6666
E-mail: no1serjeantsinn@btinternet.com
Call date: Oct 1994, Lincoln's Inn
Qualifications: [LLB (Hons)(Leic)]

CLARKE ANDREW BERTRAM QC (1997)

Littleton Chambers
3 King's Bench Walk North, Temple, London
EC4Y 7HR, Telephone: 0171 797 8600
E-mail: littletonchambers@compuserve.com
Call date: July 1980, Middle Temple
Qualifications: [LLB, AKC (Lond), BCL]

CLARKE ANDREW STANLEY ROBERT

Sedan House
Stanley Place, Chester CH1 2LU,
Telephone: 01244 320480/348282
Call date: July 1996, Gray's Inn

CLARKE MISS ANNA VICTORIA

5 Stone Buildings
Lincoln's Inn, London WC2A 3XT,
Telephone: 0171 242 6201
E-mail: clerks@5-stonebuildings.law.co.uk
Call date: Nov 1994, Inner Temple
Qualifications: [BA (Lond), CPE (Notts)]

CLARKE CHRISTOPHER SIMON COURTENAY S QC (1984)

Brick Court Chambers
15/19 Devereux Court, London WC2R 3JJ,
Telephone: 0171 583 0777
E-mail: (surname)@brickcourt.demon.co.uk
Call date: Nov 1969, Middle Temple
Recorder
Qualifications: [MA (Cantab)]

CLARKE MISS ELIZABETH ANNE

Queen Elizabeth Bldg
2nd Floor, Temple, London EC4Y 9BS,
Telephone: 0171 797 7837
Call date: Nov 1991, Gray's Inn
Qualifications: [LLB (Oxon), BA (Hons)(Oxon),
Jurisprudence]

CLARKE MISS FRANCESCA LOUISE

Forest House Chambers
15 Granville Road, Walthamstow, London
E17 9BS, Telephone: 0181 925 2240
Call date: Nov 1981, Inner Temple
Qualifications: [BA]

CLARKE GEORGE ROBERT IVAN

46/48 Essex Street
London WC2R 3GH,
Telephone: 0171 583 8899
Call date: Nov 1973, Gray's Inn
Qualifications: [LLB (Hons)]

CLARKE GERARD JOSEPH PATRICK

2 Hare Court
Ground Floor, Temple, London EC4Y 7BH,
Telephone: 0171 583 1770
E-mail: 2_Hare_Court@link.org
Call date: July 1986, Middle Temple
Qualifications: [MA (Oxon), Dip Law]

CLARKE MS HELEN

6 King's Bench Walk
Ground, Third & Fourth Floors, Temple,
London EC4Y 7DR,
Telephone: 0171 353 4931/583 0695
Call date: Nov 1988, Middle Temple
Qualifications: [BA (Hons) (Oxon), Dip Law]

CLARKE IAN JAMES

Hardwicke Building
New Square, Lincoln's Inn, London
WC2A 3SB, Telephone: 0171 242 2523
E-mail: clerks@hardwicke.co.uk
Call date: Oct 1990, Lincoln's Inn
Qualifications: [LLB (Hons)(Newc)]

CLARKE JAMIE ROY

Plowden Bldgs
2nd Floor, Temple, London EC4Y 9BU,
Telephone: 0171 583 0808
E-mail: bar@plowdenbuildings.co.uk
Call date: Nov 1995, Gray's Inn
Qualifications: [BA (Oxon)]

CLARKE JEFFREY JOHN

Gower Chambers
57 Walter Road, Swansea, West Glamorgan
SA1 5PZ, Telephone: 01792 644466
E-mail: clerk@gowerchambers.co.uk
Call date: Nov 1985, Middle Temple
Qualifications: [B.Soc.Sc (Keele)]

CLARKE MS JOANNA M

Gray's Inn Chambers
5th Floor, Gray's Inn, London WC1R 5JA,
Telephone: 0171 404 1111
Call date: Oct 1993, Gray's Inn
Qualifications: [MA (Oxon)]

CLARKE MS JOANNE ELIZABETH

33 Bedford Row
London WC1R 4JH,
Telephone: 0171 242 6476
Call date: Nov 1993, Inner Temple
Qualifications: [LLB]

CLARKE JONATHAN CHRISTOPHER ST JOHN

Old Square Chambers
Hanover House 47 Corn Street, Bristol
BS1 1HT, Telephone: 0117 9277111
Old Square Chambers
1 Verulam Buildings, Gray's Inn, London
WC1R 5LQ, Telephone: 0171 831 0801
Call date: Oct 1990, Middle Temple
Qualifications: [BA (Hons)(Ulster), Dip Law]

CLARKE KEVIN GORDON CHARLES

Francis Taylor Bldg
2nd Floor, Temple, London EC4Y 7BY,
Telephone: 0171 353 9942/3157
Call date: Feb 1983, Inner Temple
Qualifications: [LLB (Lond)(Hons)]

CLARKE MISS LISA TARIN

Clapham Chambers
21-25 Bedford Road, Clapham North, London
SW4 7SH, Telephone: 0171 978 8482/
642 5777
E-mail: 113063.632@compuserve.com
Call date: Oct 1995, Gray's Inn
Qualifications: [BA (Cantab)]

CLARKE MALCOLM JOHN

Maidstone Chambers
33 Earl Street, Maidstone, Kent ME14 1PF,
Telephone: 01622 688592
Call date: Oct 1994, Gray's Inn
Qualifications: [LLB]

CLARKE MISS MICHELLE NICOLA

Earl Street Chambers
47 Earl Street, Maidstone, Kent ME14 1PD,
Telephone: 01622 671222
E-mail: gunner-sparks@msn.com
Call date: July 1988, Inner Temple
Qualifications: [LLB (Soton)]

CLARKE NICHOLAS STEPHEN

9 St John Street
Manchester M3 4DN,
Telephone: 0161 955 9000
E-mail: ninesjs@gconnect.com
Call date: July 1981, Middle Temple
Qualifications: [LLB (Hons)]

CLARKE PETER JOHN

7 Fountain Court
Steelhouse Lane, Birmingham B4 6DR,
Telephone: 0121 236 8531
2 Harcourt Bldgs
1st Floor, Temple, London EC4Y 9DB,
Telephone: 0171 353 6961/7
Door Tenant
Harcourt Chambers
Churchill House 3 St Aldate's Courtyard, St
Aldate's, Oxford OX1 1BN,
Telephone: 01865 791559
Call date: Nov 1970, Lincoln's Inn
Qualifications: [MA (Oxon), BCL (Oxon)]

CLARKE PETER WILLIAM QC (1997)

Hollis Whiteman Chambers
3rd/4th Floor Queen Elizabeth Bldg, Temple,
London EC4Y 9BS, Telephone: 0171 583 5766
E-mail: hollis.whiteman@btinternet.com
Call date: July 1973, Lincoln's Inn
Recorder

CLARKE MISS SARAH ANNE

10 Park Square
Leeds LS1 2LH, Telephone: 0113 2455438
E-mail: chambers@bandit.legend.co.uk
Call date: Oct 1994, Inner Temple
Qualifications: [BA (Durham)]

CLARKE MISS SUSAN LESLEY

Peel House Chambers
Ground Floor, Peel House 5 Harrington Street,
Liverpool L2 9QA, Telephone: 0151 236 4321
Call date: Oct 1996, Middle Temple
Qualifications: [LLB (Hons), LLM (L'pool)]

CLARKE TIMOTHY JOHN

8 Fountain Court
Steelhouse Lane, Birmingham B4 6DR,
Telephone: 0121 236 5514/5
E-mail: clerks@no8chambers.co.uk
Call date: Oct 1992, Middle Temple
Qualifications: [MA (Cantab)]

CLARKSON PATRICK ROBERT JAMES QC (1991)

1 Serjeants' Inn
4th Floor, Temple, London EC4Y 1NH,
Telephone: 0171 583 1355
E-mail: serjeants.inn@virgin.net
Call date: July 1972, Lincoln's Inn
Assistant Recorder

CLARKSON STUART JAMES MACGREGOR

St Ive's Chambers
9 Fountain Ct, Birmingham B4 6DR,
Telephone: 0121 236 0863/0929
Call date: Nov 1987, Gray's Inn
Qualifications: [BA (L'pool)]

CLAXTON ELROY GERALDO

1 Crown Office Row
2nd Floor, Temple, London EC4Y 7HH,
Telephone: 0171 797 7111
Call date: July 1983, Inner Temple
Qualifications: [LLB (Lond)]

CLAXTON MISS JUDITH MARY

St Mary's Chambers
50 High Pavement, Lace Market, Nottingham
NG1 1HW, Telephone: 0115 9503503
E-mail: clerks@smc.law.co.uk
Call date: Oct 1991, Middle Temple
Qualifications: [LLB Hons]

CLAY JONATHAN ROGER

11 Bolt Court
London EC4A 3DQ,
Telephone: 0171 353 2300
E-mail: boltct11@aol.com
Redhill Chambers
Seloduct House 30 Station Road, Redhill
RH1 1NK, Telephone: 01737 780781
Call date: Oct 1990, Lincoln's Inn
Qualifications: [BSc, LLB]

CLAY ROBERT CHARLES

1 Atkin Building
Gray's Inn, London WC1R 5AT,
Telephone: 0171 404 0102
E-mail: clerks@atkin-chambers.co.uk
Call date: July 1989, Inner Temple
Qualifications: [D Phil (Oxon), BA (Oxon), Dip
Law]

CLAYSON TIMOTHY

6 Park Square
Leeds LS1 2LW, Telephone: 0113 2459763
E-mail: chambers@no6.co.uk
Call date: July 1974, Gray's Inn
Recorder
Qualifications: [LLB (Lond)]

CLAYTON MISS JOANNA DENISE

2 Harcourt Bldgs
2nd Floor, Temple, London EC4Y 9DB,
Telephone: 0171 353 8415
E-mail: clerks@twoharcourtbldgs.demon.co.uk
Call date: Nov 1995, Lincoln's Inn
Qualifications: [LLB (Euro)(Hons), (Bris)]

CLAYTON NIGEL GARVIN

28 St John Street
Manchester M3 4DJ,
Telephone: 0161 834 8418
E-mail: clerk@28stjohnst.co.uk
Call date: July 1987, Inner Temple
Qualifications: [LLB]

CLAYTON RICHARD ANTHONY

Devereux Chambers
Devereux Court, London WC2R 3JJ,
Telephone: 0171 353 7534
E-mail: elton@devchambers.co.uk
Call date: Nov 1977, Middle Temple
Qualifications: [MA (Oxon)]

CLAYTON MISS ROSALIND

95A Chancery Lane
London WC2A 1DT,
Telephone: 0171 405 3101
Call date: Nov 1988, Middle Temple
Qualifications: [LLB (Shef), BA (Open U), MA
(Brunel), Dip Law]

CLAYTON STEPHEN CHARLES RAYNOR

2 Harcourt Bldgs
1st Floor, Temple, London EC4Y 9DB,
Telephone: 0171 353 2112/2817
Call date: May 1973, Inner Temple

CLEASBY JOHN PAUL

Cleveland Chambers
63-65 Borough Road, Middlesbrough,
Cleveland TS1 3AA, Telephone: 01642 226036
Call date: Oct 1994, Lincoln's Inn
Qualifications: [LLB (Hons)(Leic)]

CLEAVE MRS BARBARA LESTER

1 Gray's Inn Square
1st Floor, London WC1R 5AG,
Telephone: 0171 405 3000
E-mail: clerks@onegrays.demon.co.uk
Door Tenant
Call date: July 1989, Inner Temple
Qualifications: [LLB]

CLEAVE MISS GILLIAN MARGARET

One Garden Court
Ground Floor, Temple, London EC4Y 9BJ,
Telephone: 0171 797 7900
Call date: Nov 1988, Inner Temple
Qualifications: [BA (Oxon), Dip Law (City)]

D

CLEAVER HENRY WILLIAM MANSEL

3 Temple Gardens
3rd Floor, Temple, London EC4Y 9AU,
Telephone: 0171 583 0010
Call date: July 1985, Inner Temple
Qualifications: [BA, Dip Law]

CLEAVER WAYNE DAVID

6 Gray's Inn Square
Ground Floor, Gray's Inn, London WC1R 5AZ,
Telephone: 0171 242 1052
Call date: July 1986, Inner Temple
Qualifications: [LLB Wales]

CLEE CHRISTOPHER

Angel Chambers
94 Walter Road, Swansea SA1 5QA,
Telephone: 01792 6464623/6464648
Call date: July 1983, Gray's Inn
Qualifications: [LLB Hons (Cardiff)]

CLEEVE THOMAS D'AUVERGNE

33 Bedford Row
London WC1R 4JH,
Telephone: 0171 242 6476
Call date: Feb 1993, Lincoln's Inn
Qualifications: [B.Sc, Diploma of Law]

CLEGG ADAM GORDON

Stour Chambers
Barton Mill House Barton Mill Road,
Canterbury, Kent CT1 1BP,
Telephone: 01227 764899
E-mail: clerks@stourchambers.co.uk
Call date: Nov 1994, Gray's Inn
Qualifications: [BA (Kent)]

CLEGG SEBASTIAN JAMES BARWICK

Deans Court Chambers
Cumberland House Crown Square, Manchester
M3 3HA, Telephone: 0161 834 4097
E-mail: deanscourt@compuserve.com
Call date: May 1994, Inner Temple
Qualifications: [BA (Bris), CPE]

CLEGG SIMON ROBERT JONATHAN

4 Fountain Court
Steelhouse Lane, Birmingham B4 6DR,
Telephone: 0121 236 3476
Call date: July 1980, Lincoln's Inn
Qualifications: [LLB (Lond)]

CLEGG WILLIAM QC (1991)

3 Hare Court
1st Floor, Temple, London EC4Y 7BJ,
Telephone: 0171 353 7561
Call date: July 1972, Gray's Inn
Recorder
Qualifications: [LLB]

CLEMENS ADAM

Bridewell Chambers
2 Bridewell Place, London EC4V 6AP,
Telephone: 0171 797 8800
E-mail: clerks@bridewell.law.co.uk
Call date: July 1985, Lincoln's Inn
Qualifications: [LLB (Newc)]

CLEMENT PETER GUY

2 Harcourt Bldgs
1st Floor, Temple, London EC4Y 9DB,
Telephone: 0171 353 2112/2817
Call date: Nov 1988, Inner Temple
Qualifications: [LLB,LLM(Lond)]

CLEMENTS MISS PAULA KATE

Guildford Chambers
Stoke House Leapale Lane, Guildford, Surrey
GU1 4LY, Telephone: 01483 539131
E-mail: guildford.barristers@btinternet.com
Call date: July 1985, Inner Temple
Qualifications: [LLB (So'ton)]

CLEMES ANDREW JOHN

Gower Chambers
57 Walter Road, Swansea, West Glamorgan
SA1 5PZ, Telephone: 01792 644466
E-mail: clerk@gowerchambers.co.uk
Call date: Nov 1984, Gray's Inn
Qualifications: [MA (Oxon)]

CLEMITSON MISS JULIE

Broad Chare
33 Broad Chare, Newcastle Upon Tyne
NE1 3DQ, Telephone: 0191 232 0541
Call date: Nov 1991, Inner Temple
Qualifications: [LLB (New)]

CLEVERLY CHRISTOPHER JOHN

Trafalgar Chambers
53 Fleet Street, London EC4Y 1BE,
Telephone: 0171 583 5858
E-mail: TrafalgarChambers@easynet.co.uk
Call date: Nov 1990, Middle Temple
Qualifications: [LLB (Lond)]

CLEWS RICHARD ANTHONY

6 Park Square
Leeds LS1 2LW, Telephone: 0113 2459763
E-mail: chambers@no6.co.uk
Call date: July 1986, Gray's Inn
Qualifications: [LLB]

CLIFF BARRY GEORGE

Regent Chambers
29 Regent Road, Hanley, Stoke On Trent
ST1 3BP, Telephone: 01782 286666
E-mail: regent@ftech.co.uk
Call date: July 1988, Lincoln's Inn
Qualifications: [LLB (Hons), IMEMME]

CLIFF MISS ELIZABETH DUNBAR

Chavasse Court Chambers
2nd Floor Chavasse Court, 24 Lord Street,
Liverpool L2 1TA, Telephone: 0151 707 1191
Call date: July 1975, Middle Temple

CLIFF GRAHAM HILTON

Priory Chambers
2 Fountain Court, Steelhouse Lane,
Birmingham B4 6DR,
Telephone: 0121 236 3882/1375
Call date: July 1973, Middle Temple
Qualifications: [LLB(Hons)(Lond)]

CLIFF PAUL RICHARD

Regent Chambers
29 Regent Road, Hanley, Stoke On Trent
ST1 3BP, Telephone: 01782 286666
E-mail: regent@ftech.co.uk
Call date: Nov 1992, Gray's Inn
Qualifications: [LLB]

CLIFFORD (NIGEL) JAMES

7 Stone Bldgs
Ground Floor, Lincoln's Inn, London
WC2A 3SZ, Telephone: 0171 405 3886/
242 3546
E-mail: chaldous@vossnet.co.uk
Call date: July 1984, Lincoln's Inn
Qualifications: [BA (Oxon)]

CLIFT-MATTHEWS MS AMANDA LOUISE

Victoria Chambers
3rd Floor 177 Corporation Street, Birmingham
B4 6RG, Telephone: 0121 236 9900
Call date: Nov 1995, Lincoln's Inn
Qualifications: [LLB (Lond)]

CLIMIE ROGER STEPHEN

35 Essex Street
Temple, London WC2R 3AR,
Telephone: 0171 353 6381
Call date: July 1982, Lincoln's Inn
Qualifications: [BA]

CLOMPUS JOEL

Furnival Chambers
32 Furnival Street, London EC4A 1JQ,
Telephone: 0171 405 3232
E-mail: clerks@furnivallaw.co.uk
Call date: July 1976, Inner Temple
Qualifications: [BA, PhD (Cantab)]

CLOSE DOUGLAS JONATHAN

13 Old Square
1st Floor, Lincoln's Inn, London WC2A 3UA,
Telephone: 0171 242 6105
E-mail: clerks@serlecourt.co.uk
Call date: Nov 1991, Lincoln's Inn
Qualifications: [BA (Hons) (Oxon), BCL
(Oxon)]

D

CLOUGH GEOFFREY DUNCOMBE

Coleridge Chambers
Citadel 190 Corporation Street, Birmingham
B4 6QD, Telephone: 0121 233 3303
Call date: Nov 1961, Gray's Inn
Qualifications: [BA]

CLOUGH RICHARD WILLIAM BUTLER

Gray's Inn Chambers
5th Floor, Gray's Inn, London WC1R 5JA,
Telephone: 0171 404 1111
Call date: Nov 1971, Inner Temple

CLOUT MISS EMMA MARGARET

Sussex Chambers
9 Old Steine, Brighton BN1 1FJ,
Telephone: 01273 607953
Call date: Nov 1989, Middle Temple
Qualifications: [BA Hons (Lond)]

CLOVER (THOMAS) ANTHONY

New Court Chambers
5 Verulam Buildings, Gray's Inn, London
WC1R 5LY, Telephone: 0171 831 9500
E-mail: mail@newcourtchambers.com
Call date: July 1971, Middle Temple
Recorder
Qualifications: [BA (Oxon)]

CLOVER MISS SARAH

2 Mitre Ct Bldgs
1st Floor, Temple, London EC4Y 7BX,
Telephone: 0171 353 1353
Call date: Nov 1993, Lincoln's Inn
Qualifications: [BA (Oxon)(Hons), LLM
(UPenn)]

CLUTTERBUCK ANDREW MAURICE GRAY

4 Stone Bldgs
Ground Floor, Lincoln's Inn, London
WC2A 3XT, Telephone: 0171 242 5524
E-mail: d.goddard@4stonebuildings.law.co.uk
Call date: Oct 1992, Middle Temple
Qualifications: [BA (Hons)]

COATES GEORGE ALEXANDER NIGEL

Guildford Chambers
Stoke House Leapale Lane, Guildford, Surrey
GU1 4LY, Telephone: 01483 539131
E-mail: guildford.barristers@btinternet.com
Call date: Nov 1990, Middle Temple
Qualifications: [BA (Cantab)]

COATES JOHN PAUL

1 Gray's Inn Square
Ground Floor, London WC1R 5AA,
Telephone: 0171 405 8946/7/8
Call date: Nov 1988, Middle Temple
Qualifications: [LLB (Warwick)]

COATES MISS SUZANNE

1 King's Bench Walk
2nd Floor, Temple, London EC4Y 7DB,
Telephone: 0171 936 1500
E-mail: ddear@1kbw.co.uk
Call date: July 1978, Gray's Inn
Qualifications: [LLB (Lond), SRN]

COBB STEPHEN WILLIAM SCOTT

One Garden Court
Ground Floor, Temple, London EC4Y 9BJ,
Telephone: 0171 797 7900
Call date: July 1985, Inner Temple
Qualifications: [LLB (L'pool)]

COBBS MISS LAURA SUSAN

2 Harcourt Bldgs
1st Floor, Temple, London EC4Y 9DB,
Telephone: 0171 353 2112/2817
Call date: Nov 1989, Middle Temple
Qualifications: [LLB (Hons)(Bucks)]

COBURN MICHAEL JEREMY PATRICK

20 Essex Street
London WC2R 3AL,
Telephone: 0171 583 9294
E-mail: clerks@20essexst.com
Call date: Nov 1990, Inner Temple
Qualifications: [BA (Oxon), Dip Law (City)]

COCHAND CHARLES MACLEAN

Eighteen Carlton Crescent
Southampton SO15 2XR,
Telephone: 01703 639001
Call date: Feb 1978, Middle Temple
Qualifications: [BA (Hons)]

COCHRANE CHRISTOPHER DUNCAN QC (1988)

2-3 Gray's Inn Square
Gray's Inn, London WC1R 5JH,
Telephone: 0171 242 4986
E-mail: chambers@2-3graysinnsquare.co.uk
Call date: Feb 1965, Middle Temple
Recorder
Qualifications: [BA (Oxon)]

COCKERILL MISS SARA ELIZABETH

Essex Court Chambers
24 Lincoln's Inn Fields, London WC2A 3ED,
Telephone: 0171 813 8000
E-mail: clerksroom@essexcourt-chambers.co.uk
Call date: Oct 1990, Lincoln's Inn
Qualifications: [MA (Oxon)]

COCKRILL TIMOTHY ROBERT

New Walk Chambers
27 New Walk, Leicester LE1 6TE,
Telephone: 0116 2559144
Call date: July 1991, Gray's Inn
Qualifications: [MA (Cantab)]

COCKS DAVID JOHN QC (1982)

18 Red Lion Court
(Off Fleet Street), London EC4A 3EB,
Telephone: 0171 520 6000
Thornwood House
102 New London Road, Chelmsford, Essex
CM2 0RG, Telephone: 01245 280880
Call date: June 1961, Lincoln's Inn
Recorder
Qualifications: [MA (Juris Oxon)]

CODNER PETER FYNES TIMOTHY LEIGH

Devizes Chambers
11 High Street, Potterne, Devizes, Wiltshire
SN10 5PY, Telephone: 01380 724896
E-mail: pc@devcham.demon.co.uk
Door Tenant
Staple Inn Chambers
1st Floor 9 Staple Inn, Holborn, London
WC1V 7QH, Telephone: 0171 242 5240
E-mail: clerks@staple-inn.org
Door Tenant
Call date: July 1983, Inner Temple
Qualifications: [BA]

COE MRS ROSALIND

24 The Ropewalk
Nottingham NG1 5EF,
Telephone: 0115 9472581
E-mail: clerk@ropewalk.co.uk
Call date: July 1983, Middle Temple
Qualifications: [LLB (Nott'm)]

COEN MISS YVONNE ANNE

9 Bedford Row
London WC1R 4AZ,
Telephone: 0171 242 3555
E-mail: clerks@9br.co.uk
Call date: Nov 1982, Lincoln's Inn
Assistant Recorder
Qualifications: [MA (Oxon)]

COFFEY JOHN JOSEPH QC (1996)

3 Temple Gardens
Lower Ground Floor, Temple, London
EC4Y 9AU, Telephone: 0171 353 3102/5/9297
Call date: Nov 1970, Middle Temple
Recorder
Qualifications: [LLB (Lond)(Hons)]

COFIE EDMUND KPAKPO

Somersett Chambers
52 Bedford Row, London WC1R 4LR,
Telephone: 0171 404 6701
E-mail: Somersettchambers@cocoon.co.uk
Call date: July 1980, Middle Temple
Qualifications: [LLB Hons (Lond)]

D

COGAN MICHAEL JAMES

6 King's Bench Walk
Ground, Third & Fourth Floors, Temple,
London EC4Y 7DR,
Telephone: 0171 353 4931/583 0695
Call date: Feb 1986, Middle Temple
Qualifications: [BA (Hons)]

COGGINS JONATHAN

1 Harcourt Bldgs
2nd Floor, Temple, London EC4Y 9DA,
Telephone: 0171 353 9421/9151
Call date: July 1980, Middle Temple
Qualifications: [BA]

COGHLAN TERENCE QC (1993)

1 Crown Office Row
Ground Floor, Temple, London EC4Y 7HH,
Telephone: 0171 797 7500
Crown Office Row Chambers
Blenheim House 120 Church Street, Brighton,
Sussex BN1 1WH, Telephone: 01273 625625
Call date: Nov 1968, Inner Temple
Recorder
Qualifications: [MA (Oxon)]

COGLEY STEPHEN WILLIAM

Merchant Chambers
1 North Parade, Parsonage Gardens,
Manchester M3 2NH,
Telephone: 0161 839 7070
Call date: Nov 1984, Gray's Inn
Qualifications: [LLB (Hons) (Newc)]

COGSWELL MISS FREDERICA NATASHA

Gough Square Chambers
6-7 Gough Square, London EC4A 3DE,
Telephone: 0171 353 0924
E-mail: gsc@goughsq.co.uk
Call date: Nov 1995, Lincoln's Inn
Qualifications: [BSc (Hons)(Maths), BSc
(Hons)(Chem), MSc (Lond)]

COHEN ANDREW RONALD

4 Brick Court
Ground Floor, Temple, London EC4Y 9AD,
Telephone: 0171 797 7766
E-mail: chambers@4brick.co.uk
Call date: Nov 1982, Gray's Inn
Qualifications: [BA (Hons) (Keele)]

COHEN EDWARD MERVYN

11 Stone Bldgs
Ground Floor, Lincoln's Inn, London
WC2A 3TG, Telephone: 0171 831 6381
E-mail: clerks@11StoneBuildings.law.co.uk
Call date: July 1972, Middle Temple
Qualifications: [MA (Cantab)]

COHEN JONATHAN LIONEL QC (1997)

4 Paper Bldgs
2nd Floor, Temple, London EC4Y 7EX,
Telephone: 0171 583 0816/071 353 1131
E-mail: clerks@4paperbuildings.co.uk
Call date: July 1974, Lincoln's Inn
Recorder
Qualifications: [BA]

COHEN JOSEPH MICHAEL

Old Colony House
6 South King Street, Manchester M2 6DQ,
Telephone: 0161 834 4364
Call date: Oct 1992, Gray's Inn
Qualifications: [BA (Hons)(Lancs)]

COHEN LAWRENCE FRANCIS RICHARD QC (1993)

24 Old Bldgs
Ground Floor, Lincoln's Inn, London
WC2A 3UJ, Telephone: 0171 404 0946
E-mail: clerks@24oldbuildings.law.co.uk
Call date: July 1974, Gray's Inn
Assistant Recorder
Qualifications: [LLB]

COHEN MISS LINDA

39 Windsor Road
London N3 3SN, Telephone: 0181 349 9194
E-mail: lindacohen@cobeck.clara.net
Call date: July 1985, Middle Temple
Qualifications: [MA (Wark)]

COHEN RAPHAEL GIDEON

9 Woodhouse Square
Leeds LS3 1AD, Telephone: 0113 2451986
Call date: July 1981, Lincoln's Inn
Qualifications: [LLB]

D

COHEN MISS SAMANTHA LOUISE

4 Brick Court
1st Floor, Temple, London EC4Y 9AD,
Telephone: 0171 583 8455
Call date: Nov 1995, Inner Temple
Qualifications: [BA (Soton), CPE (City)]

COKE EDWARD PETER

St Ive's Chambers
9 Fountain Ct, Birmingham B4 6DR,
Telephone: 0121 236 0863/0929
Call date: July 1976, Inner Temple
Qualifications: [LLB (Warwick)]

COKER WILLIAM JOHN QC (1994)

9 Bedford Row
London WC1R 4AZ,
Telephone: 0171 242 3555
E-mail: clerks@9br.co.uk
Call date: Nov 1973, Gray's Inn
Recorder
Qualifications: [LLB]

COLBEY RICHARD (ALAN)

Francis Taylor Bldg
3rd Floor, Temple, London EC4Y 7BY,
Telephone: 0171 797 7250
Guildhall Chambers Portsmouth
Prudential Buildings 16 Guildhall Walk,
Portsmouth, Hampshire PO1 2DE,
Telephone: 01705 752400
Call date: July 1984, Inner Temple
Qualifications: [LLB (Exon)]

COLBORNE MISS MICHELLE DIANE

Broadway House Chambers
Broadway House 9 Bank Street, Bradford,
West Yorkshire BD1 1TW,
Telephone: 01274 722560
Call date: May 1993, Gray's Inn
Qualifications: [LLB (Mid Glamorgan)]

COLE EDWARD ARTHUR

Falcon Chambers
Falcon Court, London EC4Y 1AA,
Telephone: 0171 353 2484/7
Call date: July 1980, Gray's Inn
Qualifications: [MA (Oxon)]

COLE GORDON STEWART

38 Young Street
Manchester M3 3FT,
Telephone: 0161 833 0489
E-mail: clerks@young-st-chambers.com
Call date: July 1979, Inner Temple
Qualifications: [BA (L'Pool)]

COLE JONATHAN RICHARD

Lamb Chambers
Lamb Building, Temple, London EC4Y 7AS,
Telephone: 0171 797 8300
E-mail: lambchambers@link.org
Call date: Apr 1964, Gray's Inn
Recorder
Qualifications: [BA (Dub), FCI Arb]

COLE JUSTIN MARK

5 Paper Bldgs
1st Floor, Temple, London EC4Y 7HB,
Telephone: 0171 583 6117
E-mail: clerks@5-paperbuildings.law.co.uk
Call date: May 1992, Inner Temple
Qualifications: [LLB (Notts)]

COLE MISS JUSTINE AMANDA

Bank House Chambers
Old Bank House, Hartshead, Sheffield S1 2EL,
Telephone: 0114 2751223
Call date: Nov 1994, Inner Temple
Qualifications: [LLB (Sheff) (Hons)]

COLE MISS LORNA

Wilberforce Chambers
Bishop Lane, Hull HU1 1PA,
Telephone: 01482 323264
E-mail: clerks@hullbar.demon.co.uk
Call date: Nov 1950, Lincoln's Inn
Qualifications: [LLB]

COLE MARTIN DAVID

Lamb Building
Ground Floor, Temple, London EC4Y 7AS,
Telephone: 0171 797 7788
E-mail: lamb.building@link.org
Call date: Nov 1994, Inner Temple
Qualifications: [LLB (Hons)]

COLE NICHOLAS ARTHUR

St Ive's Chambers
9 Fountain Ct, Birmingham B4 6DR,
Telephone: 0121 236 0863/0929
Call date: Oct 1993, Lincoln's Inn
Qualifications: [BSc (Hons)(B'ham), CPE]

COLE RICHARD JOHN

New Court
1st Floor, Temple, London EC4Y 9BE,
Telephone: 0171 797 8999
Lancaster Building Chambers
77 Deansgate, Manchester M3 2BW,
Telephone: 0161 661 4444
E-mail: sandra@lbnipc.com
Call date: July 1988, Gray's Inn
Qualifications: [BSc (Eng), ACGI, LLB, C.Eng,
MIEE, MBCS]

COLE ROBERT IAN GAWAIN

30 Park Square
Leeds LS1 2PF, Telephone: 0113 2436388
Call date: Oct 1991, Middle Temple
Qualifications: [LLM]

COLE MISS VANESSA ANNE

Phoenix Chambers
First Floor Gray's Inn Chambers, Gray's Inn,
London WC1R 5JA, Telephone: 0171 404 7888
Call date: Oct 1992, Lincoln's Inn
Qualifications: [LLB(Hons)(Manch)]

COLE-WILSON MS LOIS EKUNDAYO

1 Gray's Inn Square
Ground Floor, London WC1R 5AA,
Telephone: 0171 405 8946/7/8
Call date: Nov 1995, Inner Temple
Qualifications: [BA (Warwick), MA (Lond),
CPE (Lond), LLB (Hons)]

COLE-WILSON MISS YATONI IYAMIDE ELIZABETH

Lancaster Building Chambers
77 Deansgate, Manchester M3 2BW,
Telephone: 0161 661 4444
E-mail: sandra@lbnipc.com
Call date: Nov 1980, Lincoln's Inn
Qualifications: [BA (Hons)]

COLEGATE-STONE JEFFERSON MARK

2 King's Bench Walk
1st Floor, Temple, London EC4Y 7DE,
Telephone: 0171 353 9276
Call date: Nov 1975, Inner Temple

COLEMAN ANTHONY JOHN SCOTT

3 Paper Bldgs
1st Floor, Temple, London EC4Y 7EU,
Telephone: 0171 583 8055
E-mail: london@3paper.com
20 Lorne Park Road
Bournemouth BH1 1JN,
Telephone: 01202 292102 (5 Lines)
1 Alfred Street
High Street, Oxford OX1 4EH,
Telephone: 01865 793736
Call date: July 1973, Middle Temple
Qualifications: [MA (Oxon)]

COLEMAN BRUCE ROBERT

One Garden Court
Ground Floor, Temple, London EC4Y 9BJ,
Telephone: 0171 797 7900
Call date: July 1972, Inner Temple
Qualifications: [LLB]

COLEMAN CLIVE RUSSELL

199 Strand
London WC2R 1DR,
Telephone: 0171 379 9779
E-mail: chambers@199strand.co.uk
Door Tenant
Call date: July 1986, Lincoln's Inn
Qualifications: [BA (York) Dip Law]

COLEMAN MISS ELIZABETH JOANNE

4 Paper Bldgs
2nd Floor, Temple, London EC4Y 7EX,
Telephone: 0171 583 0816/071 353 1131
E-mail: clerks@4paperbuildings.co.uk
Call date: July 1985, Inner Temple
Qualifications: [MA (Cantab)]

COLEMAN NICHOLAS JOHN

1 Hare Court
Ground Floor, Temple, London EC4Y 7BE,
Telephone: 0171 353 3982/5324
Call date: July 1970, Inner Temple
Recorder
Qualifications: [LLB (Hons)]

COLEMAN RICHARD JAMES LEE

Fountain Court
Temple, London EC4Y 9DH,
Telephone: 0171 583 3335
E-mail: chambers@fountaincourt.co.uk
Call date: Feb 1994, Lincoln's Inn
Qualifications: [MA (Cantab), LLM ((Yale)]

COLEMAN RUSSELL ADAM

4 Pump Court
Temple, London EC4Y 7AN,
Telephone: 0171 353 2656/9
E-mail: 4_pump_court@compuserve.com
Call date: July 1986, Inner Temple
Qualifications: [LLB (Wales)]

COLERIDGE PAUL JAMES DUKE QC (1993)

Queen Elizabeth Bldg
2nd Floor, Temple, London EC4Y 9BS,
Telephone: 0171 797 7837
Call date: July 1970, Middle Temple
Recorder

COLES MICHAEL EDEN

Paradise Square Chambers
26 Paradise Square, Sheffield S1 2DE,
Telephone: 0114 2738951
Call date: July 1986, Inner Temple
Qualifications: [LLB (Bristol)]

COLES STEVEN FREDERICK

1 Paper Bldgs
Ground Floor, Temple, London EC4Y 7EP,
Telephone: 0171 583 7355
E-mail: clerks@1pb.co.uk
Call date: July 1983, Middle Temple
Qualifications: [MA (Cantab)]

COLEY MISS CLARE LOUISE

Clock Chambers
78 Darlington Street, Wolverhampton
WV1 4LY, Telephone: 01902 313444
Call date: Nov 1978, Middle Temple

COLEY WILLIAM LYNDALL

35 Essex Street
Temple, London WC2R 3AR,
Telephone: 0171 353 6381
Call date: July 1980, Middle Temple
Qualifications: [BA (Cantab)]

COLIN GILES DAVID

Crown Office Row Chambers
Blenheim House 120 Church Street, Brighton,
Sussex BN1 1WH, Telephone: 01273 625625
Call date: Feb 1994, Inner Temple
Qualifications: [BA (Dunelm), Dip Law]

COLLACO MORAES FRANCIS THOMAS

2 Gray's Inn Square Chambers
Gray's Inn Square, London WC1R 5AA,
Telephone: 0171 242 0328/405 1317
E-mail: clerks@2gis.co.uk
Call date: Nov 1985, Lincoln's Inn
Qualifications: [BA (Hons)]

Fax: 0171 405 3082;
Out of hours telephone: 0378 389865; DX: 43
London, Chancery Lane

Types of work: Bankruptcy; Chancery (general);
Company and commercial; Insolvency;
Professional negligence

Reported cases: *The Mayor and Burgess of the London Borough of Hounslow v Michinton*, [1997] 74 P&CR 221, 1997. Adverse possession.
Botham v TSB Plc, [1997] 73 P&CR DI, 1996. Fixtures.
Vaughan-Armatrading v Sarsah, 27 HLR 631 (CA), 1995. Landlord and tenant.
Bryan + Others v Barton + others, (1997) *TheTimes*, 20 March (CA), 1997. Estoppel.
In The Matter of the Minories Underwriting Agency Ltd, 1996. Section 14 of the Insolvency Act 1986.

D

COLLARD MICHAEL DAVID

5 Pump Court
Ground Floor, Temple, London EC4Y 7AP,
Telephone: 0171 353 2532
E-mail: fivepump@netcomuk.co.uk
Call date: July 1986, Middle Temple
Qualifications: [LLB (Bristol)]

COLLENDER ANDREW ROBERT QC (1991)

2 Temple Gardens
Temple, London EC4Y 9AY,
Telephone: 0171 583 6041 (12 Lines)
Call date: July 1969, Lincoln's Inn
Recorder
Qualifications: [LLB (Bris)]

COLLERY SHANE EDWARD

18 Red Lion Court
(Off Fleet Street), London EC4A 3EB,
Telephone: 0171 520 6000
Thornwood House
102 New London Road, Chelmsford, Essex
CM2 0RG, Telephone: 01245 280880
Call date: July 1988, Lincoln's Inn
Qualifications: [LLB (Hons) (Notts)]

COLLETT GAVIN CHARLES

Rougemont Chambers
15 Barnfield Road, Exeter EX1 1RR,
Telephone: 01392 410471
E-mail: rougemont.chambers@eclipse.co.uk
Independent Barristers Clerk
Room 5, 2nd Floor 15 Castle Street, Exeter,
Devon EX4 3PT, Telephone: 01392 210900
E-mail: cathedral.chambers@eclipse.co.uk
Call date: Oct 1993, Inner Temple
Qualifications: [LLB]

COLLETT IVOR WILLIAM

1 Serjeants' Inn
5th Floor Fleet Street, Temple, London
EC4Y 1LL, Telephone: 0171 415 6666
E-mail: no1serjeantsinn@btinternet.com
Call date: Oct 1995, Middle Temple
Qualifications: [BA (Hons)]

COLLETT MICHAEL JOHN

20 Essex Street
London WC2R 3AL,
Telephone: 0171 583 9294
E-mail: clerks@20essexst.com
Call date: Oct 1995, Gray's Inn
Qualifications: [BA]

COLLEY MISS CHRISTINE ELIZABETH

39 Park Square
Leeds LS1 2NU, Telephone: 0113 2456633
Call date: Oct 1992, Middle Temple
Qualifications: [LL.B (Hons)]

COLLEY DR PETER MCLEAN

19 Old Buildings
Lincoln's Inn, London WC2A 3UP,
Telephone: 0171 405 2001
E-mail: clerks@oldbuildingsip.com
Call date: July 1989, Gray's Inn
Qualifications: [BSc (Lond), PhD (Lond), LLB (Lond)]

Fax: 0171 405 0001; DX: 397 Chancery Lane;
Other comms: E-mail
clerks@oldbuildingsip.com

Types of work: Copyright; EC and competition law; Intellectual property; Patents; Scientific and technical disputes; Trademarks

Awards and memberships: MRI; Intellectual Property Bar Association

Publications: *Forms and Agreements on Intellectual Property and International Licensing*

Reported cases: *A Ltd v B Bank and Bank of X*, [1997] FSR 165, 1996. Do foreign bank notes alleged to infringe a British patent give rise to an act justiciable before the English courts.

COLLIER MS JANE SARAH

2 Hare Court
Ground Floor, Temple, London EC4Y 7BH,
Telephone: 0171 583 1770
E-mail: 2_Hare_Court@link.org
Call date: Nov 1994, Middle Temple
Qualifications: [BA (Hons)]

COLLIER JOHN GREENWOOD

20 Essex Street
London WC2R 3AL,
Telephone: 0171 583 9294
E-mail: clerks@20essexst.com
Door Tenant
Call date: Nov 1961, Gray's Inn
Qualifications: [MA,LLB (Cantab)]

COLLIER MARTIN MELTON

Fenners Chambers
3 Madingley Road, Cambridge CB3 OEE,
Telephone: 01223 368761
Fenners Chambers
8-12 Priestgate, Peterborough PE1 1JA,
Telephone: 01733 62030
Call date: July 1982, Gray's Inn
Qualifications: [MA(Oxon)]

COLLIER MS PATRICIA

1 Pump Court
Lower Ground Floor, Temple, London
EC4Y 7AB, Telephone: 0171 583 2012/
353 4341
E-mail: (name) @1pumpcourt.co.uk
Call date: July 1983, Gray's Inn
Qualifications: [LLB]

COLLIER PETER NEVILLE QC (1992)

30 Park Square
Leeds LS1 2PF, Telephone: 0113 2436388
Call date: July 1970, Inner Temple
Recorder
Qualifications: [MA (Cantab)]

COLLINGS ANDREW SIMON JOHN

3 Paper Bldgs
2nd Floor, Temple, London EC4Y 7EU,
Telephone: 0171 353 6208
Call date: Nov 1987, Gray's Inn
Qualifications: [LLB]

COLLINGS MATTHEW GLYNN BURKINSHAW

13 Old Square
Ground Floor, Lincoln's Inn, London
WC2A 3UA, Telephone: 0171 404 4800
Call date: July 1985, Lincoln's Inn
Qualifications: [LLB (Hons) (Lond)]

COLLINGWOOD TIMOTHY DONALD

13 Old Square
1st Floor, Lincoln's Inn, London WC2A 3UA,
Telephone: 0171 242 6105
E-mail: clerks@serlecourt.co.uk
Call date: Oct 1996, Gray's Inn
Qualifications: [BA, BCL (Oxon)]

COLLINS BENJAMIN ROGER

1 Crown Office Row
Ground Floor, Temple, London EC4Y 7HH,
Telephone: 0171 797 7500
Call date: Nov 1996, Middle Temple
Qualifications: [MA (Hons)(Cantab)]

COLLINS JAMES DOUGLAS

Essex Court Chambers
24 Lincoln's Inn Fields, London WC2A 3ED,
Telephone: 0171 813 8000
E-mail: clerksroom@essexcourt-chambers.co.uk
Call date: Feb 1995, Gray's Inn
Qualifications: [BA (Cantab)]

COLLINS MISS JENNIFER CLAIR

Eastbourne Chambers
15 Hyde Gardens, Eastbourne, East Sussex
BN21 4PR, Telephone: 01323 642102/416466
Call date: Oct 1994, Gray's Inn
Qualifications: [BSc]

COLLINS MRS JHOANN TEMLETT

South Western Chambers
Melville House 12 Middle Street, Taunton,
Somerset TA1 1SH, Telephone: 01823 331919
Call date: Nov 1991, Gray's Inn
Qualifications: [LLB (Hons)]

COLLINS JOHN JOSEPH

Westgate Chambers
144 High Street, Lewes, East Sussex BN7 1XT,
Telephone: 01273 480510
Westgate Chambers
16-17 Wellington Square, Hastings, East Sussex
TN34 1PB, Telephone: 01424 432105
1 Dr Johnson's Bldgs
Ground Floor, Temple, London EC4Y 7AX,
Telephone: 0171 353 9328
Call date: July 1971, Middle Temple

COLLINS JOHN MARTIN QC (1972)

Keating Chambers
10 Essex Street, Outer Temple, London
WC2R 3AA, Telephone: 0171 544 2600
8 King Street
Manchester M2 6AQ,
Telephone: 0161 834 9560
Door Tenant
Call date: July 1952, Gray's Inn
Qualifications: [LLB (Manch)]

COLLINS JOHN MORRIS

9 Woodhouse Square
Leeds LS3 1AD, Telephone: 0113 2451986
Door Tenant
11 King's Bench Walk
1st Floor, Temple, London EC4Y 7EQ,
Telephone: 0171 353 3337
Door Tenant
Call date: Feb 1956, Middle Temple
Recorder
Qualifications: [MA (Oxon)]

COLLINS MICHAEL GEOFFREY QC (1988)

Essex Court Chambers
24 Lincoln's Inn Fields, London WC2A 3ED,
Telephone: 0171 813 8000
E-mail: clerksroom@essexcourt-chambers.co.uk
Call date: Nov 1971, Gray's Inn
Recorder
Qualifications: [LLB (Exon)]

COLLINS PETER RICHARD

Southsea Chambers
PO Box 148, Southsea, Portsmouth,
Hampshire PO5 2TU,
Telephone: 01705 291261
Call date: Oct 1993, Gray's Inn
Qualifications: [LLB]

COLLINS ROBERT URQUHART

8 King's Bench Walk North
1 Park Square East, Leeds LS1 2NE,
Telephone: 0113 2439797
8 King's Bench Walk
2nd Floor, Temple, London EC4Y 7DU,
Telephone: 0171 797 8888
Call date: July 1978, Gray's Inn

COLLINS MISS ROSALEEN

Guildhall Chambers
23 Broad Street, Bristol BS1 2HG,
Telephone: 0117 9273366
Call date: May 1996, Inner Temple
Qualifications: [LLB (Kent), BA]

COLLINSON MISS ALICIA HESTER

2 Harcourt Bldgs
1st Floor, Temple, London EC4Y 9DB,
Telephone: 0171 353 6961/7
Harcourt Chambers
Churchill House 3 St Aldate's Courtyard, St
Aldate's, Oxford OX1 1BN,
Telephone: 01865 791559
Call date: July 1982, Middle Temple
Qualifications: [MA (Oxon), M Phil (Oxon)]

COLMAN ANDREW

1 Hare Court
Ground Floor, Temple, London EC4Y 7BE,
Telephone: 0171 353 3982/5324
Call date: July 1980, Lincoln's Inn
Qualifications: [LLB (Lond)]

COLOVER ROBERT MARK

4 Brick Court
Temple, London EC4Y 9AD,
Telephone: 0171 797 8910
Call date: Nov 1975, Middle Temple
Qualifications: [Cert of Criminology]

COLQUHOUN MISS CELINA DAPHNE MARION

11 Bolt Court
London EC4A 3DQ,
Telephone: 0171 353 2300
E-mail: boltct11@aol.com
Redhill Chambers
Seloduct House 30 Station Road, Redhill
RH1 1NK, Telephone: 01737 780781
Call date: Oct 1990, Gray's Inn
Qualifications: [LLB (Buck'm)]

COLTON MISS MARY WINIFRED

4 Brick Court
1st Floor, Temple, London EC4Y 9AD,
Telephone: 0171 583 8455
Call date: Feb 1955, Middle Temple
Recorder
Qualifications: [LLB (Lond)]

COLVILLE IAIN DAVID

Arden Chambers
27 John Street, London WC1N 2BL,
Telephone: 0171 242 4244
Call date: July 1989, Inner Temple
Qualifications: [LLB]

COLVIN ANDREW DUNCAN ROBSON

7 Norwich Street
Cambridge CB2 1ND,
Telephone: 07000 226584
1 Dr Johnson's Bldgs
Ground Floor, Temple, London EC4Y 7AX,
Telephone: 0171 353 9328
Call date: July 1972, Middle Temple
Qualifications: [BA (Hons), Dott.Giuris (Siena)]

COMAISH ANDREW JAMES CHRISTIAN

Wilberforce Chambers
Bishop Lane, Hull HU1 1PA,
Telephone: 01482 323264
E-mail: clerks@hullbar.demon.co.uk
Call date: Nov 1989, Middle Temple
Qualifications: [MA Hons (Cantab)]

COMFORT MISS POLLY-ANNE

2 Paper Bldgs
Temple, London EC4Y 7ET,
Telephone: 0171 936 2613
Call date: Feb 1988, Lincoln's Inn
Qualifications: [LLB (Hons) (Lond)]

COMPTON ALLAN SPENCER

Trinity Chambers
140 New London Road, Chelmsford, Essex
CM2 0AW, Telephone: 01245 605040
Call date: Nov 1994, Inner Temple
Qualifications: [LLB (Soton)]

COMPTON GARETH FRANCIS THOMAS

22 Old Bldgs
Lincoln's Inn, London WC2A 3UJ,
Telephone: 0171 831 0222
Call date: Mar 1997, Middle Temple
Qualifications: [BA (Hons)]

COMPTON TIMOTHY MARK

Gray's Inn Chambers
5th Floor, Gray's Inn, London WC1R 5JA,
Telephone: 0171 404 1111
Call date: July 1984, Inner Temple
Qualifications: [BA (Bristol), Dip Law]

COMPTON-RICKETT MISS MARY ANNE

Martins Building
Water Street, Liverpool L2 3SP,
Telephone: 0151 236 5818/4919
Call date: July 1972, Gray's Inn
Qualifications: [LLB]

COMPTON-WELSTEAD BENJAMIN EDWARD

2 King's Bench Walk
Ground Floor, Temple, London EC4Y 7DE,
Telephone: 0171 353 1746
E-mail: 2kbw@atlas.co.uk
King's Bench Chambers
115 North Hill, Plymouth PL4 8JY,
Telephone: 01752 221551
Call date: Nov 1979, Lincoln's Inn

COMYN TIMOTHY JOHN

2 Harcourt Bldgs
2nd Floor, Temple, London EC4Y 9DB,
Telephone: 0171 353 8415
E-mail: clerks@twoharcourtbldgs.demon.co.uk
Call date: July 1980, Inner Temple
Qualifications: [LLB (Hull)]

CONCANNON TIMOTHY THOMAS PAUL

Portsmouth Barristers'Chambers
Victory House 7 Bellevue Terrace,
Portsmouth, Hampshire PO5 3AT,
Telephone: 01705 831292
E-mail: clerks@portsmouthbar.com
Call date: May 1993, Inner Temple

CONE JOHN CRAWFORD

Erskine Chambers
30 Lincoln's Inn Fields, Lincoln's Inn, London
WC2A 3PF, Telephone: 0171 242 5532
E-mail: Clerks@Erskine-Chambers.law.co.uk
Call date: July 1975, Middle Temple
Qualifications: [LLB (L'pool)]

CONEY CHRISTOPHER RONALD RAMSDEN

4 Paper Bldgs
2nd Floor, Temple, London EC4Y 7EX,
Telephone: 0171 583 0816/071 353 1131
E-mail: clerks@4paperbuildings.co.uk
Call date: July 1979, Inner Temple
Qualifications: [LLB (Soton)]

CONLIN GEOFFREY DAVID

3 Serjeants Inn
London EC4Y 1BQ,
Telephone: 0171 353 5537
E-mail: available upon request
Call date: July 1973, Inner Temple
Recorder

CONLON MICHAEL ANTHONY

1 Essex Court
Ground Floor, Temple, London EC4Y 9AR,
Telephone: 0171 583 2000
E-mail: clerks@oneessexcourt.co.uk
Call date: July 1974, Inner Temple
Qualifications: [MA (Cantab), FT11, AIIT, FRSA]

CONLON MICHAEL JOHN PATRICK

4 Overdale Road
Knighton, Leicester LE2 3YH,
Telephone: 0116 2883930
Call date: Nov 1984, Inner Temple
Qualifications: [LLB (Hull)]

CONNELL MISS CAROLINE ANN

29 Bedford Row Chambers
London WC1R 4HE,
Telephone: 0171 831 2626
Call date: July 1984, Inner Temple
Qualifications: [LLB (Exon)]

CONNELL EDWARD SAMUEL

2 Paper Buildings
Basement, Temple, London EC4Y 7ET,
Telephone: 0171 353 0933
Call date: Oct 1996, Middle Temple
Qualifications: [BA (Hons)(Keele), CPE]

CONNERTY ANTHONY ROBIN

Lamb Chambers
Lamb Building, Temple, London EC4Y 7AS,
Telephone: 0171 797 8300
E-mail: lambchambers@link.org
Call date: July 1974, Inner Temple
Qualifications: [FCIArb]

CONNING MICHAEL CHRISTOPHER

4 Brick Court
Ground Floor, Temple, London EC4Y 9AD,
Telephone: 0171 797 7766
E-mail: chambers@4brick.co.uk
Call date: Nov 1990, Middle Temple
Qualifications: [BSc (Cardiff)]

CONNOLLY MRS BARBARA WINIFRED

9 Bedford Row
London WC1R 4AZ,
Telephone: 0171 242 3555
E-mail: clerks@9br.co.uk
Call date: July 1986, Inner Temple
Qualifications: [LLB (Hons)]

CONNOLLY MS DEIRDRE JOAN

3 Temple Gardens
Lower Ground Floor, Temple, London
EC4Y 9AU, Telephone: 0171 353 3102/5/9297
Call date: Nov 1982, Gray's Inn
Qualifications: [LLB (L'pool)]

CONNOLLY DOMINIC REGAN

1 Harcourt Bldgs
2nd Floor, Temple, London EC4Y 9DA,
Telephone: 0171 353 9421/9151
Call date: Feb 1989, Middle Temple
Qualifications: [LLB (LSE)]

CONNOLLY JAMES MARTIN PHILIP

1 Pump Court
Lower Ground Floor, Temple, London
EC4Y 7AB, Telephone: 0171 583 2012/
353 4341
E-mail: (name) @1pumpcourt.co.uk
Door Tenant
Call date: May 1985, Middle Temple
Qualifications: [MA (Dublin), LLB (Dublin)]

CONNOLLY MISS JOANNE MARIE

8 King Street
Manchester M2 6AQ,
Telephone: 0161 834 9560
Call date: Oct 1992, Middle Temple
Qualifications: [LL.B (Hons)(Nott'm)]

CONNOLLY SIMON JAMES

3 Temple Gardens
Lower Ground Floor, Temple, London
EC4Y 9AU, Telephone: 0171 353 3102/5/9297
Call date: July 1981, Middle Temple
Qualifications: [BA]

CONNOR GINO PHILIP

Furnival Chambers
32 Furnival Street, London EC4A 1JQ,
Telephone: 0171 405 3232
E-mail: clerks@furnivallaw.co.uk
Call date: Nov 1974, Gray's Inn

CONNOR MARK JONATHAN DOMINIC

21 White Friars
Chester CH1 1NZ, Telephone: 01244 323070
Call date: May 1994, Inner Temple
Qualifications: [LLB (Hons)]

CONRAD ALAN DAVID

Lincoln House Chambers
5th Floor Lincoln House, 1 Brazennose Street,
Manchester M2 5EL,
Telephone: 0161 832 5701
E-mail: LincolnHouseChambers@link.org
Call date: July 1976, Middle Temple
Recorder
Qualifications: [BA (Oxon)]

CONRATH PHILIP BERNARD

Francis Taylor Bldg
2nd Floor, Temple, London EC4Y 7BY,
Telephone: 0171 353 9942/3157
Call date: July 1972, Gray's Inn

CONROY MISS MARIAN

17 Old Bldgs
Ground Floor, Lincoln's Inn, London
WC2A 3UP, Telephone: 0171 405 9653
Call date: Nov 1991, Inner Temple
Qualifications: [LLB (Hull)]

CONRY MICHAEL HARVEY

1 Fountain Court
Steelhouse Lane, Birmingham B4 6DR,
Telephone: 0121 236 5721
Call date: July 1979, Gray's Inn
Qualifications: [LLB (Reading)]

CONSIDINE PAUL CHRISTOPHER

65-67 King Street
Leicester LE1 6RP, Telephone: 0116 2547710
Call date: Oct 1992, Middle Temple
Qualifications: [BA (Hons Oxon), Diploma in
Law(City)]

CONSTABLE ADAM MICHAEL

2 Temple Gardens
Temple, London EC4Y 9AY,
Telephone: 0171 583 6041 (12 Lines)
Call date: Oct 1995, Inner Temple
Qualifications: [BA (Oxon)]

CONSTABLE JOHN MARTYN CHESTER

Baker Street Chambers
9 Baker Street, Middlesbrough TS1 2LF,
Telephone: 01642 873873
Call date: Feb 1972, Gray's Inn
Qualifications: [LLB (Hull), LLM (Leics), MA
(York)]

CONSTANTINE STEPHEN ALLAN

Baker Street Chambers
9 Baker Street, Middlesbrough TS1 2LF,
Telephone: 01642 873873
Call date: Oct 1992, Middle Temple
Qualifications: [B.Sc. (Hons)]

CONWAY CHARLES

3 Hare Court
1st Floor, Temple, London EC4Y 7BJ,
Telephone: 0171 353 7561
Call date: July 1969, Middle Temple
Qualifications: [MA, LLB (Cantab)]

CONWAY ROBERT DAVID

7 Stone Bldgs
1st Floor, Lincoln's Inn, London WC2A 3SZ,
Telephone: 0171 242 0961
Call date: Nov 1974, Inner Temple
Qualifications: [LLB (Lond)]

D

COODE JONATHAN GRAHAM

13 King's Bench Walk
1st Floor, Temple, London EC4Y 7EN,
Telephone: 0171 353 7204
E-mail: clerks@13kbw.law.co.uk
King's Bench Chambers
32 Beaumont Street, Oxford OX1 2NP,
Telephone: 01865 311066
E-mail: clerks@kbc-oxford.law.co.uk
Call date: July 1984, Middle Temple
Qualifications: [BA (East Anglia), Dip Law]

COOK MISS ALISON NOELE

Priory Chambers
2 Fountain Court, Steelhouse Lane,
Birmingham B4 6DR,
Telephone: 0121 236 3882/1375
Call date: Feb 1989, Gray's Inn
Qualifications: [LLB (Manch) (Hons)]

COOK CHARLES STUART

33 Park Place
Cardiff CF1 3BA, Telephone: 01222 233313
Call date: Nov 1966, Lincoln's Inn
Recorder
Qualifications: [MA (Oxon)]

COOK CHRISTOPHER GRAHAM

St James's Chambers
68 Quay Street, Manchester M3 3EJ,
Telephone: 0161 834 7000
E-mail: 106241.2625@compuserve.com
Call date: Oct 1990, Inner Temple
Qualifications: [BSc, BCom (B'ham), Dip Law
(City)]

COOK GARY WILLIAM

Victoria Chambers
3rd Floor 177 Corporation Street, Birmingham
B4 6RG, Telephone: 0121 236 9900
Call date: Nov 1989, Middle Temple
Qualifications: [B.Ed Hons]

COOK IAN REGINALD BLACKLIN

1 King's Bench Walk
2nd Floor, Temple, London EC4Y 7DB,
Telephone: 0171 936 1500
E-mail: ddear@1kbw.co.uk
Call date: Nov 1994, Inner Temple
Qualifications: [BA (Hons)(Lond), CPE (City)]

COOK JEREMY DAVID

Lamb Building
Ground Floor, Temple, London EC4Y 7AS,
Telephone: 0171 797 7788
E-mail: lamb.building@link.org
Call date: July 1982, Gray's Inn
Qualifications: [BA (Keele)]

COOK JEREMY OWAIN

Cleveland Chambers
63-65 Borough Road, Middlesbrough,
Cleveland TS1 3AA, Telephone: 01642 226036
Call date: July 1982, Middle Temple
Qualifications: [LLB (Hons), M.Soc.Sc]

COOK MISS LESLEY ANN

Bank House Chambers
Old Bank House, Hartshead, Sheffield S1 2EL,
Telephone: 0114 2751223
Call date: Nov 1984, Middle Temple
Qualifications: [BA (Oxon)]

COOK MISS MARY JANE

2-3 Gray's Inn Square
Gray's Inn, London WC1R 5JH,
Telephone: 0171 242 4986
E-mail: chambers@2-3graysinnsquare.co.uk
Call date: July 1982, Inner Temple
Qualifications: [LLB (Cardiff)]

COOK PAUL GRAHAM WHALLEY

Albion Chambers
Broad Street, Bristol BS1 1DR,
Telephone: 0117 9272144
Call date: Nov 1992, Middle Temple
Qualifications: [BA (Hons)(Kent), Dip in Law]

COOK MISS TINA GAIL

22 Old Bldgs
Lincoln's Inn, London WC2A 3UJ,
Telephone: 0171 831 0222
Call date: July 1988, Middle Temple
Qualifications: [BA (Hons) (Oxon)]

COOKE GRAHAM OWEN JOHN

23 Essex Street
London WC2R 3AS,
Telephone: 0171 413 0353/353 3533
E-mail: clerks@essexstreet23.demon.co.uk
Call date: July 1983, Lincoln's Inn

COOKE JEREMY LIONEL QC (1990)

7 King's Bench Walk
Ground Floor, Temple, London EC4Y 7DS,
Telephone: 0171 583 0404
Call date: July 1976, Lincoln's Inn
Assistant Recorder
Qualifications: [MA (Oxon)]

COOKE JULIAN HUMPHREY SPENCER

20 Essex Street
London WC2R 3AL,
Telephone: 0171 583 9294
E-mail: clerks@20essexst.com
Call date: July 1965, Lincoln's Inn
Qualifications: [BA, LLB (Cantab)]

COOKE NICHOLAS ORTON

9 Park Place
Cardiff CF1 3DP, Telephone: 01222 382731
Farrar's Building
Temple, London EC4Y 7BD,
Telephone: 0171 583 9241
E-mail: chambers@farrarsbuilding.co.uk
Call date: Nov 1977, Middle Temple
Assistant Recorder
Qualifications: [LLB]

COOKE PETER RAYMOND

6 Fountain Court
Steelhouse Lane, Birmingham B4 6DR,
Telephone: 0121 233 3282
Call date: July 1985, Lincoln's Inn
Qualifications: [LLB(Manchester)]

COOKSAMMY MISS NATALIE CAMILLE

Victoria Chambers
19 Castle Street, Liverpool L2 4SX,
Telephone: 0151 236 9402
E-mail: Fa45@rapid.co.uk
Call date: Oct 1995, Lincoln's Inn
Qualifications: [LLB (Hons)(Leeds)]

COOKSLEY NIGEL JAMES

Old Square Chambers
1 Verulam Buildings, Gray's Inn, London
WC1R 5LQ, Telephone: 0171 831 0801
Old Square Chambers
Hanover House 47 Corn Street, Bristol
BS1 1HT, Telephone: 0117 9277111
Call date: July 1975, Inner Temple
Qualifications: [BA (Cantab)]

COOKSLEY MRS SUBHASHINI ANN

Lion Court
Chancery House 53-64 Chancery Lane, London
WC2A 1SJ, Telephone: 0171 404 6565
Call date: Nov 1975, Gray's Inn
Qualifications: [LLB]

COOMBE PETER MICHAEL AENEAS

2 Harcourt Bldgs
1st Floor, Temple, London EC4Y 9DB,
Telephone: 0171 353 2112/2817
Call date: Nov 1993, Middle Temple
Qualifications: [BA (Hons)(Oxon)]

COOMBES TIMOTHY JAMES

3 Paper Bldgs
1st Floor, Temple, London EC4Y 7EU,
Telephone: 0171 583 8055
E-mail: london@3paper.com
20 Lorne Park Road
Bournemouth BH1 1JN,
Telephone: 01202 292102 (5 Lines)
4 St Peter Street
Winchester SO23 8OW,
Telephone: 01962 868884
Call date: July 1980, Inner Temple
Qualifications: [BA (Dunelm)]

COOMBES DAVIES DR MAIR

30 Park Place
Cardiff CF1 3BA, Telephone: 01222 398421
E-mail: 100757.1456@compuserve.com
Call date: July 1988, Lincoln's Inn
Qualifications: [BSc(Hons), BArch, PhD
(Wales), CPE]

D

D

COONAN KIERAN BENET QC (1990)

6 Pump Court
Ground Floor, Temple, London EC4Y 7AR,
Telephone: 0171 583 6013/2510
Call date: July 1971, Gray's Inn
Recorder
Qualifications: [Dip Eur Law]

COOPER ADRIAN EDGAR MARK

2 Harcourt Bldgs
Ground Floor/Left, Temple, London
EC4Y 9DB, Telephone: 0171 583 9020
E-mail: clerks@harcourt.co.uk
Stanbrook & Henderson
2 Harcourt Bldgs 2nd Floor, Temple, London
EC4Y 9DB, Telephone: 0171 353 0101
E-mail: clerks@harcourt.co.uk
Call date: July 1970, Inner Temple
Assistant Recorder
Qualifications: [MA (Oxon)]

COOPER ALAN GEORGE

39 Essex Street
London WC2R 3AT,
Telephone: 0171 583 1111
E-mail: clerks@39essex.co.uk
Call date: July 1969, Gray's Inn

COOPER ARNOLD JAMES

3 Paper Bldgs
2nd Floor, Temple, London EC4Y 7EU,
Telephone: 0171 353 6208
Call date: July 1969, Lincoln's Inn
Qualifications: [LLB]

COOPER MISS BERYL PHYLLIS QC (1977)

9 Gough Square
London EC4A 3DE, Telephone: 0171 353 5371
Call date: Feb 1960, Gray's Inn

COOPER GILEAD PATRICK

11 New Square
Ground Floor, Lincoln's Inn, London
WC2A 3QB, Telephone: 0171 831 0081
E-mail: 11newsquare.co.uk
Call date: Nov 1983, Middle Temple
Qualifications: [MA (Oxon), Dip Law]

COOPER JOHN GORDON

7 Stone Bldgs
1st Floor, Lincoln's Inn, London WC2A 3SZ,
Telephone: 0171 242 0961
Call date: July 1983, Middle Temple
Qualifications: [LLB (Hons)(Newc),
Butterworths Law, Prizeman]

COOPER JOHN MICHAEL

11 King's Bench Walk
1st Floor, Temple, London EC4Y 7EQ,
Telephone: 0171 353 3337
3 Park Court
Leeds LS1 2QH, Telephone: 0113 297 1200
Call date: July 1985, Inner Temple
Qualifications: [LLB(Reading)]

COOPER MORRIS

Priory Chambers
2 Fountain Court, Steelhouse Lane,
Birmingham B4 6DR,
Telephone: 0121 236 3882/1375
Call date: July 1979, Gray's Inn

COOPER NIGEL STUART

4 Essex Court
Temple, London EC4Y 9AJ,
Telephone: 0171 797 7970
E-mail: clerks@4essexcourt.law.co.uk
Call date: July 1987, Lincoln's Inn
Qualifications: [LLB (Leeds),
DIPE.1(Amsterdam), LLM (Lond)]

COOPER PETER JAMES QC (1993)

2 Harcourt Bldgs
1st Floor, Temple, London EC4Y 9DB,
Telephone: 0171 353 2112/2817
Call date: Nov 1974, Gray's Inn
Recorder

COOPER PETER JOHN

St Ive's Chambers
9 Fountain Ct, Birmingham B4 6DR,
Telephone: 0121 236 0863/0929
Call date: Nov 1996, Gray's Inn
Qualifications: [MA (Oxon)]

COOPER ROGER BERNARD

Trinity Chambers
9-12 Trinity Chare, Quayside, Newcastle Upon
Tyne NE1 3DF, Telephone: 0191 232 1927
Call date: July 1989, Inner Temple
Qualifications: [BSc (L'pool), Dip Law]

COOPER MISS SARAH LUCY

Thomas More Chambers
52 Carey Street, Lincoln's Inn, London
WC2A 2JB, Telephone: 0171 404 7000
Call date: Nov 1993, Inner Temple
Qualifications: [BA (Dunelm), Dip in Law]

COOPER MISS SUSAN JOY

22 Old Bldgs
Lincoln's Inn, London WC2A 3UJ,
Telephone: 0171 831 0222
Call date: Nov 1976, Gray's Inn
Qualifications: [LLB]

COORAY TARAKNATH UPALI

Mitre House Chambers
Mitre House 44 Fleet Street, London
EC4Y 1BN, Telephone: 0171 583 8233
Call date: July 1974, Middle Temple
Qualifications: [BSc (Econ), LLB (London), MA]

COPE CHRISTOPHER DOUGLAS BAILYE

4 Paper Bldgs
2nd Floor, Temple, London EC4Y 7EX,
Telephone: 0171 583 0816/071 353 1131
E-mail: clerks@4paperbuildings.co.uk
Call date: Oct 1990, Inner Temple
Qualifications: [MA (Cantab)]

COPELAND ANDREW JOHN

46/48 Essex Street
London WC2R 3GH,
Telephone: 0171 583 8899
Call date: Nov 1992, Gray's Inn
Qualifications: [LLB]

COPEMAN IAN DAVID

1 Middle Temple Lane
Temple, London EC4Y 1LT,
Telephone: 0171 583 0659 (12 Lines)
Call date: Nov 1977, Inner Temple

COPNALL RICHARD ANTHONY

Park Lane Chambers
19 Westgate, Leeds LS1 2RD,
Telephone: 0113 2285000
Call date: Oct 1990, Inner Temple
Qualifications: [BSc, CPE (Nott'm)]

COPPEL JASON ALASTAIR

11 King's Bench Walk
Temple, London EC4Y 7EQ,
Telephone: 0171 632 8500
E-mail: clerksroom@11-kbw.law.co.uk
Call date: Nov 1994, Inner Temple
Qualifications: [BA (Oxon), LLM
(EUI,Florence)]

COPPEL PHILIP ANTONY

2-3 Gray's Inn Square
Gray's Inn, London WC1R 5JH,
Telephone: 0171 242 4986
E-mail: chambers@2-3graysinnsquare.co.uk
Call date: Nov 1994, Lincoln's Inn
Qualifications: [BA, LLB (Australia)]

COPPEL MISS YVONNE RUTH

24a St John Street
Manchester M3 4DF,
Telephone: 0161 833 9628
Call date: July 1976, Inner Temple
Assistant Recorder
Qualifications: [LL.B Hons]

COPPOLA MISS ANNA FRANCESCA

5 Raymond Buildings
1st Floor, Gray's Inn, London WC1R 5BP,
Telephone: 0171 242 2902
Call date: Nov 1996, Lincoln's Inn
Qualifications: [BA (Hons)(Lond), Dip Law]

CORBEN PAUL ANTHONY

169 Temple Chambers
Temple Avenue, London EC4Y 0DA,
Telephone: 0171 583 7644
Call date: July 1979, Gray's Inn
Qualifications: [MA (Cantab), FCIArb]

D

CORBETT JAMES PATRICK

7 Fountain Court
Steelhouse Lane, Birmingham B4 6DR,
Telephone: 0121 236 8531
Call date: July 1975, Inner Temple
Assistant Recorder
Qualifications: [LLB, LLM (Exon), ACIArb]

CORBETT MISS MICHELLE JANE

14 Gray's Inn Square
Gray's Inn, London WC1R 5JP,
Telephone: 0171 242 0858
E-mail: 100712.2134@compuserve.com
Call date: July 1987, Inner Temple
Qualifications: [LLB (Leeds)]

CORBETT MRS SANDRA MARGARET

1 New Square
Ground Floor, Lincoln's Inn, London
WC2A 3SA, Telephone: 0171 405 0884/5/6/7
E-mail: 1newsquare@compuserve.com
Call date: July 1988, Middle Temple
Qualifications: [LLB (Hons) (Lond)]

CORDARA RODERICK CHARLES QC (1994)

Essex Court Chambers
24 Lincoln's Inn Fields, London WC2A 3ED,
Telephone: 0171 813 8000
E-mail: clerksroom@essexcourt-chambers.co.uk
Call date: July 1975, Middle Temple
Qualifications: [MA (Cantab)]

CORDEY DANIEL ROE

York Chambers
14 Toft Green, York YO1 1JT,
Telephone: 01904 620048
E-mail: yorkchambers.co.uk
Call date: Nov 1990, Gray's Inn
Qualifications: [LLB (Lond)]

CORFIELD MISS SHEELAGH MARJORIE

Guildhall Chambers
23 Broad Street, Bristol BS1 2HG,
Telephone: 0117 9273366
Call date: July 1975, Middle Temple
Qualifications: [LLB (Bristol)]

CORKERY MICHAEL QC (1981)

5 Paper Bldgs
1st Floor, Temple, London EC4Y 7HB,
Telephone: 0171 583 6117
E-mail: clerks@5-paperbuildings.law.co.uk
Call date: Nov 1949, Lincoln's Inn

CORLESS JOHN VINCENT

Adrian Lyon's Chambers
14 Castle Street, Liverpool L2 0NE,
Telephone: 0151 236 4421/8240
E-mail: chambers14@aol.com
Call date: Nov 1984, Middle Temple
Qualifications: [MA (St Andrews)]

CORNAH MS EMMA LOUISE

15 Winckley Square
Preston PR1 3JJ, Telephone: 01772 252828
E-mail: clerks@winckleysq.demon.co.uk
Call date: Nov 1992, Inner Temple
Qualifications: [LLB (Hons)]

CORNER TIMOTHY FRANK

4-5 Gray's Inn Square
Ground Floor, Gray's Inn, London WC1R 5AY,
Telephone: 0171 404 5252
E-mail: chambers@4-5graysinnsquare.co.uk
Call date: Nov 1981, Gray's Inn
Qualifications: [MA, BCL (Oxon)]

CORNFORD HUGH CHARLES THOMAS

Fleet Chambers
Mitre House 44-46 Fleet Street, London
EC4Y 1BN, Telephone: 0171 936 3707
Call date: Nov 1994, Middle Temple
Qualifications: [BA (Hons) (Exon)]

CORNISH WILLIAM RUDOLPH QC (1997)

8 New Square
Lincoln's Inn, London WC2A 3QP,
Telephone: 0171 405 4321
Call date: July 1965, Gray's Inn
Qualifications: [LLB(Adelaide), BCL(Oxon)]

CORNWALL CHRISTOPHER JOHN

Exchange Chambers
Pearl Assurance House Derby Square,
Liverpool L2 9XX, Telephone: 0151 236 7747/
0458
E-mail: exchangechambers@btinternet.com
Call date: July 1975, Lincoln's Inn
Recorder
Qualifications: [BA (Oxon)]

CORNWALL MISS VIRGINIA MARGARET

2 Paper Buildings
Basement, Temple, London EC4Y 7ET,
Telephone: 0171 353 0933
Call date: Oct 1990, Middle Temple
Qualifications: [LLB (Hons)]

CORRELLA-DAVID ANDREW GEORGE EDWARD

Gower Chambers
57 Walter Road, Swansea, West Glamorgan
SA1 5PZ, Telephone: 01792 644466
E-mail: clerk@gowerchambers.co.uk
Call date: Nov 1986, Gray's Inn
Qualifications: [LLB (Wales)]

CORRIGAN PETER ANTHONY

2 Paper Bldgs
1st Floor, Temple, London EC4Y 7ET,
Telephone: 0171 936 2611 (10 Lines)
E-mail: clerks@2pbbarristers.co.uk
Call date: July 1972, Middle Temple
Qualifications: [MA (Oxon)]

CORRY MISS CAROL ELIZABETH

1 Essex Court
1st Floor, Temple, London EC4Y 9AR,
Telephone: 0171 936 3030
E-mail: one.essex_court@virgin.net
Call date: July 1981, Lincoln's Inn
Qualifications: [BA (Hons)]

CORSELLIS NICHOLAS ROBERT ALEXANDER

3 Temple Gardens
Lower Ground Floor, Temple, London
EC4Y 9AU, Telephone: 0171 353 3102/5/9297
Call date: Nov 1993, Lincoln's Inn
Qualifications: [LLB (Hons)]

CORY-WRIGHT CHARLES ALEXANDER

39 Essex Street
London WC2R 3AT,
Telephone: 0171 583 1111
E-mail: clerks@39essex.co.uk
Call date: Feb 1984, Middle Temple
Qualifications: [BA (Oxon), Dip Law (City)]

COSEDGE ANDREW JOHN

3 Stone Bldgs
Ground Floor, Lincoln's Inn, London
WC2A 3XL, Telephone: 0171 242 4937/
405 8358
Call date: July 1972, Inner Temple
Qualifications: [LLB]

COSGROVE PATRICK JOSEPH QC (1994)

Broad Chare
33 Broad Chare, Newcastle Upon Tyne
NE1 3DQ, Telephone: 0191 232 0541
11 King's Bench Walk
1st Floor, Temple, London EC4Y 7EQ,
Telephone: 0171 353 3337
Door Tenant
Call date: July 1976, Gray's Inn
Recorder

COSGROVE MR. THOMAS JAMES

2-3 Gray's Inn Square
Gray's Inn, London WC1R 5JH,
Telephone: 0171 242 4986
E-mail: chambers@2-3graysinnsquare.co.uk
Call date: Oct 1994, Inner Temple
Qualifications: [BA (Cantab)]

COSTER RONALD DAVID

22 Old Bldgs
Lincoln's Inn, London WC2A 3UJ,
Telephone: 0171 831 0222
Call date: July 1989, Lincoln's Inn
Qualifications: [BSC (Lanc), Dip Law]

COTCHER MISS ANN LOUISE

3 Temple Gardens
Lower Ground Floor, Temple, London
EC4Y 9AU, Telephone: 0171 353 3102/5/9297
Call date: July 1979, Middle Temple
Qualifications: [LLB (Soton)]

COTTAGE MISS ROSINA

9-12 Bell Yard
London WC2A 2LF,
Telephone: 0171 400 1800
Call date: Nov 1988, Inner Temple
Qualifications: [LLB (Bris)]

COTTER BARRY PAUL

Old Square Chambers
Hanover House 47 Corn Street, Bristol
BS1 1HT, Telephone: 0117 9277111
Old Square Chambers
1 Verulam Buildings, Gray's Inn, London
WC1R 5LQ, Telephone: 0171 831 0801
Call date: July 1985, Lincoln's Inn
Qualifications: [LLB (Lond)]

COTTER MARK JAMES

Holborn Chambers
6 Gate Street, Lincoln's Inn Fields, London
WC2A 3HP, Telephone: 0171 242 6060
Call date: Nov 1994, Middle Temple
Qualifications: [LLB (Hons), LLM, (Wales)]

COTTER MISS RACHEL JOSLIN ANN

5 Fountain Court
Steelhouse Lane, Birmingham B4 6DR,
Telephone: 0121 606 0500
Call date: Nov 1994, Middle Temple
Qualifications: [BA (Hons)]

COTTER MISS SARA ELIZABETH

Higher Combe
Hawkcombe, Porlock, Minehead, Somerset
TA24 8LP, Telephone: 01643 862722
Call date: Oct 1990, Middle Temple
Qualifications: [BA, Dip Law]

Fax: 01643 862871;
Out of hours telephone: 01643 862722;
DX: 117405 Minehead; Other comms: Mobile
0410 903130

Types of work: Agriculture; Chancery land law;
Common law (general); Housing; Landlord and
tenant; Personal injury; Professional negligence

Other professional experience: Pre-publication
advice to newspapers and publishing houses

Languages spoken: French

COTTERILL MISS IMOGEN KATE

Guildhall Chambers
23 Broad Street, Bristol BS1 2HG,
Telephone: 0117 9273366
Call date: Nov 1995, Gray's Inn
Qualifications: [LLB (Reading)]

COTTERILL MISS SUSAN AMANDA

Lamb Building
Ground Floor, Temple, London EC4Y 7AS,
Telephone: 0171 797 7788
E-mail: lamb.building@link.org
Call date: July 1988, Lincoln's Inn
Qualifications: [LLB (Hons) (Essex)]

COTTLE MAURICE ANTHONY HAYDEN

3 Serjeants Inn
London EC4Y 1BQ,
Telephone: 0171 353 5537
E-mail: available upon request
Call date: July 1978, Gray's Inn
Qualifications: [LLB (Lond), M.Phil (Lond)]

COTTLE STEPHEN CHARLES

2 Garden Court
1st Floor, Middle Temple, London EC4Y 9BL,
Telephone: 0171 353 1633
E-mail: barristers@2gardenct.law.co.uk
Call date: Nov 1984, Inner Temple
Qualifications: [BA, Dip Law]

COTTON MISS DIANA ROSEMARY QC (1983)

Devereux Chambers
Devereux Court, London WC2R 3JJ,
Telephone: 0171 353 7534
E-mail: elton@devchambers.co.uk
5 Fountain Court
Steelhouse Lane, Birmingham B4 6DR,
Telephone: 0121 606 0500
Call date: June 1964, Middle Temple
Recorder
Qualifications: [MA (Oxon)]

COTTRELL MATTHEW ROBERT

Oriel Chambers
14 Water Street, Liverpool L2 8TD,
Telephone: 0151 236 7191
E-mail: oriel_chambers@link.org
Call date: Oct 1996, Gray's Inn
Qualifications: [LLB (Sheff)]

COUGHLIN VINCENT WILLIAM

Furnival Chambers
32 Furnival Street, London EC4A 1JQ,
Telephone: 0171 405 3232
E-mail: clerks@furnivallaw.co.uk
Call date: July 1980, Middle Temple
Qualifications: [LLB (Lond)]

COULSON PETER DAVID WILLIAM

Keating Chambers
10 Essex Street, Outer Temple, London
WC2R 3AA, Telephone: 0171 544 2600
Call date: Nov 1982, Gray's Inn
Qualifications: [BA (Keele), ACIArb]

COULTER BARRY JOHN

1 Essex Court
1st Floor, Temple, London EC4Y 9AR,
Telephone: 0171 936 3030
E-mail: one.essex_court@virgin.net
Call date: Nov 1985, Inner Temple
Qualifications: [LLB]

COULTHARD ALAN TERENCE

Lancaster Building Chambers
77 Deansgate, Manchester M3 2BW,
Telephone: 0161 661 4444
E-mail: sandra@lbnipc.com
New Court
1st Floor, Temple, London EC4Y 9BE,
Telephone: 0171 797 8999
Call date: July 1987, Middle Temple
Qualifications: [LLB (Lond), BCL, (Oxon)]

COUNSELL EDWARD FREDERICK

South Western Chambers
Melville House 12 Middle Street, Taunton,
Somerset TA1 1SH, Telephone: 01823 331919
Call date: Nov 1990, Inner Temple
Qualifications: [BA, BCL (Oxon)]

COUNSELL JAMES HENRY

2 King's Bench Walk
Ground Floor, Temple, London EC4Y 7DE,
Telephone: 0171 353 1746
E-mail: 2kbw@atlas.co.uk
King's Bench Chambers
115 North Hill, Plymouth PL4 8JY,
Telephone: 01752 221551
Call date: July 1984, Inner Temple
Qualifications: [MA (Cantab)]

COUNSELL MISS LYNNE MARGARET

11 Stone Bldgs
1st Floor, Lincoln's Inn, London WC2A 3TG,
Telephone: 0171 404 5055
E-mail: 9stoneb@compuserve.com
Call date: Nov 1986, Inner Temple
Qualifications: [BA (Lond) Dip Law, (City)]

COUPLAND STEVEN MICHAEL EDWARD

1 High Pavement
Nottingham NG1 1HF,
Telephone: 0115 9418218
Call date: May 1993, Lincoln's Inn
Qualifications: [LLB (Hons) (Wales)]

COURTNEY MS ANN

New Court
Temple, London EC4Y 9BE,
Telephone: 0171 583 5123/0171 583 0510
Call date: Nov 1987, Inner Temple
Qualifications: [LLB (Hons)]

COURTNEY NICHOLAS PIERS

Queen's Chambers
5 John Dalton Street, Manchester M2 6ET,
Telephone: 0161 834 6875/4738
4 Camden Place
Preston PR1 3JL, Telephone: 01772 828300
Call date: Nov 1990, Middle Temple
Qualifications: [LLB (Manch)]

COUSENS MICHAEL PATRICK

1 Crown Office Row
2nd Floor, Temple, London EC4Y 7HH,
Telephone: 0171 797 7111
Call date: Feb 1973, Lincoln's Inn

COUSINS CHRISTOPHER HUGH JAMES

4 King's Bench Walk
2nd Floor, Temple, London EC4Y 7DL,
Telephone: 0171 353 3581
Call date: July 1969, Middle Temple

COUSINS EDWARD FRANCIS

11 Stone Bldgs
Ground Floor, Lincoln's Inn, London
WC2A 3TG, Telephone: 0171 831 6381
E-mail: clerks@11StoneBuildings.law.co.uk
Chichester Chambers
12 North Pallant, Chichester, West Sussex
PO19 1TQ, Telephone: 01243 784538
Door Tenant
Call date: July 1971, Gray's Inn
Qualifications: [BA (L'pool), LLM (Lo)]

COUSINS JEREMY VINCENT

4 Fountain Court
Steelhouse Lane, Birmingham B4 6DR,
Telephone: 0121 236 3476
Call date: July 1977, Middle Temple
Assistant Recorder
Qualifications: [LLB (Warks)]

COVENEY CHRISTOPHER JAMES

38 Young Street
Manchester M3 3FT,
Telephone: 0161 833 0489
E-mail: clerks@young-st-chambers.com
Call date: July 1976, Inner Temple
Qualifications: [LLB (Hons)]

COVER MISS MARTHA JUNE

4 Brick Court
Ground Floor, Temple, London EC4Y 9AD,
Telephone: 0171 797 7766
E-mail: chambers@4brick.co.uk
Call date: Nov 1979, Gray's Inn
Qualifications: [BA (W. Ontario), BA, LLM
(Lond), LLB (Lond)]

COWAN JACK

Martins Building
Water Street, Liverpool L2 3SP,
Telephone: 0151 236 5818/4919
Call date: Nov 1971, Inner Temple
Qualifications: [LLB]

COWAN PETER SHERWOOD MCCREA

Oriel Chambers
14 Water Street, Liverpool L2 8TD,
Telephone: 0151 236 7191
E-mail: oriel_chambers@link.org
Call date: July 1980, Middle Temple
Qualifications: [MA (Oxon)]

COWARD MISS ANTOINETTE CASSANDRA BERNADETTE

Clapham Chambers
21-25 Bedford Road, Clapham North, London
SW4 7SH, Telephone: 0171 978 8482/
642 5777
E-mail: 113063.632@compuserve.com
Call date: Nov 1994, Inner Temple
Qualifications: [LLB (Lond)]

COWARD JOHN STEPHEN QC (1984)

9 Bedford Row
London WC1R 4AZ,
Telephone: 0171 242 3555
E-mail: clerks@9br.co.uk
Call date: Apr 1964, Inner Temple
Recorder
Qualifications: [LLB]

COWARD MISS VICTORIA JANE

Hollis Whiteman Chambers
3rd/4th Floor Queen Elizabeth Bldg, Temple,
London EC4Y 9BS, Telephone: 0171 583 5766
E-mail: hollis.whiteman@btinternet.com
Call date: Oct 1992, Middle Temple
Qualifications: [B.Sc (Hons, Manch), Diploma
In Law(City)]

COWEN GARY ADAM

Falcon Chambers
Falcon Court, London EC4Y 1AA,
Telephone: 0171 353 2484/7
Call date: Oct 1990, Inner Temple
Qualifications: [LLB (Bris)]

COWEN JONATHAN MICHAEL

4 King's Bench Walk
2nd Floor, Temple, London EC4Y 7DL,
Telephone: 0171 353 3581
Call date: Nov 1983, Middle Temple
Qualifications: [BA (Oxon), Dip Law]

COWEN MISS SALLY EMMA

46/48 Essex Street
London WC2R 3GH,
Telephone: 0171 583 8899
Call date: Oct 1995, Inner Temple
Qualifications: [LLB (Leeds)]

COWEN TIMOTHY ARIEH

Barnard's Inn Chambers
6th Floor Halton House, 20-23 Holborn,
London EC1N 2JD, Telephone: 0171 242 8508
E-mail: clerks@barnards-inn-chambers.co.uk
Call date: Oct 1993, Inner Temple
Qualifications: [BA]

COWTON MISS CATHERINE JUDITH

Queen Elizabeth Bldg
2nd Floor, Temple, London EC4Y 9BS,
Telephone: 0171 797 7837
Call date: Nov 1995, Middle Temple
Qualifications: [BA (Hons)]

COX BRIAN ROBERT ESCOTT QC (1974)

36 Bedford Row
London WC1R 4JH,
Telephone: 0171 421 8000
E-mail: 36bedfordrow@link.org
3 Fountain Court
Steelhouse Lane, Birmingham B4 6DR,
Telephone: 0121 236 5854
Call date: July 1954, Lincoln's Inn
Qualifications: [MA (Oxon)]

COX BRYAN RICHARD

9 Woodhouse Square
Leeds LS3 1AD, Telephone: 0113 2451986
Call date: July 1979, Middle Temple
Qualifications: [LLB (Leeds)]

COX BUSTER

1 Gray's Inn Square
Ground Floor, London WC1R 5AA,
Telephone: 0171 405 8946/7/8
Call date: Nov 1993, Gray's Inn
Qualifications: [B.Sc (Manch), LLB]

COX MISS CATHERINE AILSA

Priory Chambers
2 Fountain Court, Steelhouse Lane,
Birmingham B4 6DR,
Telephone: 0121 236 3882/1375
Call date: July 1989, Middle Temple
Qualifications: [LLB (Manch)]

COX CHARLES GEOFFREY

Thomas More Chambers
52 Carey Street, Lincoln's Inn, London
WC2A 2JB, Telephone: 0171 404 7000
Call date: July 1982, Middle Temple
Qualifications: [BA (Cantab)]

COX DOMINIC

3 Temple Gardens
3rd Floor, Temple, London EC4Y 9AU,
Telephone: 0171 583 0010
Call date: Nov 1994, Lincoln's Inn
Qualifications: [BA (Hons)(Kent)]

COX JASON DAVID

24 The Ropewalk
Nottingham NG1 5EF,
Telephone: 0115 9472581
E-mail: clerk@ropewalk.co.uk
Call date: Oct 1992, Gray's Inn
Qualifications: [LLB (Nott'm)]

COX MISS KERRY AMANDA

Plowden Bldgs
2nd Floor, Temple, London EC4Y 9BU,
Telephone: 0171 583 0808
E-mail: bar@plowdenbuildings.co.uk
Call date: Oct 1990, Inner Temple
Qualifications: [MA (Hons)(St Andrew), Dip Law]

COX MISS KHARIN PAULINE

1 Gray's Inn Square
1st Floor, London WC1R 5AG,
Telephone: 0171 405 3000
E-mail: clerks@onegrays.demon.co.uk
Call date: July 1982, Middle Temple
Qualifications: [BA (Cantab)]

D

COX MS LAURA MARY QC (1994)

Cloisters
1st Floor, Temple, London EC4Y 7AA,
Telephone: 0171 827 4000
E-mail: clerks@cloisters.com
Call date: Nov 1975, Inner Temple
Recorder
Qualifications: [LLB, LLM]

COX LINDSAY RANDALL

East Anglian Chambers
Gresham House 5 Museum Street, Ipswich
IP1 1HQ, Telephone: 01473 214481
East Anglian Chambers
Sanders House 52 North Hill, Colchester
CO1 1PY, Telephone: 01206 572756
East Anglian Chambers
57 London Street, Norwich NR2 1HL,
Telephone: 01603 617351
Call date: July 1984, Middle Temple
Qualifications: [LLB (East Anglia)]

COX NICHOLAS IVAN

4 Stone Bldgs
Ground Floor, Lincoln's Inn, London
WC2A 3XT, Telephone: 0171 242 5524
E-mail: d.goddard@4stonebuildings.law.co.uk
Call date: Oct 1992, Middle Temple
Qualifications: [BA (Hons)(Oxon), MBA
(Warw)]

COX NIGEL JOHN

Gray's Inn Chambers
5th Floor, Gray's Inn, London WC1R 5JA,
Telephone: 0171 404 1111
Call date: Nov 1986, Inner Temple
Qualifications: [MA(E.Illinois), BA (Hons), Dip
Law]

COX RAYMOND EDWIN

Fountain Court
Temple, London EC4Y 9DH,
Telephone: 0171 583 3335
E-mail: chambers@fountaincourt.co.uk
Call date: July 1982, Gray's Inn
Qualifications: [BA (Oxon)]

COX SIMON FRANCIS

3 Paper Bldgs
2nd Floor, Temple, London EC4Y 7EU,
Telephone: 0171 353 6208
Call date: Nov 1992, Inner Temple
Qualifications: [LLB (Wales)]

COX MS SITA

Stour Chambers
Barton Mill House Barton Mill Road,
Canterbury, Kent CT1 1BP,
Telephone: 01227 764899
E-mail: clerks@stourchambers.co.uk
Call date: Nov 1987, Middle Temple
Qualifications: [BA (Hons)]

COY MICHAEL KEVIN

Phoenix Chambers
First Floor Gray's Inn Chambers, Gray's Inn,
London WC1R 5JA, Telephone: 0171 404 7888
Call date: Oct 1993, Middle Temple
Qualifications: [BA (Hons)(Lancs), CPE (Lond)]

CRABB RICHARD BLECHYNDEN

Colleton Chambers
Colleton Crescent, Exeter, Devon EX2 4DG,
Telephone: 01392 74898/9
Call date: Nov 1975, Middle Temple

CRABTREE RICHARD JOHN

3 Temple Gardens
Lower Ground Floor, Temple, London
EC4Y 9AU, Telephone: 0171 353 3102/5/9297
Call date: July 1974, Gray's Inn
Qualifications: [LLB]

CRABTREE SIMON JEREMY GERHARD

24a St John Street
Manchester M3 4DF,
Telephone: 0161 833 9628
Call date: Nov 1988, Lincoln's Inn
Qualifications: [LLB Hons (Leeds)]

CRACKNELL DOUGLAS GEORGE

23 Warham Road
Otford, Sevenoaks, Kent TN14 5PF,
Telephone: 01959 522325
Call date: May 1957, Middle Temple
Qualifications: [LLB]

CRAGG STEPHEN JAMES

2 Garden Court
1st Floor, Middle Temple, London EC4Y 9BL,
Telephone: 0171 353 1633
E-mail: barristers@2gardenct.law.co.uk
Call date: Nov 1996, Middle Temple
Qualifications: [LLB (Hons)(Lond), MA
(Brunel)]

CRAIG ALISTAIR TREVOR

11 New Square
Ground Floor, Lincoln's Inn, London
WC2A 3QB, Telephone: 0171 831 0081
E-mail: 11newsquare.co.uk
Call date: July 1983, Lincoln's Inn
Qualifications: [MA, (TCD)]

CRAIG AUBREY JOHN

5 Fountain Court
Steelhouse Lane, Birmingham B4 6DR,
Telephone: 0121 606 0500
Call date: Nov 1987, Inner Temple
Qualifications: [LLB]

CRAIG KENNETH ALLEN

Hardwicke Building
New Square, Lincoln's Inn, London
WC2A 3SB, Telephone: 0171 242 2523
E-mail: clerks@hardwicke.co.uk
Call date: July 1975, Lincoln's Inn
Qualifications: [BA]

CRAIL MISS (ELSPETH) ROSS

12 New Square
Ground Floor, Lincoln's Inn, London
WC2A 3SW, Telephone: 0171 419 1212
E-mail: 12newsquare@compuserve.com
25 Park Square
Leeds LS1 2PW, Telephone: 0113 2451841/2/3
E-mail: sovereignchambers@btinternet.com
Door Tenant
Call date: July 1986, Lincoln's Inn
Qualifications: [MA (Oxon), Dip Law (City)]

CRALLAN RICHARD WHARTON

Chavasse Court Chambers
2nd Floor Chavasse Court, 24 Lord Street,
Liverpool L2 1TA, Telephone: 0151 707 1191
Call date: Oct 1990, Inner Temple
Qualifications: [LLB (L'pool)]

CRAMPIN PAUL

Lamb Building
Ground Floor, Temple, London EC4Y 7AS,
Telephone: 0171 797 7788
E-mail: lamb.building@link.org
Call date: Oct 1992, Middle Temple
Qualifications: [LL.B (Hons)]

CRAMPIN PETER QC (1993)

11 New Square
Ground Floor, Lincoln's Inn, London
WC2A 3QB, Telephone: 0171 831 0081
E-mail: 11newsquare.co.uk
Call date: Nov 1976, Middle Temple
Recorder
Qualifications: [MA (Oxon)]

CRAMSIE JAMES SINCLAIR BERESFORD

13 King's Bench Walk
1st Floor, Temple, London EC4Y 7EN,
Telephone: 0171 353 7204
E-mail: clerks@13kbw.law.co.uk
King's Bench Chambers
32 Beaumont Street, Oxford OX1 2NP,
Telephone: 01865 311066
E-mail: clerks@kbc-oxford.law.co.uk
Call date: Nov 1988, Inner Temple
Qualifications: [LLB (Leeds)]

CRAN MARK DYSON GORDON QC (1988)

Brick Court Chambers
15/19 Devereux Court, London WC2R 3JJ,
Telephone: 0171 583 0777
E-mail: (surname)@brickcourt.demon.co.uk
Call date: July 1973, Gray's Inn
Qualifications: [LLB (Bris)]

CRANBROOK ALEXANDER DOUGLAS JOHN

9-12 Bell Yard
London WC2A 2LF,
Telephone: 0171 400 1800
Call date: July 1975, Gray's Inn
Qualifications: [BA (Hons)]

CRANE MICHAEL JOHN QC (1994)

5 Bell Yard
London WC2A 2JR, Telephone: 0171 333 8811
Call date: Nov 1975, Middle Temple
Qualifications: [BA (Oxon)]

CRANE MISS SUZANNE DENISE

New Court Chambers
Suite 200 Gazette Building, 168 Corporation
Street, Birmingham B4 6TZ,
Telephone: 0121 693 6656
Call date: Nov 1995, Lincoln's Inn
Qualifications: [LLB (Hons)]

CRANFIELD PETER ANTHONY

3 Verulam Buildings
London WC1R 5NT,
Telephone: 0171 831 8441
E-mail: clerks@3verulam.co.uk
Call date: July 1982, Gray's Inn
Qualifications: [BA, BCL (Oxon)]

CRANFIELD MRS ROSEMARY SHIRLEY ANNE

Sussex Chambers
9 Old Steine, Brighton BN1 1FJ,
Telephone: 01273 607953
Call date: Feb 1992, Inner Temple
Qualifications: [BA (Hons)(Oxon)]

CRANFIELD TONY

Bank House Chambers
Old Bank House, Hartshead, Sheffield S1 2EL,
Telephone: 0114 2751223
Call date: Nov 1975, Middle Temple
Qualifications: [LLB]

CRANGLE MISS CHARLOTTE MARY

Parsonage Chambers
5th Floor 3 The Parsonage, Manchester
M3 2HW, Telephone: 0161 833 1996
Call date: Oct 1995, Gray's Inn
Qualifications: [LLB (Sheff)]

CRANMER-BROWN MICHAEL TIMOTHY

King Charles House
Standard Hill, Nottingham NG1 6FX,
Telephone: 0115 9418851
E-mail: clerks@kch.co.uk
Call date: Nov 1986, Middle Temple
Qualifications: [BA (Hons)(Oxon), Dip Law
(City)]

CRANNY MISS AMANDA LOUISE

King Charles House
Standard Hill, Nottingham NG1 6FX,
Telephone: 0115 9418851
E-mail: clerks@kch.co.uk
Call date: Nov 1984, Lincoln's Inn
Qualifications: [LLB (Bristol)]

CRANSTON ROSS FREDERICK

3 Verulam Buildings
London WC1R 5NT,
Telephone: 0171 831 8441
E-mail: clerks@3verulam.co.uk
Call date: Nov 1976, Gray's Inn
Recorder
Qualifications: [D.Phil (Oxon)]

CRANSTON-MORRIS WAYNE

23 Essex Street
London WC2R 3AS,
Telephone: 0171 413 0353/353 3533
E-mail: clerks@essexstreet23.demon.co.uk
Call date: July 1986, Lincoln's Inn
Qualifications: [LLB (Brunel)]

CRASNOW MS RACHEL

Cloisters
1st Floor, Temple, London EC4Y 7AA,
Telephone: 0171 827 4000
E-mail: clerks@cloisters.com
Call date: Nov 1994, Middle Temple
Qualifications: [BA (Hons) (Oxon)]

CRAVEN RICHARD GEOFFREY

Plowden Bldgs
2nd Floor, Temple, London EC4Y 9BU,
Telephone: 0171 583 0808
E-mail: bar@plowdenbuildings.co.uk
Broad Chare
33 Broad Chare, Newcastle Upon Tyne
NE1 3DQ, Telephone: 0191 232 0541
Door Tenant
6 Pump Court
Ground Floor, Temple, London EC4Y 7AR,
Telephone: 0171 583 6013/2510
Door Tenant
Call date: July 1976, Inner Temple
Qualifications: [MA (Cantab)]

CRAVEN RICHARD JOHN

Library Chambers
Gray's Inn Chambers, Gray's Inn, London
WC1R 5JA, Telephone: 0171 404 6500
Call date: Oct 1995, Gray's Inn
Qualifications: [LLB]

CRAVEN ROBERT MICHAEL

Iscoed Chambers
86 St Helen's Road, Swansea SA1 4BQ,
Telephone: 01792 652988/9/330
Call date: Nov 1979, Gray's Inn
Qualifications: [MA, BCL (Oxon)]

CRAWFORD GRANT

11 Old Square
Ground Floor, Lincoln's Inn, London
WC2A 3TS, Telephone: 0171 430 0341
E-mail: clerks@11oldsquare.co.uk
Call date: July 1974, Middle Temple
Qualifications: [MA (Cantab)]

CRAWFORD LINCOLN SANTO

12 King's Bench Walk
Temple, London EC4Y 7EL,
Telephone: 0171 583 0811
E-mail: chambers@12kbw.co.uk
Call date: Nov 1977, Gray's Inn
Recorder

CRAWFORD MISS MARIE-BERNADETTE CLAIRE

Eastbourne Chambers
15 Hyde Gardens, Eastbourne, East Sussex
BN21 4PR, Telephone: 01323 642102/416466
Call date: Oct 1992, Lincoln's Inn
Qualifications: [LLB(Hons)(Leeds)]

CRAWFORD ROBERT DAVID

15 Winckley Square
Preston PR1 3JJ, Telephone: 01772 252828
E-mail: clerks@winckleysq.demon.co.uk
Call date: July 1976, Lincoln's Inn
Qualifications: [MA (Cantab)]

CRAWFORTH MISS EMMA

Southernhay Chambers
33 Southernhay East, Exeter EX1 1NX,
Telephone: 01392 255777
E-mail: southernhay.chambers@lineone.net
Call date: Nov 1992, Middle Temple
Qualifications: [LL.B (Hons)]

CRAWLEY GARY THOMAS BERNARD

One Garden Court
Ground Floor, Temple, London EC4Y 9BJ,
Telephone: 0171 797 7900
Call date: Feb 1988, Middle Temple
Qualifications: [LLB, LLM (Lond)]

CRAY TIMOTHY JAMES

6 King's Bench Walk
Ground Floor, Temple, London EC4Y 7DR,
Telephone: 0171 583 0410
Call date: Nov 1989, Inner Temple
Qualifications: [BA (Dunelm)]

CRAYTON PHILIP PATRICK

York Chambers
14 Toft Green, York YO1 1JT,
Telephone: 01904 620048
E-mail: yorkchambers.co.uk
Call date: July 1985, Gray's Inn
Qualifications: [LLB (Cardiff)]

D

CREAN ANTHONY

40 King Street
Manchester M2 6BA,
Telephone: 0161 832 9082
E-mail: Kingst40@aol.com
Call date: July 1987, Gray's Inn
Qualifications: [BA (Essex)]

CREAN MISS MARY ANGELA

Baker Street Chambers
9 Baker Street, Middlesbrough TS1 2LF,
Telephone: 01642 873873
Call date: Oct 1996, Gray's Inn
Qualifications: [LLB (L'pool)]

CREANER PAUL ANTHONY

15 Winckley Square
Preston PR1 3JJ, Telephone: 01772 252828
E-mail: clerks@winckleysq.demon.co.uk
Call date: Oct 1990, Lincoln's Inn
Qualifications: [BSc, LLB, ARICS]

CREGAN JOHN-PAUL FITZJAMES

Westgate Chambers
144 High Street, Lewes, East Sussex BN7 1XT,
Telephone: 01273 480510
Call date: Nov 1990, Middle Temple
Qualifications: [BCL (Ireland)]

CRICHTON-GOLD PETER LEONARD

Pall Mall Chambers
Executive House 40A Young Street,
Manchester M3 3FT,
Telephone: 0161 832 3373/4
3 Temple Gardens
2nd Floor, Temple, London EC4Y 9AU,
Telephone: 0171 583 1155
Call date: July 1972, Gray's Inn
Qualifications: [LLB (Lond), FCIArb]

CRIGMAN DAVID IAN QC (1989)

1 Fountain Court
Steelhouse Lane, Birmingham B4 6DR,
Telephone: 0121 236 5721
Call date: July 1969, Gray's Inn
Recorder
Qualifications: [LLB]

CRILLEY DR DARREL

28 St John Street
Manchester M3 4DJ,
Telephone: 0161 834 8418
E-mail: clerk@28stjohnst.co.uk
Call date: Mar 1996, Inner Temple
Qualifications: [BA (Oxon), LLB (London), PhD (London)]

CRIPPS MISS BEVERLY MARY

Newport Chambers
12 Clytha Park Road, Newport, Gwent
NP9 47L, Telephone: 01633 267403/255855
Call date: Nov 1988, Gray's Inn
Qualifications: [BA]

CRIPPS SEDDON

1 Harcourt Bldgs
2nd Floor, Temple, London EC4Y 9DA,
Telephone: 0171 353 9421/9151
Call date: Feb 1965, Middle Temple
Recorder

CRIPPS DR YVONNE MARIA

Emmanuel College
Cambridge CB2 3AP,
Telephone: 01223 334283/200
Call date: Nov 1991, Inner Temple
Qualifications: [LLM (Cantab), Ph.D (Cantab)]

CRITCHLEY JOHN STEPHEN

17 Bedford Row
London WC1R 4EB,
Telephone: 0171 831 7314
E-mail: IBoard7314@AOL.com
Call date: July 1985, Gray's Inn
Qualifications: [LLB (Bristol)]

CRITCHLOW CHRISTOPHER ALLAN

2 Crown Office Row
2nd Floor, Temple, London EC4Y 7HJ,
Telephone: 0171 797 8000
Call date: July 1973, Inner Temple
Recorder
Qualifications: [LLB (Exeter), FICArb]

CRITELLI NICHOLAS

11 Stone Bldgs
1st Floor, Lincoln's Inn, London WC2A 3TG,
Telephone: 0171 404 5055
E-mail: 9stoneb@compuserve.com
Door Tenant
Call date: July 1991, Middle Temple
Qualifications: [Juris of Drake Uni]

CROALL SIMON MARTIN

4 Essex Court
Temple, London EC4Y 9AJ,
Telephone: 0171 797 7970
E-mail: clerks@4essexcourt.law.co.uk
Call date: Nov 1986, Middle Temple
Qualifications: [MA (Cantab)]

CROALLY MILES JAMES

17 Bedford Row
London WC1R 4EB,
Telephone: 0171 831 7314
E-mail: IBoard7314@AOL.com
Call date: Nov 1987, Middle Temple
Qualifications: [BA, Dip Law]

CRONIN MISS TACEY MARGUERITE

Albion Chambers
Broad Street, Bristol BS1 1DR,
Telephone: 0117 9272144
Call date: July 1982, Middle Temple
Qualifications: [LLB (Hons) (Bris)]

CRONIN WILLIAM DAVID

Angel Chambers
94 Walter Road, Swansea SA1 5QA,
Telephone: 01792 6464623/6464648
Call date: July 1971, Inner Temple
Qualifications: [LLB]

CRONSHAW MICHAEL JOHN

2 Pump Court
1st Floor, Temple, London EC4Y 7AH,
Telephone: 0171 353 5597
Call date: Oct 1993, Middle Temple
Qualifications: [MA (Hons)(Oxon), MSc, Dip in Law (City)]

CROOK ADAM JAMES

6 Gray's Inn Square
Ground Floor, Gray's Inn, London WC1R 5AZ,
Telephone: 0171 242 1052
Call date: Nov 1994, Inner Temple
Qualifications: [BA (Keele)]

CROOKENDEN SIMON ROBERT QC (1996)

Essex Court Chambers
24 Lincoln's Inn Fields, London WC2A 3ED,
Telephone: 0171 813 8000
E-mail: clerksroom@essexcourt-chambers.co.uk
Call date: Nov 1975, Gray's Inn
Assistant Recorder
Qualifications: [MA (Cantab)]

CROSBIE MISS SUSAN MAUREEN

Paradise Square Chambers
26 Paradise Square, Sheffield S1 2DE,
Telephone: 0114 2738951
Call date: Nov 1988, Inner Temple
Qualifications: [LLB (Shef)]

CROSFILL JOHN

2 Paper Bldgs
Temple, London EC4Y 7ET,
Telephone: 0171 936 2613
Call date: Nov 1995, Middle Temple
Qualifications: [LLB (Hons), BSc]

CROSLAND JAMES BENJAMIN

Broadway House Chambers
Broadway House 9 Bank Street, Bradford,
West Yorkshire BD1 1TW,
Telephone: 01274 722560
Call date: Feb 1993, Gray's Inn
Qualifications: [MA (Cantab)]

CROSLAND TIMOTHY JOHN EDWARD

5 Paper Bldgs
Lower Ground Floor, Temple, London
EC4Y 7HB, Telephone: 0171 353 5638
E-mail: 107722,633@compuserve.com
Call date: Nov 1994, Inner Temple
Qualifications: [BA (Oxon), CPE (Lond)]

D

D

CROSS (JOSEPH) EDWARD

2 Gray's Inn Square Chambers
2nd Floor, Gray's Inn, London WC1R 5AA,
Telephone: 0171 242 0328/071 405 1317
E-mail: clerks@2gis.co.uk
Call date: July 1975, Inner Temple
Qualifications: [LLB (Bris)]

CROSS ANTHONY MAURICE

15 Winckley Square
Preston PR1 3JJ, Telephone: 01772 252828
E-mail: clerks@winckleysq.demon.co.uk
Call date: Nov 1982, Middle Temple
Qualifications: [LLB (Manc)]

CROSS GEOFFREY PAUL

New Court Chambers
3 Broad Chare, Newcastle Upon Tyne
NE1 3DQ, Telephone: 0191 232 1980
Call date: July 1981, Gray's Inn
Qualifications: [BA (Cantab)]

CROSS JAMES EDWARD MICHAEL

4 Pump Court
Temple, London EC4Y 7AN,
Telephone: 0171 353 2656/9
E-mail: 4_pump_court@compuserve.com
Call date: July 1985, Gray's Inn
Qualifications: [MA (Oxon)]

CROSS MISS JANE ELIZABETH

15 Winckley Square
Preston PR1 3JJ, Telephone: 01772 252828
E-mail: clerks@winckleysq.demon.co.uk
Call date: July 1982, Middle Temple
Qualifications: [LLB (L'pool)]

CROSS MRS JOANNA

9 Woodhouse Square
Leeds LS3 1AD, Telephone: 0113 2451986
Call date: Oct 1992, Lincoln's Inn
Qualifications: [BSc(St Andrew), MB ChB
(Manc), Dip Law]

CROSS RICHARD NOEL

Thomas More Chambers
52 Carey Street, Lincoln's Inn, London
WC2A 2JB, Telephone: 0171 404 7000
Call date: Oct 1993, Lincoln's Inn
Qualifications: [BA(Hons)(Bris)]

CROSSFIELD MISS ANNE

4 King's Bench Walk
Ground/First Floor, Temple, London
EC4Y 7DL, Telephone: 0171 822 8822
E-mail: 4kbw@barristersatlaw.com
Call date: July 1993, Lincoln's Inn
Qualifications: [LLB (B'ham), MBA (Nott'm)]

CROSSLEY SIMON JUSTIN

9 Woodhouse Square
Leeds LS3 1AD, Telephone: 0113 2451986
Call date: Nov 1993, Inner Temple
Qualifications: [LLB]

CROSSLEY STEVEN RICHARD

37 Park Square
Leeds LS1 2NY, Telephone: 0113 2439422
Call date: Nov 1992, Inner Temple
Qualifications: [LLB (Exon)]

CROSTHWAITE GRAHAM ANDREW

1 King's Bench Walk
2nd Floor, Temple, London EC4Y 7DB,
Telephone: 0171 936 1500
E-mail: ddear@1kbw.co.uk
Call date: Nov 1995, Inner Temple
Qualifications: [BA (Oxon)]

CROUCH ANDREW CHARLES MACKESAY

Fountain Chambers
Cleveland Business Centre 1 Watson Street,
Middlesbrough TS1 2RQ,
Telephone: 01642 217037
Call date: Nov 1990, Inner Temple
Qualifications: [LLB (Lancaster)]

CROUCH STEPHEN WILLIAM MICHAEL

22 Albion Place
Northampton NN1 1UD,
Telephone: 01604 36271
Call date: July 1982, Inner Temple
Qualifications: [BSc (Hons), Dip Law]

CROW JONATHAN RUPERT

4 Stone Bldgs
Ground Floor, Lincoln's Inn, London
WC2A 3XT, Telephone: 0171 242 5524
E-mail: d.goddard@4stonebuildings.law.co.uk
Call date: July 1981, Lincoln's Inn
Qualifications: [BA (Oxon)]

CROWLEY DANIEL JOHN

2 Temple Gardens
Temple, London EC4Y 9AY,
Telephone: 0171 583 6041 (12 Lines)
Call date: Oct 1990, Gray's Inn
Qualifications: [BA,LLB, BCL (Oxon)]

CROWLEY MRS JANE ELIZABETH

30 Park Place
Cardiff CF1 3BA, Telephone: 01222 398421
E-mail: 100757.1456@compuserve.com
One Garden Court
Ground Floor, Temple, London EC4Y 9BJ,
Telephone: 0171 797 7900
*Call date: July 1976, Gray's Inn
Recorder*
Qualifications: [LLB (Lond)]

CROWLEY JOHN DESMOND QC (1982)

2 Crown Office Row
Ground Floor, Temple, London EC4Y 7HJ,
Telephone: 0171 797 8100
E-mail: mail@2cor.co.uk, or to individual
barristers at: [barrister's surname]@2cor.co.uk
*Call date: May 1962, Inner Temple
Recorder*
Qualifications: [BA, LLB (Cantab)]

CROWN GILES HUMPHRY

1 Brick Court
1st Floor, Temple, London EC4Y 9BY,
Telephone: 0171 353 8845
E-mail: clerks@1brickcourt.co.uk
Call date: Oct 1993, Middle Temple
Qualifications: [MA, LLM (London)]

CROWSON HOWARD KEITH

St Paul's House
5th Floor 23 Park Square South, Leeds
LS1 2ND, Telephone: 0113 2455866
Call date: July 1987, Inner Temple
Qualifications: [LLB (Hons) (Leeds)]

CROWTHER JEREMY GAGE

9 Gough Square
London EC4A 3DE, Telephone: 0171 353 5371
Call date: Oct 1991, Middle Temple
Qualifications: [LLB Hons (Reading)]

CROWTHER THOMAS EDWARD

30 Park Place
Cardiff CF1 3BA, Telephone: 01222 398421
E-mail: 100757.1456@compuserve.com
Call date: Nov 1993, Inner Temple
Qualifications: [BSc, BA (Exon)]

CROWTHER WILLIAM RONALD HILTON QC (1980)

2 Temple Gardens
Temple, London EC4Y 9AY,
Telephone: 0171 583 6041 (12 Lines)
*Call date: July 1963, Inner Temple
Recorder*
Qualifications: [BA (Oxon)]

CROXFORD IAN LIONEL QC (1993)

Wilberforce Chambers
8 New Square, Lincoln's Inn, London
WC2A 3QP, Telephone: 0171 306 0102
E-mail: chambers@wilberforce.co.uk
Call date: July 1976, Gray's Inn
Qualifications: [LLB]

CROXFORD THOMAS HENRY

2 Hare Court
Ground Floor, Temple, London EC4Y 7BH,
Telephone: 0171 583 1770
E-mail: 2_Hare_Court@link.org
Call date: Oct 1992, Middle Temple
Qualifications: [BA (Hons)]

CROXON RAYMOND PATRICK QC (1983)

8 King's Bench Walk
2nd Floor, Temple, London EC4Y 7DU,
Telephone: 0171 797 8888
Regency Chambers
18 Cowgate, Peterborough PE1 1NA,
Telephone: 01733 315215
Regency Chambers
Sheraton House, Castle Park, Cambridge
CB3 0AX, Telephone: 01223 301517
Call date: Feb 1960, Gray's Inn
Qualifications: [LLB, MSR]

D

CROZIER RAWDON ROWLAND CRAIG

King's Bench Chambers
115 North Hill, Plymouth PL4 8JY,
Telephone: 01752 221551
2 King's Bench Walk
Ground Floor, Temple, London EC4Y 7DE,
Telephone: 0171 353 1746
E-mail: 2kbw@atlas.co.uk
Call date: Nov 1984, Middle Temple
Qualifications: [LLB (Lond)]

CRUICKSHANK MISS CYNTHIA MARILYN BENTON

1 Gray's Inn Square
Ground Floor, London WC1R 5AA,
Telephone: 0171 405 8946/7/8
Call date: Nov 1968, Lincoln's Inn

CRYSTAL JONATHAN

Cloisters
1st Floor, Temple, London EC4Y 7AA,
Telephone: 0171 827 4000
E-mail: clerks@cloisters.com
Call date: July 1972, Middle Temple
Qualifications: [LLB (Hons)(Lond)]

CRYSTAL MICHAEL QC (1984)

3/4 South Square
Gray's Inn, London WC1R 5HP,
Telephone: 0171 696 9900
E-mail: clerks@southsquare.com
Call date: Nov 1970, Middle Temple
Qualifications: [LLB (Lond), BCL (Oxon)]

CSOKA SIMON

Lloyds House Chambers
3rd Floor 18 Lloyds House, Lloyd Street,
Manchester M2 5WA,
Telephone: 0161 839 3371
Call date: Nov 1991, Gray's Inn
Qualifications: [MA (Cantab)]

CUDBY MS MARKANZA NICOLA

2 Garden Court
1st Floor, Middle Temple, London EC4Y 9BL,
Telephone: 0171 353 1633
E-mail: barristers@2gardenct.law.co.uk
Call date: July 1983, Middle Temple
Qualifications: [BA]

CULL MS LESLEY-ANNE SUSAN

4 Brick Court
Ground Floor, Temple, London EC4Y 9AD,
Telephone: 0171 797 7766
E-mail: chambers@4brick.co.uk
Call date: Oct 1995, Inner Temple
Qualifications: [BA (Cardiff), CPE]

CULLEN EDMUND WILLIAM HECTOR

7 Stone Bldgs
Ground Floor, Lincoln's Inn, London
WC2A 3SZ, Telephone: 0171 405 3886/
242 3546
E-mail: chaldous@vossnet.co.uk
Call date: Oct 1990, Lincoln's Inn
Qualifications: [BA (Bris)]

CULLEN MRS FELICITY ANN

Gray's Inn Chambers
3rd Floor, Gray's Inn, London WC1R 5JA,
Telephone: 0171 242 2642
E-mail: clerks@taxbar.com
Call date: July 1985, Lincoln's Inn
Qualifications: [LLB (B'ham) LLM, (Cantab)]

CULLUM MICHAEL

Albion Chambers
Broad Street, Bristol BS1 1DR,
Telephone: 0117 9272144
Call date: Apr 1991, Gray's Inn
Qualifications: [LLB (Warwick)]

CULVER THOMAS STATEN

Cloisters
1st Floor, Temple, London EC4Y 7AA,
Telephone: 0171 827 4000
E-mail: clerks@cloisters.com
Call date: Nov 1976, Middle Temple
Recorder
Qualifications: [LLB (Cantab)]

CUMMING GEORGE AUGUSTUS GERARD

Inns of Court School of Law
4 Grays's Inn Place, London WC1R 5DX,
Telephone: 0171 404 5787
Call date: Feb 1988, Inner Temple
Qualifications: [LLB (Lond), BA, MA, PhD]

CUMMINGS BRIAN

Exchange Chambers
Pearl Assurance House Derby Square,
Liverpool L2 9XX, Telephone: 0151 236 7747/
0458
E-mail: exchangechambers@btinternet.com
Call date: Nov 1988, Lincoln's Inn
Qualifications: [MA Hons (Cantab)]

CUMMINS BRIAN DOMINIC

Bridewell Chambers
2 Bridewell Place, London EC4V 6AP,
Telephone: 0171 797 8800
E-mail: clerks@bridewell.law.co.uk
Call date: Oct 1992, Middle Temple
Qualifications: [LL.B (Hons) & LL.M]

CUNNINGHAM MISS CLAIRE LOUISE

7 Fountain Court
Steelhouse Lane, Birmingham B4 6DR,
Telephone: 0121 236 8531
Call date: Nov 1996, Middle Temple
Qualifications: [BA (Hons)(Cantab)]

CUNNINGHAM MISS ELIZABETH ALICE

Albion Chambers
Broad Street, Bristol BS1 1DR,
Telephone: 0117 9272144
Call date: Oct 1995, Middle Temple
Qualifications: [BA (Hons)(Bris)]

CUNNINGHAM GRAHAM TAYLOR

Francis Taylor Bldg
Ground Floor, Temple, London EC4Y 7BY,
Telephone: 0171 353 7768/7769/2711
Call date: July 1976, Gray's Inn
Qualifications: [LLB (Hons)]

CUNNINGHAM MARK JAMES

13 Old Square
Ground Floor, Lincoln's Inn, London
WC2A 3UA, Telephone: 0171 404 4800
Call date: Nov 1980, Inner Temple
Qualifications: [BA (Oxon)]

CURNOW MISS (ELIZABETH) ANN (MARGUERITE) QC (1985)

6 King's Bench Walk
Ground Floor, Temple, London EC4Y 7DR,
Telephone: 0171 583 0410
Call date: Feb 1957, Gray's Inn
Recorder

CURRAN LEO

3 Paper Bldgs
1st Floor, Temple, London EC4Y 7EU,
Telephone: 0171 583 8055
E-mail: london@3paper.com
1 Alfred Street
High Street, Oxford OX1 4EH,
Telephone: 01865 793736
20 Lorne Park Road
Bournemouth BH1 1JN,
Telephone: 01202 292102 (5 Lines)
Call date: July 1972, Gray's Inn
Qualifications: [MA (Oxon)]

CURRAN PATRICK DAVID QC (1995)

9-12 Bell Yard
London WC2A 2LF,
Telephone: 0171 400 1800
30 Park Place
Cardiff CF1 3BA, Telephone: 01222 398421
E-mail: 100757.1456@compuserve.com
Door Tenant
Call date: July 1972, Gray's Inn
Recorder
Qualifications: [MA (Oxon)]

CURRAN PHILIP PETER

Lincoln House Chambers
5th Floor Lincoln House, 1 Brazennose Street,
Manchester M2 5EL,
Telephone: 0161 832 5701
E-mail: LincolnHouseChambers@link.org
Call date: May 1979, Lincoln's Inn
Qualifications: [BA (Hons)]

CURRIE FERGUS HUGH

Assize Court Chambers
14 Small Street, Bristol BS1 1DE,
Telephone: 0117 9264587
Call date: Mar 1997, Gray's Inn
Qualifications: [BA (Oxon)]

CURRY THOMAS PETER ELLISON QC (1973)

4 Stone Bldgs
Ground Floor, Lincoln's Inn, London
WC2A 3XT, Telephone: 0171 242 5524
E-mail: d.goddard@4stonebuildings.law.co.uk
Call date: June 1953, Middle Temple
Qualifications: [MA (Oxon)]

CURSHAM GEOFFREY MARK

65-67 King Street
Leicester LE1 6RP, Telephone: 0116 2547710
Call date: June 1964, Gray's Inn
Qualifications: [BA, LLB (Cantab)]

CURTIS CHARLES JOHN

1 Temple Gardens
1st Floor, Temple, London EC4Y 9BB,
Telephone: 0171 353 0407/583 1315
E-mail: clerks@1templegardens.co.uk
Call date: Oct 1992, Lincoln's Inn
Qualifications: [BA(Hons)(Dunelm)]

CURTIS MS HELEN JANE

4 Brick Court
Ground Floor, Temple, London EC4Y 9AD,
Telephone: 0171 797 7766
E-mail: chambers@4brick.co.uk
Call date: Nov 1992, Middle Temple
Qualifications: [LLB (Hons, Leic)]

CURTIS JAMES WILLIAM OCKFORD QC (1993)

6 King's Bench Walk
Ground Floor, Temple, London EC4Y 7DR,
Telephone: 0171 583 0410
Call date: July 1970, Inner Temple
Recorder
Qualifications: [MA (Oxon)]

CURTIS MICHAEL ALEXANDER

2 Crown Office Row
Ground Floor, Temple, London EC4Y 7HJ,
Telephone: 0171 797 8100
E-mail: mail@2cor.co.uk, or to individual
barristers at: [barrister's surname]@2cor.co.uk
Call date: Nov 1982, Middle Temple
Qualifications: [MA (Oxon), MSc, ACIArb]

CURTIS MISS NICOLE DIANE

1 Paper Bldgs
1st Floor, Temple, London EC4Y 7EP,
Telephone: 0171 353 3728/4953
Call date: Oct 1992, Gray's Inn
Qualifications: [MA (Cantab)]

CURTIS MISS REBECCA LOUISE

Albion Chambers
Broad Street, Bristol BS1 1DR,
Telephone: 0117 9272144
Call date: Oct 1993, Inner Temple
Qualifications: [BSc, CPE]

CURTIS-RALEIGH GILES

4 King's Bench Walk
2nd Floor, Temple, London EC4Y 7DL,
Telephone: 0171 353 3581
Call date: Oct 1992, Middle Temple
Qualifications: [BA (Hons), MA, Dip in Law]

CURWEN DAVID CHRISTIAN

Assize Court Chambers
14 Small Street, Bristol BS1 1DE,
Telephone: 0117 9264587
1 Gray's Inn Square
Ground Floor, London WC1R 5AA,
Telephone: 0171 405 8946/7/8
Door Tenant
Call date: July 1982, Gray's Inn
Qualifications: [BA (Warw), Dip Law]

CURWEN MICHAEL JONATHAN

6 Pump Court
Ground Floor, Temple, London EC4Y 7AR,
Telephone: 0171 583 6013/2510
Call date: July 1966, Inner Temple
Recorder
Qualifications: [BA (Oxon)]

CUSWORTH NICHOLAS NEVILLE GRYLLS

1 Mitre Ct Bldgs
Ground Floor, Temple, London EC4Y 7BS,
Telephone: 0171 797 7070
Call date: Nov 1986, Lincoln's Inn
Qualifications: [MA (Oxon)]

CUTTING CHRISTOPHER HUGH

11 Old Square
Ground Floor, Lincoln's Inn, London
WC2A 3TS, Telephone: 0171 242 5022/
405 1074
Call date: Nov 1973, Middle Temple
Qualifications: [LLM]

CUTTS MISS JOHANNAH

23 Essex Street
London WC2R 3AS,
Telephone: 0171 413 0353/353 3533
E-mail: clerks@essexstreet23.demon.co.uk
Call date: Nov 1986, Inner Temple
Qualifications: [LLB]

D'AIGREMONT GILLES LOUIS

Verulam Chambers
Peer House 8-14 Verulam Street, Gray's Inn,
London WC1X 8LZ,
Telephone: 0171 813 2400
Call date: July 1978, Lincoln's Inn
Qualifications: [Maitrise En Droit, Dip de
L'Institut, d'Etudes Politiques, (Paris), Avocat a
la Cour De, Paris]

D'ARCY MISS KATHARINE LOUISE

4 Brick Court
1st Floor, Temple, London EC4Y 9AD,
Telephone: 0171 583 8455
Call date: Nov 1988, Inner Temple
Qualifications: [LLB (Leic)]

D'ARCY LEO EUGENE MARY PETER CHANEL

1 Gray's Inn Square
1st Floor, London WC1R 5AG,
Telephone: 0171 405 3000
E-mail: clerks@onegrays.demon.co.uk
Call date: May 1983, Gray's Inn
Qualifications: [BA (Dublin)]

D'COTTA JOHN MILNES

4 Essex Court
Temple, London EC4Y 9AJ,
Telephone: 0171 797 7970
E-mail: clerks@4essexcourt.law.co.uk
Call date: Nov 1955, Middle Temple
Qualifications: [MA (Oxon), Licensiado de,
Derecho (Madrid)]

D'CRUZ VINOD RUPERT

10 Old Square
Ground Floor, Lincoln's Inn, London
WC2A 3SU, Telephone: 0171 405 0758
Call date: Nov 1989, Lincoln's Inn
Qualifications: [BA (Nott'm)]

D'CRUZ VIVEK RUFUS

Cloisters
1st Floor, Temple, London EC4Y 7AA,
Telephone: 0171 827 4000
E-mail: clerks@cloisters.com
Call date: Oct 1993, Lincoln's Inn
Qualifications: [BA (Hons)(B'ham), CPE
(Lond)]

D'SOUZA MISS CAROLYN AMANDA

12 King's Bench Walk
Temple, London EC4Y 7EL,
Telephone: 0171 583 0811
E-mail: chambers@12kbw.co.uk
Call date: Oct 1994, Middle Temple
Qualifications: [LLB (Hons)(Lond), LLM
(Hons)(Harvard)]

D'SOUZA DOMINIC CHARLES

2 Paper Buildings
Basement, Temple, London EC4Y 7ET,
Telephone: 0171 353 0933
Call date: Nov 1993, Inner Temple
Qualifications: [BA (Lond), CPE (City)]

DA COSTA MISS ELISSA JOSEPHINE

Verulam Chambers
Peer House 8-14 Verulam Street, Gray's Inn,
London WC1X 8LZ,
Telephone: 0171 813 2400
Call date: Oct 1990, Middle Temple
Qualifications: [BA, Dip Law, LLM]

DA SILVA DAVID VERE AUSTIN CLEMENT PETER

3 Stone Bldgs
Ground Floor, Lincoln's Inn, London
WC2A 3XL, Telephone: 0171 242 4937/
405 8358
Call date: Nov 1978, Middle Temple
Qualifications: [MA (Oxon)]

D

DABBS DAVID LESLIE

Goldsmith Chambers
Ground Floor Goldsmith Building, Temple,
London EC4Y 7BL,
Telephone: 0171 353 6802/3/4/5
E-mail: celiamonksfield@btinternet.com
Call date: July 1984, Lincoln's Inn
Qualifications: [LLB (Manchester)]

DABLE JEREMY RICHARD

New Bailey Chambers
10 Lawson Street, Preston PR1 2QT,
Telephone: 01772 258087
Call date: Nov 1987, Gray's Inn
Qualifications: [LLB (Leeds)]

DACEY MARK

3 Paper Bldgs
2nd Floor, Temple, London EC4Y 7EU,
Telephone: 0171 353 6208
Call date: Nov 1985, Middle Temple
Qualifications: [BA]

DACRE IAN THOMAS

New Bailey Chambers
10 Lawson Street, Preston PR1 2QT,
Telephone: 01772 258087
Call date: Nov 1991, Middle Temple
Qualifications: [BA;MA (Lond)]

DAGG JOHN DOUGLAS

1 Serjeants' Inn
4th Floor, Temple, London EC4Y 1NH,
Telephone: 0171 583 1355
E-mail: serjeants.inn@virgin.net
Trinity Chambers
140 New London Road, Chelmsford, Essex
CM2 0AW, Telephone: 01245 605040
Call date: July 1980, Middle Temple
Qualifications: [BSc (Dunelm), LLB (Lond),
M.C.D (L'pool), MRTPI]

DAGNALL JOHN MARSHALL ANTHONY

9 Old Square
Ground Floor, Lincoln's Inn, London
WC2A 3SR, Telephone: 0171 405 4682
E-mail: chambers@9oldsquare.co.uk
Call date: Nov 1983, Lincoln's Inn
Qualifications: [BA, BCL(Oxon)]

DAHLSEN PETER JOHN MORGAN

2 Paper Bldgs
Temple, London EC4Y 7ET,
Telephone: 0171 936 2613
Call date: Oct 1996, Gray's Inn
Qualifications: [LLB (Lond)]

DAICHES MICHAEL SALIS

22 Old Buildings
Lincoln's Inn, London WC2A 3UJ,
Telephone: 0171 831 0222
Call date: July 1977, Middle Temple

Fax: 0171 831 2239;
Out of hours telephone: 0171 831 0222;
DX: 201 London, Chancery Lane;
Other comms: E-mail
michael_daiches@link.org

Types of work: Arbitration; Chancery land law;
Commercial property; Common law (general);
Construction; Conveyancing; Housing;
Landlord and tenant; Local government;
Professional negligence

Circuit: South Eastern

Reported cases: *Austin v Windsor Life
Assurance*, [1996] 34 EG 93, 1996.
Determination of enfranchisement price -
Leasehold Reform Act 1967.
Devonshire Reid Properties Ltd v Trenaman,
[1997] 20 EG 148, 1995. Whether landlord
entitled to create additional flat in roofspace.
Hafton Properties Ltd v Camp, [1994] 03 EG
129, 1994. Implication of terms in long
residential leases involving lessees'
management company.
Staszewski v Maribella Ltd, [1998] 04 EG 149.
Lessees' right of first refusal - Landlord and
Tenant Act 1987.
*United Dominions Trust Ltd v Shellpoint
Trustees Ltd*, [1993] 4 All ER 310, 1993.
Whether mortgagee entitled to apply for relief
from forfeiture after peaceable re-entry.

Practice information

Michael Daiches practises primarily in the fields
of Property Law and Water Law, but he is
experienced in all civil matters involving
contractual, commercial and tortious disputes.
He also has experience in property-related
Professional Negligence matters and in Building
Disputes. He has a particular interest in the
management of blocks of flats, and in leasehold
enfranchisement.

He is a very experienced advocate, and regularly appears in the High Court and County Courts, and before Leasehold Valuation Tribunals, Rent Assessment Committees and Arbitrators.

He is willing to act as an Arbitrator in service charge disputes - an area with which he is particularly well acquainted. He has advised both landlords and tenants on service charge law, and he has also had direct practical experience of the problems of management at blocks of flats from the perspective of both landlord and tenant, having been a long lessee in two different blocks and having served as a committee member of a lessees' residents association, a director of a freeholding company, and a director of a lessees' management company.

He also has considerable experience in Water Law, and has acted for statutory water undertakers, local authorities, landowners and occupiers in connection with disputes relating to water and sewage legislation and damage to property interests caused by escapes from pipes and channels.

He has spoken at conferences and seminars on subjects relating to the management of blocks of flats and leasehold enfranchisement.

DAKYNS MS ISABEL ANNE FRANCES

9 Bedford Row
London WC1R 4AZ,
Telephone: 0171 242 3555
E-mail: clerks@9br.co.uk
Call date: Nov 1992, Lincoln's Inn
Qualifications: [BA (Hons)]

DALAL RAJEN CHARLES JAMES

Cobden House Chambers
19 Quay Street, Manchester M3 3HN,
Telephone: 0161 833 6000
E-mail: clerks@cobden.co.uk
Call date: Oct 1991, Lincoln's Inn
Qualifications: [LLB (Hons) (Manc)]

DALBY JOSEPH FRANCIS

Chambers of Joseph Dalby
First Floor No 28 St Stephens Road,
Winchester SO22 6DE,
Telephone: 01962 886555
Call date: July 1988, Middle Temple
Qualifications: [LLB (Hons)]

DALE DERRICK RALPH

Fountain Court
Temple, London EC4Y 9DH,
Telephone: 0171 583 3335
E-mail: chambers@fountaincourt.co.uk
Call date: Oct 1990, Middle Temple
Qualifications: [BA (Cantab), LLM (Harvard)]

DALE JONATHAN PAUL

Martins Building
Water Street, Liverpool L2 3SP,
Telephone: 0151 236 5818/4919
Call date: Oct 1991, Gray's Inn
Qualifications: [BA (Oxon)]

DALE JULIAN CHARLES RIGBY

Eastbourne Chambers
15 Hyde Gardens, Eastbourne, East Sussex
BN21 4PR, Telephone: 01323 642102/416466
Call date: Nov 1991, Middle Temple
Qualifications: [LLB (Hons)]

DALGLEISH ANTHONY JAMES

2 King's Bench Walk
1st Floor, Temple, London EC4Y 7DE,
Telephone: 0171 353 9276
Call date: Nov 1971, Inner Temple
Qualifications: [LLB]

DALLAS ANDREW THOMAS ALASTAIR

10 Park Square
Leeds LS1 2LH, Telephone: 0113 2455438
E-mail: chambers@bandit.legend.co.uk
Call date: Nov 1978, Gray's Inn
Assistant Recorder
Qualifications: [MA (Cantab)]

DALY DAVID

Francis Taylor Bldg
3rd Floor, Temple, London EC4Y 7BY,
Telephone: 0171 797 7250
Call date: July 1979, Middle Temple
Qualifications: [BA, LLB (Lond), AKC]

D

DALY DENIS MICHAEL PATRICK SHEPSTON

11 Stone Bldgs
Ground Floor, Lincoln's Inn, London
WC2A 3TG, Telephone: 0171 831 6381
E-mail: clerks@11StoneBuildings.law.co.uk
Call date: Feb 1995, Lincoln's Inn
Qualifications: [BA, LLB (Natal,S.Africa), LLM (Cantab)]

DALY NIGEL JONATHAN

13 King's Bench Walk
1st Floor, Temple, London EC4Y 7EN,
Telephone: 0171 353 7204
E-mail: clerks@13kbw.law.co.uk
King's Bench Chambers
32 Beaumont Street, Oxford OX1 2NP,
Telephone: 01865 311066
E-mail: clerks@kbc-oxford.law.co.uk
Call date: July 1979, Gray's Inn
Qualifications: [LLB (Lond)]

DALZIEL ALARIC JAMES GENGE

Park Lane Chambers
19 Westgate, Leeds LS1 2RD,
Telephone: 0113 2285000
3 Verulam Buildings
London WC1R 5NT,
Telephone: 0171 831 8441
E-mail: clerks@3verulam.co.uk
Call date: July 1967, Inner Temple
Recorder

DANGOR MRS PATRICIA MADREE TRENTON

14 Gray's Inn Square
Gray's Inn, London WC1R 5JP,
Telephone: 0171 242 0858
E-mail: 100712.2134@compuserve.com
Call date: July 1970, Middle Temple
Recorder

DANIEL (OWEN) RICHARD

Sackville Chambers
Sackville Place 44-48 Magdalen Street,
Norwich NR3 1JU, Telephone: 01603 613516/
616221
Call date: Feb 1977, Inner Temple

DANIEL LEON ROGER

14 Tooks Court
Cursitor St, London EC4A 1LB,
Telephone: 0171 405 8828
E-mail: clerks @tooks.law.co.uk
Call date: July 1992, Gray's Inn
Qualifications: [LLB]

DANIEL NIGEL

10 King's Bench Walk
1st Floor, Temple, London EC4Y 7EB,
Telephone: 0171 353 2501
Call date: Nov 1988, Inner Temple
Qualifications: [LLB (Exon)]

DANIELLS-SMITH ROGER CHARLES

8 King's Bench Walk
2nd Floor, Temple, London EC4Y 7DU,
Telephone: 0171 797 8888
8 King's Bench Walk North
1 Park Square East, Leeds LS1 2NE,
Telephone: 0113 2439797
Call date: Nov 1974, Middle Temple
Qualifications: [AKC, LLB]

DANIELS DAVID WILLIAM

Southsea Chambers
PO Box 148, Southsea, Portsmouth,
Hampshire PO5 2TU,
Telephone: 01705 291261
Call date: Oct 1995, Lincoln's Inn
Qualifications: [LLB (Hons)(Lond)]

DANIELS IAIN JAMES

10 King's Bench Walk
1st Floor, Temple, London EC4Y 7EB,
Telephone: 0171 353 2501
Call date: Oct 1992, Lincoln's Inn
Qualifications: [LLB(Hons)(Sheff)]

DANIELS NICHOLAS ANDREW

3 Dr Johnson's Bldgs
Ground Floor, Temple, London EC4Y 7BA,
Telephone: 0171 353 4854
Call date: Feb 1988, Inner Temple
Qualifications: [LLB (Bristol)]

DANIELS MISS PHILIPPA CATHERINE

Fleet Chambers
Mitre House 44-46 Fleet Street, London
EC4Y 1BN, Telephone: 0171 936 3707
Call date: Oct 1995, Inner Temple
Qualifications: [BA (Hons)(S.Africa)]

DARBISHIRE ADRIAN MUNRO

Hollis Whiteman Chambers
3rd/4th Floor Queen Elizabeth Bldg, Temple,
London EC4Y 9BS, Telephone: 0171 583 5766
E-mail: hollis.whiteman@btinternet.com
Call date: Oct 1993, Lincoln's Inn
Qualifications: [BA (Hons), Dip in Law (City),
LLM (Lond)]

DARBY PATRICK MICHAEL

3 Fountain Court
Steelhouse Lane, Birmingham B4 6DR,
Telephone: 0121 236 5854
Call date: July 1978, Middle Temple
Qualifications: [MA (Cantab)]

DARBYSHIRE WILLIAM ROBERT

9 St John Street
Manchester M3 4DN,
Telephone: 0161 955 9000
E-mail: ninesjs@gconnect.com
Call date: Nov 1995, Lincoln's Inn
Qualifications: [BA (Hons), LLM]

DARIAN MISS ANN

All Saints Chambers
9/11 Broad Street, Bristol BS1 2HP,
Telephone: 0117 921 1966
Call date: July 1974, Middle Temple
Qualifications: [LLB (Lond)]

DARLING IAN GALEN

2 Harcourt Bldgs
1st Floor, Temple, London EC4Y 9DB,
Telephone: 0171 353 2112/2817
Call date: July 1985, Middle Temple
Qualifications: [LLB (Lond)]

DARLING PAUL ANTHONY

Keating Chambers
10 Essex Street, Outer Temple, London
WC2R 3AA, Telephone: 0171 544 2600
Call date: July 1983, Middle Temple
Qualifications: [BA, BCL(Oxon)]

DARLOW MISS ANNABEL CHARLOTTE

6 King's Bench Walk
Ground Floor, Temple, London EC4Y 7DR,
Telephone: 0171 583 0410
Call date: Oct 1993, Middle Temple
Qualifications: [BA (Hons)(Cantab), Dip in Law
(City)]

DARROCH MISS FIONA CULVERWELL

7 New Square
Lincoln's Inn, London WC2A 3QS,
Telephone: 0171 430 1660
Call date: Oct 1994, Inner Temple
Qualifications: [BA (Lond), Diploma in Music,
CPE]

DARTON CLIFFORD JOHN

Chichester Chambers
12 North Pallant, Chichester, West Sussex
PO19 1TQ, Telephone: 01243 784538
Call date: July 1988, Middle Temple
Qualifications: [BA (Hons) (Oxon)]

DAS MISS KAMALA

St John's Chambers
Small Street, Bristol BS1 1DW,
Telephone: 0117 9213456/298514
E-mail: clerks@stjohns.uk.com
Door Tenant
Call date: Nov 1975, Middle Temple
Qualifications: [BA]

DASHWOOD PROFESSOR ARTHUR ALAN

2 Harcourt Bldgs
Ground Floor/Left, Temple, London
EC4Y 9DB, Telephone: 0171 583 9020
E-mail: clerks@harcourt.co.uk
Stanbrook & Henderson
2 Harcourt Bldgs 2nd Floor, Temple, London
EC4Y 9DB, Telephone: 0171 353 0101
E-mail: clerks@harcourt.co.uk
Call date: Nov 1969, Inner Temple
Qualifications: [MA (Oxon)]

DASHWOOD ROBERT THOMAS

Gray's Inn Chambers
5th Floor, Gray's Inn, London WC1R 5JA,
Telephone: 0171 404 1111
Call date: Nov 1984, Inner Temple
Qualifications: [BA (Bristol), Dip Law]

DASS PRESTON

1 Crown Office Row
2nd Floor, Temple, London EC4Y 7HH,
Telephone: 0171 797 7111
Call date: Nov 1983, Inner Temple
Qualifications: [BA Kent]

DATE JULIAN RICHARD

17 Bedford Row
London WC1R 4EB,
Telephone: 0171 831 7314
E-mail: IBoard7314@AOL.com
Call date: Nov 1988, Middle Temple
Qualifications: [BA (Oxon)]

DATTA MRS WENDY PATRICIA MIZAL

Alban Chambers
27 Old Gloucester Street, London WC1N 3XX,
Telephone: 0171 419 5051
E-mail: wpmd@clara.net
Call date: Oct 1990, Middle Temple
Qualifications: [Dip Ed (Lond), LLB (Hons)]

DAVENPORT SIMON NICHOLAS

5 Essex Court
1st Floor, Temple, London EC4Y 9AH,
Telephone: 0171 410 2000
Call date: Nov 1987, Inner Temple
Qualifications: [LLB (Leeds), ACIArb]

DAVEY (ASTLEY) CHARLES

India Buildings Chambers
Water Street, Liverpool L2 OXG,
Telephone: 0151 243 6000
Call date: Feb 1989, Middle Temple
Qualifications: [MA (Oxon)]

DAVEY BENJAMIN NICHOLAS

11 Old Square
Ground Floor, Lincoln's Inn, London
WC2A 3TS, Telephone: 0171 430 0341
E-mail: clerks@11oldsquare.co.uk
Call date: Oct 1994, Middle Temple
Qualifications: [BA (Hons)(Oxon)]

DAVEY GEOFFREY WALLACE

Fountain Chambers
Cleveland Business Centre 1 Watson Street,
Middlesbrough TS1 2RQ,
Telephone: 01642 217037
Call date: July 1954, Lincoln's Inn
Recorder
Qualifications: [MA (Oxon)]

DAVEY MISS HELEN MARGARET

2 Pump Court
1st Floor, Temple, London EC4Y 7AH,
Telephone: 0171 353 5597
Call date: July 1984, Inner Temple
Qualifications: [BSc (Cardiff)]

DAVEY MISS KATHERINE ANNE TERESA

1 Gray's Inn Square
1st Floor, London WC1R 5AG,
Telephone: 0171 405 3000
E-mail: clerks@onegrays.demon.co.uk
Call date: May 1988, Inner Temple
Qualifications: [MA (Cantab)]

DAVEY MICHAEL PHILIP

4 Field Court
Gray's Inn, London WC1R 5EA,
Telephone: 0171 440 6900
E-mail: chambers@4fieldcourt.co.uk
Call date: Nov 1990, Gray's Inn
Qualifications: [LLB (Lond), BCL (Oxon)]

DAVEY MISS MICHELLE MARIA

Adrian Lyon's Chambers
14 Castle Street, Liverpool L2 ONE,
Telephone: 0151 236 4421/8240
E-mail: chambers14@aol.com
Call date: Nov 1993, Lincoln's Inn
Qualifications: [LLB (Hons, L'pool)]

DAVEY NEIL MARTIN

39 Park Square
Leeds LS1 2NU, Telephone: 0113 2456633
Call date: July 1978, Middle Temple
Qualifications: [MA (Oxon)]

DAVEY ROGER LAWRENCE

2 Dr Johnson's Building
Temple, London EC4Y 7AY,
Telephone: 0171 353 4716
Call date: Feb 1978, Inner Temple

DAVEY MISS TINA ELAINE

9-12 Bell Yard
London WC2A 2LF,
Telephone: 0171 400 1800
Call date: Nov 1993, Middle Temple
Qualifications: [LLB (Hons)(Cardiff)]

DAVEY TOBIAS BENJAMIN

2-3 Gray's Inn Square
Gray's Inn, London WC1R 5JH,
Telephone: 0171 242 4986
E-mail: chambers@2-3graysinnsquare.co.uk
Call date: Feb 1977, Gray's Inn
Qualifications: [LLB (Lond)]

DAVIDSON ARTHUR QC (1978)

Cloisters
1st Floor, Temple, London EC4Y 7AA,
Telephone: 0171 827 4000
E-mail: clerks@cloisters.com
Call date: Feb 1953, Middle Temple

DAVIDSON EDWARD ALAN QC (1994)

11 Old Square
Ground Floor, Lincoln's Inn, London
WC2A 3TS, Telephone: 0171 430 0341
E-mail: clerks@11oldsquare.co.uk
Call date: Nov 1966, Gray's Inn
Qualifications: [MA LLB (Cantab)]

Fax: 0171 831 2469; DX: LDE 1031;
Other comms: E-mail
clerks@11oldsquare.co.uk

Types of work: Bahamas law; Chancery
(general); Commercial litigation; Company and
commercial; Equity, wills and trusts; Mining and
Mineral; Partnerships; Professional negligence;
Trusts

Awards and memberships: Member of Chancery
Bar and Professional Negligence Bar
Associations

Cases
Amongst the reported cases are *Mobil v
Rawlinson* [1981] 43 P & CR 221 (mortgage);
Gulf Oil v Page [1987] Ch 327 (conspiracy/
interlocutory injunction); *Weddell v Pearce*
[1988] Ch 26 (bankruptcy/assignment); *Eagle
Star Insurance v Provincial Insurance Plc*
[1994] 1 AC 130 (double insurance/Road Traffic
Acts/contribution); *Hunter v Moss* [1994] 1
WLR 402 (trusts certainty - company shares)
Khan v Miah [1998] 1WLR 477 (partnership)

DAVIDSON MISS KATHARINE MARY

1 Mitre Ct Bldgs
Ground Floor, Temple, London EC4Y 7BS,
Telephone: 0171 797 7070
Call date: Nov 1987, Lincoln's Inn
Qualifications: [MA (Oxon)]

DAVIDSON NICHOLAS RANKING QC (1993)

4 Paper Bldgs
Ground Floor, Temple, London EC4Y 7EX,
Telephone: 0171 353 3366/583 7155
E-mail: clerks@4paperbuildings.com
Call date: July 1974, Inner Temple
Qualifications: [BA (Cantab)]

DAVIDSON DR RANALD DUNBAR

3 Serjeants Inn
London EC4Y 1BQ,
Telephone: 0171 353 5537
E-mail: available upon request
Call date: Nov 1996, Inner Temple
Qualifications: [MB, ChB (Edinburgh), LLB
(Lond)]

DAVIE MICHAEL JAMES

4 Pump Court
Temple, London EC4Y 7AN,
Telephone: 0171 353 2656/9
E-mail: 4_pump_court@compuserve.com
Call date: Nov 1993, Middle Temple
Qualifications: [LLB (Hons)(Strathcl), D.Phil
(Oxon)]

DAVIES ANDREW

Angel Chambers
94 Walter Road, Swansea SA1 5QA,
Telephone: 01792 6464623/6464648
Call date: Oct 1992, Lincoln's Inn
Qualifications: [LLB(Hons)(Lancaster),
LLM(Hull)]

DAVIES ANDREW CHRISTOPHER

New Court Chambers
5 Verulam Buildings, Gray's Inn, London
WC1R 5LY, Telephone: 0171 831 9500
E-mail: mail@newcourtchambers.com
Call date: July 1988, Inner Temple
Qualifications: [BA (Oxon)]

DAVIES ANTHONY MARTIN

1 Paper Bldgs
1st Floor, Temple, London EC4Y 7EP,
Telephone: 0171 353 3728/4953
Call date: July 1971, Gray's Inn
Recorder

DAVIES MISS CAROL ELIZABETH

2 New Street
Leicester LE1 5NA, Telephone: 0116 2625906
Call date: Oct 1995, Middle Temple
Qualifications: [LLB (Hons)]

DAVIES DR CHARLES EDWARD

4 Field Court
Gray's Inn, London WC1R 5EA,
Telephone: 0171 440 6900
E-mail: chambers@4fieldcourt.co.uk
Call date: Nov 1995, Middle Temple
Qualifications: [BA (Hons), D.Phil]

DAVIES MISS CHARLOTTE ANNE

55 Temple Chambers
Temple Avenue, London EC4Y 0HP,
Telephone: 0171 353 7400
Call date: Nov 1996, Middle Temple
Qualifications: [LLB (Hons)(Manch)]

DAVIES DAVID COLIN

33 Park Place
Cardiff CF1 3BA, Telephone: 01222 233313
Call date: Nov 1973, Gray's Inn
Qualifications: [MA (Oxon)]

DAVIES THE RT HON DAVID JOHN DENZIL

Goldsworth Chambers
1st Floor 10-11 Gray's Inn Square, London
WC1R 5JD, Telephone: 0171 405 7117
Call date: Nov 1965, Gray's Inn
Qualifications: [MA]

DAVIES DAVID PETER

33 Park Place
Cardiff CF1 3BA, Telephone: 01222 233313
Call date: May 1996, Lincoln's Inn
Qualifications: [LLB (Hons) (Hull)]

DAVIES MISS DEBORAH SUSAN

24 The Ropewalk
Nottingham NG1 5EF,
Telephone: 0115 9472581
E-mail: clerk@ropewalk.co.uk
Call date: Oct 1993, Inner Temple
Qualifications: [LLB]

DAVIES MISS ELIZABETH JANE

1 Paper Bldgs
Ground Floor, Temple, London EC4Y 7EP,
Telephone: 0171 583 7355
E-mail: clerks@1pb.co.uk
Call date: Nov 1981, Middle Temple
Qualifications: [MA (Oxon)]

DAVIES MS ELIZABETH MARY

2 Garden Court
1st Floor, Middle Temple, London EC4Y 9BL,
Telephone: 0171 353 1633
E-mail: barristers@2gardenct.law.co.uk
Call date: Feb 1994, Inner Temple
Qualifications: [LLB (Hons)(Lond)]

DAVIES MISS EMILY JANE

Angel Chambers
94 Walter Road, Swansea SA1 5QA,
Telephone: 01792 6464623/6464648
Call date: Nov 1989, Gray's Inn
Qualifications: [LLB (Wales)]

DAVIES EVAN HUW

Essex Court Chambers
24 Lincoln's Inn Fields, London WC2A 3ED,
Telephone: 0171 813 8000
E-mail: clerksroom@essexcourt-chambers.co.uk
Call date: Nov 1985, Gray's Inn
Qualifications: [LLB (Cardiff)]

DAVIES MISS FELICITY ANNE

10 Park Square
Leeds LS1 2LH, Telephone: 0113 2455438
E-mail: chambers@bandit.legend.co.uk
Call date: July 1980, Middle Temple
Qualifications: [BA (York)]

DAVIES FRANCIS PETER

The Corn Exchange
5th Floor Fenwick Street, Liverpool L2 7QS,
Telephone: 0151 227 1081/5009
Call date: July 1986, Gray's Inn
Qualifications: [BA]

DAVIES GRAHAM BRUCE

2 Dr Johnson's Building
Temple, London EC4Y 7AY,
Telephone: 0171 353 4716
Call date: Nov 1986, Middle Temple
Qualifications: [MA, LLM Cantab]

DAVIES GRAHAM JOHN

2 Dr Johnson's Building
Temple, London EC4Y 7AY,
Telephone: 0171 353 4716
Call date: Nov 1971, Inner Temple
Qualifications: [LLM (Lond)]

DAVIES HAROLD RODNEY OLONINDIEH

Albany Chambers
91 Kentish Town Road, London NW1 8NY,
Telephone: 0171 485 5736/5758
E-mail: albanychambers@usanet
Call date: Nov 1978, Lincoln's Inn
Qualifications: [LLB (Hons), MA (Brunel)]

DAVIES MISS HELEN LOUISE

Brick Court Chambers
15/19 Devereux Court, London WC2R 3JJ,
Telephone: 0171 583 0777
E-mail: (surname)@brickcourt.demon.co.uk
Call date: Nov 1991, Inner Temple
Qualifications: [BA (Cambs)]

DAVIES HUGH CURRY

3 Raymond Buildings
Gray's Inn, London WC1R 5BH,
Telephone: 0171 831 3833
E-mail: chambers@threeraymond.demon.co.uk
Call date: Oct 1990, Lincoln's Inn
Qualifications: [BA (Oxon)]

DAVIES HUGH MICHAEL

Lincoln House Chambers
5th Floor Lincoln House, 1 Brazennose Street,
Manchester M2 5EL,
Telephone: 0161 832 5701
E-mail: LincolnHouseChambers@link.org
Call date: July 1982, Middle Temple
Qualifications: [MA (Oxon)]

DAVIES HUW

30 Park Place
Cardiff CF1 3BA, Telephone: 01222 398421
E-mail: 100757.1456@compuserve.com
Farrar's Building
Temple, London EC4Y 7BD,
Telephone: 0171 583 9241
E-mail: chambers@farrarsbuilding.co.uk
Door Tenant
Call date: Nov 1978, Gray's Inn
Assistant Recorder
Qualifications: [LLB (Wales), MPhil (Cantab)]

DAVIES HUW REES

Pendragon Chambers
124 Walter Road, Swansea SA1 5RG,
Telephone: 01792 411188
Call date: Nov 1982, Gray's Inn
Qualifications: [LLB (Wales)]

DAVIES IWAN RHUN

Iscoed Chambers
86 St Helen's Road, Swansea SA1 4BQ,
Telephone: 01792 652988/9/330
Call date: Feb 1995, Gray's Inn

Qualifications: [LLB (Wales & Cantab), LLM, PhD (Wales)]

DAVIES DR JANE ELIZABETH

East Anglian Chambers
57 London Street, Norwich NR2 1HL,
Telephone: 01603 617351
East Anglian Chambers
Sanders House 52 North Hill, Colchester
CO1 1PY, Telephone: 01206 572756
East Anglian Chambers
Gresham House 5 Museum Street, Ipswich
IP1 1HQ, Telephone: 01473 214481
Call date: July 1983, Middle Temple
Qualifications: [LLB, PhD(B'ham)]

DAVIES JOHN LLEWELLYN

24 Old Bldgs
Ground Floor, Lincoln's Inn, London
WC2A 3UJ, Telephone: 0171 404 0946
E-mail: clerks@24oldbuildings.law.co.uk
Call date: Nov 1977, Gray's Inn
Qualifications: [BA]

DAVIES JOHN MEIRION

32 Park Place
Cardiff CF1 3BA, Telephone: 01222 397364
Call date: July 1975, Gray's Inn
Qualifications: [LLB (Wales)]

DAVIES JOHN RICHARD

Littleton Chambers
3 King's Bench Walk North, Temple, London
EC4Y 7HR, Telephone: 0171 797 8600
E-mail: littletonchambers@compuserve.com
Call date: July 1981, Middle Temple
Qualifications: [MA (Cantab)]

DAVIES JOHN VERDIN

6 Pump Court
Ground Floor, Temple, London EC4Y 7AR,
Telephone: 0171 583 6013/2510
Call date: Feb 1955, Gray's Inn
Qualifications: [LLB (Manch), FCIA]

DAVIES JONATHAN NORVAL

Guildford Chambers
Stoke House Leapale Lane, Guildford, Surrey
GU1 4LY, Telephone: 01483 539131
E-mail: guildford.barristers@btinternet.com
Call date: July 1981, Inner Temple
Qualifications: [LLB (Lond)]

DAVIES JONATHAN TREFOR LLEWELYN

1 Middle Temple Lane
Temple, London EC4Y 1LT,
Telephone: 0171 583 0659 (12 Lines)
Call date: Nov 1971, Middle Temple
Recorder
Qualifications: [MA (Cantab)]

DAVIES MISS LINDSAY JANE

Fenners Chambers
3 Madingley Road, Cambridge CB3 OEE,
Telephone: 01223 368761
Fenners Chambers
8-12 Priestgate, Peterborough PE1 1JA,
Telephone: 01733 62030
Call date: July 1975, Gray's Inn
Assistant Recorder
Qualifications: [LLB (Wales)]

DAVIES MISS LOUISE GILLIAN

199 Strand
London WC2R 1DR,
Telephone: 0171 379 9779
E-mail: chambers@199strand.co.uk
Call date: Nov 1996, Lincoln's Inn
Qualifications: [BA (Hons)(E.Anglia)]

DAVIES MS MARIA CHRISTINE

Park Court Chambers
40 Park Cross Street, Leeds LS1 2QH,
Telephone: 0113 2433277
Call date: Nov 1988, Middle Temple
Qualifications: [LLB (Leeds)]

DAVIES MICHAEL IWAN

Martins Building
Water Street, Liverpool L2 3SP,
Telephone: 0151 236 5818/4919
Call date: July 1979, Middle Temple
Qualifications: [LLB (L'pool)]

DAVIES NICHOLAS JEREMY

1 Paper Bldgs
Ground Floor, Temple, London EC4Y 7EP,
Telephone: 0171 583 7355
E-mail: clerks@1pb.co.uk
Call date: July 1975, Inner Temple
Qualifications: [BA]

DAVIES MISS NICOLA VELFOR QC (1992)

3 Serjeants Inn
London EC4Y 1BQ,
Telephone: 0171 353 5537
E-mail: available upon request
Call date: July 1976, Gray's Inn
Assistant Recorder
Qualifications: [LLB]

DAVIES OWEN HANDEL

2 Garden Court
1st Floor, Middle Temple, London EC4Y 9BL,
Telephone: 0171 353 1633
E-mail: barristers@2gardenct.law.co.uk
Call date: July 1973, Inner Temple
Qualifications: [BA (Cantab)]

DAVIES MISS PENNY MAY

3 Pump Court
2nd Floor, Temple, London EC4Y 7AJ,
Telephone: 0171 353 1356 (3 Lines)
Call date: Oct 1995, Inner Temple
Qualifications: [LLB]

DAVIES PHILIP

9 Park Place
Cardiff CF1 3DP, Telephone: 01222 382731
Call date: Apr 1978, Middle Temple
Qualifications: [MA (Cantab)]

DAVIES MISS REBECCA LUCINDA

3 Temple Gardens
3rd Floor, Temple, London EC4Y 9AU,
Telephone: 0171 583 0010
Call date: Nov 1996, Lincoln's Inn
Qualifications: [LLB (Hons)(Lond)]

DAVIES RICHARD LLEWELLYN QC (1994)

39 Essex Street
London WC2R 3AT,
Telephone: 0171 583 1111
E-mail: clerks@39essex.co.uk
Call date: July 1973, Inner Temple
Qualifications: [LLB (L'pool)]

DAVIES ROBERT HOWARD

Guildhall Chambers
23 Broad Street, Bristol BS1 2HG,
Telephone: 0117 9273366
Call date: Oct 1990, Lincoln's Inn
Qualifications: [LLB (B'ham)]

DAVIES ROBERT LEIGHTON QC (1994)

Farrar's Building
Temple, London EC4Y 7BD,
Telephone: 0171 583 9241
E-mail: chambers@farrarsbuilding.co.uk
9 Park Place
Cardiff CF1 3DP, Telephone: 01222 382731
Door Tenant
Call date: Feb 1975, Gray's Inn
Recorder
Qualifications: [BA, BCL (Oxon)]

DAVIES RUSSELL DEWI THOMAS

Deans Court Chambers
Cumberland House Crown Square, Manchester
M3 3HA, Telephone: 0161 834 4097
E-mail: deanscourt@compuserve.com
Deans Court Chambers
41-43 Market Place, Preston PR1 1AH,
Telephone: 01772 555163
E-mail: deanscourt@compuserve.com
Call date: Nov 1983, Middle Temple
Qualifications: [LLB (L'pool)]

DAVIES MISS SARAH JEANETTE

2 King's Bench Walk
1st Floor, Temple, London EC4Y 7DE,
Telephone: 0171 353 9276
Call date: Feb 1984, Gray's Inn
Qualifications: [BA Hons (Kent)]

D

DAVIES MISS SARAH-JANE

4-5 Gray's Inn Square
Ground Floor, Gray's Inn, London WC1R 5AY,
Telephone: 0171 404 5252
E-mail: chambers@4-5graysinnsquare.co.uk
Call date: Oct 1996, Inner Temple
Qualifications: [BA (Cantab)]

DAVIES MISS SHEILAGH ELIZABETH

10 King's Bench Walk
1st Floor, Temple, London EC4Y 7EB,
Telephone: 0171 353 2501
Call date: Nov 1974, Middle Temple
Qualifications: [LLB (Lond)]

DAVIES STEPHEN REES

Guildhall Chambers
23 Broad Street, Bristol BS1 2HG,
Telephone: 0117 9273366
Call date: July 1983, Gray's Inn
Qualifications: [LLB (Lond) LLB, (Cantab)]

DAVIES STEPHEN RICHARD

8 King Street
Manchester M2 6AQ,
Telephone: 0161 834 9560
Call date: July 1985, Middle Temple
Qualifications: [MA (Cantab)]

DAVIES MISS SUSAN LOUISE

12 New Square
Ground Floor, Lincoln's Inn, London
WC2A 3SW, Telephone: 0171 419 1212
E-mail: 12newsquare@compuserve.com
Call date: Oct 1995, Inner Temple
Qualifications: [BA, BCL (Oxon)]

DAVIES TREFOR

Iscoed Chambers
86 St Helen's Road, Swansea SA1 4BQ,
Telephone: 01792 652988/9/330
Call date: July 1972, Inner Temple

DAVIES TREVOR GLYN

9 Gough Square
London EC4A 3DE, Telephone: 0171 353 5371
Call date: July 1978, Gray's Inn
Qualifications: [BA (Nott'm)]

DAVIES WILLIAM RHODRI

1 Essex Court
Ground Floor, Temple, London EC4Y 9AR,
Telephone: 0171 583 2000
E-mail: clerks@oneessexcourt.co.uk
Call date: July 1979, Middle Temple
Qualifications: [BA (Cantab)]

DAVIES-JONES JONATHAN

3 Verulam Buildings
London WC1R 5NT,
Telephone: 0171 831 8441
E-mail: clerks@3verulam.co.uk
Call date: Nov 1994, Middle Temple
Qualifications: [MA]

DAVIS ADAM DAVID

1 Crown Office Row
2nd Floor, Temple, London EC4Y 7HH,
Telephone: 0171 797 7111
Call date: Nov 1985, Inner Temple
Qualifications: [LLB (Lond)]

DAVIS ADRIAN MARTIN

2 Field Court
Gray's Inn, London WC1R 5BB,
Telephone: 0171 405 6114
E-mail: fieldct2@netcomuk.co.uk.
Call date: Oct 1996, Gray's Inn
Qualifications: [B.Sc (Dunelm), LLB (Notts)]

DAVIS ANDREW PAUL

2 Crown Office Row
Ground Floor, Temple, London EC4Y 7HJ,
Telephone: 0171 797 8100
E-mail: mail@2cor.co.uk, or to individual
barristers at: [barrister's surname]@2cor.co.uk
Call date: Oct 1996, Gray's Inn
Qualifications: [LLB (Hons)]

DAVIS ANTHONY JOHN

67a Westgate Road
Newcastle Upon Tyne NE1 1SQ,
Telephone: 0191 261 4407/2329785
Call date: Nov 1986, Gray's Inn
Qualifications: [BA (Hons)]

DAVIS BRENDAN JOHN

4 King's Bench Walk
2nd Floor, Temple, London EC4Y 7DL,
Telephone: 0171 353 3581
Call date: Oct 1994, Gray's Inn
Qualifications: [MA (Oxon)]

DAVIS MISS CAROL JANE

Littleton Chambers
3 King's Bench Walk North, Temple, London
EC4Y 7HR, Telephone: 0171 797 8600
E-mail: littletonchambers@compuserve.com
Call date: Oct 1996, Middle Temple
Qualifications: [BA (Hons)(Sussex), CPE]

DAVIS GLEN MILTON

3/4 South Square
Gray's Inn, London WC1R 5HP,
Telephone: 0171 696 9900
E-mail: clerks@southsquare.com
Call date: Oct 1992, Middle Temple
Qualifications: [MA (Hons)(Oxon), Dip Law
(City), MA]

DAVIS GREVILLE LEIGH BLAKEMAN

4 King's Bench Walk
Ground/First Floor, Temple, London
EC4Y 7DL, Telephone: 0171 822 8822
E-mail: 4kbw@barristersatlaw.com
Call date: July 1976, Lincoln's Inn
Qualifications: [LLB (Lond)]

DAVIS JOHN ANTHONY

Trinity Chambers
140 New London Road, Chelmsford, Essex
CM2 0AW, Telephone: 01245 605040
Call date: July 1983, Gray's Inn
Qualifications: [LLB (Hull)]

DAVIS JONATHAN MURRAY

6 Fountain Court
Steelhouse Lane, Birmingham B4 6DR,
Telephone: 0121 233 3282
Call date: July 1983, Middle Temple
Qualifications: [MA (Oxon)]

DAVIS MISS LUCINDA JANE

Chichester Chambers
12 North Pallant, Chichester, West Sussex
PO19 1TQ, Telephone: 01243 784538
Call date: Nov 1981, Gray's Inn
Qualifications: [LLB (Lond)]

DAVIS LYNDELL GEORGE MONTAGUE

Chancery Chambers
1st Floor Offices 70/72 Chancery Lane,
London WC2A 1AB,
Telephone: 0171 405 6879/6870
Call date: Nov 1963, Lincoln's Inn

DAVIS NIGEL ANTHONY LAMERT QC (1992)

7 Stone Bldgs
Ground Floor, Lincoln's Inn, London
WC2A 3SZ, Telephone: 0171 405 3886/
242 3546
E-mail: chaldous@vossnet.co.uk
Call date: July 1975, Lincoln's Inn
Assistant Recorder
Qualifications: [MA (Oxon)]

DAVIS PAUL JOHN

15 Winckley Square
Preston PR1 3JJ, Telephone: 01772 252828
E-mail: clerks@winckleysq.demon.co.uk
Call date: Nov 1996, Inner Temple
Qualifications: [BA (Trent)]

DAVIS RICHARD SIMON

23 Essex Street
London WC2R 3AS,
Telephone: 0171 413 0353/353 3533
E-mail: clerks@essexstreet23.demon.co.uk
Call date: Nov 1978, Inner Temple
Assistant Recorder
Qualifications: [LLB (Leics)]

DAVIS SIMON JOHN

6 Fountain Court
Steelhouse Lane, Birmingham B4 6DR,
Telephone: 0121 233 3282
Call date: Oct 1990, Middle Temple
Qualifications: [BA (Cantab), Dip Law]

D

DAVIS WILLIAM EASTHOPE

7 Fountain Court
Steelhouse Lane, Birmingham B4 6DR,
Telephone: 0121 236 8531
Call date: July 1975, Inner Temple
Recorder
Qualifications: [LLB]

DAVIS-WHITE MALCOLM

4 Stone Bldgs
Ground Floor, Lincoln's Inn, London
WC2A 3XT, Telephone: 0171 242 5524
E-mail: d.goddard@4stonebuildings.law.co.uk
Call date: July 1984, Middle Temple
Qualifications: [MA, BCL (Oxon)]

DAVISON RICHARD HAROLD

Thomas More Chambers
52 Carey Street, Lincoln's Inn, London
WC2A 2JB, Telephone: 0171 404 7000
Call date: July 1982, Gray's Inn
Qualifications: [BA (Oxon)]

DAVITT MISS PAULA AINE

24a St John Street
Manchester M3 4DF,
Telephone: 0161 833 9628
Call date: Nov 1988, Gray's Inn
Qualifications: [LLB Hons]

DAW CHRISTOPHER

Parsonage Chambers
5th Floor 3 The Parsonage, Manchester
M3 2HW, Telephone: 0161 833 1996
Call date: Nov 1993, Gray's Inn
Qualifications: [LLB (Manch)]

DAWAR MISS ARCHNA

Assize Court Chambers
14 Small Street, Bristol BS1 1DE,
Telephone: 0117 9264587
Call date: Oct 1996, Lincoln's Inn
Qualifications: [LLB (Hons)(L'pool)]

DAWES GORDON STEPHEN KNIGHT

Goldsmith Building
1st Floor, Temple, London EC4Y 7BL,
Telephone: 0171 353 7881
E-mail: clerks@goldsmith-building.law.co.uk
Call date: July 1989, Middle Temple
Qualifications: [MA [Oxon], Dip Law]

DAWES JAMES CHRISTOPHER

2 Harcourt Bldgs
1st Floor, Temple, London EC4Y 9DB,
Telephone: 0171 353 2112/2817
Door Tenant
Call date: Nov 1993, Inner Temple
Qualifications: [BA (Dunelm), CPE]

DAWES SIMON ROBERT

Derby Square Chambers
Merchants Court, Derby Square, Liverpool
L2 1TS, Telephone: 0151 709 4222
Call date: Oct 1990, Inner Temple
Qualifications: [LLB (Hons L'pool)]

DAWSON ALEXANDER WILLIAM

13 King's Bench Walk
1st Floor, Temple, London EC4Y 7EN,
Telephone: 0171 353 7204
E-mail: clerks@13kbw.law.co.uk
King's Bench Chambers
32 Beaumont Street, Oxford OX1 2NP,
Telephone: 01865 311066
E-mail: clerks@kbc-oxford.law.co.uk
Call date: July 1969, Middle Temple
Recorder
Qualifications: [MA (Oxon)]

DAWSON IAN JEFFERIES

67a Westgate Road
Newcastle Upon Tyne NE1 1SQ,
Telephone: 0191 261 4407/2329785
Call date: July 1971, Lincoln's Inn
Qualifications: [LLB]

DAWSON JAMES

1 Hare Court
Ground Floor, Temple, London EC4Y 7BE,
Telephone: 0171 353 3982/5324
Call date: Nov 1984, Middle Temple
Qualifications: [BA (Hons)]

DAWSON JAMES ROBERT

Oriel Chambers
14 Water Street, Liverpool L2 8TD,
Telephone: 0151 236 7191
E-mail: oriel_chambers@link.org
Call date: Nov 1994, Inner Temple
Qualifications: [LLB (Soton)]

DAWSON MISS JUDY ELIZABETH

Assize Court Chambers
14 Small Street, Bristol BS1 1DE,
Telephone: 0117 9264587
Call date: Oct 1993, Gray's Inn
Qualifications: [BA]

DAY MISS ANNELIESE MARY

2 Crown Office Row
2nd Floor, Temple, London EC4Y 7HJ,
Telephone: 0171 797 8000
Call date: Oct 1996, Inner Temple
Qualifications: [BA (Cantab)]

DAY DORIAN STEPHEN

Goldsmith Chambers
Ground Floor Goldsmith Building, Temple,
London EC4Y 7BL,
Telephone: 0171 353 6802/3/4/5
E-mail: celiamonksfield@btinternet.com
Call date: July 1987, Middle Temple
Qualifications: [BA (Hons)]

DAY DOUGLAS HENRY QC (1989)

Farrar's Building
Temple, London EC4Y 7BD,
Telephone: 0171 583 9241
E-mail: chambers@farrarsbuilding.co.uk
Call date: July 1967, Lincoln's Inn
Recorder
Qualifications: [MA (Cantab)]

DE BERTODANO MISS SYLVIA PHILIPPA THERESA

3 Gray's Inn Square
Ground Floor, London WC1R 5AH,
Telephone: 0171 520 5600
E-mail: gis3@btinternet.com
Call date: Nov 1993, Middle Temple
Qualifications: [BA (Hons)(Oxon)]

DE BONO JOHN HUGH

Derby Square Chambers
Merchants Court, Derby Square, Liverpool
L2 1TS, Telephone: 0151 709 4222
Call date: Oct 1995, Gray's Inn
Qualifications: [BA (Hons) (Oxon)]

DE BURGOS JAMIE MICHAEL ABULAFIA

36 Bedford Row
London WC1R 4JH,
Telephone: 0171 421 8000
E-mail: 36bedfordrow@link.org
Call date: July 1973, Inner Temple
Qualifications: [MA (Cantab)]

DE COSTA LEONEL LUIS

Furnival Chambers
32 Furnival Street, London EC4A 1JQ,
Telephone: 0171 405 3232
E-mail: clerks@furnivallaw.co.uk
Call date: Feb 1992, Gray's Inn
Qualifications: [BA (Hons)]

DE FREITAS ANTHONY PETER STANLEY

4 Paper Bldgs
Ground Floor, Temple, London EC4Y 7EX,
Telephone: 0171 353 3366/583 7155
E-mail: clerks@4paperbuildings.com
Call date: July 1971, Inner Temple
Assistant Recorder
Qualifications: [MA (Oxon)]

DE GARR ROBINSON ANTHONY JOHN

1 Essex Court
Ground Floor, Temple, London EC4Y 9AR,
Telephone: 0171 583 2000
E-mail: clerks@oneessexcourt.co.uk
Call date: July 1987, Lincoln's Inn
Qualifications: [BA (Oxon)]

DE HAAN KEVIN CHARLES

3 Raymond Buildings
Gray's Inn, London WC1R 5BH,
Telephone: 0171 831 3833
E-mail: chambers@threeraymond.demon.co.uk
Call date: July 1976, Inner Temple
Qualifications: [LLB (Lond), LLM (Bru)]

D

DE HAAS MISS MARGARET RUTH

The Corn Exchange
5th Floor Fenwick Street, Liverpool L2 7QS,
Telephone: 0151 227 1081/5009
12 King's Bench Walk
Temple, London EC4Y 7EL,
Telephone: 0171 583 0811
E-mail: chambers@12kbw.co.uk
Call date: July 1977, Middle Temple
Assistant Recorder
Qualifications: [LLB]

DE HAVAS CHRISTOPHER FREDERIC ERIC

Westgate Chambers
144 High Street, Lewes, East Sussex BN7 1XT,
Telephone: 01273 480510
Call date: Feb 1984, Gray's Inn
Qualifications: [BA (Kent)]

DE JEHAN DAVID

St Paul's House
5th Floor 23 Park Square South, Leeds
LS1 2ND, Telephone: 0113 2455866
Call date: Feb 1988, Inner Temple
Qualifications: [LLB (Hons), LLM (Bristol)]

DE KAUWE LALITH CHRISTOPHER

2 Garden Court
1st Floor, Middle Temple, London EC4Y 9BL,
Telephone: 0171 353 1633
E-mail: barristers@2gardenct.law.co.uk
Call date: Nov 1978, Gray's Inn
Qualifications: [BA (Hons)]

DE LA MARE THOMAS ORLANDO

2 Hare Court
Ground Floor, Temple, London EC4Y 7BH,
Telephone: 0171 583 1770
E-mail: 2_Hare_Court@link.org
Call date: Oct 1995, Middle Temple
Qualifications: [BA (Hons), LLM]

DE LA ROSA ANDREW JAMES

10 Old Square
Ground Floor, Lincoln's Inn, London
WC2A 3SU, Telephone: 0171 405 0758
Call date: July 1981, Inner Temple
Qualifications: [BA, Dip LL, JD]

DE LACY RICHARD MICHAEL

3 Verulam Buildings
London WC1R 5NT,
Telephone: 0171 831 8441
E-mail: clerks@3verulam.co.uk
Call date: July 1976, Middle Temple
Qualifications: [MA (Cantab), FCIArb]

DE LOTBINIERE HENRY JOLY

2 Temple Gardens
Temple, London EC4Y 9AY,
Telephone: 0171 583 6041 (12 Lines)
Call date: July 1968, Inner Temple
Qualifications: [MA (Cantab)]

DE LURY TERENCE WILLIAM

Pepys' Chambers
17 Fleet Street, London EC4Y 1AA,
Telephone: 0171 936 2710
Call date: July 1985, Gray's Inn
Qualifications: [F.I.Plant.E, F.C.I.Arb,
F.M.E.W.I., Forensic Eng.]

DE MELLO REMBERT JOSEPH JULIUS

6 King's Bench Walk
Ground, Third & Fourth Floors, Temple,
London EC4Y 7DR,
Telephone: 0171 353 4931/583 0695
New Court Chambers
Suite 200 Gazette Building, 168 Corporation
Street, Birmingham B4 6TZ,
Telephone: 0121 693 6656
Door Tenant
Call date: Feb 1983, Lincoln's Inn
Qualifications: [BA, MA (Madras), LLM, LLB
(Lond)]

DE MOUNTENEY JONATHAN PATRICK

East Anglian Chambers
Sanders House 52 North Hill, Colchester
CO1 1PY, Telephone: 01206 572756
East Anglian Chambers
Gresham House 5 Museum Street, Ipswich
IP1 1HQ, Telephone: 01473 214481
East Anglian Chambers
57 London Street, Norwich NR2 1HL,
Telephone: 01603 617351
Call date: Nov 1994, Gray's Inn
Qualifications: [BA (Bath)]

DE NAVARRO MICHAEL ANTONY QC (1990)

2 Temple Gardens
Temple, London EC4Y 9AY,
Telephone: 0171 583 6041 (12 Lines)
Call date: July 1968, Inner Temple
Recorder
Qualifications: [BA (Cantab)]

DE ROHAN JONATHAN STEWART

3 Paper Bldgs
2nd Floor, Temple, London EC4Y 7EU,
Telephone: 0171 353 6208
Call date: July 1989, Middle Temple
Qualifications: [BA (Read), Dip Law]

DE SILVA GEORGE DESMOND LORENZ QC (1984)

2 Paper Bldgs
1st Floor, Temple, London EC4Y 7ET,
Telephone: 0171 936 2611 (10 Lines)
E-mail: clerks@2pbbarristers.co.uk
Call date: June 1964, Middle Temple

DE SILVA HARENDRA ANEURIN DOMINGO QC (1995)

2 Paper Bldgs
1st Floor, Temple, London EC4Y 7ET,
Telephone: 0171 936 2611 (10 Lines)
E-mail: clerks@2pbbarristers.co.uk
Call date: July 1970, Middle Temple
Recorder
Qualifications: [MA, LLM (Cantab)]

DE SOUSA TURNER MISS CAMILLA ANNA MARIA

2 Harcourt Bldgs
1st Floor, Temple, London EC4Y 9DB,
Telephone: 0171 353 6961/7
Harcourt Chambers
Churchill House 3 St Aldate's Courtyard, St
Aldate's, Oxford OX1 1BN,
Telephone: 01865 791559
Call date: Nov 1989, Middle Temple
Qualifications: [BA (Cantab)]

DE VOGHELAERE PARR ADAM STEPHEN

2 Mitre Ct Bldgs
2nd Floor, Temple, London EC4Y 7BX,
Telephone: 0171 583 1380
Call date: Oct 1995, Gray's Inn
Qualifications: [MA]

DE VRIES EDO BAREND PHILIP

Guildhall Chambers Porstmouth
Prudential Buildings 16 Guildhall Walk,
Portsmouth, Hampshire PO1 2DE,
Telephone: 01705 752400
1 Appleton Road
Catisfield, Fareham, Hampshire PO15 5QH,
Telephone: 01329 847711
Call date: July 1969, Inner Temple
Qualifications: [LLM (Utrecht)]

DE WAAL JOHN HENRY LOWNDES

4 Fountain Court
Steelhouse Lane, Birmingham B4 6DR,
Telephone: 0121 236 3476
Call date: Oct 1992, Middle Temple
Qualifications: [MA (Cantab)]

DE WILDE (ALAN) ROBIN QC (1993)

199 Strand
London WC2R 1DR,
Telephone: 0171 379 9779
E-mail: chambers@199strand.co.uk
Call date: Nov 1971, Inner Temple
Assistant Recorder

DE ZONIE MISS JANE

14 Gray's Inn Square
Gray's Inn, London WC1R 5JP,
Telephone: 0171 242 0858
E-mail: 100712.2134@compuserve.com
Call date: Nov 1993, Middle Temple
Qualifications: [BA (Hons)(Lond), Dip in Law
(Westmin)]

DEACOCK ADAM JASON

Chambers of Lord Goodhart QC
Ground Floor 3 New Square, Lincoln's Inn,
London WC2A 3RS,
Telephone: 0171 405 5577
E-mail: law@threenewsquare.demon.co.uk
Call date: Nov 1991, Middle Temple
Qualifications: [BA (Oxon), Dip Law]

DEACON MS EMMA REBECCA

5 Paper Bldgs
1st Floor, Temple, London EC4Y 7HB,
Telephone: 0171 583 6117
E-mail: clerks@5-paperbuildings.law.co.uk
Call date: Nov 1993, Inner Temple
Qualifications: [LLB (Lond)]

DEACON ROBERT MURRAY

11 Stone Bldgs
Ground Floor, Lincoln's Inn, London
WC2A 3TG, Telephone: 0171 831 6381
E-mail: clerks@11StoneBuildings.law.co.uk
Chichester Chambers
12 North Pallant, Chichester, West Sussex
PO19 1TQ, Telephone: 01243 784538
Door Tenant
Call date: July 1976, Gray's Inn
Qualifications: [LL.B (Manchester)]

DEAL TIMOTHY JOHN

Chambers of Timothy Deal
First Floor 5 Eastbrook Road, Blackheath,
London SE3 8BP, Telephone: 0181 856 8738
Call date: July 1988, Gray's Inn
Qualifications: [LLB (Warwick)]

DEAN MISS ABIGAIL ELIZABETH

2 King's Bench Walk
1st Floor, Temple, London EC4Y 7DE,
Telephone: 0171 353 9276
Call date: Oct 1995, Gray's Inn
Qualifications: [BA]

DEAN BRIAN JOHN ANTHONY

7 Fountain Court
Steelhouse Lane, Birmingham B4 6DR,
Telephone: 0121 236 8531
Call date: Nov 1994, Gray's Inn
Qualifications: [LLB (Manch)]

DEAN JACOB

5 Raymond Buildings
1st Floor, Gray's Inn, London WC1R 5BP,
Telephone: 0171 242 2902
Call date: Oct 1995, Inner Temple
Qualifications: [BA (Oxon), CPE (City)]

DEAN JAMES PATRICK

1 Dr Johnson's Bldgs
Ground Floor, Temple, London EC4Y 7AX,
Telephone: 0171 353 9328
Dr Johnson's Chambers
The Atrium Court Apex Plaza, Reading
RG1 1AX, Telephone: 01734 254221
Call date: Nov 1977, Lincoln's Inn

DEAN NICHOLAS

9 Bedford Row
London WC1R 4AZ,
Telephone: 0171 242 3555
E-mail: clerks@9br.co.uk
Call date: Nov 1982, Lincoln's Inn
Qualifications: [LLB (Leeds)]

DEAN PAUL BENJAMIN

5 Bell Yard
London WC2A 2JR, Telephone: 0171 333 8811
Call date: July 1982, Inner Temple
Qualifications: [BA (Oxon)Dip Law]

DEAN PETER THOMAS

1 Crown Office Row
3rd Floor, Temple, London EC4Y 7HH,
Telephone: 0171 583 9292
E-mail: onecor@link.org
Call date: Nov 1987, Middle Temple
Qualifications: [BA (Oxon), Dip Law, (City)]

DEAN MS ROSA MARY

36 Bedford Row
London WC1R 4JH,
Telephone: 0171 421 8000
E-mail: 36bedfordrow@link.org
Call date: Oct 1993, Gray's Inn
Qualifications: [BA (Oxon)]

DEANE VINCENT

Victoria Chambers
19 Castle Street, Liverpool L2 4SX,
Telephone: 0151 236 9402
E-mail: Fa45@rapid.co.uk
Call date: July 1976, Lincoln's Inn
Qualifications: [LLB]

DEAVE JOHN JAMES

1 High Pavement
Nottingham NG1 1HF,
Telephone: 0115 9418218
Call date: July 1952, Gray's Inn
Qualifications: [MA (Oxon)]

DECAMP MISS JANE LOUISE

2 Crown Office Row
Ground Floor, Temple, London EC4Y 7HJ,
Telephone: 0171 797 8100
E-mail: mail@2cor.co.uk, or to individual
barristers at: [barrister's surname]@2cor.co.uk
Call date: Nov 1987, Gray's Inn
Qualifications: [BA (Oxon)]

DEDEZADE MISS SIBEL

Bracton Chambers
95a Chancery Lane, London WC2A 1DT,
Telephone: 0171 242 4248
Call date: Oct 1994, Gray's Inn
Qualifications: [LLB]

DEDEZADE TANER

Tindal Chambers
3/5 New Street, Chelmsford, Essex CM1 1NT,
Telephone: 01245 267742
Call date: Nov 1996, Gray's Inn
Qualifications: [LLB (Lond)]

DEDMAN PETER GEORGE

12 King's Bench Walk
Temple, London EC4Y 7EL,
Telephone: 0171 583 0811
E-mail: chambers@12kbw.co.uk
Call date: July 1968, Gray's Inn
Recorder

DEE JONATHON ANTHONY

King Charles House
Standard Hill, Nottingham NG1 6FX,
Telephone: 0115 9418851
E-mail: clerks@kch.co.uk
Call date: Nov 1989, Inner Temple
Qualifications: [LLB (Bris)]

DEEGAN LAWRENCE JEFFREY

22 Albion Place
Northampton NN1 1UD,
Telephone: 01604 36271
Call date: July 1989, Inner Temple
Qualifications: [LLB]

DEELEY MRS PATRICIA ANN

Priory Chambers
2 Fountain Court, Steelhouse Lane,
Birmingham B4 6DR,
Telephone: 0121 236 3882/1375
Call date: July 1970, Lincoln's Inn
Recorder
Qualifications: [LLB]

DEGEL MISS REBECCA EMMELINE HYDE

East Anglian Chambers
Sanders House 52 North Hill, Colchester
CO1 1PY, Telephone: 01206 572756
East Anglian Chambers
57 London Street, Norwich NR2 1HL,
Telephone: 01603 617351
East Anglian Chambers
Gresham House 5 Museum Street, Ipswich
IP1 1HQ, Telephone: 01473 214481
Call date: Nov 1987, Middle Temple
Qualifications: [LLB Hons]

DEHN CONRAD FRANCIS QC (1968)

Fountain Court
Temple, London EC4Y 9DH,
Telephone: 0171 583 3335
E-mail: chambers@fountaincourt.co.uk
Call date: July 1952, Gray's Inn
Recorder
Qualifications: [MA (Oxon)]

DEIGHTON RICHARD ANDREW GRAHAM

2 Field Court
Gray's Inn, London WC1R 5BB,
Telephone: 0171 405 6114
E-mail: fieldct2@netcomuk.co.uk.
Call date: July 1990, Middle Temple

DEIGNAN DR MARY TERESA

2 Dr Johnson's Building
Temple, London EC4Y 7AY,
Telephone: 0171 353 4716
Call date: Oct 1991, Middle Temple
Qualifications: [BSc (Aston), PhD (Belfast)]

DEIN JEREMY SYDNEY

3 Gray's Inn Square
Ground Floor, London WC1R 5AH,
Telephone: 0171 520 5600
E-mail: gis3@btinternet.com
Call date: Nov 1982, Middle Temple
Qualifications: [LLB (Lond)]

DEL FABBRO OSCAR

1 Crown Office Row
2nd Floor, Temple, London EC4Y 7HH,
Telephone: 0171 797 7111
Call date: July 1982, Gray's Inn
Qualifications: [B Com(Witwatersrand)]

DELAHUNTY MISS JOHANNE ERICA

14 Tooks Court
Cursitor St, London EC4A 1LB,
Telephone: 0171 405 8828
E-mail: clerks @tooks.law.co.uk
Call date: Nov 1986, Middle Temple
Qualifications: [BA, MA (Oxon)]

DELAMERE MISS ISABEL SARAH

9 King's Bench Walk
Ground Floor, Temple, London EC4Y 7DX,
Telephone: 0171 353 7202/3909
Call date: Nov 1985, Middle Temple
Qualifications: [BA(Hull)]

DELANEY KENNETH JOSEPH

Derby Square Chambers
Merchants Court, Derby Square, Liverpool
L2 1TS, Telephone: 0151 709 4222
Call date: Oct 1996, Inner Temple
Qualifications: [LLB, M.Phil (Cantab)]

DELANEY MS MARY EILEEN

1 Pump Court
Lower Ground Floor, Temple, London
EC4Y 7AB, Telephone: 0171 583 2012/
353 4341
E-mail: (name) @1pumpcourt.co.uk
Call date: July 1984, Gray's Inn
Qualifications: [LLB]

DELANEY ROYSTON HARLOW

38 Young Street
Manchester M3 3FT,
Telephone: 0161 833 0489
E-mail: clerks@young-st-chambers.com
Call date: Nov 1996, Lincoln's Inn
Qualifications: [MA (Hons)]

DEMETRIOU MS MARIE-ELENI

4-5 Gray's Inn Square
Ground Floor, Gray's Inn, London WC1R 5AY,
Telephone: 0171 404 5252
E-mail: chambers@4-5graysinnsquare.co.uk
Call date: Nov 1995, Middle Temple
Qualifications: [BA (Hons), BCL]

DEMPSTER MISS JENNIFER MARGARET PERT

2 Paper Bldgs
Temple, London EC4Y 7ET,
Telephone: 0171 936 2613
Call date: May 1993, Lincoln's Inn
Qualifications: [LLB (Hons)]

DENBIN JACK ARNOLD

Greenway
Sonning Lane, Sonning-on-Thames, Berkshire
RG4 6ST, Telephone: 0118 969 2484
Call date: July 1973, Inner Temple
Qualifications: [BSc (Reading), C Biol, MI Biol,
FCIArb]

DENCER MARK RICHARD

Francis Taylor Bldg
2nd Floor, Temple, London EC4Y 7BY,
Telephone: 0171 353 9942/3157
Call date: Apr 1978, Lincoln's Inn
Qualifications: [LLB (Lond)]

DENEHAN EDWARD

3 Paper Bldgs
Ground Floor, Temple, London EC4Y 7EU,
Telephone: 0171 797 7000
E-mail: clerks@3pb.co.uk
Call date: July 1981, Lincoln's Inn
Qualifications: [LLB (Warw)]

DENISON SIMON NEIL

6 King's Bench Walk
Ground Floor, Temple, London EC4Y 7DR,
Telephone: 0171 583 0410
Call date: Nov 1984, Lincoln's Inn
Qualifications: [MA (Cantab)]

DENMAN ROBERT ELLISON

5 Paper Bldgs
Ground Floor, Temple, London EC4Y 7HB,
Telephone: 0171 583 9275/583 4555
E-mail: 5paper@link.org
Call date: July 1970, Gray's Inn
Qualifications: [MA (Cantab)]

DENNETT MISS ANGELINA BRUNHILDE

24a St John Street
Manchester M3 4DF,
Telephone: 0161 833 9628
Call date: Nov 1980, Middle Temple
Qualifications: [BA (Hons), LLM (Lond)]

DENNEY STUART HENRY MACDONALD

Deans Court Chambers
Cumberland House Crown Square, Manchester
M3 3HA, Telephone: 0161 834 4097
E-mail: deanscourt@compuserve.com
Deans Court Chambers
41-43 Market Place, Preston PR1 1AH,
Telephone: 01772 555163
E-mail: deanscourt@compuserve.com
Call date: July 1982, Inner Temple
Qualifications: [MA (Cantab)]

DENNIS DAVID EDWARD

Adrian Lyon's Chambers
14 Castle Street, Liverpool L2 0NE,
Telephone: 0151 236 4421/8240
E-mail: chambers14@aol.com
5 Stone Buildings
Lincoln's Inn, London WC2A 3XT,
Telephone: 0171 242 6201
E-mail: clerks@5-stonebuildings.law.co.uk
Door Tenant
Call date: July 1979, Inner Temple
Qualifications: [LLB (Hull)]

DENNIS MARK JONATHAN

6 King's Bench Walk
Ground Floor, Temple, London EC4Y 7DR,
Telephone: 0171 583 0410
Call date: July 1977, Middle Temple
Assistant Recorder
Qualifications: [MA (Cantab)]

DENNIS MISS REBECCA LOUISE

All Saints Chambers
9/11 Broad Street, Bristol BS1 2HP,
Telephone: 0117 921 1966
Call date: July 1994, Gray's Inn
Qualifications: [LLB, LLM (Bris)]

DENNISON JAMES ANGUS

2 Paper Bldgs
Temple, London EC4Y 7ET,
Telephone: 0171 936 2613
Call date: July 1986, Inner Temple
Qualifications: [BA (Dunelm)]

DENNISON STEPHEN RANDELL

1 Atkin Building
Gray's Inn, London WC1R 5AT,
Telephone: 0171 404 0102
E-mail: clerks@atkin-chambers.co.uk
Call date: Nov 1985, Middle Temple
Qualifications: [LLB (Manch)]

DENNISS JOHN ANNEAR

4 King's Bench Walk
2nd Floor, Temple, London EC4Y 7DL,
Telephone: 0171 353 3581
Call date: July 1974, Inner Temple
Qualifications: [LLB (Hons)]

DENNY ROBIN HENRY ALISDAIR

Fountain Chambers
Cleveland Business Centre 1 Watson Street,
Middlesbrough TS1 2RQ,
Telephone: 01642 217037
Call date: May 1969, Inner Temple
Qualifications: [BA (Oxon)]

DENNYS NICHOLAS CHARLES JONATHAN QC (1991)

1 Atkin Building
Gray's Inn, London WC1R 5AT,
Telephone: 0171 404 0102
E-mail: clerks@atkin-chambers.co.uk
Call date: Nov 1975, Middle Temple
Assistant Recorder
Qualifications: [BA (Oxon)]

DENT ADRIAN RONALD

Chancery House Chambers
7 Lisbon Square, Leeds LS1 4LY,
Telephone: 0113 244 6691
E-mail: Chanceryhouse@btinternet.com
Call date: July 1974, Lincoln's Inn
Qualifications: [LLB]

DENT KEVIN JOSEPH

2 Paper Bldgs
Temple, London EC4Y 7ET,
Telephone: 0171 936 2613
Call date: Nov 1991, Inner Temple
Qualifications: [BA (Hons)(Sussex)]

DENT MS SALLY CLAIRE LEIGH

10 King's Bench Walk
Ground Floor, Temple, London EC4Y 7EB,
Telephone: 0171 353 7742
E-mail: 10kbw@lineone.net
Call date: July 1989, Lincoln's Inn
Qualifications: [BA (Reading), Dip Law]

DENT STEPHEN ROBERT CHARLES

Guildhall Chambers
23 Broad Street, Bristol BS1 2HG,
Telephone: 0117 9273366
Call date: Feb 1991, Gray's Inn
Qualifications: [LLB (Manch)]

DENTON MISS AMANDA

19 Figtree Lane
Sheffield S1 2DJ, Telephone: 0114 2759708/
2738380
Call date: Nov 1993, Lincoln's Inn
Qualifications: [LLB (Hons)]

DENTON MISS MICHELLE JAYNE

9-12 Bell Yard
London WC2A 2LF,
Telephone: 0171 400 1800
Call date: Oct 1996, Inner Temple
Qualifications: [LLB (So'ton)]

DENYER RODERICK LAWRENCE QC (1990)

St John's Chambers
Small Street, Bristol BS1 1DW,
Telephone: 0117 9213456/298514
E-mail: clerks@stjohns.uk.com
Call date: July 1970, Inner Temple
Recorder
Qualifications: [LLM]

DENYER-GREEN BARRY PETER DOUGLAS

Falcon Chambers
Falcon Court, London EC4Y 1AA,
Telephone: 0171 353 2484/7
Call date: Nov 1972, Middle Temple
Qualifications: [LLM, PhD, FRICS]

DERBYSHIRE THOMAS WILLIAM

3 Hare Court
1st Floor, Temple, London EC4Y 7BJ,
Telephone: 0171 353 7561
Call date: Nov 1989, Inner Temple
Qualifications: [LLB]

DESCHAMPSNEUFS MISS ALICE NORA

9 King's Bench Walk
Ground Floor, Temple, London EC4Y 7DX,
Telephone: 0171 353 7202/3909
Call date: July 1976, Inner Temple
Qualifications: [BA (Lond)]

DESMOND DENIS JOHN

6 Fountain Court
Steelhouse Lane, Birmingham B4 6DR,
Telephone: 0121 233 3282
Call date: Nov 1974, Middle Temple
Qualifications: [BA]

DESOUZA MS ESPERANZA LOUISA MARIA ANGELA

20 Britton Street
1st Floor, London EC1M 5NQ,
Telephone: 0171 608 3765
Call date: Nov 1994, Gray's Inn
Qualifications: [BSc (Lond), PGCE, Dip in Law]

DETHRIDGE DAVID JOHN

Verulam Chambers
Peer House 8-14 Verulam Street, Gray's Inn,
London WC1X 8LZ,
Telephone: 0171 813 2400
Call date: July 1975, Lincoln's Inn
Qualifications: [MA (Oxon)]

DETTER DE LUPIS FRANKOPAN COUNTESS (THYRA) INGRID HILDEGARD DOIMI

One Hare Court
1st Floor, Temple, London EC4Y 7BE,
Telephone: 0171 353 3171
E-mail: admin-oneharecourt@btinternet.com
Door Tenant
Call date: July 1977, Middle Temple
Qualifications: [DPhil (Oxon), Lic en droit
(Paris), CESE (Turin), Jur Kand, Jur Lic, Jur Dr
(Stockholm)]

DEVE CHRISTOPHER AGAMA

Mottingham Barrister's Chambers
43 West Park, London SE9 4RZ,
Telephone: 0181 857 5565
Call date: Nov 1990, Inner Temple
Qualifications: [LLB]

DEVINE MICHAEL BUXTON

95A Chancery Lane
London WC2A 1DT,
Telephone: 0171 405 3101
Call date: July 1995, Gray's Inn
Qualifications: [BA, JD, MPA, Diploma
Advanced Int, Legal Studies, LLM]

DEVLIN BERNARD JOSEPH

1 Harcourt Bldgs
2nd Floor, Temple, London EC4Y 9DA,
Telephone: 0171 353 9421/9151
Call date: Nov 1980, Gray's Inn
Qualifications: [LLB (Reading) LLM, (Lond)]

DEVLIN JONATHAN NICHOLAS PONTON

Park Court Chambers
40 Park Cross Street, Leeds LS1 2QH,
Telephone: 0113 2433277
Call date: Nov 1978, Inner Temple
Qualifications: [LLB (Leeds)]

DEVONSHIRE SIMON PETER

5 Paper Bldgs
Ground Floor, Temple, London EC4Y 7HB,
Telephone: 0171 583 9275/583 4555
E-mail: 5paper@link.org
Call date: Feb 1988, Gray's Inn
Qualifications: [BA(Oxon)]

DEWSBERY RICHARD MARK

St Ive's Chambers
9 Fountain Ct, Birmingham B4 6DR,
Telephone: 0121 236 0863/0929
Call date: Oct 1992, Inner Temple
Qualifications: [LLB (Essex)]

DHADLI MRS PERMINDER

King Charles House
Standard Hill, Nottingham NG1 6FX,
Telephone: 0115 9418851
E-mail: clerks@kch.co.uk
Call date: Nov 1984, Middle Temple
Qualifications: [BA (Hons)]

DHALIWAL MISS DAVINDER KAUR

New Court Chambers
Suite 200 Gazette Building, 168 Corporation
Street, Birmingham B4 6TZ,
Telephone: 0121 693 6656
Call date: Nov 1990, Middle Temple
Qualifications: [LLB (Hons)(B'ham)]

D

DHAMA SATYA PRAKASH

2 Middle Temple Lane
3rd Floor, Temple, London EC4Y 9AA,
Telephone: 0171 583 4540
Call date: July 1972, Lincoln's Inn
Qualifications: [MA]

DHILLON JASBIR SINGH

Brick Court Chambers
15/19 Devereux Court, London WC2R 3JJ,
Telephone: 0171 583 0777
E-mail: (surname)@brickcourt.demon.co.uk
Call date: Oct 1996, Gray's Inn
Qualifications: [BA (Oxon), LLM (Harvard)]

DHIR MISS ANUJA RAVINDRA

5 Paper Bldgs
1st Floor, Temple, London EC4Y 7HB,
Telephone: 0171 583 6117
E-mail: clerks@5-paperbuildings.law.co.uk
Call date: Nov 1989, Gray's Inn
Qualifications: [LLB (Dundee)]

DI MAMBRO DAVID JESSE ANDREW

Lamb Chambers
Lamb Building, Temple, London EC4Y 7AS,
Telephone: 0171 797 8300
E-mail: lambchambers@link.org
Call date: Nov 1973, Middle Temple
Qualifications: [LLB (Lond),ACIArb]

DIAMOND MISS ANNA CATRIONA

5 Fountain Court
Steelhouse Lane, Birmingham B4 6DR,
Telephone: 0121 606 0500
Call date: Oct 1995, Gray's Inn
Qualifications: [BA]

DIAMOND CHRISTOPHER LESLIE WILLIAM

18 St John Street
Manchester M3 4EA,
Telephone: 0161 278 1800
Call date: Nov 1975, Gray's Inn
Qualifications: [LLB]

DIAMOND IAN PAUL HUGH

One Raymond Buildings
Gray's Inn, London WC1R 5BH,
Telephone: 0171 430 1234
E-mail: chambers@ipbar1rb.com;
clerks@ipbar1rb.com
Call date: July 1985, Middle Temple
Qualifications: [BA (Exon), LLM (Cantab)]

DIAS CHANDRAJITH ASOKA WILLIAM

1 Gray's Inn Square
Ground Floor, London WC1R 5AA,
Telephone: 0171 405 8946/7/8
Call date: July 1989, Lincoln's Inn
Qualifications: [LLB (Warw)]

DIAS JUDE DEXTER

2 Garden Court
1st Floor, Middle Temple, London EC4Y 9BL,
Telephone: 0171 353 1633
E-mail: barristers@2gardenct.law.co.uk
Call date: Feb 1988, Inner Temple
Qualifications: [BA (Durham)]

DIAS MISS JULIA AMANDA

7 King's Bench Walk
Ground Floor, Temple, London EC4Y 7DS,
Telephone: 0171 583 0404
Call date: July 1982, Inner Temple
Qualifications: [MA (Cantab)]

DIAS MISS SAPPHO

Thomas More Chambers
52 Carey Street, Lincoln's Inn, London
WC2A 2JB, Telephone: 0171 404 7000
Call date: Nov 1982, Gray's Inn
Qualifications: [BA (Cantab)]

DICK JOHN OSWALD

3 Temple Gardens
1st Floor, Temple, London EC4Y 9AU,
Telephone: 0171 353 7884/5 8982/3
Call date: July 1974, Gray's Inn
Qualifications: [BA (Oxon)]

DICK MISS JULIA MARGARET

14 Tooks Court
Cursitor St, London EC4A 1LB,
Telephone: 0171 405 8828
E-mail: clerks @tooks.law.co.uk
Call date: Nov 1988, Middle Temple
Qualifications: [B.Tech (Bradford), Dip Law (City)]

DICKENS ANDREW WILLIAM

New Court
Temple, London EC4Y 9BE,
Telephone: 0171 583 5123/0171 583 0510
Call date: Nov 1983, Gray's Inn
Qualifications: [Dip Law]

DICKENS PAUL MICHAEL JOHN

5 New Square
1st Floor, Lincoln's Inn, London WC2A 3RJ,
Telephone: 0171 404 0404
E-mail: Chambers@FiveNewSquare.CityScape.co.uk
Call date: July 1978, Lincoln's Inn
Qualifications: [MA (Cantab),ARCO]

DICKER ROBIN MARK

3/4 South Square
Gray's Inn, London WC1R 5HP,
Telephone: 0171 696 9900
E-mail: clerks@southsquare.com
Call date: Apr 1986, Middle Temple
Qualifications: [BA, BCL (Oxon)]

DICKINSON GREGORY DAVID MARK

1 High Pavement
Nottingham NG1 1HF,
Telephone: 0115 9418218
Call date: July 1981, Gray's Inn
Assistant Recorder
Qualifications: [LLB]

DICKINSON JOHN FINCH HENEAGE

St John's Chambers
Small Street, Bristol BS1 1DW,
Telephone: 0117 9213456/298514
E-mail: clerks@stjohns.uk.com
Call date: Oct 1995, Middle Temple
Qualifications: [BA (Hons)]

DICKINSON JONATHAN DAVID

58 King Street Chambers
1st Floor, Kingsgate House 51-53 South King Street, Manchester M2 6DE,
Telephone: 0161 831 7477
Call date: Nov 1986, Inner Temple
Qualifications: [LLB (Hons) (Bristol)]

DICKS ANTHONY RICHARD

Essex Court Chambers
24 Lincoln's Inn Fields, London WC2A 3ED,
Telephone: 0171 813 8000
E-mail: clerksroom@essexcourt-chambers.co.uk
Call date: May 1961, Inner Temple
Qualifications: [MA, LLB (Cantab)]

DIGBY CHARLES SPENCER

Queen Elizabeth Bldg
Ground Floor, Temple, London EC4Y 9BS,
Telephone: 0171 353 7181 (12 Lines)
Call date: July 1982, Middle Temple
Qualifications: [BA]

DIGGINS MARTIN JOHN CARR

Rowchester Chambers
4 Rowchester Court Whittall Street,
Birmingham B4 6DH,
Telephone: 0121 233 2327/2361951
Call date: Nov 1992, Middle Temple
Qualifications: [BA (Hons)(Kent), LLM (Lond)]

DIGHT MARC DAVID

11 Stone Bldgs
Ground Floor, Lincoln's Inn, London WC2A 3TG, Telephone: 0171 831 6381
E-mail: clerks@11StoneBuildings.law.co.uk
Chichester Chambers
12 North Pallant, Chichester, West Sussex PO19 1TQ, Telephone: 01243 784538
Door Tenant
Call date: July 1984, Inner Temple
Qualifications: [LLB (Bristol)]

D

DIGNEY PETER NEIL

1 Dr Johnson's Bldgs
Ground Floor, Temple, London EC4Y 7AX,
Telephone: 0171 353 9328
Dr Johnson's Chambers
The Atrium Court Apex Plaza, Reading
RG1 1AX, Telephone: 01734 254221
Call date: July 1968, Middle Temple
Recorder
Qualifications: [BA (Cantab)]

DIGNUM MARCUS BENEDICT

1 Crown Office Row
3rd Floor, Temple, London EC4Y 7HH,
Telephone: 0171 583 9292
E-mail: onecor@link.org
Call date: Oct 1994, Middle Temple
Qualifications: [BA (Hons)(Lond)]

DILHORNE THE RT HON VISCOUNT

4 Breams Buildings
London EC4A 1AQ,
Telephone: 0171 353 5835/430 1221
Call date: Nov 1979, Inner Temple
Qualifications: [FTII]

DILLON THOMAS WILLIAM MATTHEW

1 Fountain Court
Steelhouse Lane, Birmingham B4 6DR,
Telephone: 0121 236 5721
Call date: July 1983, Middle Temple
Qualifications: [MA (Cantab), Dip IPL]

DIN SOOFI PERVAZE IQBAL

24 The Ropewalk
Nottingham NG1 5EF,
Telephone: 0115 9472581
E-mail: clerk@ropewalk.co.uk
Call date: Nov 1984, Lincoln's Inn
Qualifications: [BA (Manch)]

DINAN-HAYWARD MISS DEBORAH LOUISE

Assize Court Chambers
14 Small Street, Bristol BS1 1DE,
Telephone: 0117 9264587
Call date: Nov 1988, Inner Temple
Qualifications: [LLB (Shef)]

DINEEN MICHAEL LAURENCE

Pump Court Chambers
Upper Ground Floor 3 Pump Court, Temple,
London EC4Y 7AJ, Telephone: 0171 353 0711
Pump Court Chambers
31 Southgate Street, Winchester SO23 8EE,
Telephone: 01962 868161
All Saints Chambers
9/11 Broad Street, Bristol BS1 2HP,
Telephone: 0117 921 1966
Door Tenant
Call date: Nov 1977, Inner Temple
Qualifications: [BA (Oxon) LLB, (Cantab)]

DINES COLIN EDWARD

1 Middle Temple Lane
Temple, London EC4Y 1LT,
Telephone: 0171 583 0659 (12 Lines)
Westgate Chambers
144 High Street, Lewes, East Sussex BN7 1XT,
Telephone: 01273 480510
Call date: Nov 1970, Middle Temple
Recorder

DINES MISS SARAH ELIZABETH

3 Paper Bldgs
2nd Floor, Temple, London EC4Y 7EU,
Telephone: 0171 353 6208
Call date: July 1988, Lincoln's Inn
Qualifications: [LLB (Hons) (Brunel)]

DINGEMANS JAMES MICHAEL

1 Crown Office Row
3rd Floor, Temple, London EC4Y 7HH,
Telephone: 0171 583 9292
E-mail: onecor@link.org
Call date: July 1987, Inner Temple
Qualifications: [BA (Oxon)]

DINGLE JONATHAN CRISPIN

South Western Chambers
Melville House 12 Middle Street, Taunton,
Somerset TA1 1SH, Telephone: 01823 331919
Call date: July 1986, Middle Temple
Qualifications: [LLB (Lond)]

DINKIN ANTHONY DAVID QC (1991)

2-3 Gray's Inn Square
Gray's Inn, London WC1R 5JH,
Telephone: 0171 242 4986
E-mail: chambers@2-3graysinnsquare.co.uk
Call date: Nov 1968, Lincoln's Inn
Recorder
Qualifications: [BSc (Lond)]

DISMORR EDWARD SEEL

St Ive's Chambers
9 Fountain Ct, Birmingham B4 6DR,
Telephone: 0121 236 0863/0929
Call date: July 1983, Inner Temple
Qualifications: [MA (Oxon) Dip Law Ci]

DITCHFIELD ANTHONY MICHAEL

Trinity Chambers
9-12 Trinity Chare, Quayside, Newcastle Upon
Tyne NE1 3DF, Telephone: 0191 232 1927
Call date: Oct 1993, Middle Temple
Qualifications: [BA (Hons, Kent), LLM (Sheff)]

DIX-DYER MISS FIONA JANE

St Paul's House
5th Floor 23 Park Square South, Leeds
LS1 2ND, Telephone: 0113 2455866
Call date: July 1986, Lincoln's Inn
Qualifications: [LLB (Hons)(Leeds)]

DIXEY IAN ROGER

St John's Chambers
Small Street, Bristol BS1 1DW,
Telephone: 0117 9213456/298514
E-mail: clerks@stjohns.uk.com
Call date: Nov 1984, Inner Temple

DIXON MISS ANNE

Counsels' Chambers
2nd Floor 10-11 Gray's Inn Square, London
WC1R 5JD, Telephone: 0171 405 2576
Call date: Nov 1991, Middle Temple
Qualifications: [LLB (Hons), RGN]

DIXON DAVID STEVEN

25 Park Square
Leeds LS1 2PW, Telephone: 0113 2451841/2/3
E-mail: sovereignchambers@btinternet.com
Call date: Oct 1992, Lincoln's Inn
Qualifications: [LLB(Hons)(Newc)]

DIXON MS EMMA LOUISE

2 Hare Court
Ground Floor, Temple, London EC4Y 7BH,
Telephone: 0171 583 1770
E-mail: 2_Hare_Court@link.org
Call date: Oct 1994, Gray's Inn
Qualifications: [BA]

DIXON IAN FREDERICK

Cathedral Chambers
Milburn House Dean Street, Newcastle Upon
Tyne NE1 1LE, Telephone: 0191 232 1311
Call date: Nov 1982, Gray's Inn

DIXON JOHN

India Buildings Chambers
Water Street, Liverpool L2 OXG,
Telephone: 0151 243 6000
Call date: Nov 1995, Gray's Inn
Qualifications: [LLB (Essex)]

DIXON JOHN WATTS

2 Harcourt Bldgs
1st Floor, Temple, London EC4Y 9DB,
Telephone: 0171 353 6961/7
Harcourt Chambers
Churchill House 3 St Aldate's Courtyard, St
Aldate's, Oxford OX1 1BN,
Telephone: 01865 791559
Call date: Feb 1975, Middle Temple
Qualifications: [MA (Oxon)]

DIXON PHILIP JOHN

Francis Taylor Bldg
2nd Floor, Temple, London EC4Y 7BY,
Telephone: 0171 353 9942/3157
Call date: July 1986, Middle Temple
Qualifications: [MA(Cantab)]

DIXON RALPH JOHN PETER

St John's Chambers
Small Street, Bristol BS1 1DW,
Telephone: 0117 9213456/298514
E-mail: clerks@stjohns.uk.com
Call date: Nov 1980, Middle Temple
Qualifications: [BA (York)]

DIXON MISS SORRELL HELEN

2 Gray's Inn Square Chambers
2nd Floor, Gray's Inn, London WC1R 5AA,
Telephone: 0171 242 0328/071 405 1317
E-mail: clerks@2gis.co.uk
Call date: July 1987, Middle Temple
Qualifications: [LLB (Bristol)]

DOBBS MISS LINDA PENELOPE

18 Red Lion Court
(Off Fleet Street), London EC4A 3EB,
Telephone: 0171 520 6000
Thornwood House
102 New London Road, Chelmsford, Essex
CM2 0RG, Telephone: 01245 280880
Call date: July 1981, Gray's Inn
Qualifications: [BSc, LLM, PhD (Lond)]

DOBBYN MISS SARAH ELANARIS

199B Temple Chambers
3-7 Temple Avenue, London EC4Y 0DB,
Telephone: 0171 583 8008
Call date: Nov 1988, Middle Temple
Qualifications: [MA (Cantab), ACIArb,
M.ius.comp (Bonn)]

DOBE KULJEET SINGH

Watford Chambers
74 Mildred Avenue, Watford, Hertfordshire
WD1 7DX, Telephone: 01923 220553
Call date: Nov 1993, Lincoln's Inn
Qualifications: [LLB (Soton)]

DOCKERY PAUL

18 St John Street
Manchester M3 4EA,
Telephone: 0161 278 1800
Call date: July 1973, Gray's Inn
Qualifications: [LLB (London)]

DOCKING TONY WILFRED JAMES

1 Middle Temple Lane
Temple, London EC4Y 1LT,
Telephone: 0171 583 0659 (12 Lines)
Call date: Nov 1969, Gray's Inn

DOCTOR BRIAN ERNEST

Fountain Court
Temple, London EC4Y 9DH,
Telephone: 0171 583 3335
E-mail: chambers@fountaincourt.co.uk
Call date: July 1991, Lincoln's Inn
Qualifications: [BA (S Africa), LLB
(Witwatersand), BCL]

DODD CHRISTOPHER JOHN NICHOLAS

9 Woodhouse Square
Leeds LS3 1AD, Telephone: 0113 2451986
Call date: Nov 1984, Lincoln's Inn
Qualifications: [LLB (Leics)]

DODD JOHN STANISLAUS

3 Hare Court
1st Floor, Temple, London EC4Y 7BJ,
Telephone: 0171 353 7561
Call date: Nov 1979, Gray's Inn
Qualifications: [LLB (Leics)]

DODD MRS MARGARET ANN

3 Hare Court
1st Floor, Temple, London EC4Y 7BJ,
Telephone: 0171 353 7561
Door Tenant
Call date: July 1979, Middle Temple
Qualifications: [LLB [So'ton]]

DODD MISS SARA

58 King Street Chambers
1st Floor, Kingsgate House 51-53 South King
Street, Manchester M2 6DE,
Telephone: 0161 831 7477
Call date: July 1987, Lincoln's Inn
Qualifications: [LLB]

DODDS ROBERT STEPHEN

15 Winckley Square
Preston PR1 3JJ, Telephone: 01772 252828
E-mail: clerks@winckleysq.demon.co.uk
Call date: July 1976, Gray's Inn
Qualifications: [LLB (Lond)]

DODDS SHAUN

Baker Street Chambers
9 Baker Street, Middlesbrough TS1 2LF,
Telephone: 01642 873873
Call date: July 1990, Gray's Inn
Qualifications: [LLB (Lond)]

DODGE PETER CLIVE

11 Old Square
Ground Floor, Lincoln's Inn, London
WC2A 3TS, Telephone: 0171 430 0341
E-mail: clerks@11oldsquare.co.uk
Call date: Oct 1992, Lincoln's Inn
Qualifications: [BA(Hons), MA, Dip Law]

DODGSON PAUL

1 Hare Court
Ground Floor, Temple, London EC4Y 7BE,
Telephone: 0171 353 3982/5324
Call date: July 1975, Inner Temple
Recorder
Qualifications: [LLB]

DODSON MISS JOANNA QC (1993)

14 Gray's Inn Square
Gray's Inn, London WC1R 5JP,
Telephone: 0171 242 0858
E-mail: 100712.2134@compuserve.com
Park Court Chambers
40 Park Cross Street, Leeds LS1 2QH,
Telephone: 0113 2433277
Door Tenant
Call date: Nov 1970, Middle Temple
Qualifications: [MA (Cantab)]

DOERRIES MISS CHANTAL-AIMEE RENEE AEMELIA ANNEMARIE

1 Atkin Building
Gray's Inn, London WC1R 5AT,
Telephone: 0171 404 0102
E-mail: clerks@atkin-chambers.co.uk
Call date: Oct 1992, Middle Temple
Qualifications: [BA (Hons, Cantab)]

DOGGART PIERS GRAHAM

King's Chambers
5a Gildredge Road, Eastbourne, East Sussex
BN21 4RB, Telephone: 01323 416053
Call date: Oct 1991, Lincoln's Inn

Qualifications: [LLB (Hons) (Leeds)]

Fax: 01323 416110; DX: 6931 Eastbourne;
Other comms: E-mail
piersdoggart@compuserve.com; Mobile 0410
943326

Types of work: Administrative; Crime; Landlord
and tenant; Personal injury; Professional
negligence

Other professional qualifications: Registered
Pupil Master

Circuit: South Eastern

Awards and memberships: Administrative Law
Bar Association; Personal Injuries Bar
Association; Sussex Bar Mess

Languages spoken: French

DOGGETT RODERICK ALISTAIR MANNING

4 Paper Bldgs
Ground Floor, Temple, London EC4Y 7EX,
Telephone: 0171 353 3366/583 7155
E-mail: clerks@4paperbuildings.com
Call date: July 1969, Gray's Inn
Qualifications: [BA (Oxon)]

DOGRA MISS TANYIA ANITA

3 Pump Court
2nd Floor, Temple, London EC4Y 7AJ,
Telephone: 0171 353 1356 (3 Lines)
Call date: Oct 1994, Gray's Inn
Qualifications: [LLB, LLM]

DOHERTY BERNARD JAMES

39 Essex Street
London WC2R 3AT,
Telephone: 0171 583 1111
E-mail: clerks@39essex.co.uk
Call date: Nov 1990, Middle Temple
Qualifications: [MA (Cantab), Dip Law (City)]

DOHERTY NICHOLAS BRUDENELL

10 King's Bench Walk
1st Floor, Temple, London EC4Y 7EB,
Telephone: 0171 353 2501
Call date: July 1983, Lincoln's Inn
Qualifications: [LLB]

D

DOHMANN MISS BARBARA QC (1987)

2 Hare Court
Ground Floor, Temple, London EC4Y 7BH,
Telephone: 0171 583 1770
E-mail: 2_Hare_Court@link.org
Call date: Nov 1971, Gray's Inn
Recorder
Qualifications: [Graduate of Mainz &, Paris
Universities]

DOIG GAVIN ANDREW

St John's Chambers
Small Street, Bristol BS1 1DW,
Telephone: 0117 9213456/298514
E-mail: clerks@stjohns.uk.com
Call date: Oct 1995, Lincoln's Inn
Qualifications: [LLB (Hons)(Bris)]

DOIG MRS JEANETTA ROSE

Neston Chambers
42 Greenhill, Neston, Corsham, Wiltshire
SN13 9SQ, Telephone: 01225 811909
Call date: July 1988, Lincoln's Inn
Qualifications: [CPE, PhC, FETC, M R Pharm S]

DOMENGE MRS VICTORIA JANE

29 Bedford Row Chambers
London WC1R 4HE,
Telephone: 0171 831 2626
Call date: Nov 1993, Middle Temple
Qualifications: [BA (Hons)(Exon), Dip in Law]

DONALDSON DAVID TORRANCE QC (1984)

2 Hare Court
Ground Floor, Temple, London EC4Y 7BH,
Telephone: 0171 583 1770
E-mail: 2_Hare_Court@link.org
Call date: Nov 1968, Gray's Inn
Recorder
Qualifications: [MA (Cantab), DrJur]

DONNE ANTHONY MAURICE QC (1988)

2 King's Bench Walk
Ground Floor, Temple, London EC4Y 7DE,
Telephone: 0171 353 1746
E-mail: 2kbw@atlas.co.uk
King's Bench Chambers
115 North Hill, Plymouth PL4 8JY,
Telephone: 01752 221551
Door Tenant
All Saints Chambers
9/11 Broad Street, Bristol BS1 2HP,
Telephone: 0117 921 1966
Door Tenant
Call date: Nov 1973, Middle Temple
Recorder
Qualifications: [BA (Oxon)]

DONNE JEREMY NIGEL

Hollis Whiteman Chambers
3rd/4th Floor Queen Elizabeth Bldg, Temple,
London EC4Y 9BS, Telephone: 0171 583 5766
E-mail: hollis.whiteman@btinternet.com
Call date: Nov 1978, Middle Temple

DONNELLAN CHRISTOPHER JOHN

36 Bedford Row
London WC1R 4JH,
Telephone: 0171 421 8000
E-mail: 36bedfordrow@link.org
Call date: July 1981, Inner Temple
Qualifications: [BA (Oxon)]

DONNELLY MISS CATHERINE MARY

5 Paper Bldgs
Lower Ground Floor, Temple, London
EC4Y 7HB, Telephone: 0171 353 5638
E-mail: 107722,633@compuserve.com
Call date: Mar 1997, Middle Temple
Qualifications: [BA (Hons)(Lond)]

DONNELLY JOHN PATRICK

Counsels' Chambers
2nd Floor 10-11 Gray's Inn Square, London
WC1R 5JD, Telephone: 0171 405 2576
Call date: Nov 1983, Inner Temple
Qualifications: [LLB (Hull)]

DONNELLY KEVIN GERARD EASTWOOD

Lincoln House Chambers
5th Floor Lincoln House, 1 Brazennose Street,
Manchester M2 5EL,
Telephone: 0161 832 5701
E-mail: LincolnHouseChambers@link.org
Call date: Oct 1991, Lincoln's Inn
Qualifications: [BA (Hons) (Cambs)]

DONOGHUE STEVEN MICHAEL

9 Park Place
Cardiff CF1 3DP, Telephone: 01222 382731
Call date: Oct 1992, Middle Temple
Qualifications: [LL.B (Hons, Wales)]

DONOVAN ANTHONY FRANCIS SCOTT

Derby Square Chambers
Merchants Court, Derby Square, Liverpool
L2 1TS, Telephone: 0151 709 4222
Call date: July 1975, Gray's Inn
Assistant Recorder
Qualifications: [BA (Oxon) MA (USA)]

DONOVAN JOEL

New Court Chambers
5 Verulam Buildings, Gray's Inn, London
WC1R 5LY, Telephone: 0171 831 9500
E-mail: mail@newcourtchambers.com
Call date: July 1991, Lincoln's Inn
Qualifications: [BA (Hons) (Durham)]

DOOKHY RIYAD ABDOOL CADER

The Thames Chambers
Wickham House 10 Cleveland Way, London
E1 4TR, Telephone: 0171 790 7377
Call date: Nov 1992, Gray's Inn
Qualifications: [LLB (Sheff)]

DOOLEY ALLAN KEITH

5 Fountain Court
Steelhouse Lane, Birmingham B4 6DR,
Telephone: 0121 606 0500
Call date: Apr 1991, Lincoln's Inn
Recorder
Qualifications: [LLB (Hons) (Liver)]

DOOLEY MS CHRISTINE

2 Pump Court
1st Floor, Temple, London EC4Y 7AH,
Telephone: 0171 353 5597
Call date: July 1980, Gray's Inn
Qualifications: [BA (Hons)]

DOOTSON IAIN STUART

Furnival Chambers
32 Furnival Street, London EC4A 1JQ,
Telephone: 0171 405 3232
E-mail: clerks@furnivallaw.co.uk
Call date: Feb 1984, Gray's Inn
Qualifications: [LLB (Hons Lond)]

DORAN GERARD PATRICK

1 Gray's Inn Square
Ground Floor, London WC1R 5AA,
Telephone: 0171 405 8946/7/8
Call date: Nov 1993, Gray's Inn
Qualifications: [LLB (Hons)]

DORMAN-O'GOWAN CHRISTOPHER PATRICK DESMOND

Broad Chare
33 Broad Chare, Newcastle Upon Tyne
NE1 3DQ, Telephone: 0191 232 0541
Call date: Nov 1979, Lincoln's Inn
Qualifications: [BA (Newc)]

DORRELL MS ALISON GLENDA

19 Figtree Lane
Sheffield S1 2DJ, Telephone: 0114 2759708/
2738380
Call date: Feb 1992, Gray's Inn
Qualifications: [LLB (Sheff)]

DOUGHERTY NIGEL PETER

Erskine Chambers
30 Lincoln's Inn Fields, Lincoln's Inn, London
WC2A 3PF, Telephone: 0171 242 5532
E-mail: Clerks@Erskine-Chambers.law.co.uk
Call date: Oct 1993, Gray's Inn
Qualifications: [BA, LLM (Cantab)]

D

D

DOUGHTY PETER

17 Carlton Crescent
Southampton SO15 2XR,
Telephone: 01703 320320
E-mail: km@bar-17cc.demon.co.uk
Call date: July 1988, Lincoln's Inn
Qualifications: [LLB (Hons) (Cardiff)]

DOUGLAS MICHAEL JOHN QC (1997)

4 Pump Court
Temple, London EC4Y 7AN,
Telephone: 0171 353 2656/9
E-mail: 4_pump_court@compuserve.com
Call date: Nov 1974, Gray's Inn
Qualifications: [BA (Oxon)]

DOUGLAS STEPHEN JOHN

24a St John Street
Manchester M3 4DF,
Telephone: 0161 833 9628
Call date: Nov 1994, Inner Temple
Qualifications: [LLB (Manc), CPE
(Staffordshire)]

DOUGLASS MISS GERALDINE MAISIE

Carmarthen Chambers
30 Spilman Street, Carmarthen, Dyfed
SA31 1LQ, Telephone: 01267 234410
Chambers of Davina Gammon
Ground Floor 103 Walter Road, Swansea
SA1 5QS, Telephone: 01792 480770
Lancaster Building Chambers
77 Deansgate, Manchester M3 2BW,
Telephone: 0161 661 4444
E-mail: sandra@lbnipc.com
Door Tenant
Call date: Nov 1976, Middle Temple

DOUTHWAITE CHARLES PHILIP

2 Crown Office Row
2nd Floor, Temple, London EC4Y 7HJ,
Telephone: 0171 797 8000
Call date: July 1977, Gray's Inn
Qualifications: [MA (Cantab)]

DOVE IAN WILLIAM

5 Fountain Court
Steelhouse Lane, Birmingham B4 6DR,
Telephone: 0121 606 0500
Call date: July 1986, Inner Temple
Qualifications: [BA (Oxon)]

DOW KENNETH

5 Pump Court
Ground Floor, Temple, London EC4Y 7AP,
Telephone: 0171 353 2532
E-mail: fivepump@netcomuk.co.uk
Call date: Nov 1970, Lincoln's Inn
Qualifications: [BA]

DOWDEN ANDREW PHILIP

Harrow on the Hill Chambers
60 High Street, Harrow on the Hill, Middlesex
HA1 3LL, Telephone: 0181 423 7444
Windsor Barristers' Chambers
Windsor, Telephone: 01753 648899
Southsea Chambers
PO Box 148, Southsea, Portsmouth,
Hampshire PO5 2TU,
Telephone: 01705 291261
Call date: Oct 1991, Lincoln's Inn
Qualifications: [BA (Hons) (Manch), M Phil
(Cambs)]

DOWDING NICHOLAS ALAN TATHAM QC (1997)

Falcon Chambers
Falcon Court, London EC4Y 1AA,
Telephone: 0171 353 2484/7
Call date: July 1979, Inner Temple
Qualifications: [MA (Cantab)]

DOWELL GREGORY HAMILTON

Becket Chambers
17 New Dover Road, Canterbury, Kent
CT1 3AS, Telephone: 01227 786331
Call date: Oct 1990, Middle Temple
Qualifications: [LLB]

DOWLEY DOMINIC MYLES

One Hare Court
1st Floor, Temple, London EC4Y 7BE,
Telephone: 0171 353 3171
E-mail: admin-oneharecourt@btinternet.com
Call date: July 1983, Gray's Inn
Qualifications: [MA Oxon]

DOWN JONATHAN CHARLES

5 Fountain Court
Steelhouse Lane, Birmingham B4 6DR,
Telephone: 0121 606 0500
Call date: Nov 1993, Gray's Inn
Qualifications: [BA (Kent)]

DOWN MISS SUSAN

Devon Chambers
3 St Andrew Street, Plymouth PL1 2AH,
Telephone: 01752 661659
Call date: Nov 1984, Middle Temple
Qualifications: [LLB (Hons)(E Anglia), LLB
(Hons) (Eaton)]

DOWNES GARRY KEITH

Essex Court Chambers
24 Lincoln's Inn Fields, London WC2A 3ED,
Telephone: 0171 813 8000
E-mail: clerksroom@essexcourt-chambers.co.uk
Call date: Feb 1995, Inner Temple
Qualifications: [BA, LLB (Sydney)]

DOWNES PAUL SIMON

2 Temple Gardens
Temple, London EC4Y 9AY,
Telephone: 0171 583 6041 (12 Lines)
Call date: Oct 1991, Gray's Inn
Qualifications: [BA (Oxon)]

DOWNEY MISS AILEEN PATRICIA

9 Gough Square
London EC4A 3DE, Telephone: 0171 353 5371
Call date: Nov 1991, Lincoln's Inn
Qualifications: [LLB (Hons) (Lond)]

DOWNEY CHARLES BERNARD RAOUL DESCHAMPS

Littleton Chambers
3 King's Bench Walk North, Temple, London
EC4Y 7HR, Telephone: 0171 797 8600
E-mail: littletonchambers@compuserve.com
Call date: July 1988, Lincoln's Inn
Qualifications: [BSc (Hons) (LSE), Dip Law]

DOWNHAM MISS GILLIAN CELIA

Rougemont Chambers
15 Barnfield Road, Exeter EX1 1RR,
Telephone: 01392 410471
E-mail: rougemont.chambers@eclipse.co.uk
Call date: Nov 1993, Middle Temple
Qualifications: [BSc Soc.Sci (Hons), (So'ton),
MA Econ, (Manc)]

DOWNIE ANDREW JAMES

Martins Building
Water Street, Liverpool L2 3SP,
Telephone: 0151 236 5818/4919
Call date: Nov 1990, Gray's Inn
Qualifications: [BA, MA]

DOWNING JOHN

1 Gray's Inn Square
1st Floor, London WC1R 5AG,
Telephone: 0171 405 3000
E-mail: clerks@onegrays.demon.co.uk
Call date: June 1958, Gray's Inn
Qualifications: [LLB (Lond)]

DOWNING MISS RUTH ELIZABETH

Devereux Chambers
Devereux Court, London WC2R 3JJ,
Telephone: 0171 353 7534
E-mail: elton@devchambers.co.uk
Call date: July 1978, Gray's Inn
Qualifications: [BA (Cantab)]

DOWNS MARTIN JOHN

1 Crown Office Row
Ground Floor, Temple, London EC4Y 7HH,
Telephone: 0171 797 7500
Crown Office Row Chambers
Blenheim House 120 Church Street, Brighton,
Sussex BN1 1WH, Telephone: 01273 625625
Call date: Nov 1990, Inner Temple
Qualifications: [BA (Oxon), Dip Law (City)]

DOWNS SIMON TIMOTHY

22 Albion Place
Northampton NN1 1UD,
Telephone: 01604 36271
Call date: Oct 1996, Inner Temple
Qualifications: [BA (Warw), CPE (Exon)]

DOWOKPOR JONATHAN KUKASI

Tollgate Mews Chambers
113 Tollgate Road Tollgate Mews, North
Beckton, London E6 4JY,
Telephone: 0171 511 1838
Call date: July 1972, Lincoln's Inn
Qualifications: [MA, LLB (Lond)]

DOWSE JOHN

9 St John Street
Manchester M3 4DN,
Telephone: 0161 955 9000
E-mail: ninesjs@gconnect.com
Chambers of Lord Goodhart QC
Ground Floor 3 New Square, Lincoln's Inn,
London WC2A 3RS,
Telephone: 0171 405 5577
E-mail: law@threenewsquare.demon.co.uk
Door Tenant
Call date: July 1973, Lincoln's Inn
Recorder
Qualifications: [LLB]

DOYLE JAMES GAVIN CHARLES

Bridewell Chambers
2 Bridewell Place, London EC4V 6AP,
Telephone: 0171 797 8800
E-mail: clerks@bridewell.law.co.uk
Call date: July 1985, Middle Temple
Qualifications: [LLB]

DOYLE LOUIS GEORGE

10 Park Square
Leeds LS1 2LH, Telephone: 0113 2455438
E-mail: chambers@bandit.legend.co.uk
Call date: Nov 1996, Lincoln's Inn
Qualifications: [LLB (Hons)(Leeds), LLM (B'ham)]

DOYLE PETER JOHN

9-12 Bell Yard
London WC2A 2LF,
Telephone: 0171 400 1800
Call date: July 1975, Middle Temple
Qualifications: [LLB]

DRABBLE RICHARD JOHN BLOOR QC (1995)

4 Breams Buildings
London EC4A 1AQ,
Telephone: 0171 353 5835/430 1221
Call date: Nov 1975, Inner Temple
Qualifications: [BA (Cantab)]

DRAKE DAVID CHRISTOPHER

13 Old Square
1st Floor, Lincoln's Inn, London WC2A 3UA,
Telephone: 0171 242 6105
E-mail: clerks@serlecourt.co.uk
Call date: Nov 1994, Inner Temple
Qualifications: [BA (Oxon), BCL (Oxon)]

DRAKE MISS RACHEL ALEXIA

Wessex Chambers
48 Queens Road, Reading, Berkshire
RG1 4BD, Telephone: 01734 568856
E-mail: wessexchambers@compuserve.com
Call date: Nov 1995, Middle Temple
Qualifications: [LLB (Hons)(Brunel)]

DRAKE MISS SOPHIE HELENA

Broadway House Chambers
Broadway House 9 Bank Street, Bradford,
West Yorkshire BD1 1TW,
Telephone: 01274 722560
Call date: Oct 1990, Gray's Inn
Qualifications: [LLB (Leic)]

DRANE MISS AMANDA TERESA LOVE

4 King's Bench Walk
2nd Floor, Temple, London EC4Y 7DL,
Telephone: 0171 353 3581
Call date: Oct 1996, Lincoln's Inn
Qualifications: [BA (Hons)(Cantab)]

DRAY MARTIN BENEDICT ANTONY

Falcon Chambers
Falcon Court, London EC4Y 1AA,
Telephone: 0171 353 2484/7
Call date: Oct 1992, Gray's Inn
Qualifications: [LL.B (Bris)]

DRAYCOTT DOUGLAS QC (1965)

5 Fountain Court
Steelhouse Lane, Birmingham B4 6DR,
Telephone: 0121 606 0500
Call date: Jan 1950, Middle Temple
Qualifications: [MA (Oxon)]

DRAYCOTT MRS MARGARET JEAN BRUNTON

5 Fountain Court
Steelhouse Lane, Birmingham B4 6DR,
Telephone: 0121 606 0500
Call date: July 1980, Middle Temple
Qualifications: [LLB (B'ham)]

DRAYCOTT SIMON DOUGLAS

13 King's Bench Walk
1st Floor, Temple, London EC4Y 7EN,
Telephone: 0171 353 7204
E-mail: clerks@13kbw.law.co.uk
Call date: July 1977, Middle Temple
Assistant Recorder

DRAYTON HENRY ALEXANDER

2 Gray's Inn Square Chambers
2nd Floor, Gray's Inn, London WC1R 5AA,
Telephone: 0171 242 0328/071 405 1317
E-mail: clerks@2gis.co.uk
Call date: Feb 1993, Inner Temple
Qualifications: [BA]

DREW MRS CHERYL

Warwick House Chambers
8 Warwick Court, Gray's Inn, London
WC1R 5DJ, Telephone: 0171 430 2323
Call date: Nov 1972, Gray's Inn

DREW CHRISTOPHER THOMAS

Warwick House Chambers
8 Warwick Court, Gray's Inn, London
WC1R 5DJ, Telephone: 0171 430 2323
Call date: Nov 1969, Gray's Inn
Qualifications: [LLB (Lond)]

DREW DORIAN WARRICK SHERIDAN

Francis Taylor Bldg
3rd Floor, Temple, London EC4Y 7BY,
Telephone: 0171 797 7250
Call date: Oct 1995, Gray's Inn
Qualifications: [LLB (Hons)(Lond)]

DREW MISS JANE MARIAN

4 Brick Court
Ground Floor, Temple, London EC4Y 9AD,
Telephone: 0171 797 7766
E-mail: chambers@4brick.co.uk
Call date: July 1976, Middle Temple
Qualifications: [BA (Dunelm)]

DREW MS SANDHYA

14 Tooks Court
Cursitor St, London EC4A 1LB,
Telephone: 0171 405 8828
E-mail: clerks @tooks.law.co.uk
Call date: Oct 1993, Gray's Inn
Qualifications: [MA (Oxon), Dip Law (City)]

DREW SIMON PATRICK

5 Fountain Court
Steelhouse Lane, Birmingham B4 6DR,
Telephone: 0121 606 0500
Call date: Nov 1987, Lincoln's Inn
Qualifications: [LLB (Leeds)]

DRINKWATER PHILIP MURRAY

Colleton Chambers
Colleton Crescent, Exeter, Devon EX2 4DG,
Telephone: 01392 74898/9
Call date: Nov 1995, Inner Temple
Qualifications: [LLB (Exon)]

DRISCOLL MRS JENIFER JANE

Queen Elizabeth Bldg
Ground Floor, Temple, London EC4Y 9BS,
Telephone: 0171 353 7181 (12 Lines)
Call date: July 1989, Lincoln's Inn
Qualifications: [BA (Cantab), Dip Law (City)]

DRISCOLL MISS LYNN

Lancaster Building Chambers
77 Deansgate, Manchester M3 2BW,
Telephone: 0161 661 4444
E-mail: sandra@lbnipc.com
25 Park Square
Leeds LS1 2PW, Telephone: 0113 2451841/2/3
E-mail: sovereignchambers@btinternet.com
Call date: July 1981, Middle Temple
Qualifications: [BA, LLM (Lond), Dip Law]

D

DRISCOLL MICHAEL JOHN QC (1992)

9 Old Square
Ground Floor, Lincoln's Inn, London
WC2A 3SR, Telephone: 0171 405 4682
E-mail: chambers@9oldsquare.co.uk
Call date: July 1970, Middle Temple
Qualifications: [BA, LLB (Cantab)]

DRIVER MS EMILY ROSE

6 King's Bench Walk
Ground, Third & Fourth Floors, Temple,
London EC4Y 7DR,
Telephone: 0171 353 4931/583 0695
Call date: Nov 1988, Inner Temple
Qualifications: [BA (Oxon), Dip Law (City)]

DRIVER SIMON GREGORY

25-27 Castle Street
1st Floor, Liverpool L2 4TA,
Telephone: 0151 227 5661/051 236 5072
Call date: Nov 1991, Inner Temple
Qualifications: [BA (Reading), Dip Law]

DRIVER STUART FRANK

Adrian Lyon's Chambers
14 Castle Street, Liverpool L2 0NE,
Telephone: 0151 236 4421/8240
E-mail: chambers14@aol.com
Call date: Nov 1988, Gray's Inn
Qualifications: [BA (Oxon)]

DRUCE MICHAEL JAMES

2 Mitre Ct Bldgs
2nd Floor, Temple, London EC4Y 7BX,
Telephone: 0171 583 1380
Call date: July 1988, Inner Temple
Qualifications: [MA (Cantab)]

DRUMMOND BRUCE JONATHON HUTCHEON

40 King Street
Chester CH1 2AH, Telephone: 01244 323886
Call date: Oct 1992, Gray's Inn
Qualifications: [B.Sc (Wales)]

DRY NICHOLAS DAVID

St Paul's House
5th Floor 23 Park Square South, Leeds
LS1 2ND, Telephone: 0113 2455866
Call date: Nov 1996, Lincoln's Inn
Qualifications: [BA (Hons)(Cantab)]

DRYDEN SHAUN

Baker Street Chambers
9 Baker Street, Middlesbrough TS1 2LF,
Telephone: 01642 873873
Call date: Nov 1994, Lincoln's Inn
Qualifications: [LLB (Hons)(Lond)]

DSANE MISS VICTORIA TSOTSOO

61 Elm Grove
Sutton, Surrey SM1 4EX,
Telephone: 0181 643 9714
Call date: Nov 1971, Middle Temple
Qualifications: [BA, LLB, MA]

DU CANN CHRISTIAN DILLON LOTT

39 Essex Street
London WC2R 3AT,
Telephone: 0171 583 1111
E-mail: clerks@39essex.co.uk
Call date: July 1982, Gray's Inn
Qualifications: [BA Cantab]

DU PREEZ HENRY ROBERT

1 Crown Office Row
2nd Floor, Temple, London EC4Y 7HH,
Telephone: 0171 797 7111
Call date: Nov 1985, Inner Temple
Qualifications: [BA (Law)]

DUBARRY MS ADELE KATHERINE

Maidstone Chambers
33 Earl Street, Maidstone, Kent ME14 1PF,
Telephone: 01622 688592
Call date: Nov 1993, Middle Temple
Qualifications: [LLB (Hons), LLM (E.Anglia)]

DUBBERY MARK EDWARD

Pump Court Chambers
Upper Ground Floor 3 Pump Court, Temple,
London EC4Y 7AJ, Telephone: 0171 353 0711
Call date: Oct 1996, Middle Temple
Qualifications: [BSc (Hons)(Lond), LLB (Hons)(City)]

DUBICKA MISS ELIZABETH

14 Tooks Court
Cursitor St, London EC4A 1LB,
Telephone: 0171 405 8828
E-mail: clerks @tooks.law.co.uk
Call date: Feb 1995, Middle Temple
Qualifications: [BA (Hons)(B'ham), MA (Leic),
CPE (City)]

DUCK MICHAEL CHARLES

3 Fountain Court
Steelhouse Lane, Birmingham B4 6DR,
Telephone: 0121 236 5854
Call date: Nov 1988, Gray's Inn
Qualifications: [LLB]

DUCKWORTH (ARTHUR) PETER

29 Bedford Row Chambers
London WC1R 4HE,
Telephone: 0171 831 2626
Call date: July 1971, Middle Temple
Qualifications: [LLB]

DUDDRIDGE ROBERT JAMES

Trafalgar Chambers
53 Fleet Street, London EC4Y 1BE,
Telephone: 0171 583 5858
E-mail: TrafalgarChambers@easynet.co.uk
Call date: Feb 1992, Lincoln's Inn
Qualifications: [BA (Hons) (Oxon)]

DUDKOWSKI DOMINIC CHRISTIAN

Sussex Chambers
9 Old Steine, Brighton BN1 1FJ,
Telephone: 01273 607953
Call date: Nov 1986, Inner Temple
Qualifications: [BA(Sussex)]

DUDLEY MICHAEL JOHN

1 Fountain Court
Steelhouse Lane, Birmingham B4 6DR,
Telephone: 0121 236 5721
Call date: July 1972, Lincoln's Inn
Assistant Recorder
Qualifications: [LLB; G.Cert.Ed]

DUDLEY ROBERT MICHAEL

Exchange Chambers
Pearl Assurance House Derby Square,
Liverpool L2 9XX, Telephone: 0151 236 7747/
0458
E-mail: exchangechambers@btinternet.com
Call date: Oct 1993, Gray's Inn
Qualifications: [MA (Cantab)]

DUFF EUAN CAMERON

Broad Chare
33 Broad Chare, Newcastle Upon Tyne
NE1 3DQ, Telephone: 0191 232 0541
Call date: July 1973, Inner Temple
Qualifications: [MA (Cantab)]

DUFF MISS MORAG AILEEN

2 Paper Bldgs
1st Floor, Temple, London EC4Y 7ET,
Telephone: 0171 936 2611 (10 Lines)
E-mail: clerks@2pbbarristers.co.uk
Call date: Nov 1991, Middle Temple
Qualifications: [LLB (Hons) (Lond)]

DUFFIELD STEPHEN MICHAEL

Trinity Chambers
9-12 Trinity Chare, Quayside, Newcastle Upon
Tyne NE1 3DF, Telephone: 0191 232 1927
Call date: July 1969, Gray's Inn
Recorder
Qualifications: [BA (Oxon)]

DUFFY DEREK JAMES

St Paul's House
5th Floor 23 Park Square South, Leeds
LS1 2ND, Telephone: 0113 2455866
Call date: Mar 1997, Gray's Inn
Qualifications: [BA (Hons)(Sheffield)]

DUFFY MISS JOANNE

5 Fountain Court
Steelhouse Lane, Birmingham B4 6DR,
Telephone: 0121 606 0500
Call date: Oct 1994, Lincoln's Inn
Qualifications: [LLB (Hons)(Leic)]

DUFFY MICHAEL

Cathedral Chambers
P O Box 24 56 John Amner Close, Ely,
Cambridgeshire CB6 1DT,
Telephone: 0385 733920
Call date: July 1992, Lincoln's Inn

DUFFY PETER JOSEPH FRANCIS QC (1997)

Essex Court Chambers
24 Lincoln's Inn Fields, London WC2A 3ED,
Telephone: 0171 813 8000
E-mail: clerksroom@essexcourt-chambers.co.uk
Call date: July 1978, Lincoln's Inn
Qualifications: [MA, LLB (Cantab)]

DUGDALE JEREMY KEITH

2 Pump Court
1st Floor, Temple, London EC4Y 7AH,
Telephone: 0171 353 5597
Call date: Oct 1992, Inner Temple
Qualifications: [MA (Oxon)]

DUGDALE NICHOLAS

4 Field Court
Gray's Inn, London WC1R 5EA,
Telephone: 0171 440 6900
E-mail: chambers@4fieldcourt.co.uk
Call date: Feb 1992, Middle Temple
Qualifications: [BA (Auckland), LLB
(Auckland)]

DUGDALE PAUL DAMIAN NORWOOD

2 King's Bench Walk
Ground Floor, Temple, London EC4Y 7DE,
Telephone: 0171 353 1746
E-mail: 2kbw@atlas.co.uk
King's Bench Chambers
115 North Hill, Plymouth PL4 8JY,
Telephone: 01752 221551
Call date: Oct 1990, Gray's Inn
Qualifications: [LLB (Lond)]

DUGGAN JAMES ROSS

India Buildings Chambers
Water Street, Liverpool L2 OXG,
Telephone: 0151 243 6000
Call date: July 1978, Middle Temple
Recorder
Qualifications: [LLB (L'pool)]

DUGGAN MICHAEL

Littleton Chambers
3 King's Bench Walk North, Temple, London
EC4Y 7HR, Telephone: 0171 797 8600
E-mail: littletonchambers@compuserve.com
Call date: July 1984, Gray's Inn
Qualifications: [BA,BCL, LLM (Cantab)]

DUKE PAUL STUART

Old Colony House
6 South King Street, Manchester M2 6DQ,
Telephone: 0161 834 4364
Call date: Nov 1989, Gray's Inn
Qualifications: [LLB (Hons)]

DULOVIC MILAN

2 Gray's Inn Square Chambers
2nd Floor, Gray's Inn, London WC1R 5AA,
Telephone: 0171 242 0328/071 405 1317
E-mail: clerks@2gis.co.uk
Call date: July 1982, Gray's Inn
Qualifications: [LLB (Lond)]

DUMARESQ MS DELIA JANE

1 Atkin Building
Gray's Inn, London WC1R 5AT,
Telephone: 0171 404 0102
E-mail: clerks@atkin-chambers.co.uk
Call date: July 1984, Inner Temple
Qualifications: [MA, Dip Law]

DUMBILL ERIC ALEXANDER

King Charles House
Standard Hill, Nottingham NG1 6FX,
Telephone: 0115 9418851
E-mail: clerks@kch.co.uk
Call date: Nov 1971, Gray's Inn
Qualifications: [LLB (Nott'm)]

DUMONT THOMAS JULIAN BRADLEY

11 New Square
Ground Floor, Lincoln's Inn, London
WC2A 3QB, Telephone: 0171 831 0081
E-mail: 11newsquare.co.uk
Call date: Nov 1979, Gray's Inn
Qualifications: [MA (Cantab)]

DUNCAN JOHN CHRISTOPHER

Deans Court Chambers
Cumberland House Crown Square, Manchester
M3 3HA, Telephone: 0161 834 4097
E-mail: deanscourt@compuserve.com
Deans Court Chambers
41-43 Market Place, Preston PR1 1AH,
Telephone: 01772 555163
E-mail: deanscourt@compuserve.com
Call date: July 1971, Inner Temple
Qualifications: [BSc,BA]

DUNFORD MATTHEW SIMON

40 King Street
Chester CH1 2AH, Telephone: 01244 323886
Call date: Oct 1992, Lincoln's Inn
Qualifications: [LLB(Hons)(Newc)]

DUNFORD ROBERT CHARLES

65-67 King Street
Leicester LE1 6RP, Telephone: 0116 2547710
Call date: Nov 1995, Middle Temple
Qualifications: [BA (Hons)(Toronto)]

DUNKELS PAUL RENTON QC (1993)

Walnut House
63 St. David's Hill, Exeter, Devon EX4 4DW,
Telephone: 01392 279751
E-mail: 106627.2451@compuserve.com
Albion Chambers
Broad Street, Bristol BS1 1DR,
Telephone: 0117 9272144
Call date: May 1972, Inner Temple
Recorder

DUNLOP HAMISH MICHAEL

1 Harcourt Bldgs
2nd Floor, Temple, London EC4Y 9DA,
Telephone: 0171 353 9421/9151
Call date: Nov 1991, Middle Temple
Qualifications: [LLB Hons (Warw)]

DUNN ALEXANDER

8 King's Bench Walk
2nd Floor, Temple, London EC4Y 7DU,
Telephone: 0171 797 8888
8 King's Bench Walk North
1 Park Square East, Leeds LS1 2NE,
Telephone: 0113 2439797
Call date: Feb 1985, Middle Temple
Qualifications: [BA]

DUNN CHRISTOPHER

25 Park Square
Leeds LS1 2PW, Telephone: 0113 2451841/2/3
E-mail: sovereignchambers@btinternet.com
Call date: Oct 1996, Gray's Inn
Qualifications: [B.Sc, MA, LLM (Newc)]

DUNN MISS KATHERINE ELSPETH

40 King Street
Manchester M2 6BA,
Telephone: 0161 832 9082
E-mail: Kingst40@aol.com
Call date: Nov 1987, Middle Temple
Qualifications: [BA (Cantab)]

DUNN MISS KATHERINE LOUISE

4 King's Bench Walk
Ground/First Floor, Temple, London
EC4Y 7DL, Telephone: 0171 822 8822
E-mail: 4kbw@barristersatlaw.com
Call date: Oct 1993, Lincoln's Inn
Qualifications: [LLB (Hons)(Lond)]

DUNN STEWART WILLIAM

Chambers of Stewart Dunn
93 Millview Drive, Tynemouth, North Shields
NE30 2QJ, Telephone: 0191 258 0520
Call date: Nov 1992, Gray's Inn
Qualifications: [BSc, A.R.I.C.S., LLB]

DUNN TIMOTHY NEVILLE

Guildhall Chambers Portsmouth
Prudential Buildings 16 Guildhall Walk,
Portsmouth, Hampshire PO1 2DE,
Telephone: 01705 752400
Call date: Oct 1996, Inner Temple
Qualifications: [LLB (Hons)(Exon)]

DUNN-SHAW JASON DAVID

6 King's Bench Walk
Ground Floor, Temple, London EC4Y 7DR,
Telephone: 0171 583 0410
Call date: Oct 1992, Lincoln's Inn
Qualifications: [BA(Hons)(Manch)]

DUNNE JONATHAN ANTHONY

3 Temple Gardens
2nd Floor, Temple, London EC4Y 9AU,
Telephone: 0171 583 1155
Call date: July 1986, Inner Temple
Qualifications: [LLB (Leics)]

DUNNING FRANCIS JOHN GROVE

37 Park Square
Leeds LS1 2NY, Telephone: 0113 2439422
Call date: July 1973, Inner Temple
Qualifications: [BSc]

DUNNING GRAHAM

Essex Court Chambers
24 Lincoln's Inn Fields, London WC2A 3ED,
Telephone: 0171 813 8000
E-mail: clerksroom@essexcourt-chambers.co.uk
Call date: July 1982, Lincoln's Inn
Qualifications: [MA (Cantab), LLM (Harvard)]

DUNSTAN JAMES PETER

6 Fountain Court
Steelhouse Lane, Birmingham B4 6DR,
Telephone: 0121 233 3282
Call date: Feb 1995, Gray's Inn
Qualifications: [BA (Oxon)]

DURR JUDE PATRICK

East Anglian Chambers
Gresham House 5 Museum Street, Ipswich
IP1 1HQ, Telephone: 01473 214481
East Anglian Chambers
Sanders House 52 North Hill, Colchester
CO1 1PY, Telephone: 01206 572756
East Anglian Chambers
57 London Street, Norwich NR2 1HL,
Telephone: 01603 617351
Call date: Oct 1995, Inner Temple
Qualifications: [MA, CPE]

DURRAN MISS ALEXIA GRAINNE

23 Essex Street
London WC2R 3AS,
Telephone: 0171 413 0353/353 3533
E-mail: clerks@essexstreet23.demon.co.uk
Call date: Oct 1995, Middle Temple
Qualifications: [BA (Hons)]

DUTCHMAN-SMITH MALCOLM CHARLES

Martins Building
Water Street, Liverpool L2 3SP,
Telephone: 0151 236 5818/4919
Call date: Feb 1995, Gray's Inn
Qualifications: [LLB (Hull)]

DUTHIE MISS CATRIONA ANN MACPHERSON

Guildhall Chambers
23 Broad Street, Bristol BS1 2HG,
Telephone: 0117 9273366
Call date: July 1981, Inner Temple
Qualifications: [LLB (Nottm) MSc, (Edin)]

DUTHIE MALCOLM JAMES

5 Fountain Court
Steelhouse Lane, Birmingham B4 6DR,
Telephone: 0121 606 0500
Call date: July 1989, Inner Temple
Qualifications: [LLB [Buck], LLM [Lond]]

DUTTA MISS NANDINI

8 Fountain Court
Steelhouse Lane, Birmingham B4 6DR,
Telephone: 0121 236 5514/5
E-mail: clerks@no8chambers.co.uk
Call date: Feb 1993, Middle Temple
Qualifications: [LLB (Hons)]

DUTTON TIMOTHY CHRISTOPHER

Barnard's Inn Chambers
6th Floor Halton House, 20-23 Holborn,
London EC1N 2JD, Telephone: 0171 242 8508
E-mail: clerks@barnards-inn-chambers.co.uk
Call date: July 1985, Inner Temple
Qualifications: [BA(Durham)]

DUTTON TIMOTHY JAMES

Farrar's Building
Temple, London EC4Y 7BD,
Telephone: 0171 583 9241
E-mail: chambers@farrarsbuilding.co.uk
Call date: Nov 1979, Middle Temple
Assistant Recorder
Qualifications: [BA (Oxon)]

DUVAL ROBERT MICHAEL LOUIS

St John's Chambers
Small Street, Bristol BS1 1DW,
Telephone: 0117 9213456/298514
E-mail: clerks@stjohns.uk.com
Call date: Nov 1979, Gray's Inn
Qualifications: [LLB (Wales)]

DYBLE STEVEN JOHN

East Anglian Chambers
Sanders House 52 North Hill, Colchester
CO1 1PY, Telephone: 01206 572756
East Anglian Chambers
57 London Street, Norwich NR2 1HL,
Telephone: 01603 617351
East Anglian Chambers
Gresham House 5 Museum Street, Ipswich
IP1 1HQ, Telephone: 01473 214481
Call date: Nov 1986, Lincoln's Inn
Qualifications: [LLB (West England)]

DYE BRIAN WILLIAM

Essex Court Chambers
24 Lincoln's Inn Fields, London WC2A 3ED,
Telephone: 0171 813 8000
E-mail: clerksroom@essexcourt-chambers.co.uk
Call date: Oct 1991, Middle Temple
Qualifications: [MA (Hons) (Oxon)]

DYER ALLEN GORDON

4 Pump Court
Temple, London EC4Y 7AN,
Telephone: 0171 353 2656/9
E-mail: 4_pump_court@compuserve.com
Call date: July 1976, Inner Temple
Qualifications: [BA (Bristol)]

DYER DAVID ROGER

7 Fountain Court
Steelhouse Lane, Birmingham B4 6DR,
Telephone: 0121 236 8531
Call date: Nov 1980, Middle Temple
Qualifications: [BA, Dip Arch., RIBA, FCIArb, FFAS]

DYER JACOB JACKSON

15 Winckley Square
Preston PR1 3JJ, Telephone: 01772 252828
E-mail: clerks@winckleysq.demon.co.uk
Call date: Nov 1995, Lincoln's Inn
Qualifications: [MA (Cantab)]

DYER NIGEL INGRAM JOHN

1 Mitre Ct Bldgs
Ground Floor, Temple, London EC4Y 7BS,
Telephone: 0171 797 7070
Call date: Feb 1982, Inner Temple
Qualifications: [BA Hons (Dunelm)]

DYER SIMON CHRISTOPHER

Plowden Bldgs
2nd Floor, Temple, London EC4Y 9BU,
Telephone: 0171 583 0808
E-mail: bar@plowdenbuildings.co.uk
Call date: July 1987, Middle Temple
Qualifications: [BA (Kent)]

DYMOND ANDREW MARK

Arden Chambers
27 John Street, London WC1N 2BL,
Telephone: 0171 242 4244
Call date: Nov 1991, Middle Temple
Qualifications: [MA (Oxon)]

EADE MS PHILLIPA SARAH

New Walk Chambers
27 New Walk, Leicester LE1 6TE,
Telephone: 0116 2559144
Call date: Oct 1992, Inner Temple
Qualifications: [LLB (Leics)]

EADES ROBERT MARK

5 Fountain Court
Steelhouse Lane, Birmingham B4 6DR,
Telephone: 0121 606 0500
Call date: July 1974, Middle Temple
Recorder
Qualifications: [LLB]

EADIE JAMES RAYMOND

One Hare Court
1st Floor, Temple, London EC4Y 7BE,
Telephone: 0171 353 3171
E-mail: admin-oneharecourt@btinternet.com
Call date: July 1984, Middle Temple
Qualifications: [MA (Cantab)]

D

EADY MISS JENNIFER JANE

Old Square Chambers
1 Verulam Buildings, Gray's Inn, London
WC1R 5LQ, Telephone: 0171 831 0801
Old Square Chambers
Hanover House 47 Corn Street, Bristol
BS1 1HT, Telephone: 0117 9277111
Call date: July 1989, Inner Temple
Qualifications: [BA [Oxon], Dip Law]

EARLAM SIMON LAWRENCE

Exchange Chambers
Pearl Assurance House Derby Square,
Liverpool L2 9XX, Telephone: 0151 236 7747/
0458
E-mail: exchangechambers@btinternet.com
Call date: Feb 1975, Gray's Inn
Assistant Recorder
Qualifications: [MA (Oxon) BCL]

EARLE MISS JUDY ESTELLE

3 Paper Bldgs
1st Floor, Temple, London EC4Y 7EU,
Telephone: 0171 583 8055
E-mail: london@3paper.com
20 Lorne Park Road
Bournemouth BH1 1JN,
Telephone: 01202 292102 (5 Lines)
Call date: Oct 1994, Middle Temple
Qualifications: [LLB (Hons)(Lond)]

EARNSHAW STEPHEN

Furnival Chambers
32 Furnival Street, London EC4A 1JQ,
Telephone: 0171 405 3232
E-mail: clerks@furnivallaw.co.uk
Call date: May 1990, Middle Temple
Qualifications: [LL.B. (Brunel)]

EASTEAL ANDREW FRANCIS MARTIN

1 High Pavement
Nottingham NG1 1HF,
Telephone: 0115 9418218
Call date: Feb 1990, Inner Temple
Qualifications: [BA (Oxon)]

EASTERMAN NICHOLAS BARRIE

4 Brick Court
Temple, London EC4Y 9AD,
Telephone: 0171 797 8910
Call date: July 1975, Lincoln's Inn
Qualifications: [LLB (Lond)]

EASTMAN ROGER

2 Harcourt Bldgs
Ground Floor/Left, Temple, London
EC4Y 9DB, Telephone: 0171 583 9020
E-mail: clerks@harcourt.co.uk
Stanbrook & Henderson
2 Harcourt Bldgs 2nd Floor, Temple, London
EC4Y 9DB, Telephone: 0171 353 0101
E-mail: clerks@harcourt.co.uk
Call date: Nov 1978, Gray's Inn
Qualifications: [BA (Dunelm)]

EASTON MISS ALISON JANE

Queen Elizabeth Bldg
Ground Floor, Temple, London EC4Y 9BS,
Telephone: 0171 353 7181 (12 Lines)
Call date: Nov 1994, Inner Temple
Qualifications: [LLB (B'ham)]

EASTON JONATHAN MARK

2-3 Gray's Inn Square
Gray's Inn, London WC1R 5JH,
Telephone: 0171 242 4986
E-mail: chambers@2-3graysinnsquare.co.uk
Call date: Nov 1996, Gray's Inn
Qualifications: [LLB (Warw), LLM (Florence)]

EASTWOOD CHARLES PETER

28 St John Street
Manchester M3 4DJ,
Telephone: 0161 834 8418
E-mail: clerk@28stjohnst.co.uk
Call date: July 1988, Lincoln's Inn
Qualifications: [BA (Hons) (Oxon)]

EASTY MISS VALERIE STEPHANIE

2 Garden Court
1st Floor, Middle Temple, London EC4Y 9BL,
Telephone: 0171 353 1633
E-mail: barristers@2gardenct.law.co.uk
Call date: Oct 1992, Middle Temple
Qualifications: [B.Sc (Hons), Diploma in Law]

EATON MISS DEBORAH ANN

1 King's Bench Walk
2nd Floor, Temple, London EC4Y 7DB,
Telephone: 0171 936 1500
E-mail: ddear@1kbw.co.uk
Call date: July 1985, Inner Temple
Qualifications: [B Soc Sc (Keele),Dip]

EATON JAMES BERNARD

1 Middle Temple Lane
Temple, London EC4Y 1LT,
Telephone: 0171 583 0659 (12 Lines)
Call date: Nov 1978, Middle Temple
Qualifications: [LLB (Hons) (Liv)]

EATON NIGEL TREVOR

Essex Court Chambers
24 Lincoln's Inn Fields, London WC2A 3ED,
Telephone: 0171 813 8000
E-mail: clerksroom@essexcourt-chambers.co.uk
Call date: Nov 1991, Gray's Inn
Qualifications: [BA, BCL (Oxon)]

EATON RICHARD MARK COOPER

Westgate Chambers
144 High Street, Lewes, East Sussex BN7 1XT,
Telephone: 01273 480510
Call date: May 1982, Lincoln's Inn
Qualifications: [LLB (Hons), A.C.I.Arb]

EATON THOMAS EDWARD DAVID

Adrian Lyon's Chambers
14 Castle Street, Liverpool L2 0NE,
Telephone: 0151 236 4421/8240
E-mail: chambers14@aol.com
Call date: Nov 1976, Middle Temple
Qualifications: [LLB (Hons) (Lond)]

EATON HART ANDREW MICHAEL

Walnut House
63 St. David's Hill, Exeter, Devon EX4 4DW,
Telephone: 01392 279751
E-mail: 106627.2451@compuserve.com
Call date: July 1989, Gray's Inn
Qualifications: [LLB [Exon]]

EATON TURNER DAVID MURRAY

1 New Square
Ground Floor, Lincoln's Inn, London
WC2A 3SA, Telephone: 0171 405 0884/5/6/7
E-mail: 1newsquare@compuserve.com
Call date: July 1984, Lincoln's Inn
Qualifications: [LLB (Lond)]

EBOO ISMAIL PIRBHAI

2 Middle Temple Lane
3rd Floor, Temple, London EC4Y 9AA,
Telephone: 0171 583 4540
Call date: Nov 1970, Inner Temple

ECCLES DAVID THOMAS

8 King Street
Manchester M2 6AQ,
Telephone: 0161 834 9560
Call date: July 1976, Middle Temple
Qualifications: [MA (Cantab)]

ECCLES HUGH WILLIAM PATRICK QC (1990)

2 Harcourt Bldgs
1st Floor, Temple, London EC4Y 9DB,
Telephone: 0171 353 6961/7
Harcourt Chambers
Churchill House 3 St Aldate's Courtyard, St
Aldate's, Oxford OX1 1BN,
Telephone: 01865 791559
Call date: July 1968, Middle Temple
Recorder
Qualifications: [MA (Oxon)]

ECKERSLEY SIMON RICHARD

St Mary's Chambers
50 High Pavement, Lace Market, Nottingham
NG1 1HW, Telephone: 0115 9503503
E-mail: clerks@smc.law.co.uk
Call date: Mar 1996, Lincoln's Inn
Qualifications: [BA (Hons) (Oxon)]

ECOB MISS JOANNE ANITA

36 Bedford Row
London WC1R 4JH,
Telephone: 0171 421 8000
E-mail: 36bedfordrow@link.org
Call date: July 1985, Inner Temple
Qualifications: [LLB (Newc)]

ECONOMOU GEORGE COSTAS

4 Essex Court
Temple, London EC4Y 9AJ,
Telephone: 0171 797 7970
E-mail: clerks@4essexcourt.law.co.uk
Call date: Nov 1965, Lincoln's Inn
Qualifications: [FCIArb]

EDELMAN COLIN NEIL QC (1995)

Devereux Chambers
Devereux Court, London WC2R 3JJ,
Telephone: 0171 353 7534
E-mail: elton@devchambers.co.uk
Call date: July 1977, Middle Temple
Recorder
Qualifications: [MA (Cantab)]

EDENBOROUGH MICHAEL SIMON

One Raymond Buildings
Gray's Inn, London WC1R 5BH,
Telephone: 0171 430 1234
E-mail: chambers@ipbar1rb.com;
clerks@ipbar1rb.com
Call date: Oct 1992, Middle Temple
Qualifications: [BA (Hons), MA, M.Sc, D.Phil,
MRSC]

EDER (HENRY) BERNARD QC (1990)

Essex Court Chambers
24 Lincoln's Inn Fields, London WC2A 3ED,
Telephone: 0171 813 8000
E-mail: clerksroom@essexcourt-chambers.co.uk
Call date: July 1975, Inner Temple
Assistant Recorder
Qualifications: [BA (Cantab)]

EDEY PHILIP DAVID

20 Essex Street
London WC2R 3AL,
Telephone: 0171 583 9294
E-mail: clerks@20essexst.com
Call date: Nov 1994, Gray's Inn
Qualifications: [BA]

EDGE IAN DAVID

3 Paper Bldgs
1st Floor, Temple, London EC4Y 7EU,
Telephone: 0171 583 8055
E-mail: london@3paper.com
20 Lorne Park Road
Bournemouth BH1 1JN,
Telephone: 01202 292102 (5 Lines)
4 St Peter Street
Winchester SO23 8OW,
Telephone: 01962 868884
Call date: Feb 1981, Middle Temple
Qualifications: [BA,LLM (Cantab)]

EDGE TIMOTHY RICHARD

8 King Street
Manchester M2 6AQ,
Telephone: 0161 834 9560
Call date: Oct 1992, Gray's Inn
Qualifications: [BA]

EDGINTON HORACE RONALD

Becket Chambers
17 New Dover Road, Canterbury, Kent
CT1 3AS, Telephone: 01227 786331
Westgate Chambers
144 High Street, Lewes, East Sussex BN7 1XT,
Telephone: 01273 480510
Call date: Nov 1984, Gray's Inn
Qualifications: [RGN, BA(Hons)(Law), LLM
(Exon)]

EDHEM MISS EMMA

4 King's Bench Walk
Ground/First Floor, Temple, London
EC4Y 7DL, Telephone: 0171 822 8822
E-mail: 4kbw@barristersatlaw.com
Call date: Oct 1993, Gray's Inn
Qualifications: [BSc]

EDIE ALASTAIR SCOTT KER

2 Garden Court
1st Floor, Middle Temple, London EC4Y 9BL,
Telephone: 0171 353 1633
E-mail: barristers@2gardenct.law.co.uk
Call date: Oct 1992, Middle Temple
Qualifications: [BA(Hons)(Kent)]

EDIE ANTHONY THOMAS KER

Lamb Building
Ground Floor, Temple, London EC4Y 7AS,
Telephone: 0171 797 7788
E-mail: lamb.building@link.org
Call date: Feb 1974, Gray's Inn
Qualifications: [LLB]

EDIS ANDREW JEREMY COULTER QC (1997)

18 St John Street
Manchester M3 4EA,
Telephone: 0161 278 1800
Adrian Lyon's Chambers
14 Castle Street, Liverpool L2 0NE,
Telephone: 0151 236 4421/8240
E-mail: chambers14@aol.com
Door Tenant
Call date: July 1980, Middle Temple
Assistant Recorder
Qualifications: [MA (Oxon)]

EDIS ANGUS WILLIAM BUTLER

1 Crown Office Row
Ground Floor, Temple, London EC4Y 7HH,
Telephone: 0171 797 7500
Call date: July 1985, Lincoln's Inn
Qualifications: [BA(Oxon)]

EDLIN DAVID MILES TIMOTHY

Lamb Building
Ground Floor, Temple, London EC4Y 7AS,
Telephone: 0171 797 7788
E-mail: lamb.building@link.org
Call date: July 1971, Middle Temple
Qualifications: [MA (Oxon)]

EDMUNDS MARTIN JAMES SIMPSON

Walnut House
63 St. David's Hill, Exeter, Devon EX4 4DW,
Telephone: 01392 279751
E-mail: 106627.2451@compuserve.com
Call date: July 1983, Middle Temple
Qualifications: [MA (Cantab)]

EDUSEI FRANCIS VICTOR BURG

Chambers of Ian Macdonald QC
Waldorf House Cooper Street, Manchester
M2 2FW, Telephone: 0161 236 1840
Call date: July 1989, Inner Temple
Qualifications: [LLB]

EDWARDS (JOHN) MICHAEL QC (1981)

Verulam Chambers
Peer House 8-14 Verulam Street, Gray's Inn,
London WC1X 8LZ,
Telephone: 0171 813 2400
Call date: Nov 1949, Middle Temple
Qualifications: [BCL,MA,FCIArb]

EDWARDS MS ANN MERERID

Paradise Square Chambers
26 Paradise Square, Sheffield S1 2DE,
Telephone: 0114 2738951
Call date: Oct 1991, Gray's Inn
Qualifications: [LLB (Wales)]

EDWARDS ANTHONY HOWARD

Oriel Chambers
14 Water Street, Liverpool L2 8TD,
Telephone: 0151 236 7191
E-mail: oriel_chambers@link.org
Call date: Nov 1972, Inner Temple
Recorder
Qualifications: [LLB (L'pool)]

EDWARDS MISS CLAIRE FRANCES

Carmarthen Chambers
30 Spilman Street, Carmarthen, Dyfed
SA31 1LQ, Telephone: 01267 234410
Call date: Nov 1990, Inner Temple
Qualifications: [LLB]

EDWARDS DANIEL HUGH

York Chambers
14 Toft Green, York YO1 1JT,
Telephone: 01904 620048
E-mail: yorkchambers.co.uk
Call date: Oct 1993, Lincoln's Inn
Qualifications: [BA (Hons)(York), Dip in Law
(Lond)]

EDWARDS DAVID GARETH

Martins Building
Water Street, Liverpool L2 3SP,
Telephone: 0151 236 5818/4919
Call date: Oct 1994, Gray's Inn
Qualifications: [LLB (Warw)]

EDWARDS DAVID LESLIE

7 King's Bench Walk
Ground Floor, Temple, London EC4Y 7DS,
Telephone: 0171 583 0404
Call date: July 1989, Lincoln's Inn
Qualifications: [MA (Cantab)]

EDWARDS GLYN TUDOR

St John's Chambers
Small Street, Bristol BS1 1DW,
Telephone: 0117 9213456/298514
E-mail: clerks@stjohns.uk.com
Call date: July 1987, Lincoln's Inn
Qualifications: [MA (Cantab), LLM (Cantab)]

EDWARDS MISS HELEN JANE

32 Park Place
Cardiff CF1 3BA, Telephone: 01222 397364
Call date: July 1995, Inner Temple
Qualifications: [LLB (Middx)]

EDWARDS MISS JENNIFER MARY

2 Dr Johnson's Building
Temple, London EC4Y 7AY,
Telephone: 0171 353 4716
Call date: Oct 1992, Gray's Inn
Qualifications: [BA (Nott'm)]

EDWARDS JOHN DAVID

7 Fountain Court
Steelhouse Lane, Birmingham B4 6DR,
Telephone: 0121 236 8531
Call date: July 1983, Inner Temple
Qualifications: [BA]

EDWARDS JONATHAN GWYN
MENDUS

Pendragon Chambers
124 Walter Road, Swansea SA1 5RG,
Telephone: 01792 411188
Call date: July 1981, Lincoln's Inn

EDWARDS JONATHAN WILLIAM

Westgate Chambers
144 High Street, Lewes, East Sussex BN7 1XT,
Telephone: 01273 480510
Call date: Nov 1994, Lincoln's Inn
Qualifications: [LLB (Hons)]

EDWARDS MARTIN RICHARD

1 Serjeants' Inn
4th Floor, Temple, London EC4Y 1NH,
Telephone: 0171 583 1355
E-mail: serjeants.inn@virgin.net
Call date: Nov 1995, Inner Temple
Qualifications: [BA (Kent), MA]

EDWARDS MS NICOLA MADELAINE

12 Old Square
1st Floor, Lincoln's Inn, London WC2A 3TX,
Telephone: 0171 404 0875
Call date: Oct 1991, Lincoln's Inn
Qualifications: [LLB (Hons), RGN]

EDWARDS NIGEL ROYSTON

St Paul's House
5th Floor 23 Park Square South, Leeds
LS1 2ND, Telephone: 0113 2455866
Call date: Nov 1995, Lincoln's Inn
Qualifications: [LLB (Hons)(Sheff)]

EDWARDS OWEN MEIRION

Sedan House
Stanley Place, Chester CH1 2LU,
Telephone: 01244 320480/348282
Call date: Oct 1992, Lincoln's Inn
Qualifications: [LLB(Hons)(Wales)]

EDWARDS PERCY JOHN OSBORNE

19 Figtree Lane
Sheffield S1 2DJ, Telephone: 0114 2759708/
2738380
Call date: Nov 1994, Gray's Inn
Qualifications: [LLB (Hull), MA (Leeds)]

EDWARDS PETER ALAN

Devereux Chambers
Devereux Court, London WC2R 3JJ,
Telephone: 0171 353 7534
E-mail: elton@devchambers.co.uk
Call date: Oct 1992, Inner Temple
Qualifications: [BA (Kent)]

EDWARDS PHILIP DOUGLAS

2 Harcourt Bldgs
2nd Floor, Temple, London EC4Y 9DB,
Telephone: 0171 353 8415
E-mail: clerks@twoharcourtbldgs.demon.co.uk
Call date: Nov 1992, Lincoln's Inn
Qualifications: [LLB (Hons)(B'ham)]

EDWARDS RICHARD JULIAN HENSHAW

3 Verulam Buildings
London WC1R 5NT,
Telephone: 0171 831 8441
E-mail: clerks@3verulam.co.uk
Call date: Oct 1993, Middle Temple
Qualifications: [MA (Cantab), M.Phil (Cantab)]

EDWARDS MISS SARAH LOUISE ELIZABETH

Queen Elizabeth Bldg
2nd Floor, Temple, London EC4Y 9BS,
Telephone: 0171 797 7837
Call date: Nov 1990, Inner Temple
Qualifications: [BA (Cantab)]

EDWARDS SIMON DAVID

1 Paper Bldgs
1st Floor, Temple, London EC4Y 7EP,
Telephone: 0171 353 3728/4953
Call date: Nov 1987, Gray's Inn
Qualifications: [LLB (Leics)]

EDWARDS SIMON JOHN MAY

29 Bedford Row Chambers
London WC1R 4HE,
Telephone: 0171 831 2626
Call date: Nov 1978, Middle Temple
Qualifications: [MA (Cantab)]

EDWARDS MISS SUSAN MAY QC (1993)

23 Essex Street
London WC2R 3AS,
Telephone: 0171 413 0353/353 3533
E-mail: clerks@essexstreet23.demon.co.uk
Call date: Nov 1972, Middle Temple
Recorder
Qualifications: [LLB (Soton)]

EDWARDS-STUART ANTONY JAMES COBHAM QC (1991)

2 Crown Office Row
Ground Floor, Temple, London EC4Y 7HJ,
Telephone: 0171 797 8100
E-mail: mail@2cor.co.uk, or to individual
barristers at: [barrister's surname]@2cor.co.uk
Call date: May 1976, Gray's Inn
Assistant Recorder
Qualifications: [MA (Cantab)]

EGAN MISS CAROLINE ANN

6 Fountain Court
Steelhouse Lane, Birmingham B4 6DR,
Telephone: 0121 233 3282
Call date: Nov 1993, Gray's Inn
Qualifications: [BA]

EGAN EUGENE CHRISTOPHER

30 Park Place
Cardiff CF1 3BA, Telephone: 01222 398421
E-mail: 100757.1456@compuserve.com
Call date: Oct 1993, Lincoln's Inn
Qualifications: [MA (Oxon)]

EGAN MISS FIONA JUNE CECILE

Thomas More Chambers
52 Carey Street, Lincoln's Inn, London
WC2A 2JB, Telephone: 0171 404 7000
Call date: Nov 1987, Middle Temple
Qualifications: [LLB]

EGAN MISS MARION TERESA

1 Paper Bldgs
Ground Floor, Temple, London EC4Y 7EP,
Telephone: 0171 583 7355
E-mail: clerks@1pb.co.uk
Call date: July 1988, Middle Temple
Qualifications: [MA (Hons) (Cantab)]

EGAN MICHAEL FLYNN JOHN

9-12 Bell Yard
London WC2A 2LF,
Telephone: 0171 400 1800
Call date: Nov 1981, Gray's Inn

EGAN PATRICK MANUS DERMOT

Thomas More Chambers
52 Carey Street, Lincoln's Inn, London
WC2A 2JB, Telephone: 0171 404 7000
Call date: Nov 1991, Middle Temple
Qualifications: [LLB (Hons)]

EGBUNA ROBERT OBIORA

St Mary's Chambers
50 High Pavement, Lace Market, Nottingham
NG1 1HW, Telephone: 0115 9503503
E-mail: clerks@smc.law.co.uk
Call date: Nov 1988, Gray's Inn
Qualifications: [LLB]

EGERTON MISS CHRISTINE ANNE

39 Park Square
Leeds LS1 2NU, Telephone: 0113 2456633
Call date: Oct 1992, Inner Temple
Qualifications: [LLB (Lond), LLM (Lond)]

EGLETON RICHARD WILDMAN

Eighteen Carlton Crescent
Southampton SO15 2XR,
Telephone: 01703 639001
Call date: July 1981, Gray's Inn
Qualifications: [MA (Oxon)]

EICKE TIM

Francis Taylor Bldg
3rd Floor, Temple, London EC4Y 7BY,
Telephone: 0171 797 7250
Call date: Oct 1993, Middle Temple
Qualifications: [LLB (Hons)(Dundee)]

EIDINOW JOHN SAMUEL CHRISTOPHER

1 New Square
Ground Floor, Lincoln's Inn, London
WC2A 3SA, Telephone: 0171 405 0884/5/6/7
E-mail: 1newsquare@compuserve.com
Call date: Nov 1992, Middle Temple
Qualifications: [BA (Hons), Dip in Law]

EILLEDGE MISS AMANDA GAIL CAROLINE

1 Harcourt Bldgs
2nd Floor, Temple, London EC4Y 9DA,
Telephone: 0171 353 9421/9151
Call date: Oct 1991, Lincoln's Inn
Qualifications: [BA (Hons), BCL (Oxon)]

EISSA ADRIAN NADIR

2 Garden Court
1st Floor, Middle Temple, London EC4Y 9BL,
Telephone: 0171 353 1633
E-mail: barristers@2gardenct.law.co.uk
Call date: Nov 1988, Inner Temple
Qualifications: [LLB (Warwick)]

EKANEY NKUMBE

Albion Chambers
Broad Street, Bristol BS1 1DR,
Telephone: 0117 9272144
Call date: Oct 1990, Gray's Inn
Qualifications: [LLB (Bris)]

EKLUND GRAHAM NICHOLAS

2 Temple Gardens
Temple, London EC4Y 9AY,
Telephone: 0171 583 6041 (12 Lines)
Call date: May 1984, Inner Temple
Qualifications: [BA, LLB (Hons)(Auckland)]

EL-FALAHI SAMI DAVID

International Law Chambers
ILC House 77/79 Chepstow Road, Bayswater,
London W2 5QR, Telephone: 0171 221 5684/
5/4840
Call date: July 1972, Inner Temple
Qualifications: [MA (Oxon), MSc Econ, FCI
ARB.]

ELCOMBE NICHOLAS JOHN

East Anglian Chambers
Sanders House 52 North Hill, Colchester
CO1 1PY, Telephone: 01206 572756
East Anglian Chambers
57 London Street, Norwich NR2 1HL,
Telephone: 01603 617351
East Anglian Chambers
Gresham House 5 Museum Street, Ipswich
IP1 1HQ, Telephone: 01473 214481
Call date: July 1987, Inner Temple
Qualifications: [LLB]

ELDER MISS FIONA ANN MORAG

All Saints Chambers
9/11 Broad Street, Bristol BS1 2HP,
Telephone: 0117 921 1966
Call date: July 1988, Gray's Inn
Qualifications: [LLB (Sheffield)]

ELDERGILL EDMUND MALCOLM

Counsels' Chambers
2nd Floor 10-11 Gray's Inn Square, London
WC1R 5JD, Telephone: 0171 405 2576
Call date: Nov 1991, Inner Temple
Qualifications: [BA (East Ang), Dip Law, PCGE]

ELDRED ANDREW COLIN

College of Law
14 Store Street, London WC1E 7DE,
Telephone: 0171 291 1200
Call date: Nov 1994, Middle Temple
Qualifications: [MA (Oxon), Dip Law (City)]

ELDRIDGE MARK

114 Liverpool Road
Islington, London N1 0RE,
Telephone: 0171 226 9863
Call date: July 1982, Gray's Inn
Qualifications: [BA (Lancaster), Dip]

ELEY JOHNATHAN DESMOND HUGH

1 High Pavement
Nottingham NG1 1HF,
Telephone: 0115 9418218
Call date: July 1987, Middle Temple
Qualifications: [BA]

ELFIELD MISS LAURA ELAINE

Clapham Chambers
21-25 Bedford Road, Clapham North, London
SW4 7SH, Telephone: 0171 978 8482/
642 5777
E-mail: 113063.632@compuserve.com
Call date: Mar 1996, Gray's Inn
Qualifications: [BA]

ELGOT HOWARD CHARLES

Park Lane Chambers
19 Westgate, Leeds LS1 2RD,
Telephone: 0113 2285000
3 Paper Bldgs
Ground Floor, Temple, London EC4Y 7EU,
Telephone: 0171 797 7000
E-mail: clerks@3pb.co.uk
Door Tenant
Call date: July 1974, Gray's Inn
Qualifications: [BA, BCL (Oxon)]

ELIAS DAVID

9 Park Place
Cardiff CF1 3DP, Telephone: 01222 382731
Call date: May 1994, Inner Temple
Qualifications: [MA (Cantab)]

ELIAS GERARD QC (1984)

Farrar's Building
Temple, London EC4Y 7BD,
Telephone: 0171 583 9241
E-mail: chambers@farrarsbuilding.co.uk
9 Park Place
Cardiff CF1 3DP, Telephone: 01222 382731
Door Tenant
Call date: July 1968, Inner Temple
Recorder
Qualifications: [LLB]

ELIAS PATRICK QC (1990)

11 King's Bench Walk
Temple, London EC4Y 7EQ,
Telephone: 0171 632 8500
E-mail: clerksroom@11-kbw.law.co.uk
Call date: Feb 1973, Inner Temple
Assistant Recorder
Qualifications: [LLB (Exon), MA, PhD
(Cantab)]

ELIAS ROBERT WILLOUGHBY

Lincoln House Chambers
5th Floor Lincoln House, 1 Brazennose Street,
Manchester M2 5EL,
Telephone: 0161 832 5701
E-mail: LincolnHouseChambers@link.org
Call date: July 1979, Middle Temple
Qualifications: [LLB (Hons) (Sheff)]

D

ELKINGTON BENJAMIN MICHAEL GORDON

2 Crown Office Row
2nd Floor, Temple, London EC4Y 7HJ,
Telephone: 0171 797 8000
Call date: Oct 1996, Gray's Inn
Qualifications: [BA (Cantab), LLM (Virginia)]

ELLACOTT STUART IAN

Guildhall Chambers Porstmouth
Prudential Buildings 16 Guildhall Walk,
Portsmouth, Hampshire PO1 2DE,
Telephone: 01705 752400
Call date: Nov 1989, Inner Temple
Qualifications: [BA]

ELLENBOGEN MISS NAOMI LISA

Littleton Chambers
3 King's Bench Walk North, Temple, London
EC4Y 7HR, Telephone: 0171 797 8600
E-mail: littletonchambers@compuserve.com
Call date: Oct 1992, Gray's Inn
Qualifications: [MA (Oxon)]

ELLERAY ANTHONY JOHN QC (1993)

St James's Chambers
68 Quay Street, Manchester M3 3EJ,
Telephone: 0161 834 7000
E-mail: 106241.2625@compuserve.com
12 New Square
Lincoln's Inn, London WC2A 3SW,
Telephone: 0171 419 1212
E-mail: 12newsquare@compuserve.com
Door Tenant
Park Lane Chambers
19 Westgate, Leeds LS1 2RU,
Telephone: 0113 228 5000
Call date: July 1977, Inner Temple
Assistant Recorder
Qualifications: [MA (Cantab)]

Fax: 0161 834 2341; DX: 14350 Manchester 1

Types of work: Bankruptcy; Chancery (general);
Chancery land law; Charities; Commercial
litigation; Commercial property; Company and
commercial; Copyright; Equity, wills and trusts;
Family provision; Insolvency; Intellectual
property; Landlord and tenant; Partnerships;
Professional negligence

Circuit: Northern

Awards and memberships: Inner Temple Major
Award; CBA; PNBA; NCBA

Other professional experience: Assistant
Recorder

Languages spoken: French

Walker v Turpin (1993) CA (payments in)
Jervis v Harris (1995) CA (landlord and tenant)
Salford Van Hire v Bocholt (1995) CA (landlord
and tenant)
Bass v Latham Crossley Davis (1996) CA
(partnership)
Shah v Bolton MBC (1996) CA (compulsory
purchase)

ELLIN MISS NINA CAROLINE

6 Pump Court
1st Floor, Temple, London EC4Y 7AR,
Telephone: 0171 797 8400
E-mail: sa_hockman_qc@link.org
6-8 Mill Street
Maidstone, Kent ME15 6XH,
Telephone: 01622 688094
Call date: Nov 1994, Inner Temple
Qualifications: [LLB (Lond), Maitrise, en Droit
Francais, (Paris I, Sorg)]

ELLINS DR JULIA ELISABETH

2 Hare Court
Ground Floor, Temple, London EC4Y 7BH,
Telephone: 0171 583 1770
E-mail: 2_Hare_Court@link.org
Call date: Oct 1994, Gray's Inn
Qualifications: [LLB (Lond),LLM, Dr.Jur
(Munich)]

ELLIOTT CHRISTOPHER DAVID

38 Young Street
Manchester M3 3FT,
Telephone: 0161 833 0489
E-mail: clerks@young-st-chambers.com
Call date: July 1974, Gray's Inn
Qualifications: [BA]

ELLIOTT COLIN DOUGLAS

Godolphin Chambers
50 Castle Street, Truro, Cornwall TR1 3AF,
Telephone: 01872 276312
Call date: July 1987, Gray's Inn
Qualifications: [BSc (Lond), Dip Law]

ELLIOTT ERIC ALAN

Broad Chare
33 Broad Chare, Newcastle Upon Tyne
NE1 3DQ, Telephone: 0191 232 0541
Call date: July 1974, Gray's Inn
Recorder
Qualifications: [LLB]

ELLIOTT JASON

Barnard's Inn Chambers
6th Floor Halton House, 20-23 Holborn,
London EC1N 2JD, Telephone: 0171 242 8508
E-mail: clerks@barnards-inn-chambers.co.uk
Call date: Oct 1993, Inner Temple
Qualifications: [BA]

ELLIOTT MISS MARGOT MARY

Regency Chambers
18 Cowgate, Peterborough PE1 1NA,
Telephone: 01733 315215
Regency Chambers
Sheraton House, Castle Park, Cambridge
CB3 0AX, Telephone: 01223 301517
Call date: Nov 1989, Gray's Inn
Qualifications: [LLB (Newc)]

ELLIOTT NICHOLAS BLETHYN QC (1995)

3 Verulam Buildings
London WC1R 5NT,
Telephone: 0171 831 8441
E-mail: clerks@3verulam.co.uk
Call date: July 1972, Gray's Inn
Qualifications: [LLB]

ELLIOTT RUPERT EDMUND IVO

1 Brick Court
1st Floor, Temple, London EC4Y 9BY,
Telephone: 0171 353 8845
E-mail: clerks@1brickcourt.co.uk
Call date: July 1988, Inner Temple
Qualifications: [MA (Cantab)]

ELLIOTT TIMOTHY STANLEY QC (1992)

Keating Chambers
10 Essex Street, Outer Temple, London
WC2R 3AA, Telephone: 0171 544 2600
Call date: July 1975, Middle Temple
Qualifications: [MA (Oxon)]

ELLIS MISS CAROL JACQUELINE QC (1980)

11 Old Square
Ground Floor, Lincoln's Inn, London
WC2A 3TS, Telephone: 0171 430 0341
E-mail: clerks@11oldsquare.co.uk
Call date: Nov 1951, Gray's Inn
Qualifications: [LLB]

ELLIS MISS CATHERINE ANNE

Derby Square Chambers
Merchants Court, Derby Square, Liverpool
L2 1TS, Telephone: 0151 709 4222
Call date: July 1987, Lincoln's Inn
Qualifications: [LLB (Lanc)]

ELLIS CHRISTOPHER ANDREW

Regency Chambers
18 Cowgate, Peterborough PE1 1NA,
Telephone: 01733 315215
Regency Chambers
Sheraton House, Castle Park, Cambridge
CB3 0AX, Telephone: 01223 301517
Call date: Oct 1991, Gray's Inn
Qualifications: [LLB (Hons, Cantab), LLM
(Hons, Cantab)]

ELLIS MISS DIANA

3 Gray's Inn Square
Ground Floor, London WC1R 5AH,
Telephone: 0171 520 5600
E-mail: gis3@btinternet.com
Call date: July 1978, Inner Temple
Assistant Recorder
Qualifications: [LLB (Lond)]

ELLIS MICHAEL TYRONE

22 Albion Place
Northampton NN1 1UD,
Telephone: 01604 36271
Call date: Oct 1993, Middle Temple
Qualifications: [LLB (Hons)(Bucks)]

D

ELLIS ROGER JOHN QC (1996)

13 King's Bench Walk
1st Floor, Temple, London EC4Y 7EN,
Telephone: 0171 353 7204
E-mail: clerks@13kbw.law.co.uk
King's Bench Chambers
32 Beaumont Street, Oxford OX1 2NP,
Telephone: 01865 311066
E-mail: clerks@kbc-oxford.law.co.uk
Call date: July 1962, Gray's Inn
Qualifications: [LLB (Lond)]

ELLIS MISS ROSALIND MORAG

2-3 Gray's Inn Square
Gray's Inn, London WC1R 5JH,
Telephone: 0171 242 4986
E-mail: chambers@2-3graysinnsquare.co.uk
Call date: July 1984, Gray's Inn
Qualifications: [BA (Cantab)]

ELLIS MISS SARAH LOUISE

1 Harcourt Bldgs
2nd Floor, Temple, London EC4Y 9DA,
Telephone: 0171 353 9421/9151
Call date: Nov 1989, Gray's Inn
Qualifications: [LLB [Wales]]

ELLIS WESLEY JONATHAN

7 Stone Bldgs
1st Floor, Lincoln's Inn, London WC2A 3SZ,
Telephone: 0171 242 0961
Call date: Feb 1995, Gray's Inn
Qualifications: [MA (Cantab)]

ELLIS-JONES STEPHEN

5 Pump Court
Ground Floor, Temple, London EC4Y 7AP,
Telephone: 0171 353 2532
E-mail: fivepump@netcomuk.co.uk
Call date: Nov 1992, Middle Temple
Qualifications: [B.Eng (L'pool)]

ELLISON MARK CHRISTOPHER

Hollis Whiteman Chambers
3rd/4th Floor Queen Elizabeth Bldg, Temple,
London EC4Y 9BS, Telephone: 0171 583 5766
E-mail: hollis.whiteman@btinternet.com
Call date: Nov 1979, Gray's Inn
Qualifications: [LLB (Wales)]

ELSEY ROGER WILLIAM

Broad Chare
33 Broad Chare, Newcastle Upon Tyne
NE1 3DQ, Telephone: 0191 232 0541
Call date: May 1977, Gray's Inn
Qualifications: [LLB]

ELSOM MICHAEL ROBERT

5 Fountain Court
Steelhouse Lane, Birmingham B4 6DR,
Telephone: 0121 606 0500
Call date: July 1972, Inner Temple
Assistant Recorder
Qualifications: [BA (Dunelm)]

ELVIDGE JOHN ALLAN

1 Mitre Ct Bldgs
Ground Floor, Temple, London EC4Y 7BS,
Telephone: 0171 797 7070
Call date: Nov 1968, Lincoln's Inn
Recorder
Qualifications: [MA, LLB (Cantab)]

ELVIDGE JOHN COWIE

York Chambers
14 Toft Green, York YO1 1JT,
Telephone: 01904 620048
E-mail: yorkchambers.co.uk
Call date: Nov 1988, Gray's Inn
Qualifications: [LLB (Newc)]

ELVIN DAVID JOHN

4 Breams Buildings
London EC4A 1AQ,
Telephone: 0171 353 5835/430 1221
Call date: Nov 1983, Middle Temple
Qualifications: [BA (Oxon), BCL (Oxon)]

ELWICK BRYAN MARTIN

1 High Pavement
Nottingham NG1 1HF,
Telephone: 0115 9418218
Call date: July 1981, Middle Temple
Qualifications: [LLB (Nott'm)]

EMANUEL MARK PERING WOLFF

14 Gray's Inn Square
Gray's Inn, London WC1R 5JP,
Telephone: 0171 242 0858
E-mail: 100712.2134@compuserve.com
Call date: Nov 1985, Inner Temple
Qualifications: [BA (Hons)]

EMERSON PAUL MICHAEL

Lamb Chambers
Lamb Building, Temple, London EC4Y 7AS,
Telephone: 0171 797 8300
E-mail: lambchambers@link.org
Call date: July 1984, Middle Temple
Qualifications: [LLB]

EMERSON WILLIAM BRADLEY

Chichester Chambers
12 North Pallant, Chichester, West Sussex
PO19 1TQ, Telephone: 01243 784538
Call date: Nov 1992, Middle Temple
Qualifications: [LLB (Hons)]

EMIR MISS ASTRA

3 Temple Gardens
Lower Ground Floor, Temple, London
EC4Y 9AU, Telephone: 0171 353 3102/5/9297
Call date: Oct 1992, Gray's Inn
Qualifications: [BA (Oxon)]

EMM ROGER GARETH

Chancery House Chambers
7 Lisbon Square, Leeds LS1 4LY,
Telephone: 0113 244 6691
E-mail: Chanceryhouse@btinternet.com
Call date: July 1977, Middle Temple
Qualifications: [BA, MPhil]

EMMERSON (MICHAEL) BENEDICT

Doughty Street Chambers
11 Doughty Street, London WC1N 2PG,
Telephone: 0171 404 1313
E-mail: doughty_street@compuserve.com
Call date: Nov 1986, Middle Temple
Qualifications: [LLB (Bristol)]

ENGEL ANTHONY JOHN

3 Fountain Court
Steelhouse Lane, Birmingham B4 6DR,
Telephone: 0121 236 5854
Call date: Nov 1965, Inner Temple
Qualifications: [MA (Cantab)]

ENGELMAN PHILIP

Cloisters
1st Floor, Temple, London EC4Y 7AA,
Telephone: 0171 827 4000
E-mail: clerks@cloisters.com
Call date: July 1979, Gray's Inn
Qualifications: [LLB (Lond)]

ENGLAND GEORGE

Bank House Chambers
Old Bank House, Hartshead, Sheffield S1 2EL,
Telephone: 0114 2751223
Call date: Feb 1972, Middle Temple
Qualifications: [LLB]

ENGLAND WILLIAM EDWARD CHARLES

1 Crown Office Row
2nd Floor, Temple, London EC4Y 7HH,
Telephone: 0171 797 7111
Call date: Nov 1991, Inner Temple
Qualifications: [LLB, LLM (Lond)]

ENGLEHART ROBERT MICHAEL QC (1986)

2 Hare Court
Ground Floor, Temple, London EC4Y 7BH,
Telephone: 0171 583 1770
E-mail: 2_Hare_Court@link.org
Call date: Nov 1969, Middle Temple
Recorder
Qualifications: [MA (Oxon),LLM (Harv)]

ENGLISH MISS CAROLINE FRANCES

1 Gray's Inn Square
Ground Floor, London WC1R 5AA,
Telephone: 0171 405 8946/7/8
Call date: Nov 1989, Inner Temple
Qualifications: [LLB]

ENGLISH RICHARD WARREN

All Saints Chambers
9/11 Broad Street, Bristol BS1 2HP,
Telephone: 0117 921 1966
Call date: Nov 1995, Middle Temple
Qualifications: [LLB (Hons)(Wales)]

ENOCH DAFYDD HUW

Bridewell Chambers
2 Bridewell Place, London EC4V 6AP,
Telephone: 0171 797 8800
E-mail: clerks@bridewell.law.co.uk
Call date: Nov 1985, Gray's Inn
Qualifications: [BA Buckingham]

ENRIGHT SEAN

9-12 Bell Yard
London WC2A 2LF,
Telephone: 0171 400 1800
Call date: July 1982, Middle Temple
Qualifications: [LL.B(Nottingham)]

EPSTEIN MICHAEL PAUL

3 Hare Court
1st Floor, Temple, London EC4Y 7BJ,
Telephone: 0171 353 7561
Call date: Nov 1992, Middle Temple
Qualifications: [LLB (Hons, Manch)]

EPSTEIN PAUL JEREMY

Cloisters
1st Floor, Temple, London EC4Y 7AA,
Telephone: 0171 827 4000
E-mail: clerks@cloisters.com
Call date: Nov 1988, Middle Temple
Qualifications: [BA (Oxon)]

ERNSTZEN OLAV GUSTAV

Eurolawyer Chambers
PO Box 3621, London N7 0BQ,
Telephone: 0171 607 0075
E-mail: E-mail on Link to: OG Ernstzen
Verulam Chambers
Peer House 8-14 Verulam Street, Gray's Inn,
London WC1X 8LZ,
Telephone: 0171 813 2400
Door Tenant
Call date: July 1981, Middle Temple

ERWOOD MISS HEATHER MARY ELLISTON

3 Dr Johnson's Bldgs
Ground Floor, Temple, London EC4Y 7BA,
Telephone: 0171 353 4854
Call date: Oct 1993, Middle Temple
Qualifications: [LLB (Hons), LLM (Lond)]

ESHAGHIAN MISS YASMIN

12 Old Square
1st Floor, Lincoln's Inn, London WC2A 3TX,
Telephone: 0171 404 0875
Call date: Feb 1995, Lincoln's Inn
Qualifications: [BA (Hons)(Lond)]

ESPLEY ANDREW ROBERT

Mitre Court Chambers
3rd Floor, Temple, London EC4Y 7BP,
Telephone: 0171 353 9394
Call date: Nov 1993, Gray's Inn
Qualifications: [LLB]

ESPLEY MISS SUSAN

Fenners Chambers
3 Madingley Road, Cambridge CB3 OEE,
Telephone: 01223 368761
Fenners Chambers
8-12 Priestgate, Peterborough PE1 1JA,
Telephone: 01733 62030
Call date: July 1976, Gray's Inn
Qualifications: [LLB (Leeds)]

ESPRIT BENOIT

23 Harries Road
Hayes, Middlesex UB4 9DD,
Telephone: 0181 841 8236
Call date: Nov 1982, Inner Temple
Qualifications: [BA, BSc (Brunel), MA, LLM
(London), ADV.Dip.EDU (London)]

ESPRIT SHAUN ANDREW

1 King's Bench Walk
2nd Floor, Temple, London EC4Y 7DB,
Telephone: 0171 936 1500
E-mail: ddear@1kbw.co.uk
Call date: Nov 1996, Lincoln's Inn
Qualifications: [BA (Hons), CPE]

ETHERINGTON DAVID CHARLES LYNCH

18 Red Lion Court
(Off Fleet Street), London EC4A 3EB,
Telephone: 0171 520 6000
Thornwood House
102 New London Road, Chelmsford, Essex
CM2 0RG, Telephone: 01245 280880
Call date: Nov 1979, Middle Temple
Assistant Recorder
Qualifications: [BA, Dip Soc & Pub, Admin
(Oxon)]

ETHERTON MISS GILLIAN

2 Paper Buildings
Basement, Temple, London EC4Y 7ET,
Telephone: 0171 353 0933
Call date: July 1988, Middle Temple
Qualifications: [LLB (Hons)]

ETHERTON TERENCE MICHAEL ELKAN BARNET QC (1990)

Wilberforce Chambers
8 New Square, Lincoln's Inn, London
WC2A 3QP, Telephone: 0171 306 0102
E-mail: chambers@wilberforce.co.uk
Call date: July 1974, Gray's Inn
Qualifications: [MA, LLM (Cantab), FCIArb]

ETIENNE CLANCY ANTHONY

Chancery Chambers
1st Floor Offices 70/72 Chancery Lane,
London WC2A 1AB,
Telephone: 0171 405 6879/6870
Call date: Oct 1995, Middle Temple
Qualifications: [MA (Lond)]

EVANS ALAN

40 King Street
Manchester M2 6BA,
Telephone: 0161 832 9082
E-mail: Kingst40@aol.com
Call date: July 1978, Lincoln's Inn
Qualifications: [MA, LLB (Cantab)]

EVANS ALUN HOWARD

2 King's Bench Walk
1st Floor, Temple, London EC4Y 7DE,
Telephone: 0171 353 9276
Westgate Chambers
144 High Street, Lewes, East Sussex BN7 1XT,
Telephone: 01273 480510
Call date: Nov 1971, Gray's Inn
Qualifications: [BSc (Lond)]

EVANS ANDREW SUTHERLAND

10 King's Bench Walk
Ground Floor, Temple, London EC4Y 7EB,
Telephone: 0171 353 7742
E-mail: 10kbw@lineone.net
Call date: July 1984, Gray's Inn
Qualifications: [LLB (Manchester)]

EVANS MRS ANN

6 Gray's Inn Square
Ground Floor, Gray's Inn, London WC1R 5AZ,
Telephone: 0171 242 1052
Call date: July 1983, Gray's Inn

EVANS BARNABY ST JOHN

4 King's Bench Walk
2nd Floor, Temple, London EC4Y 7DL,
Telephone: 0171 353 3581
Call date: July 1978, Inner Temple
Qualifications: [MA (Cantab)]

EVANS MISS CAROLINE MAY

12 King's Bench Walk
Temple, London EC4Y 7EL,
Telephone: 0171 583 0811
E-mail: chambers@12kbw.co.uk
Call date: Oct 1991, Inner Temple
Qualifications: [MA (Cantab)]

EVANS MS CATRIN MIRANDA

1 Brick Court
1st Floor, Temple, London EC4Y 9BY,
Telephone: 0171 353 8845
E-mail: clerks@1brickcourt.co.uk
Call date: Nov 1994, Inner Temple
Qualifications: [BA (Essex), CPE]

D

D

EVANS CHARLES HENRY FREDERICK

Goldsmith Chambers
Ground Floor Goldsmith Building, Temple,
London EC4Y 7BL,
Telephone: 0171 353 6802/3/4/5
E-mail: celiamonksfield@btinternet.com
Call date: Nov 1988, Middle Temple
Qualifications: [LLB]

EVANS MISS CLAIRE LOUISE

Peel Court Chambers
45 Hardman Street, Manchester M3 3HA,
Telephone: 0161 832 3791
Call date: Oct 1994, Middle Temple
Qualifications: [BSc (Hons)(Manc), CPE
(Manc)]

EVANS MISS CLARE MARSHALL

1 Gray's Inn Square
1st Floor, London WC1R 5AG,
Telephone: 0171 405 3000
E-mail: clerks@onegrays.demon.co.uk
Call date: Oct 1995, Inner Temple
Qualifications: [BA (Lond), CPE]

EVANS DAVID ANTHONY QC (1983)

9-12 Bell Yard
London WC2A 2LF,
Telephone: 0171 400 1800
Iscoed Chambers
86 St Helen's Road, Swansea SA1 4BQ,
Telephone: 01792 652988/9/330
Call date: July 1965, Gray's Inn
Recorder
Qualifications: [BA (Cantab)]

EVANS DAVID HOWARD QC (1991)

Hollis Whiteman Chambers
3rd/4th Floor Queen Elizabeth Bldg, Temple,
London EC4Y 9BS, Telephone: 0171 583 5766
E-mail: hollis.whiteman@btinternet.com
Call date: Nov 1972, Middle Temple
Recorder
Qualifications: [MSc (Lond), BA (Oxon)]

EVANS DAVID HUW

32 Park Place
Cardiff CF1 3BA, Telephone: 01222 397364
Call date: July 1985, Lincoln's Inn
Qualifications: [BA (Hons)]

EVANS DAVID LEWIS

1 Crown Office Row
Ground Floor, Temple, London EC4Y 7HH,
Telephone: 0171 797 7500
Call date: July 1988, Middle Temple
Qualifications: [MA (Hons)(Cantab)]

EVANS MISS DELYTH MARY

2 Mitre Ct Bldgs
1st Floor, Temple, London EC4Y 7BX,
Telephone: 0171 353 1353
Call date: Oct 1991, Middle Temple
Qualifications: [LLB (Hons, Lond)]

EVANS DYLAN

3 Temple Gardens
3rd Floor, Temple, London EC4Y 9AU,
Telephone: 0171 583 0010
Call date: Apr 1989, Gray's Inn
Qualifications: [LLB (E Anglia), BA
(Hons)(Lond)]

EVANS MISS ELWEN MAIR

Iscoed Chambers
86 St Helen's Road, Swansea SA1 4BQ,
Telephone: 01792 652988/9/330
Call date: July 1980, Gray's Inn
Qualifications: [MA (Cantab)]

EVANS FRANCIS WALTON HERMIT QC (1994)

3 Raymond Buildings
Gray's Inn, London WC1R 5BH,
Telephone: 0171 831 3833
E-mail: chambers@threeraymond.demon.co.uk
Call date: July 1977, Middle Temple
Recorder
Qualifications: [BA]

EVANS FRANKLIN ST CLAIR MELVILLE

2 Field Court
Gray's Inn, London WC1R 5BB,
Telephone: 0171 405 6114
E-mail: fieldct2@netcomuk.co.uk.
Call date: Nov 1981, Gray's Inn
Qualifications: [BA Hons (Lancaster),]

EVANS GARETH ROBERT WILLIAM QC (1994)

5 Fountain Court
Steelhouse Lane, Birmingham B4 6DR,
Telephone: 0121 606 0500
Call date: Nov 1973, Gray's Inn
Recorder
Qualifications: [LLB (Lond)]

EVANS HUGH LEWIS

2 Crown Office Row
2nd Floor, Temple, London EC4Y 7HJ,
Telephone: 0171 797 8000
Call date: Nov 1987, Middle Temple
Qualifications: [MA (Cantab), BCL (Oxon)]

EVANS JAMES FREDERICK MEURIG

3 Verulam Buildings
London WC1R 5NT,
Telephone: 0171 831 8441
E-mail: clerks@3verulam.co.uk
Call date: Nov 1991, Gray's Inn
Qualifications: [BA (Cantab), LLM (Lond)]

EVANS MISS JANE LOIS

32 Park Place
Cardiff CF1 3BA, Telephone: 01222 397364
Call date: July 1971, Gray's Inn

EVANS MS JILL ANNALIESE

Doughty Street Chambers
11 Doughty Street, London WC1N 2PG,
Telephone: 0171 404 1313
E-mail: doughty_street@compuserve.com
Call date: July 1986, Gray's Inn
Qualifications: [BA (Hons) (Kent)]

EVANS JOHN

New Court Chambers
3 Broad Chare, Newcastle Upon Tyne
NE1 3DQ, Telephone: 0191 232 1980
Call date: Nov 1973, Gray's Inn
Assistant Recorder
Qualifications: [BA]

EVANS JOHN WAINWRIGHT

1 Fountain Court
Steelhouse Lane, Birmingham B4 6DR,
Telephone: 0121 236 5721
Call date: July 1983, Inner Temple
Qualifications: [LLB (Leic)]

EVANS JONATHAN EDWARD

Wilberforce Chambers
8 New Square, Lincoln's Inn, London
WC2A 3QP, Telephone: 0171 306 0102
E-mail: chambers@wilberforce.co.uk
Call date: Nov 1994, Middle Temple
Qualifications: [BA (Hons)]

EVANS MISS JUDI

St John's Chambers
Small Street, Bristol BS1 1DW,
Telephone: 0117 9213456/298514
E-mail: clerks@stjohns.uk.com
Call date: Nov 1996, Middle Temple
Qualifications: [LLB (Hons)(Bucks), M.Phil
(Cantab)]

EVANS KEITH ERIC

4 King's Bench Walk
Ground/First Floor, Temple, London
EC4Y 7DL, Telephone: 0171 822 8822
E-mail: 4kbw@barristersatlaw.com
Call date: Nov 1962, Middle Temple
Qualifications: [MA (Cantab)]

EVANS LEE JOHN

Farrar's Building
Temple, London EC4Y 7BD,
Telephone: 0171 583 9241
E-mail: chambers@farrarsbuilding.co.uk
Call date: Nov 1996, Gray's Inn
Qualifications: [BA (Cantab)]

EVANS MISS LISA CLAIRE

7 Fountain Court
Steelhouse Lane, Birmingham B4 6DR,
Telephone: 0121 236 8531
Call date: Oct 1991, Inner Temple
Qualifications: [LLB (Hons)]

EVANS MARK QC (1995)

All Saints Chambers
9/11 Broad Street, Bristol BS1 2HP,
Telephone: 0117 921 1966
Call date: Nov 1971, Gray's Inn
Recorder
Qualifications: [LLB]

EVANS MARTIN ALAN LANGHAM

5 Paper Bldgs
1st Floor, Temple, London EC4Y 7HB,
Telephone: 0171 583 6117
E-mail: clerks@5-paperbuildings.law.co.uk
Call date: Nov 1989, Middle Temple
Qualifications: [BA Hons (Sussex), Dip Law]

EVANS MICHAEL RITHO

1 High Pavement
Nottingham NG1 1HF,
Telephone: 0115 9418218
Call date: Nov 1988, Middle Temple
Qualifications: [LLB]

EVANS PAUL TIMOTHY

Exchange Chambers
Pearl Assurance House Derby Square,
Liverpool L2 9XX, Telephone: 0151 236 7747/
0458
E-mail: exchangechambers@btinternet.com
Call date: Nov 1992, Gray's Inn
Qualifications: [MA (Oxon), LLM (Lond), LLM
(East Anglia)]

EVANS PHILIP

6 Gray's Inn Square
Ground Floor, Gray's Inn, London WC1R 5AZ,
Telephone: 0171 242 1052
Call date: Oct 1995, Lincoln's Inn
Qualifications: [LLB (Hons)(Wales), MA
(Soton)]

EVANS RICHARD GARETH

5 Paper Bldgs
Ground Floor, Temple, London EC4Y 7HB,
Telephone: 0171 583 9275/583 4555
E-mail: 5paper@link.org
Call date: Nov 1993, Lincoln's Inn
Qualifications: [LLB (Hons, Leeds)]

EVANS ROBERT JONATHAN

Keating Chambers
10 Essex Street, Outer Temple, London
WC2R 3AA, Telephone: 0171 544 2600
Call date: July 1989, Gray's Inn
Qualifications: [MA [Cantab], LLB [Lond],
C.Eng, M.I.C.E, FCIArb, MHKIE]

EVANS ROGER KENNETH

2 Harcourt Bldgs
1st Floor, Temple, London EC4Y 9DB,
Telephone: 0171 353 6961/7
Harcourt Chambers
Churchill House 3 St Aldate's Courtyard, St
Aldate's, Oxford OX1 1BN,
Telephone: 01865 791559
Call date: Nov 1970, Middle Temple
Qualifications: [MA (Cantab)]

EVANS STEPHEN JAMES

8 King's Bench Walk
2nd Floor, Temple, London EC4Y 7DU,
Telephone: 0171 797 8888
8 King's Bench Walk North
1 Park Square East, Leeds LS1 2NE,
Telephone: 0113 2439797
Call date: Oct 1992, Middle Temple
Qualifications: [BA (Hons)]

EVANS MISS SUSAN

Harrow on the Hill Chambers
60 High Street, Harrow on the Hill, Middlesex
HA1 3LL, Telephone: 0181 423 7444
Windsor Barristers' Chambers
Windsor, Telephone: 01753 648899
Call date: Nov 1992, Inner Temple
Qualifications: [LLB (Hull)]

EVANS MISS SUSAN LOUISE CARR

St John's Chambers
Small Street, Bristol BS1 1DW,
Telephone: 0117 9213456/298514
E-mail: clerks@stjohns.uk.com
Call date: Nov 1989, Gray's Inn
Qualifications: [LLB]

EVANS MISS SUZANNE MARIE

Oriel Chambers
14 Water Street, Liverpool L2 8TD,
Telephone: 0151 236 7191
E-mail: oriel_chambers@link.org
Call date: Nov 1985, Middle Temple
Qualifications: [BA (Oxon)]

EVANS THOMAS GARETH

Rougemont Chambers
15 Barnfield Road, Exeter EX1 1RR,
Telephone: 01392 410471
E-mail: rougemont.chambers@eclipse.co.uk
Call date: Oct 1996, Middle Temple
Qualifications: [LLB (Hons)(Exon)]

EVANS TIMOTHY AYLMER

Assize Court Chambers
14 Small Street, Bristol BS1 1DE,
Telephone: 0117 9264587
Call date: July 1982, Gray's Inn
Qualifications: [LLB (Lond)]

EVANS TIMOTHY JOHN

33 Park Place
Cardiff CF1 3BA, Telephone: 01222 233313
Call date: July 1984, Gray's Inn
Qualifications: [LLB (Nottm)]

EVANS TIMOTHY WENTWORTH EYRE

13 Old Square
Ground Floor, Lincoln's Inn, London
WC2A 3UA, Telephone: 0171 404 4800
Call date: July 1979, Lincoln's Inn
Qualifications: [BA (Oxon)]

EVANS WILLIAM JAMES

4 Brick Court
Ground Floor, Temple, London EC4Y 9AD,
Telephone: 0171 797 7766
E-mail: chambers@4brick.co.uk
Call date: Nov 1988, Middle Temple
Qualifications: [LLB (L'pool)]

EVANS-GORDON MRS JANE-ANNE MARY

12 New Square
Ground Floor, Lincoln's Inn, London
WC2A 3SW, Telephone: 0171 419 1212
E-mail: 12newsquare@compuserve.com
Call date: Nov 1992, Inner Temple
Qualifications: [LLB (Reading)]

EVANS-TOVEY JASON ROBERT

2 Crown Office Row
Ground Floor, Temple, London EC4Y 7HJ,
Telephone: 0171 797 8100
E-mail: mail@2cor.co.uk, or to individual
barristers at: [barrister's surname]@2cor.co.uk
Call date: Oct 1990, Gray's Inn
Qualifications: [MA (Cantab), LLM]

EVERALL MARK ANDREW QC (1994)

1 Mitre Ct Bldgs
Ground Floor, Temple, London EC4Y 7BS,
Telephone: 0171 797 7070
Call date: Nov 1975, Inner Temple
Recorder
Qualifications: [MA (Oxon)]

EVERARD WILLIAM FIELDING

King Charles House
Standard Hill, Nottingham NG1 6FX,
Telephone: 0115 9418851
E-mail: clerks@kch.co.uk
Call date: Nov 1973, Middle Temple
Assistant Recorder
Qualifications: [LLB (Belfast)]

EVERED MRS JACLINE LANDIS

Inns of Court School of Law
39 Eagle Street, London WC1R 4AJ,
Telephone: 0171 404 5787 x422
Call date: Oct 1991, Middle Temple
Qualifications: [BA, Juris Doctorate]

EVEREST ROGER NORMAN JOSEPH

Twin Firs
P.O.Box 32, Talygarn, Pontyclun, South Wales
CF72 9BY, Telephone: 01443 229850
Call date: Nov 1968, Gray's Inn
Qualifications: [BA]

EVERETT STEVEN GEORGE

Sedan House
Stanley Place, Chester CH1 2LU,
Telephone: 01244 320480/348282
Call date: Apr 1989, Gray's Inn
Qualifications: [BA]

EVISON JOHN

5 Pump Court
Ground Floor, Temple, London EC4Y 7AP,
Telephone: 0171 353 2532
E-mail: fivepump@netcomuk.co.uk
Call date: July 1974, Lincoln's Inn
Qualifications: [LLB (Lond)]

EWART DAVID SCOTT

Pump Court Tax Chambers
16 Bedford Row, London WC1R 4EB,
Telephone: 0171 414 8080
Call date: Nov 1987, Gray's Inn
Qualifications: [BA (Oxon)]

EWINS MISS CATHERINE JANE

4 Paper Bldgs
Ground Floor, Temple, London EC4Y 7EX,
Telephone: 0171 353 3366/583 7155
E-mail: clerks@4paperbuildings.com
Call date: Nov 1995, Gray's Inn
Qualifications: [BA, Licence Speciale En, Droit
European, U.L.B. (Brussels)]

EWINS DAVID JAMES

Queen Elizabeth Bldg
2nd Floor, Temple, London EC4Y 9BS,
Telephone: 0171 797 7837
Call date: Nov 1996, Middle Temple
Qualifications: [BA (Hons)]

EXALL GORDON DAVID

10 Park Square
Leeds LS1 2LH, Telephone: 0113 2455438
E-mail: chambers@bandit.legend.co.uk
Call date: Apr 1991, Lincoln's Inn
Qualifications: [BA (Warwick)]

EYERS ANTHONY

24a St John Street
Manchester M3 4DF,
Telephone: 0161 833 9628
Call date: Nov 1994, Inner Temple
Qualifications: [BA (Oxon), CPE (Lond)]

EYRE GILES STEPHEN

2 Gray's Inn Square Chambers
2nd Floor, Gray's Inn, London WC1R 5AA,
Telephone: 0171 242 0328/071 405 1317
E-mail: clerks@2gis.co.uk
Call date: July 1974, Gray's Inn
Qualifications: [LLB]

EYRE SIR GRAHAM NEWMAN QC (1970)

2-3 Gray's Inn Square
Gray's Inn, London WC1R 5JH,
Telephone: 0171 242 4986
E-mail: chambers@2-3graysinnsquare.co.uk
Call date: Nov 1954, Middle Temple
Recorder
Qualifications: [MA, LLB (Cantab)]

EYRE STEPHEN JOHN ARTHUR

1 Fountain Court
Steelhouse Lane, Birmingham B4 6DR,
Telephone: 0121 236 5721
Call date: July 1981, Inner Temple
Qualifications: [MA, BCL (Oxon)]

EZECHIE NICHOLAS DIDEKI ASIAELUE

Odogor Chambers
14 Cairns Road, Battersea, London SW11 1ES
Call date: July 1967, Gray's Inn
Qualifications: [LLB (Lond)]

EZECHIE MISS NICHOLINA NKEMDILIM

5 Marney Road
Battersea, London SW11 1ES,
Telephone: 0171 978 4492
Call date: July 1990, Gray's Inn
Qualifications: [LLB]

FABER TREVOR MARTYN

3 Fountain Court
Steelhouse Lane, Birmingham B4 6DR,
Telephone: 0121 236 5854
Call date: July 1970, Gray's Inn
Recorder
Qualifications: [MA (Oxon)]

FADIPE GABRIEL CHARLES

Wilberforce Chambers
8 New Square, Lincoln's Inn, London
WC2A 3QP, Telephone: 0171 306 0102
E-mail: chambers@wilberforce.co.uk
Call date: Nov 1991, Inner Temple
Qualifications: [BA (Kent), M.EN.D.
(Bordeaux)]

FAGAN MISS CATHERINE JOSEPHINE

Baker Street Chambers
9 Baker Street, Middlesbrough TS1 2LF,
Telephone: 01642 873873
Call date: Oct 1993, Gray's Inn
Qualifications: [BA (Hons)]

FAIRBANK NICHOLAS JAMES

Becket Chambers
17 New Dover Road, Canterbury, Kent
CT1 3AS, Telephone: 01227 786331
Call date: Nov 1996, Lincoln's Inn
Qualifications: [MA (Hons)(Cantab)]

FAIRBURN GEORGE EDWARD HENRY

Claremont Chambers
26 Waterloo Road, Wolverhampton WV1 4BL,
Telephone: 01902 426222
Call date: Oct 1995, Lincoln's Inn
Qualifications: [BSc (Hons)]

FAIRHEAD ALLEN JOHN HUBERT

5 Paper Bldgs
Lower Ground Floor, Temple, London
EC4Y 7HB, Telephone: 0171 353 5638
E-mail: 107722,633@compuserve.com
Call date: Nov 1978, Middle Temple
Qualifications: [BA (Dunelm)]

FALK CHARLES MORTON JAMES

Staple Inn Chambers
1st Floor 9 Staple Inn, Holborn, London
WC1V 7QH, Telephone: 0171 242 5240
E-mail: clerks@staple-inn.org
Call date: Oct 1994, Middle Temple
Qualifications: [BA (Hons)(Keele), CPE
(Middx)]

FALK MISS JOSEPHINE RUTH ANN

12 Old Square
1st Floor, Lincoln's Inn, London WC2A 3TX,
Telephone: 0171 404 0875
Call date: Nov 1994, Lincoln's Inn
Qualifications: [MA (Cantab), Dip in Law]

FALKENSTEIN JOHN ROY

Chambers of Richard Bloomfield
2 Lansdowne Place, Gosforth, Newcastle
Upon Tyne NE3 1HR,
Telephone: 0191 285 4664
Call date: Oct 1996, Lincoln's Inn
Qualifications: [BA (Hons)]

FALKOWSKI DAMIAN

Littman Chambers
12 Gray's Inn Square, London WC1R 5JP,
Telephone: 0171 404 4866
E-mail: admin@littmanchambers.com
Call date: Oct 1994, Gray's Inn
Qualifications: [ARCM, B.Mus, M.Mus, LLDip]

FALLOWS MISS MARY PAULA

Cobden House Chambers
19 Quay Street, Manchester M3 3HN,
Telephone: 0161 833 6000
E-mail: clerks@cobden.co.uk
Call date: July 1981, Lincoln's Inn
Qualifications: [BA (Hons)]

FAMA MRS GUDRUN HILDEGARD

Phoenix Chambers
First Floor Gray's Inn Chambers, Gray's Inn,
London WC1R 5JA, Telephone: 0171 404 7888
Library Chambers
Gray's Inn Chambers, Gray's Inn, London
WC1R 5JA, Telephone: 0171 404 6500
Call date: Oct 1991, Gray's Inn
Qualifications: [BA, MA, LLB]

D

FANCOURT TIMOTHY MILES

Falcon Chambers
Falcon Court, London EC4Y 1AA,
Telephone: 0171 353 2484/7
Call date: Nov 1987, Lincoln's Inn
Qualifications: [MA (Cantab)]

FANE MISS ANGELA ELIZABETH

Goldsmith Building
1st Floor, Temple, London EC4Y 7BL,
Telephone: 0171 353 7881
E-mail: clerks@goldsmith-building.law.co.uk
Call date: Nov 1992, Middle Temple
Qualifications: [BA]

FANNING MISS CLAIRE ELIZABETH

95A Chancery Lane
London WC2A 1DT,
Telephone: 0171 405 3101
Call date: Oct 1993, Lincoln's Inn
Qualifications: [BA (Hons)(Lond), CPE (Lond)]

FARBER JAMES HENRY MARTIN

Lamb Chambers
Lamb Building, Temple, London EC4Y 7AS,
Telephone: 0171 797 8300
E-mail: lambchambers@link.org
Call date: July 1976, Gray's Inn

FARBEY MISS JUDITH SARAH

3 Paper Bldgs
2nd Floor, Temple, London EC4Y 7EU,
Telephone: 0171 353 6208
Call date: Oct 1992, Middle Temple
Qualifications: [BA (Hons)(Oxon), Dip Law
(City)]

FARLEY ROGER BOYD QC (1993)

40 King Street
Manchester M2 6BA,
Telephone: 0161 832 9082
E-mail: Kingst40@aol.com
*Call date: May 1974, Middle Temple
Recorder*
Qualifications: [LLB (L'pool)]

FARMER GABRIEL JOHN-HENRY

South Western Chambers
Melville House 12 Middle Street, Taunton,
Somerset TA1 1SH, Telephone: 01823 331919
Call date: Nov 1994, Gray's Inn
Qualifications: [BSc (Reading)]

FARMER JOHN MICHAEL HEREWARD

1 Paper Bldgs
1st Floor, Temple, London EC4Y 7EP,
Telephone: 0171 353 3728/4953
Octagon House
19 Colegate, Norwich NR3 1AT,
Telephone: 01603 623186
E-mail: octagon@netmatters.co.uk
*Door Tenant
Call date: Nov 1970, Gray's Inn*
Qualifications: [MA (Cantab)]

FARMER MATTHEW JONATHAN

2 Harcourt Bldgs
1st Floor, Temple, London EC4Y 9DB,
Telephone: 0171 353 2112/2817
Call date: July 1987, Inner Temple
Qualifications: [BA (Lond), Dip Law]

FARMER PRYCE MICHAEL QC (1995)

Goldsmith Building
1st Floor, Temple, London EC4Y 7BL,
Telephone: 0171 353 7881
E-mail: clerks@goldsmith-building.law.co.uk
Sedan House
Stanley Place, Chester CH1 2LU,
Telephone: 01244 320480/348282
1 Dr Johnson's Bldgs
Ground Floor, Temple, London EC4Y 7AX,
Telephone: 0171 353 9328
*Call date: July 1972, Gray's Inn
Recorder*
Qualifications: [BA (Lond)]

FARMER MS SARAH LOUISE

Thomas More Chambers
52 Carey Street, Lincoln's Inn, London
WC2A 2JB, Telephone: 0171 404 7000
Call date: Nov 1991, Lincoln's Inn
Qualifications: [BA (Hons) (Oxon)]

FARMERY PETER WILLIAM

One Raymond Buildings
Gray's Inn, London WC1R 5BH,
Telephone: 0171 430 1234
E-mail: chambers@ipbar1rb.com;
clerks@ipbar1rb.com
Call date: Nov 1979, Inner Temple
Qualifications: [BA (Dunelm), LLM (Lond),
ACIArb]

FARNON MS PATRICIA RONA GABRIELLE

1 Pump Court
Lower Ground Floor, Temple, London
EC4Y 7AB, Telephone: 0171 583 2012/
353 4341
E-mail: (name) @1pumpcourt.co.uk
Call date: Nov 1986, Inner Temple
Qualifications: [LLB (Lond)]

FARQUHAR STUART ALASTAIR

St Mary's Chambers
50 High Pavement, Lace Market, Nottingham
NG1 1HW, Telephone: 0115 9503503
E-mail: clerks@smc.law.co.uk
Call date: July 1985, Inner Temple
Qualifications: [LLB (Manchester)]

FARQUHARSON MISS JANE CAROLINE

1 Essex Court
1st Floor, Temple, London EC4Y 9AR,
Telephone: 0171 936 3030
E-mail: one.essex_court@virgin.net
Call date: Oct 1993, Inner Temple
Qualifications: [LLB]

FARQUHARSON JONATHAN

Colleton Chambers
Colleton Crescent, Exeter, Devon EX2 4DG,
Telephone: 01392 74898/9
Call date: July 1988, Inner Temple
Qualifications: [BA (Hons) (Dunelm)]

FARR MISS SUSANNAH MARGARET

5 Paper Bldgs
Lower Ground Floor, Temple, London
EC4Y 7HB, Telephone: 0171 353 5638
E-mail: 107722,633@compuserve.com
Call date: July 1990, Inner Temple
Qualifications: [BA (E Anglia), Dip Law]

FARRALL MRS PATRICIA HELEN

Holborn Chambers
6 Gate Street, Lincoln's Inn Fields, London
WC2A 3HP, Telephone: 0171 242 6060
Call date: July 1976, Inner Temple

FARRELL DAVID ANTHONY

36 Bedford Row
London WC1R 4JH,
Telephone: 0171 421 8000
E-mail: 36bedfordrow@link.org
Call date: July 1978, Inner Temple
Assistant Recorder
Qualifications: [LLB (Manch)]

FARRELL EDMUND GILBERT

36 Bedford Row
London WC1R 4JH,
Telephone: 0171 421 8000
E-mail: 36bedfordrow@link.org
Call date: July 1981, Gray's Inn
Qualifications: [LLM (Cantab), LLB Hons]

FARRELL SIMON HENRY

2 Garden Court
1st Floor, Middle Temple, London EC4Y 9BL,
Telephone: 0171 353 1633
E-mail: barristers@2gardenct.law.co.uk
Call date: Nov 1983, Lincoln's Inn
Qualifications: [MA(Cantab) Dip Law C]

FARRELLY KEVIN JAMES

10 Old Square
Ground Floor, Lincoln's Inn, London
WC2A 3SU, Telephone: 0171 405 0758
Call date: May 1993, Middle Temple
Qualifications: [BA (Hons)]

FARRER ADAM MICHAEL

4 Fountain Court
Steelhouse Lane, Birmingham B4 6DR,
Telephone: 0121 236 3476
Call date: Oct 1992, Gray's Inn
Qualifications: [LL.B (Nott'n)]

D

FARRER DAVID JOHN QC (1986)

9 Bedford Row
London WC1R 4AZ,
Telephone: 0171 242 3555
E-mail: clerks@9br.co.uk
Call date: Apr 1967, Middle Temple
Recorder
Qualifications: [MA (Cantab), LLB]

FARRER PAUL AINSWORTH

1 Fountain Court
Steelhouse Lane, Birmingham B4 6DR,
Telephone: 0121 236 5721
Call date: Feb 1988, Gray's Inn
Qualifications: [LLB (Nottm)]

FARRIMOND MISS STEPHANIE ANNE

5 Essex Court
1st Floor, Temple, London EC4Y 9AH,
Telephone: 0171 410 2000
Call date: July 1987, Middle Temple
Qualifications: [LLB (Essex)]

FARRINGTON DAVID

3 Gray's Inn Square
Ground Floor, London WC1R 5AH,
Telephone: 0171 520 5600
E-mail: gis3@btinternet.com
Call date: July 1972, Middle Temple
Qualifications: [LLB]

FARROR MISS SHELAGH ANN

Queen Elizabeth Bldg
Ground Floor, Temple, London EC4Y 9BS,
Telephone: 0171 353 7181 (12 Lines)
Call date: Nov 1970, Middle Temple
Qualifications: [MA (Oxon)]

FARROW ADRIAN JOHN

40 King Street
Manchester M2 6BA,
Telephone: 0161 832 9082
E-mail: Kingst40@aol.com
Call date: July 1997, Middle Temple
Qualifications: [LLB (Hons)(Leics)]

FARROW KENNETH JOHN

13 Old Square
1st Floor, Lincoln's Inn, London WC2A 3UA,
Telephone: 0171 242 6105
E-mail: clerks@serlecourt.co.uk
Call date: July 1966, Gray's Inn
Recorder
Qualifications: [MA, BCL (Oxon)]

FAULKS EDWARD PETER LAWLESS QC (1996)

1 Serjeants' Inn
5th Floor Fleet Street, Temple, London
EC4Y 1LL, Telephone: 0171 415 6666
E-mail: no1serjeantsinn@btinternet.com
Call date: Nov 1973, Middle Temple
Assistant Recorder
Qualifications: [MA (Oxon)]

FAUX ANDREW JOHN

Rowchester Chambers
4 Rowchester Court Whittall Street,
Birmingham B4 6DH,
Telephone: 0121 233 2327/2361951
Call date: Nov 1995, Inner Temple
Qualifications: [BA (Sheff), CPE (Manc)]

FAWCETT GARY

Eighteen Carlton Crescent
Southampton SO15 2XR,
Telephone: 01703 639001
Call date: Nov 1975, Lincoln's Inn
Qualifications: [LLB (Soton)]

FAWCETT MISS MICHELLE EVELYN

Maidstone Chambers
33 Earl Street, Maidstone, Kent ME14 1PF,
Telephone: 01622 688592
Call date: Nov 1993, Inner Temple
Qualifications: [LLB (Kent)]

FAWLS RICHARD GRANVILLE

5 Stone Buildings
Lincoln's Inn, London WC2A 3XT,
Telephone: 0171 242 6201
E-mail: clerks@5-stonebuildings.law.co.uk
Call date: July 1973, Inner Temple
Qualifications: [LLB (Hons)]

FAY CHARLES STEWART

2 Mitre Ct Bldgs
2nd Floor, Temple, London EC4Y 7BX,
Telephone: 0171 583 1380
Call date: June 1955, Inner Temple
Qualifications: [MA (Oxon)]

FAY MICHAEL JOHN

5 Fountain Court
Steelhouse Lane, Birmingham B4 6DR,
Telephone: 0121 606 0500
Call date: July 1989, Lincoln's Inn
Qualifications: [LLB]

FEATHER MISS JANET

Durham Barristers' Chambers
27 Old Elvet, Durham DH1 3HN,
Telephone: 0191 386 9199
Call date: Nov 1990, Middle Temple
Qualifications: [LLB (Leic), LLM (Florence)]

FEATHERBY WILLIAM ALAN

12 King's Bench Walk
Temple, London EC4Y 7EL,
Telephone: 0171 583 0811
E-mail: chambers@12kbw.co.uk
Call date: Nov 1978, Middle Temple
Qualifications: [MA (Oxon)]

FEATHERSTONE JASON NEIL

Forest House Chambers
15 Granville Road, Walthamstow, London
E17 9BS, Telephone: 0181 925 2240
Call date: Nov 1995, Inner Temple
Qualifications: [LLB (Newc)]

FEDER AMI

Lamb Building
Ground Floor, Temple, London EC4Y 7AS,
Telephone: 0171 797 7788
E-mail: lamb.building@link.org
Call date: July 1965, Inner Temple
Qualifications: [LLB]

FEEHAN FRANCIS THOMAS

22 Old Bldgs
Lincoln's Inn, London WC2A 3UJ,
Telephone: 0171 831 0222
Call date: July 1988, Lincoln's Inn
Qualifications: [BA (Hons) (Cantab)]

FEENY CHARLES SHERIDAN

Peel House Chambers
Ground Floor, Peel House 5 Harrington Street,
Liverpool L2 9QA, Telephone: 0151 236 4321
Call date: Nov 1977, Inner Temple
Assistant Recorder
Qualifications: [BA (Cantab)]

FEEST ADAM SEBASTIAN

2 King's Bench Walk
Ground Floor, Temple, London EC4Y 7DE,
Telephone: 0171 353 1746
E-mail: 2kbw@atlas.co.uk
King's Bench Chambers
115 North Hill, Plymouth PL4 8JY,
Telephone: 01752 221551
Call date: Feb 1994, Inner Temple
Qualifications: [BA (Oxon)]

FEETHAM DANIEL ANTHONY

Merchant Chambers
1 North Parade, Parsonage Gardens,
Manchester M3 2NH,
Telephone: 0161 839 7070
Call date: Feb 1994, Gray's Inn
Qualifications: [BA (Reading), LLB (Manc)]

FEINBERG PETER ERIC QC (1992)

1 Crown Office Row
2nd Floor, Temple, London EC4Y 7HH,
Telephone: 0171 797 7111
Call date: July 1972, Inner Temple
Recorder
Qualifications: [LLB (Lond)]

FELDMAN MATTHEW RICHARD BANKES

Staple Inn Chambers
1st Floor 9 Staple Inn, Holborn, London
WC1V 7QH, Telephone: 0171 242 5240
E-mail: clerks@staple-inn.org
Call date: Oct 1995, Inner Temple
Qualifications: [BA Joint(Hons)(Manc), CPE]

FELL ALISTAIR ALEXANDER

3 Temple Gardens (North)
Fifth Floor, Temple, London EC4Y 9AU,
Telephone: 0171 353 0853/4/7222
E-mail: 100106.1577@compuserve.com
Call date: Nov 1994, Middle Temple
Qualifications: [LLB (Hons), LLM]

D

FELLAS MISS THEKLA REBECCA

Harrow on the Hill Chambers
60 High Street, Harrow on the Hill, Middlesex
HA1 3LL, Telephone: 0181 423 7444
Windsor Barristers' Chambers
Windsor, Telephone: 01753 648899
Call date: Oct 1992, Middle Temple
Qualifications: [LLB (Hons)]

FELTHAM PIERS JONATHAN

11 New Square
Ground Floor, Lincoln's Inn, London
WC2A 3QB, Telephone: 0171 831 0081
E-mail: 11newsquare.co.uk
Call date: July 1985, Gray's Inn
Qualifications: [BA (Cantab)]

FEMI-OLA ABIODUN JOHN

2 Paper Bldgs
1st Floor, Temple, London EC4Y 7ET,
Telephone: 0171 936 2611 (10 Lines)
E-mail: clerks@2pbbarristers.co.uk
Call date: Nov 1985, Gray's Inn
Qualifications: [BA]

FENDER CARL DAVID

Regency Chambers
18 Cowgate, Peterborough PE1 1NA,
Telephone: 01733 315215
Call date: Feb 1994, Middle Temple
Qualifications: [BA (Hons)(Kent)]

FENHALLS MARK ROYDON ALLEN

23 Essex Street
London WC2R 3AS,
Telephone: 0171 413 0353/353 3533
E-mail: clerks@essexstreet23.demon.co.uk
Call date: Oct 1992, Gray's Inn
Qualifications: [BA, M.Sc]

FENN PETER JOHN

18 Red Lion Court
(Off Fleet Street), London EC4A 3EB,
Telephone: 0171 520 6000
Call date: July 1979, Middle Temple
Qualifications: [MA (Oxon)]

FENNY IAN CHARLES

Guildhall Chambers
23 Broad Street, Bristol BS1 2HG,
Telephone: 0117 9273366
Call date: July 1978, Gray's Inn
Qualifications: [LLB]

FENSTON MISS FELICIA DONOVAN

2 Harcourt Bldgs
Ground Floor/Left, Temple, London
EC4Y 9DB, Telephone: 0171 583 9020
E-mail: clerks@harcourt.co.uk
Stanbrook & Henderson
2 Harcourt Bldgs 2nd Floor, Temple, London
EC4Y 9DB, Telephone: 0171 353 0101
E-mail: clerks@harcourt.co.uk
Call date: Nov 1994, Inner Temple
Qualifications: [BA (Oxon)]

FENTON ADAM TIMOTHY DOWNS

7 King's Bench Walk
Ground Floor, Temple, London EC4Y 7DS,
Telephone: 0171 583 0404
Call date: Nov 1984, Inner Temple
Qualifications: [BA (Oxon)]

FENWICK JUSTIN FRANCIS QUINTUS QC (1993)

2 Crown Office Row
2nd Floor, Temple, London EC4Y 7HJ,
Telephone: 0171 797 8000
Call date: Nov 1980, Inner Temple
Assistant Recorder
Qualifications: [MA (Cantab)]

FERGUSON CHRISTOPHER MARK

Assize Court Chambers
14 Small Street, Bristol BS1 1DE,
Telephone: 0117 9264587
Pepys' Chambers
17 Fleet Street, London EC4Y 1AA,
Telephone: 0171 936 2710
Door Tenant
Call date: May 1979, Middle Temple

FERGUSON CRAIG CHARLES

1 Hare Court
Ground Floor, Temple, London EC4Y 7BE,
Telephone: 0171 353 3982/5324
Call date: Feb 1992, Middle Temple
Qualifications: [LLB (Hons)]

FERGUSON FREDERICK MORRIS GIFFORD

9 Gough Square
London EC4A 3DE, Telephone: 0171 353 5371
Call date: July 1978, Middle Temple
Qualifications: [BA (Oxon)]

FERGUSON MRS KATHARINE ANN

Fenners Chambers
3 Madingley Road, Cambridge CB3 OEE,
Telephone: 01223 368761
Fenners Chambers
8-12 Priestgate, Peterborough PE1 1JA,
Telephone: 01733 62030
Call date: Feb 1995, Inner Temple
Qualifications: [BA (Oxon)]

FERGUSON NIALL

36 Bedford Row
London WC1R 4JH,
Telephone: 0171 421 8000
E-mail: 36bedfordrow@link.org
Call date: July 1996, Middle Temple
Qualifications: [BA (Hons)(Dunelm)]

FERGUSON RICHARD QC (1986)

1 Crown Office Row
2nd Floor, Temple, London EC4Y 7HH,
Telephone: 0171 797 7111
Call date: July 1972, Gray's Inn
Qualifications: [LLB, BA]

FERGUSON STEPHEN MICHAEL

1 Paper Bldgs
1st Floor, Temple, London EC4Y 7EP,
Telephone: 0171 353 3728/4953
Call date: Nov 1991, Inner Temple
Qualifications: [BA (Oxon)]

FERM RODNEY ERIC

37 Park Square
Leeds LS1 2NY, Telephone: 0113 2439422
Call date: July 1972, Middle Temple
Qualifications: [BA (Oxon)]

FERN GARY

Goldsworth Chambers
1st Floor 10-11 Gray's Inn Square, London
WC1R 5JD, Telephone: 0171 405 7117
Call date: Oct 1992, Lincoln's Inn
Qualifications: [B.Eng (Hons), CPE, LLM]

FERNANDES JOHN PIEDADE AMARANTO LORENCIO

Arcadia Chambers
P O Box 16674, London W8 5ZX,
Telephone: 0171 938 1285
Call date: Nov 1979, Middle Temple
Qualifications: [LLB, LLM, FTII]

Fax: 0171 938 1285

Types of work: Chancery (general);
Discrimination; Tax - capital and income; Tax -
corporate

Circuit: South Eastern

Other professional experience: Seven years'
experience as a tax specialist in the oil sector

Publications: Various published articles in
Taxation, *Taxation Practitioner* and *Tax
Journal*; *Taxation Aspects of Oil Field
Abandonment in the UK North Sea*, 1998

FERNYHOUGH RICHARD QC (1986)

Keating Chambers
10 Essex Street, Outer Temple, London
WC2R 3AA, Telephone: 0171 544 2600
Call date: Nov 1970, Middle Temple
Recorder
Qualifications: [LLB, FCIArb]

FERRARI MS SARAH JANE

17 Carlton Crescent
Southampton SO15 2XR,
Telephone: 01703 320320
E-mail: km@bar-17cc.demon.co.uk
Call date: Nov 1993, Gray's Inn
Qualifications: [LLB]

FERRIER IAN GILBERT STRATON

8 Gray's Inn Square
Gray's Inn, London WC1R 5AZ,
Telephone: 0171 242 3529
Call date: July 1976, Middle Temple
Qualifications: [MA (Oxon)]

FERRIER MRS SUSAN

9 Park Place
Cardiff CF1 3DP, Telephone: 01222 382731
Call date: Nov 1985, Gray's Inn
Qualifications: [BSc (Hons)(Cardiff)]

FERRIS MS CAITLIN TARA

New Court
Temple, London EC4Y 9BE,
Telephone: 0171 583 5123/0171 583 0510
Call date: Mar 1996, Inner Temple
Qualifications: [BA (Leeds)]

FERRIS JONATHAN MORETON

29 Bedford Row Chambers
London WC1R 4HE,
Telephone: 0171 831 2626
Call date: Nov 1979, Middle Temple
Assistant Recorder
Qualifications: [BA (Dunelm)]

FERRIS SHAUN

1 Paper Bldgs
Ground Floor, Temple, London EC4Y 7EP,
Telephone: 0171 583 7355
E-mail: clerks@1pb.co.uk
Call date: Nov 1985, Gray's Inn
Qualifications: [BA (Oxon)]

FESSAL IGNATIUS

8 King's Bench Walk
2nd Floor, Temple, London EC4Y 7DU,
Telephone: 0171 797 8888
8 King's Bench Walk North
1 Park Square East, Leeds LS1 2NE,
Telephone: 0113 2439797
Call date: Nov 1981, Inner Temple
Qualifications: [LLB]

FETHERSTONHAUGH GUY CUTHBERT CHARLES

Falcon Chambers
Falcon Court, London EC4Y 1AA,
Telephone: 0171 353 2484/7
Call date: July 1983, Inner Temple
Qualifications: [BSc (Bris)]

FEWTRELL NICHOLAS AUSTIN

18 St John Street
Manchester M3 4EA,
Telephone: 0161 278 1800
Call date: Nov 1977, Inner Temple
Qualifications: [LLB (Lond)]

FIELD MISS AMANDA JANE

Queen Elizabeth Bldg
Ground Floor, Temple, London EC4Y 9BS,
Telephone: 0171 353 7181 (12 Lines)
Call date: Feb 1994, Middle Temple
Qualifications: [MA (Dublin)]

FIELD JULIAN NIGEL

1 Paper Bldgs
Ground Floor, Temple, London EC4Y 7EP,
Telephone: 0171 583 7355
E-mail: clerks@1pb.co.uk
Call date: Nov 1980, Gray's Inn
Qualifications: [LLB (Lond)]

FIELD MARTIN CHARLES

9-12 Bell Yard
London WC2A 2LF,
Telephone: 0171 400 1800
Call date: Nov 1966, Inner Temple
Recorder

FIELD PATRICK JOHN

Deans Court Chambers
Cumberland House Crown Square, Manchester
M3 3HA, Telephone: 0161 834 4097
E-mail: deanscourt@compuserve.com
Deans Court Chambers
41-43 Market Place, Preston PR1 1AH,
Telephone: 01772 555163
E-mail: deanscourt@compuserve.com
Call date: Nov 1981, Gray's Inn
Qualifications: [LLB (Lond)]

FIELD RICHARD ALAN QC (1987)

11 King's Bench Walk
Temple, London EC4Y 7EQ,
Telephone: 0171 632 8500
E-mail: clerksroom@11-kbw.law.co.uk
Call date: July 1977, Inner Temple
Assistant Recorder
Qualifications: [LLB (Bristol) LLM, (Lond)]

FIELD RORY DOMINIC

Hardwicke Building
New Square, Lincoln's Inn, London
WC2A 3SB, Telephone: 0171 242 2523
E-mail: clerks@hardwicke.co.uk
Call date: July 1980, Middle Temple
Qualifications: [BA (Hons) (Cantab)]

FIELD STEPHEN ANTHONY

Counsels' Chambers
2nd Floor 10-11 Gray's Inn Square, London
WC1R 5JD, Telephone: 0171 405 2576
Call date: Nov 1993, Gray's Inn
Qualifications: [LLB (Lond)]

FIELDEN DR CHRISTA MARIA

Lamb Building
Ground Floor, Temple, London EC4Y 7AS,
Telephone: 0171 797 7788
E-mail: lamb.building@link.org
Call date: Nov 1982, Lincoln's Inn
Qualifications: [BSc, MSc, PhD]

FIELDHOUSE NIGEL RICHARD ARNOLD

Cobden House Chambers
19 Quay Street, Manchester M3 3HN,
Telephone: 0161 833 6000
E-mail: clerks@cobden.co.uk
Call date: July 1976, Gray's Inn
Qualifications: [LLB (Hons)]

FIELDS MISS HELEN SARAH

Pump Court Chambers
Upper Ground Floor 3 Pump Court, Temple,
London EC4Y 7AJ, Telephone: 0171 353 0711
Call date: Oct 1993, Middle Temple
Qualifications: [LLB (Hons)(E.Ang)]

FINCH MRS NADINE ELIZABETH

Doughty Street Chambers
11 Doughty Street, London WC1N 2PG,
Telephone: 0171 404 1313
E-mail: doughty_street@compuserve.com
Call date: Oct 1991, Middle Temple
Qualifications: [BA Hons (E Anglia), Dip Law]

FINCH THOMAS MICHAEL

67a Westgate Road
Newcastle Upon Tyne NE1 1SQ,
Telephone: 0191 261 4407/2329785
Call date: Nov 1981, Lincoln's Inn
Qualifications: [BA Hons]

FINDLAY JAMES DE CARDONNEL

2-3 Gray's Inn Square
Gray's Inn, London WC1R 5JH,
Telephone: 0171 242 4986
E-mail: chambers@2-3graysinnsquare.co.uk
Call date: Nov 1984, Middle Temple
Qualifications: [BA (Cantab)]

FINDLAY MISS LORNA ANNE

Priory Chambers
2 Fountain Court, Steelhouse Lane,
Birmingham B4 6DR,
Telephone: 0121 236 3882/1375
Call date: July 1987, Middle Temple
Qualifications: [LLB (Edin)]

FINE MRS SUZANNE JOY

Queen Elizabeth Bldg
Ground Floor, Temple, London EC4Y 9BS,
Telephone: 0171 353 7181 (12 Lines)
Door Tenant
Call date: July 1976, Middle Temple
Qualifications: [BSc (Lond)]

FINLAY ANDREW STEVEN

Fountain Chambers
Cleveland Business Centre 1 Watson Street,
Middlesbrough TS1 2RQ,
Telephone: 01642 217037
Call date: Oct 1993, Gray's Inn
Qualifications: [LLB (Hons)(Manc)]

FINLAY DARREN

25 Park Square
Leeds LS1 2PW, Telephone: 0113 2451841/2/3
E-mail: sovereignchambers@btinternet.com
Call date: Oct 1994, Gray's Inn
Qualifications: [BA (Keele)]

D

D

FINN TERENCE

Eldon Chambers
Fourth Floor 30/32 Fleet Street, London
EC4Y 1AA, Telephone: 0171 353 4636
Call date: Oct 1995, Lincoln's Inn
Qualifications: [LLB (Hons)(Bournem)]

FINNERTY MISS ANGELA CATHERINE

Park Lane Chambers
19 Westgate, Leeds LS1 2RD,
Telephone: 0113 2285000
Call date: July 1976, Middle Temple
Assistant Recorder
Qualifications: [LLB (Leeds)]

FINNIGAN PETER ANTHONY

Hollis Whiteman Chambers
3rd/4th Floor Queen Elizabeth Bldg, Temple,
London EC4Y 9BS, Telephone: 0171 583 5766
E-mail: hollis.whiteman@btinternet.com
Call date: July 1978, Lincoln's Inn
Qualifications: [LLB (Newc)]

FINNIS JOHN MITCHELL

Littman Chambers
12 Gray's Inn Square, London WC1R 5JP,
Telephone: 0171 404 4866
E-mail: admin@littmanchambers.com
Door Tenant
Call date: Nov 1970, Gray's Inn
Qualifications: [LLB (Adelaide), MA,]

FINUCANE BRENDAN GODFREY EAMONN

23 Essex Street
London WC2R 3AS,
Telephone: 0171 413 0353/353 3533
E-mail: clerks@essexstreet23.demon.co.uk
Call date: July 1976, Middle Temple
Qualifications: [BSc (Lond)]

FIREMAN MARK PHILLIP

Manchester House Chambers
18-22 Bridge Street, Manchester M3 3BZ,
Telephone: 0161 834 7007
Call date: Feb 1986, Gray's Inn
Qualifications: [LLB (Lond)(Hons)]

FIRTH MISS ALISON MARY LESTER

New Court
1st Floor, Temple, London EC4Y 9BE,
Telephone: 0171 797 8999
Call date: Nov 1980, Middle Temple
Qualifications: [MA (Oxon), MSc]

FIRTH MISS CLEMENCY MARY LEE

3 Temple Gardens
Lower Ground Floor, Temple, London
EC4Y 9AU, Telephone: 0171 353 3102/5/9297
Call date: Nov 1992, Inner Temple
Qualifications: [LLB (Newc)]

FIRTH MISS GEORGINA ELIZABETH

Chambers of Ian Macdonald QC
Waldorf House Cooper Street, Manchester
M2 2FW, Telephone: 0161 236 1840
Call date: Oct 1995, Middle Temple
Qualifications: [LLB (Hons)]

FIRTH MATTHEW ALEXANDER

Queen Elizabeth Bldg
2nd Floor, Temple, London EC4Y 9BS,
Telephone: 0171 797 7837
Call date: Oct 1991, Gray's Inn
Qualifications: [MA (Oxon)]

FIRTH-BUTTERFIELD MISS KAY

1 Gray's Inn Square
1st Floor, London WC1R 5AG,
Telephone: 0171 405 3000
E-mail: clerks@onegrays.demon.co.uk
Call date: July 1980, Inner Temple
Qualifications: [BA (Sussex)]

FISCHEL ROBERT GUSTAV

5 Paper Bldgs
Lower Ground Floor, Temple, London
EC4Y 7HB, Telephone: 0171 353 5638
E-mail: 107722,633@compuserve.com
Call date: July 1975, Middle Temple
Qualifications: [LLB (Lond)]

FISH DAVID THOMAS QC (1997)

Deans Court Chambers
Cumberland House Crown Square, Manchester
M3 3HA, Telephone: 0161 834 4097
E-mail: deanscourt@compuserve.com
Deans Court Chambers
41-43 Market Place, Preston PR1 1AH,
Telephone: 01772 555163
E-mail: deanscourt@compuserve.com
Call date: July 1973, Inner Temple
Recorder
Qualifications: [LLB]

FISHER MISS CATHERINE JANE

Merchant Chambers
1 North Parade, Parsonage Gardens,
Manchester M3 2NH,
Telephone: 0161 839 7070
Call date: Oct 1990, Gray's Inn
Qualifications: [LLB (Lond), BCL (Oxon)]

FISHER DAVID

5 Bell Yard
London WC2A 2JR, Telephone: 0171 333 8811
Call date: Nov 1985, Lincoln's Inn
Qualifications: [BA (Cantab)]

FISHER DAVID PAUL QC (1996)

6 King's Bench Walk
Ground Floor, Temple, London EC4Y 7DR,
Telephone: 0171 583 0410
Call date: July 1973, Gray's Inn
Recorder

FISHER JERVIS ANDREW

Coleridge Chambers
Citadel 190 Corporation Street, Birmingham
B4 6QD, Telephone: 0121 233 3303
Call date: July 1980, Gray's Inn
Qualifications: [LLB (Lond)]

FISHER JONATHAN SIMON

18 Red Lion Court
(off Fleet Street), London EC4A 3EB,
Telephone: 0171 520 6000
Thornwood House
102 New London Road, Chelmsford, Essex
CM2 0RG, Telephone: 01245 280880
Call date: July 1980, Gray's Inn

Qualifications: [BA, LLB (Cantab)]

Fax: 0171 520 6248/9; DX: 478 LDE

Types of work: Administrative; Common law (general); Crime; Crime - corporate fraud; Financial services; Pharmacy

Other professional qualifications: Standing Counsel (Criminal) to the Inland Revenue, Central Criminal Court and London Crown Courts

Circuit: South East

Awards and memberships: Criminal Bar Association; Administrative Law Bar Association; International Bar Association

Other professional experience: Senior Visiting Fellow in Investment Law, City University Business School (PVM); UK Country Correspondent, *Journal of International Banking Law* (Sweet & Maxwell)

Publications: *The Law of Investor Protection* (Sweet & Maxwell), 1997; *Pharmacy Law & Practice* (Blackwell Science), 1997 (2nd edn); Sweet & Maxwell Practical Research Paper: *Incoming Requests for Mutual Assistance*, 1998; Sweet & Maxwell Practical Research Paper: *Out-going Letters of Request for International Assistance*, 1998

Reported cases: *R v FHSA ex parte Elmfield Drugs Ltd*, [1998] COD 33. Pharmacy/administrative law.
R v IRC ex parte Allen, [1997] STC 1141. Tax fraud/administrative law.
LB of Enfield v Castle Estate Agents Ltd, (1998) 160 JP 618. Crime/consumer law.
R v Yorkshire HA ex parte Gompels and Suri, [1996] 30 BMLR 78. Pharmacy/administrative law.
R v Secretary of State for Health ex parte Furneaux, [1994] 2 All ER 652. Pharmacy/administrative law.
R v Hunt (Nissan UK), [1994] Crim LR 747. Crime/tax fraud.

FISHER MS SANDRA

1 Gray's Inn Square
1st Floor, London WC1R 5AG,
Telephone: 0171 405 3000
E-mail: clerks@onegrays.demon.co.uk
Call date: Nov 1993, Inner Temple
Qualifications: [LLB]

D

FISHER GORDON MRS WENDY VIVIENNE

2 Paper Bldgs
Temple, London EC4Y 7ET,
Telephone: 0171 936 2613
Call date: July 1983, Gray's Inn
Qualifications: [BA (Hons), Dip Law]

FITCH-HOLLAND ANDREW ROBERT

Trinity Chambers
140 New London Road, Chelmsford, Essex
CM2 0AW, Telephone: 01245 605040
Call date: Nov 1990, Inner Temple
Qualifications: [LLB (Buck'ham)]

FITTON MICHAEL DAVID GUY

Albion Chambers
Broad Street, Bristol BS1 1DR,
Telephone: 0117 9272144
Call date: Nov 1991, Gray's Inn
Qualifications: [MA (Oxon)]

FITTON-BROWN MISS REBECCA MARY

New Walk Chambers
27 New Walk, Leicester LE1 6TE,
Telephone: 0116 2559144
Call date: July 1981, Inner Temple
Qualifications: [LLB]

FITZGERALD EDWARD HAMILTON QC (1995)

Doughty Street Chambers
11 Doughty Street, London WC1N 2PG,
Telephone: 0171 404 1313
E-mail: doughty_street@compuserve.com
Call date: Nov 1978, Inner Temple
Qualifications: [BA (Oxon), MPhil (Ca)]

FITZGERALD JOHN VINCENT

Lancaster Building Chambers
77 Deansgate, Manchester M3 2BW,
Telephone: 0161 661 4444
E-mail: sandra@lbnipc.com
New Court
1st Floor, Temple, London EC4Y 9BE,
Telephone: 0171 797 8999
Call date: July 1971, Middle Temple
Qualifications: [BSc]

FITZGERALD MICHAEL FREDERICK CLIVE QC (1980)

2 Mitre Ct Bldgs
2nd Floor, Temple, London EC4Y 7BX,
Telephone: 0171 583 1380
Call date: Feb 1961, Middle Temple
Qualifications: [MA (Cantab)]

FITZGERALD RICHARD KIERAN

11 New Square
1st Floor, Lincoln's Inn, London WC2A 3QB,
Telephone: 0171 242 4017/3981
E-mail: taxlaw@11newsquare.com
Call date: Nov 1971, Inner Temple
Qualifications: [FCA]

FITZGERALD MISS SUSANNA

1 Essex Court
Ground Floor, Temple, London EC4Y 9AR,
Telephone: 0171 583 2000
E-mail: clerks@oneessexcourt.co.uk
Call date: July 1973, Inner Temple
Qualifications: [LLB (Hons)]

FITZGERALD TOBY JONATHAN

2 Harcourt Bldgs
1st Floor, Temple, London EC4Y 9DB,
Telephone: 0171 353 2112/2817
Call date: Oct 1993, Lincoln's Inn
Qualifications: [BSc (Hons)(Bris)]

FITZGIBBON FRANCIS GEORGE HERBERT DILLON

33 Bedford Row
London WC1R 4JH,
Telephone: 0171 242 6476
Call date: Feb 1986, Middle Temple
Qualifications: [BA (Oxon)]

FITZGIBBON NEIL KEVIN

Goldsmith Chambers
Ground Floor Goldsmith Building, Temple,
London EC4Y 7BL,
Telephone: 0171 353 6802/3/4/5
E-mail: celiamonksfield@btinternet.com
Call date: Nov 1989, Lincoln's Inn
Qualifications: [LLB (Hons) (Lond)]

D

FITZHARRIS MISS GINNETTE

21 White Friars
Chester CH1 1NZ, Telephone: 01244 323070
Call date: Nov 1993, Lincoln's Inn
Qualifications: [LLB (Hons, Leeds)]

FITZMAURICE MAURICE EVELYN FORBES

2 Hare Court
Ground Floor, Temple, London EC4Y 7BH,
Telephone: 0171 583 1770
E-mail: 2_Hare_Court@link.org
Door Tenant
Call date: Nov 1969, Middle Temple
Qualifications: [BA (Cantab)]

FITZPATRICK EDWARD JAMES

1 Gray's Inn Square
Ground Floor, London WC1R 5AA,
Telephone: 0171 405 8946/7/8
Call date: Nov 1990, Gray's Inn
Qualifications: [LLB (L'pool)]

FITZPATRICK FRANCIS PAUL

11 New Square
1st Floor, Lincoln's Inn, London WC2A 3QB,
Telephone: 0171 242 4017/3981
E-mail: taxlaw@11newsquare.com
Call date: Nov 1990, Inner Temple
Qualifications: [BA (Hons)(Oxon), BCL
(Oxon)]

FITZPATRICK JEREMY PAUL

4 Brick Court
Ground Floor, Temple, London EC4Y 9AD,
Telephone: 0171 797 7766
E-mail: chambers@4brick.co.uk
Call date: Mar 1996, Middle Temple
Qualifications: [BA (Hons)]

FITZPATRICK ROSS ANTONY

King Charles House
Standard Hill, Nottingham NG1 6FX,
Telephone: 0115 9418851
E-mail: clerks@kch.co.uk
Call date: July 1972, Middle Temple

FITZPATRICK THOMAS ANDREW MICHAEL

58 King Street Chambers
1st Floor, Kingsgate House 51-53 South King
Street, Manchester M2 6DE,
Telephone: 0161 831 7477
Call date: Nov 1988, Lincoln's Inn
Qualifications: [LLB]

FLACH ROBERT THOMAS FRANCIS

3 Hare Court
1st Floor, Temple, London EC4Y 7BJ,
Telephone: 0171 353 7561
Call date: Jan 1950, Middle Temple
Qualifications: [LLB (Tas)]

FLAHIVE DANIEL MICHAEL

3 Gray's Inn Square
Ground Floor, London WC1R 5AH,
Telephone: 0171 520 5600
E-mail: gis3@btinternet.com
Call date: July 1982, Gray's Inn
Qualifications: [LLB (Lond)]

FLANAGAN MISS JULIA MARY ALICE

2 Dr Johnson's Building
Temple, London EC4Y 7AY,
Telephone: 0171 353 4716
Call date: Oct 1993, Lincoln's Inn
Qualifications: [BA (Hons), Dip in Law (Lond),
CPE]

FLATHER GARY QC (1984)

4-5 Gray's Inn Square
Ground Floor, Gray's Inn, London WC1R 5AY,
Telephone: 0171 404 5252
E-mail: chambers@4-5graysinnsquare.co.uk
Call date: May 1962, Inner Temple
Recorder
Qualifications: [MA (Oxon)]

FLATTERY MISS AMANDA NICHOLE

Durham Barristers' Chambers
27 Old Elvet, Durham DH1 3HN,
Telephone: 0191 386 9199
Call date: Oct 1993, Lincoln's Inn
Qualifications: [BA (Hons)(Lancaster), MA
(York), CPE]

D

FLAUX JULIAN MARTIN QC (1994)

7 King's Bench Walk
Ground Floor, Temple, London EC4Y 7DS,
Telephone: 0171 583 0404
Call date: July 1978, Inner Temple
Qualifications: [BA, BCL (Oxon)]

FLEISCHMANN MRS LAUREEN ANN

2 Pump Court
1st Floor, Temple, London EC4Y 7AH,
Telephone: 0171 353 5597
Call date: July 1978, Inner Temple
Qualifications: [LLB (Hons) (Lond)]

FLEMING ADRIAN

2 King's Bench Walk
Ground Floor, Temple, London EC4Y 7DE,
Telephone: 0171 353 1746
E-mail: 2kbw@atlas.co.uk
King's Bench Chambers
115 North Hill, Plymouth PL4 8JY,
Telephone: 01752 221551
Call date: Nov 1991, Middle Temple
Qualifications: [BA Hons (Cantab), Dip Law]

FLEMING PAUL STEPHEN

37 Park Square
Leeds LS1 2NY, Telephone: 0113 2439422
Call date: Nov 1983, Gray's Inn

FLENLEY WILLIAM DAVID WINGATE

4 Paper Bldgs
Ground Floor, Temple, London EC4Y 7EX,
Telephone: 0171 353 3366/583 7155
E-mail: clerks@4paperbuildings.com
Call date: Nov 1988, Middle Temple
Qualifications: [BA, BCL (Oxon), LLM
(Cornell)]

FLESCH MICHAEL CHARLES QC (1983)

Gray's Inn Chambers
3rd Floor, Gray's Inn, London WC1R 5JA,
Telephone: 0171 242 2642
E-mail: clerks@taxbar.com
Call date: May 1963, Gray's Inn
Qualifications: [LLB]

FLETCHER ANDREW FITZROY STEPHEN

4 Pump Court
Temple, London EC4Y 7AN,
Telephone: 0171 353 2656/9
E-mail: 4_pump_court@compuserve.com
Call date: Nov 1980, Inner Temple
Qualifications: [MA (Cantab)]

FLETCHER CHRISTOPHER MICHAEL

Octagon House
19 Colegate, Norwich NR3 1AT,
Telephone: 01603 623186
E-mail: octagon@netmatters.co.uk
Call date: Nov 1984, Inner Temple
Qualifications: [LLB (Exeter)]

FLETCHER DAVID HAMILTON

Albion Chambers
Broad Street, Bristol BS1 1DR,
Telephone: 0117 9272144
Call date: July 1971, Gray's Inn
Qualifications: [MA (Cantab)]

FLETCHER MARCUS ALEXANDER

1 King's Bench Walk
2nd Floor, Temple, London EC4Y 7DB,
Telephone: 0171 936 1500
E-mail: ddear@1kbw.co.uk
Call date: Oct 1990, Lincoln's Inn
Qualifications: [BA (Hons)]

FLETCHER STEPHEN JEFFERY

Somersett Chambers
52 Bedford Row, London WC1R 4LR,
Telephone: 0171 404 6701
E-mail: Somersettchambers@cocoon.co.uk
Call date: Nov 1987, Middle Temple
Qualifications: [LLB Hons (Lond)]

FLETTON MARK JOHN

Broadway House Chambers
Broadway House 9 Bank Street, Bradford,
West Yorkshire BD1 1TW,
Telephone: 01274 722560
Call date: Feb 1991, Lincoln's Inn
Qualifications: [LLB, LLM (Cantab)]

FLEWITT NEIL

The Corn Exchange
5th Floor Fenwick Street, Liverpool L2 7QS,
Telephone: 0151 227 1081/5009
Call date: July 1981, Middle Temple
Qualifications: [LLB (Hons, L'pool)]

FLINT CHARLES JOHN RAFFLES QC (1995)

2 Hare Court
Ground Floor, Temple, London EC4Y 7BH,
Telephone: 0171 583 1770
E-mail: 2_Hare_Court@link.org
Call date: July 1975, Middle Temple
Qualifications: [MA (Cantab)]

FLOOD DAVID EDWARD

India Buildings Chambers
Water Street, Liverpool L2 OXG,
Telephone: 0151 243 6000
Call date: Feb 1993, Middle Temple
Qualifications: [LLB (Hons)]

FLOOD DIARMUID BRENDAN MARTIN

Victoria Chambers
19 Castle Street, Liverpool L2 4SX,
Telephone: 0151 236 9402
E-mail: Fa45@rapid.co.uk
Call date: Apr 1989, Lincoln's Inn
Qualifications: [LLB (Lond), Maitrise (Paris)]

FLORIDA-JAMES MARK

King's Bench Chambers
175 Holdenhurst Road, Bournemouth, Dorset
BH8 8DQ, Telephone: 01202 250025
Call date: Oct 1995, Inner Temple
Qualifications: [BA (Sussex), MPhil
(Aberystwyth), Dip German Law (Bonn)]

Types of work: Civil liberties; Crime; Crime -
corporate fraud

Circuit: Western

Awards and memberships: Criminal Bar
Association, Bournemouth and Poole Medico-
Legal Society, Inner Temple

Other professional experience: Three years as
Law Lecturer, University of Wales, Aberystwyth;
German translator

Languages spoken: German

Publications: *Consent as an Element of Theft*,
24 February 1992; *Consent and Appropriation,
Has Gomez Settled the Dispute?*, June 1993;
*Foreign Radio Broadcasts & Manipulation of
the Masses in Nazi Germany*, 1993; *Prince
Harry for Wales*, 7 July 1994; *Disputed
Transcripts - Evidence or Working
Documents?*, 19 October 1996

FLOWER PHILIP RONALD

11 Stone Bldgs
1st Floor, Lincoln's Inn, London WC2A 3TG,
Telephone: 0171 404 5055
E-mail: 9stoneb@compuserve.com
Call date: Nov 1979, Inner Temple
Qualifications: [MA]

FLOYD CHRISTOPHER DAVID QC (1992)

11 South Square
2nd Floor, Gray's Inn, London WC1R 5EU,
Telephone: 0171 405 1222
*Call date: July 1975, Inner Temple
Assistant Recorder*
Qualifications: [MA (Cantab)]

FLYNN JAMES EDWARD

Brick Court Chambers
15/19 Devereux Court, London WC2R 3JJ,
Telephone: 0171 583 0777
E-mail: (surname)@brickcourt.demon.co.uk
Call date: July 1978, Middle Temple
Qualifications: [BA (Oxon)]

FLYNN VERNON JAMES HENNESSY

Essex Court Chambers
24 Lincoln's Inn Fields, London WC2A 3ED,
Telephone: 0171 813 8000
E-mail: clerksroom@essexcourt-chambers.co.uk
Call date: Oct 1991, Lincoln's Inn
Qualifications: [BA (Cantab)]

FODDER MARTIN JOHN

2 Crown Office Row
2nd Floor, Temple, London EC4Y 7HJ,
Telephone: 0171 797 8000
Call date: July 1983, Inner Temple
Qualifications: [BA (Lond) LLM, (Cantab) Dip
Law, (City)]

FOGARTY PETER DOMINIC

Oriel Chambers
14 Water Street, Liverpool L2 8TD,
Telephone: 0151 236 7191
E-mail: oriel_chambers@link.org
Call date: July 1982, Middle Temple
Qualifications: [MA (Cantab)]

FOGG ANTHONY GEORGE

2 Dr Johnson's Building
Temple, London EC4Y 7AY,
Telephone: 0171 353 4716
Call date: Nov 1970, Gray's Inn
Qualifications: [MSc]

FOINETTE IAN

1 Harcourt Bldgs
2nd Floor, Temple, London EC4Y 9DA,
Telephone: 0171 353 9421/9151
Call date: Nov 1986, Middle Temple
Qualifications: [BA (Kent)]

FOLEY MISS SHEILA MARIE

3 Paper Bldgs
Ground Floor, Temple, London EC4Y 7EU,
Telephone: 0171 797 7000
E-mail: clerks@3pb.co.uk
Call date: Nov 1988, Inner Temple
Qualifications: [BA]

FOLKES MISS SANDRA GILLIAN

2 Paper Bldgs
1st Floor, Temple, London EC4Y 7ET,
Telephone: 0171 936 2611 (10 Lines)
E-mail: clerks@2pbbarristers.co.uk
Call date: Nov 1989, Lincoln's Inn
Qualifications: [LLB]

FOOKES ROBERT LAWRENCE

2 Mitre Ct Bldgs
2nd Floor, Temple, London EC4Y 7BX,
Telephone: 0171 583 1380
Call date: July 1975, Lincoln's Inn
Qualifications: [MA (Oxon)]

FOOKS NICHOLAS DAVID

5 Paper Bldgs
1st Floor, Temple, London EC4Y 7HB,
Telephone: 0171 583 6117
E-mail: clerks@5-paperbuildings.law.co.uk
Thornwood House
102 New London Road, Chelmsford, Essex
CM2 0RG, Telephone: 01245 280880
Call date: Nov 1978, Inner Temple
Qualifications: [MA (L'pool)]

FORBES PETER GEORGE

6 Pump Court
1st Floor, Temple, London EC4Y 7AR,
Telephone: 0171 797 8400
E-mail: sa_hockman_qc@link.org
6-8 Mill Street
Maidstone, Kent ME15 6XH,
Telephone: 01622 688094
Call date: Oct 1990, Inner Temple
Qualifications: [LLB (Lond)]

FORD MISS CAROLINE EMMA

37 Park Square
Leeds LS1 2NY, Telephone: 0113 2439422
Call date: Oct 1993, Gray's Inn
Qualifications: [LLM (Buck'ham)]

FORD DAVID GRAEME

Mitre Court Chambers
3rd Floor, Temple, London EC4Y 7BP,
Telephone: 0171 353 9394
Call date: July 1972, Inner Temple
Qualifications: [LLB (Lond)]

FORD GERARD JAMES

Baker Street Chambers
9 Baker Street, Middlesbrough TS1 2LF,
Telephone: 01642 873873
Call date: July 1986, Inner Temple
Qualifications: [BSc, MA (Wark), CQSW]

FORD MISS MARGO

King Charles House
Standard Hill, Nottingham NG1 6FX,
Telephone: 0115 9418851
E-mail: clerks@kch.co.uk
Call date: July 1991, Middle Temple
Qualifications: [LLB (Hons) (Galway)]

FORD MARK STEVEN

38 Young Street
Manchester M3 3FT,
Telephone: 0161 833 0489
E-mail: clerks@young-st-chambers.com
Call date: Nov 1991, Gray's Inn
Qualifications: [LLB (B'ham)]

FORD MICHAEL DAVID

Doughty Street Chambers
11 Doughty Street, London WC1N 2PG,
Telephone: 0171 404 1313
E-mail: doughty_street@compuserve.com
Call date: July 1992, Middle Temple
Qualifications: [LLB (Hons) (Brist), MA (Sheff)]

FORD MISS MONICA DOROTHY PATIENCE

14 Gray's Inn Square
Gray's Inn, London WC1R 5JP,
Telephone: 0171 242 0858
E-mail: 100712.2134@compuserve.com
Call date: July 1984, Middle Temple
Qualifications: [LLB (Hons)(L'pool)]

FORD NEIL MURRAY QC (1997)

Albion Chambers
Broad Street, Bristol BS1 1DR,
Telephone: 0117 9272144
Call date: Nov 1976, Inner Temple
Qualifications: [BA]

FORD STEVEN CHARLES

9 Bedford Row
London WC1R 4AZ,
Telephone: 0171 242 3555
E-mail: clerks@9br.co.uk
Call date: Oct 1992, Middle Temple
Qualifications: [LLB (Hons), L.R.A.M.]

FORDE MARTIN ANDREW

1 Crown Office Row
Ground Floor, Temple, London EC4Y 7HH,
Telephone: 0171 797 7500
Call date: Feb 1984, Middle Temple
Qualifications: [BA (Oxon)]

FORDHAM MRS JUDITH

Exchange Chambers
Pearl Assurance House Derby Square,
Liverpool L2 9XX, Telephone: 0151 236 7747/
0458
E-mail: exchangechambers@btinternet.com
Call date: July 1991, Inner Temple

FORDHAM MRS MARGARET ALLISON

Staple Inn Chambers
1st Floor 9 Staple Inn, Holborn, London
WC1V 7QH, Telephone: 0171 242 5240
E-mail: clerks@staple-inn.org
Call date: Oct 1990, Gray's Inn
Qualifications: [BA (U.W.I.), LLB
(Hons)(Buck'm)]

FORDHAM MICHAEL JOHN

2 Hare Court
Ground Floor, Temple, London EC4Y 7BH,
Telephone: 0171 583 1770
E-mail: 2_Hare_Court@link.org
Call date: Feb 1990, Gray's Inn
Qualifications: [BA (Oxon), BCL (Oxon), LLM
(Virginia)]

FORDHAM ROBERT ALLAN QC (1993)

Martins Building
Water Street, Liverpool L2 3SP,
Telephone: 0151 236 5818/4919
Call date: Nov 1967, Inner Temple
Recorder
Qualifications: [LLB]

FORGAN HUGH MALCOLM

5 Paper Bldgs
Lower Ground Floor, Temple, London
EC4Y 7HB, Telephone: 0171 353 5638
E-mail: 107722,633@compuserve.com
Call date: Nov 1989, Lincoln's Inn
Qualifications: [BA (Cantab)]

FORLIN GERARD EMLYN

Phoenix Chambers
First Floor Gray's Inn Chambers, Gray's Inn,
London WC1R 5JA, Telephone: 0171 404 7888
Call date: Feb 1984, Lincoln's Inn
Qualifications: [LLB (Hons) (Lond), LLM
(Lond), M.Phil (Cantab), Diploma in Air &,
Space Law]

D

D

FORMBY MS EMILY JANE

Hardwicke Building
New Square, Lincoln's Inn, London
WC2A 3SB, Telephone: 0171 242 2523
E-mail: clerks@hardwicke.co.uk
Call date: Oct 1993, Middle Temple
Qualifications: [BA (Hons)(Oxon), CPE (City)]

FORREST ALASTAIR JOHN

18 St John Street
Manchester M3 4EA,
Telephone: 0161 278 1800
Call date: July 1972, Gray's Inn
Recorder
Qualifications: [MA (Oxon)]

FORRESTER IAN STEWART

2 Hare Court
Ground Floor, Temple, London EC4Y 7BH,
Telephone: 0171 583 1770
E-mail: 2_Hare_Court@link.org
Call date: Oct 1996, Middle Temple
Qualifications: [MA, LLB (Glasgow), MCL (Tulane)]

FORSDICK DAVID JOHN

4 Breams Buildings
London EC4A 1AQ,
Telephone: 0171 353 5835/430 1221
Call date: Oct 1993, Gray's Inn
Qualifications: [BA (Warw)]

FORSHALL MS ISABELLA LOUISE

Doughty Street Chambers
11 Doughty Street, London WC1N 2PG,
Telephone: 0171 404 1313
E-mail: doughty_street@compuserve.com
Call date: Feb 1982, Gray's Inn
Qualifications: [BA (Cantab)]

FORSHAW MISS SARAH ANNE

5 Paper Bldgs
Lower Ground Floor, Temple, London
EC4Y 7HB, Telephone: 0171 353 5638
E-mail: 107722,633@compuserve.com
Call date: Nov 1987, Middle Temple
Qualifications: [LLB (Lond)]

FORSTER BRIAN CLIVE

Trinity Chambers
9-12 Trinity Chare, Quayside, Newcastle Upon
Tyne NE1 3DF, Telephone: 0191 232 1927
Call date: July 1977, Lincoln's Inn
Recorder
Qualifications: [LLB (Newcastle)]

FORSTER MICHAEL WILLIAMS

17 Carlton Crescent
Southampton SO15 2XR,
Telephone: 01703 320320
E-mail: km@bar-17cc.demon.co.uk
Call date: Feb 1984, Gray's Inn
Qualifications: [LLB (Lond)]

FORSTER MS SARAH JUDITH

14 Gray's Inn Square
Gray's Inn, London WC1R 5JP,
Telephone: 0171 242 0858
E-mail: 100712.2134@compuserve.com
Westgate Chambers
144 High Street, Lewes, East Sussex BN7 1XT,
Telephone: 01273 480510
Call date: Nov 1976, Middle Temple
Qualifications: [LLB, Dip Law, Medical Ethics]

FORSTER THOMAS BERNARD

18 Red Lion Court
(Off Fleet Street), London EC4A 3EB,
Telephone: 0171 520 6000
Thornwood House
102 New London Road, Chelmsford, Essex
CM2 0RG, Telephone: 01245 280880
Call date: Nov 1993, Inner Temple
Qualifications: [LLB (Lond)]

FORSTER TIMOTHY SHANE CAVANAGH

Furnival Chambers
32 Furnival Street, London EC4A 1JQ,
Telephone: 0171 405 3232
E-mail: clerks@furnivallaw.co.uk
Call date: Oct 1990, Middle Temple
Qualifications: [LLB (Hons Cardiff)]

FORSTER-JONES WILFRED JENNER EMANUEL

3 Temple Gardens (North)
Fifth Floor, Temple, London EC4Y 9AU,
Telephone: 0171 353 0853/4/7222
E-mail: 100106.1577@compuserve.com
Call date: Nov 1976, Middle Temple
Qualifications: [BA (Lond)]

FORSYTH ANDREW ALLAN

Mitre Court Chambers
3rd Floor, Temple, London EC4Y 7BP,
Telephone: 0171 353 9394
Call date: Nov 1989, Inner Temple
Qualifications: [LLB (Hons) (Wales)]

FORSYTH DR CHRISTOPHER FORBES

39 Essex Street
London WC2R 3AT,
Telephone: 0171 583 1111
E-mail: clerks@39essex.co.uk
Call date: May 1987, Inner Temple
Qualifications: [BSc, LLB, LLB, PhD]

FORSYTH MISS JULIE PATRICIA

Chavasse Court Chambers
2nd Floor Chavasse Court, 24 Lord Street,
Liverpool L2 1TA, Telephone: 0151 707 1191
Call date: July 1983, Gray's Inn
Qualifications: [LLB (L'pool)]

FORSYTH MISS SAMANTHA

Coleridge Chambers
Citadel 190 Corporation Street, Birmingham
B4 6QD, Telephone: 0121 233 3303
Call date: July 1988, Inner Temple
Qualifications: [LLB (Wales)]

FORTE MARK JULIAN CARMINO

8 King Street
Manchester M2 6AQ,
Telephone: 0161 834 9560
Call date: Nov 1989, Inner Temple
Qualifications: [LLB]

FORTSON RUDI FLETCHER

3 Gray's Inn Square
Ground Floor, London WC1R 5AH,
Telephone: 0171 520 5600
E-mail: gis3@btinternet.com
Call date: Nov 1976, Middle Temple
Qualifications: [LLB (Lond)]

FORTUNE MALCOLM DONALD PORTER

3 Serjeants Inn
London EC4Y 1BQ,
Telephone: 0171 353 5537
E-mail: available upon request
Call date: July 1972, Middle Temple
Recorder

FORTUNE PETER CARL MICHAEL

2 Gray's Inn Square Chambers
2nd Floor, Gray's Inn, London WC1R 5AA,
Telephone: 0171 242 0328/071 405 1317
E-mail: clerks@2gis.co.uk
Guildhall Chambers Portsmouth
Prudential Buildings 16 Guildhall Walk,
Portsmouth, Hampshire PO1 2DE,
Telephone: 01705 752400
Call date: July 1978, Inner Temple
Qualifications: [BA (Leeds)]

FORTUNE ROBERT ANDREW

4 Brick Court
1st Floor, Temple, London EC4Y 9AD,
Telephone: 0171 583 8455
Call date: Feb 1976, Middle Temple
Qualifications: [LLB (Lond)]

FORWARD BARRY MILES

2 Mitre Ct Bldgs
1st Floor, Temple, London EC4Y 7BX,
Telephone: 0171 353 1353
Call date: July 1981, Gray's Inn
Qualifications: [BSc (Econ), Dip Law]

FORWARD MICHAEL EDMOND

Trafalgar Chambers
53 Fleet Street, London EC4Y 1BE,
Telephone: 0171 583 5858
E-mail: TrafalgarChambers@easynet.co.uk
Call date: Nov 1984, Inner Temple
Qualifications: [BA (Hons)]

D

FORWOOD NICHOLAS JAMES QC (1987)

Brick Court Chambers
15/19 Devereux Court, London WC2R 3JJ,
Telephone: 0171 583 0777
E-mail: (surname)@brickcourt.demon.co.uk
Door Tenant
8 King Street
Manchester M2 6AQ,
Telephone: 0161 834 9560
Door Tenant
Call date: July 1970, Middle Temple
Qualifications: [MA (Cantab)]

FOSKETT DAVID ROBERT QC (1991)

1 Crown Office Row
Ground Floor, Temple, London EC4Y 7HH,
Telephone: 0171 797 7500
Call date: July 1972, Gray's Inn
Recorder
Qualifications: [LLB (Lond)]

FOSTER MISS ALISON LEE CAROLINE

39 Essex Street
London WC2R 3AT,
Telephone: 0171 583 1111
E-mail: clerks@39essex.co.uk
Call date: July 1984, Inner Temple
Qualifications: [BA (Oxon), M.Phil, Dip.Law]

FOSTER BRIAN IAN

St James's Chambers
68 Quay Street, Manchester M3 3EJ,
Telephone: 0161 834 7000
E-mail: 106241.2625@compuserve.com
Park Lane Chambers
19 Westgate, Leeds LS1 2RD,
Telephone: 0113 2285000
Call date: July 1988, Lincoln's Inn
Qualifications: [LLB (Hons) Newcastle]

FOSTER MISS CATHERINE MARY

Plowden Bldgs
2nd Floor, Temple, London EC4Y 9BU,
Telephone: 0171 583 0808
E-mail: bar@plowdenbuildings.co.uk
Call date: July 1986, Inner Temple
Qualifications: [LLB (Nott'm)]

FOSTER CHARLES ANDREW

Chambers of Kieran Coonan QC
6 Pump Court, Ground Floor & Lower Ground
Floor, London EC4Y 7AR,
Telephone: 0171 583 6013/2510
Call date: July 1988, Inner Temple
Qualifications: [MA, Vet MB (Cantab), MRCVS]

Fax: 0171 353 0464; DX: 409 London,
Chancery Lane; Other comms: E-mail
charles_foster@link.org

Types of work: Common law (general);
Construction; Defamation; Medical negligence;
Personal injury; Professional negligence

Other professional qualifications: Veterinary
surgeon

Membership of foreign bars: Member of the Irish
Bar

Circuit: North Eastern

Awards and memberships: Professional
Negligence Bar Association; Medico-Legal
Society

Languages spoken: Arabic, French

Publications: *Personal Injury Toolkit* (Sweet &
Maxwell), 1997; *Disclosure and
Confidentiality* (Sweet & Maxwell), 1996;
Tripping and Slipping Cases, 2nd edn (Sweet &
Maxwell), 1996; Numerous legal articles in
Solicitors' Journal, *NLJ* and specialist medico-
legal publications, and non-legal articles in other
publications

Reported cases: *Bancroft v Harrogate HA*,
[1997] 8 Med LR 398, 1997. Whether failure to
perform total (cp sub-total) hysterectomy after
finding of certain histological changes in cervix
was negligent.
Hind v York HA, [1997] 8 Med LR 377, 1997.
Damage to anal sphincter. Immediate
knowledge of incontinence. When plaintiff
acquired knowledge for limitation purposes.
Ogden v Airedale HA, [1996] 7 Med LR 153,
1995. Liability of health authority to
radiographer for occupational asthma caused by
x-ray developing chemicals.
Kahl v Freistaat Bayern, [1995] PIQR P401,
1994. Abuse of process. Recoverability by
foreign state of sums paid under its own
legislation to foreign national injured in UK.

Fallows v Randle, [1997] 8 Med LR 160, 1996. Laparoscopic sterilisation. Fallope ring found later in incorrect position. Application of maxim *res ipsa loquitur*.

Additional Information

St John's College, Cambridge: Medical Sciences Tripos, Law Tripos and Clinical Veterinary Medicine. Research in wild animal anaesthesia and tranquilisation in Saudi Arabia and comparative anatomy at the Royal College of Surgeons. Research Fellow, Hebrew University, Jerusalem, and research assistant to Aharon Barak of the Supreme Court of Israel.

FOSTER FRANCIS ALEXANDER

St Paul's House
5th Floor 23 Park Square South, Leeds
LS1 2ND, Telephone: 0113 2455866
Call date: Oct 1990, Inner Temple
Qualifications: [LLB (Huddersfield)]

FOSTER MISS ILAINE VIVIENNE JULIA

University of Hertfordshire
7 Hatfield Road, St Albans, Herts AL1 3LS,
Telephone: 01727 286200
Call date: July 1982, Lincoln's Inn
Qualifications: [BA, LLM (Cantab)]

FOSTER JONATHAN ROWE QC (1989)

18 St John Street
Manchester M3 4EA,
Telephone: 0161 278 1800
1 Serjeants' Inn
5th Floor Fleet Street, Temple, London
EC4Y 1LL, Telephone: 0171 415 6666
E-mail: no1serjeantsinn@btinternet.com
Door Tenant
Call date: July 1970, Gray's Inn
Recorder
Qualifications: [MA (Oxon)]

FOSTER JULIEN ANDREW STEWART

Goldsmith Chambers
Ground Floor Goldsmith Building, Temple,
London EC4Y 7BL,
Telephone: 0171 353 6802/3/4/5
E-mail: celiamonksfield@btinternet.com
Call date: Oct 1995, Middle Temple
Qualifications: [BA (Hons) (York)]

FOSTER MS JULIET KATE

Southernhay Chambers
33 Southernhay East, Exeter EX1 1NX,
Telephone: 01392 255777
E-mail: southernhay.chambers@lineone.net
Call date: Nov 1989, Middle Temple
Qualifications: [LLB]

FOSTER MS MARGARET MARY

John Street Chambers
2 John Street, London WC1N 2HJ,
Telephone: 0171 242 1911
E-mail: john.street_chambers@virgin.net.uk
Call date: Feb 1993, Lincoln's Inn
Qualifications: [LLB]

FOSTER PETER

First National Building
2nd Floor 24 Fenwick Street, Liverpool
L2 7NE, Telephone: 0151 236 2098
Call date: Nov 1992, Middle Temple
Qualifications: [LLB (Hons, Manch)]

FOSTER MISS ROSALIND MARY

2 Temple Gardens
Temple, London EC4Y 9AY,
Telephone: 0171 583 6041 (12 Lines)
Call date: Nov 1969, Middle Temple
Recorder
Qualifications: [BA (Oxon)]

FOSTER SIMON HARVEY STENNETT

2 King's Bench Walk
Ground Floor, Temple, London EC4Y 7DE,
Telephone: 0171 353 1746
E-mail: 2kbw@atlas.co.uk
King's Bench Chambers
115 North Hill, Plymouth PL4 8JY,
Telephone: 01752 221551
Call date: July 1982, Middle Temple
Qualifications: [LLB (Exon)]

FOUDY MISS KIM FRANCES

8 King Street
Manchester M2 6AQ,
Telephone: 0161 834 9560
Call date: July 1982, Gray's Inn
Qualifications: [LLB]

FOULKES CHRISTOPHER DAVID

1 Hare Court
Ground Floor, Temple, London EC4Y 7BE,
Telephone: 0171 353 3982/5324
Call date: Oct 1994, Lincoln's Inn
Qualifications: [BA (Hons), LLB (Hons)(Leeds)]

FOULSER MISS JANE HELENA SUSAN

Angel Chambers
94 Walter Road, Swansea SA1 5QA,
Telephone: 01792 6464623/6464648
Call date: Feb 1994, Gray's Inn
Qualifications: [LLB (Wales), LLM (Wales)]

FOWLER EDMUND IAN CARLOSS

5 Paper Bldgs
Lower Ground Floor, Temple, London
EC4Y 7HB, Telephone: 0171 353 5638
E-mail: 107722,633@compuserve.com
Call date: Oct 1992, Gray's Inn
Qualifications: [LL.B]

FOWLER MICHAEL GLYN

36 Bedford Row
London WC1R 4JH,
Telephone: 0171 421 8000
E-mail: 36bedfordrow@link.org
Call date: July 1974, Middle Temple
Assistant Recorder
Qualifications: [LLB Lond]

FOWLER RICHARD NICHOLAS QC (1989)

Monckton Chambers
4 Raymond Buildings, Gray's Inn, London
WC1R 5BP, Telephone: 0171 405 7211
E-mail: chambers@monckton.co.uk
Call date: Nov 1969, Middle Temple
Qualifications: [BA (Oxon)]

FOWLER MISS TRACEY

Verulam Chambers
Peer House 8-14 Verulam Street, Gray's Inn,
London WC1X 8LZ,
Telephone: 0171 813 2400
Call date: Feb 1994, Inner Temple
Qualifications: [LLB (Lond)]

FOX ANDREW PATRICK

38 Young Street
Manchester M3 3FT,
Telephone: 0161 833 0489
E-mail: clerks@young-st-chambers.com
Call date: Oct 1990, Lincoln's Inn
Qualifications: [LLB (Buck'm)]

FOX MISS ANNA KATHERINE HELEN

Oriel Chambers
14 Water Street, Liverpool L2 8TD,
Telephone: 0151 236 7191
E-mail: oriel_chambers@link.org
Call date: July 1986, Middle Temple
Qualifications: [LLB (L'pool)]

FOX LADY HAZEL MARY QC (1993)

4-5 Gray's Inn Square
Ground Floor, Gray's Inn, London WC1R 5AY,
Telephone: 0171 404 5252
E-mail: chambers@4-5graysinnsquare.co.uk
Call date: June 1950, Lincoln's Inn
Qualifications: [MA (Oxon)]

FOX IAN ANTONY

2 Field Court
Gray's Inn, London WC1R 5BB,
Telephone: 0171 405 6114
E-mail: fieldct2@netcomuk.co.uk.
Call date: Oct 1990, Middle Temple
Qualifications: [LLB]

FOX JOHN HARVEY

Lamb Building
Ground Floor, Temple, London EC4Y 7AS,
Telephone: 0171 797 7788
E-mail: lamb.building@link.org
Call date: July 1973, Inner Temple
Qualifications: [LLB (Lond), BDS, LDS]

FOX MISS NICOLA SUSAN

One Garden Court
Ground Floor, Temple, London EC4Y 9BJ,
Telephone: 0171 797 7900
Call date: Oct 1996, Middle Temple
Qualifications: [BSc (Hons)(Lond), MSc, CPE
(City)]

FOX DR SIMON JAMES

Exchange Chambers
Pearl Assurance House Derby Square,
Liverpool L2 9XX, Telephone: 0151 236 7747/
0458
E-mail: exchangechambers@btinternet.com
Call date: Nov 1994, Inner Temple
Qualifications: [MB, BS, CPE (City)]

FOXTON DAVID ANDREW

Essex Court Chambers
24 Lincoln's Inn Fields, London WC2A 3ED,
Telephone: 0171 813 8000
E-mail: clerksroom@essexcourt-chambers.co.uk
Call date: Feb 1989, Gray's Inn
Qualifications: [BA, BCL (Oxon)]

FOXWELL GEORGE (AUGUSTUS)

Fenners Chambers
3 Madingley Road, Cambridge CB3 OEE,
Telephone: 01223 368761
Fenners Chambers
8-12 Priestgate, Peterborough PE1 1JA,
Telephone: 01733 62030
Call date: Nov 1987, Middle Temple
Qualifications: [LLB (Leeds)]

FOY JOHN LEONARD

9 Gough Square
London EC4A 3DE, Telephone: 0171 353 5371
Call date: July 1969, Gray's Inn
Qualifications: [LLB]

FRANCE-HAYHURST MRS JEAN GAYNOR

India Buildings Chambers
Water Street, Liverpool L2 OXG,
Telephone: 0151 243 6000
Call date: Nov 1972, Gray's Inn
Qualifications: [LLB (Hons, Wales)]

FRANCES MISS JILL

1 Pump Court
Lower Ground Floor, Temple, London
EC4Y 7AB, Telephone: 0171 583 2012/
353 4341
E-mail: (name) @1pumpcourt.co.uk
Call date: Nov 1992, Inner Temple
Qualifications: [LLB (So'ton)]

FRANCIS ADRIAN

24 Old Bldgs
Ground Floor, Lincoln's Inn, London
WC2A 3UJ, Telephone: 0171 404 0946
E-mail: clerks@24oldbuildings.law.co.uk
Call date: Nov 1988, Lincoln's Inn
Qualifications: [LLB Hons (Wales), BCL
(Oxon)]

FRANCIS ANDREW JAMES

11 New Square
Ground Floor, Lincoln's Inn, London
WC2A 3QB, Telephone: 0171 831 0081
E-mail: 11newsquare.co.uk
Call date: Nov 1977, Lincoln's Inn
Qualifications: [BA (Oxon)]

FRANCIS EDWARD GERALD FRANCIS

Enterprise Chambers
9 Old Square, Lincoln's Inn, London
WC2A 3SR, Telephone: 0171 405 9471
Enterprise Chambers
38 Park Square, Leeds LS1 2PA,
Telephone: 01132 460391
Enterprise Chambers
65 Quayside, Newcastle upon Tyne NE1 3DS,
Telephone: 0191 222 3344
Call date: Nov 1995, Inner Temple
Qualifications: [BA (Oxon), CPE (Lond)]

FRANCIS NICHOLAS

29 Bedford Row Chambers
London WC1R 4HE,
Telephone: 0171 831 2626
Call date: July 1981, Middle Temple
Qualifications: [MA (Cantab)]

FRANCIS RICHARD MAURICE

9 Park Place
Cardiff CF1 3DP, Telephone: 01222 382731
Call date: Nov 1974, Gray's Inn
Qualifications: [BA (Dunelm)]

FRANCIS ROBERT ANTHONY QC (1992)

3 Serjeants Inn
London EC4Y 1BQ,
Telephone: 0171 353 5537
E-mail: available upon request
Call date: July 1973, Inner Temple
Assistant Recorder
Qualifications: [LLB (Exon)]

FRANCK RICHARD DAVID WILLIAM

Equity Chambers
Suite 110, Gazette Buildings 168 Corporation
Street, Birmingham B4 6TS,
Telephone: 0121 233 2100
Call date: Oct 1993, Middle Temple
Qualifications: [BA (Hons)(Bris), CPE]

FRANCO GIANPIERO

2 Middle Temple Lane
3rd Floor, Temple, London EC4Y 9AA,
Telephone: 0171 583 4540
Call date: Nov 1988, Inner Temple
Qualifications: [MA (Cantab), LLB (Lond)]

FRANCOIS HERBERT DOLTON

Chancery Chambers
1st Floor Offices 70/72 Chancery Lane,
London WC2A 1AB,
Telephone: 0171 405 6879/6870
Call date: July 1972, Inner Temple
Qualifications: [BA]

FRANK IVOR RICHARD BAINTON

1 Gray's Inn Square
1st Floor, London WC1R 5AG,
Telephone: 0171 405 3000
E-mail: clerks@onegrays.demon.co.uk
Call date: July 1979, Gray's Inn
Qualifications: [LLB (Lond) LLM, (Georgetown
USA)]

FRANKLIN MISS KIM

Lamb Chambers
Lamb Building, Elm Court, Temple, London
EC4Y 7AS, Telephone: 0171 797 8300
E-mail: lambchambers@link.org
Call date: Nov 1984, Middle Temple
Qualifications: [LLB (Warwick)]

Fax: 0171 797 8308; DX: LDE 418

Types of work: Adjudication; Arbitration;
Construction; Professional negligence

Other professional qualifications: FCIArb; ORSA
Adjudicator; Approved for appointment as
arbitrator by the President of the RICS

Awards and memberships: ORBA; SCL;
Arbitration Club; Forum for Construction Law
Reform; Council Member Chartered Institute of
Arbitrators

Publications: Co-Editor, *Construction Law
Journal*, Bi-monthly; *Legal Obligations of the
Architect*, 1996; *Construction Disputes,
Liability & the Expert Witness*, 1994; *Architect's
Journal Legal Handbook*, New Edition;
Architect's Journal, Weekly Column; *'Damages
for Heartache' The award of general damages
in building cases*, 1988 and 1992

Reported cases: *Surrey Heath BC v Lovell
Construction*, (1989) 4 Const LJ 226, 1989. Fire
insurance provisions of JCT 180.
West Faulkner Associates v LB Newham, 61
BLR 81, 71 BLR, CA, 1994. Architect's duties and
determination provisions of JCT 63.
*Bernhard's Rugby Lansayres v Stockley Park
Consortium*, (1989) 14 Constr LJ, 1998.
Certifier's functions - breakdown of contract
machinery - jurisdiction.

FRANKLIN STEPHEN HALL

Fenners Chambers
3 Madingley Road, Cambridge CB3 OEE,
Telephone: 01223 368761
5 Paper Bldgs
1st Floor, Temple, London EC4Y 7HB,
Telephone: 0171 583 6117
E-mail: clerks@5-paperbuildings.law.co.uk
Door Tenant
Call date: Nov 1974, Gray's Inn
Qualifications: [BA (Dunelm)]

FRANSMAN LAURENS FRANCOIS

2 Garden Court
1st Floor, Middle Temple, London EC4Y 9BL,
Telephone: 0171 353 1633
E-mail: barristers@2gardenct.law.co.uk
Call date: July 1979, Middle Temple
Qualifications: [LLB]

FRASER ALAN RODERICK

2 Dr Johnson's Building
Temple, London EC4Y 7AY,
Telephone: 0171 353 4716
Call date: Oct 1990, Gray's Inn
Qualifications: [BSc, MSc (London), Dip Law]

FRASER NIGEL HUGH

8 King's Bench Walk
2nd Floor, Temple, London EC4Y 7DU,
Telephone: 0171 797 8888
8 King's Bench Walk North
1 Park Square East, Leeds LS1 2NE,
Telephone: 0113 2439797
Call date: Feb 1986, Inner Temple
Qualifications: [LL.B., C.N.A.A.]

FRASER ORLANDO GREGORY

4 Stone Bldgs
Ground Floor, Lincoln's Inn, London
WC2A 3XT, Telephone: 0171 242 5524
E-mail: d.goddard@4stonebuildings.law.co.uk
Call date: Nov 1994, Inner Temple
Qualifications: [BA (Cantab), CPE (Lond)]

FRASER PETER DONALD

1 Atkin Building
Gray's Inn, London WC1R 5AT,
Telephone: 0171 404 0102
E-mail: clerks@atkin-chambers.co.uk
Call date: Nov 1989, Middle Temple
Qualifications: [MA Hons, LLM (Cantab)]

FRASER VINCENT

40 King Street
Manchester M2 6BA,
Telephone: 0161 832 9082
E-mail: Kingst40@aol.com
Call date: July 1981, Gray's Inn
Qualifications: [MA (Oxon)]

FRASER-URQUHART ANDREW

4-5 Gray's Inn Square
Ground Floor, Gray's Inn, London WC1R 5AY,
Telephone: 0171 404 5252
E-mail: chambers@4-5graysinnsquare.co.uk
Call date: Oct 1993, Middle Temple
Qualifications: [MA (Hons)(Cantab)]

FRAZER CHRISTOPHER MARK

2 Harcourt Bldgs
1st Floor, Temple, London EC4Y 9DB,
Telephone: 0171 353 6961/7
Harcourt Chambers
Churchill House 3 St Aldate's Courtyard, St
Aldate's, Oxford OX1 1BN,
Telephone: 01865 791559
Call date: July 1983, Middle Temple
Qualifications: [MA, LLM (Cantab)]

FREEBORN MS SUSAN CHRISTINE

35 Essex Street
Temple, London WC2R 3AR,
Telephone: 0171 353 6381
Call date: July 1989, Gray's Inn
Qualifications: [BA [Cantab]]

FREEDLAND PROFESSOR MARK ROBERT

3 Verulam Buildings
London WC1R 5NT,
Telephone: 0171 831 8441
E-mail: clerks@3verulam.co.uk
Call date: Nov 1971, Gray's Inn
Qualifications: [LLB (Lond), MA,DPhil (Oxon)]

FREEDMAN BENJAMIN CLIVE QC (1997)

Littleton Chambers
3 King's Bench Walk North, Temple, London
EC4Y 7HR, Telephone: 0171 797 8600
E-mail: littletonchambers@compuserve.com
28 St John Street
Manchester M3 4DJ,
Telephone: 0161 834 8418
E-mail: clerk@28stjohnst.co.uk
Call date: July 1978, Middle Temple
Assistant Recorder
Qualifications: [MA (Cantab)]

FREEDMAN JEREMY STUART

New Court Chambers
3 Broad Chare, Newcastle Upon Tyne
NE1 3DQ, Telephone: 0191 232 1980
Plowden Bldgs
2nd Floor, Temple, London EC4Y 9BU,
Telephone: 0171 583 0808
E-mail: bar@plowdenbuildings.co.uk
Call date: July 1982, Middle Temple
Qualifications: [BA (Hons), Dip Law (City)]

D

FREEDMAN SAMPSON CLIVE

3 Verulam Buildings
London WC1R 5NT,
Telephone: 0171 831 8441
E-mail: clerks@3verulam.co.uk
Call date: July 1975, Gray's Inn
Qualifications: [MA (Cantab)]

FREELAND SIMON DENNIS MARSDEN

5 Essex Court
1st Floor, Temple, London EC4Y 9AH,
Telephone: 0171 410 2000
Call date: July 1978, Gray's Inn
Qualifications: [LLB (Manc)]

FREEMAN KEITH NICHOLAS

1 Crown Office Row
Ground Floor, Temple, London EC4Y 7HH,
Telephone: 0171 797 7500
York Chambers
14 Toft Green, York YO1 1JT,
Telephone: 01904 620048
E-mail: yorkchambers.co.uk
Call date: July 1985, Lincoln's Inn
Qualifications: [MA (City), BA (Reading) Dip
Law]

FREEMAN LEE ACRES

2 King's Bench Walk
1st Floor, Temple, London EC4Y 7DE,
Telephone: 0171 353 9276
Call date: Oct 1994, Lincoln's Inn
Qualifications: [LLB (Hons)(Lond), LLM
(Lond)]

FREEMAN MRS MARILYN ANNE

Gray's Inn Chambers
5th Floor, Gray's Inn, London WC1R 5JA,
Telephone: 0171 404 1111
Door Tenant
Call date: Feb 1986, Middle Temple
Qualifications: [BA (Hons), LLM Lond]

FREEMAN PETER MARK

Plowden Bldgs
2nd Floor, Temple, London EC4Y 9BU,
Telephone: 0171 583 0808
E-mail: bar@plowdenbuildings.co.uk
Call date: Oct 1992, Middle Temple
Qualifications: [LL.B (Hons)]

FREEMAN MRS SALLY JANE

East Anglian Chambers
Gresham House 5 Museum Street, Ipswich
IP1 1HQ, Telephone: 01473 214481
East Anglian Chambers
Sanders House 52 North Hill, Colchester
CO1 1PY, Telephone: 01206 572756
East Anglian Chambers
57 London Street, Norwich NR2 1HL,
Telephone: 01603 617351
Call date: Nov 1995, Lincoln's Inn
Qualifications: [LLB (Hons)]

FRENCH LOUIS CHARLES

6 Pump Court
1st Floor, Temple, London EC4Y 7AR,
Telephone: 0171 797 8400
E-mail: sa_hockman_qc@link.org
6-8 Mill Street
Maidstone, Kent ME15 6XH,
Telephone: 01622 688094
Call date: Nov 1979, Inner Temple
Qualifications: [MA (Oxon)]

FRENCH PAUL BECKINTON

Guildhall Chambers
23 Broad Street, Bristol BS1 2HG,
Telephone: 0117 9273366
Call date: July 1989, Inner Temple
Qualifications: [LLB (Hons)]

FRENCH RICHARD ANTHONY LISTER

Rougemont Chambers
15 Barnfield Road, Exeter EX1 1RR,
Telephone: 01392 410471
E-mail: rougemont.chambers@eclipse.co.uk
Call date: Nov 1995, Gray's Inn
Qualifications: [B.Eng (Exon)]

FRICKER MRS MARILYN ANN

25 Park Square
Leeds LS1 2PW, Telephone: 0113 2451841/2/3
E-mail: sovereignchambers@btinternet.com
Farrar's Building
Temple, London EC4Y 7BD,
Telephone: 0171 583 9241
E-mail: chambers@farrarsbuilding.co.uk
Door Tenant
Call date: Nov 1969, Gray's Inn

FRIDAY STEPHEN JOHN

Park Lane Chambers
19 Westgate, Leeds LS1 2RD,
Telephone: 0113 2285000
Call date: Oct 1996, Lincoln's Inn
Qualifications: [LLB (Hons)(E.Ang)]

FRIDD NICHOLAS TIMOTHY

All Saints Chambers
9/11 Broad Street, Bristol BS1 2HP,
Telephone: 0117 921 1966
Bell Yard Chambers
116/118 Chancery Lane, London WC2A 1PP,
Telephone: 0171 306 9292
Call date: Nov 1975, Inner Temple
Qualifications: [MA (Oxon)]

FRIEDMAN MS CHARLOTTE EVE

1 Pump Court
Lower Ground Floor, Temple, London
EC4Y 7AB, Telephone: 0171 583 2012/
353 4341
E-mail: (name) @1pumpcourt.co.uk
Call date: July 1982, Gray's Inn
Qualifications: [BA]

FRIEDMAN DAVID PETER QC (1990)

4 Pump Court
Temple, London EC4Y 7AN,
Telephone: 0171 353 2656/9
E-mail: 4_pump_court@compuserve.com
Call date: July 1968, Inner Temple
Assistant Recorder
Qualifications: [MA, (Oxon), BCL]

FRIEL JOHN ANTHONY

Goldsmith Building
1st Floor, Temple, London EC4Y 7BL,
Telephone: 0171 353 7881
E-mail: clerks@goldsmith-building.law.co.uk
Southsea Chambers
PO Box 148, Southsea, Portsmouth,
Hampshire PO5 2TU,
Telephone: 01705 291261
Call date: July 1974, Gray's Inn
Qualifications: [LLB (Lond)]

FRIEL MISS MICHELE

5 Fountain Court
Steelhouse Lane, Birmingham B4 6DR,
Telephone: 0121 606 0500
Call date: Oct 1991, Lincoln's Inn
Qualifications: [LLB (Hons)]

FRIESNER DAVID JONATHAN

9 St John Street
Manchester M3 4DN,
Telephone: 0161 955 9000
E-mail: ninesjs@gconnect.com
Call date: Nov 1988, Gray's Inn
Qualifications: [LLB (Hons)(Manch)]

FRIEZE DANIEL ISAAC

Victoria Chambers
19 Castle Street, Liverpool L2 4SX,
Telephone: 0151 236 9402
E-mail: Fa45@rapid.co.uk
Call date: Oct 1994, Gray's Inn
Qualifications: [BA (Manch)]

FRIEZE ROBIN BENNETT

6 Park Square
Leeds LS1 2LW, Telephone: 0113 2459763
E-mail: chambers@no6.co.uk
Call date: July 1985, Lincoln's Inn
Qualifications: [LLB (Leeds)]

FRIPP ERIC WILLIAM BURTIN

3 Pump Court
2nd Floor, Temple, London EC4Y 7AJ,
Telephone: 0171 353 1356 (3 Lines)
Call date: Oct 1994, Gray's Inn
Qualifications: [MA]

FRITH MS ALEXANDRA HELEN

Westgate Chambers
144 High Street, Lewes, East Sussex BN7 1XT,
Telephone: 01273 480510
Call date: Feb 1993, Lincoln's Inn
Qualifications: [LLB (Hons)]

FRITH MISS HEATHER VIVIEN

Kenworthy's Buildings
83 Bridge Street, Manchester M3 2RF,
Telephone: 0161 832 4036/834 6954
Call date: July 1989, Middle Temple
Qualifications: [LLB (Hons) (Bristol)]

D

FRITH NICHOLAS JOHN

30 Park Square
Leeds LS1 2PF, Telephone: 0113 2436388
Call date: Oct 1992, Gray's Inn
Qualifications: [LL.B, LL.M (Bucks)]

FRITH TIMOTHY GEORGE

Lamb Chambers
Lamb Building, Temple, London EC4Y 7AS,
Telephone: 0171 797 8300
E-mail: lambchambers@link.org
Call date: Nov 1996, Middle Temple
Qualifications: [MA (Hons), Dip Law]

FRODSHAM ALEXANDER MILES

Oriel Chambers
14 Water Street, Liverpool L2 8TD,
Telephone: 0151 236 7191
E-mail: oriel_chambers@link.org
Call date: Oct 1996, Lincoln's Inn
Qualifications: [LLB (Hons)(L'pool)]

FROST MISS GILLIAN

Mitre Court Chambers
3rd Floor, Temple, London EC4Y 7BP,
Telephone: 0171 353 9394
Call date: Nov 1979, Lincoln's Inn
Qualifications: [BA (Lond) (Hons)]

FRY NEIL JOHN

Queen Elizabeth Bldg
Ground Floor, Temple, London EC4Y 9BS,
Telephone: 0171 353 7181 (12 Lines)
Call date: Feb 1992, Inner Temple
Qualifications: [LLB (Exeter)]

FRYER ANTHONY JAMES

Priory Chambers
2 Fountain Court, Steelhouse Lane,
Birmingham B4 6DR,
Telephone: 0121 236 3882/1375
Call date: July 1995, Gray's Inn
Qualifications: [LLB (Manc)]

FRYER-SPEDDING JAMES WALTER

St James's Chambers
68 Quay Street, Manchester M3 3EJ,
Telephone: 0161 834 7000
E-mail: 106241.2625@compuserve.com
Call date: Feb 1994, Gray's Inn
Qualifications: [LLB (Lond), BCL (Oxon)]

FRYMAN NEIL

Peel Court Chambers
45 Hardman Street, Manchester M3 3HA,
Telephone: 0161 832 3791
Call date: July 1989, Middle Temple
Qualifications: [LLB [Leic]]

FRYMANN ANDREW PHILIP

Fleet Chambers
Mitre House 44-46 Fleet Street, London
EC4Y 1BN, Telephone: 0171 936 3707
Call date: Nov 1995, Inner Temple
Qualifications: [LLB (Dunelm)]

FUAD KERIM

Chambers of Helen Grindrod QC
1st Floor 95a Chancery Lane, London
WC2A 2JG, Telephone: 0171 404 4777
Call date: Nov 1992, Inner Temple
Qualifications: [LLB (Hons)(Lond)]

FULFORD ADRIAN BRUCE QC (1994)

14 Tooks Court
Cursitor St, London EC4A 1LB,
Telephone: 0171 405 8828
E-mail: clerks @tooks.law.co.uk
Call date: July 1978, Middle Temple
Assistant Recorder
Qualifications: [BA (Soton)]

FULLER ALAN PETER

Albion Chambers
Broad Street, Bristol BS1 1DR,
Telephone: 0117 9272144
Call date: Oct 1993, Gray's Inn
Qualifications: [LLB (Warw)]

FULLER JONATHAN PAUL

2 King's Bench Walk
Ground Floor, Temple, London EC4Y 7DE,
Telephone: 0171 353 1746
E-mail: 2kbw@atlas.co.uk
King's Bench Chambers
115 North Hill, Plymouth PL4 8JY,
Telephone: 01752 221551
Call date: July 1977, Lincoln's Inn
Qualifications: [LLB (Lond)]

FULLERTON MICHAEL ANDREW

Sussex Chambers
9 Old Steine, Brighton BN1 1FJ,
Telephone: 01273 607953
Call date: Feb 1990, Inner Temple
Qualifications: [BA, LLB]

FULLWOOD ADAM GARRETT

Chambers of Ian Macdonald QC
Waldorf House Cooper Street, Manchester
M2 2FW, Telephone: 0161 236 1840
Call date: Mar 1996, Gray's Inn
Qualifications: [BA, MA (Bris)]

FULTHORPE JONATHAN MARK

17 Carlton Crescent
Southampton SO15 2XR,
Telephone: 01703 320320
E-mail: km@bar-17cc.demon.co.uk
Call date: Nov 1970, Inner Temple
Qualifications: [LLB (Hons), LLM (Lond),
FRGS]

FURBER (ROBERT) JOHN QC (1995)

4 Breams Buildings
London EC4A 1AQ,
Telephone: 0171 353 5835/430 1221
Call date: July 1973, Inner Temple
Qualifications: [MA (Cantab)]

FURLONG RICHARD CRAVEN

3 Gray's Inn Square
Ground Floor, London WC1R 5AH,
Telephone: 0171 520 5600
E-mail: gis3@btinternet.com
Call date: Oct 1994, Lincoln's Inn
Qualifications: [MA (Hons), CPE (Lond)]

FURMINGER MICHAEL ASHLEY

Herons Rest
Parkham Lane, Brixham, Devon TQ5 9JR,
Telephone: 01803 882293
Call date: Oct 1991, Gray's Inn
Qualifications: [LLB (Lond)]

FURNESS (HUGH) JONATHAN

30 Park Place
Cardiff CF1 3BA, Telephone: 01222 398421
E-mail: 100757.1456@compuserve.com
Call date: July 1979, Gray's Inn
Qualifications: [MA (Cantab)]

FURNESS CORIN JOHN

Park Lane Chambers
19 Westgate, Leeds LS1 2RD,
Telephone: 0113 2285000
Call date: Oct 1994, Lincoln's Inn
Qualifications: [LLB (Hons)(Hull)]

FURNESS MARK RICHARD

30 Park Place
Cardiff CF1 3BA, Telephone: 01222 398421
E-mail: 100757.1456@compuserve.com
Call date: Nov 1970, Lincoln's Inn
Qualifications: [MA (Cantab)]

FURNESS MICHAEL JAMES

Wilberforce Chambers
8 New Square, Lincoln's Inn, London
WC2A 3QP, Telephone: 0171 306 0102
E-mail: chambers@wilberforce.co.uk
Call date: July 1982, Lincoln's Inn
Qualifications: [MA (Cantab) BCL, (Oxon)]

FURNISS RICHARD ALEXANDER

22 Old Bldgs
Lincoln's Inn, London WC2A 3UJ,
Telephone: 0171 831 0222
Call date: Oct 1991, Middle Temple
Qualifications: [MA (Cantab)]

FURST STEPHEN ANDREW QC (1991)

Keating Chambers
10 Essex Street, Outer Temple, London
WC2R 3AA, Telephone: 0171 544 2600
Call date: July 1975, Middle Temple
Assistant Recorder
Qualifications: [BA (Oxon), LLB (Hons)(Leeds)]

D

FURZE MISS CAROLINE MARY

Wilberforce Chambers
8 New Square, Lincoln's Inn, London
WC2A 3QP, Telephone: 0171 306 0102
E-mail: chambers@wilberforce.co.uk
Call date: Oct 1992, Lincoln's Inn
Qualifications: [BA (Cantab)]

FYSH MICHAEL QC (1989)

8 New Square
Lincoln's Inn, London WC2A 3QP,
Telephone: 0171 405 4321
Call date: May 1965, Inner Temple
Qualifications: [MA (Oxon)]

GABB CHARLES HENRY ESCOTT

Pump Court Chambers
Upper Ground Floor 3 Pump Court, Temple,
London EC4Y 7AJ, Telephone: 0171 353 0711
Pump Court Chambers
31 Southgate Street, Winchester SO23 8EE,
Telephone: 01962 868161
Call date: Feb 1975, Middle Temple
Qualifications: [LLB]

GABBAY EDMOND

2 Middle Temple Lane
3rd Floor, Temple, London EC4Y 9AA,
Telephone: 0171 583 4540
Call date: June 1958, Lincoln's Inn

GADD MICHAEL JOHN

24 Old Bldgs
Ground Floor, Lincoln's Inn, London
WC2A 3UJ, Telephone: 0171 404 0946
E-mail: clerks@24oldbuildings.law.co.uk
Call date: July 1981, Lincoln's Inn
Qualifications: [BA (Dunelm)]

GADD RONALD PATRICK

Newport Chambers
12 Clytha Park Road, Newport, Gwent
NP9 47L, Telephone: 01633 267403/255855
Call date: Feb 1971, Gray's Inn
Qualifications: [LL.M]

GADNEY GEORGE MUNRO

2 Crown Office Row
Ground Floor, Temple, London EC4Y 7HJ,
Telephone: 0171 797 8100
E-mail: mail@2cor.co.uk, or to individual
barristers at: [barrister's surname]@2cor.co.uk
Call date: Nov 1974, Gray's Inn
Qualifications: [BA (Cantab)]

GADSDEN MARK JEREMY

2 Harcourt Bldgs
1st Floor, Temple, London EC4Y 9DB,
Telephone: 0171 353 2112/2817
Call date: July 1980, Middle Temple
Qualifications: [BA (Oxon)]

GAINER RICHARD ST CLAIR

4 Brick Court
Temple, London EC4Y 9AD,
Telephone: 0171 797 8910
Call date: Nov 1983, Middle Temple
Qualifications: [BA (Kent)]

GAISFORD PHILIP DAVID

3 Serjeants Inn
London EC4Y 1BQ,
Telephone: 0171 353 5537
E-mail: available upon request
Call date: Nov 1969, Gray's Inn
Qualifications: [LLB (Soton)]

GAISMAN JONATHAN NICHOLAS CRISPIN QC (1995)

7 King's Bench Walk
Ground Floor, Temple, London EC4Y 7DS,
Telephone: 0171 583 0404
Call date: Nov 1979, Inner Temple
Qualifications: [MA, BCL (Oxon)]

GAITSKELL ROBERT QC (1994)

Keating Chambers
10 Essex Street, Outer Temple, London
WC2R 3AA, Telephone: 0171 544 2600
Call date: July 1978, Gray's Inn
Assistant Recorder
Qualifications: [BSc (Eng), F.I.E.E., FCIArb,
C.Eng]

GAL MS SONIA

40 King Street
Manchester M2 6BA,
Telephone: 0161 832 9082
E-mail: Kingst40@aol.com
Call date: Nov 1982, Inner Temple
Assistant Recorder
Qualifications: [BA]

GALBERG MARC KAY

33 Bedford Row
London WC1R 4JH,
Telephone: 0171 242 6476
Call date: July 1982, Middle Temple
Qualifications: [MA (Oxon)]

GALBRAITH-MARTEN JASON NICHOLAS

Cloisters
1st Floor, Temple, London EC4Y 7AA,
Telephone: 0171 827 4000
E-mail: clerks@cloisters.com
Call date: Oct 1991, Middle Temple
Qualifications: [BA Hons (Cantab)]

GALE MICHAEL QC (1979)

1 King's Bench Walk
2nd Floor, Temple, London EC4Y 7DB,
Telephone: 0171 936 1500
E-mail: ddear@1kbw.co.uk
Call date: Feb 1957, Middle Temple
Qualifications: [MA (Cantab)]

GALLAGHER BRIAN JOSEPH

12 King's Bench Walk
Temple, London EC4Y 7EL,
Telephone: 0171 583 0811
E-mail: chambers@12kbw.co.uk
Call date: July 1975, Inner Temple
Qualifications: [LLB, BL (Kings Inn)]

GALLAGHER JOHN DAVID EDMUND

Goldsmith Building
1st Floor, Temple, London EC4Y 7BL,
Telephone: 0171 353 7881
E-mail: clerks@goldsmith-building.law.co.uk
Call date: Nov 1974, Gray's Inn
Assistant Recorder
Qualifications: [BA, AKC (Lond)]

GALLAGHER PATRICK

King Charles House
Standard Hill, Nottingham NG1 6FX,
Telephone: 0115 9418851
E-mail: clerks@kch.co.uk
Call date: July 1984, Gray's Inn
Qualifications: [BSc (Econ), LLB (Lond)]

GALLAGHER STANLEY HAROLD

4 Brick Court
Temple, London EC4Y 9AD,
Telephone: 0171 797 8910
Call date: Feb 1994, Lincoln's Inn
Qualifications: [B.Ec,LLB (Austraila)]

GALLEY MRS HELEN MARGARET

24 Old Bldgs
Ground Floor, Lincoln's Inn, London
WC2A 3UJ, Telephone: 0171 404 0946
E-mail: clerks@24oldbuildings.law.co.uk
Call date: July 1987, Gray's Inn
Qualifications: [LLB (Lond)]

GALLEY ROBERT EDWARD

Cleveland Chambers
63-65 Borough Road, Middlesbrough,
Cleveland TS1 3AA, Telephone: 01642 226036
Call date: Oct 1993, Lincoln's Inn
Qualifications: [BSc (Econ)(Hons), CPE]

GALLIVAN TERENCE JOHN

6 King's Bench Walk
Ground, Third & Fourth Floors, Temple,
London EC4Y 7DR,
Telephone: 0171 353 4931/583 0695
Call date: July 1981, Inner Temple
Qualifications: [BA (Dunelm), LLB (Cantab)]

GALLOWAY MALCOLM KENNITH WILLIAM

South Western Chambers
Melville House 12 Middle Street, Taunton,
Somerset TA1 1SH, Telephone: 01823 331919
Call date: Oct 1992, Inner Temple
Qualifications: [BA (Hons)]

D

GALPIN MISS DIANA FELICITY

10 King's Bench Walk
Ground Floor, Temple, London EC4Y 7EB,
Telephone: 0171 353 7742
E-mail: 10kbw@lineone.net
Call date: Nov 1995, Middle Temple
Qualifications: [BA (Hons)]

GAMMIE MALCOLM JAMES

1 Essex Court
Ground Floor, Temple, London EC4Y 9AR,
Telephone: 0171 583 2000
E-mail: clerks@oneessexcourt.co.uk
Call date: Oct 1997, Middle Temple
Qualifications: [MA (Hons)(Cantab)]

GAMMON MRS DAVINA ANNE

Chambers of Davina Gammon
Ground Floor 103 Walter Road, Swansea
SA1 5QS, Telephone: 01792 480770
Carmarthen Chambers
30 Spilman Street, Carmarthen, Dyfed
SA31 1LQ, Telephone: 01267 234410
Call date: July 1979, Middle Temple
Qualifications: [BA (Hons)]

GANDHI MS PAULENE

Goldsworth Chambers
1st Floor 10-11 Gray's Inn Square, London
WC1R 5JD, Telephone: 0171 405 7117
Call date: Oct 1995, Inner Temple
Qualifications: [BSc (Aberdeen), BA]

GANNER JOSEPH MICHAEL

Kenworthy's Buildings
83 Bridge Street, Manchester M3 2RF,
Telephone: 0161 832 4036/834 6954
Call date: July 1983, Inner Temple
Qualifications: [LLB]

GANNON KEVIN FRANCIS

8 King's Bench Walk
2nd Floor, Temple, London EC4Y 7DU,
Telephone: 0171 797 8888
8 King's Bench Walk North
1 Park Square East, Leeds LS1 2NE,
Telephone: 0113 2439797
Call date: Nov 1993, Inner Temple
Qualifications: [BSc (Loughborough), CPE]

GARCHA AJMER SINGH

1 Argyle Road
Wolverhampton WV2 4NY,
Telephone: 01902 561047
Call date: Nov 1980, Lincoln's Inn
Qualifications: [BA]

GARCIA-MILLER MISS LAURA

Enterprise Chambers
9 Old Square, Lincoln's Inn, London
WC2A 3SR, Telephone: 0171 405 9471
Enterprise Chambers
38 Park Square, Leeds LS1 2PA,
Telephone: 01132 460391
Enterprise Chambers
65 Quayside, Newcastle upon Tyne NE1 3DS,
Telephone: 0191 222 3344
Call date: July 1989, Middle Temple
Qualifications: [LLB Hons, Dip in French]

GARDEN IAN HARRISON

Derby Square Chambers
Merchants Court, Derby Square, Liverpool
L2 1TS, Telephone: 0151 709 4222
Call date: July 1989, Lincoln's Inn
Qualifications: [LLB (Hons Wales)]

GARDINER BRUCE DOUGLAS

2 Temple Gardens
Temple, London EC4Y 9AY,
Telephone: 0171 583 6041 (12 Lines)
Call date: Oct 1994, Middle Temple
Qualifications: [BA (Hons)(Oxon)]

GARDINER CHARLES NICHOLAS

1 Middle Temple Lane
Temple, London EC4Y 1LT,
Telephone: 0171 583 0659 (12 Lines)
Call date: Apr 1967, Middle Temple

GARDINER JOHN RALPH QC (1982)

11 New Square
1st Floor, Lincoln's Inn, London WC2A 3QB,
Telephone: 0171 242 4017/3981
E-mail: taxlaw@11newsquare.com
Call date: Nov 1968, Middle Temple
Qualifications: [MA, LLM (Cantab)]

GARDINER RICHARD KINGSWELL

5 Bell Yard
London WC2A 2JR, Telephone: 0171 333 8811
Door Tenant
Call date: July 1969, Lincoln's Inn
Qualifications: [MA (Oxon), LL.M. (London)]

GARDINER WILLIAM DAVID HUGH

95A Chancery Lane
London WC2A 1DT,
Telephone: 0171 405 3101
Call date: Nov 1976, Middle Temple
Qualifications: [BSc (Chemistry)]

GARDNER MISS CATRIONA ANNE

1 Gray's Inn Square
Ground Floor, London WC1R 5AA,
Telephone: 0171 405 8946/7/8
Call date: Nov 1995, Lincoln's Inn
Qualifications: [BA (Hons)]

GARDNER CHRISTOPHER JAMES ELLIS QC (1994)

Lamb Chambers
Lamb Building, Temple, London EC4Y 7AS,
Telephone: 0171 797 8300
E-mail: lambchambers@link.org
Call date: July 1968, Gray's Inn
Recorder
Qualifications: [MA (Cantab)]

GARFIELD ROGER GLYN

33 Park Place
Cardiff CF1 3BA, Telephone: 01222 233313
Farrar's Building
Temple, London EC4Y 7BD,
Telephone: 0171 583 9241
E-mail: chambers@farrarsbuilding.co.uk
Door Tenant
Call date: July 1965, Gray's Inn
Qualifications: [MA, LLB (Cantab)]

GARGAN MISS CATHERINE JANE

36 Bedford Row
London WC1R 4JH,
Telephone: 0171 421 8000
E-mail: 36bedfordrow@link.org
Call date: July 1978, Middle Temple
Qualifications: [LLB (L'pool)]

GARGAN MARK PATRICK

6 Park Square
Leeds LS1 2LW, Telephone: 0113 2459763
E-mail: chambers@no6.co.uk
Call date: July 1983, Middle Temple
Qualifications: [MA (Oxon)]

GARLAND MS ANNA ELIZABETH MCCLENNON

4 Fountain Court
Steelhouse Lane, Birmingham B4 6DR,
Telephone: 0121 236 3476
Call date: Feb 1994, Inner Temple
Qualifications: [BA (Cantab)]

GARLAND DAVID ROBERTSON

Brick Court Chambers
15/19 Devereux Court, London WC2R 3JJ,
Telephone: 0171 583 0777
E-mail: (surname)@brickcourt.demon.co.uk
Call date: Nov 1986, Middle Temple
Qualifications: [LLB, LLM, AKC (Lond)]

GARLICK PAUL RICHARD QC (1996)

Pump Court Chambers
Upper Ground Floor 3 Pump Court, Temple,
London EC4Y 7AJ, Telephone: 0171 353 0711
Pump Court Chambers
31 Southgate Street, Winchester SO23 8EE,
Telephone: 01962 868161
Call date: July 1974, Middle Temple
Recorder

GARNER ADRIAN JOHN ROBINSON

2 Harcourt Bldgs
Ground Floor/Left, Temple, London
EC4Y 9DB, Telephone: 0171 583 9020
E-mail: clerks@harcourt.co.uk
Stanbrook & Henderson
2 Harcourt Bldgs 2nd Floor, Temple, London
EC4Y 9DB, Telephone: 0171 353 0101
E-mail: clerks@harcourt.co.uk
Call date: Nov 1985, Middle Temple
Qualifications: [LLB (Buck)]

GARNER GRAHAM HOWARD

Southsea Chambers
PO Box 148, Southsea, Portsmouth,
Hampshire PO5 2TU,
Telephone: 01705 291261
Call date: Feb 1966, Gray's Inn

GARNER MISS SOPHIE JANE

199 Strand
London WC2R 1DR,
Telephone: 0171 379 9779
E-mail: chambers@199strand.co.uk
Call date: Nov 1990, Middle Temple
Qualifications: [LLB]

GARNETT KEVIN MITCHELL QC (1991)

5 New Square
1st Floor, Lincoln's Inn, London WC2A 3RJ,
Telephone: 0171 404 0404
E-mail: Chambers@FiveNewSquare.CityScape.co.uk
Call date: Nov 1975, Middle Temple
Assistant Recorder
Qualifications: [MA (Oxon)]

GARNETT MRS SUSAN JANE LOUISA

Thomas More Chambers
52 Carey Street, Lincoln's Inn, London
WC2A 2JB, Telephone: 0171 404 7000
Call date: July 1973, Lincoln's Inn
Qualifications: [BA]

GARNHAM NEIL STEPHEN

1 Crown Office Row
Ground Floor, Temple, London EC4Y 7HH,
Telephone: 0171 797 7500
Crown Office Row Chambers
Blenheim House 120 Church Street, Brighton,
Sussex BN1 1WH, Telephone: 01273 625625
Call date: July 1982, Middle Temple
Qualifications: [MA (Cantab)]

GARNHAM TOM EDWARD KARL

Guildhall Chambers Portsmouth
Prudential Buildings 16 Guildhall Walk,
Portsmouth, Hampshire PO1 2DE,
Telephone: 01705 752400
Call date: Nov 1995, Middle Temple
Qualifications: [BA (Hons)]

GARNIER EDWARD HENRY QC (1995)

1 Brick Court
1st Floor, Temple, London EC4Y 9BY,
Telephone: 0171 353 8845
E-mail: clerks@1brickcourt.co.uk
Call date: July 1976, Middle Temple
Qualifications: [MA (Oxon)]

GARRETT MISS ANNALISSA

6 Pump Court
Ground Floor, Temple, London EC4Y 7AR,
Telephone: 0171 583 6013/2510
Call date: Nov 1991, Inner Temple
Qualifications: [BA (Hons)(Dunelm)]

GARRETT MICHAEL OWEN

Priory Chambers
2 Fountain Court, Steelhouse Lane,
Birmingham B4 6DR,
Telephone: 0121 236 3882/1375
Call date: July 1967, Gray's Inn

GARRIDO DAMIAN ROBIN LEON

2 Pump Court
1st Floor, Temple, London EC4Y 7AH,
Telephone: 0171 353 5597
Call date: Nov 1993, Middle Temple
Qualifications: [BA (Hons)(Kent), Dip Law (City)]

GARROOD JEREMY DAVID

New Court
Temple, London EC4Y 9BE,
Telephone: 0171 583 5123/0171 583 0510
Call date: May 1996, Lincoln's Inn
Qualifications: [BA (Hons)]

GARSIDE CHARLES ROGER QC (1993)

9 St John Street
Manchester M3 4DN,
Telephone: 0161 955 9000
E-mail: ninesjs@gconnect.com
Call date: Nov 1971, Gray's Inn
Recorder

GARSIDE DAVID VERNON

21 White Friars
Chester CH1 1NZ, Telephone: 01244 323070
Call date: Nov 1982, Gray's Inn
Qualifications: [LLB (Hons)]

GARSIDE MR MARK KIRKLAND

Claremont Chambers
26 Waterloo Road, Wolverhampton WV1 4BL,
Telephone: 01902 426222
Call date: Feb 1993, Inner Temple
Qualifications: [BA]

GARTH STEVEN DAVID

25 Park Square
Leeds LS1 2PW, Telephone: 0113 2451841/2/3
E-mail: sovereignchambers@btinternet.com
Call date: Nov 1983, Gray's Inn
Qualifications: [LLB (Hons) (Leeds)]

GARVIN MICHAEL

18 St John Street
Manchester M3 4EA,
Telephone: 0161 278 1800
Call date: Nov 1994, Inner Temple
Qualifications: [BA (Oxon)]

GASH WILLIAM SIMON WALKER

24 The Ropewalk
Nottingham NG1 5EF,
Telephone: 0115 9472581
E-mail: clerk@ropewalk.co.uk
Call date: July 1977, Gray's Inn

GASKELL NICHOLAS JOSEPH JAMES

4 Essex Court
Temple, London EC4Y 9AJ,
Telephone: 0171 797 7970
E-mail: clerks@4essexcourt.law.co.uk
Call date: July 1976, Inner Temple

GASKELL RICHARD CARL

65-67 King Street
Leicester LE1 6RP, Telephone: 0116 2547710
Call date: July 1971, Lincoln's Inn
Recorder
Qualifications: [LLB]

GASSMAN MISS CAROLINE DORA

8 King's Bench Walk
2nd Floor, Temple, London EC4Y 7DU,
Telephone: 0171 797 8888
8 King's Bench Walk North
1 Park Square East, Leeds LS1 2NE,
Telephone: 0113 2439797
Call date: July 1974, Inner Temple
Qualifications: [LLB (Leeds)(Hons)]

GASTON GRAEME

Plowden Bldgs
2nd Floor, Temple, London EC4Y 9BU,
Telephone: 0171 583 0808
E-mail: bar@plowdenbuildings.co.uk
Call date: Oct 1991, Lincoln's Inn
Qualifications: [LLB (Hons) (Leeds)]

GASZTOWICZ STEVEN

2 New Street
Leicester LE1 5NA, Telephone: 0116 2625906
Call date: July 1981, Gray's Inn
Qualifications: [LLB]

GATENBY JAMES MICHAEL

First National Building
2nd Floor 24 Fenwick Street, Liverpool
L2 7NE, Telephone: 0151 236 2098
Call date: Oct 1994, Middle Temple
Qualifications: [LLB (Hons)(L'pool)]

GATESHILL JOSEPH BERNARD

Wilberforce Chambers
Bishop Lane, Hull HU1 1PA,
Telephone: 01482 323264
E-mail: clerks@hullbar.demon.co.uk
Call date: July 1972, Lincoln's Inn
Assistant Recorder
Qualifications: [MA (Cantab)]

GATLAND GLENN DALE

New Court Chambers
3 Broad Chare, Newcastle Upon Tyne
NE1 3DQ, Telephone: 0191 232 1980
Call date: Nov 1972, Gray's Inn
Qualifications: [LLB (Hons) Fellow of,
Caribbean Law, Institute]

GATLEY MARK DOUGLAS

Chambers of Helen Grindrod QC
1st Floor 95a Chancery Lane, London
WC2A 2JG, Telephone: 0171 404 4777
Call date: Oct 1993, Gray's Inn
Qualifications: [BA]

GATT IAN ANDREW

Littleton Chambers
3 King's Bench Walk North, Temple, London
EC4Y 7HR, Telephone: 0171 797 8600
E-mail: littletonchambers@compuserve.com
Call date: July 1985, Lincoln's Inn
Qualifications: [BA (Oxon)]

GATTO MISS NICOLA ESTERINA

8 King's Bench Walk
2nd Floor, Temple, London EC4Y 7DU,
Telephone: 0171 797 8888
8 King's Bench Walk North
1 Park Square East, Leeds LS1 2NE,
Telephone: 0113 2439797
Call date: Nov 1987, Middle Temple
Qualifications: [LLB (B'ham)]

GATTY DANIEL SIMON

New Court Chambers
5 Verulam Buildings, Gray's Inn, London
WC1R 5LY, Telephone: 0171 831 9500
E-mail: mail@newcourtchambers.com
Call date: Oct 1990, Middle Temple
Qualifications: [BA (Manch), Dip Law]

GAU JUSTIN CHARLES

Pump Court Chambers
Upper Ground Floor 3 Pump Court, Temple,
London EC4Y 7AJ, Telephone: 0171 353 0711
Pump Court Chambers
31 Southgate Street, Winchester SO23 8EE,
Telephone: 01962 868161
Call date: July 1989, Middle Temple
Qualifications: [LLB (Lond)]

GAULT SIMON ANGUS GRAHAM LESLIE

4 Essex Court
Temple, London EC4Y 9AJ,
Telephone: 0171 797 7970
E-mail: clerks@4essexcourt.law.co.uk
Call date: Nov 1970, Gray's Inn
Recorder
Qualifications: [LLB]

GAUNT JONATHAN ROBERT QC (1991)

Falcon Chambers
Falcon Court, London EC4Y 1AA,
Telephone: 0171 353 2484/7
Call date: July 1972, Lincoln's Inn
Qualifications: [BA (Oxon)]

GAUNT MISS SARAH LEVINA

36 Bedford Row
London WC1R 4JH,
Telephone: 0171 421 8000
E-mail: 36bedfordrow@link.org
Call date: Oct 1992, Lincoln's Inn
Qualifications: [LLB(Hons)(Wales), MPhil
(Cantab)]

GAVAGHAN JONATHAN DAVID

10 Old Square
Ground Floor, Lincoln's Inn, London
WC2A 3SU, Telephone: 0171 405 0758
Call date: Oct 1992, Lincoln's Inn
Qualifications: [MA(Hons), BCL (Oxon)]

GAVRON MISS JESSICA LEAH

9-12 Bell Yard
London WC2A 2LF,
Telephone: 0171 400 1800
Call date: Oct 1995, Inner Temple
Qualifications: [BA (Cantab), CPE (City)]

GAY MISS VIVIENNE KARIN

Cloisters
1st Floor, Temple, London EC4Y 7AA,
Telephone: 0171 827 4000
E-mail: clerks@cloisters.com
Call date: July 1974, Gray's Inn
Qualifications: [LLB, LLM]

GAYLORD MRS SHEILA

2 King's Bench Walk
1st Floor, Temple, London EC4Y 7DE,
Telephone: 0171 353 9276
Westgate Chambers
144 High Street, Lewes, East Sussex BN7 1XT,
Telephone: 01273 480510
Call date: Nov 1983, Gray's Inn
Qualifications: [LLM LLB (Lond)]

GBESAN JAMES YOMI

Eldon Chambers
Fourth Floor 30/32 Fleet Street, London
EC4Y 1AA, Telephone: 0171 353 4636
Call date: Feb 1992, Lincoln's Inn
Qualifications: [LLB (Hon)]

GEARY GAVIN JOHN

7 King's Bench Walk
Ground Floor, Temple, London EC4Y 7DS,
Telephone: 0171 583 0404
Call date: Feb 1989, Gray's Inn
Qualifications: [BA (Oxon)]

GEDDES MS JOANNA FAY

One Garden Court
Ground Floor, Temple, London EC4Y 9BJ,
Telephone: 0171 797 7900
Call date: Nov 1992, Gray's Inn
Qualifications: [BA (Lond)]

GEDERON MARVIN THEOPHILUS

20 Britton Street
1st Floor, London EC1M 5NQ,
Telephone: 0171 608 3765
Call date: Nov 1979, Lincoln's Inn
Qualifications: [BA]

GEDGE SIMON JOHN FRANCIS

Chambers of Helen Grindrod QC
1st Floor 95a Chancery Lane, London
WC2A 2JG, Telephone: 0171 404 4777
Call date: Nov 1984, Inner Temple
Qualifications: [MA (Oxon)]

GEE ANTHONY HALL QC (1990)

28 St John Street
Manchester M3 4DJ,
Telephone: 0161 834 8418
E-mail: clerk@28stjohnst.co.uk
Call date: July 1972, Gray's Inn
Recorder

GEE MISS MARGARET ANN

Luton Bedford Chambers
C/O Mr Alex Reid 92 Holly Park Road, Friern
Barnet, London N11 3HB,
Telephone: 0181 361 9024/0181 444 6337
Call date: July 1979, Gray's Inn
Qualifications: [BA (Lond)]

GEE MRS PETA MARIE

2 Paper Bldgs
Temple, London EC4Y 7ET,
Telephone: 0171 936 2613
Door Tenant
Call date: Nov 1973, Gray's Inn
Qualifications: [BA (Hons), Dip Ed]

GEE RICHARD SIMON

Cobden House Chambers
19 Quay Street, Manchester M3 3HN,
Telephone: 0161 833 6000
E-mail: clerks@cobden.co.uk
Call date: Oct 1993, Lincoln's Inn
Qualifications: [MA (Oxon), Dip Law (Lond)]

GEE STEVEN MARK QC (1993)

1 Essex Court
Ground Floor, Temple, London EC4Y 9AR,
Telephone: 0171 583 2000
E-mail: clerks@oneessexcourt.co.uk
Call date: July 1975, Middle Temple
Qualifications: [MA (Oxon)]

GEE TOBY DAVID

1 Paper Bldgs
Ground Floor, Temple, London EC4Y 7EP,
Telephone: 0171 583 7355
E-mail: clerks@1pb.co.uk
Call date: Oct 1992, Inner Temple
Qualifications: [MA (Cantab), CPE]

GEEKIE CHARLES NAIRN

3 Temple Gardens
Lower Ground Floor, Temple, London
EC4Y 9AU, Telephone: 0171 353 3102/5/9297
Call date: July 1985, Inner Temple
Qualifications: [LLB(Bristol)]

GEERING IAN WALTER QC (1991)

3 Verulam Buildings
London WC1R 5NT,
Telephone: 0171 831 8441
E-mail: clerks@3verulam.co.uk
Call date: Nov 1974, Inner Temple
Recorder
Qualifications: [BVMS]

GEESON CHRISTOPHER PAUL

1 High Pavement
Nottingham NG1 1HF,
Telephone: 0115 9418218
Call date: Nov 1989, Gray's Inn
Qualifications: [BA]

GEEY DAVID SIMON

Martins Building
Water Street, Liverpool L2 3SP,
Telephone: 0151 236 5818/4919
Call date: July 1970, Inner Temple
Recorder
Qualifications: [LLB]

GELBART GEOFFREY ALAN

1 Gray's Inn Square
Ground Floor, London WC1R 5AA,
Telephone: 0171 405 8946/7/8
Call date: Nov 1982, Lincoln's Inn
Qualifications: [BA (Hons), LLM, (Lond)]

GELDART WILLIAM RALPH

6 King's Bench Walk
Ground, Third & Fourth Floors, Temple,
London EC4Y 7DR,
Telephone: 0171 353 4931/583 0695
Call date: July 1975, Inner Temple
Qualifications: [BA (Open)]

GENN MS YVETTE NAOMI

2 Garden Court
1st Floor, Middle Temple, London EC4Y 9BL,
Telephone: 0171 353 1633
E-mail: barristers@2gardenct.law.co.uk
Call date: Oct 1991, Inner Temple
Qualifications: [BA (Warw), Dip Law]

GENNEY PAUL WALTON

Wilberforce Chambers
Bishop Lane, Hull HU1 1PA,
Telephone: 01482 323264
E-mail: clerks@hullbar.demon.co.uk
Call date: May 1976, Middle Temple
Qualifications: [BDS]

GEORGE CHARLES RICHARD QC (1992)

2 Harcourt Bldgs
2nd Floor, Temple, London EC4Y 9DB,
Telephone: 0171 353 8415
E-mail: clerks@twoharcourtbldgs.demon.co.uk
Call date: July 1974, Inner Temple
Recorder
Qualifications: [MA (Oxon)]

GEORGE DONALD ERIC JOSEPH

Leone Chambers
72 Evelyn Avenue, Kingsbury, London
NW9 0JH, Telephone: 0181 931 1712
Call date: July 1973, Gray's Inn
Qualifications: [BA (Durham)]

GEORGE MISS JUDITH SARAH

7 Fountain Court
Steelhouse Lane, Birmingham B4 6DR,
Telephone: 0121 236 8531
Call date: Oct 1991, Middle Temple
Qualifications: [BA Hons (Cantab)]

GEORGE MARK MCHALLAM

2 Garden Court
1st Floor, Middle Temple, London EC4Y 9BL,
Telephone: 0171 353 1633
E-mail: barristers@2gardenct.law.co.uk
Call date: Nov 1976, Inner Temple
Qualifications: [BA (Cantab)]

GEORGE MICHAEL DAVID ROBERTS

Goldsmith Chambers
Ground Floor Goldsmith Building, Temple,
London EC4Y 7BL,
Telephone: 0171 353 6802/3/4/5
E-mail: celiamonksfield@btinternet.com
Call date: Nov 1990, Gray's Inn
Qualifications: [LLB]

GEORGE NICHOLAS FRANK RAYMOND

New Walk Chambers
27 New Walk, Leicester LE1 6TE,
Telephone: 0116 2559144
Call date: July 1983, Inner Temple
Qualifications: [LLB (Manch)]

GEORGE MISS SUSAN DEBORAH

8 King's Bench Walk
2nd Floor, Temple, London EC4Y 7DU,
Telephone: 0171 797 8888
8 King's Bench Walk North
1 Park Square East, Leeds LS1 2NE,
Telephone: 0113 2439797
Call date: Nov 1990, Gray's Inn
Qualifications: [LLB Hons (Lond)]

GEORGES ANTONIS

Martins Building
Water Street, Liverpool L2 3SP,
Telephone: 0151 236 5818/4919
Call date: July 1972, Inner Temple
Qualifications: [LLB]

GEORGHIADES ELIKKOS

Bromley Chambers
39 Durham Road, Bromley, Kent BR2 OSN,
Telephone: 0181 325 0863
Call date: July 1975, Middle Temple
Qualifications: [LLB (Lond)]

GERAGHTY MISS SARAH MARGRET

3 Paper Bldgs
1st Floor, Temple, London EC4Y 7EU,
Telephone: 0171 583 8055
E-mail: london@3paper.com
Call date: Oct 1994, Lincoln's Inn
Qualifications: [BA (Hons)]

GERALD NIGEL MORTIMER

Enterprise Chambers
9 Old Square, Lincoln's Inn, London
WC2A 3SR, Telephone: 0171 405 9471
Enterprise Chambers
38 Park Square, Leeds LS1 2PA,
Telephone: 01132 460391
Enterprise Chambers
65 Quayside, Newcastle upon Tyne NE1 3DS,
Telephone: 0191 222 3344
Call date: July 1985, Gray's Inn
Qualifications: [LLB (Lond)]

GERASIMIDIS NICOLAS

Furnival Chambers
32 Furnival Street, London EC4A 1JQ,
Telephone: 0171 405 3232
E-mail: clerks@furnivallaw.co.uk
Call date: Nov 1988, Inner Temple
Qualifications: [LLB (So'ton)]

GERMAIN RICHARD

4 Brick Court
1st Floor, Temple, London EC4Y 9AD,
Telephone: 0171 583 8455
Call date: July 1968, Inner Temple

GERRANS DANIEL

24 Old Bldgs
Ground Floor, Lincoln's Inn, London
WC2A 3UJ, Telephone: 0171 404 0946
E-mail: clerks@24oldbuildings.law.co.uk
Call date: Nov 1981, Middle Temple
Qualifications: [LLB (Cantab)]

GERRARD LEE JOHN

9 King's Bench Walk
Basement, Temple, London EC4Y 7DX,
Telephone: 0171 353 9564
E-mail: jvlee@btinternet.com
Call date: Mar 1996, Gray's Inn
Qualifications: [BA (Hons)(Newc), CPE]

GERREY DAVID CLIFF

9 Gough Square
London EC4A 3DE, Telephone: 0171 353 5371
Call date: Feb 1975, Gray's Inn
Recorder
Qualifications: [LLB]

GERRISH SIMON DAVID PETER

7 Stone Bldgs
1st Floor, Lincoln's Inn, London WC2A 3SZ,
Telephone: 0171 242 0961
Call date: Oct 1993, Gray's Inn
Qualifications: [MA (Hons)(Oxon)]

GERRY MISS FELICITY RUTH

2 New Street
Leicester LE1 5NA, Telephone: 0116 2625906
Call date: Oct 1994, Middle Temple
Qualifications: [LLB (Hons)]

GERSCH ADAM NISSEN

Trafalgar Chambers
53 Fleet Street, London EC4Y 1BE,
Telephone: 0171 583 5858
E-mail: TrafalgarChambers@easynet.co.uk
Call date: Oct 1993, Lincoln's Inn
Qualifications: [LLB (Hons)]

GESER MS ANITA

Lamb Building
Ground Floor, Temple, London EC4Y 7AS,
Telephone: 0171 797 7788
E-mail: lamb.building@link.org
Call date: Feb 1992, Middle Temple
Qualifications: [BA (Econ) (Lond)]

GETTLESON MICHAEL FRANCIS

17 Bedford Row
London WC1R 4EB,
Telephone: 0171 831 7314
E-mail: IBoard7314@AOL.com
Call date: July 1952, Middle Temple
Qualifications: [MA, BCL]

GHAFFAR ARSHAD

4 Field Court
Gray's Inn, London WC1R 5EA,
Telephone: 0171 440 6900
E-mail: chambers@4fieldcourt.co.uk
Call date: Oct 1991, Middle Temple
Qualifications: [LLB Hons (Exon), LLM (Cantab)]

GHORPADE BHASKER YESHWANT

Bracton Chambers
95a Chancery Lane, London WC2A 1DT,
Telephone: 0171 242 4248
Door Tenant
Call date: Nov 1973, Lincoln's Inn
Qualifications: [BA (Lond)]

GHOSH INDRANIL JULIAN

24 Old Bldgs
First Floor, Lincoln's Inn, London WC2A 3UJ,
Telephone: 0171 242 2744
40 King Street
Manchester M2 6BA,
Telephone: 0161 832 9082
E-mail: Kingst40@aol.com
Call date: July 1993, Lincoln's Inn

Qualifications: [LLB (Edinburgh), LLM (Lond),
Fellow of Queen Mary, & Westfield College,
University of London]

GHOSH MATILAL

Perivale Chambers
15 Colwyn Avenue, Perivale, Middlesex
UB6 8JY, Telephone: 0181 998 1935/
081 248 0246
Call date: Nov 1975, Inner Temple
Qualifications: [MA (Calcutta)]

GIBAUD MISS CATHERINE ALISON ANNETTA

3 Verulam Buildings
London WC1R 5NT,
Telephone: 0171 831 8441
E-mail: clerks@3verulam.co.uk
Call date: Oct 1996, Gray's Inn
Qualifications: [B.Bus.Sc (Hons), (Cape Town)]

GIBB MISS FIONA MARGARET

Queen Elizabeth Bldg
Ground Floor, Temple, London EC4Y 9BS,
Telephone: 0171 353 7181 (12 Lines)
Call date: July 1983, Middle Temple
Qualifications: [LLB (B'ham)]

GIBBERD MISS ANNE HEATHER

4 Brick Court
Ground Floor, Temple, London EC4Y 9AD,
Telephone: 0171 797 7766
E-mail: chambers@4brick.co.uk
Call date: Nov 1985, Gray's Inn
Qualifications: [LLB (Sheffield)]

GIBBON MISS JULIET REBECCA

9 Park Place
Cardiff CF1 3DP, Telephone: 01222 382731
Call date: Oct 1994, Lincoln's Inn
Qualifications: [LLB (Hons)(Glamorg)]

GIBBON MICHAEL NEIL

13 Old Square
Ground Floor, Lincoln's Inn, London
WC2A 3UA, Telephone: 0171 404 4800
Call date: Nov 1993, Gray's Inn
Qualifications: [BA, M.Phil]

GIBBONS CHRISTOPHER CHARLES

Rowchester Chambers
4 Rowchester Court Whittall Street,
Birmingham B4 6DH,
Telephone: 0121 233 2327/2361951
Call date: July 1977, Gray's Inn
Qualifications: [BSc (B'ham)]

GIBBONS JAMES FRANCIS

13 King's Bench Walk
1st Floor, Temple, London EC4Y 7EN,
Telephone: 0171 353 7204
E-mail: clerks@13kbw.law.co.uk
King's Bench Chambers
32 Beaumont Street, Oxford OX1 2NP,
Telephone: 01865 311066
E-mail: clerks@kbc-oxford.law.co.uk
Call date: July 1974, Gray's Inn

GIBBONS JEREMY STEWART QC (1995)

17 Carlton Crescent
Southampton SO15 2XR,
Telephone: 01703 320320
E-mail: km@bar-17cc.demon.co.uk
35 Essex Street
Temple, London WC2R 3AR,
Telephone: 0171 353 6381
Door Tenant
Call date: July 1973, Gray's Inn
Recorder

GIBBONS ORLANDO ADZIMA

10 King's Bench Walk
Ground Floor, Temple, London EC4Y 7EB,
Telephone: 0171 353 7742
E-mail: 10kbw@lineone.net
Call date: Nov 1982, Gray's Inn
Qualifications: [LLB (Lond)]

GIBBONS MRS SARAH ISOBEL

13 King's Bench Walk
1st Floor, Temple, London EC4Y 7EN,
Telephone: 0171 353 7204
E-mail: clerks@13kbw.law.co.uk
King's Bench Chambers
32 Beaumont Street, Oxford OX1 2NP,
Telephone: 01865 311066
E-mail: clerks@kbc-oxford.law.co.uk
Call date: Nov 1987, Middle Temple
Qualifications: [BA(Hons) B'ham, Dip Law
(City)]

GIBBS MRS JOCELYN IDA

8 King's Bench Walk
2nd Floor, Temple, London EC4Y 7DU,
Telephone: 0171 797 8888
Call date: Nov 1972, Lincoln's Inn
Qualifications: [LLB (Hons) (Lond)]

GIBBS MS LISA KLAIRE

Enfield Chambers
36-38 London Road, Enfield, Middlesex
EN2 6DT, Telephone: 0181 364 5627
E-mail: Enfieldchambers@compuserve.com
Call date: Oct 1995, Inner Temple
Qualifications: [BA (Lond), CPE (City)]

GIBBS PATRICK MICHAEL EVAN

2 Harcourt Bldgs
1st Floor, Temple, London EC4Y 9DB,
Telephone: 0171 353 2112/2817
Call date: Nov 1986, Middle Temple
Qualifications: [BA(Oxon) Dip Law Cit]

GIBBS PHILIP MARK

2 New Street
Leicester LE1 5NA, Telephone: 0116 2625906
Call date: Oct 1991, Inner Temple
Qualifications: [BA (E Anglia), Dip Law]

GIBNEY MALCOLM THOMAS PATRICK

17 Carlton Crescent
Southampton SO15 2XR,
Telephone: 01703 320320
E-mail: km@bar-17cc.demon.co.uk
Call date: July 1981, Inner Temple
Qualifications: [LLB (Cardiff)]

GIBSON ARTHUR GEORGE ADRIAN

Adrian Lyon's Chambers
14 Castle Street, Liverpool L2 0NE,
Telephone: 0151 236 4421/8240
E-mail: chambers14@aol.com
Call date: July 1980, Lincoln's Inn
Qualifications: [LLB Hons (Lond)]

D

GIBSON MISS CAROLINE CATHERINE ROSE

1 King's Bench Walk
2nd Floor, Temple, London EC4Y 7DB,
Telephone: 0171 936 1500
E-mail: ddear@1kbw.co.uk
Call date: Nov 1990, Inner Temple
Qualifications: [BA (Oxon), Dip Law (City)]

GIBSON CHARLES ANTHONY WARNEFORD

2 Harcourt Bldgs
Ground Floor/Left, Temple, London
EC4Y 9DB, Telephone: 0171 583 9020
E-mail: clerks@harcourt.co.uk
Call date: July 1984, Inner Temple
Qualifications: [BA (Dunelm) Dip Law]

GIBSON CHRISTOPHER ALLEN WOOD QC (1995)

2 Crown Office Row
2nd Floor, Temple, London EC4Y 7HJ,
Telephone: 0171 797 8000
Call date: July 1976, Middle Temple
Qualifications: [BA (Oxon)]

GIBSON MISS JILL MAUREEN

11 New Square
Ground Floor, Lincoln's Inn, London
WC2A 3QB, Telephone: 0171 831 0081
E-mail: 11newsquare.co.uk
Call date: July 1972, Middle Temple
Qualifications: [BA (Hons) (Bristol)]

GIBSON JOHN ARTHUR

India Buildings Chambers
Water Street, Liverpool L2 0XG,
Telephone: 0151 243 6000
Call date: Nov 1993, Lincoln's Inn
Qualifications: [LLB (Hons, B'ham)]

GIBSON JOHN WILLIAM

36 Bedford Row
London WC1R 4JH,
Telephone: 0171 421 8000
E-mail: 36bedfordrow@link.org
Call date: Nov 1991, Inner Temple
Qualifications: [LLB (Dunelm)]

GIBSON JONATHAN HEDLEY

Broadway House Chambers
Broadway House 9 Bank Street, Bradford,
West Yorkshire BD1 1TW,
Telephone: 01274 722560
Call date: July 1982, Gray's Inn
Qualifications: [LLB (Nottm)]

GIBSON MARTIN JOHN

Littman Chambers
12 Gray's Inn Square, London WC1R 5JP,
Telephone: 0171 404 4866
E-mail: admin@littmanchambers.com
Call date: Oct 1990, Lincoln's Inn
Qualifications: [BA (Oxon)]

GIBSON ROBERT MARK TIMOTHY

Peel House Chambers
Ground Floor, Peel House 5 Harrington Street,
Liverpool L2 9QA, Telephone: 0151 236 4321
Call date: Nov 1981, Middle Temple
Qualifications: [MA (Oxon)]

GIBSON-LEE DAVID MICHAEL

Bell Yard Chambers
116/118 Chancery Lane, London WC2A 1PP,
Telephone: 0171 306 9292
Call date: July 1970, Lincoln's Inn
Qualifications: [LLB]

GIDNEY JONATHAN ALFRED

Claremont Chambers
26 Waterloo Road, Wolverhampton WV1 4BL,
Telephone: 01902 426222
Call date: Oct 1991, Inner Temple
Qualifications: [BA (Hons)]

GIFFIN NIGEL DYSON

11 King's Bench Walk
Temple, London EC4Y 7EQ,
Telephone: 0171 632 8500
E-mail: clerksroom@11-kbw.law.co.uk
Call date: Nov 1986, Inner Temple
Qualifications: [MA (Oxon)]

GIFFORD ANDREW JAMES MORRIS

7 New Square
Lincoln's Inn, London WC2A 3QS,
Telephone: 0171 430 1660
Call date: July 1988, Lincoln's Inn

Qualifications: [BA (Hons) (Oxon), Dip Law (City)]

GIFFORD LORD ANTHONY MAURICE QC (1982)

8 King's Bench Walk
2nd Floor, Temple, London EC4Y 7DU,
Telephone: 0171 797 8888
8 King's Bench Walk North
1 Park Square East, Leeds LS1 2NE,
Telephone: 0113 2439797
Call date: July 1962, Middle Temple
Qualifications: [MA (Cantab)]

GIFFORD MISS CYNTHIA ALICE SOPHIE

Verulam Chambers
Peer House 8-14 Verulam Street, Gray's Inn,
London WC1X 8LZ,
Telephone: 0171 813 2400
Call date: July 1988, Gray's Inn
Qualifications: [BA (Hons)(Manc), MSc (LSE),
Dip Law]

GIFFORD ROBERT GUTHRIE

2 King's Bench Walk
1st Floor, Temple, London EC4Y 7DE,
Telephone: 0171 353 9276
Call date: Nov 1977, Inner Temple

GILBART ANDREW JAMES QC (1991)

40 King Street
Manchester M2 6BA,
Telephone: 0161 832 9082
E-mail: Kingst40@aol.com
4 Breams Buildings
London EC4A 1AQ,
Telephone: 0171 353 5835/430 1221
Door Tenant
Call date: Nov 1972, Middle Temple
Recorder
Qualifications: [MA (Cantab)]

GILBERT BARRY DAVID

10 King's Bench Walk
1st Floor, Temple, London EC4Y 7EB,
Telephone: 0171 353 2501
Call date: July 1978, Gray's Inn
Qualifications: [LLB (So'ton), Dip Ara (Lond)]

GILBERT FRANCIS HUMPHREY SHUBRICK QC (1992)

Walnut House
63 St. David's Hill, Exeter, Devon EX4 4DW,
Telephone: 01392 279751
E-mail: 106627.2451@compuserve.com
Call date: July 1970, Lincoln's Inn
Recorder
Qualifications: [MA (Dublin)]

GILBERT FRANCIS PETER

Mitre House Chambers
Mitre House 44 Fleet Street, London
EC4Y 1BN, Telephone: 0171 583 8233
Call date: July 1980, Lincoln's Inn
Qualifications: [BD, AKC, MA]

GILBERT MRS JAYNE EILEEN

3 Temple Gardens
Lower Ground Floor, Temple, London
EC4Y 9AU, Telephone: 0171 353 3102/5/9297
Call date: July 1976, Middle Temple

GILBERT MS JULIA JANE

Trinity Chambers
9-12 Trinity Chare, Quayside, Newcastle Upon
Tyne NE1 3DF, Telephone: 0191 232 1927
Call date: Nov 1994, Middle Temple
Qualifications: [LLB (Hons)]

GILBERT ROBERT JOHN

Fountain Chambers
Cleveland Business Centre 1 Watson Street,
Middlesbrough TS1 2RQ,
Telephone: 01642 217037
Call date: Apr 1986, Middle Temple
Qualifications: [LLB (L'pool), P.G.C.E.]

GILBERTSON MRS HELEN ALISON

Sackville Chambers
Sackville Place 44-48 Magdalen Street,
Norwich NR3 1JU, Telephone: 01603 613516/
616221
Call date: Nov 1993, Middle Temple
Qualifications: [LLB (Hons)(E.Anglia)]

D

GILCHRIST DAVID SOMERLED

9 St John Street
Manchester M3 4DN,
Telephone: 0161 955 9000
E-mail: ninesjs@gconnect.com
Call date: Nov 1987, Inner Temple
Qualifications: [BA (Dunelm)]

GILCHRIST MISS NAOMI ROBERTA

5 Fountain Court
Steelhouse Lane, Birmingham B4 6DR,
Telephone: 0121 606 0500
Call date: July 1996, Inner Temple
Qualifications: [LLB (Reading)]

GILCHRIST NICHOLAS JOHN

The Corn Exchange
5th Floor Fenwick Street, Liverpool L2 7QS,
Telephone: 0151 227 1081/5009
Call date: July 1975, Gray's Inn
Recorder
Qualifications: [LLB (Aberystwyth)]

GILEAD MISS BERYL LOUISE

St Mary's Chambers
50 High Pavement, Lace Market, Nottingham
NG1 1HW, Telephone: 0115 9503503
E-mail: clerks@smc.law.co.uk
Call date: Feb 1989, Inner Temple
Qualifications: [BA (Keele)]

GILES DAVID WILLIAM

Verulam Chambers
Peer House 8-14 Verulam Street, Gray's Inn,
London WC1X 8LZ,
Telephone: 0171 813 2400
Call date: Nov 1988, Lincoln's Inn
Qualifications: [LLB Hons]

GILES ROGER STEPHEN

5 Fountain Court
Steelhouse Lane, Birmingham B4 6DR,
Telephone: 0121 606 0500
Call date: July 1976, Gray's Inn
Qualifications: [BA]

GILL CLIFFORD WILLIAM

20 Essex Street
London WC2R 3AL,
Telephone: 0171 583 9294
E-mail: clerks@20essexst.com
Call date: July 1989, Inner Temple
Qualifications: [MA [Oxon], ACA]

GILL GURNAM SINGH

Rowchester Chambers
4 Rowchester Court Whittall Street,
Birmingham B4 6DH,
Telephone: 0121 233 2327/2361951
Call date: Nov 1978, Middle Temple
Qualifications: [BSc (Lond)]

GILL MISS JANE ELIZABETH

17 Bedford Row
London WC1R 4EB,
Telephone: 0171 831 7314
E-mail: IBoard7314@AOL.com
Call date: July 1973, Gray's Inn
Qualifications: [MA]

GILL MANJIT SINGH

6 King's Bench Walk
Ground, Third & Fourth Floors, Temple,
London EC4Y 7DR,
Telephone: 0171 353 4931/583 0695
Call date: July 1982, Gray's Inn
Qualifications: [LLB (Lond)]

GILL MISS MEENA

4 Brick Court
Ground Floor, Temple, London EC4Y 9AD,
Telephone: 0171 797 7766
E-mail: chambers@4brick.co.uk
Call date: July 1982, Middle Temple

GILL MISS PAMILLA

1 Dr Johnson's Bldgs
Ground Floor, Temple, London EC4Y 7AX,
Telephone: 0171 353 9328
Call date: Apr 1989, Lincoln's Inn
Qualifications: [LLB(Hons)]

GILL MS SARAH TERESA

Old Square Chambers
1 Verulam Buildings, Gray's Inn, London
WC1R 5LQ, Telephone: 0171 831 0801
Old Square Chambers
Hanover House 47 Corn Street, Bristol
BS1 1HT, Telephone: 0117 9277111
Call date: Feb 1990, Lincoln's Inn
Qualifications: [BA Hons [Manc]]

GILL SATINDER SINGH

5 Paper Bldgs
Ground Floor, Temple, London EC4Y 7HB,
Telephone: 0171 583 9275/583 4555
E-mail: 5paper@link.org
Call date: Feb 1991, Middle Temple
Qualifications: [LLB (Manch)]

GILL SIMON MURRAY

29 Bedford Row Chambers
London WC1R 4HE,
Telephone: 0171 831 2626
Call date: July 1977, Middle Temple
Qualifications: [LLB]

GILLANCE KENNETH

39 Park Square
Leeds LS1 2NU, Telephone: 0113 2456633
Call date: Nov 1977, Gray's Inn
Recorder
Qualifications: [MA (Keele) LLB, (Lond)]

GILLARD MISS ISABELLE

1 Crown Office Row
2nd Floor, Temple, London EC4Y 7HH,
Telephone: 0171 797 7111
Call date: July 1980, Middle Temple
Qualifications: [LLB (B'Ham)]

GILLESPIE CHRISTOPHER MICHAEL

3 Temple Gardens
2nd Floor, Temple, London EC4Y 9AU,
Telephone: 0171 583 1155
Call date: Nov 1991, Gray's Inn
Qualifications: [BA (Cantab)]

GILLESPIE JAMES EDWARD

Enfield Chambers
36-38 London Road, Enfield, Middlesex
EN2 6DT, Telephone: 0181 364 5627
E-mail: Enfieldchambers@compuserve.com
Call date: Nov 1991, Middle Temple
Qualifications: [BA Hons (Dunelm)]

GILLETTE JOHN CHARLES

Baker Street Chambers
9 Baker Street, Middlesbrough TS1 2LF,
Telephone: 01642 873873
Call date: Oct 1990, Middle Temple
Qualifications: [LLB (Manc)]

GILLIATT MS JACQUELINE

Francis Taylor Bldg
3rd Floor, Temple, London EC4Y 7BY,
Telephone: 0171 797 7250
Call date: Feb 1992, Middle Temple
Qualifications: [BA (Hon) (Oxon), Dip Law]

GILLIBRAND PHILIP MARTIN MANGNALL

Pump Court Chambers
Upper Ground Floor 3 Pump Court, Temple,
London EC4Y 7AJ, Telephone: 0171 353 0711
Pump Court Chambers
31 Southgate Street, Winchester SO23 8EE,
Telephone: 01962 868161
Call date: July 1975, Gray's Inn
Qualifications: [LLB (Lond)]

GILLING MISS DENISE ANN

Mitre House Chambers
Mitre House 44 Fleet Street, London
EC4Y 1BN, Telephone: 0171 583 8233
Call date: Oct 1992, Lincoln's Inn
Qualifications: [LLB(Hons)]

GILLIS RICHARD LESLIE IRVINE

1 Essex Court
Ground Floor, Temple, London EC4Y 9AR,
Telephone: 0171 583 2000
E-mail: clerks@oneessexcourt.co.uk
Call date: Nov 1982, Lincoln's Inn
Qualifications: [BA, BCL (Oxon)]

D

D

GILLMAN MISS RACHEL MARY

3 Dr Johnson's Bldgs
Ground Floor, Temple, London EC4Y 7BA,
Telephone: 0171 353 4854
Call date: July 1988, Gray's Inn
Qualifications: [LLB (Lond)]

GILLOTT PAUL ALAN ASHLEY

15 Winckley Square
Preston PR1 3JJ, Telephone: 01772 252828
E-mail: clerks@winckleysq.demon.co.uk
Call date: Oct 1996, Middle Temple
Qualifications: [BA (Hons)(Oxon), CPE (City)]

GILLYON PHILIP JEFFREY

Erskine Chambers
30 Lincoln's Inn Fields, Lincoln's Inn, London
WC2A 3PF, Telephone: 0171 242 5532
E-mail: Clerks@Erskine-Chambers.law.co.uk
Call date: July 1988, Middle Temple
Qualifications: [MA (Hons) (Cantab)]

GILMAN JONATHAN CHARLES BAGOT QC (1990)

Essex Court Chambers
24 Lincoln's Inn Fields, London WC2A 3ED,
Telephone: 0171 813 8000
E-mail: clerksroom@essexcourt-chambers.co.uk
Call date: Feb 1965, Middle Temple
Qualifications: [MA (Oxon)]

GILMARTIN JOHN

New Court
Temple, London EC4Y 9BE,
Telephone: 0171 583 5123/0171 583 0510
Call date: Nov 1972, Lincoln's Inn
Qualifications: [BA, BCom]

GILMORE IAN MARTIN

30 Park Square
Leeds LS1 2PF, Telephone: 0113 2436388
Call date: Oct 1996, Middle Temple
Qualifications: [BA (Hons)(Oxon), CPE
(Leeds)]

GILMORE MISS MARY SEANIN

2 Crown Office Row
2nd Floor, Temple, London EC4Y 7HJ,
Telephone: 0171 797 8000
Call date: Nov 1996, Gray's Inn
Qualifications: [BA (Cantab)]

GILMOUR NIGEL BENJAMIN DOUGLAS QC (1990)

Peel House Chambers
Ground Floor, Peel House 5 Harrington Street,
Liverpool L2 9QA, Telephone: 0151 236 4321
Call date: July 1970, Inner Temple
Recorder
Qualifications: [LLB (L'pool)]

GILMOUR MS SUSAN EVELYN MARY

Cobden House Chambers
19 Quay Street, Manchester M3 3HN,
Telephone: 0161 833 6000
E-mail: clerks@cobden.co.uk
Call date: Nov 1994, Inner Temple
Qualifications: [LLB (Sussex)]

GILPIN MISS ROMA ELIZABETH

Peel House Chambers
Ground Floor, Peel House 5 Harrington Street,
Liverpool L2 9QA, Telephone: 0151 236 4321
Call date: Nov 1993, Middle Temple
Qualifications: [BA (Hons)(Oxon)]

GILROY PAUL

9 St John Street
Manchester M3 4DN,
Telephone: 0161 955 9000
E-mail: ninesjs@gconnect.com
Farrar's Building
Temple, London EC4Y 7BD,
Telephone: 0171 583 9241
E-mail: chambers@farrarsbuilding.co.uk
Door Tenant
Call date: Nov 1985, Gray's Inn
Qualifications: [LLB (Dundee)]

GIMLETTE JOHN ELIOT

1 Crown Office Row
Ground Floor, Temple, London EC4Y 7HH,
Telephone: 0171 797 7500
Call date: July 1986, Inner Temple
Qualifications: [BA Cantab]

GINN MISS ALISON IRENE

Maidstone Chambers
33 Earl Street, Maidstone, Kent ME14 1PF,
Telephone: 01622 688592
Call date: July 1980, Gray's Inn
Qualifications: [BA, LL.M (Lond)]

GINN MICHAEL ANTHONY

12 King's Bench Walk
Temple, London EC4Y 7EL,
Telephone: 0171 583 0811
E-mail: chambers@12kbw.co.uk
Call date: Nov 1994, Inner Temple
Qualifications: [BA (E.Anglia), M.Phil (Oxon)]

GINNIFF NIGEL THOMAS

Adrian Lyon's Chambers
14 Castle Street, Liverpool L2 0NE,
Telephone: 0151 236 4421/8240
E-mail: chambers14@aol.com
Call date: July 1978, Inner Temple
Qualifications: [LLB]

GINNS JOHN ALFRED BERNARD

New Walk Chambers
27 New Walk, Leicester LE1 6TE,
Telephone: 0116 2559144
Call date: Nov 1977, Inner Temple
Qualifications: [LLB (Lond), ACIS]

GIOSERANO RICHARD STEPHEN

6 Park Square
Leeds LS1 2LW, Telephone: 0113 2459763
E-mail: chambers@no6.co.uk
Call date: Nov 1992, Gray's Inn
Qualifications: [LLB (Newc)]

GIOVANNETTI MISS LISA CATERINA

2 Field Court
Gray's Inn, London WC1R 5BB,
Telephone: 0171 405 6114
E-mail: fieldct2@netcomuk.co.uk.
Call date: Nov 1990, Gray's Inn
Qualifications: [LLB]

GIOVENE LAURENCE

2 Pump Court
1st Floor, Temple, London EC4Y 7AH,
Telephone: 0171 353 5597
Call date: July 1962, Lincoln's Inn
Recorder
Qualifications: [MA (Cantab)]

GIRET JOSEPH JOHN BELA LESLIE

Francis Taylor Bldg
Ground Floor, Temple, London EC4Y 7BY,
Telephone: 0171 353 7768/7769/2711
Call date: Feb 1985, Gray's Inn
Qualifications: [LLB Hons (Warwick)]

GIRET MRS JOSEPHINE JANE

11 Stone Bldgs
Ground Floor, Lincoln's Inn, London
WC2A 3TG, Telephone: 0171 831 6381
E-mail: clerks@11StoneBuildings.law.co.uk
Chichester Chambers
12 North Pallant, Chichester, West Sussex
PO19 1TQ, Telephone: 01243 784538
Door Tenant
Call date: July 1981, Inner Temple
Qualifications: [Diploma in Law]

GIRLING MISS SARAH ELIZABETH

3 Stone Bldgs
Ground Floor, Lincoln's Inn, London
WC2A 3XL, Telephone: 0171 242 4937/
405 8358
Call date: July 1986, Gray's Inn
Qualifications: [BA (Cantab)]

GIROLAMI PAUL JULIAN

13 Old Square
Ground Floor, Lincoln's Inn, London
WC2A 3UA, Telephone: 0171 404 4800
Call date: Nov 1983, Middle Temple
Qualifications: [BA (Cantab)]

GITTINS TIMOTHY JAMES

Trinity Chambers
9-12 Trinity Chare, Quayside, Newcastle Upon
Tyne NE1 3DF, Telephone: 0191 232 1927
Call date: Oct 1990, Middle Temple
Qualifications: [LLB (Manch)]

GIULIANI MARK PAUL ROBINSON

Furnival Chambers
32 Furnival Street, London EC4A 1JQ,
Telephone: 0171 405 3232
E-mail: clerks@furnivallaw.co.uk
Call date: Oct 1993, Gray's Inn
Qualifications: [BSc (Warw)]

GIZ MISS ALEV AYSE

6 King's Bench Walk
Ground, Third & Fourth Floors, Temple,
London EC4Y 7DR,
Telephone: 0171 353 4931/583 0695
Call date: Nov 1988, Gray's Inn
Qualifications: [LLB (Hons) (Lond)]

GLAH ROBERT KWAO

Equity Barristers' Chambers
50 Claude Road, London E10 6ND,
Telephone: 0181 558 6757
E-mail: equitylawyer@equitybar.co.uk
Call date: Nov 1971, Inner Temple
Qualifications: [LLM, PhD (Lond)]

GLANCY ROBERT PETER QC (1997)

Devereux Chambers
Devereux Court, London WC2R 3JJ,
Telephone: 0171 353 7534
E-mail: elton@devchambers.co.uk
Call date: July 1972, Middle Temple
Assistant Recorder
Qualifications: [MA (Cantab)]

GLANVILLE MISS SUSAN ELIZABETH

Mitre House Chambers
Mitre House 44 Fleet Street, London
EC4Y 1BN, Telephone: 0171 583 8233
Wessex Chambers
48 Queens Road, Reading, Berkshire
RG1 4BD, Telephone: 01734 568856
E-mail: wessexchambers@compuserve.com
Door Tenant
Call date: Oct 1991, Inner Temple
Qualifications: [BA (Lond), CPE]

GLASGOW EDWIN JOHN QC (1987)

39 Essex Street
London WC2R 3AT,
Telephone: 0171 583 1111
E-mail: clerks@39essex.co.uk
Call date: Nov 1969, Gray's Inn
Qualifications: [LLB (Lond)]

GLASGOW OLIVER EDWIN JAMES

1 Hare Court
Ground Floor, Temple, London EC4Y 7BE,
Telephone: 0171 353 3982/5324
Call date: Nov 1995, Middle Temple
Qualifications: [BA (Hons)]

GLASS ADAM SOLOMON

Mitre Court Chambers
3rd Floor, Temple, London EC4Y 7BP,
Telephone: 0171 353 9394
Call date: Oct 1994, Lincoln's Inn
Qualifications: [BA (Hons)(L'pool)]

GLASS ANTHONY TREVOR QC (1986)

Hollis Whiteman Chambers
3rd/4th Floor Queen Elizabeth Bldg, Temple,
London EC4Y 9BS, Telephone: 0171 583 5766
E-mail: hollis.whiteman@btinternet.com
Call date: July 1965, Inner Temple
Recorder
Qualifications: [BA (Oxon)]

GLASSBROOK ALEXANDER JAMES

1 Temple Gardens
1st Floor, Temple, London EC4Y 9BB,
Telephone: 0171 353 0407/583 1315
E-mail: clerks@1templegardens.co.uk
Call date: Oct 1995, Middle Temple
Qualifications: [BA (Hons)(Bris)]

GLASSON JONATHAN JOSEPH

Doughty Street Chambers
11 Doughty Street, London WC1N 2PG,
Telephone: 0171 404 1313
E-mail: doughty_street@compuserve.com
Call date: Mar 1996, Middle Temple
Qualifications: [MA]

GLAZE ANTHONY JOHN

Clock Chambers
78 Darlington Street, Wolverhampton
WV1 4LY, Telephone: 01902 313444
Call date: Feb 1992, Inner Temple
Qualifications: [BA, CPE (Lond)]

GLEDHILL ANDREAS NIKOLAUS

3/4 South Square
Gray's Inn, London WC1R 5HP,
Telephone: 0171 696 9900
E-mail: clerks@southsquare.com
Call date: Nov 1992, Middle Temple
Qualifications: [MA (Hons) (Cantab), CPE]

GLEDHILL KRIS

Camberwell Chambers
66 Grove Park, Camberwell, London SE5 8LF,
Telephone: 0171 274 0830
E-mail: 100622.3604@compuserve.com
Call date: July 1989, Inner Temple
Qualifications: [BA (Oxon), LLM (Virginia)]

GLEDHILL MICHAEL GEOFFREY JAMES

3 Gray's Inn Square
Ground Floor, London WC1R 5AH,
Telephone: 0171 520 5600
E-mail: gis3@btinternet.com
Call date: July 1976, Middle Temple
Assistant Recorder
Qualifications: [MA (Oxon)]

GLEN IAN DOUGLAS QC (1996)

Guildhall Chambers
23 Broad Street, Bristol BS1 2HG,
Telephone: 0117 9273366
Call date: Nov 1973, Gray's Inn
Qualifications: [LLB (Lond)]

GLEN PHILIP ALEXANDER

17 Carlton Crescent
Southampton SO15 2XR,
Telephone: 01703 320320
E-mail: km@bar-17cc.demon.co.uk
Call date: July 1983, Middle Temple
Qualifications: [LLB(Lond)]

GLENN PAUL ANTHONY

4 Fountain Court
Steelhouse Lane, Birmingham B4 6DR,
Telephone: 0121 236 3476
Call date: Nov 1983, Gray's Inn
Qualifications: [LLB (L'pool)]

GLENNIE ANDREW DAVID

13 King's Bench Walk
1st Floor, Temple, London EC4Y 7EN,
Telephone: 0171 353 7204
E-mail: clerks@13kbw.law.co.uk
King's Bench Chambers
32 Beaumont Street, Oxford OX1 2NP,
Telephone: 01865 311066
E-mail: clerks@kbc-oxford.law.co.uk
Call date: July 1982, Middle Temple
Qualifications: [MA (Oxon)]

GLENNIE ANGUS JAMES SCOTT QC (1991)

20 Essex Street
London WC2R 3AL,
Telephone: 0171 583 9294
E-mail: clerks@20essexst.com
Call date: July 1974, Lincoln's Inn
Qualifications: [MA (Cantab)]

GLENSER PETER HEATH

Eighteen Carlton Crescent
Southampton SO15 2XR,
Telephone: 01703 639001
Call date: Oct 1993, Inner Temple
Qualifications: [LLB (S'ton)]

GLICK IAN BERNARD QC (1987)

1 Essex Court
Ground Floor, Temple, London EC4Y 9AR,
Telephone: 0171 583 2000
E-mail: clerks@oneessexcourt.co.uk
Call date: Nov 1970, Inner Temple
Qualifications: [MA, BCL (Oxon)]

GLOAG ANGUS ROBIN

1 Gray's Inn Square
Ground Floor, London WC1R 5AA,
Telephone: 0171 405 8946/7/8
Call date: Oct 1992, Inner Temple
Qualifications: [LLB (Hons)]

GLOBE HENRY BRIAN QC (1994)

Exchange Chambers
Pearl Assurance House Derby Square,
Liverpool L2 9XX, Telephone: 0151 236 7747/
0458
E-mail: exchangechambers@btinternet.com
Call date: July 1972, Middle Temple
Recorder
Qualifications: [LLB]

GLOSSOP GEORGE WILLIAM

1 Harcourt Bldgs
2nd Floor, Temple, London EC4Y 9DA,
Telephone: 0171 353 9421/9151
Call date: Nov 1969, Lincoln's Inn
Qualifications: [BA (Keele)]

GLOSTER MISS ELIZABETH QC (1989)

1 Essex Court
Ground Floor, Temple, London EC4Y 9AR,
Telephone: 0171 583 2000
E-mail: clerks@oneessexcourt.co.uk
Call date: Feb 1971, Inner Temple
Recorder
Qualifications: [BA (Cantab)]

GLOVER RICHARD MICHAEL

2 Mitre Ct Bldgs
2nd Floor, Temple, London EC4Y 7BX,
Telephone: 0171 583 1380
Call date: July 1984, Inner Temple
Qualifications: [BA (Cantab)]

GLOVER STEPHEN JULIAN

37 Park Square
Leeds LS1 2NY, Telephone: 0113 2439422
Call date: July 1978, Middle Temple
Qualifications: [LLB]

GLUCKSTEIN MISS EMMA CLARE

1 Middle Temple Lane
Temple, London EC4Y 1LT,
Telephone: 0171 583 0659 (12 Lines)
Call date: Nov 1985, Lincoln's Inn
Qualifications: [BA]

GLYN CASPAR HILARY GORDON

Cloisters
1st Floor, Temple, London EC4Y 7AA,
Telephone: 0171 827 4000
E-mail: clerks@cloisters.com
Call date: Nov 1992, Inner Temple
Qualifications: [LLB (Manch)]

GLYNN MISS JOANNA ELIZABETH

23 Essex Street
London WC2R 3AS,
Telephone: 0171 413 0353/353 3533
E-mail: clerks@essexstreet23.demon.co.uk
Call date: Nov 1983, Middle Temple
Assistant Recorder
Qualifications: [BA (Lond)]

GLYNN STEPHEN PETER

9 Gough Square
London EC4A 3DE, Telephone: 0171 353 5371
Call date: Oct 1990, Middle Temple
Qualifications: [LLB (Bris)]

GOATLEY PETER SEAMUS PATRICK

5 Fountain Court
Steelhouse Lane, Birmingham B4 6DR,
Telephone: 0121 606 0500
2 Mitre Ct Bldgs
2nd Floor, Temple, London EC4Y 7BX,
Telephone: 0171 583 1380
Call date: May 1992, Inner Temple
Qualifications: [MA (Oxon)]

GODDARD ANDREW STEPHEN

1 Atkin Building
Gray's Inn, London WC1R 5AT,
Telephone: 0171 404 0102
E-mail: clerks@atkin-chambers.co.uk
Call date: Nov 1985, Inner Temple
Qualifications: [BA Law]

GODDARD CHRISTOPHER JOHN FRANCIS

Devereux Chambers
Devereux Court, London WC2R 3JJ,
Telephone: 0171 353 7534
E-mail: elton@devchambers.co.uk
Call date: July 1973, Middle Temple
Qualifications: [LLB]

GODDARD HAROLD KEITH QC (1979)

Deans Court Chambers
Cumberland House Crown Square, Manchester
M3 3HA, Telephone: 0161 834 4097
E-mail: deanscourt@compuserve.com
Deans Court Chambers
41-43 Market Place, Preston PR1 1AH,
Telephone: 01772 555163
E-mail: deanscourt@compuserve.com
4 Paper Bldgs
Ground Floor, Temple, London EC4Y 7EX,
Telephone: 0171 353 3366/583 7155
E-mail: clerks@4paperbuildings.com
Door Tenant
Call date: June 1959, Gray's Inn
Recorder
Qualifications: [MA,LLM (Cantab)]

GODDARD MISS KATHERINE LESLEY

Bank House Chambers
Old Bank House, Hartshead, Sheffield S1 2EL,
Telephone: 0114 2751223
Call date: Nov 1987, Inner Temple
Qualifications: [BA (Keele)]

GODDARD PHILIP DAMIAN

4 King's Bench Walk
2nd Floor, Temple, London EC4Y 7DL,
Telephone: 0171 353 3581
Call date: Nov 1985, Inner Temple
Qualifications: [BA (Kent)]

GODDARD MISS SUZANNE HAZEL

Lincoln House Chambers
5th Floor Lincoln House, 1 Brazennose Street,
Manchester M2 5EL,
Telephone: 0161 832 5701
E-mail: LincolnHouseChambers@link.org
Call date: Nov 1986, Gray's Inn
Qualifications: [LLB (Hons) (Manch)]

GODFREY CHRISTOPHER NICHOLAS

Queen's Chambers
5 John Dalton Street, Manchester M2 6ET,
Telephone: 0161 834 6875/4738
4 Camden Place
Preston PR1 3JL, Telephone: 01772 828300
Call date: Feb 1993, Lincoln's Inn
Qualifications: [BA (Hons)]

GODFREY MISS EMMA CHARLOTTE

2 Field Court
Gray's Inn, London WC1R 5BB,
Telephone: 0171 405 6114
E-mail: fieldct2@netcomuk.co.uk.
Call date: Nov 1995, Lincoln's Inn
Qualifications: [BA (Hons)]

GODFREY HOWARD ANTHONY QC (1991)

3 Hare Court
1st Floor, Temple, London EC4Y 7BJ,
Telephone: 0171 353 7561
Call date: Nov 1970, Middle Temple
Recorder
Qualifications: [LLB (Lond)]

GODFREY JOHN PAUL

Wilberforce Chambers
Bishop Lane, Hull HU1 1PA,
Telephone: 01482 323264
E-mail: clerks@hullbar.demon.co.uk
Call date: May 1985, Gray's Inn
Qualifications: [BSc(Econ) (Lond)]

GODFREY JONATHAN SAUL

St Paul's House
5th Floor 23 Park Square South, Leeds
LS1 2ND, Telephone: 0113 2455866
Call date: Nov 1990, Inner Temple
Qualifications: [LLB (Essex)]

GODFREY MISS LOUISE SARAH QC (1991)

Park Court Chambers
40 Park Cross Street, Leeds LS1 2QH,
Telephone: 0113 2433277
14 Gray's Inn Square
Gray's Inn, London WC1R 5JP,
Telephone: 0171 242 0858
E-mail: 100712.2134@compuserve.com
Call date: July 1972, Middle Temple
Recorder
Qualifications: [MA (Oxon)]

D

GODSMARK NIGEL GRAHAM

9 Bedford Row
London WC1R 4AZ,
Telephone: 0171 242 3555
E-mail: clerks@9br.co.uk
Call date: Nov 1979, Gray's Inn
Qualifications: [LLB (Nottm)]

GODWIN WILLIAM GEORGE HENRY

1 Atkin Building
Gray's Inn, London WC1R 5AT,
Telephone: 0171 404 0102
E-mail: clerks@atkin-chambers.co.uk
Call date: Nov 1986, Middle Temple
Qualifications: [BA (Lond), B.Phil (Oxon),
D.Phil (Oxon)]

GOFF ANTHONY THOMAS

25-27 Castle Street
1st Floor, Liverpool L2 4TA,
Telephone: 0151 227 5661/051 236 5072
Call date: July 1978, Middle Temple
Qualifications: [BA (Oxon)]

GOH ALLAN LEE GUAN

46/48 Essex Street
London WC2R 3GH,
Telephone: 0171 583 8899
Call date: July 1984, Gray's Inn
Qualifications: [LLB]

GOKHOOL VISHNU (CHANDRIKA) (SING)

King's Chambers
49a Broadway, Stratford, London E15 4BW
20 Britton Street
1st Floor, London EC1M 5NQ,
Telephone: 0171 608 3765
Call date: Nov 1978, Inner Temple

GOLD MISS DEBRA ANNE

2 Garden Court
1st Floor, Middle Temple, London EC4Y 9BL,
Telephone: 0171 353 1633
E-mail: barristers@2gardenct.law.co.uk
Call date: July 1985, Middle Temple
Qualifications: [BA (Oxon), Dip Law]

GOLD JEREMY SPENCER

Westgate Chambers
144 High Street, Lewes, East Sussex BN7 1XT,
Telephone: 01273 480510
1 Gray's Inn Square
1st Floor, London WC1R 5AG,
Telephone: 0171 405 3000
E-mail: clerks@onegrays.demon.co.uk
Call date: July 1977, Middle Temple
Qualifications: [BA]

GOLDBERG DAVID GERARD QC (1987)

Gray's Inn Chambers
3rd Floor, Gray's Inn, London WC1R 5JA,
Telephone: 0171 242 2642
E-mail: clerks@taxbar.com
Call date: July 1971, Lincoln's Inn
Qualifications: [LLM]

GOLDBERG MS ILFRA HILARY CHARLOTTE

2 Crown Office Row
2nd Floor, Temple, London EC4Y 7HJ,
Telephone: 0171 797 8000
Call date: Oct 1995, Gray's Inn
Qualifications: [BA (Hons), MA, LLM]

GOLDBERG JONATHAN JACOB QC (1989)

3 Temple Gardens
2nd Floor, Temple, London EC4Y 9AU,
Telephone: 0171 583 1155
Westgate Chambers
144 High Street, Lewes, East Sussex BN7 1XT,
Telephone: 01273 480510
Call date: Feb 1971, Middle Temple
Qualifications: [MA, LLB (Cantab)]

GOLDBLATT SIMON QC (1972)

39 Essex Street
London WC2R 3AT,
Telephone: 0171 583 1111
E-mail: clerks@39essex.co.uk
Call date: June 1953, Gray's Inn
Qualifications: [MA (Cantab)]

GOLDER-WELBY ANDREW DOMINIC

Wilberforce Chambers
Bishop Lane, Hull HU1 1PA,
Telephone: 01482 323264
E-mail: clerks@hullbar.demon.co.uk
Call date: Nov 1992, Inner Temple
Qualifications: [LLB (Leic)]

GOLDMAN MRS LINDA

7 Stone Bldgs
1st Floor, Lincoln's Inn, London WC2A 3SZ,
Telephone: 0171 242 0961
Call date: Oct 1990, Middle Temple
Qualifications: [BDS (Lond), LLB (Lond), Dip
Crim (Lond), Dip Psych (Lond)]

GOLDREIN ERIC GODFREY

Adrian Lyon's Chambers
14 Castle Street, Liverpool L2 0NE,
Telephone: 0151 236 4421/8240
E-mail: chambers14@aol.com
Call date: June 1961, Middle Temple
Qualifications: [MA (Cantab)]

GOLDREIN IAIN SAVILLE QC (1997)

The Corn Exchange
5th Floor Fenwick Street, Liverpool L2 7QS,
Telephone: 0151 227 1081/5009
12 King's Bench Walk
Temple, London EC4Y 7EL,
Telephone: 0171 583 0811
E-mail: chambers@12kbw.co.uk
Call date: July 1975, Inner Temple
Assistant Recorder
Qualifications: [MA (Cantab)]

GOLDRING MISS JENNIFER LEONIE

1 Harcourt Bldgs
2nd Floor, Temple, London EC4Y 9DA,
Telephone: 0171 353 9421/9151
Call date: Nov 1993, Middle Temple
Qualifications: [BA (Hons)(Oxon)]

GOLDRING JEREMY EDWARD

3/4 South Square
Gray's Inn, London WC1R 5HP,
Telephone: 0171 696 9900
E-mail: clerks@southsquare.com
Call date: Oct 1996, Lincoln's Inn
Qualifications: [BA (Hons)(Oxon), MA (Yale),
Dip in Law (City)]

GOLDRING JOHN BERNARD
QC (1987)

9 Bedford Row
London WC1R 4AZ,
Telephone: 0171 242 3555
E-mail: clerks@9br.co.uk
Call date: May 1969, Lincoln's Inn
Recorder
Qualifications: [LLB]

GOLDSMITH PETER HENRY
QC (1987)

Fountain Court
Temple, London EC4Y 9DH,
Telephone: 0171 583 3335
E-mail: chambers@fountaincourt.co.uk
Call date: July 1972, Gray's Inn
Recorder
Qualifications: [MA (Cantab), LLM (Lond)]

GOLDSTAUB ANTHONY JAMES
QC (1992)

24 The Ropewalk
Nottingham NG1 5EF,
Telephone: 0115 9472581
E-mail: clerk@ropewalk.co.uk
12 King's Bench Walk
Temple, London EC4Y 7EL,
Telephone: 0171 583 0811
E-mail: chambers@12kbw.co.uk
Call date: July 1972, Middle Temple
Assistant Recorder

GOLDSTONE DAVID JULIAN

4 Field Court
Gray's Inn, London WC1R 5EA,
Telephone: 0171 440 6900
E-mail: chambers@4fieldcourt.co.uk
Call date: Apr 1986, Middle Temple
Qualifications: [MA (Cantab), BCL (Oxon)]

D

GOLDSTONE LEONARD CLEMENT QC (1993)

28 St John Street
Manchester M3 4DJ,
Telephone: 0161 834 8418
E-mail: clerk@28stjohnst.co.uk
1 Crown Office Row
2nd Floor, Temple, London EC4Y 7HH,
Telephone: 0171 797 7111
Call date: July 1971, Middle Temple
Recorder
Qualifications: [BA (Cantab)]

GOLDWATER MICHAEL PHILIP

Cobden House Chambers
19 Quay Street, Manchester M3 3HN,
Telephone: 0161 833 6000
E-mail: clerks@cobden.co.uk
Call date: July 1977, Middle Temple
Qualifications: [MA (Oxon)]

GOLINSKI ROBERT FELIX

Adrian Lyon's Chambers
14 Castle Street, Liverpool L2 0NE,
Telephone: 0151 236 4421/8240
E-mail: chambers14@aol.com
Call date: Oct 1990, Middle Temple
Qualifications: [BA]

GOLLOP MS KATHARINE SUSANNAH

6 Pump Court
Ground Floor, Temple, London EC4Y 7AR,
Telephone: 0171 583 6013/2510
Call date: Nov 1993, Gray's Inn
Qualifications: [BA (Hons), CPE, ICSL]

GOMPERTZ JEREMY QC (1988)

5 Essex Court
1st Floor, Temple, London EC4Y 9AH,
Telephone: 0171 410 2000
Call date: July 1962, Gray's Inn
Recorder
Qualifications: [MA (Cantab)]

GONDAL MISS SOFIA BASHIR

9 King's Bench Walk
Basement, Temple, London EC4Y 7DX,
Telephone: 0171 353 9564
E-mail: jvlee@btinternet.com
Call date: Nov 1994, Middle Temple
Qualifications: [LLB (Hons), LLM]

GOOCH SEBASTIAN DAVID

5 Pump Court
Ground Floor, Temple, London EC4Y 7AP,
Telephone: 0171 353 2532
E-mail: fivepump@netcomuk.co.uk
Call date: July 1989, Lincoln's Inn
Qualifications: [LLB (Leic)]

GOOD ROBERT TRUST

3 Temple Gardens
3rd Floor, Temple, London EC4Y 9AU,
Telephone: 0171 353 0832
Call date: July 1979, Gray's Inn
Qualifications: [BSc (Nottm)]

GOODALL CHARLES VERNON

All Saints Chambers
9/11 Broad Street, Bristol BS1 2HP,
Telephone: 0117 921 1966
Call date: July 1986, Inner Temple
Qualifications: [BA, Dip Law]

GOODBODY PETER JAMES

Oriel Chambers
14 Water Street, Liverpool, Merseyside
L2 8TD, Telephone: 0151 236 7191
E-mail: oriel_chambers@link.org
Call date: July 1986, Lincoln's Inn
Qualifications: [LLB (Manchester)]

Fax: 0151 227 5909; DX: 14106 Liverpool

Types of work: Asset finance; Commercial litigation; Common law (general); Consumer law; Employment; Factoring; Information technology; Sale and carriage of goods

Circuit: Northern

Awards and memberships: Society for Computers and Law

Languages spoken: French

GOODCHILD MRS ELIZABETH ANN

Watford Chambers
74 Mildred Avenue, Watford, Hertfordshire
WD1 7DX, Telephone: 01923 220553
Call date: July 1981, Middle Temple
Qualifications: [LLB (Lond), ACIArb]

GOODE MISS ROWENA MARGARET

28 St John Street
Manchester M3 4DJ,
Telephone: 0161 834 8418
E-mail: clerk@28stjohnst.co.uk
1 Dr Johnson's Bldgs
Ground Floor, Temple, London EC4Y 7AX,
Telephone: 0171 353 9328
Dr Johnson's Chambers
The Atrium Court Apex Plaza, Reading
RG1 1AX, Telephone: 01734 254221
Call date: July 1974, Gray's Inn
Recorder
Qualifications: [LLB]

GOODE ROYSTON MILES QC (1990)

2 Hare Court
Ground Floor, Temple, London EC4Y 7BH,
Telephone: 0171 583 1770
E-mail: 2_Hare_Court@link.org
Call date: Feb 1988, Inner Temple
Qualifications: [LLB (Lond), LLD (Lond), FBA]

GOODFELLOW GILES WILLIAM JEREMY

Pump Court Tax Chambers
16 Bedford Row, London WC1R 4EB,
Telephone: 0171 414 8080
Call date: July 1983, Middle Temple
Qualifications: [MA (Cantab), LLM (UVa)]

GOODHART LORD QC (1979)

Chambers of Lord Goodhart QC
Ground Floor 3 New Square, Lincoln's Inn,
London WC2A 3RS,
Telephone: 0171 405 5577
E-mail: law@threenewsquare.demon.co.uk
Call date: Feb 1957, Lincoln's Inn
Qualifications: [MA (Cantab), LLM (Harvard)]

GOODISON ADAM HENRY

3/4 South Square
Gray's Inn, London WC1R 5HP,
Telephone: 0171 696 9900
E-mail: clerks@southsquare.com
Call date: Oct 1990, Middle Temple
Qualifications: [BA (Dunelm)]

GOODMAN ANDREW DAVID

199 Strand
London WC2R 1DR,
Telephone: 0171 379 9779
E-mail: chambers@199strand.co.uk
Call date: July 1978, Inner Temple
Qualifications: [LLB (Soton), ACIArb]

GOODMAN MISS BERNADETTE TRACY

Derby Square Chambers
Merchants Court, Derby Square, Liverpool
L2 1TS, Telephone: 0151 709 4222
Call date: Nov 1983, Inner Temple
Qualifications: [BA (Keele, Joint, Hons Law &
Music)]

GOODMAN SIMON CHARLES

St John's Chambers
Small Street, Bristol BS1 1DW,
Telephone: 0117 9213456/298514
E-mail: clerks@stjohns.uk.com
Call date: Nov 1996, Gray's Inn
Qualifications: [BA (Bris)]

GOODRICH MISS SIOBHAN CATHERINE

6 Pump Court
Ground Floor, Temple, London EC4Y 7AR,
Telephone: 0171 583 6013/2510
Call date: Nov 1980, Gray's Inn
Qualifications: [LLB (Lond)]

GOODWIN MISS CAROLINE TRACY

Trinity Chambers
9-12 Trinity Chare, Quayside, Newcastle Upon
Tyne NE1 3DF, Telephone: 0191 232 1927
Call date: Nov 1988, Inner Temple
Qualifications: [BA (Hons) (Newc), Dip Law]

GOODWIN MISS DEIRDRE EVELYN

13 King's Bench Walk
1st Floor, Temple, London EC4Y 7EN,
Telephone: 0171 353 7204
E-mail: clerks@13kbw.law.co.uk
King's Bench Chambers
32 Beaumont Street, Oxford OX1 2NP,
Telephone: 01865 311066
E-mail: clerks@kbc-oxford.law.co.uk
Call date: July 1974, Gray's Inn
Qualifications: [LLB]

D

D

GOODWIN MISS KATHERINE LOUISE

Verulam Chambers
Peer House 8-14 Verulam Street, Gray's Inn,
London WC1X 8LZ,
Telephone: 0171 813 2400
Call date: Nov 1993, Lincoln's Inn
Qualifications: [BA (Hons)(Oxon)]

GOODWIN NICHOLAS ALEXANDER JOHN

2 Harcourt Bldgs
1st Floor, Temple, London EC4Y 9DB,
Telephone: 0171 353 6961/7
Call date: Oct 1995, Inner Temple
Qualifications: [BA (Oxon), CPE]

GOOLAMALI MISS NINA SORAYA

2 Temple Gardens
Temple, London EC4Y 9AY,
Telephone: 0171 583 6041 (12 Lines)
Call date: Oct 1995, Middle Temple
Qualifications: [BA (Hons)]

GOOLD ALEXANDER MICHAEL

Hardwicke Building
New Square, Lincoln's Inn, London
WC2A 3SB, Telephone: 0171 242 2523
E-mail: clerks@hardwicke.co.uk
Call date: Nov 1994, Lincoln's Inn
Qualifications: [MA (Cantab)]

GOOSE JULIAN NICHOLAS

10 Park Square
Leeds LS1 2LH, Telephone: 0113 2455438
E-mail: chambers@bandit.legend.co.uk
Call date: July 1984, Lincoln's Inn
Qualifications: [LLB (Leeds)]

GOPINATHAN MISS ANUPAMA

Harrow on the Hill Chambers
60 High Street, Harrow on the Hill, Middlesex
HA1 3LL, Telephone: 0181 423 7444
Windsor Barristers' Chambers
Windsor, Telephone: 01753 648899
Call date: Nov 1994, Inner Temple
Qualifications: [LLB (Hons) (Essex)]

GORDON ASHLEY LOUIS

6 Gray's Inn Square
Ground Floor, Gray's Inn, London WC1R 5AZ,
Telephone: 0171 242 1052
Call date: Nov 1973, Inner Temple
Qualifications: [MA (Cantab)]

GORDON MISS CATHERINE ANNE

140 Cholmeley Road
Reading, Berkshire RG1 3LR,
Telephone: 01189 676318
Call date: July 1989, Middle Temple
Qualifications: [LLB]

GORDON MS CLARE

8 King's Bench Walk
2nd Floor, Temple, London EC4Y 7DU,
Telephone: 0171 797 8888
Call date: Oct 1995, Middle Temple
Qualifications: [LLB (Hons)]

GORDON DAVID MYER

25 Park Square
Leeds LS1 2PW, Telephone: 0113 2451841/2/3
E-mail: sovereignchambers@btinternet.com
Call date: July 1984, Inner Temple
Qualifications: [MA (Oxon), Dip Law (City)]

GORDON DONALD CAMERON

3 Temple Gardens
3rd Floor, Temple, London EC4Y 9AU,
Telephone: 0171 353 0832
Call date: June 1956, Middle Temple
Qualifications: [MA (Oxon)]

GORDON JEREMY

Lamb Building
Ground Floor, Temple, London EC4Y 7AS,
Telephone: 0171 797 7788
E-mail: lamb.building@link.org
Southsea Chambers
PO Box 148, Southsea, Portsmouth,
Hampshire PO5 2TU,
Telephone: 01705 291261
Call date: July 1974, Inner Temple
Qualifications: [LLB]

GORDON JOHN SANDFORD

New Court
Temple, London EC4Y 9BE,
Telephone: 0171 583 5123/0171 583 0510
Call date: Nov 1970, Gray's Inn
Qualifications: [LLB (Hons) (Lond)]

GORDON JOHN STUART

6 Pump Court
Ground Floor, Temple, London EC4Y 7AR,
Telephone: 0171 583 6013/2510
Call date: Feb 1989, Inner Temple
Qualifications: [LLB (B'ham)]

GORDON MRS KATHERINE ELIZABETH

Plowden Bldgs
2nd Floor, Temple, London EC4Y 9BU,
Telephone: 0171 583 0808
E-mail: bar@plowdenbuildings.co.uk
Call date: Feb 1988, Lincoln's Inn
Qualifications: [BA (Hons), BCL(Hons) Oxon]

GORDON MARK JOHN

11 Bolt Court
London EC4A 3DQ,
Telephone: 0171 353 2300
E-mail: boltct11@aol.com
Redhill Chambers
Seloduct House 30 Station Road, Redhill
RH1 1NK, Telephone: 01737 780781
Call date: Feb 1990, Lincoln's Inn
Qualifications: [LLB Hons (B'Ham)]

GORDON RICHARD JOHN FRANCIS QC (1994)

39 Essex Street
London WC2R 3AT,
Telephone: 0171 583 1111
E-mail: clerks@39essex.co.uk
Call date: July 1972, Middle Temple
Qualifications: [MA (Oxon), LLM (Lond)]

GORDON-SAKER ANDREW STEPHEN

4 King's Bench Walk
Ground/First Floor, Temple, London
EC4Y 7DL, Telephone: 0171 822 8822
E-mail: 4kbw@barristersatlaw.com
Call date: July 1981, Middle Temple
Qualifications: [LLB]

GORDON-SAKER MRS LIZA HELEN

Fenners Chambers
3 Madingley Road, Cambridge CB3 OEE,
Telephone: 01223 368761
Fenners Chambers
8-12 Priestgate, Peterborough PE1 1JA,
Telephone: 01733 62030
Call date: July 1982, Gray's Inn
Qualifications: [LLB (East Anglia)]

GORE ALLAN PETER

12 King's Bench Walk
Temple, London EC4Y 7EL,
Telephone: 0171 583 0811
E-mail: chambers@12kbw.co.uk
Call date: Feb 1977, Middle Temple
Qualifications: [MA, LLB (Cantab)]

GORE ANDREW JULIAN MARK

37 Park Square
Leeds LS1 2NY, Telephone: 0113 2439422
Call date: Nov 1994, Middle Temple

GORE ANDREW ROGER

Fenners Chambers
3 Madingley Road, Cambridge CB3 OEE,
Telephone: 01223 368761
Fenners Chambers
8-12 Priestgate, Peterborough PE1 1JA,
Telephone: 01733 62030
Call date: Nov 1973, Middle Temple
Qualifications: [MA (Cantab), FCIArb]

GORE MRS SUSAN DIANA

Queen Elizabeth Bldg
Ground Floor, Temple, London EC4Y 9BS,
Telephone: 0171 353 7181 (12 Lines)
Call date: Nov 1993, Middle Temple
Qualifications: [LLB (Hons)(E.Anglia)]

D

D

GORE-ANDREWS GAVIN ANGUS RUSSELL

2 Harcourt Bldgs
Ground Floor/Left, Temple, London
EC4Y 9DB, Telephone: 0171 583 9020
E-mail: clerks@harcourt.co.uk
Stanbrook & Henderson
2 Harcourt Bldgs 2nd Floor, Temple, London
EC4Y 9DB, Telephone: 0171 353 0101
E-mail: clerks@harcourt.co.uk
Call date: July 1972, Lincoln's Inn
Qualifications: [LLB (Lond)]

GORING MISS JULIA MICHELE

Mitre Court Chambers
3rd Floor, Temple, London EC4Y 7BP,
Telephone: 0171 353 9394
Call date: Oct 1991, Lincoln's Inn
Qualifications: [LLB (Hons) (Birm)]

GORNA MISS ANNE CHRISTINA

Independent Barristers Clerk
Room 5, 2nd Floor 15 Castle Street, Exeter,
Devon EX4 3PT, Telephone: 01392 210900
E-mail: cathedral.chambers@eclipse.co.uk
4 Paper Bldgs
Ground Floor, Temple, London EC4Y 7EX,
Telephone: 0171 353 3366/583 7155
E-mail: clerks@4paperbuildings.com
Call date: July 1960, Middle Temple
Qualifications: [LLB Hons]

GORTON SIMON ANTHONY

Adrian Lyon's Chambers
14 Castle Street, Liverpool L2 0NE,
Telephone: 0151 236 4421/8240
E-mail: chambers14@aol.com
Call date: July 1988, Inner Temple
Qualifications: [LLB (Lond)]

GOSLAND CHRISTOPHER ANDREW JAMES

Guildhall Chambers
23 Broad Street, Bristol BS1 2HG,
Telephone: 0117 9273366
Call date: July 1966, Middle Temple
Qualifications: [MA (Oxon)]

GOSLING JONATHAN VINCENT RONALD

4 Fountain Court
Steelhouse Lane, Birmingham B4 6DR,
Telephone: 0121 236 3476
Call date: Nov 1980, Middle Temple
Qualifications: [BA]

GOSNELL STEVEN JAMES

1 High Pavement
Nottingham NG1 1HF,
Telephone: 0115 9418218
Call date: Nov 1995, Gray's Inn
Qualifications: [BSc (Wales)]

GOSS JAMES RICHARD WILLIAM QC (1997)

6 Park Square
Leeds LS1 2LW, Telephone: 0113 2459763
E-mail: chambers@no6.co.uk
Call date: July 1975, Inner Temple
Recorder
Qualifications: [BA]

GOTHORP DAVID

19 Figtree Lane
Sheffield S1 2DJ, Telephone: 0114 2759708/
2738380
Call date: Nov 1970, Gray's Inn
Qualifications: [Gray's Inn, Prizewinner]

GOTT PAUL ANDREW

Fountain Court
Temple, London EC4Y 9DH,
Telephone: 0171 583 3335
E-mail: chambers@fountaincourt.co.uk
Call date: Oct 1991, Lincoln's Inn
Qualifications: [BA (Hons) (Cambs), BCL]

GOTTLIEB DAVID ANTHONY

Thomas More Chambers
52 Carey Street, Lincoln's Inn, London
WC2A 2JB, Telephone: 0171 404 7000
Call date: Nov 1988, Inner Temple
Qualifications: [LLB (Bris)]

GOUDIE JAMES QC (1984)

11 King's Bench Walk
Temple, London EC4Y 7EQ,
Telephone: 0171 632 8500
E-mail: clerksroom@11-kbw.law.co.uk
Call date: July 1970, Inner Temple
Recorder
Qualifications: [LLB (Lond)]

Fax: 0171 583 3690/9123;
Out of hours telephone: 0171 583 0610;
DX: LDE 368; Other comms: E-mail irvine@11-kbw.law.co.uk

Types of work: Administrative; Commercial litigation; Discrimination; Education; Employment; Entertainment; Environment; Local government; Sports

Other professional qualifications: FCI Arb

Membership of foreign bars: Antigua

Circuit: South Eastern

Awards and memberships: Past Chairman, Administrative Law Bar Association

Other professional experience: Deputy High Court Judge, Queen's Bench and Chancery Divisions; Recorder

Publications: *Judicial Review* (Co-editor), 1997 (2nd edn)

Reported cases: *Betts v Brintel*, [1997] ICR 792. Leading Court of Appeal decision on TUPE. *Timeplan Education Group Ltd v NUT*, [1997] IRLR 457. Interference by Trade Union in advertising contract for supply teachers. *Ahmed v United Kingdom*, [1997] EHRLR 670. Freedom of Association under the ECHR and restrictions on public employees. *Akinbolu v Hackney LBC*, (1997) 29 HLR 259. Whether secure tenant arrested for immigration offences could be summarily evicted. *R v Yorkshire Purchasing Organisation*, (1997) 95 LGR 727. Powers of local authority consortium to supply goods and services.

GOUDIE WILLIAM MARTIN PHILLIP

2 Dr Johnson's Building
Temple, London EC4Y 7AY,
Telephone: 0171 353 4716
Call date: Oct 1996, Inner Temple
Qualifications: [LLB (Exon)]

GOUGH MISS KAREN LOUISE

West Lodge Farm
Wrotham Road, Meopham, Kent DA13 0QG,
Telephone: 01474 812280
Arbitration Chambers
22 Willes Road, London NW5 3DS,
Telephone: 0171 267 2137
E-mail: jatqc@atack.demon.co.uk
Call date: July 1983, Inner Temple
Qualifications: [LLB (So'ton), FCIArb]

GOUGH MISS KATHERINE MARY

Lamb Chambers
Lamb Building, Temple, London EC4Y 7AS,
Telephone: 0171 797 8300
E-mail: lambchambers@link.org
Call date: Nov 1990, Inner Temple
Qualifications: [BA (Oxon)]

GOULD MISS DEBORAH SAMANTHA

Peel House Chambers
Ground Floor, Peel House 5 Harrington Street,
Liverpool L2 9QA, Telephone: 0151 236 4321
Call date: Feb 1990, Inner Temple
Qualifications: [LLB (Hons) (Warw)]

GOULD DENNIS

2 Dr Johnson's Building
Temple, London EC4Y 7AY,
Telephone: 0171 353 4716
Call date: Nov 1969, Middle Temple
Qualifications: [MA (Cantab)]

GOULDING JONATHAN STEVEN

Gough Square Chambers
6-7 Gough Square, London EC4A 3DE,
Telephone: 0171 353 0924
E-mail: gsc@goughsq.co.uk
Call date: July 1984, Inner Temple
Qualifications: [LLB (Manch)]

GOULDING PAUL ANTHONY

2 Hare Court
Ground Floor, Temple, London EC4Y 7BH,
Telephone: 0171 583 1770
E-mail: 2_Hare_Court@link.org
Call date: Nov 1984, Middle Temple
Qualifications: [MA, BCL (Oxon)]

GOURGEY ALAN

11 Stone Bldgs
Ground Floor, Lincoln's Inn, London
WC2A 3TG, Telephone: 0171 831 6381
E-mail: clerks@11StoneBuildings.law.co.uk
Call date: July 1984, Lincoln's Inn
Qualifications: [LL.B (Bristol)]

GOURLEY MISS CLAIRE ROBERTA JEAN

3 Paper Bldgs
1st Floor, Temple, London EC4Y 7EU,
Telephone: 0171 583 8055
E-mail: london@3paper.com
Call date: Oct 1996, Middle Temple
Qualifications: [BA (Hons)(Cantab)]

GOW MISS ELIZABETH SUZANNE

Iscoed Chambers
86 St Helen's Road, Swansea SA1 4BQ,
Telephone: 01792 652988/9/330
Call date: Oct 1995, Inner Temple
Qualifications: [MA (Oxon), LLM (Lond)]

GOW FERGUS BENJAMIN HARPER

22 Albion Place
Northampton NN1 1UD,
Telephone: 01604 36271
Call date: Nov 1994, Inner Temple
Qualifications: [BA (Newc), CPE (Lond)]

GOW HENRY

Victoria Chambers
19 Castle Street, Liverpool L2 4SX,
Telephone: 0151 236 9402
E-mail: Fa45@rapid.co.uk
Call date: Oct 1995, Gray's Inn
Qualifications: [LLB]

GOWEN MATTHEW ROBERT

Octagon House
19 Colegate, Norwich NR3 1AT,
Telephone: 01603 623186
E-mail: octagon@netmatters.co.uk
Call date: Oct 1992, Lincoln's Inn
Qualifications: [LLB(Hons)]

GOWER MISS HELEN CLARE

Old Square Chambers
Hanover House 47 Corn Street, Bristol
BS1 1HT, Telephone: 0117 9277111
Old Square Chambers
1 Verulam Buildings, Gray's Inn, London
WC1R 5LQ, Telephone: 0171 831 0801
Call date: Oct 1992, Middle Temple
Qualifications: [BA (Hons), LL.M]

GOWER PETER JOHN DE PEAULY

6 Pump Court
1st Floor, Temple, London EC4Y 7AR,
Telephone: 0171 797 8400
E-mail: sa_hockman_qc@link.org
6-8 Mill Street
Maidstone, Kent ME15 6XH,
Telephone: 01622 688094
Call date: July 1985, Lincoln's Inn
Qualifications: [MA (Oxon)]

GOY DAVID JOHN LISTER QC (1991)

Gray's Inn Chambers
3rd Floor, Gray's Inn, London WC1R 5JA,
Telephone: 0171 242 2642
E-mail: clerks@taxbar.com
Call date: May 1973, Middle Temple
Qualifications: [LLM]

GOYMER ANDREW ALFRED

6 Pump Court
1st Floor, Temple, London EC4Y 7AR,
Telephone: 0171 797 8400
E-mail: sa_hockman_qc@link.org
6-8 Mill Street
Maidstone, Kent ME15 6XH,
Telephone: 01622 688094
Call date: July 1970, Gray's Inn
Recorder
Qualifications: [MA (Oxon)]

GOZEM GAIAS QC (1997)

Lincoln House Chambers
5th Floor Lincoln House, 1 Brazennose Street,
Manchester M2 5EL,
Telephone: 0161 832 5701
E-mail: LincolnHouseChambers@link.org
Call date: Nov 1972, Middle Temple
Recorder
Qualifications: [LLB (Lond)]

GRABINER ANTHONY STEPHEN QC (1981)

1 Essex Court
Ground Floor, Temple, London EC4Y 9AR,
Telephone: 0171 583 2000
E-mail: clerks@oneessexcourt.co.uk
Call date: Nov 1968, Lincoln's Inn
Recorder
Qualifications: [LLB, LLM (Lond)]

GRACE JOHN OLIVER BOWMAN QC (1994)

3 Serjeants Inn
London EC4Y 1BQ,
Telephone: 0171 353 5537
E-mail: available upon request
Call date: July 1973, Middle Temple
Qualifications: [LLB (Soton)]

GRACE JONATHAN ROBERT

Deans Court Chambers
Cumberland House Crown Square, Manchester
M3 3HA, Telephone: 0161 834 4097
E-mail: deanscourt@compuserve.com
Deans Court Chambers
41-43 Market Place, Preston PR1 1AH,
Telephone: 01772 555163
E-mail: deanscourt@compuserve.com
Call date: Feb 1989, Middle Temple
Qualifications: [BA (Oxon), Dip Law]

GRACE TIMOTHY MICHAEL

Adrian Lyon's Chambers
14 Castle Street, Liverpool L2 0NE,
Telephone: 0151 236 4421/8240
E-mail: chambers14@aol.com
Call date: Nov 1993, Middle Temple
Qualifications: [BA (Hons)(Oxon)]

GRACE MISS TONIA LINDSEY

Garden Court North Chambers
2nd Floor Gregg's Building, 1 Booth Street,
Manchester M2 4DU,
Telephone: 0161 833 1774
Call date: Oct 1992, Middle Temple
Qualifications: [LL.B (Hons)]

GRAFFIUS MARK NARAYAN

Bridewell Chambers
2 Bridewell Place, London EC4V 6AP,
Telephone: 0171 797 8800
E-mail: clerks@bridewell.law.co.uk
Call date: Oct 1990, Middle Temple
Qualifications: [LLB (Leic)]

GRAHAM CHARLES ROBERT STEPHEN

1 Essex Court
Ground Floor, Temple, London EC4Y 9AR,
Telephone: 0171 583 2000
E-mail: clerks@oneessexcourt.co.uk
Call date: Nov 1986, Middle Temple
Qualifications: [MA (Oxon), Dip Law (City)]

GRAHAM IAN DAVID

New Court Chambers
3 Broad Chare, Newcastle Upon Tyne
NE1 3DQ, Telephone: 0191 232 1980
Call date: July 1978, Middle Temple
Qualifications: [MA (Oxon)]

GRAHAM JAMES HENRY FERGUS

One Raymond Buildings
Gray's Inn, London WC1R 5BH,
Telephone: 0171 430 1234
E-mail: chambers@ipbar1rb.com;
clerks@ipbar1rb.com
Call date: Nov 1994, Inner Temple
Qualifications: [B.Eng, M.Sc (Bris), CPE]

GRAHAM JOHN MALCOLM

37 Park Square
Leeds LS1 2NY, Telephone: 0113 2439422
11 King's Bench Walk
1st Floor, Temple, London EC4Y 7EQ,
Telephone: 0171 353 3337
Call date: Nov 1955, Middle Temple
Qualifications: [LLB]

GRAHAM ROGER

3 Temple Gardens
2nd Floor, Temple, London EC4Y 9AU,
Telephone: 0171 583 1155
Call date: July 1973, Middle Temple

GRAHAM MISS SANDRA CLARA

14 Tooks Court
Cursitor St, London EC4A 1LB,
Telephone: 0171 405 8828
E-mail: clerks @tooks.law.co.uk
Door Tenant
Call date: July 1982, Inner Temple
Qualifications: [BA]

GRAHAM THOMAS PATRICK HENRY

Lamb Chambers
Lamb Building, Temple, London EC4Y 7AS,
Telephone: 0171 797 8300
E-mail: lambchambers@link.org
Call date: Nov 1985, Middle Temple
Qualifications: [MA (Cantab)]

GRAHAME MISS NINA STEPHANIE

1 Hare Court
Ground Floor, Temple, London EC4Y 7BE,
Telephone: 0171 353 3982/5324
Call date: Nov 1993, Middle Temple
Qualifications: [BA (Hons)(Warwick), CPE
(City)]

GRAINGER IAN DAVID

1 Essex Court
Ground Floor, Temple, London EC4Y 9AR,
Telephone: 0171 583 2000
E-mail: clerks@oneessexcourt.co.uk
Call date: July 1978, Inner Temple
Qualifications: [MA (Oxon)]

GRAINGER NORMAN REVELL

2 Middle Temple Lane
3rd Floor, Temple, London EC4Y 9AA,
Telephone: 0171 583 4540
26 Morley Avenue
Ashgate, Chesterfield S40 4DA,
Telephone: 01246 234790/0114 2533513
Call date: July 1973, Gray's Inn
Qualifications: [M Phil (York), BA, MA (York),
DMS]

GRANSHAW MISS SARA ELIZABETH

2 Harcourt Bldgs
1st Floor, Temple, London EC4Y 9DB,
Telephone: 0171 353 6961/7
Call date: Oct 1991, Lincoln's Inn
Qualifications: [BA (Hons) (Oxon)]

GRANT DAVID EUAN BARRON

13 King's Bench Walk
1st Floor, Temple, London EC4Y 7EN,
Telephone: 0171 353 7204
E-mail: clerks@13kbw.law.co.uk
King's Bench Chambers
32 Beaumont Street, Oxford OX1 2NP,
Telephone: 01865 311066
E-mail: clerks@kbc-oxford.law.co.uk
Call date: July 1975, Middle Temple
Assistant Recorder
Qualifications: [MA, LLB (Cantab)]

GRANT EDWARD ALEXANDER GORDON

Victoria Chambers
3rd Floor 177 Corporation Street, Birmingham
B4 6RG, Telephone: 0121 236 9900
Call date: Nov 1991, Inner Temple
Qualifications: [LLB (So'ton)]

GRANT EDWARD WILLIAM

6 Pump Court
1st Floor, Temple, London EC4Y 7AR,
Telephone: 0171 797 8400
E-mail: sa_hockman_qc@link.org
6-8 Mill Street
Maidstone, Kent ME15 6XH,
Telephone: 01622 688094
Call date: Nov 1994, Inner Temple
Qualifications: [BA (Oxon), CPE]

GRANT GARY ANDREW

17 Carlton Crescent
Southampton SO15 2XR,
Telephone: 01703 320320
E-mail: km@bar-17cc.demon.co.uk
Call date: Nov 1985, Middle Temple
Qualifications: [MA (Oxon)]

GRANT GARY STEVEN

3 Temple Gardens
2nd Floor, Temple, London EC4Y 9AU,
Telephone: 0171 583 1155
Call date: Oct 1994, Gray's Inn
Qualifications: [BA]

GRANT MISS KIM AMANDA

1 Crown Office Row
Ground Floor, Temple, London EC4Y 7HH,
Telephone: 0171 797 7500
Call date: Nov 1988, Gray's Inn
Qualifications: [LLB (Cardiff)]

GRANT MARCUS H JAMES

1 Temple Gardens
1st Floor, Temple, London EC4Y 9BB,
Telephone: 0171 353 0407/583 1315
E-mail: clerks@1templegardens.co.uk
Call date: Oct 1993, Lincoln's Inn
Qualifications: [BA (Hons)(Reading)]

GRANT THOMAS PAUL WENTWORTH

New Court Chambers
5 Verulam Buildings, Gray's Inn, London
WC1R 5LY, Telephone: 0171 831 9500
E-mail: mail@newcourtchambers.com
Call date: Oct 1993, Middle Temple
Qualifications: [BA (Hons)(Bris), Dip Law
(City)]

GRANT-GARWOOD JOSHUA DAHREN

Trafalgar Chambers
53 Fleet Street, London EC4Y 1BE,
Telephone: 0171 583 5858
E-mail: TrafalgarChambers@easynet.co.uk
Call date: Nov 1992, Middle Temple
Qualifications: [BA (Hons)(Lancs)]

GRANTHAM ANDREW TIMOTHY

Deans Court Chambers
Cumberland House, Crown Square,
Manchester M3 3HA,
Telephone: 0161 834 4097
E-mail: deanscourt@compuserve.com
Deans Court Chambers
41-43 Market Place, Preston, Lancashire
PR1 1AH, Telephone: 01772 555163
E-mail: deanscourt@compuserve.com
Call date: Oct 1991, Middle Temple
Qualifications: [MA, BCL (Oxon)]

Fax: 0161 834 4805;
Out of hours telephone: 0161 428 5835;
DX: 718155 Manchester 3

Types of work: Arbitration; Banking;
Bankruptcy; Chancery (general); Commercial;
Commercial litigation; Company and
commercial; Construction; Consumer law;

Financial services; Franchising; Insolvency;
Insurance; Insurance/reinsurance; International
trade; Partnerships; Private international;
Professional negligence; Sale and carriage of
goods

Other professional qualifications: ACIArb

Circuit: Northern

Awards and memberships: Member Northern
Circuit Commercial Bar Association

Other professional experience: Lecturer in Law,
Wadham College, Oxford, 1989-90; Part-time
lecturer in Law, King's College, London 1990-1

Reported cases: *Partington v Turners Bakery
and Tomkins v Griffiths*, [1998] TLR 78. A
defence admitting negligence and some damage
was not an admission to enable an action to be
struck out under CCR Ord 9 r 10.

GRANVILLE ALEXANDER MACGREGOR

1 Dr Johnson's Bldgs
Ground Floor, Temple, London EC4Y 7AX,
Telephone: 0171 353 9328
Dr Johnson's Chambers
The Atrium Court Apex Plaza, Reading
RG1 1AX, Telephone: 01734 254221
Call date: July 1978, Lincoln's Inn
Qualifications: [LLB (Lond)]

GRANVILLE STAFFORD ANDREW

4 King's Bench Walk
2nd Floor, Temple, London EC4Y 7DL,
Telephone: 0171 353 3581
Call date: July 1987, Gray's Inn
Qualifications: [MA (Cantab)]

GRANVILLE-FALL ANTHONY

30 Park Square
Leeds LS1 2PF, Telephone: 0113 2436388
Call date: Nov 1990, Lincoln's Inn
Qualifications: [LLB]

D

GRATWICKE CHARLES JAMES PHILLIP

1 Harcourt Bldgs
2nd Floor, Temple, London EC4Y 9DA,
Telephone: 0171 353 9421/9151
Call date: July 1974, Middle Temple
Assistant Recorder
Qualifications: [LLB (Leeds)]

GRATWICKE MISS SUSAN AILEEN

Lavenham Chambers
Rookery Farm, Near Lavenham, Suffolk
CO10 0BJ, Telephone: 01787 248247
Call date: Nov 1976, Gray's Inn
Qualifications: [LLB]

GRAVES MISS CELIA TERESE ROSANNA

2 Garden Court
1st Floor, Middle Temple, London EC4Y 9BL,
Telephone: 0171 353 1633
E-mail: barristers@2gardenct.law.co.uk
Call date: July 1981, Gray's Inn
Qualifications: [BA]

GRAY CHARLES ANTHONY ST JOHN QC (1984)

5 Raymond Buildings
1st Floor, Gray's Inn, London WC1R 5BP,
Telephone: 0171 242 2902
Call date: July 1966, Lincoln's Inn
Recorder
Qualifications: [BA (Oxon)]

GRAY GILBERT QC (1971)

3 Raymond Buildings
Gray's Inn, London WC1R 5BH,
Telephone: 0171 831 3833
E-mail: chambers@threeraymond.demon.co.uk
Park Court Chambers
40 Park Cross Street, Leeds LS1 2QH,
Telephone: 0113 2433277
Door Tenant
Call date: Nov 1953, Gray's Inn
Recorder
Qualifications: [LLB]

GRAY HOWARD ROGER

Chambers of Joy Okoye
Suite 1, 2nd Floor Gray's Inn Chambers,
Gray's Inn, London WC1R 5JA,
Telephone: 0171 405 7011
Door Tenant
Call date: Nov 1980, Lincoln's Inn
Qualifications: [BSc ARICS ACI Arb]

GRAY MISS JENNIFER

11 Old Square
Ground Floor, Lincoln's Inn, London
WC2A 3TS, Telephone: 0171 242 5022/
405 1074
Call date: Oct 1992, Middle Temple
Qualifications: [LL.B (Hons)]

GRAY JOHN CHRISTOPHER

9 Gough Square
London EC4A 3DE, Telephone: 0171 353 5371
Call date: Nov 1970, Gray's Inn
Qualifications: [LLB]

GRAY JUSTIN HENRY WALFORD

Gray's Inn Chambers
5th Floor, Gray's Inn, London WC1R 5JA,
Telephone: 0171 404 1111
Call date: Nov 1993, Inner Temple
Qualifications: [BA, CPE]

GRAY MRS KAREN LOUISE

Goldsworth Chambers
1st Floor 10-11 Gray's Inn Square, London
WC1R 5JD, Telephone: 0171 405 7117
Call date: Nov 1995, Lincoln's Inn
Qualifications: [LLB (Hons)]

GRAY MISS NICHOLA JAYNE

29 Bedford Row Chambers
London WC1R 4HE,
Telephone: 0171 831 2626
Call date: Oct 1991, Lincoln's Inn
Qualifications: [BA (Hons) (Oxon)]

GRAY PETER HENRY ST JOHN

Bridewell Chambers
2 Bridewell Place, London EC4V 6AP,
Telephone: 0171 797 8800
E-mail: clerks@bridewell.law.co.uk
Call date: Nov 1984, Inner Temple
Qualifications: [BA,Dip Law PCL]

GRAY PETER LESLIE

33 Bedford Row
London WC1R 4JH,
Telephone: 0171 242 6476
Door Tenant
Call date: Nov 1983, Inner Temple
Qualifications: [LLB (So'ton)]

GRAY RICHARD

24a St John Street
Manchester M3 4DF,
Telephone: 0161 833 9628
Call date: Nov 1986, Middle Temple
Qualifications: [LLB (Liverpool)]

GRAY RICHARD PAUL QC (1993)

39 Essex Street
London WC2R 3AT,
Telephone: 0171 583 1111
E-mail: clerks@39essex.co.uk
Call date: July 1970, Inner Temple
Qualifications: [LLB]

GRAY ROBERT

Independent Barristers Clerk
Room 5, 2nd Floor 15 Castle Street, Exeter,
Devon EX4 3PT, Telephone: 01392 210900
E-mail: cathedral.chambers@eclipse.co.uk
Call date: Nov 1993, Gray's Inn
Qualifications: [BA (Hons), LLM (Exon),
DipICArb, ACIArb]

GRAY ROGER ANDERSON

2 Mitre Ct Bldgs
1st Floor, Temple, London EC4Y 7BX,
Telephone: 0171 353 1353
Call date: July 1984, Lincoln's Inn
Qualifications: [MA, Dip Law]

GRAYSON EDWARD

9–12 Bell Yard
London WC2A 2LF,
Telephone: 0171 400 1800
Call date: Nov 1948, Middle Temple
Qualifications: [MA (Oxon)]

Fax: 0171 404 1405;
Out of hours telephone: 0171 583 6207;
DX: LDE 390

Types of work: Administrative; Chancery (general); Common law (general); Copyright; Crime; EC and competition law; Intellectual property; Medical negligence; Personal injury; Sports; Sports medicine

Other professional qualifications: Visiting Professor, Sport and the Law, Anglia Law School; Fellow, Royal Society of Medicine

Circuit: South Eastern

Awards and memberships: Founding President British Association for Sport and Law; Bar Sports Law Group; Australian and New Zealand Sports Law Association; Pan-European Organisation of Personal Injury Lawyers; Association of Personal Injury Lawyers; Action for Victims of Medical Accidents; Administrative Bar Association; Criminal Bar Association; British Association of Sport and Medicine

Other professional experience: Consultant, Central Council of Physical Recreation; National Playing Fields Association; Sports Council; Former Counsel Professional Footballers' and Trainers' Association (now PFA)

Publications: *Sport and the Law*, 1978, 1988, 1994; *Ethics, Injuries and the Law in Sports Medicine*, 1998; *Medicine, Sport and the Law* (Co-editor, Co-author), 1990; *Medico-Legal Hazards of Rugby Union* (Co-editor, Co-author), 1991; *Sponsorship of Sport, Arts and Leisure* (Co-author), 1984

Reported cases: *Elliott v Saunders and Liverpool Football Club*, (1994) NLJ, 5 August, 1994. Liability for personal injury/negligence between Premier League professional footballers requires no higher duty than traditional duty of care with foreseeable risk of injury.
Morell v Owen and others, (1993) *The Times*, 14 December, 1993. Higher duty of care owed to disabled adult athlete than to able-bodied adult consistent with all persons under disability.

Worthing Rugby Football Club Trustees v IRC;
Frampton v IRC, [1985] 1 WLR; [1987] STC
273, 1985. Unincorporated association liable for
tax as distinct from individual members
notwithstanding association known to law only
through membership with no separate legal
identity.
Alder v Moore, [1961] 1 All ER 1 [1961] 2 WLR
426 [1961] 2 QB 57, 1961. Monies paid under
insurance policy described as penalty to
disabled professional footballer recoverable as
pre-existing determination of damages,
notwithstanding description as penalty.
Serville v Constance, [1954] 1 WLR 487; [1954]
1 All ER 622; 71 RPC 146, 1954. 'Welter Weight
Champion of Trinidad' failed to restrain
competitor from using title under passing off
because boxer and title unknown in United
Kingdom.

Background

'. . . acknowledged as the "founding father" of
British sports law' (per *Sports Law*, Cavendish
Publishing Limited, 1998, page 35). Accused
publicly by Chief Executive of Football
Association at 1988 Central Council Physical
Recreation Conference to have invented it.
Addressed conferences internationally and
domestically: International Athletic Federation
(Monaco); South African Sports Medicine
Congress (Cape Town); Potsdam University
(Germany); Pan-European Organisation of
Personal Injury Lawyers (Barcelona).
Contributor to legal, sporting and national
media sources on radio, television on all aspects
of sporting legal issues. Co-author with late Lord
Havers of *Royal Baccarat Scandal* - cheating at
cards Tranby Croft trial (1997; 1988). Also
author of *Corinthians and Cricketers* (4
editions:1955, 1957, 1983, 1996) and inaugural
professional lecture, Anglia Law School: *Sport
and the Law: A Return to Corinthian Values?*
(*British Association for Sport and Law
Journal*, Summer 1998): Without the Rule of
Law in Society anarchy reigns. Without the Rule
of Law in Sport chaos exists.

GREANEY PAUL RICHARD

Park Court Chambers
40 Park Cross Street, Leeds LS1 2QH,
Telephone: 0113 2433277
Call date: Oct 1993, Inner Temple
Qualifications: [BA (Hons) (Dunelm)]

GREAVES MISS ANN

East Anglian Chambers
Gresham House 5 Museum Street, Ipswich
IP1 1HQ, Telephone: 01473 214481
East Anglian Chambers
Sanders House 52 North Hill, Colchester
CO1 1PY, Telephone: 01206 572756
East Anglian Chambers
57 London Street, Norwich NR2 1HL,
Telephone: 01603 617351
Call date: Nov 1989, Inner Temple
Qualifications: [LLB (Hons)]

GREAVES JOHN

9-12 Bell Yard
London WC2A 2LF,
Telephone: 0171 400 1800
Call date: July 1973, Middle Temple
Qualifications: [LLB (Lond)]

GREAVES MICHAEL

36 Bedford Row
London WC1R 4JH,
Telephone: 0171 421 8000
E-mail: 36bedfordrow@link.org
Call date: Nov 1976, Middle Temple
Qualifications: [LLB (B'ham)]

GREEN ALAN LAURENCE

199 Strand
London WC2R 1DR,
Telephone: 0171 379 9779
E-mail: chambers@199strand.co.uk
Peel Court Chambers
45 Hardman Street, Manchester M3 3HA,
Telephone: 0161 832 3791
Door Tenant
Call date: Feb 1973, Gray's Inn
Qualifications: [BA]

GREEN MISS ALISON ANNE

4 Field Court
Gray's Inn, London WC1R 5EA,
Telephone: 0171 440 6900
E-mail: chambers@4fieldcourt.co.uk
Call date: July 1974, Middle Temple
Qualifications: [LLM (Lond)]

GREEN SIR ALLAN DAVID QC (1987)

1 Hare Court
Ground Floor, Temple, London EC4Y 7BE,
Telephone: 0171 353 3982/5324
Call date: June 1959, Inner Temple
Qualifications: [MA (Cantab)]

GREEN ANDREW

30 Park Place
Cardiff CF1 3BA, Telephone: 01222 398421
E-mail: 100757.1456@compuserve.com
Call date: July 1974, Gray's Inn
Qualifications: [BA (Oxon) (Hons)]

GREEN ANDREW JAMES

21 White Friars
Chester CH1 1NZ, Telephone: 01244 323070
Call date: Oct 1992, Gray's Inn
Qualifications: [LL.B (Sheff)]

GREEN ANDREW JAMES DOMINIC

2 Hare Court
Ground Floor, Temple, London EC4Y 7BH,
Telephone: 0171 583 1770
E-mail: 2_Hare_Court@link.org
Call date: Nov 1988, Inner Temple
Qualifications: [LLB (LSE)]

GREEN BRIAN RUSSELL QC (1997)

Wilberforce Chambers
8 New Square, Lincoln's Inn, London
WC2A 3QP, Telephone: 0171 306 0102
E-mail: chambers@wilberforce.co.uk
Call date: Nov 1980, Middle Temple
Qualifications: [BA, BCL (Oxon)]

GREEN COLIN RICHARD

Cobden House Chambers
19 Quay Street, Manchester M3 3HN,
Telephone: 0161 833 6000
E-mail: clerks@cobden.co.uk
Call date: July 1982, Lincoln's Inn
Qualifications: [BA (Leeds), Diplaw]

GREEN DAVID CAMERON

Adrian Lyon's Chambers
14 Castle Street, Liverpool L2 0NE,
Telephone: 0151 236 4421/8240
E-mail: chambers14@aol.com
Call date: Oct 1993, Lincoln's Inn
Qualifications: [LLB (Hons)(Lanc)]

GREEN DAVID JOHN MARK

18 Red Lion Court
(Off Fleet Street), London EC4A 3EB,
Telephone: 0171 520 6000
Thornwood House
102 New London Road, Chelmsford, Essex
CM2 0RG, Telephone: 01245 280880
Call date: July 1979, Inner Temple
Assistant Recorder
Qualifications: [MA (Cantab)]

GREEN DORE JOHN

2 Temple Gardens
Temple, London EC4Y 9AY,
Telephone: 0171 583 6041 (12 Lines)
Call date: Feb 1994, Lincoln's Inn
Qualifications: [BSc (Hons)]

GREEN HENRY QC (1988)

18 Red Lion Court
(Off Fleet Street), London EC4A 3EB,
Telephone: 0171 520 6000
Thornwood House
102 New London Road, Chelmsford, Essex
CM2 0RG, Telephone: 01245 280880
Call date: July 1962, Gray's Inn
Recorder
Qualifications: [LLB (Lond), MA (Cantab)]

GREEN MISS JANE ELIZABETH

Eldon Chambers
Fourth Floor 30/32 Fleet Street, London
EC4Y 1AA, Telephone: 0171 353 4636
Call date: Feb 1993, Inner Temple
Qualifications: [Designer of the, Royal College
of Art]

D

GREEN MICHAEL ANTHONY

7 Stone Bldgs
Ground Floor, Lincoln's Inn, London
WC2A 3SZ, Telephone: 0171 405 3886/
242 3546
E-mail: chaldous@vossnet.co.uk
Call date: July 1987, Lincoln's Inn
Qualifications: [MA (Cantab)]

GREEN NICHOLAS NIGEL

Brick Court Chambers
15/19 Devereux Court, London WC2R 3JJ,
Telephone: 0171 583 0777
E-mail: (surname)@brickcourt.demon.co.uk
Call date: July 1986, Inner Temple
Qualifications: [LLB, LLM, Ph.d]

GREEN PATRICK CURTIS

2 Harcourt Bldgs
Ground Floor/Left, Temple, London
EC4Y 9DB, Telephone: 0171 583 9020
E-mail: clerks@harcourt.co.uk
Stanbrook & Henderson
2 Harcourt Bldgs 2nd Floor, Temple, London
EC4Y 9DB, Telephone: 0171 353 0101
E-mail: clerks@harcourt.co.uk
Call date: Oct 1990, Middle Temple
Qualifications: [BA (Cantab), ACI.Arb]

GREEN ROBIN CHARLES DAVID MAGNUS

2-3 Gray's Inn Square
Gray's Inn, London WC1R 5JH,
Telephone: 0171 242 4986
E-mail: chambers@2-3graysinnsquare.co.uk
Call date: Oct 1992, Inner Temple
Qualifications: [LLB (Lond)]

GREEN ROGER JOHN BAILEY

Queen's Chambers
5 John Dalton Street, Manchester M2 6ET,
Telephone: 0161 834 6875/4738
4 Camden Place
Preston PR1 3JL, Telephone: 01772 828300
Call date: July 1972, Lincoln's Inn
Qualifications: [LLB (Lond)]

GREEN MISS VICTORIA LOUISE

Harrow on the Hill Chambers
60 High Street, Harrow on the Hill, Middlesex
HA1 3LL, Telephone: 0181 423 7444
Call date: Oct 1994, Gray's Inn
Qualifications: [LLB (Hons)]

GREEN MRS YVONNE

4 Field Court
Gray's Inn, London WC1R 5EA,
Telephone: 0171 440 6900
E-mail: chambers@4fieldcourt.co.uk
Call date: July 1982, Inner Temple
Qualifications: [LLB (Lond)]

GREENAN JOHN JOSEPH GILCHRIST

Hardwicke Building
New Square, Lincoln's Inn, London
WC2A 3SB, Telephone: 0171 242 2523
E-mail: clerks@hardwicke.co.uk
Call date: July 1984, Gray's Inn
Qualifications: [LLB (B'ham)]

GREENAN MISS SARAH OCTAVIA

9 Woodhouse Square
9 Woodhouse Square, Leeds LS3 1AD,
Telephone: 0113 245 1986
Call date: July 1987, Gray's Inn
Qualifications: [BA (Oxon)]

Fax: 0113 2448623; DX: 26406 Leeds Park
Square

Types of work: Family; Housing; Landlord and
tenant; Personal injury; Professional negligence

Circuit: North Eastern

Publications: 'Carbon Monoxide: A hidden
cause for Action' (*Legal Action Magazine*),
January 1997

Reported cases: *Gething v Evans*, [1997]
Current Law 4040, 1997. Housing disrepair
quantum.
Shields v Hussein, [1997] Current Law 7948,
1996. Housing disrepair quantum.
Foster v Donaghey, [1994] Current Law 1454,
1994. Housing disrepair quantum.
Barraclough v Sanders, [1994] Current Law
1752, 1994. Personal injury quantum.
Johnson v Sheffield CC, [1994] Current Law
1445, 1994. Housing disrepair liability.

GREENBERG MISS JOANNA ELISHEVER GABRIELLE QC (1994)

3 Temple Gardens
2nd Floor, Temple, London EC4Y 9AU,
Telephone: 0171 583 1155
Call date: July 1972, Gray's Inn
Recorder
Qualifications: [LLB Hons (Lond)]

GREENBOURNE JOHN HUGO

2 Crown Office Row
Ground Floor, Temple, London EC4Y 7HJ,
Telephone: 0171 797 8100
E-mail: mail@2cor.co.uk, or to individual
barristers at: [barrister's surname]@2cor.co.uk
Call date: July 1978, Gray's Inn
Qualifications: [MA (Cantab)]

GREENE MAURICE ALAN

38 Young Street
Manchester M3 3FT,
Telephone: 0161 833 0489
E-mail: clerks@young-st-chambers.com
Call date: Nov 1982, Inner Temple
Qualifications: [BA (Hons)]

GREENE PAUL MARTIN

Earl Street Chambers
47 Earl Street, Maidstone, Kent ME14 1PD,
Telephone: 01622 671222
E-mail: gunner-sparks@msn.com
Call date: Oct 1994, Middle Temple
Qualifications: [LLB (Hons)(Bris)]

GREENFIELD ALEX JEREMY

Martins Building
Water Street, Liverpool L2 3SP,
Telephone: 0151 236 5818/4919
Call date: Oct 1995, Inner Temple
Qualifications: [B.Com (L'pool), CPE (Wolves)]

GREENFIELD PETER CHARLES

King's Bench Chambers
Wellington House 175 Holdenhurst Road,
Bournemouth, Dorset BH8 8DQ,
Telephone: 01202 250025
Call date: Nov 1989, Middle Temple
Qualifications: [BA (Lond)]

GREENING RICHARD JONATHAN

Devereux Chambers
Devereux Court, London WC2R 3JJ,
Telephone: 0171 353 7534
E-mail: elton@devchambers.co.uk
Call date: Nov 1975, Middle Temple
Qualifications: [MA (Cantab)]

GREENSLADE HENRY MICHAEL

9 King's Bench Walk
Ground Floor, Temple, London EC4Y 7DX,
Telephone: 0171 353 7202/3909
Call date: Nov 1982, Gray's Inn
Qualifications: [BA (Hons)(Law), BL (Ireland)]

GREENWOOD ALAN ELIEZER

1 Crown Office Row
2nd Floor, Temple, London EC4Y 7HH,
Telephone: 0171 797 7111
Call date: July 1970, Middle Temple
Recorder
Qualifications: [LLB (Hons)]

GREENWOOD MISS CELESTINE LESLEY

Chavasse Court Chambers
2nd Floor Chavasse Court, 24 Lord Street,
Liverpool L2 1TA, Telephone: 0151 707 1191
Call date: Oct 1991, Lincoln's Inn
Qualifications: [LLB (Hons)(L'pool)]

GREENWOOD PROFESSOR CHRISTOPHER JOHN

Essex Court Chambers
24 Lincoln's Inn Fields, London WC2A 3ED,
Telephone: 0171 813 8000
E-mail: clerksroom@essexcourt-chambers.co.uk
Call date: July 1978, Middle Temple
Qualifications: [MA, LLB (Cantab)]

D

GREENWOOD JOHN

East Anglian Chambers
Gresham House 5 Museum Street, Ipswich
IP1 1HQ, Telephone: 01473 214481
East Anglian Chambers
Sanders House 52 North Hill, Colchester
CO1 1PY, Telephone: 01206 572756
East Anglian Chambers
57 London Street, Norwich NR2 1HL,
Telephone: 01603 617351
Call date: Oct 1990, Lincoln's Inn
Qualifications: [MA (Oxon)]

GREENWOOD PAUL JEROME

4 Stone Bldgs
Ground Floor, Lincoln's Inn, London
WC2A 3XT, Telephone: 0171 242 5524
E-mail: d.goddard@4stonebuildings.law.co.uk
Call date: Nov 1991, Lincoln's Inn
Qualifications: [BA (Hons), BCL (Oxon)]

GREGG WILLIAM JONATHAN

Cobden House Chambers
19 Quay Street, Manchester M3 3HN,
Telephone: 0161 833 6000
E-mail: clerks@cobden.co.uk
Call date: Oct 1990, Gray's Inn
Qualifications: [LLB (Hons)(Newc)]

GREGORY BARRY GEORGE

Furnival Chambers
32 Furnival Street, London EC4A 1JQ,
Telephone: 0171 405 3232
E-mail: clerks@furnivallaw.co.uk
Call date: Nov 1987, Gray's Inn

GREGORY JAMES HANS

Lincoln House Chambers
5th Floor Lincoln House, 1 Brazennose Street,
Manchester M2 5EL,
Telephone: 0161 832 5701
E-mail: LincolnHouseChambers@link.org
Call date: Feb 1970, Gray's Inn
Qualifications: [BA (Lond)]

GREGORY JOHN RAYMOND

Deans Court Chambers
Cumberland House Crown Square, Manchester
M3 3HA, Telephone: 0161 834 4097
E-mail: deanscourt@compuserve.com
Deans Court Chambers
41-43 Market Place, Preston PR1 1AH,
Telephone: 01772 555163
E-mail: deanscourt@compuserve.com
Call date: July 1972, Middle Temple
Qualifications: [LLB]

GREGORY MISS KAREN ANN

Exchange Chambers
Pearl Assurance House Derby Square,
Liverpool L2 9XX, Telephone: 0151 236 7747/
0458
E-mail: exchangechambers@btinternet.com
Call date: July 1985, Middle Temple
Qualifications: [BA (L'pool), Dip Law]

GREGORY PETER JOSEPH

Peel House Chambers
Ground Floor, Peel House 5 Harrington Street,
Liverpool L2 9QA, Telephone: 0151 236 4321
Call date: July 1982, Gray's Inn
Qualifications: [LLB(Manch)]

GREGORY PHILIP JOHN

6 Fountain Court
Steelhouse Lane, Birmingham B4 6DR,
Telephone: 0121 233 3282
Call date: July 1975, Middle Temple
Assistant Recorder
Qualifications: [MA (Oxon)]

GREGORY RICHARD HAMILTON

2 Harcourt Bldgs
1st Floor, Temple, London EC4Y 9DB,
Telephone: 0171 353 6961/7
Call date: Oct 1993, Middle Temple
Qualifications: [BA (Hons)(Cantab), CPE
(Notts)]

GRENFELL GIBSON QC (1994)

2 Pump Court
1st Floor, Temple, London EC4Y 7AH,
Telephone: 0171 353 5597
Call date: Nov 1969, Middle Temple
Recorder
Qualifications: [MA (Cantab)]

GRENNAN BARRY EDWARD

Kenworthy's Buildings
83 Bridge Street, Manchester M3 2RF,
Telephone: 0161 832 4036/834 6954
Call date: July 1977, Lincoln's Inn
Qualifications: [BA (Hons)]

GRENYER MARK

York Chambers
14 Toft Green, York YO1 1JT,
Telephone: 01904 620048
E-mail: yorkchambers.co.uk
Call date: Nov 1969, Gray's Inn

GRESTY MISS DENISE LYNN

25 Park Square
Leeds LS1 2PW, Telephone: 0113 2451841/2/3
E-mail: sovereignchambers@btinternet.com
Call date: Nov 1990, Inner Temple
Qualifications: [LLB (Sheff)]

GRETASON THE REVEREND MARK NICHOLAS

Eldon Chambers
Fourth Floor 30/32 Fleet Street, London
EC4Y 1AA, Telephone: 0171 353 4636
Call date: May 1992, Lincoln's Inn
Qualifications: [BA, MTA, AKC]

GREWAL MISS HARJIT

6 King's Bench Walk
Ground, Third & Fourth Floors, Temple,
London EC4Y 7DR,
Telephone: 0171 353 4931/583 0695
Call date: July 1980, Gray's Inn
Qualifications: [MA (Cantab)]

GREY MISS ELEANOR MARY GRACE

39 Essex Street
London WC2R 3AT,
Telephone: 0171 583 1111
E-mail: clerks@39essex.co.uk
Call date: Oct 1990, Gray's Inn
Qualifications: [BA (Oxon), Dip Law]

GREY MICHAEL HENRY JOHN

Coleridge Chambers
Citadel 190 Corporation Street, Birmingham
B4 6QD, Telephone: 0121 233 3303
Call date: Nov 1975, Middle Temple
Qualifications: [LLB]

GREY ROBERT WILLIAM

3 Paper Bldgs
1st Floor, Temple, London EC4Y 7EU,
Telephone: 0171 583 8055
E-mail: london@3paper.com
20 Lorne Park Road
Bournemouth BH1 1JN,
Telephone: 01202 292102 (5 Lines)
4 St Peter Street
Winchester SO23 8OW,
Telephone: 01962 868884
Call date: July 1979, Gray's Inn
Qualifications: [BA (Lancaster)]

GREY ROBIN DOUGLAS QC (1979)

Hollis Whiteman Chambers
3rd/4th Floor Queen Elizabeth Bldg, Temple,
London EC4Y 9BS, Telephone: 0171 583 5766
E-mail: hollis.whiteman@btinternet.com
Call date: Feb 1957, Gray's Inn
Recorder
Qualifications: [LLB (Lond)]

GREY MISS SIOBHAN

2 Dr Johnson's Building
Temple, London EC4Y 7AY,
Telephone: 0171 353 4716
Call date: Oct 1994, Gray's Inn
Qualifications: [BA]

GRIBBLE PETER JOHN

9 King's Bench Walk
Ground Floor, Temple, London EC4Y 7DX,
Telephone: 0171 353 7202/3909
Call date: July 1972, Gray's Inn

GRICE ALAN KEVIN

The Corn Exchange
5th Floor Fenwick Street, Liverpool L2 7QS,
Telephone: 0151 227 1081/5009
Call date: July 1977, Gray's Inn
Assistant Recorder
Qualifications: [LLB]

D

GRICE MISS JOANNA HARRISON

1 King's Bench Walk
2nd Floor, Temple, London EC4Y 7DB,
Telephone: 0171 936 1500
E-mail: ddear@1kbw.co.uk
Call date: Oct 1991, Middle Temple
Qualifications: [MA Hons (Cantab)]

GRICE PETER ROBERT

St Ive's Chambers
9 Fountain Ct, Birmingham B4 6DR,
Telephone: 0121 236 0863/0929
Call date: July 1984, Gray's Inn
Qualifications: [LLB]

GRICE TIMOTHY JAMES

St John's Chambers
Small Street, Bristol BS1 1DW,
Telephone: 0117 9213456/298514
E-mail: clerks@stjohns.uk.com
Call date: July 1975, Middle Temple
Qualifications: [MA (Oxon)]

GRIEF MISS ALISON SARAH

2 Garden Court
1st Floor, Middle Temple, London EC4Y 9BL,
Telephone: 0171 353 1633
E-mail: barristers@2gardenct.law.co.uk
Call date: Oct 1990, Inner Temple
Qualifications: [LLB]

GRIERSON JACOB

1 Essex Court
Ground Floor, Temple, London EC4Y 9AR,
Telephone: 0171 583 2000
E-mail: clerks@oneessexcourt.co.uk
Call date: Oct 1993, Lincoln's Inn
Qualifications: [BA (Hons) (Oxon), Dip in Law (City)]

GRIERSON ROBERT JAMES

24 Old Bldgs
First Floor, Lincoln's Inn, London WC2A 3UJ,
Telephone: 0171 242 2744
Call date: Oct 1991, Middle Temple
Qualifications: [MA, LLM (Cantab)]

GRIEVE DOMINIC CHARLES ROBERTS

1 Temple Gardens
1st Floor, Temple, London EC4Y 9BB,
Telephone: 0171 353 0407/583 1315
E-mail: clerks@1templegardens.co.uk
Call date: Nov 1980, Middle Temple
Qualifications: [BA (Oxon)]

GRIEVE MICHAEL ROBERTSON CRICHTON

Doughty Street Chambers
11 Doughty Street, London WC1N 2PG,
Telephone: 0171 404 1313
E-mail: doughty_street@compuserve.com
Call date: Nov 1975, Middle Temple
Assistant Recorder
Qualifications: [BA (Oxon)]

GRIEVES-SMITH PETER MICHAEL

6 King's Bench Walk
Ground Floor, Temple, London EC4Y 7DR,
Telephone: 0171 583 0410
Call date: Nov 1989, Middle Temple
Qualifications: [LLB (Hons)(Leic)]

GRIFFIN MISS LYNN MYFANWY

5 Paper Bldgs
1st Floor, Temple, London EC4Y 7HB,
Telephone: 0171 583 6117
E-mail: clerks@5-paperbuildings.law.co.uk
Call date: Oct 1991, Gray's Inn
Qualifications: [LLB (Brunel)]

GRIFFIN NEIL PATRICK LUKE

9-12 Bell Yard
London WC2A 2LF,
Telephone: 0171 400 1800
Call date: Oct 1996, Gray's Inn
Qualifications: [LLB (Hons) (Lond)]

GRIFFIN NICHOLAS JOHN

5 Paper Bldgs
1st Floor, Temple, London EC4Y 7HB,
Telephone: 0171 583 6117
E-mail: clerks@5-paperbuildings.law.co.uk
Call date: Oct 1992, Inner Temple
Qualifications: [LLB (Hons) (Bristol)]

GRIFFIN PAUL

4 Essex Court
Temple, London EC4Y 9AJ,
Telephone: 0171 797 7970
E-mail: clerks@4essexcourt.law.co.uk
Call date: Nov 1979, Gray's Inn
Qualifications: [MA, BCL (Oxon)]

GRIFFITH MARTIN LEONARD

1 Harcourt Bldgs
2nd Floor, Temple, London EC4Y 9DA,
Telephone: 0171 353 9421/9151
Call date: July 1977, Inner Temple
Qualifications: [LLB (Lond)]

GRIFFITH PETER MALCOLM

3 Temple Gardens
3rd Floor, Temple, London EC4Y 9AU,
Telephone: 0171 583 0010
Call date: Feb 1964, Inner Temple
Qualifications: [MA (Cantab),MIPD]

GRIFFITH-JONES DAVID ERIC

Devereux Chambers
Devereux Court, London WC2R 3JJ,
Telephone: 0171 353 7534
E-mail: elton@devchambers.co.uk
Call date: Nov 1975, Middle Temple
Recorder
Qualifications: [LLB (Bristol), FCI Arb]

GRIFFITH-JONES RICHARD HAYDN

1 Fountain Court
Steelhouse Lane, Birmingham B4 6DR,
Telephone: 0121 236 5721
Call date: July 1974, Middle Temple
Recorder
Qualifications: [LLB (Leeds)]

GRIFFITHS (JOHN) PETER (GWYNNE) QC (1995)

30 Park Place
Cardiff CF1 3BA, Telephone: 01222 398421
E-mail: 100757.1456@compuserve.com
Call date: Nov 1970, Gray's Inn
Recorder
Qualifications: [LLB (Lond)]

GRIFFITHS (WILLIAM) ROBERT QC (1993)

4-5 Gray's Inn Square
Ground Floor, Gray's Inn, London WC1R 5AY,
Telephone: 0171 404 5252
E-mail: chambers@4-5graysinnsquare.co.uk
Call date: Nov 1974, Middle Temple
Qualifications: [MA, BCL (Oxon)]

GRIFFITHS ALAN PAUL

1 Essex Court
Ground Floor, Temple, London EC4Y 9AR,
Telephone: 0171 583 2000
E-mail: clerks@oneessexcourt.co.uk
Call date: Feb 1981, Gray's Inn
Qualifications: [MA, BCL (Oxon)]

GRIFFITHS CONRAD PAUL RADCLIFFE

2 Harcourt Bldgs
Ground Floor/Left, Temple, London
EC4Y 9DB, Telephone: 0171 583 9020
E-mail: clerks@harcourt.co.uk
Stanbrook & Henderson
2 Harcourt Bldgs 2nd Floor, Temple, London
EC4Y 9DB, Telephone: 0171 353 0101
E-mail: clerks@harcourt.co.uk
Call date: Nov 1986, Gray's Inn
Qualifications: [LLB(E.Anglia)]

GRIFFITHS COURTENAY

2 Garden Court
1st Floor, Middle Temple, London EC4Y 9BL,
Telephone: 0171 353 1633
E-mail: barristers@2gardenct.law.co.uk
Call date: July 1980, Gray's Inn
Qualifications: [LLB (Hons)(Lond)]

GRIFFITHS HUGH ROBERT JAMES

Furnival Chambers
32 Furnival Street, London EC4A 1JQ,
Telephone: 0171 405 3232
E-mail: clerks@furnivallaw.co.uk
Call date: Nov 1972, Inner Temple

GRIFFITHS JOHN ALFRED

2 King's Bench Walk
Ground Floor, Temple, London EC4Y 7DE,
Telephone: 0171 353 1746
E-mail: 2kbw@atlas.co.uk
Door Tenant
Call date: Nov 1948, Lincoln's Inn
Qualifications: [MA (Oxon)]

GRIFFITHS LAWRENCE

Iscoed Chambers
86 St Helen's Road, Swansea SA1 4BQ,
Telephone: 01792 652988/9/330
Call date: Nov 1957, Inner Temple
Qualifications: [MA (Cantab)]

GRIFFITHS MARTIN ALEXANDER

Essex Court Chambers
24 Lincoln's Inn Fields, London WC2A 3ED,
Telephone: 0171 813 8000
E-mail: clerksroom@essexcourt-chambers.co.uk
Call date: Nov 1986, Inner Temple
Qualifications: [MA (Oxon), Dip Law (City)]

GRIFFITHS MICHAEL DAVID

33 Park Place
Cardiff CF1 3BA, Telephone: 01222 233313
Call date: May 1993, Middle Temple
Qualifications: [LLB (Hons)(Cardiff)]

GRIFFITHS PATRICK THOMAS JOHN

Iscoed Chambers
86 St Helen's Road, Swansea SA1 4BQ,
Telephone: 01792 652988/9/330
Call date: Nov 1972, Gray's Inn
Qualifications: [MA (Oxon)]

GRIFFITHS PETER ROBERT

4 Stone Bldgs
Ground Floor, Lincoln's Inn, London
WC2A 3XT, Telephone: 0171 242 5524
E-mail: d.goddard@4stonebuildings.law.co.uk
Call date: July 1977, Inner Temple
Qualifications: [MA (Cantab)]

GRIFFITHS RICHARD STEPHEN

Carmarthen Chambers
30 Spilman Street, Carmarthen, Dyfed
SA31 1LQ, Telephone: 01267 234410
Call date: Nov 1983, Gray's Inn
Qualifications: [BA]

GRIFFITHS ROBIN CLIVE

2 Paper Bldgs
Temple, London EC4Y 7ET,
Telephone: 0171 936 2613
Call date: Nov 1970, Middle Temple
Qualifications: [BA (Hons)(Oxon), Dip Crim (Cantab)]

GRIFFITHS ROGER VAUGHAN

32 Park Place
Cardiff CF1 3BA, Telephone: 01222 397364
Call date: July 1983, Gray's Inn
Qualifications: [LLB (Wales)]

GRIFFITHS MISS SIAN HAYLEY

17 Carlton Crescent
Southampton SO15 2XR,
Telephone: 01703 320320
E-mail: km@bar-17cc.demon.co.uk
South Western Chambers
Melville House 12 Middle Street, Taunton,
Somerset TA1 1SH, Telephone: 01823 331919
Call date: Oct 1990, Inner Temple
Qualifications: [LLB (Cardiff)]

GRIFFITHS MISS TANIA VERONICA

Exchange Chambers
Pearl Assurance House Derby Square,
Liverpool L2 9XX, Telephone: 0151 236 7747/
0458
E-mail: exchangechambers@btinternet.com
Call date: July 1982, Gray's Inn
Qualifications: [BA]

GRIME MARK STEPHEN EASTBURN QC (1987)

Deans Court Chambers
Cumberland House Crown Square, Manchester
M3 3HA, Telephone: 0161 834 4097
E-mail: deanscourt@compuserve.com
2 Pump Court
1st Floor, Temple, London EC4Y 7AH,
Telephone: 0171 353 5597
Call date: Feb 1970, Middle Temple
Recorder
Qualifications: [MA (Oxon)]

GRIMSHAW MISS ELIZABETH ANNE

King Charles House
Standard Hill, Nottingham NG1 6FX,
Telephone: 0115 9418851
E-mail: clerks@kch.co.uk
Call date: Oct 1993, Gray's Inn
Qualifications: [LLB (Buck'ham)]

GRIMSHAW NICHOLAS EDWARD

Deans Court Chambers
Cumberland House Crown Square, Manchester
M3 3HA, Telephone: 0161 834 4097
E-mail: deanscourt@compuserve.com
Deans Court Chambers
41-43 Market Place, Preston PR1 1AH,
Telephone: 01772 555163
E-mail: deanscourt@compuserve.com
Call date: Nov 1988, Inner Temple
Qualifications: [BA (Oxon)]

GRINDROD MRS HELEN M QC (1982)

Chambers of Helen Grindrod QC
1st Floor 95a Chancery Lane, London
WC2A 2JG, Telephone: 0171 404 4777
18 St John Street
Manchester M3 4EA,
Telephone: 0161 278 1800
Door Tenant
Call date: July 1966, Lincoln's Inn
Qualifications: [MA (Oxon)]

GRIPTON DAVID JOHN

York Chambers
14 Toft Green, York YO1 1JT,
Telephone: 01904 620048
E-mail: yorkchambers.co.uk
Call date: July 1969, Middle Temple
Qualifications: [LLB]

GROBEL PETER

12 King's Bench Walk
Temple, London EC4Y 7EL,
Telephone: 0171 583 0811
E-mail: chambers@12kbw.co.uk
Call date: July 1967, Lincoln's Inn
Recorder
Qualifications: [LLB (Lond)]

GROCOTT MISS SUSAN

Queen's Chambers
5 John Dalton Street, Manchester M2 6ET,
Telephone: 0161 834 6875/4738
4 Camden Place
Preston PR1 3JL, Telephone: 01772 828300
Call date: Nov 1986, Middle Temple
Qualifications: [BA (Oxon)]

GRODZINSKI SAMUEL MARC

39 Essex Street
London WC2R 3AT,
Telephone: 0171 583 1111
E-mail: clerks@39essex.co.uk
Call date: Mar 1996, Middle Temple
Qualifications: [BA (Hons)]

GROOM IAN JOHN

Paradise Square Chambers
26 Paradise Square, Sheffield S1 2DE,
Telephone: 0114 2738951
Call date: Nov 1990, Middle Temple
Qualifications: [LLB (Wales)]

GROOME DAVID

5 Paper Bldgs
1st Floor, Temple, London EC4Y 7HB,
Telephone: 0171 583 6117
E-mail: clerks@5-paperbuildings.law.co.uk
Call date: Nov 1987, Middle Temple
Qualifications: [LLB (London)]

GROSS PETER HENRY QC (1992)

20 Essex Street
London WC2R 3AL,
Telephone: 0171 583 9294
E-mail: clerks@20essexst.com
Call date: July 1977, Gray's Inn
Recorder
Qualifications: [MA, BCL (Oxon)]

D

GROUND REGINALD PATRICK QC (1981)

2-3 Gray's Inn Square
Gray's Inn, London WC1R 5JH,
Telephone: 0171 242 4986
E-mail: chambers@2-3graysinnsquare.co.uk
Call date: Feb 1960, Inner Temple
Qualifications: [MA]

GROUND RICHARD WILLIAM SCOTT

2-3 Gray's Inn Square
Gray's Inn, London WC1R 5JH,
Telephone: 0171 242 4986
E-mail: chambers@2-3graysinnsquare.co.uk
Call date: Oct 1994, Inner Temple
Qualifications: [BA (Cantab), CPE]

GROUT-SMITH JEREMY GAYWOOD

Peel Court Chambers
45 Hardman Street, Manchester M3 3HA,
Telephone: 0161 832 3791
Call date: July 1986, Inner Temple
Qualifications: [LLB, LLM (Bristol)]

GROVER TIM RUSSELL

Martins Building
Water Street, Liverpool L2 3SP,
Telephone: 0151 236 5818/4919
Call date: Nov 1991, Inner Temple
Qualifications: [LLB (Essex)]

GROVES HUGO GERARD

Enterprise Chambers
9 Old Square, Lincoln's Inn, London
WC2A 3SR, Telephone: 0171 405 9471
Enterprise Chambers
38 Park Square, Leeds LS1 2PA,
Telephone: 01132 460391
Enterprise Chambers
65 Quayside, Newcastle upon Tyne NE1 3DS,
Telephone: 0191 222 3344
Call date: July 1980, Gray's Inn
Qualifications: [LLB (Leic), LLM (Lond)]

GRUBB PROFESSOR ANDREW

3 Serjeants Inn
London EC4Y 1BQ,
Telephone: 0171 353 5537
E-mail: available upon request
Call date: July 1980, Inner Temple
Qualifications: [MA (Cantab)]

GRUCHY SIMON GEOFFREY

1 Crown Office Row
2nd Floor, Temple, London EC4Y 7HH,
Telephone: 0171 797 7111
Call date: May 1993, Middle Temple
Qualifications: [BSc(Nautical Studies,),
Diploma in Law]

GRUDER JEFFREY NIGEL QC (1997)

1 Essex Court
Ground Floor, Temple, London EC4Y 9AR,
Telephone: 0171 583 2000
E-mail: clerks@oneessexcourt.co.uk
Call date: July 1977, Middle Temple
Qualifications: [MA (Cantab)]

GRUFFYDD JOHN

Oriel Chambers
14 Water Street, Liverpool L2 8TD,
Telephone: 0151 236 7191
E-mail: oriel_chambers@link.org
Call date: Feb 1992, Gray's Inn
Qualifications: [LLB (Lond)]

GRUMBAR PAUL HARRY JULIAN

St John's Chambers
Small Street, Bristol BS1 1DW,
Telephone: 0117 9213456/298514
E-mail: clerks@stjohns.uk.com
Call date: Nov 1974, Middle Temple
Qualifications: [BA]

GRUNDY MISS ARABELLA ELIZABETH LOUISE

College Chambers
19 Carlton Cresent, Southampton, Hants
SO15 2ET, Telephone: 01703 230338
Call date: Oct 1995, Inner Temple
Qualifications: [MA, CPE (City)]

GRUNDY MS CLARE

28 St John Street
Manchester M3 4DJ,
Telephone: 0161 834 8418
E-mail: clerk@28stjohnst.co.uk
Call date: July 1989, Gray's Inn
Qualifications: [LLB (B'ham)]

GRUNDY JAMES MILTON

Gray's Inn Chambers
3rd Floor, Gray's Inn, London WC1R 5JA,
Telephone: 0171 242 2642
E-mail: clerks@taxbar.com
Call date: Nov 1954, Inner Temple
Qualifications: [MA (Cantab)]

GRUNDY LIAM

Adrian Lyon's Chambers
14 Castle Street, Liverpool L2 0NE,
Telephone: 0151 236 4421/8240
E-mail: chambers14@aol.com
Call date: July 1995, Inner Temple
Qualifications: [LLB (Hull), LLM (Cantab)]

GRUNDY NICHOLAS JOHN

1 Essex Court
1st Floor, Temple, London EC4Y 9AR,
Telephone: 0171 936 3030
E-mail: one.essex_court@virgin.net
Call date: Oct 1993, Gray's Inn
Qualifications: [MA (Cantab), MSc, Dip Law]

GRUNDY NIGEL LAWRENCE JOHN

9 St John Street
Manchester M3 4DN,
Telephone: 0161 955 9000
E-mail: ninesjs@gconnect.com
Call date: July 1983, Middle Temple
Qualifications: [MA (Oxon)]

GRUNDY PHILIP MICHAEL DAVID

28 St John Street
Manchester M3 4DJ,
Telephone: 0161 834 8418
E-mail: clerk@28stjohnst.co.uk
Call date: July 1980, Middle Temple
Assistant Recorder
Qualifications: [LLB (Wales)]

GRUNWALD HENRY CYRIL

1 Crown Office Row
2nd Floor, Temple, London EC4Y 7HH,
Telephone: 0171 797 7111
Call date: July 1972, Gray's Inn
Qualifications: [LLB (Lond)]

GUBBAY JEFFREY

Chambers of Raana Sheikh
Gray's Inn Chambers, Gray's Inn, London
WC1R, Telephone: 0171 831 5344
E-mail: s.mcblain@btinternet.com
Call date: Oct 1992, Inner Temple
Qualifications: [LLB (Bucks)]

GUEST MS HELEN

3 Temple Gardens
2nd Floor, Temple, London EC4Y 9AU,
Telephone: 0171 583 1155
Call date: Oct 1996, Lincoln's Inn
Qualifications: [BA (Hons)(Lond)]

GUEST NEIL

3 Temple Gardens
2nd Floor, Temple, London EC4Y 9AU,
Telephone: 0171 583 1155
Call date: July 1989, Lincoln's Inn
Qualifications: [LLB (Hons)]

GUEST PETER LIAM

Cloisters
1st Floor, Temple, London EC4Y 7AA,
Telephone: 0171 827 4000
E-mail: clerks@cloisters.com
Call date: July 1975, Inner Temple
Qualifications: [BA (Hons) (Dunelm)]

GUEST DR STEPHEN FRANCIS DEXTER

199 Strand
London WC2R 1DR,
Telephone: 0171 379 9779
E-mail: chambers@199strand.co.uk
Door Tenant
Call date: Nov 1980, Inner Temple
Qualifications: [BA, LLB, B Litt, PhD]

GUGGENHEIM MISS ANNA MAEVE

2 Crown Office Row
Ground Floor, Temple, London EC4Y 7HJ,
Telephone: 0171 797 8100
E-mail: mail@2cor.co.uk, or to individual
barristers at: [barrister's surname]@2cor.co.uk
Call date: July 1982, Gray's Inn
Qualifications: [BA (Oxon)]

GUIRGUIS MISS SHEREN

21 White Friars
Chester CH1 1NZ, Telephone: 01244 323070
Call date: Oct 1996, Inner Temple
Qualifications: [LLB (B'ham)]

GUISHARD DAVID ELSWORTH KELLY

Rowchester Chambers
4 Rowchester Court Whittall Street,
Birmingham B4 6DH,
Telephone: 0121 233 2327/2361951
Call date: Feb 1978, Middle Temple
Qualifications: [LLB]

GULLICK STEPHEN JOHN

25 Park Square
Leeds LS1 2PW, Telephone: 0113 2451841/2/3
E-mail: sovereignchambers@btinternet.com
Call date: Feb 1971, Gray's Inn
Qualifications: [LLB]

GULLIFER MRS LOUISE JOAN

3 Verulam Buildings
London WC1R 5NT,
Telephone: 0171 831 8441
E-mail: clerks@3verulam.co.uk
Call date: July 1984, Gray's Inn
Qualifications: [MA (Oxon), BCL]

GULLIVER MISS ALISON LOUISE

4 Paper Buildings
Ground Floor, Temple, London EC4Y 7EX,
Telephone: 0171 353 3366/583 7155
E-mail: clerks@4paperbuildings.com
Call date: Nov 1989, Middle Temple
Qualifications: [BA Hons (Oxon)]

Fax: 0171 353 5778; DX: 1036 London

Types of work: Medical negligence; Personal
injury; Professional negligence

Other professional qualifications: MA

Awards and memberships: Member of PNBA

Other professional experience: Chair of an
independent inquiry team into a homicide

Reported cases: *Ritchie v Chichester Health
Authority*, [1994] 5 Med LR, 1994. Medical
negligence - obstetrics - administration of
epidural causing permanent paralysis - doctrine
of *res ipsa loquitur* in medical negligence cases.

GUMBEL MISS ELIZABETH ANNE

199 Strand
London WC2R 1DR,
Telephone: 0171 379 9779
E-mail: chambers@199strand.co.uk
Call date: Nov 1974, Inner Temple
Qualifications: [MA (Oxon)]

GUMBITI-ZIMUTO ANDREW

6 King's Bench Walk
Ground, Third & Fourth Floors, Temple,
London EC4Y 7DR,
Telephone: 0171 353 4931/583 0695
Call date: Nov 1983, Inner Temple
Qualifications: [BA (Hons)(Sussex)]

GUMBS MISS ANNETTE PATRICIA

28 St John Street
Manchester M3 4DJ,
Telephone: 0161 834 8418
E-mail: clerk@28stjohnst.co.uk
Call date: Oct 1994, Gray's Inn
Qualifications: [LLB]

GUMPERT RUSSELL BENJAMIN WALLACE

4 King's Bench Walk
2nd Floor, Temple, London EC4Y 7DL,
Telephone: 0171 353 3581
Call date: Feb 1987, Inner Temple
Qualifications: [MA (Cantab)]

GUMSLEY CARL JOHN

Broad Chare
33 Broad Chare, Newcastle Upon Tyne
NE1 3DQ, Telephone: 0191 232 0541
Call date: Nov 1989, Inner Temple
Qualifications: [LLB (Sheff)]

GUN CUNINGHAME JULIAN ARTHUR

Gough Square Chambers
6-7 Gough Square, London EC4A 3DE,
Telephone: 0171 353 0924
E-mail: gsc@goughsq.co.uk
Call date: Nov 1989, Lincoln's Inn
Qualifications: [MA (Edin)]

Fax: 0171 353 2221; DX: 476 London

Types of work: Commercial litigation; Limitation and striking out for delay; Private international; Professional negligence; Sale and carriage of goods

Other professional qualifications: Former solicitor

Circuit: Midland and Oxford

Awards and memberships: Professional Negligence Bar Association; London Common Law and Commercial Bar Association; Personal Injury Bar Association

Other professional experience: Practising as a solicitor for a year before going to the bar

Languages spoken: French, Italian

Publications: *Delay in Legal Proceedings: Responses and Remedies*, 1994; Matrimonial and Jointly Owned Property section of *Encloypaedia of Forms and Precedents*, 1990; *Compliance Case Law*, 1990

GUNASEKARA PRINS

12 Old Square
1st Floor, Lincoln's Inn, London WC2A 3TX,
Telephone: 0171 404 0875
Call date: Nov 1993, Middle Temple
Qualifications: [BA (Hons) (Lond)]

GUNNING ALEXANDER RUPERT

4 Pump Court
Temple, London EC4Y 7AN,
Telephone: 0171 353 2656/9
E-mail: 4_pump_court@compuserve.com
Call date: Nov 1994, Inner Temple
Qualifications: [LLB, LLM (Lond)]

GUNTHER MISS ELIZABETH ANN

Pump Court Chambers
Upper Ground Floor 3 Pump Court, Temple,
London EC4Y 7AJ, Telephone: 0171 353 0711
Pump Court Chambers
31 Southgate Street, Winchester SO23 8EE,
Telephone: 01962 868161
Call date: Oct 1993, Lincoln's Inn
Qualifications: [LLB (Hons)(B'ham)]

GUPTA TEERTHA

1 Gray's Inn Square
1st Floor, London WC1R 5AG,
Telephone: 0171 405 3000
E-mail: clerks@onegrays.demon.co.uk
Call date: Nov 1990, Inner Temple
Qualifications: [LLB (Leeds)]

GUPTA MISS USHA

New Chambers
3 Sadleir Road, St Albans, Hertfordshire
AL1 2BL, Telephone: 0966 212126
Call date: July 1984, Middle Temple
Qualifications: [BA (Modern Studies, Dip Law), BA (Hons)]

GURSOY RAMIZ ALI

3 Temple Gardens
3rd Floor, Temple, London EC4Y 9AU,
Telephone: 0171 353 0832
Call date: Nov 1991, Middle Temple
Qualifications: [BA Hons (Essex), Dip Law (City)]

GUTHRIE JAMES DALGLISH QC (1993)

1 Crown Office Row
3rd Floor, Temple, London EC4Y 7HH,
Telephone: 0171 583 9292
E-mail: onecor@link.org
Call date: July 1975, Inner Temple
Assistant Recorder
Qualifications: [BA (Oxon)]

GUTHRIE MARK JONATHAN

14 Tooks Court
Cursitor St, London EC4A 1LB,
Telephone: 0171 405 8828
E-mail: clerks @tooks.law.co.uk
Call date: July 1984, Middle Temple
Qualifications: [LLB (Manch)]

GUTTERIDGE MISS BEVERLEY JANE

Chambers of Beverley Gutteridge
36 Dunmore Road, Wimbledon, London
SW20 8TN, Telephone: 0181 947 0717
Call date: July 1987, Middle Temple
Qualifications: [BA (Keele)]

GUY JOHN DAVID COLIN

Francis Taylor Bldg
3rd Floor, Temple, London EC4Y 7BY,
Telephone: 0171 797 7250
Call date: July 1972, Gray's Inn
Qualifications: [BA, FCIArb]

GUY RICHARD PERRAN

Queen Elizabeth Bldg
Ground Floor, Temple, London EC4Y 9BS,
Telephone: 0171 353 7181 (12 Lines)
Godolphin Chambers
50 Castle Street, Truro, Cornwall TR1 3AF,
Telephone: 01872 276312
Call date: Nov 1970, Inner Temple
Qualifications: [MA (Oxon)]

GUY-DAVIES MRS JUDITH MARY

Bell Yard Chambers
116/118 Chancery Lane, London WC2A 1PP,
Telephone: 0171 306 9292
Call date: Nov 1976, Gray's Inn
Qualifications: [LLB]

HABBOO MISS CAMILLE FRANCES

1 Dr Johnson's Bldgs
Ground Floor, Temple, London EC4Y 7AX,
Telephone: 0171 353 9328
Dr Johnson's Chambers
The Atrium Court Apex Plaza, Reading
RG1 1AX, Telephone: 01734 254221
Call date: July 1987, Gray's Inn
Qualifications: [LLB (L'pool)]

HABEL MRS JESSICA JENNET

College Chambers
19 Carlton Cresent, Southampton, Hants
SO15 2ET, Telephone: 01703 230338
Call date: July 1991, Middle Temple
Qualifications: [MA (Oxon)]

HABIB DR MUSTAFA SALMAN

10 King's Bench Walk
Ground Floor, Temple, London EC4Y 7EB,
Telephone: 0171 353 7742
E-mail: 10kbw@lineone.net
Call date: Nov 1980, Lincoln's Inn
Qualifications: [BPharm (Lond), PhD]

HACKER RICHARD DANIEL

3/4 South Square
Gray's Inn, London WC1R 5HP,
Telephone: 0171 696 9900
E-mail: clerks@southsquare.com
Call date: July 1977, Lincoln's Inn
Qualifications: [MA (Cantab)]

HACKETT MARTIN JOHN

15 Winckley Square
Preston PR1 3JJ, Telephone: 01772 252828
E-mail: clerks@winckleysq.demon.co.uk
Call date: Feb 1995, Middle Temple
Qualifications: [LLB (Hons)(Wales)]

HACKETT PHILIP GEORGE

3 Hare Court
1st Floor, Temple, London EC4Y 7BJ,
Telephone: 0171 353 7561
Call date: Nov 1978, Middle Temple
Qualifications: [BA]

HACKING ANTHONY STEPHEN QC (1983)

1 King's Bench Walk
2nd Floor, Temple, London EC4Y 7DB,
Telephone: 0171 936 1500
E-mail: ddear@1kbw.co.uk
Call date: Nov 1965, Inner Temple
Recorder
Qualifications: [MA (Oxon)]

HACKMAN CARL

Mitre Court Chambers
3rd Floor, Temple, London EC4Y 7BP,
Telephone: 0171 353 9394
Call date: Nov 1990, Gray's Inn
Qualifications: [LLB]

HACON RICHARD DAVID

11 South Square
2nd Floor, Gray's Inn, London WC1R 5EU,
Telephone: 0171 405 1222
Call date: Nov 1979, Gray's Inn
Qualifications: [BSc (Leeds)]

HADDON-CAVE CHARLES ANTHONY

4 Essex Court
Temple, London EC4Y 9AJ,
Telephone: 0171 797 7970
E-mail: clerks@4essexcourt.law.co.uk
Call date: July 1978, Gray's Inn
Qualifications: [MA (Cantab)]

HADLEY STEVEN FRANK

2 Paper Buildings
Basement, Temple, London EC4Y 7ET,
Telephone: 0171 353 0933
Call date: July 1987, Inner Temple
Qualifications: [BA (Hons)(Wales), BIB Studies/
Phil, BD (Hons)(Wales), Dip Law]

HADRILL KEITH PAUL

9-12 Bell Yard
London WC2A 2LF,
Telephone: 0171 400 1800
Call date: July 1977, Lincoln's Inn

HAGE JOSEPH

1 Essex Court
Ground Floor, Temple, London EC4Y 9AR,
Telephone: 0171 583 2000
E-mail: clerks@oneessexcourt.co.uk
Call date: Oct 1991, Lincoln's Inn
Qualifications: [BA (York)]

HAGGAN NICHOLAS SOMERSET

17 Carlton Crescent
Southampton SO15 2XR,
Telephone: 01703 320320
E-mail: km@bar-17cc.demon.co.uk
Call date: July 1977, Middle Temple

HAGGERTY MISS ELIZABETH FRANCES

Lamb Chambers
Lamb Building, Temple, London EC4Y 7AS,
Telephone: 0171 797 8300
E-mail: lambchambers@link.org
Call date: Feb 1994, Lincoln's Inn
Qualifications: [LLB (Hons)]

HAGUE PAUL FRANCIS

15 Winckley Square
Preston PR1 3JJ, Telephone: 01772 252828
E-mail: clerks@winckleysq.demon.co.uk
Call date: July 1983, Lincoln's Inn
Qualifications: [BA]

HAIDEMENOS STAVROS

Warwick House Chambers
8 Warwick Court, Gray's Inn, London
WC1R 5DJ, Telephone: 0171 430 2323
Call date: Oct 1992, Lincoln's Inn
Qualifications: [LLB(Hons)(Lond), LLM(Lond),
Maitrise (Paris II), ACIArb]

HAIG-HADDOW JOHN ALASTAIR HAIG

Eighteen Carlton Crescent
Southampton SO15 2XR,
Telephone: 01703 639001
Call date: July 1972, Middle Temple
Qualifications: [BA]

HAIGH MARTIN JAMES

30 Park Square
Leeds LS1 2PF, Telephone: 0113 2436388
Call date: Nov 1970, Gray's Inn
Qualifications: [LLB]

HAILSTONE MISS CATHARINE ELIZABETH

Albion Chambers
Broad Street, Bristol BS1 1DR,
Telephone: 0117 9272144
Call date: July 1962, Middle Temple
Qualifications: [LLB (Lond)]

D

HAINES GEOFFREY RALPH

55 Temple Chambers
Temple Avenue, London EC4Y 0HP,
Telephone: 0171 353 7400
136B Vine Lane
Hillingdon, Uxbridge, Middlesex UB10 0BQ,
Telephone: 01895 270221
Call date: June 1949, Lincoln's Inn

HAINES JOHN WILLIAM

2-3 Gray's Inn Square
Gray's Inn, London WC1R 5JH,
Telephone: 0171 242 4986
E-mail: chambers@2-3graysinnsquare.co.uk
Call date: Nov 1967, Middle Temple
Recorder
Qualifications: [BA (Oxon)]

HAITINK MRS PATRICIA

Devereux Chambers
Devereux Court, London WC2R 3JJ,
Telephone: 0171 353 7534
E-mail: elton@devchambers.co.uk
Call date: Nov 1995, Middle Temple
Qualifications: [BA (Hons)]

HAJIMITSIS ANTHONY PAUL

39 Park Square
Leeds LS1 2NU, Telephone: 0113 2456633
Call date: Nov 1984, Inner Temple
Qualifications: [BA (Oxon)]

HALE CHARLES STANLEY

2 Dr Johnson's Building
Temple, London EC4Y 7AY,
Telephone: 0171 353 4716
Call date: Oct 1992, Middle Temple
Qualifications: [LL.B (Hons)]

HALE SEAN MARTIN PHILIP

St Mary's Chambers
50 High Pavement, Lace Market, Nottingham
NG1 1HW, Telephone: 0115 9503503
E-mail: clerks@smc.law.co.uk
Call date: Nov 1988, Inner Temple
Qualifications: [BA (Dunelm)]

HALEEMA MISS SAFINA

Trafalgar Chambers
53 Fleet Street, London EC4Y 1BE,
Telephone: 0171 583 5858
E-mail: TrafalgarChambers@easynet.co.uk
Call date: Oct 1993, Lincoln's Inn
Qualifications: [LLB (Hons)(L'pool), MA (Leic)]

HALES MISS SALLY ANN

9 Gough Square
London EC4A 3DE, Telephone: 0171 353 5371
Call date: July 1988, Gray's Inn
Qualifications: [LLB (Hons)]

HALKERSTON GRAEME ALEXANDER

1 Essex Court
Ground Floor, Temple, London EC4Y 9AR,
Telephone: 0171 583 2000
E-mail: clerks@oneessexcourt.co.uk
Call date: Nov 1994, Middle Temple
Qualifications: [BA (Hons), LLM
(Pennsylvania)]

HALKERSTON MISS SALLY

2 Harcourt Bldgs
1st Floor, Temple, London EC4Y 9DB,
Telephone: 0171 353 2112/2817
Door Tenant
Call date: Oct 1994, Middle Temple
Qualifications: [LLB (Hons)]

HALKYARD MISS (ALYSON) KAY

One Garden Court
Ground Floor, Temple, London EC4Y 9BJ,
Telephone: 0171 797 7900
Call date: July 1980, Gray's Inn
Qualifications: [LLB (Lond)]

HALL ADRIAN

Enfield Chambers
36-38 London Road, Enfield, Middlesex
EN2 6DT, Telephone: 0181 364 5627
E-mail: Enfieldchambers@compuserve.com
Southsea Chambers
PO Box 148, Southsea, Portsmouth,
Hampshire PO5 2TU,
Telephone: 01705 291261
Call date: July 1989, Inner Temple
Qualifications: [LLB (Hull), B.Ed (Hull)]

HALL ANDREW JOSEPH

Doughty Street Chambers
11 Doughty Street, London WC1N 2PG,
Telephone: 0171 404 1313
E-mail: doughty_street@compuserve.com
Call date: Feb 1991, Gray's Inn
Qualifications: [LLB (B'ham), MA (Sheff)]

HALL DAVID PERCY

9 Woodhouse Square
Leeds LS3 1AD, Telephone: 0113 2451986
Call date: July 1980, Gray's Inn
Qualifications: [BA]

HALL DEREK

York House
Borough Road, Middlesbrough, Cleveland
TS1 2HJ, Telephone: 01642 213000
Call date: Nov 1994, Middle Temple
Qualifications: [LLB (Hons)]

HALL MISS JACQUELINE ANN

18 Red Lion Court
(Off Fleet Street), London EC4A 3EB,
Telephone: 0171 520 6000
Thornwood House
102 New London Road, Chelmsford, Essex
CM2 0RG, Telephone: 01245 280880
Call date: Nov 1994, Lincoln's Inn
Qualifications: [BA (Hons)(Warw)]

HALL JEREMY JOHN

Becket Chambers
17 New Dover Road, Canterbury, Kent
CT1 3AS, Telephone: 01227 786331
Call date: Feb 1988, Gray's Inn
Qualifications: [LLB (Hons) (East, Anglia)]

HALL MISS JOANNA MARY

14 Gray's Inn Square
Gray's Inn, London WC1R 5JP,
Telephone: 0171 242 0858
E-mail: 100712.2134@compuserve.com
Call date: Nov 1973, Inner Temple
Qualifications: [LLB (Lond)]

HALL JOHN ANTHONY SANDERSON QC (1967)

Francis Taylor Bldg
3rd Floor, Temple, London EC4Y 7BY,
Telephone: 0171 797 7250
Call date: Nov 1948, Inner Temple
Qualifications: [MA (Cantab), FCI Arb]

HALL JONATHAN DAVID DURHAM QC (1995)

Bank House Chambers
Old Bank House, Hartshead, Sheffield S1 2EL,
Telephone: 0114 2751223
New Walk Chambers
27 New Walk, Leicester LE1 6TE,
Telephone: 0116 2559144
Door Tenant
Call date: July 1975, Gray's Inn
Recorder
Qualifications: [LLB (Hons)]

HALL JONATHAN RUPERT

5 Paper Bldgs
Lower Ground Floor, Temple, London
EC4Y 7HB, Telephone: 0171 353 5638
E-mail: 107722,633@compuserve.com
Call date: Nov 1994, Inner Temple
Qualifications: [BA (Oxon), CPE (City)]

HALL MRS MELANIE RUTH

Monckton Chambers
4 Raymond Buildings, Gray's Inn, London
WC1R 5BP, Telephone: 0171 405 7211
E-mail: chambers@monckton.co.uk
Call date: Nov 1982, Inner Temple
Qualifications: [BA Law (Dunelm)]

HALL MICHAEL LEBERT

2 Garden Court
1st Floor, Middle Temple, London EC4Y 9BL,
Telephone: 0171 353 1633
E-mail: barristers@2gardenct.law.co.uk
Call date: July 1983, Middle Temple
Qualifications: [BA]

HALL NICHOLAS

Sussex Chambers
9 Old Steine, Brighton BN1 1FJ,
Telephone: 01273 607953
Call date: July 1973, Gray's Inn
Qualifications: [MA (Oxon)]

D

HALL PETER STEPHEN

34 Graham Road
Wood Green, London N15 3NL,
Telephone: 0181 889 7671
Call date: July 1983, Gray's Inn
Qualifications: [BA (Manch), Dip Law]

HALL PHILIP JOHN

Peel House Chambers
Ground Floor, Peel House 5 Harrington Street,
Liverpool L2 9QA, Telephone: 0151 236 4321
Call date: Nov 1973, Gray's Inn
Qualifications: [LLB (Lond)]

HALL RICHARD ANDREW

Eighteen Carlton Crescent
Southampton SO15 2XR,
Telephone: 01703 639001
Call date: Nov 1995, Inner Temple
Qualifications: [LLB (Soton)]

HALL RICHARD ARTHUR

Adrian Lyon's Chambers
14 Castle Street, Liverpool L2 0NE,
Telephone: 0151 236 4421/8240
E-mail: chambers14@aol.com
Call date: Nov 1991, Lincoln's Inn
Qualifications: [MA (Oxon)]

HALL TAYLOR ALEXANDER EDWARD

11 Old Square
Ground Floor, Lincoln's Inn, London
WC2A 3TS, Telephone: 0171 430 0341
E-mail: clerks@11oldsquare.co.uk
Call date: Oct 1996, Inner Temple
Qualifications: [BA (Hons)(Bris), CPE (Lond)]

HALL-SMITH MARTIN CLIVE WILLIAM

Goldsmith Building
1st Floor, Temple, London EC4Y 7BL,
Telephone: 0171 353 7881
E-mail: clerks@goldsmith-building.law.co.uk
Call date: July 1972, Inner Temple
Qualifications: [LLB (Edin), MA (Cantab)]

HALLAM MISS RONA MARY LOUISE

30 Park Square
Leeds LS1 2PF, Telephone: 0113 2436388
Call date: July 1984, Inner Temple
Qualifications: [MA (Edinburgh), LLB]

HALLETT MISS HEATHER CAROL QC (1989)

23 Essex Street
London WC2R 3AS,
Telephone: 0171 413 0353/353 3533
E-mail: clerks@essexstreet23.demon.co.uk
Call date: July 1972, Inner Temple
Recorder
Qualifications: [MA (Oxon)]

HALLIDAY HAROLD DAVID

40 King Street
Manchester M2 6BA,
Telephone: 0161 832 9082
E-mail: Kingst40@aol.com
Call date: July 1972, Gray's Inn
Qualifications: [MA (Oxon)]

HALLIGAN RODNEY LEWTON

Martins Building
Water Street, Liverpool L2 3SP,
Telephone: 0151 236 5818/4919
Call date: July 1972, Gray's Inn
Qualifications: [LLB]

HALLIWELL MARK GARETH

40 King Street
Manchester M2 6BA,
Telephone: 0161 832 9082
E-mail: Kingst40@aol.com
Call date: July 1985, Lincoln's Inn
Qualifications: [B.Sc(Econ), Diploma]

HALLIWELL TOBY GEORGE

Assize Court Chambers
14 Small Street, Bristol BS1 1DE,
Telephone: 0117 9264587
Call date: Nov 1992, Middle Temple
Qualifications: [LLB (Hons, Manch)]

HALLORAN MS CEILIDH ANN

Arden Chambers
27 John Street, London WC1N 2BL,
Telephone: 0171 242 4244
Call date: Nov 1992, Lincoln's Inn
Qualifications: [MA (Psych), MEd (Psych),
Dip.TEFL (Psych)]

HALLOWES RUPERT JOHN MICHAEL

20 Britton Street
1st Floor, London EC1M 5NQ,
Telephone: 0171 608 3765
Call date: Oct 1995, Inner Temple
Qualifications: [BA (Bris), CPE]

HALPERN DAVID ANTHONY

Enterprise Chambers
9 Old Square, Lincoln's Inn, London
WC2A 3SR, Telephone: 0171 405 9471
Enterprise Chambers
38 Park Square, Leeds LS1 2PA,
Telephone: 01132 460391
Enterprise Chambers
65 Quayside, Newcastle upon Tyne NE1 3DS,
Telephone: 0191 222 3344
Call date: July 1978, Gray's Inn
Qualifications: [MA (Oxon)]

HALPIN THOMAS GAVIN

Earl Street Chambers
47 Earl Street, Maidstone, Kent ME14 1PD,
Telephone: 01622 671222
E-mail: gunner-sparks@msn.com
Call date: Nov 1994, Inner Temple
Qualifications: [LLB (Lond)]

HALSALL MISS LOUISE KIM

3 Temple Gardens
Lower Ground Floor, Temple, London
EC4Y 9AU, Telephone: 0171 353 3102/5/9297
Call date: July 1982, Middle Temple

HALSEY MARK STEPHEN

3 Hare Court
1st Floor, Temple, London EC4Y 7BJ,
Telephone: 0171 353 7561
Call date: Feb 1974, Inner Temple
Qualifications: [LLB (Bris)]

HALSTEAD ROBIN BERNARD

Fleet Chambers
Mitre House 44-46 Fleet Street, London
EC4Y 1BN, Telephone: 0171 936 3707
Call date: Oct 1996, Inner Temple
Qualifications: [BA (Oxon)]

HAM ROBERT WALLACE QC (1994)

Wilberforce Chambers
8 New Square, Lincoln's Inn, London
WC2A 3QP, Telephone: 0171 306 0102
E-mail: chambers@wilberforce.co.uk
Call date: Nov 1973, Middle Temple
Qualifications: [BCL, BA (Oxon)]

HAMBLEN NICHOLAS ARCHIBALD QC (1997)

20 Essex Street
London WC2R 3AL,
Telephone: 0171 583 9294
E-mail: clerks@20essexst.com
Call date: July 1981, Lincoln's Inn
Qualifications: [MA (Oxon),LLM (Harv)]

HAMBLIN STEWART WAYNE

2 Harcourt Bldgs
1st Floor, Temple, London EC4Y 9DB,
Telephone: 0171 353 2112/2817
Call date: Oct 1990, Middle Temple
Qualifications: [BA (Leic), Dip Law]

HAMER GEORGE CLEMENS

8 New Square
Lincoln's Inn, London WC2A 3QP,
Telephone: 0171 405 4321
Call date: Nov 1974, Gray's Inn
Qualifications: [BSc, ARCS (Lond)]

HAMER MICHAEL HOWARD KENNETH

2 Harcourt Bldgs
Ground Floor/Left, Temple, London
EC4Y 9DB, Telephone: 0171 583 9020
E-mail: clerks@harcourt.co.uk
Westgate Chambers
144 High Street, Lewes, East Sussex BN7 1XT,
Telephone: 01273 480510
Call date: Apr 1975, Inner Temple
Assistant Recorder

D

HAMES CHRISTOPHER WILLIAM

3 Dr Johnson's Bldgs
Ground Floor, Temple, London EC4Y 7BA,
Telephone: 0171 353 4854
Call date: July 1987, Inner Temple
Qualifications: [LLB (Sheffield)]

HAMEY JOHN ANTHONY

East Anglian Chambers
57 London Street, Norwich NR2 1HL,
Telephone: 01603 617351
East Anglian Chambers
Sanders House 52 North Hill, Colchester
CO1 1PY, Telephone: 01206 572756
East Anglian Chambers
Gresham House 5 Museum Street, Ipswich
IP1 1HQ, Telephone: 01473 214481
Call date: July 1979, Inner Temple
Qualifications: [MA (Cantab)]

HAMID MRS BEEBEE NAZMOON

Clapham Chambers
21-25 Bedford Road, Clapham North, London
SW4 7SH, Telephone: 0171 978 8482/
642 5777
E-mail: 113063.632@compuserve.com
Call date: July 1980, Lincoln's Inn
Qualifications: [BA (Hons) (Lond)]

HAMILL HUGH ANTHONY

12 King's Bench Walk
Temple, London EC4Y 7EL,
Telephone: 0171 583 0811
E-mail: chambers@12kbw.co.uk
Call date: July 1988, Inner Temple
Qualifications: [BA (Dublin), Dip Law (City)]

HAMILTON ADRIAN WALTER QC (1973)

7 King's Bench Walk
Ground Floor, Temple, London EC4Y 7DS,
Telephone: 0171 583 0404
Call date: June 1949, Lincoln's Inn
Qualifications: [MA (Oxon)]

HAMILTON ANDREW NINIAN ROBERTS

St Mary's Chambers
50 High Pavement, Lace Market, Nottingham
NG1 1HW, Telephone: 0115 9503503
E-mail: clerks@smc.law.co.uk
Call date: Nov 1970, Gray's Inn
Assistant Recorder
Qualifications: [LLB (B'ham)]

HAMILTON MS CAROLYN PAULA

One Garden Court
Ground Floor, Temple, London EC4Y 9BJ,
Telephone: 0171 797 7900
Call date: July 1996, Gray's Inn
Qualifications: [LLB (Bristol)]

HAMILTON DOUGLAS WILLIAM SETH

55 Temple Chambers
Temple Avenue, London EC4Y 0HP,
Telephone: 0171 353 7400
Call date: Oct 1990, Inner Temple
Qualifications: [BA (Sussex), Dip, Law, Dip
Management, Studies]

HAMILTON EBEN WILLIAM QC (1981)

1 New Square
Ground Floor, Lincoln's Inn, London
WC2A 3SA, Telephone: 0171 405 0884/5/6/7
E-mail: 1newsquare@compuserve.com
Call date: May 1962, Inner Temple
Qualifications: [MA (Cantab)]

HAMILTON MISS ELEANOR WARWICK

6 Park Square
Leeds LS1 2LW, Telephone: 0113 2459763
E-mail: chambers@no6.co.uk
Call date: July 1979, Inner Temple
Assistant Recorder
Qualifications: [LLB (Hull)]

HAMILTON GAVIN

2 Crown Office Row
2nd Floor, Temple, London EC4Y 7HJ,
Telephone: 0171 797 8000
Call date: July 1979, Gray's Inn
Qualifications: [BA (Oxon)]

HAMILTON MISS GEORGINA CAROLINE

3 Temple Gardens
3rd Floor, Temple, London EC4Y 9AU,
Telephone: 0171 583 0010
Call date: July 1989, Middle Temple
Qualifications: [LLB]

HAMILTON GRAEME MONTAGU QC (1978)

2 Crown Office Row
Ground Floor, Temple, London EC4Y 7HJ,
Telephone: 0171 797 8100
E-mail: mail@2cor.co.uk, or to individual
barristers at: [barrister's surname]@2cor.co.uk
Call date: Feb 1959, Gray's Inn
Recorder
Qualifications: [MA (Cantab)]

HAMILTON JAIME RICHARD

9 St John Street
Manchester M3 4DN,
Telephone: 0161 955 9000
E-mail: ninesjs@gconnect.com
Call date: Oct 1993, Gray's Inn
Qualifications: [LLB (Wales)]

HAMILTON JOHN CONRAD

3 Temple Gardens
3rd Floor, Temple, London EC4Y 9AU,
Telephone: 0171 583 0010
Call date: Nov 1988, Gray's Inn
Qualifications: [BSc (City),Dip Law]

HAMILTON NIGEL JOHN MAWDESLEY QC (1981)

St John's Chambers
Small Street, Bristol BS1 1DW,
Telephone: 0117 9213456/298514
E-mail: clerks@stjohns.uk.com
Call date: Nov 1965, Inner Temple
Qualifications: [MA (Cantab)]

HAMILTON PETER BERNARD

4 Pump Court
Temple, London EC4Y 7AN,
Telephone: 0171 353 2656/9
E-mail: 4_pump_court@compuserve.com
Call date: Feb 1968, Inner Temple
Qualifications: [BA (Rhodes), MA (Cantab)]

HAMILTON MISS PHILIPPA ANNE

Fountain Court
Temple, London EC4Y 9DH,
Telephone: 0171 583 3335
E-mail: chambers@fountaincourt.co.uk
Call date: Oct 1996, Lincoln's Inn
Qualifications: [MA (Hons)(Oxon), Dip in Law
(City)]

HAMILTON MISS SUSAN QC (1993)

2 Mitre Ct Bldgs
2nd Floor, Temple, London EC4Y 7BX,
Telephone: 0171 583 1380
Call date: Nov 1975, Middle Temple

HAMILTON-HAGUE MISS RACHAEL ELIZABETH

The Corn Exchange
5th Floor Fenwick Street, Liverpool L2 7QS,
Telephone: 0151 227 1081/5009
Call date: Oct 1993, Gray's Inn
Qualifications: [BA (Hons)(Keele)]

HAMILTON-SHIELD MISS ANNA-MARIA

2 Dr Johnson's Building
Temple, London EC4Y 7AY,
Telephone: 0171 353 4716
Call date: Nov 1989, Middle Temple
Qualifications: [LLb Hons]

HAMLIN PATRICK LINDOP

22 Old Bldgs
Lincoln's Inn, London WC2A 3UJ,
Telephone: 0171 831 0222
Call date: Nov 1970, Gray's Inn
Recorder

HAMMERTON ALASTAIR ROLF

1 Serjeants' Inn
5th Floor Fleet Street, Temple, London
EC4Y 1LL, Telephone: 0171 415 6666
E-mail: no1serjeantsinn@btinternet.com
Call date: July 1983, Inner Temple
Qualifications: [MA (Cantab), LLM (Virginia)]

D

HAMMERTON MISS VERONICA LESLEY

1 Serjeants' Inn
5th Floor Fleet Street, Temple, London
EC4Y 1LL, Telephone: 0171 415 6666
E-mail: no1serjeantsinn@btinternet.com
Call date: July 1977, Inner Temple
Assistant Recorder
Qualifications: [MA (Cantab)]

HAMMOND MISS KAREN ANN

3 Gray's Inn Square
Ground Floor, London WC1R 5AH,
Telephone: 0171 520 5600
E-mail: gis3@btinternet.com
Call date: July 1985, Middle Temple
Qualifications: [LLB(Notts)]

HAMMOND KOBINA TAHIR

Chancery Chambers
1st Floor Offices 70/72 Chancery Lane,
London WC2A 1AB,
Telephone: 0171 405 6879/6870
Call date: Nov 1991, Gray's Inn
Qualifications: [BA (Ghana)]

HAMMOND SEAN FRANCIS

18 Red Lion Court
(Off Fleet Street), London EC4A 3EB,
Telephone: 0171 520 6000
Thornwood House
102 New London Road, Chelmsford, Essex
CM2 0RG, Telephone: 01245 280880
Call date: Oct 1991, Lincoln's Inn
Qualifications: [LLB (Hons)]

HAMPTON MISS ALISON WENDY

24 The Ropewalk
Nottingham NG1 5EF,
Telephone: 0115 9472581
E-mail: clerk@ropewalk.co.uk
Call date: July 1977, Gray's Inn
Assistant Recorder
Qualifications: [LLB]

HANBURY WILLIAM EDMUND

Park Lane Chambers
19 Westgate, Leeds LS1 2RD,
Telephone: 0113 2285000
Call date: Nov 1985, Inner Temple
Qualifications: [LLB (Manch)]

HANCOCK CHRISTOPHER PATRICK

20 Essex Street
London WC2R 3AL,
Telephone: 0171 583 9294
E-mail: clerks@20essexst.com
Call date: July 1983, Middle Temple
Qualifications: [MA (Cantab), LLM (Harvard)]

HANCOCK MS MARIA

Westgate Chambers
144 High Street, Lewes, East Sussex BN7 1XT,
Telephone: 01273 480510
Westgate Chambers
16-17 Wellington Square, Hastings, East Sussex
TN34 1PB, Telephone: 01424 432105
Call date: Oct 1995, Gray's Inn
Qualifications: [BA (Hons)]

HANCOX MISS SALLY ELIZABETH

2 Paper Bldgs
Temple, London EC4Y 7ET,
Telephone: 0171 936 2613
Call date: Oct 1996, Lincoln's Inn
Qualifications: [BSc (Hons)(Bath)]

HANCOX STEPHEN HARRY

Francis Taylor Bldg
3rd Floor, Temple, London EC4Y 7BY,
Telephone: 0171 797 7250
Newport Chambers
12 Clytha Park Road, Newport, Gwent
NP9 47L, Telephone: 01633 267403/255855
Call date: Nov 1986, Inner Temple
Qualifications: [BD (Lond), Dip Law]

HAND ANTHONY RICHARD

College Chambers
19 Carlton Cresent, Southampton, Hants
SO15 2ET, Telephone: 01703 230338
Call date: July 1989, Lincoln's Inn
Qualifications: [LLB (Lond)]

HAND JOHN LESTER QC (1988)

9 St John Street
Manchester M3 4DN,
Telephone: 0161 955 9000
E-mail: ninesjs@gconnect.com
Old Square Chambers
1 Verulam Buildings, Gray's Inn, London
WC1R 5LQ, Telephone: 0171 831 0801
Old Square Chambers
Hanover House 47 Corn Street, Bristol
BS1 1HT, Telephone: 0117 9277111
Call date: July 1972, Gray's Inn
Recorder
Qualifications: [LLB (Nott'm)]

HAND JONATHAN ELLIOTT SHEERMAN

35 Essex Street
Temple, London WC2R 3AR,
Telephone: 0171 353 6381
Call date: Nov 1990, Inner Temple
Qualifications: [BA (Oxon)]

HANDS DAVID RICHARD GRANVILLE QC (1988)

4 Breams Buildings
London EC4A 1AQ,
Telephone: 0171 353 5835/430 1221
40 King Street
Manchester M2 6BA,
Telephone: 0161 832 9082
E-mail: Kingst40@aol.com
Call date: July 1965, Inner Temple

HANDS MISS JANE ELIZABETH

Wilberforce Chambers
Bishop Lane, Hull HU1 1PA,
Telephone: 01482 323264
E-mail: clerks@hullbar.demon.co.uk
Call date: July 1978, Inner Temple
Qualifications: [BA (Lond)]

HANDYSIDE RICHARD NEIL

Fountain Court
Temple, London EC4Y 9DH,
Telephone: 0171 583 3335
E-mail: chambers@fountaincourt.co.uk
Call date: Oct 1993, Lincoln's Inn
Qualifications: [LLB (Hons)(Bris), BCL (Oxon)]

HANHAM JAMES CHARLES FERGUSON

3 Paper Bldgs
Ground Floor, Temple, London EC4Y 7EU,
Telephone: 0171 797 7000
E-mail: clerks@3pb.co.uk
Call date: Oct 1996, Middle Temple
Qualifications: [BA (Hons)(Oxon), CPE (City)]

HANKIN JONAS KEITH

Coleridge Chambers
Citadel 190 Corporation Street, Birmingham
B4 6QD, Telephone: 0121 233 3303
Call date: Nov 1994, Middle Temple
Qualifications: [BA (Hons)]

HANLON MISS JACQUELINE PATRICIA

East Anglian Chambers
57 London Street, Norwich NR2 1HL,
Telephone: 01603 617351
East Anglian Chambers
Gresham House 5 Museum Street, Ipswich
IP1 1HQ, Telephone: 01473 214481
East Anglian Chambers
Sanders House 52 North Hill, Colchester
CO1 1PY, Telephone: 01206 572756
Call date: Nov 1994, Gray's Inn
Qualifications: [LLB]

HANNAFORD MISS SARAH JANE

Keating Chambers
10 Essex Street, Outer Temple, London
WC2R 3AA, Telephone: 0171 544 2600
Call date: July 1989, Middle Temple
Qualifications: [BA [Oxon]]

HANNAM TIMOTHY JAMES

4 Fountain Court
Steelhouse Lane, Birmingham B4 6DR,
Telephone: 0121 236 3476
Call date: Oct 1995, Gray's Inn
Qualifications: [BA (Hons)]

HANSEN WILLIAM JOSEPH

5 Bell Yard
London WC2A 2JR, Telephone: 0171 333 8811
Call date: Nov 1992, Lincoln's Inn
Qualifications: [BSc (Econ)(Hons), M.Phil (Cantab)]

HANSON TIMOTHY VINCENT RICHARD

7 Fountain Court
Steelhouse Lane, Birmingham B4 6DR,
Telephone: 0121 236 8531
Call date: July 1989, Inner Temple
Qualifications: [LLB Hons]

HANTUSCH ROBERT ANTHONY

3 Stone Buildings
Ground Floor, Lincoln's Inn, London
WC2A 3XL, Telephone: 0171 242 4937/
405 8358
Call date: July 1982, Inner Temple
Qualifications: [MA (Cantab)]

Fax: 0171 405 3896/01302 752 662;
Out of hours telephone: 01302 743 261;
DX: 317 London; Other comms: Mobile 0860
302460; E-mail RAHantusch@link.org;
RAHantusch@compuserve.com

Types of work: Banking; Bankruptcy; Chancery
(general); Chancery land law; Commercial
litigation; Company and commercial;
Construction; Equity, wills and trusts; Financial
services; Insolvency; Landlord and tenant;
Partnerships; Professional negligence; Sale and
carriage of goods

Awards and memberships: Chancery Bar
Association

Reported cases: *John Dee Group v WMH (21)
Ltd (formerly Magnet Ltd)*, [1997] BCC 518,
1996. The application of non-insolvency set off
in the context of administrative receivership.
*Wake and Eastgate Motor Company v Renault
UK Ltd*, (1996) *The Times* 1 August, 1996.
Mandatory injunctive relief granted to enforce a
collateral contract preventing the termination
of a motor dealer's franchise.
Moon v Franklin, [1996] BPIL 196, 1990.
Consideration of the form of relief to be granted
on an application under s423 of the Insolvency
Act 1986.
IRC v Woolen, [1992] STC 944, 1992.
Consideration of whether tax is recoverable as a
preferential debt in insolvency following a back
duty settlement agreement.
Re Barrow Borough Transport, [1990] Ch 227,
1989. Whether a debenture can be registered
out of time after the grantor is subject to an
administration order.

HAPGOOD MARK BERNARD QC (1994)

Brick Court Chambers
15/19 Devereux Court, London WC2R 3JJ,
Telephone: 0171 583 0777
E-mail: (surname)@brickcourt.demon.co.uk
Call date: Feb 1979, Gray's Inn
Qualifications: [LLB (Nott'm)]

HAQ MAHMOODUL RAJA

2 Middle Temple Lane
3rd Floor, Temple, London EC4Y 9AA,
Telephone: 0171 583 4540
Call date: Feb 1981, Middle Temple
Qualifications: [BA, LLB]

HAQUE GAZI MOSTA GAWSAL

197 Ellesmere Road
London NW10 1LG,
Telephone: 0181 208 1663
Call date: July 1970, Inner Temple
Qualifications: [MA]

HARBAGE WILLIAM JOHN HIRONS

36 Bedford Row
London WC1R 4JH,
Telephone: 0171 421 8000
E-mail: 36bedfordrow@link.org
Call date: July 1983, Middle Temple
Qualifications: [MA (Cantab)]

HARBOTTLE GWILYM THOMAS

5 New Square
1st Floor, Lincoln's Inn, London WC2A 3RJ,
Telephone: 0171 404 0404
E-mail: Chambers@FiveNewSquare.CityScape.co.uk
Call date: Nov 1987, Lincoln's Inn
Qualifications: [BA (Oxon), Dip Law, (City)]

HARDIMAN ADRIAN PATRICK

Doughty Street Chambers
11 Doughty Street, London WC1N 2PG,
Telephone: 0171 404 1313
E-mail: doughty_street@compuserve.com
Door Tenant
Call date: May 1988, Middle Temple
Qualifications: [BA(Hons) Dublin]

HARDING MISS CHERRY JACINTA

Gray's Inn Chambers
5th Floor, Gray's Inn, London WC1R 5JA,
Telephone: 0171 404 1111
Call date: Nov 1978, Gray's Inn
Qualifications: [LLB (Lond)]

HARDING MRS CHRISTINE LAURETTA AYODELE

Leone Chambers
72 Evelyn Avenue, Kingsbury, London
NW9 OJH, Telephone: 0181 931 1712
Call date: Feb 1966, Lincoln's Inn

HARDING CHRISTOPHER JAMES

10 King's Bench Walk
1st Floor, Temple, London EC4Y 7EB,
Telephone: 0171 353 2501
Call date: Nov 1992, Inner Temple
Qualifications: [LLB (Lond)]

HARDING MISS FIONA SUZANNE

Claremont Chambers
26 Waterloo Road, Wolverhampton WV1 4BL,
Telephone: 01902 426222
Door Tenant
Call date: Feb 1993, Gray's Inn
Qualifications: [BA]

HARDING MISS PATRICIA JANE

10 King's Bench Walk
Ground Floor, Temple, London EC4Y 7EB,
Telephone: 0171 353 7742
E-mail: 10kbw@lineone.net
Call date: Nov 1994, Lincoln's Inn
Qualifications: [BSc (Hons)(Bris)]

HARDING RICHARD ANTHONY

Keating Chambers
10 Essex Street, Outer Temple, London
WC2R 3AA, Telephone: 0171 544 2600
Call date: Oct 1992, Middle Temple
Qualifications: [MA (Hons), Common
Profesional, Examination]

HARDWICK MATTHEW RICHARD

Enterprise Chambers
9 Old Square, Lincoln's Inn, London
WC2A 3SR, Telephone: 0171 405 9471
Enterprise Chambers
38 Park Square, Leeds LS1 2PA,
Telephone: 01132 460391
Enterprise Chambers
65 Quayside, Newcastle upon Tyne NE1 3DS,
Telephone: 0191 222 3344
Call date: Oct 1994, Gray's Inn
Qualifications: [MA, Licence Speciale, En Droit
Europeen]

HARDY MRS AMANDA JANE

24 Old Bldgs
First Floor, Lincoln's Inn, London WC2A 3UJ,
Telephone: 0171 242 2744
Call date: Nov 1993, Middle Temple
Qualifications: [LLB (Hons), LLM (Lond), AKC]

HARDY DAVID ROBERT

33 Park Place
Cardiff CF1 3BA, Telephone: 01222 233313
Call date: Oct 1993, Lincoln's Inn
Qualifications: [LLB (Hons)(Bris), BCL (Oxon)]

HARDY JOHN SYDNEY

3 Raymond Buildings
Gray's Inn, London WC1R 5BH,
Telephone: 0171 831 3833
E-mail: chambers@threeraymond.demon.co.uk
Call date: Nov 1988, Gray's Inn
Qualifications: [BA (Hons) (Oxon), Dip Law]

HARDY PAUL CHRISTIAN KINNEAR

18 Red Lion Court
(Off Fleet Street), London EC4A 3EB,
Telephone: 0171 520 6000
Thornwood House
102 New London Road, Chelmsford, Essex
CM2 ORG, Telephone: 01245 280880
Call date: Nov 1992, Inner Temple
Qualifications: [MA (St.Andrews), Dip in Law]

D

HARE MISS ROSINA SELINA ALICE QC (1976)

10 King's Bench Walk
Ground Floor, Temple, London EC4Y 7EB,
Telephone: 0171 353 7742
E-mail: 10kbw@lineone.net
Call date: Feb 1956, Middle Temple
Recorder

HARE WILLIAM RICHARD

67a Westgate Road
Newcastle Upon Tyne NE1 1SQ,
Telephone: 0191 261 4407/2329785
Call date: Nov 1994, Inner Temple
Qualifications: [BA (Newc)]

HARFORD-BELL MISS NERIDA

2 Garden Court
1st Floor, Middle Temple, London EC4Y 9BL,
Telephone: 0171 353 1633
E-mail: barristers@2gardenct.law.co.uk
Call date: Nov 1984, Middle Temple
Qualifications: [MA (Sussex), BA (Hons)]

HARGAN JAMES JOHN

30 Park Square
Leeds LS1 2PF, Telephone: 0113 2436388
Call date: Feb 1990, Middle Temple
Qualifications: [LLB (Hons)]

HARGAN JOHN CARL

1 Gray's Inn Square
Ground Floor, London WC1R 5AA,
Telephone: 0171 405 8946/7/8
Call date: Nov 1995, Lincoln's Inn
Qualifications: [LLB (Hons)]

HARGAN MARTIN CAMPBELL MCLAREN

Paradise Square Chambers
26 Paradise Square, Sheffield S1 2DE,
Telephone: 0114 2738951
Call date: Nov 1964, Gray's Inn
Qualifications: [LLB (Lond)]

HARGRAVE HENRY BRIAN

Westgate Chambers
4 Copse Close, Northwood, Middlesex
HA6 2XG, Telephone: 01923 823671
Call date: May 1988, Inner Temple
Qualifications: [LLB (Lond)]

HARGREAVES BENJAMIN THOMAS

Goldsmith Chambers
Ground Floor Goldsmith Building, Temple,
London EC4Y 7BL,
Telephone: 0171 353 6802/3/4/5
E-mail: celiamonksfield@btinternet.com
Call date: Nov 1989, Lincoln's Inn
Qualifications: [LLB (Hons) (Wales)]

HARGREAVES MISS KATIE JANE

1 High Pavement
Nottingham NG1 1HF,
Telephone: 0115 9418218
Call date: Nov 1991, Gray's Inn
Qualifications: [LLB (L'pool)]

HARGREAVES MISS SARA JANE

12 New Square
Ground Floor, Lincoln's Inn, London
WC2A 3SW, Telephone: 0171 419 1212
E-mail: 12newsquare@compuserve.com
25 Park Square
Leeds LS1 2PW, Telephone: 0113 2451841/2/3
E-mail: sovereignchambers@btinternet.com
Door Tenant
Call date: July 1979, Middle Temple
Qualifications: [LLB (Lond)]

HARGREAVES SIMON JOHN ROBERT

Keating Chambers
10 Essex Street, Outer Temple, London
WC2R 3AA, Telephone: 0171 544 2600
Call date: Oct 1991, Inner Temple
Qualifications: [BA (Oxon)]

HARGROVE JEREMY JOHN LOVEDAY

Trinity Chambers
9-12 Trinity Chare, Quayside, Newcastle Upon
Tyne NE1 3DF, Telephone: 0191 232 1927
Call date: Nov 1970, Inner Temple
Qualifications: [LLB]

HARING SIMON NICHOLAS

30 Park Square
Leeds LS1 2PF, Telephone: 0113 2436388
Call date: July 1982, Lincoln's Inn
Qualifications: [LLB (Leeds)]

HARINGTON MISS AMANDA

24 Old Bldgs
Ground Floor, Lincoln's Inn, London
WC2A 3UJ, Telephone: 0171 404 0946
E-mail: clerks@24oldbuildings.law.co.uk
Call date: July 1989, Inner Temple
Qualifications: [BA (Cantab)]

HARINGTON MICHAEL KENNETH

6 Pump Court
1st Floor, Temple, London EC4Y 7AR,
Telephone: 0171 797 8400
E-mail: sa_hockman_qc@link.org
6-8 Mill Street
Maidstone, Kent ME15 6XH,
Telephone: 01622 688094
Call date: July 1974, Inner Temple
Recorder
Qualifications: [MA (Oxon)]

HARKUS GEORGE EVERARD

Goldsmith Chambers
Ground Floor Goldsmith Building, Temple,
London EC4Y 7BL,
Telephone: 0171 353 6802/3/4/5
E-mail: celiamonksfield@btinternet.com
Call date: Nov 1975, Inner Temple
Qualifications: [LLB (Leeds), DPA, MA]

HARLE ALAN

Cleveland Chambers
63-65 Borough Road, Middlesbrough,
Cleveland TS1 3AA, Telephone: 01642 226036
Call date: July 1982, Middle Temple
Qualifications: [BA Hons]

HARMAN ROBERT DONALD QC (1974)

2 Harcourt Bldgs
1st Floor, Temple, London EC4Y 9DB,
Telephone: 0171 353 2112/2817
Call date: Feb 1954, Gray's Inn
Recorder
Qualifications: [BA (Oxon)]

HARMAN MISS SARAH JANE

4 Stone Bldgs
Ground Floor, Lincoln's Inn, London
WC2A 3XT, Telephone: 0171 242 5524
E-mail: d.goddard@4stonebuildings.law.co.uk
Call date: Nov 1987, Lincoln's Inn
Qualifications: [BA (Oxon)]

HARMER MISS CHRISTINE

Broad Chare
33 Broad Chare, Newcastle Upon Tyne
NE1 3DQ, Telephone: 0191 232 0541
Call date: July 1973, Middle Temple
Qualifications: [BA]

HAROLD FERGUS DOUGAL

Tindal Chambers
3/5 New Street, Chelmsford, Essex CM1 1NT,
Telephone: 01245 267742
Call date: Oct 1996, Gray's Inn
Qualifications: [BA (Dunelm)]

HAROUNOFF DAVID

4 King's Bench Walk
Ground/First Floor, Temple, London
EC4Y 7DL, Telephone: 0171 822 8822
E-mail: 4kbw@barristersatlaw.com
Call date: Nov 1984, Middle Temple
Qualifications: [BA (Sussex)]

HARPER ANDREW GRAHAM

65-67 King Street
Leicester LE1 6RP, Telephone: 0116 2547710
Call date: Feb 1989, Middle Temple
Qualifications: [LLB (Leic)]

HARPER JAMES NORMAN

Broad Chare
33 Broad Chare, Newcastle Upon Tyne
NE1 3DQ, Telephone: 0191 232 0541
Call date: July 1957, Gray's Inn
Qualifications: [BA (Oxon)]

HARPER JOSEPH CHARLES QC (1992)

4 Breams Buildings
London EC4A 1AQ,
Telephone: 0171 353 5835/430 1221
Call date: July 1970, Gray's Inn
Qualifications: [BA, LLM (Lond)]

HARPER MARK ELIOT GEORGE

40 King Street
Manchester M2 6BA,
Telephone: 0161 832 9082
E-mail: Kingst40@aol.com
Call date: Oct 1993, Lincoln's Inn
Qualifications: [BA (Hons)]

HARPER ROGER ALAN

All Saints Chambers
9/11 Broad Street, Bristol BS1 2HP,
Telephone: 0117 921 1966
Call date: May 1994, Lincoln's Inn
Qualifications: [LLB (Hons, B'ham)]

HARPWOOD MRS VIVIENNE MARGARET

30 Park Place
Cardiff CF1 3BA, Telephone: 01222 398421
E-mail: 100757.1456@compuserve.com
Call date: July 1969, Gray's Inn
Qualifications: [LLB]

HARRAP GILES THRESHER

Pump Court Chambers
Upper Ground Floor, 3 Pump Court, London
EC4Y 7AJ, Telephone: 0171 353 0711
Pump Court Chambers
31 Southgate Street, Winchester SO23 9EE,
Telephone: 01962 868161
Call date: Nov 1971, Inner Temple
Recorder
Qualifications: [LLB (Lond)]

Fax: 01962 867645;
Out of hours telephone: 01420 22359

Types of work: Family provision on death;
Medical negligence; Personal injury;
Professional negligence

Circuit: Western

Awards and memberships: Professional
Negligence Bar Association; Family Law Bar
Association; Personal Injury Bar Association

Publications: 'Update: Inheritance (Provision
for Family and Dependants' Act 1975' *Solicitors
Journal*, 23 January 1993; 'Provision for Co-
habitants on Death' *Family Law*, June 1997

Reported cases: *Re Coventry, deceased*, [1980]
Ch 461, 1979. Application for provision on
death by adult son in work.

Re Callaghan, deceased, [1985] Fam 1, 1984.
Application for provision on death by man
treated as a child of the deceased.
Re Dawkins, deceased, [1986] 2 FLR 360, 1986.
Application to set aside disposition intended to
defeat family provision claim.
Jessop v Jessop, [1992] 1 FLR 591, 1991.
Exercise of Court's power in family provision
cases to treat deceased's share of jointly held
property as part of estate.
Peach Grey & Co v Sommers, [1995] 2 AllER
513, 1995. Power of Divisional Court to commit
for contempt following interference with
witnesses before industrial tribunal.

HARRIES MARK ROBERT

6 Gray's Inn Square
Ground Floor, Gray's Inn, London WC1R 5AZ,
Telephone: 0171 242 1052
Call date: Oct 1995, Lincoln's Inn
Qualifications: [LLB (Hons)(Lond)]

HARRIES NICHOLAS JOHN SAMUEL

10 Old Square
Ground Floor, Lincoln's Inn, London
WC2A 3SU, Telephone: 0171 405 0758
Call date: Nov 1995, Lincoln's Inn
Qualifications: [BA (Hons)]

HARRIES RAYMOND ELWYN

Bracton Chambers
95a Chancery Lane, London WC2A 1DT,
Telephone: 0171 242 4248
Call date: July 1988, Lincoln's Inn
Qualifications: [BA (Hons) (Cardiff), Dip Law
(City), FCA, ATII, ACIArb, ATII, ACIArb]

HARRILL MISS JAYNE ANNE

8 King's Bench Walk
2nd Floor, Temple, London EC4Y 7DU,
Telephone: 0171 797 8888
8 King's Bench Walk North
1 Park Square East, Leeds LS1 2NE,
Telephone: 0113 2439797
Call date: Oct 1990, Middle Temple
Qualifications: [BA]

HARRINGTON PATRICK JOHN QC (1993)

Farrar's Building
Temple, London EC4Y 7BD,
Telephone: 0171 583 9241
E-mail: chambers@farrarsbuilding.co.uk
30 Park Place
Cardiff CF1 3BA, Telephone: 01222 398421
E-mail: 100757.1456@compuserve.com
Door Tenant
Call date: July 1973, Gray's Inn
Recorder
Qualifications: [LLB (Lond)]

HARRINGTON MISS TINA AMANDA

Trinity Chambers
140 New London Road, Chelmsford, Essex
CM2 0AW, Telephone: 01245 605040
9 Gough Square
London EC4A 3DE, Telephone: 0171 353 5371
Call date: Nov 1985, Middle Temple
Qualifications: [BA]

HARRIS MS ALEXANDRA JANE

Holborn Chambers
6 Gate Street, Lincoln's Inn Fields, London
WC2A 3HP, Telephone: 0171 242 6060
Call date: July 1989, Gray's Inn
Qualifications: [LLB]

HARRIS MISS ANNMARIE

3 Dr Johnson's Bldgs
Ground Floor, Temple, London EC4Y 7BA,
Telephone: 0171 353 4854
Call date: July 1975, Middle Temple
Qualifications: [BA]

HARRIS MS BETHAN ELEANOR

1 Pump Court
Lower Ground Floor, Temple, London
EC4Y 7AB, Telephone: 0171 583 2012/
353 4341
E-mail: (name) @1pumpcourt.co.uk
Call date: May 1990, Middle Temple
Qualifications: [B.A. (Oxon)]

HARRIS BRIAN THOMAS QC (1982)

4-5 Gray's Inn Square
Ground Floor, Gray's Inn, London WC1R 5AY,
Telephone: 0171 404 5252
E-mail: chambers@4-5graysinnsquare.co.uk
Call date: Nov 1960, Gray's Inn
Qualifications: [LLB (Lond)]

HARRIS DAVID ANDREW WALLACE

Iscoed Chambers
86 St Helen's Road, Swansea SA1 4BQ,
Telephone: 01792 652988/9/330
Call date: Oct 1990, Gray's Inn
Qualifications: [BA (Sussex)]

HARRIS REV DAVID JAMES

32 Park Place
Cardiff CF1 3BA, Telephone: 01222 397364
Call date: Nov 1979, Gray's Inn
Qualifications: [BA (Wales)]

HARRIS DAVID MICHAEL QC (1989)

India Buildings Chambers
Water Street, Liverpool L2 OXG,
Telephone: 0151 243 6000
3 Paper Bldgs
1st Floor, Temple, London EC4Y 7EU,
Telephone: 0171 583 8055
E-mail: london@3paper.com
4 St Peter Street
Winchester SO23 8OW,
Telephone: 01962 868884
Call date: Nov 1969, Middle Temple
Recorder
Qualifications: [MA (Oxon), PhD, (Cantab)]

HARRIS DAVID RAYMOND

Prince Henry's Chambers
17 Fleet Street, London EC4Y 1AA,
Telephone: 0171 353 1183/1190
Call date: Nov 1973, Lincoln's Inn
Qualifications: [LLM (Lond)]

HARRIS DONALD RENSHAW

Littleton Chambers
3 King's Bench Walk North, Temple, London
EC4Y 7HR, Telephone: 0171 797 8600
E-mail: littletonchambers@compuserve.com
Door Tenant
Call date: June 1958, Inner Temple

D

HARRIS MISS ELIZABETH MARY

Angel Chambers
94 Walter Road, Swansea SA1 5QA,
Telephone: 01792 6464623/6464648
Call date: Nov 1992, Inner Temple
Qualifications: [LLB (Hull)]

HARRIS GLENN PETER

Trafalgar Chambers
53 Fleet Street, London EC4Y 1BE,
Telephone: 0171 583 5858
E-mail: TrafalgarChambers@easynet.co.uk
Call date: Oct 1994, Lincoln's Inn
Qualifications: [LLB (Hons)(Hull)]

HARRIS IAN ROBERT

25-27 Castle Street
1st Floor, Liverpool L2 4TA,
Telephone: 0151 227 5661/051 236 5072
Call date: Nov 1990, Inner Temple

HARRIS JAMES

1 Harcourt Bldgs
2nd Floor, Temple, London EC4Y 9DA,
Telephone: 0171 353 9421/9151
Call date: Nov 1975, Gray's Inn
Qualifications: [MA (Oxon)]

HARRIS MISS JOANNE OLGA CHARLOTTE

2 Garden Court
1st Floor, Middle Temple, London EC4Y 9BL,
Telephone: 0171 353 1633
E-mail: barristers@2gardenct.law.co.uk
Call date: Oct 1991, Gray's Inn
Qualifications: [BA (L'pool), MSc (London),
Diploma in Law]

HARRIS JOHN HENRY EDGAR

Forest House Chambers
15 Granville Road, Walthamstow, London
E17 9BS, Telephone: 0181 925 2240
Call date: Oct 1993, Lincoln's Inn
Qualifications: [MSc, LLB (Hons)(Sheff)]

HARRIS MISS LAURA

Queen Elizabeth Bldg
Ground Floor, Temple, London EC4Y 9BS,
Telephone: 0171 353 7181 (12 Lines)
Call date: Nov 1977, Middle Temple
Qualifications: [BA (Oxon)]

HARRIS MARK GEOFFREY CHARLES

3 Raymond Buildings
Gray's Inn, London WC1R 5BH,
Telephone: 0171 831 3833
E-mail: chambers@threeraymond.demon.co.uk
Call date: July 1980, Gray's Inn
Qualifications: [BA (Oxon)]

HARRIS MICHAEL PETER

10 King's Bench Walk
Ground Floor, Temple, London EC4Y 7EB,
Telephone: 0171 353 7742
E-mail: 10kbw@lineone.net
Call date: Oct 1993, Gray's Inn
Qualifications: [BA (Hons)(Cantab)]

HARRIS MISS NICOLA JANE

33 Park Place
Cardiff CF1 3BA, Telephone: 01222 233313
Call date: Oct 1992, Middle Temple
Qualifications: [MA (Hons, Cantab), MA
(Toronto)]

HARRIS PAUL BEST

Monckton Chambers
4 Raymond Buildings, Gray's Inn, London
WC1R 5BP, Telephone: 0171 405 7211
E-mail: chambers@monckton.co.uk
Call date: Oct 1994, Gray's Inn
Qualifications: [LLB, LLM]

HARRIS PHILIP JOSEPH ALBERT

10 King's Bench Walk
Ground Floor, Temple, London EC4Y 7EB,
Telephone: 0171 353 7742
E-mail: 10kbw@lineone.net
Call date: July 1968, Inner Temple
Qualifications: [LLB (Lond)]

D

HARRIS ROGER CHARLES JAMES

2 Temple Gardens
Temple, London EC4Y 9AY,
Telephone: 0171 583 6041 (12 Lines)
Call date: Oct 1996, Inner Temple
Qualifications: [BA (Exeter)]

HARRIS RUSSELL JAMES

1 Serjeants' Inn
4th Floor, Temple, London EC4Y 1NH,
Telephone: 0171 583 1355
E-mail: serjeants.inn@virgin.net
33 Park Place
Cardiff CF1 3BA, Telephone: 01222 233313
Door Tenant
Call date: Nov 1986, Gray's Inn
Qualifications: [MA (Cantab)]

HARRIS MISS SARAH KATHARINE HOLTBY

3 Gray's Inn Square
Ground Floor, London WC1R 5AH,
Telephone: 0171 520 5600
E-mail: gis3@btinternet.com
Call date: Nov 1989, Middle Temple
Qualifications: [BA (Hons), Dip.Law]

HARRIS WILBERT ARTHURLYN

Rowchester Chambers
4 Rowchester Court Whittall Street,
Birmingham B4 6DH,
Telephone: 0121 233 2327/2361951
Call date: Nov 1973, Inner Temple
Qualifications: [BA, FCIArb]

HARRIS-JENKINS PHILIP LEIGH

Angel Chambers
94 Walter Road, Swansea SA1 5QA,
Telephone: 01792 6464623/6464648
Call date: Nov 1990, Gray's Inn
Qualifications: [LLB (Hons)(Wales)]

HARRISON (JOHN) KEITH

24a St John Street
Manchester M3 4DF,
Telephone: 0161 833 9628
Call date: Nov 1983, Lincoln's Inn
Qualifications: [LLB (Hons) (Newc)]

HARRISON MS AVERIL

2 Harcourt Bldgs
Ground Floor/Left, Temple, London
EC4Y 9DB, Telephone: 0171 583 9020
E-mail: clerks@harcourt.co.uk
Call date: Oct 1990, Gray's Inn
Qualifications: [BA (Lond)]

HARRISON CHRISTOPHER JOHN

4 Stone Bldgs
Ground Floor, Lincoln's Inn, London
WC2A 3XT, Telephone: 0171 242 5524
E-mail: d.goddard@4stonebuildings.law.co.uk
Call date: Nov 1988, Gray's Inn
Qualifications: [MA (Cantab)]

HARRISON JOHN FOSTER

St Paul's House
5th Floor 23 Park Square South, Leeds
LS1 2ND, Telephone: 0113 2455866
Call date: Oct 1994, Lincoln's Inn
Qualifications: [BA (Hons)(Notts), LLB
(Hons)(Leeds), M.Soc.Sc.(B'ham)]

HARRISON MISS LEONA MELANIE

India Buildings Chambers
Water Street, Liverpool L2 OXG,
Telephone: 0151 243 6000
Call date: Oct 1993, Middle Temple
Qualifications: [LLB (Hons)(Manc)]

HARRISON MICHAEL LEE

New Court
Temple, London EC4Y 9BE,
Telephone: 0171 583 5123/0171 583 0510
Call date: Nov 1979, Inner Temple
Qualifications: [LLB (Hons) (Sheff)]

HARRISON MICHAEL THOMAS

199 Strand
London WC2R 1DR,
Telephone: 0171 379 9779
E-mail: chambers@199strand.co.uk
Call date: July 1986, Lincoln's Inn
Qualifications: [MA (Oxon), Dip Law (City)]

HARRISON NICHOLAS FRANCIS

13 Old Square
1st Floor, Lincoln's Inn, London WC2A 3UA,
Telephone: 0171 242 6105
E-mail: clerks@serlecourt.co.uk
Call date: July 1988, Lincoln's Inn
Qualifications: [BA (Hons) (Oxon)]

HARRISON PETER JOHN

6 Pump Court
1st Floor, Temple, London EC4Y 7AR,
Telephone: 0171 797 8400
E-mail: sa_hockman_qc@link.org
6-8 Mill Street
Maidstone, Kent ME15 6XH,
Telephone: 01622 688094
Call date: July 1987, Inner Temple
Qualifications: [BA (Hons) (Dunelm)]

HARRISON PETER JOHN

24a St John Street
Manchester M3 4DF,
Telephone: 0161 833 9628
Call date: July 1983, Middle Temple
Qualifications: [LLB Hons (L'pool)]

HARRISON MISS PHILOMENA MARY

199 Strand
London WC2R 1DR,
Telephone: 0171 379 9779
E-mail: chambers@199strand.co.uk
Call date: Nov 1985, Middle Temple
Qualifications: [BA (Lond), Dip Law (City)]

HARRISON MISS RACHAEL

Paradise Square Chambers
26 Paradise Square, Sheffield S1 2DE,
Telephone: 0114 2738951
Call date: Nov 1993, Inner Temple
Qualifications: [LLB (Hons)]

HARRISON MRS REZIYA

11 Old Square
Ground Floor, Lincoln's Inn, London
WC2A 3TS, Telephone: 0171 430 0341
E-mail: clerks@11oldsquare.co.uk
Call date: July 1975, Lincoln's Inn
Qualifications: [MA (Oxon), FCI Arb]

HARRISON RICHARD ANDREW

Devereux Chambers
Devereux Court, London WC2R 3JJ,
Telephone: 0171 353 7534
E-mail: elton@devchambers.co.uk
Call date: Nov 1991, Lincoln's Inn
Qualifications: [BA (Hons)(Cantab)]

HARRISON RICHARD TRISTAN

1 King's Bench Walk
2nd Floor, Temple, London EC4Y 7DB,
Telephone: 0171 936 1500
E-mail: ddear@1kbw.co.uk
Call date: Nov 1993, Inner Temple
Qualifications: [MA (Hons)(Cantab), Dip law
(City)]

HARRISON ROBERT JOHN MACKINTOSH

30 Park Place
Cardiff CF1 3BA, Telephone: 01222 398421
E-mail: 100757.1456@compuserve.com
Call date: Feb 1988, Lincoln's Inn
Qualifications: [LLB (Cardiff)]

HARRISON ROBERT MICHAEL QC (1987)

Park Court Chambers
40 Park Cross Street, Leeds LS1 2QH,
Telephone: 0113 2433277
Call date: Nov 1969, Gray's Inn
Recorder
Qualifications: [LLB]

HARRISON ROGER DONALD

1 Paper Bldgs
1st Floor, Temple, London EC4Y 7EP,
Telephone: 0171 353 3728/4953
Octagon House
19 Colegate, Norwich NR3 1AT,
Telephone: 01603 623186
E-mail: octagon@netmatters.co.uk
Door Tenant
Call date: Feb 1970, Gray's Inn
Assistant Recorder
Qualifications: [LLB]

HARRISON MISS SALLY

40 King Street
Manchester M2 6BA,
Telephone: 0161 832 9082
E-mail: Kingst40@aol.com
Call date: Oct 1992, Gray's Inn
Qualifications: [B.Sc (Reading), Dip Law (City)]

HARRISON MS SARAH LOUISE

Cobden House Chambers
19 Quay Street, Manchester M3 3HN,
Telephone: 0161 833 6000
E-mail: clerks@cobden.co.uk
Call date: Nov 1989, Lincoln's Inn
Qualifications: [LLB (Leic)]

HARRISON MS STEPHANIE JAYNE

2 Garden Court
1st Floor, Middle Temple, London EC4Y 9BL,
Telephone: 0171 353 1633
E-mail: barristers@2gardenct.law.co.uk
Call date: Nov 1991, Middle Temple
Qualifications: [BSc Hons (Bris), MSc (Lond), Dip Law]

HARRISON MISS SUSAN KATHRYN

18 St John Street
Manchester M3 4EA,
Telephone: 0161 278 1800
Call date: Oct 1993, Middle Temple
Qualifications: [BA (Hons)(Bris)]

HARRISON-HALL GILES ARTHUR

1 Fountain Court
Steelhouse Lane, Birmingham B4 6DR,
Telephone: 0121 236 5721
Call date: July 1977, Gray's Inn
Qualifications: [MA (Oxon)]

HARROD HENRY MARK

5 Stone Buildings
Lincoln's Inn, London WC2A 3XT,
Telephone: 0171 242 6201
E-mail: clerks@5-stonebuildings.law.co.uk
Call date: July 1963, Lincoln's Inn
Recorder
Qualifications: [MA (Oxon)]

HARROP-GRIFFITHS HILTON

2 Field Court
Gray's Inn, London WC1R 5BB,
Telephone: 0171 405 6114
E-mail: fieldct2@netcomuk.co.uk.
Call date: July 1978, Inner Temple
Qualifications: [BA Hons (Manchester)]

HARRY TIMOTHY HAWKINS

9 Old Square
Ground Floor, Lincoln's Inn, London
WC2A 3SR, Telephone: 0171 405 4682
E-mail: chambers@9oldsquare.co.uk
Call date: July 1983, Lincoln's Inn
Qualifications: [MA, BCL (Oxon)]

HARRY THOMAS MISS CAROLINE JANE

Littleton Chambers
3 King's Bench Walk North, Temple, London
EC4Y 7HR, Telephone: 0171 797 8600
E-mail: littletonchambers@compuserve.com
Call date: Feb 1981, Middle Temple
Qualifications: [LLB (Exon)]

HART COLIN JOHN JEFFREY DINE

10 King's Bench Walk
Ground Floor, Temple, London EC4Y 7EB,
Telephone: 0171 353 7742
E-mail: 10kbw@lineone.net
Call date: Nov 1966, Middle Temple
Qualifications: [MA (Oxon), Dip Ecom]

HART DAVID TIMOTHY NELSON

1 Crown Office Row
Ground Floor, Temple, London EC4Y 7HH,
Telephone: 0171 797 7500
Crown Office Row Chambers
Blenheim House 120 Church Street, Brighton,
Sussex BN1 1WH, Telephone: 01273 625625
Call date: July 1982, Middle Temple
Qualifications: [BA (Cantab)]

HART MS JENNIFER ANN

2 Paper Buildings
Basement, Temple, London EC4Y 7ET,
Telephone: 0171 353 0933
Call date: Oct 1993, Middle Temple
Qualifications: [BA (Hons)(Lond), LLB (Reading)]

HART MICHAEL CHRISTOPHER CAMPBELL QC (1987)

5 Stone Buildings
Lincoln's Inn, London WC2A 3XT,
Telephone: 0171 242 6201
E-mail: clerks@5-stonebuildings.law.co.uk
Call date: Nov 1970, Gray's Inn
Qualifications: [MA, BCL (Oxon)]

HART PAUL

15 Winckley Square
Preston PR1 3JJ, Telephone: 01772 252828
E-mail: clerks@winckleysq.demon.co.uk
Call date: July 1982, Gray's Inn
Qualifications: [LLB (Newc)]

HART WILLIAM STEPHEN

Albion Chambers
Broad Street, Bristol BS1 1DR,
Telephone: 0117 9272144
Call date: July 1979, Middle Temple
Qualifications: [LLB (Exon)]

HART-LEVERTON COLIN ALLEN QC (1979)

8 King's Bench Walk
2nd Floor, Temple, London EC4Y 7DU,
Telephone: 0171 797 8888
8 King's Bench Walk North
1 Park Square East, Leeds LS1 2NE,
Telephone: 0113 2439797
Call date: May 1957, Middle Temple

HARTE JOHN DAVID CHESTERS

Broad Chare
33 Broad Chare, Newcastle Upon Tyne
NE1 3DQ, Telephone: 0191 232 0541
Call date: July 1967, Gray's Inn
Qualifications: [MA (Cantab), Dip Crim (Cantab)]

HARTLEY ANTONY ARNOLD

8 Fountain Court
Steelhouse Lane, Birmingham B4 6DR,
Telephone: 0121 236 5514/5
E-mail: clerks@no8chambers.co.uk
Call date: Feb 1991, Gray's Inn
Qualifications: [LLB (Bris)]

HARTLEY RICHARD ANTHONY

Cobden House Chambers
19 Quay Street, Manchester M3 3HN,
Telephone: 0161 833 6000
E-mail: clerks@cobden.co.uk
Call date: July 1985, Middle Temple
Qualifications: [LLB (Hons)]

HARTLEY RICHARD LESLIE CLIFFORD QC (1976)

1 Brick Court
1st Floor, Temple, London EC4Y 9BY,
Telephone: 0171 353 8845
E-mail: clerks@1brickcourt.co.uk
Call date: June 1956, Gray's Inn
Qualifications: [MA (Cantab)]

HARTLEY ROBERT EDWARD

Bell Yard Chambers
116/118 Chancery Lane, London WC2A 1PP,
Telephone: 0171 306 9292
Call date: Oct 1995, Middle Temple
Qualifications: [BA (Hon), LLM]

HARTLEY TIMOTHY GUY

Park Court Chambers
40 Park Cross Street, Leeds LS1 2QH,
Telephone: 0113 2433277
9-12 Bell Yard
London WC2A 2LF,
Telephone: 0171 400 1800
Call date: July 1970, Gray's Inn
Qualifications: [LLB]

HARTLEY-DAVIES PAUL KEVIL

30 Park Place
Cardiff CF1 3BA, Telephone: 01222 398421
E-mail: 100757.1456@compuserve.com
Call date: July 1977, Gray's Inn
Qualifications: [LLB (Hons) (Wales)]

HARTMAN MICHAEL

9 King's Bench Walk
Ground Floor, Temple, London EC4Y 7DX,
Telephone: 0171 353 7202/3909
Call date: Nov 1975, Lincoln's Inn

HARVEY COLIN TREVOR

St Paul's House
5th Floor 23 Park Square South, Leeds
LS1 2ND, Telephone: 0113 2455866
Call date: July 1975, Middle Temple
Qualifications: [LLB (Lond)]

HARVEY MISS JAYNE DENISE

Goldsworth Chambers
1st Floor 10-11 Gray's Inn Square, London
WC1R 5JD, Telephone: 0171 405 7117
Call date: Feb 1992, Middle Temple
Qualifications: [LLB (Hons), LLM (Lond)]

HARVEY JOHN GILBERT

4 King's Bench Walk
2nd Floor, Temple, London EC4Y 7DL,
Telephone: 0171 353 3581
Call date: July 1973, Gray's Inn
Recorder
Qualifications: [LLB (Hons), FCIArb]

HARVEY JONATHAN ROBERT WILLIAM

2 Harcourt Bldgs
Ground Floor/Left, Temple, London
EC4Y 9DB, Telephone: 0171 583 9020
E-mail: clerks@harcourt.co.uk
Call date: July 1974, Inner Temple
Qualifications: [BA (Cantab)]

HARVEY MISS LOUISE BARBARA

15 Winckley Square
Preston PR1 3JJ, Telephone: 01772 252828
E-mail: clerks@winckleysq.demon.co.uk
Call date: Oct 1991, Lincoln's Inn
Qualifications: [LLB (Hons)]

HARVEY MICHAEL LLEWELLYN TUCKER QC (1982)

2 Crown Office Row
Ground Floor, Temple, London EC4Y 7HJ,
Telephone: 0171 797 8100
E-mail: mail@2cor.co.uk, or to individual
barristers at: [barrister's surname]@2cor.co.uk
Call date: July 1966, Gray's Inn
Recorder
Qualifications: [MA, LLB (Cantab)]

HARVEY SIMON GRANT

3 Fountain Court
Steelhouse Lane, Birmingham B4 6DR,
Telephone: 0121 236 5854
Call date: Oct 1994, Lincoln's Inn
Qualifications: [LLB (Hons)(Leeds)]

HARVEY STEPHEN FRANK

18 Red Lion Court
(Off Fleet Street), London EC4A 3EB,
Telephone: 0171 520 6000
Thornwood House
102 New London Road, Chelmsford, Essex
CM2 0RG, Telephone: 01245 280880
Call date: July 1979, Gray's Inn
Qualifications: [LLB (Lond)]

HARVIE JONATHAN ALEXANDER QC (1992)

2 Hare Court
Ground Floor, Temple, London EC4Y 7BH,
Telephone: 0171 583 1770
E-mail: 2_Hare_Court@link.org
Call date: July 1973, Middle Temple
Assistant Recorder
Qualifications: [MA (Oxon)]

HARWOOD RICHARD JOHN

1 Serjeants' Inn
4th Floor, Temple, London EC4Y 1NH,
Telephone: 0171 583 1355
E-mail: serjeants.inn@virgin.net
Call date: Nov 1993, Middle Temple
Qualifications: [MA, LLM (Cantab)]

HARWOOD-STEVENSON JOHN FRANCIS RICHARD

9-12 Bell Yard
London WC2A 2LF,
Telephone: 0171 400 1800
East Anglian Chambers
57 London Street, Norwich NR2 1HL,
Telephone: 01603 617351
Call date: Nov 1975, Inner Temple
Qualifications: [MA (Oxon)]

D

HASAN MISS AYESHA

3 Dr Johnson's Bldgs
Ground Floor, Temple, London EC4Y 7BA,
Telephone: 0171 353 4854
Call date: July 1987, Gray's Inn
Qualifications: [LLB (Nigeria) LLM, (Cantab)]

HASAN MISS TAZEEN

5 Pump Court
Ground Floor, Temple, London EC4Y 7AP,
Telephone: 0171 353 2532
E-mail: fivepump@netcomuk.co.uk
Call date: Nov 1988, Lincoln's Inn
Qualifications: [BA Hons (Oxon), LLM (LSE)]

HASELHURST IAN SHAND

Adrian Lyon's Chambers
14 Castle Street, Liverpool L2 0NE,
Telephone: 0151 236 4421/8240
E-mail: chambers14@aol.com
Call date: July 1976, Gray's Inn
Qualifications: [LLB (L'pool)]

HASLAM ANDREW PETER

25 Park Square
Leeds LS1 2PW, Telephone: 0113 2451841/2/3
E-mail: sovereignchambers@btinternet.com
Call date: Oct 1991, Gray's Inn
Qualifications: [LLB (Leics)]

HASSALL JAMES CHRISTOPHER

Southernhay Chambers
33 Southernhay East, Exeter EX1 1NX,
Telephone: 01392 255777
E-mail: southernhay.chambers@lineone.net
Call date: Nov 1995, Lincoln's Inn
Qualifications: [LLB (Hons)]

HASSLACHER JAMES MICHAEL ROCHE

New Court
Temple, London EC4Y 9BE,
Telephone: 0171 583 5123/0171 583 0510
Call date: Nov 1993, Middle Temple
Qualifications: [LLB (Hons)(Keele)]

HASTINGS MISS FRANCES MARIA

2 Dr Johnson's Building
Temple, London EC4Y 7AY,
Telephone: 0171 353 4716
Call date: Oct 1990, Inner Temple
Qualifications: [BA (L'pool), Dip Law]

HATCHER MS NICHOLA JANE

Guildford Chambers
Stoke House Leapale Lane, Guildford, Surrey
GU1 4LY, Telephone: 01483 539131
E-mail: guildford.barristers@btinternet.com
Call date: Oct 1995, Inner Temple
Qualifications: [LLB (B'ham)]

HATFIELD MS SALLY ANNE

Doughty Street Chambers
11 Doughty Street, London WC1N 2PG,
Telephone: 0171 404 1313
E-mail: doughty_street@compuserve.com
Call date: Nov 1988, Inner Temple
Qualifications: [BA (Oxon)]

HATTON ANDREW JOHN

Paradise Square Chambers
26 Paradise Square, Sheffield S1 2DE,
Telephone: 0114 2738951
Plowden Bldgs
2nd Floor, Temple, London EC4Y 9BU,
Telephone: 0171 583 0808
E-mail: bar@plowdenbuildings.co.uk
Call date: July 1987, Gray's Inn
Qualifications: [LLB]

HATTON DAVID WILLIAM QC (1996)

Park Court Chambers
40 Park Cross Street, Leeds LS1 2QH,
Telephone: 0113 2433277
Call date: July 1976, Gray's Inn
Recorder
Qualifications: [LLB (Hons)]

HAUGHTY JEREMY NICHOLAS

Lamb Building
Ground Floor, Temple, London EC4Y 7AS,
Telephone: 0171 797 7788
E-mail: lamb.building@link.org
Call date: Nov 1989, Lincoln's Inn
Qualifications: [LLB, LLM (Exon)]

HAUKELAND MARTIN JONATHAN

3 Paper Bldgs
2nd Floor, Temple, London EC4Y 7EU,
Telephone: 0171 353 6208
Call date: Feb 1989, Middle Temple
Qualifications: [Dip Law,BA]

HAVELOCK-ALLAN ANTHONY MARK DAVID QC (1993)

20 Essex Street
London WC2R 3AL,
Telephone: 0171 583 9294
E-mail: clerks@20essexst.com
Call date: July 1974, Inner Temple
Assistant Recorder
Qualifications: [BA (Dunelm), LLB (Cantab)]

HAVEN KEVIN

2 Gray's Inn Square Chambers
2nd Floor, Gray's Inn, London WC1R 5AA,
Telephone: 0171 242 0328/071 405 1317
E-mail: clerks@2gis.co.uk
Call date: July 1982, Gray's Inn
Qualifications: [BA (Kent)]

HAVERS THE HON PHILIP NIGEL QC (1995)

1 Crown Office Row
Ground Floor, Temple, London EC4Y 7HH,
Telephone: 0171 797 7500
Crown Office Row Chambers
Blenheim House 120 Church Street, Brighton,
Sussex BN1 1WH, Telephone: 01273 625625
Call date: July 1974, Inner Temple
Recorder
Qualifications: [BA (Cantab)]

HAVEY PETER SUNIL

4-5 Gray's Inn Square
Ground Floor, Gray's Inn, London WC1R 5AY,
Telephone: 0171 404 5252
E-mail: chambers@4-5graysinnsquare.co.uk
Call date: July 1984, Gray's Inn
Qualifications: [MA (Oxon)]

HAWES NEIL ASHLEY

2 Dr Johnson's Building
Temple, London EC4Y 7AY,
Telephone: 0171 353 4716
Call date: Nov 1989, Inner Temple
Qualifications: [LLB]

HAWKER GEOFFREY FORT

46/48 Essex Street
London WC2R 3GH,
Telephone: 0171 583 8899
Call date: Apr 1970, Gray's Inn
Qualifications: [BSc(Eng) FEng FICE, C Eng
FIEI, FIStructE, MSocIS(France), MConsE
FCIArb]

HAWKES MISS NAOMI NANTEZA ASTRID WALLUSIMBI

22 Old Bldgs
Lincoln's Inn, London WC2A 3UJ,
Telephone: 0171 831 0222
Call date: Oct 1994, Middle Temple
Qualifications: [BA (Hons)(Cantab)]

HAWKESWORTH (THOMAS) SIMON ASHWELL QC (1982)

York Chambers
14 Toft Green, York YO1 1JT,
Telephone: 01904 620048
E-mail: yorkchambers.co.uk
199 Strand
London WC2R 1DR,
Telephone: 0171 379 9779
E-mail: chambers@199strand.co.uk
Call date: Feb 1967, Gray's Inn
Recorder
Qualifications: [BA (Oxon)]

HAWKESWORTH (WALTER) GARETH

Fenners Chambers
3 Madingley Road, Cambridge CB3 OEE,
Telephone: 01223 368761
Fenners Chambers
8-12 Priestgate, Peterborough PE1 1JA,
Telephone: 01733 62030
5 Paper Bldgs
1st Floor, Temple, London EC4Y 7HB,
Telephone: 0171 583 6117
E-mail: clerks@5-paperbuildings.law.co.uk
Door Tenant
Call date: Nov 1972, Gray's Inn
Recorder
Qualifications: [MA (Cantab)]

HAWKINS DAVID JAMES

Bank House Chambers
Old Bank House, Hartshead, Sheffield S1 2EL,
Telephone: 0114 2751223
Call date: Oct 1991, Gray's Inn
Qualifications: [B Ed (Exeter), LLB (Sheff)]

D

HAWKINS MISS LUCY ELIZABETH

St Ive's Chambers
9 Fountain Ct, Birmingham B4 6DR,
Telephone: 0121 236 0863/0929
Call date: Nov 1994, Lincoln's Inn
Qualifications: [BA (Hons)(Durham), CPE]

HAWKS ANTHONY JOSEPH VINCENT

Broad Chare
33 Broad Chare, Newcastle Upon Tyne
NE1 3DQ, Telephone: 0191 232 0541
Call date: Nov 1975, Middle Temple
Qualifications: [LLB]

HAWLEY MS CAROL ANNE

14 Tooks Court
Cursitor St, London EC4A 1LB,
Telephone: 0171 405 8828
E-mail: clerks @tooks.law.co.uk
Call date: Oct 1990, Gray's Inn
Qualifications: [LLB (Hons, Lond)]

HAWORTH RICHARD ANTHONY

15 Winckley Square
Preston PR1 3JJ, Telephone: 01772 252828
E-mail: clerks@winckleysq.demon.co.uk
Call date: Nov 1978, Inner Temple
Qualifications: [LLB (Leeds)]

HAWTHORNE MRS PATRICIA VERONICA

Chancery Chambers
1st Floor Offices 70/72 Chancery Lane,
London WC2A 1AB,
Telephone: 0171 405 6879/6870
Call date: May 1995, Middle Temple
Qualifications: [BA (Hons)]

HAY MS DEBORAH JANE

Goldsmith Building
1st Floor, Temple, London EC4Y 7BL,
Telephone: 0171 353 7881
E-mail: clerks@goldsmith-building.law.co.uk
Call date: Apr 1991, Middle Temple
Qualifications: [BA]

HAY MISS FIONA RUTH

13 King's Bench Walk
1st Floor, Temple, London EC4Y 7EN,
Telephone: 0171 353 7204
E-mail: clerks@13kbw.law.co.uk
King's Bench Chambers
32 Beaumont Street, Oxford OX1 2NP,
Telephone: 01865 311066
E-mail: clerks@kbc-oxford.law.co.uk
Call date: Nov 1989, Inner Temple
Qualifications: [BSc, BA (Exon)]

HAY MALCOLM JOHN MARSHALL

3 Dr Johnson's Bldgs
Ground Floor, Temple, London EC4Y 7BA,
Telephone: 0171 353 4854
Call date: Nov 1972, Gray's Inn
Qualifications: [BA (Oxon)]

HAY ROBIN WILLIAM PATRICK HAMILTON

Goldsmith Building
1st Floor, Temple, London EC4Y 7BL,
Telephone: 0171 353 7881
E-mail: clerks@goldsmith-building.law.co.uk
Call date: Nov 1964, Inner Temple
Recorder
Qualifications: [MA, LLB (Cantab)]

HAYATALLY TARIK RUMI

2 Paper Buildings
Basement, Temple, London EC4Y 7ET,
Telephone: 0171 353 0933
Call date: Feb 1990, Gray's Inn
Qualifications: [BA, LLB (Lond)]

HAYCROFT ANTHONY MARK

Queen Elizabeth Bldg
Ground Floor, Temple, London EC4Y 9BS,
Telephone: 0171 353 7181 (12 Lines)
Call date: Nov 1982, Middle Temple
Qualifications: [LLB (Reading), BCL (Oxon)]

HAYDEN ANTHONY PAUL

28 St John Street
Manchester M3 4DJ,
Telephone: 0161 834 8418
E-mail: clerk@28stjohnst.co.uk
Call date: Nov 1987, Middle Temple
Qualifications: [BA (Manch) Dip Law, (City)]

HAYDEN RICHARD

2 Paper Bldgs
Temple, London EC4Y 7ET,
Telephone: 0171 936 2613
Call date: June 1964, Gray's Inn
Qualifications: [LLB (Lond)]

HAYDON ALEC GUY

Brick Court Chambers
15/19 Devereux Court, London WC2R 3JJ,
Telephone: 0171 583 0777
E-mail: (surname)@brickcourt.demon.co.uk
Call date: Oct 1993, Gray's Inn
Qualifications: [BA (Cantab), LLM (Harvard)]

HAYES JEREMY JOSEPH JAMES

2 Paper Bldgs
1st Floor, Temple, London EC4Y 7ET,
Telephone: 0171 936 2611 (10 Lines)
E-mail: clerks@2pbbarristers.co.uk
Call date: Nov 1977, Middle Temple
Qualifications: [LLB]

HAYES JOHN ALLAN

10 Park Square
Leeds LS1 2LH, Telephone: 0113 2455438
E-mail: chambers@bandit.legend.co.uk
Call date: Nov 1992, Lincoln's Inn
Qualifications: [BA (Hons)]

HAYES MISS JOSEPHINE MARY

Chambers of Lord Goodhart QC
Ground Floor 3 New Square, Lincoln's Inn,
London WC2A 3RS,
Telephone: 0171 405 5577
E-mail: law@threenewsquare.demon.co.uk
Call date: July 1980, Lincoln's Inn
Qualifications: [MA (Oxon), LLM (Yale)]

HAYES RICHARD JAMES

Lamb Chambers
Lamb Building, Temple, London EC4Y 7AS,
Telephone: 0171 797 8300
E-mail: lambchambers@link.org
Call date: Oct 1995, Lincoln's Inn
Qualifications: [LLB (Hons)(Durham)]

HAYES MISS SUSAN MARY

3 Temple Gardens
2nd Floor, Temple, London EC4Y 9AU,
Telephone: 0171 583 1155
Call date: Oct 1990, Inner Temple
Qualifications: [LLB (Lond)]

HAYGARTH EDMUND BRUCE

25-27 Castle Street
1st Floor, Liverpool L2 4TA,
Telephone: 0151 227 5661/051 236 5072
Call date: Nov 1988, Gray's Inn
Qualifications: [LLB (Lond)]

HAYHOE JUSTIN OLIVER

Parsonage Chambers
5th Floor 3 The Parsonage, Manchester
M3 2HW, Telephone: 0161 833 1996
Call date: Oct 1994, Gray's Inn
Qualifications: [BA]

HAYHOW MRS LYNDSAY JILL

5 Essex Court
1st Floor, Temple, London EC4Y 9AH,
Telephone: 0171 410 2000
Call date: Nov 1990, Inner Temple
Qualifications: [LLB]

HAYNE MISS JANETTE ELIZABETH

Tindal Chambers
3/5 New Street, Chelmsford, Essex CM1 1NT,
Telephone: 01245 267742
Call date: Nov 1991, Inner Temple
Qualifications: [BA (Lond)]

HAYNES JOHN CHARLES

3 Paper Bldgs
1st Floor, Temple, London EC4Y 7EU,
Telephone: 0171 583 8055
E-mail: london@3paper.com
20 Lorne Park Road
Bournemouth BH1 1JN,
Telephone: 01202 292102 (5 Lines)
4 St Peter Street
Winchester SO23 8OW,
Telephone: 01962 868884
Call date: Nov 1968, Middle Temple

D

HAYNES MATTHEW THOMAS BONIFACE

St Ive's Chambers
9 Fountain Ct, Birmingham B4 6DR,
Telephone: 0121 236 0863/0929
Call date: Nov 1991, Lincoln's Inn
Qualifications: [BA (Oxon)]

HAYNES MICHAEL JOHN

4 Brick Court
Temple, London EC4Y 9AD,
Telephone: 0171 797 8910
Call date: July 1979, Gray's Inn
Qualifications: [LLB (Leic)]

HAYNES PETER

7 Fountain Court
Steelhouse Lane, Birmingham B4 6DR,
Telephone: 0121 236 8531
Call date: July 1983, Gray's Inn
Qualifications: [LLB (B'ham)]

HAYNES MISS REBECCA

Monckton Chambers
4 Raymond Buildings, Gray's Inn, London
WC1R 5BP, Telephone: 0171 405 7211
E-mail: chambers@monckton.co.uk
Call date: Nov 1994, Inner Temple
Qualifications: [LLB (Lond), LLM (Lond)]

HAYTER MRS KATHLEEN

Merriemore Cottage
Sawbridge, Nr Rugby, Warwickshire
CV23 8BB, Telephone: 01788 891832
Call date: July 1982, Middle Temple
Qualifications: [LLB (leics)]

HAYTON PROFESSOR DAVID JOHN

5 Stone Buildings
Lincoln's Inn, London WC2A 3XT,
Telephone: 0171 242 6201
E-mail: clerks@5-stonebuildings.law.co.uk
Door Tenant
Call date: Nov 1968, Inner Temple
Qualifications: [LLD (Newc)]

HAYTON MRS LINDA PATRICIA

Arden Chambers
27 John Street, London WC1N 2BL,
Telephone: 0171 242 4244
Call date: Nov 1975, Lincoln's Inn
Qualifications: [LLB]

HAYTON MICHAEL PEARSON

Queen's Chambers
5 John Dalton Street, Manchester M2 6ET,
Telephone: 0161 834 6875/4738
4 Camden Place
Preston PR1 3JL, Telephone: 01772 828300
Call date: Oct 1993, Lincoln's Inn
Qualifications: [BA (Hons)]

HAYWARD JAMES GERALD STEPHEN

Independent Barristers Clerk
Room 5, 2nd Floor 15 Castle Street, Exeter,
Devon EX4 3PT, Telephone: 01392 210900
E-mail: cathedral.chambers@eclipse.co.uk
Call date: July 1985, Middle Temple
Qualifications: [MA (Cantab)]

HAYWARD PETER MICHAEL

The Outer Temple
Room 26, 222/225 Strand, London
WC2R 1BQ, Telephone: 0171 353 4647
Call date: July 1974, Gray's Inn
Qualifications: [BA, BCL (Oxon)]

HAYWARD-SMITH RODGER QC (1988)

1 King's Bench Walk
2nd Floor, Temple, London EC4Y 7DB,
Telephone: 0171 936 1500
E-mail: ddear@1kbw.co.uk
Call date: July 1967, Gray's Inn
Recorder
Qualifications: [MA (Oxon)]

HAYWOOD MISS JANET

Guildford Chambers
Stoke House Leapale Lane, Guildford, Surrey
GU1 4LY, Telephone: 01483 539131
E-mail: guildford.barristers@btinternet.com
Call date: July 1985, Inner Temple
Qualifications: [BA, Dip Law City]

HAYWOOD MISS JANETTE

Gray's Inn Chambers
5th Floor, Gray's Inn, London WC1R 5JA,
Telephone: 0171 404 1111
Call date: Nov 1977, Middle Temple
Qualifications: [LLM (Lond) LLB, (Cardiff)]

HEAD JOHN PHILIP TREVELYAN

9 Bedford Row
London WC1R 4AZ,
Telephone: 0171 242 3555
E-mail: clerks@9br.co.uk
Call date: July 1976, Middle Temple
Assistant Recorder
Qualifications: [MA (Oxon), LLM, (Virginia)]

HEAD JOHN SEBASTIAN

2 King's Bench Walk
Ground Floor, Temple, London EC4Y 7DE,
Telephone: 0171 353 1746
E-mail: 2kbw@atlas.co.uk
King's Bench Chambers
115 North Hill, Plymouth PL4 8JY,
Telephone: 01752 221551
Call date: Nov 1987, Gray's Inn
Qualifications: [BA (Cantab)]

HEADLAM ROY WASHINGTON

Furnival Chambers
32 Furnival Street, London EC4A 1JQ,
Telephone: 0171 405 3232
E-mail: clerks@furnivallaw.co.uk
Call date: Nov 1983, Gray's Inn
Qualifications: [BA]

HEAL MISS JOANNA MARY

Devereux Chambers
Devereux Court, London WC2R 3JJ,
Telephone: 0171 353 7534
E-mail: elton@devchambers.co.uk
Call date: July 1988, Inner Temple
Qualifications: [MA (Cantab)]

HEALD OLIVER

Fenners Chambers
3 Madingley Road, Cambridge CB3 OEE,
Telephone: 01223 368761
Fenners Chambers
8-12 Priestgate, Peterborough PE1 1JA,
Telephone: 01733 62030
Call date: July 1977, Middle Temple
Qualifications: [MA (Cantab)]

HEALEY MS SUSAN HILARY

Trafalgar Chambers
53 Fleet Street, London EC4Y 1BE,
Telephone: 0171 583 5858
E-mail: TrafalgarChambers@easynet.co.uk
Call date: Nov 1995, Middle Temple
Qualifications: [BA (Hons)]

HEALING MISS YVONNE MARY

38 Young Street
Manchester M3 3FT,
Telephone: 0161 833 0489
E-mail: clerks@young-st-chambers.com
Call date: May 1987, Inner Temple
Qualifications: [LLB (L'pool)]

HEALY MISS ALEXANDRA

9-12 Bell Yard
London WC2A 2LF,
Telephone: 0171 400 1800
Call date: Oct 1992, Gray's Inn
Qualifications: [MA (Cantab)]

HEALY BRIAN PATRICK JAMES

Priory Chambers
2 Fountain Court, Steelhouse Lane,
Birmingham B4 6DR,
Telephone: 0121 236 3882/1375
Call date: Nov 1967, Gray's Inn
Qualifications: [LLB (Lond), LLM (Lond)]

HEALY MISS SIOBAN

7 King's Bench Walk
Ground Floor, Temple, London EC4Y 7DS,
Telephone: 0171 583 0404
Call date: July 1993, Inner Temple
Qualifications: [BA, LLM]

HEAP GERARD MILES

25 Park Square
Leeds LS1 2PW, Telephone: 0113 2451841/2/3
E-mail: sovereignchambers@btinternet.com
Call date: July 1985, Gray's Inn
Qualifications: [MA (Cantab)]

HEAP WALTER RICHARD CARTWRIGHT

Kenworthy's Buildings
83 Bridge Street, Manchester M3 2RF,
Telephone: 0161 832 4036/834 6954
Call date: Nov 1963, Inner Temple
Qualifications: [LLB]

HEATH STEPHEN DAVID

Francis Taylor Bldg
2nd Floor, Temple, London EC4Y 7BY,
Telephone: 0171 353 9942/3157
Call date: Feb 1992, Lincoln's Inn
Qualifications: [BA (Hons) (Cambs), Dip Law]

HEATON CLIVE WILLIAM

10 Park Square
Leeds LS1 2LH, Telephone: 0113 2455438
E-mail: chambers@bandit.legend.co.uk
Call date: July 1992, Gray's Inn
Qualifications: [MA (Oxon)]

HEATON DAVID MICHAEL

18 St John Street
Manchester M3 4EA,
Telephone: 0161 278 1800
Call date: July 1983, Middle Temple
Qualifications: [MA (Cantab)]

HEATON MISS FRANCES MARGARET

Deans Court Chambers
Cumberland House Crown Square, Manchester
M3 3HA, Telephone: 0161 834 4097
E-mail: deanscourt@compuserve.com
Deans Court Chambers
41-43 Market Place, Preston PR1 1AH,
Telephone: 01772 555163
E-mail: deanscourt@compuserve.com
4 Brick Court
Ground Floor, Temple, London EC4Y 9AD,
Telephone: 0171 797 7766
E-mail: chambers@4brick.co.uk
Call date: Nov 1985, Gray's Inn
Qualifications: [LLB (Hons)]

HEATON-ARMSTRONG ANTHONY EUSTACE JOHN

9-12 Bell Yard
London WC2A 2LF,
Telephone: 0171 400 1800
Call date: July 1973, Gray's Inn
Qualifications: [LLB]

HEAVEY MISS CIARA

3 Temple Gardens
3rd Floor, Temple, London EC4Y 9AU,
Telephone: 0171 353 0832
Call date: Nov 1992, Middle Temple
Qualifications: [BA (Hons)(Lond), Dip in Law]

HEBRON HAROLD

3 Paper Bldgs
1st Floor, Temple, London EC4Y 7EU,
Telephone: 0171 583 8055
E-mail: london@3paper.com
20 Lorne Park Road
Bournemouth BH1 1JN,
Telephone: 01202 292102 (5 Lines)
4 St Peter Street
Winchester SO23 8OW,
Telephone: 01962 868884
Call date: Feb 1960, Middle Temple

HEDGECOE JOHN PHILIP

21 White Friars
Chester CH1 1NZ, Telephone: 01244 323070
Call date: Nov 1972, Inner Temple
Qualifications: [LLB (Hull)]

HEDGELAND ROGER

18 St John Street
Manchester M3 4EA,
Telephone: 0161 278 1800
Call date: Nov 1972, Gray's Inn
Assistant Recorder
Qualifications: [MA (Cantab)]

HEDLEY RICHARD PHILIP

St Mary's Chambers
50 High Pavement, Lace Market, Nottingham
NG1 1HW, Telephone: 0115 9503503
E-mail: clerks@smc.law.co.uk
Call date: Nov 1983, Middle Temple
Qualifications: [LLB (Leic)]

HEDWORTH ALAN TOBY QC (1996)

Trinity Chambers
9-12 Trinity Chare, Quayside, Newcastle Upon
Tyne NE1 3DF, Telephone: 0191 232 1927
11 King's Bench Walk
1st Floor, Temple, London EC4Y 7EQ,
Telephone: 0171 353 3337
Call date: July 1975, Inner Temple
Recorder
Qualifications: [MA (Cantab)]

HEDWORTH LEONARD

10 King's Bench Walk
Ground Floor, Temple, London EC4Y 7EB,
Telephone: 0171 353 7742
E-mail: 10kbw@lineone.net
Call date: July 1979, Lincoln's Inn
Qualifications: [BSc (Lond)]

HEER MISS DEANNA MARY

Hardwicke Building
New Square, Lincoln's Inn, London
WC2A 3SB, Telephone: 0171 242 2523
E-mail: clerks@hardwicke.co.uk
Call date: Oct 1994, Gray's Inn
Qualifications: [LLB]

HEGARTY KEVIN JOHN

7 Fountain Court
Steelhouse Lane, Birmingham B4 6DR,
Telephone: 0121 236 8531
Call date: Nov 1982, Middle Temple
Qualifications: [LLB (Hons) (Newc)]

HEHIR CHRISTOPHER JOSEPH

1 Hare Court
Ground Floor, Temple, London EC4Y 7BE,
Telephone: 0171 353 3982/5324
Call date: Oct 1990, Inner Temple
Qualifications: [BA (Oxon)]

HEILBRON MISS HILARY NORA QC (1987)

Brick Court Chambers
15/19 Devereux Court, London WC2R 3JJ,
Telephone: 0171 583 0777
E-mail: (surname)@brickcourt.demon.co.uk
Call date: July 1971, Gray's Inn
Qualifications: [MA (Oxon)]

HEIM PAUL EMIL

3 Verulam Buildings
London WC1R 5NT,
Telephone: 0171 831 8441
E-mail: clerks@3verulam.co.uk
Call date: June 1956, Lincoln's Inn
Qualifications: [LLB Dunelm]

HEIMLER GEORGE ERNEST

6 Gray's Inn Square
Ground Floor, Gray's Inn, London WC1R 5AZ,
Telephone: 0171 242 1052
Call date: July 1978, Inner Temple
Qualifications: [LLB]

HEINZ VOLKER GUSTAV STEFAN

3 Verulam Buildings
London WC1R 5NT,
Telephone: 0171 831 8441
E-mail: clerks@3verulam.co.uk
Call date: Nov 1989, Inner Temple
Qualifications: [Dip Law, First &, Second
German Legal, State Examinations]

HELLENS MATTHEW JAMES

3 Dr Johnson's Bldgs
Ground Floor, Temple, London EC4Y 7BA,
Telephone: 0171 353 4854
Call date: Oct 1992, Lincoln's Inn
Qualifications: [MA (Cantab)]

HELLER MRS ANNE

John Street Chambers
2 John Street, London WC1N 2HJ,
Telephone: 0171 242 1911
E-mail: john.street_chambers@virgin.net.uk
Call date: Nov 1995, Gray's Inn
Qualifications: [BA (Kent), LLB]

HELY MICHAEL HAMILTON MCMATH

Helions Chambers
Pilgrims' Way Camps Road, Helions
Bumpstead, Haverhill, Suffolk CB9 7AS,
Telephone: 01440 730523
E-mail: helionslaw@aol.com
Call date: July 1975, Middle Temple
Qualifications: [MA (Cantab), C Eng, MIEE]

HELY HUTCHINSON MRS CAROLINE DEBORAH

One Garden Court
Ground Floor, Temple, London EC4Y 9BJ,
Telephone: 0171 797 7900
Call date: July 1983, Gray's Inn
Qualifications: [LLB (Bristol)]

HENDERSON (ANTHONY) MARK

Mitre House Chambers
Mitre House 44 Fleet Street, London
EC4Y 1BN, Telephone: 0171 583 8233
Call date: Oct 1994, Gray's Inn
Qualifications: [BA (Oxon)]

HENDERSON MISS CAMILLA SOPHIE

Queen Elizabeth Bldg
2nd Floor, Temple, London EC4Y 9BS,
Telephone: 0171 797 7837
Call date: Oct 1992, Inner Temple
Qualifications: [BA (Hons)(Cantab)]

HENDERSON MISS FIONA ELIZABETH

2 Paper Bldgs
1st Floor, Temple, London EC4Y 7ET,
Telephone: 0171 936 2611 (10 Lines)
E-mail: clerks@2pbbarristers.co.uk
Call date: Oct 1993, Lincoln's Inn
Qualifications: [BA (Hons)(Bris)]

HENDERSON IAN FRANCIS

8 King's Bench Walk
2nd Floor, Temple, London EC4Y 7DU,
Telephone: 0171 797 8888
8 King's Bench Walk North
1 Park Square East, Leeds LS1 2NE,
Telephone: 0113 2439797
Call date: Nov 1990, Inner Temple
Qualifications: [LLB]

HENDERSON JAMES FROWYKE

4 Brick Court
1st Floor, Temple, London EC4Y 9AD,
Telephone: 0171 583 8455
Call date: July 1984, Middle Temple
Qualifications: [LLB]

HENDERSON MISS JOSEPHINE

Arden Chambers
27 John Street, London WC1N 2BL,
Telephone: 0171 242 4244
Call date: Nov 1990, Inner Temple
Qualifications: [BSc (Bris), Dip Law (PCL)]

HENDERSON LAUNCELOT DINADAN JAMES QC (1995)

5 Stone Buildings
Lincoln's Inn, London WC2A 3XT,
Telephone: 0171 242 6201
E-mail: clerks@5-stonebuildings.law.co.uk
Call date: Nov 1977, Lincoln's Inn
Qualifications: [MA (Oxon)]

Fax: 0171 831 8102; DX: 304 London,
Chancery Lane

Types of work: Charities; Equity, wills and trusts;
Pensions; Tax - capital and income; Tax -
corporate

Other professional qualifications: Standing
Junior Counsel to the Inland Revenue, 1991-5

Membership of foreign bars: Hong Kong (1998)

Awards and memberships: Member of Chancery
and Revenue Bar Associations; Member of STEP;
Fellow of All Souls College, Oxford, 1974-81 and
1982-9

Languages spoken: French, Italian

Reported cases: *IRC v McGuckian*, [1997] 1
WLR 991 (HL), 1997. Tax avoidance and the
Ramsay principle.
IRC v Willoughby, [1997] 1 WLR 1071 (HL),
1997. Tax avoidance, transfers of assets abroad.
Bricom Holdings v IRC, [1997] STC 1179 (CA),
1997. Controlled foreign companies and double
taxation relief.
EMI Group Electronics v Coldicott, [1997] STC
1372, 1997. Payments in lieu of notice taxable
as emoluments from employment.
L M Tenancies 1 Plc v IRC, [1998] STC 326
(CA), 1998. Stamp duty and the contingency
principle.

HENDERSON LAWRENCE MARK

11 Bolt Court
London EC4A 3DQ,
Telephone: 0171 353 2300
E-mail: boltct11@aol.com
Redhill Chambers
Seloduct House 30 Station Road, Redhill
RH1 1NK, Telephone: 01737 780781
Call date: Nov 1990, Middle Temple
Qualifications: [LLB]

HENDERSON MISS LYNNE MCLEOD

All Saints Chambers
9/11 Broad Street, Bristol BS1 2HP,
Telephone: 0117 921 1966
Call date: Nov 1993, Inner Temple
Qualifications: [LLB (So'ton)]

HENDERSON RODERICK ST CLAIR MAWSON

St Ive's Chambers
9 Fountain Ct, Birmingham B4 6DR,
Telephone: 0121 236 0863/0929
Call date: Nov 1978, Middle Temple
Qualifications: [BA (Oxon)]

HENDERSON ROGER ANTHONY QC (1980)

2 Harcourt Bldgs
Ground Floor/Left, Temple, London
EC4Y 9DB, Telephone: 0171 583 9020
E-mail: clerks@harcourt.co.uk
Stanbrook & Henderson
2 Harcourt Bldgs 2nd Floor, Temple, London
EC4Y 9DB, Telephone: 0171 353 0101
E-mail: clerks@harcourt.co.uk
Call date: Nov 1964, Inner Temple
Recorder
Qualifications: [MA (Cantab)]

HENDERSON SIMON ALEXANDER

4 Pump Court
Temple, London EC4Y 7AN,
Telephone: 0171 353 2656/9
E-mail: 4_pump_court@compuserve.com
Call date: Oct 1993, Inner Temple
Qualifications: [BA (Dunelm), Dip Law (City)]

HENDERSON MISS SOPHIE

3 Paper Bldgs
2nd Floor, Temple, London EC4Y 7EU,
Telephone: 0171 353 6208
Call date: Oct 1990, Middle Temple
Qualifications: [BA (Hons), Dip Law]

HENDERSON WILLIAM HUGO

13 Old Square
1st Floor, Lincoln's Inn, London WC2A 3UA,
Telephone: 0171 242 6105
E-mail: clerks@serlecourt.co.uk
East Anglian Chambers
57 London Street, Norwich NR2 1HL,
Telephone: 01603 617351
East Anglian Chambers
Sanders House 52 North Hill, Colchester
CO1 1PY, Telephone: 01206 572756
Call date: July 1978, Inner Temple
Qualifications: [BA (Cantab)]

HENDRON GERALD JAMES

Broadway House Chambers
Broadway House 9 Bank Street, Bradford,
West Yorkshire BD1 1TW,
Telephone: 01274 722560
Call date: Oct 1992, Lincoln's Inn
Qualifications: [LLB(Hons)(Leeds)]

HENDRY MISS HELEN MARY LOW

9 Woodhouse Square
Leeds LS3 1AD, Telephone: 0113 2451986
Call date: Nov 1983, Middle Temple
Qualifications: [BSc (Lond), Dip Law]

HENDY JOHN GILES QC (1987)

Old Square Chambers
1 Verulam Buildings, Gray's Inn, London
WC1R 5LQ, Telephone: 0171 831 0801
Old Square Chambers
Hanover House 47 Corn Street, Bristol
BS1 1HT, Telephone: 0117 9277111
Call date: July 1972, Gray's Inn
Qualifications: [LLB, LLM]

HENDY MRS PAULINE FRANCES

Cloisters
1st Floor, Temple, London EC4Y 7AA,
Telephone: 0171 827 4000
E-mail: clerks@cloisters.com
Call date: Nov 1985, Lincoln's Inn
Qualifications: [BA(Lond)]

HENKE MISS RUTH SARA MARGARET

Iscoed Chambers
86 St Helen's Road, Swansea SA1 4BQ,
Telephone: 01792 652988/9/330
Call date: Nov 1987, Inner Temple
Qualifications: [MA (Oxon)]

HENLEY ANDREW MICHAEL

Furnival Chambers
32 Furnival Street, London EC4A 1JQ,
Telephone: 0171 405 3232
E-mail: clerks@furnivallaw.co.uk
Call date: Oct 1992, Middle Temple
Qualifications: [LLB(Hons)(Lond)]

HENLEY MR CHRISTOPHER MICHAEL

1 Crown Office Row
2nd Floor, Temple, London EC4Y 7HH,
Telephone: 0171 797 7111
Call date: July 1989, Gray's Inn
Qualifications: [LLB [Bris]]

HENLEY MARK ROBERT DANIEL

9 Woodhouse Square
Leeds LS3 1AD, Telephone: 0113 2451986
Call date: Oct 1994, Lincoln's Inn
Qualifications: [MA (Cantab)]

HENNELL PETER GORDON

Queen's Chambers
5 John Dalton Street, Manchester M2 6ET,
Telephone: 0161 834 6875/4738
4 Camden Place
Preston PR1 3JL, Telephone: 01772 828300
Call date: July 1982, Middle Temple
Qualifications: [MA (Cantab)]

HENRIQUES CECIL QUIXANO

Deans Court Chambers
Cumberland House Crown Square, Manchester
M3 3HA, Telephone: 0161 834 4097
E-mail: deanscourt@compuserve.com
Deans Court Chambers
41-43 Market Place, Preston PR1 1AH,
Telephone: 01772 555163
E-mail: deanscourt@compuserve.com
Call date: June 1936, Inner Temple
Qualifications: [MA, BCL (Oxon)]

HENRIQUES RICHARD HENRY QUIXANO QC (1986)

Deans Court Chambers
Cumberland House Crown Square, Manchester
M3 3HA, Telephone: 0161 834 4097
E-mail: deanscourt@compuserve.com
1 Crown Office Row
2nd Floor, Temple, London EC4Y 7HH,
Telephone: 0171 797 7111
Deans Court Chambers
41-43 Market Place, Preston PR1 1AH,
Telephone: 01772 555163
E-mail: deanscourt@compuserve.com
Call date: Nov 1967, Inner Temple
Recorder
Qualifications: [MA (Oxon)]

HENRY MISS ANNETTE PHYLLIS

10 King's Bench Walk
1st Floor, Temple, London EC4Y 7EB,
Telephone: 0171 353 2501
Call date: July 1984, Gray's Inn
Qualifications: [LLB (Manch)]

HENRY EDWARD JOSEPH ALOYSIUS

Hollis Whiteman Chambers
3rd/4th Floor Queen Elizabeth Bldg, Temple,
London EC4Y 9BS, Telephone: 0171 583 5766
E-mail: hollis.whiteman@btinternet.com
Call date: Nov 1988, Lincoln's Inn
Qualifications: [BA Hons (Cantab), Dip Law
(City)]

HENRY MISS JENNIFER LORRAINE

Mitre House Chambers
Mitre House 44 Fleet Street, London
EC4Y 1BN, Telephone: 0171 583 8233
Call date: Oct 1990, Middle Temple
Qualifications: [BA (Kent)]

HENRY PETER CLIFFORD

3 Paper Bldgs
1st Floor, Temple, London EC4Y 7EU,
Telephone: 0171 583 8055
E-mail: london@3paper.com
4 St Peter Street
Winchester SO23 8OW,
Telephone: 01962 868884
20 Lorne Park Road
Bournemouth BH1 1JN,
Telephone: 01202 292102 (5 Lines)
Call date: Nov 1977, Inner Temple
Qualifications: [LLB (Exon)]

HENRY PHILIP BRUCE

15 Winckley Square
Preston PR1 3JJ, Telephone: 01772 252828
E-mail: clerks@winckleysq.demon.co.uk
Call date: Nov 1988, Middle Temple
Qualifications: [LLB (Lond), AKC]

HENSHELL MICHAEL JOHN

25-27 Castle Street
1st Floor, Liverpool L2 4TA,
Telephone: 0151 227 5661/051 236 5072
Call date: July 1975, Inner Temple
Qualifications: [LLB (Hull)]

HENSON MISS CHRISTINE RUTH

3 Hare Court
1st Floor, Temple, London EC4Y 7BJ,
Telephone: 0171 353 7561
Call date: Oct 1994, Middle Temple
Qualifications: [LLB (Hons)(Warw)]

HENSON GRAHAM STANLEY

Furnival Chambers
32 Furnival Street, London EC4A 1JQ,
Telephone: 0171 405 3232
E-mail: clerks@furnivallaw.co.uk
Call date: July 1976, Gray's Inn
Qualifications: [BA (Cantab)]

HENTHORN MRS AISHA

Watford Chambers
74 Mildred Avenue, Watford, Hertfordshire
WD1 7DX, Telephone: 01923 220553
Call date: July 1981, Middle Temple
Qualifications: [BA (Hons) Law]

HEPHER PAUL ARTHUR RICHARD

King's Bench Chambers
Wellington House 175 Holdenhurst Road,
Bournemouth, Dorset BH8 8DQ,
Telephone: 01202 250025
Call date: Oct 1994, Gray's Inn
Qualifications: [MA (Oxon)]

HEPPENSTALL MISS CLAIRE NORAH

3 Dr Johnson's Bldgs
Ground Floor, Temple, London EC4Y 7BA,
Telephone: 0171 353 4854
Call date: Nov 1990, Inner Temple
Qualifications: [LLM (Lond)]

HEPPLE PROFESSOR BOB ALEXANDER QC (1996)

2 Hare Court
Ground Floor, Temple, London EC4Y 7BH,
Telephone: 0171 583 1770
E-mail: 2_Hare_Court@link.org
Call date: July 1966, Gray's Inn
Qualifications: [MA, LLD (Camb)]

HERAGHTY DAVID ANDREW PAUL

Mitre House Chambers
Mitre House 44 Fleet Street, London
EC4Y 1BN, Telephone: 0171 583 8233
Call date: Oct 1995, Inner Temple
Qualifications: [BSc (Hons), CPE]

HERBERG JAVAN WILLIAM

2 Hare Court
Ground Floor, Temple, London EC4Y 7BH,
Telephone: 0171 583 1770
E-mail: 2_Hare_Court@link.org
Call date: Oct 1992, Lincoln's Inn
Qualifications: [LLB(Hons)(Lond), BCL]

HERBERT (DONALD) PETER

14 Tooks Court
Cursitor St, London EC4A 1LB,
Telephone: 0171 405 8828
E-mail: clerks @tooks.law.co.uk
Call date: Nov 1982, Gray's Inn
Qualifications: [LLB (Lond)]

D

HERBERT DAVID RICHARD

2 New Street
Leicester LE1 5NA, Telephone: 0116 2625906
Call date: Nov 1992, Gray's Inn
Qualifications: [BA (So'ton)]

HERBERT DOUGLAS CHURCHILL

24 The Ropewalk
Nottingham NG1 5EF,
Telephone: 0115 9472581
E-mail: clerk@ropewalk.co.uk
Devereux Chambers
Devereux Court, London WC2R 3JJ,
Telephone: 0171 353 7534
E-mail: elton@devchambers.co.uk
Call date: July 1973, Middle Temple
Assistant Recorder
Qualifications: [LLB]

HERBERT GARRY GERARD PAUL

10 King's Bench Walk
1st Floor, Temple, London EC4Y 7EB,
Telephone: 0171 353 2501
Call date: Nov 1995, Lincoln's Inn
Qualifications: [MBE, BA (Hons), Dip in Law]

HERBERT MARK JEREMY QC (1995)

5 Stone Buildings
Lincoln's Inn, London WC2A 3XT,
Telephone: 0171 242 6201
E-mail: clerks@5-stonebuildings.law.co.uk
Call date: July 1974, Lincoln's Inn
Qualifications: [BA (Lond)]

Fax: 0171 831 8102; DX: 304 London

Types of work: Chancery (general); Equity, wills and trusts; Pensions; Probate and administration; Tax - capital and income

Awards and memberships: Member: Chancery Bar Association; Revenue Bar Association; Association of Pension Lawyers; Society of Trust and Estate Practitioners

Publications: *Whiteman on Capital Gains Tax* (Co-editor), 1988; *Drafting and Variation of Wills*, 1989

Reported cases: *IRC v Fitzwilliam*, [1993] 1 WLR 1189, 1993. Application of the *Ramsay* principle to capital transfer tax.
Mettoy Pension Trustees v Evans, [1990] 1 WLR 1587, 1989. Exercise of fiduciary powers conferred by pension scheme.

R v OPRA ex parte Littlewoods, [1998] PLR 63, 1997. Entitlement to cash equivalent from occupational pension scheme.

HERBERT MRS REBECCA MARY

2 New Street
Leicester LE1 5NA, Telephone: 0116 2625906
Call date: Oct 1993, Gray's Inn
Qualifications: [LLB (Manch)]

HERMAN RAYMOND CHARLES

India Buildings Chambers
Water Street, Liverpool L2 OXG,
Telephone: 0151 243 6000
Call date: Feb 1972, Inner Temple
Recorder
Qualifications: [LLB]

HERMER RICHARD SIMON

Doughty Street Chambers
11 Doughty Street, London WC1N 2PG,
Telephone: 0171 404 1313
E-mail: doughty_street@compuserve.com
30 Park Place
Cardiff CF1 3BA, Telephone: 01222 398421
E-mail: 100757.1456@compuserve.com
Door Tenant
Call date: Oct 1993, Middle Temple
Qualifications: [BA (Hons)(Manc)]

HERNANDEZ DAVID ANTHONY

38 Young Street
Manchester M3 3FT,
Telephone: 0161 833 0489
E-mail: clerks@young-st-chambers.com
Call date: Nov 1976, Lincoln's Inn
Assistant Recorder
Qualifications: [MA (Oxon)]

HERRING MISS WENDY JANE

1 Serjeants' Inn
5th Floor Fleet Street, Temple, London
EC4Y 1LL, Telephone: 0171 415 6666
E-mail: no1serjeantsinn@btinternet.com
Call date: Nov 1993, Lincoln's Inn
Qualifications: [BA (Hons)]

HERRITY PETER

Holborn Chambers
6 Gate Street, Lincoln's Inn Fields, London
WC2A 3HP, Telephone: 0171 242 6060
Door Tenant
Call date: July 1982, Lincoln's Inn
Qualifications: [BSc (Social Science, Lond)]

HERSHMAN DAVID ALLAN

Priory Chambers
2 Fountain Court, Steelhouse Lane,
Birmingham B4 6DR,
Telephone: 0121 236 3882/1375
Call date: July 1981, Gray's Inn
Qualifications: [LLB (Lond)]

HESLOP MARTIN SYDNEY QC (1995)

1 Hare Court
Ground Floor, Temple, London EC4Y 7BE,
Telephone: 0171 353 3982/5324
Call date: July 1972, Lincoln's Inn
Recorder
Qualifications: [LLB (Hons)]

HESLOP PHILIP LINNELL QC (1985)

4 Stone Bldgs
Ground Floor, Lincoln's Inn, London
WC2A 3XT, Telephone: 0171 242 5524
E-mail: d.goddard@4stonebuildings.law.co.uk
Call date: Nov 1970, Lincoln's Inn
Qualifications: [BA, LLM (Cantab)]

HESS EDWARD JOHN WATKIN

2 Harcourt Bldgs
1st Floor, Temple, London EC4Y 9DB,
Telephone: 0171 353 6961/7
Harcourt Chambers
Churchill House 3 St Aldate's Courtyard, St
Aldate's, Oxford OX1 1BN,
Telephone: 01865 791559
Call date: Nov 1985, Middle Temple
Qualifications: [MA (Cantab)]

HESTER PAUL STEPHEN

3 Paper Bldgs
1st Floor, Temple, London EC4Y 7EU,
Telephone: 0171 583 8055
E-mail: london@3paper.com
20 Lorne Park Road
Bournemouth BH1 1JN,
Telephone: 01202 292102 (5 Lines)
4 St Peter Street
Winchester SO23 8OW,
Telephone: 01962 868884
Call date: July 1989, Middle Temple
Qualifications: [BA (Warw), Dip Law]

HETHERINGTON ROGER ROOKE

2 Temple Gardens
Temple, London EC4Y 9AY,
Telephone: 0171 583 6041 (12 Lines)
Call date: July 1973, Middle Temple
Assistant Recorder
Qualifications: [BA (Cantab)]

HETT JAMES

St Mary's Chambers
50 High Pavement, Lace Market, Nottingham
NG1 1HW, Telephone: 0115 9503503
E-mail: clerks@smc.law.co.uk
Call date: Nov 1991, Middle Temple
Qualifications: [LLB (Hons) (Birm)]

HEWITSON WILLIAM ANDREW

1 Crown Office Row
3rd Floor, Temple, London EC4Y 7HH,
Telephone: 0171 583 9292
E-mail: onecor@link.org
Call date: July 1975, Gray's Inn
Qualifications: [MB, BS, FRCS]

HEWITT MISS ALEXANDRA HELEN

40 King Street
Chester CH1 2AH, Telephone: 01244 323886
Call date: Oct 1995, Middle Temple
Qualifications: [BA (Hons)]

HEWITT MISS ALISON BRYDIE

1 Temple Gardens
1st Floor, Temple, London EC4Y 9BB,
Telephone: 0171 353 0407/583 1315
E-mail: clerks@1templegardens.co.uk
Call date: July 1984, Middle Temple
Qualifications: [LLB (lond)]

D

HEWITT DAVID EDWARD MILES

1 Harcourt Bldgs
2nd Floor, Temple, London EC4Y 9DA,
Telephone: 0171 353 9421/9151
Call date: Feb 1991, Middle Temple
Qualifications: [BSc (Cardiff)]

HEWITT MISS MONICA DIANE

20 Britton Street
1st Floor, London EC1M 5NQ,
Telephone: 0171 608 3765
Call date: Nov 1994, Inner Temple
Qualifications: [LLB (Lond)]

HEWITT TIMOTHY

Broad Chare
33 Broad Chare, Newcastle Upon Tyne
NE1 3DQ, Telephone: 0191 232 0541
Call date: July 1973, Middle Temple
Recorder
Qualifications: [LLB]

HEWSON MISS BARBARA MARY

Littman Chambers
12 Gray's Inn Square, London WC1R 5JP,
Telephone: 0171 404 4866
E-mail: admin@littmanchambers.com
Call date: Nov 1985, Middle Temple
Qualifications: [MA (Cantab)]

HEXT NEIL FRASER

2 Temple Gardens
Temple, London EC4Y 9AY,
Telephone: 0171 583 6041 (12 Lines)
Call date: Oct 1995, Gray's Inn
Qualifications: [LLB (Bris)]

HEYWOOD MARK ADRIAN

5 Paper Bldgs
Lower Ground Floor, Temple, London
EC4Y 7HB, Telephone: 0171 353 5638
E-mail: 107722,633@compuserve.com
Call date: July 1985, Gray's Inn
Qualifications: [BA(Cantab)]

HEYWOOD MARK STEPHEN

5 Fountain Court
Steelhouse Lane, Birmingham B4 6DR,
Telephone: 0121 606 0500
Call date: July 1986, Gray's Inn
Qualifications: [LLB (Newcastle)]

HEYWOOD MICHAEL EDMUNDSON

Chambers of Lord Goodhart QC
Ground Floor 3 New Square, Lincoln's Inn,
London WC2A 3RS,
Telephone: 0171 405 5577
E-mail: law@threenewsquare.demon.co.uk
Cobden House Chambers
19 Quay Street, Manchester M3 3HN,
Telephone: 0161 833 6000
E-mail: clerks@cobden.co.uk
Door Tenant
Call date: July 1975, Inner Temple
Qualifications: [BSc Soc(Lond)]

HEYWOOD PETER LESLIE

All Saints Chambers
9/11 Broad Street, Bristol BS1 2HP,
Telephone: 0117 921 1966
Call date: Nov 1988, Gray's Inn
Qualifications: [LLB (Wales), MA (City)]

HEYWORTH MISS CATHERINE LOUISE

Iscoed Chambers
86 St Helen's Road, Swansea SA1 4BQ,
Telephone: 01792 652988/9/330
Call date: Nov 1991, Inner Temple
Qualifications: [LLB (Hons)]

HIBBERT WILLIAM JOHN

Gough Square Chambers
6-7 Gough Square, London EC4A 3DE,
Telephone: 0171 353 0924
E-mail: gsc@goughsq.co.uk
Call date: July 1979, Inner Temple
Qualifications: [BA (Oxon)]

HICK MICHAEL ANDREW

5 Paper Bldgs
1st Floor, Temple, London EC4Y 7HB,
Telephone: 0171 583 6117
E-mail: clerks@5-paperbuildings.law.co.uk
Call date: Oct 1995, Gray's Inn
Qualifications: [BA]

HICKEY ALEXANDER FREDERICK

Littman Chambers
12 Gray's Inn Square, London WC1R 5JP,
Telephone: 0171 404 4866
E-mail: admin@littmanchambers.com
Call date: Nov 1995, Lincoln's Inn
Qualifications: [BA (Hons) (Oxon)]

HICKEY EUGENE JAMES

5 Fountain Court
Steelhouse Lane, Birmingham B4 6DR,
Telephone: 0121 606 0500
Call date: July 1988, Lincoln's Inn
Qualifications: [LLB (Hons) (Leeds)]

HICKEY SIMON ROGER GREENWOOD

10 Park Square
Leeds LS1 2LH, Telephone: 0113 2455438
E-mail: chambers@bandit.legend.co.uk
Call date: Nov 1985, Gray's Inn
Qualifications: [LLB]

HICKLAND MISS MARGARET

Peel House Chambers
Ground Floor, Peel House 5 Harrington Street,
Liverpool L2 9QA, Telephone: 0151 236 4321
Call date: July 1988, Gray's Inn
Qualifications: [LLB (Wales)]

HICKLING MISS SALLY BARBARA

1 Paper Bldgs
1st Floor, Temple, London EC4Y 7EP,
Telephone: 0171 353 3728/4953
Call date: Oct 1993, Gray's Inn
Qualifications: [M.Soc.Sci (B'ham)]

HICKMAN MISS CLAIRE LOUISE

1 Dr Johnson's Bldgs
Ground Floor, Temple, London EC4Y 7AX,
Telephone: 0171 353 9328
Call date: Nov 1994, Inner Temple
Qualifications: [LLB (Hons) (Lond)]

HICKMAN MRS SALLY LOUISE

8 Fountain Court
Steelhouse Lane, Birmingham B4 6DR,
Telephone: 0121 236 5514/5
E-mail: clerks@no8chambers.co.uk
Call date: Nov 1987, Middle Temple
Qualifications: [LLB (Hons)]

HICKMET RICHARD SALADIN

South Western Chambers
Melville House 12 Middle Street, Taunton,
Somerset TA1 1SH, Telephone: 01823 331919
Call date: July 1974, Inner Temple
Qualifications: [BA]

HICKS MARTIN LESLIE ARTHUR

1 Hare Court
Ground Floor, Temple, London EC4Y 7BE,
Telephone: 0171 353 3982/5324
Call date: May 1977, Inner Temple
Qualifications: [LLB (Lond)]

HICKS MICHAEL CHARLES

19 Old Buildings
Lincoln's Inn, London WC2A 3UP,
Telephone: 0171 405 2001
E-mail: clerks@oldbuildingsip.com
Call date: Nov 1976, Inner Temple
Qualifications: [BA (Cantab)]

Fax: 0171 405 0001; DX: 397 London,
Chancery Lane

Types of work: Competition; Copyright; EC and
competition law; Entertainment; Film, cable,
TV; Franchising; Intellectual property; Patents;
Trademarks

Awards and memberships: Intellectual Property
Bar Association; Chancery Bar Association

Reported cases: *PCR Ltd v Don Jones*, [1998]
FSR 170, 1997. Confidential information,
copyright and fair dealing.
Designers Guild v Russell Williams, [1998] FSR
275, 1997. Textile copyright infringement.
Roger Bance's Application, [1996] RPC 667,
1996. Copyright licence of right case.
BL v Armstrong, [1986] AC 577, 1986. Spare
parts monopoly case.

HICKS WILLIAM DAVID ANTHONY QC (1995)

1 Serjeants' Inn
4th Floor, Temple, London EC4Y 1NH,
Telephone: 0171 583 1355
E-mail: serjeants.inn@virgin.net
Call date: July 1975, Inner Temple
Qualifications: [MA (Cantab)]

HIDDLESTON ADAM WALLACE

17 Carlton Crescent
Southampton SO15 2XR,
Telephone: 01703 320320
E-mail: km@bar-17cc.demon.co.uk
Call date: Oct 1990, Inner Temple
Qualifications: [LLB (Newc)]

HIGGINS ADRIAN JOHN

13 King's Bench Walk
1st Floor, Temple, London EC4Y 7EN,
Telephone: 0171 353 7204
E-mail: clerks@13kbw.law.co.uk
King's Bench Chambers
32 Beaumont Street, Oxford OX1 2NP,
Telephone: 01865 311066
E-mail: clerks@kbc-oxford.law.co.uk
Call date: Oct 1990, Lincoln's Inn
Qualifications: [BA (Oxon)]

HIGGINS ANTHONY PAUL

Goldsmith Building
1st Floor, Temple, London EC4Y 7BL,
Telephone: 0171 353 7881
E-mail: clerks@goldsmith-building.law.co.uk
Call date: Nov 1978, Gray's Inn
Qualifications: [BA (Oxon), LLM]

HIGGINS KEVIN

4 King's Bench Walk
2nd Floor, Temple, London EC4Y 7DL,
Telephone: 0171 353 3581
Call date: Oct 1990, Inner Temple
Qualifications: [LLB (Hons)]

HIGGINS PAUL ANDREW

Old Colony House
6 South King Street, Manchester M2 6DQ,
Telephone: 0161 834 4364
Call date: Mar 1996, Lincoln's Inn
Qualifications: [BA (Hons), BA (Hons)]

HIGGINS RUPERT JAMES HALE

Littman Chambers
12 Gray's Inn Square, London WC1R 5JP,
Telephone: 0171 404 4866
E-mail: admin@littmanchambers.com
Call date: Oct 1991, Inner Temple
Qualifications: [BA (Cantab)]

HIGGINSON MISS LUCY VERNON MARIE

33 Park Place
Cardiff CF1 3BA, Telephone: 01222 233313
Call date: Oct 1992, Gray's Inn
Qualifications: [LLB (Hons)(Cardiff)]

HIGGINSON PETER ST GEORGE

2 Dr Johnson's Building
Temple, London EC4Y 7AY,
Telephone: 0171 353 4716
Call date: July 1975, Lincoln's Inn
Qualifications: [BA (Queens Canada)]

HIGGINSON TIMOTHY NICHOLAS BENNETT

Littleton Chambers
3 King's Bench Walk North, Temple, London
EC4Y 7HR, Telephone: 0171 797 8600
E-mail: littletonchambers@compuserve.com
Call date: Nov 1977, Inner Temple
Qualifications: [LLB]

HIGGO JUSTIN BERESFORD

13 Old Square
1st Floor, Lincoln's Inn, London WC2A 3UA,
Telephone: 0171 242 6105
E-mail: clerks@serlecourt.co.uk
Call date: Feb 1995, Gray's Inn
Qualifications: [BA (Oxon)]

HIGGS BRIAN JAMES QC (1974)

5 Paper Bldgs
Lower Ground Floor, Temple, London
EC4Y 7HB, Telephone: 0171 353 5638
E-mail: 107722,633@compuserve.com
Call date: Nov 1955, Gray's Inn
Recorder

HIGGS JONATHAN ALEXANDER CAMERON

5 Paper Bldgs
Lower Ground Floor, Temple, London
EC4Y 7HB, Telephone: 0171 353 5638
E-mail: 107722,633@compuserve.com
Call date: Nov 1987, Middle Temple
Recorder
Qualifications: [BA]

HIGGS ROLAND FRANCIS

11 Stone Bldgs
Ground Floor, Lincoln's Inn, London
WC2A 3TG, Telephone: 0171 831 6381
E-mail: clerks@11StoneBuildings.law.co.uk
Call date: Feb 1984, Gray's Inn
Qualifications: [MA (Oxon)]

HIGHAM JOHN ARTHUR QC (1992)

3/4 South Square
Gray's Inn, London WC1R 5HP,
Telephone: 0171 696 9900
E-mail: clerks@southsquare.com
Call date: July 1976, Lincoln's Inn
Assistant Recorder
Qualifications: [MA, LLM (Cantab)]

HIGHAM PAUL JOSEPH FRANCIS

1 Pump Court
Lower Ground Floor, Temple, London
EC4Y 7AB, Telephone: 0171 583 2012/
353 4341
E-mail: (name) @1pumpcourt.co.uk
Call date: Feb 1982, Gray's Inn
Qualifications: [MA (Cantab)]

HIGNETT RICHARD JAMES

Chartlands Chambers
3 St Giles Terrace, Northampton NN1 2BN,
Telephone: 01604 603322
Call date: Nov 1995, Inner Temple
Qualifications: [BA (Keele)]

HIGSON-SMITH MISS GILLIAN MARY

Gray's Inn Chambers
5th Floor, Gray's Inn, London WC1R 5JA,
Telephone: 0171 404 1111
Call date: Nov 1973, Inner Temple

HILDER MISS CAROLYN HAYLEY-JANE

3 Fountain Court
Steelhouse Lane, Birmingham B4 6DR,
Telephone: 0121 236 5854
Call date: Oct 1991, Lincoln's Inn
Qualifications: [BA (Cambs)]

HILDYARD MISS MARIANNA CATHERINE THOROTON

4 Brick Court
Temple, London EC4Y 9AD,
Telephone: 0171 797 8910
Call date: Nov 1977, Inner Temple

HILDYARD ROBERT HENRY THOROTON QC (1994)

4 Stone Bldgs
Ground Floor, Lincoln's Inn, London
WC2A 3XT, Telephone: 0171 242 5524
E-mail: d.goddard@4stonebuildings.law.co.uk
Call date: Nov 1977, Inner Temple
Qualifications: [BA (Oxon)]

HILKEN MS ALICE MARY

1 Pump Court
Lower Ground Floor, Temple, London
EC4Y 7AB, Telephone: 0171 583 2012/
353 4341
E-mail: (name) @1pumpcourt.co.uk
Call date: Nov 1994, Middle Temple
Qualifications: [BA (Hons)]

HILL (ELIOT) MICHAEL QC (1979)

23 Essex Street
London WC2R 3AS,
Telephone: 0171 413 0353/353 3533
E-mail: clerks@essexstreet23.demon.co.uk
Call date: June 1958, Gray's Inn
Qualifications: [MA (Oxon)]

HILL ANDREW CHARLES ROWLAND

8 King's Bench Walk
2nd Floor, Temple, London EC4Y 7DU,
Telephone: 0171 797 8888
Harrow on the Hill Chambers
60 High Street, Harrow on the Hill, Middlesex
HA1 3LL, Telephone: 0181 423 7444
Door Tenant
8 King's Bench Walk North
1 Park Square East, Leeds LS1 2NE,
Telephone: 0113 2439797
Call date: Nov 1982, Gray's Inn
Qualifications: [LLB]

D

HILL MISS CANDIDA TAMARA LOUISE

18 Red Lion Court
(Off Fleet Street), London EC4A 3EB,
Telephone: 0171 520 6000
Call date: Oct 1990, Middle Temple
Qualifications: [LLB (Hons)]

HILL MISS CAROL JANE

22 Old Bldgs
Lincoln's Inn, London WC2A 3UJ,
Telephone: 0171 831 0222
Call date: Nov 1980, Gray's Inn
Qualifications: [LLB B'ham]

HILL MISS CATHERINE LOUISE

30 Park Square
Leeds LS1 2PF, Telephone: 0113 2436388
Call date: July 1988, Gray's Inn
Qualifications: [BA (Hons)(Dunelm)]

HILL MISS CATHERINE MARY

2 Paper Bldgs
1st Floor, Temple, London EC4Y 7ET,
Telephone: 0171 936 2611 (10 Lines)
E-mail: clerks@2pbbarristers.co.uk
Call date: Nov 1991, Inner Temple
Qualifications: [BA (Newc), Dip Law]

HILL GREGORY JOHN SUMMERS

17 Old Bldgs
Ground Floor, Lincoln's Inn, London
WC2A 3UP, Telephone: 0171 405 9653
Call date: July 1972, Lincoln's Inn
Qualifications: [MA, BCL (Oxon)]

HILL JAMES MICHAEL

Fountain Chambers
Cleveland Business Centre 1 Watson Street,
Middlesbrough TS1 2RQ,
Telephone: 01642 217037
Call date: July 1984, Inner Temple
Qualifications: [LLB (Manch)]

HILL JASON

Bank House Chambers
Old Bank House, Hartshead, Sheffield S1 2EL,
Telephone: 0114 2751223
Call date: Oct 1995, Lincoln's Inn
Qualifications: [BSc (Hons)(Sheff)]

HILL MAX BENJAMIN ROWLAND

18 Red Lion Court
(Off Fleet Street), London EC4A 3EB,
Telephone: 0171 520 6000
Call date: Nov 1987, Middle Temple
Qualifications: [BA (Oxon)]

HILL NICHOLAS IAN

6 Park Square
Leeds LS1 2LW, Telephone: 0113 2459763
E-mail: chambers@no6.co.uk
Call date: Oct 1993, Lincoln's Inn
Qualifications: [BA (Hons)]

HILL NICHOLAS MARK

Pump Court Chambers
Upper Ground Floor 3 Pump Court, Temple,
London EC4Y 7AJ, Telephone: 0171 353 0711
Pump Court Chambers
31 Southgate Street, Winchester SO23 8EE,
Telephone: 01962 868161
Call date: July 1987, Middle Temple
Qualifications: [LLB (Lond), AKC]

HILL PEREGRINE EDWARD

169 Temple Chambers
Temple Avenue, London EC4Y 0DA,
Telephone: 0171 583 7644
Call date: Nov 1995, Inner Temple
Qualifications: [BA (Manc)]

HILL PIERS NICHOLAS

37 Park Square
Leeds LS1 2NY, Telephone: 0113 2439422
2 Paper Bldgs
1st Floor, Temple, London EC4Y 7ET,
Telephone: 0171 936 2611 (10 Lines)
E-mail: clerks@2pbbarristers.co.uk
Call date: July 1987, Inner Temple
Qualifications: [LLB (Hull)]

HILL RAYMOND

Monckton Chambers
4 Raymond Buildings, Gray's Inn, London
WC1R 5BP, Telephone: 0171 405 7211
E-mail: chambers@monckton.co.uk
Call date: Oct 1992, Lincoln's Inn
Qualifications: [BA(Hons)]

HILL RICHARD GEOFFREY

4 Stone Bldgs
Ground Floor, Lincoln's Inn, London
WC2A 3XT, Telephone: 0171 242 5524
E-mail: d.goddard@4stonebuildings.law.co.uk
Call date: Oct 1993, Gray's Inn
Qualifications: [BA (Cantab)]

HILL ROBERT DOUGLAS

Pump Court Chambers
Upper Ground Floor 3 Pump Court, Temple,
London EC4Y 7AJ, Telephone: 0171 353 0711
Pump Court Chambers
31 Southgate Street, Winchester SO23 8EE,
Telephone: 01962 868161
Call date: July 1980, Gray's Inn
Qualifications: [LLB (Wales)]

HILL THOMAS PATRICK JAMES

4-5 Gray's Inn Square
Ground Floor, Gray's Inn, London WC1R 5AY,
Telephone: 0171 404 5252
E-mail: chambers@4-5graysinnsquare.co.uk
Call date: July 1988, Lincoln's Inn
Qualifications: [MA (Hons) (Cantab)]

HILL TIMOTHY JOHN

4 Field Court
Gray's Inn, London WC1R 5EA,
Telephone: 0171 440 6900
E-mail: chambers@4fieldcourt.co.uk
Call date: Oct 1990, Middle Temple
Qualifications: [LLB (Lond), DLS (Cantab), BCL
(Oxon)]

HILL-BAKER JEREMY ROBERT

6 Park Square
Leeds LS1 2LW, Telephone: 0113 2459763
E-mail: chambers@no6.co.uk
Call date: July 1983, Inner Temple
Qualifications: [LLB Leeds]

HILL-SMITH ALEXANDER GEORGE LEVANDER

12 King's Bench Walk
Temple, London EC4Y 7EL,
Telephone: 0171 583 0811
E-mail: chambers@12kbw.co.uk
Call date: July 1978, Gray's Inn
Qualifications: [LLB, MA (Cantab)]

HILLEN JOHN MALCOLM

5 Paper Bldgs
Lower Ground Floor, Temple, London
EC4Y 7HB, Telephone: 0171 353 5638
E-mail: 107722,633@compuserve.com
Call date: Nov 1976, Middle Temple
Qualifications: [MA (Oxon)]

HILLIARD MISS (PIERS) ALEXANDRA

3/4 South Square
Gray's Inn, London WC1R 5HP,
Telephone: 0171 696 9900
E-mail: clerks@southsquare.com
Call date: Nov 1987, Middle Temple
Qualifications: [LLB (Lond)]

HILLIARD NICHOLAS RICHARD MAYBURY

6 King's Bench Walk
Ground Floor, Temple, London EC4Y 7DR,
Telephone: 0171 583 0410
Call date: July 1981, Middle Temple
Qualifications: [MA (Oxon)]

HILLIARD SPENSER RODNEY

Lamb Building
Ground Floor, Temple, London EC4Y 7AS,
Telephone: 0171 797 7788
E-mail: lamb.building@link.org
Southsea Chambers
PO Box 148, Southsea, Portsmouth,
Hampshire PO5 2TU,
Telephone: 01705 291261
Call date: Nov 1975, Middle Temple
Qualifications: [LLB]

HILLIER ANDREW CHARLES

5 Bell Yard
London WC2A 2JR, Telephone: 0171 333 8811
Call date: July 1972, Gray's Inn
Qualifications: [BA]

HILLIER MRS NANCY ROSE

65-67 King Street
Leicester LE1 6RP, Telephone: 0116 2547710
Call date: July 1984, Inner Temple
Qualifications: [LEU (LLB)]

D

HILLIER NICOLAS PETER

9 Gough Square
London EC4A 3DE, Telephone: 0171 353 5371
Call date: July 1982, Inner Temple
Qualifications: [LLB (So'ton)]

HILLIS JOHN

Bank House Chambers
Old Bank House, Hartshead, Sheffield S1 2EL,
Telephone: 0114 2751223
Call date: July 1982, Gray's Inn
Qualifications: [LLB (Sheff)]

HILLMAN BASIL

4 King's Bench Walk
2nd Floor, Temple, London EC4Y 7DL,
Telephone: 0171 353 3581
Call date: Nov 1968, Gray's Inn
Qualifications: [MA (MOD)]

HILLMAN ROGER JOHN

Exchange Chambers
Pearl Assurance House Derby Square,
Liverpool L2 9XX, Telephone: 0151 236 7747/
0458
E-mail: exchangechambers@btinternet.com
Call date: July 1983, Gray's Inn
Qualifications: [LLB (L'Pool)]

HILLS TIMOTHY JAMES

Albion Chambers
Broad Street, Bristol BS1 1DR,
Telephone: 0117 9272144
Call date: July 1968, Lincoln's Inn

HILSDON JAMES SPENCER

Cobden House Chambers
19 Quay Street, Manchester M3 3HN,
Telephone: 0161 833 6000
E-mail: clerks@cobden.co.uk
Call date: Nov 1993, Lincoln's Inn
Qualifications: [MA (Hons)]

HILTON ALAN JOHN HOWARD QC (1990)

Hollis Whiteman Chambers
3rd/4th Floor Queen Elizabeth Bldg, Temple,
London EC4Y 9BS, Telephone: 0171 583 5766
E-mail: hollis.whiteman@btinternet.com
Call date: Nov 1964, Middle Temple
Recorder
Qualifications: [LLB (Manch)]

HILTON MS SAISAMPAN

95A Chancery Lane
London WC2A 1DT,
Telephone: 0171 405 3101
Call date: Oct 1994, Gray's Inn
Qualifications: [BA, MA]

HILTON SIMON JONATHAN

40 King Street
Manchester M2 6BA,
Telephone: 0161 832 9082
E-mail: Kingst40@aol.com
Call date: Nov 1987, Gray's Inn
Qualifications: [BA (Oxon)]

HIMSWORTH MISS EMMA KATHERINE

1 Essex Court
Ground Floor, Temple, London EC4Y 9AR,
Telephone: 0171 583 2000
E-mail: clerks@oneessexcourt.co.uk
Call date: Oct 1993, Gray's Inn
Qualifications: [BSc (Edin), Dip Law, (City),
Dip EC Law, (Kings)]

HINCHCLIFFE DR DOREEN

2 Paper Bldgs
1st Floor, Temple, London EC4Y 7ET,
Telephone: 0171 936 2611 (10 Lines)
E-mail: clerks@2pbbarristers.co.uk
Gray's Inn Chambers
5th Floor, Gray's Inn, London WC1R 5JA,
Telephone: 0171 404 1111
Door Tenant
Call date: Nov 1953, Gray's Inn
Qualifications: [LLB, PhD]

HINCHLIFF BENJAMIN JOHN

1 Brick Court
1st Floor, Temple, London EC4Y 9BY,
Telephone: 0171 353 8845
E-mail: clerks@1brickcourt.co.uk
Call date: Nov 1992, Gray's Inn
Qualifications: [MA (Oxon)]

HINCHLIFFE PHILIP NICHOLAS

9 St John Street
Manchester M3 4DN,
Telephone: 0161 955 9000
E-mail: ninesjs@gconnect.com
Call date: Nov 1980, Middle Temple
Qualifications: [LLB (Manch)]

HIND KENNETH HARVARD

3 Temple Gardens
2nd Floor, Temple, London EC4Y 9AU,
Telephone: 0171 583 1155
Call date: July 1973, Gray's Inn
Qualifications: [LLB (Hons)]

HINDLE MISS RACHEL FRANCES

Lamb Building
Ground Floor, Temple, London EC4Y 7AS,
Telephone: 0171 797 7788
E-mail: lamb.building@link.org
Call date: Oct 1990, Inner Temple
Qualifications: [LLB]

HINDMARSH MISS ELIZABETH

Plowden Bldgs
2nd Floor, Temple, London EC4Y 9BU,
Telephone: 0171 583 0808
E-mail: bar@plowdenbuildings.co.uk
Call date: July 1974, Inner Temple
Qualifications: [BA (Dunelm)]

HINDS ORIEL GLENVERE

66 Worthington Road
Surbiton, Kingston, Surrey KT6
Call date: July 1988, Inner Temple
Qualifications: [LLB]

HINE CHARLES RODERICK JOHN

King's Bench Chambers
Wellington House 175 Holdenhurst Road,
Bournemouth, Dorset BH8 8DQ,
Telephone: 01202 250025
Call date: Nov 1985, Gray's Inn
Qualifications: [B.Com (B'ham), Dip in Law, Cert Ed]

HINE MISS RUTH ALISON

55 Temple Chambers
Temple Avenue, London EC4Y 0HP,
Telephone: 0171 353 7400
Call date: Oct 1992, Gray's Inn
Qualifications: [LL.B]

HINES JAMES PHILIP

3 Raymond Buildings
Gray's Inn, London WC1R 5BH,
Telephone: 0171 831 3833
E-mail: chambers@threeraymond.demon.co.uk
Call date: July 1982, Gray's Inn
Qualifications: [BA]

HINKS FRANK PETER

13 Old Square
1st Floor, Lincoln's Inn, London WC2A 3UA,
Telephone: 0171 242 6105
E-mail: clerks@serlecourt.co.uk
Call date: July 1973, Lincoln's Inn
Qualifications: [MA, BCL (Oxon)]

HIORNS ROGER MARTIN FAIRCHILD

9 Gough Square
London EC4A 3DE, Telephone: 0171 353 5371
Call date: July 1983, Middle Temple
Qualifications: [LLB (B'ham)]

HIPKIN JOHN LESLIE

Iscoed Chambers
86 St Helen's Road, Swansea SA1 4BQ,
Telephone: 01792 652988/9/330
Call date: Nov 1989, Gray's Inn
Qualifications: [LLB [Manch]]

D

HIRST JONATHAN WILLIAM QC (1990)

Brick Court Chambers
15/19 Devereux Court, London WC2R 3JJ,
Telephone: 0171 583 0777
E-mail: (surname)@brickcourt.demon.co.uk
Call date: July 1975, Inner Temple
Qualifications: [MA (Cantab)]

HIRST SIMON DAVID

Wilberforce Chambers
Bishop Lane, Hull HU1 1PA,
Telephone: 01482 323264
E-mail: clerks@hullbar.demon.co.uk
Call date: Oct 1993, Lincoln's Inn
Qualifications: [LLB (Hons)(Hull)]

HIRST WILLIAM TIMOTHY JOHN

Park Court Chambers
40 Park Cross Street, Leeds LS1 2QH,
Telephone: 0113 2433277
Call date: Nov 1970, Inner Temple
Recorder
Qualifications: [BA (Oxon), IDIL (German)]

HISLOP DAVID SEYMOUR

1 Crown Office Row
2nd Floor, Temple, London EC4Y 7HH,
Telephone: 0171 797 7111
Call date: Feb 1989, Gray's Inn
Qualifications: [LLB (Auckland)]

HITCHCOCK MS PATRICIA ANN

Cloisters
1st Floor, Temple, London EC4Y 7AA,
Telephone: 0171 827 4000
E-mail: clerks@cloisters.com
Call date: Nov 1988, Inner Temple
Qualifications: [BA (Oxon)]

HITCHCOCK RICHARD GUY

35 Essex Street
Temple, London WC2R 3AR,
Telephone: 0171 353 6381
Call date: Nov 1989, Gray's Inn
Qualifications: [BA [Oxon]]

HITCHCOCK TIMOTHY JOHN

5 Paper Bldgs
Lower Ground Floor, Temple, London
EC4Y 7HB, Telephone: 0171 353 5638
E-mail: 107722,633@compuserve.com
Call date: Nov 1986, Inner Temple
Qualifications: [BA(Durham)]

HITCHEN JOHN DAVID

6 Park Square
Leeds LS1 2LW, Telephone: 0113 2459763
E-mail: chambers@no6.co.uk
Call date: June 1961, Lincoln's Inn
Recorder
Qualifications: [BA (Oxon)]

HITCHING MISS ISABEL JOY

5 Fountain Court
Steelhouse Lane, Birmingham B4 6DR,
Telephone: 0121 606 0500
Call date: Oct 1992, Middle Temple
Qualifications: [BA(Hons)(Oxon), BCL(Oxon)]

HITCHMOUGH ANDREW JOHN

Pump Court Tax Chambers
16 Bedford Row, London WC1R 4EB,
Telephone: 0171 414 8080
Call date: Oct 1991, Inner Temple
Qualifications: [LLB (So'ton)]

HOARE GREGORY BLAKE

Martins Building
Water Street, Liverpool L2 3SP,
Telephone: 0151 236 5818/4919
Call date: Nov 1992, Gray's Inn
Qualifications: [LLB]

HOBBS MISS EMMA-JANE

1 Temple Gardens
1st Floor, Temple, London EC4Y 9BB,
Telephone: 0171 353 0407/583 1315
E-mail: clerks@1templegardens.co.uk
Call date: Oct 1996, Gray's Inn
Qualifications: [BA (Bris)]

HOBBS GEOFFREY WILLIAM QC (1991)

1 Essex Court
Ground Floor, Temple, London EC4Y 9AR,
Telephone: 0171 583 2000
E-mail: clerks@oneessexcourt.co.uk
Call date: July 1977, Inner Temple
Qualifications: [LLB (So'ton)]

HOBBS MS NAOMI JOSEPHINE

Claremont Chambers
26 Waterloo Road, Wolverhampton WV1 4BL,
Telephone: 01902 426222
Call date: Oct 1993, Gray's Inn
Qualifications: [LLB]

HOBHOUSE MS HELEN ROSAMUND

Farrar's Building
Temple, London EC4Y 7BD,
Telephone: 0171 583 9241
E-mail: chambers@farrarsbuilding.co.uk
Call date: Oct 1990, Inner Temple
Qualifications: [B.Soc Sci, Dip Law]

HOBSON MISS HEATHER FIONA

Queen's Chambers
5 John Dalton Street, Manchester M2 6ET,
Telephone: 0161 834 6875/4738
4 Camden Place
Preston PR1 3JL, Telephone: 01772 828300
Call date: Nov 1987, Lincoln's Inn
Qualifications: [LLB (Hons) (Lond)]

HOBSON JOHN GRAHAM

4-5 Gray's Inn Square
Ground Floor, Gray's Inn, London WC1R 5AY,
Telephone: 0171 404 5252
E-mail: chambers@4-5graysinnsquare.co.uk
Call date: July 1980, Inner Temple
Qualifications: [LLM (Cantab)]

HOCHBERG DANIEL ALAN

9 Old Square
Ground Floor, Lincoln's Inn, London
WC2A 3SR, Telephone: 0171 405 4682
E-mail: chambers@9oldsquare.co.uk
Call date: July 1982, Lincoln's Inn
Qualifications: [MA (Oxon)]

HOCHHAUSER ANDREW ROMAIN QC (1997)

Essex Court Chambers
24 Lincoln's Inn Fields, London WC2A 3ED,
Telephone: 0171 813 8000
E-mail: clerksroom@essexcourt-chambers.co.uk
Call date: July 1977, Middle Temple
Qualifications: [LLB (Bris), LLM (Lond)]

HOCKADAY MISS ANNIE

3 Verulam Buildings
London WC1R 5NT,
Telephone: 0171 831 8441
E-mail: clerks@3verulam.co.uk
Call date: Oct 1990, Gray's Inn
Qualifications: [MA (Cantab), LLM
Commercial, (Lond)]

HOCKMAN STEPHEN ALEXANDER QC (1990)

6 Pump Court
1st Floor, Temple, London EC4Y 7AR,
Telephone: 0171 797 8400
E-mail: sa_hockman_qc@link.org
6-8 Mill Street
6-8 Mill Street, Maidstone, Kent ME15 6XH,
Telephone: 01622 688 094
Call date: July 1970, Middle Temple
Recorder
Qualifications: [MA (Cantab)]

Fax: 0171 797 8401;
Out of hours telephone: 0836 744 939;
DX: LDE 293; Other comms: E-mail
sa_hockman_qc@link.org

Types of work: Administrative; Common law
(general); Environment; Local government;
Town and country planning

Circuit: South Eastern

Languages spoken: French

HOCKTON ANDREW IAN CALLINAN

6 Pump Court
Ground Floor, Temple, London EC4Y 7AR,
Telephone: 0171 583 6013/2510
Call date: Nov 1984, Middle Temple
Qualifications: [BA (Oxon), Dip Law]

HODES MISS ANGELA EVE

Lamb Building
Ground Floor, Temple, London EC4Y 7AS,
Telephone: 0171 797 7788
E-mail: lamb.building@link.org
Call date: Nov 1979, Middle Temple
Qualifications: [BA]

HODGE DAVID RALPH QC (1997)

9 Old Square
Ground Floor, Lincoln's Inn, London
WC2A 3SR, Telephone: 0171 405 4682
E-mail: chambers@9oldsquare.co.uk
Call date: July 1979, Inner Temple
Qualifications: [BA, BCL (Oxon)]

HODGES MISS VICTORIA LESLEY

St Mary's Chambers
50 High Pavement, Lace Market, Nottingham
NG1 1HW, Telephone: 0115 9503503
E-mail: clerks@smc.law.co.uk
Call date: July 1980, Gray's Inn
Qualifications: [LLB (B'ham)]

HODGKIN HARRY JOHN

South Western Chambers
Melville House 12 Middle Street, Taunton,
Somerset TA1 1SH, Telephone: 01823 331919
Call date: July 1983, Middle Temple
Qualifications: [LLB]

HODGKINSON JOHN ROBERT

1 Fountain Court
Steelhouse Lane, Birmingham B4 6DR,
Telephone: 0121 236 5721
1 Crown Office Row
3rd Floor, Temple, London EC4Y 7HH,
Telephone: 0171 583 9292
E-mail: onecor@link.org
Call date: Nov 1968, Inner Temple
Qualifications: [MA (Cantab)]

HODGKINSON TRISTRAM PATRICK

5 Pump Court
Ground Floor, Temple, London EC4Y 7AP,
Telephone: 0171 353 2532
E-mail: fivepump@netcomuk.co.uk
Call date: July 1982, Middle Temple

Qualifications: [LLB, LLM]

Fax: 0171 353 5321;
Out of hours telephone: 0171 622 4680;
DX: LDE 497 Chancery Lane

Types of work: Commercial litigation; Consumer credit; Consumer law; Financial services; Personal injury; Professional negligence

Circuit: South Eastern

Awards and memberships: Middle Temple Winston Churchill Prize

Other professional experience: Speaker at legal conferences and seminars

Languages spoken: French

Publications: *Expert Evidence: Law and Practice* (Sweet & Maxwell), 1990; Various articles in newspapers and legal journals

Reported cases: *City Mortgage Corporation v Baptiste*, [1997] CCLR 64, 1997. Consumer credit - extortionate credit bargain - mortgage possession.
Sparks v Harland, [1997] 1 WLR 143, 1997. Damages for sexual abuse - European Human Rights Convention - limitation - stay of proceedings. (Recent cases).

HODGSON MISS ELIZABETH JANE

24 The Ropewalk
Nottingham NG1 5EF,
Telephone: 0115 9472581
E-mail: clerk@ropewalk.co.uk
Call date: Oct 1993, Gray's Inn
Qualifications: [LLB (L'Pool)]

HODGSON MS JANE

9 Woodhouse Square
Leeds LS3 1AD, Telephone: 0113 2451986
Call date: July 1989, Gray's Inn
Qualifications: [BA [Oxon]]

HODGSON JOHN ARNOLD

3 Dr Johnson's Bldgs
Ground Floor, Temple, London EC4Y 7BA,
Telephone: 0171 353 4854
Call date: Feb 1963, Gray's Inn
Qualifications: [LLB (Lond)]

HODGSON MISS MARGARET JULIA

St Ive's Chambers
9 Fountain Ct, Birmingham B4 6DR,
Telephone: 0121 236 0863/0929
Call date: July 1975, Lincoln's Inn
Qualifications: [LLB (Hons)(Warw)]

HODGSON MARTIN DERRICK

8 King's Bench Walk
2nd Floor, Temple, London EC4Y 7DU,
Telephone: 0171 797 8888
8 King's Bench Walk North
1 Park Square East, Leeds LS1 2NE,
Telephone: 0113 2439797
Call date: July 1980, Middle Temple
Qualifications: [BA]

HODGSON RICHARD ANDREW

New Court
1st Floor, Temple, London EC4Y 9BE,
Telephone: 0171 797 8999
Call date: Nov 1980, Inner Temple
Qualifications: [BSc (Eng) (Lond)]

HODGSON MISS SUSAN ANN

2 Crown Office Row
Ground Floor, Temple, London EC4Y 7HJ,
Telephone: 0171 797 8100
E-mail: mail@2cor.co.uk, or to individual
barristers at: [barrister's surname]@2cor.co.uk
Call date: July 1989, Middle Temple
Qualifications: [BA (Oxon), LLM (Toronto)]

HODGSON TIMOTHY PAUL

8 King Street
Manchester M2 6AQ,
Telephone: 0161 834 9560
Call date: Nov 1991, Inner Temple
Qualifications: [BA (Victoria, New, Zealand),
BA, D.Phil, (Oxon), Dip Law]

HODSON MICHAEL JOHN

New Court Chambers
3 Broad Chare, Newcastle Upon Tyne
NE1 3DQ, Telephone: 0191 232 1980
Call date: Feb 1977, Middle Temple

HODSON PETER DAVID

1 Pump Court
Lower Ground Floor, Temple, London
EC4Y 7AB, Telephone: 0171 583 2012/
353 4341
E-mail: (name) @1pumpcourt.co.uk
Call date: Nov 1994, Inner Temple
Qualifications: [LLB (Hons), Dip CE]

HOFFMANN MISS JOCELYN CLARE

13 Old Square
1st Floor, Lincoln's Inn, London WC2A 3UA,
Telephone: 0171 242 6105
E-mail: clerks@serlecourt.co.uk
Call date: Oct 1990, Gray's Inn
Qualifications: [BA]

HOFFORD PETER JOHN

Mitre Court Chambers
3rd Floor, Temple, London EC4Y 7BP,
Telephone: 0171 353 9394
Call date: Nov 1979, Gray's Inn
Qualifications: [BA (Hons) (Wales), Dip Law
(City)]

HOFMEYR STEPHEN MURRAY

7 King's Bench Walk
Ground Floor, Temple, London EC4Y 7DS,
Telephone: 0171 583 0404
Call date: July 1982, Gray's Inn
Qualifications: [MA (Oxon), LLB, (Cape
Town), B.Com]

HOGARTH ANDREW ALLAN

12 King's Bench Walk
Temple, London EC4Y 7EL,
Telephone: 0171 583 0811
E-mail: chambers@12kbw.co.uk
Call date: July 1974, Lincoln's Inn
Qualifications: [MA (Cantab)]

HOGBEN PAUL RAYMOND

Chambers of Paul Hogben
199 Kingsworth Road, Ashford, Kent
TN23 6NB, Telephone: 01233 645805
Call date: Feb 1993, Gray's Inn
Qualifications: [LLB]

D

D

HOGG THE HON DOUGLAS MARTIN QC (1990)

4 Paper Bldgs
Ground Floor, Temple, London EC4Y 7EX,
Telephone: 0171 353 3366/583 7155
E-mail: clerks@4paperbuildings.com
37 Park Square
Leeds LS1 2NY, Telephone: 0113 2439422
Call date: July 1968, Lincoln's Inn
Qualifications: [BA (Oxon)]

HOGG MISS KATHARINE ELIZABETH

1 Crown Office Row
Ground Floor, Temple, London EC4Y 7HH,
Telephone: 0171 797 7500
Call date: Oct 1996, Middle Temple
Qualifications: [BA (Hons)(Cantab), CPE
(Westminster)]

HOGGETT ANTHONY JOHN CHRISTOPHER QC (1986)

40 King Street
Manchester M2 6BA,
Telephone: 0161 832 9082
E-mail: Kingst40@aol.com
Call date: July 1969, Gray's Inn
Recorder
Qualifications: [MA, LLB, PhD]

HOLBECH CHARLES EDWARD

11 Stone Bldgs
Ground Floor, Lincoln's Inn, London
WC2A 3TG, Telephone: 0171 831 6381
E-mail: clerks@11StoneBuildings.law.co.uk
Call date: July 1988, Lincoln's Inn
Qualifications: [BA (Hons) (Oxon)]

HOLBORN DAVID REGINALD

18 Red Lion Court
(Off Fleet Street), London EC4A 3EB,
Telephone: 0171 520 6000
Thornwood House
102 New London Road, Chelmsford, Essex
CM2 0RG, Telephone: 01245 280880
Call date: Oct 1991, Inner Temple
Qualifications: [LLB (Essex)]

HOLBROOK JON

2 Garden Court
1st Floor, Middle Temple, London EC4Y 9BL,
Telephone: 0171 353 1633
E-mail: barristers@2gardenct.law.co.uk
Call date: Nov 1991, Inner Temple
Qualifications: [BA (Sheff)]

HOLDER MISS CLAIRE ALISON

243 Westbourne Grove
London W11 2SE, Telephone: 0171 229 3819
Call date: July 1978, Lincoln's Inn
Qualifications: [MA]

HOLDER SIMON MICHAEL

India Buildings Chambers
Water Street, Liverpool L2 OXG,
Telephone: 0151 243 6000
Call date: July 1989, Inner Temple
Qualifications: [LLB [Lond]]

HOLDER TERENCE

Colleton Chambers
Powlett House 34 High Street, Taunton,
Somerset TA1 3PN, Telephone: 01823 324252
Colleton Chambers
Colleton Crescent, Exeter, Devon EX2 4DG,
Telephone: 01392 74898/9
Call date: Nov 1984, Gray's Inn

HOLDHAM MISS SUSAN PAULINE

3 Paper Bldgs
2nd Floor, Temple, London EC4Y 7EU,
Telephone: 0171 353 6208
Call date: July 1983, Gray's Inn
Qualifications: [LLB (Hons) (Bristol)]

HOLDSWORTH JAMES ARTHUR

2 Crown Office Row
Ground Floor, Temple, London EC4Y 7HJ,
Telephone: 0171 797 8100
E-mail: mail@2cor.co.uk, or to individual
barristers at: [barrister's surname]@2cor.co.uk
Call date: Feb 1977, Middle Temple
Qualifications: [MA (Oxon)]

HOLGATE DAVID JOHN QC (1997)

4 Breams Buildings
London EC4A 1AQ,
Telephone: 0171 353 5835/430 1221
Call date: July 1978, Middle Temple
Qualifications: [BA (Oxon)]

HOLL-ALLEN JONATHAN GUY

3 Serjeants Inn
London EC4Y 1BQ,
Telephone: 0171 353 5537
E-mail: available upon request
Call date: Nov 1990, Inner Temple
Qualifications: [MA, LLM (Cantab)]

HOLLAND MRS ANNE ROSEMARY

Godolphin Chambers
50 Castle Street, Truro, Cornwall TR1 3AF,
Telephone: 01872 276312
Call date: Nov 1994, Middle Temple
Qualifications: [LLB (Hons), RGN]

HOLLAND CHARLES CHRISTOPHER

Trinity Chambers
9-12 Trinity Chare, Quayside, Newcastle Upon
Tyne NE1 3DF, Telephone: 0191 232 1927
Call date: Nov 1994, Inner Temple
Qualifications: [LLB (Notts)]

HOLLAND MISS CHARLOTTE KATE

Old Colony House
6 South King Street, Manchester M2 6DQ,
Telephone: 0161 834 4364
Call date: Oct 1996, Lincoln's Inn
Qualifications: [BA (Hons)(B'ham), CPE
(Manc)]

HOLLAND DAVID MOORE

29 Bedford Row Chambers
London WC1R 4HE,
Telephone: 0171 831 2626
Call date: July 1986, Inner Temple
Qualifications: [MA (Cantab) LLM, (Toronto)]

HOLLAND MISS KATHARINE JANE

9 Old Square
Ground Floor, Lincoln's Inn, London
WC2A 3SR, Telephone: 0171 405 4682
E-mail: chambers@9oldsquare.co.uk
Call date: July 1989, Middle Temple
Qualifications: [BA [Oxon], BCL [Oxon]]

HOLLAND MICHAEL FREDERICK RICHARD

1 Hare Court
Ground Floor, Temple, London EC4Y 7BE,
Telephone: 0171 353 3982/5324
Call date: Nov 1984, Inner Temple
Qualifications: [BA (Dunelm)]

HOLLAND RICKY JOHN

Lincoln House Chambers
5th Floor Lincoln House, 1 Brazennose Street,
Manchester M2 5EL,
Telephone: 0161 832 5701
E-mail: LincolnHouseChambers@link.org
Call date: Nov 1994, Gray's Inn
Qualifications: [LLB]

HOLLAND MRS ROBERTA

17 Carlton Crescent
Southampton SO15 2XR,
Telephone: 01703 320320
E-mail: km@bar-17cc.demon.co.uk
Call date: Nov 1989, Lincoln's Inn
Qualifications: [BSc (Bath), LLB]

HOLLAND WILLIAM

Francis Taylor Bldg
2nd Floor, Temple, London EC4Y 7BY,
Telephone: 0171 353 9942/3157
Call date: July 1982, Gray's Inn
Qualifications: [LLB (Lond)]

HOLLANDER CHARLES SIMON

Brick Court Chambers
15/19 Devereux Court, London WC2R 3JJ,
Telephone: 0171 583 0777
E-mail: (surname)@brickcourt.demon.co.uk
Call date: July 1978, Gray's Inn
Qualifications: [MA (Cantab)]

D

HOLLIER MARK ANTHONY

All Saints Chambers
9/11 Broad Street, Bristol BS1 2HP,
Telephone: 0117 921 1966
Call date: May 1994, Inner Temple
Qualifications: [LLB]

HOLLINGTON ROBIN FRANK

1 New Square
Ground Floor, Lincoln's Inn, London
WC2A 3SA, Telephone: 0171 405 0884/5/6/7
E-mail: 1newsquare@compuserve.com
Call date: July 1979, Lincoln's Inn
Qualifications: [MA (Oxon), LLM (Penn)]

HOLLINGWORTH PETER JAMES MICHAEL

22 Albion Place
Northampton NN1 1UD,
Telephone: 01604 36271
Call date: May 1993, Lincoln's Inn
Qualifications: [BA, MA]

HOLLIS MRS KIM

2 Paper Bldgs
1st Floor, Temple, London EC4Y 7ET,
Telephone: 0171 936 2611 (10 Lines)
E-mail: clerks@2pbbarristers.co.uk
Call date: July 1979, Gray's Inn
Qualifications: [LLB (Lond)]

HOLLORAN MS FIONA ANNE

58 King Street Chambers
1st Floor, Kingsgate House 51-53 South King
Street, Manchester M2 6DE,
Telephone: 0161 831 7477
Call date: Nov 1989, Gray's Inn
Qualifications: [LLB (Warw)]

HOLLOW PAUL JOHN

Fenners Chambers
3 Madingley Road, Cambridge CB3 OEE,
Telephone: 01223 368761
Fenners Chambers
8-12 Priestgate, Peterborough PE1 1JA,
Telephone: 01733 62030
Call date: Nov 1981, Gray's Inn
Qualifications: [LLB (E.Ang)]

HOLLOWAY RICHARD MARK

22 Albion Place
Northampton NN1 1UD,
Telephone: 01604 36271
Call date: Nov 1993, Gray's Inn
Qualifications: [BA (B'ham)]

HOLLOWAY MS SHARON LOUISE

Mitre House Chambers
Mitre House 44 Fleet Street, London
EC4Y 1BN, Telephone: 0171 583 8233
Call date: Oct 1994, Inner Temple
Qualifications: [BA (York), CPE (Staffordshire)]

HOLLOWAY TIMOTHY RICHARD

Derby Square Chambers
Merchants Court, Derby Square, Liverpool
L2 1TS, Telephone: 0151 709 4222
Call date: Nov 1991, Inner Temple
Qualifications: [MA (Cantab)]

HOLMAN MISS TAMSIN PERDITA

19 Old Buildings
Lincoln's Inn, London WC2A 3UP,
Telephone: 0171 405 2001
E-mail: clerks@oldbuildingsip.com
Call date: Oct 1995, Middle Temple
Qualifications: [MA (Oxon)]

HOLMES JONATHAN MAURICE

Plowden Bldgs
2nd Floor, Temple, London EC4Y 9BU,
Telephone: 0171 583 0808
E-mail: bar@plowdenbuildings.co.uk
Call date: July 1985, Inner Temple
Qualifications: [LLB (Newcastle), ACIARB]

HOLMES JUSTIN FRANCIS

Chambers of Lord Goodhart QC
Ground Floor 3 New Square, Lincoln's Inn,
London WC2A 3RS,
Telephone: 0171 405 5577
E-mail: law@threenewsquare.demon.co.uk
Call date: Feb 1994, Inner Temple
Qualifications: [MA (Cantab)]

HOLMES PAUL CYRIL

Queen's Chambers
5 John Dalton Street, Manchester M2 6ET,
Telephone: 0161 834 6875/4738
4 Camden Place
Preston PR1 3JL, Telephone: 01772 828300
Call date: July 1979, Gray's Inn
Qualifications: [MA (Cantab)]

HOLMES PHILIP JOHN

8 King Street
Manchester M2 6AQ,
Telephone: 0161 834 9560
Call date: July 1980, Lincoln's Inn
Qualifications: [MA (Cantab)]

HOLMES MISS SUSAN ELIZABETH MICHAELA

2 King's Bench Walk
Ground Floor, Temple, London EC4Y 7DE,
Telephone: 0171 353 1746
E-mail: 2kbw@atlas.co.uk
King's Bench Chambers
115 North Hill, Plymouth PL4 8JY,
Telephone: 01752 221551
Call date: July 1989, Middle Temple
Qualifications: [LLB Hons (Bris)]

HOLMES-MILNER JAMES NEIL

2 Mitre Ct Bldgs
1st Floor, Temple, London EC4Y 7BX,
Telephone: 0171 353 1353
Call date: July 1989, Middle Temple
Qualifications: [MA (Cantab), Dip Law]

HOLROYD MS JOANNE

37 Park Square
Leeds LS1 2NY, Telephone: 0113 2439422
Call date: Nov 1994, Middle Temple
Qualifications: [BA (Hons)]

HOLROYD JOHN JAMES

9 Woodhouse Square
9 Woodhouse Square, Leeds LS3 1AD,
Telephone: 0113 245 1986
Call date: Nov 1989, Gray's Inn

Qualifications: [BSc (Nott'm), LLB, MICE, C
Eng, ACI Arb]

Fax: 0113 244 8623;
Out of hours telephone: 01924 270784;
DX: 26406 PKSQ

Types of work: Arbitration; Construction;
Environment; Housing; Landlord and tenant;
Personal injury; Planning; Professional
negligence; Town and country planning; Water

Other professional qualifications: Chartered
Civil Engineer

Circuit: North Eastern

Awards and memberships: Member of the
Institution of Civil Engineers

Other professional experience: 25 years as a Civil
Engineer, the last five as Assistant County
Surveyor, Clwyd County Council

HOLROYDE TIMOTHY VICTOR QC (1996)

Exchange Chambers
Pearl Assurance House Derby Square,
Liverpool L2 9XX, Telephone: 0151 236 7747/
0458
E-mail: exchangechambers@btinternet.com
Call date: Nov 1977, Middle Temple
Assistant Recorder
Qualifications: [BA (Oxon)]

HOLT MISS ABIGAIL CLAIRE

24a St John Street
Manchester M3 4DF,
Telephone: 0161 833 9628
Call date: Oct 1993, Lincoln's Inn
Qualifications: [BA (Hons)(Oxon)]

HOLT JOHN FREDERICK

East Anglian Chambers
57 London Street, Norwich NR2 1HL,
Telephone: 01603 617351
East Anglian Chambers
Gresham House 5 Museum Street, Ipswich
IP1 1HQ, Telephone: 01473 214481
East Anglian Chambers
Sanders House 52 North Hill, Colchester
CO1 1PY, Telephone: 01206 572756
Call date: Feb 1970, Lincoln's Inn
Qualifications: [LLB (Bris)]

HOLT MISS KAREN JANE

Queen Elizabeth Bldg
Ground Floor, Temple, London EC4Y 9BS,
Telephone: 0171 353 7181 (12 Lines)
Call date: Nov 1987, Lincoln's Inn
Qualifications: [LLB (Leeds)]

HOLT MISS MARGARET EVELYN

First National Building
2nd Floor 24 Fenwick Street, Liverpool
L2 7NE, Telephone: 0151 236 2098
Call date: Feb 1978, Lincoln's Inn
Qualifications: [BA, LLB]

HOLT MICHAEL JULIAN

Parsonage Chambers
5th Floor 3 The Parsonage, Manchester
M3 2HW, Telephone: 0161 833 1996
Call date: Feb 1982, Middle Temple
Qualifications: [BA]

HOLT ROBERT CHARLES STEPHEN

Furnival Chambers
32 Furnival Street, London EC4A 1JQ,
Telephone: 0171 405 3232
E-mail: clerks@furnivallaw.co.uk
Call date: Nov 1978, Gray's Inn
Qualifications: [BSc]

HOLTUM IAN ROBERT

2 Crown Office Row
2nd Floor, Temple, London EC4Y 7HJ,
Telephone: 0171 797 8000
Call date: July 1985, Gray's Inn
Qualifications: [BA (Oxon), Dip Law, (City)]

HOLWILL DEREK PAUL WINSOR

4 Paper Bldgs
Ground Floor, Temple, London EC4Y 7EX,
Telephone: 0171 353 3366/583 7155
E-mail: clerks@4paperbuildings.com
Call date: July 1982, Gray's Inn
Qualifications: [MA (Cantab)]

HOMER MISS MADELINE JANE

Mendhir Chambers
38 Priest Avenue, Wokingham, Berkshire
RG40 2LX, Telephone: 0118 9771274
Call date: Oct 1994, Gray's Inn
Qualifications: [LLB]

HONE RICHARD MICHAEL QC (1997)

1 Paper Bldgs
Ground Floor, Temple, London EC4Y 7EP,
Telephone: 0171 583 7355
E-mail: clerks@1pb.co.uk
Call date: July 1970, Middle Temple
Recorder
Qualifications: [MA (Oxon)]

HONEY JOHN FRANCIS

Lion Court
Chancery House 53-64 Chancery Lane, London
WC2A 1SJ, Telephone: 0171 404 6565
Call date: Nov 1990, Inner Temple
Qualifications: [BA (Cantab), Dip Law (PCL)]

HOOD DAVID

90 Overstrand Mansions
Prince of Wales Drive, London SW11 4EU,
Telephone: 0171 622 7415
Call date: Nov 1980, Inner Temple
Qualifications: [LLB (Lond)]

HOOD NIGEL ANTHONY

4 King's Bench Walk
Ground/First Floor, Temple, London
EC4Y 7DL, Telephone: 0171 822 8822
E-mail: 4kbw@barristersatlaw.com
Call date: Oct 1993, Inner Temple
Qualifications: [BA (Bournemouth), MBA
(Missouri), CPE]

HOOKWAY RICHARD AELRED

39 Park Square
Leeds LS1 2NU, Telephone: 0113 2456633
Call date: Nov 1990, Gray's Inn
Qualifications: [LLB (B'ham)]

HOOLEY RICHARD JOHN ALEXANDER

Fountain Court
Temple, London EC4Y 9DH,
Telephone: 0171 583 3335
E-mail: chambers@fountaincourt.co.uk
Door Tenant
Call date: July 1984, Middle Temple
Qualifications: [MA (Cantab)]

HOON PRITHVIJIT NOTU SINGH

2 Paper Bldgs
1st Floor, Temple, London EC4Y 7ET,
Telephone: 0171 936 2611 (10 Lines)
E-mail: clerks@2pbbarristers.co.uk
Call date: Nov 1975, Inner Temple

HOOPER DAVID JOHN

3 Gray's Inn Square
Ground Floor, London WC1R 5AH,
Telephone: 0171 520 5600
E-mail: gis3@btinternet.com
Call date: Feb 1971, Middle Temple

HOOPER GOPAL ARTHUR JOHN

1 Middle Temple Lane
Temple, London EC4Y 1LT,
Telephone: 0171 583 0659 (12 Lines)
Call date: July 1973, Middle Temple
Assistant Recorder
Qualifications: [LLB]

HOOPER MARTIN CHARLES

3 Temple Gardens
3rd Floor, Temple, London EC4Y 9AU,
Telephone: 0171 583 0010
Call date: July 1988, Middle Temple
Qualifications: [LLB (Hons)]

HOOPER TOBY JULIEN ANDERSON

12 King's Bench Walk
Temple, London EC4Y 7EL,
Telephone: 0171 583 0811
E-mail: chambers@12kbw.co.uk
Call date: July 1973, Inner Temple
Assistant Recorder
Qualifications: [BA]

HOPE ANTONY DERWIN

3 Paper Bldgs
1st Floor, Temple, London EC4Y 7EU,
Telephone: 0171 583 8055
E-mail: london@3paper.com
4 St Peter Street
Winchester SO23 8OW,
Telephone: 01962 868884
20 Lorne Park Road
Bournemouth BH1 1JN,
Telephone: 01202 292102 (5 Lines)
Call date: Nov 1970, Middle Temple
Recorder
Qualifications: [BSc (Lond) Est Man, (Lond)]

HOPE MISS HEATHER ROSALIND

Trafalgar Chambers
53 Fleet Street, London EC4Y 1BE,
Telephone: 0171 583 5858
E-mail: TrafalgarChambers@easynet.co.uk
Call date: Oct 1993, Gray's Inn
Qualifications: [LLB]

HOPE MISS NADINE SAMANTHA

Victoria Chambers
19 Castle Street, Liverpool L2 4SX,
Telephone: 0151 236 9402
E-mail: Fa45@rapid.co.uk
Enfield Chambers
36-38 London Road, Enfield, Middlesex
EN2 6DT, Telephone: 0181 364 5627
E-mail: Enfieldchambers@compuserve.com
Call date: Feb 1988, Lincoln's Inn
Qualifications: [LLB (Hons), MA]

HOPEWELL GREGORY TURTLE

John Street Chambers
2 John Street, London WC1N 2HJ,
Telephone: 0171 242 1911
E-mail: john.street_chambers@virgin.net.uk
Call date: Feb 1992, Inner Temple
Qualifications: [BA, LLB (Hons)]

HOPKINS ADRIAN MARK

3 Serjeants Inn
London EC4Y 1BQ,
Telephone: 0171 353 5537
E-mail: available upon request
Call date: Nov 1984, Lincoln's Inn
Qualifications: [BA (Oxon)]

HOPKINS MISS ANDREA LOUISE

St John's Chambers
Small Street, Bristol BS1 1DW,
Telephone: 0117 9213456/298514
E-mail: clerks@stjohns.uk.com
Call date: Nov 1992, Gray's Inn
Qualifications: [LLB (Exeter)]

HOPKINS PAUL ANDREW

9 Park Place
Cardiff CF1 3DP, Telephone: 01222 382731
Call date: July 1989, Gray's Inn
Qualifications: [LLB (B'ham)]

HOPKINS MISS PHILIPPA MARY

Essex Court Chambers
24 Lincoln's Inn Fields, London WC2A 3ED,
Telephone: 0171 813 8000
E-mail: clerksroom@essexcourt-chambers.co.uk
Call date: Oct 1994, Middle Temple
Qualifications: [BA (Hons), BCL (Oxon)]

HOPKINS ROWLAND RHYS

Rowchester Chambers
4 Rowchester Court Whittall Street,
Birmingham B4 6DH,
Telephone: 0121 233 2327/2361951
Call date: Nov 1970, Inner Temple
Qualifications: [LLB (Lond)]

HOPKINS SIMEON FRANCIS MCKAY

5 Pump Court
Ground Floor, Temple, London EC4Y 7AP,
Telephone: 0171 353 2532
E-mail: fivepump@netcomuk.co.uk
Call date: Nov 1968, Inner Temple

HOPKINS STEPHEN JOHN

30 Park Place
Cardiff CF1 3BA, Telephone: 01222 398421
E-mail: 100757.1456@compuserve.com
Call date: Nov 1973, Gray's Inn
Recorder
Qualifications: [LLB (Wales)]

HOPMEIER MICHAEL ANDREW PHILIP

Hardwicke Building
New Square, Lincoln's Inn, London
WC2A 3SB, Telephone: 0171 242 2523
E-mail: clerks@hardwicke.co.uk
Call date: July 1974, Middle Temple
Recorder
Qualifications: [MA (Oxon), LLM (Lond)]

HORAN JOHN PATRICK

22 Old Bldgs
Lincoln's Inn, London WC2A 3UJ,
Telephone: 0171 831 0222
Call date: Feb 1993, Inner Temple
Qualifications: [BA, Diploma in Law]

HORGAN PETER THOMAS

Queen's Chambers
5 John Dalton Street, Manchester M2 6ET,
Telephone: 0161 834 6875/4738
4 Camden Place
Preston PR1 3JL, Telephone: 01772 828300
Call date: Oct 1993, Middle Temple
Qualifications: [BA (Hons)(Manc), Dip in Law (City)]

HORGAN TIMOTHY GEORGE

Cloisters
1st Floor, Temple, London EC4Y 7AA,
Telephone: 0171 827 4000
E-mail: clerks@cloisters.com
Call date: July 1982, Inner Temple
Qualifications: [LLB (Leeds)]

HORLICK LADY FIONA

23 Essex Street
London WC2R 3AS,
Telephone: 0171 413 0353/353 3533
E-mail: clerks@essexstreet23.demon.co.uk
Call date: May 1992, Middle Temple
Qualifications: [LLB (Hons) (Lond)]

HORLOCK TIMOTHY JOHN QC (1997)

9 St John Street
Manchester M3 4DN,
Telephone: 0161 955 9000
E-mail: ninesjs@gconnect.com
Call date: July 1981, Middle Temple
Assistant Recorder
Qualifications: [BA (Cantab), MA]

HORNBY ROBERT CHRISTOPHER

Sedan House
Stanley Place, Chester CH1 2LU,
Telephone: 01244 320480/348282
Call date: Oct 1990, Lincoln's Inn
Qualifications: [LLB]

HORNE CHARLES HUGH WILSON

40 King Street
Manchester M2 6BA,
Telephone: 0161 832 9082
E-mail: Kingst40@aol.com
Call date: Oct 1992, Lincoln's Inn
Qualifications: [LLB(Hons)(Leeds)]

HORNE KENDERIK THOMAS CLARKE

Adrian Lyon's Chambers
14 Castle Street, Liverpool L2 0NE,
Telephone: 0151 236 4421/8240
E-mail: chambers14@aol.com
Call date: Mar 1996, Lincoln's Inn
Qualifications: [BA (Hons)]

HORNE MICHAEL ANDREW

3 Serjeants Inn
London EC4Y 1BQ,
Telephone: 0171 353 5537
E-mail: available upon request
Call date: Oct 1992, Gray's Inn
Qualifications: [BA]

HORNE ROGER COZENS-HARDY

11 New Square
Ground Floor, Lincoln's Inn, London
WC2A 3QB, Telephone: 0171 831 0081
E-mail: 11newsquare.co.uk
Call date: July 1967, Lincoln's Inn
Qualifications: [LLB (St Andrews)]

HORNE-ROBERTS MRS JENNIFER

1 Dr Johnson's Bldgs
Ground Floor, Temple, London EC4Y 7AX,
Telephone: 0171 353 9328
Westgate Chambers
144 High Street, Lewes, East Sussex BN7 1XT,
Telephone: 01273 480510
Westgate Chambers
16-17 Wellington Square, Hastings, East Sussex
TN34 1PB, Telephone: 01424 432105
Call date: Nov 1976, Middle Temple
Qualifications: [BA (Hons)(Lond)]

HORNER ROBIN MICHAEL

Broad Chare
33 Broad Chare, Newcastle Upon Tyne
NE1 3DQ, Telephone: 0191 232 0541
Call date: July 1975, Lincoln's Inn
Qualifications: [LLB]

HORNETT STUART IAN

29 Bedford Row Chambers
London WC1R 4HE,
Telephone: 0171 831 2626
Call date: Oct 1992, Middle Temple
Qualifications: [LL.B (Hons) & M.Phil, (Leic)]

HORNSBY WALTON FRANCIS PETRE

Queen Elizabeth Bldg
Ground Floor, Temple, London EC4Y 9BS,
Telephone: 0171 353 7181 (12 Lines)
Call date: July 1980, Lincoln's Inn
Qualifications: [BA (Oxon)]

HOROWITZ MICHAEL QC (1990)

1 Mitre Ct Bldgs
Ground Floor, Temple, London EC4Y 7BS,
Telephone: 0171 797 7070
Call date: July 1968, Lincoln's Inn
Recorder
Qualifications: [MA, LLB (Cantab)]

HORROCKS PETER LESLIE

One Garden Court
Ground Floor, Temple, London EC4Y 9BJ,
Telephone: 0171 797 7900
Call date: Nov 1977, Middle Temple
Qualifications: [MA (Cantab)]

HORSPOOL ANTHONY BERNARD GRAEME

Hardwicke Building
New Square, Lincoln's Inn, London
WC2A 3SB, Telephone: 0171 242 2523
E-mail: clerks@hardwicke.co.uk
Call date: Nov 1991, Middle Temple
Qualifications: [BA Hons (Oxon), Dip Law]

D

HORTON MISS CAROLINE ANN

Fenners Chambers
3 Madingley Road, Cambridge CB3 OEE,
Telephone: 01223 368761
Fenners Chambers
8-12 Priestgate, Peterborough PE1 1JA,
Telephone: 01733 62030
Call date: Oct 1993, Middle Temple
Qualifications: [LLB (Hons, Nott)]

HORTON MARK ANTHONY

St John's Chambers
Small Street, Bristol BS1 1DW,
Telephone: 0117 9213456/298514
E-mail: clerks@stjohns.uk.com
Call date: July 1976, Middle Temple
Qualifications: [LLB]

HORTON MARK VARNEY

Colleton Chambers
Colleton Crescent, Exeter, Devon EX2 4DG,
Telephone: 01392 74898/9
Call date: July 1981, Middle Temple
Qualifications: [LLB (Lond)]

HORTON MATTHEW BETHELL
QC (1989)

2 Mitre Ct Bldgs
2nd Floor, Temple, London EC4Y 7BX,
Telephone: 0171 583 1380
Call date: July 1969, Middle Temple
Qualifications: [MA, LLB (Cantab)]

HORTON MICHAEL JOHN EDWARD

4 Brick Court
Ground Floor, Temple, London EC4Y 9AD,
Telephone: 0171 797 7766
E-mail: chambers@4brick.co.uk
Call date: Nov 1993, Gray's Inn
Qualifications: [BA]

HORWELL RICHARD ERIC

Hollis Whiteman Chambers
3rd/4th Floor Queen Elizabeth Bldg, Temple,
London EC4Y 9BS, Telephone: 0171 583 5766
E-mail: hollis.whiteman@btinternet.com
Call date: Nov 1976, Gray's Inn

HORWOOD MISS ANYA LOUISE

25-27 Castle Street
1st Floor, Liverpool L2 4TA,
Telephone: 0151 227 5661/051 236 5072
Call date: Nov 1991, Inner Temple
Qualifications: [LLB (Lancs)]

HORWOOD-SMART MISS ROSAMUND
QC (1996)

18 Red Lion Court
(Off Fleet Street), London EC4A 3EB,
Telephone: 0171 520 6000
Thornwood House
102 New London Road, Chelmsford, Essex
CM2 0RG, Telephone: 01245 280880
Call date: July 1974, Inner Temple
Recorder

HOSER PHILIP JACOB

13 Old Square
1st Floor, Lincoln's Inn, London WC2A 3UA,
Telephone: 0171 242 6105
E-mail: clerks@serlecourt.co.uk
Call date: Nov 1982, Lincoln's Inn
Qualifications: [BA (Cantab)]

HOSFORD-TANNER (JOSEPH)
MICHAEL

Queen Elizabeth Bldg
2nd Floor, Temple, London EC4Y 9BS,
Telephone: 0171 797 7837
Call date: Nov 1974, Inner Temple
Qualifications: [BA, LLB]

HOSKING STEVE

Lion Court
Chancery House 53-64 Chancery Lane, London
WC2A 1SJ, Telephone: 0171 404 6565
Call date: Nov 1988, Inner Temple
Qualifications: [BA (Nott'm)]

HOSKINS MARK GEORGE

Brick Court Chambers
15/19 Devereux Court, London WC2R 3JJ,
Telephone: 0171 583 0777
E-mail: (surname)@brickcourt.demon.co.uk
Call date: Nov 1991, Gray's Inn
Qualifications: [MA (Oxon),BCL (Oxon),
Lic.Spec Dr Eur, (Brussels)]

HOSKINS WILLIAM GUERIN

1 Temple Gardens
1st Floor, Temple, London EC4Y 9BB,
Telephone: 0171 353 0407/583 1315
E-mail: clerks@1templegardens.co.uk
Call date: Nov 1980, Middle Temple
Qualifications: [MA (Oxon)]

HOSSAIN AJMALUL

29 Bedford Row Chambers
London WC1R 4HE,
Telephone: 0171 831 2626
Call date: Nov 1976, Lincoln's Inn
Qualifications: [LLB (Hons)LLM (Lond),
FCIArb]

HOSSAIN SYED MOHAMMAD SA'AD ANSARUL

1 Essex Court
Ground Floor, Temple, London EC4Y 9AR,
Telephone: 0171 583 2000
E-mail: clerks@oneessexcourt.co.uk
Call date: Nov 1995, Gray's Inn
Qualifications: [BA]

HOTTEN CHRISTOPHER PETER QC (1994)

9 Bedford Row
London WC1R 4AZ,
Telephone: 0171 242 3555
E-mail: clerks@9br.co.uk
7 Fountain Court
Steelhouse Lane, Birmingham B4 6DR,
Telephone: 0121 236 8531
Door Tenant
Call date: Nov 1972, Inner Temple
Recorder
Qualifications: [LLB (Leics)]

HOTTEN KEITH ROBERT

23 Essex Street
London WC2R 3AS,
Telephone: 0171 413 0353/353 3533
E-mail: clerks@essexstreet23.demon.co.uk
Call date: Nov 1990, Middle Temple
Qualifications: [MA PhD (Lond)]

HOUGH CHRISTOPHER SIMON

199 Strand
London WC2R 1DR,
Telephone: 0171 379 9779
E-mail: chambers@199strand.co.uk
Call date: July 1981, Middle Temple
Qualifications: [LLB]

HOUGH RICHARD ANTHONY

Devon Chambers
3 St Andrew Street, Plymouth PL1 2AH,
Telephone: 01752 661659
Call date: Nov 1979, Gray's Inn

HOUGHTON MISS KIRSTEN ANNETTE

4 Pump Court
Temple, London EC4Y 7AN,
Telephone: 0171 353 2656/9
E-mail: 4_pump_court@compuserve.com
Call date: July 1989, Inner Temple
Qualifications: [BA (Cantab)]

HOUGHTON MISS LISA JAYNE

58 King Street Chambers
1st Floor, Kingsgate House 51-53 South King
Street, Manchester M2 6DE,
Telephone: 0161 831 7477
Call date: Oct 1994, Gray's Inn
Qualifications: [BA (Lancs)]

HOUGHTON MARK

33 Bedford Row
London WC1R 4JH,
Telephone: 0171 242 6476
Door Tenant
Call date: Nov 1980, Middle Temple
Qualifications: [BA]

HOULDER BRUCE QC (1994)

6 King's Bench Walk
Ground Floor, Temple, London EC4Y 7DR,
Telephone: 0171 583 0410
Call date: July 1969, Gray's Inn
Recorder

HOUSE JAMES MICHAEL

2 New Street
Leicester LE1 5NA, Telephone: 0116 2625906
Call date: Oct 1995, Inner Temple
Qualifications: [BA (Lanc), CPE]

D

HOUSE MICHAEL JOHN

2 Garden Court
1st Floor, Middle Temple, London EC4Y 9BL,
Telephone: 0171 353 1633
E-mail: barristers@2gardenct.law.co.uk
Call date: July 1972, Inner Temple
Qualifications: [MA (Oxon)]

HOUSEMAN STEPHEN TERENCE

Essex Court Chambers
24 Lincoln's Inn Fields, London WC2A 3ED,
Telephone: 0171 813 8000
E-mail: clerksroom@essexcourt-chambers.co.uk
Call date: Nov 1995, Inner Temple
Qualifications: [BA, BCL (Oxon)]

HOUSTON ANDREW

Eighteen Carlton Crescent
Southampton SO15 2XR,
Telephone: 01703 639001
Call date: July 1989, Inner Temple
Qualifications: [LLB (So'ton)]

HOUSTON DAVID JOHN

Gray's Inn Chambers
5th Floor, Gray's Inn, London WC1R 5JA,
Telephone: 0171 404 1111
Call date: Nov 1976, Gray's Inn
Qualifications: [BA (Dunelm)]

HOUSTON DAVID MARTIN RUSSELL

3 Dr Johnson's Bldgs
Ground Floor, Temple, London EC4Y 7BA,
Telephone: 0171 353 4854
Call date: Nov 1973, Gray's Inn
Qualifications: [LLB (Lond)]

HOWARD MISS AMANDA JAYNE

Derby Square Chambers
Merchants Court, Derby Square, Liverpool
L2 1TS, Telephone: 0151 709 4222
Call date: Nov 1994, Inner Temple
Qualifications: [LLB (Hons)]

HOWARD ANTHONY JOHN

9 St John Street
Manchester M3 4DN,
Telephone: 0161 955 9000
E-mail: ninesjs@gconnect.com
Call date: Oct 1992, Inner Temple
Qualifications: [LLB (Lancs)]

HOWARD CHARLES ANTHONY FREDERICK

New Court Chambers
5 Verulam Buildings, Gray's Inn, London
WC1R 5LY, Telephone: 0171 831 9500
E-mail: mail@newcourtchambers.com
Call date: July 1975, Inner Temple
Qualifications: [MA (Cantab)]

HOWARD GRAHAM JOHN

Queen Elizabeth Bldg
Ground Floor, Temple, London EC4Y 9BS,
Telephone: 0171 353 7181 (12 Lines)
Call date: Nov 1987, Lincoln's Inn
Qualifications: [LLB (Hons)]

HOWARD IAN

Broadway House Chambers
Broadway House 9 Bank Street, Bradford,
West Yorkshire BD1 1TW,
Telephone: 01274 722560
Call date: Nov 1987, Lincoln's Inn
Qualifications: [LLB(Hons) Newcastle]

HOWARD JONATHAN ROY

12 King's Bench Walk
Temple, London EC4Y 7EL,
Telephone: 0171 583 0811
E-mail: chambers@12kbw.co.uk
Call date: Nov 1983, Middle Temple
Qualifications: [MA (Cantab)]

HOWARD MISS MARGARET JOAN

4 King's Bench Walk
Ground/First Floor, Temple, London
EC4Y 7DL, Telephone: 0171 822 8822
E-mail: 4kbw@barristersatlaw.com
Call date: July 1977, Middle Temple
Qualifications: [LLB(B'ham)]

HOWARD MARK STEVEN QC (1996)

Brick Court Chambers
15/19 Devereux Court, London WC2R 3JJ,
Telephone: 0171 583 0777
E-mail: (surname)@brickcourt.demon.co.uk
Call date: July 1980, Gray's Inn
Qualifications: [LLB, LLM (Lond)]

HOWARD MICHAEL NEWMAN QC (1986)

4 Essex Court
Temple, London EC4Y 9AJ,
Telephone: 0171 797 7970
E-mail: clerks@4essexcourt.law.co.uk
Call date: May 1971, Gray's Inn
Recorder
Qualifications: [MA, BCL]

HOWARD ROBIN WILLIAM JOHN

Trinity Chambers
140 New London Road, Chelmsford, Essex
CM2 0AW, Telephone: 01245 605040
Call date: Feb 1986, Middle Temple
Qualifications: [BA (Oxon)]

HOWARD TIMOTHY DOUGLAS

17 Carlton Crescent
Southampton SO15 2XR,
Telephone: 01703 320320
E-mail: km@bar-17cc.demon.co.uk
Call date: July 1981, Lincoln's Inn
Qualifications: [LLB (Manch)]

HOWARD-JONES MISS SARAH RACHEL

8 Stone Buildings
Lincoln's Inn, London WC2A 3TA,
Telephone: 0171 831 9881
Call date: Nov 1994, Middle Temple
Qualifications: [BA (Hons)(Cantab)]

HOWARTH ANDREW

36 Bedford Row
London WC1R 4JH,
Telephone: 0171 421 8000
E-mail: 36bedfordrow@link.org
Call date: Nov 1988, Lincoln's Inn
Qualifications: [BA (Oxon)]

HOWARTH SIMON STUART

2 Crown Office Row
Ground Floor, Temple, London EC4Y 7HJ,
Telephone: 0171 797 8100
E-mail: mail@2cor.co.uk, or to individual
barristers at: [barrister's surname]@2cor.co.uk
Call date: Oct 1991, Gray's Inn
Qualifications: [BA (Oxon)]

HOWAT ROBIN DAVID CHALMERS

6 King's Bench Walk
Ground, Third & Fourth Floors, Temple,
London EC4Y 7DR,
Telephone: 0171 353 4931/583 0695
Call date: Nov 1986, Inner Temple
Qualifications: [BA(Dunelm)]

HOWD STEPHEN EDMUND JEFFERSON

5 Fountain Court
Steelhouse Lane, Birmingham B4 6DR,
Telephone: 0121 606 0500
Call date: July 1989, Middle Temple
Qualifications: [BA (Oxon), Dip Law]

HOWE MISS CAROLE ANNE

8 King's Bench Walk North
1 Park Square East, Leeds LS1 2NE,
Telephone: 0113 2439797
8 King's Bench Walk
2nd Floor, Temple, London EC4Y 7DU,
Telephone: 0171 797 8888
Call date: Nov 1984, Gray's Inn
Qualifications: [DMS]

HOWE DARREN FRANCIS

Sussex Chambers
9 Old Steine, Brighton BN1 1FJ,
Telephone: 01273 607953
Call date: Oct 1992, Gray's Inn
Qualifications: [LL.B (Hull)]

HOWE MARTIN RUSSELL THOMSON QC (1996)

8 New Square
Lincoln's Inn, London WC2A 3QP,
Telephone: 0171 405 4321
Call date: July 1978, Middle Temple
Qualifications: [BA (Cantab)]

D

HOWE MISS PENELOPE ANNE MACGREGOR

Pump Court Chambers
Upper Ground Floor 3 Pump Court, Temple,
London EC4Y 7AJ, Telephone: 0171 353 0711
Call date: Nov 1991, Inner Temple
Qualifications: [BA (Cambs)]

HOWE PETER ST JOHN

9 King's Bench Walk
Ground Floor, Temple, London EC4Y 7DX,
Telephone: 0171 353 7202/3909
Call date: July 1992, Middle Temple

HOWE ROBERT PAUL THOMPSON

2 Hare Court
Ground Floor, Temple, London EC4Y 7BH,
Telephone: 0171 583 1770
E-mail: 2_Hare_Court@link.org
Call date: Nov 1988, Middle Temple
Qualifications: [MA (Cantab), BCL (Oxon)]

HOWE MISS RUTH ALYSON

Derby Square Chambers
Merchants Court, Derby Square, Liverpool
L2 1TS, Telephone: 0151 709 4222
Call date: July 1983, Lincoln's Inn
Qualifications: [BA (Hons)]

HOWE MISS SARA-LISE ANGELIQUE

Westgate Chambers
16-17 Wellington Square, Hastings, East Sussex
TN34 1PB, Telephone: 01424 432105
Westgate Chambers
144 High Street, Lewes, East Sussex BN7 1XT,
Telephone: 01273 480510
Call date: Oct 1993, Lincoln's Inn
Qualifications: [BA (Hons)(Leic)]

HOWE TIMOTHY JEAN-PAUL

Fountain Court
Temple, London EC4Y 9DH,
Telephone: 0171 583 3335
E-mail: chambers@fountaincourt.co.uk
Call date: Nov 1987, Middle Temple
Qualifications: [MA (Oxon)]

HOWELL JOHN QC (1993)

4 Breams Buildings
London EC4A 1AQ,
Telephone: 0171 353 5835/430 1221
Call date: Feb 1979, Middle Temple
Qualifications: [BA (Oxon)]

HOWELL WILLIAMS CRAIG

2 Harcourt Bldgs
2nd Floor, Temple, London EC4Y 9DB,
Telephone: 0171 353 8415
E-mail: clerks@twoharcourtbldgs.demon.co.uk
Call date: July 1983, Gray's Inn
Qualifications: [BA (Leeds)]

HOWELLS MISS CATHERINE JANE

Exchange Chambers
Pearl Assurance House Derby Square,
Liverpool L2 9XX, Telephone: 0151 236 7747/
0458
E-mail: exchangechambers@btinternet.com
Call date: July 1989, Gray's Inn
Qualifications: [LLB [L'pool]]

HOWELLS CENYDD IORWERTH

11 Stone Bldgs
1st Floor, Lincoln's Inn, London WC2A 3TG,
Telephone: 0171 404 5055
E-mail: 9stoneb@compuserve.com
33 Park Place
Cardiff CF1 3BA, Telephone: 01222 233313
Door Tenant
Call date: June 1964, Lincoln's Inn
Recorder
Qualifications: [MA LLM (Cantab), FCIArb]

HOWELLS JAMES RICHARD

1 Atkin Building
Gray's Inn, London WC1R 5AT,
Telephone: 0171 404 0102
E-mail: clerks@atkin-chambers.co.uk
Call date: Nov 1995, Middle Temple
Qualifications: [BA (Hons), BCL]

HOWELLS JOHN JULIAN

Assize Court Chambers
14 Small Street, Bristol BS1 1DE,
Telephone: 0117 9264587
Call date: Nov 1985, Gray's Inn
Qualifications: [LLB (Lond)]

HOWELLS MISS KATHERINE JANE

7 New Square
Lincoln's Inn, London WC2A 3QS,
Telephone: 0171 430 1660
Call date: Oct 1994, Gray's Inn
Qualifications: [BA (Oxon)]

HOWES MISS SALLY MARGARET

1 Hare Court
Ground Floor, Temple, London EC4Y 7BE,
Telephone: 0171 353 3982/5324
Call date: Nov 1983, Middle Temple
Qualifications: [BA (Newc), Dip Law]

HOWKER DAVID THOMAS

1 Hare Court
Ground Floor, Temple, London EC4Y 7BE,
Telephone: 0171 353 3982/5324
Call date: July 1982, Inner Temple
Assistant Recorder
Qualifications: [LLB (B'ham)]

HOWLETT JAMES ANTHONY

King Charles House
Standard Hill, Nottingham NG1 6FX,
Telephone: 0115 9418851
E-mail: clerks@kch.co.uk
Call date: July 1980, Middle Temple
Qualifications: [LLB (Bris)]

HOWLING REX ANDREW

2 Field Court
Gray's Inn, London WC1R 5BB,
Telephone: 0171 405 6114
E-mail: fieldct2@netcomuk.co.uk.
Call date: Oct 1991, Middle Temple
Qualifications: [BSc (Hons) (Sussex), Dip Law]

HOYAL MS JANE

1 Pump Court
Temple, London EC4Y 7AB,
Telephone: 0171 583 2012/353 4341
E-mail: (name) @1pumpcourt.co.uk
Call date: Nov 1976, Middle Temple
Qualifications: [LLB MA]

Fax: 0171 353 4944

Types of work: Administrative; Care proceedings; Civil liberties; Crime; European human rights; Family; Private international

Circuit: South Eastern

Awards and memberships: Management Committee Grandparents' Federation; Trustees of PAIN (Parents against injustice); *Member:* FLBA; Family Rights Group; Association of Lawyers for Children; The Haldane Society; Rights of Women; Liberty; Association of Women Barristers; The Howard League for Penal Reform; BASPCAN; Commonwealth Lawyers' Association; International Bar Association; Amnesty International; Justice; Fawcett Society; Society of Labour Lawyers; National Council for Family Proceedings; *Friend:* Mothers apart from their children

Other professional experience: Member of Social Security Appeals Tribunals for 14 years to 1991

Reported Cases
Rv Woodgreen Crown Court ex parte P [1983] 1 FLR 206,
Re J (a minor) (Care Order: Wardship) [1984] FLR 43,
Re BA (Wardship and Adoption) [1985] FLR 1008,
M v Westminster CC [1985] FLR 325,
R v Salisbury and Tisbury and Mere Combined JC ex parte B [1986] FLR 1,
R v the United Kingdom Government [1988] 2 FLR 445,
Re F (minors) (denial of contact) [1993] 2 FLR 667,
Re P (minors) (contact with children in care) [1993] 2 FLR 156,
Re D (a minor) (Care or Supervision order) [1993] 2 FLR 423,
R v LB Brent ex parte S [1994] 1 FLR 203,
R v LB Barnet ex parte B [1994] 1 FLR 592,
Re W (minors) (Removal from Jurisdiction) [1994] 1 FLR 842,
Re H (a minor) (Adoption Proceedings) [1994] 2 FLR 437,
Re W (Wardship: discharge: publicity) [1995] 2 FLR 466,
Re E (Parental responsibility: blood tests) [1995] 1 FLR 392,
Re M (Care: Contact: Grandmother's Application) [1995] 2 FLR 81,
Re C (a minor) (Grandfather's application) [1997] Fam Law 456,
Re D (abduction: aquiescence) [1998] I FLR 686

JANE HOYAL is a founder member of Chambers, and Head of the 20 strong family law team. She writes articles and reviews for various publications including *Family Law*, *Legal Action*, *Childright*, *Representing Children*, and the *Association of Lawyers for Children*. She has advised the media and appeared in some TV and radio documentaries. She writes legal submissions in respect of family law-related issues and proof-reads some legal publications and DoH sponsored research. She is committed to the implementation of equality throughout the legal system. Jane lives in Kent with her husband and their three sons.

HOYLE MARK STANLEY WADIH

1 Gray's Inn Square
1st Floor, London WC1R 5AG,
Telephone: 0171 405 3000
E-mail: clerks@onegrays.demon.co.uk
Call date: July 1978, Inner Temple
Qualifications: [BA,PhD,ACIArb, MBIM]

HUBBARD MARK IAIN

1 New Square
Ground Floor, Lincoln's Inn, London
WC2A 3SA, Telephone: 0171 405 0884/5/6/7
E-mail: 1newsquare@compuserve.com
Call date: Nov 1991, Middle Temple

HUBBARD MICHAEL JOSEPH QC (1985)

1 Paper Bldgs
1st Floor, Temple, London EC4Y 7EP,
Telephone: 0171 353 3728/4953
Call date: May 1972, Gray's Inn
Recorder

HUBBLE BENEDICT JOHN WAKELIN

2 Crown Office Row
2nd Floor, Temple, London EC4Y 7HJ,
Telephone: 0171 797 8000
Call date: Nov 1992, Middle Temple
Qualifications: [BA (Hons), Dip in Law]

HUCKLE THEODORE DAVID

33 Park Place
Cardiff CF1 3BA, Telephone: 01222 233313
Call date: July 1985, Lincoln's Inn
Qualifications: [BA, LLM (Cantab)]

HUDA MISS ABIDA ALIA JEHAN

8 King's Bench Walk
2nd Floor, Temple, London EC4Y 7DU,
Telephone: 0171 797 8888
8 King's Bench Walk North
1 Park Square East, Leeds LS1 2NE,
Telephone: 0113 2439797
Call date: Nov 1989, Middle Temple
Qualifications: [LLB Hons]

HUDA SHAMSUL

1 Wensley Avenue
Woodford Green, Essex IG8 9HE,
Telephone: 0181 505 9259
9 King's Bench Walk
Basement, Temple, London EC4Y 7DX,
Telephone: 0171 353 9564
E-mail: jvlee@btinternet.com
Call date: July 1976, Lincoln's Inn
Qualifications: [MA]

HUDSON ANTHONY SEAN

Doughty Street Chambers
11 Doughty Street, London WC1N 2PG,
Telephone: 0171 404 1313
E-mail: doughty_street@compuserve.com
Call date: Nov 1996, Middle Temple
Qualifications: [LLB (Hons)(Exon)]

HUDSON CHRISTOPHER JOHN

Deans Court Chambers
Cumberland House Crown Square, Manchester
M3 3HA, Telephone: 0161 834 4097
E-mail: deanscourt@compuserve.com
Deans Court Chambers
41-43 Market Place, Preston PR1 1AH,
Telephone: 01772 555163
E-mail: deanscourt@compuserve.com
Call date: May 1987, Lincoln's Inn
Qualifications: [MA (Oxon)]

HUDSON MISS ELISABETH HELEN

3 Paper Bldgs
1st Floor, Temple, London EC4Y 7EU,
Telephone: 0171 583 8055
E-mail: london@3paper.com
20 Lorne Park Road
Bournemouth BH1 1JN,
Telephone: 01202 292102 (5 Lines)
4 St Peter Street
Winchester SO23 8OW,
Telephone: 01962 868884
Call date: Nov 1987, Gray's Inn
Qualifications: [LLB (Bucks)]

HUDSON MS EMMA CAROLYN VAUGHAN

One Garden Court
Ground Floor, Temple, London EC4Y 9BJ,
Telephone: 0171 797 7900
Call date: Feb 1995, Inner Temple
Qualifications: [MA (Edinburgh), CPE (Lond)]

HUDSON MISS KATHRYN JANE

14 Gray's Inn Square
Gray's Inn, London WC1R 5JP,
Telephone: 0171 242 0858
E-mail: 100712.2134@compuserve.com
Call date: July 1981, Middle Temple
Qualifications: [LLB (Bris)]

HUDSON MISS RACHEL SOPHIA MARGARET

Trinity Chambers
9-12 Trinity Chare, Quayside, Newcastle Upon
Tyne NE1 3DF, Telephone: 0191 232 1927
Call date: July 1985, Middle Temple
Qualifications: [LLB (Lond)]

HUFFER THOMAS IAN

38 Young Street
Manchester M3 3FT,
Telephone: 0161 833 0489
E-mail: clerks@young-st-chambers.com
Call date: Nov 1979, Gray's Inn
Qualifications: [MA (Oxon)]

HUFFORD MISS VICTORIA RACHEL

Assize Court Chambers
14 Small Street, Bristol BS1 1DE,
Telephone: 0117 9264587
Call date: Oct 1994, Gray's Inn
Qualifications: [BA]

HUGH-JONES GEORGE

3 Serjeants Inn
London EC4Y 1BQ,
Telephone: 0171 353 5537
E-mail: available upon request
Call date: Nov 1983, Middle Temple
Qualifications: [MA (Cantab), Dip Law]

HUGHES ADRIAN WARWICK

4 Pump Court
Temple, London EC4Y 7AN,
Telephone: 0171 353 2656/9
E-mail: 4_pump_court@compuserve.com
Call date: July 1984, Middle Temple
Qualifications: [MA (Oxon)]

HUGHES MISS ANNA GABRIEL

Wilberforce Chambers
8 New Square, Lincoln's Inn, London
WC2A 3QP, Telephone: 0171 306 0102
E-mail: chambers@wilberforce.co.uk
Call date: Apr 1978, Lincoln's Inn
Qualifications: [BA (Cantab)]

HUGHES DR CONSTANCE MARY

46/48 Essex Street
London WC2R 3GH,
Telephone: 0171 583 8899
Call date: Oct 1994, Inner Temple
Qualifications: [BA (Hull), MPhil (Notts), PhD,
CPE (Middx)]

HUGHES DAVID LLOYD

2 Gray's Inn Square Chambers
2nd Floor, Gray's Inn, London WC1R 5AA,
Telephone: 0171 242 0328/071 405 1317
E-mail: clerks@2gis.co.uk
Call date: July 1980, Inner Temple
Qualifications: [LLB (Hull)]

D

D

HUGHES DERMOT FRANCIS

Paradise Square Chambers
26 Paradise Square, Sheffield S1 2DE,
Telephone: 0114 2738951
Call date: Nov 1993, Gray's Inn
Qualifications: [LLB, LLM]

HUGHES GARETH DUNCAN

1 Gray's Inn Square
1st Floor, London WC1R 5AG,
Telephone: 0171 405 3000
E-mail: clerks@onegrays.demon.co.uk
Call date: Nov 1985, Gray's Inn
Qualifications: [LLB (Lond)]

HUGHES HYWEL TUDOR

30 Park Place
Cardiff CF1 3BA, Telephone: 01222 398421
E-mail: 100757.1456@compuserve.com
Call date: Oct 1995, Gray's Inn
Qualifications: [LLB (Wales)]

HUGHES IAIN HAMILTON-DOUGLAS QC (1996)

2 Crown Office Row
2nd Floor, Temple, London EC4Y 7HJ,
Telephone: 0171 797 8000
Call date: July 1974, Inner Temple
Qualifications: [LLB]

HUGHES IGNATIUS LOYOLA

Albion Chambers
Broad Street, Bristol BS1 1DR,
Telephone: 0117 9272144
Call date: Apr 1986, Middle Temple
Qualifications: [LLB (N'Castle)]

HUGHES MISS JUDITH CAROLINE ANNE QC (1994)

1 Mitre Ct Bldgs
Ground Floor, Temple, London EC4Y 7BS,
Telephone: 0171 797 7070
Call date: July 1974, Inner Temple
Recorder
Qualifications: [LLB]

HUGHES MISS KATHRYN ANN

Iscoed Chambers
86 St Helen's Road, Swansea SA1 4BQ,
Telephone: 01792 652988/9/330
Call date: Nov 1992, Inner Temple
Qualifications: [LLB (Bris)]

HUGHES LEIGHTON ALEXANDER

Newport Chambers
12 Clytha Park Road, Newport, Gwent
NP9 47L, Telephone: 01633 267403/255855
Call date: July 1989, Inner Temple
Qualifications: [LLB Hons]

HUGHES MISS MARY JOSEPHINE

Chambers of Lord Goodhart QC
Ground Floor 3 New Square, Lincoln's Inn,
London WC2A 3RS,
Telephone: 0171 405 5577
E-mail: law@threenewsquare.demon.co.uk
Call date: Feb 1995, Gray's Inn
Qualifications: [BA (L'pool)]

HUGHES MRS MELANIE CATHERINE

3 Paper Bldgs
1st Floor, Temple, London EC4Y 7EU,
Telephone: 0171 583 8055
E-mail: london@3paper.com
20 Lorne Park Road
Bournemouth BH1 1JN,
Telephone: 01202 292102 (5 Lines)
1 Alfred Street
High Street, Oxford OX1 4EH,
Telephone: 01865 793736
Call date: Nov 1995, Middle Temple
Qualifications: [BA (Hons)(W.Indies)]

HUGHES MISS MERYL ELIZABETH

Fenners Chambers
3 Madingley Road, Cambridge CB3 OEE,
Telephone: 01223 368761
Fenners Chambers
8-12 Priestgate, Peterborough PE1 1JA,
Telephone: 01733 62030
Call date: Nov 1987, Gray's Inn
Qualifications: [LLB (Leeds)]

HUGHES PETER THOMAS QC (1993)

3 Paper Bldgs
1st Floor, Temple, London EC4Y 7EU,
Telephone: 0171 583 8055
E-mail: london@3paper.com
40 King Street
Chester CH1 2AH, Telephone: 01244 323886
20 Lorne Park Road
Bournemouth BH1 1JN,
Telephone: 01202 292102 (5 Lines)
Call date: July 1971, Gray's Inn
Qualifications: [LLB (Hons)(Bris), Tribunals]

HUGHES MISS RACHEL

Peel House Chambers
Ground Floor, Peel House 5 Harrington Street,
Liverpool L2 9QA, Telephone: 0151 236 4321
Call date: Nov 1995, Gray's Inn
Qualifications: [BA]

HUGHES ROBERT PHILIP

40 King Street
Chester CH1 2AH, Telephone: 01244 323886
Call date: Nov 1971, Gray's Inn
Recorder

HUGHES SIMON DAVID

Keating Chambers
10 Essex Street, Outer Temple, London
WC2R 3AA, Telephone: 0171 544 2600
Call date: Nov 1995, Gray's Inn
Qualifications: [BA]

HUGHES SIMON HENRY WARD

13 King's Bench Walk
1st Floor, Temple, London EC4Y 7EN,
Telephone: 0171 353 7204
E-mail: clerks@13kbw.law.co.uk
King's Bench Chambers
32 Beaumont Street, Oxford OX1 2NP,
Telephone: 01865 311066
E-mail: clerks@kbc-oxford.law.co.uk
Call date: July 1974, Inner Temple
Qualifications: [BA (Cantab)]

HUGHES STANLEY GEORGE

5 Paper Bldgs
1st Floor, Temple, London EC4Y 7HB,
Telephone: 0171 583 6117
E-mail: clerks@5-paperbuildings.law.co.uk
Call date: July 1971, Lincoln's Inn

HUGHES THOMAS MERFYN QC (1994)

Goldsmith Building
1st Floor, Temple, London EC4Y 7BL,
Telephone: 0171 353 7881
E-mail: clerks@goldsmith-building.law.co.uk
40 King Street
Chester CH1 2AH, Telephone: 01244 323886
Call date: Nov 1971, Inner Temple
Recorder
Qualifications: [LLB (L'pool)]

HUGHES WILLIAM LLOYD

9-12 Bell Yard
London WC2A 2LF,
Telephone: 0171 400 1800
Call date: Nov 1989, Gray's Inn
Qualifications: [BSc (Leic)]

HUGHES YWAIN GWYDION

9 Park Place
Cardiff CF1 3DP, Telephone: 01222 382731
Call date: Nov 1994, Gray's Inn
Qualifications: [LLB (Wales)]

HULL LESLIE DAVID

9 St John Street
Manchester M3 4DN,
Telephone: 0161 955 9000
E-mail: ninesjs@gconnect.com
Call date: Nov 1972, Middle Temple
Recorder
Qualifications: [MA (Oxon)]

HULME GRAHAM ERNEST

4 King's Bench Walk
Ground/First Floor, Temple, London
EC4Y 7DL, Telephone: 0171 822 8822
E-mail: 4kbw@barristersatlaw.com
Call date: Nov 1977, Lincoln's Inn
Qualifications: [LLB (Leeds)]

HULME JOHN TRELAWNEY STEWART

Goldsmith Chambers
Ground Floor Goldsmith Building, Temple,
London EC4Y 7BL,
Telephone: 0171 353 6802/3/4/5
E-mail: celiamonksfield@btinternet.com
Call date: Nov 1983, Middle Temple
Qualifications: [BSC, Dip Law]

D

HUMBERSTONE MRS PEARL EDITH

Verulam Chambers
Peer House 8-14 Verulam Street, Gray's Inn,
London WC1X 8LZ,
Telephone: 0171 813 2400
Call date: Nov 1987, Middle Temple
Qualifications: [LLB]

HUMPHREYS MS JACQUELINE LOUISE

St John's Chambers
Small Street, Bristol BS1 1DW,
Telephone: 0117 9213456/298514
E-mail: clerks@stjohns.uk.com
Call date: Oct 1994, Lincoln's Inn
Qualifications: [BA (Hons)]

HUMPHREYS MISS JANE CHARLOTTE

New Court
Temple, London EC4Y 9BE,
Telephone: 0171 583 5123/0171 583 0510
Call date: Oct 1990, Inner Temple
Qualifications: [BA (Newc), Dip Law]

HUMPHREYS RICHARD WILLIAM

4-5 Gray's Inn Square
Ground Floor, Gray's Inn, London WC1R 5AY,
Telephone: 0171 404 5252
E-mail: chambers@4-5graysinnsquare.co.uk
Call date: July 1986, Inner Temple
Qualifications: [LLB (Notts), LLM (Cantab)]

HUMPHRIES DAVID JOHN

28 St John Street
Manchester M3 4DJ,
Telephone: 0161 834 8418
E-mail: clerk@28stjohnst.co.uk
Call date: July 1988, Middle Temple
Qualifications: [LLB (Hons)]

HUMPHRIES MICHAEL JOHN

2 Mitre Ct Bldgs
2nd Floor, Temple, London EC4Y 7BX,
Telephone: 0171 583 1380
Call date: July 1982, Inner Temple
Qualifications: [LLB (Leic)]

HUMPHRIES PAUL BENEDICT

Deans Court Chambers
Cumberland House Crown Square, Manchester
M3 3HA, Telephone: 0161 834 4097
E-mail: deanscourt@compuserve.com
Deans Court Chambers
41-43 Market Place, Preston PR1 1AH,
Telephone: 01772 555163
E-mail: deanscourt@compuserve.com
Call date: Nov 1986, Middle Temple
Qualifications: [BA (Oxon)]

HUMPHRY RICHARD MICHAEL

28 St John Street
Manchester M3 4DJ,
Telephone: 0161 834 8418
E-mail: clerk@28stjohnst.co.uk
Call date: July 1972, Gray's Inn
Qualifications: [MA (Cantab), LLB]

HUMPHRYES MISS JANE CAROLE

3 Raymond Buildings
Gray's Inn, London WC1R 5BH,
Telephone: 0171 831 3833
E-mail: chambers@threeraymond.demon.co.uk
Call date: July 1983, Middle Temple
Qualifications: [BA (Kent)]

HUNGERFORD WALTER GUY BECHER

1 Harcourt Bldgs
2nd Floor, Temple, London EC4Y 9DA,
Telephone: 0171 353 9421/9151
Call date: Nov 1971, Middle Temple

HUNJAN SATINDER PAL SINGH

5 Fountain Court
Steelhouse Lane, Birmingham B4 6DR,
Telephone: 0121 606 0500
Call date: July 1984, Gray's Inn
Qualifications: [LLB (B'ham)]

HUNT MISS ALISON JANET

St Paul's House
5th Floor 23 Park Square South, Leeds
LS1 2ND, Telephone: 0113 2455866
Call date: July 1986, Gray's Inn
Qualifications: [BA (Cantab)]

HUNT DAVID RODERIC NOTLEY QC (1987)

2 Hare Court
Ground Floor, Temple, London EC4Y 7BH,
Telephone: 0171 583 1770
E-mail: 2_Hare_Court@link.org
Call date: July 1969, Gray's Inn
Recorder
Qualifications: [MA (Hons) (Cantab)]

HUNT JAMES QC (1987)

36 Bedford Row
London WC1R 4JH,
Telephone: 0171 421 8000
E-mail: 36bedfordrow@link.org
Call date: July 1968, Gray's Inn
Recorder
Qualifications: [MA (Oxon)]

HUNT MURRAY ROBERT

4-5 Gray's Inn Square
Ground Floor, Gray's Inn, London WC1R 5AY,
Telephone: 0171 404 5252
E-mail: chambers@4-5graysinnsquare.co.uk
Call date: Nov 1992, Middle Temple
Qualifications: [BA (Hons), BCL, LLM]

HUNT PETER JOHN

2 Mitre Ct Bldgs
1st Floor, Temple, London EC4Y 7BX,
Telephone: 0171 353 1353
Door Tenant
Call date: Nov 1964, Lincoln's Inn
Qualifications: [MA (Cantab)]

HUNT RICHARD MARK

15 Winckley Square
Preston PR1 3JJ, Telephone: 01772 252828
E-mail: clerks@winckleysq.demon.co.uk
Call date: July 1985, Lincoln's Inn
Qualifications: [LLB]

HUNT RODERICK IRWIN

Fountain Chambers
Cleveland Business Centre 1 Watson Street,
Middlesbrough TS1 2RQ,
Telephone: 01642 217037
Call date: July 1981, Middle Temple
Qualifications: [MA (Cantab)]

HUNT STEPHEN

4 Stone Bldgs
Ground Floor, Lincoln's Inn, London
WC2A 3XT, Telephone: 0171 242 5524
E-mail: d.goddard@4stonebuildings.law.co.uk
Call date: July 1968, Lincoln's Inn
Qualifications: [MA (Oxon)]

HUNT MISS VICTORIA KATHARINE

Queen Elizabeth Bldg
2nd Floor, Temple, London EC4Y 9BS,
Telephone: 0171 797 7837
Call date: Nov 1995, Gray's Inn
Qualifications: [BA]

HUNT WILFRED

Chambers of Raana Sheikh
Gray's Inn Chambers, Gray's Inn, London
WC1R, Telephone: 0171 831 5344
E-mail: s.mcblain@btinternet.com
Call date: July 1979, Gray's Inn
Qualifications: [LLB (Lond)]

HUNTER (JAMES) MARTIN HUGH

Essex Court Chambers
24 Lincoln's Inn Fields, London WC2A 3ED,
Telephone: 0171 813 8000
E-mail: clerksroom@essexcourt-chambers.co.uk
Call date: May 1994, Lincoln's Inn
Qualifications: [BA (Cantab)]

HUNTER ANDREW MICHAEL

2 Hare Court
Ground Floor, Temple, London EC4Y 7BH,
Telephone: 0171 583 1770
E-mail: 2_Hare_Court@link.org
Call date: Oct 1993, Middle Temple
Qualifications: [BA (Hons)(Oxon)]

HUNTER ANTHONY CHARLES BRYAN

5 Pump Court
Ground Floor, Temple, London EC4Y 7AP,
Telephone: 0171 353 2532
E-mail: fivepump@netcomuk.co.uk
Call date: Nov 1962, Inner Temple
Qualifications: [BA (Oxon)]

D

HUNTER MISS CAROLINE MARGARET

Arden Chambers
27 John Street, London WC1N 2BL,
Telephone: 0171 242 4244
Call date: Nov 1985, Middle Temple
Qualifications: [BA (Oxon)]

HUNTER GEOFFREY MARTIN

67a Westgate Road
Newcastle Upon Tyne NE1 1SQ,
Telephone: 0191 261 4407/2329785
Call date: Feb 1979, Gray's Inn
Qualifications: [LLB (Newc)]

HUNTER IAN GERALD ADAMSON QC (1980)

Essex Court Chambers
24 Lincoln's Inn Fields, London WC2A 3ED,
Telephone: 0171 813 8000
E-mail: clerksroom@essexcourt-chambers.co.uk
Call date: Nov 1967, Inner Temple
Recorder
Qualifications: [MA, LLB (Cantab), LLM (Harvard)]

HUNTER JOHN DAVID

2 Pump Court
1st Floor, Temple, London EC4Y 7AH,
Telephone: 0171 353 5597
1 Gray's Inn Square
Ground Floor, London WC1R 5AA,
Telephone: 0171 405 8946/7/8
Call date: Feb 1991, Lincoln's Inn
Qualifications: [LLB (Buck'ham)]

HUNTER MACK ROBERT

1 Crown Office Row
2nd Floor, Temple, London EC4Y 7HH,
Telephone: 0171 797 7111
Call date: Nov 1979, Gray's Inn
Qualifications: [MA (Oxon)]

HUNTER MUIR VANE SKERRETT QC (1965)

3/4 South Square
Gray's Inn, London WC1R 5HP,
Telephone: 0171 696 9900
E-mail: clerks@southsquare.com
Call date: Nov 1938, Gray's Inn
Qualifications: [MA, MRI]

HUNTER MISS SUSAN CLARE

Pump Court Chambers
Upper Ground Floor 3 Pump Court, Temple,
London EC4Y 7AJ, Telephone: 0171 353 0711
Pump Court Chambers
31 Southgate Street, Winchester SO23 8EE,
Telephone: 01962 868161
Call date: July 1985, Inner Temple
Qualifications: [MA (Cantab) Dip Law]

HUNTER WILLIAM EDWARD HENRY

Veritas Chambers
33 Corn Street, Bristol BS1 1HT,
Telephone: 0117 930 8802
Call date: July 1982, Gray's Inn
Qualifications: [BA (Hons)]

HUNTER WILLIAM QUIGLEY

1 Serjeants' Inn
5th Floor Fleet Street, Temple, London
EC4Y 1LL, Telephone: 0171 415 6666
E-mail: no1serjeantsinn@btinternet.com
Call date: July 1972, Inner Temple
Qualifications: [MA (Cantab)]

HUNTER MISS WINIFRED

6 Gray's Inn Square
Ground Floor, Gray's Inn, London WC1R 5AZ,
Telephone: 0171 242 1052
Call date: Nov 1990, Middle Temple
Qualifications: [LLB (Lond)]

HUNTER WINSTON RONALD

28 St John Street
Manchester M3 4DJ,
Telephone: 0161 834 8418
E-mail: clerk@28stjohnst.co.uk
Call date: July 1985, Lincoln's Inn
Qualifications: [LLB (Leeds)]

HURD JAMES ROBERT

St James's Chambers
68 Quay Street, Manchester M3 3EJ,
Telephone: 0161 834 7000
E-mail: 106241.2625@compuserve.com
Call date: Oct 1994, Gray's Inn
Qualifications: [LLB]

HURD MARK DUNSDON

New Walk Chambers
27 New Walk, Leicester LE1 6TE,
Telephone: 0116 2559144
Call date: Feb 1993, Gray's Inn
Qualifications: [LLB]

HURLOCK LUGARD JOHN

3 Hare Court
1st Floor, Temple, London EC4Y 7BJ,
Telephone: 0171 353 7561
Call date: Oct 1993, Gray's Inn
Qualifications: [LLB (Coventry)]

HURST ANDREW ROBERT

23 Essex Street
London WC2R 3AS,
Telephone: 0171 413 0353/353 3533
E-mail: clerks@essexstreet23.demon.co.uk
Call date: Nov 1992, Inner Temple
Qualifications: [BA (Oxon)]

HURST BRIAN

17 Bedford Row
London WC1R 4EB,
Telephone: 0171 831 7314
E-mail: IBoard7314@AOL.com
Call date: July 1983, Middle Temple
Qualifications: [MA (Oxon)]

HURST MARTIN RICHARD JOHN

4 King's Bench Walk
Ground/First Floor, Temple, London
EC4Y 7DL, Telephone: 0171 822 8822
E-mail: 4kbw@barristersatlaw.com
Call date: July 1985, Middle Temple
Qualifications: [LLB (L'pool)]

HURTLEY MISS DIANE ELAINE

Furnival Chambers
32 Furnival Street, London EC4A 1JQ,
Telephone: 0171 405 3232
E-mail: clerks@furnivallaw.co.uk
Call date: Oct 1990, Gray's Inn
Qualifications: [LLB]

HURWORTH MISS JILLIAN MARY

10 King's Bench Walk
Ground Floor, Temple, London EC4Y 7EB,
Telephone: 0171 353 7742
E-mail: 10kbw@lineone.net
Call date: Oct 1993, Inner Temple
Qualifications: [BA (Cantab)]

HUSAIN SYED RAZA

2 Garden Court
1st Floor, Middle Temple, London EC4Y 9BL,
Telephone: 0171 353 1633
E-mail: barristers@2gardenct.law.co.uk
Call date: Nov 1993, Middle Temple
Qualifications: [BA (Hons)(Oxon), CPE
(London), LLM (Lond)]

HUSCROFT RICHARD MICHAEL

Westgate Chambers
144 High Street, Lewes, East Sussex BN7 1XT,
Telephone: 01273 480510
1 Dr Johnson's Bldgs
Ground Floor, Temple, London EC4Y 7AX,
Telephone: 0171 353 9328
Dr Johnson's Chambers
The Atrium Court Apex Plaza, Reading
RG1 1AX, Telephone: 01734 254221
Call date: Nov 1990, Middle Temple
Qualifications: [BA (Oxon), Dip Law (PCL)]

HUSEYIN MARTIN TREVOR

14 Tooks Court
Cursitor St, London EC4A 1LB,
Telephone: 0171 405 8828
E-mail: clerks @tooks.law.co.uk
Call date: Nov 1988, Inner Temple
Qualifications: [BA (Sussex),Dip Law]

HUSKINSON GEORGE NICHOLAS NEVIL

4-5 Gray's Inn Square
Ground Floor, Gray's Inn, London WC1R 5AY,
Telephone: 0171 404 5252
E-mail: chambers@4-5graysinnsquare.co.uk
Call date: July 1971, Gray's Inn
Assistant Recorder
Qualifications: [MA (Cantab)]

D

HUSSAIN MISS FRIDA KHANAM

17 Carlton Crescent
Southampton SO15 2XR,
Telephone: 01703 320320
E-mail: km@bar-17cc.demon.co.uk
Call date: Oct 1995, Inner Temple
Qualifications: [LLB (Hons), (Huddersfield)]

HUSSAIN MUKHTAR QC (1992)

Lincoln House Chambers
5th Floor Lincoln House, 1 Brazennose Street,
Manchester M2 5EL,
Telephone: 0161 832 5701
E-mail: LincolnHouseChambers@link.org
Call date: July 1971, Middle Temple
Recorder

HUSSEIN TIMUR

Phoenix Chambers
First Floor Gray's Inn Chambers, Gray's Inn,
London WC1R 5JA, Telephone: 0171 404 7888
5 Essex Court
1st Floor, Temple, London EC4Y 9AH,
Telephone: 0171 410 2000
Call date: Oct 1993, Inner Temple
Qualifications: [LLB]

HUSSEY MISS ANN ELIZABETH

29 Bedford Row Chambers
London WC1R 4HE,
Telephone: 0171 831 2626
Call date: July 1981, Middle Temple
Qualifications: [BA (Hons)]

HUSTON GRAHAM MARTIN

4 King's Bench Walk
Ground/First Floor, Temple, London
EC4Y 7DL, Telephone: 0171 822 8822
E-mail: 4kbw@barristersatlaw.com
Call date: Feb 1991, Inner Temple
Qualifications: [LLB (PCL)]

HUTCHINGS MARTIN ANTHONY

199 Strand
London WC2R 1DR,
Telephone: 0171 379 9779
E-mail: chambers@199strand.co.uk
Call date: Feb 1986, Middle Temple
Qualifications: [MA (Oxon)]

HUTCHINGS MATTHEW HOWARD OLSEN

22 Old Bldgs
Lincoln's Inn, London WC2A 3UJ,
Telephone: 0171 831 0222
Call date: Nov 1993, Inner Temple
Qualifications: [BA (Oxon), LLB (City)]

HUTCHINSON COLIN THOMAS

2 Garden Court
1st Floor, Middle Temple, London EC4Y 9BL,
Telephone: 0171 353 1633
E-mail: barristers@2gardenct.law.co.uk
Call date: Oct 1990, Middle Temple
Qualifications: [LLB (Hons)]

HUTT MICHAEL ARTHUR

6 Fountain Court
Steelhouse Lane, Birmingham B4 6DR,
Telephone: 0121 233 3282
Call date: Nov 1968, Middle Temple
Qualifications: [BA, LLB (Cantab)]

HUTTON ALEXANDER FORBES

6 Pump Court
Ground Floor, Temple, London EC4Y 7AR,
Telephone: 0171 583 6013/2510
Call date: Oct 1992, Gray's Inn
Qualifications: [B.Sc (Bris)]

HUTTON MISS CAROLINE

Enterprise Chambers
9 Old Square, Lincoln's Inn, London
WC2A 3SR, Telephone: 0171 405 9471
Enterprise Chambers
38 Park Square, Leeds LS1 2PA,
Telephone: 01132 460391
Enterprise Chambers
65 Quayside, Newcastle upon Tyne NE1 3DS,
Telephone: 0191 222 3344
Call date: Nov 1979, Middle Temple
Qualifications: [MA (Cantab)]

HUYTON BRIAN JAMES

17 Bedford Row
London WC1R 4EB,
Telephone: 0171 831 7314
E-mail: IBoard7314@AOL.com
Call date: July 1977, Inner Temple
Qualifications: [BA, LLB (Lond)]

HYAM JEREMY RUPERT DANIEL

1 Crown Office Row
Ground Floor, Temple, London EC4Y 7HH,
Telephone: 0171 797 7500
Call date: Nov 1995, Gray's Inn
Qualifications: [BA (Hons)]

HYAMS OLIVER MARKS

New Court
Temple, London EC4Y 9BE,
Telephone: 0171 583 5123/0171 583 0510
Call date: July 1989, Middle Temple
Qualifications: [LLB]

HYAMS-PARISH ANTONY ROBERT

Acre Lane Neighbourhood Chambers
30A Acre Lane, London SW2 5SG,
Telephone: 0171 274 4400
Call date: May 1995, Gray's Inn
Qualifications: [B.ED]

HYDE CHARLES GORDON

Albion Chambers
Broad Street, Bristol BS1 1DR,
Telephone: 0117 9272144
Call date: July 1988, Middle Temple
Qualifications: [LLB (Hons) (Manch)]

HYDE MISS CHRISTIANA VICTORIA MARY

14 Tooks Court
Cursitor St, London EC4A 1LB,
Telephone: 0171 405 8828
E-mail: clerks @tooks.law.co.uk
Call date: May 1982, Gray's Inn
Qualifications: [MA (Cantab)]

HYDE MS MARCIA

22 Old Bldgs
Lincoln's Inn, London WC2A 3UJ,
Telephone: 0171 831 0222
Call date: Oct 1992, Inner Temple
Qualifications: [BA (Leeds), MA, Dip Law]

HYLAND JAMES GRAHAM KEITH

Broadway House Chambers
Broadway House 9 Bank Street, Bradford,
West Yorkshire BD1 1TW,
Telephone: 01274 722560
Call date: July 1978, Inner Temple
Recorder
Qualifications: [BA]

HYMANSON MISS DEANNA SUSAN

Cobden House Chambers
19 Quay Street, Manchester M3 3HN,
Telephone: 0161 833 6000
E-mail: clerks@cobden.co.uk
Door Tenant
Call date: Feb 1988, Middle Temple
Qualifications: [LLB (Hons) (Lond)]

HYNES PAUL RICHARD

Goldsmith Chambers
Ground Floor Goldsmith Building, Temple,
London EC4Y 7BL,
Telephone: 0171 353 6802/3/4/5
E-mail: celiamonksfield@btinternet.com
Call date: Nov 1987, Lincoln's Inn
Qualifications: [BA (Hons)]

HYTNER BENET ALAN QC (1970)

22 Old Bldgs
Lincoln's Inn, London WC2A 3UJ,
Telephone: 0171 831 0222
25 Byrom Street
Manchester M3 4PF,
Telephone: 0161 829 2100
E-mail: Byromst25@aol.com
Call date: Feb 1952, Middle Temple
Qualifications: [MA (Cantab)]

IFE MISS LINDEN ELIZABETH

Enterprise Chambers
9 Old Square, Lincoln's Inn, London
WC2A 3SR, Telephone: 0171 405 9471
Enterprise Chambers
38 Park Square, Leeds LS1 2PA,
Telephone: 01132 460391
Enterprise Chambers
65 Quayside, Newcastle upon Tyne NE1 3DS,
Telephone: 0191 222 3344
Call date: Nov 1982, Middle Temple
Qualifications: [MA (Oxon)]

D

IGORI KINGSLEY IZEHIUWA

8 King's Bench Walk
2nd Floor, Temple, London EC4Y 7DU,
Telephone: 0171 797 8888
Call date: Feb 1993, Inner Temple
Qualifications: [LLB]

IHUOMAH MISS BIBIANA CHIWUBA

10 King's Bench Walk
1st Floor, Temple, London EC4Y 7EB,
Telephone: 0171 353 2501
Call date: Nov 1986, Lincoln's Inn
Qualifications: [LLB(Hons)]

ILES ADRIAN

5 Paper Bldgs
Ground Floor, Temple, London EC4Y 7HB,
Telephone: 0171 583 9275/583 4555
E-mail: 5paper@link.org
Call date: July 1980, Inner Temple
Qualifications: [MA (Cantab)]

ILES DAVID

5 Fountain Court
Steelhouse Lane, Birmingham B4 6DR,
Telephone: 0121 606 0500
Call date: July 1977, Inner Temple
Qualifications: [LLB (Lond)]

ILLINGWORTH STEPHEN JOHN

Mitre House Chambers
Mitre House 44 Fleet Street, London
EC4Y 1BN, Telephone: 0171 583 8233
Call date: Feb 1993, Gray's Inn
Qualifications: [LLB (Hons)]

IMONA-RUSSEL ALFRED OMOAFENA

Essex House Chambers
Essex House 375-377 Stratford High Street,
Stratford, London E15 4QZ,
Telephone: 0181 536 1077
Call date: Nov 1992, Inner Temple
Qualifications: [LLB (Lond)]

INFIELD PAUL LOUIS

5 Paper Bldgs
Ground Floor, Temple, London EC4Y 7HB,
Telephone: 0171 583 9275/583 4555
E-mail: 5paper@link.org
Call date: July 1980, Inner Temple
Qualifications: [LLB (Sheff)]

INGHAM MISS ELIZABETH CLAIRE

Walnut House
63 St. David's Hill, Exeter, Devon EX4 4DW,
Telephone: 01392 279751
E-mail: 106627.2451@compuserve.com
36 Bedford Row
London WC1R 4JH,
Telephone: 0171 421 8000
E-mail: 36bedfordrow@link.org
Door Tenant
Call date: Nov 1989, Middle Temple
Qualifications: [BA (Hons) (Oxon)]

INGHAM RICHARD LEE

32 Park Place
Cardiff CF1 3BA, Telephone: 01222 397364
Call date: Nov 1994, Lincoln's Inn
Qualifications: [LLB (Hons)(B'ham)]

INGLIS ALAN

One Garden Court
Ground Floor, Temple, London EC4Y 9BJ,
Telephone: 0171 797 7900
Call date: July 1989, Middle Temple
Qualifications: [BA (Essex), MA (Warw), Dip
Law, C.Q.S.W]

INGLIS-JONES NIGEL JOHN
QC (1982)

35 Essex Street
Temple, London WC2R 3AR,
Telephone: 0171 353 6381
Call date: June 1959, Inner Temple
Recorder
Qualifications: [BA (Oxon)]

INGRAM JONATHAN ANTONY

Francis Taylor Bldg
Ground Floor, Temple, London EC4Y 7BY,
Telephone: 0171 353 7768/7769/2711
Call date: July 1984, Inner Temple
Qualifications: [BA (Lond)]

INGRAM NIGEL COLQUHOUN

3 Hare Court
1st Floor, Temple, London EC4Y 7BJ,
Telephone: 0171 353 7561
Call date: July 1972, Inner Temple

INMAN MELBOURNE DONALD

1 Fountain Court
Steelhouse Lane, Birmingham B4 6DR,
Telephone: 0121 236 5721
Call date: July 1979, Inner Temple
Assistant Recorder
Qualifications: [MA (Oxon)]

INSALL RICHARD STUART

65-67 King Street
Leicester LE1 6RP, Telephone: 0116 2547710
Call date: Nov 1952, Gray's Inn

INWARD MS LOUISE JANE

Sussex Chambers
9 Old Steine, Brighton BN1 1FJ,
Telephone: 01273 607953
Call date: Nov 1995, Middle Temple
Qualifications: [LLB (Hons)]

IOANNOU MISS ANASTASIA

18 St John Street
Manchester M3 4EA,
Telephone: 0161 278 1800
Call date: July 1982, Inner Temple
Qualifications: [LLB Hons]

IQBAL ABDUL SHAFFAQ

10 Park Square
Leeds LS1 2LH, Telephone: 0113 2455438
E-mail: chambers@bandit.legend.co.uk
Call date: Oct 1994, Gray's Inn
Qualifications: [B.Pharm (Brad), Dip Law]

IRELAND MISS PENELOPE JANE

Wessex Chambers
48 Queens Road, Reading, Berkshire
RG1 4BD, Telephone: 01734 568856
E-mail: wessexchambers@compuserve.com
Call date: Oct 1996, Gray's Inn
Qualifications: [LLB (Bris)]

IRO AUGUSTINE OKEVURUMBA

First National Building
2nd Floor 24 Fenwick Street, Liverpool
L2 7NE, Telephone: 0151 236 2098
Call date: May 1995, Gray's Inn
Qualifications: [LLB]

IRONFIELD MISS JANET RUTH

Deans Court Chambers
Cumberland House Crown Square, Manchester
M3 3HA, Telephone: 0161 834 4097
E-mail: deanscourt@compuserve.com
Deans Court Chambers
41-43 Market Place, Preston PR1 1AH,
Telephone: 01772 555163
E-mail: deanscourt@compuserve.com
Call date: Oct 1992, Gray's Inn
Qualifications: [BA]

IRONSIDE JULIAN C

St John's Chambers
Small Street, Bristol BS1 1DW,
Telephone: 0117 9213456/298514
E-mail: clerks@stjohns.uk.com
Call date: Nov 1985, Gray's Inn
Qualifications: [BA (Cantab)]

IRVIN PETER

Brick Court Chambers
15/19 Devereux Court, London WC2R 3JJ,
Telephone: 0171 583 0777
E-mail: (surname)@brickcourt.demon.co.uk
Call date: July 1972, Gray's Inn
Qualifications: [BA (Oxon)]

IRVINE MICHAEL FRASER

1 Crown Office Row
3rd Floor, Temple, London EC4Y 7HH,
Telephone: 0171 583 9292
E-mail: onecor@link.org
Call date: Feb 1964, Inner Temple
Qualifications: [BA (Oxon)]

D

IRVING EDWARD

East Anglian Chambers
Gresham House 5 Museum Street, Ipswich
IP1 1HQ, Telephone: 01473 214481
East Anglian Chambers
57 London Street, Norwich NR2 1HL,
Telephone: 01603 617351
East Anglian Chambers
Sanders House 52 North Hill, Colchester
CO1 1PY, Telephone: 01206 572756
Call date: Feb 1976, Inner Temple
Qualifications: [BA (Oxon)]

IRVING MISS GILLIAN

9 St John Street
Manchester M3 4DN,
Telephone: 0161 955 9000
E-mail: ninesjs@gconnect.com
Call date: July 1984, Inner Temple
Qualifications: [BA (Hons)]

IRWIN STEPHEN JOHN QC (1997)

Doughty Street Chambers
11 Doughty Street, London WC1N 2PG,
Telephone: 0171 404 1313
E-mail: doughty_street@compuserve.com
Call date: Nov 1976, Gray's Inn
Qualifications: [BA (Hons) (Cantab)]

ISAAC NICHOLAS DUDLEY

199 Strand
London WC2R 1DR,
Telephone: 0171 379 9779
E-mail: chambers@199strand.co.uk
Call date: Oct 1993, Gray's Inn
Qualifications: [BA (Leeds)]

ISAACS BARRY RUSSELL

3/4 South Square
Gray's Inn, London WC1R 5HP,
Telephone: 0171 696 9900
E-mail: clerks@southsquare.com
Call date: Nov 1994, Inner Temple
Qualifications: [MA (Oxon), MA (Harvard),
ASA]

ISAACS PAUL RICHARD

9 Woodhouse Square
Leeds LS3 1AD, Telephone: 0113 2451986
Call date: Feb 1974, Middle Temple
Qualifications: [MA (Cantab)]

ISAACS STUART LINDSAY QC (1991)

4-5 Gray's Inn Square
Ground Floor, Gray's Inn, London WC1R 5AY,
Telephone: 0171 404 5252
E-mail: chambers@4-5graysinnsquare.co.uk
Call date: July 1975, Lincoln's Inn
Assistant Recorder
Qualifications: [MA (Cantab), Licencie special
en, droit eur (Brussels)]

ISAACSON RICHARD QC (1997)

Exchange Chambers
Pearl Assurance House Derby Square,
Liverpool L2 9XX, Telephone: 0151 236 7747/
0458
E-mail: exchangechambers@btinternet.com
Call date: Nov 1972, Middle Temple
Qualifications: [LLB]

ISHERWOOD JOHN STANLEY

Assize Court Chambers
14 Small Street, Bristol BS1 1DE,
Telephone: 0117 9264587
Call date: July 1978, Gray's Inn
Qualifications: [MA (Cantab)]

ISHMAEL COLIN

4 Brick Court
Temple, London EC4Y 9AD,
Telephone: 0171 797 8910
Call date: Feb 1989, Lincoln's Inn
Qualifications: [BA]

ISLAM MOHAMMED NURAL

45 Ullswater Crescent
Kingston Vale, London SW15 3RG,
Telephone: 0181 546 9284
Call date: June 1959, Lincoln's Inn
Qualifications: [MA]

ISLAM-CHOUDHURY MUGNI

11 Bolt Court
London EC4A 3DQ,
Telephone: 0171 353 2300
E-mail: boltct11@aol.com
Call date: Oct 1996, Lincoln's Inn
Qualifications: [LLB (Hons)(Lond)]

ISLES MS MARY PATRICIA THERESA

1 Pump Court
Lower Ground Floor, Temple, London
EC4Y 7AB, Telephone: 0171 583 2012/
353 4341
E-mail: (name) @1pumpcourt.co.uk
Call date: Nov 1984, Inner Temple
Qualifications: [BSc, BA]

ISMAIL MISS NAZMUN NISHA

Garden Court North Chambers
2nd Floor Gregg's Building, 1 Booth Street,
Manchester M2 4DU,
Telephone: 0161 833 1774
Call date: Oct 1992, Lincoln's Inn
Qualifications: [BA(Hons)]

ISMAIL MISS ROXANNE

3/4 South Square
Gray's Inn, London WC1R 5HP,
Telephone: 0171 696 9900
E-mail: clerks@southsquare.com
Call date: Oct 1993, Lincoln's Inn
Qualifications: [LLB (Hons)(Lond)]

ISSA MISS ALEXANDRA HANNAH

1 Temple Gardens
1st Floor, Temple, London EC4Y 9BB,
Telephone: 0171 353 0407/583 1315
E-mail: clerks@1templegardens.co.uk
Call date: Nov 1993, Lincoln's Inn
Qualifications: [MA (Hons)(Oxon)]

IVENS MS JEMIMA

8 King's Bench Walk
2nd Floor, Temple, London EC4Y 7DU,
Telephone: 0171 797 8888
8 King's Bench Walk North
1 Park Square East, Leeds LS1 2NE,
Telephone: 0113 2439797
Call date: Feb 1994, Lincoln's Inn
Qualifications: [LLB (Hons)]

IVERS MICHAEL JOSEPH

Counsels' Chambers
2nd Floor 10-11 Gray's Inn Square, London
WC1R 5JD, Telephone: 0171 405 2576
Call date: Nov 1991, Middle Temple
Qualifications: [LLB Hons (Lond)]

IVES MRS ANNE ELIZABETH

3 Temple Gardens
3rd Floor, Temple, London EC4Y 9AU,
Telephone: 0171 353 0832
Independent Barristers Clerk
Room 5, 2nd Floor 15 Castle Street, Exeter,
Devon EX4 3PT, Telephone: 01392 210900
E-mail: cathedral.chambers@eclipse.co.uk
Call date: Feb 1994, Gray's Inn
Qualifications: [BSc (Econ)(Wales)]

IVIMY MS CECILIA RACHEL

11 King's Bench Walk
Temple, London EC4Y 7EQ,
Telephone: 0171 632 8500
E-mail: clerksroom@11-kbw.law.co.uk
Call date: Nov 1995, Middle Temple
Qualifications: [BA (Hons) (Oxon)]

IVORY THOMAS PETER GERARD

1 Essex Court
Ground Floor, Temple, London EC4Y 9AR,
Telephone: 0171 583 2000
E-mail: clerks@oneessexcourt.co.uk
Call date: July 1978, Lincoln's Inn
Qualifications: [MA (Cantab)]

IWI IAN DAVID

11 Stone Bldgs
1st Floor, Lincoln's Inn, London WC2A 3TG,
Telephone: 0171 404 5055
E-mail: 9stoneb@compuserve.com
Call date: Feb 1961, Gray's Inn
Qualifications: [MA (Cantab)]

IWI QUINTIN JOSEPH

2 Harcourt Bldgs
Ground Floor/Left, Temple, London
EC4Y 9DB, Telephone: 0171 583 9020
E-mail: clerks@harcourt.co.uk
Stanbrook & Henderson
2 Harcourt Bldgs 2nd Floor, Temple, London
EC4Y 9DB, Telephone: 0171 353 0101
E-mail: clerks@harcourt.co.uk
Call date: Feb 1956, Gray's Inn
Qualifications: [MA (Oxon)]

D

D

IYER SUNIL KRISHNA

2 New Street
Leicester LE1 5NA, Telephone: 0116 2625906
Call date: July 1988, Gray's Inn
Qualifications: [LLB (Dundee)]

JABATI MISS MARIA HANNAH

2 Middle Temple Lane
3rd Floor, Temple, London EC4Y 9AA,
Telephone: 0171 583 4540
Door Tenant
Call date: Nov 1986, Lincoln's Inn
Qualifications: [BA, LLM (Lond)]

JACK ADRIAN LAURENCE ROBERT

Enterprise Chambers
9 Old Square, Lincoln's Inn, London
WC2A 3SR, Telephone: 0171 405 9471
Call date: Nov 1986, Middle Temple
Qualifications: [MA(Oxon)]

JACK MISS KATRINA MABEL

Prince Henry's Chambers
17 Fleet Street, London EC4Y 1AA,
Telephone: 0171 353 1183/1190
Call date: July 1978, Lincoln's Inn

JACK SIMON MICHAEL

9 Woodhouse Square
Leeds LS3 1AD, Telephone: 0113 2451986
Call date: July 1974, Middle Temple
Recorder
Qualifications: [BA (Cantab)]

JACKLIN MISS SUSAN ELIZABETH

St John's Chambers
Small Street, Bristol BS1 1DW,
Telephone: 0117 9213456/298514
E-mail: clerks@stjohns.uk.com
Call date: Nov 1980, Inner Temple
Assistant Recorder
Qualifications: [BA (Dunelm)]

JACKSON ADRIAN PHILIP

King Charles House
Standard Hill, Nottingham NG1 6FX,
Telephone: 0115 9418851
E-mail: clerks@kch.co.uk
Call date: Oct 1990, Lincoln's Inn
Qualifications: [MA (Hons)(Cantab)]

JACKSON ANDREW FRASER

East Anglian Chambers
Sanders House 52 North Hill, Colchester
CO1 1PY, Telephone: 01206 572756
East Anglian Chambers
57 London Street, Norwich NR2 1HL,
Telephone: 01603 617351
East Anglian Chambers
Gresham House 5 Museum Street, Ipswich
IP1 1HQ, Telephone: 01473 214481
Call date: Oct 1990, Inner Temple
Qualifications: [BA (Hons)]

JACKSON ANDREW JOHN

3 Fountain Court
Steelhouse Lane, Birmingham B4 6DR,
Telephone: 0121 236 5854
Call date: July 1986, Lincoln's Inn
Qualifications: [BA (Manch), Dip Law]

JACKSON ANTHONY WARREN

3 Serjeants Inn
London EC4Y 1BQ,
Telephone: 0171 353 5537
E-mail: available upon request
Call date: Oct 1995, Inner Temple
Qualifications: [MA, M.Phil (Cantab), LLM
(Illinois)]

JACKSON DAVID

St Ive's Chambers
9 Fountain Ct, Birmingham B4 6DR,
Telephone: 0121 236 0863/0929
Call date: July 1986, Gray's Inn

JACKSON DIRIK GEORGE ALLAN

Chambers of Mr Peter Crampin QC
11 New Square, Lincoln's Inn, London
WC2A 3QB, Telephone: 0171 831 0081
E-mail: 11newsquare.co.uk
Call date: Nov 1969, Lincoln's Inn
Recorder
Qualifications: [BA, LLB (Cantab)]

Fax: 0171 405 2560;
Out of hours telephone: 0181 299 2100;
DX: 319 London, Chancery Lane;
Other comms: E-mail
djackson@netcomuk.co.uk

Types of work: Agriculture; Chancery (general);
Chancery land law; Commercial property;
Common land; Conveyancing; Directors'

disqualification; Equity, wills and trusts; Family provision; Insolvency; Landlord and tenant; Mental health; Partnerships; Pensions; Probate and administration; Professional negligence

Awards and memberships: Chancery Bar Association; Professional Negligence Bar Association; Association of Contentious Trust and Probate Specialists

Reported cases: *Hastingwood Property Ltd v Saunders Bearman Anselm Ltd*, [1991] Ch 114, 1990. Liability of solicitor as stakeholder of deposit.
Gran Gelato Ltd v Richcliff (Group) Ltd, [1992] Ch 560, 1991. Liability of landlord's solicitor for negligent misrepresentation to tenant.
Murphy v Sawyer-Hoare, [1993] 2 EGLR 61, 1992. Liability of guarantor of assignee on disclaimer of lease.
Hannaford v Smallacombe, [1994] 1 EGLR 9, 1993. Validity of notice to quit agricultural holding.
Frankland v IRC, [1997] STC 1450, 1997. Inheritance tax on distribution out of discretionary trust within three months of death.

JACKSON HUGH WOODWARD

Hardwicke Building
New Square, Lincoln's Inn, London
WC2A 3SB, Telephone: 0171 242 2523
E-mail: clerks@hardwicke.co.uk
Call date: July 1981, Middle Temple
Qualifications: [LLB Sheff]

JACKSON JOHN EDGAR

40 King Street
Manchester M2 6BA,
Telephone: 0161 832 9082
E-mail: Kingst40@aol.com
Call date: July 1970, Middle Temple

JACKSON MISS JUDITH QC (1994)

9 Old Square
Ground Floor, Lincoln's Inn, London
WC2A 3SR, Telephone: 0171 405 4682
E-mail: chambers@9oldsquare.co.uk
Call date: Nov 1975, Inner Temple
Qualifications: [LLB (Hons), LLM (Lond)]

JACKSON KEVIN ROY

Becket Chambers
17 New Dover Road, Canterbury, Kent
CT1 3AS, Telephone: 01227 786331
Call date: Nov 1984, Middle Temple
Qualifications: [BA (Hons)(Law)]

JACKSON MATTHEW DAVID EVERARD

4 Paper Bldgs
Ground Floor, Temple, London EC4Y 7EX,
Telephone: 0171 353 3366/583 7155
E-mail: clerks@4paperbuildings.com
Call date: July 1986, Middle Temple
Qualifications: [MA(Cantab)]

JACKSON NICHOLAS DAVID KINGSLEY

Adrian Lyon's Chambers
14 Castle Street, Liverpool L2 0NE,
Telephone: 0151 236 4421/8240
E-mail: chambers14@aol.com
Call date: Nov 1992, Lincoln's Inn
Qualifications: [LLB (Hons)(Newc)]

JACKSON PETER ARTHUR BRIAN

4 Paper Bldgs
2nd Floor, Temple, London EC4Y 7EX,
Telephone: 0171 583 0816/071 353 1131
E-mail: clerks@4paperbuildings.co.uk
Call date: July 1978, Inner Temple
Assistant Recorder
Qualifications: [BA (Oxon)]

JACKSON MISS ROSEMARY ELIZABETH

Keating Chambers
10 Essex Street, Outer Temple, London
WC2R 3AA, Telephone: 0171 544 2600
Call date: July 1981, Middle Temple
Qualifications: [LLB (Lond), AKC]

JACKSON RUPERT MATTHEW QC (1987)

2 Crown Office Row
2nd Floor, Temple, London EC4Y 7HJ,
Telephone: 0171 797 8000
Call date: July 1972, Middle Temple
Recorder
Qualifications: [MA, LLB (Cantab)]

JACKSON SIMON MALCOLM DERMOT

Park Court Chambers
40 Park Cross Street, Leeds LS1 2QH,
Telephone: 0113 2433277
Call date: Nov 1982, Gray's Inn
Qualifications: [LLB (Leeds)]

JACKSON MISS STEPHANIE

Queen Elizabeth Bldg
Ground Floor, Temple, London EC4Y 9BS,
Telephone: 0171 353 7181 (12 Lines)
Call date: Oct 1992, Inner Temple
Qualifications: [LLB (Reading)]

JACKSON WAYNE THOMAS

Manchester House Chambers
18-22 Bridge Street, Manchester M3 3BZ,
Telephone: 0161 834 7007
Call date: Nov 1984, Middle Temple
Qualifications: [LLB (Sheff)]

JACKSON WILLIAM GORDON

1 King's Bench Walk
2nd Floor, Temple, London EC4Y 7DB,
Telephone: 0171 936 1500
E-mail: ddear@1kbw.co.uk
Call date: Nov 1989, Lincoln's Inn
Qualifications: [LLB (St Andrew's)]

JACKSON DR WILLIAM THOMAS

Westgate Chambers
144 High Street, Lewes, East Sussex BN7 1XT,
Telephone: 01273 480510
Call date: Nov 1975, Lincoln's Inn
Qualifications: [MRCVS, DVSM, FCIARb]

JACOB ISAAC ELLIS

3 Paper Bldgs
Ground Floor, Temple, London EC4Y 7EU,
Telephone: 0171 797 7000
E-mail: clerks@3pb.co.uk
Call date: July 1963, Lincoln's Inn
Recorder
Qualifications: [LLB (Manchester), FCIArb]

JACOBS CHRISTOPHER PETER

9 King's Bench Walk
Ground Floor, Temple, London EC4Y 7DX,
Telephone: 0171 353 7202/3909
Call date: Oct 1994, Lincoln's Inn
Qualifications: [LLB (Hons)(Hull)]

JACOBS MS CLAIRE VANESSA

4 King's Bench Walk
2nd Floor, Temple, London EC4Y 7DL,
Telephone: 0171 353 3581
Call date: July 1989, Gray's Inn
Qualifications: [LLB (Hons)]

JACOBS NIGEL ROBERT

4 Essex Court
Temple, London EC4Y 9AJ,
Telephone: 0171 797 7970
E-mail: clerks@4essexcourt.law.co.uk
Call date: Nov 1983, Middle Temple
Qualifications: [BA, LLM (Cantab)]

JACOBS RICHARD DAVID

Essex Court Chambers
24 Lincoln's Inn Fields, London WC2A 3ED,
Telephone: 0171 813 8000
E-mail: clerksroom@essexcourt-chambers.co.uk
Call date: Nov 1979, Middle Temple
Qualifications: [BA (Cantab)]

JACOBS STEVEN NEIL

Lion Court
Chancery House 53-64 Chancery Lane, London
WC2A 1SJ, Telephone: 0171 404 6565
Call date: Nov 1974, Middle Temple
Qualifications: [LLB]

JACOBSON LAWRENCE

5 Paper Bldgs
Ground Floor, Temple, London EC4Y 7HB,
Telephone: 0171 583 9275/583 4555
E-mail: 5paper@link.org
Call date: Nov 1985, Gray's Inn
Qualifications: [BA, LLB (UCT), Dip Law
(PCL)]

JACOBSON MS MARY INGE

Maidstone Chambers
33 Earl Street, Maidstone, Kent ME14 1PF,
Telephone: 01622 688592
Call date: Oct 1992, Middle Temple
Qualifications: [MA (Cantab), LLB (Hons)]

JACONELLI JOSEPH

St James's Chambers
68 Quay Street, Manchester M3 3EJ,
Telephone: 0161 834 7000
E-mail: 106241.2625@compuserve.com
Door Tenant
Call date: Feb 1972, Lincoln's Inn
Qualifications: [BA, LLB (Cantab)]

JAFFA RONALD MERVYN

3 Gray's Inn Square
Ground Floor, London WC1R 5AH,
Telephone: 0171 520 5600
E-mail: gis3@btinternet.com
Call date: July 1974, Gray's Inn
Qualifications: [LLB]

JAFFERJEE AFTAB ASGER

2 Harcourt Bldgs
1st Floor, Temple, London EC4Y 9DB,
Telephone: 0171 353 2112/2817
Call date: Nov 1980, Inner Temple
Qualifications: [BA (Dunelm)]

JAGO MISS ANN LOUISE

Verulam Chambers
Peer House 8-14 Verulam Street, Gray's Inn,
London WC1X 8LZ,
Telephone: 0171 813 2400
Call date: Nov 1991, Middle Temple
Qualifications: [LLB (Hons)]

JAISRI SHASHI SATYENDRA

Chancery Chambers
1st Floor Offices 70/72 Chancery Lane,
London WC2A 1AB,
Telephone: 0171 405 6879/6870
Call date: Nov 1995, Lincoln's Inn
Qualifications: [LLB (Hons)]

JAKENS MISS CLAIRE

Westgate Chambers
144 High Street, Lewes, East Sussex BN7 1XT,
Telephone: 01273 480510
Goldsmith Chambers
Ground Floor Goldsmith Building, Temple,
London EC4Y 7BL,
Telephone: 0171 353 6802/3/4/5
E-mail: celiamonksfield@btinternet.com
Door Tenant
Call date: July 1988, Middle Temple
Qualifications: [BA (Hons) (Reading), MPhil
(Lond), Dip Law]

JAMES ALUN EDWARD

3 Temple Gardens
1st Floor, Temple, London EC4Y 9AU,
Telephone: 0171 353 7884/5 8982/3
Exchange Chambers
Pearl Assurance House Derby Square,
Liverpool L2 9XX, Telephone: 0151 236 7747/
0458
E-mail: exchangechambers@btinternet.com
Call date: Nov 1986, Middle Temple
Qualifications: [MA (Oxon), BCL]

JAMES ARTHUR RONALD ALFRED

Abbey Chambers
PO Box 47 47 Ashurst Drive, Shepperton,
Middlesex TW17 0LD,
Telephone: 01932 560913
Call date: Nov 1975, Middle Temple
Qualifications: [LLB]

JAMES MISS DELYTH ANGHARAD

2 Paper Bldgs
1st Floor, Temple, London EC4Y 7ET,
Telephone: 0171 936 2611 (10 Lines)
E-mail: clerks@2pbbarristers.co.uk
Call date: July 1990, Lincoln's Inn
Qualifications: [LLB, MA(Keele)]

JAMES ERNEST PARKER

Bridewell Chambers
2 Bridewell Place, London EC4V 6AP,
Telephone: 0171 797 8800
E-mail: clerks@bridewell.law.co.uk
Call date: Nov 1977, Gray's Inn

D

JAMES GEORGE CHRISTOPHER MOHUN

5 Fountain Court
Steelhouse Lane, Birmingham B4 6DR,
Telephone: 0121 606 0500
Call date: July 1977, Middle Temple
Qualifications: [LLB]

JAMES GRAHAME HOWARD

Goldsmith Chambers
Ground Floor Goldsmith Building, Temple,
London EC4Y 7BL,
Telephone: 0171 353 6802/3/4/5
E-mail: celiamonksfield@btinternet.com
Call date: Apr 1989, Gray's Inn
Qualifications: [LLB]

JAMES IAN FREDERICK

Octagon House
19 Colegate, Norwich NR3 1AT,
Telephone: 01603 623186
E-mail: octagon@netmatters.co.uk
1 Paper Bldgs
1st Floor, Temple, London EC4Y 7EP,
Telephone: 0171 353 3728/4953
Call date: July 1981, Gray's Inn
Qualifications: [LLB Lond]

JAMES MARK DAVID BARTON

5 Pump Court
Ground Floor, Temple, London EC4Y 7AP,
Telephone: 0171 353 2532
E-mail: fivepump@netcomuk.co.uk
Call date: Nov 1987, Middle Temple
Qualifications: [BA (Oxon)]

JAMES MICHAEL FRANK

Enterprise Chambers
9 Old Square, Lincoln's Inn, London
WC2A 3SR, Telephone: 0171 405 9471
Enterprise Chambers
38 Park Square, Leeds LS1 2PA,
Telephone: 01132 460391
Enterprise Chambers
65 Quayside, Newcastle upon Tyne NE1 3DS,
Telephone: 0191 222 3344
Call date: Feb 1976, Lincoln's Inn

JAMES MICHAEL PETER

Plowden Bldgs
2nd Floor, Temple, London EC4Y 9BU,
Telephone: 0171 583 0808
E-mail: bar@plowdenbuildings.co.uk
Call date: Nov 1989, Gray's Inn
Qualifications: [LLB]

JAMES MISS RACHAEL ELIZABETH

2 Paper Bldgs
Temple, London EC4Y 7ET,
Telephone: 0171 936 2613
Call date: Oct 1992, Middle Temple
Qualifications: [BA (Hons, Leic), Diploma in Law(City)]

JAMES MISS REBECCA ELIZABETH ANGELA

1 King's Bench Walk
2nd Floor, Temple, London EC4Y 7DB,
Telephone: 0171 936 1500
E-mail: ddear@1kbw.co.uk
Call date: Oct 1992, Gray's Inn
Qualifications: [BA (Hons) Dip in Law]

JAMES RODERICK MORRICE

23 Essex Street
London WC2R 3AS,
Telephone: 0171 413 0353/353 3533
E-mail: clerks@essexstreet23.demon.co.uk
Call date: July 1979, Gray's Inn
Qualifications: [BA (Cantab)]

JAMES MISS SHARON ANN SARAH

Angel Chambers
94 Walter Road, Swansea SA1 5QA,
Telephone: 01792 6464623/6464648
Call date: Oct 1995, Gray's Inn
Qualifications: [LLB (Wales), LLM (Bris)]

JAMES SIMON JOHN

9 St John Street
Manchester M3 4DN,
Telephone: 0161 955 9000
E-mail: ninesjs@gconnect.com
Call date: Nov 1988, Lincoln's Inn
Qualifications: [LLB Hons (Leeds)]

JAMES MRS VENICE IMOGEN

Rowchester Chambers
4 Rowchester Court Whittall Street,
Birmingham B4 6DH,
Telephone: 0121 233 2327/2361951
24 Old Bldgs
Ground Floor, Lincoln's Inn, London
WC2A 3UJ, Telephone: 0171 404 0946
E-mail: clerks@24oldbuildings.law.co.uk
Call date: July 1983, Lincoln's Inn
Qualifications: [BA (Warw) Dip Law, (City)]

JAMESON BARNABY LUKE CONRAD

18 Red Lion Court
(Off Fleet Street), London EC4A 3EB,
Telephone: 0171 520 6000
Thornwood House
102 New London Road, Chelmsford, Essex
CM2 0RG, Telephone: 01245 280880
Call date: Nov 1993, Middle Temple
Qualifications: [BA (Hons)(Lond), CPE (City)]

JAMESON RODNEY MELLOR MAPLES

6 Park Square
Leeds LS1 2LW, Telephone: 0113 2459763
E-mail: chambers@no6.co.uk
Call date: July 1976, Middle Temple
Assistant Recorder
Qualifications: [BA (Hons) (York)]

JAMIESON ANTHONY GEORGE

21 White Friars
Chester CH1 1NZ, Telephone: 01244 323070
Call date: July 1974, Gray's Inn
Qualifications: [BA, LLB (Wales)]

JAMIL MISS AISHA

Broadway House Chambers
Broadway House 9 Bank Street, Bradford,
West Yorkshire BD1 1TW,
Telephone: 01274 722560
Call date: Nov 1995, Lincoln's Inn
Qualifications: [LLB (Hons)]

JANES JEREMY NICHOLAS

King Charles House
Standard Hill, Nottingham NG1 6FX,
Telephone: 0115 9418851
E-mail: clerks@kch.co.uk
Call date: Oct 1992, Lincoln's Inn
Qualifications: [BA(Hons)(Bris), Dip Law]

JANNER DANIEL JOSEPH MITCHELL

23 Essex Street
London WC2R 3AS,
Telephone: 0171 413 0353/353 3533
E-mail: clerks@essexstreet23.demon.co.uk
Call date: July 1980, Middle Temple
Qualifications: [MA (Cantab)]

JANUSZ PIERRE PHILIP

1 Crown Office Row
3rd Floor, Temple, London EC4Y 7HH,
Telephone: 0171 583 9292
E-mail: onecor@link.org
Call date: July 1979, Middle Temple
Qualifications: [BA (Lond)]

JAQUES GEOFFREY WILFRED

17 Old Bldgs
Ground Floor, Lincoln's Inn, London
WC2A 3UP, Telephone: 0171 405 9653
Call date: Nov 1963, Lincoln's Inn
Qualifications: [LLB]

JARAND GODFREY WILLIAM MACKENZIE

24 The Ropewalk
Nottingham NG1 5EF,
Telephone: 0115 9472581
E-mail: clerk@ropewalk.co.uk
Call date: Nov 1965, Inner Temple
Qualifications: [BA, LLB (Dub)]

JARMAN JOHN MILWYN

9 Park Place
Cardiff CF1 3DP, Telephone: 01222 382731
Call date: July 1980, Gray's Inn
Qualifications: [LLM (Cantab), LLB, (Wales)]

JARMAN MARK CHRISTOPHER

14 Gray's Inn Square
Gray's Inn, London WC1R 5JP,
Telephone: 0171 242 0858
E-mail: 100712.2134@compuserve.com
Call date: Nov 1989, Inner Temple
Qualifications: [LLB (Hons)]

D

D

JARMAN NICHOLAS FRANCIS BARNABY QC (1985)

4 King's Bench Walk
2nd Floor, Temple, London EC4Y 7DL,
Telephone: 0171 353 3581
Call date: Feb 1965, Inner Temple
Recorder
Qualifications: [MA (Oxon)]

JARMAN SAMUEL JAMES GUTHRIE

4 King's Bench Walk
Ground/First Floor, Temple, London
EC4Y 7DL, Telephone: 0171 822 8822
E-mail: 4kbw@barristersatlaw.com
Call date: July 1989, Inner Temple
Qualifications: [LLB (Lond)]

JARRON MISS STEPHANIE ALLAN

67a Westgate Road
Newcastle Upon Tyne NE1 1SQ,
Telephone: 0191 261 4407/2329785
Call date: Oct 1990, Lincoln's Inn
Qualifications: [BA, ACIArb]

JARVIS JOHN MANNERS QC (1989)

3 Verulam Buildings
London WC1R 5NT,
Telephone: 0171 831 8441
E-mail: clerks@3verulam.co.uk
Call date: July 1970, Lincoln's Inn
Recorder
Qualifications: [MA (Cantab)]

JARVIS OLIVER MARTIN

Lloyds House Chambers
3rd Floor 18 Lloyds House, Lloyd Street,
Manchester M2 5WA,
Telephone: 0161 839 3371
Call date: Nov 1992, Inner Temple
Qualifications: [LLB]

JARZABKOWSKI MISS JULIA MARIE ANTIONETTE

Hardwicke Building
New Square, Lincoln's Inn, London
WC2A 3SB, Telephone: 0171 242 2523
E-mail: clerks@hardwicke.co.uk
Call date: Oct 1993, Middle Temple
Qualifications: [BA (Hons)(Cantab), MA (Cantab)]

JAY ADAM MARC

1 King's Bench Walk
2nd Floor, Temple, London EC4Y 7DB,
Telephone: 0171 936 1500
E-mail: ddear@1kbw.co.uk
Call date: Nov 1995, Gray's Inn
Qualifications: [LLB (Hons)(Bris)]

JAY GRENVILLE RICHARD

38 Young Street
Manchester M3 3FT,
Telephone: 0161 833 0489
E-mail: clerks@young-st-chambers.com
Call date: Nov 1975, Inner Temple
Qualifications: [MA (Cantab)]

JAY ROBERT MAURICE

39 Essex Street
London WC2R 3AT,
Telephone: 0171 583 1111
E-mail: clerks@39essex.co.uk
Call date: July 1981, Middle Temple
Qualifications: [BA (Oxon)]

JAYANATHAN MISS SHAMINI

30 Park Place
Cardiff CF1 3BA, Telephone: 01222 398421
E-mail: 100757.1456@compuserve.com
Call date: Nov 1996, Lincoln's Inn
Qualifications: [LLB (Hons)(Wales)]

JEANS CHRISTOPHER JAMES MARWOOD QC (1997)

11 King's Bench Walk
Temple, London EC4Y 7EQ,
Telephone: 0171 632 8500
E-mail: clerksroom@11-kbw.law.co.uk
Call date: July 1980, Gray's Inn
Qualifications: [LLB (Lond), BCL, (Oxon)]

JEARY STEPHEN JOHN

32 Park Place
Cardiff CF1 3BA, Telephone: 01222 397364
Call date: July 1987, Inner Temple
Qualifications: [LLB, APMI]

JEBB ANDREW JOHN

40 King Street
Chester CH1 2AH, Telephone: 01244 323886
Call date: Oct 1993, Gray's Inn
Qualifications: [LLB (Hons, Exon)]

JEFFERIES ANDREW

1 Pump Court
Lower Ground Floor, Temple, London
EC4Y 7AB, Telephone: 0171 583 2012/
353 4341
E-mail: (name) @1pumpcourt.co.uk
Call date: Oct 1990, Middle Temple
Qualifications: [LLB (E Anglia)]

JEFFERIES THOMAS ROBERT

Chambers of Lord Goodhart QC
Ground Floor 3 New Square, Lincoln's Inn,
London WC2A 3RS,
Telephone: 0171 405 5577
E-mail: law@threenewsquare.demon.co.uk
Call date: Nov 1981, Middle Temple
Qualifications: [BA, Dip Law]

JEFFERIS ARTHUR MICHAEL QUENTIN

11 New Square
Ground Floor, Lincoln's Inn, London
WC2A 3QB, Telephone: 0171 831 0081
E-mail: 11newsquare.co.uk
Call date: July 1976, Middle Temple
Qualifications: [LLB (Hons) (Lond), AKC]

JEFFORD MISS NERYS ANGHARAD

Keating Chambers
10 Essex Street, Outer Temple, London
WC2R 3AA, Telephone: 0171 544 2600
Call date: Nov 1986, Gray's Inn
Qualifications: [MA (Oxon), LLM (UVA)]

JEFFREYS ALAN HOWARD QC (1996)

Farrar's Building
Temple, London EC4Y 7BD,
Telephone: 0171 583 9241
E-mail: chambers@farrarsbuilding.co.uk
Call date: July 1970, Gray's Inn
Recorder
Qualifications: [LLB]

JEFFREYS DAVID ALFRED QC (1981)

Hollis Whiteman Chambers
3rd/4th Floor Queen Elizabeth Bldg, Temple,
London EC4Y 9BS, Telephone: 0171 583 5766
E-mail: hollis.whiteman@btinternet.com
Call date: Nov 1958, Gray's Inn
Recorder
Qualifications: [BA (Cantab)]

JEGARAJAH MISS SHIVANI

1 Gray's Inn Square
Ground Floor, London WC1R 5AA,
Telephone: 0171 405 8946/7/8
Call date: July 1993, Middle Temple
Qualifications: [BA (Hons)(Lond)]

JENKALA ADRIAN ALEKSANDER

11 Bolt Court
London EC4A 3DQ,
Telephone: 0171 353 2300
E-mail: boltct11@aol.com
Redhill Chambers
Seloduct House 30 Station Road, Redhill
RH1 1NK, Telephone: 01737 780781
Call date: July 1984, Middle Temple
Qualifications: [BSc LLB ACIArb]

JENKINS ALAN MICHAEL

6 Pump Court
Ground Floor, Temple, London EC4Y 7AR,
Telephone: 0171 583 6013/2510
Call date: Feb 1984, Middle Temple
Qualifications: [BA Warw, DipLaw City]

JENKINS ALUN AUSTEN

New Court
Temple, London EC4Y 9BE,
Telephone: 0171 583 5123/0171 583 0510
Call date: May 1981, Gray's Inn
Qualifications: [LLB (Warw)]

JENKINS MISS CATHERINE PHILLIDA

One Garden Court
Ground Floor, Temple, London EC4Y 9BJ,
Telephone: 0171 797 7900
Call date: Nov 1990, Middle Temple
Qualifications: [BA (Keele)]

JENKINS DAVID CROFTON

2 King's Bench Walk
Ground Floor, Temple, London EC4Y 7DE,
Telephone: 0171 353 1746
E-mail: 2kbw@atlas.co.uk
King's Bench Chambers
115 North Hill, Plymouth PL4 8JY,
Telephone: 01752 221551
Call date: Nov 1967, Inner Temple
Qualifications: [LLB]

JENKINS DAVID MORGAN

32 Park Place
Cardiff CF1 3BA, Telephone: 01222 397364
Call date: Oct 1990, Gray's Inn
Qualifications: [LLB (Cardiff)]

JENKINS EDWARD NICHOLAS

5 Paper Bldgs
1st Floor, Temple, London EC4Y 7HB,
Telephone: 0171 583 6117
E-mail: clerks@5-paperbuildings.law.co.uk
Call date: July 1977, Middle Temple
Qualifications: [BA (Cantab)]

JENKINS MISS ELIZABETH

12 Old Square
1st Floor, Lincoln's Inn, London WC2A 3TX,
Telephone: 0171 404 0875
Call date: Oct 1995, Lincoln's Inn
Qualifications: [LLB (Hons)(Newc)]

JENKINS HYWEL IESTYN

35 Essex Street
Temple, London WC2R 3AR,
Telephone: 0171 353 6381
Call date: July 1974, Inner Temple
Qualifications: [LLB]

JENKINS JAMES JOHN

Iscoed Chambers
86 St Helen's Road, Swansea SA1 4BQ,
Telephone: 01792 652988/9/330
Farrar's Building
Temple, London EC4Y 7BD,
Telephone: 0171 583 9241
E-mail: chambers@farrarsbuilding.co.uk
Door Tenant
Call date: Nov 1974, Gray's Inn
Assistant Recorder
Qualifications: [LLB]

JENKINS DR JANET CAROLINE

6 Pump Court
Ground Floor, Temple, London EC4Y 7AR,
Telephone: 0171 583 6013/2510
Call date: Nov 1994, Middle Temple
Qualifications: [MB, BS]

JENKINS JEREMY DAVID

33 Park Place
Cardiff CF1 3BA, Telephone: 01222 233313
Call date: July 1984, Inner Temple
Qualifications: [BA]

JENKINS JOHN DAVID QC (1990)

30 Park Place
Cardiff CF1 3BA, Telephone: 01222 398421
E-mail: 100757.1456@compuserve.com
Call date: July 1970, Gray's Inn
Recorder
Qualifications: [LLB (Lond) (Hons)]

JENKINS MARTIN STEPHEN

Coleridge Chambers
Citadel 190 Corporation Street, Birmingham
B4 6QD, Telephone: 0121 233 3303
Call date: Nov 1994, Gray's Inn
Qualifications: [BA (Keele)]

JENKINS MISS MELANIE KIM

1 Gray's Inn Square
1st Floor, London WC1R 5AG,
Telephone: 0171 405 3000
E-mail: clerks@onegrays.demon.co.uk
Call date: July 1982, Gray's Inn
Qualifications: [BA (Keele)]

JENKINS PHILIP DUNSFORD

33 Park Place
Cardiff CF1 3BA, Telephone: 01222 233313
Call date: Nov 1970, Lincoln's Inn
Qualifications: [LLB (Lond)]

JENKINS ROWAN MATTHEW

King's Bench Chambers
Wellington House 175 Holdenhurst Road,
Bournemouth, Dorset BH8 8DQ,
Telephone: 01202 250025
Call date: Nov 1994, Lincoln's Inn
Qualifications: [MA (Botany), D.Phil (Botany), CPE]

JENKINS THOMAS ALUN QC (1996)

All Saints Chambers
9/11 Broad Street, Bristol BS1 2HP,
Telephone: 0117 921 1966
3 Hare Court
1st Floor, Temple, London EC4Y 7BJ,
Telephone: 0171 353 7561
Door Tenant
Call date: July 1972, Lincoln's Inn
Assistant Recorder
Qualifications: [LLB]

JENNINGS ANTHONY FRANCIS

2 Garden Court
1st Floor, Middle Temple, London EC4Y 9BL,
Telephone: 0171 353 1633
E-mail: barristers@2gardenct.law.co.uk
Call date: July 1983, Gray's Inn
Qualifications: [LLB (Warw)]

JENNINGS NIGEL CALVERLEY

17 Bedford Row
London WC1R 4EB,
Telephone: 0171 831 7314
E-mail: IBoard7314@AOL.com
Call date: Nov 1967, Gray's Inn

JENNINGS PETER NIGEL

3 Paper Bldgs
1st Floor, Temple, London EC4Y 7EU,
Telephone: 0171 583 8055
E-mail: london@3paper.com
20 Lorne Park Road
Bournemouth BH1 1JN,
Telephone: 01202 292102 (5 Lines)
4 St Peter Street
Winchester SO23 8OW,
Telephone: 01962 868884
Call date: July 1972, Middle Temple
Qualifications: [MA (Cantab), LLM (Lond)]

JENNINGS TIMOTHY ROBIN FINNEGAN

Enterprise Chambers
9 Old Square, Lincoln's Inn, London
WC2A 3SR, Telephone: 0171 405 9471
Enterprise Chambers
38 Park Square, Leeds LS1 2PA,
Telephone: 01132 460391
Enterprise Chambers
65 Quayside, Newcastle upon Tyne NE1 3DS,
Telephone: 0191 222 3344
Call date: Nov 1962, Gray's Inn
Qualifications: [LLM (Lond)]

JENRICK MISS KATE HENRIETTA

Arden Chambers
27 John Street, London WC1N 2BL,
Telephone: 0171 242 4244
Call date: Nov 1990, Inner Temple
Qualifications: [LLB (So'ton)]

JEREMY DAVID HUGH THOMAS

Queen Elizabeth Bldg
Ground Floor, Temple, London EC4Y 9BS,
Telephone: 0171 353 7181 (12 Lines)
Call date: July 1977, Middle Temple
Qualifications: [LLB]

JERMAN ANTHONY IVAN

22 Old Bldgs
Lincoln's Inn, London WC2A 3UJ,
Telephone: 0171 831 0222
Call date: Nov 1989, Middle Temple
Qualifications: [BA Hons [Lond], Dip in Law]

JERVIS CHRISTOPHER ROBERT

Albion Chambers
Broad Street, Bristol BS1 1DR,
Telephone: 0117 9272144
Call date: July 1966, Inner Temple
Qualifications: [MA (Oxon)]

JESS DIGBY CHARLES

8 King Street Chambers
8 King Street, Manchester M2 6AQ,
Telephone: 0161 834 9560
Call date: July 1978, Gray's Inn
Qualifications: [BSc.Hons, LLM, (Manchester), FCIArb]

Fax: 0161 834 2733; DX: 14354 Manchester

Types of work: Arbitration; Commercial litigation; Construction; Insurance; Insurance/reinsurance; Professional negligence

Circuit: Northern

Other professional experience: Arbitrator

Publications: *The Insurance of Commercial Risks: Law and Practice* (Butterworths), 1993 (2nd edn); *The Insurance of Professional Negligence Risks: Law and Practice* (Butterworths), 1989 (2nd edn); *The Encyclopaedia of Forms and Precedents - Vol. 20 Insurance*, 1988 (5th edn); *Butterworths Insurance Law Handbook*, 1992 (3rd edn)

Reported cases: *CTN Cash & Carry Ltd v General Accident Fire and Life Assurance Co Ltd*, [1989] 1 Lloyd's Rep 229, 1989. Insurance - breach of warranty - clause delimiting scope of indemnity.
Hitchins (Hatfield) Ltd v Prudential Assurance Co Ltd, [1991] 2 Lloyd's Rep 580, CA, 1991. Contractor's all risks insurance - construction of exclusion within inclusive clause.
Curtis v Wild, [1991] 4 All ER 172, 1991. Personal Injury time bar - whether boating accident in 'navigable waters'.
CTN Cash & Carry Ltd v Gallaher Ltd, [1994] 4 All ER 714, CA, 1994. Economic duress in commercial contract.
Barratts (Manchester) Ltd v Bolton MBC and Attorney General, [1998] 1 All ER 1 [1998] 1 WLR 1003, CA, 1997. Inquiry into damages - grounds upon which inquiry can be struck out for delay.

JESSEL MRS PHILIPPA BRIGID

6 King's Bench Walk
Ground Floor, Temple, London EC4Y 7DR,
Telephone: 0171 583 0410
Call date: July 1978, Inner Temple
Qualifications: [BSc (Hons)(Lond)]

JESSUP MISS ANNE ELIZABETH

2 Garden Court
1st Floor, Middle Temple, London EC4Y 9BL,
Telephone: 0171 353 1633
E-mail: barristers@2gardenct.law.co.uk
Call date: Nov 1981, Gray's Inn
Qualifications: [BA (Lond)]

JESUDASON MISS CHRISTINE PREMILA

40 King Street
Chester CH1 2AH, Telephone: 01244 323886
Call date: Oct 1993, Middle Temple
Qualifications: [BA (Juris, Oxon)]

JEWELL MATTHEW

1 Paper Bldgs
1st Floor, Temple, London EC4Y 7EP,
Telephone: 0171 353 3728/4953
Call date: Nov 1989, Lincoln's Inn
Qualifications: [BA (Oxon), Dip Law (City)]

JIBOWU OLUMUYIWA OLUBUKUNOLA A.O.

Chancery Chambers
1st Floor Offices 70/72 Chancery Lane,
London WC2A 1AB,
Telephone: 0171 405 6879/6870
Call date: Oct 1993, Middle Temple
Qualifications: [LLB (Hons)(Lond)]

JINADU ABDUL-LATEEF ABODURIN OLAYINKA

Keating Chambers
10 Essex Street, Outer Temple, London
WC2R 3AA, Telephone: 0171 544 2600
Call date: Nov 1995, Middle Temple
Qualifications: [BA (Hons), LLM (Hons) (Cantab)]

JOBANPUTRA SANDIP MUKUND

Keating Chambers
10 Essex Street, Outer Temple, London
WC2R 3AA, Telephone: 0171 544 2600
Call date: Oct 1996, Gray's Inn
Qualifications: [BA (Oxon)]

JOBLING IAN MICHAEL THOMAS

3 Gray's Inn Square
Ground Floor, London WC1R 5AH,
Telephone: 0171 520 5600
E-mail: gis3@btinternet.com
Call date: Nov 1982, Gray's Inn
Qualifications: [LLB (Lond)]

JOFFE MISS NATASHA JULIET LOUISE

Devereux Chambers
Devereux Court, London WC2R 3JJ,
Telephone: 0171 353 7534
E-mail: elton@devchambers.co.uk
Call date: Oct 1992, Gray's Inn
Qualifications: [BA (Hons)]

JOFFE VICTOR HOWARD

13 Old Square
1st Floor, Lincoln's Inn, London WC2A 3UA,
Telephone: 0171 242 6105
E-mail: clerks@serlecourt.co.uk
Call date: Nov 1975, Middle Temple
Qualifications: [MA (Cantab) LLB]

JOHAL MISS DEVINDER KAUR

Holborn Chambers
6 Gate Street, Lincoln's Inn Fields, London
WC2A 3HP, Telephone: 0171 242 6060
Call date: Oct 1995, Gray's Inn
Qualifications: [LLB]

JOHAL MISS SUKHJINDER KAUR

4 King's Bench Walk
2nd Floor, Temple, London EC4Y 7DL,
Telephone: 0171 353 3581
Call date: Nov 1991, Middle Temple
Qualifications: [LLB Hons (Wales)]

JOHN MISS (EMMA) CATRIN

30 Park Place
Cardiff CF1 3BA, Telephone: 01222 398421
E-mail: 100757.1456@compuserve.com
Call date: Oct 1992, Gray's Inn
Qualifications: [LL.B (Wales)]

JOHN PETER CHARLES

1 Essex Court
1st Floor, Temple, London EC4Y 9AR,
Telephone: 0171 936 3030
E-mail: one.essex_court@virgin.net
Call date: Nov 1989, Inner Temple
Qualifications: [LLB (Lond)]

JOHN STEPHEN ALUN

9-12 Bell Yard
London WC2A 2LF,
Telephone: 0171 400 1800
Call date: July 1975, Middle Temple
Qualifications: [MA (Oxon)]

JOHN-JULES CHARLES

Somersett Chambers
52 Bedford Row, London WC1R 4LR,
Telephone: 0171 404 6701
E-mail: Somersettchambers@cocoon.co.uk
Call date: July 1983, Gray's Inn
Qualifications: [LLB Hons (Soton)]

JOHNS ALAN GRANT

9 Old Square
Ground Floor, Lincoln's Inn, London
WC2A 3SR, Telephone: 0171 405 4682
E-mail: chambers@9oldsquare.co.uk
Call date: Oct 1994, Gray's Inn
Qualifications: [BA]

JOHNSON ALAN MICHAEL BORTHWICK

1 Gray's Inn Square
Ground Floor, London WC1R 5AA,
Telephone: 0171 405 8946/7/8
Call date: July 1971, Middle Temple
Qualifications: [MA (Oxon)]

JOHNSON MISS AMANDA

9 Park Place
Cardiff CF1 3DP, Telephone: 01222 382731
Call date: Oct 1992, Gray's Inn
Qualifications: [LL.B (Wales)]

JOHNSON MISS AMANDA JANE

36 Bedford Row
London WC1R 4JH,
Telephone: 0171 421 8000
E-mail: 36bedfordrow@link.org
Call date: Nov 1990, Middle Temple
Qualifications: [LLB (Lond)]

D

D

JOHNSON MISS CHRISTINE MARGARET

Adrian Lyon's Chambers
14 Castle Street, Liverpool L2 0NE,
Telephone: 0151 236 4421/8240
E-mail: chambers14@aol.com
Call date: Nov 1991, Middle Temple
Qualifications: [LLB (Hons)]

JOHNSON DAVID BURNHAM QC (1978)

20 Essex Street
London WC2R 3AL,
Telephone: 0171 583 9294
E-mail: clerks@20essexst.com
Call date: July 1967, Inner Temple
Recorder

JOHNSON EDWIN GEOFFREY

9 Old Square
Ground Floor, Lincoln's Inn, London
WC2A 3SR, Telephone: 0171 405 4682
E-mail: chambers@9oldsquare.co.uk
Call date: Nov 1987, Lincoln's Inn
Qualifications: [BA (Oxon)]

JOHNSON IAN FREDERICK

Adrian Lyon's Chambers
14 Castle Street, Liverpool L2 0NE,
Telephone: 0151 236 4421/8240
E-mail: chambers14@aol.com
5 Stone Buildings
Lincoln's Inn, London WC2A 3XT,
Telephone: 0171 242 6201
E-mail: clerks@5-stonebuildings.law.co.uk
Door Tenant
Call date: July 1982, Gray's Inn
Qualifications: [LLB (Reading)]

JOHNSON MRS JANICE COSIE

2 King's Bench Walk
1st Floor, Temple, London EC4Y 7DE,
Telephone: 0171 353 9276
Call date: Nov 1994, Inner Temple
Qualifications: [LLB (Anglia)]

JOHNSON JEREMY CHARLES

5 Essex Court
1st Floor, Temple, London EC4Y 9AH,
Telephone: 0171 410 2000
Call date: Oct 1994, Middle Temple
Qualifications: [BA (Hons)(Oxon), CPE
(Middx)]

JOHNSON JOHN RICHARD HENESEY

Regent Chambers
29 Regent Road, Hanley, Stoke On Trent
ST1 3BP, Telephone: 01782 286666
E-mail: regent@ftech.co.uk
Call date: Oct 1993, Middle Temple
Qualifications: [MA (Hons)(Oxon),
Dip.B.Admin, CPE]

JOHNSON MS KATHYRN MARGARET

15 Winckley Square
Preston PR1 3JJ, Telephone: 01772 252828
E-mail: clerks@winckleysq.demon.co.uk
Call date: July 1989, Gray's Inn
Qualifications: [LLB (Sheff)]

JOHNSON MATTHEW STUART

1 Hare Court
Ground Floor, Temple, London EC4Y 7BE,
Telephone: 0171 353 3982/5324
Call date: Oct 1995, Lincoln's Inn
Qualifications: [LLB (Hons)(Leic)]

JOHNSON MICHAEL SLOAN

9 St John Street
Manchester M3 4DN,
Telephone: 0161 955 9000
E-mail: ninesjs@gconnect.com
Call date: Nov 1971, Lincoln's Inn
Assistant Recorder
Qualifications: [MA, LLM (Cantab)]

JOHNSON NICHOLAS JAMES

Park Court Chambers
40 Park Cross Street, Leeds LS1 2QH,
Telephone: 0113 2433277
Call date: Nov 1994, Inner Temple
Qualifications: [BA (York), CPE]

JOHNSON NICHOLAS ROBERT

25-27 Castle Street
1st Floor, Liverpool L2 4TA,
Telephone: 0151 227 5661/051 236 5072
Call date: July 1987, Inner Temple
Qualifications: [BA (Leeds)]

JOHNSON PETER TIMOTHY

York Chambers
14 Toft Green, York YO1 1JT,
Telephone: 01904 620048
E-mail: yorkchambers.co.uk
Call date: July 1986, Inner Temple
Qualifications: [BA (Durham)]

JOHNSON ROBIN PETER

5 Paper Bldgs
Lower Ground Floor, Temple, London
EC4Y 7HB, Telephone: 0171 353 5638
E-mail: 107722,633@compuserve.com
Call date: Nov 1979, Gray's Inn
Qualifications: [BA (Exon)]

JOHNSON RODERICK STOWERS

2 Paper Bldgs
1st Floor, Temple, London EC4Y 7ET,
Telephone: 0171 936 2611 (10 Lines)
E-mail: clerks@2pbbarristers.co.uk
Call date: Nov 1975, Lincoln's Inn
Qualifications: [MA (Oxon)]

JOHNSON MISS RUTH

Chambers of Helen Grindrod QC
1st Floor 95a Chancery Lane, London
WC2A 2JG, Telephone: 0171 404 4777
Call date: July 1984, Lincoln's Inn
Qualifications: [LLB (Lond)]

JOHNSON SIMON NICHOLAS

Stour Chambers
Barton Mill House Barton Mill Road,
Canterbury, Kent CT1 1BP,
Telephone: 01227 764899
E-mail: clerks@stourchambers.co.uk
Call date: July 1987, Gray's Inn
Qualifications: [LLB (Hons) (Wales)]

JOHNSON STEVEN

9 St John Street
Manchester M3 4DN,
Telephone: 0161 955 9000
E-mail: ninesjs@gconnect.com
Call date: July 1984, Middle Temple
Qualifications: [LLB (Hons) (Lond)]

JOHNSON MISS SUSANNAH MALEHLOHONOLO

9 Bedford Row
London WC1R 4AZ,
Telephone: 0171 242 3555
E-mail: clerks@9br.co.uk
Call date: Nov 1996, Middle Temple
Qualifications: [LLB (Hons)(Kent)]

JOHNSON MISS ZOE ELISABETH

Hollis Whiteman Chambers
3rd/4th Floor Queen Elizabeth Bldg, Temple,
London EC4Y 9BS, Telephone: 0171 583 5766
E-mail: hollis.whiteman@btinternet.com
Call date: Nov 1990, Inner Temple
Qualifications: [BA (Oxon), Dip Law (City)]

JOHNSTON MISS ANNE-MARIE

1 Paper Bldgs
1st Floor, Temple, London EC4Y 7EP,
Telephone: 0171 353 3728/4953
Call date: Oct 1990, Inner Temple
Qualifications: [LLB]

JOHNSTON ANTHONY PAUL

1 Fountain Court
Steelhouse Lane, Birmingham B4 6DR,
Telephone: 0121 236 5721
Call date: Nov 1993, Middle Temple
Qualifications: [BA (Hons)(Cantab)]

JOHNSTON MISS CAREY ANN

18 Red Lion Court
(Off Fleet Street), London EC4A 3EB,
Telephone: 0171 520 6000
Thornwood House
102 New London Road, Chelmsford, Essex
CM2 0RG, Telephone: 01245 280880
Call date: July 1977, Middle Temple
Qualifications: [LLM (Warwick)]

JOHNSTON CHRISTOPHER GEORGE

3 Serjeants Inn
London EC4Y 1BQ,
Telephone: 0171 353 5537
E-mail: available upon request
Call date: Nov 1990, Gray's Inn
Qualifications: [MA (Cantab) (Hons)]

JOHNSTON CHRISTOPHER MARK

Chambers of Helen Grindrod QC
1st Floor 95a Chancery Lane, London
WC2A 2JG, Telephone: 0171 404 4777
Call date: Nov 1983, Gray's Inn
Qualifications: [BA, LLB]

JOHNSTON MISS JILL

13 Old Square
1st Floor, Lincoln's Inn, London WC2A 3UA,
Telephone: 0171 242 6105
E-mail: clerks@serlecourt.co.uk
Call date: Oct 1990, Lincoln's Inn
Qualifications: [MA (Cantab)]

JOHNSTON MS KAREN ANN

36 Bedford Row
London WC1R 4JH,
Telephone: 0171 421 8000
E-mail: 36bedfordrow@link.org
Call date: Nov 1994, Inner Temple
Qualifications: [MA (Oxon), CPE (City)]

JOHNSTONE MARK ANTHONY

4 Paper Bldgs
2nd Floor, Temple, London EC4Y 7EX,
Telephone: 0171 583 0816/071 353 1131
E-mail: clerks@4paperbuildings.co.uk
Call date: July 1984, Inner Temple
Qualifications: [LLB (Lond)]

JOLOWICZ JOHN ANTHONY QC (1990)

Brick Court Chambers
15/19 Devereux Court, London WC2R 3JJ,
Telephone: 0171 583 0777
E-mail: (surname)@brickcourt.demon.co.uk
Door Tenant
Call date: Nov 1952, Inner Temple

JONATHAN-JONES GARETH

32 Park Place
Cardiff CF1 3BA, Telephone: 01222 397364
Call date: Oct 1991, Inner Temple

JONES MISS (CATHERINE) CHARLOTTE

5 Bell Yard
London WC2A 2JR, Telephone: 0171 333 8811
Call date: July 1982, Middle Temple
Qualifications: [MA (Cantab)]

JONES ANDREW CRAIG

30 Park Place
Cardiff CF1 3BA, Telephone: 01222 398421
E-mail: 100757.1456@compuserve.com
Call date: Oct 1996, Inner Temple
Qualifications: [LLB (Bris)]

JONES BENJAMIN WILLIAM

India Buildings Chambers
Water Street, Liverpool L2 OXG,
Telephone: 0151 243 6000
Call date: Feb 1993, Middle Temple
Qualifications: [LLB (Hons)(L'pool)]

JONES BRIAN LLOYD

9 Park Place
Cardiff CF1 3DP, Telephone: 01222 382731
Call date: July 1992, Gray's Inn
Qualifications: [BA (Wales)]

JONES MISS CAROLYN NERYS

Clock Chambers
78 Darlington Street, Wolverhampton
WV1 4LY, Telephone: 01902 313444
Call date: Oct 1995, Lincoln's Inn
Qualifications: [LLB (Hons)(Lond)]

JONES CARWYN HOWELL

Gower Chambers
57 Walter Road, Swansea, West Glamorgan
SA1 5PZ, Telephone: 01792 644466
E-mail: clerk@gowerchambers.co.uk
Call date: Nov 1989, Gray's Inn
Qualifications: [LLB [Wales]]

JONES MISS CATHERINE ANNE

Angel Chambers
94 Walter Road, Swansea SA1 5QA,
Telephone: 01792 6464623/6464648
Call date: Oct 1992, Gray's Inn
Qualifications: [BA (Hons)(Swansea), Dip in Law]

JONES MS CHERYL STEPHANIE

Fleet Chambers
Mitre House 44-46 Fleet Street, London
EC4Y 1BN, Telephone: 0171 936 3707
Call date: Oct 1996, Gray's Inn
Qualifications: [LLB (Lancs)]

JONES CLIVE HUGH

1 New Square
Ground Floor, Lincoln's Inn, London
WC2A 3SA, Telephone: 0171 405 0884/5/6/7
E-mail: 1newsquare@compuserve.com
Call date: July 1981, Middle Temple
Qualifications: [BA (Oxon),ACIA]

JONES DANIEL OSKAR

2 Dr Johnson's Building
Temple, London EC4Y 7AY,
Telephone: 0171 353 4716
Call date: Oct 1994, Gray's Inn
Qualifications: [BA (Hons), CPE]

JONES DAVID ALAN FREEBORN

3 Fountain Court
Steelhouse Lane, Birmingham B4 6DR,
Telephone: 0121 236 5854
Call date: July 1967, Gray's Inn
Recorder
Qualifications: [LLB(Nottm)]

JONES DAVID JAMES

8 King's Bench Walk
2nd Floor, Temple, London EC4Y 7DU,
Telephone: 0171 797 8888
8 King's Bench Walk North
1 Park Square East, Leeds LS1 2NE,
Telephone: 0113 2439797
Call date: Nov 1994, Lincoln's Inn
Qualifications: [LLB (Hons), LLM (Lond)]

JONES DAVID LLOYD

Brick Court Chambers
15/19 Devereux Court, London WC2R 3JJ,
Telephone: 0171 583 0777
E-mail: (surname)@brickcourt.demon.co.uk
Call date: July 1975, Middle Temple
Recorder
Qualifications: [MA, LLB (Cantab)]

JONES DAVID NICHOLAS

Broadway House Chambers
Broadway House 9 Bank Street, Bradford,
West Yorkshire BD1 1TW,
Telephone: 01274 722560
Call date: July 1985, Gray's Inn
Qualifications: [LLB (Hons, Lond)]

JONES DOUGLAS PETER RICHARD

King Charles House
Standard Hill, Nottingham NG1 6FX,
Telephone: 0115 9418851
E-mail: clerks@kch.co.uk
Call date: Oct 1991, Lincoln's Inn
Qualifications: [BSc (Hons) (Notts), Dip Law]

JONES EDWARD BARTLEY QC (1997)

Exchange Chambers
Pearl Assurance House Derby Square,
Liverpool L2 9XX, Telephone: 0151 236 7747/
0458
E-mail: exchangechambers@btinternet.com
Call date: July 1975, Lincoln's Inn
Assistant Recorder
Qualifications: [BA (Hons)(Oxon)]

JONES MISS ELAINE THOMSON

The Corn Exchange
5th Floor Fenwick Street, Liverpool L2 7QS,
Telephone: 0151 227 1081/5009
Call date: July 1984, Lincoln's Inn
Qualifications: [BA (Hons)]

JONES MISS ELIZABETH SIAN

13 Old Square
1st Floor, Lincoln's Inn, London WC2A 3UA,
Telephone: 0171 242 6105
E-mail: clerks@serlecourt.co.uk
Call date: Nov 1984, Middle Temple
Qualifications: [BA (Cantab)]

JONES FRANCIS HUMPHREY

Iscoed Chambers
86 St Helen's Road, Swansea SA1 4BQ,
Telephone: 01792 652988/9/330
Call date: July 1980, Inner Temple
Qualifications: [MA (Oxon)]

D

JONES GARETH DARYL

India Buildings Chambers
Water Street, Liverpool L2 OXG,
Telephone: 0151 243 6000
1 Dr Johnson's Bldgs
Ground Floor, Temple, London EC4Y 7AX,
Telephone: 0171 353 9328
Call date: Nov 1984, Gray's Inn
Qualifications: [LLB (Wales)]

JONES GARETH JOHN

33 Park Place
Cardiff CF1 3BA, Telephone: 01222 233313
Call date: Feb 1992, Inner Temple
Qualifications: [MA (Camb)]

JONES GERAINT ANTHONY

9 Park Place
Cardiff CF1 3DP, Telephone: 01222 382731
Farrar's Building
Temple, London EC4Y 7BD,
Telephone: 0171 583 9241
E-mail: chambers@farrarsbuilding.co.uk
Door Tenant
Call date: July 1976, Middle Temple
Qualifications: [MA (Cantab)]

JONES GERAINT MARTYN

Fenners Chambers
3 Madingley Road, Cambridge CB3 OEE,
Telephone: 01223 368761
Fenners Chambers
8-12 Priestgate, Peterborough PE1 1JA,
Telephone: 01733 62030
Call date: Nov 1972, Gray's Inn
Qualifications: [MA, LLM (Cantab)]

JONES GERALD WILLIAM

Exchange Chambers
Pearl Assurance House Derby Square,
Liverpool L2 9XX, Telephone: 0151 236 7747/
0458
E-mail: exchangechambers@btinternet.com
Call date: July 1995, Gray's Inn
Qualifications: [LLB (Sheff)]

JONES MISS GILLIAN HUNTER

18 Red Lion Court
(Off Fleet Street), London EC4A 3EB,
Telephone: 0171 520 6000
Thornwood House
102 New London Road, Chelmsford, Essex
CM2 0RG, Telephone: 01245 280880
Call date: Oct 1996, Lincoln's Inn
Qualifications: [LLB (Hons)(Leic)]

JONES GREGORY PERCY

2 Harcourt Buildings
Temple, London EC4Y 9DB,
Telephone: 0171 353 8415
E-mail: clerks@twoharcourtbldgs.demon.co.uk
Call date: Nov 1991, Lincoln's Inn
Qualifications: [MA (Hons) (Oxon)]

Fax: 0171 353 8415; DX: 402 London;
Other comms: E-mail
clerks@twoharcourtbldgs.demon.co.uk

Types of work: Administrative; Chancery
(general); Chancery land law; Common land;
Common law (general); Compulsory purchase;
EC and competition law; Education; Energy;
Environment; Licensing; Local government;
Parliamentary; Town and country planning

Membership of foreign bars: King's Inns, Dublin

Awards and memberships: Planning and
Environment Bar Association; Bar European
Group; Administrative Law Bar Association;
Association for Regulated Procurement;
Education Law Society

Other professional experience: Director of the
Lothian Foundation; Visiting Senior Lecturer in
European Law at South Bank University (1993-7)

Publications: *Education Case Reports* (Editor),
1998-; *Planning and Environmental Law
Bulletin* (Assistant Editor), 1993-

Reported Cases

R v Sandhu (CA) (1997) *The Times*, 2 January;
[1997] JPL 853; [1997] Crim LR 288
Listed buildings prosecution; admissibility of
evidence of *mens rea* in strict liability offences

*Lady Berkeley v Secretary of State for the
Environment and Fulham Football Club (CA)*
(1998) *The Times*, 2 March; see also (1998) *The
Times*, 7 April re: Costs;
s 54A Town and Country Planning Act 1990,

Environmental Impact Assessment EC Directive 85/337

R v Somerset County Council ex parte Harcombe (1997) The Times, 7 May; [1998] COD 71
National assistance, exercise of local authority's discretion to recover nursing home costs

O'Brien v Hertsmere Borough Council [No 1] [1997] 74 P&CR 264
Burden of proof in prosecution for display of advertisement without consent

O'Brien v Hertsmere Borough Council [No 2] [1998] JPL B73
Whether defendant can be convicted of continuing offence while appeal to High Court against the original conviction is pending

R v Elmbridge Borough Council ex parte Active Office (1997) *The Times*, 29 December
Judicial review of council's decision to prosecute for breach of a listed building enforcement notice

R v Local Government Ombudsman ex parte Turpin [1998] EGCS 18
Judicial review

R v Essex County Council ex parte Jackson Projects [1995] COD 155
Compulsory purchase

Charles Church Developments v Hart District Council [1995] JPLB 133
Planning, local plan

Torbay v Mills and Cross [1995] JP 13
Highways

Houghton v Secretary of State for the Environment [1995] P&CR 178; [1996] PLR 6
Planning, green belt

Background

School: Colfe's; *University*: New College Oxford, MA; University College, London LLM (Euro).

Member of the National Council of the United Kingdom Environmental Law Association. Jean Pierre Warner Scholar to the European Court of Justice (*Cabinet of Advocate General Jacobs*). Gave expert evidence before House of Commons Environment Committee's report into the burning of Secondary Liquid Fuels in Cement Kilns (1997).

JONES GUY TREHARN HOWEL

32 Park Place
Cardiff CF1 3BA, Telephone: 01222 397364
Call date: July 1975, Gray's Inn
Qualifications: [LLB]

JONES HOWARD PETER

Francis Taylor Bldg
2nd Floor, Temple, London EC4Y 7BY,
Telephone: 0171 353 9942/3157
Call date: Oct 1992, Gray's Inn
Qualifications: [MA (Hons)(Cantab)]

JONES IFAN WYN LLOYD

Sedan House
Stanley Place, Chester CH1 2LU,
Telephone: 01244 320480/348282
Call date: Nov 1979, Lincoln's Inn
Qualifications: [LLB (Wales), BCL, (Oxon)]

JONES MISS JENNIFER CLAIRE

5 Fountain Court
Steelhouse Lane, Birmingham B4 6DR,
Telephone: 0121 606 0500
Call date: Oct 1991, Lincoln's Inn
Qualifications: [LLB (Hons) (Birm)]

JONES MISS JESSICA FAY

One Raymond Buildings
Gray's Inn, London WC1R 5BH,
Telephone: 0171 430 1234
E-mail: chambers@ipbar1rb.com;
clerks@ipbar1rb.com
Call date: Nov 1991, Inner Temple
Qualifications: [BSc (So'ton), Dip Law]

JONES JOHN EVAN

10 King's Bench Walk
1st Floor, Temple, London EC4Y 7EB,
Telephone: 0171 353 2501
Call date: July 1982, Inner Temple
Qualifications: [BA (Hons) (Dunelm)]

JONES JOHN RICHARD

28 St John Street
Manchester M3 4DJ,
Telephone: 0161 834 8418
E-mail: clerk@28stjohnst.co.uk
Call date: July 1981, Middle Temple
Qualifications: [LLB]

JONES JONATHAN ARTHUR DAVID

3 Fountain Court
Steelhouse Lane, Birmingham B4 6DR,
Telephone: 0121 236 5854
Call date: Oct 1994, Gray's Inn
Qualifications: [MA]

JONES MISS KAY MARY

2 Field Court
Gray's Inn, London WC1R 5BB,
Telephone: 0171 405 6114
E-mail: fieldct2@netcomuk.co.uk.
Call date: July 1974, Gray's Inn
Qualifications: [BA (Hons) (Sussex), Cert
Universit, d'Aix/Marseille]

JONES LAWRENCE VICTOR

3 Paper Bldgs
2nd Floor, Temple, London EC4Y 7EU,
Telephone: 0171 353 6208
Call date: July 1988, Lincoln's Inn
Qualifications: [LLB (Hons)]

JONES MISS LESLIE ANN

Trafalgar Chambers
53 Fleet Street, London EC4Y 1BE,
Telephone: 0171 583 5858
E-mail: TrafalgarChambers@easynet.co.uk
Call date: Oct 1995, Inner Temple
Qualifications: [LLB (Lond)]

JONES MISS MARGARET EMMA

2 Garden Court
1st Floor, Middle Temple, London EC4Y 9BL,
Telephone: 0171 353 1633
E-mail: barristers@2gardenct.law.co.uk
Call date: Nov 1990, Middle Temple
Qualifications: [BA (Dunelm)]

JONES MARTIN WYNNE

8 King's Bench Walk
2nd Floor, Temple, London EC4Y 7DU,
Telephone: 0171 797 8888
8 King's Bench Walk North
1 Park Square East, Leeds LS1 2NE,
Telephone: 0113 2439797
Call date: Nov 1977, Inner Temple
Qualifications: [MA (Warwick), LLB (Lond)]

JONES MICHAEL ADRIAN LYSTER

Sussex Chambers
9 Old Steine, Brighton BN1 1FJ,
Telephone: 01273 607953
Call date: July 1972, Inner Temple
Qualifications: [BA]

JONES MICHAEL SELWYN TUDOR

Gower Chambers
57 Walter Road, Swansea, West Glamorgan
SA1 5PZ, Telephone: 01792 644466
E-mail: clerk@gowerchambers.co.uk
Call date: July 1995, Middle Temple
Qualifications: [BA (Hons)]

JONES NICHOLAS DAVID JULIAN

33 Park Place
Cardiff CF1 3BA, Telephone: 01222 233313
Call date: Nov 1987, Gray's Inn
Qualifications: [BSc Econ (Wales), LLM
(Cantab)]

JONES NICHOLAS GARETH

33 Park Place
Cardiff CF1 3BA, Telephone: 01222 233313
Goldsmith Building
1st Floor, Temple, London EC4Y 7BL,
Telephone: 0171 353 7881
E-mail: clerks@goldsmith-building.law.co.uk
Door Tenant
Call date: Nov 1970, Gray's Inn
Assistant Recorder

JONES NICHOLAS GRAHAM

4 Brick Court
1st Floor, Temple, London EC4Y 9AD,
Telephone: 0171 583 8455
Call date: July 1975, Inner Temple
Recorder
Qualifications: [MA (Oxon)]

JONES MS NICOLA JANE

Coleridge Chambers
Citadel 190 Corporation Street, Birmingham
B4 6QD, Telephone: 0121 233 3303
Call date: Oct 1996, Gray's Inn
Qualifications: [BA (Oxon), MA (Sussex)]

JONES NIGEL DOUGLAS

Hardwicke Building
New Square, Lincoln's Inn, London
WC2A 3SB, Telephone: 0171 242 2523
E-mail: clerks@hardwicke.co.uk
Call date: July 1976, Gray's Inn
Qualifications: [LLB (Lond)]

JONES PAUL ALAN

1 Essex Court
1st Floor, Temple, London EC4Y 9AR,
Telephone: 0171 936 3030
E-mail: one.essex_court@virgin.net
Call date: July 1981, Inner Temple
Qualifications: [BA (Hons)]

JONES PETER ALFRED

Guildhall Chambers
23 Broad Street, Bristol BS1 2HG,
Telephone: 0117 9273366
Call date: July 1973, Inner Temple
Qualifications: [BSc]

JONES PETER WILLIAM WARBURTON

4 Brick Court
Ground Floor, Temple, London EC4Y 9AD,
Telephone: 0171 797 7766
E-mail: chambers@4brick.co.uk
Call date: July 1969, Gray's Inn
Qualifications: [BA (Cantab)]

JONES PHILIP ALUN

9 Gough Square
London EC4A 3DE, Telephone: 0171 353 5371
Call date: Nov 1990, Middle Temple
Qualifications: [BA (Cantab), LLM (Lond)]

JONES PHILIP JOHN

13 Old Square
1st Floor, Lincoln's Inn, London WC2A 3UA,
Telephone: 0171 242 6105
E-mail: clerks@serlecourt.co.uk
Call date: July 1985, Lincoln's Inn
Qualifications: [MA,BCL (Oxon) LLM,
(Dalhousie Canada)]

JONES MISS PHILIPPA NANCY HUDSON

Derby Square Chambers
Merchants Court, Derby Square, Liverpool
L2 1TS, Telephone: 0151 709 4222
Call date: Oct 1992, Gray's Inn
Qualifications: [LLB]

JONES MISS RHIANNON

Lamb Chambers
Lamb Building, Temple, London EC4Y 7AS,
Telephone: 0171 797 8300
E-mail: lambchambers@link.org
Call date: Nov 1993, Inner Temple
Qualifications: [B Mus AKC Dip Law, MA]

JONES RHYS CHARLES MANSEL

33 Bedford Row
London WC1R 4JH,
Telephone: 0171 242 6476
Call date: May 1990, Middle Temple
Qualifications: [MA (Cantab)]

JONES RICHARD ALAN

33 Park Place
Cardiff CF1 3BA, Telephone: 01222 233313
Farrar's Building
Temple, London EC4Y 7BD,
Telephone: 0171 583 9241
E-mail: chambers@farrarsbuilding.co.uk
Door Tenant
Call date: Nov 1969, Gray's Inn
Qualifications: [MA (Oxon), LLB (Cantab)]

JONES RICHARD FREDERICK THOMAS

All Saints Chambers
9/11 Broad Street, Bristol BS1 2HP,
Telephone: 0117 921 1966
8 Fountain Court
Steelhouse Lane, Birmingham B4 6DR,
Telephone: 0121 236 5514/5
E-mail: clerks@no8chambers.co.uk
Door Tenant
Call date: July 1979, Gray's Inn
Qualifications: [LLB (Bris) MICE, FCIArb]

D

JONES RICHARD HENRY QC (1996)

1 Crown Office Row
3rd Floor, Temple, London EC4Y 7HH,
Telephone: 0171 583 9292
E-mail: onecor@link.org
Call date: Nov 1972, Inner Temple
Qualifications: [MA (Oxon)]

JONES RICHARD HUW FRANKLYN

Francis Taylor Bldg
Ground Floor, Temple, London EC4Y 7BY,
Telephone: 0171 353 7768/7769/2711
Call date: July 1984, Gray's Inn
Qualifications: [LLB (Wales)]

JONES ROBERT ALUN QC (1989)

3 Raymond Buildings
Gray's Inn, London WC1R 5BH,
Telephone: 0171 831 3833
E-mail: chambers@threeraymond.demon.co.uk
Call date: Nov 1972, Gray's Inn
Recorder
Qualifications: [BSc]

JONES ROBERT FFRANCON WYN

1 Middle Temple Lane
Temple, London EC4Y 1LT,
Telephone: 0171 583 0659 (12 Lines)
Call date: Nov 1993, Lincoln's Inn
Qualifications: [BA (Hons)]

JONES RODERICK JAMES WATSON

4 Brick Court
Ground Floor, Temple, London EC4Y 9AD,
Telephone: 0171 797 7766
E-mail: chambers@4brick.co.uk
Guildhall Chambers Porstmouth
Prudential Buildings 16 Guildhall Walk,
Portsmouth, Hampshire PO1 2DE,
Telephone: 01705 752400
Call date: July 1983, Gray's Inn
Qualifications: [BA]

JONES MISS SARAH ELIZABETH

9 Park Place
Cardiff CF1 3DP, Telephone: 01222 382731
Call date: July 1989, Gray's Inn
Qualifications: [BA (Exon), MA (Cantab)]

JONES MISS SARAH FRANCES

2 King's Bench Walk
Ground Floor, Temple, London EC4Y 7DE,
Telephone: 0171 353 1746
E-mail: 2kbw@atlas.co.uk
Call date: Nov 1996, Lincoln's Inn
Qualifications: [BA (Hons)]

JONES SEAN WILLIAM PAUL

11 King's Bench Walk
Temple, London EC4Y 7EQ,
Telephone: 0171 632 8500
E-mail: clerksroom@11-kbw.law.co.uk
Call date: Oct 1991, Inner Temple
Qualifications: [BA,BCL (Oxon)]

JONES STEPHEN HUGH

Farrar's Building
Temple, London EC4Y 7BD,
Telephone: 0171 583 9241
E-mail: chambers@farrarsbuilding.co.uk
Call date: Nov 1978, Inner Temple
Qualifications: [MA (Oxon)]

Fax: 0171 583 0090; DX: 406 London

Types of work: Common law (general); Housing;
Landlord and tenant; Professional negligence

Circuit: South Eastern

Publications: *Butterworths County Court
Pleadings and Precedents* - Joint Contributing
Editor of Landlord and Tenant Division

Reported cases: *Capital and City Holdings v
Dean Warburg Ltd*, [1989] 1 EGLR 90, 1989.
Landlord and tenant - liability of guarantors -
mode of forfeiture.
Foalquest Ltd v Roberts, [1990] 1 EGLR 50,
1990. Agency - whether agent personally liable.
*William Hill (Southern) Ltd v Waller and
Russell*, [1991] 1 EGLR 271, 1991. Landlord and
tenant - liability of guarantors.
National Westminster Bank Plc v Daniel,
[1993] 1 WLR 1493, 1993. Procedure - Order 14
- credibility of affidavits.
Fox and Widley v Guram, [1998] 03 EG 142,
1997. Landlord and tenant - rent review clause -
effect of s12 of Arbitration Act 1996.

JONES STEVEN CHARLES

South Western Chambers
Melville House 12 Middle Street, Taunton,
Somerset TA1 1SH, Telephone: 01823 331919
Call date: Oct 1994, Middle Temple
Qualifications: [LLB (Hons)(Exeter)]

JONES STEWART ELGAN QC (1994)

3 Paper Bldgs
1st Floor, Temple, London EC4Y 7EU,
Telephone: 0171 583 8055
E-mail: london@3paper.com
20 Lorne Park Road
Bournemouth BH1 1JN,
Telephone: 01202 292102 (5 Lines)
4 St Peter Street
Winchester SO23 8OW,
Telephone: 01962 868884
Call date: Nov 1972, Gray's Inn
Recorder
Qualifications: [MA (Oxon)]

JONES THOMAS GLANVILLE

Angel Chambers
94 Walter Road, Swansea SA1 5QA,
Telephone: 01792 6464623/6464648
Call date: Nov 1956, Gray's Inn
Recorder
Qualifications: [LLB (Lond)]

JONES TIMOTHY ARTHUR

St Philip's Chambers
Fountain Court, Steelhouse Lane, Birmingham,
West Midlands B4 6DR,
Telephone: 0121 246 7000
Arden Chambers
27 John Street, London WC1N 2BL,
Telephone: 0171 242 4244
Call date: July 1975, Inner Temple
Qualifications: [LLB (Lond), ACIArb]

Fax: 0171 242 3224; 0121 246 7001;
Out of hours telephone: 0966 195228;
DX: 16073 Birmingham 4/29 Chancery Lane;
Other comms: E-mail timjones@link.org; Link:
Timothy Jones

Types of work: Administrative; Environment;
European Convention on Human Rights; Local
government; Town and country planning

Other professional qualifications: ACIArb

Membership of foreign bars: Ireland and
Northern Ireland

Circuit: Midland and Oxford

Awards and memberships: Member: Planning
and Environment Bar Association;
Administrative Law Bar Association; UK
Environmental Law Association; Fellow Royal
Geographical Society

Languages spoken: French

Publications: 'Property Rights, Planning Law
and the European Convention', *European
Human Rights Law Review* 233, 1996;
'Travellers' Tales' (the impact of the Criminal
Justice and Public Order Bill on Romanies),
Gazette, 7 September 1994

Cases
Buckley v United Kingdom 23 EHRR 101
[1996] JPL 1018 [1995] JPL 633 (ECtHR)
Burton v United Kingdom 22 EHRR CD134
(ECommHR)
Henderson v Law 17 HLR 237 (CA)
Hughes v Environment Secretary 71 P&CR 168
NHBC v Sandwell MBC [1991] COD 17 (DC)
R v Bexley LBC ex parte B [1995] CLY 3225
R v Bristol CC ex parte McDonough [1993] CLY
3891
R v Duckworth 16 CrAppR(S) 529 (CA)
R v Hereford & Worcester CC ex parte Smith
[1994] COD 129 (CA)
*R v Housing Benefit Review Board ex parte
Smith* 19 HLR 217
R v Oldbury Justices ex parte Smith [1995]
7AdminLR 315
R v Sandwell MBC ex parte Lyn 34 RVR 126
R v Environment Secretary ex parte Davies 61
P&CR 487 (CA)
R v Environment Secretary ex parte Smith
[1988] COD 3
R v South Herefordshire DC ex parte Miles 17
HLR 82
R v Warley Justices ex parte Callis [1994] COD
240
Safeways v Greenwich LBC [1995] JPL 865
Sainsbury v Greenwich LBC [1997] JPL 774
South Northamptonshire DC v Power [1987] 1
WLR 1433 (CA)
Stirk v Bridgnorth DC 73 P&CR 439 (CA)
Stirrup v Environment Secretary LA Law 1/94
Turner v United Kingdom 23 EHRR CD 181
Webb v Environment Secretary 71 P&CR 411
Webb v United Kingdom [1977] EHRLR 680
(EComm HR)
Woodhouse v Walsall MBC [1994] EnvLR 30
Woolhead v Environment Secretary 71 P&CR
419
Wychavon DC v Environment Secretary [1994]
2 EnvLR 239
Wyre Forest DC v Bostock [1993] 1 EnvLR 235
(CA)

Wyre Forest DC v Environment Secretary
[1990] 2 AC 357 (HL)

JONES WILLIAM JOHN

1 Hare Court
Ground Floor, Temple, London EC4Y 7BE,
Telephone: 0171 353 3982/5324
Call date: Nov 1972, Inner Temple
Recorder

JORDAN ANDREW

2 Harcourt Bldgs
Ground Floor/Left, Temple, London
EC4Y 9DB, Telephone: 0171 583 9020
E-mail: clerks@harcourt.co.uk
Stanbrook & Henderson
2 Harcourt Bldgs 2nd Floor, Temple, London
EC4Y 9DB, Telephone: 0171 353 0101
E-mail: clerks@harcourt.co.uk
Call date: July 1973, Lincoln's Inn
Qualifications: [LLB (Warwick)]

JORDAN MS FIONA CLARE

The Corn Exchange
5th Floor Fenwick Street, Liverpool L2 7QS,
Telephone: 0151 227 1081/5009
Call date: Oct 1991, Gray's Inn
Qualifications: [LLB (Hons, Lond)]

JORDAN MICHAEL JOSEPH

21 Colless Road
Seven Sisters, London N15 4NR,
Telephone: 0181 365 1706
Call date: July 1974, Middle Temple
Qualifications: [MA (Oxon)]

JORY RICHARD NORMAN

9-12 Bell Yard
London WC2A 2LF,
Telephone: 0171 400 1800
Call date: Oct 1993, Middle Temple
Qualifications: [BA (Hons)(Reading), CPE
(Middx)]

JORY ROBERT JOHN HUGH

Enterprise Chambers
9 Old Square, Lincoln's Inn, London
WC2A 3SR, Telephone: 0171 405 9471
Enterprise Chambers
38 Park Square, Leeds LS1 2PA,
Telephone: 01132 460391
Enterprise Chambers
65 Quayside, Newcastle upon Tyne NE1 3DS,
Telephone: 0191 222 3344
Call date: Oct 1992, Lincoln's Inn
Qualifications: [MA, Dip Law]

JOSE RICHARD CALDER

St Mary's Chambers
50 High Pavement, Lace Market, Nottingham
NG1 1HW, Telephone: 0115 9503503
E-mail: clerks@smc.law.co.uk
Call date: Nov 1971, Gray's Inn
Assistant Recorder
Qualifications: [BA (Hons)]

JOSEPH CHARLES HENRY

4 Paper Bldgs
2nd Floor, Temple, London EC4Y 7EX,
Telephone: 0171 583 0816/071 353 1131
E-mail: clerks@4paperbuildings.co.uk
Call date: July 1980, Lincoln's Inn
Qualifications: [BA (Hons), FCIArb]

JOSEPH CLIFFORD DEREK

Pepys' Chambers
17 Fleet Street, London EC4Y 1AA,
Telephone: 0171 936 2710
Call date: Apr 1975, Gray's Inn
Qualifications: [MA (Oxon), LMRTPI]

JOSEPH DAVID PHILIP

Essex Court Chambers
24 Lincoln's Inn Fields, London WC2A 3ED,
Telephone: 0171 813 8000
E-mail: clerksroom@essexcourt-chambers.co.uk
Call date: Nov 1984, Middle Temple
Qualifications: [MA (Cantab)]

D

JOSEPH MRS ELIZABETH ANN AYODELE

Acre Lane Neighbourhood Chambers
30A Acre Lane, London SW2 5SG,
Telephone: 0171 274 4400
66 Daubeney Road
London E5 0EF, Telephone: 0181 985 3030
Call date: July 1983, Gray's Inn
Qualifications: [BA, LLM]

JOSEPH SELLAPPH JOB

2 Middle Temple Lane
3rd Floor, Temple, London EC4Y 9AA,
Telephone: 0171 583 4540
Call date: Nov 1983, Middle Temple
Qualifications: [LLB (Lond), LLB (Sri Lanka)]

JOSEPH MISS SUSANNE

20 Britton Street
1st Floor, London EC1M 5NQ,
Telephone: 0171 608 3765
Call date: Nov 1995, Middle Temple
Qualifications: [LLB (Hons)]

JOSEPH MS WENDY ROSE

6 King's Bench Walk
Ground Floor, Temple, London EC4Y 7DR,
Telephone: 0171 583 0410
Call date: Nov 1975, Gray's Inn
Assistant Recorder
Qualifications: [MA (Cantab)]

JOSHI PRAMOD KUMAR

Wessex Chambers
48 Queens Road, Reading, Berkshire
RG1 4BD, Telephone: 01734 568856
E-mail: wessexchambers@compuserve.com
Call date: Nov 1992, Inner Temple
Qualifications: [LLB (Hons), MBA]

JOSLING WILLIAM HENRY CHARLES

Fenners Chambers
3 Madingley Road, Cambridge CB3 0EE,
Telephone: 01223 368761
Fenners Chambers
8-12 Priestgate, Peterborough PE1 1JA,
Telephone: 01733 62030
Call date: Nov 1995, Lincoln's Inn
Qualifications: [MA (Cantab), Dip.Law]

JOSS NORMAN JAMES

1 Essex Court
1st Floor, Temple, London EC4Y 9AR,
Telephone: 0171 936 3030
E-mail: one.essex_court@virgin.net
Call date: July 1982, Lincoln's Inn
Qualifications: [BA (Hons)]

JOSSE DAVID BENJAMIN

Bridewell Chambers
2 Bridewell Place, London EC4V 6AP,
Telephone: 0171 797 8800
E-mail: clerks@bridewell.law.co.uk
Call date: July 1985, Middle Temple
Qualifications: [BA (Lond)]

JOURDAN STEPHEN ERIC

Falcon Chambers
Falcon Court, London EC4Y 1AA,
Telephone: 0171 353 2484/7
Call date: Nov 1989, Gray's Inn
Qualifications: [MA (Cantab)]

JOWELL DANIEL SIMON SUZMAN

1 Essex Court
Ground Floor, Temple, London EC4Y 9AR,
Telephone: 0171 583 2000
E-mail: clerks@oneessexcourt.co.uk
Call date: Nov 1995, Middle Temple
Qualifications: [BA (Hons), LLM]

JOWELL PROFESSOR JEFFREY LIONEL QC (1993)

2 Hare Court
Ground Floor, Temple, London EC4Y 7BH,
Telephone: 0171 583 1770
E-mail: 2_Hare_Court@link.org
Call date: Feb 1965, Middle Temple
Qualifications: [BA, LLB (C.Town), MA (Oxon),
LLM, SJD (Harvard), LLD]

JOWITT MATTHEW THOMAS

9 Bedford Row
London WC1R 4AZ,
Telephone: 0171 242 3555
E-mail: clerks@9br.co.uk
Call date: Nov 1994, Middle Temple
Qualifications: [MA (Oxons)]

JOY HENRY MARTIN

6 Pump Court
1st Floor, Temple, London EC4Y 7AR,
Telephone: 0171 797 8400
E-mail: sa_hockman_qc@link.org
6-8 Mill Street
Maidstone, Kent ME15 6XH,
Telephone: 01622 688094
Call date: July 1971, Lincoln's Inn
Qualifications: [LLB (Soton)]

JOYCE MICHAEL JOHN

9 Gough Square
London EC4A 3DE, Telephone: 0171 353 5371
Call date: Nov 1976, Gray's Inn
Qualifications: [LLB (Lond)]

JOYCE PETER STUART LANGFORD QC (1991)

1 High Pavement
Nottingham NG1 1HF,
Telephone: 0115 9418218
36 Bedford Row
London WC1R 4JH,
Telephone: 0171 421 8000
E-mail: 36bedfordrow@link.org
Door Tenant
Call date: July 1968, Inner Temple
Recorder

JUBB BRIAN PATRICK

Gray's Inn Chambers
5th Floor, Gray's Inn, London WC1R 5JA,
Telephone: 0171 404 1111
Call date: Nov 1971, Gray's Inn

JUCKES ROBERT WILLIAM SOMERVILLE

3 Fountain Court
Steelhouse Lane, Birmingham B4 6DR,
Telephone: 0121 236 5854
Call date: July 1974, Inner Temple
Recorder
Qualifications: [BA (Exon)]

JUDD MISS FRANCES JEAN

2 Harcourt Bldgs
1st Floor, Temple, London EC4Y 9DB,
Telephone: 0171 353 6961/7
Harcourt Chambers
Churchill House 3 St Aldate's Courtyard, St
Aldate's, Oxford OX1 1BN,
Telephone: 01865 791559
Call date: Nov 1984, Middle Temple
Qualifications: [BA(Cantab)]

JUDGE ANDREW JOHN

Westgate Chambers
144 High Street, Lewes, East Sussex BN7 1XT,
Telephone: 01273 480510
Door Tenant
Call date: July 1986, Middle Temple
Qualifications: [BA (Hons)]

JUDGE CHARLES JOSEPH

5 Paper Bldgs
1st Floor, Temple, London EC4Y 7HB,
Telephone: 0171 583 6117
E-mail: clerks@5-paperbuildings.law.co.uk
Call date: July 1981, Inner Temple
Qualifications: [BA (Hons)]

JUDGE MISS LISA JANE

Manchester House Chambers
18-22 Bridge Street, Manchester M3 3BZ,
Telephone: 0161 834 7007
Call date: Oct 1993, Gray's Inn
Qualifications: [LLB (Hons)]

JULIEN MISS CHRISTINE HELEN

3 Temple Gardens
3rd Floor, Temple, London EC4Y 9AU,
Telephone: 0171 583 0010
Call date: Nov 1991, Inner Temple
Qualifications: [LLB (Hons)(L'pool)]

JUNAID-ADAMSON MISS SHEKINAH ADEBISI

Chancery Chambers
1st Floor Offices 70/72 Chancery Lane,
London WC2A 1AB,
Telephone: 0171 405 6879/6870
Call date: Nov 1994, Lincoln's Inn
Qualifications: [LLB (Hons)]

JUPP JEFFREY ERNEST

36 Bedford Row
London WC1R 4JH,
Telephone: 0171 421 8000
E-mail: 36bedfordrow@link.org
Call date: Nov 1994, Inner Temple
Qualifications: [BA, CPE]

JURENKO MISS RENATA ANNA

95A Chancery Lane
London WC2A 1DT,
Telephone: 0171 405 3101
Call date: Oct 1993, Middle Temple
Qualifications: [B.Ed (Hons)]

JUSS DR SATVINDER SINGH

4 King's Bench Walk
2nd Floor, Temple, London EC4Y 7DL,
Telephone: 0171 353 3581
Call date: Nov 1989, Gray's Inn
Qualifications: [BA, Ph.D (Cantab)]

KADRI SADAKAT

Doughty Street Chambers
11 Doughty Street, London WC1N 2PG,
Telephone: 0171 404 1313
E-mail: doughty_street@compuserve.com
Call date: Nov 1989, Inner Temple
Qualifications: [BA (Cantab), LLM (Harvard)]

KADRI SIBGHATULLAH QC (1989)

6 King's Bench Walk
Ground, Third & Fourth Floors, Temple,
London EC4Y 7DR,
Telephone: 0171 353 4931/583 0695
Call date: Nov 1969, Inner Temple
Qualifications: [FRSA]

KAFFEL PAUL ELLIOTT

Lion Court
Chancery House 53-64 Chancery Lane, London
WC2A 1SJ, Telephone: 0171 404 6565
Call date: Nov 1993, Inner Temple
Qualifications: [BSc (Manc), CPE]

KAIHIVA ABIUD KARATE

Eldon Chambers
Fourth Floor 30/32 Fleet Street, London
EC4Y 1AA, Telephone: 0171 353 4636
Call date: Feb 1993, Inner Temple
Qualifications: [BCOM, LLB,]

KALER MISS MANJEET KAUR

11 Old Square
Ground Floor, Lincoln's Inn, London
WC2A 3TS, Telephone: 0171 242 5022/
405 1074
Call date: Feb 1993, Middle Temple
Qualifications: [LLB (Hons)(Middx)]

KALLIPETIS MICHEL LOUIS QC (1989)

Littleton Chambers
3 King's Bench Walk North, Temple, London
EC4Y 7HR, Telephone: 0171 797 8600
E-mail: littletonchambers@compuserve.com
Call date: July 1968, Gray's Inn
Recorder
Qualifications: [LLB (Lond)]

KALSI MRS MANINDER

New Court Chambers
Suite 200 Gazette Building, 168 Corporation
Street, Birmingham B4 6TZ,
Telephone: 0121 693 6656
Call date: Nov 1992, Inner Temple
Qualifications: [LLB]

KAMILL MISS LOUISE NAIMA RACHEL

1 Hare Court
Ground Floor, Temple, London EC4Y 7BE,
Telephone: 0171 353 3982/5324
Call date: July 1974, Inner Temple
Recorder

KAMLISH STEPHEN MICHAEL ADRIAN

14 Tooks Court
Cursitor St, London EC4A 1LB,
Telephone: 0171 405 8828
E-mail: clerks @tooks.law.co.uk
Call date: July 1979, Gray's Inn
Qualifications: [BA (Hons)]

D

KANE ADAM VINCENT SIMON

1 Dr Johnson's Bldgs
Ground Floor, Temple, London EC4Y 7AX,
Telephone: 0171 353 9328
Call date: Nov 1993, Gray's Inn
Qualifications: [BA (Oxon), CPE]

KAPLAN MRS BARBARA JANE

2 Crown Office Row
2nd Floor, Temple, London EC4Y 7HJ,
Telephone: 0171 797 8000
Call date: Nov 1980, Inner Temple
Qualifications: [MA (Cantab) ACIArb]

KAPUR DEEPAK KUMAR

2 King's Bench Walk
1st Floor, Temple, London EC4Y 7DE,
Telephone: 0171 353 9276
Call date: July 1984, Lincoln's Inn
Qualifications: [BA (Hons)]

KARALLIS MISS CONSTANTINA DINA

10 King's Bench Walk
1st Floor, Temple, London EC4Y 7EB,
Telephone: 0171 353 2501
Call date: Nov 1989, Gray's Inn
Qualifications: [LLB (Kingston), LLM]

KARAS JONATHAN MARCUS

4 Breams Buildings
London EC4A 1AQ,
Telephone: 0171 353 5835/430 1221
Call date: July 1986, Middle Temple
Qualifications: [MA (Oxon), Dip Law]

KARK THOMAS VICTOR WILLIAM

Hollis Whiteman Chambers
3rd/4th Floor Queen Elizabeth Bldg, Temple,
London EC4Y 9BS, Telephone: 0171 583 5766
E-mail: hollis.whiteman@btinternet.com
Call date: July 1982, Inner Temple

KARMY-JONES MISS RIEL MEREDITH

1 Hare Court
Ground Floor, Temple, London EC4Y 7BE,
Telephone: 0171 353 3982/5324
Call date: Nov 1995, Lincoln's Inn
Qualifications: [BA (Alberta), LLB (Hons)]

KARSTEN IAN GEORGE FRANCIS QC (1990)

Queen Elizabeth Bldg
2nd Floor, Temple, London EC4Y 9BS,
Telephone: 0171 797 7837
Door Tenant
Exchange Chambers
Pearl Assurance House Derby Square,
Liverpool L2 9XX, Telephone: 0151 236 7747/
0458
E-mail: exchangechambers@btinternet.com
Call date: Nov 1967, Gray's Inn
Assistant Recorder
Qualifications: [MA, BCL (Oxon)]

KARU LEE N

2 Paper Bldgs
1st Floor, Temple, London EC4Y 7ET,
Telephone: 0171 936 2611 (10 Lines)
E-mail: clerks@2pbbarristers.co.uk
Call date: July 1985, Lincoln's Inn
Qualifications: [BA (Hons)]

KASHMIRI MISS SOPHIA

Chambers of Raana Sheikh
Gray's Inn Chambers, Gray's Inn, London
WC1R, Telephone: 0171 831 5344
E-mail: s.mcblain@btinternet.com
Call date: Oct 1994, Gray's Inn
Qualifications: [LLB]

KATAN JONATHAN MAX

Goldsmith Chambers
Ground Floor Goldsmith Building, Temple,
London EC4Y 7BL,
Telephone: 0171 353 6802/3/4/5
E-mail: celiamonksfield@btinternet.com
Call date: Oct 1990, Gray's Inn
Qualifications: [LLB]

KATKOWSKI CHRISTOPHER ANDREW MARK

4 Breams Buildings
London EC4A 1AQ,
Telephone: 0171 353 5835/430 1221
Call date: Feb 1982, Gray's Inn
Qualifications: [MA, LLB (Cantab)]

KATRAK CYRUS PESI

Gough Square Chambers
6-7 Gough Square, London EC4A 3DE,
Telephone: 0171 353 0924
E-mail: gsc@goughsq.co.uk
Call date: Oct 1991, Gray's Inn
Qualifications: [LLB]

KATYAR ARUN KUMAR

2 King's Bench Walk
1st Floor, Temple, London EC4Y 7DE,
Telephone: 0171 353 9276
Call date: Nov 1993, Lincoln's Inn
Qualifications: [LLB (Hons)]

KATZ PHILIP ALEC JACKSON

9-12 Bell Yard
London WC2A 2LF,
Telephone: 0171 400 1800
Call date: Nov 1976, Middle Temple
Qualifications: [MA (Oxon)]

KAUFMANN MS PHILLIPPA JANE

Doughty Street Chambers
11 Doughty Street, London WC1N 2PG,
Telephone: 0171 404 1313
E-mail: doughty_street@compuserve.com
Call date: Oct 1991, Gray's Inn
Qualifications: [MA (Sheffield), LLB (Bris)]

KAUL MISS KALYANI

3 Gray's Inn Square
Ground Floor, London WC1R 5AH,
Telephone: 0171 520 5600
E-mail: gis3@btinternet.com
Call date: July 1983, Middle Temple
Qualifications: [LLB]

KAUR MISS HARINDER

New Walk Chambers
27 New Walk, Leicester LE1 6TE,
Telephone: 0116 2559144
Call date: May 1995, Inner Temple
Qualifications: [LLB (Hons), LLM]

KAUR MISS RANI

Acre Lane Neighbourhood Chambers
30A Acre Lane, London SW2 5SG,
Telephone: 0171 274 4400
Call date: Nov 1993, Gray's Inn
Qualifications: [LLB (Hull)]

KAVANAGH GILES WILFRED CONOR

5 Bell Yard
London WC2A 2JR, Telephone: 0171 333 8811
Call date: Feb 1984, Middle Temple
Qualifications: [MA, LLM (Cantab)]

Fax: 0171 333 8831;
Out of hours telephone: 0181 549 7391;
DX: LDE 400

Types of work: Aviation; Commercial litigation;
Insurance/reinsurance; Professional negligence;
Town and country planning

Circuit: Western

Awards and memberships: Commercial Bar
Association (COMBAR); Professional
Negligence Bar Association (PNBA); Planning
and Environmental Bar Association (PEBA)

Languages spoken: French

Publications: *Coroners Rules and Statutes*,
1984

Reported cases: *R v West Berks Coroner, ex
parte Thomas*, (1991) *The Times* 25 April, 1991.
Challenge to coroner's inquisition both by
judicial review and s13 Coroners Act 1988.
Philcox v CAA, (1995) *The Times*, 5 June, 1995.
Duty of care of CAA as aviation regulator.
Wall v Lefever, (1997) *The Times*, 1 August,
1997. Wasted costs - the appropriateness of
appeals against refusals to make wasted costs
orders.
*R v North Somerset Council ex parte Garnett
and Another*, [1997] EGCS 48, 1997. Right of
third parties to challenge planning decisions.

KAY MICHAEL JACK DAVID

3 Verulam Buildings
London WC1R 5NT,
Telephone: 0171 831 8441
E-mail: clerks@3verulam.co.uk
Park Lane Chambers
19 Westgate, Leeds LS1 2RD,
Telephone: 0113 2285000
Call date: July 1981, Lincoln's Inn
Qualifications: [MA (Cantab)]

D

KAY ROBERT JERVIS QC (1996)

4 Field Court
Gray's Inn, London WC1R 5EA,
Telephone: 0171 440 6900
E-mail: chambers@4fieldcourt.co.uk
Call date: Nov 1972, Lincoln's Inn
Qualifications: [LLB]

KAY STEVEN WALTON QC (1997)

3 Gray's Inn Square
Ground Floor, London WC1R 5AH,
Telephone: 0171 520 5600
E-mail: gis3@btinternet.com
Call date: Nov 1977, Inner Temple
Assistant Recorder
Qualifications: [LLB (Leeds)]

KAYANI (MOHAMMED) ASAF (REHMAT)

3 Stone Bldgs
Ground Floor, Lincoln's Inn, London
WC2A 3XL, Telephone: 0171 242 4937/
405 8358
Call date: Nov 1991, Lincoln's Inn
Qualifications: [LLB (Hons) (Leeds), BCL
(Oxon)]

KAYE MISS LARAINE

Lion Court
Chambers House 53-64 Chancery Lane, London
WC2A 1SJ, Telephone: 0171 404 6565
Call date: July 1971, Middle Temple
Qualifications: [LLB (Lond), LLM (Lon)]

KAYE ROGER GODFREY QC (1989)

24 Old Bldgs
Ground Floor, Lincoln's Inn, London
WC2A 3UJ, Telephone: 0171 404 0946
E-mail: clerks@24oldbuildings.law.co.uk
St John's Chambers
Small Street, Bristol BS1 1DW,
Telephone: 0117 9213456/298514
E-mail: clerks@stjohns.uk.com
Call date: Nov 1970, Lincoln's Inn
Recorder
Qualifications: [LLB]

KAYMAN MRS ESTHER LEBE

10 King's Bench Walk
1st Floor, Temple, London EC4Y 7EB,
Telephone: 0171 353 2501
Call date: July 1974, Gray's Inn

KAYNE CHARLES ADRIAN

1 Gray's Inn Square
Ground Floor, London WC1R 5AA,
Telephone: 0171 405 8946/7/8
Call date: Nov 1989, Inner Temple
Qualifications: [LLB (Hons)]

KEALEY GAVIN SEAN JAMES QC (1994)

7 King's Bench Walk
Ground Floor, Temple, London EC4Y 7DS,
Telephone: 0171 583 0404
Call date: Feb 1977, Inner Temple
Qualifications: [BA (Oxon)]

KEALEY SIMON THOMAS

10 Park Square
Leeds LS1 2LH, Telephone: 0113 2455438
E-mail: chambers@bandit.legend.co.uk
Call date: Apr 1991, Inner Temple
Qualifications: [LLB (Liverpool)]

KEALY CHARLES BRIAN

10 Park Square
Leeds LS1 2LH, Telephone: 0113 2455438
E-mail: chambers@bandit.legend.co.uk
Call date: Nov 1965, Middle Temple
Recorder

KEANE DESMOND ST JOHN QC (1981)

Bracton Chambers
95a Chancery Lane, London WC2A 1DT,
Telephone: 0171 242 4248
Pepys' Chambers
17 Fleet Street, London EC4Y 1AA,
Telephone: 0171 936 2710
Call date: June 1964, Middle Temple
Qualifications: [MA (Oxon)]

KEANE MICHAEL LEO

4 Paper Bldgs
Ground Floor, Temple, London EC4Y 7EX,
Telephone: 0171 353 3366/583 7155
E-mail: clerks@4paperbuildings.com
Call date: Nov 1963, Middle Temple
Recorder
Qualifications: [MA (Cantab)]

KEANE MICHAEL PETER

29 Bedford Row Chambers
London WC1R 4HE,
Telephone: 0171 831 2626
Call date: July 1979, Gray's Inn
Qualifications: [MA (Cantab)]

KEANY BRENDAN JOSEPH

3 Gray's Inn Square
Ground Floor, London WC1R 5AH,
Telephone: 0171 520 5600
E-mail: gis3@btinternet.com
Call date: July 1974, Middle Temple
Qualifications: [BA (Lond)]

KEARL GUY ALEXANDER

St Paul's House
5th Floor 23 Park Square South, Leeds
LS1 2ND, Telephone: 0113 2455866
Call date: July 1982, Middle Temple
Qualifications: [BA]

KEARNEY JAMES MARTIN

Lamb Building
Ground Floor, Temple, London EC4Y 7AS,
Telephone: 0171 797 7788
E-mail: lamb.building@link.org
Call date: Feb 1992, Gray's Inn
Qualifications: [LLB (Dublin)]

KEARNEY JOHN

2 Paper Bldgs
1st Floor, Temple, London EC4Y 7ET,
Telephone: 0171 936 2611 (10 Lines)
E-mail: clerks@2pbbarristers.co.uk
Call date: Nov 1994, Middle Temple
Qualifications: [LLB (Hons)]

KEEGAN LESLIE FRANCIS

1 Pump Court
Lower Ground Floor, Temple, London
EC4Y 7AB, Telephone: 0171 583 2012/
353 4341
E-mail: (name) @1pumpcourt.co.uk
Call date: Nov 1989, Middle Temple
Qualifications: [BA [Dub], B.Sc [Dun], Dip in Law]

KEEHAN MICHAEL JOSEPH

St Ive's Chambers
9 Fountain Ct, Birmingham B4 6DR,
Telephone: 0121 236 0863/0929
Call date: July 1982, Middle Temple
Qualifications: [LLB B'ham]

KEELEY JAMES FRANCIS

25 Park Square
Leeds LS1 2PW, Telephone: 0113 2451841/2/3
E-mail: sovereignchambers@btinternet.com
Call date: Oct 1993, Middle Temple
Qualifications: [LLB (Hons)(Kingston)]

KEELING ADRIAN FRANCIS

3 Fountain Court
Steelhouse Lane, Birmingham B4 6DR,
Telephone: 0121 236 5854
Call date: Oct 1990, Inner Temple
Qualifications: [BA (Cantab)]

KEEN GRAEME

4 Breams Buildings
London EC4A 1AQ,
Telephone: 0171 353 5835/430 1221
Call date: Oct 1995, Middle Temple
Qualifications: [LLB (Hons)]

KEEN KENNETH ROGER QC (1991)

Paradise Square Chambers
26 Paradise Square, Sheffield S1 2DE,
Telephone: 0114 2738951
Call date: Feb 1976, Gray's Inn
Recorder

D

KEENAN PETER BERNARD

Cobden House Chambers
19 Quay Street, Manchester M3 3HN,
Telephone: 0161 833 6000
E-mail: clerks@cobden.co.uk
Call date: Nov 1962, Gray's Inn
Qualifications: [LLB, B (Litt)]

KEENE MRS GILLIAN MARGARET

Fountain Court
Temple, London EC4Y 9DH,
Telephone: 0171 583 3335
E-mail: chambers@fountaincourt.co.uk
Call date: Nov 1980, Gray's Inn
Qualifications: [MA (Oxon)]

KEFFORD ANTHONY JOHN ROLAND

East Anglian Chambers
57 London Street, Norwich NR2 1HL,
Telephone: 01603 617351
East Anglian Chambers
Sanders House 52 North Hill, Colchester
CO1 1PY, Telephone: 01206 572756
East Anglian Chambers
Gresham House 5 Museum Street, Ipswich
IP1 1HQ, Telephone: 01473 214481
Call date: Nov 1980, Middle Temple
Qualifications: [BSc]

KEIGAN MISS LINDA DIONE

Chambers of Helen Grindrod QC
1st Floor 95a Chancery Lane, London
WC2A 2JG, Telephone: 0171 404 4777
Call date: Nov 1992, Inner Temple
Qualifications: [LLB]

KEITH ALISTAIR JOHN

5 Pump Court
Ground Floor, Temple, London EC4Y 7AP,
Telephone: 0171 353 2532
E-mail: fivepump@netcomuk.co.uk
Call date: Nov 1974, Middle Temple
Qualifications: [BD (Lond)]

KEITH HUGO GEORGE

3 Raymond Buildings
Gray's Inn, London WC1R 5BH,
Telephone: 0171 831 3833
E-mail: chambers@threeraymond.demon.co.uk
Call date: Nov 1989, Gray's Inn
Qualifications: [MA (Oxon)]

KEITH THOMAS HAMILTON

Fountain Court
Temple, London EC4Y 9DH,
Telephone: 0171 583 3335
E-mail: chambers@fountaincourt.co.uk
Call date: July 1983, Gray's Inn
Qualifications: [BA (Oxon)]

KELBRICK ANTHONY MICHAEL

37 Park Square
Leeds LS1 2NY, Telephone: 0113 2439422
Call date: Feb 1992, Gray's Inn
Qualifications: [BA]

KELEHER PAUL ROBERT

3 Gray's Inn Square
Ground Floor, London WC1R 5AH,
Telephone: 0171 520 5600
E-mail: gis3@btinternet.com
Call date: July 1980, Gray's Inn
Qualifications: [BA (Cantab)]

KELLEHER BENEDICT PETER JOHN

2 Harcourt Bldgs
1st Floor, Temple, London EC4Y 9DB,
Telephone: 0171 353 2112/2817
Call date: Nov 1994, Inner Temple
Qualifications: [LLB, MSc (Bris)]

KELLEHER KEITH ROY

Eaton House
1st Floor 4 Eaton Road, Branksome Park,
Poole, Dorset BH13 6DG,
Telephone: 01202 766301/768068
Door Tenant
Call date: Nov 1987, Gray's Inn
Qualifications: [LLB (Hons)]

KELLETT JOHN CHARLES

1 Paper Bldgs
1st Floor, Temple, London EC4Y 7EP,
Telephone: 0171 353 3728/4953
Octagon House
19 Colegate, Norwich NR3 1AT,
Telephone: 01603 623186
E-mail: octagon@netmatters.co.uk
Door Tenant
Call date: Nov 1971, Middle Temple
Qualifications: [BA (Cantab)]

KELLY BRENDAN DAMIEN

1 Hare Court
Ground Floor, Temple, London EC4Y 7BE,
Telephone: 0171 353 3982/5324
Call date: July 1988, Gray's Inn
Qualifications: [LLB]

KELLY CHARLES LAYTON

Trinity Chambers
9-12 Trinity Chare, Quayside, Newcastle Upon
Tyne NE1 3DF, Telephone: 0191 232 1927
Call date: Feb 1965, Inner Temple
Qualifications: [MA (Cantab)]

KELLY DAVID

Broadway House Chambers
Broadway House 9 Bank Street, Bradford,
West Yorkshire BD1 1TW,
Telephone: 01274 722560
Call date: July 1980, Gray's Inn
Qualifications: [LLB (L'pool)]

KELLY GEOFFREY ROBERT

Pump Court Chambers
Upper Ground Floor 3 Pump Court, Temple,
London EC4Y 7AJ, Telephone: 0171 353 0711
Pump Court Chambers
31 Southgate Street, Winchester SO23 8EE,
Telephone: 01962 868161
Call date: Feb 1992, Middle Temple
Qualifications: [LLB (Hons) (Lond)]

KELLY MARK

Francis Taylor Bldg
3rd Floor, Temple, London EC4Y 7BY,
Telephone: 0171 797 7250
Call date: Nov 1985, Gray's Inn
Qualifications: [LLB (Bristol), Dip in Law
(Belgium)]

KELLY MARTYN ALEXANDER

9 Park Place
Cardiff CF1 3DP, Telephone: 01222 382731
Call date: Nov 1972, Inner Temple
Qualifications: [MA (Oxon)]

KELLY MATTHIAS JOHN

Old Square Chambers
1 Verulam Buildings, Gray's Inn, London
WC1R 5LQ, Telephone: 0171 831 0801
Old Square Chambers
Hanover House 47 Corn Street, Bristol
BS1 1HT, Telephone: 0117 9277111
Call date: Feb 1979, Gray's Inn
Qualifications: [BA (Hons), LLB (Dub)]

KELLY MRS PATRICIA ANN

3 Paper Bldgs
1st Floor, Temple, London EC4Y 7EU,
Telephone: 0171 583 8055
E-mail: london@3paper.com
4 St Peter Street
Winchester SO23 8OW,
Telephone: 01962 868884
20 Lorne Park Road
Bournemouth BH1 1JN,
Telephone: 01202 292102 (5 Lines)
Call date: July 1988, Inner Temple
Qualifications: [LLB (Soton)]

KELLY RICHARD BERNARD

East Anglian Chambers
Sanders House 52 North Hill, Colchester
CO1 1PY, Telephone: 01206 572756
East Anglian Chambers
57 London Street, Norwich NR2 1HL,
Telephone: 01603 617351
East Anglian Chambers
Gresham House 5 Museum Street, Ipswich
IP1 1HQ, Telephone: 01473 214481
Call date: Oct 1994, Gray's Inn
Qualifications: [BA]

KELLY MISS SANDRA MARIE

3 Paper Bldgs
1st Floor, Temple, London EC4Y 7EU,
Telephone: 0171 583 8055
E-mail: london@3paper.com
4 St Peter Street
Winchester SO23 8OW,
Telephone: 01962 868884
20 Lorne Park Road
Bournemouth BH1 1JN,
Telephone: 01202 292102 (5 Lines)
Call date: Nov 1992, Inner Temple
Qualifications: [LLB (Hons) (Glas), Dip in
Higher, European Studies, College of Europe]

D

KELLY SEAN

Cobden House Chambers
19 Quay Street, Manchester M3 3HN,
Telephone: 0161 833 6000
E-mail: clerks@cobden.co.uk
Call date: Oct 1990, Gray's Inn
Qualifications: [MA (Cantab)]

KELLY MISS SHERON

Chancery Chambers
1st Floor Offices 70/72 Chancery Lane,
London WC2A 1AB,
Telephone: 0171 405 6879/6870
Call date: Nov 1982, Middle Temple
Qualifications: [BA]

KELLY MS SIOBHAN FRANCES

Trafalgar Chambers
53 Fleet Street, London EC4Y 1BE,
Telephone: 0171 583 5858
E-mail: TrafalgarChambers@easynet.co.uk
Call date: Oct 1995, Middle Temple
Qualifications: [BA (Hons)]

KELLY MISS SIOBHAN MARIE

Paradise Square Chambers
26 Paradise Square, Sheffield S1 2DE,
Telephone: 0114 2738951
Call date: Oct 1995, Gray's Inn
Qualifications: [BA]

KELLY THOMAS ANDREW

2 Harcourt Bldgs
2nd Floor, Temple, London EC4Y 9DB,
Telephone: 0171 353 8415
E-mail: clerks@twoharcourtbldgs.demon.co.uk
Call date: July 1978, Lincoln's Inn
Qualifications: [MA (Oxon)]

KELMAN ALISTAIR BRUCE

Lancaster Building Chambers
77 Deansgate, Manchester M3 2BW,
Telephone: 0161 661 4444
E-mail: sandra@lbnipc.com
Call date: July 1977, Middle Temple
Qualifications: [BSc (Eng), ACIArb, AMBCS]

KELSEY-FRY JOHN

Hollis Whiteman Chambers
3rd/4th Floor Queen Elizabeth Bldg, Temple,
London EC4Y 9BS, Telephone: 0171 583 5766
E-mail: hollis.whiteman@btinternet.com
Call date: Nov 1978, Gray's Inn

KELSON PETER JOHN

Bank House Chambers
Old Bank House, Hartshead, Sheffield S1 2EL,
Telephone: 0114 2751223
Call date: July 1981, Middle Temple
Assistant Recorder
Qualifications: [LLB]

KEMBER RICHARD

32 Park Place
Cardiff CF1 3BA, Telephone: 01222 397364
Call date: Oct 1993, Middle Temple
Qualifications: [BA (Hons)(Oxon)]

KEMP CHARLES JAMES BOWRING

1 King's Bench Walk
2nd Floor, Temple, London EC4Y 7DB,
Telephone: 0171 936 1500
E-mail: ddear@1kbw.co.uk
Call date: July 1973, Gray's Inn
Recorder
Qualifications: [LLB (Lond)]

KEMP CHRISTOPHER MARK

35 Essex Street
Temple, London WC2R 3AR,
Telephone: 0171 353 6381
Call date: Nov 1984, Middle Temple
Qualifications: [BA (Oxon) Dip Law]

KEMPSTER IVOR TOBY CHALMERS

Old Square Chambers
Hanover House 47 Corn Street, Bristol
BS1 1HT, Telephone: 0117 9277111
Old Square Chambers
1 Verulam Buildings, Gray's Inn, London
WC1R 5LQ, Telephone: 0171 831 0801
Call date: July 1980, Inner Temple
Qualifications: [LLB (Leic)]

KENDAL MARK GILES

Phoenix Chambers
First Floor Gray's Inn Chambers, Gray's Inn,
London WC1R 5JA, Telephone: 0171 404 7888
Call date: Feb 1993, Inner Temple
Qualifications: [LLB]

KENDALL JOEL CAMILO TEPLITZ

12 King's Bench Walk
Temple, London EC4Y 7EL,
Telephone: 0171 583 0811
E-mail: chambers@12kbw.co.uk
Call date: Oct 1993, Middle Temple
Qualifications: [BA (Hons)(Oxon)]

KENDALL TIMOTHY JAMES

3 Hare Court
1st Floor, Temple, London EC4Y 7BJ,
Telephone: 0171 353 7561
Call date: Nov 1985, Gray's Inn
Qualifications: [LLB]

KENDRICK DOMINIC JOHN QC (1997)

7 King's Bench Walk
Ground Floor, Temple, London EC4Y 7DS,
Telephone: 0171 583 0404
Call date: July 1981, Middle Temple
Qualifications: [MA (Cantab)]

KENEFICK TIMOTHY

7 King's Bench Walk
Ground Floor, Temple, London EC4Y 7DS,
Telephone: 0171 583 0404
Call date: Oct 1996, Gray's Inn
Qualifications: [BA (Cantab)]

KENNEDY ANDREW IAN

6 Pump Court
Ground Floor, Temple, London EC4Y 7AR,
Telephone: 0171 583 6013/2510
Call date: Nov 1989, Middle Temple
Qualifications: [BA Hons (Newc), Dip Law]

KENNEDY BERESFORD ROLAND GEORGE

King's Bench Chambers
Wellington House 175 Holdenhurst Road,
Bournemouth, Dorset BH8 8DQ,
Telephone: 01202 250025
Call date: Oct 1995, Middle Temple
Qualifications: [LLB (Hons)]

KENNEDY BRIAN JOSEPH

2 King's Bench Walk
1st Floor, Temple, London EC4Y 7DE,
Telephone: 0171 353 9276
Call date: Oct 1992, Middle Temple
Qualifications: [LL.B (Hons)]

KENNEDY CHRISTOPHER LAURENCE PAUL

9 St John Street
Manchester M3 4DN,
Telephone: 0161 955 9000
E-mail: ninesjs@gconnect.com
Call date: July 1989, Gray's Inn
Qualifications: [BA [Cantab]]

KENNEDY MATTHEW ANTHONY

4 Brick Court
1st Floor, Temple, London EC4Y 9AD,
Telephone: 0171 583 8455
Call date: Nov 1981, Gray's Inn
Qualifications: [BSc]

KENNEDY MICHAEL JOHN

India Buildings Chambers
Water Street, Liverpool L2 OXG,
Telephone: 0151 243 6000
Call date: May 1985, Middle Temple
Qualifications: [LLB (Bristol)]

KENNEDY MICHAEL KIRK INCHES

1 New Square
Ground Floor, Lincoln's Inn, London
WC2A 3SA, Telephone: 0171 405 0884/5/6/7
E-mail: 1newsquare@compuserve.com
Call date: July 1967, Middle Temple
Qualifications: [BA (Cantab)]

D

D

KENNEDY PAUL GILBERT

Warwick House Chambers
8 Warwick Court, Gray's Inn, London
WC1R 5DJ, Telephone: 0171 430 2323
Call date: Nov 1991, Lincoln's Inn
Qualifications: [MA (Cantab), FIA, FCII, ACCA]

KENNEDY PETER NICHOLAS DODGSON

15 Winckley Square
Preston PR1 3JJ, Telephone: 01772 252828
E-mail: clerks@winckleysq.demon.co.uk
Call date: July 1977, Lincoln's Inn
Qualifications: [LLB (Lond)]

KENNEDY OF THE SHAWS BARONESS QC (1991)

Doughty Street Chambers
11 Doughty Street, London WC1N 2PG,
Telephone: 0171 404 1313
E-mail: doughty_street@compuserve.com
Call date: July 1972, Gray's Inn

KENNEDY-MCGREGOR MS MARILYN

11 Stone Bldgs
Ground Floor, Lincoln's Inn, London
WC2A 3TG, Telephone: 0171 831 6381
E-mail: clerks@11StoneBuildings.law.co.uk
Call date: July 1989, Gray's Inn
Qualifications: [BA (Newc), Dip in Law]

KENNEDY-MORRISON MISS CAROLINE LOUISE

3 Temple Gardens
2nd Floor, Temple, London EC4Y 9AU,
Telephone: 0171 583 1155
Call date: Feb 1990, Middle Temple
Qualifications: [BA Hons]

KENNERLEY IAN LESLIE

Broad Chare
33 Broad Chare, Newcastle Upon Tyne
NE1 3DQ, Telephone: 0191 232 0541
Call date: July 1983, Gray's Inn
Qualifications: [BA]

KENNING THOMAS PATRICK

New Court Chambers
Suite 200 Gazette Building, 168 Corporation
Street, Birmingham B4 6TZ,
Telephone: 0121 693 6656
Call date: Feb 1989, Lincoln's Inn
Qualifications: [BSc (Cardiff)]

KENNY MISS CHARLOTTE

Exchange Chambers
Pearl Assurance House Derby Square,
Liverpool L2 9XX, Telephone: 0151 236 7747/
0458
E-mail: exchangechambers@btinternet.com
Call date: Nov 1993, Gray's Inn
Qualifications: [BA (Hull), Dip in Law (City)]

KENNY DAVID JOSEPH

15 Winckley Square
Preston PR1 3JJ, Telephone: 01772 252828
E-mail: clerks@winckleysq.demon.co.uk
Call date: Nov 1982, Middle Temple
Qualifications: [BA, MPhil (Nott'm)]

KENNY STEPHEN CHARLES WILFRID

7 King's Bench Walk
Ground Floor, Temple, London EC4Y 7DS,
Telephone: 0171 583 0404
Call date: July 1987, Inner Temple
Qualifications: [MA, BCL (Oxon)]

KENT ALAN PETER

23 Essex Street
London WC2R 3AS,
Telephone: 0171 413 0353/353 3533
E-mail: clerks@essexstreet23.demon.co.uk
Call date: Nov 1986, Inner Temple
Qualifications: [LLB]

KENT MISS GEORGINA

5 Essex Court
1st Floor, Temple, London EC4Y 9AH,
Telephone: 0171 410 2000
Call date: Nov 1989, Gray's Inn
Qualifications: [LLB (Lond)]

KENT MISS JENNY MARY

Park Court Chambers
40 Park Cross Street, Leeds LS1 2QH,
Telephone: 0113 2433277
Call date: Oct 1993, Lincoln's Inn
Qualifications: [BA (Hons) (Oxon), Dip in Law
(Lond)]

KENT MICHAEL HARCOURT QC (1996)

2 Crown Office Row
Ground Floor, Temple, London EC4Y 7HJ,
Telephone: 0171 797 8100
E-mail: mail@2cor.co.uk, or to individual
barristers at: [barrister's surname]@2cor.co.uk
Call date: July 1975, Middle Temple
Qualifications: [BA (Sussex)]

KENT PETER BRYAN CARLYLE

3 Paper Bldgs
1st Floor, Temple, London EC4Y 7EU,
Telephone: 0171 583 8055
E-mail: london@3paper.com
1 Alfred Street
High Street, Oxford OX1 4EH,
Telephone: 01865 793736
20 Lorne Park Road
Bournemouth BH1 1JN,
Telephone: 01202 292102 (5 Lines)
Call date: Nov 1978, Gray's Inn
Qualifications: [LLB, FCI (Arb)]

KENTRIDGE SYDNEY QC (1984)

Brick Court Chambers
15/19 Devereux Court, London WC2R 3JJ,
Telephone: 0171 583 0777
E-mail: (surname)@brickcourt.demon.co.uk
Call date: July 1977, Lincoln's Inn
Qualifications: [BA (Witw), MA (Oxon)]

KENWARD RICHARD FRANCIS

Watford Chambers
74 Mildred Avenue, Watford, Hertfordshire
WD1 7DX, Telephone: 01923 220553
Call date: Oct 1990, Inner Temple
Qualifications: [LLB]

KENWARD TIMOTHY DAVID NELSON

25-27 Castle Street
1st Floor, Liverpool L2 4TA,
Telephone: 0151 227 5661/051 236 5072
Call date: Nov 1987, Gray's Inn
Qualifications: [MA (Oxon)]

KEOGH ANDREW JOHN

8 King's Bench Walk
2nd Floor, Temple, London EC4Y 7DU,
Telephone: 0171 797 8888
8 King's Bench Walk North
1 Park Square East, Leeds LS1 2NE,
Telephone: 0113 2439797
Call date: Nov 1978, Inner Temple
Qualifications: [BSc (Econ)]

KEOGH RICHARD THOMAS

46/48 Essex Street
London WC2R 3GH,
Telephone: 0171 583 8899
Call date: Nov 1991, Middle Temple
Qualifications: [LLB (Hons) (Essex)]

KER-REID JOHN

Pump Court Chambers
Upper Ground Floor 3 Pump Court, Temple,
London EC4Y 7AJ, Telephone: 0171 353 0711
Pump Court Chambers
31 Southgate Street, Winchester SO23 8EE,
Telephone: 01962 868161
Call date: Nov 1974, Inner Temple
Qualifications: [MA (Cantab)]

KERNER MRS ANGELA

Bell Yard Chambers
116/118 Chancery Lane, London WC2A 1PP,
Telephone: 0171 306 9292
Call date: July 1965, Inner Temple
Qualifications: [LLB (Lond)]

KERR CHRISTOPHER RICHARD

5 Essex Court
1st Floor, Temple, London EC4Y 9AH,
Telephone: 0171 410 2000
Call date: Nov 1988, Middle Temple
Qualifications: [MA (Oxon)]

KERR DAVID MILNE

Martins Building
Water Street, Liverpool L2 3SP,
Telephone: 0151 236 5818/4919
Call date: Nov 1971, Inner Temple
Recorder
Qualifications: [LLB (Lond)]

KERR DEREK WILLIAM

Francis Taylor Bldg
Ground Floor, Temple, London EC4Y 7BY,
Telephone: 0171 353 7768/7769/2711
Call date: Oct 1994, Middle Temple
Qualifications: [LLB (Hons)(Reading)]

KERR TIM JULIAN

4-5 Gray's Inn Square
Ground Floor, Gray's Inn, London WC1R 5AY,
Telephone: 0171 404 5252
E-mail: chambers@4-5graysinnsquare.co.uk
Call date: Nov 1983, Gray's Inn
Qualifications: [BA (Oxon)]

KERRIGAN HERBERT AIRD

9-12 Bell Yard
London WC2A 2LF,
Telephone: 0171 400 1800
Call date: July 1990, Middle Temple
Qualifications: [LLB (Hons), MA (Keele)]

KERSHAW ANDREW

30 Park Square
Leeds LS1 2PF, Telephone: 0113 2436388
Call date: July 1975, Middle Temple
Qualifications: [LLB (Lond)]

KERSHAW MRS JENNIFER CHRISTINE

6 Park Square
Leeds LS1 2LW, Telephone: 0113 2459763
E-mail: chambers@no6.co.uk
Call date: Nov 1974, Lincoln's Inn
Assistant Recorder
Qualifications: [LLB]

KERSHEN LAWRENCE DAVID QC (1992)

Cloisters
1st Floor, Temple, London EC4Y 7AA,
Telephone: 0171 827 4000
E-mail: clerks@cloisters.com
Call date: July 1967, Middle Temple

KESSLER JAMES RICHARD

24 Old Bldgs
First Floor, Lincoln's Inn, London WC2A 3UJ,
Telephone: 0171 242 2744
Call date: July 1984, Gray's Inn
Qualifications: [MA (Oxon)]

KESSLER MARK

King's Bench Chambers
Wellington House 175 Holdenhurst Road,
Bournemouth, Dorset BH8 8DQ,
Telephone: 01202 250025
Call date: Nov 1988, Inner Temple
Qualifications: [LLB]

KESSLING CHRISTOPHER DAVID

65-67 King Street
Leicester LE1 6RP, Telephone: 0116 2547710
Call date: Oct 1992, Middle Temple
Qualifications: [LL.B (Hons)]

KEVAN TIMOTHY LOWIS

1 Temple Gardens
1st Floor, Temple, London EC4Y 9BB,
Telephone: 0171 353 0407/583 1315
E-mail: clerks@1templegardens.co.uk
Call date: Oct 1996, Middle Temple
Qualifications: [BA (Hons)(Cantab)]

KEWLEY MISS SARAH HELEN

22 Old Bldgs
Lincoln's Inn, London WC2A 3UJ,
Telephone: 0171 831 0222
Call date: Nov 1994, Lincoln's Inn
Qualifications: [BA (Hons)(B'ham), Dip in Law (City)]

KEY DR PAUL ANTHONY

Essex Court Chambers
24 Lincoln's Inn Fields, London WC2A 3ED,
Telephone: 0171 813 8000
E-mail: clerksroom@essexcourt-chambers.co.uk
Call date: July 1997, Inner Temple
Qualifications: [PhD (Cantab), LLB (Auckland)]

KEYSER ANDREW JOHN

9 Park Place
Cardiff CF1 3DP, Telephone: 01222 382731
Call date: Nov 1986, Middle Temple
Qualifications: [MA (Oxon)]

KHALIL KARIM SHAKIR

1 Paper Bldgs
1st Floor, Temple, London EC4Y 7EP,
Telephone: 0171 353 3728/4953
Octagon House
19 Colegate, Norwich NR3 1AT,
Telephone: 01603 623186
E-mail: octagon@netmatters.co.uk
Door Tenant
Call date: July 1984, Lincoln's Inn
Qualifications: [MA (Cantab)]

KHALIQUE MISS NAGEENA

5 Fountain Court
Steelhouse Lane, Birmingham B4 6DR,
Telephone: 0121 606 0500
Call date: Oct 1994, Gray's Inn
Qualifications: [BDS, LDSRCS]

KHAMISA MOHAMMED JAFFER

9-12 Bell Yard
London WC2A 2LF,
Telephone: 0171 400 1800
Call date: Nov 1985, Middle Temple
Qualifications: [BA (Hons) (Lond)]

KHAN (KARIMULLA HYAT) AKBAR

Verulam Chambers
Peer House 8-14 Verulam Street, Gray's Inn,
London WC1X 8LZ,
Telephone: 0171 813 2400
Call date: Oct 1990, Middle Temple
Qualifications: [LLB (Hons) Reading, LLM
(Cambs), Postgrad Cert in, Human Rights]

KHAN MISS ANIKA PRAVEEN

2 Mitre Ct Bldgs
1st Floor, Temple, London EC4Y 7BX,
Telephone: 0171 353 1353
Call date: Nov 1987, Gray's Inn
Qualifications: [LLB (Manch)]

KHAN ANWAR WILLIAM

Eastbourne Chambers
15 Hyde Gardens, Eastbourne, East Sussex
BN21 4PR, Telephone: 01323 642102/416466
Wessex Chambers
48 Queens Road, Reading, Berkshire
RG1 4BD, Telephone: 01734 568856
E-mail: wessexchambers@compuserve.com
Call date: Nov 1971, Gray's Inn
Qualifications: [LLB (Lond)]

KHAN ASHRAF

A K Chambers
19 Headlands Drive, Hessle, Hull, East
Yorkshire HU13 0JP,
Telephone: 01482 641180
Call date: July 1960, Middle Temple
Qualifications: [LLM]

KHAN AVICENNA ALKINDI CORNELIUS

55 Temple Chambers
Temple Avenue, London EC4Y 0HP,
Telephone: 0171 353 7400
Call date: July 1993, Lincoln's Inn
Qualifications: [BA (Hons)]

KHAN BASHARAT JAMIL

The Corn Exchange
5th Floor Fenwick Street, Liverpool L2 7QS,
Telephone: 0151 227 1081/5009
Call date: July 1986, Lincoln's Inn
Qualifications: [LLB (Hons)]

KHAN FAUZ MOHAMMAD

Garden Court North Chambers
2nd Floor Gregg's Building, 1 Booth Street,
Manchester M2 4DU,
Telephone: 0161 833 1774
Call date: July 1988, Middle Temple
Qualifications: [LLB (Hons)(Lond)]

D

KHAN MISS HELEN MARY GRACE

2 King's Bench Walk
1st Floor, Temple, London EC4Y 7DE,
Telephone: 0171 353 9276
Call date: Nov 1990, Middle Temple
Qualifications: [LLB (Hons)(Leic)]

KHAN MS JUDITH

2 Garden Court
1st Floor, Middle Temple, London EC4Y 9BL,
Telephone: 0171 353 1633
E-mail: barristers@2gardenct.law.co.uk
Call date: Nov 1989, Middle Temple
Qualifications: [LLB (Hons)]

KHAN MOHAMED WAHID

9 King's Bench Walk
Basement, Temple, London EC4Y 7DX,
Telephone: 0171 353 9564
E-mail: jvlee@btinternet.com
Call date: Nov 1969, Lincoln's Inn
Qualifications: [MA Econ agra]

KHAN MOHAMMAD TAYYAB

Melbury House
55 Manor Road, Oadby, Leicester LE2 2LL,
Telephone: 0116 2711848
Call date: Feb 1972, Lincoln's Inn

KHAN MOHAMMED ASIF

Claremont Chambers
26 Waterloo Road, Wolverhampton WV1 4BL,
Telephone: 01902 426222
Call date: Nov 1983, Lincoln's Inn
Qualifications: [LLB, DPL]

KHAN SAADALLAH FRANS HASSAN

55 Temple Chambers
Temple Avenue, London EC4Y 0HP,
Telephone: 0171 353 7400
Call date: Nov 1991, Lincoln's Inn
Qualifications: [BSc, LLB (Hons)]

KHAN SHAUKAT ALI

2 Middle Temple Lane
3rd Floor, Temple, London EC4Y 9AA,
Telephone: 0171 583 4540
Call date: July 1971, Lincoln's Inn
Qualifications: [BA, LLB]

KHAN SHOKAT

40 King Street
Manchester M2 6BA,
Telephone: 0161 832 9082
E-mail: Kingst40@aol.com
Call date: Nov 1979, Middle Temple
Qualifications: [LLB (Warw) LLM (Lond]

KHAN TAHIR

Broadway House Chambers
Broadway House 9 Bank Street, Bradford,
West Yorkshire BD1 1TW,
Telephone: 01274 722560
Call date: July 1986, Lincoln's Inn
Qualifications: [LLB (Hons)]

KHANGURE AVTAR AMARJIT SINGH

6 Fountain Court
Steelhouse Lane, Birmingham B4 6DR,
Telephone: 0121 233 3282
Call date: Nov 1985, Gray's Inn
Qualifications: [BA, LLM (Cantab)]

KHANZADA MS NAJMA SABRA RAHMAN

1 Pump Court
Lower Ground Floor, Temple, London
EC4Y 7AB, Telephone: 0171 583 2012/
353 4341
E-mail: (name) @1pumpcourt.co.uk
Call date: Oct 1992, Inner Temple
Qualifications: [BA, LLB]

KHAWAR AFTAB

24a St John Street
Manchester M3 4DF,
Telephone: 0161 833 9628
Call date: July 1983, Gray's Inn
Qualifications: [LLB Hons (Lancaster)]

KHAYAT GEORGES MARIO QC (1992)

10 King's Bench Walk
1st Floor, Temple, London EC4Y 7EB,
Telephone: 0171 353 2501
Call date: Nov 1967, Lincoln's Inn
Recorder

KHOKHAR MUSHTAQ AHMED

25 Park Square
Leeds LS1 2PW, Telephone: 0113 2451841/2/3
E-mail: sovereignchambers@btinternet.com
Call date: July 1982, Lincoln's Inn
Assistant Recorder
Qualifications: [LLB, LLM (Lond)]

KHUBLALL NATURAM

Chancery Chambers
1st Floor Offices 70/72 Chancery Lane,
London WC2A 1AB,
Telephone: 0171 405 6879/6870
Call date: July 1981, Lincoln's Inn

KHURSHID JAWDAT

7 King's Bench Walk
Ground Floor, Temple, London EC4Y 7DS,
Telephone: 0171 583 0404
Call date: Oct 1994, Lincoln's Inn
Qualifications: [BA (Hons)(Oxon)]

KIBLING THOMAS

Cloisters
1st Floor, Temple, London EC4Y 7AA,
Telephone: 0171 827 4000
E-mail: clerks@cloisters.com
Call date: Nov 1990, Middle Temple
Qualifications: [LLB]

KIDD MISS JOANNE TERESA

39 Park Square
Leeds LS1 2NU, Telephone: 0113 2456633
Call date: Oct 1995, Lincoln's Inn
Qualifications: [BA (Hons)(Cantab)]

KIDD PETER WILLIAM

Martins Building
Water Street, Liverpool L2 3SP,
Telephone: 0151 236 5818/4919
Call date: July 1987, Lincoln's Inn
Qualifications: [LLB (L'pool)]

KILCOYNE PATRICK DESMOND OLIVER

Arden Chambers
27 John Street, London WC1N 2BL,
Telephone: 0171 242 4244
Call date: May 1990, Inner Temple
Qualifications: [LL.B. (So'ton), LL.M. (Lond)]

KILCOYNE PAUL ANTHONY JAMES

1 Temple Gardens
1st Floor, Temple, London EC4Y 9BB,
Telephone: 0171 353 0407/583 1315
E-mail: clerks@1templegardens.co.uk
Call date: Nov 1985, Lincoln's Inn
Qualifications: [LLB (B'ham)]

KILGOUR PETER JAMES

Cleveland Chambers
63-65 Borough Road, Middlesbrough,
Cleveland TS1 3AA, Telephone: 01642 226036
Call date: July 1984, Lincoln's Inn
Qualifications: [STB Comillas, (Madrid) Dip Law]

KILLALEA STEPHEN JOSEPH

Devereux Chambers
Devereux Court, London WC2R 3JJ,
Telephone: 0171 353 7534
E-mail: elton@devchambers.co.uk
Call date: July 1981, Middle Temple
Qualifications: [LLB]

KILLEEN ROBERT WILLIAM

1 Pump Court
Lower Ground Floor, Temple, London
EC4Y 7AB, Telephone: 0171 583 2012/
353 4341
E-mail: (name) @1pumpcourt.co.uk
Call date: Oct 1995, Middle Temple
Qualifications: [LLB (Hons)]

KILLEEN SIMON JOHN

The Corn Exchange
5th Floor Fenwick Street, Liverpool L2 7QS,
Telephone: 0151 227 1081/5009
Call date: July 1984, Inner Temple
Qualifications: [BA]

KILLEN GEOFFREY JAMES

3 Paper Bldgs
Ground Floor, Temple, London EC4Y 7EU,
Telephone: 0171 797 7000
E-mail: clerks@3pb.co.uk
Call date: Oct 1990, Inner Temple
Qualifications: [LLB]

D

KILPATRICK MISS ALYSON

Arden Chambers
27 John Street, London WC1N 2BL,
Telephone: 0171 242 4244
Call date: July 1991, Middle Temple
Qualifications: [LLB (Hons) (Belfast), Advanced Dip]

KILPATRICK MRS JEAN MARY

3 Paper Bldgs
1st Floor, Temple, London EC4Y 7EU,
Telephone: 0171 583 8055
E-mail: london@3paper.com
1 Alfred Street
High Street, Oxford OX1 4EH,
Telephone: 01865 793736
4 St Peter Street
Winchester SO23 8OW,
Telephone: 01962 868884
Call date: Oct 1990, Middle Temple
Qualifications: [BA (Sheff)]

KILVINGTON SIMON CHARLES

18 St John Street
Manchester M3 4EA,
Telephone: 0161 278 1800
Call date: Nov 1995, Lincoln's Inn
Qualifications: [BA (Hons) (Oxon)]

KIMBELL JOHN ASHLEY

5 Bell Yard
London WC2A 2JR, Telephone: 0171 333 8811
Call date: Nov 1995, Inner Temple
Qualifications: [BA, M.Phil (Cantab)]

KIME MATTHEW JONATHAN

New Court
1st Floor, Temple, London EC4Y 9BE,
Telephone: 0171 797 8999
Cobden House Chambers
19 Quay Street, Manchester M3 3HN,
Telephone: 0161 833 6000/6001
E-mail: clerks@cobden.co.uk
Door Tenant
Call date: July 1988, Middle Temple
Qualifications: [MA, DPhil (Oxon), LLB (Lond), Dip Law (City)]

Fax: 0171 583 5885;
Out of hours telephone: 0171 797 8981;
DX: 420 LDE; Other comms: E-mail
matthewkime@ipbarristermjk.softnet.co.uk;
Web Site: http://www.matthewkime.com

Types of work: Commercial litigation; Competition; Copyright; EC and competition law; Entertainment; Film, cable, TV; Franchising; Information technology; Intellectual property; International trade; Patents; Private international; Telecommunications; Trademarks

Awards and memberships: Intellectual Property Bar Association; Chancery Bar Association; NATO/SERC Postdoctoral Research Fellowship

Other professional experience: Six years as a research scientist

Reported cases: *Games Workshop v Transworld Publishers*, FSR 705 CA, [1993]. An appeal against an interlocutory injunction for infringement of a trademark used as the title of a series of books. Passing off was also in issue. *Valeo Vision v Flexible Lamps*, RPC 205 Patents Court, [1995]. An action between manufacturers of lamps for commercial vehicles involving claims based on causes of action including infringement of copyright in industrial designs, infringement of registered design and breach of confidence.

Mr Kime (an IP specialist with a science and engineering background and a law degree) has a specialist practice across the full range of intellectual property and related areas. He handles contractual matters where the contract involves intellectual property (the various forms of licences such as publishing agreements) or computer-related matters and he has worked on many disputes involving computers.

Mr Kime's background, his scientific education studying chemistry (with biophysics) and his subsequent experience in advanced multi-disciplinary scientific research in England (at Oxford University, as a SRC research student) and in the United States (at Yale University, as a NATO/SERC postdoctoral research fellow and as a postdoctoral research associate on work supported by NIH) in biophysics equipped him to handle the most technical of subject matter. He has been an author of several publications describing research studies of material of interest in molecular biology, botany and biochemistry. He has practical experience of applying and developing physical techniques in research (particularly as a nuclear magnetic resonance spectroscopist) and of exploiting preparative and analytical techniques for isolating and handling large quantities of biological macromolecules, including proteins and overproduced nucleic acids of natural isotopic abundance or enriched in stable isotopes or radio-isotopically labelled.

Mr Kime has applied and applies the practical problem-solving approach developed in his education and young professional scientific research career in England and North America to his legal professional work whether in soft IP (copyright and designs, trade marks and passing off) or patent or trade secrets matters and irrespective of whether his professional clients are intellectual property specialists from large firms of solicitors, patent or trade mark agents, sole practitioners with little or no experience of IP or professionals with direct access.

Geographically Mr Kime's practice involves a significant proportion of work for clients in the North West where he has been associated with chambers in Manchester specialising in chancery and commercial work. He is pleased to act for clients from elsewhere, particularly for clients from London and East Anglia.

KIMMINS CHARLES DOMINIC

20 Essex Street
London WC2R 3AL,
Telephone: 0171 583 9294
E-mail: clerks@20essexst.com
Call date: Nov 1994, Inner Temple
Qualifications: [BA (Cantab)]

KIMSEY MARK FENTON

Harrow on the Hill Chambers
60 High Street, Harrow on the Hill, Middlesex
HA1 3LL, Telephone: 0181 423 7444
Windsor Barristers' Chambers
Windsor, Telephone: 01753 648899
Call date: Oct 1990, Inner Temple
Qualifications: [LLB (Hons)]

KINCADE MS JULIE-ANNE

1 Crown Office Row
2nd Floor, Temple, London EC4Y 7HH,
Telephone: 0171 797 7111
Call date: Nov 1991, Inner Temple
Qualifications: [LLB]

KINCH CHRISTOPHER ANTHONY

23 Essex Street
London WC2R 3AS,
Telephone: 0171 413 0353/353 3533
E-mail: clerks@essexstreet23.demon.co.uk
Call date: July 1976, Lincoln's Inn
Assistant Recorder
Qualifications: [MA (Oxon)]

KING MISS ANNE FAWZIA

2 Gray's Inn Square Chambers
2nd Floor, Gray's Inn, London WC1R 5AA,
Telephone: 0171 242 0328/071 405 1317
E-mail: clerks@2gis.co.uk
Call date: Nov 1985, Middle Temple
Qualifications: [BA.Law]

KING MISS BARBARA MAXINE

3 Dr Johnson's Bldgs
Ground Floor, Temple, London EC4Y 7BA,
Telephone: 0171 353 4854
Call date: Nov 1980, Gray's Inn
Qualifications: [BA (Hons)]

KING CHARLES GRANVILLE

Goldsworth Chambers
1st Floor 10-11 Gray's Inn Square, London
WC1R 5JD, Telephone: 0171 405 7117
Call date: Nov 1995, Middle Temple
Qualifications: [LLB (Hons)]

KING GELAGA PERRY

3 Hare Court
1st Floor, Temple, London EC4Y 7BJ,
Telephone: 0171 353 7561
Call date: July 1985, Gray's Inn
Qualifications: [LLB (Hull)]

KING JOHN PATRICK

1 Gray's Inn Square
Ground Floor, London WC1R 5AA,
Telephone: 0171 405 8946/7/8
Call date: July 1983, Gray's Inn

KING JOHN SAWREY

12 King's Bench Walk
Temple, London EC4Y 7EL,
Telephone: 0171 583 0811
E-mail: chambers@12kbw.co.uk
Call date: Nov 1973, Inner Temple
Qualifications: [LLB (Lond)]

KING KARL ERROL

Hardwicke Building
New Square, Lincoln's Inn, London
WC2A 3SB, Telephone: 0171 242 2523
E-mail: clerks@hardwicke.co.uk
Call date: Nov 1985, Gray's Inn
Qualifications: [BA (Lond)]

D

KING MICHAEL RICHARD

24 Old Bldgs
Ground Floor, Lincoln's Inn, London
WC2A 3UJ, Telephone: 0171 404 0946
E-mail: clerks@24oldbuildings.law.co.uk
Call date: July 1971, Gray's Inn
Qualifications: [BA (Cantab)]

KING NEIL GERALD ALEXANDER

2 Mitre Ct Bldgs
2nd Floor, Temple, London EC4Y 7BX,
Telephone: 0171 583 1380
Call date: July 1980, Inner Temple
Qualifications: [MA (Oxon)]

KING PAUL STUART

1 High Pavement
Nottingham NG1 1HF,
Telephone: 0115 9418218
Call date: July 1992, Inner Temple
Qualifications: [LLB (Leeds)]

KING PETER DUNCAN

Fenners Chambers
3 Madingley Road, Cambridge CB3 OEE,
Telephone: 01223 368761
5 Pump Court
Ground Floor, Temple, London EC4Y 7AP,
Telephone: 0171 353 2532
E-mail: fivepump@netcomuk.co.uk
Door Tenant
Call date: Nov 1970, Gray's Inn
Qualifications: [LLB MA (Cantab) AKC]

KING PHILLIP HENRY RUSSELL

1 Middle Temple Lane
Temple, London EC4Y 1LT,
Telephone: 0171 583 0659 (12 Lines)
Call date: Nov 1974, Inner Temple
Qualifications: [BA]

KING RICHARD

5 Paper Bldgs
Ground Floor, Temple, London EC4Y 7HB,
Telephone: 0171 583 9275/583 4555
E-mail: 5paper@link.org
Call date: July 1978, Inner Temple
Qualifications: [BA (Dunelm)]

KING MISS SAMANTHA LEONIE

14 Gray's Inn Square
Gray's Inn, London WC1R 5JP,
Telephone: 0171 242 0858
E-mail: 100712.2134@compuserve.com
Call date: Nov 1990, Middle Temple
Qualifications: [BA (Cantab)]

KING SIMON PAUL

9 Bedford Row
London WC1R 4AZ,
Telephone: 0171 242 3555
E-mail: clerks@9br.co.uk
Call date: Nov 1987, Gray's Inn
Qualifications: [MA (Oxon)]

KING TIMOTHY ROGER ALAN QC (1991)

22 Old Bldgs
Lincoln's Inn, London WC2A 3UJ,
Telephone: 0171 831 0222
25 Byrom Street
Manchester M3 4PF,
Telephone: 0161 829 2100
E-mail: Byromst25@aol.com
Call date: Nov 1973, Lincoln's Inn
Recorder
Qualifications: [BCL, MA (Oxon)]

KING-SMITH JAMES

1 Crown Office Row
Ground Floor, Temple, London EC4Y 7HH,
Telephone: 0171 797 7500
Crown Office Row Chambers
Blenheim House 120 Church Street, Brighton,
Sussex BN1 1WH, Telephone: 01273 625625
Call date: Nov 1980, Middle Temple
Qualifications: [BA (Oxon)]

KINGHORN ANDREW DAVID

College Chambers
19 Carlton Cresent, Southampton, Hants
SO15 2ET, Telephone: 01703 230338
Call date: Nov 1991, Gray's Inn
Qualifications: [LLB]

KINGSCOTE GEOFFREY LLEWELYN WOODWARD

1 Mitre Ct Bldgs
Ground Floor, Temple, London EC4Y 7BS,
Telephone: 0171 797 7070
Call date: Nov 1993, Inner Temple
Qualifications: [BA (Oxon), M.Phil (Cantab)]

KINGSLAND LORD QC (1988)

4 Breams Buildings
London EC4A 1AQ,
Telephone: 0171 353 5835/430 1221
Call date: Nov 1972, Middle Temple
Qualifications: [DPhil]

KINGSLEY DANIEL

3 Temple Gardens
3rd Floor, Temple, London EC4Y 9AU,
Telephone: 0171 583 0010
Call date: Oct 1994, Lincoln's Inn
Qualifications: [MA (Hons)(Cantab)]

KINGSLEY RICHARD CHARLES

New Court
Temple, London EC4Y 9BE,
Telephone: 0171 583 5123/0171 583 0510
Call date: July 1977, Inner Temple
Qualifications: [LLB (Hons)]

KINGSTON WILLIAM MARTIN QC (1992)

5 Fountain Court
Steelhouse Lane, Birmingham B4 6DR,
Telephone: 0121 606 0500
Call date: July 1972, Middle Temple
Recorder
Qualifications: [LLB]

KINLEY GEOFFREY DORAN

4 Essex Court
Temple, London EC4Y 9AJ,
Telephone: 0171 797 7970
E-mail: clerks@4essexcourt.law.co.uk
Call date: Nov 1970, Gray's Inn
Qualifications: [BA (L'pool) MA, (Oxon)]

KINNEAR JONATHAN SHEA

9-12 Bell Yard
London WC2A 2LF,
Telephone: 0171 400 1800
Call date: Oct 1994, Gray's Inn
Qualifications: [LLB]

KINNIER ANDREW JOHN

2 Harcourt Bldgs
Ground Floor/Left, Temple, London
EC4Y 9DB, Telephone: 0171 583 9020
E-mail: clerks@harcourt.co.uk
Call date: Oct 1996, Middle Temple
Qualifications: [BA (Hons)(Cantab)]

KINSKY CYRIL (NORMAN)(FRANCIS)

Brick Court Chambers
15/19 Devereux Court, London WC2R 3JJ,
Telephone: 0171 583 0777
E-mail: (surname)@brickcourt.demon.co.uk
Call date: Nov 1988, Middle Temple
Qualifications: [BA (Cantab), Dip Law (City)]

KINSLER MISS MARIE LOUISE

2 Temple Gardens
Temple, London EC4Y 9AY,
Telephone: 0171 583 6041 (12 Lines)
Call date: July 1992, Inner Temple
Qualifications: [BA (Cambs), Dip Ad Eur
Studies]

KIRBY JAMES PATRICK

Phoenix Chambers
First Floor Gray's Inn Chambers, Gray's Inn,
London WC1R 5JA, Telephone: 0171 404 7888
Call date: Oct 1994, Gray's Inn
Qualifications: [BA (Manch)]

KIRBY PETER JOHN

Hardwicke Building
New Square, Lincoln's Inn, London
WC2A 3SB, Telephone: 0171 242 2523
E-mail: clerks@hardwicke.co.uk
Call date: July 1989, Inner Temple
Qualifications: [LLB (Hull)]

Fax: 0171 691 1234; DX: LDE 393;
Other comms: E-mail pjkirby9@aol.com

Types of work: Chancery (general); Common law (general); Employment; Professional negligence

Awards and memberships: Member of Employment Law Bar Association; Professional Negligence Bar Association; London Commercial and Common Law Bar Association

Other professional experience: Former solicitor, admitted 1983

Reported cases: *National Home Loans Corporation v Giffen Couch and Archer*, [1997] 3 All ER 808, 1997. Duties of solicitor to lender client when acting for lender and mortgagor.
UCB Home Loans v Roger North, [1995] EGCS 149, 1995. The approach to the appropriate margin of error in valuation cases.
Re Cedar Developments Ltd, [1994] BCLC 714; [1995] BCC 220, 1994. Application refused for leave to apply out of time under Company Directors Disqualification Act 1986.
Duckwari v Offerventure Ltd, [1995] BCC 89, 1993. Whether company could avoid substantial property transaction involving directors.
Tramp Leasing Ltd v Turnbull, (1991)*The Times*, 12 June, 1991. The right to appeal a taxation of Sheriff's fees.

KIRBY MISS RUTH MARY ANTHONY

Mitre House Chambers
Mitre House 44 Fleet Street, London EC4Y 1BN, Telephone: 0171 583 8233
Call date: Oct 1994, Middle Temple
Qualifications: [BCL, LLM (Lond), CPE]

KIRK ANTHONY JAMES NIGEL

1 King's Bench Walk
2nd Floor, Temple, London EC4Y 7DB,
Telephone: 0171 936 1500
E-mail: ddear@1kbw.co.uk
Call date: July 1981, Gray's Inn
Qualifications: [LLB (Lond), AKC]

KIRK JONATHAN

36 Bedford Row
London WC1R 4JH,
Telephone: 0171 421 8000
E-mail: 36bedfordrow@link.org
Call date: Nov 1995, Lincoln's Inn
Qualifications: [LLB (Hons)]

KIRK ROBERT WILSON

Littman Chambers
12 Gray's Inn Square, London WC1R 5JP,
Telephone: 0171 404 4866
E-mail: admin@littmanchambers.com
Call date: Nov 1972, Lincoln's Inn
Qualifications: [MA (Cantab), FCIArb]

KIRKPATRICK MRS KRYSTYNA MARIA

3 Paper Bldgs
1st Floor, Temple, London EC4Y 7EU,
Telephone: 0171 583 8055
E-mail: london@3paper.com
20 Lorne Park Road
Bournemouth BH1 1JN,
Telephone: 01202 292102 (5 Lines)
4 St Peter Street
Winchester SO23 8OW,
Telephone: 01962 868884
Call date: Feb 1965, Gray's Inn

KIRSTEN ADRIAN RICHARD CALTHORPE

Manchester House Chambers
18-22 Bridge Street, Manchester M3 3BZ,
Telephone: 0161 834 7007
Call date: Nov 1962, Gray's Inn
Qualifications: [LLM]

KIRTLEY PAUL GEORGE

37 Park Square
Leeds LS1 2NY, Telephone: 0113 2439422
Call date: July 1982, Middle Temple
Qualifications: [MA (Cantab)]

KIRWAN MRS HELEN ANN HERMIONE

Stour Chambers
Barton Mill House Barton Mill Road,
Canterbury, Kent CT1 1BP,
Telephone: 01227 764899
E-mail: clerks@stourchambers.co.uk
Call date: Nov 1983, Middle Temple
Qualifications: [BSS (Hons), LLB (Dublin)]

KIRWIN MS TRACEY

King Charles House
Standard Hill, Nottingham NG1 6FX,
Telephone: 0115 9418851
E-mail: clerks@kch.co.uk
Call date: Oct 1995, Middle Temple
Qualifications: [LLB (Hons)]

KISHORE PAUL JEWANLALL

Chancery Chambers
1st Floor Offices 70/72 Chancery Lane,
London WC2A 1AB,
Telephone: 0171 405 6879/6870
Call date: Nov 1982, Lincoln's Inn
Qualifications: [LLB (Lond), BA, ACP, ACIArb]

KITCHEN SIMON DUGALD OWEN RALPH

8 King's Bench Walk
2nd Floor, Temple, London EC4Y 7DU,
Telephone: 0171 797 8888
8 King's Bench Walk North
1 Park Square East, Leeds LS1 2NE,
Telephone: 0113 2439797
Call date: Nov 1988, Lincoln's Inn
Qualifications: [LLB Hons]

KITCHENER NEIL DAVID

1 Essex Court
Ground Floor, Temple, London EC4Y 9AR,
Telephone: 0171 583 2000
E-mail: clerks@oneessexcourt.co.uk
Call date: Oct 1991, Middle Temple
Qualifications: [BA (Oxon)]

KITCHIN DAVID JAMES TYSON QC (1994)

8 New Square
Lincoln's Inn, London WC2A 3QP,
Telephone: 0171 405 4321
Call date: July 1977, Gray's Inn
Qualifications: [MA (Cantab)]

KITCHING ROBIN MILES

Cobden House Chambers
19 Quay Street, Manchester M3 3HN,
Telephone: 0161 833 6000
E-mail: clerks@cobden.co.uk
Call date: Nov 1989, Middle Temple
Qualifications: [BA (Hons) (Manc), C.P.E]

KIVDEH SHAHROKH-SEAN

3 Temple Gardens (North)
Fifth Floor, Temple, London EC4Y 9AU,
Telephone: 0171 353 0853/4/7222
E-mail: 100106.1577@compuserve.com
Call date: Nov 1992, Middle Temple
Qualifications: [LLB (Hons, Lond), LLM (UCL)]

KLEIN JONATHAN SIMON

Chancery House Chambers
7 Lisbon Square, Leeds LS1 4LY,
Telephone: 0113 244 6691
E-mail: Chanceryhouse@btinternet.com
Call date: Oct 1992, Lincoln's Inn
Qualifications: [LLB(Hons)(Essex), BCL]

KLEIN MS LEONORA JANE

1 Gray's Inn Square
1st Floor, London WC1R 5AG,
Telephone: 0171 405 3000
E-mail: clerks@onegrays.demon.co.uk
Call date: Nov 1989, Gray's Inn
Qualifications: [BA (Lond)]

KLEVAN RODNEY CONRAD QC (1984)

18 St John Street
Manchester M3 4EA,
Telephone: 0161 278 1800
Call date: May 1966, Gray's Inn
Recorder
Qualifications: [LLB (B'ham)]

KLONIN MISS SUSAN JANE

Old Colony House
6 South King Street, Manchester M2 6DQ,
Telephone: 0161 834 4364
Call date: Nov 1970, Gray's Inn
Qualifications: [LLB (Hons)]

KLOSS ALEXANDER WOLFGANG

28 St John Street
Manchester M3 4DJ,
Telephone: 0161 834 8418
E-mail: clerk@28stjohnst.co.uk
Call date: Oct 1993, Gray's Inn
Qualifications: [BA (Bris)]

D

KLOSS MRS DIANA MARY

28 St John Street
Manchester M3 4DJ,
Telephone: 0161 834 8418
E-mail: clerk@28stjohnst.co.uk
Call date: July 1986, Gray's Inn
Qualifications: [LLB Lond LLM Tulane]

KNAFLER STEPHEN

6 King's Bench Walk
Ground, Third & Fourth Floors, Temple,
London EC4Y 7DR,
Telephone: 0171 353 4931/583 0695
Call date: May 1993, Lincoln's Inn
Qualifications: [MA (Cantab)]

KNAPP EDWARD IAN

4 Brick Court
Temple, London EC4Y 9AD,
Telephone: 0171 797 8910
Call date: Feb 1992, Lincoln's Inn
Qualifications: [LLB (Hons)]

KNAPP MISS SOPHIE JACQUELINE

2 Pump Court
1st Floor, Temple, London EC4Y 7AH,
Telephone: 0171 353 5597
Call date: Feb 1990, Gray's Inn
Qualifications: [BA [Lond]]

KNAPP STEPHEN JOHN

Martins Building
Water Street, Liverpool L2 3SP,
Telephone: 0151 236 5818/4919
Call date: July 1986, Gray's Inn
Qualifications: [LLB (Lond)]

KNIFTON DAVID ALAN

Chavasse Court Chambers
2nd Floor Chavasse Court, 24 Lord Street,
Liverpool L2 1TA, Telephone: 0151 707 1191
Call date: July 1986, Inner Temple
Qualifications: [LLB (Nottingahm)]

KNIGHT MISS ADRIENNE

Bridewell Chambers
2 Bridewell Place, London EC4V 6AP,
Telephone: 0171 797 8800
E-mail: clerks@bridewell.law.co.uk
Call date: July 1981, Gray's Inn
Qualifications: [LLB]

KNIGHT BRIAN JOSEPH QC (1981)

1 Atkin Building
Gray's Inn, London WC1R 5AT,
Telephone: 0171 404 0102
E-mail: clerks@atkin-chambers.co.uk
Call date: Nov 1964, Gray's Inn
Recorder
Qualifications: [LLB, LLM (Lond)]

KNIGHT MISS CAROLINE SARAH DARLEY

1 Harcourt Bldgs
2nd Floor, Temple, London EC4Y 9DA,
Telephone: 0171 353 9421/9151
Call date: July 1985, Inner Temple
Qualifications: [LLB (B'ham), Diplome D'etudes, Juridiques, Francaises]

KNIGHT CHRISTOPHER HARRINGTON

Chartlands Chambers
3 St Giles Terrace, Northampton NN1 2BN,
Telephone: 01604 603322
Call date: Oct 1994, Gray's Inn
Qualifications: [BA (York)]

KNIGHT CHRISTOPHER MICHAEL ST JOHN

9 St John Street
Manchester M3 4DN,
Telephone: 0161 955 9000
E-mail: ninesjs@gconnect.com
Call date: Nov 1966, Middle Temple
Qualifications: [BA (Cantab)]

KNIGHT KEITH LESLIE FRANCIS

2 Gray's Inn Square Chambers
2nd Floor, Gray's Inn, London WC1R 5AA,
Telephone: 0171 242 0328/071 405 1317
E-mail: clerks@2gis.co.uk
Call date: Nov 1969, Gray's Inn
Qualifications: [BCL]

KNIGHT MISS SARAH LOUISE

St Mary's Chambers
50 High Pavement, Lace Market, Nottingham
NG1 1HW, Telephone: 0115 9503503
E-mail: clerks@smc.law.co.uk
Call date: July 1996, Middle Temple
Qualifications: [BA (Hons)(Notts), Dip Law
(Lond)]

KNIGHTON MISS CLAIRE LOUISE

65-67 King Street
Leicester LE1 6RP, Telephone: 0116 2547710
Call date: Oct 1996, Lincoln's Inn
Qualifications: [LLB (Hons)(Leic)]

KNIGHTS MISS SAMANTHA JANE

3/4 South Square
Gray's Inn, London WC1R 5HP,
Telephone: 0171 696 9900
E-mail: clerks@southsquare.com
Call date: Nov 1996, Lincoln's Inn
Qualifications: [BA (Hons)(Oxon)]

KNOTT MALCOLM STEPHEN

New Court Chambers
5 Verulam Buildings, Gray's Inn, London
WC1R 5LY, Telephone: 0171 831 9500
E-mail: mail@newcourtchambers.com
Call date: July 1968, Inner Temple
Recorder

KNOWLES GRAHAM ROY

Peel Court Chambers
45 Hardman Street, Manchester M3 3HA,
Telephone: 0161 832 3791
Call date: Oct 1990, Middle Temple
Qualifications: [MA (Cantab)]

KNOWLES MS GWYNNETH FRANCES

4 Brick Court
Temple, London EC4Y 9AD,
Telephone: 0171 797 8910
Call date: Oct 1993, Gray's Inn
Qualifications: [BA, M.Sc]

KNOWLES JULIAN BERNARD

3 Raymond Buildings
Gray's Inn, London WC1R 5BH,
Telephone: 0171 831 3833
E-mail: chambers@threeraymond.demon.co.uk
Call date: Nov 1994, Inner Temple
Qualifications: [BA (Oxon), CPE]

KNOWLES MISS LINDA

Sedan House
Stanley Place, Chester CH1 2LU,
Telephone: 01244 320480/348282
Call date: Oct 1993, Gray's Inn
Qualifications: [LLB (Hons)]

KNOWLES MARK DAVID

Equity Chambers
Suite 110, Gazette Buildings 168 Corporation
Street, Birmingham B4 6TS,
Telephone: 0121 233 2100
Call date: Nov 1989, Middle Temple
Qualifications: [LLB Hons [Leic]]

KNOWLES ROBIN ST JOHN

3/4 South Square
Gray's Inn, London WC1R 5HP,
Telephone: 0171 696 9900
E-mail: clerks@southsquare.com
Call date: July 1982, Middle Temple
Qualifications: [MA (Cantab)]

KNOX CHRISTOPHER JOHN

Trinity Chambers
9-12 Trinity Chare, Quayside, Newcastle Upon
Tyne NE1 3DF, Telephone: 0191 232 1927
Call date: July 1974, Inner Temple
Recorder
Qualifications: [BA (Dunelm)]

KNOX SIMON CHRISTOPHER PETER

1 Crown Office Row
3rd Floor, Temple, London EC4Y 7HH,
Telephone: 0171 583 9292
E-mail: onecor@link.org
Call date: Nov 1983, Middle Temple
Qualifications: [BA (Oxon)]

D

KODAGODA FRITZ ST CLAIR

9 King's Bench Walk
Basement, Temple, London EC4Y 7DX,
Telephone: 0171 353 9564
E-mail: jvlee@btinternet.com
Call date: Nov 1993, Lincoln's Inn

KOGAN BARRY ISAAC

33 Bedford Row
London WC1R 4JH,
Telephone: 0171 242 6476
Call date: July 1973, Inner Temple
Assistant Recorder
Qualifications: [LLB (Hull)]

KOLANKO MICHAEL PHILIP

17 Carlton Crescent
Southampton SO15 2XR,
Telephone: 01703 320320
E-mail: km@bar-17cc.demon.co.uk
Call date: July 1975, Middle Temple
Qualifications: [LLB (Manch)]

KOLODYNSKI STEFAN RICHARD

New Court Chambers
Suite 200 Gazette Building, 168 Corporation
Street, Birmingham B4 6TZ,
Telephone: 0121 693 6656
Call date: Oct 1993, Lincoln's Inn
Qualifications: [BSc (Hons)(Lond), CPE
(Huddesfield)]

KOLODZIEJ ANDRZEJ JOZEF

Littman Chambers
12 Gray's Inn Square, Gray's Inn, London
WC1R 5JP, Telephone: 0171 404 4866
E-mail: admin@littmanchambers.com
Call date: Nov 1978, Gray's Inn
Qualifications: [BA (Oxon), FCIArb]

Fax: 0171 404 4812; DX: 0055 CH/LN;
Other comms: Lix: Lon 041; E-mail
100617.504@compuserve.com

Types of work: Arbitration; Banking; Chancery
(general); Commercial litigation; Common law
(general); Company and commercial;
Construction; Defamation; EC and competition
law; Employment; Franchising; Insurance;
International trade; Private international;
Professional negligence; Sale and carriage of
goods

Other professional qualifications: Fellow of
Chartered Institute of Arbitrators; LLM (Kings)

Membership of foreign bars: New South Wales,
Australia

Awards and memberships: Bar European Group;
British Polish Legal Association; COMBAR

Other professional experience: Sits as an
arbitrator, domestically and internationally;
registered on the list of arbitrators of
International Arbitral Centre of the Austrian
Federal Economic Chamber, Vienna

Languages spoken: French, Polish

KOLVIN PHILIP ALAN

2-3 Gray's Inn Square
Gray's Inn, London WC1R 5JH,
Telephone: 0171 242 4986
E-mail: chambers@2-3graysinnsquare.co.uk
Call date: July 1985, Inner Temple
Qualifications: [BA (Oxon)]

KOPIECZEK ALOYSIUS MICHAEL

6 Gray's Inn Square
Ground Floor, Gray's Inn, London WC1R 5AZ,
Telephone: 0171 242 1052
Call date: Nov 1983, Gray's Inn
Qualifications: [LLB]

KORAH PROF VALENTINE

Guildford Chambers
Stoke House Leapale Lane, Guildford, Surrey
GU1 4LY, Telephone: 01483 539131
E-mail: guildford.barristers@btinternet.com
Call date: Nov 1952, Lincoln's Inn
Qualifications: [LL.M (Lond), PhD]

KORDA ANTHONY

1 Middle Temple Lane
Temple, London EC4Y 1LT,
Telephone: 0171 583 0659 (12 Lines)
Call date: July 1988, Inner Temple
Qualifications: [LLB (Lond)]

KORN ADAM RICHARD

Park Lane Chambers
19 Westgate, Leeds LS1 2RD,
Telephone: 0113 2285000
Call date: Oct 1992, Middle Temple

Qualifications: [BA (Hons), MA, Diploma in Law, A.K.C.]

KORN ANTHONY HENRY

Barnard's Inn Chambers
6th Floor Halton House, 20-23 Holborn, London EC1N 2JD, Telephone: 0171 242 8508
E-mail: clerks@barnards-inn-chambers.co.uk
Call date: Nov 1978, Gray's Inn
Qualifications: [BA (Oxon)]

KORNER MISS JOANNA CHRISTIAN MARY QC (1993)

6 King's Bench Walk
Ground Floor, Temple, London EC4Y 7DR, Telephone: 0171 583 0410
Call date: Nov 1974, Inner Temple
Recorder

KOROL MS KATHRYN MARGARET

Kenworthy's Buildings
83 Bridge Street, Manchester M3 2RF, Telephone: 0161 832 4036/834 6954
Call date: Mar 1996, Middle Temple
Qualifications: [LLB (Hons)]

KOSMIN LESLIE GORDON QC (1994)

Erskine Chambers
30 Lincoln's Inn Fields, Lincoln's Inn, London WC2A 3PF, Telephone: 0171 242 5532
E-mail: Clerks@Erskine-Chambers.law.co.uk
Call date: July 1976, Middle Temple
Qualifications: [MA, LLM (Cantab), LLM (Harvard)]

KOTHARI MISS SIMA

1 Pump Court
Lower Ground Floor, Temple, London EC4Y 7AB, Telephone: 0171 583 2012/ 353 4341
E-mail: (name) @1pumpcourt.co.uk
Call date: Oct 1992, Gray's Inn
Qualifications: [LLB (Lond)]

KOTHARI VASANT CHUNILAL

2 Paper Bldgs
1st Floor, Temple, London EC4Y 7ET, Telephone: 0171 936 2611 (10 Lines)
E-mail: clerks@2pbbarristers.co.uk
Call date: July 1960, Lincoln's Inn
Qualifications: [BA (Hons)]

KOVALEVSKY RICHARD TARAS

18 Red Lion Court
(Off Fleet Street), London EC4A 3EB, Telephone: 0171 520 6000
Thornwood House
102 New London Road, Chelmsford, Essex CM2 0RG, Telephone: 01245 280880
Call date: July 1983, Gray's Inn
Qualifications: [LLB Manchester]

KOVATS STEVEN LASZLO

39 Essex Street
London WC2R 3AT, Telephone: 0171 583 1111
E-mail: clerks@39essex.co.uk
Call date: July 1989, Middle Temple
Qualifications: [BA [Cantab]]

KRAMER PHILIP ANTHONY

New Court Chambers
3 Broad Chare, Newcastle Upon Tyne NE1 3DQ, Telephone: 0191 232 1980
Call date: July 1982, Inner Temple
Qualifications: [LLB (Newc)]

KRAMER STEPHEN ERNEST QC (1995)

1 Hare Court
Ground Floor, Temple, London EC4Y 7BE, Telephone: 0171 353 3982/5324
Call date: July 1970, Gray's Inn
Recorder
Qualifications: [MA (Oxon)]

Fax: 0171 353 0667; DX: LDE 444 Chancery Lane

Types of work: Crime; Crime - corporate fraud

Circuit: South Eastern

Other professional experience: Standing Counsel
(Crime) HM Customs and Excise (1989-95) SE
Circuit

Languages spoken: French

KREMEN PHILIP MICHAEL

Hardwicke Building
New Square, Lincoln's Inn, London
WC2A 3SB, Telephone: 0171 242 2523
E-mail: clerks@hardwicke.co.uk
Call date: Nov 1975, Gray's Inn
Qualifications: [BSc (Hons)]

KRiKLER MISS SUSAN

3 Temple Gardens
Lower Ground Floor, Temple, London
EC4Y 9AU, Telephone: 0171 353 3102/5/9297
Call date: Nov 1988, Middle Temple
Qualifications: [BA (Oxon), Dip Law (City)]

KRISH MISS JULIA ROSALIE

4 Brick Court
Ground Floor, Temple, London EC4Y 9AD,
Telephone: 0171 797 7766
E-mail: chambers@4brick.co.uk
Call date: Feb 1992, Middle Temple
Qualifications: [MA (Oxon)]

KRISHNADASAN MISS DOUSHKA

New Court
Temple, London EC4Y 9BE,
Telephone: 0171 583 5123/0171 583 0510
Call date: July 1991, Middle Temple
Qualifications: [LLB (Hons) (Lond)]

KROLICK IVAN

Lamb Building
Ground Floor, Temple, London EC4Y 7AS,
Telephone: 0171 797 7788
E-mail: lamb.building@link.org
Call date: Nov 1966, Gray's Inn
Qualifications: [LLB (Dunelm), FCIArb]

KRONE MRS MAXINE JANE

2 New Street
Leicester LE1 5NA, Telephone: 0116 2625906
Call date: July 1980, Middle Temple
Qualifications: [BA (Leics) (Hons)]

KUBIK MISS HEIDI MARIE

3 Fountain Court
Steelhouse Lane, Birmingham B4 6DR,
Telephone: 0121 236 5854
Call date: Oct 1993, Lincoln's Inn
Qualifications: [BA (Hons)(Notts)]

KULATILAKE INDRA SEMAGE

52 Wembley Park Drive
Wembley, Middlesex HA9 8HB,
Telephone: 0181 902 5629
Call date: July 1971, Inner Temple

KUMALO DABI SIMON

New Court
Temple, London EC4Y 9BE,
Telephone: 0171 583 5123/0171 583 0510
Call date: Nov 1974, Inner Temple
Qualifications: [MA (Oxon)]

KUMAR MISS MOUSUMI

Chambers of Joy Okoye
Suite 1, 2nd Floor Gray's Inn Chambers,
Gray's Inn, London WC1R 5JA,
Telephone: 0171 405 7011
Call date: Oct 1992, Gray's Inn
Qualifications: [LLB (Lond)]

KUMAR UMESH

1 Crown Office Row
3rd Floor, Temple, London EC4Y 7HH,
Telephone: 0171 583 9292
E-mail: onecor@link.org
Call date: Oct 1995, Inner Temple
Qualifications: [BA (Oxon)]

KUMI ISHMAEL JOB

Cromwell-Ayeh-Kumi Chambers
1st Floor Suite 119 Cricklewood Broadway,
London NW2 3JG, Telephone: 0181 450 6620
Call date: Nov 1977, Gray's Inn
Qualifications: [MA (Oxon) Maitrise,
(Sorbonne)]

KURREIN MARTIN GEORGE

199 Strand
London WC2R 1DR,
Telephone: 0171 379 9779
E-mail: chambers@199strand.co.uk
Call date: July 1981, Middle Temple
Qualifications: [BA (Hons)]

KUSCHKE LEON SIEGFRIED

Erskine Chambers
30 Lincoln's Inn Fields, Lincoln's Inn, London
WC2A 3PF, Telephone: 0171 242 5532
E-mail: Clerks@Erskine-Chambers.law.co.uk
Call date: July 1993, Lincoln's Inn
Qualifications: [B.Comm, LLB]

KUSHNER MISS LINDSEY JOY QC (1992)

28 St John Street
Manchester M3 4DJ,
Telephone: 0161 834 8418
E-mail: clerk@28stjohnst.co.uk
14 Gray's Inn Square
Gray's Inn, London WC1R 5JP,
Telephone: 0171 242 0858
E-mail: 100712.2134@compuserve.com
Call date: July 1974, Middle Temple
Recorder
Qualifications: [LLB]

KUSHNER MISS MARTINE

36 Bedford Row
London WC1R 4JH,
Telephone: 0171 421 8000
E-mail: 36bedfordrow@link.org
Call date: July 1980, Middle Temple
Qualifications: [LLB (B'ham)]

KVERNDAL SIMON RICHARD

4 Essex Court
Temple, London EC4Y 9AJ,
Telephone: 0171 797 7970
E-mail: clerks@4essexcourt.law.co.uk
Call date: Nov 1982, Middle Temple
Qualifications: [MA (Cantab)]

KWIATKOWSKI FELIKS JERZY

Goldsworth Chambers
1st Floor 10-11 Gray's Inn Square, London
WC1R 5JD, Telephone: 0171 405 7117
Call date: July 1977, Middle Temple
Qualifications: [LLB (Hons)(Bris)]

KYNOCH DUNCAN STUART SANDERSON

29 Bedford Row Chambers
London WC1R 4HE,
Telephone: 0171 831 2626
Call date: Nov 1994, Gray's Inn
Qualifications: [LLB (Bris)]

KYRIACOU KYRIACOS PHILIPPOU

Enfield Chambers
36-38 London Road, Enfield, Middlesex
EN2 6DT, Telephone: 0181 364 5627
E-mail: Enfieldchambers@compuserve.com
Call date: Feb 1994, Lincoln's Inn
Qualifications: [LLB (Hons)]

KYRIAKIDES MISS TINA

11 Stone Bldgs
Ground Floor, Lincoln's Inn, London
WC2A 3TG, Telephone: 0171 831 6381
E-mail: clerks@11StoneBuildings.law.co.uk
Call date: July 1984, Lincoln's Inn
Qualifications: [MA(Cantab)]

KYTE PETER ERIC QC (1996)

Hollis Whiteman Chambers
3rd/4th Floor Queen Elizabeth Bldg, Temple,
London EC4Y 9BS, Telephone: 0171 583 5766
E-mail: hollis.whiteman@btinternet.com
Call date: July 1970, Gray's Inn
Recorder
Qualifications: [MA (Cantab)]

LABAN ALEXANDER

Mitre Court Chambers
3rd Floor, Temple, London EC4Y 7BP,
Telephone: 0171 353 9394
Call date: Nov 1981, Inner Temple
Qualifications: [BA Dip Law]

D

LABELLE JEAN-MARIE

John Street Chambers
2 John Street, London WC1N 2HJ,
Telephone: 0171 242 1911
E-mail: john.street_chambers@virgin.net.uk
Call date: Nov 1992, Inner Temple
Qualifications: [MSc (Surrey), Dip in Law]

LACEY MISS ROISIN MARY

6 Pump Court
Ground Floor, Temple, London EC4Y 7AR,
Telephone: 0171 583 6013/2510
Call date: Nov 1991, Middle Temple
Qualifications: [BA (Hons) (Dublin), BL
(Dublin)]

LACEY MISS SARAH HELEN

3 Stone Bldgs
Ground Floor, Lincoln's Inn, London
WC2A 3XL, Telephone: 0171 242 4937/
405 8358
Call date: Nov 1991, Middle Temple
Qualifications: [LLB Hons (Cantab)]

LACHKOVIC JAMES ADRIAN GEORGE

1 Middle Temple Lane
Temple, London EC4Y 1LT,
Telephone: 0171 583 0659 (12 Lines)
Call date: Nov 1987, Gray's Inn
Qualifications: [LLB (Hull)]

LACHKOVIC MISS VERONICA MARGARET MARY

One Garden Court
Ground Floor, Temple, London EC4Y 9BJ,
Telephone: 0171 797 7900
Call date: July 1982, Gray's Inn
Qualifications: [LLB (Lond)]

LADAK MISS TAHERA

8 King's Bench Walk
2nd Floor, Temple, London EC4Y 7DU,
Telephone: 0171 797 8888
8 King's Bench Walk North
1 Park Square East, Leeds LS1 2NE,
Telephone: 0113 2439797
Call date: Nov 1986, Gray's Inn
Qualifications: [LLB (Essex)]

LADDIE JAMES MATTHEW LANG

Cloisters
1st Floor, Temple, London EC4Y 7AA,
Telephone: 0171 827 4000
E-mail: clerks@cloisters.com
Call date: Nov 1995, Middle Temple
Qualifications: [BA (Hons) (Cantab)]

LADMORE RICHARD JAMES

9 King's Bench Walk
Ground Floor, Temple, London EC4Y 7DX,
Telephone: 0171 353 7202/3909
Call date: Feb 1995, Middle Temple
Qualifications: [BA (Hons)(Sussex)]

LAHIFFE MARTIN PATRICK JOSEPH

3 Temple Gardens
Lower Ground Floor, Temple, London
EC4Y 9AU, Telephone: 0171 353 3102/5/9297
Call date: Nov 1984, Middle Temple
Qualifications: [BA (Hons)]

LAIDLAW JONATHAN JAMES

1 Hare Court
Ground Floor, Temple, London EC4Y 7BE,
Telephone: 0171 353 3982/5324
Call date: July 1982, Inner Temple
Assistant Recorder
Qualifications: [LLB (Hull)]

LAING MISS CHRISTINE KATHERINE

9-12 Bell Yard
London WC2A 2LF,
Telephone: 0171 400 1800
Call date: July 1984, Lincoln's Inn
Qualifications: [LLB]

LAING MISS ELISABETH MARY CAROLINE

11 King's Bench Walk
Temple, London EC4Y 7EQ,
Telephone: 0171 632 8500
E-mail: clerksroom@11-kbw.law.co.uk
Call date: July 1980, Middle Temple
Qualifications: [BA (Cantab)]

LAIRD FRANCIS JOSEPH

3 Fountain Court
Steelhouse Lane, Birmingham B4 6DR,
Telephone: 0121 236 5854
Call date: Nov 1986, Gray's Inn
Qualifications: [LLB (N'Castle)]

LAKE MRS LISA (JANE)

1 Essex Court
Ground Floor, Temple, London EC4Y 9AR,
Telephone: 0171 583 2000
E-mail: clerks@oneessexcourt.co.uk
Call date: Oct 1994, Inner Temple
Qualifications: [MA (Cantab)]

LAKHA ABBAS

4 Brick Court
1st Floor, Temple, London EC4Y 9AD,
Telephone: 0171 583 8455
Call date: Nov 1984, Inner Temple
Qualifications: [BA (Hons)]

LAKHA MURTAZA AHMED

3 Pump Court
2nd Floor, Temple, London EC4Y 7AJ,
Telephone: 0171 353 1356 (3 Lines)
Call date: Nov 1961, Lincoln's Inn

LAKHA SHABBIR

7 Stone Bldgs
1st Floor, Lincoln's Inn, London WC2A 3SZ,
Telephone: 0171 242 0961
Call date: July 1989, Lincoln's Inn
Qualifications: [LLB (Hons), M.Phil (Cantab)]

LAKIN GORDON

6 Park Square
Leeds LS1 2LW, Telephone: 0113 2459763
E-mail: chambers@no6.co.uk
Call date: July 1972, Middle Temple
Qualifications: [LLB (Leeds)]

LAKIN MISS TRACY

Victoria Chambers
3rd Floor 177 Corporation Street, Birmingham
B4 6RG, Telephone: 0121 236 9900
Call date: Oct 1993, Inner Temple
Qualifications: [LLB]

LAL SANJAY

Warwick House Chambers
8 Warwick Court, Gray's Inn, London
WC1R 5DJ, Telephone: 0171 430 2323
Call date: Oct 1993, Lincoln's Inn
Qualifications: [LLB (Hons), LLM (Lond)]

LAM CHUEN FAT

King's Chambers
49a Broadway, Stratford, London E15 4BW
Call date: Nov 1994, Lincoln's Inn
Qualifications: [BA (Hons)(Wolves)]

LAMACRAFT IAN RICHARD

Bracton Chambers
95a Chancery Lane, London WC2A 1DT,
Telephone: 0171 242 4248
Call date: July 1989, Lincoln's Inn
Qualifications: [LLB]

LAMB DAVID STEPHEN

York Chambers
14 Toft Green, York YO1 1JT,
Telephone: 01904 620048
E-mail: yorkchambers.co.uk
Call date: Nov 1987, Middle Temple
Qualifications: [LLB Hons (Cardiff)]

LAMB ERIC ALAN

Exchange Chambers
Pearl Assurance House Derby Square,
Liverpool L2 9XX, Telephone: 0151 236 7747/
0458
E-mail: exchangechambers@btinternet.com
Call date: July 1975, Lincoln's Inn
Qualifications: [LLB]

LAMB JEFFREY THOMAS

3 Paper Bldgs
2nd Floor, Temple, London EC4Y 7EU,
Telephone: 0171 353 6208
Call date: Oct 1992, Middle Temple
Qualifications: [BA(Hons)(Sussex), MA(Susex),
Dip Law]

D

LAMB JOHN RICHARD

New Court
Temple, London EC4Y 9BE,
Telephone: 0171 583 5123/0171 583 0510
Call date: May 1990, Middle Temple
Qualifications: [B.A.]

LAMB MISS MARIA-JANE CARMEL

1 Paper Bldgs
1st Floor, Temple, London EC4Y 7EP,
Telephone: 0171 353 3728/4953
Call date: Nov 1984, Gray's Inn
Qualifications: [MA (Cantab)]

LAMB ROBERT GLASSON

13 King's Bench Walk
1st Floor, Temple, London EC4Y 7EN,
Telephone: 0171 353 7204
E-mail: clerks@13kbw.law.co.uk
King's Bench Chambers
32 Beaumont Street, Oxford OX1 2NP,
Telephone: 01865 311066
E-mail: clerks@kbc-oxford.law.co.uk
Call date: July 1973, Middle Temple
Qualifications: [MA (Cantab)]

LAMB TIMOTHY ROBERT QC (1995)

2 Temple Gardens
Temple, London EC4Y 9AY,
Telephone: 0171 583 6041 (12 Lines)
Call date: Nov 1974, Gray's Inn
Assistant Recorder
Qualifications: [MA (Oxon)]

LAMBERT MISS CHRISTINA CAROLINE

6 Pump Court
Ground Floor, Temple, London EC4Y 7AR,
Telephone: 0171 583 6013/2510
Call date: Nov 1988, Inner Temple
Qualifications: [MA (Cantab), Dip Law (City)]

LAMBERT MISS DEBORAH MARY

Kenworthy's Buildings
83 Bridge Street, Manchester M3 2RF,
Telephone: 0161 832 4036/834 6954
Call date: May 1977, Lincoln's Inn
Qualifications: [BA (Oxon)]

LAMBERT JOHN

New Court
1st Floor, Temple, London EC4Y 9BE,
Telephone: 0171 797 8999
25 Park Square
Leeds LS1 2PW, Telephone: 0113 2451841/2/3
E-mail: sovereignchambers@btinternet.com
Lancaster Building Chambers
77 Deansgate, Manchester M3 2BW,
Telephone: 0161 661 4444
E-mail: sandra@lbnipc.com
Call date: July 1977, Lincoln's Inn
Qualifications: [MA, FCIArb]

LAMBERT NIGEL ROBERT WOOLF

1 Crown Office Row
2nd Floor, Temple, London EC4Y 7HH,
Telephone: 0171 797 7111
Call date: Nov 1974, Gray's Inn
Recorder
Qualifications: [also Inn of Court I]

LAMBERT PAUL JULIAN LAY

Albion Chambers
Broad Street, Bristol BS1 1DR,
Telephone: 0117 9272144
Call date: July 1983, Middle Temple
Qualifications: [LLB (Lond)]

LAMBERT MISS SARAH KATRINA

1 Crown Office Row
Ground Floor, Temple, London EC4Y 7HH,
Telephone: 0171 797 7500
Call date: Oct 1994, Gray's Inn
Qualifications: [BA]

LAMBERT STUART GRAY

Sussex Chambers
9 Old Steine, Brighton BN1 1FJ,
Telephone: 01273 607953
Call date: July 1965, Gray's Inn
Assistant Recorder
Qualifications: [MA (Oxon)]

LAMBERTY MARK JULIAN HARKER

Queen's Chambers
5 John Dalton Street, Manchester M2 6ET,
Telephone: 0161 834 6875/4738
4 Camden Place
Preston PR1 3JL, Telephone: 01772 828300
Call date: Nov 1970, Gray's Inn
Qualifications: [BCL, MA (Oxon)]

LAMBIE DONALD GOODWYN

13 King's Bench Walk
1st Floor, Temple, London EC4Y 7EN,
Telephone: 0171 353 7204
E-mail: clerks@13kbw.law.co.uk
King's Bench Chambers
32 Beaumont Street, Oxford OX1 2NP,
Telephone: 01865 311066
E-mail: clerks@kbc-oxford.law.co.uk
Call date: July 1978, Lincoln's Inn
Qualifications: [LLB (Lond)]

LAMBIS MARIOS PAMBOS

2 Paper Bldgs
1st Floor, Temple, London EC4Y 7ET,
Telephone: 0171 936 2611 (10 Lines)
E-mail: clerks@2pbbarristers.co.uk
Call date: Nov 1989, Middle Temple
Qualifications: [BA Hons (Sus), Dip in Law]

LAMING MS NORMA YVONNE

New Court
Temple, London EC4Y 9BE,
Telephone: 0171 583 5123/0171 583 0510
Call date: July 1990, Middle Temple

LAMMING DAVID JOHN

2-3 Gray's Inn Square
Gray's Inn, London WC1R 5JH,
Telephone: 0171 242 4986
E-mail: chambers@2-3graysinnsquare.co.uk
Call date: Nov 1972, Gray's Inn
Qualifications: [LLB (Lond), LLM (Lon)]

LAMONT MISS CAMILLA ROSE

Chambers of Lord Goodhart QC
Ground Floor 3 New Square, Lincoln's Inn,
London WC2A 3RS,
Telephone: 0171 405 5577
E-mail: law@threenewsquare.demon.co.uk
Call date: Nov 1995, Middle Temple
Qualifications: [BA (Hons)]

LAMS BARNABAS JEFFREY

3 Temple Gardens (North)
Fifth Floor, Temple, London EC4Y 9AU,
Telephone: 0171 353 0853/4/7222
E-mail: 100106.1577@compuserve.com
Call date: Oct 1995, Gray's Inn
Qualifications: [BA (Bris), MA]

LANCASTER PHILIP STUART

39 Park Square
Leeds LS1 2NU, Telephone: 0113 2456633
Call date: July 1982, Inner Temple
Qualifications: [BA (Cantab)]

LANDALE MISS TINA JEANETTE

Old Colony House
6 South King Street, Manchester M2 6DQ,
Telephone: 0161 834 4364
Call date: July 1988, Middle Temple
Qualifications: [LLB (Hons)]

LANDAU TOBY THOMAS

Essex Court Chambers
24 Lincoln's Inn Fields, London WC2A 3ED,
Telephone: 0171 813 8000
E-mail: clerksroom@essexcourt-chambers.co.uk
Call date: Nov 1993, Middle Temple
Qualifications: [MA (Hons), BCL (Oxon), LLM
(Harvard)]

LANDAW JOHN NICHOLAS

Hardwicke Building
New Square, Lincoln's Inn, London
WC2A 3SB, Telephone: 0171 242 2523
E-mail: clerks@hardwicke.co.uk
Call date: Feb 1976, Gray's Inn
Qualifications: [BA (Oxon), MA]

LANDER CHARLES GIDEON

25-27 Castle Street
1st Floor, Liverpool L2 4TA,
Telephone: 0151 227 5661/051 236 5072
Call date: Nov 1993, Lincoln's Inn
Qualifications: [LLB (Leeds)]

D

D

LANDER RICHARD MARK

40 King Street
Manchester M2 6BA,
Telephone: 0161 832 9082
E-mail: Kingst40@aol.com
Call date: Oct 1993, Lincoln's Inn
Qualifications: [BA (Hons)]

LANDES MISS ANNA-ROSE

7 Fountain Court
Steelhouse Lane, Birmingham B4 6DR,
Telephone: 0121 236 8531
Call date: Nov 1986, Gray's Inn
Qualifications: [BA (Oxon)]

LANDSBURY ALAN PAUL

6 Gray's Inn Square
Ground Floor, Gray's Inn, London WC1R 5AZ,
Telephone: 0171 242 1052
Call date: Nov 1975, Gray's Inn

LANE DAVID GOODWIN QC (1991)

11 Bolt Court
London EC4A 3DQ,
Telephone: 0171 353 2300
E-mail: boltct11@aol.com
All Saints Chambers
9/11 Broad Street, Bristol BS1 2HP,
Telephone: 0117 921 1966
Door Tenant
Call date: Nov 1968, Gray's Inn
Recorder
Qualifications: [LLB]

LANE MS LINDSAY RUTH BUSFIELD

8 New Square
Lincoln's Inn, London WC2A 3QP,
Telephone: 0171 405 4321
Call date: Oct 1996, Middle Temple
Qualifications: [BA (Hons) (Camb), MA
(Florence)]

LANE MICHAEL JOHN

East Anglian Chambers
Sanders House 52 North Hill, Colchester
CO1 1PY, Telephone: 01206 572756
East Anglian Chambers
Gresham House 5 Museum Street, Ipswich
IP1 1HQ, Telephone: 01473 214481
East Anglian Chambers
57 London Street, Norwich NR2 1HL,
Telephone: 01603 617351
Call date: July 1983, Middle Temple
Qualifications: [BA (Cantab), Dip.Soc (Kent)]

LANE PATRICK MICHAEL MACE

1 Atkin Building
Gray's Inn, London WC1R 5AT,
Telephone: 0171 404 0102
E-mail: clerks@atkin-chambers.co.uk
Door Tenant
Call date: July 1997, Gray's Inn
Qualifications: [BA, LLB]

LANG MISS BEVERLEY ANN MACNAUGHTON

2 Hare Court
Ground Floor, Temple, London EC4Y 7BH,
Telephone: 0171 583 1770
E-mail: 2_Hare_Court@link.org
Call date: Nov 1978, Inner Temple
Qualifications: [BA (Oxon)]

LANGDALE ADRIAN MARK

Enfield Chambers
36-38 London Road, Enfield, Middlesex
EN2 6DT, Telephone: 0181 364 5627
E-mail: Enfieldchambers@compuserve.com
Call date: Mar 1996, Gray's Inn
Qualifications: [LLB (L'pool)]

LANGDALE MISS RACHEL

9 Bedford Row
London WC1R 4AZ,
Telephone: 0171 242 3555
E-mail: clerks@9br.co.uk
Call date: Oct 1990, Middle Temple
Qualifications: [LLB (Hons), M Phil (Cantab)]

LANGDALE TIMOTHY JAMES QC (1992)

Hollis Whiteman Chambers
3rd/4th Floor Queen Elizabeth Bldg, Temple,
London EC4Y 9BS, Telephone: 0171 583 5766
E-mail: hollis.whiteman@btinternet.com
Call date: July 1966, Lincoln's Inn
Recorder
Qualifications: [MA (St Andrews)]

LANGDON ANDREW DOMINIC

Guildhall Chambers
23 Broad Street, Bristol BS1 2HG,
Telephone: 0117 9273366
Call date: July 1986, Middle Temple
Qualifications: [LLB (Bristol)]

LANGHAM RICHARD GEOFFREY

1 Serjeants' Inn
4th Floor, Temple, London EC4Y 1NH,
Telephone: 0171 583 1355
E-mail: serjeants.inn@virgin.net
Call date: Nov 1986, Lincoln's Inn
Qualifications: [BA (Oxon)]

LANGLOIS PETER JOHN

Assize Court Chambers
14 Small Street, Bristol BS1 1DE,
Telephone: 0117 9264587
Call date: Oct 1991, Lincoln's Inn
Qualifications: [LLB (Hons) (E.Ang)]

LANGRIDGE MS NICOLA DAWN

Hardwicke Building
New Square, Lincoln's Inn, London
WC2A 3SB, Telephone: 0171 242 2523
E-mail: clerks@hardwicke.co.uk
Call date: Nov 1993, Lincoln's Inn
Qualifications: [LLB (Hons, Sheff)]

LANGSTAFF BRIAN FREDERICK JAMES QC (1994)

Cloisters
1st Floor, Temple, London EC4Y 7AA,
Telephone: 0171 827 4000
E-mail: clerks@cloisters.com
Call date: July 1971, Middle Temple
Recorder
Qualifications: [BA (Cantab)]

LANIGAN WILLIAM CHARLES

10 King's Bench Walk
Ground Floor, Temple, London EC4Y 7EB,
Telephone: 0171 353 7742
E-mail: 10kbw@lineone.net
Call date: July 1980, Middle Temple

LANLEHIN OLAJIDE ADEBOLA

20 Britton Street
1st Floor, London EC1M 5NQ,
Telephone: 0171 608 3765
Call date: Nov 1994, Inner Temple
Qualifications: [LLB (Lond)]

LAPRELL MARK DIETER

18 St John Street
Manchester M3 4EA,
Telephone: 0161 278 1800
Call date: Nov 1979, Gray's Inn
Assistant Recorder
Qualifications: [BA (Oxon)]

LARGE ALAN MACDONALD

South Western Chambers
Melville House 12 Middle Street, Taunton,
Somerset TA1 1SH, Telephone: 01823 331919
Call date: July 1988, Middle Temple
Qualifications: [LLB (Hons) (Manch)]

LARIZADEH CYRUS RAIS

4 Paper Bldgs
2nd Floor, Temple, London EC4Y 7EX,
Telephone: 0171 583 0816/071 353 1131
E-mail: clerks@4paperbuildings.co.uk
Call date: Nov 1992, Inner Temple
Qualifications: [BA (Kent), Certificat De Droit,
Francais (Bordeaux)]

LARKIN SEAN

Hollis Whiteman Chambers
3rd/4th Floor Queen Elizabeth Bldg, Temple,
London EC4Y 9BS, Telephone: 0171 583 5766
E-mail: hollis.whiteman@btinternet.com
Call date: July 1987, Inner Temple
Qualifications: [LLB (London)]

D

D

LASKER JEREMY STEWART

Lincoln House Chambers
5th Floor Lincoln House, 1 Brazennose Street,
Manchester M2 5EL,
Telephone: 0161 832 5701
E-mail: LincolnHouseChambers@link.org
Call date: July 1976, Inner Temple
Qualifications: [LLB (B'ham)]

LASOK DOMINIK QC (1982)

35 Essex Street
Temple, London WC2R 3AR,
Telephone: 0171 353 6381
Door Tenant
Call date: Nov 1954, Middle Temple
Qualifications: [LLM, PhD, Dr juris,]

LASOK KAROL PAUL EDWARD QC (1994)

Monckton Chambers
4 Raymond Buildings, Gray's Inn, London
WC1R 5BP, Telephone: 0171 405 7211
E-mail: chambers@monckton.co.uk
Call date: July 1977, Middle Temple
Qualifications: [MA (Cantab), LLM,PhD (Exon)]

LASSMAN LIONEL KING

1 Crown Office Row
2nd Floor, Temple, London EC4Y 7HH,
Telephone: 0171 797 7111
Call date: Feb 1955, Middle Temple

LATHAM MICHAEL RAYMOND HENRI

Furnival Chambers
32 Furnival Street, London EC4A 1JQ,
Telephone: 0171 405 3232
E-mail: clerks@furnivallaw.co.uk
Call date: Nov 1975, Gray's Inn
Qualifications: [LLB]

LATHAM RICHARD BRUNTON QC (1991)

9 Bedford Row
London WC1R 4AZ,
Telephone: 0171 242 3555
E-mail: clerks@9br.co.uk
Call date: July 1971, Gray's Inn
Recorder
Qualifications: [LLB (B'ham)]

LATHAM ROBERT JAMES

1 Pump Court
Lower Ground Floor, Temple, London
EC4Y 7AB, Telephone: 0171 583 2012/
353 4341
E-mail: (name) @1pumpcourt.co.uk
Call date: July 1976, Middle Temple
Qualifications: [MA (Cantab)]

LATIF MOHAMMED

Equity Chambers
Suite 110, Gazette Buildings 168 Corporation
Street, Birmingham B4 6TS,
Telephone: 0121 233 2100
Call date: July 1985, Lincoln's Inn
Qualifications: [BA]

LATIMER ANDREW GERARD

40 King Street
Manchester M2 6BA,
Telephone: 0161 832 9082
E-mail: Kingst40@aol.com
Call date: Nov 1995, Gray's Inn
Qualifications: [BA, BCL]

LATTIMER MISS JUSTINE ADELE

3 Fountain Court
Steelhouse Lane, Birmingham B4 6DR,
Telephone: 0121 236 5854
Call date: May 1992, Inner Temple
Qualifications: [BA (Oxon)]

LAUGHLAND JAMES RUSSELL

1 Temple Gardens
1st Floor, Temple, London EC4Y 9BB,
Telephone: 0171 353 0407/583 1315
E-mail: clerks@1templegardens.co.uk
Call date: Nov 1991, Inner Temple
Qualifications: [BA (Kent)]

LAUGHTON SAMUEL DENNIS

17 Old Bldgs
Ground Floor, Lincoln's Inn, London
WC2A 3UP, Telephone: 0171 405 9653
Call date: Feb 1993, Middle Temple
Qualifications: [MA (Cantab), Dip in Law]

LAURENCE GEORGE FREDERICK QC (1991)

12 New Square
Ground Floor, Lincoln's Inn, London
WC2A 3SW, Telephone: 0171 419 1212
E-mail: 12newsquare@compuserve.com
25 Park Square
Leeds LS1 2PW, Telephone: 0113 2451841/2/3
E-mail: sovereignchambers@btinternet.com
Door Tenant
Call date: Nov 1972, Middle Temple
Assistant Recorder
Qualifications: [MA (Oxon), BA (Cape Town)]

LAUTERPACHT ELIHU QC (1970)

20 Essex Street
London WC2R 3AL,
Telephone: 0171 583 9294
E-mail: clerks@20essexst.com
Call date: Nov 1950, Gray's Inn
Qualifications: [MA, LLB (Cantab)]

LAVENDER NICHOLAS

One Hare Court
1st Floor, Temple, London EC4Y 7BE,
Telephone: 0171 353 3171
E-mail: admin-oneharecourt@btinternet.com
Call date: July 1989, Inner Temple
Qualifications: [MA (Cantab), BCL (Oxon)]

LAVERS MICHAEL

2 Dr Johnson's Building
Temple, London EC4Y 7AY,
Telephone: 0171 353 4716
Call date: Oct 1990, Middle Temple
Qualifications: [BA (Sussex), Dip Law (City)]

LAVERY MICHAEL JAMES

24a St John Street
Manchester M3 4DF,
Telephone: 0161 833 9628
Call date: Feb 1990, Gray's Inn
Qualifications: [LLB]

LAW JOHN EDWARD

33 Bedford Row
London WC1R 4JH,
Telephone: 0171 242 6476
Call date: Oct 1996, Lincoln's Inn
Qualifications: [BA (Hons)(Oxon)]

LAWE MRS SUSAN PATRICIA

Verulam Chambers
Peer House 8-14 Verulam Street, Gray's Inn,
London WC1X 8LZ,
Telephone: 0171 813 2400
Call date: July 1982, Middle Temple
Qualifications: [BA (Hons)]

LAWLER SIMON WILLIAM QC (1993)

6 Park Square
Leeds LS1 2LW, Telephone: 0113 2459763
E-mail: chambers@no6.co.uk
11 King's Bench Walk
1st Floor, Temple, London EC4Y 7EQ,
Telephone: 0171 353 3337
Door Tenant
Call date: Nov 1971, Inner Temple
Qualifications: [LLB]

LAWRENCE DR HEATHER BUNTING ELIZABETH

11 South Square
2nd Floor, Gray's Inn, London WC1R 5EU,
Telephone: 0171 405 1222
Call date: Oct 1990, Middle Temple
Qualifications: [MA, D Phil (Oxon)]

LAWRENCE SIR IVAN JOHN QC (1981)

1 Essex Court
1st Floor, Temple, London EC4Y 9AR,
Telephone: 0171 936 3030
E-mail: one.essex_court@virgin.net
Call date: Feb 1962, Inner Temple
Recorder
Qualifications: [MA (Oxon)]

LAWRENCE NALLATHAMBY MEROLIS KARUPIAH

Victoria Chambers
3rd Floor 177 Corporation Street, Birmingham
B4 6RG, Telephone: 0121 236 9900
Call date: May 1987, Middle Temple
Qualifications: [LLB (Hons)]

LAWRENCE NIGEL STUART

Martins Building
Water Street, Liverpool L2 3SP,
Telephone: 0151 236 5818/4919
Call date: July 1988, Lincoln's Inn
Qualifications: [LLB (Hons) (Leics)]

LAWRENCE MISS PAMELA AVRIL

Albany Chambers
91 Kentish Town Road, London NW1 8NY,
Telephone: 0171 485 5736/5758
E-mail: albanychambers@usanet
Call date: Nov 1975, Inner Temple
Qualifications: [LLB (Lond)]

LAWRENCE THE HON PATRICK JOHN TRISTRAM

4 Paper Bldgs
Ground Floor, Temple, London EC4Y 7EX,
Telephone: 0171 353 3366/583 7155
E-mail: clerks@4paperbuildings.com
Call date: Feb 1985, Inner Temple
Qualifications: [BA (Oxon)]

LAWRENCE MISS RACHEL CAMILLA

1 Essex Court
1st Floor, Temple, London EC4Y 9AR,
Telephone: 0171 936 3030
E-mail: one.essex_court@virgin.net
Call date: Oct 1992, Inner Temple
Qualifications: [LLB (LSE)]

LAWRENSON MRS MARY CHRISTINE

Mitre House Chambers
Mitre House 44 Fleet Street, London
EC4Y 1BN, Telephone: 0171 583 8233
Call date: Nov 1994, Lincoln's Inn
Qualifications: [B.Ed (Hons)(Lanc)_, LLB
(Hons)(Northumb)]

LAWRIE IAN DOUGLAS

Bridewell Chambers
2 Bridewell Place, London EC4V 6AP,
Telephone: 0171 797 8800
E-mail: clerks@bridewell.law.co.uk
Call date: Nov 1985, Gray's Inn
Qualifications: [LLB (Wark)]

LAWS MISS ELEANOR JANE

5 Paper Bldgs
Lower Ground Floor, Temple, London
EC4Y 7HB, Telephone: 0171 353 5638
E-mail: 107722,633@compuserve.com
Call date: Oct 1990, Inner Temple
Qualifications: [BA (B'ham), Dip Law]

LAWS SIMON REGINALD

6 King's Bench Walk
Ground Floor, Temple, London EC4Y 7DR,
Telephone: 0171 583 0410
Call date: Oct 1991, Inner Temple
Qualifications: [BA (York), Dip Law]

LAWSON ANDREW CHARLES

24a St John Street
Manchester M3 4DF,
Telephone: 0161 833 9628
Call date: Oct 1995, Inner Temple
Qualifications: [BA (Leeds), CPE (Lanc)]

LAWSON DANIEL GEORGE

Goldsmith Building
1st Floor, Temple, London EC4Y 7BL,
Telephone: 0171 353 7881
E-mail: clerks@goldsmith-building.law.co.uk
Call date: Nov 1994, Inner Temple
Qualifications: [BA (Oxon), MA (Lond), CPE]

LAWSON EDMUND JAMES QC (1988)

9-12 Bell Yard
London WC2A 2LF,
Telephone: 0171 400 1800
Call date: Feb 1971, Gray's Inn
Qualifications: [BA (Cantab)]

LAWSON MISS ELIZABETH ANN QC (1989)

Cloisters
1st Floor, Temple, London EC4Y 7AA,
Telephone: 0171 827 4000
E-mail: clerks@cloisters.com
Call date: July 1969, Gray's Inn
Qualifications: [LLB]

LAWSON MATTHEW CHRISTOPHER

1 Gray's Inn Square
Ground Floor, London WC1R 5AA,
Telephone: 0171 405 8946/7/8
Call date: Nov 1995, Gray's Inn
Qualifications: [LLB]

LAWSON MICHAEL HENRY QC (1991)

23 Essex Street
London WC2R 3AS,
Telephone: 0171 413 0353/353 3533
E-mail: clerks@essexstreet23.demon.co.uk
Call date: Nov 1969, Inner Temple
Recorder
Qualifications: [LLB (Lond)]

LAWSON ROBERT JOHN

5 Bell Yard
London WC2A 2JR, Telephone: 0171 333 8811
Call date: Nov 1989, Inner Temple
Qualifications: [BA (Oxon), Dip Law (City)]

LAWSON MISS SARA LUCY JANE

18 Red Lion Court
(Off Fleet Street), London EC4A 3EB,
Telephone: 0171 520 6000
Thornwood House
102 New London Road, Chelmsford, Essex
CM2 0RG, Telephone: 01245 280880
Call date: Oct 1990, Inner Temple
Qualifications: [LLB]

LAWSON ROGERS GEORGE STUART QC (1994)

23 Essex Street
London WC2R 3AS,
Telephone: 0171 413 0353/353 3533
E-mail: clerks@essexstreet23.demon.co.uk
Call date: July 1969, Gray's Inn
Recorder
Qualifications: [LLB Hons]

LAWTON PAUL ANTHONY

38 Young Street
Manchester M3 3FT,
Telephone: 0161 833 0489
E-mail: clerks@young-st-chambers.com
Call date: Nov 1987, Lincoln's Inn
Qualifications: [LLB(Hons) Manchester]

LAYNE RONALD BALFOUR ROBERT

12 Old Square
1st Floor, Lincoln's Inn, London WC2A 3TX,
Telephone: 0171 404 0875
Call date: Oct 1992, Lincoln's Inn
Qualifications: [LLB (Hons)(Lond), LLM
(Comm & Corp)]

LAYTON ALEXANDER WILLIAM QC (1995)

2 Temple Gardens
Temple, London EC4Y 9AY,
Telephone: 0171 583 6041 (12 Lines)
Call date: July 1976, Middle Temple
Assistant Recorder
Qualifications: [MA (Oxon)]

LAZARUS GRANT PHILIP

The Corn Exchange
5th Floor Fenwick Street, Liverpool L2 7QS,
Telephone: 0151 227 1081/5009
Call date: Nov 1981, Gray's Inn
Qualifications: [LLB (Hons)]

LAZARUS MISS MARY HELEN

22 Old Bldgs
Lincoln's Inn, London WC2A 3UJ,
Telephone: 0171 831 0222
Call date: Oct 1991, Middle Temple
Qualifications: [BA (Cantab), CPE]

LAZARUS MICHAEL STEVEN

1 Crown Office Row
3rd Floor, Temple, London EC4Y 7HH,
Telephone: 0171 583 9292
E-mail: onecor@link.org
Call date: Nov 1987, Middle Temple
Qualifications: [MA (Cantab)]

LE BROCQ MARK WILLIAM

40 King Street
Chester CH1 2AH, Telephone: 01244 323886
Call date: Nov 1982, Middle Temple
Qualifications: [MA (Cantab)]

LE CHEVALIER DE LA PIQUERIE PAUL ANDRE LEO ALPHONSE

Falcon Chambers
Falcon Court, London EC4Y 1AA,
Telephone: 0171 353 2484/7
Call date: July 1966, Gray's Inn
Recorder
Qualifications: [LLB (B'ham)(Hons)]

D

LE CORNU PHILIP JOHN

Priory Chambers
2 Fountain Court, Steelhouse Lane,
Birmingham B4 6DR,
Telephone: 0121 236 3882/1375
Call date: Oct 1992, Middle Temple
Qualifications: [LL.B (Hons, B'ham)]

LE FOE MISS SARAH HARRIET

2 Paper Buildings
Basement, Temple, London EC4Y 7ET,
Telephone: 0171 353 0933
Call date: Nov 1989, Middle Temple
Qualifications: [BA (Hons, Lond), Dip in Law]

LE GRICE VALENTINE

1 Mitre Ct Bldgs
Ground Floor, Temple, London EC4Y 7BS,
Telephone: 0171 797 7070
Southernhay Chambers
33 Southernhay East, Exeter EX1 1NX,
Telephone: 01392 255777
E-mail: southernhay.chambers@lineone.net
Door Tenant
Call date: July 1977, Middle Temple
Qualifications: [BA (Dunelm)]

LE POIDEVIN NICHOLAS PETER

12 New Square
Ground Floor, Lincoln's Inn, London
WC2A 3SW, Telephone: 0171 419 1212
E-mail: 12newsquare@compuserve.com
25 Park Square
Leeds LS1 2PW, Telephone: 0113 2451841/2/3
E-mail: sovereignchambers@btinternet.com
Door Tenant
Call date: Nov 1975, Middle Temple
Qualifications: [MA, LLB (Cantab)]

LE PREVOST MRS AVIVA

Westgate Chambers
144 High Street, Lewes, East Sussex BN7 1XT,
Telephone: 01273 480510
Maidstone Chambers
33 Earl Street, Maidstone, Kent ME14 1PF,
Telephone: 01622 688592
Call date: Nov 1990, Inner Temple
Qualifications: [BA (Manch), Dip Law (PCL)]

LE QUESNE MS CATHERINE MARY

7 Stone Bldgs
1st Floor, Lincoln's Inn, London WC2A 3SZ,
Telephone: 0171 242 0961
Call date: Nov 1993, Inner Temple
Qualifications: [BA (Manc), Dip in Periodical,
Journalism, CPE (City)]

LE QUESNE SIR JOHN GODFRAY QC (1962)

1 Crown Office Row
3rd Floor, Temple, London EC4Y 7HH,
Telephone: 0171 583 9292
E-mail: onecor@link.org
Call date: Nov 1947, Inner Temple
Qualifications: [MA (Oxon)]

LEA JEREMY HUGH CHALONER

St Mary's Chambers
50 High Pavement, Lace Market, Nottingham
NG1 1HW, Telephone: 0115 9503503
E-mail: clerks@smc.law.co.uk
Call date: July 1978, Middle Temple
Qualifications: [BA, LLB (Sussex)]

LEACH ROBIN ANTHONY LANGLEY

2 Harcourt Bldgs
1st Floor, Temple, London EC4Y 9DB,
Telephone: 0171 353 2112/2817
Call date: July 1979, Lincoln's Inn
Qualifications: [MA (St Andrews)]

LEADBETTER IAIN WILLIAM

Walnut House
63 St. David's Hill, Exeter, Devon EX4 4DW,
Telephone: 01392 279751
E-mail: 106627.2451@compuserve.com
Call date: Nov 1975, Middle Temple
Qualifications: [LLB (So'ton)]

LEADER PROFESSOR SHELDON LAWRENCE

33 Bedford Row
London WC1R 4JH,
Telephone: 0171 242 6476
Door Tenant
East Anglian Chambers
Sanders House 52 North Hill, Colchester
CO1 1PY, Telephone: 01206 572756
Call date: May 1980, Gray's Inn
Qualifications: [BA (Yale), BA, DPhil, (Oxon)]

LEADER TIMOTHY JAMES

5 Fountain Court
Steelhouse Lane, Birmingham B4 6DR,
Telephone: 0121 606 0500
Call date: Oct 1994, Middle Temple
Qualifications: [BSc (Hons)(B'ham), MA
(Sheff), CPE (B'ham)]

LEAVER PETER LAWRENCE OPPENHEIM QC (1987)

1 Essex Court
Ground Floor, Temple, London EC4Y 9AR,
Telephone: 0171 583 2000
E-mail: clerks@oneessexcourt.co.uk
Call date: July 1967, Lincoln's Inn
Assistant Recorder

LEBASCI MS JETSUN RYONEN

St John's Chambers
Small Street, Bristol BS1 1DW,
Telephone: 0117 9213456/298514
E-mail: clerks@stjohns.uk.com
Call date: July 1995, Inner Temple
Qualifications: [LLB (Wales)]

LECKIE DAVID ERIC WILLIAM

Hardwicke Building
New Square, Lincoln's Inn, London
WC2A 3SB, Telephone: 0171 242 2523
E-mail: clerks@hardwicke.co.uk
Call date: Oct 1994, Gray's Inn
Qualifications: [LLB (Hons)]

LECKIE JAMES HARRY LAIRD

Westleigh Chambers
Westleigh Wiltown, Curry Rivel, Langport,
Somerset TA10 OJE, Telephone: 01458 251261
Door Tenant
Verulam Chambers
Peer House 8-14 Verulam Street, Gray's Inn,
London WC1X 8LZ,
Telephone: 0171 813 2400
Door Tenant
Call date: June 1964, Gray's Inn
Qualifications: [MA, LLM, FCIArb]

LECOINTE MS ELPHA MARY

1 Pump Court
Lower Ground Floor, Temple, London
EC4Y 7AB, Telephone: 0171 583 2012/
353 4341
E-mail: (name) @1pumpcourt.co.uk
Call date: Nov 1988, Lincoln's Inn
Qualifications: [LLB Hons]

LEDERMAN DAVID QC (1990)

18 Red Lion Court
(Off Fleet Street), London EC4A 3EB,
Telephone: 0171 520 6000
Thornwood House
102 New London Road, Chelmsford, Essex
CM2 0RG, Telephone: 01245 280880
Call date: July 1966, Inner Temple
Recorder
Qualifications: [BA (Cantab)]

LEDERMAN HOWARD DAVID

22 Old Bldgs
Lincoln's Inn, London WC2A 3UJ,
Telephone: 0171 831 0222
Call date: July 1982, Gray's Inn
Qualifications: [BA (Hons) (Oxon)]

LEE DAVID CHARLES

36 Bedford Row
London WC1R 4JH,
Telephone: 0171 421 8000
E-mail: 36bedfordrow@link.org
Call date: July 1973, Gray's Inn
Qualifications: [BA (Cantab), BA (Har]

LEE IAN

Devereux Chambers
Devereux Court, London WC2R 3JJ,
Telephone: 0171 353 7534
E-mail: elton@devchambers.co.uk
Call date: July 1973, Gray's Inn
Qualifications: [LLM]

LEE JOHN MICHAEL HUBERT

Bell Yard Chambers
116/118 Chancery Lane, London WC2A 1PP,
Telephone: 0171 306 9292
9 Gough Square
London EC4A 3DE, Telephone: 0171 353 5371
Call date: May 1960, Middle Temple

D

D

LEE JONATHAN JAMES WILTON

Keating Chambers
10 Essex Street, Outer Temple, London
WC2R 3AA, Telephone: 0171 544 2600
Call date: Oct 1993, Gray's Inn
Qualifications: [B.Eng (Sheff)]

LEE MICHAEL HAL

10 King's Bench Walk
1st Floor, Temple, London EC4Y 7EB,
Telephone: 0171 353 2501
Call date: July 1987, Middle Temple
Qualifications: [BA (Cal) JD (USA), LLM (LSE)]

LEE RICHARD THOMAS

5 Fountain Court
Steelhouse Lane, Birmingham B4 6DR,
Telephone: 0121 606 0500
Call date: May 1993, Gray's Inn
Qualifications: [LLB (Belfast)]

LEE ROSSLYN ALEXANDER

York Chambers
14 Toft Green, York YO1 1JT,
Telephone: 01904 620048
E-mail: yorkchambers.co.uk
Call date: Nov 1987, Gray's Inn
Qualifications: [BA, MA (Oxon)]

LEE MISS SARAH JOANNE

Brick Court Chambers
15/19 Devereux Court, London WC2R 3JJ,
Telephone: 0171 583 0777
E-mail: (surname)@brickcourt.demon.co.uk
Call date: Nov 1990, Middle Temple
Qualifications: [BA, BCL (Oxon)]

LEE MISS TARYN JANE

37 Park Square
Leeds LS1 2NY, Telephone: 0113 2439422
Call date: July 1992, Inner Temple
Qualifications: [LLB]

LEECH BRIAN WALTER THOMAS

1 Serjeants' Inn
5th Floor Fleet Street, Temple, London
EC4Y 1LL, Telephone: 0171 415 6666
E-mail: no1serjeantsinn@btinternet.com
Call date: Nov 1967, Middle Temple
Recorder

LEECH GEOFFREY ANTHONY

Advolex Chambers
70 Coulsdon Road, Coulsdon, Surrey CR5 2LB,
Telephone: 0181 763 2345
Call date: Nov 1992, Lincoln's Inn
Qualifications: [BSc (Hons)(Lough), CPE
(City)]

LEECH STEWART

Queen Elizabeth Bldg
2nd Floor, Temple, London EC4Y 9BS,
Telephone: 0171 797 7837
Call date: Oct 1992, Lincoln's Inn
Qualifications: [MA(Oxon)]

LEECH THOMAS ALEXANDER CRISPIN

9 Old Square
Ground Floor, Lincoln's Inn, London
WC2A 3SR, Telephone: 0171 405 4682
E-mail: chambers@9oldsquare.co.uk
Call date: Nov 1988, Middle Temple
Qualifications: [MA, BCL (Oxon)]

LEEK MISS SAMANTHA LOUISE

5 Essex Court
1st Floor, Temple, London EC4Y 9AH,
Telephone: 0171 410 2000
Call date: Oct 1993, Gray's Inn
Qualifications: [BA (Oxon)]

LEEMING IAN QC (1988)

9 St John Street
Manchester M3 4DN,
Telephone: 0161 955 9000
E-mail: ninesjs@gconnect.com
Lamb Chambers
Lamb Building, Temple, London EC4Y 7AS,
Telephone: 0171 797 8300
E-mail: lambchambers@link.org
Call date: Nov 1970, Gray's Inn
Recorder
Qualifications: [LLB (Manch)]

LEEMING MICHAEL PETER GEORGE

9 St John Street
Manchester M3 4DN,
Telephone: 0161 955 9000
E-mail: ninesjs@gconnect.com
Call date: July 1983, Inner Temple
Qualifications: [LLB (Hons) (Leeds)]

LEEPER THOMAS RICHARD GEOFFREY

35 Essex Street
Temple, London WC2R 3AR,
Telephone: 0171 353 6381
Call date: Nov 1991, Middle Temple
Qualifications: [BA Hons (Dunelm)]

LEES ANDREW JAMES

St Paul's House
5th Floor 23 Park Square South, Leeds
LS1 2ND, Telephone: 0113 2455866
Call date: July 1984, Gray's Inn
Qualifications: [LLB (Liverpool)]

LEES MISS PATRICIA SUSAN VIRGINIA

Furnival Chambers
32 Furnival Street, London EC4A 1JQ,
Telephone: 0171 405 3232
E-mail: clerks@furnivallaw.co.uk
Call date: Nov 1988, Lincoln's Inn
Qualifications: [LLB Hons]

LEGARD EDWARD THOMAS

York Chambers
14 Toft Green, York YO1 1JT,
Telephone: 01904 620048
E-mail: yorkchambers.co.uk
Call date: Oct 1996, Gray's Inn
Qualifications: [MA (St Andrews)]

LEGGATT GEORGE ANDREW MIDSOMER QC (1997)

Brick Court Chambers
15/19 Devereux Court, London WC2R 3JJ,
Telephone: 0171 583 0777
E-mail: (surname)@brickcourt.demon.co.uk
Call date: July 1983, Middle Temple
Qualifications: [MA (Cantab)]

LEGGE HENRY

5 Stone Buildings
Lincoln's Inn, London WC2A 3XT,
Telephone: 0171 242 6201
E-mail: clerks@5-stonebuildings.law.co.uk
Call date: Nov 1993, Middle Temple
Qualifications: [MA (Hons)(Oxon), CPE (City)]

LEGH-JONES PIERS NICHOLAS QC (1987)

20 Essex Street
20 Essex Street, London WC2R 3AL,
Telephone: 0171 583 9294
E-mail: clerks@20essexst.com
Call date: Nov 1968, Lincoln's Inn
Qualifications: [MA (Oxon)]

Fax: 0171 583 1341

Types of work: Arbitration; Commercial; Commodities; Insurance; Insurance/reinsurance; Sale and carriage of goods; Shipping, admiralty

Awards and memberships: Supporting Member London Maritime Arbitrators Association; eligible for appointment under Lloyd's Arbitration Scheme, Tier 2

Other professional experience: Visiting professor in Commercial Law, King's College University of London from 1 January 1998

Languages spoken: French

Publications: *MacGillivray and Parkington on Insurance Law* (Editor), 1975; *MacGillivray and Parkington on Insurance Law* (Editor), 1981; *MacGillivray and Parkington on Insurance Law* (Editor), 1988; *MacGillivray on Insurance Law* (General Editor) (9th edn), 1997

Reported cases: *Ackman v Policyholders' Protection Board*, [1994] 2 AC 57, HL. Ambit of cover provided by the Policyholders' Protection Act 1975 when insurer insolvent.
The 'Wondrous', [1992] 2 Lloyd's Rep 566, CA. Application of institute time clauses to maritime insurance.
SOFI v Prudential Assurance, [1993] 2 Lloyd's Rep 559, CA. Interpretation of exclusion clauses in all risks consumer insurance policy.
Yona v La Reunion Francaise, [1996] 2 Lloyd's Rep 84, Commercial Court. Political risks insurance cover and the operation of a specialist insurance pool.
The 'Zeus', [1993] 2 Lloyd's Rep 497, Commercial Court. Whether adjustment by average adjuster conclusive.

D

LEHAIN PHILIP PETER

199 Strand
London WC2R 1DR,
Telephone: 0171 379 9779
E-mail: chambers@199strand.co.uk
Call date: July 1978, Inner Temple
Qualifications: [LLB (Lond)]

LEIGH CHRISTOPHER HUMPHREY DE VERD QC (1989)

1 Paper Bldgs
1st Floor, Temple, London EC4Y 7EP,
Telephone: 0171 353 3728/4953
Call date: Nov 1967, Lincoln's Inn
Recorder

LEIGH EDWARD JULIAN EGERTON

Goldsmith Chambers
Ground Floor Goldsmith Building, Temple,
London EC4Y 7BL,
Telephone: 0171 353 6802/3/4/5
E-mail: celiamonksfield@btinternet.com
Call date: Nov 1977, Inner Temple
Qualifications: [BA (Dunelm)]

LEIGH KEVIN

10 King's Bench Walk
1st Floor, Temple, London EC4Y 7EB,
Telephone: 0171 353 2501
Regency Chambers
18 Cowgate, Peterborough PE1 1NA,
Telephone: 01733 315215
Door Tenant
Westgate Chambers
144 High Street, Lewes, East Sussex BN7 1XT,
Telephone: 01273 480510
Call date: July 1986, Lincoln's Inn
Qualifications: [LLB (Leics)]

LEIGH MISS SAMANTHA CERI

East Anglian Chambers
Sanders House 52 North Hill, Colchester
CO1 1PY, Telephone: 01206 572756
East Anglian Chambers
57 London Street, Norwich NR2 1HL,
Telephone: 01603 617351
East Anglian Chambers
Gresham House 5 Museum Street, Ipswich
IP1 1HQ, Telephone: 01473 214481
Call date: Nov 1995, Inner Temple
Qualifications: [BA (Essex), CPE]

LEIGH MISS SARAH SIOBHAN

21 White Friars
Chester CH1 1NZ, Telephone: 01244 323070
Call date: July 1983, Inner Temple
Qualifications: [LLB (Hull)]

LEIGH-MORGAN (DAVID) PAUL

Fenners Chambers
3 Madingley Road, Cambridge CB3 OEE,
Telephone: 01223 368761
Fenners Chambers
8-12 Priestgate, Peterborough PE1 1JA,
Telephone: 01733 62030
Call date: Nov 1978, Gray's Inn
Qualifications: [LLB (Exon)]

LEIGHTON PETER LEONARD

2 Gray's Inn Square Chambers
2nd Floor, Gray's Inn, London WC1R 5AA,
Telephone: 0171 242 0328/071 405 1317
E-mail: clerks@2gis.co.uk
Call date: July 1966, Inner Temple
Qualifications: [LLB (Lond)]

LEIPER RICHARD THOMAS

11 King's Bench Walk
Temple, London EC4Y 7EQ,
Telephone: 0171 632 8500
E-mail: clerksroom@11-kbw.law.co.uk
Call date: Oct 1996, Gray's Inn
Qualifications: [LLB (B'ham), M.Iuris]

LEIST IAN DOUGLAS

1 Hare Court
Ground Floor, Temple, London EC4Y 7BE,
Telephone: 0171 353 3982/5324
Call date: July 1981, Inner Temple
Qualifications: [BA]

LEMMY MICHAEL DAVID

Old Colony House
6 South King Street, Manchester M2 6DQ,
Telephone: 0161 834 4364
Call date: Nov 1994, Middle Temple
Qualifications: [LLB (Hons)]

LEMON MISS JANE KATHERINE

Keating Chambers
10 Essex Street, Outer Temple, London
WC2R 3AA, Telephone: 0171 544 2600
Call date: Nov 1993, Inner Temple
Qualifications: [BA (Hons), CPE]

LEMON ROY

Devereux Chambers
Devereux Court, London WC2R 3JJ,
Telephone: 0171 353 7534
E-mail: elton@devchambers.co.uk
Call date: July 1970, Gray's Inn
Qualifications: [LLB]

LENNARD STEPHEN CHARLES

Hardwicke Building
New Square, Lincoln's Inn, London
WC2A 3SB, Telephone: 0171 242 2523
E-mail: clerks@hardwicke.co.uk
Call date: July 1976, Gray's Inn
Qualifications: [LLB (Manch), Dip Crim
(Cantab)]

LENNON DESMOND JOSEPH

25-27 Castle Street
1st Floor, Liverpool L2 4TA,
Telephone: 0151 227 5661/051 236 5072
Call date: Nov 1986, Gray's Inn
Qualifications: [BA]

LENNON JOHN FRANCIS

1 Gray's Inn Square
Ground Floor, London WC1R 5AA,
Telephone: 0171 405 8946/7/8
Call date: Mar 1997, Lincoln's Inn
Qualifications: [BA (Hons)]

LENON ANDREW RALPH FITZMAURICE

1 Essex Court
Ground Floor, Temple, London EC4Y 9AR,
Telephone: 0171 583 2000
E-mail: clerks@oneessexcourt.co.uk
Call date: Nov 1982, Lincoln's Inn
Qualifications: [BA (Oxon), Dip Law (City)]

LEON MARC EDWARD

Lloyds House Chambers
3rd Floor 18 Lloyds House, Lloyd Street,
Manchester M2 5WA,
Telephone: 0161 839 3371
Call date: May 1988, Middle Temple
Qualifications: [LLB (Hons)]

LEONARD ANTHONY JAMES

6 King's Bench Walk
Ground Floor, Temple, London EC4Y 7DR,
Telephone: 0171 583 0410
Call date: July 1978, Inner Temple
Assistant Recorder

LEONARD CHARLES ROBERT WESTON

Goldsmith Building
1st Floor, Temple, London EC4Y 7BL,
Telephone: 0171 353 7881
E-mail: clerks@goldsmith-building.law.co.uk
Call date: July 1976, Inner Temple
Qualifications: [BA (Dublin)]

LEONARD MS EDNA JEAN

King Charles House
Standard Hill, Nottingham NG1 6FX,
Telephone: 0115 9418851
E-mail: clerks@kch.co.uk
Call date: Oct 1992, Gray's Inn
Qualifications: [BSc Hons (Oxon)]

LEONARD JAMES ALEXANDER

2 King's Bench Walk
Ground Floor, Temple, London EC4Y 7DE,
Telephone: 0171 353 1746
E-mail: 2kbw@atlas.co.uk
King's Bench Chambers
115 North Hill, Plymouth PL4 8JY,
Telephone: 01752 221551
Call date: Nov 1989, Inner Temple
Qualifications: [BA]

LEREGO MICHAEL JOHN QC (1995)

Fountain Court
Temple, London EC4Y 9DH,
Telephone: 0171 583 3335
E-mail: chambers@fountaincourt.co.uk
Call date: July 1972, Inner Temple
Qualifications: [MA (Oxon), BCL, FCIArb]

D

D

LESLIE NIGEL TERENCE

3 Pump Court
2nd Floor, Temple, London EC4Y 7AJ,
Telephone: 0171 353 1356 (3 Lines)
Call date: Nov 1994, Gray's Inn
Qualifications: [BA (Sheff)]

LESLIE STEPHEN WINDSOR QC (1993)

1 Crown Office Row
2nd Floor, Temple, London EC4Y 7HH,
Telephone: 0171 797 7111
Call date: Feb 1971, Lincoln's Inn
Qualifications: [LLB (Lond)]

LESTER OF HERNE HILL LORD QC (1975)

2 Hare Court
Ground Floor, Temple, London EC4Y 7BH,
Telephone: 0171 583 1770
E-mail: 2_Hare_Court@link.org
Call date: Feb 1963, Lincoln's Inn
Qualifications: [BA (Cantab), LLM (Harvard)]

LETHBRIDGE MISS NEMONE SUSAN

Bell Yard Chambers
116/118 Chancery Lane, London WC2A 1PP,
Telephone: 0171 306 9292
Call date: June 1956, Gray's Inn
Qualifications: [BA (Oxon)]

LETMAN PAUL ST JOHN

3 Paper Bldgs
1st Floor, Temple, London EC4Y 7EU,
Telephone: 0171 583 8055
E-mail: london@3paper.com
20 Lorne Park Road
Bournemouth BH1 1JN,
Telephone: 01202 292102 (5 Lines)
4 St Peter Street
Winchester SO23 8OW,
Telephone: 01962 868884
Call date: Nov 1987, Middle Temple
Qualifications: [BSc, Dip Law]

LETT HUGH BRIAN GORDON

South Western Chambers
Melville House 12 Middle Street, Taunton,
Somerset TA1 1SH, Telephone: 01823 331919
Call date: Nov 1971, Inner Temple
Recorder

LEVENE MISS JACQUELINE DIANE

3 Temple Gardens
3rd Floor, Temple, London EC4Y 9AU,
Telephone: 0171 583 0010
Call date: Nov 1970, Inner Temple
Qualifications: [LLB (Lond)]

LEVENE SIMON

199 Strand
London WC2R 1DR,
Telephone: 0171 379 9779
E-mail: chambers@199strand.co.uk
Call date: July 1977, Middle Temple
Assistant Recorder
Qualifications: [MA (Cantab)]

LEVENE VICTOR

Lamb Building
Ground Floor, Temple, London EC4Y 7AS,
Telephone: 0171 797 7788
E-mail: lamb.building@link.org
Call date: Nov 1961, Middle Temple
Qualifications: [LLB]

LEVER THE HON BERNARD LEWIS

Peel Court Chambers
45 Hardman Street, Manchester M3 3HA,
Telephone: 0161 832 3791
2 Harcourt Bldgs
1st Floor, Temple, London EC4Y 9DB,
Telephone: 0171 353 6961/7
Door Tenant
Call date: July 1975, Middle Temple
Recorder
Qualifications: [MA (Oxon)]

LEVER JOHN

40 King Street
Chester CH1 2AH, Telephone: 01244 323886
Call date: Nov 1978, Middle Temple
Qualifications: [LLB (L'pool)]

LEVESON BRIAN HENRY QC (1986)

22 Old Bldgs
Lincoln's Inn, London WC2A 3UJ,
Telephone: 0171 831 0222
25 Byrom Street
Manchester M3 4PF,
Telephone: 0161 829 2100
E-mail: Byromst25@aol.com
Call date: Nov 1970, Middle Temple
Recorder
Qualifications: [MA (Oxon)]

LEVETT MARTYN NEALE

East Anglian Chambers
Sanders House 52 North Hill, Colchester
CO1 1PY, Telephone: 01206 572756
East Anglian Chambers
57 London Street, Norwich NR2 1HL,
Telephone: 01603 617351
East Anglian Chambers
Gresham House 5 Museum Street, Ipswich
IP1 1HQ, Telephone: 01473 214481
Call date: Nov 1978, Middle Temple
Qualifications: [BSc (Leeds)]

LEVINE STEVEN ADRIAN

Parsonage Chambers
5th Floor 3 The Parsonage, Manchester
M3 2HW, Telephone: 0161 833 1996
Call date: Nov 1989, Lincoln's Inn
Qualifications: [LLB (Hons), LLM (Lond)]

LEVINE SYDNEY

Broadway House Chambers
Broadway House 9 Bank Street, Bradford,
West Yorkshire BD1 1TW,
Telephone: 01274 722560
Call date: Nov 1952, Inner Temple
Qualifications: [LLB]

LEVINSON JUSTIN MAURICE

1 Dr Johnson's Bldgs
Ground Floor, Temple, London EC4Y 7AX,
Telephone: 0171 353 9328
Call date: Oct 1994, Middle Temple
Qualifications: [LLB (Hons)]

LEVISEUR NICHOLAS TEMPLAR

3 Paper Bldgs
1st Floor, Temple, London EC4Y 7EU,
Telephone: 0171 583 8055
E-mail: london@3paper.com
20 Lorne Park Road
Bournemouth BH1 1JN,
Telephone: 01202 292102 (5 Lines)
4 St Peter Street
Winchester SO23 8OW,
Telephone: 01962 868884
Call date: Nov 1979, Gray's Inn
Qualifications: [MA(Oxon)]

LEVITT MISS ALISON FRANCES JOSEPHINE

3 Gray's Inn Square
Ground Floor, London WC1R 5AH,
Telephone: 0171 520 5600
E-mail: gis3@btinternet.com
Call date: July 1988, Inner Temple
Qualifications: [MA (St Andrews), Dip Law]

LEVY ALLAN EDWARD QC (1989)

17 Bedford Row
London WC1R 4EB,
Telephone: 0171 831 7314
E-mail: IBoard7314@AOL.com
Call date: Nov 1969, Inner Temple
Recorder
Qualifications: [LLB]

LEVY ANTHONY JULIAN

2 King's Bench Walk
1st Floor, Temple, London EC4Y 7DE,
Telephone: 0171 353 9276
Call date: Nov 1983, Middle Temple
Qualifications: [LLB]

LEVY BENJAMIN KEITH

Enterprise Chambers
9 Old Square, Lincoln's Inn, London
WC2A 3SR, Telephone: 0171 405 9471
Enterprise Chambers
38 Park Square, Leeds LS1 2PA,
Telephone: 01132 460391
Enterprise Chambers
65 Quayside, Newcastle upon Tyne NE1 3DS,
Telephone: 0191 222 3344
Call date: Nov 1956, Lincoln's Inn
Qualifications: [MA, LLB (Cantab)]

LEVY GERALD

2 Hare Court
Ground Floor, Temple, London EC4Y 7BH,
Telephone: 0171 583 1770
E-mail: 2_Hare_Court@link.org
Call date: Apr 1964, Gray's Inn
Qualifications: [MA (Oxon)]

LEVY JACOB

9 Gough Square
London EC4A 3DE, Telephone: 0171 353 5371
Call date: July 1986, Inner Temple
Qualifications: [LLB (Lond)]

LEVY MISS JULIETTE

New Court
Temple, London EC4Y 9BE,
Telephone: 0171 583 5123/0171 583 0510
Call date: Nov 1992, Middle Temple
Qualifications: [BA (Hons), MA (Lond)]

LEVY MICHAEL PETER

3 Hare Court
1st Floor, Temple, London EC4Y 7BJ,
Telephone: 0171 353 7561
Call date: Nov 1979, Gray's Inn
Qualifications: [LLB Hons]

LEVY NEIL HOWARD

St John's Chambers
Small Street, Bristol BS1 1DW,
Telephone: 0117 9213456/298514
E-mail: clerks@stjohns.uk.com
Call date: July 1986, Lincoln's Inn
Qualifications: [LLB (Exeter)]

LEVY PHILIP GRENVILLE

3 Temple Gardens
2nd Floor, Temple, London EC4Y 9AU,
Telephone: 0171 583 1155
Call date: Nov 1968, Inner Temple
Qualifications: [LLB (Manch)]

LEVY ROBERT STUART

11 Stone Bldgs
1st Floor, Lincoln's Inn, London WC2A 3TG,
Telephone: 0171 404 5055
E-mail: 9stoneb@compuserve.com
Assize Court Chambers
14 Small Street, Bristol BS1 1DE,
Telephone: 0117 9264587
Call date: Nov 1988, Middle Temple
Qualifications: [LLB, LLM (Cantab)]

LEWER MICHAEL EDWARD QC (1983)

Farrar's Building
Temple, London EC4Y 7BD,
Telephone: 0171 583 9241
E-mail: chambers@farrarsbuilding.co.uk
Call date: June 1958, Gray's Inn
Recorder
Qualifications: [MA (Oxon)]

LEWERS NIGEL CHRISTOPHER

12 King's Bench Walk
Temple, London EC4Y 7EL,
Telephone: 0171 583 0811
E-mail: chambers@12kbw.co.uk
Call date: Nov 1986, Gray's Inn
Qualifications: [BA(Oxon)]

LEWIN LT CDR NICHOLAS ANTON

2 King's Bench Walk
Ground Floor, Temple, London EC4Y 7DE,
Telephone: 0171 353 1746
E-mail: 2kbw@atlas.co.uk
King's Bench Chambers
115 North Hill, Plymouth PL4 8JY,
Telephone: 01752 221551
Call date: July 1989, Gray's Inn
Qualifications: [BA]

LEWINSKI STEFAN ANDREW

Merchant Chambers
1 North Parade, Parsonage Gardens,
Manchester M3 2NH,
Telephone: 0161 839 7070
Call date: Nov 1995, Gray's Inn
Qualifications: [LLB (Bris), LLB (Euro)]

LEWIS ADAM VALENTINE SHERVEY

2 Hare Court
Ground Floor, Temple, London EC4Y 7BH,
Telephone: 0171 583 1770
E-mail: 2_Hare_Court@link.org
Call date: July 1985, Gray's Inn
Qualifications: [MA (Cantab)]

LEWIS ALUN KYNRIC QC (1978)

8 New Square
Lincoln's Inn, London WC2A 3QP,
Telephone: 0171 405 4321
9 Park Place
Cardiff CF1 3DP, Telephone: 01222 382731
Door Tenant
Call date: Nov 1954, Middle Temple
Qualifications: [B.Sc, LLB]

LEWIS ANDREW SIMON

Francis Taylor Bldg
Ground Floor, Temple, London EC4Y 7BY,
Telephone: 0171 353 7768/7769/2711
Call date: Nov 1986, Middle Temple
Qualifications: [BA(Oxon)]

LEWIS ANDREW WILLIAM

25 Park Square
Leeds LS1 2PW, Telephone: 0113 2451841/2/3
E-mail: sovereignchambers@btinternet.com
Call date: July 1985, Lincoln's Inn
Qualifications: [BA]

LEWIS MISS CAROLINE SUSANNAH

3 Verulam Buildings
London WC1R 5NT,
Telephone: 0171 831 8441
E-mail: clerks@3verulam.co.uk
Call date: July 1988, Middle Temple
Qualifications: [BA (Oxon)]

LEWIS CHARLES JAMES

Old Square Chambers
1 Verulam Buildings, Gray's Inn, London
WC1R 5LQ, Telephone: 0171 831 0801
Old Square Chambers
Hanover House 47 Corn Street, Bristol
BS1 1HT, Telephone: 0117 9277111
Call date: July 1963, Inner Temple
Qualifications: [MA (Oxon)]

LEWIS CHARLES WILLIAM

36 Bedford Row
London WC1R 4JH,
Telephone: 0171 421 8000
E-mail: 36bedfordrow@link.org
Call date: July 1977, Inner Temple
Qualifications: [MA (Oxon)]

LEWIS MRS CHERRY ANNE

Verulam Chambers
Peer House 8-14 Verulam Street, Gray's Inn,
London WC1X 8LZ,
Telephone: 0171 813 2400
Door Tenant
Call date: July 1973, Inner Temple
Qualifications: [FCIArb]

LEWIS CLIVE BUCKLAND

4-5 Gray's Inn Square
Ground Floor, Gray's Inn, London WC1R 5AY,
Telephone: 0171 404 5252
E-mail: chambers@4-5graysinnsquare.co.uk
Call date: Nov 1987, Middle Temple
Qualifications: [MA (Cambs), LLM (Dalhousie Uni), Fellow Selwyn Cambs]

LEWIS DAVID RALPH

5 Fountain Court
Steelhouse Lane, Birmingham B4 6DR,
Telephone: 0121 606 0500
Call date: July 1978, Middle Temple
Assistant Recorder
Qualifications: [BA (Oxon)]

LEWIS EDWARD TREVOR GWYN

Francis Taylor Bldg
Ground Floor, Temple, London EC4Y 7BY,
Telephone: 0171 353 7768/7769/2711
Call date: July 1972, Gray's Inn

LEWIS MISS ELERI VODDEN

2 Field Court
Gray's Inn, London WC1R 5BB,
Telephone: 0171 405 6114
E-mail: fieldct2@netcomuk.co.uk.
Call date: Nov 1989, Middle Temple
Qualifications: [LLB (Lond)]

D

LEWIS HUGH WILSON

Southernhay Chambers
33 Southernhay East, Exeter EX1 1NX,
Telephone: 01392 255777
E-mail: southernhay.chambers@lineone.net
Call date: July 1970, Middle Temple
Qualifications: [LLB]

LEWIS IAN ANTHONY

Gray's Inn Chambers
5th Floor, Gray's Inn, London WC1R 5JA,
Telephone: 0171 404 1111
Call date: Feb 1989, Middle Temple
Qualifications: [MA (Cantab)]

LEWIS JAMES THOMAS

3 Raymond Buildings
Gray's Inn, London WC1R 5BH,
Telephone: 0171 831 3833
E-mail: chambers@threeraymond.demon.co.uk
Call date: July 1987, Gray's Inn
Qualifications: [BSc (Hons), Dip Law]

LEWIS MISS JANE ALEXIS

1 Hare Court
Ground Floor, Temple, London EC4Y 7BE,
Telephone: 0171 353 3982/5324
Call date: Nov 1990, Middle Temple
Qualifications: [BA (McGill), Dip Law (PCL)]

LEWIS JEFFREY ALLAN

9 Woodhouse Square
Leeds LS3 1AD, Telephone: 0113 2451986
Call date: July 1978, Middle Temple
Recorder
Qualifications: [BA, LLB]

LEWIS JEREMY STEPHEN

Littleton Chambers
3 King's Bench Walk North, Temple, London
EC4Y 7HR, Telephone: 0171 797 8600
E-mail: littletonchambers@compuserve.com
Call date: May 1992, Lincoln's Inn
Qualifications: [BA, BCL]

LEWIS JONATHAN MARK

3 Paper Bldgs
Ground Floor, Temple, London EC4Y 7EU,
Telephone: 0171 797 7000
E-mail: clerks@3pb.co.uk
Call date: Mar 1996, Inner Temple
Qualifications: [LLB (Manch)]

LEWIS MISS MARIAN ELENA

30 Park Place
Cardiff CF1 3BA, Telephone: 01222 398421
E-mail: 100757.1456@compuserve.com
Farrar's Building
Temple, London EC4Y 7BD,
Telephone: 0171 583 9241
E-mail: chambers@farrarsbuilding.co.uk
Door Tenant
Call date: Nov 1977, Middle Temple
Qualifications: [LLB (Lond) (Hons)]

LEWIS MISS MELANIE ELIZABETH

4 Brick Court
Ground Floor, Temple, London EC4Y 9AD,
Telephone: 0171 797 7766
E-mail: chambers@4brick.co.uk
Call date: Nov 1980, Gray's Inn
Qualifications: [LLB (L'pool), LLM (Leic)]

LEWIS MEYRIC

2 Harcourt Bldgs
2nd Floor, Temple, London EC4Y 9DB,
Telephone: 0171 353 8415
E-mail: clerks@twoharcourtbldgs.demon.co.uk
Call date: Nov 1986, Gray's Inn
Qualifications: [BA (Bris)]

LEWIS MICHAEL AP GWILYM QC (1975)

3 Hare Court
1st Floor, Temple, London EC4Y 7BJ,
Telephone: 0171 353 7561
Call date: Nov 1956, Gray's Inn
Recorder
Qualifications: [MA (Oxon)]

LEWIS OWEN PRYS

9 Park Place
Cardiff CF1 3DP, Telephone: 01222 382731
Call date: July 1985, Middle Temple
Qualifications: [LLM (Cantab), LLB, (Wales)]

LEWIS PAUL KEITH

30 Park Place
Cardiff CF1 3BA, Telephone: 01222 398421
E-mail: 100757.1456@compuserve.com
Call date: Feb 1981, Gray's Inn
Qualifications: [LLB (Leic) (Hons)]

LEWIS PETER REES

Francis Taylor Bldg
Ground Floor, Temple, London EC4Y 7BY,
Telephone: 0171 353 7768/7769/2711
Call date: June 1964, Gray's Inn
Qualifications: [LLM]

LEWIS PHILIP SIMON COLEMAN

Littman Chambers
12 Gray's Inn Square, London WC1R 5JP,
Telephone: 0171 404 4866
E-mail: admin@littmanchambers.com
Door Tenant
Call date: Feb 1958, Lincoln's Inn
Qualifications: [MA (Oxon)]

LEWIS RAYMOND JOSEPH

2 Paper Bldgs
1st Floor, Temple, London EC4Y 7ET,
Telephone: 0171 936 2611 (10 Lines)
E-mail: clerks@2pbbarristers.co.uk
Call date: July 1971, Middle Temple

LEWIS RAYMOND SPENCER

32 Park Place
Cardiff CF1 3BA, Telephone: 01222 397364
Call date: July 1994, Inner Temple
Recorder

LEWIS PROFESSOR ROY MALCOLM

Old Square Chambers
1 Verulam Buildings, Gray's Inn, London
WC1R 5LQ, Telephone: 0171 831 0801
Old Square Chambers
Hanover House 47 Corn Street, Bristol
BS1 1HT, Telephone: 0117 9277111
Call date: May 1992, Lincoln's Inn
Qualifications: [LLB, MSc (Econ)]

LEWIS THOMAS ROBIN ARWEL

Priory Chambers
2 Fountain Court, Steelhouse Lane,
Birmingham B4 6DR,
Telephone: 0121 236 3882/1375
Call date: Nov 1991, Inner Temple
Qualifications: [MA (Cantab)]

LEWIS WAYNE ANTHONY

Chambers of Raana Sheikh
Gray's Inn Chambers, Gray's Inn, London
WC1R, Telephone: 0171 831 5344
E-mail: s.mcblain@btinternet.com
Call date: Nov 1982, Lincoln's Inn
Qualifications: [LLB]

LEWIS-JONES MEIRION

Sedan House
Stanley Place, Chester CH1 2LU,
Telephone: 01244 320480/348282
1 Dr Johnson's Bldgs
Ground Floor, Temple, London EC4Y 7AX,
Telephone: 0171 353 9328
Call date: Nov 1971, Gray's Inn
Qualifications: [LLB (Lond)]

LEWISON KIM MARTIN JORDAN QC (1991)

Falcon Chambers
Falcon Court, London EC4Y 1AA,
Telephone: 0171 353 2484/7
Call date: July 1975, Lincoln's Inn
Recorder
Qualifications: [MA (Cantab)]

LEWSLEY CHRISTOPHER STANTON

4 Breams Buildings
London EC4A 1AQ,
Telephone: 0171 353 5835/430 1221
Call date: July 1976, Lincoln's Inn
Qualifications: [BSc PhD CEng, MiStructE]

LEWTHWAITE MISS JOANNE ELIZABETH

Peel House Chambers
Ground Floor, Peel House 5 Harrington Street,
Liverpool L2 9QA, Telephone: 0151 236 4321
Call date: Oct 1990, Inner Temple
Qualifications: [LLB (L'pool)]

LEY (NIGEL) SPENCER

Farrar's Building
Temple, London EC4Y 7BD,
Telephone: 0171 583 9241
E-mail: chambers@farrarsbuilding.co.uk
Call date: July 1985, Middle Temple
Qualifications: [MA (Cantab)]

LEY NIGEL JOSEPH

Chambers of Nigel Ley
Second Floor South Gray's Inn Chambers,
Gray's Inn, London WC1R 5JA,
Telephone: 0171 831 7888
Call date: Nov 1969, Gray's Inn
Qualifications: [LLM (Manch)]

LEY-MORGAN MARK JOHN

3 Serjeants Inn
London EC4Y 1BQ,
Telephone: 0171 353 5537
E-mail: available upon request
Call date: Oct 1994, Gray's Inn
Qualifications: [BSc, LLB]

LICKERT EDWARD MARTIN

2 Pump Court
1st Floor, Temple, London EC4Y 7AH,
Telephone: 0171 353 5597
Call date: Nov 1986, Middle Temple
Qualifications: [LLB (Hons)]

LICKLEY NIGEL JAMES DOMINIC

3 Paper Bldgs
1st Floor, Temple, London EC4Y 7EU,
Telephone: 0171 583 8055
E-mail: london@3paper.com
4 St Peter Street
Winchester SO23 8OW,
Telephone: 01962 868884
20 Lorne Park Road
Bournemouth BH1 1JN,
Telephone: 01202 292102 (5 Lines)
Call date: July 1983, Gray's Inn
Qualifications: [LLB (Lond)]

LIDDIARD MARTIN THOMAS

5 Fountain Court
Steelhouse Lane, Birmingham B4 6DR,
Telephone: 0121 606 0500
Call date: Nov 1989, Inner Temple
Qualifications: [LLB (B'ham)]

LIDDY SIMON TERENCE

New Walk Chambers
27 New Walk, Leicester LE1 6TE,
Telephone: 0116 2559144
Call date: July 1979, Middle Temple
Qualifications: [LLM]

LIEBRECHT JOHN MICHAEL

One Garden Court
Ground Floor, Temple, London EC4Y 9BJ,
Telephone: 0171 797 7900
Call date: Nov 1989, Inner Temple
Qualifications: [BA (Oxon), LLM (Cantab)]

LIEVEN MS NATHALIE MARIE DANIELLA

4 Breams Buildings
London EC4A 1AQ,
Telephone: 0171 353 5835/430 1221
Call date: July 1989, Gray's Inn
Qualifications: [BA [Cantab]]

LIGHT PROFESSOR ROY ALAN

St John's Chambers
Small Street, Bristol BS1 1DW,
Telephone: 0117 9213456/298514
E-mail: clerks@stjohns.uk.com
Call date: Feb 1992, Gray's Inn
Qualifications: [LLB (Lond), LLM (Lond), MPhil (Cambs), PhD (Cambs)]

LIGHTMAN DANIEL

13 Old Square
1st Floor, Lincoln's Inn, London WC2A 3UA,
Telephone: 0171 242 6105
E-mail: clerks@serlecourt.co.uk
Call date: Oct 1995, Lincoln's Inn
Qualifications: [BA (Hons)(Oxon), CPE]

LIGHTWING STUART

York House
Borough Road, Middlesbrough, Cleveland
TS1 2HJ, Telephone: 01642 213000
22 Old Bldgs
Lincoln's Inn, London WC2A 3UJ,
Telephone: 0171 831 0222
Call date: July 1972, Middle Temple
Qualifications: [LLB, FCIS, MBIM,FRSA, FCIArb]

LILLINGTON SIMON DOUGLAS

1 Gray's Inn Square
1st Floor, London WC1R 5AG,
Telephone: 0171 405 3000
E-mail: clerks@onegrays.demon.co.uk
Call date: Nov 1980, Middle Temple
Qualifications: [BA, LLM]

LIM MALCOLM KIAN-LENG

3 Serjeants Inn
London EC4Y 1BQ,
Telephone: 0171 353 5537
E-mail: available upon request
Call date: July 1989, Inner Temple
Qualifications: [BA (Keele), LLM (Lond)]

LIMB CHRISTOPHER

38 Young Street
Manchester M3 3FT,
Telephone: 0161 833 0489
E-mail: clerks@young-st-chambers.com
Call date: July 1975, Gray's Inn
Qualifications: [LLB]

LIMB PATRICK FRANCIS

24 The Ropewalk
Nottingham NG1 5EF,
Telephone: 0115 9472581
E-mail: clerk@ropewalk.co.uk
Call date: July 1987, Middle Temple
Qualifications: [BA (Cantab)]

LIMBREY BERNARD MARTIN

Staple Inn Chambers
1st Floor 9 Staple Inn, Holborn, London
WC1V 7QH, Telephone: 0171 242 5240
E-mail: clerks@staple-inn.org
Call date: Nov 1980, Middle Temple
Qualifications: [MSc (Lond)]

LIMONT WILLIAM ANTHONY

Chavasse Court Chambers
2nd Floor Chavasse Court, 24 Lord Street,
Liverpool L2 1TA, Telephone: 0151 707 1191
Call date: Nov 1964, Gray's Inn
Qualifications: [LLB (L'pool)]

LINCOLN (FREDMAN) ASHE QC (1947)

9 King's Bench Walk
Ground Floor, Temple, London EC4Y 7DX,
Telephone: 0171 353 7202/3909
Call date: Nov 1929, Inner Temple
Recorder
Qualifications: [MA, BCL]

LINDBLOM KEITH JOHN QC (1996)

2 Harcourt Bldgs
2nd Floor, Temple, London EC4Y 9DB,
Telephone: 0171 353 8415
E-mail: clerks@twoharcourtbldgs.demon.co.uk
Call date: July 1980, Gray's Inn
Qualifications: [MA (Oxon)]

LINDEN THOMAS DOMINIC

4-5 Gray's Inn Square
Ground Floor, Gray's Inn, London WC1R 5AY,
Telephone: 0171 404 5252
E-mail: chambers@4-5graysinnsquare.co.uk
Call date: Nov 1989, Gray's Inn
Qualifications: [BA,(Oxon), BCL]

LINDOP MISS SARAH LOUISE

2 Paper Buildings
Basement, Temple, London EC4Y 7ET,
Telephone: 0171 353 0933
Call date: Nov 1989, Gray's Inn
Qualifications: [LLB (Hons)]

LINDQVIST ANDREW NILS GUNNAR

Octagon House
19 Colegate, Norwich NR3 1AT,
Telephone: 01603 623186
E-mail: octagon@netmatters.co.uk
Call date: Nov 1968, Middle Temple
Qualifications: [MA (Cantab)]

LINDSAY MISS CLAIRE LOUISE

Plowden Bldgs
2nd Floor, Temple, London EC4Y 9BU,
Telephone: 0171 583 0808
E-mail: bar@plowdenbuildings.co.uk
Call date: Oct 1991, Middle Temple
Qualifications: [LLB (Leic)]

D

LINDSAY CRAWFORD CALLUM DOUGLAS QC (1987)

1 Serjeants' Inn
5th Floor Fleet Street, Temple, London
EC4Y 1LL, Telephone: 0171 415 6666
E-mail: no1serjeantsinn@btinternet.com
Call date: June 1961, Lincoln's Inn
Recorder
Qualifications: [MA (Oxon)]

LINDSAY JEREMY MARK HENRY

37 Park Square
Leeds LS1 2NY, Telephone: 0113 2439422
Call date: July 1986, Gray's Inn
Qualifications: [LLB (Hons)(Nott'm),
Postgraduate Diploma, in Radio Journalism]

LINDSAY MARTIN ROSS

York Chambers
14 Toft Green, York YO1 1JT,
Telephone: 01904 620048
E-mail: yorkchambers.co.uk
Call date: July 1977, Gray's Inn

LINDSAY RONALD BLENNERHASSETT

Westgate Chambers
144 High Street, Lewes, East Sussex BN7 1XT,
Telephone: 01273 480510
9-12 Bell Yard
London WC2A 2LF,
Telephone: 0171 400 1800
Call date: Nov 1975, Gray's Inn
Qualifications: [BA, LLB (TCD)]

LINEHAN STEPHEN JOHN QC (1993)

5 Fountain Court
Steelhouse Lane, Birmingham B4 6DR,
Telephone: 0121 606 0500
Call date: Feb 1970, Lincoln's Inn
Recorder
Qualifications: [LLB (Lond)]

LINFORD ROBERT FRANK

Devon Chambers
3 St Andrew Street, Plymouth PL1 2AH,
Telephone: 01752 661659
Call date: Nov 1987, Gray's Inn
Qualifications: [LLB (Hons) (Wales)]

LINKLATER MISS LISA MARGARET

Chancery House Chambers
7 Lisbon Square, Leeds LS1 4LY,
Telephone: 0113 244 6691
E-mail: Chanceryhouse@btinternet.com
Call date: Oct 1995, Inner Temple
Qualifications: [BA (Cantab)]

LINNEMANN BERNARD MARIA

3 Fountain Court
Steelhouse Lane, Birmingham B4 6DR,
Telephone: 0121 236 5854
Call date: Nov 1980, Gray's Inn
Qualifications: [BA (Tcd)]

LINSTEAD PETER JAMES

11 Bolt Court
London EC4A 3DQ,
Telephone: 0171 353 2300
E-mail: boltct11@aol.com
Call date: Oct 1994, Gray's Inn
Qualifications: [BA]

LINTOTT DAVID JAMES

2-3 Gray's Inn Square
Gray's Inn, London WC1R 5JH,
Telephone: 0171 242 4986
E-mail: chambers@2-3graysinnsquare.co.uk
Call date: Oct 1996, Gray's Inn
Qualifications: [BA (Cantab)]

LIPSTEIN KURT

13 Old Square
Ground Floor, Lincoln's Inn, London
WC2A 3UA, Telephone: 0171 404 4800
Door Tenant
Call date: Jan 1950, Middle Temple
Qualifications: [PhD]

LISSACK RICHARD ANTHONY QC (1994)

35 Essex Street
Temple, London WC2R 3AR,
Telephone: 0171 353 6381
Call date: Nov 1978, Inner Temple
Assistant Recorder

LISTER MISS CAROLINE JANE

1 King's Bench Walk
2nd Floor, Temple, London EC4Y 7DB,
Telephone: 0171 936 1500
E-mail: ddear@1kbw.co.uk
Call date: Nov 1980, Middle Temple
Qualifications: [BSc (Lond)]

LITCHFIELD MISS LINDA

3 Paper Bldgs
1st Floor, Temple, London EC4Y 7EU,
Telephone: 0171 583 8055
E-mail: london@3paper.com
20 Lorne Park Road
Bournemouth BH1 1JN,
Telephone: 01202 292102 (5 Lines)
4 St Peter Street
Winchester SO23 8OW,
Telephone: 01962 868884
Call date: July 1974, Inner Temple
Qualifications: [BA (Kingston), BCL (Oxon)]

LITHERLAND MISS REBECCA JANE

Fenners Chambers
3 Madingley Road, Cambridge CB3 OEE,
Telephone: 01223 368761
Fenners Chambers
8-12 Priestgate, Peterborough PE1 1JA,
Telephone: 01733 62030
Call date: July 1987, Middle Temple
Qualifications: [LLB (Bham)]

LITHMAN NIGEL LLOYD QC (1997)

3 Hare Court
1st Floor, Temple, London EC4Y 7BJ,
Telephone: 0171 353 7561
Call date: Nov 1976, Inner Temple
Assistant Recorder
Qualifications: [LLB (Hons)]

LITTLE GEOFFREY WILLIAM

Sedan House
Stanley Place, Chester CH1 2LU,
Telephone: 01244 320480/348282
1 Dr Johnson's Bldgs
Ground Floor, Temple, London EC4Y 7AX,
Telephone: 0171 353 9328
Dr Johnson's Chambers
The Atrium Court Apex Plaza, Reading
RG1 1AX, Telephone: 01734 254221
Door Tenant
Call date: July 1973, Middle Temple
Assistant Recorder
Qualifications: [MA (Cantab) LLM, (Warwick)]

LITTLE IAN

9 St John Street
Manchester M3 4DN,
Telephone: 0161 955 9000
E-mail: ninesjs@gconnect.com
Call date: Feb 1989, Middle Temple
Qualifications: [BA (Oxon), Dip Law (City)]

LITTLER MARTIN GORDON

Cobden House Chambers
19 Quay Street, Manchester M3 3HN,
Telephone: 0161 833 6000
E-mail: clerks@cobden.co.uk
Call date: Nov 1989, Gray's Inn
Qualifications: [LLB]

LITTLER RICHARD MARK

Kenworthy's Buildings
83 Bridge Street, Manchester M3 2RF,
Telephone: 0161 832 4036/834 6954
Call date: Oct 1994, Gray's Inn
Qualifications: [LLB]

LITTLEWOOD MISS REBECCA MAE

Trafalgar Chambers
53 Fleet Street, London EC4Y 1BE,
Telephone: 0171 583 5858
E-mail: TrafalgarChambers@easynet.co.uk
Call date: Nov 1988, Inner Temple
Qualifications: [LLB (Soton)]

D

LITTLEWOOD ROBERT

2 Garden Court
1st Floor, Middle Temple, London EC4Y 9BL,
Telephone: 0171 353 1633
E-mail: barristers@2gardenct.law.co.uk
Call date: Oct 1993, Inner Temple
Qualifications: [BA, CPE]

LITTMAN JEFFREY JAMES

2 Field Court
Gray's Inn, London WC1R 5BB,
Telephone: 0171 405 6114
E-mail: fieldct2@netcomuk.co.uk.
Call date: July 1974, Middle Temple
Qualifications: [MA (Cantab)]

LITTMAN MARK QC (1961)

Littman Chambers
12 Gray's Inn Square, London WC1R 5JP,
Telephone: 0171 404 4866
E-mail: admin@littmanchambers.com
Call date: June 1947, Middle Temple
Qualifications: [MA (Oxon), BSc (Econ]

LITTON JOHN LETABLERE

4 Breams Buildings
London EC4A 1AQ,
Telephone: 0171 353 5835/430 1221
Call date: July 1989, Middle Temple
Qualifications: [LLB (So'ton)]

LIVESEY BERNARD JOSEPH EDWARD QC (1990)

2 Crown Office Row
2nd Floor, Temple, London EC4Y 7HJ,
Telephone: 0171 797 8000
Call date: July 1969, Lincoln's Inn
Recorder
Qualifications: [MA, LLB (Cantab)]

LIVESEY FRASER MICHAEL STANIER

15 Winckley Square
Preston PR1 3JJ, Telephone: 01772 252828
E-mail: clerks@winckleysq.demon.co.uk
Call date: Oct 1992, Lincoln's Inn
Qualifications: [LLB(Hons)(Newc)]

LIVESEY JOHN WILLIAM ALLAN

Albion Chambers
Broad Street, Bristol BS1 1DR,
Telephone: 0117 9272144
Call date: Nov 1990, Lincoln's Inn
Qualifications: [LLB (Bris)]

LIVESEY SIMON PETER

169 Temple Chambers
Temple Avenue, London EC4Y 0DA,
Telephone: 0171 583 7644
Call date: July 1987, Inner Temple
Qualifications: [BSc (Leicester)]

LIVING MARC STEPHEN

Holborn Chambers
6 Gate Street, Lincoln's Inn Fields, London
WC2A 3HP, Telephone: 0171 242 6060
Call date: July 1983, Middle Temple
Qualifications: [BA (Hons) (Kent),]

LIVINGSTON RICHARD JOHN

3 Hare Court
1st Floor, Temple, London EC4Y 7BJ,
Telephone: 0171 353 7561
Call date: July 1980, Gray's Inn
Qualifications: [BA (Oxon),LLM (Lond)]

LIVINGSTONE SIMON JOHN

11 Bolt Court
London EC4A 3DQ,
Telephone: 0171 353 2300
E-mail: boltct11@aol.com
Redhill Chambers
Seloduct House 30 Station Road, Redhill
RH1 1NK, Telephone: 01737 780781
Call date: Oct 1990, Inner Temple
Qualifications: [LLB (Bris)]

LIVINGSTONE THOMAS DOUGLAS

New Court
Temple, London EC4Y 9BE,
Telephone: 0171 583 5123/0171 583 0510
Call date: Nov 1989, Inner Temple
Qualifications: [LLB (Lond)]

LLEWELLYN CHARLES IVOR

Staple Inn Chambers
1st Floor 9 Staple Inn, Holborn, London
WC1V 7QH, Telephone: 0171 242 5240
E-mail: clerks@staple-inn.org
Call date: July 1978, Gray's Inn
Qualifications: [LLB (Hons) (Lond)]

LLEWELLYN-JONES CHRISTOPHER GEOFFREY QC (1990)

Goldsmith Building
1st Floor, Temple, London EC4Y 7BL,
Telephone: 0171 353 7881
E-mail: clerks@goldsmith-building.law.co.uk
9 Park Place
Cardiff CF1 3DP, Telephone: 01222 382731
Door Tenant
Call date: Nov 1965, Middle Temple
Recorder
Qualifications: [MA (Cantab)]

LLEWELYN MISS JANE RHIANNON

1 Temple Gardens
1st Floor, Temple, London EC4Y 9BB,
Telephone: 0171 353 0407/583 1315
E-mail: clerks@1templegardens.co.uk
Call date: July 1989, Middle Temple
Qualifications: [MA [Cantab]]

LLOYD (DAVID) HUW

3 Serjeants Inn
London EC4Y 1BQ,
Telephone: 0171 353 5537
E-mail: available upon request
Call date: July 1975, Middle Temple
Qualifications: [LLB (Leics)]

LLOYD FRANCIS ZACHARY

Hardwicke Building
New Square, Lincoln's Inn, London
WC2A 3SB, Telephone: 0171 242 2523
E-mail: clerks@hardwicke.co.uk
Call date: July 1987, Inner Temple
Qualifications: [BA (Exon), Dip Law]

LLOYD MISS GAYNOR ELIZABETH

Sedan House
Stanley Place, Chester CH1 2LU,
Telephone: 01244 320480/348282
Call date: Oct 1992, Lincoln's Inn
Qualifications: [LLB(Hons)(Nott'm)]

LLOYD MISS HEATHER CLAIRE

Peel House Chambers
Ground Floor, Peel House 5 Harrington Street,
Liverpool L2 9QA, Telephone: 0151 236 4321
Call date: July 1979, Gray's Inn
Qualifications: [LLB (L'pool)]

LLOYD JAMES DAVID

5 Paper Bldgs
Lower Ground Floor, Temple, London
EC4Y 7HB, Telephone: 0171 353 5638
E-mail: 107722,633@compuserve.com
Call date: Feb 1985, Middle Temple
Qualifications: [MA (Oxon)]

LLOYD JOHN NESBITT

11 Old Square
Ground Floor, Lincoln's Inn, London
WC2A 3TS, Telephone: 0171 242 5022/
405 1074
Call date: Nov 1988, Inner Temple
Qualifications: [BA (Natal), MA, LLB (Exon)]

LLOYD JULIAN ALASTAIR

21 White Friars
Chester CH1 1NZ, Telephone: 01244 323070
Call date: July 1985, Gray's Inn
Qualifications: [MA, LLM (Cantab)]

LLOYD LLOYD

4 Field Court
Gray's Inn, London WC1R 5EA,
Telephone: 0171 440 6900
E-mail: chambers@4fieldcourt.co.uk
Call date: July 1973, Gray's Inn
Qualifications: [MA (Cantab), LLM (Lond)]

LLOYD MISS PATRICIA

2 King's Bench Walk
1st Floor, Temple, London EC4Y 7DE,
Telephone: 0171 353 9276
Call date: July 1979, Gray's Inn
Qualifications: [LLB(Hons)]

LLOYD STEPHEN JAMES GEORGE

11 New Square
Ground Floor, Lincoln's Inn, London
WC2A 3QB, Telephone: 0171 831 0081
E-mail: 11newsquare.co.uk
Call date: July 1971, Middle Temple

D

LLOYD MISS WENDY-JANE

25-27 Castle Street
1st Floor, Liverpool L2 4TA,
Telephone: 0151 227 5661/051 236 5072
Call date: July 1983, Middle Temple
Qualifications: [LLB (L'pool)]

LLOYD-DAVIES ANDREW

17 Old Bldgs
Ground Floor, Lincoln's Inn, London
WC2A 3UP, Telephone: 0171 405 9653
St Mary's Chambers
50 High Pavement, Lace Market, Nottingham
NG1 1HW, Telephone: 0115 9503503
E-mail: clerks@smc.law.co.uk
Call date: July 1973, Lincoln's Inn
Qualifications: [BA (Oxon)]

LLOYD-ELEY ANDREW JAMES

1 Hare Court
Ground Floor, Temple, London EC4Y 7BE,
Telephone: 0171 353 3982/5324
Call date: Nov 1979, Middle Temple
Qualifications: [LLB]

LLOYD-JACOB MISS CAMPASPE CLARE HELEN

3 Raymond Buildings
Gray's Inn, London WC1R 5BH,
Telephone: 0171 831 3833
E-mail: chambers@threeraymond.demon.co.uk
Call date: Nov 1990, Gray's Inn
Qualifications: [MA (Oxon)]

LLOYD-JONES JOHN BENEDICT

36 Bedford Row
London WC1R 4JH,
Telephone: 0171 421 8000
E-mail: 36bedfordrow@link.org
Call date: Nov 1993, Inner Temple
Qualifications: [BA (Hons) (Dunelm), CPE]

LLOYD-SMITH MISS REBECCA JANE

Peel Court Chambers
45 Hardman Street, Manchester M3 3HA,
Telephone: 0161 832 3791
Call date: Oct 1994, Lincoln's Inn
Qualifications: [BA (Hons)(Leic), CPE (Leic)]

LO BERNARD NORMAN

17 Bedford Row
London WC1R 4EB,
Telephone: 0171 831 7314
E-mail: IBoard7314@AOL.com
Call date: Nov 1991, Inner Temple
Qualifications: [BA (Bristol), Dip Law]

LOADES JONATHAN CHARLES

9 Gough Square
London EC4A 3DE, Telephone: 0171 353 5371
Call date: Nov 1986, Middle Temple
Qualifications: [BSc (Bradford) Dip, Law]

LOBBENBERG NICHOLAS

6 Gray's Inn Square
Ground Floor, Gray's Inn, London WC1R 5AZ,
Telephone: 0171 242 1052
Call date: Nov 1987, Gray's Inn
Qualifications: [BA (Oxon)]

LOBO MATTHEW JOSEPH EDWIN

Fenners Chambers
3 Madingley Road, Cambridge CB3 0EE,
Telephone: 01223 368761
Fenners Chambers
8-12 Priestgate, Peterborough PE1 1JA,
Telephone: 01733 62030
Call date: Oct 1995, Middle Temple
Qualifications: [BA (Hons) (Cantab)]

LOCHRANE DAMIEN HORATIO ROSS

Pump Court Chambers
Upper Ground Floor 3 Pump Court, Temple,
London EC4Y 7AJ, Telephone: 0171 353 0711
Pump Court Chambers
31 Southgate Street, Winchester SO23 8EE,
Telephone: 01962 868161
Call date: Nov 1983, Gray's Inn
Qualifications: [MA (Oxon)]

LOCKEY JOHN CHARLTON GERARD

Essex Court Chambers
24 Lincoln's Inn Fields, London WC2A 3ED,
Telephone: 0171 813 8000
E-mail: clerksroom@essexcourt-chambers.co.uk
Call date: July 1987, Middle Temple
Qualifications: [MA (Cantab) LLM, (Harvard)]

LOCKHART ANDREW WILLIAM JARDINE

Priory Chambers
2 Fountain Court, Steelhouse Lane,
Birmingham B4 6DR,
Telephone: 0121 236 3882/1375
Call date: Oct 1991, Lincoln's Inn
Qualifications: [LLB (Hons) (Lond)]

LOCKHART-MUMMERY CHRISTOPHER JOHN QC (1986)

4 Breams Buildings
London EC4A 1AQ,
Telephone: 0171 353 5835/430 1221
Call date: July 1971, Inner Temple
Qualifications: [BA (Cantab)]

LOCKYER MISS BARBARA JANE

4 Brick Court
1st Floor, Temple, London EC4Y 9AD,
Telephone: 0171 583 8455
Call date: July 1970, Gray's Inn
Qualifications: [LLB (Soton)]

LODDER PETER NORMAN

3 Hare Court
1st Floor, Temple, London EC4Y 7BJ,
Telephone: 0171 353 7561
Call date: July 1981, Middle Temple
Qualifications: [LLB (B'ham)]

LODGE ANTON JAMES CORDUFF QC (1989)

Park Court Chambers
40 Park Cross Street, Leeds LS1 2QH,
Telephone: 0113 2433277
Call date: Nov 1966, Gray's Inn
Recorder
Qualifications: [MA (Cantab)]

LODGE GRAHAM

Francis Taylor Bldg
Ground Floor, Temple, London EC4Y 7BY,
Telephone: 0171 353 7768/7769/2711
Call date: July 1971, Middle Temple
Qualifications: [LLB (Lond)]

LODGE JOHN ROBERT

Park Court Chambers
40 Park Cross Street, Leeds LS1 2QH,
Telephone: 0113 2433277
Call date: July 1980, Middle Temple
Qualifications: [MA (Oxon)]

LODGE NICHOLAS CHARLES GARA

65-67 King Street
Leicester LE1 6RP, Telephone: 0116 2547710
Call date: July 1979, Gray's Inn
Qualifications: [BA, MT.heal, Dip Law]

LODY TUSTIAN STUART

St Mary's Chambers
50 High Pavement, Lace Market, Nottingham
NG1 1HW, Telephone: 0115 9503503
E-mail: clerks@smc.law.co.uk
Call date: Nov 1991, Gray's Inn
Qualifications: [BA]

LOFTHOUSE JOHN CHARLES

2 King's Bench Walk
Ground Floor, Temple, London EC4Y 7DE,
Telephone: 0171 353 1746
E-mail: 2kbw@atlas.co.uk
King's Bench Chambers
115 North Hill, Plymouth PL4 8JY,
Telephone: 01752 221551
Call date: May 1979, Middle Temple
Qualifications: [MA (Oxon)]

LOFTHOUSE SIMON TIMOTHY

1 Atkin Building
Gray's Inn, London WC1R 5AT,
Telephone: 0171 404 0102
E-mail: clerks@atkin-chambers.co.uk
Call date: Nov 1988, Gray's Inn
Qualifications: [LLB (Lond)]

LOFTUS MISS TERESA ANNE MARTINE

25-27 Castle Street
1st Floor, Liverpool L2 4TA,
Telephone: 0151 227 5661/051 236 5072
Call date: Feb 1995, Lincoln's Inn
Qualifications: [LLB (Hull)]

D

LOGAN MISS MAURA

St John's Chambers
One High Elm Drive, Hale Barns, Cheshire
WA15 0JD, Telephone: 0161 980 7379
Call date: July 1971, Inner Temple

LOGSDON MICHAEL ANTHONY

1 Hare Court
Ground Floor, Temple, London EC4Y 7BE,
Telephone: 0171 353 3982/5324
Call date: Feb 1988, Inner Temple
Qualifications: [LLB (Soton)]

LOMAS MARK HENRY

Littleton Chambers
3 King's Bench Walk North, Temple, London
EC4Y 7HR, Telephone: 0171 797 8600
E-mail: littletonchambers@compuserve.com
Call date: Nov 1977, Middle Temple
Qualifications: [MA (Cantab)]

LOMAS MARK STEPHEN

3 Paper Bldgs
1st Floor, Temple, London EC4Y 7EU,
Telephone: 0171 583 8055
E-mail: london@3paper.com
4 St Peter Street
Winchester SO23 8OW,
Telephone: 01962 868884
20 Lorne Park Road
Bournemouth BH1 1JN,
Telephone: 01202 292102 (5 Lines)
Call date: July 1983, Middle Temple
Qualifications: [BA (Keele)]

LOMNICKA MISS EVA ZOFIA

2 Crown Office Row
2nd Floor, Temple, London EC4Y 7HJ,
Telephone: 0171 797 8000
Call date: July 1974, Middle Temple
Qualifications: [MA, LLB (Cantab)]

LONERGAN PAUL HENRY

22 Old Bldgs
Lincoln's Inn, London WC2A 3UJ,
Telephone: 0171 831 0222
Call date: Oct 1991, Lincoln's Inn
Qualifications: [BA (Hons, Cantab)]

LONG ANDREW PETER

Peel Court Chambers
45 Hardman Street, Manchester M3 3HA,
Telephone: 0161 832 3791
Call date: July 1981, Inner Temple
Qualifications: [LLB (Sheff)]

LONG TOBIAS CHARLES

4 Brick Court
Temple, London EC4Y 9AD,
Telephone: 0171 797 8910
Call date: Nov 1988, Inner Temple
Qualifications: [BA(E.Anglia),Dip Law]

LONGDEN ANTHONY GORDON

Hollis Whiteman Chambers
3rd/4th Floor Queen Elizabeth Bldg, Temple,
London EC4Y 9BS, Telephone: 0171 583 5766
E-mail: hollis.whiteman@btinternet.com
Call date: Nov 1967, Inner Temple
Qualifications: [BA (Oxon)]

LONGHURST-WOODS MS LESLEY

Forest House Chambers
15 Granville Road, Walthamstow, London
E17 9BS, Telephone: 0181 925 2240
Call date: Nov 1992, Gray's Inn
Qualifications: [BA]

LONGMAN MICHAEL JAMES

St John's Chambers
Small Street, Bristol BS1 1DW,
Telephone: 0117 9213456/298514
E-mail: clerks@stjohns.uk.com
Call date: July 1978, Middle Temple
Qualifications: [MA (Cantab)]

LONGWORTH ANTONY STEPHEN

Old Colony House
6 South King Street, Manchester M2 6DQ,
Telephone: 0161 834 4364
Call date: July 1978, Middle Temple
Qualifications: [BA (Oxon)]

LONSDALE DAVID JAMES

33 Bedford Row
London WC1R 4JH,
Telephone: 0171 242 6476
Call date: Nov 1988, Inner Temple
Qualifications: [BA (Oxon)(Hons)]

LONSDALE MISS MARION MARY

46/48 Essex Street
London WC2R 3GH,
Telephone: 0171 583 8899
Call date: July 1984, Gray's Inn
Qualifications: [BSC Hons (Nott'm), LLB Hons (Lond), ATII]

LOOSEMORE MRS MARY

Chichester Chambers
12 North Pallant, Chichester, West Sussex
PO19 1TQ, Telephone: 01243 784538
Call date: May 1992, Inner Temple
Qualifications: [BSc (Lond)]

LOPEZ PAUL ANTHONY

St Ive's Chambers
9 Fountain Ct, Birmingham B4 6DR,
Telephone: 0121 236 0863/0929
Call date: July 1982, Middle Temple
Qualifications: [LLB (B'ham)]

LOPEZ RONALD

Forest House Chambers
15 Granville Road, Walthamstow, London
E17 9BS, Telephone: 0181 925 2240
Call date: Nov 1992, Lincoln's Inn
Qualifications: [LLB (Hons)]

LOPIAN DR JONATHAN BERNARD

11 Stone Bldgs
Ground Floor, Lincoln's Inn, London
WC2A 3TG, Telephone: 0171 831 6381
E-mail: clerks@11StoneBuildings.law.co.uk
Call date: Nov 1994, Middle Temple
Qualifications: [MA, Ph.D (Cantab), Dip Law (City)]

LORAINE-SMITH NICHOLAS GEORGE EDWARD

2 Harcourt Bldgs
1st Floor, Temple, London EC4Y 9DB,
Telephone: 0171 353 2112/2817
Call date: Nov 1977, Inner Temple
Qualifications: [BA (Oxon)]

LORAM MISS MARY CAROLINE

Victoria Chambers
3rd Floor 177 Corporation Street, Birmingham
B4 6RG, Telephone: 0121 236 9900
Call date: Nov 1995, Inner Temple
Qualifications: [BA (Oxon), M.Phil (Cantab)]

LORD DAVID WILLIAM

3 Stone Bldgs
Ground Floor, Lincoln's Inn, London
WC2A 3XL, Telephone: 0171 242 4937/
405 8358
Call date: July 1987, Middle Temple
Qualifications: [LLB (Bristol)]

LORD RICHARD DENYER

Brick Court Chambers
15/19 Devereux Court, London WC2R 3JJ,
Telephone: 0171 583 0777
E-mail: (surname)@brickcourt.demon.co.uk
Call date: Nov 1981, Inner Temple
Qualifications: [MA (Cantab)]

LORD TIMOTHY MICHAEL

2 Temple Gardens
Temple, London EC4Y 9AY,
Telephone: 0171 583 6041 (12 Lines)
Call date: Nov 1992, Inner Temple
Qualifications: [MA (Cantab)]

LORENZO MS CLAUDIA

2 King's Bench Walk
1st Floor, Temple, London EC4Y 7DE,
Telephone: 0171 353 9276
Call date: Apr 1991, Inner Temple
Qualifications: [BA (Hons), LLB (Hons), LLM]

LORIE ANDREW GIDEON

College Chambers
19 Carlton Cresent, Southampton, Hants
SO15 2ET, Telephone: 01703 230338
Call date: Oct 1996, Middle Temple
Qualifications: [BA (Hons)(Bris), CPE (Westminster)]

D

LOUGHRAN PAUL VINCENT

Bracton Chambers
95a Chancery Lane, London WC2A 1DT,
Telephone: 0171 242 4248
Call date: Feb 1988, Gray's Inn
Qualifications: [LLB (Hons) Belfast]

LOVE DUDLEY MARK

2 Paper Bldgs
Temple, London EC4Y 7ET,
Telephone: 0171 936 2613
Call date: Nov 1979, Gray's Inn
Qualifications: [BSc (Lond)]

LOVEDAY MARK ALAN

Francis Taylor Bldg
3rd Floor, Temple, London EC4Y 7BY,
Telephone: 0171 797 7250
Call date: July 1986, Inner Temple
Qualifications: [BA (Hons)(Kent)]

LOVEGROVE RICHARD QUENTIN CLOUDESLEY

Sussex Chambers
9 Old Steine, Brighton BN1 1FJ,
Telephone: 01273 607953
Call date: July 1986, Middle Temple
Qualifications: [LLB (Hons)(Bris)]

LOVELL MISS MILDRED JEANETTE

20 Britton Street
1st Floor, London EC1M 5NQ,
Telephone: 0171 608 3765
Call date: July 1976, Middle Temple

LOVELL-PANK DORIAN CHRISTOPHER QC (1993)

6 King's Bench Walk
Ground Floor, Temple, London EC4Y 7DR,
Telephone: 0171 583 0410
Call date: July 1971, Inner Temple
Recorder

LOVERIDGE ANDREW ROBERT

The Corn Exchange
5th Floor Fenwick Street, Liverpool L2 7QS,
Telephone: 0151 227 1081/5009
Call date: July 1983, Lincoln's Inn
Qualifications: [LLB (Newc)]

LOWCOCK ANDREW CHARLES

28 St John Street
Manchester M3 4DJ,
Telephone: 0161 834 8418
E-mail: clerk@28stjohnst.co.uk
Call date: July 1973, Middle Temple
Recorder
Qualifications: [MA (Oxon)]

LOWE ALAN VAUGHAN

Essex Court Chambers
24 Lincoln's Inn Fields, London WC2A 3ED,
Telephone: 0171 813 8000
E-mail: clerksroom@essexcourt-chambers.co.uk
Call date: Feb 1993, Gray's Inn
Qualifications: [LLB, LLM, Ph.D (Cardiff)]

LOWE ANTHONY MARSHALL

6 Fountain Court
Steelhouse Lane, Birmingham B4 6DR,
Telephone: 0121 233 3282
Call date: July 1976, Middle Temple
Qualifications: [MA (Oxon)]

LOWE CRAIG DAVID

New Walk Chambers
27 New Walk, Leicester LE1 6TE,
Telephone: 0116 2559144
Call date: Oct 1994, Lincoln's Inn
Qualifications: [LLB (Hons)(Lond)]

LOWE DAVID ALEXANDER QC (1984)

Wilberforce Chambers
8 New Square, Lincoln's Inn, London
WC2A 3QP, Telephone: 0171 306 0102
E-mail: chambers@wilberforce.co.uk
Call date: July 1965, Middle Temple
Qualifications: [MA (Cantab)]

LOWE GEOFFREY JAMES

India Buildings Chambers
Water Street, Liverpool L2 OXG,
Telephone: 0151 243 6000
Call date: July 1975, Gray's Inn
Qualifications: [LLB]

LOWE GEORGE WILLIAM QC (1997)

Plowden Bldgs
2nd Floor, Temple, London EC4Y 9BU,
Telephone: 0171 583 0808
E-mail: bar@plowdenbuildings.co.uk
Broad Chare
33 Broad Chare, Newcastle Upon Tyne
NE1 3DQ, Telephone: 0191 232 0541
Door Tenant
Call date: July 1972, Lincoln's Inn
Recorder
Qualifications: [LLB]

LOWE JOHN

Trinity Chambers
9-12 Trinity Chare, Quayside, Newcastle Upon
Tyne NE1 3DF, Telephone: 0191 232 1927
Plowden Bldgs
2nd Floor, Temple, London EC4Y 9BU,
Telephone: 0171 583 0808
E-mail: bar@plowdenbuildings.co.uk
Call date: July 1976, Gray's Inn
Qualifications: [LLB]

LOWE MATTHEW JUSTIN

36 Bedford Row
London WC1R 4JH,
Telephone: 0171 421 8000
E-mail: 36bedfordrow@link.org
Call date: Nov 1991, Inner Temple
Qualifications: [LLb (Exeter)]

LOWE NICHOLAS MARK QC (1996)

2-3 Gray's Inn Square
Gray's Inn, London WC1R 5JH,
Telephone: 0171 242 4986
E-mail: chambers@2-3graysinnsquare.co.uk
Call date: July 1972, Gray's Inn
Qualifications: [LLB]

LOWE MISS SARAH LOUISE

4 Paper Bldgs
2nd Floor, Temple, London EC4Y 7EX,
Telephone: 0171 583 0816/071 353 1131
E-mail: clerks@4paperbuildings.co.uk
Call date: Nov 1995, Middle Temple
Qualifications: [BA (Hons)]

LOWE THOMAS WILLIAM GORDON

Wilberforce Chambers
8 New Square, Lincoln's Inn, London
WC2A 3QP, Telephone: 0171 306 0102
E-mail: chambers@wilberforce.co.uk
Call date: Nov 1985, Inner Temple
Qualifications: [LLB (Lond), LLM (Cantab)]

LOWEN JONATHAN ANDREW MICHAEL

Queen Elizabeth Bldg
Ground Floor, Temple, London EC4Y 9BS,
Telephone: 0171 353 7181 (12 Lines)
Call date: Nov 1972, Gray's Inn
Recorder
Qualifications: [MA (Oxon), BA (Rand)]

LOWENSTEIN PAUL DAVID

Littleton Chambers
3 King's Bench Walk North, Temple, London
EC4Y 7HR, Telephone: 0171 797 8600
E-mail: littletonchambers@compuserve.com
Call date: Nov 1988, Middle Temple
Qualifications: [LLB (Manch), LLM (Cantab)]

LOWNE STEPHEN MARK

King Charles House
Standard Hill, Nottingham NG1 6FX,
Telephone: 0115 9418851
E-mail: clerks@kch.co.uk
Call date: July 1981, Inner Temple
Qualifications: [BA (Hons)]

LOWRY MISS ANNE-MARIE SUZANNE

9 King's Bench Walk
Ground Floor, Temple, London EC4Y 7DX,
Telephone: 0171 353 7202/3909
Call date: Oct 1995, Middle Temple
Qualifications: [LLB (Hons) (Exon)]

LOWRY CHARLES STEPHEN

Colleton Chambers
Colleton Crescent, Exeter, Devon EX2 4DG,
Telephone: 01392 74898/9
Call date: Feb 1960, Inner Temple
Qualifications: [MA (Oxon)]

D

LOWRY MISS EMMA MARGARET COLLINS

Hollis Whiteman Chambers
3rd/4th Floor Queen Elizabeth Bldg, Temple,
London EC4Y 9BS, Telephone: 0171 583 5766
E-mail: hollis.whiteman@btinternet.com
Call date: Oct 1991, Inner Temple
Qualifications: [MA (Oxon)]

LOWSON NORMAN LAURENCE

New Bailey Chambers
10 Lawson Street, Preston PR1 2QT,
Telephone: 01772 258087
Call date: July 1989, Lincoln's Inn
Qualifications: [Dip Law]

LOWTHER MRS SAMANTHA SARAH-ANNE

Library Chambers
Gray's Inn Chambers, Gray's Inn, London
WC1R 5JA, Telephone: 0171 404 6500
Call date: July 1995, Lincoln's Inn
Qualifications: [BCL, BL]

LUBA JAN MICHAEL ANDREW

2 Garden Court
1st Floor, Middle Temple, London EC4Y 9BL,
Telephone: 0171 353 1633
E-mail: barristers@2gardenct.law.co.uk
Call date: July 1980, Middle Temple
Qualifications: [LLB (Lond), LLM (Leics)]

LUCAS MISS BRIDGET ANN

13 Old Square
1st Floor, Lincoln's Inn, London WC2A 3UA,
Telephone: 0171 242 6105
E-mail: clerks@serlecourt.co.uk
Call date: Nov 1989, Inner Temple
Qualifications: [BA (Oxon)]

LUCAS EDWARD ALLAN

All Saints Chambers
9/11 Broad Street, Bristol BS1 2HP,
Telephone: 0117 921 1966
Call date: Oct 1991, Middle Temple
Qualifications: [MA, MLitt, D.Phil (Oxon)]

LUCAS NOEL JOHN MAC

1 Middle Temple Lane
Temple, London EC4Y 1LT,
Telephone: 0171 583 0659 (12 Lines)
Call date: July 1979, Middle Temple
Qualifications: [BSc (Lond)]

LUCAS PHILLIP JOHN

1 Gray's Inn Square
Ground Floor, London WC1R 5AA,
Telephone: 0171 405 8946/7/8
Call date: Oct 1995, Middle Temple
Qualifications: [LLB (Hons)]

LUCIE GARY ALLAN

Clock Chambers
78 Darlington Street, Wolverhampton
WV1 4LY, Telephone: 01902 313444
Call date: Oct 1994, Middle Temple
Qualifications: [LLB (Hons)(Manc)]

LUCKING MRS ADRIENNE SIMONE

65-67 King Street
Leicester LE1 6RP, Telephone: 0116 2547710
Call date: Nov 1989, Inner Temple
Qualifications: [LLB (Hons)]

LUCRAFT MARK

18 Red Lion Court
(Off Fleet Street), London EC4A 3EB,
Telephone: 0171 520 6000
Thornwood House
102 New London Road, Chelmsford, Essex
CM2 0RG, Telephone: 01245 280880
Call date: July 1984, Inner Temple
Qualifications: [BA (Kent)]

LUGG MISS ELIZABETH CLAIRE

Broad Chare
33 Broad Chare, Newcastle Upon Tyne
NE1 3DQ, Telephone: 0191 232 0541
Call date: Oct 1994, Gray's Inn
Qualifications: [BA]

LUMLEY GERALD

9 Woodhouse Square
Leeds LS3 1AD, Telephone: 0113 2451986
Call date: July 1972, Inner Temple
Qualifications: [LLB (Lond)]

LUMLEY NICHOLAS JAMES HENRY

25 Park Square
Leeds LS1 2PW, Telephone: 0113 2451841/2/3
E-mail: sovereignchambers@btinternet.com
Call date: Oct 1992, Lincoln's Inn
Qualifications: [LLB(Hons)(Newc)]

LUMSDON JOHN STUART

Goldsworth Chambers
1st Floor 10-11 Gray's Inn Square, London
WC1R 5JD, Telephone: 0171 405 7117
Call date: July 1991, Inner Temple
Qualifications: [BA (Notts), MSc (Warwick),
LLB]

LUMSDON MISS KATHERINE JANE

2 King's Bench Walk
Ground Floor, Temple, London EC4Y 7DE,
Telephone: 0171 353 1746
E-mail: 2kbw@atlas.co.uk
King's Bench Chambers
115 North Hill, Plymouth PL4 8JY,
Telephone: 01752 221551
Call date: Oct 1993, Middle Temple
Qualifications: [BA (Hons)(Manc), CPE (Lond)]

LUND MRS CELIA

Adrian Lyon's Chambers
14 Castle Street, Liverpool L2 0NE,
Telephone: 0151 236 4421/8240
E-mail: chambers14@aol.com
5 Stone Buildings
Lincoln's Inn, London WC2A 3XT,
Telephone: 0171 242 6201
E-mail: clerks@5-stonebuildings.law.co.uk
Door Tenant
Call date: Nov 1988, Lincoln's Inn
Qualifications: [LLB Hons]

LUNDIE CHRISTOPHER CARLTON

1 Harcourt Bldgs
2nd Floor, Temple, London EC4Y 9DA,
Telephone: 0171 353 9421/9151
Call date: Nov 1991, Inner Temple
Qualifications: [MA (Cantab)]

LUNT MISS BEVERLY ANNE

58 King Street Chambers
1st Floor, Kingsgate House 51-53 South King
Street, Manchester M2 6DE,
Telephone: 0161 831 7477
Call date: July 1977, Gray's Inn
Qualifications: [BA (Lond)]

LUNT STEVEN

9 Woodhouse Square
Leeds LS3 1AD, Telephone: 0113 2451986
Call date: Oct 1991, Inner Temple
Qualifications: [LLB (Leeds)]

LURIE SYDNEY JONATHAN JOSEPH

10 King's Bench Walk
1st Floor, Temple, London EC4Y 7EB,
Telephone: 0171 353 2501
Call date: Nov 1972, Middle Temple

LYDIARD ANDREW JOHN

5 Bell Yard
London WC2A 2JR, Telephone: 0171 333 8811
Call date: July 1980, Inner Temple
Qualifications: [BA (Oxon), LLM]

LYELL THE RT HON SIR NICHOLAS WALTER QC (1980)

Brick Court Chambers
15/19 Devereux Court, London WC2R 3JJ,
Telephone: 0171 583 0777
E-mail: (surname)@brickcourt.demon.co.uk
Call date: Feb 1965, Inner Temple
Qualifications: [MA (Oxon)]

LYGO CARL RAYMOND

Mitre House Chambers
Mitre House 44 Fleet Street, London
EC4Y 1BN, Telephone: 0171 583 8233
Call date: Oct 1991, Middle Temple
Qualifications: [LLB (Hons), LLM (E Anglia)]

D

D

LYNAGH RICHARD DUDLEY QC (1996)

2 Crown Office Row
Ground Floor, Temple, London EC4Y 7HJ,
Telephone: 0171 797 8100
E-mail: mail@2cor.co.uk, or to individual
barristers at: [barrister's surname]@2cor.co.uk
Call date: July 1975, Gray's Inn
Qualifications: [LLB]

LYNCH ADRIAN CHARLES EDMUND

11 King's Bench Walk
Temple, London EC4Y 7EQ,
Telephone: 0171 632 8500
E-mail: clerksroom@11-kbw.law.co.uk
Call date: Nov 1983, Gray's Inn
Qualifications: [LLB (Lond)]

LYNCH DERMOT MICHAEL

Field Court Chambers
2nd Floor 3 Field Court, Gray's Inn, London
WC1R 4EP, Telephone: 0171 404 7474
E-mail: Clerks@FieldCourtChambers.law.co.uk
Call date: Nov 1994, Gray's Inn
Qualifications: [LLB (Kent)]

LYNCH JEROME

Cloisters
1st Floor, Temple, London EC4Y 7AA,
Telephone: 0171 827 4000
E-mail: clerks@cloisters.com
Call date: July 1983, Lincoln's Inn
Qualifications: [BA (Hons)]

LYNCH JULIAN

7 Stone Bldgs
1st Floor, Lincoln's Inn, London WC2A 3SZ,
Telephone: 0171 242 0961
Call date: Nov 1976, Inner Temple
Qualifications: [LLB (Lond)]

LYNCH MISS PATRICIA

18 Red Lion Court
(Off Fleet Street), London EC4A 3EB,
Telephone: 0171 520 6000
Thornwood House
102 New London Road, Chelmsford, Essex
CM2 0RG, Telephone: 01245 280880
Call date: Nov 1979, Inner Temple
Assistant Recorder
Qualifications: [LLB (Hull)]

LYNCH PATRICK DENIS

Clock Chambers
78 Darlington Street, Wolverhampton
WV1 4LY, Telephone: 01902 313444
Call date: July 1988, Inner Temple
Qualifications: [BEd (Lond), Dip Law]

LYNCH PETER GARETH

4 Brick Court
Temple, London EC4Y 9AD,
Telephone: 0171 797 8910
Call date: July 1985, Lincoln's Inn
Qualifications: [BSc, Dip Law]

LYNCH TERRY JOHN

22 Albion Place
Northampton NN1 1UD,
Telephone: 01604 36271
Call date: Nov 1989, Inner Temple
Qualifications: [BA]

LYNDON-STANFORD MICHAEL ANDREW FLEMYNG QC (1979)

13 Old Square
Ground Floor, Lincoln's Inn, London
WC2A 3UA, Telephone: 0171 404 4800
Call date: Feb 1962, Inner Temple
Qualifications: [MA (Cantab)]

LYNE MARK HILARY

1 Essex Court
1st Floor, Temple, London EC4Y 9AR,
Telephone: 0171 936 3030
E-mail: one.essex_court@virgin.net
Call date: Nov 1981, Inner Temple
Qualifications: [MA (Cantab)]

LYNESS SCOTT EDWARD

1 Serjeants' Inn
4th Floor, Temple, London EC4Y 1NH,
Telephone: 0171 583 1355
E-mail: serjeants.inn@virgin.net
Call date: Oct 1996, Lincoln's Inn
Qualifications: [LLB (Hons)(Hull)]

LYNN JEREMY DAVID

2 King's Bench Walk
1st Floor, Temple, London EC4Y 7DE,
Telephone: 0171 353 9276
Call date: Nov 1983, Inner Temple
Qualifications: [BSc Cardiff]

LYON ADRIAN PIRRIE

Adrian Lyon's Chambers
14 Castle Street, Liverpool L2 0NE,
Telephone: 0151 236 4421/8240
E-mail: chambers14@aol.com
Call date: July 1975, Gray's Inn
Assistant Recorder
Qualifications: [LLB (Lond)]

LYON MRS SHANE VALERIE

Walnut House
63 St. David's Hill, Exeter, Devon EX4 4DW,
Telephone: 01392 279751
E-mail: 106627.2451@compuserve.com
Call date: Nov 1976, Middle Temple
Qualifications: [LLB (Exon)]

LYON STEPHEN JOHN

14 Gray's Inn Square
Gray's Inn, London WC1R 5JP,
Telephone: 0171 242 0858
E-mail: 100712.2134@compuserve.com
Westgate Chambers
144 High Street, Lewes, East Sussex BN7 1XT,
Telephone: 01273 480510
Call date: July 1987, Inner Temple
Qualifications: [LLB (Notts)]

LYON VICTOR LAWRENCE

Essex Court Chambers
24 Lincoln's Inn Fields, London WC2A 3ED,
Telephone: 0171 813 8000
E-mail: clerksroom@essexcourt-chambers.co.uk
Call date: July 1980, Gray's Inn
Qualifications: [MA (Cantab)]

LYONS DAVID WAKEFIELD

3 Paper Bldgs
2nd Floor, Temple, London EC4Y 7EU,
Telephone: 0171 353 6208
Call date: July 1987, Middle Temple
Qualifications: [BA (Hons)]

LYONS EDWARD QC (1974)

4 Brick Court
Temple, London EC4Y 9AD,
Telephone: 0171 797 8910
6 Park Square
Leeds LS1 2LW, Telephone: 0113 2459763
E-mail: chambers@no6.co.uk
Call date: Nov 1952, Lincoln's Inn
Recorder
Qualifications: [LLB(Hons)]

LYONS GRAHAM ANTHONY

2 Pump Court
1st Floor, Temple, London EC4Y 7AH,
Telephone: 0171 353 5597
Call date: July 1972, Inner Temple

LYONS JOHN ADAM

4 Brick Court
Ground Floor, Temple, London EC4Y 9AD,
Telephone: 0171 797 7766
E-mail: chambers@4brick.co.uk
Call date: July 1986, Middle Temple
Qualifications: [BA (Dunelm) Dip Law]

LYONS TIMOTHY JOHN

24 Old Bldgs
First Floor, Lincoln's Inn, London WC2A 3UJ,
Telephone: 0171 242 2744
St James's Chambers
68 Quay Street, Manchester M3 3EJ,
Telephone: 0161 834 7000
E-mail: 106241.2625@compuserve.com
Call date: July 1980, Inner Temple
Qualifications: [LLB (Bris), LLM Phd, (Lon)]

MABB DAVID MICHAEL

Erskine Chambers
30 Lincoln's Inn Fields, Lincoln's Inn, London
WC2A 3PF, Telephone: 0171 242 5532
E-mail: Clerks@Erskine-Chambers.law.co.uk
Call date: July 1979, Lincoln's Inn
Qualifications: [MA (Cantab)]

MACADAM JASON ANGUS ALAISTER ROBERT L

37 Park Square
Leeds LS1 2NY, Telephone: 0113 2439422
Call date: Nov 1990, Lincoln's Inn
Qualifications: [LLB (Wales), B.TEC]

D

MACAULAY BERTHAN

1 Gray's Inn Square
Ground Floor, London WC1R 5AA,
Telephone: 0171 405 8946/7/8
Call date: Nov 1953, Gray's Inn
Qualifications: [MA, LLB]

MACAULAY MISS DONORA MARIE

3 Temple Gardens (North)
Fifth Floor, Temple, London EC4Y 9AU,
Telephone: 0171 353 0853/4/7222
E-mail: 100106.1577@compuserve.com
Call date: Nov 1982, Middle Temple
Qualifications: [LLB (Bucks)]

MACCABE IRVINE JOHN

3 Paper Bldgs
1st Floor, Temple, London EC4Y 7EU,
Telephone: 0171 583 8055
E-mail: london@3paper.com
20 Lorne Park Road
Bournemouth BH1 1JN,
Telephone: 01202 292102 (5 Lines)
4 St Peter Street
Winchester SO23 8OW,
Telephone: 01962 868884
Call date: July 1983, Gray's Inn
Qualifications: [MA (Cantab)]

MACDONALD ALISTAIR NEIL

Park Court Chambers
40 Park Cross Street, Leeds LS1 2QH,
Telephone: 0113 2433277
Call date: July 1983, Gray's Inn
Assistant Recorder
Qualifications: [BSc (Bath), Dip Law (City)]

MACDONALD ALISTAIR WILLIAM ORCHARD

Priory Chambers
2 Fountain Court, Steelhouse Lane,
Birmingham B4 6DR,
Telephone: 0121 236 3882/1375
Call date: Nov 1995, Inner Temple
Qualifications: [BA (Hons)(Notts), Dip in Law
(Lond)]

MACDONALD CHARLES ADAM QC (1992)

4 Essex Court
Temple, London EC4Y 9AJ,
Telephone: 0171 797 7970
E-mail: clerks@4essexcourt.law.co.uk
Call date: Nov 1972, Lincoln's Inn
Assistant Recorder
Qualifications: [MA (Oxon)]

MACDONALD IAIN

Gough Square Chambers
6-7 Gough Square, London EC4A 3DE,
Telephone: 0171 353 0924
E-mail: gsc@goughsq.co.uk
Call date: July 1996, Middle Temple
Qualifications: [BA (Hons)(Oxon)]

MACDONALD IAN ALEXANDER QC (1988)

2 Garden Court
1st Floor, Middle Temple, London EC4Y 9BL,
Telephone: 0171 353 1633
E-mail: barristers@2gardenct.law.co.uk
Chambers of Ian Macdonald QC
Waldorf House Cooper Street, Manchester
M2 2FW, Telephone: 0161 236 1840
Call date: Feb 1963, Middle Temple
Qualifications: [MA, LLB]

MACDONALD JOHN REGINALD QC (1976)

12 New Square
Ground Floor, Lincoln's Inn, London
WC2A 3SW, Telephone: 0171 419 1212
E-mail: 12newsquare@compuserve.com
25 Park Square
Leeds LS1 2PW, Telephone: 0113 2451841/2/3
E-mail: sovereignchambers@btinternet.com
Door Tenant
Call date: June 1955, Lincoln's Inn
Qualifications: [MA (Cantab)]

MACDONALD KENNETH DONALD JOHN QC (1997)

2 Garden Court
1st Floor, Middle Temple, London EC4Y 9BL,
Telephone: 0171 353 1633
E-mail: barristers@2gardenct.law.co.uk
Call date: July 1978, Inner Temple
Qualifications: [BA (Oxon)]

MACDONALD MISS LINDSEY RACHEL

Hardwicke Building
New Square, Lincoln's Inn, London
WC2A 3SB, Telephone: 0171 242 2523
E-mail: clerks@hardwicke.co.uk
Call date: Feb 1985, Lincoln's Inn
Qualifications: [LLB (Bris)]

MACDONALD MISS SHELIA HAMILTON

11 Stone Bldgs
Ground Floor, Lincoln's Inn, London
WC2A 3TG, Telephone: 0171 831 6381
E-mail: clerks@11StoneBuildings.law.co.uk
Call date: Feb 1993, Middle Temple
Qualifications: [MA (Hons)(Glas), LLB (Hons)(Lond)]

MACEY-DARE THOMAS CHARLES

4 Essex Court
Temple, London EC4Y 9AJ,
Telephone: 0171 797 7970
E-mail: clerks@4essexcourt.law.co.uk
Call date: Feb 1994, Middle Temple
Qualifications: [MA (Cantab), LLM, (Cantab), LLM (USA)]

MACFARLANE MRS ALISON JANE

St Mary's Chambers
50 High Pavement, Lace Market, Nottingham
NG1 1HW, Telephone: 0115 9503503
E-mail: clerks@smc.law.co.uk
Call date: Oct 1993, Middle Temple
Qualifications: [LLB (Hons, Nott'm)]

MACFARLANE ANDREW LENNOX

Guildhall Chambers
23 Broad Street, Bristol BS1 2HG,
Telephone: 0117 9273366
Call date: May 1995, Inner Temple

MACGREGOR ALASTAIR RANKIN QC (1994)

1 Essex Court
Ground Floor, Temple, London EC4Y 9AR,
Telephone: 0171 583 2000
E-mail: clerks@oneessexcourt.co.uk
Call date: July 1974, Lincoln's Inn
Qualifications: [MA (Oxon)]

MACGREGOR MRS HEATHER MARGARET

Gray's Inn Chambers
5th Floor, Gray's Inn, London WC1R 5JA,
Telephone: 0171 404 1111
Call date: July 1982, Gray's Inn
Qualifications: [BA, Dip Law (Lond)]

MACHELL JOHN WILLIAM

13 Old Square
1st Floor, Lincoln's Inn, London WC2A 3UA,
Telephone: 0171 242 6105
E-mail: clerks@serlecourt.co.uk
Call date: Oct 1993, Inner Temple
Qualifications: [LLB (So'ton)]

MACHELL RAYMOND DONATUS QC (1988)

Deans Court Chambers
Cumberland House Crown Square, Manchester
M3 3HA, Telephone: 0161 834 4097
E-mail: deanscourt@compuserve.com
2 Pump Court
1st Floor, Temple, London EC4Y 7AH,
Telephone: 0171 353 5597
Call date: July 1973, Gray's Inn
Recorder
Qualifications: [MA, LLB (Cantab)]

MACHIN CHARLES KIM

Cobden House Chambers
19 Quay Street, Manchester M3 3HN,
Telephone: 0161 833 6000
E-mail: clerks@cobden.co.uk
Call date: Nov 1973, Lincoln's Inn
Qualifications: [MA (Oxon)]

MACHIN GRAHAM EDWARD

24 The Ropewalk
Nottingham NG1 5EF,
Telephone: 0115 9472581
E-mail: clerk@ropewalk.co.uk
Call date: July 1965, Gray's Inn

D

MACKAY COLIN CRICHTON QC (1989)

39 Essex Street
London WC2R 3AT,
Telephone: 0171 583 1111
E-mail: clerks@39essex.co.uk
Call date: July 1967, Middle Temple
Recorder
Qualifications: [MA (Oxon)]

MACKEAN MS SARAH SUTTON

All Saints Chambers
9/11 Broad Street, Bristol BS1 2HP,
Telephone: 0117 921 1966
Call date: Nov 1992, Inner Temple
Qualifications: [MA (Oxon), Dip in Law (City)]

MACKENZIE MISS ANNA KAREEN

3 Paper Bldgs
2nd Floor, Temple, London EC4Y 7EU,
Telephone: 0171 353 6208
Call date: Nov 1994, Lincoln's Inn
Qualifications: [LLB (Hons)(L'pool)]

MACKENZIE CHARLES WILLIAM TAAFFE MUNRO

20 Essex Street
London WC2R 3AL,
Telephone: 0171 583 9294
E-mail: clerks@20essexst.com
Call date: Oct 1990, Middle Temple
Qualifications: [MA (Oxon), Dip Law (City)]

MACKENZIE MISS JULIE FIONA

Colleton Chambers
Colleton Crescent, Exeter, Devon EX2 4DG,
Telephone: 01392 74898/9
Colleton Chambers
Powlett House 34 High Street, Taunton,
Somerset TA1 3PN, Telephone: 01823 324252
Call date: Nov 1978, Lincoln's Inn

MACKENZIE SMITH MRS CATHERINE JOANNA

3 Paper Bldgs
2nd Floor, Temple, London EC4Y 7EU,
Telephone: 0171 353 6208
Call date: Nov 1960, Inner Temple

MACKESON-SANDBACH MISS ANTOINETTE GERALDINE

4 Brick Court
1st Floor, Temple, London EC4Y 9AD,
Telephone: 0171 583 8455
Call date: Oct 1993, Lincoln's Inn
Qualifications: [BA (Hons)(Notts), LLM (Notts)]

MACKIE MS JEANNIE

1 Dr Johnson's Bldgs
Ground Floor, Temple, London EC4Y 7AX,
Telephone: 0171 353 9328
Call date: July 1995, Inner Temple
Qualifications: [BA (Cantab)]

MACKILLOP NORMAN MALCOLM

Chartlands Chambers
3 St Giles Terrace, Northampton NN1 2BN,
Telephone: 01604 603322
Call date: Oct 1994, Gray's Inn
Qualifications: [MA]

Other professional qualifications: MA (Police &
Criminal Justice Studies) Exeter

Fax: 01604 603388;
Out of hours telephone: 01480 861811;
DX: 12408 Northampton 1;
Other comms: 0468 472 676

Types of work: Care proceedings; Common law
(general); Crime; Family; Family provision;
Licensing

Membership of foreign bars: Hong Kong

Circuit: Midland and Oxford

Other professional experience: Ex Senior
Superintendent of Police RHKP

Languages spoken: Cantonese

MACKINNON THOMAS JOSEPH

8 King's Bench Walk
2nd Floor, Temple, London EC4Y 7DU,
Telephone: 0171 797 8888
8 King's Bench Walk North
1 Park Square East, Leeds LS1 2NE,
Telephone: 0113 2439797
Call date: July 1982, Middle Temple
Qualifications: [LLB,LLM (Sheff)]

MACKINTOSH ANDREW STUART

Warwick House Chambers
8 Warwick Court, Gray's Inn, London
WC1R 5DJ, Telephone: 0171 430 2323
Call date: Nov 1990, Middle Temple
Qualifications: [BA (Keele), MPhil (Cantab)]

MACKINTOSH COLIN RICHARD

3 Fountain Court
Steelhouse Lane, Birmingham B4 6DR,
Telephone: 0121 236 5854
Call date: July 1976, Inner Temple
Qualifications: [LLB (B'ham)]

MACLAREN MS CATRIONA LONGUEVILLE

Francis Taylor Bldg
2nd Floor, Temple, London EC4Y 7BY,
Telephone: 0171 353 9942/3157
Call date: Oct 1993, Inner Temple
Qualifications: [MA (Cantab)]

MACLEAN ALAN JOHN

39 Essex Street
London WC2R 3AT,
Telephone: 0171 583 1111
E-mail: clerks@39essex.co.uk
Call date: Oct 1993, Gray's Inn
Qualifications: [BA (Oxon)]

MACLEAN KENNETH WALTER

1 Essex Court
Ground Floor, Temple, London EC4Y 9AR,
Telephone: 0171 583 2000
E-mail: clerks@oneessexcourt.co.uk
Call date: May 1985, Gray's Inn
Qualifications: [MA (Cantab) LLM, (Harvard)]

MACLEOD DUNCAN

9 Gough Square
London EC4A 3DE, Telephone: 0171 353 5371
Call date: July 1980, Middle Temple
Qualifications: [BA (Lond), LLB (Cardiff)]

MACLEOD NIGEL RONALD BUCHANAN QC (1979)

4 Breams Buildings
London EC4A 1AQ,
Telephone: 0171 353 5835/430 1221
40 King Street
Manchester M2 6BA,
Telephone: 0161 832 9082
E-mail: Kingst40@aol.com
Call date: Feb 1961, Gray's Inn
Recorder
Qualifications: [MA, BCL (Oxon)]

MACLEOD MATTHEWS FRANCIS SPENCER

12 King's Bench Walk
Temple, London EC4Y 7EL,
Telephone: 0171 583 0811
E-mail: chambers@12kbw.co.uk
Call date: Nov 1982, Inner Temple
Qualifications: [BA (Oxon)]

MACLEOD-JAMES NICHOLAS MARK

11 Old Square
Ground Floor, Lincoln's Inn, London
WC2A 3TS, Telephone: 0171 242 5022/
405 1074
Call date: Nov 1986, Lincoln's Inn
Qualifications: [BA, BSc (Lond)]

MACNAB ALEXANDER ANDREW

Monckton Chambers
4 Raymond Buildings, Gray's Inn, London
WC1R 5BP, Telephone: 0171 405 7211
E-mail: chambers@monckton.co.uk
Call date: July 1986, Middle Temple
Qualifications: [MA,LLM (Cantab)]

MACPHERSON ANGUS JOHN

5 Bell Yard
London WC2A 2JR, Telephone: 0171 333 8811
Call date: July 1977, Inner Temple
Qualifications: [MA (Cantab)]

MACPHERSON DUNCAN CHARLES STEWART

Bracton Chambers
95a Chancery Lane, London WC2A 1DT,
Telephone: 0171 242 4248
Call date: May 1994, Middle Temple
Qualifications: [BA (Hons)]

MACPHERSON THE HON MARY STEWART

2 Mitre Ct Bldgs
2nd Floor, Temple, London EC4Y 7BX,
Telephone: 0171 583 1380
Call date: July 1984, Inner Temple
Qualifications: [MA (Hons) (Edin), Dip Law]

MACRAE ROBERT JAMES

Walnut House
63 St. David's Hill, Exeter, Devon EX4 4DW,
Telephone: 01392 279751
E-mail: 106627.2451@compuserve.com
Call date: Oct 1990, Middle Temple
Qualifications: [LLB (Exon)]

MACRORY RICHARD BRABAZON

Brick Court Chambers
15/19 Devereux Court, London WC2R 3JJ,
Telephone: 0171 583 0777
E-mail: (surname)@brickcourt.demon.co.uk
Door Tenant
Call date: Nov 1974, Gray's Inn
Qualifications: [MA (Oxon)]

MACUR MISS JULIA

St Ive's Chambers
9 Fountain Ct, Birmingham B4 6DR,
Telephone: 0121 236 0863/0929
Call date: July 1979, Lincoln's Inn
Qualifications: [LLB (Sheff)]

MADDICK FRANCIS BRUCE

2 King's Bench Walk
Ground Floor, Temple, London EC4Y 7DE,
Telephone: 0171 353 1746
E-mail: 2kbw@atlas.co.uk
King's Bench Chambers
115 North Hill, Plymouth PL4 8JY,
Telephone: 01752 221551
Call date: July 1970, Gray's Inn

MADDOX PETER

Gower Chambers
57 Walter Road, Swansea, West Glamorgan
SA1 5PZ, Telephone: 01792 644466
E-mail: clerk@gowerchambers.co.uk
Call date: Feb 1994, Gray's Inn
Qualifications: [LLB (Wales)]

MAGARIAN MICHAEL

4 Brick Court
Ground Floor, Temple, London EC4Y 9AD,
Telephone: 0171 797 7766
E-mail: chambers@4brick.co.uk
Call date: July 1988, Gray's Inn
Qualifications: [BA (Hons, Cantab)]

MAGEE MISS ROSEIN MOIRA

Chichester Chambers
12 North Pallant, Chichester, West Sussex
PO19 1TQ, Telephone: 01243 784538
Call date: Oct 1994, Gray's Inn
Qualifications: [BA (Hons)(Keele)]

MAGILL CIARAN SEOSA

Counsels' Chambers
2nd Floor 10-11 Gray's Inn Square, London
WC1R 5JD, Telephone: 0171 405 2576
Call date: Nov 1988, Middle Temple
Qualifications: [LLB (Hons), BL]

MAGLOIRE MICHAEL

Chancery Chambers
1st Floor Offices 70/72 Chancery Lane,
London WC2A 1AB,
Telephone: 0171 405 6879/6870
Call date: Nov 1982, Middle Temple
Qualifications: [BA, LLB]

MAGUIRE ALBERT MICHAEL QC (1967)

Goldsmith Building
1st Floor, Temple, London EC4Y 7BL,
Telephone: 0171 353 7881
E-mail: clerks@goldsmith-building.law.co.uk
Call date: Jan 1949, Middle Temple
Qualifications: [BA (Cantab)]

MAGUIRE ANDREW JAMES

St Ive's Chambers
9 Fountain Ct, Birmingham B4 6DR,
Telephone: 0121 236 0863/0929
Call date: Nov 1988, Inner Temple
Qualifications: [LLB (Hull)]

MAGUIRE MARTIN BENN

4 King's Bench Walk
2nd Floor, Temple, London EC4Y 7DL,
Telephone: 0171 353 3581
Call date: Nov 1994, Inner Temple
Qualifications: [BA (Hons), MA]

MAGUIRE MS SARAH RUTH

14 Tooks Court
Cursitor St, London EC4A 1LB,
Telephone: 0171 405 8828
E-mail: clerks @tooks.law.co.uk
Call date: Nov 1990, Inner Temple
Qualifications: [BA, Dip Law (PCL)]

MAHER MS MARTHA JOHANNA DOROTHY

Guildhall Chambers
23 Broad Street, Bristol BS1 2HG,
Telephone: 0117 9273366
Call date: Nov 1987, Inner Temple
Qualifications: [BCL,LLB (Cork), LLM (Cantab)]

MAHER MICHAEL JAMES

4 Brick Court
1st Floor, Temple, London EC4Y 9AD,
Telephone: 0171 583 8455
Call date: Nov 1995, Gray's Inn
Qualifications: [BA (Dunelm), LLM (Edinburgh)]

MAHMOOD ABID

8 Fountain Court
Steelhouse Lane, Birmingham B4 6DR,
Telephone: 0121 236 5514/5
E-mail: clerks@no8chambers.co.uk
Call date: Nov 1992, Inner Temple
Qualifications: [LLB (Hons)]

MAHMOOD IMRAN WASEEM

Holborn Chambers
6 Gate Street, Lincoln's Inn Fields, London
WC2A 3HP, Telephone: 0171 242 6060
Call date: July 1992, Middle Temple
Qualifications: [LLB (Hons)]

MAHMOOD SALIM HUSSAIN

Law Chambers
2nd Floor 5 Cardiff Road, Luton, Bedfordshire
LU1 1PP,
Telephone: 01582 431352 or 0958 674785
Call date: July 1979, Lincoln's Inn
Qualifications: [BA]

MAHON BRIAN PATRICK

Equity Chambers
Suite 110, Gazette Buildings 168 Corporation
Street, Birmingham B4 6TS,
Telephone: 0121 233 2100
Call date: Oct 1996, Lincoln's Inn
Qualifications: [LLB (Hons)(B'ham)]

MAIDMENT KIERAN FRANCIS

Doughty Street Chambers
11 Doughty Street, London WC1N 2PG,
Telephone: 0171 404 1313
E-mail: doughty_street@compuserve.com
Call date: Nov 1989, Gray's Inn
Qualifications: [LLB (LSE), MA (KCL)]

MAIDMENT MRS SUSAN RACHEL

1 King's Bench Walk
2nd Floor, Temple, London EC4Y 7DB,
Telephone: 0171 936 1500
E-mail: ddear@1kbw.co.uk
Call date: July 1968, Lincoln's Inn
Assistant Recorder
Qualifications: [LLB, LLM (Lond), LLD]

MAILER CLIFFORD ROWLAND

1 Dr Johnson's Bldgs
Ground Floor, Temple, London EC4Y 7AX,
Telephone: 0171 353 9328
Dr Johnson's Chambers
The Atrium Court Apex Plaza, Reading
RG1 1AX, Telephone: 01734 254221
Call date: July 1987, Middle Temple
Qualifications: [BA, LLB (Witwater), LLB (Cantab), LLM]

MAIN PETER RAMSAY

8 King Street
Manchester M2 6AQ,
Telephone: 0161 834 9560
Call date: July 1981, Inner Temple
Qualifications: [LLB (LSE), Dip Pet Law (Dundee)]

D

MAINDS ALLAN GILFILLAN

36 Bedford Row
London WC1R 4JH,
Telephone: 0171 421 8000
E-mail: 36bedfordrow@link.org
Call date: Feb 1977, Inner Temple
Recorder

MAINWARING [ROBERT] PAUL CLASON

Carmarthen Chambers
30 Spilman Street, Carmarthen, Dyfed
SA31 1LQ, Telephone: 01267 234410
Call date: Nov 1996, Gray's Inn
Qualifications: [LLM (Bris)]

MAIRS ROBIN GORDON JAMES

Victoria Chambers
19 Castle Street, Liverpool L2 4SX,
Telephone: 0151 236 9402
E-mail: Fa45@rapid.co.uk
Call date: Oct 1992, Gray's Inn
Qualifications: [LL.B (Manch)]

MAITLAND ANDREW HENRY REAVELY

King's Bench Chambers
115 North Hill, Plymouth PL4 8JY,
Telephone: 01752 221551
2 King's Bench Walk
Ground Floor, Temple, London EC4Y 7DE,
Telephone: 0171 353 1746
E-mail: 2kbw@atlas.co.uk
Call date: July 1970, Lincoln's Inn
Recorder
Qualifications: [LLB (St Andrews)]

MAITLAND MARC CLAUDE

11 Old Square
Ground Floor, Lincoln's Inn, London
WC2A 3TS, Telephone: 0171 242 5022/
405 1074
Call date: July 1988, Middle Temple
Qualifications: [LLB (Hons), LLM [Cantab]]

MAITLAND JONES MARK GRIFFITH

Goldsmith Building
1st Floor, Temple, London EC4Y 7BL,
Telephone: 0171 353 7881
E-mail: clerks@goldsmith-building.law.co.uk
Call date: Nov 1986, Middle Temple

Qualifications: [MA (Edinburgh) Dip, Law (City)]

MAJUMDAR SHANTANU

13 King's Bench Walk
1st Floor, Temple, London EC4Y 7EN,
Telephone: 0171 353 7204
E-mail: clerks@13kbw.law.co.uk
King's Bench Chambers
32 Beaumont Street, Oxford OX1 2NP,
Telephone: 01865 311066
E-mail: clerks@kbc-oxford.law.co.uk
Call date: Nov 1992, Middle Temple
Qualifications: [BA (Hons)]

MAKEPEACE PETER ANTHONY

York Chambers
14 Toft Green, York YO1 1JT,
Telephone: 01904 620048
E-mail: yorkchambers.co.uk
Call date: July 1988, Lincoln's Inn
Qualifications: [LLB (Hons) (Wales)]

MAKEY CHRISTOPHER DOUGLAS

Old Square Chambers
1 Verulam Buildings, Gray's Inn, London
WC1R 5LQ, Telephone: 0171 831 0801
Old Square Chambers
Hanover House 47 Corn Street, Bristol
BS1 1HT, Telephone: 0117 9277111
Call date: July 1975, Middle Temple
Qualifications: [LLB, ACIArb]

MALCOLM ALASTAIR RICHARD QC (1996)

1 Paper Bldgs
1st Floor, Temple, London EC4Y 7EP,
Telephone: 0171 353 3728/4953
Call date: Feb 1971, Inner Temple
Recorder
Qualifications: [BA (Oxon)]

MALCOLM MISS HELEN KATHARINE LUCY

3 Raymond Buildings
Gray's Inn, London WC1R 5BH,
Telephone: 0171 831 3833
E-mail: chambers@threeraymond.demon.co.uk
Call date: Nov 1986, Gray's Inn
Qualifications: [MA (Oxon)]

MALCOLM MISS ROSALIND NIVEN

Field Court Chambers
2nd Floor 3 Field Court, Gray's Inn, London
WC1R 4EP, Telephone: 0171 404 7474
E-mail: Clerks@FieldCourtChambers.law.co.uk
Door Tenant
Call date: July 1977, Middle Temple
Qualifications: [LLB (Lond)]

MALCOLM MRS ROZANNA

Gray's Inn Chambers
5th Floor, Gray's Inn, London WC1R 5JA,
Telephone: 0171 404 1111
Call date: Nov 1974, Gray's Inn

MALDEN MISS GRACE

35 Essex Street
Temple, London WC2R 3AR,
Telephone: 0171 353 6381
Call date: Nov 1993, Gray's Inn
Qualifications: [BA]

MALE JOHN MARTIN

4 Breams Buildings
London EC4A 1AQ,
Telephone: 0171 353 5835/430 1221
Call date: July 1976, Lincoln's Inn
Qualifications: [BA (Cantab)]

MALECKA DR MARY MARGARET

Goldsworth Chambers
1st Floor 10-11 Gray's Inn Square, London
WC1R 5JD, Telephone: 0171 405 7117
Call date: Oct 1994, Inner Temple
Qualifications: [BA (Illinois), PGCE (Leicester),
PhD (Notts), CPE (City)]

MALEK ALI QC (1996)

3 Verulam Buildings
London WC1R 5NT,
Telephone: 0171 831 8441
E-mail: clerks@3verulam.co.uk
Call date: July 1980, Gray's Inn
Assistant Recorder
Qualifications: [MA, BCL (Oxon)]

MALEK MEHDI (HODGE)

4-5 Gray's Inn Square
Ground Floor, Gray's Inn, London WC1R 5AY,
Telephone: 0171 404 5252
E-mail: chambers@4-5graysinnsquare.co.uk
Call date: July 1983, Gray's Inn
Qualifications: [BA, BCL (Oxon)]

MALES STEPHEN MARTIN

20 Essex Street
London WC2R 3AL,
Telephone: 0171 583 9294
E-mail: clerks@20essexst.com
Call date: July 1978, Middle Temple
Qualifications: [MA (Cantab)]

MALEY WILLIAM RAYMOND

3 Gray's Inn Square
Ground Floor, London WC1R 5AH,
Telephone: 0171 520 5600
E-mail: gis3@btinternet.com
Call date: July 1982, Gray's Inn
Qualifications: [LLB (Warw)]

MALHOTRA RAGHUBIR SINGH

Perivale Chambers
15 Colwyn Avenue, Perivale, Middlesex
UB6 8JY, Telephone: 0181 998 1935/
081 248 0246
Call date: July 1994, Lincoln's Inn
Qualifications: [BA, LLB, MA (India), LLM
(Lond)]

MALIK AMJAD RAZA

36 Bedford Row
London WC1R 4JH,
Telephone: 0171 421 8000
E-mail: 36bedfordrow@link.org
Call date: Nov 1987, Lincoln's Inn
Qualifications: [LLM (UCL)]

MALIK OMAR LATIF

Eighteen Carlton Crescent
Southampton SO15 2XR,
Telephone: 01703 639001
Call date: Nov 1990, Inner Temple
Qualifications: [LLB (So'ton)]

D

D

MALINS JULIAN HENRY QC (1991)

One Hare Court
1st Floor, Temple, London EC4Y 7BE,
Telephone: 0171 353 3171
E-mail: admin-oneharecourt@btinternet.com
Call date: July 1972, Middle Temple
Qualifications: [MA (Oxon)]

MALLALIEU THE BARONESS ANN QC (1988)

6 King's Bench Walk
Ground Floor, Temple, London EC4Y 7DR,
Telephone: 0171 583 0410
Call date: July 1970, Inner Temple
Qualifications: [MA, LLM (Cantab)]

MALLENDER PAUL NIGEL

2 Pump Court
1st Floor, Temple, London EC4Y 7AH,
Telephone: 0171 353 5597
Call date: Nov 1974, Lincoln's Inn
Qualifications: [LLB (Lond)]

MALLETT MISS SARAH JANE VICTORIA

67a Westgate Road
Newcastle Upon Tyne NE1 1SQ,
Telephone: 0191 261 4407/2329785
Call date: Nov 1988, Inner Temple
Qualifications: [BA (Dunelm)]

MALLETT SIMON JEREMY

11 King's Bench Walk
1st Floor, Temple, London EC4Y 7EQ,
Telephone: 0171 353 3337
3 Park Court
Leeds LS1 2QH, Telephone: 0113 297 1200
Call date: July 1986, Inner Temple
Qualifications: [LLB(Sheffield)]

MALLICK MISS NABILA HANI

Clapham Chambers
21-25 Bedford Road, Clapham North, London
SW4 7SH, Telephone: 0171 978 8482/
642 5777
E-mail: 113063.632@compuserve.com
Call date: Nov 1992, Gray's Inn
Qualifications: [LLB (Lond), LLM]

MALLIN MAXWELL JAMES

11 Stone Bldgs
Ground Floor, Lincoln's Inn, London
WC2A 3TG, Telephone: 0171 831 6381
E-mail: clerks@11StoneBuildings.law.co.uk
Call date: Oct 1993, Inner Temple
Qualifications: [BA (Cantab), CPE (Coventry)]

MALLISON MISS CATHERINE MARY HELEN

Francis Taylor Bldg
2nd Floor, Temple, London EC4Y 7BY,
Telephone: 0171 353 9942/3157
Call date: Nov 1974, Middle Temple

MALLON MISS JOANNA

Derby Square Chambers
Merchants Court, Derby Square, Liverpool
L2 1TS, Telephone: 0151 709 4222
Call date: Oct 1996, Lincoln's Inn
Qualifications: [BA (Hons)(Dunelm)]

MALONE MICHAEL JULIAN

1 Essex Court
Ground Floor, Temple, London EC4Y 9AR,
Telephone: 0171 583 2000
E-mail: clerks@oneessexcourt.co.uk
Call date: Nov 1975, Gray's Inn
Qualifications: [BA]

MANASSE MRS ANNE KATHERINE

Cathedral Chambers
Milburn House Dean Street, Newcastle Upon
Tyne NE1 1LE, Telephone: 0191 232 1311
Call date: Nov 1994, Inner Temple
Qualifications: [BA (Durham), CPE
(Northumbria)]

MANASSE DR PAUL REUBEN

38 Young Street
Manchester M3 3FT,
Telephone: 0161 833 0489
E-mail: clerks@young-st-chambers.com
Call date: Oct 1995, Gray's Inn
Qualifications: [B.Sc, Ph.D (L'pool)]

MANDEL RICHARD

11 Bolt Court
London EC4A 3DQ,
Telephone: 0171 353 2300
E-mail: boltct11@aol.com
Redhill Chambers
Seloduct House 30 Station Road, Redhill
RH1 1NK, Telephone: 01737 780781
Call date: July 1972, Gray's Inn
Qualifications: [MA, BCL (Oxon)]

MANDIL-WADE MISS ROSALYNE HELEN

East Anglian Chambers
Sanders House 52 North Hill, Colchester
CO1 1PY, Telephone: 01206 572756
East Anglian Chambers
57 London Street, Norwich NR2 1HL,
Telephone: 01603 617351
East Anglian Chambers
Gresham House 5 Museum Street, Ipswich
IP1 1HQ, Telephone: 01473 214481
Call date: Nov 1988, Inner Temple
Qualifications: [BA (Hons)]

MANGAT DR TEJINA KIRAN

New Court Chambers
5 Verulam Buildings, Gray's Inn, London
WC1R 5LY, Telephone: 0171 831 9500
E-mail: mail@newcourtchambers.com
Call date: Oct 1990, Middle Temple
Qualifications: [BSc,MBBS (Lond)]

MANLEY DAVID ERIC

40 King Street
Manchester M2 6BA,
Telephone: 0161 832 9082
E-mail: Kingst40@aol.com
Call date: July 1981, Inner Temple
Qualifications: [BA (Hons) (Leeds)]

MANLEY MS HILARY

Cobden House Chambers
19 Quay Street, Manchester M3 3HN,
Telephone: 0161 833 6000
E-mail: clerks@cobden.co.uk
Call date: Nov 1996, Gray's Inn
Qualifications: [LLB (Lond)]

MANLEY MISS LESLEY PATRICA

Chambers of Helen Grindrod QC
1st Floor 95a Chancery Lane, London
WC2A 2JG, Telephone: 0171 404 4777
Call date: Nov 1983, Middle Temple
Qualifications: [BA (Liverpool)]

MANN MISS DAYA LUCIENNE CATHERINE

Devon Chambers
3 St Andrew Street, Plymouth PL1 2AH,
Telephone: 01752 661659
Call date: Feb 1995, Lincoln's Inn
Qualifications: [BA (Joint Hons)(Lon), Dip
Law, CPE]

MANN GEORGE ANTHONY QC (1992)

Enterprise Chambers
9 Old Square, Lincoln's Inn, London
WC2A 3SR, Telephone: 0171 405 9471
Enterprise Chambers
38 Park Square, Leeds LS1 2PA,
Telephone: 01132 460391
Enterprise Chambers
65 Quayside, Newcastle upon Tyne NE1 3DS,
Telephone: 0191 222 3344
Call date: July 1974, Lincoln's Inn
Qualifications: [MA (Oxon)]

MANN JONATHAN SIMON

8 King's Bench Walk
2nd Floor, Temple, London EC4Y 7DU,
Telephone: 0171 797 8888
8 King's Bench Walk North
1 Park Square East, Leeds LS1 2NE,
Telephone: 0113 2439797
Call date: Nov 1989, Inner Temple
Qualifications: [LLB (Essex)]

MANN MARTIN EDWARD QC (1983)

24 Old Bldgs
Ground Floor, Lincoln's Inn, London
WC2A 3UJ, Telephone: 0171 404 0946
E-mail: clerks@24oldbuildings.law.co.uk
Call date: July 1968, Gray's Inn
Recorder

D

MANN PAUL

1 High Pavement
Nottingham NG1 1HF,
Telephone: 0115 9418218
Call date: Nov 1980, Gray's Inn
Qualifications: [BA]

MANN MISS REBECCA CLAIRE

Pendragon Chambers
124 Walter Road, Swansea SA1 5RG,
Telephone: 01792 411188
Call date: Oct 1995, Lincoln's Inn
Qualifications: [LLB (Hons)(Leic)]

MANN MISS SARA ANGELA

India Buildings Chambers
Water Street, Liverpool L2 OXG,
Telephone: 0151 243 6000
Call date: Nov 1994, Middle Temple
Qualifications: [LLB (Hons)]

MANNAN MADANI FUAD

Clapham Chambers
21-25 Bedford Road, Clapham North, London
SW4 7SH, Telephone: 0171 978 8482/
642 5777
E-mail: 113063.632@compuserve.com
Call date: Nov 1993, Lincoln's Inn
Qualifications: [BSc (Econ, Hons)]

MANNERS MISS HENRIETTA LOUISE

Francis Taylor Bldg
2nd Floor, Temple, London EC4Y 7BY,
Telephone: 0171 353 9942/3157
Call date: July 1981, Middle Temple
Qualifications: [LLB]

MANNING COLIN

Littleton Chambers
3 King's Bench Walk North, Temple, London
EC4Y 7HR, Telephone: 0171 797 8600
E-mail: littletonchambers@compuserve.com
Call date: July 1970, Gray's Inn
Qualifications: [LLB]

MANNING JONATHAN DAVID GRANT

Arden Chambers
27 John Street, London WC1N 2BL,
Telephone: 0171 242 4244
Call date: July 1989, Inner Temple
Qualifications: [MA (Cantab)]

MANNING ROBERT MICHAEL JONATHAN

1 High Pavement
Nottingham NG1 1HF,
Telephone: 0115 9418218
Call date: Nov 1992, Inner Temple
Qualifications: [LLB]

MANNION JOHN DENNIS

Westgate Chambers
144 High Street, Lewes, East Sussex BN7 1XT,
Telephone: 01273 480510
Frederick Place Chambers
9 Frederick Place, Clifton, Bristol BS8 1AS,
Telephone: 0117 9738667
Call date: May 1987, Middle Temple
Qualifications: [BA LLM]

MANSELL RICHARD AUSTIN

6 Park Square
Leeds LS1 2LW, Telephone: 0113 2459763
E-mail: chambers@no6.co.uk
Call date: Oct 1991, Gray's Inn
Qualifications: [LLB (Hons)(Leeds)]

MANSFIELD MS ELEANOR CLARE

Warwick House Chambers
8 Warwick Court, Gray's Inn, London
WC1R 5DJ, Telephone: 0171 430 2323
Call date: Oct 1995, Inner Temple
Qualifications: [LLB (Lond)]

MANSFIELD GAVIN HARRISON

4 Paper Bldgs
2nd Floor, Temple, London EC4Y 7EX,
Telephone: 0171 583 0816/071 353 1131
E-mail: clerks@4paperbuildings.co.uk
Call date: Nov 1992, Middle Temple
Qualifications: [BA (Hons)(Cantab)]

MANSFIELD THE HON GUY RHYS JOHN QC (1994)

1 Crown Office Row
Ground Floor, Temple, London EC4Y 7HH,
Telephone: 0171 797 7500
Call date: Nov 1972, Middle Temple
Recorder
Qualifications: [MA (Oxon)]

MANSFIELD MICHAEL QC (1989)

14 Tooks Court
Cursitor St, London EC4A 1LB,
Telephone: 0171 405 8828
E-mail: clerks @tooks.law.co.uk
Acre Lane Neighbourhood Chambers
30A Acre Lane, London SW2 5SG,
Telephone: 0171 274 4400
Call date: Nov 1967, Gray's Inn
Qualifications: [BA, LLB]

MANSON MISS JULIE-ANN

11 Bolt Court
London EC4A 3DQ,
Telephone: 0171 353 2300
E-mail: boltct11@aol.com
Redhill Chambers
Seloduct House 30 Station Road, Redhill
RH1 1NK, Telephone: 01737 780781
Call date: July 1985, Middle Temple
Qualifications: [BA (Bris) Dip Law]

MANTELL-SAYER PETER GEORGE

Sackville Chambers
Sackville Place 44-48 Magdalen Street,
Norwich NR3 1JU, Telephone: 01603 613516/
616221
Tindal Chambers
3/5 New Street, Chelmsford, Essex CM1 1NT,
Telephone: 01245 267742
Call date: Oct 1992, Lincoln's Inn
Qualifications: [LLB(Hons)(Lond)]

MANTLE PETER JOHN

Monckton Chambers
4 Raymond Buildings, Gray's Inn, London
WC1R 5BP, Telephone: 0171 405 7211
E-mail: chambers@monckton.co.uk
Call date: July 1989, Inner Temple
Qualifications: [BA (Oxon), LLM (Cantab)]

MANUEL MISS ELIZABETH

Eighteen Carlton Crescent
Southampton SO15 2XR,
Telephone: 01703 639001
Call date: Nov 1987, Middle Temple
Qualifications: [LLB (B'ham)]

MANZONI CHARLES PETER

39 Essex Street
London WC2R 3AT,
Telephone: 0171 583 1111
E-mail: clerks@39essex.co.uk
Call date: July 1988, Middle Temple
Qualifications: [B.Sc, A.M.I, Mech Eng
(Bristol)]

MARGOLIN DANIEL GEORGE

11 New Square
Ground Floor, Lincoln's Inn, London
WC2A 3QB, Telephone: 0171 831 0081
E-mail: 11newsquare.co.uk
Call date: Nov 1995, Gray's Inn
Qualifications: [BA]

MARGREE MISS SARAH LOUISE

11 King's Bench Walk
1st Floor, Temple, London EC4Y 7EQ,
Telephone: 0171 353 3337
3 Park Court
Leeds LS1 2QH, Telephone: 0113 297 1200
Call date: Oct 1996, Lincoln's Inn
Qualifications: [LLB (Hons)(Leic)]

MARK ANDREW BRIAN

67a Westgate Road
Newcastle Upon Tyne NE1 1SQ,
Telephone: 0191 261 4407/2329785
Call date: Nov 1981, Inner Temple
Qualifications: [BA (N'castle)]

MARK MICHAEL

10 Old Square
Ground Floor, Lincoln's Inn, London
WC2A 3SU, Telephone: 0171 405 0758
Call date: Nov 1964, Inner Temple
Qualifications: [MA, BCL (Oxon)]

MARKE ERIC OLUWOLE MERVYN

Essex House Chambers
Essex House 375-377 Stratford High Street,
Stratford, London E15 4QZ,
Telephone: 0181 536 1077
Call date: Nov 1980, Inner Temple
Qualifications: [LLB (Lond)]

MARKESINIS DR BASIL SPYRIDONOS

Essex Court Chambers
24 Lincoln's Inn Fields, London WC2A 3ED,
Telephone: 0171 813 8000
E-mail: clerksroom@essexcourt-chambers.co.uk
Call date: July 1972, Gray's Inn
Qualifications: [MA, PhD (Cantab)]

MARKHAM MISS ANNA VICTORIA

4 Stone Bldgs
Ground Floor, Lincoln's Inn, London
WC2A 3XT, Telephone: 0171 242 5524
E-mail: d.goddard@4stonebuildings.law.co.uk
Call date: Oct 1996, Lincoln's Inn
Qualifications: [BA (Hons), MA (Hons)(Oxon)]

MARKHAM DAVID HAROLD

2 King's Bench Walk
1st Floor, Temple, London EC4Y 7DE,
Telephone: 0171 353 9276
Call date: Nov 1983, Gray's Inn
Qualifications: [BA, MA Business Law]

MARKLEW LEE JONATHON

6 Fountain Court
Steelhouse Lane, Birmingham B4 6DR,
Telephone: 0121 233 3282
Call date: May 1993, Gray's Inn
Qualifications: [BA (Sheff)]

MARKS DAVID GEORGES MAINFROY

3/4 South Square
Gray's Inn, London WC1R 5HP,
Telephone: 0171 696 9900
E-mail: clerks@southsquare.com
Call date: Nov 1974, Gray's Inn
Qualifications: [MA, BCL (Oxon)]

MARKS MISS GILLIAN

Gray's Inn Chambers
5th Floor, Gray's Inn, London WC1R 5JA,
Telephone: 0171 404 1111
Call date: July 1981, Gray's Inn
Qualifications: [BA(Sussex)]

MARKS MISS JACQUELINE STEPHANIE

2 Gray's Inn Square Chambers
2nd Floor, Gray's Inn, London WC1R 5AA,
Telephone: 0171 242 0328/071 405 1317
E-mail: clerks@2gis.co.uk
Call date: July 1984, Middle Temple
Qualifications: [BA]

MARKS JONATHAN CLIVE QC (1995)

4 Pump Court
Temple, London EC4Y 7AN,
Telephone: 0171 353 2656/9
E-mail: 4_pump_court@compuserve.com
Call date: July 1975, Inner Temple
Qualifications: [BA (Oxon)]

MARKS JONATHAN HAROLD

3 Verulam Buildings
London WC1R 5NT,
Telephone: 0171 831 8441
E-mail: clerks@3verulam.co.uk
Call date: Oct 1992, Inner Temple
Qualifications: [BA (Oxon), BCL]

MARKS LEWIS

Queen Elizabeth Bldg
2nd Floor, Temple, London EC4Y 9BS,
Telephone: 0171 797 7837
Call date: July 1984, Middle Temple
Qualifications: [BA Hons (Oxon)]

MARKS PETER

Goldsworth Chambers
1st Floor 10-11 Gray's Inn Square, London
WC1R 5JD, Telephone: 0171 405 7117
Call date: Nov 1987, Middle Temple
Qualifications: [MB, ChB, MRCP & MSc, LLB, MA]

MARKS RICHARD LEON

Peel Court Chambers
45 Hardman Street, Manchester M3 3HA,
Telephone: 0161 832 3791
Call date: July 1975, Gray's Inn
Recorder
Qualifications: [LLB (Manch)]

MARKSON JONATHAN

4 Brick Court
1st Floor, Temple, London EC4Y 9AD,
Telephone: 0171 583 8455
Call date: July 1980, Middle Temple
Qualifications: [BA (Oxon)]

MARKUS MS KATE

Doughty Street Chambers
11 Doughty Street, London WC1N 2PG,
Telephone: 0171 404 1313
E-mail: doughty_street@compuserve.com
Call date: Nov 1981, Gray's Inn
Qualifications: [LLB (Manch)]

MARLEY MISS SARAH ANNE

5 Pump Court
Ground Floor, Temple, London EC4Y 7AP,
Telephone: 0171 353 2532
E-mail: fivepump@netcomuk.co.uk
Call date: Oct 1995, Lincoln's Inn
Qualifications: [LLB (Hons)(Leic)]

MARLOW MS CLAIRE DEBORAH

All Saints Chambers
9/11 Broad Street, Bristol BS1 2HP,
Telephone: 0117 921 1966
Call date: July 1983, Gray's Inn
Qualifications: [BA]

MARQUAND CHARLES NICHOLAS HILARY

Chambers of Lord Goodhart QC
Ground Floor 3 New Square, Lincoln's Inn,
London WC2A 3RS,
Telephone: 0171 405 5577
E-mail: law@threenewsquare.demon.co.uk
Call date: Nov 1987, Inner Temple
Qualifications: [MA (Oxon), MA LAW, (City),
Dip E C Law, (Lond)]

MARRACHE ISAAC SAMUEL

1 Crown Office Row
Ground Floor, Temple, London EC4Y 7HH,
Telephone: 0171 797 7500
Call date: July 1982, Inner Temple
Qualifications: [LLB, LLM (Lond)]

MARRIAGE MRS HENRIETTA-JANE

Counsels' Chambers
2nd Floor 10-11 Gray's Inn Square, London
WC1R 5JD, Telephone: 0171 405 2576
Call date: Oct 1993, Inner Temple
Qualifications: [LLB (Hons)(Lond)]

MARRIN JOHN WHEELER QC (1990)

Keating Chambers
10 Essex Street, Outer Temple, London
WC2R 3AA, Telephone: 0171 544 2600
Call date: Nov 1974, Inner Temple
Recorder
Qualifications: [MA (Cantab)]

MARRIS MISS SARAH SELENA RIXAR

1 Serjeants' Inn
5th Floor Fleet Street, Temple, London
EC4Y 1LL, Telephone: 0171 415 6666
E-mail: no1serjeantsinn@btinternet.com
Call date: Nov 1991, Inner Temple
Qualifications: [BA (Oxon), Dip Law]

MARRON AIDAN STEPHEN QC (1993)

York Chambers
14 Toft Green, York YO1 1JT,
Telephone: 01904 620048
E-mail: yorkchambers.co.uk
Call date: July 1973, Lincoln's Inn
Recorder

MARRS ANDREW CHARLES

Kenworthy's Buildings
83 Bridge Street, Manchester M3 2RF,
Telephone: 0161 832 4036/834 6954
Call date: Nov 1995, Inner Temple
Qualifications: [BA (Oxon), CPE (Manc)]

D

D

MARSDEN ANDREW CHARLES

All Saints Chambers
9/11 Broad Street, Bristol BS1 2HP,
Telephone: 0117 921 1966
Call date: May 1994, Lincoln's Inn
Qualifications: [BA, BCL Hons)]

MARSDEN ANDREW GUY

East Anglian Chambers
Sanders House 52 North Hill, Colchester
CO1 1PY, Telephone: 01206 572756
East Anglian Chambers
57 London Street, Norwich NR2 1HL,
Telephone: 01603 617351
East Anglian Chambers
Gresham House 5 Museum Street, Ipswich
IP1 1HQ, Telephone: 01473 214481
Call date: July 1975, Middle Temple
Assistant Recorder
Qualifications: [MA (Oxon)]

MARSDEN-LYNCH JOHN FRANCIS

Sussex Chambers
9 Old Steine, Brighton BN1 1FJ,
Telephone: 01273 607953
Call date: Nov 1988, Middle Temple
Qualifications: [BA (Sydney), LLB (Lond), MA
(Lond)]

MARSH MISS CAROLYN DEBORAH

2 Dr Johnson's Building
Temple, London EC4Y 7AY,
Telephone: 0171 353 4716
Call date: July 1985, Inner Temple
Qualifications: [LLB (Bris)]

MARSH MISS ELIZABETH ANN

4 Brick Court
1st Floor, Temple, London EC4Y 9AD,
Telephone: 0171 583 8455
Call date: Nov 1979, Gray's Inn
Qualifications: [BA]

MARSH JOHN

Parsonage Chambers
5th Floor 3 The Parsonage, Manchester
M3 2HW, Telephone: 0161 833 1996
Call date: July 1977, Gray's Inn

MARSH LAURENCE JOHN

4 Pump Court
Temple, London EC4Y 7AN,
Telephone: 0171 353 2656/9
E-mail: 4_pump_court@compuserve.com
Call date: July 1975, Middle Temple
Qualifications: [BA (Oxon)]

MARSH PETER PAUL

9 King's Bench Walk
Ground Floor, Temple, London EC4Y 7DX,
Telephone: 0171 353 7202/3909
Abbey Chambers
PO Box 47 47 Ashurst Drive, Shepperton,
Middlesex TW17 0LD,
Telephone: 01932 560913
Call date: July 1975, Middle Temple
Qualifications: [MA (Cantab), DipPols (Oxon)]

MARSHALL ANDREW

1 Middle Temple Lane
Temple, London EC4Y 1LT,
Telephone: 0171 583 0659 (12 Lines)
Call date: July 1986, Inner Temple
Qualifications: [LLB (UCL)]

MARSHALL ANDREW DAVID MICHAEL CREAGH

3 Paper Bldgs
Ground Floor, Temple, London EC4Y 7EU,
Telephone: 0171 797 7000
E-mail: clerks@3pb.co.uk
Call date: July 1981, Lincoln's Inn
Qualifications: [MA (Oxon)]

MARSHALL DAVID

18 Red Lion Court
(Off Fleet Street), London EC4A 3EB,
Telephone: 0171 520 6000
Thornwood House
102 New London Road, Chelmsford, Essex
CM2 0RG, Telephone: 01245 280880
Call date: July 1985, Gray's Inn
Qualifications: [LLB (Leeds)]

MARSHALL DEREK STANLEY

College Chambers
19 Carlton Cresent, Southampton, Hants
SO15 2ET, Telephone: 01703 230338
Call date: July 1980, Inner Temple
Qualifications: [LLB (Soton)]

MARSHALL MISS ELOISE MARY KATHERINE SELINA

23 Essex Street
London WC2R 3AS,
Telephone: 0171 413 0353/353 3533
E-mail: clerks@essexstreet23.demon.co.uk
Call date: Oct 1994, Gray's Inn
Qualifications: [BA]

MARSHALL MISS ITA DELORIS

Horizon Chambers
95a Chancery Lane, London WC2A 1DT,
Telephone: 0171 242 2440
Call date: July 1980, Middle Temple
Qualifications: [LLB (Hons), MA]

MARSHALL MISS NICOLA JANE

Pall Mall Chambers
Executive House 40A Young Street,
Manchester M3 3FT,
Telephone: 0161 832 3373/4
Call date: Oct 1991, Middle Temple

MARSHALL PAUL DAVID JOHN

1 Crown Office Row
3rd Floor, Temple, London EC4Y 7HH,
Telephone: 0171 583 9292
E-mail: onecor@link.org
Call date: Oct 1991, Inner Temple
Qualifications: [BA (Cantab), BSc (Lond)]

MARSHALL PAUL ROBERT

Lloyds House Chambers
3rd Floor 18 Lloyds House, Lloyd Street,
Manchester M2 5WA,
Telephone: 0161 839 3371
Call date: Nov 1982, Middle Temple
Qualifications: [B.Ed (Manch)]

MARSHALL PETER DAVID

Trafalgar Chambers
53 Fleet Street, London EC4Y 1BE,
Telephone: 0171 583 5858
E-mail: TrafalgarChambers@easynet.co.uk
Call date: Nov 1991, Lincoln's Inn
Qualifications: [LLB (Hons)(Warw)]

MARSHALL PHILIP DEREK

Iscoed Chambers
86 St Helen's Road, Swansea SA1 4BQ,
Telephone: 01792 652988/9/330
Farrar's Building
Temple, London EC4Y 7BD,
Telephone: 0171 583 9241
E-mail: chambers@farrarsbuilding.co.uk
Door Tenant
Call date: Nov 1975, Middle Temple
Assistant Recorder
Qualifications: [MA (Cantab)]

MARSHALL PHILIP JOHN

1 King's Bench Walk
2nd Floor, Temple, London EC4Y 7DB,
Telephone: 0171 936 1500
E-mail: ddear@1kbw.co.uk
Call date: July 1989, Gray's Inn
Qualifications: [LLB [L'pool]]

MARSHALL PHILIP SCOTT

13 Old Square
1st Floor, Lincoln's Inn, London WC2A 3UA,
Telephone: 0171 242 6105
E-mail: clerks@serlecourt.co.uk
Call date: July 1987, Lincoln's Inn
Qualifications: [MA (Hons) (Cantab),
LLM(Harvard)]

MARSHALL MISS VANESSA JULIETTE

9 Bedford Row
London WC1R 4AZ,
Telephone: 0171 242 3555
E-mail: clerks@9br.co.uk
Call date: Oct 1994, Gray's Inn
Qualifications: [RGN, LLB]

MARSHALL-ANDREWS ROBERT GRAHAM QC (1987)

4 Paper Bldgs
Ground Floor, Temple, London EC4Y 7EX,
Telephone: 0171 353 3366/583 7155
E-mail: clerks@4paperbuildings.com
Call date: Feb 1967, Gray's Inn
Recorder
Qualifications: [LLB (Bris)]

D

D

MARSON GEOFFREY CHARLES QC (1997)

25 Park Square
Leeds LS1 2PW, Telephone: 0113 2451841/2/3
E-mail: sovereignchambers@btinternet.com
Call date: Nov 1975, Gray's Inn
Recorder
Qualifications: [LLB (Lond)]

MARSTON NICHOLAS RICHARD

St John's Chambers
Small Street, Bristol BS1 1DW,
Telephone: 0117 9213456/298514
E-mail: clerks@stjohns.uk.com
Call date: July 1975, Middle Temple
Assistant Recorder
Qualifications: [LLB (Wales)]

MARSTON-PARCHMENT MS MURZILINE

2 Mitre Ct Bldgs
2nd Floor, Temple, London EC4Y 7BX,
Telephone: 0171 583 1380
Call date: Nov 1989, Inner Temple
Qualifications: [LLB (So'ton)]

MARTEN RICHARD HEDLEY WESTWOOD

Chambers of Lord Goodhart QC
Ground Floor 3 New Square, Lincoln's Inn,
London WC2A 3RS,
Telephone: 0171 405 5577
E-mail: law@threenewsquare.demon.co.uk
Call date: Nov 1966, Lincoln's Inn
Qualifications: [MA (Cantab)]

MARTIGNETTI IAN R

Regency Chambers
18 Cowgate, Peterborough PE1 1NA,
Telephone: 01733 315215
Regency Chambers
Sheraton House, Castle Park, Cambridge
CB3 0AX, Telephone: 01223 301517
Call date: Nov 1990, Inner Temple
Qualifications: [LLB]

MARTIN BRADLEY DAVID

2 Temple Gardens
Temple, London EC4Y 9AY,
Telephone: 0171 583 6041 (12 Lines)
Call date: Oct 1990, Lincoln's Inn
Qualifications: [LLB (Leic)]

MARTIN DAVID JOHN

Cathedral Chambers
Milburn House Dean Street, Newcastle Upon
Tyne NE1 1LE, Telephone: 0191 232 1311
Call date: Oct 1994, Gray's Inn
Qualifications: [BSc]

MARTIN MRS DIANNE JOAN ABEGAIL

St John's Chambers
Small Street, Bristol BS1 1DW,
Telephone: 0117 9213456/298514
E-mail: clerks@stjohns.uk.com
Call date: Oct 1992, Gray's Inn
Qualifications: [LL.B]

MARTIN MRS GAY MADELEINE ANNESLEY

7 Stone Bldgs
1st Floor, Lincoln's Inn, London WC2A 3SZ,
Telephone: 0171 242 0961
Call date: July 1970, Inner Temple

MARTIN GERARD JAMES

Exchange Chambers
Pearl Assurance House Derby Square,
Liverpool L2 9XX, Telephone: 0151 236 7747/
0458
E-mail: exchangechambers@btinternet.com
Call date: July 1978, Middle Temple
Assistant Recorder
Qualifications: [MA (Cantab)]

MARTIN MRS JILL ELIZABETH

Barnard's Inn Chambers
6th Floor Halton House, 20-23 Holborn,
London EC1N 2JD, Telephone: 0171 242 8508
E-mail: clerks@barnards-inn-chambers.co.uk
Call date: Nov 1993, Lincoln's Inn
Qualifications: [LLB(Hons) LLM (Lond)]

MARTIN JOHN VANDELEUR QC (1991)

Wilberforce Chambers
8 New Square, Lincoln's Inn, London
WC2A 3QP, Telephone: 0171 306 0102
E-mail: chambers@wilberforce.co.uk
Call date: July 1972, Lincoln's Inn
Qualifications: [MA (Cantab)]

MARTIN JONATHAN DAVID

10 King's Bench Walk
Ground Floor, Temple, London EC4Y 7EB,
Telephone: 0171 353 7742
E-mail: 10kbw@lineone.net
Call date: Nov 1994, Middle Temple
Qualifications: [BA (Hons)]

MARTIN PETER

9 Fountains Way
Pinders Heath, Wakefield, West Yorkshire
WF1 4TQ, Telephone: 01924 378631
Call date: Feb 1990, Gray's Inn
Qualifications: [LLB (Lond), MA (Sheff)]

MARTIN PETER JOHN

2 Paper Bldgs
1st Floor, Temple, London EC4Y 7ET,
Telephone: 0171 936 2611 (10 Lines)
E-mail: clerks@2pbbarristers.co.uk
Call date: July 1969, Gray's Inn
Qualifications: [BSc, MSc]

MARTIN PHILIP ROGER

Albany Chambers
91 Kentish Town Road, London NW1 8NY,
Telephone: 0171 485 5736/5758
E-mail: albanychambers@usanet
Call date: Oct 1995, Inner Temple
Qualifications: [BA (York), CPE (Lond)]

MARTIN RICHARD HENRY BOLAM

Rowchester Chambers
4 Rowchester Court Whittall Street,
Birmingham B4 6DH,
Telephone: 0121 233 2327/2361951
Call date: Nov 1978, Inner Temple
Qualifications: [BSc (Econ)]

MARTIN ROY LOGAN

1 Serjeants' Inn
4th Floor, Temple, London EC4Y 1NH,
Telephone: 0171 583 1355
E-mail: serjeants.inn@virgin.net
Call date: July 1990, Lincoln's Inn
Qualifications: [LLB (Glas)]

MARTIN MISS ZOE VICTORIA

2 Paper Bldgs
1st Floor, Temple, London EC4Y 7ET,
Telephone: 0171 936 2611 (10 Lines)
E-mail: clerks@2pbbarristers.co.uk
Call date: Oct 1990, Gray's Inn
Qualifications: [LLB]

MARTIN-SPERRY DAVID ANTHONY

1 Crown Office Row
2nd Floor, Temple, London EC4Y 7HH,
Telephone: 0171 797 7111
Call date: Nov 1971, Inner Temple
Qualifications: [MA (Cantab)]

MARTINEAU HENRY RALPH ADEANE

Goldsmith Building
1st Floor, Temple, London EC4Y 7BL,
Telephone: 0171 353 7881
E-mail: clerks@goldsmith-building.law.co.uk
Call date: Nov 1966, Inner Temple
Recorder
Qualifications: [BA (Cantab)]

MARTINO ANTHONY R.

5 New Square
1st Floor, Lincoln's Inn, London WC2A 3RJ,
Telephone: 0171 404 0404
E-mail: Chambers@FiveNewSquare.CityScape.co.uk
Call date: Nov 1982, Inner Temple
Qualifications: [MA]

MARTINS MISS YETUNDE TOKUNBO

Albany Chambers
91 Kentish Town Road, London NW1 8NY,
Telephone: 0171 485 5736/5758
E-mail: albanychambers@usanet
Call date: July 1989, Middle Temple
Qualifications: [BA (Hons)]

MARVEN ROBERT

Assize Court Chambers
14 Small Street, Bristol BS1 1DE,
Telephone: 0117 9264587
Call date: Oct 1994, Middle Temple
Qualifications: [BA (Hons)(Cantab)]

MARYNIAK RUPERT ANDREW WARD

1 Gray's Inn Square
Ground Floor, London WC1R 5AA,
Telephone: 0171 405 8946/7/8
Door Tenant
Call date: Nov 1991, Inner Temple
Qualifications: [BSc, MSc (Lond), Dip Law]

MARZEC MS ALEXANDRA

5 Raymond Buildings
1st Floor, Gray's Inn, London WC1R 5BP,
Telephone: 0171 242 2902
Call date: Nov 1990, Middle Temple
Qualifications: [LLB (Warw)]

MASEFIELD ROGER FRANCIS

Brick Court Chambers
15/19 Devereux Court, London WC2R 3JJ,
Telephone: 0171 583 0777
E-mail: (surname)@brickcourt.demon.co.uk
Call date: Nov 1994, Middle Temple
Qualifications: [MA (Cantab), BCL, (Oxon)]

MASKREY SIMEON ANDREW
QC (1995)

9 Bedford Row
London WC1R 4AZ,
Telephone: 0171 242 3555
E-mail: clerks@9br.co.uk
Call date: July 1977, Gray's Inn
Recorder
Qualifications: [LLB]

MASNIUK PETER

Staple Inn Chambers
1st Floor 9 Staple Inn, Holborn, London
WC1V 7QH, Telephone: 0171 242 5240
E-mail: clerks@staple-inn.org
Call date: July 1983, Inner Temple
Qualifications: [BA (Hons), BA (Econ)]

MASON MISS ALEXANDRA

3 Stone Bldgs
Ground Floor, Lincoln's Inn, London
WC2A 3XL, Telephone: 0171 242 4937/
405 8358
Call date: Nov 1981, Gray's Inn
Qualifications: [BA (Lond)]

MASON DAVID BUCHANAN

3 Fountain Court
Steelhouse Lane, Birmingham B4 6DR,
Telephone: 0121 236 5854
11 Bolt Court
London EC4A 3DQ,
Telephone: 0171 353 2300
E-mail: boltct11@aol.com
Call date: July 1986, Middle Temple
Qualifications: [LLB (Leics)]

MASON DAVID HUGH ROTHWELL

67a Westgate Road
Newcastle Upon Tyne NE1 1SQ,
Telephone: 0191 261 4407/2329785
Call date: Feb 1984, Middle Temple
Qualifications: [LLB Notts]

MASON DAVID JOHN

Bank House Chambers
Old Bank House, Hartshead, Sheffield S1 2EL,
Telephone: 0114 2751223
Call date: July 1979, Gray's Inn
Qualifications: [LLB]

MASON IAN DOUGLAS

11 Bolt Court
London EC4A 3DQ,
Telephone: 0171 353 2300
E-mail: boltct11@aol.com
Redhill Chambers
Seloduct House 30 Station Road, Redhill
RH1 1NK, Telephone: 01737 780781
Call date: Nov 1978, Lincoln's Inn
Qualifications: [BA]

MASON JAMES WILLIAM

Francis Taylor Bldg
Ground Floor, Temple, London EC4Y 7BY,
Telephone: 0171 353 7768/7769/2711
Call date: July 1969, Gray's Inn

MASON JOHN JOSEPH

6 Fountain Court
Steelhouse Lane, Birmingham B4 6DR,
Telephone: 0121 233 3282
Call date: Nov 1971, Inner Temple
Qualifications: [LLB]

MASON NICHOLAS ALAN

40 King Street
Chester CH1 2AH, Telephone: 01244 323886
Call date: July 1984, Gray's Inn
Qualifications: [B.A., Dip Law]

MASON PATRICK DAVID ANTHONY

South Western Chambers
Melville House 12 Middle Street, Taunton,
Somerset TA1 1SH, Telephone: 01823 331919
Call date: Oct 1997, Inner Temple

MASSEY ANDREW HUGH

Eighteen Carlton Crescent
Southampton SO15 2XR,
Telephone: 01703 639001
Call date: July 1969, Gray's Inn
Qualifications: [BA (Cantab)]

MASSEY RUPERT JOHN

Eaton House
1st Floor 4 Eaton Road, Branksome Park,
Poole, Dorset BH13 6DG,
Telephone: 01202 766301/768068
Call date: July 1972, Inner Temple
Qualifications: [BA (Oxon)]

MASSEY MISS STELLA MARIA

Garden Court North Chambers
2nd Floor Gregg's Building, 1 Booth Street,
Manchester M2 4DU,
Telephone: 0161 833 1774
Acre Lane Neighbourhood Chambers
30A Acre Lane, London SW2 5SG,
Telephone: 0171 274 4400
Call date: Feb 1990, Middle Temple
Qualifications: [BA Hons, PGCE]

MASSEY WAYNE RICHARD

Parsonage Chambers
5th Floor 3 The Parsonage, Manchester
M3 2HW, Telephone: 0161 833 1996
Call date: July 1986, Inner Temple
Qualifications: [BA (Hons)]

MASSEY WILLIAM GREVILLE SALE QC (1996)

Pump Court Tax Chambers
16 Bedford Row, London WC1R 4EB,
Telephone: 0171 414 8080
Call date: July 1977, Middle Temple
Qualifications: [BA (Oxon)]

MASSIH MICHAEL GEORGES ABDEL

2 Paper Bldgs
1st Floor, Temple, London EC4Y 7ET,
Telephone: 0171 936 2611 (10 Lines)
E-mail: clerks@2pbbarristers.co.uk
Call date: Nov 1979, Middle Temple
Qualifications: [LLB (Lond)]

MASTERS ALAN BRUCE RAYMOND

Counsels' Chambers
2nd Floor 10-11 Gray's Inn Square, London
WC1R 5JD, Telephone: 0171 405 2576
Call date: July 1979, Middle Temple
Qualifications: [LLB (Wales), BL]

MASTERS LEE AUBREY GEORGE

Victoria Chambers
3rd Floor 177 Corporation Street, Birmingham
B4 6RG, Telephone: 0121 236 9900
Call date: Nov 1984, Middle Temple
Qualifications: [BA]

MASTERS MISS SARA ALAYNA

20 Essex Street
London WC2R 3AL,
Telephone: 0171 583 9294
E-mail: clerks@20essexst.com
Call date: Oct 1993, Middle Temple
Qualifications: [BA (Hons)(Cantab)]

MATES THOMAS RORY

Peel House Chambers
Ground Floor, Peel House 5 Harrington Street,
Liverpool L2 9QA, Telephone: 0151 236 4321
Call date: Oct 1993, Middle Temple
Qualifications: [BA (Hons)(Kent)]

MATHER MISS KATE

4 King's Bench Walk
2nd Floor, Temple, London EC4Y 7DL,
Telephone: 0171 353 3581
Call date: Oct 1990, Gray's Inn
Qualifications: [LLB (Lond)]

MATHER-LEES MICHAEL ANTHONY

Albion Chambers
Broad Street, Bristol BS1 1DR,
Telephone: 0117 9272144
Call date: Feb 1981, Inner Temple
Qualifications: [LLB (Lond)]

MATHESON DUNCAN QC (1989)

1 Crown Office Row
Ground Floor, Temple, London EC4Y 7HH,
Telephone: 0171 797 7500
Crown Office Row Chambers
Blenheim House 120 Church Street, Brighton,
Sussex BN1 1WH, Telephone: 01273 625625
Call date: July 1965, Inner Temple
Recorder
Qualifications: [MA, LLM (Cantab)]

MATHEW JOHN CHARLES QC (1977)

5 Paper Bldgs
1st Floor, Temple, London EC4Y 7HB,
Telephone: 0171 583 6117
E-mail: clerks@5-paperbuildings.law.co.uk
Call date: June 1949, Lincoln's Inn

MATHEW MISS NERGIS-ANNE

2 Gray's Inn Square Chambers
2nd Floor, Gray's Inn, London WC1R 5AA,
Telephone: 0171 242 0328/071 405 1317
E-mail: clerks@2gis.co.uk
Call date: Nov 1981, Inner Temple
Qualifications: [BSc (Hons)]

MATHEW ROBERT KNOX QC (1992)

5 Bell Yard
London WC2A 2JR, Telephone: 0171 333 8811
Call date: Nov 1974, Lincoln's Inn
Qualifications: [BA (Dublin)]

MATHEWS DENI

8 Fountain Court
Steelhouse Lane, Birmingham B4 6DR,
Telephone: 0121 236 5514/5
E-mail: clerks@no8chambers.co.uk
Call date: Oct 1996, Gray's Inn
Qualifications: [BSc (B'ham), LLB (Bucks)]

MATHIAS MISS ANNA

11 Bolt Court
London EC4A 3DQ,
Telephone: 0171 353 2300
E-mail: boltct11@aol.com
Call date: Oct 1994, Lincoln's Inn
Qualifications: [LLB (Hons)(Warw)]

MATHIESON GUY ALASTAIR DAVID

28 St John Street
Manchester M3 4DJ,
Telephone: 0161 834 8418
E-mail: clerk@28stjohnst.co.uk
Call date: Oct 1993, Middle Temple
Qualifications: [BA (Hons)]

MATOVU DANIEL MBUSI SAJABI

Farrar's Building
Temple, London EC4Y 7BD,
Telephone: 0171 583 9241
E-mail: chambers@farrarsbuilding.co.uk
Call date: Nov 1985, Inner Temple
Qualifications: [BA(Oxon)]

MATOVU HAROLD NSAMBA

Brick Court Chambers
15/19 Devereux Court, London WC2R 3JJ,
Telephone: 0171 583 0777
E-mail: (surname)@brickcourt.demon.co.uk
Call date: July 1988, Inner Temple
Qualifications: [BA (Oxon), Dip Law]

MATSUSHIMA MISS MASUMI

Monckton Chambers
4 Raymond Buildings, Gray's Inn, London
WC1R 5BP, Telephone: 0171 405 7211
E-mail: chambers@monckton.co.uk
Door Tenant
Call date: Oct 1990, Lincoln's Inn
Qualifications: [BA (Cantab)]

MATTHEW ALFRED DAVID HUGH

9 Bedford Row
London WC1R 4AZ,
Telephone: 0171 242 3555
E-mail: clerks@9br.co.uk
Call date: Nov 1987, Inner Temple
Qualifications: [MA (E'burgh),Dip Law]

MATTHEWS MISS ALISON REBECCA

11 Bolt Court
London EC4A 3DQ,
Telephone: 0171 353 2300
E-mail: boltct11@aol.com
Redhill Chambers
Seloduct House 30 Station Road, Redhill
RH1 1NK, Telephone: 01737 780781
Call date: Nov 1989, Middle Temple
Qualifications: [LLB Hons (Wales)]

MATTHEWS MRS ANN MARIE

King's Bench Chambers
Wellington House 175 Holdenhurst Road,
Bournemouth, Dorset BH8 8DQ,
Telephone: 01202 250025
Call date: Oct 1994, Middle Temple
Qualifications: [LLB (Hons)]

MATTHEWS DENNIS ROLAND

5 Bell Yard
London WC2A 2JR, Telephone: 0171 333 8811
Call date: July 1973, Middle Temple
Qualifications: [LLM]

MATTHEWS DUNCAN HENRY ROWLAND

20 Essex Street
London WC2R 3AL,
Telephone: 0171 583 9294
E-mail: clerks@20essexst.com
Call date: Nov 1986, Gray's Inn
Qualifications: [BA (Hons) (Oxon)]

MATTHEWS MISS GILLIAN

York Chambers
14 Toft Green, York YO1 1JT,
Telephone: 01904 620048
E-mail: yorkchambers.co.uk
Call date: July 1985, Inner Temple
Qualifications: [LLB (Hull)]

MATTHEWS JANEK PAUL

Pump Court Tax Chambers
16 Bedford Row, London WC1R 4EB,
Telephone: 0171 414 8080
Call date: July 1972, Gray's Inn
Qualifications: [MA (Cantab), FCA]

MATTHEWS JULIAN DAVID

9 Bedford Row
London WC1R 4AZ,
Telephone: 0171 242 3555
E-mail: clerks@9br.co.uk
Call date: July 1979, Middle Temple
Qualifications: [LLB (Lond)]

MATTHEWS MISS LISA

Furnival Chambers
32 Furnival Street, London EC4A 1JQ,
Telephone: 0171 405 3232
E-mail: clerks@furnivallaw.co.uk
Call date: Nov 1974, Gray's Inn

MATTHEWS PHILLIP ROWLAND

Francis Taylor Bldg
2nd Floor, Temple, London EC4Y 7BY,
Telephone: 0171 353 9942/3157
Call date: July 1974, Inner Temple
Recorder
Qualifications: [MA (Cantab)]

MATTHEWS RICHARD ANDREW

3 Hare Court
1st Floor, Temple, London EC4Y 7BJ,
Telephone: 0171 353 7561
Call date: Feb 1989, Inner Temple
Qualifications: [MA (Cantab)]

D

D

MATTHEWS MRS SUZAN PATRICIA QC (1993)

Guildford Chambers
Stoke House Leapale Lane, Guildford, Surrey
GU1 4LY, Telephone: 01483 539131
E-mail: guildford.barristers@btinternet.com
Call date: July 1974, Middle Temple
Recorder
Qualifications: [BSc]

MATTHEWS-STROUD MISS JACQUELINE

Francis Taylor Bldg
2nd Floor, Temple, London EC4Y 7BY,
Telephone: 0171 353 9942/3157
Call date: Nov 1984, Gray's Inn
Qualifications: [LLB (Bris)]

MATTHEWSON SCOTT

1 Gray's Inn Square
1st Floor, London WC1R 5AG,
Telephone: 0171 405 3000
E-mail: clerks@onegrays.demon.co.uk
Call date: Oct 1996, Inner Temple
Qualifications: [BA (Lond), CPE]

MATTHIAS DAVID HUW

Hardwicke Building
New Square, Lincoln's Inn, London
WC2A 3SB, Telephone: 0171 242 2523
E-mail: clerks@hardwicke.co.uk
Call date: July 1980, Inner Temple
Qualifications: [BA]

MATTISON ANDREW

Chavasse Court Chambers
2nd Floor Chavasse Court, 24 Lord Street,
Liverpool L2 1TA, Telephone: 0151 707 1191
Call date: Nov 1963, Gray's Inn
Qualifications: [LLB (L'pool)]

MATUK MS HELEN ANTOINETTE

58 King Street Chambers
1st Floor, Kingsgate House 51-53 South King
Street, Manchester M2 6DE,
Telephone: 0161 831 7477
Call date: July 1990, Gray's Inn
Qualifications: [LLB]

MAUGER MISS CLAIRE SHANTI ANDREA

Enterprise Chambers
9 Old Square, Lincoln's Inn, London
WC2A 3SR, Telephone: 0171 405 9471
Call date: Oct 1996, Inner Temple
Qualifications: [BA (Oxon)]

MAULEVERER PETER BRUCE QC (1985)

4 Pump Court
Temple, London EC4Y 7AN,
Telephone: 0171 353 2656/9
E-mail: 4_pump_court@compuserve.com
Call date: July 1969, Inner Temple
Recorder
Qualifications: [BA (Dunelm), FCIArb]

MAUNDER DAVID JAMES

St John's Chambers
Small Street, Bristol BS1 1DW,
Telephone: 0117 9213456/298514
E-mail: clerks@stjohns.uk.com
Call date: Oct 1993, Middle Temple
Qualifications: [BA(Hons)(Oxon), Dip in Law
(City), ISCL]

MAURICI JAMES PATRICK

4 Breams Buildings
London EC4A 1AQ,
Telephone: 0171 353 5835/430 1221
Call date: Oct 1996, Inner Temple
Qualifications: [BA, BCL (Oxon)]

MAWDSLEY MATTHEW EDWARD

Manchester House Chambers
18-22 Bridge Street, Manchester M3 3BZ,
Telephone: 0161 834 7007
Call date: Nov 1991, Inner Temple
Qualifications: [LLB (Hons)]

MAWHINNEY RICHARD MARTIN

35 Essex Street
Temple, London WC2R 3AR,
Telephone: 0171 353 6381
Call date: Nov 1977, Middle Temple
Qualifications: [BA (Oxon)]

MAWREY RICHARD BROOKS QC (1986)

2 Harcourt Bldgs
Ground Floor/Left, Temple, London
EC4Y 9DB, Telephone: 0171 583 9020
E-mail: clerks@harcourt.co.uk
Stanbrook & Henderson
2 Harcourt Bldgs 2nd Floor, Temple, London
EC4Y 9DB, Telephone: 0171 353 0101
E-mail: clerks@harcourt.co.uk
Call date: Feb 1964, Gray's Inn
Recorder
Qualifications: [MA (Oxon)]

MAWSON STEPHEN JOHN CHRISTOPHER

3 Temple Gardens
3rd Floor, Temple, London EC4Y 9AU,
Telephone: 0171 353 0832
Call date: Oct 1994, Gray's Inn
Qualifications: [MA]

MAX MISS SALLY ANN

2 Harcourt Bldgs
1st Floor, Temple, London EC4Y 9DB,
Telephone: 0171 353 6961/7
Call date: Oct 1991, Lincoln's Inn
Qualifications: [BA (Hons) (Cambs)]

MAXWELL ADRIAN ROBERT JOHN

4 King's Bench Walk
Ground/First Floor, Temple, London
EC4Y 7DL, Telephone: 0171 822 8822
E-mail: 4kbw@barristersatlaw.com
Call date: Nov 1993, Middle Temple
Qualifications: [MA (Hons)(Oxon)]

MAXWELL DAVID

Claremont Chambers
26 Waterloo Road, Wolverhampton WV1 4BL,
Telephone: 01902 426222
Call date: Feb 1994, Inner Temple
Qualifications: [LLB (Warw)]

MAXWELL JOHN FREDERICK MICHAEL

4 Fountain Court
Steelhouse Lane, Birmingham B4 6DR,
Telephone: 0121 236 3476
Call date: Feb 1965, Inner Temple
Recorder
Qualifications: [MA (Oxon)]

MAXWELL JOHN JOSEPH

Old Colony House
6 South King Street, Manchester M2 6DQ,
Telephone: 0161 834 4364
Call date: July 1985, Inner Temple
Qualifications: [BA]

MAXWELL MISS JUDITH MARY ANGELA

The Garden House
14 New Square, Lincoln's Inn, London
WC2A 3SH, Telephone: 0171 404 6150
Call date: July 1988, Lincoln's Inn
Qualifications: [LLB (Hons) (B'ham)]

MAXWELL MISS KAREN LAETITIA

20 Essex Street
London WC2R 3AL,
Telephone: 0171 583 9294
E-mail: clerks@20essexst.com
Call date: Oct 1992, Lincoln's Inn
Qualifications: [BA(Hons), BCL]

MAXWELL RICHARD QC (1988)

24 The Ropewalk
Nottingham NG1 5EF,
Telephone: 0115 9472581
E-mail: clerk@ropewalk.co.uk
Doughty Street Chambers
11 Doughty Street, London WC1N 2PG,
Telephone: 0171 404 1313
E-mail: doughty_street@compuserve.com
Call date: July 1968, Inner Temple
Recorder
Qualifications: [BA (Oxon)]

D

MAXWELL-SCOTT JAMES HERBERT

2 Crown Office Row
Ground Floor, Temple, London EC4Y 7HJ,
Telephone: 0171 797 8100
E-mail: mail@2cor.co.uk, or to individual
barristers at: [barrister's surname]@2cor.co.uk
Call date: Nov 1995, Gray's Inn
Qualifications: [MA (Cantab), BCL]

MAY (WILLIAM) NIGEL

33 Bedford Row
London WC1R 4JH,
Telephone: 0171 242 6476
Call date: July 1974, Inner Temple
Assistant Recorder
Qualifications: [BA, Dip Criminology,
(Cantab)]

MAY ALAN

23 Essex Street
London WC2R 3AS,
Telephone: 0171 413 0353/353 3533
E-mail: clerks@essexstreet23.demon.co.uk
Call date: Oct 1995, Inner Temple
Qualifications: [LLB (Plymouth)]

MAY MISS CHARLOTTE LOUISA

8 New Square
Lincoln's Inn, London WC2A 3QP,
Telephone: 0171 405 4321
Call date: Nov 1995, Inner Temple
Qualifications: [BA (Oxon), CPE (City)]

MAY CHRISTOPHER JOHN

1 Harcourt Bldgs
2nd Floor, Temple, London EC4Y 9DA,
Telephone: 0171 353 9421/9151
Call date: Nov 1983, Middle Temple
Qualifications: [MA (Cantab)]

MAY MISS JULIET MARY

3 Verulam Buildings
London WC1R 5NT,
Telephone: 0171 831 8441
E-mail: clerks@3verulam.co.uk
Call date: July 1988, Inner Temple
Qualifications: [BA (Oxon), M Phil (Lond), Dip
Law (City)]

MAY KIERAN LAURENCE

199 Strand
London WC2R 1DR,
Telephone: 0171 379 9779
E-mail: chambers@199strand.co.uk
Call date: Feb 1971, Middle Temple
Qualifications: [BA (Oxon)]

MAY MISS NICOLA JANE

Trinity Chambers
140 New London Road, Chelmsford, Essex
CM2 0AW, Telephone: 01245 605040
Call date: Nov 1993, Gray's Inn
Qualifications: [LLB]

MAY MRS PATRICIA ROSEMARY

4 Brick Court
1st Floor, Temple, London EC4Y 9AD,
Telephone: 0171 583 8455
Call date: July 1965, Gray's Inn
Recorder
Qualifications: [LLB (Lond)]

MAYALL DAVID WILLIAM

Francis Taylor Bldg
Ground Floor, Temple, London EC4Y 7BY,
Telephone: 0171 353 7768/7769/2711
Call date: July 1979, Gray's Inn
Qualifications: [MA (Cantab)]

MAYER MRS VERA

4 Brick Court
Ground Floor, Temple, London EC4Y 9AD,
Telephone: 0171 797 7766
E-mail: chambers@4brick.co.uk
Call date: July 1978, Inner Temple
Qualifications: [BA (Israel), MSc (Lond)]

MAYES IAN QC (1993)

Littleton Chambers
3 King's Bench Walk North, Temple, London
EC4Y 7HR, Telephone: 0171 797 8600
E-mail: littletonchambers@compuserve.com
Call date: July 1974, Middle Temple
Qualifications: [BA (Cantab)]

MAYHEW JEROME PATRICK BURKE

Goldsmith Building
1st Floor, Temple, London EC4Y 7BL,
Telephone: 0171 353 7881
E-mail: clerks@goldsmith-building.law.co.uk
Call date: Nov 1995, Middle Temple

MAYLIN MS KERRY FIONA

Chambers of Helen Grindrod QC
1st Floor 95a Chancery Lane, London
WC2A 2JG, Telephone: 0171 404 4777
Call date: Oct 1994, Gray's Inn
Qualifications: [LLB]

MAYNARD CHRISTOPHER HOWARD

New Court
Temple, London EC4Y 9BE,
Telephone: 0171 583 5123/0171 583 0510
Call date: July 1988, Gray's Inn
Qualifications: [BA Hons (York), Dip Law]

MAYNARD-CONNOR GILES

St James's Chambers
68 Quay Street, Manchester M3 3EJ,
Telephone: 0161 834 7000
E-mail: 106241.2625@compuserve.com
Call date: Nov 1992, Inner Temple
Qualifications: [LLB (Lancs)]

MAYO KHUDA BAKHSH KAHN

Forest House Chambers
15 Granville Road, Walthamstow, London
E17 9BS, Telephone: 0181 925 2240
Call date: Nov 1979, Lincoln's Inn

MAYO RUPERT CHARLES

9 Bedford Row
London WC1R 4AZ,
Telephone: 0171 242 3555
E-mail: clerks@9br.co.uk
Call date: Nov 1987, Gray's Inn
Qualifications: [BA (Dunelm)]

MAYO SIMON PETER

1 Middle Temple Lane
Temple, London EC4Y 1LT,
Telephone: 0171 583 0659 (12 Lines)
Call date: Nov 1985, Inner Temple
Qualifications: [BA (Lond)]

MAZZAG ANTHONY JAMES

Peel Court Chambers
45 Hardman Street, Manchester M3 3HA,
Telephone: 0161 832 3791
Call date: Nov 1996, Lincoln's Inn
Qualifications: [LLB (Hons)(Nott'm), MA
(Sheff)]

MBATHA MRS MYRTLE

54 Anne Way
Ilford, Essex IG6 2RL,
Telephone: 0181 501 4311
Call date: Nov 1977, Lincoln's Inn
Qualifications: [BA, LLM]

MCALINDEN BARRY O'NEILL

17 Bedford Row
London WC1R 4EB,
Telephone: 0171 831 7314
E-mail: IBoard7314@AOL.com
Call date: Oct 1993, Inner Temple
Qualifications: [BA (Hons) (Cantab)]

MCALLISTER MISS EIMEAR JANE

9 Woodhouse Square
Leeds LS3 1AD, Telephone: 0113 2451986
Call date: Oct 1992, Gray's Inn
Qualifications: [LLB (Hull)]

MCALLISTER MISS ELIZABETH ANN

Enterprise Chambers
9 Old Square, Lincoln's Inn, London
WC2A 3SR, Telephone: 0171 405 9471
Enterprise Chambers
38 Park Square, Leeds LS1 2PA,
Telephone: 01132 460391
Enterprise Chambers
65 Quayside, Newcastle upon Tyne NE1 3DS,
Telephone: 0191 222 3344
Call date: Nov 1982, Lincoln's Inn
Qualifications: [MA (Cantab), LLM (Lond)]

MCATASNEY MISS PHILIPPA MARY

9-12 Bell Yard
London WC2A 2LF,
Telephone: 0171 400 1800
Call date: Nov 1985, Lincoln's Inn
Qualifications: [LLB (Lond)]

D

MCATEER MISS SHANDA LOUISE

Phoenix Chambers
First Floor Gray's Inn Chambers, Gray's Inn,
London WC1R 5JA, Telephone: 0171 404 7888
Call date: Oct 1994, Gray's Inn
Qualifications: [BA (Hons)(Oxon)]

MCAULAY MARK JOHN

6 Gray's Inn Square
Ground Floor, Gray's Inn, London WC1R 5AZ,
Telephone: 0171 242 1052
Call date: Oct 1993, Inner Temple
Qualifications: [LLB (Hons)]

MCBRIDE GAVIN JOHN

Peel Court Chambers
45 Hardman Street, Manchester M3 3HA,
Telephone: 0161 832 3791
Call date: Oct 1996, Middle Temple
Qualifications: [BA (Cantab), CPE Dip Law]

MCCABE MS MARGARET ANN

2 King's Bench Walk
Ground Floor, Temple, London EC4Y 7DE,
Telephone: 0171 353 1746
E-mail: 2kbw@atlas.co.uk
King's Bench Chambers
115 North Hill, Plymouth PL4 8JY,
Telephone: 01752 221551
Door Tenant
Call date: July 1981, Middle Temple
Qualifications: [BA, LLB Lond]

MCCAHEY MISS CATHERINE ANNE MARY

7 Fountain Court
Steelhouse Lane, Birmingham B4 6DR,
Telephone: 0121 236 8531
Call date: Oct 1996, Inner Temple
Qualifications: [LLB (Notts)]

MCCAHILL DOMINIC TERENCE JOHN

4 Pump Court
Temple, London EC4Y 7AN,
Telephone: 0171 353 2656/9
E-mail: 4_pump_court@compuserve.com
Call date: Oct 1991, Lincoln's Inn
Qualifications: [BA (Hons)]

MCCAHILL PATRICK GERARD QC (1996)

Priory Chambers
2 Fountain Court, Steelhouse Lane,
Birmingham B4 6DR,
Telephone: 0121 236 3882/1375
Call date: July 1975, Gray's Inn
Assistant Recorder
Qualifications: [MA (Cantab), FCIArb]

MCCALL CHRISTOPHER HUGH QC (1987)

13 Old Square
Ground Floor, Lincoln's Inn, London
WC2A 3UA, Telephone: 0171 404 4800
Call date: Nov 1966, Lincoln's Inn
Qualifications: [BA (Oxon)]

MCCALL DUNCAN JAMES

4 Pump Court
Temple, London EC4Y 7AN,
Telephone: 0171 353 2656/9
E-mail: 4_pump_court@compuserve.com
Call date: Feb 1988, Gray's Inn
Qualifications: [BA (Oxon)]

MCCALLA TARQUIN JEFFREY

2 Dr Johnson's Building
Temple, London EC4Y 7AY,
Telephone: 0171 353 4716
Call date: Oct 1994, Lincoln's Inn
Qualifications: [BA (Hons)(Hull)]

MCCANDLESS PAUL JAMES

2 New Street
Leicester LE1 5NA, Telephone: 0116 2625906
Call date: Nov 1991, Lincoln's Inn
Qualifications: [LLB (Hons) (Manch)]

MCCANN MISS CATRYN ANNE

2 Paper Buildings
Basement, Temple, London EC4Y 7ET,
Telephone: 0171 353 0933
Call date: July 1988, Lincoln's Inn
Qualifications: [LLM, LLB (Hons) SOAS]

MCCANN MISS COLLEEN MARIA

Angel Chambers
94 Walter Road, Swansea SA1 5QA,
Telephone: 01792 6464623/6464648
Call date: Nov 1988, Inner Temple
Qualifications: [LLB (Wales)]

MCCANN JOHN MICHAEL

65-67 King Street
Leicester LE1 6RP, Telephone: 0116 2547710
Call date: Nov 1983, Gray's Inn
Qualifications: [LLB L'pool]

MCCANN SIMON HOWARD

Deans Court Chambers
Cumberland House Crown Square, Manchester
M3 3HA, Telephone: 0161 834 4097
E-mail: deanscourt@compuserve.com
Call date: Nov 1996, Gray's Inn
Qualifications: [BA (Leeds)]

MCCARRAHER COLIN FRASER

1 Paper Bldgs
1st Floor, Temple, London EC4Y 7EP,
Telephone: 0171 353 3728/4953
Call date: Oct 1990, Lincoln's Inn
Qualifications: [MA (Cantab)]

MCCARROLL JOHN JOHNSTON

Exchange Chambers
Pearl Assurance House Derby Square,
Liverpool L2 9XX, Telephone: 0151 236 7747/
0458
E-mail: exchangechambers@btinternet.com
Call date: Nov 1988, Inner Temple
Qualifications: [LLB (Dub)]

MCCARTHY DAMIAN PAUL

Mitre House Chambers
Mitre House 44 Fleet Street, London
EC4Y 1BN, Telephone: 0171 583 8233
Call date: Nov 1994, Gray's Inn
Qualifications: [LLB (Warw)]

MCCARTHY MARTIN RAYMOND

8 King's Bench Walk
2nd Floor, Temple, London EC4Y 7DU,
Telephone: 0171 797 8888
8 King's Bench Walk North
1 Park Square East, Leeds LS1 2NE,
Telephone: 0113 2439797
Call date: Nov 1994, Gray's Inn
Qualifications: [LLB]

MCCARTHY MISS MARY ANN

Walnut House
63 St. David's Hill, Exeter, Devon EX4 4DW,
Telephone: 01392 279751
E-mail: 106627.2451@compuserve.com
Call date: Oct 1994, Middle Temple
Qualifications: [LLB (Hons)(Exeter)]

MCCARTHY MISS NIAMH JANE

Littman Chambers
12 Gray's Inn Square, London WC1R 5JP,
Telephone: 0171 404 4866
E-mail: admin@littmanchambers.com
Call date: Nov 1991, Gray's Inn
Qualifications: [LLB (Dublin), Dip De Hantes
Etudes, Europeenes (Bruges)]

MCCARTHY ROGER JOHN QC (1996)

Cloisters
1st Floor, Temple, London EC4Y 7AA,
Telephone: 0171 827 4000
E-mail: clerks@cloisters.com
Call date: July 1975, Gray's Inn
Qualifications: [BA (Hons)]

MCCARTHY WILLIAM

New Bailey Chambers
10 Lawson Street, Preston PR1 2QT,
Telephone: 01772 258087
Call date: Nov 1996, Middle Temple
Qualifications: [LLB (Hons)(Leeds)]

MCCARTNEY MISS JOANNE

Enfield Chambers
36-38 London Road, Enfield, Middlesex
EN2 6DT, Telephone: 0181 364 5627
E-mail: Enfieldchambers@compuserve.com
Call date: Nov 1990, Inner Temple
Qualifications: [LLB (Warw), LLM]

MCCARTNEY JOHN KEVIN

Hardwicke Building
New Square, Lincoln's Inn, London
WC2A 3SB, Telephone: 0171 242 2523
E-mail: clerks@hardwicke.co.uk
Call date: Nov 1991, Middle Temple
Qualifications: [LLB Hons (Manch)]

MCCARTNEY PETER

7 Fountain Court
Steelhouse Lane, Birmingham B4 6DR,
Telephone: 0121 236 8531
Call date: Nov 1983, Inner Temple
Qualifications: [BA]

MCCAUGHRAN JOHN

1 Essex Court
Ground Floor, Temple, London EC4Y 9AR,
Telephone: 0171 583 2000
E-mail: clerks@oneessexcourt.co.uk
Call date: July 1982, Gray's Inn
Qualifications: [MA (Cantab)]

MCCAUL COLIN BROWNLIE

39 Essex Street
London WC2R 3AT,
Telephone: 0171 583 1111
E-mail: clerks@39essex.co.uk
Call date: July 1978, Gray's Inn
Qualifications: [LLB (Lond)]

MCCLUGGAGE BRIAN THOMAS

9 St John Street
Manchester M3 4DN,
Telephone: 0161 955 9000
E-mail: ninesjs@gconnect.com
Call date: Oct 1995, Middle Temple
Qualifications: [BA (Hons)]

MCCLURE BRIAN DAVID

Littman Chambers
12 Gray's Inn Square, London WC1R 5JP,
Telephone: 0171 404 4866
E-mail: admin@littmanchambers.com
Call date: May 1976, Gray's Inn
Qualifications: [BA (Cantab)]

MCCLURE JOHN PATRICK

24a St John Street
Manchester M3 4DF,
Telephone: 0161 833 9628
Call date: Nov 1975, Middle Temple
Qualifications: [LL.B Hons]

MCCOMBE RICHARD GEORGE BRAMWELL QC (1989)

13 Old Square
Ground Floor, Lincoln's Inn, London
WC2A 3UA, Telephone: 0171 404 4800
Call date: July 1975, Lincoln's Inn
Recorder
Qualifications: [MA (Cantab)]

MCCONNELL CHRISTOPHER RONALD

2 Gray's Inn Square Chambers
2nd Floor, Gray's Inn, London WC1R 5AA,
Telephone: 0171 242 0328/071 405 1317
E-mail: clerks@2gis.co.uk
Call date: July 1979, Lincoln's Inn
Qualifications: [MA (Oxon)]

MCCONVILLE DONALD ALEXANDER

3 Fountain Court
Steelhouse Lane, Birmingham B4 6DR,
Telephone: 0121 236 5854
24 Old Bldgs
Ground Floor, Lincoln's Inn, London
WC2A 3UJ, Telephone: 0171 404 0946
E-mail: clerks@24oldbuildings.law.co.uk
Call date: Feb 1963, Lincoln's Inn
Qualifications: [LLM]

MCCORMACK ALAN

Staple Inn Chambers
1st Floor 9 Staple Inn, Holborn, London
WC1V 7QH, Telephone: 0171 242 5240
E-mail: clerks@staple-inn.org
Call date: Oct 1990, Lincoln's Inn
Qualifications: [LLB (Hons)]

MCCORMACK MISS HELEN

10 King's Bench Walk
1st Floor, Temple, London EC4Y 7EB,
Telephone: 0171 353 2501
Call date: Feb 1986, Middle Temple
Qualifications: [LLB(L'pool)]

MCCORMACK PHILIP ALEXANDER

2 Mitre Ct Bldgs
1st Floor, Temple, London EC4Y 7BX,
Telephone: 0171 353 1353
Call date: Oct 1994, Gray's Inn
Qualifications: [LLB (Wales)]

MCCORMICK MISS ALISON CLAIRE

35 Essex Street
Temple, London WC2R 3AR,
Telephone: 0171 353 6381
Call date: Nov 1988, Middle Temple
Qualifications: [BA (Hons)]

MCCORMICK DR PAUL MARTIN

Malton House
24 Hampshire Terrace, Portsmouth,
Hampshire PO1 2QF,
Telephone: 01705 826636/826426
Call date: July 1983, Middle Temple
Qualifications: [Dip Soc Stud, MA, MPhil, DPhil (Oxon)]

MCCORMICK WILLIAM THOMAS

10 King's Bench Walk
1st Floor, Temple, London EC4Y 7EB,
Telephone: 0171 353 2501
Call date: July 1985, Gray's Inn
Qualifications: [LLB (Hons) (Cardiff)]

MCCOURT CHRISTOPHER

Francis Taylor Bldg
Ground Floor, Temple, London EC4Y 7BY,
Telephone: 0171 353 7768/7769/2711
Call date: Nov 1993, Inner Temple
Qualifications: [LLB (Nott'm)]

MCCOWAN MISS HESTER XANTHE JANE

24 The Ropewalk
Nottingham NG1 5EF,
Telephone: 0115 9472581
E-mail: clerk@ropewalk.co.uk
Call date: Nov 1995, Gray's Inn
Qualifications: [BA]

MCCOY GERARD JOHN XAVIER

2 Paper Bldgs
1st Floor, Temple, London EC4Y 7ET,
Telephone: 0171 936 2611 (10 Lines)
E-mail: clerks@2pbbarristers.co.uk
Call date: Nov 1986, Middle Temple
Qualifications: [BA, LLB, MSc]

MCCRACKEN ROBERT HENRY JOY

2 Harcourt Buildings
Temple, London EC4Y 9DB,
Telephone: 0171 353 8415
E-mail: clerks@twoharcourtbldgs.demon.co.uk
Call date: July 1973, Inner Temple
Qualifications: [MA (Oxon)]

Fax: 0171 353 7622; DX: LDE 402

Types of work: Administrative; Energy; Environment; Local government; Planning; Town and country planning

Circuit: South Eastern

Awards and memberships: Forster Boulton Prizeman; Kenneth H Solomon Prizeman

Publications: *Liability of Funding Institutions for Contaminated Land*, 1992

Reported cases: *Berkeley v SSE and Fulham FC (CA)*, (1998) *The Times*, 27 February, 1998. Environmental assessment.
R v Northumbria Water ex parte Able UK, [1996] COD 187, 1996. Compulsory acquisition: withdrawal of notice to quit.
LB of Newham v Secretary of State for Environment, [1986] JPL 607, 1986. Internal noise insulation as a planning consideration.
LB Merton v Lowe (CA), 18 Build LR 130. Architect's duties.
Flegg v City of London Building Society, [1988] (HL) AC 453, 1988. Occupier's rights.

Practice

Specialises in all aspects of environmental law and land use planning. Acts for a wide range of clients from multinational corporations and regulatory authorities to small entrepreneurs and groups of active citizens.

Chairman of the United Kingdom Environmental Law Association 1995-7. Secretary of the Planning and Environmental Bar Association 1992-4, whose *pro bono* advocacy service he established. Standing Counsel to the Council for National Parks. Member of the Legal

Advisory Panel to the Council for the Protection of Rural England and of the DoE's steering group for PPGs.

Lectures for bodies such as the RICS, ISVA, Law Society, Academy of European Environmental Law, National Society for Clean Air and Environmental Protection and the Institute of Waste and Environmental Management.

Wide experience includes petrochemical industry, power, water retail and transport sectors, waste and contaminated land. Promoted at public inquiry the LB Harrow UDP, the Ipswich Local Plan and the King's Lynn Local Plan. Opposed the MoD Otterburn proposals for the Northumberland County Council and Northumberland National Park Authority May to November 1997.

Interesting cases include Windermere Speed Limit Inquiry, National Grid East London Overhead Power Lines Hearing, Heathrow Terminal 5 Inquiry. Background in general property litigation provides useful depth.

MCCRAE MISS FIONA

Trinity Chambers
9-12 Trinity Chare, Quayside, Newcastle Upon Tyne NE1 3DF, Telephone: 0191 232 1927
Call date: July 1986, Gray's Inn
Qualifications: [LLB Newcastle]

MCCREATH MS FIONA MARY

4 King's Bench Walk
2nd Floor, Temple, London EC4Y 7DL,
Telephone: 0171 353 3581
Call date: Oct 1991, Gray's Inn
Qualifications: [LLB (Lond)]

MCCREATH MISS JEAN ALEXANDER

Counsels' Chambers
2nd Floor 10-11 Gray's Inn Square, London WC1R 5JD, Telephone: 0171 405 2576
Call date: July 1978, Gray's Inn
Qualifications: [BA (Hons) (Hull), AFBPsS]

MCCREDIE MISS FIONNUALA MARY CONSTANCE

3 Serjeants Inn
London EC4Y 1BQ,
Telephone: 0171 353 5537
E-mail: available upon request
Call date: Oct 1992, Middle Temple

Qualifications: [B.Sc (Hons, Manch), MA (Brunel), Common Profesional, Examination]

MCCRIMMON MISS CATHRYN JANE

Counsels' Chambers
2nd Floor 10-11 Gray's Inn Square, London WC1R 5JD, Telephone: 0171 405 2576
Call date: Nov 1991, Middle Temple
Qualifications: [LLB (Hons)]

MCCRINDELL JAMES DERREY

Mitre House Chambers
Mitre House 44 Fleet Street, London EC4Y 1BN, Telephone: 0171 583 8233
Call date: Oct 1993, Middle Temple
Qualifications: [BSc (Hons)(Lond), Dip in Law (City)]

MCCUE DONALD

11 Stone Bldgs
Ground Floor, Lincoln's Inn, London WC2A 3TG, Telephone: 0171 831 6381
E-mail: clerks@11StoneBuildings.law.co.uk
Call date: July 1974, Lincoln's Inn
Qualifications: [MA (Cantab)]

MCCULLOCH IAN

Bracton Chambers
95a Chancery Lane, London WC2A 1DT,
Telephone: 0171 242 4248
Lloyds House Chambers
3rd Floor 18 Lloyds House, Lloyd Street, Manchester M2 5WA,
Telephone: 0161 839 3371
Door Tenant
Claremont Chambers
26 Waterloo Road, Wolverhampton WV1 4BL,
Telephone: 01902 426222
Call date: Nov 1951, Middle Temple
Qualifications: [BA, LLB (Cantab)]

MCCULLOUGH ANGUS MAXWELL THOMAS

1 Crown Office Row
Ground Floor, Temple, London EC4Y 7HH,
Telephone: 0171 797 7500
Call date: Oct 1990, Middle Temple
Qualifications: [BA (Oxon), Dip Law]

MCCULLOUGH MISS JUDITH ANN

Queen's Chambers
5 John Dalton Street, Manchester M2 6ET,
Telephone: 0161 834 6875/4738
4 Camden Place
Preston PR1 3JL, Telephone: 01772 828300
Call date: Apr 1991, Middle Temple
Qualifications: [LLB (Hons)]

MCCULLOUGH MISS LOUISE CLARE

Lion Court
Chancery House 53-64 Chancery Lane, London
WC2A 1SJ, Telephone: 0171 404 6565
Call date: Oct 1991, Middle Temple
Qualifications: [LLB Hons (Lond)]

MCCUTCHEON BARRY DUFF

8 Gray's Inn Square
Gray's Inn, London WC1R 5AZ,
Telephone: 0171 242 3529
Call date: Nov 1975, Inner Temple
Qualifications: [BA, LLM, FTII]

MCDERMOTT GERARD FRANCIS

8 King Street
Manchester M2 6AQ,
Telephone: 0161 834 9560
2 Pump Court
1st Floor, Temple, London EC4Y 7AH,
Telephone: 0171 353 5597
Call date: July 1978, Middle Temple
Assistant Recorder
Qualifications: [LLB (Manchester)]

MCDERMOTT JOHN RAYMUND

Chavasse Court Chambers
2nd Floor Chavasse Court, 24 Lord Street,
Liverpool L2 1TA, Telephone: 0151 707 1191
Call date: Nov 1976, Gray's Inn
Qualifications: [LLB]

MCDERMOTT THOMAS FRANCIS

Farrar's Building
Temple, London EC4Y 7BD,
Telephone: 0171 583 9241
E-mail: chambers@farrarsbuilding.co.uk
Call date: July 1980, Gray's Inn
Qualifications: [LLB (Lond), MPhil, (Cantab)]

MCDEVITT COLIN JOHN

Wessex Chambers
48 Queens Road, Reading, Berkshire
RG1 4BD, Telephone: 01734 568856
E-mail: wessexchambers@compuserve.com
Call date: Oct 1995, Inner Temple
Qualifications: [BSc (Reading), CPE (City)]

MCDONAGH MATTHEW BARTLY ANTHONY

2 Paper Buildings
Basement, Temple, London EC4Y 7ET,
Telephone: 0171 353 0933
Call date: Oct 1994, Middle Temple
Qualifications: [LLB (Hons)(B'ham)]

MCDONALD ANDREW

Martins Building
Water Street, Liverpool L2 3SP,
Telephone: 0151 236 5818/4919
Call date: July 1971, Gray's Inn
Qualifications: [LLB (L'pool)]

MCDONALD MISS JANET

9 Park Place
Cardiff CF1 3DP, Telephone: 01222 382731
Call date: July 1984, Gray's Inn
Qualifications: [LLB]

MCDONALD JOHN WILLIAM

2 Temple Gardens
Temple, London EC4Y 9AY,
Telephone: 0171 583 6041 (12 Lines)
Call date: Nov 1981, Middle Temple
Qualifications: [MA (St Andrews) FRSA]

MCDONALD MS MELANIE SHARON

5 Fountain Court
Steelhouse Lane, Birmingham B4 6DR,
Telephone: 0121 606 0500
Call date: Nov 1990, Inner Temple
Qualifications: [MA (Kent), Dip Law (City)]

MCDONALD PAUL

Old Colony House
6 South King Street, Manchester M2 6DQ,
Telephone: 0161 834 4364
Call date: July 1975, Lincoln's Inn
Qualifications: [LLB (Hons)]

D

MCDONNELL CONRAD MORTIMER

Gray's Inn Chambers
3rd Floor, Gray's Inn, London WC1R 5JA,
Telephone: 0171 242 2642
E-mail: clerks@taxbar.com
Call date: Oct 1994, Lincoln's Inn
Qualifications: [BA (Hons), Dip in Law]

MCDONNELL JOHN BERESFORD WILLIAM QC (1984)

1 New Square
Ground Floor, Lincoln's Inn, London
WC2A 3SA, Telephone: 0171 405 0884/5/6/7
E-mail: 1newsquare@compuserve.com
Call date: July 1968, Inner Temple
Assistant Recorder
Qualifications: [MA (Oxon), LLM (Harvard)]

MCDOWALL ANDREW GORDON

1 King's Bench Walk
2nd Floor, Temple, London EC4Y 7DB,
Telephone: 0171 936 1500
E-mail: ddear@1kbw.co.uk
Call date: July 1972, Gray's Inn
Recorder
Qualifications: [MA, BCL (Oxon)]

MCELROY MISS JOSEPHINE ANN

1 Gray's Inn Square
Ground Floor, London WC1R 5AA,
Telephone: 0171 405 8946/7/8
Call date: Feb 1995, Inner Temple
Qualifications: [BSc (Ulster), CPE (Middx)]

MCEVILLY GERARD MARTIN

Furnival Chambers
32 Furnival Street, London EC4A 1JQ,
Telephone: 0171 405 3232
E-mail: clerks@furnivallaw.co.uk
Call date: Oct 1994, Lincoln's Inn
Qualifications: [LLB (Hons)(Wolves)]

MCEWAN MALCOLM CHARLES

18 St John Street
Manchester M3 4EA,
Telephone: 0161 278 1800
15 Winckley Square
Preston PR1 3JJ, Telephone: 01772 252828
E-mail: clerks@winckleysq.demon.co.uk
Call date: July 1976, Middle Temple
Qualifications: [MA (Oxon)]

MCEWAN MISS VERA GEORGINA

Durham Barristers' Chambers
27 Old Elvet, Durham DH1 3HN,
Telephone: 0191 386 9199
Call date: Nov 1979, Inner Temple
Qualifications: [MA, LLM, M.Sc, Dip.Ed]

MCFARLAND MISS DENISE

3 New Square
Lincoln's Inn, London WC2A 3RS,
Telephone: 0171 405 1111
Call date: July 1987, Inner Temple
Qualifications: [MA (Cantab)]

MCFARLANE ALASTAIR DUNCAN JAMES

Francis Taylor Bldg
Ground Floor, Temple, London EC4Y 7BY,
Telephone: 0171 353 7768/7769/2711
Call date: July 1985, Middle Temple
Qualifications: [LLB]

MCFARLANE ANDREW EWART

1 King's Bench Walk
2nd Floor, Temple, London EC4Y 7DB,
Telephone: 0171 936 1500
E-mail: ddear@1kbw.co.uk
Priory Chambers
2 Fountain Court, Steelhouse Lane,
Birmingham B4 6DR,
Telephone: 0121 236 3882/1375
Door Tenant
Call date: July 1977, Gray's Inn
Assistant Recorder
Qualifications: [BA (Dunelm)]

MCGAHEY MISS CATHRYN MARGARET

9 Bedford Row
London WC1R 4AZ,
Telephone: 0171 242 3555
E-mail: clerks@9br.co.uk
Call date: Nov 1990, Inner Temple
Qualifications: [MA (Cantab)]

MCGAHEY MISS ELIZABETH CLARE

30 Park Place
Cardiff CF1 3BA, Telephone: 01222 398421
E-mail: 100757.1456@compuserve.com
Call date: Nov 1994, Inner Temple
Qualifications: [BA (Wales), CPE (Glamorgan)]

MCGEORGE ANTHONY WILLIAM

13 King's Bench Walk
1st Floor, Temple, London EC4Y 7EN,
Telephone: 0171 353 7204
E-mail: clerks@13kbw.law.co.uk
King's Bench Chambers
32 Beaumont Street, Oxford OX1 2NP,
Telephone: 01865 311066
E-mail: clerks@kbc-oxford.law.co.uk
Call date: Nov 1969, Inner Temple
Qualifications: [MA (Cantab)]

MCGHEE JOHN ALEXANDER

9 Old Square
Ground Floor, Lincoln's Inn, London
WC2A 3SR, Telephone: 0171 405 4682
E-mail: chambers@9oldsquare.co.uk
Call date: July 1984, Lincoln's Inn
Qualifications: [MA (Oxon)]

MCGINN DOMINIC STUART

3 Temple Gardens
2nd Floor, Temple, London EC4Y 9AU,
Telephone: 0171 583 1155
Call date: Nov 1990, Gray's Inn
Qualifications: [LLB (Cardiff)]

MCGINTY ROBERT FRASER

New Bailey Chambers
10 Lawson Street, Preston PR1 2QT,
Telephone: 01772 258087
Call date: Nov 1994, Inner Temple
Qualifications: [BA (Oxon)]

MCGIVERN WILLIAM JOSEPH

9 King's Bench Walk
Ground Floor, Temple, London EC4Y 7DX,
Telephone: 0171 353 7202/3909
Call date: Nov 1987, Inner Temple
Qualifications: [LLB (Hull)]

MCGLYNE JOHN EDWARD

9 Park Place
Cardiff CF1 3DP, Telephone: 01222 382731
Call date: May 1993, Gray's Inn
Qualifications: [LLB (Lond)]

MCGONIGAL DAVID AMBROSE

30 Park Square
Leeds LS1 2PF, Telephone: 0113 2436388
Call date: July 1982, Gray's Inn
Qualifications: [BA]

MCGOVERN EDMOND TERENCE

4-5 Gray's Inn Square
Ground Floor, Gray's Inn, London WC1R 5AY,
Telephone: 0171 404 5252
E-mail: chambers@4-5graysinnsquare.co.uk
Call date: Nov 1966, Middle Temple
Qualifications: [LLB (B'ham)]

MCGOVERN SEAN PATRICK

New Walk Chambers
27 New Walk, Leicester LE1 6TE,
Telephone: 0116 2559144
Call date: Nov 1990, Inner Temple
Qualifications: [LLB]

MCGOWAN MISS MAURA PATRICIA

3 Hare Court
1st Floor, Temple, London EC4Y 7BJ,
Telephone: 0171 353 7561
Call date: Nov 1980, Middle Temple
Assistant Recorder
Qualifications: [LLB (Manch)]

MCGRAIL PETER RONALD

1 Crown Office Row
2nd Floor, Temple, London EC4Y 7HH,
Telephone: 0171 797 7111
Call date: July 1977, Gray's Inn
Qualifications: [LLB (Lond)]

MCGRATH ANDREW JOHN

5 Fountain Court
Steelhouse Lane, Birmingham B4 6DR,
Telephone: 0121 606 0500
Call date: Nov 1983, Gray's Inn
Qualifications: [BA]

MCGRATH DAVID THOMAS

1 Crown Office Row
2nd Floor, Temple, London EC4Y 7HH,
Telephone: 0171 797 7111
Call date: Nov 1993, Inner Temple
Qualifications: [LLB (Bris)]

MCGRATH MISS ELIZABETH ANN

7 Fountain Court
Steelhouse Lane, Birmingham B4 6DR,
Telephone: 0121 236 8531
Call date: Nov 1987, Inner Temple
Qualifications: [LLB (Hull)]

MCGRATH PATRICK JOHN

33 Bedford Row
London WC1R 4JH,
Telephone: 0171 242 6476
Call date: Nov 1991, Middle Temple
Qualifications: [BCL (N.U.I.)]

MCGRATH PAUL ANTHONY

Essex Court Chambers
24 Lincoln's Inn Fields, London WC2A 3ED,
Telephone: 0171 813 8000
E-mail: clerksroom@essexcourt-chambers.co.uk
Call date: Nov 1994, Inner Temple
Qualifications: [BA (Hons), BCL (Oxon)]

MCGRATH SIMON JAMES

Portsmouth Barristers'Chambers
Victory House 7 Bellevue Terrace,
Portsmouth, Hampshire PO5 3AT,
Telephone: 01705 831292
E-mail: clerks@portsmouthbar.com
Call date: Oct 1995, Inner Temple
Qualifications: [MA (Edinburgh), CPE (City)]

MCGRATH MISS SIOBHAN EVELYN

Arden Chambers
27 John Street, London WC1N 2BL,
Telephone: 0171 242 4244
Door Tenant
Call date: July 1982, Middle Temple
Qualifications: [BA (Sussex)]

MCGREGOR ALEXANDER SCOTT

3 Temple Gardens
3rd Floor, Temple, London EC4Y 9AU,
Telephone: 0171 353 0832
Call date: Oct 1996, Lincoln's Inn
Qualifications: [BA (Oxon)]

MCGREGOR ALISTAIR JOHN QC (1997)

11 King's Bench Walk
Temple, London EC4Y 7EQ,
Telephone: 0171 632 8500
E-mail: clerksroom@11-kbw.law.co.uk
Call date: July 1974, Middle Temple
Qualifications: [LLB (Lond)]

MCGREGOR HARVEY QC (1978)

4 Paper Bldgs
Ground Floor, Temple, London EC4Y 7EX,
Telephone: 0171 353 3366/583 7155
E-mail: clerks@4paperbuildings.com
Call date: Feb 1955, Inner Temple
Qualifications: [MA, DCL, SJD (Harv)]

MCGREGOR MISS HELEN MARGARET

Eastern Chambers
Badgers Bottom Dysons Wood Lane, Tokers
Green, Oxford RG4 9EY,
Telephone: 0118 972 3722
Call date: July 1980, Inner Temple
Qualifications: [BSc, LLB (Lond)]

MCGREGOR-JOHNSON RICHARD JOHN

Queen Elizabeth Bldg
Ground Floor, Temple, London EC4Y 9BS,
Telephone: 0171 353 7181 (12 Lines)
Call date: July 1973, Inner Temple
Qualifications: [LLB]

MCGUINNESS JOHN FRANCIS

9-12 Bell Yard
London WC2A 2LF,
Telephone: 0171 400 1800
Call date: July 1980, Lincoln's Inn
Qualifications: [BA (Lond)]

MCGUINNESS-WAY ANDREW JEFFREY SEBASTIAN B

3 Temple Gardens
3rd Floor, Temple, London EC4Y 9AU,
Telephone: 0171 353 0832
Call date: Oct 1992, Middle Temple
Qualifications: [BA (Hons)(Cantab)]

MCGUIRE BRYAN NICHOLAS

2 Field Court
Gray's Inn, London WC1R 5BB,
Telephone: 0171 405 6114
E-mail: fieldct2@netcomuk.co.uk.
Call date: July 1983, Middle Temple
Qualifications: [LLB (Lond), M Phil, (Cantab)]

MCGUIRE MISS DEIRDRE MARIA

Martins Building
Water Street, Liverpool L2 3SP,
Telephone: 0151 236 5818/4919
Call date: Nov 1983, Inner Temple
Qualifications: [LLB (Leeds)]

MCGUIRE DONAL PATRICK

The Corn Exchange
5th Floor Fenwick Street, Liverpool L2 7QS,
Telephone: 0151 227 1081/5009
Call date: July 1983, Gray's Inn
Qualifications: [LLB (L'pool), BL (Dub)]

MCHUGH DENIS DAVID

Bracton Chambers
95a Chancery Lane, London WC2A 1DT,
Telephone: 0171 242 4248
Call date: Oct 1994, Lincoln's Inn
Qualifications: [LLB (Hons)(Hull)]

MCHUGH MISS KAREN

4 Breams Buildings
London EC4A 1AQ,
Telephone: 0171 353 5835/430 1221
Call date: Nov 1992, Middle Temple
Qualifications: [BA (Hons) (Keele), Dip in Law]

MCILROY MR DAVID HALLIDAY

3 Paper Bldgs
1st Floor, Temple, London EC4Y 7EU,
Telephone: 0171 583 8055
E-mail: london@3paper.com
1 Alfred Street
High Street, Oxford OX1 4EH,
Telephone: 01865 793736
4 St Peter Street
Winchester SO23 8OW,
Telephone: 01962 868884
Call date: Nov 1995, Inner Temple
Qualifications: [BA (Cantab)]

MCILROY WILLIAM EWART PATRICK

7 Wilton Road
Redhill, Surrey RH1 6QR,
Telephone: 01737 760264
Call date: Nov 1952, Gray's Inn
Qualifications: [MA (Oxon)]

MCILWAIN SYLVESTER DAVID

1 Dr Johnson's Bldgs
Ground Floor, Temple, London EC4Y 7AX,
Telephone: 0171 353 9328
Dr Johnson's Chambers
The Atrium Court Apex Plaza, Reading
RG1 1AX, Telephone: 01734 254221
Call date: July 1985, Lincoln's Inn
Qualifications: [LLB (Warwick)]

MCINTOSH MISS JACQUELINE LORRAINE

Verulam Chambers
Peer House 8-14 Verulam Street, Gray's Inn,
London WC1X 8LZ,
Telephone: 0171 813 2400
Call date: July 1987, Inner Temple
Qualifications: [LLB]

MCINTYRE BRUCE MACGILLIVRAY

Plowden Bldgs
2nd Floor, Temple, London EC4Y 9BU,
Telephone: 0171 583 0808
E-mail: bar@plowdenbuildings.co.uk
Plowden Buildings
1 Jesmond Dene Terrace, Newcastle upon
Tyne NE2 2ET, Telephone: 0191 281 2096
Call date: Nov 1969, Middle Temple
Recorder
Qualifications: [LLB (Cantab), LLB (Manch)]

MCIVOR MISS (FRANCES) JANE

3 Hare Court
1st Floor, Temple, London EC4Y 7BJ,
Telephone: 0171 353 7561
Call date: July 1983, Inner Temple
Qualifications: [LLB (E Anglia)]

D

MCIVOR MISS HELEN SUSANNAH

38 Young Street
Manchester M3 3FT,
Telephone: 0161 833 0489
E-mail: clerks@young-st-chambers.com
Call date: Oct 1992, Gray's Inn
Qualifications: [LLB (Hons)(Leic)]

MCIVOR IAN WALKER

334 Deansgate
Manchester M3 4LY,
Telephone: 0161 834 3767
Call date: July 1973, Inner Temple
Qualifications: [LLB (Hons)(Lond)]

MCKAY MISS ANNMARIE

6 Gray's Inn Square
Ground Floor, Gray's Inn, London WC1R 5AZ,
Telephone: 0171 242 1052
Call date: Nov 1992, Lincoln's Inn
Qualifications: [LLB (Hons)(Lond)]

MCKAY CHRISTOPHER ALEXANDER

Angel Chambers
94 Walter Road, Swansea SA1 5QA,
Telephone: 01792 6464623/6464648
Call date: Nov 1976, Gray's Inn
Qualifications: [LLB (Lond)]

MCKAY HUGH JOSEPH PETER

Gray's Inn Chambers
3rd Floor, Gray's Inn, London WC1R 5JA,
Telephone: 0171 242 2642
E-mail: clerks@taxbar.com
Call date: Oct 1990, Lincoln's Inn
Qualifications: [LLM, MA, FTII]

MCKEE HUGH ANTHONY

Manchester House Chambers
18-22 Bridge Street, Manchester M3 3BZ,
Telephone: 0161 834 7007
Call date: Nov 1983, Middle Temple
Qualifications: [BA]

MCKEEVER MISS FRANCES MORAG

3 Temple Gardens
Lower Ground Floor, Temple, London
EC4Y 9AU, Telephone: 0171 353 3102/5/9297
Call date: July 1988, Gray's Inn
Qualifications: [LLB (B'ham)]

MCKENNA MISS ANNA LOUISE

Queen Elizabeth Bldg
Ground Floor, Temple, London EC4Y 9BS,
Telephone: 0171 353 7181 (12 Lines)
Call date: Nov 1994, Middle Temple
Qualifications: [BA (Hons) (Leeds)]

MCKENNA BRIAN MALACHY

Manchester House Chambers
18-22 Bridge Street, Manchester M3 3BZ,
Telephone: 0161 834 7007
Call date: July 1983, Middle Temple
Qualifications: [LLB (Liverpool)]

MCKENZIE MISS LESLEY SHARON

Broad Chare
33 Broad Chare, Newcastle Upon Tyne
NE1 3DQ, Telephone: 0191 232 0541
Call date: Feb 1983, Lincoln's Inn
Qualifications: [LLB (Newc)]

MCKEON JAMES PATRICK

Peel House Chambers
Ground Floor, Peel House 5 Harrington Street,
Liverpool L2 9QA, Telephone: 0151 236 4321
Call date: Nov 1982, Lincoln's Inn
Qualifications: [LLB (L'pool)]

MCKEONE MS MARY BRENDA

2 Garden Court
1st Floor, Middle Temple, London EC4Y 9BL,
Telephone: 0171 353 1633
E-mail: barristers@2gardenct.law.co.uk
Call date: Feb 1986, Gray's Inn
Qualifications: [LLB]

MCKIE MISS JACQUELINE

Cleveland Chambers
63-65 Borough Road, Middlesbrough,
Cleveland TS1 3AA, Telephone: 01642 226036
Call date: Oct 1995, Inner Temple
Qualifications: [LLB (Northumbria)]

MCKIERNAN EDWARD JOSEPH

Holborn Chambers
6 Gate Street, Lincoln's Inn Fields, London
WC2A 3HP, Telephone: 0171 242 6060
Watford Chambers
74 Mildred Avenue, Watford, Hertfordshire
WD1 7DX, Telephone: 01923 220553
Middlesex Chambers
Suite 3 & 4 Stanley House Stanley Avenue,
Wembley, Middlesex HA0 4SB,
Telephone: 0181 902 1499
Call date: Nov 1981, Lincoln's Inn
Qualifications: [LLB(Lond)]

MCKINLEY GREGOR CHARLES

Holborn Chambers
6 Gate Street, Lincoln's Inn Fields, London
WC2A 3HP, Telephone: 0171 242 6060
Call date: Oct 1992, Gray's Inn
Qualifications: [BA (Hons)(Belfast), Dip Law]

MCKINNELL MISS SORAYA JANE

Enterprise Chambers
9 Old Square, Lincoln's Inn, London
WC2A 3SR, Telephone: 0171 405 9471
Enterprise Chambers
65 Quayside, Newcastle upon Tyne NE1 3DS,
Telephone: 0191 222 3344
Enterprise Chambers
38 Park Square, Leeds LS1 2PA,
Telephone: 01132 460391
Call date: Oct 1991, Middle Temple
Qualifications: [LLB Hons (Exon)]

MCKINNON RODNEY GORDON

2 Pump Court
1st Floor, Temple, London EC4Y 7AH,
Telephone: 0171 353 5597
Call date: July 1967, Lincoln's Inn
Qualifications: [MA (Cantab)]

MCKINNON WARWICK NAIRN

Hollis Whiteman Chambers
3rd/4th Floor Queen Elizabeth Bldg, Temple,
London EC4Y 9BS, Telephone: 0171 583 5766
E-mail: hollis.whiteman@btinternet.com
Call date: July 1970, Lincoln's Inn
Qualifications: [MA (Cantab)]

MCKONE MARK DESMOND

25 Park Square
Leeds LS1 2PW, Telephone: 0113 2451841/2/3
E-mail: sovereignchambers@btinternet.com
Call date: Nov 1988, Lincoln's Inn
Qualifications: [LLB Hons (Leeds)]

MCLAREN IAN ALBAN BRYANT QC (1993)

24 The Ropewalk
Nottingham NG1 5EF,
Telephone: 0115 9472581
E-mail: clerk@ropewalk.co.uk
Call date: Nov 1962, Gray's Inn
Recorder
Qualifications: [LLB (Nott'm)]

MCLAREN THE HON MICHAEL DUNCAN

Fountain Court
Temple, London EC4Y 9DH,
Telephone: 0171 583 3335
E-mail: chambers@fountaincourt.co.uk
Call date: Nov 1981, Middle Temple
Qualifications: [MA (Cantab)]

MCLAREN MISS NICOLA RUTH

1 Harcourt Bldgs
2nd Floor, Temple, London EC4Y 9DA,
Telephone: 0171 353 9421/9151
Call date: Nov 1991, Inner Temple
Qualifications: [LLB (Hull)]

MCLAUCHLAN IAN JOHN GERALD

Paradise Square Chambers
26 Paradise Square, Sheffield S1 2DE,
Telephone: 0114 2738951
Call date: Oct 1992, Lincoln's Inn
Qualifications: [LLB(Hons)]

MCLAUGHLIN ANDREW PETER

St John's Chambers
Small Street, Bristol BS1 1DW,
Telephone: 0117 9213456/298514
E-mail: clerks@stjohns.uk.com
Call date: Nov 1993, Middle Temple
Qualifications: [BA (Hons)(York), CPE (Lancs)]

MCLAUGHLIN MISS ELAINE

Trafalgar Chambers
53 Fleet Street, London EC4Y 1BE,
Telephone: 0171 583 5858
E-mail: TrafalgarChambers@easynet.co.uk
Call date: Nov 1993, Middle Temple
Qualifications: [LLB (Hons)]

MCLAUGHLIN MISS KAREN JANET

14 Gray's Inn Square
Gray's Inn, London WC1R 5JP,
Telephone: 0171 242 0858
E-mail: 100712.2134@compuserve.com
Call date: July 1982, Middle Temple
Qualifications: [BA (Hons)]

MCLEAN MRS MANDY RACHEL

5 Essex Court
1st Floor, Temple, London EC4Y 9AH,
Telephone: 0171 410 2000
Call date: Oct 1996, Middle Temple
Qualifications: [LLB (Hons)(Kent)]

MCLEOD IAIN

1 Crown Office Row
3rd Floor, Temple, London EC4Y 7HH,
Telephone: 0171 583 9292
E-mail: onecor@link.org
Call date: July 1969, Inner Temple
Recorder
Qualifications: [LLB]

MCLEVY MS TRACEY

Goldsmith Chambers
Ground Floor Goldsmith Building, Temple,
London EC4Y 7BL,
Telephone: 0171 353 6802/3/4/5
E-mail: celiamonksfield@btinternet.com
Call date: Nov 1993, Lincoln's Inn
Qualifications: [LLB (Hons)]

MCLINDEN JOHN VINCENT BARRY

17 Bedford Row
London WC1R 4EB,
Telephone: 0171 831 7314
E-mail: IBoard7314@AOL.com
Call date: Apr 1991, Inner Temple
Qualifications: [LLB (Hons), LLM (New,
Zealand)]

MCLOUGHLIN IAN

Francis Taylor Bldg
Ground Floor, Temple, London EC4Y 7BY,
Telephone: 0171 353 7768/7769/2711
Call date: Nov 1993, Lincoln's Inn
Qualifications: [B.Soc.Sci (Hons)]

MCLOUGHLIN TIMOTHY PATRICK

East Anglian Chambers
57 London Street, Norwich NR2 1HL,
Telephone: 01603 617351
East Anglian Chambers
Sanders House 52 North Hill, Colchester
CO1 1PY, Telephone: 01206 572756
East Anglian Chambers
Gresham House 5 Museum Street, Ipswich
IP1 1HQ, Telephone: 01473 214481
Call date: Nov 1978, Lincoln's Inn
Qualifications: [BA]

MCMANUS JONATHAN RICHARD

4-5 Gray's Inn Square
Ground Floor, Gray's Inn, London WC1R 5AY,
Telephone: 0171 404 5252
E-mail: chambers@4-5graysinnsquare.co.uk
Call date: July 1982, Middle Temple
Qualifications: [MA (Cantab)]

MCMANUS MISS REBECCA JANE

Staple Inn Chambers
1st Floor 9 Staple Inn, Holborn, London
WC1V 7QH, Telephone: 0171 242 5240
E-mail: clerks@staple-inn.org
Call date: Nov 1994, Middle Temple
Qualifications: [BA (Hons)]

MCMASTER PETER

3 Paper Bldgs
Ground Floor, Temple, London EC4Y 7EU,
Telephone: 0171 797 7000
E-mail: clerks@3pb.co.uk
Call date: July 1981, Middle Temple
Qualifications: [LLB (Lond)]

MCMEEKIN IAN

58 King Street Chambers
1st Floor, Kingsgate House 51-53 South King
Street, Manchester M2 6DE,
Telephone: 0161 831 7477
Call date: July 1987, Middle Temple

Qualifications: [BA (Hons) (Leeds), Dip Law (City)]

MCMEEL GERARD PATRICK

Guildhall Chambers
23 Broad Street, Bristol BS1 2HG,
Telephone: 0117 9273366
Call date: Nov 1993, Inner Temple
Qualifications: [BCL, MA (Oxon)]

MCMILLAN MRS CAROL ANN

Paradise Square Chambers
26 Paradise Square, Sheffield S1 2DE,
Telephone: 0114 2738951
Call date: Nov 1996, Middle Temple
Qualifications: [BA (Hons)(So'ton), MPhil (Lond)]

MCMINN MISS VALERIE KATHLEEN

Baker Street Chambers
9 Baker Street, Middlesbrough TS1 2LF,
Telephone: 01642 873873
Call date: Oct 1990, Gray's Inn
Qualifications: [BA (Hons), LLB (Lond)]

MCMULLAN MANUS ANTHONY

1 Atkin Building
Gray's Inn, London WC1R 5AT,
Telephone: 0171 404 0102
E-mail: clerks@atkin-chambers.co.uk
Call date: Nov 1994, Middle Temple
Qualifications: [BA (Hons)]

MCMULLEN JEREMY JOHN QC (1994)

Old Square Chambers
1 Verulam Buildings, Gray's Inn, London
WC1R 5LQ, Telephone: 0171 831 0801
Old Square Chambers
Hanover House 47 Corn Street, Bristol
BS1 1HT, Telephone: 0117 9277111
Call date: Nov 1971, Middle Temple
Recorder, Assistant Recorder
Qualifications: [MA (Oxon), MSc (Lond)]

MCNAB MISS MHAIRI SHUNA ELSPETH

14 Gray's Inn Square
Gray's Inn, London WC1R 5JP,
Telephone: 0171 242 0858
E-mail: 100712.2134@compuserve.com
Call date: July 1974, Middle Temple

MCNALLY JOHN JOSEPH

10 King's Bench Walk
Ground Floor, Temple, London EC4Y 7EB,
Telephone: 0171 353 7742
E-mail: 10kbw@lineone.net
Call date: Nov 1996, Gray's Inn
Qualifications: [BSc (Surrey), LLM (Lond)]

MCNAMARA ANDREW DAVID

St Mary's Chambers
50 High Pavement, Lace Market, Nottingham
NG1 1HW, Telephone: 0115 9503503
E-mail: clerks@smc.law.co.uk
Call date: Nov 1992, Inner Temple
Qualifications: [BA (So'ton), LLB (Leeds)]

MCNAMARA JAMES

1 High Pavement
Nottingham NG1 1HF,
Telephone: 0115 9418218
Call date: May 1990, Inner Temple
Qualifications: [B.A.]

MCNEILE ANTHONY MICHAEL

Lamb Chambers
Lamb Building, Temple, London EC4Y 7AS,
Telephone: 0171 797 8300
E-mail: lambchambers@link.org
Call date: July 1970, Gray's Inn

MCNEILIS MISS SHARRON DAWN

King Charles House
Standard Hill, Nottingham NG1 6FX,
Telephone: 0115 9418851
E-mail: clerks@kch.co.uk
Call date: Oct 1990, Gray's Inn
Qualifications: [LLB]

MCNEILL MISS ELIZABETH JANE

Old Square Chambers
1 Verulam Buildings, Gray's Inn, London
WC1R 5LQ, Telephone: 0171 831 0801
Old Square Chambers
Hanover House 47 Corn Street, Bristol
BS1 1HT, Telephone: 0117 9277111
Call date: Nov 1982, Lincoln's Inn
Qualifications: [BA (Oxon), Dip Law (City)]

MCNEILL MISS FIONA KIRSTY

Peel House Chambers
Ground Floor, Peel House 5 Harrington Street,
Liverpool L2 9QA, Telephone: 0151 236 4321
Call date: Oct 1992, Lincoln's Inn
Qualifications: [LLB(Hons)(Nott'm)]

MCNEILL JOHN SEDDON

24a St John Street
Manchester M3 4DF,
Telephone: 0161 833 9628
Old Square Chambers
Hanover House 47 Corn Street, Bristol
BS1 1HT, Telephone: 0117 9277111
Call date: July 1974, Gray's Inn
Qualifications: [BSc]

MCNICHOLAS EAMON JOHN

3 Temple Gardens
1st Floor, Temple, London EC4Y 9AU,
Telephone: 0171 353 7884/5 8982/3
Call date: Oct 1994, Lincoln's Inn
Qualifications: [BA (Hons)(Leic), Dip in Law
(City), ACMA]

MCNIFF MATTHEW JAMES

2 Paper Buildings
Basement, Temple, London EC4Y 7ET,
Telephone: 0171 353 0933
Call date: Oct 1992, Gray's Inn
Qualifications: [LLB (Hons)]

MCNULTY LAWRENCE JAMES

3 Paper Bldgs
2nd Floor, Temple, London EC4Y 7EU,
Telephone: 0171 353 6208
Call date: Nov 1985, Middle Temple
Qualifications: [BA (Kent), BCL (Oxon)]

MCPARLAND MICHAEL JOSEPH

New Court Chambers
5 Verulam Buildings, Gray's Inn, London
WC1R 5LY, Telephone: 0171 831 9500
E-mail: mail@newcourtchambers.com
Call date: July 1983, Inner Temple
Qualifications: [BA (Oxon)]

MCPHERSON GRAEME PAUL

2 Crown Office Row
2nd Floor, Temple, London EC4Y 7HJ,
Telephone: 0171 797 8000
Call date: Oct 1993, Gray's Inn
Qualifications: [BA (Hons)]

MCQUAIL MS KATHERINE EMMA

11 Old Square
Ground Floor, Lincoln's Inn, London
WC2A 3TS, Telephone: 0171 430 0341
E-mail: clerks@11oldsquare.co.uk
Call date: Nov 1989, Middle Temple
Qualifications: [BA (Hons) (Oxon)]

MCQUATER EWAN ALAN

3 Verulam Buildings
London WC1R 5NT,
Telephone: 0171 831 8441
E-mail: clerks@3verulam.co.uk
Call date: July 1985, Middle Temple
Qualifications: [MA (Cantab)]

MCSHANE MISS ANNE

10 King's Bench Walk
Ground Floor, Temple, London EC4Y 7EB,
Telephone: 0171 353 7742
E-mail: 10kbw@lineone.net
Call date: Oct 1992, Middle Temple
Qualifications: [LLB (Hons, Leic)]

MCVAY MS BRIDGET SIOBHAN

Mitre House Chambers
Mitre House 44 Fleet Street, London
EC4Y 1BN, Telephone: 0171 583 8233
Call date: Feb 1990, Inner Temple
Qualifications: [LLB (Hons)]

MEACHIN MISS (SARAH) VANESSA VERONICA

7 Fountain Court
Steelhouse Lane, Birmingham B4 6DR,
Telephone: 0121 236 8531
Call date: Oct 1990, Inner Temple
Qualifications: [LLB (B'ham)]

MEAD JOHN PHILIP

Old Square Chambers
1 Verulam Buildings, Gray's Inn, London
WC1R 5LQ, Telephone: 0171 831 0801
Old Square Chambers
Hanover House 47 Corn Street, Bristol
BS1 1HT, Telephone: 0117 9277111
Call date: July 1989, Lincoln's Inn
Qualifications: [LLB (B'ham), LLM (EUI
Florence)]

MEADE RICHARD DAVID

8 New Square
Lincoln's Inn, London WC2A 3QP,
Telephone: 0171 405 4321
Call date: Nov 1991, Lincoln's Inn
Qualifications: [BA (Hons) (Oxon)]

MEADOWCROFT GREGORY JOHN

2 King's Bench Walk
1st Floor, Temple, London EC4Y 7DE,
Telephone: 0171 353 9276
Call date: Nov 1990, Middle Temple
Qualifications: [LLB]

MEADOWCROFT STEPHEN CHRISTIAN

Peel Court Chambers
45 Hardman Street, Manchester M3 3HA,
Telephone: 0161 832 3791
Call date: Nov 1973, Gray's Inn

MEADWAY MISS SUSANNAH LAWTON

10 Old Square
Ground Floor, Lincoln's Inn, London
WC2A 3SU, Telephone: 0171 405 0758
Call date: July 1988, Middle Temple
Qualifications: [MA (Oxon), Dip Law (City)]

MEAKIN TIMOTHY WILLIAM

Fenners Chambers
3 Madingley Road, Cambridge CB3 OEE,
Telephone: 01223 368761
Fenners Chambers
8-12 Priestgate, Peterborough PE1 1JA,
Telephone: 01733 62030
Call date: July 1989, Middle Temple
Qualifications: [BA (Leeds), Dip Law, LLM
(LSE)]

MEARES NIGEL LESLIE VELLACOTT

11 Stone Bldgs
Ground Floor, Lincoln's Inn, London
WC2A 3TG, Telephone: 0171 831 6381
E-mail: clerks@11StoneBuildings.law.co.uk
Call date: Nov 1975, Middle Temple
Qualifications: [BA (Cantab)]

MEDD JAMES POWYS

1 Paper Bldgs
Ground Floor, Temple, London EC4Y 7EP,
Telephone: 0171 583 7355
E-mail: clerks@1pb.co.uk
Call date: July 1985, Middle Temple
Qualifications: [MA (Cantab)]

MEDHURST DAVID CHARLES

4 Brick Court
Temple, London EC4Y 9AD,
Telephone: 0171 797 8910
Call date: Nov 1969, Gray's Inn
Qualifications: [LLB (Manch)]

MEDLAND SIMON EDWARD

23 Essex Street
London WC2R 3AS,
Telephone: 0171 413 0353/353 3533
E-mail: clerks@essexstreet23.demon.co.uk
Call date: Oct 1991, Middle Temple
Qualifications: [BA (Hull), Dip Law]

D

D

MEE PAUL MICHAEL

6 Pump Court
1st Floor, Temple, London EC4Y 7AR,
Telephone: 0171 797 8400
E-mail: sa_hockman_qc@link.org
6-8 Mill Street
Maidstone, Kent ME15 6XH,
Telephone: 01622 688094
Call date: Nov 1992, Middle Temple
Qualifications: [B.Sc (Hons)(Aston)]

MEECH MISS ANITA ELLEN

All Saints Chambers
9/11 Broad Street, Bristol BS1 2HP,
Telephone: 0117 921 1966
Call date: Oct 1991, Lincoln's Inn
Qualifications: [LLB (Hons), M Phil (Cantab)]

MEEKE ROBERT MARTIN JAMES

Colleton Chambers
Colleton Crescent, Exeter, Devon EX2 4DG,
Telephone: 01392 74898/9
Call date: July 1973, Gray's Inn
Assistant Recorder
Qualifications: [LLB (Bristol)]

MEESON NIGEL KEITH

4 Field Court
Gray's Inn, London WC1R 5EA,
Telephone: 0171 440 6900
E-mail: chambers@4fieldcourt.co.uk
Call date: Nov 1982, Middle Temple
Qualifications: [MA (Oxon)]

MEHENDALE MS NEELIMA KRISHNA

Stour Chambers
Barton Mill House Barton Mill Road,
Canterbury, Kent CT1 1BP,
Telephone: 01227 764899
E-mail: clerks@stourchambers.co.uk
Call date: Oct 1993, Inner Temple
Qualifications: [BA]

MEHIGAN SIMON PETER

5 Paper Bldgs
1st Floor, Temple, London EC4Y 7HB,
Telephone: 0171 583 6117
E-mail: clerks@5-paperbuildings.law.co.uk
Call date: July 1980, Lincoln's Inn
Qualifications: [LLB (Lond)]

MEHTA SAILESH

Verulam Chambers
Peer House 8-14 Verulam Street, Gray's Inn,
London WC1X 8LZ,
Telephone: 0171 813 2400
Call date: July 1986, Lincoln's Inn
Qualifications: [LLB (Manch)]

MEIKLE ROBERT WILLIAM

Goldsmith Chambers
Ground Floor Goldsmith Building, Temple,
London EC4Y 7BL,
Telephone: 0171 353 6802/3/4/5
E-mail: celiamonksfield@btinternet.com
Call date: July 1970, Gray's Inn
Qualifications: [LLB (B'ham)]

MEJZNER STEPHEN JOHN

2 Dr Johnson's Building
Temple, London EC4Y 7AY,
Telephone: 0171 353 4716
Call date: Nov 1978, Middle Temple
Qualifications: [LLB (Sheff)]

MELLOR EDWARD JAMES WILSON

8 New Square
Lincoln's Inn, London WC2A 3QP,
Telephone: 0171 405 4321
Call date: July 1986, Middle Temple
Qualifications: [MA (Cantab)]

MELLOR JOHN WALTER

30 Park Square
Leeds LS1 2PF, Telephone: 0113 2436388
Call date: Feb 1953, Gray's Inn
Qualifications: [LLB]

MELTON CHRISTOPHER

Peel Court Chambers
45 Hardman Street, Manchester M3 3HA,
Telephone: 0161 832 3791
199 Strand
London WC2R 1DR,
Telephone: 0171 379 9779
E-mail: chambers@199strand.co.uk
Door Tenant
Call date: July 1982, Gray's Inn
Qualifications: [LLB (Bristol)]

MELVILLE MISS ELIZABETH EMMA JANE

Old Square Chambers
1 Verulam Buildings, Gray's Inn, London
WC1R 5LQ, Telephone: 0171 831 0801
Old Square Chambers
Hanover House 47 Corn Street, Bristol
BS1 1HT, Telephone: 0117 9277111
Call date: Oct 1994, Gray's Inn
Qualifications: [BA]

MELVILLE RICHARD DAVID

39 Essex Street
London WC2R 3AT,
Telephone: 0171 583 1111
E-mail: clerks@39essex.co.uk
Call date: July 1975, Inner Temple
Qualifications: [MA (Cantab)]

MELVILLE-SHREEVE MICHAEL DAVID

Walnut House
63 St. David's Hill, Exeter, Devon EX4 4DW,
Telephone: 01392 279751
E-mail: 106627.2451@compuserve.com
Call date: July 1986, Gray's Inn
Qualifications: [LLB (Exeter)]

MELWANI MISS POONAM ARJANDAS

4 Essex Court
Temple, London EC4Y 9AJ,
Telephone: 0171 797 7970
E-mail: clerks@4essexcourt.law.co.uk
Call date: Nov 1989, Inner Temple
Qualifications: [MA (Cantab)]

MENARY ANDREW GWYN

Martins Building
Water Street, Liverpool L2 3SP,
Telephone: 0151 236 5818/4919
Call date: Nov 1982, Inner Temple
Qualifications: [BA]

MENDEL MS PHILIPPA

3 Pump Court
2nd Floor, Temple, London EC4Y 7AJ,
Telephone: 0171 353 1356 (3 Lines)
Call date: May 1992, Inner Temple
Qualifications: [LLB (Newcastle)]

MENDELLE PAUL MICHAEL

3 Gray's Inn Square
Ground Floor, London WC1R 5AH,
Telephone: 0171 520 5600
E-mail: gis3@btinternet.com
Call date: July 1981, Lincoln's Inn
Qualifications: [LLB Lond]

MENDELSON PROFESSOR MAURICE HARVEY QC (1992)

2 Hare Court
Ground Floor, Temple, London EC4Y 7BH,
Telephone: 0171 583 1770
E-mail: 2_Hare_Court@link.org
Call date: Nov 1965, Lincoln's Inn
Qualifications: [MA,DPhil (Oxon)]

MENDES DA COSTA DAVID

2 King's Bench Walk
1st Floor, Temple, London EC4Y 7DE,
Telephone: 0171 353 9276
Call date: Nov 1976, Inner Temple

MENDHIR MRS MANJEET

Mendhir Chambers
38 Priest Avenue, Wokingham, Berkshire
RG40 2LX, Telephone: 0118 9771274
Call date: Nov 1980, Lincoln's Inn
Qualifications: [BA Law]

MENDOZA COLIN JOHN

Lamb Chambers
Lamb Building, Temple, London EC4Y 7AS,
Telephone: 0171 797 8300
E-mail: lambchambers@link.org
Call date: Nov 1983, Inner Temple
Qualifications: [BA (Kent), LLM (Cantab)]

MENDOZA NEIL DAVID PEREIRA

Hardwicke Building
New Square, Lincoln's Inn, London
WC2A 3SB, Telephone: 0171 242 2523
E-mail: clerks@hardwicke.co.uk
Call date: July 1982, Inner Temple
Qualifications: [MA (Cantab)]

D

D

MENON HARIGOVIND

New Court Chambers
3 Broad Chare, Newcastle Upon Tyne
NE1 3DQ, Telephone: 0191 232 1980
Call date: July 1989, Gray's Inn
Qualifications: [BSc (Aberdeen), LLB (Newc)]

MENON RAJIV

2 Garden Court
1st Floor, Middle Temple, London EC4Y 9BL,
Telephone: 0171 353 1633
E-mail: barristers@2gardenct.law.co.uk
Call date: Nov 1993, Middle Temple
Qualifications: [MSc (Lond), CPE]

MENSAH MISS BARBARA

1 Gray's Inn Square
Ground Floor, London WC1R 5AA,
Telephone: 0171 405 8946/7/8
Door Tenant
Call date: July 1984, Lincoln's Inn
Qualifications: [BSc (lond), Dip Law]

MENZIES RICHARD MARK

8 Stone Buildings
Lincoln's Inn, London WC2A 3TA,
Telephone: 0171 831 9881
Call date: Nov 1993, Middle Temple
Qualifications: [BA (Hons)(Cantab), MA
(Cantab)]

MERCER DAVID PAUL

Queen's Chambers
5 John Dalton Street, Manchester M2 6ET,
Telephone: 0161 834 6875/4738
4 Camden Place
Preston PR1 3JL, Telephone: 01772 828300
Call date: July 1980, Lincoln's Inn
Qualifications: [BA (Oxon) Dip Law]

MERCER GEOFFREY MICHAEL

Walnut House
63 St. David's Hill, Exeter, Devon EX4 4DW,
Telephone: 01392 279751
E-mail: 106627.2451@compuserve.com
Call date: Nov 1975, Inner Temple
Assistant Recorder
Qualifications: [LLB (Soton)]

MERCER HUGH CHARLES

Essex Court Chambers
24 Lincoln's Inn Fields, London WC2A 3ED,
Telephone: 0171 813 8000
E-mail: clerksroom@essexcourt-chambers.co.uk
Call date: July 1985, Middle Temple
Qualifications: [MA (Cantab) Licence, Speciale
en droit, europeen (Brux)]

MERCER NEIL STANLEY

Mitre Court Chambers
3rd Floor, Temple, London EC4Y 7BP,
Telephone: 0171 353 9394
Call date: Nov 1988, Lincoln's Inn
Qualifications: [LLB Hons (Wales)]

MERCER NICHOLAS JOHN

Staple Inn Chambers
1st Floor 9 Staple Inn, Holborn, London
WC1V 7QH, Telephone: 0171 242 5240
E-mail: clerks@staple-inn.org
Call date: Nov 1994, Lincoln's Inn
Qualifications: [BA (Hons)(Lond), CPE
(Sussex)]

MEREDITH CHRISTOPHER WILLIAM

1 Gray's Inn Square
1st Floor, London WC1R 5AG,
Telephone: 0171 405 3000
E-mail: clerks@onegrays.demon.co.uk
Call date: Nov 1988, Inner Temple
Qualifications: [LLB]

MEREDITH GEORGE HUBBARD

Southernhay Chambers
33 Southernhay East, Exeter EX1 1NX,
Telephone: 01392 255777
E-mail: southernhay.chambers@lineone.net
Call date: July 1969, Gray's Inn

MEREDITH PHILIP GRANVILLE

Westgate Chambers
144 High Street, Lewes, East Sussex BN7 1XT,
Telephone: 01273 480510
Call date: July 1979, Inner Temple
Qualifications: [BA (Dunelm)]

MEREDITH-HARDY JOHN OCTAVIAN

2 King's Bench Walk
Ground Floor, Temple, London EC4Y 7DE,
Telephone: 0171 353 1746
E-mail: 2kbw@atlas.co.uk
King's Bench Chambers
115 North Hill, Plymouth PL4 8JY,
Telephone: 01752 221551
Call date: Nov 1989, Inner Temple
Qualifications: [MA (St Andrews), Dip Law]

MERRETT MISS LOUISE ANN

Fountain Court
Temple, London EC4Y 9DH,
Telephone: 0171 583 3335
E-mail: chambers@fountaincourt.co.uk
Call date: Oct 1995, Gray's Inn
Qualifications: [BA]

MERRETT RICHARD JAMES

Colleton Chambers
Colleton Crescent, Exeter, Devon EX2 4DG,
Telephone: 01392 74898/9
5 Paper Bldgs
Ground Floor, Temple, London EC4Y 7HB,
Telephone: 0171 583 9275/583 4555
E-mail: 5paper@link.org
Call date: June 1959, Inner Temple
Qualifications: [MA (Oxon)]

MERRICK MISS NICOLA

Furnival Chambers
32 Furnival Street, London EC4A 1JQ,
Telephone: 0171 405 3232
E-mail: clerks@furnivallaw.co.uk
Call date: Nov 1983, Gray's Inn
Qualifications: [BA, LLB]

MERRIMAN NICHOLAS FLAVELLE QC (1988)

3 Verulam Buildings
London WC1R 5NT,
Telephone: 0171 831 8441
E-mail: clerks@3verulam.co.uk
Call date: Feb 1969, Inner Temple
Recorder

MERRITT JOHN RICHARD

Fountain Chambers
Cleveland Business Centre 1 Watson Street,
Middlesbrough TS1 2RQ,
Telephone: 01642 217037
Call date: May 1981, Middle Temple
Qualifications: [LLB (Manch)]

MERRY HUGH GAIRNS

17 Carlton Crescent
Southampton SO15 2XR,
Telephone: 01703 320320
E-mail: km@bar-17cc.demon.co.uk
Call date: July 1979, Inner Temple
Qualifications: [LLB (Bris)]

MERRYLEES RICHARD GAVIN

Francis Taylor Bldg
2nd Floor, Temple, London EC4Y 7BY,
Telephone: 0171 353 9942/3157
Call date: Nov 1964, Gray's Inn
Qualifications: [LLB (Lond)]

MERZ RICHARD JAMES

9-12 Bell Yard
London WC2A 2LF,
Telephone: 0171 400 1800
Call date: July 1972, Inner Temple
Qualifications: [LLB (So'ton)]

MESSLING LAWRENCE DAVID

Priory Chambers
2 Fountain Court, Steelhouse Lane,
Birmingham B4 6DR,
Telephone: 0121 236 3882/1375
Call date: July 1983, Middle Temple
Qualifications: [BA (Keele)]

MESTON LORD QC (1996)

Queen Elizabeth Bldg
2nd Floor, Temple, London EC4Y 9BS,
Telephone: 0171 797 7837
Call date: July 1973, Middle Temple
Qualifications: [MA (Cantab), LLM (Leic)]

METAXA WILLIAM ALEXANDER

Gray's Inn Chambers
5th Floor, Gray's Inn, London WC1R 5JA,
Telephone: 0171 404 1111
Call date: Nov 1995, Middle Temple
Qualifications: [BA (Hons)]

METCALF CHRISTOPHER SHERWOOD JOHN

36 Bedford Row
London WC1R 4JH,
Telephone: 0171 421 8000
E-mail: 36bedfordrow@link.org
Call date: Feb 1972, Middle Temple
Recorder

METCALF JOHN CHARLES

4 King's Bench Walk
2nd Floor, Temple, London EC4Y 7DL,
Telephone: 0171 353 3581
Call date: Feb 1990, Inner Temple
Qualifications: [BSc (Hons), MSc]

METCALFE IAN MICHAEL

Cobden House Chambers
19 Quay Street, Manchester M3 3HN,
Telephone: 0161 833 6000
E-mail: clerks@cobden.co.uk
Call date: Nov 1985, Middle Temple
Qualifications: [LLB (Hons)]

METHUEN RICHARD ST BARBE QC (1997)

12 King's Bench Walk
Temple, London EC4Y 7EL,
Telephone: 0171 583 0811
E-mail: chambers@12kbw.co.uk
Call date: Nov 1972, Lincoln's Inn

METZER ANTHONY DAVID ERWIN

Doughty Street Chambers
11 Doughty Street, London WC1N 2PG,
Telephone: 0171 404 1313
E-mail: doughty_street@compuserve.com
Call date: Nov 1987, Middle Temple
Qualifications: [MA (Oxon)]

METZGER KEVIN ALBERT

3 Temple Gardens (North)
Fifth Floor, Temple, London EC4Y 9AU,
Telephone: 0171 353 0853/4/7222
E-mail: 100106.1577@compuserve.com
Call date: Nov 1984, Middle Temple
Qualifications: [BA (Hons)]

METZGER KEVIN RAYMOND

Horizon Chambers
95a Chancery Lane, London WC2A 1DT,
Telephone: 0171 242 2440
Call date: Apr 1986, Gray's Inn
Qualifications: [LLB (Cardiff)]

MEUSZ MISS AMANDA JANE

2 Garden Court
1st Floor, Middle Temple, London EC4Y 9BL,
Telephone: 0171 353 1633
E-mail: barristers@2gardenct.law.co.uk
Call date: July 1986, Gray's Inn
Qualifications: [LLB (UCL)]

MEW GRAEME STEUART

1 Essex Court
1st Floor, Temple, London EC4Y 9AR,
Telephone: 0171 936 3030
E-mail: one.essex_court@virgin.net
Door Tenant
Call date: July 1982, Middle Temple
Qualifications: [BA, LLB(Windsor)]

MEYER MISS BIRGITTA SARAH GRACE

11 Stone Bldgs
Ground Floor, Lincoln's Inn, London
WC2A 3TG, Telephone: 0171 831 6381
E-mail: clerks@11StoneBuildings.law.co.uk
Call date: Nov 1992, Middle Temple
Qualifications: [BA (Hons, Cantab)]

MEYER MISS LORNA GILLIAN

5 Fountain Court
Steelhouse Lane, Birmingham B4 6DR,
Telephone: 0121 606 0500
Call date: July 1986, Inner Temple
Qualifications: [LLB (Sheffield)]

MIAH ZACHARIAS AZAD AFZAL

9 King's Bench Walk
Ground Floor, Temple, London EC4Y 7DX,
Telephone: 0171 353 7202/3909
Call date: Nov 1990, Inner Temple
Qualifications: [LLB]

MICHAEL SIMON LAURENCE

Bedford Chambers
The Clock House, 2 Bedford Street, Ampthill,
Bedford, Bedfordshire MK45 2NB,
Telephone: 0870 733 7333
Call date: Nov 1978, Middle Temple
Qualifications: [LLB Hons (Lond)]

Fax: 01234 741237;
Out of hours telephone: 070500 99557;
DX: 36901 Ampthill; Other comms: E-mail
simon_michael@link.org;
pilawyer.demon.co.uk

Types of work: Medical negligence; Personal
injury

Circuit: South Eastern

Awards and memberships: Member: Association
of Personal Injury Lawyers; Personal Injury Bar
Association; Professional Negligence Bar
Association

Other professional experience: Lecturer in Law
(Business Law and Contract)

Languages spoken: French

MICHAELS MISS AMANDA LOUISE

5 New Square
1st Floor, Lincoln's Inn, London WC2A 3RJ,
Telephone: 0171 404 0404
E-mail: Chambers@FiveNewSquare.CityScape.co.uk
Call date: July 1981, Gray's Inn
Qualifications: [BA (Dunelm) MA, (Bruges)]

MICHALOS MISS CHRISTINA ANTIGONE DIANA

17 Bedford Row
London WC1R 4EB,
Telephone: 0171 831 7314
E-mail: IBoard7314@AOL.com
Call date: Oct 1994, Gray's Inn
Qualifications: [LLB]

MICHELL MICHAEL JOHN

17 Old Bldgs
Ground Floor, Lincoln's Inn, London
WC2A 3UP, Telephone: 0171 405 9653
St Mary's Chambers
50 High Pavement, Lace Market, Nottingham
NG1 1HW, Telephone: 0115 9503503
E-mail: clerks@smc.law.co.uk
Call date: July 1984, Inner Temple
Qualifications: [MA (Oxon)]

MICHELL PAUL JOSEPH

Bridewell Chambers
2 Bridewell Place, London EC4V 6AP,
Telephone: 0171 797 8800
E-mail: clerks@bridewell.law.co.uk
Call date: Nov 1991, Middle Temple
Qualifications: [MA (Cantab), Dip Law]

MICKLETHWAIT DAVID JOHN

One Raymond Buildings
Gray's Inn, London WC1R 5BH,
Telephone: 0171 430 1234
E-mail: chambers@ipbar1rb.com;
clerks@ipbar1rb.com
Call date: Nov 1970, Middle Temple
Qualifications: [MA (Cantab)]

MIDDLEBURGH JONATHAN SIMON

11 Stone Bldgs
Ground Floor, Lincoln's Inn, London
WC2A 3TG, Telephone: 0171 831 6381
E-mail: clerks@11StoneBuildings.law.co.uk
Call date: Nov 1990, Inner Temple
Qualifications: [BA (Oxon)]

MIDDLETON MS CLAIRE LOUISE

67a Westgate Road
Newcastle Upon Tyne NE1 1SQ,
Telephone: 0191 261 4407/2329785
Call date: Oct 1991, Lincoln's Inn
Qualifications: [LLB (Hons) (New)]

MIDDLETON MISS GEORGINA CLAIRE

New Court Chambers
5 Verulam Buildings, Gray's Inn, London
WC1R 5LY, Telephone: 0171 831 9500
E-mail: mail@newcourtchambers.com
Call date: Nov 1989, Middle Temple
Qualifications: [BA Hons [Bris]]

D

MIDDLETON SEAN

Goldsworth Chambers
1st Floor 10-11 Gray's Inn Square, London
WC1R 5JD, Telephone: 0171 405 7117
Call date: Nov 1991, Lincoln's Inn
Qualifications: [BA (Hons) (Keele), Dip Law,
LLM (Osnabruck)]

MIFFLIN MISS HELEN

30 Park Place
Cardiff CF1 3BA, Telephone: 01222 398421
E-mail: 100757.1456@compuserve.com
Call date: July 1982, Lincoln's Inn
Qualifications: [LLB (Hons) (Leics)]

MIGDAL STEPHEN DAVID

Victoria Chambers
3rd Floor 177 Corporation Street, Birmingham
B4 6RG, Telephone: 0121 236 9900
Call date: July 1974, Inner Temple
Qualifications: [BA]

MILDON DAVID WALLIS

Essex Court Chambers
24 Lincoln's Inn Fields, London WC2A 3ED,
Telephone: 0171 813 8000
E-mail: clerksroom@essexcourt-chambers.co.uk
Call date: July 1980, Middle Temple
Qualifications: [MA, LLB (Cantab)]

MILES EDWARD NAPIER TREMAYNE

2 Harcourt Bldgs
1st Floor, Temple, London EC4Y 9DB,
Telephone: 0171 353 6961/7
Harcourt Chambers
Churchill House 3 St Aldate's Courtyard, St
Aldate's, Oxford OX1 1BN,
Telephone: 01865 791559
Call date: Feb 1989, Inner Temple
Qualifications: [BA (Oxon)]

MILES ROBERT JOHN

4 Stone Bldgs
Ground Floor, Lincoln's Inn, London
WC2A 3XT, Telephone: 0171 242 5524
E-mail: d.goddard@4stonebuildings.law.co.uk
Call date: Nov 1987, Lincoln's Inn
Qualifications: [BA, BCL (Oxon)]

MILFORD JOHN TILLMAN QC (1989)

Trinity Chambers
9-12 Trinity Chare, Quayside, Newcastle Upon
Tyne NE1 3DF, Telephone: 0191 232 1927
Call date: Nov 1969, Inner Temple
Recorder
Qualifications: [LLB (Exon)]

MILL IAN ALEXANDER

2 Hare Court
Ground Floor, Temple, London EC4Y 7BH,
Telephone: 0171 583 1770
E-mail: 2_Hare_Court@link.org
Call date: July 1981, Middle Temple
Qualifications: [MA (Cantab)]

MILLAR MS ALISON MARY

2 Crown Office Row
2nd Floor, Temple, London EC4Y 7HJ,
Telephone: 0171 797 8000
Call date: Nov 1995, Inner Temple
Qualifications: [BA (Cantab)]

MILLAR GAVIN JAMES

Doughty Street Chambers
11 Doughty Street, London WC1N 2PG,
Telephone: 0171 404 1313
E-mail: doughty_street@compuserve.com
Call date: July 1981, Lincoln's Inn
Qualifications: [BA (Oxon)]

MILLARD MARTIN RICHARD

Chambers of Raana Sheikh
Gray's Inn Chambers, Gray's Inn, London
WC1R, Telephone: 0171 831 5344
E-mail: s.mcblain@btinternet.com
Call date: Oct 1995, Middle Temple
Qualifications: [BA (New York), Dip in Law]

MILLER ANDREW

2 Temple Gardens
Temple, London EC4Y 9AY,
Telephone: 0171 583 6041 (12 Lines)
Call date: July 1989, Inner Temple
Qualifications: [LLB [So'ton]]

MILLER MRS CELIA FRANCES

East Anglian Chambers
Gresham House 5 Museum Street, Ipswich
IP1 1HQ, Telephone: 01473 214481
East Anglian Chambers
Sanders House 52 North Hill, Colchester
CO1 1PY, Telephone: 01206 572756
East Anglian Chambers
57 London Street, Norwich NR2 1HL,
Telephone: 01603 617351
Call date: July 1978, Inner Temple
Qualifications: [BA, LLB (Lond)]

MILLER MS HAYLEY JANE

Library Chambers
Gray's Inn Chambers, Gray's Inn, London
WC1R 5JA, Telephone: 0171 404 6500
Call date: Oct 1995, Inner Temple
Qualifications: [LLB (Sussex)]

MILLER MISS JANE ELIZABETH MACKAY

Pump Court Chambers
Upper Ground Floor 3 Pump Court, Temple,
London EC4Y 7AJ, Telephone: 0171 353 0711
Pump Court Chambers
31 Southgate Street, Winchester SO23 8EE,
Telephone: 01962 868161
Call date: Nov 1979, Inner Temple
Assistant Recorder
Qualifications: [LLB (Bris)]

MILLER JOHN NICHOLAS

Guildhall Chambers
23 Broad Street, Bristol BS1 2HG,
Telephone: 0117 9273366
Call date: July 1994, Inner Temple
Qualifications: [LLB]

MILLER KEITH STEWART HUNTER

Fountain Chambers
Cleveland Business Centre 1 Watson Street,
Middlesbrough TS1 2RQ,
Telephone: 01642 217037
Call date: July 1973, Middle Temple
Recorder
Qualifications: [LLB]

MILLER PAUL WAIND

Wilberforce Chambers
Bishop Lane, Hull HU1 1PA,
Telephone: 01482 323264
E-mail: clerks@hullbar.demon.co.uk
Call date: July 1974, Lincoln's Inn
Assistant Recorder
Qualifications: [MA (Oxon)]

MILLER PETER OWEN MICHAEL

2-3 Gray's Inn Square
Gray's Inn, London WC1R 5JH,
Telephone: 0171 242 4986
E-mail: chambers@2-3graysinnsquare.co.uk
Call date: Oct 1993, Lincoln's Inn
Qualifications: [LLB (Hons)(Lond)]

MILLER RICHARD HUGH QC (1995)

3 New Square
Lincoln's Inn, London WC2A 3RS,
Telephone: 0171 405 1111
Call date: July 1976, Middle Temple
Qualifications: [BSc]

MILLER RICHARD JAMES

Newport Chambers
12 Clytha Park Road, Newport, Gwent
NP9 47L, Telephone: 01633 267403/255855
Call date: Oct 1991, Gray's Inn
Qualifications: [LLB (Wales)]

MILLER ROBIN ANTHONY

2 King's Bench Walk
Ground Floor, Temple, London EC4Y 7DE,
Telephone: 0171 353 1746
E-mail: 2kbw@atlas.co.uk
King's Bench Chambers
115 North Hill, Plymouth PL4 8JY,
Telephone: 01752 221551
Call date: Nov 1960, Middle Temple
Recorder
Qualifications: [BA (Oxon)]

MILLER MISS SARAH ELIZABETH BARBARA

4 Field Court
Gray's Inn, London WC1R 5EA,
Telephone: 0171 440 6900
E-mail: chambers@4fieldcourt.co.uk
Call date: Nov 1971, Gray's Inn

D

MILLER SIMON RICHARD ANDREW

Enfield Chambers
36-38 London Road, Enfield, Middlesex
EN2 6DT, Telephone: 0181 364 5627
E-mail: Enfieldchambers@compuserve.com
Call date: Oct 1996, Lincoln's Inn
Qualifications: [LLB (Hons)(Leic)]

MILLER STEPHEN MACKENZIE QC (1990)

1 Crown Office Row
Ground Floor, Temple, London EC4Y 7HH,
Telephone: 0171 797 7500
Crown Office Row Chambers
Blenheim House 120 Church Street, Brighton,
Sussex BN1 1WH, Telephone: 01273 625625
Call date: July 1971, Middle Temple
Recorder
Qualifications: [BA Hons (Oxon)]

MILLETT KENNETH JAMES

1 Hare Court
Ground Floor, Temple, London EC4Y 7BE,
Telephone: 0171 353 3982/5324
Call date: July 1988, Inner Temple
Qualifications: [LLB]

MILLETT RICHARD LESTER

Essex Court Chambers
24 Lincoln's Inn Fields, London WC2A 3ED,
Telephone: 0171 813 8000
E-mail: clerksroom@essexcourt-chambers.co.uk
Call date: July 1985, Lincoln's Inn
Qualifications: [BA Cantab]

MILLIGAN IAIN ANSTRUTHER QC (1991)

20 Essex Street
London WC2R 3AL,
Telephone: 0171 583 9294
E-mail: clerks@20essexst.com
Call date: July 1973, Inner Temple
Qualifications: [MA (Cantab)]

MILLIKEN-SMITH MARK GORDON

3 Hare Court
1st Floor, Temple, London EC4Y 7BJ,
Telephone: 0171 353 7561
Call date: Nov 1986, Gray's Inn
Qualifications: [LLB(Bristol)]

MILLINGTON CHRISTOPHER JOHN

1 Fountain Court
Steelhouse Lane, Birmingham B4 6DR,
Telephone: 0121 236 5721
Call date: July 1976, Gray's Inn
Assistant Recorder
Qualifications: [LLM(B'ham)]

MILLS MISS BARBARA

4 Paper Bldgs
2nd Floor, Temple, London EC4Y 7EX,
Telephone: 0171 583 0816/071 353 1131
E-mail: clerks@4paperbuildings.co.uk
Call date: Oct 1990, Inner Temple
Qualifications: [LLB (Hull)]

MILLS CHRISTOPHER DAVID

19 Figtree Lane
Sheffield S1 2DJ, Telephone: 0114 2759708/
2738380
Call date: July 1972, Inner Temple
Qualifications: [LLB (Lond)]

MILLS COREY ARTHUR

Becket Chambers
17 New Dover Road, Canterbury, Kent
CT1 3AS, Telephone: 01227 786331
Call date: Nov 1987, Middle Temple
Qualifications: [LLB]

MILLS REGINALD STUART

First National Building
2nd Floor 24 Fenwick Street, Liverpool
L2 7NE, Telephone: 0151 236 2098
Call date: Oct 1992, Middle Temple
Qualifications: [LL.B (Hons)]

MILLS SIMON MARK

21 White Friars
Chester CH1 1NZ, Telephone: 01244 323070
Call date: Nov 1986, Inner Temple
Qualifications: [LLB(Birm)]

MILLS SIMON THOMAS

1 Essex Court
1st Floor, Temple, London EC4Y 9AR,
Telephone: 0171 936 3030
E-mail: one.essex_court@virgin.net
Call date: Nov 1994, Lincoln's Inn
Qualifications: [MA (Cantab)]

MILMO JOHN BOYLE MARTIN QC (1984)

1 High Pavement
Nottingham NG1 1HF,
Telephone: 0115 9418218
Door Tenant
9 Bedford Row
London WC1R 4AZ,
Telephone: 0171 242 3555
E-mail: clerks@9br.co.uk
Call date: Nov 1966, Lincoln's Inn
Qualifications: [MA, LLB (Dub)]

MILMO PATRICK HELENUS QC (1985)

5 Raymond Buildings
1st Floor, Gray's Inn, London WC1R 5BP,
Telephone: 0171 242 2902
Call date: July 1962, Middle Temple
Qualifications: [MA (Cantab)]

MILNE ALEXANDER HUGH

18 Red Lion Court
(Off Fleet Street), London EC4A 3EB,
Telephone: 0171 520 6000
Thornwood House
102 New London Road, Chelmsford, Essex
CM2 0RG, Telephone: 01245 280880
Call date: Nov 1981, Gray's Inn
Qualifications: [BA]

MILNE DAVID CALDER QC (1987)

Pump Court Tax Chambers
16 Bedford Row, London WC1R 4EB,
Telephone: 0171 414 8080
Call date: July 1970, Lincoln's Inn
Qualifications: [MA (Oxon), FCA]

MILNE MICHAEL

Resolution Chambers
Oak Lodge 55 Poolbrook Road, Malvern,
Worcestershire WR14 3JN,
Telephone: 01684 561279
46/48 Essex Street
London WC2R 3GH,
Telephone: 0171 583 8899
Door Tenant
Call date: July 1987, Lincoln's Inn
Qualifications: [BA, Dip Law, FRICS, FCIAr]

MILNE RICHARD JAMES

23 Essex Street
London WC2R 3AS,
Telephone: 0171 413 0353/353 3533
E-mail: clerks@essexstreet23.demon.co.uk
Call date: Oct 1992, Middle Temple
Qualifications: [MA (Hons)(Oxon), Diploma in Law]

MILNER JONATHAN DAVID BENJAMIN

2 Harcourt Bldgs
2nd Floor, Temple, London EC4Y 9DB,
Telephone: 0171 353 8415
E-mail: clerks@twoharcourtbldgs.demon.co.uk
Call date: July 1977, Inner Temple
Qualifications: [LLB (Lond)]

MILSOM MS CATHERINE MARY

3 Temple Gardens
3rd Floor, Temple, London EC4Y 9AU,
Telephone: 0171 353 0832
Call date: Nov 1994, Inner Temple
Qualifications: [BA, Cert.ED]

MINHAS MS RAFHAT

Northeastern Law Chambers
The Chocolate Factory B305 Clarendon Road /
Western Road, Wood Green, London
N22 6UN, Telephone: 0181 881 3890
Call date: Nov 1994, Gray's Inn
Qualifications: [BSc, LLB]

MINIHAN SEAN THOMAS

6 Gray's Inn Square
Ground Floor, Gray's Inn, London WC1R 5AZ,
Telephone: 0171 242 1052
Call date: Nov 1988, Gray's Inn
Qualifications: [LLB]

MINTZ SIMON HAROLD

Chavasse Court Chambers
2nd Floor Chavasse Court, 24 Lord Street,
Liverpool L2 1TA, Telephone: 0151 707 1191
Call date: Nov 1996, Inner Temple
Qualifications: [BA (Newcastle)]

MIRIC ROBIN

10 King's Bench Walk
1st Floor, Temple, London EC4Y 7EB,
Telephone: 0171 353 2501
Call date: July 1978, Gray's Inn
Qualifications: [LLB]

MIRWITCH MISS JANE

4 Brick Court
1st Floor, Temple, London EC4Y 9AD,
Telephone: 0171 583 8455
Call date: Nov 1974, Middle Temple
Qualifications: [LLM (Lond)]

MIRZA MISS SAIRA

169 Temple Chambers
Temple Avenue, London EC4Y 0DA,
Telephone: 0171 583 7644
Call date: Oct 1996, Gray's Inn
Qualifications: [LLB]

MISCAMPBELL NORMAN ALEXANDER QC (1974)

1 Temple Gardens
1st Floor, Temple, London EC4Y 9BB,
Telephone: 0171 353 0407/583 1315
E-mail: clerks@1templegardens.co.uk
Call date: May 1952, Inner Temple
Recorder
Qualifications: [MA (Oxon)]

MISCAMPBELL MISS P. BERNADETTE

10 King's Bench Walk
Ground Floor, Temple, London EC4Y 7EB,
Telephone: 0171 353 7742
E-mail: 10kbw@lineone.net
Call date: Nov 1980, Middle Temple
Qualifications: [LLB (Lond), M.Sc (Lond)]

MISHCON MISS JANE MALCA

4 Paper Bldgs
Ground Floor, Temple, London EC4Y 7EX,
Telephone: 0171 353 3366/583 7155
E-mail: clerks@4paperbuildings.com
Call date: July 1979, Gray's Inn
Qualifications: [BA (Oxon)]

MISHCON OLIVER ZEBEDEE

4 King's Bench Walk
Ground/First Floor, Temple, London
EC4Y 7DL, Telephone: 0171 822 8822
E-mail: 4kbw@barristersatlaw.com
Call date: Nov 1993, Gray's Inn
Qualifications: [LLB]

MISKIN CHARLES JAMES MONCKTON

23 Essex Street
London WC2R 3AS,
Telephone: 0171 413 0353/353 3533
E-mail: clerks@essexstreet23.demon.co.uk
Call date: July 1975, Gray's Inn
Assistant Recorder
Qualifications: [MA (Oxon)]

MISKIN MISS CLAIRE MARIANNE

39 Essex Street
London WC2R 3AT,
Telephone: 0171 583 1111
E-mail: clerks@39essex.co.uk
Call date: Nov 1970, Middle Temple
Qualifications: [LLM (Lond)]

MISNER PHILIP LAWRENCE IAN

6 Gray's Inn Square
Ground Floor, Gray's Inn, London WC1R 5AZ,
Telephone: 0171 242 1052
Call date: July 1984, Middle Temple
Qualifications: [LLB (B'ham)]

MISZKIEL MISS URSULA

3 Pump Court
2nd Floor, Temple, London EC4Y 7AJ,
Telephone: 0171 353 1356 (3 Lines)
Call date: Oct 1994, Gray's Inn
Qualifications: [LLB (Leeds)]

MITCHELL (RICHARD) JOHN

One Garden Court
Ground Floor, Temple, London EC4Y 9BJ,
Telephone: 0171 797 7900
Call date: July 1972, Middle Temple
Qualifications: [MA (Cantab)]

MITCHELL ANDREW EDWARD

Fountain Court
Temple, London EC4Y 9DH,
Telephone: 0171 583 3335
E-mail: chambers@fountaincourt.co.uk
Call date: Nov 1992, Middle Temple
Qualifications: [MA Hons (Cantab), BCL
(Oxon)]

MITCHELL ANDREW JONATHAN MILLS

6 Park Square
Leeds LS1 2LW, Telephone: 0113 2459763
E-mail: chambers@no6.co.uk
Call date: Nov 1991, Lincoln's Inn
Qualifications: [LLB (Hons) (Leeds)]

MITCHELL ANDREW ROBERT

Furnival Chambers
32 Furnival Street, London EC4A 1JQ,
Telephone: 0171 405 3232
E-mail: clerks@furnivallaw.co.uk
Call date: July 1976, Gray's Inn
Assistant Recorder

MITCHELL MS ANNE CUMMING

Cleveland Chambers
63-65 Borough Road, Middlesbrough,
Cleveland TS1 3AA, Telephone: 01642 226036
Call date: Oct 1994, Gray's Inn
Qualifications: [LLB]

MITCHELL BRENTON BALLINGTINE

Bell Yard Chambers
116/118 Chancery Lane, London WC2A 1PP,
Telephone: 0171 306 9292
Call date: July 1973, Lincoln's Inn
Qualifications: [DipCrim]

MITCHELL CHRISTOPHER RICHARD

Hollis Whiteman Chambers
3rd/4th Floor Queen Elizabeth Bldg, Temple,
London EC4Y 9BS, Telephone: 0171 583 5766
E-mail: hollis.whiteman@btinternet.com
Call date: Nov 1968, Gray's Inn
Recorder
Qualifications: [LLB, MA (Oxon)]

MITCHELL DAVID CHARLES

Broadway House Chambers
Broadway House 9 Bank Street, Bradford,
West Yorkshire BD1 1TW,
Telephone: 01274 722560
Call date: July 1972, Inner Temple
Recorder
Qualifications: [MA (Oxon)]

MITCHELL GREGORY CHARLES MATHEW QC (1997)

3 Verulam Buildings
London WC1R 5NT,
Telephone: 0171 831 8441
E-mail: clerks@3verulam.co.uk
Call date: July 1979, Gray's Inn
Qualifications: [BA (Lond), PhD]

MITCHELL IAN MARCUS

Phoenix Chambers
First Floor Gray's Inn Chambers, Gray's Inn,
London WC1R 5JA, Telephone: 0171 404 7888
Call date: Nov 1995, Lincoln's Inn
Qualifications: [B.Eng (Hons)]

MITCHELL JAMES RONALD

Broad Chare
33 Broad Chare, Newcastle Upon Tyne
NE1 3DQ, Telephone: 0191 232 0541
Call date: July 1973, Inner Temple
Recorder

MITCHELL MISS JANET VIVIAN

4 Brick Court
Temple, London EC4Y 9AD,
Telephone: 0171 797 8910
Call date: Feb 1978, Middle Temple
Qualifications: [BA (Lond)]

MITCHELL JONATHAN HOWARD

24 The Ropewalk
Nottingham NG1 5EF,
Telephone: 0115 9472581
E-mail: clerk@ropewalk.co.uk
Call date: Oct 1992, Gray's Inn
Qualifications: [LL.B (Wales)]

MITCHELL JONATHAN STUART

3 Gray's Inn Square
Ground Floor, London WC1R 5AH,
Telephone: 0171 520 5600
E-mail: gis3@btinternet.com
Call date: Nov 1974, Middle Temple
Qualifications: [MA]

MITCHELL MISS JULIANA MARIE

2 Harcourt Bldgs
Ground Floor/Left, Temple, London
EC4Y 9DB, Telephone: 0171 583 9020
E-mail: clerks@harcourt.co.uk
Call date: Oct 1994, Lincoln's Inn
Qualifications: [LLB (Hons)(B'ham), BCL
(Oxon)]

MITCHELL KEITH ARNO

3 Hare Court
1st Floor, Temple, London EC4Y 7BJ,
Telephone: 0171 353 7561
Call date: Nov 1981, Inner Temple
Qualifications: [BA]

MITCHELL MS LESLEY

Chambers of Lesley Mitchell
Stapleton Lodge 71 Hamilton Road, Brentford,
Middlesex TW8 0QJ,
Telephone: 0181 568 2164
Call date: Nov 1987, Inner Temple
Qualifications: [B.Sc (Lond), Dip in Law]

MITCHELL MISS MARIE CATHLEEN

15 Winckley Square
Preston PR1 3JJ, Telephone: 01772 252828
E-mail: clerks@winckleysq.demon.co.uk
Call date: Oct 1991, Gray's Inn
Qualifications: [LLB]

MITCHELL NIGEL CAMPBELL

3 Paper Bldgs
1st Floor, Temple, London EC4Y 7EU,
Telephone: 0171 583 8055
E-mail: london@3paper.com
20 Lorne Park Road
Bournemouth BH1 1JN,
Telephone: 01202 292102 (5 Lines)
4 St Peter Street
Winchester SO23 8OW,
Telephone: 01962 868884
Call date: Feb 1978, Lincoln's Inn
Qualifications: [LLB (Lond)]

MITCHELL PAUL

13 King's Bench Walk
1st Floor, Temple, London EC4Y 7EN,
Telephone: 0171 353 7204
E-mail: clerks@13kbw.law.co.uk
King's Bench Chambers
32 Beaumont Street, Oxford OX1 2NP,
Telephone: 01865 311066
E-mail: clerks@kbc-oxford.law.co.uk
Call date: Nov 1994, Inner Temple
Qualifications: [BA (York), CPE (City)]

MITCHELL PETER

29 Bedford Row Chambers
London WC1R 4HE,
Telephone: 0171 831 2626
Call date: Oct 1996, Inner Temple
Qualifications: [LLB (Lond)]

MITCHELL MRS SALLY

Counsels' Chambers
2nd Floor 10-11 Gray's Inn Square, London
WC1R 5JD, Telephone: 0171 405 2576
Door Tenant
Call date: Oct 1990, Inner Temple
Qualifications: [LLB]

MITCHELL THOMAS JARLETH DAVID

The Corn Exchange
5th Floor Fenwick Street, Liverpool L2 7QS,
Telephone: 0151 227 1081/5009
Call date: Oct 1995, Lincoln's Inn
Qualifications: [BA (Hons) MA (Oxon), CPE
(Manc)]

MITCHELL-HEGGS CHRISTOPHER KENNETH

Francis Taylor Bldg
3rd Floor, Temple, London EC4Y 7BY,
Telephone: 0171 797 7250
Call date: Feb 1966, Inner Temple
Qualifications: [diplome D'etudes sup]

MITCHESON THOMAS GEORGE MOSELEY

3 New Square
Lincoln's Inn, London WC2A 3RS,
Telephone: 0171 405 1111
Call date: Oct 1996, Inner Temple
Qualifications: [BA (Cantab), CPE (Lond)]

MITROPOULOS MS GEORGIA

46/48 Essex Street
London WC2R 3GH,
Telephone: 0171 583 8899
Call date: July 1989, Gray's Inn
Qualifications: [BA (Wales), DipLaw]

MITTING JOHN EDWARD QC (1987)

4 Fountain Court
Steelhouse Lane, Birmingham B4 6DR,
Telephone: 0121 236 3476
Call date: July 1970, Gray's Inn
Recorder
Qualifications: [BA, LLB (Cantab)]

MOAT FRANK ROBERT

Pump Court Chambers
Upper Ground Floor 3 Pump Court, Temple,
London EC4Y 7AJ, Telephone: 0171 353 0711
Pump Court Chambers
31 Southgate Street, Winchester SO23 8EE,
Telephone: 01962 868161
Call date: Nov 1970, Lincoln's Inn
Recorder
Qualifications: [LLB]

MOAT RICHARD MARK

4 Fountain Court
Steelhouse Lane, Birmingham B4 6DR,
Telephone: 0121 236 3476
Call date: July 1985, Lincoln's Inn
Qualifications: [BA (Oxon)]

MOBEDJI FIRDAUS JEHANGIR

7 Stone Bldgs
1st Floor, Lincoln's Inn, London WC2A 3SZ,
Telephone: 0171 242 0961
Call date: July 1977, Lincoln's Inn
Qualifications: [BA (Hons)]

MODGIL MISS SANGITA

1 Crown Office Row
2nd Floor, Temple, London EC4Y 7HH,
Telephone: 0171 797 7111
Call date: Oct 1990, Gray's Inn
Qualifications: [LLB (Leic)]

MOERAN FENNER OLANDO

3 Stone Bldgs
Ground Floor, Lincoln's Inn, London
WC2A 3XL, Telephone: 0171 242 4937/
405 8358
Call date: Oct 1996, Lincoln's Inn
Qualifications: [BSc (Hons)(Bris), Dip in Law
(City)]

MOFFETT JONATHAN KEITH

4-5 Gray's Inn Square
Ground Floor, Gray's Inn, London WC1R 5AY,
Telephone: 0171 404 5252
E-mail: chambers@4-5graysinnsquare.co.uk
Call date: Oct 1996, Inner Temple
Qualifications: [BA, LLM (Cantab)]

MOGER CHRISTOPHER RICHARD DERWENT QC (1992)

4 Pump Court
Temple, London EC4Y 7AN,
Telephone: 0171 353 2656/9
E-mail: 4_pump_court@compuserve.com
Call date: July 1972, Inner Temple
Recorder
Qualifications: [LLB (Bris), FCIArb]

MOGRIDGE FRASER MCLEAN

Chichester Chambers
12 North Pallant, Chichester, West Sussex
PO19 1TQ, Telephone: 01243 784538
Call date: Nov 1995, Inner Temple
Qualifications: [LLB (Soton)]

D

MOIR MRS JUDITH PATRICIA

Broad Chare
33 Broad Chare, Newcastle Upon Tyne
NE1 3DQ, Telephone: 0191 232 0541
Call date: Nov 1978, Gray's Inn
Recorder
Qualifications: [BA (Oxon)]

MOLE DAVID RICHARD PENTON QC (1990)

4-5 Gray's Inn Square
Ground Floor, Gray's Inn, London WC1R 5AY,
Telephone: 0171 404 5252
E-mail: chambers@4-5graysinnsquare.co.uk
Call date: Nov 1970, Inner Temple
Recorder
Qualifications: [MA (TCD) LLM (Lond)]

MOLL CHRISTIAAN ERIC

55 Temple Chambers
Temple Avenue, London EC4Y 0HP,
Telephone: 0171 353 7400
Call date: July 1986, Middle Temple
Qualifications: [BA (Hons) (Oxon)]

MOLONEY PATRICK MARTIN JOSEPH

1 Brick Court
1st Floor, Temple, London EC4Y 9BY,
Telephone: 0171 353 8845
E-mail: clerks@1brickcourt.co.uk
Call date: July 1976, Middle Temple
Qualifications: [BA, BCL (Oxon)]

MOLONEY TIMOTHY JOHN

14 Tooks Court
Cursitor St, London EC4A 1LB,
Telephone: 0171 405 8828
E-mail: clerks @tooks.law.co.uk
Call date: Nov 1993, Middle Temple
Qualifications: [LLB (Hons)(B'ham), Ph.D
(B'ham)]

MOLYNEUX BRENTON JOHN

29 Bedford Row Chambers
London WC1R 4HE,
Telephone: 0171 831 2626
Call date: Feb 1994, Lincoln's Inn
Qualifications: [BA (Hons, Oxon), Dip. in Law]

MOLYNEUX SIMON ROWLEY

4 Brick Court
Temple, London EC4Y 9AD,
Telephone: 0171 797 8910
Call date: Apr 1986, Inner Temple
Qualifications: [BSc (Econ) MA, (Wales)
M.Phil]

MONAGHAN MS KARON

14 Tooks Court
Cursitor St, London EC4A 1LB,
Telephone: 0171 405 8828
E-mail: clerks @tooks.law.co.uk
Call date: July 1989, Inner Temple
Qualifications: [LLB]

MONAGHAN MARK TERENCE

Cobden House Chambers
19 Quay Street, Manchester M3 3HN,
Telephone: 0161 833 6000
E-mail: clerks@cobden.co.uk
Call date: July 1987, Lincoln's Inn
Qualifications: [LLB (Hons) (Sheff)]

MONAGHAN MS SUSAN MARY

Enfield Chambers
36-38 London Road, Enfield, Middlesex
EN2 6DT, Telephone: 0181 364 5627
E-mail: Enfieldchambers@compuserve.com
Call date: Oct 1995, Inner Temple
Qualifications: [BA (Galway), LLB (Wales)]

MONDAIR RASHPAL SINGH

Claremont Chambers
26 Waterloo Road, Wolverhampton WV1 4BL,
Telephone: 01902 426222
Call date: Nov 1995, Middle Temple
Qualifications: [Dip Law, BDS]

MONEY ERNLE DAVID DRUMMOND

1 Gray's Inn Square
Ground Floor, London WC1R 5AA,
Telephone: 0171 405 8946/7/8
Call date: Feb 1958, Lincoln's Inn
Qualifications: [MA (Oxon)]

MONK DAVID KENNETH

2 New Street
Leicester LE1 5NA, Telephone: 0116 2625906
Call date: July 1991, Middle Temple
Qualifications: [BA (Hons)]

MONKCOM STEPHEN PHILIP

Francis Taylor Bldg
3rd Floor, Temple, London EC4Y 7BY,
Telephone: 0171 797 7250
Call date: Nov 1974, Middle Temple
Qualifications: [BA (Oxon)]

MONRO DAVIES MS TIFFANY LEE

4 Brick Court
1st Floor, Temple, London EC4Y 9AD,
Telephone: 0171 583 8455
Call date: July 1984, Gray's Inn
Qualifications: [LLB Hons (Lond)]

MONSON THE HON ANDREW ANTHONY JOHN

5 Raymond Buildings
1st Floor, Gray's Inn, London WC1R 5BP,
Telephone: 0171 242 2902
Call date: Nov 1983, Middle Temple
Qualifications: [MA (Oxon)]

MONTAGUE MS SUSAN

1 Pump Court
Lower Ground Floor, Temple, London
EC4Y 7AB, Telephone: 0171 583 2012/
353 4341
E-mail: (name) @1pumpcourt.co.uk
Call date: Nov 1981, Inner Temple
Qualifications: [BA]

MONTEITH KEIR BARTLEY

Acre Lane Neighbourhood Chambers
30A Acre Lane, London SW2 5SG,
Telephone: 0171 274 4400
Call date: May 1994, Lincoln's Inn
Qualifications: [LLB (Hons, Essex)]

MONTGOMERY MISS CLARE PATRICIA QC (1996)

3 Raymond Buildings
Gray's Inn, London WC1R 5BH,
Telephone: 0171 831 3833
E-mail: chambers@threeraymond.demon.co.uk
Call date: Nov 1980, Gray's Inn
Qualifications: [LLB (Lond)]

MONTGOMERY JAMES ARDRAN

1 Crown Office Row
2nd Floor, Temple, London EC4Y 7HH,
Telephone: 0171 797 7111
Call date: Nov 1989, Lincoln's Inn
Qualifications: [LLB]

MONTGOMERY PROFESSOR JOHN WARWICK

Francis Taylor Bldg
3rd Floor, Temple, London EC4Y 7BY,
Telephone: 0171 797 7250
Call date: July 1984, Middle Temple
Qualifications: [MA Calif PhD Chicago, STM
Wittenberg, MPhil Essex, Dip Intl Inst Human,
Rights Strasbourg, D d'U Strasbourg]

MONTGOMERY MISS KRISTINA (AILEEN)

8 Fountain Court
Steelhouse Lane, Birmingham B4 6DR,
Telephone: 0121 236 5514/5
E-mail: clerks@no8chambers.co.uk
Call date: Oct 1993, Middle Temple
Qualifications: [LLB (Hons)(Lond)]

MONTGOMERY ROBERT MICHAEL

Pump Court Chambers
Upper Ground Floor 3 Pump Court, Temple,
London EC4Y 7AJ, Telephone: 0171 353 0711
Pump Court Chambers
31 Southgate Street, Winchester SO23 8EE,
Telephone: 01962 868161
Chavasse Court Chambers
2nd Floor Chavasse Court, 24 Lord Street,
Liverpool L2 1TA, Telephone: 0151 707 1191
Call date: July 1972, Inner Temple
Qualifications: [MA (Cantab)]

D

MONTGOMERY TONY KEVIN

Fleet Chambers
Mitre House 44-46 Fleet Street, London
EC4Y 1BN, Telephone: 0171 936 3707
Call date: Nov 1987, Inner Temple
Qualifications: [LLB (Brunel)]

MONTROSE RODNEY STUART

Cloisters
1st Floor, Temple, London EC4Y 7AA,
Telephone: 0171 827 4000
E-mail: clerks@cloisters.com
Call date: May 1972, Middle Temple
Qualifications: [LLB]

MONTY SIMON TREVOR

2 Crown Office Row
2nd Floor, Temple, London EC4Y 7HJ,
Telephone: 0171 797 8000
Call date: July 1982, Middle Temple
Qualifications: [LLB]

MOODY NEIL ROBERT

2 Temple Gardens
Temple, London EC4Y 9AY,
Telephone: 0171 583 6041 (12 Lines)
Call date: Nov 1989, Gray's Inn
Qualifications: [MA (Oxon)]

MOODY-STUART THOMAS

8 New Square
Lincoln's Inn, London WC2A 3QP,
Telephone: 0171 405 4321
Call date: Nov 1995, Middle Temple
Qualifications: [BA (Hons)]

MOON PHILIP CHARLES ANGUS

3 Serjeants Inn
London EC4Y 1BQ,
Telephone: 0171 353 5537
E-mail: available upon request
Call date: Nov 1986, Middle Temple
Qualifications: [MA (Cantab)]

MOONCEY EBRAHAM MOHAMED

9 Bedford Row
London WC1R 4AZ,
Telephone: 0171 242 3555
E-mail: clerks@9br.co.uk
Call date: Nov 1983, Gray's Inn
Qualifications: [LLB]

MOONEY STEPHEN JOHN

Albion Chambers
Broad Street, Bristol BS1 1DR,
Telephone: 0117 9272144
Call date: Nov 1987, Inner Temple
Qualifications: [LLB (Hull)]

MOOR PHILIP DRURY

1 Mitre Ct Bldgs
Ground Floor, Temple, London EC4Y 7BS,
Telephone: 0171 797 7070
Call date: July 1982, Inner Temple
Qualifications: [MA (Oxon)]

MOOR MISS SARAH KATHRYN

Old Square Chambers
1 Verulam Buildings, Gray's Inn, London
WC1R 5LQ, Telephone: 0171 831 0801
Old Square Chambers
Hanover House 47 Corn Street, Bristol
BS1 1HT, Telephone: 0117 9277111
Call date: Oct 1991, Middle Temple
Qualifications: [BA Hons (Cantab)]

MOORE MISS ALISON DENISE

Counsels' Chambers
2nd Floor 10-11 Gray's Inn Square, London
WC1R 5JD, Telephone: 0171 405 2576
Call date: Oct 1994, Middle Temple
Qualifications: [BA (Hons)(Oxon)]

MOORE ANDREW DAVID

18 St John Street
Manchester M3 4EA,
Telephone: 0161 278 1800
Call date: Nov 1996, Inner Temple
Qualifications: [BA, PHd (Manch)]

MOORE ARTHUR JAMES

Arden Chambers
27 John Street, London WC1N 2BL,
Telephone: 0171 242 4244
Call date: Oct 1992, Gray's Inn
Qualifications: [BA (Oxon), Dip Law (City)]

MOORE MR CRAIG IAN

Barnard's Inn Chambers
6th Floor Halton House, 20-23 Holborn,
London EC1N 2JD, Telephone: 0171 242 8508
E-mail: clerks@barnards-inn-chambers.co.uk
Call date: July 1989, Middle Temple
Qualifications: [LLB [Lond]]

MOORE DANNY GEORGE

5 Paper Bldgs
Lower Ground Floor, Temple, London
EC4Y 7HB, Telephone: 0171 353 5638
E-mail: 107722,633@compuserve.com
Call date: Nov 1994, Middle Temple
Qualifications: [LLB (Hons)]

MOORE DAVID JAMES

Tindal Chambers
3/5 New Street, Chelmsford, Essex CM1 1NT,
Telephone: 01245 267742
Tindal Chambers
3 Waxhouse Gate, St Albans, Herts AL5 4DU,
Telephone: 01727 843383
Call date: July 1983, Middle Temple
Qualifications: [BA, MA (Lond)]

MOORE DOUGLAS MARKS

6 King's Bench Walk
Ground Floor, Temple, London EC4Y 7DR,
Telephone: 0171 583 0410
Call date: Nov 1979, Gray's Inn
Assistant Recorder
Qualifications: [BA (Belfast), Dip.Soc.Anth]

MOORE JAMES ANTHONY

2 Gray's Inn Square Chambers
2nd Floor, Gray's Inn, London WC1R 5AA,
Telephone: 0171 242 0328/071 405 1317
E-mail: clerks@2gis.co.uk
Call date: July 1984, Lincoln's Inn
Qualifications: [BA]

MOORE MISS JENNIFER MARY

Independent Barristers Clerk
Room 5, 2nd Floor 15 Castle Street, Exeter,
Devon EX4 3PT, Telephone: 01392 210900
E-mail: cathedral.chambers@eclipse.co.uk
Call date: Oct 1992, Gray's Inn
Qualifications: [LL.B (Brunel)]

MOORE MISS JOAN YVETTE

Verulam Chambers
Peer House 8-14 Verulam Street, Gray's Inn,
London WC1X 8LZ,
Telephone: 0171 813 2400
Call date: Nov 1986, Lincoln's Inn
Qualifications: [LLB]

MOORE MISS KATHERINE ELIZABETH

East Anglian Chambers
57 London Street, Norwich NR2 1HL,
Telephone: 01603 617351
Call date: Oct 1995, Middle Temple
Qualifications: [BA (Hons)]

MOORE MISS KIRSTIE ELIZABETH

Regent Chambers
29 Regent Road, Hanley, Stoke On Trent
ST1 3BP, Telephone: 01782 286666
E-mail: regent@ftech.co.uk
Call date: Oct 1994, Middle Temple
Qualifications: [LLB (Hons)(Lond), LLM
(Sheff)]

MOORE MARTIN LUKE

Erskine Chambers
30 Lincoln's Inn Fields, Lincoln's Inn, London
WC2A 3PF, Telephone: 0171 242 5532
E-mail: Clerks@Erskine-Chambers.law.co.uk
Call date: July 1982, Lincoln's Inn
Qualifications: [BA (Oxon)]

MOORE MISS MIRANDA JAYNE

5 Paper Bldgs
1st Floor, Temple, London EC4Y 7HB,
Telephone: 0171 583 6117
E-mail: clerks@5-paperbuildings.law.co.uk
Call date: July 1983, Lincoln's Inn
Qualifications: [BSc (Aston)]

D

MOORE NEIL PATRICK

13 King's Bench Walk
1st Floor, Temple, London EC4Y 7EN,
Telephone: 0171 353 7204
E-mail: clerks@13kbw.law.co.uk
King's Bench Chambers
32 Beaumont Street, Oxford OX1 2NP,
Telephone: 01865 311066
E-mail: clerks@kbc-oxford.law.co.uk
Call date: July 1986, Gray's Inn
Qualifications: [LLB (Hons) (Notts)]

MOORE RODERICK ANDREW MCGOWAN

Warwick House Chambers
8 Warwick Court, Gray's Inn, London
WC1R 5DJ, Telephone: 0171 430 2323
Call date: Nov 1993, Inner Temple
Qualifications: [LLB (So'ton)]

MOORE ROGER ANSON

New Court Chambers
3 Broad Chare, Newcastle Upon Tyne
NE1 3DQ, Telephone: 0191 232 1980
Call date: July 1969, Lincoln's Inn
Qualifications: [LLM]

MOORE MISS SARAH ELIZABETH

4-5 Gray's Inn Square
Ground Floor, Gray's Inn, London WC1R 5AY,
Telephone: 0171 404 5252
E-mail: chambers@4-5graysinnsquare.co.uk
Call date: Nov 1990, Middle Temple
Qualifications: [BA, LLM (Cantab)]

MOORE MRS THERESE FINOLA

3 Dr Johnson's Bldgs
Ground Floor, Temple, London EC4Y 7BA,
Telephone: 0171 353 4854
Call date: July 1988, Lincoln's Inn
Qualifications: [MA, BA (Hons) Soton]

MOORE PROFESSOR VICTOR WILLIAM EDWARD

2 Mitre Ct Bldgs
2nd Floor, Temple, London EC4Y 7BX,
Telephone: 0171 583 1380
Call date: May 1992, Gray's Inn
Qualifications: [LLB (Lond), LLM (Lond)]

MOORE-GRAHAM MISS FIONA ADELE

3 Paper Bldgs
2nd Floor, Temple, London EC4Y 7EU,
Telephone: 0171 353 6208
Call date: Nov 1986, Gray's Inn
Qualifications: [LLB (Hons)(Leic)]

MOORES TIMOTHY KIERON

17 Carlton Crescent
Southampton SO15 2XR,
Telephone: 01703 320320
E-mail: km@bar-17cc.demon.co.uk
Call date: July 1987, Lincoln's Inn
Qualifications: [LLB (Bristol)]

MOORMAN MISS LUCINDA CLAIRE

Farrar's Building
Temple, London EC4Y 7BD,
Telephone: 0171 583 9241
E-mail: chambers@farrarsbuilding.co.uk
Call date: Nov 1992, Inner Temple
Qualifications: [LLM (Cantab)]

MORAN ANDREW GERARD QC (1994)

22 Old Bldgs
Lincoln's Inn, London WC2A 3UJ,
Telephone: 0171 831 0222
25 Byrom Street
Manchester M3 4PF,
Telephone: 0161 829 2100
E-mail: Byromst25@aol.com
Call date: Nov 1976, Gray's Inn
Recorder
Qualifications: [MA (Oxon)]

MORAN ANDREW JOHN

One Hare Court
1st Floor, Temple, London EC4Y 7BE,
Telephone: 0171 353 3171
E-mail: admin-oneharecourt@btinternet.com
Call date: Feb 1989, Middle Temple
Qualifications: [LLB (Lond), BCL (Oxon)]

MORAN THOMAS

New Court Chambers
3 Broad Chare, Newcastle Upon Tyne
NE1 3DQ, Telephone: 0191 232 1980
Call date: Nov 1996, Gray's Inn
Qualifications: [LLB (B'ham)]

MORAN VINCENT JOHN

12 King's Bench Walk
Temple, London EC4Y 7EL,
Telephone: 0171 583 0811
E-mail: chambers@12kbw.co.uk
Call date: Oct 1991, Gray's Inn
Qualifications: [MA (Cantab), Dip Law (City)]

MORCOM CHRISTOPHER QC (1991)

One Raymond Buildings
Gray's Inn, London WC1R 5BH,
Telephone: 0171 430 1234
E-mail: chambers@ipbar1rb.com;
clerks@ipbar1rb.com
Call date: July 1963, Middle Temple
Qualifications: [MA (Cantab)]

MORE O'FERRALL MISS GERALDINE ANN

1 Pump Court
Lower Ground Floor, Temple, London
EC4Y 7AB, Telephone: 0171 583 2012/
353 4341
E-mail: (name) @1pumpcourt.co.uk
Call date: July 1983, Middle Temple

MOREL PETER HOWITT EDWARD

Counsels' Chambers
2nd Floor 10-11 Gray's Inn Square, London
WC1R 5JD, Telephone: 0171 405 2576
Call date: Oct 1993, Inner Temple
Qualifications: [BA (Manch), CPE]

MORELAND MISS PENELOPE JANE

New Court Chambers
3 Broad Chare, Newcastle Upon Tyne
NE1 3DQ, Telephone: 0191 232 1980
Call date: July 1986, Gray's Inn
Qualifications: [MA (Cantab)]

MORELLI MISS LUISA TERESA

Westgate Chambers
16-17 Wellington Square, Hastings, East Sussex
TN34 1PB, Telephone: 01424 432105
Call date: Nov 1993, Middle Temple
Qualifications: [BA (Hons)(Sussex), CPE
(Brighton), Dip in Law]

MORGAN (THOMAS) JEREMY

6 Pump Court
Ground Floor, Temple, London EC4Y 7AR,
Telephone: 0171 583 6013/2510
Call date: Apr 1989, Middle Temple
Qualifications: [BA (Oxon), BA (Kent)]

MORGAN ADAM GEOFFREY

2 Dr Johnson's Building
Temple, London EC4Y 7AY,
Telephone: 0171 353 4716
Call date: Nov 1996, Gray's Inn
Qualifications: [LLB, LLM (Lond)]

MORGAN MS ADRIENNE

4 King's Bench Walk
2nd Floor, Temple, London EC4Y 7DL,
Telephone: 0171 353 3581
Call date: Nov 1988, Gray's Inn
Qualifications: [BA (Hons) (Lond)]

MORGAN ANDREW JAMES

Priory Chambers
2 Fountain Court, Steelhouse Lane,
Birmingham B4 6DR,
Telephone: 0121 236 3882/1375
Call date: Oct 1996, Inner Temple
Qualifications: [BA (Cantab)]

MORGAN DR AUSTEN JUDE

3 Temple Gardens
3rd Floor, Temple, London EC4Y 9AU,
Telephone: 0171 353 0832
Call date: Oct 1995, Lincoln's Inn
Qualifications: [BSc (Hons)(Bris), PhD
(Belfast)]

MORGAN CHARLES JAMES ARTHUR

Enterprise Chambers
9 Old Square, Lincoln's Inn, London
WC2A 3SR, Telephone: 0171 405 9471
Enterprise Chambers
65 Quayside, Newcastle upon Tyne NE1 3DS,
Telephone: 0191 222 3344
Enterprise Chambers
38 Park Square, Leeds LS1 2PA,
Telephone: 01132 460391
Call date: July 1978, Middle Temple
Qualifications: [MA, FCIArb]

MORGAN CHRISTOPHER JOHN

1 Paper Bldgs
1st Floor, Temple, London EC4Y 7EP,
Telephone: 0171 353 3728/4953
Call date: July 1987, Middle Temple
Qualifications: [LLB (Hons)]

MORGAN COLIN THOMAS PATRICK

Chichester Chambers
12 North Pallant, Chichester, West Sussex
PO19 1TQ, Telephone: 01243 784538
Call date: Nov 1989, Middle Temple
Qualifications: [BA (Oxon), Dip Law]

MORGAN DAVID SIMON SELBY

St John's Chambers
Small Street, Bristol BS1 1DW,
Telephone: 0117 9213456/298514
E-mail: clerks@stjohns.uk.com
Call date: Nov 1988, Gray's Inn

MORGAN DAVID WYNN

30 Park Place
Cardiff CF1 3BA, Telephone: 01222 398421
E-mail: 100757.1456@compuserve.com
Farrar's Building
Temple, London EC4Y 7BD,
Telephone: 0171 583 9241
E-mail: chambers@farrarsbuilding.co.uk
Door Tenant
Call date: Nov 1976, Gray's Inn
Recorder
Qualifications: [BA (Oxon) (Hons)]

MORGAN DYLAN ROBERT

17 Carlton Crescent
Southampton SO15 2XR,
Telephone: 01703 320320
E-mail: km@bar-17cc.demon.co.uk
Call date: July 1986, Gray's Inn
Qualifications: [LLB (CNAA)]

MORGAN EDWARD PATRICK

Deans Court Chambers
Cumberland House Crown Square, Manchester
M3 3HA, Telephone: 0161 834 4097
E-mail: deanscourt@compuserve.com
4 King's Bench Walk
Ground/First Floor, Temple, London
EC4Y 7DL, Telephone: 0171 822 8822
E-mail: 4kbw@barristersatlaw.com
Call date: July 1989, Lincoln's Inn
Qualifications: [LLB]

MORGAN MISS HELEN ELIZABETH

1 Gray's Inn Square
1st Floor, London WC1R 5AG,
Telephone: 0171 405 3000
E-mail: clerks@onegrays.demon.co.uk
Call date: Nov 1993, Gray's Inn
Qualifications: [BA]

MORGAN MS LYNNE MARY

32 Park Place
Cardiff CF1 3BA, Telephone: 01222 397364
Call date: July 1984, Middle Temple
Qualifications: [LLB (Wales)]

MORGAN PAUL QC (1992)

Falcon Chambers
Falcon Court, London EC4Y 1AA,
Telephone: 0171 353 2484/7
Call date: July 1975, Lincoln's Inn
Qualifications: [MA (Cantab)]

MORGAN RICHARD HUGO LYNDON

13 Old Square
Ground Floor, Lincoln's Inn, London
WC2A 3UA, Telephone: 0171 404 4800
Call date: Nov 1988, Gray's Inn
Qualifications: [LLB UBucks), LLM (Cantab)]

MORGAN MISS SARAH MARY

Francis Taylor Bldg
Ground Floor, Temple, London EC4Y 7BY,
Telephone: 0171 353 7768/7769/2711
Call date: Nov 1988, Gray's Inn
Qualifications: [LLB (Brunel)]

MORGAN STEPHEN FRANCIS

1 Serjeants' Inn
4th Floor, Temple, London EC4Y 1NH,
Telephone: 0171 583 1355
E-mail: serjeants.inn@virgin.net
Call date: Nov 1983, Gray's Inn
Qualifications: [LLB (Warw), MA, (Nottm)]

MORGAN MRS TINA JANE

20 Britton Street
1st Floor, London EC1M 5NQ,
Telephone: 0171 608 3765
Call date: Oct 1995, Middle Temple
Qualifications: [LLB (Hons)]

MORGANS JOHN MORGAN

East Anglian Chambers
57 London Street, Norwich NR2 1HL,
Telephone: 01603 617351
East Anglian Chambers
Sanders House 52 North Hill, Colchester
CO1 1PY, Telephone: 01206 572756
East Anglian Chambers
Gresham House 5 Museum Street, Ipswich
IP1 1HQ, Telephone: 01473 214481
Call date: Nov 1996, Middle Temple
Qualifications: [LLB (Hons)(Lancs), LLM]

MORIARTY GERALD EVELYN QC (1974)

2 Mitre Ct Bldgs
2nd Floor, Temple, London EC4Y 7BX,
Telephone: 0171 583 1380
Call date: June 1951, Lincoln's Inn
Recorder

MORIARTY STEPHEN

Fountain Court
Temple, London EC4Y 9DH,
Telephone: 0171 583 3335
E-mail: chambers@fountaincourt.co.uk
Call date: Nov 1986, Middle Temple
Qualifications: [BCL, MA (Oxon)]

MORLEY GARETH EDWARD

3 Temple Gardens
3rd Floor, Temple, London EC4Y 9AU,
Telephone: 0171 583 0010
Call date: July 1982, Middle Temple
Qualifications: [LLB]

MORLEY IAIN CHARLES

1 Hare Court
Ground Floor, Temple, London EC4Y 7BE,
Telephone: 0171 353 3982/5324
Call date: July 1988, Inner Temple
Qualifications: [BA (Oxon)]

MORPUSS GUY

20 Essex Street
London WC2R 3AL,
Telephone: 0171 583 9294
E-mail: clerks@20essexst.com
Call date: Oct 1991, Lincoln's Inn
Qualifications: [LLB (Hons) (Birm)]

MORRIS MISS ANGELA JANE

18 Red Lion Court
(Off Fleet Street), London EC4A 3EB,
Telephone: 0171 520 6000
Thornwood House
102 New London Road, Chelmsford, Essex
CM2 0RG, Telephone: 01245 280880
Call date: July 1984, Middle Temple
Qualifications: [LLB]

MORRIS ANTHONY JOSEPH

Parsonage Chambers
5th Floor 3 The Parsonage, Manchester
M3 2HW, Telephone: 0161 833 1996
Call date: Nov 1986, Gray's Inn

MORRIS ANTHONY PAUL QC (1991)

Peel Court Chambers
45 Hardman Street, Manchester M3 3HA,
Telephone: 0161 832 3791
Call date: July 1970, Gray's Inn
Recorder
Qualifications: [MA (Oxon)]

MORRIS MISS ANTONIA LOUISE

Trafalgar Chambers
53 Fleet Street, London EC4Y 1BE,
Telephone: 0171 583 5858
E-mail: TrafalgarChambers@easynet.co.uk
Call date: Nov 1993, Inner Temple
Qualifications: [BA (Lond)]

MORRIS BEN

Victoria Chambers
19 Castle Street, Liverpool L2 4SX,
Telephone: 0151 236 9402
E-mail: Fa45@rapid.co.uk
Call date: Oct 1996, Middle Temple
Qualifications: [LLB (Hons)(L'pool)]

MORRIS MISS BRENDA ALISON

14 Gray's Inn Square
Gray's Inn, London WC1R 5JP,
Telephone: 0171 242 0858
E-mail: 100712.2134@compuserve.com
Call date: July 1978, Middle Temple
Qualifications: [BSc (Lond), P.G.C.E.]

MORRIS BRENDAN ANTHONY

18 Red Lion Court
(Off Fleet Street), London EC4A 3EB,
Telephone: 0171 520 6000
Thornwood House
102 New London Road, Chelmsford, Essex
CM2 0RG, Telephone: 01245 280880
Call date: July 1985, Middle Temple
Qualifications: [BA, Dip Law (Lond)]

MORRIS MS CHRISTINA GAYE

5 Pump Court
Ground Floor, Temple, London EC4Y 7AP,
Telephone: 0171 353 2532
E-mail: fivepump@netcomuk.co.uk
Call date: Nov 1983, Gray's Inn
Qualifications: [BA (Warw)]

MORRIS CHRISTOPHER

New Court Chambers
Suite 200 Gazette Building, 168 Corporation
Street, Birmingham B4 6TZ,
Telephone: 0121 693 6656
Call date: July 1977, Lincoln's Inn
Qualifications: [BA (Hons)]

MORRIS DAVID PAUL

6 Pump Court
Ground Floor, Temple, London EC4Y 7AR,
Telephone: 0171 583 6013/2510
Call date: July 1976, Inner Temple
Qualifications: [LLB (Bris)]

MORRIS MISS DEBORAH ANNE

1 Gray's Inn Square
Ground Floor, London WC1R 5AA,
Telephone: 0171 405 8946/7/8
Call date: July 1989, Gray's Inn
Qualifications: [BEd (Hons), Dip Law]

MORRIS DERRICK

Arbitration Chambers
22 Willes Road, London NW5 3DS,
Telephone: 0171 267 2137
E-mail: jatqc@atack.demon.co.uk
Call date: Nov 1983, Lincoln's Inn
Qualifications: [LLB (Cardiff), FRICS]

MORRIS MISS FENELLA

4 Brick Court
Ground Floor, Temple, London EC4Y 9AD,
Telephone: 0171 797 7766
E-mail: chambers@4brick.co.uk
Call date: Oct 1990, Middle Temple
Qualifications: [BA (Hons) (Oxon), Dip Law
(City)]

MORRIS GRAHAM PAUL

Martins Building
Water Street, Liverpool L2 3SP,
Telephone: 0151 236 5818/4919
Call date: July 1975, Gray's Inn
Qualifications: [LLB]

MORRIS IEUAN JOHN

9 Park Place
Cardiff CF1 3DP, Telephone: 01222 382731
Call date: July 1979, Gray's Inn
Qualifications: [LLB (Lond)]

MORRIS MISS JANE PENELOPE KATRIN

King Charles House
Standard Hill, Nottingham NG1 6FX,
Telephone: 0115 9418851
E-mail: clerks@kch.co.uk
Call date: Oct 1991, Gray's Inn
Qualifications: [LLB]

MORRIS THE RT HON JOHN QC (1973)

3 Hare Court
1st Floor, Temple, London EC4Y 7BJ,
Telephone: 0171 353 7561
Call date: Feb 1954, Gray's Inn
Recorder
Qualifications: [LLM]

MORRIS MISS JUNE VICTORIA

Peel Court Chambers
45 Hardman Street, Manchester M3 3HA,
Telephone: 0161 832 3791
Call date: Oct 1995, Lincoln's Inn
Qualifications: [BA (Hons)(Manc), CPE (Manc)]

MORRIS MICHAEL HARVEY

Goldsmith Chambers
Ground Floor Goldsmith Building, Temple,
London EC4Y 7BL,
Telephone: 0171 353 6802/3/4/5
E-mail: celiamonksfield@btinternet.com
Call date: July 1984, Gray's Inn
Qualifications: [BSc (Eng) (Lond)]

MORRIS PAUL HOWARD

Chancery House Chambers
7 Lisbon Square, Leeds LS1 4LY,
Telephone: 0113 244 6691
E-mail: Chanceryhouse@btinternet.com
5 Stone Buildings
Lincoln's Inn, London WC2A 3XT,
Telephone: 0171 242 6201
E-mail: clerks@5-stonebuildings.law.co.uk
Door Tenant
Call date: Nov 1986, Lincoln's Inn
Qualifications: [MA (Cantab)]

MORRIS MISS SARAH

4 Brick Court
Temple, London EC4Y 9AD,
Telephone: 0171 797 8910
Call date: Mar 1996, Lincoln's Inn
Qualifications: [LLB (Hons)(L'pool)]

MORRIS SEAN ROBERT

6 Park Square
Leeds LS1 2LW, Telephone: 0113 2459763
E-mail: chambers@no6.co.uk
Call date: Nov 1983, Lincoln's Inn
Qualifications: [BA]

MORRIS MISS SHAN ELIZABETH

33 Park Place
Cardiff CF1 3BA, Telephone: 01222 233313
Call date: Oct 1991, Middle Temple
Qualifications: [LLB Hons (Hull)]

MORRIS STEPHEN NATHAN

20 Essex Street
London WC2R 3AL,
Telephone: 0171 583 9294
E-mail: clerks@20essexst.com
Call date: July 1981, Lincoln's Inn
Assistant Recorder
Qualifications: [MA (Cantab)]

MORRIS-COOLE CHRISTOPHER

Goldsmith Building
1st Floor, Temple, London EC4Y 7BL,
Telephone: 0171 353 7881
E-mail: clerks@goldsmith-building.law.co.uk
Call date: July 1974, Inner Temple
Recorder

MORRISH PETER JEFFERY

Goldsmith Chambers
Ground Floor Goldsmith Building, Temple,
London EC4Y 7BL,
Telephone: 0171 353 6802/3/4/5
E-mail: celiamonksfield@btinternet.com
Call date: May 1962, Gray's Inn

MORRISON CHRISTOPHER JAMES

Chambers of Christopher J Morrison
5 Gladeside, Chessington, Surrey KT9 2JQ
Call date: Nov 1990, Inner Temple
Qualifications: [BA (Hons)(Oxon), Dip Law]

MORRISON CHRISTOPHER QUINTIN

Durham Barristers' Chambers
27 Old Elvet, Durham DH1 3HN,
Telephone: 0191 386 9199
Call date: Nov 1986, Inner Temple
Qualifications: [LLB (Leic), DBA (Dunelm)]

MORRISON HOWARD ANDREW CLIVE

36 Bedford Row
London WC1R 4JH,
Telephone: 0171 421 8000
E-mail: 36bedfordrow@link.org
7 Fountain Court
Steelhouse Lane, Birmingham B4 6DR,
Telephone: 0121 236 8531
Call date: July 1977, Gray's Inn
Recorder
Qualifications: [LLB (Lond)]

MORROW GRAHAM ERIC QC (1996)

Exchange Chambers
Pearl Assurance House Derby Square,
Liverpool L2 9XX, Telephone: 0151 236 7747/
0458
E-mail: exchangechambers@btinternet.com
12 King's Bench Walk
Temple, London EC4Y 7EL,
Telephone: 0171 583 0811
E-mail: chambers@12kbw.co.uk
Call date: July 1974, Lincoln's Inn
Assistant Recorder
Qualifications: [LLB (Hons)]

MORSE CHRISTOPHER GEORGE JOHN

2 Hare Court
Ground Floor, Temple, London EC4Y 7BH,
Telephone: 0171 583 1770
E-mail: 2_Hare_Court@link.org
Door Tenant
Call date: July 1972, Middle Temple
Qualifications: [BA, BCL (Oxon)]

MORSE MALCOLM GEORGE MCEWAN

1 Fountain Court
Steelhouse Lane, Birmingham B4 6DR,
Telephone: 0121 236 5721
Call date: July 1967, Inner Temple
Qualifications: [MA (Cantab)]

MORSHEAD TIMOTHY FRANCIS

4 Breams Buildings
London EC4A 1AQ,
Telephone: 0171 353 5835/430 1221
Call date: Feb 1995, Lincoln's Inn
Qualifications: [BA (Hons), Dip in Law (City)]

MORT JUSTIN JOHN GLASBROOK

2 Temple Gardens
Temple, London EC4Y 9AY,
Telephone: 0171 583 6041 (12 Lines)
Call date: Oct 1994, Middle Temple
Qualifications: [BA (Hons)(Durham)]

MORTIMORE MISS CLAUDIA

18 Red Lion Court
(Off Fleet Street), London EC4A 3EB,
Telephone: 0171 520 6000
Thornwood House
102 New London Road, Chelmsford, Essex
CM2 0RG, Telephone: 01245 280880
Call date: Oct 1994, Middle Temple
Qualifications: [LLB (Hons)(Leeds), LLM
(Lond)]

MORTIMORE SIMON ANTHONY QC (1991)

3/4 South Square
Gray's Inn, London WC1R 5HP,
Telephone: 0171 696 9900
E-mail: clerks@southsquare.com
Call date: July 1972, Inner Temple
Qualifications: [LLB (Exon)]

MORTON GARY DAVID

Pepys' Chambers
17 Fleet Street, London EC4Y 1AA,
Telephone: 0171 936 2710
Call date: Nov 1993, Gray's Inn
Qualifications: [B.Sc (Econ), MA (Warw)]

MORTON KEITH FARRANCE

1 Temple Gardens
1st Floor, Temple, London EC4Y 9BB,
Telephone: 0171 353 0407/583 1315
E-mail: clerks@1templegardens.co.uk
Call date: Oct 1990, Lincoln's Inn
Qualifications: [BSc (Hull), Dip Law (City)]

MORTON PETER JOHN

Plowden Bldgs
2nd Floor, Temple, London EC4Y 9BU,
Telephone: 0171 583 0808
E-mail: bar@plowdenbuildings.co.uk
Call date: Nov 1988, Middle Temple
Qualifications: [LLB (Lanc), LLM (Cantab)]

MORTON MISS RACHAEL JOANNA EADEN

4 Brick Court
Temple, London EC4Y 9AD,
Telephone: 0171 797 8910
Call date: Feb 1995, Lincoln's Inn
Qualifications: [LLB (Hons)(Warw)]

MOSELEY MISS JULIE RUTH

7 Fountain Court
Steelhouse Lane, Birmingham B4 6DR,
Telephone: 0121 236 8531
Call date: Oct 1992, Inner Temple
Qualifications: [LLB (Leics)]

MOSER PHILIP CURT HAROLD

Warwick House Chambers
8 Warwick Court, Gray's Inn, London
WC1R 5DJ, Telephone: 0171 430 2323
Call date: Oct 1992, Inner Temple
Qualifications: [MA (Cantab)]

MOSES MISS REBECCA

Barrister's Common Law Chambers
57 Whitechapel Road, Aldgate East, London
E1 1DU, Telephone: 0171 375 3012
E-mail: barristers@hotmail:com
Lion Court
Chancery House 53-64 Chancery Lane, London
WC2A 1SJ, Telephone: 0171 404 6565
Call date: Nov 1996, Inner Temple
Qualifications: [LLB (Hons)]

MOSHI RICHARD JOSEPH

4 Breams Buildings
London EC4A 1AQ,
Telephone: 0171 353 5835/430 1221
Call date: Feb 1955, Middle Temple
Qualifications: [LLM]

MOSS CHRISTOPHER JOHN QC (1994)

5 Essex Court
1st Floor, Temple, London EC4Y 9AH,
Telephone: 0171 410 2000
Call date: July 1972, Gray's Inn
Recorder
Qualifications: [LLB (Lond)]

MOSS GABRIEL STEPHEN QC (1989)

3/4 South Square
Gray's Inn, London WC1R 5HP,
Telephone: 0171 696 9900
E-mail: clerks@southsquare.com
Call date: July 1974, Lincoln's Inn
Qualifications: [MA, BCL (Oxon)]

MOSS MS JOANNE ROSEMARY

Falcon Chambers
Falcon Court, London EC4Y 1AA,
Telephone: 0171 353 2484/7
Call date: July 1976, Inner Temple
Qualifications: [MA (Cantab), FCI Arb, LLM (Lond)]

MOSS NICHOLAS SIMON

1 Temple Gardens
1st Floor, Temple, London EC4Y 9BB,
Telephone: 0171 353 0407/583 1315
E-mail: clerks@1templegardens.co.uk
Call date: Nov 1995, Middle Temple
Qualifications: [BA (Hons)(Cantab)]

MOSS NORMAN WILLIAM

Goldsmith Chambers
Ground Floor Goldsmith Building, Temple,
London EC4Y 7BL,
Telephone: 0171 353 6802/3/4/5
E-mail: celiamonksfield@btinternet.com
Call date: Oct 1990, Inner Temple
Qualifications: [LLB (Hons Wales)]

MOSS PETER

Sedan House
Stanley Place, Chester CH1 2LU,
Telephone: 01244 320480/348282
Call date: Nov 1980, Middle Temple

MOSS PETER JONATHAN

9-12 Bell Yard
London WC2A 2LF,
Telephone: 0171 400 1800
Call date: Nov 1976, Lincoln's Inn

D

D

MOSTESHAR SA'ID

Hardwicke Building
New Square, Lincoln's Inn, London
WC2A 3SB, Telephone: 0171 242 2523
E-mail: clerks@hardwicke.co.uk
Door Tenant
Call date: July 1975, Lincoln's Inn
Qualifications: [DPhil, FCA, B.SC, M.Sc (Econ)]

MOSTYN NICHOLAS ANTHONY JOSEPH GHISLAIN QC (1997)

1 Mitre Ct Bldgs
Ground Floor, Temple, London EC4Y 7BS,
Telephone: 0171 797 7070
Call date: Nov 1980, Middle Temple
Assistant Recorder
Qualifications: [LLB]

MOSTYN PIERS NICHOLAS

4 Brick Court
Ground Floor, Temple, London EC4Y 9AD,
Telephone: 0171 797 7766
E-mail: chambers@4brick.co.uk
Call date: Nov 1989, Middle Temple
Qualifications: [B.Sc Hons [Bris], Dip in Law]

MOTT GEOFFREY EDWARD

Gray's Inn Chambers
5th Floor, Gray's Inn, London WC1R 5JA,
Telephone: 0171 404 1111
Call date: July 1982, Gray's Inn
Qualifications: [Ba, Dip Law]

MOTT PHILIP CHARLES QC (1991)

35 Essex Street
Temple, London WC2R 3AR,
Telephone: 0171 353 6381
Call date: July 1970, Inner Temple
Recorder
Qualifications: [BA (Oxon)]

MOULD TIMOTHY JAMES

4 Breams Buildings
London EC4A 1AQ,
Telephone: 0171 353 5835/430 1221
Call date: Nov 1987, Gray's Inn
Qualifications: [BA (Oxon), Dip Law]

MOULDER MISS PAULINE MARY

Broad Chare
33 Broad Chare, Newcastle Upon Tyne
NE1 3DQ, Telephone: 0191 232 0541
Call date: July 1983, Lincoln's Inn
Qualifications: [LLB (Newc)]

MOULSON PETER CHARLES EDWARD

10 Park Square
Leeds LS1 2LH, Telephone: 0113 2455438
E-mail: chambers@bandit.legend.co.uk
Call date: Oct 1991, Gray's Inn
Qualifications: [LLB, MBA]

MOUNTFIELD MS HELEN

4-5 Gray's Inn Square
Ground Floor, Gray's Inn, London WC1R 5AY,
Telephone: 0171 404 5252
E-mail: chambers@4-5graysinnsquare.co.uk
Call date: Oct 1991, Gray's Inn
Qualifications: [BA (Oxon), Dip Law (City),
Dip European Law]

MOUSLEY TIMOTHY JOHN

2 King's Bench Walk
Ground Floor, Temple, London EC4Y 7DE,
Telephone: 0171 353 1746
E-mail: 2kbw@atlas.co.uk
King's Bench Chambers
115 North Hill, Plymouth PL4 8JY,
Telephone: 01752 221551
Call date: July 1979, Middle Temple
Qualifications: [BA (Keele)]

MOUSLEY WILLIAM HOWARD

2 King's Bench Walk
Ground Floor, Temple, London EC4Y 7DE,
Telephone: 0171 353 1746
E-mail: 2kbw@atlas.co.uk
King's Bench Chambers
115 North Hill, Plymouth PL4 8JY,
Telephone: 01752 221551
Call date: July 1986, Middle Temple
Qualifications: [LLB (Warks)]

MOVERLEY SMITH STEPHEN PHILIP

24 Old Bldgs
Ground Floor, Lincoln's Inn, London
WC2A 3UJ, Telephone: 0171 404 0946
E-mail: clerks@24oldbuildings.law.co.uk
Call date: Feb 1985, Middle Temple
Qualifications: [MA (Oxon)]

MOWBRAY (WILLIAM) JOHN QC (1974)

12 New Square
Ground Floor, Lincoln's Inn, London
WC2A 3SW, Telephone: 0171 419 1212
E-mail: 12newsquare@compuserve.com
25 Park Square
Leeds LS1 2PW, Telephone: 0113 2451841/2/3
E-mail: sovereignchambers@btinternet.com
Door Tenant
Call date: June 1953, Lincoln's Inn
Qualifications: [BA (Oxon)]

MOWSCHENSON TERENCE RENNIE QC (1995)

1 Essex Court
Ground Floor, Temple, London EC4Y 9AR,
Telephone: 0171 583 2000
E-mail: clerks@oneessexcourt.co.uk
Call date: July 1977, Middle Temple
Qualifications: [LLB (Lond), BCL (Oxon),
FCIArb]

MOXON BROWNE ROBERT WILLIAM QC (1990)

2 Temple Gardens
Temple, London EC4Y 9AY,
Telephone: 0171 583 6041 (12 Lines)
Call date: July 1969, Gray's Inn
Recorder
Qualifications: [BA (Oxon)]

MOYLAN ANDREW JOHN GREGORY

Queen Elizabeth Bldg
2nd Floor, Temple, London EC4Y 9BS,
Telephone: 0171 797 7837
Call date: Nov 1978, Inner Temple
Qualifications: [BA (Oxon)]

MPANGA DAVID FREDERICK KISITU

5 Paper Bldgs
1st Floor, Temple, London EC4Y 7HB,
Telephone: 0171 583 6117
E-mail: clerks@5-paperbuildings.law.co.uk
Call date: Nov 1993, Middle Temple
Qualifications: [LLB (Hons)(Exon)]

MUCHLINSKI PETER THOMAS

Brick Court Chambers
15/19 Devereux Court, London WC2R 3JJ,
Telephone: 0171 583 0777
E-mail: (surname)@brickcourt.demon.co.uk
Door Tenant
Call date: July 1981, Lincoln's Inn
Qualifications: [LLB (Cantab), LLB (Lond)]

MUIR ANDREW CHARLES

3 Raymond Buildings
Gray's Inn, London WC1R 5BH,
Telephone: 0171 831 3833
E-mail: chambers@threeraymond.demon.co.uk
Call date: Nov 1975, Lincoln's Inn
Qualifications: [BA (Hons)]

MUIR JOHN HENRY

25 Park Square
Leeds LS1 2PW, Telephone: 0113 2451841/2/3
E-mail: sovereignchambers@btinternet.com
12 New Square
Ground Floor, Lincoln's Inn, London
WC2A 3SW, Telephone: 0171 419 1212
E-mail: 12newsquare@compuserve.com
Door Tenant
Call date: Nov 1969, Lincoln's Inn
Recorder
Qualifications: [BA, BSc (Econ), FCIS, ACIArb]

MUKHERJEE AVIK

1 High Pavement
Nottingham NG1 1HF,
Telephone: 0115 9418218
Call date: Oct 1990, Gray's Inn
Qualifications: [LLB]

MULCAHY MS JANE SUZANNE

2 Hare Court
Ground Floor, Temple, London EC4Y 7BH,
Telephone: 0171 583 1770
E-mail: 2_Hare_Court@link.org
Call date: Oct 1995, Middle Temple
Qualifications: [BA (Hons)]

MULCAHY MISS LEIGH-ANN MARIA

2 Crown Office Row
Ground Floor, Temple, London EC4Y 7HJ,
Telephone: 0171 797 8100
E-mail: mail@2cor.co.uk, or to individual
barristers at: [barrister's surname]@2cor.co.uk
Call date: Oct 1993, Inner Temple
Qualifications: [BA, MA, LLM]

MULHOLLAND JAMES MALACHI

3 Gray's Inn Square
Ground Floor, London WC1R 5AH,
Telephone: 0171 520 5600
E-mail: gis3@btinternet.com
Call date: July 1986, Inner Temple
Qualifications: [LLB (Leeds)]

MULHOLLAND MS KATHRYN SHONA

1 King's Bench Walk
2nd Floor, Temple, London EC4Y 7DB,
Telephone: 0171 936 1500
E-mail: ddear@1kbw.co.uk
Call date: Nov 1994, Inner Temple
Qualifications: [BA (Oxon)]

MULHOLLAND MICHAEL

St James's Chambers
68 Quay Street, Manchester M3 3EJ,
Telephone: 0161 834 7000
E-mail: 106241.2625@compuserve.com
Call date: Nov 1976, Gray's Inn
Qualifications: [MA (Oxon) Dip Crim,
(Cantab)]

MULLALLY MRS MAUREEN VINCENT

Lamb Building
Ground Floor, Temple, London EC4Y 7AS,
Telephone: 0171 797 7788
E-mail: lamb.building@link.org
Westgate Chambers
144 High Street, Lewes, East Sussex BN7 1XT,
Telephone: 01273 480510
Call date: July 1957, Gray's Inn

MULLAN RICHARD FRANCIS

Sedan House
Stanley Place, Chester CH1 2LU,
Telephone: 01244 320480/348282
Call date: Oct 1994, Gray's Inn
Qualifications: [BA (Wales)]

MULLEN MISS JAYNE ALISON

St Ive's Chambers
9 Fountain Ct, Birmingham B4 6DR,
Telephone: 0121 236 0863/0929
Call date: July 1989, Gray's Inn
Qualifications: [BA (Hons)(Cantab)]

MULLEN PATRICK ANTHONY

1 Essex Court
1st Floor, Temple, London EC4Y 9AR,
Telephone: 0171 936 3030
E-mail: one.essex_court@virgin.net
Call date: July 1967, Gray's Inn
Qualifications: [MA (Cantab)]

MULLEN PETER

Verulam Chambers
Peer House 8-14 Verulam Street, Gray's Inn,
London WC1X 8LZ,
Telephone: 0171 813 2400
Call date: July 1977, Lincoln's Inn
Qualifications: [BA (Lond)]

MULLER ANTONIE SEAN

4 Fountain Court
Steelhouse Lane, Birmingham B4 6DR,
Telephone: 0121 236 3476
Call date: July 1990, Middle Temple
Qualifications: [MA (Cantab)]

MULLER FRANZ JOSEPH QC (1978)

11 King's Bench Walk
1st Floor, Temple, London EC4Y 7EQ,
Telephone: 0171 353 3337
3 Park Court
Leeds LS1 2QH, Telephone: 0113 297 1200
Call date: Feb 1961, Gray's Inn
Recorder
Qualifications: [LLB Hons]

MULLER MARK OLIVER BENJAMIN

Counsels' Chambers
2nd Floor 10-11 Gray's Inn Square, London
WC1R 5JD, Telephone: 0171 405 2576
Call date: Apr 1991, Lincoln's Inn
Qualifications: [BSC(Econ) LLB(Dip)]

MULLIGAN MS ANN COLLETTE

Hardwicke Building
New Square, Lincoln's Inn, London
WC2A 3SB, Telephone: 0171 242 2523
E-mail: clerks@hardwicke.co.uk
Call date: July 1989, Gray's Inn
Qualifications: [BA (Oxon), PPE]

MULLINS MARK

4 Brick Court
Ground Floor, Temple, London EC4Y 9AD,
Telephone: 0171 797 7766
E-mail: chambers@4brick.co.uk
Call date: Nov 1988, Lincoln's Inn
Qualifications: [BA Hons (Oxon), Dip in Law
(City)]

MULLINS MARK LOVEL RUPERT

1 Harcourt Bldgs
2nd Floor, Temple, London EC4Y 9DA,
Telephone: 0171 353 9421/9151
Call date: Nov 1995, Inner Temple
Qualifications: [BA (Dunelm), CPE (Lond)]

MULLIS ANTHONY ROGER

Chambers of Lord Goodhart QC
Ground Floor 3 New Square, Lincoln's Inn,
London WC2A 3RS,
Telephone: 0171 405 5577
E-mail: law@threenewsquare.demon.co.uk
Call date: Nov 1987, Lincoln's Inn
Qualifications: [BA (Oxon),BCL]

MULRENNAN MISS MARIA HELEN ANNE

St Mary's Chambers
50 High Pavement, Lace Market, Nottingham
NG1 1HW, Telephone: 0115 9503503
E-mail: clerks@smc.law.co.uk
Call date: Nov 1990, Inner Temple
Qualifications: [BA (Sussex), LLM (Nott'm)]

MULROONEY MARK TERENCE DANIEL

Exchange Chambers
Pearl Assurance House Derby Square,
Liverpool L2 9XX, Telephone: 0151 236 7747/
0458
E-mail: exchangechambers@btinternet.com
Call date: July 1988, Middle Temple
Qualifications: [BA (Hons) Kent, MPhil
(Cantab)]

MULVEIN MISS HELEN JANE

24 The Ropewalk
Nottingham NG1 5EF,
Telephone: 0115 9472581
E-mail: clerk@ropewalk.co.uk
Call date: Oct 1994, Lincoln's Inn
Qualifications: [MA (Cantab), LLM]

MUNASINGHE LEELANANDA SEPALA

235 London Road
Twickenham, London TW1 1ES,
Telephone: 0181 892 5947
Call date: Feb 1963, Lincoln's Inn

MUNBY JAMES LAWRENCE QC (1988)

1 New Square
Ground Floor, Lincoln's Inn, London
WC2A 3SA, Telephone: 0171 405 0884/5/6/7
E-mail: 1newsquare@compuserve.com
Call date: Nov 1971, Middle Temple
Qualifications: [BA (Oxon)]

MUNDAY ANDREW HUGH QC (1996)

3 Hare Court
1st Floor, Temple, London EC4Y 7BJ,
Telephone: 0171 353 7561
Call date: Nov 1973, Middle Temple
Assistant Recorder
Qualifications: [LLB]

MUNDAY MISS ANNE MARGARET

8 King's Bench Walk North
1 Park Square East, Leeds LS1 2NE,
Telephone: 0113 2439797
8 King's Bench Walk
2nd Floor, Temple, London EC4Y 7DU,
Telephone: 0171 797 8888
Call date: Oct 1994, Lincoln's Inn
Qualifications: [LLB (Hons)(L'pool)]

MUNDY ROBERT GEOFFREY

St James's Chambers
68 Quay Street, Manchester M3 3EJ,
Telephone: 0161 834 7000
E-mail: 106241.2625@compuserve.com
Call date: Nov 1966, Middle Temple
Qualifications: [LLB]

MUNIR DR ASHLEY EDWARD

1 Harcourt Bldgs
2nd Floor, Temple, London EC4Y 9DA,
Telephone: 0171 353 9421/9151
Call date: June 1956, Gray's Inn
Qualifications: [MA (Cantab), PhD (Lond),
M.Phil]

MUNKMAN JOHN

10 Park Square
Leeds LS1 2LH, Telephone: 0113 2455438
E-mail: chambers@bandit.legend.co.uk
Call date: Jan 1948, Middle Temple
Qualifications: [LLB]

MUNKS MRS CHRISTINE ANN

Eighteen Carlton Crescent
Southampton SO15 2XR,
Telephone: 01703 639001
Call date: Nov 1991, Inner Temple
Qualifications: [LLB (So'ton)]

MUNONYEDI MISS IFEYINWA

Goldsmith Chambers
Ground Floor Goldsmith Building, Temple,
London EC4Y 7BL,
Telephone: 0171 353 6802/3/4/5
E-mail: celiamonksfield@btinternet.com
Call date: July 1985, Gray's Inn
Qualifications: [BA(Lond), Dip Law]

MUNRO MISS FIONA CAROLINE

Queen Elizabeth Bldg
Ground Floor, Temple, London EC4Y 9BS,
Telephone: 0171 353 7181 (12 Lines)
Call date: July 1986, Lincoln's Inn
Qualifications: [LLB]

MUNRO KENNETH STUART

5 Bell Yard
London WC2A 2JR, Telephone: 0171 333 8811
Call date: Nov 1973, Inner Temple
Qualifications: [MA (Cantab)]

MUNRO SANDERSON WILSON

8 King's Bench Walk
2nd Floor, Temple, London EC4Y 7DU,
Telephone: 0171 797 8888
8 King's Bench Walk North
1 Park Square East, Leeds LS1 2NE,
Telephone: 0113 2439797
Call date: July 1981, Gray's Inn
Qualifications: [LLB (Scots)(Hons), Dip Law]

MUNRO MISS SARAH BELINDA MCLEOD

Walnut House
63 St. David's Hill, Exeter, Devon EX4 4DW,
Telephone: 01392 279751
E-mail: 106627.2451@compuserve.com
Call date: Nov 1984, Inner Temple
Assistant Recorder
Qualifications: [BA (Exon)]

MUNRO MISS SARAH TIFFANY

1 High Pavement
Nottingham NG1 1HF,
Telephone: 0115 9418218
Call date: Oct 1990, Middle Temple
Qualifications: [LLB]

MUNROE MISS VERONICA ALLISON

14 Tooks Court
Cursitor St, London EC4A 1LB,
Telephone: 0171 405 8828
E-mail: clerks @tooks.law.co.uk
Call date: Oct 1992, Middle Temple
Qualifications: [BA (Hons)(Cantab), Diploma in
Law]

MUNT ALASTAIR HENRY MCLAREN

King Charles House
Standard Hill, Nottingham NG1 6FX,
Telephone: 0115 9418851
E-mail: clerks@kch.co.uk
Call date: July 1989, Gray's Inn
Qualifications: [LLB (Reading), LLM (Cantab),
MPhil (Cantab)]

MUNYARD TERRY

2 Garden Court
1st Floor, Middle Temple, London EC4Y 9BL,
Telephone: 0171 353 1633
E-mail: barristers@2gardenct.law.co.uk
Call date: July 1972, Gray's Inn
Qualifications: [LLB (Lond)]

MURCH STEPHEN JAMES

11 Bolt Court
London EC4A 3DQ,
Telephone: 0171 353 2300
E-mail: boltct11@aol.com
Call date: Oct 1991, Lincoln's Inn
Qualifications: [LLB (Hons) (Bucks)]

Fax: 0171 353 1878; DX: 00 22 LDE

Types of work: Common law (general);
Environment; Highways; Housing; Landlord and
tenant; Planning; Town and country planning

Languages spoken: German

Publications: *Atkins Court Forms*, contributor
to Vol 38 - *Town and Country Planning*, 1995

MURDOCH GORDON STUART QC (1995)

4 Paper Bldgs
2nd Floor, Temple, London EC4Y 7EX,
Telephone: 0171 583 0816/071 353 1131
E-mail: clerks@4paperbuildings.co.uk
Call date: July 1970, Inner Temple
Recorder
Qualifications: [MA, LLB (Cantab)]

MURFITT MISS CATRIONA ANNE CAMPBELL

1 Mitre Ct Bldgs
Ground Floor, Temple, London EC4Y 7BS,
Telephone: 0171 797 7070
Call date: Nov 1981, Gray's Inn
Assistant Recorder
Qualifications: [BA]

MURPHY MISS CRESSIDA JANE

4 King's Bench Walk
2nd Floor, Temple, London EC4Y 7DL,
Telephone: 0171 353 3581
Call date: Feb 1991, Gray's Inn
Qualifications: [BA (Cantab)]

MURPHY IAN PATRICK QC (1992)

9 Park Place
Cardiff CF1 3DP, Telephone: 01222 382731
Farrar's Building
Temple, London EC4Y 7BD,
Telephone: 0171 583 9241
E-mail: chambers@farrarsbuilding.co.uk
Door Tenant
Call date: July 1972, Middle Temple
Qualifications: [LLB (Lond)]

MURPHY JAMES ST JOHN

Park Lane Chambers
19 Westgate, Leeds LS1 2RD,
Telephone: 0113 2285000
Call date: Nov 1993, Inner Temple
Qualifications: [BA (L'pool), CPE]

MURPHY MICHAEL JOSEPH ADRIAN QC (1993)

Paradise Square Chambers
26 Paradise Square, Sheffield S1 2DE,
Telephone: 0114 2738951
Call date: July 1973, Inner Temple
Recorder
Qualifications: [LLB, MA]

MURPHY MICHAEL PATRICK

9 King's Bench Walk
Ground Floor, Temple, London EC4Y 7DX,
Telephone: 0171 353 7202/3909
Call date: Nov 1992, Inner Temple
Qualifications: [LLB (Essex)]

MURPHY MISS NICOLA JANE

4 King's Bench Walk
Ground/First Floor, Temple, London
EC4Y 7DL, Telephone: 0171 822 8822
E-mail: 4kbw@barristersatlaw.com
Call date: Oct 1995, Gray's Inn
Qualifications: [LLB (Hull)]

MURPHY PETER JOHN

30 Park Place
Cardiff CF1 3BA, Telephone: 01222 398421
E-mail: 100757.1456@compuserve.com
Call date: Nov 1980, Gray's Inn
Assistant Recorder
Qualifications: [LLB (Leics)]

D

MURPHY MISS PHILOMENA CATHERINE

1 Middle Temple Lane
Temple, London EC4Y 1LT,
Telephone: 0171 583 0659 (12 Lines)
Call date: Oct 1992, Gray's Inn
Qualifications: [BA (Hons)]

MURPHY MISS SHEILA MARY

Holborn Chambers
6 Gate Street, Lincoln's Inn Fields, London
WC2A 3HP, Telephone: 0171 242 6060
Call date: Oct 1992, Middle Temple
Qualifications: [LL.B (Hons)]

MURRAY ANIL PETER

Wilberforce Chambers
Bishop Lane, Hull HU1 1PA,
Telephone: 01482 323264
E-mail: clerks@hullbar.demon.co.uk
Call date: July 1989, Middle Temple
Qualifications: [LLB (Hull)]

MURRAY ASHLEY CHARLES

Oriel Chambers
14 Water Street, Liverpool L2 8TD,
Telephone: 0151 236 7191
E-mail: oriel_chambers@link.org
Call date: July 1974, Middle Temple
Assistant Recorder
Qualifications: [LLB (Birmingham)]

MURRAY MS CAROLE JEANNE

1 Gray's Inn Square
1st Floor, London WC1R 5AG,
Telephone: 0171 405 3000
E-mail: clerks@onegrays.demon.co.uk
Call date: Nov 1989, Middle Temple
Qualifications: [MA Hons [Cantab], Dip in
Law]

MURRAY MISS HARRIET CAROLINE JANE

2-3 Gray's Inn Square
Gray's Inn, London WC1R 5JH,
Telephone: 0171 242 4986
E-mail: chambers@2-3graysinnsquare.co.uk
Call date: Nov 1992, Middle Temple
Qualifications: [B.Sc (Hons)]

MURRAY JOHN MICHAEL ANDREW

9 St John Street
Manchester M3 4DN,
Telephone: 0161 955 9000
E-mail: ninesjs@gconnect.com
Call date: Nov 1979, Middle Temple
Qualifications: [BA]

MURRAY MISS JUDITH ROWENA

New Court
Temple, London EC4Y 9BE,
Telephone: 0171 583 5123/0171 583 0510
Call date: Oct 1994, Middle Temple
Qualifications: [BA (Hons)(Oxon)]

MURRAY STEPHEN JOHN

8 Fountain Court
Steelhouse Lane, Birmingham B4 6DR,
Telephone: 0121 236 5514/5
E-mail: clerks@no8chambers.co.uk
Call date: July 1986, Inner Temple
Qualifications: [LLB (Leic)]

MURRAY-SMITH JAMES MICHAEL

8 King's Bench Walk
2nd Floor, Temple, London EC4Y 7DU,
Telephone: 0171 797 8888
8 King's Bench Walk North
1 Park Square East, Leeds LS1 2NE,
Telephone: 0113 2439797
Call date: May 1990, Middle Temple
Qualifications: [B.A.]

MUSAHEB IKBAL KEVIN

New Bailey Chambers
10 Lawson Street, Preston PR1 2QT,
Telephone: 01772 258087
Call date: Oct 1990, Middle Temple
Qualifications: [LLB]

MUSTAFA BIN SA'AD

146 Carshalton Park Road
Carshalton, Surrey SM5 3SG,
Telephone: 0181 773 0531
Call date: Nov 1981, Lincoln's Inn
Qualifications: [LLB (Hons)(LSE)]

MUSTAKIM ABDUL YUNUS AL

New Bailey Chambers
10 Lawson Street, Preston PR1 2QT,
Telephone: 01772 258087
Call date: May 1997, Lincoln's Inn
Qualifications: [LLB (Hons), BCL]

MUTCH MISS ALISON JANE

Library Chambers
Gray's Inn Chambers, Gray's Inn, London
WC1R 5JA, Telephone: 0171 404 6500
Call date: Oct 1995, Middle Temple
Qualifications: [B.Sc (Hons)]

MYATT CHARLES EDWARD

Fenners Chambers
3 Madingley Road, Cambridge CB3 OEE,
Telephone: 01223 368761
Fenners Chambers
8-12 Priestgate, Peterborough PE1 1JA,
Telephone: 01733 62030
Call date: Nov 1993, Gray's Inn
Qualifications: [BA (Dunelm)]

MYDEEN KALANDAR

11 Old Square
Ground Floor, Lincoln's Inn, London
WC2A 3TS, Telephone: 0171 242 5022/
405 1074
Call date: Nov 1973, Lincoln's Inn
Qualifications: [LLB]

MYERS ALLAN JAMES

4 Field Court
Gray's Inn, London WC1R 5EA,
Telephone: 0171 440 6900
E-mail: chambers@4fieldcourt.co.uk
Call date: May 1988, Lincoln's Inn
Qualifications: [BCL (Hons) Oxon, BA, LLB
(Hons), Melbourne]

MYERS BARRY

3 Temple Gardens
3rd Floor, Temple, London EC4Y 9AU,
Telephone: 0171 583 0010
Call date: Nov 1988, Inner Temple
Qualifications: [BA (Hull), Dip Law]

MYERS BENJAMIN JOHN

38 Young Street
Manchester M3 3FT,
Telephone: 0161 833 0489
E-mail: clerks@young-st-chambers.com
Call date: Oct 1994, Inner Temple
Qualifications: [BA (Leeds), CPE (Lond)]

MYERS KEITH

Chambers of Raana Sheikh
Gray's Inn Chambers, Gray's Inn, London
WC1R, Telephone: 0171 831 5344
E-mail: s.mcblain@btinternet.com
Call date: Nov 1996, Inner Temple
Qualifications: [LLB (Middx)]

MYERS SIMON MARTIN

1 Gray's Inn Square
1st Floor, London WC1R 5AG,
Telephone: 0171 405 3000
E-mail: clerks@onegrays.demon.co.uk
Call date: Nov 1987, Middle Temple
Qualifications: [BA (Bristol) Dip. Law (City)]

MYERSON DAVID SIMON

Park Court Chambers
40 Park Cross Street, Leeds LS1 2QH,
Telephone: 0113 2433277
Call date: July 1986, Middle Temple
Qualifications: [MA (Cantab)]

MYERSON MISS VICTORIA

Lion Court
Chancery House 53-64 Chancery Lane, London
WC2A 1SJ, Telephone: 0171 404 6565
Call date: Nov 1994, Inner Temple
Qualifications: [BA (Lond), CPE]

MYLNE NIGEL JAMES QC (1984)

2 Harcourt Bldgs
1st Floor, Temple, London EC4Y 9DB,
Telephone: 0171 353 2112/2817
Call date: Feb 1963, Middle Temple
Recorder

MYLONAS-WIDDALL MICHAEL JOHN

4 Brick Court
Temple, London EC4Y 9AD,
Telephone: 0171 797 8910
Call date: July 1988, Gray's Inn
Qualifications: [LLB (Bucks)]

MYLVAGANAM MS JANAKI INDRANI

14 Tooks Court
Cursitor St, London EC4A 1LB,
Telephone: 0171 405 8828
E-mail: clerks @tooks.law.co.uk
Call date: July 1983, Gray's Inn
Qualifications: [BA (Kent)]

MYLVAGANAM PAUL JOSEPH PARAM SOTHY

2 Paper Bldgs
1st Floor, Temple, London EC4Y 7ET,
Telephone: 0171 936 2611 (10 Lines)
E-mail: clerks@2pbbarristers.co.uk
Call date: Nov 1993, Middle Temple
Qualifications: [BA (Hons)(Oxon), CPE (Lond)]

MYNORS CHARLES BASKERVILLE

2 Harcourt Bldgs
2nd Floor, Temple, London EC4Y 9DB,
Telephone: 0171 353 8415
E-mail: clerks@twoharcourtbldgs.demon.co.uk
Call date: Nov 1988, Middle Temple
Qualifications: [MA (Cantab), MA (Shef), Dip
Law, FRTPI, ARICS]

MYTTON PAUL VINCENT

Furnival Chambers
32 Furnival Street, London EC4A 1JQ,
Telephone: 0171 405 3232
E-mail: clerks@furnivallaw.co.uk
Call date: July 1982, Lincoln's Inn
Qualifications: [LLB]

NABI ZIA UL-HAQ

1 Pump Court
Lower Ground Floor, Temple, London
EC4Y 7AB, Telephone: 0171 583 2012/
353 4341
E-mail: (name) @1pumpcourt.co.uk
Call date: Nov 1991, Middle Temple
Qualifications: [LLB Hons (Essex)]

NADIM AHMED

38 Young Street
Manchester M3 3FT,
Telephone: 0161 833 0489
E-mail: clerks@young-st-chambers.com
Call date: July 1982, Lincoln's Inn
Qualifications: [BA]

NAIDOO SEAN VAN

Littman Chambers
12 Gray's Inn Square, London WC1R 5JP,
Telephone: 0171 404 4866
E-mail: admin@littmanchambers.com
Call date: July 1990, Lincoln's Inn
Qualifications: [B.Proc,LLB (Wits), BA,BCL
(Oxon)]

NAIK GAURANG RAMANLAL

9 Gough Square
London EC4A 3DE, Telephone: 0171 353 5371
Call date: July 1985, Gray's Inn
Qualifications: [BSc, Dip Law]

NAIK TIMOTHY ANIL

Holborn Chambers
6 Gate Street, Lincoln's Inn Fields, London
WC2A 3HP, Telephone: 0171 242 6060
Call date: Nov 1994, Gray's Inn
Qualifications: [LLB]

NAISH CHRISTOPHER JOHN

Southernhay Chambers
33 Southernhay East, Exeter EX1 1NX,
Telephone: 01392 255777
E-mail: southernhay.chambers@lineone.net
Call date: July 1980, Inner Temple
Qualifications: [LLB]

NAISH RICHARD DENNIS MACAVOY

Francis Taylor Bldg
2nd Floor, Temple, London EC4Y 7BY,
Telephone: 0171 353 9942/3157
Call date: Nov 1966, Middle Temple
Qualifications: [BA (Oxon)]

NAJAND MS MARYAM

6 King's Bench Walk
Ground, Third & Fourth Floors, Temple,
London EC4Y 7DR,
Telephone: 0171 353 4931/583 0695
Call date: Nov 1993, Middle Temple
Qualifications: [BSc (Hons)(City), Dip in Law (City)]

NANCE FRANCIS PETER

Exchange Chambers
Pearl Assurance House Derby Square,
Liverpool L2 9XX, Telephone: 0151 236 7747/0458
E-mail: exchangechambers@btinternet.com
Call date: Nov 1970, Gray's Inn

NAPIER PROFESSOR BRIAN WILLIAM

Fountain Court
Temple, London EC4Y 9DH,
Telephone: 0171 583 3335
E-mail: chambers@fountaincourt.co.uk
Call date: July 1990, Middle Temple
Qualifications: [MA, PhD (Cantab), LLB (Edin)]

NAPTHINE (GODFREY) JOHN

1 High Pavement
Nottingham NG1 1HF,
Telephone: 0115 9418218
Call date: July 1983, Inner Temple
Qualifications: [BA]

NAPTHINE DAVID ROBERT GUY

1 High Pavement
Nottingham NG1 1HF,
Telephone: 0115 9418218
Call date: Nov 1979, Inner Temple
Qualifications: [BA]

NARAYAN HIRANYA GARBHA

Cobden House Chambers
19 Quay Street, Manchester M3 3HN,
Telephone: 0161 833 6000
E-mail: clerks@cobden.co.uk
Call date: Nov 1970, Lincoln's Inn
Recorder

NARDECCHIA NICHOLAS CHARLES

2-3 Gray's Inn Square
Gray's Inn, London WC1R 5JH,
Telephone: 0171 242 4986
E-mail: chambers@2-3graysinnsquare.co.uk
Call date: Nov 1974, Middle Temple
Qualifications: [MA (Cantab)]

NASH JONATHAN SCOTT

3 Verulam Buildings
London WC1R 5NT,
Telephone: 0171 831 8441
E-mail: clerks@3verulam.co.uk
Call date: Nov 1986, Gray's Inn
Qualifications: [BA(Oxon)]

NASHASHIBI ANWAR DAVID

9 Bedford Row
London WC1R 4AZ,
Telephone: 0171 242 3555
E-mail: clerks@9br.co.uk
Call date: Nov 1995, Middle Temple
Qualifications: [BA (Hons)(Manch)]

NASIR JAMAL JAMIL

2 Stone Bldgs
1st Floor, Lincoln's Inn, London WC2A 3XB,
Telephone: 0171 405 3818/9
Call date: Jan 1948, Lincoln's Inn
Qualifications: [BA, PhD (Lond)]

NASSAR MISS VICTORIA KATIE

1 Gray's Inn Square
Ground Floor, London WC1R 5AA,
Telephone: 0171 405 8946/7/8
Call date: Feb 1994, Gray's Inn
Qualifications: [BSc (B'ham), CPE (Manch)]

NATHAN MISS APARNA

Gray's Inn Chambers
3rd Floor, Gray's Inn, London WC1R 5JA,
Telephone: 0171 242 2642
E-mail: clerks@taxbar.com
Call date: Nov 1994, Middle Temple
Qualifications: [LLB (Hons), LLM]

D

D

NATHAN DAVID BRIAN

10 King's Bench Walk
1st Floor, Temple, London EC4Y 7EB,
Telephone: 0171 353 2501
Call date: Nov 1971, Middle Temple
Qualifications: [LLB]

NATHAN PETER JOSEPH

One Garden Court
Ground Floor, Temple, London EC4Y 9BJ,
Telephone: 0171 797 7900
Call date: July 1973, Inner Temple
Qualifications: [LLM (Lond)]

NATHAN PHILIP GABRIEL

Earl Street Chambers
47 Earl Street, Maidstone, Kent ME14 1PD,
Telephone: 01622 671222
E-mail: gunner-sparks@msn.com
Call date: Mar 1996, Lincoln's Inn
Qualifications: [LLB (Hons)]

NATHAN STEPHEN ANDREW QC (1993)

2 Hare Court
Ground Floor, Temple, London EC4Y 7BH,
Telephone: 0171 583 1770
E-mail: 2_Hare_Court@link.org
Call date: Nov 1969, Middle Temple
Assistant Recorder
Qualifications: [MA (Oxon)]

NAUGHTON PHILIP ANTHONY QC (1988)

3 Serjeants Inn
London EC4Y 1BQ,
Telephone: 0171 353 5537
E-mail: available upon request
Call date: Apr 1970, Gray's Inn
Qualifications: [LLB (Nott'm)]

NAVARATNE MR FRANCIS REGINALD

9 King's Bench Walk
Basement, Temple, London EC4Y 7DX,
Telephone: 0171 353 9564
E-mail: jvlee@btinternet.com
Call date: Nov 1990, Lincoln's Inn
Qualifications: [Bsc (Lond), MSc (Manchester),
LLM (Leic), MA (Lond), C.Eng, MICE,
MISTRUCTE, FCIArb]

NAWAZ AMJAD

Coleridge Chambers
Citadel 190 Corporation Street, Birmingham
B4 6QD, Telephone: 0121 233 3303
Call date: July 1983, Lincoln's Inn
Qualifications: [BA (Aston)]

NAWAZ MOHAMMED

Lincoln House Chambers
5th Floor Lincoln House, 1 Brazennose Street,
Manchester M2 5EL,
Telephone: 0161 832 5701
E-mail: LincolnHouseChambers@link.org
Call date: Nov 1995, Lincoln's Inn
Qualifications: [LLB, LLM (Cantab)]

NAYLOR JONATHAN PETER

King's Chambers
5a Gildredge Road, Eastbourne, East Sussex
BN21 4RB, Telephone: 01323 416053
Call date: Oct 1995, Lincoln's Inn
Qualifications: [LLB (Hons)(Lond)]

NAYLOR KEVIN MICHAEL THOMAS

8 King Street
Manchester M2 6AQ,
Telephone: 0161 834 9560
Call date: Oct 1992, Lincoln's Inn
Qualifications: [MB.ChB, LLB(Hons)(Sheff)]

NAZARETH MISS MELANIE BERNADETTE

Gray's Inn Chambers
5th Floor, Gray's Inn, London WC1R 5JA,
Telephone: 0171 404 1111
Call date: July 1984, Inner Temple
Qualifications: [BSc (Lond), Dip Law]

NAZIR KAISER

Park Lane Chambers
19 Westgate, Leeds LS1 2RD,
Telephone: 0113 2285000
Call date: Nov 1991, Lincoln's Inn
Qualifications: [LLB (Hons)]

NDLOVU LAZARUS

12 Old Square
1st Floor, Lincoln's Inn, London WC2A 3TX,
Telephone: 0171 404 0875
Call date: July 1979, Lincoln's Inn
Qualifications: [BA,LLM (Lond)]

NDUKA-EZE CHUKWUEMEKA CECIL

New Court Chambers
Suite 200 Gazette Building, 168 Corporation
Street, Birmingham B4 6TZ,
Telephone: 0121 693 6656
Door Tenant
Call date: Oct 1990, Middle Temple
Qualifications: [LLB (Warw)]

NEAL ALAN CHRISTOPHER

2 New Street
Leicester LE1 5NA, Telephone: 0116 2625906
Call date: July 1975, Gray's Inn
Qualifications: [LLB (Warks), LLM (Lond),
DGLS (Stockholm)]

NEALE MISS FIONA ROSALIND

3 Serjeants Inn
London EC4Y 1BQ,
Telephone: 0171 353 5537
E-mail: available upon request
Call date: July 1981, Middle Temple
Qualifications: [LLB (Lond)]

NEALE NICHOLAS LAWRENCE

Paradise Square Chambers
26 Paradise Square, Sheffield S1 2DE,
Telephone: 0114 2738951
Call date: July 1972, Gray's Inn
Qualifications: [BA]

NEALE STUART RONALD

Cobden House Chambers
19 Quay Street, Manchester M3 3HN,
Telephone: 0161 833 6000
E-mail: clerks@cobden.co.uk
Call date: July 1976, Middle Temple
Qualifications: [MA (Cantab)]

NEAMAN SAMUEL LISTER

4 Paper Bldgs
2nd Floor, Temple, London EC4Y 7EX,
Telephone: 0171 583 0816/071 353 1131
E-mail: clerks@4paperbuildings.co.uk
Call date: July 1988, Inner Temple
Qualifications: [MA (Oxon), Dip Law (City)]

NEATHEY MISS RONA VANESSA

6 King's Bench Walk
Ground, Third & Fourth Floors, Temple,
London EC4Y 7DR,
Telephone: 0171 353 4931/583 0695
Call date: Nov 1990, Inner Temple
Qualifications: [LLB (Hons)]

NEAVES ANDREW MICHAEL

36 Bedford Row
London WC1R 4JH,
Telephone: 0171 421 8000
E-mail: 36bedfordrow@link.org
Call date: July 1977, Gray's Inn
Qualifications: [LLB]

NEBHRAJANI MISS MEL

11 Stone Bldgs
1st Floor, Lincoln's Inn, London WC2A 3TG,
Telephone: 0171 404 5055
E-mail: 9stoneb@compuserve.com
Call date: Nov 1994, Middle Temple
Qualifications: [BA (Hons) (Dunelm), Dip Law
(City)]

NEENAN MISS LESLEY

3 Temple Gardens
3rd Floor, Temple, London EC4Y 9AU,
Telephone: 0171 353 0832
Call date: Nov 1990, Inner Temple
Qualifications: [LLB (Hons)]

NEILL ROBERT JAMES MACGILLIVRAY

3 Hare Court
1st Floor, Temple, London EC4Y 7BJ,
Telephone: 0171 353 7561
Call date: July 1975, Middle Temple
Qualifications: [LLB (Lond)]

D

D

NEILL OF BLADEN LORD QC (1966)

One Hare Court
1st Floor, Temple, London EC4Y 7BE,
Telephone: 0171 353 3171
E-mail: admin-oneharecourt@btinternet.com
Call date: Nov 1951, Gray's Inn
Qualifications: [BCL, MA, DCL (Oxon)]

NEILSON MISS LOUISE

9 Gough Square
London EC4A 3DE, Telephone: 0171 353 5371
Call date: Oct 1994, Middle Temple
Qualifications: [BA (Hons), LLM (Cantab)]

NEISH ANDREW GRAHAM

4 Pump Court
Temple, London EC4Y 7AN,
Telephone: 0171 353 2656/9
E-mail: 4_pump_court@compuserve.com
Call date: July 1988, Lincoln's Inn
Qualifications: [MA (Hons) St Andrews, Dip
Law]

NELSON CAIRNS LOUIS DAVID

5 Paper Bldgs
Lower Ground Floor, Temple, London
EC4Y 7HB, Telephone: 0171 353 5638
E-mail: 107722,633@compuserve.com
Call date: Nov 1987, Gray's Inn
Qualifications: [LLB (Lond)]

NELSON GILES YORICK

5 Paper Bldgs
Lower Ground Floor, Temple, London
EC4Y 7HB, Telephone: 0171 353 5638
E-mail: 107722,633@compuserve.com
Call date: Feb 1995, Inner Temple
Qualifications: [BSc (Bris), CPE]

NELSON MS JULIA MARIA

Broadway House Chambers
Broadway House 9 Bank Street, Bradford,
West Yorkshire BD1 1TW,
Telephone: 01274 722560
Call date: Nov 1993, Gray's Inn
Qualifications: [BA (Manch)]

NELSON MICHAEL PAUL

4 King's Bench Walk
Ground/First Floor, Temple, London
EC4Y 7DL, Telephone: 0171 822 8822
E-mail: 4kbw@barristersatlaw.com
Call date: Oct 1992, Lincoln's Inn
Qualifications: [LLB(Hons)]

NELSON MISS MICHELLE

18 Red Lion Court
(Off Fleet Street), London EC4A 3EB,
Telephone: 0171 520 6000
Thornwood House
102 New London Road, Chelmsford, Essex
CM2 0RG, Telephone: 01245 280880
Call date: Oct 1994, Middle Temple
Qualifications: [BSc (Hons)(Brunel), LLB
(Hons)(Lond)]

NELSON VINCENT LEONARD

39 Essex Street
London WC2R 3AT,
Telephone: 0171 583 1111
E-mail: clerks@39essex.co.uk
Call date: Nov 1980, Inner Temple
Qualifications: [LLB (Birmingham)]

NESBITT TIMOTHY JOHN ROBERT

199 Strand
London WC2R 1DR,
Telephone: 0171 379 9779
E-mail: chambers@199strand.co.uk
Call date: Feb 1991, Middle Temple
Qualifications: [BA (Dunelm), Dip Law (PCL)]

NEUBERT JOLYON NICHOLAS

3 Temple Gardens
3rd Floor, Temple, London EC4Y 9AU,
Telephone: 0171 353 0832
Call date: July 1989, Middle Temple
Qualifications: [LLB (Hons)]

NEUFELD MISS MICHAELA

95A Chancery Lane
London WC2A 1DT,
Telephone: 0171 405 3101
Call date: July 1990, Middle Temple
Qualifications: [LLB (Lond)]

NEVILLE STEPHEN JOHN

Gough Square Chambers
6-7 Gough Square, London EC4A 3DE,
Telephone: 0171 353 0924
E-mail: gsc@goughsq.co.uk
Call date: Nov 1986, Middle Temple
Qualifications: [MA(Cantab)]

NEVILLE-CLARKE SEBASTIAN ADRIAN BENNETT

1 Crown Office Row
3rd Floor, Temple, London EC4Y 7HH,
Telephone: 0171 583 9292
E-mail: onecor@link.org
Call date: Nov 1973, Inner Temple
Qualifications: [BA (Oxon)]

NEWBERRY CLIVE DOUGLAS QC (1993)

4-5 Gray's Inn Square
Ground Floor, Gray's Inn, London WC1R 5AY,
Telephone: 0171 404 5252
E-mail: chambers@4-5graysinnsquare.co.uk
Call date: July 1978, Inner Temple

NEWBERRY DAVID JOHN

17a Barclay Road
Walthamstow, London E17 9JH,
Telephone: 0181 521 3112
Call date: Oct 1990, Middle Temple
Qualifications: [BA, Dip Law]

NEWBERY MISS FREYA PATRICIA

12 King's Bench Walk
Temple, London EC4Y 7EL,
Telephone: 0171 583 0811
E-mail: chambers@12kbw.co.uk
Call date: Nov 1986, Middle Temple
Qualifications: [MA (Cantab)]

NEWBOLD RONALD EDGAR

Priory Chambers
2 Fountain Court, Steelhouse Lane,
Birmingham B4 6DR,
Telephone: 0121 236 3882/1375
Call date: July 1965, Inner Temple
Recorder
Qualifications: [MA (Oxon), DIP.ED]

NEWBON IAN

Broadway House Chambers
Broadway House 9 Bank Street, Bradford,
West Yorkshire BD1 1TW,
Telephone: 01274 722560
Call date: Feb 1977, Middle Temple
Qualifications: [LL.B]

NEWBURY RICHARD LENNOX

25 Park Square
Leeds LS1 2PW, Telephone: 0113 2451841/2/3
E-mail: sovereignchambers@btinternet.com
Call date: July 1976, Gray's Inn
Qualifications: [LLB (Hons) (New)]

NEWCOMBE ANDREW BENNETT

2 Harcourt Buildings
Temple, London EC4Y 9DB,
Telephone: 0171 353 8415
E-mail: clerks@twoharcourtbldgs.demon.co.uk
Call date: July 1987, Middle Temple
Qualifications: [BA (Dunelm)]

Fax: 0171 353 7622; DX: LDE 402

Types of work: Administrative; Ecclesiastical;
Environment; Local government; Parliamentary;
Town and country planning

Membership of foreign bars: Irish Bar

Awards and memberships: Member of the
Planning and Environment Bar Association;
Member of the Parliamentary Bar Mess; Member
of the Equine Lawyers Association

Languages spoken: French, Russian

NEWCOMBE PAUL ANTHONY

Baker Street Chambers
9 Baker Street, Middlesbrough TS1 2LF,
Telephone: 01642 873873
Call date: Feb 1991, Inner Temple
Qualifications: [LLB (Hons)]

NEWCOMBE TIMOTHY RICHARD

St Paul's House
5th Floor 23 Park Square South, Leeds
LS1 2ND, Telephone: 0113 2455866
Call date: Nov 1972, Inner Temple
Qualifications: [TD]

NEWDICK CHRISTOPHER

No published address
Call date: Feb 1983, Gray's Inn
Qualifications: [BA, LLM (Lond)]

NEWELL MISS CHARLOTTE ANNE

Mitre Court Chambers
3rd Floor, Temple, London EC4Y 7BP,
Telephone: 0171 353 9394
Call date: Oct 1994, Gray's Inn
Qualifications: [LLB]

NEWELL SIMON PETER

15 Winckley Square
Preston PR1 3JJ, Telephone: 01772 252828
E-mail: clerks@winckleysq.demon.co.uk
Call date: Nov 1973, Inner Temple
Qualifications: [LLB]

NEWEY GUY RICHARD

7 Stone Bldgs
Ground Floor, Lincoln's Inn, London
WC2A 3SZ, Telephone: 0171 405 3886/
242 3546
E-mail: chaldous@vossnet.co.uk
Call date: July 1982, Middle Temple
Qualifications: [MA, LLM (Cantab)]

NEWMAN ALAN RONALD HARVEY QC (1989)

Cloisters
1st Floor, Temple, London EC4Y 7AA,
Telephone: 0171 827 4000
E-mail: clerks@cloisters.com
Call date: Nov 1968, Middle Temple
Qualifications: [MA, LLB (Cantab)]

NEWMAN AUSTIN ERIC

9 Woodhouse Square
Leeds LS3 1AD, Telephone: 0113 2451986
Call date: Nov 1987, Inner Temple
Qualifications: [LLB, LLM]

NEWMAN BENEDICT GEORGE

1 Paper Bldgs
Ground Floor, Temple, London EC4Y 7EP,
Telephone: 0171 583 7355
E-mail: clerks@1pb.co.uk
Call date: Nov 1991, Middle Temple
Qualifications: [LLB Hons (Bris)]

NEWMAN MISS CATHERINE MARY QC (1995)

13 Old Square
Lincoln's Inn, London WC2A 3UA,
Telephone: 0171 404 4800
Call date: July 1979, Middle Temple
Assistant Recorder
Qualifications: [LLB (Hons) (Lond)]

Fax: 0171 405 4267;
Out of hours telephone: 0171 823 1232;
DX: LDE 326

Types of work: Chancery (general); Chancery land law; Commercial; Commercial litigation; Company and commercial; Crime - corporate fraud; Equity, wills and trusts; Financial services; Insolvency; Partnerships; Probate and administration; Professional negligence

Awards and memberships: Harmsworth Scholar of the Middle Temple 1979-81

Languages spoken: French

Reported cases: *Trident International v Hamlet Plc*, (1998) *The Times* 13 March, 1998. Lien or floating charge; insolvency.
Richbell Strategic Holdings Plc, [1997] 2 BCLC 429, 1997. Winding up.
Hazell v Hammersmith and Fulham LBC, [1992] 2 AC 1, 1992. Powers of local authorities to enter interest rate swap contracts.
Nemgia Ltd v AGF (UK) Ltd, [1997] LRLR 159, 1997. Net loss approach to damages.
Harrods Ltd v Schwartz-Sackin & Co Ltd, [1991] FSR 209, CA, 1991. Breach of contract, passing off.

Additional Information

Considerable experience in insolvency matters (Maxwell, BCCI) including the insolvency of insurance companies (see, for example, *Transit Casualty Co v The Policyholders' Protection Board* [1992] 2 Lloyd's Rep 358). Undertakes broad range of work including statutory construction (see for example *NRDC v The Wellcome Foundation* [1991] FSR 663), the operation of commercial contracts; professional negligence (especially lawyers, accountants and financial advisers), partnership disputes; contentious trusts work, land law. Accepts appointments to arbitrate.

NEWMAN MS INGRID

Hardwicke Building
New Square, Lincoln's Inn, London
WC2A 3SB, Telephone: 0171 242 2523
E-mail: clerks@hardwicke.co.uk
Call date: Oct 1992, Inner Temple
Qualifications: [LLB (Lond)]

NEWMAN MISS JANET MARGARET

St Ive's Chambers
9 Fountain Ct, Birmingham B4 6DR,
Telephone: 0121 236 0863/0929
Call date: Oct 1990, Inner Temple
Qualifications: [LLB (L'pool)]

NEWMAN MALCOLM RICHARD ANTHONY

10 Park Square
Leeds LS1 2LH, Telephone: 0113 2455438
E-mail: chambers@bandit.legend.co.uk
Call date: Feb 1972, Gray's Inn
Qualifications: [LLB (Hons)]

NEWMAN PAUL LANCE

Wilberforce Chambers
8 New Square, Lincoln's Inn, London
WC2A 3QP, Telephone: 0171 306 0102
E-mail: chambers@wilberforce.co.uk
Call date: Oct 1991, Lincoln's Inn
Qualifications: [MA (Hons) (Cantab), LLM (Harvard)]

NEWMAN PHILIP ADRIAN

1 Gray's Inn Square
1st Floor, London WC1R 5AG,
Telephone: 0171 405 3000
E-mail: clerks@onegrays.demon.co.uk
Call date: Nov 1977, Gray's Inn
Qualifications: [LLM (Lond), FCIArb]

NEWMAN TIMOTHY JOHN

5 Fountain Court
Steelhouse Lane, Birmingham B4 6DR,
Telephone: 0121 606 0500
Call date: July 1981, Gray's Inn
Qualifications: [BA]

NEWSOM GEORGE LUCIEN

Guildhall Chambers
23 Broad Street, Bristol BS1 2HG,
Telephone: 0117 9273366
Door Tenant
17 Old Bldgs
Ground Floor, Lincoln's Inn, London
WC2A 3UP, Telephone: 0171 405 9653
Door Tenant
Call date: Nov 1973, Lincoln's Inn
Qualifications: [MA (Oxon) FCIArb]

NEWTON ANDREW DAVID

10 King's Bench Walk
1st Floor, Temple, London EC4Y 7EB,
Telephone: 0171 353 2501
Call date: Nov 1989, Inner Temple
Qualifications: [MA (Oxon), Dip Law (City), LLM]

NEWTON MISS CLAIRE ELAINE MARIA BAILEY

Goldsmith Building
1st Floor, Temple, London EC4Y 7BL,
Telephone: 0171 353 7881
E-mail: clerks@goldsmith-building.law.co.uk
Call date: Oct 1992, Gray's Inn
Qualifications: [LL.B (Lond)]

NEWTON CLIVE RICHARD

1 King's Bench Walk
2nd Floor, Temple, London EC4Y 7DB,
Telephone: 0171 936 1500
E-mail: ddear@1kbw.co.uk
Call date: Nov 1968, Middle Temple
Qualifications: [MA, BCL (Oxon)]

NEWTON JOHN SIMON

Derby Square Chambers
Merchants Court, Derby Square, Liverpool
L2 1TS, Telephone: 0151 709 4222
12 King's Bench Walk
Temple, London EC4Y 7EL,
Telephone: 0171 583 0811
E-mail: chambers@12kbw.co.uk
Call date: July 1970, Middle Temple
Qualifications: [LLB, Diplome de, l'ecole Int'l de, droit du travail, compare]

D

NEWTON MISS LESLEY ANNE

38 Young Street
Manchester M3 3FT,
Telephone: 0161 833 0489
E-mail: clerks@young-st-chambers.com
Call date: Nov 1977, Middle Temple
Assistant Recorder
Qualifications: [LLB]

NEWTON PHILIP

Becket Chambers
17 New Dover Road, Canterbury, Kent
CT1 3AS, Telephone: 01227 786331
Call date: July 1984, Middle Temple
Qualifications: [BA (Hons), LLM,
Dip.Int.Human Rights, (Strasbourg)]

NEWTON RODERICK BRIAN

East Anglian Chambers
Gresham House 5 Museum Street, Ipswich
IP1 1HQ, Telephone: 01473 214481
East Anglian Chambers
Sanders House 52 North Hill, Colchester
CO1 1PY, Telephone: 01206 572756
East Anglian Chambers
57 London Street, Norwich NR2 1HL,
Telephone: 01603 617351
Call date: July 1982, Middle Temple
Assistant Recorder
Qualifications: [BA (Hons)]

NEWTON STUART RICHARD JAMES

19 Figtree Lane
Sheffield S1 2DJ, Telephone: 0114 2759708/
2738380
Call date: Nov 1993, Middle Temple
Qualifications: [BA (Hons)(Lond), CPE]

NEWTON-PRICE JAMES EDWARD

Pump Court Chambers
Upper Ground Floor 3 Pump Court, Temple,
London EC4Y 7AJ, Telephone: 0171 353 0711
Pump Court Chambers
31 Southgate Street, Winchester SO23 8EE,
Telephone: 01962 868161
Call date: Oct 1992, Middle Temple
Qualifications: [BA (Hons)]

NG RAY KIAN HIN

5 Bell Yard
London WC2A 2JR, Telephone: 0171 333 8811
Call date: July 1987, Inner Temple
Qualifications: [BA (Dunelm)]

NIBLETT ANTHONY IAN

1 Crown Office Row
Ground Floor, Temple, London EC4Y 7HH,
Telephone: 0171 797 7500
Crown Office Row Chambers
Blenheim House 120 Church Street, Brighton,
Sussex BN1 1WH, Telephone: 01273 625625
Call date: July 1976, Inner Temple
Assistant Recorder
Qualifications: [LLB.]

NICE GEOFFREY QC (1990)

Farrar's Building
Temple, London EC4Y 7BD,
Telephone: 0171 583 9241
E-mail: chambers@farrarsbuilding.co.uk
Call date: July 1971, Inner Temple
Recorder
Qualifications: [MA (Oxon)]

NICHOL SIMON BEDE

Cobden House Chambers
19 Quay Street, Manchester M3 3HN,
Telephone: 0161 833 6000
E-mail: clerks@cobden.co.uk
Call date: May 1994, Lincoln's Inn
Qualifications: [BSc (Hons, Manch)]

NICHOLAS MISS GEORGINA MARY

Lion Court
Chancery House 53-64 Chancery Lane, London
WC2A 1SJ, Telephone: 0171 404 6565
Call date: July 1983, Gray's Inn
Qualifications: [BA]

NICHOLES MS CATHERINE MARGARET ELIZABETH

4 Brick Court
Ground Floor, Temple, London EC4Y 9AD,
Telephone: 0171 797 7766
E-mail: chambers@4brick.co.uk
Call date: May 1977, Inner Temple
Qualifications: [LLB (Lond)]

NICHOLLS MRS (DEBORAH) JANE

Oriel Chambers
14 Water Street, Liverpool L2 8TD,
Telephone: 0151 236 7191
E-mail: oriel_chambers@link.org
Call date: Nov 1989, Inner Temple
Qualifications: [BA (Keele)]

NICHOLLS CHRISTOPHER BENJAMIN

1 Fountain Court
Steelhouse Lane, Birmingham B4 6DR,
Telephone: 0121 236 5721
Call date: July 1978, Gray's Inn
Qualifications: [BA (Cantab), Dip ECL (Lond)]

NICHOLLS CLIVE VICTOR QC (1982)

3 Raymond Buildings
Gray's Inn, London WC1R 5BH,
Telephone: 0171 831 3833
E-mail: chambers@threeraymond.demon.co.uk
Call date: May 1957, Gray's Inn
Recorder
Qualifications: [MA, LLM]

NICHOLLS COLIN ALFRED ARTHUR QC (1981)

3 Raymond Buildings
Gray's Inn, London WC1R 5BH,
Telephone: 0171 831 3833
E-mail: chambers@threeraymond.demon.co.uk
Call date: July 1957, Gray's Inn
Recorder
Qualifications: [MA, LLB]

NICHOLLS MISS ELIZABETH JANE

Lincoln House Chambers
5th Floor Lincoln House, 1 Brazennose Street,
Manchester M2 5EL,
Telephone: 0161 832 5701
E-mail: LincolnHouseChambers@link.org
Call date: July 1984, Inner Temple
Qualifications: [BA (Manch), Dip Law]

NICHOLLS JOHN PETER

13 Old Square
Ground Floor, Lincoln's Inn, London
WC2A 3UA, Telephone: 0171 404 4800
Call date: July 1986, Middle Temple
Qualifications: [MA (Cantab)]

NICHOLLS PAUL RICHARD

11 King's Bench Walk
Temple, London EC4Y 7EQ,
Telephone: 0171 632 8500
E-mail: clerksroom@11-kbw.law.co.uk
Call date: Oct 1992, Inner Temple
Qualifications: [LLB (Sheffield), BCL (Oxon)]

NICHOLLS PETER JOHN

5 Pump Court
Ground Floor, Temple, London EC4Y 7AP,
Telephone: 0171 353 2532
E-mail: fivepump@netcomuk.co.uk
Call date: Nov 1991, Inner Temple
Qualifications: [BA(Hons)(Dunelm)]

NICHOLLS RICHARD JOHN

New Walk Chambers
27 New Walk, Leicester LE1 6TE,
Telephone: 0116 2559144
Call date: Oct 1994, Gray's Inn
Qualifications: [LLB (Manch)]

NICHOLS STUART RICHARD

New Court
Temple, London EC4Y 9BE,
Telephone: 0171 583 5123/0171 583 0510
Call date: Nov 1989, Lincoln's Inn
Qualifications: [LLB (Leic)]

NICHOLSON ANTHONY THOMAS CUTHBERTSON

Tindal Chambers
3/5 New Street, Chelmsford, Essex CM1 1NT,
Telephone: 01245 267742
Tindal Chambers
3 Waxhouse Gate, St Albans, Herts AL5 4DU,
Telephone: 01727 843383
Call date: Nov 1962, Gray's Inn
Recorder

NICHOLSON JEREMY MARK

4 Pump Court
Temple, London EC4Y 7AN,
Telephone: 0171 353 2656/9
E-mail: 4_pump_court@compuserve.com
Call date: July 1977, Middle Temple
Qualifications: [MA (Cantab)]

D

NICHOLSON MICHAEL HUGH

2 Field Court
Gray's Inn, London WC1R 5BB,
Telephone: 0171 405 6114
E-mail: fieldct2@netcomuk.co.uk.
Call date: Oct 1993, Middle Temple
Qualifications: [LLB (Hons)(Lond)]

NICHOLSON MISS ROSALIND VERONICA

4 Stone Bldgs
Ground Floor, Lincoln's Inn, London
WC2A 3XT, Telephone: 0171 242 5524
E-mail: d.goddard@4stonebuildings.law.co.uk
Call date: July 1987, Gray's Inn
Qualifications: [MA (Oxon)]

NICHOLSON PRATT THOMAS HYCY

Hardwicke Building
New Square, Lincoln's Inn, London
WC2A 3SB, Telephone: 0171 242 2523
E-mail: clerks@hardwicke.co.uk
Call date: July 1986, Lincoln's Inn
Qualifications: [LLB (Lond)]

NICKLIN MATTHEW JAMES

5 Raymond Buildings
1st Floor, Gray's Inn, London WC1R 5BP,
Telephone: 0171 242 2902
Call date: Oct 1993, Lincoln's Inn
Qualifications: [LLB (Hons)(Newc)]

NICOL ANDREW GEORGE LINDSAY QC (1995)

Doughty Street Chambers
11 Doughty Street, London WC1N 2PG,
Telephone: 0171 404 1313
E-mail: doughty_street@compuserve.com
Call date: July 1978, Middle Temple
Assistant Recorder
Qualifications: [BA, LLB (Cantab), LLM (Harvard)]

NICOL ANDREW ROBERT

2 Crown Office Row
2nd Floor, Temple, London EC4Y 7HJ,
Telephone: 0171 797 8000
Call date: Nov 1991, Inner Temple
Qualifications: [MA (Cantab)]

NICOL ANGUS SEBASTIAN TORQUIL EYERS

5 Paper Bldgs
Ground Floor, Temple, London EC4Y 7HB,
Telephone: 0171 583 9275/583 4555
E-mail: 5paper@link.org
Call date: July 1963, Middle Temple
Recorder

NICOL NICHOLAS KEITH

Staple Inn Chambers
1st Floor 9 Staple Inn, Holborn, London
WC1V 7QH, Telephone: 0171 242 5240
E-mail: clerks@staple-inn.org
Call date: Nov 1986, Inner Temple
Qualifications: [LLB (Lond)]

NICOL-GENT WILLIAM PHILIP TRAHAIR

King's Chambers
5a Gildredge Road, Eastbourne, East Sussex
BN21 4RB, Telephone: 01323 416053
Call date: Oct 1991, Inner Temple
Qualifications: [LLB (Bucks)]

NICOLSON ARIS TONY

23 Bracken Gardens
Barnes, London SW13 9HW,
Telephone: 0181 748 4924
Call date: July 1981, Gray's Inn
Qualifications: [LLB]

NIELD MICHAEL WILLIAM

7 Stone Bldgs
Ground Floor, Lincoln's Inn, London
WC2A 3SZ, Telephone: 0171 405 3886/
242 3546
E-mail: chaldous@vossnet.co.uk
Call date: Nov 1969, Lincoln's Inn
Qualifications: [MA (Oxon)]

NIGHTINGALE MS JANE ANN

12 Old Square
1st Floor, Lincoln's Inn, London WC2A 3TX,
Telephone: 0171 404 0875
Call date: Nov 1995, Lincoln's Inn
Qualifications: [BA (Hons)]

NIGHTINGALE PETER VINCENT JOSEPH

4 King's Bench Walk
2nd Floor, Temple, London EC4Y 7DL,
Telephone: 0171 353 3581
Call date: July 1986, Inner Temple

NIJABAT MISS SHAMA BATOOL

Paradise Square Chambers
26 Paradise Square, Sheffield S1 2DE,
Telephone: 0114 2738951
Call date: Nov 1993, Middle Temple
Qualifications: [LLB (Hons), LLM (Lond)]

NIMMO ADRIAN

Bank House Chambers
Old Bank House, Hartshead, Sheffield S1 2EL,
Telephone: 0114 2751223
Call date: Nov 1971, Gray's Inn
Qualifications: [LLB]

NISBETT JAMES THEOPHILUS

7 Westmeath Avenue
Evington, Leicester LE5 6SS,
Telephone: 0116 2412003
Call date: July 1973, Lincoln's Inn
Qualifications: [LLB]

NISSEN ALEXANDER DAVID

Keating Chambers
10 Essex Street, Outer Temple, London
WC2R 3AA, Telephone: 0171 544 2600
Call date: July 1985, Middle Temple
Qualifications: [LLB (Manch)]

NIXON COLIN ROSSINGTON

1 Paper Bldgs
Ground Floor, Temple, London EC4Y 7EP,
Telephone: 0171 583 7355
E-mail: clerks@1pb.co.uk
Call date: July 1973, Lincoln's Inn
Qualifications: [BA (Natal)]

NIXON-MOSS GARETH JAMES

Tindal Chambers
3/5 New Street, Chelmsford, Essex CM1 1NT,
Telephone: 01245 267742
Tindal Chambers
3 Waxhouse Gate, St Albans, Herts AL5 4DU,
Telephone: 01727 843383
Call date: Oct 1994, Inner Temple
Qualifications: [LLB (Bucks)]

NOBLE ANDREW

Merchant Chambers
1 North Parade, Parsonage Gardens,
Manchester M3 2NH,
Telephone: 0161 839 7070
Eldon Chambers
Fourth Floor 30/32 Fleet Street, London
EC4Y 1AA, Telephone: 0171 353 4636
Call date: Nov 1992, Lincoln's Inn
Qualifications: [LLB (Hons)(Manc), FRICS]

NOBLE MISS ANTONIA CARTER

3 Pump Court
2nd Floor, Temple, London EC4Y 7AJ,
Telephone: 0171 353 1356 (3 Lines)
Call date: Nov 1995, Middle Temple
Qualifications: [BA (Hons)]

NOBLE ARTHUR EDWIN RANDALL

Peel House Chambers
Ground Floor, Peel House 5 Harrington Street,
Liverpool L2 9QA, Telephone: 0151 236 4321
Call date: July 1965, Inner Temple
Recorder
Qualifications: [BA (Dub)]

NOBLE PHILIP ROBERT

Thomas More Chambers
52 Carey Street, Lincoln's Inn, London
WC2A 2JB, Telephone: 0171 404 7000
Call date: July 1978, Inner Temple

NOBLE RODERICK GRANT

39 Essex Street
London WC2R 3AT,
Telephone: 0171 583 1111
E-mail: clerks@39essex.co.uk
Call date: Nov 1977, Gray's Inn
Qualifications: [BSc]

D

NOLAN BENJAMIN QC (1992)

9 Woodhouse Square
Leeds LS3 1AD, Telephone: 0113 2451986
Call date: July 1971, Middle Temple
Qualifications: [LLB (Lond)]

NOLAN DAMIAN FRANCIS

25-27 Castle Street
1st Floor, Liverpool L2 4TA,
Telephone: 0151 227 5661/051 236 5072
Call date: Oct 1994, Lincoln's Inn
Qualifications: [BSc (Hons)(Cardiff)]

NOLAN DOMINIC THOMAS

24 The Ropewalk
Nottingham NG1 5EF,
Telephone: 0115 9472581
E-mail: clerk@ropewalk.co.uk
Call date: July 1985, Lincoln's Inn
Qualifications: [LLB (Nott'm)]

NOLAN MICHAEL ALFRED ANTHONY

4 Essex Court
Temple, London EC4Y 9AJ,
Telephone: 0171 797 7970
E-mail: clerks@4essexcourt.law.co.uk
Call date: July 1981, Middle Temple
Qualifications: [MA (Oxon)]

NOORDEEN MS SAMIYA SALAMATH SAHABDEEN

169 Temple Chambers
Temple Avenue, London EC4Y 0DA,
Telephone: 0171 583 7644
Call date: Oct 1994, Middle Temple
Qualifications: [BSc (Hons)(Lond), CPE]

NORBURY HUGH ROBERT

13 Old Square
1st Floor, Lincoln's Inn, London WC2A 3UA,
Telephone: 0171 242 6105
E-mail: clerks@serlecourt.co.uk
Call date: Nov 1995, Lincoln's Inn
Qualifications: [BA (Hons), Dip Law]

NORBURY LUKE EDWARD

17 Old Bldgs
Ground Floor, Lincoln's Inn, London
WC2A 3UP, Telephone: 0171 405 9653
Call date: Oct 1995, Inner Temple
Qualifications: [MA (Cantab)]

NORIE-MILLER JEFFREY REGINALD

55 Temple Chambers
Temple Avenue, London EC4Y 0HP,
Telephone: 0171 353 7400
Call date: July 1996, Inner Temple
Qualifications: [LLB (Soton)]

NORMAN MISS CHARITY JOANNA

York Chambers
14 Toft Green, York YO1 1JT,
Telephone: 01904 620048
E-mail: yorkchambers.co.uk
Call date: July 1988, Lincoln's Inn
Qualifications: [LLB (Hons) (Exon)]

NORMAN CHRISTOPHER JOHN GEORGE

1 Serjeants' Inn
5th Floor Fleet Street, Temple, London
EC4Y 1LL, Telephone: 0171 415 6666
E-mail: no1serjeantsinn@btinternet.com
Call date: Nov 1979, Lincoln's Inn
Qualifications: [LLB (Hons) (Lond)]

NORMAN MISS ELIZABETH ANNE

Rowchester Chambers
4 Rowchester Court Whittall Street,
Birmingham B4 6DH,
Telephone: 0121 233 2327/2361951
Call date: Nov 1977, Middle Temple
Qualifications: [MA (Cantab)]

NORMAN MARK ANDREW

1 Paper Bldgs
1st Floor, Temple, London EC4Y 7EP,
Telephone: 0171 353 3728/4953
Call date: Apr 1989, Inner Temple
Qualifications: [BA (Lond), Dip Law]

NORMAN MICHAEL CHARLES

3 Paper Bldgs
1st Floor, Temple, London EC4Y 7EU,
Telephone: 0171 583 8055
E-mail: london@3paper.com
20 Lorne Park Road
Bournemouth BH1 1JN,
Telephone: 01202 292102 (5 Lines)
4 St Peter Street
Winchester SO23 8OW,
Telephone: 01962 868884
Call date: Feb 1971, Gray's Inn
Recorder
Qualifications: [MA (Hons), LLB (Cantab)]

NORMAN PHILIP FRANCIS

95A Chancery Lane
London WC2A 1DT,
Telephone: 0171 405 3101
Call date: Oct 1995, Lincoln's Inn
Qualifications: [LLB (Hons)(Bucks)]

NORRIS ALASTAIR HUBERT QC (1997)

5 Stone Buildings
Lincoln's Inn, London WC2A 3XT,
Telephone: 0171 242 6201
E-mail: clerks@5-stonebuildings.law.co.uk
Southernhay Chambers
33 Southernhay East, Exeter, Devon EX1 1NX,
Telephone: 01392 255777
E-mail: southernhay.chambers@lineone.net
Door Tenant
Call date: July 1973, Lincoln's Inn
Assistant Recorder
Qualifications: [MA (Cantab), FCIArb]

Fax: 0171 831 8102; DX: 304 LDE;
Other comms: E-mail clerks@5-
stonebuildings.law.co.uk

Types of work: Arbitration; Chancery (general);
Chancery land law; Charities; Commercial
property; Conveyancing; Equity, wills and
trusts; Family provision; Landlord and tenant;
Partnerships; Pensions; Probate and
administration; Professional negligence

Other professional qualifications: FCIArb

Circuit: Western

NORRIS ANDREW JAMES STEEDSMAN

5 New Square
1st Floor, Lincoln's Inn, London WC2A 3RJ,
Telephone: 0171 404 0404
E-mail: Chambers@FiveNewSquare.CityScape.co.uk
Call date: Nov 1995, Middle Temple
Qualifications: [BSc (Hons)]

NORRIS JAMES LESLIE

Goldsmith Chambers
Ground Floor Goldsmith Building, Temple,
London EC4Y 7BL,
Telephone: 0171 353 6802/3/4/5
E-mail: celiamonksfield@btinternet.com
Call date: May 1984, Inner Temple
Qualifications: [LLB Soton]

NORRIS JOHN GERAINT

Albion Chambers
Broad Street, Bristol BS1 1DR,
Telephone: 0117 9272144
Call date: July 1980, Lincoln's Inn
Qualifications: [MA (Oxon)]

NORRIS PAUL HOWARD

1 Essex Court
1st Floor, Temple, London EC4Y 9AR,
Telephone: 0171 936 3030
E-mail: one.essex_court@virgin.net
Call date: May 1963, Middle Temple
Recorder
Qualifications: [BA (Oxon)]

NORRIS WILLIAM JOHN QC (1997)

Farrar's Building
Temple, London EC4Y 7BD,
Telephone: 0171 583 9241
E-mail: chambers@farrarsbuilding.co.uk
Call date: July 1974, Middle Temple
Qualifications: [MA (Oxon)]

NORRIS WILLIAM VERNON WESTWORTH

9 Old Square
Ground Floor, Lincoln's Inn, London
WC2A 3SR, Telephone: 0171 405 4682
E-mail: chambers@9oldsquare.co.uk
Call date: July 1997, Lincoln's Inn

D

NORTHROP KEITH DOUGLAS

199 Strand
London WC2R 1DR,
Telephone: 0171 379 9779
E-mail: chambers@199strand.co.uk
Door Tenant
Call date: Nov 1989, Inner Temple
Qualifications: [BA (Hull), Dip Law]

NORTON ANDREW DAVID

One Garden Court
Ground Floor, Temple, London EC4Y 9BJ,
Telephone: 0171 797 7900
Call date: Oct 1992, Inner Temple
Qualifications: [BSc (S'ton), CPE]

NORTON MISS HEATHER SOPHIA

23 Essex Street
London WC2R 3AS,
Telephone: 0171 413 0353/353 3533
E-mail: clerks@essexstreet23.demon.co.uk
Call date: Nov 1988, Middle Temple
Qualifications: [LLB (B'ham)]

NORTON RICHARD DAMIAN

28 St John Street
Manchester M3 4DJ,
Telephone: 0161 834 8418
E-mail: clerk@28stjohnst.co.uk
Call date: Nov 1992, Lincoln's Inn
Qualifications: [LLB (Hons)(Leeds)]

NOTHER DANIEL ROBERT

College Chambers
19 Carlton Cresent, Southampton, Hants
SO15 2ET, Telephone: 01703 230338
Call date: Nov 1994, Inner Temple
Qualifications: [BA (Oxon)]

NOURSE EDMUND ALEXANDER MARTIN

1 Essex Court
Ground Floor, Temple, London EC4Y 9AR,
Telephone: 0171 583 2000
E-mail: clerks@oneessexcourt.co.uk
Call date: Nov 1994, Lincoln's Inn
Qualifications: [BA (Hons)(Oxon), Dip in Law (City)]

NSUGBE OBA ERIC

Pump Court Chambers
Upper Ground Floor 3 Pump Court, Temple,
London EC4Y 7AJ, Telephone: 0171 353 0711
Pump Court Chambers
31 Southgate Street, Winchester SO23 8EE,
Telephone: 01962 868161
Call date: July 1985, Gray's Inn
Qualifications: [LLB (Hull)]

NUGEE CHRISTOPHER GEORGE

Wilberforce Chambers
8 New Square, Lincoln's Inn, London
WC2A 3QP, Telephone: 0171 306 0102
E-mail: chambers@wilberforce.co.uk
Call date: July 1983, Inner Temple
Qualifications: [BA (Oxon), Dip Law (City)]

NUGEE EDWARD GEORGE QC (1977)

Wilberforce Chambers
8 New Square, Lincoln's Inn, London
WC2A 3QP, Telephone: 0171 306 0102
E-mail: chambers@wilberforce.co.uk
Call date: June 1955, Inner Temple
Qualifications: [TD, MA (Oxon)]

NUGENT COLM GERARD

Hardwicke Building
New Square, Lincoln's Inn, London
WC2A 3SB, Telephone: 0171 242 2523
E-mail: clerks@hardwicke.co.uk
Call date: Oct 1992, Inner Temple
Qualifications: [BA (Kent)]

NUGENT PETER FRANCIS

Harrow on the Hill Chambers
60 High Street, Harrow on the Hill, Middlesex
HA1 3LL, Telephone: 0181 423 7444
Windsor Barristers' Chambers
Windsor, Telephone: 01753 648899
Call date: Feb 1994, Middle Temple
Qualifications: [BA (Hons)(Lond)]

NURSE GORDON BRAMWELL WILLIAM

11 Old Square
Ground Floor, Lincoln's Inn, London
WC2A 3TS, Telephone: 0171 430 0341
E-mail: clerks@11oldsquare.co.uk
Call date: Nov 1973, Middle Temple
Qualifications: [MA (Cantab)]

NUSRAT MAHMOOD ALI

9 King's Bench Walk
Basement, Temple, London EC4Y 7DX,
Telephone: 0171 353 9564
E-mail: jvlee@btinternet.com
Call date: July 1977, Lincoln's Inn
Qualifications: [MA]

NUSSEY RICHARD JOHN GEORGE

Farrar's Building
Temple, London EC4Y 7BD,
Telephone: 0171 583 9241
E-mail: chambers@farrarsbuilding.co.uk
Call date: Nov 1971, Lincoln's Inn
Qualifications: [BA]

NUTTALL ANDREW PETER

Lincoln House Chambers
5th Floor Lincoln House, 1 Brazennose Street,
Manchester M2 5EL,
Telephone: 0161 832 5701
E-mail: LincolnHouseChambers@link.org
Call date: Nov 1978, Lincoln's Inn
Qualifications: [LLB]

NUTTALL EVAN CALEB

3 Temple Gardens
Lower Ground Floor, Temple, London
EC4Y 9AU, Telephone: 0171 353 3102/5/9297
Call date: Oct 1993, Gray's Inn
Qualifications: [BA, MSc (Econ)]

NUTTER JULIAN ANDREW

3 Athol Street
Douglas, Isle of Man,
Telephone: 01624 897 420
Call date: Nov 1979, Gray's Inn
Qualifications: [LLB (L'pool)]

NUTTING JOHN GRENFELL QC (1995)

3 Raymond Buildings
Gray's Inn, London WC1R 5BH,
Telephone: 0171 831 3833
E-mail: chambers@threeraymond.demon.co.uk
Call date: Nov 1968, Middle Temple
Recorder
Qualifications: [BA]

NUVOLONI STEFANO VINCENZO

22 Old Bldgs
Lincoln's Inn, London WC2A 3UJ,
Telephone: 0171 831 0222
Call date: Nov 1994, Inner Temple
Qualifications: [LLB (Lond), MA (Lond)]

O'BRIEN BERNARD NICHOLAS

Albion Chambers
Broad Street, Bristol BS1 1DR,
Telephone: 0117 9272144
Call date: July 1968, Middle Temple
Qualifications: [MA (Dub)]

O'BRIEN MR. DAVID

Trinity Chambers
140 New London Road, Chelmsford, Essex
CM2 0AW, Telephone: 01245 605040
Call date: Nov 1994, Middle Temple
Qualifications: [LLB (Hons) Dips.W, C.Q.S.W,
ASW]

O'BRIEN DERMOD PATRICK QC (1983)

2 Temple Gardens
Temple, London EC4Y 9AY,
Telephone: 0171 583 6041 (12 Lines)
Call date: July 1962, Inner Temple
Recorder
Qualifications: [MA (Oxon)]

O'BRIEN MISS HAYLEE FIONA

2 Pump Court
1st Floor, Temple, London EC4Y 7AH,
Telephone: 0171 353 5597
Call date: Nov 1984, Middle Temple
Qualifications: [LLB (Hons)(Lond)]

O'BRIEN JOHN

3 Pump Court
2nd Floor, Temple, London EC4Y 7AJ,
Telephone: 0171 353 1356 (3 Lines)
Call date: May 1976, Middle Temple
Qualifications: [MA,LLB (Cantab),LLM]

D

O'BRIEN JOSEPH PATRICK ANTONY PETER

67a Westgate Road
Newcastle Upon Tyne NE1 1SQ,
Telephone: 0191 261 4407/2329785
Call date: Nov 1989, Inner Temple
Qualifications: [LLB (Newc)]

O'BRIEN NICHOLAS JOHN

4 Brick Court
Ground Floor, Temple, London EC4Y 9AD,
Telephone: 0171 797 7766
E-mail: chambers@4brick.co.uk
Call date: Nov 1985, Middle Temple
Qualifications: [BA (Oxon), ACIArb]

O'BRIEN PAUL

18 St John Street
Manchester M3 4EA,
Telephone: 0161 278 1800
Call date: Nov 1974, Gray's Inn
Assistant Recorder
Qualifications: [BA]

O'BRIEN WILLIAM ANTHONY PATRICK

2 Mitre Ct Bldgs
1st Floor, Temple, London EC4Y 7BX,
Telephone: 0171 353 1353
Call date: Nov 1994, Gray's Inn
Qualifications: [BA]

O'BYRNE ANDREW JOHN MARTIN

Peel Court Chambers
45 Hardman Street, Manchester M3 3HA,
Telephone: 0161 832 3791
Call date: July 1978, Gray's Inn
Qualifications: [LLB (L'pool)]

O'CALLAGHAN DECLAN MATHEW DENIS MARK

10 King's Bench Walk
Ground Floor, Temple, London EC4Y 7EB,
Telephone: 0171 353 7742
E-mail: 10kbw@lineone.net
Call date: Oct 1995, Gray's Inn
Qualifications: [LLB (Exon), LLM]

O'CONNELL MICHAEL ALFRED

King Charles House
Standard Hill, Nottingham NG1 6FX,
Telephone: 0115 9418851
E-mail: clerks@kch.co.uk
Call date: Nov 1966, Inner Temple
Qualifications: [LLB (Lond)]

O'CONNOR ANDREW MCDOUGAL

2 Crown Office Row
Ground Floor, Temple, London EC4Y 7HJ,
Telephone: 0171 797 8100
E-mail: mail@2cor.co.uk, or to individual
barristers at: [barrister's surname]@2cor.co.uk
Call date: Oct 1996, Gray's Inn
Qualifications: [BA (Cantab), Dip in Law]

O'CONNOR GERARD MICHAEL

Verulam Chambers
Peer House 8-14 Verulam Street, Gray's Inn,
London WC1X 8LZ,
Telephone: 0171 813 2400
Call date: Nov 1993, Lincoln's Inn
Qualifications: [MA (Oxon)]

O'CONNOR MARK

12 Old Square
1st Floor, Lincoln's Inn, London WC2A 3TX,
Telephone: 0171 404 0875
Call date: Oct 1994, Inner Temple
Qualifications: [LLB (Lond)]

O'CONNOR MISS MAUREEN THERESA

6 Gray's Inn Square
Ground Floor, Gray's Inn, London WC1R 5AZ,
Telephone: 0171 242 1052
Call date: Nov 1988, Gray's Inn
Qualifications: [LLB (Lond)]

O'CONNOR PATRICK MICHAEL JOSEPH QC (1993)

1 Crown Office Row
2nd Floor, Temple, London EC4Y 7HH,
Telephone: 0171 797 7111
Call date: Nov 1970, Inner Temple
Qualifications: [LLB (Lond)]

O'CONNOR MISS SARAH BERNADETTE ELIZABETH

1 King's Bench Walk
2nd Floor, Temple, London EC4Y 7DB,
Telephone: 0171 936 1500
E-mail: ddear@1kbw.co.uk
Call date: Nov 1986, Inner Temple
Qualifications: [LLB (Hons) (Soton)]

O'DEMPSEY DECLAN JOHN

4 Brick Court
Ground Floor, Temple, London EC4Y 9AD,
Telephone: 0171 797 7766
E-mail: chambers@4brick.co.uk
Call date: Nov 1987, Middle Temple
Qualifications: [BA (Hons) (Cantab), Dip Law (City)]

O'DONNELL DUNCAN GERARD

1 Paper Bldgs
1st Floor, Temple, London EC4Y 7EP,
Telephone: 0171 353 3728/4953
Call date: Oct 1992, Gray's Inn
Qualifications: [MA]

O'DONOGHUE FLORENCE

2 Mitre Ct Bldgs
1st Floor, Temple, London EC4Y 7BX,
Telephone: 0171 353 1353
Call date: Feb 1959, Inner Temple
Qualifications: [MA (Dub),FCIArb]

O'DONOHOE ANTHONY FRANCIS

Chavasse Court Chambers
2nd Floor Chavasse Court, 24 Lord Street,
Liverpool L2 1TA, Telephone: 0151 707 1191
Call date: July 1983, Middle Temple
Qualifications: [LLB (L'pool)]

O'DONOVAN JOHN MARTIN

1 Gray's Inn Square
1st Floor, London WC1R 5AG,
Telephone: 0171 405 3000
E-mail: clerks@onegrays.demon.co.uk
Call date: Nov 1993, Inner Temple
Qualifications: [BA, CPE]

O'DONOVAN KEVIN JOHN

5 Fountain Court
Steelhouse Lane, Birmingham B4 6DR,
Telephone: 0121 606 0500
Call date: July 1978, Middle Temple
Qualifications: [BA]

O'DONOVAN PAUL GODFREY

2 Paper Bldgs
1st Floor, Temple, London EC4Y 7ET,
Telephone: 0171 936 2611 (10 Lines)
E-mail: clerks@2pbbarristers.co.uk
Call date: Nov 1975, Inner Temple

O'DWYER MARTIN PATRICK

One Garden Court
Ground Floor, Temple, London EC4Y 9BJ,
Telephone: 0171 797 7900
Call date: Nov 1978, Middle Temple
Qualifications: [MA (Oxon)]

O'FARRELL MS FINOLA MARY

Keating Chambers
10 Essex Street, Outer Temple, London
WC2R 3AA, Telephone: 0171 544 2600
Call date: July 1983, Inner Temple
Qualifications: [BA Dunelm]

O'FLAHERTY MISS NORA

One Garden Court
Ground Floor, Temple, London EC4Y 9BJ,
Telephone: 0171 797 7900
Call date: Oct 1991, Lincoln's Inn
Qualifications: [BA (Hons) (Cambs), Dip Law]

O'FLYNN TIMOTHY JAMES

Pump Court Chambers
Upper Ground Floor 3 Pump Court, Temple,
London EC4Y 7AJ, Telephone: 0171 353 0711
Call date: July 1979, Gray's Inn
Qualifications: [LLB (Bris)]

O'GORMAN CHRISTOPHER FRANCIS

Clock Chambers
78 Darlington Street, Wolverhampton
WV1 4LY, Telephone: 01902 313444
Call date: Nov 1987, Gray's Inn
Qualifications: [LLB (Sheff)]

D

O'HALLORAN MISS JILL

First National Building
2nd Floor 24 Fenwick Street, Liverpool
L2 7NE, Telephone: 0151 236 2098
Call date: Oct 1994, Gray's Inn
Qualifications: [LLB]

O'HARA MISS SARAH LOUISE

3 Paper Bldgs
1st Floor, Temple, London EC4Y 7EU,
Telephone: 0171 583 8055
E-mail: london@3paper.com
20 Lorne Park Road
Bournemouth BH1 1JN,
Telephone: 01202 292102 (5 Lines)
1 Alfred Street
High Street, Oxford OX1 4EH,
Telephone: 01865 793736
Call date: July 1984, Middle Temple
Qualifications: [MA (Cantab)]

O'HARE MISS ELIZABETH ANNE

Park Lane Chambers
19 Westgate, Leeds LS1 2RD,
Telephone: 0113 2285000
Call date: July 1980, Middle Temple
Qualifications: [LLB]

O'HIGGINS JOHN GERARD

Chambers of Helen Grindrod QC
1st Floor 95a Chancery Lane, London
WC2A 2JG, Telephone: 0171 404 4777
Call date: Nov 1990, Middle Temple
Qualifications: [MA (Cantab)]

O'KEEFFE DARREN PHILIP DE VOIELS

Derby Square Chambers
Merchants Court, Derby Square, Liverpool
L2 1TS, Telephone: 0151 709 4222
Call date: July 1984, Inner Temple
Qualifications: [MA (Oxon)]

O'LEARY MISS CATHERINE ELIZABETH

40 King Street
Chester CH1 2AH, Telephone: 01244 323886
3 Paper Bldgs
1st Floor, Temple, London EC4Y 7EU,
Telephone: 0171 583 8055
E-mail: london@3paper.com
Call date: July 1979, Gray's Inn
Qualifications: [LLB (L'pool)]

O'LEARY MS MICHELE ANN

Goldsmith Chambers
Ground Floor Goldsmith Building, Temple,
London EC4Y 7BL,
Telephone: 0171 353 6802/3/4/5
E-mail: celiamonksfield@btinternet.com
Call date: Nov 1983, Gray's Inn
Qualifications: [LLB (Hons)(Wales)]

O'LEARY ROBERT MICHAEL

33 Park Place
Cardiff CF1 3BA, Telephone: 01222 233313
Call date: Oct 1990, Inner Temple
Qualifications: [LLB (Cardiff)]

O'MAHONY DECLAN LIAM

Arden Chambers
27 John Street, London WC1N 2BL,
Telephone: 0171 242 4244
Call date: July 1980, Inner Temple
Qualifications: [BA (Hons, Hull), Dip Law,
FCIArb]

O'MAHONY PATRICK JAMES MARTIN

5 Paper Bldgs
Lower Ground Floor, Temple, London
EC4Y 7HB, Telephone: 0171 353 5638
E-mail: 107722,633@compuserve.com
Call date: July 1973, Inner Temple
Assistant Recorder
Qualifications: [LLB (Lond)]

O'MALLEY MS JULIE BERNADETTE

10 King's Bench Walk
1st Floor, Temple, London EC4Y 7EB,
Telephone: 0171 353 2501
Call date: Nov 1983, Gray's Inn
Qualifications: [LLB (Sheff)]

O'MALLEY MISS MARY HELLEN

Holborn Chambers
6 Gate Street, Lincoln's Inn Fields, London
WC2A 3HP, Telephone: 0171 242 6060
Call date: Oct 1991, Lincoln's Inn
Qualifications: [Ba (Hons) (Kent)]

O'MAOILEOIN MICHAEL BRENDAN

3 Temple Gardens
3rd Floor, Temple, London EC4Y 9AU,
Telephone: 0171 353 0832
Call date: Feb 1986, Inner Temple
Qualifications: [BCL,LLB (Dub), ACI.Arb]

O'NEILL BRIAN PATRICK

1 Hare Court
Ground Floor, Temple, London EC4Y 7BE,
Telephone: 0171 353 3982/5324
Call date: Nov 1987, Gray's Inn
Qualifications: [LLB Hons (Brunel)]

O'NEILL MISS LOUISE CATHERINE

St John's Chambers
Small Street, Bristol BS1 1DW,
Telephone: 0117 9213456/298514
E-mail: clerks@stjohns.uk.com
Call date: Feb 1989, Gray's Inn
Qualifications: [BA (Dublin), LLM (Cantab)]

O'NEILL MICHAEL ALISTAIR HUGH

York Chambers
14 Toft Green, York YO1 1JT,
Telephone: 01904 620048
E-mail: yorkchambers.co.uk
Call date: July 1979, Inner Temple
Qualifications: [MA (Oxon)]

O'NEILL PAUL GERARD

Parsonage Chambers
5th Floor 3 The Parsonage, Manchester
M3 2HW, Telephone: 0161 833 1996
Call date: Oct 1994, Gray's Inn
Qualifications: [LLB (Leeds)]

O'NEILL PHILIP JOHN

The Corn Exchange
5th Floor Fenwick Street, Liverpool L2 7QS,
Telephone: 0151 227 1081/5009
Call date: Nov 1983, Gray's Inn
Qualifications: [LLB (Hons)(L'pool)]

O'NEILL MISS SALLY JANE QC (1997)

Furnival Chambers
32 Furnival Street, London EC4A 1JQ,
Telephone: 0171 405 3232
E-mail: clerks@furnivallaw.co.uk
Call date: Nov 1976, Gray's Inn
Qualifications: [LLB (Lond)]

O'NEILL TADHG JOSEPH

1 Crown Office Row
3rd Floor, Temple, London EC4Y 7HH,
Telephone: 0171 583 9292
E-mail: onecor@link.org
Call date: Nov 1987, Middle Temple
Qualifications: [BA (Cantab)]

O'RAWE MISS DOLORES

John Street Chambers
2 John Street, London WC1N 2HJ,
Telephone: 0171 242 1911
E-mail: john.street_chambers@virgin.net.uk
Call date: Nov 1992, Middle Temple
Qualifications: [LLB (Hons) (Lond)]

O'REILLY JAMES

Essex Court Chambers
24 Lincoln's Inn Fields, London WC2A 3ED,
Telephone: 0171 813 8000
E-mail: clerksroom@essexcourt-chambers.co.uk
Door Tenant
Call date: July 1983, Lincoln's Inn
Qualifications: [BCL, LLB (Dublin), LLM (Yale)]

O'REILLY MISS JANE ANN ELIZABETH

Rowchester Chambers
4 Rowchester Court Whittall Street,
Birmingham B4 6DH,
Telephone: 0121 233 2327/2361951
Call date: Nov 1991, Lincoln's Inn
Qualifications: [LLB (Hons)]

O'REILLY MICHAEL PATRICK

Paradise Square Chambers
26 Paradise Square, Sheffield S1 2DE,
Telephone: 0114 2738951
Call date: Nov 1988, Gray's Inn
Qualifications: [BEng (Shef), PhD (Nott'm), LLB (Lond)]

D

O'REILLY WALTER ANTHONY PAUL

3 Aisby Drive
Rossington, Doncaster DN11 OYY,
Telephone: 01302 866495
Call date: Nov 1978, Lincoln's Inn
Qualifications: [BA]

O'ROURKE MISS MARY BERNADETTE

3 Serjeants Inn
London EC4Y 1BQ,
Telephone: 0171 353 5537
E-mail: available upon request
Call date: Nov 1981, Gray's Inn
Qualifications: [Cert des Hautes, Etudes
Europeenes, (Bruges), LLB (Lond)]

O'SHEA EOIN FINBARR

4 Field Court
Gray's Inn, London WC1R 5EA,
Telephone: 0171 440 6900
E-mail: chambers@4fieldcourt.co.uk
Call date: Oct 1996, Inner Temple
Qualifications: [BA (N.U.I), BA (Cantab)]

O'SHEA JOHN ANTHONY ANDREW

58 King Street Chambers
1st Floor, Kingsgate House 51-53 South King
Street, Manchester M2 6DE,
Telephone: 0161 831 7477
Call date: Nov 1983, Middle Temple
Qualifications: [BA (Hons)]

O'SHEA PAUL ANDREW

19 Figtree Lane
Sheffield S1 2DJ, Telephone: 0114 2759708/
2738380
Call date: July 1989, Inner Temple
Qualifications: [LLB (L'pool)]

O'SULLIVAN BERNARD ANTHONY

2 Harcourt Bldgs
Ground Floor/Left, Temple, London
EC4Y 9DB, Telephone: 0171 583 9020
E-mail: clerks@harcourt.co.uk
Stanbrook & Henderson
2 Harcourt Bldgs 2nd Floor, Temple, London
EC4Y 9DB, Telephone: 0171 353 0101
E-mail: clerks@harcourt.co.uk
Call date: July 1971, Inner Temple
Qualifications: [MA (Cantab), MBA (Open
Univ)]

O'SULLIVAN DEREK ANTHONY

5 Pump Court
Ground Floor, Temple, London EC4Y 7AP,
Telephone: 0171 353 2532
E-mail: fivepump@netcomuk.co.uk
Call date: Oct 1990, Lincoln's Inn
Qualifications: [BA (Dunelm), Dip Law]

O'SULLIVAN JOHN

Broad Chare
33 Broad Chare, Newcastle Upon Tyne
NE1 3DQ, Telephone: 0191 232 0541
Call date: Nov 1984, Middle Temple
Qualifications: [LLB (Warwick)]

O'SULLIVAN MICHAEL KENNETH

Chambers of Raana Sheikh
Gray's Inn Chambers, Gray's Inn, London
WC1R, Telephone: 0171 831 5344
E-mail: s.mcblain@btinternet.com
Door Tenant
Call date: Oct 1991, Lincoln's Inn
Qualifications: [LLB (Hons)]

O'SULLIVAN MICHAEL MORTON

5 Stone Buildings
Lincoln's Inn, London WC2A 3XT,
Telephone: 0171 242 6201
E-mail: clerks@5-stonebuildings.law.co.uk
Call date: July 1986, Lincoln's Inn
Qualifications: [MA (Cantab), BCL (Oxon)]

O'SULLIVAN MICHAEL NEIL

5 Paper Bldgs
Lower Ground Floor, Temple, London
EC4Y 7HB, Telephone: 0171 353 5638
E-mail: 107722,633@compuserve.com
Call date: Nov 1970, Gray's Inn
Recorder

O'SULLIVAN ROBERT MICHAEL

5 Paper Bldgs
1st Floor, Temple, London EC4Y 7HB,
Telephone: 0171 583 6117
E-mail: clerks@5-paperbuildings.law.co.uk
Call date: July 1988, Lincoln's Inn
Qualifications: [LLB (Hons) (Lond)]

O'SULLIVAN MISS ZOE SIOBHAN

1 Essex Court
Ground Floor, Temple, London EC4Y 9AR,
Telephone: 0171 583 2000
E-mail: clerks@oneessexcourt.co.uk
Call date: Oct 1993, Middle Temple
Qualifications: [BA (Hons)(Oxon), Dip Law
(City)]

O'TOOLE ANTHONY JAMES

40 King Street
Chester CH1 2AH, Telephone: 01244 323886
Call date: Feb 1993, Gray's Inn
Qualifications: [LLB]

O'TOOLE BARTHOLOMEW VINCENT

Mitre Court Chambers
3rd Floor, Temple, London EC4Y 7BP,
Telephone: 0171 353 9394
Call date: Nov 1980, Middle Temple
Qualifications: [BSc (Lond), Dip Law]

O'TOOLE SIMON GERARD

2 Mitre Ct Bldgs
1st Floor, Temple, London EC4Y 7BX,
Telephone: 0171 353 1353
Call date: July 1984, Inner Temple
Qualifications: [BA (B'ham), Dip Law (City)]

OAKES MISS ALISON DENISE

4 Breams Buildings
London EC4A 1AQ,
Telephone: 0171 353 5835/430 1221
Call date: Oct 1996, Inner Temple
Qualifications: [BA (Dunelm), CPE (Lond)]

OAKES CHRISTOPHER NEIL

Cobden House Chambers
19 Quay Street, Manchester M3 3HN,
Telephone: 0161 833 6000
E-mail: clerks@cobden.co.uk
Call date: Oct 1996, Lincoln's Inn
Qualifications: [B.Eng (Hons)(L'pool)]

OAKLEY PAUL JAMES

3 Temple Gardens
3rd Floor, Temple, London EC4Y 9AU,
Telephone: 0171 353 0832
Call date: Nov 1995, Gray's Inn
Qualifications: [LLB, MSc (Bris)]

OAKLEY TONY

11 Old Square
Ground Floor, Lincoln's Inn, London
WC2A 3TS, Telephone: 0171 430 0341
E-mail: clerks@11oldsquare.co.uk
Call date: Feb 1994, Lincoln's Inn
Qualifications: [BA, LLB, MA]

Fax: 0171 831 2469;
Out of hours telephone: 0860 441135;
DX: LDE 1031; LIX LON042; Other comms: E-
mail clerks@11oldsquare.co.uk

Types of work: Chancery (general); Chancery
land law; Charities; Conveyancing; Equity, wills
and trusts; Foreign law; Pensions; Probate and
administration; Tax - capital and income

Other professional qualifications: TEP

Other professional experience: 27 years as
university teacher (London 1971-5, Cambridge
1975 to date)

Languages spoken: French, Spanish

Publications: *Constructive Trusts* (3rd edn),
1997; *Parker and Mellows: The Modern Law of
Trusts* (7th edn), 1998; *Trends in
Contemporary Trust Law*, 1996; *More Trends
in Contemporary Trust Law*, due 1999

OATES JOHN RICHARD

21 White Friars
Chester CH1 1NZ, Telephone: 01244 323070
Call date: July 1987, Gray's Inn

OBI ONYEABO C

Trafalgar Chambers
53 Fleet Street, London EC4Y 1BE,
Telephone: 0171 583 5858
E-mail: TrafalgarChambers@easynet.co.uk
Call date: Nov 1962, Gray's Inn

OBUKA MS OBIJUO AGWU

9 King's Bench Walk
Ground Floor, Temple, London EC4Y 7DX,
Telephone: 0171 353 7202/3909
Call date: Oct 1993, Inner Temple
Qualifications: [LLB]

D

D

ODGERS JOHN ARTHUR

3 Verulam Buildings
London WC1R 5NT,
Telephone: 0171 831 8441
E-mail: clerks@3verulam.co.uk
Call date: Oct 1990, Gray's Inn
Qualifications: [BA (Hons)(Oxon)]

ODITAH DR FIDELIS HILARY IZUKA

3/4 South Square
Gray's Inn, London WC1R 5HP,
Telephone: 0171 696 9900
E-mail: clerks@southsquare.com
Call date: July 1992, Lincoln's Inn
Qualifications: [MA, BCL, D.Phil]

OFFEH JOHN KOFI

12 Old Square
1st Floor, Lincoln's Inn, London WC2A 3TX,
Telephone: 0171 404 0875
Call date: Nov 1969, Inner Temple
Qualifications: [LLB (Lond)]

OFFENBACH ROGER LEON

3 Gray's Inn Square
Ground Floor, London WC1R 5AH,
Telephone: 0171 520 5600
E-mail: gis3@btinternet.com
Call date: July 1978, Inner Temple
Qualifications: [ARICS]

OFFOH JOHNSON IFEANYI

9 King's Bench Walk
Basement, Temple, London EC4Y 7DX,
Telephone: 0171 353 9564
E-mail: jvlee@btinternet.com
Call date: Nov 1972, Inner Temple

OFORI GEORGE EDWARD

ACMHA Chambers
44 Yarnfield Square Clayton Road, London
SE15 5JD, Telephone: 0181 639 7817/
0958 301089
Chancery Chambers
1st Floor Offices 70/72 Chancery Lane,
London WC2A 1AB,
Telephone: 0171 405 6879/6870
Call date: Nov 1982, Gray's Inn
Qualifications: [LLB Lond]

OGDEN ERIC

2 Paper Bldgs
Temple, London EC4Y 7ET,
Telephone: 0171 936 2613
Call date: July 1983, Inner Temple
Qualifications: [BA]

OGLE MISS REBECCA THEODOSIA ABIGAIL

Southernhay Chambers
33 Southernhay East, Exeter EX1 1NX,
Telephone: 01392 255777
E-mail: southernhay.chambers@lineone.net
Call date: July 1989, Inner Temple
Qualifications: [BA, Dip Law]

OGUNBIYI OLUWOLE AFOLABI

Horizon Chambers
95a Chancery Lane, London WC2A 1DT,
Telephone: 0171 242 2440
Call date: July 1995, Lincoln's Inn
Qualifications: [LLB (Hons)]

OGUNMUYIWA MISS FADEKEMI OMOTAYO

Goldsworth Chambers
1st Floor 10-11 Gray's Inn Square, London
WC1R 5JD, Telephone: 0171 405 7117
Call date: Oct 1994, Lincoln's Inn
Qualifications: [BA (Hons)(Nigeria), LLB
(Hons)(Lond)]

OHRENSTEIN DOV

Chambers of Lord Goodhart QC
Ground Floor 3 New Square, Lincoln's Inn,
London WC2A 3RS,
Telephone: 0171 405 5577
E-mail: law@threenewsquare.demon.co.uk
Call date: Oct 1995, Gray's Inn
Qualifications: [BA]

OJI MISS ATIM ANENE IFEOMA

John Street Chambers
2 John Street, London WC1N 2HJ,
Telephone: 0171 242 1911
E-mail: john.street_chambers@virgin.net.uk
Call date: Nov 1992, Inner Temple
Qualifications: [BA, LLB (Lond)]

OKAI ANTHONY SETH

Chancery Chambers
1st Floor Offices 70/72 Chancery Lane,
London WC2A 1AB,
Telephone: 0171 405 6879/6870
Call date: July 1973, Inner Temple
Qualifications: [LLB (Lond)]

OKE OLANREWAJU OLADIPUPO

Kingsway Chambers
88 Kingsway, Holborn, London WC2B 6AA,
Telephone: 07000 653529
E-mail: lanreoke@lineone.net
Call date: July 1979, Lincoln's Inn
Qualifications: [MA(Oxon)]

OKOYA WILLIAM EDIKISE

Arden Chambers
27 John Street, London WC1N 2BL,
Telephone: 0171 242 4244
Call date: Nov 1989, Gray's Inn
Qualifications: [LLM]

OKOYE MISS JOY NWAMALA

Chambers of Joy Okoye
Suite 1, 2nd Floor Gray's Inn Chambers,
Gray's Inn, London WC1R 5JA,
Telephone: 0171 405 7011
Call date: July 1981, Inner Temple
Qualifications: [BA (Hons)]

OLDHAM MS (ELIZABETH) JANE

4-5 Gray's Inn Square
Ground Floor, Gray's Inn, London WC1R 5AY,
Telephone: 0171 404 5252
E-mail: chambers@4-5graysinnsquare.co.uk
Call date: July 1985, Middle Temple
Qualifications: [MA (Cantab)]

OLDHAM MRS FRANCES MARY THERESA QC (1994)

36 Bedford Row
London WC1R 4JH,
Telephone: 0171 421 8000
E-mail: 36bedfordrow@link.org
Call date: July 1977, Gray's Inn
Recorder

OLDHAM PETER ROBERT

11 King's Bench Walk
Temple, London EC4Y 7EQ,
Telephone: 0171 632 8500
E-mail: clerksroom@11-kbw.law.co.uk
Call date: Oct 1990, Gray's Inn
Qualifications: [BA (Cantab), Dip Law (City)]

OLDLAND ANDREW RICHARD

Walnut House
63 St. David's Hill, Exeter, Devon EX4 4DW,
Telephone: 01392 279751
E-mail: 106627.2451@compuserve.com
Call date: Nov 1990, Inner Temple
Qualifications: [MSc (Lond), Dip Law (City)]

OLDLAND MISS JENNIFER JANE

1 Dr Johnson's Bldgs
Ground Floor, Temple, London EC4Y 7AX,
Telephone: 0171 353 9328
Dr Johnson's Chambers
The Atrium Court Apex Plaza, Reading
RG1 1AX, Telephone: 01734 254221
Call date: Nov 1978, Inner Temple

OLIVER PROFESSOR (ANN) DAWN (HARRISON)

2 Hare Court
Ground Floor, Temple, London EC4Y 7BH,
Telephone: 0171 583 1770
E-mail: 2_Hare_Court@link.org
Call date: July 1965, Middle Temple
Qualifications: [MA (Cantab), PhD (Cantab)]

OLIVER ANDREW JAMES

Octagon House
19 Colegate, Norwich NR3 1AT,
Telephone: 01603 623186
E-mail: octagon@netmatters.co.uk
Call date: Nov 1993, Lincoln's Inn
Qualifications: [LLB (Hons)]

OLIVER CRISPIN ARTHUR

Trinity Chambers
9-12 Trinity Chare, Quayside, Newcastle Upon
Tyne NE1 3DF, Telephone: 0191 232 1927
Call date: Nov 1990, Middle Temple
Qualifications: [MA (St Andrews), Dip Law]

OLIVER DAVID KEIGHTLEY RIDEAL QC (1986)

13 Old Square
Ground Floor, Lincoln's Inn, London
WC2A 3UA, Telephone: 0171 404 4800
Call date: July 1972, Lincoln's Inn
Qualifications: [BA (Cantab), Licenci Spec en, droit European, Brussels]

OLIVER MISS JULIET DIANNE

Bridewell Chambers
2 Bridewell Place, London EC4V 6AP,
Telephone: 0171 797 8800
E-mail: clerks@bridewell.law.co.uk
Call date: Nov 1974, Gray's Inn
Qualifications: [LLB]

OLIVER MICHAEL RICHARD

Hardwicke Building
New Square, Lincoln's Inn, London
WC2A 3SB, Telephone: 0171 242 2523
E-mail: clerks@hardwicke.co.uk
Call date: July 1977, Inner Temple
Qualifications: [MA (Oxon)]

OLIVER SIMON JONATHAN

Guildford Chambers
Stoke House Leapale Lane, Guildford, Surrey
GU1 4LY, Telephone: 01483 539131
E-mail: guildford.barristers@btinternet.com
Call date: July 1981, Inner Temple
Qualifications: [LLB (Exon)]

OLIVER-JONES STEPHEN QC (1996)

5 Fountain Court
Steelhouse Lane, Birmingham B4 6DR,
Telephone: 0121 606 0500
Call date: Apr 1970, Inner Temple
Recorder
Qualifications: [BA (Dunelm)]

OLLENNU ASHITEY KWAME NII-AMAA

Horizon Chambers
95a Chancery Lane, London WC2A 1DT,
Telephone: 0171 242 2440
Westgate Chambers
144 High Street, Lewes, East Sussex BN7 1XT,
Telephone: 01273 480510
Call date: July 1981, Lincoln's Inn
Qualifications: [BA]

OLUPITAN-RUBAN MRS YETUNDE

Chancery Chambers
1st Floor Offices 70/72 Chancery Lane,
London WC2A 1AB,
Telephone: 0171 405 6879/6870
Call date: Nov 1996, Inner Temple
Qualifications: [BA]

OMAMBALA MISS IJEOMA CHINYELU

Old Square Chambers
1 Verulam Buildings, Gray's Inn, London
WC1R 5LQ, Telephone: 0171 831 0801
Old Square Chambers
Hanover House 47 Corn Street, Bristol
BS1 1HT, Telephone: 0117 9277111
Call date: Apr 1989, Gray's Inn
Qualifications: [BA, MPhil (Cantab)]

OMAR MISS ROBINA

Wessex Chambers
48 Queens Road, Reading, Berkshire
RG1 4BD, Telephone: 01734 568856
E-mail: wessexchambers@compuserve.com
Call date: Oct 1991, Lincoln's Inn
Qualifications: [LLB (Hons)]

ONG DR COLIN YEE CHENG

Essex Court Chambers
24 Lincoln's Inn Fields, London WC2A 3ED,
Telephone: 0171 813 8000
E-mail: clerksroom@essexcourt-chambers.co.uk
Call date: Nov 1991, Inner Temple
Qualifications: [LLB (Sheff), LLM, PhD (Lond), ACIArb]

ONG MISS GRACE YU MAE

1 Essex Court
1st Floor, Temple, London EC4Y 9AR,
Telephone: 0171 936 3030
E-mail: one.essex_court@virgin.net
Call date: July 1985, Lincoln's Inn
Qualifications: [LLB (London)]

ONIONS JEFFERY PETER

1 Essex Court
Ground Floor, Temple, London EC4Y 9AR,
Telephone: 0171 583 2000
E-mail: clerks@oneessexcourt.co.uk
Call date: July 1981, Middle Temple
Qualifications: [MA, LLM (Cantab)]

ONSLOW ANDREW GEORGE

3 Verulam Buildings
London WC1R 5NT,
Telephone: 0171 831 8441
E-mail: clerks@3verulam.co.uk
Call date: July 1982, Middle Temple
Qualifications: [MA (Oxon)]

ONSLOW RICHARD ALAN DOUGLAS

2 King's Bench Walk
Ground Floor, Temple, London EC4Y 7DE,
Telephone: 0171 353 1746
E-mail: 2kbw@atlas.co.uk
King's Bench Chambers
115 North Hill, Plymouth PL4 8JY,
Telephone: 01752 221551
Call date: July 1982, Inner Temple
Qualifications: [MA (Oxon)]

ONSLOW ROBERT DENZIL

8 New Square
Lincoln's Inn, London WC2A 3QP,
Telephone: 0171 405 4321
Call date: Oct 1991, Lincoln's Inn
Qualifications: [BA (Hons) (Oxon), Dip Law]

ONUAGULUCHI JONES

Southsea Chambers
PO Box 148, Southsea, Portsmouth,
Hampshire PO5 2TU,
Telephone: 01705 291261
Call date: Feb 1971, Inner Temple
Qualifications: [LLM (Lond)]

OON MISS PAMELA BENG SUE

2 Dr Johnson's Building
Temple, London EC4Y 7AY,
Telephone: 0171 353 4716
Call date: July 1982, Inner Temple
Qualifications: [LL.L]

OPENSHAW CHARLES PETER LAWFORD QC (1991)

Peel Court Chambers
45 Hardman Street, Manchester M3 3HA,
Telephone: 0161 832 3791
Call date: July 1970, Inner Temple
Recorder
Qualifications: [MA (Cantab)]

OPPENHEIM ROBIN FRANK

Doughty Street Chambers
11 Doughty Street, London WC1N 2PG,
Telephone: 0171 404 1313
E-mail: doughty_street@compuserve.com
Call date: Nov 1988, Middle Temple
Qualifications: [BA Hons (Manch), Dip Law]

OPPERMAN GUY THOMAS

3 Paper Bldgs
1st Floor, Temple, London EC4Y 7EU,
Telephone: 0171 583 8055
E-mail: london@3paper.com
4 St Peter Street
Winchester SO23 8OW,
Telephone: 01962 868884
20 Lorne Park Road
Bournemouth BH1 1JN,
Telephone: 01202 292102 (5 Lines)
Call date: Nov 1989, Middle Temple
Qualifications: [LLB (Hons)(Bucks)]

ORCHARD ANTHONY EDWARD

1 Crown Office Row
2nd Floor, Temple, London EC4Y 7HH,
Telephone: 0171 797 7111
Call date: Oct 1991, Inner Temple
Qualifications: [LLB (So'ton)]

ORCHOVER MS FRANCES RACHEL

4 Brick Court
Ground Floor, Temple, London EC4Y 9AD,
Telephone: 0171 797 7766
E-mail: chambers@4brick.co.uk
Call date: July 1989, Middle Temple
Qualifications: [BA (Hons) (Lond), Dip Law]

ORME RICHARD ANDREW

Peel Court Chambers
45 Hardman Street, Manchester M3 3HA,
Telephone: 0161 832 3791
Call date: Oct 1993, Lincoln's Inn
Qualifications: [BA (Hons)(Leeds), CPE (Lond)]

ORNSBY MISS SUZANNE DOREEN

2 Harcourt Buildings
Temple, London EC4Y 9DB,
Telephone: 0171 353 8415
E-mail: clerks@twoharcourtbldgs.demon.co.uk
Call date: Nov 1986, Middle Temple

Qualifications: [LLB (UCL)]

Fax: 0171 353 7622; DX: LDE 402

Types of work: Administrative; Arbitration; Chancery land law; Energy; Environment; Licensing; Local government; Professional negligence; Town and country planning

Awards and memberships: Secretary of the Planning and Environment Bar Association (PEBA); Member of the United Kingdom Environmental Law Association (UKELA)

Other professional experience: Three years' employment in the electricity supply industry

ORR CRAIG WYNDHAM

Fountain Court
Temple, London EC4Y 9DH,
Telephone: 0171 583 3335
E-mail: chambers@fountaincourt.co.uk
Call date: July 1986, Middle Temple
Qualifications: [MA (Cantab), BCL (Oxon)]

ORR JULIAN BOYD

Cobden House Chambers
19 Quay Street, Manchester M3 3HN,
Telephone: 0161 833 6000
E-mail: clerks@cobden.co.uk
Call date: Oct 1995, Lincoln's Inn
Qualifications: [LLB (Hons)(L'pool)]

ORR NICHOLAS GUY

Adrian Lyon's Chambers
14 Castle Street, Liverpool L2 0NE,
Telephone: 0151 236 4421/8240
E-mail: chambers14@aol.com
5 Stone Buildings
Lincoln's Inn, London WC2A 3XT,
Telephone: 0171 242 6201
E-mail: clerks@5-stonebuildings.law.co.uk
Door Tenant
Call date: Nov 1970, Gray's Inn
Qualifications: [LLB (Bris)]

ORSULIK MICHAEL ANTHONY

9-12 Bell Yard
London WC2A 2LF,
Telephone: 0171 400 1800
Call date: Nov 1978, Middle Temple
Qualifications: [BA, LLM (Lond)]

ORTON PAUL WALTER

3 Paper Bldgs
2nd Floor, Temple, London EC4Y 7EU,
Telephone: 0171 353 6208
Call date: Nov 1988, Gray's Inn
Qualifications: [BA (Hons)]

OSBORNE DAVID THOMAS

South Western Chambers
Melville House 12 Middle Street, Taunton,
Somerset TA1 1SH, Telephone: 01823 331919
Call date: July 1974, Gray's Inn
Qualifications: [BA (Hons) (McGill), CSS (Granada)]

OSBORNE MISS KATIE ANTOINETTE

Holborn Chambers
6 Gate Street, Lincoln's Inn Fields, London
WC2A 3HP, Telephone: 0171 242 6060
Call date: Nov 1993, Middle Temple
Qualifications: [BA (Hons), CPE]

OSBORNE NIGEL JOHN

33 Park Place
Cardiff CF1 3BA, Telephone: 01222 233313
Call date: Nov 1993, Middle Temple
Qualifications: [LLB (Hons)(Wales)]

OSBORNE-HALSEY MRS THELMA EDWINA

Northeastern Law Chambers
The Chocolate Factory B305 Clarendon Road /
Western Road, Wood Green, London
N22 6UN, Telephone: 0181 881 3890
Call date: July 1982, Gray's Inn
Qualifications: [BA,MA (West Indies), LLB (Hons)]

OSMAN OSMAN HASAN

Mitre House Chambers
Mitre House 44 Fleet Street, London
EC4Y 1BN, Telephone: 0171 583 8233
Call date: Feb 1995, Inner Temple
Qualifications: [LLB (Hons) (Middx)]

OSMAN ROBERT WALTER

Queen's Chambers
5 John Dalton Street, Manchester M2 6ET,
Telephone: 0161 834 6875/4738
4 Camden Place
Preston PR1 3JL, Telephone: 01772 828300
Call date: July 1974, Middle Temple
Qualifications: [LLB (Lond)]

OSMAN MISS SONA KAARINA PIA

Mitre House Chambers
Mitre House 44 Fleet Street, London
EC4Y 1BN, Telephone: 0171 583 8233
Call date: Nov 1986, Middle Temple
Qualifications: [BA(Keele) Dip Law]

OSSACK MRS TANYA RACHELLE ELISE

3 Temple Gardens
3rd Floor, Temple, London EC4Y 9AU,
Telephone: 0171 583 0010
Call date: Oct 1993, Gray's Inn
Qualifications: [MA (Brunel)]

OTENG EMMANUEL ALDO

The Thames Chambers
Wickham House 10 Cleveland Way, London
E1 4TR, Telephone: 0171 790 7377
Call date: Feb 1963, Middle Temple
Qualifications: [Diploma Legal, Administration,
(Hebrew University, of Jerusalem 1966)]

OTTON-GOULDER MISS CATHARINE ANNE

Brick Court Chambers
15/19 Devereux Court, London WC2R 3JJ,
Telephone: 0171 583 0777
E-mail: (surname)@brickcourt.demon.co.uk
Call date: Nov 1983, Lincoln's Inn
Qualifications: [MA (Oxon)]

OTTY TIMOTHY JOHN

2 Temple Gardens
Temple, London EC4Y 9AY,
Telephone: 0171 583 6041 (12 Lines)
Call date: Oct 1990, Lincoln's Inn
Qualifications: [MA (Cantab)]

OTWAL MUKHTIAR SINGH

Mitre Court Chambers
3rd Floor, Temple, London EC4Y 7BP,
Telephone: 0171 353 9394
Call date: Nov 1991, Lincoln's Inn
Qualifications: [LLB (Hons) (Leeds)]

OUDKERK DANIEL RICHARD

22 Old Bldgs
Lincoln's Inn, London WC2A 3UJ,
Telephone: 0171 831 0222
Call date: Nov 1992, Inner Temple
Qualifications: [LLB (Bris)]

OUGH DR RICHARD NORMAN

Hardwicke Building
New Square, Lincoln's Inn, London
WC2A 3SB, Telephone: 0171 242 2523
E-mail: clerks@hardwicke.co.uk
Call date: July 1985, Inner Temple
Qualifications: [MA Law (City), MB, BS (Lond),
MRCS (Eng), LRCP (Lond), Dip Law (City),
LMCC, FCIArb, MSc]

Fax: 0171 691 1234; DX: LDE 393;
Other comms: E-mail ough@ough.com;
www.ough.com

Types of work: Arbitration; Commercial;
Common law (general); Ecclesiastical; Family;
Medical negligence; Personal injury;
Professional negligence

Circuit: North Eastern

Awards and memberships: Fellow of the Royal
Society of Medicine; Sloan Fellow. London
Business School

Other professional experience: Qualified as a
doctor in London and after being Resident in
Obstetrics and Gynaecology at University of
British Coloumbia in Vancouver, entered
private practice in Ontario, where his hospital
experience included all major specialties.

Languages spoken: French

Publications: *The Mareva Injunction and
Anton Piller Order*, Butterworths 1998; *MS
Sufferers: can they bring a claim?*, 1997;
*Automatic Strike Out [A European Court of
Human Rights perspective]*, 1996

Reported cases: *Ratcliffe v Plymouth and
Torbay HA CA*, [1998] 3 PIQR 170, 1998.
Leading case on *res ipsa* in medical negligence.

Appleton and Ors v Garrett, [1997] 8 Med LR 75. £2 million group action of over 100 plaintiffs: dental negligence, consent, trespass to person, aggravated damages.
Rhodes v Spokes and Farbridge, [1996] Med LR 135. Medical negligence failure to diagnose blocked cerebral shunt.
Fletcher v Sheffield HA, [1994] Med LR 156 CA. Limitation in medical negligence actions.
Stobart v Nottingham HA, Yaffi v North Lincs HA, [1992] 3 Med LR 284, 1992. Medical negligence/discovery, whether discovery should precede inquest.

OUGHTON RICHARD DONALD

Cobden House Chambers
19 Quay Street, Manchester M3 3HN,
Telephone: 0161 833 6000
E-mail: clerks@cobden.co.uk
Call date: July 1978, Lincoln's Inn
Qualifications: [MA (Cantab), LLM (Pennsylvania)]

OULTON RICHARD ARTHUR COURTNEY

2 King's Bench Walk
Ground Floor, Temple, London EC4Y 7DE,
Telephone: 0171 353 1746
E-mail: 2kbw@atlas.co.uk
King's Bench Chambers
115 North Hill, Plymouth PL4 8JY,
Telephone: 01752 221551
Call date: Nov 1995, Middle Temple
Qualifications: [MA]

OUSELEY DUNCAN BRIAN WALTER QC (1992)

4-5 Gray's Inn Square
Ground Floor, Gray's Inn, London WC1R 5AY,
Telephone: 0171 404 5252
E-mail: chambers@4-5graysinnsquare.co.uk
Call date: Feb 1973, Gray's Inn
Recorder
Qualifications: [MA (Cantab) LLM, (Lond)]

OUTHWAITE MRS WENDY-JANE TIVNAN

2 Harcourt Bldgs
Ground Floor/Left, Temple, London
EC4Y 9DB, Telephone: 0171 583 9020
E-mail: clerks@harcourt.co.uk
Stanbrook & Henderson
2 Harcourt Bldgs 2nd Floor, Temple, London
EC4Y 9DB, Telephone: 0171 353 0101
E-mail: clerks@harcourt.co.uk
Call date: May 1990, Lincoln's Inn
Qualifications: [MA (Oxon), License Speciale en, Droit Europeen]

OVERBURY RUPERT SIMON

18 Red Lion Court
(Off Fleet Street), London EC4A 3EB,
Telephone: 0171 520 6000
Thornwood House
102 New London Road, Chelmsford, Essex
CM2 0RG, Telephone: 01245 280880
Call date: July 1984, Middle Temple
Qualifications: [BA (Hons)]

OVERS MS ESTELLE FAE

New Court Chambers
5 Verulam Buildings, Gray's Inn, London
WC1R 5LY, Telephone: 0171 831 9500
E-mail: mail@newcourtchambers.com
Call date: Oct 1994, Gray's Inn
Qualifications: [BA]

OVEY MISS ELIZABETH HELEN

11 Old Square
Ground Floor, Lincoln's Inn, London
WC2A 3TS, Telephone: 0171 430 0341
E-mail: clerks@11oldsquare.co.uk
Call date: July 1978, Middle Temple
Qualifications: [BA (Oxon)]

OWEN DAVID CHRISTOPHER

20 Essex Street
London WC2R 3AL,
Telephone: 0171 583 9294
E-mail: clerks@20essexst.com
Call date: Nov 1983, Middle Temple
Qualifications: [BA (Oxon), Dip Law (City)]

OWEN DAVID MEURIG

25-27 Castle Street
1st Floor, Liverpool L2 4TA,
Telephone: 0151 227 5661/051 236 5072
Call date: July 1981, Gray's Inn
Qualifications: [BA (Keele)]

OWEN ERIC CYRIL HAMMERSLEY

40 King Street
Manchester M2 6BA,
Telephone: 0161 832 9082
E-mail: Kingst40@aol.com
4 Breams Buildings
London EC4A 1AQ,
Telephone: 0171 353 5835/430 1221
Door Tenant
Call date: Nov 1969, Gray's Inn
Qualifications: [LLB (L'pool)]

OWEN MISS GAIL ANN

India Buildings Chambers
Water Street, Liverpool L2 OXG,
Telephone: 0151 243 6000
Call date: Nov 1980, Gray's Inn
Qualifications: [LLB (L'pool)]

OWEN MISS HELEN NNONYELUM

Forest House Chambers
15 Granville Road, Walthamstow, London
E17 9BS, Telephone: 0181 925 2240
Call date: Nov 1994, Inner Temple
Qualifications: [BA]

OWEN JAMES ALEXANDER DALZIEL

Rougemont Chambers
15 Barnfield Road, Exeter EX1 1RR,
Telephone: 01392 410471
E-mail: rougemont.chambers@eclipse.co.uk
Call date: Mar 1996, Gray's Inn
Qualifications: [BA (Dunelm)]

OWEN PHILIP LOSCOMBE WINTRINGHAM QC (1963)

Brick Court Chambers
15/19 Devereux Court, London WC2R 3JJ,
Telephone: 0171 583 0777
E-mail: (surname)@brickcourt.demon.co.uk
Call date: Jan 1949, Middle Temple
Qualifications: [MA (Oxon)]

OWEN ROBERT FRANK QC (1996)

24 The Ropewalk
Nottingham NG1 5EF,
Telephone: 0115 9472581
E-mail: clerk@ropewalk.co.uk
Call date: July 1977, Inner Temple
Assistant Recorder
Qualifications: [LLB (Lond)]

OWEN ROBERT MICHAEL QC (1988)

1 Crown Office Row
Ground Floor, Temple, London EC4Y 7HH,
Telephone: 0171 797 7500
Crown Office Row Chambers
Blenheim House 120 Church Street, Brighton,
Sussex BN1 1WH, Telephone: 01273 625625
Call date: Nov 1968, Inner Temple
Recorder
Qualifications: [LLB (Exon)]

OWEN MS SARA JANE

Carmarthen Chambers
30 Spilman Street, Carmarthen, Dyfed
SA31 1LQ, Telephone: 01267 234410
Call date: Oct 1995, Inner Temple
Qualifications: [BA (Cantab)]

OWEN TIMOTHY WYNN

Doughty Street Chambers
11 Doughty Street, London WC1N 2PG,
Telephone: 0171 404 1313
E-mail: doughty_street@compuserve.com
Call date: July 1983, Middle Temple
Qualifications: [BA (Lond), Dip Law]

OWEN TUDOR WYN

9-12 Bell Yard
London WC2A 2LF,
Telephone: 0171 400 1800
Call date: July 1974, Gray's Inn
Recorder
Qualifications: [LLB (Lond)]

OWEN-JONES DAVID RODERIC

3 Temple Gardens
2nd Floor, Temple, London EC4Y 9AU,
Telephone: 0171 583 1155
Call date: July 1972, Inner Temple
Qualifications: [LLM (Lond)]

D

OWENS MISS HILARY JANE

7 Fountain Court
Steelhouse Lane, Birmingham B4 6DR,
Telephone: 0121 236 8531
Call date: Feb 1994, Middle Temple
Qualifications: [BA (Hons)(Dunelm)]

OWENS MATTHEW JOHN

7 Stone Bldgs
1st Floor, Lincoln's Inn, London WC2A 3SZ,
Telephone: 0171 242 0961
Call date: Nov 1988, Gray's Inn
Qualifications: [LLB (Lond)]

OWUSU KWABENA

Chancery Chambers
1st Floor Offices 70/72 Chancery Lane,
London WC2A 1AB,
Telephone: 0171 405 6879/6870
Call date: Nov 1983, Gray's Inn
Qualifications: [LLB (Warks)]

OWUSU-YIANOMA DAVID KWASI DARTEY

3 Temple Gardens (North)
Fifth Floor, Temple, London EC4Y 9AU,
Telephone: 0171 353 0853/4/7222
E-mail: 100106.1577@compuserve.com
Call date: Nov 1992, Inner Temple
Qualifications: [LLB (Hons)]

OXLADE MISS JOANNE ELIZABETH

33 Bedford Row
London WC1R 4JH,
Telephone: 0171 242 6476
Call date: July 1988, Middle Temple
Qualifications: [LLB (Hons)]

OYEBANJI ADAM

5 Fountain Court
Steelhouse Lane, Birmingham B4 6DR,
Telephone: 0121 606 0500
Call date: July 1987, Inner Temple
Qualifications: [LLB (B'ham)]

OZIN PAUL DAVID

23 Essex Street
London WC2R 3AS,
Telephone: 0171 413 0353/353 3533
E-mail: clerks@essexstreet23.demon.co.uk
Call date: Nov 1987, Middle Temple
Qualifications: [BA (Oxon)]

PACK MISS MELISSA ELIZABETH JANE

Farrar's Building
Temple, London EC4Y 7BD,
Telephone: 0171 583 9241
E-mail: chambers@farrarsbuilding.co.uk
Call date: Nov 1995, Middle Temple
Qualifications: [BA (Hons)]

PACKMAN MISS CLAIRE GERALDINE VANCE

4 Pump Court
Temple, London EC4Y 7AN,
Telephone: 0171 353 2656/9
E-mail: 4_pump_court@compuserve.com
Call date: Oct 1996, Inner Temple
Qualifications: [BA (Oxon), CPE (Lond)]

PADFIELD MS ALISON MARY

One Hare Court
1st Floor, Temple, London EC4Y 7BE,
Telephone: 0171 353 3171
E-mail: admin-oneharecourt@btinternet.com
Call date: Oct 1992, Lincoln's Inn
Qualifications: [BA (Oxon), BCL (Oxon,), Lic
Spec Dr Eur, (Brussels)]

PADFIELD NICHOLAS DAVID QC (1991)

One Hare Court
1st Floor, Temple, London EC4Y 7BE,
Telephone: 0171 353 3171
E-mail: admin-oneharecourt@btinternet.com
Call date: Nov 1972, Inner Temple
Recorder
Qualifications: [MA (Oxon), LLB (Cantab),
FCIArb]

PADLEY MISS CLARE MELANIE

9 Gough Square
London EC4A 3DE, Telephone: 0171 353 5371
Call date: Oct 1991, Inner Temple
Qualifications: [BA (Cantab)]

PADMAN ANTHONY

Crystal Chambers
25A Cintra Park, London SE19 2LH,
Telephone: 0181 402 5801
Call date: Nov 1972, Lincoln's Inn
Qualifications: [LLB (Wales)]

PAGE MISS ADRIENNE MAY

5 Raymond Buildings
1st Floor, Gray's Inn, London WC1R 5BP,
Telephone: 0171 242 2902
Call date: July 1974, Middle Temple
Assistant Recorder
Qualifications: [BA (Kent)]

PAGE ARTHUR HUGO MICKLEM

2 Hare Court
Ground Floor, Temple, London EC4Y 7BH,
Telephone: 0171 583 1770
E-mail: 2_Hare_Court@link.org
Call date: Nov 1977, Inner Temple
Qualifications: [MA (Cantab)]

PAGE DAVID MARK

2 King's Bench Walk
Ground Floor, Temple, London EC4Y 7DE,
Telephone: 0171 353 1746
E-mail: 2kbw@atlas.co.uk
King's Bench Chambers
115 North Hill, Plymouth PL4 8JY,
Telephone: 01752 221551
Call date: Nov 1984, Middle Temple
Qualifications: [LLB (Brunel)]

PAGE HOWARD WILLIAM BARRETT QC (1987)

One Hare Court
1st Floor, Temple, London EC4Y 7BE,
Telephone: 0171 353 3171
E-mail: admin-oneharecourt@btinternet.com
Call date: July 1967, Lincoln's Inn
Qualifications: [MA, LLB (Cantab), FCIArb]

PAGE MRS JANE ELIZABETH

Chartlands Chambers
3 St Giles Terrace, Northampton NN1 2BN,
Telephone: 01604 603322
Call date: July 1982, Inner Temple
Qualifications: [LLB]

PAGE JONATHAN ROWLAND THOMAS

Guildford Chambers
Stoke House Leapale Lane, Guildford, Surrey
GU1 4LY, Telephone: 01483 539131
E-mail: guildford.barristers@btinternet.com
Call date: Oct 1996, Middle Temple
Qualifications: [B.Eng, PhD (Lond), CPE (City)]

PAGE NIGEL BERNARD

St Mary's Chambers
50 High Pavement, Lace Market, Nottingham
NG1 1HW, Telephone: 0115 9503503
E-mail: clerks@smc.law.co.uk
Call date: July 1976, Gray's Inn
Qualifications: [LLB (Lond)]

PAGET TERENCE

St George's Chambers
32/33 Foregate Street, Worcester WR1 1EE,
Telephone: 0345 413635
Call date: Oct 1990, Middle Temple
Qualifications: [LLB (B'ham), FCII, ACIArb]

PAIN KENNETH WILLIAM

College Chambers
19 Carlton Cresent, Southampton, Hants
SO15 2ET, Telephone: 01703 230338
Call date: Nov 1969, Gray's Inn

PAINES NICHOLAS PAUL BILLOT QC (1997)

Monckton Chambers
4 Raymond Buildings, Gray's Inn, London
WC1R 5BP, Telephone: 0171 405 7211
E-mail: chambers@monckton.co.uk
Call date: Apr 1978, Gray's Inn
Qualifications: [MA, Licence Speciale en, droit
European]

PAINTER IAN DAVID

Counsels' Chambers
2nd Floor 10-11 Gray's Inn Square, London
WC1R 5JD, Telephone: 0171 405 2576
Call date: Nov 1993, Lincoln's Inn
Qualifications: [BA (Hons)]

D

D

PALFREY MONTAGUE MARK

Hardwicke Building
New Square, Lincoln's Inn, London
WC2A 3SB, Telephone: 0171 242 2523
E-mail: clerks@hardwicke.co.uk
Call date: Nov 1985, Middle Temple
Qualifications: [LLB (Bucks)]

PALMER ADRIAN OLIVER QC (1992)

Guildhall Chambers
23 Broad Street, Bristol BS1 2HG,
Telephone: 0117 9273366
Call date: July 1972, Middle Temple
Recorder
Qualifications: [MA (Cantab)]

PALMER ANTHONY WHEELER QC (1979)

3 Fountain Court
Steelhouse Lane, Birmingham B4 6DR,
Telephone: 0121 236 5854
9 Gough Square
London EC4A 3DE, Telephone: 0171 353 5371
Call date: July 1962, Gray's Inn
Recorder

PALMER MISS GILLIAN

7 New Square
Lincoln's Inn, London WC2A 3QS,
Telephone: 0171 430 1660
Call date: Feb 1993, Gray's Inn
Qualifications: [BA]

PALMER HOWARD WILLIAM ARTHUR

2 Temple Gardens
Temple, London EC4Y 9AY,
Telephone: 0171 583 6041 (12 Lines)
Call date: July 1977, Inner Temple
Qualifications: [MA (Oxon)]

PALMER JAMES SAVILL

2 Harcourt Bldgs
Ground Floor/Left, Temple, London
EC4Y 9DB, Telephone: 0171 583 9020
E-mail: clerks@harcourt.co.uk
Call date: Nov 1983, Middle Temple
Qualifications: [MA (Cantab)]

PALMER NATHAN EMMANUEL

3 Temple Gardens (North)
Fifth Floor, Temple, London EC4Y 9AU,
Telephone: 0171 353 0853/4/7222
E-mail: 100106.1577@compuserve.com
Call date: Oct 1994, Middle Temple
Qualifications: [LLB (Hons)(Lond)]

PALMER NORMAN ERNEST

2 Field Court
Gray's Inn, London WC1R 5BB,
Telephone: 0171 405 6114
E-mail: fieldct2@netcomuk.co.uk.
Call date: July 1973, Gray's Inn
Qualifications: [MA, BCL (Oxon)]

PALMER PATRICK JOHN STEVEN

25 Park Square
Leeds LS1 2PW, Telephone: 0113 2451841/2/3
E-mail: sovereignchambers@btinternet.com
Call date: July 1978, Inner Temple
Assistant Recorder
Qualifications: [LLB (Lond)]

PALMER MISS SUZANNE ELIZABETH JOSEPHINE

Field Court Chambers
2nd Floor 3 Field Court, Gray's Inn, London
WC1R 4EP, Telephone: 0171 404 7474
E-mail: Clerks@FieldCourtChambers.law.co.uk
Call date: Nov 1995, Middle Temple
Qualifications: [BA (Hons)]

PALMER TIMOTHY NIGEL JOHN

1 High Pavement
Nottingham NG1 1HF,
Telephone: 0115 9418218
Call date: July 1982, Middle Temple
Qualifications: [LLB]

PALTENGHI MARK FRANCIS

2 Dr Johnson's Building
Temple, London EC4Y 7AY,
Telephone: 0171 353 4716
Call date: July 1979, Middle Temple
Qualifications: [LLB]

PANAGIOTOPOULOU MISS SOPHIE THALIA

Staple Inn Chambers
1st Floor 9 Staple Inn, Holborn, London
WC1V 7QH, Telephone: 0171 242 5240
E-mail: clerks@staple-inn.org
Call date: Oct 1995, Middle Temple
Qualifications: [LLB (Hons), LLM (Hons)]

PANAGIOTOPOULOU MISS TANIA

Staple Inn Chambers
1st Floor 9 Staple Inn, Holborn, London
WC1V 7QH, Telephone: 0171 242 5240
E-mail: clerks@staple-inn.org
Call date: Oct 1994, Middle Temple
Qualifications: [LLB (Hons), LLM (Bucks)]

PANAYI PAVLOS PAUL

2 Paper Bldgs
1st Floor, Temple, London EC4Y 7ET,
Telephone: 0171 936 2611 (10 Lines)
E-mail: clerks@2pbbarristers.co.uk
Call date: Oct 1995, Gray's Inn
Qualifications: [LLB]

PANAYIOTOU MISS ELEFTHERIA

Furnival Chambers
32 Furnival Street, London EC4A 1JQ,
Telephone: 0171 405 3232
E-mail: clerks@furnivallaw.co.uk
Call date: Oct 1992, Gray's Inn
Qualifications: [LL.B (Lond)]

PANESAR DESHPAL SINGH

13 King's Bench Walk
1st Floor, Temple, London EC4Y 7EN,
Telephone: 0171 353 7204
E-mail: clerks@13kbw.law.co.uk
King's Bench Chambers
32 Beaumont Street, Oxford OX1 2NP,
Telephone: 01865 311066
E-mail: clerks@kbc-oxford.law.co.uk
Call date: Feb 1993, Inner Temple
Qualifications: [LLB (Hons)(Lond)]

PANESAR MANJIT SINGH

6 King's Bench Walk
Ground, Third & Fourth Floors, Temple,
London EC4Y 7DR,
Telephone: 0171 353 4931/583 0695
Call date: Nov 1989, Middle Temple
Qualifications: [LLB Hons]

PANETH MISS SARAH RUTH

1 Serjeants' Inn
5th Floor Fleet Street, Temple, London
EC4Y 1LL, Telephone: 0171 415 6666
E-mail: no1serjeantsinn@btinternet.com
Call date: Nov 1985, Gray's Inn
Qualifications: [BA (York) Dip Law]

PANFORD FRANK HAIG

Doughty Street Chambers
11 Doughty Street, London WC1N 2PG,
Telephone: 0171 404 1313
E-mail: doughty_street@compuserve.com
Call date: Nov 1972, Middle Temple
Qualifications: [LLB (Lond), LLB (Cantab), Dip Droit Prive, (Hague Academy)]

PANNICK DAVID PHILIP QC (1992)

2 Hare Court
Ground Floor, Temple, London EC4Y 7BH,
Telephone: 0171 583 1770
E-mail: 2_Hare_Court@link.org
Call date: July 1979, Gray's Inn
Recorder
Qualifications: [MA, BCL (Oxon)]

PANTON ALASTAIR HOWARD

Fleet Chambers
Mitre House 44-46 Fleet Street, London
EC4Y 1BN, Telephone: 0171 936 3707
Call date: Oct 1996, Inner Temple
Qualifications: [MA (Cantab), CPE]

PANTON WILLIAM DWIGHT

Horizon Chambers
95a Chancery Lane, London WC2A 1DT,
Telephone: 0171 242 2440
Call date: Nov 1977, Inner Temple

PAPAGEORGIS GEORGE MICHAEL

2 King's Bench Walk
1st Floor, Temple, London EC4Y 7DE,
Telephone: 0171 353 9276
Call date: July 1981, Middle Temple

PAPAZIAN MISS CLIONA CONCEPTA

Warwick House Chambers
8 Warwick Court, Gray's Inn, London
WC1R 5DJ, Telephone: 0171 430 2323
Call date: Nov 1994, Inner Temple
Qualifications: [BA (Wales), MA, LLB (Ireland)]

PARCHMENT NOLLIS REGINALD

16 Tatnell Road
Forest Hill, London SE23 1JY,
Telephone: 0181 699 3818
Call date: Nov 1974, Lincoln's Inn
Qualifications: [LLB (Lond)]

PARDOE ALAN DOUGLAS WILLIAM QC (1988)

Devereux Chambers
Devereux Court, London WC2R 3JJ,
Telephone: 0171 353 7534
E-mail: elton@devchambers.co.uk
Call date: Nov 1971, Lincoln's Inn
Recorder
Qualifications: [MA, LLB (Cantab)]

PARDOE MATTHEW JAMES

Counsels' Chambers
2nd Floor 10-11 Gray's Inn Square, London
WC1R 5JD, Telephone: 0171 405 2576
Call date: Feb 1992, Inner Temple
Qualifications: [BA (Hons), CPE]

PARDOE RUPERT ADAM CORIN

23 Essex Street
London WC2R 3AS,
Telephone: 0171 413 0353/353 3533
E-mail: clerks@essexstreet23.demon.co.uk
Call date: July 1984, Inner Temple
Qualifications: [MA (Cantab)]

PARFITT NICHOLAS JOHN

11 Stone Bldgs
Ground Floor, Lincoln's Inn, London
WC2A 3TG, Telephone: 0171 831 6381
E-mail: clerks@11StoneBuildings.law.co.uk
Call date: Oct 1993, Middle Temple
Qualifications: [BA (Hons)(Bris), CPE (Lond)]

PARISH STEPHEN ADRIAN BURGIS

2 King's Bench Walk
Ground Floor, Temple, London EC4Y 7DE,
Telephone: 0171 353 1746
E-mail: 2kbw@atlas.co.uk
King's Bench Chambers
115 North Hill, Plymouth PL4 8JY,
Telephone: 01752 221551
Call date: July 1966, Inner Temple
Recorder
Qualifications: [LLB]

PARK DAVID JOHN

5 Fountain Court
Steelhouse Lane, Birmingham B4 6DR,
Telephone: 0121 606 0500
Call date: May 1992, Lincoln's Inn
Qualifications: [LLB (Lond)]

PARKER ALAN PHILIP

Coleridge Chambers
Citadel 190 Corporation Street, Birmingham
B4 6QD, Telephone: 0121 233 3303
Call date: May 1995, Gray's Inn
Qualifications: [LLB (Manch)]

PARKER MRS ANTHEA ELIZABETH

4 Brick Court
Ground Floor, Temple, London EC4Y 9AD,
Telephone: 0171 797 7766
E-mail: chambers@4brick.co.uk
Call date: Nov 1990, Middle Temple
Qualifications: [BA (Hons) (E Anglia), Dip Law (PCL)]

PARKER CHRISTOPHER JAMES FRANCIS

3 Paper Bldgs
1st Floor, Temple, London EC4Y 7EU,
Telephone: 0171 583 8055
E-mail: london@3paper.com
4 St Peter Street
Winchester SO23 8OW,
Telephone: 01962 868884
20 Lorne Park Road
Bournemouth BH1 1JN,
Telephone: 01202 292102 (5 Lines)
Call date: July 1986, Gray's Inn
Qualifications: [LLB (Hons)(Exon)]

PARKER CHRISTOPHER ROY

7 Stone Bldgs
Ground Floor, Lincoln's Inn, London
WC2A 3SZ, Telephone: 0171 405 3886/
242 3546
E-mail: chaldous@vossnet.co.uk
Call date: Nov 1984, Lincoln's Inn
Qualifications: [BCL, MA (Oxon) LLM, (Ill)
LLM (Harv)]

PARKER HUGH CHRISTOPHER

King's Bench Chambers
115 North Hill, Plymouth PL4 8JY,
Telephone: 01752 221551
2 King's Bench Walk
Ground Floor, Temple, London EC4Y 7DE,
Telephone: 0171 353 1746
E-mail: 2kbw@atlas.co.uk
Call date: Nov 1973, Gray's Inn
Qualifications: [MA (Cantab)]

PARKER JOHN

2 Mitre Ct Bldgs
1st Floor, Temple, London EC4Y 7BX,
Telephone: 0171 353 1353
Call date: July 1975, Inner Temple
Qualifications: [BSc (Lond)]

PARKER MISS JUDITH MARY FRANCES QC (1991)

1 King's Bench Walk
2nd Floor, Temple, London EC4Y 7DB,
Telephone: 0171 936 1500
E-mail: ddear@1kbw.co.uk
Call date: Nov 1973, Middle Temple
Assistant Recorder
Qualifications: [BA (Oxon)]

PARKER KENNETH BLADES QC (1992)

Monckton Chambers
4 Raymond Buildings, Gray's Inn, London
WC1R 5BP, Telephone: 0171 405 7211
E-mail: chambers@monckton.co.uk
Call date: Nov 1975, Gray's Inn
Qualifications: [MA, BCL (Oxon)]

PARKER PAUL ANDREW

2 Crown Office Row
2nd Floor, Temple, London EC4Y 7HJ,
Telephone: 0171 797 8000
Call date: July 1986, Middle Temple
Qualifications: [MA(Cantab)]

PARKER PHILIP LAURENCE

3 Fountain Court
Steelhouse Lane, Birmingham B4 6DR,
Telephone: 0121 236 5854
Call date: July 1976, Middle Temple
Assistant Recorder
Qualifications: [LLB (B'ham)]

PARKER STEVEN NIGEL

The Corn Exchange
5th Floor Fenwick Street, Liverpool L2 7QS,
Telephone: 0151 227 1081/5009
Call date: Nov 1987, Gray's Inn
Qualifications: [LLB]

PARKER TIMOTHY TERENCE

2 Mitre Ct Bldgs
1st Floor, Temple, London EC4Y 7BX,
Telephone: 0171 353 1353
Call date: Nov 1995, Gray's Inn
Qualifications: [BA (Lond)]

PARKER MISS WENDY (WOO)

Francis Taylor Bldg
Ground Floor, Temple, London EC4Y 7BY,
Telephone: 0171 353 7768/7769/2711
Call date: July 1978, Middle Temple
Qualifications: [MA]

D

PARKES MALCOLM FRANK

4 Fountain Court
Steelhouse Lane, Birmingham B4 6DR,
Telephone: 0121 236 3476
Call date: July 1984, Lincoln's Inn
Qualifications: [BA (Notts) LLM, (Cantab)]

PARKES RICHARD JOHN BYERLEY

5 Raymond Buildings
1st Floor, Gray's Inn, London WC1R 5BP,
Telephone: 0171 242 2902
Call date: Nov 1977, Gray's Inn
Qualifications: [MA (Cantab)]

PARKIN MISS FIONA JANE

1 Atkin Building
Gray's Inn, London WC1R 5AT,
Telephone: 0171 404 0102
E-mail: clerks@atkin-chambers.co.uk
Call date: Oct 1993, Inner Temple
Qualifications: [BA]

PARKIN JONATHAN

Chambers of John Hand QC
9 St John Street, Manchester M3 4DN,
Telephone: 0161 955 9000
E-mail: ninesjs@gconnect.com
Call date: Nov 1978, Middle Temple
Qualifications: [MA (Cantab)]

Fax: 0161 955 9001; DX: MDX 14326;
Other comms: E-mail ninesjs@gconnect.com

Types of work: Commercial; Discrimination;
Employment; Professional negligence

Other professional qualifications: Part-time
Chairman of Employment Tribunals

Circuit: Northern

Awards and memberships: ELBA, PNBA, ELA

Languages spoken: French

PARKIN TIMOTHY CHARLES

New Court Chambers
3 Broad Chare, Newcastle Upon Tyne
NE1 3DQ, Telephone: 0191 232 1980
Call date: Nov 1971, Inner Temple
Qualifications: [LLB]

PARKINS GRAHAM CHARLES QC (1990)

18 Red Lion Court
(Off Fleet Street), London EC4A 3EB,
Telephone: 0171 520 6000
Thornwood House
102 New London Road, Chelmsford, Essex
CM2 0RG, Telephone: 01245 280880
Call date: July 1972, Inner Temple
Recorder
Qualifications: [LLB (Hons)]

PARKINSON FREDERICK BECK

Old Colony House
6 South King Street, Manchester M2 6DQ,
Telephone: 0161 834 4364
Call date: July 1981, Middle Temple
Qualifications: [LLB]

PARKINSON MISS HELEN ESTHER

3 Temple Gardens
3rd Floor, Temple, London EC4Y 9AU,
Telephone: 0171 583 0010
Call date: July 1986, Middle Temple
Qualifications: [LLB (Hons)]

PARNELL GRAHAM

East Anglian Chambers
Gresham House 5 Museum Street, Ipswich
IP1 1HQ, Telephone: 01473 214481
East Anglian Chambers
Sanders House 52 North Hill, Colchester
CO1 1PY, Telephone: 01206 572756
East Anglian Chambers
57 London Street, Norwich NR2 1HL,
Telephone: 01603 617351
Call date: Nov 1982, Middle Temple
Qualifications: [MA (Oxon)]

PARR JOHN EDWARD

8 King Street
Manchester M2 6AQ,
Telephone: 0161 834 9560
Call date: July 1989, Middle Temple
Qualifications: [LLB (Reading)]

PARR MS JUDITH MARGARET

2 Gray's Inn Square Chambers
2nd Floor, Gray's Inn, London WC1R 5AA,
Telephone: 0171 242 0328/071 405 1317
E-mail: clerks@2gis.co.uk
Call date: Feb 1994, Inner Temple
Qualifications: [LLB (Canterbury, New,
Zealand), Diploma Child, Protection (ICCL &,
LSE)]

PARRISH SAMUEL NEVILLE

3 Paper Bldgs
2nd Floor, Temple, London EC4Y 7EU,
Telephone: 0171 353 6208
Call date: Feb 1962, Inner Temple
Qualifications: [LLB (Hons)]

PARROY MICHEL PICTON QC (1991)

3 Paper Bldgs
1st Floor, Temple, London EC4Y 7EU,
Telephone: 0171 583 8055
E-mail: london@3paper.com
20 Lorne Park Road
Bournemouth BH1 1JN,
Telephone: 01202 292102 (5 Lines)
4 St Peter Street
Winchester SO23 8OW,
Telephone: 01962 868884
Call date: Nov 1969, Middle Temple
Qualifications: [BA (Oxon), MA (Oxon)]

PARRY CHARLES ROBERT

Pump Court Chambers
Upper Ground Floor 3 Pump Court, Temple,
London EC4Y 7AJ, Telephone: 0171 353 0711
Pump Court Chambers
31 Southgate Street, Winchester SO23 8EE,
Telephone: 01962 868161
Call date: Nov 1973, Middle Temple
Qualifications: [LLB (Lond)]

PARRY DAVID JULIAN THOMAS

Chambers of Lord Goodhart QC
Ground Floor 3 New Square, Lincoln's Inn,
London WC2A 3RS,
Telephone: 0171 405 5577
E-mail: law@threenewsquare.demon.co.uk
Call date: July 1972, Inner Temple
Recorder

PARRY DESMOND WYNN

40 King Street
Chester CH1 2AH, Telephone: 01244 323886
Call date: July 1995, Inner Temple
Qualifications: [LLB (L'pool)]

PARRY MISS ISABEL CLARE

9 Park Place
Cardiff CF1 3DP, Telephone: 01222 382731
Call date: July 1979, Gray's Inn
Assistant Recorder
Qualifications: [MA (Cantab)]

PARRY RICHARD GWYNEDD

Angel Chambers
94 Walter Road, Swansea SA1 5QA,
Telephone: 01792 6464623/6464648
Call date: Oct 1993, Gray's Inn
Qualifications: [LLB (Hons)(Wales)]

PARRY MISS SIAN RACHEL

Gower Chambers
57 Walter Road, Swansea, West Glamorgan
SA1 5PZ, Telephone: 01792 644466
E-mail: clerk@gowerchambers.co.uk
Call date: Oct 1994, Gray's Inn
Qualifications: [LLB (Hons)(Wales)]

PARRY EVANS MS MARY ALETHEA

33 Park Place
Cardiff CF1 3BA, Telephone: 01222 233313
Call date: June 1953, Inner Temple
Recorder
Qualifications: [BCL, MA]

PARRY-JONES MRS CAROLE ANN

East Anglian Chambers
Sanders House 52 North Hill, Colchester
CO1 1PY, Telephone: 01206 572756
East Anglian Chambers
57 London Street, Norwich NR2 1HL,
Telephone: 01603 617351
East Anglian Chambers
Gresham House 5 Museum Street, Ipswich
IP1 1HQ, Telephone: 01473 214481
Call date: Nov 1992, Middle Temple
Qualifications: [LLB (Hons, Westmin)]

D

PARRY-JONES JOHN TREVOR

The Corn Exchange
5th Floor Fenwick Street, Liverpool L2 7QS,
Telephone: 0151 227 1081/5009
Call date: Feb 1992, Gray's Inn
Qualifications: [LLB (Hons, Wales)]

PARSLEY CHARLES RONALD

33 Park Place
Cardiff CF1 3BA, Telephone: 01222 233313
Door Tenant
Goldsmith Building
1st Floor, Temple, London EC4Y 7BL,
Telephone: 0171 353 7881
E-mail: clerks@goldsmith-building.law.co.uk
Door Tenant
Call date: July 1973, Inner Temple
Qualifications: [LLB (Exon)]

PARSONS ANDREW JAMES

Portsmouth Barristers'Chambers
Victory House 7 Bellevue Terrace,
Portsmouth, Hampshire PO5 3AT,
Telephone: 01705 831292
E-mail: clerks@portsmouthbar.com
Call date: July 1985, Inner Temple
Qualifications: [LLB (Hons)(Lond)]

PARSONS LUKE ARTHUR

4 Essex Court
Temple, London EC4Y 9AJ,
Telephone: 0171 797 7970
E-mail: clerks@4essexcourt.law.co.uk
Call date: July 1985, Inner Temple
Qualifications: [LLB (Bris)]

PARSONS SIMON PETER

New Walk Chambers
27 New Walk, Leicester LE1 6TE,
Telephone: 0116 2559144
Call date: Nov 1993, Inner Temple
Qualifications: [MA (Oxon)]

PARTINGTON DAVID JOHN

Chancery House Chambers
7 Lisbon Square, Leeds LS1 4LY,
Telephone: 0113 244 6691
E-mail: Chanceryhouse@btinternet.com
10 Old Square
Ground Floor, Lincoln's Inn, London
WC2A 3SU, Telephone: 0171 405 0758
Door Tenant
15 Winckley Square
Preston PR1 3JJ, Telephone: 01772 252828
E-mail: clerks@winckleysq.demon.co.uk
Call date: July 1987, Middle Temple
Qualifications: [MA (Cantab)]

PARTINGTON MISS LISA SHIRLEY

24a St John Street
Manchester M3 4DF,
Telephone: 0161 833 9628
Call date: July 1989, Inner Temple
Qualifications: [LLB (Hons)]

PARTINGTON PROF THOMAS MARTIN

Arden Chambers
27 John Street, London WC1N 2BL,
Telephone: 0171 242 4244
Call date: Nov 1984, Middle Temple
Qualifications: [BA, LLB (Cantab)]

PARTRIDGE IAN SIMON

3 Paper Bldgs
1st Floor, Temple, London EC4Y 7EU,
Telephone: 0171 583 8055
E-mail: london@3paper.com
20 Lorne Park Road
Bournemouth BH1 1JN,
Telephone: 01202 292102 (5 Lines)
4 St Peter Street
Winchester SO23 8OW,
Telephone: 01962 868884
Call date: July 1979, Inner Temple
Qualifications: [MA (Oxon)]

PARTRIDGE DR RICHARD CHARLES

3 Serjeants Inn
London EC4Y 1BQ,
Telephone: 0171 353 5537
E-mail: available upon request
Call date: July 1994, Lincoln's Inn
Qualifications: [MBBch, LLB (Hons), (Cardiff)]

D

PASCALL MATTHEW STEPHEN

Guildford Chambers
Stoke House Leapale Lane, Guildford, Surrey
GU1 4LY, Telephone: 01483 539131
E-mail: guildford.barristers@btinternet.com
Call date: July 1984, Middle Temple
Qualifications: [BA]

PASCOE MARTIN MICHAEL

3/4 South Square
Gray's Inn, London WC1R 5HP,
Telephone: 0171 696 9900
E-mail: clerks@southsquare.com
Call date: July 1977, Lincoln's Inn
Qualifications: [BA, BCL (Oxon)]

PASCOE NIGEL SPENCER KNIGHT QC (1988)

Pump Court Chambers
Upper Ground Floor 3 Pump Court, Temple,
London EC4Y 7AJ, Telephone: 0171 353 0711
Pump Court Chambers
31 Southgate Street, Winchester SO23 8EE,
Telephone: 01962 868161
All Saints Chambers
9/11 Broad Street, Bristol BS1 2HP,
Telephone: 0117 921 1966
Door Tenant
Call date: July 1966, Inner Temple
Recorder

PASIUK MS JANINA STEFANIA

2 Paper Bldgs
1st Floor, Temple, London EC4Y 7ET,
Telephone: 0171 936 2611 (10 Lines)
E-mail: clerks@2pbbarristers.co.uk
Call date: July 1983, Middle Temple
Qualifications: [LLB (B'ham)]

PASS GEOFFREY JAMES

40 King Street
Manchester M2 6BA,
Telephone: 0161 832 9082
E-mail: Kingst40@aol.com
Call date: July 1975, Middle Temple
Qualifications: [LLB (Lond)]

PASSMORE JOHN WILLIAM

Verulam Chambers
Peer House 8-14 Verulam Street, Gray's Inn,
London WC1X 8LZ,
Telephone: 0171 813 2400
Call date: Oct 1992, Lincoln's Inn
Qualifications: [LLB(Hons)(Bris)]

PATCHETT-JOYCE MICHAEL THURSTON

Monckton Chambers
4 Raymond Buildings, Gray's Inn, London
WC1R 5BP, Telephone: 0171 405 7211
E-mail: chambers@monckton.co.uk
Call date: July 1981, Middle Temple
Qualifications: [MA (Cantab)]

PATEL BHAVIN VINUBHAI

Eldon Chambers
Fourth Floor 30/32 Fleet Street, London
EC4Y 1AA, Telephone: 0171 353 4636
Call date: Nov 1991, Lincoln's Inn
Qualifications: [BA (Oxon)]

PATEL ELYAS MOHAMMED

Park Court Chambers
40 Park Cross Street, Leeds LS1 2QH,
Telephone: 0113 2433277
Call date: Nov 1991, Gray's Inn
Qualifications: [LLB (Hons), LLM (Cantab)]

PATEL MISS GITA

Kenworthy's Buildings
83 Bridge Street, Manchester M3 2RF,
Telephone: 0161 832 4036/834 6954
Call date: July 1988, Inner Temple
Qualifications: [LLB (B'ham)]

PATEL MISS JAYABEN

Warwick House Chambers
8 Warwick Court, Gray's Inn, London
WC1R 5DJ, Telephone: 0171 430 2323
Call date: Oct 1990, Inner Temple
Qualifications: [BA (Sussex), LLM (UCL)]

D

PATEL PARISHIL JAYANTILAL

39 Essex Street
London WC2R 3AT,
Telephone: 0171 583 1111
E-mail: clerks@39essex.co.uk
Call date: Nov 1996, Middle Temple
Qualifications: [BA (Hons)(Cantab)]

PATEL SANDIP

Furnival Chambers
32 Furnival Street, London EC4A 1JQ,
Telephone: 0171 405 3232
E-mail: clerks@furnivallaw.co.uk
Call date: July 1991, Middle Temple
Qualifications: [LLB (Hons) (Essex)]

PATERSON DAVID

2 King's Bench Walk
Ground Floor, Temple, London EC4Y 7DE,
Telephone: 0171 353 1746
E-mail: 2kbw@atlas.co.uk
King's Bench Chambers
115 North Hill, Plymouth PL4 8JY,
Telephone: 01752 221551
Call date: Nov 1961, Lincoln's Inn

PATES RICHARD ANDREW

Queen Elizabeth Bldg
2nd Floor, Temple, London EC4Y 9BS,
Telephone: 0171 797 7837
Call date: Oct 1993, Lincoln's Inn
Qualifications: [LLB (Hons)(Wales), LLM]

PATHAK PANKAJ KUMAR

2 Paper Bldgs
Temple, London EC4Y 7ET,
Telephone: 0171 936 2613
Call date: Oct 1992, Lincoln's Inn
Qualifications: [MA (Cantab), LLM (Lond)]

PATIENCE ANDREW QC (1990)

5 Paper Bldgs
Lower Ground Floor, Temple, London
EC4Y 7HB, Telephone: 0171 353 5638
E-mail: 107722,633@compuserve.com
Call date: Nov 1966, Gray's Inn
Recorder
Qualifications: [MA (Oxon)]

PATON IAN FRANCIS

Hollis Whiteman Chambers
3rd/4th Floor Queen Elizabeth Bldg, Temple,
London EC4Y 9BS, Telephone: 0171 583 5766
E-mail: hollis.whiteman@btinternet.com
Call date: Apr 1975, Middle Temple

PATRICK JAMES HARRY JOHNSON

Guildhall Chambers
23 Broad Street, Bristol BS1 2HG,
Telephone: 0117 9273366
Call date: Nov 1989, Inner Temple
Qualifications: [LLB]

PATTEN BENEDICT JOSEPH

2 Crown Office Row
Ground Floor, Temple, London EC4Y 7HJ,
Telephone: 0171 797 8100
E-mail: mail@2cor.co.uk, or to individual
barristers at: [barrister's surname]@2cor.co.uk
Call date: July 1986, Middle Temple
Qualifications: [BA (Oxon)]

PATTEN NICHOLAS JOHN QC (1988)

9 Old Square
Ground Floor, Lincoln's Inn, London
WC2A 3SR, Telephone: 0171 405 4682
E-mail: chambers@9oldsquare.co.uk
Call date: July 1974, Lincoln's Inn
Qualifications: [MA (Oxon), BCL]

PATTENDEN MATHEW SHAUN

Eastbourne Chambers
15 Hyde Gardens, Eastbourne, East Sussex
BN21 4PR, Telephone: 01323 642102/416466
Call date: Nov 1995, Middle Temple
Qualifications: [BA (Hons), MA (Cantab)]

PATTERSON MISS FRANCES SILVIA

40 King Street
Manchester M2 6BA,
Telephone: 0161 832 9082
E-mail: Kingst40@aol.com
Call date: Nov 1977, Middle Temple
Assistant Recorder
Qualifications: [BA]

PATTERSON GARETH THOMAS

3 Temple Gardens
Lower Ground Floor, Temple, London
EC4Y 9AU, Telephone: 0171 353 3102/5/9297
Call date: July 1995, Gray's Inn
Qualifications: [BA]

PATTERSON MISS JO-ANNE CLAIR

Newport Chambers
12 Clytha Park Road, Newport, Gwent
NP9 47L, Telephone: 01633 267403/255855
Call date: Nov 1993, Inner Temple
Qualifications: [LLB (Bris)]

PATTERSON NORMAN WILLIAM

14 Gray's Inn Square
Gray's Inn, London WC1R 5JP,
Telephone: 0171 242 0858
E-mail: 100712.2134@compuserve.com
Call date: July 1971, Middle Temple
Qualifications: [LLB (Lond)]

PATTERSON STEWART

Pump Court Chambers
Upper Ground Floor, 3 Pump Court, London
EC4Y 7AJ, Telephone: 0171 353 0711
Pump Court Chambers
31 Southgate Street, Winchester SO23 9EE,
Telephone: 01962 868161
Call date: Nov 1967, Middle Temple
Assistant Recorder
Qualifications: [BA (Oxon)]

Fax: 01962 867 645; DX: 2514;
Other comms: E-mail
stewartpatterson@compuserve.com; Direct
Line and Voicemail 01962 833221; Mobile
0498 811752

Types of work: Arbitration; Computer contracts;
Construction; Crime; Crime - corporate fraud;
Information technology; Mediation;
Professional negligence; Sports

Other professional qualifications: MSc (Courts
Law), FCIArb, Accredited Mediator (ADR)

Circuit: Western

Awards and memberships: Member of Society of
Construction Lawyers; Criminal Bar Association

Other professional experience: Writing and
broadcasting on legal matters

PATTON ROBIN MICHAEL

New Court Chambers
3 Broad Chare, Newcastle Upon Tyne
NE1 3DQ, Telephone: 0191 232 1980
Call date: July 1983, Inner Temple
Qualifications: [BA]

PAUFFLEY MISS ANNA EVELYN HAMILTON QC (1995)

4 Paper Bldgs
2nd Floor, Temple, London EC4Y 7EX,
Telephone: 0171 583 0816/071 353 1131
E-mail: clerks@4paperbuildings.co.uk
Call date: July 1979, Middle Temple
Recorder
Qualifications: [BA (Hons)(Lond)]

PAUL NICHOLAS MARTIN

Doughty Street Chambers
11 Doughty Street, London WC1N 2PG,
Telephone: 0171 404 1313
E-mail: doughty_street@compuserve.com
Westgate Chambers
144 High Street, Lewes, East Sussex BN7 1XT,
Telephone: 01273 480510
Call date: July 1980, Gray's Inn
Qualifications: [BA (York)]

PAULUSZ JAN GILBERT

8 King's Bench Walk
2nd Floor, Temple, London EC4Y 7DU,
Telephone: 0171 797 8888
Call date: July 1957, Lincoln's Inn
Recorder

PAVLOU PAVLOS KYRIACOU

9 King's Bench Walk
Ground Floor, Temple, London EC4Y 7DX,
Telephone: 0171 353 7202/3909
Call date: Nov 1993, Lincoln's Inn
Qualifications: [LLB (Hons)]

PAVRY JAMES FRANCIS

Queen Elizabeth Bldg
Ground Floor, Temple, London EC4Y 9BS,
Telephone: 0171 353 7181 (12 Lines)
Call date: July 1974, Inner Temple
Qualifications: [BA (Oxon)]

PAWLAK WITOLD EXPEDYT

9 Bedford Row
London WC1R 4AZ,
Telephone: 0171 242 3555
E-mail: clerks@9br.co.uk
Call date: Nov 1970, Inner Temple
Recorder
Qualifications: [MA (Cantab)]

PAWLOWSKI MARK

Pepys' Chambers
17 Fleet Street, London EC4Y 1AA,
Telephone: 0171 936 2710
Door Tenant
Call date: July 1978, Middle Temple
Qualifications: [LLB (Hons), BCL (Oxon)]

PAWSON ROBERT EDWARD CRUICKSHANK

Pump Court Chambers
Upper Ground Floor 3 Pump Court, Temple,
London EC4Y 7AJ, Telephone: 0171 353 0711
Pump Court Chambers
31 Southgate Street, Winchester SO23 8EE,
Telephone: 01962 868161
Call date: Nov 1994, Inner Temple
Qualifications: [BA, MA (Lond), CPE]

PAXTON CHRISTOPHER

2 Pump Court
1st Floor, Temple, London EC4Y 7AH,
Telephone: 0171 353 5597
Call date: Nov 1991, Gray's Inn
Qualifications: [LLB]

PAYNE BRIAN WYNDHAM

Phoenix Chambers
First Floor Gray's Inn Chambers, Gray's Inn,
London WC1R 5JA, Telephone: 0171 404 7888
Call date: Nov 1993, Inner Temple
Qualifications: [BSc (Bris), Dip.L. (City)]

PAYNE RICHARD ANTHONY DOUGLAS

24 The Ropewalk
Nottingham NG1 5EF,
Telephone: 0115 9472581
E-mail: clerk@ropewalk.co.uk
Call date: June 1964, Gray's Inn

PAYNE MISS TRACEY ELIZABETH

Mitre House Chambers
Mitre House 44 Fleet Street, London
EC4Y 1BN, Telephone: 0171 583 8233
Call date: Oct 1991, Inner Temple
Qualifications: [BA (Lanc), Dip Law]

PAYTON BARRY ARNOLD

95A Chancery Lane
London WC2A 1DT,
Telephone: 0171 405 3101
Call date: Jan 1951, Middle Temple
Qualifications: [LLB, LMRTPI]

PAYTON CLIFFORD CONINGSBY

Verulam Chambers
Peer House 8-14 Verulam Street, Gray's Inn,
London WC1X 8LZ,
Telephone: 0171 813 2400
Call date: July 1972, Inner Temple
Qualifications: [BCL,MA]

PEACOCK IAN CHRISTOPHER

12 New Square
Ground Floor, Lincoln's Inn, London
WC2A 3SW, Telephone: 0171 419 1212
E-mail: 12newsquare@compuserve.com
25 Park Square
Leeds LS1 2PW, Telephone: 0113 2451841/2/3
E-mail: sovereignchambers@btinternet.com
Door Tenant
Call date: Oct 1990, Gray's Inn
Qualifications: [BA (Cantab)]

PEACOCK JONATHAN DAVID

11 New Square
1st Floor, Lincoln's Inn, London WC2A 3QB,
Telephone: 0171 242 4017/3981
E-mail: taxlaw@11newsquare.com
Call date: July 1987, Middle Temple
Qualifications: [MA (Oxon)]

PEACOCK MISS LISA JAYNE

3 Dr Johnson's Bldgs
Ground Floor, Temple, London EC4Y 7BA,
Telephone: 0171 353 4854
Call date: Oct 1992, Lincoln's Inn
Qualifications: [MA (Hons)(Cantab)]

PEACOCK NICHOLAS

67a Westgate Road
Newcastle Upon Tyne NE1 1SQ,
Telephone: 0191 261 4407/2329785
Call date: Oct 1996, Gray's Inn
Qualifications: [LLB (Coventry)]

PEACOCK NICHOLAS ALLEN

6 Pump Court
Ground Floor, Temple, London EC4Y 7AR,
Telephone: 0171 583 6013/2510
Call date: Oct 1992, Gray's Inn
Qualifications: [MA (Cantab)]

PEACOCK NICHOLAS CHRISTOPHER

13 Old Square
Ground Floor, Lincoln's Inn, London
WC2A 3UA, Telephone: 0171 404 4800
Call date: Nov 1989, Middle Temple
Qualifications: [BA [Oxon]]

PEACOCKE MRS TERESA ANNE ROSEN

Enterprise Chambers
9 Old Square, Lincoln's Inn, London
WC2A 3SR, Telephone: 0171 405 9471
Enterprise Chambers
38 Park Square, Leeds LS1 2PA,
Telephone: 01132 460391
Enterprise Chambers
65 Quayside, Newcastle upon Tyne NE1 3DS,
Telephone: 0191 222 3344
Call date: Nov 1982, Lincoln's Inn
Qualifications: [BA, MA (Michigan)]

PEARCE FREDERICK MICHAEL

1 High Pavement
Nottingham NG1 1HF,
Telephone: 0115 9418218
Call date: Feb 1975, Middle Temple
Assistant Recorder

PEARCE IVAN JAMES

Furnival Chambers
32 Furnival Street, London EC4A 1JQ,
Telephone: 0171 405 3232
E-mail: clerks@furnivallaw.co.uk
Call date: Oct 1994, Gray's Inn
Qualifications: [LLB, Ndarb]

PEARCE MISS LINDA ANN

6 King's Bench Walk
Ground, Third & Fourth Floors, Temple,
London EC4Y 7DR,
Telephone: 0171 353 4931/583 0695
Call date: July 1982, Inner Temple
Qualifications: [LLB (Soton)]

PEARCE MARCUS STEWART

East Anglian Chambers
57 London Street, Norwich NR2 1HL,
Telephone: 01603 617351
East Anglian Chambers
Sanders House 52 North Hill, Colchester
CO1 1PY, Telephone: 01206 572756
East Anglian Chambers
Gresham House 5 Museum Street, Ipswich
IP1 1HQ, Telephone: 01473 214481
Call date: July 1972, Inner Temple

PEARCE RICHARD WILLIAM

Peel Court Chambers
45 Hardman Street, Manchester M3 3HA,
Telephone: 0161 832 3791
Call date: July 1985, Middle Temple
Qualifications: [BA (Cantab)]

PEARCE ROBERT EDGAR

11 New Square
Ground Floor, Lincoln's Inn, London
WC2A 3QB, Telephone: 0171 831 0081
E-mail: 11newsquare.co.uk
Call date: July 1977, Middle Temple
Qualifications: [MA, BCL (Oxon)]

PEARCE WALTER REID

10 King's Bench Walk
Ground Floor, Temple, London EC4Y 7EB,
Telephone: 0171 353 7742
E-mail: 10kbw@lineone.net
Call date: Nov 1979, Middle Temple
Qualifications: [BA (Toronto), LLB (Lond)]

PEARCE-HIGGINS DANIEL JOHN

2 Temple Gardens
Temple, London EC4Y 9AY,
Telephone: 0171 583 6041 (12 Lines)
Call date: July 1973, Middle Temple
Assistant Recorder
Qualifications: [BSc (Bristol)]

D

PEARL DAVID ANTHONY

4 King's Bench Walk
2nd Floor, Temple, London EC4Y 7DL,
Telephone: 0171 353 3581
Call date: Nov 1977, Inner Temple
Qualifications: [MA (Cantab)]

PEARS DERRICK ALLAN

Francis Taylor Bldg
2nd Floor, Temple, London EC4Y 7BY,
Telephone: 0171 353 9942/3157
Call date: July 1975, Inner Temple
Qualifications: [MA (Oxon)]

PEARSE WHEATLEY ROBIN JOHN

2 Paper Bldgs
1st Floor, Temple, London EC4Y 7ET,
Telephone: 0171 936 2611 (10 Lines)
E-mail: clerks@2pbbarristers.co.uk
Call date: July 1971, Inner Temple
Recorder

PEARSON MS CAROLYN JAYNE

3 Temple Gardens
Lower Ground Floor, Temple, London
EC4Y 9AU, Telephone: 0171 353 3102/5/9297
Call date: Nov 1990, Gray's Inn
Qualifications: [LLB (Warw), MA (Lond)]

PEARSON CHRISTOPHER

169 Temple Chambers
Temple Avenue, London EC4Y 0DA,
Telephone: 0171 583 7644
Call date: Oct 1995, Inner Temple
Qualifications: [BSc (Dunelm), CPE]

PEARSON DAVID EDWARD

Victoria Chambers
3rd Floor 177 Corporation Street, Birmingham
B4 6RG, Telephone: 0121 236 9900
Call date: Feb 1983, Gray's Inn

PEARSON MICHAEL

2 Mitre Ct Bldgs
1st Floor, Temple, London EC4Y 7BX,
Telephone: 0171 353 1353
Call date: July 1952, Inner Temple
Qualifications: [BCL, MA (Oxon)]

PEARSON MICHAEL

30 Park Square
Leeds LS1 2PF, Telephone: 0113 2436388
Call date: Nov 1984, Lincoln's Inn
Qualifications: [BA Hons]

PEARSON THOMAS ADAM SPENSER

Pump Court Chambers
Upper Ground Floor 3 Pump Court, Temple,
London EC4Y 7AJ, Telephone: 0171 353 0711
Pump Court Chambers
31 Southgate Street, Winchester SO23 8EE,
Telephone: 01962 868161
Call date: Nov 1969, Middle Temple
Qualifications: [BA, LLB (Cantab)]

PEARSON MRS WENDY

Queen's Chambers
5 John Dalton Street, Manchester M2 6ET,
Telephone: 0161 834 6875/4738
4 Camden Place
Preston PR1 3JL, Telephone: 01772 828300
Call date: Nov 1996, Lincoln's Inn
Qualifications: [LLB (Hons)(Lancs)]

PEART ICAH DELANO EVERARD

2 Garden Court
1st Floor, Middle Temple, London EC4Y 9BL,
Telephone: 0171 353 1633
E-mail: barristers@2gardenct.law.co.uk
Call date: Nov 1978, Middle Temple
Assistant Recorder
Qualifications: [LLB (LSE)]

PEAY DR JILL VALERIE

Doughty Street Chambers
11 Doughty Street, London WC1N 2PG,
Telephone: 0171 404 1313
E-mail: doughty_street@compuserve.com
Door Tenant
Call date: Oct 1991, Gray's Inn
Qualifications: [BSc (Birm), PhD (Birm), MA
(Oxon)]

D

PECK MISS CATHERINE MARY ELIZABETH

12 King's Bench Walk
Temple, London EC4Y 7EL,
Telephone: 0171 583 0811
E-mail: chambers@12kbw.co.uk
Call date: Oct 1995, Gray's Inn
Qualifications: [LLB]

PEDDIE IAN JAMES CROFTON QC (1992)

One Garden Court
Ground Floor, Temple, London EC4Y 9BJ,
Telephone: 0171 797 7900
Call date: July 1971, Inner Temple
Recorder
Qualifications: [LLB]

PEEBLES ANDREW JAMES

Farrar's Building
Temple, London EC4Y 7BD,
Telephone: 0171 583 9241
E-mail: chambers@farrarsbuilding.co.uk
Call date: Nov 1987, Inner Temple
Qualifications: [MA (Cantab) Dip Law, (City)]

PEEL ROBERT ROGER

29 Bedford Row Chambers
London WC1R 4HE,
Telephone: 0171 831 2626
Call date: Oct 1990, Middle Temple
Qualifications: [BA (Oxon), Dip Law (City)]

PEEL STUART JAMES

Bell Yard Chambers
116/118 Chancery Lane, London WC2A 1PP,
Telephone: 0171 306 9292
Call date: Nov 1994, Inner Temple
Qualifications: [LLB (Wolverhampton)]

PEERS MS HEATHER LOUISE

Guildhall Chambers
23 Broad Street, Bristol BS1 2HG,
Telephone: 0117 9273366
Call date: Oct 1991, Gray's Inn
Qualifications: [BA (Durham), M Phil (Camb)]

PEERS MISS NICOLA JANE

Broadway House Chambers
Broadway House 9 Bank Street, Bradford,
West Yorkshire BD1 1TW,
Telephone: 01274 722560
Call date: Oct 1996, Inner Temple
Qualifications: [BA (Oxon)]

PEET ANDREW GERAINT

2 New Street
Leicester LE1 5NA, Telephone: 0116 2625906
Call date: Oct 1991, Inner Temple
Qualifications: [LLB (Manch)(Hons)]

PEGDEN JEFFREY VINCENT QC (1996)

3 Temple Gardens
Lower Ground Floor, Temple, London
EC4Y 9AU, Telephone: 0171 353 3102/5/9297
Call date: July 1973, Inner Temple
Recorder
Qualifications: [LLB]

PEGLOW DR MICHAEL ALFRED HERMAN

46/48 Essex Street
London WC2R 3GH,
Telephone: 0171 583 8899
Call date: July 1993, Middle Temple
Qualifications: [D.Phil (Oxon), Dr.ivr. (Saarb),
M.Sc (Saarb)]

PEIRSON OLIVER JAMES

Pump Court Chambers
Upper Ground Floor 3 Pump Court, Temple,
London EC4Y 7AJ, Telephone: 0171 353 0711
Pump Court Chambers
31 Southgate Street, Winchester SO23 8EE,
Telephone: 01962 868161
Call date: Oct 1993, Lincoln's Inn
Qualifications: [LLB (Hons)(Lond)]

PELLING (PHILIP) MARK

Monckton Chambers
4 Raymond Buildings, Gray's Inn, London
WC1R 5BP, Telephone: 0171 405 7211
E-mail: chambers@monckton.co.uk
Call date: July 1979, Middle Temple
Qualifications: [LLB, AKC (Lond)]

PELLING RICHARD ALEXANDER

New Court Chambers
5 Verulam Buildings, Gray's Inn, London
WC1R 5LY, Telephone: 0171 831 9500
E-mail: mail@newcourtchambers.com
Call date: Oct 1995, Middle Temple
Qualifications: [MA (Hons), D.Phil]

PEMA ANES BHUMIN LALOO

9 Woodhouse Square
Leeds LS3 1AD, Telephone: 0113 2451986
Call date: Nov 1994, Middle Temple
Qualifications: [BA (Hons)]

PENDLEBURY JEREMY JOHN STRINGFELLOW

9 Bedford Row
London WC1R 4AZ,
Telephone: 0171 242 3555
E-mail: clerks@9br.co.uk
Call date: July 1980, Inner Temple
Qualifications: [BA (Kent)]

PENGELLY MS SARAH KATHARINE

Arden Chambers
27 John Street, London WC1N 2BL,
Telephone: 0171 242 4244
Call date: Oct 1996, Inner Temple
Qualifications: [BA (Oxon), CPE (Lond)]

PENNICOTT IAN

Keating Chambers
10 Essex Street, Outer Temple, London
WC2R 3AA, Telephone: 0171 544 2600
Call date: July 1982, Middle Temple
Qualifications: [BA, LLM (Cantab)]

PENNIFER MISS KELLY

Exchange Chambers
Pearl Assurance House Derby Square,
Liverpool L2 9XX, Telephone: 0151 236 7747/
0458
E-mail: exchangechambers@btinternet.com
Call date: Nov 1994, Middle Temple
Qualifications: [LLB (Hons), Maitrise en Droit]

PENNY DUNCAN JOHN WILLIAM

6 King's Bench Walk
Ground Floor, Temple, London EC4Y 7DR,
Telephone: 0171 583 0410
Call date: Oct 1992, Middle Temple
Qualifications: [BA (Hons)(Oxon)]

PENNY JOHN CORNELIUS

Veritas Chambers
33 Corn Street, Bristol BS1 1HT,
Telephone: 0117 930 8802
Call date: Oct 1995, Middle Temple
Qualifications: [BA (Hons)]

PENNY TIMOTHY CHARLES

11 Stone Bldgs
Ground Floor, Lincoln's Inn, London
WC2A 3TG, Telephone: 0171 831 6381
E-mail: clerks@11StoneBuildings.law.co.uk
Call date: July 1988, Inner Temple
Qualifications: [LLB (Hons)]

PENTOL SIMON ALEX

3 Gray's Inn Square
Ground Floor, London WC1R 5AH,
Telephone: 0171 520 5600
E-mail: gis3@btinternet.com
Call date: Nov 1982, Middle Temple
Qualifications: [LLB (Lond)]

PEPPER MISS THERESA

Chavasse Court Chambers
2nd Floor Chavasse Court, 24 Lord Street,
Liverpool L2 1TA, Telephone: 0151 707 1191
Call date: Nov 1973, Gray's Inn
Assistant Recorder

PEPPER DR WILLIAM FRANCIS

20 Britton Street
1st Floor, London EC1M 5NQ,
Telephone: 0171 608 3765
Door Tenant
Call date: Feb 1991, Lincoln's Inn
Qualifications: [BA,MA (Columbia), EdD, JD (Univ.Mass.), ACIArb]

PEPPERALL EDWARD BRIAN

Priory Chambers
2 Fountain Court, Steelhouse Lane,
Birmingham B4 6DR,
Telephone: 0121 236 3882/1375
Call date: July 1989, Lincoln's Inn
Qualifications: [LLB (B'ham)]

PERCIVAL THE RT HON SIR IAN QC (1963)

5 Paper Bldgs
Ground Floor, Temple, London EC4Y 7HB,
Telephone: 0171 583 9275/583 4555
E-mail: 5paper@link.org
Call date: Jan 1948, Inner Temple
Recorder
Qualifications: [MA (Cantab) FCI Arb, FTII R Econs]

PERCIVAL ROBERT ELDON

5 Paper Bldgs
Ground Floor, Temple, London EC4Y 7HB,
Telephone: 0171 583 9275/583 4555
E-mail: 5paper@link.org
Call date: Nov 1971, Inner Temple
Qualifications: [MA (Cantab)]

PEREIRA JAMES ALEXANDER

2 Harcourt Bldgs
2nd Floor, Temple, London EC4Y 9DB,
Telephone: 0171 353 8415
E-mail: clerks@twoharcourtbldgs.demon.co.uk
Call date: Oct 1996, Middle Temple
Qualifications: [MA (Hons)(Cantab), LLM (Lond)]

PERIAN STEVEN SUPPIAH

Chambers of Raana Sheikh
Gray's Inn Chambers, Gray's Inn, London
WC1R, Telephone: 0171 831 5344
E-mail: s.mcblain@btinternet.com
Call date: Nov 1987, Lincoln's Inn
Qualifications: [LLB (Lond)]

PERKINS ALISTAIR GEOFFREY

Gray's Inn Chambers
5th Floor, Gray's Inn, London WC1R 5JA,
Telephone: 0171 404 1111
Call date: July 1986, Middle Temple
Qualifications: [BA (Keele)]

PERKINS JONATHAN DAVID

8 Fountain Court
Steelhouse Lane, Birmingham B4 6DR,
Telephone: 0121 236 5514/5
E-mail: clerks@no8chambers.co.uk
Call date: Nov 1980, Middle Temple
Qualifications: [LLB (Wales)]

PERKOFF RICHARD MICHAEL

Littleton Chambers
3 King's Bench Walk North, Temple, London
EC4Y 7HR, Telephone: 0171 797 8600
E-mail: littletonchambers@compuserve.com
Call date: July 1971, Middle Temple
Qualifications: [MA (Oxon)]

PERKS JOLYON ANTHONY

4 Brick Court
Temple, London EC4Y 9AD,
Telephone: 0171 797 8910
Call date: Nov 1994, Lincoln's Inn
Qualifications: [BA (Jnt Hons)(Hull), Dip in Law (Leeds)]

PERKS RICHARD HOWARD

7 Fountain Court
Steelhouse Lane, Birmingham B4 6DR,
Telephone: 0121 236 8531
Call date: Nov 1977, Lincoln's Inn
Qualifications: [LLB (B'ham)]

PERRY MISS AMANDA

Fountain Chambers
Cleveland Business Centre 1 Watson Street,
Middlesbrough TS1 2RQ,
Telephone: 01642 217037
Call date: Nov 1987, Lincoln's Inn
Qualifications: [LLB(B'ham)]

PERRY CHRISTOPHER ALAN

Godolphin Chambers
50 Castle Street, Truro, Cornwall TR1 3AF,
Telephone: 01872 276312
Call date: Nov 1980, Gray's Inn
Qualifications: [BA (Hons) (Oxon)]

D

PERRY CHRISTOPHER DAVID WILSON

20 Essex Street
London WC2R 3AL,
Telephone: 0171 583 9294
E-mail: clerks@20essexst.com
Call date: Nov 1965, Middle Temple

PERRY DAVID

6 King's Bench Walk
Ground Floor, Temple, London EC4Y 7DR,
Telephone: 0171 583 0410
Call date: July 1980, Lincoln's Inn
Qualifications: [LLB, MA]

PERRY MISS JACQUELINE ANNE

Lamb Building
Ground Floor, Temple, London EC4Y 7AS,
Telephone: 0171 797 7788
E-mail: lamb.building@link.org
Call date: Feb 1975, Gray's Inn
Qualifications: [MA (Oxon)]

PERRY JOHN QC (1989)

3 Gray's Inn Square
Ground Floor, London WC1R 5AH,
Telephone: 0171 520 5600
E-mail: gis3@btinternet.com
Call date: Nov 1975, Middle Temple
Recorder
Qualifications: [LLB (Lond), MA, LLM]

PERRY MRS NAOMI MELANIE

3 Temple Gardens
3rd Floor, Temple, London EC4Y 9AU,
Telephone: 0171 583 0010
Call date: July 1974, Middle Temple
Qualifications: [BA (B'ham)]

PERRY NIGEL JOHN

Hickstead Cottage
Brighton Road, Hickstead, West Sussex
RH17 5NU, Telephone: 01444 881182
Call date: July 1984, Gray's Inn
Qualifications: [LLB (Lond)]

PERSAD SATYANAND ALAN

Clapham Chambers
21-25 Bedford Road, Clapham North, London
SW4 7SH, Telephone: 0171 978 8482/
642 5777
E-mail: 113063.632@compuserve.com
Call date: Feb 1968, Inner Temple

PERSEY LIONEL EDWARD QC (1997)

4 Field Court
Gray's Inn, London WC1R 5EA,
Telephone: 0171 440 6900
E-mail: chambers@4fieldcourt.co.uk
Call date: July 1981, Gray's Inn
Qualifications: [LLB, DEJF (Limoges)]

PERSHAD ROHAN

2 Crown Office Row
Ground Floor, Temple, London EC4Y 7HJ,
Telephone: 0171 797 8100
E-mail: mail@2cor.co.uk, or to individual
barristers at: [barrister's surname]@2cor.co.uk
Call date: Oct 1991, Lincoln's Inn
Qualifications: [LLB (Hons) (Lond)]

PERT MICHAEL QC (1992)

36 Bedford Row
London WC1R 4JH,
Telephone: 0171 421 8000
E-mail: 36bedfordrow@link.org
Call date: Apr 1970, Gray's Inn
Recorder
Qualifications: [LLB (Manchester)]

PETCHEY PHILIP NEIL

2 Harcourt Bldgs
2nd Floor, Temple, London EC4Y 9DB,
Telephone: 0171 353 8415
E-mail: clerks@twoharcourtbldgs.demon.co.uk
Call date: July 1976, Middle Temple
Qualifications: [MA (Oxon)]

PETER LEVI ANDREW

4 Brick Court
Temple, London EC4Y 9AD,
Telephone: 0171 797 8910
Call date: Nov 1993, Lincoln's Inn
Qualifications: [LLB (Hons)]

PETERS NIGEL MELVIN QC (1997)

18 Red Lion Court
(Off Fleet Street), London EC4A 3EB,
Telephone: 0171 520 6000
Thornwood House
102 New London Road, Chelmsford, Essex
CM2 0RG, Telephone: 01245 280880
Call date: July 1976, Lincoln's Inn
Assistant Recorder
Qualifications: [LLB]

PETERS WILLIAM JOHN STEPHEN CHARLES

Iscoed Chambers
86 St Helen's Road, Swansea SA1 4BQ,
Telephone: 01792 652988/9/330
Call date: Nov 1992, Lincoln's Inn

PETERSEN LEWIS NEIL

2 Paper Bldgs
Temple, London EC4Y 7ET,
Telephone: 0171 936 2613
Call date: July 1983, Middle Temple
Qualifications: [BA LLB (Capetown), Dip Crim (Cantab)]

PETO ANTHONY NICHOLAS GEORGE

2 Hare Court
Ground Floor, Temple, London EC4Y 7BH,
Telephone: 0171 583 1770
E-mail: 2_Hare_Court@link.org
Call date: Feb 1985, Middle Temple
Qualifications: [MA,BCL (Oxon)]

PETTS TIMOTHY DAVID

12 King's Bench Walk
Temple, London EC4Y 7EL,
Telephone: 0171 583 0811
E-mail: chambers@12kbw.co.uk
Call date: Oct 1996, Inner Temple
Qualifications: [BA, M.Jur (Oxon)]

PHELAN MS MARGARET

Mitre House Chambers
Mitre House 44 Fleet Street, London
EC4Y 1BN, Telephone: 0171 583 8233
Call date: Oct 1993, Inner Temple
Qualifications: [LLB (Hons)]

PHELPS MARK

East Anglian Chambers
Gresham House 5 Museum Street, Ipswich
IP1 1HQ, Telephone: 01473 214481
East Anglian Chambers
Sanders House 52 North Hill, Colchester
CO1 1PY, Telephone: 01206 572756
East Anglian Chambers
57 London Street, Norwich NR2 1HL,
Telephone: 01603 617351
Call date: Nov 1994, Lincoln's Inn
Qualifications: [BA (Jnt Hons), MA (Notts), CPE (Notts)]

PHELVIN BERNARD JOHN

2 Harcourt Bldgs
1st Floor, Temple, London EC4Y 9DB,
Telephone: 0171 353 2112/2817
Call date: July 1971, Middle Temple
Qualifications: [BA (Cantab)]

PHIL-EBOSIE MISS EUNICE SHEILA NNEKA

Francis Taylor Bldg
3rd Floor, Temple, London EC4Y 7BY,
Telephone: 0171 797 7250
Call date: Nov 1988, Gray's Inn
Qualifications: [LLB (Nigeria), LLM (Lond), BL (Nigeria)]

PHILCOX MISS BARBARA ANNE

Queen Elizabeth Bldg
Ground Floor, Temple, London EC4Y 9BS,
Telephone: 0171 353 7181 (12 Lines)
Call date: July 1988, Inner Temple
Qualifications: [LLB (Soton)]

PHILIPPS GUY WOGAN

Fountain Court
Temple, London EC4Y 9DH,
Telephone: 0171 583 3335
E-mail: chambers@fountaincourt.co.uk
Call date: July 1986, Inner Temple
Qualifications: [MA (Oxon), Dip Law]

D

D

PHILIPSON JOHN TREVOR GRAHAM QC (1989)

Fountain Court
Temple, London EC4Y 9DH,
Telephone: 0171 583 3335
E-mail: chambers@fountaincourt.co.uk
Call date: Nov 1972, Middle Temple
Qualifications: [BA, BCL (Oxon)]

PHILLIMORE LORD FRANCIS STEPHEN

Queen Elizabeth Bldg
2nd Floor, Temple, London EC4Y 9BS,
Telephone: 0171 797 7837
Call date: July 1972, Middle Temple
Qualifications: [BA (Cantab)]

PHILLIPS ANDREW CHARLES

2 Crown Office Row
Ground Floor, Temple, London EC4Y 7HJ,
Telephone: 0171 797 8100
E-mail: mail@2cor.co.uk, or to individual
barristers at: [barrister's surname]@2cor.co.uk
Call date: July 1978, Middle Temple
Qualifications: [BA (Oxon), MA (Cantab)]

PHILLIPS DAVID JOHN QC (1997)

199 Strand
London WC2R 1DR,
Telephone: 0171 379 9779
E-mail: chambers@199strand.co.uk
30 Park Place
Cardiff CF1 3BA, Telephone: 01222 398421
E-mail: 100757.1456@compuserve.com
Door Tenant
Call date: Nov 1976, Gray's Inn
Assistant Recorder
Qualifications: [MA (Oxon)]

PHILLIPS FRANK

Iscoed Chambers
86 St Helen's Road, Swansea SA1 4BQ,
Telephone: 01792 652988/9/330
Call date: Nov 1972, Lincoln's Inn
Qualifications: [LLB (Bris)]

PHILLIPS MISS JANE ROSE

1 Brick Court
1st Floor, Temple, London EC4Y 9BY,
Telephone: 0171 353 8845
E-mail: clerks@1brickcourt.co.uk
Call date: July 1989, Inner Temple
Qualifications: [BA (Oxon)(Hons)]

PHILLIPS JEREMY PATRICK MANFRED QC (1980)

2 Temple Gardens
Temple, London EC4Y 9AY,
Telephone: 0171 583 6041 (12 Lines)
Call date: Feb 1964, Gray's Inn

PHILLIPS JOHN ANDREW

28 St John Street
Manchester M3 4DJ,
Telephone: 0161 834 8418
E-mail: clerk@28stjohnst.co.uk
Call date: July 1976, Gray's Inn
Recorder
Qualifications: [MA (Cantab)]

PHILLIPS JOHN CHRISTOPHER

2 Field Court
Gray's Inn, London WC1R 5BB,
Telephone: 0171 405 6114
E-mail: fieldct2@netcomuk.co.uk.
Call date: Feb 1975, Middle Temple
Qualifications: [MA (Cantab), LLM
(Queensland), PhD (Queensland)]

PHILLIPS JONATHAN MARK

3 Verulam Buildings
London WC1R 5NT,
Telephone: 0171 831 8441
E-mail: clerks@3verulam.co.uk
Call date: Nov 1991, Inner Temple
Qualifications: [BA (Hons)(Cantab)]

PHILLIPS MARK PAUL

3/4 South Square
Gray's Inn, London WC1R 5HP,
Telephone: 0171 696 9900
E-mail: clerks@southsquare.com
Call date: July 1984, Inner Temple
Qualifications: [LLB, LLM (Bris)]

PHILLIPS MATTHEW JAMES

35 Essex Street
Temple, London WC2R 3AR,
Telephone: 0171 353 6381
Call date: Nov 1993, Lincoln's Inn
Qualifications: [BA (Hons)]

PHILLIPS MICHAEL CHARLES

Lamb Building
Ground Floor, Temple, London EC4Y 7AS,
Telephone: 0171 797 7788
E-mail: lamb.building@link.org
Call date: Feb 1980, Middle Temple
Qualifications: [LLB (Lond)]

PHILLIPS NEVIL DAVID

4 Essex Court
Temple, London EC4Y 9AJ,
Telephone: 0171 797 7970
E-mail: clerks@4essexcourt.law.co.uk
Call date: Oct 1992, Gray's Inn
Qualifications: [BA (So'ton), Dip Law (City),
LLM (Lond)]

PHILLIPS PAUL STUART

2 Dr Johnson's Building
Temple, London EC4Y 7AY,
Telephone: 0171 353 4716
Call date: Feb 1991, Gray's Inn
Qualifications: [LLB (Wales)]

PHILLIPS RICHARD CHARLES JONATHAN QC (1990)

2 Harcourt Bldgs
2nd Floor, Temple, London EC4Y 9DB,
Telephone: 0171 353 8415
E-mail: clerks@twoharcourtbldgs.demon.co.uk
Call date: Nov 1970, Inner Temple
Qualifications: [MA (Cantab)]

PHILLIPS RORY ANDREW LIVINGSTONE

3 Verulam Buildings
London WC1R 5NT,
Telephone: 0171 831 8441
E-mail: clerks@3verulam.co.uk
Call date: July 1984, Inner Temple
Qualifications: [MA (Cantab)]

PHILLIPS SIMON BENJAMIN

Park Court Chambers
40 Park Cross Street, Leeds LS1 2QH,
Telephone: 0113 2433277
Call date: July 1985, Inner Temple
Qualifications: [BA (Sussex), LLM, (Cantab)]

PHILLIPS STEPHEN EDMUND

3 Verulam Buildings
London WC1R 5NT,
Telephone: 0171 831 8441
E-mail: clerks@3verulam.co.uk
Call date: July 1984, Gray's Inn
Qualifications: [BA (Oxon)]

PHILLIPS STEPHEN JAMES

7 King's Bench Walk
Ground Floor, Temple, London EC4Y 7DS,
Telephone: 0171 583 0404
Call date: Oct 1993, Lincoln's Inn
Qualifications: [BA (Oxon), BCL]

PHILLIPS WILLIAM BERNARD

Paradise Square Chambers
26 Paradise Square, Sheffield S1 2DE,
Telephone: 0114 2738951
Call date: July 1970, Inner Temple
Recorder
Qualifications: [MA (Oxon)]

PHILO NOEL PHILIP

St Mary's Chambers
50 High Pavement, Lace Market, Nottingham
NG1 1HW, Telephone: 0115 9503503
E-mail: clerks@smc.law.co.uk
Call date: Feb 1975, Gray's Inn
Qualifications: [MA (Oxon)]

PHILPOTT FREDERICK ALAN

Gough Square Chambers
6-7 Gough Square, London EC4A 3DE,
Telephone: 0171 353 0924
E-mail: gsc@goughsq.co.uk
Call date: July 1974, Gray's Inn
Qualifications: [LLB (Lond)]

D

PHILPOTTS ROBERT JOHN

40 King Street
Chester CH1 2AH, Telephone: 01244 323886
Call date: Oct 1990, Gray's Inn
Qualifications: [BA, MPhil (L'pool)]

PHIPPS CHARLES MACKENZIE

2 Crown Office Row
2nd Floor, Temple, London EC4Y 7HJ,
Telephone: 0171 797 8000
Call date: Nov 1992, Middle Temple
Qualifications: [BA (Oxon), Dip in Law (City)]

PICARDA HUBERT ALISTAIR PAUL QC (1992)

Chambers of Lord Goodhart QC
Ground Floor 3 New Square, Lincoln's Inn,
London WC2A 3RS,
Telephone: 0171 405 5577
E-mail: law@threenewsquare.demon.co.uk
Call date: Feb 1962, Inner Temple
Qualifications: [MA, BCL (Oxon)]

PICKAVANCE GRAHAM MICHAEL

Chavasse Court Chambers
2nd Floor Chavasse Court, 24 Lord Street,
Liverpool L2 1TA, Telephone: 0151 707 1191
Call date: Nov 1973, Gray's Inn
Qualifications: [LLB]

PICKAVANCE MICHAEL JOHN

The Corn Exchange
5th Floor Fenwick Street, Liverpool L2 7QS,
Telephone: 0151 227 1081/5009
Call date: July 1974, Middle Temple
Qualifications: [LLB (Hons)]

PICKEN SIMON DEREK

7 King's Bench Walk
Ground Floor, Temple, London EC4Y 7DS,
Telephone: 0171 583 0404
30 Park Place
Cardiff CF1 3BA, Telephone: 01222 398421
E-mail: 100757.1456@compuserve.com
Door Tenant
Call date: July 1989, Middle Temple
Qualifications: [LLB [Cardiff], LLM (Cantab)]

PICKERING JAMES PATRICK

Enterprise Chambers
9 Old Square, Lincoln's Inn, London
WC2A 3SR, Telephone: 0171 405 9471
Enterprise Chambers
38 Park Square, Leeds LS1 2PA,
Telephone: 01132 460391
Enterprise Chambers
65 Quayside, Newcastle upon Tyne NE1 3DS,
Telephone: 0191 222 3344
Call date: Oct 1991, Middle Temple
Qualifications: [BSc Hons (So'ton)]

PICKERING MURRAY ASHLEY QC (1985)

20 Essex Street
London WC2R 3AL,
Telephone: 0171 583 9294
E-mail: clerks@20essexst.com
Call date: Nov 1963, Inner Temple
Recorder
Qualifications: [MA (NZ), LLM (Lond)]

PICKERING RICHARD ANDREW

12 King's Bench Walk
Temple, London EC4Y 7EL,
Telephone: 0171 583 0811
E-mail: chambers@12kbw.co.uk
Call date: Nov 1987, Lincoln's Inn
Qualifications: [BA(Hons) Cantab, Dip Law
(City)]

PICKERSGILL DAVID WILLIAM

Bell Yard Chambers
116/118 Chancery Lane, London WC2A 1PP,
Telephone: 0171 306 9292
Call date: Nov 1996, Middle Temple
Qualifications: [LLB (Hons)(Kingston)]

PICKFORD ANTHONY JAMES

Prince Henry's Chambers
17 Fleet Street, London EC4Y 1AA,
Telephone: 0171 353 1183/1190
Call date: June 1951, Lincoln's Inn
Qualifications: [LLB (Lond)]

PICKLES SIMON ROBERT

1 Serjeants' Inn
4th Floor, Temple, London EC4Y 1NH,
Telephone: 0171 583 1355
E-mail: serjeants.inn@virgin.net
Call date: July 1978, Inner Temple
Qualifications: [MA (Cantab)]

PICKUP DAVID MICHAEL WALKER

Peel Court Chambers
45 Hardman Street, Manchester M3 3HA,
Telephone: 0161 832 3791
Call date: July 1984, Inner Temple
Qualifications: [LLB (Leeds)]

PICKUP JAMES KENNETH

Lincoln House Chambers
5th Floor Lincoln House, 1 Brazennose Street,
Manchester M2 5EL,
Telephone: 0161 832 5701
E-mail: LincolnHouseChambers@link.org
Call date: July 1976, Gray's Inn
Recorder
Qualifications: [MA (Oxon), BCL]

PICTON JULIAN MARK

4 Paper Bldgs
Ground Floor, Temple, London EC4Y 7EX,
Telephone: 0171 353 3366/583 7155
E-mail: clerks@4paperbuildings.com
Call date: Feb 1988, Middle Temple
Qualifications: [BA (Oxon)]

PICTON MARTIN THOMAS

Albion Chambers
Broad Street, Bristol BS1 1DR,
Telephone: 0117 9272144
Call date: July 1981, Middle Temple
Qualifications: [LLB (Lond)]

PIERCY MISS ARLETTE MARY

3 Gray's Inn Square
Ground Floor, London WC1R 5AH,
Telephone: 0171 520 5600
E-mail: gis3@btinternet.com
Call date: Nov 1990, Lincoln's Inn
Qualifications: [LLB (Leeds)]

PIERCY HON MARK EDWARD PELHAM

Francis Taylor Bldg
Ground Floor, Temple, London EC4Y 7BY,
Telephone: 0171 353 7768/7769/2711
Call date: July 1976, Lincoln's Inn
Qualifications: [BA (Oxon)]

PIGOT MISS DIANA MARGUERITE

2 Pump Court
1st Floor, Temple, London EC4Y 7AH,
Telephone: 0171 353 5597
Call date: Nov 1978, Inner Temple
Qualifications: [BA (Lond)]

PILKINGTON MRS MAVIS PATRICIA

9 Woodhouse Square
Leeds LS3 1AD, Telephone: 0113 2451986
Call date: Oct 1990, Lincoln's Inn
Qualifications: [LLB, LLM (B'ham)]

PILLING MISS ANNABEL LUCY

6 King's Bench Walk
Ground Floor, Temple, London EC4Y 7DR,
Telephone: 0171 583 0410
Call date: Oct 1995, Middle Temple
Qualifications: [BA (Hons)]

PIMENTEL CARLOS DE SERPA ALBERTO LEGG

3 Stone Bldgs
Ground Floor, Lincoln's Inn, London
WC2A 3XL, Telephone: 0171 242 4937/
405 8358
Call date: Oct 1990, Inner Temple
Qualifications: [LLB, LLM (Exon)]

PIMM PETER JULIAN

Bank House Chambers
Old Bank House, Hartshead, Sheffield S1 2EL,
Telephone: 0114 2751223
Door Tenant
Cloisters
1st Floor, Temple, London EC4Y 7AA,
Telephone: 0171 827 4000
E-mail: clerks@cloisters.com
Door Tenant
Call date: Apr 1991, Gray's Inn
Qualifications: [BSC (Bristol)]

PINDER MISS MARY ELIZABETH

1 Serjeants' Inn
5th Floor Fleet Street, Temple, London
EC4Y 1LL, Telephone: 0171 415 6666
E-mail: no1serjeantsinn@btinternet.com
Call date: July 1989, Gray's Inn
Qualifications: [LLB (Bris)]

PINE-COFFIN MISS MARGARET ANN

17 Carlton Crescent
Southampton SO15 2XR,
Telephone: 01703 320320
E-mail: km@bar-17cc.demon.co.uk
Call date: July 1981, Inner Temple
Qualifications: [BA (Leeds)]

PINI JOHN PETER JULIAN

9 Bedford Row
London WC1R 4AZ,
Telephone: 0171 242 3555
E-mail: clerks@9br.co.uk
Call date: July 1981, Gray's Inn
Qualifications: [BA]

PINKHAM MRS JOY EMMA

Chartlands Chambers
3 St Giles Terrace, Northampton NN1 2BN,
Telephone: 01604 603322
Call date: Feb 1993, Gray's Inn
Qualifications: [LLB (Buckingham)]

PINKNEY ANDREW GILES FREDERICK

Fountain Chambers
Cleveland Business Centre 1 Watson Street,
Middlesbrough TS1 2RQ,
Telephone: 01642 217037
Door Tenant
Call date: Nov 1978, Gray's Inn
Qualifications: [BA (Hons)]

PINTO MISS AMANDA EVE

5 Paper Bldgs
1st Floor, Temple, London EC4Y 7HB,
Telephone: 0171 583 6117
E-mail: clerks@5-paperbuildings.law.co.uk
Call date: Nov 1983, Middle Temple
Qualifications: [MA (Cantab)]

PIPE GREGORY SIMON

Chancery House Chambers
7 Lisbon Square, Leeds LS1 4LY,
Telephone: 0113 244 6691
E-mail: Chanceryhouse@btinternet.com
Call date: Oct 1995, Lincoln's Inn
Qualifications: [BA (Hons)(Oxon), LLM (Cantab)]

PIPER ANGUS RICHARD

3 Paper Bldgs
Ground Floor, Temple, London EC4Y 7EU,
Telephone: 0171 797 7000
E-mail: clerks@3pb.co.uk
Call date: Nov 1991, Lincoln's Inn
Qualifications: [BA (Hons) (York), Dip Law]

PIPI CHUKWUEMEKA EZEKIEL

Bell Yard Chambers
116/118 Chancery Lane, London WC2A 1PP,
Telephone: 0171 306 9292
Call date: Apr 1991, Inner Temple
Qualifications: [LLB]

PIRANI ROHAN CARL

Old Square Chambers
Hanover House 47 Corn Street, Bristol
BS1 1HT, Telephone: 0117 9277111
Call date: Oct 1995, Middle Temple
Qualifications: [MA (Oxon), BCL (Oxon), LLM (Toronto)]

PIRIE MISS FERNANDA

13 Old Square
Ground Floor, Lincoln's Inn, London
WC2A 3UA, Telephone: 0171 404 4800
Call date: Nov 1988, Middle Temple
Qualifications: [BA (Oxon), Dip Law (City)]

PIROTTA MISS MONICA JOSEPHINE

8 Fountain Court
Steelhouse Lane, Birmingham B4 6DR,
Telephone: 0121 236 5514/5
E-mail: clerks@no8chambers.co.uk
Call date: Nov 1976, Middle Temple
Qualifications: [LLB]

PITCHERS HENRY WILLIAM STODART

22 Old Bldgs
Lincoln's Inn, London WC2A 3UJ,
Telephone: 0171 831 0222
Call date: Nov 1996, Inner Temple
Qualifications: [BA (Oxon)]

PITCHFORD CHRISTOPHER JOHN QC (1987)

Farrar's Building
Temple, London EC4Y 7BD,
Telephone: 0171 583 9241
E-mail: chambers@farrarsbuilding.co.uk
30 Park Place
Cardiff CF1 3BA, Telephone: 01222 398421
E-mail: 100757.1456@compuserve.com
Door Tenant
Call date: July 1969, Middle Temple
Recorder
Qualifications: [LLB]

PITHERS CLIVE ROBERT

Fenners Chambers
3 Madingley Road, Cambridge CB3 OEE,
Telephone: 01223 368761
Fenners Chambers
8-12 Priestgate, Peterborough PE1 1JA,
Telephone: 01733 62030
Call date: Feb 1989, Gray's Inn
Qualifications: [LLB (Reading)]

PITT MISS ANDREA ELAINE

Cleveland Chambers
63-65 Borough Road, Middlesbrough,
Cleveland TS1 3AA, Telephone: 01642 226036
Call date: July 1987, Inner Temple
Qualifications: [LLB]

PITT THE HON BRUCE MICHAEL DAVID

Phoenix Chambers
First Floor Gray's Inn Chambers, Gray's Inn,
London WC1R 5JA, Telephone: 0171 404 7888
Door Tenant
Holborn Chambers
6 Gate Street, Lincoln's Inn Fields, London
WC2A 3HP, Telephone: 0171 242 6060
Door Tenant
Call date: Nov 1970, Gray's Inn
Qualifications: [LLB(Lond)]

PITT COLIN GEORGE

3 Raymond Buildings
Gray's Inn, London WC1R 5BH,
Telephone: 0171 831 3833
E-mail: chambers@threeraymond.demon.co.uk
Call date: Nov 1968, Gray's Inn
Qualifications: [BA (Econ) LLB (Lond)]

PITT-LEWIS MRS JANET REBECCA

6 Fountain Court
Steelhouse Lane, Birmingham B4 6DR,
Telephone: 0121 233 3282
Call date: July 1976, Middle Temple
Qualifications: [MA (Oxon)]

PITT-PAYNE TIMOTHY SHERIDAN

11 King's Bench Walk
Temple, London EC4Y 7EQ,
Telephone: 0171 632 8500
E-mail: clerksroom@11-kbw.law.co.uk
Call date: Nov 1989, Inner Temple
Qualifications: [BA, BCL (Oxon)]

Fax: 0171 583 9123/3690; DX: LDE 368

Types of work: Administrative; Commercial
litigation; Discrimination; Employment; Local
government

Languages spoken: French

Publications: *Judicial Review* (Eds Supperstone
and Goudie), 1997

PITTAWAY MISS AMANDA MICHELLE

6 Fountain Court
Steelhouse Lane, Birmingham B4 6DR,
Telephone: 0121 233 3282
Call date: July 1980, Gray's Inn
Qualifications: [LLB (B'ham)]

PITTAWAY DAVID MICHAEL

1 Serjeants' Inn
5th Floor Fleet Street, Temple, London
EC4Y 1LL, Telephone: 0171 415 6666
E-mail: no1serjeantsinn@btinternet.com
Call date: July 1977, Inner Temple
Qualifications: [MA (Cantab)]

D

D

PITTER JASON KARL

Park Court Chambers
40 Park Cross Street, Leeds LS1 2QH,
Telephone: 0113 2433277
Call date: Oct 1994, Gray's Inn
Qualifications: [LLB]

PITTS ANTHONY BRIAN

4 Brick Court
1st Floor, Temple, London EC4Y 9AD,
Telephone: 0171 583 8455
Call date: Nov 1975, Gray's Inn
Assistant Recorder
Qualifications: [BA (Oxon)]

PIYADASA MISS SURANGANI DEVI

4 Brick Court
Temple, London EC4Y 9AD,
Telephone: 0171 797 8910
Call date: Oct 1994, Lincoln's Inn
Qualifications: [LLB (Hons)(Lond)]

PLANGE MISS JANET NYANCH

14 Tooks Court
Cursitor St, London EC4A 1LB,
Telephone: 0171 405 8828
E-mail: clerks @tooks.law.co.uk
Call date: July 1981, Gray's Inn
Qualifications: [LLB (B'ham)]

PLANTEROSE ROWAN MICHAEL

Littman Chambers
12 Gray's Inn Square, London WC1R 5JP,
Telephone: 0171 404 4866
E-mail: admin@littmanchambers.com
Call date: Nov 1978, Middle Temple
Qualifications: [MA, LLB (Cantab), FCIARB]

PLASCHKES MS SARAH GEORGINA

Hollis Whiteman Chambers
3rd/4th Floor Queen Elizabeth Bldg, Temple,
London EC4Y 9BS, Telephone: 0171 583 5766
E-mail: hollis.whiteman@btinternet.com
Call date: July 1988, Inner Temple
Qualifications: [LLB (Soton)]

PLATFORD GRAHAM ROY

5 Paper Bldgs
Ground Floor, Temple, London EC4Y 7HB,
Telephone: 0171 583 9275/583 4555
E-mail: 5paper@link.org
Call date: Nov 1970, Gray's Inn
Qualifications: [BA]

PLATT DAVID WALLACE

1 Paper Bldgs
Ground Floor, Temple, London EC4Y 7EP,
Telephone: 0171 583 7355
E-mail: clerks@1pb.co.uk
Call date: July 1987, Middle Temple
Qualifications: [MA (Cantab)]

PLATT MISS ELEANOR FRANCES QC (1982)

One Garden Court
Ground Floor, Temple, London EC4Y 9BJ,
Telephone: 0171 797 7900
Call date: Feb 1960, Gray's Inn
Recorder
Qualifications: [LLB (Lond)]

PLATTS CHARLES GRAHAM GREGORY

28 St John Street
Manchester M3 4DJ,
Telephone: 0161 834 8418
E-mail: clerk@28stjohnst.co.uk
Call date: July 1978, Gray's Inn
Qualifications: [MA (Cantab)]

PLATTS MISS RACHEL ELIZABETH

1 Mitre Ct Bldgs
Ground Floor, Temple, London EC4Y 7BS,
Telephone: 0171 797 7070
Call date: Nov 1989, Inner Temple
Qualifications: [LLB (Hons)(Lond)]

PLATTS ROBERT

Lincoln House Chambers
5th Floor Lincoln House, 1 Brazennose Street,
Manchester M2 5EL,
Telephone: 0161 832 5701
E-mail: LincolnHouseChambers@link.org
Call date: July 1973, Lincoln's Inn
Recorder
Qualifications: [LLB (Hons) Lond, MSc (Bradford)]

PLATTS-MILLS JOHN FAITHFUL FORTESCUE QC (1964)

Cloisters
1st Floor, Temple, London EC4Y 7AA,
Telephone: 0171 827 4000
E-mail: clerks@cloisters.com
Call date: Jan 1932, Inner Temple
Qualifications: [MA BCL (Oxon) LLM, (NZ)]

PLATTS-MILLS MARK FORTESCUE QC (1995)

8 New Square
Lincoln's Inn, London WC2A 3QP,
Telephone: 0171 405 4321
Call date: July 1974, Inner Temple
Qualifications: [BA (Oxon)]

PLAYFORD JONATHAN RICHARD QC (1982)

2 Harcourt Bldgs
Ground Floor/Left, Temple, London
EC4Y 9DB, Telephone: 0171 583 9020
E-mail: clerks@harcourt.co.uk
Call date: Nov 1962, Inner Temple
Recorder
Qualifications: [LLB (Lond)]

PLEMING NIGEL PETER QC (1992)

39 Essex Street
London WC2R 3AT,
Telephone: 0171 583 1111
E-mail: clerks@39essex.co.uk
Call date: Feb 1971, Inner Temple
Qualifications: [LLM (Lond)]

PLENDER DR RICHARD OWEN QC (1989)

20 Essex Street
London WC2R 3AL,
Telephone: 0171 583 9294
E-mail: clerks@20essexst.com
Call date: Nov 1972, Inner Temple
Recorder
Qualifications: [PhD (Sheff), JSD,LLM (Illinois), BA,LLB (Cantab)]

PLIMMER MISS MELANIE ANN

Chambers of Ian Macdonald QC
Waldorf House Cooper Street, Manchester
M2 2FW, Telephone: 0161 236 1840
Call date: Mar 1996, Gray's Inn
Qualifications: [LLB (Bris), LLM (Lond)]

PLUMSTEAD JOHN CHARLES

1 Middle Temple Lane
Temple, London EC4Y 1LT,
Telephone: 0171 583 0659 (12 Lines)
Call date: July 1975, Middle Temple
Qualifications: [LLB]

PLUNKETT (ANDREW) CHRISTOPHER

36 Bedford Row
London WC1R 4JH,
Telephone: 0171 421 8000
E-mail: 36bedfordrow@link.org
Call date: July 1983, Gray's Inn
Qualifications: [LLB (Warw)]

POCOCK CHRISTOPHER JAMES

1 King's Bench Walk
2nd Floor, Temple, London EC4Y 7DB,
Telephone: 0171 936 1500
E-mail: ddear@1kbw.co.uk
Call date: July 1984, Inner Temple
Qualifications: [BA (Hons) Law (Oxon)]

POINTER MARTIN JOHN QC (1996)

1 Mitre Ct Bldgs
Ground Floor, Temple, London EC4Y 7BS,
Telephone: 0171 797 7070
Call date: July 1976, Gray's Inn
Qualifications: [LLB]

POINTING JOHN ERIC

Field Court Chambers
2nd Floor 3 Field Court, Gray's Inn, London
WC1R 4EP, Telephone: 0171 404 7474
E-mail: Clerks@FieldCourtChambers.law.co.uk
Call date: Oct 1992, Middle Temple
Qualifications: [BA (Hons, Keele), M.Phil, Diploma In Law]

D

POINTON MISS CAROLINE JANE

Fenners Chambers
3 Madingley Road, Cambridge CB3 OEE,
Telephone: 01223 368761
Fenners Chambers
8-12 Priestgate, Peterborough PE1 1JA,
Telephone: 01733 62030
Call date: July 1976, Gray's Inn
Qualifications: [LLB (Hons) (Lond)]

POKU MISS MARY LAUREEN

12 Old Square
1st Floor, Lincoln's Inn, London WC2A 3TX,
Telephone: 0171 404 0875
Call date: Nov 1993, Lincoln's Inn
Qualifications: [LLB (Hons)]

POLGLASE DAVID SUTHERLAND

Victoria Chambers
19 Castle Street, Liverpool L2 4SX,
Telephone: 0151 236 9402
E-mail: Fa45@rapid.co.uk
Call date: Oct 1993, Middle Temple
Qualifications: [BA (Hons)(Oxon), MA (Oxon)]

POLLARD MISS JOANNA KATE

2 Hare Court
Ground Floor, Temple, London EC4Y 7BH,
Telephone: 0171 583 1770
E-mail: 2_Hare_Court@link.org
Call date: Oct 1993, Gray's Inn
Qualifications: [BA]

POLLOCK ALAN GORDON SETON QC (1979)

Essex Court Chambers
24 Lincoln's Inn Fields, London WC2A 3ED,
Telephone: 0171 813 8000
E-mail: clerksroom@essexcourt-chambers.co.uk
Call date: Nov 1968, Gray's Inn
Qualifications: [MA, LLB (Cantab)]

POLLOCK DR EVELYN MARIAN MARGARET

5 Essex Court
1st Floor, Temple, London EC4Y 9AH,
Telephone: 0171 410 2000
Call date: Oct 1991, Inner Temple
Qualifications: [BSc, MBChB MD (Edin), Dip Law]

POLLOCK MISS ROBERTA HILARY

1 Dr Johnson's Bldgs
Ground Floor, Temple, London EC4Y 7AX,
Telephone: 0171 353 9328
Dr Johnson's Chambers
The Atrium Court Apex Plaza, Reading
RG1 1AX, Telephone: 01734 254221
Call date: Nov 1993, Inner Temple
Qualifications: [LLB (Brunel)]

POLSON ALISTAIR JAMES

1 Pump Court
Lower Ground Floor, Temple, London
EC4Y 7AB, Telephone: 0171 583 2012/
353 4341
E-mail: (name) @1pumpcourt.co.uk
Call date: Nov 1989, Middle Temple
Qualifications: [MA Hons (Glas), Dip in Law]

PONS GARY STEPHEN

Holborn Chambers
6 Gate Street, Lincoln's Inn Fields, London
WC2A 3HP, Telephone: 0171 242 6060
Call date: Oct 1995, Gray's Inn
Qualifications: [BA (Kent)]

PONTAC MRS SANDRA GAIL

Mitre House Chambers
Mitre House 44 Fleet Street, London
EC4Y 1BN, Telephone: 0171 583 8233
Call date: Nov 1981, Middle Temple
Qualifications: [BA(Law)]

PONTER IAN MICHAEL

2-3 Gray's Inn Square
Gray's Inn, London WC1R 5JH,
Telephone: 0171 242 4986
E-mail: chambers@2-3graysinnsquare.co.uk
Call date: Oct 1993, Middle Temple
Qualifications: [BA (Hons, Keele), LLM (Aberdeen)]

POOLE CHRISTOPHER ROBERT

New Court
Temple, London EC4Y 9BE,
Telephone: 0171 583 5123/0171 583 0510
Call date: Nov 1996, Lincoln's Inn
Qualifications: [LLB (Hons)(Lond)]

POOLE NIGEL DAVID

18 St John Street
Manchester M3 4EA,
Telephone: 0161 278 1800
Call date: Nov 1989, Middle Temple
Qualifications: [BA (Oxon), Dip in Law]

POOLES MICHAEL PHILIP HOLMES

4 Paper Bldgs
Ground Floor, Temple, London EC4Y 7EX,
Telephone: 0171 353 3366/583 7155
E-mail: clerks@4paperbuildings.com
Call date: July 1978, Inner Temple
Qualifications: [LLB (Lond)]

POOLEY MRS MOIRA HELEN

4 King's Bench Walk
2nd Floor, Temple, London EC4Y 7DL,
Telephone: 0171 353 3581
Call date: Nov 1974, Middle Temple
Qualifications: [LLB (Hons) (Lond)]

POOTS MISS CAROLYN ELIZABETH

All Saints Chambers
9/11 Broad Street, Bristol BS1 2HP,
Telephone: 0117 921 1966
Call date: Oct 1995, Inner Temple
Qualifications: [LLB (Huddersfield)]

POPAT PRASHANT

2 Harcourt Bldgs
Ground Floor/Left, Temple, London
EC4Y 9DB, Telephone: 0171 583 9020
E-mail: clerks@harcourt.co.uk
Stanbrook & Henderson
2 Harcourt Bldgs 2nd Floor, Temple, London
EC4Y 9DB, Telephone: 0171 353 0101
E-mail: clerks@harcourt.co.uk
Call date: Feb 1992, Gray's Inn
Qualifications: [MA (Oxon)]

POPAT SURENDRA

9 King's Bench Walk
Ground Floor, Temple, London EC4Y 7DX,
Telephone: 0171 353 7202/3909
Call date: July 1969, Lincoln's Inn
Assistant Recorder
Qualifications: [LLB (Lond),LLM (Cal)]

POPE DAVID JAMES

3 Verulam Buildings
London WC1R 5NT,
Telephone: 0171 831 8441
E-mail: clerks@3verulam.co.uk
Call date: Feb 1995, Lincoln's Inn
Qualifications: [LLB (Hons)(Edinbur), LLM
(Harvard)]

POPE MRS HEATHER

1 Mitre Ct Bldgs
Ground Floor, Temple, London EC4Y 7BS,
Telephone: 0171 797 7070
Call date: July 1977, Inner Temple
Qualifications: [BA (Hons) (Wales), Dip Ed
(Wales)]

POPERT MISS CATHERINE TERESA MARIE

3 Temple Gardens
Lower Ground Floor, Temple, London
EC4Y 9AU, Telephone: 0171 353 3102/5/9297
Call date: Nov 1987, Middle Temple
Qualifications: [LLB (London)]

POPLAWSKI ROMAN

169 Temple Chambers
Temple Avenue, London EC4Y 0DA,
Telephone: 0171 583 7644
Call date: Nov 1989, Lincoln's Inn
Qualifications: [LLB (B'ham)]

POPLE MISS ALISON RUTH

3 Hare Court
1st Floor, Temple, London EC4Y 7BJ,
Telephone: 0171 353 7561
Call date: Nov 1993, Middle Temple
Qualifications: [LLB (Hons)]

POPPLEWELL ANDREW JOHN QC (1997)

Brick Court Chambers
15/19 Devereux Court, London WC2R 3JJ,
Telephone: 0171 583 0777
E-mail: (surname)@brickcourt.demon.co.uk
Call date: Nov 1981, Inner Temple
Qualifications: [MA (Cantab)]

D

PORTEN ANTHONY RALPH QC (1988)

2-3 Gray's Inn Square
Gray's Inn, London WC1R 5JH,
Telephone: 0171 242 4986
E-mail: chambers@2-3graysinnsquare.co.uk
Call date: July 1969, Inner Temple
Recorder
Qualifications: [BA (Cantab)]

PORTER DAVID LEONARD

St James's Chambers
68 Quay Street, Manchester M3 3EJ,
Telephone: 0161 834 7000
E-mail: 106241.2625@compuserve.com
Park Lane Chambers
19 Westgate, Leeds LS1 2RD,
Telephone: 0113 2285000
Call date: July 1980, Lincoln's Inn
Qualifications: [LLB (Manch)]

PORTER MARTIN HUGH

2 Temple Gardens
Temple, London EC4Y 9AY,
Telephone: 0171 583 6041 (12 Lines)
Call date: July 1986, Inner Temple
Qualifications: [MA (Cantab), LLM]

PORTER NIGEL JOHN

11 King's Bench Walk
Temple, London EC4Y 7EQ,
Telephone: 0171 632 8500
E-mail: clerksroom@11-kbw.law.co.uk
Call date: Nov 1994, Middle Temple
Qualifications: [MA (Cantab), LLM
(Hons)(Cantab)]

PORTER ROBERT GEOFFREY WALDEGRAVE

3 Temple Gardens
3rd Floor, Temple, London EC4Y 9AU,
Telephone: 0171 353 0832
Call date: Nov 1988, Middle Temple
Qualifications: [BA (Dunelm), Dip Law, LLM
(Pennsylvania)]

PORTER MISS SARAH RUTH

11 Bolt Court
London EC4A 3DQ,
Telephone: 0171 353 2300
E-mail: boltct11@aol.com
Call date: Nov 1996, Gray's Inn
Qualifications: [LLB (Teeside), MA (Sheff)]

PORTNOY LESLIE REUBEN

9 St John Street
Manchester M3 4DN,
Telephone: 0161 955 9000
E-mail: ninesjs@gconnect.com
Call date: June 1961, Gray's Inn
Recorder
Qualifications: [LLB (Hons)]

PORTWOOD TIMOTHY GORDON

Old Square Chambers
1 Verulam Buildings, Gray's Inn, London
WC1R 5LQ, Telephone: 0171 831 0801
Call date: Nov 1988, Gray's Inn
Qualifications: [BA (Cantab)]

POSNANSKY JEREMY ROSS LEON QC (1994)

1 Mitre Ct Bldgs
Ground Floor, Temple, London EC4Y 7BS,
Telephone: 0171 797 7070
Southernhay Chambers
33 Southernhay East, Exeter EX1 1NX,
Telephone: 01392 255777
E-mail: southernhay.chambers@lineone.net
Door Tenant
Call date: July 1972, Gray's Inn
Assistant Recorder

POSNER MISS GABRIELLE JAN

2 Gray's Inn Square Chambers
2nd Floor, Gray's Inn, London WC1R 5AA,
Telephone: 0171 242 0328/071 405 1317
E-mail: clerks@2gis.co.uk
Call date: July 1984, Inner Temple
Qualifications: [LLB (Soton) LLM, (Indiana)]

POST ANDREW JOHN

6 Pump Court
Ground Floor, Temple, London EC4Y 7AR,
Telephone: 0171 583 6013/2510
Call date: July 1988, Middle Temple
Qualifications: [BA (Cantab), Dip Law (City)]

POSTA ADRIAN MARK

South Western Chambers
Melville House 12 Middle Street, Taunton,
Somerset TA1 1SH, Telephone: 01823 331919
Call date: Oct 1996, Middle Temple
Qualifications: [LLB (Hons)(Warw)]

POSTILL MS JULIA DALE

2 Paper Bldgs
1st Floor, Temple, London EC4Y 7ET,
Telephone: 0171 936 2611 (10 Lines)
E-mail: clerks@2pbbarristers.co.uk
Call date: Nov 1982, Inner Temple
Qualifications: [BA]

POTTER ANTHONY JOHN

3 Paper Bldgs
2nd Floor, Temple, London EC4Y 7EU,
Telephone: 0171 353 6208
Call date: July 1994, Gray's Inn
Qualifications: [BA (Wales)]

POTTER DAVID ANDREW

21 White Friars
Chester CH1 1NZ, Telephone: 01244 323070
Call date: Oct 1990, Lincoln's Inn
Qualifications: [LLB (E.Anglia)]

POTTER REV HARRY DRUMMOND

Barnard's Inn Chambers
6th Floor Halton House, 20-23 Holborn,
London EC1N 2JD, Telephone: 0171 242 8508
E-mail: clerks@barnards-inn-chambers.co.uk
Call date: Oct 1993, Gray's Inn
Qualifications: [BA, MA, M Phil, LLB]

POTTER MISS LOUISE

1 Mitre Ct Bldgs
Ground Floor, Temple, London EC4Y 7BS,
Telephone: 0171 797 7070
Call date: Nov 1993, Inner Temple
Qualifications: [MA (Oxon), CPE]

POTTINGER GAVIN JAMES

Maidstone Chambers
33 Earl Street, Maidstone, Kent ME14 1PF,
Telephone: 01622 688592
Call date: Oct 1991, Inner Temple
Qualifications: [BScECON, Diploma in, Law]

POTTS JAMES RUPERT

Erskine Chambers
30 Lincoln's Inn Fields, Lincoln's Inn, London
WC2A 3PF, Telephone: 0171 242 5532
E-mail: Clerks@Erskine-Chambers.law.co.uk
Call date: Oct 1994, Gray's Inn
Qualifications: [BA (Oxon)]

POTTS RICHARD ANDREW

Octagon House
19 Colegate, Norwich NR3 1AT,
Telephone: 01603 623186
E-mail: octagon@netmatters.co.uk
1 Paper Bldgs
1st Floor, Temple, London EC4Y 7EP,
Telephone: 0171 353 3728/4953
Call date: Nov 1991, Inner Temple
Qualifications: [LLB (Birm)]

POTTS ROBIN QC (1982)

Erskine Chambers
30 Lincoln's Inn Fields, Lincoln's Inn, London
WC2A 3PF, Telephone: 0171 242 5532
E-mail: Clerks@Erskine-Chambers.law.co.uk
Call date: Nov 1968, Gray's Inn
Qualifications: [BA,BCL (Oxon)]

POTTS WARREN NIGEL

Queen's Chambers
5 John Dalton Street, Manchester M2 6ET,
Telephone: 0161 834 6875/4738
4 Camden Place
Preston PR1 3JL, Telephone: 01772 828300
Call date: July 1995, Middle Temple
Qualifications: [BA (Hons)]

POULET MRS REBECCA MARIA QC (1995)

Hollis Whiteman Chambers
3rd/4th Floor Queen Elizabeth Bldg, Temple,
London EC4Y 9BS, Telephone: 0171 583 5766
E-mail: hollis.whiteman@btinternet.com
Call date: Nov 1975, Lincoln's Inn
Recorder

POUNDER GERARD

5 Essex Court
1st Floor, Temple, London EC4Y 9AH,
Telephone: 0171 410 2000
Call date: July 1980, Lincoln's Inn
Qualifications: [LLB (Lond), BA (Lond)]

POVOAS SIMON JOHN SPENCER

Chavasse Court Chambers
2nd Floor Chavasse Court, 24 Lord Street,
Liverpool L2 1TA, Telephone: 0151 707 1191
Call date: Oct 1996, Lincoln's Inn
Qualifications: [LLB (Hons), MA]

POWELL BERNARD HILSON

Newport Chambers
12 Clytha Park Road, Newport, Gwent
NP9 47L, Telephone: 01633 267403/255855
Call date: Oct 1991, Gray's Inn
Qualifications: [BSc, PhD]

POWELL DEAN

10 King's Bench Walk
Ground Floor, Temple, London EC4Y 7EB,
Telephone: 0171 353 7742
E-mail: 10kbw@lineone.net
Call date: Nov 1982, Gray's Inn
Qualifications: [BSc (Cardiff)]

POWELL MISS DEBRA ANN

3 Serjeants Inn
London EC4Y 1BQ,
Telephone: 0171 353 5537
E-mail: available upon request
Call date: Oct 1995, Middle Temple
Qualifications: [BA (Hons)]

POWELL JOHN LEWIS QC (1990)

2 Crown Office Row
2nd Floor, Temple, London EC4Y 7HJ,
Telephone: 0171 797 8000
Call date: July 1974, Middle Temple
Assistant Recorder
Qualifications: [MA, LLB (Cantab)]

POWELL JONATHAN DAVID

95A Chancery Lane
London WC2A 1DT,
Telephone: 0171 405 3101
Durham Barristers' Chambers
27 Old Elvet, Durham DH1 3HN,
Telephone: 0191 386 9199
Call date: Nov 1984, Inner Temple
Qualifications: [LLM, Legal, Assoc.RTPI]

POWELL RICHARD FREDERIC

Victoria Chambers
3rd Floor 177 Corporation Street, Birmingham
B4 6RG, Telephone: 0121 236 9900
Call date: Nov 1991, Inner Temple
Qualifications: [BA (Surrey), LLM (Warw)]

POWELL ROBIN EDWARD

New Court
Temple, London EC4Y 9BE,
Telephone: 0171 583 5123/0171 583 0510
Call date: Nov 1993, Inner Temple
Qualifications: [BA, CPE, LLM (Lond)]

POWELL WILLIAM GILES HUGH

5 Essex Court
1st Floor, Temple, London EC4Y 9AH,
Telephone: 0171 410 2000
Call date: Nov 1990, Gray's Inn
Qualifications: [LLB (Cardiff)]

POWER MISS ERICA MARGARET

1 Paper Bldgs
Ground Floor, Temple, London EC4Y 7EP,
Telephone: 0171 583 7355
E-mail: clerks@1pb.co.uk
Call date: Oct 1990, Lincoln's Inn
Qualifications: [MA (Cantab), LLM]

POWER LEWIS NIALL

Cloisters
1st Floor, Temple, London EC4Y 7AA,
Telephone: 0171 827 4000
E-mail: clerks@cloisters.com
Call date: Nov 1990, Gray's Inn
Qualifications: [LLB (Hons)]

POWER NIGEL JOHN

25-27 Castle Street
1st Floor, Liverpool L2 4TA,
Telephone: 0151 227 5661/051 236 5072
Call date: Nov 1992, Inner Temple
Qualifications: [LLB (Reading)]

POWER PIERCE DECLEAN KIERAN

Westgate Chambers
144 High Street, Lewes, East Sussex BN7 1XT,
Telephone: 01273 480510
Call date: Apr 1989, Gray's Inn
Qualifications: [BA (Hons)]

POWER RICHARD MICHAEL ARTHUR

6 Pump Court
Ground Floor, Temple, London EC4Y 7AR,
Telephone: 0171 583 6013/2510
Call date: Nov 1983, Middle Temple
Qualifications: [BA (Oxon)]

POWERS DR MICHAEL JOHN QC (1995)

1 Paper Bldgs
Ground Floor, Temple, London EC4Y 7EP,
Telephone: 0171 583 7355
E-mail: clerks@1pb.co.uk
Call date: July 1979, Lincoln's Inn
Qualifications: [BSc, MB, BS, DA]

POWIS MISS LUCY ELIZABETH

40 King Street
Manchester M2 6BA,
Telephone: 0161 832 9082
E-mail: Kingst40@aol.com
Call date: Oct 1992, Gray's Inn
Qualifications: [LLB (L'pool)]

POWIS MISS SAMANTHA INEZ

7 Fountain Court
Steelhouse Lane, Birmingham B4 6DR,
Telephone: 0121 236 8531
Call date: Nov 1985, Lincoln's Inn
Qualifications: [LLB (UC Cardiff)]

POWLES JOHN LAMBERT

1 Paper Bldgs
Ground Floor, Temple, London EC4Y 7EP,
Telephone: 0171 583 7355
E-mail: clerks@1pb.co.uk
Call date: July 1975, Middle Temple
Qualifications: [MA (Oxon)]

POWLES STEPHEN ROBERT QC (1995)

2 Harcourt Bldgs
Ground Floor/Left, Temple, London
EC4Y 9DB, Telephone: 0171 583 9020
E-mail: clerks@harcourt.co.uk
Stanbrook & Henderson
2 Harcourt Bldgs 2nd Floor, Temple, London
EC4Y 9DB, Telephone: 0171 353 0101
E-mail: clerks@harcourt.co.uk
Call date: July 1972, Middle Temple
Recorder
Qualifications: [MA (Oxon)]

POWNALL STEPHEN ORLANDO FLETCHER

1 Crown Office Row
2nd Floor, Temple, London EC4Y 7HH,
Telephone: 0171 797 7111
Call date: July 1975, Inner Temple

POYER-SLEEMAN MS PATRICIA

Pump Court Chambers
Upper Ground Floor 3 Pump Court, Temple,
London EC4Y 7AJ, Telephone: 0171 353 0711
Pump Court Chambers
31 Southgate Street, Winchester SO23 8EE,
Telephone: 01962 868161
Call date: Nov 1992, Gray's Inn
Qualifications: [BA (Manc)]

PRAIS EDGAR

4 Brick Court
Ground Floor, Temple, London EC4Y 9AD,
Telephone: 0171 797 7766
E-mail: chambers@4brick.co.uk
Call date: Nov 1990, Lincoln's Inn
Qualifications: [MA (Glas), LLB (Edin)]

PRASAD KRISHNA

21 Craven Road
Kingston-Upon-Thames, Surrey KT2 6LW,
Telephone: 0181 974 6799
Call date: May 1958, Gray's Inn
Qualifications: [LLB]

PRATT ALLAN DUNCAN

New Court Chambers
5 Verulam Buildings, Gray's Inn, London
WC1R 5LY, Telephone: 0171 831 9500
E-mail: mail@newcourtchambers.com
Call date: Nov 1971, Middle Temple
Qualifications: [BA (Oxon)]

PRATT MRS PATRICIA MARY

India Buildings Chambers
Water Street, Liverpool L2 0XG,
Telephone: 0151 243 6000
Call date: Oct 1991, Lincoln's Inn
Qualifications: [LLB (Hons)(L'pool)]

PRATT RICHARD CAMDEN QC (1992)

1 King's Bench Walk
2nd Floor, Temple, London EC4Y 7DB,
Telephone: 0171 936 1500
E-mail: ddear@1kbw.co.uk
Call date: July 1970, Gray's Inn
Recorder
Qualifications: [MA (Oxon)]

PRATT RICHARD JAMES

The Corn Exchange
5th Floor Fenwick Street, Liverpool L2 7QS,
Telephone: 0151 227 1081/5009
Call date: July 1980, Gray's Inn
Assistant Recorder
Qualifications: [BA]

PREEN MISS CATHERINE LOUISE

St Ive's Chambers
9 Fountain Ct, Birmingham B4 6DR,
Telephone: 0121 236 0863/0929
Call date: Nov 1988, Middle Temple
Qualifications: [LLB (Lond)]

PRENTICE PROFESSOR DANIEL DAVID

Erskine Chambers
30 Lincoln's Inn Fields, Lincoln's Inn, London
WC2A 3PF, Telephone: 0171 242 5532
E-mail: Clerks@Erskine-Chambers.law.co.uk
Call date: Nov 1982, Lincoln's Inn
Qualifications: [LLB (Hons)(Belfast), JD
(Chicago), MA (Oxon)]

PRENTIS SEBASTIAN HUGH RUNTON

1 New Square
Ground Floor, Lincoln's Inn, London
WC2A 3SA, Telephone: 0171 405 0884/5/6/7
E-mail: 1newsquare@compuserve.com
Call date: Oct 1996, Middle Temple
Qualifications: [BA (Hons) (Cantab)]

PRESCOTT PETER RICHARD KYLE QC (1990)

8 New Square
Lincoln's Inn, London WC2A 3QP,
Telephone: 0171 405 4321
Call date: Nov 1970, Lincoln's Inn
Qualifications: [BSc, MSc]

PRESLAND FREDERICK JAMES ADRIAN

2 Field Court
Gray's Inn, London WC1R 5BB,
Telephone: 0171 405 6114
E-mail: fieldct2@netcomuk.co.uk.
Call date: July 1985, Gray's Inn
Qualifications: [BA Hons (E Anglia),]

PRESS BARRY

21 Colless Road
Seven Sisters, London N15 4NR,
Telephone: 0181 365 1706
Call date: July 1975, Inner Temple
Qualifications: [BA, MSc (Oxon)]

PRESSDEE PIERS CHARLES WILLIAM

2 Harcourt Bldgs
1st Floor, Temple, London EC4Y 9DB,
Telephone: 0171 353 6961/7
Call date: Oct 1991, Middle Temple
Qualifications: [MA (Hons)(Cantab)]

PRESTON (RICHARD) DOMINIC

Arden Chambers
27 John Street, London WC1N 2BL,
Telephone: 0171 242 4244
Call date: Feb 1995, Inner Temple
Qualifications: [BA (Lond), CPE (City)]

D

PRESTON DARREN SAMUEL

Kenworthy's Buildings
83 Bridge Street, Manchester M3 2RF,
Telephone: 0161 832 4036/834 6954
Call date: Oct 1991, Gray's Inn
Qualifications: [LLB (Liverpool)]

PRESTON DAVID HENRY

Hardwicke Building
New Square, Lincoln's Inn, London
WC2A 3SB, Telephone: 0171 242 2523
E-mail: clerks@hardwicke.co.uk
Call date: Nov 1993, Lincoln's Inn
Qualifications: [LLB (Auckland)]

PRESTON HUGH GEOFFREY

Trinity Chambers
140 New London Road, Chelmsford, Essex
CM2 0AW, Telephone: 01245 605040
Call date: Oct 1994, Middle Temple
Qualifications: [BA (Hons)(Durham), CPE]

PRESTON MISS KIM DEBORAH

4 King's Bench Walk
2nd Floor, Temple, London EC4Y 7DL,
Telephone: 0171 353 3581
Call date: Nov 1991, Inner Temple
Qualifications: [BSc (Hons), Dip Law]

PRESTON NICHOLAS JOHN HOLMAN

3 Temple Gardens
3rd Floor, Temple, London EC4Y 9AU,
Telephone: 0171 353 0832
Call date: July 1986, Gray's Inn
Qualifications: [MA]

PRESTON MRS NICOLA

5 Fountain Court
Steelhouse Lane, Birmingham B4 6DR,
Telephone: 0121 606 0500
Call date: Nov 1992, Lincoln's Inn
Qualifications: [LLB (Hons)(Manc), LLM
(B'ham)]

PRESTON TIMOTHY WILLIAM QC (1982)

2 Temple Gardens
Temple, London EC4Y 9AY,
Telephone: 0171 583 6041 (12 Lines)
Call date: June 1964, Inner Temple
Recorder
Qualifications: [BA (Oxon)]

PRESTWICH ANDREW

24 The Ropewalk
Nottingham NG1 5EF,
Telephone: 0115 9472581
E-mail: clerk@ropewalk.co.uk
Call date: Nov 1986, Gray's Inn
Qualifications: [LLB (B'ham)]

PREVATT MISS BEATRICE HILARY ROSE

2 Garden Court
1st Floor, Middle Temple, London EC4Y 9BL,
Telephone: 0171 353 1633
E-mail: barristers@2gardenct.law.co.uk
Call date: Nov 1985, Gray's Inn
Qualifications: [BA (Oxon)]

PREVEZER MS SUSAN RACHEL

Essex Court Chambers
24 Lincoln's Inn Fields, London WC2A 3ED,
Telephone: 0171 813 8000
E-mail: clerksroom@essexcourt-chambers.co.uk
Call date: July 1983, Inner Temple
Qualifications: [MA (Cantab)]

PRICE (ARTHUR) LEOLIN QC (1968)

10 Old Square
Ground Floor, Lincoln's Inn, London
WC2A 3SU, Telephone: 0171 405 0758
Call date: Nov 1949, Middle Temple
Qualifications: [MA(Oxon)]

PRICE ALBERT JOHN

23 Essex Street
London WC2R 3AS,
Telephone: 0171 413 0353/353 3533
E-mail: clerks@essexstreet23.demon.co.uk
Call date: July 1982, Inner Temple
Qualifications: [BA (Oxon)]

PRICE MISS ANNA VICTORIA

40 King Street
Chester CH1 2AH, Telephone: 01244 323886
Call date: Oct 1996, Lincoln's Inn
Qualifications: [LLB (Hons)(Lond)]

PRICE MISS DEBORA JANET

Queen Elizabeth Bldg
Ground Floor, Temple, London EC4Y 9BS,
Telephone: 0171 353 7181 (12 Lines)
Call date: Feb 1987, Gray's Inn
Qualifications: [MA (Cantab)]

PRICE GERALD ALEXANDER LEWIN QC (1992)

33 Park Place
Cardiff CF1 3BA, Telephone: 01222 233313
Goldsmith Building
1st Floor, Temple, London EC4Y 7BL,
Telephone: 0171 353 7881
E-mail: clerks@goldsmith-building.law.co.uk
Door Tenant
Call date: Nov 1969, Middle Temple
Recorder

PRICE JAMES RICHARD KENRICK QC (1995)

5 Raymond Buildings
1st Floor, Gray's Inn, London WC1R 5BP,
Telephone: 0171 242 2902
Call date: July 1974, Inner Temple
Qualifications: [BA(Oxon)]

PRICE JEFFREY WILLIAM

10 Old Square
Ground Floor, Lincoln's Inn, London
WC2A 3SU, Telephone: 0171 405 0758
Door Tenant
Call date: Nov 1975, Lincoln's Inn
Qualifications: [BA (Oxon) BCL (Oxon), MA
(Oxon)]

PRICE JOHN ALAN QC (1980)

22 Old Bldgs
Lincoln's Inn, London WC2A 3UJ,
Telephone: 0171 831 0222
25 Byrom Street
Manchester M3 4PF,
Telephone: 0161 829 2100
E-mail: Byromst25@aol.com
Call date: Feb 1961, Gray's Inn
Recorder
Qualifications: [LLB]

PRICE JOHN CHARLES

Priory Chambers
2 Fountain Court, Steelhouse Lane,
Birmingham B4 6DR,
Telephone: 0121 236 3882/1375
Call date: Nov 1969, Gray's Inn
Recorder
Qualifications: [LLB (B'ham)]

PRICE JOHN SCOTT

10 Launceston Avenue
Caversham Park Village, Reading, Berkshire
RG4 6SW, Telephone: 01189 479548
Southsea Chambers
PO Box 148, Southsea, Portsmouth,
Hampshire PO5 2TU,
Telephone: 01705 291261
Call date: Oct 1990, Inner Temple
Qualifications: [LLB (Hons)(Reading)]

PRICE MISS KATHARINE CLARE HARDING

4 Paper Bldgs
Ground Floor, Temple, London EC4Y 7EX,
Telephone: 0171 353 3366/583 7155
E-mail: clerks@4paperbuildings.com
Call date: July 1988, Middle Temple
Qualifications: [LLB (Hons) (Lond), LLM
(Cantab)]

PRICE MRS LOUISE THERESE

Guildhall Chambers
23 Broad Street, Bristol BS1 2HG,
Telephone: 0117 9273366
Call date: Nov 1972, Middle Temple
Qualifications: [MA (Oxon)]

PRICE NICHOLAS PETER LEES QC (1992)

3 Raymond Buildings
Gray's Inn, London WC1R 5BH,
Telephone: 0171 831 3833
E-mail: chambers@threeraymond.demon.co.uk
Call date: Nov 1968, Gray's Inn
Recorder
Qualifications: [LLB (Edin)]

PRICE PETER NICHOLAS

York Chambers
14 Toft Green, York YO1 1JT,
Telephone: 01904 620048
E-mail: yorkchambers.co.uk
Call date: Nov 1987, Inner Temple
Qualifications: [LLB (Hull)]

PRICE MISS RACHAEL ELIZABETH

5 Fountain Court
Steelhouse Lane, Birmingham B4 6DR,
Telephone: 0121 606 0500
Call date: Oct 1994, Inner Temple
Qualifications: [LLB (B'ham)]

PRICE RICHARD MERVYN QC (1996)

Littleton Chambers
3 King's Bench Walk North, Temple, London
EC4Y 7HR, Telephone: 0171 797 8600
E-mail: littletonchambers@compuserve.com
Call date: Nov 1969, Gray's Inn
Qualifications: [LLB (Lond)]

PRICE ROBERT SAMUEL

6 Fountain Court
Steelhouse Lane, Birmingham B4 6DR,
Telephone: 0121 233 3282
Call date: Oct 1990, Middle Temple
Qualifications: [LLB (Leic)]

PRICE RODERICK MICHAEL THOMAS

Cloisters
1st Floor, Temple, London EC4Y 7AA,
Telephone: 0171 827 4000
E-mail: clerks@cloisters.com
Call date: Nov 1971, Inner Temple
Qualifications: [LLB]

PRICE THOMAS

6 Gray's Inn Square
Ground Floor, Gray's Inn, London WC1R 5AZ,
Telephone: 0171 242 1052
Call date: Nov 1985, Inner Temple
Qualifications: [LLB(S'ampton)]

PRICE WAYNE

32 Park Place
Cardiff CF1 3BA, Telephone: 01222 397364
Call date: July 1982, Gray's Inn
Qualifications: [BA]

PRICE LEWIS RHODRI

1 Serjeants' Inn
4th Floor, Temple, London EC4Y 1NH,
Telephone: 0171 583 1355
E-mail: serjeants.inn@virgin.net
33 Park Place
Cardiff CF1 3BA, Telephone: 01222 233313
Door Tenant
Call date: July 1975, Middle Temple
Assistant Recorder
Qualifications: [MA (Oxon), Dip.Crim
(Cantab)]

PRICE ROWLANDS GWYNN

Peel House Chambers
Ground Floor, Peel House 5 Harrington Street,
Liverpool L2 9QA, Telephone: 0151 236 4321
Call date: May 1985, Inner Temple
Qualifications: [LLB (L'pool), MBA, Dip
E.C.Law (Lond)]

PRICHARD GUY HESKETH

Frederick Place Chambers
9 Frederick Place, Clifton, Bristol BS8 1AS,
Telephone: 0117 9738667
Call date: Nov 1986, Gray's Inn
Qualifications: [BA(Oxon)]

PRICHARD MICHAEL JOHN

4 Stone Bldgs
Ground Floor, Lincoln's Inn, London
WC2A 3XT, Telephone: 0171 242 5524
E-mail: d.goddard@4stonebuildings.law.co.uk
Call date: June 1951, Gray's Inn

PRIDAY CHARLES NICHOLAS BRUTON

7 King's Bench Walk
Ground Floor, Temple, London EC4Y 7DS,
Telephone: 0171 583 0404
Call date: Nov 1982, Middle Temple
Qualifications: [BA (Oxon)]

PRIDEAUX-BRUNE PETER JOHN NICHOLAS

Queen Elizabeth Bldg
Ground Floor, Temple, London EC4Y 9BS,
Telephone: 0171 353 7181 (12 Lines)
Call date: Nov 1972, Inner Temple
Qualifications: [MA (Oxon)]

PRIEST JOHN RAYMOND

York Chambers
14 Toft Green, York YO1 1JT,
Telephone: 01904 620048
E-mail: yorkchambers.co.uk
Call date: July 1973, Inner Temple
Qualifications: [LLB]

PRIEST JULIAN WERNET QC (1974)

Lamb Chambers
Lamb Building, Temple, London EC4Y 7AS,
Telephone: 0171 797 8300
E-mail: lambchambers@link.org
Call date: Feb 1954, Inner Temple
Qualifications: [MA (Cantab)]

PRIESTLEY MS REBECCA JANET

2 Gray's Inn Square Chambers
2nd Floor, Gray's Inn, London WC1R 5AA,
Telephone: 0171 242 0328/071 405 1317
E-mail: clerks@2gis.co.uk
Call date: Nov 1989, Middle Temple
Qualifications: [BA Hons [Oxon]]

PRIESTLEY RODERICK CHARLES

Lincoln House Chambers
5th Floor Lincoln House, 1 Brazennose Street,
Manchester M2 5EL,
Telephone: 0161 832 5701
E-mail: LincolnHouseChambers@link.org
Call date: Nov 1996, Gray's Inn
Qualifications: [BSc (Bris)]

PRIMOST NORMAN BASIL

5 Pump Court
Ground Floor, Temple, London EC4Y 7AP,
Telephone: 0171 353 2532
E-mail: fivepump@netcomuk.co.uk
Call date: July 1954, Middle Temple
Qualifications: [LLB (Lond)]

PRINCE CHRISTOPHER JOHN

New Court Chambers
3 Broad Chare, Newcastle Upon Tyne
NE1 3DQ, Telephone: 0191 232 1980
Call date: Nov 1981, Lincoln's Inn
Qualifications: [BA]

PRINCE EDWIN JACOB

Falcon Chambers
Falcon Court, London EC4Y 1AA,
Telephone: 0171 353 2484/7
12 Old Square
1st Floor, Lincoln's Inn, London WC2A 3TX,
Telephone: 0171 404 0875
Call date: Nov 1955, Inner Temple
Qualifications: [BA]

PRINCE DR ETHLYN AGATHA

12 Old Square
1st Floor, Lincoln's Inn, London WC2A 3TX,
Telephone: 0171 404 0875
Call date: July 1970, Gray's Inn
Qualifications: [LLB, D.Phil]

PRINGLE GORDON ALEXANDER

Bridewell Chambers
2 Bridewell Place, London EC4V 6AP,
Telephone: 0171 797 8800
E-mail: clerks@bridewell.law.co.uk
Call date: Nov 1973, Inner Temple
Qualifications: [BA (Oxon)]

PRINGLE IAN DEREK

Guildhall Chambers
23 Broad Street, Bristol BS1 2HG,
Telephone: 0117 9273366
Call date: July 1979, Gray's Inn
Qualifications: [MA (Cantab)]

PRINN MISS HELEN ELIZABETH

Octagon House
19 Colegate, Norwich NR3 1AT,
Telephone: 01603 623186
E-mail: octagon@netmatters.co.uk
Call date: Oct 1993, Middle Temple
Qualifications: [BA (Hons)(Lond), CPE (City)]

PRIOR CHARLES ROBERT CHRISTOPHER

Adrian Lyon's Chambers
14 Castle Street, Liverpool L2 0NE,
Telephone: 0151 236 4421/8240
E-mail: chambers14@aol.com
Call date: Oct 1995, Lincoln's Inn
Qualifications: [BA (Hons)(Oxon), Dip in Law (City)]

PRITCHARD MISS DAWN MARIE

1 High Pavement
Nottingham NG1 1HF,
Telephone: 0115 9418218
Call date: Feb 1992, Inner Temple
Qualifications: [LLB (Sheff)]

PRITCHARD RODNEY

Kenworthy's Buildings
83 Bridge Street, Manchester M3 2RF,
Telephone: 0161 832 4036/834 6954
Call date: June 1964, Inner Temple
Qualifications: [LLB]

PRITCHARD MISS SARAH JANE

40 King Street
Manchester M2 6BA,
Telephone: 0161 832 9082
E-mail: Kingst40@aol.com
Call date: Oct 1993, Gray's Inn
Qualifications: [LLB (Manch)]

PRITCHARD MRS TERESA JULIA

2 Mitre Ct Bldgs
1st Floor, Temple, London EC4Y 7BX,
Telephone: 0171 353 1353
Call date: Oct 1994, Lincoln's Inn
Qualifications: [MA (Hons)(St Andrew), Dip in Law (City)]

PRITCHETT STEPHEN JOHN

40 King Street
Manchester M2 6BA,
Telephone: 0161 832 9082
E-mail: Kingst40@aol.com
5 Stone Buildings
Lincoln's Inn, London WC2A 3XT,
Telephone: 0171 242 6201
E-mail: clerks@5-stonebuildings.law.co.uk
Door Tenant
Call date: July 1989, Lincoln's Inn
Qualifications: [LLB (Hons) (L'pool)]

PRIVETT FRANK SIMON KENNETH

1 Paper Bldgs
1st Floor, Temple, London EC4Y 7EP,
Telephone: 0171 353 3728/4953
Call date: July 1976, Middle Temple
Assistant Recorder
Qualifications: [LLB (Edin)]

PROBERT-WOOD TIMOTHY BLAIR

2 Harcourt Bldgs
1st Floor, Temple, London EC4Y 9DB,
Telephone: 0171 353 2112/2817
Call date: July 1983, Inner Temple
Qualifications: [LLB (Hull)]

PROBYN MISS CALISTA JANE

Queen Elizabeth Bldg
Ground Floor, Temple, London EC4Y 9BS,
Telephone: 0171 353 7181 (12 Lines)
Call date: Feb 1988, Middle Temple
Qualifications: [LLB]

PROCTER MICHAEL

Fleet Chambers
Mitre House 44-46 Fleet Street, London
EC4Y 1BN, Telephone: 0171 936 3707
Call date: Nov 1993, Gray's Inn
Qualifications: [BA]

D

PROGHOULIS PHILIP GEORGE

Roehampton Chambers
30 Stoughton Close, Roehampton, London
SW15 4LS, Telephone: 0181 788 1238
1 Dr Johnson's Bldgs
Ground Floor, Temple, London EC4Y 7AX,
Telephone: 0171 353 9328
Westgate Chambers
144 High Street, Lewes, East Sussex BN7 1XT,
Telephone: 01273 480510
Call date: Nov 1963, Inner Temple

PROOPS MISS HELEN JEANETTE

York Chambers
14 Toft Green, York YO1 1JT,
Telephone: 01904 620048
E-mail: yorkchambers.co.uk
Call date: July 1986, Middle Temple
Qualifications: [LLB Exeter]

PROSSER ANTHONY GRIFFITH THOMAS

1 Harcourt Bldgs
2nd Floor, Temple, London EC4Y 9DA,
Telephone: 0171 353 9421/9151
Call date: July 1985, Inner Temple
Qualifications: [LLB (Lond)]

PROSSER HENRY WILLIAM

Park Court Chambers
40 Park Cross Street, Leeds LS1 2QH,
Telephone: 0113 2433277
Call date: July 1969, Middle Temple
Recorder
Qualifications: [MA]

PROSSER KEVIN JOHN QC (1996)

Pump Court Tax Chambers
16 Bedford Row, London WC1R 4EB,
Telephone: 0171 414 8080
8 King Street
Manchester M2 6AQ,
Telephone: 0161 834 9560
Door Tenant
Call date: July 1982, Lincoln's Inn
Qualifications: [LLB (Lond), BCL, (Oxon)]

PROUDMAN MISS SONIA ROSEMARY SUSAN QC (1994)

11 New Square
Ground Floor, Lincoln's Inn, London
WC2A 3QB, Telephone: 0171 831 0081
E-mail: 11newsquare.co.uk
Call date: July 1972, Lincoln's Inn
Qualifications: [MA (Oxon)]

PROWSE JAMES BARRINGTON

Derby Square Chambers
Merchants Court, Derby Square, Liverpool
L2 1TS, Telephone: 0151 709 4222
Call date: July 1986, Inner Temple
Qualifications: [LLB, MIMgt, Assoc IPD]

PRUDHOE TIMOTHY NIXON

Queen's Chambers
5 John Dalton Street, Manchester M2 6ET,
Telephone: 0161 834 6875/4738
4 Camden Place
Preston PR1 3JL, Telephone: 01772 828300
Call date: Oct 1994, Gray's Inn
Qualifications: [LLB (Hons)(Manc)]

PRYCE GREGORY HUGH

36 Bedford Row
London WC1R 4JH,
Telephone: 0171 421 8000
E-mail: 36bedfordrow@link.org
Call date: July 1988, Gray's Inn
Qualifications: [BA (Hons)]

PRYKE STUART

Trinity Chambers
9-12 Trinity Chare, Quayside, Newcastle Upon
Tyne NE1 3DF, Telephone: 0191 232 1927
Call date: Oct 1994, Lincoln's Inn
Qualifications: [BEng (Lond), MSc (Econ), Dip
in Law (City)]

D

PRYNNE ANDREW GEOFFREY LOCKYER QC (1995)

2 Harcourt Bldgs
Ground Floor/Left, Temple, London
EC4Y 9DB, Telephone: 0171 583 9020
E-mail: clerks@harcourt.co.uk
Stanbrook & Henderson
2 Harcourt Bldgs 2nd Floor, Temple, London
EC4Y 9DB, Telephone: 0171 353 0101
E-mail: clerks@harcourt.co.uk
Call date: July 1975, Middle Temple
Qualifications: [LLB (Soton)]

PRYOR MICHAEL ROBERT

9 Old Square
Ground Floor, Lincoln's Inn, London
WC2A 3SR, Telephone: 0171 405 4682
E-mail: chambers@9oldsquare.co.uk
Call date: Oct 1992, Inner Temple
Qualifications: [LLB (Hons)]

PUCKRIN CEDRIC ELDRED

19 Old Buildings
Lincoln's Inn, London WC2A 3UP,
Telephone: 0171 405 2001
E-mail: clerks@oldbuildingsip.com
Call date: Nov 1990, Middle Temple
Qualifications: [BA, LLB (S Africa)]

PUGH ANDREW CARTWRIGHT QC (1988)

2 Hare Court
Ground Floor, Temple, London EC4Y 7BH,
Telephone: 0171 583 1770
E-mail: 2_Hare_Court@link.org
Call date: Nov 1961, Inner Temple
Recorder
Qualifications: [MA (Oxon)]

PUGH DAVID SAMUEL

East Anglian Chambers
Sanders House 52 North Hill, Colchester
CO1 1PY, Telephone: 01206 572756
East Anglian Chambers
57 London Street, Norwich NR2 1HL,
Telephone: 01603 617351
East Anglian Chambers
Gresham House 5 Museum Street, Ipswich
IP1 1HQ, Telephone: 01473 214481
Call date: July 1978, Middle Temple
Qualifications: [B Sc (Salford)]

PUGH GLANVILLE VERNON QC (1986)

2-3 Gray's Inn Square
Gray's Inn, London WC1R 5JH,
Telephone: 0171 242 4986
E-mail: chambers@2-3graysinnsquare.co.uk
33 Park Place
Cardiff CF1 3BA, Telephone: 01222 233313
Door Tenant
Call date: Nov 1969, Lincoln's Inn
Recorder
Qualifications: [LLB (Wales), LLB (Cantab)]

PUGH JOHN BISHOP

John Pugh's Chambers
3rd Floor 14 Castle Street, Liverpool L2 0NE,
Telephone: 0151 236 5415
Call date: July 1972, Lincoln's Inn
Qualifications: [LLB (Hons)]

PUGH MICHAEL CHARLES

Old Square Chambers
1 Verulam Buildings, Gray's Inn, London
WC1R 5LQ, Telephone: 0171 831 0801
Old Square Chambers
Hanover House 47 Corn Street, Bristol
BS1 1HT, Telephone: 0117 9277111
Call date: Nov 1975, Gray's Inn
Qualifications: [BSc (Econ), C Dip AF]

PUGH-SMITH JOHN EDGAR

1 Serjeants' Inn
4th Floor, Temple, London EC4Y 1NH,
Telephone: 0171 583 1355
E-mail: serjeants.inn@virgin.net
East Anglian Chambers
57 London Street, Norwich NR2 1HL,
Telephone: 01603 617351
Call date: July 1977, Gray's Inn
Qualifications: [MA (Oxon)]

PULLEN TIMOTHY JOHN

33 Bedford Row
London WC1R 4JH,
Telephone: 0171 242 6476
Call date: Nov 1993, Middle Temple
Qualifications: [BSc (Plymouth), CPE (Lond)]

PULLING DEAN

Gower Chambers
57 Walter Road, Swansea, West Glamorgan
SA1 5PZ, Telephone: 01792 644466
E-mail: clerk@gowerchambers.co.uk
Call date: Nov 1993, Middle Temple
Qualifications: [LLB (Hons)(Wales)]

PULMAN GEORGE FREDERICK QC (1989)

Hardwicke Building
New Square, Lincoln's Inn, London
WC2A 3SB, Telephone: 0171 242 2523
E-mail: clerks@hardwicke.co.uk
Stour Chambers
Barton Mill House, Barton Mill Road,
Canterbury, Kent CT1 1BP,
Telephone: 01227 764899
E-mail: clerks@stourchambers.co.uk
Door Tenant
Call date: July 1971, Middle Temple
Recorder
Qualifications: [MA (Cantab)]

Fax: 0171 691 1234;
Out of hours telephone: 01892 782402;
DX: LDE 393; Other comms: Fax (private)
01892 784622

Types of work: Crime; Ecclesiastical; Insurance;
Medical negligence; Personal injury;
Professional negligence; Radiation induced
injuries

Circuit: South Eastern

Awards and memberships: Fellow of the Royal
Society of Medicine; Formerly Board Member,
Legal Aid Board; Formerly Junior Counsel to the
Crown (Common Law); Deputy Chancellor,
Diocese of Peterborough

Other professional experience: Adviser to Hong
Kong Government (SAR) Legal Aid Study (1997-
8); Member of PIBAR Committee on Conditional
Fees; Member of Justice Committee on Funding
Civil Litigation

Publications: *Shaping the Future* (Part Author),
LAG: 1996

Reported cases: *Corrigan v Breadon*, (1998) 17
April, QBD (unreported as yet), 1998. Cost of
financial management of large awards of
damages recovered as separate head of damage.

R v DPQT ex parte Caswell, [1990] 2 AC 738,
1990. Delay in judicial review: relief refused
(when otherwise entitled) because application
delayed.
McDonnell v Woodhouse and Jones, [1995]
The Times, 25 May, 1995. Plaintiff's payment in
- 'if the plaintiff recovers more, indemnity costs
to be awarded' - form of draft letter.
Somasundaram v M Julius Melchior and Co,
[1988] 1 WLR 1394, 1988. Liability of solicitor
where negligence alleged in conduct of criminal
defence.
Molinari v Ministry of Defence, [1994] PIQR
Q33, 1994. Provisional damages: radiation
induced cancer (final award: discretion in court
to award).
Davies v Eli Lilly, [1987] 1 WLR 1136, 1987.
Costs sharing order in multi-party actions -
('open order') - *amicus curiae* - 'invented the
order'.

PUNWAR PURVAISE PHILIP JAMES

Francis Taylor Bldg
3rd Floor, Temple, London EC4Y 7BY,
Telephone: 0171 797 7250
Call date: Nov 1989, Inner Temple
Qualifications: [BA (B'ham), Dip Law (City)]

PURCHAS CHRISTOPHER PATRICK BROOKS QC (1990)

2 Crown Office Row
Ground Floor, Temple, London EC4Y 7HJ,
Telephone: 0171 797 8100
E-mail: mail@2cor.co.uk, or to individual
barristers at: [barrister's surname]@2cor.co.uk
Call date: July 1966, Inner Temple
Recorder
Qualifications: [MA (Cantab)]

PURCHAS ROBIN MICHAEL QC (1987)

2 Harcourt Buildings
Temple, London EC4Y 9DB,
Telephone: 0171 353 8415
E-mail: clerks@twoharcourtbldgs.demon.co.uk
Call date: Nov 1968, Inner Temple
Recorder
Qualifications: [MA (Cantab)]

Fax: 0171 353 7622; DX: LDE 402

Types of work: Administrative; Common land;
Compulsory purchase/compensation; Environment; Licensing; Local government;
Parliamentary; Planning; Professional
negligence; Town and country planning

Other professional qualifications: Queen's Counsel

Circuit: South Eastern

Awards and memberships: Senior Exhibitioner; Member of the Administrative Law Bar Association, Parliamentary Bar and Planning and Environment Bar Associations, Fellow of the Society for Advanced Legal Studies

Other professional experience: Recorder (1989); sits as Deputy High Court Judge (1994); Master of Bench of Inner Temple (1996); previously on Attorney General's Supplementary Panel - Common Law

Recent Cases:

Bolton MBC v Secretary of State for the Environment (HL) [1995] 1 WLR 1176; [1995] 3 PLR 37
Reasons - approach to decisions - validity - costs

English Property Corporation v Kingston upon Thames RBC [1998] EGCS 35 (CA)
Compensation - severance - re Land Compensation Act 1961

Wards v Barclays Bank Plc (CA) [1994] 68 PCR 391
Compensation - principle in Pointe Gourde - application of the Stokes principle

Prudential Assurance v Waterloo Real Estate [1998] EGCS 51
Construction/Title - adverse possession - proprietary/convention estoppel - injunctive relief

R v Newbury DC ex parte Chieveley PC [1997] JPL 1137
Validity of planning permission - outline and approval of details - delay - discretion

Fletcher v SS for Transport 10 June 1997; CA 11 June 1998
Land Compensation Act 1961 s 17 - Certificate of alternative development - date for determination - scope of scheme to be ignored

Braintree DC v SSE [1996] 71 PCR 323
Scope of outline planning permission - material considerations

Batchelor v Kent County Council [1990] 59 PCR 357 (CA)
Land Compensation Act 1961 - Rule 3 - Stokes principle - Pointe Gourde - reasons

Pye (Oxford) Ltd v Kingswood BC (CA) 6 March 1998
Compensation - scheme - collateral highway benefits - ransom - reasons

Pickering v Kettering BC [1996] EGCS 130 (CA)
Local Plan - mistake in Inspector's Report - local authority duties and discretion

Government promotions include: Channel Tunnel Rail Link and Channel Tunnel Bills.

PURDIE ROBERT ANTHONY JAMES

28 Western Road
Oxford OX1 4LG, Telephone: 01865 204911
Call date: July 1979, Middle Temple
Qualifications: [LLB]

PURDY QUENTIN ALEXANDER

2 Paper Bldgs
Temple, London EC4Y 7ET,
Telephone: 0171 936 2613
Call date: July 1983, Gray's Inn
Qualifications: [BA (Leic), LLM, (Lond)]

PURKIS MS KATHRYN MIRANDA

13 Old Square
1st Floor, Lincoln's Inn, London WC2A 3UA,
Telephone: 0171 242 6105
E-mail: clerks@serlecourt.co.uk
Call date: Oct 1991, Lincoln's Inn
Qualifications: [BA (Hons) (Cape Twn), BA (Hons) (Oxon)]

PURKISS MISS CATHLEEN KAREN

Goldsmith Building
1st Floor, Temple, London EC4Y 7BL,
Telephone: 0171 353 7881
E-mail: clerks@goldsmith-building.law.co.uk
Call date: July 1988, Lincoln's Inn
Qualifications: [BA (Hons) (Lond), Dip Law]

D

PURLE CHARLES LAMBERT QC (1989)

12 New Square
Ground Floor, Lincoln's Inn, London
WC2A 3SW, Telephone: 0171 419 1212
E-mail: 12newsquare@compuserve.com
25 Park Square
Leeds LS1 2PW, Telephone: 0113 2451841/2/3
E-mail: sovereignchambers@btinternet.com
Door Tenant
Call date: Nov 1970, Gray's Inn
Qualifications: [LLB (Nottm), BCL (Oxon)]

PURNELL NICHOLAS ROBERT QC (1985)

23 Essex Street
London WC2R 3AS,
Telephone: 0171 413 0353/353 3533
E-mail: clerks@essexstreet23.demon.co.uk
Call date: July 1968, Middle Temple
Recorder
Qualifications: [MA (Cantab)]

PURNELL PAUL OLIVER QC (1982)

1 Crown Office Row
2nd Floor, Temple, London EC4Y 7HH,
Telephone: 0171 797 7111
Call date: Nov 1962, Inner Temple
Recorder
Qualifications: [MA (Oxon)]

PURVES GAVIN BOWMAN

Swan House
P.O.Box 8749, London W13 9WQ,
Telephone: 0181 998 3035
Call date: July 1979, Gray's Inn
Qualifications: [LLB (Hons)(Brunel), DEI (Amsterdam)]

PURVIS IAIN YOUNIE

11 South Square
2nd Floor, Gray's Inn, London WC1R 5EU,
Telephone: 0171 405 1222
Call date: July 1986, Gray's Inn
Qualifications: [MA (Cantab) BCL, (Oxon)]

PUSEY WILLIAM JAMES

Priory Chambers
2 Fountain Court, Steelhouse Lane,
Birmingham B4 6DR,
Telephone: 0121 236 3882/1375
Call date: Nov 1977, Inner Temple
Qualifications: [LLB (Leeds)]

PUTNAM MRS SHEELAGH

North London Chambers
14 Keyes Road, London NW2 3XA,
Telephone: 0181 208 4651
Verulam Chambers
Peer House 8-14 Verulam Street, Gray's Inn,
London WC1X 8LZ,
Telephone: 0171 813 2400
Door Tenant
Call date: Nov 1976, Middle Temple

PUTNAM THOMAS DREW

Verulam Chambers
Peer House 8-14 Verulam Street, Gray's Inn,
London WC1X 8LZ,
Telephone: 0171 813 2400
North London Chambers
14 Keyes Road, London NW2 3XA,
Telephone: 0181 208 4651
Call date: July 1976, Gray's Inn

PUTTICK ANTHONY DAVID

Colleton Chambers
Colleton Crescent, Exeter, Devon EX2 4DG,
Telephone: 01392 74898/9
Godolphin Chambers
50 Castle Street, Truro, Cornwall TR1 3AF,
Telephone: 01872 276312
Call date: May 1971, Middle Temple

PUZEY JAMES RODERICK

1 Fountain Court
Steelhouse Lane, Birmingham B4 6DR,
Telephone: 0121 236 5721
Call date: Oct 1990, Inner Temple
Qualifications: [LLB (L'pool)]

PYE MISS MARGARET JANE

25 Park Square
Leeds LS1 2PW, Telephone: 0113 2451841/2/3
E-mail: sovereignchambers@btinternet.com
Call date: May 1995, Middle Temple
Qualifications: [BA (Hons)]

PYLE MISS SUSAN DEBORAH

7 Stone Bldgs
1st Floor, Lincoln's Inn, London WC2A 3SZ,
Telephone: 0171 242 0961
Call date: Nov 1985, Gray's Inn
Qualifications: [LLB(Newcastle)]

PYMONT CHRISTOPHER HOWARD QC (1996)

13 Old Square
Ground Floor, Lincoln's Inn, London
WC2A 3UA, Telephone: 0171 404 4800
Call date: July 1979, Gray's Inn
Qualifications: [MA (Oxon)]

PYNE RUSSELL DAVID

2 King's Bench Walk
Ground Floor, Temple, London EC4Y 7DE,
Telephone: 0171 353 1746
E-mail: 2kbw@atlas.co.uk
King's Bench Chambers
115 North Hill, Plymouth PL4 8JY,
Telephone: 01752 221551
Call date: Oct 1991, Inner Temple
Qualifications: [LLB (Bris)]

QADRI KHALID

Holborn Chambers
6 Gate Street, Lincoln's Inn Fields, London
WC2A 3HP, Telephone: 0171 242 6060
Call date: Nov 1993, Middle Temple
Qualifications: [BA (Hons), CPE
(Wolverhampton)]

QAZI MOHAMMED AYAZ

Garden Court North Chambers
2nd Floor Gregg's Building, 1 Booth Street,
Manchester M2 4DU,
Telephone: 0161 833 1774
Call date: Feb 1993, Gray's Inn
Qualifications: [LLB]

QUADRAT SIMON VICTOR

All Saints Chambers
9/11 Broad Street, Bristol BS1 2HP,
Telephone: 0117 921 1966
Call date: Nov 1969, Inner Temple
Qualifications: [LLB (Bris)]

QUDDUS KHANDAKAR ABDUL

19 Chestnut Drive
Pinner, Middlesex HA5 1LX,
Telephone: 0181 866 7603/933 2382
Call date: July 1968, Inner Temple
Qualifications: [MA]

QUEST DAVID CHARLES

3 Verulam Buildings
London WC1R 5NT,
Telephone: 0171 831 8441
E-mail: clerks@3verulam.co.uk
Call date: Oct 1993, Gray's Inn
Qualifications: [BA (Cantab)]

QUIGLEY MISS CAMILLA JACINTH CALVERT

Plowden Bldgs
2nd Floor, Temple, London EC4Y 9BU,
Telephone: 0171 583 0808
E-mail: bar@plowdenbuildings.co.uk
Call date: July 1988, Inner Temple
Qualifications: [BSc (Durham), Dip Law (City)]

QUIGLEY CONOR

Brick Court Chambers
15/19 Devereux Court, London WC2R 3JJ,
Telephone: 0171 583 0777
E-mail: (surname)@brickcourt.demon.co.uk
Call date: Nov 1985, Gray's Inn
Qualifications: [LLB (Lond), Dip.E.I.
(Amsterdam), MA (Oxon)]

QUINLAN CHRISTOPHER JOHN

30 Park Place
Cardiff CF1 3BA, Telephone: 01222 398421
E-mail: 100757.1456@compuserve.com
Call date: Nov 1992, Inner Temple
Qualifications: [LLB (Hons)]

QUINN CHRISTOPHER JOHN

Cloisters
1st Floor, Temple, London EC4Y 7AA,
Telephone: 0171 827 4000
E-mail: clerks@cloisters.com
Call date: Oct 1992, Middle Temple
Qualifications: [LL.B (Hons, Cantab), LL.M
(Queens Uni., Canada)]

D

D

QUINN HUGH DAVID O'BRIEN

5 Fountain Court
Steelhouse Lane, Birmingham B4 6DR,
Telephone: 0121 606 0500
Call date: Feb 1992, Gray's Inn
Qualifications: [LLB (Wales)]

QUINN JOSEPH MICHAEL

1 Gray's Inn Square
Ground Floor, London WC1R 5AA,
Telephone: 0171 405 8946/7/8
Call date: Nov 1987, Inner Temple
Qualifications: [BA]

QUINN MS SUSAN ANN

4 Brick Court
Temple, London EC4Y 9AD,
Telephone: 0171 797 8910
Call date: Nov 1983, Gray's Inn
Qualifications: [LLB (lond)]

QUINN MISS VICTORIA KATHLEEN

Verulam Chambers
Peer House 8-14 Verulam Street, Gray's Inn,
London WC1X 8LZ,
Telephone: 0171 813 2400
Call date: Oct 1995, Lincoln's Inn
Qualifications: [BA (Hons)(Abery)]

QUINT MRS JOAN FRANCESCA RAE

11 Old Square
Ground Floor, Lincoln's Inn, London
WC2A 3TS, Telephone: 0171 242 5022/
405 1074
Call date: July 1970, Gray's Inn
Qualifications: [LLB [Lond], A.K.C]

QUIRKE GERARD MARTIN

13 King's Bench Walk
1st Floor, Temple, London EC4Y 7EN,
Telephone: 0171 353 7204
E-mail: clerks@13kbw.law.co.uk
King's Bench Chambers
32 Beaumont Street, Oxford OX1 2NP,
Telephone: 01865 311066
E-mail: clerks@kbc-oxford.law.co.uk
Call date: Nov 1988, Middle Temple
Qualifications: [BA (Hull), Dip Law (City)]

QUIRKE JAMES KEIRON

6 Fountain Court
Steelhouse Lane, Birmingham B4 6DR,
Telephone: 0121 233 3282
Call date: Nov 1974, Gray's Inn
Qualifications: [BA (Oxon)]

QURESHI ABDUL SALEEM

Barclay Chambers
2a Barclay Road, Leytonstone, London
E11 3DG, Telephone: 0181 558 2289/
925 0688
Call date: July 1972, Middle Temple
Qualifications: [BA,LLB]

QURESHI KHAWAR MEHMOOD

One Hare Court
1st Floor, Temple, London EC4Y 7BE,
Telephone: 0171 353 3171
E-mail: admin-oneharecourt@btinternet.com
Call date: Oct 1990, Middle Temple
Qualifications: [LLB, LLM (Cantab)]

QURESHI SHAMIM AHMED

Assize Court Chambers
14 Small Street, Bristol BS1 1DE,
Telephone: 0117 9264587
Call date: July 1982, Gray's Inn
Qualifications: [BA (Bris)]

RABEY MISS CATHERINE MARY

2 Temple Gardens
Temple, London EC4Y 9AY,
Telephone: 0171 583 6041 (12 Lines)
Call date: July 1987, Middle Temple
Qualifications: [BA (Oxon) Dip Law]

RABIE GERALD ALLEN

Devereux Chambers
Devereux Court, London WC2R 3JJ,
Telephone: 0171 353 7534
E-mail: elton@devchambers.co.uk
Call date: Feb 1973, Inner Temple
Qualifications: [BA, LLB]

RABINOWITZ LAURENCE ANTON

1 Essex Court
Ground Floor, Temple, London EC4Y 9AR,
Telephone: 0171 583 2000
E-mail: clerks@oneessexcourt.co.uk
Call date: Nov 1987, Middle Temple
Qualifications: [BA, LLB (Wits), BA, BCL
(Oxon)]

RADBURN MARK CHARLES CRISPIN

5 Fountain Court
Steelhouse Lane, Birmingham B4 6DR,
Telephone: 0121 606 0500
Call date: Oct 1991, Lincoln's Inn
Qualifications: [LLB (Hons)]

RADCLIFFE ANDREW ALLEN

1 Hare Court
Ground Floor, Temple, London EC4Y 7BE,
Telephone: 0171 353 3982/5324
Call date: Nov 1975, Middle Temple
Assistant Recorder
Qualifications: [BA (Oxon)]

RADCLIFFE DAVID ANDREW

18 Red Lion Court
(Off Fleet Street), London EC4A 3EB,
Telephone: 0171 520 6000
Thornwood House
102 New London Road, Chelmsford, Essex
CM2 0RG, Telephone: 01245 280880
Call date: July 1966, Inner Temple
Recorder
Qualifications: [MA (Cantab)]

RADCLIFFE FRANCIS CHARLES JOSEPH

11 King's Bench Walk
1st Floor, Temple, London EC4Y 7EQ,
Telephone: 0171 353 3337
3 Park Court
Leeds LS1 2QH, Telephone: 0113 297 1200
Call date: Nov 1962, Gray's Inn
Qualifications: [MA (Cantab)]

RADCLIFFE MS PAMELA JOAN

Holborn Chambers
6 Gate Street, Lincoln's Inn Fields, London
WC2A 3HP, Telephone: 0171 242 6060
Call date: July 1979, Gray's Inn
Qualifications: [LLB (Warwick)]

RADEVSKY ANTHONY ERIC

5 Bell Yard
London WC2A 2JR, Telephone: 0171 333 8811
Call date: July 1978, Inner Temple
Qualifications: [LLB (Soton)]

Fax: 0171 333 8831;
Out of hours telephone: 314 0605; DX: LDE
400

Types of work: Chancery land law; Commercial
property; Conveyancing; Equity, wills and
trusts; Housing; Landlord and tenant;
Professional negligence

Circuit: South Eastern

Awards and memberships: Member, Chancery
Bar Association; COMBAR

Publications: *Service of Documents*, 2nd edn
(Longman), 1989; *Drafting Pleadings*, 2nd edn
(Tolley), 1995; *Instructing Counsel (Landlord
and Tenant)* (Tolley), 1994

Reported cases: *Belvedere Court Management
v Frogmore Developments*, [1997] QB 858,
1995. Landlord and Tenant Act 1987 - right of
first refusal - avoidance scheme.
*Dean and Chapter of Canterbury Cathedral v
Whitbread*, [1995] 1 EGLR 82, 1995. Mesne
profits at end of business lease.
*R v London Rent Assessment Committee ex
parte Cadogan Estates*, [1997] 3 WLR 833,
1997. Judicial review of rent assessment
committee - rent under assured tenancy.
John Lyon v Mayhew, [1997] 1 EGLR 88, 1997.
Defective notice under Section 25 of Landlord
and Tenant Act 1954 - estoppel.
*Donath v Second Duke of Westminster's
Trustees*, [1997] 1 EGLR 96. Collective
enfranchisement - valuation.

RADFORD MRS NADINE POGGIOLI QC (1995)

3 Gray's Inn Square
Ground Floor, London WC1R 5AH,
Telephone: 0171 520 5600
E-mail: gis3@btinternet.com
Call date: Nov 1974, Lincoln's Inn
Recorder

D

RAE JAMES ROBERT

Exchange Chambers
Pearl Assurance House Derby Square,
Liverpool L2 9XX, Telephone: 0151 236 7747/
0458
E-mail: exchangechambers@btinternet.com
Call date: July 1976, Inner Temple

RAE JOHN WILLIAM

16a Campden Hill Court
Campden Hill Road, London W8 7HS,
Telephone: 0171 937 3492
Call date: Nov 1961, Inner Temple
Qualifications: [MA (Oxon)]

RAESIDE MARK ANDREW

1 Atkin Building
Gray's Inn, London WC1R 5AT,
Telephone: 0171 404 0102
E-mail: clerks@atkin-chambers.co.uk
Call date: Nov 1982, Middle Temple
Qualifications: [BA, MPhil (Cantab)]

RAFATI ALI REZA

2 King's Bench Walk
Ground Floor, Temple, London EC4Y 7DE,
Telephone: 0171 353 1746
E-mail: 2kbw@atlas.co.uk
King's Bench Chambers
115 North Hill, Plymouth PL4 8JY,
Telephone: 01752 221551
Call date: Nov 1993, Gray's Inn
Qualifications: [LLB]

RAFFELL ANDREW JOHN

Mitre House Chambers
Mitre House 44 Fleet Street, London
EC4Y 1BN, Telephone: 0171 583 8233
Call date: Feb 1983, Middle Temple
Qualifications: [LLB (Lond), LLM (Leic)]

RAFFERTY MISS ANGELA MARGARET MARY

1 Paper Bldgs
1st Floor, Temple, London EC4Y 7EP,
Telephone: 0171 353 3728/4953
Call date: Feb 1995, Lincoln's Inn
Qualifications: [BA (Cantab)]

RAFFERTY MISS ANNE JUDITH QC (1990)

4 Brick Court
1st Floor, Temple, London EC4Y 9AD,
Telephone: 0171 583 8455
Call date: July 1973, Gray's Inn
Recorder
Qualifications: [LLB]

RAFFERTY STUART

1 High Pavement
Nottingham NG1 1HF,
Telephone: 0115 9418218
Call date: July 1975, Gray's Inn
Qualifications: [BA]

RAFFRAY FREDERIC JOSEPH

17 Bedford Row
London WC1R 4EB,
Telephone: 0171 831 7314
E-mail: IBoard7314@AOL.com
Call date: Feb 1991, Middle Temple
Qualifications: [LLB (Lond), Maitrise en Droit,
(Paris I)]

RAFIQUE SYED TARIQ DAUD

6 King's Bench Walk
Ground, Third & Fourth Floors, Temple,
London EC4Y 7DR,
Telephone: 0171 353 4931/583 0695
Call date: Nov 1961, Lincoln's Inn
Qualifications: [BA (Cantab)]

RAGGATT TIMOTHY WALTER HAROLD QC (1993)

36 Bedford Row
London WC1R 4JH,
Telephone: 0171 421 8000
E-mail: 36bedfordrow@link.org
3 Fountain Court
Steelhouse Lane, Birmingham B4 6DR,
Telephone: 0121 236 5854
Call date: July 1972, Inner Temple
Recorder
Qualifications: [LLB (Lond)]

RAHAL MISS RAVINDER KAUR

2 Garden Court
1st Floor, Middle Temple, London EC4Y 9BL,
Telephone: 0171 353 1633
E-mail: barristers@2gardenct.law.co.uk
Call date: Nov 1983, Middle Temple
Qualifications: [LLB, LLM (Cantab)]

RAHMAN IMRAN

Essex House Chambers
Essex House 375-377 Stratford High Street,
Stratford, London E15 4QZ,
Telephone: 0181 536 1077
Call date: July 1974, Middle Temple

RAHMAN MD ANISUR

12 Old Square
1st Floor, Lincoln's Inn, London WC2A 3TX,
Telephone: 0171 404 0875
Call date: Nov 1990, Inner Temple
Qualifications: [MA (Bangladesh), Dip Law
(PCL)]

RAHMAN MUHAMMAD ALTAFUR

Barrister's Common Law Chambers
57 Whitechapel Road, Aldgate East, London
E1 1DU, Telephone: 0171 375 3012
E-mail: barristers@hotmail:com
Call date: Nov 1970, Inner Temple
Qualifications: [MA]

RAHMAN MS SADEQA SHAHEEN

1 Crown Office Row
Ground Floor, Temple, London EC4Y 7HH,
Telephone: 0171 797 7500
Call date: Nov 1996, Gray's Inn
Qualifications: [BA (B'ham)]

RAHMAN YAQUB

Peel House Chambers
Ground Floor, Peel House 5 Harrington Street,
Liverpool L2 9QA, Telephone: 0151 236 4321
Call date: Oct 1991, Gray's Inn
Qualifications: [BA (Hons) (Oxon), Dip Law
(PCL)]

RAI AMARJIT SINGH

7 Fountain Court
Steelhouse Lane, Birmingham B4 6DR,
Telephone: 0121 236 8531
Call date: July 1989, Middle Temple
Qualifications: [LLB]

RAI RAJESH KUMAR

12 Old Square
1st Floor, Lincoln's Inn, London WC2A 3TX,
Telephone: 0171 404 0875
Call date: Feb 1993, Lincoln's Inn
Qualifications: [LLB (Hons)]

RAILTON DAVID QC (1996)

Fountain Court
Temple, London EC4Y 9DH,
Telephone: 0171 583 3335
E-mail: chambers@fountaincourt.co.uk
Call date: July 1979, Gray's Inn
Qualifications: [BA (Oxon)]

RAINEY PHILIP CARSLAKE

Francis Taylor Bldg
2nd Floor, Temple, London EC4Y 7BY,
Telephone: 0171 353 9942/3157
Call date: Oct 1990, Middle Temple
Qualifications: [LLB (Leic)]

RAINEY SIMON PIERS NICHOLAS

4 Essex Court
Temple, London EC4Y 9AJ,
Telephone: 0171 797 7970
E-mail: clerks@4essexcourt.law.co.uk
Call date: July 1982, Lincoln's Inn
Qualifications: [MA (Cantab) LSDE, (Brussels)]

RAINS RICHARD EDWIN RANDOLPH STEPHEN

Colleton Chambers
Colleton Crescent, Exeter, Devon EX2 4DG,
Telephone: 01392 74898/9
35 Essex Street
Temple, London WC2R 3AR,
Telephone: 0171 353 6381
Door Tenant
Call date: May 1963, Gray's Inn
Qualifications: [LLB]

RAINSFORD MARK DAVID

1 Middle Temple Lane
Temple, London EC4Y 1LT,
Telephone: 0171 583 0659 (12 Lines)
Call date: Nov 1985, Lincoln's Inn
Qualifications: [LLB (Hons) (LSE)]

RAJAH EASON THURAI

10 Old Square
Ground Floor, Lincoln's Inn, London
WC2A 3SU, Telephone: 0171 405 0758
Call date: July 1989, Gray's Inn
Qualifications: [LLB]

RAJAK HARRY HYMAN

13 Old Square
1st Floor, Lincoln's Inn, London WC2A 3UA,
Telephone: 0171 242 6105
E-mail: clerks@serlecourt.co.uk
Call date: Nov 1968, Inner Temple
Qualifications: [LLM (Lond), BA, LLB]

RALLS PETER JOHN HENRY QC (1997)

29 Bedford Row Chambers
London WC1R 4HE,
Telephone: 0171 831 2626
Call date: July 1972, Middle Temple
Qualifications: [LLB (Hons)]

RALPH MISS CAROLINE SUSAN

Assize Court Chambers
14 Small Street, Bristol BS1 1DE,
Telephone: 0117 9264587
Call date: July 1990, Inner Temple
Qualifications: [BA (B'ham)]

RALPHS MISS ANNE

22 Old Bldgs
Lincoln's Inn, London WC2A 3UJ,
Telephone: 0171 831 0222
Call date: Nov 1977, Middle Temple
Assistant Recorder
Qualifications: [BSc, AcDipEd (Lond),]

RALTON ALEXANDER JULIUS

Albion Chambers
Broad Street, Bristol BS1 1DR,
Telephone: 0117 9272144
Call date: Oct 1990, Lincoln's Inn
Qualifications: [LLB (E. Anglia)]

RAMACHANDRAN MS ARUNA

2 Paper Bldgs
1st Floor, Temple, London EC4Y 7ET,
Telephone: 0171 936 2611 (10 Lines)
E-mail: clerks@2pbbarristers.co.uk
Call date: July 1985, Gray's Inn
Qualifications: [LLB (Lond)]

RAMASAMY SELVARAJU

Hollis Whiteman Chambers
3rd/4th Floor Queen Elizabeth Bldg, Temple,
London EC4Y 9BS, Telephone: 0171 583 5766
E-mail: hollis.whiteman@btinternet.com
Call date: Nov 1992, Inner Temple
Qualifications: [LLB (Lond), LLM (Lond)]

RAMDEEN MISS KAMALA BERNADETTE

20 Britton Street
1st Floor, London EC1M 5NQ,
Telephone: 0171 608 3765
Call date: Nov 1978, Lincoln's Inn
Qualifications: [LLB (Hons) (Brunel)]

RAMDHUN PRUSRAM JAMES

Clapham Chambers
21-25 Bedford Road, Clapham North, London
SW4 7SH, Telephone: 0171 978 8482/
642 5777
E-mail: 113063.632@compuserve.com
Call date: July 1980, Lincoln's Inn
Qualifications: [BA]

RAMPERSAD DEVAN

7 Fountain Court
Steelhouse Lane, Birmingham B4 6DR,
Telephone: 0121 236 8531
Call date: Feb 1994, Inner Temple
Qualifications: [LLB (Lancs)]

RAMPTON (JOHN) RICHARD (ANTHONY) QC (1987)

1 Brick Court
1st Floor, Temple, London EC4Y 9BY,
Telephone: 0171 353 8845
E-mail: clerks@1brickcourt.co.uk
Call date: Nov 1965, Inner Temple
Qualifications: [BA (Oxon)]

RAMSAHOYE MISS INDIRA KIM

Hardwicke Building
New Square, Lincoln's Inn, London
WC2A 3SB, Telephone: 0171 242 2523
E-mail: clerks@hardwicke.co.uk
Call date: Nov 1980, Lincoln's Inn
Qualifications: [BA]

RAMSDEN JAMES MICHAEL SCOTT

4-5 Gray's Inn Square
Ground Floor, Gray's Inn, London WC1R 5AY,
Telephone: 0171 404 5252
E-mail: chambers@4-5graysinnsquare.co.uk
Call date: Nov 1987, Middle Temple
Qualifications: [LLB (Leics)]

RAMSDEN MISS VERONICA MARY

Staple Inn Chambers
1st Floor 9 Staple Inn, Holborn, London
WC1V 7QH, Telephone: 0171 242 5240
E-mail: clerks@staple-inn.org
Call date: July 1979, Gray's Inn
Qualifications: [LLB (Hons) (Wales)]

RAMSEY VIVIAN ARTHUR QC (1992)

Keating Chambers
10 Essex Street, Outer Temple, London
WC2R 3AA, Telephone: 0171 544 2600
Call date: July 1979, Middle Temple
Qualifications: [MA, C Eng, MICE]

RAMZAN MOHAMMED ANWAR

2 Middle Temple Lane
3rd Floor, Temple, London EC4Y 9AA,
Telephone: 0171 583 4540
Call date: Oct 1995, Lincoln's Inn
Qualifications: [LLB (Hons)(Wolves)]

RANA MOHAMMED AKRAM

Chancery Chambers
1st Floor Offices 70/72 Chancery Lane,
London WC2A 1AB,
Telephone: 0171 405 6879/6870
Call date: Nov 1995, Lincoln's Inn
Qualifications: [BSc (Hons), LLB (Hons)]

RANDALL JOHN YEOMAN QC (1995)

7 Fountain Court
Steelhouse Lane, Birmingham B4 6DR,
Telephone: 0121 236 8531
7 Stone Bldgs
Ground Floor, Lincoln's Inn, London
WC2A 3SZ, Telephone: 0171 405 3886/
242 3546
E-mail: chaldous@vossnet.co.uk
Door Tenant
Call date: July 1978, Lincoln's Inn
Assistant Recorder
Qualifications: [MA (Cantab)]

RANDALL MISS LOUISE ELIZABETH

Keating Chambers
10 Essex Street, Outer Temple, London
WC2R 3AA, Telephone: 0171 544 2600
Call date: July 1988, Middle Temple
Qualifications: [BA (Hons) (Keele)]

RANDALL NICHOLAS CLIVE

Devereux Chambers
Devereux Court, London WC2R 3JJ,
Telephone: 0171 353 7534
E-mail: elton@devchambers.co.uk
Call date: Oct 1990, Middle Temple
Qualifications: [LLB (Lond)]

RANDHAWA MISS RAVINDER KAUR

York Chambers
14 Toft Green, York YO1 1JT,
Telephone: 01904 620048
E-mail: yorkchambers.co.uk
Call date: Oct 1995, Lincoln's Inn
Qualifications: [LLB (Hons)(Leeds)]

D

RANDLE SIMON PATRICK

11 Bolt Court
London EC4A 3DQ,
Telephone: 0171 353 2300
E-mail: boltct11@aol.com
Redhill Chambers
Seloduct House 30 Station Road, Redhill
RH1 1NK, Telephone: 01737 780781
Call date: July 1982, Inner Temple
Qualifications: [LLB (Hull)]

RANDOLPH FERGUS MARK HARRY

Brick Court Chambers
15/19 Devereux Court, London WC2R 3JJ,
Telephone: 0171 583 0777
E-mail: (surname)@brickcourt.demon.co.uk
Call date: July 1985, Middle Temple
Qualifications: [LLB, Dip French Law]

RANDOLPH PAUL LESLIE

New Court
Temple, London EC4Y 9BE,
Telephone: 0171 583 5123/0171 583 0510
Call date: Nov 1971, Inner Temple
Qualifications: [LLB (Lond)]

RANK PETER MICHAEL

Regent Chambers
29 Regent Road, Hanley, Stoke On Trent
ST1 3BP, Telephone: 01782 286666
E-mail: regent@ftech.co.uk
Call date: July 1976, Middle Temple
Qualifications: [BCL (Oxon) LLB]

RANKIN ANDREW QC (1968)

4 Field Court
Gray's Inn, London WC1R 5EA,
Telephone: 0171 440 6900
E-mail: chambers@4fieldcourt.co.uk
Call date: May 1950, Gray's Inn
Recorder
Qualifications: [BA (Cantab), BL (Edi)]

RANKIN CIARAN EMMANUEL

58 King Street Chambers
1st Floor, Kingsgate House 51-53 South King
Street, Manchester M2 6DE,
Telephone: 0161 831 7477
Call date: Nov 1988, Lincoln's Inn
Qualifications: [LLB Hons]

RANKIN JAMES ROWLAND EVELYN

3 Raymond Buildings
Gray's Inn, London WC1R 5BH,
Telephone: 0171 831 3833
E-mail: chambers@threeraymond.demon.co.uk
Call date: July 1983, Inner Temple
Qualifications: [LLB (Bucks)]

RANKIN WILLIAM KERR

Peel House Chambers
Ground Floor, Peel House 5 Harrington Street,
Liverpool L2 9QA, Telephone: 0151 236 4321
Call date: Oct 1994, Gray's Inn
Qualifications: [LLB]

RANKIN WILLIAM PETER

Oriel Chambers
14 Water Street, Liverpool L2 8TD,
Telephone: 0151 236 7191
E-mail: oriel_chambers@link.org
Call date: Nov 1972, Gray's Inn
Qualifications: [BA (Cantab)]

RAPPO PATRICK JAMES

4 Brick Court
1st Floor, Temple, London EC4Y 9AD,
Telephone: 0171 583 8455
Call date: Nov 1995, Gray's Inn
Qualifications: [MA (Oxon)]

RASHID MIRZA ABDUL

Commonwealth Chambers
354 Moseley Road, Birmingham B12 9AZ,
Telephone: 0121 446 5732
Call date: Nov 1981, Lincoln's Inn
Qualifications: [BA, MA, LLB (Hons)]

RASHID SHAHID

Middlesex Chambers
Suite 3 & 4 Stanley House Stanley Avenue,
Wembley, Middlesex HA0 4SB,
Telephone: 0181 902 1499
Call date: Nov 1982, Middle Temple
Qualifications: [BA (Hons), LLM]

RATCLIFFE MISS ANNE KIRKPATRICK

5 Pump Court
Ground Floor, Temple, London EC4Y 7AP,
Telephone: 0171 353 2532
E-mail: fivepump@netcomuk.co.uk
Call date: Feb 1981, Inner Temple
Qualifications: [BSc (Soton), Dip Law]

RATHBONE BRIAN BENSON

Richmond Green Chambers
Greyhound House 23-24 George Street,
Richmond-upon-Thames, Surrey TW9 1HY,
Telephone: 0181 940 1841
Call date: July 1960, Lincoln's Inn
Qualifications: [BA (Hons)]

RATLIFF JOHN HARRISON

2 Harcourt Bldgs
Ground Floor/Left, Temple, London
EC4Y 9DB, Telephone: 0171 583 9020
E-mail: clerks@harcourt.co.uk
Stanbrook & Henderson
2 Harcourt Bldgs 2nd Floor, Temple, London
EC4Y 9DB, Telephone: 0171 353 0101
E-mail: clerks@harcourt.co.uk
Call date: July 1980, Middle Temple
Qualifications: [BA (Oxon), Diploma in
European, Intergration (NDR), (Amsterdam)]

RATTIGAN MICHAEL PAUL WILLIAM

Chambers of Raana Sheikh
Gray's Inn Chambers, Gray's Inn, London
WC1R, Telephone: 0171 831 5344
E-mail: s.mcblain@btinternet.com
Call date: Oct 1991, Lincoln's Inn
Qualifications: [LLB (Hons) (Lond)]

RAUDNITZ PAUL NIKOLAI

2 Dr Johnson's Building
Temple, London EC4Y 7AY,
Telephone: 0171 353 4716
Call date: Nov 1994, Inner Temple
Qualifications: [BA (Oxon), CPE]

RAW EDWARD

Francis Taylor Bldg
3rd Floor, Temple, London EC4Y 7BY,
Telephone: 0171 797 7250
Call date: July 1963, Inner Temple
Qualifications: [MA (Oxon)]

RAWAT BILAL MAHMAD

9 Bedford Row
London WC1R 4AZ,
Telephone: 0171 242 3555
E-mail: clerks@9br.co.uk
Call date: Oct 1995, Middle Temple
Qualifications: [B.Sc (Hons), PhD, Dip Law]

RAWCLIFFE ANTHONY MARK WILSON

Adrian Lyon's Chambers
14 Castle Street, Liverpool L2 0NE,
Telephone: 0151 236 4421/8240
E-mail: chambers14@aol.com
Call date: Nov 1996, Middle Temple
Qualifications: [BA (Hons)]

RAWLEY ALAN DAVID QC (1977)

35 Essex Street
Temple, London WC2R 3AR,
Telephone: 0171 353 6381
Call date: June 1958, Middle Temple
Recorder
Qualifications: [MA (Oxon)]

RAWLEY MISS DOMINIQUE JANE

1 Atkin Building
Gray's Inn, London WC1R 5AT,
Telephone: 0171 404 0102
E-mail: clerks@atkin-chambers.co.uk
Call date: Nov 1991, Middle Temple
Qualifications: [BA Hons (Cantab)]

RAWLINGS CLIVE PATRICK

Goldsmith Building
1st Floor, Temple, London EC4Y 7BL,
Telephone: 0171 353 7881
E-mail: clerks@goldsmith-building.law.co.uk
Call date: Nov 1994, Inner Temple
Qualifications: [BA (Bradford), CPE (Middx)]

RAWLINSON MICHAEL EDWARD

28 St John Street
Manchester M3 4DJ,
Telephone: 0161 834 8418
E-mail: clerk@28stjohnst.co.uk
Call date: Nov 1991, Inner Temple
Qualifications: [LLB (Manch)]

D

RAY JONATHAN RICHARD

Thomas More Chambers
52 Carey Street, Lincoln's Inn, London
WC2A 2JB, Telephone: 0171 404 7000
Call date: July 1980, Gray's Inn
Qualifications: [BA (Hons)]

RAY-CROSBY MISS IRENA WYVIS

6 King's Bench Walk
Ground Floor, Temple, London EC4Y 7DR,
Telephone: 0171 583 0410
Call date: Nov 1990, Middle Temple
Qualifications: [MA (Oxon)]

RAYBAUD MRS JUNE ROSE

Goldsworth Chambers
1st Floor 10-11 Gray's Inn Square, London
WC1R 5JD, Telephone: 0171 405 7117
Call date: Nov 1990, Inner Temple
Qualifications: [BA (Kent)]

RAYMENT MR. BENEDICK MICHAEL

1 King's Bench Walk
2nd Floor, Temple, London EC4Y 7DB,
Telephone: 0171 936 1500
E-mail: ddear@1kbw.co.uk
Call date: Oct 1996, Inner Temple
Qualifications: [MA (Hons), BCL (Oxon)]

RAYMOND JEAN-GILLES

John Street Chambers
2 John Street, London WC1N 2HJ,
Telephone: 0171 242 1911
E-mail: john.street_chambers@virgin.net.uk
Call date: Nov 1982, Lincoln's Inn
Qualifications: [LLB (Wales)]

RAYNER JAMES JONATHAN ELWYN QC (1988)

5 New Square
1st Floor, Lincoln's Inn, London WC2A 3RJ,
Telephone: 0171 404 0404
E-mail: Chambers@FiveNewSquare.CityScape.co.uk
Call date: Nov 1971, Lincoln's Inn
Assistant Recorder
Qualifications: [MA LLM (Cantab), Lic.Sp.en droit, Europeen]

RAYNOR PHILIP RONALD QC (1994)

40 King Street
Manchester M2 6BA,
Telephone: 0161 832 9082
E-mail: Kingst40@aol.com
Hardwicke Building
New Square, Lincoln's Inn, London
WC2A 3SB, Telephone: 0171 242 2523
E-mail: clerks@hardwicke.co.uk
Call date: July 1973, Inner Temple
Recorder
Qualifications: [MA (Cantab)]

RAYSON MISS JANE VIVIENNE

2 Gray's Inn Square Chambers
2nd Floor, Gray's Inn, London WC1R 5AA,
Telephone: 0171 242 0328/071 405 1317
E-mail: clerks@2gis.co.uk
Call date: July 1982, Gray's Inn
Qualifications: [LLB (Hons)]

REA MISS KAREN MARIE-JEANNE

1 Serjeants' Inn
5th Floor Fleet Street, Temple, London
EC4Y 1LL, Telephone: 0171 415 6666
E-mail: no1serjeantsinn@btinternet.com
Call date: July 1980, Gray's Inn
Qualifications: [BA, RGN]

READ GRAHAM STEPHEN

Devereux Chambers
Devereux Court, London WC2R 3JJ,
Telephone: 0171 353 7534
E-mail: elton@devchambers.co.uk
Call date: July 1981, Gray's Inn
Qualifications: [MA (Cantab)]

READ PROFESSOR JAMES STRACEY

2 Paper Bldgs
1st Floor, Temple, London EC4Y 7ET,
Telephone: 0171 936 2611 (10 Lines)
E-mail: clerks@2pbbarristers.co.uk
Call date: Feb 1954, Gray's Inn

READ LIONEL FRANK QC (1973)

1 Serjeants' Inn
4th Floor, Temple, London EC4Y 1NH,
Telephone: 0171 583 1355
E-mail: serjeants.inn@virgin.net
Call date: Feb 1954, Gray's Inn
Recorder
Qualifications: [MA (Cantab)]

READ SIMON ERIC

8 King's Bench Walk
2nd Floor, Temple, London EC4Y 7DU,
Telephone: 0171 797 8888
8 King's Bench Walk North
1 Park Square East, Leeds LS1 2NE,
Telephone: 0113 2439797
Call date: Nov 1989, Inner Temple
Qualifications: [LLB (Warc)]

READE DAVID JARRETT

4 Paper Bldgs
2nd Floor, Temple, London EC4Y 7EX,
Telephone: 0171 583 0816/071 353 1131
E-mail: clerks@4paperbuildings.co.uk
Call date: July 1983, Middle Temple
Qualifications: [LLB (B'ham)]

READE KEVIN

Martins Building
Water Street, Liverpool L2 3SP,
Telephone: 0151 236 5818/4919
Call date: July 1983, Gray's Inn
Qualifications: [LLB (L'pool)]

READHEAD SIMON JOHN HOWARD

1 Serjeants' Inn
5th Floor Fleet Street, Temple, London
EC4Y 1LL, Telephone: 0171 415 6666
E-mail: no1serjeantsinn@btinternet.com
Call date: July 1979, Middle Temple
Assistant Recorder
Qualifications: [BCL, MA (Oxon)]

READINGS DOUGLAS GEORGE

Priory Chambers
2 Fountain Court, Steelhouse Lane,
Birmingham B4 6DR,
Telephone: 0121 236 3882/1375
Call date: July 1972, Middle Temple
Assistant Recorder
Qualifications: [MA (Cantab)]

REANEY MISS JANET ELIZABETH

The Corn Exchange
5th Floor Fenwick Street, Liverpool L2 7QS,
Telephone: 0151 227 1081/5009
Call date: July 1987, Middle Temple
Qualifications: [MA (Cantab)]

RECTOR MISS PENELOPE JANE

2 Paper Bldgs
Temple, London EC4Y 7ET,
Telephone: 0171 936 2613
Call date: Nov 1980, Gray's Inn
Qualifications: [LLB (Hons) (Lond)]

REDDIFORD ANTHONY JAMES

Guildhall Chambers
23 Broad Street, Bristol BS1 2HG,
Telephone: 0117 9273366
Call date: Nov 1991, Inner Temple
Qualifications: [BA (Warw), Dip Law]

REDDIHOUGH JOHN HARGREAVES

9 Gough Square
London EC4A 3DE, Telephone: 0171 353 5371
Call date: July 1969, Gray's Inn
Recorder
Qualifications: [LLB]

REDDISH JOHN WILSON

1 King's Bench Walk
2nd Floor, Temple, London EC4Y 7DB,
Telephone: 0171 936 1500
E-mail: ddear@1kbw.co.uk
Call date: July 1973, Middle Temple
Qualifications: [MA (Oxon)]

REDFERN DAVID ALAN

1 Essex Court
Ground Floor, Temple, London EC4Y 9AR,
Telephone: 0171 583 2000
E-mail: clerks@oneessexcourt.co.uk
Call date: May 1995, Middle Temple
Qualifications: [MA (Cantab), FCIArb]

REDFERN MISS LYNDA

2 New Street
Leicester LE1 5NA, Telephone: 0116 2625906
Call date: Oct 1993, Middle Temple
Qualifications: [BA, Dip Law, M.I.L.]

REDFERN MICHAEL HOWARD QC (1993)

28 St John Street
Manchester M3 4DJ,
Telephone: 0161 834 8418
E-mail: clerk@28stjohnst.co.uk
Call date: July 1970, Inner Temple
Assistant Recorder
Qualifications: [LLB (Leeds)]

REDFORD MISS JESSICA KATE

3 Dr Johnson's Bldgs
Ground Floor, Temple, London EC4Y 7BA,
Telephone: 0171 353 4854
Call date: Nov 1994, Inner Temple
Qualifications: [BA (Hons) (Oxon), CPE]

REDGRAVE ADRIAN ROBERT FRANK QC (1992)

1 Serjeants' Inn
5th Floor Fleet Street, Temple, London
EC4Y 1LL, Telephone: 0171 415 6666
E-mail: no1serjeantsinn@btinternet.com
Call date: Nov 1968, Inner Temple
Recorder
Qualifications: [LLB]

REDGRAVE MISS DIANE CATHERINE

Gray's Inn Chambers
5th Floor, Gray's Inn, London WC1R 5JA,
Telephone: 0171 404 1111
Call date: Nov 1977, Middle Temple
Qualifications: [BA]

REDGRAVE WILLIAM ALEXANDER FRANK

9 Bedford Row
London WC1R 4AZ,
Telephone: 0171 242 3555
E-mail: clerks@9br.co.uk
Call date: Oct 1995, Inner Temple
Qualifications: [BA (Hons), Dip Law]

REDHEAD LEROY PETER BASIL

3 Gray's Inn Square
Ground Floor, London WC1R 5AH,
Telephone: 0171 520 5600
E-mail: gis3@btinternet.com
Call date: Nov 1982, Lincoln's Inn
Qualifications: [LLB (Lond), LLM]

REDMAYNE SIMON MARK

East Anglian Chambers
57 London Street, Norwich NR2 1HL,
Telephone: 01603 617351
East Anglian Chambers
Sanders House 52 North Hill, Colchester
CO1 1PY, Telephone: 01206 572756
East Anglian Chambers
Gresham House 5 Museum Street, Ipswich
IP1 1HQ, Telephone: 01473 214481
Call date: July 1982, Inner Temple
Qualifications: [BA (Oxon)]

REDMOND STEVEN

4 Fountain Court
Steelhouse Lane, Birmingham B4 6DR,
Telephone: 0121 236 3476
Call date: July 1975, Gray's Inn
Qualifications: [BA]

REECE BRIAN ALFRED WILLIAM

1 Middle Temple Lane
Temple, London EC4Y 1LT,
Telephone: 0171 583 0659 (12 Lines)
Call date: July 1974, Middle Temple
Qualifications: [LLB (Lond)]

REECE RUPERT VAUGHAN PAYNTER

2 Temple Gardens
Temple, London EC4Y 9AY,
Telephone: 0171 583 6041 (12 Lines)
Call date: Oct 1992, Inner Temple
Qualifications: [BA (Cambs), DESS (Paris-Assas), Examen D'aptitude, (Paris)]

REED JASON LESLIE RICHARD

Phoenix Chambers
First Floor Gray's Inn Chambers, Gray's Inn,
London WC1R 5JA, Telephone: 0171 404 7888
Call date: Oct 1994, Lincoln's Inn
Qualifications: [BA (Hons)(Leeds)]

REED JOHN WILLIAM RUPERT

Wilberforce Chambers
8 New Square, Lincoln's Inn, London
WC2A 3QP, Telephone: 0171 306 0102
E-mail: chambers@wilberforce.co.uk
Call date: Oct 1996, Lincoln's Inn
Qualifications: [BA (Hons)(Oxon), BA (Hons)(Cantab), LLM (Harvard)]

REED JULIAN WINN

32 Park Place
Cardiff CF1 3BA, Telephone: 01222 397364
Call date: Nov 1991, Inner Temple
Qualifications: [LLB]

REED MATTHEW ROBERT

1 Serjeants' Inn
4th Floor, Temple, London EC4Y 1NH,
Telephone: 0171 583 1355
E-mail: serjeants.inn@virgin.net
Call date: Nov 1995, Middle Temple
Qualifications: [MA (Hons)]

REED PAUL STUART MALCOLM

Hardwicke Building
New Square, Lincoln's Inn, London
WC2A 3SB, Telephone: 0171 242 2523
E-mail: clerks@hardwicke.co.uk
Call date: July 1988, Inner Temple
Qualifications: [LLB, MSC]

REED MISS PENELOPE JANE

11 Stone Bldgs
1st Floor, Lincoln's Inn, London WC2A 3TG,
Telephone: 0171 404 5055
E-mail: 9stoneb@compuserve.com
Call date: July 1983, Inner Temple
Qualifications: [LLB (Lond)]

REED PHILIP JAMES WILLIAM

5 Bell Yard
London WC2A 2JR, Telephone: 0171 333 8811
Call date: July 1985, Lincoln's Inn
Qualifications: [MA (Oxon)]

REED PIERS KNOWLE MOORHOUSE

3 Temple Gardens
Lower Ground Floor, Temple, London
EC4Y 9AU, Telephone: 0171 353 3102/5/9297
Call date: Nov 1974, Lincoln's Inn

REED ROBERT JOHN

Brick Court Chambers
15/19 Devereux Court, London WC2R 3JJ,
Telephone: 0171 583 0777
E-mail: (surname)@brickcourt.demon.co.uk
Door Tenant
Call date: July 1991, Inner Temple
Qualifications: [LLB (Edin), D.Phil (Oxford)]

REED MISS SUSAN CATHERINE

9 Bedford Row
London WC1R 4AZ,
Telephone: 0171 242 3555
E-mail: clerks@9br.co.uk
Call date: July 1984, Gray's Inn
Qualifications: [LLB (Manch)]

REEDER JOHN QC (1989)

4 Field Court
Gray's Inn, London WC1R 5EA,
Telephone: 0171 440 6900
E-mail: chambers@4fieldcourt.co.uk
Call date: July 1971, Gray's Inn
Qualifications: [LLM, PhD]

REEDER STEPHEN

1 Pump Court
Lower Ground Floor, Temple, London
EC4Y 7AB, Telephone: 0171 583 2012/
353 4341
E-mail: (name) @1pumpcourt.co.uk
Call date: Nov 1991, Middle Temple
Qualifications: [LLB Hons]

REEDS GRAHAM JOSEPH

11 King's Bench Walk
1st Floor, Temple, London EC4Y 7EQ,
Telephone: 0171 353 3337
3 Park Court
Leeds LS1 2QH, Telephone: 0113 297 1200
Call date: Nov 1984, Middle Temple
Qualifications: [LLB (Sheff)]

REEDS MISS MADELEINE LUCIA

6 Park Square
Leeds LS1 2LW, Telephone: 0113 2459763
E-mail: chambers@no6.co.uk
Call date: Nov 1988, Lincoln's Inn
Qualifications: [LLB Hons (Sheff)]

REES MISS CAROLINE ELIZABETH

33 Park Place
Cardiff CF1 3BA, Telephone: 01222 233313
Call date: Oct 1994, Gray's Inn
Qualifications: [LLB]

D

REES CHRISTOPHER LLOYD

33 Park Place
Cardiff CF1 3BA, Telephone: 01222 233313
Call date: Nov 1996, Lincoln's Inn
Qualifications: [BA (Cantab)]

REES DAVID BENJAMIN

5 Stone Buildings
Lincoln's Inn, London WC2A 3XT,
Telephone: 0171 242 6201
E-mail: clerks@5-stonebuildings.law.co.uk
Call date: Oct 1994, Lincoln's Inn
Qualifications: [BA (Hons) (Oxon)]

REES EDWARD PARRY

Doughty Street Chambers
11 Doughty Street, London WC1N 2PG,
Telephone: 0171 404 1313
E-mail: doughty_street@compuserve.com
Call date: Feb 1973, Gray's Inn
Qualifications: [LLB (Wales)]

REES GARETH DAVID

Hollis Whiteman Chambers
3rd/4th Floor Queen Elizabeth Bldg, Temple,
London EC4Y 9BS, Telephone: 0171 583 5766
E-mail: hollis.whiteman@btinternet.com
Call date: July 1981, Gray's Inn
Qualifications: [BA]

REES HEFIN EDNYFED

4 King's Bench Walk
2nd Floor, Temple, London EC4Y 7DL,
Telephone: 0171 353 3581
Call date: Nov 1992, Inner Temple
Qualifications: [BA (Hons)]

REES IEUAN

Angel Chambers
94 Walter Road, Swansea SA1 5QA,
Telephone: 01792 6464623/6464648
10 King's Bench Walk
1st Floor, Temple, London EC4Y 7EB,
Telephone: 0171 353 2501
Door Tenant
Call date: Nov 1982, Gray's Inn
Qualifications: [BSc (Cardiff)]

REES JAMES WILLIAM STEWART

2 King's Bench Walk
Ground Floor, Temple, London EC4Y 7DE,
Telephone: 0171 353 1746
E-mail: 2kbw@atlas.co.uk
King's Bench Chambers
115 North Hill, Plymouth PL4 8JY,
Telephone: 01752 221551
Call date: Nov 1994, Gray's Inn
Qualifications: [BA (Dumelm)]

REES JOHN CHARLES QC (1991)

33 Park Place
Cardiff CF1 3BA, Telephone: 01222 233313
Call date: July 1972, Lincoln's Inn
Assistant Recorder
Qualifications: [LLB (Cantab)]

REES JONATHAN DAVID

2 Harcourt Bldgs
1st Floor, Temple, London EC4Y 9DB,
Telephone: 0171 353 2112/2817
Call date: Nov 1987, Gray's Inn
Qualifications: [BA (Oxon)]

REES OWEN HUW

Iscoed Chambers
86 St Helen's Road, Swansea SA1 4BQ,
Telephone: 01792 652988/9/330
Call date: July 1983, Gray's Inn
Qualifications: [LLB (Wales)]

REES PAUL STUART

1 Crown Office Row
Ground Floor, Temple, London EC4Y 7HH,
Telephone: 0171 797 7500
Call date: Nov 1980, Gray's Inn
Qualifications: [MA, M Phil, BCL (Oxon)]

REES PHILLIP

9 Park Place
Cardiff CF1 3DP, Telephone: 01222 382731
Door Tenant
Farrar's Building
Temple, London EC4Y 7BD,
Telephone: 0171 583 9241
E-mail: chambers@farrarsbuilding.co.uk
Door Tenant
Call date: Feb 1965, Middle Temple
Qualifications: [LLB (Bris)]

REES ROBERT CHARLES DAVID

New Walk Chambers
27 New Walk, Leicester LE1 6TE,
Telephone: 0116 2559144
Call date: Feb 1978, Middle Temple
Qualifications: [BA, LLB]

REES STEPHEN ROBERT TRISTRAM

Iscoed Chambers
86 St Helen's Road, Swansea SA1 4BQ,
Telephone: 01792 652988/9/330
Call date: Nov 1979, Gray's Inn
Qualifications: [LLB (Wales)]

REES PROFESSOR WILLIAM MICHAEL

4 King's Bench Walk
Ground/First Floor, Temple, London
EC4Y 7DL, Telephone: 0171 822 8822
E-mail: 4kbw@barristersatlaw.com
Call date: July 1973, Inner Temple
Qualifications: [MA (Cantab)]

REESE COLIN EDWARD QC (1987)

1 Atkin Building
Gray's Inn, London WC1R 5AT,
Telephone: 0171 404 0102
E-mail: clerks@atkin-chambers.co.uk
Call date: July 1973, Gray's Inn
Recorder
Qualifications: [MA (Cantab)]

REEVE MATTHEW FRANCIS

5 Bell Yard
London WC2A 2JR, Telephone: 0171 333 8811
Call date: Nov 1987, Inner Temple
Qualifications: [MA (Cantab)]

REEVE MISS SUZANNE MARY

9-12 Bell Yard
London WC2A 2LF,
Telephone: 0171 400 1800
Call date: Nov 1993, Middle Temple
Qualifications: [BA (Hons)(Oxon)]

REEVELL SIMON JUSTIN

39 Park Square
Leeds LS1 2NU, Telephone: 0113 2456633
Call date: Oct 1990, Lincoln's Inn
Qualifications: [BA (Econs), Dip Law]

REFFIN MISS CLARE ALYSON

1 Essex Court
Ground Floor, Temple, London EC4Y 9AR,
Telephone: 0171 583 2000
E-mail: clerks@oneessexcourt.co.uk
Call date: July 1981, Middle Temple
Qualifications: [MA (Cantab)]

REGAN DAVID ROBERT

Chichester Chambers
12 North Pallant, Chichester, West Sussex
PO19 1TQ, Telephone: 01243 784538
Call date: Nov 1994, Inner Temple
Qualifications: [MA (Oxon), CPE (City)]

REICHERT KLAUS

5 Paper Bldgs
Ground Floor, Temple, London EC4Y 7HB,
Telephone: 0171 583 9275/583 4555
E-mail: 5paper@link.org
Call date: Nov 1996, Middle Temple
Qualifications: [BCL (Dublin)]

REID BRIAN CHRISTOPHER

19 Old Buildings
Lincoln's Inn, London WC2A 3UP,
Telephone: 0171 405 2001
E-mail: clerks@oldbuildingsip.com
Call date: Nov 1971, Middle Temple
Qualifications: [MA (Cantab), LLM (Lond)]

REID MISS CAROLINE OLDCORN

14 Gray's Inn Square
Gray's Inn, London WC1R 5JP,
Telephone: 0171 242 0858
E-mail: 100712.2134@compuserve.com
Call date: Nov 1982, Middle Temple
Qualifications: [BA PhD (Sheff) Dip, Law (City)]

REID MISS CLAUDETTE PATRICIA

Chancery Chambers
1st Floor Offices 70/72 Chancery Lane,
London WC2A 1AB,
Telephone: 0171 405 6879/6870
Call date: Oct 1990, Gray's Inn
Qualifications: [BA, LLM]

D

D

REID DAVID DONALD WILLIAM

3 Paper Bldgs
1st Floor, Temple, London EC4Y 7EU,
Telephone: 0171 583 8055
E-mail: london@3paper.com
4 St Peter Street
Winchester SO23 8OW,
Telephone: 01962 868884
Call date: Nov 1994, Gray's Inn
Qualifications: [BA (Oxon)]

REID GRAHAM MATTHEW

4 Paper Bldgs
Ground Floor, Temple, London EC4Y 7EX,
Telephone: 0171 353 3366/583 7155
E-mail: clerks@4paperbuildings.com
Call date: Feb 1993, Middle Temple
Qualifications: [BA (Hons)(Oxon), Dip in Law
(City)]

REID HOWARD BARRINGTON

New Court Chambers
Suite 200 Gazette Building, 168 Corporation
Street, Birmingham B4 6TZ,
Telephone: 0121 693 6656
Call date: Feb 1991, Middle Temple
Qualifications: [BA (Hons)]

REID MISS JACQUELINE CLAIRE

11 South Square
2nd Floor, Gray's Inn, London WC1R 5EU,
Telephone: 0171 405 1222
Call date: Oct 1992, Middle Temple
Qualifications: [BSc (Surrey), MPhil (Lond)]

REID JAMES ROBERT QC (1980)

9 Old Square
Ground Floor, Lincoln's Inn, London
WC2A 3SR, Telephone: 0171 405 4682
E-mail: chambers@9oldsquare.co.uk
Call date: Nov 1965, Lincoln's Inn
Recorder
Qualifications: [MA (Oxon), FCI Arb]

REID PAUL CAMPBELL

Lincoln House Chambers
5th Floor Lincoln House, 1 Brazennose Street,
Manchester M2 5EL,
Telephone: 0161 832 5701
E-mail: LincolnHouseChambers@link.org
Call date: July 1973, Gray's Inn
Recorder
Qualifications: [MA (Cantab)]

REID PAUL WILLIAM

13 King's Bench Walk
1st Floor, Temple, London EC4Y 7EN,
Telephone: 0171 353 7204
E-mail: clerks@13kbw.law.co.uk
King's Bench Chambers
32 Beaumont Street, Oxford OX1 2NP,
Telephone: 01865 311066
E-mail: clerks@kbc-oxford.law.co.uk
Call date: July 1975, Inner Temple
Qualifications: [MA (Cantab)]

REID SEBASTIAN PETER SCOTT

Francis Taylor Bldg
2nd Floor, Temple, London EC4Y 7BY,
Telephone: 0171 353 9942/3157
Call date: July 1982, Gray's Inn
Qualifications: [BA (Lond) AKC Dip, Law]

REID-CHALMERS MISS EMMA LOUISE

Chambers of Joy Okoye
Suite 1, 2nd Floor Gray's Inn Chambers,
Gray's Inn, London WC1R 5JA,
Telephone: 0171 405 7011
Call date: July 1996, Lincoln's Inn
Qualifications: [LLB (Hons)]

REIFF-MUSGROVE MISS KAJA

Phoenix Chambers
First Floor Gray's Inn Chambers, Gray's Inn,
London WC1R 5JA, Telephone: 0171 404 7888
Call date: Nov 1992, Middle Temple
Qualifications: [BA (Hons, Sussex)]

D

REILLY MR. DANIEL EDWARD

Tindal Chambers
3/5 New Street, Chelmsford, Essex CM1 1NT,
Telephone: 01245 267742
Tindal Chambers
3 Waxhouse Gate, St Albans, Herts AL5 4DU,
Telephone: 01727 843383
Call date: Nov 1995, Middle Temple
Qualifications: [LLB (Hons)]

REILLY JOHN JOSEPH

14 Tooks Court
Cursitor St, London EC4A 1LB,
Telephone: 0171 405 8828
E-mail: clerks @tooks.law.co.uk
Call date: Nov 1972, Inner Temple
Qualifications: [BL (Dublin)]

REILLY MRS LAXMI DEVI

4 Brick Court
Ground Floor, Temple, London EC4Y 9AD,
Telephone: 0171 797 7766
E-mail: chambers@4brick.co.uk
Call date: Nov 1972, Middle Temple

RENFREE PETER GERALD STANLEY

Harbour Court Chambers
11 William Price Gardens, Fareham,
Hampshire PO16 7PD,
Telephone: 01329 827828
Call date: July 1992, Middle Temple
Qualifications: [LLB (Hons)]

RENNIE DAVID JAMES

1 King's Bench Walk
2nd Floor, Temple, London EC4Y 7DB,
Telephone: 0171 936 1500
E-mail: ddear@1kbw.co.uk
Call date: July 1976, Inner Temple
Assistant Recorder
Qualifications: [BA]

RENOUF GERARD JOHN PETER

2 Pump Court
1st Floor, Temple, London EC4Y 7AH,
Telephone: 0171 353 5597
Call date: July 1977, Inner Temple

RENTON THE HON CLARE OLIVIA

29 Bedford Row Chambers
London WC1R 4HE,
Telephone: 0171 831 2626
Call date: Nov 1972, Lincoln's Inn

RESTELL THOMAS GEORGE

Granary Chambers
4 Glenleigh Park Road, Bexhill-on-Sea, East
Sussex TN39 4EH, Telephone: 01424 733008
E-mail: restell@granary-law.prestel.co.uk
Call date: Nov 1976, Middle Temple
Qualifications: [FCIArb]

RESTRICK ALEXANDER THOMAS

11 King's Bench Walk
Temple, London EC4Y 7EQ,
Telephone: 0171 632 8500
E-mail: clerksroom@11-kbw.law.co.uk
Call date: Nov 1995, Middle Temple
Qualifications: [BA (Hons) (Oxon)]

REVELL MARCUS JOHN

Field Court Chambers
2nd Floor 3 Field Court, Gray's Inn, London
WC1R 4EP, Telephone: 0171 404 7474
E-mail: Clerks@FieldCourtChambers.law.co.uk
Door Tenant
Call date: Nov 1992, Middle Temple
Qualifications: [BA (Hons, Kent), LLB (Hons)]

REYNOLD FREDERIC QC (1982)

New Court Chambers
5 Verulam Buildings, Gray's Inn, London
WC1R 5LY, Telephone: 0171 831 9500
E-mail: mail@newcourtchambers.com
Call date: July 1960, Gray's Inn
Qualifications: [BA (Oxon)]

REYNOLDS ADRIAN LEONARD

St Mary's Chambers
50 High Pavement, Lace Market, Nottingham
NG1 1HW, Telephone: 0115 9503503
E-mail: clerks@smc.law.co.uk
Call date: Nov 1982, Gray's Inn
Qualifications: [MA (Oxon)]

D

REYNOLDS PROFESSOR FRANCIS MARTIN BAILLIE

7 King's Bench Walk
Ground Floor, Temple, London EC4Y 7DS,
Telephone: 0171 583 0404
Call date: Feb 1961, Inner Temple
Qualifications: [DCL]

REYNOLDS GARY WILLIAM

Manchester House Chambers
18-22 Bridge Street, Manchester M3 3BZ,
Telephone: 0161 834 7007
Call date: Nov 1994, Lincoln's Inn
Qualifications: [BSc (Hons)(Portsm), Dip in Law (Staff)]

REYNOLDS JONATHAN JAMES

2 Middle Temple Lane
3rd Floor, Temple, London EC4Y 9AA,
Telephone: 0171 583 4540
Door Tenant
Call date: Nov 1992, Inner Temple
Qualifications: [LLB (Lond)]

REYNOLDS KIRK QC (1993)

Falcon Chambers
Falcon Court, London EC4Y 1AA,
Telephone: 0171 353 2484/7
Call date: July 1974, Middle Temple
Qualifications: [MA (Cantab)]

REYNOLDS MISS STELLA LOUISE

3 Temple Gardens
Lower Ground Floor, Temple, London
EC4Y 9AU, Telephone: 0171 353 3102/5/9297
Call date: July 1983, Gray's Inn
Qualifications: [LLB (Liverpool)]

REYNOLDS STEPHEN ALAN

29 Bedford Row Chambers
London WC1R 4HE,
Telephone: 0171 831 2626
Call date: Nov 1987, Inner Temple
Qualifications: [BA]

REZA HASHIM

17 Bedford Row
London WC1R 4EB,
Telephone: 0171 831 7314
E-mail: IBoard7314@AOL.com
Call date: July 1981, Middle Temple
Qualifications: [LLB (Leics)]

RHIND MARK ALEXANDER

24a St John Street
Manchester M3 4DF,
Telephone: 0161 833 9628
Call date: Nov 1989, Middle Temple
Qualifications: [LLB Hons (Manc)]

RHODES MISS AMANDA LOUISE

Holborn Chambers
6 Gate Street, Lincoln's Inn Fields, London
WC2A 3HP, Telephone: 0171 242 6060
Call date: May 1990, Lincoln's Inn
Qualifications: [LL.B.]

RHODES COLIN HARVEY

1 Gray's Inn Square
Ground Floor, London WC1R 5AA,
Telephone: 0171 405 8946/7/8
Call date: Nov 1994, Lincoln's Inn
Qualifications: [LLB (Hons)(Leic)]

RHODES MISS KAREN

2 Paper Buildings
Basement, Temple, London EC4Y 7ET,
Telephone: 0171 353 0933
Call date: Oct 1990, Gray's Inn
Qualifications: [BH (Hons), Dip Law]

RHODES NICHOLAS PIERS

2 Dr Johnson's Building
Temple, London EC4Y 7AY,
Telephone: 0171 353 4716
Call date: July 1981, Lincoln's Inn
Qualifications: [LLB (E Anglia)]

RHODES ROBERT ELLIOTT QC (1989)

4 King's Bench Walk
Ground/First Floor, Temple, London
EC4Y 7DL, Telephone: 0171 822 8822
E-mail: 4kbw@barristersatlaw.com
Call date: July 1968, Inner Temple
Recorder
Qualifications: [MA (Oxon)]

RHYS JOHN OWEN

17 Old Bldgs
Ground Floor, Lincoln's Inn, London
WC2A 3UP, Telephone: 0171 405 9653
St Mary's Chambers
50 High Pavement, Lace Market, Nottingham
NG1 1HW, Telephone: 0115 9503503
E-mail: clerks@smc.law.co.uk
Call date: July 1976, Gray's Inn
Qualifications: [MA (Cantab)]

RHYS MS MEGAN JILL

Paradise Square Chambers
26 Paradise Square, Sheffield S1 2DE,
Telephone: 0114 2738951
Call date: Nov 1994, Inner Temple
Qualifications: [LLB (Sheff)]

RICE CHRISTOPHER DOUGLAS

2 Gray's Inn Square Chambers
2nd Floor, Gray's Inn, London WC1R 5AA,
Telephone: 0171 242 0328/071 405 1317
E-mail: clerks@2gis.co.uk
Call date: July 1991, Middle Temple
Qualifications: [BA (Hons)]

RICH MISS ANN BARBARA

5 Stone Buildings
Lincoln's Inn, London WC2A 3XT,
Telephone: 0171 242 6201
E-mail: clerks@5-stonebuildings.law.co.uk
Call date: Oct 1990, Gray's Inn
Qualifications: [MA (Cantab), Dip Law]

RICH CHARLES STEPHEN ANTHONY

67a Westgate Road
Newcastle Upon Tyne NE1 1SQ,
Telephone: 0191 261 4407/2329785
Call date: July 1972, Gray's Inn
Qualifications: [LLB (Hons), LLM]

RICH JONATHAN BERNARD GEORGE

5 Paper Bldgs
Ground Floor, Temple, London EC4Y 7HB,
Telephone: 0171 583 9275/583 4555
E-mail: 5paper@link.org
Call date: July 1989, Middle Temple
Qualifications: [BA (Cantab)]

RICH SIMEON PAUL

Assize Court Chambers
14 Small Street, Bristol BS1 1DE,
Telephone: 0117 9264587
Call date: Nov 1991, Lincoln's Inn
Qualifications: [LLB (Hons)]

RICHARD LORD IVOR SEWARD QC (1971)

2 Paper Bldgs
1st Floor, Temple, London EC4Y 7ET,
Telephone: 0171 936 2611 (10 Lines)
E-mail: clerks@2pbbarristers.co.uk
Call date: Nov 1955, Inner Temple
Qualifications: [BA (Oxon)]

RICHARDS DAVID ANTHONY STEWART QC (1992)

Erskine Chambers
30 Lincoln's Inn Fields, Lincoln's Inn, London
WC2A 3PF, Telephone: 0171 242 5532
E-mail: Clerks@Erskine-Chambers.law.co.uk
Call date: Nov 1974, Inner Temple
Qualifications: [MA (Cantab)]

RICHARDS CAPTAIN DAVID JAMES MARTIN

East Anglian Chambers
Sanders House 52 North Hill, Colchester
CO1 1PY, Telephone: 01206 572756
East Anglian Chambers
Gresham House 5 Museum Street, Ipswich
IP1 1HQ, Telephone: 01473 214481
East Anglian Chambers
57 London Street, Norwich NR2 1HL,
Telephone: 01603 617351
Call date: July 1989, Middle Temple
Qualifications: [LLB (Cantab), MA (Cantab),
LLM]

RICHARDS DAVID RAWSON

1 Harcourt Bldgs
2nd Floor, Temple, London EC4Y 9DA,
Telephone: 0171 353 9421/9151
Call date: July 1981, Inner Temple
Qualifications: [LLB (Brunel)]

RICHARDS DAVID WYN

Iscoed Chambers
86 St Helen's Road, Swansea SA1 4BQ,
Telephone: 01792 652988/9/330
Call date: Nov 1968, Inner Temple
Recorder
Qualifications: [MA (Cantab), LLB (Lond)]

RICHARDS HUGH ALAN

5 Fountain Court
Steelhouse Lane, Birmingham B4 6DR,
Telephone: 0121 606 0500
Call date: Nov 1992, Inner Temple
Qualifications: [BSc (Wales), Dip in Law]

RICHARDS IAN

Pump Court Tax Chambers
16 Bedford Row, London WC1R 4EB,
Telephone: 0171 414 8080
Call date: Nov 1971, Lincoln's Inn
Qualifications: [BA]

RICHARDS MISS JENNIFER

39 Essex Street
London WC2R 3AT,
Telephone: 0171 583 1111
E-mail: clerks@39essex.co.uk
Call date: Oct 1991, Middle Temple
Qualifications: [MA (Hons) (Cantab), LLM
(Toronto)]

RICHARDS JEREMY SIMON

Octagon House
19 Colegate, Norwich NR3 1AT,
Telephone: 01603 623186
E-mail: octagon@netmatters.co.uk
Call date: July 1981, Gray's Inn
Assistant Recorder
Qualifications: [LLB (Wales)]

RICHARDS MS JOANNE

John Street Chambers
2 John Street, London WC1N 2HJ,
Telephone: 0171 242 1911
E-mail: john.street_chambers@virgin.net.uk
Call date: Nov 1992, Inner Temple
Qualifications: [BA, Dip in Law (City)]

RICHARDS DR JONATHAN NICHOLAS

Godolphin Chambers
50 Castle Street, Truro, Cornwall TR1 3AF,
Telephone: 01872 276312
Call date: Oct 1995, Middle Temple
Qualifications: [MB, Ch.B (Bris), CPE]

RICHARDS MISS KATHY JANINE

York House
Borough Road, Middlesbrough, Cleveland
TS1 2HJ, Telephone: 01642 213000
Call date: Oct 1995, Lincoln's Inn
Qualifications: [LLB (Hons)(Northumb)]

RICHARDS PHILIP BRIAN

30 Park Place
Cardiff CF1 3BA, Telephone: 01222 398421
E-mail: 100757.1456@compuserve.com
Call date: July 1969, Inner Temple
Assistant Recorder
Qualifications: [LLB (Bris) (Hons)]

RICHARDS STEPHEN THOMAS

All Saints Chambers
9/11 Broad Street, Bristol BS1 2HP,
Telephone: 0117 921 1966
Call date: Oct 1993, Middle Temple
Qualifications: [BA (Hons))L'pool), BA
(Hons)(Cantab), Dip History Studies]

RICHARDSON (PETER) JAMES

23 Essex Street
London WC2R 3AS,
Telephone: 0171 413 0353/353 3533
E-mail: clerks@essexstreet23.demon.co.uk
Call date: July 1975, Gray's Inn
Qualifications: [LLM LLB (Lond) Dip, Crim
(Cantab)]

RICHARDSON MISS ANNE LYDIA

Broad Chare
33 Broad Chare, Newcastle Upon Tyne
NE1 3DQ, Telephone: 0191 232 0541
Call date: July 1986, Inner Temple
Qualifications: [LLB (B'ham)]

RICHARDSON DAVID JOHN

13 King's Bench Walk
1st Floor, Temple, London EC4Y 7EN,
Telephone: 0171 353 7204
E-mail: clerks@13kbw.law.co.uk
King's Bench Chambers
32 Beaumont Street, Oxford OX1 2NP,
Telephone: 01865 311066
E-mail: clerks@kbc-oxford.law.co.uk
Call date: July 1973, Middle Temple
Recorder
Qualifications: [MA, LLB (Cantab)]

RICHARDSON GARTH DOUGLAS ANTHONY

3 Paper Bldgs
1st Floor, Temple, London EC4Y 7EU,
Telephone: 0171 583 8055
E-mail: london@3paper.com
20 Lorne Park Road
Bournemouth BH1 1JN,
Telephone: 01202 292102 (5 Lines)
4 St Peter Street
Winchester SO23 8OW,
Telephone: 01962 868884
Call date: July 1975, Middle Temple
Qualifications: [LLB]

RICHARDSON JAMES DAVID

Trinity Chambers
9-12 Trinity Chare, Quayside, Newcastle Upon
Tyne NE1 3DF, Telephone: 0191 232 1927
Call date: Nov 1982, Gray's Inn
Qualifications: [LLB (Leic)]

RICHARDSON JEREMY WILLIAM

11 King's Bench Walk
1st Floor, Temple, London EC4Y 7EQ,
Telephone: 0171 353 3337
3 Park Court
Leeds LS1 2QH, Telephone: 0113 297 1200
Call date: July 1980, Inner Temple
Qualifications: [LLB (Lond)]

RICHARDSON PAUL

New Court Chambers
3 Broad Chare, Newcastle Upon Tyne
NE1 3DQ, Telephone: 0191 232 1980
Call date: Nov 1986, Middle Temple
Qualifications: [BA]

RICHARDSON PAUL ANDREW

Bell Yard Chambers
116/118 Chancery Lane, London WC2A 1PP,
Telephone: 0171 306 9292
Call date: Feb 1993, Inner Temple
Qualifications: [LLB (So'ton)]

RICHARDSON PAUL BRAYSHAW

Peel Court Chambers
45 Hardman Street, Manchester M3 3HA,
Telephone: 0161 832 3791
Call date: Nov 1972, Middle Temple
Qualifications: [MA (Oxon)]

RICHARDSON MISS SARAH JANE

Enterprise Chambers
9 Old Square, Lincoln's Inn, London
WC2A 3SR, Telephone: 0171 405 9471
Enterprise Chambers
38 Park Square, Leeds LS1 2PA,
Telephone: 01132 460391
Enterprise Chambers
65 Quayside, Newcastle upon Tyne NE1 3DS,
Telephone: 0191 222 3344
Call date: Oct 1993, Inner Temple
Qualifications: [BA (Nott'm)]

RICHMAN MRS HELENE PINES

11 Stone Bldgs
1st Floor, Lincoln's Inn, London WC2A 3TG,
Telephone: 0171 404 5055
E-mail: 9stoneb@compuserve.com
Call date: July 1992, Middle Temple
Qualifications: [BA (Hons)(University, of
Pennsylvania)]

RICHMOND BERNARD GRANT

Lamb Building
Ground Floor, Temple, London EC4Y 7AS,
Telephone: 0171 797 7788
E-mail: lamb.building@link.org
Call date: July 1988, Middle Temple
Qualifications: [LLB (Hons)]

D

RICKARBY WILLIAM EDMUND

6 Fountain Court
Steelhouse Lane, Birmingham B4 6DR,
Telephone: 0121 233 3282
Call date: July 1975, Gray's Inn
Qualifications: [LLB (Hons)]

RIDD DAVID IAN MCGREGOR

4 Paper Bldgs
2nd Floor, Temple, London EC4Y 7EX,
Telephone: 0171 583 0816/071 353 1131
E-mail: clerks@4paperbuildings.co.uk
Call date: July 1975, Middle Temple
Qualifications: [BA (Hons)(Oxon), FCIArb]

RIDDELL DAVID ANDREW

Cobden House Chambers
19 Quay Street, Manchester M3 3HN,
Telephone: 0161 833 6000
E-mail: clerks@cobden.co.uk
Call date: Oct 1993, Middle Temple
Qualifications: [MA (Hons)(Cantab)]

RIDDLE NICHOLAS FINDLAY

Adrian Lyon's Chambers
14 Castle Street, Liverpool L2 0NE,
Telephone: 0151 236 4421/8240
E-mail: chambers14@aol.com
Call date: July 1970, Gray's Inn
Qualifications: [MA (Cantab)]

RIDING HENRY

The Corn Exchange
5th Floor Fenwick Street, Liverpool L2 7QS,
Telephone: 0151 227 1081/5009
Call date: July 1981, Middle Temple
Qualifications: [LLB (Hons)]

RIDLEY STEPHEN RONALD

Sackville Chambers
Sackville Place 44-48 Magdalen Street,
Norwich NR3 1JU, Telephone: 01603 613516/
616221
Call date: July 1977, Middle Temple
Qualifications: [LLB (Hons)(Lond)]

RIFAT MAURICE ALAN

Verulam Chambers
Peer House 8-14 Verulam Street, Gray's Inn,
London WC1X 8LZ,
Telephone: 0171 813 2400
Call date: Nov 1990, Inner Temple
Qualifications: [LLB]

RIGBY MISS CHARITY ELIZABETH

25 Park Square
Leeds LS1 2PW, Telephone: 0113 2451841/2/3
E-mail: sovereignchambers@btinternet.com
Call date: Oct 1993, Lincoln's Inn
Qualifications: [LLB (Hons)(Leic)]

RIGBY TERENCE

9 St John Street
Manchester M3 4DN,
Telephone: 0161 955 9000
E-mail: ninesjs@gconnect.com
Call date: May 1971, Gray's Inn
Recorder
Qualifications: [LLB (Nottm), BCL (Ox)]

RIGNEY ANDREW JAMES

2 Crown Office Row
Ground Floor, Temple, London EC4Y 7HJ,
Telephone: 0171 797 8100
E-mail: mail@2cor.co.uk, or to individual
barristers at: [barrister's surname]@2cor.co.uk
Call date: Oct 1992, Gray's Inn
Qualifications: [MA (Cantab), Dip Law (City)]

RILEY BRIAN DOUGLAS

Francis Taylor Bldg
3rd Floor, Temple, London EC4Y 7BY,
Telephone: 0171 797 7250
Call date: July 1986, Gray's Inn
Qualifications: [MSc, LLB]

RILEY MISS CHRISTINE ANNE

9 St John Street
Manchester M3 4DN,
Telephone: 0161 955 9000
E-mail: ninesjs@gconnect.com
Call date: July 1974, Gray's Inn
Qualifications: [LLB]

RILEY JAMIE SPENCER

11 Stone Bldgs
Ground Floor, Lincoln's Inn, London
WC2A 3TG, Telephone: 0171 831 6381
E-mail: clerks@11StoneBuildings.law.co.uk
Call date: Nov 1995, Lincoln's Inn
Qualifications: [BA (Hons)]

RILEY MICHAEL JOHN

4 King's Bench Walk
2nd Floor, Temple, London EC4Y 7DL,
Telephone: 0171 353 3581
Call date: Nov 1983, Middle Temple
Qualifications: [BA (Hons)]

RILEY-SMITH TOBIAS AUGUSTINE WILLIAM

2 Harcourt Bldgs
Ground Floor/Left, Temple, London
EC4Y 9DB, Telephone: 0171 583 9020
E-mail: clerks@harcourt.co.uk
Call date: Nov 1995, Middle Temple
Qualifications: [MA (Cantab)]

RIMMER ANTHONY MICHAEL

Counsels' Chambers
2nd Floor 10-11 Gray's Inn Square, London
WC1R 5JD, Telephone: 0171 405 2576
Call date: July 1983, Gray's Inn
Qualifications: [BA]

RIORDAN KEVIN

Iscoed Chambers
86 St Helen's Road, Swansea SA1 4BQ,
Telephone: 01792 652988/9/330
Call date: Nov 1972, Gray's Inn
Qualifications: [BCL (Cork)]

RIORDAN STEPHEN VAUGHAN QC (1992)

25-27 Castle Street
1st Floor, Liverpool L2 4TA,
Telephone: 0151 227 5661/051 236 5072
Call date: July 1972, Inner Temple
Recorder
Qualifications: [LLB (L'pool)]

RIPPON MRS AMANDA JAYNE

East Anglian Chambers
Sanders House 52 North Hill, Colchester
CO1 1PY, Telephone: 01206 572756
East Anglian Chambers
57 London Street, Norwich NR2 1HL,
Telephone: 01603 617351
East Anglian Chambers
Gresham House 5 Museum Street, Ipswich
IP1 1HQ, Telephone: 01473 214481
Call date: Oct 1993, Gray's Inn
Qualifications: [BA, Dip Law]

RIPPON PAUL HOWARD

One Garden Court
Ground Floor, Temple, London EC4Y 9BJ,
Telephone: 0171 797 7900
Call date: Nov 1985, Gray's Inn

RITCHIE ANDREW GEORGE

9 Gough Square
London EC4A 3DE, Telephone: 0171 353 5371
Call date: Feb 1985, Inner Temple
Qualifications: [MA (Cantab)]

RITCHIE DAVID JOHN

10 Old Square
Ground Floor, Lincoln's Inn, London
WC2A 3SU, Telephone: 0171 405 0758
Call date: Nov 1970, Middle Temple
Qualifications: [MA (Oxon)]

RITCHIE MISS JEAN HARRIS QC (1992)

4 Paper Bldgs
Ground Floor, Temple, London EC4Y 7EX,
Telephone: 0171 353 3366/583 7155
E-mail: clerks@4paperbuildings.com
Call date: July 1970, Gray's Inn
Recorder
Qualifications: [LLM (McGill) LLB, (Lond)]

RITCHIE RICHARD BULKELEY

24 Old Bldgs
Ground Floor, Lincoln's Inn, London
WC2A 3UJ, Telephone: 0171 404 0946
E-mail: clerks@24oldbuildings.law.co.uk
Call date: July 1978, Middle Temple
Qualifications: [BA (Oxon)]

RITCHIE STUART MARTIN

Littleton Chambers
3 King's Bench Walk North, Temple, London
EC4Y 7HR, Telephone: 0171 797 8600
E-mail: littletonchambers@compuserve.com
Call date: Oct 1995, Middle Temple
Qualifications: [BA (Oxon)]

RITSON PROFESSOR JOHN

Clock Chambers
78 Darlington Street, Wolverhampton
WV1 4LY, Telephone: 01902 313444
Call date: July 1967, Lincoln's Inn
Qualifications: [LLB (Hons)]

RIVALLAND MARC-EDOUARD

1 Serjeants' Inn
5th Floor Fleet Street, Temple, London
EC4Y 1LL, Telephone: 0171 415 6666
E-mail: no1serjeantsinn@btinternet.com
Call date: July 1987, Middle Temple
Qualifications: [B.Com, LLB (Witwatersrand),
Dip Law, LLM]

RIVERS MRS ANDREA LOUISE

2 Gray's Inn Square Chambers
2nd Floor, Gray's Inn, London WC1R 5AA,
Telephone: 0171 242 0328/071 405 1317
E-mail: clerks@2gis.co.uk
Call date: Nov 1990, Middle Temple
Qualifications: [MA (Cantab)]

RIZA ALPER ALI QC (1991)

10 King's Bench Walk
1st Floor, Temple, London EC4Y 7EB,
Telephone: 0171 353 2501
Lloyds House Chambers
3rd Floor 18 Lloyds House, Lloyd Street,
Manchester M2 5WA,
Telephone: 0161 839 3371
Door Tenant
Call date: Nov 1973, Gray's Inn
Recorder, Assistant Recorder

ROACH MICHAEL WILLIAM

Albion Chambers
Broad Street, Bristol BS1 1DR,
Telephone: 0117 9272144
Call date: July 1975, Middle Temple
Qualifications: [LLB]

ROACH MISS SUSAN

169 Temple Chambers
Temple Avenue, London EC4Y 0DA,
Telephone: 0171 583 7644
Call date: Oct 1993, Inner Temple
Qualifications: [BA (Hons)]

ROBB ADAM DUNCAN

39 Essex Street
London WC2R 3AT,
Telephone: 0171 583 1111
E-mail: clerks@39essex.co.uk
Call date: Nov 1995, Inner Temple
Qualifications: [BA (Oxon)]

ROBBINS IAN GEOFFREY

One Garden Court
Ground Floor, Temple, London EC4Y 9BJ,
Telephone: 0171 797 7900
Call date: Feb 1991, Middle Temple
Qualifications: [LLB]

ROBERTS ADRIAN PAUL

2 Gray's Inn Square Chambers
2nd Floor, Gray's Inn, London WC1R 5AA,
Telephone: 0171 242 0328/071 405 1317
E-mail: clerks@2gis.co.uk
Call date: July 1988, Middle Temple
Qualifications: [BA (Cantab)]

ROBERTS ADRIAN PAUL

Phoenix Chambers
First Floor Gray's Inn Chambers, Gray's Inn,
London WC1R 5JA, Telephone: 0171 404 7888
Call date: Feb 1993, Lincoln's Inn
Qualifications: [LLB (Hons)]

ROBERTS MISS CATHERINE ANN

Erskine Chambers
30 Lincoln's Inn Fields, Lincoln's Inn, London
WC2A 3PF, Telephone: 0171 242 5532
E-mail: Clerks@Erskine-Chambers.law.co.uk
Call date: Nov 1986, Lincoln's Inn
Qualifications: [MA, LLM (Cantab)]

ROBERTS MISS CLARE JUSTINE

Francis Taylor Bldg
2nd Floor, Temple, London EC4Y 7BY,
Telephone: 0171 353 9942/3157
Call date: Nov 1988, Middle Temple
Qualifications: [LLB (Lond)]

ROBERTS DOMINIC DEOGRATIAS PERDITUS

3 Temple Gardens (North)
Fifth Floor, Temple, London EC4Y 9AU,
Telephone: 0171 353 0853/4/7222
E-mail: 100106.1577@compuserve.com
Call date: July 1977, Gray's Inn
Qualifications: [LLB (Lond)]

ROBERTS HILARY LLEWELYN ARTHUR

Newport Chambers
12 Clytha Park Road, Newport, Gwent
NP9 47L, Telephone: 01633 267403/255855
Call date: Nov 1978, Gray's Inn
Qualifications: [LLB (Aberystwyth)]

ROBERTS HUW EIFION

Sedan House
Stanley Place, Chester CH1 2LU,
Telephone: 01244 320480/348282
Call date: Nov 1993, Gray's Inn
Qualifications: [LLB, LLM]

ROBERTS JAMES MCCLINTOCK

1 King's Bench Walk
2nd Floor, Temple, London EC4Y 7DB,
Telephone: 0171 936 1500
E-mail: ddear@1kbw.co.uk
Call date: Oct 1993, Gray's Inn
Qualifications: [BA (Hons)(Oxon)]

ROBERTS JAMES PHILIP

Littman Chambers
12 Gray's Inn Square, London WC1R 5JP,
Telephone: 0171 404 4866
E-mail: admin@littmanchambers.com
Call date: Nov 1996, Middle Temple
Qualifications: [LLB (Hons)(Hull), MA (Sheff)]

ROBERTS MRS JENNIFER MARY

Queen Elizabeth Bldg
2nd Floor, Temple, London EC4Y 9BS,
Telephone: 0171 797 7837
Call date: July 1988, Inner Temple
Qualifications: [LLB (Soton)]

ROBERTS JEREMY MICHAEL GRAHAM QC (1982)

9 Gough Square
London EC4A 3DE, Telephone: 0171 353 5371
Call date: July 1965, Inner Temple
Recorder
Qualifications: [BA (Oxon)]

ROBERTS DR JOHN ANTHONY QC (1988)

20 Richmond Way
1st Floor, London W12 8LY,
Telephone: 0181 749 2004
12 Old Square
1st Floor, Lincoln's Inn, London WC2A 3TX,
Telephone: 0171 404 0875
Call date: Nov 1969, Gray's Inn
Recorder
Qualifications: [FCIArb, Doctor of Civil Law]

ROBERTS JOHN MERVYN

5 Essex Court
1st Floor, Temple, London EC4Y 9AH,
Telephone: 0171 410 2000
Call date: May 1963, Inner Temple
Recorder
Qualifications: [LLB]

ROBERTS DR JULIAN FRANCIS

Monckton Chambers
4 Raymond Buildings, Gray's Inn, London
WC1R 5BP, Telephone: 0171 405 7211
E-mail: chambers@monckton.co.uk
Door Tenant
Call date: July 1987, Lincoln's Inn
Qualifications: [BA, MA, PhD (Cantab),
Rechtsanwalt]

D

D

ROBERTS MISS LISA

Lincoln House Chambers
5th Floor Lincoln House, 1 Brazennose Street,
Manchester M2 5EL,
Telephone: 0161 832 5701
E-mail: LincolnHouseChambers@link.org
Call date: Oct 1993, Lincoln's Inn
Qualifications: [LLB]

ROBERTS MARC ALEXANDER

4 Brick Court
Temple, London EC4Y 9AD,
Telephone: 0171 797 8910
Call date: Nov 1984, Inner Temple
Qualifications: [BA]

ROBERTS MARK VAUGHAN

21 White Friars
Chester CH1 1NZ, Telephone: 01244 323070
Call date: Nov 1991, Inner Temple
Qualifications: [LLB (Sheff)]

ROBERTS MICHAEL CHARLES

1 New Square
Ground Floor, Lincoln's Inn, London
WC2A 3SA, Telephone: 0171 405 0884/5/6/7
E-mail: 1newsquare@compuserve.com
Call date: July 1978, Lincoln's Inn
Qualifications: [BA (Cantab)]

ROBERTS MISS PATRICIA

Bridewell Chambers
2 Bridewell Place, London EC4V 6AP,
Telephone: 0171 797 8800
E-mail: clerks@bridewell.law.co.uk
Call date: Nov 1987, Gray's Inn
Qualifications: [LLB (L'pool)]

ROBERTS RICHARD JAMES LLOYD

Lamb Building
Ground Floor, Temple, London EC4Y 7AS,
Telephone: 0171 797 7788
E-mail: lamb.building@link.org
Call date: July 1983, Middle Temple
Qualifications: [BA]

ROBERTS STUART ROYD

37 Park Square
Leeds LS1 2NY, Telephone: 0113 2439422
Call date: Nov 1994, Middle Temple
Qualifications: [BA (Hons)]

ROBERTS TIMOTHY DAVID

Fountain Chambers
Cleveland Business Centre 1 Watson Street,
Middlesbrough TS1 2RQ,
Telephone: 01642 217037
Call date: July 1978, Gray's Inn
Recorder
Qualifications: [LLB (Soton)]

ROBERTSHAW MARTIN ANDREW

39 Park Square
Leeds LS1 2NU, Telephone: 0113 2456633
Call date: Nov 1977, Middle Temple
Qualifications: [LLB (Sheff)]

ROBERTSHAW MISS MIRANDA-LOUISE

2 King's Bench Walk
Ground Floor, Temple, London EC4Y 7DE,
Telephone: 0171 353 1746
E-mail: 2kbw@atlas.co.uk
King's Bench Chambers
115 North Hill, Plymouth PL4 8JY,
Telephone: 01752 221551
Call date: Nov 1985, Gray's Inn
Qualifications: [BA, Dip Law]

ROBERTSON AIDAN MALCOLM DAVID

Monckton Chambers
4 Raymond Buildings, Gray's Inn, London
WC1R 5BP, Telephone: 0171 405 7211
E-mail: chambers@monckton.co.uk
Call date: July 1995, Middle Temple
Qualifications: [MA, LLM (Cantab)]

ROBERTSON MS ALICE MICHELLE

6 Pump Court
Ground Floor, Temple, London EC4Y 7AR,
Telephone: 0171 583 6013/2510
Call date: Oct 1996, Gray's Inn
Qualifications: [LLB (Sussex)]

ROBERTSON ANDREW JAMES QC (1996)

11 King's Bench Walk
1st Floor, Temple, London EC4Y 7EQ,
Telephone: 0171 353 3337
3 Park Court
Leeds LS1 2QH, Telephone: 0113 297 1200
Call date: July 1975, Middle Temple
Recorder
Qualifications: [MA (Cantab)]

ROBERTSON ANGUS FREDERICK

Eighteen Carlton Crescent
Southampton SO15 2XR,
Telephone: 01703 639001
Call date: July 1978, Middle Temple
Qualifications: [BA]

ROBERTSON GEOFFREY RONALD QC (1988)

Doughty Street Chambers
11 Doughty Street, London WC1N 2PG,
Telephone: 0171 404 1313
E-mail: doughty_street@compuserve.com
Call date: July 1973, Middle Temple
Assistant Recorder
Qualifications: [BA, LLB, BCL]

ROBERTSON JAMES GRAHAM

New Bailey Chambers
10 Lawson Street, Preston PR1 2QT,
Telephone: 01772 258087
Door Tenant
Call date: Feb 1991, Gray's Inn
Qualifications: [BSc, LLB]

ROBERTSON JAMES JOLLYON

10 King's Bench Walk
1st Floor, Temple, London EC4Y 7EB,
Telephone: 0171 353 2501
Call date: Feb 1983, Middle Temple
Qualifications: [BA]

ROBERTSON MISS PATRICIA GRACE

Fountain Court
Temple, London EC4Y 9DH,
Telephone: 0171 583 3335
E-mail: chambers@fountaincourt.co.uk
Call date: Nov 1988, Inner Temple
Qualifications: [BA (Oxon), Dip Law (City)]

ROBERTSON MS SALLY ELIZABETH

Cloisters
1st Floor, Temple, London EC4Y 7AA,
Telephone: 0171 827 4000
E-mail: clerks@cloisters.com
Call date: Nov 1995, Inner Temple
Qualifications: [BA (Hons) (Reading), MSc (LSE)]

ROBINS MISS ALISON ELIZABETH

10 King's Bench Walk
Ground Floor, Temple, London EC4Y 7EB,
Telephone: 0171 353 7742
E-mail: 10kbw@lineone.net
Call date: Feb 1987, Gray's Inn
Qualifications: [BA Law (Dunelm)]

ROBINS MISS IMOGEN

Eighteen Carlton Crescent
Southampton SO15 2XR,
Telephone: 01703 639001
Call date: Oct 1991, Inner Temple
Qualifications: [LLB]

ROBINSON ADRIAN CARINS

Park Court Chambers
40 Park Cross Street, Leeds LS1 2QH,
Telephone: 0113 2433277
Call date: July 1981, Inner Temple
Qualifications: [MA (Oxon)]

ROBINSON MISS ALICE

4 Breams Buildings
London EC4A 1AQ,
Telephone: 0171 353 5835/430 1221
Call date: July 1983, Gray's Inn
Qualifications: [LLB (Cardiff)]

ROBINSON MISS CLAIRE MARIA

2 Dr Johnson's Building
Temple, London EC4Y 7AY,
Telephone: 0171 353 4716
Call date: Oct 1991, Gray's Inn
Qualifications: [BA (Oxon)]

D

ROBINSON DANIEL MICHAEL

Bell Yard Chambers
116/118 Chancery Lane, London WC2A 1PP,
Telephone: 0171 306 9292
Call date: Nov 1993, Lincoln's Inn
Qualifications: [BSc (Hons, Wales), CPE]

ROBINSON DAVID GARIN ALEXANDER

Regent Chambers
29 Regent Road, Hanley, Stoke On Trent
ST1 3BP, Telephone: 01782 286666
E-mail: regent@ftech.co.uk
Call date: Oct 1992, Middle Temple
Qualifications: [BA (Hons, Wales)]

ROBINSON GRAHAM

Paradise Square Chambers
26 Paradise Square, Sheffield S1 2DE,
Telephone: 0114 2738951
Plowden Bldgs
2nd Floor, Temple, London EC4Y 9BU,
Telephone: 0171 583 0808
E-mail: bar@plowdenbuildings.co.uk
Call date: July 1981, Inner Temple
Qualifications: [LLB (Hull)]

ROBINSON JAMES DOUGLAS

Council of Legal Education
39 Eagle Street, London WC1 4AJ
Call date: Nov 1991, Inner Temple
Qualifications: [LLB (Reading)]

ROBINSON JAMES EDWARD

York Chambers
14 Toft Green, York YO1 1JT,
Telephone: 01904 620048
E-mail: yorkchambers.co.uk
Call date: Oct 1992, Middle Temple
Qualifications: [MA (St.Andrews), Diploma in
Law]

ROBINSON MATTHEW JAMIE

Chartlands Chambers
3 St Giles Terrace, Northampton NN1 2BN,
Telephone: 01604 603322
Call date: Nov 1994, Inner Temple
Qualifications: [LLB (Lond)]

ROBINSON MICHAEL JOHN

Tower Hamlets Barristers Chambers
First Floor 45 Brick Lane, London E1 6PU,
Telephone: 0171 247 9825
Tower Hamlets Barristers Chambers
37B Princelet Street, London E1 5LP,
Telephone: 0171 377 8090
Call date: Nov 1976, Middle Temple
Qualifications: [LLB (Lond)]

ROBINSON RICHARD JOHN

2 Gray's Inn Square Chambers
2nd Floor, Gray's Inn, London WC1R 5AA,
Telephone: 0171 242 0328/071 405 1317
E-mail: clerks@2gis.co.uk
Call date: July 1977, Middle Temple
Qualifications: [BA (Cantab) LLM, (Lond)]

ROBINSON MISS SARA JANE

Broad Chare
33 Broad Chare, Newcastle Upon Tyne
NE1 3DQ, Telephone: 0191 232 0541
Call date: Nov 1994, Inner Temple
Qualifications: [LLB]

ROBINSON SIMON ROBERT

Chambers of Ian Macdonald QC
Waldorf House Cooper Street, Manchester
M2 2FW, Telephone: 0161 236 1840
Call date: Oct 1991, Lincoln's Inn
Qualifications: [LLB (Hons)]

ROBINSON VIVIAN QC (1986)

Hollis Whiteman Chambers
3rd/4th Floor Queen Elizabeth Bldg, Temple,
London EC4Y 9BS, Telephone: 0171 583 5766
E-mail: hollis.whiteman@btinternet.com
Call date: July 1967, Inner Temple
Recorder
Qualifications: [BA (Cantab)]

ROBLIN MISS LARAINE ARIANWEN

2 King's Bench Walk
Ground Floor, Temple, London EC4Y 7DE,
Telephone: 0171 353 1746
E-mail: 2kbw@atlas.co.uk
King's Bench Chambers
115 North Hill, Plymouth PL4 8JY,
Telephone: 01752 221551
Call date: July 1981, Lincoln's Inn
Qualifications: [LLB (Wales)]

D

ROBOTHAM JOHN ANSEL

Victoria Chambers
3rd Floor 177 Corporation Street, Birmingham
B4 6RG, Telephone: 0121 236 9900
Call date: Feb 1990, Inner Temple
Qualifications: [LLB (Manch)]

ROBSON DAVID ERNEST HENRY QC (1980)

New Court Chambers
3 Broad Chare, Newcastle Upon Tyne
NE1 3DQ, Telephone: 0191 232 1980
11 King's Bench Walk
1st Floor, Temple, London EC4Y 7EQ,
Telephone: 0171 353 3337
Call date: Feb 1965, Inner Temple
Recorder
Qualifications: [MA (Oxon)]

ROBSON JOHN MALCOLM

2 Gray's Inn Square Chambers
2nd Floor, Gray's Inn, London WC1R 5AA,
Telephone: 0171 242 0328/071 405 1317
E-mail: clerks@2gis.co.uk
Assize Court Chambers
14 Small Street, Bristol BS1 1DE,
Telephone: 0117 9264587
Door Tenant
Call date: July 1974, Inner Temple
Qualifications: [LLB (Lond), FCIArb]

ROBSON NICHOLAS DAVID

Baker Street Chambers
9 Baker Street, Middlesbrough TS1 2LF,
Telephone: 01642 873873
Call date: Oct 1994, Lincoln's Inn
Qualifications: [LLB (Hons)(L'pool)]

ROCHE BRENDAN KENNETH

9 Bedford Row
London WC1R 4AZ,
Telephone: 0171 242 3555
E-mail: clerks@9br.co.uk
Call date: July 1989, Middle Temple
Qualifications: [MA (Oxon), Dip Law]

ROCHE PATRICK RICHARD REDMOND

14 Tooks Court
Cursitor St, London EC4A 1LB,
Telephone: 0171 405 8828
E-mail: clerks @tooks.law.co.uk
Call date: July 1977, Middle Temple
Qualifications: [BA (Oxon)]

ROCHFORD THOMAS NICHOLAS BEVERLEY

Priory Chambers
2 Fountain Court, Steelhouse Lane,
Birmingham B4 6DR,
Telephone: 0121 236 3882/1375
Call date: July 1984, Inner Temple
Qualifications: [MA (Cantab)]

RODDICK (GEORGE) WINSTON QC (1986)

10 King's Bench Walk
1st Floor, Temple, London EC4Y 7EB,
Telephone: 0171 353 2501
9 Park Place
Cardiff CF1 3DP, Telephone: 01222 382731
Door Tenant
Call date: Nov 1968, Gray's Inn
Recorder
Qualifications: [LLM]

RODDY MISS MAUREEN BERNADETTE

India Buildings Chambers
Water Street, Liverpool L2 0XG,
Telephone: 0151 243 6000
Call date: July 1977, Middle Temple
Recorder
Qualifications: [LLB, LLM (Lond)]

RODGER ANDREW CHARLES JAMES

5 Paper Bldgs
Lower Ground Floor, Temple, London
EC4Y 7HB, Telephone: 0171 353 5638
E-mail: 107722,633@compuserve.com
Call date: July 1993, Gray's Inn
Qualifications: [LLB]

D

RODGER MISS CAROLINE BANKIER

Gray's Inn Chambers
5th Floor, Gray's Inn, London WC1R 5JA,
Telephone: 0171 404 1111
Call date: Nov 1968, Gray's Inn
Qualifications: [BA (Oxon)]

RODGER MARK STUART

30 Park Square
Leeds LS1 2PF, Telephone: 0113 2436388
Call date: Nov 1983, Gray's Inn
Qualifications: [LLB (Hons) (Bris)]

RODGER MARTIN OWEN

Falcon Chambers
Falcon Court, London EC4Y 1AA,
Telephone: 0171 353 2484/7
Call date: July 1986, Middle Temple
Qualifications: [BA (Oxon)]

RODGERS MISS DORIS JUNE

2 Harcourt Bldgs
1st Floor, Temple, London EC4Y 9DB,
Telephone: 0171 353 6961/7
Harcourt Chambers
Churchill House 3 St Aldate's Courtyard, St
Aldate's, Oxford OX1 1BN,
Telephone: 01865 791559
Call date: Nov 1971, Middle Temple
Recorder
Qualifications: [MA (Dub), MA (Oxon)]

RODHAM MISS SUSAN ANNE

1 Gray's Inn Square
1st Floor, London WC1R 5AG,
Telephone: 0171 405 3000
E-mail: clerks@onegrays.demon.co.uk
Call date: Nov 1989, Gray's Inn
Qualifications: [LLB]

RODIKIS MISS JOANNA

Old Colony House
6 South King Street, Manchester M2 6DQ,
Telephone: 0161 834 4364
Call date: Oct 1993, Middle Temple
Qualifications: [LLB (Hons)]

RODWAY MISS SUSAN CAROLINE

2 Temple Gardens
Temple, London EC4Y 9AY,
Telephone: 0171 583 6041 (12 Lines)
Call date: July 1981, Middle Temple
Qualifications: [BA (Lond)]

ROE THOMAS IDRIS

Goldsmith Building
1st Floor, Temple, London EC4Y 7BL,
Telephone: 0171 353 7881
E-mail: clerks@goldsmith-building.law.co.uk
Call date: Oct 1995, Middle Temple
Qualifications: [BA (Hons)]

ROEBUCK ROY DELVILLE

Bell Yard Chambers
116/118 Chancery Lane, London WC2A 1PP,
Telephone: 0171 306 9292
Call date: Nov 1974, Gray's Inn

ROGERS MISS BEVERLY-ANN

13 Old Square
1st Floor, Lincoln's Inn, London WC2A 3UA,
Telephone: 0171 242 6105
E-mail: clerks@serlecourt.co.uk
Call date: July 1978, Middle Temple
Qualifications: [LLB (Lond)]

ROGERS DONALD HALEY

Mitre House Chambers
Mitre House 44 Fleet Street, London
EC4Y 1BN, Telephone: 0171 583 8233
Call date: Nov 1991, Middle Temple
Qualifications: [LLB (Hons)]

ROGERS GREGORY CHARLES

St Ive's Chambers
9 Fountain Ct, Birmingham B4 6DR,
Telephone: 0121 236 0863/0929
Call date: Nov 1992, Gray's Inn
Qualifications: [BA]

ROGERS MS HEATHER

5 Raymond Buildings
1st Floor, Gray's Inn, London WC1R 5BP,
Telephone: 0171 242 2902
Call date: July 1983, Middle Temple
Qualifications: [LLB (LSE)]

ROGERS IAN PAUL

1 Crown Office Row
3rd Floor, Temple, London EC4Y 7HH,
Telephone: 0171 583 9292
E-mail: onecor@link.org
Call date: Oct 1995, Gray's Inn
Qualifications: [BA]

ROGERS JOHN MICHAEL THOMAS QC (1979)

9 Gough Square
London EC4A 3DE, Telephone: 0171 353 5371
40 King Street
Chester CH1 2AH, Telephone: 01244 323886
7 Fountain Court
Steelhouse Lane, Birmingham B4 6DR,
Telephone: 0121 236 8531
Call date: July 1963, Gray's Inn
Recorder
Qualifications: [MA, LLB (Cantab)]

ROGERS MARK NICHOLAS

St Mary's Chambers
50 High Pavement, Lace Market, Nottingham
NG1 1HW, Telephone: 0115 9503503
E-mail: clerks@smc.law.co.uk
Call date: July 1980, Middle Temple
Qualifications: [BA (Oxon)]

ROGERS PAUL JOHN

1 Crown Office Row
Ground Floor, Temple, London EC4Y 7HH,
Telephone: 0171 797 7500
Crown Office Row Chambers
Blenheim House 120 Church Street, Brighton,
Sussex BN1 1WH, Telephone: 01273 625625
Call date: July 1989, Inner Temple
Qualifications: [LLB (L'pool)]

ROGERS PHILIP CLIFFORD

22 Old Bldgs
Lincoln's Inn, London WC2A 3UJ,
Telephone: 0171 831 0222
Call date: May 1994, Inner Temple

ROGERSON ANDREW GORDON

Trafalgar Chambers
53 Fleet Street, London EC4Y 1BE,
Telephone: 0171 583 5858
E-mail: TrafalgarChambers@easynet.co.uk
Call date: July 1981, Middle Temple

ROLFE PATRICK JOHN BENEDICT

Lamb Chambers
Lamb Building, Temple, London EC4Y 7AS,
Telephone: 0171 797 8300
E-mail: lambchambers@link.org
Call date: Nov 1987, Middle Temple
Qualifications: [LLB (Lond)]

ROLLASON MICHAEL CHRISTOPHER

1 Essex Court
Ground Floor, Temple, London EC4Y 9AR,
Telephone: 0171 583 2000
E-mail: clerks@oneessexcourt.co.uk
Call date: Nov 1992, Inner Temple
Qualifications: [MA (Cantab)]

ROMAIN MISS CHARAN MARGARET HELENA

Martins Building
Water Street, Liverpool L2 3SP,
Telephone: 0151 236 5818/4919
Call date: Oct 1991, Inner Temple
Qualifications: [LLB (Hons) (Leics)]

ROMANS PHILIP RUTHERS

Furnival Chambers
32 Furnival Street, London EC4A 1JQ,
Telephone: 0171 405 3232
E-mail: clerks@furnivallaw.co.uk
Call date: Nov 1982, Gray's Inn
Qualifications: [MA Oxon]

ROMER MISS EMMA EVELYN MARTINDALE

22 Old Bldgs
Lincoln's Inn, London WC2A 3UJ,
Telephone: 0171 831 0222
Call date: Nov 1992, Lincoln's Inn
Qualifications: [BA (Hons), CPE]

ROMILLY EDMUND HUMPHREY SAMUEL

3 Temple Gardens
3rd Floor, Temple, London EC4Y 9AU,
Telephone: 0171 583 0010
Call date: Nov 1983, Gray's Inn
Qualifications: [BA (Lond)]

ROMNEY MISS DAPHNE IRENE

4 Field Court
Gray's Inn, London WC1R 5EA,
Telephone: 0171 440 6900
E-mail: chambers@4fieldcourt.co.uk
Call date: Nov 1979, Inner Temple
Qualifications: [BA (Cantab)]

RONKSLEY ANDREW PETER

Library Chambers
Gray's Inn Chambers, Gray's Inn, London
WC1R 5JA, Telephone: 0171 404 6500
Call date: Oct 1995, Gray's Inn
Qualifications: [BA]

ROOCHOVE MARK NATHAN

Trinity Chambers
140 New London Road, Chelmsford, Essex
CM2 0AW, Telephone: 01245 605040
Call date: Oct 1994, Gray's Inn
Qualifications: [BSc (Wales)]

ROOK PETER FRANCIS GROSVENOR QC (1991)

18 Red Lion Court
(Off Fleet Street), London EC4A 3EB,
Telephone: 0171 520 6000
Thornwood House
102 New London Road, Chelmsford, Essex
CM2 0RG, Telephone: 01245 280880
Call date: July 1973, Gray's Inn
Recorder
Qualifications: [MA (Cantab)]

ROOM STEWART

8 Stone Buildings
Lincoln's Inn, London WC2A 3TA,
Telephone: 0171 831 9881
Call date: Nov 1991, Middle Temple
Qualifications: [LLB Hons (B'ham)]

ROOTS GUY ROBERT GODFREY QC (1989)

2 Mitre Ct Bldgs
2nd Floor, Temple, London EC4Y 7BX,
Telephone: 0171 583 1380
Call date: July 1969, Middle Temple
Assistant Recorder
Qualifications: [MA (Oxon)]

ROPER MISS SOPHIA

5 Raymond Buildings
1st Floor, Gray's Inn, London WC1R 5BP,
Telephone: 0171 242 2902
Call date: Oct 1990, Middle Temple
Qualifications: [MA (Cantab), BCL (Oxon)]

ROSARIO DESMOND DAVID LUKE

Paradise Square Chambers
26 Paradise Square, Sheffield S1 2DE,
Telephone: 0114 2738951
Call date: Nov 1990, Inner Temple
Qualifications: [LLB (Sheff)]

ROSE ANTHONY KENNETH

Chavasse Court Chambers
2nd Floor Chavasse Court, 24 Lord Street,
Liverpool L2 1TA, Telephone: 0151 707 1191
Call date: Nov 1978, Middle Temple
Qualifications: [LLM (Lond)]

ROSE DAVID LESLIE

6 Park Square
Leeds LS1 2LW, Telephone: 0113 2459763
E-mail: chambers@no6.co.uk
Call date: July 1977, Middle Temple
Qualifications: [MA, LLB (Cantab)]

ROSE MISS DINAH GWEN LISON

2 Hare Court
Ground Floor, Temple, London EC4Y 7BH,
Telephone: 0171 583 1770
E-mail: 2_Hare_Court@link.org
Call date: July 1989, Gray's Inn
Qualifications: [BA (Oxon)]

ROSE PROFESSOR FRANCIS DENNIS

4 Essex Court
Temple, London EC4Y 9AJ,
Telephone: 0171 797 7970
E-mail: clerks@4essexcourt.law.co.uk
Call date: Nov 1983, Gray's Inn
Qualifications: [MA BCL PhD]

ROSE JONATHAN LEE

St Paul's House
5th Floor 23 Park Square South, Leeds
LS1 2ND, Telephone: 0113 2455866
Call date: July 1981, Middle Temple
Qualifications: [BA (Hons)]

ROSE JONATHAN PETER

2 Dr Johnson's Building
Temple, London EC4Y 7AY,
Telephone: 0171 353 4716
Call date: Nov 1986, Middle Temple
Qualifications: [LLB (London)]

ROSE MISS PAMELA SUSAN

8 King's Bench Walk
2nd Floor, Temple, London EC4Y 7DU,
Telephone: 0171 797 8888
8 King's Bench Walk North
1 Park Square East, Leeds LS1 2NE,
Telephone: 0113 2439797
Call date: July 1980, Inner Temple
Qualifications: [BA]

ROSE PAUL TELFER

Old Square Chambers
1 Verulam Buildings, Gray's Inn, London
WC1R 5LQ, Telephone: 0171 831 0801
Old Square Chambers
Hanover House 47 Corn Street, Bristol
BS1 1HT, Telephone: 0117 9277111
Call date: Nov 1981, Gray's Inn
Qualifications: [LLB (Reading)]

ROSE STEPHEN PAUL

5 Essex Court
1st Floor, Temple, London EC4Y 9AH,
Telephone: 0171 410 2000
Call date: Nov 1995, Gray's Inn
Qualifications: [BA (Oxon)]

ROSE WILLIAM MICHAEL

Verulam Chambers
Peer House 8-14 Verulam Street, Gray's Inn,
London WC1X 8LZ,
Telephone: 0171 813 2400
Call date: Nov 1972, Middle Temple
Qualifications: [LLB (Soton)]

ROSEN MURRAY HILARY QC (1993)

11 Stone Bldgs
Ground Floor, Lincoln's Inn, London
WC2A 3TG, Telephone: 0171 831 6381
E-mail: clerks@11StoneBuildings.law.co.uk
Call date: Nov 1976, Inner Temple
Qualifications: [BA (Cantab)]

ROSENBLATT JEREMY GEORGE

4 Paper Bldgs
2nd Floor, Temple, London EC4Y 7EX,
Telephone: 0171 583 0816/071 353 1131
E-mail: clerks@4paperbuildings.co.uk
Call date: July 1985, Gray's Inn
Qualifications: [LLB (Hons) (LSE)]

ROSS ANTHONY JOHN

3 Temple Gardens
3rd Floor, Temple, London EC4Y 9AU,
Telephone: 0171 583 0010
Call date: Oct 1991, Lincoln's Inn
Qualifications: [LLB (Hons) (Leeds)]

ROSS DAVID JOHN

1 Harcourt Bldgs
2nd Floor, Temple, London EC4Y 9DA,
Telephone: 0171 353 9421/9151
Call date: Nov 1974, Middle Temple
Qualifications: [LLB (Lond)]

ROSS GORDON MACRAE

2 Dr Johnson's Building
Temple, London EC4Y 7AY,
Telephone: 0171 353 4716
Call date: July 1986, Inner Temple
Qualifications: [LLB]

ROSS IAIN ALASDAIR

3 Paper Bldgs
1st Floor, Temple, London EC4Y 7EU,
Telephone: 0171 583 8055
E-mail: london@3paper.com
20 Lorne Park Road
Bournemouth BH1 1JN,
Telephone: 01202 292102 (5 Lines)
4 St Peter Street
Winchester SO23 8OW,
Telephone: 01962 868884
Call date: Nov 1991, Inner Temple
Qualifications: [LLB (Glasgow), Dip Law]

ROSS MISS JACQUELINE GORDON

Crown Office Row Chambers
Blenheim House 120 Church Street, Brighton,
Sussex BN1 1WH, Telephone: 01273 625625
Call date: Nov 1985, Middle Temple
Qualifications: [BA(Lond)]

D

ROSS JOHN GRAFFIN

1 Serjeants' Inn
5th Floor Fleet Street, Temple, London
EC4Y 1LL, Telephone: 0171 415 6666
E-mail: no1serjeantsinn@btinternet.com
Call date: July 1971, Inner Temple
Recorder
Qualifications: [LLM (Lond)]

ROSS MISS SALLY-ANN

28 St John Street
Manchester M3 4DJ,
Telephone: 0161 834 8418
E-mail: clerk@28stjohnst.co.uk
Call date: Oct 1990, Gray's Inn
Qualifications: [BA]

ROSS SIDNEY DAVID

11 Stone Bldgs
Ground Floor, Lincoln's Inn, London
WC2A 3TG, Telephone: 0171 831 6381
E-mail: clerks@11StoneBuildings.law.co.uk
Call date: July 1983, Middle Temple
Qualifications: [LLB, M.Sc, Ph.D]

ROSS MARTYN JOHN GREAVES

5 New Square
1st Floor, Lincoln's Inn, London WC2A 3RJ,
Telephone: 0171 404 0404
E-mail: Chambers@FiveNewSquare.CityScape.co.uk
Octagon House
19 Colegate, Norwich, Norfolk NR3 1AT,
Telephone: 01603 623186
E-mail: octagon@netmatters.co.uk
Door Tenant
Call date: July 1969, Middle Temple
Recorder
Qualifications: [MA, LLM (Cantab), FCIArb]

Fax: 0171 831 6016;
Out of hours telephone: 0181 467 9444;
DX: 272 London, Chancery Lane;
Other comms: E-mail
chambers@fivenewsquare.cityscape.co.uk

Types of work: Arbitration; Bankruptcy;
Chancery (general); Chancery land law;
Charities; Commercial property; Common land;
Conveyancing; Equity, wills and trusts; Family
provision; Insolvency; Landlord and tenant;
Partnerships; Pensions; Probate and
administration; Professional negligence

Other professional qualifications: Fellow of the
Chartered Institute of Arbitrators (Panel
Member)

Circuit: South Eastern

Awards and memberships: Member, Chancery
Bar Association; Professional Negligence Bar
Association; Society of Trust and Estate
Practitioners

Other professional experience: Recorder sitting
in the County Court and the Crown Court

Publications: *Williams, Mortimer and
Sunnucks on Executors, Administration and
Probate* (Joint Editor), 1993; *Theobald on Wills*
(Joint Editor), 1993; *Family Provision: Law
and Practice*, 1985

Reported cases: *Jones (AE) v Jones (EW)*,
[1997] 1 WLR 438, 1976. Co-ownership of land;
proprietary estoppel; tenants in common not
liable to pay rent.
Re Beaumont, [1980] Ch 444, 1979.
Inheritance (Provision for Family and
Dependants) Act 1975; person maintained by
deceased; assumption of responsibility.
Re Hetherington, [1990] Ch 1, 1989. Gift for
Roman Catholic Masses construed as gift for
public Masses and so charitable.
Re Finnemore, [1991] 1WLR 793, 1990.
Doctrine of Conditional Revocation can
preserve part of earlier will to take effect with
valid part of later will.
Taylor v Dickens, [1998] 1FLR 806, 1997.
Promise to leave house to gardener gave rights
neither under contract nor by proprietary
estoppel.

ROSS-MUNRO COLIN WILLIAM GORDON QC (1972)

2 Hare Court
Ground Floor, Temple, London EC4Y 7BH,
Telephone: 0171 583 1770
E-mail: 2_Hare_Court@link.org
Call date: June 1951, Middle Temple
Qualifications: [MA (Cantab)]

ROSSDALE PHILIP SAMUEL ANTHONY

10 Old Square
Ground Floor, Lincoln's Inn, London
WC2A 3SU, Telephone: 0171 405 0758
Call date: June 1948, Inner Temple
Qualifications: [MA, LLM (Cantab)]

ROTH PETER MARCEL QC (1997)

Monckton Chambers
4 Raymond Buildings, Gray's Inn, London
WC1R 5BP, Telephone: 0171 405 7211
E-mail: chambers@monckton.co.uk
Call date: July 1976, Middle Temple
Qualifications: [LLM, MA (Oxon)]

ROTHERY PETER

Queen's Chambers
5 John Dalton Street, Manchester M2 6ET,
Telephone: 0161 834 6875/4738
4 Camden Place
Preston PR1 3JL, Telephone: 01772 828300
Call date: Oct 1994, Lincoln's Inn
Qualifications: [BA (Hons)(Oxon)]

ROTHWELL MISS CAROLYN ANN

Bridewell Chambers
2 Bridewell Place, London EC4V 6AP,
Telephone: 0171 797 8800
E-mail: clerks@bridewell.law.co.uk
Call date: Oct 1991, Lincoln's Inn
Qualifications: [LLB (Hons)]

ROTHWELL MRS JOANNE LESLEY

Lamb Building
Ground Floor, Temple, London EC4Y 7AS,
Telephone: 0171 797 7788
E-mail: lamb.building@link.org
Call date: Oct 1993, Inner Temple
Qualifications: [LLB (Hons)]

ROTHWELL STEPHEN JOHN

28 St John Street
Manchester M3 4DJ,
Telephone: 0161 834 8418
E-mail: clerk@28stjohnst.co.uk
Call date: July 1977, Gray's Inn
Qualifications: [LLB (L'pool)]

ROUCH PETER CHRISTOPHER QC (1996)

9-12 Bell Yard
London WC2A 2LF,
Telephone: 0171 400 1800
Iscoed Chambers
86 St Helen's Road, Swansea SA1 4BQ,
Telephone: 01792 652988/9/330
Door Tenant
Call date: July 1972, Gray's Inn
Recorder
Qualifications: [LLB (Wales)]

ROUGHTON ASHLEY WENTWORTH

One Raymond Buildings
Gray's Inn, London WC1R 5BH,
Telephone: 0171 430 1234
E-mail: chambers@ipbar1rb.com;
clerks@ipbar1rb.com
Call date: Oct 1992, Inner Temple
Qualifications: [BSc (Eng)(Lond), PhD (Cantab), Dip. Law]

ROUSE JUSTIN CLIVE DOUGLAS

4 Brick Court
1st Floor, Temple, London EC4Y 9AD,
Telephone: 0171 583 8455
Call date: July 1982, Lincoln's Inn
Qualifications: [BA]

ROUSE NIGEL PHILIP

38 Young Street
Manchester M3 3FT,
Telephone: 0161 833 0489
E-mail: clerks@young-st-chambers.com
Call date: Feb 1993, Gray's Inn
Qualifications: [LLB (Manc)]

ROUTLEDGE SHAUN WILLIAM

Trinity Chambers
9-12 Trinity Chare, Quayside, Newcastle Upon
Tyne NE1 3DF, Telephone: 0191 232 1927
Call date: Nov 1988, Gray's Inn
Qualifications: [LLB (L'pool)]

ROUTLEY PATRICK

Goldsmith Building
1st Floor, Temple, London EC4Y 7BL,
Telephone: 0171 353 7881
E-mail: clerks@goldsmith-building.law.co.uk
Call date: July 1979, Inner Temple
Qualifications: [MA (Cantab)]

ROW CHARLES PHILIP

All Saints Chambers
9/11 Broad Street, Bristol BS1 2HP,
Telephone: 0117 921 1966
Call date: Oct 1993, Lincoln's Inn
Qualifications: [BA (Hons)(Portsmth)]

ROWE MISS DEBORAH JOY

Warwick House Chambers
8 Warwick Court, Gray's Inn, London
WC1R 5DJ, Telephone: 0171 430 2323
Call date: Nov 1990, Inner Temple
Qualifications: [BSC (Hons)(Surrey), MSc
(Lond), Dip Law (City), Cert Ed]

ROWE JOHN JERMYN QC (1982)

8 King Street
Manchester M2 6AQ,
Telephone: 0161 834 9560
Call date: Feb 1960, Middle Temple
Recorder
Qualifications: [MA (Oxon)]

ROWE MISS JUDITH MAY

One Garden Court
Ground Floor, Temple, London EC4Y 9BJ,
Telephone: 0171 797 7900
Call date: July 1979, Gray's Inn
Qualifications: [LLB (Lond)]

ROWELL DAVID STEWART

Chambers of Lord Goodhart QC
Ground Floor 3 New Square, Lincoln's Inn,
London WC2A 3RS,
Telephone: 0171 405 5577
E-mail: law@threenewsquare.demon.co.uk
Call date: July 1972, Gray's Inn
Qualifications: [BA (Oxon)]

ROWLAND MISS DERVILLE ANN

Sussex Chambers
9 Old Steine, Brighton BN1 1FJ,
Telephone: 01273 607953
Call date: Oct 1996, Inner Temple
Qualifications: [LLB]

ROWLAND JOHN PETER QC (1996)

4 Pump Court
Temple, London EC4Y 7AN,
Telephone: 0171 353 2656/9
E-mail: 4_pump_court@compuserve.com
Call date: Nov 1979, Middle Temple
Qualifications: [LLB (Lond), BA (W.Aust)]

ROWLAND NICHOLAS EDWARD

3 Paper Bldgs
1st Floor, Temple, London EC4Y 7EU,
Telephone: 0171 583 8055
E-mail: london@3paper.com
20 Lorne Park Road
Bournemouth BH1 1JN,
Telephone: 01202 292102 (5 Lines)
4 St Peter Street
Winchester SO23 8OW,
Telephone: 01962 868884
Call date: July 1988, Inner Temple
Qualifications: [BA (Bristol), Dip Law (City)]

ROWLANDS MS CATHERINE JANET

Victoria Chambers
3rd Floor 177 Corporation Street, Birmingham
B4 6RG, Telephone: 0121 236 9900
Call date: Nov 1992, Gray's Inn
Qualifications: [LLB (Lond), Maitrise en Droit,
(Paris)]

ROWLANDS DAVID PETER ANDREW

Broad Chare
33 Broad Chare, Newcastle Upon Tyne
NE1 3DQ, Telephone: 0191 232 0541
Call date: Nov 1988, Middle Temple
Qualifications: [LLB (Manch)]

ROWLANDS MARC HUMPHREYS

4 Pump Court
Temple, London EC4Y 7AN,
Telephone: 0171 353 2656/9
E-mail: 4_pump_court@compuserve.com
Call date: Nov 1990, Gray's Inn
Qualifications: [BA Hons (Oxon)]

ROWLANDS PETER FRANCIS CLEVELAND

4 Brick Court
Ground Floor, Temple, London EC4Y 9AD,
Telephone: 0171 797 7766
E-mail: chambers@4brick.co.uk
Call date: Feb 1990, Middle Temple
Qualifications: [BA Hons (Oxon)]

ROWLANDS RHYS PRICE

Sedan House
Stanley Place, Chester CH1 2LU,
Telephone: 01244 320480/348282
1 Dr Johnson's Bldgs
Ground Floor, Temple, London EC4Y 7AX,
Telephone: 0171 353 9328
Call date: July 1986, Gray's Inn
Qualifications: [MSc (Wales) LLB, (Lond)]

ROWLEY MRS ALISON CLAIRE

4 Fountain Court
Steelhouse Lane, Birmingham B4 6DR,
Telephone: 0121 236 3476
Call date: Nov 1987, Middle Temple
Qualifications: [MA (Cantab)]

ROWLEY JOHN JAMES

28 St John Street
Manchester M3 4DJ,
Telephone: 0161 834 8418
E-mail: clerk@28stjohnst.co.uk
Call date: July 1987, Lincoln's Inn
Qualifications: [MA (Cantab) Dip Law]

ROWLEY KARL JOHN

38 Young Street
Manchester M3 3FT,
Telephone: 0161 833 0489
E-mail: clerks@young-st-chambers.com
Call date: Nov 1994, Middle Temple
Qualifications: [BA (Hons)(Hons)]

ROWLEY KEITH NIGEL

11 Old Square
Ground Floor, Lincoln's Inn, London
WC2A 3TS, Telephone: 0171 430 0341
E-mail: clerks@11oldsquare.co.uk
Call date: July 1979, Gray's Inn
Qualifications: [LLB (Lond)]

ROWLEY MISS LESLEY LENORA JANE

32 Park Place
Cardiff CF1 3BA, Telephone: 01222 397364
Call date: July 1988, Gray's Inn
Qualifications: [LLB (Wales)]

ROWLING MISS FIONA JANE

Chambers of Helen Grindrod QC
1st Floor 95a Chancery Lane, London
WC2A 2JG, Telephone: 0171 404 4777
Call date: July 1980, Inner Temple
Qualifications: [LLB (Lond)]

ROWLINSON MISS WENDY JULIA

Chichester Chambers
12 North Pallant, Chichester, West Sussex
PO19 1TQ, Telephone: 01243 784538
Call date: July 1981, Gray's Inn
Qualifications: [BA]

ROWSELL MISS CLAIRE LOUISE

Albion Chambers
Broad Street, Bristol BS1 1DR,
Telephone: 0117 9272144
Call date: Feb 1991, Middle Temple
Qualifications: [LLB]

ROWSELL PAUL JOHN

2 King's Bench Walk
Ground Floor, Temple, London EC4Y 7DE,
Telephone: 0171 353 1746
E-mail: 2kbw@atlas.co.uk
King's Bench Chambers
115 North Hill, Plymouth PL4 8JY,
Telephone: 01752 221551
Call date: July 1971, Inner Temple
Qualifications: [LLB]

ROXBURGH ALAN JOHN NORTON

Brick Court Chambers
15/19 Devereux Court, London WC2R 3JJ,
Telephone: 0171 583 0777
E-mail: (surname)@brickcourt.demon.co.uk
Call date: Oct 1992, Middle Temple
Qualifications: [MA (Hons Oxon), Diploma in Law(City)]

D

ROY-TOOLE CHRISTOPHER LAWRENCE

Durham Barristers' Chambers
27 Old Elvet, Durham DH1 3HN,
Telephone: 0191 386 9199
Call date: Oct 1990, Middle Temple
Qualifications: [BA (Oxon), Dip Law (City)]

ROYCE DARRYL FRASER

1 Atkin Building
Gray's Inn, London WC1R 5AT,
Telephone: 0171 404 0102
E-mail: clerks@atkin-chambers.co.uk
Call date: Nov 1976, Gray's Inn
Qualifications: [BA]

ROYCE R JOHN QC (1987)

Guildhall Chambers
23 Broad Street, Bristol BS1 2HG,
Telephone: 0117 9273366
Call date: Nov 1970, Gray's Inn
Qualifications: [BA (Cantab)]

ROZHAN ARIFF

One Garden Court
Ground Floor, Temple, London EC4Y 9BJ,
Telephone: 0171 797 7900
Call date: Feb 1990, Inner Temple
Qualifications: [LLB (Read)]

RUBENS MRS JACQUELINE ANN

Trafalgar Chambers
53 Fleet Street, London EC4Y 1BE,
Telephone: 0171 583 5858
E-mail: TrafalgarChambers@easynet.co.uk
Eldon Chambers
Fourth Floor 30/32 Fleet Street, London
EC4Y 1AA, Telephone: 0171 353 4636
Call date: Nov 1989, Inner Temple
Qualifications: [BA (Florida), LLB (Lond)]

RUBERY PHILIP ALAN

8 King's Bench Walk
2nd Floor, Temple, London EC4Y 7DU,
Telephone: 0171 797 8888
8 King's Bench Walk North
1 Park Square East, Leeds LS1 2NE,
Telephone: 0113 2439797
Call date: July 1973, Lincoln's Inn

RUBIN ANTHONY JOHN MEEK

St James's Chambers
68 Quay Street, Manchester M3 3EJ,
Telephone: 0161 834 7000
E-mail: 106241.2625@compuserve.com
Door Tenant
Call date: May 1960, Gray's Inn

RUBIN STEPHEN CHARLES

Farrar's Building
Temple, London EC4Y 7BD,
Telephone: 0171 583 9241
E-mail: chambers@farrarsbuilding.co.uk
Call date: July 1977, Middle Temple
Qualifications: [MA (Oxon)]

RUCK MS MARY IDA

10 King's Bench Walk
1st Floor, Temple, London EC4Y 7EB,
Telephone: 0171 353 2501
Call date: Oct 1993, Gray's Inn
Qualifications: [BA (Hons), MA]

RUDD MATTHEW ALLAN

11 Bolt Court
London EC4A 3DQ,
Telephone: 0171 353 2300
E-mail: boltct11@aol.com
Redhill Chambers
Seloduct House 30 Station Road, Redhill
RH1 1NK, Telephone: 01737 780781
Call date: Nov 1994, Inner Temple
Qualifications: [BA (Hons)(Sheff)]

RUDLAND MARTIN WILLIAM

10 Park Square
Leeds LS1 2LH, Telephone: 0113 2455438
E-mail: chambers@bandit.legend.co.uk
Call date: July 1977, Middle Temple
Recorder
Qualifications: [LLB (Hons)]

RUDMAN MISS SARA ANN

4 King's Bench Walk
2nd Floor, Temple, London EC4Y 7DL,
Telephone: 0171 353 3581
Call date: Nov 1992, Inner Temple
Qualifications: [LLB (Hons)]

RUEFF PHILIP EDMOND BRUNO MARCUS

2 King's Bench Walk
1st Floor, Temple, London EC4Y 7DE,
Telephone: 0171 353 9276
Call date: Nov 1969, Gray's Inn
Recorder
Qualifications: [BA (Oxon) LLM (New, York)]

RUFFELL MARK BERESFORD

Trafalgar Chambers
53 Fleet Street, London EC4Y 1BE,
Telephone: 0171 583 5858
E-mail: TrafalgarChambers@easynet.co.uk
Call date: Nov 1992, Middle Temple
Qualifications: [BA (Hons), Diploma in Law]

RULE JONATHAN DANIEL

Merchant Chambers
1 North Parade, Parsonage Gardens,
Manchester M3 2NH,
Telephone: 0161 839 7070
Call date: Nov 1993, Gray's Inn
Qualifications: [BA (Hons, Oxon)]

RUMBELOW ARTHUR ANTHONY QC (1990)

28 St John Street
Manchester M3 4DJ,
Telephone: 0161 834 8418
E-mail: clerk@28stjohnst.co.uk
1 Serjeants' Inn
4th Floor, Temple, London EC4Y 1NH,
Telephone: 0171 583 1355
E-mail: serjeants.inn@virgin.net
Call date: July 1967, Middle Temple
Recorder
Qualifications: [BA (Cantab)]

RUMFITT NIGEL JOHN QC (1994)

9 Bedford Row
London WC1R 4AZ,
Telephone: 0171 242 3555
E-mail: clerks@9br.co.uk
Call date: July 1974, Middle Temple
Recorder
Qualifications: [BCL (Oxon), MA (Oxon)]

RUMNEY CONRAD WILLIAM ARTHUR

7 Fountain Court
Steelhouse Lane, Birmingham B4 6DR,
Telephone: 0121 236 8531
Call date: Feb 1988, Inner Temple
Qualifications: [MA (Oxon), Dip Law]

RUNDELL RICHARD JOHN

2-3 Gray's Inn Square
Gray's Inn, London WC1R 5JH,
Telephone: 0171 242 4986
E-mail: chambers@2-3graysinnsquare.co.uk
Call date: Feb 1971, Gray's Inn
Recorder
Qualifications: [LLB]

RUPASINHA SUNIL JAYANTHA

1 Harcourt Bldgs
2nd Floor, Temple, London EC4Y 9DA,
Telephone: 0171 353 9421/9151
Call date: Nov 1983, Inner Temple
Qualifications: [LLB (Cardiff)]

RUSCOE MISS JANET CAROLINE

New Walk Chambers
27 New Walk, Leicester LE1 6TE,
Telephone: 0116 2559144
Call date: Oct 1995, Lincoln's Inn
Qualifications: [LLB (Hons)(Northumb), LLM (Manch)]

RUSH CRAIG PETER

3 Hare Court
1st Floor, Temple, London EC4Y 7BJ,
Telephone: 0171 353 7561
Call date: Nov 1989, Inner Temple
Qualifications: [LLB]

RUSHBROOKE JUSTIN CHARLES NEIL

5 Raymond Buildings
1st Floor, Gray's Inn, London WC1R 5BP,
Telephone: 0171 242 2902
Call date: Oct 1992, Middle Temple
Qualifications: [MA (Oxon)]

RUSHTON MS NICOLA JANE

5 Paper Bldgs
Ground Floor, Temple, London EC4Y 7HB,
Telephone: 0171 583 9275/583 4555
E-mail: 5paper@link.org
Call date: Oct 1993, Gray's Inn
Qualifications: [BA (Cantab), LLM (Canada)]

RUSSELL MS ALISON ELIZABETH

King's Chambers
5a Gildredge Road, Eastbourne, East Sussex
BN21 4RB, Telephone: 01323 416053
Call date: Oct 1993, Middle Temple
Qualifications: [LLB (Hons, Essex)]

RUSSELL MS ALISON HUNTER

1 Pump Court
Lower Ground Floor, Temple, London
EC4Y 7AB, Telephone: 0171 583 2012/
353 4341
E-mail: (name) @1pumpcourt.co.uk
Call date: July 1983, Gray's Inn
Qualifications: [BA (Hons)]

RUSSELL ANTHONY PATRICK

Peel Court Chambers
45 Hardman Street, Manchester M3 3HA,
Telephone: 0161 832 3791
Call date: July 1974, Middle Temple
Qualifications: [MA (Oxon)]

RUSSELL MISS CHRISTINA MARTHA

9-12 Bell Yard
London WC2A 2LF,
Telephone: 0171 400 1800
Call date: Oct 1994, Gray's Inn
Qualifications: [MA (Cantab)]

RUSSELL CHRISTOPHER GARNET

12 New Square
Ground Floor, Lincoln's Inn, London
WC2A 3SW, Telephone: 0171 419 1212
E-mail: 12newsquare@compuserve.com
25 Park Square
Leeds LS1 2PW, Telephone: 0113 2451841/2/3
E-mail: sovereignchambers@btinternet.com
Door Tenant
Call date: Nov 1971, Middle Temple
Qualifications: [MA (Oxon)]

RUSSELL CHRISTOPHER JOHN

2 Temple Gardens
Temple, London EC4Y 9AY,
Telephone: 0171 583 6041 (12 Lines)
Call date: Nov 1982, Gray's Inn
Qualifications: [LLB (Exon)]

RUSSELL MISS FERN

2 King's Bench Walk
Ground Floor, Temple, London EC4Y 7DE,
Telephone: 0171 353 1746
E-mail: 2kbw@atlas.co.uk
King's Bench Chambers
115 North Hill, Plymouth PL4 8JY,
Telephone: 01752 221551
Call date: Nov 1994, Middle Temple
Qualifications: [BA (Hons)]

RUSSELL GUY JONOTHON

Westgate Chambers
144 High Street, Lewes, East Sussex BN7 1XT,
Telephone: 01273 480510
Door Tenant
Call date: Nov 1985, Gray's Inn
Qualifications: [BA]

RUSSELL MISS JENNIFER ANNE

Victoria Chambers
3rd Floor 177 Corporation Street, Birmingham
B4 6RG, Telephone: 0121 236 9900
Call date: Oct 1990, Middle Temple
Qualifications: [LLB (Hons)]

RUSSELL JEREMY FRANCIS JOHN

2 Pump Court
1st Floor, Temple, London EC4Y 7AH,
Telephone: 0171 353 5597
Call date: Nov 1973, Middle Temple
Qualifications: [MA (Cantab) LLB]

RUSSELL JEREMY JONATHAN
QC (1994)

4 Essex Court
Temple, London EC4Y 9AJ,
Telephone: 0171 797 7970
E-mail: clerks@4essexcourt.law.co.uk
Call date: Nov 1975, Middle Temple
Qualifications: [BA, LLM (Lond)]

RUSSELL MISS MARGUERITE

2 Garden Court
1st Floor, Middle Temple, London EC4Y 9BL,
Telephone: 0171 353 1633
E-mail: barristers@2gardenct.law.co.uk
Call date: July 1972, Lincoln's Inn

RUSSELL MARTIN HOWARD

17 Bedford Row
London WC1R 4EB,
Telephone: 0171 831 7314
E-mail: IBoard7314@AOL.com
Call date: Nov 1977, Inner Temple
Qualifications: [LLB]

RUSSELL PAUL ANTHONY WELLINGTON

12 King's Bench Walk
Temple, London EC4Y 7EL,
Telephone: 0171 583 0811
E-mail: chambers@12kbw.co.uk
Call date: July 1984, Middle Temple
Qualifications: [BA (Dunelm)]

RUSSELL ROBERT JOHN FINLAY

5 Bell Yard
London WC2A 2JR, Telephone: 0171 333 8811
Call date: Oct 1993, Middle Temple
Qualifications: [BA (Hons)(Oxon)]

RUSSELL FLINT SIMON COLERIDGE

23 Essex Street
London WC2R 3AS,
Telephone: 0171 413 0353/353 3533
E-mail: clerks@essexstreet23.demon.co.uk
Call date: Nov 1980, Inner Temple
Assistant Recorder
Qualifications: [BA]

RUSSEN JONATHAN HUW SINCLAIR

13 Old Square
Ground Floor, Lincoln's Inn, London
WC2A 3UA, Telephone: 0171 404 4800
Call date: July 1986, Lincoln's Inn
Qualifications: [LLB Wales, LLM, Cantab.]

RUSSEN SIMON NICHOLAS SINCLAIR

2 Crown Office Row
2nd Floor, Temple, London EC4Y 7HJ,
Telephone: 0171 797 8000
Call date: July 1976, Lincoln's Inn
Qualifications: [BA, FCIArb]

RUTHERFORD MARTIN

3 Temple Gardens
Lower Ground Floor, Temple, London
EC4Y 9AU, Telephone: 0171 353 3102/5/9297
Call date: Oct 1990, Lincoln's Inn
Qualifications: [BA (Cardiff), Dip Law]

RUTLEDGE KELVIN ALBERT

2 Field Court
Gray's Inn, London WC1R 5BB,
Telephone: 0171 405 6114
E-mail: fieldct2@netcomuk.co.uk.
Call date: July 1989, Middle Temple
Qualifications: [LLB (Essex), LLB (Lond)]

RUTTER ANDREW MICHAEL

3 Temple Gardens
2nd Floor, Temple, London EC4Y 9AU,
Telephone: 0171 583 1155
Call date: July 1990, Middle Temple
Qualifications: [LLB (Lond)]

RUTTLE STEPHEN QC (1997)

Brick Court Chambers
15/19 Devereux Court, London WC2R 3JJ,
Telephone: 0171 583 0777
E-mail: (surname)@brickcourt.demon.co.uk
Call date: Nov 1976, Gray's Inn
Qualifications: [BA (Cantab)]

RYAN DAVID PATRICK

46/48 Essex Street
London WC2R 3GH,
Telephone: 0171 583 8899
Call date: Nov 1985, Inner Temple
Qualifications: [LLB (Hons)]

RYAN MISS EITHNE MARY CATHERINE

Hardwicke Building
New Square, Lincoln's Inn, London
WC2A 3SB, Telephone: 0171 242 2523
E-mail: clerks@hardwicke.co.uk
Call date: July 1990, Inner Temple
Qualifications: [LLB (Dublin)]

RYAN GERARD CHARLES QC (1981)

2 Harcourt Bldgs
2nd Floor, Temple, London EC4Y 9DB,
Telephone: 0171 353 8415
E-mail: clerks@twoharcourtbldgs.demon.co.uk
Call date: June 1955, Middle Temple
Recorder
Qualifications: [MA (Cantab)]

RYAN NICHOLAS JOSEPH

Adrian Lyon's Chambers
14 Castle Street, Liverpool L2 0NE,
Telephone: 0151 236 4421/8240
E-mail: chambers14@aol.com
Call date: July 1984, Gray's Inn
Qualifications: [BA (Lond)]

RYAN THOMAS PATRICK FRANCIS

Derby Square Chambers
Merchants Court, Derby Square, Liverpool
L2 1TS, Telephone: 0151 709 4222
Goldsmith Building
1st Floor, Temple, London EC4Y 7BL,
Telephone: 0171 353 7881
E-mail: clerks@goldsmith-building.law.co.uk
Door Tenant
Call date: July 1979, Gray's Inn
Qualifications: [BA Hons (Keele)]

RYAN TIMOTHY JOHN

8 King's Bench Walk
2nd Floor, Temple, London EC4Y 7DU,
Telephone: 0171 797 8888
8 King's Bench Walk North
1 Park Square East, Leeds LS1 2NE,
Telephone: 0113 2439797
Call date: Nov 1991, Inner Temple
Qualifications: [LLB (Lond)]

RYAN WILLIAM

8 King's Bench Walk
2nd Floor, Temple, London EC4Y 7DU,
Telephone: 0171 797 8888
8 King's Bench Walk North
1 Park Square East, Leeds LS1 2NE,
Telephone: 0113 2439797
Call date: Oct 1994, Gray's Inn
Qualifications: [LLB (Hons)]

RYDE RICHARD ALEXANDER

3 Temple Gardens
3rd Floor, Temple, London EC4Y 9AU,
Telephone: 0171 353 0832
Call date: July 1986, Middle Temple
Qualifications: [BA (Hons) (Oxon)]

RYDER ERNEST NIGEL QC (1997)

8 King Street
Manchester M2 6AQ,
Telephone: 0161 834 9560
Call date: July 1981, Gray's Inn
Assistant Recorder
Qualifications: [MA (Cantab)]

RYDER JOHN

6 King's Bench Walk
Ground Floor, Temple, London EC4Y 7DR,
Telephone: 0171 583 0410
Call date: Nov 1980, Inner Temple
Assistant Recorder
Qualifications: [BA Hons]

RYDER MATTHEW CONRAD

Cloisters
1st Floor, Temple, London EC4Y 7AA,
Telephone: 0171 827 4000
E-mail: clerks@cloisters.com
Call date: Nov 1992, Gray's Inn
Qualifications: [BA]

RYDER TIMOTHY ROBERT

Queen's Chambers
5 John Dalton Street, Manchester M2 6ET,
Telephone: 0161 834 6875/4738
4 Camden Place
Preston PR1 3JL, Telephone: 01772 828300
Call date: July 1977, Middle Temple
Qualifications: [MA (Cantab)]

RYLANCE JOHN RANDOLPH TREVOR

Francis Taylor Bldg
Ground Floor, Temple, London EC4Y 7BY,
Telephone: 0171 353 7768/7769/2711
Call date: Nov 1968, Lincoln's Inn
Recorder

RYLANDS MISS MARGARET ELIZABETH

8 King Street
Manchester M2 6AQ,
Telephone: 0161 834 9560
Call date: Nov 1973, Middle Temple
Assistant Recorder
Qualifications: [LLB (Hons) (Bris)]

SABBEN-CLARE MISS REBECCA MARY

7 King's Bench Walk
Ground Floor, Temple, London EC4Y 7DS,
Telephone: 0171 583 0404
Call date: Oct 1993, Gray's Inn
Qualifications: [MA (Oxon)]

SABIDO JOHN HARRIES

1 Dr Johnson's Bldgs
Ground Floor, Temple, London EC4Y 7AX,
Telephone: 0171 353 9328
Dr Johnson's Chambers
The Atrium Court Apex Plaza, Reading
RG1 1AX, Telephone: 01734 254221
Call date: July 1976, Lincoln's Inn

SABINE JOHN ALEXANDER

College Chambers
19 Carlton Cresent, Southampton, Hants
SO15 2ET, Telephone: 01703 230338
Call date: July 1979, Gray's Inn
Qualifications: [MA BCL]

SABISTON PETER JOHN

Baker Street Chambers
9 Baker Street, Middlesbrough TS1 2LF,
Telephone: 01642 873873
Call date: Feb 1992, Gray's Inn
Qualifications: [LLB (N'Castle)]

SABRY KARIM SAMIR

Manchester House Chambers
18-22 Bridge Street, Manchester M3 3BZ,
Telephone: 0161 834 7007
Call date: Nov 1992, Inner Temple
Qualifications: [BA (Hons)]

SADD PATRICK JAMES THOMAS

199 Strand
London WC2R 1DR,
Telephone: 0171 379 9779
E-mail: chambers@199strand.co.uk
Call date: Nov 1984, Middle Temple
Qualifications: [BA]

SADIQ TARIQ MAHMOOD

9 St John Street
Manchester M3 4DN,
Telephone: 0161 955 9000
E-mail: ninesjs@gconnect.com
Call date: Nov 1993, Gray's Inn
Qualifications: [BA (Hons) (Kent)]

SAFFIAN MS LEAH SUSAN

Hollis Whiteman Chambers
3rd/4th Floor Queen Elizabeth Bldg, Temple,
London EC4Y 9BS, Telephone: 0171 583 5766
E-mail: hollis.whiteman@btinternet.com
Call date: July 1992, Gray's Inn
Qualifications: [BA, JD, LLM]

SAGAR (EDWARD) LEIGH

12 New Square
Ground Floor, Lincoln's Inn, London
WC2A 3SW, Telephone: 0171 419 1212
E-mail: 12newsquare@compuserve.com
Newport Chambers
12 Clytha Park Road, Newport, Gwent
NP9 47L, Telephone: 01633 267403/255855
Door Tenant
25 Park Square
Leeds LS1 2PW, Telephone: 0113 2451841/2/3
E-mail: sovereignchambers@btinternet.com
Door Tenant
Call date: July 1983, Lincoln's Inn
Qualifications: [BA (Lond)]

SAGGERSON ALAN DAVID

Barnard's Inn Chambers
6th Floor Halton House, 20-23 Holborn,
London EC1N 2JD, Telephone: 0171 242 8508
E-mail: clerks@barnards-inn-chambers.co.uk
Call date: July 1981, Lincoln's Inn
Qualifications: [MA, BCL (Oxon)]

SAHONTE RAJINDER KUMAR

22 Old Bldgs
Lincoln's Inn, London WC2A 3UJ,
Telephone: 0171 831 0222
Call date: Nov 1986, Lincoln's Inn
Qualifications: [LLB (Hons)]

SAHOTA MISS SUKHJINDER

30 Park Place
Cardiff CF1 3BA, Telephone: 01222 398421
E-mail: 100757.1456@compuserve.com
Call date: Feb 1992, Lincoln's Inn
Qualifications: [LLB (Hons) (Bucks), LLM]

SAINI PUSHPINDER

2 Hare Court
Ground Floor, Temple, London EC4Y 7BH,
Telephone: 0171 583 1770
E-mail: 2_Hare_Court@link.org
Call date: Oct 1991, Gray's Inn
Qualifications: [BA (Oxon), BCL (Oxon)]

SALEEM SARWAR

9 Woodhouse Square
Leeds LS3 1AD, Telephone: 0113 2451986
Call date: Feb 1960, Lincoln's Inn
Qualifications: [LLM (Manch), BSc]

SALES PHILIP JAMES

11 King's Bench Walk
Temple, London EC4Y 7EQ,
Telephone: 0171 632 8500
E-mail: clerksroom@11-kbw.law.co.uk
Call date: July 1985, Lincoln's Inn
Qualifications: [MA (Cantab), BCL, (Oxon)]

SALLON CHRISTOPHER ROBERT QC (1994)

Doughty Street Chambers
11 Doughty Street, London WC1N 2PG,
Telephone: 0171 404 1313
E-mail: doughty_street@compuserve.com
Westgate Chambers
144 High Street, Lewes, East Sussex BN7 1XT,
Telephone: 01273 480510
Call date: July 1973, Gray's Inn
Recorder

SALMON CHARLES NATHAN QC (1996)

1 Hare Court
Ground Floor, Temple, London EC4Y 7BE,
Telephone: 0171 353 3982/5324
Call date: Nov 1972, Inner Temple
Recorder
Qualifications: [LLB (Hons)]

SALMON JONATHAN CARL

1 Fountain Court
Steelhouse Lane, Birmingham B4 6DR,
Telephone: 0121 236 5721
Call date: Nov 1987, Inner Temple
Qualifications: [LLB (Nottm)]

SALMON KEVIN

King Charles House
Standard Hill, Nottingham NG1 6FX,
Telephone: 0115 9418851
E-mail: clerks@kch.co.uk
Call date: Nov 1984, Gray's Inn
Qualifications: [MA (St Andrews)]

SALMON MISS LOUISE MELISSA

Bell Yard Chambers
116/118 Chancery Lane, London WC2A 1PP,
Telephone: 0171 306 9292
Call date: Nov 1991, Middle Temple
Qualifications: [BA Hons, LLM (Lond)]

SALOMAN TIMOTHY PETER (DAYRELL) QC (1993)

7 King's Bench Walk
Ground Floor, Temple, London EC4Y 7DS,
Telephone: 0171 583 0404
Call date: Nov 1975, Middle Temple
Assistant Recorder
Qualifications: [BA (Oxon)]

SALTER ADRIAN NICHOLAS

11 Stone Bldgs
Ground Floor, Lincoln's Inn, London
WC2A 3TG, Telephone: 0171 831 6381
E-mail: clerks@11StoneBuildings.law.co.uk
Chichester Chambers
12 North Pallant, Chichester, West Sussex
PO19 1TQ, Telephone: 01243 784538
Door Tenant
Call date: July 1973, Middle Temple
Qualifications: [BA (Cantab)]

SALTER CHARLES PHILIP ARTHUR

8 King's Bench Walk
2nd Floor, Temple, London EC4Y 7DU,
Telephone: 0171 797 8888
8 King's Bench Walk North
1 Park Square East, Leeds LS1 2NE,
Telephone: 0113 2439797
Call date: July 1981, Lincoln's Inn
Qualifications: [BSc]

SALTER RICHARD STANLEY QC (1995)

3 Verulam Buildings
London WC1R 5NT,
Telephone: 0171 831 8441
E-mail: clerks@3verulam.co.uk
Call date: July 1975, Inner Temple
Assistant Recorder
Qualifications: [MA (Oxon), ACIArb]

SALTER MISS SIBBY ANNE VICTORIA

1 Gray's Inn Square
Ground Floor, London WC1R 5AA,
Telephone: 0171 405 8946/7/8
Call date: Oct 1991, Middle Temple
Qualifications: [BA Hons (Cantab)]

SALTS NIGEL THOMAS QC (1983)

2 Paper Bldgs
1st Floor, Temple, London EC4Y 7ET,
Telephone: 0171 936 2611 (10 Lines)
E-mail: clerks@2pbbarristers.co.uk
Call date: June 1961, Inner Temple

SALVESEN KEITH NEVILLE

Queen Elizabeth Bldg
Ground Floor, Temple, London EC4Y 9BS,
Telephone: 0171 353 7181 (12 Lines)
Call date: Nov 1974, Inner Temple
Qualifications: [MA (Cantab)]

SALZEDO SIMON LOPEZ

Brick Court Chambers
15/19 Devereux Court, London WC2R 3JJ,
Telephone: 0171 583 0777
E-mail: (surname)@brickcourt.demon.co.uk
Call date: Nov 1995, Lincoln's Inn
Qualifications: [BA (Hons)(Oxon), ACA Dip
Law (City)]

SAMAT DAREN ARMAND CAMERON

2 Paper Bldgs
1st Floor, Temple, London EC4Y 7ET,
Telephone: 0171 936 2611 (10 Lines)
E-mail: clerks@2pbbarristers.co.uk
Call date: Oct 1992, Middle Temple
Qualifications: [LL.B (Hons)]

SAMEK CHARLES STEPHEN

Littleton Chambers
3 King's Bench Walk North, Temple, London
EC4Y 7HR, Telephone: 0171 797 8600
E-mail: littletonchambers@compuserve.com
Call date: Nov 1989, Middle Temple
Qualifications: [BA (Oxon), Dip Law (City)]

SAMILOFF JULIAN

Southsea Chambers
PO Box 148, Southsea, Portsmouth,
Hampshire PO5 2TU,
Telephone: 01705 291261
Call date: July 1988, Inner Temple
Qualifications: [BSc, Dip Law]

SAMMON MISS SARAH BRIDGET

40 King Street
Chester CH1 2AH, Telephone: 01244 323886
Call date: Oct 1991, Middle Temple
Qualifications: [BA (Hons), Dip Law]

D

SAMPSON GRAEME WILLIAM

46/48 Essex Street
London WC2R 3GH,
Telephone: 0171 583 8899
Call date: Nov 1981, Gray's Inn
Qualifications: [BA]

SAMPSON JAMES

Wilberforce Chambers
Bishop Lane, Hull HU1 1PA,
Telephone: 01482 323264
E-mail: clerks@hullbar.demon.co.uk
Call date: Nov 1985, Inner Temple
Qualifications: [LLB (Nott'm)]

SAMUEL DAVID GERWYN

Lamb Chambers
Lamb Building, Temple, London EC4Y 7AS,
Telephone: 0171 797 8300
E-mail: lambchambers@link.org
Call date: July 1986, Gray's Inn
Qualifications: [MA (Oxon)]

SAMUEL GLYN ROSS

7 Fountain Court
Steelhouse Lane, Birmingham B4 6DR,
Telephone: 0121 236 8531
Call date: Oct 1991, Lincoln's Inn
Qualifications: [LLB (Hons)]

SAMUEL MISS JACQUELINE ELEANOR

1 Hare Court
Ground Floor, Temple, London EC4Y 7BE,
Telephone: 0171 353 3982/5324
Call date: July 1971, Gray's Inn
Qualifications: [LLB (Hons)(Lond)]

SAMUELS JEFFREY KEITH

28 St John Street
Manchester M3 4DJ,
Telephone: 0161 834 8418
E-mail: clerk@28stjohnst.co.uk
Call date: July 1988, Middle Temple
Qualifications: [LLB (Hons) (Leeds)]

SAMUELS LESLIE JOHN

Pump Court Chambers
Upper Ground Floor 3 Pump Court, Temple,
London EC4Y 7AJ, Telephone: 0171 353 0711
Pump Court Chambers
31 Southgate Street, Winchester SO23 8EE,
Telephone: 01962 868161
Call date: July 1989, Gray's Inn
Qualifications: [BA (Cantab), MA (Toronto)]

SANDALL MS GILLIAN DORIS

12 Old Square
1st Floor, Lincoln's Inn, London WC2A 3TX,
Telephone: 0171 404 0875
Call date: Nov 1992, Inner Temple
Qualifications: [BA (E.Anglia), Dip in law]

SANDBROOK-HUGHES STEWERT KARL ANTHONY

Iscoed Chambers
86 St Helen's Road, Swansea SA1 4BQ,
Telephone: 01792 652988/9/330
Call date: Nov 1980, Lincoln's Inn
Qualifications: [BSc Econ (Wales), Dip Law]

SANDELLS MS NICOLE

17 Old Bldgs
Ground Floor, Lincoln's Inn, London
WC2A 3UP, Telephone: 0171 405 9653
Call date: Nov 1994, Inner Temple
Qualifications: [BA (Oxon)]

SANDEMAN DAVID MCEWEN

2 King's Bench Walk
1st Floor, Temple, London EC4Y 7DE,
Telephone: 0171 353 9276
Call date: Nov 1993, Middle Temple
Qualifications: [LLB (Hons)(Kingston)]

SANDER ANDREW THOMAS

Oriel Chambers
14 Water Street, Liverpool L2 8TD,
Telephone: 0151 236 7191
E-mail: oriel_chambers@link.org
Goldsmith Building
1st Floor, Temple, London EC4Y 7BL,
Telephone: 0171 353 7881
E-mail: clerks@goldsmith-building.law.co.uk
Door Tenant
Call date: Nov 1970, Middle Temple
Recorder
Qualifications: [LLB (L'pool)]

SANDERS (JAMES) DAMIAN

India Buildings Chambers
Water Street, Liverpool L2 OXG,
Telephone: 0151 243 6000
Call date: Nov 1988, Middle Temple
Qualifications: [LLB]

SANDERS NEIL JOHN TAIT

29 Bedford Row Chambers
London WC1R 4HE,
Telephone: 0171 831 2626
Call date: July 1975, Inner Temple
Qualifications: [MA (Cantab)]

SANDERSON DAVID FRANK

3 Paper Bldgs
1st Floor, Temple, London EC4Y 7EU,
Telephone: 0171 583 8055
E-mail: london@3paper.com
20 Lorne Park Road
Bournemouth BH1 1JN,
Telephone: 01202 292102 (5 Lines)
4 St Peter Street
Winchester SO23 8OW,
Telephone: 01962 868884
Call date: Nov 1985, Inner Temple
Qualifications: [BA (Sussex)]

SANDFORD SIMON JOHN AUSTIN

3 Paper Bldgs
2nd Floor, Temple, London EC4Y 7EU,
Telephone: 0171 353 6208
Call date: Nov 1979, Gray's Inn
Qualifications: [MA (Cantab)]

SANDHU SUNIT

Equity Chambers
Suite 110, Gazette Buildings 168 Corporation
Street, Birmingham B4 6TS,
Telephone: 0121 233 2100
Call date: Feb 1990, Middle Temple
Qualifications: [LLB(Hons)(B'ham), BA]

SANDIFORD DAVID CHARLES

8 King Street
Manchester M2 6AQ,
Telephone: 0161 834 9560
Call date: Oct 1995, Gray's Inn
Qualifications: [BA]

SANDIFORD JONATHAN

St Paul's House
5th Floor 23 Park Square South, Leeds
LS1 2ND, Telephone: 0113 2455866
Call date: Oct 1992, Gray's Inn
Qualifications: [LLB (Hons) (Newc)]

SANDS MR PHILIPPE JOSEPH

3 Verulam Buildings
London WC1R 5NT,
Telephone: 0171 831 8441
E-mail: clerks@3verulam.co.uk
Call date: Nov 1985, Middle Temple
Qualifications: [MA, LLM (Cantab)]

SANGSTER NIGEL

St Paul's House
5th Floor 23 Park Square South, Leeds
LS1 2ND, Telephone: 0113 2455866
Call date: Nov 1976, Middle Temple
Assistant Recorder
Qualifications: [LLB (Hons)]

SANKEY GUY RICHARD QC (1991)

1 Temple Gardens
1st Floor, Temple, London EC4Y 9BB,
Telephone: 0171 353 0407/583 1315
E-mail: clerks@1templegardens.co.uk
Call date: July 1966, Inner Temple
Recorder
Qualifications: [MA (Oxon)]

D

SAPIECHA DAVID JOHN

Veritas Chambers
33 Corn Street, Bristol BS1 1HT,
Telephone: 0117 930 8802
Call date: Oct 1990, Gray's Inn
Qualifications: [LLB]

SAPNARA MISS KHATUN

8 King's Bench Walk
2nd Floor, Temple, London EC4Y 7DU,
Telephone: 0171 797 8888
8 King's Bench Walk North
1 Park Square East, Leeds LS1 2NE,
Telephone: 0113 2439797
Call date: Nov 1990, Middle Temple
Qualifications: [LLB (Lond)]

SAPSARD JAMAL PARVEZ

2 Paper Bldgs
Temple, London EC4Y 7ET,
Telephone: 0171 936 2613
Call date: July 1987, Lincoln's Inn
Qualifications: [LLB (Hons)]

SAPSFORD PHILIP ANTHONY CHALKLIN QC (1992)

Goldsmith Chambers
Ground Floor Goldsmith Building, Temple,
London EC4Y 7BL,
Telephone: 0171 353 6802/3/4/5
E-mail: celiamonksfield@btinternet.com
Call date: Nov 1974, Inner Temple
Assistant Recorder

SASSE TOBY WILLIAM

18 St John Street
Manchester M3 4EA,
Telephone: 0161 278 1800
Call date: July 1988, Middle Temple
Qualifications: [LLB (Hons) (Exon)]

SASTRY BOB AJAY DWARAKANATH

Garden Court North Chambers
2nd Floor Gregg's Building, 1 Booth Street,
Manchester M2 4DU,
Telephone: 0161 833 1774
Call date: Oct 1996, Inner Temple
Qualifications: [LLB (Exon)]

SAUNDERS JOHN HENRY BOULTON QC (1991)

4 Fountain Court
Steelhouse Lane, Birmingham B4 6DR,
Telephone: 0121 236 3476
Call date: July 1972, Gray's Inn
Recorder
Qualifications: [BA (Oxon)]

SAUNDERS NEIL

3 Raymond Buildings
Gray's Inn, London WC1R 5BH,
Telephone: 0171 831 3833
E-mail: chambers@threeraymond.demon.co.uk
Call date: Nov 1983, Middle Temple
Qualifications: [BA]

SAUNDERS NICHOLAS JOSEPH

4 Field Court
Gray's Inn, London WC1R 5EA,
Telephone: 0171 440 6900
E-mail: chambers@4fieldcourt.co.uk
Call date: July 1989, Middle Temple
Qualifications: [LLB (Hull), LLM (Cantab)]

SAUNDERS WILLIAM ANTHONY

3 Temple Gardens
Lower Ground Floor, Temple, London
EC4Y 9AU, Telephone: 0171 353 3102/5/9297
Westgate Chambers
144 High Street, Lewes, East Sussex BN7 1XT,
Telephone: 01273 480510
Call date: Nov 1980, Gray's Inn
Qualifications: [LLB (B'ham)]

SAUNT THOMAS WILLIAM GATTY

2 Crown Office Row
Ground Floor, Temple, London EC4Y 7HJ,
Telephone: 0171 797 8100
E-mail: mail@2cor.co.uk, or to individual
barristers at: [barrister's surname]@2cor.co.uk
Call date: July 1974, Inner Temple
Qualifications: [LLB]

SAUVAIN STEPHEN JOHN QC (1995)

40 King Street
Manchester M2 6BA,
Telephone: 0161 832 9082
E-mail: Kingst40@aol.com
Call date: July 1977, Lincoln's Inn
Qualifications: [MA, LLB (Cantab)]

SAVAGE MISS AYISHA CAROL

20 Britton Street
1st Floor, London EC1M 5NQ,
Telephone: 0171 608 3765
Call date: July 1995, Inner Temple
Qualifications: [BA (Leic)]

SAVAGE TIMOTHY JOHN

Paradise Square Chambers
26 Paradise Square, Sheffield S1 2DE,
Telephone: 0114 2738951
Call date: Nov 1991, Inner Temple

SAVILL MARK ASHLEY

Deans Court Chambers
Cumberland House Crown Square, Manchester
M3 3HA, Telephone: 0161 834 4097
E-mail: deanscourt@compuserve.com
Call date: Nov 1993, Inner Temple
Qualifications: [BA (Dunelm)]

SAVILL PETER JOHN

17 Carlton Crescent
Southampton SO15 2XR,
Telephone: 01703 320320
E-mail: km@bar-17cc.demon.co.uk
Call date: Nov 1995, Inner Temple
Qualifications: [BA (Warw), CPE]

SAVLA SANDEEP

55 Temple Chambers
Temple Avenue, London EC4Y 0HP,
Telephone: 0171 353 7400
Call date: Oct 1992, Middle Temple
Qualifications: [BA (Hons)]

SAVVIDES MISS MARIA

22 Albion Place
Northampton NN1 1UD,
Telephone: 01604 36271
Call date: July 1986, Middle Temple
Qualifications: [BA (Hons)]

SAWHNEY MISS DEBBIE JANE

Lamb Building
Ground Floor, Temple, London EC4Y 7AS,
Telephone: 0171 797 7788
E-mail: lamb.building@link.org
Call date: Nov 1987, Middle Temple
Qualifications: [BA (Keele)]

SAWYERR MISS SHARON ROSE

Queen Elizabeth Bldg
Ground Floor, Temple, London EC4Y 9BS,
Telephone: 0171 353 7181 (12 Lines)
Call date: Nov 1992, Inner Temple
Qualifications: [LLB]

SAXBY OLIVER CHARLES JOHN

6 Pump Court
1st Floor, Temple, London EC4Y 7AR,
Telephone: 0171 797 8400
E-mail: sa_hockman_qc@link.org
6-8 Mill Street
6-8 Mill Street, Maidstone, Kent ME15 6XH,
Telephone: 01622 688 094
Call date: Nov 1992, Inner Temple
Qualifications: [LLB (So'ton)]

Fax: 0171 797 8401;
Out of hours telephone: 01233 820485;
DX: LDE 293; Other comms: 0410 851045

Types of work: Crime

Other professional qualifications: Duke of Edinburgh Scholar; Member Kent Bar Mess

Circuit: South Eastern

SAXTON MISS NICOLA HELEN

St Paul's House
5th Floor 23 Park Square South, Leeds
LS1 2ND, Telephone: 0113 2455866
Call date: Nov 1992, Inner Temple
Qualifications: [MA (Cantab)]

SAY BRADLEY JOHN

5 Pump Court
Ground Floor, Temple, London EC4Y 7AP,
Telephone: 0171 353 2532
E-mail: fivepump@netcomuk.co.uk
Call date: Oct 1993, Inner Temple
Qualifications: [LLB]

SAYEED MUHAMMAD ABU

10 Highlever Road
North Kensington, London W10 6PS,
Telephone: 0181 969 8514
Call date: July 1973, Inner Temple
Qualifications: [B.A.]

SAYER MR PETER EDWIN

Gough Square Chambers
6-7 Gough Square, London EC4A 3DE,
Telephone: 0171 353 0924
E-mail: gsc@goughsq.co.uk
Call date: July 1975, Middle Temple
Qualifications: [MA (Cantab)]

SAYERS MICHAEL PATRICK
QC (1988)

2 King's Bench Walk
Ground Floor, Temple, London EC4Y 7DE,
Telephone: 0171 353 1746
E-mail: 2kbw@atlas.co.uk
King's Bench Chambers
115 North Hill, Plymouth PL4 8JY,
Telephone: 01752 221551
Call date: Nov 1970, Inner Temple
Recorder
Qualifications: [MA (Cantab)]

SCAMELL ERNEST HAROLD

5 New Square
1st Floor, Lincoln's Inn, London WC2A 3RJ,
Telephone: 0171 404 0404
E-mail: Chambers@FiveNewSquare.CityScape.co.uk
Call date: Nov 1949, Lincoln's Inn
Qualifications: [LLM]

SCANNELL RICHARD PAUL

2 Garden Court
1st Floor, Middle Temple, London EC4Y 9BL,
Telephone: 0171 353 1633
E-mail: barristers@2gardenct.law.co.uk
Call date: Nov 1986, Middle Temple
Qualifications: [BA, LLM]

SCARRATT RICHARD JOHN

One Garden Court
Ground Floor, Temple, London EC4Y 9BJ,
Telephone: 0171 797 7900
Call date: July 1979, Lincoln's Inn
Qualifications: [LLB (B'ham)]

SCHAFF ALISTAIR GRAHAM

7 King's Bench Walk
Ground Floor, Temple, London EC4Y 7DS,
Telephone: 0171 583 0404
Call date: July 1983, Inner Temple
Qualifications: [MA (Cantab)]

SCHAFFER LOUIS

10 King's Bench Walk
1st Floor, Temple, London EC4Y 7EB,
Telephone: 0171 353 2501
Call date: Nov 1955, Middle Temple
Qualifications: [MA, LLB (Cantab)]

SCHAW-MILLER STEPHEN GRANT

5 Bell Yard
London WC2A 2JR, Telephone: 0171 333 8811
Call date: Nov 1988, Inner Temple
Qualifications: [BA (Oxon), Dip Law (City)]

SCHENKENBERG MISS BARBARA

St Ive's Chambers
9 Fountain Ct, Birmingham B4 6DR,
Telephone: 0121 236 0863/0929
Call date: July 1993, Inner Temple
Qualifications: [BSc, Juris Doctorate]

SCHIFFER MISS CORINNA ANNE

5 Pump Court
Ground Floor, Temple, London EC4Y 7AP,
Telephone: 0171 353 2532
E-mail: fivepump@netcomuk.co.uk
Call date: Nov 1989, Middle Temple
Qualifications: [BA Hons (Cantab)]

SCHMITZ DAVID REUBEN

10 Old Square
Ground Floor, Lincoln's Inn, London
WC2A 3SU, Telephone: 0171 405 0758
Call date: Nov 1976, Lincoln's Inn
Qualifications: [BA]

SCHOFIELD ALEXANDER GEORGE

4 Paper Bldgs
2nd Floor, Temple, London EC4Y 7EX,
Telephone: 0171 583 0816/071 353 1131
E-mail: clerks@4paperbuildings.co.uk
Call date: Mar 1997, Middle Temple
Qualifications: [BA (Hons)(Oxon)]

SCHOFIELD PETER ANDREW

New Court Chambers
3 Broad Chare, Newcastle Upon Tyne
NE1 3DQ, Telephone: 0191 232 1980
Call date: Nov 1982, Gray's Inn
Qualifications: [BA]

SCHOLES MICHAEL HOWARD

India Buildings Chambers
Water Street, Liverpool L2 OXG,
Telephone: 0151 243 6000
Call date: July 1996, Inner Temple
Qualifications: [LLB (Hons)(L'pool)]

SCHOLES RODNEY JAMES QC (1987)

22 Old Bldgs
Lincoln's Inn, London WC2A 3UJ,
Telephone: 0171 831 0222
25 Byrom Street
Manchester M3 4PF,
Telephone: 0161 829 2100
E-mail: Byromst25@aol.com
Call date: July 1968, Lincoln's Inn
Recorder
Qualifications: [BA, BCL (Oxon)]

SCHOLZ KARL HUBERTUS

3 Temple Gardens
Lower Ground Floor, Temple, London
EC4Y 9AU, Telephone: 0171 353 3102/5/9297
Call date: July 1973, Gray's Inn
Qualifications: [LLB (Lond)]

SCHOOLING SIMON JOHN

3 Pump Court
2nd Floor, Temple, London EC4Y 7AJ,
Telephone: 0171 353 1356 (3 Lines)
Call date: Nov 1995, Lincoln's Inn
Qualifications: [BA (Hons)]

SCHUSMAN STEVEN PAUL

Chambers of Helen Grindrod QC
1st Floor 95a Chancery Lane, London
WC2A 2JG, Telephone: 0171 404 4777
Call date: July 1985, Middle Temple
Qualifications: [LLB (Manch)]

SCOBIE JAMES TIMOTHY NORMAN

Francis Taylor Bldg
Ground Floor, Temple, London EC4Y 7BY,
Telephone: 0171 353 7768/7769/2711
Call date: July 1984, Gray's Inn
Qualifications: [BA (Exon) Dip Law, (City)]

SCORAH CHRISTOPHER JAMES

8 King Street
Manchester M2 6AQ,
Telephone: 0161 834 9560
Call date: Nov 1991, Middle Temple
Qualifications: [BA Hons (Oxon), Dip Law]

SCOTLAND OF ASTRAL BARONESS QC (1991)

1 Gray's Inn Square
1st Floor, London WC1R 5AG,
Telephone: 0171 405 3000
E-mail: clerks@onegrays.demon.co.uk
Call date: July 1977, Middle Temple
Recorder
Qualifications: [LLB (Lond)]

SCOTT MISS ALEXANDRA ELISABETH

2 New Street
Leicester LE1 5NA, Telephone: 0116 2625906
Call date: July 1983, Gray's Inn
Qualifications: [LLB (Leic)]

SCOTT CHARLES EDWIN

169 Temple Chambers
Temple Avenue, London EC4Y 0DA,
Telephone: 0171 583 7644
Call date: July 1980, Middle Temple
Qualifications: [LLB (Lond), FCIArb]

SCOTT MISS CHRISTINE RUTH

Francis Taylor Bldg
Ground Floor, Temple, London EC4Y 7BY,
Telephone: 0171 353 7768/7769/2711
Call date: Nov 1986, Gray's Inn
Qualifications: [LLB(Reading)]

SCOTT IAN RICHARD

Old Square Chambers
1 Verulam Buildings, Gray's Inn, London
WC1R 5LQ, Telephone: 0171 831 0801
Old Square Chambers
Hanover House 47 Corn Street, Bristol
BS1 1HT, Telephone: 0117 9277111
Call date: Oct 1991, Lincoln's Inn
Qualifications: [BA (Hons) (Newc), MSc (LSE),
Dip Law (City)]

D

D

SCOTT JOHN ALSTON

4 Stone Bldgs
Ground Floor, Lincoln's Inn, London
WC2A 3XT, Telephone: 0171 242 5524
E-mail: d.goddard@4stonebuildings.law.co.uk
Call date: July 1982, Middle Temple
Qualifications: [MA LLM (Cantab), FCIArb]

SCOTT MATTHEW JOHN

Pump Court Chambers
Upper Ground Floor 3 Pump Court, Temple,
London EC4Y 7AJ, Telephone: 0171 353 0711
Pump Court Chambers
31 Southgate Street, Winchester SO23 8EE,
Telephone: 01962 868161
Call date: Nov 1985, Inner Temple
Qualifications: [BA (York)]

SCOTT PETER DENYS JOHN
QC (1978)

Fountain Court
Temple, London EC4Y 9DH,
Telephone: 0171 583 3335
E-mail: chambers@fountaincourt.co.uk
Call date: May 1960, Middle Temple
Qualifications: [MA (Oxon)]

SCOTT RICHARD MARK

York Chambers
14 Toft Green, York YO1 1JT,
Telephone: 01904 620048
E-mail: yorkchambers.co.uk
Call date: Nov 1992, Middle Temple
Qualifications: [LLB (Hons)]

SCOTT TIMOTHY JOHN WHITTAKER
QC (1995)

29 Bedford Row Chambers
London WC1R 4HE,
Telephone: 0171 831 2626
Call date: Nov 1975, Gray's Inn
Assistant Recorder
Qualifications: [BA (Oxon)]

SCOTT BELL MRS ROSALIND SARA

Trinity Chambers
9-12 Trinity Chare, Quayside, Newcastle Upon
Tyne NE1 3DF, Telephone: 0191 232 1927
Call date: Oct 1993, Middle Temple
Qualifications: [LLB (Hons)(Manc)]

SCOTT-JONES MISS ALISON CLAIRE

Equity Chambers
Suite 110, Gazette Buildings 168 Corporation
Street, Birmingham B4 6TS,
Telephone: 0121 233 2100
Call date: Feb 1991, Middle Temple
Qualifications: [LLB (Cardiff)]

SCOTT-MANDERSON MARCUS
CHARLES WILLIAM

4 Paper Bldgs
2nd Floor, Temple, London EC4Y 7EX,
Telephone: 0171 583 0816/071 353 1131
E-mail: clerks@4paperbuildings.co.uk
Call date: July 1980, Lincoln's Inn
Qualifications: [BA, BCL (Oxon)]

SCOTT-PHILLIPS ALEXANDER
JAMES

Earl Street Chambers
47 Earl Street, Maidstone, Kent ME14 1PD,
Telephone: 01622 671222
E-mail: gunner-sparks@msn.com
Call date: Oct 1995, Inner Temple
Qualifications: [BA (Hons)(Durham), CPE
(Leic)]

SCRIVEN MISS PAMELA QC (1992)

1 King's Bench Walk
2nd Floor, Temple, London EC4Y 7DB,
Telephone: 0171 936 1500
E-mail: ddear@1kbw.co.uk
Call date: Nov 1970, Inner Temple
Assistant Recorder
Qualifications: [LLB (Lond)]

SCRIVENER ANTHONY FRANK
BERTRAM QC (1975)

2-3 Gray's Inn Square
Gray's Inn, London WC1R 5JH,
Telephone: 0171 242 4986
E-mail: chambers@2-3graysinnsquare.co.uk
Call date: Nov 1958, Gray's Inn
Recorder

SCUTT DAVID ROBERT

11 Bolt Court
London EC4A 3DQ,
Telephone: 0171 353 2300
E-mail: boltct11@aol.com
Redhill Chambers
Seloduct House 30 Station Road, Redhill
RH1 1NK, Telephone: 01737 780781
Call date: Nov 1989, Middle Temple
Qualifications: [BA (Keele)]

SEABROOK RICHARD MICHAEL

24 The Ropewalk
Nottingham NG1 5EF,
Telephone: 0115 9472581
E-mail: clerk@ropewalk.co.uk
Call date: July 1987, Inner Temple
Qualifications: [LLB]

SEABROOK ROBERT JOHN QC (1983)

1 Crown Office Row
Ground Floor, Temple, London EC4Y 7HH,
Telephone: 0171 797 7500
Crown Office Row Chambers
Blenheim House 120 Church Street, Brighton,
Sussex BN1 1WH, Telephone: 01273 625625
Call date: June 1964, Middle Temple
Recorder
Qualifications: [LLB]

SEAL JULIUS DAMIEN

189 Randolph Avenue
London W9 1DJ, Telephone: 0171 624 9139
3 Temple Gardens
3rd Floor, Temple, London EC4Y 9AU,
Telephone: 0171 353 0832
Call date: Nov 1967, Lincoln's Inn

SEARLE BARRIE

St James's Chambers
68 Quay Street, Manchester M3 3EJ,
Telephone: 0161 834 7000
E-mail: 106241.2625@compuserve.com
Call date: July 1975, Middle Temple
Qualifications: [LLB (Hons)]

SEARLE MISS CORINNE LOUISE TEAGUE

Walnut House
63 St. David's Hill, Exeter, Devon EX4 4DW,
Telephone: 01392 279751
E-mail: 106627.2451@compuserve.com
Call date: July 1982, Gray's Inn
Qualifications: [LLB (Lond)]

SEARS ROBERT DAVID MURRAY

4 Pump Court
Temple, London EC4Y 7AN,
Telephone: 0171 353 2656/9
E-mail: 4_pump_court@compuserve.com
Call date: Nov 1984, Middle Temple
Qualifications: [MA (Oxon)]

SEAWARD MARTIN VINCENT

4 Brick Court
Ground Floor, Temple, London EC4Y 9AD,
Telephone: 0171 797 7766
E-mail: chambers@4brick.co.uk
Call date: Nov 1978, Gray's Inn
Qualifications: [BA (Dunelm)]

SECHIARI MISS HELEN LOUISE PANDIA

Manchester House Chambers
18-22 Bridge Street, Manchester M3 3BZ,
Telephone: 0161 834 7007
Call date: Nov 1991, Lincoln's Inn
Qualifications: [LLB (Hons)]

SECONDE DAVID GORDON

Coleridge Chambers
Citadel 190 Corporation Street, Birmingham
B4 6QD, Telephone: 0121 233 3303
Call date: July 1968, Middle Temple
Qualifications: [BA (Oxon)]

SEDDON MISS DOROTHY

6 Fountain Court
Steelhouse Lane, Birmingham B4 6DR,
Telephone: 0121 233 3282
Call date: July 1974, Middle Temple
Qualifications: [LLB (B'ham)]

D

SEDDON JAMES DURAN

2 Garden Court
1st Floor, Middle Temple, London EC4Y 9BL,
Telephone: 0171 353 1633
E-mail: barristers@2gardenct.law.co.uk
Call date: Feb 1994, Middle Temple
Qualifications: [BA (Hons)(Oxon), CPE
(Manc)]

SEEBORUTH ROYLN JEAN-PAUL

Tower Hamlets Barristers Chambers
First Floor 45 Brick Lane, London E1 6PU,
Telephone: 0171 247 9825
Call date: Nov 1986, Middle Temple
Qualifications: [LLB (Hons)(Bucks)]

SEED NIGEL JOHN

3 Paper Bldgs
1st Floor, Temple, London EC4Y 7EU,
Telephone: 0171 583 8055
E-mail: london@3paper.com
20 Lorne Park Road
Bournemouth BH1 1JN,
Telephone: 01202 292102 (5 Lines)
4 St Peter Street
Winchester SO23 8OW,
Telephone: 01962 868884
Call date: Nov 1978, Inner Temple
Assistant Recorder
Qualifications: [BA (Dunelm)]

SEED STEPHEN NICHOLAS

Martins Building
Water Street, Liverpool L2 3SP,
Telephone: 0151 236 5818/4919
Call date: Oct 1991, Gray's Inn
Qualifications: [LLB]

SEELY JONATHAN SEBASTIAN

East Anglian Chambers
Sanders House 52 North Hill, Colchester
CO1 1PY, Telephone: 01206 572756
East Anglian Chambers
57 London Street, Norwich NR2 1HL,
Telephone: 01603 617351
East Anglian Chambers
Gresham House 5 Museum Street, Ipswich
IP1 1HQ, Telephone: 01473 214481
Call date: Nov 1987, Inner Temple
Qualifications: [BA,Dip Law]

SEFI BENEDICT JOHN

2 Harcourt Bldgs
1st Floor, Temple, London EC4Y 9DB,
Telephone: 0171 353 6961/7
Harcourt Chambers
Churchill House 3 St Aldate's Courtyard, St
Aldate's, Oxford OX1 1BN,
Telephone: 01865 791559
Call date: July 1972, Inner Temple
Qualifications: [BA (Oxon)]

SEFTON MARK THOMAS DUNBLANE

199 Strand
London WC2R 1DR,
Telephone: 0171 379 9779
E-mail: chambers@199strand.co.uk
Call date: Nov 1996, Middle Temple
Qualifications: [BA (Hons)(Cantab)]

SEFTON-SMITH LLOYD

Bridewell Chambers
2 Bridewell Place, London EC4V 6AP,
Telephone: 0171 797 8800
E-mail: clerks@bridewell.law.co.uk
Call date: Oct 1993, Lincoln's Inn
Qualifications: [BA (Hons)(Lond)]

SEGAL OLIVER LEON

Old Square Chambers
1 Verulam Buildings, Gray's Inn, London
WC1R 5LQ, Telephone: 0171 831 0801
Old Square Chambers
Hanover House 47 Corn Street, Bristol
BS1 1HT, Telephone: 0117 9277111
Call date: Oct 1992, Middle Temple
Qualifications: [BA (Hons)]

SEIFERT MISS ANNE MIRIAM

4 Breams Buildings
London EC4A 1AQ,
Telephone: 0171 353 5835/430 1221
Call date: July 1975, Inner Temple

SEITLER MS DEBORAH

1 Gray's Inn Square
1st Floor, London WC1R 5AG,
Telephone: 0171 405 3000
E-mail: clerks@onegrays.demon.co.uk
Call date: Nov 1991, Inner Temple
Qualifications: [BA (Leeds, Dip Law]

SEITLER JONATHAN SIMON

Wilberforce Chambers
8 New Square, Lincoln's Inn, London
WC2A 3QP, Telephone: 0171 306 0102
E-mail: chambers@wilberforce.co.uk
Call date: Nov 1985, Inner Temple
Qualifications: [BA (Oxon)]

SEKAR CHANDRA

Acre Lane Neighbourhood Chambers
30A Acre Lane, London SW2 5SG,
Telephone: 0171 274 4400
Call date: Mar 1996, Gray's Inn
Qualifications: [BA (Bris)]

SELF GARY PETER

College Chambers
19 Carlton Cresent, Southampton, Hants
SO15 2ET, Telephone: 01703 230338
Call date: Oct 1991, Lincoln's Inn
Qualifications: [BA (Hons)(Manc), Dip Law]

SELF HUGH MICHAEL QC (1973)

4 Brick Court
1st Floor, Temple, London EC4Y 9AD,
Telephone: 0171 583 8455
Call date: Jan 1951, Lincoln's Inn
Qualifications: [BA (Oxon)]

SELFE MICHAEL ROSS

2 King's Bench Walk
Ground Floor, Temple, London EC4Y 7DE,
Telephone: 0171 353 1746
E-mail: 2kbw@atlas.co.uk
King's Bench Chambers
115 North Hill, Plymouth PL4 8JY,
Telephone: 01752 221551
Call date: Nov 1965, Middle Temple
Recorder
Qualifications: [LLB (Soton)]

SELIGMAN MATTHEW THOMAS ARTHUR

39 Essex Street
London WC2R 3AT,
Telephone: 0171 583 1111
E-mail: clerks@39essex.co.uk
Call date: Oct 1994, Middle Temple
Qualifications: [BA (Hons)(Oxon), CPE (Lond)]

SELIGMAN RALPH DAVID

4 Stone Bldgs
Ground Floor, Lincoln's Inn, London
WC2A 3XT, Telephone: 0171 242 5524
E-mail: d.goddard@4stonebuildings.law.co.uk
Call date: Nov 1996, Gray's Inn
Qualifications: [BA, LLB, MA (Dublin)]

SELLARS MICHAEL JOHN

Adrian Lyon's Chambers
14 Castle Street, Liverpool L2 0NE,
Telephone: 0151 236 4421/8240
E-mail: chambers14@aol.com
Call date: July 1980, Inner Temple
Qualifications: [BA (Dunelm)]

SELLERS ALAN MITCHELL

Peel House Chambers
Ground Floor, Peel House 5 Harrington Street,
Liverpool L2 9QA, Telephone: 0151 236 4321
Call date: July 1991, Gray's Inn
Qualifications: [LLB (Lanc)]

SELLERS GRAHAM

Adrian Lyon's Chambers
14 Castle Street, Liverpool L2 0NE,
Telephone: 0151 236 4421/8240
E-mail: chambers14@aol.com
Call date: Oct 1990, Middle Temple
Qualifications: [LLB, LLM (Cantab)]

SELLERS ROBIN ST. JOHN

Guildford Chambers
Stoke House Leapale Lane, Guildford, Surrey
GU1 4LY, Telephone: 01483 539131
E-mail: guildford.barristers@btinternet.com
Call date: Nov 1994, Inner Temple
Qualifications: [LLB (Reading)]

SELLICK WILLIAM PATRICK LLEWELLYN

King's Bench Chambers
115 North Hill, Plymouth PL4 8JY,
Telephone: 01752 221551
2 King's Bench Walk
Ground Floor, Temple, London EC4Y 7DE,
Telephone: 0171 353 1746
E-mail: 2kbw@atlas.co.uk
Call date: July 1973, Middle Temple
Recorder
Qualifications: [LLB]

D

SELLS OLIVER MATTHEW QC (1995)

5 Paper Bldgs
1st Floor, Temple, London EC4Y 7HB,
Telephone: 0171 583 6117
E-mail: clerks@5-paperbuildings.law.co.uk
Fenners Chambers
3 Madingley Road, Cambridge CB3 OEE,
Telephone: 01223 368761
Door Tenant
Call date: July 1972, Inner Temple
Recorder

SELMAN MISS ELIZABETH

1 King's Bench Walk
2nd Floor, Temple, London EC4Y 7DB,
Telephone: 0171 936 1500
E-mail: ddear@1kbw.co.uk
Call date: Nov 1989, Inner Temple
Qualifications: [LLB (Lond)]

SELVARATNAM MISS VASANTI EMILY INDRANI

4 Field Court
Gray's Inn, London WC1R 5EA,
Telephone: 0171 440 6900
E-mail: chambers@4fieldcourt.co.uk
Call date: July 1983, Middle Temple
Qualifications: [LLM, LLB (Lond), AKC]

SELWAY DR KATHERINE EMMA

11 Old Square
Ground Floor, Lincoln's Inn, London
WC2A 3TS, Telephone: 0171 430 0341
E-mail: clerks@11oldsquare.co.uk
Call date: Nov 1995, Inner Temple
Qualifications: [BA (Hons)(Bris), D.Phil (Oxon), CPE (City)]

SELWYN SHARPE RICHARD CHARLES

67a Westgate Road
Newcastle Upon Tyne NE1 1SQ,
Telephone: 0191 261 4407/2329785
5 Bell Yard
London WC2A 2JR, Telephone: 0171 333 8811
Door Tenant
Call date: Nov 1985, Lincoln's Inn
Qualifications: [LLB(Bristol)]

SEMKEN CHRISTOPHER RICHARD

1 New Square
Ground Floor, Lincoln's Inn, London
WC2A 3SA, Telephone: 0171 405 0884/5/6/7
E-mail: 1newsquare@compuserve.com
Call date: July 1977, Lincoln's Inn
Qualifications: [MA (Oxon)]

SEMPLE ANDREW BLAIR

25 Park Square
Leeds LS1 2PW, Telephone: 0113 2451841/2/3
E-mail: sovereignchambers@btinternet.com
Call date: Oct 1993, Inner Temple
Qualifications: [BA (Dunelm)]

SEN ADITYA KUMAR

4 Brick Court
Ground Floor, Temple, London EC4Y 9AD,
Telephone: 0171 797 7766
E-mail: chambers@4brick.co.uk
Call date: July 1977, Lincoln's Inn
Qualifications: [MA, LLB (Cantab), BA (Hons) (Dehli), FCA]

SENDALL ANTONY JOHN CHRISTMAS

Littleton Chambers
3 King's Bench Walk North, Temple, London
EC4Y 7HR, Telephone: 0171 797 8600
E-mail: littletonchambers@compuserve.com
Call date: July 1984, Lincoln's Inn
Qualifications: [MA (Cantab)]

SEPHTON CRAIG GARDNER

Deans Court Chambers
Cumberland House Crown Square, Manchester
M3 3HA, Telephone: 0161 834 4097
E-mail: deanscourt@compuserve.com
Deans Court Chambers
41-43 Market Place, Preston PR1 1AH,
Telephone: 01772 555163
E-mail: deanscourt@compuserve.com
Call date: July 1981, Middle Temple
Qualifications: [MA, BCL (Oxon)]

SERLE MS DIANA COLEMAN

10 King's Bench Walk
Ground Floor, Temple, London EC4Y 7EB,
Telephone: 0171 353 7742
E-mail: 10kbw@lineone.net
Call date: Nov 1992, Inner Temple
Qualifications: [BA (Hons), Dip in Law]

SERLIN RICHARD ANTHONY

199 Strand
London WC2R 1DR,
Telephone: 0171 379 9779
E-mail: chambers@199strand.co.uk
Call date: Nov 1987, Lincoln's Inn
Qualifications: [BA (Oxon) Dip Law, (City)]

SEROTA DANIEL QC (1989)

Littleton Chambers
3 King's Bench Walk North, Temple, London
EC4Y 7HR, Telephone: 0171 797 8600
E-mail: littletonchambers@compuserve.com
Call date: Nov 1969, Lincoln's Inn
Recorder
Qualifications: [MA (Oxon)]

SERUGO-LUGO YOSEFALY NDAULA KIKWANGWIRA SE

Essex House Chambers
Essex House 375-377 Stratford High Street,
Stratford, London E15 4QZ,
Telephone: 0181 536 1077
Call date: Nov 1973, Inner Temple
Qualifications: [BA]

SETRIGHT HENRY JOHN

1 Gray's Inn Square
1st Floor, London WC1R 5AG,
Telephone: 0171 405 3000
E-mail: clerks@onegrays.demon.co.uk
Call date: Nov 1979, Middle Temple
Qualifications: [MA (Oxon), DipGerms]

SEWELL TIMOTHY WILLIAM

10 King's Bench Walk
1st Floor, Temple, London EC4Y 7EB,
Telephone: 0171 353 2501
Call date: May 1976, Gray's Inn
Qualifications: [LLB (Hons) (Leics)]

SEYMOUR MISS JUDIT EMESE AGNES

Gray's Inn Chambers
5th Floor, Gray's Inn, London WC1R 5JA,
Telephone: 0171 404 1111
Call date: Oct 1990, Inner Temple
Qualifications: [LLB (Lond)]

SEYMOUR MARK WILLIAM

9-12 Bell Yard
London WC2A 2LF,
Telephone: 0171 400 1800
Call date: Oct 1992, Middle Temple
Qualifications: [MA (Hons)]

SEYMOUR RICHARD WILLIAM QC (1991)

Monckton Chambers
4 Raymond Buildings, Gray's Inn, London
WC1R 5BP, Telephone: 0171 405 7211
E-mail: chambers@monckton.co.uk
Call date: July 1972, Gray's Inn
Recorder
Qualifications: [MA (Cantab)]

SEYMOUR THOMAS OLIVER

Wilberforce Chambers
8 New Square, Lincoln's Inn, London
WC2A 3QP, Telephone: 0171 306 0102
E-mail: chambers@wilberforce.co.uk
Call date: July 1975, Inner Temple
Qualifications: [MA (Cantab)]

SEYS LLEWELLYN ANTHONY JOHN

Farrar's Building
Temple, London EC4Y 7BD,
Telephone: 0171 583 9241
E-mail: chambers@farrarsbuilding.co.uk
Call date: Nov 1972, Gray's Inn
Recorder
Qualifications: [MA, BCL (Oxon)]

SHACKLEFORD MISS SUSAN ANGELA

New Court
Temple, London EC4Y 9BE,
Telephone: 0171 583 5123/0171 583 0510
Call date: Nov 1980, Inner Temple
Qualifications: [BA (Lond)]

SHADAREVIAN PAUL

East Anglian Chambers
Sanders House 52 North Hill, Colchester
CO1 1PY, Telephone: 01206 572756
East Anglian Chambers
Gresham House 5 Museum Street, Ipswich
IP1 1HQ, Telephone: 01473 214481
East Anglian Chambers
57 London Street, Norwich NR2 1HL,
Telephone: 01603 617351
Call date: July 1984, Gray's Inn
Qualifications: [BA (Essex)]

SHAH AKHIL

5 Bell Yard
London WC2A 2JR, Telephone: 0171 333 8811
Call date: Nov 1990, Inner Temple
Qualifications: [BA (Cantab)]

SHAH BAJUL AMRATLAL SOMCHAND

24 Old Bldgs
Ground Floor, Lincoln's Inn, London
WC2A 3UJ, Telephone: 0171 404 0946
E-mail: clerks@24oldbuildings.law.co.uk
Call date: Oct 1996, Lincoln's Inn
Qualifications: [BA (Hons), BCL (Oxon)]

SHAH FERDOUS

1 Garfield Road
Battersea, London SW11 5PL,
Telephone: 0171 228 1137
Call date: July 1969, Lincoln's Inn
Qualifications: [BCom]

SHAH MISS SHEENA

Phoenix Chambers
First Floor Gray's Inn Chambers, Gray's Inn,
London WC1R 5JA, Telephone: 0171 404 7888
Call date: Nov 1993, Inner Temple
Qualifications: [LLB (Hons)(Lond)]

SHAIKH EUR.ING. (JAIKUMAR) CHRISTOPHER (SAMUEL

Avondale Chambers
2 Avondale Avenue, London N12 8EJ,
Telephone: 0181 445 9984
Equity Chambers
Suite 110, Gazette Buildings 168 Corporation
Street, Birmingham B4 6TS,
Telephone: 0121 233 2100
Door Tenant
Call date: July 1980, Gray's Inn
Qualifications: [BSc Eng (Hons)(Lond), C.Eng,
M.R.I.N.A., MI.MAR.E]

SHAIKH MOHAMMAD RASHID

9 King's Bench Walk
Basement, Temple, London EC4Y 7DX,
Telephone: 0171 353 9564
E-mail: jvlee@btinternet.com
Call date: Nov 1968, Inner Temple
Qualifications: [BA (Hons), MA, LLB (Karachi)]

SHAKOOR TARIQ BIN

6 Fountain Court
Steelhouse Lane, Birmingham B4 6DR,
Telephone: 0121 233 3282
Call date: Feb 1992, Inner Temple
Qualifications: [BA (Lancs), CPE]

SHALDON MISS NICOLA

2 Crown Office Row
2nd Floor, Temple, London EC4Y 7HJ,
Telephone: 0171 797 8000
Call date: Oct 1994, Middle Temple
Qualifications: [MA (Cantab), LLB
(Hons)(Lond)]

SHALE JUSTIN ANTON

4 King's Bench Walk
Ground/First Floor, Temple, London
EC4Y 7DL, Telephone: 0171 822 8822
E-mail: 4kbw@barristersatlaw.com
King's Bench Chambers
Wellington House 175 Holdenhurst Road,
Bournemouth, Dorset BH8 8DQ,
Telephone: 01202 250025
Call date: July 1982, Inner Temple
Qualifications: [LLB (Soton)]

SHAMASH MISS ANNE MARION

14 Tooks Court
Cursitor St, London EC4A 1LB,
Telephone: 0171 405 8828
E-mail: clerks @tooks.law.co.uk
Call date: Nov 1986, Gray's Inn
Qualifications: [BA]

SHANKARDASS VIJAY SOHAG TRILOKNATH

13 Old Square
Ground Floor, Lincoln's Inn, London
WC2A 3UA, Telephone: 0171 404 4800
Door Tenant
Call date: Nov 1972, Lincoln's Inn
Qualifications: [B.Sc.(Delhi), MA,LLM (Cantab)]

SHANKS MURRAY GEORGE

Fountain Court
Temple, London EC4Y 9DH,
Telephone: 0171 583 3335
E-mail: chambers@fountaincourt.co.uk
Call date: Nov 1984, Middle Temple
Qualifications: [MA (Cantab)]

SHANNON THOMAS ERIC

Queen's Chambers
5 John Dalton Street, Manchester M2 6ET,
Telephone: 0161 834 6875/4738
4 Camden Place
Preston PR1 3JL, Telephone: 01772 828300
Call date: Nov 1974, Middle Temple
Qualifications: [BA (Oxon)]

SHANT MISS NIRMAL KANTA

1 High Pavement
Nottingham NG1 1HF,
Telephone: 0115 9418218
Call date: July 1984, Gray's Inn
Qualifications: [LLB (Leics)]

SHAPIRO SELWYN

Guildford Chambers
Stoke House Leapale Lane, Guildford, Surrey
GU1 4LY, Telephone: 01483 539131
E-mail: guildford.barristers@btinternet.com
Call date: July 1979, Inner Temple
Qualifications: [LLB (Lond)]

SHARDA ASHOK KUMAR

Chambers of Raana Sheikh
Gray's Inn Chambers, Gray's Inn, London
WC1R, Telephone: 0171 831 5344
E-mail: s.mcblain@btinternet.com
Call date: Nov 1979, Inner Temple
Qualifications: [BA]

SHARIF MS NADIA

Berkeley Chambers
321 Stratford Road, Shirley, Solihull, West
Midlands B90 3BL, Telephone: 0121 733 6925
Call date: Nov 1985, Lincoln's Inn
Qualifications: [BA (Hons)]

SHARLAND ANDREW JOHN

4-5 Gray's Inn Square
Ground Floor, Gray's Inn, London WC1R 5AY,
Telephone: 0171 404 5252
E-mail: chambers@4-5graysinnsquare.co.uk
Call date: Oct 1996, Gray's Inn
Qualifications: [LLB (Lond), BCL (Oxon)]

SHARMA BHAWANI PERSAUD

Primrose Chambers
5 Primrose Way, Alperton, Middlesex
HA0 1DS, Telephone: 0181 998 1806
Call date: July 1975, Inner Temple
Qualifications: [FIArb]

SHARMA KISHORE

4-5 Gray's Inn Square
Ground Floor, Gray's Inn, London WC1R 5AY,
Telephone: 0171 404 5252
E-mail: chambers@4-5graysinnsquare.co.uk
Call date: Nov 1986, Gray's Inn
Qualifications: [LLB (London)]

SHARMA PAVAN

Fleet Chambers
Mitre House 44-46 Fleet Street, London
EC4Y 1BN, Telephone: 0171 936 3707
Call date: Oct 1993, Middle Temple
Qualifications: [LLB (Hons)(Lond)]

D

D

SHARMA MISS RAKHEE

Kingsway Chambers
88 Kingsway, Holborn, London WC2B 6AA,
Telephone: 07000 653529
E-mail: lanreoke@lineone.net
Call date: Nov 1995, Gray's Inn
Qualifications: [LLB]

SHARMA MRS SUMAN

3 Temple Gardens (North)
Fifth Floor, Temple, London EC4Y 9AU,
Telephone: 0171 353 0853/4/7222
E-mail: 100106.1577@compuserve.com
Call date: May 1994, Middle Temple
Qualifications: [LLB (Hons)]

SHARP ALASTAIR RICHARD FRANCIS

2 Pump Court
1st Floor, Temple, London EC4Y 7AH,
Telephone: 0171 353 5597
Call date: Nov 1968, Middle Temple
Recorder
Qualifications: [MA (Cantab)]

SHARP CHRISTOPHER FRANCIS

St John's Chambers
Small Street, Bristol BS1 1DW,
Telephone: 0117 9213456/298514
E-mail: clerks@stjohns.uk.com
Call date: July 1975, Inner Temple
Qualifications: [MA (Oxon)]

SHARP DAVID IAN

Francis Taylor Bldg
3rd Floor, Temple, London EC4Y 7BY,
Telephone: 0171 797 7250
Call date: Nov 1986, Middle Temple
Qualifications: [BA (Oxon), MA, Dip Law]

SHARP JONATHAN JEREMY GRANVILLE

2 King's Bench Walk
Ground Floor, Temple, London EC4Y 7DE,
Telephone: 0171 353 1746
E-mail: 2kbw@atlas.co.uk
King's Bench Chambers
115 North Hill, Plymouth PL4 8JY,
Telephone: 01752 221551
Call date: July 1987, Inner Temple
Qualifications: [BA (Oxon) Dip Law]

SHARP THE HON VICTORIA MADELEINE

1 Brick Court
1st Floor, Temple, London EC4Y 9BY,
Telephone: 0171 353 8845
E-mail: clerks@1brickcourt.co.uk
Call date: July 1979, Inner Temple
Qualifications: [LLB (Bris)]

SHARPE ANDREW

Spon Chambers
13 Spon Street, Coventry, Warwickshire
CV1 3BA, Telephone: 01203 632977
Call date: Nov 1972, Gray's Inn

SHARPE DENNIS NIGEL

17 Bedford Row
London WC1R 4EB,
Telephone: 0171 831 7314
E-mail: IBoard7314@AOL.com
Call date: July 1976, Inner Temple
Qualifications: [LLB (Exon), BCL (Oxon)]

SHARPE MALCOLM DAVID

Adrian Lyon's Chambers
14 Castle Street, Liverpool L2 0NE,
Telephone: 0151 236 4421/8240
E-mail: chambers14@aol.com
Call date: July 1989, Lincoln's Inn
Qualifications: [LLB (Sheff), LLM (Belfast)]

SHARPE MARTIN LAURENCE

1 Pump Court
Lower Ground Floor, Temple, London
EC4Y 7AB, Telephone: 0171 583 2012/
353 4341
E-mail: (name) @1pumpcourt.co.uk
Call date: Nov 1989, Middle Temple
Qualifications: [BA Hons (Manc), MA (L'pool)]

SHARPE THOMAS ANTHONY EDWARD QC (1994)

1 Essex Court
Ground Floor, Temple, London EC4Y 9AR,
Telephone: 0171 583 2000
E-mail: clerks@oneessexcourt.co.uk
Call date: May 1976, Lincoln's Inn
Qualifications: [MA(Cantab)]

SHARPLES JOHN EDMUND

St John's Chambers
Small Street, Bristol BS1 1DW,
Telephone: 0117 9213456/298514
E-mail: clerks@stjohns.uk.com
Call date: Nov 1992, Middle Temple
Qualifications: [BA (Oxon), LLM
(Pennsylvania), LLM (Cantab)]

SHARPSTON MISS ELEANOR VERONICA ELIZABETH

4 Paper Bldgs
Ground Floor, Temple, London EC4Y 7EX,
Telephone: 0171 353 3366/583 7155
E-mail: clerks@4paperbuildings.com
Call date: Nov 1980, Middle Temple
Qualifications: [MA (Cantab)]

SHAW (RICHARD) JULIAN (FRANKLYN)

21 White Friars
Chester CH1 1NZ, Telephone: 01244 323070
Call date: Nov 1984, Gray's Inn
Qualifications: [LLB (Wales)]

SHAW ANTONY MICHAEL NINIAN QC (1994)

4 Brick Court
Ground Floor, Temple, London EC4Y 9AD,
Telephone: 0171 797 7766
E-mail: chambers@4brick.co.uk
Call date: July 1975, Middle Temple
Qualifications: [BA (Oxon)]

SHAW CHARLES NOEL

1 Gray's Inn Square
Ground Floor, London WC1R 5AA,
Telephone: 0171 405 8946/7/8
Call date: Feb 1991, Inner Temple
Qualifications: [MA (Cantab), MSc (Lond)]

SHAW MISS ELIZABETH

Wilberforce Chambers
Bishop Lane, Hull HU1 1PA,
Telephone: 01482 323264
E-mail: clerks@hullbar.demon.co.uk
Call date: Nov 1986, Middle Temple
Qualifications: [BA]

SHAW GEOFFREY PETER QC (1991)

1 Brick Court
1st Floor, Temple, London EC4Y 9BY,
Telephone: 0171 353 8845
E-mail: clerks@1brickcourt.co.uk
Call date: Nov 1968, Gray's Inn
Qualifications: [BA, BCL (Oxon)]

SHAW JAMES NICHOLAS

10 King's Bench Walk
1st Floor, Temple, London EC4Y 7EB,
Telephone: 0171 353 2501
Call date: Nov 1988, Inner Temple
Qualifications: [LLB (Reading)]

SHAW MISS JENNIFER BRIDGET

Francis Taylor Bldg
Ground Floor, Temple, London EC4Y 7BY,
Telephone: 0171 353 7768/7769/2711
Call date: Nov 1990, Inner Temple
Qualifications: [LLB (Lond)]

SHAW JOHN HOWARD

29 Bedford Row Chambers
London WC1R 4HE,
Telephone: 0171 831 2626
Call date: July 1973, Inner Temple
Qualifications: [LLB (Lond)]

SHAW PROF MALCOLM NATHAN

Essex Court Chambers
24 Lincoln's Inn Fields, London WC2A 3ED,
Telephone: 0171 813 8000
E-mail: clerksroom@essexcourt-chambers.co.uk
Call date: July 1988, Gray's Inn
Qualifications: [LLB (L'pool), LLM (Israel), PhD
(Keele)]

SHAW MARK RICHARD

2 Hare Court
Ground Floor, Temple, London EC4Y 7BH,
Telephone: 0171 583 1770
E-mail: 2_Hare_Court@link.org
Call date: July 1987, Inner Temple
Qualifications: [BA (Durham) LLM, (Cantab)]

SHAW MICHAEL JOHN

2 Mitre Ct Bldgs
1st Floor, Temple, London EC4Y 7BX,
Telephone: 0171 353 1353
Call date: Nov 1994, Middle Temple
Qualifications: [LLB (Hons)]

SHAW PETER FRANCIS

Cloisters
1st Floor, Temple, London EC4Y 7AA,
Telephone: 0171 827 4000
E-mail: clerks@cloisters.com
Call date: Nov 1992, Inner Temple
Qualifications: [LLB (Brunel)]

SHAW PETER MAURICE

4 King's Bench Walk
Ground/First Floor, Temple, London
EC4Y 7DL, Telephone: 0171 822 8822
E-mail: 4kbw@barristersatlaw.com
Call date: Nov 1995, Middle Temple
Qualifications: [BA (Hons)]

SHAW SAMUEL BENJAMIN BARNABY

1 Paper Bldgs
1st Floor, Temple, London EC4Y 7EP,
Telephone: 0171 353 3728/4953
Call date: Nov 1996, Middle Temple
Qualifications: [MA (Hons)(Edinburgh)]

SHAW STEPHEN

Lamb Chambers
Lamb Building, Temple, London EC4Y 7AS,
Telephone: 0171 797 8300
E-mail: lambchambers@link.org
Call date: July 1975, Gray's Inn
Qualifications: [LLB, ACIArb]

SHAY STEPHEN EVERETT

1 King's Bench Walk
2nd Floor, Temple, London EC4Y 7DB,
Telephone: 0171 936 1500
E-mail: ddear@1kbw.co.uk
Call date: Nov 1984, Middle Temple
Qualifications: [BA Hons (Oxon)]

SHEA MS CAROLINE MARY

Falcon Chambers
Falcon Court, London EC4Y 1AA,
Telephone: 0171 353 2484/7
Call date: Nov 1994, Middle Temple
Qualifications: [MA (Cantab)]

SHEARS PHILIP PETER QC (1996)

9 Bedford Row
London WC1R 4AZ,
Telephone: 0171 242 3555
E-mail: clerks@9br.co.uk
Call date: July 1972, Middle Temple
Recorder
Qualifications: [LLB (Nottm) LLB, (Cantab)]

SHEEHAN MISS ANNE-MARIE

Bell Yard Chambers
116/118 Chancery Lane, London WC2A 1PP,
Telephone: 0171 306 9292
Call date: July 1994, Lincoln's Inn
Qualifications: [LLB (Hons)]

SHEEHAN MALCOLM PETER

2 Harcourt Bldgs
Ground Floor/Left, Temple, London
EC4Y 9DB, Telephone: 0171 583 9020
E-mail: clerks@harcourt.co.uk
Stanbrook & Henderson
2 Harcourt Bldgs 2nd Floor, Temple, London
EC4Y 9DB, Telephone: 0171 353 0101
E-mail: clerks@harcourt.co.uk
Call date: Oct 1993, Lincoln's Inn
Qualifications: [MA (Hons)(Oxon)]

SHEFF MS JANINE RACHEL

18 Red Lion Court
(Off Fleet Street), London EC4A 3EB,
Telephone: 0171 520 6000
Thornwood House
102 New London Road, Chelmsford, Essex
CM2 0RG, Telephone: 01245 280880
Call date: July 1983, Middle Temple
Qualifications: [LLB (B'ham)]

SHEFFI MISS BOSMATH

9 King's Bench Walk
Ground Floor, Temple, London EC4Y 7DX,
Telephone: 0171 353 7202/3909
Call date: Nov 1991, Middle Temple
Qualifications: [BA Hons (Kent)]

SHEIKH AMJAD IQBAL

20 Britton Street
1st Floor, London EC1M 5NQ,
Telephone: 0171 608 3765
Call date: Nov 1988, Gray's Inn
Qualifications: [BA]

SHEIKH IRSHAD AHMED

2 Paper Buildings
Basement, Temple, London EC4Y 7ET,
Telephone: 0171 353 0933
Call date: July 1983, Lincoln's Inn
Qualifications: [LLB (Hons, Hull)]

SHEIKH KHALID FADHAL-RAHMAN

Harrow on the Hill Chambers
60 High Street, Harrow on the Hill, Middlesex
HA1 3LL, Telephone: 0181 423 7444
Call date: Feb 1993, Middle Temple
Qualifications: [LLB (Hons)(Lond), LLM
(Lond)]

SHEIKH MS RAANA

Chambers of Raana Sheikh
Gray's Inn Chambers, Gray's Inn, London
WC1R, Telephone: 0171 831 5344
E-mail: s.mcblain@btinternet.com
Call date: Nov 1977, Middle Temple
Qualifications: [LLB]

SHEKERDEMIAN MISS MARCIA ANNA-MARIA

11 Stone Bldgs
Ground Floor, Lincoln's Inn, London
WC2A 3TG, Telephone: 0171 831 6381
E-mail: clerks@11StoneBuildings.law.co.uk
Call date: July 1987, Middle Temple
Qualifications: [MA (Cantab)]

SHELDON CLIVE DAVID

11 King's Bench Walk
Temple, London EC4Y 7EQ,
Telephone: 0171 632 8500
E-mail: clerksroom@11-kbw.law.co.uk
Call date: Nov 1991, Inner Temple
Qualifications: [BA (Cantab), LLM
(Philadelphia)]

SHELDON RICHARD MICHAEL QC (1996)

3/4 South Square
Gray's Inn, London WC1R 5HP,
Telephone: 0171 696 9900
E-mail: clerks@southsquare.com
Call date: July 1979, Gray's Inn
Qualifications: [MA (Cantab)]

SHELDON RICHARD NEIL

Bank House Chambers
Old Bank House, Hartshead, Sheffield S1 2EL,
Telephone: 0114 2751223
Call date: July 1984, Lincoln's Inn
Qualifications: [LLB (Leeds)]

SHELDRAKE MISS CHRISTINE ANNE

3 Dr Johnson's Bldgs
Ground Floor, Temple, London EC4Y 7BA,
Telephone: 0171 353 4854
Call date: July 1977, Middle Temple
Qualifications: [LLB (Lond)]

SHELLARD ROBIN JAMES SPENCER

All Saints Chambers
9/11 Broad Street, Bristol BS1 2HP,
Telephone: 0117 921 1966
Call date: Nov 1992, Inner Temple
Qualifications: [BA (Wales), Dip in Law]

SHELTON GORDON EDWARD

Broadway House Chambers
Broadway House 9 Bank Street, Bradford,
West Yorkshire BD1 1TW,
Telephone: 01274 722560
Call date: Nov 1981, Inner Temple
Qualifications: [LLB (Leics)]

SHELTON-AGAR CHARLES WEDDERBURN SHELTON

"Rydal Mount"
164 Heaton Moor Road, Heaton Moor,
Stockport, Cheshire SK4 4HS,
Telephone: 0161 432 8875
Call date: July 1965, Gray's Inn
Qualifications: [BA (Cantab)]

D

SHENTON MISS RACHEL CLAIRE

21 White Friars
Chester CH1 1NZ, Telephone: 01244 323070
Call date: Nov 1993, Middle Temple
Qualifications: [LLB (Hons)(Lancs)]

SHENTON MISS SUZANNE HELENE

One Garden Court
Ground Floor, Temple, London EC4Y 9BJ,
Telephone: 0171 797 7900
Call date: July 1973, Middle Temple
Qualifications: [LLB (Manch)]

SHEPHERD NIGEL PATRICK

8 King's Bench Walk North
1 Park Square East, Leeds LS1 2NE,
Telephone: 0113 2439797
8 King's Bench Walk
2nd Floor, Temple, London EC4Y 7DU,
Telephone: 0171 797 8888
Call date: July 1973, Inner Temple
Qualifications: [LLB]

SHEPHERD PHILIP ALEXANDER

5 Bell Yard
London WC2A 2JR, Telephone: 0171 333 8811
Call date: Nov 1975, Gray's Inn
Assistant Recorder
Qualifications: [BSc (Econ)]

Fax: 0171 333 8831;
Out of hours telephone: 0181 870 8008

Types of work: Arbitration; Aviation;
Commercial litigation; Insurance; Insurance/
reinsurance; Private international; Sale and
carriage of goods

Other professional qualifications: Royal
Aeronautical Society; European Air Law Group;
Lawyers Flying Association; Commercial Bar
Association

Membership of foreign bars: Isle of Man

Circuit: Western

Other professional experience: Former
insurance broker at Lloyd's

Languages spoken: French, Italian

Reported cases: *Sidhu v British Airways*,
[1997] 1 WLR 26. Exclusivity of remedy under
Warsaw Convention - availability of common
law remedy (House of Lords).
McCausland v SIS Securities, [1997] 1 WLR.
Variation of contract - sale of land - formalities
required (CP).
*TGA Chapman v Christopher and Sun Alliance
Plc*, [1998] 1 WLR 12, 1997. Costs against
insurers in excess of limit of indemnity (leave to
appeal granted by House of Lords).
Thomas Cook v Air Malta, [1997] Lloyd's Rep,
1997. Carriage by air - armed robbery - wilful
misconduct - Article 25 Warsaw Convention.
H 5 Air Services Norway AS v CAA, [1998] 1
Lloyd's Rep 364, 1997. Carriage by air - cabotage
- restriction on night flights - effect of
Community Law 'open skies' Directive.

SHEPPARD MISS ABIGAIL RUTH ALICE

4 Brick Court
Temple, London EC4Y 9AD,
Telephone: 0171 797 8910
Call date: Nov 1990, Inner Temple
Qualifications: [BA, Dip Law (PCL)]

SHEPPARD TIMOTHY DERIE

Bracton Chambers
95a Chancery Lane, London WC2A 1DT,
Telephone: 0171 242 4248
Call date: Nov 1995, Inner Temple
Qualifications: [BSc (Edinburgh), CPE (Lond)]

SHER JULES QC (1981)

Wilberforce Chambers
8 New Square, Lincoln's Inn, London
WC2A 3QP, Telephone: 0171 306 0102
E-mail: chambers@wilberforce.co.uk
Call date: July 1968, Inner Temple
Qualifications: [BCom, LLB (Rand), BCL
(Oxon)]

SHER MISS SHAMIM AKHTAR

2 Middle Temple Lane
3rd Floor, Temple, London EC4Y 9AA,
Telephone: 0171 583 4540
Call date: May 1995, Lincoln's Inn
Qualifications: [LLB (Hons)]

SHERBORNE DAVID ALEXANDER

5 Raymond Buildings
1st Floor, Gray's Inn, London WC1R 5BP,
Telephone: 0171 242 2902
Call date: Oct 1992, Gray's Inn
Qualifications: [BA (Oxon)]

SHERBORNE MONTAGUE QC (1993)

3 Raymond Buildings
Gray's Inn, London WC1R 5BH,
Telephone: 0171 831 3833
E-mail: chambers@threeraymond.demon.co.uk
Call date: Feb 1960, Middle Temple
Qualifications: [BA (Oxon)]

SHERIDAN FRANCIS ANTHONY

Furnival Chambers
32 Furnival Street, London EC4A 1JQ,
Telephone: 0171 405 3232
E-mail: clerks@furnivallaw.co.uk
Call date: July 1980, Inner Temple
Qualifications: [BA Hons]

SHERIDAN MAURICE BERNARD GERARD

3 Verulam Buildings
London WC1R 5NT,
Telephone: 0171 831 8441
E-mail: clerks@3verulam.co.uk
Call date: July 1984, Middle Temple
Qualifications: [LLM (Cantab)]

Fax: 0171 831 8479; DX: LDE 331;
Other comms: E-mail
msheridan@mbgs.demon.co.uk

Types of work: Agriculture; Banking;
Commercial; Commercial litigation; EC and
competition law; Environment; Private
international; Waste management

Other professional qualifications: Member of the
Bar European Group; British Italian Law
Association; British Bulgarian Law Association;
Associate with the Foundation for International
Environmental Law and Development (FIELD)

Other professional experience: British Assistant
to the President of the Italian Constitutional
Court (over two and a half years); Assistant to
the Italian Minister for European Affairs (two
years)

Languages spoken: French, Italian

Publications: *EC Legal Systems: An
Introductory Guide*, 1993; *EFTA Legal Systems:
An Introductory Guide*, 1994; *Italian
Yearbook of Civil Procedure* [1991-6] (English
Editor)

SHERIDAN NORMAN PATRICK

11 Bolt Court
London EC4A 3DQ,
Telephone: 0171 353 2300
E-mail: boltct11@aol.com
Redhill Chambers
Seloduct House, 30 Station Road, Redhill,
Surrey RH1 1NF, Telephone: 01737 780781
Call date: Oct 1990, Middle Temple
Qualifications: [BSc (Lond), MPhil, Dip Law
(City)]

Fax: 0171 353 1878; DX: LDE 0022

Types of work: Common law (general);
Environment; Personal injury

Other professional qualifications: LLM
(Environmental Law)

Awards and memberships: Member of the
United Kingdom Environmental Law
Association; Member of the Environmental Law
Foundation

Other professional experience: Prior to being
called to the Bar I was a research biochemist for
ten years in the UK and the USA

Languages spoken: French

SHERIDAN PAUL ADRIAN

Manchester House Chambers
18-22 Bridge Street, Manchester M3 3BZ,
Telephone: 0161 834 7007
Call date: Nov 1984, Lincoln's Inn
Qualifications: [LLB(Belfast)]

SHERIDAN PETER QC (1977)

11 Stone Bldgs
Ground Floor, Lincoln's Inn, London
WC2A 3TG, Telephone: 0171 831 6381
E-mail: clerks@11StoneBuildings.law.co.uk
Call date: June 1955, Middle Temple
Qualifications: [BA (Oxon)]

SHERIDAN SHANE PETER BRIGHT

4 Brick Court
1st Floor, Temple, London EC4Y 9AD,
Telephone: 0171 583 8455
Call date: Feb 1973, Inner Temple
Qualifications: [BSc (Hons)(Lond)]

SHERMAN ROBERT LESLIE

2 Dr Johnson's Building
Temple, London EC4Y 7AY,
Telephone: 0171 353 4716
Call date: July 1977, Gray's Inn
Qualifications: [LLB (Leeds)]

SHERMAN MISS SUSAN ELIZABETH

Chavasse Court Chambers
2nd Floor Chavasse Court, 24 Lord Street,
Liverpool L2 1TA, Telephone: 0151 707 1191
Call date: Nov 1993, Middle Temple
Qualifications: [LLB (Hons)(Lancs)]

SHERRARD CHARLES ISAAC

Furnival Chambers
32 Furnival Street, London EC4A 1JQ,
Telephone: 0171 405 3232
E-mail: clerks@furnivallaw.co.uk
Call date: Nov 1986, Middle Temple
Qualifications: [LLB]

SHERRATT MATTHEW JOHN

Thomas More Chambers
52 Carey Street, Lincoln's Inn, London
WC2A 2JB, Telephone: 0171 404 7000
Call date: July 1994, Inner Temple
Qualifications: [LLB (New Zealand), LLM
(Miami, USA)]

SHERRY EAMONN MARTIN

1 Gray's Inn Square
Ground Floor, London WC1R 5AA,
Telephone: 0171 405 8946/7/8
Call date: Nov 1990, Gray's Inn
Qualifications: [LLB (Hons)]

SHERRY MICHAEL GABRIEL

3 Temple Gardens Tax Chambers
1st Floor, Temple, London EC4Y 9AU,
Telephone: 0171 353 7884
Peel Court Chambers
45 Hardman Street, Manchester M3 3PL,
Telephone: 0161 832 3791
Door Tenant
Call date: Nov 1978, Gray's Inn
Qualifications: [MA (Oxon), FCA, ATII]

Fax: 0171 583 2044; Other comms: E-mail
sherry@taxlawchambers.demon.co.uk

Types of work: Tax - capital and income; Tax -
corporate; VAT

Awards and memberships: President, Institute
of Indirect Taxation; Deputy Chairman, Faculty
of Taxation, ICAEW

Other professional experience: Secretary,
Revenue Bar Association (1986-94); Ernst &
Young (1978-83)

Publications: *Whiteman on Income Tax* (Sweet
& Maxwell 3rd edn), (Co-editor), 1988; *Tax
Planning for Family Company Shareholders*
(Keyhaven), 1993

Reported cases: *R v Customs & Excise
Commissioners ex parte Kay & others*, [1996]
STC 1500, Nov 1996. The anticipation by the
Commissioners of a change in the law was held
to be unlawful.

Practice:
Time divides (i) one-third planning etc; (ii) half
resolving dispute (including litigation); (iii) one-
sixth back duty; and (iv) the balance including
tax-related judicial review, professional
negligence in relation to tax etc. Approximately
one-third of turnover is value added tax with
corporate matters dominating both direct and
indirect tax work. Approximately half of
turnover arises from DPA. A particular interest is
the impact of accountancy evidence on
measuring taxable profit.

SHERWIN MISS DEBORAH ANN

Fountain Chambers
Cleveland Business Centre 1 Watson Street,
Middlesbrough TS1 2RQ,
Telephone: 01642 217037
Call date: July 1979, Inner Temple
Assistant Recorder
Qualifications: [LLB (Exon)]

SHETTY RAJEEV RAMA

Harrow on the Hill Chambers
60 High Street, Harrow on the Hill, Middlesex
HA1 3LL, Telephone: 0181 423 7444
Windsor Barristers' Chambers
Windsor, Telephone: 01753 648899
Call date: Mar 1996, Inner Temple
Qualifications: [LLB (S'ton)]

SHIELD MISS DEBORAH

21 White Friars
Chester CH1 1NZ, Telephone: 01244 323070
Call date: Nov 1991, Inner Temple
Qualifications: [LLB]

SHIELDS MISS SONJA MARION

1 Crown Office Row
2nd Floor, Temple, London EC4Y 7HH,
Telephone: 0171 797 7111
Call date: July 1977, Inner Temple
Qualifications: [BA (Cantab)]

SHIELDS THOMAS MCGREGOR QC (1993)

1 Brick Court
1st Floor, Temple, London EC4Y 9BY,
Telephone: 0171 353 8845
E-mail: clerks@1brickcourt.co.uk
Call date: July 1973, Inner Temple
Qualifications: [LLB]

SHIELS IAN

30 Park Square
Leeds LS1 2PF, Telephone: 0113 2436388
Call date: Nov 1992, Inner Temple
Qualifications: [BA (Leeds), Dip in Law (City)]

SHIER FRANCIS PETER

Mitre Court Chambers
3rd Floor, Temple, London EC4Y 7BP,
Telephone: 0171 353 9394
Call date: July 1952, Gray's Inn

SHIKDER KUTUB UDDIN AHMED

Tower Hamlets Barristers Chambers
First Floor 45 Brick Lane, London E1 6PU,
Telephone: 0171 247 9825
Tower Hamlets Barristers Chambers
37B Princelet Street, London E1 5LP,
Telephone: 0171 377 8090
Call date: Nov 1990, Lincoln's Inn
Qualifications: [LLB (Hons), MA]

SHILLINGFORD GEORGE MILES

11 New Square
Ground Floor, Lincoln's Inn, London
WC2A 3QB, Telephone: 0171 831 0081
E-mail: 11newsquare.co.uk
Call date: Apr 1964, Inner Temple
Qualifications: [MA Jurisp (Oxon)]

SHILSON STUART JAMES

Guildhall Chambers
23 Broad Street, Bristol BS1 2HG,
Telephone: 0117 9273366
Call date: Oct 1992, Middle Temple
Qualifications: [BA (Hons) (Oxon), MSc
(Oxon), MPhil (Cantab)]

SHINER BRENDAN ELIAS JOHN

All Saints Chambers
9/11 Broad Street, Bristol BS1 2HP,
Telephone: 0117 921 1966
Call date: June 1955, Middle Temple
Qualifications: [MA (Oxon)]

SHIPLEY MISS JANE

6 Park Square
Leeds LS1 2LW, Telephone: 0113 2459763
E-mail: chambers@no6.co.uk
Call date: July 1974, Gray's Inn
Recorder
Qualifications: [MA (Oxon)]

SHIPLEY NORMAN GRAHAM

19 Old Buildings
Lincoln's Inn, London WC2A 3UP,
Telephone: 0171 405 2001
E-mail: clerks@oldbuildingsip.com
Call date: July 1973, Lincoln's Inn

Qualifications: [MA (Cantab) Dip, Comp Sci (Cantab)]

Fax: 0171 405 0001; DX: 397 London, Chancery Lane

Types of work: Competition; Copyright; EC and competition law; Entertainment; Film, cable, TV; Information technology; Intellectual property; Patents; Trademarks

Awards and memberships: Intellectual Property Bar Association; Chancery Bar Association

Reported cases: *British Sugar v James Robertson and Sons Ltd*, [1996] RPC 281, 1996. The 'Treat' trademark case.
Circuit Systems Ltd v Zuken Redac Ltd, [1997] 3 WLR 1177, 1997. Validity of assigning causes of action.
Roger Bance's Application, [1996] RPC 667, 1996. Copyright licence of right case.
Roger Bullivat Ltd v Ellis, [1987] FSR 172, 1987. Confidential information case and 'leap frog' injunctions.

SHIPSEY MISS HELEN JUDITH

55 Temple Chambers
Temple Avenue, London EC4Y 0HP,
Telephone: 0171 353 7400
Call date: Nov 1991, Inner Temple
Qualifications: [LLB (Hons)(Lond)]

SHIPWRIGHT ADRIAN JOHN

Pump Court Tax Chambers
16 Bedford Row, London WC1R 4EB,
Telephone: 0171 414 8080
Call date: Feb 1993, Lincoln's Inn
Qualifications: [BCL, MA]

SHOKER MAKKAN SINGH

Priory Chambers
2 Fountain Court, Steelhouse Lane,
Birmingham B4 6DR,
Telephone: 0121 236 3882/1375
Call date: May 1981, Inner Temple
Qualifications: [LLB (Lond)]

SHORROCK JOHN MICHAEL QC (1988)

Peel Court Chambers
45 Hardman Street, Manchester M3 3HA,
Telephone: 0161 832 3791
Call date: July 1966, Inner Temple
Recorder
Qualifications: [MA (Cantab)]

SHORROCK PHILIP GEOFFREY

2 Harcourt Bldgs
1st Floor, Temple, London EC4Y 9DB,
Telephone: 0171 353 2112/2817
Call date: Nov 1978, Middle Temple
Qualifications: [BA (Cantab)]

SHORT ANDREW JOHN

4 Brick Court
Ground Floor, Temple, London EC4Y 9AD,
Telephone: 0171 797 7766
E-mail: chambers@4brick.co.uk
Call date: Nov 1990, Gray's Inn
Qualifications: [LLB (Bristol)]

SHRIMPTON MS CLAIRE ALISON

Guildford Chambers
Stoke House Leapale Lane, Guildford, Surrey
GU1 4LY, Telephone: 01483 539131
E-mail: guildford.barristers@btinternet.com
Call date: July 1983, Inner Temple
Qualifications: [LLB (Hull)]

SHRIMPTON MICHAEL

Francis Taylor Bldg
3rd Floor, Temple, London EC4Y 7BY,
Telephone: 0171 797 7250
Call date: Nov 1983, Gray's Inn
Qualifications: [LLB(Cardiff)]

SHRIMPTON ROBERT JAMES

3 Paper Bldgs
2nd Floor, Temple, London EC4Y 7EU,
Telephone: 0171 353 6208
Call date: July 1981, Middle Temple
Qualifications: [LLB (Hons) (Hull)]

D

SHUMAN MISS KAREN ANN ELIZABETH

Bracton Chambers
95a Chancery Lane, London WC2A 1DT,
Telephone: 0171 242 4248
Call date: Oct 1991, Lincoln's Inn
Qualifications: [LLB (Hons) (Birm)]

SHUTTLEWORTH TIMOTHY WILLIAM

Francis Taylor Bldg
3rd Floor, Temple, London EC4Y 7BY,
Telephone: 0171 797 7250
Call date: July 1971, Gray's Inn
Qualifications: [LLB]

SIBERRY (WILLIAM) RICHARD QC (1989)

Essex Court Chambers
24 Lincoln's Inn Fields, London WC2A 3ED,
Telephone: 0171 813 8000
E-mail: clerksroom@essexcourt-chambers.co.uk
Call date: July 1974, Middle Temple
Assistant Recorder
Qualifications: [MA, LLB (Cantab)]

SIDDIQI FAIZUL AQTAB

Justice Court Chambers
75 Kendal Road, Willesden Green, London
NW10 1JE, Telephone: 0181 830 7786
Call date: July 1990, Lincoln's Inn
Qualifications: [LLB]

SIDDIQUE BILAL MOHAMMED

9 King's Bench Walk
Basement, Temple, London EC4Y 7DX,
Telephone: 0171 353 9564
E-mail: jvlee@btinternet.com
Call date: Nov 1996, Gray's Inn
Qualifications: [LLB, LLM (Bucks)]

SIDDLE TREVOR BRYAN

Verulam Chambers
Peer House 8-14 Verulam Street, Gray's Inn,
London WC1X 8LZ,
Telephone: 0171 813 2400
Call date: Oct 1991, Gray's Inn
Qualifications: [LLB (Hons)]

SIDHU NAVJOT

Cloisters
1st Floor, Temple, London EC4Y 7AA,
Telephone: 0171 827 4000
E-mail: clerks@cloisters.com
Call date: Nov 1993, Lincoln's Inn
Qualifications: [MA (Oxon), MSc (Econ)
(London)]

SIDHU-BRAR NISHARN SINGH

6 Gray's Inn Square
Ground Floor, Gray's Inn, London WC1R 5AZ,
Telephone: 0171 242 1052
Call date: Oct 1991, Gray's Inn

SIGSWORTH GEORGE PEREGRINE

Park Lane Chambers
19 Westgate, Leeds LS1 2RD,
Telephone: 0113 2285000
Call date: May 1977, Middle Temple
Qualifications: [MA (Cantab)]

SILLIS MS LOUISE ANN

Library Chambers
Gray's Inn Chambers, Gray's Inn, London
WC1R 5JA, Telephone: 0171 404 6500
Call date: Nov 1994, Middle Temple
Qualifications: [MA (Cantab)]

SILSOE THE LORD QC (1972)

2 Mitre Ct Bldgs
2nd Floor, Temple, London EC4Y 7BX,
Telephone: 0171 583 1380
Call date: Nov 1955, Inner Temple

SILVERBECK MISS RACHEL NAOMI

Exchange Chambers
Pearl Assurance House Derby Square,
Liverpool L2 9XX, Telephone: 0151 236 7747/
0458
E-mail: exchangechambers@btinternet.com
Call date: Oct 1996, Middle Temple
Qualifications: [BA (Hons)(Newc), CPE]

SILVERLEAF MICHAEL QC (1996)

11 South Square
2nd Floor, Gray's Inn, London WC1R 5EU,
Telephone: 0171 405 1222
Call date: May 1980, Gray's Inn

D

Qualifications: [BSc (Lond)]

Fax: 0171 242 4282;
Out of hours telephone: 0171 405 1222;
DX: LDE 433 Chancery Lane; Other comms: E-mail michael@silverleaf.co.uk

Types of work: Computer disputes; Copyright; EC and competition law; Entertainment; Film, cable, TV; Information technology; Intellectual property; Patents

Other professional qualifications: QC 1996

Languages spoken: French

SILVESTER BRUCE ROSS

Lamb Chambers
Lamb Building, Temple, London EC4Y 7AS,
Telephone: 0171 797 8300
E-mail: lambchambers@link.org
Call date: July 1983, Inner Temple
Qualifications: [LLB (Lond)]

SIMBLET STEPHEN JOHN

2 Garden Court
1st Floor, Middle Temple, London EC4Y 9BL,
Telephone: 0171 353 1633
E-mail: barristers@2gardenct.law.co.uk
Call date: Oct 1991, Inner Temple
Qualifications: [MA (Cantab), LLM]

SIME STUART JOHN

169 Temple Chambers
Temple Avenue, London EC4Y 0DA,
Telephone: 0171 583 7644
Call date: Nov 1983, Gray's Inn
Qualifications: [LLB]

SIMISON JEREMY CHARLES

Trinity Chambers
140 New London Road, Chelmsford, Essex
CM2 0AW, Telephone: 01245 605040
Call date: Oct 1993, Inner Temple
Qualifications: [BA (B'ham), CPE]

SIMKIN IAIN JAMES

7 Stone Bldgs
1st Floor, Lincoln's Inn, London WC2A 3SZ,
Telephone: 0171 242 0961
Call date: Feb 1995, Inner Temple
Qualifications: [BA, CPE (Staffs)]

SIMLER MISS INGRID ANN

Devereux Chambers
Devereux Court, London WC2R 3JJ,
Telephone: 0171 353 7534
E-mail: elton@devchambers.co.uk
Call date: July 1987, Inner Temple
Qualifications: [MA (Cantab), Dip EEC Law]

SIMMONDS ANDREW JOHN

5 Stone Buildings
Lincoln's Inn, London WC2A 3XT,
Telephone: 0171 242 6201
E-mail: clerks@5-stonebuildings.law.co.uk
Call date: Nov 1980, Middle Temple
Qualifications: [MA (Cantab)]

SIMMONDS NICHOLAS HAROLD

Peel Court Chambers
45 Hardman Street, Manchester M3 3HA,
Telephone: 0161 832 3791
Call date: July 1969, Gray's Inn
Qualifications: [LLB (Manch)]

SIMMONS MISS MARION ADELE QC (1994)

3/4 South Square
Gray's Inn, London WC1R 5HP,
Telephone: 0171 696 9900
E-mail: clerks@southsquare.com
Call date: Nov 1970, Gray's Inn
Assistant Recorder
Qualifications: [LLB (Hons) LLM(Lond)]

SIMMS ALAN JOHN GORDON

Chavasse Court Chambers
2nd Floor Chavasse Court, 24 Lord Street,
Liverpool L2 1TA, Telephone: 0151 707 1191
Call date: Nov 1976, Lincoln's Inn
Qualifications: [LLB (Lond)]

SIMON MICHAEL HENRY

4 Brick Court
Temple, London EC4Y 9AD,
Telephone: 0171 797 8910
Call date: Nov 1992, Inner Temple
Qualifications: [LLB (L'pool)]

SIMON THE HON PEREGRINE CHARLES HUGO QC (1991)

Brick Court Chambers
15/19 Devereux Court, London WC2R 3JJ,
Telephone: 0171 583 0777
E-mail: (surname)@brickcourt.demon.co.uk
Call date: July 1973, Middle Temple
Assistant Recorder
Qualifications: [MA (Cantab)]

SIMONS MRS ANGELA MARY

1 Gray's Inn Square
Ground Floor, London WC1R 5AA,
Telephone: 0171 405 8946/7/8
Call date: July 1985, Gray's Inn
Qualifications: [BA(Oxon)]

SIMONS RICHARD GRAHAM

Lincoln House Chambers
5th Floor Lincoln House, 1 Brazennose Street,
Manchester M2 5EL,
Telephone: 0161 832 5701
E-mail: LincolnHouseChambers@link.org
Call date: Feb 1991, Gray's Inn
Qualifications: [LLB (Hons)]

SIMOR MISS JESSICA MARGARET POPPAEA

Monckton Chambers
4 Raymond Buildings, Gray's Inn, London
WC1R 5BP, Telephone: 0171 405 7211
E-mail: chambers@monckton.co.uk
Call date: Nov 1992, Middle Temple
Qualifications: [BA (Hons), Dip in Law]

SIMPKISS (RICHARD) JONATHAN

11 Old Square
Ground Floor, Lincoln's Inn, London
WC2A 3TS, Telephone: 0171 430 0341
E-mail: clerks@11oldsquare.co.uk
Call date: July 1975, Middle Temple
Qualifications: [MA (Cantab)]

SIMPSON MRS ALEXANDRA KATHERINE

24a St John Street
Manchester M3 4DF,
Telephone: 0161 833 9628
Call date: Nov 1989, Lincoln's Inn
Qualifications: [LLB (Hons)]

SIMPSON DAVID JOSEPH

9 King's Bench Walk
Basement, Temple, London EC4Y 7DX,
Telephone: 0171 353 9564
E-mail: jvlee@btinternet.com
Call date: Oct 1992, Gray's Inn
Qualifications: [LLB (Hons)]

SIMPSON EDWIN JOHN FLETCHER

12 New Square
Ground Floor, Lincoln's Inn, London
WC2A 3SW, Telephone: 0171 419 1212
E-mail: 12newsquare@compuserve.com
Call date: Nov 1990, Lincoln's Inn
Qualifications: [MA, BCL (Oxon)]

SIMPSON GRAEME MICHAEL

Harrow on the Hill Chambers
60 High Street, Harrow on the Hill, Middlesex
HA1 3LL, Telephone: 0181 423 7444
Windsor Barristers' Chambers
Windsor, Telephone: 01753 648899
Call date: Nov 1994, Middle Temple
Qualifications: [LLB (Hons)]

SIMPSON JAMES

Bell Yard Chambers
116/118 Chancery Lane, London WC2A 1PP,
Telephone: 0171 306 9292
Call date: Feb 1990, Middle Temple
Qualifications: [LLB (Lond)]

SIMPSON JONATHAN DAVID

Verulam Chambers
Peer House 8-14 Verulam Street, Gray's Inn,
London WC1X 8LZ,
Telephone: 0171 813 2400
Call date: Nov 1993, Gray's Inn
Qualifications: [LLB (Hons)]

SIMPSON KEITH

2 Gray's Inn Square Chambers
2nd Floor, Gray's Inn, London WC1R 5AA,
Telephone: 0171 242 0328/071 405 1317
E-mail: clerks@2gis.co.uk
Call date: Nov 1995, Gray's Inn
Qualifications: [BA (Sheff), MA (Sheff)]

SIMPSON MARK TAYLOR

4 Paper Bldgs
Ground Floor, Temple, London EC4Y 7EX,
Telephone: 0171 353 3366/583 7155
E-mail: clerks@4paperbuildings.com
Call date: Oct 1992, Middle Temple
Qualifications: [BA (Hons, Oxon)]

SIMPSON MRS NICOLA JANE

Queen Elizabeth Bldg
Ground Floor, Temple, London EC4Y 9BS,
Telephone: 0171 353 7181 (12 Lines)
Call date: July 1982, Inner Temple
Qualifications: [LLB (Hons) (B'ham)]

SIMPSON PAUL RICHARD

First National Building
2nd Floor 24 Fenwick Street, Liverpool
L2 7NE, Telephone: 0151 236 2098
Call date: Nov 1980, Lincoln's Inn
Qualifications: [LLB (L'pool)]

SIMPSON MS RAQUEL

18 St John Street
Manchester M3 4EA,
Telephone: 0161 278 1800
Call date: Oct 1990, Inner Temple
Qualifications: [LLB (LSE)]

SIMS PAUL LLYSTYN

Bell Yard Chambers
116/118 Chancery Lane, London WC2A 1PP,
Telephone: 0171 306 9292
Call date: Nov 1990, Gray's Inn
Qualifications: [LLB]

SINAN IZZET MAHMUT

Fountain Court
Temple, London EC4Y 9DH,
Telephone: 0171 583 3335
E-mail: chambers@fountaincourt.co.uk
Door Tenant
Call date: July 1981, Inner Temple
Qualifications: [MA, LLM (Cantab), Licence
Speciale En, Droit European Grand,
Distinction, ULB, Brussels]

SINCLAIR BRIAN

Fyfield Chambers
Field Cottage, Fyfield, Southrop,
Gloucestershire GL7 3NT,
Telephone: 01367 850304
Call date: Feb 1959, Middle Temple
Qualifications: [MA (Tinity College, Dublin
University)]

SINCLAIR MISS FIONA JANE

9 Gough Square
London EC4A 3DE, Telephone: 0171 353 5371
Call date: Oct 1990, Gray's Inn
Qualifications: [BA (Oxon)]

SINCLAIR MISS FIONA MARY

2 Crown Office Row
2nd Floor, Temple, London EC4Y 7HJ,
Telephone: 0171 797 8000
Call date: July 1989, Inner Temple
Qualifications: [MA (Cantab), LLM (Cantab)]

SINCLAIR GRAHAM KELSO

East Anglian Chambers
57 London Street, Norwich NR2 1HL,
Telephone: 01603 617351
East Anglian Chambers
Sanders House 52 North Hill, Colchester
CO1 1PY, Telephone: 01206 572756
East Anglian Chambers
Gresham House 5 Museum Street, Ipswich
IP1 1HQ, Telephone: 01473 214481
Call date: July 1979, Gray's Inn
Qualifications: [LLB (Hons) (Lond)]

SINCLAIR SIR IAN MACTAGGART QC (1979)

2 Hare Court
Ground Floor, Temple, London EC4Y 7BH,
Telephone: 0171 583 1770
E-mail: 2_Hare_Court@link.org
Call date: July 1952, Middle Temple
Qualifications: [BA, LL B Cantab]

SINCLAIR JEAN-PAUL MEEHAN

33 Bedford Row
London WC1R 4JH,
Telephone: 0171 242 6476
Call date: Feb 1989, Middle Temple
Qualifications: [MA (Cantab)]

SINCLAIR MISS LISA ANNE

7 New Square
Lincoln's Inn, London WC2A 3QS,
Telephone: 0171 430 1660
Call date: July 1993, Gray's Inn
Qualifications: [LLB (Leic), MBA]

SINCLAIR MALCOLM DAVID

11 Old Square
Ground Floor, Lincoln's Inn, London
WC2A 3TS, Telephone: 0171 242 5022/
405 1074
Call date: July 1978, Lincoln's Inn
Qualifications: [LLB (Lond), BA]

SINCLAIR SIR PATRICK ROBERT RICHARD

5 New Square
1st Floor, Lincoln's Inn, London WC2A 3RJ,
Telephone: 0171 404 0404
E-mail: Chambers@FiveNewSquare.CityScape.co.uk
Call date: May 1961, Lincoln's Inn
Qualifications: [MA (Oxon)]

SINCLAIR MR. PHILIP JUSTYN

Maidstone Chambers
33 Earl Street, Maidstone, Kent ME14 1PF,
Telephone: 01622 688592
Call date: Oct 1995, Gray's Inn
Qualifications: [LLB (Hons)]

SINCLAIR-MORRIS CHARLES ROBERT

9 Woodhouse Square
Leeds LS3 1AD, Telephone: 0113 2451986
Call date: Nov 1966, Lincoln's Inn

SINGER ANDREW MICHAEL

40 King Street
Manchester M2 6BA,
Telephone: 0161 832 9082
E-mail: Kingst40@aol.com
Call date: Nov 1990, Gray's Inn
Qualifications: [BA (Cantab)]

SINGER HARRY DAVID

Forest House Chambers
15 Granville Road, Walthamstow, London
E17 9BS, Telephone: 0181 925 2240
Call date: Nov 1969, Middle Temple
Qualifications: [LLB (Hons)]

SINGER PHILIP FRANCIS QC (1994)

2 Pump Court
1st Floor, Temple, London EC4Y 7AH,
Telephone: 0171 353 5597
Call date: Feb 1964, Inner Temple
Recorder
Qualifications: [MA, LLM (Cantab)]

SINGH BALBIR

Equity Chambers
153A Corporation Street, Birmingham, West
Midlands B4 6PH, Telephone: 0121 233 2100
Call date: July 1984, Lincoln's Inn
Qualifications: [BA, LLB (Hons), Dip M.R.S]

Fax: 0121 233 2102;
Out of hours telephone: 01543 677321 (Chief
Clerk); DX: 23531 Birmingham 3

Types of work: Administrative; Bankruptcy; Care
proceedings; Commercial; Common law
(general); Crime; Crime - corporate fraud;
Family; Landlord and tenant; Licensing; Mental
health; Partnerships; Personal injury; Sports

Circuit: Midland and Oxford

Awards and memberships: Student advocate of
the year 1984 at Lincoln's Inn; chosen to moot
for the university and debate for the Inn

Other professional experience: Director of (1) a
housing association (2) the Institute of Punjabi
Art and Culture (3) an investment company; I
also have extensive experience of the catering
industry having owned a highly rated restaurant

Languages spoken: Bengali, Gujarati, Hindi,
Punjabi, Urdu

Reported cases: *R v Telford JJ's ex parte
Badhan*, [1991] 2 QB 78; 2 WLR 866, 1990. One
of the leading authorities on staying
proceedings as being an abuse of process - the
tests to be applied.
R v Dhillon, (1997) 2 Cr App Rep 104, CA,
1996. Murder conviction quashed - when
provocation should be left as an issue for the
jury.

R v Rungzabe Khan, (1998) *The Times*, 7 March, 1998. Conviction for manslaughter - quashed after a review of authority's overlap between unlawful act and breach of duty. Prosecution seeking leave to appeal to House of Lords.
R v Redgaurd, [1991] Crim LR 213, 1990. Rape conviction quashed - CA consider when evidence relevant only to credit - even past alleged rape inadmissible.
R v Brown et al, 161 JP 345 DC, 1997. Custody time limits.

SINGH GURDIAL

Goldsmith Chambers
Ground Floor Goldsmith Building, Temple, London EC4Y 7BL,
Telephone: 0171 353 6802/3/4/5
E-mail: celiamonksfield@btinternet.com
Call date: July 1989, Lincoln's Inn
Qualifications: [LLB (Leeds)]

SINGH HARJIT

3 Pump Court
2nd Floor, Temple, London EC4Y 7AJ,
Telephone: 0171 353 1356 (3 Lines)
Call date: Nov 1956, Lincoln's Inn
Qualifications: [LLB, LLM (Lond)]

SINGH KULDIP QC (1993)

5 Paper Bldgs
1st Floor, Temple, London EC4Y 7HB,
Telephone: 0171 583 6117
E-mail: clerks@5-paperbuildings.law.co.uk
Call date: July 1975, Middle Temple

SINGH RABINDER

4-5 Gray's Inn Square
Ground Floor, Gray's Inn, London WC1R 5AY,
Telephone: 0171 404 5252
E-mail: chambers@4-5graysinnsquare.co.uk
Call date: July 1989, Lincoln's Inn
Qualifications: [BA (Cantab), LLM (California)]

SINGH RAJ KUMAR

Beresford Chambers
21 King Street, Luton, Bedfordshire LU1 2DW,
Telephone: 01582 429111
E-mail: info@it-law.com
Call date: May 1992, Gray's Inn
Qualifications: [LLB]

SINGH MISS RANJANA

Holborn Chambers
6 Gate Street, Lincoln's Inn Fields, London WC2A 3HP, Telephone: 0171 242 6060
Call date: Oct 1995, Middle Temple
Qualifications: [LLB (Hons)]

SINGH-HAYER BANSA

58 King Street Chambers
1st Floor, Kingsgate House 51-53 South King Street, Manchester M2 6DE,
Telephone: 0161 831 7477
Call date: Nov 1988, Gray's Inn
Qualifications: [LLB (Hons)]

SINGLETON BARRY NEILL QC (1989)

1 King's Bench Walk
2nd Floor, Temple, London EC4Y 7DB,
Telephone: 0171 936 1500
E-mail: ddear@1kbw.co.uk
Call date: July 1968, Gray's Inn
Qualifications: [MA (Cantab)]

SINGLETON MICHAEL JOHN

St Ive's Chambers
9 Fountain Ct, Birmingham B4 6DR,
Telephone: 0121 236 0863/0929
Call date: July 1987, Middle Temple
Qualifications: [LLB (Leics)]

SINGLETON MISS SARAH LOUISE

28 St John Street
Manchester M3 4DJ,
Telephone: 0161 834 8418
E-mail: clerk@28stjohnst.co.uk
Call date: July 1983, Middle Temple
Qualifications: [BA (Oxon)]

SINKER ANDREW TENNANT

Victoria Chambers
19 Castle Street, Liverpool L2 4SX,
Telephone: 0151 236 9402
E-mail: Fa45@rapid.co.uk
Call date: Oct 1991, Lincoln's Inn
Qualifications: [LLB (Hons) (Leeds)]

SINNATT SIMON PETER RANDALL

Crown Office Row Chambers
Blenheim House 120 Church Street, Brighton,
Sussex BN1 1WH, Telephone: 01273 625625
Call date: Oct 1993, Lincoln's Inn
Qualifications: [BA (Hons)(York), CPE]

SISLEY TIMOTHY JULIAN CRISPIN

11 Stone Bldgs
1st Floor, Lincoln's Inn, London WC2A 3TG,
Telephone: 0171 404 5055
E-mail: 9stoneb@compuserve.com
Westgate Chambers
144 High Street, Lewes, East Sussex BN7 1XT,
Telephone: 01273 480510
Call date: Feb 1989, Middle Temple
Qualifications: [BA (Lond), BA (Lond)]

SIVA KANNAN SARAVANAPAVAANANTHAN

Bell Yard Chambers
116/118 Chancery Lane, London WC2A 1PP,
Telephone: 0171 306 9292
Call date: Nov 1996, Gray's Inn
Qualifications: [BA]

SKELLEY MICHAEL DAVID

4 King's Bench Walk
2nd Floor, Temple, London EC4Y 7DL,
Telephone: 0171 353 3581
Call date: Oct 1991, Inner Temple
Qualifications: [BA (Oxon)]

SKELLORN MISS KATHRYN MAIR

St John's Chambers
Small Street, Bristol BS1 1DW,
Telephone: 0117 9213456/298514
E-mail: clerks@stjohns.uk.com
Call date: Nov 1993, Gray's Inn
Qualifications: [BA (Hons)(Oxon)]

SKELLY ANDREW JON

3 Temple Gardens
3rd Floor, Temple, London EC4Y 9AU,
Telephone: 0171 353 0832
Call date: Oct 1994, Inner Temple
Qualifications: [LLB]

SKELT IAN STUART

11 King's Bench Walk
1st Floor, Temple, London EC4Y 7EQ,
Telephone: 0171 353 3337
3 Park Court
Leeds LS1 2QH, Telephone: 0113 297 1200
Call date: Oct 1994, Lincoln's Inn
Qualifications: [LLB (Hons)(Newc)]

SKILBECK MRS JENNIFER SETH

Monckton Chambers
4 Raymond Buildings, Gray's Inn, London
WC1R 5BP, Telephone: 0171 405 7211
E-mail: chambers@monckton.co.uk
Call date: Oct 1991, Lincoln's Inn
Qualifications: [BSc (Econ), MSc (Econ), Dip
Law]

SKILBECK RUPERT HUGH

36 Bedford Row
London WC1R 4JH,
Telephone: 0171 421 8000
E-mail: 36bedfordrow@link.org
Call date: Mar 1996, Gray's Inn
Qualifications: [BA (York)]

SKINNER MISS KATHERINE JOY

King Charles House
Standard Hill, Nottingham NG1 6FX,
Telephone: 0115 9418851
E-mail: clerks@kch.co.uk
Call date: Nov 1988, Inner Temple
Qualifications: [LLB (L'pool)]

SKINNER TOM MILNE

Francis Taylor Bldg
3rd Floor, Temple, London EC4Y 7BY,
Telephone: 0171 797 7250
Call date: May 1992, Gray's Inn
Qualifications: [BA (Oxon), LLM (Exeter), Lic
Sp en Droit Eur, (Brussels)]

SLACK IAN

2 King's Bench Walk
1st Floor, Temple, London EC4Y 7DE,
Telephone: 0171 353 9276
Call date: Nov 1974, Middle Temple
Qualifications: [BA]

SLADE MISS ELIZABETH ANN QC (1992)

11 King's Bench Walk
Temple, London EC4Y 7EQ,
Telephone: 0171 632 8500
E-mail: clerksroom@11-kbw.law.co.uk
Call date: July 1972, Inner Temple
Assistant Recorder
Qualifications: [MA (Oxon)]

Fax: 0171 583 3690/9123;
Out of hours telephone: 0171 583 0610;
DX: LDE 368; Other comms: E-mail irvine@11-kbw.law.co.uk

Types of work: Discrimination; Employment

Other professional qualifications: Assistant Recorder; Authorised to sit as Deputy High Court Judge 1998

Awards and memberships: Employment Law Bar Association; Employment Lawyers' Association; Industrial Law Society

Other professional experience: Bencher of Inner Temple

Languages spoken: French

Publications: *Tolley's Employment Handbook* (Joint Editor), 1978 to 7th edn

Reported cases: *Crees v Royal London Mutual Insurance Society Ltd*, [1998] IRLR 245. Whether the right to return to work is lost if there is no physical return to work by the end of the statutory period of maternity absence.
Foster v British Gas, [1991] ICR 463. Decision of the European Court on the type of body against which European Directives may be relied upon for direct effect.
Westminster City Council v Haywood and another, [1997] 2 All ER 84. The case concerned the jurisdiction and powers of the Pensions Ombudsman.
Rastell and others v Midlands Electricity and others, [1996] ICR 644. Time limits for claim based on Equal Treatment Directive (76/207) and the exercise of discretion under Sex Discrimination Act 1975 to extend time.
Newns v British Airways, [1992] IRLR 575. No injunctive relief available to restrain a transfer of an undertaking where consultation with union is allegedly defective.

SLADE RICHARD PENKIVIL

Brick Court Chambers
15/19 Devereux Court, London WC2R 3JJ,
Telephone: 0171 583 0777
E-mail: (surname)@brickcourt.demon.co.uk
Call date: Nov 1987, Lincoln's Inn
Qualifications: [BA (Hons) (Cantab)]

SLADE JONES ROBIN

Chartlands Chambers
3 St Giles Terrace, Northampton NN1 2BN,
Telephone: 01604 603322
Call date: Oct 1993, Gray's Inn
Qualifications: [M.Eng]

SLATER IAIN JAMES

Victoria Chambers
19 Castle Street, Liverpool L2 4SX,
Telephone: 0151 236 9402
E-mail: Fa45@rapid.co.uk
Call date: Oct 1991, Lincoln's Inn
Qualifications: [LLB (Hons)]

SLATER JOHN CHRISTOPHER NASH QC (1987)

1 Paper Bldgs
Ground Floor, Temple, London EC4Y 7EP,
Telephone: 0171 583 7355
E-mail: clerks@1pb.co.uk
Call date: Nov 1969, Middle Temple
Recorder
Qualifications: [MA (Oxon)]

SLATER MISS JULIE ANN

Victoria Chambers
3rd Floor 177 Corporation Street, Birmingham B4 6RG, Telephone: 0121 236 9900
Call date: July 1988, Lincoln's Inn
Qualifications: [LLB (Hons)]

SLATER MICHAEL NEAL

Paradise Square Chambers
26 Paradise Square, Sheffield S1 2DE,
Telephone: 0114 2738951
Plowden Bldgs
2nd Floor, Temple, London EC4Y 9BU,
Telephone: 0171 583 0808
E-mail: bar@plowdenbuildings.co.uk
Call date: July 1983, Inner Temple
Qualifications: [LLB (Sheff)]

SLAUGHTER ANDREW FRANCIS
Bridewell Chambers
2 Bridewell Place, London EC4V 6AP,
Telephone: 0171 797 8800
E-mail: clerks@bridewell.law.co.uk
Call date: Oct 1993, Middle Temple
Qualifications: [BA (Hons)]

SLEEMAN MISS RACHEL SARAH ELIZABETH
1 Essex Court
1st Floor, Temple, London EC4Y 9AR,
Telephone: 0171 936 3030
E-mail: one.essex_court@virgin.net
Call date: Nov 1996, Gray's Inn
Qualifications: [LLB (Lond)]

SLEIGHTHOLME JOHN TREVOR
37 Park Square
Leeds LS1 2NY, Telephone: 0113 2439422
Call date: Nov 1982, Gray's Inn
Qualifications: [LLB (Leeds)]

SLEVIN FRANK
9 King's Bench Walk
Basement, Temple, London EC4Y 7DX,
Telephone: 0171 353 9564
E-mail: jvlee@btinternet.com
Call date: July 1985, Lincoln's Inn
Qualifications: [BA]

SLIWINSKI ROBERT ANDREW
46/48 Essex Street
London WC2R 3GH,
Telephone: 0171 583 8899
Call date: Oct 1990, Middle Temple
Qualifications: [BSc, LLB (Hons), ARICS, ACIArb]

SLOAM MISS DENISE
4 King's Bench Walk
2nd Floor, Temple, London EC4Y 7DL,
Telephone: 0171 353 3581
Call date: July 1979, Inner Temple
Qualifications: [MA (Oxon)]

SLOAN PAUL KAY
Trinity Chambers
9-12 Trinity Chare, Quayside, Newcastle Upon Tyne NE1 3DF, Telephone: 0191 232 1927
Call date: July 1981, Inner Temple
Qualifications: [LLB (Lond)]

SLOMNICKA MISS BARBARA IRENA
14 Gray's Inn Square
Gray's Inn, London WC1R 5JP,
Telephone: 0171 242 0858
E-mail: 100712.2134@compuserve.com
Call date: Nov 1976, Middle Temple
Qualifications: [LLB MJur]

SLOWE MISS EMILY JANE
Chancery Chambers
1st Floor Offices 70/72 Chancery Lane,
London WC2A 1AB,
Telephone: 0171 405 6879/6870
Call date: Nov 1996, Inner Temple
Qualifications: [LLB]

SMAIL ALASTAIR HAROLD KURT
4 Fountain Court
Steelhouse Lane, Birmingham B4 6DR,
Telephone: 0121 236 3476
Call date: Nov 1987, Gray's Inn
Qualifications: [BA, BCL (Oxon)]

SMALES MRS SUZANNE
6 Park Square
Leeds LS1 2LW, Telephone: 0113 2459763
E-mail: chambers@no6.co.uk
Call date: Oct 1990, Inner Temple
Qualifications: [LLB (Hons) (Essex)]

SMALL DEVON
2 Middle Temple Lane
3rd Floor, Temple, London EC4Y 9AA,
Telephone: 0171 583 4540
Call date: Nov 1990, Inner Temple
Qualifications: [LLB]

D

SMALL MISS GINA LEE

King's Bench Chambers
115 North Hill, Plymouth PL4 8JY,
Telephone: 01752 221551
2 King's Bench Walk
Ground Floor, Temple, London EC4Y 7DE,
Telephone: 0171 353 1746
E-mail: 2kbw@atlas.co.uk
Call date: Oct 1991, Lincoln's Inn
Qualifications: [BA (Hons) (Lond), Dip Law]

SMALL JONATHAN EDWIN

Falcon Chambers
Falcon Court, London EC4Y 1AA,
Telephone: 0171 353 2484/7
Call date: Oct 1990, Lincoln's Inn
Qualifications: [BA (Nott'm), Dip Law (City)]

SMALL MISS PENELOPE SUSAN

1 Paper Bldgs
1st Floor, Temple, London EC4Y 7EP,
Telephone: 0171 353 3728/4953
Call date: Oct 1992, Inner Temple
Qualifications: [BA (Warw), Dip
Law(Westminster)]

SMALLWOOD MISS ANNE ELIZABETH

5 Fountain Court
Steelhouse Lane, Birmingham B4 6DR,
Telephone: 0121 606 0500
Call date: Nov 1977, Middle Temple
Qualifications: [LLB]

SMALLWOOD MISS LAURA JANE

Guildford Chambers
Stoke House Leapale Lane, Guildford, Surrey
GU1 4LY, Telephone: 01483 539131
E-mail: guildford.barristers@btinternet.com
Call date: July 1987, Middle Temple
Qualifications: [MA (Cantab), Dip Law (City)]

SMALLWOOD ROBERT ANDREW

5 Fountain Court
Steelhouse Lane, Birmingham B4 6DR,
Telephone: 0121 606 0500
Call date: Oct 1994, Lincoln's Inn
Qualifications: [LLB (Hons)(Sheff)]

SMART DAVID PETER ROSS

St Mary's Chambers
50 High Pavement, Lace Market, Nottingham
NG1 1HW, Telephone: 0115 9503503
E-mail: clerks@smc.law.co.uk
Call date: Nov 1977, Middle Temple
Qualifications: [LLB (Bris)]

SMART MISS JACQUELINE ANNE

Trinity Chambers
9-12 Trinity Chare, Quayside, Newcastle Upon
Tyne NE1 3DF, Telephone: 0191 232 1927
Call date: Nov 1981, Middle Temple
Qualifications: [LLB (Lond)]

SMART JOHN ANDREW CHARLES

11 Stone Bldgs
1st Floor, Lincoln's Inn, London WC2A 3TG,
Telephone: 0171 404 5055
E-mail: 9stoneb@compuserve.com
Call date: Nov 1989, Middle Temple
Qualifications: [B.Sc Hons (Bris), Dip Law
(City)]

SMART MISS JULIA ELIZABETH

Verulam Chambers
Peer House 8-14 Verulam Street, Gray's Inn,
London WC1X 8LZ,
Telephone: 0171 813 2400
Call date: Oct 1993, Gray's Inn
Qualifications: [LLB]

SMART ROGER BERNARD

4 Brick Court
1st Floor, Temple, London EC4Y 9AD,
Telephone: 0171 583 8455
Call date: July 1989, Inner Temple
Qualifications: [LLB (Hons)]

SMITH MISS ABIGAIL

Godolphin Chambers
50 Castle Street, Truro, Cornwall TR1 3AF,
Telephone: 01872 276312
Call date: July 1989, Middle Temple
Qualifications: [LLB (B'ham)]

SMITH ADAM JOHN

Crown Office Row Chambers
Blenheim House 120 Church Street, Brighton,
Sussex BN1 1WH, Telephone: 01273 625625
Call date: Nov 1987, Inner Temple
Qualifications: [LLB (Hull)]

SMITH ALAN ARTHUR

Hardwicke Building
New Square, Lincoln's Inn, London
WC2A 3SB, Telephone: 0171 242 2523
E-mail: clerks@hardwicke.co.uk
Call date: July 1981, Middle Temple
Qualifications: [BA]

SMITH ALISDAIR ROBERT MACSORLEY

3 Temple Gardens
Lower Ground Floor, Temple, London
EC4Y 9AU, Telephone: 0171 353 3102/5/9297
Call date: July 1981, Gray's Inn
Qualifications: [LLB (Lond)]

SMITH ANDREW CHARLES QC (1990)

Fountain Court
Temple, London EC4Y 9DH,
Telephone: 0171 583 3335
E-mail: chambers@fountaincourt.co.uk
Call date: Nov 1974, Middle Temple
Recorder
Qualifications: [BA (Oxon)]

SMITH ANDREW DESMOND

Bank House Chambers
Old Bank House, Hartshead, Sheffield S1 2EL,
Telephone: 0114 2751223
Call date: Oct 1991, Middle Temple
Qualifications: [LLB Hons (Sheff)]

SMITH ANDREW WILLIAM

24a St John Street
Manchester M3 4DF,
Telephone: 0161 833 9628
Call date: Oct 1996, Lincoln's Inn
Qualifications: [LLB (Hons)(Manc)]

SMITH ANTHONY THOMAS QC (1977)

Berkeley Chambers
321 Stratford Road, Shirley, Solihull, West
Midlands B90 3BL, Telephone: 0121 733 6925
Call date: Feb 1958, Inner Temple
Recorder
Qualifications: [MA (Cantab)]

SMITH MISS CATHERINE EMMA

5 Pump Court
Ground Floor, Temple, London EC4Y 7AP,
Telephone: 0171 353 2532
E-mail: fivepump@netcomuk.co.uk
Call date: Nov 1994, Middle Temple
Qualifications: [LLB (Hons) (Kent), Dip French
Law, (Grenoble)]

SMITH CHRISTOPHER FRANK

4 Field Court
Gray's Inn, London WC1R 5EA,
Telephone: 0171 440 6900
E-mail: chambers@4fieldcourt.co.uk
Call date: July 1989, Inner Temple
Qualifications: [LLB (So'ton)]

SMITH DAVID ANDREW

Goldsmith Chambers
Ground Floor Goldsmith Building, Temple,
London EC4Y 7BL,
Telephone: 0171 353 6802/3/4/5
E-mail: celiamonksfield@btinternet.com
Call date: July 1988, Middle Temple
Qualifications: [LLB (Hons)]

SMITH DAVID ANTHONY

4 Breams Buildings
London EC4A 1AQ,
Telephone: 0171 353 5835/430 1221
Call date: Nov 1980, Inner Temple
Qualifications: [LLM (Lond) LLB, (Brunel)]

SMITH DUNCAN

Trinity Chambers
9-12 Trinity Chare, Quayside, Newcastle Upon
Tyne NE1 3DF, Telephone: 0191 232 1927
Call date: July 1979, Inner Temple
Assistant Recorder
Qualifications: [LLB]

SMITH MISS ELEANOR RACHEL

Broad Chare
33 Broad Chare, Newcastle Upon Tyne
NE1 3DQ, Telephone: 0191 232 0541
Call date: Feb 1992, Middle Temple
Qualifications: [LLB (Hons) (Sheff)]

SMITH MISS EMMA LOUISE

Old Square Chambers
1 Verulam Buildings, Gray's Inn, London
WC1R 5LQ, Telephone: 0171 831 0801
Old Square Chambers
Hanover House 47 Corn Street, Bristol
BS1 1HT, Telephone: 0117 9277111
Call date: Oct 1995, Lincoln's Inn
Qualifications: [LLB (Hons)(Leic)]

SMITH MISS HELEN MARY

6 Gray's Inn Square
Ground Floor, Gray's Inn, London WC1R 5AZ,
Telephone: 0171 242 1052
Call date: Nov 1990, Inner Temple
Qualifications: [LLB]

SMITH HOWARD JAMES

11 New Square
Ground Floor, Lincoln's Inn, London
WC2A 3QB, Telephone: 0171 831 0081
E-mail: 11newsquare.co.uk
Call date: July 1986, Inner Temple
Qualifications: [BA (Oxon)]

SMITH IAN TRUMAN

Devereux Chambers
Devereux Court, London WC2R 3JJ,
Telephone: 0171 353 7534
E-mail: elton@devchambers.co.uk
Call date: July 1972, Gray's Inn
Qualifications: [MA, LLB (Cantab)]

SMITH J STEPHEN

12 New Square
Ground Floor, Lincoln's Inn, London
WC2A 3SW, Telephone: 0171 419 1212
E-mail: 12newsquare@compuserve.com
25 Park Square
Leeds LS1 2PW, Telephone: 0113 2451841/2/3
E-mail: sovereignchambers@btinternet.com
Door Tenant
Call date: July 1983, Middle Temple
Qualifications: [BA (Oxon)]

SMITH JAMIE CHARLES

2 Crown Office Row
2nd Floor, Temple, London EC4Y 7HJ,
Telephone: 0171 797 8000
Call date: Oct 1995, Lincoln's Inn
Qualifications: [BA (Hons)(Cantab)]

SMITH JASON

25-27 Castle Street
1st Floor, Liverpool L2 4TA,
Telephone: 0151 227 5661/051 236 5072
Call date: July 1989, Middle Temple
Qualifications: [LLB [L'pool]]

SMITH MISS JOANNA ANGELA

Wilberforce Chambers
8 New Square, Lincoln's Inn, London
WC2A 3QP, Telephone: 0171 306 0102
E-mail: chambers@wilberforce.co.uk
Call date: Nov 1990, Lincoln's Inn
Qualifications: [BA (Hons)(Oxon)]

SMITH JONATHAN MICHAEL

Cobden House Chambers
19 Quay Street, Manchester M3 3HN,
Telephone: 0161 833 6000
E-mail: clerks@cobden.co.uk
Call date: Oct 1991, Gray's Inn
Qualifications: [LLB]

SMITH MISS JULIA MAIR WHELDON

Gough Square Chambers
6-7 Gough Square, London EC4A 3DE,
Telephone: 0171 353 0924
E-mail: gsc@goughsq.co.uk
Call date: Nov 1988, Inner Temple
Qualifications: [LLB (L'pool)]

SMITH JULIAN WILLIAM

New Court Chambers
3 Broad Chare, Newcastle Upon Tyne
NE1 3DQ, Telephone: 0191 232 1980
Call date: Nov 1991, Inner Temple
Qualifications: [LLB (New)]

SMITH MS KATHERINE EMMA

Monckton Chambers
4 Raymond Buildings, Gray's Inn, London
WC1R 5BP, Telephone: 0171 405 7211
E-mail: chambers@monckton.co.uk
Call date: Nov 1995, Inner Temple
Qualifications: [BA (Oxon), BCL (Oxon)]

SMITH MISS LEONORAH PATRICIA DOLORES

Verulam Chambers
Peer House 8-14 Verulam Street, Gray's Inn,
London WC1X 8LZ,
Telephone: 0171 813 2400
Call date: Nov 1993, Inner Temple
Qualifications: [BA (Surrey), CPE (Sussex)]

SMITH MARCUS ALEXANDER

Fountain Court
Temple, London EC4Y 9DH,
Telephone: 0171 583 3335
E-mail: chambers@fountaincourt.co.uk
Call date: Oct 1991, Lincoln's Inn
Qualifications: [MA, BCL (Oxon)]

SMITH MISS MARION HELEN

4 Essex Court
Temple, London EC4Y 9AJ,
Telephone: 0171 797 7970
E-mail: clerks@4essexcourt.law.co.uk
Call date: July 1981, Gray's Inn
Qualifications: [LLB, LLM (Lond)]

SMITH MARK VALENTINE

Essex Court Chambers
24 Lincoln's Inn Fields, London WC2A 3ED,
Telephone: 0171 813 8000
E-mail: clerksroom@essexcourt-chambers.co.uk
Call date: July 1981, Lincoln's Inn
Qualifications: [MA (Cantab)]

SMITH MARK WILLIAM

Kenworthy's Buildings
83 Bridge Street, Manchester M3 2RF,
Telephone: 0161 832 4036/834 6954
Call date: Mar 1997, Gray's Inn
Qualifications: [LLB (Nott'm)]

SMITH MATTHEW JAMES

40 King Street
Manchester M2 6BA,
Telephone: 0161 832 9082
E-mail: Kingst40@aol.com
Call date: Oct 1991, Lincoln's Inn
Qualifications: [BA (Hons)(Cantab)]

SMITH MATTHEW ROBERT

25 Park Square
Leeds LS1 2PW, Telephone: 0113 2451841/2/3
E-mail: sovereignchambers@btinternet.com
Call date: Nov 1996, Inner Temple
Qualifications: [BA (Dunelm), MPhil (Cantab)]

SMITH MICHAEL ANTHONY

6 Park Square
Leeds LS1 2LW, Telephone: 0113 2459763
E-mail: chambers@no6.co.uk
Call date: July 1980, Inner Temple
Qualifications: [LLB (Newc)]

SMITH MICHAEL JOSEPH

8 King Street
Manchester M2 6AQ,
Telephone: 0161 834 9560
Call date: July 1989, Lincoln's Inn
Qualifications: [MA, BCL (Oxon)]

SMITH NICHOLAS GILBERT

Assize Court Chambers
14 Small Street, Bristol BS1 1DE,
Telephone: 0117 9264587
Call date: Nov 1990, Lincoln's Inn
Qualifications: [LLB]

SMITH NICHOLAS MARTIN

1 Fountain Court
Steelhouse Lane, Birmingham B4 6DR,
Telephone: 0121 236 5721
Call date: Oct 1994, Gray's Inn
Qualifications: [BA]

SMITH MISS NICOLA JANE

22 Albion Place
Northampton NN1 1UD,
Telephone: 01604 36271
Call date: Oct 1994, Gray's Inn
Qualifications: [LLB (Hons)]

D

SMITH PAUL ANDREW

One Hare Court
1st Floor, Temple, London EC4Y 7BE,
Telephone: 0171 353 3171
E-mail: admin-oneharecourt@btinternet.com
Call date: July 1978, Middle Temple
Qualifications: [BA (Hons) MA, FCIArb]

SMITH PETER GEOGHEGAN

Exchange Chambers
Pearl Assurance House Derby Square,
Liverpool L2 9XX, Telephone: 0151 236 7747/
0458
E-mail: exchangechambers@btinternet.com
Call date: July 1954, Middle Temple
Qualifications: [MA, BCL]

SMITH PETER RICHARD

24a St John Street
Manchester M3 4DF,
Telephone: 0161 833 9628
Call date: Nov 1988, Inner Temple
Qualifications: [LLB Hons (Lancaster)]

SMITH PETER WINSTON QC (1992)

40 King Street
Manchester M2 6BA,
Telephone: 0161 832 9082
E-mail: Kingst40@aol.com
11 Old Square
Ground Floor, Lincoln's Inn, London
WC2A 3TS, Telephone: 0171 430 0341
E-mail: clerks@11oldsquare.co.uk
Call date: July 1975, Lincoln's Inn
Recorder
Qualifications: [MA (Cantab)]

SMITH MISS RACHEL CATHERINE

Peel Court Chambers
45 Hardman Street, Manchester M3 3HA,
Telephone: 0161 832 3791
Call date: Oct 1990, Lincoln's Inn
Qualifications: [BA (Leeds), Dip Law (City)]

SMITH RAYMOND KENNETH

East Anglian Chambers
57 London Street, Norwich NR2 1HL,
Telephone: 01603 617351
East Anglian Chambers
Sanders House 52 North Hill, Colchester
CO1 1PY, Telephone: 01206 572756
East Anglian Chambers
Gresham House 5 Museum Street, Ipswich
IP1 1HQ, Telephone: 01473 214481
Call date: Apr 1991, Lincoln's Inn

SMITH RICHARD LLOYD

Guildhall Chambers
23 Broad Street, Bristol BS1 2HG,
Telephone: 0117 9273366
Call date: July 1986, Middle Temple
Qualifications: [LLB (Lond)]

SMITH ROBERT ANTHONY

2 Eastwood Road
South Woodford, London E18 1BW,
Telephone: 0181 491 0980
Call date: Nov 1980, Inner Temple
Qualifications: [BA (Hons, Kent)]

SMITH ROBERT CLIVE

Bank House Chambers
Old Bank House, Hartshead, Sheffield S1 2EL,
Telephone: 0114 2751223
Call date: July 1974, Middle Temple
Qualifications: [MA (Cantab)]

SMITH ROBERT IAN

New Bailey Chambers
10 Lawson Street, Preston PR1 2QT,
Telephone: 01772 258087
Call date: Oct 1995, Lincoln's Inn
Qualifications: [LLB (Hons)(Northum)]

SMITH ROBERT STEEN QC (1986)

Park Court Chambers
40 Park Cross Street, Leeds LS1 2QH,
Telephone: 0113 2433277
3 Serjeants Inn
London EC4Y 1BQ,
Telephone: 0171 353 5537
E-mail: available upon request
Call date: July 1971, Inner Temple
Recorder
Qualifications: [LLB]

SMITH ROGER DENZIL HOWARD QC (1992)

6 Fountain Court
Steelhouse Lane, Birmingham B4 6DR,
Telephone: 0121 233 3282
Call date: Feb 1972, Gray's Inn
Recorder
Qualifications: [LLM]

SMITH ROGER GAVIN ABBEY

1 Mitre Ct Bldgs
Ground Floor, Temple, London EC4Y 7BS,
Telephone: 0171 797 7070
Call date: Nov 1981, Middle Temple
Qualifications: [BA (Oxon)]

SMITH ROGER HUGH TRAYLEN

4 Paper Bldgs
2nd Floor, Temple, London EC4Y 7EX,
Telephone: 0171 583 0816/071 353 1131
E-mail: clerks@4paperbuildings.co.uk
Call date: Nov 1968, Gray's Inn
Qualifications: [BA (Oxon)]

SMITH MISS RUTH ELIZABETH ANNE

32 Park Place
Cardiff CF1 3BA, Telephone: 01222 397364
Call date: July 1987, Gray's Inn
Qualifications: [LLB (Cardiff)]

SMITH MISS SALLY ELIZABETH QC (1997)

1 Crown Office Row
Ground Floor, Temple, London EC4Y 7HH,
Telephone: 0171 797 7500
Call date: Nov 1977, Inner Temple
Qualifications: [LLB (Lond)]

SMITH MISS SALLY-ANN

Crown Office Row Chambers
Blenheim House 120 Church Street, Brighton,
Sussex BN1 1WH, Telephone: 01273 625625
Call date: Oct 1996, Inner Temple
Qualifications: [LLB (Bris)]

SMITH SHAUN MALDEN

1 High Pavement
Nottingham NG1 1HF,
Telephone: 0115 9418218
Call date: July 1981, Gray's Inn
Qualifications: [LLB (Sheff)]

SMITH SIMON NOEL

3 Temple Gardens
Lower Ground Floor, Temple, London
EC4Y 9AU, Telephone: 0171 353 3102/5/9297
Call date: July 1981, Gray's Inn
Qualifications: [LLB (Lond)]

SMITH TYRONE GREGORY

3 Gray's Inn Square
Ground Floor, London WC1R 5AH,
Telephone: 0171 520 5600
E-mail: gis3@btinternet.com
Call date: Oct 1994, Gray's Inn
Qualifications: [LLB]

SMITH WARWICK TIMOTHY CRESSWELL

Deans Court Chambers
Cumberland House, Crown Square,
Manchester M3 3HA,
Telephone: 0161 834 4097
E-mail: deanscourt@compuserve.com
Deans Court Chambers
41-43 Market Place, Preston, Lancashire
PR1 1AH, Telephone: 01772 555163
E-mail: deanscourt@compuserve.com
Call date: July 1982, Middle Temple
Qualifications: [MA (Cantab)]

Types of work: Arbitration; Commercial;
Commercial litigation; Common law (general);
Construction; Insurance; Medical negligence;
Personal injury; Professional negligence; Sale
and carriage of goods

Other professional qualifications: Fellow of the
Chartered Institute of Arbitrators (FCIArb)

Circuit: Northern

Awards and memberships: Professional
Negligence Bar Association (PNBA); Northern
Circuit Commercial Bar Association (NCCBA);
Personal Injury Bar Association (PIBA);
Northern Circuit Official Referees Bar
Association (NCORBA)

SMITH WAYNE LEONARD

2 New Street
Leicester LE1 5NA, Telephone: 0116 2625906
Call date: July 1991, Gray's Inn
Qualifications: [LLB]

SMITH MS ZOE PHILIPPA

Hardwicke Building
New Square, Lincoln's Inn, London
WC2A 3SB, Telephone: 0171 242 2523
E-mail: clerks@hardwicke.co.uk
Call date: July 1970, Gray's Inn
Recorder

SMITHERS DR ROGER HOWARD

Wessex Chambers
48 Queens Road, Reading, Berkshire
RG1 4BD, Telephone: 01734 568856
E-mail: wessexchambers@compuserve.com
Call date: Oct 1990, Inner Temple
Qualifications: [BSc,PhD (Lond), Dip Law]

SMOKER MISS KATHLEEN MARY

All Saints Chambers
9/11 Broad Street, Bristol BS1 2HP,
Telephone: 0117 921 1966
Call date: May 1974, Gray's Inn
Qualifications: [LLB (B'ham)]

SMOUHA JOSEPH

Essex Court Chambers
24 Lincoln's Inn Fields, London WC2A 3ED,
Telephone: 0171 813 8000
E-mail: clerksroom@essexcourt-chambers.co.uk
Call date: July 1986, Middle Temple
Qualifications: [MA (Cantab), LLM (New York)]

SMULLEN MRS MARION

Chambers of Helen Grindrod QC
1st Floor 95a Chancery Lane, London
WC2A 2JG, Telephone: 0171 404 4777
Call date: July 1985, Gray's Inn
Qualifications: [BA, LLB (Lond)]

SMYTH CHRISTOPHER JACKSON

1 Crown Office Row
Ground Floor, Temple, London EC4Y 7HH,
Telephone: 0171 797 7500
Crown Office Row Chambers
Blenheim House 120 Church Street, Brighton,
Sussex BN1 1WH, Telephone: 01273 625625
Call date: July 1972, Inner Temple
Recorder
Qualifications: [MA (Cantab)]

SMYTH MISS JULIA MADELEINE

1 Temple Gardens
1st Floor, Temple, London EC4Y 9BB,
Telephone: 0171 353 0407/583 1315
E-mail: clerks@1templegardens.co.uk
Call date: Oct 1996, Inner Temple
Qualifications: [LLB (Lond), Dip in Law]

SMYTH STEPHEN MARK JAMES ATHELSTAN

2 Harcourt Bldgs
1st Floor, Temple, London EC4Y 9DB,
Telephone: 0171 353 2112/2817
Call date: July 1974, Inner Temple

SNELL JOHN

New Walk Chambers
27 New Walk, Leicester LE1 6TE,
Telephone: 0116 2559144
Call date: July 1973, Inner Temple
Qualifications: [LLB]

SNELL JOHN MICHAEL

2 Temple Gardens
Temple, London EC4Y 9AY,
Telephone: 0171 583 6041 (12 Lines)
Call date: Oct 1991, Lincoln's Inn
Qualifications: [BA (Hons) (Oxon), Dip Law]

SNELLER MISS ELAINE RUTH

9 King's Bench Walk
Ground Floor, Temple, London EC4Y 7DX,
Telephone: 0171 353 7202/3909
Call date: Feb 1994, Middle Temple
Qualifications: [LLB (Hons)(Bris)]

SNELSON ANTHONY MARTIN

Thomas More Chambers
52 Carey Street, Lincoln's Inn, London
WC2A 2JB, Telephone: 0171 404 7000
Call date: Nov 1982, Gray's Inn
Qualifications: [LLB (L'pool)]

SNIDER JOHN LEOPOLD

Essex Court Chambers
24 Lincoln's Inn Fields, London WC2A 3ED,
Telephone: 0171 813 8000
E-mail: clerksroom@essexcourt-chambers.co.uk
Call date: July 1982, Middle Temple
Qualifications: [MA (Hons) (Oxon), MBA]

SNOWDEN JOHN STEVENSON

2 Crown Office Row
Ground Floor, Temple, London EC4Y 7HJ,
Telephone: 0171 797 8100
E-mail: mail@2cor.co.uk, or to individual
barristers at: [barrister's surname]@2cor.co.uk
Call date: July 1989, Inner Temple
Qualifications: [BA (Nott'm)]

SNOWDEN RICHARD ANDREW

Erskine Chambers
30 Lincoln's Inn Fields, Lincoln's Inn, London
WC2A 3PF, Telephone: 0171 242 5532
E-mail: Clerks@Erskine-Chambers.law.co.uk
Call date: July 1986, Lincoln's Inn
Qualifications: [MA (Cantab), LLM (Harvard)]

SOARES PATRICK CLAUDE

8 Gray's Inn Square
Gray's Inn, London WC1R 5AZ,
Telephone: 0171 242 3529
Call date: Nov 1983, Lincoln's Inn
Qualifications: [LLB LLM (Lond) FTII]

SOFAER MISS MOIRA

Verulam Chambers
Peer House 8-14 Verulam Street, Gray's Inn,
London WC1X 8LZ,
Telephone: 0171 813 2400
Call date: July 1975, Middle Temple
Qualifications: [BSc (Lond)]

SOFER JONATHAN

46/48 Essex Street
London WC2R 3GH,
Telephone: 0171 583 8899
Call date: Apr 1942, Inner Temple
Qualifications: [BA, LLB (Cantab)]

SOFFA MISS HELEN ROSEMARY

New Court
Temple, London EC4Y 9BE,
Telephone: 0171 583 5123/0171 583 0510
Call date: Nov 1990, Inner Temple

SOKOL CHRISTOPHER JOHN FRANCIS

24 Old Bldgs
First Floor, Lincoln's Inn, London WC2A 3UJ,
Telephone: 0171 242 2744
Call date: July 1975, Lincoln's Inn
Qualifications: [MA (Cantab)]

SOLARI MISS YOLANDA ELLEN

Counsels' Chambers
2nd Floor 10-11 Gray's Inn Square, London
WC1R 5JD, Telephone: 0171 405 2576
Call date: Nov 1992, Gray's Inn
Qualifications: [LLB (Hons)]

SOLLEY STEPHEN MALCOLM QC (1989)

Cloisters
1st Floor, Temple, London EC4Y 7AA,
Telephone: 0171 827 4000
E-mail: clerks@cloisters.com
Call date: Nov 1969, Inner Temple
Qualifications: [LLB (Lond)]

SOLMAN ROBERT FREDERICK

5 Fountain Court
Steelhouse Lane, Birmingham B4 6DR,
Telephone: 0121 606 0500
Call date: May 1958, Middle Temple
Qualifications: [LLB]

SOLOMON REUBEN

12 Old Square
1st Floor, Lincoln's Inn, London WC2A 3TX,
Telephone: 0171 404 0875
Call date: Oct 1993, Lincoln's Inn
Qualifications: [LLB (Hons)]

SOLOMON MISS SUSAN ISABEL BARBARA

3 Paper Bldgs
Ground Floor, Temple, London EC4Y 7EU,
Telephone: 0171 797 7000
E-mail: clerks@3pb.co.uk
Call date: July 1967, Middle Temple
Qualifications: [MA (Oxon)]

SOLOMONS MRS ELLEN BETTY

One Garden Court
Ground Floor, Temple, London EC4Y 9BJ,
Telephone: 0171 797 7900
Call date: Feb 1964, Inner Temple

SOLOMONS GEOFFREY

36 Bedford Row
London WC1R 4JH,
Telephone: 0171 421 8000
E-mail: 36bedfordrow@link.org
Call date: July 1974, Gray's Inn
Qualifications: [LLB]

SOMERSET JONES ERIC QC (1978)

Goldsmith Building
1st Floor, Temple, London EC4Y 7BL,
Telephone: 0171 353 7881
E-mail: clerks@goldsmith-building.law.co.uk
Call date: May 1952, Middle Temple
Recorder
Qualifications: [MA (Oxon)]

SOMERSET-JONES MISS FELICITY

Oriel Chambers
14 Water Street, Liverpool L2 8TD,
Telephone: 0151 236 7191
E-mail: oriel_chambers@link.org
Call date: Oct 1994, Middle Temple
Qualifications: [BA (Hons)(L'pool), Dip in Law (City)]

SOMERVILLE BRYCE EDWARD

6 Fountain Court
Steelhouse Lane, Birmingham B4 6DR,
Telephone: 0121 233 3282
Call date: July 1980, Middle Temple
Qualifications: [BA (Cantab)]

SOMERVILLE THOMAS CLINTON

Peel House Chambers
Ground Floor, Peel House 5 Harrington Street,
Liverpool L2 9QA, Telephone: 0151 236 4321
Call date: July 1979, Middle Temple
Qualifications: [BA (Bris)]

SONES RICHARD

5 Paper Bldgs
Lower Ground Floor, Temple, London
EC4Y 7HB, Telephone: 0171 353 5638
E-mail: 107722,633@compuserve.com
Call date: Nov 1969, Inner Temple
Qualifications: [LLB (Lond)]

SOOD MRS USHA RANI

70 Charlecote Drive
Wollaton, Nottingham NG8 2SB,
Telephone: 0115 928 8901
Call date: July 1974, Gray's Inn
Qualifications: [LLB, M.Phil]

SOOLE MICHAEL ALEXANDER

5 Bell Yard
London WC2A 2JR, Telephone: 0171 333 8811
Call date: July 1977, Inner Temple
Assistant Recorder
Qualifications: [MA (Oxon)]

SOOR SMAIR SINGH

33 Bedford Row
London WC1R 4JH,
Telephone: 0171 242 6476
Call date: July 1988, Gray's Inn
Qualifications: [LLB]

SOORJOO MARTIN

14 Tooks Court
Cursitor St, London EC4A 1LB,
Telephone: 0171 405 8828
E-mail: clerks @tooks.law.co.uk
Call date: Oct 1990, Lincoln's Inn
Qualifications: [LLB]

SOPPITT NIGEL

Cleveland Chambers
63-65 Borough Road, Middlesbrough,
Cleveland TS1 3AA, Telephone: 01642 226036
Call date: Nov 1996, Gray's Inn

SOUBRY MS ANNA MARY

St Mary's Chambers
50 High Pavement, Lace Market, Nottingham
NG1 1HW, Telephone: 0115 9503503
E-mail: clerks@smc.law.co.uk
Call date: Nov 1995, Inner Temple
Qualifications: [LLB (B'ham)]

SOULSBY EDWARD WILLIAM

Clock Chambers
78 Darlington Street, Wolverhampton
WV1 4LY, Telephone: 01902 313444
Call date: Oct 1996, Gray's Inn
Qualifications: [LLB (Staffs)]

SOUTHALL RICHARD ANTHONY

17 Bedford Row
London WC1R 4EB,
Telephone: 0171 831 7314
E-mail: IBoard7314@AOL.com
Call date: Nov 1983, Middle Temple
Qualifications: [LLB (Buckingham)]

SOUTHERN PROFESSOR DAVID BOARDMAN

3 Temple Gardens Tax Chambers
1st Floor, Temple, London EC4Y 9AU,
Telephone: 0171 353 7884
Call date: July 1982, Lincoln's Inn
Qualifications: [LLB (Hons)(Lond), MA, M.Phil, D.Phil (Oxon), FTII]

Fax: 0171 583 2044;
Out of hours telephone: 01273 555542;
Other comms: 0411 578612

Types of work: Banking; Corporate finance; Equity, wills and trusts; Tax - capital and income; Tax - corporate

Other professional qualifications: Fellow of Chartered Institute of Taxation (FTII); Visiting Professor, Centre for Commercial Law Studies, Queen Mary and Westfield College, University of London

Other professional experience: Senior Legal Adviser, Lloyds TSB; Inland Revenue Solicitor's Office

Languages spoken: French, German

Publications: *Tolley's Taxation of Corporate Debt and Financial Instruments* (2nd edn), 1998; *Gore-Browne on Companies* (Contributor); *Simon's Direct Tax Service* (Contributor); *De Voil's Indirect Tax Service* (Contributor)

Reported cases: *IRC v Lloyd's Private Banking Ltd*, [1998] STC 559

SOUTHERN RICHARD MICHAEL

7 King's Bench Walk
Ground Floor, Temple, London EC4Y 7DS,
Telephone: 0171 583 0404
Call date: Nov 1987, Middle Temple
Qualifications: [MA (Cantab)]

SOUTHEY DAVID HUGH

14 Tooks Court
Cursitor St, London EC4A 1LB,
Telephone: 0171 405 8828
E-mail: clerks @tooks.law.co.uk
Call date: Nov 1996, Inner Temple
Qualifications: [MEng (Lond)]

SOUTHGATE JONATHAN BLAKE

29 Bedford Row Chambers
London WC1R 4HE,
Telephone: 0171 831 2626
Call date: Nov 1992, Middle Temple
Qualifications: [LLB]

SOUTHWELL RICHARD CHARLES QC (1977)

One Hare Court
1st Floor, Temple, London EC4Y 7BE,
Telephone: 0171 353 3171
E-mail: admin-oneharecourt@btinternet.com
Call date: June 1959, Inner Temple
Recorder
Qualifications: [MA (Cantab)]

D

SOUTHWELL RICHARD CHARLES EDWARD

Farrar's Building
Temple, London EC4Y 7BD,
Telephone: 0171 583 9241
E-mail: chambers@farrarsbuilding.co.uk
Call date: July 1970, Inner Temple
Recorder

SOWERBY MATTHEW GILES

Verulam Chambers
Peer House 8-14 Verulam Street, Gray's Inn,
London WC1X 8LZ,
Telephone: 0171 813 2400
Call date: July 1987, Middle Temple
Qualifications: [BA (Sussex)]

SPACKMAN MARK ANDREW

Iscoed Chambers
86 St Helen's Road, Swansea SA1 4BQ,
Telephone: 01792 652988/9/330
Call date: Nov 1986, Lincoln's Inn
Qualifications: [LLB (Leic)]

SPAIN TIMOTHY HARRISSON

Trinity Chambers
9-12 Trinity Chare, Quayside, Newcastle Upon
Tyne NE1 3DF, Telephone: 0191 232 1927
Call date: July 1983, Gray's Inn
Qualifications: [LLB (Newc)]

SPARKS MISS JOCELYN MARGARET

Hollis Whiteman Chambers
3rd/4th Floor Queen Elizabeth Bldg, Temple,
London EC4Y 9BS, Telephone: 0171 583 5766
E-mail: hollis.whiteman@btinternet.com
Call date: Nov 1987, Inner Temple
Qualifications: [LLB]

SPARKS KEVIN LAURENCE

Earl Street Chambers
47 Earl Street, Maidstone, Kent ME14 1PD,
Telephone: 01622 671222
E-mail: gunner-sparks@msn.com
Call date: July 1983, Gray's Inn
Qualifications: [BEd (Lond), LLM]

SPARROW ALBERT CHARLES QC (1966)

13 Old Square
1st Floor, Lincoln's Inn, London WC2A 3UA,
Telephone: 0171 242 6105
E-mail: clerks@serlecourt.co.uk
Call date: Nov 1950, Gray's Inn
Qualifications: [LLB (Lond), FSA]

SPARROW MISS JULIE ELIZABETH

8 Fountain Court
Steelhouse Lane, Birmingham B4 6DR,
Telephone: 0121 236 5514/5
E-mail: clerks@no8chambers.co.uk
Call date: Oct 1992, Lincoln's Inn
Qualifications: [LLB(Hons)]

SPARROW MRS MARIE-CLAIRE

95A Chancery Lane
London WC2A 1DT,
Telephone: 0171 405 3101
Call date: Nov 1977, Lincoln's Inn
Qualifications: [Maitrise en droit, (Paris),
Chevalier de L'Ordre, du Merite]

SPEAIGHT ANTHONY HUGH QC (1995)

12 King's Bench Walk
Temple, London EC4Y 7EL,
Telephone: 0171 583 0811
E-mail: chambers@12kbw.co.uk
Call date: July 1973, Middle Temple
Qualifications: [MA (Oxon)]

SPEAK MICHAEL NORMAN

4 Brick Court
1st Floor, Temple, London EC4Y 9AD,
Telephone: 0171 583 8455
Call date: July 1983, Lincoln's Inn
Qualifications: [BA (Hull), Dip Law]

SPEARMAN RICHARD QC (1996)

5 Raymond Buildings
1st Floor, Gray's Inn, London WC1R 5BP,
Telephone: 0171 242 2902
Call date: Nov 1977, Middle Temple
Qualifications: [MA (Cantab)]

SPECK ADRIAN

8 New Square
Lincoln's Inn, London WC2A 3QP,
Telephone: 0171 405 4321
Call date: Oct 1993, Gray's Inn
Qualifications: [BA]

SPEDDING MISS CATHERINE ANN

All Saints Chambers
9/11 Broad Street, Bristol BS1 2HP,
Telephone: 0117 921 1966
Call date: Nov 1995, Inner Temple
Qualifications: [LLB (Hons)]

SPEIRS ALISTAIR CHARLES

Plowden Bldgs
2nd Floor, Temple, London EC4Y 9BU,
Telephone: 0171 583 0808
E-mail: bar@plowdenbuildings.co.uk
Call date: Oct 1995, Middle Temple
Qualifications: [LLB (Newcastle)]

SPELLER BRUCE CHRISTOPHER NORMAN

4 Field Court
Gray's Inn, London WC1R 5EA,
Telephone: 0171 440 6900
E-mail: chambers@4fieldcourt.co.uk
Call date: July 1976, Inner Temple
Qualifications: [MA (Oxon)]

SPENCE MALCOLM HUGH QC (1979)

2-3 Gray's Inn Square
Gray's Inn, London WC1R 5JH,
Telephone: 0171 242 4986
E-mail: chambers@2-3graysinnsquare.co.uk
Call date: June 1958, Gray's Inn
Recorder

SPENCE SIMON PETER

18 Red Lion Court
(Off Fleet Street), London EC4A 3EB,
Telephone: 0171 520 6000
Thornwood House
102 New London Road, Chelmsford, Essex
CM2 0RG, Telephone: 01245 280880
Call date: July 1985, Inner Temple
Qualifications: [LLB (Leics)]

SPENCE STEPHEN NICHOLAS

1 Paper Bldgs
1st Floor, Temple, London EC4Y 7EP,
Telephone: 0171 353 3728/4953
Call date: July 1983, Gray's Inn
Qualifications: [BSc (Cardiff)]

SPENCER SIR DEREK HAROLD QC (1980)

18 Red Lion Court
(Off Fleet Street), London EC4A 3EB,
Telephone: 0171 520 6000
Thornwood House
102 New London Road, Chelmsford, Essex
CM2 0RG, Telephone: 01245 280880
Call date: Feb 1961, Gray's Inn
Recorder
Qualifications: [MA, BCL (Oxon)]

SPENCER MISS HANNAH KATYA

9 St John Street
Manchester M3 4DN,
Telephone: 0161 955 9000
E-mail: ninesjs@gconnect.com
5 Pump Court
Ground Floor, Temple, London EC4Y 7AP,
Telephone: 0171 353 2532
E-mail: fivepump@netcomuk.co.uk
Door Tenant
Call date: Feb 1993, Inner Temple
Qualifications: [BA]

SPENCER JAMES QC (1991)

11 King's Bench Walk
1st Floor, Temple, London EC4Y 7EQ,
Telephone: 0171 353 3337
3 Park Court
Leeds LS1 2QH, Telephone: 0113 297 1200
Call date: Nov 1975, Gray's Inn
Recorder
Qualifications: [LLB (Newc)]

SPENCER MRS MARGARET MARY

Enfield Chambers
36-38 London Road, Enfield, Middlesex
EN2 6DT, Telephone: 0181 364 5627
E-mail: Enfieldchambers@compuserve.com
Call date: Nov 1992, Lincoln's Inn
Qualifications: [LLB (Hons)(Lond)]

D

SPENCER MARTIN BENEDICT

4 Paper Bldgs
Ground Floor, Temple, London EC4Y 7EX,
Telephone: 0171 353 3366/583 7155
E-mail: clerks@4paperbuildings.com
Call date: July 1979, Inner Temple
Qualifications: [MA, BCL (Oxon)]

SPENCER MISS MELANIE DAWN

Field Court Chambers
2nd Floor 3 Field Court, Gray's Inn, London
WC1R 4EP, Telephone: 0171 404 7474
E-mail: Clerks@FieldCourtChambers.law.co.uk
Call date: July 1986, Inner Temple
Qualifications: [BA (Leeds) Dip Law]

SPENCER MICHAEL GERALD
QC (1989)

1 Paper Bldgs
Ground Floor, Temple, London EC4Y 7EP,
Telephone: 0171 583 7355
E-mail: clerks@1pb.co.uk
Call date: July 1970, Inner Temple
Recorder
Qualifications: [MA (Oxon)]

SPENCER PAUL ANTHONY

2 New Street
Leicester LE1 5NA, Telephone: 0116 2625906
Call date: Nov 1965, Inner Temple
Qualifications: [LLB]

SPENCER PAUL ANTHONY

Cloisters
1st Floor, Temple, London EC4Y 7AA,
Telephone: 0171 827 4000
E-mail: clerks@cloisters.com
Call date: Nov 1988, Middle Temple
Qualifications: [LLB]

SPENCER ROBIN GODFREY

Sedan House
Stanley Place, Chester CH1 2LU,
Telephone: 01244 320480/348282
1 Dr Johnson's Bldgs
Ground Floor, Temple, London EC4Y 7AX,
Telephone: 0171 353 9328
Call date: July 1978, Gray's Inn
Assistant Recorder
Qualifications: [MA (Cantab)]

SPENCER SHAUN MICHAEL QC (1988)

6 Park Square
Leeds LS1 2LW, Telephone: 0113 2459763
E-mail: chambers@no6.co.uk
11 King's Bench Walk
1st Floor, Temple, London EC4Y 7EQ,
Telephone: 0171 353 3337
Call date: July 1968, Lincoln's Inn
Recorder
Qualifications: [LLB]

SPENCER TIMOTHY JOHN

9 Bedford Row
London WC1R 4AZ,
Telephone: 0171 242 3555
E-mail: clerks@9br.co.uk
Call date: July 1982, Middle Temple
Qualifications: [MA (Cantab)]

SPENCER TIMOTHY ROBERT

9-12 Bell Yard
London WC2A 2LF,
Telephone: 0171 400 1800
Call date: July 1976, Lincoln's Inn

SPENCER BERNARD ROBERT VERE

4 King's Bench Walk
2nd Floor, Temple, London EC4Y 7DL,
Telephone: 0171 353 3581
Call date: Nov 1969, Inner Temple
Recorder
Qualifications: [MA (Oxon)]

SPENCER-LEWIS NEVILLE JULIAN

12 King's Bench Walk
Temple, London EC4Y 7EL,
Telephone: 0171 583 0811
E-mail: chambers@12kbw.co.uk
Call date: July 1970, Inner Temple
Qualifications: [MA (Oxon)]

SPENS DAVID PATRICK QC (1995)

6 King's Bench Walk
Ground Floor, Temple, London EC4Y 7DR,
Telephone: 0171 583 0410
Call date: Nov 1973, Inner Temple
Recorder
Qualifications: [BA]

SPENS WILLIAM DAVID RALPH

Albion Chambers
Broad Street, Bristol BS1 1DR,
Telephone: 0117 9272144
Call date: July 1972, Inner Temple
Qualifications: [MA (Cantab)]

SPICER ROBERT HADEN

Frederick Place Chambers
9 Frederick Place, Clifton, Bristol BS8 1AS,
Telephone: 0117 9738667
Call date: July 1970, Inner Temple
Qualifications: [MA (Cantab),
Dip.LegStuds(Cantab)]

SPIER MISS SIAN

10 King's Bench Walk
Ground Floor, Temple, London EC4Y 7EB,
Telephone: 0171 353 7742
E-mail: 10kbw@lineone.net
Call date: Nov 1989, Inner Temple
Qualifications: [LLB (Buck)]

SPINK ANDREW JOHN MURRAY

35 Essex Street
Temple, London WC2R 3AR,
Telephone: 0171 353 6381
Call date: Nov 1985, Middle Temple
Qualifications: [BA (Cantab)]

SPINK PETER JOHN WILLIAM

5 Essex Court
1st Floor, Temple, London EC4Y 9AH,
Telephone: 0171 410 2000
Call date: July 1979, Gray's Inn

SPIRO MISS DAFNA MIRIAM

6 Gray's Inn Square
Ground Floor, Gray's Inn, London WC1R 5AZ,
Telephone: 0171 242 1052
Call date: Nov 1994, Inner Temple
Qualifications: [BA (Sussex), CPE]

SPOLLON GUY MERTON

7 Fountain Court
Steelhouse Lane, Birmingham B4 6DR,
Telephone: 0121 236 8531
Call date: Nov 1976, Gray's Inn
Qualifications: [BA]

SPON-SMITH ROBIN WITTERICK

1 Mitre Ct Bldgs
Ground Floor, Temple, London EC4Y 7BS,
Telephone: 0171 797 7070
Call date: Nov 1976, Inner Temple
Recorder
Qualifications: [LLM]

SPOONER HENRY NEVILLE

Westgate Chambers
144 High Street, Lewes, East Sussex BN7 1XT,
Telephone: 01273 480510
Frederick Place Chambers
9 Frederick Place, Clifton, Bristol BS8 1AS,
Telephone: 0117 9738667
1 Dr Johnson's Bldgs
Ground Floor, Temple, London EC4Y 7AX,
Telephone: 0171 353 9328
Call date: Nov 1971, Lincoln's Inn

SPOONER MISS JUDITH ANN

Hardwicke Building
New Square, Lincoln's Inn, London
WC2A 3SB, Telephone: 0171 242 2523
E-mail: clerks@hardwicke.co.uk
Call date: July 1987, Middle Temple
Qualifications: [LLB (Hons)(Reading)]

SPRACK JOHN MAURICE

1 Pump Court
Lower Ground Floor, Temple, London
EC4Y 7AB, Telephone: 0171 583 2012/
353 4341
E-mail: (name) @1pumpcourt.co.uk
Door Tenant
Call date: July 1984, Gray's Inn
Qualifications: [BA, LLB (Rhodes)]

SPRATLING MRS ANNE VIRGINIA

4 Brick Court
Ground Floor, Temple, London EC4Y 9AD,
Telephone: 0171 797 7766
E-mail: chambers@4brick.co.uk
Call date: July 1980, Lincoln's Inn
Qualifications: [BA (Cantab)]

SPRATT CHRISTOPHER DAVID RICHARD DEAN

33 Bedford Row
London WC1R 4JH,
Telephone: 0171 242 6476
Call date: Nov 1986, Gray's Inn
Qualifications: [LLB(Dundee)]

SPRATT-DAWSON MISS JOSEPHINE MARGERY

Trinity Chambers
140 New London Road, Chelmsford, Essex
CM2 0AW, Telephone: 01245 605040
Call date: Oct 1993, Gray's Inn
Qualifications: [LLB (Anglia)]

SPROSTON-MATTHEWS MRS LYNNE TERESA

Assize Court Chambers
14 Small Street, Bristol BS1 1DE,
Telephone: 0117 9264587
Call date: Nov 1987, Inner Temple
Qualifications: [LLB (Nottm)]

SPROULL NICHOLAS

Albion Chambers
Broad Street, Bristol BS1 1DR,
Telephone: 0117 9272144
Call date: Nov 1992, Gray's Inn
Qualifications: [LLB (Bris)]

SPRUNKS JAMES EDWARD

32 Park Place
Cardiff CF1 3BA, Telephone: 01222 397364
Call date: Oct 1995, Lincoln's Inn
Qualifications: [LLB (Hons)(Notts)]

SQUIRRELL BENJAMIN

1 Crown Office Row
2nd Floor, Temple, London EC4Y 7HH,
Telephone: 0171 797 7111
Call date: Oct 1990, Inner Temple
Qualifications: [BA (Lond), Dip Law]

ST JOHN-STEVENS PHILIP SIMEON

Queen Elizabeth Bldg
Ground Floor, Temple, London EC4Y 9BS,
Telephone: 0171 353 7181 (12 Lines)
Call date: July 1985, Inner Temple
Qualifications: [LLB (Cardiff)]

ST LOUIS BRIAN LLOYD

Hardwicke Building
New Square, Lincoln's Inn, London
WC2A 3SB, Telephone: 0171 242 2523
E-mail: clerks@hardwicke.co.uk
Call date: Oct 1994, Middle Temple
Qualifications: [LLB (Hons), LLM (Lond)]

ST VILLE LAURENCE AUGUSTIN ISAIAH

Chancery Chambers
1st Floor Offices 70/72 Chancery Lane,
London WC2A 1AB,
Telephone: 0171 405 6879/6870
Call date: June 1955, Gray's Inn

ST VILLE LAURENCE JAMES

8 New Square
Lincoln's Inn, London WC2A 3QP,
Telephone: 0171 405 4321
Call date: Oct 1995, Gray's Inn
Qualifications: [MA, C.Eng, MIEE]

STABLES CHRISTOPHER HILTON

Exchange Chambers
Pearl Assurance House Derby Square,
Liverpool L2 9XX, Telephone: 0151 236 7747/
0458
E-mail: exchangechambers@btinternet.com
Call date: Oct 1990, Gray's Inn
Qualifications: [LLB (L'pool)]

STABLES GORDON

Paradise Square Chambers
26 Paradise Square, Sheffield S1 2DE,
Telephone: 0114 2738951
Call date: Oct 1995, Lincoln's Inn
Qualifications: [BA (Hons), MA, CPE
(Huddersfield)]

STADDON MISS CLAIRE ANN

12 New Square
Ground Floor, Lincoln's Inn, London
WC2A 3SW, Telephone: 0171 419 1212
E-mail: 12newsquare@compuserve.com
25 Park Square
Leeds LS1 2PW, Telephone: 0113 2451841/2/3
E-mail: sovereignchambers@btinternet.com
Door Tenant
Call date: July 1985, Middle Temple
Qualifications: [LLB (Lond)]

STADDON PAUL

Francis Taylor Bldg
2nd Floor, Temple, London EC4Y 7BY,
Telephone: 0171 353 9942/3157
Call date: July 1976, Inner Temple
Qualifications: [BSc (Econ) Lond.]

STADLEN NICHOLAS FELIX QC (1991)

Fountain Court
Temple, London EC4Y 9DH,
Telephone: 0171 583 3335
E-mail: chambers@fountaincourt.co.uk
Call date: Nov 1976, Inner Temple
Assistant Recorder
Qualifications: [BA (Cantab)]

STAFFORD ANDREW BRUCE

2 Crown Office Row
2nd Floor, Temple, London EC4Y 7HJ,
Telephone: 0171 797 8000
Call date: July 1980, Middle Temple
Qualifications: [MA (Cantab)]

STAFFORD PAUL RINALDO

10 Old Square
Ground Floor, Lincoln's Inn, London
WC2A 3SU, Telephone: 0171 405 0758
Call date: Nov 1987, Gray's Inn
Qualifications: [MA (Oxon), D Phil (Oxon),
Dip Law]

STAFFORD-MICHAEL SIMON ALEXANDER

4 King's Bench Walk
Ground/First Floor, Temple, London
EC4Y 7DL, Telephone: 0171 822 8822
E-mail: 4kbw@barristersatlaw.com
Call date: Nov 1982, Gray's Inn
Qualifications: [LLB(Bristol)]

STAGE PETER JAMES

Queen Elizabeth Bldg
Ground Floor, Temple, London EC4Y 9BS,
Telephone: 0171 353 7181 (12 Lines)
Call date: July 1971, Lincoln's Inn
Qualifications: [LLB]

STAGG PAUL ANDREW

1 Serjeants' Inn
5th Floor Fleet Street, Temple, London
EC4Y 1LL, Telephone: 0171 415 6666
E-mail: no1serjeantsinn@btinternet.com
Call date: Oct 1994, Gray's Inn
Qualifications: [LLB (Warw)]

STAITE MISS SARA ELIZABETH

2 Harcourt Bldgs
Ground Floor/Left, Temple, London
EC4Y 9DB, Telephone: 0171 583 9020
E-mail: clerks@harcourt.co.uk
Stanbrook & Henderson
2 Harcourt Bldgs 2nd Floor, Temple, London
EC4Y 9DB, Telephone: 0171 353 0101
E-mail: clerks@harcourt.co.uk
Call date: July 1979, Inner Temple
Assistant Recorder
Qualifications: [LLB (Leeds)]

STALKER MISS MONICA

Queen's Chambers
5 John Dalton Street, Manchester M2 6ET,
Telephone: 0161 834 6875/4738
4 Camden Place
Preston PR1 3JL, Telephone: 01772 828300
Call date: July 1967, Gray's Inn
Qualifications: [LLB (Manch)]

D

STALLEBRASS PAUL

5 Paper Bldgs
Ground Floor, Temple, London EC4Y 7HB,
Telephone: 0171 583 9275/583 4555
E-mail: 5paper@link.org
Call date: Oct 1991, Inner Temple
Qualifications: [BA (Cantab)]

STALLWORTHY NICOLAS KYD

35 Essex Street
Temple, London WC2R 3AR,
Telephone: 0171 353 6381
Call date: Oct 1993, Middle Temple
Qualifications: [BA (Hons)(Oxon)]

STANBROOK CLIVE ST GEORGE QC (1989)

2 Harcourt Bldgs
Ground Floor/Left, Temple, London
EC4Y 9DB, Telephone: 0171 583 9020
E-mail: clerks@harcourt.co.uk
Stanbrook & Henderson
2 Harcourt Bldgs 2nd Floor, Temple, London
EC4Y 9DB, Telephone: 0171 353 0101
E-mail: clerks@harcourt.co.uk
Call date: Nov 1972, Inner Temple
Qualifications: [LLB (Lond)]

STANCOMBE BARRY TERRENCE

Gough Square Chambers
6-7 Gough Square, London EC4A 3DE,
Telephone: 0171 353 0924
E-mail: gsc@goughsq.co.uk
Call date: July 1983, Gray's Inn
Qualifications: [LLB (Hons) (Lond)]

STANDFAST PHILIP ARTHUR

St Paul's House
5th Floor 23 Park Square South, Leeds
LS1 2ND, Telephone: 0113 2455866
Call date: July 1980, Inner Temple
Qualifications: [BA (Sheff)]

STANFIELD MISS SANDRA GASCOYNE

5 Paper Bldgs
Lower Ground Floor, Temple, London
EC4Y 7HB, Telephone: 0171 353 5638
E-mail: 107722,633@compuserve.com
Call date: Nov 1984, Gray's Inn
Qualifications: [BA (Hons)]

STANFORD DAVID RALPH

3 Stone Bldgs
Ground Floor, Lincoln's Inn, London
WC2A 3XL, Telephone: 0171 242 4937/
405 8358
Call date: Nov 1951, Middle Temple
Qualifications: [MA, LLB (Cantab)]

STANGER MISS NINA VERA MARY

1 Gray's Inn Square
1st Floor, London WC1R 5AG,
Telephone: 0171 405 3000
E-mail: clerks@onegrays.demon.co.uk
Door Tenant
Call date: Nov 1965, Middle Temple
Qualifications: [LLB (Lond)]

STANISLAS PAUL JUNIOR

Somersett Chambers
52 Bedford Row, London WC1R 4LR,
Telephone: 0171 404 6701
E-mail: Somersettchambers@cocoon.co.uk
Call date: Feb 1989, Middle Temple
Qualifications: [LLB (PCL)]

STANLEY MISS CLARE FIONA LOUISE

24 Old Bldgs
Ground Floor, Lincoln's Inn, London
WC2A 3UJ, Telephone: 0171 404 0946
E-mail: clerks@24oldbuildings.law.co.uk
Call date: Nov 1994, Middle Temple
Qualifications: [BA (Hons) (Cantab)]

STANLEY PAUL MALLALIEU

Essex Court Chambers
24 Lincoln's Inn Fields, London WC2A 3ED,
Telephone: 0171 813 8000
E-mail: clerksroom@essexcourt-chambers.co.uk
Call date: Nov 1993, Middle Temple
Qualifications: [BA (Hons)(Cantab), LLM
(Harvard)]

STANNILAND JONATHAN PETER

Assize Court Chambers
14 Small Street, Bristol BS1 1DE,
Telephone: 0117 9264587
Call date: Nov 1993, Inner Temple
Qualifications: [LLB]

STANSBY MRS HILARY ALEXANDRA

Kenworthy's Buildings
83 Bridge Street, Manchester M3 2RF,
Telephone: 0161 832 4036/834 6954
Call date: Nov 1985, Middle Temple
Qualifications: [MA (Cantab)]

STANSFIELD PIERS ALISTAIR

Keating Chambers
10 Essex Street, Outer Temple, London
WC2R 3AA, Telephone: 0171 544 2600
Call date: Nov 1993, Inner Temple
Qualifications: [LLB (Bris)]

STANTON MRS CAROLYN VERITY

Sedan House
Stanley Place, Chester CH1 2LU,
Telephone: 01244 320480/348282
Call date: Oct 1993, Middle Temple
Qualifications: [LLB (Hons)(L'pool)]

STANTON DAVID RONALD

33 Bedford Row
London WC1R 4JH,
Telephone: 0171 242 6476
Call date: July 1979, Gray's Inn
Qualifications: [BA]

STANTON MISS LISA HELEN

Francis Taylor Bldg
3rd Floor, Temple, London EC4Y 7BY,
Telephone: 0171 797 7250
Call date: Oct 1993, Inner Temple
Qualifications: [MA (Cantab)]

STANTON NICHOLAS PHILIP

169 Temple Chambers
Temple Avenue, London EC4Y 0DA,
Telephone: 0171 583 7644
Call date: Feb 1991, Inner Temple
Qualifications: [BA (Oxon)]

STARCEVIC PETAR

7 Fountain Court
Steelhouse Lane, Birmingham B4 6DR,
Telephone: 0121 236 8531
Call date: July 1983, Inner Temple
Qualifications: [LLB (Bris)]

STARKIE MISS CLAIRE ELIZABETH

Priory Chambers
2 Fountain Court, Steelhouse Lane,
Birmingham B4 6DR,
Telephone: 0121 236 3882/1375
Call date: Nov 1991, Lincoln's Inn
Qualifications: [MA (Hons) (Cambs)]

STARKS NICHOLAS ERNSHAW

8 Fountain Court
Steelhouse Lane, Birmingham B4 6DR,
Telephone: 0121 236 5514/5
E-mail: clerks@no8chambers.co.uk
Call date: July 1989, Middle Temple
Qualifications: [LLB (Hons)(Manch)]

STARMER KEIR

Doughty Street Chambers
11 Doughty Street, London WC1N 2PG,
Telephone: 0171 404 1313
E-mail: doughty_street@compuserve.com
Call date: Nov 1987, Middle Temple
Qualifications: [LLB (Leeds), BCL, (Oxon)]

START MISS VICTORIA LOUISE

2 King's Bench Walk
Ground Floor, Temple, London EC4Y 7DE,
Telephone: 0171 353 1746
E-mail: 2kbw@atlas.co.uk
Call date: Oct 1996, Middle Temple
Qualifications: [BA (Hons)(Oxon), LLM (Lond)]

STARTE HARVEY NICHOLAS ADRIAN

1 Brick Court
1st Floor, Temple, London EC4Y 9BY,
Telephone: 0171 353 8845
E-mail: clerks@1brickcourt.co.uk
Call date: Nov 1985, Gray's Inn
Qualifications: [MA (Cantab)]

STATMAN PHILIP RICHARD

3 Gray's Inn Square
Ground Floor, London WC1R 5AH,
Telephone: 0171 520 5600
E-mail: gis3@btinternet.com
Call date: July 1975, Middle Temple
Assistant Recorder
Qualifications: [LLB (Lond)]

D

STAUNTON (THOMAS) ULICK (PATRICK)

11 New Square
Ground Floor, Lincoln's Inn, London
WC2A 3QB, Telephone: 0171 831 0081
E-mail: 11newsquare.co.uk
65-67 King Street
Leicester LE1 6RP, Telephone: 0116 2547710
Call date: July 1984, Middle Temple
Qualifications: [LLB (Lond)]

STAUNTON WILLIAM JOHN PAUL

58 King Street Chambers
1st Floor, Kingsgate House 51-53 South King
Street, Manchester M2 6DE,
Telephone: 0161 831 7477
Call date: Feb 1986, Middle Temple
Qualifications: [MA (Cantab)]

STEAD MISS KATE REBECCA

Barrister's Common Law Chambers
57 Whitechapel Road, Aldgate East, London
E1 1DU, Telephone: 0171 375 3012
E-mail: barristers@hotmail:com
Call date: Oct 1996, Lincoln's Inn
Qualifications: [LLB (Hons)(Middx), M.Phil
(Cantab)]

STEAD RICHARD JAMES

St John's Chambers
Small Street, Bristol BS1 1DW,
Telephone: 0117 9213456/298514
E-mail: clerks@stjohns.uk.com
Call date: July 1979, Middle Temple
Assistant Recorder
Qualifications: [MA (Cantab)]

STEAD TIMOTHY HAROLD

6 Park Square
Leeds LS1 2LW, Telephone: 0113 2459763
E-mail: chambers@no6.co.uk
Call date: Nov 1979, Gray's Inn
Qualifications: [BA]

STEADMAN RUSSELL CHARLES

Mitre House Chambers
Mitre House 44 Fleet Street, London
EC4Y 1BN, Telephone: 0171 583 8233
Call date: Nov 1995, Inner Temple
Qualifications: [BA (Essex), CPE]

STEEL JOHN BRYCHAN QC (1993)

4-5 Gray's Inn Square
Ground Floor, Gray's Inn, London WC1R 5AY,
Telephone: 0171 404 5252
E-mail: chambers@4-5graysinnsquare.co.uk
Call date: July 1978, Gray's Inn
Qualifications: [BSc Hons]

STEELE DAVID MARK

Colleton Chambers
Colleton Crescent, Exeter, Devon EX2 4DG,
Telephone: 01392 74898/9
Call date: Nov 1975, Gray's Inn
Qualifications: [LLB (B'ham)]

STEEN MARTIN GAMPER

Albion Chambers
Broad Street, Bristol BS1 1DR,
Telephone: 0117 9272144
Call date: July 1976, Inner Temple
Qualifications: [LLB (Hons)]

STEENSON DAVID SAMUEL

3 Paper Bldgs
1st Floor, Temple, London EC4Y 7EU,
Telephone: 0171 583 8055
E-mail: london@3paper.com
4 St Peter Street
Winchester SO23 8OW,
Telephone: 01962 868884
20 Lorne Park Road
Bournemouth BH1 1JN,
Telephone: 01202 292102 (5 Lines)
Call date: Nov 1991, Lincoln's Inn
Qualifications: [LLB (Hons) (Belfast)]

STEER DAVID QC (1993)

The Corn Exchange
5th Floor Fenwick Street, Liverpool L2 7QS,
Telephone: 0151 227 1081/5009
Call date: Nov 1974, Middle Temple
Recorder
Qualifications: [BA (Hons)]

STEER WILFRED REED QC (1972)

Park Court Chambers
40 Park Cross Street, Leeds LS1 2QH,
Telephone: 0113 2433277
Call date: Nov 1950, Gray's Inn
Qualifications: [LLB (Lond)]

STEIGER MARTIN THOMAS QC (1994)

18 St John Street
Manchester M3 4EA,
Telephone: 0161 278 1800
Call date: Nov 1969, Inner Temple
Recorder
Qualifications: [LLB (Nottm)]

STEIN SAMUEL

1 Pump Court
Lower Ground Floor, Temple, London
EC4Y 7AB, Telephone: 0171 583 2012/
353 4341
E-mail: (name) @1pumpcourt.co.uk
Call date: Nov 1988, Inner Temple
Qualifications: [LLB (Hons)]

STEINERT JONATHAN

New Court Chambers
5 Verulam Buildings, Gray's Inn, London
WC1R 5LY, Telephone: 0171 831 9500
E-mail: mail@newcourtchambers.com
Call date: Feb 1986, Middle Temple
Qualifications: [BA (Oxon) Dip Law, (PCL)]

STEINFELD ALAN GEOFFREY QC (1987)

24 Old Bldgs
Ground Floor, Lincoln's Inn, London
WC2A 3UJ, Telephone: 0171 404 0946
E-mail: clerks@24oldbuildings.law.co.uk
Call date: Nov 1968, Lincoln's Inn
Qualifications: [BA, LLB (Cantab)]

STELLING NIGEL ROY

Coleridge Chambers
Citadel 190 Corporation Street, Birmingham
B4 6QD, Telephone: 0121 233 3303
Call date: July 1987, Inner Temple
Qualifications: [BA]

STEMBRIDGE DAVID HARRY QC (1990)

5 Fountain Court
Steelhouse Lane, Birmingham B4 6DR,
Telephone: 0121 606 0500
199 Strand
London WC2R 1DR,
Telephone: 0171 379 9779
E-mail: chambers@199strand.co.uk
Call date: Nov 1955, Gray's Inn
Recorder
Qualifications: [LLB]

STEMMER-BALDWIN MARCUS STEPHEN

8 Stone Buildings
Lincoln's Inn, London WC2A 3TA,
Telephone: 0171 831 9881
Call date: Nov 1994, Inner Temple
Qualifications: [LLB (Kent)]

STENHOUSE JOHN ALEXANDER

6 Fountain Court
Steelhouse Lane, Birmingham B4 6DR,
Telephone: 0121 233 3282
Call date: Nov 1986, Lincoln's Inn
Qualifications: [LLB]

STENT MISS CAROLINE MARGARET

Newport Chambers
12 Clytha Park Road, Newport, Gwent
NP9 47L, Telephone: 01633 267403/255855
Call date: May 1993, Lincoln's Inn
Qualifications: [LLB (Hons)]

STEPHENS JOHN LEWIS

35 Essex Street
Temple, London WC2R 3AR,
Telephone: 0171 353 6381
Call date: July 1975, Middle Temple
Qualifications: [BA (Oxon)]

STEPHENS MICHAEL ALLEN

5 Fountain Court
Steelhouse Lane, Birmingham B4 6DR,
Telephone: 0121 606 0500
Call date: July 1983, Middle Temple
Qualifications: [BA (Keele), A.C.I.ARB]

D

STEPHENSON CHRISTOPHER JAMES

9 Gough Square
London EC4A 3DE, Telephone: 0171 353 5371
Call date: Nov 1994, Lincoln's Inn
Qualifications: [MA (Hons)(Edinburgh)]

STEPHENSON GEOFFREY CHARLES

2-3 Gray's Inn Square
Gray's Inn, London WC1R 5JH,
Telephone: 0171 242 4986
E-mail: chambers@2-3graysinnsquare.co.uk
Call date: Nov 1971, Gray's Inn

STEPHENSON WILLIAM BENEDICT

3 Paper Bldgs
1st Floor, Temple, London EC4Y 7EU,
Telephone: 0171 583 8055
E-mail: london@3paper.com
20 Lorne Park Road
Bournemouth BH1 1JN,
Telephone: 01202 292102 (5 Lines)
4 St Peter Street
Winchester SO23 8OW,
Telephone: 01962 868884
Call date: July 1973, Inner Temple
Qualifications: [MA (Oxon)]

STERLING JOHN ADRIAN LAWRENCE

Lamb Chambers
Lamb Building, Temple, London EC4Y 7AS,
Telephone: 0171 797 8300
E-mail: lambchambers@link.org
Call date: Feb 1953, Middle Temple
Qualifications: [LLB]

STERLING ROBERT ALAN

St James's Chambers
68 Quay Street, Manchester M3 3EJ,
Telephone: 0161 834 7000
E-mail: 106241.2625@compuserve.com
12 New Square
Ground Floor, Lincoln's Inn, London
WC2A 3SW, Telephone: 0171 419 1212
E-mail: 12newsquare@compuserve.com
Door Tenant
Park Lane Chambers
19 Westgate, Leeds LS1 2RD,
Telephone: 0113 2285000
Call date: July 1970, Gray's Inn
Qualifications: [MA (Cantab)]

STERN DAVID PATRICK JULIAN

4 King's Bench Walk
Ground/First Floor, Temple, London
EC4Y 7DL, Telephone: 0171 822 8822
E-mail: 4kbw@barristersatlaw.com
Call date: July 1989, Lincoln's Inn
Qualifications: [LLB (Lond)]

STERN IAN MICHAEL

Hollis Whiteman Chambers
3rd/4th Floor Queen Elizabeth Bldg, Temple,
London EC4Y 9BS, Telephone: 0171 583 5766
E-mail: hollis.whiteman@btinternet.com
Call date: July 1983, Inner Temple
Qualifications: [BA (Warw) Dip Law, (City)]

STERN DR KRISTINA ANNE

39 Essex Street
London WC2R 3AT,
Telephone: 0171 583 1111
E-mail: clerks@39essex.co.uk
Call date: Nov 1996, Inner Temple
Qualifications: [LLB (Melbourne), PhD
(Cantab)]

STERN MRS LINDA JOY QC (1991)

18 Red Lion Court
(Off Fleet Street), London EC4A 3EB,
Telephone: 0171 520 6000
Thornwood House
102 New London Road, Chelmsford, Essex
CM2 0RG, Telephone: 01245 280880
Call date: July 1971, Gray's Inn
Recorder

STERN MARK RICHARD ALEXANDER

2 Paper Bldgs
Temple, London EC4Y 7ET,
Telephone: 0171 936 2613
Call date: Feb 1988, Lincoln's Inn
Qualifications: [MA (Hons) (Cantab)]

STERN MICHAEL ADAM

4 Paper Bldgs
2nd Floor, Temple, London EC4Y 7EX,
Telephone: 0171 583 0816/071 353 1131
E-mail: clerks@4paperbuildings.co.uk
Call date: July 1983, Lincoln's Inn
Qualifications: [BA (Lond), Dip Law]

STERN THOMAS WILLIAM PAUL

Maidstone Chambers
33 Earl Street, Maidstone, Kent ME14 1PF,
Telephone: 01622 688592
Call date: Nov 1995, Gray's Inn
Qualifications: [LLB (Hons)]

STERNBERG MISS LESLI EDEN

Warwick House Chambers
8 Warwick Court, Gray's Inn, London
WC1R 5DJ, Telephone: 0171 430 2323
Call date: Nov 1994, Gray's Inn
Qualifications: [BA]

STERNBERG MICHAEL VIVIAN

4 Paper Bldgs
2nd Floor, Temple, London EC4Y 7EX,
Telephone: 0171 583 0816/071 353 1131
E-mail: clerks@4paperbuildings.co.uk
Call date: July 1975, Gray's Inn
Qualifications: [MA (Cantab), LLM (Cantab)]

STEVENS HOWARD LINTON

1 Crown Office Row
3rd Floor, Temple, London EC4Y 7HH,
Telephone: 0171 583 9292
E-mail: onecor@link.org
Call date: Oct 1990, Middle Temple
Qualifications: [BA (Dunelm), Dip Law (City)]

STEVENS MISS NINA PAULINE

3 Temple Gardens (North)
Fifth Floor, Temple, London EC4Y 9AU,
Telephone: 0171 353 0853/4/7222
E-mail: 100106.1577@compuserve.com
Call date: Oct 1994, Lincoln's Inn
Qualifications: [BA (Hons)]

STEVENS STUART STANDISH

Holborn Chambers
6 Gate Street, Lincoln's Inn Fields, London
WC2A 3HP, Telephone: 0171 242 6060
Middlesex Chambers
Suite 3 & 4 Stanley House Stanley Avenue,
Wembley, Middlesex HA0 4SB,
Telephone: 0181 902 1499
Call date: July 1970, Gray's Inn

STEVENS-HOARE MISS MICHELLE

Hardwicke Building
New Square, Lincoln's Inn, London
WC2A 3SB, Telephone: 0171 242 2523
E-mail: clerks@hardwicke.co.uk
Call date: July 1986, Middle Temple
Qualifications: [LLB (Lond), LLM (Property)(Lond)]

Fax: 0171 691 1234; DX: LDE 393;
Other comms: E-mail brieol@globalnet.co.uk

Types of work: Chancery land law; Commercial property; Equity, wills and trusts; Intellectual property; Landlord and tenant; Partnerships; Professional negligence

Circuit: South Eastern

Awards and memberships: PNBA; London Commercial & Common Law Bar Association

Reported cases: *R v London Borough of Newham ex parte Ugbo*, (1993) 26 HLR 263, 1993. Judicial review of decision that applicant was intentionally homeless.
Huwyler v Ruddy, [1996] EGCS 8, 1996. Residential property, flat sharing whether tenant or licensee.
BNP Mortgages Ltd v Goadsby & Harding Ltd, [1994] 2 EGLR 168, 1994. Professional negligence, negligent or fraudulent valuation, quantification of damages.
Onelife Ltd (in liquidation) v Roy, (1996) *The Times*, 12 July, 1996. Gaming, unlawful lottery snow-ball scheme.
Sheffield v Pickfords, (1997) *The Times*, 17 March, 1997. Pleading of UCTA.

STEVENSON ARTHUR WILLIAM QC (1996)

1 Paper Bldgs
Ground Floor, Temple, London EC4Y 7EP,
Telephone: 0171 583 7355
E-mail: clerks@1pb.co.uk
Call date: Nov 1968, Lincoln's Inn
Recorder
Qualifications: [MA (Oxon)]

STEVENSON JOHN MELFORD

2 Crown Office Row
Ground Floor, Temple, London EC4Y 7HJ,
Telephone: 0171 797 8100
E-mail: mail@2cor.co.uk, or to individual
barristers at: [barrister's surname]@2cor.co.uk
Call date: Nov 1975, Inner Temple
Qualifications: [MA (Oxon)]

STEVENSON JOSEPH GIBBS

62 Cortworth Road
Ecclesall, Sheffield S11 9LP,
Telephone: 0114 236 0988
Call date: Feb 1960, Inner Temple

STEVENSON ROBERT ANTHONY

Wilberforce Chambers
Bishop Lane, Hull HU1 1PA,
Telephone: 01482 323264
E-mail: clerks@hullbar.demon.co.uk
Call date: July 1972, Inner Temple
Qualifications: [MA (Cantab)]

STEVENSON-WATT NEVILLE WILLIAM

2 Field Court
Gray's Inn, London WC1R 5BB,
Telephone: 0171 405 6114
E-mail: fieldct2@netcomuk.co.uk.
Call date: Nov 1985, Middle Temple
Qualifications: [MA (Cantab), LLB, (Lond)]

STEVENTON MRS ELIZABETH ANNE

Chambers of Elizabeth Steventon
50 Firle Road, Brighton, Sussex BN2 2YH,
Telephone: 01273 670394
Call date: Oct 1991, Middle Temple
Qualifications: [LLB (Lond Ext)]

STEWART ALEXANDER JOSEPH

5 New Square
1st Floor, Lincoln's Inn, London WC2A 3RJ,
Telephone: 0171 404 0404
E-mail: Chambers@FiveNewSquare.CityScape.co.uk
Call date: July 1975, Gray's Inn
Qualifications: [BA, BCL (Oxon)]

STEWART GEORGE BARRY

Cleveland Chambers
63-65 Borough Road, Middlesbrough,
Cleveland TS1 3AA, Telephone: 01642 226036
Call date: July 1968, Gray's Inn
Qualifications: [LLB (Notts) Dip Crim, JD]

STEWART JAMES SIMEON HAMILTON QC (1982)

Park Court Chambers
40 Park Cross Street, Leeds LS1 2QH,
Telephone: 0113 2433277
18 Red Lion Court
(Off Fleet Street), London EC4A 3EB,
Telephone: 0171 520 6000
Call date: July 1966, Inner Temple
Recorder
Qualifications: [LLB]

STEWART MISS LINDSEY KATHLEEN

7 Stone Bldgs
Ground Floor, Lincoln's Inn, London
WC2A 3SZ, Telephone: 0171 405 3886/
242 3546
E-mail: chaldous@vossnet.co.uk
Call date: Nov 1983, Lincoln's Inn
Qualifications: [MA (Oxon)]

STEWART MARK COURTNEY

College Chambers
19 Carlton Cresent, Southampton, Hants
SO15 2ET, Telephone: 01703 230338
Call date: July 1989, Middle Temple
Qualifications: [BA (Hons), LLM [Anglia]]

STEWART NEILL ALASTAIR

Hollis Whiteman Chambers
3rd/4th Floor Queen Elizabeth Bldg, Temple,
London EC4Y 9BS, Telephone: 0171 583 5766
E-mail: hollis.whiteman@btinternet.com
Call date: July 1973, Middle Temple
Recorder
Qualifications: [BA (Cantab)]

STEWART NICHOLAS JOHN CAMERON QC (1987)

Hardwicke Building
New Square, Lincoln's Inn, London
WC2A 3SB, Telephone: 0171 242 2523
E-mail: clerks@hardwicke.co.uk
Call date: July 1971, Inner Temple
Recorder
Qualifications: [BA (Oxon),C Dip,A.F., CEDR
Accredited, Mediator]

STEWART RICHARD PAUL

New Court Chambers
5 Verulam Buildings, Gray's Inn, London
WC1R 5LY, Telephone: 0171 831 9500
E-mail: mail@newcourtchambers.com
Call date: July 1975, Gray's Inn
Qualifications: [BA (Belfast)]

STEWART ROBIN MILTON QC (1978)

199 Strand
London WC2R 1DR,
Telephone: 0171 379 9779
E-mail: chambers@199strand.co.uk
Call date: Feb 1963, Middle Temple
Recorder
Qualifications: [MA (Oxon)]

STEWART ROGER PAUL DAVIDSON

2 Crown Office Row
2nd Floor, Temple, London EC4Y 7HJ,
Telephone: 0171 797 8000
Call date: July 1986, Inner Temple
Qualifications: [MA (Cantab) LLM]

STEWART STEPHEN PAUL QC (1996)

22 Old Bldgs
Lincoln's Inn, London WC2A 3UJ,
Telephone: 0171 831 0222
25 Byrom Street
Manchester M3 4PF,
Telephone: 0161 829 2100
E-mail: Byromst25@aol.com
Call date: July 1975, Middle Temple
Assistant Recorder
Qualifications: [MA (Oxon)]

STEWART TOBY ALASDAIR CHARLES

24 The Ropewalk
Nottingham NG1 5EF,
Telephone: 0115 9472581
E-mail: clerk@ropewalk.co.uk
Call date: July 1989, Middle Temple
Qualifications: [LLB (Sheff)]

STEWART-SMITH WILLIAM RODNEY

1 New Square
Ground Floor, Lincoln's Inn, London
WC2A 3SA, Telephone: 0171 405 0884/5/6/7
E-mail: 1newsquare@compuserve.com
Call date: June 1964, Middle Temple
Recorder
Qualifications: [BA, LLB]

STEYN MS KAREN MARGARET

4-5 Gray's Inn Square
Ground Floor, Gray's Inn, London WC1R 5AY,
Telephone: 0171 404 5252
E-mail: chambers@4-5graysinnsquare.co.uk
Call date: Oct 1995, Middle Temple
Qualifications: [BA (Hons) (L'pool), Dip Law]

STEYNOR ALAN CHARLES

Keating Chambers
10 Essex Street, Outer Temple, London
WC2R 3AA, Telephone: 0171 544 2600
Call date: July 1975, Gray's Inn
Recorder
Qualifications: [MA (Cantab), FCIArb]

STILES JOHN ERNEST

9 Woodhouse Square
Leeds LS3 1AD, Telephone: 0113 2451986
Call date: July 1986, Middle Temple
Qualifications: [LLB]

STILGOE RUFUS NATHANIEL ABBOTT

23 Essex Street
London WC2R 3AS,
Telephone: 0171 413 0353/353 3533
E-mail: clerks@essexstreet23.demon.co.uk
Call date: Oct 1994, Inner Temple
Qualifications: [BA (Durham), CPE
(Huddersfield)]

D

STILITZ DANIEL MALACHI

11 King's Bench Walk
Temple, London EC4Y 7EQ,
Telephone: 0171 632 8500
E-mail: clerksroom@11-kbw.law.co.uk
Call date: Oct 1992, Lincoln's Inn
Qualifications: [BA (Hons)(Oxon), MA (City)]

STILL GEOFFREY JOHN CHURCHILL

Pump Court Chambers
Upper Ground Floor 3 Pump Court, Temple,
London EC4Y 7AJ, Telephone: 0171 353 0711
Pump Court Chambers
31 Southgate Street, Winchester SO23 8EE,
Telephone: 01962 868161
Call date: Feb 1966, Gray's Inn
Recorder
Qualifications: [LLB]

STIMPSON MICHAEL EDWARD

Littman Chambers
12 Gray's Inn Square, London WC1R 5JP,
Telephone: 0171 404 4866
E-mail: admin@littmanchambers.com
Call date: Nov 1969, Lincoln's Inn

STINCHCOMBE PAUL DAVID

4-5 Gray's Inn Square
Ground Floor, Gray's Inn, London WC1R 5AY,
Telephone: 0171 404 5252
E-mail: chambers@4-5graysinnsquare.co.uk
Call date: July 1985, Lincoln's Inn
Qualifications: [MA (Cantab), LLM (Harv)]

STIRLING CHRISTOPHER WILLIAM

Bell Yard Chambers
116/118 Chancery Lane, London WC2A 1PP,
Telephone: 0171 306 9292
Call date: Oct 1993, Inner Temple
Qualifications: [LLB]

STIRLING MR SIMON

4 Brick Court
1st Floor, Temple, London EC4Y 9AD,
Telephone: 0171 583 8455
Call date: July 1989, Gray's Inn
Qualifications: [BA (Hull)]

STITCHER MALCOLM DAVID

199 Strand
London WC2R 1DR,
Telephone: 0171 379 9779
E-mail: chambers@199strand.co.uk
Call date: Nov 1971, Lincoln's Inn
Qualifications: [LLB]

STOBART JOHN

King Charles House
Standard Hill, Nottingham NG1 6FX,
Telephone: 0115 9418851
E-mail: clerks@kch.co.uk
Call date: July 1974, Gray's Inn
Qualifications: [LLB (B'ham)]

STOCKDALE DAVID ANDREW
QC (1995)

Deans Court Chambers
Cumberland House Crown Square, Manchester
M3 3HA, Telephone: 0161 834 4097
E-mail: deanscourt@compuserve.com
Deans Court Chambers
41-43 Market Place, Preston PR1 1AH,
Telephone: 01772 555163
E-mail: deanscourt@compuserve.com
9 Bedford Row
London WC1R 4AZ,
Telephone: 0171 242 3555
E-mail: clerks@9br.co.uk
Call date: July 1975, Middle Temple
Recorder
Qualifications: [MA (Oxon)]

STOCKDALE SIR THOMAS MINSHULL

Erskine Chambers
30 Lincoln's Inn Fields, Lincoln's Inn, London
WC2A 3PF, Telephone: 0171 242 5532
E-mail: Clerks@Erskine-Chambers.law.co.uk
Call date: Nov 1966, Inner Temple
Qualifications: [MA (Oxon)]

STOCKER JOHN CRISPIN

One Garden Court
Ground Floor, Temple, London EC4Y 9BJ,
Telephone: 0171 797 7900
Call date: Nov 1985, Inner Temple
Qualifications: [LLB (Exon), LLM (Cantab)]

STOCKILL DAVID ANDREW

5 Fountain Court
Steelhouse Lane, Birmingham B4 6DR,
Telephone: 0121 606 0500
Call date: Nov 1985, Lincoln's Inn
Qualifications: [MA (Cantab)]

STOCKLEY MISS RUTH ANGELA

40 King Street
Manchester M2 6BA,
Telephone: 0161 832 9082
E-mail: Kingst40@aol.com
Call date: July 1988, Lincoln's Inn
Qualifications: [LLB (Hons)(Notts)]

STOCKWELL GRAHAM CLIVE

1 High Pavement
Nottingham NG1 1HF,
Telephone: 0115 9418218
Call date: Nov 1988, Inner Temple
Qualifications: [LLB]

STOKELL ROBERT

2 Crown Office Row
Ground Floor, Temple, London EC4Y 7HJ,
Telephone: 0171 797 8100
E-mail: mail@2cor.co.uk, or to individual
barristers at: [barrister's surname]@2cor.co.uk
Call date: Oct 1995, Lincoln's Inn
Qualifications: [BA (Hons)(Oxon)]

STOKER GRAHAM KENNETH ROBERT

2-3 Gray's Inn Square
Gray's Inn, London WC1R 5JH,
Telephone: 0171 242 4986
E-mail: chambers@2-3graysinnsquare.co.uk
Call date: Nov 1977, Middle Temple
Qualifications: [LLB, LLM]

STOKES DAVID MAYHEW ALLEN QC (1989)

5 Paper Bldgs
1st Floor, Temple, London EC4Y 7HB,
Telephone: 0171 583 6117
E-mail: clerks@5-paperbuildings.law.co.uk
Fenners Chambers
3 Madingley Road, Cambridge CB3 OEE,
Telephone: 01223 368761
Door Tenant
Call date: July 1968, Gray's Inn
Recorder
Qualifications: [MA (Cantab)]

STOKES MISS MARY ELIZABETH

Erskine Chambers
30 Lincoln's Inn Fields, Lincoln's Inn, London
WC2A 3PF, Telephone: 0171 242 5532
E-mail: Clerks@Erskine-Chambers.law.co.uk
Call date: July 1989, Lincoln's Inn
Qualifications: [MA BCL (Oxon), LLM
(Harvard)]

STOKES MICHAEL GEORGE THOMAS QC (1994)

36 Bedford Row
London WC1R 4JH,
Telephone: 0171 421 8000
E-mail: 36bedfordrow@link.org
7 Fountain Court
Steelhouse Lane, Birmingham B4 6DR,
Telephone: 0121 236 8531
Call date: Nov 1971, Gray's Inn
Recorder
Qualifications: [LLB]

STOLL JAMES ANDREW

Portsmouth Barristers'Chambers
Victory House 7 Bellevue Terrace,
Portsmouth, Hampshire PO5 3AT,
Telephone: 01705 831292
E-mail: clerks@portsmouthbar.com
Call date: Nov 1994, Inner Temple
Qualifications: [LLB (Hons)(Soton)]

STONE EVAN DAVID ROBERT QC (1979)

29 Bedford Row Chambers
London WC1R 4HE,
Telephone: 0171 831 2626
Call date: July 1954, Inner Temple
Assistant Recorder
Qualifications: [MA (Oxon)]

STONE GREGORY QC (1994)

4-5 Gray's Inn Square
Ground Floor, Gray's Inn, London WC1R 5AY,
Telephone: 0171 404 5252
E-mail: chambers@4-5graysinnsquare.co.uk
Call date: July 1976, Inner Temple
Qualifications: [MA (Oxon)]

Fax: 0171 242 7803; DX: 1029 London;
Other comms: E-mail chambers@4-
5graysinnsquare.co.uk

Types of work: Administrative; Environment;
Local government; Parliamentary; Town and
country planning

Other professional qualifications: MA (Econ)

Circuit: South Eastern

Awards and memberships: Local Government
Planning and Environmental Bar Association;
Standing Counsel to DTI for SE Circuit 1989-90

Other professional experience: Senior
Economist Morgan Grenfell & Co (1973-6)

Languages spoken: French

Publications: *Architects Journal Legal
Handbook*, 1997

STONE JOSEPH

2 Paper Bldgs
Temple, London EC4Y 7ET,
Telephone: 0171 936 2613
Call date: July 1989, Inner Temple
Qualifications: [BA [Manch], Dip Law [City]]

STONE MISS LUCILLE MADELINE

29 Bedford Row Chambers
London WC1R 4HE,
Telephone: 0171 831 2626
Call date: July 1983, Middle Temple
Qualifications: [MA (Cantab)]

STONE RICHARD FREDERICK QC (1968)

4 Field Court
Gray's Inn, London WC1R 5EA,
Telephone: 0171 440 6900
E-mail: chambers@4fieldcourt.co.uk
Call date: Nov 1952, Gray's Inn
Qualifications: [MA (Cantab)]

STONE RUSSELL CLIVE ANDREW

10 King's Bench Walk
1st Floor, Temple, London EC4Y 7EB,
Telephone: 0171 353 2501
Call date: Oct 1992, Inner Temple
Qualifications: [BA (Oxon)]

STONE MISS SALLY VICTORIA

Francis Taylor Bldg
Ground Floor, Temple, London EC4Y 7BY,
Telephone: 0171 353 7768/7769/2711
Call date: Nov 1994, Inner Temple
Qualifications: [BA (Hons) (Kent)]

STONEFROST MS HILARY

3/4 South Square
Gray's Inn, London WC1R 5HP,
Telephone: 0171 696 9900
E-mail: clerks@southsquare.com
Call date: Nov 1991, Middle Temple
Qualifications: [MSc (Lond)]

STONER CHRISTOPHER PAUL

9 Old Square
Ground Floor, Lincoln's Inn, London
WC2A 3SR, Telephone: 0171 405 4682
E-mail: chambers@9oldsquare.co.uk
Call date: Oct 1991, Lincoln's Inn
Qualifications: [LLB (Hons)(E.Anglia)]

STONES KEITH WILLIAM

9 King's Bench Walk
Ground Floor, Temple, London EC4Y 7DX,
Telephone: 0171 353 7202/3909
Call date: Nov 1975, Gray's Inn
Qualifications: [LLB]

STONOR NICHOLAS WILLIAM

Trinity Chambers
9-12 Trinity Chare, Quayside, Newcastle Upon
Tyne NE1 3DF, Telephone: 0191 232 1927
Door Tenant
Call date: Oct 1993, Middle Temple
Qualifications: [LLB (Hons)]

STOPA CHRISTOPHER PAUL MICHAEL

2 King's Bench Walk
Ground Floor, Temple, London EC4Y 7DE,
Telephone: 0171 353 1746
E-mail: 2kbw@atlas.co.uk
King's Bench Chambers
115 North Hill, Plymouth PL4 8JY,
Telephone: 01752 221551
Call date: Nov 1976, Middle Temple
Qualifications: [LLB (Leeds), FCA]

STOREY CHRISTOPHER THOMAS QC (1995)

Park Lane Chambers
19 Westgate, Leeds LS1 2RD,
Telephone: 0113 2285000
3 Serjeants Inn
London EC4Y 1BQ,
Telephone: 0171 353 5537
E-mail: available upon request
Call date: July 1979, Lincoln's Inn
Assistant Recorder

STOREY IAN FRANCIS

19 Figtree Lane
Sheffield S1 2DJ, Telephone: 0114 2759708/
2738380
Call date: Feb 1986, Gray's Inn
Qualifications: [LLB (Manch)]

STOREY JEREMY BRIAN QC (1994)

4 Pump Court
Temple, London EC4Y 7AN,
Telephone: 0171 353 2656/9
E-mail: 4_pump_court@compuserve.com
Call date: July 1974, Inner Temple
Recorder
Qualifications: [MA (Cantab)]

STOREY NICHOLAS JOHN

7 New Square
Lincoln's Inn, London WC2A 3QS,
Telephone: 0171 430 1660
Call date: July 1982, Gray's Inn
Qualifications: [LLB London]

STOREY PAUL MARK

29 Bedford Row Chambers
London WC1R 4HE,
Telephone: 0171 831 2626
Call date: July 1982, Lincoln's Inn
Qualifications: [BA]

STOREY THOMAS SEBASTIAN

10 Park Square
Leeds LS1 2LH, Telephone: 0113 2455438
E-mail: chambers@bandit.legend.co.uk
Call date: Feb 1993, Gray's Inn
Qualifications: [BA (Oxon)]

STOREY-REA MRS ALEXA ROSEANN

4 Brick Court
Temple, London EC4Y 9AD,
Telephone: 0171 797 8910
Call date: Feb 1990, Middle Temple
Qualifications: [LLB]

STORK BRIAN RAYMOND

2 Dr Johnson's Building
Temple, London EC4Y 7AY,
Telephone: 0171 353 4716
Call date: July 1981, Inner Temple
Qualifications: [LLB (Lond)]

STORRIE TIMOTHY JAMES

Old Colony House
6 South King Street, Manchester M2 6DQ,
Telephone: 0161 834 4364
Call date: Oct 1993, Middle Temple
Qualifications: [BA (Hons)(Oxon), CPE]

STOTESBURY DAVID CHARLES

21 Lauderdale Tower
Barbican, London EC2Y 8BY,
Telephone: 0171 920 9308
Call date: Feb 1980, Gray's Inn
Qualifications: [LLB (Lond), MA (Cantab)]

STOUT ROGER CHARLES

18 St John Street
Manchester M3 4EA,
Telephone: 0161 278 1800
Call date: Nov 1976, Gray's Inn
Qualifications: [BA (Exeter)]

STOW TIMOTHY MONTAGUE FENWICK QC (1989)

12 King's Bench Walk
Temple, London EC4Y 7EL,
Telephone: 0171 583 0811
E-mail: chambers@12kbw.co.uk
Call date: Nov 1965, Gray's Inn
Recorder

STRACHAN MISS BARBARA HELEN

1 Middle Temple Lane
Temple, London EC4Y 1LT,
Telephone: 0171 583 0659 (12 Lines)
Call date: July 1986, Inner Temple
Qualifications: [LLB]

STRACHAN CHRISTOPHER WILLIAM CHARLES

2 Paper Bldgs
1st Floor, Temple, London EC4Y 7ET,
Telephone: 0171 936 2611 (10 Lines)
E-mail: clerks@2pbbarristers.co.uk
Westgate Chambers
144 High Street, Lewes, East Sussex BN7 1XT,
Telephone: 01273 480510
Call date: July 1975, Inner Temple
Qualifications: [MA (Exon)]

STRACHAN DOUGLAS MARK ARTHUR QC (1987)

1 Crown Office Row
3rd Floor, Temple, London EC4Y 7HH,
Telephone: 0171 583 9292
E-mail: onecor@link.org
Call date: July 1969, Inner Temple
Recorder
Qualifications: [MA, BCL (Oxon)]

STRACHAN MS ELAINE JUNE

3 Paper Bldgs
1st Floor, Temple, London EC4Y 7EU,
Telephone: 0171 583 8055
E-mail: london@3paper.com
1 Alfred Street
High Street, Oxford OX1 4EH,
Telephone: 01865 793736
Call date: Nov 1995, Middle Temple
Qualifications: [BA (Hons)]

STRACHAN JAMES OLIVER JOHN

4-5 Gray's Inn Square
Ground Floor, Gray's Inn, London WC1R 5AY,
Telephone: 0171 404 5252
E-mail: chambers@4-5graysinnsquare.co.uk
Call date: Oct 1996, Middle Temple
Qualifications: [BA (Hons)]

STRAKER TIMOTHY DERRICK QC (1996)

2-3 Gray's Inn Square
2-3 Gray's Inn Square, Gray's Inn, London
WC1R 5JH, Telephone: 0171 242 4986
E-mail: chambers@2-3graysinnsquare.co.uk
Call date: July 1977, Gray's Inn
Assistant Recorder
Qualifications: [MA (Cantab)]

Fax: 0181 341 4158;
Out of hours telephone: 0181 341 0413;
Other comms: E-mail halsbury@msn.com

Types of work: Administrative; Civil liberties; Compulsory purchase; Discrimination; Education; Housing; Local government; Planning; Town and country planning

Circuit: South Eastern

Awards and memberships: Administrative Law Bar Association; Planning Bar Association; Downing College Prize for Law; Senior Harris Scholar; Holt Scholar of Gray's Inn; Lord Justice Holker Senior Award

Publications: *Rights of Way Law Review*, 1996; *Intelligence Services Act 1994*, 1994; *Evidence at Inquiries*, 1995

Reported cases: *R v Oldham ex parte Garlick*, [1993] AC 509, 1992-3. Determined position of children under the homelessness legislation (House of Lords).

Gillenden v Surrey, (1997) 74 P&CR 119, 1997.
Extent of reasoning to be given in adopting
Local Plan (Court of Appeal).
Reckley v Minister of Public Safety, [1996] AC
527; [1995] 2 AC 491, 1995-6. Whether judicial
review available to prerogative of mercy (Privy
Council).
R v Cornwall ex parte Huntingdon, [1994] 1
All ER 694, 1993. Statutory provision prevents
judicial review.
Hollis v Dudley, [1998] 1 All ER 759, 1997.
Compulsory costs in certain environmental
cases.

STRANGE MS (KAREN) MICHELLE

Doughty Street Chambers
11 Doughty Street, London WC1N 2PG,
Telephone: 0171 404 1313
E-mail: doughty_street@compuserve.com
Call date: July 1989, Lincoln's Inn
Qualifications: [BA (Oxon)]

STRATFORD MISS JEMIMA LUCY

Brick Court Chambers
15/19 Devereux Court, London WC2R 3JJ,
Telephone: 0171 583 0777
E-mail: (surname)@brickcourt.demon.co.uk
Call date: Oct 1993, Middle Temple
Qualifications: [BA (Hons)(Oxon), CPE (City)]

STRAUSS NICHOLAS ALBERT QC (1984)

1 Essex Court
Ground Floor, Temple, London EC4Y 9AR,
Telephone: 0171 583 2000
E-mail: clerks@oneessexcourt.co.uk
Call date: Nov 1965, Middle Temple
Assistant Recorder
Qualifications: [MA, LLB (Cantab)]

STRAW JONATHAN JAMES

King Charles House
Standard Hill, Nottingham NG1 6FX,
Telephone: 0115 9418851
E-mail: clerks@kch.co.uk
Call date: Oct 1992, Lincoln's Inn
Qualifications: [LLB(Hons)(Newc)]

STREATFEILD-JAMES DAVID STEWART

1 Atkin Building
Gray's Inn, London WC1R 5AT,
Telephone: 0171 404 0102
E-mail: clerks@atkin-chambers.co.uk
Call date: July 1986, Inner Temple
Qualifications: [BA(Oxon)]

STREEK JOSEPH ALEXANDER

22 Old Bldgs
Lincoln's Inn, London WC2A 3UJ,
Telephone: 0171 831 0222
Call date: Oct 1990, Gray's Inn
Qualifications: [LLB (Lond)]

STREETS MRS CAROLINE JANE HAMPSON

One Garden Court
Ground Floor, Temple, London EC4Y 9BJ,
Telephone: 0171 797 7900
Call date: Nov 1986, Middle Temple
Qualifications: [MA (Cantab)]

STRICKLAND MISS CLARE ELIZABETH

23 Essex Street
London WC2R 3AS,
Telephone: 0171 413 0353/353 3533
E-mail: clerks@essexstreet23.demon.co.uk
Call date: Oct 1995, Lincoln's Inn
Qualifications: [LLB (Hons)(B'ham)]

STRINGER LEON

Clapham Chambers
21-25 Bedford Road, Clapham North, London
SW4 7SH, Telephone: 0171 978 8482/
642 5777
E-mail: 113063.632@compuserve.com
Call date: Oct 1996, Lincoln's Inn
Qualifications: [BSc (Hons)(Newc), Dip in
Computer, Studies (Aberdeen), Dip in Law
(Northum)]

STRONGMAN IAN MELVILLE

8 Fountain Court
Steelhouse Lane, Birmingham B4 6DR,
Telephone: 0121 236 5514/5
E-mail: clerks@no8chambers.co.uk
Call date: July 1981, Lincoln's Inn
Qualifications: [LLB (Hons)]

STRUDWICK MISS LINDA DIANE

Hollis Whiteman Chambers
3rd/4th Floor Queen Elizabeth Bldg, Temple,
London EC4Y 9BS, Telephone: 0171 583 5766
E-mail: hollis.whiteman@btinternet.com
Call date: July 1973, Lincoln's Inn
Qualifications: [BA]

STRUTT MARTIN ANDREW

3 Paper Bldgs
1st Floor, Temple, London EC4Y 7EU,
Telephone: 0171 583 8055
E-mail: london@3paper.com
20 Lorne Park Road
Bournemouth BH1 1JN,
Telephone: 01202 292102 (5 Lines)
4 St Peter Street
Winchester SO23 8OW,
Telephone: 01962 868884
Call date: Nov 1981, Inner Temple
Qualifications: [BA (Cantab)]

STUART BRUCE IAN

4 King's Bench Walk
Ground/First Floor, Temple, London
EC4Y 7DL, Telephone: 0171 822 8822
E-mail: 4kbw@barristersatlaw.com
Call date: Nov 1977, Gray's Inn

STUART DOUGLAS MARK

15 Winckley Square
Preston PR1 3JJ, Telephone: 01772 252828
E-mail: clerks@winckleysq.demon.co.uk
Call date: Nov 1985, Gray's Inn
Qualifications: [BA (Newc)]

STUART JAMES WILLIAM

Lamb Chambers
Lamb Building, Temple, London EC4Y 7AS,
Telephone: 0171 797 8300
E-mail: lambchambers@link.org
Call date: Oct 1990, Gray's Inn
Qualifications: [MA (Cantab)]

STUART-SMITH JEREMY HUGH QC (1997)

2 Temple Gardens
Temple, London EC4Y 9AY,
Telephone: 0171 583 6041 (12 Lines)
Call date: July 1978, Gray's Inn
Assistant Recorder
Qualifications: [MA (Cantab)]

STUBBS ANDREW JAMES

St Paul's House
5th Floor 23 Park Square South, Leeds
LS1 2ND, Telephone: 0113 2455866
Call date: July 1988, Lincoln's Inn
Qualifications: [LLB (Hons) (Notts)]

STUBBS MISS REBECCA

13 Old Square
Ground Floor, Lincoln's Inn, London
WC2A 3UA, Telephone: 0171 404 4800
Call date: Oct 1994, Middle Temple
Qualifications: [BA (Hons)(Cantab)]

STUBBS WILLIAM FREDERICK QC (1978)

Erskine Chambers
30 Lincoln's Inn Fields, Lincoln's Inn, London
WC2A 3PF, Telephone: 0171 242 5532
E-mail: Clerks@Erskine-Chambers.law.co.uk
Call date: July 1957, Gray's Inn
Qualifications: [MA, LLB (Cantab)]

STUDD MISS ANNE ELIZABETH

5 Essex Court
1st Floor, Temple, London EC4Y 9AH,
Telephone: 0171 410 2000
Call date: July 1988, Gray's Inn
Qualifications: [BA (Lond)]

STUDER MARK EDGAR WALTER

11 New Square
Ground Floor, Lincoln's Inn, London
WC2A 3QB, Telephone: 0171 831 0081
E-mail: 11newsquare.co.uk
Call date: July 1976, Lincoln's Inn
Qualifications: [BA (Oxon)]

STURMAN JAMES ANTHONY

3 Hare Court
1st Floor, Temple, London EC4Y 7BJ,
Telephone: 0171 353 7561
Call date: July 1982, Gray's Inn
Qualifications: [LLB (Reading)]

STUTTARD ARTHUR RUPERT DAVIES

Manchester House Chambers
18-22 Bridge Street, Manchester M3 3BZ,
Telephone: 0161 834 7007
Call date: Feb 1967, Middle Temple
Qualifications: [MA (Oxon)]

STYLES CLIVE RICHARD

Becket Chambers
17 New Dover Road, Canterbury, Kent
CT1 3AS, Telephone: 01227 786331
Call date: Oct 1990, Gray's Inn
Qualifications: [LLB (Hons)]

STYLES MARK PATRICK

Broad Chare
33 Broad Chare, Newcastle Upon Tyne
NE1 3DQ, Telephone: 0191 232 0541
Call date: July 1988, Inner Temple
Qualifications: [LLB (Lancaster)]

SUCH FREDERICK RUDOLPH CHARLES

Broad Chare
33 Broad Chare, Newcastle Upon Tyne
NE1 3DQ, Telephone: 0191 232 0541
Call date: Feb 1960, Gray's Inn
Recorder
Qualifications: [MA, FCIArb]

SUCKLING ALAN BLAIR QC (1983)

Hollis Whiteman Chambers
3rd/4th Floor Queen Elizabeth Bldg, Temple,
London EC4Y 9BS, Telephone: 0171 583 5766
E-mail: hollis.whiteman@btinternet.com
Call date: July 1963, Middle Temple
Recorder
Qualifications: [BA, LLB (Cantab)]

SUDDABY JOHN ANDREW

7 New Square
Lincoln's Inn, London WC2A 3QS,
Telephone: 0171 430 1660
Call date: Nov 1990, Inner Temple
Qualifications: [BA (Hons), Dip Law]

SUGAR SIMON GARETH

5 New Square
1st Floor, Lincoln's Inn, London WC2A 3RJ,
Telephone: 0171 404 0404
E-mail: Chambers@FiveNewSquare.CityScape.co.uk
Call date: Nov 1990, Middle Temple
Qualifications: [LLB (Warw)]

SUGARMAN JASON ASHLEY

2 Pump Court
1st Floor, Temple, London EC4Y 7AH,
Telephone: 0171 353 5597
Call date: July 1995, Inner Temple
Qualifications: [BA (Dunelm), CPE (Lond)]

SUGGETT IAIN ROBERT OTTAR

Equity Chambers
Suite 110, Gazette Buildings 168 Corporation
Street, Birmingham B4 6TS,
Telephone: 0121 233 2100
Call date: Nov 1989, Lincoln's Inn
Qualifications: [LLB (Hons)]

SUKUL RABI SHANKAR

The Courts
8 Abbotsleigh Road, Streatham, London
SW16 1SP, Telephone: 0181 769 6243
Call date: July 1988, Lincoln's Inn
Qualifications: [LLB (Hons)]

SULLIVAN MS JANE TERESA

Hollis Whiteman Chambers
3rd/4th Floor Queen Elizabeth Bldg, Temple,
London EC4Y 9BS, Telephone: 0171 583 5766
E-mail: hollis.whiteman@btinternet.com
Call date: July 1984, Inner Temple
Qualifications: [LLB, BA (Lond)]

D

D

SULLIVAN MISS LINDA ELIZABETH QC (1994)

35 Essex Street
Temple, London WC2R 3AR,
Telephone: 0171 353 6381
Call date: July 1973, Middle Temple
Recorder
Qualifications: [BA]

SULLIVAN MICHAEL JEROME

5 Bell Yard
London WC2A 2JR, Telephone: 0171 333 8811
Call date: July 1983, Middle Temple
Qualifications: [LLB Hons (Manch)]

SULLIVAN PATRICK CLEMENT

Assize Court Chambers
14 Small Street, Bristol BS1 1DE,
Telephone: 0117 9264587
Call date: Nov 1992, Middle Temple
Qualifications: [LLB (Hons)(Lond)]

SULLIVAN RORY MYLES

19 Old Buildings
Lincoln's Inn, London WC2A 3UP,
Telephone: 0171 405 2001
E-mail: clerks@oldbuildingsip.com
Call date: Oct 1992, Gray's Inn
Qualifications: [MA (Oxon)]

SULLIVAN SCOTT

Barnard's Inn Chambers
6th Floor Halton House, 20-23 Holborn,
London EC1N 2JD, Telephone: 0171 242 8508
E-mail: clerks@barnards-inn-chambers.co.uk
Call date: Nov 1991, Inner Temple
Qualifications: [LLB (So'ton)]

SULTAN AMIR

9 King's Bench Walk
Ground Floor, Temple, London EC4Y 7DX,
Telephone: 0171 353 7202/3909
Call date: July 1983, Lincoln's Inn
Qualifications: [BA (Law)]

SULTAN MS NEELIM

Acre Lane Neighbourhood Chambers
30A Acre Lane, London SW2 5SG,
Telephone: 0171 274 4400
Call date: Nov 1993, Gray's Inn
Qualifications: [BA (Hull), LLM (Lond)]

SUMERAY MRS CAROLINE SARAH

Chambers of Raana Sheikh
Gray's Inn Chambers, Gray's Inn, London
WC1R, Telephone: 0171 831 5344
E-mail: s.mcblain@btinternet.com
Call date: July 1993, Middle Temple
Qualifications: [LLB (Hons)(Wolver)]

SUMMERS BENJAMIN DYLAN JAMES

Hollis Whiteman Chambers
3rd/4th Floor Queen Elizabeth Bldg, Temple,
London EC4Y 9BS, Telephone: 0171 583 5766
E-mail: hollis.whiteman@btinternet.com
Call date: Nov 1994, Inner Temple
Qualifications: [LLB (Sussex)]

SUMNER DAVID MOORCROFT

Lincoln House Chambers
5th Floor Lincoln House, 1 Brazennose Street,
Manchester M2 5EL,
Telephone: 0161 832 5701
E-mail: LincolnHouseChambers@link.org
Call date: May 1963, Lincoln's Inn
Recorder

SUMPTION JONATHAN PHILIP CHADWICK QC (1986)

Brick Court Chambers
15/19 Devereux Court, London WC2R 3JJ,
Telephone: 0171 583 0777
E-mail: (surname)@brickcourt.demon.co.uk
Call date: July 1975, Inner Temple
Recorder
Qualifications: [MA (Oxon)]

SUMPTON CHRISTOPHER MARTIN WILSON

19 Figtree Lane
Sheffield S1 2DJ, Telephone: 0114 2759708/
2738380
Call date: Nov 1991, Inner Temple
Qualifications: [LLB (Warw)]

SUNNUCKS JAMES HORACE GEORGE

5 New Square
1st Floor, Lincoln's Inn, London WC2A 3RJ,
Telephone: 0171 404 0404
E-mail: Chambers@FiveNewSquare.CityScape.co.uk
Octagon House
19 Colegate, Norwich, Norfolk NR3 1AT,
Telephone: 01603 623186
E-mail: octagon@netmatters.co.uk
Door Tenant
Call date: Jan 1950, Lincoln's Inn
Qualifications: [MA (Cantab)]

Fax: 0171 831 6016; DX: LDE 272

Types of work: Chancery (general); Chancery land law; Charities; Conveyancing; Local government; Partnerships; Planning; Probate and administration; Tax - capital and income; Town and country planning; Wills and trusts

Other professional qualifications: Bencher Lincoln's Inn

Circuit: South Eastern

Publications: Williams Mortimer and Sunnucks *Executors, Administrators and Probate*, 1993 Supp 1997; *Halsbury's Law of England*, title *Executors*, 1976

Reported cases: *Re Goodchild*, [1997] 1 WLR 1226, CA, 1997. Mutual wills - family provision - Wills Act s18.
Re Benham, [1995] STC 210, 1995. Will construction - charities - incidence of inheritance tax.
Re Finnemore, [1991] 1 WLR 793. Conditional revocation of wills.
Re Hetherington, [1990] Ch 1, 1990. Will - religious charity - gift for saying of Masses for the dead.
Re Grant, [1980] 1 WLR 360. Effect of non-charitable gift to a political party - purpose gifts.

SUPPERSTONE MICHAEL ALAN QC (1991)

11 King's Bench Walk
Temple, London EC4Y 7EQ,
Telephone: 0171 632 8500
E-mail: clerksroom@11-kbw.law.co.uk
Call date: Nov 1973, Middle Temple
Recorder
Qualifications: [MA, BCL (Oxon)]

SURI YASIN UL RAHMAN KHAN

2 Salvia Gardens
Perivale, Middlesex UB6 7PG,
Telephone: 0181 997 9905
Call date: Nov 1963, Lincoln's Inn
Qualifications: [BA, LLB]

SUSMAN PETER JOSEPH QC (1997)

New Court Chambers
5 Verulam Buildings, Gray's Inn, London WC1R 5LY, Telephone: 0171 831 9500
E-mail: mail@newcourtchambers.com
Call date: Nov 1966, Middle Temple
Recorder
Qualifications: [MA (Oxon) JD, (Chicago)]

SUSSEX CHARLES ANTHONY

4 Essex Court
Temple, London EC4Y 9AJ,
Telephone: 0171 797 7970
E-mail: clerks@4essexcourt.law.co.uk
Call date: May 1982, Middle Temple
Qualifications: [LLB (Lond)]

SUTCLIFFE ANDREW HAROLD WENTWORTH

3 Verulam Buildings
London WC1R 5NT,
Telephone: 0171 831 8441
E-mail: clerks@3verulam.co.uk
Call date: Nov 1983, Inner Temple
Qualifications: [MA (Oxon)]

SUTHERLAND PAUL JEFFREY JOHN-PAUL

2 Crown Office Row
2nd Floor, Temple, London EC4Y 7HJ,
Telephone: 0171 797 8000
Call date: Nov 1992, Middle Temple
Qualifications: [MA (Oxon), MA (Cantab)]

D

SUTHERLAND WILLIAMS MARK

King's Bench Chambers
Wellington House 175 Holdenhurst Road,
Bournemouth, Dorset BH8 8DQ,
Telephone: 01202 250025
4 King's Bench Walk
Ground/First Floor, Temple, London
EC4Y 7DL, Telephone: 0171 822 8822
E-mail: 4kbw@barristersatlaw.com
Call date: Oct 1995, Inner Temple
Qualifications: [LLB (Exon)]

SUTTLE STEPHEN JOHN

1 Brick Court
1st Floor, Temple, London EC4Y 9BY,
Telephone: 0171 353 8845
E-mail: clerks@1brickcourt.co.uk
Call date: July 1980, Gray's Inn
Qualifications: [MA (Oxon)]

SUTTON ALASTAIR MORRIS

2 Hare Court
Ground Floor, Temple, London EC4Y 7BH,
Telephone: 0171 583 1770
E-mail: 2_Hare_Court@link.org
Call date: May 1972, Middle Temple
Qualifications: [LLB (Aberdeen), LLM (Lond),
Dip Int Air Law]

SUTTON CLIVE RAYMOND

22 Albion Place
Northampton NN1 1UD,
Telephone: 01604 36271
Call date: July 1987, Inner Temple
Qualifications: [LLB]

SUTTON MRS KAROLINE ROSEMARIE

14 Gray's Inn Square
Gray's Inn, London WC1R 5JP,
Telephone: 0171 242 0858
E-mail: 100712.2134@compuserve.com
Call date: Nov 1986, Middle Temple
Qualifications: [LLB (Hons)]

SUTTON KEITH ANDREW

The Corn Exchange
5th Floor Fenwick Street, Liverpool L2 7QS,
Telephone: 0151 227 1081/5009
Call date: Nov 1988, Gray's Inn
Qualifications: [LLB]

SUTTON MARK

4 Field Court
Gray's Inn, London WC1R 5EA,
Telephone: 0171 440 6900
E-mail: chambers@4fieldcourt.co.uk
Call date: July 1982, Middle Temple
Qualifications: [BA]

SUTTON PAUL EDMUND

Holborn Chambers
6 Gate Street, Lincoln's Inn Fields, London
WC2A 3HP, Telephone: 0171 242 6060
Call date: July 1973, Middle Temple
Qualifications: [LLB (Lond)]

SUTTON PHILIP JULIAN

Bell Yard Chambers
116/118 Chancery Lane, London WC2A 1PP,
Telephone: 0171 306 9292
Call date: Nov 1971, Inner Temple
Qualifications: [LLB (Hons)]

SUTTON RICHARD PATRICK QC (1993)

18 Red Lion Court
(Off Fleet Street), London EC4A 3EB,
Telephone: 0171 520 6000
Thornwood House
102 New London Road, Chelmsford, Essex
CM2 0RG, Telephone: 01245 280880
Call date: July 1969, Middle Temple
Recorder
Qualifications: [BA (Oxon)]

SUTTON RICHARD WILLIAM WALLACE

10 Park Square
Leeds LS1 2LH, Telephone: 0113 2455438
E-mail: chambers@bandit.legend.co.uk
Call date: July 1968, Inner Temple
Qualifications: [BA (Oxon)]

SUTTON MISS RUTH DEBORAH

24a St John Street
Manchester M3 4DF,
Telephone: 0161 833 9628
Call date: Nov 1994, Middle Temple
Qualifications: [LLB (Hons)]

SUTTON-MATTOCKS CHRISTOPHER JOHN

2 Paper Bldgs
1st Floor, Temple, London EC4Y 7ET,
Telephone: 0171 936 2611 (10 Lines)
E-mail: clerks@2pbbarristers.co.uk
Call date: July 1975, Middle Temple
Recorder
Qualifications: [MA (Oxon)]

SWAIN MRS FIONA PATRICIA

11 King's Bench Walk
1st Floor, Temple, London EC4Y 7EQ,
Telephone: 0171 353 3337
3 Park Court
Leeds LS1 2QH, Telephone: 0113 297 1200
Call date: July 1983, Gray's Inn
Qualifications: [BA]

SWAIN MISS HANNAH

23 Essex Street
London WC2R 3AS,
Telephone: 0171 413 0353/353 3533
E-mail: clerks@essexstreet23.demon.co.uk
Call date: Oct 1994, Gray's Inn
Qualifications: [BA]

SWAIN JON DAVID

Furnival Chambers
32 Furnival Street, London EC4A 1JQ,
Telephone: 0171 405 3232
E-mail: clerks@furnivallaw.co.uk
Call date: Nov 1983, Lincoln's Inn
Qualifications: [BSc (Hons)]

SWAIN RICHARD HENRY

24 The Ropewalk
Nottingham NG1 5EF,
Telephone: 0115 9472581
E-mail: clerk@ropewalk.co.uk
Call date: July 1969, Gray's Inn
Assistant Recorder
Qualifications: [LLB (B'ham)]

SWAINSON RICHARD JOSEPH

10 King's Bench Walk
Ground Floor, Temple, London EC4Y 7EB,
Telephone: 0171 353 7742
E-mail: 10kbw@lineone.net
Call date: Oct 1994, Lincoln's Inn
Qualifications: [LLB (Hons)(Lond)]

SWAINSTON MICHAEL GEORGE

Brick Court Chambers
15/19 Devereux Court, London WC2R 3JJ,
Telephone: 0171 583 0777
E-mail: (surname)@brickcourt.demon.co.uk
Call date: Nov 1985, Lincoln's Inn
Qualifications: [MA (Cantab), BCL, (Oxon)]

SWALLOW MISS JODIE

40 King Street
Chester CH1 2AH, Telephone: 01244 323886
Call date: Nov 1989, Inner Temple
Qualifications: [LLB]

SWAN IAN CHRISTOPHER

2 Crown Office Row
Ground Floor, Temple, London EC4Y 7HJ,
Telephone: 0171 797 8100
E-mail: mail@2cor.co.uk, or to individual
barristers at: [barrister's surname]@2cor.co.uk
Call date: July 1985, Middle Temple
Qualifications: [BA (Oxon)]

SWAN TIMOTHY ROBERT MUNGO

1 Paper Bldgs
1st Floor, Temple, London EC4Y 7EP,
Telephone: 0171 353 3728/4953
Call date: Nov 1983, Gray's Inn
Qualifications: [BA (Oxon)]

SWEENEY CHRISTIAN NOEL

3 Paper Bldgs
1st Floor, Temple, London EC4Y 7EU,
Telephone: 0171 583 8055
E-mail: london@3paper.com
20 Lorne Park Road
Bournemouth BH1 1JN,
Telephone: 01202 292102 (5 Lines)
4 St Peter Street
Winchester SO23 8OW,
Telephone: 01962 868884
Call date: Oct 1992, Gray's Inn
Qualifications: [LL.B (Reading)]

SWEENEY NIGEL HAMILTON

6 King's Bench Walk
Ground Floor, Temple, London EC4Y 7DR,
Telephone: 0171 583 0410
Call date: July 1976, Middle Temple
Recorder
Qualifications: [LLB (Hons)]

D

SWEENEY NOEL CHRISTOPHER

Veritas Chambers
33 Corn Street, Bristol BS1 1HT,
Telephone: 0117 930 8802
Call date: July 1975, Gray's Inn
Qualifications: [LLB]

SWEET MISS LOUISE JUNE

1 Crown Office Row
2nd Floor, Temple, London EC4Y 7HH,
Telephone: 0171 797 7111
Call date: Oct 1994, Gray's Inn
Qualifications: [LLB (Hull)]

SWEETING DEREK ANTHONY

9 Bedford Row
London WC1R 4AZ,
Telephone: 0171 242 3555
E-mail: clerks@9br.co.uk
Call date: July 1983, Middle Temple
Qualifications: [MA (Cantab)]

SWERLING ROBERT HARRY

13 Old Square
Ground Floor, Lincoln's Inn, London
WC2A 3UA, Telephone: 0171 404 4800
Call date: Nov 1996, Lincoln's Inn
Qualifications: [BA (Hons)]

SWIFFEN GUY CHARLES

58 King Street Chambers
1st Floor, Kingsgate House 51-53 South King
Street, Manchester M2 6DE,
Telephone: 0161 831 7477
Call date: Nov 1991, Lincoln's Inn
Qualifications: [BA (Hons), Dip Law]

SWIFT ANTONY

Harrow on the Hill Chambers
60 High Street, Harrow on the Hill, Middlesex
HA1 3LL, Telephone: 0181 423 7444
Windsor Barristers' Chambers
Windsor, Telephone: 01753 648899
Call date: Nov 1984, Inner Temple
Qualifications: [BA (Hons) (Grad),
Inst.F.W.R.I.]

SWIFT MISS CAROLINE JANE QC (1993)

22 Old Bldgs
Lincoln's Inn, London WC2A 3UJ,
Telephone: 0171 831 0222
25 Byrom Street
Manchester M3 4PF,
Telephone: 0161 829 2100
E-mail: Byromst25@aol.com
Call date: Nov 1977, Inner Temple
Recorder
Qualifications: [BA (Dunelm)]

SWIFT JONATHAN MARK

11 King's Bench Walk
Temple, London EC4Y 7EQ,
Telephone: 0171 632 8500
E-mail: clerksroom@11-kbw.law.co.uk
Call date: July 1989, Inner Temple
Qualifications: [BA [Oxon], LLM [Cantab]]

SWIFT JONATHAN PETER

College Chambers
19 Carlton Cresent, Southampton, Hants
SO15 2ET, Telephone: 01703 230338
1 Mitre Ct Bldgs
Ground Floor, Temple, London EC4Y 7BS,
Telephone: 0171 797 7070
Door Tenant
Call date: Nov 1977, Inner Temple
Assistant Recorder
Qualifications: [LLB (Hons)(Lond)]

SWIFT LIONEL QC (1975)

4 Paper Bldgs
2nd Floor, Temple, London EC4Y 7EX,
Telephone: 0171 583 0816/071 353 1131
E-mail: clerks@4paperbuildings.co.uk
Call date: Feb 1959, Inner Temple
Qualifications: [LLB (lond), BCL, (Oxon), JD
(Chicago)]

SWIFT MALCOLM ROBIN QC (1988)

Park Court Chambers
40 Park Cross Street, Leeds LS1 2QH,
Telephone: 0113 2433277
6 Gray's Inn Square
Ground Floor, Gray's Inn, London WC1R 5AZ,
Telephone: 0171 242 1052
Call date: July 1970, Gray's Inn
Recorder
Qualifications: [LLB, AKC]

SWIFT STEVEN GEOFFREY

India Buildings Chambers
Water Street, Liverpool L2 OXG,
Telephone: 0151 243 6000
Call date: Nov 1991, Inner Temple
Qualifications: [LLB (Lan)]

SWINDELLS MISS HEATHER HUGHSON QC (1995)

36 Bedford Row
London WC1R 4JH,
Telephone: 0171 421 8000
E-mail: 36bedfordrow@link.org
Call date: Nov 1974, Middle Temple
Recorder
Qualifications: [MA (Oxon)]

SWINHOE LUKE FRANCIS

York House
Borough Road, Middlesbrough, Cleveland
TS1 2HJ, Telephone: 01642 213000
Call date: Nov 1987, Inner Temple
Qualifications: [BA (Hons), LLM]

SWINNERTON DAVID MICHAEL

6 Fountain Court
Steelhouse Lane, Birmingham B4 6DR,
Telephone: 0121 233 3282
Call date: Nov 1995, Lincoln's Inn
Qualifications: [BA (Hons)]

SWINSTEAD DAVID LLOYD

3 Paper Bldgs
1st Floor, Temple, London EC4Y 7EU,
Telephone: 0171 583 8055
E-mail: london@3paper.com
4 St Peter Street
Winchester SO23 8OW,
Telephone: 01962 868884
20 Lorne Park Road
Bournemouth BH1 1JN,
Telephone: 01202 292102 (5 Lines)
Call date: July 1970, Inner Temple

SWIRSKY ADAM ABRAHAM BURL BRADBURY

7 Stone Bldgs
1st Floor, Lincoln's Inn, London WC2A 3SZ,
Telephone: 0171 242 0961
Call date: Nov 1989, Middle Temple
Qualifications: [B.Sc, M.Sc [Lond]]

SWIRSKY JOSHUA MAX BRADBURY

2 Field Court
Gray's Inn, London WC1R 5BB,
Telephone: 0171 405 6114
E-mail: fieldct2@netcomuk.co.uk.
Call date: Nov 1987, Middle Temple
Qualifications: [BA (Dunelm)]

SYDENHAM COLIN PETER

4 Breams Buildings
London EC4A 1AQ,
Telephone: 0171 353 5835/430 1221
Call date: July 1963, Middle Temple
Qualifications: [MA (Cantab)]

SYED GULZAR SHAH

Bank House Chambers
Old Bank House, Hartshead, Sheffield S1 2EL,
Telephone: 0114 2751223
Call date: July 1983, Gray's Inn
Qualifications: [LLB (Lanc)]

SYED MISS MARYAM HASSAN

2 Paper Bldgs
Temple, London EC4Y 7ET,
Telephone: 0171 936 2613
Call date: Oct 1993, Lincoln's Inn
Qualifications: [LLB (Hons)(Lond)]

SYED MOHAMMAD ALI

39 Park Avenue
Mitcham, Surrey CR4 2ER,
Telephone: 0181 648 1684
Call date: July 1970, Lincoln's Inn
Qualifications: [BA, MA]

SYED MUZAHID ALI

10 Millfields Road
London E5 OSB, Telephone: 0181 986 8059
Call date: Nov 1971, Inner Temple
Qualifications: [B.Com, LLB]

D

SYFRET NICHOLAS

13 King's Bench Walk
1st Floor, Temple, London EC4Y 7EN,
Telephone: 0171 353 7204
E-mail: clerks@13kbw.law.co.uk
King's Bench Chambers
32 Beaumont Street, Oxford OX1 2NP,
Telephone: 01865 311066
E-mail: clerks@kbc-oxford.law.co.uk
Call date: July 1979, Middle Temple
Qualifications: [MA (Cantab)]

SYKES (JAMES) RICHARD QC (1981)

Erskine Chambers
30 Lincoln's Inn Fields, Lincoln's Inn, London
WC2A 3PF, Telephone: 0171 242 5532
E-mail: Clerks@Erskine-Chambers.law.co.uk
Call date: June 1958, Lincoln's Inn
Qualifications: [MA (Cantab)]

SYLVESTER MIO PAUL

Pall Mall Chambers
Executive House 40A Young Street,
Manchester M3 3FT,
Telephone: 0161 832 3373/4
3 Temple Gardens
2nd Floor, Temple, London EC4Y 9AU,
Telephone: 0171 583 1155
Call date: July 1980, Middle Temple
Qualifications: [MA, LLB (Cantab)]

SYMMS MISS KATHRYN ANN

Martins Building
Water Street, Liverpool L2 3SP,
Telephone: 0151 236 5818/4919
Call date: Oct 1990, Gray's Inn
Qualifications: [BA (Cantab)]

SYMONS CHRISTOPHER JOHN MAURICE QC (1989)

3 Verulam Buildings
London WC1R 5NT,
Telephone: 0171 831 8441
E-mail: clerks@3verulam.co.uk
Call date: July 1972, Middle Temple
Recorder
Qualifications: [BA (Kent)]

SYRIL GEORGE CARMEL

2 Middle Temple Lane
3rd Floor, Temple, London EC4Y 9AA,
Telephone: 0171 583 4540
Call date: July 1980, Lincoln's Inn
Qualifications: [MA,LLB]

SZANTO GREGORY JOHN MICHAEL

Eastbourne Chambers
15 Hyde Gardens, Eastbourne, East Sussex
BN21 4PR, Telephone: 01323 642102/416466
Call date: July 1967, Inner Temple

SZERARD ANDREI MICHAEL

Goldsmith Chambers
Ground Floor Goldsmith Building, Temple,
London EC4Y 7BL,
Telephone: 0171 353 6802/3/4/5
E-mail: celiamonksfield@btinternet.com
Call date: Apr 1986, Inner Temple
Qualifications: [LLB (Hull)]

SZUMOWSKA MISS HELENA CECILIA

Westgate Chambers
144 High Street, Lewes, East Sussex BN7 1XT,
Telephone: 01273 480510
Call date: July 1989, Inner Temple
Qualifications: [BSc, Dip Law]

SZWED MISS ELIZABETH MARIA

One Garden Court
Ground Floor, Temple, London EC4Y 9BJ,
Telephone: 0171 797 7900
Call date: Nov 1974, Middle Temple
Qualifications: [LLB (Leeds)]

TABACHNIK ANDREW DANIEL

4-5 Gray's Inn Square
Ground Floor, Gray's Inn, London WC1R 5AY,
Telephone: 0171 404 5252
E-mail: chambers@4-5graysinnsquare.co.uk
Call date: Nov 1991, Inner Temple
Qualifications: [MA (Cambs), LLM (Columbia)]

TABACHNIK ELDRED QC (1982)

11 King's Bench Walk
Temple, London EC4Y 7EQ,
Telephone: 0171 632 8500
E-mail: clerksroom@11-kbw.law.co.uk
Call date: July 1970, Inner Temple
Assistant Recorder
Qualifications: [BA, LLB (Cape, Town), LLM
(Lond)]

TABOR JAMES PATRICK QC (1995)

Albion Chambers
Broad Street, Bristol BS1 1DR,
Telephone: 0117 9272144
Door Tenant
5 Paper Bldgs
1st Floor, Temple, London EC4Y 7HB,
Telephone: 0171 583 6117
E-mail: clerks@5-paperbuildings.law.co.uk
Door Tenant
Call date: July 1974, Middle Temple

TACKABERRY JOHN ANTONY QC (1982)

Arbitration Chambers
22 Willes Road, London NW5 3DS,
Telephone: 0171 267 2137
E-mail: jatqc@atack.demon.co.uk
40 King Street
Manchester M2 6BA,
Telephone: 0161 832 9082
E-mail: Kingst40@aol.com
Assize Court Chambers
14 Small Street, Bristol BS1 1DE,
Telephone: 0117 9264587
Door Tenant
Call date: July 1967, Gray's Inn
Recorder
Qualifications: [MA, LLM, FCIARB, FFB]

TAELOR START MISS ANGHARAD JOCELYN

3 Verulam Buildings
London WC1R 5NT,
Telephone: 0171 831 8441
E-mail: clerks@3verulam.co.uk
Call date: Nov 1988, Lincoln's Inn
Qualifications: [BA (Dunelm)]

TAGER ROMIE QC (1995)

Hardwicke Building
New Square, Lincoln's Inn, London
WC2A 3SB, Telephone: 0171 242 2523
E-mail: clerks@hardwicke.co.uk
Call date: Nov 1970, Middle Temple
Recorder
Qualifications: [LLM]

TAGGART NICHOLAS

4 Breams Buildings
London EC4A 1AQ,
Telephone: 0171 353 5835/430 1221
Call date: Oct 1991, Middle Temple
Qualifications: [LLB (Hons)(Lond), BCL
(Oxon)]

TAGGART SAMUEL NICHOLAS

Clapham Chambers
21-25 Bedford Road, Clapham North, London
SW4 7SH, Telephone: 0171 978 8482/
642 5777
E-mail: 113063.632@compuserve.com
Call date: Nov 1992, Middle Temple
Qualifications: [LLB (Hons, Manch)]

TAGHAVI SHAHRAM

6 King's Bench Walk
Ground, Third & Fourth Floors, Temple,
London EC4Y 7DR,
Telephone: 0171 353 4931/583 0695
Call date: Oct 1994, Gray's Inn
Qualifications: [LLB]

TAGLIAVINI MS LORNA MARIE

6 King's Bench Walk
Ground, Third & Fourth Floors, Temple,
London EC4Y 7DR,
Telephone: 0171 353 4931/583 0695
Call date: Nov 1989, Inner Temple
Qualifications: [BA (Hons) (Brad), Dip Law
(City), LLM (LSE)]

TAIT ANDREW CHARLES GORDON

2 Harcourt Bldgs
2nd Floor, Temple, London EC4Y 9DB,
Telephone: 0171 353 8415
E-mail: clerks@twoharcourtbldgs.demon.co.uk
Call date: July 1981, Inner Temple
Qualifications: [MA (Oxon)]

TAIT CAMPBELL

Lincoln House Chambers
5th Floor Lincoln House, 1 Brazennose Street,
Manchester M2 5EL,
Telephone: 0161 832 5701
E-mail: LincolnHouseChambers@link.org
Call date: Nov 1979, Middle Temple
Assistant Recorder
Qualifications: [LLB (Hons) (Lond)]

TAIT DONALD

All Saints Chambers
9/11 Broad Street, Bristol BS1 2HP,
Telephone: 0117 921 1966
Call date: Feb 1987, Inner Temple
Qualifications: [BA (Leic)]

TALACCHI CARLO GIANCARLO

10 King's Bench Walk
Ground Floor, Temple, London EC4Y 7EB,
Telephone: 0171 353 7742
E-mail: 10kbw@lineone.net
Call date: July 1986, Lincoln's Inn
Qualifications: [BSc (B'ham) LLM, (Cantab)]

TALBOT DENNIS

Exchange Chambers
Pearl Assurance House Derby Square,
Liverpool L2 9XX, Telephone: 0151 236 7747/
0458
E-mail: exchangechambers@btinternet.com
Call date: July 1985, Gray's Inn
Qualifications: [ACMA]

TALBOT KENNEDY VERNON

Furnival Chambers
32 Furnival Street, London EC4A 1JQ,
Telephone: 0171 405 3232
E-mail: clerks@furnivallaw.co.uk
Call date: Nov 1984, Gray's Inn
Qualifications: [BA]

TALBOT PATRICK JOHN QC (1990)

13 Old Square
1st Floor, Lincoln's Inn, London WC2A 3UA,
Telephone: 0171 242 6105
E-mail: clerks@serlecourt.co.uk
Call date: July 1969, Lincoln's Inn
Assistant Recorder
Qualifications: [MA (Oxon)]

TALBOT RICHARD KEVIN KENT

Deans Court Chambers
Cumberland House Crown Square, Manchester
M3 3HA, Telephone: 0161 834 4097
E-mail: deanscourt@compuserve.com
Deans Court Chambers
41-43 Market Place, Preston PR1 1AH,
Telephone: 01772 555163
E-mail: deanscourt@compuserve.com
Call date: July 1970, Inner Temple
Recorder
Qualifications: [LLB]

TALBOT RICE MRS (ALICE) ELSPETH MIDDLETON

24 Old Bldgs
Ground Floor, Lincoln's Inn, London
WC2A 3UJ, Telephone: 0171 404 0946
E-mail: clerks@24oldbuildings.law.co.uk
Call date: Oct 1990, Lincoln's Inn
Qualifications: [BA (Dunelm)]

TALBOT-BAGNALL JOHN RICHARD

2 Paper Bldgs
Temple, London EC4Y 7ET,
Telephone: 0171 936 2613
Call date: Nov 1988, Inner Temple
Qualifications: [LLB (Shef)]

TALLON JOHN MARK

Pump Court Tax Chambers
16 Bedford Row, London WC1R 4EB,
Telephone: 0171 414 8080
4 Fountain Court
Steelhouse Lane, Birmingham B4 6DR,
Telephone: 0121 236 3476
Call date: July 1975, Middle Temple
Qualifications: [F.C.A.]

TAM ROBIN BING-KUEN

1 Temple Gardens
1st Floor, Temple, London EC4Y 9BB,
Telephone: 0171 353 0407/583 1315
E-mail: clerks@1templegardens.co.uk
Call date: July 1986, Middle Temple
Qualifications: [MA (Cantab)]

TAMLYN LLOYD JEFFREY

3/4 South Square
Gray's Inn, London WC1R 5HP,
Telephone: 0171 696 9900
E-mail: clerks@southsquare.com
Call date: Nov 1991, Gray's Inn
Qualifications: [BA (Hons, Cantab)]

TAN MISS CHENG SIOH

1 Gray's Inn Square
Ground Floor, London WC1R 5AA,
Telephone: 0171 405 8946/7/8
Call date: Nov 1970, Middle Temple

TANKEL MRS RUTH SHOSHANA

St James's Chambers
68 Quay Street, Manchester M3 3EJ,
Telephone: 0161 834 7000
E-mail: 106241.2625@compuserve.com
Call date: July 1990, Middle Temple
Qualifications: [LLB (Manch)]

TANNEY ANTHONY

Falcon Chambers
Falcon Court, London EC4Y 1AA,
Telephone: 0171 353 2484/7
Call date: Oct 1994, Lincoln's Inn
Qualifications: [BA (Hons), M.Jur (Durham)]

TANSEY ROCK BENEDICT QC (1990)

3 Gray's Inn Square
Ground Floor, London WC1R 5AH,
Telephone: 0171 520 5600
E-mail: gis3@btinternet.com
Call date: July 1966, Lincoln's Inn
Recorder
Qualifications: [Dip Soc (Bristol), LLB (Bristol) (Hons)]

TANZER JOHN BRIAN CAMILLE

1 King's Bench Walk
2nd Floor, Temple, London EC4Y 7DB,
Telephone: 0171 936 1500
E-mail: ddear@1kbw.co.uk
Call date: Nov 1975, Gray's Inn
Assistant Recorder
Qualifications: [BA]

TAPPER PAUL KENNEDY

Chartlands Chambers
3 St Giles Terrace, Northampton NN1 2BN,
Telephone: 01604 603322
Call date: July 1991, Middle Temple
Qualifications: [LLB (Hons)]

TAPPIN MICHAEL JOHN

8 New Square
Lincoln's Inn, London WC2A 3QP,
Telephone: 0171 405 4321
Call date: Oct 1991, Middle Temple
Qualifications: [BA Hons, DPhil (Oxon, CPE]

TAPPING MISS SUSAN

10 King's Bench Walk
Ground Floor, Temple, London EC4Y 7EB,
Telephone: 0171 353 7742
E-mail: 10kbw@lineone.net
Call date: July 1975, Middle Temple
Assistant Recorder
Qualifications: [LLB]

TAPSELL PAUL RICHARD

Becket Chambers
17 New Dover Road, Canterbury, Kent
CT1 3AS, Telephone: 01227 786331
Call date: Oct 1991, Middle Temple
Qualifications: [LLB Hons (Lanc)]

TAPSON MISS LESLEY KATHERINE

Francis Taylor Bldg
Ground Floor, Temple, London EC4Y 7BY,
Telephone: 0171 353 7768/7769/2711
Call date: Nov 1982, Gray's Inn
Qualifications: [LLB (Newc)]

TARBITT NICHOLAS EDWARD HENRY

6 Fountain Court
Steelhouse Lane, Birmingham B4 6DR,
Telephone: 0121 233 3282
Call date: July 1988, Inner Temple
Qualifications: [LLB]

TASKIS MISS CATHERINE LOUISE

Falcon Chambers
Falcon Court, London EC4Y 1AA,
Telephone: 0171 353 2484/7
Call date: Nov 1995, Inner Temple
Qualifications: [BA, BCL (Oxon)]

D

D

TATFORD WARWICK HENRY PATRICK

9-12 Bell Yard
London WC2A 2LF,
Telephone: 0171 400 1800
Call date: Oct 1993, Lincoln's Inn
Qualifications: [BA (Hons)(Oxon)]

TATLOW NICHOLAS MARK

4 Fountain Court
Steelhouse Lane, Birmingham B4 6DR,
Telephone: 0121 236 3476
Call date: May 1996, Gray's Inn
Qualifications: [BA (Wales)]

TATTERSALL GEOFFREY FRANK QC (1992)

22 Old Bldgs
Lincoln's Inn, London WC2A 3UJ,
Telephone: 0171 831 0222
25 Byrom Street
Manchester M3 4PF,
Telephone: 0161 829 2100
E-mail: Byromst25@aol.com
Call date: July 1970, Lincoln's Inn
Recorder
Qualifications: [MA (Oxon)]

TATTERSALL SIMON MARK ROGERS

Fenners Chambers
3 Madingley Road, Cambridge CB3 OEE,
Telephone: 01223 368761
Fenners Chambers
8-12 Priestgate, Peterborough PE1 1JA,
Telephone: 01733 62030
Call date: Nov 1977, Middle Temple
Qualifications: [LLB (Lond)]

TATTON-BROWN DANIEL NICHOLAS

Littleton Chambers
3 King's Bench Walk North, Temple, London
EC4Y 7HR, Telephone: 0171 797 8600
E-mail: littletonchambers@compuserve.com
Call date: Nov 1994, Middle Temple
Qualifications: [BA (Hons)]

TAUBE SIMON AXEL ROBIN

10 Old Square
Ground Floor, Lincoln's Inn, London
WC2A 3SU, Telephone: 0171 405 0758
Call date: July 1980, Middle Temple
Qualifications: [MA (Oxon)]

TAURAH MS SHEILA DOOLARY

Godolphin Chambers
50 Castle Street, Truro, Cornwall TR1 3AF,
Telephone: 01872 276312
Call date: Oct 1991, Lincoln's Inn
Qualifications: [LLB (Hons)]

TAUSSIG ANTHONY CHRISTOPHER

Wilberforce Chambers
8 New Square, Lincoln's Inn, London
WC2A 3QP, Telephone: 0171 306 0102
E-mail: chambers@wilberforce.co.uk
Call date: Nov 1966, Gray's Inn
Qualifications: [MA (Oxon)]

TAVARES NATHAN WARREN

35 Essex Street
Temple, London WC2R 3AR,
Telephone: 0171 353 6381
Call date: Oct 1992, Middle Temple
Qualifications: [BSE (Hons), Common
Professional, Examination]

TAVERNER MARCUS LOUIS

Keating Chambers
10 Essex Street, Outer Temple, London
WC2R 3AA, Telephone: 0171 544 2600
Call date: July 1981, Gray's Inn
Qualifications: [LLB, LLM (Lond), ACIArb]

TAY ROBERT KOCUVIE

The Ralek
66 Carshalton Park Road, Carshalton, Surrey
SM5 3SS, Telephone: 0181 669 1777
Call date: July 1972, Lincoln's Inn
Qualifications: [LLB]

TAYLER RICHARD JAMES

Devereux Chambers
Devereux Court, London WC2R 3JJ,
Telephone: 0171 353 7534
E-mail: elton@devchambers.co.uk
Call date: Nov 1989, Middle Temple
Qualifications: [BA (Oxon), Dip in Law]

TAYLOR ADRIAN

4 Brick Court
Ground Floor, Temple, London EC4Y 9AD,
Telephone: 0171 797 7766
E-mail: chambers@4brick.co.uk
Call date: July 1977, Inner Temple
Qualifications: [MA, LLB (Cantab)]

TAYLOR ALAN JEREMY

Furnival Chambers
32 Furnival Street, London EC4A 1JQ,
Telephone: 0171 405 3232
E-mail: clerks@furnivallaw.co.uk
Call date: July 1986, Lincoln's Inn
Qualifications: [BA(Bristol) Dip Law, MPhil (Oxon)]

TAYLOR ANDREW PETER

Fenners Chambers
3 Madingley Road, Cambridge CB3 OEE,
Telephone: 01223 368761
Fenners Chambers
8-12 Priestgate, Peterborough PE1 1JA,
Telephone: 01733 62030
Call date: Nov 1989, Gray's Inn
Qualifications: [BA (E.Anglia)]

TAYLOR ANDREW ROBERT

Newport Chambers
12 Clytha Park Road, Newport, Gwent
NP9 47L, Telephone: 01633 267403/255855
Call date: Nov 1985, Gray's Inn
Qualifications: [BSc Econ (Cardiff)]

TAYLOR MISS ARABA ARBA KURANKYIWA

11 Stone Bldgs
1st Floor, Lincoln's Inn, London WC2A 3TG,
Telephone: 0171 404 5055
E-mail: 9stoneb@compuserve.com
Call date: July 1985, Middle Temple
Qualifications: [MA (Cantab)]

TAYLOR CHARLES SPENCER

Chichester Chambers
12 North Pallant, Chichester, West Sussex
PO19 1TQ, Telephone: 01243 784538
Call date: July 1974, Middle Temple
Qualifications: [LLB Hons]

TAYLOR CHRISTOPHER JOHN

All Saints Chambers
9/11 Broad Street, Bristol BS1 2HP,
Telephone: 0117 921 1966
Call date: Nov 1982, Gray's Inn
Qualifications: [BA (Hons)]

TAYLOR DAVID BARTHOLOMEW

5 Fountain Court
Steelhouse Lane, Birmingham B4 6DR,
Telephone: 0121 606 0500
Call date: Nov 1993, Lincoln's Inn
Qualifications: [BA (Hons)]

TAYLOR DAVID EDWARD

37 Park Square
Leeds LS1 2NY, Telephone: 0113 2439422
Call date: May 1995, Inner Temple

TAYLOR MRS DEBBIE

Hardwicke Building
New Square, Lincoln's Inn, London
WC2A 3SB, Telephone: 0171 242 2523
E-mail: clerks@hardwicke.co.uk
Call date: July 1984, Lincoln's Inn
Qualifications: [BA]

TAYLOR MISS DEBORAH FRANCES

2 Crown Office Row
Ground Floor, Temple, London EC4Y 7HJ,
Telephone: 0171 797 8100
E-mail: mail@2cor.co.uk, or to individual
barristers at: [barrister's surname]@2cor.co.uk
Call date: July 1983, Inner Temple
Qualifications: [BA (Oxon)]

TAYLOR DOUGLAS JAMES

College Chambers
19 Carlton Cresent, Southampton, Hants
SO15 2ET, Telephone: 01703 230338
Call date: July 1981, Middle Temple
Qualifications: [BA (Hons) (Sheff)]

D

TAYLOR MISS GEMMA MARY

22 Old Bldgs
Lincoln's Inn, London WC2A 3UJ,
Telephone: 0171 831 0222
Call date: Feb 1988, Inner Temple
Qualifications: [LLB (London)]

TAYLOR GREGORY LYNN

9 Park Place
Cardiff CF1 3DP, Telephone: 01222 382731
Call date: July 1974, Middle Temple
Qualifications: [BA (Keele)]

TAYLOR MISS HELEN PATRICIA MARY

3 Temple Gardens
3rd Floor, Temple, London EC4Y 9AU,
Telephone: 0171 583 0010
Call date: Nov 1990, Inner Temple
Qualifications: [LLB (Hons)(Lond)]

TAYLOR IAN FREDERICK

Devon Chambers
3 St Andrew Street, Plymouth PL1 2AH,
Telephone: 01752 661659
Call date: July 1986, Gray's Inn
Qualifications: [BA (Sydney)]

TAYLOR JASON

Albion Chambers
Broad Street, Bristol BS1 1DR,
Telephone: 0117 9272144
Call date: Nov 1995, Gray's Inn
Qualifications: [LLB (Wales)]

TAYLOR JOHN CHARLES

Fountain Court
Temple, London EC4Y 9DH,
Telephone: 0171 583 3335
E-mail: chambers@fountaincourt.co.uk
Call date: Oct 1993, Middle Temple
Qualifications: [MA (Hons)(Cantab)]

TAYLOR JOHN CHARLES QC (1983)

2 Mitre Ct Bldgs
2nd Floor, Temple, London EC4Y 7BX,
Telephone: 0171 583 1380
Call date: Feb 1958, Middle Temple
Qualifications: [MA, LLB (Cantab), LLM Harvard]

TAYLOR JOHN DAVID

2 Dr Johnson's Building
Temple, London EC4Y 7AY,
Telephone: 0171 353 4716
Call date: July 1986, Gray's Inn
Qualifications: [LLB (Cardiff)]

TAYLOR JONATHAN ANDREW

Godolphin Chambers
50 Castle Street, Truro, Cornwall TR1 3AF,
Telephone: 01872 276312
Call date: Nov 1987, Gray's Inn
Qualifications: [BA (Manch)]

TAYLOR JONATHAN FORD

India Buildings Chambers
Water Street, Liverpool L2 OXG,
Telephone: 0151 243 6000
Call date: Nov 1991, Middle Temple
Qualifications: [LLB Hons (Reading)]

TAYLOR JONATHAN MORRIS

29a Lambs Conduit Street
Holborn, London WC1N 3NG,
Telephone: 0171 831 9907
Call date: July 1983, Gray's Inn
Qualifications: [BA (Hons)]

TAYLOR JULIAN MARK

4 Field Court
Gray's Inn, London WC1R 5EA,
Telephone: 0171 440 6900
E-mail: chambers@4fieldcourt.co.uk
Call date: Oct 1994, Gray's Inn
Qualifications: [BA, Dip Law]

TAYLOR JULIAN RICHARD

Peel Court Chambers
45 Hardman Street, Manchester M3 3HA,
Telephone: 0161 832 3791
Call date: July 1986, Middle Temple
Qualifications: [LLB (Bristol)]

TAYLOR MISS JULIE

15 Winckley Square
Preston PR1 3JJ, Telephone: 01772 252828
E-mail: clerks@winckleysq.demon.co.uk
Call date: Nov 1992, Inner Temple
Qualifications: [LLB]

TAYLOR MARTIN JOHN

6 King's Bench Walk
Ground, Third & Fourth Floors, Temple,
London EC4Y 7DR,
Telephone: 0171 353 4931/583 0695
Call date: July 1988, Middle Temple
Qualifications: [BA (Hons) (Leeds), Dip Law]

TAYLOR MATTHEW JAMES

5 Fountain Court
Steelhouse Lane, Birmingham B4 6DR,
Telephone: 0121 606 0500
Call date: Oct 1996, Gray's Inn
Qualifications: [BA (Cantab)]

TAYLOR MISS MAUREEN JOAN

Enfield Chambers
36-38 London Road, Enfield, Middlesex
EN2 6DT, Telephone: 0181 364 5627
E-mail: Enfieldchambers@compuserve.com
Call date: Oct 1993, Lincoln's Inn
Qualifications: [LLB (Hons)(Lond)]

TAYLOR MICHAEL PAUL

28 St John Street
Manchester M3 4DJ,
Telephone: 0161 834 8418
E-mail: clerk@28stjohnst.co.uk
Call date: Nov 1985, Gray's Inn
Qualifications: [LL.B (Leeds)]

TAYLOR MICHAEL RICHARD

Park Court Chambers
40 Park Cross Street, Leeds LS1 2QH,
Telephone: 0113 2433277
Call date: July 1980, Gray's Inn
Qualifications: [LLB (Hons)]

TAYLOR NEIL QC (1975)

Lion Court
Chancery House 53-64 Chancery Lane, London
WC2A 1SJ, Telephone: 0171 404 6565
Call date: Jan 1949, Inner Temple
Recorder
Qualifications: [MA (Oxon)]

TAYLOR NIGEL STUART

New Court
Temple, London EC4Y 9BE,
Telephone: 0171 583 5123/0171 583 0510
Call date: Oct 1993, Inner Temple
Qualifications: [BA, LLB (Lond)]

TAYLOR PAUL RICHARD

Doughty Street Chambers
11 Doughty Street, London WC1N 2PG,
Telephone: 0171 404 1313
E-mail: doughty_street@compuserve.com
Call date: Nov 1989, Middle Temple
Qualifications: [LLB, LLM (Cantab), CNAA]

TAYLOR PHILLIP BRIAN

Richmond Green Chambers
Greyhound House 23-24 George Street,
Richmond-upon-Thames, Surrey TW9 1HY,
Telephone: 0181 940 1841
Watford Chambers
74 Mildred Avenue, Watford, Hertfordshire
WD1 7DX, Telephone: 01923 220553
Call date: Nov 1991, Lincoln's Inn
Qualifications: [LLB (Hons) (Lond)]

TAYLOR REUBEN MALLINSON

2 Mitre Ct Bldgs
2nd Floor, Temple, London EC4Y 7BX,
Telephone: 0171 583 1380
Call date: Oct 1990, Gray's Inn
Qualifications: [LLB (Hons) (Wales)]

TAYLOR RHYS STEADMAN

33 Park Place
Cardiff CF1 3BA, Telephone: 01222 233313
Call date: Nov 1996, Inner Temple
Qualifications: [LLB (Reading)]

TAYLOR RUPERT LADD

Devon Chambers
3 St Andrew Street, Plymouth PL1 2AH,
Telephone: 01752 661659
Call date: July 1990, Gray's Inn
Qualifications: [LLB (Hons), LLM (Lond)]

TAYLOR SIMON

Francis Taylor Bldg
Ground Floor, Temple, London EC4Y 7BY,
Telephone: 0171 353 7768/7769/2711
Call date: Oct 1993, Inner Temple
Qualifications: [BSc (Hons), CPE]

TAYLOR SIMON WHELDON

Cloisters
1 Pump Court, Temple, London EC4Y 7AA,
Telephone: 0171 827 4000
E-mail: clerks@cloisters.com
Call date: July 1984, Middle Temple
Qualifications: [BA (Cantab), MA (Cantab),
MB.B Chir]

Fax: 0171 827 4100; DX: 452 London,
Chancery Lane

Types of work: Common law (general); Medical
negligence; Mental health; Personal injury;
Professional negligence; Tribunals/Inquiries

Circuit: South Eastern

Other professional experience: Qualified doctor

Reported cases: *R v Thanet and Canterbury
District Health Authority and others, ex parte F
and W*, [1994] 5 Med LR 132, 1993. Health
Service administrative law case, concerning
patient's right to an inquiry.
*Williamson v East London and the City Health
Authority and others*, [1998] Lloyd's Rep Med
6, 1997. Medical negligence case concerning
silicone breast implants and consent to
treatment.
Hooper v Young, [1998] Lloyd's Rep Med 61
(CA), 1996. Medical negligence case concerning
ureteric damage during hysterectomy and
applicability of maxim *res ipsa loquitur*.
Taylor v West Kent Health Authority, [1997] 8
Med LR 251, 1997. Medical negligence case
concerning delay in diagnosis of breast cancer,
and in particular the effect of delay on
prognosis.
Crouchman v Burke and others, 40 BMLR 163,
1997. Medical negligence case concerning
dilatation and curettage and subsequent
unwanted pregnancy.

TAYLOR STEVEN JAMES

8 King's Bench Walk North
1 Park Square East, Leeds LS1 2NE,
Telephone: 0113 2439797
8 King's Bench Walk
2nd Floor, Temple, London EC4Y 7DU,
Telephone: 0171 797 8888
Call date: Oct 1992, Lincoln's Inn
Qualifications: [LLB(Hons)]

TAYLOR MRS SUSAN

New Court Chambers
3 Broad Chare, Newcastle Upon Tyne
NE1 3DQ, Telephone: 0191 232 1980
Call date: Nov 1987, Middle Temple
Qualifications: [BA]

TAYLOR WILLIAM JAMES

3 Gray's Inn Square
Ground Floor, London WC1R 5AH,
Telephone: 0171 520 5600
E-mail: gis3@btinternet.com
Call date: July 1990, Inner Temple
Qualifications: [MA, LLB (Aberdeen)]

TAYLOR-CAMARA ALEXANDER ABDU RAHMAN

6 King's Bench Walk
Ground, Third & Fourth Floors, Temple,
London EC4Y 7DR,
Telephone: 0171 353 4931/583 0695
Call date: Nov 1989, Middle Temple
Qualifications: [LLB (Hons)]

TAYO MISS ANN IBILOLA

1 Crown Office Row
2nd Floor, Temple, London EC4Y 7HH,
Telephone: 0171 797 7111
Call date: Oct 1991, Gray's Inn
Qualifications: [LLB]

TAYTON MISS LYNN MARGARET

36 Bedford Row
London WC1R 4JH,
Telephone: 0171 421 8000
E-mail: 36bedfordrow@link.org
Call date: July 1981, Gray's Inn
Qualifications: [LLB (Lond)]

TEAGUE EDWARD THOMAS HENRY

40 King Street
Chester CH1 2AH, Telephone: 01244 323886
Call date: July 1977, Inner Temple
Qualifications: [MA (Cantab)]

TEARE JONATHAN JAMES

1 High Pavement
Nottingham NG1 1HF,
Telephone: 0115 9418218
Call date: July 1970, Middle Temple

TEARE NIGEL JOHN MARTIN QC (1991)

4 Essex Court
Temple, London EC4Y 9AJ,
Telephone: 0171 797 7970
E-mail: clerks@4essexcourt.law.co.uk
Call date: July 1974, Lincoln's Inn
Recorder
Qualifications: [MA (Oxon)]

TECKS JONATHAN HOWARD

Littman Chambers
12 Gray's Inn Square, London WC1R 5JP,
Telephone: 0171 404 4866
E-mail: admin@littmanchambers.com
Call date: July 1978, Gray's Inn
Qualifications: [MA (Cantab), FCIArb, CEDR
Accredited, Mediator]

TEDD REX HILARY QC (1993)

St Philip's Chambers
Fountain Court, Steelhouse Lane, Birmingham,
West Midlands B4 6DR,
Telephone: 0121 246 7000
22 Albion Place
Northampton NN1 1UD,
Telephone: 01604 636271
Door Tenant
Call date: Feb 1970, Inner Temple
Recorder
Qualifications: [MA, BCL (Oxon)]

Fax: 0121 236 4408; DX: 16073 Birmingham

Types of work: Aviation; Banking; Chancery
(general); Commercial litigation; Common law
(general); Company and commercial;
Construction; Crime; Crime - corporate fraud;
Education; Employment; Film, cable, TV;
Insolvency; Partnerships; Personal injury;
Professional negligence; Tax - capital and
income; Tax - corporate; Town and country
planning

Circuit: Midland and Oxford

Additional Information
*Educated King Edwards School - Birmingham;
Yarborough-Anderson Scholarship - Inner
Temple; Chairman of Council of Malvern
Girls' College; Former Lecturer in Law -
Nottingham University; Former Teaching
Fellow - Osgoode Hall Law School - Toronto.*

TEDORE MS AMANDA JANE

2 Paper Buildings
Basement, Temple, London EC4Y 7ET,
Telephone: 0171 353 0933
Call date: Nov 1992, Middle Temple
Qualifications: [BA (Hons)(Warw), Dip in Law]

TEEMAN MISS MIRIAM JOY

30 Park Square
Leeds LS1 2PF, Telephone: 0113 2436388
Call date: Feb 1993, Gray's Inn
Qualifications: [LLB (L'pool)]

TEGGIN MISS VICTORIA HELEN

Mitre House Chambers
Mitre House 44 Fleet Street, London
EC4Y 1BN, Telephone: 0171 583 8233
Call date: Nov 1990, Inner Temple
Qualifications: [BA (Hons) (UCL), Dip Law
(PCL)]

TEHRANI CHRISTOPHER

8 King's Bench Walk North
1 Park Square East, Leeds LS1 2NE,
Telephone: 0113 2439797
8 King's Bench Walk
2nd Floor, Temple, London EC4Y 7DU,
Telephone: 0171 797 8888
Call date: Nov 1990, Inner Temple
Qualifications: [LLB]

TEJI MISS USHA DEVI

1 Pump Court
Lower Ground Floor, Temple, London
EC4Y 7AB, Telephone: 0171 583 2012/
353 4341
E-mail: (name) @1pumpcourt.co.uk
Call date: July 1981, Lincoln's Inn
Qualifications: [LLB (Lond)]

TELFORD PETER

Devon Chambers
3 St Andrew Street, Plymouth PL1 2AH,
Telephone: 01752 661659
Call date: July 1985, Lincoln's Inn
Qualifications: [BA (Joint Hons), (Keele)]

TEMBLETT ROBERT HAROLD

517 Bunyan Court
Barbican, London EC2Y 8DH,
Telephone: 0171 638 5076
Call date: Nov 1980, Middle Temple
Qualifications: [LLB]

TEMMINK ROBERT-JAN

35 Essex Street
Temple, London WC2R 3AR,
Telephone: 0171 353 6381
Call date: Oct 1996, Middle Temple
Qualifications: [BA (Hons)(Cantab)]

TEMPLE ANTHONY DOMINIC QC (1986)

4 Pump Court
Temple, London EC4Y 7AN,
Telephone: 0171 353 2656/9
E-mail: 4_pump_court@compuserve.com
Call date: July 1968, Inner Temple
Recorder
Qualifications: [MA (Oxon)]

TEMPLE MISS MICHELLE JEAN

Broad Chare
33 Broad Chare, Newcastle Upon Tyne
NE1 3DQ, Telephone: 0191 232 0541
Call date: Oct 1992, Lincoln's Inn
Qualifications: [MA (Hons) (Oxon)]

TEMPLE SIMON ERNEST WILLIAM

9 St John Street
Manchester M3 4DN,
Telephone: 0161 955 9000
E-mail: ninesjs@gconnect.com
Call date: July 1977, Gray's Inn
Qualifications: [BA]

TEMPLE VICTOR BEVIS AFAMADO QC (1993)

6 King's Bench Walk
Ground Floor, Temple, London EC4Y 7DR,
Telephone: 0171 583 0410
Call date: July 1971, Inner Temple
Recorder

TEMPLE-BONE MISS GILLIAN ELIZABETH

7 Stone Bldgs
1st Floor, Lincoln's Inn, London WC2A 3SZ,
Telephone: 0171 242 0961
Call date: Nov 1978, Gray's Inn
Qualifications: [BA (Durham)]

TEMPLEMAN MARK JEREMY

Essex Court Chambers
24 Lincoln's Inn Fields, London WC2A 3ED,
Telephone: 0171 813 8000
E-mail: clerksroom@essexcourt-chambers.co.uk
Call date: Nov 1981, Middle Temple
Qualifications: [MA BCL (Oxon)]

TEMPLEMAN MICHAEL RICHARD

5 Stone Buildings
Lincoln's Inn, London WC2A 3XT,
Telephone: 0171 242 6201
E-mail: clerks@5-stonebuildings.law.co.uk
Door Tenant
Southernhay Chambers
33 Southernhay East, Exeter EX1 1NX,
Telephone: 01392 255777
E-mail: southernhay.chambers@lineone.net
Call date: Nov 1973, Lincoln's Inn
Qualifications: [MA (Oxon)]

TENNET MICHAEL JOHN

Wilberforce Chambers
8 New Square, Lincoln's Inn, London
WC2A 3QP, Telephone: 0171 306 0102
E-mail: chambers@wilberforce.co.uk
Call date: July 1985, Inner Temple
Qualifications: [BA (Oxon)]

TEPER CARL WOLF

1 Gray's Inn Square
Ground Floor, London WC1R 5AA,
Telephone: 0171 405 8946/7/8
Call date: July 1980, Middle Temple
Qualifications: [LLB (Warw)]

TER HAAR ROGER EDUARD LOUND QC (1992)

2 Crown Office Row
Ground Floor, Temple, London EC4Y 7HJ,
Telephone: 0171 797 8100
E-mail: mail@2cor.co.uk, or to individual
barristers at: [barrister's surname]@2cor.co.uk
Call date: July 1974, Inner Temple
Qualifications: [BA (Oxon)]

TERRAS NICHOLAS CHARLES

12 New Square
Ground Floor, Lincoln's Inn, London
WC2A 3SW, Telephone: 0171 419 1212
E-mail: 12newsquare@compuserve.com
Call date: Oct 1993, Lincoln's Inn
Qualifications: [BA (Hons)(Lond), PhD (Lond),
Dip in Law (City)]

TERRY MISS MICHELLE JANE EVELYN

Lamb Building
Ground Floor, Temple, London EC4Y 7AS,
Telephone: 0171 797 7788
E-mail: lamb.building@link.org
Call date: July 1988, Lincoln's Inn
Qualifications: [LLB (Hons)]

TERRY ROBERT EDWARD LEETHAM

York Chambers
14 Toft Green, York YO1 1JT,
Telephone: 01904 620048
E-mail: yorkchambers.co.uk
Call date: Nov 1986, Gray's Inn
Qualifications: [BA (Leeds)]

TERRY ROBERT JEFFREY

8 King Street
Manchester M2 6AQ,
Telephone: 0161 834 9560
Call date: July 1976, Lincoln's Inn
Qualifications: [LLB, MA (Lond)]

TESTAR PETER THOMAS

4 Brick Court
1st Floor, Temple, London EC4Y 9AD,
Telephone: 0171 583 8455
Call date: July 1974, Middle Temple
Qualifications: [LLB (Soton)]

TETHER MS MELANIE GEORGIA KIM

Old Square Chambers
1 Verulam Buildings, Gray's Inn, London
WC1R 5LQ, Telephone: 0171 831 0801
Old Square Chambers
Hanover House 47 Corn Street, Bristol
BS1 1HT, Telephone: 0117 9277111
Call date: July 1995, Inner Temple
Qualifications: [MA (Oxon)]

TETLOW BERNARD GEOFFREY

2 Dr Johnson's Building
Temple, London EC4Y 7AY,
Telephone: 0171 353 4716
Call date: Nov 1984, Middle Temple
Qualifications: [BA, LLM (Cantab)]

TETTENBORN ANDREW MARTIN

Regency Chambers
18 Cowgate, Peterborough PE1 1NA,
Telephone: 01733 315215
Regency Chambers
Sheraton House, Castle Park, Cambridge
CB3 0AX, Telephone: 01223 301517
Call date: Nov 1988, Lincoln's Inn
Qualifications: [BA Hons,LLB (Cantab), MA
(Cantab)]

TEVERSON PAUL RICHARD

24 Old Bldgs
Ground Floor, Lincoln's Inn, London
WC2A 3UJ, Telephone: 0171 404 0946
E-mail: clerks@24oldbuildings.law.co.uk
Call date: July 1976, Inner Temple
Qualifications: [BA (Cantab)]

THACKER RAJEEV KUMAR

4 Brick Court
Ground Floor, Temple, London EC4Y 9AD,
Telephone: 0171 797 7766
E-mail: chambers@4brick.co.uk
Call date: Oct 1993, Gray's Inn
Qualifications: [LLB (Wales)]

THACKRAY JOHN RICHARD DOMINIC

Wilberforce Chambers
Bishop Lane, Hull HU1 1PA,
Telephone: 01482 323264
E-mail: clerks@hullbar.demon.co.uk
Call date: Oct 1994, Lincoln's Inn
Qualifications: [LLB (Hons)(Leeds)]

D

THANKI BANKIM

Fountain Court
Temple, London EC4Y 9DH,
Telephone: 0171 583 3335
E-mail: chambers@fountaincourt.co.uk
Call date: July 1988, Middle Temple
Qualifications: [MA (Oxon), Dip Law (City)]

THATCHER RICHARD DAVID

1 High Pavement
Nottingham NG1 1HF,
Telephone: 0115 9418218
Call date: July 1989, Inner Temple
Qualifications: [LLB]

THEIS MISS LUCY MORGAN

2 Field Court
Gray's Inn, London WC1R 5BB,
Telephone: 0171 405 6114
E-mail: fieldct2@netcomuk.co.uk.
Call date: July 1982, Gray's Inn
Assistant Recorder
Qualifications: [LLB (B'ham)]

THEMIS SAM

Verulam Chambers
Peer House 8-14 Verulam Street, Gray's Inn,
London WC1X 8LZ,
Telephone: 0171 813 2400
Call date: Oct 1995, Inner Temple
Qualifications: [LLB (Lond)]

THIND MISS ANITA

Regency Chambers
18 Cowgate, Peterborough PE1 1NA,
Telephone: 01733 315215
Regency Chambers
Sheraton House, Castle Park, Cambridge
CB3 0AX, Telephone: 01223 301517
Call date: Nov 1988, Inner Temple
Qualifications: [LLB]

THIRLWALL MISS KATHRYN MARY

9 Bedford Row
London WC1R 4AZ,
Telephone: 0171 242 3555
E-mail: clerks@9br.co.uk
Call date: July 1982, Middle Temple
Assistant Recorder
Qualifications: [BA (Bris)]

THOKA MICHAEL

Lloyds House Chambers
3rd Floor 18 Lloyds House, Lloyd Street,
Manchester M2 5WA,
Telephone: 0161 839 3371
Call date: Nov 1983, Middle Temple
Qualifications: [BA (Hons)]

THOM JAMES ALEXANDER FRANCIS

4 Field Court
Gray's Inn, London WC1R 5EA,
Telephone: 0171 440 6900
E-mail: chambers@4fieldcourt.co.uk
Call date: Nov 1974, Middle Temple
Qualifications: [MA (Oxon), BCL (Oxon)]

THOM MICHAEL

Eighteen Carlton Crescent
Southampton SO15 2XR,
Telephone: 01703 639001
Call date: Nov 1994, Inner Temple
Qualifications: [LLB (Soton)]

THOMAS (ROBERT) NEVILLE QC (1975)

3 Verulam Buildings
London WC1R 5NT,
Telephone: 0171 831 8441
E-mail: clerks@3verulam.co.uk
Call date: July 1962, Inner Temple
Qualifications: [MA (Oxon), BCL]

THOMAS MISS (YVETTE) BERNADETTE

Chancery Chambers
1st Floor Offices 70/72 Chancery Lane,
London WC2A 1AB,
Telephone: 0171 405 6879/6870
Call date: July 1993, Middle Temple
Qualifications: [LLB (Hons)]

THOMAS ADRIAN FRANCIS TREVELYAN

2-3 Gray's Inn Square
Gray's Inn, London WC1R 5JH,
Telephone: 0171 242 4986
E-mail: chambers@2-3graysinnsquare.co.uk
Call date: July 1974, Gray's Inn

THOMAS ANDREW (MARTIN)

Sedan House
Stanley Place, Chester CH1 2LU,
Telephone: 01244 320480/348282
1 Dr Johnson's Bldgs
Ground Floor, Temple, London EC4Y 7AX,
Telephone: 0171 353 9328
Call date: Nov 1989, Gray's Inn
Qualifications: [MA (Cantab)]

THOMAS ANDREW RICHARD

Brick Court Chambers
15/19 Devereux Court, London WC2R 3JJ,
Telephone: 0171 583 0777
E-mail: (surname)@brickcourt.demon.co.uk
Call date: Oct 1996, Inner Temple

THOMAS MS ANNA LOUISE

22 Old Bldgs
Lincoln's Inn, London WC2A 3UJ,
Telephone: 0171 831 0222
Call date: Nov 1995, Inner Temple
Qualifications: [BA (Oxon), CPE (City)]

THOMAS BRYAN MICHAEL

Gower Chambers
57 Walter Road, Swansea, West Glamorgan
SA1 5PZ, Telephone: 01792 644466
E-mail: clerk@gowerchambers.co.uk
10 King's Bench Walk
1st Floor, Temple, London EC4Y 7EB,
Telephone: 0171 353 2501
Door Tenant
Call date: July 1978, Gray's Inn
Qualifications: [LLB Hons (Wales)]

THOMAS CHARLES AUBREY MORGAN

1 Paper Bldgs
1st Floor, Temple, London EC4Y 7EP,
Telephone: 0171 353 3728/4953
Call date: Oct 1990, Middle Temple
Qualifications: [BA (Oxon)]

THOMAS CHRISTOPHER SYDNEY QC (1989)

Keating Chambers
10 Essex Street, Outer Temple, London
WC2R 3AA, Telephone: 0171 544 2600
Call date: July 1973, Lincoln's Inn
Assistant Recorder

Qualifications: [BA, Dip de Droit Compare,
Phd]

THOMAS DR DAVID ARTHUR QC (1996)

Cloisters
1st Floor, Temple, London EC4Y 7AA,
Telephone: 0171 827 4000
E-mail: clerks@cloisters.com
Door Tenant
Call date: Feb 1992, Lincoln's Inn
Qualifications: [LLD (Cambs)]

THOMAS DAVID ERYL

32 Park Place
Cardiff CF1 3BA, Telephone: 01222 397364
Call date: July 1975, Gray's Inn
Qualifications: [MA (Oxon)]

THOMAS DAVID OWEN QC (1972)

6 Gray's Inn Square
Ground Floor, Gray's Inn, London WC1R 5AZ,
Telephone: 0171 242 1052
Assize Court Chambers
14 Small Street, Bristol BS1 1DE,
Telephone: 0117 9264587
Door Tenant
Call date: July 1952, Middle Temple
Recorder

THOMAS MISS DOROTHY ANN

Victoria Chambers
3rd Floor 177 Corporation Street, Birmingham
B4 6RG, Telephone: 0121 236 9900
Call date: Nov 1991, Inner Temple
Qualifications: [LLB (Hull)]

THOMAS DYFED LLION

Angel Chambers
94 Walter Road, Swansea SA1 5QA,
Telephone: 01792 6464623/6464648
Call date: Oct 1992, Middle Temple
Qualifications: [BA (Hons)(Oxon)]

D

THOMAS GARETH

Oriel Chambers
14 Water Street, Liverpool L2 8TD,
Telephone: 0151 236 7191
E-mail: oriel_chambers@link.org
Call date: July 1977, Gray's Inn
Qualifications: [LLB (Wales) ACII]

THOMAS GARETH DAVID

Pendragon Chambers
124 Walter Road, Swansea SA1 5RG,
Telephone: 01792 411188
Call date: Nov 1993, Inner Temple
Qualifications: [LLB (Wales)]

THOMAS GEORGE LLEWELLYN

3 Serjeants Inn
London EC4Y 1BQ,
Telephone: 0171 353 5537
E-mail: available upon request
Call date: Oct 1995, Gray's Inn
Qualifications: [BA]

THOMAS GERAINT WYNN

10 Old Square
Ground Floor, Lincoln's Inn, London
WC2A 3SU, Telephone: 0171 405 0758
Door Tenant
Call date: July 1976, Inner Temple
Qualifications: [BA (Wales) DPhil, (Oxon)]

THOMAS IAN

St Ive's Chambers
9 Fountain Ct, Birmingham B4 6DR,
Telephone: 0121 236 0863/0929
Call date: Oct 1993, Gray's Inn
Qualifications: [LLB (Wolver'ton)]

THOMAS MISS KATIE

Clock Chambers
78 Darlington Street, Wolverhampton
WV1 4LY, Telephone: 01902 313444
Call date: Oct 1994, Gray's Inn
Qualifications: [LLB]

THOMAS KEITH GARFIELD

9 Park Place
Cardiff CF1 3DP, Telephone: 01222 382731
Call date: July 1977, Gray's Inn
Assistant Recorder
Qualifications: [BA]

THOMAS KEITH SINCLAIR

New Bailey Chambers
10 Lawson Street, Preston PR1 2QT,
Telephone: 01772 258087
Call date: July 1969, Gray's Inn
Qualifications: [BA (Oxon)]

THOMAS KENNETH LLOYD

Iscoed Chambers
86 St Helen's Road, Swansea SA1 4BQ,
Telephone: 01792 652988/9/330
Call date: July 1966, Lincoln's Inn
Qualifications: [MA, LLB (Cantab)]

THOMAS LESLIE

2 Garden Court
1st Floor, Middle Temple, London EC4Y 9BL,
Telephone: 0171 353 1633
E-mail: barristers@2gardenct.law.co.uk
Call date: Nov 1988, Inner Temple
Qualifications: [LLB]

THOMAS MISS MEGAN MOIRA

1 Serjeants' Inn
4th Floor, Temple, London EC4Y 1NH,
Telephone: 0171 583 1355
E-mail: serjeants.inn@virgin.net
Call date: July 1987, Gray's Inn
Qualifications: [BA (Hons)(Shef)]

THOMAS MICHAEL DAVID QC (1973)

Essex Court Chambers
24 Lincoln's Inn Fields, London WC2A 3ED,
Telephone: 0171 813 8000
E-mail: clerksroom@essexcourt-chambers.co.uk
Call date: May 1955, Middle Temple
Qualifications: [LLB (Lond), BA]

THOMAS NIGEL MATTHEW

13 Old Square
Ground Floor, Lincoln's Inn, London
WC2A 3UA, Telephone: 0171 404 4800
Call date: July 1976, Gray's Inn
Qualifications: [LLB (Wales) LLB, (Cantab)]

THOMAS OWEN HUW

9 Park Place
Cardiff CF1 3DP, Telephone: 01222 382731
Call date: Oct 1994, Gray's Inn
Qualifications: [BA (Oxon)]

THOMAS PATRICK ANTHONY

4 Fountain Court
Steelhouse Lane, Birmingham B4 6DR,
Telephone: 0121 236 3476
Call date: July 1973, Gray's Inn
Recorder
Qualifications: [BA (Oxon)]

THOMAS PAUL HUW

Iscoed Chambers
86 St Helen's Road, Swansea SA1 4BQ,
Telephone: 01792 652988/9/330
Farrar's Building
Temple, London EC4Y 7BD,
Telephone: 0171 583 9241
E-mail: chambers@farrarsbuilding.co.uk
Door Tenant
Call date: July 1979, Gray's Inn
Qualifications: [MA (Cantab)]

THOMAS PHILIP

Pendragon Chambers
124 Walter Road, Swansea SA1 5RG,
Telephone: 01792 411188
Call date: July 1982, Inner Temple
Qualifications: [LLB (Soton)]

THOMAS ROBERT GREGORY

Guildhall Chambers
23 Broad Street, Bristol BS1 2HG,
Telephone: 0117 9273366
Call date: Apr 1991, Gray's Inn
Qualifications: [LLB]

THOMAS ROBERT OWAIN PHILIP

4 Essex Court
Temple, London EC4Y 9AJ,
Telephone: 0171 797 7970
E-mail: clerks@4essexcourt.law.co.uk
Call date: Nov 1992, Lincoln's Inn
Qualifications: [MA (Cantab), BCL (Oxon),
LIC.SP.Dr.Eur., (Bruxelles)]

THOMAS ROGER CHRISTOPHER

Pump Court Tax Chambers
16 Bedford Row, London WC1R 4EB,
Telephone: 0171 414 8080
Call date: July 1979, Lincoln's Inn
Qualifications: [MA, BCL (Oxon)]

THOMAS ROGER LLOYD QC (1994)

9 Park Place
Cardiff CF1 3DP, Telephone: 01222 382731
Farrar's Building
Temple, London EC4Y 7BD,
Telephone: 0171 583 9241
E-mail: chambers@farrarsbuilding.co.uk
Door Tenant
Call date: July 1969, Gray's Inn
Qualifications: [LLB (Wales)]

THOMAS ROGER MARTIN

Broadway House Chambers
Broadway House 9 Bank Street, Bradford,
West Yorkshire BD1 1TW,
Telephone: 01274 722560
Call date: Nov 1976, Inner Temple
Recorder
Qualifications: [LLB]

THOMAS ROYDON URQUHART QC (1985)

1 Essex Court
Ground Floor, Temple, London EC4Y 9AR,
Telephone: 0171 583 2000
E-mail: clerks@oneessexcourt.co.uk
Call date: July 1960, Middle Temple
Recorder
Qualifications: [BA (Cantab)]

D

THOMAS MISS SIAN CAROLINE MARTHA

11 Old Square
Ground Floor, Lincoln's Inn, London
WC2A 3TS, Telephone: 0171 430 0341
E-mail: clerks@11oldsquare.co.uk
Call date: July 1981, Inner Temple
Qualifications: [BA (Oxon)]

THOMAS STEPHEN EDWARD OWEN

7 Fountain Court
Steelhouse Lane, Birmingham B4 6DR,
Telephone: 0121 236 8531
Call date: July 1980, Gray's Inn
Qualifications: [LLB (Exon)]

THOMAS STEPHEN JOHN

32 Park Place
Cardiff CF1 3BA, Telephone: 01222 397364
Call date: Feb 1993, Gray's Inn
Qualifications: [LLB (Hons)(Wales)]

THOMAS MISS SYBIL MILWYN

3 Fountain Court
Steelhouse Lane, Birmingham B4 6DR,
Telephone: 0121 236 5854
Call date: July 1976, Gray's Inn
Assistant Recorder
Qualifications: [LLB (Bris)]

THOMAS WILLIAM DAVID

2 Temple Gardens
Temple, London EC4Y 9AY,
Telephone: 0171 583 6041 (12 Lines)
Call date: July 1982, Middle Temple
Qualifications: [MA (Oxon)]

THOMAS WILLIAM OWAIN

1 Crown Office Row
Ground Floor, Temple, London EC4Y 7HH,
Telephone: 0171 797 7500
Call date: Oct 1995, Inner Temple
Qualifications: [BA (Oxon), BCL]

THOMAS OF GRESFORD LORD QC (1979)

1 Dr Johnson's Bldgs
Ground Floor, Temple, London EC4Y 7AX,
Telephone: 0171 353 9328
Dr Johnson's Chambers
The Atrium Court Apex Plaza, Reading
RG1 1AX, Telephone: 01734 254221
Sedan House
Stanley Place, Chester CH1 2LU,
Telephone: 01244 320480/348282
Call date: Nov 1967, Gray's Inn
Recorder
Qualifications: [MA, LLB]

THOMPSON MISS (HELEN) (LOUISE) POLLY

2 Pump Court
1st Floor, Temple, London EC4Y 7AH,
Telephone: 0171 353 5597
Call date: Nov 1990, Middle Temple
Qualifications: [BA, Dip Law (Lond)]

THOMPSON ANDREW EDWARD COURTNEY

Francis Taylor Bldg
3rd Floor, Temple, London EC4Y 7BY,
Telephone: 0171 797 7250
Call date: Nov 1969, Inner Temple
Qualifications: [BA (Hons), LLB (Dublin)]

THOMPSON ANDREW IAN

2 Paper Buildings
Basement, Temple, London EC4Y 7ET,
Telephone: 0171 353 0933
Call date: Oct 1991, Gray's Inn
Qualifications: [MA (Oxon)]

THOMPSON ANDREW PETER

Park Court Chambers
40 Park Cross Street, Leeds LS1 2QH,
Telephone: 0113 2433277
Call date: July 1989, Inner Temple
Qualifications: [LLB (Hons)]

THOMPSON ANDREW RICHARD

Erskine Chambers
30 Lincoln's Inn Fields, Lincoln's Inn, London
WC2A 3PF, Telephone: 0171 242 5532
E-mail: Clerks@Erskine-Chambers.law.co.uk
Call date: Nov 1991, Inner Temple
Qualifications: [MA, LLM (Cantab)]

THOMPSON MISS BLONDELLE MARGUERITE

1 Fountain Court
Steelhouse Lane, Birmingham B4 6DR,
Telephone: 0121 236 5721
Call date: July 1987, Middle Temple
Qualifications: [LLB]

THOMPSON CEDRIC AUGUSTUS

Somersett Chambers
52 Bedford Row, London WC1R 4LR,
Telephone: 0171 404 6701
E-mail: Somersettchambers@cocoon.co.uk
Call date: Nov 1984, Gray's Inn
Qualifications: [BA Hons]

THOMPSON COLLINGWOOD FORSTER JAMES

9 Bedford Row
London WC1R 4AZ,
Telephone: 0171 242 3555
E-mail: clerks@9br.co.uk
Call date: July 1975, Gray's Inn
Recorder
Qualifications: [LLB (Lond)]

THOMPSON DERMOT MICHAEL MAIN

1 Gray's Inn Square
1st Floor, London WC1R 5AG,
Telephone: 0171 405 3000
E-mail: clerks@onegrays.demon.co.uk
Call date: July 1977, Gray's Inn
Qualifications: [MA, LLB (Cantab)]

THOMPSON MS GLENNA

3 Temple Gardens (North)
Fifth Floor, Temple, London EC4Y 9AU,
Telephone: 0171 353 0853/4/7222
E-mail: 100106.1577@compuserve.com
Call date: Nov 1993, Inner Temple
Qualifications: [BSc (Hons)]

THOMPSON HOWARD NEIL

5 Fountain Court
Steelhouse Lane, Birmingham B4 6DR,
Telephone: 0121 606 0500
Call date: July 1982, Lincoln's Inn
Qualifications: [BA]

THOMPSON JONATHAN RICHARD

8 King Street
Manchester M2 6AQ,
Telephone: 0161 834 9560
Call date: Oct 1990, Inner Temple
Qualifications: [MA, LLM (Cantab)]

THOMPSON LYALL NORRIS

Tindal Chambers
3/5 New Street, Chelmsford, Essex CM1 1NT,
Telephone: 01245 267742
Tindal Chambers
3 Waxhouse Gate, St Albans, Herts AL5 4DU,
Telephone: 01727 843383
Call date: Oct 1995, Inner Temple
Qualifications: [LLB (Aberdeen), CPE (City)]

THOMPSON MARCUS ELLIOT GERARD

Queen Elizabeth Bldg
Ground Floor, Temple, London EC4Y 9BS,
Telephone: 0171 353 7181 (12 Lines)
Call date: Oct 1996, Inner Temple
Qualifications: [BA (Cantab), CPE]

THOMPSON PATRICK MILES

Queen's Chambers
5 John Dalton Street, Manchester M2 6ET,
Telephone: 0161 834 6875/4738
4 Camden Place
Preston PR1 3JL, Telephone: 01772 828300
Call date: Oct 1990, Gray's Inn
Qualifications: [LLB (Hons)(Manch)]

THOMPSON RHODRI WILLIAM RALPH

Monckton Chambers
4 Raymond Buildings, Gray's Inn, London
WC1R 5BP, Telephone: 0171 405 7211
E-mail: chambers@monckton.co.uk
Call date: July 1989, Middle Temple
Qualifications: [MA (Oxon), BPhil (Oxon)]

THOMPSON MISS SALLY

2 Harcourt Bldgs
1st Floor, Temple, London EC4Y 9DB,
Telephone: 0171 353 2112/2817
Call date: Oct 1994, Middle Temple
Qualifications: [Dip in Music, CPE (Lond)]

THOMPSON SIMON

3 Temple Gardens
3rd Floor, Temple, London EC4Y 9AU,
Telephone: 0171 353 0832
Call date: July 1988, Lincoln's Inn
Qualifications: [LLB (Hons) (Leics)]

THOMPSON STEVEN LIM

24 Old Bldgs
Ground Floor, Lincoln's Inn, London
WC2A 3UJ, Telephone: 0171 404 0946
E-mail: clerks@24oldbuildings.law.co.uk
Call date: Oct 1996, Inner Temple
Qualifications: [BA (Cantab)]

THOMSON DR DAVID JAMES RAMSAY GIBB

Barnard's Inn Chambers
6th Floor Halton House, 20-23 Holborn,
London EC1N 2JD, Telephone: 0171 242 8508
E-mail: clerks@barnards-inn-chambers.co.uk
Call date: Nov 1994, Inner Temple
Qualifications: [MB, Ch.B (Sheff), LLB (Lond), LLM (Cantab)]

THOMSON MARTIN HALDANE AHMAD

Wynne Chambers
1 Wynne Road, London SW9 0BB,
Telephone: 0171 737 7266
E-mail: m_h_a.thomson_esq@which.net
Call date: July 1979, Gray's Inn
Qualifications: [LLB (Hons, Exeter), Dip Law (City)]

THORESBY ROBERT MCCALL

Lamb Chambers
Lamb Building, Temple, London EC4Y 7AS,
Telephone: 0171 797 8300
E-mail: lambchambers@link.org
Call date: July 1978, Inner Temple
Qualifications: [MA (Cantab)]

THORLEY SIMON JOE QC (1989)

3 New Square
Lincoln's Inn, London WC2A 3RS,
Telephone: 0171 405 1111
Call date: July 1972, Inner Temple
Qualifications: [MA (Oxon)]

THORN ROGER ERIC QC (1990)

New Court Chambers
3 Broad Chare, Newcastle Upon Tyne
NE1 3DQ, Telephone: 0191 232 1980
Call date: Nov 1970, Middle Temple
Assistant Recorder
Qualifications: [LLB]

THORNBERRY MISS EMILY ANNE

14 Tooks Court
Cursitor St, London EC4A 1LB,
Telephone: 0171 405 8828
E-mail: clerks @tooks.law.co.uk
Call date: Nov 1983, Gray's Inn
Qualifications: [BA (Kent)]

THORNDIKE ANTHONY EDWARD

Claremont Chambers
26 Waterloo Road, Wolverhampton WV1 4BL,
Telephone: 01902 426222
Bracton Chambers
95a Chancery Lane, London WC2A 1DT,
Telephone: 0171 242 4248
Call date: Oct 1994, Lincoln's Inn
Qualifications: [BSc (Econ), MSc, PhD]

THORNE MS KATHERINE HARRIET

Counsels' Chambers
2nd Floor 10-11 Gray's Inn Square, London
WC1R 5JD, Telephone: 0171 405 2576
Call date: Nov 1994, Inner Temple
Qualifications: [BA (Leeds), CPE]

THORNE MISS SARAH LOUISE

Westgate Chambers
144 High Street, Lewes, East Sussex BN7 1XT,
Telephone: 01273 480510
Call date: Feb 1995, Middle Temple
Qualifications: [LLB (Hons)(Lond)]

THORNE TIMOTHY PETER

33 Bedford Row
London WC1R 4JH,
Telephone: 0171 242 6476
Call date: Nov 1987, Gray's Inn
Qualifications: [MA (Oxon)]

THORNETT GARY PAUL

1 Fountain Court
Steelhouse Lane, Birmingham B4 6DR,
Telephone: 0121 236 5721
Call date: Nov 1991, Middle Temple
Qualifications: [B Mus (Lond)]

THORNHILL ANDREW ROBERT QC (1985)

Pump Court Tax Chambers
16 Bedford Row, London WC1R 4EB,
Telephone: 0171 414 8080
Call date: July 1969, Middle Temple
Qualifications: [BA (Oxon)]

THORNHILL MS TERESA

29 Gwilliam Street
Bristol BS3 4LT, Telephone: 0117 966 8997
Call date: July 1986, Middle Temple
Qualifications: [BA (Hons) (Oxon), Dip Law
(City)]

THORNLEY DAVID

Eldon Chambers
Fourth Floor 30/32 Fleet Street, London
EC4Y 1AA, Telephone: 0171 353 4636
Call date: July 1988, Inner Temple
Qualifications: [BA (Kent)]

THORNTON ANDREW JAMES

Erskine Chambers
30 Lincoln's Inn Fields, Lincoln's Inn, London
WC2A 3PF, Telephone: 0171 242 5532
E-mail: Clerks@Erskine-Chambers.law.co.uk
Call date: Nov 1994, Lincoln's Inn
Qualifications: [LLB (Hons)(Hull)]

THORNTON MISS ANNE REBECCA

9 Woodhouse Square
Leeds LS3 1AD, Telephone: 0113 2451986
Call date: July 1976, Middle Temple
Qualifications: [LLB]

THORNTON PETER RIBBLESDALE QC (1992)

Doughty Street Chambers
11 Doughty Street, London WC1N 2PG,
Telephone: 0171 404 1313
E-mail: doughty_street@compuserve.com
*Call date: July 1969, Middle Temple
Assistant Recorder*
Qualifications: [BA (Cantab)]

THORNTON PHILIP CHARLES

Devereux Chambers
Devereux Court, London WC2R 3JJ,
Telephone: 0171 353 7534
E-mail: elton@devchambers.co.uk
Call date: Nov 1988, Middle Temple
Qualifications: [MA (Cantab)]

THOROGOOD BERNARD

5 Fountain Court
Steelhouse Lane, Birmingham B4 6DR,
Telephone: 0121 606 0500
Call date: July 1986, Gray's Inn
Qualifications: [LLB Leeds]

THOROLD OLIVER

Doughty Street Chambers
11 Doughty Street, London WC1N 2PG,
Telephone: 0171 404 1313
E-mail: doughty_street@compuserve.com
Call date: Nov 1971, Inner Temple
Qualifications: [BA (Oxon)]

THOROWGOOD MAX CAMPBELL DE WARRENNE

Mitre Court Chambers
3rd Floor, Temple, London EC4Y 7BP,
Telephone: 0171 353 9394
Call date: Nov 1995, Lincoln's Inn
Qualifications: [MA (Hons)]

THORP IAN SIMON

Park Lane Chambers
19 Westgate, Leeds LS1 2RD,
Telephone: 0113 2285000
Call date: July 1988, Inner Temple
Qualifications: [BA (Hull)]

D

THORPE ALEXANDER LAMBERT

Queen Elizabeth Bldg
2nd Floor, Temple, London EC4Y 9BS,
Telephone: 0171 797 7837
Call date: Oct 1995, Inner Temple
Qualifications: [BA (Lond), CPE (Lond)]

THRELFALL RICHARD WILLIAM GEORGE

All Saints Chambers
9/11 Broad Street, Bristol BS1 2HP,
Telephone: 0117 921 1966
Call date: July 1972, Gray's Inn

THROP MISS ALISON

2 Mitre Ct Bldgs
1st Floor, Temple, London EC4Y 7BX,
Telephone: 0171 353 1353
Door Tenant
Call date: Oct 1992, Middle Temple
Qualifications: [BA (Hons)(York), Common Profeional, Examination]

THROWER JAMES SIMEON

11 Old Square
Ground Floor, Lincoln's Inn, London
WC2A 3TS, Telephone: 0171 242 5022/
405 1074
Call date: July 1973, Middle Temple
Qualifications: [LLB]

THURBIN MRS DAYE BARBOT

Westgate Chambers
144 High Street, Lewes, East Sussex BN7 1XT,
Telephone: 01273 480510
Call date: Nov 1991, Gray's Inn
Qualifications: [BSc (Florida), Juris Doctor (Nova)]

THWAITES RONALD QC (1987)

10 King's Bench Walk
1st Floor, Temple, London EC4Y 7EB,
Telephone: 0171 353 2501
Call date: Nov 1970, Gray's Inn
Qualifications: [LLB (Lond)]

TICCIATI OLIVER

4 Pump Court
Temple, London EC4Y 7AN,
Telephone: 0171 353 2656/9
E-mail: 4_pump_court@compuserve.com
Call date: July 1979, Inner Temple
Qualifications: [MA (Cantab)]

TIDBURY ANDREW HUGH

Queen Elizabeth Bldg
2nd Floor, Temple, London EC4Y 9BS,
Telephone: 0171 797 7837
Call date: July 1976, Inner Temple
Qualifications: [BA (Cantab)]

TIDMARSH CHRISTOPHER RALPH FRANCIS

5 Stone Buildings
Lincoln's Inn, London WC2A 3XT,
Telephone: 0171 242 6201
E-mail: clerks@5-stonebuildings.law.co.uk
Call date: Nov 1985, Lincoln's Inn
Qualifications: [BA (Oxon)]

TIGHE MISS DAWN

37 Park Square
Leeds LS1 2NY, Telephone: 0113 2439422
Call date: Nov 1989, Lincoln's Inn
Qualifications: [LLB (Newc)]

TILBURY JAMES RICHARD

2 Paper Bldgs
1st Floor, Temple, London EC4Y 7ET,
Telephone: 0171 936 2611 (10 Lines)
E-mail: clerks@2pbbarristers.co.uk
Call date: Mar 1996, Gray's Inn
Qualifications: [LLB]

TILLETT MICHAEL BURN QC (1996)

39 Essex Street
London WC2R 3AT,
Telephone: 0171 583 1111
E-mail: clerks@39essex.co.uk
Call date: July 1965, Inner Temple
Recorder
Qualifications: [MA (Cantab)]

TILLYARD JAMES HENRY HUGH

30 Park Place
Cardiff CF1 3BA, Telephone: 01222 398421
E-mail: 100757.1456@compuserve.com
Farrar's Building
Temple, London EC4Y 7BD,
Telephone: 0171 583 9241
E-mail: chambers@farrarsbuilding.co.uk
Call date: July 1978, Middle Temple
Qualifications: [BSc (Leeds)]

TIPPETT GILES PETER

1 Gray's Inn Square
Ground Floor, London WC1R 5AA,
Telephone: 0171 405 8946/7/8
Call date: Oct 1992, Middle Temple
Qualifications: [LL.B (Hons)]

TIPPLES MISS AMANDA JANE

13 Old Square
Ground Floor, Lincoln's Inn, London
WC2A 3UA, Telephone: 0171 404 4800
Call date: Oct 1991, Gray's Inn
Qualifications: [MA (Cambs)]

TITHERIDGE ROGER NOEL
QC (1973)

1 Paper Bldgs
1st Floor, Temple, London EC4Y 7EP,
Telephone: 0171 353 3728/4953
Call date: July 1954, Gray's Inn
Recorder
Qualifications: [MA (Oxon)]

TIWANA PARDEEP SINGH

4 Fountain Court
Steelhouse Lane, Birmingham B4 6DR,
Telephone: 0121 236 3476
Call date: Nov 1993, Lincoln's Inn
Qualifications: [LLB (Hons)]

TIZZANO FRANCO SALVATORE

8 King's Bench Walk
2nd Floor, Temple, London EC4Y 7DU,
Telephone: 0171 797 8888
8 King's Bench Walk North
1 Park Square East, Leeds LS1 2NE,
Telephone: 0113 2439797
Call date: Feb 1989, Middle Temple
Qualifications: [LLB]

TOAL DAVID JOHN

Old Colony House
6 South King Street, Manchester M2 6DQ,
Telephone: 0161 834 4364
Call date: Feb 1990, Gray's Inn
Qualifications: [LLB (Hons)0]

TOBIN DANIEL ALPHONSUS JOSEPH

46/48 Essex Street
London WC2R 3GH,
Telephone: 0171 583 8899
Call date: Oct 1994, Middle Temple
Qualifications: [LLB (Hons)(Lond)]

TOCH MISS JOANNA PATRICIA

3 Dr Johnson's Bldgs
Ground Floor, Temple, London EC4Y 7BA,
Telephone: 0171 353 4854
Warwick House Chambers
8 Warwick Court, Gray's Inn, London
WC1R 5DJ, Telephone: 0171 430 2323
Call date: Nov 1988, Middle Temple
Qualifications: [LLB (Hons)(Lond)]

TOD JONATHAN ALAN

7 Stone Bldgs
1st Floor, Lincoln's Inn, London WC2A 3SZ,
Telephone: 0171 242 0961
Call date: Nov 1990, Inner Temple
Qualifications: [LLB (Hons)]

TODD ALAN JAMES

Farrar's Building
Temple, London EC4Y 7BD,
Telephone: 0171 583 9241
E-mail: chambers@farrarsbuilding.co.uk
Call date: Nov 1990, Gray's Inn
Qualifications: [MA (Cantab)]

TODD CHARLES LOUIS

1 Mitre Ct Bldgs
Ground Floor, Temple, London EC4Y 7BS,
Telephone: 0171 797 7070
Trinity Chambers
9-12 Trinity Chare, Quayside, Newcastle Upon
Tyne NE1 3DF, Telephone: 0191 232 1927
Call date: July 1983, Gray's Inn
Qualifications: [BA,ACA]

D

TODD MRS ELISABETH HELEN MARGARET

1 Mitre Ct Bldgs
Ground Floor, Temple, London EC4Y 7BS,
Telephone: 0171 797 7070
Call date: Oct 1990, Middle Temple
Qualifications: [LLB (Lond) (Hons)]

TODD MARTIN RUSSELL

York Chambers
14 Toft Green, York YO1 1JT,
Telephone: 01904 620048
E-mail: yorkchambers.co.uk
Call date: Nov 1991, Inner Temple
Qualifications: [LLB (Hons)]

TODD MICHAEL ALAN QC (1997)

Erskine Chambers
30 Lincoln's Inn Fields, Lincoln's Inn, London
WC2A 3PF, Telephone: 0171 242 5532
E-mail: Clerks@Erskine-Chambers.law.co.uk
Call date: July 1977, Lincoln's Inn
Qualifications: [BA (Keele)]

TODD RICHARD FRAZER

1 Mitre Ct Bldgs
Ground Floor, Temple, London EC4Y 7BS,
Telephone: 0171 797 7070
Call date: July 1988, Middle Temple
Qualifications: [MA (Hons) (Oxon)]

TODMAN MRS DEBORAH

New Court
Temple, London EC4Y 9BE,
Telephone: 0171 583 5123/0171 583 0510
Call date: Oct 1991, Gray's Inn
Qualifications: [LLB (Hons)]

TOLANEY MISS SONIA

3 Verulam Buildings
London WC1R 5NT,
Telephone: 0171 831 8441
E-mail: clerks@3verulam.co.uk
Call date: Oct 1995, Middle Temple
Qualifications: [BA (Hons)]

TOLEDANO DANIEL ZE'EV

1 Essex Court
Ground Floor, Temple, London EC4Y 9AR,
Telephone: 0171 583 2000
E-mail: clerks@oneessexcourt.co.uk
Call date: Oct 1993, Inner Temple
Qualifications: [MA (Hons) (Cantab)]

TOLHURST ROBERT LEIGH DOUGLAS

3 Temple Gardens
2nd Floor, Temple, London EC4Y 9AU,
Telephone: 0171 583 1155
Call date: Oct 1992, Middle Temple
Qualifications: [Ba (Hons)]

TOLKIEN SIMON MARIO REUEL

2 Paper Bldgs
Temple, London EC4Y 7ET,
Telephone: 0171 936 2613
Call date: July 1994, Middle Temple
Qualifications: [BA (Hons)(Oxon)]

TOLLEY ADAM RICHARD

Fountain Court
Temple, London EC4Y 9DH,
Telephone: 0171 583 3335
E-mail: chambers@fountaincourt.co.uk
Call date: Oct 1994, Inner Temple

TOLSON ROBIN STEWART

35 Essex Street
Temple, London WC2R 3AR,
Telephone: 0171 353 6381
Call date: Nov 1980, Inner Temple
Qualifications: [BA (Cantab)]

TOMASSI MARK DAVID

2 Dr Johnson's Building
Temple, London EC4Y 7AY,
Telephone: 0171 353 4716
Call date: Nov 1981, Middle Temple
Qualifications: [BA (Hons)]

TOMLINSON DAVID REDVERS

5 Paper Bldgs
Lower Ground Floor, Temple, London
EC4Y 7HB, Telephone: 0171 353 5638
E-mail: 107722,633@compuserve.com
Call date: July 1977, Inner Temple
Assistant Recorder
Qualifications: [LLB (Leeds)]

TOMLINSON HUGH RICHARD EDWARD

New Court Chambers
5 Verulam Buildings, Gray's Inn, London
WC1R 5LY, Telephone: 0171 831 9500
E-mail: mail@newcourtchambers.com
Call date: Nov 1983, Gray's Inn
Qualifications: [BA (Oxon), MA(Sussex]

TOMLINSON STEPHEN MILES QC (1988)

7 King's Bench Walk
Ground Floor, Temple, London EC4Y 7DS,
Telephone: 0171 583 0404
Call date: July 1974, Inner Temple
Recorder
Qualifications: [MA (Oxon)]

TOMS NICHOLAS ROBERT

Mitre House Chambers
Mitre House 44 Fleet Street, London
EC4Y 1BN, Telephone: 0171 583 8233
Call date: Nov 1996, Middle Temple
Qualifications: [LLB (Hons), LLM (Cantab)]

TONGE CHRISTOPHER PAUL

19 Figtree Lane
Sheffield S1 2DJ, Telephone: 0114 2759708/
2738380
Call date: July 1988, Inner Temple
Qualifications: [LLB (Sheffield)]

TONGE MISS RUTH MARGARET HAYES

Claremont Chambers
26 Waterloo Road, Wolverhampton WV1 4BL,
Telephone: 01902 426222
Call date: Oct 1993, Gray's Inn
Qualifications: [LLB (Hons)]

TONNA JOHN PRINGLE NODWELL

29 Bedford Row Chambers
London WC1R 4HE,
Telephone: 0171 831 2626
Call date: July 1974, Gray's Inn
Qualifications: [BA (Oxon)]

TOOGOOD MISS CLAIRE VICTORIA

1 Paper Bldgs
Ground Floor, Temple, London EC4Y 7EP,
Telephone: 0171 583 7355
E-mail: clerks@1pb.co.uk
Call date: Oct 1995, Middle Temple
Qualifications: [BA (Hons)]

TOOGOOD JOHN

4 King's Bench Walk
Ground/First Floor, Temple, London
EC4Y 7DL, Telephone: 0171 822 8822
E-mail: 4kbw@barristersatlaw.com
Call date: July 1957, Gray's Inn
Qualifications: [LLM]

TOOKEY MICHAEL JOHN

95A Chancery Lane
London WC2A 1DT,
Telephone: 0171 405 3101
Call date: Oct 1992, Lincoln's Inn
Qualifications: [LLB (Hons)]

TOOMBS RICHARD JOHN

King Charles House
Standard Hill, Nottingham NG1 6FX,
Telephone: 0115 9418851
E-mail: clerks@kch.co.uk
Call date: July 1983, Gray's Inn
Qualifications: [LLB (B'ham)]

TOONE ROBERT FRANCIS

11 King's Bench Walk
1st Floor, Temple, London EC4Y 7EQ,
Telephone: 0171 353 3337
3 Park Court
Leeds LS1 2QH, Telephone: 0113 297 1200
Call date: Oct 1993, Inner Temple
Qualifications: [BA]

TOPHAM GEOFFREY JOHN

3 Stone Bldgs
Ground Floor, Lincoln's Inn, London
WC2A 3XL, Telephone: 0171 242 4937/
405 8358
Call date: June 1964, Lincoln's Inn
Qualifications: [BA (Cantab)]

TOPHAM JOHN DAVID

Broadway House Chambers
Broadway House 9 Bank Street, Bradford,
West Yorkshire BD1 1TW,
Telephone: 01274 722560
Call date: July 1970, Gray's Inn
Qualifications: [LLB (Lond)]

TOPLISS MISS MEGAN LOUISE

1 Paper Bldgs
1st Floor, Temple, London EC4Y 7EP,
Telephone: 0171 353 3728/4953
Call date: Oct 1994, Gray's Inn
Qualifications: [LLB (Wales)]

TOPOLSKI MICHAEL JONATHAN

14 Tooks Court
Cursitor St, London EC4A 1LB,
Telephone: 0171 405 8828
E-mail: clerks @tooks.law.co.uk
Call date: Apr 1986, Inner Temple

TORRANCE HUGH MYER BERNARD

Goldsmith Chambers
Ground Floor Goldsmith Building, Temple,
London EC4Y 7BL,
Telephone: 0171 353 6802/3/4/5
E-mail: celiamonksfield@btinternet.com
Call date: May 1956, Lincoln's Inn
Qualifications: [MA, LLB (Cantab)]

TOUBE MS FELICITY ROSALIND

3/4 South Square
Gray's Inn, London WC1R 5HP,
Telephone: 0171 696 9900
E-mail: clerks@southsquare.com
Call date: Nov 1995, Inner Temple
Qualifications: [BA, BCL (Oxon)]

TOUSSAINT MISS DEBORAH

46/48 Essex Street
London WC2R 3GH,
Telephone: 0171 583 8899
Call date: July 1988, Middle Temple
Qualifications: [LLB (Hons)]

TOWLER PETER JEREMY HAMILTON

17 Carlton Crescent
Southampton SO15 2XR,
Telephone: 01703 320320
E-mail: km@bar-17cc.demon.co.uk
3 Paper Bldgs
1st Floor, Temple, London EC4Y 7EU,
Telephone: 0171 583 8055
E-mail: london@3paper.com
Call date: July 1974, Middle Temple
Recorder
Qualifications: [MA (Cantab), FCI Arb]

TOWN-GINSBURG MRS AMANDA

37 Park Square
Leeds LS1 2NY, Telephone: 0113 2439422
Call date: July 1986, Lincoln's Inn
Qualifications: [LLB (London)]

TOWNEND JAMES BARRIE STANLEY QC (1978)

1 King's Bench Walk
2nd Floor, Temple, London EC4Y 7DB,
Telephone: 0171 936 1500
E-mail: ddear@1kbw.co.uk
Call date: Feb 1962, Middle Temple
Recorder
Qualifications: [MA (Oxon)]

TOWNSEND JAMES NEVILLE

Guildhall Chambers
23 Broad Street, Bristol BS1 2HG,
Telephone: 0117 9273366
Call date: July 1980, Inner Temple
Qualifications: [MA (Oxon)]

TOWNSHEND TIMOTHY JOHN HUME

Octagon House
19 Colegate, Norwich NR3 1AT,
Telephone: 01603 623186
E-mail: octagon@netmatters.co.uk
Call date: Nov 1972, Lincoln's Inn
Qualifications: [MA (Cantab)]

TOZER MISS STEPHANIE

9 Old Square
Ground Floor, Lincoln's Inn, London
WC2A 3SR, Telephone: 0171 405 4682
E-mail: chambers@9oldsquare.co.uk
Call date: Oct 1996, Lincoln's Inn
Qualifications: [BA (Hons)(Oxon)]

TOZZI NIGEL KENNETH

4 Pump Court
Temple, London EC4Y 7AN,
Telephone: 0171 353 2656/9
E-mail: 4_pump_court@compuserve.com
Call date: July 1980, Gray's Inn
Qualifications: [LLB (Exon)]

TRACE ANTHONY JOHN QC (1998)

13 Old Square
Lincoln's Inn, London WC2A 3UA,
Telephone: 0171 404 4800
Call date: July 1981, Lincoln's Inn
Qualifications: [MA (Hons) (Cantab)]

Fax: 0171 405 4267;
Out of hours telephone: 01992 441374 (Clerk
- John Moore); DX: LDE 326

Types of work: Arbitration; Banking;
Bankruptcy; Chancery (general); Chancery land
law; Commercial; Commercial litigation;
Commercial property; Company and
commercial; Equity, wills and trusts; Insolvency;
Insurance/reinsurance; Landlord and tenant;
Partnerships; Probate and administration;
Professional negligence; Sports

Awards and memberships: Bundy Scholarship
(Magdalene College, Cambridge University);
Hardwick Scholar, Tancred Studentship and
Droop Scholar of Lincoln's Inn; Honorary
Secretary, Chancery Bar Association; Member
Bar Sports Law Group, COMBAR and ACTAPS
(Association of Contentious Trust and Probate
Specialists)

Languages spoken: French, Swahili

Publications: *Butterworths European Law
Service (Company Law)*, (Contributor), 1992;
*Receivers, Administrators and Liquidators
Quarterly* (RALQ), (Deputy Managing Editor),
1993 to date

Practice

After graduating from Cambridge in 1980 with
First Class Honours in Law, Anthony Trace was

a pupil to David Oliver (now The Hon David
Oliver QC) and Colin Rimer (now The Hon Mr
Justice Rimer). In 1981 he was joint winner of
the Observer Mace Debating Competition and
won the Crowther Advocacy Shield. He went on
to develop a very substantial junior practice,
both in England and in foreign jurisdictions. (He
was involved in a number of cases in the
Cayman Islands, The Bahamas, the Isle of Man
and Hong Kong.) Having taken silk in 1998 he is
building on that practice, and is currently
involved in cases going to the Court of Appeal
and the House of Lords.

**Reported cases in which he has appeared
include**:

*Annangel Glory Compania Naviera SA v
Golodetz Ltd* 1988 PCC 37 (company charges)

Gomba Holdings UK Ltd v Homan [1986] 3 All
ER 94 (receivers' duties)

Kemmis v Kemmis [1988] 1 WLR 1307
(constructive notice)

*Haarhaus & Co GmbH v Law Debenture Trust
Corp plc* [1988] BCLC 640 (company meetings)

*Ronald Preston & Partners v Markheath
Securities plc* [1988] 31 EG 50 (estate agents)

Re A Debtor (No 222 of 1990) [1992] BCLC 137
(voting at creditors' meetings)

Harrison v Thompson [1989] 1 WLR 1325
(equitable interest)

Re Unisoft Group Ltd (No 2) [1992] BCC 494
(security for costs against limited companies)

*BBMB Finance (Hong Kong) Ltd v Eda
Holdings Ltd* [1991] 2 All ER 129 (conversion)

*Bank of Credit and Commerce International
SA v Aboody* [1990] 1 QB 923 (undue influence)

Lee Panavision Ltd v Lee Lighting Ltd [1991]
BCLC 575 (directors' duties)

Jelson (Estates) Ltd v Harvey [1984] 1 All ER 12
(contempt)

Re Jeffrey S Levitt Ltd [1992] BCLC 250
(privilege against self-incrimination)

*Gomba Holdings (UK) Ltd v Minories Finance
Ltd (No 2)* [1993] BCLC 7 (mortgagee's costs)

Re Mirror Group (Holdings) Ltd [1993] BCLC
538 (liability of assignees on liquidation)

D

Lotteryking Ltd v AMEC Properties Ltd [1995] 28 EG 100 (set-off against assignees)

Re BCCI SA (No 10) [1996] 4 All ER 796 (insolvency set-off)

Slough Estates plc v Welwyn Hatfield District Council [1996] EGCS 132 (measure of damages for fraudulent misrepresentation)

Grand Metropolitan plc v The William Hill Group Ltd [1997] 1 BCLC 390 (rectification)

Jordan Grand Prix Ltd v Baltic Insurance Group [1998] 1 WLR 1049 (Brussels Convention)

Bogg v Raper [1998] *The Times Law Reports* 22 April (will drafting and exclusion clauses)

Plant v Plant [1998] 1 BCLC (individual voluntary arrangements)

TRACY FORSTER MISS JANE ELIZABETH

13 King's Bench Walk
1st Floor, Temple, London EC4Y 7EN,
Telephone: 0171 353 7204
E-mail: clerks@13kbw.law.co.uk
King's Bench Chambers
32 Beaumont Street, Oxford OX1 2NP,
Telephone: 01865 311066
E-mail: clerks@kbc-oxford.law.co.uk
Call date: July 1975, Inner Temple
Qualifications: [LLB (L'pool)]

TRAFFORD MARK RUSSELL

2 King's Bench Walk
Ground Floor, Temple, London EC4Y 7DE,
Telephone: 0171 353 1746
E-mail: 2kbw@atlas.co.uk
King's Bench Chambers
115 North Hill, Plymouth PL4 8JY,
Telephone: 01752 221551
Call date: May 1992, Lincoln's Inn
Qualifications: [BSc (Hons) (Brunel), Dip Law (City)]

TRAVERS DAVID

3 Fountain Court
Steelhouse Lane, Birmingham B4 6DR,
Telephone: 0121 236 5854
Call date: July 1981, Middle Temple
Qualifications: [LLB, LLM, AKC]

TRAVERS HUGH

Pump Court Chambers
Upper Ground Floor 3 Pump Court, Temple,
London EC4Y 7AJ, Telephone: 0171 353 0711
Pump Court Chambers
31 Southgate Street, Winchester SO23 8EE,
Telephone: 01962 868161
Call date: Nov 1988, Middle Temple
Qualifications: [MA (Cantab)]

TRAVERS RICHARD ETTORE NICHOLAS

Maidstone Chambers
33 Earl Street, Maidstone, Kent ME14 1PF,
Telephone: 01622 688592
Call date: Feb 1985, Lincoln's Inn
Qualifications: [BA (Lond), Dip Law]

TRAVERSI JOHN DAVID STEPHEN ANTONA

4 Brick Court
1st Floor, Temple, London EC4Y 9AD,
Telephone: 0171 583 8455
Call date: July 1977, Gray's Inn
Qualifications: [MA (Oxon)]

TREACY COLMAN MAURICE QC (1990)

3 Fountain Court
Steelhouse Lane, Birmingham B4 6DR,
Telephone: 0121 236 5854
36 Bedford Row
London WC1R 4JH,
Telephone: 0171 421 8000
E-mail: 36bedfordrow@link.org
Door Tenant
Call date: July 1971, Middle Temple
Recorder
Qualifications: [MA (Cantab)]

TREASURE FRANCIS SETON

199 Strand
London WC2R 1DR,
Telephone: 0171 379 9779
E-mail: chambers@199strand.co.uk
Call date: Feb 1980, Gray's Inn
Qualifications: [MA (Oxon)]

TREBLE PAUL JOSEPH

58 King Street Chambers
1st Floor, Kingsgate House 51-53 South King Street, Manchester M2 6DE,
Telephone: 0161 831 7477
Call date: Nov 1994, Lincoln's Inn
Qualifications: [BSc (Hons)(Sheff), CPE (Manc)]

TREGEAR FRANCIS BENEDICT WILLIAM

24 Old Bldgs
Ground Floor, Lincoln's Inn, London
WC2A 3UJ, Telephone: 0171 404 0946
E-mail: clerks@24oldbuildings.law.co.uk
Call date: July 1980, Middle Temple
Qualifications: [BA (Cantab)]

TREHARNE MISS JENNET MARY LLOYD

33 Park Place
Cardiff CF1 3BA, Telephone: 01222 233313
Hardwicke Building
New Square, Lincoln's Inn, London
WC2A 3SB, Telephone: 0171 242 2523
E-mail: clerks@hardwicke.co.uk
Door Tenant
Call date: July 1975, Middle Temple
Qualifications: [LLB (Lond)]

TREIP MICHAEL ANTHONY JOHN

Chambers of Joy Okoye
Suite 1, 2nd Floor Gray's Inn Chambers,
Gray's Inn, London WC1R 5JA,
Telephone: 0171 405 7011
Call date: Nov 1995, Inner Temple
Qualifications: [LLB (Lond), M.Phil (Cantab)]

TREMBATH GRAHAM ROBERT

5 Paper Bldgs
1st Floor, Temple, London EC4Y 7HB,
Telephone: 0171 583 6117
E-mail: clerks@5-paperbuildings.law.co.uk
Call date: July 1978, Middle Temple
Qualifications: [LLB (Soton)]

TREMBERG DAVID

Wilberforce Chambers
Bishop Lane, Hull HU1 1PA,
Telephone: 01482 323264
E-mail: clerks@hullbar.demon.co.uk
Call date: July 1985, Lincoln's Inn
Qualifications: [LLB (Hull) Dip de, Hautes Etudes, Europeenne]

TRENEER EDWARD MARK

Walnut House
63 St. David's Hill, Exeter, Devon EX4 4DW,
Telephone: 01392 279751
E-mail: 106627.2451@compuserve.com
Call date: July 1987, Inner Temple
Qualifications: [BA (Soton), Dip Law (City), MA (City)]

TREPTE PETER ARMIN

Littleton Chambers
3 King's Bench Walk North, Temple, London
EC4Y 7HR, Telephone: 0171 797 8600
E-mail: littletonchambers@compuserve.com
Call date: July 1987, Gray's Inn
Qualifications: [BA (Hons), Licence en Droit]

TRESMAN LEWIS ROBERT SIMON

Staple Inn Chambers
1st Floor 9 Staple Inn, Holborn, London
WC1V 7QH, Telephone: 0171 242 5240
E-mail: clerks@staple-inn.org
Call date: Nov 1980, Gray's Inn
Qualifications: [LLB (Hons) (Reading)]

TREVERTON-JONES GREGORY DENNIS

Farrar's Building
Temple, London EC4Y 7BD,
Telephone: 0171 583 9241
E-mail: chambers@farrarsbuilding.co.uk
Call date: Nov 1977, Inner Temple
Assistant Recorder
Qualifications: [MA (Oxon)]

D

TREVETHAN MISS SUSAN WENDY

3 Paper Bldgs
1st Floor, Temple, London EC4Y 7EU,
Telephone: 0171 583 8055
E-mail: london@3paper.com
20 Lorne Park Road
Bournemouth BH1 1JN,
Telephone: 01202 292102 (5 Lines)
4 St Peter Street
Winchester SO23 8OW,
Telephone: 01962 868884
Call date: Nov 1967, Middle Temple

TREVETT PETER GEORGE QC (1992)

11 New Square
1st Floor, Lincoln's Inn, London WC2A 3QB,
Telephone: 0171 242 4017/3981
E-mail: taxlaw@11newsquare.com
Call date: July 1971, Lincoln's Inn
Qualifications: [MA, LLM (Cantab)]

TREVIS ROBERT JAMES

Counsels' Chambers
2nd Floor 10-11 Gray's Inn Square, London
WC1R 5JD, Telephone: 0171 405 2576
Call date: Feb 1990, Inner Temple
Qualifications: [LLB]

TREVOR-JONES ROBERT DAVID

40 King Street
Chester CH1 2AH, Telephone: 01244 323886
Call date: July 1977, Gray's Inn
Qualifications: [LLB]

TRIGG MILES HADDON

9 King's Bench Walk
Ground Floor, Temple, London EC4Y 7DX,
Telephone: 0171 353 7202/3909
Call date: July 1987, Inner Temple
Qualifications: [LLB (Hons) (Lond)]

TRIMMER MS CAROL JANE

Wilberforce Chambers
Bishop Lane, Hull HU1 1PA,
Telephone: 01482 323264
E-mail: clerks@hullbar.demon.co.uk
Call date: Nov 1993, Gray's Inn
Qualifications: [LLB (Hull)]

TRIMMER STUART ALAN

6 Gray's Inn Square
Ground Floor, Gray's Inn, London WC1R 5AZ,
Telephone: 0171 242 1052
Call date: July 1977, Gray's Inn
Qualifications: [LLB (Lond)]

TRIPPIER LADY

Deans Court Chambers
Cumberland House Crown Square, Manchester
M3 3HA, Telephone: 0161 834 4097
E-mail: deanscourt@compuserve.com
Deans Court Chambers
41-43 Market Place, Preston PR1 1AH,
Telephone: 01772 555163
E-mail: deanscourt@compuserve.com
Call date: July 1978, Gray's Inn
Qualifications: [LLB (Manch)]

TRITTON ROBERT GUY HENTON

One Raymond Buildings
Gray's Inn, London WC1R 5BH,
Telephone: 0171 430 1234
E-mail: chambers@ipbar1rb.com;
clerks@ipbar1rb.com
Call date: July 1987, Inner Temple
Qualifications: [BSc (Dunelm), Dip Law]

TROLLOPE ANDREW DAVID HEDDERWICK QC (1991)

1 Middle Temple Lane
Temple, London EC4Y 1LT,
Telephone: 0171 583 0659 (12 Lines)
Westgate Chambers
144 High Street, Lewes, East Sussex BN7 1XT,
Telephone: 01273 480510
Call date: Nov 1971, Inner Temple
Recorder

TROTMAN PAUL EDWARD

Gower Chambers
57 Walter Road, Swansea, West Glamorgan
SA1 5PZ, Telephone: 01792 644466
E-mail: clerk@gowerchambers.co.uk
Call date: July 1988, Gray's Inn
Qualifications: [LLB (Cardiff)]

TROTMAN TIMOTHY OLIVER

Deans Court Chambers
Cumberland House Crown Square, Manchester
M3 3HA, Telephone: 0161 834 4097
E-mail: deanscourt@compuserve.com
Deans Court Chambers
41-43 Market Place, Preston PR1 1AH,
Telephone: 01772 555163
E-mail: deanscourt@compuserve.com
Call date: July 1983, Middle Temple
Qualifications: [MA (Cantab)]

TROTT RONALD JOHN

3 Hare Court
1st Floor, Temple, London EC4Y 7BJ,
Telephone: 0171 353 7561
Door Tenant
Call date: June 1956, Gray's Inn

TROTTER DAVID JOHN BURNELL

Plowden Bldgs
2nd Floor, Temple, London EC4Y 9BU,
Telephone: 0171 583 0808
E-mail: bar@plowdenbuildings.co.uk
Call date: July 1975, Inner Temple
Qualifications: [BA (Cantab), MA (Manch)]

TROUSDALE MALCOLM RAYMOND

Fountain Chambers
Cleveland Business Centre 1 Watson Street,
Middlesbrough TS1 2RQ,
Telephone: 01642 217037
Call date: Oct 1993, Middle Temple
Qualifications: [BA (Hons)(Newc), MA (Exon),
CPE (Lond)]

TROWELL STEPHEN MARK

1 Mitre Ct Bldgs
Ground Floor, Temple, London EC4Y 7BS,
Telephone: 0171 797 7070
Call date: Oct 1995, Middle Temple
Qualifications: [BA (Hons) (Oxon), D.Phil]

TROWER WILLIAM SPENCER PHILIP

3/4 South Square
Gray's Inn, London WC1R 5HP,
Telephone: 0171 696 9900
E-mail: clerks@southsquare.com
Call date: July 1983, Lincoln's Inn
Qualifications: [MA (Oxon)]

TROWLER MS REBECCA

4 Brick Court
Ground Floor, Temple, London EC4Y 9AD,
Telephone: 0171 797 7766
E-mail: chambers@4brick.co.uk
Call date: Oct 1995, Gray's Inn
Qualifications: [B.Sc]

TROY ALAN LAURENCE

Newport Chambers
12 Clytha Park Road, Newport, Gwent
NP9 47L, Telephone: 01633 267403/255855
Call date: Oct 1990, Gray's Inn
Qualifications: [LLB (Aberystwyth)]

TROY MRS JILL MARY

6 Park Square
Leeds LS1 2LW, Telephone: 0113 2459763
E-mail: chambers@no6.co.uk
Call date: July 1986, Middle Temple
Qualifications: [BA (Oxon)]

TROY-DAVIES MRS (CHRISTINE) KAREN

Essex Court Chambers
24 Lincoln's Inn Fields, London WC2A 3ED,
Telephone: 0171 813 8000
E-mail: clerksroom@essexcourt-chambers.co.uk
Call date: July 1981, Lincoln's Inn
Qualifications: [BA (Oxon), LLM (Virginia)]

TRUMPER MISS SARA KATHERINE

Holborn Chambers
6 Gate Street, Lincoln's Inn Fields, London
WC2A 3HP, Telephone: 0171 242 6060
Call date: Nov 1996, Lincoln's Inn
Qualifications: [BA (Hons)(Lond)]

TRUMPINGTON JOHN HENRY

Staple Inn Chambers
1st Floor 9 Staple Inn, Holborn, London
WC1V 7QH, Telephone: 0171 242 5240
E-mail: clerks@staple-inn.org
Call date: Feb 1985, Middle Temple
Qualifications: [BA (Hons)]

TRUSCOTT IAN DEREK

Old Square Chambers
1 Verulam Buildings, Gray's Inn, London
WC1R 5LQ, Telephone: 0171 831 0801
Old Square Chambers
Hanover House 47 Corn Street, Bristol
BS1 1HT, Telephone: 0117 9277111
Call date: Nov 1995, Gray's Inn
Qualifications: [LLB (Edinburgh), LLM (Leeds)]

TRUSSLER JONATHAN ANDREW

2 Middle Temple Lane
3rd Floor, Temple, London EC4Y 9AA,
Telephone: 0171 583 4540
Call date: Nov 1987, Gray's Inn
Qualifications: [LLB (Hons) (Wales), F.Inst BA]

TRUSTED JAMES HARRY

35 Essex Street
Temple, London WC2R 3AR,
Telephone: 0171 353 6381
Call date: July 1985, Inner Temple
Qualifications: [MA (Cantab)]

TRUSTMAN MRS JUDITH ANN

Watford Chambers
74 Mildred Avenue, Watford, Hertfordshire
WD1 7DX, Telephone: 01923 220553
Call date: Oct 1996, Middle Temple
Qualifications: [LLB (Hons)(Notts)]

TSE NICHOLAS HON KEUNG

29 Bedford Row Chambers
London WC1R 4HE,
Telephone: 0171 831 2626
Call date: Nov 1995, Inner Temple
Qualifications: [BA (Oxon), CPE, Maitre de
Lettres, (Sorbonne)]

TSELENTIS MICHAEL

20 Essex Street
London WC2R 3AL,
Telephone: 0171 583 9294
E-mail: clerks@20essexst.com
Call date: Nov 1995, Gray's Inn
Qualifications: [BA, LLB (Cape Town), BCL]

TUCKER ANDREW RICHARD SMETHURST

6 Fountain Court
Steelhouse Lane, Birmingham B4 6DR,
Telephone: 0121 233 3282
Call date: July 1977, Middle Temple
Qualifications: [LLB (Sheffield)]

TUCKER ASHLEY RUSSELL

Park Court Chambers
40 Park Cross Street, Leeds LS1 2QH,
Telephone: 0113 2433277
Call date: Nov 1990, Middle Temple
Qualifications: [BA (Manch), Dip Law (City)]

TUCKER DAVID WILLIAM

2 Crown Office Row
Ground Floor, Temple, London EC4Y 7HJ,
Telephone: 0171 797 8100
E-mail: mail@2cor.co.uk, or to individual
barristers at: [barrister's surname]@2cor.co.uk
Call date: Nov 1973, Middle Temple
Assistant Recorder
Qualifications: [MA (Oxon)]

TUCKER MISS KATHERINE JANE GREENING

7 Fountain Court
Steelhouse Lane, Birmingham B4 6DR,
Telephone: 0121 236 8531
Call date: Oct 1993, Lincoln's Inn
Qualifications: [LLB (Hons)(Leic)]

TUCKER LYNTON ANTHONY

12 New Square
Ground Floor, Lincoln's Inn, London
WC2A 3SW, Telephone: 0171 419 1212
E-mail: 12newsquare@compuserve.com
25 Park Square
Leeds LS1 2PW, Telephone: 0113 2451841/2/3
E-mail: sovereignchambers@btinternet.com
Door Tenant
Call date: Feb 1971, Lincoln's Inn
Qualifications: [MA, BCL (Oxon)]

TUCKER NICHOLAS JAMES

Lincoln House Chambers
5th Floor Lincoln House, 1 Brazennose Street,
Manchester M2 5EL,
Telephone: 0161 832 5701
E-mail: LincolnHouseChambers@link.org
Call date: Oct 1993, Inner Temple
Qualifications: [BA]

TUCKER PAUL GEOFFREY

40 King Street
Manchester M2 6BA,
Telephone: 0161 832 9082
E-mail: Kingst40@aol.com
Call date: Nov 1990, Gray's Inn
Qualifications: [MA (Cantab)]

TUCKER PETER LOUIS

Leone Chambers
72 Evelyn Avenue, Kingsbury, London
NW9 0JH, Telephone: 0181 931 1712
12 Old Square
1st Floor, Lincoln's Inn, London WC2A 3TX,
Telephone: 0171 404 0875
Call date: Nov 1970, Gray's Inn
Qualifications: [MA (Oxon), MA (Dunelm),
DCL, USL]

TUCKER TREVOR LAWTON

Iscoed Chambers
86 St Helen's Road, Swansea SA1 4BQ,
Telephone: 01792 652988/9/330
Call date: Feb 1971, Lincoln's Inn
Qualifications: [MA (Cantab)]

TUDOR-EVANS QUINTIN JOHN

199 Strand
London WC2R 1DR,
Telephone: 0171 379 9779
E-mail: chambers@199strand.co.uk
Call date: July 1977, Lincoln's Inn

TUGENDHAT MICHAEL GEORGE QC (1986)

5 Raymond Buildings
1st Floor, Gray's Inn, London WC1R 5BP,
Telephone: 0171 242 2902
Call date: July 1969, Inner Temple
Recorder
Qualifications: [MA (Cantab)]

TUGHAN JOHN CHARLES RONALD

9 Gough Square
London EC4A 3DE, Telephone: 0171 353 5371
Call date: Nov 1991, Inner Temple
Qualifications: [LLB (L'pool)]

TULLY MS ANNE MARGARET

Eastbourne Chambers
15 Hyde Gardens, Eastbourne, East Sussex
BN21 4PR, Telephone: 01323 642102/416466
Call date: July 1989, Gray's Inn
Qualifications: [MA (Cantab), LLM (Cantab)]

TULLY RAYMOND PETER

All Saints Chambers
9/11 Broad Street, Bristol BS1 2HP,
Telephone: 0117 921 1966
Call date: Nov 1987, Inner Temple
Qualifications: [BA (Keele), Dip Law, (City)]

TUNKEL ALAN MICHAEL

3 Stone Bldgs
Ground Floor, Lincoln's Inn, London
WC2A 3XL, Telephone: 0171 242 4937/
405 8358
Call date: July 1976, Middle Temple
Qualifications: [BA (Oxon)]

TURAY MISS FATMATA

12 Old Square
1st Floor, Lincoln's Inn, London WC2A 3TX,
Telephone: 0171 404 0875
Call date: July 1994, Gray's Inn
Qualifications: [LLB]

TURCAN HENRY WATSON

4 Paper Bldgs
2nd Floor, Temple, London EC4Y 7EX,
Telephone: 0171 583 0816/071 353 1131
E-mail: clerks@4paperbuildings.co.uk
Call date: July 1965, Inner Temple
Recorder
Qualifications: [MA (Oxon)]

D

D

TURNBULL CHARLES EMERSON LOVETT

Wilberforce Chambers
8 New Square, Lincoln's Inn, London
WC2A 3QP, Telephone: 0171 306 0102
E-mail: chambers@wilberforce.co.uk
Call date: July 1975, Inner Temple
Qualifications: [BA (Oxon)]

TURNER ADRIAN JOHN

Eastbourne Chambers
15 Hyde Gardens, Eastbourne, East Sussex
BN21 4PR, Telephone: 01323 642102/416466
Call date: Feb 1978, Gray's Inn

TURNER ALAN JOSEPH

46/48 Essex Street
London WC2R 3GH,
Telephone: 0171 583 8899
Call date: Nov 1984, Gray's Inn
Qualifications: [LLB, BSc, MSc(Wales)]

TURNER AMEDEE EDWARD QC (1976)

One Raymond Buildings
Gray's Inn, London WC1R 5BH,
Telephone: 0171 430 1234
E-mail: chambers@ipbar1rb.com;
clerks@ipbar1rb.com
Door Tenant
Call date: Nov 1954, Inner Temple
Qualifications: [MA (Oxon)]

TURNER DAVID ANDREW QC (1991)

Exchange Chambers
Pearl Assurance House Derby Square,
Liverpool L2 9XX, Telephone: 0151 236 7747/
0458
E-mail: exchangechambers@btinternet.com
Door Tenant
Call date: Feb 1971, Gray's Inn
Recorder
Qualifications: [MA, LLM (Cantab)]

TURNER DAVID BENJAMIN

2 Temple Gardens
Temple, London EC4Y 9AY,
Telephone: 0171 583 6041 (12 Lines)
Call date: Nov 1992, Gray's Inn
Qualifications: [BA (Cantab)]

TURNER DAVID GEORGE PATRICK

14 Gray's Inn Square
Gray's Inn, London WC1R 5JP,
Telephone: 0171 242 0858
E-mail: 100712.2134@compuserve.com
Call date: Nov 1976, Gray's Inn
Assistant Recorder
Qualifications: [LLB, (Lond), AKC]

TURNER JAMES

1 King's Bench Walk
2nd Floor, Temple, London EC4Y 7DB,
Telephone: 0171 936 1500
E-mail: ddear@1kbw.co.uk
Call date: July 1976, Inner Temple
Qualifications: [LLB Hons (Hull)]

TURNER JAMES MICHAEL

4 Essex Court
Temple, London EC4Y 9AJ,
Telephone: 0171 797 7970
E-mail: clerks@4essexcourt.law.co.uk
Call date: Oct 1990, Inner Temple
Qualifications: [BA (Dunelm), LLM(Tubingen),
M.I.L.]

TURNER MISS JANET MARY QC (1996)

3 Verulam Buildings
London WC1R 5NT,
Telephone: 0171 831 8441
E-mail: clerks@3verulam.co.uk
Call date: Nov 1979, Middle Temple
Qualifications: [LLB (Bris)]

TURNER JONATHAN CHADWICK

6 King's Bench Walk
Ground Floor, Temple, London EC4Y 7DR,
Telephone: 0171 583 0410
Call date: July 1974, Gray's Inn
Assistant Recorder

TURNER JONATHAN DAVID CHATTYN

4 Field Court
Gray's Inn, London WC1R 5EA,
Telephone: 0171 440 6900
E-mail: chambers@4fieldcourt.co.uk
Call date: Feb 1982, Gray's Inn

Qualifications: [MA (Cantab), Lic Sp, Dr Eur (Brussels)]

Fax: 0171 242 0197; DX: LDE 483;
Other comms: Mobile 0467 428129; E-Mail jonathan_dc_turner@link.org

Types of work: EC and competition law; Information technology; Intellectual property

Awards and memberships: Member of Intellectual Property Bar Association; Associate of the Chartered Institute of Patent Agents; Fellow of the Chartered Institute of Arbitrators

Other professional experience: Head of IP and IT Law at Coopers & Lybrand (1995-7)

Languages spoken: French

Publications: *Vaughan's Law of the European Communities*, 1986-97; *Halsbury's Laws of England - EC Competition Law*, 1985; *EU Rules on the Exploitation of Intellectual Property*, 1998; *Countdown to 2000 - A Guide to the Legal Issues*, 1998; *European Patent Office Reports*, 1986-95

Reported cases: *PLG Research v Ardon*, [1995] RPC 287, 1990-4. A major patent infringement case - scope of claims under the European Patent Convention, prior use and obviousness.
Reckitt and Colman v Borden, [1990] RPC 341, 1985-9. The Jif Lemon case - passing off in relation to visual branding.
C&H v Klucznik, [1992] FSR 421, 1991. Leading case on design right.
Potton v York Close, [1990] FSR 11, 1989. Copyright in plans of houses - account of builder's profits.
British Sky Broadcasting v Lyons, [1995] FSR 357, 1994. Rights in television signals - EC law.

TURNER JONATHAN RICHARD

Monckton Chambers
4 Raymond Buildings, Gray's Inn, London WC1R 5BP, Telephone: 0171 405 7211
E-mail: chambers@monckton.co.uk
Call date: Nov 1988, Middle Temple
Qualifications: [BA (Cantab), LLM (Harvard)]

TURNER JUSTIN JOHN

3 New Square
Lincoln's Inn, London WC2A 3RS,
Telephone: 0171 405 1111
Call date: Nov 1992, Middle Temple

Qualifications: [Vet.Med (Lond), Ph.D (Cantab), AFRC, Dip in Law]

TURNER MARK GEORGE

Deans Court Chambers
Cumberland House Crown Square, Manchester M3 3HA, Telephone: 0161 834 4097
E-mail: deanscourt@compuserve.com
Deans Court Chambers
41-43 Market Place, Preston PR1 1AH,
Telephone: 01772 555163
E-mail: deanscourt@compuserve.com
Call date: July 1981, Gray's Inn
Assistant Recorder
Qualifications: [BA (Oxon)]

TURNER MICHAEL

Cloisters
1st Floor, Temple, London EC4Y 7AA,
Telephone: 0171 827 4000
E-mail: clerks@cloisters.com
Call date: July 1981, Gray's Inn
Qualifications: [BA (Hons)]

TURNER ROGER BURTON

Mitre Court Chambers
3rd Floor, Temple, London EC4Y 7BP,
Telephone: 0171 353 9394
Call date: Nov 1982, Gray's Inn
Qualifications: [MA (Kent) BD MTh, (Lond)]

TURNER STEVEN MURRAY

Park Lane Chambers
19 Westgate, Leeds LS1 2RD,
Telephone: 0113 2285000
Call date: Nov 1993, Middle Temple
Qualifications: [LLB (Hons)(Kent), CPE (Notts)]

TURNER MRS TARYN JONES

Park Court Chambers
40 Park Cross Street, Leeds LS1 2QH,
Telephone: 0113 2433277
Call date: Feb 1990, Gray's Inn
Qualifications: [LLB (Hons)]

D

TURRALL-CLARKE ROBERT TURRALL FACER

Bond Street Chambers
Standbrook House 2-5 Old Bond Street,
Mayfair, London W1X 3TB,
Telephone: 01932 342951
Crayshott House
Woodlands Road, West Byfleet, Surrey
KT14 6JW, Telephone: 01932 342951
Call date: July 1971, Middle Temple
Qualifications: [MA (Oxon), AInst Arb]

TURTLE ALISTER MARK

Wessex Chambers
48 Queens Road, Reading, Berkshire
RG1 4BD, Telephone: 01734 568856
E-mail: wessexchambers@compuserve.com
Door Tenant
Call date: Nov 1994, Inner Temple
Qualifications: [LLB (Bris)]

TURTON ANDREW PHILIP

1 Crown Office Row
2nd Floor, Temple, London EC4Y 7HH,
Telephone: 0171 797 7111
Call date: July 1977, Middle Temple
Qualifications: [LLB (Lond), AKC]

TURTON PHILIP JOHN

24 The Ropewalk
Nottingham NG1 5EF,
Telephone: 0115 9472581
E-mail: clerk@ropewalk.co.uk
Call date: Nov 1989, Gray's Inn
Qualifications: [LLB (Wales)]

TWANA EKWALL SINGH

New Court Chambers
Suite 200 Gazette Building, 168 Corporation
Street, Birmingham B4 6TZ,
Telephone: 0121 693 6656
Call date: Nov 1988, Middle Temple
Qualifications: [LLB(Hons)]

TWIGG PATRICK ALAN QC (1986)

2 Temple Gardens
Temple, London EC4Y 9AY,
Telephone: 0171 583 6041 (12 Lines)
Call date: July 1967, Inner Temple
Recorder
Qualifications: [LLB (Bristol) LLM, (Virginia)]

TWIGGER ANDREW MARK

3 Stone Bldgs
Ground Floor, Lincoln's Inn, London
WC2A 3XL, Telephone: 0171 242 4937/
405 8358
Call date: Nov 1994, Inner Temple
Qualifications: [BA (Oxon), CPE (City)]

TWIST STEPHEN JOHN

York Chambers
14 Toft Green, York YO1 1JT,
Telephone: 01904 620048
E-mail: yorkchambers.co.uk
Call date: July 1979, Middle Temple
Qualifications: [LLB (L'pool), CACDPI]

TWOMEY MARK JAMES JOHN

Bell Yard Chambers
116/118 Chancery Lane, London WC2A 1PP,
Telephone: 0171 306 9292
Call date: Nov 1990, Inner Temple
Qualifications: [LLB (Bris)]

TWOMLOW RICHARD WILLIAM

9 Park Place
Cardiff CF1 3DP, Telephone: 01222 382731
Call date: July 1976, Gray's Inn
Assistant Recorder
Qualifications: [BA (Cantab)]

TYACK DAVID GUY

7 Fountain Court
Steelhouse Lane, Birmingham B4 6DR,
Telephone: 0121 236 8531
Call date: Nov 1994, Middle Temple
Qualifications: [BA (Hons)]

TYRELL GLEN

2 Crown Office Row
2nd Floor, Temple, London EC4Y 7HJ,
Telephone: 0171 797 8000
Call date: July 1977, Inner Temple
Qualifications: [LLB]

TYRRELL ALAN RUPERT QC (1976)

Francis Taylor Bldg
3rd Floor, Temple, London EC4Y 7BY,
Telephone: 0171 797 7250
Call date: Feb 1956, Gray's Inn
Qualifications: [LLB (Lond)]

TYRRELL RICHARD MARK LAWRENCE

28 St John Street
Manchester M3 4DJ,
Telephone: 0161 834 8418
E-mail: clerk@28stjohnst.co.uk
Call date: Nov 1993, Gray's Inn
Qualifications: [LLB (Sheff)]

TYSON RICHARD THEODORE

3 Paper Bldgs
1st Floor, Temple, London EC4Y 7EU,
Telephone: 0171 583 8055
E-mail: london@3paper.com
20 Lorne Park Road
Bournemouth BH1 1JN,
Telephone: 01202 292102 (5 Lines)
4 St Peter Street
Winchester SO23 8OW,
Telephone: 01962 868884
Call date: Nov 1975, Inner Temple
Assistant Recorder
Qualifications: [BA (Exon)]

TYSON THOMAS DAVID

2 Field Court
Gray's Inn, London WC1R 5BB,
Telephone: 0171 405 6114
E-mail: fieldct2@netcomuk.co.uk.
Call date: Oct 1995, Gray's Inn
Qualifications: [LLB (Bris)]

TYTHCOTT MISS ELISABETH CLAIRE

18 St John Street
Manchester M3 4EA,
Telephone: 0161 278 1800
Call date: Nov 1989, Inner Temple
Qualifications: [LLB]

TYZACK DAVID IAN HESLOP

Southernhay Chambers
33 Southernhay East, Exeter EX1 1NX,
Telephone: 01392 255777
E-mail: southernhay.chambers@lineone.net
1 Mitre Ct Bldgs
Ground Floor, Temple, London EC4Y 7BS,
Telephone: 0171 797 7070
Door Tenant
Call date: July 1970, Inner Temple
Assistant Recorder
Qualifications: [MA (Cantab)]

UDUJE BENJAMIN ELLIOTT

Somersett Chambers
52 Bedford Row, London WC1R 4LR,
Telephone: 0171 404 6701
E-mail: Somersettchambers@cocoon.co.uk
Call date: Nov 1992, Middle Temple
Qualifications: [LLB (Hons)]

UFF DAVID CHARLES

Cobden House Chambers
19 Quay Street, Manchester M3 3HN,
Telephone: 0161 833 6000
E-mail: clerks@cobden.co.uk
Call date: July 1981, Gray's Inn
Qualifications: [LLB (Hons)]

UFF JOHN FRANCIS QC (1983)

Keating Chambers
10 Essex Street, Outer Temple, London
WC2R 3AA, Telephone: 0171 544 2600
Call date: July 1970, Gray's Inn
Assistant Recorder
Qualifications: [PhD, BScEng, F.Eng, FCIArb]

ULLAH MOHAMMED HASH MOT

72 Brick Lane
1st Floor, London E1 6RL,
Telephone: 0171 377 0119
Call date: Apr 1989, Middle Temple
Qualifications: [LLB (Bangladesh)]

ULLSTEIN AUGUSTUS RUPERT PATRICK A QC (1992)

29 Bedford Row Chambers
London WC1R 4HE,
Telephone: 0171 831 2626
Call date: July 1970, Inner Temple
Assistant Recorder
Qualifications: [LLB (Lond)]

UME CYRIL OBIORA

12 Old Square
1st Floor, Lincoln's Inn, London WC2A 3TX,
Telephone: 0171 404 0875
Call date: July 1972, Gray's Inn
Qualifications: [LLB (Lond), ACIArb]

UMEZURUIKE CHIMA NNADOZIE

Trafalgar Chambers
53 Fleet Street, London EC4Y 1BE,
Telephone: 0171 583 5858
E-mail: TrafalgarChambers@easynet.co.uk
Call date: July 1991, Inner Temple
Qualifications: [LLB (Nigeria), LLM (Lond)]

UNDERHILL NICHOLAS EDWARD QC (1992)

Fountain Court
Temple, London EC4Y 9DH,
Telephone: 0171 583 3335
E-mail: chambers@fountaincourt.co.uk
Call date: July 1976, Gray's Inn
Recorder
Qualifications: [MA (Oxon)]

UNDERWOOD ASHLEY GRENVILLE

2 Field Court
Gray's Inn, London WC1R 5BB,
Telephone: 0171 405 6114
E-mail: fieldct2@netcomuk.co.uk.
Call date: July 1976, Gray's Inn
Qualifications: [LLB Hons (Lond)]

UNDERWOOD ROBERT ANTHONY

36 Bedford Row
London WC1R 4JH,
Telephone: 0171 421 8000
E-mail: 36bedfordrow@link.org
Call date: July 1986, Lincoln's Inn
Qualifications: [BA]

UNSWORTH IAN STEPHEN

38 Young Street
Manchester M3 3FT,
Telephone: 0161 833 0489
E-mail: clerks@young-st-chambers.com
Call date: Oct 1992, Lincoln's Inn
Qualifications: [LLB(Hons)]

UNWIN DAVID CHARLES QC (1995)

7 Stone Bldgs
Ground Floor, Lincoln's Inn, London
WC2A 3SZ, Telephone: 0171 405 3886/
242 3546
E-mail: chaldous@vossnet.co.uk
Call date: Nov 1971, Middle Temple
Qualifications: [BA (Oxon)]

UPEX PROFESSOR ROBERT VAUGHAN

29 Bedford Row Chambers
London WC1R 4HE,
Telephone: 0171 831 2626
Call date: July 1973, Middle Temple
Qualifications: [MA, LLM (Cantab)]

UPPAL MISS BALJINDER KAUR

College Chambers
19 Carlton Cresent, Southampton, Hants
SO15 2ET, Telephone: 01703 230338
Call date: Oct 1996, Lincoln's Inn
Qualifications: [LLB (Hons)(Warw)]

UPSON MICHAEL JAMES

Bank House Chambers
Old Bank House, Hartshead, Sheffield S1 2EL,
Telephone: 0114 2751223
Call date: Oct 1993, Lincoln's Inn
Qualifications: [LLB (Hons)]

UPTON JAMES WILLIAM DAVID

1 Serjeants' Inn
4th Floor, Temple, London EC4Y 1NH,
Telephone: 0171 583 1355
E-mail: serjeants.inn@virgin.net
Call date: Nov 1990, Inner Temple
Qualifications: [MA (Cantab), LLM (Cantab)]

UPWARD PATRICK CHARLES QC (1996)

9 Gough Square
London EC4A 3DE, Telephone: 0171 353 5371
Call date: July 1972, Inner Temple
Assistant Recorder
Qualifications: [LLB (Lond)]

URQUHART ANDREW ROBERT HILDYARD

36 Bedford Row
London WC1R 4JH,
Telephone: 0171 421 8000
E-mail: 36bedfordrow@link.org
Call date: Nov 1963, Middle Temple
Qualifications: [BA (Oxon)]

URQUHART MRS DORIS

10 King's Bench Walk
Ground Floor, Temple, London EC4Y 7EB,
Telephone: 0171 353 7742
E-mail: 10kbw@lineone.net
Call date: July 1967, Middle Temple
Qualifications: [BA (Michigan)]

USHER NEIL MORRIS

Kenworthy's Buildings
83 Bridge Street, Manchester M3 2RF,
Telephone: 0161 832 4036/834 6954
Call date: Oct 1993, Middle Temple
Qualifications: [BA (Hons)(Hull), CPE (City)]

UTLEY CHARLES EDWARD

22 Old Bldgs
Lincoln's Inn, London WC2A 3UJ,
Telephone: 0171 831 0222
Call date: Nov 1979, Middle Temple

VAGG HOWARD VICTOR

6 King's Bench Walk
Ground Floor, Temple, London EC4Y 7DR,
Telephone: 0171 583 0410
Call date: July 1974, Inner Temple
Assistant Recorder
Qualifications: [LL.B Hons (Bristol)]

VAIN RICHARD PETER

3 Dr Johnson's Bldgs
Ground Floor, Temple, London EC4Y 7BA,
Telephone: 0171 353 4854
Call date: Nov 1970, Middle Temple
Qualifications: [MA (Cantab)]

VAJDA CHRISTOPHER STEPHEN QC (1997)

Monckton Chambers
4 Raymond Buildings, Gray's Inn, London
WC1R 5BP, Telephone: 0171 405 7211
E-mail: chambers@monckton.co.uk
Call date: July 1979, Gray's Inn
Qualifications: [MA]

VAKIL JIMMY

Staple Inn Chambers
1st Floor 9 Staple Inn, Holborn, London
WC1V 7QH, Telephone: 0171 242 5240
E-mail: clerks@staple-inn.org
Call date: May 1993, Middle Temple
Qualifications: [LLB (Hons)(Lond)]

VALDER PAUL

1 Harcourt Bldgs
2nd Floor, Temple, London EC4Y 9DA,
Telephone: 0171 353 9421/9151
Call date: Nov 1994, Inner Temple
Qualifications: [BA (B'ham), CPE (City)]

VALENTIN BEN MATTHEW

3/4 South Square
Gray's Inn, London WC1R 5HP,
Telephone: 0171 696 9900
E-mail: clerks@southsquare.com
Call date: Nov 1995, Inner Temple
Qualifications: [BA, BCL (Oxon), LLM (Cornell)]

VALENTINE DONALD GRAHAM

1 Atkin Building
Gray's Inn, London WC1R 5AT,
Telephone: 0171 404 0102
E-mail: clerks@atkin-chambers.co.uk
Call date: June 1956, Lincoln's Inn
Qualifications: [MA, LLB (Cantab), Dr Jur (Utrecht)]

VALIOS NICHOLAS PAUL QC (1991)

Francis Taylor Bldg
Ground Floor, Temple, London EC4Y 7BY,
Telephone: 0171 353 7768/7769/2711
Call date: June 1964, Inner Temple
Recorder

VALKS MICHAEL

King's Chambers
5a Gildredge Road, Eastbourne, East Sussex
BN21 4RB, Telephone: 01323 416053
Call date: Oct 1994, Gray's Inn
Qualifications: [LLB (Hons)(Bucks)]

D

VALLACK MISS JULIE ANN

Gower Chambers
57 Walter Road, Swansea, West Glamorgan
SA1 5PZ, Telephone: 01792 644466
E-mail: clerk@gowerchambers.co.uk
Call date: Oct 1993, Gray's Inn
Qualifications: [BA (Bath),LLB (Lond)]

VALLANCE PHILIP IAN FERGUS QC (1989)

1 Crown Office Row
Ground Floor, Temple, London EC4Y 7HH,
Telephone: 0171 797 7500
Call date: July 1968, Inner Temple
Qualifications: [BA (Oxon)]

VALLEY MISS HELEN MARIA

3 Gray's Inn Square
Ground Floor, London WC1R 5AH,
Telephone: 0171 520 5600
E-mail: gis3@btinternet.com
Call date: Oct 1990, Middle Temple
Qualifications: [BA, Dip Law (Lond)]

VALLI YUNUS

6 Park Square
Leeds LS1 2LW, Telephone: 0113 2459763
E-mail: chambers@no6.co.uk
Call date: Nov 1994, Lincoln's Inn
Qualifications: [LLB (Hons)(Leeds)]

VAN BESOUW EUFRON

Chartlands Chambers
3 St Giles Terrace, Northampton NN1 2BN,
Telephone: 01604 603322
Call date: Nov 1988, Middle Temple
Qualifications: [LLB]

VAN BUEREN MS GERALDINE LEA

Doughty Street Chambers
11 Doughty Street, London WC1N 2PG,
Telephone: 0171 404 1313
E-mail: doughty_street@compuserve.com
Door Tenant
Call date: Nov 1979, Middle Temple
Qualifications: [LLB (Hons) (Wales), LLM (Lond)]

VAN DEN BERG BARRIE PATRICK

Godolphin Chambers
50 Castle Street, Truro, Cornwall TR1 3AF,
Telephone: 01872 276312
Call date: July 1978, Middle Temple
Qualifications: [BA]

VAN DER BIJL NIGEL CHARLES

1 Harcourt Bldgs
2nd Floor, Temple, London EC4Y 9DA,
Telephone: 0171 353 9421/9151
Call date: July 1973, Inner Temple
Recorder
Qualifications: [BA, LLB]

VAN DER ZWART MARK ANDREW

King Charles House
Standard Hill, Nottingham NG1 6FX,
Telephone: 0115 9418851
E-mail: clerks@kch.co.uk
Call date: Feb 1988, Middle Temple
Qualifications: [BA (Hons) (Essex)]

VAN HAGEN CHRISTOPHER SEYMOUR NIGEL

4 King's Bench Walk
Ground/First Floor, Temple, London
EC4Y 7DL, Telephone: 0171 822 8822
E-mail: 4kbw@barristersatlaw.com
King's Bench Chambers
Wellington House 175 Holdenhurst Road,
Bournemouth, Dorset BH8 8DQ,
Telephone: 01202 250025
Call date: Nov 1980, Middle Temple
Qualifications: [BA]

VAN STONE GRANT FREDERICK

6 Gray's Inn Square
Ground Floor, Gray's Inn, London WC1R 5AZ,
Telephone: 0171 242 1052
Call date: Nov 1988, Middle Temple
Qualifications: [LLB (Hons)]

VAN TONDER GERARD DIRK

Lamb Chambers
Lamb Building, Temple, London EC4Y 7AS,
Telephone: 0171 797 8300
E-mail: lambchambers@link.org
Call date: Nov 1990, Middle Temple
Qualifications: [BA, LLB (Witwatersrand)]

D

VANDYCK WILLIAM GEORGE

1 Paper Bldgs
Ground Floor, Temple, London EC4Y 7EP,
Telephone: 0171 583 7355
E-mail: clerks@1pb.co.uk
Call date: July 1988, Lincoln's Inn
Qualifications: [BA (Hons) (Cantab)]

VANE THE HON CHRISTOPHER JOHN FLETCHER

Trinity Chambers
9-12 Trinity Chare, Quayside, Newcastle Upon
Tyne NE1 3DF, Telephone: 0191 232 1927
Call date: Nov 1976, Inner Temple
Qualifications: [MA (Cantab)]

VANHEGAN MARK JAMES

11 South Square
2nd Floor, Gray's Inn, London WC1R 5EU,
Telephone: 0171 405 1222
Call date: Nov 1990, Lincoln's Inn
Qualifications: [MA (Cantab)]

VARDON RICHARD STANHOPE

18 St John Street
Manchester M3 4EA,
Telephone: 0161 278 1800
Call date: Nov 1985, Gray's Inn
Qualifications: [LLB (B'ham)]

VARTY MISS LOUISE JANE

9 Bedford Row
London WC1R 4AZ,
Telephone: 0171 242 3555
E-mail: clerks@9br.co.uk
Call date: Nov 1986, Middle Temple
Qualifications: [LLB (Birmingham)]

VASS HUGH PATRICK

East Anglian Chambers
Gresham House 5 Museum Street, Ipswich
IP1 1HQ, Telephone: 01473 214481
East Anglian Chambers
57 London Street, Norwich NR2 1HL,
Telephone: 01603 617351
East Anglian Chambers
Sanders House 52 North Hill, Colchester
CO1 1PY, Telephone: 01206 572756
Call date: Nov 1983, Gray's Inn
Qualifications: [BA]

VATER JOHN ALISTAIR PITT

2 Harcourt Bldgs
1st Floor, Temple, London EC4Y 9DB,
Telephone: 0171 353 6961/7
Call date: Feb 1995, Gray's Inn
Qualifications: [BA (Oxon)]

VAUGHAN DAVID ARTHUR JOHN QC (1981)

Brick Court Chambers
15/19 Devereux Court, London WC2R 3JJ,
Telephone: 0171 583 0777
E-mail: (surname)@brickcourt.demon.co.uk
Call date: Nov 1963, Inner Temple
Recorder
Qualifications: [MA (Cantab)]

VAUGHAN KEITH VICTOR

8 Fountain Court
Steelhouse Lane, Birmingham B4 6DR,
Telephone: 0121 236 5514/5
E-mail: clerks@no8chambers.co.uk
Call date: July 1968, Gray's Inn
Qualifications: [LLB (B'ham)]

VAUGHAN KIERAN PATRICK

Francis Taylor Bldg
Ground Floor, Temple, London EC4Y 7BY,
Telephone: 0171 353 7768/7769/2711
Call date: Nov 1993, Middle Temple
Qualifications: [LLB (Hons)]

VAUGHAN SIMON PETER

Manchester House Chambers
18-22 Bridge Street, Manchester M3 3BZ,
Telephone: 0161 834 7007
Call date: Nov 1989, Gray's Inn
Qualifications: [LLB,LLM (Lond)]

VAUGHAN TERENCE PAUL

Watford Chambers
74 Mildred Avenue, Watford, Hertfordshire
WD1 7DX, Telephone: 01923 220553
Call date: Oct 1996, Middle Temple
Qualifications: [BSc (Salford), CPE (B'Ham)]

VAUGHAN-JONES MISS SARAH JANE

2 Temple Gardens
Temple, London EC4Y 9AY,
Telephone: 0171 583 6041 (12 Lines)
Call date: Nov 1983, Middle Temple
Qualifications: [MA (Cantab)]

VAUGHAN-NEIL MISS CATHERINE MARY BERNARDINE

5 Bell Yard
London WC2A 2JR, Telephone: 0171 333 8811
Call date: Oct 1994, Inner Temple
Qualifications: [BA (Oxon), LLM (Cantab)]

VAUGHAN-WILLIAMS ARTHUR LAURENCE

Southsea Chambers
PO Box 148, Southsea, Portsmouth,
Hampshire PO5 2TU,
Telephone: 01705 291261
Call date: Nov 1988, Lincoln's Inn
Qualifications: [LLB (Bucks)]

VAVRECKA DAVID PAUL FRANK

14 Gray's Inn Square
Gray's Inn, London WC1R 5JP,
Telephone: 0171 242 0858
E-mail: 100712.2134@compuserve.com
Call date: Oct 1992, Middle Temple
Qualifications: [LLB (Lond), LLM]

VEATS MISS ELIZABETH CLEA

2 Garden Court
1st Floor, Middle Temple, London EC4Y 9BL,
Telephone: 0171 353 1633
E-mail: barristers@2gardenct.law.co.uk
Call date: July 1986, Middle Temple
Qualifications: [LLB (B'ham), LLM]

VEEDER VAN VECHTEN QC (1986)

Essex Court Chambers
24 Lincoln's Inn Fields, London WC2A 3ED,
Telephone: 0171 813 8000
E-mail: clerksroom@essexcourt-chambers.co.uk
Call date: Nov 1971, Inner Temple
Assistant Recorder
Qualifications: [MA (Cantab)]

VENABLES ROBERT QC (1990)

24 Old Bldgs
First Floor, Lincoln's Inn, London WC2A 3UJ,
Telephone: 0171 242 2744
Call date: July 1973, Middle Temple
Qualifications: [MA (Oxon), LLM, FTII]

VENMORE JOHN

30 Park Place
Cardiff CF1 3BA, Telephone: 01222 398421
E-mail: 100757.1456@compuserve.com
Call date: Nov 1971, Lincoln's Inn

VENTHAM ANTHONY MICHAEL

1 Crown Office Row
2nd Floor, Temple, London EC4Y 7HH,
Telephone: 0171 797 7111
Call date: Apr 1991, Middle Temple
Qualifications: [B.Sc (Hons)]

VERDAN ALEXANDER

9 Gough Square
London EC4A 3DE, Telephone: 0171 353 5371
Call date: Nov 1987, Inner Temple
Qualifications: [BA, Dip Law]

VERDUYN DR ANTHONY JAMES

Priory Chambers
2 Fountain Court, Steelhouse Lane,
Birmingham B4 6DR,
Telephone: 0121 236 3882/1375
Call date: Oct 1993, Lincoln's Inn
Qualifications: [BA (Hons)(Dunelm), D.Phil (Oxon), Dip Law (City)]

VERE-HODGE MICHAEL JOHN DAVY QC (1993)

2 King's Bench Walk
Ground Floor, Temple, London EC4Y 7DE,
Telephone: 0171 353 1746
E-mail: 2kbw@atlas.co.uk
Assize Court Chambers
14 Small Street, Bristol BS1 1DE,
Telephone: 0117 9264587
Door Tenant
King's Bench Chambers
115 North Hill, Plymouth PL4 8JY,
Telephone: 01752 221551
Call date: Nov 1970, Gray's Inn
Recorder

VICKERS EDMUND BENEDICT BLYTH

3 Temple Gardens
2nd Floor, Temple, London EC4Y 9AU,
Telephone: 0171 583 1155
Call date: Nov 1993, Middle Temple
Qualifications: [BA (Hons)(Dunelm), CPE
(City)]

VICKERS GUY JULIAN COURTNEY

28 St John Street
Manchester M3 4DJ,
Telephone: 0161 834 8418
E-mail: clerk@28stjohnst.co.uk
Call date: Nov 1986, Middle Temple
Qualifications: [BA (Oxon)]

VICKERS MISS RACHEL CLARE

199 Strand
London WC2R 1DR,
Telephone: 0171 379 9779
E-mail: chambers@199strand.co.uk
Call date: Oct 1992, Lincoln's Inn
Qualifications: [LLB(Hons)(Bris)]

VICKERY NEIL MICHAEL

13 King's Bench Walk
1st Floor, Temple, London EC4Y 7EN,
Telephone: 0171 353 7204
E-mail: clerks@13kbw.law.co.uk
King's Bench Chambers
32 Beaumont Street, Oxford OX1 2NP,
Telephone: 01865 311066
E-mail: clerks@kbc-oxford.law.co.uk
Call date: July 1985, Gray's Inn
Qualifications: [BA (Cantab)]

VIDAL MS MAVELYN KATHLEEN

Northeastern Law Chambers
The Chocolate Factory B305 Clarendon Road /
Western Road, Wood Green, London
N22 6UN, Telephone: 0181 881 3890
Call date: Nov 1986, Inner Temple
Qualifications: [LLB]

VIGARS MRS ANNA LILIAN

Guildhall Chambers
23 Broad Street, Bristol BS1 2HG,
Telephone: 0117 9273366
Call date: Nov 1996, Gray's Inn
Qualifications: [BA (Oxon)]

VILLAGE PETER MALCOLM

4-5 Gray's Inn Square
Ground Floor, Gray's Inn, London WC1R 5AY,
Telephone: 0171 404 5252
E-mail: chambers@4-5graysinnsquare.co.uk
Call date: July 1983, Inner Temple
Qualifications: [LLB (Leeds)]

Fax: 0171 242 7803;
Out of hours telephone: 038 5503 038;
DX: 1029 London

Types of work: Administrative; Arbitration;
Environment; Local government; Parliamentary;
Planning; Town and country planning

Membership of foreign bars: Bar of Northern
Ireland 1997

Reported cases: *R v LDDC and CWI Holdings
Ltd ex parte Sister Frost*, [1997] 73 P&CR 199,
1997. Judicial review - variation of a time limit
condition - renewal of planning permission -
correct approach.
Jones v Secretary of State for Wales, [1995] 2
PLR 26, 1995. Inquiry - allegation of bias and
breach of rules of natural justice - establishing
that planning inspector can be cross-examined.
R v Thurrock BC ex parte Tesco Stores Ltd,
[1993] 2 PLR 114, 1993. Challenge to grant of
planning permission for a warehouse club -
whether within Class A1of Use Classes Order.
*R v Secretary of State for the Environment ex
parte Bolton MBC*, [1990] 61 P&CR 343, 1990.
Compulsory purchase - whether failure to take
into account relevant considerations - statement
of principles.
*R v Secretary of State for the Environment ex
parte Rose Theatre Trust Co*, [1990] 1 QB 504,
1989. Judicial review - *locus standi*.

Practice
Specialises in all aspects of planning litigation
and advice particularly inquiries, challenges to
the grant of planning permission and challenges
to the adoption of Local Plans.
Retail: he has undertaken many retail foodstore
inquiries for promotors and objectors, and has
appeared in a number of notable retail cases, eg
*Tesco Stores Ltd v North Norfolk District
Council* - relating to the alleged implementation
of a foodstore permission, as well as the Costco
litigation.
Housing: he appears regularly at s 78 and Local
Plan inquiries for the county's largest volume
housebuilder (Wimpey) and acts for other
housebuilders (large and small) as well as local
authorities.
Commercial/Office: he acted for Pearl
Assurance in the s 78 inquiry into

D

redevelopment proposals of its former headquarters in Holborn. He appeared on behalf of Deutsche Morgan Grenfell and Wates Construction in the High Court challenge to the grant of permission for DMG'S new HQ in London Wall.

Major Infrastructure Projects: he appeared for the major objector in the East London River Crossing Inquiry (No 1) and the M40 Inquiry (No 2). He has acted for promotors and objectors in major road schemes, all involving CPOs.

Electricity: he appeared on behalf of the Department of Energy at the Hinchley Point C Inquiry, and regularly advises in wayleave matters and power and transmission line proposals.

Local Plans: as well as appearing very frequently in Local Plan inquiries, he specialises in challenges to the adoption of Local Plans: see eg *BRB v Slough BC [1993] 2 PLR 42; also Milton Keynes, Wycombe.*

Minerals/Waste/Contaminated Land: he often appears at mineral extraction and waste disposal inquiries, and has been involved in several cases involving development of contaminated land.

Other areas of practice: he has appeared in professional negligence and contractual disputes, all planning related.

In 1997 he advised the Conservative Party on its proposals for constitutional reform of the party, and he drafted the Party's Constitution and the Rules for all Constituency Associations.

VILLAROSA MISS ANNUNZIATA

9 King's Bench Walk
Ground Floor, Temple, London EC4Y 7DX,
Telephone: 0171 353 7202/3909
Call date: July 1995, Middle Temple
Qualifications: [BA, PGCE (Adelaide), LLB]

VINCENT MISS CLAIRE

Phoenix Chambers
First Floor Gray's Inn Chambers, Gray's Inn,
London WC1R 5JA, Telephone: 0171 404 7888
Call date: Nov 1993, Middle Temple
Qualifications: [LLB (Hons)(Lond)]

VINCENT PATRICK BENJAMIN

12 King's Bench Walk
Temple, London EC4Y 7EL,
Telephone: 0171 583 0811
E-mail: chambers@12kbw.co.uk
Call date: Oct 1992, Middle Temple
Qualifications: [BA (Hons)(Bris), Dip Law]

VINCENT MISS RUTH CAROLYN

Colleton Chambers
Colleton Crescent, Exeter, Devon EX2 4DG,
Telephone: 01392 74898/9
Call date: Oct 1995, Gray's Inn
Qualifications: [LLB (Manch)]

VINE AIDAN JAMES WILSON

2 Harcourt Bldgs
1st Floor, Temple, London EC4Y 9DB,
Telephone: 0171 353 6961/7
Harcourt Chambers
Churchill House 3 St Aldate's Courtyard, St
Aldate's, Oxford OX1 1BN,
Telephone: 01865 791559
Call date: Oct 1995, Middle Temple
Qualifications: [BA (Hons), MA]

VINE JAMES PETER STOCKMAN

Hardwicke Building
New Square, Lincoln's Inn, London
WC2A 3SB, Telephone: 0171 242 2523
E-mail: clerks@hardwicke.co.uk
Call date: Nov 1977, Middle Temple

VINEALL NICHOLAS EDWARD JOHN

12 King's Bench Walk
Temple, London EC4Y 7EL,
Telephone: 0171 583 0811
E-mail: chambers@12kbw.co.uk
Call date: Nov 1988, Middle Temple
Qualifications: [BA (Cantab), MA (Pittsburgh),
Dip Law (City)]

VINES ANTHONY ROBERT FRANCIS

Gough Square Chambers
6-7 Gough Square, London EC4A 3DE,
Telephone: 0171 353 0924
E-mail: gsc@goughsq.co.uk
Call date: Nov 1993, Gray's Inn
Qualifications: [BA (Cantab)]

VINEY RICHARD JOHN

12 King's Bench Walk
Temple, London EC4Y 7EL,
Telephone: 0171 583 0811
E-mail: chambers@12kbw.co.uk
Call date: Feb 1994, Middle Temple
Qualifications: [BA (Hons)(Cantab)]

VIRDI MISS PRABHJOT KAUR

5 Essex Court
1st Floor, Temple, London EC4Y 9AH,
Telephone: 0171 410 2000
Call date: Oct 1995, Lincoln's Inn
Qualifications: [LLB (Hons)(Leic)]

VIRGO JOHN ANTHONY

Guildhall Chambers
23 Broad Street, Bristol BS1 2HG,
Telephone: 0117 9273366
Call date: Nov 1983, Inner Temple
Qualifications: [MA (Oxon)]

VITORIA MISS MARY CHRISTINE QC (1997)

8 New Square
Lincoln's Inn, London WC2A 3QP,
Telephone: 0171 405 4321
Call date: Nov 1975, Lincoln's Inn
Qualifications: [BSc, PhD, LLB]

VOKES STEPHEN JOHN

Rowchester Chambers
4 Rowchester Court Whittall Street,
Birmingham B4 6DH,
Telephone: 0121 233 2327/2361951
Call date: July 1989, Lincoln's Inn
Qualifications: [BA (Wales)]

VOLZ KARL ANDREW

46/48 Essex Street
London WC2R 3GH,
Telephone: 0171 583 8899
Call date: Nov 1993, Middle Temple
Qualifications: [BA (Hons)(Newc), CPE (City)]

VON SANTEN-PAGAVA MAXIMILIAN KASIMIR

Forest House Chambers
15 Granville Road, Walthamstow, London
E17 9BS, Telephone: 0181 925 2240
Call date: Nov 1993, Middle Temple
Qualifications: [LLB (Hons)(Lond)]

VOS GEOFFREY CHARLES QC (1993)

3 Stone Bldgs
Ground Floor, Lincoln's Inn, London
WC2A 3XL, Telephone: 0171 242 4937/
405 8358
Call date: July 1977, Inner Temple
Qualifications: [MA (Cantab)]

VOSPER CHRISTOPHER JOHN

Angel Chambers
94 Walter Road, Swansea SA1 5QA,
Telephone: 01792 6464623/6464648
Farrar's Building
Temple, London EC4Y 7BD,
Telephone: 0171 583 9241
E-mail: chambers@farrarsbuilding.co.uk
Door Tenant
Call date: Nov 1977, Middle Temple
Assistant Recorder
Qualifications: [MA (Oxon)]

WADDICOR MISS JANET

1 Crown Office Row
Ground Floor, Temple, London EC4Y 7HH,
Telephone: 0171 797 7500
Crown Office Row Chambers
Blenheim House 120 Church Street, Brighton,
Sussex BN1 1WH, Telephone: 01273 625625
Call date: Nov 1985, Gray's Inn
Qualifications: [MA (Oxon)]

WADDINGTON MRS ANNE LOUISE

Pump Court Chambers
Upper Ground Floor 3 Pump Court, Temple,
London EC4Y 7AJ, Telephone: 0171 353 0711
Pump Court Chambers
31 Southgate Street, Winchester SO23 8EE,
Telephone: 01962 868161
Call date: Nov 1988, Middle Temple
Qualifications: [BA (Kent)]

D

D

WADDINGTON JAMES CHARLES

2 Pump Court
1st Floor, Temple, London EC4Y 7AH,
Telephone: 0171 353 5597
Call date: July 1983, Gray's Inn
Qualifications: [LLB (Exon)]

WADDINGTON NIGEL WILLIAM JAMES

8 Stone Buildings
Lincoln's Inn, London WC2A 3TA,
Telephone: 0171 831 9881
Call date: Oct 1992, Middle Temple
Qualifications: [MSc, Dip Law]

WADE MISS CLARE CATHERINE

2 Dr Johnson's Building
Temple, London EC4Y 7AY,
Telephone: 0171 353 4716
Call date: Nov 1990, Inner Temple
Qualifications: [BA (Dunelm), Dip Law (City)]

WADE PROFESSOR SIR HENRY WILLIAM RAWSON QC (1968)

4-5 Gray's Inn Square
Ground Floor, Gray's Inn, London WC1R 5AY,
Telephone: 0171 404 5252
E-mail: chambers@4-5graysinnsquare.co.uk
Call date: July 1946, Lincoln's Inn
Qualifications: [MA, LLD (Cantab)]

WADE IAN

5 Paper Bldgs
1st Floor, Temple, London EC4Y 7HB,
Telephone: 0171 583 6117
E-mail: clerks@5-paperbuildings.law.co.uk
Call date: Nov 1977, Gray's Inn
Qualifications: [MA (Cantab)]

WADLING ANTHONY NEAL

4 Brick Court
Ground Floor, Temple, London EC4Y 9AD,
Telephone: 0171 797 7766
E-mail: chambers@4brick.co.uk
Call date: Feb 1977, Inner Temple
Qualifications: [BA (Hons), Dip EC Law]

WADOODI MISS AISHA

Fountain Chambers
Cleveland Business Centre 1 Watson Street,
Middlesbrough TS1 2RQ,
Telephone: 01642 217037
Call date: Oct 1994, Middle Temple
Qualifications: [LLB (Hons)(Newc)]

WADSLEY PETER JOHN CAMPBELL

St John's Chambers
Small Street, Bristol BS1 1DW,
Telephone: 0117 9213456/298514
E-mail: clerks@stjohns.uk.com
Call date: July 1984, Middle Temple
Qualifications: [BA LLB (Cantab)]

WADSWORTH JAMES PATRICK QC (1981)

4 Paper Bldgs
Ground Floor, Temple, London EC4Y 7EX,
Telephone: 0171 353 3366/583 7155
E-mail: clerks@4paperbuildings.com
Call date: Feb 1963, Inner Temple
Recorder
Qualifications: [MA (Oxon)]

WADSWORTH NICHOLAS STEPHEN

Clock Chambers
78 Darlington Street, Wolverhampton
WV1 4LY, Telephone: 01902 313444
Southsea Chambers
PO Box 148, Southsea, Portsmouth,
Hampshire PO5 2TU,
Telephone: 01705 291261
Call date: Feb 1993, Gray's Inn
Qualifications: [LLB]

WAGNER MRS LINDA ANN

Goldsworth Chambers
1st Floor 10-11 Gray's Inn Square, London
WC1R 5JD, Telephone: 0171 405 7117
Call date: Nov 1990, Middle Temple
Qualifications: [LLB (Hons)]

WAGNER MISS LYNN

Westgate Chambers
16-17 Wellington Square, Hastings, East Sussex
TN34 1PB, Telephone: 01424 432105
Call date: July 1975, Lincoln's Inn
Qualifications: [BA, MA (Cantab), BA
(Australia)]

WAGSTAFFE CHRISTOPHER DAVID

Watford Chambers
74 Mildred Avenue, Watford, Hertfordshire
WD1 7DX, Telephone: 01923 220553
Call date: Nov 1992, Inner Temple
Qualifications: [LLB (Essex)]

WAIN PETER

East Anglian Chambers
Gresham House 5 Museum Street, Ipswich
IP1 1HQ, Telephone: 01473 214481
East Anglian Chambers
57 London Street, Norwich NR2 1HL,
Telephone: 01603 617351
East Anglian Chambers
Sanders House 52 North Hill, Colchester
CO1 1PY, Telephone: 01206 572756
Call date: July 1972, Gray's Inn
Qualifications: [LLB]

WAINE STEPHEN PHILLIP

36 Bedford Row
London WC1R 4JH,
Telephone: 0171 421 8000
E-mail: 36bedfordrow@link.org
Call date: Nov 1969, Lincoln's Inn
Recorder
Qualifications: [LLB (Soton)]

WAINWRIGHT JEREMY PATRICK

Westgate Chambers
144 High Street, Lewes, East Sussex BN7 1XT,
Telephone: 01273 480510
1 Dr Johnson's Bldgs
Ground Floor, Temple, London EC4Y 7AX,
Telephone: 0171 353 9328
Call date: Oct 1990, Gray's Inn
Qualifications: [BA (Hons), Dip Law]

WAINWRIGHT JOHN PATRICK HADEN

St Mary's Chambers
50 High Pavement, Lace Market, Nottingham
NG1 1HW, Telephone: 0115 9503503
E-mail: clerks@smc.law.co.uk
Call date: Oct 1994, Lincoln's Inn
Qualifications: [MA (Oxon)]

WAITE JONATHAN GILBERT STOKES

1 Paper Bldgs
Ground Floor, Temple, London EC4Y 7EP,
Telephone: 0171 583 7355
E-mail: clerks@1pb.co.uk
Call date: July 1978, Inner Temple
Qualifications: [MA (Cantab)]

WAITHE JOHN ALBERT

12 Old Square
1st Floor, Lincoln's Inn, London WC2A 3TX,
Telephone: 0171 404 0875
Call date: Nov 1972, Lincoln's Inn
Qualifications: [LLB (Lond), LLM (Lond), MA
(Business Law), (Guildhall)]

WAKEFIELD MISS ANNE PRUDENCE

3 Verulam Buildings
London WC1R 5NT,
Telephone: 0171 831 8441
E-mail: clerks@3verulam.co.uk
Call date: Nov 1968, Gray's Inn
Recorder
Qualifications: [LLM (Cantab), LLB (Lond)]

WAKEHAM PHILIP JOHN LE MESSURIER

Hardwicke Building
New Square, Lincoln's Inn, London
WC2A 3SB, Telephone: 0171 242 2523
E-mail: clerks@hardwicke.co.uk
Call date: July 1978, Middle Temple
Qualifications: [BA]

WAKERLEY PAUL CHARLES MACLENNON

4 King's Bench Walk
2nd Floor, Temple, London EC4Y 7DL,
Telephone: 0171 353 3581
Call date: Nov 1990, Gray's Inn
Qualifications: [LLB (Hons)]

WAKERLEY RICHARD MACLENNON QC (1982)

4 Fountain Court
Steelhouse Lane, Birmingham B4 6DR,
Telephone: 0121 236 3476
Call date: Feb 1965, Gray's Inn
Recorder
Qualifications: [MA (Cantab)]

D

WAKSMAN DAVID MICHAEL

3 Verulam Buildings
London WC1R 5NT,
Telephone: 0171 831 8441
E-mail: clerks@3verulam.co.uk
Call date: Nov 1982, Middle Temple
Qualifications: [LLB (Manch) BCL, (Oxon)]

WALBANK DAVID NICHOLAS

5 Essex Court
1st Floor, Temple, London EC4Y 9AH,
Telephone: 0171 410 2000
Call date: Nov 1987, Inner Temple
Qualifications: [MA (Cantab)]

WALDEN-SMITH DAVID EDWARD

6 Pump Court
1st Floor, Temple, London EC4Y 7AR,
Telephone: 0171 797 8400
E-mail: sa_hockman_qc@link.org
6-8 Mill Street
Maidstone, Kent ME15 6XH,
Telephone: 01622 688094
Call date: July 1985, Lincoln's Inn
Qualifications: [MA (Cantab)]

WALDEN-SMITH MISS KAREN JANE

Lamb Chambers
Lamb Building, Temple, London EC4Y 7AS,
Telephone: 0171 797 8300
E-mail: lambchambers@link.org
Call date: Oct 1990, Lincoln's Inn
Qualifications: [MA (Cantab)]

WALDRON WILLIAM FRANCIS

Exchange Chambers
Pearl Assurance House Derby Square,
Liverpool L2 9XX, Telephone: 0151 236 7747/
0458
E-mail: exchangechambers@btinternet.com
Call date: Nov 1986, Gray's Inn
Qualifications: [LLB]

WALDRON WILLIAM HENRY QC (1982)

Exchange Chambers
Pearl Assurance House Derby Square,
Liverpool L2 9XX, Telephone: 0151 236 7747/
0458
E-mail: exchangechambers@btinternet.com
Call date: Feb 1970, Gray's Inn
Recorder

WALES ANDREW NIGEL MALCOLM

7 King's Bench Walk
Ground Floor, Temple, London EC4Y 7DS,
Telephone: 0171 583 0404
Call date: Nov 1992, Gray's Inn
Qualifications: [MA (Cantab), LLM (Virginia USA)]

WALES MATTHEW JAMES

Guildhall Chambers
23 Broad Street, Bristol BS1 2HG,
Telephone: 0117 9273366
Call date: Oct 1993, Inner Temple
Qualifications: [BA (Dunelm)]

WALEY ERIC RICHARD THOMAS

Assize Court Chambers
14 Small Street, Bristol BS1 1DE,
Telephone: 0117 9264587
Call date: Nov 1976, Inner Temple
Qualifications: [MA Hons (Cantab)]

WALEY SIMON FELIX

39 Park Square
Leeds LS1 2NU, Telephone: 0113 2456633
Call date: Feb 1988, Middle Temple
Qualifications: [LLB (Exon)]

WALFORD RICHARD HENRY HOWARD

13 Old Square
1st Floor, Lincoln's Inn, London WC2A 3UA,
Telephone: 0171 242 6105
E-mail: clerks@serlecourt.co.uk
Call date: July 1984, Middle Temple
Qualifications: [LLB (Exon)]

WALKER ALLISTER DAVID

5 Pump Court
Ground Floor, Temple, London EC4Y 7AP,
Telephone: 0171 353 2532
E-mail: fivepump@netcomuk.co.uk
Call date: Nov 1990, Inner Temple
Qualifications: [LLB (Essex)]

WALKER ANDREW ANGUS

Chambers of Helen Grindrod QC
1st Floor 95a Chancery Lane, London
WC2A 2JG, Telephone: 0171 404 4777
Call date: Oct 1994, Middle Temple
Qualifications: [LLB (Hons)(Lond)]

WALKER ANDREW GREENFIELD

Chambers of Lord Goodhart QC
Ground Floor 3 New Square, Lincoln's Inn,
London WC2A 3RS,
Telephone: 0171 405 5577
E-mail: law@threenewsquare.demon.co.uk
Call date: July 1975, Lincoln's Inn
Qualifications: [MA (Cantab)]

WALKER ANDREW PAUL DALTON

9 Old Square
Ground Floor, Lincoln's Inn, London
WC2A 3SR, Telephone: 0171 405 4682
E-mail: chambers@9oldsquare.co.uk
Call date: Nov 1991, Lincoln's Inn
Qualifications: [MA (Cantab)]

WALKER MISS ANWEN ELIZABETH

Rowchester Chambers
4 Rowchester Court Whittall Street,
Birmingham B4 6DH,
Telephone: 0121 233 2327/2361951
Call date: July 1992, Inner Temple
Qualifications: [LLB]

WALKER CHRISTOPHER DAVID BESTWICK

Old Square Chambers
Hanover House 47 Corn Street, Bristol
BS1 1HT, Telephone: 0117 9277111
Old Square Chambers
1 Verulam Buildings, Gray's Inn, London
WC1R 5LQ, Telephone: 0171 831 0801
Call date: Oct 1990, Middle Temple
Qualifications: [BA (Cantab), Licence Speciale
en, Droit Europeer]

WALKER EDWARD JEREMY BRUCE

St John's Chambers
Small Street, Bristol BS1 1DW,
Telephone: 0117 9213456/298514
E-mail: clerks@stjohns.uk.com
Call date: Nov 1994, Gray's Inn
Qualifications: [BSc]

WALKER MRS ELIZABETH ANNABEL QC (1997)

Paradise Square Chambers
26 Paradise Square, Sheffield S1 2DE,
Telephone: 0114 2738951
Call date: Nov 1976, Gray's Inn
Recorder
Qualifications: [LLB]

WALKER MRS ELIZABETH MARY

Priory Chambers
2 Fountain Court, Steelhouse Lane,
Birmingham B4 6DR,
Telephone: 0121 236 3882/1375
Call date: Oct 1994, Gray's Inn
Qualifications: [BA (Hons)(Dunelm)]

WALKER MRS FIONA

Bank House Chambers
Old Bank House, Hartshead, Sheffield S1 2EL,
Telephone: 0114 2751223
Call date: Feb 1992, Inner Temple
Qualifications: [LLB (Manc)]

WALKER JAMES

1 Gray's Inn Square
Ground Floor, London WC1R 5AA,
Telephone: 0171 405 8946/7/8
Call date: Oct 1994, Lincoln's Inn
Qualifications: [LLB (Hons)(Anglia)]

WALKER MISS JANE

9 St John Street
Manchester M3 4DN,
Telephone: 0161 955 9000
E-mail: ninesjs@gconnect.com
Call date: July 1987, Middle Temple
Qualifications: [MA (Oxon)]

D

WALKER MISS JANE SHARMAN

43 Eglantine Road
London SW18 2DE,
Telephone: 0181 874 3469
6 Fountain Court
Steelhouse Lane, Birmingham B4 6DR,
Telephone: 0121 233 3282
Door Tenant
Call date: Nov 1974, Middle Temple
Qualifications: [LLB (B'ham)]

WALKER MARK JONATHAN JASON

Chancery House Chambers
7 Lisbon Square, Leeds LS1 4LY,
Telephone: 0113 244 6691
E-mail: Chanceryhouse@btinternet.com
Call date: Nov 1986, Middle Temple
Qualifications: [LLB(Leeds)]

WALKER PATRICK HOWARD

Chancery House Chambers
7 Lisbon Square, Leeds LS1 4LY,
Telephone: 0113 244 6691
E-mail: Chanceryhouse@btinternet.com
Call date: July 1979, Lincoln's Inn
Qualifications: [LLB (Sheff)]

WALKER PAUL CHRISTOPHER

Bridewell Chambers
2 Bridewell Place, London EC4V 6AP,
Telephone: 0171 797 8800
E-mail: clerks@bridewell.law.co.uk
Call date: Oct 1993, Lincoln's Inn
Qualifications: [LLB (Hons)(Lond)]

WALKER PAUL JAMES

Brick Court Chambers
15/19 Devereux Court, London WC2R 3JJ,
Telephone: 0171 583 0777
E-mail: (surname)@brickcourt.demon.co.uk
Call date: Nov 1979, Gray's Inn
Qualifications: [BCL,MA (Oxon)]

WALKER PETER BRIAN

Broadway House Chambers
Broadway House 9 Bank Street, Bradford,
West Yorkshire BD1 1TW,
Telephone: 01274 722560
Call date: July 1985, Inner Temple

WALKER RAYMOND AUGUSTUS QC (1988)

1 Harcourt Bldgs
2nd Floor, Temple, London EC4Y 9DA,
Telephone: 0171 353 9421/9151
Call date: July 1966, Middle Temple
Recorder
Qualifications: [BA (Cantab)]

WALKER RONALD JACK QC (1983)

12 King's Bench Walk
Temple, London EC4Y 7EL,
Telephone: 0171 583 0811
E-mail: chambers@12kbw.co.uk
Call date: July 1962, Gray's Inn
Recorder
Qualifications: [LLB]

WALKER STEVEN JOHN

1 Atkin Building
Gray's Inn, London WC1R 5AT,
Telephone: 0171 404 0102
E-mail: clerks@atkin-chambers.co.uk
Call date: Nov 1993, Lincoln's Inn
Qualifications: [LLB (Hons)]

WALKER STUART JAMES

Mitre House Chambers
Mitre House 44 Fleet Street, London
EC4Y 1BN, Telephone: 0171 583 8233
Call date: Oct 1990, Gray's Inn
Qualifications: [BA (Oxon)]

WALKER MRS SUSANNAH MARY

One Garden Court
Ground Floor, Temple, London EC4Y 9BJ,
Telephone: 0171 797 7900
Call date: July 1985, Inner Temple
Qualifications: [BSocSc, Dip Law (City), Dip
Social Work]

WALKER MISS SUZANNE

Trinity Chambers
140 New London Road, Chelmsford, Essex
CM2 0AW, Telephone: 01245 605040
Call date: Oct 1995, Lincoln's Inn
Qualifications: [LLB (Hons)(Manc)]

WALKER TERENCE CARR

1 Crown Office Row
3rd Floor, Temple, London EC4Y 7HH,
Telephone: 0171 583 9292
E-mail: onecor@link.org
Call date: July 1973, Inner Temple
Qualifications: [MA (Oxon)]

WALKER TIMOTHY JOHN

29 Bedford Row Chambers
London WC1R 4HE,
Telephone: 0171 831 2626
Call date: July 1984, Inner Temple
Qualifications: [MA (Cantab)]

WALKER-KANE JONATHAN CHARLES

Paradise Square Chambers
26 Paradise Square, Sheffield S1 2DE,
Telephone: 0114 2738951
Call date: July 1994, Gray's Inn
Qualifications: [BA]

WALKER-SMITH SIR JOHN JONAH

Doughty Street Chambers
11 Doughty Street, London WC1N 2PG,
Telephone: 0171 404 1313
E-mail: doughty_street@compuserve.com
Call date: Nov 1963, Middle Temple
Assistant Recorder
Qualifications: [MA (Oxon)]

WALL (DARYL) WILLIAM

3 Fountain Court
Steelhouse Lane, Birmingham B4 6DR,
Telephone: 0121 236 5854
Call date: Nov 1985, Inner Temple
Qualifications: [BA (York), Dip Law (City)]

WALL MRS CARMEL MIRIAM

4 Fountain Court
Steelhouse Lane, Birmingham B4 6DR,
Telephone: 0121 236 3476
Call date: Nov 1986, Lincoln's Inn
Qualifications: [BA (Hons)(Cantab)]

WALL CHRISTOPHER JAMES LYNTON

Becket Chambers
17 New Dover Road, Canterbury, Kent
CT1 3AS, Telephone: 01227 786331
Call date: Nov 1987, Lincoln's Inn
Qualifications: [LLB (Hons)]

WALL MISS JACQUELINE FRANCOISE

India Buildings Chambers
Water Street, Liverpool L2 OXG,
Telephone: 0151 243 6000
Call date: July 1986, Gray's Inn
Qualifications: [LLB (Lanc)]

WALL MARK ARTHUR

4 Fountain Court
Steelhouse Lane, Birmingham B4 6DR,
Telephone: 0121 236 3476
Call date: Nov 1985, Lincoln's Inn
Qualifications: [MA (Cantab)]

WALLACE ADRIAN ROBERT

Peel Court Chambers
45 Hardman Street, Manchester M3 3HA,
Telephone: 0161 832 3791
Call date: July 1979, Middle Temple
Qualifications: [BA (Cantab)]

WALLACE ANDREW DUNCAN GRAY

3 Fountain Court
Steelhouse Lane, Birmingham B4 6DR,
Telephone: 0121 236 5854
Call date: Nov 1988, Gray's Inn
Qualifications: [LLB]

WALLACE MS ANN CHRISTINE

Godolphin Chambers
50 Castle Street, Truro, Cornwall TR1 3AF,
Telephone: 01872 276312
1 Pump Court
Lower Ground Floor, Temple, London
EC4Y 7AB, Telephone: 0171 583 2012/
353 4341
E-mail: (name) @1pumpcourt.co.uk
Door Tenant
Call date: July 1979, Inner Temple
Qualifications: [LLB]

D

WALLACE HUGH GEORGE

9 Park Place
Cardiff CF1 3DP, Telephone: 01222 382731
Call date: July 1993, Gray's Inn

WALLACE IAN NORMAN DUNCAN QC (1973)

1 Atkin Building
Gray's Inn, London WC1R 5AT,
Telephone: 0171 404 0102
E-mail: clerks@atkin-chambers.co.uk
Call date: June 1948, Middle Temple
Qualifications: [MA (Oxon)]

WALLACE MRS JANE SCOTT

1a Middle Temple Lane
Ground Floor, Temple, London EC4Y 9AA,
Telephone: 0171 353 8815
Call date: July 1974, Inner Temple

WALLACE SHAUN ANTHONY

20 Britton Street
1st Floor, London EC1M 5NQ,
Telephone: 0171 608 3765
Call date: Nov 1984, Inner Temple
Qualifications: [BA]

WALLER RICHARD BEAUMONT

7 King's Bench Walk
Ground Floor, Temple, London EC4Y 7DS,
Telephone: 0171 583 0404
Call date: Oct 1994, Gray's Inn
Qualifications: [MA]

WALLING PHILIP THOMAS GEORGE

67a Westgate Road
Newcastle Upon Tyne NE1 1SQ,
Telephone: 0191 261 4407/2329785
Call date: Nov 1986, Lincoln's Inn
Qualifications: [LLB(Lanc), BL (Dublin)]

WALLINGTON PETER THOMAS

11 King's Bench Walk
Temple, London EC4Y 7EQ,
Telephone: 0171 632 8500
E-mail: clerksroom@11-kbw.law.co.uk
Call date: July 1987, Gray's Inn
Qualifications: [MA, LLM (Cantab)]

WALLINGTON RICHARD ANTHONY

10 Old Square
Ground Floor, Lincoln's Inn, London
WC2A 3SU, Telephone: 0171 405 0758
Call date: July 1972, Middle Temple
Qualifications: [MA (Cantab)]

WALLWORK BERNARD GRAHAM FRANK

28 St John Street
Manchester M3 4DJ,
Telephone: 0161 834 8418
E-mail: clerk@28stjohnst.co.uk
Call date: Nov 1976, Middle Temple
Assistant Recorder
Qualifications: [MA (Oxon)]

WALMSLEY ALAN

Bridewell Chambers
2 Bridewell Place, London EC4V 6AP,
Telephone: 0171 797 8800
E-mail: clerks@bridewell.law.co.uk
Call date: Nov 1991, Inner Temple
Qualifications: [BSc]

WALMSLEY KEITH BERNARD RUPERT

199 Strand
London WC2R 1DR,
Telephone: 0171 379 9779
E-mail: chambers@199strand.co.uk
Call date: July 1973, Inner Temple
Qualifications: [LLB (Bris), DCrim (Cantab)]

WALMSLEY PETER JEREMY

1 High Pavement
Nottingham NG1 1HF,
Telephone: 0115 9418218
Call date: June 1964, Inner Temple

WALSH BRIAN JOSEPH

12 Old Square
1st Floor, Lincoln's Inn, London WC2A 3TX,
Telephone: 0171 404 0875
Call date: Feb 1994, Gray's Inn
Qualifications: [BA (Dublin)]

WALSH JOHN PATRICK

3 Paper Bldgs
2nd Floor, Temple, London EC4Y 7EU,
Telephone: 0171 353 6208
Call date: Nov 1993, Inner Temple
Qualifications: [BA, MA (Ireland), LLB (Lond)]

WALSH MARTIN FRASER

Peel Court Chambers
45 Hardman Street, Manchester M3 3HA,
Telephone: 0161 832 3791
Call date: Nov 1990, Gray's Inn
Qualifications: [LLB (Manch)]

WALSH MICHAEL STEVEN

St Ive's Chambers
9 Fountain Ct, Birmingham B4 6DR,
Telephone: 0121 236 0863/0929
Call date: Oct 1996, Middle Temple
Qualifications: [BA (Hons) (Lond)]

WALSH MISS PATRICIA CLAIRE

East Anglian Chambers
Sanders House 52 North Hill, Colchester
CO1 1PY, Telephone: 01206 572756
East Anglian Chambers
57 London Street, Norwich NR2 1HL,
Telephone: 01603 617351
East Anglian Chambers
Gresham House 5 Museum Street, Ipswich
IP1 1HQ, Telephone: 01473 214481
Call date: Nov 1993, Lincoln's Inn
Qualifications: [LLB (Hons)]

WALSH PETER ANTHONY JOSEPH

Queen Elizabeth Bldg
Ground Floor, Temple, London EC4Y 9BS,
Telephone: 0171 353 7181 (12 Lines)
Call date: Nov 1978, Middle Temple
Qualifications: [LLB (Hons) (Lond)]

WALSH PETER PAUL

New Court Chambers
3 Broad Chare, Newcastle Upon Tyne
NE1 3DQ, Telephone: 0191 232 1980
Call date: May 1982, Gray's Inn
Qualifications: [BA (Hons)]

WALSH SIMON

Bridewell Chambers
2 Bridewell Place, London EC4V 6AP,
Telephone: 0171 797 8800
E-mail: clerks@bridewell.law.co.uk
Call date: Nov 1987, Middle Temple
Qualifications: [MA (Oxon), Dip Law, (City),
ACIArb]

WALSH STEPHEN PAUL

3 Raymond Buildings
Gray's Inn, London WC1R 5BH,
Telephone: 0171 831 3833
E-mail: chambers@threeraymond.demon.co.uk
Call date: Nov 1983, Middle Temple
Qualifications: [LL.B]

WALSH STEVEN JAMES FRANKLYN

5 Paper Bldgs
Ground Floor, Temple, London EC4Y 7HB,
Telephone: 0171 583 9275/583 4555
E-mail: 5paper@link.org
Call date: Feb 1965, Lincoln's Inn
Qualifications: [BA, LLB (Cantab)]

WALSHE MS ANNIE PATRICIA

Holborn Chambers
6 Gate Street, Lincoln's Inn Fields, London
WC2A 3HP, Telephone: 0171 242 6060
Call date: Oct 1993, Inner Temple
Qualifications: [LLB]

WALTER MISS FRANCESCA ELIZABETH

East Anglian Chambers
Sanders House 52 North Hill, Colchester
CO1 1PY, Telephone: 01206 572756
East Anglian Chambers
57 London Street, Norwich NR2 1HL,
Telephone: 01603 617351
East Anglian Chambers
Gresham House 5 Museum Street, Ipswich
IP1 1HQ, Telephone: 01473 214481
Call date: Oct 1994, Middle Temple
Qualifications: [BA (Hons)(Oxon)]

WALTER PHILIP LEWIS

2 Field Court
Gray's Inn, London WC1R 5BB,
Telephone: 0171 405 6114
E-mail: fieldct2@netcomuk.co.uk.
Call date: July 1975, Inner Temple
Qualifications: [MA (Cantab)]

WALTERS EDMUND JOHN

13 King's Bench Walk
1st Floor, Temple, London EC4Y 7EN,
Telephone: 0171 353 7204
E-mail: clerks@13kbw.law.co.uk
King's Bench Chambers
32 Beaumont Street, Oxford OX1 2NP,
Telephone: 01865 311066
E-mail: clerks@kbc-oxford.law.co.uk
Call date: Nov 1991, Middle Temple
Qualifications: [BA Hons (Bris), Dip Law]

WALTERS GARETH RUPEL

7 Fountain Court
Steelhouse Lane, Birmingham B4 6DR,
Telephone: 0121 236 8531
Call date: Nov 1986, Middle Temple
Qualifications: [LLB (Wales)]

WALTERS GERAINT WYN

Angel Chambers
94 Walter Road, Swansea SA1 5QA,
Telephone: 01792 6464623/6464648
Call date: Nov 1981, Gray's Inn
Qualifications: [LLB (Wales)]

WALTERS GRAHAM ANTHONY

33 Park Place
Cardiff CF1 3BA, Telephone: 01222 233313
Call date: July 1986, Gray's Inn
Qualifications: [MA (Oxon)]

WALTERS MISS JILL MARY

33 Park Place
Cardiff CF1 3BA, Telephone: 01222 233313
Call date: July 1979, Middle Temple
Qualifications: [LLB (Wales)]

WALTERS JOHN LATIMER QC (1997)

Gray's Inn Chambers
3rd Floor, Gray's Inn, London WC1R 5JA,
Telephone: 0171 242 2642
E-mail: clerks@taxbar.com
Call date: July 1977, Middle Temple
Qualifications: [MA (Oxon)]

WALTERS JONATHAN GWYNNE

33 Park Place
Cardiff CF1 3BA, Telephone: 01222 233313
Call date: July 1984, Inner Temple
Qualifications: [LLB (Lond)]

WALTERS PROFESSOR TERENCE CHARLES

St Mary's Chambers
50 High Pavement, Lace Market, Nottingham
NG1 1HW, Telephone: 0115 9503503
E-mail: clerks@smc.law.co.uk
Call date: Nov 1993, Inner Temple
Qualifications: [LLB (Wales), M.Phil (Notts),
MiMgt]

WALTERS MISS VIVIAN IRENE ELIZABETH

13 King's Bench Walk
1st Floor, Temple, London EC4Y 7EN,
Telephone: 0171 353 7204
E-mail: clerks@13kbw.law.co.uk
King's Bench Chambers
32 Beaumont Street, Oxford OX1 2NP,
Telephone: 01865 311066
E-mail: clerks@kbc-oxford.law.co.uk
Call date: Nov 1991, Middle Temple
Qualifications: [BA Hons (Leic)]

WALTON ALASTAIR HENRY

7 Stone Bldgs
Ground Floor, Lincoln's Inn, London
WC2A 3SZ, Telephone: 0171 405 3886/
242 3546
E-mail: chaldous@vossnet.co.uk
Call date: July 1977, Lincoln's Inn
Qualifications: [BA (Oxon)]

WALTON MISS CAROLYN MARGERY

13 Old Square
Ground Floor, Lincoln's Inn, London
WC2A 3UA, Telephone: 0171 404 4800
Call date: July 1980, Gray's Inn
Qualifications: [LLB (Lond)]

WAN DAUD MALEK

6 King's Bench Walk
Ground, Third & Fourth Floors, Temple,
London EC4Y 7DR,
Telephone: 0171 353 4931/583 0695
Call date: Nov 1991, Inner Temple
Qualifications: [LLB]

WARBURTON MISS JULIE

King Charles House
Standard Hill, Nottingham NG1 6FX,
Telephone: 0115 9418851
E-mail: clerks@kch.co.uk
Call date: Oct 1993, Middle Temple
Qualifications: [LLB (Hons)(Lond)]

WARBY MARK DAVID JOHN

5 Raymond Buildings
1st Floor, Gray's Inn, London WC1R 5BP,
Telephone: 0171 242 2902
Call date: Nov 1981, Gray's Inn
Qualifications: [MA (Oxon)]

WARD ANTHONY DOUGLAS

3 Paper Bldgs
1st Floor, Temple, London EC4Y 7EU,
Telephone: 0171 583 8055
E-mail: london@3paper.com
4 St Peter Street
Winchester SO23 8OW,
Telephone: 01962 868884
20 Lorne Park Road
Bournemouth BH1 1JN,
Telephone: 01202 292102 (5 Lines)
Call date: July 1971, Inner Temple
Qualifications: [LLB (Lond)]

WARD MARTIN STUART

3 Temple Gardens
3rd Floor, Temple, London EC4Y 9AU,
Telephone: 0171 353 0832
Call date: Oct 1992, Lincoln's Inn
Qualifications: [BA(Hons)(Warw)]

WARD MS ORLA MARY

3 Serjeants Inn
London EC4Y 1BQ,
Telephone: 0171 353 5537
E-mail: available upon request
Call date: Oct 1996, Gray's Inn
Qualifications: [BA (Cantab)]

WARD PETER MARK

Garden Court North Chambers
2nd Floor Gregg's Building, 1 Booth Street,
Manchester M2 4DU,
Telephone: 0161 833 1774
Call date: Oct 1996, Inner Temple
Qualifications: [LLB (Lond)]

WARD ROBERT WARWICK ROURKE

5 Paper Bldgs
Lower Ground Floor, Temple, London
EC4Y 7HB, Telephone: 0171 353 5638
E-mail: 107722,633@compuserve.com
Call date: July 1977, Inner Temple
Qualifications: [LLB (Hons) (Lond)]

WARD SIMON JOHN

1 Fountain Court
Steelhouse Lane, Birmingham B4 6DR,
Telephone: 0121 236 5721
Call date: July 1986, Inner Temple
Qualifications: [LLB (B'ham)]

WARD SIMON KENNETH

2 Paper Bldgs
1st Floor, Temple, London EC4Y 7ET,
Telephone: 0171 936 2611 (10 Lines)
E-mail: clerks@2pbbarristers.co.uk
Call date: Nov 1984, Middle Temple
Qualifications: [BA (Durham), MA (City)]

WARD MISS SIOBHAN MARIE LUCIA

11 King's Bench Walk
Temple, London EC4Y 7EQ,
Telephone: 0171 632 8500
E-mail: clerksroom@11-kbw.law.co.uk
Call date: Nov 1984, Inner Temple
Qualifications: [MA, LLM (Cantab)]

D

D

WARD TIMOTHY JUSTIN

39 Essex Street
London WC2R 3AT,
Telephone: 0171 583 1111
E-mail: clerks@39essex.co.uk
Call date: Oct 1994, Gray's Inn
Qualifications: [BA, MA]

WARD TREVOR ROBERT EDWARD

17 Carlton Crescent
Southampton SO15 2XR,
Telephone: 01703 320320
E-mail: km@bar-17cc.demon.co.uk
Call date: Apr 1991, Middle Temple
Qualifications: [LLB (Hons), MSc]

WARD-JACKSON CHARLES

1 Crown Office Row
2nd Floor, Temple, London EC4Y 7HH,
Telephone: 0171 797 7111
Call date: Nov 1985, Middle Temple
Qualifications: [BA (Edin) Dip Law]

WARDELL JOHN DAVID MEREDITH

New Court Chambers
5 Verulam Buildings, Gray's Inn, London
WC1R 5LY, Telephone: 0171 831 9500
E-mail: mail@newcourtchambers.com
Call date: July 1979, Gray's Inn
Qualifications: [LLB (Exon) MPhil, (Cantab)]

WARDLOW JAN JEFFERY

East Anglian Chambers
57 London Street, Norwich NR2 1HL,
Telephone: 01603 617351
East Anglian Chambers
Sanders House 52 North Hill, Colchester
CO1 1PY, Telephone: 01206 572756
East Anglian Chambers
Gresham House 5 Museum Street, Ipswich
IP1 1HQ, Telephone: 01473 214481
Call date: July 1971, Gray's Inn
Recorder

WARE MRS SUSAN PAMELA

Lancaster Building Chambers
77 Deansgate, Manchester M3 2BW,
Telephone: 0161 661 4444
E-mail: sandra@lbnipc.com
Call date: Nov 1990, Inner Temple
Qualifications: [LLB (Sheff), LLM (Exon)]

WARITAY SAMUEL

Trafalgar Chambers
53 Fleet Street, London EC4Y 1BE,
Telephone: 0171 583 5858
E-mail: TrafalgarChambers@easynet.co.uk
Call date: Nov 1993, Inner Temple
Qualifications: [BA (Hons)(Sussex)]

WARNE PETER LAWRENCE

Hollis Whiteman Chambers
3rd/4th Floor Queen Elizabeth Bldg, Temple,
London EC4Y 9BS, Telephone: 0171 583 5766
E-mail: hollis.whiteman@btinternet.com
Call date: Nov 1993, Inner Temple
Qualifications: [BA (Manch), CPE]

WARNE ROY LESLIE

Stour Chambers
Barton Mill House Barton Mill Road,
Canterbury, Kent CT1 1BP,
Telephone: 01227 764899
E-mail: clerks@stourchambers.co.uk
Call date: Nov 1979, Gray's Inn
Qualifications: [MA (Cantab)]

WARNER ANTHONY CHARLES BROUGHTON

7 Fountain Court
Steelhouse Lane, Birmingham B4 6DR,
Telephone: 0121 236 8531
Call date: July 1979, Gray's Inn
Qualifications: [BA]

WARNER BRIAN BEN

1 Hare Court
Ground Floor, Temple, London EC4Y 7BE,
Telephone: 0171 353 3982/5324
Call date: May 1969, Inner Temple
Assistant Recorder
Qualifications: [LLB (Lond)]

WARNER MALCOLM DIGBY

Guildhall Chambers
23 Broad Street, Bristol BS1 2HG,
Telephone: 0117 9273366
24 Old Bldgs
Ground Floor, Lincoln's Inn, London
WC2A 3UJ, Telephone: 0171 404 0946
E-mail: clerks@24oldbuildings.law.co.uk
Call date: July 1979, Lincoln's Inn
Qualifications: [BScEcon (Wales)]

WARNER MISS SHARAN PAMELA

14 Gray's Inn Square
Gray's Inn, London WC1R 5JP,
Telephone: 0171 242 0858
E-mail: 100712.2134@compuserve.com
Call date: Feb 1985, Gray's Inn
Qualifications: [BA (Hons)]

WARNER STEPHEN CLIFFORD

Hardwicke Building
New Square, Lincoln's Inn, London
WC2A 3SB, Telephone: 0171 242 2523
E-mail: clerks@hardwicke.co.uk
Call date: July 1976, Lincoln's Inn
Qualifications: [MA (Oxon)]

WARNOCK ALASTAIR ROBERT LYON

Adrian Lyon's Chambers
14 Castle Street, Liverpool L2 0NE,
Telephone: 0151 236 4421/8240
E-mail: chambers14@aol.com
Call date: Nov 1977, Lincoln's Inn
Assistant Recorder

WARNOCK ANDREW RONALD

1 Serjeants' Inn
5th Floor Fleet Street, Temple, London
EC4Y 1LL, Telephone: 0171 415 6666
E-mail: no1serjeantsinn@btinternet.com
Call date: Nov 1993, Inner Temple
Qualifications: [BA, Dip in French, (Cantab)]

WARNOCK MISS CERI AILSA

38 Young Street
Manchester M3 3FT,
Telephone: 0161 833 0489
E-mail: clerks@young-st-chambers.com
Call date: Oct 1993, Gray's Inn
Qualifications: [LLB (Hons)(Wales)]

WARNOCK-SMITH MRS SHAN

5 Stone Buildings
Lincoln's Inn, London WC2A 3XT,
Telephone: 0171 242 6201
E-mail: clerks@5-stonebuildings.law.co.uk
Call date: July 1971, Gray's Inn
Qualifications: [LLM]

WARREN JOHN QC (1994)

1 High Pavement
Nottingham NG1 1HF,
Telephone: 0115 9418218
Call date: July 1968, Gray's Inn
Recorder
Qualifications: [LLB]

WARREN MS LYNNETTE KATHLEEN

1 Pump Court
Lower Ground Floor, Temple, London
EC4Y 7AB, Telephone: 0171 583 2012/
353 4341
E-mail: (name) @1pumpcourt.co.uk
Call date: Nov 1987, Gray's Inn
Qualifications: [Dip Law]

WARREN MICHAEL JOHN DAVID

1 King's Bench Walk
2nd Floor, Temple, London EC4Y 7DB,
Telephone: 0171 936 1500
E-mail: ddear@1kbw.co.uk
Call date: Nov 1971, Middle Temple
Qualifications: [MA (Oxon)]

WARREN NICHOLAS ROGER QC (1993)

Wilberforce Chambers
8 New Square, Lincoln's Inn, London
WC2A 3QP, Telephone: 0171 306 0102
E-mail: chambers@wilberforce.co.uk
Call date: Nov 1972, Middle Temple
Qualifications: [BA (Oxon)]

WARREN PHILIP DAVID CHARLES

Assize Court Chambers
14 Small Street, Bristol BS1 1DE,
Telephone: 0117 9264587
Door Tenant
Call date: May 1988, Gray's Inn
Qualifications: [LLB (Wales)]

WARREN RUPERT MILES

2 Mitre Ct Bldgs
2nd Floor, Temple, London EC4Y 7BX,
Telephone: 0171 583 1380
Call date: Oct 1994, Gray's Inn
Qualifications: [BA]

WARREN MISS SASHA

Portsmouth Barristers'Chambers
Victory House 7 Bellevue Terrace,
Portsmouth, Hampshire PO5 3AT,
Telephone: 01705 831292
E-mail: clerks@portsmouthbar.com
Call date: Oct 1996, Gray's Inn
Qualifications: [BA (Wales), LLB (City)]

WARRENDER MISS NICHOLA MARY

New Court Chambers
5 Verulam Buildings, Gray's Inn, London
WC1R 5LY, Telephone: 0171 831 9500
E-mail: mail@newcourtchambers.com
Call date: Nov 1995, Inner Temple
Qualifications: [LLB (Bris)]

WARSHAW JUSTIN ALEXANDER EDWARD

1 Mitre Ct Bldgs
Ground Floor, Temple, London EC4Y 7BS,
Telephone: 0171 797 7070
Call date: Nov 1995, Gray's Inn
Qualifications: [MA (Oxon)]

WARWICK MARK GRANVILLE

29 Bedford Row Chambers
Bedford Row, London WC1R 4HE,
Telephone: 0171 831 2626
Call date: July 1974, Inner Temple
Qualifications: [LLB (Hons)]

Fax: 0171 831 0626; DX: 1044 London

Types of work: Commercial property; Landlord
and tenant

Other professional qualifications: PNBA

Circuit: South Eastern

Reported cases: *Ashley Guarantee v Zacaria*,
[1993] 1 WLR 62. Mortgagee's right to
possession.
Connaught v Indoor Leisure, [1994] 1 WLR
501. Exclusion of equitable set off.
Mercantile Group v Aiyela, [1994] QB 366.
Discovery - injunction against third parties.
Romulus Trading v Comet, [1996] 2 EGLR 70.
Letting adjacent premises for competing use not
a derogation from grant.
Rainbow Estates v Tokenhold, [1998] 2 All ER
860. Specific performance of tenant's repairing
covenant.

WASS MISS SASHA

6 King's Bench Walk
Ground Floor, Temple, London EC4Y 7DR,
Telephone: 0171 583 0410
Call date: Nov 1981, Gray's Inn
Assistant Recorder
Qualifications: [LLB (L'pool)]

WASTIE WILLIAM GRANVILLE

Hollis Whiteman Chambers
3rd/4th Floor Queen Elizabeth Bldg, Temple,
London EC4Y 9BS, Telephone: 0171 583 5766
E-mail: hollis.whiteman@btinternet.com
Call date: Oct 1993, Middle Temple
Qualifications: [LLB (Hons)(Bris)]

WATERMAN ADRIAN MARK

11 King's Bench Walk
1st Floor, Temple, London EC4Y 7EQ,
Telephone: 0171 353 3337
3 Park Court
Leeds LS1 2QH, Telephone: 0113 297 1200
Call date: July 1988, Inner Temple
Qualifications: [LLB (Lond)]

WATERS ANDREW JOHN

5 Essex Court
1st Floor, Temple, London EC4Y 9AH,
Telephone: 0171 410 2000
Call date: Nov 1987, Inner Temple
Qualifications: [LLB]

WATERS DAVID EBSWORTH

1 Hare Court
Ground Floor, Temple, London EC4Y 7BE,
Telephone: 0171 353 3982/5324
Call date: May 1973, Middle Temple
Recorder

WATERS JOHN CLOUGH

Lamb Building
Ground Floor, Temple, London EC4Y 7AS,
Telephone: 0171 797 7788
E-mail: lamb.building@link.org
Call date: May 1974, Lincoln's Inn

WATERS JULIAN WILLIAM PENROSE

1 Serjeants' Inn
5th Floor Fleet Street, Temple, London
EC4Y 1LL, Telephone: 0171 415 6666
E-mail: no1serjeantsinn@btinternet.com
Call date: Nov 1986, Middle Temple
Qualifications: [MA (Cantab)]

WATERS MALCOLM IAN QC (1997)

11 Old Square
Ground Floor, Lincoln's Inn, London
WC2A 3TS, Telephone: 0171 430 0341
E-mail: clerks@11oldsquare.co.uk
Call date: July 1977, Lincoln's Inn
Qualifications: [MA, BCL (Oxon)]

Fax: 0171 831 2469; DX: LDE 1031

Types of work: Banking; Building societies;
Chancery (general); Chancery land law;
Charities; Conveyancing; Equity, wills and
trusts; Professional negligence

Awards and memberships: Member of the
Working Party responsible for drafting the
Standard Conditions of Sale; Member of the
Committee responsible for drafting the Standard
Commercial Property Conditions

Publications: *Wurtzburg and Mills, Building
Society Law* (Joint Author) (and annual
looseleaf releases), 1989; *The Building Societies
Act 1986* (Co-author), 1987

Reported cases: *Peggs v Lamb*, [1994] Ch 172,
1993. Charities.
BSC v Halifax BS and Leeds PBS, [1997] Ch
255, 1995. Conversion to Plc.
C & G v Grattidge, 25 HLR 454, 1993.
Mortgages.
Halifax v Thomas, [1996] Ch 217, 1995.
Mortgages/restitution.
C & G v Norgan, [1996] 1 WLR 343, 1995.
Mortgages.

WATERWORTH MICHAEL CHRISTOPHER

10 Old Square
Ground Floor, Lincoln's Inn, London
WC2A 3SU, Telephone: 0171 405 0758
Call date: Oct 1994, Lincoln's Inn
Qualifications: [MA (Cantab), Dip in Law
(City)]

WATKINS MYLES KENNETH GEORGE

Assize Court Chambers
14 Small Street, Bristol BS1 1DE,
Telephone: 0117 9264587
2 Gray's Inn Square Chambers
2nd Floor, Gray's Inn, London WC1R 5AA,
Telephone: 0171 242 0328/071 405 1317
E-mail: clerks@2gis.co.uk
Call date: Feb 1990, Middle Temple
Qualifications: [LLB]

WATKINS PETER WILLIAM

Cobden House Chambers
19 Quay Street, Manchester M3 3HN,
Telephone: 0161 833 6000
E-mail: clerks@cobden.co.uk
Call date: Feb 1952, Lincoln's Inn
Qualifications: [MA, BCL]

WATKINSON DAVID ROBERT

2 Garden Court
1st Floor, Middle Temple, London EC4Y 9BL,
Telephone: 0171 353 1633
E-mail: barristers@2gardenct.law.co.uk
Call date: July 1972, Middle Temple
Qualifications: [MA, LLB (Cantab)]

WATSON ANTHONY DENNIS

Lincoln House Chambers
5th Floor Lincoln House, 1 Brazennose Street,
Manchester M2 5EL,
Telephone: 0161 832 5701
E-mail: LincolnHouseChambers@link.org
Call date: July 1985, Inner Temple
Qualifications: [BA (Hons)]

WATSON ANTONY EDWARD DOUGLAS QC (1986)

3 New Square
Lincoln's Inn, London WC2A 3RS,
Telephone: 0171 405 1111
Call date: Nov 1968, Inner Temple
Qualifications: [MA (Cantab)]

WATSON MISS BARBARA JOAN

15 Winckley Square
Preston PR1 3JJ, Telephone: 01772 252828
E-mail: clerks@winckleysq.demon.co.uk
Call date: July 1973, Gray's Inn
Qualifications: [LLB]

D

WATSON BRIAN JAMES ROBB

Guildhall Chambers
23 Broad Street, Bristol BS1 2HG,
Telephone: 0117 9273366
Call date: July 1978, Lincoln's Inn
Qualifications: [MA, LLB (Cantab)]

WATSON MS CLAIRE

55 Temple Chambers
Temple Avenue, London EC4Y 0HP,
Telephone: 0171 353 7400
Call date: Nov 1991, Lincoln's Inn
Qualifications: [LLB (Hons)]

WATSON DAVID JAMES

6 Fountain Court
Steelhouse Lane, Birmingham B4 6DR,
Telephone: 0121 233 3282
Call date: Nov 1994, Gray's Inn
Qualifications: [BA (Bris), BA (Manch)]

WATSON DAVID WILLIAM

Adrian Lyon's Chambers
14 Castle Street, Liverpool L2 0NE,
Telephone: 0151 236 4421/8240
E-mail: chambers14@aol.com
3 Temple Gardens
3rd Floor, Temple, London EC4Y 9AU,
Telephone: 0171 583 0010
Call date: Oct 1990, Middle Temple
Qualifications: [LLB (Brunel)]

WATSON FRANCIS PAUL

Paradise Square Chambers
26 Paradise Square, Sheffield S1 2DE,
Telephone: 0114 2738951
Call date: Nov 1978, Gray's Inn
Assistant Recorder
Qualifications: [BA (Leeds)]

WATSON MISS HILARY JANE

St Mary's Chambers
50 High Pavement, Lace Market, Nottingham
NG1 1HW, Telephone: 0115 9503503
E-mail: clerks@smc.law.co.uk
Call date: July 1979, Gray's Inn
Qualifications: [LLB (Bris)]

WATSON MISS ISABELLE MARGARET

Francis Taylor Bldg
Ground Floor, Temple, London EC4Y 7BY,
Telephone: 0171 353 7768/7769/2711
Call date: Oct 1991, Middle Temple
Qualifications: [BA Hons (Cantab), Dip Law]

WATSON SIR JAMES ANDREW

4 Fountain Court
Steelhouse Lane, Birmingham B4 6DR,
Telephone: 0121 236 3476
Door Tenant
1 Crown Office Row
3rd Floor, Temple, London EC4Y 7HH,
Telephone: 0171 583 9292
E-mail: onecor@link.org
Call date: July 1966, Inner Temple
Recorder

WATSON JAMES VERNON

3 Serjeants Inn
London EC4Y 1BQ,
Telephone: 0171 353 5537
E-mail: available upon request
Call date: July 1979, Middle Temple
Qualifications: [BA (Cantab)]

WATSON MISS KIRSTIE ANN

St Paul's House
5th Floor 23 Park Square South, Leeds
LS1 2ND, Telephone: 0113 2455866
Call date: Oct 1995, Middle Temple
Qualifications: [LLB (Hons)(Leeds)]

WATSON MARK

6 Pump Court
1st Floor, Temple, London EC4Y 7AR,
Telephone: 0171 797 8400
E-mail: sa_hockman_qc@link.org
6-8 Mill Street
Maidstone, Kent ME15 6XH,
Telephone: 01622 688094
Call date: Oct 1994, Gray's Inn
Qualifications: [BA]

WATSON DR PHILIPPA

Essex Court Chambers
24 Lincoln's Inn Fields, London WC2A 3ED,
Telephone: 0171 813 8000
E-mail: clerksroom@essexcourt-chambers.co.uk
Call date: July 1988, Middle Temple

Qualifications: [MA (Dublin), LLM, PhD (Cantab), BL (Kings Inn)]

WATSON ROBERT JEFFREY

3 Temple Gardens
2nd Floor, Temple, London EC4Y 9AU,
Telephone: 0171 583 1155
Call date: July 1963, Inner Temple

WATSON MS SHARON

New Bailey Chambers
10 Lawson Street, Preston PR1 2QT,
Telephone: 01772 258087
Call date: Nov 1994, Middle Temple
Qualifications: [BA (Hons)]

WATSON TOM BRADLEY

Chavasse Court Chambers
2nd Floor Chavasse Court, 24 Lord Street,
Liverpool L2 1TA, Telephone: 0151 707 1191
Call date: Oct 1990, Inner Temple
Qualifications: [BA (N Wales), MA (Keele), Dip Law]

WATSON-GANDY MARK

3 Paper Bldgs
2nd Floor, Temple, London EC4Y 7EU,
Telephone: 0171 353 6208
Call date: Oct 1990, Inner Temple
Qualifications: [LLB (Hons)]

WATSON-HOPKINSON MS GHISLAINE ELIZABETH CLARE

Guildford Chambers
Stoke House Leapale Lane, Guildford, Surrey
GU1 4LY, Telephone: 01483 539131
E-mail: guildford.barristers@btinternet.com
Call date: Nov 1991, Inner Temple
Qualifications: [LLB]

WATT-PRINGLE JONATHAN HELIER

Farrar's Building
Temple, London EC4Y 7BD,
Telephone: 0171 583 9241
E-mail: chambers@farrarsbuilding.co.uk
Call date: July 1987, Middle Temple
Qualifications: [MA, BCL (Oxon), BA, LLB, (Stellenbosch)]

WATTS MISS ALISON ELFRIDA

4 King's Bench Walk
Ground/First Floor, Temple, London
EC4Y 7DL, Telephone: 0171 822 8822
E-mail: 4kbw@barristersatlaw.com
Call date: July 1981, Middle Temple
Qualifications: [LLB (Lond)]

WATTS SIR ARTHUR DESMOND QC (1988)

20 Essex Street
London WC2R 3AL,
Telephone: 0171 583 9294
E-mail: clerks@20essexst.com
Call date: Nov 1957, Gray's Inn
Qualifications: [MA,LLM]

WATTS LAWRENCE PETER

7 Fountain Court
Steelhouse Lane, Birmingham B4 6DR,
Telephone: 0121 236 8531
Call date: July 1988, Inner Temple
Qualifications: [LLB]

WATTS MR. MARTIN WILLIAM

1 Crown Office Row
2nd Floor, Temple, London EC4Y 7HH,
Telephone: 0171 797 7111
Call date: Oct 1995, Middle Temple
Qualifications: [MA (Oxon)]

WAUCHOPE PIERS ANDREW CHARLES

3 Temple Gardens
3rd Floor, Temple, London EC4Y 9AU,
Telephone: 0171 583 0010
Call date: July 1985, Gray's Inn
Qualifications: [BA (Manchester)]

WAUGH ANDREW PETER

3 New Square
Lincoln's Inn, London WC2A 3RS,
Telephone: 0171 405 1111
Call date: July 1982, Gray's Inn
Qualifications: [BSc (City), Dip Law (City)]

D

WAUGH MS JANE

Fountain Chambers
Cleveland Business Centre 1 Watson Street,
Middlesbrough TS1 2RQ,
Telephone: 01642 217037
Call date: Oct 1992, Inner Temple
Qualifications: [LLB]

WAY IAN LEONARD

King Charles House
Standard Hill, Nottingham NG1 6FX,
Telephone: 0115 9418851
E-mail: clerks@kch.co.uk
Call date: Nov 1988, Inner Temple
Qualifications: [BA (Lond)]

WAY PATRICK EDWARD

8 Gray's Inn Square
Gray's Inn, London WC1R 5AZ,
Telephone: 0171 242 3529
Call date: May 1994, Lincoln's Inn
Qualifications: [BA (Hons, Leeds)]

WAYLEN BARNABY JAMES

1 Gray's Inn Square
1st Floor, London WC1R 5AG,
Telephone: 0171 405 3000
E-mail: clerks@onegrays.demon.co.uk
Call date: July 1968, Inner Temple
Recorder
Qualifications: [MA (Cantab)]

WAYNE NICHOLAS

1 Gray's Inn Square
Ground Floor, London WC1R 5AA,
Telephone: 0171 405 8946/7/8
Call date: July 1994, Middle Temple
Qualifications: [BA (Hons)(Oxon)]

WEATHERALL MISS JULIA

Cleveland Chambers
63-65 Borough Road, Middlesbrough,
Cleveland TS1 3AA, Telephone: 01642 226036
Call date: July 1985, Inner Temple
Qualifications: [LLB (Brunel)]

WEATHERBY PETER FRANCIS

2 Garden Court
1st Floor, Middle Temple, London EC4Y 9BL,
Telephone: 0171 353 1633
E-mail: barristers@2gardenct.law.co.uk
Chambers of Ian Macdonald QC
Waldorf House Cooper Street, Manchester
M2 2FW, Telephone: 0161 236 1840
Call date: Nov 1992, Gray's Inn
Qualifications: [BSc (Hons)]

WEATHERILL BERNARD RICHARD QC (1996)

Chambers of Lord Goodhart QC
Ground Floor 3 New Square, Lincoln's Inn,
London WC2A 3RS,
Telephone: 0171 405 5577
E-mail: law@threenewsquare.demon.co.uk
Call date: July 1974, Middle Temple
Qualifications: [BA]

WEAVER MISS ELIZABETH ANNE

24 Old Bldgs
Ground Floor, Lincoln's Inn, London
WC2A 3UJ, Telephone: 0171 404 0946
E-mail: clerks@24oldbuildings.law.co.uk
Call date: July 1982, Lincoln's Inn
Qualifications: [LLB (Bris)]

WEBB ANTHONY RONALD

Farrar's Building
Temple, London EC4Y 7BD,
Telephone: 0171 583 9241
E-mail: chambers@farrarsbuilding.co.uk
Call date: July 1970, Inner Temple
Recorder
Qualifications: [LLB, Dip Soc]

WEBB GERAINT TIMOTHY

2 Harcourt Bldgs
Ground Floor/Left, Temple, London
EC4Y 9DB, Telephone: 0171 583 9020
E-mail: clerks@harcourt.co.uk
Call date: Oct 1995, Inner Temple
Qualifications: [BA (Oxon), CPE (City)]

WEBB MISS LORRAINE ELIZABETH

Tindal Chambers
3/5 New Street, Chelmsford, Essex CM1 1NT,
Telephone: 01245 267742
Flat 4, Churston Mansions
Churston Mansions 176 Gray's Inn Road,
London WC1R 4DB,
Telephone: 0171 837 1596
Call date: July 1980, Middle Temple
Qualifications: [BA]

WEBB NICHOLAS JOHN DAVID

4 Fountain Court
Steelhouse Lane, Birmingham B4 6DR,
Telephone: 0121 236 3476
Call date: July 1972, Middle Temple
Qualifications: [BA (Cantab)]

WEBB ROBERT STOPFORD QC (1988)

5 Bell Yard
London WC2A 2JR, Telephone: 0171 333 8811
Call date: July 1971, Inner Temple
Recorder
Qualifications: [LLB]

Fax: 0171 333 8811; DX: LDE 400

Types of work: Arbitration; Aviation;
Commercial litigation; Common law (general);
Competition; EC and competition law;
Insurance; Insurance/reinsurance; Mass
disasters; Medical negligence; Personal injury;
Professional negligence; Sale and carriage of
goods

Other professional qualifications: Fellow Royal
Aeronautical Society

Circuit: Western

Reported cases: *Sidhu v British Airways Plc*,
[1997] AC 430, HL, 1996. Gulf War - hostages
taken by Iraq - Warsaw Convention did not
permit recovery against carrier.
Philcox v CAA, (1995) *The Times*, 8 June, CA,
1995. Civil Aviation Authority owes no duty of
care to public when certifying aircraft.
Kuwait Airways Corp v Kuwait Insurance Co,
[1997] 2 Lloyd's Rep 687, CA, 1997. Kuwait
Airways' recovery of over £300 million for loss
of aircraft fleet.
Virgin Atlantic v British Airways Plc, 1995-8.
Numerous skirmishes.
EasyJet v BA, 1998. Competition law -
lawfulness of subsidies.

WEBB STANLEY GEORGE

9 King's Bench Walk
Basement, Temple, London EC4Y 7DX,
Telephone: 0171 353 9564
E-mail: jvlee@btinternet.com
Call date: Oct 1993, Gray's Inn
Qualifications: [B.Sc (Hons)(Eng)]

WEBBER DOMINIC DENZIL FERNANDEZ

Verulam Chambers
Peer House 8-14 Verulam Street, Gray's Inn,
London WC1X 8LZ,
Telephone: 0171 813 2400
Call date: Nov 1985, Gray's Inn
Qualifications: [BA, Dip Law]

WEBBER MISS FRANCES GAIL

2 Garden Court
1st Floor, Middle Temple, London EC4Y 9BL,
Telephone: 0171 353 1633
E-mail: barristers@2gardenct.law.co.uk
Call date: July 1978, Gray's Inn
Qualifications: [BSc]

WEBBER GARY NEIL

33 Bedford Row
London WC1R 4JH,
Telephone: 0171 242 6476
Call date: July 1979, Inner Temple
Qualifications: [LLB (Lond)]

WEBSTER ALISTAIR STEVENSON QC (1995)

Lincoln House Chambers
5th Floor Lincoln House, 1 Brazennose Street,
Manchester M2 5EL,
Telephone: 0161 832 5701
E-mail: LincolnHouseChambers@link.org
Call date: July 1976, Middle Temple
Recorder
Qualifications: [BA (Oxon)]

WEBSTER DAVID FRANCIS

32 Park Place
Cardiff CF1 3BA, Telephone: 01222 397364
Call date: Oct 1993, Gray's Inn
Qualifications: [B.Sc (Econ, Wales)]

D

WEBSTER MISS ELIZABETH JANE

18 Red Lion Court
(Off Fleet Street), London EC4A 3EB,
Telephone: 0171 520 6000
Thornwood House
102 New London Road, Chelmsford, Essex
CM2 0RG, Telephone: 01245 280880
Call date: Nov 1995, Middle Temple
Qualifications: [BA (Hons)]

WEBSTER JUSTIN

Hardwicke Building
New Square, Lincoln's Inn, London
WC2A 3SB, Telephone: 0171 242 2523
E-mail: clerks@hardwicke.co.uk
Call date: Feb 1985, Inner Temple
Qualifications: [BA]

WEBSTER LEONARD

Cobden House Chambers
19 Quay Street, Manchester M3 3HN,
Telephone: 0161 833 6000
E-mail: clerks@cobden.co.uk
Call date: July 1984, Lincoln's Inn
Qualifications: [BA]

WEBSTER ROBERT MARTIN CHRISTOPHER

1 Harcourt Bldgs
2nd Floor, Temple, London EC4Y 9DA,
Telephone: 0171 353 9421/9151
Door Tenant
Call date: July 1979, Inner Temple
Qualifications: [BA (Sussex)]

WEBSTER WILLIAM HOWARD

17 Carlton Crescent
Southampton SO15 2XR,
Telephone: 01703 320320
E-mail: km@bar-17cc.demon.co.uk
Call date: July 1975, Middle Temple
Qualifications: [LLB (Bristol)]

WEDDELL GEOFFREY DAVID ANDREW

2 King's Bench Walk
Ground Floor, Temple, London EC4Y 7DE,
Telephone: 0171 353 1746
E-mail: 2kbw@atlas.co.uk
King's Bench Chambers
115 North Hill, Plymouth PL4 8JY,
Telephone: 01752 221551
Call date: Nov 1989, Inner Temple
Qualifications: [LLB]

WEDDERBURN OF CHARLTON LORD QC (1990)

Old Square Chambers
1 Verulam Buildings, Gray's Inn, London
WC1R 5LQ, Telephone: 0171 831 0801
Old Square Chambers
Hanover House 47 Corn Street, Bristol
BS1 1HT, Telephone: 0117 9277111
Call date: Feb 1953, Middle Temple
Qualifications: [MA (Cantab), LLB, FBA, Hon D
GIUR, (Pavia)(Siena), HonD.Econ (Siena), LLD
(Stockholm)]

WEDDERSPOON MISS RACHEL LEONE

9 St John Street
Manchester M3 4DN,
Telephone: 0161 955 9000
E-mail: ninesjs@gconnect.com
Call date: Oct 1993, Middle Temple
Qualifications: [LLB (Hons)(Manc)]

WEDDLE STEVEN EDGAR

Hardwicke Building
New Square, Lincoln's Inn, London
WC2A 3SB, Telephone: 0171 242 2523
E-mail: clerks@hardwicke.co.uk
Call date: Nov 1977, Gray's Inn
Qualifications: [BA]

WEEKES MISS ANESTA GLENDORA

36 Bedford Row
London WC1R 4JH,
Telephone: 0171 421 8000
E-mail: 36bedfordrow@link.org
Call date: July 1981, Gray's Inn

WEEKS MS JANET KATHLEEN

Queen Elizabeth Bldg
Ground Floor, Temple, London EC4Y 9BS,
Telephone: 0171 353 7181 (12 Lines)
Call date: Oct 1993, Inner Temple
Qualifications: [LLB (Exon)]

WEERERATNE MS RUFINA ASWINI

Doughty Street Chambers
11 Doughty Street, London WC1N 2PG,
Telephone: 0171 404 1313
E-mail: doughty_street@compuserve.com
Call date: July 1986, Gray's Inn
Qualifications: [BSc (Sussex), Dip Law]

WEHRLE MISS JACQUELINE

Goldsmith Chambers
Ground Floor Goldsmith Building, Temple,
London EC4Y 7BL,
Telephone: 0171 353 6802/3/4/5
E-mail: celiamonksfield@btinternet.com
Call date: Nov 1984, Lincoln's Inn
Qualifications: [LLB (Reading)]

WEINIGER NORMAN NOAH

Gray's Inn Chambers
5th Floor, Gray's Inn, London WC1R 5JA,
Telephone: 0171 404 1111
Call date: Nov 1984, Gray's Inn
Qualifications: [LLB (Manch)]

WEINSTEIN MISS LINDSAY

Lamb Building
Ground Floor, Temple, London EC4Y 7AS,
Telephone: 0171 797 7788
E-mail: lamb.building@link.org
Call date: Oct 1992, Middle Temple
Qualifications: [LLB (Hons)]

WEIR MISS OLIVIA

John Street Chambers
2 John Street, London WC1N 2HJ,
Telephone: 0171 242 1911
E-mail: john.street_chambers@virgin.net.uk
Call date: Nov 1995, Inner Temple
Qualifications: [BA]

WEIR ROBERT THOMAS MACDONALD

3 Paper Bldgs
1st Floor, Temple, London EC4Y 7EU,
Telephone: 0171 583 8055
E-mail: london@3paper.com
1 Alfred Street
High Street, Oxford OX1 4EH,
Telephone: 01865 793736
4 St Peter Street
Winchester SO23 8OW,
Telephone: 01962 868884
Call date: Nov 1992, Middle Temple
Qualifications: [MA (Hons)]

WEISMAN MALCOLM

1 Gray's Inn Square
Ground Floor, London WC1R 5AA,
Telephone: 0171 405 8946/7/8
Call date: June 1961, Middle Temple
Recorder
Qualifications: [MA (Oxon)]

WEISSELBERG TOM

2 Hare Court
Ground Floor, Temple, London EC4Y 7BH,
Telephone: 0171 583 1770
E-mail: 2_Hare_Court@link.org
Call date: Oct 1995, Inner Temple
Qualifications: [BA (Oxon), CPE (City)]

WEITZMAN ADAM JOHN

9 Bedford Row
London WC1R 4AZ,
Telephone: 0171 242 3555
E-mail: clerks@9br.co.uk
Call date: Nov 1993, Middle Temple
Qualifications: [BA (Hons)(Cantab), MA
(Manc), CPE (Lond)]

WEITZMAN PETER QC (1973)

Devereux Chambers
Devereux Court, London WC2R 3JJ,
Telephone: 0171 353 7534
E-mail: elton@devchambers.co.uk
5 Fountain Court
Steelhouse Lane, Birmingham B4 6DR,
Telephone: 0121 606 0500
Call date: July 1952, Gray's Inn
Recorder
Qualifications: [MA (Oxon)]

D

WEITZMAN THOMAS EDWARD BENJAMIN

3 Verulam Buildings
London WC1R 5NT,
Telephone: 0171 831 8441
E-mail: clerks@3verulam.co.uk
Call date: July 1984, Gray's Inn
Qualifications: [BA (Oxon)]

WELCH EDWARD BRETT

Verulam Chambers
Peer House 8-14 Verulam Street, Gray's Inn,
London WC1X 8LZ,
Telephone: 0171 813 2400
Call date: Oct 1996, Lincoln's Inn
Qualifications: [BA (Hons)(Manc), Dip in Law
(City), CPE]

WELCHMAN CHARLES STUART

199 Strand
London WC2R 1DR,
Telephone: 0171 379 9779
E-mail: chambers@199strand.co.uk
Call date: July 1966, Gray's Inn
Qualifications: [LLB (Lond)]

WELLESLEY-COLE MISS PATRICE SUZANNE

11 Old Square
Ground Floor, Lincoln's Inn, London
WC2A 3TS, Telephone: 0171 242 5022/
405 1074
Call date: Nov 1975, Inner Temple
Qualifications: [BA (Oxon)]

WELLS COLIN JOHN

3 Gray's Inn Square
Ground Floor, London WC1R 5AH,
Telephone: 0171 520 5600
E-mail: gis3@btinternet.com
Call date: Nov 1987, Inner Temple
Qualifications: [BSc, MA (Warwick), Dip Law]

WELLS DAVID MARLON

Cleveland Chambers
63-65 Borough Road, Middlesbrough,
Cleveland TS1 3AA, Telephone: 01642 226036
Call date: Nov 1995, Gray's Inn
Qualifications: [LLB]

WELLS GRAHAM HOLLAND

Derby Square Chambers
Merchants Court, Derby Square, Liverpool
L2 1TS, Telephone: 0151 709 4222
Call date: July 1982, Middle Temple
Qualifications: [MA (Oxon)]

WELLS NICHOLAS THOMAS CLINTON

Thomas More Chambers
52 Carey Street, Lincoln's Inn, London
WC2A 2JB, Telephone: 0171 404 7000
Call date: Nov 1990, Lincoln's Inn
Qualifications: [BA (Cantab), Dip Law (City)]

WELSH JAMES ANTHONY KIRKMAN

Devon Chambers
3 St Andrew Street, Plymouth PL1 2AH,
Telephone: 01752 661659
Call date: Nov 1994, Middle Temple
Qualifications: [BA (Hons) (Dunelm), Dip Law]

WELSH PASCHAL JUDE RICHARD

3 Temple Gardens
3rd Floor, Temple, London EC4Y 9AU,
Telephone: 0171 353 0832
Call date: July 1974, Lincoln's Inn

WENLOCK MISS HEATHER

13 King's Bench Walk
1st Floor, Temple, London EC4Y 7EN,
Telephone: 0171 353 7204
E-mail: clerks@13kbw.law.co.uk
King's Bench Chambers
32 Beaumont Street, Oxford OX1 2NP,
Telephone: 01865 311066
E-mail: clerks@kbc-oxford.law.co.uk
Call date: Oct 1991, Middle Temple
Qualifications: [BA Hons (Hull), MPhil, DPhil
(Oxon)]

WENTWORTH MISS ANNABEL HENRIETTE

4 Brick Court
Temple, London EC4Y 9AD,
Telephone: 0171 797 8910
Call date: Oct 1990, Inner Temple
Qualifications: [BA (Nott'm), Dip Law]

WERNHAM STEWART FREDERICK

1 Dr Johnson's Bldgs
Ground Floor, Temple, London EC4Y 7AX,
Telephone: 0171 353 9328
Call date: July 1984, Middle Temple
Qualifications: [LLB (Warwick)]

WEST IAN HERBERT

Bank House Chambers
Old Bank House, Hartshead, Sheffield S1 2EL,
Telephone: 0114 2751223
Call date: Nov 1996, Middle Temple
Qualifications: [LLB (Hons)(Auckland)]

WEST IAN STUART

Plowden Bldgs
2nd Floor, Temple, London EC4Y 9BU,
Telephone: 0171 583 0808
E-mail: bar@plowdenbuildings.co.uk
Call date: Nov 1985, Inner Temple
Qualifications: [LLB (Hull)]

WEST JOHN REDVERS

5 Fountain Court
Steelhouse Lane, Birmingham B4 6DR,
Telephone: 0121 606 0500
Call date: Feb 1965, Middle Temple
Qualifications: [BA (Cantab)]

WEST LAWRENCE JOSEPH

2 Harcourt Bldgs
Ground Floor/Left, Temple, London
EC4Y 9DB, Telephone: 0171 583 9020
E-mail: clerks@harcourt.co.uk
Stanbrook & Henderson
2 Harcourt Bldgs 2nd Floor, Temple, London
EC4Y 9DB, Telephone: 0171 353 0101
E-mail: clerks@harcourt.co.uk
Call date: May 1979, Gray's Inn
Assistant Recorder
Qualifications: [LLM (Lond), LLB, BA
(Toronto)]

WEST MARK

11 Old Square
Ground Floor, Lincoln's Inn, London
WC2A 3TS, Telephone: 0171 430 0341
E-mail: clerks@11oldsquare.co.uk
Call date: July 1987, Middle Temple

Qualifications: [MA, LLM (Cantab)]

Fax: 0171 831 2469; DX: LDE 1031;
Other comms: E-mail
clerks@11oldsquare.co.uk

Types of work: Bankruptcy; Chancery (general); Chancery land law; Charities; Commercial litigation; Commercial property; Common law (general); Company and commercial; Conveyancing; Equity, wills and trusts; Family provision; Insolvency; Landlord and tenant; Partnerships; Probate and administration; Professional negligence; Restitution

Awards and memberships: Chancery Bar Association; Professional Negligence Bar Association; Bar European Group

Languages spoken: French

Publications: 'Swaps & Local Authorities: A Mistake?' (with Catherine Newman QC) in *Swaps & Off-exchange Derivatives Trading: Law & Regulation* (edited by Bettelheim, Parry & Rees) (FT Law & Tax), 1996

Reported cases: *Kleinwort Benson v Sandwell BC*, [1994] 4 All ER 890, 1993. Restitution of monies paid under *ultra vires* interest rate swap contracts.
Morgan Grenfell v Welwyn Hatfield DC; Islington LBC (third party), [1995] 1 All ER 1, 1993. Whether interest rate swap contracts are wagers within s18 of the Gaming Act 1845/s1 of the Gaming Act 1892.
Kleinwort Benson v Birmingham CC, [1997] QB 380, 1996. Whether passing on is a defence to restitution of monies paid under a void interest rate swap contract.
Chong Kai Tai Ringo v Lee Gee Kee, [1997] HKLRD 491, 1997. Provisional agreement for sale of flat; whether obligations of purchaser and vendor concurrent; whether liquidated damage clause a bar to specific performance.

WEST MARK ROGER

Lamb Chambers
Lamb Building, Temple, London EC4Y 7AS,
Telephone: 0171 797 8300
E-mail: lambchambers@link.org
Call date: May 1973, Inner Temple
Assistant Recorder
Qualifications: [LLB]

WEST MICHAEL CHARLES BERESFORD QC (1975)

3 & 4 Farnham Hall
Farnham, Saxmundham, Suffolk IP17 1LB,
Telephone: 01728 602758
8 Lambert Jones Mews
Barbican, London EC2Y 8DP,
Telephone: 0171 638 8804
Call date: Nov 1952, Lincoln's Inn

WEST MISS STEPHANIE

Bell Yard Chambers
116/118 Chancery Lane, London WC2A 1PP,
Telephone: 0171 306 9292
Call date: May 1993, Gray's Inn
Qualifications: [LLB (Huddersfield)]

WEST-KNIGHTS LAURENCE JAMES

4 Paper Bldgs
Ground Floor, Temple, London EC4Y 7EX,
Telephone: 0171 353 3366/583 7155
E-mail: clerks@4paperbuildings.com
Call date: Nov 1977, Gray's Inn
Assistant Recorder
Qualifications: [MA (Cantab)]

WESTCOTT DAVID GUY

35 Essex Street
Temple, London WC2R 3AR,
Telephone: 0171 353 6381
Call date: Nov 1982, Middle Temple
Qualifications: [BA (Oxon)]

WESTERLAND MISS REBECCA ABIGAIL

Queen Elizabeth Bldg
Ground Floor, Temple, London EC4Y 9BS,
Telephone: 0171 353 7181 (12 Lines)
Call date: Feb 1992, Inner Temple
Qualifications: [LLB (LSE)]

WESTERN ADAM JOHN BROOKS

Coleridge Chambers
Citadel 190 Corporation Street, Birmingham
B4 6QD, Telephone: 0121 233 3303
Call date: Mar 1997, Gray's Inn
Qualifications: [BA (L'pool)]

WESTGATE MARTIN TREVOR

Doughty Street Chambers
11 Doughty Street, London WC1N 2PG,
Telephone: 0171 404 1313
E-mail: doughty_street@compuserve.com
Call date: Nov 1985, Middle Temple
Qualifications: [BA (Oxon)]

WESTON MS AMANDA

Chambers of Ian Macdonald QC
Waldorf House Cooper Street, Manchester
M2 2FW, Telephone: 0161 236 1840
Call date: Oct 1995, Inner Temple
Qualifications: [LLB (Hons)]

WESTON CLIVE AUBREY RICHARD

2 Crown Office Row
Ground Floor, Temple, London EC4Y 7HJ,
Telephone: 0171 797 8100
E-mail: mail@2cor.co.uk, or to individual
barristers at: [barrister's surname]@2cor.co.uk
Call date: Nov 1993, Middle Temple
Qualifications: [MA (Hons)(Cantab), CPE
(City)]

WESTON JEREMY PAUL

St Ive's Chambers
9 Fountain Ct, Birmingham B4 6DR,
Telephone: 0121 236 0863/0929
Call date: Oct 1991, Inner Temple
Qualifications: [LLB]

WESTON LOUIS ROY PAUL

King's Bench Chambers
115 North Hill, Plymouth PL4 8JY,
Telephone: 01752 221551
Call date: Nov 1994, Lincoln's Inn
Qualifications: [BA (Hons)(Bris), CPE]

WESTWOOD ANDREW DAVID

7 Stone Bldgs
Ground Floor, Lincoln's Inn, London
WC2A 3SZ, Telephone: 0171 405 3886/
242 3546
E-mail: chaldous@vossnet.co.uk
Call date: Nov 1994, Inner Temple
Qualifications: [BA (Oxon), CPE
(Huddersfield)]

WETTON PAUL NICHOLAS

1 Gray's Inn Square
Ground Floor, London WC1R 5AA,
Telephone: 0171 405 8946/7/8
Call date: Nov 1992, Middle Temple
Qualifications: [HND Business Studies, CPE]

WHAITES MISS EMMA LOUISE

2 Paper Buildings
Basement, Temple, London EC4Y 7ET,
Telephone: 0171 353 0933
Call date: Nov 1994, Gray's Inn
Qualifications: [LLB (Hons)]

WHALAN MARK ANDREW

2 Gray's Inn Square Chambers
2nd Floor, Gray's Inn, London WC1R 5AA,
Telephone: 0171 242 0328/071 405 1317
E-mail: clerks@2gis.co.uk
Call date: Nov 1988, Middle Temple
Qualifications: [BA (Leeds), Dip Law (City)]

WHEATLEY DEREK PETER FRANCIS QC (1981)

Verulam Chambers
Peer House 8-14 Verulam Street, Gray's Inn,
London WC1X 8LZ,
Telephone: 0171 813 2400
Door Tenant
Call date: Apr 1951, Middle Temple
Qualifications: [MA (Oxon)]

WHEATLEY SIMON DEREK JOHN

9 Bedford Row
London WC1R 4AZ,
Telephone: 0171 242 3555
E-mail: clerks@9br.co.uk
Call date: July 1979, Middle Temple
Qualifications: [LLB]

WHEATLY IAN NEVILL

2 Dr Johnson's Building
Temple, London EC4Y 7AY,
Telephone: 0171 353 4716
Call date: July 1977, Inner Temple
Qualifications: [BA (Hons)(Kent)]

WHEELDON MISS SARAH HELEN ELIZABETH

St James's Chambers
68 Quay Street, Manchester M3 3EJ,
Telephone: 0161 834 7000
E-mail: 106241.2625@compuserve.com
Call date: Oct 1990, Gray's Inn
Qualifications: [MA (Hons), Dip Law]

WHEELER ANDREW GEORGE

9 Gough Square
London EC4A 3DE, Telephone: 0171 353 5371
Call date: July 1988, Lincoln's Inn
Qualifications: [LLB (Hons)]

WHEELER KENNETH RICHARD

Lamb Building
Ground Floor, Temple, London EC4Y 7AS,
Telephone: 0171 797 7788
E-mail: lamb.building@link.org
Fenners Chambers
3 Madingley Road, Cambridge CB3 OEE,
Telephone: 01223 368761
Door Tenant
Fenners Chambers
8-12 Priestgate, Peterborough PE1 1JA,
Telephone: 01733 62030
Door Tenant
Call date: Nov 1956, Lincoln's Inn

WHEELER MISS MARINA CLAIRE

2 Harcourt Bldgs
Ground Floor/Left, Temple, London
EC4Y 9DB, Telephone: 0171 583 9020
E-mail: clerks@harcourt.co.uk
Stanbrook & Henderson
2 Harcourt Bldgs 2nd Floor, Temple, London
EC4Y 9DB, Telephone: 0171 353 0101
E-mail: clerks@harcourt.co.uk
Call date: Nov 1987, Gray's Inn
Qualifications: [MA (Cantab), Licence Speciale en, Droit Enrop]

WHEELER MISS SUVI DAWN

Sussex Chambers
9 Old Steine, Brighton BN1 1FJ,
Telephone: 01273 607953
Call date: Oct 1994, Lincoln's Inn
Qualifications: [BA (Hons)(Oxon)]

WHEETMAN ALAN

East Anglian Chambers
57 London Street, Norwich NR2 1HL,
Telephone: 01603 617351
East Anglian Chambers
Sanders House 52 North Hill, Colchester
CO1 1PY, Telephone: 01206 572756
East Anglian Chambers
Gresham House 5 Museum Street, Ipswich
IP1 1HQ, Telephone: 01473 214481
Call date: Oct 1995, Middle Temple
Qualifications: [LLB (Hons)]

WHELAN MISS ROMA FELICITY

Goldsmith Chambers
Ground Floor Goldsmith Building, Temple,
London EC4Y 7BL,
Telephone: 0171 353 6802/3/4/5
E-mail: celiamonksfield@btinternet.com
Call date: May 1984, Gray's Inn
Qualifications: [LLB (Belfast)]

WHIPPLE MRS PHILIPPA JANE EDWARDS

1 Crown Office Row
Ground Floor, Temple, London EC4Y 7HH,
Telephone: 0171 797 7500
Call date: Feb 1994, Middle Temple
Qualifications: [MA (Oxon)]

WHIPPMAN MRS CONSTANCE

33 Bedford Row
London WC1R 4JH,
Telephone: 0171 242 6476
Call date: Nov 1978, Gray's Inn
Qualifications: [BA,MA]

WHITAKER JOHN STEPHEN

5 Fountain Court
Steelhouse Lane, Birmingham B4 6DR,
Telephone: 0121 606 0500
Call date: Nov 1970, Lincoln's Inn
Qualifications: [MA, BCL (Oxon)]

WHITAKER MS QUINCY RACHEL SUZY

Doughty Street Chambers
11 Doughty Street, London WC1N 2PG,
Telephone: 0171 404 1313
E-mail: doughty_street@compuserve.com
Call date: Nov 1991, Middle Temple
Qualifications: [BA Hons (Oxon)]

WHITAKER STEVEN DIXON

199 Strand
London WC2R 1DR,
Telephone: 0171 379 9779
E-mail: chambers@199strand.co.uk
All Saints Chambers
9/11 Broad Street, Bristol BS1 2HP,
Telephone: 0117 921 1966
Call date: July 1973, Middle Temple
Qualifications: [MA (Cantab)]

WHITBY CHARLES HARLEY QC (1970)

12 King's Bench Walk
Temple, London EC4Y 7EL,
Telephone: 0171 583 0811
E-mail: chambers@12kbw.co.uk
Call date: July 1952, Middle Temple
Recorder
Qualifications: [MA (Cantab)]

WHITCOMBE MARK DAVID

Old Square Chambers
Hanover House 47 Corn Street, Bristol
BS1 1HT, Telephone: 0117 9277111
Old Square Chambers
1 Verulam Buildings, Gray's Inn, London
WC1R 5LQ, Telephone: 0171 831 0801
Call date: Nov 1994, Middle Temple
Qualifications: [BA (Hons)(Oxon), BCL
(Oxon)]

WHITE MISS ADELE SUSANNAH

Westgate Chambers
144 High Street, Lewes, East Sussex BN7 1XT,
Telephone: 01273 480510
Call date: Mar 1996, Lincoln's Inn
Qualifications: [BA (Hons)(Hull)]

WHITE MISS AMANDA JANE

8 Fountain Court
Steelhouse Lane, Birmingham B4 6DR,
Telephone: 0121 236 5514/5
E-mail: clerks@no8chambers.co.uk
Call date: Nov 1976, Gray's Inn
Qualifications: [BA, CNAA]

WHITE ANDREW QC (1997)

1 Atkin Building
Gray's Inn, London WC1R 5AT,
Telephone: 0171 404 0102
E-mail: clerks@atkin-chambers.co.uk
Call date: July 1980, Lincoln's Inn
Qualifications: [LLB (Wales)]

WHITE ANTONY DENIS LOWNDES

Cloisters
1st Floor, Temple, London EC4Y 7AA,
Telephone: 0171 827 4000
E-mail: clerks@cloisters.com
Call date: Nov 1983, Middle Temple
Qualifications: [BA (Cantab)]

WHITE DARREN PAUL

Independent Barristers Clerk
Room 5, 2nd Floor 15 Castle Street, Exeter,
Devon EX4 3PT, Telephone: 01392 210900
E-mail: cathedral.chambers@eclipse.co.uk
Call date: Oct 1996, Lincoln's Inn
Qualifications: [LLB (Hons)(Notts)]

WHITE MISS GEMMA SOPHIE GOLDER

2 Hare Court
Ground Floor, Temple, London EC4Y 7BH,
Telephone: 0171 583 1770
E-mail: 2_Hare_Court@link.org
Call date: Nov 1994, Inner Temple
Qualifications: [LLB (Lond), BA (Oxon)]

WHITE GEOFFREY GEORGE NOBLE

Chambers of Raana Sheikh
Gray's Inn Chambers, Gray's Inn, London
WC1R, Telephone: 0171 831 5344
E-mail: s.mcblain@btinternet.com
Door Tenant
Call date: Nov 1985, Middle Temple
Qualifications: [BSc (L'pool), Dip, Law
(Westminster)]

WHITE MISS JOANNE ELIZABETH

Verulam Chambers
Peer House 8-14 Verulam Street, Gray's Inn,
London WC1X 8LZ,
Telephone: 0171 813 2400
Call date: July 1987, Middle Temple
Qualifications: [BA (Hons)]

WHITE PETER-JOHN SPENCER

Pembroke House
18 The Crescent, Leatherhead, Surrey
KT22 8EE, Telephone: 01372 376160/376493
Call date: July 1977, Inner Temple
Qualifications: [BA]

WHITE ROBERT DOUGLAS

1 Serjeants' Inn
4th Floor, Temple, London EC4Y 1NH,
Telephone: 0171 583 1355
E-mail: serjeants.inn@virgin.net
Call date: Nov 1993, Inner Temple
Qualifications: [LLB (LSE)]

WHITE MR. ROBIN MARK

Field Court Chambers
2nd Floor 3 Field Court, Gray's Inn, London
WC1R 4EP, Telephone: 0171 404 7474
E-mail: Clerks@FieldCourtChambers.law.co.uk
Call date: Nov 1995, Gray's Inn
Qualifications: [BSc, LLB (Exon)]

WHITE SASHA NICHOLAS

1 Serjeants' Inn
4th Floor, Temple, London EC4Y 1NH,
Telephone: 0171 583 1355
E-mail: serjeants.inn@virgin.net
Call date: Oct 1991, Inner Temple
Qualifications: [BA (Cantab)]

WHITE MRS TANYA

Pembroke House
18 The Crescent, Leatherhead, Surrey
KT22 8EE, Telephone: 01372 376160/376493
Call date: Feb 1983, Middle Temple
Qualifications: [BA]

WHITE TIMOTHY GORDON

15 Winckley Square
Preston PR1 3JJ, Telephone: 01772 252828
E-mail: clerks@winckleysq.demon.co.uk
Call date: July 1978, Middle Temple
Qualifications: [BA]

WHITE TIMOTHY RICHARD

30 Park Square
Leeds LS1 2PF, Telephone: 0113 2436388
Call date: Oct 1993, Middle Temple
Qualifications: [LLB (Hons), MA (Keele)]

WHITEHALL MARK ANTHONY

Colleton Chambers
Colleton Crescent, Exeter, Devon EX2 4DG,
Telephone: 01392 74898/9
Call date: July 1983, Inner Temple
Qualifications: [LLB (Exon)]

WHITEHEAD DARRON MARCUS

Chichester Chambers
12 North Pallant, Chichester, West Sussex
PO19 1TQ, Telephone: 01243 784538
Call date: Nov 1995, Inner Temple
Qualifications: [LLB (Sheff)]

WHITEHOUSE CHRISTOPHER JOHN

8 Gray's Inn Square
Gray's Inn, London WC1R 5AZ,
Telephone: 0171 242 3529
Call date: May 1972, Inner Temple
Qualifications: [BA, BCL (Oxon)]

WHITEHOUSE DAVID RAE BECKWITH QC (1990)

3 Raymond Buildings
Gray's Inn, London WC1R 5BH,
Telephone: 0171 831 3833
E-mail: chambers@threeraymond.demon.co.uk
Call date: Nov 1969, Gray's Inn
Recorder
Qualifications: [MA (Cantab)]

WHITEHOUSE MRS SARAH ALICE

6 King's Bench Walk
Ground Floor, Temple, London EC4Y 7DR,
Telephone: 0171 583 0410
Call date: Oct 1993, Lincoln's Inn
Qualifications: [MA (Hons)]

WHITEHOUSE STUART COLIN

New Court
Temple, London EC4Y 9BE,
Telephone: 0171 583 5123/0171 583 0510
Call date: July 1987, Middle Temple
Qualifications: [LLB(Hons), LLM (Exon)]

WHITEHOUSE-VAUX WILLIAM EDWARD

4 Field Court
Gray's Inn, London WC1R 5EA,
Telephone: 0171 440 6900
E-mail: chambers@4fieldcourt.co.uk
Call date: Nov 1977, Inner Temple
Qualifications: [Dr. Jur (Bologna)]

WHITEHURST IAN JOHN

New Bailey Chambers
10 Lawson Street, Preston PR1 2QT,
Telephone: 01772 258087
Call date: Nov 1994, Inner Temple
Qualifications: [LLB (Hull)]

WHITELEY MISS MIRANDA BLYTH

4 Field Court
Gray's Inn, London WC1R 5EA,
Telephone: 0171 440 6900
E-mail: chambers@4fieldcourt.co.uk
Call date: Nov 1985, Middle Temple
Qualifications: [MA (Cantab)]

WHITEMAN PETER GEORGE QC (1977)

Hollis Whiteman Chambers
3rd/4th Floor Queen Elizabeth Bldg, Temple,
London EC4Y 9BS, Telephone: 0171 583 5766
E-mail: hollis.whiteman@btinternet.com
Call date: July 1967, Lincoln's Inn
Recorder
Qualifications: [LLB, LLM]

WHITFIELD ADRIAN QC (1983)

3 Serjeants Inn
London EC4Y 1BQ,
Telephone: 0171 353 5537
E-mail: available upon request
Call date: June 1964, Middle Temple
Recorder
Qualifications: [MA (Oxon)]

WHITFIELD JONATHAN

Hardwicke Building
New Square, Lincoln's Inn, London
WC2A 3SB, Telephone: 0171 242 2523
E-mail: clerks@hardwicke.co.uk
Call date: July 1985, Middle Temple
Qualifications: [BA]

WHITING RICHARD JAMES

Newport Chambers
12 Clytha Park Road, Newport, Gwent
NP9 47L, Telephone: 01633 267403/255855
Call date: July 1976, Middle Temple

WHITLEY JONATHAN DENTON

Harrow on the Hill Chambers
60 High Street, Harrow on the Hill, Middlesex
HA1 3LL, Telephone: 0181 423 7444
Windsor Barristers' Chambers
Windsor, Telephone: 01753 648899
Call date: Nov 1993, Inner Temple
Qualifications: [LLB (Hons) (Exon)]

WHITMORE JOHN

21 Portland Road
Clarendon Park, Leicester LE2 3AB,
Telephone: 0116 2706235
Door Tenant
Cloisters
1st Floor, Temple, London EC4Y 7AA,
Telephone: 0171 827 4000
E-mail: clerks@cloisters.com
Door Tenant
Call date: May 1976, Lincoln's Inn
Qualifications: [BA, BCL (Oxon)]

WHITNEY IAIN DOUGLAS

St George's Chambers
32/33 Foregate Street, Worcester WR1 1EE,
Telephone: 0345 413635
Clock Chambers
78 Darlington Street, Wolverhampton
WV1 4LY, Telephone: 01902 313444
Call date: July 1980, Lincoln's Inn

WHITTAKER DAVID JOHN

4 Brick Court
1st Floor, Temple, London EC4Y 9AD,
Telephone: 0171 583 8455
Call date: Nov 1986, Middle Temple
Qualifications: [BA (Lond) Dip Law]

WHITTAKER MISS DORNE JOANNA

Park Lane Chambers
19 Westgate, Leeds LS1 2RD,
Telephone: 0113 2285000
Call date: Nov 1994, Middle Temple
Qualifications: [BA (Hons), MBA]

WHITTAKER JOHN PERCIVAL

13 Old Square
1st Floor, Lincoln's Inn, London WC2A 3UA,
Telephone: 0171 242 6105
E-mail: clerks@serlecourt.co.uk
Call date: Nov 1969, Lincoln's Inn
Qualifications: [MA, BCL (Oxon)]

WHITTAKER ROBERT MICHAEL

3 Temple Gardens
Lower Ground Floor, Temple, London
EC4Y 9AU, Telephone: 0171 353 3102/5/9297
Call date: July 1977, Middle Temple
Qualifications: [LLB (Lond)]

WHITTAM MS SAMANTHA ABIGAIL

14 Gray's Inn Square
Gray's Inn, London WC1R 5JP,
Telephone: 0171 242 0858
E-mail: 100712.2134@compuserve.com
Call date: Nov 1995, Middle Temple
Qualifications: [BA (Hons)(Bris), MA (Lond)]

WHITTAM WILLIAM RICHARD LAMONT

Furnival Chambers
32 Furnival Street, London EC4A 1JQ,
Telephone: 0171 405 3232
E-mail: clerks@furnivallaw.co.uk
Call date: July 1983, Gray's Inn
Qualifications: [LLB (Hons) (Lond)]

WHITTING JOHN JUSTIN

1 Crown Office Row
Ground Floor, Temple, London EC4Y 7HH,
Telephone: 0171 797 7500
Call date: Oct 1991, Middle Temple
Qualifications: [BA (Hons)(Oxon), LLM (Lond)]

D

WHITTLE CHRISTOPHER DAVID

11 South Square
2nd Floor, Gray's Inn, London WC1R 5EU,
Telephone: 0171 405 1222
Call date: July 1975, Gray's Inn
Qualifications: [BSc, PhD (Lond)]

WHITTLE-MARTIN MISS LUCIA

2 Harcourt Bldgs
1st Floor, Temple, London EC4Y 9DB,
Telephone: 0171 353 2112/2817
Call date: Nov 1985, Middle Temple
Qualifications: [BSc (Lond), Dip Law]

WHITTLESTONE MISS KIM

3 Temple Gardens
2nd Floor, Temple, London EC4Y 9AU,
Telephone: 0171 583 1155
Call date: Nov 1994, Middle Temple
Qualifications: [LLB (Hons)]

WHYATT MICHAEL GEORGE

15 Winckley Square
Preston PR1 3JJ, Telephone: 01772 252828
E-mail: clerks@winckleysq.demon.co.uk
Call date: Feb 1992, Gray's Inn
Qualifications: [LLB]

WHYBROW CHRISTOPHER JOHN QC (1992)

1 Serjeants' Inn
4th Floor, Temple, London EC4Y 1NH,
Telephone: 0171 583 1355
E-mail: serjeants.inn@virgin.net
Call date: July 1965, Inner Temple
Qualifications: [LLB (Lond)]

WHYSALL MISS CAROLINE SARA

2 Paper Bldgs
Temple, London EC4Y 7ET,
Telephone: 0171 936 2613
Call date: July 1993, Inner Temple
Qualifications: [LLB (E.Anglia)]

WHYTE MISS ANNE LYNNE

Adrian Lyon's Chambers
14 Castle Street, Liverpool L2 0NE,
Telephone: 0151 236 4421/8240
E-mail: chambers14@aol.com
Call date: Feb 1993, Lincoln's Inn
Qualifications: [BA, Diploma in Law]

WICHEREK MISS ANN MARIE

One Garden Court
Ground Floor, Temple, London EC4Y 9BJ,
Telephone: 0171 797 7900
Call date: July 1978, Inner Temple
Qualifications: [LLB (So'ton)]

WICKINS MISS STEFANIE LORRAINE

Trinity Chambers
140 New London Road, Chelmsford, Essex
CM2 0AW, Telephone: 01245 605040
Call date: Nov 1994, Lincoln's Inn
Qualifications: [LLB (Hons)(Anglia), LLM
(Bristol)]

WICKREMERATNE DR UPALI CHANDRABHAYE

Warwick House Chambers
8 Warwick Court, Gray's Inn, London
WC1R 5DJ, Telephone: 0171 430 2323
Call date: July 1962, Lincoln's Inn
Qualifications: [BA (Hons)(Ceylon), BA
(Hons)(London), PhD (London)]

WICKS DAVID CHARLES

Farrar's Building
Temple, London EC4Y 7BD,
Telephone: 0171 583 9241
E-mail: chambers@farrarsbuilding.co.uk
Call date: July 1989, Middle Temple
Qualifications: [BA]

WICKS IAIN GEORGE MACKENZIE

4 Brick Court
1st Floor, Temple, London EC4Y 9AD,
Telephone: 0171 583 8455
Call date: Nov 1990, Middle Temple
Qualifications: [LLB (Hons)]

WICKS MS JOANNE

Wilberforce Chambers
8 New Square, Lincoln's Inn, London
WC2A 3QP, Telephone: 0171 306 0102
E-mail: chambers@wilberforce.co.uk
Call date: Nov 1990, Lincoln's Inn
Qualifications: [BA (Hons)(Oxon), BCL]

WIDDICOMBE DAVID GRAHAM QC (1965)

2 Mitre Ct Bldgs
2nd Floor, Temple, London EC4Y 7BX,
Telephone: 0171 583 1380
Call date: Nov 1950, Inner Temple
Qualifications: [MA, LL.B (Cantab)]

WIDDUP STANLEY JEFFREY PONSONBY

Guildford Chambers
Stoke House Leapale Lane, Guildford, Surrey
GU1 4LY, Telephone: 01483 539131
E-mail: guildford.barristers@btinternet.com
Call date: Nov 1973, Gray's Inn
Assistant Recorder

WIDE CHARLES THOMAS QC (1995)

9 Bedford Row
London WC1R 4AZ,
Telephone: 0171 242 3555
E-mail: clerks@9br.co.uk
Call date: Feb 1974, Inner Temple
Recorder

WIGGANS MISS AMANDA JANE

Rowchester Chambers
4 Rowchester Court Whittall Street,
Birmingham B4 6DH,
Telephone: 0121 233 2327/2361951
Call date: Nov 1986, Middle Temple
Qualifications: [LLB (Warw)]

WIGGLESWORTH RAYMOND

18 St John Street
Manchester M3 4EA,
Telephone: 0161 278 1800
Call date: July 1974, Gray's Inn
Recorder
Qualifications: [LLB (Hons) (Manch)]

WIGHTWICK (WILLIAM) IAIN

Assize Court Chambers
14 Small Street, Bristol BS1 1DE,
Telephone: 0117 9264587
Call date: Nov 1985, Inner Temple
Qualifications: [BSc (Bris), Dip Law]

WIGIN MISS CAROLINE ROSEMARY

Park Court Chambers
40 Park Cross Street, Leeds LS1 2QH,
Telephone: 0113 2433277
Call date: July 1984, Inner Temple
Qualifications: [BA (Exon)]

WIGNALL EDWARD GORDON

1 Dr Johnson's Buildings
Ground Floor, Temple, London EC4Y 7AX,
Telephone: 0171 353 9328
Dr Johnson's Chambers
The Atrium Court, Apex Plaza, Reading,
Berkshire RG1 1AX, Telephone: 01189 254221
Call date: July 1987, Gray's Inn
Qualifications: [MA (Oxon)]

Fax: 0118 951 0559; DX: 117880 Reading
(Apex Plaza); Other comms: E-mail
gordon.wignall@wiglaw.co.uk

Types of work: Administrative; Common law
(general); Employment; Health and safety;
Licensing; Local government; Medical
negligence; Personal injury

Other professional qualifications: CEDR
accredited mediator

Circuit: South Eastern

Awards and memberships: Norman Tapp
Prizewinner (Gray's Inn 1988); Karmel
Scholarship Prizewinner (Gray's Inn 1988)

Publications: *Nuisances* (Sweet & Maxwell),
1998

Reported cases: *Mills v R*, [1995] 1 WLR 511
(PC), 1994. Murder - identification.
Chan Wai-Keung v R, [1995] 1 WLR 251 (PC),
1995. Murder - abuse of process.
R v Wycombe DC ex parte Hazeltine, [1993]
FLR 417; (1993) 25 HLR 313. Judicial review -
homelessness.
Warner v Adnet, [1998] *The Times*, 12 March,
1998. TUPE - redundancy - dismissal -
consultation.

WIGODER THE HON LEWIS JUSTIN

1 High Pavement
Nottingham NG1 1HF,
Telephone: 0115 9418218
Call date: July 1977, Gray's Inn
Qualifications: [MA, DPhil (Oxon)]

WILBY DAVID CHRISTOPHER QC (1998)

199 Strand
London WC2R 1DR,
Telephone: 0171 379 9779
E-mail: chambers@199strand.co.uk
Park Lane Chambers
19 Westgate, Leeds LS1 2RU,
Telephone: 0113 228 5000
Call date: July 1974, Inner Temple
Qualifications: [MA (Cantab)]

Fax: 0171 379 9481;
Out of hours telephone: 01423 547786/Fax:
01423 547786; DX: 322 London, Chancery
Lane/11999 Harrogate 1; Other comms: E-mail
davidwilby@lawyer.demon.co.uk

Types of work: Commercial litigation; Family
provision; Medical negligence; Personal injury;
Professional negligence

Membership of foreign bars: American Bar
Association

Circuit: North Eastern

Awards and memberships: Member of Bar
Council; Member Executive Committee
Professional Negligence Bar Association

Publications: *Professional Negligence and
Liability Law Reports* (Editor)

Reported cases: *Ramsden v Lee*, [1992] 2 All ER
205, CA, 1992. Approach to exercise of
discretion under section 33 Limitation Act 1980.
United Norwest Co-operatives Ltd v Johnson,
(1994) *The Times*, 24 Feb, CA; SCP 024/5/4,
1994. Right of silence of defendant in Mareva
injunction proceedings.
*Landall v Dennis Faulkner and Alsop,
Maskrey, Scott-Ferguson*, [1994] 5 Med LR 268,
1994. Liability of lawyer and doctors in respect
of compromise of civil claim, solicitor and
barrister immunity from suit.
Re Port (a Bankrupt), [1994] 1 WLR 862, 1993.
Basis of and grounds for striking out a claim in
respect of misconduct of trustee in bankruptcy.
Re W (a Minor), [1988] 1 FLR175, CA, 1988.
Adoption where access to child appropriate.

WILCKEN ANTHONY DAVID FELIX

Hollis Whiteman Chambers
3rd/4th Floor Queen Elizabeth Bldg, Temple,
London EC4Y 9BS, Telephone: 0171 583 5766
E-mail: hollis.whiteman@btinternet.com
Call date: Nov 1966, Middle Temple
Recorder

WILCOCK PETER LAZENBY

14 Tooks Court
Cursitor St, London EC4A 1LB,
Telephone: 0171 405 8828
E-mail: clerks @tooks.law.co.uk
Call date: July 1988, Middle Temple
Qualifications: [LLB (Hons) (LSE)]

WILCOX JEROME CARL JEAN

Guildford Chambers
Stoke House Leapale Lane, Guildford, Surrey
GU1 4LY, Telephone: 01483 539131
E-mail: guildford.barristers@btinternet.com
Call date: Nov 1988, Middle Temple
Qualifications: [LLB(Bucks), Dip Law]

WILCOX NICHOLAS HUGH

5 Essex Court
1st Floor, Temple, London EC4Y 9AH,
Telephone: 0171 410 2000
Call date: July 1977, Gray's Inn
Qualifications: [LLB]

WILD SIMON PETER

Queen Elizabeth Bldg
Ground Floor, Temple, London EC4Y 9BS,
Telephone: 0171 353 7181 (12 Lines)
Call date: July 1977, Inner Temple
Qualifications: [BA (Lond)]

WILD STEVEN

Parsonage Chambers
5th Floor 3 The Parsonage, Manchester
M3 2HW, Telephone: 0161 833 1996
Call date: Oct 1994, Gray's Inn
Qualifications: [LLB]

WILDBLOOD STEPHEN ROGER

Albion Chambers
Broad Street, Bristol BS1 1DR,
Telephone: 0117 9272144
Call date: July 1980, Inner Temple
Qualifications: [LLB (Sheff)]

WILDING KEITH

65-67 King Street
Leicester LE1 6RP, Telephone: 0116 2547710
Call date: Oct 1990, Inner Temple
Qualifications: [BA, Dip Law]

WILDING MISS LISA MARIE

2 Harcourt Bldgs
1st Floor, Temple, London EC4Y 9DB,
Telephone: 0171 353 2112/2817
Call date: Nov 1993, Inner Temple
Qualifications: [BA Hons (Cantab)]

WILEY MISS FRANCESCA PETRA DENNING

10 King's Bench Walk
1st Floor, Temple, London EC4Y 7EB,
Telephone: 0171 353 2501
Call date: May 1996, Gray's Inn
Qualifications: [MA]

WILKEN SEAN DAVID HENRY

39 Essex Street
London WC2R 3AT,
Telephone: 0171 583 1111
E-mail: clerks@39essex.co.uk
Call date: Nov 1991, Middle Temple
Qualifications: [BA Hons (Oxon), Dip Law]

WILKINS ANDREW LEWIS

Harrow on the Hill Chambers
60 High Street, Harrow on the Hill, Middlesex
HA1 3LL, Telephone: 0181 423 7444
Windsor Barristers' Chambers
Windsor, Telephone: 01753 648899
Call date: Oct 1995, Lincoln's Inn
Qualifications: [MA (Hons)(Oxon)]

WILKINS CHRISTOPHER JOHN

11 Stone Bldgs
Ground Floor, Lincoln's Inn, London
WC2A 3TG, Telephone: 0171 831 6381
E-mail: clerks@11StoneBuildings.law.co.uk
Call date: May 1993, Lincoln's Inn
Qualifications: [MA (Oxon)]

WILKINS MRS COLETTE ANN

1 New Square
Ground Floor, Lincoln's Inn, London
WC2A 3SA, Telephone: 0171 405 0884/5/6/7
E-mail: 1newsquare@compuserve.com
Call date: Nov 1989, Lincoln's Inn
Qualifications: [BA, Dip Law (City)]

WILKINS THOMAS ALEXANDER

2 Harcourt Bldgs
1st Floor, Temple, London EC4Y 9DB,
Telephone: 0171 353 2112/2817
Call date: Oct 1993, Middle Temple
Qualifications: [BSc (Hons)(Bris), CPE (Lond)]

WILKINSON MARC ASHLEY

5 Fountain Court
Steelhouse Lane, Birmingham B4 6DR,
Telephone: 0121 606 0500
Call date: Nov 1992, Lincoln's Inn
Qualifications: [BA (Hons)]

WILKINSON MICHAEL JOHN

Trinity Chambers
9-12 Trinity Chare, Quayside, Newcastle Upon
Tyne NE1 3DF, Telephone: 0191 232 1927
Call date: July 1979, Gray's Inn
Qualifications: [LLB (Exon)]

WILKINSON NIGEL VIVIAN MARSHALL QC (1990)

2 Crown Office Row
Ground Floor, Temple, London EC4Y 7HJ,
Telephone: 0171 797 8100
E-mail: mail@2cor.co.uk, or to individual
barristers at: [barrister's surname]@2cor.co.uk
Call date: July 1972, Middle Temple
Recorder
Qualifications: [MA (Oxon)]

D

WILKINSON RICHARD JOHN

1 Temple Gardens
1st Floor, Temple, London EC4Y 9BB,
Telephone: 0171 353 0407/583 1315
E-mail: clerks@1templegardens.co.uk
Call date: Oct 1992, Lincoln's Inn
Qualifications: [LLB(Hons)(Bris)]

WILLANS DAVID

22 Albion Place
Northampton NN1 1UD,
Telephone: 01604 36271
Call date: Oct 1995, Lincoln's Inn
Qualifications: [BSc (Hons)(Lond), LLB (Hons)(City)]

WILLARD NEVILLE FREDERICK MORGAN

Bridewell Chambers
2 Bridewell Place, London EC4V 6AP,
Telephone: 0171 797 8800
E-mail: clerks@bridewell.law.co.uk
Call date: July 1976, Gray's Inn
Qualifications: [LLB]

WILLBOURNE MISS CAROLINE CATCHPOLE

One Garden Court
Ground Floor, Temple, London EC4Y 9BJ,
Telephone: 0171 797 7900
Call date: Nov 1970, Inner Temple
Qualifications: [BA]

WILLEMS MARC PAUL BERNARD ALFRED

Cobden House Chambers
19 Quay Street, Manchester M3 3HN,
Telephone: 0161 833 6000
E-mail: clerks@cobden.co.uk
Call date: Nov 1990, Lincoln's Inn
Qualifications: [BA (Nott'm)]

WILLER ROBERT MICHAEL

Hardwicke Building
New Square, Lincoln's Inn, London
WC2A 3SB, Telephone: 0171 242 2523
E-mail: clerks@hardwicke.co.uk
Call date: July 1970, Middle Temple
Qualifications: [BA (Oxon)]

WILLERS MARC LAWRENCE GEORGE

Counsels' Chambers
2nd Floor 10-11 Gray's Inn Square, London
WC1R 5JD, Telephone: 0171 405 2576
Call date: Nov 1987, Lincoln's Inn
Qualifications: [LLB, BL]

WILLIAMS A JOHN

13 King's Bench Walk
Temple, London EC4Y 7EN,
Telephone: 0171 353 7204
E-mail: clerks@13kbw.law.co.uk
King's Bench Chambers
32 Beaumont Street, Oxford OX1 2NP,
Telephone: 01865 311066
E-mail: clerks@kbc-oxford.law.co.uk
Call date: July 1983, Lincoln's Inn
Qualifications: [MA (Cantab)]

Fax: 0171 582 0252; DX: LDE 359

Types of work: Common law (general);
Consumer law; Environment; Licensing;
Personal injury; Professional negligence;
Statutory nuisance

Circuit: Midland and Oxford

Awards and memberships: Megarry Scholar
(Lincoln's Inn)

Reported cases: *Jarrett v Royal Bank of
Scotland*, [1997] 2 All ER 484, 1996. Consumer
credit - foreign timeshares.
Husseyin v Crumplin, [1997] PIQR P481, 1997.
Personal injury - extension of time for serving
writ - more than one extension.

WILLIAMS ALAN RONALD

8 King's Bench Walk
2nd Floor, Temple, London EC4Y 7DU,
Telephone: 0171 797 8888
8 King's Bench Walk North
1 Park Square East, Leeds LS1 2NE,
Telephone: 0113 2439797
Call date: July 1978, Middle Temple
Qualifications: [BSc]

WILLIAMS ALEXANDER JAMES HYATT

3 Temple Gardens
Lower Ground Floor, Temple, London
EC4Y 9AU, Telephone: 0171 353 3102/5/9297
Call date: Nov 1995, Middle Temple
Qualifications: [BA (Hons)]

WILLIAMS ANDREW ARTHUR

Adrian Lyon's Chambers
14 Castle Street, Liverpool L2 0NE,
Telephone: 0151 236 4421/8240
E-mail: chambers14@aol.com
Call date: Oct 1994, Gray's Inn
Qualifications: [LLB]

WILLIAMS ANDREW EDWARD

3 Hare Court
1st Floor, Temple, London EC4Y 7BJ,
Telephone: 0171 353 7561
Call date: Nov 1975, Lincoln's Inn
Qualifications: [MA Crim, LLB]

WILLIAMS MISS ANNA

Trinity Chambers
140 New London Road, Chelmsford, Essex
CM2 0AW, Telephone: 01245 605040
Call date: Nov 1990, Gray's Inn
Qualifications: [LLB]

WILLIAMS MISS ANNE MARGARET

4 Breams Buildings
London EC4A 1AQ,
Telephone: 0171 353 5835/430 1221
37 Park Square
Leeds LS1 2NY, Telephone: 0113 2439422
Call date: Nov 1980, Gray's Inn
Qualifications: [BA (Manch) MPhil, (Lond),
R.T.P.I.]

WILLIAMS MRS BARBARA ELIZABETH

22 Albion Place
Northampton NN1 1UD,
Telephone: 01604 36271
Call date: Oct 1995, Lincoln's Inn
Qualifications: [LLB (Hons)(Coventry)]

WILLIAMS BENJAMIN JAMES

3 Paper Bldgs
1st Floor, Temple, London EC4Y 7EU,
Telephone: 0171 583 8055
E-mail: london@3paper.com
1 Alfred Street
High Street, Oxford OX1 4EH,
Telephone: 01865 793736
4 St Peter Street
Winchester SO23 8OW,
Telephone: 01962 868884
Call date: Nov 1994, Lincoln's Inn
Qualifications: [BA (Hons)(Oxon), Dip in Law
(City)]

WILLIAMS BRIAN DAVID

18 St John Street
Manchester M3 4EA,
Telephone: 0161 278 1800
Call date: July 1986, Inner Temple
Qualifications: [LLB (Manch)]

WILLIAMS MISS CHERYL ANNE

7 Stone Bldgs
1st Floor, Lincoln's Inn, London WC2A 3SZ,
Telephone: 0171 242 0961
Call date: July 1982, Inner Temple
Qualifications: [BA (Oxon), LLM (Lond)]

WILLIAMS CHRISTOPHER DAVID CURNOW

York Chambers
14 Toft Green, York YO1 1JT,
Telephone: 01904 620048
E-mail: yorkchambers.co.uk
Call date: July 1981, Gray's Inn

WILLIAMS CHRISTOPHER MICHAEL

32 Park Place
Cardiff CF1 3BA, Telephone: 01222 397364
Call date: Nov 1972, Middle Temple
Qualifications: [MA (Oxon)]

WILLIAMS CHRISTOPHER PAUL

1 Gray's Inn Square
Ground Floor, London WC1R 5AA,
Telephone: 0171 405 8946/7/8
Call date: Feb 1988, Inner Temple
Qualifications: [LLB]

D

WILLIAMS DANIEL VAUGHAN

33 Park Place
Cardiff CF1 3BA, Telephone: 01222 233313
Call date: May 1993, Gray's Inn
Qualifications: [LLB (B'ham)]

WILLIAMS DAVID ALAN

12 Old Square
1st Floor, Lincoln's Inn, London WC2A 3TX,
Telephone: 0171 404 0875
Call date: Oct 1992, Middle Temple
Qualifications: [LL.B (Hons), RGN, RSCN,
RNT]

WILLIAMS DAVID BASIL

2 Dr Johnson's Building
Temple, London EC4Y 7AY,
Telephone: 0171 353 4716
Call date: Oct 1990, Inner Temple
Qualifications: [LLB (Leic)]

WILLIAMS DAVID BEVERLEY

4 Brick Court
1st Floor, Temple, London EC4Y 9AD,
Telephone: 0171 583 8455
Call date: Nov 1972, Middle Temple

WILLIAMS DAVID DEVOY

10 King's Bench Walk
Ground Floor, Temple, London EC4Y 7EB,
Telephone: 0171 353 7742
E-mail: 10kbw@lineone.net
Call date: July 1989, Middle Temple
Qualifications: [BA (Oxon), MA (Cantab)]

WILLIAMS DAVID ESSEX

9 Park Place
Cardiff CF1 3DP, Telephone: 01222 382731
Call date: July 1975, Middle Temple
Qualifications: [LLB (Wales), ACIB]

WILLIAMS DAVID HENRY

Chavasse Court Chambers
2nd Floor Chavasse Court, 24 Lord Street,
Liverpool L2 1TA, Telephone: 0151 707 1191
Call date: Feb 1990, Gray's Inn
Assistant Recorder
Qualifications: [BA (Hons)]

WILLIAMS DAVID HUW ANTHONY

18 Red Lion Court
(Off Fleet Street), London EC4A 3EB,
Telephone: 0171 520 6000
Thornwood House
102 New London Road, Chelmsford, Essex
CM2 0RG, Telephone: 01245 280880
Call date: July 1988, Inner Temple
Qualifications: [BSc (Wales), Dip Law (Lond),
GRSC]

WILLIAMS GRAEME QC (1983)

13 King's Bench Walk
1st Floor, Temple, London EC4Y 7EN,
Telephone: 0171 353 7204
E-mail: clerks@13kbw.law.co.uk
King's Bench Chambers
32 Beaumont Street, Oxford OX1 2NP,
Telephone: 01865 311066
E-mail: clerks@kbc-oxford.law.co.uk
Call date: June 1959, Inner Temple
Recorder
Qualifications: [MA (Oxon)]

WILLIAMS MS HEATHER JEAN

Doughty Street Chambers
11 Doughty Street, London WC1N 2PG,
Telephone: 0171 404 1313
E-mail: doughty_street@compuserve.com
Call date: July 1985, Gray's Inn
Qualifications: [LLB (Lond)]

WILLIAMS HUGH DAVID HAYDN

7 Fountain Court
Steelhouse Lane, Birmingham B4 6DR,
Telephone: 0121 236 8531
Call date: July 1992, Gray's Inn
Qualifications: [BA]

WILLIAMS DR JASON SCOTT

3 Dr Johnson's Bldgs
Ground Floor, Temple, London EC4Y 7BA,
Telephone: 0171 353 4854
Call date: Oct 1995, Lincoln's Inn
Qualifications: [BA (Hons)(Oxon), D.Phil
(Oxon), Dip Law]

WILLIAMS MISS JEAN ADELE

6 Pump Court
1st Floor, Temple, London EC4Y 7AR,
Telephone: 0171 797 8400
E-mail: sa_hockman_qc@link.org
6-8 Mill Street
Maidstone, Kent ME15 6XH,
Telephone: 01622 688094
Call date: July 1972, Gray's Inn
Recorder
Qualifications: [LLB (Lond)]

WILLIAMS MISS JEANETTE MARY

Coleridge Chambers
Citadel 190 Corporation Street, Birmingham
B4 6QD, Telephone: 0121 233 3303
Call date: July 1985, Gray's Inn
Qualifications: [BA]

WILLIAMS JOHN ALBAN

9-12 Bell Yard
London WC2A 2LF,
Telephone: 0171 400 1800
Call date: Nov 1979, Middle Temple

WILLIAMS JOHN GLYN

15 Winckley Square
Preston PR1 3JJ, Telephone: 01772 252828
E-mail: clerks@winckleysq.demon.co.uk
Call date: Nov 1981, Inner Temple
Qualifications: [BA (Manch)]

WILLIAMS JOHN GRIFFITH QC (1985)

Goldsmith Building
1st Floor, Temple, London EC4Y 7BL,
Telephone: 0171 353 7881
E-mail: clerks@goldsmith-building.law.co.uk
33 Park Place
Cardiff CF1 3BA, Telephone: 01222 233313
Door Tenant
Call date: Nov 1968, Gray's Inn
Recorder
Qualifications: [BA (Oxon)]

WILLIAMS JOHN LEIGHTON QC (1986)

Farrar's Building
Temple, London EC4Y 7BD,
Telephone: 0171 583 9241
E-mail: chambers@farrarsbuilding.co.uk
Call date: Apr 1964, Gray's Inn
Recorder
Qualifications: [MA, LLB]

WILLIAMS THE HON JOHN MELVILLE QC (1977)

Old Square Chambers
1 Verulam Buildings, Gray's Inn, London
WC1R 5LQ, Telephone: 0171 269 0300
Old Square Chambers
Hanover House, 47 Corn Street, Bristol
BS1 1HT, Telephone: 0117 927 7111
Call date: Jun 1955, Inner Temple
Recorder
Qualifications: [BA (Cantab)]

Fax: 0171 405 1387;
Out of hours telephone: 01306 730331 Out of
hours fax: 01306 730 913; DX: 1046 London;
Other comms: E-mail jmwqe@dial.pipex.com

Types of work: Environment; Medical
negligence; Personal injury; Private
international; Product liability; Professional
negligence

Awards and memberships: Association Of
Personal Injury Lawyers (President 1990-4);
Personal Injury Bar Association; Environment
Law Foundation; Association of Trial Lawyers of
America (Chair International Practice Section
1991-2)

Other professional experience: Legal Assessor to
General Medical Council and General Dental
Council; Member CICB

WILLIAMS JOHN ROBERT SELWYN

2 Harcourt Bldgs
1st Floor, Temple, London EC4Y 9DB,
Telephone: 0171 353 2112/2817
Call date: Nov 1973, Middle Temple
Qualifications: [LLB]

D

WILLIAMS JOHN WYN

Sedan House
Stanley Place, Chester CH1 2LU,
Telephone: 01244 320480/348282
Call date: Nov 1992, Gray's Inn
Qualifications: [LLB (Wales)]

WILLIAMS JON FREDERICK

6 Pump Court
Ground Floor, Temple, London EC4Y 7AR,
Telephone: 0171 583 6013/2510
Call date: Nov 1970, Inner Temple
Qualifications: [LLB (Lond)]

WILLIAMS KARL

9 Park Place
Cardiff CF1 3DP, Telephone: 01222 382731
Call date: July 1982, Middle Temple
Qualifications: [LLB (Lond)]

WILLIAMS LEIGH MICHAEL

7 King's Bench Walk
Ground Floor, Temple, London EC4Y 7DS,
Telephone: 0171 583 0404
Call date: July 1996, Inner Temple
Qualifications: [BA, BCL (Oxon)]

WILLIAMS LLOYD

30 Park Place
Cardiff CF1 3BA, Telephone: 01222 398421
E-mail: 100757.1456@compuserve.com
Call date: July 1981, Inner Temple
Qualifications: [BA]

WILLIAMS NEAL MARTON

1 Fountain Court
Steelhouse Lane, Birmingham B4 6DR,
Telephone: 0121 236 5721
Call date: July 1984, Lincoln's Inn
Qualifications: [LLB (Leeds)]

WILLIAMS NICHOLAS MICHAEL HEATHCOTE

12 King's Bench Walk
Temple, London EC4Y 7EL,
Telephone: 0171 583 0811
E-mail: chambers@12kbw.co.uk
Call date: Nov 1976, Inner Temple
Qualifications: [MA (Cantab)]

WILLIAMS MS NICOLA EGERSIS

8 King's Bench Walk
2nd Floor, Temple, London EC4Y 7DU,
Telephone: 0171 797 8888
Call date: Nov 1985, Lincoln's Inn
Qualifications: [BA (Law)]

WILLIAMS OWEN JOHN

4 Brick Court
1st Floor, Temple, London EC4Y 9AD,
Telephone: 0171 583 8455
Call date: July 1974, Middle Temple
Qualifications: [MA (Oxon)]

WILLIAMS PAUL KENNETH

3 Temple Gardens
3rd Floor, Temple, London EC4Y 9AU,
Telephone: 0171 583 0010
Call date: July 1990, Inner Temple
Qualifications: [BA (Wales)]

WILLIAMS PAUL ROBERT

8 King's Bench Walk North
1 Park Square East, Leeds LS1 2NE,
Telephone: 0113 2439797
8 King's Bench Walk
2nd Floor, Temple, London EC4Y 7DU,
Telephone: 0171 797 8888
Call date: Oct 1994, Inner Temple
Qualifications: [BA (Hons), CPE (Lond)]

WILLIAMS RHODRI JOHN

30 Park Place
Cardiff CF1 3BA, Telephone: 01222 398421
E-mail: 100757.1456@compuserve.com
Call date: July 1987, Gray's Inn
Qualifications: [BA (Oxon), Dip Law]

WILLIAMS RICHARD EVAN HUW

All Saints Chambers
9/11 Broad Street, Bristol BS1 2HP,
Telephone: 0117 921 1966
Call date: Nov 1992, Lincoln's Inn
Qualifications: [LLB (Hons)(Bris)]

WILLIAMS RICHARD NOEL

Goldsmith Chambers
Ground Floor Goldsmith Building, Temple,
London EC4Y 7BL,
Telephone: 0171 353 6802/3/4/5
E-mail: celiamonksfield@btinternet.com
Call date: Nov 1988, Gray's Inn
Qualifications: [LLB]

WILLIAMS ROBERT CHARLES

1 Crown Office Row
2nd Floor, Temple, London EC4Y 7HH,
Telephone: 0171 797 7111
Call date: July 1973, Inner Temple
Qualifications: [MA (Oxon)]

WILLIAMS MISS SARA HELEN

5 Fountain Court
Steelhouse Lane, Birmingham B4 6DR,
Telephone: 0121 606 0500
Call date: Feb 1989, Gray's Inn
Qualifications: [LLB (Lond)]

WILLIAMS MISS SARAH VICTORIA

18 St John Street
Manchester M3 4EA,
Telephone: 0161 278 1800
Call date: Nov 1995, Inner Temple
Qualifications: [BA (Bris), CPE]

WILLIAMS SIMON PAUL

2 Pump Court
1st Floor, Temple, London EC4Y 7AH,
Telephone: 0171 353 5597
Call date: Nov 1984, Inner Temple
Qualifications: [LLB (Soton)]

WILLIAMS MISS SUSAN FRANCES

2 Dr Johnson's Building
Temple, London EC4Y 7AY,
Telephone: 0171 353 4716
Call date: Nov 1978, Middle Temple
Qualifications: [LLB (Bristol)]

WILLIAMS THOMAS CHRISTOPHER CHARLES

1 Fountain Court
Steelhouse Lane, Birmingham B4 6DR,
Telephone: 0121 236 5721
Call date: Nov 1995, Middle Temple
Qualifications: [BA (Hons)]

WILLIAMS THOMAS ELLIS

30 Park Place
Cardiff CF1 3BA, Telephone: 01222 398421
E-mail: 100757.1456@compuserve.com
Call date: Oct 1996, Middle Temple
Qualifications: [LLB (Hons)(Kent), Licence En
Droit, (Grenoble)]

WILLIAMS VINCENT ALLAN

Bridewell Chambers
2 Bridewell Place, London EC4V 6AP,
Telephone: 0171 797 8800
E-mail: clerks@bridewell.law.co.uk
Call date: July 1985, Middle Temple
Qualifications: [BA (Cantab)]

WILLIAMS WYN LEWIS QC (1992)

33 Park Place
Cardiff CF1 3BA, Telephone: 01222 233313
Goldsmith Building
1st Floor, Temple, London EC4Y 7BL,
Telephone: 0171 353 7881
E-mail: clerks@goldsmith-building.law.co.uk
Door Tenant
Call date: July 1974, Inner Temple
Recorder
Qualifications: [MA (Oxon)]

WILLIAMSON ADRIAN JOHN GERARD HUGHES

Keating Chambers
10 Essex Street, Outer Temple, London
WC2R 3AA, Telephone: 0171 544 2600
Call date: Nov 1983, Middle Temple
Qualifications: [MA (Cantab)]

D

WILLIAMSON ALISDAIR GEORGE JAMES

3 Raymond Buildings
Gray's Inn, London WC1R 5BH,
Telephone: 0171 831 3833
E-mail: chambers@threeraymond.demon.co.uk
Call date: Nov 1994, Middle Temple
Qualifications: [MA (Oxon), DipLL, (City)]

WILLIAMSON MISS BRIDGET SUSAN

Enterprise Chambers
9 Old Square, Lincoln's Inn, London
WC2A 3SR, Telephone: 0171 405 9471
Enterprise Chambers
38 Park Square, Leeds LS1 2PA,
Telephone: 01132 460391
Enterprise Chambers
65 Quayside, Newcastle upon Tyne NE1 3DS,
Telephone: 0191 222 3344
Call date: Feb 1993, Lincoln's Inn
Qualifications: [BA (Hons)]

WILLIAMSON MISS HAZEL ELEANOR QC (1988)

13 Old Square
Ground Floor, Lincoln's Inn, London
WC2A 3UA, Telephone: 0171 404 4800
Call date: July 1972, Gray's Inn
Recorder
Qualifications: [BA (Oxon)]

WILLIAMSON MISS MELANIE JANE

Chancery House Chambers
7 Lisbon Square, Leeds LS1 4LY,
Telephone: 0113 244 6691
E-mail: Chanceryhouse@btinternet.com
Call date: Oct 1990, Inner Temple
Qualifications: [LLB (Sheff)]

WILLIAMSON PATRICK LAWRENCE VICTOR

Old Colony House
6 South King Street, Manchester M2 6DQ,
Telephone: 0161 834 4364
Call date: Nov 1989, Inner Temple
Qualifications: [BSc (Keele)]

WILLIAMSON STEPHEN WRIGHT QC (1981)

6 Park Square
Leeds LS1 2LW, Telephone: 0113 2459763
E-mail: chambers@no6.co.uk
Francis Taylor Bldg
2nd Floor, Temple, London EC4Y 7BY,
Telephone: 0171 353 9942/3157
Call date: Feb 1964, Inner Temple
Recorder
Qualifications: [MA (Cantab)]

WILLIAMSON MISS TESSA LOUISE

Verulam Chambers
Peer House 8-14 Verulam Street, Gray's Inn,
London WC1X 8LZ,
Telephone: 0171 813 2400
Door Tenant
Call date: Nov 1990, Inner Temple
Qualifications: [LLB (Hons)(Bris)]

WILLIS MISS ELIZABETH EDITH PEARL

22 Albion Place
Northampton NN1 1UD,
Telephone: 01604 36271
Call date: July 1986, Inner Temple
Qualifications: [LLB (Hull)]

WILLIS MISS RHYDDIAN ELIZABETH

2 Harcourt Bldgs
1st Floor, Temple, London EC4Y 9DB,
Telephone: 0171 353 2112/2817
Call date: July 1984, Gray's Inn
Qualifications: [LLB (Nott'm)]

WILLITTS TIMOTHY LEONARD

Cobden House Chambers
19 Quay Street, Manchester M3 3HN,
Telephone: 0161 833 6000
E-mail: clerks@cobden.co.uk
Call date: Nov 1989, Gray's Inn
Qualifications: [LLB (Hons) (B'Ham)]

WILLMOT MISS ELISABETH RACHEL

35 Essex Street
Temple, London WC2R 3AR,
Telephone: 0171 353 6381
Call date: Oct 1994, Lincoln's Inn
Qualifications: [BA (Hons), BCL]

WILLMOTT WILLIAM DEREK IAN

Chambers of Derek Willmott
8 Links Crescent, St Marys Bay, Romney
Marsh, Kent TN29 0RS,
Telephone: 01303 87 3899
Call date: Nov 1966, Inner Temple
Qualifications: [BA, Dip Ed]

WILLS MISS JANICE MARIE

Kenworthy's Buildings
83 Bridge Street, Manchester M3 2RF,
Telephone: 0161 832 4036/834 6954
Call date: Oct 1991, Gray's Inn
Qualifications: [LLB]

WILLS-GOLDINGHAM MISS CLAIRE LOUISE MARGARET

Albion Chambers
Broad Street, Bristol BS1 1DR,
Telephone: 0117 9272144
Call date: July 1988, Inner Temple
Qualifications: [LLB (B'ham)]

WILMOT-SMITH RICHARD JAMES CROSBIE QC (1994)

39 Essex Street
London WC2R 3AT,
Telephone: 0171 583 1111
E-mail: clerks@39essex.co.uk
Call date: July 1978, Middle Temple
Qualifications: [AB (N Carolina)]

WILSHIRE SIMON VINCENT

1 Gray's Inn Square
1st Floor, London WC1R 5AG,
Telephone: 0171 405 3000
E-mail: clerks@onegrays.demon.co.uk
Call date: Oct 1994, Gray's Inn
Qualifications: [BSc]

WILSON (ALAN) MARTIN QC (1982)

1 Serjeants' Inn
5th Floor Fleet Street, Temple, London
EC4Y 1LL, Telephone: 0171 415 6666
E-mail: no1serjeantsinn@btinternet.com
Priory Chambers
2 Fountain Court, Steelhouse Lane,
Birmingham B4 6DR,
Telephone: 0121 236 3882/1375
Door Tenant
Call date: Nov 1963, Gray's Inn
Recorder
Qualifications: [LLB (Nottm)]

WILSON ADAM

6 Park Square
Leeds LS1 2LW, Telephone: 0113 2459763
E-mail: chambers@no6.co.uk
Call date: Nov 1994, Inner Temple
Qualifications: [LLB (Lond)]

WILSON ALASDAIR JOHN

Fenners Chambers
3 Madingley Road, Cambridge CB3 0EE,
Telephone: 01223 368761
Fenners Chambers
8-12 Priestgate, Peterborough PE1 1JA,
Telephone: 01733 62030
Call date: Nov 1988, Gray's Inn
Qualifications: [LLB (Wales)]

WILSON ALASTAIR JAMES DRYSDALE QC (1987)

19 Old Buildings
Lincoln's Inn, London WC2A 3UP,
Telephone: 0171 405 2001
E-mail: clerks@oldbuildingsip.com
Call date: July 1968, Middle Temple
Recorder
Qualifications: [MA (Cantab)]

Fax: 0171 405 0001; DX: 397 London,
Chancery Lane; Other comms: E-mail
alw@oldbuildingsip.com

Types of work: Competition; Copyright; EC and
competition law; Entertainment; Film, cable,
TV; Franchising; Information technology;
Intellectual property; Patents;
Telecommunications; Trademarks

Membership of foreign bars: Northern Ireland,
Eire

Awards and memberships: Intellectual Property Bar Association; Chancery Bar Association; Chartered Institute of Patent Agents (Associate)

Other professional experience: Recorder

Languages spoken: French

Reported cases: *Designers Guild v Russell Williams*, [1998] FSR 275, 1997. Textile copyright infringement.
PLG Research v Ardon International, [1995] RPC 287, 1995. Patent infringement and European law.
Lock International v Beswick, [1989] 3 All ER 373, 1989. Confidential information, ex-employees and Anton Pillers.

WILSON ANDREW ROBERT

9 Woodhouse Square
Leeds LS3 1AD, Telephone: 0113 2451986
Call date: Nov 1995, Gray's Inn
Qualifications: [BA]

WILSON CHARLES JONATHAN

Warwick House Chambers
8 Warwick Court, Gray's Inn, London WC1R 5DJ, Telephone: 0171 430 2323
Call date: Oct 1995, Gray's Inn
Qualifications: [BA (Wales), LLB (Lond), LLM (Cantab)]

WILSON CHRISTOPHER JOHN

9 Gough Square
London EC4A 3DE, Telephone: 0171 353 5371
Call date: July 1980, Gray's Inn
Qualifications: [LLB (Hons)]

WILSON DAVID WILLIAM

East Anglian Chambers
57 London Street, Norwich NR2 1HL, Telephone: 01603 617351
East Anglian Chambers
Sanders House 52 North Hill, Colchester CO1 1PY, Telephone: 01206 572756
East Anglian Chambers
Gresham House 5 Museum Street, Ipswich IP1 1HQ, Telephone: 01473 214481
Call date: Oct 1996, Gray's Inn
Qualifications: [LLB (E.Anglia)]

WILSON MISS ELIZABETH HELEN

3 Temple Gardens
3rd Floor, Temple, London EC4Y 9AU, Telephone: 0171 353 0832
Call date: Nov 1989, Gray's Inn
Qualifications: [LLB (Hons)]

WILSON GERALD SIMON JOHN

Francis Taylor Bldg
2nd Floor, Temple, London EC4Y 7BY, Telephone: 0171 353 9942/3157
Call date: Nov 1989, Gray's Inn
Qualifications: [BA [Oxon]]

WILSON GRAEME JOHN

3 Temple Gardens
3rd Floor, Temple, London EC4Y 9AU, Telephone: 0171 583 0010
Call date: Feb 1987, Inner Temple
Qualifications: [LLB (London)]

WILSON IAN ROBERT

3 Verulam Buildings
London WC1R 5NT, Telephone: 0171 831 8441
E-mail: clerks@3verulam.co.uk
Call date: Oct 1995, Middle Temple
Qualifications: [BA (Hons), LLM]

WILSON JAMES MASON

Fenners Chambers
3 Madingley Road, Cambridge CB3 OEE, Telephone: 01223 368761
Fenners Chambers
8-12 Priestgate, Peterborough PE1 1JA, Telephone: 01733 62030
Call date: Nov 1991, Inner Temple
Qualifications: [LLB (Hons)(Leeds)]

WILSON JAMES WILLIAM

King's Bench Chambers
Wellington House 175 Holdenhurst Road, Bournemouth, Dorset BH8 8DQ, Telephone: 01202 250025
Call date: Nov 1994, Middle Temple
Qualifications: [LLB (Hons), ACIS]

WILSON MISS JENNIFER MARY PENTREATH

All Saints Chambers
9/11 Broad Street, Bristol BS1 2HP,
Telephone: 0117 921 1966
Call date: July 1979, Gray's Inn
Qualifications: [LLB (Hons)(LSE)]

WILSON JOHN ARMSTRONG

29 Bedford Row Chambers
London WC1R 4HE,
Telephone: 0171 831 2626
Call date: July 1981, Inner Temple
Qualifications: [MA (Cantab)]

WILSON JOHN BARKER

24a St John Street
Manchester M3 4DF,
Telephone: 0161 833 9628
Call date: July 1988, Inner Temple
Qualifications: [LLB (Lancaster)]

WILSON JULIAN MARTIN

11 King's Bench Walk
Temple, London EC4Y 7EQ,
Telephone: 0171 632 8500
E-mail: clerksroom@11-kbw.law.co.uk
Call date: Oct 1997, Inner Temple
Qualifications: [BA (Oxon)]

WILSON LACHLAN BAYARD

2 King's Bench Walk
1st Floor, Temple, London EC4Y 7DE,
Telephone: 0171 353 9276
Call date: Oct 1996, Inner Temple
Qualifications: [BA (Oxon), CPE (Westminster)]

WILSON MS MARION JANET

5 Fountain Court
Steelhouse Lane, Birmingham B4 6DR,
Telephone: 0121 606 0500
Call date: Oct 1991, Middle Temple
Qualifications: [LLB Hons (Lanc)]

WILSON MISS MARY ELIZABETH FRANCES

Pump Court Tax Chambers
16 Bedford Row, London WC1R 4EB,
Telephone: 0171 414 8080
Call date: Oct 1995, Middle Temple
Qualifications: [BA (Hons)]

WILSON MYLES BRENNAND

21 White Friars
Chester CH1 1NZ, Telephone: 01244 323070
Call date: Oct 1993, Lincoln's Inn
Qualifications: [LLB (Hons)(Leeds)]

WILSON PAUL RICHARD

Broadway House Chambers
Broadway House 9 Bank Street, Bradford,
West Yorkshire BD1 1TW,
Telephone: 01274 722560
Call date: Nov 1989, Lincoln's Inn
Qualifications: [BA (Oxon)]

WILSON RICHARD CARVER

36 Bedford Row
London WC1R 4JH,
Telephone: 0171 421 8000
E-mail: 36bedfordrow@link.org
Call date: Nov 1981, Lincoln's Inn
Qualifications: [BA, LLM (Cantab)]

WILSON SCOTT

Park Court Chambers
40 Park Cross Street, Leeds LS1 2QH,
Telephone: 0113 2433277
Call date: Nov 1993, Lincoln's Inn
Qualifications: [LLB (Hons, Leic)]

WILSON STEPHEN MARK

4 Field Court
Gray's Inn, London WC1R 5EA,
Telephone: 0171 440 6900
E-mail: chambers@4fieldcourt.co.uk
Call date: Oct 1990, Inner Temple
Qualifications: [LLB (UCL)]

WILSON-BARNES MISS LUCY EMMA

St James's Chambers
68 Quay Street, Manchester M3 3EJ,
Telephone: 0161 834 7000
E-mail: 106241.2625@compuserve.com
Call date: July 1989, Inner Temple
Qualifications: [BA (Warw)]

WILSON-SMITH CHRISTOPHER QC (1986)

35 Essex Street
Temple, London WC2R 3AR,
Telephone: 0171 353 6381
Albion Chambers
Broad Street, Bristol BS1 1DR,
Telephone: 0117 9272144
Call date: Nov 1965, Gray's Inn
Recorder

WILTON SIMON DANIEL

4 Paper Bldgs
Ground Floor, Temple, London EC4Y 7EX,
Telephone: 0171 353 3366/583 7155
E-mail: clerks@4paperbuildings.com
Call date: Oct 1993, Gray's Inn
Qualifications: [BA (Sussex)]

WILTSHIRE BERNARD

Horizon Chambers
95a Chancery Lane, London WC2A 1DT,
Telephone: 0171 242 2440
Call date: Nov 1984, Gray's Inn
Qualifications: [BA (York),MA (Lond), M.Phil
(Columbia)]

WINBERG STEPHEN ALEXANDER

1 Crown Office Row
2nd Floor, Temple, London EC4Y 7HH,
Telephone: 0171 797 7111
Call date: Nov 1974, Inner Temple
Qualifications: [BA]

WINCH JOHN

Cleveland Chambers
63-65 Borough Road, Middlesbrough,
Cleveland TS1 3AA, Telephone: 01642 226036
Door Tenant
11 King's Bench Walk
1st Floor, Temple, London EC4Y 7EQ,
Telephone: 0171 353 3337
Door Tenant
Call date: July 1973, Gray's Inn
Qualifications: [LLM, FCIT, Post.Grad Dip,
(Employment Law)]

WINDSOR MISS EMILY MAY

Falcon Chambers
Falcon Court, London EC4Y 1AA,
Telephone: 0171 353 2484/7
Call date: Oct 1995, Gray's Inn
Qualifications: [BA, DSU (Paris)]

WING CHRISTOPHER JOHN

Eighteen Carlton Crescent
Southampton SO15 2XR,
Telephone: 01703 639001
Call date: July 1985, Gray's Inn
Qualifications: [BSc (Kent), BA]

WINGATE-SAUL GILES WINGATE QC (1983)

22 Old Bldgs
Lincoln's Inn, London WC2A 3UJ,
Telephone: 0171 831 0222
25 Byrom Street
Manchester M3 4PF,
Telephone: 0161 829 2100
E-mail: Byromst25@aol.com
Call date: Nov 1967, Inner Temple
Recorder
Qualifications: [LLB]

WINGERT MISS RACHEL THOMAS

Gray's Inn Chambers
5th Floor, Gray's Inn, London WC1R 5JA,
Telephone: 0171 404 1111
Call date: July 1980, Middle Temple
Qualifications: [LLB (Lond), LLM (Lond)]

WINSHIP JULIAN ABDULLA

Furnival Chambers
32 Furnival Street, London EC4A 1JQ,
Telephone: 0171 405 3232
E-mail: clerks@furnivallaw.co.uk
Call date: Oct 1995, Gray's Inn
Qualifications: [LLB]

WINTELER JOHN FRIDOLIN

6 Park Square
Leeds LS1 2LW, Telephone: 0113 2459763
E-mail: chambers@no6.co.uk
Call date: July 1969, Inner Temple
Qualifications: [MA (Cantab)]

WINTER IAN DAVID

Hollis Whiteman Chambers
3rd/4th Floor Queen Elizabeth Bldg, Temple,
London EC4Y 9BS, Telephone: 0171 583 5766
E-mail: hollis.whiteman@btinternet.com
Call date: July 1988, Inner Temple
Qualifications: [LLB (Hons)]

WINTER MISS MELANIE JANE

1 Gray's Inn Square
Ground Floor, London WC1R 5AA,
Telephone: 0171 405 8946/7/8
Call date: Oct 1996, Middle Temple
Qualifications: [LLB (Hons)(Wales)]

WISE IAN

Doughty Street Chambers
11 Doughty Street, London WC1N 2PG,
Telephone: 0171 404 1313
E-mail: doughty_street@compuserve.com
Call date: Oct 1992, Gray's Inn
Qualifications: [BA]

WISE LESLIE MICHAEL

Mitre Court Chambers
3rd Floor, Temple, London EC4Y 7BP,
Telephone: 0171 353 9394
Call date: Nov 1985, Middle Temple
Qualifications: [F.C.A]

WISE OLIVER DACRES

Queen Elizabeth Bldg
2nd Floor, Temple, London EC4Y 9BS,
Telephone: 0171 797 7837
Call date: July 1981, Lincoln's Inn
Qualifications: [MA (Cantab)]

WISEMAN ADAM PHILIP PASTERNAK

18 Red Lion Court
(Off Fleet Street), London EC4A 3EB,
Telephone: 0171 520 6000
Thornwood House
102 New London Road, Chelmsford, Essex
CM2 0RG, Telephone: 01245 280880
Call date: Nov 1994, Inner Temple
Qualifications: [MSc (Exon), CPE (Lond)]

WISHART JOHN DUCKWORTH SCOTT

Manchester House Chambers
18-22 Bridge Street, Manchester M3 3BZ,
Telephone: 0161 834 7007
Call date: July 1974, Gray's Inn
Qualifications: [HNC (Mechanical &,
Production Eng)]

WITCOMB HENRY JAMES

199 Strand
London WC2R 1DR,
Telephone: 0171 379 9779
E-mail: chambers@199strand.co.uk
Call date: Apr 1989, Lincoln's Inn
Qualifications: [BA (Dunelm)]

WITHERS MISS MICHELLE JEAN MARY

Windsor Chambers
2 Penuel Lane, Pontypridd, Mid Glamorgan,
South Wales CF37 4UF,
Telephone: 01443 402067
Call date: Nov 1991, Inner Temple
Qualifications: [LLB (Wales)]

WITHINGTON ANGUS RICHARD

22 Old Bldgs
Lincoln's Inn, London WC2A 3UJ,
Telephone: 0171 831 0222
Call date: Nov 1995, Gray's Inn
Qualifications: [BA (Dunelm)]

D

D

WOLANSKI ADAM MICHAEL VENANTIUS

5 Raymond Buildings
1st Floor, Gray's Inn, London WC1R 5BP,
Telephone: 0171 242 2902
Call date: Feb 1995, Lincoln's Inn
Qualifications: [MA Hons (Cantab)]

WOLCHOVER CHAIM DAVID HIRSCH

Ridgeway Chambers
6 The Ridgeway, Golders Green, London
NW11 8TB, Telephone: 0181 455 2939
E-mail: 101337.1722@compuserve.com
Call date: July 1971, Gray's Inn

WOLFE DR DAVID FREDERICK HARRIS

4-5 Gray's Inn Square
Ground Floor, Gray's Inn, London WC1R 5AY,
Telephone: 0171 404 5252
E-mail: chambers@4-5graysinnsquare.co.uk
Call date: Nov 1992, Middle Temple
Qualifications: [B.Sc M.Eng (Manch), Ph.D
(Cantab), Dip Law]

WOLFF MICHAEL EMANUEL

India Buildings Chambers
Water Street, Liverpool L2 0XG,
Telephone: 0151 243 6000
Call date: June 1964, Gray's Inn
Qualifications: [LLB]

WOLFIN JOLYON HOWARD

Eldon Chambers
Fourth Floor 30/32 Fleet Street, London
EC4Y 1AA, Telephone: 0171 353 4636
Call date: Oct 1992, Middle Temple
Qualifications: [BA (Hons)]

WOLFSON DAVID

3 Verulam Buildings
London WC1R 5NT,
Telephone: 0171 831 8441
E-mail: clerks@3verulam.co.uk
Call date: Nov 1992, Inner Temple
Qualifications: [MA (Cantab)]

WOLKIND MICHAEL IAN

10 King's Bench Walk
1st Floor, Temple, London EC4Y 7EB,
Telephone: 0171 353 2501
Call date: Nov 1976, Middle Temple

WOLLNER ERNEST JOHN

21 Lauderdale Tower
Barbican, London EC2Y 8BY,
Telephone: 0171 920 9308
Call date: Nov 1988, Inner Temple
Qualifications: [Dip Law]

WOLSTENHOLME ALAN JAMES

Lincoln House Chambers
5th Floor Lincoln House, 1 Brazennose Street,
Manchester M2 5EL,
Telephone: 0161 832 5701
E-mail: LincolnHouseChambers@link.org
Call date: July 1989, Lincoln's Inn
Qualifications: [LLB (Leeds)]

WOLTON HARRY QC (1982)

5 Fountain Court
Steelhouse Lane, Birmingham B4 6DR,
Telephone: 0121 606 0500
Devereux Chambers
Devereux Court, London WC2R 3JJ,
Telephone: 0171 353 7534
E-mail: elton@devchambers.co.uk
Call date: July 1969, Gray's Inn
Recorder

WONG MISS NATASHA PUI-WAI

1 Middle Temple Lane
Temple, London EC4Y 1LT,
Telephone: 0171 583 0659 (12 Lines)
Call date: Nov 1993, Middle Temple
Qualifications: [BSc (Hons)(Kingston), CPE
(Middx)]

WONG RENE

2 King's Bench Walk
1st Floor, Temple, London EC4Y 7DE,
Telephone: 0171 353 9276
Call date: Nov 1973, Inner Temple

WONNACOTT MARK ANDREW

199 Strand
London WC2R 1DR,
Telephone: 0171 379 9779
E-mail: chambers@199strand.co.uk
Call date: July 1989, Lincoln's Inn
Qualifications: [LLB (Lond)]

WOOD MISS CATHERINE

4 Paper Bldgs
2nd Floor, Temple, London EC4Y 7EX,
Telephone: 0171 583 0816/071 353 1131
E-mail: clerks@4paperbuildings.co.uk
Call date: July 1985, Middle Temple
Qualifications: [LLB (Lond)]

WOOD CHRISTOPHER MARK BRUCE

1 Mitre Ct Bldgs
Ground Floor, Temple, London EC4Y 7BS,
Telephone: 0171 797 7070
Call date: Feb 1986, Middle Temple
Qualifications: [MA (Oxon), DESU Aix-Marseille, III]

WOOD DEREK ALEXANDER QC (1978)

Falcon Chambers
Falcon Court, London EC4Y 1AA,
Telephone: 0171 353 2484/7
Call date: Feb 1964, Middle Temple
Recorder
Qualifications: [MA, BCL (Oxon)]

WOOD GRAEME CRESSWELL

Assize Court Chambers
14 Small Street, Bristol BS1 1DE,
Telephone: 0117 9264587
New Bailey Chambers
10 Lawson Street, Preston PR1 2QT,
Telephone: 01772 258087
Door Tenant
Call date: July 1968, Middle Temple
Qualifications: [MA, LLM (Cantab)]

WOOD GRAHAM NASH

India Buildings Chambers
Water Street, Liverpool L2 0XG,
Telephone: 0151 243 6000
Door Tenant
3 Paper Bldgs
1st Floor, Temple, London EC4Y 7EU,
Telephone: 0171 583 8055
E-mail: london@3paper.com
Door Tenant
Call date: July 1979, Middle Temple
Assistant Recorder
Qualifications: [LLB (Leeds)]

WOOD GUY NICHOLAS MARSHALL

Hollis Whiteman Chambers
3rd/4th Floor Queen Elizabeth Bldg, Temple,
London EC4Y 9BS, Telephone: 0171 583 5766
E-mail: hollis.whiteman@btinternet.com
Call date: Nov 1980, Middle Temple
Qualifications: [MA (Oxon), LLM, (Indianna)]

WOOD IAN ROBERT

8 King Street
Manchester M2 6AQ,
Telephone: 0161 834 9560
Call date: Oct 1990, Middle Temple
Qualifications: [BA (Manch)]

WOOD JAMES ALEXANDER DOUGLAS

Doughty Street Chambers
11 Doughty Street, London WC1N 2PG,
Telephone: 0171 404 1313
E-mail: doughty_street@compuserve.com
Call date: Nov 1975, Middle Temple
Assistant Recorder
Qualifications: [LLB]

WOOD MISS JOANNA LINDA IRIS

Gower Chambers
57 Walter Road, Swansea, West Glamorgan
SA1 5PZ, Telephone: 01792 644466
E-mail: clerk@gowerchambers.co.uk
Call date: Nov 1989, Inner Temple
Qualifications: [LLB]

WOOD MS LANA CLAIRE

3 Paper Bldgs
Ground Floor, Temple, London EC4Y 7EU,
Telephone: 0171 797 7000
E-mail: clerks@3pb.co.uk
Call date: Oct 1993, Gray's Inn
Qualifications: [BA]

WOOD MARTIN

1 Serjeants' Inn
4th Floor, Temple, London EC4Y 1NH,
Telephone: 0171 583 1355
E-mail: serjeants.inn@virgin.net
Call date: July 1972, Inner Temple
Qualifications: [LLB (Lond)]

WOOD MARTIN JOHN

Broadway House Chambers
Broadway House 9 Bank Street, Bradford,
West Yorkshire BD1 1TW,
Telephone: 01274 722560
Call date: July 1973, Inner Temple
Qualifications: [MA (Cantab)]

WOOD MICHAEL JOHN

Exchange Chambers
Pearl Assurance House Derby Square,
Liverpool L2 9XX, Telephone: 0151 236 7747/
0458
E-mail: exchangechambers@btinternet.com
Call date: Nov 1989, Lincoln's Inn
Qualifications: [BA (Sheff), DipIA (Bradford),
LLB (Hons I)(Sheff)]

WOOD MICHAEL MURE

23 Essex Street
London WC2R 3AS,
Telephone: 0171 413 0353/353 3533
E-mail: clerks@essexstreet23.demon.co.uk
Call date: July 1976, Middle Temple
Assistant Recorder
Qualifications: [LLB]

WOOD NICHOLAS ANDREW

5 Paper Bldgs
Ground Floor, Temple, London EC4Y 7HB,
Telephone: 0171 583 9275/583 4555
E-mail: 5paper@link.org
Call date: July 1970, Inner Temple
Recorder

WOOD PERCY

St James's Chambers
68 Quay Street, Manchester M3 3EJ,
Telephone: 0161 834 7000
E-mail: 106241.2625@compuserve.com
Call date: Feb 1961, Gray's Inn
Qualifications: [MA (Cantab)]

WOOD RICHARD GILLIES

20 Essex Street
London WC2R 3AL,
Telephone: 0171 583 9294
E-mail: clerks@20essexst.com
Call date: July 1975, Lincoln's Inn
Qualifications: [MA (Cantab), BCL (Oxon)]

WOOD RICHARD MICHAEL

Sackville Chambers
Sackville Place 44-48 Magdalen Street,
Norwich NR3 1JU, Telephone: 01603 613516/
616221
Call date: Nov 1995, Gray's Inn
Qualifications: [BA]

WOOD RODERIC LIONEL JAMES QC (1993)

1 King's Bench Walk
2nd Floor, Temple, London EC4Y 7DB,
Telephone: 0171 936 1500
E-mail: ddear@1kbw.co.uk
Call date: July 1974, Middle Temple
Assistant Recorder
Qualifications: [MA (Oxon)]

WOOD SIMON EDWARD

Trinity Chambers
9-12 Trinity Chare, Quayside, Newcastle Upon
Tyne NE1 3DF, Telephone: 0191 232 1927
Plowden Bldgs
2nd Floor, Temple, London EC4Y 9BU,
Telephone: 0171 583 0808
E-mail: bar@plowdenbuildings.co.uk
Call date: Nov 1981, Middle Temple
Qualifications: [LLB]

WOOD SIMON RICHARD HENRY

Lamb Chambers
Lamb Building, Temple, London EC4Y 7AS,
Telephone: 0171 797 8300
E-mail: lambchambers@link.org
Call date: July 1987, Middle Temple
Qualifications: [BA (Bristol), Dip Law (City)]

WOOD STEPHEN

Broadway House Chambers
Broadway House 9 Bank Street, Bradford,
West Yorkshire BD1 1TW,
Telephone: 01274 722560
Call date: Nov 1991, Inner Temple
Qualifications: [LLB (Hons)]

WOOD WILLIAM JAMES

Brick Court Chambers
15/19 Devereux Court, London WC2R 3JJ,
Telephone: 0171 583 0777
E-mail: (surname)@brickcourt.demon.co.uk
Call date: Nov 1980, Middle Temple
Qualifications: [BA, BCL (Oxon), LLM]

WOOD WILLIAM ROWLEY QC (1997)

5 Fountain Court
Steelhouse Lane, Birmingham B4 6DR,
Telephone: 0121 606 0500
Call date: July 1970, Gray's Inn
Recorder
Qualifications: [BA (Oxon)]

WOODALL PETER

Goldsmith Chambers
Ground Floor Goldsmith Building, Temple,
London EC4Y 7BL,
Telephone: 0171 353 6802/3/4/5
E-mail: celiamonksfield@btinternet.com
Call date: July 1983, Middle Temple
Qualifications: [LLB (Leeds)]

WOODBRIDGE JULIAN GUY

1 King's Bench Walk
2nd Floor, Temple, London EC4Y 7DB,
Telephone: 0171 936 1500
E-mail: ddear@1kbw.co.uk
Call date: Nov 1981, Middle Temple
Qualifications: [LLB (Warwick)]

WOODCOCK JONATHAN

10 King's Bench Walk
1st Floor, Temple, London EC4Y 7EB,
Telephone: 0171 353 2501
Call date: Nov 1981, Middle Temple
Qualifications: [LLB, LLM (Lond)]

WOODCOCK ROBERT ANDREW PHILIP

New Court Chambers
3 Broad Chare, Newcastle Upon Tyne
NE1 3DQ, Telephone: 0191 232 1980
Call date: Feb 1978, Inner Temple
Qualifications: [BA]

WOODCRAFT MISS ELIZABETH JANE

14 Tooks Court
Cursitor St, London EC4A 1LB,
Telephone: 0171 405 8828
E-mail: clerks @tooks.law.co.uk
Call date: July 1980, Middle Temple
Qualifications: [BA (Hons)(B'ham)]

WOODLEY LEONARD GASTON QC (1988)

8 King's Bench Walk
2nd Floor, Temple, London EC4Y 7DU,
Telephone: 0171 797 8888
8 King's Bench Walk North
1 Park Square East, Leeds LS1 2NE,
Telephone: 0113 2439797
Call date: July 1963, Inner Temple
Recorder
Qualifications: [Dip Int Aff (Lond)]

WOODLEY MISS SONIA QC (1996)

9-12 Bell Yard
London WC2A 2LF,
Telephone: 0171 400 1800
Call date: July 1968, Gray's Inn
Recorder

WOODS JONATHAN

2 Crown Office Row
Ground Floor, Temple, London EC4Y 7HJ,
Telephone: 0171 797 8100
E-mail: mail@2cor.co.uk, or to individual
barristers at: [barrister's surname]@2cor.co.uk
Call date: July 1965, Middle Temple
Recorder
Qualifications: [BA (Oxon)]

WOODS TERENCE MCCARTAN

2 Gray's Inn Square Chambers
2nd Floor, Gray's Inn, London WC1R 5AA,
Telephone: 0171 242 0328/071 405 1317
E-mail: clerks@2gis.co.uk
Call date: Nov 1989, Middle Temple
Qualifications: [LLB Hons [Lond]]

WOODWARD MISS ALISON JANE

Cobden House Chambers
19 Quay Street, Manchester M3 3HN,
Telephone: 0161 833 6000
E-mail: clerks@cobden.co.uk
Call date: Oct 1992, Gray's Inn
Qualifications: [LL.B (Sheff)]

WOODWARD MISS JOANNE CLAIRE

Cobden House Chambers
19 Quay Street, Manchester M3 3HN,
Telephone: 0161 833 6000
E-mail: clerks@cobden.co.uk
Call date: Nov 1989, Gray's Inn
Qualifications: [LLB (Hons)]

WOODWARD JOHN EDWARD

15 Winckley Square
Preston PR1 3JJ, Telephone: 01772 252828
E-mail: clerks@winckleysq.demon.co.uk
Call date: Nov 1984, Lincoln's Inn
Qualifications: [LLB]

WOODWARD NICHOLAS FREDERICK

21 White Friars
Chester CH1 1NZ, Telephone: 01244 323070
Call date: Nov 1975, Lincoln's Inn
Assistant Recorder
Qualifications: [BA]

WOODWARD WILLIAM CHARLES QC (1985)

24 The Ropewalk
Nottingham NG1 5EF,
Telephone: 0115 9472581
E-mail: clerk@ropewalk.co.uk
22 Old Bldgs
Lincoln's Inn, London WC2A 3UJ,
Telephone: 0171 831 0222
Call date: Feb 1964, Inner Temple
Recorder
Qualifications: [BA (Oxon)]

WOODWARD-CARLTON DAMIAN

22 Old Bldgs
Lincoln's Inn, London WC2A 3UJ,
Telephone: 0171 831 0222
Call date: Oct 1995, Inner Temple
Qualifications: [BSc, MA (Durham), CPE (City)]

WOODWARK MS JANE ELIZABETH

Milburn House Chambers
"A" Floor Milburn House, Dean Street,
Newcastle Upon Tyne NE1 1LE,
Telephone: 0191 230 5511
E-mail: milburnhousechambers@btinternet.com
Call date: Nov 1995, Middle Temple
Qualifications: [BA (Hons), MSc]

WOOLF ELIOT CHARLES ANTHONY

199 Strand
London WC2R 1DR,
Telephone: 0171 379 9779
E-mail: chambers@199strand.co.uk
Call date: Oct 1993, Inner Temple
Qualifications: [BA, CPE]

WOOLF THE HON JEREMY RICHARD GEORGE

Pump Court Tax Chambers
16 Bedford Row, London WC1R 4EB,
Telephone: 0171 414 8080
Call date: July 1986, Inner Temple
Qualifications: [BA (Sussex), LLM (Cantab)]

WOOLF STEVEN JEREMY

Hardwicke Building
New Square, Lincoln's Inn, London
WC2A 3SB, Telephone: 0171 242 2523
E-mail: clerks@hardwicke.co.uk
Call date: July 1989, Inner Temple
Qualifications: [LLB]

WOOLFALL RICHARD IAN

Wilberforce Chambers
Bishop Lane, Hull HU1 1PA,
Telephone: 01482 323264
E-mail: clerks@hullbar.demon.co.uk
Call date: Nov 1992, Middle Temple
Qualifications: [LLB (Hons)]

WOOLFENDEN IVAN PETER

Adrian Lyon's Chambers
14 Castle Street, Liverpool L2 0NE,
Telephone: 0151 236 4421/8240
E-mail: chambers14@aol.com
Call date: July 1985, Middle Temple
Qualifications: [BA(Oxon)]

WOOLGAR DERMOT GERVASE BECKET

3 Paper Bldgs
1st Floor, Temple, London EC4Y 7EU,
Telephone: 0171 583 8055
E-mail: london@3paper.com
1 Alfred Street
High Street, Oxford OX1 4EH,
Telephone: 01865 793736
20 Lorne Park Road
Bournemouth BH1 1JN,
Telephone: 01202 292102 (5 Lines)
Call date: July 1988, Inner Temple
Qualifications: [LLB (Manch)]

WOOLLEY DAVID RORIE QC (1980)

1 Serjeants' Inn
4th Floor, Temple, London EC4Y 1NH,
Telephone: 0171 583 1355
E-mail: serjeants.inn@virgin.net
Call date: July 1962, Middle Temple
Qualifications: [MA (Cantab)]

Fax: 0171 583 1672; DX: 440 Chancery Lane

Types of work: Administrative; Environment;
Housing; Parliamentary; Planning; Tax - capital
and income; Tax - corporate; Town and country
planning

Membership of foreign bars: Western

Awards and memberships: Bencher, Middle
Temple

Languages spoken: French, German

Publications: *Town Hall & The Property
Owner*, 1967; *Environmental Law and
Practice*, 1998

Reported cases: *Lovell v Bristol Corporation*,
[1998] AC (HL), 1998. Right to buy Local
Authority housing - extent of court's discretion.
Great Portland Estates v Westminster Corpn,
[1985] AC 661 (HL), 1985. Extent of planning
authority discretion in preparing local
development plan.

Nothman v Barnet LBC, [1979] 1 All ER 142
(HL), 1979. Right of female teacher to bring
proceedings for unfair dismissal.
Re Elm Avenue, New Milton, [1984] 1 WLR
1398, 1984. Procedure to be followed in
applying to High Court on construction of
restrictive covenant.
Vibroplant v Holland, [1981] 1 All ER 146 (CA),
1981. Liability to corporation tax.

WOOLLS MISS TANYA JANE

Furnival Chambers
32 Furnival Street, London EC4A 1JQ,
Telephone: 0171 405 3232
E-mail: clerks@furnivallaw.co.uk
Call date: Feb 1991, Middle Temple
Qualifications: [LLB (Hons)]

WOOLMAN ANDREW PAUL LANDER

10 Park Square
Leeds LS1 2LH, Telephone: 0113 2455438
E-mail: chambers@bandit.legend.co.uk
Call date: Nov 1973, Inner Temple
Recorder
Qualifications: [MA (Cantab)]

WOOLRICH MISS SARAH

Trinity Chambers
9-12 Trinity Chare, Quayside, Newcastle Upon
Tyne NE1 3DF, Telephone: 0191 232 1927
Call date: Nov 1994, Middle Temple
Qualifications: [LLB]

WOOSEY MISS ELIZABETH JANE

Victoria Chambers
19 Castle Street, Liverpool L2 4SX,
Telephone: 0151 236 9402
E-mail: Fa45@rapid.co.uk
Call date: July 1993, Lincoln's Inn
Qualifications: [LLB (Hons)]

WOOTLIFF MISS BARBARA JACQUELINE

37 Park Square
Leeds LS1 2NY, Telephone: 0113 2439422
Call date: May 1956, Middle Temple

D

WORDSWORTH MRS PHILIPPA LINDSEY

10 Park Square
Leeds LS1 2LH, Telephone: 0113 2455438
E-mail: chambers@bandit.legend.co.uk
Call date: Oct 1995, Gray's Inn
Qualifications: [LLB (Manch)]

WORMALD RICHARD

3 Raymond Buildings
Gray's Inn, London WC1R 5BH,
Telephone: 0171 831 3833
E-mail: chambers@threeraymond.demon.co.uk
Call date: Oct 1993, Gray's Inn
Qualifications: [BA (York)]

WORMINGTON TIMOTHY MICHAEL

Fountain Court
Temple, London EC4Y 9DH,
Telephone: 0171 583 3335
E-mail: chambers@fountaincourt.co.uk
Call date: Nov 1977, Middle Temple
Qualifications: [BA, BCL (Oxon)]

WORRALL MISS ANNA MAUREEN QC (1989)

Cloisters
1st Floor, Temple, London EC4Y 7AA,
Telephone: 0171 827 4000
E-mail: clerks@cloisters.com
8 King Street
Manchester M2 6AQ,
Telephone: 0161 834 9560
Door Tenant
Call date: Nov 1959, Middle Temple
Recorder
Qualifications: [LLB]

WORRALL JOHN RAYMOND GUY

10 Park Square
Leeds LS1 2LH, Telephone: 0113 2455438
E-mail: chambers@bandit.legend.co.uk
Call date: July 1984, Gray's Inn
Qualifications: [BA (Hons) LLB (Hons)]

WORRALL MISS SHIRLEY VERA FRANCES

8 King Street
Manchester M2 6AQ,
Telephone: 0161 834 9560
Call date: Nov 1987, Gray's Inn
Qualifications: [LLB (Hons)]

WORSLEY DANIEL

2 Harcourt Bldgs
Ground Floor/Left, Temple, London
EC4Y 9DB, Telephone: 0171 583 9020
E-mail: clerks@harcourt.co.uk
Stanbrook & Henderson
2 Harcourt Bldgs 2nd Floor, Temple, London
EC4Y 9DB, Telephone: 0171 353 0101
E-mail: clerks@harcourt.co.uk
Call date: May 1971, Gray's Inn
Recorder
Qualifications: [BA (Cantab)]

WORSLEY MARK INDRA

Guildhall Chambers
23 Broad Street, Bristol BS1 2HG,
Telephone: 0117 9273366
Call date: Nov 1994, Inner Temple
Qualifications: [LLB (Newc)]

WORSLEY MICHAEL DOMINIC LAURENCE QC (1985)

6 King's Bench Walk
Ground Floor, Temple, London EC4Y 7DR,
Telephone: 0171 583 0410
Call date: June 1955, Inner Temple

WORSLEY PAUL FREDERICK QC (1990)

Park Court Chambers
40 Park Cross Street, Leeds LS1 2QH,
Telephone: 0113 2433277
1 Hare Court
Ground Floor, Temple, London EC4Y 7BE,
Telephone: 0171 353 3982/5324
Door Tenant
Call date: July 1970, Middle Temple
Recorder
Qualifications: [MA (Oxon)]

WORSTER DAVID JAMES STEWART

7 Fountain Court
Steelhouse Lane, Birmingham B4 6DR,
Telephone: 0121 236 8531
Call date: Nov 1980, Lincoln's Inn
Qualifications: [MA (Cantab)]

WORTHINGTON STEPHEN

12 King's Bench Walk
Temple, London EC4Y 7EL,
Telephone: 0171 583 0811
E-mail: chambers@12kbw.co.uk
Call date: Nov 1976, Gray's Inn
Qualifications: [MA (Cantab)]

WRAY NIGEL HUBERT

Wilberforce Chambers
Bishop Lane, Hull HU1 1PA,
Telephone: 01482 323264
E-mail: clerks@hullbar.demon.co.uk
Call date: July 1986, Middle Temple
Qualifications: [LLB(Lond)]

WRENN MISS HELEN MARGARET

Martins Building
Water Street, Liverpool L2 3SP,
Telephone: 0151 236 5818/4919
Call date: Nov 1994, Inner Temple
Qualifications: [BA (Leeds), CPE
(Wolverhampton)]

WRIGHT ALASTAIR DAVID

28 St John Street
Manchester M3 4DJ,
Telephone: 0161 834 8418
E-mail: clerk@28stjohnst.co.uk
Call date: Oct 1991, Lincoln's Inn
Qualifications: [MA (Oxon), Dip Law]

WRIGHT MISS CAROLINE JANE

Albion Chambers
Broad Street, Bristol BS1 1DR,
Telephone: 0117 9272144
Door Tenant
6 Gray's Inn Square
Ground Floor, Gray's Inn, London WC1R 5AZ,
Telephone: 0171 242 1052
Call date: July 1983, Gray's Inn
Qualifications: [BSc (York) Dip Law]

WRIGHT MISS CLARE ELIZABETH

6 Pump Court
1st Floor, Temple, London EC4Y 7AR,
Telephone: 0171 797 8400
E-mail: sa_hockman_qc@link.org
Call date: Oct 1995, Inner Temple
Qualifications: [LLB (Bris)]

WRIGHT COLIN JOHN

4 Field Court
Gray's Inn, London WC1R 5EA,
Telephone: 0171 440 6900
E-mail: chambers@4fieldcourt.co.uk
Call date: July 1987, Middle Temple
Qualifications: [LLB (Leics)]

WRIGHT DERMOT JOHN FETHERSTONHAUGH

3 Temple Gardens
3rd Floor, Temple, London EC4Y 9AU,
Telephone: 0171 583 0010
Call date: July 1967, Inner Temple
Qualifications: [MA (Cantab)]

WRIGHT DESMOND GARFORTH QC (1974)

1 Atkin Building
Gray's Inn, London WC1R 5AT,
Telephone: 0171 404 0102
E-mail: clerks@atkin-chambers.co.uk
Call date: Jan 1950, Lincoln's Inn
Qualifications: [MA (Oxon)]

WRIGHT FREDERICK GEORGE IAN

3 Serjeants' Inn
London EC4Y 1BQ,
Telephone: 0171 353 5537
E-mail: available upon request
Call date: July 1989, Inner Temple
Qualifications: [BSc(Hons), MSc, DIC,
Chartered Engineer, MICE, MIStruct E, Dip.
Law]

Fax: 0171 353 0425; DX: LDE 421

Types of work: Arbitration; Construction;
Professional negligence

Other professional qualifications: Chartered
Civil Engineer; Chartered Structural Engineer

Membership of foreign bars: Northern Ireland
Bar

Awards and memberships: Committee Member of Official Referees' Bar Association; Fellow of the Chartered Institute of Arbitrators; Member of the Institution of Civil Engineers; Member of the Institution of Structural Engineers

Other professional experience: Consulting civil and structural engineer in private practice before being called to the Bar

Reported cases: *Bennell's Electrical Contractors Ltd v London Underground Ltd*, (1995) CILL 1110, 1995. Exclusivity of contract - period of notice for term contract - effect of signing contract after repudiation.

WRIGHT GERARD HENRY QC (1973)

25-27 Castle Street
1st Floor, Liverpool L2 4TA,
Telephone: 0151 227 5661/051 236 5072
Call date: Feb 1954, Gray's Inn
Qualifications: [BCL, BA (Oxon)]

WRIGHT IAN

5 Paper Bldgs
Ground Floor, Temple, London EC4Y 7HB,
Telephone: 0171 583 9275/583 4555
E-mail: 5paper@link.org
Call date: Nov 1983, Middle Temple
Qualifications: [BSc (Dundee) LLB, (Leic)]

WRIGHT MR. IAN BERNARD

Iscoed Chambers
86 St Helen's Road, Swansea SA1 4BQ,
Telephone: 01792 652988/9/330
Call date: Nov 1994, Middle Temple
Qualifications: [LLB (Hons) (Wales)]

WRIGHT MISS JACQUELINE LESLEY

Holborn Chambers
6 Gate Street, Lincoln's Inn Fields, London
WC2A 3HP, Telephone: 0171 242 6060
Door Tenant
Call date: Nov 1975, Gray's Inn

WRIGHT JEREMY JOHN

2 King's Bench Walk
Ground Floor, Temple, London EC4Y 7DE,
Telephone: 0171 353 1746
E-mail: 2kbw@atlas.co.uk
King's Bench Chambers
115 North Hill, Plymouth PL4 8JY,
Telephone: 01752 221551
Call date: July 1970, Inner Temple
Recorder
Qualifications: [BA (Oxon)]

WRIGHT JEREMY PAUL

5 Fountain Court
Steelhouse Lane, Birmingham B4 6DR,
Telephone: 0121 606 0500
Call date: Oct 1996, Inner Temple
Qualifications: [LLB (Exon)]

WRIGHT NORMAN ALFRED

Oriel Chambers
14 Water Street, Liverpool L2 8TD,
Telephone: 0151 236 7191
E-mail: oriel_chambers@link.org
Call date: Nov 1974, Gray's Inn
Assistant Recorder
Qualifications: [LLB (L'pool)]

WRIGHT PAUL WAYNE

Brick Court Chambers
15/19 Devereux Court, London WC2R 3JJ,
Telephone: 0171 583 0777
E-mail: (surname)@brickcourt.demon.co.uk
Call date: Nov 1990, Inner Temple
Qualifications: [LLB (So'ton)]

WRIGHT PETER DUNCAN

Lincoln House Chambers
5th Floor Lincoln House, 1 Brazennose Street,
Manchester M2 5EL,
Telephone: 0161 832 5701
E-mail: LincolnHouseChambers@link.org
Call date: July 1981, Inner Temple
Qualifications: [LLB (Hull)]

WRIGHT PETER MALCOLM

Queen Elizabeth Bldg
2nd Floor, Temple, London EC4Y 9BS,
Telephone: 0171 797 7837
Call date: July 1974, Middle Temple
Qualifications: [MA (Cantab)]

WRIGHT ROBERT ANTHONY KENT QC (1973)

Erskine Chambers
30 Lincoln's Inn Fields, Lincoln's Inn, London
WC2A 3PF, Telephone: 0171 242 5532
E-mail: Clerks@Erskine-Chambers.law.co.uk
Call date: Jan 1949, Lincoln's Inn
Qualifications: [MA (Oxon)]

WRIGHT MS SADIE

Goldsmith Building
1st Floor, Temple, London EC4Y 7BL,
Telephone: 0171 353 7881
E-mail: clerks@goldsmith-building.law.co.uk
Call date: Oct 1994, Lincoln's Inn
Qualifications: [BA (Hons)]

WRIGHT MISS SARAH CAROLYN

Paradise Square Chambers
26 Paradise Square, Sheffield S1 2DE,
Telephone: 0114 2738951
Call date: Nov 1984, Gray's Inn
Qualifications: [BA]

WRIGHT STEWART MACDONALD

1 Pump Court
Lower Ground Floor, Temple, London
EC4Y 7AB, Telephone: 0171 583 2012/
353 4341
E-mail: (name) @1pumpcourt.co.uk
Call date: Oct 1993, Gray's Inn
Qualifications: [MA (Glasgow)]

WRIGHT TREVOR

Bell Yard Chambers
116/118 Chancery Lane, London WC2A 1PP,
Telephone: 0171 306 9292
Call date: Nov 1992, Middle Temple
Qualifications: [LL.B (Hons, Lond)]

WRIGHT MRS YASMIN TAJDIN

New Bailey Chambers
10 Lawson Street, Preston PR1 2QT,
Telephone: 01772 258087
Call date: Nov 1990, Inner Temple
Qualifications: [LLB]

WULWIK PETER DAVID

Devereux Chambers
Devereux Court, London WC2R 3JJ,
Telephone: 0171 353 7534
E-mail: elton@devchambers.co.uk
Call date: July 1972, Gray's Inn
Assistant Recorder

WURTZEL DAVID IRA

2 Dr Johnson's Building
Temple, London EC4Y 7AY,
Telephone: 0171 353 4716
Call date: Nov 1974, Middle Temple
Qualifications: [MA (Cantab), MA (Lond)]

WYAND ROGER NICHOLAS LEWES QC (1997)

One Raymond Buildings
Gray's Inn, London WC1R 5BH,
Telephone: 0171 430 1234
E-mail: chambers@ipbar1rb.com;
clerks@ipbar1rb.com
Call date: May 1973, Middle Temple
Assistant Recorder
Qualifications: [MA (Cantab)]

WYATT DERRICK ARTHUR QC (1993)

Brick Court Chambers
15/19 Devereux Court, London WC2R 3JJ,
Telephone: 0171 583 0777
E-mail: (surname)@brickcourt.demon.co.uk
Door Tenant
Call date: July 1972, Lincoln's Inn
Qualifications: [MA, LLB (Cantab), JD
(Chicago)]

WYATT GUY PETER JAMES

Earl Street Chambers
47 Earl Street, Maidstone, Kent ME14 1PD,
Telephone: 01622 671222
E-mail: gunner-sparks@msn.com
Call date: July 1981, Inner Temple
Qualifications: [BA (Hons) Law]

WYATT JONATHAN MARTIN

Assize Court Chambers
14 Small Street, Bristol BS1 1DE,
Telephone: 0117 9264587
Call date: July 1973, Gray's Inn
Qualifications: [LLB (Lond), FCIArb]

D

WYATT MARK

2 New Street
Leicester LE1 5NA, Telephone: 0116 2625906
Call date: July 1976, Middle Temple
Qualifications: [MA (Oxon)]

WYATT MICHAEL CHRISTOPHER

10 Winterbourne Grove
Weybridge, Surrey KT13 OPP,
Telephone: 0181 941 3939
E-mail: wyatt_taxco@compuserve.com
Call date: July 1975, Gray's Inn
Qualifications: [LLB Hons (Bris), ATII]

WYETH MARK CHARLES

2 Paper Bldgs
Temple, London EC4Y 7ET,
Telephone: 0171 936 2613
Call date: July 1983, Inner Temple
Qualifications: [BA (Hons), LLM, ACI (arb)]

WYLES MISS LUCY ANNE

2 Temple Gardens
Temple, London EC4Y 9AY,
Telephone: 0171 583 6041 (12 Lines)
Call date: Oct 1994, Lincoln's Inn
Qualifications: [BA (Hons), Licence Speciale,
Droit, (Bruxelles)]

WYLIE KEITH FRANCIS

Eighteen Carlton Crescent
Southampton SO15 2XR,
Telephone: 01703 639001
Call date: July 1976, Gray's Inn
Qualifications: [MA (Cantab)]

WYLIE NEIL RICHARD

King Charles House
Standard Hill, Nottingham NG1 6FX,
Telephone: 0115 9418851
E-mail: clerks@kch.co.uk
Call date: Nov 1996, Gray's Inn
Qualifications: [LLB (Manch)]

WYNN TOBY

11 King's Bench Walk
1st Floor, Temple, London EC4Y 7EQ,
Telephone: 0171 353 3337
3 Park Court
Leeds LS1 2QH, Telephone: 0113 297 1200
Call date: July 1982, Gray's Inn
Qualifications: [LLB (Lond)]

WYNNE ASHLEY JOHN

5 Fountain Court
Steelhouse Lane, Birmingham B4 6DR,
Telephone: 0121 606 0500
Call date: Nov 1990, Gray's Inn
Qualifications: [LLB (Cardiff)]

WYNNE-GRIFFITHS RALPH RICHARD DAVID

Guildhall Chambers
23 Broad Street, Bristol BS1 2HG,
Telephone: 0117 9273366
Door Tenant
Call date: July 1981, Gray's Inn
Qualifications: [MA (Cantab)]

WYNTER COLIN PETER

Devereux Chambers
Devereux Court, London WC2R 3JJ,
Telephone: 0171 353 7534
E-mail: elton@devchambers.co.uk
Call date: Nov 1984, Inner Temple
Qualifications: [LLB MPhil]

XYDIAS NICHOLAS

5 Fountain Court
Steelhouse Lane, Birmingham B4 6DR,
Telephone: 0121 606 0500
Call date: Oct 1992, Lincoln's Inn
Qualifications: [LLB(Hons)(Lond), LLM(Lond)]

YAJNIK RAM

6 Gray's Inn Square
Ground Floor, Gray's Inn, London WC1R 5AZ,
Telephone: 0171 242 1052
Call date: Nov 1965, Inner Temple
Qualifications: [BA, BCom (Bombay), LLB
(Lond)]

YAKUBU EMMANUEL MAHAMA

74 Chancery Lane
First Floor, London WC2A 1AA,
Telephone: 0171 430 0667
Call date: July 1970, Middle Temple
Qualifications: [LLB (Lond), J.B Montague Award, Winner]

YAQUB ZAHD

2 King's Bench Walk
1st Floor, Temple, London EC4Y 7DE,
Telephone: 0171 353 9276
Call date: Feb 1991, Inner Temple
Qualifications: [BA, LLM (Lond)]

YATES NICHOLAS GILMORE

1 Mitre Ct Bldgs
Ground Floor, Temple, London EC4Y 7BS,
Telephone: 0171 797 7070
Call date: Oct 1996, Inner Temple
Qualifications: [BA (Cantab), CPE (Lond)]

YAZAWA YUTAKA

4 King's Bench Walk
Ground/First Floor, Temple, London
EC4Y 7DL, Telephone: 0171 822 8822
E-mail: 4kbw@barristersatlaw.com
Call date: Oct 1994, Middle Temple
Qualifications: [LLB (Hons)(Lond)]

YAZDANI GHULAM

6 King's Bench Walk
Ground, Third & Fourth Floors, Temple,
London EC4Y 7DR,
Telephone: 0171 353 4931/583 0695
Call date: Feb 1963, Lincoln's Inn
Qualifications: [MA, LLB (Karachi)]

YEARWOOD JEFFREY RYEBURN

8 King's Bench Walk
2nd Floor, Temple, London EC4Y 7DU,
Telephone: 0171 797 8888
8 King's Bench Walk North
1 Park Square East, Leeds LS1 2NE,
Telephone: 0113 2439797
Call date: Nov 1975, Inner Temple
Assistant Recorder
Qualifications: [BA]

YEBOAH MISS YAA FREMPOMAA

14 Tooks Court
Cursitor St, London EC4A 1LB,
Telephone: 0171 405 8828
E-mail: clerks @tooks.law.co.uk
Door Tenant
Westgate Chambers
144 High Street, Lewes, East Sussex BN7 1XT,
Telephone: 01273 480510
Call date: Nov 1977, Gray's Inn
Qualifications: [LLB (Ghana) LLM, (Harvard)]

YELL NICHOLAS ANTHONY

1 Serjeants' Inn
5th Floor Fleet Street, Temple, London
EC4Y 1LL, Telephone: 0171 415 6666
E-mail: no1serjeantsinn@btinternet.com
Call date: July 1979, Middle Temple
Qualifications: [LLB (Lond)]

YELTON MICHAEL PAUL

Fenners Chambers
3 Madingley Road, Cambridge CB3 OEE,
Telephone: 01223 368761
Fenners Chambers
8-12 Priestgate, Peterborough PE1 1JA,
Telephone: 01733 62030
Call date: July 1972, Middle Temple
Recorder
Qualifications: [MA (Cantab)]

YEUNG STUART ROY

22 Albion Place
Northampton NN1 1UD,
Telephone: 01604 36271
Call date: Nov 1989, Inner Temple
Qualifications: [LLB]

YIP MRS AMANDA LOUISE

Exchange Chambers
Pearl Assurance House Derby Square,
Liverpool L2 9XX, Telephone: 0151 236 7747/0458
E-mail: exchangechambers@btinternet.com
Call date: Oct 1991, Gray's Inn
Qualifications: [MA (Cantab)]

YONG YING KEONG

Chancery Chambers
1st Floor Offices 70/72 Chancery Lane,
London WC2A 1AB,
Telephone: 0171 405 6879/6870
Call date: Oct 1993, Middle Temple
Qualifications: [LLB (Hons)(Notts)]

YOULL MISS JOANNA ISABEL

2 Field Court
Gray's Inn, London WC1R 5BB,
Telephone: 0171 405 6114
E-mail: fieldct2@netcomuk.co.uk.
Call date: Nov 1989, Gray's Inn
Qualifications: [LLB (Lond)]

YOUNG ANDREW GEORGE

1 Crown Office Row
3rd Floor, Temple, London EC4Y 7HH,
Telephone: 0171 583 9292
E-mail: onecor@link.org
Call date: July 1977, Lincoln's Inn
Qualifications: [BA (Oxon)]

YOUNG CHRISTOPHER REGINALD BOYD

24 Old Bldgs
Ground Floor, Lincoln's Inn, London
WC2A 3UJ, Telephone: 0171 404 0946
E-mail: clerks@24oldbuildings.law.co.uk
Call date: July 1988, Lincoln's Inn
Qualifications: [BA (Hons) (Sussex)]

YOUNG DAVID ANTHONY

3 Gray's Inn Square
Ground Floor, London WC1R 5AH,
Telephone: 0171 520 5600
E-mail: gis3@btinternet.com
Call date: July 1986, Middle Temple
Qualifications: [BA (Hons) LLM (Lond)]

YOUNG DAVID EDWARD MICHAEL QC (1980)

3 New Square
Lincoln's Inn, London WC2A 3RS,
Telephone: 0171 405 1111
Call date: July 1966, Lincoln's Inn
Recorder
Qualifications: [MA (Oxon)]

YOUNG EDWARD WILLIAM

Cleveland Chambers
63-65 Borough Road, Middlesbrough,
Cleveland TS1 3AA, Telephone: 01642 226036
Call date: Nov 1988, Gray's Inn
Qualifications: [LLB (Manch)]

YOUNG LEE TERENCE

Guildhall Chambers Portsmouth
Prudential Buildings 16 Guildhall Walk,
Portsmouth, Hampshire PO1 2DE,
Telephone: 01705 752400
Call date: Oct 1991, Middle Temple
Qualifications: [LLB (Hons)]

YOUNG MARTIN FORD

3 Paper Bldgs
Ground Floor, Temple, London EC4Y 7EU,
Telephone: 0171 797 7000
E-mail: clerks@3pb.co.uk
Call date: Nov 1984, Middle Temple
Qualifications: [LLB, LLM (Lond)]

YOUNG MISS REBECCA LEAH

39 Park Square
Leeds LS1 2NU, Telephone: 0113 2456633
Call date: Nov 1993, Inner Temple
Qualifications: [LLB]

YOUNG TIMOTHY NICHOLAS QC (1996)

20 Essex Street
London WC2R 3AL,
Telephone: 0171 583 9294
E-mail: clerks@20essexst.com
Call date: July 1977, Gray's Inn
Qualifications: [BA, BCL (Oxon)]

YOXALL BASIL JOSHUA

Francis Taylor Bldg
3rd Floor, Temple, London EC4Y 7BY,
Telephone: 0171 797 7250
Call date: July 1975, Inner Temple
Qualifications: [MA (Cantab), FCIArb]

ZACAROLI ANTONY JAMES

3/4 South Square
Gray's Inn, London WC1R 5HP,
Telephone: 0171 696 9900
E-mail: clerks@southsquare.com
Call date: Nov 1987, Middle Temple
Qualifications: [BA,BCL (Oxon)]

ZAHED YASREEB

Phoenix Chambers
First Floor Gray's Inn Chambers, Gray's Inn,
London WC1R 5JA, Telephone: 0171 404 7888
Call date: May 1993, Lincoln's Inn
Qualifications: [BSc (Hons)(City), LLM (Lond)]

ZAMAN MOHAMMED KHALIL

King Charles House
Standard Hill, Nottingham NG1 6FX,
Telephone: 0115 9418851
E-mail: clerks@kch.co.uk
Call date: Nov 1985, Gray's Inn
Qualifications: [LLB (Warwick)]

ZEIDMAN MARTYN KEITH

33 Bedford Row
London WC1R 4JH,
Telephone: 0171 242 6476
Call date: July 1974, Middle Temple
Assistant Recorder
Qualifications: [LLB (Lond), ACIArb]

ZEITLIN DEREK JAMES

4 Brick Court
1st Floor, Temple, London EC4Y 9AD,
Telephone: 0171 583 8455
Call date: July 1974, Lincoln's Inn
Qualifications: [BSc]

ZELIN GEOFFREY ANDREW

Enterprise Chambers
9 Old Square, Lincoln's Inn, London
WC2A 3SR, Telephone: 0171 405 9471
Enterprise Chambers
38 Park Square, Leeds LS1 2PA,
Telephone: 01132 460391
Enterprise Chambers
65 Quayside, Newcastle upon Tyne NE1 3DS,
Telephone: 0191 222 3344
Call date: July 1984, Middle Temple
Qualifications: [MA (Cantab)]

ZIEGER JOHN HARRY

29 Bedford Row Chambers
London WC1R 4HE,
Telephone: 0171 831 2626
Call date: July 1962, Middle Temple

ZIMBLER MISS ALEXIA

2 King's Bench Walk
Ground Floor, Temple, London EC4Y 7DE,
Telephone: 0171 353 1746
E-mail: 2kbw@atlas.co.uk
King's Bench Chambers
115 North Hill, Plymouth PL4 8JY,
Telephone: 01752 221551
Call date: Oct 1993, Lincoln's Inn
Qualifications: [BSc (Hons)(Lond)]

ZORBAS PANAYLOTIS CHRISTOPHOROU

2 Paper Bldgs
1st Floor, Temple, London EC4Y 7ET,
Telephone: 0171 936 2611 (10 Lines)
E-mail: clerks@2pbbarristers.co.uk
Call date: June 1964, Lincoln's Inn

ZORNOZA MISS ISABELLE

2 Harcourt Bldgs
Ground Floor/Left, Temple, London
EC4Y 9DB, Telephone: 0171 583 9020
E-mail: clerks@harcourt.co.uk
Stanbrook & Henderson
2 Harcourt Bldgs 2nd Floor, Temple, London
EC4Y 9DB, Telephone: 0171 353 0101
E-mail: clerks@harcourt.co.uk
Call date: Oct 1993, Inner Temple
Qualifications: [BA (Hons), CPE]

ZORNOZA PHILIP

One Raymond Buildings
Gray's Inn, London WC1R 5BH,
Telephone: 0171 430 1234
E-mail: chambers@ipbar1rb.com;
clerks@ipbar1rb.com
Door Tenant
Call date: July 1983, Middle Temple
Qualifications: [BSc (Nottm), Dip Law]

D

ZUCKER DAVID GRAHAM

Park Lane Chambers
19 Westgate, Leeds LS1 2RD,
Telephone: 0113 2285000
Call date: July 1986, Middle Temple
Qualifications: [LLB]

Individual Barristers in Employment and Non-practising

This section lists those barristers who are in employment and those who do not practise. Barristers are listed alphabetically by surname, and details include their date of call to the Bar, their Inn of Court and academic qualifications. Barristers who are currently employed have details of their position of employment with a full address.

The symbol ● indicates that a barrister is in employment.

E

E

Abai *Miss Joyce Ola*
Called: Feb 1995, Middle Temple, LLB
(Hons), LLM (Lond)

Abanulo *Miss Annette Obiageli*
Called: Oct 1997, Gray's Inn, LLB (Essex)

Abbas *Nigel* ●
Lawyer, Channel 4 Television Corp., 124
Horseferry Road, London SW1P 2TS, 0171
306 8731, Fax: 0171 306 9367. Called: Nov
1995, Lincoln's Inn, BA (Hons)

Abbasi *Miss Sufiah Naz*
Called: Nov 1997, Gray's Inn, LLB (Manch)

Abbots *Robert Patrick* ●
Principal Legal Officer, HM Customs &
Excise, Solicitor's Office, New King's Beam
House, 22 Upper Ground, London SE1 9PS,
0171 620 1313, Fax: 0171 865 5164.
Called: Nov 1988, Inner Temple, BA
(Warwick)

Abbott *David Michael*
Called: Nov 1995, Inner Temple, LLB
(Soton), LLM (Lond)

Abbott *Miss Emma-Jane Amelia*
Called: Nov 1996, Gray's Inn, MA
(Edinburgh), LLB (Leeds)

Abbott *Miss Helen Louise*
9 Park Place, Cardiff, CF1 3DP. Called: Nov
1988, Gray's Inn, LLB (Lond)

Abbott *Stephen George*
Director of Legal Services, Birmingham
Magistrates Court, Victoria Law Courts,
Corporation Street, Birmingham B4 6QJ,
0121 212 6611, Fax: 0121 212 6766.
Called: July 1983, Inner Temple, LLB (Sheff),
MA

Abd. Karim *Miss Ida Hanani*
Called: July 1994, Lincoln's Inn, LLB (Hons)

Abdin *Miss Romana* ●
Group Legal Advisor, Black Horse Agencies
Ltd, Salisbury Square, Hatfield, Herts
AL9 5DD, 01707 275371, Fax: 01707
274053. Called: July 1988, Gray's Inn, LLB
(Wales)

Abdul Ghafor *Miss Siti Norishan*
Legal Advisor, Brunei Attorney General's
Chamber, 51 Jalan Madewa, Jalan Tutong,
Bandar Seri Begawan 2688, 00673 (2)
651732. Called: July 1996, Lincoln's Inn,
LLB (Hons) (LSE)

Abdul Hamid *Miss Muslin*
Called: July 1993, Middle Temple, LLB
(Hons, Warw)

Abdul Haque *Miss Nasreen Begum*
and Member Malaysia Bar. Called: Nov 1994,
Lincoln's Inn, LLB (Hons)(Lond)

Abdul Jabid *Miss Soraya*
Called: Nov 1995, Lincoln's Inn, LLB (Hons)

Abdul Kadir *Rizal*
Legal Adviser, Shell Malaysia Ltd, Legal
Department, Bangunan Shell, Off Jalan
Semantan, P.O.Box 11027, 50732 Kuala
Lumpur, 60 - 3 - 2512891, Fax: 60 - 3 -
2512732. Called: Nov 1993, Lincoln's Inn,
LLB (Hons, Leic)

Abdul Karim *Miss Yasmeen*
Called: July 1997, Lincoln's Inn, LLB
(Hons)(Lond)

Abdul Majid Khan *Miss Sabriya*
and Member Malaysia Bar. Called: Nov 1992,
Lincoln's Inn, LLB (Hons)(Sheff)

Abdul Malek *Faisal Ramza*
Called: July 1995, Middle Temple, LLB
(Hons)

Abdul Rahman *Mrs Ramzidah*
Called: Mar 1998, Lincoln's Inn, LLB (Hons)

Abdul Rashid *Miss Zaidatul Mazwin*
Called: Nov 1996, Lincoln's Inn, LLB
(Hons)(Manch)

Abdul Shukor *Miss Shazwan*
Called: July 1996, Lincoln's Inn, LLB
(Hons)(Sheff)

Abdul-Rasool *Miss Leila*
Called: Nov 1994, Lincoln's Inn, LLB
(Hons)(Lond), Dip in Intellectual, Property

Abdulhusein *Shamsuddin Taherali*
5 Overbury Close, Weymouth, Dorset
DT4 9UE. Called: Feb 1963, Lincoln's Inn

Abdullah *Arshad*
Advocate, BAP 35-C, Cantonment Plaza,
Sadmar Road, Peshawar, N W F P, 00 92 91
285 277, Fax: 00 92 91 285 277, and
Member Pakistan. Called: Nov 1996,
Lincoln's Inn, LLM (Staff), MA (Pakistan)

Abdullah *Miss Azleena*
Called: Nov 1997, Gray's Inn, LLB (Bris)

Abdullah *Miss Hajah Pauziah*
Called: July 1996, Lincoln's Inn, LLB
(Hons)(Kent)

Abdulrahim *Miss Nor Rejina*
Legal Officer, (603) 253 4852, Fax: (603)
253 4537. Called: July 1997, Lincoln's Inn,
LLB (Hons)(Kent)

Abecassis *Dr David William*
28 Ravenswood Road, Bristol BS6 6BW,
0117 9735680, Fax: 0117 9467754.
Called: Apr 1975, Middle Temple, MA
(Cantab), PhD (Cantab)

Abedi *Ali Abbas Welayat Husain*
Abbas F.Ghazzawi Law Firm, P O Box 2335,
Jeddah 21451, (+9662) 6654646, Fax:
(+9662) 6659155, and Member New York.
Called: Nov 1988, Middle Temple, LLB
(Lond), LLM (NY)

Abedin *Miss Syeda Khadizatulkubra*
Administrative Officer. Called: Nov 1995,
Lincoln's Inn, LLB (Hons)

Abelson *Ivor Gordon*
16 Gunners Grove, London E4 9SS, 0181
529 5090. Called: Nov 1974, Gray's Inn

Aber *Gordon*
and Member South Africa 4 Paper Bldgs,
2nd Floor, Temple, London, EC4Y 7EX.
Called: Mar 1996, Lincoln's Inn,
BA,LLM(Johannesburg), LLM (Lond)

Abercrombie *Ian Ralph*
7 Lauder Road, Edinburgh EH9 2EW, 0131
668 2489, Fax: 0131 668 3037, QC Scottish
Bar and Member Scottish Bar. Called: Apr
1991, Lincoln's Inn, LLB (Hons)

Abiola *Mrs Oluremilekun Onabolu*
Part-time Chairman of Tribunal, 266 Etim
Inyang Cre, Victoria Island, Lagos Nigeria,
0171 328 0941, and Member Nigerian Bar.
Called: July 1990, Middle Temple, LLB
(Lond), LLM (Lond)(KCL)

Abraham *Dr Chakalamannil Mathew*
Advocate of India, High Court of Kerala and
Member Indian Bar. Called: July 1996,
Lincoln's Inn, BA, LLB, LLM, Ph.D (Lond)

Abrahams *Anthony Claude Walter*
Partner, Top Floor, Goldsmith Building,
Temple, London EC4Y 7BL, 0171 353 7913,
Fax: 0171 353 2756, Advocate and Solicitor
of Brunei Darussalam. Called: Nov 1950,
Middle Temple, MA (Cantab)

Abrahams *Ms Paula Anita* ●
Principle Crown Prosecutor, Crown
Prosecution Service, County House, 100
New London Road, Chelmsford, Essex,
01245 252939, Fax: 01245 490476.
Called: Nov 1987, Middle Temple, BA.

Abrahamson *Miss Debbie*
Principal Lecturer, Inns of Court School of
Law, 39 Eagle Street, London WC1R 4AJ,
0171 404 5787. Called: July 1981, Lincoln's
Inn, BA TCD

Abrams *Daniel*
Group Finance Director, Xenova Group
PLC, 240 Bath Road, Slough SL1 4EF, 01753
706 600, Fax: 01753 811 001. Called: July
1979, Inner Temple, FCA, MA (Cantab)

Abu Bakar *Mustaffa*
Called: July 1996, Lincoln's Inn, LLB
(Hons)(L'pool)

Abu Bakar *Miss Nor'ain Binte*
Called: July 1996, Middle Temple, LLB
(Hons)(Lond)

Acton *Ms Victoria Jane*
6 Chilcombe Heights, Quarry Road,
Winchester SO23 0HE. Called: Oct 1995,
Inner Temple, BA (Kent), M.Phil (Leeds),
Dip Law (City)

Acton-Bond *Jonathan Edward*
and Member Hong Kong Bar. Called: July
1971, Gray's Inn, BA

Adaikalasamy *Miss Jeyanthy*
Called: Nov 1997, Lincoln's Inn, LLB
(Hons)(N'Castle)

Adam *Michael William* ●
Senior Legal Officer, Department of Social
Security, New Court, Carey Street, London
WC2A 2LS. Called: Oct 1990, Middle
Temple, BA (Lond), Dip Law (City)

Adamec *Richard Vaclav* ●
Senior Court Clerk, West Glam Magistrates
Ct Comm, Swansea Magistrates' Court,
Grove Place, Swansea, West Glamorgan
SA1 5DB, 01792 655171, Fax: 01792
651066. Called: Nov 1988, Gray's Inn

Adamidou *Miss Effie*
Legal Advisor, P.O.Box 1211, Nicosia, Cyprus, 357 2 318995, Fax: 357 2 314869, and Member Cyprus Bar. Called: Feb 1993, Middle Temple, LLB (Hons)(Leic), Dip in Shipping Law, (UCL)

Adams *Mrs Catherine Elizabeth Stella*
Court Clerk at Banbury Court. Called: Feb 1994, Gray's Inn, LLB (Dundee)

Adams *Mrs Hazel Caroline*
Legal Adviser at Southampton Magistrates' Court, Justices' Clerks Office, 51-59 Commercial Road, Southampton SO15 1BQ, 01703 635911, Fax: 01703 233882. Called: July 1994, Inner Temple, LLB (Hons)(Lond)

Adams *Ms Hester Rose*
Called: July 1997, Lincoln's Inn, LLB (Hons)

Adams *Mrs Hilary* •
Specialist Lawyer & Legal Training & Development Manager, Criminal Appeal Office, Royal Courts of Justice, The Strand, London WC2A 2LL, 0171 936 6631, Fax: 0171 936 6900. Called: July 1976, Gray's Inn, LLB

Adams *Howard James* •
Crown Prosecution Service, C/O 50 Ludgate Hill, London EC4M 7EX. Called: July 1988, Gray's Inn, LLB (Wales)

Adams *Ijaz* •
Grade 6 Lawyer, Dept of the Environment,, Transport & the Regions, St Christopher House, Southwark Street, London SE1 0TE, 0171 921 2219. Called: Feb 1969, Lincoln's Inn, BA, LLB, LLM

Adams *James David Seton* •
Legal Adviser, Eagle Star Holdings Plc, 60 St Mary Axe, London EC3, 0171 929 1111, Fax: 0171 626 0311. Called: July 1989, Middle Temple, MA (Oxon)

Adams *John Frederick* •
Special Adviser to the Secretary of State of Wales. Called: Nov 1995, Middle Temple, LLB (Hons)(L'Pool)

Adams *John McPhillamy*
c/o Lloyds Bank plc, Law Courts Branch, 222 Strand, London WC2R 1BB, and Member New South Wales Bar. Called: June 1944, Inner Temple, MA LLB(Cantab), Dip. Trans. IoL. AIL

Adams *Miss Linda Christine*
Called: Nov 1987, Gray's Inn, BA (Kent)

Adams *Mrs Linda Judith* •
Head of Corporate Legal Services, The Automobile Association, Norfolk House, Priestley Road, Basingstoke, Hants RG24 9NY, 01256 20123. Called: Nov 1994, Inner Temple, LLB (Lond)

Adamson *Norman Joseph CB QC*
Faculty of Advocates, QC (Scotland) and Member Scottish Bar. Called: Feb 1959, Gray's Inn, MA, LLB (Glas)

Adatia *Kamal*
Called: Nov 1995, Gray's Inn, LLB (B'ham)

Adcock *Thomas Christopher Augustine* •
Legal Officer, The Treasury Solicitor, Queen Anne's Chambers, 28 Broadway, London SW1H 9JS. Called: Nov 1974, Inner Temple, LLB

Addae *Ms Sandra Anita* •
UK General Counsel, Unisys Ltd, Bakers Court, Bakers Road, Uxbridge, Middlesex UB8 1RG, 01895 862517, Fax: 01895 862010. Called: Nov 1988, Middle Temple, LLB (Essex)

Adderley *Miss Paula Anne Lilith*
Graham Thompson & Co, P O Box N272, Nassau, 242 322 4130, Fax: 242 328 1069, and Member Bahamas Bar. Called: July 1997, Middle Temple, BA (Hons)

Addo *Miss Cynthia Pamela (Akotaa)*
Called: Nov 1989, Lincoln's Inn, LLB (Lond), LLM

Adeane *The Hon George Edward CVO* •
Hambros Plc - Group Compliance Director, B4 Albany, Piccadilly, London W1V 9RE, Gray's Inn - Ad Eudem and Member Gibraltar Bar. Called: July 1962, Middle Temple, MA

Aderonmu *Miss Louisa*
Called: Mar 1998, Gray's Inn, LLB (Warw)

Adeusi *Ms Siobhan*
Called: Nov 1994, Lincoln's Inn, LLB (Hons)

Adie *Miss Diana Madelaine* •
Head of Intellectual Property, Intellectual Property, British Broadcasting Corp, White City, 201 Wood Lane, London W12 7TS, 0181 752 5252, Fax: 0181 752 5080. Called: Nov 1979, Middle Temple, MA, BCL (Oxon)

Adimoolam *Anpualagan*
Called: July 1996, Middle Temple, LLB (Hons)(Lond)

Adjaye *Charles Robert*
Unit 51A, Eurolink Business Centre, 49 Effra Road, London SW9 2BZ, 0171 274 8952, Fax: 0171 274 7883. Called: Feb 1962, Middle Temple

Adutt *James Ian* •
Treasury Solicitors Dept., Queen Anne's Chambers, 28 Broadway, London SW1H 9JS. Called: Oct 1992, Lincoln's Inn, MA (Cantab)

Advani *Ajay Jiwat*
Called: July 1997, Middle Temple, LLB (Hons)(Nott'm)

Aepli *Peter Andrew*
16 A, Chemin du Grand Communal, CH-1222 Vesenaz, Geneva, (41 22) 855 07 23, Fax: (41 22) 855 07 24. Called: July 1974, Inner Temple

Afariogun *Miss Oluremi Rushidat Abiono*
Called: Mar 1998, Gray's Inn, LLB (Middx)

Afiari *Charles Timothy*
and Member Nigeria. Called: Mar 1996, Gray's Inn, LLB, LLM (Lagos)

Agace *Christopher Paul*
Executive Director, Winkworth & Co (Holdings) Ltd, 118 Kensington Church Street, London W8, 0171 727 1117. Called: Nov 1990, Inner Temple, LLB (So'ton)

Agarwala *Surendra Kumar*
Senior Legal Advisor, Norfolk Mag Crts Committee, The Court House, Old Bury Road, Thetford, Norfolk IP24 3AQ, 01842 754941, Fax: 01842 766068. Called: Nov 1975, Gray's Inn, MA (Cantab), Cert Ed

Agathangelou *Angelos Marcianos* •
Senior Principal Legal Officer, HM Customs & Excise, New King's Beam House, 22 Upper Ground, London SE1 9PJ. Called: Nov 1983, Middle Temple, BA

Agati *Kwame Amponsah*
Legal Adviser, Newham Rights Centre, 285 Romford Road, Forest Gate, London E7 9HJ, 0181 555 3331, Fax: 0181 519 7348. Called: Feb 1992, Middle Temple, LLB (Hons) Ghana, LLM (Lond), ACIS

Aghadiuno *Charles*
Deputy Chief Clerk, Inner London Magistrates', Courts Service, 65 Romney Street, London SW1P 3RD, 0171 799 3332, Fax: 0171 799 3072. Called: Nov 1987, Inner Temple, LLB

Aghadiuno *Miss Patricia Nnonye* •
and Member Nigerian Bar. Called: July 1993, Gray's Inn, LLB, LLM

Agutu *Solomon Ochaye* •
Assistant Borough Solicitor and Head of Contracts, London Borough of Southwark, The Town Hall, Peckham Road, London SE15 8UB, 0171 525 7512. Called: July 1980, Inner Temple, LLB (S'ton), LLM (Lon/LSE)

Agyeman *Pierre*
Called: Oct 1995, Gray's Inn, LLB (Leeds)

Agyeman *Miss Roselyn Michelle Serwa Bonsu*
Called: Nov 1996, Inner Temple, LLB (Wales)

Agyemang *Augustus Osei*
and Member Ghana, Zimbabwe. Called: May 1992, Inner Temple, LLB (Ghana)

Ahluwalia *Miss Rupina*
Called: Nov 1994, Lincoln's Inn, LLB (Hons)(Notts)

Ahmad *Adi Satria*
Called: Nov 1994, Lincoln's Inn, LLB (Hons)(Wales)

Ahmad *Miss Aysha*
Called: Oct 1996, Middle Temple, BA (Hons)(Lond)

Ahmad *Azlin*
Called: July 1996, Gray's Inn, LLB (Warwick)

Ahmad *Mirza Farakh Navid* •
Head of Legal Services, Bolton Metropolitan,
Borough Council Town Hall, Bolton
BL1 1RU, 01204 22311 ext1111, Fax: 01204
39 2808, Elected Member of Bar Council.
Called: July 1984, Gray's Inn, BSoc Sci
(Keele), MBA, MIMgt

Ahmad *Mohd Faizal*
Called: July 1994, Lincoln's Inn, LLB (Hons,
Leeds)

Ahmad *Miss Sahia*
Called: Nov 1994, Lincoln's Inn, LLB
(Hons)(Lond)

Ahmad *Miss Sakinah*
Called: Nov 1997, Middle Temple, LLB
(Hons)(Lond)

Ahmed *Miss Ayla*
Associate, Rizvi, Isa & Co, 517/518 Clifton
Centre, DC - 1, Block 5, Clifton, Karachi
75600, (92)(21) 570727. Called: July 1997,
Lincoln's Inn, LLB (Hons)(Lond), LLM
(Cantab)

Ahmed *Gulam Mortuza*
Called: Oct 1997, Lincoln's Inn, LLB
(Hons)(B'ham)

Ahmed *Ms Rachael Amaya* •
Solicitor's Office, Inland Revenue, East Wing,
Somerset House, London WC2R 1LB, 0171
438 6377. Called: Oct 1995, Inner Temple,
LLB (Lond)

Ahmed *Salahuddin*
16 Hawthorn Road, Wallington, Surrey
SM6 0SX, 0181 647 7469. Called: Nov 1956,
Middle Temple

Ahmed *Mrs Shahnaz*
Called: Feb 1994, Gray's Inn, LLB (Bucks)

Ahmed *Miss Shazia*
Called: Oct 1997, Middle Temple, LLB
(Hons)(Luton)

Ahmed *Ms Sima*
Called: Nov 1997, Inner Temple, LLB

Ahmed *Sultan Tanvir*
and Member Punjab Bar. Called: Nov 1996,
Lincoln's Inn, BA (Punjab), LLB (Bucks)

Ahuja *Raju Neil* •
Senior Crown Prosecutor, Crown
Prosecution Service, 2nd Floor,Blackburn
House, Newcastle-Under-Lyme, Staffs
ST5 1TB, 01782 611877, Fax: 01782
711026. Called: Nov 1990, Inner Temple,
LLB Law

Ahyow *Miss Dorothee Paola Cathie*
Called: Nov 1996, Lincoln's Inn, BSc
(Hons)(Wales), Dip Law

Aiken *Jason Robert* •
Company Legal Advisor, Blick PLC, Blick
House, Bramble Road, Swindon, Wilts
SN2 6ER, 01793 692401, Fax: 01793
615848. Called: Oct 1992, Lincoln's Inn,
LLB(Hons)

Aiken *Nigel Alexander Carlisle*
9 Bedford Row, London, WC1R 4AZ.
Called: July 1974, Inner Temple, BA

Ainslie *Mrs Rosemary Caroline
Patricia*
"Glenbeigh", The Lane, Gate Helmsley,
York, North Yorkshire, 01759 372686, Fax:
01759 372686, Inn of Court of N Ireland
and Member Northern Ireland Bar.
Called: Nov 1990, Middle Temple, BA
(Belfast), BL (Belfast)

Airey *Anthony Maurice*
Managing Director, Airey & Wheeler Ltd, 8
Sackville street, London W12X 1DD, 0171
734 7461, Fax: 0171 734 8616. Called: July
1988, Inner Temple, LLB

Ajayi *Dr Olukonyinsola*
Consultant to United Nations Centre for
Transnational Corporations, 70 Lorne Road,
London E7 0LL, 0181 502 2944, Fax: 0181
502 0125, and 31 Marina, Lagos Nigeria. Tel
00234-1-2642551 Assoc Member American
Bar Association and Member Nigerian Bar.
Called: July 1989, Middle Temple, LLB, LLM
(Harvard), PhD (Cantab)

Ajoh *Anthony Afamefune*
Contract Officer, London Borough of Ealing,
Contract & Property Services, Percival
House, 1st Floor NE, 14/16 Uxbridge Road,
London W5 2HL, 0181 280 1242.
Called: Feb 1994, Gray's Inn, Btech (Hons),
MSc (Reading), LLB (Lond), ARICS, MCIOB

Ajose *Ms Oladunni Ayodele* •
Advocate, Criminal Injuries Compensation,
Board, Whittington House, 19 Alfred Place,
London WC1E 7LG, 0171 355 6802, Fax:
0171 436 0804. Called: Nov 1988, Middle
Temple, LLB

Akbar *Anwar* •
Assistant Counsel to the, Speaker, House of
Commons, London SW1A 0AA, 0171 219
5552. Called: Nov 1966, Middle Temple,
BCL (Oxon), MA (Oxon)

Akbar *Ms Ruby*
4 Shenton Way, [H]21-03A, 2240100, Fax:
2276002, and Member Singapore.
Called: July 1992, Gray's Inn, LLB (Brist)

Akel *Richard Livingstone*
Royal New Zealand Infantry (Hon.
Discharge), Richard L Akel,Attorney at Law,
151 Meeting Street, Suite 600, Charleston
S.C. 29401, U.S.A., 803.720.9142, Fax:
803.577.7513, American Trial Lawyers
Association, Trial Lawyers' Associations of
Washington DC & California & South
Carolina American Bar Association.
International Bar Association U.S.Supreme
Court, U.S. Courts of Appeal for District of
Columbia and 3rd, 4th, 5th. Called: July
1992, Lincoln's Inn, LLB (Hons, N.Z.), LLM
(Cantab), Dip., of Trial Advocacy, (U.S.)

Akeroyd *Timothy John*
Commercial/International Consultant, 21
Bunker Street, Freckleton, Nr Preston
PR4 1HA, 01772 634342, Fax: 01772
634342. Called: Nov 1971, Lincoln's Inn,
LLB

Akhand *Shahnawaz*
Called: Nov 1996, Lincoln's Inn, LLB
(Hons)(Lond)

Akhtar *Suhail Abdul Qadir* •
Crown Prosecutor, Crown Prosecution
Service, The Cooperage, Gainsford Street,
London SE1, 0171 962 2788. Called: Nov
1984, Middle Temple, LLB (Lond)

Akif *Alkan*
Head of Legal Services, Tewkesbury
Magistrates' Court, Gander Lane,
Tewkesbury, Glos GL20 5DR, 01684
294632, Fax: 01684 274596. Called: Nov
1975, Middle Temple

Akil *Munir Mehmet*
Called: Nov 1972, Middle Temple

Akiwumi *Christopher Stephen Akilano*
Daly & Figgis Advocates, P O Box 40034,
8th Floor, Lonrho House, Standard Street,
Nairobi, Kenya, 336332/1, Fax: 334892, and
Member Kenya. Called: Nov 1992, Lincoln's
Inn, BA (Rhode Island), LLB (Hons)(Bucks),
Dip Law (Kenya)

Akonta *Victor Solomon Kudzo* •
Senior Principal Legal Officer, Department
of Social Security, New Court, 48 Carey
Street, London WC2A 2LS. Called: Nov
1975, Inner Temple, MA

Akosile *Adeleke Jacob*
Called: Mar 1997, Lincoln's Inn, LLB (Hons)

Akpan *Samuel Sunday*
and Member Nigeria. Called: Mar 1996,
Inner Temple, LLB, LLM (Nigeria)

Al-Attas *Syed Reza Helmy*
and Member Malaysia Bar. Called: Oct 1994,
Lincoln's Inn, LLB (Hons)(Sheff)

Al-Harith *Sinclair Muhammad
Abdullah*
Called: Oct 1996, Middle Temple, BA
(Hons)(Lond)

Al-Saleem *Ms Sally Asil*
Called: Oct 1997, Inner Temple, BSc
(London), CPE

Alabi *Babatunde Omotoso* •
Senior Crown Prosecutor, Crown
Prosecution Service, Barking & Newham
Branch, 1-9 Romford Row, Stratford,
London E15 4LJ, 0181 534 6601, Fax: 0181
519 9690, and Member Nigerian Bar.
Called: Oct 1992, Lincoln's Inn, LLB(Hons),
LLM(Lond)

Alam *Kazi Mohammad Tanjibul*
Called: Nov 1997, Lincoln's Inn, LLB
(Hons)(Lond)

Alam *Miss Zaiban Nassa*
Called: Mar 1998, Lincoln's Inn, LLB
(Hons)(Sheff)

Alban-Davies *John Lewis* •
Senior Crown Prosecutor, Crown
Prosecution Service, Severn Thames,
Artillery House, Heritage Way, Droitwich,
Worcestershire WR8 8YB, 01905 779502.
Called: Nov 1973, Inner Temple, MA (Lond),
LLB (Wales)

E

Albery *Oliver Peter*
Messrs de Beristain Humphrey, 13
Woodbridge Street, London EC1R 0LL, 0171
250 0276, Fax: 0171 250 0278. Called: July
1972, Lincoln's Inn

Albon *Commander Ross RN* •
Legal Advisor, Royal Navy, HMS Seahawk,
RNAS, Culdrose, Helston, Cornwall
TR12 7RH, 01326 552198. Called: Nov
1988, Inner Temple, BSc (Aston)

Albury *Ms Candia Aubyn Patricia*
Called: July 1994, Inner Temple, LLB (Keele)

Alcock *Alistair Robert*
6 Bristle Hill, Buckingham MK18 1EZ,
01280 812059. Called: Nov 1977, Middle
Temple, MA (Cantab), MSI (Dip)

Alderman *Richard John* •
Room F1, Solicitor's Office, Inland Revenue,
East Wing, Somerset House, London
WC2R 1LB, 0171 438 7262. Called: June
1974, Gray's Inn, LLB [Lond]

Alderson *Christopher James*
Called: Oct 1993, Lincoln's Inn, LLB
(Hons)(Notts)

Alexander *Miss Josephine Anne* •
Called: Feb 1994, Middle Temple, LLB
(Hons)(Lond)

Alexander *Richard Charles Henry*
Research Officer, Institute od Advanced
Legal, Studies, 17 Russell Square, London
WC1B 5DR, 0171 637 1731, Fax: 0171 580
9613. Called: Feb 1991, Middle Temple, MA
(Cantab), Dip Law (City)

Alexander *Miss Rosemarie Simone*
Olswang, 90 Long Acre, London WC2E 9TT,
0171 208 8888, Fax: 0171 208 8800.
Called: Nov 1993, Inner Temple, MA (St
Andrews), CPE

Alexander of Weedon *Lord QC (1973)*
QC (NSW) Judge, Courts of Appeal Jersey &
Guernsey Chairman, Bar Council 1985-86,
Chairman's Office, National Westminster
Bank PLC, 41 Lothbury, London EC2P 2BP,
0171 726 1950, Fax: 0171 726 1704.
Called: Nov 1961, Middle Temple, MA
(Cantab)

Alexander-Jack *Mrs Juliana Marie*
Education Committee, Bermuda Bar
Council, Mello,Hollis,Jones & Martin, Reid
House, Church Street, Hamilton, Bermuda,
(441) 292 1345, Fax: (441) 292 2277, and
Member Bermuda Bar. Called: Oct 1994,
Inner Temple, BA (California), BA (Oxon)

Alexander-Wall *Michael Graeme*
Called: Feb 1994, Inner Temple, BA (Oxon),
Dip in Law

Alexandrou *Miss Maria*
Called: Mar 1996, Gray's Inn, LLB (East
Anglia)

Alfrey *Mrs Penelope Ann*
01509 261515. Called: Oct 1995, Middle
Temple, MA (Hons)

Alg *Miss Bhupinder Kaur* •
London Borough of Merton, Crown House,
London Road, Morden, Surrey SM4 5DX,
0181 545 3341, Fax: 0181 543 7126.
Called: Nov 1974, Inner Temple, LLB

Ali *Ahmed*
219 Dialstone Lane, Stockport, Cheshire
SK2 7LF, 0161 483 7642. Called: Jan 1945,
Middle Temple, BA, LLB

Ali *Azad*
Called: Oct 1996, Inner Temple, BA (Exon)

Ali *Ifther* •
Merrill Lynch Europe, Ropemaker Place, 25
Ropemaker Street, London EC2Y 9LY, 0171
867 4961, Fax: 0171 573 0990. Called: Nov
1994, Inner Temple, LLB (Lond)

Ali *Ishtiyaq*
Called: Nov 1996, Lincoln's Inn, LLB (Hons)

Ali *Muhammad Imman*
Advocate of the Supreme Court of
Bangladesh, High Court Division and
Appellate Divisio, Lee Khan & Associates,
City Heart Suit [H] 5/7, Naya Paltan (4th
Floor), V.I.P. Road, Motijheel, Dhaka - 1000,
88-02- 865412/933508, Fax: 88-02- 865412,
and Member Dhaka Supreme Court Bar.
Called: July 1978, Inner Temple, BA, LLM

Ali *Miss Rukhsana Akhtar*
Called: Oct 1995, Lincoln's Inn, LLB
(Hons)(Lond)

Ali *Sham Shudin*
Called: July 1994, Lincoln's Inn, LLB (Hons)

Ali *Zubair* •
NCR Limited, 206 Marylebone Road,
London NW1 6LY, 0171 725 88590, Fax:
0171 725 8120. Called: May 1993, Lincoln's
Inn, LLB (Hons), LLM (Lond)

Ali-Khan *Leigh Robert Nigel*
Called: Nov 1995, Inner Temple, LLB
(Soton)

Ali-Selvaratnam *Mrs Rasheeda*
Housing Lawyer, South Islington Law
Centre, 131-132 Upper Street, London
N1 1QP, 0171 354 3207, Fax: 0171 354
8155. Called: Nov 1981, Middle Temple

Aling *Miss Jenny Li Ting Chin*
Called: July 1995, Middle Temple, LLB
(Hons)

Alizond *Mrs Tamara Leigh*
Called: Nov 1995, Lincoln's Inn, BA (Hons),
Dip Law, MA (Hons) (Cantab)

Allan *Robert John*
Director of Legal Services, Haringey
Magistrates Court, Bishops Road, Archway
Road, Highgate, London N6 4HS, 0181 340
3472, Fax: 0181 348 3343. Called: July
1980, Lincoln's Inn, BA

Alland *Brian David*
Called: July 1976, Lincoln's Inn, B.Eng,MSc

Allen *Capt Albert Eric OBE RN*
Greysands, 29 Beach Road, Emsworth,
Hants PO10 7HR, 01243 372028.
Called: Nov 1961, Middle Temple

Allen *Andrew Clifford*
Called: Nov 1996, Gray's Inn, LLB (Hull)

Allen *Bernard Robert*
10 Cavaye House, Cavaye Place, London
SW10 9PT, 0171 373 1471. Called: Nov
1950, Gray's Inn

Allen *Christian Darrel* •
Legal Adviser/Assistant Company Secretary,
AIG Europe (UK) Ltd, 120 Fenchurch Street,
London EC3M 5BP, 0171 280 3645, Fax:
0171 280 8815. Called: Nov 1992, Inner
Temple, LLB (Lancs), LLM (Nott'm)

Allen *Christopher*
Assistant Legal Secretary. Called: Nov 1975,
Inner Temple, BA (Wales)

Allen *David John*
General Business Consultant, 38 South Hill,
Catteshall Lane, Godalming, Surrey
GU22 0JX, 01483 421767. Called: Nov 1989,
Middle Temple, LLB (So'ton)

Allen *Mrs Diana*
43 Halsey Street, London SW3 2PT.
Called: Nov 1972, Inner Temple

Allen *Harold Davis*
Called: July 1995, Middle Temple, LLB
(Hons)

Allen *Ms Heather Muriel*
63 Goldstone Crescent, Hove, East Sussex
BN3 6LR, 01273 553523, Fax: 01273
553523. Called: Nov 1977, Inner Temple,
BA (Lond), CEDR Accredited, Mediator

Allen *Leonard Charles*
Clerk to the Justices Somerset Magistrates
Courts County of Somerset, Somerset
Magistrates Court, The Courthouse,
Northgate, Bridgwater, Somerset TA6 3EU,
01278 452182, Fax: 01278 453667.
Called: July 1980, Inner Temple, DML

Allen *Neil Edward* •
Senior Lawyer, Lewisham Legal Services,
London Borough of Lewisham, Town Hall,
Lewisham, London. Called: Feb 1993, Inner
Temple, LLB (Reading)

Allen *Miss Tawanna Cherrel*
Called: July 1995, Gray's Inn, BA (Ottawa),
LLB (Hull)

Allen *William Edwin*
Called: Nov 1978, Gray's Inn, BA (Kent)

Allgrove *Jeffrey William*
Vice President - Finance, Unilever United
States, 390 Park Avenue, New York, NY
10022 USA. Called: July 1976, Lincoln's Inn,
LLB, FCCA

Allison *Clifford Howard* •
Senior Crown Prosecutor, Crown
Prosecution Service, Central Casework
(Fraud), 50 Ludgate Hill, London EC4M 7EX,
0171 273 1349, Fax: 0171 329 8164, and
Member Hong Kong Bar. Called: July 1976,
Inner Temple, LLB

Allison *Mrs Gillian Margaret Clarkson*
Magistrates' Courts Clerk, Inner London
Magistrates', Courts Service, 65 Romney
Street, London SW1P 3DR, 0171 799 3332.
Called: Oct 1990, Gray's Inn

• Barristers in employment

Allison *Richard Christopher*
Called: May 1997, Inner Temple, BA (Reading), MA (Lond)

Allison *Samuel Austin* ●
Compliance and Legal Director, West Merchant Bank, 33/36 Gracechurch Street, London EC3V 0AX, 0171 623 8711, Fax: 0171 588 1346. Called: Nov 1969, Middle Temple, BA, BCL(Oxon), FCIArb

Allnatt *Peter Brian*
30 Seymour Road, East Molesey, Surrey KT8 0PB, 0181 979 2490. Called: Feb 1953, Gray's Inn, LLB

Allott *Stephen Anthony*
Associate, Micromuse PLC, Disraeli House, 90 Putney Bridge Road, London SW18 1DA, 0181 875 9500, Fax: 0181 875 9995. Called: Nov 1981, Gray's Inn, MA (Cantab)

Allsebrook *Geoffrey Pole*
The Green, Cark-in-Cartmel, Grange-over-Sands, Cumbria LA11 7NJ, 015395 58258. Called: Feb 1955, Inner Temple, MA (Oxon), PPE

Allsop *David James*
Writer & Journalist, 22 Prince of Wales Drive, London SW11 4SF, 0171 738 9965, Fax: 0171 738 9328. Called: July 1981, Middle Temple, LLB (Dundee)

Alltree *Miss Eileen Mary* ●
23 Turnberry Grove, Leeds, West Yorkshire LS17 7TD. Called: July 1972, Middle Temple, LLB

Almond *Roger Buckley*
Called: June 1958, Middle Temple, MA, BCL, FCIS, frsa

Alvarez *Manuel* ●
Group Legal Adviser, GEC-Marconi Limited, The Grove, Warren Lane, Stanmore HA7 4LY, 0181 420 3399, Fax: 0181 420 3860. Called: Nov 1969, Gray's Inn, LLB (Hons)

Alway *Lorne Victor*
Quantity Surveyor, Alway Associates, Howard House, The Runway, South Ruislip, Middlesex HA4 6SE, 0181 842 0028, Fax: 0181 842 0003. Called: Nov 1990, Middle Temple, LLB (Lond), Dip QS, FRICS

Amah *Stanley Chikanene*
Senior Court Clerk, Ealing Magistrates Court, Court House, Green Man Lane, West Ealing, London W13 OSD, 0181 579 9311, Fax: 0181 579 2985. Called: July 1991, Gray's Inn, BA (Nigeria), LLB (Lond)

Amako *William C.N.B.*
Called: Mar 1997, Lincoln's Inn, LLB (Hons), LLM

Amarasinha *Revantha Arjuna*
Called: Oct 1996, Middle Temple, LLB (Hons)(Lond)

Amaratunga *Mrs Praveen Dharshini* ●
Chief Programme Officer, Commonwealth Secretariat, Marlborough House, Pall Mall, London SW1Y 5HX, 0171 747 6435. Called: Oct 1995, Gray's Inn, BA (Hons), LLM

Ameen *Mahmud Riad*
Called: Mar 1998, Lincoln's Inn, LLB (Hons)(Lond)

Ameer *Mohammed Ameen Chezard*
Called: July 1996, Middle Temple, LLB (Hons)(Lond)

Ames *Mrs Tracey Amanda* ●
Stratford Office, Solar House, 1-9 Romford Road, London E15, 0181 534 6601. Called: Nov 1987, Inner Temple, LLB (Essex)

Amess *Ms Naomi Anne*
10 Trenic Crescent, Headingly, Leeds LS6 3DL. Called: Mar 1996, Middle Temple, BA (Hons)

Amin *Ms Neeta* ●
Senior Crown Prosecutor, Crown Prosecution Service, 1st Floor, 8 Gainsford Street, London SE1 2EN, 0171 357 7010, Fax: 0171 962 0905. Called: Oct 1990, Inner Temple, LLB (Hons)

Amin *Omar Kemal Shaikh Mohamed*
Nairobi Hilton, Mama Ngina Street, P O Box 25241, Nairobi, Kenya, 254 (2) 334000, Fax: 254 (2) 339462, and Member Kenya Bar. Called: Nov 1991, Lincoln's Inn, LLB (Hons) (Bucks)

Amin *Miss Saiqa*
Called: Nov 1991, Inner Temple, LLB (Hons), LLM

Amin *Salah-El-Din Mohamed*
First Floor, Nairobi Hilton Building, P O Box 25241, Nairobi, 254-2-242443/254-2-48453, Advocate of the High Court of Kenya. Called: Oct 1993, Lincoln's Inn, LLB (Hons)(Bucks)

Amir *Miss Nasim Akhtar* ●
Senior Crown Prosecutor, Crown Prosecution Service, The Cooperage, Gainsford Street, London SE1, 0171 357 7010. Called: Nov 1990, Gray's Inn, LLB

Amirfazli *Miss Farinaz* ●
Crown Prosecution Service, C/O 50 Ludgate Hill, London EC4M 7EX. Called: Nov 1991, Lincoln's Inn, LLB (Hons)

Amisu *Adekunle Oluwagbeminiyi*
Locum Lawyer Solicitor, London Borough of Hackney, 183-187 Stoke Newington, High Street, London N16 0LU, 0171 275 6187, Fax: 0171 275 6193. Called: Nov 1992, Lincoln's Inn, LLB (Hons)(Lond)

Amoh *Miss Christine Omenaa*
Called: Nov 1994, Middle Temple, LLB (Hons)

Amos *William John*
Called: Nov 1966, Gray's Inn

Amstell *Anthony David* ●
Crown Prosecutor, Crown Prosecution Service, River Park house, High Road, Wood Green, London N22, 0181 888 8889. Called: Nov 1968, Lincoln's Inn, LLB

Anahory *Moses Jacob*
138 Main Street, Gibraltar, 78804/79000, Fax: 71966, and Member Gibraltar Bar. Called: Oct 1994, Middle Temple, LLB (Hons)(Middx)

Anandakrishna *Thiagu*
Called: Nov 1997, Middle Temple, LLB (Hons)(Manch)

Anastassiou *Miss Maria Andreas*
Called: July 1997, Gray's Inn, LLB (Lond)

Ancill *Miss Karen Cecile*
Called: Oct 1995, Lincoln's Inn, MA (Hons)(Edinburgh), Dip in Law (Lond)

Andall *Hogarth Christopher*
Biddle & Co, 1 Gresham Street, London EC2V 7BU. Called: Oct 1993, Lincoln's Inn, BA (Hons)(Oxon)

Anderson *David Heywood CMG*
Member of the International Tribunal for the Law of the Sea (part-time), International Tribunal for the Law of the Sea, Wexstrasse 4, 20355 Hamburg, +49 40 35 60 7261, Fax: +49 40 35 60 7245. Called: Feb 1963, Gray's Inn, LLM (Lond), LLB (Leeds)

Anderson *Lt Cdr Hugh Alastair*
The Ward Room, HMS Gloucester, BFPO 289. Called: Oct 1996, Middle Temple, LLB (Hons)(Lond)

Anderson *Iain Massey*
Called: Oct 1995, Lincoln's Inn, LLB (Hons)(Newc)

Anderson *Ian George* ●
Leeds City Council, Civic Hall, Leeds LS1 1UR. Called: July 1984, Gray's Inn, B.Soc.Sc

Anderson *John Victor Ronald OBE*
Caer Rhun Hall, Conwy, Gwynedd, N Wales LL32 8HX, 01492 650 012, Fax: 01492 650 593. Called: July 1972, Gray's Inn, FCA, MA

Anderson *Miss Lisa Jayne*
Called: Oct 1996, Inner Temple, LLB (S'ton)

Anderson *Miss Maxanne Javita*
Called: May 1997, Lincoln's Inn, LLB (Hons)(Kent), BA (Atlanta)

Anderson *Nicholas Guy*
Called: Oct 1995, Gray's Inn, LLB

Anderson *Peter Lawrence*
49 The Avenue, London W13 8JR. Called: July 1970, Gray's Inn, FCCA

Anderson *Peter Robert*
Part Time Chairman of Industrial Tribunals, The Swallows, 12A Little Knowle, Budleigh Salterton, Devon EX9 6QS. Called: July 1969, Middle Temple, MA

Anderson *Richard Neil Macdiarmid*
Chairman of Social Security Tribunal, 2 Nicolson Square, Edinburgh, Scotland EH8 9BH, 01831 830 893, Fax: 0131 668 4880, Advocate,Chartered Accountant Attorney and Member New York Bar Scottish Bar. Called: Apr 1991, Gray's Inn, LLB (Hons), CA, FSA (Scot)

Anderson *Miss Sheila Drummond*
Called: Nov 1957, Gray's Inn, LLB

Andreou *Andreas*
8 Rigas Fereos Str, Libra Chambers, 3095
Limassol, 00357 5 363154, Fax: 00357 5
342887, and Member Cyprus Bar.
Called: Nov 1995, Lincoln's Inn, LLB
(Hons)(Leic)

Andrew *Ms Carolyn Ruth*
Called: Oct 1997, Inner Temple, LLB
(London)

Andrew *Edward Alexander*
Sheffield International Ltd, 5th Floor,
Aldermary House, 10-15 Queen Street,
London EC4N 1TX. Called: Oct 1993,
Middle Temple, LLB (Hons)

Andrew *Mrs Margaret ●*
Crown Prosecutor, Crown Prosecution
Service, Prospect West, Station Road,
Croydon, Surrey CR0 2RD. Called: Feb 1987,
Middle Temple, Dip Law, CPE

Andrews *Edward Whybrow*
Manor House Farm, Barningham, Richmond,
North Yorkshire DL11 7DW. Called: July
1972, Lincoln's Inn

Andrews *Miss Gillian Margaret*
Clerk to the Justices, Reading & Newbury,
Berkshire & Oxfordshire, Magistrates Court,
Easby House, Northfield House, Henley-on-
Thames, Oxfordshire RG9 2NB, 01491
412720, Fax: 01491 412762. Called: Nov
1987, Gray's Inn

Andrews *Nicholas William*
0171 731 2910. Called: Nov 1995, Inner
Temple, BSc, CPE (Sussex)

Andrews *Robert Craig*
Chairman, Appeal Tribunal (Buildings),
Admiralty centre, 1405 Tower 2, 18
Harcourt Road, 00852 25273082, Fax:
00852 25298226, and Member Hong Kong
Bar. Called: May 1971, Middle Temple, BA

Aneke *Lloyd Chukwuma ●*
Court Clerk, Bromley Magistrates' Court,
The Court House, London Road, Bromley
BR1 1BY, 0181 325 4000, Fax: 0181 325
4006, and Member Nigerian Bar. Called: July
1987, Inner Temple, LLB

Ang *Miss Alexia Hui Tsun*
Called: July 1997, Middle Temple, LLB
(Hons)

Ang *Andrew Lye Whatt*
Called: July 1996, Middle Temple, LLB
(Hons)(Leic)

Ang *Cheng Yong*
Legal Assistant, Blk 503 *03-233, Pasir Ris
Street 52, Singapore 1851, Singapore, 583-
3559, Fax: 583-3559, and Member Singapore
Bar. Called: July 1991, Gray's Inn, LLB
(Hons) (Lond), ACII, LM(Lond)

Ang *Kah Soon*
Messrs Gregory Chan, Tam Moo &, Ang,
M2-D-6 Jalan Pandan Indah 4/6, Pahdan
Indah, 55100 Kuala Lumpur, 603-4943186,
Fax: 603-4948186, and Member Malaysia
Bar. Called: July 1994, Middle Temple, LLB
(Hons)(Lond)

Ang *Khoon Cheong*
c/o Messrs C P Ang & Co, 18 Lebuh
Kampung Benggali, 12000 Butterworth,
Penang, 04 3313009, Fax: 04 3328115, and
Member Malaysia. Called: July 1995, Middle
Temple, LLB (Hons) (Wales)

Ang *Miss Kim Noi*
Called: July 1995, Middle Temple, LLB
(Hons)

Ang *Miss Ru-Lin*
Called: July 1997, Middle Temple, LLB
(Hons)(Nott'm)

Ang *Miss Sue Khoon*
and Member Malaysia Bar. Called: July 1994,
Middle Temple, LLB (Hons)(Bris)

Ang *Miss Valerie Freda Mei-Ling*
Messrs Derrick, Ravi & Partner, 133 New
Bridge Road, [H]16-03/04 Chinatown Point,
Singapore 059413, 538 1300, Fax: 538
1311, and Member Singapore Bar.
Called: July 1994, Middle Temple, LLB
(Hons)(Hull)

Ang *Wen Po Andrew*
Called: July 1997, Gray's Inn, LLB (Notts)

Ang *Woon Kherk*
Called: July 1996, Lincoln's Inn, LLB (Hons)

Angelides *Savvas*
Called: Nov 1997, Gray's Inn, LLB

Angelides *Ms Zoma*
Called: Nov 1997, Inner Temple, LLB

Angeloglou *George*
15 Oakfield Court, 252 Pampisford Rd,
South Croydon, Surrey CR2 6DD, 0181 680
0547, Fax: 0181 680 0547. Called: June
1939, Inner Temple, MA (Oxon)

Annanth *Mrs Parvathi*
Called: Nov 1996, Middle Temple, LLB
(Hons)

Anning *Miss Barbara Mary*
15 Fawley Road, West Hampstead, London
NW6 1SJ, 0171 794 4335, Fax: 0171 794
4335. Called: Nov 1992, Gray's Inn, LLB
(Buckingham), Licence Speciale en,
Sciences de (ULB), L'Environnement

Anniss *Mrs Jane Ellen ●*
Called: Nov 1984, Gray's Inn, LLB
(Lancaster)

Ansari *Askar Humayun ●*
Principal Legal Officer, The Inland Revenue,
Solicitor's Office, Somerset House (East
Wing), The Strand, London WC2R 1LB,
0171 438 6248. Called: July 1973, Middle
Temple, BA

Ansari *Daniyal*
Called: Oct 1995, Inner Temple, LLB (Exon),
LLM (Cantab)

Antao *Mrs Alexia Gertrude*
Barrister & Attorney at Law in La Poudriere
Law of Comsultancy Chambers (Legal
Advisor, Litigation etc), 355b Romford
Road, Forest Gate, London E7 8AA, 0181
519 8658, and Member Seychelles Bar.
Called: May 1996, Inner Temple, LLB
(Hons)(Lond), LLM (LSE)

Antell *John Jason*
Integral Computing Ltd, Ringmarsh House,
Horsington, Temple Combe, Somerset
BA8 OEL, 01963 370544, Chartered
Information Systems Engineer. Called: Oct
1992, Middle Temple, LL.B (Hons Lond),
MBCS, CEng

Antelme *Leopold John TD*
Winchcombe Lodge, Bucklebury, Berkshire
RG7 6NS, 0118 9713261, Fax: 0118
9714696. Called: July 1952, Inner Temple,
MA

Anthony *Farid Ray*
89 Saxon Street, Gillingham, Kent ME7 5EG,
01634 578649, Fax: 01634 578649, and
Member Sierra Leone Bar and Gambian Bar.
Called: Nov 1963, Inner Temple

Anthoson *Jason Lawrence*
Called: May 1985, Lincoln's Inn, BA Keele

Anuar *Miss Ifa Mutiara*
Called: Nov 1997, Lincoln's Inn, LLB
(Hons)(Nott'm)

Anuar *Miss Zeti Azita*
Called: Nov 1997, Lincoln's Inn, LLB
(Hons)(Warw)

Anwar *Miss Fatema*
Called: Nov 1997, Lincoln's Inn, LLB (Hons)
(Lond)

Anyiam *Izomor Herbert ●*
Adviser, Plumstead Community Law Centre,
105 Plumstead High Street, London
SE18 1SB, 0181 244 4951, Fax: 0181 316
7903, and Member Nigeria Bar. Called: Nov
1996, Lincoln's Inn, LLB (Hons)(Lagos)

Apostolou *Evangelos Christopher*
Called: Mar 1998, Lincoln's Inn, BA (Hons)
(Lond)

Appadoo *Miss Danista*
Called: July 1996, Gray's Inn, BA (Hons),
Dip Law

Appaduray *Miss Nina Urmilla*
Called: July 1996, Middle Temple, LLB
(Hons)(Lond)

Appiah *Kofi*
Freeman of the City of London, 57
Chambord Street, London E2 7NJ, 0171 729
4803, Fax: 0171 729 4803, and Member
Ghana Bar. Called: Nov 1974, Inner Temple,
LLB (Lond)

Appleby *Charles Mark ●*
Senior Crown Prosecutor, Crown
Prosecution Service, Heritage House,
Fisherman's Wharf, Grimsby DN31 1SY,
Kings Inn, Dublin (Dec 1970) and Member
Southern Ireland Bar. Called: July 1975,
Gray's Inn

Arbel *Mrs Caroline Emma*
Called: July 1994, Middle Temple, LLB
(Hons)(Lond)

Arbuthnot *James Norwich MP*
Assistant Recorder, also Lincolns Inn 1977
10 Old Square, Ground Floor, Lincoln's Inn,
London, WC2A 3SU. Called: July 1975, Inner
Temple, BA (Cantab)

Archer *David John* •
Principal Crown Prosecutor, Crown
Prosecution Service, 24th Floor, Portland
House, Stag Place, London SW1E 5BH, 0171
828 9050. Called: Feb 1988, Gray's Inn, BA
(Oxon)

Archer *Mrs Jacqueline Ann*
Deputy Chief Clerk, Inner London
Magistrates Crt, 65 Romney Street, London
SW1P 3RD. Called: Feb 1988, Gray's Inn,
BA(Hons)

Archer *Mrs Lorna Helen*
Deputy Chief Clerk, Inner London
Magistrates', Courts Service, Inner London
& City Proceeding, 59-65 Wells Street,
London W1A 3AE, 0171 323 1649, Fax:
0171 636 0617. Called: Nov 1986, Gray's
Inn, BA (Hons)

Archer *Mark David*
Called: Oct 1995, Inner Temple, LLB
(Hons)(Hudds)

Arfon-Jones *Miss Elisabeth*
Full-time Immigration Adjudicator, Part-Time
Chairman, Social Security Appeal Tribunal.
Lay Chairman NHS Complaints Panel (vol),
and Member Bermuda Bar. Called: July
1972, Gray's Inn, LLB (Lond)

Arian *Chinsamy Chagadeven*
Legal Advisor. Called: Nov 1994, Gray's Inn,
LLB (Lon)

Armbrister *Allan Ramsay*
Clerk to the Justices, Teesside Law Courts,
Victoria Square, Middlesbrough, Cleveland
TS1 2AS, 01642 240301, Fax: 01642
224010. Called: Nov 1984, Inner Temple,
BA, D.M.S., D.M.L.

Armitage *Robert*
12 Milner St, London SW3 2PU, 0171 584
0162. Called: June 1948, Inner Temple, MA
(Cantab)

Armitage *Roderick Donald* •
Legal Director and Secretary Staveley
Industries Plc, Staveley Industries plc, 11
Dingwall Road, Croydon CR9 1BY, 0181
688 4404, Fax: 0181 760 0563. Called: Feb
1979, Middle Temple, FCIS

Armson *Miss Barbara Ann* •
Senior Legal Adviser, Texaco Ltd, Legal
Dept, 1 Westferry Circus, Canary Wharf,
London E14 4HA, 0171 719 3402, Fax: 0171
719 5124. Called: Nov 1985, Inner Temple,
BA Hons

Armstrong *Henry Napier DL*
Adv High Ct Kenya Chairman Legal &
Commercial Committee. Ulster Farmers
Union. Called: June 1961, Inner Temple, BA

Armstrong *Rear Admiral John Herbert
Arthur James RN* •
Royal College of Defence, Studies, Seaford
House, 37 Belgrave Square, London
SW1X 8NS, 0171 915 4834, Fax: 0171 915
4999. Called: July 1976, Middle Temple, MA
(Oxon)

Armstrong *Martin Robert* •
Legal Adviser, Philips Electronics UK, The
Philips Centre, 420-430 London Road,
Croydon CR9 3QR, 0181 781 8471, Fax:
0181 781 8888. Called: July 1979, Inner
Temple, BA [Camb]

Arnold *Mrs Anne Mary*
Director of Legal Services Acting Provincial
Stipendiary Magistrate, P O Box 15, Law
Courts, Stafford Road, Bournemouth
BH1 1LA, 01202 745309, Fax: 01202
711994. Called: Nov 1981, Inner Temple,
BA Hons, MBA

Arnold *John Irwin Ernest*
p/t Chairman Ind Trib-Retired p/t
Adjudicator Imm App Retired Part-time Asst
Recorder Retired, 128 Worcester Road,
Chichester, West Sussex PO19 4EE.
Called: June 1949, Lincoln's Inn

Arnold *Piers John* •
Crown Prosecutor, Crown Prosecution
Service, Lombard Street, Abingdon, Oxon
OX14 5SE, 01235 555678, Fax: 01235
554144. Called: Nov 1992, Inner Temple,
BA (Oxon), Dip in Law

Arnold-Baker *Professor Charles OBE*
Former Dep.Traffic Commissioner &
Licensing Authority, Editor 'Road Law'
Visiting Professor, City Uni, Top Floor, 2
Paper Bldgs, Inner Temple, London
EC4Y 7ET, 0171 353 3490. Called: June
1948, Inner Temple, BA(Oxon)

Arnot *Graham Robert Erwin* •
Commercial Lawyer, Thames Water Utilities
Limited, Nugent House, Vastern Road,
Reading RG1 8DB, 01734 399283, Fax:
01734 566913. Called: July 1973, Inner
Temple, MA (Oxon)

Arnot *Simon Richard Cranstoun* •
Legal Department, Allied Dunbar Assurance
plc, Allied Dunbar Centre, Swindon
SN1 1EL, 01793 514514. Called: Nov 1987,
Gray's Inn, BA, LLB

Arowojolu *Olutayo Olaniran*
Legal Advisor, Newham Rights Centre, 285
Romford Road, Forest Gate, London E7 9HJ,
0181 5553331, Fax: 0181 5197348, and
Member Nigerian Bar. Called: Nov 1993,
Lincoln's Inn, LLB (Hons, Lagos), LLM
(Lond)

Arrif *Ms Hawa Bibi Bahemia*
The Thames Chambers, Wickham House, 10
Cleveland Way, London, E1 4TR. Called: July
1996, Gray's Inn, BSc. (Hertfordshire)

Arrowsmith *Christopher John*
Advocate, Mann & Partners, 20 Finch Road,
Douglas, Isle of Man IM1 2PS, 01624
622221, Fax: 01624 627222, Partner and
Member Manx Bar. Called: Oct 1990, Gray's
Inn, LLB (Hons) (Brunel)

Arthur *Michael David*
Called: Nov 1997, Middle Temple, BA
(Hons)(Lond)

Arthur *Robin Anthony* •
The Manor Hse, The Green, Hilton,
Huntingdon, Cambridgeshire PE18 9NA.
Called: Nov 1976, Gray's Inn, LLB (Lond)

Arthur *Mrs Susannah Jane*
Called: Nov 1997, Middle Temple, BSc
(Hons)(Wales), LLB (Hons)(Lond)

Asare *Kwame Ohene*
Consumer/Debt Advisor. Called: Nov 1995,
Lincoln's Inn, BSc (Hons), LLB (Hons)
(Lond)

Ascroft *Richard Geoffrey*
Called: Nov 1995, Lincoln's Inn, LLB
(Hons)(New, Zealand), BCL (Oxon)

Asekun *Miss Diane Omolola*
Called: Mar 1998, Middle Temple, BA
(Psyc)(Virginia), LLB (Hons), LLM, (Bucks)

Asghar *Miss Shermine*
Called: July 1997, Lincoln's Inn, LLB
(Hons)(City)

Ashby *Peter Marcus* •
Principal Crown Prosecutor, Crown
Prosecution Service, 2 Kimbrose Way,
Gloucester GL1 2DB, 01452 308989, Also
Inn of Court G. Called: Nov 1978, Middle
Temple, BA (Hons)

Ashcroft *Miss Sophie Laura*
Called: Mar 1997, Inner Temple, BA

Ashenden *Michael Roy Edward*
25 Melrose Road, Merton Park, London
SW19, 0181 542 5019. Called: Jan 1949,
Middle Temple, MA (Cantab)

Asher *Peter John*
5 Garth Road, Kingston 8, Jamaica, West
Indies, and Member Jamaican Bar.
Called: July 1994, Lincoln's Inn, LLB (Hons),
BA

Ashford *Stephen James* •
Director - Legal & Corporate Affairs,
Deminex UK Oil and Gas Ltd, Bowater Hse,
114 Knightsbridge, London SW1X 7LD,
0171 225 7100, Fax: 0171 584 6459.
Called: July 1973, Gray's Inn, LLB (Lond),
AKC

Ashhab *Bazul*
Called: July 1997, Lincoln's Inn, LLB
(Hons)(Lond)

Ashley *Miss Gayle Beverley*
Called: Oct 1997, Middle Temple, LLB
(Hons)(Sussex)

Ashley *Dr Graham William* •
Patent Examiner, European Patent Office,
Bayerstrasse 34, 80335 Munich, 00 49 89
2399 8420. Called: Oct 1996, Lincoln's Inn,
B.Tech (Brunel), PhD (Cantab), MSc (Lond)

Ashman *Peter Frank* •
Director, European Human Rights,
Foundation, 70 Ave Michel-Ange, 1000
Brussels, Belgium, 32-2 734 9424, Fax: 32-2
734 6831. Called: Nov 1974, Middle
Temple, LLB (Lond)

Ashmore *Anthony John*
Called: Nov 1996, Middle Temple, LLB
(Hons), F.P.M.I., F.I.P.D., A.C.I.I.

Ashplant *Anthony John* •
Head of Legal & Compliance, M & G
Limited, 7th Floor, 3 Minster Court, Great
Tower Street, London EC3R 7HX, 0171 621
8903, Fax: 0171 283 4293. Called: July
1977, Middle Temple, LLB Hons (Lond)

Ashra *Jay Kanji*
Called: Oct 1995, Gray's Inn, BA (Keele)

Ashraf *Ms Leila*
Called: July 1995, Gray's Inn, LLB (E.Anglia)

Ashraf *Miss Nida*
Called: July 1996, Lincoln's Inn, BA
(Hons)(Kent)

Ashton *Barry Philip* •
Senior Crown Prosecutor, Crown
Prosecution Service, East Kent Branch, 3rd
Floor, Queen's House, Guildhall St,
Folkestone, Kent CT20 2DT, 01303 50533,
Fax: 01303 250521. Called: Nov 1985,
Gray's Inn, BSc (Bradford), LLB

Ashton *Miss Bridget Lesley* •
Senior Crown Prosecutor, Crown
Prosecution Service, 3rd Floor, Black Horse
House, 8-10 Leigh Road, Eastleigh
SO50 4FH, 01703 614622, Fax: 01703
644258. Called: Feb 1990, Inner Temple,
LLB (Hons) Bucks

Ashton *Dr Raymond Keighley*
01494 725330, Fax: 01494 432165, and
Member Guernsey Bar, Channel Islands.
Called: July 1979, Lincoln's Inn, BSC (Econ,
Lond), FCA, MSc (Econ,Lond), LLM FTII
ACMA ACIS, PHD (Lond)

Ashton *Roy*
Called: Feb 1954, Lincoln's Inn, LL.B

Ashton-Jones *Philip* •
Principal Legal Adviser, Associated British
Foods plc, NEM House, 3-5 Rickmansworth
Road, Watford, Herts WD1 7HG, 01923
252050, Fax: 01923 223542. Called: Nov
1986, Middle Temple, LLB (E Anglia)

Ashworth *John Nigel Laurence* •
Legal Adviser to the British Forces
Germany., Legal Adviser, External Affairs
Division, Joint Headquarters, British Forces
Germany, BFPO 140. Called: July 1973,
Inner Temple, BA (Lond)

Ashworth *Mark Heddle* •
National Westminster Bank Plc, Company
Secretary's Office, 41 Lothbury, London
EC2P 2BP, 0171 726 1177, Fax: 0171 726
1035. Called: Nov 1987, Lincoln's Inn, MA
(Oxon), Dip Law, (City)

Askew *Richard John Aldis* •
Group Legal Adviser Refined Sugar Assoc
Arbitrator ICC Arbitration Appointments, E
D & F Man Ltd, Sugar Quay, Lower Thames
Street, London EC3R 6DU, 0171 285 3000,
Fax: 0171 285 3518. Called: July 1978, Inner
Temple, MA (Oxon), ACIArb

Aslam *Ms Saiqa Naureen* •
Legal Advisor, Avon & Bristol Law Centre, 2
Moon Street, Stokes Court, Bristol BS2 8QE,
0117 924 8662, Fax: 0117 924 8020.
Called: July 1995, Inner Temple, LLB
(Wolverhampton), MA (Oxon)

Aslam *Miss Sharen*
Block 554, [H] 11-219, Bedok North Street
3, Singapore 460554, 2436057. Called: July
1995, Middle Temple, LLB (Hons)

Asnani *Shankar Ram Pohumall*
197 Taman Star (Lorong 4), 93150 Kuching,
Sarawak, Malaysia, 245421, Fax: 255758.
Called: July 1995, Middle Temple, LLB
(Hons) (Wales)

Aspinall *Michael* •
Legal Adviser, Legal Secretariat to Law,
Officers, 9 Buckingham Gate, London
SW1E 6JP, 0171 828 8134. Called: Nov
1986, Gray's Inn, BSocSci, MA (Keele)

Astbury *Malcolm John*
Chief Executive, Humberside Magistrates
Court, Court House, Station Road, Brough,
East Yorkshire HU15 1DY, 01482 666007,
Fax: 01482 666476. Called: Nov 1980,
Gray's Inn, D.M.L

Astbury *Mrs Margaret*
Deputy Chairman of the South West
Agricultural Land Tribunal. Called: Nov
1970, Gray's Inn, FCIArb

Astbury *Michael Henry Richardson*
Three Way's, Boneashe Lane, St Mary's Platt,
Sevenoaks, Kent TN15 8NW, 01732 884163,
Fax: 01732 780713. Called: Nov 1953,
Middle Temple, MA (Cantab), ACIArb

Aston *Lee Anthony*
Called: Mar 1996, Gray's Inn, BA

Aston *Simon Richard*
Called: Mar 1996, Middle Temple, BA
(Hons), M.Phil, (N. Wales)

Astor *Richard Joseph*
also Inn of Court L. Called: July 1982,
Middle Temple, BA (Kent), ACIArb

Atikpakpa *Ogheneovo Joshua*
Consultant, Usman & Co Solicitors, 6A
Blenheim Grove, Peckham, London
SE15 4QL, 0171 732 9101, Fax: 0171 732
9181. Called: Nov 1994, Lincoln's Inn, LLB
(Lanc), LLM (L'pool)

Atkins *John Edward*
Called: Nov 1997, Middle Temple, BA
(Hons)(Lancs)

Atkinson *Alexander Peter David*
3 Quick Street, Islington, London N1 8HL,
0171 837 8001, Fax: 0171 833 3555.
Called: July 1967, Inner Temple, MA, LLB,
FCA

Atkinson *Daniel Maria Teresa
Solferino*
Director - James R Knowles, 53 Bedford
Square, London WC1B 3DP, 0171 580 4434,
Fax: 0171 436 4860. Called: July 1994,
Lincoln's Inn, LLB (Hons), BSc (Hons)

Atkinson *Ms Esther Mary*
Called: Mar 1997, Gray's Inn, LLB (Warw)

Atkinson-Lyon *Mrs Ruth* •
Senior Crown Prosecutor, The Crown
Prosecution Service, 2nd Floor, Windsor
House, Pepper Street, Chester CH1 1TD,
01244 348043. Called: Nov 1988, Lincoln's
Inn, LLB (Hons)

Attaur-Rehman *Ahmad*
Orr Dignam & Co Advocates, 3 Street 32 F-
8/1, Islamabad, Pakistan, 260517/253086/
260518, Fax: 260653, and Member Lahore
High Court Bar. Called: Nov 1993, Lincoln's
Inn, LLB (Hons), LLM

Attygalle *Miss Amila Sita*
Called: July 1996, Lincoln's Inn, LLB
(Hons)(LSE)

Au *Cheen Kuan*
Called: July 1995, Middle Temple, LLB
(Hons)

Au *Seng Heng*
Called: Mar 1996, Middle Temple, LLB
(Hons)

Au *Tony Thye Chuen*
111 North Bridge Road, [H]22-04, Singapore
0617, 4338102, Fax: 3395436. Called: July
1995, Lincoln's Inn, LLB (Hons)

Au Yong *Miss Pei Yi*
Called: July 1996, Lincoln's Inn, LLB
(Hons)(Sheff)

Aubeelack *Dhirajdass*
and Member Mauritius Bar. Called: Nov
1982, Middle Temple, BA

August *Mrs Rosemarie*
August Associates, 31 Walmers Avenue,
Higham, Rochester, Kent ME3 7EH,
0147482 2194, Fax: 0147482 2194.
Called: July 1977, Middle Temple

Aussant *Mrs Jill Amaryllis*
Legal Adviser, Council of the European
Union, Legal Dept, Rue de la Loi 175, 1049
Bruxelles, Belgium, 02 285 7919, Fax: 285
6743. Called: Nov 1966, Inner Temple, MA
(Cantab), LLB

Austen-Baker *Richard Lindsay
Peregrine St Joh*
Called: Oct 1997, Gray's Inn, LLB (Wales)

Austen-Peters *Oludotun* •
Senior Lawyer, Eastern Group plc,
Wherstead Park, Wherstead, Ipswich
IP9 2AQ, 01473 553623, Fax: 01473
533617, and Member Nigerian Bar.
Called: July 1983, Inner Temple, BA (Hons),
LLM

Austin *Mrs Angela Catherine Anne*
Fellow of Royal Institution of Chartered
Surveyors. Called: Mar 1998, Gray's Inn, BSc
(Not'ham), LLB (Lond)

Austin *Anthony Charles*
Called: Feb 1960, Gray's Inn

Austin *Christopher Bound*
Bedell & Cristin, Advocates & Notaries
Public, P.O.Box 75, One The Forum,
Grenville Street, St Helier, Jersey JE4 8PP,
01534 814814, Fax: 01534 814815.
Called: May 1996, Inner Temple, LLB (Hons)

Austin *Miss Jane Margaret*
Deputy Clerk to the Justices, The Court
House, Shotfield, Wallington, Surrey
SM6 OJA, 0181 770 5950, Fax: 0181 770
5977. Called: Nov 1977, Gray's Inn, LLB

Austin *Miss Patricia Mary*
Called: Nov 1955, Gray's Inn

Austin *Colonel Richard Peter Meredith* •
Officer, Army Legal Services, Directorate of Army Legal, Services,, Trenchard Lines, Upavon, Pewsey, Wiltshire SN9 6BE, 01980 615968, Fax: 01980 615978, Attorney & Counsellor of the United States Army Court of Military Review. Called: July 1976, Inner Temple

Avery *Miss Katrina*
Called: Oct 1993, Inner Temple, BA (Kent), CPE

Avgousti *Avgoustinos Andreas* •
Manager, Fair Trading Group, Office of Telecommunications, 50 Ludgate Hill, London EC4M 7JJ, 0171 634 8700, Fax: 0171 634 8943, and Member Cyprus Bar. Called: Nov 1989, Lincoln's Inn, LLM

Avraamides *Nicos*
10 Mylinae Str, Off 22, Nicosia, 766156 or 766157, Fax: 766123. Called: Nov 1995, Middle Temple, LLB (Hons)(Hull)

Aw *Dominic Kian-Wee*
Assistant General Manager, DKH Management & Sdn Bhd, 20th Floor, Mewara Multi, Purpose, 8 Jalan Munshi Abdullah, 50100 Kuala Lumpur, 603 2982611, Fax: 603 2928112, and Member Malaysia Bar. Called: July 1992, Middle Temple, LLB (Hons) (Hull)

Awad *Anthony Joseph*
Called: Nov 1991, Middle Temple, Bsc (Hons), Dip Law

Awoonor-Renner *Miss Loraine Beatrice*
Called: Nov 1996, Middle Temple, LLB (Hons)(Sheff)

Ayaduray *Jeyapalan*
Called: July 1997, Lincoln's Inn, LLB (Hons)(Lond)

Aylett *Anthony Peter Michael* •
Grade 6 Legal Oficer, Treasury Solicitor's Dept, Queen Anne's Chambers, 28 Broadway, London SW1H 9JS, 0171 210 3496, Fax: 0171 210 3410. Called: May 1971, Middle Temple, LLB

Ayre *Marcus Logan*
Called: Oct 1997, Middle Temple, LLB (Hons)(B'Ham)

Ayres *Andrew John*
Court Place, St Peter Port, Guernsey, Channel Islands, (01481) 723191, Fax: (01481) 711880/711881, and Member Guernsey Bar. Called: Nov 1992, Inner Temple, LLB (Warw)

Ayres *George Leslie CBE*
19 West Way, Pinner, Middlesex HA5 3NX, 0181 866 2055. Called: Jan 1941, Middle Temple, MSc

Azhar *Miss Marina* •
Essex County Council, County Secretary's Dept, P O Box 11, County Hall, Chelmsford CM1 1LX, 01245 430436, Fax: 01245 364994/352710. Called: Nov 1990, Lincoln's Inn, LLB (PCL)

Azhar *Miss Ruby Tayyaba* •
Legal Officer, Dept of Trade & Industry, 1-19 Victoria Street, London SW1H 0NN. Called: Nov 1987, Middle Temple, BA (Hons) (Lond), Dip Law (City)

Azis *Osman Abdul*
Parke & Co Ltd, 6 Vigo Street, London W1X 1AH, 0171 494 2700, Fax: 0171 494 2800. Called: July 1952, Lincoln's Inn, MA (Oxon)

Aziz *Imran*
Called: July 1977, Lincoln's Inn, LLB (Lond), LLM (Lond)

Aziz *Miss Miriam*
Mommsentrabe 47, 10629 Berlin. Called: July 1994, Inner Temple, LLB (Manch)

Aziz *Munir Mydin Abdul*
8 Jalan Desa Ria, Taman Desa, 58100 Kuala Lumpur, 00 603 7803766. Called: July 1997, Lincoln's Inn, BA (Hons)

Aziz *Miss Noor Afizah*
Called: Oct 1992, Middle Temple, BA (Hons)

Aziz *Miss Noraini*
Advocate & Solcitor, Khattar Wong & Partners, 80 Raffles Place [H]25-01, Plaza 1, and Member Singapore. Called: Nov 1993, Gray's Inn, LLB, LLM

Aziz *Shahzad*
Called: Oct 1997, Lincoln's Inn, LLB (Hons)(Brunel)

Aziz *Miss Tengku Azrina Bt Raja Abdul*
Called: July 1997, Lincoln's Inn, BA (Hons)

Azlan *Miss Nor Azrini*
Called: July 1995, Lincoln's Inn, BA (Hons)

Azopardi *The Hon Keith MHA*
Minister for the Environment & Health, Government of Gibraltar. Member of the House of Assembly, 213 Rosia Plaza, Rosia Bay, (350) 50294, Fax: (350) 71143, and Member Gibraltar Bar. Called: Nov 1990, Middle Temple, BA (Keele)

Baars *Adriaan Willem*
Assistant, Winward Fearon, 33 Bow Street, London WC2E 7AU, 0171 420 2800, Fax: 0171 420 2801. Called: Feb 1993, Middle Temple, LLB (Hons)(Bucks), LLM (Bucks)

Babalola *Chief Emmanuel Afe*
and Member Nigerian Bar. Called: July 1963, Lincoln's Inn, B.Sc (Econ)(Lond), LLB (Hons)(Lond), B.L

Babar *Jawad Altahir*
Called: Oct 1997, Lincoln's Inn, LLB (Hons)(Lond)

Baboolal *Miss Maureen* •
Principal Legal Officer, Department of Social Security, Office of the Solicitor, Block 2, Spurr Gout Buildings, Honeypot Lane, Stanmore, Middlesex HA7 1AY, 0171 972 3625, Fax: 0171 972 3671. Called: Nov 1987, Middle Temple, BSc (Hons), LLB (Hons)

Bacarese *George Alan* •
Senior Crown Prosecutor, Crown Prosecution Service, Princes Court, 34 York Road, Leicester LE1 5TU. Called: July 1988, Middle Temple, LLB (Hons)

Bacik *Ms Ivana Catherine Alexis*
Reid Professor of Criminal Law and Criminology, Trinity College Dublin, Law School, Trinity College, Dublin 6, 608 2299, Fax: 677 0449, Member of King's Inns, Dublin and Member Southern Ireland Bar. Called: Nov 1992, Middle Temple, LLB, LLM

Backus *Duncan William Torquil* •
Senior Associate, Legal Operations, Electronic Arts Limited, Mead Field Road, Langley, Slough, Berkshire SL3 8AL, 01753 549442. Called: Oct 1990, Middle Temple, LLB

Bacon *Bernard Matthew*
9 Wisley Court, West Avenue, Worthing, W Sussex BN11 5LY. Called: Nov 1952, Gray's Inn, MA (Cantab)

Bacon *Stephen Francis Theodore* •
Legal Adviser, Express Newspapers plc, Ludgate House, 245 Blackfriars Road, London SE1 9UX, 0171 922 7784, Fax: 0171 922 7967. Called: July 1969, Gray's Inn, LLB (Lond), A.K.C

Badaruddin *Nabil Daraina*
Deputy Public Prosecutor Counsel, Attorney General's Chambers, Jalan Tutong, Bandar Seri, Begawan 2016, Brunei, (673)(2)227959. Called: Nov 1996, Lincoln's Inn, LLB (Hons)(Bucks)

Badejo *Abimbola Rafiu* •
Legal Adviser/Advocate, London Borough of Camden, Legal Services, Town Hall, Judd Street, London WC1H 9LP, 0171 278 4444 x 5223, Fax: 0171 860 5659. Called: Nov 1993, Lincoln's Inn, LLB (Hons)

Badham *Christopher Andrew* •
Mayer Brown & Platt, Bucklesbury House, Queen Victoria Street, London, 2 Dr Johnson's Building, Temple, London, EC4Y 7AY. Called: Oct 1994, Lincoln's Inn, LLB (Hons)(Wales)

Badom *Ms Helen*
Called: Oct 1997, Inner Temple, LLB

Badrudin *Nizam* •
Barry House, 20-22 Worple Road, Wimbledon, London SW19 4DH, 0181 947 0088, Fax: 0181 947 6827. Called: Nov 1969, Middle Temple, FRICS

Baggs *David John* •
County Solicitors Office, County Hall, Colliton Park, Dorchester, Dorset, 01305 251000. Called: Nov 1975, Lincoln's Inn, LLB

Baggs *John William*
Company Chairman, 10 St Margaret's Close, Southampton SO18 5NE, 0850 40100 5, Formerly a Legal Executive. Called: July 1996, Lincoln's Inn, LLB (Hons)

Bagnall *Kenneth Reginald* QC (1973)
Chairman, The New Law Publishing Co
PLC, QC Hong Kong 1983. Called: Jan 1950,
Gray's Inn, LLB

Bagshaw *Miss Joan Ernestine*
Porte Bonheur, 87 Park Road, Brentwood,
Essex CM14 4TU, 01277 221939, Fax:
01277 221939. Called: Jan 1950, Gray's Inn

Bahadursingh *Ravi Ananta*
2 Main Street, New Amsterdam, Berbice,
(592) 3 2841, and Member Guyana Bar.
Called: Nov 1995, Gray's Inn, LLB (Dublin)

Bahrin *Awangku Izad-Ryan*
Skrine & Co, 303B Wisma Jaya, 406A Jalan
Pemancha, Bandar Seri Begawan 2085,
Brunei, 23 29 46/48, Fax: 23 29 49, and
Member Brunei Darussalam. Called: Nov
1994, Lincoln's Inn, BA (Hons)(Keele)

Bahrin *Miss Dayangku Nina Jasmine*
Called: Mar 1998, Lincoln's Inn, LLB
(Hons)(E.Anglia)

Bailey *Anthony Lee*
Called: Nov 1997, Inner Temple, LLB
(Reading)

Bailey *Barry Raymond*
9 Trafford Road, Hinckley, Leics LE10,
01455 610439. Called: Feb 1975, Lincoln's
Inn, LLB

Bailey *Mrs Doreen Patricia* •
Called: Nov 1983, Gray's Inn, BA

Bailey *Miss Helen Clare*
Called: Oct 1994, Inner Temple, LLB (Nott),
LLM (Nott)

Bailey *Miss Jane Angela Tabitha* •
Legal Officer, Solicitor of Inland Revenue,
Somerset House, Strand, London WC2R 1LB,
0171 438 7041, Fax: 0171 438 6246.
Called: Oct 1993, Inner Temple, LLB

Bailey *Miss Rebecca Anne*
Called: Oct 1994, Lincoln's Inn, LLB
(Hons)(Leic)

Bailey *Sam*
45c Crouch Hill, London N4 4AJ.
Called: Oct 1995, Lincoln's Inn, LLB
(Hons)(L'pool)

Baily *Christopher Hugh*
Bailys, Land Agents, Ullswater Road,
Penrith, Cumbria CA11 7EH, 01768 890222,
Fax: 01768 890989. Called: July 1979,
Gray's Inn, BA (Cantab), FRICS, ACIArb

Bainbridge *Dr David Ian*
Reader in Law, Aston University, Aston
Triangle, Birmingham B4 7ET, 0121 359
3611, Fax: 0121 333 4313. Called: Oct
1996, Lincoln's Inn, BSc (Wales), LLB
(Hons), PhD (B'ham), MICE, MBCS

Bainbridge *Garth Tristan Athelstan*
Ozannes, 1 Le Marchant St, St Peter Port4,
Guernsey, 01481 723466, Fax: 01481
727935/720378, and Member Guernsey Bar.
Called: Nov 1978, Gray's Inn, LLB

Baines *Dr Arnold Herbert John*
District and Town Councillor, Finmere, 90
Eskdale Avenue, Chesham, Bucks HP5 3AY.
Called: June 1951, Gray's Inn, MA, PhD,
FSA, FR Hist S, FRSA, C Stat

Baines *Paul Harold*
Detective Superintendent, Merseyside
Police, PO Box 69, Liverpool L69 1JD, 0151
709 6010. Called: May 1988, Lincoln's Inn,
LLB (L'Pool)

Bajaj *Harpal Singh*
Called: Nov 1997, Middle Temple, LLB
(Hons)(Lond)

Bajwa *Azfar Naseem*
Called: July 1996, Gray's Inn, LLB (London),
LLM

Bakar *Miss Falisa Abu*
Called: July 1996, Gray's Inn, LLB
(Manchester)

Bakar *Mohamad Husini*
Assistant Legal Adviser & Assistant Company
Secretary, Brunei Shell Petroleum Company,
Sendirian Berhad, Seria 7082, Brunei,
Darussalam, 673 3 373375, Fax: 673 3
373996, and Member Supreme Court of
Brunei. Called: July 1994, Lincoln's Inn, BA
(Hons) (Keele)

Baker *Mrs Caroline Frances*
Called: July 1988, Gray's Inn, BSc
(Lancaster), MA (Bristol)

Baker *Miss Elisabeth Sara*
10 Park Square, Leeds, LS1 2LH. Called: Nov
1970, Middle Temple, LLB (Leeds)

Baker *Mrs Elizabeth Anne* •
Senior Crown Prosecutor. Called: July 1982,
Middle Temple, BA (Lond), Dip Law

Baker *Ellis David*
Called: Oct 1991, Inner Temple, BA
(Cantab)

Baker *Mrs Helen Lesley*
The Hill, Tair Croes, Ewenny, Nr Bridgend,
Mid Glamorgan CF35 5AG, 01656 654073.
Called: Feb 1980, Gray's Inn, LLB (Wales)

Baker *John Victor Robert*
Clerk to the Justices, Surrey Magistrates'
Court, Court House, London Road, Dorking,
Surrey RH4 1SX. Called: July 1981, Middle
Temple

Baker *John Walter*
2 Richil Court, Ayston Road, Uppingham,
Rutland LE15 9RL, 01572 821729.
Called: July 1966, Gray's Inn, MB,ChB

Baker *Mrs Margaret Daphne*
Called: Nov 1994, Middle Temple, LLB
(Hons)

Baker *Michael Johnathan Charles*
Head of Regulatory Affairs, PAGB, Vernon
House, Sicilian Avenue, London WC1A 2QH,
071 242 8331, Fax: 071 405 7719.
Called: July 1983, Middle Temple, LLB
(Newc)

Baker *Paul MBE*
57 Kingswood Road, Shortlands, Bromley,
Kent BR2 0NL, 0181 460 0612, Hon Lt
Colonel. Called: Nov 1949, Middle Temple

Baker *Peter Tustin*
Kingsclere, Groombridge, Nr Tunbridge
Wells, Kent TN3 9SH, 01892 863220, Fax:
01892 861349. Called: June 1956, Middle
Temple, MA

Baker *Roger* •
Grade 7 Lawyer (Nominated Officer), Office
of the Social Security, & Child Support
Commissioners, Harp House, 83 Farringdon
Street, London EC4A 4DH, 0171 353 5145,
Fax: 0171 936 2171. Called: Nov 1966,
Gray's Inn

Baker *Stuart* •
Justices Chief Executive, West Riding,
Metropolitan Magistrates' Crt, 1st Floor,
Colbeck House, Bradford Rd, Birstall, Batley
WF17 9NR, 01924 424030, Fax: 01924
427910. Called: Nov 1976, Gray's Inn,
B.Tech (Law)

Baker-Layton *Miss Elizabeth Ann
Millicent R* •
Principal Legal Officer, HM Customs &
Excise, New Kings Beam House, 22 Upper
Ground, London SE1 9PJ, 0171 620 1313,
Fax: 0171 865 5243. Called: Nov 1983,
Middle Temple, BA (Hons)

Bakshi *Miss Irvinder Kaur*
Head of Construction Department, Howard
Kennedy, Harcourt House, 19 Cavendish
Square, London W1A 2AW, 0171 546 8821,
Fax: 0171 491 2899. Called: Nov 1987,
Lincoln's Inn, LLB(Hons), DipICArb, ACIArb

Bal *Miss Karen Kaur*
Called: July 1995, Inner Temple, LLB
(Northumbria)

Balasamy *Kasturi Kesveren*
Kas & Co, Advocates & Solicitors, 19b
Wisma Chye Hin, Jalan Sultain Idris, Shah
Ipoh 30,000, 241 4635, Fax: 241 5776, and
Member Malaysia Bar. Called: July 1994,
Lincoln's Inn, LLB (Hons)

Baldry *John Charles*
Allen & Overy, One New Change, London
EC4M 9QQ, 0171 330 3000, Fax: 0171 330
9999. Called: Nov 1993, Middle Temple, LLB
(Hons)(Lond), LLM (Lond)

Baldwyn *Anthony Shaw* •
Senior Adviser to EC, Commission of the
European, Communities, CSM2 4/75 Rue de
la Loi 200, B-1049 Brussels, Belgium, 00 322
2965476, Fax: 00 322 2956451, Contracted
to European Commission. Called: July 1977,
Middle Temple, LLB

Bale *Mrs Katherine Geraldine*
Called: Oct 1993, Gray's Inn, BA (Sheff), LLB

Balen *Miss Bernadette*
and Member Singapore. Called: Nov 1993,
Lincoln's Inn, LLB (Hons)

Balendra *Miss Natasha Thiruni
Jayasekara*
Called: July 1994, Lincoln's Inn, LLB (Hons)

Balfour *James Selby*
Called: Nov 1997, Inner Temple, BA

Balia *Miss Sabwati Shukrin*
Called: July 1996, Lincoln's Inn, LLB
(Hons)(Soton)

Ball *Andrew Charles Manton*
VAT Partner, Deloitte & Touche, Stonecutter Court, Stonecutter Street, London EC4A 3TR, 0171 303 6365, Fax: 0171 303 5109. Called: Nov 1979, Gray's Inn, LLB (Lond)

Ball *Andrew Nicholas*
Principal Court Clerk, Stockport Magistrates' Court, P O Box 155, Edward Street, Stockport, Cheshire SK1 3NF, 0161 477 2020, Fax: 0161 474 1115. Called: May 1993, Middle Temple, LLB (Hons)(Aberystw)

Ball *Brian Anthony*
Called: July 1996, Lincoln's Inn, LLB (Hons)(Wales), LLM (Lond)

Ball *Mrs Deborah Elizabeth*
Called: Nov 1992, Middle Temple, BA (Hons)

Ball *Mrs Jane* ●
Senior Crown Prosecutor, CPS, 4-12 Queen Anne'a Gate, London SW1H 9AZ. Called: July 1986, Inner Temple, Dip Magisterial Law

Ball *Ms Sally Anne*
1 Alfred Street, High Street, Oxford OX1 4EH, 01865 793736, 3 Paper Bldgs, 1st Floor, Temple, London, EC4Y 7EU. Called: Nov 1989, Middle Temple, BA Hons (Oxon)

Ballard *David Edward*
Director, Glass and Glazing Federation, 44-48 Borough High Street, London SE1 1XB, 0171 403 7177, Fax: 0171 357 7458. Called: July 1988, Middle Temple, BSc (City),MSc (Lon), CEng., LLB, FICE, FCIArb

Ballard *Peter*
Compton Developments, 13 Compton Avenue, Skewen, Swansea SA10 6BB, 01792 790934, Fax: 01792 702930. Called: Nov 1976, Middle Temple, MA (Cantab), ACA, ATII, MBA

Ballingal *Alexander James*
Called: Jan 1946, Middle Temple, MA (Oxon)

Balogun *Mrs Kirsten Victoria*
Called: July 1997, Lincoln's Inn, LLB (Hons)(Manch)

Balonwu *Stephen*
Called: Oct 1993, Middle Temple, BA (Hons)(Kent)

Baltaian *Miss Anna Alice*
Called: Feb 1995, Gray's Inn, BA (Newcastle)

Bamforth *Miss Ruth Alexandra* ●
Office of Solicitor for DHSS, New Court, 48 Carey Street, London. Called: Nov 1996, Lincoln's Inn, LLB (Hons)(Leeds), LLM (Cantab)

Bamieh *Miss Thuraya Maria* ●
Senior Crown Prosecutor, Crown Prosecution Service, 23rd Floor, Portland House, Stag Place, London SW1E 5BH. Called: Nov 1984, Lincoln's Inn, BA

Banerji *Ratnanko*
Called: July 1994, Inner Temple, LLB

Banham *Mark Richard Middlecott*
Called: Nov 1994, Inner Temple, BA (Cantab), CPE

Banjoko *Ademunyiwa Monyayo*
Called: May 1997, Inner Temple, LLB (Anglia)

Bapu *David Salim*
P O Box 1042, Blantyre, Malawi, (265) 624820, Fax: (265) 622105, and Member Malawi Bar. Called: Nov 1991, Gray's Inn, LLB (Wales), LLM (Lond)

Baranski *Mrs Gillian Elizabeth*
Clerk to the Cardiff Justices, Fitzalan Place, Cardiff CF2 1RZ, 01222 463040, Fax: 01222 456224. Called: July 1981, Gray's Inn, LLB, MBA

Barber *Anthony Paul*
Broomhall Manor, Norton, Nr Worcester WR5 2NU, Secretary to Lloyd's Disciplinary Committees & Appeal Tribunal. Called: Feb 1972, Middle Temple, LLM

Barber *Miss Julie Greta*
Called: Oct 1996, Middle Temple, BA (Hons)(Keele)

Barber *Keith George*
Called: July 1973, Lincoln's Inn, MA, F.C.I.B

Barber *Paul Edward Stephen* ●
Legal Officer, Catholic Education Service, 39 Eccleston Square, London SW1V 1BX, 0171 828 7604, Fax: 0171 233 9802, Visiting Fellow, University of Westminster. Called: Oct 1992, Middle Temple, MA (Cantab)

Barber *Philip James*
Called: Nov 1996, Middle Temple, LLB(Hons)(Edinburgh)

Barber *Miss Ruth May*
Trainee Solicitor, Tuckers Solicitors, 35 Queen Anne Street, London W1M 9FB, 0171 580 1764, Fax: 0171 637 8738. Called: Oct 1996, Inner Temple, LLB (South Bank)

Barbour *David Stephen Peter*
90 Ennerdale Road, Kew Gardens, Richmond, Surrrey TW9 2DL, 0181 940 3088. Called: July 1984, Lincoln's Inn, BA (Oxon), LLM (Lond)

Barby *Ian Christopher Simon*
Called: July 1969, Middle Temple, MA (Cantab)

Barclay *Rene James* ●
Branch Crown Prosecutor, Crown Prosecution Service, Portland House, Stag Place, London SW1E 5BH, 0171 915 5700. Called: July 1977, Gray's Inn, LLB (Lond)

Bard *Dr Basil Joseph Asher CBE*
23 Mourne House, Maresfield Gardens, London NW3 5SL, 0171 435 5340. Called: June 1938, Gray's Inn, PhD, BSc, M.D., N.R.D.C. (1972-5)

Barit *Ms Georgette De Stefanis*
Appleby, Spurling & Kempe, 41 Cedar Avenue, Hamilton, 441 295 7563, and Member Bermuda Bar. Called: Feb 1995, Middle Temple, MBA, BA, CPE (City), Dip Law

Bark-Jones *Antony Giles*
Also Inn of Court "I". Called: Nov 1990, Middle Temple, BA (Hons)(L'pool), Dip Law (City)

Barker *Mrs Andrea June*
Called: July 1995, Gray's Inn, LLB (Leeds)

Barker *David John*
Called: Mar 1996, Inner Temple, LLB (Leeds)

Barker *Miss Deborah Jayne*
Lecturer, College of Law, Store Street, London. Called: Nov 1994, Middle Temple, LLB (Hons)

Barker *Miss Geraldine Mary*
17 Bedford Road, Twickenham, Middlesex. Called: Nov 1992, Gray's Inn, LLB (Lond)

Barker *Glenn Preston*
Called: Nov 1994, Inner Temple, BA (Manc), CPE (Wolverhampton)

Barker *Grenville Stuart* ●
Principal Crown Prosecutor, Crown Prosecution Service, Pearl Assurance House, 20th Floor, Greyfriars Road, Cardiff CF1 3PL. Called: Nov 1984, Middle Temple, LLB (Cardiff)

Barker *Jeremy*
28 High Riggs, Barnard Castle, Co Durham DL12 8HU, 01833 631299. Called: Nov 1996, Gray's Inn, LLB (Bucks)

Barker *John Roger*
Called: Oct 1992, Inner Temple, BA (Hons)(B'mth)

Barker *Nicolas Michael Anthony*
Called: July 1986, Lincoln's Inn, LLB (Hons) (Reading)

Barker *Ramsey*
Deputy Clerk to the Justices, Cumbria Magistrates' Court, Carlyle's Court, 1 St Mary's Gate, Carlisle CA3 8RN, 01228 592111, Fax: 01228 598968. Called: Nov 1989, Middle Temple, LLB (Manc), DMS

Barker *Richard John*
Legal Adviser, Hampshire Magistrates Court, Court House, Elmleigh Road, Havant PO9 2AL, 01252 366000, Fax: 01256 811447. Called: Feb 1986, Middle Temple, BA, DMS

Barlay *Miss Yema*
Called: Mar 1998, Middle Temple, LLB (Hons)(Middx)

Barlen *Miss Catherine Veronica*
Lovell White Durrant, Avenue Louise 523, Boite 24, 1050 Brussels, 00 32 2 647 0660, Fax: 00 32 2 647 1124. Called: Oct 1990, Inner Temple, BA (Oxon), Dip Law, LLM EC Law (Bruges)

Barlow *Nigel Douglas*
Senior Court Clerk, Birmingham Magistrates Court, Victoria Law Courts, Corporation Street, Birmingham B4 6QA, 0121 212 6608. Called: July 1985, Gray's Inn, BA, LLB

Barlow *Philip Thomas*
Legal Adviser, Hempsons Solicitors, Portland Tower, Portland street, Manchester M1 3LF, 0161 228 0011. Called: Nov 1994, Inner Temple, MB, ChB (Sheff), BA (Cantab)

Barma *Aarif Tyebjee*
and Member Hong Kong Bar 3 Verulam Buildings, London, WC1R 5NT. Called: July 1983, Middle Temple, BA, BCL (Oxon)

Barma *Hussein*
Called: Feb 1995, Middle Temple, BA (Hons), BCL (Oxon), ACA

Barnard *Anthony Christopher* •
Senior Crown Prosecutor, The Cooperage, Gainsford Street, London SE1, 0171 962 2697. Called: Oct 1992, Gray's Inn, BA (Uni E.Anglia), Dip Law (PCL)

Barnatt *Mrs Karen Elizabeth* •
Senior Crown Prosecutor, Crown Prosecution Service, King Edward Court, King Edward Street, Nottingham NG1 1EL, 0115 9480480. Called: July 1983, Gray's Inn, BSc (Econ),Dip Law

Barnes *Adrian Francis Patrick CVO* •
City Remembrancer, Corporation of London, PO Box 270, Guildhall, London EC2P 2EJ, 0171 332 1200, Fax: 0171 332 1895, Doyen of the Seniors in hall at Gray's Inn since 1992. Called: July 1973, Gray's Inn, MA

Barnes *Alexander Ian*
Called: Nov 1996, Lincoln's Inn, LLB (Hons)(L'pool)

Barnes *Miss Barbara Lucinda*
Senior Deputy Chief Clerk, Bow Street Magistrates' Court, 28 Bow Street, London WC2, 0171 379 4713. Called: July 1976, Gray's Inn, LLB (Lond)

Barnes *Miss Kathleen Georgina*
Deputy Chief Clerk, Inner London Magistrates', Courts Service. Called: Nov 1969, Middle Temple, LLB (Lond)

Barnes *Nicholas Gerard Hugh*
Eric Robinson & Co Solicitors, Cooper House, 9-10 New Road, Hythe, Southampton, Hampshire SO45 6RP, 01703 844304. Called: Oct 1996, Inner Temple, LLB (Westminster)

Barnett *Ian Simon* •
IBSA House, The Ridgeway, London NW7 1RP, 0181 906 2211. Called: Apr 1991, Lincoln's Inn, LLB (Hons)

Barnett *Ivor David*
Called: July 1971, Gray's Inn

Baron *Christopher John Clifford*
Called: Nov 1958, Lincoln's Inn

Baron *Miss Francis Althea*
Called: July 1995, Middle Temple, LLB (Hons)

Baron *William Robert* •
Commercial Lawyer, Costain Engineering &, Construction Limited, Costain House, Nicholsons Walk, Maidenhead, Berks SL6 1LN, 01628 842258, Fax: 01628 842271. Called: Feb 1984, Inner Temple, LLB

Barraclough *David Norman Gregory*
Called: Nov 1976, Inner Temple, BA Hons

Barratt *Miss Julie Ann* •
Vale of Glamorgan, Civic Offices, Holton Road, Barry, South Glamorgan, 01446 709405, Fax: 01446 745566. Called: Oct 1993, Gray's Inn, B.Sc (Ulster), LLB (Lond)

Barrett *Ms Catherine Wendy* •
Crown Prosecution Service, King's House, Kimberley Road, Harrow, Middlesex HA1 1YH. Called: Nov 1994, Middle Temple, BA (Hons)

Barrett *Ms Jill Mary* •
Assistant Legal Adviser, Legal Advisers, Foreign & Commonwealth Office, King Charles Street, London SW1A 2AH, Fax: 0171 270 2767, First Secretary (Legal Adviser) to the United Kingdom Mission to the United Nations, New York 1994-1997. Called: July 1989, Gray's Inn, BA [Dunelm], LLM [Cantab]

Barrett *Marcus Morton*
Called: Oct 1996, Inner Temple, LLB (So'ton)

Barrett *Michael John* •
Counsel & Assistant Company Secretary. Called: Nov 1991, Middle Temple, BA (Hons) (Cambs), Dip Law, ACIS

Barrett *Paul James* •
Legal Assistant, Argos Plc, Avebury, 489-499 Avebury, Boulevard, Saxon Gate West, Central Milton Keynes MK9 2NW, 01908 600538, Fax: 01908 600721. Called: Feb 1993, Lincoln's Inn, LLB (Hons)

Barrett *Richard*
Second Legal Assistant in the Office of the Attorney General Dublin, and Member Northern Ireland Bar Southern Ireland Bar. Called: Feb 1988, Middle Temple, BCL, LLB (Ireland), LLM (Lond)

Barrett-Brown *Miss Sophia Aleka*
Called: Nov 1997, Gray's Inn, LLB (Wales)

Barrett-Williams *Dr Jacqueline Sally* •
Legal Manager UK Commercial Business., National Power PLC, Windmill Hill Business Park, Whitehill Way, Swindon, Wiltshire SN5 6PB, 01793 892852, Fax: 01793 892851. Called: July 1985, Inner Temple, BA (Lond), DPhil (Oxon), Dip Law

Barretto *Ruy Octavio*
Part-Time Chairman, Pollution Control Appeal Boards, Member (Part Time) Legal Aid Services Council, Director (Part Time) Kadoorie Farm & Botanic Garden, Temple Chambers, 16/F One Pacific Place, 88 Queensway, 5-2 32003, Fax: 8 100302, and Member New South Wales Bar Hong Kong Bar. Called: Nov 1974, Middle Temple, LLB (Lond), AKC

Barron *Justin Simon* •
Clerk to the Justices, Swansea Magistrates' Court, Grove Place, Swansea SA1 5DB, 01792 655171, Fax: 01792 651066. Called: Nov 1985, Lincoln's Inn, BA

Barrow *Charles Anthony*
Senior Lecturer, University of North London, C/O Law School, UNL, Ladbroke House, 62-66 Highbury Grove, London N5 2AD, 0171 607 2789 Ext 5133. Called: Feb 1993, Lincoln's Inn, BSc (Econ), (Wales), LLM (LSE), Cert Ed

Barrowclough *Sir Anthony Richard QC (1974)*
Called: Nov 1949, Inner Temple, MA (Oxon)

Barry *Anthony* •
Crown Prosecutor, Crown Prosecution Service, United House, York YO1 1PQ. Called: July 1986, Gray's Inn, BA

Barry *Miss Margaret Mary*
8 Rushbury Court, Station Road, Hampton, Middlesex TW1 2DD, 0181 941 0134. Called: Nov 1984, Gray's Inn, BA MA (Dublin), Dip., in European Law, (Dublin)

Barsby *Andrew Walter* •
Senior Principal Legal Adviser, The Treasury Solicitor, Room 80/G, H.M.Treasury, Parliment Street, London SW1P 3AG. Called: July 1975, Gray's Inn, LLB (Lond)

Barsby *Mrs Clare* •
Law Reporter, 2 Lynwood Avenue, Epsom, Surrey KT17 4LQ, 01372 742372, Fax: 01372 721900. Called: Nov 1977, Gray's Inn

Bartfeld *Jason Maurice*
Called: Oct 1995, Middle Temple, BA (Hons)

Bartlet *Michael James George*
Parliamentary Liason Officer, Religions Society of Friends, (Quakers), 173-177 Euston Road, London NW1 2BJ, 0171 663 1000, Fax: 0171 663 1001. Called: Oct 1992, Middle Temple, BA (Hons), Diploma in Law

Bartlett *Robert* •
H M Customs & Excise, Solicitors Office, New King's Beam House, 22 Upper Ground, London SE1 9PJ. Called: Nov 1983, Lincoln's Inn, LLB Hons [Lond]

Barton *Charles Neville* •
Grade 6 (Legal), Her Majesty's Treasury, Parliament Street, London SW1P 3AG, 0171 270 1662, Fax: 0171 270 1668. Called: July 1986, Inner Temple, LLB (Lond)

Barton *Nigel John*
2 Stapleford Court, Sevenoaks, Kent TN13 2LB, 0171 234 2726, Fax: 0171 234 2762. Called: July 1977, Lincoln's Inn, BA (Hons) Bus Law

Barton-Hanson *Mrs Renu*
Called: Nov 1991, Middle Temple, LLB Hons, LLM

Barwick *Glynn*
Simmons & Simmons, 21 Wilson Street, London EC2M 2TX, 0171 825 4015. Called: Oct 1992, Lincoln's Inn, BA(Hons)

Basah *Miss Nashah*
Called: Mar 1998, Middle Temple, LLB (Hons)(Staffs)

Basaran *Halil Attila* •
Prosecution Team Leader, Crown Prosecution Service, The Cooperage, Gainsford Street, London SE1 2NG, 0171 357 7010. Called: Nov 1978, Gray's Inn, Cert Ed

Basaran *Mrs Sandra Judith* •
Company Secretary Legal Director Compliance Officer, Consolidated Financial Ins, Vantage West, Great West Road, Brentford, Middlesex TW8 9AG, 0181 380 3054, Fax: 0181 380 3065. Called: July 1984, Gray's Inn, LLB

Bascoe *Miss Ingrid*
Called: Mar 1997, Lincoln's Inn, LLB (Hons), LLM

Bashford *Keith* •
Senior Legal Adviser, J Sainsbury Plc, Stamford House, Stamford Street, London SE1 9LL, 0171 695 6798. Called: July 1980, Lincoln's Inn, LLB

Baskett *Arno Romer*
13 Orchard Close, Bardsea, Ulverston, Cumbria LA12 9QP, 01229 869681. Called: June 1951, Inner Temple, LLB

Basnayake *Miss Bridget Philomena*
Messrs Sohal & Co Solicitors, 10 Church Road, London W3 8PP, 0181 896 1626, Fax: 0181 896 1628. Called: Apr 1991, Lincoln's Inn, LLB (Hons)

Bassil *Jeremy Nevil Charles*
Titmuss Sainer Dechert, 2 Serjeant's Inn, London EC4Y 1LT. Called: Nov 1987, Lincoln's Inn, LLB Hons

Bastos G Martin *Philip John*
Dorsey & Whitney LLP, 35 Square de Meeus, B-100 Brussels, (32-2) 5044611, Fax: (32-2) 5044646. Called: Nov 1993, Gray's Inn, LLB (Essex), DEA (France)

Bastow *Antony*
Called: Nov 1997, Gray's Inn, BA

Basu *Angelo* •
Legal & Regulatory Adviser, Telstra UK Limited, 44-52 Paul Street, London EC2A 4LB, 0171 858 8800, Fax: 0171 858 8801. Called: Nov 1994, Inner Temple, MA, BCL (Oxon)

Batchelor *Miss Alexandra Mary*
Called: July 1996, Middle Temple, LLB (Hons)(Lond)

Bateman *Lucas William*
Pinsent Curtis Solicitors, 41 Park Square, Leeds LS1 2NS, 0113 244 5000, Fax: 0113 244 8000, Also Qualified as a Solicitor in England & Wales. Called: Oct 1994, Middle Temple, BA (Hons)(Oxon), CPE

Bates *Mrs Alba Heather Phyllida*
Called: July 1968, Lincoln's Inn

Bates *John Gerald Higgs*
140 Mortlake Road, Kew Gardens, Surrey TW9 4EW. Called: Nov 1959, Middle Temple, MA (Cantab), LLM (Harvard)

Bates *Peter Spensley*
and Member New South Wales Bar New Walk Chambers, 27 New Walk, Leicester, LE1 6TE. Called: July 1978, Lincoln's Inn, BA

Bates *Ronald Adrian*
Head of Legal Services, North West Gwent Magistrates Courts, Gwent Magistrates' Court Comm, 2nd Floor, Gwent House, Gwent Square, Cwmbran, Gwent NP44 1PL, 01633 645132, Fax: 01633 645177. Called: July 1978, Gray's Inn, LLB (Exon), DMS

Batstone *Rodney Karl CBE*
Called: June 1961, Inner Temple, MA, LLB (Cantab)

Batteson *Alexander*
Freshfields Solicitors, 65 Fleet Street, London EC4Y 1HS, 0171 832 7678. Called: Nov 1995, Gray's Inn, BSc (L'pool)

Battle *John Gerard Stephen* •
Group Legal Adviser, Associated Newspapers Limited, North Cliffe House, 2 Derry Street, Kensington, London W8 5EE, 0171 938 7223, Fax: 0171 938 1092. Called: July 1985, Lincoln's Inn, LLB

Batuk *Sanjay*
Called: Oct 1997, Middle Temple, LLB (Hons)(Wales)

Baty *Paul Raymond* •
Senior Crown Prosecutor, Crown Prosecution Service, Colmore Gate, Colmore Circus, Birmingham, 0121 629 7200. Called: Nov 1980, Middle Temple, BA (Hons)

Baudains *Martyn*
Called: Mar 1998, Gray's Inn, LLB (W'hampton)

Bauer *Christian Rudolf Johann*
Called: Oct 1996, Lincoln's Inn, LLB (Hons)(Lond)

Bavidge *Giles David* •
Clerk to the Justices, Sunderland Magistrates Cts Com, Justices Clerks Office, The Villa, Dairy Lane, Houghton-Le-Spring, Tyne & Wear DH4 5BL, 0191 5842392, Fax: 0191 5845809, Broad Chare, 33 Broad Chare, Newcastle Upon Tyne, NE1 3DQ. Called: July 1968, Inner Temple, LLB

Baxter-Phillips *Miss Felicity Dawn* •
Lawyer, Ministry of Agriculture,, Fisheries & Food, 55 Whitehall, London SW1A 2EY, 0171 270 3000. Called: Feb 1964, Gray's Inn, Diploma in Field, Archaeology (Lond)

Bay *Miss Chern Chieh*
Called: July 1995, Middle Temple, LLB (Hons)

Bayer *Tufan*
Called: Oct 1997, Lincoln's Inn, LLB (Hons)(Lond)

Bayley *John Richard* •
Company Secretary & Group General Counsel. Called: July 1962, Middle Temple, LLB

Bayliss *Neil McKenzie* •
Called: July 1986, Gray's Inn, LLB (Hons)

Bayly *Mrs Julia Mary* •
Crown Prosecutor, Crown Prosecution Service, 1st Floor Offices, Lowther Arcade, Lowther Street, Carlisle. Called: Nov 1972, Gray's Inn, LLB (Lond)

Bayman *Keith William* •
Called: July 1987, Lincoln's Inn, MA, LLM (Cantab)

Baytug *Denizhan*
Hammond Suddards Solicitors, 2 Park Lane, Leeds LS3 1ES, 0113 284 7000, Fax: 0113 284 7001. Called: Oct 1992, Lincoln's Inn, LB(Hons)(Sheff)

Bazley *Stuart Richard*
45 Vicarage Road, Old Moulsham, Chelmsford, Essex, 01245 609206. Called: Nov 1991, Middle Temple, LLB (Hons) (Lond)

Beach *Nicholas Peter* •
Treasury Solicitors Department, Queen Anne's Chambers, 28 Broadway, London SW1H 9JS. Called: Nov 1983, Middle Temple, BA (Hons)(Oxon)

Beale *Professor Hugh Gurney*
School of Law, University of Warwick, Coventry CV4 7AL, 01203 523185, Fax: 01203 524105. Called: Nov 1971, Lincoln's Inn, BA (Oxon)

Beale *Noel Joseph*
Called: Oct 1997, Middle Temple, BA (Hons)(Notts), CPE (Lond)

Beamer-Downie *Mrs Darcy*
Flat 8, Cross Deep, Twickenham TW1 4QL, 0181 892 1537, Fax: 0181 892 1537. Called: Nov 1996, Middle Temple, LLB (Hons)

Bean *Miss Alison Margaret* •
Child Care Lawyer, Oxfordshire County Council, Chief Executives Dept, Social Services, County Hall, New Road, Oxford OX1 1ND, 01865 815452, Fax: 01865 815447. Called: Oct 1990, Middle Temple, LLB (Lond)

Beardmore *Miss Alison Claire*
Court Clerk, The Court House, Field Street, Leek, Staffs ST13 5ST, 01538 372858, Fax: 0538 385129. Called: Oct 1991, Gray's Inn, LLB (B'ham)

Beardwell *Philip Norman*
Wace Morgan Solicitors, 2 Belmont, Shrewsbury, Shropshire SY1 1TD, 01743 361451, Fax: 01743 231708. Called: Nov 1994, Inner Temple, LLB (Hons)

Bearn *Miss Natasha Victoria*
Called: Nov 1995, Middle Temple, BA (Hons)

Beattie *Cameron Robert*
Legal Adviser, North Avon Magistrates, Court House, Kennedy Way, Yate, Bristol BS17 4PY, 01454 310505. Called: Feb 1991, Lincoln's Inn, LLB

• Barristers in employment

Beaumont *David Anthony* ●
Financial Services Lawyer, Halifax Building
Society, Trinity Road, Halifax, West
Yorkshire, 01422 333492, Fax: 01422
333453. Called: July 1987, Lincoln's Inn, BA
(Durham)

Beaumont *Miss Louise Ann* ●
Executive Legal & Administrative Manager,
Secretary to Merseyside Passenger
Transport, Mersey Travel, 24 Hatton
Garden, Liverpool L3 2AN, 0151 224 7020,
Fax: 0151 224 7022. Called: July 1989,
Middle Temple, BA (Keele) (Hons)

Beaven *Gregory Paul* ●
Crown Prosecution Service, Princes Court,
York Road, Leicester, 0116 2549333, Fax:
0116 2550855. Called: Nov 1991, Inner
Temple, MA (Oxon), MPHIL (York), Pst Grd
Cert Ed, LLB

Beavers *David John*
Called: Nov 1992, Middle Temple, LLB
(Hons, L'pool)

Beazer *Dominic William Jesse*
Called: Feb 1994, Inner Temple, BA (Lond),
Dip in Law

Beck *Miss Sandra Mary* ●
Crown Prosecution Service, Berkshire
Branch, Eaton Court, 112 Oxford Road,
Reading RG1 7LL, 01734 503771.
Called: Nov 1982, Lincoln's Inn, BA

Beck *Stephen James*
Called: Oct 1996, Inner Temple, LLB

Becker *Paul Antony* ●
Senior Crown Prosecutor, Crown
Prosecution Service, Heron House,
Houghoumont Avenue, Crosby, Merseyside
L22 0LL, 0151 920 8711, Fax: 0151 920
8244. Called: Nov 1990, Gray's Inn, LLB
(Hons)(Leeds)

Beckless *Ms Jo-Anne*
Called: Oct 1997, Inner Temple, LLB
(Middx)

Beckwith *Miss Gillian*
Assistant Deputy Clerk to the Justices,
Oldham Magistrates Court, St Domingo
Place, West Street, Oldham OL1 1YY, 0161
624 2331, Fax: 0161 652 0172. Called: Feb
1982, Middle Temple, DML, Dip Training &,
Development.

Beckwith *Silas Walter Lawrence*
Called: Oct 1993, Lincoln's Inn, LLB
(Hons)(Lond)

Bedford *John Edgar* ●
Grade 7 (Europe), European Commission,
DG VI.B.I.1, Office L130 5/212, rue de la
Loi 200, B-1049 Bruxelles, +322 299 5414,
Fax: +322 296 5195. Called: Nov 1993,
Middle Temple, BA (Hons)(Oxon), CPE

Beel *Robert William Trevor*
Called: May 1996, Gray's Inn, LLB (Lond)

Beer *Charles Esmond*
KPMG, One Canada Square, London
E14 5AG, 0171 311 4193, Fax: 0171 311
4088. Called: July 1978, Middle Temple, MA
(Cantab), ATII

Beetham *James Edward*
Called: Oct 1994, Lincoln's Inn, BA
(Hons)(Exeter)

Beg *Miss Mosion Shazadi* ●
Special Immigration Adjudicator, Advisor to
the Dept of International Development and
IBA Human Rights Institute, Immigration
Appellate Auth., Myddleton Place, Roseberry
Avenue, Islington, London, 0181 829 2405,
Fax: 0181 829 2402. Called: Nov 1984,
Inner Temple, BA (B'ham) LLM, (So'ton)

Beggs *Miss Danielle Ann* ●
McKenna & Company, Mitre House, 160
Aldersgate Street, London EC1A 4DD, 0171
606 9000. Called: July 1983, Inner Temple,
LLB (Leeds)

Begum-Baig *Miss Farah*
Called: Nov 1994, Inner Temple, LLB (Hons)

Beharrylal *Satyanand Sarju*
Called: Oct 1997, Lincoln's Inn, LLB
(Hons)(Herts)

Behrouzi *Miss Parisa*
Called: Nov 1996, Middle Temple, LLB
(Hons)

Behzadi *Miss Shayesteh* ●
Fellow in European Community Law,
Ministry of Agriculture,, Fisheries & Food,
Legal Department, 55 Whitehall, London
SW1A 2EY, 0171 270 8541, Fax: 0171 270
8270. Called: Nov 1988, Middle Temple, LLB
(Hons), LLM

Belch *Michael Andrew*
Counsel and Commercial Director, Joniq
(UK) Ltd, SBC House, Restmor Way,
Wallington, Surrey SM6 7AH, 0181 288
0424, Fax: 0181 288 0425. Called: Nov
1993, Middle Temple, BSc (Hons)(Wales),
CPE

Beldam *Ms Alexander Gay* ●
Lawyer, Criminal Appeal Office, Royal
Courts of Justice, Strand, London
WC2A 2LL, 0171 936 6314, Fax: 0171 936
6900. Called: Nov 1981, Inner Temple, BA
(Hons)

Bell *Andrew John*
19 Elms Road, Clapham, London SW4 9ER,
0171 627 1763, Fax: 0171 627 1764.
Called: Nov 1986, Gray's Inn, MA (Cantab),
MBA (Insead)

Bell *Miss Catherine Isobel* ●
Head of Business Affairs, The Chrysalis
Group Plc, The Chrysalis Building, Bramley
Road, London W10 6SP. Called: Oct 1992,
Inner Temple, LLB (Hons)

Bell *Miss Helen Suzanne*
4 King's Bench Walk, 2nd Floor, Temple,
London, EC4Y 7DL. Called: July 1985,
Middle Temple, BA (Cantab)

Bell *Ms Kerrie Olivia* ●
Principle Crown Prosecutor Team Leader,
Crown Prosecution Service, The Cooperage,
Gainsford Street, London SE1. Called: July
1986, Inner Temple, LLB (Lond)

Bell *Nigel John* ●
Senior Principal Legal Officer, HM Customs
& Excise, New King's Beam House, 22
Upper Ground, London SE1 9PJ, 0171 865
5167. Called: Nov 1976, Middle Temple, LLB
(Lond)

Bell *Simon Richard*
Called: Nov 1994, Inner Temple, BA, BCL
(Oxon)

Bell *Mrs Susan Josephine*
Butterworths Division of Reed, Elsevier
(UK) ltd, Halsbury House, 35 Chancery
Lane, London WC2A 1EL, 0171 400 2800,
Fax: 0171 400 2598. Called: Nov 1992,
Lincoln's Inn, LLB (Hons)

Belle *Mrs Berthalee Louise*
Called: Oct 1997, Gray's Inn, BA (Ohio), LLB
(Leeds)

Belle-Fortune *Roger James Alexander*
Called: July 1988, Lincoln's Inn, LLB (Hons)

Bellis *Neil Graham*
Called: July 1976, Gray's Inn, LLB

Belton *Mrs Valerie Pak Lian*
Court Clerk, Wimbledon Magistrates' Court,
Alexandra Road, Wimbledon, London
SW19 7JP, 0181 946 8622, Fax: 0181 946
7030. Called: July 1984, Inner Temple, LLB
(buckingham)

Beltrami *Edwin Joseph* ●
Crown Prosecutor, Crown Prosecution
Service, Thames/Wells Branch, 2nd Floor,
Portland House, Stag Place, London
SW1E 5BH. Called: July 1988, Middle
Temple, LLB (Hons)

Benady *Miss Yael Horabuena Simha*
Called: Oct 1994, Middle Temple, LLB
(Hons)(Manc)

Benest *David John*
Bailache Labesse, 14/16 Hill Street, St
Helier, Jersey JE2 3ZB, 01534 888777, Fax:
01534 888778. Called: Nov 1995, Inner
Temple, BA (Sussex)

Benest *Frederick John*
Called: July 1996, Middle Temple

Benest *Miss Nina Sophie Hacquoil*
Bois & Bois, 2 Bond Street, P.O.Box 429, St
Helier, Jersey JE4 5QR, 01534 601010, Fax:
01534 601011. Called: July 1996, Middle
Temple, LLB (Hons)(Kent)

Beng *Miss Li-Sher*
Called: July 1996, Middle Temple, BA
(Hons)(Notts)

Benjamin *Miss Gaynor*
Called: Feb 1994, Lincoln's Inn, LLB (Hons)

Benjamin *Ian Leroy Colin*
1 Crown Office Row, Ground Floor,
Temple, London, EC4Y 7HH. Called: July
1988, Middle Temple, BA, LLM (Cantab)

Bennett *Ms Alexandra Catherine*
Called: Nov 1997, Inner Temple, BA (Lond)

Bennett *Ms Helen Rachel* •
Senior Principal Lawyer, Civil Service
College, Sunningdale, Ascot, Berks, 01344
634088. Called: Nov 1982, Middle Temple,
MA (Oxon), Dip Law

Bennett *Julian Frank Lawrence*
Called: Oct 1994, Middle Temple, LLB
(Hons)(Lond)

Bennett *Lee Anthony*
Called: May 1997, Inner Temple, LLB (Lond)

Bennett *Patrick* QC (1969)
Recorder. Called: Nov 1949, Gray's Inn, MA,
BCL (Oxon)

Bennett *Paul Richard*
Called: Nov 1995, Inner Temple, LLB (Exon)

Bennett *Thomas Christopher* •
Principal Crown Prosecutor, Crown
Prosecution Service, Hawkins House, Rydon
Lane, Pynes Hill, Exeter, Devon EX2 5SS,
01392 422555, Fax: 01392 422111.
Called: Nov 1980, Middle Temple, BA

Benney *Mark William* •
Legal Adviser's Office, Department of
Employment, Caxton House, Tothill Street,
London SW1H 9NF, 0171 273 6072.
Called: July 1982, Inner Temple, BA
(Dunelm)

Bennion *Francis Alan Roscoe*
5 Old Nursery View, Kennington, Oxford
OX1 5NT, 01865 735365, Fax: 01865
736807, Former Parliamentary Counsel
Member of Oxford University Law faculty.
Called: Jan 1951, Middle Temple, MA
(Oxon)

Bennison *Craig Jeffrey*
Called: Oct 1997, Lincoln's Inn, LLB
(Hons)(Anglia)

Benns *Miss Elizabeth Susan*
Manager, Fin & Gen Bank Plc, Age Concern
Bedfordshire, Disability Resource Centre,
Poynters House, Poynters Road, Dunstable,
Bedfordshire LU5 4PT, 01582 470900, Fax:
01582 470977. Called: July 1979, Middle
Temple, LLB, A.C.I.B

Bensadon *Mrs Janine Yvette*
Called: Oct 1994, Lincoln's Inn, LLB
(Hons)(Hudders)

Bentall *Miss Georgina Mary* •
Contracts Lawyer, International
Management Group, (UK) Ltd, Pier House,
Strand on the Green, Chiswick W4 3NN.
Called: Mar 1996, Inner Temple, BSc
(Manch)

Bentick-Owens *Ms Pia Anne Maria* •
Company Secretary, Presdner Kleinwort
Benson, P.O.Box 560, 20 Fenchurch Street,
London EC3P 3DB, 0171 956 6410, Fax:
0171 621 1481. Called: July 1997, Gray's
Inn, ACIS, LL Dip

Bentley *Mrs Anne Louise* •
Called: July 1987, Lincoln's Inn, LLB
(London)

Bentley *David Jeffrey* CB
Consultant, Foreign & Commonwealth
Office, King Charles Street, London
SW1A 2AH, 0171 270 3075, Fax: 0171 270
2767. Called: Nov 1963, Lincoln's Inn,
MA,BCL (Oxon)

Bentley *John Graham*
Sundowners, Picaterre, Alderney GY9 3UP,
0148 182 2698, Fax: 0148 182 3559, and
Member Malaysia Bar Nigerian Bar
Cameroon Bar. Called: June 1953, Lincoln's
Inn, MA (Oxon)

Benzaquen *Joseph Pinhas*
350 78534, Fax: 350 73201, and Member
Gibraltar Bar. Called: July 1992, Middle
Temple, LLB (Hons)

Benzaquen *Rafael Jacob*
Law Draftsman, Legislation Support Unit, 13
Town Range, + (350) 41821, Fax: + (350)
41822. Called: July 1995, Middle Temple,
LLB (Hons), Maitre en Droit, (Paris)

Berger *Jonathan Charles*
Called: Nov 1993, Inner Temple, LLB
(Lond), MA (Westminster)

Bergin *Gerard Patrick*
Principal, Gerard Bergin Associates, 9
Barnacre Drive, Parkgate, South Wirral,
Cheshire L64 6RJ, 0151 336 4643, Fax:
0151 336 4643. Called: July 1995, Middle
Temple, LLB (Hons), FRICS, FCIOB

Bergman *Mrs Sophie*
1 Sneath Avenue, London NW11 9AJ.
Called: Nov 1958, Lincoln's Inn

Berish *Joseph Michael*
13 Waters Edge, Sandside, Milnthorpe,
Cumbria LA7 7HN, 015395 62195.
Called: Nov 1964, Gray's Inn

Berk *Deniz Andrew*
Called: Nov 1996, Inner Temple, LLB
(Essex), LLM (Germany)

Berkeley-Hill *Michael Amar Samuel*
Legal Assistant, Squadron Ellenoff Plesent &,
Sheinfeld LLP, 551 Fifth Avenue, New York,
NY 10176-0001, 00 1 212 661 6500, Fax: 00
1 212 697 6686. Called: Oct 1994, Middle
Temple, LLB (Hons)(Lond), AKC (Lond),
LLM (Lond)

Berman *David Michael*
Called: Nov 1997, Gray's Inn, BSc (Leeds),
LLM, (Lond)

Berman *Sir Franklin Delow* KCMG QC
(1992) •
Legal Adviser to the Foreign &
Commonwealth Office, Foreign &
Commonwealth Office, King Charles Street,
London SW1A 2AH, 0171 270 3000, Fax:
0171 270 3071. Called: Nov 1966, Middle
Temple, MA (Oxon), BA, BSc (Capetown)

Berman *Paul Richard* •
Legal Adviser, Advisory Service. Called: Nov
1990, Gray's Inn, BA (Oxon), Dip Law
(City), D.E.S.(Geneva)

Berman *Ms Yvonne Marie* •
Intellectual Prop Lawyer. Called: May 1988,
Middle Temple, LLB (Hons)

Bernacchi *Brook Antony* OBE JP
Arbitration Panel Hong Kong, 1103 Prince's
Building, Central, 5 2 20066, Fax: 8 450851,
QC, Hong Kong. Called: Jan 1943, Middle
Temple, FCIArb

Bernasko *Frank George*
Barrister and Solicitor Supreme Court of
Ghana (1970) and Member Ghana Bar.
Called: Nov 1988, Gray's Inn, LLB (Hons)
Ghana, BSc (Lond)

Berney *Nigel Philip*
17 Tylers Close, Kings Langley,
Hertfordshire WD4 9QA. Called: Feb 1990,
Inner Temple, LLB (Lond)

Bernstein *Miss Elizabeth Diane
Melanie*
5 Corringway, London W5 3AB. Called: Nov
1986, Lincoln's Inn, BA Law

Bernstein *Ronald Harold* DFC QC
(1969)
Vice-President Emeritus. The Chartered
Institute of Arbitrators, Bencher 1975-,
Handbook of Rene Review (1981-1997),
Handbook of Arbitration Practice 1987/
1993/1997). Called: Jan 1948, Middle
Temple, MA (Oxon), FCIArb, ARICS (Hon),
F.S.V.A (Hon)

Berrill-Cox *Adrian Leigh* •
Legal Advisor, Legal Unit, Bank of England
HO-4, Threadneedle Street, London
EC2R 8AH, 0171 601 5070, Fax: 0171 601
3865. Called: July 1986, Inner Temple, LLB
(Reading)

Berry *George*
Called: July 1967, Gray's Inn, BSc Econ, Dip
Religious Studie

Berry *John Graham* •
Company Secretary, Iceland Group Plc,
Deeside Industrial Park, Second Avenue,
Deeside, Flintshire CH5 2NW, 01244
842329, Fax: 01244 842684. Called: Nov
1976, Lincoln's Inn, BA

Berry *John Percival*
Called: July 1960, Gray's Inn

Berry *Miss Julia Mary*
Legal Adviser, Richards Butler, Beaufort
House, 15 St Botolph Street, London
EC3A 7EE, 0171 247 6555, Fax: 0171 247
5091. Called: Nov 1988, Gray's Inn, LLB
(Lond)

Berry *Mark Joseph*
Legal Adviser, DJ Freeman, 43 Fetter Lane,
London EC4A 1NA, 0171 583 4055, Fax:
0171 353 7377. Called: Nov 1995, Lincoln's
Inn, BEng(Hons), CEng

Berry *Thomas Hugh Kirk*
Called: July 1935, Inner Temple, BA

Besomi *Michael John Guy*
Charles Russell Solicitors, 36/38 Leadenhall
Street, London EC3A 1AT, 0171 458 3306,
Fax: 0171 480 6640. Called: July 1981,
Gray's Inn, LLB (Warw), LLM (Lond)

Bessell *William Gregory*
Called: Oct 1997, Lincoln's Inn, BSc
(Hons)(Lond)

Betteley *Jason Paul* •
Legal Officer, The Treasury Solicitor, Queen
Anne's Chambers, 28 Broadway, LondoN.
Called: Oct 1990, Inner Temple, LLB

Bettelheim *Eric Christopher*
Partner, Mayer Brown & Platt, Mayer Brown
& Platt, Bucklersbury House, 3 Queen
Victoria Street, London EC4N 8EL, 0171 246
6208, Fax: 0171 329 4465, and Member
New York, California. Called: Nov 1979,
Inner Temple, BA (Oxon), JD (Chicago)

Betts *Mrs Christine Rosemary* •
Family & Community Law Manager, Bath &
NE Somerset Council, Riverside, Temple
Street, Keynsham, Bristol, 01225 395223,
Fax: 01225 395128. Called: Nov 1971,
Middle Temple, LLB (Hons)

Bevan *Mrs Anne* •
Consultant, Wansbroughs, Willey Hargrave,
St Swithins House, 1a St Cross Road,
Winchester, Hants, 01962 841444.
Called: Nov 1979, Middle Temple, BA

Bevan *Miss Sally Frances* •
Called: Nov 1982, Middle Temple,
BA(Reading) Dip Law

Bexley *Simon Mark*
Called: Oct 1993, Inner Temple, LLB (Hull)

Bhagobati *Ruben Kumar*
Called: Nov 1995, Gray's Inn, BA (Oxon)

Bhakta *Miss Nilema* •
Principal Legal Officer, Solicitors Office,
H.M.Customs & Excise, New King's Beam
House, 22 Upper Ground, London SE1 9PJ,
0171 865 5139, Fax: 0171 865 5987.
Called: Oct 1994, Inner Temple, LLB (Notts)

Bhalla *Tajinder Singh*
Smithkline Beecham Plc, One New Horizons
Court, Middlesex TW8 9EP, 0181 975 2353,
Fax: 0181 975 2360. Called: July 1988,
Middle Temple, BA (Hons) (Keele), Dip Law
(City), AIIT

Bhambri *Miss Sunita*
Called: Nov 1991, Lincoln's Inn, LLB (Hons)

Bhamra *Miss Meena Kaur*
Called: Nov 1997, Middle Temple, LLB
(Hons)

Bhar *Miss Sherina*
Called: Nov 1997, Lincoln's Inn, LLB (Hons)

Bhatia *Anil*
Called: Nov 1994, Middle Temple, LLB
(Hons)

Bhatia *Ms Anita*
Called: Nov 1997, Inner Temple, LLB (Lond)

Bheeroo *Khumrajsing Sunil*
Called: July 1996, Gray's Inn, LLB
(Wolverhampton)

Bhimjee *Anwar Ali*
244 Juanita Way, San Francisco, California
94107, (415) 242 1734, Chartered
Accountant. Called: July 1965, Lincoln's Inn,
MA, FCA, LLB

Bhimji *Mrs Mumtaz Begum*
64 Mount Stewart Avenue, Kenton, Harrow,
Middlesex HA3 0JU, 0181 907 4882, Fax:
0181 907 0787. Called: July 1971, Gray's
Inn, LLB

Bhola *Miss Susan*
Supreme Court of Trinidad & Tobago.
Called: Nov 1993, Lincoln's Inn, LLB (Hons,
Buck'ham)

Bibby *John Benjamin*
Kirby Mount, Warwick Drive, West Kirby,
Wirral, Merseyside L48 2HT, 0151 625
8071, Fax: 0151 625 8071. Called: July
1981, Gray's Inn, MA (Cantab)

Bibby *Peter James*
62 Oakhurst Grove, London SE22 9AQ,
0181 693 8752. Called: Oct 1992, Middle
Temple

Bickerstaff *Miss Anthea Mary*
Called: Oct 1990, Gray's Inn, BA (Keele)

Bicknell *Mrs Louise Jean* •
Director,, Swiss Bank Corporation, 2
Finsbury Avenue, London EC2M 2PP, 0171
568 0859. Called: Nov 1984, Middle
Temple, BA

Biddulph *Ms Jemima Jane*
Called: Oct 1996, Middle Temple, BA (Hons)
(Camb)

Bielby *Richard Mark* •
Legal Officer, Transport & General Workers,
Union, "Woodberry", 218 Green Lanes,
London N4 2HB, 0181 800 4281, Fax: 0181
809 6501. Called: Oct 1994, Gray's Inn, BA,
Dip Law

Biesmans *John Robert*
Deputy Secretary General, European
Parliament, Rue Belliard 97, 1040 Brussels,
02 284 30 26, Fax: 02 231 11 83/ 02 284
9877. Called: July 1979, Middle Temple, MA
(Oxon), LLB (Cantab) LLM

Bignall *Mrs Gillian Meryl* •
Crown Prosecutor, CPS, 4-12 Queen Anne's
Gate, London SW1H 9AZ. Called: Nov 1978,
Middle Temple, LLB

Biker *Andrew Dunkin* •
Lawyer, HM Customs & Excise, Solicitors
Office, New Kings Beam House, 22 Upper
Ground, London SE1 9PJ, 0171 865 5184,
Fax: 0171 865 5164. Called: Nov 1978,
Gray's Inn, MA (Cantab)

Bilewycz *Michael Domenico* •
Legal Adviser, Unilever (UK) Limited, Legal
Department, Unilever House, Blackfriars,
London EC4P 4BQ, 0171 822 5252 X5655,
Fax: 0171 822 6539. Called: Nov 1988,
Middle Temple, BA Hons

Binder *Mrs Joanne*
Senior Court Clerk, Bucks County Council,
Berkley House, Walton Street, Aylesbury,
Bucks HP21 7QG, 01296 383058, Fax:
01296 383436. Called: July 1985, Gray's Inn,
BA

Binder *Miss Naveen Kaur*
Called: July 1995, Middle Temple, LLB
(Hons)

Binding *David Wyn* •
Group Secretary/Group Compliance Officer,
Legal & General Group Plc, Temple Court,
11 Queen Victoria Street, London
EC4N 4TP, 0171 528 6200, Fax: 0171 528
6221. Called: July 1978, Middle Temple, BA

Binet *Miss Francoise Charlotte*
Called: Mar 1998, Lincoln's Inn, LLB (Hons),
LLM, (Bucks)

Biney *Kwamina Aubyn* •
Senior Court Clerk, Redbridge Magistrates'
Court, 850 Cranbrook Road, Barkingside,
Ilford, Essex IG6 1HW, 0181 551 4461, Fax:
0181 550 2101. Called: July 1989, Lincoln's
Inn, LLB (Ghana), Dip Law (City), LLM
(Lond)

Binns *Miss Quinell Maria*
Called: Nov 1997, Lincoln's Inn, LLB (Hons)

Biondi *Alessandro* •
Legal Adviser, Shell UK Limited, Shellmex
House, Strand, London WC2R 0DX, 0171
257 3000. Called: Feb 1994, Lincoln's Inn,
LLB (Hons)

Birch *Miss Karen Margaret* •
Deputy General Counsel, Price Waterhouse,
Southwark Towers, 32 London Bridge
Street, London SE1 9SY, 0171 939 3000,
Fax: 0171 939 2673, and Member Bermuda
Bar New South Wales Bar. Called: July 1984,
Inner Temple, LLB (Wales)

Birch *Keith Jeffrey*
Called: Nov 1994, Lincoln's Inn, BA (Hons),
LLM (Warw)

Birch *Paul Ronald*
Senior Court Clerk, North Sefton
Magistrates, Courts Committee, Law Courts,
Albert Road, Southport, Merseyside PR9 0LJ,
01704 534141, Fax: 01704 500226.
Called: Feb 1988, Middle Temple, LLB
(Hons), Dip Magistrates Law

Bird *Charles Ashley Richard* •
Legal Adviser Grade 6, Health & Safety
Executive, Solicitor's Office, Rose Court, 2
Southwark Bridge, London SE1 9HS, 0171
717 6654, Fax: 0171 717 6661. Called: Nov
1977, Middle Temple, MA [Cantab]

Bird *Miss Elizabeth Margaret*
Sub-Editor at Halsbury's Statutes,
Butterworths, Halsbury House, 35 Chancery
Lane, London WC2A 1EL, 0171 400 2516,
Fax: 0171 400 2559. Called: Nov 1996,
Lincoln's Inn, LLB (Hons)(Brunel)

Bird *Nicholas David*
Called: Oct 1993, Middle Temple, BA
(Hons)(York), CPE

Bird *Miss Penelope Hamilton*
Called: July 1982, Inner Temple, BA

Birdi *Ms Tarnjit*
Called: Nov 1995, Inner Temple, LLB (Lond)

Birikorang *Charles Seth Addo* •
Principal Legal Officer, HM Customs &
Excise, Solicitors Office, New King's Beam
House, 22 Upper Ground, London SE1 9PJ,
0171 865 4832, Fax: 0171 865 5248, and
Member Ghana Bar. Called: July 1987,
Lincoln's Inn, LLB (Ghana) LLM, (Lond)

Birkin *James Francis Richard*
Called: Feb 1992, Inner Temple, LLB

Birrell *Duncan MacCallum* •
LLB (Hons), Crown Prosecution Service, 2nd Floor, Calder House, St James St, Burnley, Lancs BB11 1XG, 01282 412298, Fax: 01282 412239. Called: May 1984, Lincoln's Inn

Birt *Michael Cameron St John*
H M Attorney General of Jersey, Law Officer's Department, Royal Court House, Jersey JE1 1DD, 0534 502200, Fax: 0534 502299, QC 1995 and Member Jersey Bar 9 Bedford Row, London, WC1R 4AZ. Called: Nov 1970, Middle Temple, MA (Cantab)

Birtwistle *Daniel James*
Called: July 1996, Middle Temple, LLB (Hons)(Wales)

Bishop *Miss Angela Mary*
Called: July 1981, Lincoln's Inn, LLB (Lond)

Bishop *Miss Helen Susan* •
Senior Crown Prosecutor, Crown Prosecution Service, 9th Floor, RAS House, Alencon Link, Basingstoke, Hampshire. Called: July 1988, Lincoln's Inn, LLB (Hons)

Bishop *Mrs Janice Elaine*
Deputy Chief Clerk. Called: July 1979, Gray's Inn

Bishop *Mrs Pauline* •
Senior Crown Prosecutor, Crown Prosecution Service, Eaton Court, Oxford Road, Reading, Berks. Called: July 1980, Inner Temple

Biswas *Manoranjan*
81 Gorwel, Llanfairfechan, Gwynedd, North Wales LL33 ODT, 01248 680757. Called: Nov 1954, Lincoln's Inn, BA

Biswas *Miss Nisha Sujata*
Called: Oct 1996, Lincoln's Inn, LLB (Hons)(L'pool)

Black *Charles Michael Andrew*
Called: Oct 1996, Gray's Inn, LLB

Black *James Walter* QC (1979)
Edmund Barton Chambers, Level 44 MLC Centre, Martin Place, Sydney 2000, 02 9220 6100, Fax: 02 9232 3949, and Member Australian Capitol Territory New South Wales Bar. Called: Feb 1964, Middle Temple, MA (Cantab)

Black *Julian Neil*
Called: Oct 1995, Lincoln's Inn, LLB (Hons)(Leic)

Black-Branch *Dr Jonathan Lee*
Called: Mar 1998, Lincoln's Inn, BA (Canada), B.Ed (Canada), MA (Oxon), LLB (Hons)(Oxon), M.Ed, Ph.D (Toronto)

Blackburn *Barry John* •
Vice President & Chief Legal Adviser, Sun Life Assurance Company of, Canada, Basingview, Basingstoke, Hampshire RG21 2DZ, 01256 841414, Fax: 01256 460067. Called: Nov 1977, Gray's Inn, MA (Oxon)

Blackburn *Mrs Diana Jeanette*
P O Box 748, Belgrave, Victoria 3160, and Member New Zealand Bar. Called: Nov 1991, Middle Temple, BA Hons (Kent), ACIArb, AArbInz

Blackburn *Lieut-Cdr George Richard VRD, RNR*
Company Secretary Consultant, 26 Pearl Ct, Cornfield Terrace, Eastbourne, E Sussex BN21 4AA, 01323 411096. Called: Nov 1948, Inner Temple, MA (Cantab), ALAM, ARAES

Blackburn *John Roger* •
Principal Legal Officer, HM Customs & Excise, New King's Beam House, 22 Upper Ground, London SE1 9PJ, 0171 865 5169. Called: Nov 1971, Middle Temple, LLB, AKC

Blackburn-Lindley *Mrs Claire Ann* •
Principal Crown Prosecutor, CPS (Sth London & Surrey), 17th Floor, Tolworth Tower, Surbiton, Surrey KT6 7DS. Called: Nov 1986, Gray's Inn, LLB (Nott'm), LLM (LSE)

Blacker *James*
Called: Nov 1986, Gray's Inn, S.T.L., B.A., M.B.A.

Blackett *Captain Jeffrey RN* •
Acting Metropolitan Stipendiary Magistrate, 10 Blount Road, Pembroke Park, Portsmouth PO1 2TD, 01705 815398. Called: July 1983, Gray's Inn, LLB (Lond)

Blackman *Colin*
M Inst P, Wharf Cable, 8/F Wharf Cable Tower, 9 Hoi Shing Road, Tsuen Wan, 2112 6222, Fax: 2112 7824. Called: July 1988, Gray's Inn, BSc (Lond), MSc (Reading), C Phys

Blackman *Miss Sharon Annette* •
Colonial, Colonial House, Quayside, Chatham Maritime, Kent ME4 4YY, 01634 898017. Called: Oct 1997, Lincoln's Inn, LLB (Brunel)

Blackmore *Miss Wendie Helen*
Called: Mar 1996, Inner Temple, LLB (LSE)

Blackshaw *Miss Gail*
Called: Oct 1997, Middle Temple, BSc (Hons)(Bris), CPE

Blagburn *Ms Alison*
Called: Oct 1997, Inner Temple, LLB (Northumbria)

Blain *Lt Cdr Roderick Graham RN* •
Assistant Naval Adviser OTTAWA, BDL (S) Ottawa, Naval Party 1010 BFPO 487, 613 237 1530 X 234, Fax: 613 232 4030. Called: Oct 1991, Middle Temple, BA (Stirling)

Blair *Anthony Charles Lynton MP*
11 King's Bench Walk, Temple, London, EC4Y 7EQ. Called: July 1976, Lincoln's Inn, BA (Oxon)

Blair *Ms Linda Susan*
Housing Advisor, Central London Law Centre, 19 Whitcomb Street, London WC2H 7HA, 0181 969 2433, Fax: 0181 968 0345. Called: Oct 1993, Gray's Inn, LLB (Hons)

Blair *Michael Campbell* QC (1996) •
Deputy Chief Executive and General Counsel, Securities and Investments Board, Gavrelle House, 2-14 Bunhill Row, London EC1Y 8RA, 0171 638 1240, Fax: 0171 382 5903, Treasurer of the Bar Council 1995, 1996,1997,1998 Bencher, Middle Temple 3 Verulam Buildings, London, WC1R 5NT. Called: July 1965, Middle Temple, MA, LLM (Cantab), MA (Yale)

Blake *Leslie Leonard*
Also Inn of Court G. Called: July 1974, Middle Temple

Blake *Leslie William*
Lecturer in Law, Dept of Linguistic &, International Studies, University of Surrey, Guildford, Surrey GU2 5XH, 01483 300800 Ext 2830, Fax: 01483 259527. Called: Nov 1972, Lincoln's Inn, LLM, AKC

Blake *Ms Penelope Natasha*
Called: July 1996, Gray's Inn, BA (Sussex)

Blake *Miss Susan Heather*
Course Director Bar Vocational Course, Inns of Court School of Law, 39 Eagle Street, London WC1R 4AJ, 0171 404 5787. Called: Nov 1976, Inner Temple, MA, LLM (Cantab)

Blake-James *Hugh Desmond*
Called: Mar 1998, Middle Temple, BA (Hons)(Lond)

Blakebrough *Philip David* •
Principal Crown Prosecutor, Crown Prosecution Service, Stoke Mill, Woking Road, Guildford, Surrey GU1 1AQ. Called: July 1987, Middle Temple, LLB (Lond)

Blakeley *John Christopher* •
Corporate Development Director, Glynwed International plc, Headland Hse, New Coventry Rd, Birmingham B26 3AZ, 0121 742 2366, Fax: 0121 742 0403. Called: July 1967, Lincoln's Inn, MA

Blakesley *Major John Cadman MBE*
Shepherds Hill House, Pinnock, Winchcombe, Cheltenham GL54 5AX, 01242 602620, Fax: 01242 602620. Called: Nov 1966, Middle Temple

Blanche *Martin James*
Called: Nov 1997, Middle Temple, BA (Hons)(Manch)

Blanco White *Thomas Anthony* QC (1969)
0171 405 4321, Fax: 0171 405 9955, 8 New Square, Lincoln's Inn, London, WC2A 3QP. Called: June 1937, Lincoln's Inn, BA (Cantab)

Blankson *Harry Douglas*
Called: Nov 1992, Inner Temple, BSc (Nigeria), LLB (Lond)

Blatchford *Charles Robert*
Called: July 1997, Inner Temple, BSc (Dunelm), Dip in Law

E

Blatchford *Trevor John*
Deputy Clerk to the Justices, East Cornwall
Magistrates' Crt, Launceston Road, Bodmin,
Cornwall, 01208 73873, Fax: 01208 77198.
Called: July 1979, Gray's Inn, BA

Blin *Roger Louis*
Called: July 1962, Middle Temple, LLB
(Lond)

Blincow *Peter Stanley Adrian*
22 Easton Street, High Wycombe,
Buckinghamshire HP11 1LT, 01494 473240,
Fax: 01494 473233. Called: Oct 1996,
Lincoln's Inn, MSc (Reading), LLB (Hons)
(Lond), Dip in Building Econ, (DSTN),
FRICS

Blizzard *Keith Anthony*
Called: Nov 1997, Gray's Inn, BA

Blom-Cooper *Sir Louis Jacques KB*
QC (1970)
Independant Commissioner for the Holding
Centre (NI), 2 Ripplevale Grove, London
N1 1HU, 0171 607 8045, Fax: 0171 609
3350, Doughty Street Chambers, 11
Doughty Street, London, WC1N 2PG.
Called: July 1952, Middle Temple, LLB
(Lond), Dr Jur (Amsterdam)

Blood *Ms Alison Jane*
Called: Oct 1990, Gray's Inn, BA (Lond),
Dip Law

Bloom *Bryan Neville Irving*
Called: May 1997, Middle Temple, BPharm
(Hons), MSc (Sheff), LLB (Hons)

Blow *Detmar Hamilton Lorenz Arthur*
Called: Apr 1989, Middle Temple, BA (LSE),
Dip Law

Blumenthal *David* •
Called: Feb 1993, Middle Temple, BA
(Hons)(Lond), Dip in Law (City)

Blunden *Mrs Anne-Marie* •
Crown Prosecution Service, Horsham
Branch, P.O.Box 229, Horsham, West
Sussex RH12 1YB, Fax: 01403 272 923.
Called: Nov 1992, Inner Temple, BA, Dip in
Law (City)

Blunden *Mark Edward*
Called: Nov 1996, Lincoln's Inn, LLB
(Hons)(Herts)

Blythe *Mark Andrew* •
Legal Advisor, HM Treasury, Treasury
Chambers, Parliament Street, London SW1,
0171 270 1666, Lincoln's Inn (Ad Eundem)
and Member New York. Called: Nov 1966,
Inner Temple, BCL, MA (Oxon)

Boadita-Cormican *Miss Aedeen*
1 Crown Office Row, 3rd Floor, Temple,
London, EC4Y 7HH. Called: Oct 1990,
Gray's Inn, LLB (Dub), LLM (Cantab)

Boafo *Yaw Acheampong*
Called: July 1994, Inner Temple, LLB (Lond),
LLM

Boase *Charles Nigel*
Vauxhall House, Monmouth NP5 4AX,
01600 715076. Called: Mar 1996, Lincoln's
Inn, BA (Hons)

Bodden *Truman Murray OBE*
Truman Bodden & Co, P O Box 1796,
Anderson Square Building, Grand Cayman,
British West Indies, 809 949 7555, Fax: 809
949 8492, and Member Cayman Islands.
Called: July 1969, Inner Temple, ACIB, FFA,
FICM, FCI, MBIM, ACIArB, FBSC, LLB
(Hons) (Lond)

Boden *Peter Horrox*
19 Station Road, Chinley, High Peak,
Derbyshire SK23 6AR. Called: Feb 1965,
Gray's Inn, BSc (Econ), LLB

Bodruddoza *Md*
Hall Room, No 3, Supreme Court Bar
Association, Building, Dhaka-1000,
Bangladesh, Chamber 45/Kha, New Eskaton
2nd Floor, Dhaka, 88-02-9340080, and
Member Bangladesh Bar Council Dhaka Bar.
Called: Nov 1995, Lincoln's Inn, LLB
(Hons)(Lond), LLB (Hons)(Banglade), LLM
(Bangladesh)

Bogaert *Peter Willy Luc*
Kunstlaan 44, 1040 Brussel, 32-2-5495230,
Fax: 32-2-5021598, and Member Brussels
Bar. Called: May 1995, Gray's Inn, Licenciaat
in de, Rechten, BA

Bogle *Paul Wakefield* •
Essex County Council, County Secretary's
Department, P O Box 11, County Hall,
Chelmsford CM1 1LX, 01245 430528, Fax:
01245 346994. Called: Oct 1995, Lincoln's
Inn, LLB (Hons)(Bris)

Boh *Miss Wah Boon*
Called: July 1996, Middle Temple, LLB
(Hons)(Glamorg)

Bokszczanin *Ryszard*
34 Bradley Gardens, Ealing, London W13,
0181 998 2874, Fax: 0181 998 2873.
Called: Nov 1995, Middle Temple, LLB
(Hons) (Lond), BSc (Hons)

Bolt *Miss Annabelle Elizabeth* •
HM Customs & Excise, Room 3.43, New
King's Beam House, 22 Upper Ground,
London SE1 9PJ, 0171 620 1313/865 5157,
Fax: 0171 865 5822. Called: July 1970,
Gray's Inn

Bolton *Miss Sally Margaret*
and Member Manx Bar. Called: July 1988,
Gray's Inn, BA (E Anglia), Dip Law

Bolton *Miss Susan Anne*
Called• Oct 1997, Gray's Inn, BA
(Edinburgh)

Bon *Edmund*
Called: July 1997, Lincoln's Inn, LLB
(Hons)(Lond)

Bonage *Ms Isabella*
Called: Nov 1997, Lincoln's Inn, LLB (Hons),
LLM, (Essex)

Bondy *Rupert Mark Boden* •
SmithKline Beecham Plc, One New
Horizons Court, Brentford, Middlesex
TW8 9EP, 0181 975 2080, Fax: 0181 975
2090, and Member California. Called: July
1987, Middle Temple, BA (Cantab)

Bonney *Charles John*
Called: Nov 1969, Lincoln's Inn, MA (Oxon)

Bontoux *Mrs Virginie Francoise
Ghislaine P*
92 Chesson Road, Baron's Court, London
W14 9QU. Called: Nov 1995, Lincoln's Inn,
LLB (Hons), LLM

Boo *Moh Cheh*
Called: July 1994, Lincoln's Inn, LLB (Hons)

Boodia *Miss Anuradha Devi* •
Called: Oct 1994, Gray's Inn, LLB

Boon *Swan Ngee*
Called: Nov 1994, Middle Temple, LLB
(Hons)

Boone *Miss Caroline Anne* •
Legal Adviser, British Airways Plc, Speedbird
House, PO Box 10,Heathrow Airport,
Hounslow, Middlesex TW6 2JA. Called: Feb
1980, Middle Temple, LLB (Soton)

Booth *Miss Amanda Jane*
0171 603 6623. Called: July 1979, Gray's
Inn, LLB (L'pool)

Booth *Nigel Robert* •
Crown Prosecutor, CPS North West Area,
Manchester South Branch, Sunlight House,
Quay Street, Manchester M60 3PT, 0161
908 2600, Fax: 0161 908 2617. Called: Oct
1994, Gray's Inn, LLB, Diploma in German,
Law

Boothroyd *Paul*
Called: May 1995, Lincoln's Inn, BSc (Econ),
FCA

Borenius *Lars Ulric*
Karelia, Stocksbridge Lane, Coombe Bissett,
Salisbury, Wiltshire SP5 4LZ, 01722 718
466. Called: June 1941, Lincoln's Inn

Borge *Paul Louis Anthony*
Called: Mar 1998, Gray's Inn, BA (Derby)

Borrett *Louis Albert Frank*
54 Farm Close, East Grinstead, West Sussex
RH19 3QG, 01342 312350. Called: Nov
1955, Gray's Inn, LLB (Lond)

Borrie *Lord QC (1986)*
1 Plowden Buildings, Temple, London
EC4Y 9BU, 0171 353 4434. Called: Nov
1952, Middle Temple, LLM, FCI Arb

Boss *Miss Bernadette Carmel*
Senior Legal Officer, Dept of Defence -
Army, Defence Centre Melbourne, Victoria
Barracks, St Kilda Road, Melbourne 3006, 00
617 364 4455, and Member Queensland
Bar. Called: Oct 1992, Middle Temple, B.Sc
(Hons, Lond), Diploma in Law

Boss *Ronald William OBE*
The Old Coach House, River Lane, Alfriston,
East Sussex BN26 5SX, 01323 870813.
Called: Nov 1958, Middle Temple

Bossino *Damon James*
Suite C, 2nd Floor, Regal House,
Queensway, 010 350 79423, Fax: 010 350
71405, and Member Gibraltar. Called: Nov
1995, Middle Temple, LLB (Hons)

Bossino *Stephen Richard*
2 Hadfield House, P.O.Box 659, Library
Street, Gibraltar, 74998/73316, Fax: 73074,
and Member Gibraltar. Called: Oct 1994,
Lincoln's Inn, LLB (Hons)(Leic)

Bostwick *Ms Janet Lissette Racquel*
Bostwick & Bostwick, Attorneys at Law, 50
George Street, PO Box N-1605, Nassau N.P.,
(809) 322 2039/2038, Fax: (809) 328 2521,
and Member Bahamas Bar Association.
Called: July 1996, Gray's Inn, BA (McGill,
Canada), LLB (Buckingham)

Bostwick *John Henry*
Called: Nov 1995, Gray's Inn, BA (Keele)

Boswell *Peter Douglas*
18 Market Place, Market Bosworth,
Nuneaton, Warks CV13 0LE, 01455 291851,
Fax: 01455 291637. Called: Nov 1994,
Gray's Inn, BA

Botros *John Michael*
Called: Feb 1992, Middle Temple, MA
(Oxon)

Bottrell *Eric Perry* •
Legal Advisor, Mid Essex Hospital Services,
NHS Trust, Collingwood Road, Witham,
Essex CM8 2TT, 01376 532625, Fax: 01376
532590. Called: Mar 1997, Middle Temple,
LLB (Hons)

Boucly *Miss Nathalie*
Called: Nov 1996, Middle Temple, LLB
(Hons)(LSE)

Bough *Mrs Jennifer Christine*
Lecturer in Law, Wye College Univ. of
London, Departmetn of Agriculture,
Economics & Business Mngmnt., Wye
College, University of London, Wye,
Ashford, Kent TN25 5AH. Called: July 1978,
Gray's Inn, LLM (Lond)

Boughton *David Allan*
Deputy Chief Clerk, Inner London
Magistrates', Courts Service, 65 Romney
Street, London SW1P 3RD. Called: Nov
1970, Gray's Inn

Boulter *Christopher Nigel Jarvis* •
Deputy Clerk to the Justices, Magistrates'
Clerk's Office, Law Courts, County Civic
Centre, Mold, Flintshire CH7 1AQ, 01352
752757, Fax: 01352 753551. Called: Nov
1975, Middle Temple, LLB (Lond)

Boulton *Sir William Whytehead Bt, Kt,
CBE, TD*
The Quarters Hse, Alresford, Colchester,
Essex CO7 8AY, 01206 82 2450.
Called: Nov 1936, Inner Temple, BA

Bourke *Ms Sarah Victoria Norma*
Called: Oct 1996, Gray's Inn, LLB (Lond)

Bourne *Miss Judith Pullen*
Called: Oct 1993, Lincoln's Inn, LLB
(Hons)(Lond)

Bourne *Professor Nicholas*
Pendragon Chambers, 124 Walter Road,
Swansea, SA1 5RG. Called: July 1976, Gray's
Inn, LLB, LLM (Wales), LLM (Cantab)

Bourne *Mrs Sharon Elsie Mary* •
Senior Crown Prosecutor, Crown
Prosecution Service, 7th Floor (South),
Royal Liver Building, Pier Head, Liverpool
L3 1HN, 0151 2367575. Called: July 1985,
Gray's Inn, LLB (Liverpool)

Bousher *Stephen* •
Assistant Solicitor, The Inland Revenue,
Solicitor's Office, Somerset House, The
Strand, London WC2R 1LB, 0171 438 7085.
Called: Nov 1975, Gray's Inn, LLB

Boustred *Mrs Anne Mary* •
County Council Employed Barrister,
Childcare Litigation Unit, Dept of Law &
Admin, Hertfordshire County Council,
County Hall, Hertford SG13 8DE, 01992
555524/5, Fax: 01992 555541, (nee
Norman). Called: July 1975, Inner Temple,
LLB

Bowden *Gerald Francis*
Principal Lecturer in Law, 2 Paper Bldgs, 1st
Floor, Temple, London, EC4Y 7ET.
Called: July 1962, Gray's Inn, MA (Oxon)
FRICS

Bowden *Mrs Gwyneth Margaret*
Senior Deputy Chief Clerk, Inner London
Magistrates', Courts Service, Clerkenwell
Magistrates' Court, London WC1, 0171 278
6541, Fax: 0171 837 4526. Called: July
1968, Gray's Inn, LLB

Bowen *David James Jeffreys* •
Senior Crown Prosecutor, CPS, Cumbria
House, Merthyr Tydfil Industrial Est,
Pentrebach, Merthyr Tydfil, Mid Glamorgan,
01443 693240. Called: July 1975, Gray's Inn,
LLB, MA

Bowen *Justin* •
GEC plc, 1 Stanhope Gate, London
W1A 1EH, 0171 493 8484. Called: Oct 1994,
Lincoln's Inn, MA (Cantab)

Bower *Alastair Ross*
Called: July 1986, Inner Temple, LLB (Leeds)

Bower *David Bartlett*
Obstetric & Gynaecological Surgeon Chelsea
& Westminster Hospital, 42 Harley Street,
London W1N 1AB, 0171 636 1952.
Called: Nov 1950, Inner Temple, FRCS,
FRCOG

Bower *Marcus Himan*
14 Camelot Close, London SW19 7EA.
Called: Nov 1946, Middle Temple, MA, LLM
(Cantab)

Bowers *Miss Deborah*
Alberton Richelieu & Associate, P.O.Box
2130, Gros-Islet, St Lucia, 001 758 4524515,
Fax: 001 758 4523329, and Member St
Lucia. Called: July 1997, Middle Temple, LLB
(Hons)(Lond)

Bowett *Prof. Derek William CBE QC
(1978)*
01223 414618, Fax: 01223 414617.
Called: Nov 1953, Middle Temple, LLD
(Cantab), FBA

Bowker *Miss Cathryn Anne* •
Principal Crown Prosecutor, Crown
Prosecution Service, Unit 3, Clifton Mews,
Clifton Hill, Brighton, East Sussex BN1 3HR,
01273 207171, Fax: 01273 207849.
Called: July 1983, Gray's Inn, BA (Keele)

Bowler *Christopher Fairfax*
Justices' Clerk, Justices Clerks Office, Shire
Hall, Bury St Edmunds, Suffolk IP33 1HF,
01284 3522300, Fax: 01284 352343.
Called: July 1978, Gray's Inn, LLB (L'pool)

Bowler-Smith *Mark*
Called: Nov 1997, Middle Temple, LLB
(Hons)(Exon)

Bowles *Edward Raymond* •
Senior Crown Prosecutor, Crown
Prosecution Service, Camberwell Branch,
2nd Floor, The Cooperage, 8 Gainsford
Street, London SE1 2NE, 0171 357 2760.
Called: Oct 1993, Middle Temple, LLB
(Hons)(Lond)

Bowles *Philip Cranton*
Called: Nov 1950, Inner Temple, MA

Bowman *Miss Catherine*
Called: Nov 1992, Lincoln's Inn, BA (Hons)

Bowman *Edwin Geoffrey CB* •
Parliamentary Counsel, Law Commission,
Conquest House, 37/38 John Street,
Theobalds Road, London WC1N 2BQ, 0171
453 1206. Called: Nov 1968, Lincoln's Inn,
MA, LLM (Cantab)

Bowman *Mrs Georgina June*
Called: July 1973, Gray's Inn, MA (Cantab)

Bowman *Timothy James Elliott*
Called: May 1993, Lincoln's Inn, B.MUS
(Hons)(Sheff), LLB (Hons)(Sheff)

Bowman-Boyles *Ms Chantal Marie
Brenda*
Head of Communications, Misis Infocom
Group plc, 1 Epsom Square, White Horse
Business Park, Trowbridge, Wilts BA14 0XG,
01225 752200, Fax: 01225 775527.
Called: Oct 1994, Middle Temple, BA
(Hons)(Lond), CPE (City)

Boxall *Randolph Leonard*
Lamb Chambers, Lamb Building, Temple,
London, EC4Y 7AS. Called: Nov 1952, Inner
Temple

Boy *David Raymond*
QC (Hong Kong). Called: May 1954, Gray's
Inn

Boyd *David John QC (1982)*
Member of Monopolies and Mergers
Commission Immigration Adjudicator
Chairman Axxia Systems Ltd, Beeches,
Upton Bishop, Ross-on-Wye, Herefordshire
HR9 7UD, 01989 780214, Fax: 01989
780538. Called: Nov 1963, Gray's Inn, MA
(Cantab), FCIArb

Boyd *Duncan Rodney Lecington*
0171 723 2630, Fax: 0171 724 1460.
Called: Nov 1994, Lincoln's Inn, BA (Hons)

Boyd *Henry Marlow*
Director NYK Intl PLC, Chairman Coalgas
olc & Dominion Energy PLC, Secretary UK
Onshore Operators Group, Director Oil
Management Services Limited Secretary
General, The Gas Forum, 63 Duke Street,
London W1M 5DH, 0171 355 3393, Fax:
0171 355 3704. Called: Nov 1964, Middle
Temple, MA (Oxon)

Boyd *Miss Marian Elizabeth* ●
Senior Crown Prosecutor. Called: July 1983,
Middle Temple, BA

Boydell *Peter Thomas Sherrington QC*
(1965)
Chanc Dioc of Truro, Oxford Worcester.
Called: Jan 1948, Middle Temple, LLB

Boyle *Charles Gerard*
Called: Nov 1994, Middle Temple, LLB
(Hons)

Boyle *Professor Christopher Kevin*
and Member Northern Ireland Bar Southern
Ireland Bar. Called: May 1992, Gray's Inn,
LLB (Belfast), Dip Crim (Cantab)

Boyle *Miss Jane Kerr*
Via S Martino E Solferino 90, Padova, (049)
65 40 58. Called: Feb 1992, Middle Temple,
MA (Lond), LLB (Hons)

Boyle *Dr John Charles*
Legal Adviser, Kvaerner PLC, 55/F Central
Plaza, 18 Harbour Road, Wanchai, (852)
28681100, Fax: (852) 28681522. Called: July
1974, Lincoln's Inn, B.Sc, PhD, C.Eng,
M.I.C.E

Boyle *Jonathan Gavin*
Called: Oct 1995, Inner Temple, BA (Manc),
CPE

Boyton *David Rex*
Flat 4-H, Ventris Court, 15 Ventris Road,
(832) 2521 5544, Fax: (832) 2524 5912, and
Member Hong Kong. Called: July 1997,
Gray's Inn, BA (Newc), LLB (Lond), LLM
(Lond)

Braby-Pavitt *Mrs Lynne Louise* ●
Assistant Solicitor, Essex County Council,
Chief Executive & Clerk's Dept, PO Box 11,
County Hall, Chelmsford, Essex CM1 1LX,
01245 492211, Fax: 01245 352710.
Called: Nov 1986, Gray's Inn, LLB (Hons)

Bracewell *Miss Julia Helen*
Senior Associate, Brobeck Hale & Dorr,
Hasilwood House, 60 Bishopsgate, London
EC2N 4AJ, 0171 638 6688, Fax: 0171 638
5888. Called: July 1987, Lincoln's Inn, LLB
(Bristol)

Bradbury *Christopher William*
Called: May 1997, Inner Temple, BA (Leics),
MA (Keele)

Bradbury *Ms Jeanne Brenda*
1 Old Dock Close, Kew Green, Surrey
TW9 3BL, 0181 948 8688, Fax: 0181 948
8688. Called: Nov 1992, Inner Temple, LLB

Bradbury *John Arthur*
Cot Hoy, Buckland, Nr Faversham, Kent
ME13 0TP. Called: June 1953, Lincoln's Inn

Bradbury *Trevor* ●
Group Legal & Commercial Advisor, HOW
Group plc, Intersection House, Birmingham
Road, West Bromwich, West Midland
B70 6RX, 0121 500 5000, Fax: 0121 580
1037. Called: Nov 1995, Middle Temple, LLB
(Hons), FRICS, ARIArb

Bradford *Paul Andrew*
Called: Mar 1996, Lincoln's Inn, BA (Hons)

Bradley *Miss Celia Anne*
Legal Adviser, Kent Magistrates Courts
Cmmtte, The Court House, Tufton Street,
Ashford, Kent TN23 1QS, 01233 663203,
Fax: 01233 663206. Called: Feb 1992,
Middle Temple, LLB (Hons)

Bradley *Clive CBE*
8 Northumberland Place, Richmond, Surrey
TW10 6TS, 0181 940 7172, Fax: 0181 940
7603. Called: Feb 1961, Middle Temple, MA

Bradley *David Robert*
Called: Nov 1995, Middle Temple, LLB
(Hons), BSc (L'pool)

Bradley *Nigel Frank* ●
Legal Director, British Aerospace, Systems &
Services, Mill Lane, Warton Aerodrome,
Preston, Lancashire PR4 1AX, 01772
852095, Fax: 01772 856262. Called: July
1981, Lincoln's Inn, LLB Hons (Sheffield)

Bradley *Paul David*
Justices' Chief Executive, The Courthouse,
Church Hill, Easingwold, York YO6 3JX,
01347 821776, Fax: 01347 823776.
Called: July 1979, Gray's Inn, LLB (Exon)

Bradshaw *Mrs Caron Louise*
Called: Oct 1994, Lincoln's Inn, LLB
(Hons)(Lond)

Brady *Kevin Joseph*
Lecturer in Law, 47 Hervey Close, Finchley,
London N3 O6H. Called: July 1984, Gray's
Inn, BA (Belfast) LLB, (Lond)

Brady *Paul James*
Called: May 1995, Inner Temple, BA

Braggins *James Richard John* ●
Treasury Solicitor's Department, Queen
Anne's Chambers, 28 Broadway, London
SW1, 0171 210 3000. Called: July 1972,
Gray's Inn, MA (Cantab)

Braich *Stephen Harmit Singh*
Bench Legal Adviser, Northampton
Magistrates' Court, Regents Pavilion,
Summerhouse Road, Moulton Park,
Northampton, 01604 497000, Fax: 01604
497010. Called: Nov 1987, Gray's Inn, LLB,
LLM (Cantab)

Braine *Richard Michael Allix*
109 Cheyne Walk, London SW10 0DJ, 0171
352 0030, Fax: 0171 352 0030, and Member
Turks & Caicos Islands. Called: July 1952,
Gray's Inn, BA (Hons, Oxon)

Bramall *Sir Ashley*
2 Egerton House, 59/63 Belgrave Road,
London SW1N 2BE, 0171 828 0973, Fax:
0171 828 0973. Called: Nov 1949, Inner
Temple, MA (Oxon)

Bramley *Steven Michael Stuart* ●
Assistant Legal Adviser, THe Home Office,
50 Queen Anne's Gate, London SW1H 9AT.
Called: July 1983, Gray's Inn, LLB

Bramwell *Christopher Paul*
Called: Nov 1996, Gray's Inn, LLB (Lancs)

Bramwell *Mrs Elizabeth Anne Oxley* ●
7 Penwerris Terrace, Falmouth, Cornwall
TR11 2PA, 01326 314465, Fax: 01326
314465. Called: July 1971, Lincoln's Inn,
LLB

Bramwell *Philip Nicholas*
Managing Director, DDV
Telecommunications, Strategy, Woluwe
Garden, Woluwedal 26,65, 1932 Brussels,
00 322 715 0930, Fax: 00 322 715 0931.
Called: Nov 1983, Lincoln's Inn, BA (Hons)

Brandon *Michael*
P O Box 200, 1291 Commugny, Vaud, 0041
22 776 14 00/776 15 00, Fax: 0041 22 776
55 18. Called: Nov 1952, Inner Temple, MA,
LLM (Cantab), MA (Yale), FCIArb

Brandt *Howard Patrick* ●
Legal Officer at the Personal Investment
Authority, 7th Floor, One Canada Square,
London E14 5AZ, 0171 538 8860, Fax: 0171
418 9300. Called: Feb 1993, Middle Temple,
BA (Hons)(Oxon)

Brankin *Sean-Paul*
Called: Oct 1993, Lincoln's Inn, BA (Hons),
LLM (Virginia)

Branson *David John*
Middlesbrough College, Roman Road,
Middlesbrough TS5 5PJ, 01642 333333, Fax:
01642 333310, Lecturer. Called: July 1992,
Middle Temple, BA (Hons) (Camb), LLB
(Hons) (Lond)

Brantingham *Leslie Andrew*
Called: Mar 1998, Gray's Inn, BSc
(Loughborough), MSc

Brassil *Michael Joseph*
Trainee Legal Adviser, Derbyshire
Magistrates' Court, Westbank House, Albion
Road, Chesterfield. Called: Nov 1994, Gray's
Inn, LLB

Braune *Mrs Janet Valerie* ●
Called: May 1980, Gray's Inn

Braviner *Stephen Thomas* ●
Legal Adviser, Department of the
Environment, Transport and the Regions,
Great Minster House, 76 Marsham Street,
London SW1, 0171 271 4458, Fax: 0171 271
4462. Called: Oct 1992, Gray's Inn, BA

Brawn *Daniel Hugh* ●
Assistant Lawyer, Peter Kerrigan Associates,
4 Abbots Quay, Monks Ferry, Birkenhead,
Merseyside L41 5LH, 0151 647 8862.
Called: Oct 1996, Gray's Inn, BA (Manc), BA
(Greenwich)

Bray *Alan Hornby*
4th Floor, South Flat, 2 Garden Court,
Temple, London EC4Y 9BL, 0171 353 3437.
Called: June 1934, Middle Temple, MA
(Oxon)

Bray-Deacon *Terence Philip*
Called: Nov 1975, Middle Temple, LL.B.,
LL.M.

Brazier *Martin* •
Commercial Director, Jarvis PLC, Best
House, Grange Business Park, Enderby
Road, Whetstone, Leicester LE8 6EP, 0116
278 0808. Called: Nov 1997, Middle
Temple, BSc (Hons)

Breckon *Miss Carolyn Constance*
Court Clerk. Called: Oct 1992, Gray's Inn,
LL.B

Brenan *George Patrick*
Called: Nov 1994, Gray's Inn, BA, MSc

Brennan *Christopher John*
Called: Oct 1996, Middle Temple, LLB
(Hons)(Lond)

Brennan *John*
6 Park Square, Leeds, LS1 2LW. Called: Nov
1973, Lincoln's Inn, LLB (Lond)

Brennan *Dr John Lester*
16 Butterfield Road, Wheathampstead, Herts
AL4 8PU, 01582 832230. Called: July 1971,
Middle Temple, MD, MRCP, FRCPath, LLM

Brennan *Michael Barry* •
Manager, Trading Legal Service, Citibank,
N.A., 336 Strand, London Ec2R 1HB, 0171
500 0027. Called: Nov 1996, Lincoln's Inn,
LLB (Hons)(Dublin)

Brereton *Miss Anita Helen*
The British Occupational, Health Research
Foundation, at Whitbread PLC, 52 Chiswell
Street, London EC1Y 4SD. Called: July 1979,
Gray's Inn, BSc

Breslin *Miss Brigid Claire*
Called: Nov 1995, Inner Temple, LLB
(Soton)

Brett-Holt *Ms Alexis Fayrer* •
Director of Legal Services, Department of
Trade & Industry, Room 309, 10 Victoria
Street, London SW1H 0NN, 0171 215 3247,
Fax: 0171 215 3248. Called: July 1973,
Lincoln's Inn, BA Hons (Oxon)

Brew *Richard Maddock CBE,DL*
The Abbey, Coggeshall, Essex CO6 1RD,
01376 561246, Fax: 01376 562773.
Called: June 1956, Inner Temple, BA
[Cantab]

Brewer *David Leonard*
Justices Clerk, Swindon Magistrates' Court,
Princes Street, Swindon, Wiltshire SN1 2JB,
01793 527281, Fax: 01793 488525.
Called: July 1976, Gray's Inn

Brewer *Miss Imogen Melanie Fleur*
27 Hortensia House, Hortensia Road,
London SW10 0QP, 0171 351 5306, and
Member New York Bar. Called: Nov 1994,
Middle Temple, LLB (Hons)

Brewis *Mark*
Senior Common Room, Ranmoor House,
University of Sheffield, Shore Lane,
Sheffield, 0114 2663165. Called: Oct 1993,
Lincoln's Inn, LLB (Hons)(Sheff)

Brewster *David John* •
Director, Legal & Policy, IMRO, Lloyds
Chambers, 1 Portsoken Street, London
E1 8BT, 0171 390 5000, Fax: 0171 480
5861. Called: June 1961, Gray's Inn, MA
(Cantab)

Bridge *Mrs Anabelle Jane*
Le Haugard, La Ville de l'Eglise, St Ouen,
Jersey JE3 2LR, 01534 482671, Fax: 01534
481675. Called: Nov 1981, Gray's Inn, LLB
(Nott'm)

Bridge *Mark David*
Professor of Taxation, University of Victoria,
Canada, 3395 Cadboro Bay Road, Victoria,
BC, Canada V8R 5K4, 604-592 9457, and
Member British Columbia. Called: July 1992,
Lincoln's Inn, LLB (Canada), BSc (Canada),
LLM (Lond)

Bridge *Maximilian Paul Martin*
Called: Nov 1997, Middle Temple, LLB
(Hons)

Bridgeford *William Andrew Macrae*
Crills, 44 The Esplanade, St Helier, Jersey,
Channel Islands, 01534 873521, Advocate of
the Royal Court of Jersey. Called: July 1986,
Middle Temple, LLB (Dundee) MPhil,
(Cantab)

Bridger *Henry Chris*
62 Baring Road, Hengistbury, Bournemouth
BH6 4DT, 01202 421050. Called: July 1967,
Inner Temple, BCom, BCL, FCIS

Bridges *Mrs Clare Jane*
Deputy Clerk to the Justices, The
Magistrate's Court, Barclay Road, Croydon,
Surrey CR9 3NG, 0181 686 8680, Fax: 0181
680 9801. Called: Oct 1992, Middle Temple,
B.Sc (Hons, Dunelm)

Bridges *Dr Paul William* •
Dept of Health & Social, Security, New
Court, 48 Carey Street, London WC2A 2LS.
Called: July 1984, Gray's Inn, BA, Ph.D

Briggs *Mark Edward*
Court Clerk, Stockport Magistrates Court,
PO Box 155, Court House, Edward Street,
Stockport SK1 3NF, 0161 477 2020, Fax:
0161 474 1115. Called: July 1982, Inner
Temple, BA

Briggs *Timothy Roy*
Herbert Smith, Exchange House, Primrose
Street, London EC2A 2HS, 0171 466 2506,
Fax: 0171 496 0043. Called: Oct 1995,
Middle Temple, BA (Hons)

Brighton *Miss Pamela Dallas*
14 Tooks Court, Cursitor St, London, EC4A
1LB. Called: Nov 1986, Gray's Inn,
B.Sc(Econ) Dip Law

Bristol *Anthony Fitzgerald Le Varrie*
Called: Oct 1997, Gray's Inn, BSc (West
Indies)

Bristol *James Anthony Louis*
Chairman, Air Transport & Licensing Board,
Henry, Henry & Bristol, P.O.Box 386, St.
Georges, Grenada, 809 440 2500/2809, Fax:
809 440 4128, and Member Grenada,
Trinidad & Tobago, St Lucia, Barbados.
Called: July 1989, Middle Temple, LLB

Bristow *Miss Clare* •
Commercial & Legal Adviser, HVCA, Esca
House, Palace Court, London W2 4JG, 0171
229 2488, Fax: 0171 727 9268. Called: Oct
1996, Lincoln's Inn, LLB (Hons)(Leeds), MA
(Leeds)

Britton *His Honour Judge Ian Robert*
District Judge, The Law Courts, Harbour
Road, Wan Chai, 5824106, Formerly a
Solicitor admitted 1965. Called: May 1977,
Inner Temple

Britton *James Robert*
Called: Nov 1996, Inner Temple, LLB
(So'ton)

Broadbent *Keith* •
Justices' Chief Executive for West
Glamorgan. Training Officer for Justices and
Staff Secretary to the Lord Chancellor's
Advisory Committee, West Glam Magistrates
Cts Comm, Magistrates' Court, Cramic Way,
Port Talbot SA13 1RU, 01639 896718, Fax:
01639 893855. Called: Nov 1965, Gray's Inn

Broadberry *Miss Alison Lesley
Caroline* •
Financial Planning Manager, Sun Life
Technical Services, Ltd, 100 Borough High
Street, London SE1 1LD. Called: Oct 1991,
Lincoln's Inn, BA (Hons), ATT, TEP, ACII

Broadley *Clive*
Called: Nov 1982, Middle Temple, LLB
(Nott'm)

Broadway *Dennis*
87 Newdigate Road, Watnall, Nottingham
NG16 1HN, 0115 945 9097. Called: Oct
1993, Inner Temple, LLB

Brock *Mrs (Patricia) Ann*
Called: Nov 1969, Gray's Inn

Brock *Miss Carolyn Anne* •
Commercial Lawyer, British
Telecommunications PLC, C3004, Westside,
London Road, Hemel Hempstead HP3 9YF,
01442 296097. Called: July 1987, Lincoln's
Inn, LLB

Brock *Richard Selig Joseph*
Called: July 1957, Inner Temple, MA (Oxon)

Brockway *Stephen Peter* •
Legal Advisor to the Housing Corporation,
The Housing Corporation, 149 Tottenham
Court Road, London W1P 0BN, 0171 393
2107, Fax: 0171 393 2111. Called: July
1985, Lincoln's Inn, BA (Hons)

Broder *Milton Joseph*
Called: Nov 1993, Middle Temple, BA
(Hons), MA, CPE

Brodie *Philip Hope*
Part Time Chairman, Medical Appeal
Tribunal, Advocates Library, Parliament
House, Edinburgh, Scotland EH1 1RF, 031
226 5071, Fax: 031 225 3642, Scottish
Advocate Queens Counsel, Scotland.
Called: Nov 1991, Lincoln's Inn, LLB (Hons)
(Edin), LLM Virginia

Brohi *Miss Saleema Kate*
Cameron McKenna, Sceptre Court, Tower Hill, London EC3N 4BB, 0171 367 3000, Fax: 0171 367 2000. Called: Feb 1995, Lincoln's Inn, LLB (Hons)(Lond)

Bromley-Challenor *James Roland*
170 Holland Park Avenue, London W11 4UH, 0171 610 5416. Called: May 1988, Inner Temple, LLB (Bristol)

Brooke *Miss Abigail*
Legal Advisor. Called: Oct 1995, Middle Temple, LLB (Hons)

Brooke *Nicholas Mark*
Called: Nov 1991, Inner Temple, BSc (Bristol), Dip Law

Brookes *Miss Melanie*
Called: Oct 1995, Gray's Inn, LLB, BA (Leeds)

Brooks *David Michael William*
Called: Nov 1977, Middle Temple

Brooks *Mrs Karen Anne* •
Senior Crown Prosecutor, Crown Prosecution Service, 8th Floor, Sunlight House, Quay Street, Manchester M60 3LU, 0161 837 7402, Fax: 0161 835 2663. Called: July 1983, Middle Temple, LLB (Manch)

Brooks *Miss Sarah Anne* •
Crown Prosecutor, Crown Prosecution Service, Princes Court, 34 York Road, Leicester LE1 5TU. Called: Nov 1985, Middle Temple, Dip Mag Law

Brooks *Miss Shelagh* •
Legal Counsellor, Foreign & Commonwealth Office, King Charles Street, London SW1, and Member Hong Kong Bar. Called: Nov 1978, Inner Temple, MA (Oxon), BCL(Oxon), Licence en Droit, European, Universite, Libre de Bruselles

Brookwell *Paul* •
Crown Prosecutor, Crown Prosecution Service, 1st Floor, Redrose House, Lancaster Road, Preston, Lancashire PO1 1DH, 01772 555015. Called: Feb 1985, Middle Temple, BA

Brosnan *Mrs Teresa Sook Hian* •
Legal Adviser, The British Petroleum Co plc, Legal Group, Britannic House, 1 Finsbury Circus, London EC2M 7BA, 0171 496 4000. Called: Nov 1983, Gray's Inn, B.S.Sc (Hons)

Brotherton *Matthew Sean de la Haye Browne*
Former Solicitor. Called: July 1995, Lincoln's Inn, MA (Cantab), PGCE

Brough *Philip*
The Potters, Abernant, Aberdare, Mid Glamorgan CF44 0ST, 01685 874320. Called: May 1977, Gray's Inn

Brough *Simon*
Senior Court Clerk, Sheffield Magistrates' Court, Castle Street, Sheffield S3 8LU, 0114 276 0760, Fax: 0114 272 0129. Called: May 1987, Gray's Inn, B.A.

Brown *Miss Angela Adorkor* •
First Interstate, Bank of California, 6 Agar Street, London WC2H 4HN, 0171 836 3560. Called: July 1984, Middle Temple, LLB, LLM

Brown *Anthony Roger Ernest* •
Company Secretary, T R Brown & Sons, 54-62 Clouds Hill Road, St George, Bristol BS5 7LB, 0117 955 7441, Fax: 0117 941 3068. Called: July 1978, Lincoln's Inn, BA (Cantab), MA (Cantab), ACIS

Brown *Mrs Caroline Louise*
Called: May 1997, Lincoln's Inn, LLB (Hons), MSc (Econ)

Brown *Mrs Elaine Maude* •
Lawyer (Grade 7), The Public Trust Office, Stewart House, 24 Kingsway, London WC2B 6JX, 0171 269 7121. Called: July 1983, Middle Temple, LLM (Lond), LLB (Lond)

Brown *Eric Crichton*
Advocate's Library, Parliment House, Edinburgh, Scotland EH1 1RF, 0131 226 5071, Fax: 0131 225 3642, and Member Scottish Bar. Called: Nov 1990, Lincoln's Inn, LLB (Hons) (Edin)

Brown *George Gordon*
Called: Nov 1966, Inner Temple

Brown *Mrs Grace Kwee-Yoke*
Called: Nov 1993, Middle Temple, LLB (Hons)(Lond)

Brown *Graham* •
Chief Crown Prosecutor, Crown Prosecution Service, 7th Floor South, Royal Liver BuildinG, Liverpool L3 1HN, 0151 236 7575, Fax: 0151 255 0642. Called: Nov 1982, Gray's Inn, BA

Brown *Ian Davis* •
Called: Nov 1987, Middle Temple, M.Phil, MA (Oxon), Dip Law

Brown *Ian Keith Rae* •
Senior Legal Adviser, Shell International, Legal Services, Shell Centre SE1 7NA, 0171 934 6133, Fax: 0171 934 7043. Called: Nov 1971, Middle Temple

Brown *Miss Joanna Diana*
Called: Nov 1990, Inner Temple, BSc (Cardiff)

Brown *Miss Juliette Kathrine* •
Buisiness Development Manager, Aqumen Services Limited, 127 Clerkenwell Road, London, 0171 405 2211, Fax: 0171 405 3344. Called: Nov 1995, Lincoln's Inn, BSc (Hons), Dip Law

Brown *Keith William*
Justices Chief Executive, Windsor House, Spitfire close, Ermine Business Park, Huntingdon PE18 6XY, 01480 414455, Fax: 01480 414499. Called: July 1980, Gray's Inn, D.M.L.

Brown *Kenneth*
Called: July 1972, Gray's Inn

Brown *Ms Mandy* •
Legal Officer, The Treasury Solicitor, Queen Anne's Chambers, 28 Broadway, London SW1, 0171 210 3148, Fax: 0171 210 3310. Called: Nov 1991, Lincoln's Inn, LLB (Hons) (Essex)

Brown *Martin Frederick John* •
Court Clerk, Stoke-on-Trent Magistrates Crt, Albert Square, Fenton, Stoke-on-Trent ST4 3BX, 01782 845353, Fax: 01782 744782. Called: Feb 1990, Gray's Inn, BA (Hons), LLM

Brown *Matthew James*
Called: Nov 1994, Middle Temple, LLB (Hons)

Brown *Miss Michelle Diane* •
Prosecutor, Crown Prosecution Service, 11a Princes Street, Stratford, 01785 223414, Fax: 01785 59132. Called: Feb 1992, Inner Temple, LLB (Hons, So'ton)

Brown *Lt Commander RN Neil Logan* •
Naval Prosecuting Officer, Naval Prosecuting Authority, HMS Nelson, Queen Street, Portsmouth PO1 3HH, 01705 727269, Fax: 01705 727189. Called: Oct 1992, Middle Temple, LLB (Hons)(Queens)

Brown *Norman Francis Graham*
Baring Asset Management Ltd, 155 Bishopsgate, London EC2M 3XY. Called: July 1981, Middle Temple, MA (Cantab)

Brown *Mrs Pauline Carol*
Called: Nov 1990, Lincoln's Inn, LLB (PCL)

Brown *Roger William*
Head of Legal Services, The Law Courts, Magistrates' Court, Bishopgate, Norwich NR3 1UP, 01603 632421, Fax: 01603 663263. Called: Nov 1975, Middle Temple, LLB (Manch)

Brown *Miss Samantha Emma Ravenhill*
Called: Oct 1995, Inner Temple, LLB (Manc)

Brown *Steven David*
Called: Oct 1994, Inner Temple, BA (Lond), MA (Reading)

Browne *Michael Brendan*
Called: May 1996, Middle Temple, BA (Hons) (York)

Browning *Miss Anna Jane*
Called: Nov 1997, Lincoln's Inn, LLB (Hons)

Browning *Colin Allister*
Called: Nov 1958, Gray's Inn, MA (Cantab)

Browning *Robert Andre* •
Legal Adviser, Sir Robert McAlpine Limited, Yorkshire House, Grosvenor Crescent, London SW1X 7EP, 0171 225 0064, Fax: 0171 838 9162. Called: Nov 1995, Gray's Inn, LLB (Hons), FRICS, ACIArb

Browning *Robert Mark* •
Consultant, 59 Pelham Street, South Kensington, London SW7 2NJ, 0171 581 8801, and Member Turks & Caicos Islands Bar. Called: Nov 1986, Inner Temple, LLB (S'hampton)

Bruce *Malcolm Gray*
House of Commons, London SW1A 0AA,
0171 219 4580, Fax: 0171 219 2334.
Called: Nov 1995, Gray's Inn, MA, MSc

Bruce *Peter Richard* •
Called: Oct 1996, Inner Temple, BSc
(Greenwich), MSc (South Bank), CPE
(Lond), FRICS, MCIOB, ACIArb

Brudenell *Miss Kim Elaine* •
Grade 7 Lawyer, Treasury Solicitor's Dept,
28 Broadway, London SW1H 9JS, 0171 210
3270. Called: Nov 1992, Inner Temple, BA
(Hons), CPE

Bruggemann *Miss Emma Hamilton*
Called: Mar 1996, Lincoln's Inn, LLB (Hons)

Brunning *Peter David*
Deputy Chief Clerk, Inner London
Magistrates', Court Committee, Magistrates
Court, Bow Street, London WC2E 7AS, 0171
379 4713, Fax: 0171 379 5634. Called: Nov
1987, Gray's Inn, BA, MA, LLB.

Brunt *Mrs Dracaena Ann*
Called: Nov 1989, Middle Temple, LLB
(Hons)

Brunton *Captain Ian Arthur Joseph*
Airline Captain/Private Law practice Rep of
Trinidad & Tobago., 6 La Boiselle Road, La
Baja, St Joseph, Trinidad, West Indies, 868-
645 5693, Fax: 868-662 4822, and Member
Trinidad & Tobago Bar Antigua Bar
Bermuda Bar. Called: July 1990, Lincoln's
Inn, LLB (Lond)

Bruton *Thomas Howard*
Called: Oct 1996, Middle Temple, BSc
(Hons)(Lond), CPE (B'ham)

Bryan *Mrs Ethna Rose*
01283 585484, Fax: 01283 585. Called: Feb
1975, Middle Temple

Bryan *Ms Niamh Myra*
Disability Rights Development Worker, The
Law Centre Federation, 3rd Floor, Arundel
Court, 177 Arundel Street, Sheffield S1 2NU,
0114 2787088, Fax: 0114 2787004.
Called: July 1986, Middle Temple, LLB
(Hons)

Bryan-Brown *Michael John*
Called: July 1996, Gray's Inn, BA (Dunelm)

Bryn Davies *Mrs Mary*
Called: Nov 1969, Middle Temple

Bryson *David Thomas* •
Senior Crown Prosecutor, Crown
Prosecution Service, Coniston House,
District 4, Washington, Tyne and Wear
NE38 7RN. Called: Nov 1979, Lincoln's Inn,
MA (Cantab)

Buchanan *Angus*
Court Clerk, Inner London Magistrates',
Courts Service, 3rd Floor, North West Wing,
Bush House, Aldwych, London WC2.
Called: July 1979, Gray's Inn

Buchanan *Mrs Charissa Siew-Fong*
Messrs Rodyk & Davidson, 9 Raffles Place
[H]55-01, Republic Plaza, Singapore 048619,
(65) 5399247/22552626, Fax: (65) 2251838
& 2257511, and Member Singapore Bar.
Called: July 1993, Inner Temple, LLB
(Hons)(Notts)

Buchanan *Mark Philip*
Called: Nov 1991, Inner Temple, LLB

Buckenham *Giles Edward* •
Legal Adviser, D.T.I., 10 Victoria Street,
London SW1H 0NN, 0171 215 3184, Fax:
0171 215 3235. Called: Feb 1995, Lincoln's
Inn, BA (Hons)(Warw)

Buckhurst *Brian Alfred*
Justices Chief Executive and Clerk to the
Justices, Somerset Magistrates' Cts Comm,
The Court House, Northgate, Bridgwater,
Somerset TA6 3EU, 01278 452182, Fax:
01278 453667. Called: July 1975, Gray's Inn,
BA (Wales)

Buckingham *Miss Lise Merie*
Court Clerk. Called: Feb 1992, Gray's Inn,
LLB

Buckingham *Paul Richard*
Clifford Chance Solicitors, 200 Aldersgate
Street, London EC1A 4JJ, 0171 600 1000,
Fax: 0171 282 7000. Called: Nov 1995,
Middle Temple, BSc (Hons), CEng,
MIChemE

Buckingham *Stewart John*
Called: Nov 1996, Middle Temple, BA
(Hons), BCL

Buckland *Miss Alexandra Elizabeth Mary*
Called: Oct 1996, Inner Temple, LLB (Leic)

Buckley *James Rice Kempthorne*
Flat 10, 89 Onslow Square, London
SW7 3LT, 0171 584 8436. Called: Feb 1952,
Middle Temple, MA, LLB

Buckman *Mrs Akosua Asaa*
Research Officer, Industrial Relations
Services, Limited, 18-20 Highbury Place,
London N5 1QP. Called: July 1986, Lincoln's
Inn, LLB (Ghana), DipLaw

Bucknell *Patrick John*
Called: June 1956, Inner Temple, MA
(Cantab)

Buckrell *Jonathan Mark*
Called: Nov 1995, Inner Temple, BA
(Cantab), CPE

Bucksey *Nicholas Richard*
Called: July 1995, Inner Temple, LLB

Buckwell *William Dominic Heymanson*
Solicitor Advocate, Holman Fenwick &
Willan, Marlow House, Lloyds Avenue,
London EC3N 3AL, 0171 488 2300, Fax:
0171 481 0316. Called: Oct 1993, Middle
Temple, BA (Hons)

Budd *Bernard Wilfred* QC (1969)
Highlands, Elham, Canterbury, Kent
CT4 6UG, (01303) 840350, Also Inn of
Court M (1968). Called: July 1952, Gray's
Inn, MA (Cantab)

Budd *Dr Jeremy David*
Called: Oct 1996, Inner Temple, MA
(Cantab), CPE (Oxon)

Budden *Dr Ian*
Director of Estates & Legal Affairs,
University of London, University of London,
Senate House, Malet Street, London
WC1E 7HU, 0171 636 8000, Fax: 0171 255
2171. Called: July 1993, Middle Temple, MA,
Ph.D, LLB

Bueno *Miss Nicola Anna Christina* •
Kleinwort Benson, 10 Fenchurch Street,
London EC3M 3LB, 0171 956 6066.
Called: Nov 1990, Middle Temple, LLB (Bris)

Bugeja *Albert John* •
Head of Legal Services, Rochford District
Council, Council Offices, South St,
Rochford, Essex SS4 1BW, 01702 546366,
Fax: 01702 545737. Called: Nov 1981,
Lincoln's Inn, BA Hons

Bukhari *Syed Mustafa Ali*
Called: July 1997, Lincoln's Inn, LLB
(Hons)(Lond)

Bulbeck *Miss Nicola Jane* •
Grade 6 HQ Prosecutor, Crown Prosecution
Service, C/O 50 Ludgate Hill, LondoN
EC4M 7EX. Called: July 1983, Inner Temple,
LLB (Leeds)

Bulgin *Kenneth Arthur*
Called: Nov 1980, Lincoln's Inn, MA (Oxon),
FCII, ATII

Bull *Cavinder*
Drew & Napier, 20 Raffles Place, Ocean
Towers [H]17-00, (65) 535 0733, Fax: (65)
532 7149, and Member Singapore Bar, New
York. Called: July 1993, Gray's Inn, BA
(Oxon), LLM (Harv)

Bull *Colin Reginald*
Called: July 1966, Gray's Inn

Bullas *Justin Adrian*
Called: Oct 1996, Middle Temple, LLB
(Hons) (Bucks), LLM (Sheff)

Bulleid *Michael Leonard John*
Also Inn of Court G and Member Hong
Kong Bar. Called: July 1973, Inner Temple,
LLB(Lond)

Bullimore *Timothy Michael Duncan*
Former Solicitor. Called: Feb 1995, Inner
Temple, BA (Cantab)

Bunker *Mrs Barbara Reece*
Called: Nov 1960, Inner Temple, LLB (Lond)

Bunting *Michael Robert Daniel*
Temple Chambers, 16th Floor, 1 Pacific
Place, 88 Queensway, 5-2 32003, Fax: 5-8
400711, and Member Hong Kong Bar Falcon
Chambers, Falcon Court, London, EC4Y
1AA. Called: Nov 1972, Middle Temple, MA
(Oxon)

Bunton *John*
3rd Floor Flat, 4 Stone Bldgs, Lincoln's Inn,
London WC2A 3XT, 0171 242 7971.
Called: Nov 1952, Lincoln's Inn, MA
(Cantab), C.Eng, FIEE, C.Phys, F.inst P.

E

Burch *Miss Rosalyn*
Called: Oct 1997, Middle Temple, BA (Hons)(Keele)

Burchill *David Jeremy Michael* ●
Company Secretary Compliance Officer Legal Adviser, M & G Group plc, 7th Floor, 3 Minster Court, Gt Tower Street, London EC3R 7XH, 0171 621 8904, Fax: 0171 621 8860, Also Inn of Court N.Ireland. Called: May 1983, Gray's Inn, LL.B(Belfast)

Burdess *Andrew George*
Called: Mar 1996, Lincoln's Inn, B.Ed (Hons)

Burge *Miss Natalie Heidi*
Flat 2, 42 Clanricarde Gardens, London W2 4JW, 0171 727 8938. Called: Nov 1994, Inner Temple, BA (Oxon), CPE (Lond)

Burger *Schalk Frederick*
Practising Advocate, South Africa, Botswana & Namibia, 621 Innes Chambers, Pritchard Street, Johannesburg, 11-333 8903, Fax: 11-333 0626, and Member Johannesburg Bar; Senior Counsel Cape Town; Senior Counsel. Called: Feb 1990, Lincoln's Inn, B.Comm, LLB, (Stellenbosch), LLM (Lond)

Burgess *Brian Neil* ●
Senior Crown Prosecutor, Crown Prosecution Service, Sceptre House, Luton, Bedfordshire LU1 3AJ, 015821 404808. Called: July 1989, Lincoln's Inn, BA (Warw)

Burgess *David Brian* ●
Senior Crown Prosecutor, Crown Prosecution Service, Hawkins House, Pynes Hill, Rydon Lane, Exeter,Devon EX2 5SS. Called: Nov 1989, Inner Temple, LLB

Burgess *Keith John* ●
Group Company Secretary, Queens Moat Houses Plc, Queens Court, 9-17 Eastern Road, Romford, Essex RM1 3NG, 01708 730522, Fax: 01708 734848. Called: Nov 1977, Inner Temple, BA [Bus Law], FCIS

Burke *Miss Andrea Faith*
Called: Oct 1994, Lincoln's Inn, LLB (Hons)(Sheff)

Burke *Mrs Catherine Lucy* ●
ICI Chemicals & Polymers Ltd, P O Box 90, Wilton, Middlesborough TS6 8JE, 01642 454144, Fax: 01642 432971. Called: Nov 1990, Lincoln's Inn, LLB (Sheff)

Burke *Christopher Michael* ●
HM Customs & Excise, New King's Beam House, 22 Upper Ground, London SE1 9PJ, 0171 865 5138, Fax: 0171 865 5822. Called: July 1985, Inner Temple, BA, Dip Law

Burke *James David*
Called: Oct 1996, Middle Temple, BA (Hons)(Lond), CPE

Burke *John Stewart*
Called: Oct 1994, Gray's Inn, BA

Burke *Malachy Columba*
Called: Nov 1997, Inner Temple, LLB (Lond), BEng, (South Bank)

Burke *Miss Rosalie Elizabeth*
Called: Nov 1995, Lincoln's Inn, BA (Hons)

Burke *Miss Vanessa Samantha* ●
Principal Legal Officer, Room 439B, New Court, 48 Carey Street, London WC2. Called: Nov 1989, Lincoln's Inn, LLB

Burke-Gaffney *John Campion Anthony*
94 Copse Hill, London SW20. Called: Feb 1956, Gray's Inn

Burkill *John Ernest*
Senior Deputy Chief Clerk, Inner London Magistrates', Courts Service, 65 Romney Street, London SW1P 3RD. Called: July 1976, Gray's Inn, LLB

Burling *Julian Michael* ●
Counsel to Lloyds, Corporation of Lloyds, 51 Lime Street, London EC3M 7HA, 0171 327 5601/327 1000, Fax: 0171 327 5414, Also Inn of Court G. Called: July 1976, Middle Temple, MA,LLB [Cantab]

Burman *Keith William S.B.St.J*
Senior Deputy Chief Clerk Inner London Mag's Court Service. Called: Nov 1984, Middle Temple, Dip Mag Law

Burn *Nicholas George Orwin* ●
Principal Crown Prosecutor, Crown Prosecution Service, (Midlands), 11a Princes Street, Stafford ST17 9UQ, 01785 223423. Called: July 1982, Gray's Inn, BA (Hons)

Burnett *Miss Alice Margaret* ●
Assistant Legal Adviser to H M Diplomatic Service., Foreign & Commonwealth Office, London SW1A 2AH, 0171 270 3283, Fax: 0171 270 2767. Called: Oct 1991, Middle Temple, BA Hons (Cantab), MA

Burnett *John Wyndham MBE*
Grafton, Albury, Nr Guildford, Surrey GU5 9AE. Called: July 1962, Middle Temple, LLB

Burnett Rae *Jeremy Alexander James Fraser* ●
Legal Director, Fax: 0171 626 1184. Called: Nov 1977, Middle Temple, MA (Oxon), MSI

Burney *Ali Hasan*
Called: Nov 1997, Lincoln's Inn, BA (Hons)(Tennessee)

Burney *Miss Margaret Mitchell*
Principal Court Clerk, Victoria Law Courts, Corporation Street, Birmingham, 0121 212 6655. Called: Nov 1986, Gray's Inn, DML

Burnham *James Pitt* ●
Prosecution Team Leader (West Berks), Crown Prosecution Service, Eaton Court, 112 Oxford Road, Reading, Berkshire, 0118 9503771, Fax: 0118 9508192. Called: July 1984, Gray's Inn, LLB (Reading)

Burns *Miss Lorna Marie* ●
Principal Crown Prosecutor, Crown Prosecution Service, The Cooperage, 8 Gainsford Street, London SE1 2NG. Called: Nov 1986, Inner Temple, LLB (Leic)

Burns *Miss Rebecca Jane Katherine*
Called: Nov 1991, Lincoln's Inn, LLB (Hons)

Burrell *Michael John*
Also Inn of Court G. Called: Feb 1965, Inner Temple, MA (Cantab)

Burrell *The Hon Mr Justice Michael Peter*
District Court Judge 1991 High Court Judge 1995 (HK), Supreme Court, Queensway, Hong Kong, 28254316, Fax: 28495494, and Member Hong Kong Bar. Called: July 1971, Inner Temple, MA (Cantab)

Burrell *Mrs Sarah Maureen Rose* ●
Regulatory Legal Affairs, BBC WHite Cite, London W12 7TS, 0181 752 4149. Called: Oct 1990, Lincoln's Inn, LLB (Lond)

Burridge *Roger Henry Moore*
Senior Lecturer, University of Warwick, School of Law, University of Warwick, Coventry CV4 7AL, 01203 523094, Fax: 01203 524105. Called: Feb 1973, Gray's Inn, LLB

Burriss *Rhys*
0191 383 1641, Member Institute of Management. Called: May 1979, Gray's Inn, BA (Oxon), Dip Uni Lisbon

Burrows *Mrs Carol Jane*
Senior Legal Adviser, Justices' Clerks Office, The Court House, South Walls, Stafford, Staffs ST16 3DW, 01785 223144. Called: Apr 1989, Gray's Inn, LLB

Burrows *Christon Jon* ●
Legal Adviser, Axa Equity & Law, Victory House, Prospect Hill, Douglas IM1 1QP, 01624 683683. Called: July 1996, Middle Temple, BA (Hons)(Lond), Dip in Law, ACII

Burrows *Dr Fred CMG*
Called: June 1950, Gray's Inn, MA (Cantab), PhD

Burrows *Nicholas James*
Called: Nov 1997, Inner Temple, MA (St Andrews)

Burrows *Miss Tameka Shevone*
Attorney at Law, Attorney Generals Office, P.O.Box N3007, Nassau N.P., and Member Bahamas. Called: July 1997, Middle Temple, LLB (Hons)

Burt *Arthur Norman*
Pen-y-Bryn Farm, Ffordd y Blaenau, Treuddyn, Mold, Flintshire CH7 4NS, 01352 770473. Called: June 1953, Lincoln's Inn, LLB

Burton *Miss Denise Patricia*
Called: Apr 1989, Gray's Inn, LLB (B'ham), FCIS

Burton *John*
Called: Nov 1979, Gray's Inn

Burton *Dr John David Keith CBE*
Coroner of the Queen's Household, HM Coroner for West London, The Coroners Court, Western District, 25 Bagleys Lane, London SW6 2QA, 0171 371 9938. Called: June 1964, Middle Temple, MB, MRCS, FFA, RCS,

● Barristers in employment

Burton *Ralph Dennis*
Graham Miller Carvallo SA, Argentina, Av Cordoba 836 (Office 1304), (1054) Buenos Aires, Argentina, 00 54 1 393 3209/6539, Fax: 00 54 1 393 6242. Called: Nov 1985, Inner Temple, BA (Oxon)

Burton *Raymond* •
Solicitor's Office, Dept Of Trade and Industry, 10-18 Victoria Street, London SW1H 0NN. Called: Nov 1968, Gray's Inn

Burton *Dr Rosemary Ann*
Deputy Coroner - W. London, 7 Orchard Rise, Richmond, Surrey TW10 5BX, 0181 876 5386. Called: July 1971, Middle Temple, MB, BS, MRCS, LRCP, DA

Bury *Miss Claire Louise*
Member of the Legal Service of the European Commission, Rue de la Loi 200, 1040 Brussels, 00 32 2 296 0499, Fax: 00 32 2 295 2483. Called: July 1988, Middle Temple, LLB (Hons) (Lond)

Bush *Miss Rosalind Hilary*
Assistant Recorder. Called: Nov 1978, Gray's Inn, LLB(B'ham)

Bushell *Jonathan David* •
Senior Crown Prosecutor, Crown Prosecution Service, Cambria House, Merthyr Tydfil Industrial Prk, Pentrebach, Metrthyr Tydfil, Mid Glam CF48 4XA, 01443 693240, Fax: 01443 692965. Called: July 1990, Lincoln's Inn, MA (Oxon)

Bushnell *David Edward* •
Legal Advisor, 5 Bodenham Road, Folkestone, Kent CT20 2NU, 01303 255803. Called: May 1953, Middle Temple

Butcher *Anthony John* QC (1977)
Recorder, 1 Atkin Building, Gray's Inn, London, WC1R 5AT. Called: Feb 1957, Gray's Inn, MA (Cantab), LLB

Butcher *Michael* •
General Counsel to General Utilities PLC. Director of Central Railway PLC. General Secretary of the Franco-British Lawyers Society Ltd. Consultant to Reynolds Porter Chamberlain, & to Tripler & Associes. Director; Leigh Interests plc, General Utilities PLC, 37-41 Old Queen Street, Westminster, London SW1H 9JA, 0171 393 2700, Fax: 0171 222 2376, Member of Commercial Panel of American Arbitration Assoc.. Called: July 1975, Gray's Inn, BA Hons (Keele)

Butler *Adam Michael*
Called: Oct 1997, Lincoln's Inn, LLB (Hons)(Manc)

Butler *Miss Anne Kathleen*
Lawyer Special Casework (Retired), and Member Southern Ireland Bar Nigerian Bar. Called: July 1972, Gray's Inn, MA, LLB, B Comm

Butler *Miss Bernadette Mae Evelyn*
Called: July 1995, Lincoln's Inn, LLB (Hons)

Butler *Miss Brenda Mary* •
"PRIVATE & CONFIDENTIAL", Legal & Contracts Adviser, c/o Talisman Energy (UK) Ltd, Belmont House, 1 Berry Street, Aberdeen AB1 1DL, 01224 413200, Fax: 01224 413450. Called: Nov 1992, Gray's Inn, LLB (Buckingham), LLM (Buckingham)

Butler *Miss Frances Helen*
Called: Nov 1975, Lincoln's Inn

Butler *Miss Jacinda Pomona*
Called: Nov 1995, Gray's Inn, LLB (Lond)

Butler *John Spencer*
Consultant, Messrs Barlow Lyle & Gilbert, Beaufort House, 15 St Botolph Street, London EC3A 7NJ, 0171 247 2277, Fax: 0171 782 8500. Called: Feb 1963, Lincoln's Inn, LLB (Lond)

Butler *Miss Judith Lynne*
Called: Oct 1997, Middle Temple, BA (Hons)(Oxon)

Butler *Mark*
Martin Murray & Associates, 138 High Street, Yiewsley, Middlesex UB7 7BD, 01895 431332, Fax: 01895 448343. Called: Oct 1995, Middle Temple, LLB (Hons)

Butler *Miss Megan Veronica*
7th Floor, London Stock Exchange Limited, Old Broad Street, London EC2N 1HP. Called: July 1987, Inner Temple, LLB (Sheff)

Butler *Truman Kirkland*
Called: July 1996, Middle Temple, LLB (Hons)(Wolves)

Butt *Naeem*
32 Onslow Gardens, London SW7 3AH, and Member Lahore Bar. Called: Nov 1966, Lincoln's Inn, BA

Butt *Ms Saiqa Jamil*
Local Government Officer. Called: Feb 1991, Middle Temple, LLB

Butt *Zahur-Ud-Din*
9a High Street, Southall, Middlesex UB1 3HA, 0181 574 1119/571 6264, Fax: 0181 571 6132, High Court, Punjab, Pakistan. Called: Nov 1959, Lincoln's Inn, BA

Butter *Timothy* •
Senior Crown Prosecutor, CPS (Inner London), 1st Floor, The Cooperage, Gainsford Street, London SE1 2NE, 0171 962 2605, Fax: 0171 962 0906. Called: Oct 1991, Inner Temple, BA (Warw), MSc (Lond), Dip Law

Butterfield *Charles Harris*
QC Singapore 1952. Called: June 1934, Middle Temple, MA

Butterfield *Cleveland Michael Geoffrey*
Called: Nov 1954, Gray's Inn, MA (Cantab) LLM, (Cantab)

Butterfield *Toby Michael John*
Secretary, Cemorc Ltd, Kay Collyer & Boose LLP, One Dag Hammarskjold Plaza, New York, NY 10017-2299, USA, (212) 940 8369, Fax: (212) 755 0921, and Member New York. Called: July 1989, Lincoln's Inn, BA (Oxon), LLM (Int'l)

Butterworth *Adrian Ernest*
Financial Regulatory Group, DIBB Lupton, Alsop Solicitors 125 London Wall, London, EC2Y 5AE, 98 Whitley Close, Stanwell Village, Middlesex TW19 7EY, 0171 814 6177. Called: Nov 1995, Middle Temple, BA (Hons)(Hull), ACIS

Butterworth *Mrs Barbara Susan*
Legal Adviser. Company Secretary, Janssen Cilag Limited, P O Box 79, Saunderton, High Wycombe, Bucks HP14 4HJ, 01494 567567, Fax: 01494 567568. Called: July 1989, Lincoln's Inn, BA (York), Grad ICSA, LLB

Butterworth *Miss Pamela*
Called: Nov 1995, Middle Temple, LLB (Hons)(Dundee)

Buttery *Miss Alison Tracey*
Assistant Company Secretary, Millenium Place, 2 Swiftfields, Welwyn Garden City, Herts AL1 1HP, 01707 288000, Fax: 01707 288001. Called: July 1997, Lincoln's Inn, BA (Jnt Hons)(Hull), ACIS

Buttery *Miss Louise*
Called: Oct 1997, Gray's Inn, BA (Leic)

Buttler *Miss Rosalind Pamela* •
Crown Prosecutor, Crown Prosecution Service, Dale House, Dale End, Birmingham, West Midlands. Called: Feb 1987, Gray's Inn, LLB (B'ham)

Byatt *James Robert* •
Senior Crown Prosecutor, Crown Prosecution Service, King William House, 2nd Floor, Lowgate, Hull, Humberside. Called: July 1983, Gray's Inn, LLB (E Anglia), LLB (Hons)

Byford *Neville Paul*
Called: July 1987, Inner Temple, LLB (Soton)

Byng *Julian Michael Edmund*
15a Chemin Rieu, 1208 Geneva. Called: Feb 1954, Inner Temple, MA (Cantab)

Byrne *Dr John Patrick* •
Legal Advisor, Company Secretary, Company Director, 2 Sloane Terrace, London SW1X 9DQ, 0171 823 4146, Fax: 0171 823 6764. Called: Feb 1995, Lincoln's Inn, BSc (Syracuse), MBA (Lond Busn. Sch), PhD (Lond Busn. Sch), Dip in Law

Byrne *Miss Josephine Mary* •
Senior Crown Prosecutor, CPS (Highbury), Solar House, 1-9 Romford Road, London E15 4LJ, 0181 534 6601. Called: Nov 1981, Lincoln's Inn, BA (Hons) (Law)

Byrne *Miss Kathryn Anne* •
Company Secretary and Legal Adviser. Called: July 1978, Lincoln's Inn, LLB (Lond)

Byrne *Kevin Mowbray*
Head of Legal Services, The Magistrates
Court, Old Bury Road, Thetford, Norfolk
IP24 3AQ, 01842 754941, Fax: 01842
766068. Called: Nov 1983, Middle Temple,
BA (Kent)

Bywater *Andre Edward*
85 Broadmead, Tunbridge Wells, Kent
TN2 5NW, 01892 542335. Called: Oct 1993,
Middle Temple, MA (Sussex), BA (Hull), BA
(Cantab)

Cabeza *Mrs Ruth Roberta Elizabeth*
Called: Mar 1998, Middle Temple, LLB
(Hons)(Kent)

Cable *Miss Aida Anna*
Called: Oct 1995, Middle Temple, BA (Hons)

Cagan *John Wright*
Called: Oct 1997, Inner Temple, BA
(Columbia), LLB (London)

Cahalan *Michael James*
and Member Northern Ireland Bar.
Called: July 1996, Middle Temple, CPE,
B.S.Sc, M.Sc (Belfast)

Cahill *Brian Francis* •
Director, Group Legal Services, Glaxo
Wellcome Plc, Glaxo Wellcome House,
Berkeley Ave, Greenford, Middlesex
UB6 0NN, 0181 966 8752, Fax: 0181 966
8330. Called: Nov 1977, Gray's Inn, LLB

Cain *Daniel John* •
Senior Court Clerk, Ipswich Magistrates
Court, Elm Street, Ipswich, Suffolk IP1 2AP,
01473 217261, Fax: 01473 231249.
Called: Feb 1990, Inner Temple, LLB (Hons)

Cain *Oliver James*
Curtis Davis Garrard, Lancaster House,
Northumberland Close, Heathrow Airport,
Staines TW19 7LN, 0181 400 2400, Fax:
0181 400 2420. Called: Nov 1994, Lincoln's
Inn, LLB (Hons)(Sheff)

Cairncross *Neil Francis CB*
Little Grange, The Green, Olveston, Bristol
BS35 4EJ, 01454 613060. Called: June 1948,
Lincoln's Inn, MA

Cairney *Miss Lorna Elizabeth*
Called: Oct 1997, Middle Temple, BSc
(Hons), CPE

Cala *Miss Maryse Desiree Therese*
and Member Mauritius Bar. Called: Nov
1976, Lincoln's Inn, B.D Hons, MA

Calcroft *Christopher John*
Called: Oct 1996, Middle Temple, BA
(Hons), B.Arch (Manc), CPE

Caldicott *Martyn Stephen*
4 North View, Gouilon, Apergavenny,
Gwent NP7 9PW, 01873 832088.
Called: Nov 1994, Inner Temple, BSc

Caldwell *Andrew Frew*
Mitre House Chambers, Mitre House, 44
Fleet Street, London, EC4Y 1BN. Called: July
1984, Middle Temple, MA (Edinburgh) Dip.

Caldwell *Dr Helen Janet* •
Parliamentary Counsel, The Law
Commission, London, 0171 453 1207.
Called: Nov 1975, Lincoln's Inn, BA
(Cantab), D.Phil (Oxon)

Caldwell *Miss Marion Allan*
Standing Junior to the Accountant of Court,
Advocates' Library, Parliament, House,
Parliament Square, Edinburgh EH1 1RF,
0131 226 5071, Scottish Advocate.
Called: July 1991, Inner Temple, LLB
(Aberdeen), Dip Law P (Glasgow)

Callaghan *Lee Patrick* •
Legal Adviser (Senior), Albright & Wilson
PLC, Corporate Headquarters, Legal
Department, 210-222 Hagley Road West,
Oldbury, Warley, West Midlands B68 0NN,
0121 420 5361, Fax: 0121 420 5139.
Called: Feb 1988, Gray's Inn, BA, LLM, Dip
EC, Dip COMP

Callaghan *Valentine Edward*
Legal Advisor, Guillermo Golding Abogados
S.L, Bethencourt Alfonso, 33-3o, 38002
Santa Cruz De Tenerife, 24 12 85/38 40 17,
Fax: 24 25 27/37 03 78, King's Inns.
Called: Nov 1979, Lincoln's Inn, MA, BCL
(Dub), Post Grad Dip Eu Law

Callan *Miss Joan Margaret*
Called: Mar 1997, Lincoln's Inn, BCL, LLM
(Dublin)

Callaway *Ian Paul* •
Senior Crown Prosecutor, Crown
Prosecution Service, Queens House,
Guildhall Street, Folkestone, Kent.
Called: July 1987, Middle Temple, LLB
(Lond)

Callender *Jason Colin*
Callenders & Co, One Millars Court, PO Box
N-7117, Nassau, 809 322 2511, Fax: 809
326 7666, and Member Bahamas Bar (1996).
Called: July 1996, Middle Temple, LLB
(Hons)(Soton)

Callender *Sean Bradley*
P O Box N-7117, Nassau, Bahamas, (809)
322 2511, Fax: (809) 326 7666, and
Member Bahamas Bar. Called: Nov 1994,
Lincoln's Inn, LLB (Kent)

Callender Smith *Robin* •
Prosecution Team Leader, Crown
Prosecution Service, Youth Branch, The
Cooperage, Gainsford Street, London
SE1 2NG. Called: July 1977, Gray's Inn, LLB
(Lond)

Caller *Mitchell Bernard* •
Vice-President & Legal Adviser, The Chase
Manhattan Bank NA, Woolgate House,
Coleman Street, London EC2P 2HD, 0171
962 5478, Fax: 0171 962 5088. Called: July
1978, Middle Temple, BA (Oxon)

Callow *Duncan Alexander* •
House Counsel, C/O Callow's Law Limited,
24 Bourne Road, South Merstham, Surrey
RH1 3HF, 01737 645983. Called: Feb 1993,
Inner Temple, LLB

Calvert *Philip Alan* •
Director Legal Services, Sea Containers
Services Ltd, Sea Containers Hse, 20 Upper
Ground, London SE1, 0171 928 6969, Fax:
0171 401 3417, and Member New York Bar.
Called: July 1977, Middle Temple, BA

Calvert-Lee *Miss Georgina Eliza Jane*
Sonnenschein, Nath & Rosenthal, 8000
Sears Tower, Chicago, Illinois 60606, (USA)
312 876 8964, Fax: (USA) 312 876 7934.
Called: Oct 1993, Middle Temple, MA
(Hons)(Oxon), CPE (City)

Cam *David Edward* •
Group Company Secretary and Director,
Blackpool Pleasure Beach Ltd, Ocean
Boulevard, Blackpool, Lancs FY4 1EZ, 01253
341033 Ext 206, Fax: 01253 401098.
Called: May 1981, Middle Temple, BA

Cameron *Ms Jean McKillop* •
Assistant Solicitor. Called: July 1989, Inner
Temple, BA [Sheff], Dip Law, MA [Lond]

Cameron *Mrs Sarah Louise* •
D.T.I., 10-18 Victoria Street, London SW1.
Called: July 1985, Inner Temple, BA
(Cantab)

Camilletti *Peter Alfred Laurence*
Superintendent, New Scotland Yard, 0171
230 4761. Called: Feb 1989, Middle Temple,
MA (Cantab)

Camp *Mrs Caroline Helen* •
Principal Crown Prosecutor, Crown
Prosecution Service, Greenfield House, 39
Scotland Street, Sheffield S3 7DQ, 0114 291
2000. Called: July 1973, Inner Temple

Camp *The Reverend John Edward*
1 Brick Court, 1st Floor, Temple, London,
EC4Y 9BY. Called: May 1969, Inner Temple,
MA (Oxon) MTech, (Brunel)

Campbell *Alistair Peter*
Advocates Library, Parliment House,
Parliment Square, Edinburgh EH1 1RF, 0131
226 2881, QC, Scotland. Called: Apr 1991,
Inner Temple, MA (Aberdeen), LLB
(Strathclyde)

Campbell *Andrew Neil*
Called: Nov 1988, Middle Temple, BA
(Cantab)

Campbell *Charles Grigor Gordon*
45 Avenue Montaigne, 75008 Paris, 0147-23-
64-82, Fax: 0147-23-37-74, Avocat in France
and Member Paris Bar. Called: Feb 1965,
Gray's Inn, BA (Cantab), Cert Comm Mkt
Law, (Paris)

Campbell *Colin Hugh*
Called: July 1987, Lincoln's Inn, MA (Oxon),
D Phil, FCA

Campbell *Ms Elizabeth Cameron*
Called: Mar 1998, Gray's Inn, BA

Campbell *Mrs Kerry*
Called: Mar 1998, Middle Temple, BA
(Hons)(Portsmouth

Campbell *Miss Michelle Yvonne*
P.O. Box N-9180, Nassau, (809) 393 5551,
Fax: (809) 393 5116, and Member Member
of the Bar of the Commonwealth of The
Bahamas. Called: July 1996, Inner Temple,
LLB (Lond)

Campbell *Mrs Patricia Dorothy*
Deputy Clerk to the Justices, Bedfordshire
Magistrates Court, Stuart Street, Shire Hall,
Luton, Beds, 01582 402333, Fax: 01582
24852. Called: Nov 1982, Gray's Inn, Dip
Law

Campbell *Miss Susanne Allison*
Called: Oct 1995, Middle Temple, BA
(Canada)

Campion *Donald John Martin*
11 Stone Bldgs, 1st Floor, Lincoln's Inn,
London, WC2A 3TG. Called: June 1956,
Gray's Inn, MA (Cantab)

Campos *Miss Helen*
Called: July 1994, Middle Temple, LLB
(Hons)(Lond)

Campos *Miss Pamela Jennifer*
Called: Nov 1996, Middle Temple, LLB
(Hons)(Wales)

Canavan *David Douglass*
Called: Nov 1978, Gray's Inn, BA (Hons)

Candilio *Miss Maria Elena*
Called: Mar 1998, Middle Temple, BSc
(Hons)(LSE), M.Phil (Cantab), LLB, LLM
(Bucks)

Canepa *James Silvio*
Called: May 1996, Inner Temple, LLB (Lond)

Caney *Howard Bernard*
Called: May 1997, Lincoln's Inn, LLB (Hons)

Canlin *James Patrick*
Called: July 1967, Middle Temple, LLB
(Lond)

Cannell *Alfred Edward*
Called: July 1968, Gray's Inn, LLB, ACIS,
FIArb

Canner *Gordon Richard*
Acerhill, Berry Lane, Beer, East Devon
EX12 3JS, 01297 23118. Called: May 1950,
Inner Temple, MA (Cantab)

Canning *Edward* •
Senior Crown Prosecutor, Crown
Prosecution Service, Hawkins House, Pynes
Lane, Rydon Lane, Exeter, Devon EX2 5SS,
01392 422555, Fax: 01392 422111.
Called: July 1985, Lincoln's Inn, BA, LRAM,
DSA, Dip App Soc Studies

Cannon *Miss Claire Jacqueline* •
Senior Crown Prosecutor, Crown
Prosecution Service, County House, 100
New London Road, Chelmsford, Essex
CM2 0BR, 01245 252939, Fax: 01245
490476. Called: Nov 1983, Middle Temple,
LLB (Lond)

Caplan *Harold*
3 The Pennards, Sunbury on Thames
TW16 5JZ, 01932 781200, Fax: 01932
779694. Called: Nov 1955, Middle Temple,
MSc, CEng, ACII, FRAes, FCIArb

Caplin *Ian*
Called: Oct 1995, Lincoln's Inn, BA
(Hons)(Oxon)

Capon *Julius Piers* •
Crown Prosecution Service, Crown
Prosecution Service, C/O 50 Ludgate Hill,
London EC4M 7EX. Called: Nov 1990,
Lincoln's Inn, LLB (Newc)

Capp *Jonathan Charles*
High Garth, Heathwaite, Windermere,
Cumbria LA23 2DH, and Member New York
Bar California BaR. Called: Oct 1990,
Lincoln's Inn, LLB (Lond), LLM (Paris)

Capps *Deveral Carmichael*
Lecturer, University of Northumbria, at
Newcastle, Sutherland Building, Newcastle,
0191 227 3027, Fax: 0191 227 4557.
Called: Oct 1995, Inner Temple, LLB (Sheff),
LLM (Belfast)

Capstick *Robert Adrian* •
Called: Feb 1987, Gray's Inn, LLB (Lond)

Cardovillis *Ms Helen Jacqueline* •
Legal and Business Affairs Manager, British
Broadcasting Corp., Independant
Commissions, White City, 201 Wood Lane,
London W12 7TS, 0181 752 5212, Fax:
0181 752 5237. Called: Nov 1995, Inner
Temple, BA (Hons)

Cardwell *Paul Graham* •
Principal Crown Prosecutor, Crown
Prosecution Service, St John's House, Union
Street, Dudley. Called: July 1986, Inner
Temple, LLB Wolverhampton

Carey *Miss Mary Frances*
Called: Nov 1990, Lincoln's Inn, BA (Dub),
Dip Law

Carey *Paul*
Called: Nov 1995, Gray's Inn, BA

Carey-Yard *Gordon Michael* •
Principal Legal Officer, Solicitors
Department, Wellington House, New
Scotland Yard, London SW1H 0BG, 0171
230 7346. Called: Nov 1982, Gray's Inn, LLB
(Lond) (Hons)

Cargill *Miss Marie*
P O Box SS-5569, Nassau, Bahamas.
Called: Nov 1993, Gray's Inn, BA, MBA, LLB

Carins *Duncan*
Called: Mar 1996, Lincoln's Inn, BSc, LLB
(Hons)

Cariou *Marcel Robert*
Les Queux, Ruette Des Effards, Castel,
Guernsey. Called: Nov 1987, Gray's Inn,
LLB(Hons)

Carle *Peter Charles* •
Senior Crown Prosecutor, CPS (Exeter
Office), Hawkins House, Pynes Hill, Rydon
Lane, Exeter, Devon EX2 5SS DX 8363,
01392 422555, Fax: 01392 422111.
Called: Oct 1991, Gray's Inn, BA
(Hons)(Sheff)

Carne *Philip Austin*
5 Bingham Place, London W1M 3FH, 0171
486 1115, Solicitor (1943),Notary (1944)
Lincoln's Inn (1976). Called: Jan 1949,
Gray's Inn

Carpenter *Michael Charles
Lancaster* •
Legal Adviser Cabinet Office / Office of
Public Service & Science, Treasury
Solicitor's Dept, Queen Anne's Chambers,
28 Broadway, London SW1H 9JS, 0171 210
3450, Fax: 0171 210 3503. Called: July
1971, Inner Temple, MA (Oxon)

Carpenter *Richard John*
Called: July 1981, Gray's Inn, BSc

Carpenter *Miss Susan Caroline*
15 Edwardes Square, London W8 6HE, 0171
603 2987, and Member New York State Bar.
Called: Nov 1982, Middle Temple, LLB, LLM
(Lond)

Carr *Alexandria Pirie*
Called: Oct 1997, Inner Temple, LLB
(Nottingham)

Carr *Anthony Paul*
Area Justices' Clerk, Essex Magistrates
Courts Cmtte, Greenwood House, P.O.Box
3010, 91-99 New London Road, Chelmsford
CM2 0SN, 01245 346989, Fax: 01245
349058. Called: July 1976, Middle Temple,
M.A. (Cantab)

Carr *Mrs Caroline*
Jockey Club Official, The Jockey Club, 42
Portman square, London W1H 0EN, 0171
486 4921. Called: July 1976, Gray's Inn, LLB

Carr *Miss Chelon Marie*
Associate, Lennox Paton, Devonshire House,
Queens Street, P O Box N-4875, Nassau,
(809) 328 0563, Fax: (809) 328 0566, and
Member Bahamas Bar. Called: July 1996,
Lincoln's Inn, LLB (Hons)(Leeds)

Carr *Richard Charles Lascelles*
Recorder. Called: July 1963, Inner Temple,
MA (Cantab)

Carr *William Forsyth Emsley*
Called: June 1964, Inner Temple, BA
(Hons)(Cantab)

Carrier *David James*
Justices' Clerk, Norwich Magistrates' Court,
Bishopsgate, Norwich, Norfolk NR3 1UP,
01603 632421, Fax: 01603 663263.
Called: July 1980, Gray's Inn, D.M.S.

Carrington *Mrs Margaret Elaine* •
Senior Crown Prosecutor Chairman Milk &
Dairies Tribunal Eastern Region (P/t),
Crown Prosecution Service, Justinian House,
Spitfire Close, Ermine Business Park,
Huntingdon Cambs PE17 4HJ, 01480
432333, Fax: 01482 432404. Called: Nov
1970, Gray's Inn

Carrington *Mark Anthony* •
Senior Crown Prosecutor, Crown
Prosecution Service, Priory Gate, 29 Union
Street, Maidstone, Kent ME14 1PT.
Called: Oct 1991, Inner Temple, BA (Kent),
Dip Soc (Kent)

Carrolan *Adam*
Called: Oct 1996, Inner Temple, LLB
(Wales)

Carroll *Benedick James*
Called: Nov 1994, Inner Temple, LLB
(Soton)

Carroll *Mrs Janice* ●
Senior Crown Prosecutor, Crown
Prosecution Service, County House, County
Square, 100 New London Road, Chelmsford,
Essex, 01245 252939, Fax: 01245 490476.
Called: July 1987, Inner Temple, LLB (Hons)

Carroll *Professor William Alexander*
1 Paper Bldgs, Ground Floor, Temple,
London, EC4Y 7EP. Called: July 1980,
Middle Temple

Carrow *Robert Duane*
Goldstein & Philips, Embarcadero Center,
Suite 880 San Francisco, CA94111, and
Member California Bar New York Bar 33
Bedford Row, London, WC1R 4JH.
Called: Nov 1981, Middle Temple, BA
(Minnesota), JD, (Stanford)

Carruthers *Stephen Robert*
Legal Adviser, European Investment Bank,
32 Southborough Road, London E9 7EF.
Called: Nov 1981, Gray's Inn, MA (Cantab),
Licence in EEC Law, DSU (Paris II)

Carsley *Robert Clive* ●
Boulders, Beckenham Place Park,
Beckenham, Kent BR3 5BP, 0181 658 1300,
Fax: 0181 658 1300. Called: Nov 1966,
Middle Temple, MA (Oxon)

Carson *Stuart Crosbie* ●
Corporate Counsel, Irish Life International.
Called: Feb 1982, Inner Temple, LLB
(Wales), LLM (Lond)

Carter *Christopher Richard*
Called: Oct 1996, Lincoln's Inn, BA
(Hons)(Keele)

Carter *Miss Connie*
International Consultant. Called: Oct 1997,
Lincoln's Inn, LLB (Hons)(Lond)

Carter *Harold Mark* ●
Lawyer Grade 6, The Home Office, 50
Queen Anne's Gate, London SW1H 9AT.
Called: July 1984, Gray's Inn, LLB

Carter *Howard Ernest* ●
Legal Director, English Heritage, 23 Savile
Row, London W1X 1AB, 0171 973 3360.
Called: Nov 1989, Middle Temple, LLB
(Hons) (Manch), LLM

Carter *Miss Jacqueline Anne* ●
Senior Legal Adviser, Royal & Sun Alliance,
Insurance Group plc, Bartholomew Lane,
London EC2N 2AB, 0171 588 2345, Fax:
0171 826 1078. Called: Nov 1978, Inner
Temple, LLB

Carter *Mrs Janet* ●
Magistrates Principal Court Clerk, Leeds
Magistrate's Court, Westgate, Leeds LS1 3JP,
0113 2459653. Called: Feb 1992, Middle
Temple, LLB (Hons) (Lond), MIPD, DMS

Carter *Ms Melanie Catherine* ●
Legal Adviser Grade 6 Treasury Solicitor,
Health & Safety Executive, Rose Court, 2
Southwark Bridge Road, London SE1 9HS.
Called: July 1984, Middle Temple, BA

Carter *Mrs Natalie Jane* ●
Queens House, 58 Victoria Street, St Albans,
Hertfordshire AL1 3HZ, 01727 818100, Fax:
01727 851080. Called: Nov 1991, Inner
Temple, LLB

Carter *Patrick James*
Called: Feb 1994, Gray's Inn, LLB (Sheff),
ACA

Carter *Robert James*
Licensing Lawyer, Shell International B.V.,
Carel Van Bylandtlaan 30, 2501 An The
Hague, 31 (0)70 377 1822, Fax: 31 (0) 70
377 6141. Called: July 1995, Inner Temple,
BSc (Leeds), CPE (Notts)

Cartledge *Stanley*
Called: July 1957, Gray's Inn

Cartwright *Mrs Monique Ruth*
and Member Bahamas. Called: July 1994,
Lincoln's Inn, LLB (Hons, Bris), LLM (LSE)

Carvalho Gomes *Miss Ana Alexandra*
Called: Oct 1996, Middle Temple, LLB
(Hons)(Wales)

Casely-Hayford *Ms Margaret
Henrietta Augusta*
Denton Hall, 5 Chancery Lane, London
EC4A 1BU, 0171 242 1212/071 320 6136,
Fax: 0171 404 0087/071 320 6645.
Called: July 1983, Gray's Inn, BA (Hons)
(Oxon)

Casey *Miss Niamh Ann*
Called: Nov 1993, Middle Temple, BCL, LLM

Casserley *Miss Catherine*
Legal Officer at Royal National Institute for
the Blind, Royal National Institute, for the
Blind, 224 Great Portland Street, London
W1N 6AA, 0171 388 1266, Fax: 0171 388
2034. Called: Feb 1991, Gray's Inn, LLB
(Leic)

Cassidy *Dominic* ●
Legal Assistant, Securities & Investments
Board, Gavrelle House, 2-14 Bunhill Row,
London EC1Y 8RA, 0171 638 1240, Fax:
0171 382 5900. Called: Nov 1991, Lincoln's
Inn, BA (Hons) (Kent)

Cassidy *Hugh John Alexander*
35 Broadwater Down, Tunbridge Wells,
Kent TN2 5NU, 01892 532988. Called: Nov
1961, Inner Temple

Cassidy *Ian*
Called: Nov 1990, Gray's Inn, LLB

Cassidy *Mrs Linda Jean* ●
Principal Crown Prosecutor, Crown
Prosecution Service, Fox Talbot House,
Bellingham Close, Malmesbury Road,
Chippenham SN15 1BN, 01249 443443,
Fax: 01249 440800. Called: Feb 1975,
Middle Temple, LLB (Lond)

Castleman *Joseph Benjamin*
and Member New York Bar 1 Paper Bldgs,
Ground Floor, Temple, London, EC4Y 7EP.
Called: Nov 1950, Middle Temple

Catliff *Geoffrey Charles*
Brook House, Berrick Salome, Nr
Wallingford, Oxfordshire OX10 6JQ, 01844
352280. Called: Feb 1967, Gray's Inn, LLB
(Lond)

Catlin *David Hamilton*
Called: June 1953, Gray's Inn, BA Hons
[Oxon]

Catterall *Michael James*
Called: Oct 1995, Lincoln's Inn, BA
(Hons)(Oxon)

Causton *Ms Catherine Mary* ●
CPS, Gemini Centre,, 88 New London Road,
Chelmsford, Essex CM2 OBR. Called: July
1990, Gray's Inn, BA

Causton *Peter Anthony Leo*
Pinsent Curtis Solicitors, 3 Colmore Circus,
Birmingham B4 6BH, 0121 200 1050, Fax:
0121 626 1040. Called: Oct 1995, Middle
Temple, MA (Cantab), Dip Law

Cavanagh *Vincent Lawrence*
Called: Oct 1996, Inner Temple, BA (Oxon),
CPE (Manch)

Cave *Miss Valerie Helen* ●
Deputy Clerk to the Justices, Devon
Magistrates', Courts Committee, County
Hall, Exeter EX2 4QD, 01392 70081, Fax:
01392 420913. Called: July 1984, Middle
Temple, BA (Hons)

Cavenagh *Prof Winifred Elizabeth
OBE, JP*
20 Lingfield Court, High Street, Harborne,
West Midlands B17 9NE, 0121 428 2400.
Called: Nov 1964, Gray's Inn,
PhD(B'ham),BSc(Econ)

Caveney *John* ●
Senior Court Clerk, The Magistrates' Court,
Corporation Street, St Helens, Merseyside
WA10 1SZ, 01744 20244, Fax: 01744
451697. Called: Feb 1990, Middle Temple,
Dip Mag

Cawley *Mrs Serene Chor Joo*
Senior Court Clerk, Buckhamshire
Magistrates' Crt, C/O Milton Keynes
Magistrates', Crt, 301 Silbury Boulevard,
Witan Gate East, Milton Keynes, Bucks
MK9 2AJ, 01908 684901, Fax: 01908
684904. Called: Nov 1990, Inner Temple,
LLB (Lond), MSc

Cawse *Arthur Douglas*
Woodlands, Aldwick, Wrington, Bristol
BS18 7RF, 01934 862235. Called: June 1950,
Middle Temple, MA (Oxon)

Cawthra *Bruce Illingworth*
Erich-Holthaus Str 1, 82211 Herrsching
Ammersee, 0 81 52 17 52. Called: Feb 1962,
Middle Temple, BA

Ch'ng *Frank Eng Hing*
Called: July 1995, Middle Temple, LLB
(Hons)

Ch'ng *Miss Li-Ling*
Called: July 1996, Lincoln's Inn, LLB (Hons)(Lond)

Chacko *Miss Grace*
Called: Feb 1994, Lincoln's Inn, LLB (Hons)

Chadha *Miss Selina Kim*
Called: Nov 1996, Gray's Inn, LLB (Hull)

Chadwick *Neville*
Principal State Counsel, Attorney General's Chambers, Private Bag 62, Francistown, 212 342, Fax: 213 402, Advocate of the High Court of Botswana. Called: July 1972, Middle Temple, BA, LLM (Lond)

Chadwick *Stephen Paul*
Called: Oct 1997, Inner Temple, LLB (Sheffield)

Chahil *Ravinder*
Bird & Bird, 90 Fetter Lane, London WC2 4JP, 0171 415 6000, Fax: 0171 415 6111. Called: Nov 1994, Middle Temple, B.Sc (Leeds), Parmaology, Dip IP, Law (Bris)

Chai *Hean Leong*
Called: July 1996, Lincoln's Inn, LLB (Hons)(Lond)

Chai *Jen Chiew*
Called: Nov 1994, Middle Temple, LLB (Hons) (Sheff)

Chai *Miss Yoke Peng*
Called: July 1995, Lincoln's Inn, LLB (Hons)

Chair *Yong Huang Adrian*
Called: July 1996, Gray's Inn, LLB (Leicester)

Chakrabarti *Miss Shami* •
Principal Legal Officer, The Home Office, 50 Queen Anne's Gate, London SW1H 9AT, 0171 273 3000, Fax: 0171 273 4075. Called: Oct 1994, Middle Temple, LLB (Hons)(Lond)

Chakrabortty *Ashis Ranjan* •
Counsellor, Immigration Advisory Service, County House, 190 Great Dover Street, London SE1 4YB, 0171 357 6917, West Bengal Bar association, India. Called: July 1970, Inner Temple, B.Com, LLB

Chalk *David John*
Called: May 1997, Gray's Inn, LLB (Wales)

Chamberlain *Kevin John CMG* •
Deputy Legal Adviser, Foreign & Commonwealth Office, King Charles Street, London SW1A 2AH. Called: July 1965, Inner Temple, LLB (Lond)

Chamberlain *Nigel*
9 Hasted Drive, Alresford, Hampshire SO24 9PX. Called: July 1975, Middle Temple, MA (Cantab)

Chamberlain *Paul* •
Senior Crown Prosecutor, Crown Prosecution Service, The Cooperage, Gainsford Street, London, 0171 357 7010, Fax: 0171 962 0904. Called: Nov 1993, Inner Temple, BA (Reading), CPE

Chambers *Dr Douglas Robert*
HM Coroner London City, 4 Ormond Avenue, Richmond, Surrey TW10 6TN, 0181 940 7745. Called: May 1965, Lincoln's Inn, MB, BS, LLB, MA, CBiol, F Inst Biol

Chambers *Richard Morgan*
S J Berwin & Co, 222 Gray's Inn Road, London WC1X 8HB, 0171 533 2216, Fax: 0171 533 2000. Called: Nov 1993, Gray's Inn, LLB (Hons) (Wales)

Champion *Ronan Henry*
Northcrofts Management, Services Limited, 12 Grosvenor Place, London SW1X 7HH, 0171 839 7858, Fax: 0171 235 4401, Chartered Quantity Surveyor. Called: Nov 1992, Middle Temple, B.Sc, LLB, ARICS, MCIOB

Chan *Allan Chun Hwee*
Called: July 1996, Middle Temple, LLB (Hons)(Lond)

Chan *Miss Amanda Yuk Ying*
Called: July 1996, Middle Temple, LLB (Hons)(Wolves)

Chan *Anthony Hung-Chiu* •
Principal Crown Prosecutor, Crown Prosecution Service, 50 Ludgate Hill, London EC4M 7EX, 0171 273 8322, Fax: 0171 273 8016. Called: Nov 1984, Middle Temple, BSc (Hons) (Dundee), Diplaw

Chan *Bo Ching*
Called: July 1995, Gray's Inn, LLB, LLM (Lond)

Chan *Ms Charmaine Poh Meng*
Called: July 1997, Gray's Inn, LLB (Notts)

Chan *Che Bun Anderson*
Called: Nov 1997, Gray's Inn, LLB, LLM (Lond), LLM (Deakin, Australia)

Chan *Chee Choong*
Called: Nov 1997, Lincoln's Inn, LLB (Hons)

Chan *Miss Ching Fan*
Room B, 12/F, Yee Cheung Mansion, Lei King Wan, Sai Wan Ho, (852) 2535 6251, Fax: (852) 2539 5416, and Member Hong Kong Bar. Called: July 1996, Middle Temple, BA (Hons)(Hong Kong), CPE (Manc)

Chan *Ms Christine Mei-An*
Messrs Khattar Wong & Partners, 80 Raffles Place, [H]25-01 UOB Plaza 1, 65-5356844 65-5314022, Fax: 65-5351030. Called: Nov 1994, Middle Temple, LLB (Hons)

Chan *David Ming Onn*
Called: July 1996, Middle Temple, LLB (Hons)(Lond)

Chan *Mrs Dora Kit Ho*
and Member Hong Kong. Called: July 1996, Middle Temple, BSc (Hons)(Lond), MSc (City), CPE (Manc)

Chan *Eu Gene*
Called: Nov 1996, Middle Temple, LLB (Hons)

Chan *Miss Evelyn Lillian Swee Lian*
12 Lorong Taman Pantai 6, Bukit Pantai, 59100 Kuala Lumpur, Malaysia, 603-2821636. Called: July 1995, Lincoln's Inn, LLB (Hons)

Chan *Miss Fiona Foong Ling*
Called: July 1996, Lincoln's Inn, LLB (Hons)(Leics)

Chan *Fu Kit Brian*
and Member Hong Kong Bar. Called: July 1996, Gray's Inn, LLB (Wolverhampton)

Chan *Hing Wai*
and Member Hong Kong Bar. Called: July 1990, Gray's Inn, B.Pharm (Brad), MRPharmS, LLB (Lond)

Chan *Hock Keng*
Called: July 1993, Middle Temple, LLB (Hons, Bris)

Chan *Hon Wan Edwin*
Department of Building & Real, Estate, Hong Kong Polytechnic Uni, Hung Hom, Kowloon, Hong Kong, (HK) 27665800, Fax: (HK) 27645131, and Member Hong Kong Bar. Called: July 1993, Inner Temple, BA, Dip. Arch., MA, LLB, RIBA, ACIArb, Pg.D Prc law

Chan *Ms Ifan*
Publisher, Hong Kong Transit Publishing Co Ltd, Temple Chambers, 1607-1612 One Pacific Place, 88 Queensway, 852 25232003, Fax: 852 28179326, and Member Hong Kong Bar. Called: July 1996, Inner Temple, BA, CPE

Chan *Ka Sing Louise*
Called: Nov 1997, Inner Temple, LLB, LLM

Chan *Miss Keng Yean*
Called: Nov 1997, Lincoln's Inn, LLB (Hons)(L'pool)

Chan *Kia Khuang*
Called: July 1996, Middle Temple, LLB (Hons)(Bris)

Chan *Kong Meng Lawrence*
Called: July 1997, Middle Temple, LLB (Hons)(Keele)

Chan *Kun Ming*
Called: Nov 1994, Middle Temple, LLB (Hons)

Chan *Kwai Chun Charles*
Senior Administrative Officer (Hong-Kong Government), and Member Hong-Kong Bar. Called: July 1993, Gray's Inn, B.BA, LLB

Chan *Kwok-Chun*
Called: Nov 1997, Gray's Inn, LLB (Lond), BSc, MSc, (Hong Kong)

Chan *Miss Lin Wai Ruth*
Called: July 1995, Gray's Inn, LLB (Bris)

Chan *Miss Lin-Mei*
Called: July 1996, Lincoln's Inn, LLB (Hons)(Lond)

Chan *LLoyd Kah Seng*
Called: July 1996, Middle Temple, LLB (Hons)(Lond)

Chan *Miss Michelle Geraldine Chui-Wah*
20 Cecil Street, [H]25-02 to 05, The Exchange, (65) 534 1711, Fax: (65) 534 3331, and Member Singapore Bar. Called: Nov 1993, Middle Temple, LLB (Hons)(B'ham)

Chan *Ming-Ki*
and Member Barrister, Supreme Court of Hong Kong. Called: Oct 1995, Middle Temple, LLB (Hons), LLM

Chan *Nicholas Kei Cheong*
Orrick, Herrington & Sutcliffe, 10 Collyer Quay, [H]23-08 Ocean Building, Singapore 049315, (65) 538 6116, Fax: (65) 538 0606, and Member Singapore Bar. Called: Feb 1993, Inner Temple, MA (Cantab)

Chan *Pat Lun*
Des Voeux Chambers, 10th Floor, Bank of East Asia Building, 10 Des Voeux Road, Central, (852) 2526 3071, Fax: (852) 2810 5287, and Member Hong Kong Bar. Called: July 1994, Lincoln's Inn, BA (Hons)

Chan *Peter Chi-Kwan*
Fellow of the Chartered Institute of Arbitrators, 604 Cosmos Bldg, 8-11 Lan Kwai Fong, D'Aguilar St, 852 25230858, Fax: 852 28684673, and Member Hong Kong Bar. Called: Nov 1965, Middle Temple

Chan *Miss Pik Dzee*
Called: July 1995, Middle Temple, LLB (Hons)

Chan *Miss Shui Ping Peggy*
Called: July 1997, Middle Temple, LLB (Hons)(Lond)

Chan *Miss Suk-Wai Winsome*
Room 545, High Block, Queensway Government Offices, Admiralty, (852) 28672231, Fax: (852) 25368423. Called: Nov 1994, Gray's Inn, BA (Hong Kong)

Chan *Tak Pun*
Called: Nov 1997, Gray's Inn, BSc (Hong Kong)

Chan *Thomas Chun Yee*
Called: Oct 1995, Middle Temple, LLB (Hons)

Chan *Wa Shing*
Called: Nov 1994, Middle Temple, B.Sc (Hons)

Chan *Wing-Cheong*
Lecturer at National University of Singapore, 5 Cluny Hill, Singapore 1025, Republic of Singapore, 468 1188, and Member Singapore Bar New York Bar. Called: July 1991, Gray's Inn, BA, LLM (Cornell)

Chan *Yee Kwong*
Called: Mar 1998, Middle Temple, LLB (Hons)(Lond)

Chan *Miss Yew Ping*
J5, 2nd Floor, Bangunan Khas, Lorong 8/1E, 46050 petaling Jaya, Selangor, Malaysia, 03 7552466, Fax: 603 7552405, and Member Malaysia Bar. Called: Nov 1994, Lincoln's Inn, LLB (Hons)(Lond)

Chan *Yoong Heng*
Called: July 1997, Lincoln's Inn, LLB (Hons)(Lond)

Chanda *Satwaki*
Called: Oct 1992, Inner Temple, BSc, Dip Law

Chandarana *Yogain Jitendra*
Called: Oct 1997, Lincoln's Inn, LLB (Hons)(Lond)

Chandler *Miss Esme Katharine* •
European Vocational College, Dukes House, 32-38 Dukes Place, London EC3A 7CP, 0171 929 0102, Fax: 0171 929 0103. Called: July 1982, Inner Temple, LLB (B'ham)

Chandler *Dr William John*
FCybS, 3 Willow Grove, Welwyn Garden City, Herts AL8 7NA, 01707 324600, Fax: 01707 376003. Called: Feb 1956, Middle Temple, MA, PhD, ASCA

Chandrakesan *Prabakaran*
Called: Mar 1998, Middle Temple, LLB (Hons)

Chandran *Miss Parosha*
Called: Oct 1997, Lincoln's Inn, LLB (Hons), LLM (Lond), Dip. Human Rights, (Strasborg)

Chandranayagam *Daniel Masillamaney*
Called: July 1997, Gray's Inn, LLB (Glamorgan)

Chang *Chi Hoong*
Called: July 1995, Lincoln's Inn, LLB (Hons)

Chang *Choon Chuen Kevin*
PVD-2 G-08 Jln Perdana 2/1, Pandan Perdana, 55300 Kuala Lumpur, Malaysia, 603-9826722. Called: July 1994, Lincoln's Inn, LLB (Hons)

Chang *Miss Jo-Anne*
Called: Nov 1996, Lincoln's Inn, LLB (Hons)(Lond), AKC Diploma

Chang *Kin Hui*
Called: Nov 1995, Middle Temple, BA (Hons)

Chang *Miss Laura Vun Tzin*
Called: Nov 1992, Lincoln's Inn, LLB (Hons)

Chang *Miss Wai Yoong*
Called: Nov 1996, Middle Temple, LLB (Hons)(Lond)

Changaroth *Anil M*
Legal Assistant, Lim & Lim, 63 Market Street, [H]13-03/05, Tat Lee Bank Building, Singapore 048942, 5358626, Fax: 5356736, and Member Singapore Bar. Called: Nov 1993, Middle Temple, LLB (Hons)(Bucks)

Channing *Michael David*
Consultant, Asia Pacific Associates, Melrose Cottage, Mellersh Hill Road, Wonersh Park, Wonersh, Surrey GU5 OQJ, 01483 892032, Fax: 01483 898633. Called: Nov 1976, Lincoln's Inn, MA (Oxon)

Chao *Bernard Wee Chun*
J S Yeh & Company, 133 New Bridge Road, [H]18-03/04/05 Chinatown Point, 065 533 1188, Fax: 065 535 0388, and Member Singapore. Called: July 1993, Lincoln's Inn, LLB (Hons)

Chao *Miss Elaine Wen Su*
Drew & Napier, 20 Raffles Place, [H]17-00, Ocean Towers, (65) 531 2496, Fax: (65) 532 7149, and Member Singapore. Called: July 1996, Middle Temple, LLB (Hons)(Lond)

Chapaneri *Mrs Dipika*
Principal Legal Adviser, Watford Magistrates' Court, The Court House, Clarendon Road, Watford, Herts WD1 1ST, 01923 238111, Fax: 01923 251273. Called: Feb 1989, Inner Temple, LLB Hons

Chaplin *Miss Amanda Jane* •
Prosecution Lawyer, Department of Trade & Industry, 10-18 Victoria Street, London SW1H 0NN, 0171 215 3124, Fax: 0171 215 3235. Called: Nov 1993, Gray's Inn, LLB (Hons)

Chaplin *Richard James* •
Legal Manager (UK), OMV (UK) Limited, 14 Ryder Street, London SW1Y 6QB, 0171 333 1600, Fax: 0171 333 1610. Called: Feb 1992, Middle Temple, LLB (Hons), LLM (Cantab)

Chapman *Christopher Scott*
Buddle Findlay, P O Box 2694, 1 Willis Street, Wellington, 00 644 499 4242, Fax: 00 644 499 4141, Barrister & Solicitor, High Court of New Zealand (1983) Formerly a solicitor of the Supreme court and Member New Zealand Bar. Called: July 1980, Inner Temple, BSc, LLM (Vic, Wellington)

Chapman *David Nathan*
Court Clerk, 4/5 Quay Street, Carmarthen, Dyfed, 01267 221658, Fax: 01267 221812. Called: Nov 1989, Middle Temple, LLB Hons (Wales)

Chapman *Mrs Geraldine Claire*
Enfin, Quartier Bujalon, 32230 Marciac, 00 33 562082510. Called: Nov 1973, Gray's Inn, BA, LLM

Chapman *James Charles Begg-Hempton*
P O Box 1234 GT, Grand Cayman, 345 949 9876, Fax: 345 949 9877, and Member Cayman Islands. Called: Nov 1987, Inner Temple, LLM, MA (Cantab), BSc, BA

Chapman *Keith Anthony*
Cheif Executive, Padiham Group Limited, Redbrook House, 29 Bollin Hill, Wilmslow, Cheshire SK9 4AN, 01625 251891, Fax: 01625 251893. Called: Nov 1978, Gray's Inn, MA (Oxon)

Chapman *Peter Howard John*
Arbitrator, Chartered Civil Engineer, 46/48 Essex Street, London, WC2R 3GH. Called: Apr 1991, Gray's Inn, BSc, LLB, FCI Arb, FICE, FHKIE, FIHT, MSI Arb

Chapman *Richard Kenneth*
2 Route De La Cascade, 78110 Le Vesinet, 00 33 1 34801234, Fax: 00 33 1 34801263. Called: Nov 1976, Lincoln's Inn, FCA

Chapman *Robin Denis*
Called: Mar 1998, Middle Temple, LLB (Hons)

Chapman *Roderick Alan Keith* •
Senior Crown Prosecutor,, CPS East Midlands, 2 King Edward Court, King Edward Street, Nottingham NG1 1EL, 0115 9480480, Fax: 0115 9364562. Called: Nov 1983, Middle Temple, LLB Nott'm

Chapman Stanley John
Also Inn of Court G. Called: Feb 1954, Lincoln's Inn, BSc,MSc

Chapple Darran Mark
Called: Mar 1996, Middle Temple, LLB (Hons), LLM

Chapple David Anthony
Legal Consultant, 106 Park Avenue, Ruislip, Middlesex HA4 7UP, 01895 635171. Called: July 1971, Middle Temple, BA Hons, A.C.I.S

Charalambous Andreas
Called: Nov 1997, Gray's Inn, LLB (Sheff)

Charitonos Miss Panayiota Costa
Called: Nov 1995, Middle Temple, LLB (Hons)

Charkham Jonathan Philip
Director, The Great Universal Stores PLC, Crestacare PLC, CLM Plc, Leopold Joseph Holdings PLC Visiting Professor City University Business School, The Yellow House, 22 Montpelier Place, Knightsbridge, London SW7 1HL, 0171 589 9879, Fax: 0171 581 8520, Sheriff of the City of London 1994-95. Called: June 1953, Inner Temple, MA (Cantab)

Charles Mrs Jacqueline Fay JP ●
Chairman of Social Security Appeals Tribunals and Rent Assessment Committees, 38 Chester Close North, London NW1 4JE, 0171 935 6968. Called: June 1956, Gray's Inn, LLB

Charles Kevin Lawrence
Called: Oct 1996, Middle Temple, LLB (Hons)(Essex)

Charlton Robert Craig
Called: Nov 1988, Middle Temple, Dip in Mag Law, Dip in Law, DMG. MIMgt

Charnley Philip James ●
Principal Crown Prosecutor, Crown Prosecution Service, Lovell House, St Nicholas Street, Kings Lynn, Norfolk, 01553 776622. Called: July 1983, Gray's Inn, LLB (E.Ang)

Charters Andrew Philip
Called: Oct 1995, Lincoln's Inn, BA (Hons)(Oxon)

Chase Miss Charlotte Elizabeth Diana ●
Senior Crown Prosecutor, Crown Prosecution Service, St Georges House, Lever Street, Wolverhampton WV2 1EZ, 01902 870900. Called: July 1976, Lincoln's Inn, LLB

Chastney Ms Carol Anne ●
Crown Prosecutor, Crown Prosecution Service, Riding Gate House, Old Dover Road, Canterbury, Kent, 01227 451144. Called: Oct 1993, Gray's Inn, LLB (Hons)

Chataway Benjamin Thomas Mary
Called: Nov 1995, Lincoln's Inn, BA (Hons)

Chatfield Mrs Rebecca Jane
Called: Mar 1996, Inner Temple, BA (N'ham), MA (Bris)

Chau Miss Catherine Siew Ping
40 Luyang Phase 4, Jalan Kijang, 88100 Koya Kinabalu, Sabah, and Member Advocate, Sabah Bar. Called: Nov 1991, Gray's Inn, BA (Hons) (Kent), LLM (Lond)

Chau Kwok Leung Raymond
Called: Oct 1997, Middle Temple, BSc (Hons)(Lond)

Chau Philip
South China Chambers, 16 Harcourt Road, Far East Finance Centre, Room 1101, 2528 2378, Fax: 2520 1512, and Member Hong Kong Bar. Called: May 1995, Inner Temple, LLB

Chaudhri Ferhan Munir
Called: Nov 1995, Lincoln's Inn, LLB (Hons)(Warw)

Chaudhry Muhammad Alfaz
Called: Nov 1997, Lincoln's Inn, BA, LLB (Punjab), LLM (Lond)

Chaudhry Miss Safina Habib ●
Lawyer, Department of Employment, Eland House, Bresenden Place, London SW1E 5DU, 0171 890 4809, Fax: 0171 890 4804. Called: Nov 1994, Lincoln's Inn, BA (Hons)

Chaudhry Tanveer Hussain
Called: Nov 1997, Lincoln's Inn, LLB (Hons)(B'ham)

Chaundy Mrs Vicki Ann ●
Senior Crown Prosecutor, Crown Prosecution Service, Friars House, Manor House Drive, Coventry CV1 2TE, 01203 520421. Called: July 1976, Gray's Inn, LLB

Chauvin Mrs Joanne Aun Leng
Court Clerk, Kingston Magistrates Court, 19-23 High Street, Kingston, Surrey KT1 1JW, 0181 546 5603. Called: July 1982, Middle Temple, LLB

Chawner John Lovatt
Rosecroft, Hylands Road, Epsom, Surrey KT18 7ED, 01372 722110, Fax: 01372 812926. Called: Nov 1966, Gray's Inn, BSc, BA (Lond)

Chay Miss Kum Yoon
Block 68, Dakota Crescent [H]12-600, 346 2990. Called: July 1996, Middle Temple, LLB (Hons)(Leeds)

Che Shu Fai
Called: Nov 1992, Lincoln's Inn, LLB (Hons)

Cheah Peng Kun
Called: July 1995, Middle Temple, LLB (Hons) (Wales)

Cheah Sau Voon
Messrs Mohd Noor & SY Lee, Room 110, 1st Floor, Asia Life Building, 45-B Jalan Tun Sambanthan, 30000 Ipoh, Perak, 05 2543589/9823, Fax: 05 2542611, and Member Malaysia. Called: Nov 1995, Middle Temple, LLB (Hons)

Cheah Soo Chuan
Called: July 1995, Lincoln's Inn, LLB (Hons)

Cheah Tien Eu
Called: July 1996, Lincoln's Inn, LLB (Hons)(Leeds)

Cheah Mrs Wai Mun
and Member Singapore Bar. Called: July 1986, Lincoln's Inn, BA (Kent)

Cheam Miss Phaik Ling
Nordin Hamid & Co, 9th Floor, Campbell Complex, Jalan DanG Wangi, 50100 Kuala Lumpur, 03-2944677, Fax: 03-2944418, and Member Malaysia Bar. Called: July 1992, Middle Temple, LLB (Hons) (Leics)

Chechatwala Shabbir Ismail
Called: July 1997, Middle Temple, LLB (Hons)(Keele)

Chedumbarum Pillay Neil Radhakrishna
Called: July 1997, Middle Temple, LLB (Hons)(Wales)

Chee Miss Julie Suk-Yuen
Called: Nov 1996, Gray's Inn, LLB (LSE), MA (Lond)

Chee Ms Kit Wai
Called: Nov 1990, Lincoln's Inn, LLB (Nott'm)(Hons)

Chee Yew Chung
Ling Koh & Partners, 7500a Beach Road, 04-332/333 The Plaza, Int ++ (65) 2953335, Fax: Int ++ (65) 2950102, and Member Singapore Bar. Called: July 1996, Inner Temple, LLB (Hull)

Cheema Miss Harminder Kaur
Stephen Fidler & Co, 39 Doughty Street, London WC1 2LF. Called: Oct 1995, Inner Temple, LLB (Lond)

Cheeseman John William
23 Castle View Park, Mawnan Smith, Falmouth, Cornwall TR11 5HB, 01326 250601. Called: June 1953, Gray's Inn

Cheesman Clive Edwin Alexander
38c Grove Park Gardens, London W4 3RZ, 0181 994 7567. Called: Nov 1996, Middle Temple, MA (Hons)(Oxon)

Cheesman William James
Chief Superintendent, Northern Constabulary, Police Headquarters, Inverness, 01463 720300. Called: Nov 1990, Lincoln's Inn, LLB (Lond)

Chelliah Kumarendran
Called: July 1995, Middle Temple, LLB (Hons)

Chen Mian Kuang
Messrs Raja, Darryl & Loh, 18th Floor, Wisma Sime Darby, Jalan Raja Laut, 50350, Kuala Lumpur, (Malaysia) 03 2949999, and Member Malaysia Bar. Called: July 1995, Lincoln's Inn, LLB (Hons)

Chen Miss Moi Kooi
Called: July 1972, Lincoln's Inn

Chen Mrs Moira Yang-Cher
Deputy Chief Clerk, Inner London Magistrates', Courts Service, 65 Romney Street, London SW1P 3RD, 0171 799 3332. Called: Nov 1973, Inner Temple

Chen Simon Adam
Called: Nov 1994, Gray's Inn, LLB (Bris)

Cheng *Alvin Sun Cheok*
Legal Assistant, 7th Floor, Maybank
Chambers, 2 Battery Road, 3366533, Fax:
3370906, and Member Singapore Bar.
Called: Nov 1993, Lincoln's Inn, LLB (Hons)

Cheng *Miss Angelina Tan*
Called: July 1996, Middle Temple, LLB
(Hons)(Kent)

Cheng *Francis Ming Bun*
Called: Nov 1994, Middle Temple, LLB
(Hons)

Cheng *Glenn Li Huei*
Called: Nov 1995, Middle Temple, LLB
(Hons)(Wales)

Cheng *Hock Hua*
Called: Oct 1993, Middle Temple, LLB
(Hons)(Lond)

Cheng *Kim Kuan*
Advocate & Solicitor, Billy Ng Chua &
Partners, Advocates & Solicitors, No 17
Upper Circular Road, [H]02-01, 5366382,
Fax: 5366387, and Member Singapore.
Called: July 1996, Middle Temple, BA
(Hons)(Keele)

Cheng *Miss Kitty Kit Yee*
Assistant Legal Adviser, c/o Legal Service
Division, Legislative Council Secretaria, 8
Jackson Road, Central, Hong Kong,
8699209, Fax: 8775029, and Member Hong
Kong Bar Australian Capital Territory Bar.
Called: Apr 1991, Gray's Inn, LLB, PCLL,
MIL

Cheng *Miss Mai*
Measat Broadcast Network SDN, BHD, All
Asia Broadcast Centre, Lebuhraya Puchong -
SG Besi, Bukit Jalil, Kuala Lumpur, 603-
5836688, Fax: 603-5836872, and Member
Malaysia Bar. Called: July 1993, Middle
Temple, LLB (Hons)(Lond)

Cheng *Miss Patricia May Li*
Advocate & Solicitor, M/S C C Choo & Co,
Suite D33 & D34, 3rd Floor, Pekeliling
Plaza, Jalan Tun Razak, 50400 Kuala
Lumour, 603 4411481, Fax: 603 4411481,
and Member Malaysia Bar. Called: July 1995,
Middle Temple, LLB (Hons)

Cheng *Peter Kwock Kwan*
Called: Mar 1996, Lincoln's Inn, LLB (Hons)
(Sussex), LLM (Lond)

Cheng *Peter Ong Lip*
and Member Malaysia Bar. Called: Nov 1995,
Inner Temple, LLB (Lond)

Cheng *Tak Ying*
Called: Nov 1996, Middle Temple, LLB
(Hons)

Cheng *Miss Teresa Chin Pei*
Called: July 1994, Middle Temple, LLB
(Hons)(Sheff)

Cheng *Miss Wei Lin*
Legal Assistant, Toh Tan & Partners,
Advocates & Solicitors, 79 Robinson Road,
[H] 21-03, CPF Building, 225 6446, Fax: 225
2356, and Member Singapore Bar.
Called: July 1993, Lincoln's Inn, LLB (Hons,
Bris)

Cheng *Miss Wei Min*
Called: Nov 1995, Middle Temple, LLB
(Hons)

Cheng *Miss Yen Lin*
and Member Singapore Bar. Called: July
1993, Lincoln's Inn, LLB (Hons, L'pool)

Cheng *Miss Yvonne Wai Sum*
2B Goldson Place, 11 Shouson Hill Road
West, Deep Water Bay, and Member Hong
Kong Bar. Called: July 1996, Gray's Inn, BA
(Oxon)

Cheok *Robin Van Kee*
Abrahams, Davidson & Co, Room 516, 5th
Floor, Plaza Athirah, Jalan Kubah Makam
Diraja, Bandar Seri Begawan, Brunei
Darussala, 673 2 242840, Fax: 673 2
242836, and Member Brunei Darussalam.
Called: July 1995, Inner Temple, LLB (Essex)

Cheong *Chin Min*
Called: July 1996, Middle Temple, LLB
(Hons)(Lond)

Cheong *Goh Boon Wilfred*
Barrister/Arbitrator Advocate & Solicitor,
Apt Block 75, Whampoa Drive, [H]10-368,
Singapore 320075, Republic of Singapore,
5365334/98277457, Fax: 5365134, and
Member Supreme Court of Australian
Capital Territory, Supreme Court of Brunei
Darrussalam Singapore Bar Supreme Court
of Singapore. Called: Nov 1990, Lincoln's
Inn, LLb (Lond) (Hons)

Cheong *Miss Seok Wah*
7500 Beach Road, [H] 07-301 The Plaza, 65
2985755, Fax: 65 2988390, and Member
Singapore Bar. Called: July 1993, Middle
Temple, LLB (Hons, Bris)

Cheong *Miss Whye Mun*
Called: July 1995, Lincoln's Inn, LLB (Hons)

Cheong *Yuk Leung*
and Member Malaysian Bar. Called: July
1996, Lincoln's Inn, LLB (Hons)(Warw)

Chern *Aik Hua*
and Member Singapore Bar. Called: July
1992, Lincoln's Inn, LLB (Hons) (Lond)

Chern *Miss Chyi Ching*
15 Tagore Avenue, Singapore 787650,
Republic of Singapore, and Member
Singapore Bar. Called: July 1994, Lincoln's
Inn, LLB (Hons)

Chesney *George Cecil TD*
Bar Library, Royal Courts of Justice,
Chichester Street, Belfast, N Ireland, 0232
241523, Fax: 0232 231850, and Member
Northern Ireland Bar. Called: May 1988,
Middle Temple, LLB (Hons) Bristol

Cheung *Adonis Kam Wing*
Suite 401, Printing House, 6 Duddell Street,
Central, 852 2526 0888, Fax: 852 2869
8320, and Member Hong Kong Bar.
Called: July 1994, Inner Temple, LLB

Cheung *K-John*
7208 Queenston Court, Burnaby, B.C.
V5A 3M4, (604) 299 8193, Fax: (604) 299
8365, and Member British Columbia Law
Society (Canada), Canada, Hong Kong &
Victoria (Austraila) Bars Hong Kong Bar.
Called: July 1973, Lincoln's Inn, BSc, LLB,
JD, Dip Comp Law, Dip Ch Law

Cheung *Miss Kuan Swan*
Called: Nov 1994, Middle Temple, BA in
Law & Econ, (Joint Hons)

Cheung *Miss Man Ching*
Called: Nov 1996, Lincoln's Inn, LLB (Hons)

Cheung *Man To Raymond*
Called: Nov 1997, Lincoln's Inn,
Postgraduate Diploma, In Law

Cheung *Sir Oswald Victor CBE, LLD*
New Henry House, 10th Floor, 10 Ice
House Street, 2524-2156, Fax: 2810-5656,
QC Hong Kong. Called: Jan 1950, Lincoln's
Inn, MA (Oxon)

Cheung *Phei Chiet*
Called: July 1994, Gray's Inn, BA, LLM

Cheung *Miss Susan*
Called: July 1996, Lincoln's Inn, LLB (Hons)

Cheung *Miss Tania Su Li*
Called: July 1995, Lincoln's Inn, LLB (Hons)

Cheung *Wen Ping*
Deloitte & Touche Corporate, Finance,
Stonecutter Court, London EC4A 4TR, 0171
303 6425, Fax: 0171 303 5949. Called: Nov
1993, Lincoln's Inn, LLB (Hons), ACA

Chew *Miss Chin Yean*
Called: Nov 1996, Lincoln's Inn, LLB
(Hons)(Kent)

Chew *Eng Ghee*
Messrs P S Ranjan & Co, Advocates &
Solicitors, 12th Floor MUI Plaza, Jalan P
Ramlee, 50250 Kuala Lumpur, 03 2489200,
Fax: 03 2423758, and Member Malaysia Bar.
Called: Nov 1992, Lincoln's Inn, LLB (Hons)

Chew *Hew Wearn*
Called: Nov 1997, Lincoln's Inn, LLB
(Hons)(Sheff)

Chew *Kei-Jin*
Legal Assistant, 9 Battery Road, Straits
Trading Building, [H]15-00, Singapore
049910, 65 5322271, Fax: 65 5352975, and
Member Singapore Bar. Called: July 1993,
Middle Temple, BA (Cantab), MA (Cantab)

Chew *Kok Liang*
2 Jalan SS 20/22, Damansara Utama, 47400
Petaling Jaya, Selangor, Malaysia, 03
7180095, and Member Malaysia Bar.
Called: July 1991, Inner Temple, BSc Econ
(Wales), LLM (Leic), Dip in Shariah Law &,
Practice (IIU)

Chew *Kok Liang*
Called: May 1994, Middle Temple, LLB
(Hons)

Chew *Kok Wye*
Called: Nov 1997, Middle Temple, BA
(Hons)(Kent)

Chew *Kwee-San*
Advocate & Solicitor of the Supreme Court in Singapore. Called: July 1994, Middle Temple, LLB (Hons)(Notts)

Chew *Miss Lynette Mei Lin*
4 Shenton Way, [H]15-07 Shing Kwan House, 220 6888, Fax: 223 1736, and Member Singapore. Called: July 1995, Lincoln's Inn, LLB (Hons)

Chew *Miss Mong Fei Vivian*
Called: Nov 1997, Middle Temple, LLB (Hons)(Lond)

Chew *Miss Pitt Har*
and Member Malaysia Bar. Called: July 1992, Lincoln's Inn, LLB (Hons) (Lanc)

Chew *Miss Soo San*
Messrs Tang & Yoges, 8b Jalan Raja Haroun, 43000 Kajang, Selangor Darul Ehsan, 60-3-8376510, Fax: 60-3-8376515, and Member Malaysia Bar. Called: July 1992, Middle Temple, LLB (Hons) (Warw)

Chew *Yee Teck Eric*
Blk 113, Clementi Street 13, [H]06-25, 8728562. Called: July 1997, Gray's Inn, LLB (Sheff), ACIArb

Cheyne *Miss Ilona Claire* •
Senior Lecturer in Law, Newcastle Law School, Newcastle University, Newcastle upon Tyne NE1 7RU, 0191 232 8511, Fax: 0191 212 0064. Called: July 1986, Gray's Inn, LLB (Edinburgh), LLM (Lond)

Chhabra *Sunit*
Called: July 1997, Lincoln's Inn, LLB (Hons)(Lond)

Chhabra *Vinit*
Called: July 1996, Middle Temple, LLB (Hons)(Lond)

Chia *Boon Teck*
Legal Assistant in Lee & Lee, 5 Shenton Way, UIC Building, Level 19, 2200666/3295322 (Direct), Fax: 2219712, and Member Singapore Bar. Called: July 1994, Lincoln's Inn, LLB (Hons)

Chia *Miss Carolyn Anne Cheow Hiang*
Partner, Tan Rajah & Cheah, (Advocates & Solicitors), 9 Battery Road, Straits Trading Building, [H]15-00, (65) 532 2271, Fax: (65) 5322633/5352475, and Member Singapore Bar. Called: July 1989, Middle Temple, (Cantab) MA(Cantab)

Chia *Miss Corrinne Ee-Lynn*
Legal Officer, Port of Singapore Authority, 460 Alexandra Road, PSA Building, (65) 279 4049, Fax: (65) 279 5811, and Member Singapore. Called: Nov 1994, Lincoln's Inn, LLB (Hons)(Lond)

Chia *Miss En-Lin*
151 Cavenagh Road, [H]09-159, 0065 7340697/7384245. Called: Nov 1996, Gray's Inn, LLB (Nott'm)

Chia *Miss Gillian Hsu-Lien*
Called: July 1997, Gray's Inn, LLB (Bris)

Chia *Miss Jeanette Shau Ken*
Called: July 1996, Lincoln's Inn, LLB (Hons)(Leeds)

Chia *Peng Chuang*
Block 7, Teck Whye Avenue [H]04-102, Singapore 680007, 7647753, and Member Singapore Bar. Called: Nov 1993, Middle Temple, LLB (Hons)(Lond), BSc (Hons), ARICS

Chia *Soo Michael*
Called: July 1997, Middle Temple, LLB (Hons)

Chia *Yau Hoong*
Called: July 1994, Lincoln's Inn, LLB (Hons)

Chiah *Miss Yoke Li*
Called: July 1997, Lincoln's Inn, LLB (Hons)(Wales)

Chiang *Pak Chien*
Legal Assistant, 17 Goldhill Drive, (65) 3520821, and Member Singapore. Called: Nov 1995, Middle Temple, LLB (Hons)

Chiang *Steven Joon Heng*
Called: Nov 1995, Middle Temple, LLB (Hons)

Chiang *Wee Sean*
Called: July 1995, Middle Temple, LLB (Hons)

Chiang *Miss Wen-Shan*
and Member Singapore Bar. Called: July 1990, Gray's Inn, LLB (Leic)

Chibwana *Enock Daniel Alfred*
Chief State Advocate, Ministry of Justice, P/B 333, Lilongwe 3, 782411. Called: Feb 1994, Gray's Inn, LLB, LLM

Chien *Hoe Yong*
Director, Lippo Securities Ltd, 2302 Lippo Tower, Lippo Centre, 89 Queensway, Central, Hong Kong, 25337434/28457711, Fax: 25337435. Called: Nov 1988, Middle Temple, LLB (Lanc), ACA, HKSA

Chieng *Miss Stephanie Lun Tying*
Awang Lai & Co Advocates, Lots 432 & 434, 2nd Floor, Jalan Bendahara, 98000 Miri, Sarawak, Malaysia, 085-416688, Fax: 085-416684, and Member Sarawak Bar. Called: July 1995, Inner Temple, LLB (Kent)

Chiew *Ean Vooi*
Called: July 1997, Middle Temple, LLB (Hons)(Leeds)

Chijner *David*
Called: Oct 1993, Inner Temple, Diplome de Droit, Francais (Paris), BA (Kent), LLM (European, University Institut)

Chilton *Miss Melorie Anne*
Sole Practitioner - Legal & Business Media Consultancy, Chilton Media Law, 8 West Street, London WC2H 9NG, 0171 836 2764, Fax: 0171 836 2765. Called: Nov 1980, Gray's Inn, LLB (Lond), LLM (Lond)

Chim *Ms Sook Heng*
Messrs Royds Treadwell, 2 Crane Court, Fleet Street, London EC4A 2BL, 0171 583 2222, Fax: 0171 583 2034. Called: July 1996, Lincoln's Inn, LLB (Hons)

Chin *Miss Beatrice Choon Hwa*
Chooi & Co, Penthouse, Bangunan Ming, Jalan Bukit Nanas, 50250 Kuala Lumpur, Malaysia, 03-2327344, Fax: 03-2382915/03-2380708, and Member Malaysia Bar. Called: July 1994, Lincoln's Inn, LLB (Hons)

Chin *Chee Chien*
No 20 Jalan SS 21/32, Damansara Utama, 47400 Petaling Jaya, Selangor Darul Ehsan, 603-716-9285, Fax: 603-716-9287, and Member Malaysian Bar. Called: Nov 1993, Gray's Inn, LLB

Chin *Miss Emily Mei Fong*
Group Legal Officer, and Member Singapore Bar. Called: July 1990, Gray's Inn, LLB,ICSA,GRAD

Chin *Hein Choong*
Called: July 1995, Lincoln's Inn, LLB (Hons)

Chin *Miss Jia Huey*
7-4 Lorong Teratai 4, Off Jalan Haji Jaib, 84000 Muar, Johor, Malaysia, 06 921367, Fax: 03 2301768, and Member Malaysia Bar. Called: July 1992, Lincoln's Inn, LLB (Hons), LLM

Chin *Julian Ye-Fung*
Legal Counsel, Asia Pulp & Paper Co Ltd, 1 Maritime Square, [H]10-01 (Lobby 13), World Trade Centre, (65) 2729288, Fax: (65) 3749388, and Member Singapore Bar. Called: July 1992, Middle Temple, LLB (Hons) (Leics)

Chin *Keith Hsiun*
C/O Yong Wong & Chin Advocates, 1st Floor, Bangunan Chin Fook, Lot 382 South Yu Seng Road, P O Box 736 98007 Miri, Sarawak, 085 414348, Fax: 085 415602, and Member Brunei Darrusalam (High Court of Brunei) Malaya (Kuala Lumpur Bar). Called: July 1995, Lincoln's Inn, LLB (Hons) (Sheff)

Chin *Miss Mye-Ling*
Legal Advisor, and Member High Court of Malaya. Called: Nov 1994, Middle Temple, LLB

Chin *Miss Oi Jean*
123 Jalan SS22/37, Damansara Jaya, 47400 Petaling Jaya, Selangor, (60)(3) 7189 232. Called: Nov 1995, Lincoln's Inn, LLB (Hons), LLM

Chin *Miss Pek Khen*
Called: July 1994, Middle Temple, LLB (Hons)(Lond)

Chin *Miss Pheik Lin Elaine*
Called: Nov 1997, Lincoln's Inn, LLB (Hons)

Chin *Miss Pik Khiun*
Legal Assistant, M/S Kean Chye & Sivalingam, 42 Jalan Medan Ipoh 6, Bandar Baru Medan Ipoh, 31400 Ipoh, Perak, 05-545 6010, Fax: 05-545 6359, and Member High Court of Malaya. Called: July 1995, Lincoln's Inn, LLB (Hons)

Chin *Miss Tze Jin*
Called: July 1996, Lincoln's Inn, LLB (Hons) (Kent)

Chin *Tze Jone*
Called: July 1995, Middle Temple, LLB (Hons)

Chin *Yuen Fong*
Called: Nov 1995, Middle Temple, BA (Hons)(Keele)

Chin *Miss Yvonne Mei Oy*
Called: Nov 1989, Lincoln's Inn, LLB, LLM (Lond)

Ching *Miss Fiona Pui Yeng*
and Member Singapore. Called: July 1994, Middle Temple, LLB (Hons)(Notts)

Ching *Kim Chuah*
Called: Nov 1994, Middle Temple, LLB (Hons)

Ching *Leonard Tchi Pang*
Called: Nov 1994, Middle Temple, LLB (Hons)

Chiok *Beng Piow*
724 Bedok Reservoir Road, [H]06-5232 Singapore 470724, 065 449 3121, and Member Singapore Bar. Called: July 1993, Middle Temple, LLB (Hons)

Chionh *Miss Mavis Sze-Chyi*
Called: July 1993, Middle Temple, BA (Hons)

Chisholm *Miss Marcela*
Senior Lecturer in Law, Glasgow Caledonian University, Dept of Law and Public Admin, Cowcaddens Road, Glasgow G4 OBA, 041 331 3427, Fax: 041 331 3798. Called: July 1991, Gray's Inn, JUDr (Prague), LLM (Manch)

Chitsaka *John*
Called: Apr 1975, Gray's Inn, LLB(Lond)

Chittenden *Timothy Paul* •
Called: Oct 1990, Gray's Inn, LLB (Lond)

Chitthu *Arut*
Called: July 1995, Middle Temple, LLB (Hons)

Chitty *Mrs Anne Louise* •
Principal Crown Prosecutor, Crown Prosecution Service, 4,5,6,& 7 Prendal Court, Aylesbury, Bucks, 01296 436441. Called: July 1983, Inner Temple, LLB (Exon)

Chiu *Hsu-Hwee*
and Member Singapore. Called: July 1995, Middle Temple, LLB (Hons) (Hull)

Chiu *Kwok Kit*
Senior Assessor (Appeals Section), C/O Hong Kong Inland Revenue, Appeals Section, 36/F Wanchai Tower 3, 5 Gloucester Road, Hong Kong, 852 2594 5038, Fax: 852 2877 1131. Called: Nov 1990, Lincoln's Inn, LLB (Lond), LLM, (Lond), LLB (Peking), MCom, FCCA, AHKSA, CPA (Aust), Graduate, Diploma in Taxation

Chiu *Michael Kai Ting*
Called: Nov 1996, Middle Temple, LLB (Hons), MA (Hull)

Chiu *Paul Hung Shun*
F.I.S.M., Room 1931, Swire House, 11 Chater Road, Central, Hong Kong, (852) 2522 9168, Fax: (852) 2845 2072, Barrister & Solicitor Supreme Court and High Court of Australian Capital Territory and Barrister of Supreme Court of Hong Kong and Member Australia Bar Hong Kong Bar. Called: Nov 1971, Middle Temple

Chiu *Ms Yong Yong*
Called: July 1997, Lincoln's Inn, LLB (Hons)(Lond)

Chng *Miss Angeline Kim-Ann*
3 Astrid Hill, Singapore 269926, 65-4697011, Fax: 65-4697012. Called: July 1995, Middle Temple, LLB (Hons)

Cho *Chi-kong*
10/F, 2 Murray Road, Central, Hong Kong, 28264397, Fax: 25626912, Barrister Supreme Court of Hong Kong and Member Canberra, Australia. Called: Nov 1989, Lincoln's Inn, LLB (Lond)

Choa *Brendon Sn-Yien*
Partner, 133 New Bridge Road, China Point [H]15-09, 5382687, Fax: 5380287, Advocate & Solicitor Supreme Court of Singapore and Member Singapore. Called: July 1991, Inner Temple, BA (Sussex)

Choa *Miss Deborah Deb-Bie*
Legal Assistant, Messrs Lee Choon Wan & Co, No 12, Lorong Dungun, Damansara Heights, 50490 Kuala Lumpur, 03 2530078, Fax: 03 2541750, and Member Malaysian Bar. Called: July 1994, Lincoln's Inn, LLB (Hons)

Choh *Irving Thian Chee*
Legal Assistant, No 9 Jalan Rengkam, Singapore 537566, 65 3361878, Fax: 65 2242270, and Member Singapore Bar. Called: July 1993, Middle Temple, LLB (Hons)(Bucks)

Choi *Sheung Kong*
Called: Nov 1997, Lincoln's Inn, LLB (Hons)(Lond)

Chok *Miss Hong-Fui A*
Principal Court Clerk, Coventry Magistrates Court, Little Park Street, Coventry CV1 1SQ, 01203 630666/500 676, Fax: 01203 500699. Called: July 1987, Middle Temple, LLB (Lanc)

Chok *Miss Ketty Li Ket*
Called: July 1997, Middle Temple, LLB (Hons)(Wales)

Chong *Miss Ann Ching*
Called: July 1997, Middle Temple, LLB (Hons)(Leics)

Chong *Avery Soon Yong*
Called: July 1996, Inner Temple, LLB (Warwick)

Chong *Miss Boon Chin*
Called: July 1997, Lincoln's Inn, LLB (Hons)(Leics)

Chong *Miss Chee Er*
20 Margoliouth Road, (+65) 732 2603, Fax: (+65) 261 7075. Called: Nov 1994, Middle Temple, LLB (Hons) (Warw), MBA

Chong *Chi On*
Called: Nov 1997, Lincoln's Inn, LLB (Hons)

Chong *Christopher Fook Choy*
Called: July 1993, Lincoln's Inn, LLB (Hons, Bris)

Chong *Miss Fiona Yeo-Peen*
Called: July 1993, Lincoln's Inn, LLB (Hons)

Chong *Gerald Siak Yen*
20 Malacca Street [H]05-00, Malacca Centre, Singapore 048979, (65) 536 5369, Fax: (65) 536 5811, and Member Singapore Bar. Called: Nov 1994, Middle Temple, BA (Joint Hons)

Chong *Miss Jia Ling*
Called: July 1996, Lincoln's Inn, LLB (Hons)

Chong *Kah Heng*
Called: July 1996, Gray's Inn, LLB (Leicester)

Chong *Karl Shang Chin*
Called: July 1994, Middle Temple, LLB (Hons)

Chong *Kenneth Yun Kien*
c/o Chin Lau Wong & Foo, A818, 8th Floor, Wisma Merdeka, 88000 Kota Kinabalu, Sabah, 088 238111, Fax: 088 238222, and Member Sabah. Called: July 1993, Lincoln's Inn, LLB (Hons, Leeds)

Chong *Kuok Peng*
Called: July 1997, Lincoln's Inn, LLB (Hons)(Exon)

Chong *Miss Mae Shan*
35 Jelutong Villas, Lorong Jelutong Kanan, Damansara Heights, 50490 Kuala Lumpur, 254 8111. Called: July 1996, Middle Temple, BA (Hons)(Cantab)

Chong *Mark Choong Weng*
Called: July 1996, Lincoln's Inn, LLB (Hons)(Lond)

Chong *Miss May Yean*
Called: July 1996, Lincoln's Inn, LLB (Hons)(Wales)

Chong *Michael Wai Yen*
Called: Mar 1998, Middle Temple, LLB (Hons)(Keele)

Chong *Miss Su Ping Cecilia*
Called: July 1997, Middle Temple, LLB (Hons)(Hull)

Chong *Victor Thien Loi*
Called: July 1995, Middle Temple, BA (Hons) (Keele)

Choo *Miss Audrey Pao Lin*
Called: Nov 1997, Lincoln's Inn, LLB (Nott'm)

Choo *Miss Josephine Poh Hua*
Called: Nov 1996, Middle Temple, LLB (Hons)(Lond)

Choo *Raymond Choon Sheng*
and Member Singapore. Called: Nov 1995, Middle Temple, LLB (Hons)(Hull), LLM (King's College, Lond)

Choo *Miss Yuin*
Called: July 1996, Lincoln's Inn, LLB (Hons)(Leeds)

Choo Simons *Mrs Mei Ling*
Called: Oct 1994, Middle Temple, LLB
(Hons)(Lond)

Choong *Allen Ching Yet*
Called: Nov 1997, Lincoln's Inn, LLB
(Hons)(Lond)

Choong *Miss Kartina Abdullah*
Called: July 1995, Lincoln's Inn, LLB (Hons)

Chope *Christopher Robert OBE MP*
House of Commons, London SW1A 0AA.
Called: July 1972, Inner Temple, LLB

Chopra *Gerald*
1242 519 169, and Member Alberta, Canada
Bar. Called: Nov 1948, Middle Temple, MA
(Cantab)

Chorlton *Miss Margaret Denise*
Deans Court Chambers, Cumberland House,
Crown Square, Manchester, M3 3HA.
Called: Nov 1935, Inner Temple, MA (Oxon)

Chou *Sean Yu*
Messrs Wong Partnership, 80 Raffles Place,
[H]58-01, UOB Plaza 1, Singapore 0106, 532
7488, Fax: (65) 532 5722, and Member
Singapore Bar. Called: July 1993, Middle
Temple, LLB (Hons, Bris)

Choudhury *Bhaskar* •
In House Barrister, Hambro Legal Protection
Ltd, Hambro House, Stephenson Road,
Business Park, Colchester, Essex CO4 4QR,
0990 234600, Fax: 0990 234880, and
Member Calcutta. Called: Nov 1988,
Lincoln's Inn, BSc (Calcutta), BA (Hons),
MSc, LLB, (Hons), ACMA, AICWA

Choudhury *Ms Roxana Idris*
Called: Mar 1996, Inner Temple, LLB

Choudhury *Tuyfal Ahmed*
Called: Oct 1997, Inner Temple, BA
(London)

Chow *Miss Ee-Chin*
Associate Solicitor Paralegal, Fong & Ng
Solicitors, 7th Floor, China Building, 29
Queen's Road Central, Central, 852
28484848, Fax: 852 28452995, and Member
Malaysia Bar. Called: July 1994, Gray's Inn,
LLB (Reading)

Chow *Miss Fung Kwan*
Called: Oct 1997, Middle Temple, BSc
(Hong Kong), CPE (Hong Kong)

Chow *Kenneth Charn Ki*
11/F Flat G, Skyline Mansion, 51 Conduit
Road, Hong Kong, 25212555, Fax:
28691527, Formerly Solicitor. Called: May
1988, Middle Temple, LLB (Hons), LLM
(London)

Chow *Kenneth Kok Wee*
Called: July 1995, Lincoln's Inn, LLB (Hons)

Chow *Kenny Yin Wo*
Superintendent, Hong Kong Police Force,
Flat 12h, Braemar Terrace, 1 Pak Fuk Road,
28950025, Fax: 28950025, and Member
Supreme Court of the Australia Capital
Territory. Called: July 1990, Gray's Inn, LLB
(Lond)

Chow *Miss Lai Yin*
Called: July 1994, Lincoln's Inn, LLB (Hons)

Chow *Miss Letty Yu Shu*
and Member Hong Kong Bar. Called: Nov
1985, Lincoln's Inn, LLB

Chow *Miss Min Wei*
Called: July 1995, Middle Temple, LLB
(Hons) (Hull)

Chow *Miss Nona Swee Li*
Called: Nov 1997, Lincoln's Inn, LLB
(Hons)(Wales)

Chow *Wai Lun*
Called: Nov 1997, Gray's Inn, BSc
(Eng)(Hong Kong), Diplome d'ingenieur,
(Ecole Nationale des, Treavaux Publics)

Chowdhury *Fazle Karim*
Called: Mar 1998, Lincoln's Inn, BSc
(Hons)(B'ham), CPE (Sussex)

Chowdhury *Khaled Hamid*
Asfia House, Road 36, House 13, Ghulshan,
Dhaka 1212, 880 2 885872/017525542, Fax:
880 2 885736, and Member Dhaka,
Bangladesh. Called: July 1995, Lincoln's Inn,
LLB (Hons), MA (Legal Studies), LLM (Int'l
Bus Law), (KCL)

Chowdhury *Md Moinal Islam*
and Member Bangladesh Bar. Called: Nov
1994, Lincoln's Inn, BA (Hons), MA, LLB
(Dhaka), LLB (Hons)

Choy *Montague Wing Kin*
Called: July 1997, Lincoln's Inn, LLB
(Hons)(L'pool)

Chrimes *David Francis William* •
Senior Crown Prosecutor, Crown
Prosecution Service, 5th Floor, St Peter's
House, Derby, 01332 621600. Called: Oct
1990, Gray's Inn, LLB(Hons) (London)

Christian *John Charles*
Editor "Graya", Ferndale House, Harling
Road, North Lopham, Diss, Norfolk
IP22 2NQ, 01379 687518, Fax: 01379
687704. Called: July 1975, Gray's Inn, BA

Christie *Iain Robert* •
Assistant Legal Adviser, Foreign &
Commonwealth Office, King Charles Street,
London SW1A 2AH, 0171 270 2576, Fax:
0171 270 2767, Member of the High Court
of Australia and Member Australian Capital
Territory. Called: July 1989, Inner Temple,
BA [Dunelm]

Christie *Professor Richard Hunter*
President, Association of Arbitrators (SA)
Vice-President, All Africa Council, LCIA, 30
Harman Road, Claremont 7700, South
Africa, (27) 021 61 1928, Fax: 927) 021 61
1928, QC Zimbabwe & Zambia. Called: June
1949, Lincoln's Inn, MA LLB (Cantab),
FCIArb, FAArb

Christie *Robert Harold McLeod Hunter*
Bronderi, Llandovery Road, Llanwrtyd Wells,
Powys LD5 4TA. Called: July 1974, Lincoln's
Inn, MA

Christie *Victor Benjamin* •
10 Capstan Square, London E14 3EU, 0171
987 2893/01 706 0183. Called: Nov 1965,
Inner Temple, MA (Oxon), FCA, ATII

Christie-Miller *Roderick Wallace*
Called: Nov 1994, Inner Temple, BA (Lond),
CPE

Christofides *Miss Anna Maria*
Hollis Whiteman Chambers, 3rd/4th Floor,
Queen Elizabeth Bldg, Temple, London,
EC4Y 9BS. Called: Nov 1983, Lincoln's Inn,
BA (Lond)

Christofides *Miss Etta*
Called: Feb 1993, Gray's Inn, LLB (Anglia),
LLM

Christoforou *Mrs Stella Tanta*
Called: Nov 1991, Middle Temple, BA Hons
(Kent)

Chronias *Nicholas John*
Legal Adviser, Beachcroft Stanleys Solicitors,
20 Furnival Street, London EC4A 1BN, 0171
242 1011, Fax: 0171 894 6530. Called: Nov
1991, Inner Temple, LLB (Lond)

Chrysanthou *Nicos*
Partner, 4 Demosthenes Str, P.O.Box 1762,
1513 Nicosia, (3572) 447443, Fax: (3572)
472075, and Member Cyprus. Called: Nov
1996, Inner Temple, LLB (Lond), LLM
(So'ton)

Chrysostomides *Mrs Eleni*
Dr K Chrysostomides & Co, PO Box 2119, 1
Lambousa Street, Nicosia, 448 278, Fax: 02
451391. Called: Nov 1973, Gray's Inn, LLB

Chu *Chung Keung*
Called: Nov 1996, Middle Temple, LLB
(Hons)

Chu *Miss Yuen Yee*
Called: July 1995, Middle Temple, LLB
(Hons)

Chu *Miss Yvonne Siok Teang*
Suite 2, Montagu Pavilion, 10 Queensway,
Gibraltar, 45467/40824, Fax: 45467/40931,
and Member Gibraltar Bar. Called: Nov
1993, Gray's Inn, LLB (Manch)

Chua *Boon Thien*
Called: July 1994, Lincoln's Inn, LLB (Hons)

Chua *Miss Cynthia Cher Lan*
and Member Singapore Bar. Called: July
1995, Middle Temple, LLB (Hons)

Chua *Miss Geok Hong*
Called: Nov 1995, Middle Temple, LLB
(Hons)

Chua *Miss Grace Hwee Bin*
and Member Malaysia Bar. Called: Nov 1992,
Lincoln's Inn, LLB (Hons)(Wales)

Chua *Miss Huey Sian*
Legal Assistant, M/S Chooi & Company,
Penthouse, Ming Building PH-O1, Jalan
Bukit Nanas, 50200 Kuala Lumpur, 03
2327344, and Member Malaysia. Called: July
1996, Lincoln's Inn, LLB (Hons)(Sheff)

Chua *Miss Hui Peng*
and Member Malaysian Bar. Called: July
1995, Middle Temple, LLB (Hons)

Chua *Kok Wan*
Called: July 1995, Middle Temple, B.Ec, LLB

Chua *Miss Lay Kuang*
Called: Nov 1994, Middle Temple, B.Pharm
(Hons)

Chua *Miss Lik Teng*
Yeo-Leong & Peh, 20 McCallum Street, 12-
03, Asia Chambers, Singapore, 65 2238168,
Fax: 65 2207888, Advocate & Solicitor of
the Supreme Court of Singapore.
Called: July 1992, Middle Temple, LLB
(Hons) LSe

Chua *Lincoln*
Legal Advisor, 579 L Lorong Utama 6, Air
Keroh Heights, 75450 Malacca, West
Malaysia, 06 326860, and Member Malaysia
Bar. Called: July 1992, Inner Temple, LLB

Chua *Miss Lucianna Mei Ling*
2 Ridgewood Close, [H]05-02, Himiko
Court, and Member Singapore. Called: July
1996, Middle Temple, LLB (Hons)(Sheff)

Chua *Miss Siew Gaik*
Called: July 1996, Lincoln's Inn, BA (Hons)

Chua *Miss Soo Fon*
Called: July 1995, Lincoln's Inn, LLB (Hons)

Chua *Miss Suzanie May-Li*
501-1155 Mainland Street, Vancouver V6B
5P2, (604) 6828231, Fax: (604) 6828231,
International Bar Association, Chartered
Accountant (ICAEW) Honorary Legal
Scholar (Centre for Int'l Legal Studies) and
Member Singapore Bar. Called: July 1988,
Gray's Inn, LLB Hons (Bris)

Chua *Tze Wei*
Called: July 1990, Gray's Inn, LLB(Bris), BCL
(Oxon)

Chua *Miss Yak Hoon*
15 N Kang Choo Bin Road, Singapore
548285. Called: July 1991, Middle Temple,
LLB (Hons) (Lond)

Chuah *Miss Hooi Bien*
Called: July 1997, Middle Temple, LLB
(Hons)(Leics)

Chuah *Jern Ern*
Legal Associate, Shearn Delamore & Co, 7th
Floor, Wisma Hamzah, Kwong-Hing, 2
Leboh Ampang, 50100 Kuala Lumpur,
2300644 (0603), Fax: 2386525, and Member
Malaysia Bar. Called: July 1993, Lincoln's
Inn, LLB (Hons, N'ham)

Chuah *Miss Joo Ee*
No 79 Jalan Labrooy, Merdeka Garden,
30100 Ipoh, Perak, 5060192. Called: July
1997, Gray's Inn, LLB (Lond)

Chuah *Miss Sheena Sze Ching*
Called: July 1997, Middle Temple, LLB
(Hons)

Chuah *Miss Yean Ping*
Legal Assistant, Messrs Shook Lin & Bok,
Advocates & Solicitors, 20th Floor, Arab -
Malaysian, Building, 55 Jalan Raja Chulan,
50200 Kuala Lumpur, 03 2011788, Fax: 03
2011778/779/775, and Member Malaysia.
Called: July 1996, Lincoln's Inn, LLB
(Hons)(Leics)

Chuang *Miss Effie Twan Phey*
Called: Nov 1997, Lincoln's Inn, LLB
(Hons)(Leeds)

Chuang *Keng Chiew*
2 Battery Road, Maybank Chambers, 7th
Floor, 3366533, Fax: 3370906. Called: July
1996, Middle Temple, LLB (Hons)(Lond)

Chubb *Francis Edward Vaudrey*
Called: Oct 1996, Middle Temple, BA
(Hons)(L'pool), CPE

Chuhan *Maluk Singh*
and Member Punjab & Haryana Bars.
Called: Nov 1974, Lincoln's Inn, BA LLB

Chui *Miss Yee Mei Ivy*
Called: July 1996, Middle Temple, LLB
(Hons)(Wales)

Chularojmontri *Prathan*
Called: July 1995, Gray's Inn, LLB (Wales)

Chun *Lim Whei*
Called: Nov 1997, Inner Temple, LLB (Lond)

Chung *Miss Jillian*
Lawrence Graham Solicitors, 190 Strand,
London WC2R 1JN, 0171 379 0000, Fax:
0171 379 6854. Called: Nov 1989, Gray's
Inn, LLB [Brunel]

Chung *Kee Ying*
and Member Hong Kong Bar Supreme Court
of the Australian Capital Territory.
Called: Nov 1990, Gray's Inn, LLB (Lond)

Chung *Ming (Chit)*
Associate Director, Corporate Finance, SBC
Warburg Dillon Read, 2 Finsbury Avenue,
London EC2M 2PP, and Member Hong Kong
Bar. Called: Nov 1993, Inner Temple, LLB

Chung *Miss Rebecca Wan-Yi*
64 Jalan Lembah Thomson, 4544266, Fax:
4544766, and Member Singapore Bar.
Called: Nov 1992, Middle Temple, LLB
(Hons, Hull)

Chung *Yiu Ming*
26d South Bay Towers, 59 South Bay Road,
(852) 25769090, and Member Hong Kong
Bar. Called: July 1991, Lincoln's Inn, BSc
(Hons), Dip Law (City Uni), ACIArb, FRICS,
FHKIS

Churaman *Miss Deborah Sirojini* •
Grade 6, Dept of Trade & Industry,
Ashdown House, 123 Victoria Street,
Victoria, London, 0171 215 3130.
Called: Nov 1984, Middle Temple, LLB

Churaman *Miss Simone Gail* •
Senior Principal Legal Officer, DSS, 5th
Floor, Southend House, 29/37 Brighton
Road, Sutton, Surrey SM2 5AN, 0181 652
6000 X 6500. Called: Nov 1987, Middle
Temple, BA(Hons), LLM

Church *Lucas Jacques Richard* •
Called: Feb 1990, Middle Temple, LLB

Church *Thomas Henry*
Called: Oct 1994, Gray's Inn, BA

Chwee *Han Sin*
Called: Nov 1995, Middle Temple, LLB
(Hons)

Cladingbowl *Rodney* •
Senior Crown Prosecutor, Crown
Prosecution Service, Queens House, 58
Victoria Street, St Albans, Herts AL1 3HZ,
01727 844753. Called: Nov 1970, Gray's
Inn, LLB (Lond)

Claiborne *Louis Fenner*
12 Park Road, Wivenhoe, Colchester, Essex
CO7 9NB, (01206) 822430, Fax: (01206)
824300, US Supreme Court and Member
Louisiana Bar District of Columbia Bar.
Called: Nov 1974, Middle Temple, LLB

Claire *Rajinder Kumar*
Called: Oct 1997, Inner Temple, LLB
(Wolverhampton)

Claisse *Victor BEM*
11 Cambridge Drive, Bognor Regis, W
Sussex PO21 5RJ, 01243 826678.
Called: July 1971, Gray's Inn, LLB (Lond)

Clark *Alastair Trevor CBE LVO*
11 Ramsay Garden, Edinburgh EH1 2NA,
0131 225 8070, Fax: 0131 225 8070.
Called: Nov 1963, Middle Temple, MA
(Oxon), FSAScot

Clark *David Andrew* •
Principal Crown Prosecutor, Crown
Prosecution Service, Colmore Gate, 2
Colmore Row, Birmingham B3 2QA, 0121
629 7200, Fax: 0121 629 7335. Called: Nov
1987, Middle Temple, LLB

Clark *Mrs Elizabeth Anne* •
Principal Crown Prosecutor, Crown
Prosecution Service, Brighton Branch
Office, 3 Clifton Mews, Clifton Hill,
Brighton, East Sussex BN1 3HR, 01273
207171, Fax: 01273 207849. Called: July
1984, Gray's Inn, BA

Clark *Julian James*
Lawyer, Clifford Chance, 200 Aldersgate
Street, London EC1A 4JJ, 0171 600 1000,
Fax: 0171 600 5555. Called: Nov 1988,
Inner Temple, LLB

Clark *Dr Margaret Lynda*
Advocates Library, Parliament Square,
Edinburgh, Scotland, 031 226 2881, QC
Scotland and Member Scottish Bar.
Called: July 1988, Inner Temple, PhD
(Edinburgh), LLB (St Andrews)

Clark *Ms Samantha Claire*
Called: Mar 1996, Lincoln's Inn, LLB (Hons)

Clarke *Andrew Terence*
Vice-President Business Development - Asia
Pacific Mobil Power Inc., Mobil Power Inc.,
[H] 10-00 Winsland House, 3 Killiney Road,
65 739 5574, Fax: 65 739 5640. Called: July
1982, Middle Temple, MA (Cantab)

Clarke *Mrs Antonette Oluwatoyin* •
Senior Crown Prosecutor, Crown
Prosecution Service, Portland House, Stag
Place, London SW1, 0171 915 5700.
Called: Nov 1986, Lincoln's Inn, BA

Clarke *Dominic Tobias*
40 King Street West, Suite 2100, Toronto
M5H 3C2, (416) 869 5300, Fax: (416) 360
8877, and Member Ontario Bar. Called: July
1988, Middle Temple, MA, LLM (Cantab)

Clarke *Gerald*
The Old School House, Slaugham, near Haywards Heath, Sussex RH17 6AG, 01444 400800/400575, and Member Brunei. Called: Feb 1956, Inner Temple, MA, BCL

Clarke *Giles Nevill*
62 Westbourne Park Villas, London W2 1EB, 0171 221 8557. Called: Nov 1976, Middle Temple, MA (Cantab) PhD, (Lond), FTII

Clarke *Miss Gillian Marjorie* •
Legal Director, UBS Asset Management, London Limited, Triton Court, 14 Finsbury Square, London EC2A 1PD, 0171 901 5000. Called: July 1982, Middle Temple, MA (Oxon)

Clarke *Miss Gina Maria* •
Principal Lawyer, London Borough of Islington, Town Hall, Upper Hall, Islington, London N1 2UD, 0171 477 3213, Fax: 0171 477 3243. Called: Feb 1983, Gray's Inn, BA

Clarke *Mrs Jennifer* •
Senior Lawyer, HM Customs & Excise, New King's Beam House, 22 Upper Ground, London SE1 9PJ, 0171 865 5172. Called: July 1971, Gray's Inn, LLB, P.G.Cert.Ed, Dip in Counselling

Clarke *Miss Juliana Patience*
Called: July 1978, Lincoln's Inn, LLB (Lond)

Clarke *Keith Cutts*
52 Holly Hill, Bassett, Southampton SO16 7EW, 01703 769029, Formerly a Solicitor, Also Inn of Court L Formerly Clerk to City of Southampton Justices and Clerk to Hampshire Magistrates' Courts Committee. Called: May 1977, Middle Temple, Hon LLD (S'ton), FTCL, FRSA

Clarke *Keith Stanley*
Lleweni, 16 Queens Walk, Rhyl, Denbighshire LL18 3NG, 01745 337088. Called: July 1992, Inner Temple, BA (Kent)

Clarke *The Rt Hon Kenneth Harry MP* QC (1980)
Bencher of Gray's Inn 9 Gough Square, London, EC4A 3DE. Called: Nov 1963, Gray's Inn, BA, LLB (Cantab)

Clarke *Malcolm Raymond*
16 Bythorne Close, Lower Earley, Reading RG6 3BH, 0118 9667507, Fax: 0118 9261241. Called: July 1976, Inner Temple

Clarke *Mrs Maria Anne*
11a Craigleith Drive, Edinburgh EH4 3HR, and Member Scottish Bar. Called: Apr 1991, Inner Temple, LLB (Glasgow), BA (Hons) Open

Clarke *Mrs Mollie Marguerite*
Arbitrator, 33 The Street, Uley, Nr Dursley, Glos GL11 5TE, 01453 860245. Called: June 1950, Middle Temple, FCIArb

Clarke *Patrick James* •
Senior Principal Legal Officer, HM Customs & Excise, New Kings Beam House, 22 Upper Ground, London SE1 9PJ. Called: July 1975, Middle Temple, LLB

Clarke *Patrick James*
Called: Oct 1997, Gray's Inn, BSc

Clarke *Paul*
Called: Feb 1995, Inner Temple, BSc (Leic)

Clarke *Paul Matthew*
IT Consultant, Greythorn Plc, 6 Southampton Place, London WC1A 2DA, 0171 576 6020, Fax: 0171 831 2233. Called: Feb 1995, Gray's Inn, LLB (Warwick)

Clarke *Miss Petra Cecilia*
and Member Trinidad & Tobago Bar. Called: Nov 1989, Middle Temple, BA, Dip Int. Law

Clarke *Richard Thomas Edward*
Jones Miller & Co, 7 George St, Luton, Beds LU1 2BS, 01582 730098. Called: Feb 1992, Inner Temple, LLB (Hons)(Hull)

Clarke *Ms Theresa Mary* •
Grade 6, Department of the Environment, 2 Marsham Street, London SW1P 3EB. Called: Nov 1970, Middle Temple, LLB

Clarke-Jervoise *Miss Caroline Sarah*
Lovell White Durrant, 65 Holborn Viaduct, London EC1A 2DY, 0171 236 0066, Fax: 0171 248 4212. Called: July 1986, Inner Temple, LLB

Clarke-Melville *Dr Betty Elizabeth*
and Member Barbados Bar. Called: July 1996, Inner Temple, LLB, BA

Clarke-Wills *Mrs Auriol Paulina*
Equal Opps Sub-Comm of FDA, and Member Trinidad and Tobago. Called: July 1969, Inner Temple, LLB (Hons)

Clasper *Stephen Reid*
65 Campden Hill Court, Campden Hill Road, Kensington, London W8 7HL, and Member California, USA. Called: July 1971, Gray's Inn, MA (Cantab)

Claughton-Rugg *Mrs Claire Lilian Margaret* •
Principal Crown Prosecutor. Called: Feb 1983, Inner Temple, BA Lond

Claypoole *Charles Henry*
Called: Nov 1997, Inner Temple, BA (Cantab), LLM (Germany)

Clayton *Cedric*
Called: Nov 1960, Middle Temple, MA, LLB

Clayton *Peter David*
2302 Diamond Exchange Bldg, 8-10 Duddell Street, Central, Hong Kong, and Member Hong Kong Bar 11 Stone Bldgs, 1st Floor, Lincoln's Inn, London, WC2A 3TG. Called: July 1977, Middle Temple

Clayton *Richard John* •
Assistant Legal Adviser, The Home Office, 50 Queen Anne's Gate, London SW1H 9AT. Called: Nov 1969, Middle Temple, MA, BCL

Cleare *Miss Camille Amanda*
Called: Nov 1997, Gray's Inn, LLB (Kent)

Cleary *Edmund*
Deputy Clerk to the Justices, Magistrates Court, Gillbridge Avenue, Sunderland SR1 3AP, 0191 5141621. Called: Apr 1986, Gray's Inn, BA

Cleave *Mrs Celia Valentine* •
Legal Officer, GMB, 205 Hook Road, Chessington, Surrey KT9 1EA, 0181 397 8881. Called: Nov 1985, Gray's Inn, MA (St Andrews), Dip Law (City)

Clegg *Richard Ninian Barwick* QC (1979)
Called: July 1960, Inner Temple, MA (Oxon)

Clemens *Ms Julie*
Called: Nov 1997, Gray's Inn, BA (N.E.Lond), MA (Middx), LLB (Lond)

Clement *Ryan Wayne* •
Legal Adviser, Taylor Woodrow, Legal Department, Taywood House, 345 Ruislip Road, Southall, Middlesex UB1 2QX, 0181 578 2366, Fax: 0181 575 4096. Called: Oct 1996, Middle Temple, B.Sc (Hons), LLM (Wolverhampton), LLDip, LLM, ACIArb

Clements *Miss Fiona Anne*
Called: Oct 1996, Middle Temple, MA (Oxon), M.Mus (Sheff)

Clements *Simon Anthony* •
Legal Director, Department of Trade & Industry, 10-18 Victoria Street, London SW1, 0171 215 3132, Fax: 0171 215 3235. Called: Nov 1982, Gray's Inn, BA (Hull)

Cleminson *Craig Derrick* •
Legal Adviser, Stratford Magistrates Court, The Court House, 389/397 High Street, Stratford, London E15 4SB, 0181 522 5000, Fax: 0181 519 9214. Called: Oct 1993, Lincoln's Inn, LLB (Hons)(L'pool)

Clifford *Colin Raymond*
Justices' Chief Executive, Buckinghamshire Magistrates, Courts Committee, The Magistrates' Court, Walton Street, Aylesbury, Bucks HP21 7QG, 01296 338959, Fax: 01296 338960. Called: July 1980, Gray's Inn, MBA

Clifford *Nigel Robert Leslie*
Admitted as Attorney-at-Law Cayman Islands. Called: July 1973, Middle Temple, LLB (Hons)

Clifford *Steven Butler* •
Legal Counsel, Toshiba Electronics (UK) Ltd, Riverside Way, Camberley, Surrey GU15 3YA, 01276 694600, Fax: 01276 691583. Called: Nov 1981, Gray's Inn, BA, LLM

Clifton *Roger Cheston*
Company Secretary & Chief Legal Officer London & Continental Railways Limited, 3-5 Rathbone Place, London W1P 1DA, 0171 314 1000, Fax: 0171 436 2886. Called: July 1996, Gray's Inn, F.C.I.S

Clinch *Timothy Michael Edward*
Called: July 1997, Inner Temple, LLB (Lond)

Closs *Adrian Kenneth* •
Lawyer (Grade 6), MAFF, Legal Department, 55 Whitehall, London SW1A 2EY, 0171 270 8774, Fax: 0171 270 8755. Called: July 1982, Gray's Inn, BA (Lond)

E

Clough *Miss Pamela*
Advocates Library, Parliament House,
Edinburgh EH1 1RF, 0131 226 5071, and
Member Scottish Bar 4 Brick Court, Ground
Floor, Temple, London, EC4Y 9AD.
Called: July 1973, Middle Temple

Clowes *Andrew Mark*
Called: Oct 1996, Inner Temple, LLB
(Wolves)

Clowry *Karl Joseph Konrad*
Associate, Allen & Overy, One New Change,
London EC4M 9QE, 0171 330 3000, Fax:
0171 330 9999. Called: Nov 1994, Inner
Temple, BA (Dublin), LLM (Lond), Dip Law

Clynes *Gordon*
Called: July 1980, Gray's Inn

Coakley *Miss Jamaine*
Called: July 1994, Lincoln's Inn, LLB (Hons,
Manch)

Coast-Powell *Mrs Susan Mary*
Legal Advisor, Director, Cater Allen Trust
Co Ltd, 01534 828000. Called: Nov 1994,
Middle Temple, LLB (Hons), TEP

Coates *Reginald Ian*
61 Wharfedale, Runcorn, Cheshire
WA7 6PS, 01928 717206. Called: Nov 1984,
Gray's Inn, DML, MIMgt

Cocker *Daniel Richard*
104 Crosslet Vale, Greenwich, London
SE10 8DL, 0181 694 0973/0976 742779,
Fax: 0181 694 0973. Called: Oct 1996,
Lincoln's Inn, LLB (Hons)(Leeds)

Cocker *Robert Glenville* •
Crown Prosecutor, Crown Prosecution
Service, Gemini Centre, 88 New London
Road, Chelmsford, Essex CM2 0BR, 01245
252939. Called: Nov 1977, Gray's Inn, BA

Cockrell *Miss Teresa* •
Lawyer, Lord Chancellor's Department,
Selbourne House, 54-60 Victoria Street,
London SW1E 6QW, 0171 210 0719, Fax:
0171 210 0725. Called: Nov 1988, Lincoln's
Inn, BA Hons (Lond), Dip Law, MPhil
(Cantab)

Cockshutt *Ms Emma Elizabeth* •
Head of Legal & Business Affairs, Talkback
Productions Limited, 36 Percy Street,
London W1P 0LN, 0171 323 9777, Fax:
0171 637 5105. Called: Nov 1983, Inner
Temple, LLB Lond, LLB (Hons)(Lond)

Codd *Michael Richard* •
Called: Nov 1989, Gray's Inn, BA [Oxon]

Coddington *Nicholas James*
Called: Oct 1997, Middle Temple, LLB
(Hons)(Sheff)

Codrai *Christian Augustus*
Senior Legal Adviser, International Fund for
Agricultural Development (IFAD), Legal
Services, I.F.A.D. of the United Nations, 107
Via Del Serafico, 00142 Roma, (396) 5459
2457, Fax: (396) 504-3463. Called: Nov
1979, Inner Temple, LLB,LLM

Coe *Roger Graham*
Called: Nov 1994, Middle Temple, LLB
(Hons), LLM

Coelho *Oswaldo Gerardo*
Rua Garrett 21, PO Box 91, 8600 Lagos, 82
762408, Fax: 82 767258, and Member
Portugal. Called: Nov 1979, Lincoln's Inn,
MA (Hons) (Bombay), Licentiate in Law,
(Lisbon)

Coffer *Ian*
Principal Court Clerk, Justices' Clerk's
Office, Market Street (East), Newcastle
Upon Tyne NE99 1TB, 0191 232 7326.
Called: Nov 1985, Inner Temple, LLB (Lond)

Coffey *Nicholas Alexander*
Called: Nov 1994, Inner Temple, LLB, LLM
(Lond)

Coffey *Paul Michael Matthew*
Law Library, Four Courts, Dublin, Republic
of Ireland, 720622, Fax: 722254, King's Inns
(Dublin) and Member Southern Ireland Bar.
Called: Feb 1988, Middle Temple, BCL
(Ireland), LLM (Dublin

Coford *Frederic John* •
Assistant Director, Serious Fraud Office, Elm
House, 10-16 Elm Street, London WC1X 0BJ.
Called: July 1971, Middle Temple, BA
(Cantab)

Coghlan *Christopher David Francis*
5/F 10 Queen's Road, Central, (852) 2525
0221, Fax: (852) 2845 2441, and Member
Hong Kong Bar. Called: Nov 1972, Inner
Temple, BCL

Cohen *Adrian Leon*
Clifford Chance, 200 Aldersgate Street,
London EC1A 4SS, 0171 600 1000, Fax:
0171 600 5555. Called: Nov 1988, Middle
Temple, LLB (LSE), LLM (Lond)

Cohen *Clive Zev*
and Member Member of the Bars of
Johannesburg, Swaziland and Zimbabwe 3/4
South Square, Gray's Inn, London, WC1R
5HP. Called: Feb 1989, Lincoln's Inn, BA,
LLB, (Witwatersrand)

Cohen *Daniel James Marcus* •
Warner/Chappell Music Ltd. Called: Oct
1995, Middle Temple, LLB (Hons)(Bris)

Cohen *Dr Harvey* •
Principal Lecturer In Law, London Guildhall
University, Department of Law, 84
Moorgate, London EC2M 6SQ, 0171 320
1455, Fax: 0171 320 1439, Formerly a
Solicitor. Called: Nov 1969, Lincoln's Inn,
LLB, PhD (Lond)

Cohen *Howard Lawrence* •
Branch Crown Prosecutor, Crown
Prosecution Service, Barnet & Haringey
Branch, River Park House, 225 High Road,
Wood Green, London N22 4HQ, 0181 888
8889, Fax: 0181 888 0746. Called: July
1980, Inner Temple, BA(Hons)

Cohen *Mrs Jacqueline Susan*
Called: Nov 1973, Middle Temple, LLB, PhD

Cohen *Mrs Lenora Annette* •
Legal Advisor Company Secretary.
Called: July 1977, Middle Temple, LLB
(Hons)

Cohen *Michael Alan* •
Chairman; British Academy of Experts, 2
South Square, Gray's Inn, London
WC1R 5HP, 0171 637 0333, Fax: 0171 637
1893. Called: June 1955, Gray's Inn, LLB,
FCIArb, FBAE

Cohen *Ms Susan Elizabeth*
Director of Legal & Business Affairs,
Polygram Pty Ltd, 3 Munn Reserve, Millers
Point, Sydney 2000, N.S.W. Australia, (02)
9207 0519, Fax: (02) 9241 1497. Called: July
1981, Gray's Inn, LLB (B'ham),MA

Colclough *Mrs Leslie Ann*
Lobosky & Lobosky, P O Box N-7123,
Nassau, (242) 323 1317, Fax: (242) 323
1318, and Member Bahamas Bar.
Called: Nov 1996, Lincoln's Inn, LLB
(Hons)(Bucks)

Coldstream *Sir George Phillips KCB,
KCVO* QC (1960)
The Gate Hse, Blatchington Hill, Seaford,
Sussex BN25 2AH, 01323 892801, American
College of Trial Lawyers American Institute
of Judicial Administration Chairman,
Council of Legal Education 1970-73 and
Member American Bar Association.
Called: Nov 1930, Lincoln's Inn, LLD Hon,
Columbia, MA (Oxon)

Cole *Sir Alexander Colin KCB, KCVO,
TD*
Sheriff, City of London 1976-77, Former
Garter King of Arms. Called: Nov 1949,
Inner Temple, BCL, MA (Oxon)

Cole *Miss Justine Mary-Louisa*
Called: Nov 1997, Gray's Inn, LLB (Thames
V)

Cole *Mrs Sally Margaret* •
Principal Crown Prosecutor, Crown
Prosecution Service H/Q, 50 Ludgate Hill,
London EC4M 7EX, 0171 273 8000, Fax:
0171 329 8166. Called: July 1982, Gray's
Inn, BA Hons (Keele)

Cole *Miss Sarah Helen*
28 Kendal Court, Shoot Up Hill, London
NW2 3PD, 0181 452 2077. Called: Feb
1995, Inner Temple, LLB

Colebrook *Miss Ashlar Shikell*
Trust Officer, and Member Bahamas Bar,
Sept 1996. Called: July 1996, Lincoln's Inn,
BBA (Miami), MA (Bris)

Coleman *Mrs Anne Elizabeth*
Principal Court Clerk, S.E. Surrey
Magistrates Court, The Law Courts,
Hatchlands Road, Redhill, Surrey RH1 6DH,
01737 765581, Fax: 01737 764972.
Called: July 1982, Inner Temple, LLB
(Bristol)

Coleman *Miss Sarah Catherine Mary*
Former Solicitor. Called: July 1996, Gray's
Inn, BA (Oxon)

Colenso *John Adam*
Called: Oct 1995, Lincoln's Inn, BA
(Hons)(Newcastle), MA (York)

Colesworthy *Peter Harry*
Flat 9, Muster Court, Muster Green,
Haywards heath, W Sussex RH16 4AW,
01444 417223. Called: Nov 1951, Inner
Temple, BA, LLB MHCIMA

Collett *Dr Philip Michel Rene*
46 Station Way, Buckhurst Hill, Essex
IG9 6LN, Fax: 0181 504 3303. Called: Oct
1991, Inner Temple, MB BS (Lond), Dip Law
(City), D.O. MRCOphth

Colley *Ms Lita Susan*
Called: Mar 1997, Gray's Inn, LLB (Derby)

Colley *Ms Rachel Elizabeth*
Called: Nov 1997, Inner Temple, LLB, LLM

Collie *Ellison Isaac*
Michael A Dean & Co, 94 Dowdeswell
Street, P O Box N7521, Nassau, 809 322
3997, Fax: 809 325 3345, Counsel and
Attorney-at-Law and Member Bahamas Bar
Association. Called: July 1996, Lincoln's Inn,
CPE (City)

Collie *Peter Andrew* •
Legal Adviser, Tarmac Construction Limited,
Construction House, Birch Street,
Wolverhampton WV1 4HY. Called: July
1994, Middle Temple, LLB (Hons)(Notts),
MCIOB, ACIArb, LCGI

Collier *Leigh Howard*
46 Vallance Road, Alexandra Park, London
N22 4UB, 0181 881 9293. Called: Oct 1995,
Inner Temple, MA (Cantab), CPE, M.I.Mgt,
M.B.C.S.

Collier *Miss Naomi Lawson*
Called: July 1982, Middle Temple, LLB
So'ton, ACA

Collier *Ms Shirley Diane*
Called: Nov 1984, Middle Temple, Dip
Mag.Law

Collier *Stephen John* •
Director of Legal Services, General
Healthcare Group Ltd, Legal Department,
210 Euston Road, London NW1 2DA, 0171
419 6021. Called: July 1980, Lincoln's Inn,
LLB (Hons), Dip Ae Law, LLM

Collier-Wright *Charles Edward
Hurrell* •
Group Legal Manager, MGN Ltd, 1 Canada
Square, London E14 5AD, 0171 293 3747,
Fax: 0171 293 3613. Called: July 1976,
Middle Temple, MA (Oxon)

Collinge *Ronald Ashton Hilton OBE* •
The Manchester Ship Canal Co, Collier
Street, Runcorn, Cheshire WA7 1HR,
019285 67465, Fax: 019285 67469.
Called: June 1950, Inner Temple, MA
(Oxon)

Collinge *Thomas Roden*
Called: Oct 1997, Gray's Inn, BA (Dunelm),
MBA (Edinburgh)

Collings *Andrew John*
Called: Nov 1995, Middle Temple, LLB
(Hons)

Collins *Ms Beverley Bernice*
JP Salford Bench, 0161 707 4616.
Called: Nov 1995, Inner Temple, BA (York),
Dip Law (City)

Collins *James*
Called: Mar 1997, Gray's Inn, BA (Lond)

Collins *Michael Geoffrey* •
General Manager, Lloyds Policy Signing
Office, Chairman Broker Network Limited,
Three Oaks, 7 Manor Park Drive,
Westorning, Bedfordfordshire MK45 5LS,
01525 717852, Fax: 01525 717584.
Called: Nov 1981, Inner Temple, LLB
(Lond), FCII, MBA

Collins *Miss Nadia Anouchka*
Called: Nov 1994, Middle Temple, BA
(Hons), LLM

Collins *Miss Nicolette* •
Senior Crown Prosecutor, Crown
Prosecuton Service, Kings House, Kimberley
Road, Harrow, Middlesex, 0181 424 8688.
Called: Oct 1990, Middle Temple, LLB (Bris)

Collins *Richard Alexander* •
Director - Divisional Legal Services, U.G.C
Limited, Unipart House, Garsington Road,
Cowley, Oxford OX4 2PG, 01865 383643,
Fax: 01865 384672. Called: Nov 1982,
Middle Temple, BA (Hons)

Collins *Ruaidhri Jolyon McCracken*
Called: Oct 1994, Middle Temple, BA
(Hons)(Cantab), LLM (Lond)

Collins *Miss Sara Jane*
W S Walker & Co, P O Box 26SGT, Grand
Cayman, 1-809-949-0100, Fax: 1-809-949-
7886, and Member Cayman Islands Bar.
Called: July 1995, Lincoln's Inn, LLB (Hons)

Collins *Scott*
Called: Nov 1994, Gray's Inn, BA
(Queensland), LLB (Sydney), LLM (Lond)

Collon *Michael Hyde* •
Head of Legal Advice & Litigation Division,
Lord Chancellor's Department, Selborne
House, 54/60 Victoria Street, London
SW1E 6QW, 0171 210 0716, Fax: 0171 210
0725. Called: July 1970, Middle Temple, MA

Collu *Miss Melissa*
Called: Oct 1997, Middle Temple, BA
(Hons)(Notts), CPE (Lond)

Colombo *Kevin Joseph*
Called: Mar 1996, Gray's Inn, LLB

Colpstein *Miss Lisa Laya*
Deputy Chief Clerk, Thames Magistrates
Court, 58 Bow Road, London E3 4DJ.
Called: Nov 1990, Inner Temple, BA
(Hons)(Kent)

Colquitt *Robert Ian*
Dickinson Cruickshank & Co, Advocates,
33-37 Athol Street, Douglas, Isle of Man
IM1 1LB, 01624 673391, Fax: 01624
620992. Called: July 1995, Inner Temple,
LLB

Comber *John Leslie* •
Assistant Solicitor, Department of the
Environment, 2 Marsham Street, London
SW1P 3EB. Called: July 1970, Gray's Inn,
LLB

Commissioning *Miss Mira Elisabet*
(809) 457 1293, Fax: (809) 456 2696.
Called: July 1997, Lincoln's Inn, LLB
(Hons)(City)

Comonte *Crispin Matthew Morton*
Called: Oct 1996, Lincoln's Inn, BA
(Hons)(Oxon)

Compton *Jonathan Robert*
Called: Feb 1995, Gray's Inn, LLB (Warwick)

Compton *Petrus*
Honourable Attorney General, Attorney
General's Chambers, Erdiston Place, Mandel
Street, Castries, St Lucia, 758 45 23622/
23772, Fax: 758 45 36315, Eastern
Caribbean Supreme Court. Called: July 1992,
Gray's Inn, BA, LLB, LLM (Lond)

Conboy *Andrew* •
Crown Prosecutor, CPS, 2 King Edward
Court, King Edward Street, Nottinghham,
0115 9480480. Called: July 1983, Lincoln's
Inn, LLB (Hons)

Conceicao *Carlos Manuel* •
Deputy Legal Adviser, Ministry of Defence.
Called: July 1987, Middle Temple, LLB
(Hons) (Manch)

Concisom *Miss Audry*
Legal Adviser, Concisom & Co, 2 Jalan
Seenivasagam, 30450 Ipoh, Perak, and
Member Malaysia Bar. Called: Nov 1996,
Middle Temple, LLB (Hons)

Condon *Miss Denise Lynn* •
British Medical Association, BMA HOuse,
Tavistock Square, London, WC1H 9JP, 0171
383 6909, Fax: 0171 383 6911. Called: Oct
1994, Gray's Inn, LLB, MA, AKC

Condon *Ms Elizabeth Esther Patricia*
Called: Feb 1994, Inner Temple, BEd, BA,
MSc, MPhil, (Lond), CPE (Nott'm)

Conlan *James Aloysius*
Called: Nov 1984, Gray's Inn, LLB (Lond)

Conlon *Benjamin Vincenzo Rosario*
Arbitrator to US District Court for the
Northern District of New York, Conlon Law
Offices, P.O.Box 937, Keene Road,
Elizabethtown, New York 12932-0937, 00 1
(518) 873 6887, Fax: 00 1 (518) 873 6897,
US. Supreme Court, US. Court of Appeals
for 2nd, 3rd and 9th Circuits, US. District
Courts for Northern, Southern, Eastern and
Western Districts of New York. US. District
Court of Vermont, US. Tax Court, US Court
of International Trade and Member New.
Called: Nov 1975, Gray's Inn, LLB (Hons)

Conlon Mrs Loraine
Member of Committee for Special
Education, Member of Committee for Pre-
School Special Education, Member of Shared
Decision Making Team, Conlon Law Offices,
Keene Road, Elizabethtown, New York
12932-0937, (518) 873 6887, Fax: (518) 873
6897, Essex County Bar Assoc 1 Crown
Office Row, 2nd Floor, Temple, London,
EC4Y 7HH. Called: Nov 1977, Gray's Inn

Conn Miss Gillian Dallas
Furnival Chambers, 32 Furnival Street,
London, EC4A 1JQ. Called: Nov 1992,
Middle Temple, BA (Hons, Keele)

Connal Ms Sulina Larissa
Called: Nov 1993, Lincoln's Inn, BA (Hons),
Dip in Law

Connell Anthony Edward •
Branch Crown Prosecutor, Crown
Prosecution Service, Solar House, Romford
Road, London E15 4LJ, 0181 534 6601.
Called: July 1982, Gray's Inn, LLB (B'ham)

Connell Miss Joan Agnes
33 Bedford Row, London, WC1R 4JH.
Called: July 1985, Middle Temple, BA
(Hons)

Connell Squadron Leader Paul
James •
Legal Officer, DDLS, RAF STRICKE
COMMAND, SUPPORT SERVICES
(GERMANY), 02161 474683, Fax: 02161
474505, Barrister of Northern Ireland (Sep
1985) and Member Hong Kong. Called: Apr
1991, Middle Temple, BA (Dublin)

Connell William Howard •
Assistant Director of Legal Services, The
Office of the Solicitor, Department of
Health &, Social Security, New Court, 48
Carey Street, London WC2A 2LS, 0171 412
1399, Fax: 0171 412 1415. Called: July
1979, Inner Temple, BA [Dunelm]

Connelly Paul Michael
Called: Nov 1989, Middle Temple, BSc
[Exon], Dip in Law, M Phil (Cantab)

Conner Graham
Called: Feb 1995, Lincoln's Inn, LLB (Hons)

Connick Miss Jillian Rachael
Called: Oct 1992, Middle Temple, BA
(Hons), PGCE &, MA (Leeds), Diploma in
Law

Connolly David
Called: Nov 1996, Lincoln's Inn, BA
(Hons)(Manch)

Connolly Oliver Joseph
and Member Ireland. Called: July 1997,
Middle Temple, LLB (Hons)(Dublin)

Connor Miss Amanda Jane
Called: Oct 1993, Lincoln's Inn, LLB
(Hons)(Lond), A.K.C.

Connor Laurence Joseph
Principal Clerk, Coventry Magistrates Court,
Court House, Little Park Street, Coventry
CV1 2SQ, 01203 630666, Fax: 01203
256513. Called: Dec 1973, Middle Temple,
LLB, MA, Assoc IPD

Conroy Miles Christopher
Called: Feb 1995, Middle Temple, LLB
(Hons)(Lond)

Conroy Mrs Rashidah
Called: July 1995, Lincoln's Inn, LLB (Hons)

Conroy Harris Michael James
Berwin Leighton Solicitors, Adelaide House,
London Bridge, London EC4R 9HA, 0171
623 3144, Fax: 0171 623 4416. Called: Oct
1996, Inner Temple, LLB (Kingston), ARICS,
ACIArb

Cons The Hon Sir Derek Kt
Called: June 1953, Gray's Inn, LLB, FCIArb

Constantinides Miss Rania
Called: Oct 1997, Gray's Inn, BA (Warks),
LLM

Constantinidou Ms Eleni Adoni
Legal Advisor of Offshore Company,
P.O.Box 897, Larnaca, Cyprus, 04-620400,
Fax: 04-620860, and Member Cyprus Bar.
Called: July 1992, Lincoln's Inn, LLB (Hons)
(Leics)

Constantinou Miss Maria
Called: Feb 1994, Lincoln's Inn, LLB (Hons)

Conti John Patrick
Conti, 17 Circular Road, Douglas, Isle of
Man IM1 1AF, 01624 670003, Fax: 01624
612281, Member International Bar
Association and Member Isle of Man Bar.
Called: Nov 1988, Inner Temple, LLB
(Wales)

Conyngham John Stafford •
Director, Control Risks Ltd Legal Advisor,
Control Risks Group Ltd, 83 Victoria Street,
London SW1H OHW, 0171 222 1552, Fax:
0171 222 2296, and Member Hong Kong
Bar. Called: Nov 1975, Gray's Inn, LLB

Coogan Michael Joseph •
Director General, Council of Mortgage
Lenders, 3 Savile Row, London W1X 1AF,
0171 440 2230, Fax: 0171 434 3791.
Called: July 1981, Middle Temple, LLB

Cook Andrew John OBE
Parkway Avenue, Sheffield S9 4UL, 0114
2700895, Fax: 0114 2724553. Called: July
1972, Gray's Inn, LLB (Lond)

Cook Ms Katherine Helen •
Grade 7 (International & EC Division), The
Department of the, Environment, Eland
House, London SW1E 5DU, 0171 890 4815,
Fax: 0171 890 4804. Called: Nov 1990,
Middle Temple, BA (Oxon)

Cooke Christopher George •
In-House Lawyer, Warner Bros Productions
Ltd, 135 Wardour Street, London
WC1V 4AP, 0171 465 4812, Fax: 0171 465
4810. Called: Oct 1993, Inner Temple, LLB
(Bris)

Cooke Peter John
Called: Mar 1998, Lincoln's Inn, LLB
(Hons)(Leeds)

Cooke of Thorndon The Rt Hon. The
Lord KBE QC,
QC New Zealand, PO Box 1530, Wellington,
President of Court of Appeal, New Zealand
Brick Court Chambers, 15/19 Devereux
Court, London, WC2R 3JJ. Called: May 1954,
Inner Temple, MA, PhD (Cantab), LLM (NZ)

Coomansingh Miss Anamarie •
Senior Crown Prosecutor, Crown
Prosecution Service, Branch 2, Birmingham,
12th Floor, 2 Colmore Gate, Birmingham.
Called: Nov 1987, Gray's Inn, LLB (Wales)

Coomaraswamy Punch
Judge, Supreme Court Singapore, Judge's
Chambers, Supreme Court. Called: Feb
1956, Lincoln's Inn, LLB (Nottm)

Coombs Miss Geraldine
Called: Oct 1995, Gray's Inn, BA (Kent)

Coombs John Sebastian
11th Floor, Garfield Barwick Chambers, 53
Martin Place, Sydney NSW 2000, (02) 232
7754, Fax: (02) 221 8006, QC (Australia)
and Member New South Wales Bar 1
Temple Gardens, 1st Floor, Temple,
London, EC4Y 9BB. Called: Apr 1989,
Middle Temple, LLB (Sydney)

Coonan Miss Delia M.
Inns of Court School of Law, 39 Eagle
Street, London WC1R 4AJ, 0171 404 5787,
Fax: 0171 831 4188. Called: July 1973,
Gray's Inn, LLB, LLM, FCIArb

Coope Simon Paul
547 Pacific Street, Brooklyn, NY 11217,
(718) 875 1355, and Member New York
State Bar. Called: Oct 1991, Middle Temple,
LLB Hons

Cooper Miss Dawn •
Treasury Solicitor Department, Queen
Anne's Chambers, 28 The Broadway,
London SW1H 9JS, 0171 210 3375.
Called: July 1989, Lincoln's Inn, BCL
(Oxon), LLB

Cooper Edmund Robert Roy
Called: May 1997, Lincoln's Inn, BA (Hons)

Cooper Geoffrey William
Called: July 1967, Lincoln's Inn, LLB (Lond)

Cooper Miss Helen Elizabeth
Called: Oct 1994, Lincoln's Inn, BA (New
York), CPE

Cooper James Joseph •
Legal Adviser, H M Treasury, Parliament
Street, London SW1P 3AG, 0171 270 1712,
Fax: 0171 270 1668. Called: July 1986, Inner
Temple, MA, BCL (Oxon)

Cooper John Peter •
Assistant Legal Adviser, Off. of Electricity
Regulation, Hagley House, Hagley Road,
Edgbaston, Birmingham B16 8QG, 0121 456
6218, Fax: 0121 456 6464. Called: Oct
1993, Lincoln's Inn, BA (Hons)(Oxon)

Cooper Jonathan Paul •
Legal Director, Liberty, 21 Tabbard Street,
London SE1 4LA, 0171 403 3888, Doughty
Street Chambers, 11 Doughty Street,
London, WC1N 2PG. Called: Nov 1992,
Gray's Inn, BA (Kent)

Cooper *Lieutenant Kevin Simon RN* •
Captain's Secretary, HMS Illustrious, BFPO
305. Called: July 1989, Lincoln's Inn, MA
(Oxon)

Cooper *Mrs Mahtab*
Called: July 1996, Gray's Inn, LLB
(Middlesex)

Cooper *Mark*
Deputy Chief Clerk, Inner London and City
Family, Proceeding & Courts, 59-65 Wells
Street, London W1A 3AE, 0171 323 1649,
Fax: 0171 636 0617. Called: Nov 1989,
Inner Temple, BA, Dip Law

Cooper *Martin Anthony*
17 Privett Road, Fareham, Hants PO15 6SE,
01329 847079. Called: June 1959, Lincoln's
Inn, MA

Cooper *Ms Penelope Elisabeth* •
Borough Council Legal Dept., Wandsworth
Borough Council, Administration
Department, The Town Hall, Wandsworth
High Street, London SW18 2PU, 0181 871
6130, Fax: 0181 871 7506. Called: Nov
1990, Inner Temple, BSc (Hons)

Cooper *Richard Vaughan* •
General Counsel, Bat Mark Limited, Export
House, Cawsey Way, Woking, Surrey
GU21 1YB, 01483 792944, Fax: 01483
792982. Called: July 1971, Gray's Inn, BSc
MSc

Cooper *Commander Simon Nicholas
RN* •
Deputy Chief Naval Judge Advocate.
Called: July 1982, Middle Temple, LLB
(Bristol)

Coopman *Mrs Patricia Mary* •
Senior Principal Legal Officer, HM Customs
& Excise, New King's Beam House, 22
Upper Ground, London SE1 9PJ. Called: July
1970, Middle Temple

Coote *Mrs Shirley Ann*
Called: July 1977, Middle Temple, BA
(Lond), MSc

Cope *John Thomas*
Called: Oct 1997, Middle Temple, BA
(Hons)(Leeds)

Corbett *Adrian Charles*
Called: Oct 1997, Lincoln's Inn, LLB
(Hons)(Lond)

Corbett *Anthony Ian* •
Grade 5 (Prosecutions), Ministry of
Agriculture,, Fisheries and Food, 55
Whitehall, London SW1, 0171 270 8305,
Fax: 0171 270 8755. Called: Nov 1973,
Lincoln's Inn, LLB (Hons)

Corcos *Edward David* •
Senior Legal Adviser, Sun Life Assurance
Society PLC, Chief Office, 107 Cheapside,
London EC2V 6DU, 0171 606 7788, Fax:
0171 378 1865. Called: July 1980, Gray's
Inn, LLB (Soton)

Corcut *Andrew*
Called: Feb 1994, Lincoln's Inn, LLB (Hons)

Corderoy *Conor Simon Ivor Mark*
Called: Oct 1996, Inner Temple, LLB
(Westminster)

Corfield *The Rt Hon. Sir Frederick
Vernon QC* (1972)
Recorder, Wordings Orchard, Sheepscombe,
Stroud, Glos GL6 7RE. Called: June 1945,
Middle Temple

Coriat *Christopher Archibald*
Coriats Trustees, Bristol House, PO Box
171, Providenciales, Turks & Caicos Islands,
+1 649 946 4800, Fax: +1 649 946 4850,
Attorney at Law, Turks & Caicos Islands and
Member Turks & Caicos Islands. Called: July
1977, Lincoln's Inn, TEP

Corke *Donald Stevenson*
Part-time Special Adjudicator (Immigration
Appeals), Advocates Library, Parliament
House, Edinburgh EH1 1RF, 0131 226 5071,
Fax: 0131 225 3642, and Member Scottish
Bar. Called: July 1995, Middle Temple, BA
(Cape Town), LLB (Witwatersrand)

Corless-Smith *David*
Called: Oct 1993, Inner Temple, BDS
(L'pool), Dip, Law, LLM (UCL)

Corn *Matthew Adam*
Called: Oct 1995, Gray's Inn, BA

Cornelius *Marc*
Called: Oct 1997, Inner Temple, LLB
(Thames Valley)

Corness *Sir Colin Ross*
Chairman, Glaxo Wellcome Pension
Trustees, Glaxo Wellcome Plc, Lansdowne
House, Berkeley Square, London W1X 6BQ,
0171 408 8901, Fax: 0171 408 8603.
Called: Nov 1956, Inner Temple, MA

Corning *Miss Elizbeth Ann*
Called: Nov 1995, Middle Temple, BA
(Hons)

Cornish *Miss Emma Rachael*
Called: Oct 1996, Middle Temple, BA (Hons)
(Keele)

Coroneos *Miss Georgina*
B Logothetidis 23, Athens 115-24, 6928040,
Fax: 6928040. Called: Oct 1996, Middle
Temple, BA (Hons) (Keele)

Corrie *Hugh Robert La Touche*
Director Legal Services, Mirror Group
Newspapers (Retired), Waterperry House,
Wineham, Nr Henfield, West Sussex
BN5 9BT, 01403 710294. Called: June 1951,
Gray's Inn, BA, LLB (Cantab)

Corrigan *Anthony John QC*
15/F Printing House, 6 Duddell Street,
Central, 25212 616, Fax: 28450260.
Called: July 1962, Gray's Inn, LLB

Corrin *Miss Alexandra Jane*
5 Wrightons Hill, Helmdon, Northants
NN13 5UF. Called: July 1977, Gray's Inn,
LLB (Wales)

Corsan *James David Martin*
10 Richmond Bridge Mansions, Willoughby
Road, Twickenham, Middlesex TW1 2QJ,
0181 744 9677, Fax: 0181 744 9677.
Called: July 1977, Gray's Inn, BA

Corston *Ms Jean Ann MP*
St John's Chambers, Small Street, Bristol,
BS1 1DW. Called: Feb 1991, Inner Temple,
LLB

Cort *Dr Leon Errol*
Adviser to Government of Antigua &
Barbuda Chairman of the St John's
Development Corporation, Chambers, 44
Church Street, PO Box 260, St John's,
Antigua, 809 462 5232, Fax: 809 462 5234,
Eastern Caribbean. Called: Nov 1990, Middle
Temple, B Comm, MA, PhD (Canada), MA
(Oxon)

Cort *Miss Sharon May*
Called: Nov 1997, Middle Temple, LLB
(Hons)

Cory *Mrs Joanna Gethin JP DL O st J*
Penllyn Castle, Cowbridge, South
Glamorgan CF7 7RQ. Called: June 1956,
Inner Temple, MA

Cosma *Miss Maria*
Called: Oct 1994, Middle Temple, LLB
(Hons)(Reading)

Cossar *Bruce James*
Called: Oct 1995, Inner Temple, LLB (Staffs)

Costin *Miss Emma Rebecca*
Legal Advisor, Simpson Millar Solicitors, 20
Church Road, Lawrence Hill, Bristol
BS5 9JA, 0117 955 9800, Fax: 0117 955
7915. Called: Nov 1992, Lincoln's Inn, LLB
(Hons)(B'ham)

Cotsen *Stuart Hugh*
15/F Printing House, 6 Duddell Street,
Central, Hong Kong, 25212616, Fax:
28450260, Formerly Solicitor of the
Supreme Court of England & Wales and
Member Australia Bar Hong Kong Bar
Victoria Bar New South Wales Bar.
Called: Apr 1986, Middle Temple

Cottam *Graeme Robin*
Partner, International Tax Services, Price
Waterhouse, No 1 London Bridge, London
SE1 9QL, 0171 939 4594, Fax: 0171 378
0676, Associate; American Bar Association.
Called: July 1978, Middle Temple, LLB Hons
(Bris), FCA

Cottis *Crispus Peter*
21 Campion Road, London SW15 6NN,
0181 788 9714. Called: Feb 1958, Lincoln's
Inn, MA, B Litt

Cotton *Stephen David*
Called: Mar 1998, Lincoln's Inn, LLB
(Hons)(So'ton)

Coucouni *Miss Dimitria*
Called: Mar 1996, Lincoln's Inn, LLB
(Hons)(Leics)

Coughlin *Mrs Elizabeth Anne*
Furnival Chambers, 32 Furnival Street,
London, EC4A 1JQ. Called: Nov 1989,
Middle Temple, LLB (Hons)

Coughtrey *Keith Andrew*
Called: Nov 1993, Inner Temple, BSc
(E.Anglia), Dip Law

Couldrey *The Hon Mr Justice John Alexander OBE*
Advisory Committee on the Prerogative of Mercy, PO Box 43323, Nairobi, 882 227, High Court Judge, Kenya (Retired) Advocates Complaints Commission, Commissioner and Member Victoria, Australia Kenya. Called: June 1948, Middle Temple, MA (Cantab)

Coulson *Francis Owen Harrison* •
Export Credits Guarantee Dept, P O Box 22000, 2 Exchange Tower, Harbour Exchange Square, London E14 9GS, 0171 512 7849, Fax: 0171 512 7649. Called: Nov 1971, Middle Temple, MA (Cantab)

Counihan *Miss Caroline Jeanne Mary*
Chambers of Raana Sheikh, Gray's Inn Chambers, Gray's Inn, London, WC1R. Called: Oct 1992, Middle Temple, BA French & German, BSc Psychology

Course *Ms Lindy*
and Member Hong Kong Bar. Called: July 1994, Middle Temple, BA (Hons)(Lanc), CPE (Manc)

Courtney *Mark St John* •
European General Counsel, Viatel Incorporated, 197 Knightsbridge, London SW7 1RB, 0171 589 3333, Fax: 0171 589 6333. Called: July 1981, Middle Temple, LLB

Coussey *James Romaine Henley* •
Lawyer, C/O Crown Prosecution Service, 50 Ludgate Hill, London EC4M 7EX. Called: July 1971, Middle Temple

Coutts *Thomas Gordon QC*
Part-time Chairman Industrial Tribunals 1972· M.A.T., 1984 Temporary Judge, Court of Session 1991. Vice President (Scot) VAT & Duties Tribunals 1996. Special Commission Income Tax., 6 Heriot Row, Edinburgh, Scotland EH3 6HU, 0131 556 3042, Fax: 0131 556 3042, A Scottish Advocate and Member Scottish Bar. Called: July 1995, Lincoln's Inn, MA, LLB, FCI(Arb)

Coventry *Roger James* •
Principal Crown Prosecutor, Crown Prosecution Service, The Courtyard, Lombard Street, Abingdon, Oxfordshire OX14 5SE, 01235 555678, Fax: 01235 554144. Called: July 1971, Gray's Inn, LLM(Lond)

Covill *Richard Vernon*
51 Elgin RoaD, Talbot Woods, Bournemouth BH3 7DJ, 01202 529301. Called: Feb 1963, Inner Temple

Cowan *Mrs Veronica*
Called: July 1984, Middle Temple, LLM (Lond), LLB, SRN, OHN

Coward *Gerald Anthony Fenwick*
Licensed Insolvency Pract'er, 16 Croftdown Road, Harborne, Birmingham B17 8RB, 0121 427 2324, Fax: 0121 428 2599. Called: Feb 1959, Gray's Inn, LLB, FIPA

Cowdell *James Michael*
Called: Feb 1994, Inner Temple, BA (Oxon), CPE

Cowderoy *Miss Brenda*
Called: Nov 1949, Gray's Inn, MA (Oxon)

Cowdroy *Dennis Antill*
Wentworth Chambers, 12/180 Phillip Street, Sydney, New South Wales 2000, 012 221 71 83, Queen's Counsel Australia and Member Australian New South Wales, Victorian, Queensland and Republic of Ireland Bars 2 Crown Office Row, Ground Floor, Temple, London, EC4Y 7HJ. Called: July 1994, Lincoln's Inn, LLB (Sydney), LLM (Lond)

Cowen *Timothy Robert William*
Called: July 1985, Inner Temple, BA Cantab

Cowgill *John Keith*
8 Corrie Drive, Kearsley, Bolton BL4 8RG, 0161 794 4803. Called: Mar 1996, Inner Temple, BA (Lond), M.ED (Manch), LLB (Lond)

Cowgill *Nigel Geoffrey* •
Principal Crown Prosecutor, Crown Prosecution Service, Windsor House, Manchester Road, Bradford, 01274 742530. Called: Nov 1985, Middle Temple, Dip Law

Cowhey *Miss Jennifer Marie*
Called: Nov 1996, Lincoln's Inn, LLB (Hons)(Essex)

Cowie *Matthew John*
Called: Nov 1995, Inner Temple, LLB (Warw), MA (Sheff)

Cowley *Miss Allison Maria*
Called: Oct 1995, Inner Temple, LLB

Cowley *Peter John*
Senior Legal Adviser, Berkshire Magistrates Court, Easby House, Northfield End, Henley-on-Thames, Oxon RG9 2NB, 01491 412720, Fax: 01491 412762. Called: Nov 1983, Middle Temple, BA (Hons)

Cownie *Miss Fiona Caird*
Senior Lecturer in Law. Part-time Chairman Special Education Needs Tribunal., Faculty of Law, The University, University Road, Leicester LE1 7RH, 0116 252 2372, Fax: 0116 252 5023. Called: Nov 1985, Lincoln's Inn, LLB (Leic) BA, (Bristol), LLM(Lond)

Cox *Andrew John*
Chartered Institute of Arbitrators - London Branch Committee Member & Hon Treasurer, 8 Vale Royal House, Newport Court, London WC2H 7PS, 0171 437 3179, Fax: 0171 437 3179, Chartered Surveyor. Called: Oct 1996, Gray's Inn, BSc, ARICS, FCIArB

Cox *Miss Charise Felicia Vanessa*
Higgs & Johnson Chambers, 83 Sandringham House, Shirley Street, Nassau, Bahamas, 1-809-32-28571-9, Fax: 1-809-32-87727, and Member Bahamas Bar. Called: July 1991, Lincoln's Inn, BA (Hons) (Cant), LLM (Lond)

Cox *David Rupert Fenwick*
Called: July 1970, Middle Temple, MA

Cox *Ms Iona Maxine*
Called: Nov 1997, Lincoln's Inn, LLB (Hons)

Cox *Nicholas William* •
Legal Adviser, Financial Services Authority, Gavrelle House, 2-14 Bunhill Row, London EC1Y 8RA, 0171 638 1240, Fax: 0171 382 5903. Called: Nov 1993, Middle Temple, LLB (Hons), LLM (Lond)

Cox *Oliver Ivor Zeus*
Called: Nov 1996, Middle Temple, BA (Hons)(Manch)

Cox *Philip Joseph DSC QC (1967)*
Honorary Recorder of Northampton. Chairman:Code of Practice Appeal Board of Prescription Medicine Code of Practice Auth Legal Assessor to the Disciplinary Committee of the Royal College of Veterinary Surgeons., 9 Sir Harrys Road, Edgbaston, Birmingham B15 2UY, 0121 440 0278. Called: Nov 1949, Gray's Inn, BA (Cantab)

Cox *Miss Rosemary Jennifer*
Called: July 1978, Inner Temple, BA (Dunelm)

Cox *Sidney Lewis*
Branch Crown Prosecutor, Whiteacre, Low Street, Elston, Nr Newark-On-Trent, Notts NG23 5PA. Called: July 1971, Middle Temple, LLB

Coy *Glyn*
1 Deacon Court, Windsor, Berkshire SL4 4LN. Called: July 1995, Lincoln's Inn, LLB (Hons)

Coyle *Miss Susanne* •
F.A.O. Mrs S Breach, Flemings Private Asset, Management Limited, 20 Finsbury Street, London EC2Y 9AQ, 0171 814 2700, Fax: 0171 814 2800. Called: Nov 1994, Middle Temple, LLB (Hons)

Coyte *Anthony Christopher* •
Director, Towry Law Trustee Company Ltd, 57 High Street, Windsor, Berks SL4 1LX, 01753 868244, Fax: 01753 621710. Called: Nov 1984, Middle Temple, BA (Lanc), Dip Law

Crabbe *The Hon Mr Justice Vincent Cyril Richard Arthur C CV*
Professor of Legislative Drafting, Director, Legislative Drafting Programme, Faculty of Law, University of The West Indies, Cave Hill Campus, Bridgetown, (246) 417 4236, Fax: (246) 424 1788. Called: Feb 1955, Inner Temple, LLD

Crabtree *Commander Peter Dixon RN, OBE* •
Senior Legal Adviser, Commander (S), HMS Invincible, BFPO 308. Called: July 1985, Gray's Inn, BA

Craig *Mrs Muriel Margaret*
Called: May 1979, Inner Temple, LLB

Craigen *Mrs Carolyn Ann* •
Senior Crown Prosecutor, Crown Prosecution Service, Aalbourg Square, Lancaster, Lancashire LA1 1GG, 01524 847676. Called: July 1985, Gray's Inn, LLB (Hons)

Cramp *Laurence George Charles*
Part Time Chairman, Social Security Appeals Tribunal. Called: Nov 1979, Gray's Inn, DML

Crampton *Nicholas Paul Deverell* ●
Senior Crown Prosecutor, Crown Prosecution Service, Haldin House, Old Bank of England Court, Queen Street, Norwich NR2 4SX, 01603 666491, Fax: 01603 617989. Called: May 1976, Gray's Inn, LLB (Soton)

Crane *Miss Candys Samantha*
Called: Nov 1995, Inner Temple, BSc, CPE (B'ham)

Crane *Malcolm* ●
Legal Member, Mental Health Review Tribunal, Winsford, Main Street, Beckley, Rye, East Sussex TN31 6RN, 01797 260 385. Called: Nov 1967, Gray's Inn, MA

Crane *Miss Nicola Louise*
Called: Nov 1995, Inner Temple, LLB (B'ham), LLM (Bris)

Cranfield *Ms Freda Elizabeth*
Called: Mar 1998, Gray's Inn, LLB (Lond)

Craven *Thomas Jock*
Called: Nov 1961, Lincoln's Inn, MA (Oxon)

Crawford *Miss Jacqueline* ●
Assistant Parliamentary Counsel. Called: Nov 1993, Lincoln's Inn, MA (Hons)

Crawford *John Gerald* ●
Senior Crown Prosecutor, CPS, 4-12 Queen Anne's Gate, London SW1H 9AZ. Called: Nov 1980, Lincoln's Inn, BA, LLM

Crawford *Marcel Christopher*
Called: June 1964, Lincoln's Inn

Crayford *Patrick John Augustine*
Halliday Crayford Balcombe, Chambers, 21 Victoria Avenue, Harrogate HG1 5RD, 01423 523252, Fax: 01423 523838. Called: July 1977, Middle Temple, LLB (Hons)

Crayford-Brown *Mrs Sarah Jane* ●
Crown Prosecution Service, Grantham Office, The Old Barracks, Sandon Road, Grantham, Lincs NG31 9AS, 01476 401177, Fax: 01476 401188. Called: Nov 1988, Gray's Inn, LLB

Crean *Ms Catherine*
Law Library, P.O. Box 2424, Four Courts, Dublin 7, 0103531 720 622, Fax: 0103531 722 254, and Member Irish Bar. Called: May 1982, Middle Temple, BA, HDE, LLB, ALCM

Creasey *Miss Barbara*
Trainee Court Clerk. Called: Oct 1994, Inner Temple, LLB

Creasy *Richard Andrew* ●
Legal Advisor, The Treasury Solicitor, Queen Anne's Chambers, 28 Broadway, London SW1H 9JS. Called: Oct 1990, Inner Temple, LLB (So'ton), LLM (Leics)

Crew *Michael Edwin John AE*
32 St Ann's Road, Chertsey, Surrey KT16 9DQ. Called: July 1977, Middle Temple, BA (Lond), MA (Dublin), BA (Mod, Dublin), BA (Hons, O.U)

Crichlow *Carl Ulrick*
Middle Chambers, Cr Crichlow's Alley & Maidens, Lane, Roebuck Street, Bridgetown, Barbados W I, 246 427 8191, Fax: 246 427 8213, and Member Barbados Bar Association,Barbados,West Indies. Called: July 1987, Middle Temple, BSc (Boston), LLB, (Lond), FCCA, LLM (Lond)

Cridge *Philip James*
Called: Nov 1992, Lincoln's Inn, LLB (Hons)

Crimp *Michael William Jason* ●
Principal Crown Prosecutor, Crown Prosecution Service, Saxon House, 1 Cromwell Square, Ipswich, Suffolk IP1 1TS, 01473 230332. Called: Nov 1980, Gray's Inn, BA, MA

Crinnion *Mrs Neena Latifa*
Called: Oct 1997, Gray's Inn

Crisham *Ms Catherine Ann* ●
Lawyer (Grade 3), Ministry of Agriculture, Whitehall Place, London SW1, 0171 270 8553, Fax: 0171 270 8166. Called: Nov 1981, Gray's Inn, BA, LLM

Crisp *Peter Charles*
Called: Oct 1995, Inner Temple, BA (Lond), CPE (Lond)

Crocker *Gavin Anthony*
29 Biggin Avenue, Mitcham, Surrey CR4 3HN, 0181 646 4955. Called: July 1989, Inner Temple, BSc, Dip Law [City]

Crockford *Gary Brett* ●
Head of legal Department, Chartered Association of, Certified Accountants, 29 Lincoln's Inn Fields, London WC2A 3EE, 0171 242 6855, Fax: 0171 831 8054. Called: July 1980, Inner Temple, BA

Crockford *Peter Michael*
The Garden Cottage, Boxley, Nr Maidstone, Kent ME14 3DX, 01622 677079. Called: Nov 1974, Gray's Inn, LLB

Croft *Ms Caroline Charlotte Ann* ●
Department of Trade & Industry, Room 207, 10 Victoria Street, London SW1H 0NN, 0171 215 3472, Fax: 0171 215 3141. Called: Nov 1991, Gray's Inn, BA (Oxon), Dip. Law

Croft *Frederick Lister* ●
Assistant Treasury Solicitor, Legal Adviser, Department for Education &, Employment, Caxton House, 6-12 Tothill St, London sw1h 9na, 0171 273 5865, Fax: 0171 273 5605. Called: July 1975, Middle Temple, MA (Oxon)

Crone *Thomas Gerald* ●
News International, Legal Department, 1 Virginia Street, London E1 9BD. Called: July 1975, Gray's Inn, LLB

Cronk *John Julian Tristam* ●
Group Company Secretary, The Hartstone Group PLC, 4 Brent Cross Gardens, London NW4 3RJ, 0181 359 1000, Fax: 0181 359 1010. Called: Nov 1972, Inner Temple, LLB

Croot *Wayne David* ●
Crown Prosecutor, Crown Prosecution Service, 21st Floor, Pearl Assurance House, Greyfriars Road, Cardiff CF1 3PL. Called: Oct 1993, Gray's Inn, BA, LLB

Cross *Charles Albert*
Called: June 1949, Gray's Inn, MA, LLB, DPA

Cross *Donald*
79 Albert Road West, Bolton BL1 5HW. Called: Feb 1955, Gray's Inn

Cross *Ian Grenville*
Deputy Director of Public Prosecutions, Attorney General's Chambers, Prosecutions Division, 6/f High Block, Queensway Government Offices, 66 Queensway, Hong Kong, 867 2263, Fax: 852-845-1609, QC (1990) (Hong Kong) 3 Temple Gardens, 2nd Floor, Temple, London, EC4Y 9AU. Called: July 1974, Middle Temple, LLB (So'ton)

Cross *Jonathan Peter* ●
Sony Music Entertainment (UK), Limited, 10 Great Marlborough Street, London W1V 2LP, 0171 911 8200, Fax: 0171 911 8600. Called: Nov 1992, Middle Temple, LLB (Hons)

Cross *Kenneth*
Frondiron Uchaf, Cilgwyn, Carmel, Caernarfon, Gwynedd LL54 7SE, Chartered Engineer. Called: Nov 1989, Inner Temple, BSc, LLB (Lond), MSc (B'ham), C Eng, MIMech E, MIEE

Crossley *Anthony Dominic*
Chief Operating Officer Officer, Reinsurance Australia Corp Ltd, Level 41, Tower Building, Australia Square, 264 George Street, Sydney 2000, New South Wales, Australia, 9247 6565, Fax: 9252 1614. Called: Nov 1977, Lincoln's Inn, LLB (Lond), ACA

Crossley *Ashley Roger* ●
Clifford Chance, 200 Aldersgate Road, London. Called: Oct 1995, Lincoln's Inn, BA (Hons)(Oxon)

Crossley *Miss Vanessa Anne* ●
Crown Prosecution Service, Rossmore House, 10 Newbold Terrace, Warwickshire CV32 4EA, 01926 450444. Called: Nov 1992, Lincoln's Inn, BA (Hons)

Crosthwaite-Eyre *Oliver Nicholas* ●
Eyre Holdings Ltd, The Estate Office, Warrens House, Bramshaw, Nr Lyndhurst, Hampshire SO43 7JH, 01703 812954, Fax: 01703 813956. Called: Nov 1986, Inner Temple, LLB (Exon)

Croston *George Roy* ●
Prosecution Team Leader, Crown Prosecution Service, 4th Floor, United House, Piccadilly, York YO1 1PQ, 01904 45 6595. Called: July 1987, Middle Temple, MA (Cantab)

Crouch *Kevin*
Called: Oct 1996, Middle Temple, BA (Hons)(Lanc), CPE (Northumbria)

Crouch *Miss Sonia Jane*
Deputy Chief Clerk, Inner London Magistrates', Courts Service, 65 Romney Street, London SW1P 3RD. Called: Nov 1984, Inner Temple, BA

Crow *Michael Richard Stanley* •
Head of Group Taxation, Nat West Group,
41 Lothbury, London EC2P 2BP, 0171 726
1500, Fax: 0171 726 1599. Called: July
1976, Gray's Inn, BA Hons

Crowley *Dale Michael*
Maples & Calder, P O Box 309, Cayman
Islands, (345) 949 8066, Fax: (345) 949
8080, and Member Attorney-at-Law, Cayman
Islands. Called: July 1996, Middle Temple,
LLB (Hons)(L'pool)

Crown *Simon David*
Called: Mar 1997, Middle Temple, BA
(Hons), LLM (Lond)

Crozier *Mrs Mairi*
Bench Legal Adviser, Warwickshire
Magistrates Crt, P O Box 16, 14 Hammilton
Terrace, Leamington Spa, Warwickshire
CV32 4XG, 01926 883350, Fax: 01926
335051. Called: Nov 1985, Middle Temple,
BA

Crozier *Stuart Ross McDonald* •
Legal Advisor (Royal Navy), SLA to FOSNNI,
HM Naval Base Clyde, Faslane,
Dunbartonshire G84 8HL. Called: Nov 1991,
Gray's Inn, LLB

Cubbon *John Edward*
Legal Adviser, United Nations Mission in
Bosnia & Herzegovina. Called: Oct 1993,
Middle Temple, BA (Hons)(Oxon), MSc, B
Phil

Cubitt Sowden *Patrick Flinn*
44 The Esplanade, St Helier, Jersey JE2 3QB,
01534 871415, Fax: 01534 872699,
Advocate of Royal Court of Jersey Notary
Public and Member Jersey Bar. Called: Nov
1960, Middle Temple

Cucchi *Frederick*
Via F. Civinini, 111, 00197 Rome, 39-6-
8085460, Fax: 39-6-8072793. Called: Nov
1978, Middle Temple, MA (Oxon)

Culbard *Ms Karen Cecilia*
Inn Chambers, "Inga Lodge", Pinfold Street,
Bridgetown, Barbados, (246) 427-7192, Fax:
(246) 429-2771, and Member Barbados Bar.
Called: Nov 1994, Inner Temple, LLB
(W.Indies), LLM (Lond), CPE (Lond)

Cullen *Miss Deborah Elizabeth* •
CSC Computer Services Limited, 279
Farnborough Road, Farnborough, Hants
GU14 7LS, 01252 363052, Fax: 01252
372577. Called: Nov 1989, Gray's Inn, LLB,
MA (European, Business Law)

Cullen *John Gerard* •
Legal Advisor. Called: Nov 1992, Inner
Temple, LLB (Hons Warw)

Cullen *Terence Lindsay Graham* QC
(1978)
and Member Hong Kong Bar Singapore Bar
Malaysian Bar Bermuda Bar. Called: Feb
1961, Lincoln's Inn

Cully *Ms Louise Dorothy*
Called: Nov 1994, Inner Temple, LLB
(Belfast)

Cumberbatch *Miss Sherrylyn Kathlean*
Called: July 1997, Middle Temple, LLB
(Hons)

Cumlajee *Mrs Angelay*
10 Shelley Gardens, Wembley, Midlesex
HA0 3QG, 0181 904 2097, Fax: 0181 908
1184, and Member Mauritius Bar.
Called: Nov 1985, Gray's Inn, BA, MA

Cumming *Robert Scott*
22 Charlton Place, London N1 8AJ.
Called: Feb 1963, Middle Temple, MA

Cumpsty *Professor John Sutherland*
University of Cape Town, 27 21 650 3454,
Fax: 27 21 689 7575. Called: Feb 1956,
Middle Temple, BSc,PhD & Grad Dip, Thel
(Dunelm), MS (USA)

Cunliffe *John Alfred*
10 Garratts Lane, Banstead, Surrey SM7 2DZ.
Called: July 1968, Lincoln's Inn

Cunningham *Andrew John*
Called: Nov 1991, Gray's Inn, LLB (Bris)

Cunningham *Charles Joseph*
Called: Nov 1970, Gray's Inn, MA, MEd
(Glasgow)

Cunningham *Redvers Paul* •
Thomas Miller & Co, International House,
26 Creechurch Lane, London EC3A 5BA,
0171 204 2531, Fax: 0171 283 5988.
Called: Feb 1993, Middle Temple, LLB
(Hons)(Reading)

Curran *Mrs Andria Dawn*
Called: Oct 1991, Gray's Inn, LLB (Leics)

Curran *Sean Patrick*
Called: Oct 1990, Gray's Inn, LLB, MA

Currie *Heriot Whitson*
Advocates Library, Edinburgh EH1 1RF,
0131 226 5071, Fax: 0131 225 3642,
Q.C.Scotland 1992 and Member Scottish
Bar. Called: Apr 1991, Gray's Inn, MA
(Oxford), LLb (Edin)

Currie *Sean*
Deputy Clerk to the Justices, Shropshire
Magistrates Court, The Magistrates Court,
Preston Street, Shrewsbury SY2 5NX, 01743
458511, Fax: 01743 458502. Called: Nov
1982, Middle Temple, BA (Hons), MBA

Curry *Mrs Anne Louise*
1 Ashley Close, Bookham, Leatherhead,
Surrey KT23 3QJ, 01372 451709, Fax:
01372 451709. Called: Oct 1991, Lincoln's
Inn, LLB (Hons (Warw), LLM (Lond)

Curtice Hillen *Mrs Monica Lilian Marie*
Deputy Chief Clerk to Inner London
Magistrates' Court Service and Parking
Adjudicator, Inner London Magistrates',
Courts Service, 65 Romney Street, London
WC2B 4PJ, 0171 233 2000. Called: Nov
1975, Gray's Inn

Curtin *Miss Nathalie Yasmin*
Called: Oct 1996, Inner Temple, BA
(Dunelm)

Curtin *Richard John Edward* •
Trade mark Administrator & Trainee Trade
Mark Attorney, Rothmans International
Service, Limited, Denham Place, Village
Road, Denham, Uxbridge, Middlesex
UB9 5BL, 01895 834949 x 2363, Fax: 01895
834757. Called: Oct 1996, Inner Temple,
LLB (De Montfort)

Curtis *Mrs Deborah Sarah*
Called: Oct 1995, Inner Temple, LLB (Hons)

Curtis *John William James*
Called: July 1996, Middle Temple, BA
(Hons)(Warw), CPE

Curtis *Richard Anthony* •
Group Investigator, Standard Chartered
Bank, 1 Aldermanbury Square, London
EV2V 7SB, 0171 280 7343, Fax: 0171 280
7274. Called: July 1984, Inner Temple, LLB
(Wales)

Cush *Martin Stuart*
Senior Principal Court Clerk, Avon
Magistrates Crts Comm, Bristol Magistrates
Court, PO Box 107, Nelson Street, Bristol
BS99 7BJ, 0117 943 5100. Called: July 1981,
Lincoln's Inn, BA

Cushen *Mrs Helen Margaret*
Crills, 44 Esplanade, St Helier, Jersey
JE4 8PZ, (0) 534 611055, Fax: (0) 534
611066, and Member Jersey Bar. Called: Nov
1993, Middle Temple, BA (Hons)(Lond), MA
(Kent), CPE (City)

Cushen *Peter Roy*
Advocate, Crills, P.O. Box No 72, 44
Esplanade, St Helier, Jersey JE4 8PN, 01534
611055, Fax: 01534 611066, Admitted to
the Jersey Bar (Oct 1984) and Member
Jersey Bar. Called: July 1981, Inner Temple,
LLB (Soton)

Cusworth *Paul Goodwin*
Called: Mar 1997, Inner Temple, LLB

Cyrus *Willan Julius* •
Berkshire County Council, County
Solicitors' Office, PO Box 189, Shire Hall,
Shinfield Park, Reading, Berks RG2 9DU,
01734 233118, Fax: 01734 873521.
Called: Nov 1984, Lincoln's Inn, BA (Hons,
Reading), Diploma in Law(City)

D'Alton *Edward Dermot Quan*
Woodcote Grove House, Woodcote Park,
Coulsdon CR5 2XL, 0181 660 2867.
Called: July 1979, Gray's Inn, FCA

D'Alton *Richard John*
Called: July 1979, Lincoln's Inn, BA (Hons)

D'Cruz *Miss Nalini Claris*
Interchange Legal Advisory, Service,
Interchange Studios, Dalby Street, London
NW5 3NQ. Called: Oct 1993, Lincoln's Inn,
LLB (Hons)(Leeds)

D'Cruz *Rodney Gerard*
Called: July 1994, Lincoln's Inn, LLB (Hons)

D'Sa *Professor Rose Maria*
Professor of European Law, European Law Unit, Law School, University of Glamorgan, Pontypridd, Mid Glamorgan, Wales CF37 1DL, (01443) 480480, Fax: (01443) 483008. Called: July 1981, Middle Temple, LLB PHD

D'Souza *Miss Mavis Mathilda Ursula* •
Editor in Chief Lloyd's Law Reports, Lloyd's of London Press Ltd, 69-77 Paul Street, London EC2A 4LQ, 0171 553 1000, Fax: 0171 553 1106. Called: Nov 1975, Middle Temple, LLB (Lond)

Da Costa *Christopher Luis Athaide*
43 Jalan Jambu Ayer, Singapore 2158, 00 65 4692170, and Member Singapore Bar. Called: July 1993, Inner Temple, LLB

Da Silva *Miss Rosalind*
Called: Oct 1994, Lincoln's Inn, BSc (Hons)(Bradford), LLB (Hons)(Leeds)

Dabbs *Ian Peter Frank* •
Trainee Court Clerk, Leeds Magistrates' Court, P O Box 97, Westgate, Leeds LS1 3JP, 0113 2476870. Called: Oct 1993, Gray's Inn, LLB

Daber *Timothy Mark*
Clerk to the Justices, The Magistrates' Court, Bridge Street, Peterborough PE1 1ED, 01733 63971, Fax: 01733 313749. Called: Nov 1981, Gray's Inn, LLB, DMS, MIMgt

Dachs *Miss Katherine Mary*
Called: Nov 1988, Lincoln's Inn, BA Hons (Cantab), AT11

Dadial *Harpartap Singh*
Called: Oct 1995, Inner Temple, LLB (Lond)

Dagnall *Miss Jane Mary* •
Senior Crown Prosecutor, Crown Prosecution Service, 8th Floor, Sunlight House, Quay Street, Manchester M60 3LU, 0161 837 7402, Fax: 0161 835 2663. Called: Nov 1987, Inner Temple, LLB (Hons)

Daintith *Professor Terence Charles*
Institute of Advanced Legal, Studies, 17 Russell Square, London WC1B 5DR, 0171 637 1731, Fax: 0171 580 9613. Called: Nov 1966, Lincoln's Inn, MA (Oxon)

Dalby *Marc Charles* •
Group Legal Director & Company Secretary, Merck Sharp & Dohme, Hertford Road, Hoddesdon EN11 9BU, 01992 452014, Fax: 01992 470189. Called: July 1986, Inner Temple, MA (Oxon)

Dalby *Thomas James*
Deloitte & Touche, 1 Woodborough Road, Nottingham NG1 3FG, 0115 950 0511. Called: Oct 1995, Lincoln's Inn, LLB (Hons)(Notts)

Dale *Sir William Leonard KCMG*
20 Old Buildings, Lincoln's Inn, London WC2A 3UP, 0171 242 9365, Also Inn of Court L. Called: June 1931, Gray's Inn, LL.D

Dallow *Richard Julian*
Clerk to the Commissioners of Taxes,Wolverhampton & Dudley Divisions, St Mary's House, St Mary's Street, Bridgnorth, Shropshire WV16 4DW, 01746 765061. Called: Nov 1991, Inner Temple, MA (Oxon)

Dalton *Nicholas David* •
Legal & Business Affairs Manager. Called: Oct 1993, Lincoln's Inn, BA (Hons)(Exon), Dip in Law (Lond)

Daly *The Hon Francis Lenton*
Judge of District Court, Queensland,Australia, Judges Chambers District Court, Cairns, Queensland, 070 528904, Fax: 070 515173. Called: June 1961, Gray's Inn, LLB (Lond)

Daly *Guy Sebastian Sawle*
Called: Nov 1997, Gray's Inn, LLB (Lond)

Daly *Miss Jeanette Susan*
Called: Oct 1995, Middle Temple, LLB (Hons)

Daly *Martin Geoffrey*
and Member Trinidad & Tobago Bar Essex Court Chambers, 24 Lincoln's Inn Fields, London, WC2A 3ED. Called: Nov 1967, Gray's Inn, LLB (Lond)

Daly *Thomas Charles*
Construction Law Consultant, Haley Somerset Consulting Ltd, 118 High Street, Purley, Surrey CR8 2AD, 0181 645 9707, Fax: 0181 668 2155. Called: July 1995, Inner Temple, LLB, ACIArb

Damazer *Miss Audrey Faith*
Senior Deputy Chief Clerk Training Officer, Inner London Magistrates', Courts Service, Romney Street, London SW1P 3RD. Called: Nov 1980, Gray's Inn, BA (Hons) Law

Danbury *Richard*
Called: Oct 1994, Lincoln's Inn, MA (Cantab), CPE

Danby *Gerald Alwyn* •
Assistant Director (Legal), City of Bradford Metropolitan District, Council. Directorate of, Corporate Services, City Hall, Bradford BD1 1HY, 01274 752236, Fax: 01274 730337. Called: July 1980, Middle Temple, BSc (Hull), Dip Law, MBA, MIMgt

Dance *Mrs Iona Lorraine* •
Regional Counsel & Company Secretary, Dow Chemical Company Limited, Lakeside House, Stockley Park, Uxbridge, Middlesex UB11 1BG, 0181 848 5001, Fax: 0181 848 5426. Called: Nov 1982, Middle Temple, LLB (Hons) (Brunel)

Dang *Miss Lee Boon*
Called: July 1997, Middle Temple, LLB (Hons)

Dangerfield *Jeremy George Bubb*
3P-300 Roslyn Road, Winnipeg, Manituba R3L0H4, (204) 453-8340, QC Canada and Member Manituba Bar. Called: Nov 1983, Gray's Inn, BSc,LLM (Manitoba)

Daniel-Selvaratnam *Aruchunan*
Called: Nov 1997, Middle Temple, LLB (Hons)(Kent)

Daniels *Adrian Maurice*
Called: Oct 1993, Lincoln's Inn, LLB (Hons)(Leeds), MA (Lond)

Daniels *Paul Dominic* •
Senior Court Clerk, Sandwell Court Committee, Lombard Street West, West Bromwich, West Midlands, 0121 569 5805. Called: Nov 1990, Gray's Inn, BA

Daniels *Miss Tanya Collette* •
European Legal Advisor, Amdahl International Group, Services, Dogmersfield Park, Hartley Wintney, Hampshire RG27 8TE, 01252 344400, Fax: 01252 334211. Called: Nov 1985, Lincoln's Inn, LLB (Exon)

Danker *Miss Geralyn Germaine*
34 Jalan Chelagi, 542 6684. Called: July 1995, Middle Temple, LLB (Hons)

Dann *Geoffrey Leonard Keith*
Deputy Clerk to the Justices, The Court House, Stafford Street, Walsall, West Midlands WS2 8HA, 01922 38222, Fax: 01922 35657. Called: Nov 1978, Gray's Inn, MA (Cantab)

Danny *John Patrick Cyril*
Notley Abbey, Chearsley Road, Long Crendon, Aylesbury, Bucks HP18 9ES. Called: Jan 1945, Gray's Inn, FCIS

Danou *Miss Georgia*
Assistant Legal Advisor, The Cyprus Popular Bank Ltd, The Cyprus Popular Bank Ltd, Popular Bank Building, 154 Limassol Avenue, P O Box 2032 CY-1598, Nicosia, 02 81 1187, Fax: 02 81 1492, and Member Cyprus Bar. Called: Feb 1991, Lincoln's Inn, LLB (Leic), LLM (Lond)

Darley *Miss Gillian Elizabeth Anne*
Director General, O'Connor & Company, European Lawyers, rue de Spa 30, 1000 Brussels, (0032) 2 285 46 85, Fax: (0032) 2 285 46 90. Called: July 1981, Inner Temple, LLB (Lond), AKC

Darnton *Mrs Hazel* •
Senior Crown Prosecutor, Crown Prosecution Service, 5-7 South Parade, Wakefield. Called: July 1985, Gray's Inn

Darr *Miss Amber*
Called: July 1997, Lincoln's Inn, BA (Pennsylvania), CPE

Darvell *Mrs Julia Frances Stockbridge*
Called: July 1983, Middle Temple, BA

Darville *Miss Camille Diane*
Called: July 1995, Gray's Inn, BA (Soc)(Ontario), LLB (Leeds)

Darwyne *Michael Thurston*
Group Legal Director, Overseas Company Registration, Agents Ltd, Companies House, Tower Street, Ramsey, 01624 816 800, Fax: 01624 816 300, and Member Hong Kong Bar Fiji Bar New York Bar. Called: July 1969, Inner Temple, MA, BCL (Oxon), LLM (Harvard)

DaSilva *Douglas Gerald St Elmo*
24 Greenway, Kenton, Harrow, Middlesex
HA3 0TT, 0181 204 3264. Called: Nov
1971, Inner Temple, MA (Oxon), BA (Lond),
LLB (Lond)

Daswani *Jeevan*
Attorney General Chambers, 17 Town
Range, Gibraltar, 78882, Fax: 79891.
Called: Nov 1994, Middle Temple, LLB
(Hons)

Dato Haji Abdul Razak *Miss Rahayu*
02-61025 3, and Member Brunei Bar.
Called: July 1994, Lincoln's Inn, LLB (Hons)
(Manch)

Dato Hj Abdul Rahman *Mohd
Rozaiman*
Legal Adviser, Attorney General Chambers,
Ministry of Law, B.S.B., Brunei, Darussalam
2016, 6732 244872 Ext 174, Fax: 6732
222720, and Member Brunei Bar.
Called: July 1995, Lincoln's Inn, LLB (Hons),
LLM (Exeter)

Dato Hj Zaidan *Miss Hanariza*
Called: Nov 1997, Lincoln's Inn, LLB
(Hons)(Wales)

Davda *Mrs Anjani* •
Court Clerk, Secretariat Offices, The Court
House, London Road, Dorking, Surrey
RH4 1SX, 01306 885544. Called: July 1969,
Lincoln's Inn

David *Miss Audra Catherine*
Called: Nov 1997, Middle Temple, LLB
(Hons)(E.Lond)

David *Derrick Huw* •
Senior Crown Prosecutor, Crown
Prosecution Service, Cambria House,
Pentrebach Ind. Est, Pentrebach, Merthyr
Tgdfil, Mid Glamorgan, 01222 378201.
Called: July 1989, Middle Temple, LLB

David *Paul Wilson*
Farrar's Building, Temple, London, EC4Y
7BD. Called: Nov 1981, Inner Temple,
BA,LLM (Cantab)

Davidson *Alasdair Michael*
Attorney at Law, Dempsey & Company,
Caribbean Place, P.O.Box 97, Leeward
Highway, Providenciales, Turks & Caicos
Islands, 00 649 94 64344, Fax: 00 649 94
65464, and Member Turks & Caicos Islands.
Called: Oct 1992, Gray's Inn, LL.B (Newc)

Davidson *Miss Fiona Ann*
Called: Feb 1995, Lincoln's Inn, LLB
(Hons)(Hudders), LLM (Huddersfield)

Davidson *Miss Laura Anne*
Called: Oct 1996, Lincoln's Inn, MA
(Hons)(Edinburgh)

Davidson *Neil Forbes*
Director-City Disputes Panel, Advocates'
Library, Parliament House, Edinburgh
EH1 1RF, 031 226 5071, Fax: 031 220 4440,
QC (Scotland) and Member Scottish Bar.
Called: May 1990, Inner Temple, B.A. (Stirl),
M.Sc. (Brad), LL.B.& LL.M. (Edin)

Davidson *Thomas David*
10/11 Gray's Inn Square, London WC1R 5JP,
0171 405 2576, Fax: 0171 889 0875.
Called: July 1973, Middle Temple, LLB
(Hons), LLM

Davidson-Hood *Simon*
Called: Oct 1995, Lincoln's Inn, LLB
(Hons)(Middx)

Davies *Miss Anne Margaret* •
Crown Prosecutor, Crown Prosecution
Service, 17th Floor, Tolworth Tower,
Surbiton, Surrey, 0181 399 5171, Fax: 0181
390 3474. Called: Nov 1989, Inner Temple,
LLB (Hull)

Davies *Ashleigh Bevan* •
Crown Prosecutor. Called: July 1981, Middle
Temple, LLB (Wales)

Davies *Mrs Asta Clara*
LL.B(Hons), 24 Pine Grove, Prestwich,
Manchester M25 3DR. Called: June 1955,
Gray's Inn

Davies *Miss Charlotte Lisa*
Called: Nov 1995, Gray's Inn, LLB

Davies *Christopher Alan Robertshaw*
Called: Nov 1971, Lincoln's Inn, MA
(Cantab)

Davies *David Ioan*
General Caseworker Kirklees Law Centre.
Called: Oct 1992, Lincoln's Inn, LLB(Hons),
MA

Davies *David Martyn JP*
Wray Park Lodge, 59 Alma Road, Reigate,
Surrey RH2 0DN. Called: Feb 1958, Inner
Temple

Davies *Mrs Elizabeth Caroline Sian* •
C/O CPS Headquarters, 50 Ludgate Hill,
London EC4M 7EX, 0171 273 8000, Also
Inn of Court L. Called: July 1980, Gray's Inn,
LLB (Bristol) MA

Davies *Frederick George*
Deputy Justices' Clerk, Cambridgeshire
Mgistrates' Crt, C/O Windsor House, Ermine
Park, Spitfire Close, Huntingdon, Cambs,
01733 63971 Ext 511, Editor, Justice of the
Peace. Called: July 1979, Inner Temple, BA
(Hons) Law

Davies *Gareth Trevor*
Called: Oct 1995, Middle Temple, BA (Hons)

Davies *Dr Gillian*
Hon. Professor, University of Wales,
Aberystwyth, European Patent Office, DG
III, Erhardtstrasse 27, D-80298 Munich,
Germany, 4989 2399 3230, Fax: 4989 2399
4460, Chairman, Technical Board of Appeal
and Member, Enlarged Board of Appeal,
EPO. Called: Nov 1961, Lincoln's Inn, Ph.D

Davies *Jeremy David*
Morlandes Mead, 56 Croham Manor Road,
Addington Village, South Croydon, Surrey
CR2 7BE, 0181 688 6060, Fax: 0181 667
0260. Called: July 1974, Inner Temple, BSc
Chem

Davies *Miss Julie Louise*
Former Solicitor. Called: Nov 1995, Inner
Temple, LLB (Hull)

Davies *Keith* •
Legal Adviser, British Aerospace Airbus Ltd,
New Filton House, PO Box 77, Bristol
BS99 7AR, 0117 9362224, Fax: 0117
9362680. Called: Nov 1976, Inner Temple,
MA (Cantab) MIL

Davies *Keith Frederick RD* •
Under-Secretary - Professional Conduct
Dept, Institute of Chartered, Accountants in
England & Wales, Gloucester House, 399
Silbury Boulevard, Milton Keynes MK9 2HL,
01908 248352, Fax: 01908 248002.
Called: July 1980, Gray's Inn

Davies *Miss Nia Martin* •
Crown Prosecutor, Crown Prosecution
Service, Pearl Assurance House, 20th Floor,
Greyfriars Road, Cardiff CF1 3PL.
Called: Feb 1988, Middle Temple, MA
(Hull), LLB (Wales)

Davies *Mrs Nicola Jane* •
Principal Crown Prosecutor, Mersey/
Lancashire Crown Prosecution Service,
Liverpool South Branch, 7th Floor South,
Royal Liver Building, Liverpool L3 1HN,
0151 236 7575. Called: July 1978, Middle
Temple, MA (Oxon)

Davies *Paul Richard*
Trainee Accountant, Ernst & Young, 1
Colmore Row, Birmingham B3 2DB, 0121
232 4018. Called: Oct 1994, Lincoln's Inn,
LLB (Hons)(Notts)

Davies *Peter* •
Advisor, Office of Telecommunications, 50
Ludgate Hill, London EC4M 7JJ, 0171 634
8923, Fax: 0171 634 8847. Called: Nov
1990, Middle Temple, LLB (Lond), FRSA

Davies *Philip John* •
Parliamentary Counsel, Office of the
Parliamentary, Counsel, 36 Whitehall,
London SW1A 2AY, 0171 210 6630, Fax:
0171 210 6632. Called: Feb 1981, Middle
Temple, MA (Oxon), BCL (Oxon)

Davies *Mrs Rachel Valerie* •
Legal Adviser, Dorset Magistrates' Courts,
Committee, The Law Courts, Park Road,
Poole, Dorset, 01202 745309, Fax: 01202
711999. Called: July 1995, Gray's Inn, LLB

Davies *Robert Stephen*
Called: Nov 1994, Gray's Inn, BA, LLM
(LSE), Dip, in Law

Davies *Robin Hunkin*
19 The Common, Ealing, London W5.
Called: Nov 1960, Inner Temple, LLB

Davies *Miss Susan Wendy* •
The Courtyard, Lombard Street, Abingdon,
Oxon OX14 5SE. Called: Nov 1984, Gray's
Inn, BA

Davis *Andrew Raj*
Called: July 1997, Lincoln's Inn, LLB
(Hons)(Nott'm), LLM (Nott'm)

Davis *Bernard James* •
Judge Advocate & Legal Advisor. Called: July
1982, Gray's Inn, LLB (B'ham)

Davis *Mrs Emma Elizabeth*
Called: Nov 1995, Inner Temple, BA
(Australia), M.Phil (Cantab), CPE

Davis *Francis Patrick Reginald Peter* ●
Senior Crown Prosecutor, Crown
Prosecution Service, 2nd Floor, Kings
House, Kymberley Road, Harrow, Middlesex
HA1 1YH, 0181 424 8688, Fax: 0181 424
9134. Called: Oct 1991, Middle Temple, BA
Hons (L'pool), Dip Law, DMS (Dip in
Management Studies)

Davis *Gerald Hugh Blakeman ERD*
The Athenaeum, Pall Mall, London
SW1Y 5ER, 0171 930 4843. Called: Feb
1959, Lincoln's Inn

Davis *James Charles Aylmer* ●
Senior Crown Prosecutor. Called: Nov 1990,
Gray's Inn, LLB (Hons)(Essex)

Davis *James Joseph*
Legal Adviser, The Stone House, Church
Street, West Chiltington, West Sussex
RH20 2JW, 01798 812316. Called: July
1952, Lincoln's Inn, MA (Cantab)

Davis *Miss Janet Elizabeth Maria*
Called: Nov 1994, Lincoln's Inn, LLB
(Hons)(Bucks)

Davis *John Atkins RD*
Called: July 1975, Gray's Inn

Davis *Julian Mark*
Called: July 1973, Middle Temple, LLB

Davis *Mark*
Called: Nov 1996, Gray's Inn, LLB (Hull)

Davis *Peter Andrew*
S G Archibald, Archibald Andersen
Association, d'Avocats, 41 rue Ybry, 92576
Newilly-sur-seine, 331 55 61 12 69, Fax: 331
55 61 15 15. Called: Oct 1994, Lincoln's
Inn, LLB (Hons)(Leic)

Davis *Philip Richard* ●
Group Legal Adviser, GEC Marconi Avionics
Ltd., Airport Works, Maidstone Road,
Rochester, Kent ME1 2XX, 01634 816024,
Fax: 01634 816752. Called: Nov 1971,
Gray's Inn, BSc LiB

Davis *Richard Jolyon Harold* ●
Beresford & Co, 2-5 Warwick Court, High
Holborn, London WC1R 5DJ, 0171 831
2290, Fax: 0171 405 4092. Called: Oct
1992, Gray's Inn, BA (Cantab), Dip Law,
AM.I.E.E.

Davis *Mrs Sally Janine* ●
Government Lawyer, Lord Chancellor's
Department, Selborne House, 54-60 Victoria
Street, London SW1E 6QW, 0171 210 1300.
Called: Nov 1987, Inner Temple, Dip Comm
Studies, Dip Law

Davis *Miss Sarah Luise* ●
Contracts Oficer, Electrical Contractors
Assoc, ESCA House, 34 Palace Court,
London W2. Called: July 1987, Middle
Temple, BA (Kent), Dip Law (City)

Davis *Miss Susan Lynn*
Called: Mar 1998, Gray's Inn, LLB (Bucks)

Davison *Andrew Michael*
Justices' Clerk/ Chief Executive, Rotherham
Magistrates Court, P O Box 15, The Statutes,
Rotherham S60 1YW, 01709 839339, Fax:
01709 370082. Called: Nov 1986, Middle
Temple, Dip Law

Davison *James Edward*
Called: Nov 1996, Gray's Inn, LLB (Wales)

Daw *Roger Keith* ●
Lead Inspector, Directorate of Casework
Evaluation. Senior Civil Service., CPS
Headquarters, 50 Ludgate Hill, London
EC4M 7EX, 0171 273 8000. Called: July
1982, Middle Temple, LLB (B'ham)

Dawes *Alistair Nicholas Louis*
Called: Feb 1995, Inner Temple, BA
(Cantab)

Dawkins *James Stephen*
Called: Nov 1994, Inner Temple, LLB
(Soton), LLM (Soton)

Dawson *Miss Anne Diana*
Called: July 1996, Middle Temple, LLB
(Hons)(Lond)

Dawson *Peter MBE* ●
Clerk to the Justices, Bolton Magistrates'
Court, P O Box 24, Civic Centre, Le Mans
Crescent, Bolton BL1 1QX, 01204 522244,
Fax: 01204 364373. Called: Feb 1971, Gray's
Inn

Dawson *Peter Anthony Hawkins*
Fant Cottage, Garford, Nr Abingdon,
Oxfordshire OX13 5PF, 01865 391405.
Called: Nov 1971, Inner Temple

Dawson *Peter Henry* ●
Legal Adviser, Friend & Falcke Limited, 293
Brompton Road, Chelsea, London SW3 2DZ,
01604 643173, Fax: 01604 643173.
Called: Feb 1976, Middle Temple, MA, LLB
(Lond)

Dawson *Stephen Peter*
1 Reeve Gardens, Ipswich IP5 2FG, 01473
611193, Fax: 01473 631221. Called: Mar
1997, Lincoln's Inn, BA (Hons)(Sheff)

Day *Harold*
Examiner, Ecclesiastical Jurisdiction Measure
1963 Manchester Diocese. Called: June
1948, Gray's Inn

Day *Nicholas John* ●
Company Secretary, WT Partnership Group,
Leon House, High Street, Croydon, Surrey
CR9 1YY, 0181 686 0431, Fax: 0181 686
3195. Called: July 1982, Lincoln's Inn, BA
(Lond), Dip Law, FCIS

Day *Robert* ●
33 Poundfield Way, Broad Hinton, Twyford,
Berkshire RG10 0XR, 0118 9321087, Fax:
0118 9321087. Called: Feb 1991, Lincoln's
Inn, B Pharm, M Phil, LLB, MR Pharm S

Daya-Winterbottom *Trevor*
Senior Solicitor, Chapman Tripp Sheffield
Young, Level 35, Coopers & Lybrand
Tower, 23-29 Albert Street, Auckland, 00 64
9 357 9000, Fax: 00 64 9 357 9099, and
Member Barrister & Solicitor of the High
Court of New Zealand (Admitted November
1996). Called: Nov 1985, Lincoln's Inn, BA
(Hons), Diplome de Droit, International et
De, Droit Compares des, Droits de
l'Homme, MA, Legal Associate of, the Royal
Town, Planning Institute, FRSA, Affiliate
Member of, the New Zealand, Planning
Institute

Dayer *Mrs Penelope Andrea* ●
Assistant Treasury Solicitor, Treasury
Solicitor's, Queen Anne's Chambers, 28
Broadway, London SW1. Called: July 1976,
Gray's Inn, LLB (Lond)

De *Miss Zoe Monica*
Called: Nov 1994, Inner Temple, BA (Warw)

De Alwis *Miss Claire Louise*
Called: Nov 1997, Middle Temple, LLB
(Hons) (Kent)

De Basto *Gerald Arthur QC*
Canterbury Lodge, 21 Canterbury Drive,
Bishopscourt 7700, (021)762 5626, Fax:
(021)762 5627, and Member New South
Wales Hong Kong Bar. Called: Nov 1955,
Lincoln's Inn, LLB (Syd)

De Berti *Giovanni*
De Berti & Jacchia, Foro Buonaparte 20,
20121 Milano, 39- 2-725541, Fax: 39- 2-
72554600, and Member Italy Bar.
Called: Nov 1970, Gray's Inn

de Bruir *Rory*
Law Library, Four Courts, Dublin 7, 045
521881, Fax: 045 521881, and Member
Southern Ireland Bar Northern Ireland Bar.
Called: Oct 1992, Middle Temple, Diploma
in Legal, Studies (Kings Inns), Dip US Army
Command, & General Staff, College,
Commission, Irish Army, BL, FCIArb

De Cruz *Miss Clares*
Advocate & Solicitor, 24 Raffles Place,
[H]18-00 Clifford Centre, 533 2323, Fax:
533 1579, and Member Singapore Bar.
Called: July 1995, Middle Temple, LLB
(Hons), BA (Singapore)

De Friend *Richard Henry Max*
Called: Nov 1992, Middle Temple, BA
(Kent), LLM, Lecturer

de Graft-Johnson *Dr Edward Victor
Collins*
28a Hallswelle Road, Temple Fortune,
London NW11 ODJ, 0181 458 0421, Fax:
0181 209 1105, and Member Ghana Bar.
Called: June 1958, Lincoln's Inn, LLM, PhD

De Guise *Rupert James*
Called: Feb 1995, Middle Temple, MA (St
Andrews), CPE (Wolves)

de Havillande *Mrs Jane Elizabeth*
Senior Lecturer in Law, Kingston University,
School of Law, Kingston University,
Kingston Hill, Kingston-Upon-Thames,
Surrey KT2 7LB, 0181 547 2000 Ext 5318,
Fax: 0181 547 7038. Called: July 1992, Inner
Temple, MA (Oxon), CPE

De May *Ferdinand Leopold*
1 Edith Terrace, London SW10 0TQ, 0171
352 4465. Called: June 1950, Middle
Temple, MA

De Menezes *Raul Antonio* •
Legal Adviser, Bournemouth Magistrates
Court, The Law Courts, Stafford Road,
Bournemouth, Dorset, 01202 711905.
Called: Feb 1994, Lincoln's Inn, BA (Hons),
LLM

De Rijke *Hugo Tate*
FLBA Committee. Called: Oct 1990,
Lincoln's Inn, BA (Keele)

De Rozario *Miss Lynette Rita*
Called: Nov 1992, Middle Temple, BA
(Hons, Kent)

De Silva *Miss Natasha Esther*
Called: July 1997, Middle Temple, LLB
(Hons)(Warw)

De Silva *Suren Charitha*
Called: July 1996, Gray's Inn, LLB (Wales)

De Smith *Mrs Barbara*
17 Cavendish Avenue, Cambridge CB1 4UP.
Called: Nov 1957, Gray's Inn, LLB (Lond),
MA (Oxon)

De Souza *Miss Vanessa-Anne*
Straits Tradine Building, 9 Battery Road,
[H]15-00, (65) 5322271, Fax: (65) 5352475,
and Member Singapore. Called: July 1996,
Middle Temple, LLB (Hons)(Leeds)

De Speville *Andre Patrice Doger*
605 Chancery House, Lislet Geoffroy Street,
Port Louis, (230) 208 8618/210 3467/210
0174, Fax: (230) 210 3440, Pepys'
Chambers, 17 Fleet Street, London, EC4Y
1AA. Called: July 1978, Middle Temple

de Speville *Bertrand Edouard Doger*
Anti-Corruption Consultant, 55 The Avenue,
Richmond, Surrey TW9 2AL, 0181 940
1771, Fax: 0181 948 5176, Formerly
Solicitor General, Hong Kong Commissioner
Against Corruption, Hong Kong. Called: July
1967, Middle Temple, LLB (Lond)

De Ste Croix *Miss Emma Rebecca*
Ogier & Le Masurier, P O Box 404, Pirouet
House, Union Street, St Helier, Jersey,
Channel Islands, 01534 504000, Fax: 01534
35328. Called: May 1995, Inner Temple, LLB

De Val *Peter Robert* •
Legal Adviser, The Treasury Solicitors Dept,
Central Advisory Division, Queen Annes
Chambers, 28 Broadway, London SW1.
Called: Nov 1988, Inner Temple, LLB, MPhil
(Leic)

De Vall *David Spencer* •
78 Brackenbury Road, London W6 0BD,
0181 932 1234. Called: July 1988, Inner
Temple, BSc (Bath), Dip Law (City)

De Warrene *Ms Diane Trudy*
Performer's Diploma of the Royal College of
Music. Called: Oct 1997, Inner Temple, CPE
(Westminster)

De-Grey Homer *Ms Sarah Justine*
Called: Oct 1996, Inner Temple, LLB

Deakin *George Anthony Hartley CBE*
Chairman Addenbrooke's NHS Trust,
Manting Hse, Meldreth, Nr Royston, Herts
SG8 6NU, 01763 260276, Fax: 01763
260276. Called: Nov 1963, Gray's Inn, MA
(Oxon), MBA (INSEAD)

Deakin *Paul Kingsley*
Called: Nov 1972, Middle Temple, LLM
(Lond)

Deal *Alexander Marc*
Called: Nov 1992, Inner Temple, LLB

Dealy *Nicholas John*
Called: Oct 1996, Middle Temple, BSc
(Hons)(Hull), CPE

Dean *James Thomas*
Called: Nov 1997, Middle Temple, LLB
(Hons)(Manch)

Dean *Ms Margaret*
Called: Nov 1992, Middle Temple, B.Sc
(Hons, Wales)

Deane *Michael Boyd*
Called: Mar 1998, Middle Temple, BSc
(Hons)(LSE)

Deans *Miss Jacqueline Elaine*
Called: July 1997, Lincoln's Inn, LLB
(Hons)(L'pool)

Dearnley *Trevor David*
Justices Clerk, Cumbria Magistrates Crts
Comm., Magistrates Clerks Office,
Rickergate, Carlisle, Cumbria CA3 8QH,
01228 27534, Fax: 01228 515624.
Called: Nov 1969, Gray's Inn

Deason *Christopher John* •
Contracts Administrator Dip QS FRICS
FCIArb Dip EU Law, Taylor Woodrow
International, 345 Ruislip Road, Southall,
Middlesex UB1 2QP, 0181 231 1062, Fax:
0181 231 1085. Called: Nov 1995, Middle
Temple, LLB (Hons)(Lond)

Debono *Marius Paul Anthony*
22 Avenue De Suffren, 75015 Paris.
Called: May 1956, Lincoln's Inn, Licence en
droit, (Paris), AIB

Deby *John Bedford QC (1980)*
Recorder. Called: Nov 1954, Inner Temple,
MA (Cantab)

Decker-Kingston *Mrs Micheline
Hildegard Franziska*
16 Alwyne Villas, London N1 2HQ, 0171
354 2046, and Member Avocat a la Cour
D'appel de Paris. Called: July 1997, Gray's
Inn, Maitrise, DEA (Paris), Dip Law

Dee *Nicholas* •
Director of Taxation, SmithKline Beecham
plc, One New Horizons Court, Great West
Road, Brentford, Middlesex TW8 9EP, 0181
975 2350, Fax: 0181 975 2360. Called: July
1973, Lincoln's Inn, BA, F.C.A

Deeley *Jeremy John* •
Senior Legal Advisor. Called: Nov 1980,
Gray's Inn

Deeny *Donnell Justin JP*
Bar Library, Royal Courts of Justice, Belfast,
0232 241523/323243, Fax: 0232 231850,
QC Northern Ireland Senior Counsel
Republic of Ireland and Member Northern
Ireland Bar. Called: July 1986, Middle
Temple, BA Dublin

DeGale *David Otway*
Dernford Barn, Sweffling, Saxmundham,
Suffolk IP17 2BQ, 01728 663 402, Fax:
01728 663 402. Called: Nov 1956, Middle
Temple, BA (Oxon)

Degirmenci *Mrs Kyriacoulla*
Called: Feb 1995, Inner Temple, LLB
(Sussex)

Delaney *Barry Douglas*
P O Box 36, Orchasrd Point. Called: Oct
1993, Inner Temple, LLB (Lond)

Delbourgo *Mrs Angela Marie*
Also Inn of Court I. Called: July 1980,
Lincoln's Inn, LLB

Delip Singh *Tara Singh*
Called: Nov 1995, Lincoln's Inn, LLB (Hons)

Dellimore *Wayne*
Called: Oct 1996, Lincoln's Inn, BSc
(Hons)(Lond), LLB (Hons)(Wales), llm
(London)

Demetriades *Demetris*
P.O.Box 47, 8100 Pafos, 06-232689, 235755,
Fax: 06-2322313, and Member Cyprus Bar.
Called: Nov 1994, Gray's Inn, LLB

Demetriou *Antonis*
Called: Oct 1996, Gray's Inn, LLB (Kent)

Demetriou *Miss Elina*
Called: Nov 1995, Lincoln's Inn, LLB (Hons)
(So'ton)

Demetriou *Miss Natasha*
Called: Oct 1996, Middle Temple, BA
(Hons)(Dunelm), CPE

Dempsey *Miss Karen Marie*
Called: Mar 1996, Lincoln's Inn, LLB (Hons),
LLM (Lond)

den Brinker *Miss Melanie Jane
Margaret*
West House, Town Row, East Sussex
TN6 3QU. Called: July 1984, Inner Temple,
LLB (Liverpool)

Dendroff *Jason Peter*
Called: Nov 1993, Middle Temple, LLB
(Hons)(Lond)

Denham *Grey* •
Group Secretary, GKN Plc, P O Box 55
Ipsley Hse, Ipsley Church Lane, Redditch,
Worcs B98 0TL, 01527 517715, Fax: 01527
517700. Called: Nov 1972, Inner Temple,
LLB ((Lond)

Denham *Paul Victor* •
Senior Lecturer, The Law School, University
of Central England, in Birmingham, Perry
Barr, Birmingham B42 2SU, 0121 331 5102.
Called: July 1996, Inner Temple, BA (Soton),
LLB (W.Eng)

Dening *Richard Dacre Lewis*
Called: Nov 1968, Middle Temple, BA, BCL
(Oxon)

Denman *Daniel Jeremy* •
Principal Legal Officer, Office of the
Solicitor, DHSS, New Court, 48 Carey Street,
London WC2A 2LS, 0171 412 1357.
Called: Nov 1995, Gray's Inn, MA (Cantab)

Dennis *Miss Lucy Henrietta Wesley*
6 Pump Court, Ground Floor, Temple,
London, EC4Y 7AR. Called: Nov 1988, Inner
Temple, LLB

Dennis *Philip William Coleridge*
230 Greys Road, Henley on Thames, Oxon
RG9 1QY, 01491 573554. Called: June 1948,
Inner Temple, MA (Oxon)

Denny *Miss Susan Louise* •
Law Reporter, Incorporated Council of Law,
Reporting for England & Wales, Room
W234, Royal Courts of Justice, Strand,
London WC2A 2LL, 0171 936 6609, Fax:
0171 405 1978. Called: July 1977, Middle
Temple, BA, MA, LLB

Denton *Douglas*
Called: Oct 1997, Lincoln's Inn, LLB
(Hons)(L'pool)

Denza *Mrs Eileen CMG* •
Visiting Professor University College
London. Called: Jan 1963, Lincoln's Inn, MA
(Ab & Oxon), LLM (Harvard)

Deo *Jagdeep Singh*
Legal Assistant, C/O Karpal Singh & Co, 17
Green Hall, 10200 Penang, Malaysia, 04
2638543/2639558, Fax: 04 2630461, and
Member Malaysia Bar. Called: July 1993,
Gray's Inn, LLB (Warw)

Derham *Gerald Bernard Samuel*
Clerk to the Justices. Called: May 1969,
Inner Temple, LLB

Derriman *James Parkyns*
34 Mossville Gardens, Morden, Surrey
SM4 4DG, 0181 542 4548. Called: June
1947, Lincoln's Inn

Derry *Ms Caroline Louise*
Called: Nov 1994, Inner Temple, BA (Oxon)

Desai *Jayant Nichhabhai*
Called: Nov 1956, Lincoln's Inn, LLB (Lond)

Desai *Sadananda Shankrappa*
46 Parkfield Road, Harrow, Middlesex
HA2 8LB, 0181 422 2855. Called: July 1970,
Inner Temple, BA, LLB, BIM Dip

Desbruslais *Mr Anthony David*
Clerk to the Justices Justices Chief
Executive, Magistrates' Court, Carrington
Street, Nottingham NG2 1EE, 0115 955
8111, Fax: 0115 955 8131. Called: July
1976, Middle Temple, LLB

DeSilva *Miss Joanne*
Associate, Morgan, Lewis & Badans LLP, 80
Raffles Place, [H]14-20 UOB Plaza 2, (010)
(65) 438 2188, Fax: (010) (65) 230 7100,
and Member Singapore Bar. Called: Oct
1992, Gray's Inn, BA

Dessain *Anthony James*
Advocate, Notary Public, Crown Advocate,
Bedell & Cristin, P.O. Box 75, One the
Forum, Grenville Street, St Helier,Jersey
JE4 8PP, 01534 814814, Fax: 01534 814815.
Called: July 1974, Middle Temple, LLB

Devadasan *Miss Valentina*
Called: Oct 1996, Middle Temple, LLB
(Hons) (Lond)

Devendarajah *Vivekananda*
Called: July 1995, Middle Temple, LLB
(Hons) (Wales)

Deverell *William Shirley*
Kaplan & Stratton, Advocates, PO Box
40111, Nairobi, Kenya, 335 333, Fax: 340
827, and Member Advocate of the High
Court of Kenya. Called: Nov 1961, Gray's
Inn, BA

Devine-Baillie *Mrs Francesca Maria* •
Senior Crown Prosecutor, Crown
Prosecution Service, St Johns House, Merton
Road, Bootle, Liverpool L20, 0151 922
8711. Called: Feb 1984, Gray's Inn, BA
(Hons)

Devitt *Miss Clare Oonagh-Jane*
Legal Advisor, Squire & Co, 49 St John Sq,
London EC1V 4JL, 0171 490 3444, Fax:
0171 250 4087. Called: Oct 1991, Gray's
Inn, BA (Lond), Dip Law

Devitt *Stephen John*
Called: Nov 1994, Lincoln's Inn, BA (Hons)

Dewan *Miss Sharene*
Called: Oct 1995, Inner Temple, LLB (Lond)

Dewar *John Kinley*
Called: May 1995, Gray's Inn, MA, BCL

Dewar *Mrs Sarah Alison* •
Prosecution Team Leader, Crown
Prosecution Service, 8th Floor, Prospect
West, Station Road, Croydon, Surrey, 0181
251 5425. Called: July 1986, Middle Temple,
LLB

Dewhirst *Nicholas Michael* •
Unijet Group PLC, Sandrocks, Rocky Lane,
Haywards Heath, West Sussex RH16 4RH,
01444 255600, Fax: 01444 417799.
Called: Nov 1990, Lincoln's Inn, BA (Hull)

Dewick *Mrs Chiew Yin* •
Senior Crown Prosecutor, Crown
Prosecution Service, Harrow Branch, 2nd
Floor, King's House, Kymberley Road,
Harrow, Middlesex HA1 1YH, 0181 424
8688, Fax: 0181 424 9134. Called: Nov
1990, Lincoln's Inn, LLB (Reading)

Dhaniram *Mahendranath*
5 Gordon Street (North), San Fernando,
Trinidad, (809) 652 6806, Fax: (809) 652
6806, and Member Trinidad & Tobago Bar.
Called: Feb 1994, Gray's Inn, LLB (Lond),
LLM (Lond), LEC (Trinidad &, Tobago)

Dhanoo *David Devanand* •
Legal Advisor, Trade Indemnity plc, 1
Canada Square, London E14 5DX, 0171 739
4311, Fax: 0171 729 7682, and Member
Attorney of the Supreme Court of Trinidad
& Tobago. Called: Nov 1988, Lincoln's Inn,
LLB Hons (Lond)

Dhargalkar *Mrs Jean*
Called: Nov 1985, Inner Temple, BA (Hull)

Dharsan *Miss Kiranjit Kaur*
Called: July 1997, Middle Temple, LLB
(Hons)(Lond)

Dhesi *Miss Tejpal* •
North of England Protecting, and Indemnity
Association Ltd, The Quayside, Newcastle
Upon Tyne NE1 3DU, 0191 232 5221, Fax:
0191 261 0540. Called: Nov 1989, Inner
Temple, LLB

Dhillon *Balkar Singh* •
Assistant Legal Adviser, The Retail Motor
Industry, Federation, 201 Great POrtland
Street, London NW1N 6AB, 0171 580 9122.
Called: Feb 1992, Lincoln's Inn, LLB (Hons)
(Lond), LLM (Lond)

Dhillon *Gurmit Singh* •
Called: Nov 1996, Lincoln's Inn, LLB (Hons)

Dhillon *Gursharan Singh*
Called: Nov 1996, Middle Temple, LLB
(Hons)(Leeds)

Dhillon *Surinder Singh*
Chua Dhillon Tan & Partners, 71 Robinson
Road, [H]03-03, 32332320, Fax: 2213211,
and Member Singapore Bar. Called: Nov
1991, Lincoln's Inn, LLB (Hons) (Lond)

Dhir *Mark Christiaan*
Trident Trust Company (UK) Ltd, 7
Welbeck Street, London W1M 7PB, 0171
935 1503, Fax: 0171 935 7242. Called: July
1996, Middle Temple, LLB (Hons)(Lanc)

di Mambro *Mrs Louise Jane* •
Secretary, Supreme Court, Family
Proceedings and County Court Rule
Committees., Lord Chancellor's Department,
Selborne House, 6th Floor, 54/60 Victoria
Street, London SW1E 6QB, 0171 210 0731.
Called: July 1976, Middle Temple, LLB

Di Rienzo *Matthew James*
Called: Feb 1994, Lincoln's Inn, MA
(Cantab)

Dias *Reginald Walter Michael*
13 Old Square, Ground Floor, Lincoln's Inn,
London, WC2A 3UA. Called: June 1945,
Inner Temple, MA LLB (Cantab)

Dibble *Kenneth Michael* •
Manager, Legal Department London Office,
Charity Commission, St Alban's House, 57-
60 Haymarket, London SW1Y 4QX, 0171
210 4542. Called: July 1977, Lincoln's Inn,
LLB, LLM, AIB, AKC

Dickens *Miss Deirdre Dawn* •
Senior Crown Prosecutor, Crown
Prosecution Service, 2nd Floor, Portland
House, Stag Place, Victoria, London SW1,
0171 915 5800, Fax: 0171 915 5795.
Called: July 1990, Inner Temple, LLB
(Hons), LLM (Lond)

E

Dickie *Andrew Valentine Acworth*
Councillor, Ward member for Hale Ward
Chair Economic Development Committee,
London Borough of Barnet, Members Room,
Town Hall, Hendon, London NW4 4BG,
0181 359 2000. Called: Oct 1994, Lincoln's
Inn, MA, Dip in Management, Studies
(Middx), LLB (Hons)

Dickinson *Ms Georgina Ann* •
Principal Crown Prosecutor, Crown
Prosecution Service, Wakefield Branch
Office, 4/5 South Parade, Wakefield, West
Yorkshire WF1 1LR, 01924 290620, Fax:
01924 369360. Called: July 1977, Lincoln's
Inn, B.A. (Kent)

Dickinson *Mrs Melanie Jane*
Called: Oct 1996, Middle Temple, B.Sc
(Hons) (Bucks)

Dickson *Christopher William* •
Senior Assistant Director Senior Fraud
Office, Serious Fraud Office, Elm House, 10-
16 Elm Street, London WC1X 0BJ, 0171 239
7155, Fax: 0171 833 5440, and Member
Northern Ireland Bar. Called: July 1986,
Middle Temple, BA Cantab

Dickson *Donald John Kurt*
L'Ardailler, 87230 Bussiere-Galant, France,
(+33) 05 55 78 85 77, Fax: (+33) 05 55 78
85 33. Called: Nov 1966, Inner Temple, LLB
(Leeds)

Dickson *Ian* •
Creative Labs (UK) Ltd, Unit 2, The
Pavilions, Ruscombe Business Park,
Ruscombe, Berks RG10 9NN, 01189
344322, Fax: 01189 320137. Called: Nov
1978, Inner Temple, LLB (Lond)

Dignan *Ms Noleen Patricia* •
Legal Adviser, Sun Life Assurance Society
Plc, 107 Cheapside, London EC2V 6DU,
0171 606 7788, Fax: 0171 378 1865.
Called: Nov 1989, Gray's Inn, LLB

Dilbert *Miss Sophia Armanda*
Called: July 1996, Middle Temple, LLB
(Hons)(L'pool)

Dilks *Miss Tracy Elizabeth* •
Assistant Vice President, Credit Suisse First
Boston, One Cabot Square, London
E14 4QJ, 0171 888 8927. Called: Nov 1997,
Middle Temple, BA (New Brunswick), MA
(Reading)

Dilworth *John* •
Senior Crown Prosecutor, Crown
Prosecution Service, 3rd Floor, Unicentre,
Lords Walk, Preston, Lancashire PR1 1DH,
01772 555015. Called: Nov 1987, Gray's
Inn, LLB (Hons) DML

Dilworth *Ms Kristin*
Called: July 1980, Lincoln's Inn, BA

Dinan-Hayward *Miss Jacqueline Anne
Catherine*
Called: Mar 1998, Middle Temple, LLB
(Hons)

Dingsdale *George Neville*
56 Cloncurry Street, London SW6, 0171 736
8199. Called: July 1966, Inner Temple, LLB
(Lond), BA

Dingwall *Howard John*
Justices' Clerk, Ealing P.S.A. Justices Chief
Executive Ealing MCC, Ealing Magistrates'
Court, The Courthouse, Green Man Lane,
London W13, 0181 579 9311. Called: Nov
1974, Lincoln's Inn, MA LLB

Dingwall *Richard Andrew* •
Senior Crown Prosecutor, Crown
Prosecution Service, 2nd floor, Portland
House, Stag Lane, London SW1. Called: Oct
1991, Gray's Inn, LLB

Diplock *Mrs Ann*
Senior Court Clerk, Wolverhampton
Magistrates Ct, The Law Courts, North
Street, Wolverhampton WV1 1RA, 01902
773151, Fax: 01902 27875. Called: Nov
1985, Lincoln's Inn, BA (Hons)

Ditchburn *Mathew James*
Called: Mar 1996, Lincoln's Inn, LLB (Hons)

Dixon *Mrs Christine Angela*
Court Clerk, Barnet Magistrates Court
Comm, Justice's Clerk's Office, 7C High
Street, Barnet, Herts EN5 5UE, 0181 441
9042. Called: Nov 1989, Gray's Inn, LLB

Dixon *Mrs Colette Yvonne* •
Senior Crown Prosecutor, Crown
Prosecution Service, Ryedale House, 60
Piccadilly, York YO1 1NS, 01904 610726,
Fax: 01904 610394. Called: Nov 1987,
Lincoln's Inn, LLB

Dixon *Dennis Joseph* •
Legal Officer, Inland Revenue Solicitor's,
Office, Somersets House, Strand, London
WC2R 4RD, 0171 438 6107, Fax: 0171 438
62488. Called: Nov 1995, Middle Temple,
BA (Hons) (Cantab)

Dixon *Keith Owen*
Ogier & Le Masurier, Pirouet House, Union
Street, St Helier, Jersey, Channel Islands,
01534 504000, Fax: 01534 35238, and
Member Jersey Bar. Called: May 1994,
Middle Temple, MA (Hons)

Dixon *Miss Shelley*
Called: Oct 1997, Inner Temple, LLB (Leeds)

Dobbin *William-Wallace* •
Director, Corporate & Strategic Affairs.,
British American Financial, Services, 22
Arlington Street, London SW1A 1RW, 0171
495 5563. Called: July 1982, Gray's Inn, BA

Dobry *Ms Josephine Carola*
Called: Oct 1995, Inner Temple, BA (Oxon),
MA (Bris)

Dobson *Miss Amanda Jane-Marie* •
Senior Crown Prosecutor, Crown
Prosecution Service, C/O 50 Ludgate Hill,
London EC4M 7EX. Called: Nov 1991, Inner
Temple, LLB (So'ton)

Docksey *Christopher* •
Legal Adviser, Legal Service, Commission of,
the European Communities, Rue de la Loi
200, B-1049 Brussels, Belgium, 32-2-
2955717, Fax: 32-2-2965971. Called: July
1976, Inner Temple, MA (Cantab), LLM
(Virginia)

Dodd *Peter Wellesley*
Called: Nov 1965, Gray's Inn, FCIS

Dodd *Miss Philippa Alice May*
Simmons & Simmons, 21 Wilson Street,
London EC2M 2TX, 0171 628 2020, Fax:
0171 628 2070. Called: Oct 1995, Inner
Temple, LLB (Sheff), LLM (Lond)

Dodds *Malcolm Douglas*
Deputy Clerk to the Justices, Secretariat
Offices, Court House, Tufton Street,
Ashford, Kent TN23 1QS, 01233 663203,
Fax: 01233 663206. Called: Nov 1984,
Middle Temple, BA (Kent), LLM.(Manch)

Dodgshon *Simon Earl*
Deputy Clerk to the Justices, Stockport
Magistrates Court, P.O.Box. 155, Court
House, Edward Street, Stockport SK1 3NF,
0161 477 2020, Fax: 0161 474 1115.
Called: July 1986, Middle Temple, BA Hons,
D.M.S.

Dodson *Timothy Charles*
Principal Court Clerk, Cardiff Magistrates
Court, Fitzalan Place, Cardiff CR2 1RZ,
01222 463040, Fax: 01222 456224.
Called: Jan 1980, Gray's Inn

Doggart *Anthony Hamilton*
Chairman of Fleming Fund Management
(Luxembourg)SA. Finance Director of
Robert Fleming Asset Management Ltd, 23
Ovington Gardens, London SW3 1LE, 0171
880 3297, Fax: 0171 880 3294, also Inn of
Court L. Called: July 1962, Middle Temple

Doggett *John Clayton CBE*
Called: May 1941, Middle Temple

Dogra-Brazell *Ms Julia Marisa*
Called: Oct 1995, Lincoln's Inn, BA (Hons),
MA (Lond)

Doherty *John*
Barrister of Ireland. Called: Nov 1995,
Middle Temple, BL (King's Inn)

Dolby-Stevens *Mrs Wendy Elizabeth*
Visiting Law Lecturer. Called: Oct 1996,
Middle Temple, LLB (Hons)

Dolphin *Miss Kelly Louise*
Called: Oct 1996, Inner Temple, BA (Oxon),
CPE (City)

Don *Andrew George*
Part-time Chairman S.S.A.T, M.A.T., D.A.T.,
Deputy Chairman A.L.T. (S.E.), Examiner
(Ecclesiastial Jurisdiction - Norwich Diocese
), The Old Rectory, Little Dunham, Kings
Lynn, Norfolk PE32 2DG, 01760 722584,
Fax: 01760 720709. Called: Nov 1960, Inner
Temple, MA (Cantab)

Don *Brendan Robert*
Called: July 1994, Middle Temple, LLB
(Hons)(Leic), LLM (Boston)

Donald *Keith Malcolm Hamilton* •
General Counsel, International Water
Limited, New Zealand House, 10th Floor, 80
Haymarket, London SW1Y 4TE, 0171 766
5100/5160, Fax: 0171 766 5180. Called: July
1978, Gray's Inn, LLB (Sheff)

• Barristers in employment

Donaldson *Nicholas John*
Credit Lyonnais Securities, Broadwalk
House, 5 Appold Street, London EC2A 2DA,
0171 588 4000, Fax: 0171 588 0278.
Called: July 1976, Middle Temple, LLB
(Lond)

Donegan *Ms Sally Frances Averill* •
Crown Prosecution Service, Crown
Prosecution Service, River Park House, High
Road, London N22, 0181 888 8889, Fax:
0181 888 0746. Called: Oct 1992, Gray's
Inn, LL.B (Lond)

Donnabella *Miss Rosemary*
Blythe Liggins Solicitors, Edmund House,
Rugby Road, Leamington Spa CV32 6EL, 1
Dr Johnson's Bldgs, Ground Floor, Temple,
London, EC4Y 7AX. Called: Feb 1991,
Middle Temple, LLB

Donnelly *Brian OBE*
44 Main Street, Ledston, Castleford, W.
Yorkshire WF10 2AB, 01977 516563.
Called: July 1976, Gray's Inn, LLB, FRICS

Donnelly *William Howard* •
Prosecution Team Leader, Crown
Prosecution Service, 1st Floor, Churchgate
House, Bolton BL1 1JG, 01204 535202, Fax:
01204 364569. Called: Nov 1981, Gray's
Inn, BA

Donovan *Allan James*
LLB Hons. Called: Nov 1991, Middle Temple

Donovan *The Hon Hugh Desmond*
Called: Apr 1959, Middle Temple, MA
(Oxon)

Doody *Richard James*
Called: Oct 1995, Inner Temple, LLB
(Huddersfield)

Dookhee *Mohamade Ally Noorooddin*
Called: Nov 1997, Middle Temple, LLB
(Hons)

Dorai Raj *Dinesh Pragasam*
Called: Nov 1995, Middle Temple, LLB
(Hons)(Wales)

Doraisamy *Raghunath Ramachandran*
Called: Nov 1997, Middle Temple, LLB
(Hons)(Nott'm)

Doran *James Christopher*
Beachcroft Stanleys, 20 Furnival Street,
London EC4A 1BN, 0171 242 1011, Fax:
0171 831 6630. Called: Oct 1990, Lincoln's
Inn, LLB (Essex)

Doran *Kevin Reginald*
Clerk to the Justices, Hampshire Magistrates
Court, Committee, The Court House,
Elmleigh Road, Havant, Hants PO9 2AL,
01705 819421, Fax: 01705 293085.
Called: Nov 1979, Gray's Inn, DML

Dorey *Sir Graham Martyn*
Bailiff of Guernsey, President Guernsey
Court of Appeal, The Bailiff's Chambers,
Royal Court, Guernsey, 0481 726161, Fax:
0481 713861, Former Solicitor and Member
Member of the Jersey Court of Appeal.
Called: Feb 1992, Gray's Inn, BA (Bristol)

Dorey *Robert Graham*
Called: Nov 1996, Inner Temple, LLB
(So'ton)

Dorey *Thomas Alan*
Le Haugard, Rue De Sorel, St John, Jersey
JE3 4AA, 01534 862258, Formerly Judicial
Greffier Formerly Commissioner of the
Royal Court of Jersey Formerly Police Court
Magistrate & Judge of the Petty Debts
Courts. and Member Jersey. Called: May
1958, Gray's Inn, MA, PhD

Dorner *Miss Irene Mitchell*
Chief Operating Officer, HSBC MIDLAND,
Thames Exchange, 10 Queen Street Place,
London EC4R 1BQ, 0171 336 3300, Fax:
0171 336 2738. Called: July 1977, Middle
Temple, MA (Oxon)

Dorrington *Miles Hamilton*
Called: Nov 1996, Lincoln's Inn, BA(Jnt
Hons)(Dunelm)

Dorsett *Kenred Michael Ansara*
Executive Director, Providence Consulting
Group, P.O.Box N-1527, Nassau, (240) 394
0886, Fax: (240) 394 0573, and Member
Bahamas Bar. Called: July 1995, Middle
Temple, BA (Hons) (Keele)

Double *Paul Robert Edgar* •
Counsel to City Remembrancer (Parl & Bill
drafting work), City Remembrancer's Office,
PO Box 270, London EC2P 2EJ, 0171 332
1207, Fax: 0171 332 1895. Called: July
1981, Middle Temple, BSc, LLM

Douer *Ariel*
Suite 301, 1170 N Federal Hwy, Fort
Lauderdale, Florida 33304, 954-463 1670,
954 761 8280 Residence. Called: Nov 1975,
Lincoln's Inn, LLB

Dougall *Alistair Ross*
Called: July 1983, Inner Temple, LLB (Lond)

Dougall *Mrs Anne Louise Borisova*
3 Etheldene Avenue, Muswell Hill, London
N10 3QG, 0181 444 9551, Fax: 0181 444
9551. Called: Nov 1981, Inner Temple, LL.B

Douglas *Miss Mary*
Called: July 1976, Middle Temple, MBA, LLB

Dourado *Mrs Maria Alba Aldonca*
Senior Court Clerk, Coventry Magistrates
Court, Little Park Street, Coventry CV1 2SQ,
01203 630666, Fax: 01203 256513, and
Member Kenya Bar. Called: July 1967, Inner
Temple

Dove-Edwin *Bassey Tokumboh*
Lehman Brothers, One Broadgate, London
EC2M 7HA, 0171 260 2053, Fax: 0171 260
2207. Called: Feb 1995, Inner Temple, BA
(Notts), ACA

Dow *Harold Peter Bourner QC (1971)*
Mustow House, Mustow Street, Bury St
Edmunds, Suffolk IP33 1XL, 01284 725093,
Fax: 01284 704227. Called: Nov 1946,
Middle Temple, MA (Cantab)

Dowd *Miss Carmen Jane Louise* •
Crown Prosecutor, Crown Prosecution
Service, 50 Ludgate Hill, London EC4M 7EX,
0181 273 8000. Called: July 1989, Gray's
Inn, BA

Dowell *Ms Nita Mary* •
Senior Crown Prosecutor, Crown
Prosecution Service, 491 Abergele Road,
Old Colwyn, Colwyn Bay, Clwyd.
Called: July 1982, Gray's Inn, LLB (L'pool)

Dowle *Michael Joseph*
Called: May 1995, Lincoln's Inn, LLB (Hons)

Down *Miss Sara Lydia*
Assistant Ombudsman (Legal), Prisons
Ombudsmans Office, St Vincent House, 30
Orange Street, London W1V 7HH, 0171 389
1527. Called: Oct 1991, Gray's Inn, LLB
(L'pool)

Downes *Miss Charlotte Sara*
Called: May 1997, Lincoln's Inn, BA
(Hons)(Cantab), LLB (Hons), LLM

Downes *Ms Christine Beverley*
Monplaisir & Co, Floissac Building, Brazil
Street, PO Box 256, Castries, St Lucia, 809-
45 22837/22803, Fax: 32358, and Member
St Lucian Bar. Called: Nov 1989, Gray's Inn,
BA, LLB (Lond)

Downey *Mrs Sally-Ann* •
Senior Principal Legal Officer, D.S.S., Block
2, Spur R, Room 20, Government Buildings,
Honeypot Lane, Stanmore, Middlesex
HA7 1AY, 0171 972 3849. Called: Nov 1985,
Gray's Inn, BA

Downie *Anthony Robert* •
Group Secretary & Legal Adviser, Anglo-
Norden Limited, Orwell Terminal, Duke
Street, Ipswich IP3 0AJ, 01473 220120, Fax:
01473 230805. Called: Oct 1995, Gray's Inn,
BA (L'Pool), MBA (Sheff), Dip Law
(Westminst), MIMgt

Doyle *Mrs Kim Jane* •
Crown Prosecutor, Crown Prosecution
Service, 8th Floor, Sunlight House, Quay
Street, Manchester M60 3LU, 0161 908
2611, Fax: 0161 908 2686. Called: Apr
1986, Middle Temple, B.A

Drabble *John William David*
Called: Nov 1997, Gray's Inn, LLB (Sussex)

Drage *Mrs Lesley Anne*
Legal Adviser, Rochford and Southend,
Magistrates Court, The Court House,
Victoria Avenue, Southend on Sea, Essex
SS2 6EU, 01702 348491. Called: Apr 1991,
Middle Temple, BA (Hons), Cert Ed

Drahaman *Ms Cirami Mastura*
Called: Nov 1996, Gray's Inn, LLB (Lond)

Draper *Miss Jeannette* •
Senior Crown Prosecutor, Solar House, 1-9
Romford Road, Stratford, London E15, 0181
534 6601, Fax: 0181 522 1236. Called: Oct
1992, Middle Temple, LL.B (Hons)

Draper *Norman Henry* •
Clerk to the Justices/Justices Chief
Executive, Knowsley Magistrates', Courts
Committee, The Court House, Lathom Road,
Huyton, Merseyside L36 9XY, 0151 481
4400, Fax: 0151 449 2841. Called: Nov
1978, Inner Temple, BA (Hons)

Draycott *Paul Richard*
Advice Worker - Employment Law,
Tameside Welfare Rights Unit, 200 Market
Street, Hyde, Cheshire SK14 1HB, (0161)
367 0085, Fax: (0161) 366 1731.
Called: Nov 1994, Gray's Inn, LLB (Hull)

Drayton *Fitzroy* •
Prosecution Team Leader, Crown
Prosecution Service, Central Confiscation
Branch, Central Casework, 50 Ludgate Hill,
London EC4M 7EX, 0171 273 1314, Fax:
0171 273 1325. Called: July 1983, Middle
Temple, BA

Dreelan *Ian Christopher James*
Called: Oct 1995, Inner Temple, LLB (Sheff)

Drewry *Nigel* •
Court Clerk, Bromley Magistrates Court,
London Road, Bromley, Kent BR1 1BY,
0181 325 4000, Fax: 0181 325 4006.
Called: Oct 1991, Lincoln's Inn, LLB (Hons)

Driu *Miss Sera Palu*
Legal Officer, The Ministry of Justice,
Attorney General's Chambers,
Rogorogoivuda House, Lautoka, 679
667710, Fax: 679 668077, and Member The
Fiji Bar. Called: July 1995, Inner Temple,
LLB (Wolverhampton)

Driver *Miss Shirley* •
Senior Crown Prosecutor, Crown
Prosecution Service, 8th Floor, Prospect
West, 81 Station Road, Croydon, Surrey
CR0 2RD, 0181 251 5430. Called: May 1993,
Middle Temple, LLB (Hons)

Drury *Jonathan Michael*
Criminal Clerk. Called: Nov 1995, Lincoln's
Inn, LLB (Hons)

Drury *Michael John* •
Lawyer, CESG, M Block, Priors Road,
Cheltenham GL52 5AJ, 01242 221 491 x
2349. Called: July 1982, Middle Temple, LLB
(Hons), LLM

Drybrough-Smith *Robert Ian* •
Assistant Chief Crown Prosecutor, CPS
(South East Area), One Onslow Street,
Guildford, Surrey GU1 4YA, 01483 882600,
Fax: 01483 882606. Called: July 1975, Inner
Temple, LLB (Leeds)

Drysdale *John Gillespie*
Called: July 1965, Gray's Inn, MA,
M.Sc(Oxon)

Drysdale Wilson *Alexander*
C/O 8 New Square, Lincoln's Inn, London
WC2A 3QP, Also Inn of Court L. Called: July
1981, Gray's Inn, BSc Eng RMCS

Du Boulay *Ms Raquel Jane*
Called: Oct 1997, Gray's Inn, BA (Ontario),
LLB (Wolves)

Du Toit *Dr Emma Jeanne*
300 Innes Chambers, 84 Pritchard Street,
Johannesburg 2001, +27 11 337 2370, Fax:
+27 11 333 8425, and Member
Johannesburg Bar. Called: Nov 1995, Middle
Temple, BA, M.Phil, D.Phil

Dubljevic *Alexander Salvatore* •
Senior Crown Prosecutor, Crown
Prosecution Service, Pearl Assurance House,
20th Floor, Greyfriars Road, Cardiff
CF1 3PL, 01222 378201. Called: July 1979,
Middle Temple, LLB (Cardiff)

Duck *Hywel Ivor*
Director, The General Secretariat of the,
Council of Ministers of the, European
Union, 175 rue de la Loi, 1048 Brussels
Belgium, 010322 2856267, Fax: 010322
2858261. Called: June 1956, Gray's Inn, MA,
Diplome D'Etudes, Superieures,
Europeennes

Duckworth *Mrs Margaret Ashworth* •
Senior Crown Prosecutor, Crown
Prosecution Service, 2nd Floor, Calder
House, St James Street, Burnley, Lancashire
BB11 1XG, 01282 412298. Called: Feb 1990,
Middle Temple, LLB Hons

Duckworth *Miss Shirley Lynne*
Called: Oct 1997, Gray's Inn, LLB (De
Montfort)

Duddington *John Gabriel*
6 Hanbury Park Road, St John's, Worcester
WR2 4PB, 01905 423131, Fax: 01905
423131. Called: July 1976, Middle Temple,
LLB (Hull)

Dudley *Anthony Edward*
Called: Nov 1989, Middle Temple, LLB Hons
[Hull]

Dudley *Mrs Julia Jill*
Called: Nov 1982, Middle Temple, Dip Law
Poly of, Central London

Duff *Graham* •
Director, Casework Services, Crown
Prosecution Service, 50 Ludgate Hill,
London EC4M 7EX, 0171 273 8146, Fax:
0171 273 8016. Called: July 1976, Lincoln's
Inn, BA, PGCE

Duff *Miss Jacki Kim*
Called: Nov 1997, Middle Temple, LLB
(Hons)

Duff *Mrs Jayne Peta*
Called: Nov 1992, Inner Temple, LLB

Duffett *Peter Lionel*
General Management Consultant, c/o Allianz
Shanghai, Representative Office, 707 Office
Complex, Hotel Equatorial Shangai, 65
Yanan Xi Lu, Shanghai 2000040, 0086 21
6248 8148, Fax: 0086 21 6248 8240.
Called: Feb 1980, Middle Temple, MA, FIA,
FCCA, FCII

Duffield *Mrs Janet Rachel*
Senior Court Clerk, Calderdale Magistrates
Court, PO Box 32, Harrison Road, Halifax,
Yorks HX1 2AN, 01422 360695, Fax: 01422
347874. Called: Nov 1990, Middle Temple,
LLB (Lancaster)

Duffill *David William*
Called: Feb 1973, Gray's Inn

Duffus *Howard James* •
Called: July 1969, Gray's Inn

Duffy *Simon John* •
Legal Officer, Office of the Solicitor, Room
510, East Wing, Somerset House, London
WC2R 1LB, 0171 438 7147, Fax: 0171 438
6246. Called: Oct 1996, Lincoln's Inn, BSc
(Hons)(Sheff), CPE (Northumbria)

Dugan *Humphrey John Aurelius*
Goodwyn House, 12 High Street, Datchet,
Berkshire SL3 9EQ, 01753 542904, Fax:
01753 582585. Called: Feb 1957, Gray's Inn,
MA, LLB (Cantab)

Dukes *Christopher James Noel*
Yolaw Trust & Corporate, Services Limited,
P O Box 415, Templar House, Don Road, St
Helier, Jersey JE4 8WH, 01534 500419, Fax:
01534 500450. Called: July 1983, Middle
Temple, LLB

Dulwich *David John*
Clerk to the Justices, Wiltshire Magistrates
Court, 43-55 Milford Street, Salisbury,
Wiltshire SP1 2BP, 0722 333225, Fax: 0722
413395. Called: July 1970, Gray's Inn

Duma *Alexander Agim*
13 Coulson Street, London SW3, 0171 823
7422, Fax: 0171 581 0982. Called: Nov
1969, Gray's Inn, LLB, FCA

Dumbuya *Ibrahim Pierre Hassan* •
Called: Nov 1981, Gray's Inn

Duncan *Benjamin Paul*
Scotland Europa, 35 Square de Meeus, B-
1040, Brussels, (32-2) 502 50 28, Fax: (32-2)
502 51 56. Called: Oct 1990, Lincoln's Inn,
LLB (Lanc), LLM (Edin)

Duncan *Delroy*
Messrs Trott & Duncan, 1st Floor, Sea
Venture, Building 19, Parliament Street,
Hamilton, 441 295 7444, Fax: 441 295
6600, and Member Bermuda. Called: Nov
1984, Gray's Inn, MA, LLB, FCIArb

Duncan *Ms Denise*
Deputy Chief Clerk, Inner London
Magistrates', Courts Service, 65 Romney
Street, London SW1P 3RD, 0171 799 3332.
Called: Nov 1985, Gray's Inn, LLB

Duncan *Douglas John Stewart*
Legislative Counsel, 86 Cromwell Road,
Winchester, Hants S023 4AE, 01962 856048,
Fax: 01962 856048, and Member Scottish
Bar. Called: Nov 1990, Inner Temple, LLB
(Aberdeen)

Duncan *Miss Gracie Sharon*
Called: Feb 1995, Gray's Inn, LLB

Duncan *Kenneth Stroud* •
European Tax Manager, Gillette Industries
PLC, Gillette Corner, Great West Road,
Isleworth, Middlesex TW7 5NP, 0181 847
8982, Fax: 0181 758 0818. Called: Feb 1976,
Gray's Inn, LLB (Lond), F.T.I.I, F.C.C.A.

Duncan *Miss Marjorie Camille*
Called: Mar 1996, Gray's Inn, BA (West
Indies), LLB (Lond)

Duncan *Mrs Sarah*
Called: Nov 1996, Gray's Inn, LLB

Duncan *Simon Ross* ●
Senior Crown Prosecutor, Crown
Prosecution Service, 7th Floor South, Royal
Liver Building, Pier Head, Liverpool.
Called: May 1987, Lincoln's Inn, LLB

Duncan *Miss Susan Elizabeth Ramsay* ●
Principal Legal Officer, HM Customs &
Excise, New Kings Beam House, 22 Upper
Ground, London SE1 9PJ. Called: Nov 1987,
Gray's Inn, BA (Newc)

Duncanson *Beryn Sigurd*
Called: Mar 1997, Gray's Inn, BA (Toronto),
LLB (Bucks)

Dundas *James Frederick Trevor*
Director, 16 Norland Square, London
W11 6PX, 0171 727 3781, Fax: 0171 792
1089. Called: Nov 1972, Inner Temple, BA
(Oxon)

Dunham *Michael John*
29 Spring Street, Sandringham, Victoria, 9
336 1917, Fax: 9 320 4178, and Member
Australia Bar. Called: Nov 1980, Middle
Temple, Master Mariner

Dunk *David Frederick* ●
Senior Crown Prosecutor, Crown
Prosecution Service, New Magistrates Court
Building, Burneside Road, Kendal, Cumbria
LA9 4RT, 01539 728999 Ext 25, Fax: 01539
725270. Called: July 1977, Middle Temple,
LLB (Sheff)

Dunleavy *Miss Ann Geraldine* ●
Legal Adviser & Company Secretary, Mace
Limited, 7 Plough Yard, London EC2A 3LP,
0171 375 0375, Fax: 0171 375 1606.
Called: Nov 1988, Inner Temple, B.Ed
(Newc), LLB

Dunn *John Christie CPM*
The Cloisters Apartment, The Elms, Weston
Park West, Bath BA1 4AR, 01225 483912,
and Member Hong Kong Bar. Called: July
1989, Inner Temple, LLB (Lond), M.SocSc

Dunn *Philip* ●
Deputy Company Secretary, James Walker
Group Ltd, Lion House, Woking, Surrey
GU22 9LL, 01483 757757, Fax: 01483
757715. Called: July 1975, Gray's Inn, LLB

Dunne *Ms Lynn Noelle*
Called: Oct 1997, Inner Temple, BA
(Cantab)

Dunnett *Denzil Roderick Rawcliffe*
Head of Division, European Investment
Bank, L-2950 Luxembourg, 352 43791, Fax:
352 437704. Called: Nov 1970, Middle
Temple, MA (Oxon)

Dunstan *Mrs Tessa Jane* ●
Legal Advisor, Dept of Trade & Industry, 10
Victoria Street, London SW1E 0NN, 0171
215 3144, Fax: 0171 215 3221. Called: Nov
1967, Middle Temple, MA (Oxon)

Dunt *Robert John*
Called: May 1997, Middle Temple, BA
(Hons)(Bris)

Dupplin *The Viscount Charles William Harley Hay*
Director, Hiscox Underwriting Limited, 52
Leadenhall Street, London EC3A 2BJ, 0171
423 4000, Fax: 0171 488 1702. Called: Oct
1990, Middle Temple, MA (Oxon), Dip Law
(City)

Durack *John Francis* ●
Special Casework Lawyer, Crown
Prosecution Service, River Park House, 225
High Road, Wood Green, London N22 4HQ,
0181 345 7752. Called: Nov 1970, Middle
Temple, MA (Cantab)

Duraipandi *Miss Ganaselvarani*
M.N.Swami & Yap, No 1 North Bridge Road,
[H]18-05 High Street Centre, 3361677, Fax:
3371737, and Member Singapore Bar.
Called: Feb 1994, Lincoln's Inn, LLB (Hons,
Lond)

Durance *Alexander Christian John*
Called: Nov 1997, Middle Temple, BA
(Hons)

During *Miss Jacqueline Alison*
Called: Oct 1996, Inner Temple, BA (Lond)

Durnin *Martin Laurence* ●
Clerk to the Justices South East Surrey,
Surrey Magistrates Court, The Law Courts,
Hatchlands Road, Redhill, Surrey RH1 6DH,
01737 765581, Fax: 01737 764972.
Called: Nov 1978, Lincoln's Inn, BA

Durston *Gregory John*
Senior Lecturer Kingston Law School,
Associate Professor of Law Niigata
University Japan, Kingston Law School,
Kingston Hill, Kingston Upon Thames,
Surrey KT2 7LB, 081 549 1141 Ext 5330,
Fax: 081 547 1440. Called: Nov 1985,
Middle Temple, MA (St Andrews), Dip Law,
LLM (Lond)

Dusun *Marcus*
Called: Nov 1996, Lincoln's Inn, LLB
(Hons)(Lond)

Dutnall *Julian Richard*
Called: Oct 1995, Inner Temple, LLB (Exon)

Dutton *James Alexander* ●
Assistant Solicitor, Charity Commission, St
Albans House, 57/60 Haymarket, London
SW1Y 4QX, 0171 210 4406, Fax: 0171 210
4604. Called: Nov 1971, Middle Temple, BA
(Hons)

Dwan *Francis Eugene*
The Law Library, The Four Courts, Inns
Quay, Dublin 7, 00 353 1 702 3925, Fax: 00
353 1 872 0455, Barrister of Ireland.
Called: Mar 1996, Middle Temple, BA
(Hons), BL (Kings Inn)

Dwyer *John Augustine*
Called: Nov 1986, Gray's Inn, LLB(Lond)

Dwyer *Timothy John*
Called: Oct 1993, Inner Temple

Dyer *Christopher Guy*
29 Charnwood Drive, South Woodford,
London E18 1PF, 0181 989 0676.
Called: Oct 1993, Gray's Inn, LLB

Dyer *Miss Sandra Penelope* ●
Senior Crown Prosecutor, Crown
Prosecution Service, Chartist Tower, Dock
Street, Newport, Gwent. Called: Nov 1983,
Middle Temple, BA (Hons)

Dykes *Jonathan Hugh Elwand Maxwell*
Offshore Finacne Inspector, P.O.Box 1407,
Queen's Drive, London WC1X 8NF, 0171
404 5566, Fax: 0171 404 2244. Called: Nov
1994, Inner Temple, LLB (Lond), ACCA

Dykes *Philip John*
Suite 1517-1522, Two Pacific Place,
Queensway, 2810 7222, Fax: 2845 0439,
Queen's Counsel (Hong Kong 1997), Senior
Counsel, (1997) and Member Hong Kong
Bar. Called: July 1977, Lincoln's Inn, BA
(Oxon)

Dymond *Anthony Simon*
Called: Feb 1993, Inner Temple, BA

Dyson *Robert Frank* ●
Principal Crown Prosecutor, CPS (London),
18th Floor, Tolworth Tower, Surbiton,
Surrey KT6 7DS, 0181 399 5171, Fax: 0181
390 3474. Called: Nov 1973, Lincoln's Inn,
LLB (Lond)

Dyson *Mr Stephen John*
Deputy Clerk to the Justices, Northampton
Magistrates' Court, Regent's Pavillion,
Summerhouse Road, Moulton Park,
Northampton NN3 6AS, 01604 497011, Fax:
01604 497010. Called: Feb 1986, Gray's Inn,
MBA (Bham)

Dzakpasu *Lucas Kwami Wenceslav*
Called: Nov 1997, Middle Temple, LLB
(Hons)(Lond)

Eades *Christopher Nicholas*
Principal Court Clerk, Coventry Magistrates
Court, Little Park Street, Coventry, West
Midlands CV1 2SQ, 01203 630666 Ext 2176,
Fax: 01203 256513. Called: Nov 1984,
Lincoln's Inn, LLB

Eaglestone *Dr Frank Nelson*
Senior Examiner to the Chartered Insurance
Institute, 5 St Michael's Avenue, Bramhall,
Stockport, Cheshire SK7 2PT, 0161 439
4628. Called: Nov 1972, Gray's Inn, LLB
(Lond), FCII, FCIArb, PhD

Eames *Anthony John*
Called: July 1981, Gray's Inn

Earles *Charles Graham*
Slaughter & May, 35 Basinghall Street,
London EC2 3DB, 0171 710 5028.
Called: Oct 1990, Lincoln's Inn, MA
(Cantab)

Easton *Dr Susan Margaret*
Senior Lecturer, Department of Law, Brunel
University, Uxbridge, Middlesex UB8 3PH,
01895 274000, Fax: 01895 810476 (Law
Dept). Called: Nov 1988, Inner Temple, BSc
(Econ, Wales), LLM (Lond), PhD (Soton),
Dip Law (City)

E

Easton *Miss Tracy* •
Senior Crown Prosecutor, Crown
Prosecution Service, 2nd Floor, Froomsgate
House, Rupert Street, Bristol BS1 2DJ, 0117
927 3093. Called: Nov 1992, Inner Temple,
BA (Hons), Dip in Law

Eastwood *Mrs Hilary Ann* •
Director of Administration, Liverpool City
Magistrates Crt, 107-109 Dale Street,
Liverpool L2 2JQ, 0151 243 5672, Fax: 0151
243 5685. Called: Feb 1991, Middle Temple,
LLB

Eatwell *Nikolai Jonathan*
Called: Nov 1995, Lincoln's Inn, BA (Hons)

Eberwein *Irving James* •
Trust & Taxation Director, CMI Financial
Services Ltd, Narrow Plain, Bristol BS2 0JH,
0181 520 0123, Fax: 0181 520 7501,
Associate Fellow of the Society of Advanced
Legal Studies. Called: Nov 1975, Inner
Temple, LLB, LLM (Lond), TEP

Eble *Keith James* •
Called: Oct 1994, Lincoln's Inn, LLB
(Hons)(Wales)

Eborn *Andrew Martin James*
Managing Director, Eborn & Associates Ltd,
Law & Buisiness Offices, Sponsorship &
Rights Mngment, 195 Euston Road, London
NW1 2BN, 0171 383 5884, Fax: 0171 753
8648, Former Solicitor. Called: July 1985,
Inner Temple, BA (Dunelm)

Ebulue *Emmanuel Reginald
Ordiranachuh* •
Health & Safety Executive, Rose Court, 2
Southwark Bridge, London SE1 9HS, 0171
717 6666, Fax: 0171 717 6661. Called: Feb
1979, Middle Temple, LLB (Lond), MA

Eccles *Alan Michael* •
Clerk to the Justices, Dudley Magistrates'
Court, The Inhedge, Dudley, West Midlands
DY1 1RY, 01384 211411, Fax: 01384
211415. Called: July 1981, Middle Temple,
BA Hons

Eckersley *Basil Stuart MBE*
Called: Jan 1949, Lincoln's Inn, MA (Oxon)

Eckersley *Simon James*
Goldman Sachs International, Limited, 133
Fleet Street, London EC4A 2BB, 0171 774
5275, Fax: 0171 774 1700. Called: Nov
1988, Lincoln's Inn, LLB Hons (LSE), Dip
D'Etudes Jur, MBA

Ede *Ronald George* •
Senior Crown Prosecutor, Crown
Prosecution Service, Lysnoweth, Infirmary
Hill, Truro, Cornwall TRi 2XG, 01872
70127, Fax: 01872 42495. Called: July 1981,
Middle Temple, BA, DMS

Eden *Edgar*
8 Woodcote, Maidenhead, Berkshire
SL6 4DU, 01628 783678. Called: Nov 1950,
Inner Temple, MA (Oxon)

Eden-Shallcross *Mrs Deborah Doreen*
Court Clerk, North Sefton Magistrates'Court,
The Law Courts, Albert road, Southport
PR9 0LJ, 01704 534141, Fax: 01704 500226.
Called: Feb 1991, Middle Temple, LLB
(L'pool)

Edgar *Effrem Owen*
Edgar & Co Chambers, P.O.Box 500,
Castries, St Lucia, 758 452 2405, Fax: 758
451 8979, and Member East Caribbean
Supreme Court (St Lucia). Called: July 1995,
Lincoln's Inn, BA (Hons), LLM

Edgell *Mrs Shobha Goriah*
Magistrates' Court Clerk, Justices' Clerk's
Office, The Court House, Civic Centre, St
Peter Street, St Albans AL1 3LB, 01727
816823/36, Fax: 01727 816829. Called: July
1988, Inner Temple, LLB (Wales)

Edila *Ms Gifty* •
Head of Legal Services, Legal Division,
London Borough of Newham, Barking Road,
London E6 2RP, 0181 472 1430 x 23003,
Fax: 0181 472 0480, and Member Nigerian
Bar. Called: July 1979, Inner Temple,
LLB,LLM (Lond)

Edlington *Crawford Ian Anthony*
Called: Nov 1997, Middle Temple, LLB
(Hons)

Edmonds *Mrs Mary Xue-Ying*
Called: Nov 1996, Lincoln's Inn, LLB
(Hons)(Lond)

Edmonds *Mrs Vanessa Moragh* •
Legal Advisor. Called: July 1994, Lincoln's
Inn, LLB (Hons, Bucks)

Edmondson *James Douglas*
Called: Oct 1997, Gray's Inn, BA, MBA
(Belfast)

Edney *Miss Sarah Mary*
4 Field Court, Gray's Inn, London, WC1R
5EA. Called: July 1982, Inner Temple, MA
(Oxon)

Edusei *John Roger* •
Associate at Andrade & Co, Bank Chambers,
48 Onslow Gardens, London SW7 3AH,
0171 581 2871, Fax: 0171 581 0275.
Called: Oct 1991, Gray's Inn, LLB (Lond)

Edward Jnr *Fred*
Cain & Abel Law Firm, 239 Missenden,
Inville Road, London SE17 2HX, 0171 701
2327, Fax: 0171 201 2327. Called: Nov
1996, Lincoln's Inn, LLB (Hons), LLM (Lond)

Edwards *Miss Benita Ava*
Called: Oct 1997, Middle Temple, LLB
(Hons)(Lond)

Edwards *David Charles* •
Senior Lawyer, The Greenalls Group plc,
Wilderspool House, Greenalls Avenue,
Warrington WA4 6RH, 01925 51234, Fax:
01925 244957. Called: Nov 1978, Gray's
Inn, LLB (Nottm)

Edwards *David William* •
Senior Crown Prosecutor, Crown
Prosecution Service, River Park House, 225
High Road, London N22 4HQ, 0181 888
8889, Fax: 0181 365 7752. Called: July
1988, Middle Temple, LLB (Hons)

Edwards *Miss Jacqueline Elizabeth
Anne*
Called: Mar 1997, Lincoln's Inn, BA (Jnt
Hons)(Keele)

Edwards *Miss Jane Grace Wyn* •
Garretts Law Firm, 180 Strand, London
WC2R 2NN. Called: Nov 1994, Lincoln's
Inn, BA (Hons)(Belfast), MA (Durham), Dip
in Law (City)

Edwards *Miss Joanne Louise*
Called: Nov 1996, Lincoln's Inn, LLB (Hons)

Edwards *Miss Judith Caroline* •
Tax Consultant, Tusons, 29/30 Newbury
Street, London EC1A 7HU, 0171 600 0203,
Fax: 0171 600 0795. Called: Nov 1989,
Inner Temple, BA (Dunelm)

Edwards *Mrs Katherine Louise* •
Counsel, Goldman Sachs International,
Peterborough Court, 133 Fleet Street,
London EC4A 2BB, 0171 774 1000, Fax:
0171 774 1313. Called: July 1987, Inner
Temple, BA Sheffield

Edwards *Miss Luisa Francesca*
Theodore Goddard Solicitors, 150
Aldersgate Street, London EC1A 4EJ, 0171
606 8855, Fax: 0171 606 4390. Called: Oct
1992, Lincoln's Inn, MA (Hons) (Oxon),
Lic.Spec Dr Eur, (Brussels)

Edwards *Martin Russell*
Court Clerk, Derbyshire Magistrates' Court,
The Court House, Derwent Street, Derby
DE1 2EP, 01332 292 100. Called: Nov 1992,
Lincoln's Inn, LLB (Hons)

Edwards *Michael George* •
Crown Prosecution Service, C/O 50 Ludgate
Hill, London EC4M 7EX. Called: Feb 1988,
Lincoln's Inn, LLB (UC Wales)

Edwards *Miss Patricia Anne* •
Legal Director, Office of Fair Trading, Office
of Fair Trading, Field House, 15-25 Bream's
Buildings, London EC4A 1PR. Called: July
1967, Middle Temple, LLB

Edwards *Peter Alfred Howard*
Legal Assistant. Called: Oct 1996, Inner
Temple, LLB (Hons)

Edwards *Mrs Sheila Therese Sarah* •
Senior Crown Prosecutor, Crown
Prosecution Service, Reading, Berkshire
RG1 7LL, 0118 950 3771. Called: Nov 1980,
Gray's Inn, LLB Hons

Edwards *Steven John* •
Abbey National Treasury, Services plc, Legal
& Documentation, Abbey House, Baker
Street, London NW1 6XL, 0171 612 4487,
Fax: 0171 612 4581. Called: Oct 1995, Inner
Temple, BA, LLB

Edwards *Mrs Susan* •
Assistant Director, Legal Services, Office of
the Solicitor, Dept of Health & Social,
Security, New Court, 48 Carey Street,
London WC2A 2LS, 0171 412 1402.
Called: Nov 1972, Gray's Inn, LLB (Lond)

Edwards *Miss Teresa Louise*
Called: Oct 1996, Lincoln's Inn, LLB
(Hons)(L'pool)

Edwards Timothy
Called: Nov 1994, Middle Temple, BA (Hons)

Ee Miss Annie Yeok Leng
Called: Mar 1998, Lincoln's Inn, LLB (Hons)(Keele)

Efrem Mrs Eleni Andreas
District Court Judge, District Court of Larnaca, Larnaca, 04 630531. Called: July 1990, Gray's Inn, LLB (E Ang), LLM (Lond)

Efstathiou Miss Antigoni
Called: May 1995, Inner Temple, LLB (Wales)

Ehamparam Santhirasegaram
Called: July 1995, Inner Temple, LLB

Ehiribe Ike
Arbitrator & Medator, Part Time Lecturer, 4/24 Britannia House, Britannia Street, London WC1X 9JD, 0171 278 5961, Fax: 0171 278 5961, and Member Nigeria. Called: Nov 1996, Lincoln's Inn, LLB (Hons)(Lagos), BL (Lagos), FCIArb

Eidinow John Allan Lindsay
68 North Road, London N6, 0181 340 0835. Called: May 1961, Middle Temple, MA, LLM (Cantab)

Eimer Mrs Vivien Ruth
Called: Nov 1969, Gray's Inn, LLB (Hons)(Leeds)

Ejindu Mrs Virginia Obiageli •
Senior Crown Prosecutor, Crown Prosecution Service, Youth Branch, The Cooperage, Gainsford Street, London SE1 2NG. Called: July 1987, Lincoln's Inn, LLB Hons [Lond], BL Hons [Nigeria]

Ekins Charles Wareing
Assistant Recorder, 25 Park Square, Leeds, LS1 2PW. Called: July 1980, Gray's Inn, LLB (Leeds)

Elahi Rizwan •
Crown Prosecution Service, Inner London-Central Branch, Portland House, Stag Place, London SW1E 5BM, 0171 828 9050, Fax: 0171 630 0157. Called: May 1990, Middle Temple, LLB (Hons)

Elcock Julian Edward •
Senior Crown Prosecutor, St George's House, Lever Street, Wolverhampton, West Midlands, 01902 870900. Called: Oct 1992, Middle Temple, LLB (Hons)

Eldridge Mark Graham
Justices' Chief Executive & Joint Justices' Clerk, Warwickshire Magistrates', Courts Committee, PO Box 16, Leamington Spa, Warwickshire CV32 4XG, 01926 883350, Fax: 01926 335051. Called: Nov 1975, Gray's Inn, LLB

Eliot Smith Ms Valerie •
Senior Crown Prosecutor, Crown Prosecution Service, Solar House, 1-9 Romford Road, Stratford, London E15, 0181 534 6601, Fax: 0181 522 1236. Called: Nov 1987, Gray's Inn, BA (Lond), Dip Law

Elkeles Mrs Arran
11 Askew Road, Moor Park, Northwood, Middlesex HA6 2JF, 01923 827341. Called: July 1969, Gray's Inn, MA, MIPD

Elkin Alexander CMG, LLD
70 Apsley House, Finchley Road, St John's Wood, London NW8 ONZ, 0171 483 2475. Called: June 1937, Middle Temple, LLM (Lond) Dr jur, (Kiel)

Elkinson Jeffrey Philip
Conyers Dill & Pearman, Clarendon House, Church Street, Hamilton HM CX, 809 295 1422, Fax: 809 292 4720, and Member Southern Ireland (1978) Hong Kong (1985), New South Wales, Australia (1985), New York (1987), Bermuda (1989) New York (1987) and Bermuda (1989) Bars. Called: Feb 1982, Middle Temple, BL, MA, LLB, FCIArb

Elles Baroness Diana Louie
3 Verulam Buildings, London, WC1R 5NT. Called: June 1956, Lincoln's Inn, BA (Lond)

Ellicott Peter Richard •
Legal Advisor, International Chamber of, Commerce, Linton House, 1 Linton Road, Barking, Essex IG11 8HG, 0181 591 3000, Fax: 0181 594 2833. Called: May 1997, Middle Temple, LLB (Hons)(Lond)

Ellinas Miss Evanthia
Called: Nov 1995, Inner Temple, LLB (Lond)

Elliott Miss Carol Ann
Called: Oct 1997, Gray's Inn

Elliott Miss Catherine •
Called: Nov 1990, Lincoln's Inn, LLB (B'ham)

Elliott John Mark •
Principal Crown Prosecutor, Crown Prosecution Service, Justian House, Spitfire Close, Ermine Business Park, Huntingdon Cambs, 01480 432333. Called: Nov 1978, Gray's Inn, BA (Keele)

Elliott Sebastion Michael Garcia
Called: Oct 1996, Lincoln's Inn, BA (Hons)(Essex), Dip in Law (City)

Ellis David Leon
Development Director, Johnson Fry, 20 Regent Street, London SW1Y 4PZ, 0171 451 1000, Fax: 0171 321 0505. Called: July 1981, Gray's Inn, MA (Cantab), LLM (Lond)

Ellis Edward David
Attorney in Guyana Attorney in New York, Lot 2809, Church Avenue, Brooklyn, New York 11226, and Member Guyana Bar New York Bar. Called: July 1979, Lincoln's Inn, BA

Ellis Mrs Edwina Francesca •
Principal Legal Advisor, Stratford Magistrates' Court, The Courthouse, 389-397 High Street, Stratford, London E15 4SB, 0181 522 5000, Fax: 0181 519 9214. Called: Nov 1984, Middle Temple, BA

Ellis Professor Evelyn Daphne •
Professor of Public Law, Faculty of Law, University of Birmingham, Edgbaston, Birmingham B15 2TT, 0121 414 6306. Called: Nov 1972, Middle Temple, MA, LLM, PhD

Ellis Patrick John Cleverly
Called: May 1965, Gray's Inn, MA (Oxon)

Ellis Paul David d'Andria
Senior Court Clerk, Ealing Magistrates Court, The Court House, Green Man Lane, West Ealing, London W13 OSD, 0181 579 9311, Fax: 0181 579 2935. Called: Nov 1990, Inner Temple, LLB (Lond)

Ellis Ralph Lewis •
Chairman; of the Urban Renewal Foundation. Chairman & Chief Executive of Western Water Highway, Nettle Beds, Old Alresford, Hants SO24 9RF, 01962 734761. Called: July 1972, Middle Temple, LLB, FCIArb, MILDM, FCIPS

Ellis Miss Rebecca Lisa •
Law Commission, Conquest House, 37/38 John Street, Theobalds Road, London WC1N, 0171 453 1221, Fax: 0171 453 1297. Called: Nov 1992, Inner Temple, BA (Oxon), BCL

Ellis William Rowland •
Managing Director, Temple Lectures Ltd, Charter House, Bexhill-on-Sea, East Sussex TN40 1JA, 01424 212021, Fax: 01424 730074. Called: Nov 1976, Gray's Inn, LLB Lond

Ellison Ms Alice Louise
Called: Oct 1994, Gray's Inn, LLB (Manch)

Ellison John Anthony
c/o Conyers Dill & Pearman, Clarendon House, Church Street, Hamilton HM CX, 441 295-1422, Fax: 441 292-4720, and Member Bahamas Bar Bermuda Bar. Called: May 1957, Inner Temple, MA

Ellison Michael
10 Deanscourt Road, West Knighton, Leicester LE2 6GH, 0533 810345, 9 Bedford Row, London, WC1R 4AZ. Called: Nov 1984, Inner Temple, BA, LLM in Welfare Law

Elliston Miss Sarah Joanne
Lecturer in Medical Law, Medical Law Unit, School of Law, Stair Building, University of Glasgow, Glasgow G12 8QQ, 0141 339 8855 x 8397/8028, Fax: 0141 330 4698. Called: Feb 1993, Lincoln's Inn, MA (Hons), LLM

Ellul Marc Xavier
Suite 7, Hadfield House, Library Street, 00 (350) 70921, Fax: 00 (350) 74969, and Member Gibratar. Called: Nov 1993, Inner Temple, BA (Hons)(Cardiff)

Elphick Timothy
Publisher, 23 Lilyville Road, London SW6 5DP, 0171 371 8532. Called: Nov 1988, Middle Temple, MA (Cantab)

Elphicke *Brett Charles Anthony*
Wilde Sapte, 1 Fleet Street, London, 0171 246 7676, Fax: 0171 246 7777. Called: Nov 1994, Middle Temple, LLB (Hons)

Elphicke *Mrs Natalie Cecilia*
Wilde Sapte, 1 Fleet Place, London, 0171 246 7000, Fax: 0171 246 7777. Called: Oct 1994, Lincoln's Inn, LLB (Hons)(Kent)

Elsey *Derek William* •
Head of Legal Services, Division of Legal Services, Secretriat, University of Teesside, Middlesbrough, Cleveland, 01642 218121 X2027/342027, Fax: 01642 342067 or 342071. Called: July 1980, Middle Temple, LLB(Hons) (Wales)

Elvy *Phillip James*
Called: Oct 1997, Inner Temple, LLB (Southampton)

Ely *Jonathan Michael Charles*
Called: Apr 1991, Gray's Inn, LLB

Emanuel *Miss Justina Omowunmi*
Called: Nov 1990, Inner Temple, BA (Kent)

Emberton *Miss Judith Elizabeth* •
Called: Oct 1992, Middle Temple, LL.B (Hons, Nott'm)

Emerson *Ms Fernandez Tina Mary*
Seventrees, Coolham Road, West Chiltington, West Sussex RH20 2LH, 01403 741154, Fax: 01403 741154. Called: July 1992, Lincoln's Inn, LLB (Hons) (Lond)

Emerton *Lieutenant Commander Mark Simon RN* •
Deputy Chief Naval Judge Advocate, Deputy Chief Naval Judge, Advocate., Royal Naval College, King William Walk, Greenwich, London SE10 9NN, 0181 858 2154 x 4368, Fax: 0181 293 1985. Called: Oct 1991, Gray's Inn, MA (Oxon), Dip Law (City)

Emeruwa *John* •
Legal Advisor, Department of Trade & Industry, Ashdown House, 123 Victoria Street, London SW1E 6RB, 0171 215 6979. Called: July 1989, Inner Temple, LLM (S'ton)

Emmanuel *Ms Christine Lorna*
Called: July 1995, Lincoln's Inn, LLB (Hons)

Emmanuel *Miss Eileen Elizabeth*
Called: Nov 1990, Gray's Inn, LLB (Bristol)

Emodi *Miss Rosemary*
Called: Feb 1994, Inner Temple, LLB, LLM (Lond)

Empson *Gordon Everett*
Canterbury Gate House, Sandwich, Kent CT13 9HZ, 01304 612178. Called: Nov 1948, Middle Temple

Endicott *David Nigel*
Called: Feb 1994, Lincoln's Inn, LLB (Hons, Bucks)

Eng *Ms Audrey Cher Hwee*
Legal Assistant, Messrs Drew & Napier, 20 Raffles Place, [H]17-00 Ocean Towers, Fax: 65 535 0733, Advocate & Solicitor of the Supreme Court of the Republic of Singapore. Called: July 1993, Gray's Inn, LLB (Leeds)

Engelman *Mark Trevor* •
Head of Intellectual Property Treasury of the Bar Association for Commerce Finance & Industry, Member of the Bar Council, The Body Shop International, Plc, Watermead, Littlehampton, West Sussex, 01903 731500, Fax: 01903 731275. Called: Nov 1987, Gray's Inn, BSc, Dip Law

England *James* •
Branch Crown Prosecutor, Central Casework, Crown Prosecution Service, 50 Ludgate Hill, London EC4M 7EX. Called: July 1981, Gray's Inn, LLB (Lond)

England *Mrs Lisa Johanna Louise*
84A Oakwood Court, Holland park, London W14 8JF, 0171 602 5877, Fax: 0171 603 1219. Called: Nov 1992, Gray's Inn, LLB (Hons)(Lond)

English *Ms Helen Warnock*
32 Ellington Street, London N7 8PL, 0171 607 1628, Fax: 0171 609 6451, Phi Beta Kappa and Member New York Bar (Called 1979). Called: May 1988, Middle Temple, BA, Juris Doctor (US), Dip Law (City)

English *Miss Katherine Louise*
Called: Oct 1994, Gray's Inn, LLB (Manch)

English *Miss Kathryn Bridget Margaret*
3 Temple Gardens, 3rd Floor, Temple, London, EC4Y 9AU. Called: July 1985, Gray's Inn, BA (Cardiff)

English *Lawrence James* •
Senior Crown Prosecutor, Crown Prosecution Service, Solar House, 1-9 Romford Road, Stratford, London E15, 0181 534 6601 X 316, Fax: 0181 522 1236. Called: Nov 1988, Lincoln's Inn, LLB (Nott'm)

English *Ms Rosalind Catherine*
Part-time BBC Presenter Lecturer in Law, Merton College, Oxford, 15 Fentiman Road, London SW8 1LF, 0171 582 7592, Fax: 0171 793 8741, Former Solicitor. Called: July 1993, Gray's Inn, MA, LLM

Enright *Guy Thomas*
Schroders, 120 Cheapside, London EC2V 6DS, 0171 658 2137, Fax: 0171 658 6459. Called: Nov 1993, Middle Temple, BA (Hons)(Oxon)

Enser *Miss Juliette Corinne*
Weil, Gotshal and Manges LLP, 81 Avenue Louise, P.O.Box 9-10, 1050 Brussels, 00 32 2 543 7484. Called: Oct 1991, Inner Temple, BA (Oxon), Dip EC LAW

Entwistle *Miss Janet Anne Catherine* •
Called: July 1984, Gray's Inn, BA (Keele), LLM (Lond)

Entwistle *John Reid*
Called: Nov 1995, Gray's Inn, LLB

Entwistle *Robert Mark*
Called: May 1997, Lincoln's Inn, LLB (Hons)(Lond), B.Tech, FRICS, FCIOB, FCIArb, FFB

Envis *Gary*
Eastern Caribbean. Called: Nov 1992, Inner Temple, LLB

Ephraim *Miss Pamela*
Called: July 1997, Middle Temple, LLB (Hons)(Lond)

Er *Miss Joanna Wuan Sher*
Called: July 1995, Lincoln's Inn, LLB (Hons)

Erdeljan *Branislav*
Called: Oct 1991, Inner Temple, LLB, LLM (Lond)

Ern *Lai Daryl Chee*
Called: July 1997, Inner Temple, LLB (Lond)

Eronen *Mrs Gonul*
Supreme Court Judge, Supreme Court, Lefkosa, TRNC, 90 392 2273690, Fax: 90 392 2286001. Called: Nov 1975, Gray's Inn

Erotocritou *Miss Elena*
Called: Nov 1996, Lincoln's Inn, LLB (Hons)(Leics)

Erotokritou *Miss Christianna A*
A.P.Erotokritou & Co, Advocate, P.O.Box 2154, Nicosia, 357 2 452466. Called: Nov 1997, Lincoln's Inn, LLB (Hons)

Erriah *Ramdeo*
Called: Nov 1995, Gray's Inn, LLB (Lond)

Ershad *Miss Jennifer*
Akainyaj & Co, 308 Seven Sisters Road, London N4. Called: Oct 1994, Middle Temple, LLB (Hons)(Lond)

Ershad *Sheikh Monsore Habib*
Deputy Chief Clerk, Inner London Magistrates', Courts Service, 3rd Floor, North West Wing, Bush House, Aldwych, London WC2B 4PJ. Called: Nov 1988, Middle Temple, LLB

Erskine *Alexander Jude*
Assistant Director (Legal & Compliance) Deputy Company Secretary. Called: Nov 1996, Inner Temple, LLB (Wales)

Erskine *Thomas Ralph CB*
Office of the Legislative Csl., Parliament Bldgs, Stormont, Belfast, Northern Ireland BT4 3SW. Called: Feb 1962, Gray's Inn, LLB

Eshun *Yaw Fenyi*
Called: July 1995, Lincoln's Inn, BA (Hons) (Ghana)

Esmail *Miss Lubna*
Called: Mar 1997, Inner Temple, BA

Espiner *Miss Claire Anne*
Called: Oct 1995, Middle Temple, BA (Hons)

Essayan *Michael QC (1976)*
Also Inn of Court I. Called: Feb 1957, Middle Temple, MA (Oxon)

Essien *Carl Anthony Ekong*
Leasehold Advisor, Leasehold Enfranchisement, Advisory Service, 8 Maddox Street, London W1R 9PN, 0171 493 3116, Fax: 0171 493 4318. Called: Oct 1991, Gray's Inn, LLB (Bucks), LLM (Lond)

Essien *Mrs Olive* •
Called: July 1990, Gray's Inn, LLB

Etherton *Michael Robert*
Called: July 1996, Middle Temple, BA (Hons)(Oxon), LTCL

Etican *Ramsay Roy*
Called: July 1997, Lincoln's Inn, LLB
(Hons)(Hull)

Eubank *Miss Nicole Ruth*
Called: Oct 1997, Middle Temple, LLB
(Hons)(Lond)

Evangelou *Miss Theano Alexandros*
Called: July 1995, Gray's Inn, LLB (Lond)

Evans *Sir (William) Vincent John*
GCMG, MBE QC (1973)
4 Bedford Road, Moor Park, Northwood,
Middlesex HA6 2BB, 01923 824085.
Called: June 1939, Lincoln's Inn, MA, BCL
(Hons)

Evans *Alastair Mackenzie*
Manager, International Affairs, Lloyd's of
London, 1 Lime Street, London EC3M 7HA,
0171 327 6682, Fax: 0171 327 5255.
Called: Feb 1995, Inner Temple, MA
(Oxon), LLB (Lond), A.C.I.S.

Evans *Miss Alison*
Senior Legal Adviser, Berkshire Courts
Committee, Easby House, Northfield End,
Henley on Thames, Oxon RG9 2NB, 01491
412720, Fax: 01491 412762. Called: Nov
1991, Gray's Inn, LLB

Evans *Christian William Philip Roe*
Called: May 1996, Gray's Inn, LLB (Hull)

Evans *Edward Owen* •
Legal Officer, University of Salford, Salford
M5 4WT, 0161 745 5035, Fax: 0161 745
5016. Called: May 1987, Lincoln's Inn, LLB
(Lond), LLM (Lond), FCIS, ACIArb

Evans *Guy St John*
Legal Affairs Officer, World Trade
Organisation, Geneva. Called: Nov 1992,
Inner Temple, BA (Hons)(Kent), MA
(Bruges)

Evans *Miss Gwawr*
Called: Mar 1996, Inner Temple, LLB
(Wales)

Evans *Gwilym Thomas*
18 The Rath, Milford Haven, Dyfed
SA73 2QA. Called: Feb 1973, Middle
Temple, Extra Master, (Mariner)

Evans *Henry Wilson*
The Waggon Hole, Market Overton, Rutland
LE15 7PH, 01572 767607. Called: Nov 1955,
Gray's Inn

Evans *Ian Michael Probyn*
Bridge Farm House, Chelsworth, Ipswich,
Suffolk IP7 7HX. Called: Feb 1955, Inner
Temple, BCL, MA (Oxon)

Evans *James Martin Crispin* •
Director of Legal & Business Affairs,
Polygram International Music, Publishing
Ltd, 8 St James Square, London SW1Y 4JU,
0171 747 4000, Fax: 0171 747 4467.
Called: July 1977, Inner Temple, B.A.

Evans *Jeremy Roger*
Called: Nov 1997, Middle Temple, BSc
(Hons)(Sheff)

Evans *Jonathan Dominic David*
46/48 Essex Street, London, WC2R 3GH.
Called: Oct 1990, Gray's Inn, LLB

Evans *Nicholas John*
Called: Nov 1997, Gray's Inn, LLB, LLM
(Warw)

Evans *Miss Penelope Caroline* •
Legal Advisor, BBC, 0181 752 5734, Fax:
0181 752 5080. Called: July 1987, Gray's
Inn, BA (Durham)

Evans *Mrs Penelope Susan*
Senior Court Clerk, The Court House,
Oldbury Ringway, Oldbury, Warley, West
Midlands B69 4JN, 0121 511 2222, Fax:
0121 544 8492. Called: Feb 1993, Gray's
Inn, LLB (B'ham)

Evans *Peter Norman*
01703 252667, Fax: 01703 252667, and
Member New York Bar. Called: May 1963,
Gray's Inn, MA (Oxon)

Evans *Peter William* •
Legal Services (Prosecution), Department of
Trade & Industry, 10 Victoria Street, London
SW1H 0NN, 0171 215 3173, Fax: 0171 215
3235. Called: Nov 1994, Middle Temple, BA
(Hons)

Evans *Robert James Francis*
Senior Deputy Chief Clerk, Inner London
Magistrates', Courts Service, 65 Romney
Street, London SW1P 3RD. Called: Nov
1975, Middle Temple, LLB

Evans *Mrs Sally Anne* •
Deputy Legal Adviser, The Home Office, 50
Queen Anne's Gate, London SW1H 9AT.
Called: Feb 1971, Gray's Inn, LLB

Evans *Miss Sian Amanda*
Called: Oct 1997, Lincoln's Inn, LLB
(Hons)(Greenwic), LLM (Lond)

Evans *Ms Susan Elizabeth* •
Senior Legal Adviser, Inland Revenue
Solicitor's, Office, Somerset House, London
WC2R 1LB, 0171 438 6905, Fax: 0171 438
6246, and Member Washington DC State &
Federal Bars, Maryland Federal Bar.
Called: July 1985, Lincoln's Inn, BA, Dip
Law, MCL, (Amer Practice)

Evans-Lombe *Miss Sarah Frances*
Called: Nov 1992, Inner Temple, LLB (Bris)

Everett *Henry Wentworth*
Called: Mar 1996, Gray's Inn, BA (Reading)

Everett-Heath *Miss Catharine Rose*
Called: Nov 1989, Lincoln's Inn, MA
(Cantab)

Everington *Dr Anthony Herbert*
GP, Stepney, London, 28 Rhondda Grove,
London E3 5AP, 0181 981 6996. Called: July
1978, Gray's Inn, MB, BS, MRCGP

Everson *Mrs Susan Lilian*
2 Fernsdale Cottages, Rays Lane, Tylers
Green Common, Penn, Bucks HP10 8LH,
0149 481 4637. Called: July 1988, Middle
Temple, LLB (Hons)

Eveson *Trevor John*
Called: Feb 1986, Gray's Inn

Evie *Mrs Georgiou Antoniou*
Legal Adviser to the President of the
Supreme Court, Supreme Court, Nicosia, 02-
302391, and Member Cyprus Bar.
Called: Nov 1995, Gray's Inn, LLB (Leic),
LLM

Ewen *Mrs Lorna Sylvia* •
Principal Crown Prosecutor (part time),
Crown Prosecution Service, 1st Floor, The
Cooperage, 8 Gainsford Street, London
SE1 2NE, 0171 357 7010, Fax: 0171 962
0906. Called: Nov 1983, Gray's Inn, BA, LLM

Ewing *Miss Michelle* •
Treasury Solicitor, Queen Anne's Chambers,
28 Broadway, London SW1H 9JS, 0171 210
3216, Fax: 0171 210 3433. Called: Oct
1994, Middle Temple, BA (Hons)(Oxon),
LLM (Canada)

Exton *Miss Lesley Mary*
Called: Oct 1992, Middle Temple,
BA(Oxon), LLB(Lond)

Eyeington *Miss Louise Rebecca* •
Legal Adviser, Dept of Environment,
Transport, & the Regions, 76 Marsham
Street, London SW1, 0171 271 4421, Fax:
0171 271 4496. Called: Nov 1993, Inner
Temple, LLB (Warw)

Eyles *Alan James* •
C/O CPS Headquarters, 50 Ludgate Hill,
London EC4M 7EX, 0171 273 8000.
Called: Feb 1989, Gray's Inn, LLB

Eyles *Keith* •
Legal Adviser, Travers Morgan, Cantelupe
Road, E Grinstead, W Sussex RH19 3DG,
01342 327161, Fax: 01342 315927.
Called: July 1983, Inner Temple, BA (Keele)

Eyre *Edward*
1 Serjeants' Inn, 5th Floor, Fleet Street,
Temple, London, EC4Y 1LL. Called: July
1957, Inner Temple, LLB (Harvard)

Eyre *Philip James*
Called: Nov 1994, Middle Temple, LLB
(Hons), ARICS

Eyres *Raymond John* •
Company Secretary, Cummins Engine Co
Ltd, 46-50 Coombe Rd, New Malden, Surrey
KT3 4QL, 0181 949 6171, Fax: 0181 949
5604. Called: Nov 1973, Inner Temple, LLB,
MA, MBA

Eyton *Mrs Nik Mariah Zainab*
Abdullah A Rahman & Co, Suite 1803, 18th
Floor, Wisma Hamzah-Kwong, No 1 Leboh
Ampang, 50100 Kuala Lumpur, Fellow,
Institute of Legal Executives and Member
Malaysia Bar. Called: July 1971, Lincoln's
Inn, LLB

Eze *Miss Ugoji Adanma*
and Member Nigerian Bar. Called: Oct 1994,
Gray's Inn, BA

Ezekiel *Solomon Jonathan*
Called: Nov 1993, Lincoln's Inn, LLB (Hons)

E

Faal *Dr Edirissa Mohammad Omar*
Professor of Law, Private Practitioner, 222
S.Harbor Blvd, Suite 830, Anaheim,
California 92805, 714 502 1900, Fax: 714
502 1909, Attorney at Law(USA) and
Member Bar of U.S. Supreme Court,
California Bar, Indiana Bar. Called: July
1992, Middle Temple, BSc, Dr of Juris
Prudence

Fadden *Dr Kathleen*
0171 367 3000, Fax: 0171 367 2000.
Called: Oct 1993, Inner Temple, BSc, PhD,
LLB

Faherty *Miss Mary*
and Member Irish Bar. Called: Nov 1996,
Middle Temple, BA, LLB (Galway), BL
(King's Inn)

Fahy *Ms Sheila Catherine Elise*
Called: Nov 1994, Inner Temple, LLB (Lond)

Faidz *Miss Saliza*
Called: July 1994, Lincoln's Inn, LLB (Hons,
Sheff)

Faiers *Andrew Clive* •
Lawyer, Crown Prosecution Service, 50
Ludgate Hill, London EC4. Called: July 1976,
Gray's Inn

Fair *James Dale*
29154 Jefferson Ct, St Clair Shores,
Michigan 48081, 810 415 0625, Fax: 810
294 1811, and Member State of Kansas USA.
Called: Nov 1980, Lincoln's Inn, AB
(Princeton), MA, (Oxon) JD (Stanford)

Fairclough *Murray Simon Charles*
Associate (Employment Law),
Sonnenscheins Solicitors, Royex House,
Aldermanbury Square, London EC2V 7HR,
0171 600 2222, Fax: 0171 600 2221.
Called: Nov 1993, Inner Temple, LLB, LLM

Fairey *Hamish Webster*
Called: Nov 1997, Lincoln's Inn, LLB (Hons)

Fairweather *Anthony Charles*
Called: Nov 1994, Inner Temple, MA, Dip
Law

Falconer of Thoroton *Lord QC (1991)*
Solicitor General Recorder, Fountain Court,
Temple, London, EC4Y 9DH. Called: July
1974, Inner Temple, MA (Cantab)

Falk *Andrew Michael Pope* •
Solicitor to the Metropolitan, Police, New
Scotland, Broadway, London SW1.
Called: Nov 1977, Inner Temple, MA
(Cantab)

Falsafi *Miss Laya*
Legal Associate, Pullig & Co Solicitors,
Bridewell House, 9 Bridewell Place, London
EC4V 6AP, 0171 353 0505. Called: Feb
1991, Lincoln's Inn, LLB (Buck'ham)

Falshaw *William Fredrick* •
Senior Crown Prosecutor, Crown
Prosecution Service, Level 3, Beaumont
House, Cliftonville, Northampton NN1 5BN,
01604 230220, Fax: 01604 232081.
Called: July 1987, Inner Temple, Dip Law
(City), BA (Hons)

Fan *Edward*
and Member Hong Kong. Called: July 1997,
Inner Temple, BDS (Lond), MGDSRCS
(Edinburgh), Dip.F.Od (LHMC), LLB
(Westminster)

Fan *Miss Yuen Chi Edwina*
Called: July 1995, Middle Temple, LLB
(Hons)

Fanner *Roger Martin*
Deputy Clerk to the Justices, The Court
House, Homer Road, Solihull B91 3RD, 0121
705 8101, Fax: 0121 711 2045. Called: July
1978, Gray's Inn

Faraway *Michael John David* •
Justices' Chief Executive & Clerk to the
Justices, Redbridge Magistrates' Court, 850
Cranbrook Road, Barkingside, Ilford
IG6 1HW, 0181 551 4461, Fax: 0181 550
2101. Called: Nov 1971, Middle Temple

Farazi *Shahin*
Called: Mar 1997, Lincoln's Inn, BA
(Hons)(L'pool), MA, MPhil (Kent), CPE
(Lond)

Farid *Ms Fuzet*
2 Lorong Abang Haji Openg 3, Taman Tun
Dr Ismail, 60000 Kuala Lumpur, 603-718
2198, Fax: 603-201 4257, and Member
Malaysia Bar. Called: July 1993, Middle
Temple, BA (Hons)

Farley *Peter John* •
Legal Director & Company Secretary, Fiat
Auto (UK) Ltd, Fiat House, 266 Bath Road,
Slough, Berks SL1 4HJ, 01753 511431, Fax:
01753 512432. Called: July 1982, Middle
Temple, BA (Hons), LLM (Lond)

Farmiloe *Mrs Collette Marie* •
Assistant Group Legal Advisor Burton Group
Plc, The Burton Group Plc, 214 Oxford
Street, London W1N 9DF. Called: Nov 1990,
Middle Temple, BA (PCL)

Farnsworth *Miss Joanne*
Legal Information Consultant, 59 St Martin's
Lane, London WC2N 4JS, 0171 379 4441,
Fax: 0171 240 3982, and Member Canadian
Bar. Called: May 1983, Middle Temple, BA
(Hons), LLB, LLM (Lond)

Farooq *Mohammed Khan* •
Senior Lawyer, Dudley Metropolitian
Borough, Council, Legal & Property
Services, 3 St James Road, Dudley DY1 1HL,
01384 815333, Fax: 01384 815325.
Called: Oct 1993, Lincoln's Inn, LLB
(Hons)(Warw)

Farr *Alastair Richard*
Trett Consulting, Cap House, 9-12 Long
Lane, London EC1A 9HA, 0171 600 2211,
Fax: 0171 600 3818. Called: Oct 1995,
Middle Temple, LLB (Hons)

Farr *Sebastian Charles Arthur David* •
Office of Telecommunications, 50 Ludgate
Hill, London, Belgium EC4M 7JJ, 02 511
7270, Fax: 02 513 4220. Called: July 1981,
Gray's Inn, BA

Farran *Ms Denise Margaret*
Called: Mar 1996, Gray's Inn, B.Soc.Sci, MA,
PhD, (Manch)

Farrar *John Jewell*
22 Sylvan Way, West Wickham, Kent
BR4 9HB. Called: July 1970, Gray's Inn,
Chartered Chemist, Fellow, Royal Soc of,
Chemistry & Royal, Soc of Arts

Farren *Brendan Martin* •
Citibank International plc, St Martin's
House, 1 Grove Road, Hammersmith,
London, 0171 500 3814. Called: Nov 1988,
Middle Temple, LLB (Warwick)

Farren *Joseph Michael* •
Executive, KPMG Corporate Finance, 8
Salisbury Square, London EC4Y 8BB, 0171
311 8509. Called: Mar 1997, Lincoln's Inn,
BA (Hons) (Oxon)

Farthing *Richard Bruce Crosby*
Commander Royal Norwegian Order of
Merit, 44 St George's Drive, London
SW1V 4BT, 0171 834 1211, Fax: 0171 834
1211. Called: Feb 1954, Inner Temple, MA
(Cantab), FIMgt

Fateh *Anatul*
General Counsel, KAFCO Limited Dhaka,
KAFCO Limited, GPO Box 3049, Uttara
Bank Building, 15th F, 90-91 Motijeel
Commercial Area, Dhaka 1000, 00 880 2
956 5055/56, Fax: 00 880 2 956 5063, and
Member Bangladesh Bar. Called: Feb 1983,
Lincoln's Inn, BSc (Econ)(LSE), Dip Law
(City)

Faulkner *Miss Angela Elizabeth* •
Deputy Legal Services Manager, General
Accident, Life Services Ltd, 2 Rougier Street,
York YO1 1HR, 01904 452403, Fax: 01904
452422. Called: Nov 1988, Middle Temple,
LLB (L'pool)

Faulkner *Mrs Sabrina Louise* •
Official Solicitor of, The Supreme Court, 81
Chancery Lane, London WC2A 1DD, 0171
911 7124, Fax: 0171 911 7105. Called: July
1974, Gray's Inn

Faure *Trevor* •
European Legal Counsel, Apple Computer
Europe Inc, European H.Q., Paris, (331)
4714 6412, Fax: (331) 4714 6443.
Called: July 1988, Middle Temple, LLB
(Hons) (Lond)

Fawcett *Miss Alison Jane*
Called: Nov 1992, Lincoln's Inn, BA
(Hons)(Wales)

Fawcett *Miss Donna Marie*
Customer Services Manager/ Board
Secretary, Lincolnshire Health Authority,
Cross O'Cliff, Bracebridge Heath,
Lincolnshire LN4 2HN, 01522 515326.
Called: Feb 1994, Gray's Inn, LLB

Fayers *Roger Darley*
UK Delegate on Uncitral Working Group, 16
Grove Way, Esher, Surrey KT10 8HL, 0181
398 4744. Called: July 1966, Middle Temple,
LLB

Feaster *Miss Trudy Dawn*
Bristows Cooke and Carpmael, 10 Lincoln's
Inn Fields, London WC2A 3BP, 0171 400
8000, Fax: 0171 400 8050. Called: Oct
1993, Inner Temple, LLB (Warw), Diplome
Special en, Droit

Fedrick *Mrs Janet* •
Prosecutor for the Environment Agency,
King Meadows House, Kings Meadow Road,
Reading, Berks RG1 8DQ. Called: Nov 1974,
Gray's Inn

Feely *Miss Teresa Mary* •
Senior Crown Prosecutor, 7th Floor (South),
Royal Liver Building, Liverpool L3 1HN,
0151 236 7575. Called: Nov 1989, Gray's
Inn, LLB

Feeney *Thomas Francis Patrick*
Called: Nov 1992, Lincoln's Inn, LLB (Hons)

Feijao *Miss Sara Bettencourt Portella*
Called: Nov 1996, Inner Temple, LLB
(Sussex), LLM (Brussels)

Fellingham *Paul*
Clerk to the Justices, Hertfordshire
Magistrates Crt, Bayley House, Sish Lane,
Stevenage SG1 3SS, 01438 730430, Fax:
01438 730413. Called: Nov 1982, Middle
Temple, Dip Mag Law

Fennelly *Nial (Michael Patrick)*
Advocate General, European Court, 84 Rue
du Kirchberg, L-1858 Luxemborg, Senior
Counsel, Ireland (1978) and Member
Southern Ireland Bar Northern Ireland Bar.
Called: July 1988, Middle Temple, MA
(Dublin)

Fennemore *Miss Camilla Marianne*
Called: Nov 1993, Middle Temple, BA
(Hons)(Cantab), MA (Cantab)

Fenwick *Daniel Fitzgerald*
Called: Oct 1993, Lincoln's Inn, BA
(Hons)(Manc), CPE (Manc)

Ferguson *Francis John* •
Senior Crown Prosecutor, Crown
Prosecution Service, Haldin House, Old
Bank of England Court, Queen Street,
Norwich NR2 4SX, 01603 666491.
Called: Nov 1992, Gray's Inn, BA (Hons)

Ferguson *Gerald Patrick*
Court Clerk/Legal Adviser, Bedfordshire
Magistrates Court, St Paul's Square, Shire
Hall, Bedford MK40 1SQ, 01234 359426,
Fax: 01234 210607. Called: Nov 1991,
Gray's Inn, BA (Dub), LLB (Lond)

Ferguson *Gregor James*
Called: Nov 1995, Lincoln's Inn, BA (Hons),
LLM (Canada), LLM

Ferguson *Miss Joyann Louise*
Called: Nov 1997, Gray's Inn, BA, MA
(Morgan State,) LLB (Bucks)

Ferguson *Samuel William*
Barrister in N Ireland Employed barrister.
Called: July 1991, Gray's Inn, LLB (Belfast)

Ferley *Mrs Joyce Mary*
Justices' Clerk, Inner London Magistrates',
Courts Service, Bow Street Magistrates'
Court, Bow Street, London WC2, 0171 379
4713, Fax: 0171 379 5634. Called: Feb 1964,
Gray's Inn

Fernandes *Nicholas John Damian* •
Lawyer, Ministry of Agriculture,, Fisheries &
Food, Legal Dept, 55 Whitehall, London
SW1A 2EY, 0171 270 8093, Fax: 0171 270
8096. Called: Nov 1984, Lincoln's Inn, LLM,
BA, Dip French, Law

Fernandez *Christopher*
and Member Singapore. Called: Nov 1994,
Middle Temple, LLB (Hons)

Fernandez *James*
Called: July 1996, Lincoln's Inn, LLB
(Hons)(Lond)

Ferrari *Cesare Maria Primo* •
Senior Crown Prosecutor, 9 Clifford House,
Edith Villas, London W14 8UG, 0171 603
6099. Called: Feb 1979, Middle Temple, BA
(Oxon)

Ferrari *Mrs Lesley Jane*
Called: Nov 1996, Lincoln's Inn, LLB
(Hons)(Brunel)

Ferreira *Clive Joaquim* •
Medley, Kingston Hill, Kingston-Upon-
Thames, Surrey KT2 7IU. Called: Nov 1985,
Gray's Inn, LLB - Hons (Brunel)

Ferry *John Edward*
Called: Feb 1956, Gray's Inn, MA (Oxon)

Fesel *Christopher*
Called: Nov 1997, Inner Temple, LLB (Lond)

Field *Mrs Frances Myra*
10 Thornton Way, London NW11 6RY.
Called: Nov 1970, Gray's Inn

Field *Miss Sally Ann* •
Company Secretary, De La Rue Plc, 6 Agar
Street, London WC2N 4DE, 0171 836 8383,
Fax: 0171 240 4224. Called: July 1970,
Gray's Inn, MA (Cantab)

Field *Miss Sara Jean* •
Crown Prosecutor, Crown Prosecution
Service, Guildford Branch, Stoke Mill,
Woking Road, Guildford. Called: July 1985,
Middle Temple, LLB (Lond)

Field *Terence Robert* •
Legal Advisor, Brown & Root Limited, Hill
Park Court, Springfield Drive, Leatherhead,
Surrey KT24 7NL, 0181 544 5000, Fax:
0181 544 4400. Called: July 1973, Gray's
Inn, BA (Hons) (Lond)

Field-Fisher *Thomas Gilbert TD QC
(1969)*
Chairman Police Disciplinary Tribunals, 2
King's Bench Walk, Ground Floor, Temple,
London, EC4Y 7DE. Called: Nov 1942,
Middle Temple, MA (Cantab)

Fields *Mrs Fiona Catharine*
Ogier & le Masurier, Pirouet House, Union
Street, St Helier, Jersey JE4 9WG, 01534
504000, Fax: 01534 35328. Called: Nov
1984, Middle Temple, BA (Kent)

Fife *Richard Ian Macduff*
Senior Court Clerk, Nottinghamshire
Magistrates', Carrington Street, Nottingham
NG2 1EE, 0115 955 8111, Fax: 0115 955
8131. Called: July 1973, Inner Temple

Figgest *Lee*
Called: May 1996, Lincoln's Inn, LLB (Hons)
(Dunelm)

Finch *Michael Anthony*
Called: Nov 1971, Gray's Inn, LLB

Finch *Paul John*
and Member Australia, California and New
York Bars 2 Field Court, Gray's Inn,
London, WC1R 5BB. Called: Nov 1990,
Lincoln's Inn, LLB, B.Comm (NSW)

Findlay *The Hon Mr Justice James
Kerr OBE*
Judge of the High Court Hong Kong,
Supreme Court, Queensway, 2825 432534,
Fax: 2523 4253, Formerly a Solicitor
(Scotland) QC Hong Kong and Member
Zimbabwe Bar Victoria Bar Hong Kong Bar.
Called: May 1985, Inner Temple, LLB
(Lond), FCIA

Findlay *John Harley Sefton Max*
3 Lainson Street, London SW18 5RS, 0181
870 0466. Called: Nov 1974, Middle
Temple, MA (Oxon)

Fine *Miss Pamela Margaret*
Called: Nov 1983, Lincoln's Inn, LLB
(Bristol)

Finigan *John Patrick*
Chief Executive, Qatar National Bank SAQ,
P O Box 1000, Doha, 00974 430240, Fax:
00974 438349. Called: July 1980, Lincoln's
Inn, FCIB, ACIS, FRSA, MSI

Finlay *Fabian John Adam*
Audley House, 9 North Audley Street,
London W1Y 1NF, 0171 629 7821, Fax:
0171 408 1581, Lincoln's Inn Ad Eundem
Jan 1978. Called: July 1976, Middle Temple,
LLB, FCA

Finn *Miss Sally Frances* •
Called: Nov 1972, Gray's Inn, BA, LLM

Finn *Sean Brendan* •
Called: May 1996, Lincoln's Inn, LLB
(Hons)(L'pool), LLM (Manc)

Finnegan *Joseph Gerald*
Senior Counsel,Republic of Ireland, Ardara,
Killarney Road, Bray, Co Wicklow, 2868
108, Fax: 2867 306. Called: Nov 1986,
Middle Temple, BCL LLB (Dublin)

Finnegan *Ms Lorna Ann*
Called: Feb 1994, Inner Temple, BA, LLB
(Ireland)

Finney *John Stephen*
Called: July 1970, Middle Temple, MA
(Oxon), Dip Ed

Finney *Mark Matyas Veszy* •
Head of Legal Department, Yamaichi
International, (Europe) Limited, Finsbury
Court, 111-117 Finsbury Pavement, London
EC2A 1EQ, 0171 330 8138, Fax: 0171 628
8365. Called: Nov 1983, Gray's Inn, LLB
(Reading)

E

Finnigan John Anthony
Justices' Chief Executive, Gloucestershire, Magistrates Courts Committee, Tewkesbury Magistrates Court, Gander Lane, Tewksbury, Gloucestershire GL20 5TR, 01684 294632, Fax: 01684 274596. Called: July 1970, Gray's Inn, FIMgt

Firman Miss Avril Mary
Called: May 1987, Middle Temple, LLB, ACIS

Firth Miss Sheila Ruth •
Barnet Magistrates Court, 7c High Street, Barnet, Herts. Called: Nov 1996, Lincoln's Inn, LLB (Hons)(Hull)

Fish James Andrew
Trade Mark Agent, Page White Farrer, 54 Doughty Street, London WC1N 2LS, 0171 831 7929, Fax: 0171 831 8040. Called: Nov 1996, Inner Temple, LLB (Huddersfield), LLM (Manch)

Fisher Miss Angela Patricia
Called: Oct 1996, Lincoln's Inn, LLB (Hons)(Brunel)

Fisher Miss Brigitte Jane
Called: Nov 1991, Inner Temple, LLB, LLM

Fisher Charles Nicholas
and Member New Mexico Bar 4 Brick Court, Ground Floor, Temple, London, EC4Y 9AD. Called: Nov 1973, Middle Temple, BA (Oxon)

Fisher John Charles
Called: Nov 1995, Inner Temple, BA (Kent)

Fisher Michael John
Called: July 1992, Gray's Inn, LLB (Manch), MA (Brunel)

Fitzgerald Miss Elizabeth Anne •
Called: July 1982, Inner Temple, LLB (Hull), LLM (Lond)

Fitzgerald Tyrone Leon Easton
Called: July 1995, Lincoln's Inn, LLB (Hons)

Fitzgibbon Terence
Executive Director, James R Knowles, 128 Newport Road, Cardiff, 01222 471144, Fax: 01222 471658. Called: Nov 1995, Lincoln's Inn, LLB (Hons) (Wales), BSc (Hons) (Aston), ARICS, FCI Arb

Fitzlyon Ms Anastasia Catya
Called: Nov 1982, Gray's Inn, LLB (Lond)

Fitzpatrick David
1001 Far East Finance Centre, 16 Harcourt Road, Central, Hong Kong, 28668233, Fax: 28663932, Barrister of Hong Kong Barrister & Solicitor of Supreme Court of Victoria. Called: July 1992, Middle Temple, MA (Cambs)

Fitzpatrick Desmond Christopher
Called: July 1983, Inner Temple, BA (York)

Fitzpatrick Edward Peter
Verulam Chambers, Peer House, 8-14 Verulam Street, Gray's Inn, London, WC1X 8LZ. Called: Nov 1985, Gray's Inn, BA

Fitzpatrick John Anthony •
Legal Adviser, Legal Services Dept, International Stock Exchange, The Tower, Old Broad Street, London EC2N 1HP. Called: Nov 1983, Gray's Inn, BA, LLB

Fitzpatrick Mark John
Scottish Advocate. Called: July 1991, Lincoln's Inn, BA (Oxon), MA (Oxon)

Fitzsimmons Roy Dunsmore •
Sales & Marketing Director, William Ransom & Son plc, Bancroft, Hitchin, Herts SG5 1LY, 01462 437615, Fax: 01462 420528. Called: Nov 1982, Lincoln's Inn, B Pharm (Brad), LLB (Lond), MR Pharm, LLM (Wales), MCIM, MIM

Fitzsimons Eoghan Patrick
Law Library, Four Courts, Dublin 7, Ireland, 01 8720622, Fax: 01 8720455, S.C.(Ireland) and Member Southern Ireland Bar New South Wales Bar. Called: Feb 1986, Middle Temple, BCL (U C Dublin), LLM (Yale), Doct de l'Univ, (Paris)

Flaherty Ms Maureen
Called: Nov 1995, Lincoln's Inn, BA (Hons)

Flaherty Michael Francis
Adams Blair Cox Solicitors, 29/31 Guildhall Walk, Portsmouth PO1 2RU, 01705 296705. Called: Oct 1995, Inner Temple, LLB

Flanagan Lt Cdr John RN •
Royal Navy Officer, Staff Legal Adviser to the, Flag Officer, Training &, Recruiting, Admiralty House, North, HM Naval Base, Portsmouth PO1 3NH, 01705 722918. Called: Oct 1991, Middle Temple, BA Hons (Dunelm), Dip Law

Fleisch Mrs Anna Margot Gertrud
Called: July 1980, Inner Temple, LLB

Fleming Ms Annabel Clare
Called: Oct 1995, Middle Temple, BA (Hons)

Fleming Martin Dominic •
Crown Prosecutor, Crown Prosecution Service, 8th Floor, Sunlight House, Quay Street, Manchester M60 3LU, 0161 837 7402, Fax: 0161 835 2663. Called: July 1983, Inner Temple

Fleming Peter James •
72 Leybourne Road, Leytonstone, London E11 3BT, 0181 530 2515. Called: July 1988, Middle Temple, LLB (Hons)

Fletcher Alan Philip QC (1984)
26 Hollies Close, Royston, Herts SG8 7DZ, 01763 248580. Called: Nov 1940, Inner Temple, MA

Fletcher Clifford Daniel St Quentin MBE
42A Cyncoed Road, Cardiff CF2 6BH, 01222 464790. Called: July 1946, Gray's Inn, LLB

Fletcher Peter Grey
Charlotte House Nassau, P.O.Box N3950, Nassau NP, 809 322 2871, Fax: 809 322 2874, and Member Commonwealth of the Bahamas. Called: Nov 1992, Lincoln's Inn, LLB (Hons)(E Anglia)

Fletcher Rogers Mrs Helen Susan •
Company Secretary, European Legal Director, Kodak Ltd, Kodak Hse, Station Rd, Hemel Hempstead, Herts HP1 1JU, 01442 844413, Fax: 01442 844807. Called: July 1965, Gray's Inn, LLB (Hons) (Lond)

Fletcher-Cooke Sir Charles Fletcher QC (1958)
Gray's Inn Chambers, Gray's Inn Road, London WC1R 5JA, 0171 404 1111, Fax: 0171 430 1522, DATO of Sovereign of Brunei and Member Gambia & Sierra Leone Bars Gray's Inn Chambers, 5th Floor, Gray's Inn, London, WC1R 5JA. Called: Nov 1938, Lincoln's Inn, MA A.R.I.Arb

Flood John •
Senior Civil Service, Solicitor's Office, H M Customs & Excise, 22 Upper Ground, London SE1 9PJ, 0171 865 5530, Fax: 0171 865 5022. Called: July 1975, Middle Temple, LLB

Flood Miss Sarah-Lucy
1 809 453 6966, Fax: 1 809 452 5655, Minister for Health, Human Services Family Affairs, Women's Affairs. Called: July 1995, Lincoln's Inn, LLB (Hons), MP

Florendine Miss Sarah Ann •
Legal Advisor, RAC Legal Services, P.O.Box 700, Bristol, Avon, 0345 300 400. Called: July 1996, Gray's Inn, LLB (West of England

Florin Miss Catherine France
Called: Feb 1995, Middle Temple, BA (Hons)(Cantab)

Flower Philip Harvey
Chief Inspector of Police. Called: Nov 1995, Inner Temple, LLB (Lond)

Flowitt Mrs Nicola •
Court Clerk/Legal Advisor, Justices' Clerk's Office, Shire Hall, Bury St Edmunds IP33 1HF, 01284 352300, Fax: 01284 352345. Called: Nov 1986, Inner Temple, LLB

Floy Geoffrey Alan
Old Farmhouse, Whitlenge Lane, Hartlebury, Worcestershire DY10 4HD, 01299 251643. Called: July 1974, Gray's Inn, LLB, BA, M.PHIL

Floyd Robert Hamilton
Avocat Au Barreau De Grasse 06 France, 22-24 Boulevard Alexander 111, 06400 Cannes, 00 334 93 43 93 55, Fax: 00 334 93 43 40 26. Called: Nov 1971, Middle Temple, LLM (Lond)

Fluker Miss Christine Louise •
Senior Legal Adviser, De La Rue plc, 6 Agar Street, London WC2 4DN, 0171 836 8383, Fax: 0171 240 4224. Called: Nov 1976, Gray's Inn, MA [Cantab], LLB (Cantab)

Flynn Mr. Paul Francis
Called: Oct 1994, Middle Temple, BSc (Lond), LLB (Hons)(Lond)

Foakes *Ms Joanne Sarah* •
Legal Counsellor, Foreign & Commonwealth
Office, King Charles Street, London
SW1A 2AH, 0171 270 3075/01580 754710,
Fax: 0171 270 2767/01580 754710.
Called: July 1979, Inner Temple, MA (Oxon)

Fock *Miss Yin Ling*
Called: July 1996, Middle Temple, LLB
(Hons)(Bris)

Fodor *Dr Neil Harris* •
Crown Prosecution Service, Cuthbert
House, All Saints Office Centre, Newcastle
on Tyne, 0191 232 6602. Called: Nov 1991,
Inner Temple, MA (Dundee), PHD (Glas),
Dip Law

Fogaard *Ms Alexandra Katherine*
Called: Nov 1997, Inner Temple, BA (Bris)

Fogarty *Paul*
The Bar Library, Four Courts, Dublin 7,
Ireland, 283 3513/677 8373, Fax: 677 8375,
and Member Southern Ireland Bar.
Called: May 1988, Middle Temple, BCL
(Dublin), BA, BL (Kings Inn), ACIArb

Foggin *Miss Erica*
Called: July 1980, Middle Temple, MA
(Oxon)

Foggitt *Eben Robin* •
Joint Managing Director, Ardent Productions
Limited, Ariel House, 74a Charlotte Street,
London W1P 2DA, 0171 636 5010, Fax:
0171 636 5574. Called: July 1978, Gray's
Inn, BA

Foley *Benedict James*
Called: Mar 1996, Gray's Inn, BA (Wales)

Foley *John Sheldon*
Principal Court Clerk, Tameside Magistrates,
Courts Committee, Magistrates' Court,
Manchester Road, Ashton-under-Lyne
OL7 OBG, 0161 330 2023. Called: July 1981,
Lincoln's Inn, LLB

Foley *Michael Timothy* •
Legal Director, W S Atkins plc, Woodcote
Grove, Ashley Road, Epsom, Surrey
KT18 5BW, 01372 726140, Fax: 01372
740055. Called: Nov 1970, Gray's Inn, BSc
[Eng] (Lond), C.Eng, F.I.C.E, F Cons E

Folland *David James*
Deputy Clerk to the Justices, Mansfield
Magistrates Court, Rosemary Street,
Mansfield, Nottinghamshire NG19 6EE,
01623 451500, Fax: 01623 451648.
Called: Oct 1976, Lincoln's Inn

Follows *Terence John*
Lecturer. Called: July 1992, Middle Temple,
LLB (Hons) (Leeds), FCIArb

Fong *Miss Cornelia Siew Ping*
Legal Assistant, 13 Crichton Close,
Singapore 557990, 0065 2888365, and
Member Singapore Bar. Called: July 1994,
Inner Temple, LLB (Nott'm)

Fong *Miss Gwendolyn Teen-Li*
Company Secretary, Messrs Shook Lin &
Bok, 1 Robinson Road, AIA Tower, [H]18-
00, and Member Singapore. Called: July
1995, Middle Temple, LLB (Hons)(Hull)

Fong *Kelvin Kai Tong*
325k Bukit Timah Road, Singapore 259714,
(65) 2355120, Fax: (65) 2353500.
Called: July 1996, Middle Temple, LLB
(Hons)(Newc)

Fong *Philip Yeng Fatt*
Messrs Harry Elias & Partners, No 79
Robinson Road, [H]16-03, Singapore 06, 65-
2235006 Ext 359, Fax: 65-2270281, and
Member Singapore Bar. Called: July 1994,
Inner Temple, LLB (Lond), B.Econs (Hons)

Fong *Ms Shin Ni*
Called: Nov 1997, Lincoln's Inn, LLB
(Hons)(Sheff)

Fong *Miss Yuke Ching*
Called: July 1994, Lincoln's Inn, LLB (Hons)

Foo *Ms Chiew Eng*
479 River Valley Road, [H]13-07, Valley
Park. Called: July 1996, Inner Temple, LLB
(Lond)

Foo *Miss Fiona Wei Ling*
Called: July 1997, Lincoln's Inn, LLB (Lond)

Foo *Frederick Kong Tuck*
Called: July 1996, Lincoln's Inn, LLB
(Hons)(Lond)

Foo *Miss Jon-Hui Amanda*
Khattar Wong & Partners, 80 Raffles Place,
[H]25-01 UOB Plaza 1, Singapore 048624,
535 6844, Fax: 533 0585, and Member
Singapore Bar. Called: Oct 1990, Gray's Inn,
LLB (Lond), LLM (Lond), AKC

Foo *Ms Li Mei*
27 Jalan Telawi 8, Bangsar Baru, 59100
Kuala Lumpur, 09 7474 653. Called: July
1996, Lincoln's Inn, LLB (Hons)(Cardiff)

Foo *Say Tun*
Messrs David Lim & Partners, Advocates &
Solicitors, 50 Raffles Place, [H]17-01
Singapore Land Tower, Singapore 048623,
65 532 2122, Fax: 65 532 0122, and
Member Malaysia Bar Singapore Bar.
Called: Nov 1991, Middle Temple, LLB Hons
(E Ang)

Foo *Yoke Yan* •
M & A Commercial Lawyer, British
Telecommunications plc, Group Legal
Services, BT Centre, 81 Newgate Street,
London EC1A 7AJ, 0171 356 5545, Fax:
0171 356 4012. Called: July 1989, Lincoln's
Inn, BSc (Keele)

Foo *Yong Teng*
Called: Nov 1995, Lincoln's Inn, LLB (Hons)

Footring *Mrs Marika Everdina*
01206 825310. Called: Nov 1985, Inner
Temple, LLB(Essex)

Ford *Miss Patricia Ann* •
Legal Adviser, Young & Rubicam Group
Limited, Greater London House, Hampstead
Road, London NW1 7QP, 0171 611 6835,
Fax: 0171 611 6915. Called: Oct 1995,
Middle Temple, LLB (Hons)

Ford *Richard Andrew* •
In House Lawyer. Called: Oct 1993, Middle
Temple, BSc Econ (Hons)

Forde *Dr Michael Patrick*
33 Mountainview Rd, Dublin 6, 00353 14
978349, Fax: 00353 14 966835, King's Inn,
Dublin (1984), Senior Counsel (1995) and
Member Southern Ireland Bar. Called: Nov
1987, Middle Temple, BA, LLB (Dublin),
LLM (Brussels), PhD (Cantab)

Forde *Patrick Bernard*
Brook Hse, Moreton Morrell, Warwicks
CV35 9AN, 01926 651733, Irish Bar 1951.
Called: July 1966, Gray's Inn, BCom (Dub)

Forder *Kenneth John*
Registrar of UK Architects Freeman of the
City of London, Napier Cottage, 2a Napier
Avenue, Hurlingham, London SW6 3NJ,
0171 736 3958. Called: May 1963, Gray's
Inn, MA (Oxon), BA (Cantab)

Fordjour *Oscar*
Called: Nov 1994, Middle Temple, BA
(Hons), LLB (Hons)

Foreman *Frederick Christopher* •
Senior Legal Advisor, Legal & General
Assurance, Society Limited, Legal & General
House, Kingsworth,Tadworth, Surrey
KT20 6EU, 01737 376129, Fax: 01737
376144. Called: Feb 1991, Inner Temple,
LLB

Foreman *Mrs Marguerite Alyce*
Saint Christopher & Nevis (Eastern
Caribbean Supreme Court), Seaton &
Foreman, Chambers P O Box 82, Central
Street, Basseterre, St Kitts, (809) 465 9292,
Fax: (809) 465 7373, and Member Saint
Christopher & Nevis. Called: Oct 1991,
Inner Temple, MA (Edin), LLB (Hons),
D.M.S.

Forer *Lt Cdr Timothy John RN* •
Commodore's Secretary, HMS Nelson,
Queen Street, Portsmouth, Hants PO1 3HH,
01705 723830, Fax: 01705 724757.
Called: Oct 1993, Gray's Inn, BA (Dunelm)

Forman *John Wilson* •
Chase House, Scarletts Chase, West
Bergholt, Essex CO6 3DH, 01206 240300.
Called: Nov 1970, Lincoln's Inn, ACI.Arb
MCIT

Forrest *Ms Gabrielle*
Called: Nov 1993, Gray's Inn, MA (Oxon)

Forrester *Stephen Kenneth*
Called: Nov 1993, Lincoln's Inn, BA (Hons)

Forster *Brian Howard OBE*
Justices' Chief Executive, Gwent
Magistrates' Court Comm, 2nd Floor, Gwent
House, Gwent Square, Cwmbran, Gwent
NP44 IPL, 01633 645000, Fax: 01633
645015. Called: July 1966, Middle Temple,
MA (Oxon), M I Mgt

Forsyth *Alistair James Menteith*
O.St.J.
Director,Hargreaves,Reiss & Quinn Ltd,
Ethie Castle, By Arbroath, Angus DD11 5SP,
01241 830458, Fax: 01241 830477, Also Inn
of Court L and Member Scottish Bar.
Called: July 1990, Inner Temple, MTh (St
Andrews), LLB (Buck), LLB,
(Edinburgh),FSA.Scot, DipLp (Edinburgh),
ACII, Chartered, Insurance Practioner

Forsyth *Anthony Stewart Karl*
Called: Nov 1995, Lincoln's Inn, LLB (Hons)

Forsyth *Iain Grant*
Legal Advisor to the Office Communaitaire des Varietes Vegetales, C.P.V.O., PO Box 2141, F-40921 ANgers, Cedex 02. Called: Feb 1988, Inner Temple, LLB (Notts)

Forth *David Alexander*
Finance Controller, British-American Tobacco Co, Limited, Millbank, Knowle Green, Staines TW18 1DY, 01784 448074, Fax: 01784 448653. Called: Nov 1976, Inner Temple, LLB, FCA

Fortunato *Miss Karen* •
Company Secretary, Abbey National Treasury Services plc, Abbey National Treasury, Services plc, Abbey House, Baker Street, London NW1 6XL, 0171 612 4677, Fax: 0171 612 4319, and Member Gibraltar Bar. Called: July 1986, Lincoln's Inn, LLB (Lond)

Foster *Adrian Gavin* •
Crown Prosecutor, Crown Prosecution Service, 4 Artillery Row, Victoria, London SW1, 0171 976 5699, Fax: 0171 233 2043. Called: Oct 1993, Inner Temple, LLB

Foster *David Christopher*
Environmental Health Officer, North Devon District Council, Civic Centre, Barnstaple, Devon EX31 1EA, 01271 388335, Fax: 01271 388451. Called: Oct 1992, Inner Temple, LLB (Warwick), Dip in Enviromental, Health

Foster *Desmond Roy*
Called: Oct 1996, Lincoln's Inn, BSc (Hons)(W.Indies), LLB (Hons)(Warw)

Foster *Miss Elizabeth Anne*
Assistant Solicitor, Clifford Chance, 200 Aldersgate Street, London EC2A 4JJ, 0171 600 1000, Fax: 0171 600 5555. Called: Oct 1992, Middle Temple, LLB (Hons, Leic)

Foster *Guy Robert* •
Simmons & Simmons, 21 Wilson Street, London EC2M 2TX, 0171 628 2020, Fax: 0171 628 2070. Called: Oct 1995, Inner Temple, LLB (Lond)

Foster *Jonathan Robert Melville*
0181 670 4754, Fax: 0181 670 4754. Called: Feb 1978, Middle Temple, BA

Fosuhene *Miss Amelia Tracy*
Called: Nov 1996, Middle Temple, LLB (Hons)(Lond)

Fotherby *Gordon* •
Senior Civil Service (Formerly Grade 3), HM Customs & Excise, Solicitor's Office, New King's Beam House, Upper Ground, London SE1, 0171 865 5124, Fax: 0171 865 5022. Called: Nov 1973, Inner Temple, LLB

Fotheringham *Mrs Emma Clark*
Area Intelligence Analyst, Kent Police Authority, Police Headquarters, Sutton Road, Maidstone, Kent, 01622 654682. Called: Nov 1992, Gray's Inn, LLB

Foucar *Antony Emile*
Called: Jan 1949, Middle Temple

Foudy *Ms Denise* •
Group Legal Advisor & Company Secretary, Isode Ltd, The Dome, The Square, Richmond, Surrey TW9 1DT, 0181 332 9091, Fax: 0181 332 9019. Called: July 1983, Gray's Inn, BSc (Bath), Dip Law

Foulkes *Dyfed Charles*
Justices' Clerk, The Law Courts, Alfred Gelder Street, Kingston Upon Hull HU1 2AD, 01482 328914. Called: July 1986, Gray's Inn, LLB, Dip.Mgt (Open), MIMgt

Fountain *Jonathan William*
Called: May 1994, Middle Temple, BSc (Hons, Dunelm)

Fovargue *Ms Sara Jane*
Called: Oct 1994, Lincoln's Inn, LLB (Hons)(Leic)

Fowler *Christopher Stephen* •
Legal Assistant, Volkswagen Financial Services, (UK) Limited, Yeomans Drive, Blakelands, Milton Keynes MK14 5AN, 01908 601452, Fax: 01908 601873. Called: Feb 1994, Lincoln's Inn, LLB (Hons)

Fowler *Geoffrey Alan*
Justices Chief Executive, Derbyshire Magistrates' Court, West Bank House, Albion Road, Chesterfield, Derby, 01246 220008. Called: Nov 1977, Gray's Inn, LLB (Lond)

Fowler *Ian OBE*
Deputy Traffic Commissioner, 6 Dence Park, Herne Bay, Kent CT6 6BG, 01227 375530. Called: July 1957, Gray's Inn, MA (Oxon)

Fox *Miss Claire Louise* •
Legal Advisor, Southend & Rochford, Magistrates' Court, 80 Victoria Avenue,, Southend-on-Sea, Essex SS2 6EU, 01702 348491. Called: Oct 1993, Lincoln's Inn, LLB (Hons), MSC

Fox *Martin George* •
Senior Crown Prosecutor, Crown Prosecution Service, 17th Floor, Tolworth Tower, Surbiton, Surrey KT6 7DS, 0181 399 5171. Called: July 1981, Middle Temple, LLB

Fox *Nicholas Russell Philip*
Called: Oct 1994, Lincoln's Inn, BA (Hons)

Fox *Ms Victoria Charlotte* •
Principal Legal Officer, Department of Social Security, 48 Carey Street, London WC2A 2LS, 0171 962 8000. Called: Nov 1995, Middle Temple, LLB (Hons), LLM

Foxall-Smedley *Miss Diana*
Called: Nov 1972, Gray's Inn, MA (TCD)

Foy *Miss Agnes*
Barrister of Ireland. Called: Nov 1996, Middle Temple, BA (Dublin), BL (King's Inn)

Frame *Stuart James*
Called: May 1997, Gray's Inn, LLB (Kingston), MA (Brunel)

Francis *Ms Angela Pamela*
Former Solicitor. Called: Feb 1995, Middle Temple, BA (Hons)(Kent)

Francis *Ms Angela Valerie*
Insurance Ombudsman Asst, Insurance Ombudsman Bureau, City Gate One, 135 Park Street, London SE1 9EA, 0171 928 4488. Called: Nov 1989, Middle Temple, LLM, LLB

Francis *Benedict Peter Beauchamp*
The Ackerson Group, 1275 Pennsylvania Avenue, N.W., Suite 1100, Washington DC 20004-2417, 001 202 628 1100, Fax: 001 202 628 0242, and Member New York. Called: Nov 1989, Lincoln's Inn, MA (Edin), Dip Law (City), LLM (USA)

Francis *Miss Bridget Cecile*
Called: Nov 1997, Gray's Inn, LLB (Lond), LLM

Francis *Ms Charmaine*
Called: July 1995, Middle Temple, LLB (Hons)

Francis *Ms Claire Louise* •
Senior Legal Officer, Solicitors Office, Somerset House, London, 0171 438 7410. Called: Nov 1987, Inner Temple, BA, BCL (Oxon)

Francis *Derek Roy Lebert*
Advocates' Library, Parliament House, Edinburgh, Scottish Advocate. Called: Feb 1991, Lincoln's Inn, LLB (Edin)

Francis *Miss Kenrah Nicole Philippa*
Associate, Chancery Law Associates, P.O.Box N-8199, Nassau, 1-242 356 6108, Fax: 1-242 356 6109, and Member Bahamas. Called: July 1996, Lincoln's Inn, LLB (Hons)(Reading)

Francis *Ms Margaret Ayodele*
Called: Oct 1997, Inner Temple, BSc (Nigeria), CPE

Francis *Michael Anthony*
Called: Oct 1996, Gray's Inn, LLB

Francombe *Miss Susan Jane*
Construction Lawyer, Hammond Suddards Solicitors, 7 Devonshire Square, Cutlers Gardens, London EC2M 4YH, 0171 655 1157, Fax: 0171 655 1001. Called: May 1997, Inner Temple, BSc (Wales), C.Eng, MICE, LLDip

Frankham *David Mark* •
Deputy Justices Clerk, Devon Magistrates Court, County Hall, Exeter EX2 4QJ, 01271 388461. Called: Feb 1988, Gray's Inn

Frankl *Dr Anna Maria*
102 East Sheen Avenue, London SW14 8AU, 0181 876 6108. Called: Feb 1956, Lincoln's Inn, LLD (Prague), LLB (Wales)

Franklin *Mrs Helen Jane* •
Counsel, Mobil North Sea Ltd, Mobil Court, 3 Clements Inn, London WC2A 2GB, 0171 412 2517, Fax: 0171 404 0035. Called: July 1985, Lincoln's Inn, BA (Law), Dip Pet. Law (Dundee)

Fraser *Anthony Kenneth* •
Grade 6, Treasury Solicitor's Dept, Queen
Anne's Chambers, 28 Broadway, London
SW1H 9JS, 0171 210 3000, Fax: 0171 222
6006, and Member British Columbia Bar.
Called: Nov 1986, Lincoln's Inn, BA
(Victoria), LLB (Brit Columbia), BA (Oxon)

Fraser *Commander Robert William
MVO, RN* •
DNSD, Ministry of Defence, Whitehall,
London SW1A 2HB, 0171 218 3079, Fax:
0171 218 4207. Called: July 1984, Gray's
Inn, LLB

Frazer *Miss Lucy Claire*
Called: Oct 1996, Middle Temple, BA
(Hons)(Cantab)

Frazer *Ms Onike Letitia*
Holborn College, 200 Greyhound Road,
London W14 9RY, 0171 385 3377, Fax:
0171 381 3377, and Member Sierra Leone.
Called: Nov 1995, Middle Temple, LLB
(Hons)

Frederick *Richard*
Private Legal Practitioner, [H] 13 Bridge
Street, Castries, St. Lucia, West Indies, 809
451 7773, Fax: 809 451 7373, and Member
St Lucia Bar. Called: July 1994, Lincoln's
Inn, BSc (Hons)

Freeland *Sir John Redvers KCMG QC*
(1987)
Judge, European Crt of Human Rights, Also
Inn of Court M. Called: Feb 1952, Lincoln's
Inn, MA

Freeland *Richard Daniel*
Called: May 1997, Gray's Inn, BA (Lond)

Freeman *Mrs Elizabeth Mary*
College Lecturer, Clare College, Cambridge
CB2 1TL, 01223 333200. Called: Nov 1970,
Middle Temple, MA, LLB, LLM, Lic en, droit
europeen

Freeman *Miss Lucy Mekhala
Catherine*
and Member Republic of Ireland.
Called: Oct 1990, Middle Temple, BA
(Oxon), Dip Law

Freemantle *Clive James Francis* •
Senior Crown Prosecutor, Crown
Prosecution Service, 3rd Floor, Cuthbert
House, All Saints Office Centre, Newcastle
upon Tyne NE1 2DW, 0191 232 6602.
Called: July 1982, Inner Temple, BA Hons

Freij *Miss Deema Mounir*
Called: Nov 1996, Lincoln's Inn, BA (Hons)

French *Alan Van* •
Senior Crown Prosecutor, Crown
Prosecution Service, St George's House,
Lever Street, Wolverhampton WVZ 1EZ,
01902 870900. Called: July 1984, Middle
Temple, BA

French *John*
Councillor Legal Advisor for Carassist, 35
Hinckley Road, Stoke Golding, Warks
CV13 6DU, (01455) 212359. Called: July
1996, Lincoln's Inn, LLB (Hons)

French *Michael Alan* •
Prosecution Team Leader, Crown
Prosecution Service, St Andrew's Court, 12
St Andrew's Street, Plymouth PL1 2AH,
01752 668700. Called: Nov 1986, Middle
Temple, LLB (Nott'm)

Frend *Captain David Peter* •
Called: Nov 1994, Inner Temple, BA (Keele)

Frias *Miss Cristina Samantha*
Called: Mar 1997, Middle Temple, BA
(Hons)

Frida *Miss Samantha*
Called: July 1996, Lincoln's Inn, LLB
(Hons)(Leeds)

Friend *Alasdair James Christopher* •
Called: Oct 1993, Lincoln's Inn, MA
(Cantab), Dip Law

Frisby *Roger Harry Kilbourne QC*
(1969)
0171 589 5100 X 709. Called: Jan 1950,
Lincoln's Inn, MA (Oxon), LLB (Lond

Fritchie *Andrew Peel* •
Group Counsel-Head of Legal Affairs,
Company Secretary, Marlborough Stirling,
16 Imperial Square, Cheltenham,
Gloucestershire GL50 1QZ, 01242 221973,
Fax: 01242 520329. Called: July 1988, Inner
Temple, LLB (Wales)

Froomkin *Saul Morten*
Senior Litigation Partner, Mello,Hollis,Jones
& Martin, Reid House, 31 Church Street, PO
Box HM 1564, Hamilton,Bermuda, 441-292
1345, Fax: 441-292 2277, QC (Canada &
Bermuda) and Member Canada, Bermuda,
Anguilla. Called: Apr 1989, Middle Temple,
LLB, LLM (Manitoba), FCIArb

Frost *Frank Reginald*
Called: Apr 1951, Middle Temple

Frost *Peter* •
Principal Crown Prosecutor, CPS, St Mark
House, 2 Conway Street, Birkenhead,
Merseyside L41 6QD, 0151 647 4681.
Called: Feb 1985, Gray's Inn, DML

Frudd *Mrs Stephanie Julia*
Deputy Justices' Chief Executive, Richmond
Upon Thames Mag Crt, Richmond
Magistrates Court, Parkshot, Richmond,
Surrey TW9 2RF, 0181 948 2101, Fax: 0181
332 2628. Called: Nov 1981, Gray's Inn, LLB
(Hons)

Fry *Laurence Frederick* •
Legal Manager, Monument Exploration and,
Production Limited, Kierran Cross, 11
Strand, London WC2N 5HR, 0171 891 2294,
Fax: 0171 891 2222, and Member California
Bar. Called: Nov 1989, Middle Temple, LLB
Hons (Nott'm)

Fuchs *Miss Iris*
Called: Oct 1997, Middle Temple, LLB
(Hons)(Lond), BA (New York)

Fulbrook *Dr Julian George Holder*
London School of Economics &, Political
Science, Houghton Street, London
WC2A 2AE, 0171 955 7244, Fax: 0171 955
7366. Called: July 1977, Inner Temple, PhD
(Cantab)

Fullalove *Mrs Elizabeth Anne*
Called: Oct 1995, Inner Temple, BA (Oxon)

Fullarton *Patrick James John* •
BSc (Wales), GEC Alsthom Limited, P.O.Box
449, Trabford Park, Manchester M60 1GA,
0161 875 2406, Fax: 0161 875 4550.
Called: Nov 1979, Gray's Inn

Fullbrook *Ms Suzanne Dorothy*
35a Silvester Road, East Dulwich, London
SE22 9PB, 0181 299 3928, Fax: 0181 299
2522. Called: Nov 1994, Middle Temple, LLB
(Hons), M.Phil, RGN

Fuller *Graham Francis* •
Senior Legal Advisor, Rolls-Royce plc, PO
Box 3, Filton, Bristol, Avon BS12 7QE, 0117
9795161, Fax: 0117 9797575. Called: July
1969, Gray's Inn, LLB

Fuller *Nicolas Alan*
Called: July 1995, Middle Temple, LLB
(Hons)

Fullman *Peter Michael*
Called: Nov 1997, Middle Temple, MB.BS.,
FRCS (Ed), FRCOG (Royal Lond., Hosp.
Med. School), LLB (Hons)(Lond)

Fulthorpe *Mrs Elizabeth Clare*
Sutton Associates, 60 Avenue de Wagram,
75017 Paris, 331 4440 0232/46681 0159,
Fax: 331 4440 0232/46681 0159.
Called: Nov 1974, Gray's Inn, LLB Hons

Fulton *Mrs Kathryn Mary* •
Chief Counsel, Young & Rubicam Group
Ltd, Greater London House, Hampstead
Road, London NW1 7QP, 0171 611 6374,
Fax: 0171 611 6915. Called: July 1987, Inner
Temple, LLB (Lond)(Hons)

Fung *Miss Catherine Shuk Yin*
Senior Crown Counsel, Department of
Justice, Queensway Govt Offices, 66
Queensway, 28672356, Fax: 28690236, and
Member Australian Capital Territory, 1988 &
Northern Territory, Australia 1991 Australia
Bar Hong Kong Bar. Called: July 1987,
Middle Temple, BA (Manitoba) LLB, (Bucks)

Fung *Daniel Richard JP*
Solicitor General, Member of China
International Economic & Trade Arbitration
Commission, 4th Floor, High Block,
Queensway Government Offices, 66
Queensway, (852) 2867 2003, Fax: (852)
2501 0371, Q.C., S.C., Hong Kong and
Member Victoria, Australian Capital
Territory Bar Hong Kong Bar. Called: Nov
1975, Middle Temple, LLB LLM

Fung *Eugene Ting Sek*
Temple Chambers, 16/F One Pacific Place,
88 Queensway, (852) 2523 2003, Fax: (852)
2810 0302, and Member Hong Kong.
Called: Mar 1997, Lincoln's Inn, BA
(Cantab), LLM, (Cantab)

Fung *Leonard Shui-Kei*
Called: Nov 1995, Gray's Inn, BA

Fung *Miss Lucille Yun Sim*
A2-19 Evergreen Villa, 43 Stubbs Road, and
Member Brunei, and Victoria Bars Hong
Kong Bar New South Wales. Called: July
1960, Middle Temple, BA, MCI Arb

Fung *Miss Nora Yin Ling*
18 Goldhaze Close, Woodford Green, Essex
IG8 7LE, 0181 506 1634, and Member
Malaysia Bar. Called: Nov 1993, Gray's Inn,
LLB (Lond)

Fung *Patrick Chee Yuen*
and Member Singapore Bar. Called: July
1992, Middle Temple, LLB (Hons) (Leics)

Fung *Patrick Pak-Tung*
10/F, New Henry House, 10 Ice House
Street, Central, (852) 2524 2156, Fax: (852)
2810 5656, Queen's Counsel 1995 (Hong
Kong) and Member Hong Kong Bar.
Called: Nov 1968, Inner Temple, LLB
(Lond), FCI Arb

Furlonger *Miss Lesley Margaret*
Stocks Farm, New Road, Rayne, Essex
CM7 8SY, (0376) 61109. Called: July 1968,
Inner Temple

Furness *Clive William*
11 Fisher Street, London E16 4DS, 0171 474
5262. Called: Feb 1993, Gray's Inn, LLB
(Sheff), D.M.S.

Fussell *Charles Edward Roger*
Called: Nov 1994, Lincoln's Inn, BA
(Hons)(Exon), Dip in Law

Futerman *Samuel*
Called: Nov 1996, Middle Temple, LLB
(Hons)(Manch)

Gabathuler *David*
Called: Nov 1996, Inner Temple, LLB
(Nott'm), LLM (Lond)

Gabbert *Dale* •
J P Morgan Investment Mngment, 28 King
Street, London SW1Y 6XA, 0171 451 8000,
Fax: 0171 451 8693. Called: Oct 1993, Inner
Temple, LLB, LLM

Gabriel *Mrs Wendy Alicia*
Company Secretary. Called: Oct 1995,
Lincoln's Inn, BA (Hons)

Gabrielczyk *Mrs Maria Genowefa*
Principal Court Clerk, Mansfield Magistrates
Court, Rosemary Street, Mansfield,
Nottinghamshire NG19 6EE, 01623 451500,
Fax: 01623 451648. Called: Nov 1975,
Gray's Inn, MA

Gadd *Miss Suzanne Heather*
Deputy Clerk to the Justices, North & East
Hertfordshire, Magistrates' Court, Bayley
House, Sish Lane, Stevenage SG1 3SS, 01438
730431, Fax: 01438 730413. Called: July
1984, Lincoln's Inn, LLB

Gadras *Mrs Susan Elizabeth* •
Court Clerk, West Hertfordshire Magistrates,
Court, The Court House, Clarendon Road,
Watford, Herts WD1 1ST, 01923 297500,
Fax: 01923 297528. Called: July 1989, Inner
Temple, LLB

Gafoor *Anthony David Jalil* •
Legal Adviser, Dept of Trade & Industry,
Solicitor's Office, Room 114, 10 Victoria
Street, London SW1H 0NN, 0171 215 3412,
Fax: 0171 215 3479, Member of the
International Bar Association Member of the
Bar Association for Commerce,Finance &
Industry (BACFI) Member of the
Administrative Bar Association and Member
Trinidad & Tobago. Called: July 1987, Gray's
Inn, LLB (UWI),LLM (Lond), MA, Dip
Commercial, Law, Dip European,
Community Law (Lond), Cert in Air Law,
(Lond), Cert in Corporate &, Investment
Law, Dip Copyright Law &, Related rights

Gagg *Mrs Lesley Florence*
Deputy Clerk to the Justices, Somerset
Magistrates Court, The Courthouse,
Northgate, Bridgwater, Somerset TA6 3EU,
01278 452182, Fax: 01278 453667.
Called: Nov 1984, Inner Temple, M.Soc.Sc

Gaik *Miss Anne Ooi*
Called: July 1994, Middle Temple, LLB
(Hons)(Sheff)

Gairdner *Ms Margaret Christine*
Called: Mar 1998, Inner Temple, LLB
(Sussex)

Gajadhar *Jerome*
Called: Nov 1996, Lincoln's Inn, BA, MA
(Ontario), LLM (Leeds)

Galgani *Padraig*
Called: Nov 1997, Middle Temple, BA
(Buck), MA

Gallagher *David Leslie* •
Occupational Pensions, Regulatory
Authority, Invicta House, Trafalgar Place,
Brighton BN1 4DW, 01273 627600, Fax:
01273 627631. Called: Oct 1992, Gray's Inn,
BA (Hons)(Cantab)

Gallagher *Miss Grace Marie Walsh*
Called: Nov 1997, Lincoln's Inn, BA, LLB
(Galway), BL (King's Inn)

Gallagher *Dr Margaret Sutherland* •
Treasury Solicitors Chambers, Queen Anne's
Chambers, Broadway, London SW1, 0171
210 3390. Called: July 1989, Inner Temple,
LLB (Glas), D Phil (Oxon)

Gallagher *Martin John*
No 1 Arran Square, Arran Quay, Dublin 7,
872 5908, Fax: 872 8963, Senior Counsel.
Called: Nov 1981, Middle Temple, BA,
FCIArb

Gallagher *Mrs Sarah Jane* •
Principal Crown Prosecutor Prosecution
Team Leader, Crown Prosecution Service, St
Andrews Court, 12 St Andrew Street,
Plymouth, Devon PL1 2AH, 01752 668700.
Called: July 1976, Inner Temple, B.A.
(Dunelm)

Gallagher *Mrs Susan Wendy*
Lecturer in Law. Called: Nov 1994, Lincoln's
Inn, LLB (Hons)(Sheff)

Galliford *Leslie Bertram*
Coppinside, 11 Kenwith Road, Raleigh,
Bideford, Devon EX39 3NW. Called: Feb
1952, Lincoln's Inn, LLB

Galligan *Denis James*
Called: July 1996, Gray's Inn, LLB
(Queensland), BCL, MA (Oxon)

Gallimore *Patrick James*
University of Northumbria, at Newcastle,
School of Law, Sutherland Building,
Newcastle upon Tyne NE1 8ST. Called: Oct
1992, Middle Temple, LLB (Hons) (Lond),
LLM (Lond)

Galloway *Miss Natasha Clare*
Called: Feb 1993, Middle Temple, BA
(Hons)(Oxon), Dip in Law (City)

Gammanpila *Miss Dakshina Kumudu*
Tutor in Criminology, Centre for Criminal
Justice, Studies, University of Leeds, West
Yorkshire, Undertaking Firensic Medicine
PhD. Called: Oct 1992, Inner Temple, LLB
(Hons), MA

Gammon *Jonathan Michael Hugh*
Team Leader, Court House, Bishops Road,
Highgate, London N6 4HS, 0181 340 3472,
Fax: 0181 348 3343. Called: Oct 1990,
Middle Temple, LLB (Bris)

Gan *Mr David Chern Ning*
7601218. Called: Nov 1992, Middle Temple,
LLB (Hons, B'ham), LLM (Southampton)

Gan *Gerry Kian Koon*
Called: July 1997, Middle Temple, LLB
(Hons)

Gan *Miss Huey Piin*
C/O M/S Gulam & Wong, Advocates &
Solicitors, Suite 1103-1106, 11th Floor, 15
Jalan Gereja, 80100 Johor, West Malaysia,
07-2246851/2 2245963, Fax: 07-2246854
2245460. Called: July 1994, Lincoln's Inn,
LLB

Gan *Miss Jui Chui*
Called: July 1995, Lincoln's Inn, LLB (Hons)

Gan *Miss Jui Fui*
Called: July 1997, Gray's Inn, LLB (Notts)

Gan *Miss Sye Ni*
Called: July 1997, Lincoln's Inn, LLB
(Hons)(Wales)

Gan *Miss Yee Min*
Called: July 1995, Middle Temple, LLB
(Hons)

Ganatra *Hargovind Gorhandas*
"Vrindavan", 1 Wentworth Avenue, Elstree,
Herts WD6 3PX, 0181 207 4321. Called: July
1967, Lincoln's Inn

Gandham *Bopinder Paul Singh*
Called: Nov 1997, Lincoln's Inn, LLB

Gandolfi *Mrs Joan*
Called: May 1997, Lincoln's Inn, LLB (Hons)

Gandy *Geoffrey Harold*
Vice President, Montell Polyolefins
Intellectual Property, Montell Polyolefins,
Centro Ricerche "G Natta", P.Le G Donegani
12, 44100 Ferrara, 00 39 532 468205, Fax:
00 39 532 467675. Called: Feb 1963, Inner
Temple, MA, LLM (Cantab)

Ganesan *Anandan*
Called: July 1996, Middle Temple, LLB
(Hons)(Bris)

Ganesan *Miss Susila*
Called: July 1995, Lincoln's Inn, LLB (Hons)

Ganeson *Miss Visahini*
Called: July 1995, Lincoln's Inn, LLB (Hons)

Gangadharan *Miss Prasanna Devi*
Called: Nov 1996, Middle Temple, LLB
(Hons)(Lond)

Gannon *Miss Catherine*
Legal Advisor, Baker & McKenzie Solicitors,
100 New Bridge Street, London EC4V 6JA,
0171 919 1000, Fax: 0171 919 1999,
Member of Chartered Institute of Taxation.
Called: Feb 1994, Lincoln's Inn, LLB (Hons),
ATII

Gans-Lartey *Joseph Kojo* •
Principal Crown Prosecutor, Crown
Prosecution Service, Western Branch, 4
Artillery Row, London SW1P 1RZ, 0171 976
5699 x 2144, Fax: 0171 233 2039, and
Member Bar of Trinidad & Tobago.
Called: July 1983, Lincoln's Inn, LLB, LLM
(Lond)

Garcha *Gurdeep Singh*
Called: Nov 1997, Lincoln's Inn, LLB
(Hons)(Warw)

Gardam *David Hill QC (1968)*
Called: Nov 1949, Inner Temple, MA (Oxon)

Gardiner *Miss Carolyn Edith*
Called: Oct 1997, Middle Temple, BA
(Hons)(Soton), CPE (Northumbria)

Gardiner *Miss Joanna Marie*
Called: Oct 1996, Middle Temple, LLB
(Hons)(Kent)

Gardner *Alan George*
23 The Daedings, Deddington, Banbury,
Oxon OX15 ORT, 01869 338138.
Called: Nov 1973, Middle Temple, LLB, ACIS

Gardner *Carl Martin* •
Called: Nov 1993, Gray's Inn, BA

Gardner *David Andrew* •
Called: Oct 1992, Middle Temple, BA(Hons)
& MA (Exen)

Gardner *Sir Edward Lucas QC (1960)*
Arbitrator, Sparrows, Hatfield Broad Oak,
Bishop's Stortford, Hert CM22 7HN, 01279
718265. Called: Nov 1947, Gray's Inn

Gardner *Dr John Blair*
Reader in Legal Philosophy in the University
of London, School of Law, King's College
London, Strand, London WC2R 2LS, 0171
873 2203. Called: July 1988, Inner Temple,
MA, BCL (Oxon), D.Phil

Gardner *John Willoughby*
Rowancroft, Upton Grey, Hants RG25 2RJ,
01256 862476. Called: Apr 1964, Middle
Temple

Gardner *Mrs Pamela Jeannette Noall*
Called: Nov 1974, Inner Temple

Gardner-Bougaard *Paul Frederick
Francis*
Managing Director, Cornerstone, Abbey
National Estate Agents, Abbey House, Baker
Street, London NW1 6XL, 0171 486 5555,
Fax: 0171 486 8822. Called: July 1972,
Middle Temple, LLB, LLM

Garen *Edgar*
The Thames Chambers, Wickham House, 10
Cleveland Way, London, E1 4TR.
Called: May 1994, Inner Temple

Garfield *Scott Kennedy*
Called: Nov 1996, Middle Temple, LLB
(Hons), LLM (Lond)

Garland *Gary John Richard* •
Senior Crown Prosecutor. Called: Nov 1989,
Inner Temple, LLB (Hons), F.T.C.

Garland *Peter William*
1501, Two Pacific Place, 88 Queensway,
852-28401130, Fax: 852-28100612, QC
(Hong Kong 1995), SC (Hong Kong 1997),
Supreme Court of the Australian Capital
Territory, High Court of Australia and
Member Hong Kong Bar. Called: Nov 1978,
Middle Temple

Garland *Stuart* •
Legal Adviser. Called: Feb 1992, Lincoln's
Inn, BA (Hons) (Oxon)

Garland-Collins *Francis*
Senior Deputy Chief Clerk, Inner London
Magistrates', Courts Committee, Tower
Bridge Magistrates'Court, Tooley Street,
London SE1, 0171 407 4232, Fax: 0171 403
9378. Called: July 1974, Middle Temple

Garlick *Mrs Helen Mary* •
Serious Fraud Office, Elm House, 10-16 Elm
Street, London WC1X 0BJ. Called: Nov
1974, Middle Temple, LLB

Garlick *Neil Harvey*
9 Windsor Road, Gee Cross, Hyde, Cheshire
SK14 5JB, 0161 367 7663. Called: Nov 1983,
Middle Temple, BA, ALCM

Garmon-Jones *Richard* •
The Citibank Private Bank, 41 Berkeley
Square, London W1X 6NA, 0171 409 5000.
Called: Feb 1993, Middle Temple, LLB
(Hons)(Lond), ACIB

Garner *Miss Margaret Theresa* •
Head of Group Legal Services (London),
Legal Dept, Banque Indosuez, 122
Leadenhall Street, London EC3V 4QH, 0171
971 4000, Fax: 0171 971 4407, Director,
L'Association Des Juristes France-
Britanniques. Called: Nov 1968, Gray's Inn

Garnett *David Michael* •
Senior Crown Prosecutor, Crown
Prosecution Service, The Ryedale Building,
60 Piccadilly, York, 01904 610726, Fax:
01904 610394. Called: July 1981, Gray's Inn,
LLB

Garratt *Basil Sanders*
Called: Feb 1971, Gray's Inn, LLB

Garraway *Colonel Charles Henry
Barre* •
Legal Officer in Armed Forces, Directorate
of Army Legal, Services (ALS 2), Metropole
Building, Northumberland Avenue, London
WC2N 5BL, 0171 218 4766, Fax: 0171 218
9944. Called: July 1972, Inner Temple, MA
(Cantab)

Garside *John-Paul*
Kingsley Napley Solicitors, St Johns Lane,
London EC1. Called: Oct 1996, Inner
Temple, LLB (Lond)

Garvey *Ms Sarah*
Called: Oct 1994, Gray's Inn, BA

Gaskell *Mrs Vera Norma*
Called: Nov 1985, Gray's Inn

Gasper *Michael Charles Kinahan* •
Senior Lawyer Employed by the Solicitor for
Customs & Excise, Solicitor's Office, HM
Customs & Excise, New King's Beam
House, 22 Upper Ground, London SE1 9PJ,
0171 865 5201, Fax: 0171 865 5194.
Called: Feb 1964, Gray's Inn

Gasson *John Gustav Haycraft CB,*
The White House, Candys Lane, Blandford
Road, Shillingstone Road, Dorset DT11 OSF,
01258 861690. Called: Feb 1957, Gray's Inn,
BA (Cape Town), MA, BCL (Oxford)

Gates *Peter Leslie*
94 St Margarets, Stevenage, Herts SG2 8RE.
Called: Feb 1987, Gray's Inn, LLB (E Anglia)

Gau *Miss Susan*
Called: July 1996, Lincoln's Inn, LLB
(Hons)(Hull)

Gaudin *James Harman*
Called: Nov 1996, Middle Temple, LLB
(Hons)

Gaunt *Stephen Alistair*
Ford & Warren Solicitors, Westgate Point,
Westgate, Leeds LS1 2AX, 0113 243 6601,
Fax: 0113 242 0905. Called: Nov 1995,
Gray's Inn, BA (Manc)

Gauntlett *Jeremy John SC*
Acting Judge, Cape Supreme Court (1991 &
1994), 1114 Huguenot Chambers, 40 Queen
Victoria St, Cape Town, South Africa,
249340, Fax: 245666, Senior Counsel, South
Africa, Lesotho & Namibia. Called: May
1994, Gray's Inn, BA, LLB, BCL

Gautama *Miss Nisha*
Deputy Justices Clerk, Church End, 448
High Road, Willesden, London NW10 2DZ,
0181 451 7111, Fax: 0181 451 2040.
Called: Nov 1988, Middle Temple, LLB
(B'ham)

Gavaloo *Miss Vedna*
Called: Nov 1995, Lincoln's Inn, LLB (Hons)

Gavin *Alastair Douglas MC*
2 Phillimore Terrace, Allen Street, London
W8. Called: Nov 1957, Inner Temple, BA

Gavin *Miss Georgia Henrietta Bulkely*
Called: Nov 1989, Inner Temple, BA
(Manch), Dip Law

Gavin *Jake Alfred Bulkeley*
Called: Oct 1993, Inner Temple, BA, CPE

Gawne *Miss Anne Maria*
Called: Oct 1990, Middle Temple, LLB
(Lond)

Gaymer *Mrs Vivien Murray* •
Company Secretary, Enterprise Oil Plc,
Grand Buildings, Trafalgar Square, London
WC2N 5EJ, 0171 925 4194, Fax: 0171 925
4606. Called: Feb 1971, Middle Temple, LLB
Hons

Gbondo *Joseph Dominic Andrew* •
Principal Contracts Lawyer, London
Borough of Islington, The Town Hall, Upper
Street, Islington, London N1 2UD, 0171 477
3314. Called: Nov 1983, Gray's Inn, BA
Dip.Construction, Law & Arbitration, (Kings
College Lon)

Geater *Miss Sara Kate*
Called: Mar 1998, Middle Temple, LLB
(Hons)

Gebbie *Mrs Sarah Jane*
Called: Oct 1992, Middle Temple, LL.B
(Hons, Brunel)

Geddes *Miss Gillian Mary*
Called: Oct 1997, Gray's Inn, LLB

Geer *David John Granville*
European Human Rights, Foundation,
Avenue Michelange 70, Brussels 1049, (322)
732 6653, Fax: (322) 7346831. Called: Nov
1988, Middle Temple, BA (Cantab), Dip
Law, LLM

Geering *Philip James* •
Legal Adviser, Legal Secretariat to the Law,
Officers, Attorney General's Chambers, 9
Buckingham Gate, London SW1E 6JP.
Called: July 1984, Middle Temple, LLB
(Hons)

Gemmell *Mrs Marie Cecile*
Called: Oct 1994, Gray's Inn, LLB

Genkatharan *Mrs Kala Malar*
Called: Mar 1998, Middle Temple, LLB
(Hons)(Lond)

George *Miss Caroline Mary*
Called: Nov 1996, Lincoln's Inn, LLB (Hons)

George *Gareth Richard Llewellyn*
9 Park Place, Cardiff, CF1 3DP. Called: Nov
1977, Middle Temple, MA (Oxon)

George *Mrs Judy Ava*
Assistant Director (Strategy & Support
Services), Social Services Department,
Corporation of London, Milton Court, Moor
Lane, London EC2Y 9BL, 0171 332 1211,
Fax: 0171 588 9173. Called: May 1977,
Middle Temple, BA (Hons)

George *Laurence Christopher Tyacke*
Steptoe & Johnson, Box 174, c/o Post
International, 2 Gales Gardens, Birkbeck
Street, London E2 0EJ. Called: Nov 1976,
Middle Temple, LLB,MA

George *Rynholdt*
Advocate of Supreme Court of South Africa,
Group 500, Innes Chambers, P.O.Box 1073,
Johannesburg 2000, (2711) 337 4355, Fax:
(2711) 333 1602, and Member
Johannesburg Bar. Called: July 1996,
Lincoln's Inn, LLB (Hons), BA(Hon), (Oxon)

George *Miss Sara Dawn*
Called: Oct 1996, Middle Temple, BA
(Hons)(Cantab), CPE (City)

Georghiadou *Miss Chrysso Souli*
Company Secretary/Legal Advise.
Called: July 1983, Middle Temple, BA

Georgiadis *Byron Nicholas*
Arbitrator, P.O.Box 42851, Nairobi, Kenya,
Nairobi 882319/884037, Fax: 884037, and
Member Kenya Bar Seychelles Bar.
Called: Nov 1951, Inner Temple, MA
(Oxon), MCA Arb

Georgiou *Ms Angela Kyriacos*
Called: Oct 1997, Inner Temple, LLB
(Sheffield)

Georgiou *Miss Chloe*
Called: Nov 1997, Gray's Inn, LLB (Leics)

Georgis Taylor *Miss Vivian*
Peter I Foster & Associates, 35 Jeremie
Street, Castries, 758 4531100, Fax: 758
4524940, and Member St Lucia. Called: Nov
1995, Middle Temple, LLB (Hons)

Georgulas *Miss Efrocynne*
Called: Nov 1995, Gray's Inn, BA, LLB (City)

Geraghty *Miss Toni* •
Lincolnshire County Council, Lincoln,
01522 552222, Fax: 01522 552138.
Called: Oct 1993, Middle Temple, LLB
(Hons)(Lond)

Germain *Mrs Jadwiga Anne Teresa*
ILMCS, 65 Romney Street, London
SW1P 3RD. Called: July 1966, Inner Temple,
LLB

Germany *Mrs Alison* •
Court Clerk. Called: Nov 1985, Gray's Inn,
LLB

Gerrard *Stephen*
Called: Mar 1997, Gray's Inn, LLB (Manch)

Gethin *Mrs Susan Jane* •
Senior Crown Prosecutor, Crown
Prosecution Service, Froomsgate House, 1st
Floor, Rupert Street, Bristol BS1 2QJ.
Called: Oct 1990, Inner Temple, LLB (Hons)

Getley *Miss Kate Ann Cameron*
87 Lionel Road, Brentford, Middlesex
TW8 9QZ, 0181 847 0735, Fax: 0181 758
1181. Called: Feb 1988, Inner Temple, BA
(Oxon)

Gevisser *Antony James*
12 Montrose Road, Hurlingham, Sandton
2196, South Africa, 0171 730 9371, Fax:
011 7831317, and Member Johannesburg
Bar. Called: Nov 1993, Gray's Inn, BA, LLB
(Cape)

Ghandinesen *Kanarasan*
Called: July 1995, Lincoln's Inn, LLB (Hons)

Ghani *Ahmad Shukri Abdul*
Called: Nov 1997, Gray's Inn, LLB (Wales)

Ghani *Miss Marianne Antoinette*
00 60 88 218667/218663, Fax: 00 60 88
239627, and Member Sabah & Sarawak,
Malaysia. Called: Oct 1995, Gray's Inn, LLB

Gheera *Ms Manjit*
Called: Oct 1997, Inner Temple, LLB
(Reading)

Ghosh *Dhruba*
Called: July 1995, Lincoln's Inn, LLB (Hons)

Ghows-Retnam *Jiva*
Deputy Chief Clerk, Inner London
Magistrates', Courts Service, 65 Romney
Street, London SW1P 3RD, 0171 799 3332,
Fax: 0171 799 3072. Called: July 1989,
Middle Temple, LLB (Newc)

Ghumman *Mohammed-Khurram*
Called: Nov 1997, Lincoln's Inn, BA, LLM
(Punjab), LLM (Lond)

Giaquinto *Martino John*
Called: Oct 1996, Lincoln's Inn, BSc
(Hons)(Aston)

Gibb *Jeremy Roderick* •
Immigration Advisor, Tower Hamlets Law
Centre, 341 Commercial Road, London
E1 2PS, 0171 791 0741, Fax: 0171 702
7301. Called: July 1989, Middle Temple, BA
(Oxon) MST(Oxon), Dip Law

Gibbard-Jones *David Mark*
Called: Oct 1993, Middle Temple, LLB
(Hons, B'ham)

Gibbins *Brian Richard* •
Senior Crown Prosecutor, International,
Civil and, Appellate Branch, CPS Central
Casework, 50 Ludgate Hill, London
EC4M 7EX, 0171 273 1250, Fax: 0171 329
8171, and Member Northern Ireland Bar.
Called: Nov 1986, Middle Temple,
LLB(Hons) London, Assoc of Inst of,
Linguists

Gibbons *(Ronald) Peter*
Called: May 1958, Gray's Inn, BA (Oxon)

Gibbons *John Thomas*
Law Library, Four Courts, Inns Quay, Dublin
7, 01 872 0622, Barrister of Ireland and
Member Kings Inn, Dublin. Called: Nov
1991, Middle Temple, BL (Dublin), BE,
(NUI), DIP. LScEng, FIEI, FCIArb, LAM, RTPI

Gibbons *Miss Linda Marie*
Called: Oct 1996, Inner Temple, LLB
(L'pool)

Gibbs *David*
Clerk to the Justices, Justices' Clerk's Office,
The Court House, Civic Centre, St Peter's
Street, St Albans AL1 3LB, 01727 816822,
Fax: 01727 816829. Called: Nov 1984,
Gray's Inn, DML, DMS

Gibbs *Nigel James* •
Senior Crown Prosecutor, Crown
Prosecution Service, 5th Floor, River Park
House, High Road, Wood Green, London
N22. Called: July 1985, Inner Temple, LLB
(Brunel)

Gibbs *Peter Christopher Colston*
Called: July 1974, Lincoln's Inn, LLB

Gibbs *Simon Thomas Bernard*
Legal Costs Negotiator, Legal Costs
Negotiator, 56 Marsh Wall, London E14.
Called: Oct 1995, Middle Temple, LLB
(Hons)

Gibson *Bryan Donald*
Waterside, Domum Road, Winchester
SO23 9NN, 01256 882250, Fax: 01256
882250. Called: July 1976, Gray's Inn, BA
(Hons)

Gibson *John Philip Robson*
Called: July 1990, Inner Temple, MA,
Dip.Information, & Library Management,
LLM

Gibson *Kenyatta Mboya*
Called: July 1994, Lincoln's Inn, LLB (Hons,
Bucks)

Gibson *Mrs Mavis Dorothy*
Called: Nov 1965, Lincoln's Inn

Gibson *Mrs Sally Ann Safeena*
Kiln Wood, Huntsland Drive, Crawley
Down, West Sussex RH10 4HB, 01342 717
533. Called: Nov 1979, Lincoln's Inn, BA
(Hons)

Gibson *Scott William*
Called: Oct 1996, Gray's Inn, LLB (Wales)

Gibson *Miss Susan Eile*
Wilde Sapte, 1 Fleet Place, London
EC4M 7WS, 0171 246 7168. Called: Oct
1995, Lincoln's Inn, LLB (Hons)(Lond),
ACIS, AGSM

Giglioli *George*
P.O.Box 1316, George Town, Grand
Cayman, Cayman Islands, 12 New Square,
Ground Floor, Lincoln's Inn, London, WC2A
3SW. Called: July 1982, Lincoln's Inn, BSc
(Exon),Dip Law

Gilbert *Carl St. John* •
United Bank of Kuwait, 7 Baker Street,
London W1M 1AB, 0171 487 6591.
Called: Oct 1996, Middle Temple, BA
(Hons)(Exon), CPE (Notts)

Gilbert *David Richard TD*
Consultant/Secretary of Horizon IJUC Ltd,
Little Orchard, Littlewick Green, Berks
SL6 3RA, 01628 828462, Fax: 01628
828462. Called: Feb 1957, Middle Temple,
MA, LLM

Gilbert *Miss Dionne*
Crill Canavan, La Chasse Chambers, La
Chasse, St Helier, Jersey, 01534 888933,
Fax: 01534 887040. Called: July 1996, Inner
Temple, LLB (Bucks)

Gilbert *Ms Helen Marie*
and Member New Zealand. Called: July
1996, Inner Temple, LLB

Gilbert *Mrs Jeanine Bryony*
Lecturer in Law, University of Exeter,
Faculty of Law, Amory Building, Rennes
Drive, Exeter EX4 4RJ, 01392 263263.
Called: Nov 1987, Lincoln's Inn, BD (Hons)
(Lond), Dip Law, AKC, LLM (Leic)

Gilbert *Ms Lorianne Darnelle*
Called: Nov 1994, Gray's Inn, BA (USA), LLB

Gilbert *Robert Greenway*
5 Orchid Avenue, Kingsteignton, Newton
Abbot, Devon TQ12 3HG, 01626 61718.
Called: Nov 1950, Lincoln's Inn, MA

Giles *Derryck Peter Fitzgibbon*
Governor of BFWG Charitable Foundation
(p/t), 22 Petworth Road, Haslemere, Surrey
GU27 2HR, 01428 644425. Called: July
1954, Gray's Inn, LLB

Giles *Peter*
Called: Oct 1997, Inner Temple, LLB
(Southampton)

Gilhespy *Mrs Sonia* •
Senior Crown Prosecutor, Crown
Prosecution Service, York House, 34 Princes
Street, Leicester LE1 5TU, 0116 254 9333.
Called: Oct 1990, Gray's Inn, LLB (Newc)

Giliker *Ms Paula Rosalind*
Called: Oct 1994, Gray's Inn, MA (Oxon),
BCL (Oxon), PHD (Cantab)

Gill *The Honourable Lord*
Senator of the College of Justice in Scotland.
Chairman, Scottish Law Commission., Court
of Session, Parliament House, Edinburgh
EH1 1RQ, 0131 225 2595, Fax: 0131 225
8213. Called: Apr 1991, Lincoln's Inn, MA
(Glas), LLB (Glas), PH.D (Edinburgh)

Gill *Amarick Singh*
Called: Mar 1998, Middle Temple, LLB
(Hons)

Gill *Miss Baljinder*
Called: Oct 1996, Inner Temple, BA
(Wolves)

Gill *David Edwin*
Called: July 1983, Middle Temple,
BA(Cantab), Dip Law

Gill *Mrs Elizabeth Jane*
Principal Legal Adviser, Basildon
Magistrates' Court, Great Oaks, Basildon,
Essex, 01268 293129, Fax: 01268 293187.
Called: Feb 1987, Middle Temple, BA
(Hons), Dip MLaw

Gill *Ian Charles*
Clerk to the Magistrates, N.E. Essex
Magistrates Courts, Stanwell House,
Stanwell Street, Colchester, Essex CO2 7DL,
01206 563057, Fax: 01206 563694.
Called: May 1984, Middle Temple, Dip
MLaw

Gill *Jagjit Singh*
Advocate & Solicitor, Legal Assistant,
Chinese Chambers of Commerce, &
Industry Building, 47 Hill Street, [H]04-03,
3382622, Fax: 3392386, and Member
Singapore. Called: July 1996, Lincoln's Inn,
LLB (Hons)(Lond)

Gill *Julian Clive* •
Principal Team Leader, Crown Prosecution
Service, Princes House, 34 York Road, Leic,
0116 2549333. Called: July 1987, Gray's Inn,
LLB

Gill *Maninder Singh*
6 Cedar Drive, London N2 0PS. Called: Nov
1992, Gray's Inn, LLB (Bris), LLM (Lond)

Gill *Mrs Naranderjit*
Litigation Manager, First National Bank Plc,
First National House, College Road, Harrow,
Middlesex HA1 1FB. Called: Nov 1988,
Inner Temple, LLM (Lond), LLB

Gill *Miss Susan Eveline*
Deputy Chief Clerk, Inner London
Magistrates', Courts Service, 65 Romney
Street, London SW1P 3RD, 0171 799 3332,
Fax: 0171 799 3072. Called: Nov 1987,
Gray's Inn, BA

Gill *Mrs Susan Li-Tseng*
Legal Advisor, OMLX, The London Securities
& Derivatives Exchange, 107 Cannon
Street, London EC4N 5AD, 0171 283 0678,
Fax: 0171 815 8508. Called: Nov 1993,
Gray's Inn, LLB, LLM

Gill *Zaminder Singh*
No 87 Beach Road, [H]04-01 Chye Sing
Building, 3387225, Fax: 3388815, and
Member Singapore. Called: Nov 1993,
Middle Temple, LLB (Hons)(Lanc)

Gillanders *Roderick Colin Fabian* •
Senior Advisory Lawyer, Senior Fraud
Office, Serious Fraud Office, Elm House, 10-
16 Elm Street, London WC1X 0BJ, 0171 239
7106, Fax: 0171 239 7323. Called: July
1976, Middle Temple, LLB (Lond)

Gillard *The Hon Mr Justice Eugene
William*
Chairman; Victorian Bar Council 1988-1990.
President; Australian Bar Association 1989-
1990. Justice of the Supreme Court of
Victoria, Judges' Chambers, Supreme Court
of Victoria, 210 William Street, Melbourne,
Vic.3000, (03) 9603 6222, Fax: (03) 9670
8408, QC (Australia) and Member Victorian,
Tasmania, New South Wales, Queensland 4
Stone Bldgs, Ground Floor, Lincoln's Inn,
London, WC2A 3XT. Called: Feb 1991,
Gray's Inn, LLB (Melbourne)

Gillespie *Alisdair Allan*
Called: Oct 1996, Middle Temple, LLB
(Hons)

Gillespie *Brian David*
2 Glenvar Park, Blackrock, Co. Dublin,
2882887, Fax: 720455, and Member
Southern Ireland Bar. Called: July 1989,
Middle Temple, MA [Dub], MAI [Dub], B
Comm [Dub], FIEE

Gillett *Ms Tonia Jane*
Called: Oct 1997, Inner Temple, LLB
(Birmingham)

Gilliland *David Jeremy*
Theodore Goddard, 150 Aldersgate Street,
London EC1A 4EJ, 0171 606 8855, Fax:
0171 606 4390. Called: Oct 1994, Gray's
Inn, BSc, MSc, CEng, MIChem E

Gilling *Simon Jolyon* •
Legal Adviser & Partnership Secretary &
Legal Director, Mercury Personal
Communication, T/A One to One, Imperial
Place, Maxwell Road, Borehamwood, Herts
WD6 1EA, 0181 214 2310, Fax: 0181 214
3441. Called: July 1981, Middle Temple,
BSc, Dip Law

Gilmore *Stephen*
University Lecturer. Called: Nov 1993,
Lincoln's Inn, LLB (Hons, Leic), LLM

Gilpin *Matthew Thomas Diarmuid*
Assistant, Securities Group, Corporate
Finance Department, S J Berwin & Co, 222
Gray's Inn Road, LondoN WC1X 8HB, 0171
533 2222, Fax: 0171 533 2000. Called: Nov
1993, Middle Temple, MA (Hons)(Oxon)

Gilthorpe *Miss Charlotte Emma
Tiffany* •
Head of Competition Policy, Cable &
Wireless Communication, 26 Red Lion
Square, London WC1R 4HQ, 0171 528
3712, Fax: 0171 528 2163. Called: July
1996, Middle Temple, BSc (Hons)

Gingell *Miss Melanie Ann*
Mitre House Chambers, Mitre House, 44
Fleet Street, London, EC4Y 1BN. Called: Nov
1988, Middle Temple, LLB (Hons Lond)

Gingell *Miss Virginia Carol*
Called: Nov 1990, Inner Temple, LLB

Ginn *Mrs Ginn Adeline-Marie Odile
Claude*
Called: Nov 1994, Inner Temple, LLB
(Warw), LLM (Canada)

Girvin *Miss Cecelia Ann*
Called: Nov 1994, Middle Temple, LLB
(Hons)

Gittens *Miss Chrystine Louise* •
London Borough of Newham, 0181 472
1430. Called: Feb 1994, Inner Temple, BA
(Lond), CPE

Gittens *Ms Janet Dianne* •
Court Clerk, Bexley Magistrates Court,
Norwich Place, Bexleyheath, Kent
DA5 7NB, 0181 304 5211, Fax: 0181 303
6849. Called: Nov 1989, Gray's Inn, LLB

Gittings *Daniel John*
Associate Editor, South China Morning Post,
29/F Dorset House, 979 King's Road, + 852
28653584, Fax: + 852 28653464, and
Member High Court of Hong Kong.
Called: July 1997, Gray's Inn, MA

Gittings *David Howard*
Director, Regulatory Services, Lloyd's of
London, Lloyd's of London, One Lime
Street, London EC3. Called: July 1977,
Middle Temple, LLB Hons (Lond)

Gittins *David James* •
Senior Crown Prosecutor, Crown
Prosecution Service, Plymouth Branch
Office, St Andrews Court, 12 St Andrews
Street, Plymouth PL1 2AH, 01752 668700,
Fax: 01752 672093. Called: July 1971, Inner
Temple, MA (Cantab)

Gladwell *David John* •
Head of Civil Justice Division, Lord
Chancellor's Department, Selbourne House,
54-60 Victoria Street, London SW1E 6QW,
0171 210 8789, Fax: 0171 210 0682.
Called: July 1972, Gray's Inn, LLM (Exon),
Dip IP Law (Lond), CEDR, Accredited
Mediator

Glanvill *Dr Michael Edward OStJ*
Jocelyn Mews, 18A High Street, Chard,
Somerset TA20 1QL, 01460 63348.
Called: Nov 1956, Middle Temple, BA,
MRCS, LRCP, MRCGP, DMJ

Gleave *Edward Ernest James*
31 Winston Drive, Noctorum, Birkenhead,
Wirral, Liverpool L43 9RU, 0151 678 4030.
Called: July 1968, Lincoln's Inn, BCom

Gleave *Miss Justina Louise* •
Trogan Television Limited, Queen Anne
House, Charlotte Street, Bath BA1 2NE,
01795 536969. Called: May 1988, Gray's
Inn, LLB (SOAS)

Gledhill *Lee*
Called: Mar 1998, Lincoln's Inn, BA
(Hons)(Leeds)

Gleeson *Donough Patrick*
and Member Irish Bar. Called: July 1963,
Gray's Inn, BA

Gleeson *Mark Anthony John* •
Office of the Solicitor, Dept of Social
Security, New Court, 48 Carey Street,
London WC2A 2LS, 0171 962 8000.
Called: Oct 1995, Middle Temple, B.Sc
(Hons) (Manch)

Glenister *Richard Edwin* •
Lawyer Special Casework, Crown
Prosecution Service, 10 Furnival Street,
London EC4A 1PE. Called: July 1972, Gray's
Inn, MA (Oxon)_

Glenn *Miss Angela Veronica*
01703 559770. Called: Nov 1981, Gray's
Inn, BA

Glenn *Miss Christine Mary*
Justices' Chief Executive, Inner London
Magistrates' Crts, Committee, 65 Romney
Street, London SW1P 3RD, 0171 799 3332,
Fax: 0171 799 3072. Called: July 1980,
Gray's Inn, BA (L'pool)

Glenn *Miss Nicola Louise* •
Principal Legal Officer, H M Customs &
Excise, New Kings Beam House, 22 Upper
Ground, London SE1, 0171 865 5247.
Called: Nov 1992, Lincoln's Inn, LLB (Hons)

Glitzenhirn-Augustin *Mrs Natalie
Elaine*
P O Box 1695, Castries, Fax: (758) 451
8409, and Member St Lucia Bar Association.
Called: July 1996, Middle Temple, BA
(Hons)(Warw), CPE

Glover *Mrs Audrey Frances* •
Legal Counsellor, Foreign & Commonwealth
Office, Kings Charles Street, London SW1.
Called: Feb 1961, Gray's Inn

Glover *Kevin Peter*
London Borough of Islington, 222 Uper
Street, London N1. Called: Nov 1980, Inner
Temple, BA

Glover *Nigel David*
Called: July 1985, Gray's Inn, BA (Cantab)

Glover *William James QC (1969)*
Called: Jan 1950, Inner Temple, BA (Cantab)

Gnanapragasam *Miss Christina Olivia*
Called: Nov 1997, Middle Temple, LLB
(Hons)(Wales)

Go *Tiong Siew*
Called: July 1997, Lincoln's Inn, LLB (Hons)

Goad *Ms Donna Elizabeth*
Called: Nov 1995, Inner Temple, LLB

Goddard *David John*
Chapman Tripp Sheffield Young, Barristers
& Solicitors, P O Box 993, Wellington, 64 4
499 5999, Fax: 64 4 472 7111, Barrister &
Solicitor of the High Court of New Zealand.
Called: July 1988, Lincoln's Inn, BA (Hons)
(Victoria), BA (Oxon)

Goddard *Ian Lester* •
Manager, Legal Dept, 3i plc, Legal Dept,
Trinity Park, Bickenhill, Birmingham
B37 7ES, 0121 782 3131, Fax: 0121 782
6161. Called: July 1974, Gray's Inn, BA
Oxon

Goddard *Peter Andrew George*
Managing Director of ATC Trustees (BVI)
Limited, ATC Trustees (BVI) Limited, P O
Box 933, Road Town Tortola, (809) 494
6122, Fax: (809) 494 6124, Formerly a
solicitor. Called: Nov 1987, Middle Temple,
LLB (Wales)

Godding *John Peter*
15 Sunbury Avenue, London SW14 8RA,
0181 876 5064, Fax: 0181 876 5064.
Called: Nov 1978, Gray's Inn, ACII

Goggins *Michael Eugene*
Called: Feb 1995, Gray's Inn, LLB (Coventry)

Gogo *Emmanuel Markwei Kofi* •
Senior Assistant Solicitor, Legal Services
Division, Newham Borough Council, Town
Hall, East Ham, London E6 2RP, 0181 472
1430 ext 23069, Fax: 0181 472 0480.
Called: July 1984, Middle Temple, LL.B,
LL.M

Goh *Aik Leng*
Goh Aik Leng & Partners, No 50A Temple
Street, 065 222 6330, Fax: 065 222 4262,
and Member Singapore Bar. Called: Nov
1991, Middle Temple, LLB Hons (Buck'm)

Goh *Boon Yee*
Called: July 1996, Middle Temple, LLB
(Hons)(Lond)

Goh *Miss Christina Choy Boon*
Block 7, Teck Whye Ave [H]04-102,
Singapore 680007, 7647753. Called: July
1995, Middle Temple, LLB (Hons)(Lond),
BSC (Est Mg+)(Hons)

Goh *Chuan Huat*
Called: July 1996, Middle Temple, LLB
(Hons)(Lond)

Goh *Hoon Huar*
Called: July 1996, Middle Temple, LLB
(Hons)(Notts)

Goh *Miss Hui Nee*
Called: Nov 1996, Lincoln's Inn, BA
(Hons)(Keele)

Goh *Miss Joan Penn Nee*
Called: July 1996, Lincoln's Inn, LLB
(Hons)(Wales)

Goh *Joseph Chye Hock*
Blk 146 Pasir Ris Street 11, [H] 02-61
Singapore 510146, (65) 5840843, and
Member Singapore Bar. Called: Nov 1994,
Middle Temple, LLB (Hons)

Goh *Miss Justine Soo Hsien*
Called: Nov 1997, Gray's Inn, LLB (LSE)

Goh *Kien Ping*
Called: Nov 1993, Lincoln's Inn, LLB (Hons)

Goh *Lam Chuan*
Called: May 1994, Middle Temple, LLB (Hons)

Goh *Laurence Eng Yau*
Legal Advisor, Company Secretary, Director, 47 Saraca Road, Singapore 807392, Republic of Singapore, 4822285/ 3240727, Fax: 4841060/ 3240703, Advocate & Solicitor, Singapore and Member Singapore Bar. Called: July 1989, Lincoln's Inn, LLB (Hons)(Lond)

Goh *Li Kian*
Called: July 1995, Middle Temple, LLB (Hons)

Goh *Miss Li Peen*
546 Ang Mo Kio Avenue 10, [H]03-2252, Singapore 560546, 65 4578225, and Member Singapore Bar. Called: July 1994, Gray's Inn, LLB (Lond)

Goh *Miss Li Yen*
Associate, 17 Thomson View, Singapore 2057, (65) 455 4883, and Member Singapore Bar. Called: July 1994, Middle Temple, BA (Hons)(Oxon)

Goh *Miss Maxine Whui Min*
Called: Nov 1995, Middle Temple, LLB (Hons)(Hull)

Goh *Miss Pricilla May Lih*
Legal Assistant, 2175-J Taman Tunku Habsah, 05100, Alor Setar, Kedah, 04 7317154, Fax: 04 7311375, and Member Malaysia Bar. Called: July 1995, Lincoln's Inn, LLB (Hons)

Goh *Miss Sen Fong*
Called: July 1995, Lincoln's Inn, BA (Hons)

Goh *Seng Leong Christopher*
Harry Elias & Partners, 9 Raffles Place, [H]12-00 Republic Plaza, 535 0550, Fax: 438 0550, and Member Singapore. Called: July 1996, Middle Temple, LLB (Hons)(Lond)

Goh *Miss Susan Guat Eng*
Called: Mar 1997, Gray's Inn, LLB (L'pool)

Goh *Miss Susan Hui San*
Called: July 1992, Lincoln's Inn, LLB (Hons) (Notts)

Goh *Miss Swee Hua Phylina*
Called: July 1997, Middle Temple, LLB (Hons)(Lond)

Goh *Miss Wei Lin*
Called: Nov 1994, Lincoln's Inn, LLB (Hons)(Sheff)

Goh *Miss Yolande Hui Lynn*
Called: July 1996, Lincoln's Inn, LLB (Hons)

Goins *Ms Debra Lynn*
Legal Analyst, Bermuda Monetary Authority, Burnaby House, 26 Burnaby Street, Hamilton, 441 295 5278, Fax: 441 292 7471, and Member Bermuda. Called: Nov 1996, Inner Temple, LLB (Lond)

Golamaully *Abdus Samad*
Called: Nov 1995, Lincoln's Inn, LLB (Hons)

Golan *Miss Alin Ayelet*
Lawyer, Legal Department, ING Barings, ING Barings, 60 London Wall, London EC2, 0171 767 6991, Fax: 0171 767 7780. Called: Nov 1992, Middle Temple, LLB (Hons, Manch)

Gold *William Duncan*
30 Oakwood Drive, Fulwood, Preston, Lancs PR2 3LY. Called: Nov 1964, Gray's Inn, LLM (Lond), A.C.I.S

Goldberg *Ms Joy Paula*
Called: Nov 1994, Middle Temple, BA (Hons)

Goldberg *Mrs Rhoda Joyce*
Called: Oct 1997, Middle Temple, BA (Hons)(Boston), MA (Chicago), LLB (Lond)

Golden *Mrs Aviva*
Called: Nov 1969, Middle Temple, BA (S.Africa)

Goldie *Charles William Homan*
2 Myddylton Place, Saffron Walden, Essex CB10 1BB. Called: Nov 1965, Middle Temple, MA, LLB

Goldie *Gainneos Jacob*
Messrs Yusoff Shamsuddin &, Partners, 5th Floor, Straits Trading, Building No 4 Lebow Pasar, Besar 50050, Kuala Lumpur Malaysia, 03 2938244, Fax: 03 2938381, and Member Malaysia Bar. Called: Nov 1992, Middle Temple, LLB (Hons)

Golding *Ms Jane Lindsey*
Brosio Casati e Associati, Corso Vittorio Emanuele II, 68, 10121 Torino, 00 39 11 5155300, Fax: 00 39 11 541018. Called: Nov 1989, Lincoln's Inn, LLB (Lond), Maitrise (Paris)

Golding *Timothy John*
Called: July 1994, Gray's Inn, LLB (Wolv)

Goldman *James Simon Mark*
Called: Nov 1994, Middle Temple, B.Sc

Goldring *Jonathan Derek*
Called: Oct 1997, Middle Temple, LLB (Hons)(Lond)

Goldring *Mrs Judith Ann*
Managing Director, Clark Goldring & Page Ltd, Beech House, St Swithun Street, Winchester, Hampshire SO23 9HU, 01962 842726, Fax: 01962 842726. Called: Nov 1979, Gray's Inn, LLB

Goldsmith *Immanuel*
QC Canada, Smart & Biggar, 439 University Avenue, Suite 1500, Box 111, Toronto, Ontario, 416 593 5514, Fax: 416 591 1690, and Member Ontario Bar. Called: Jan 1950, Middle Temple, LLB

Goldsmith *Mrs Joy*
7 Hanover Terrace, Regents Park, London NW1 4RJ. Called: July 1973, Lincoln's Inn, BA (Hons), LLB, LLM

Goldspink *Justin Stephen*
Called: Nov 1994, Inner Temple, BA (Oxon), LLM (Notts)

Goldstein *Ms Sara Jayne* •
London Borough of Lewisham, Town Hall, London SE6 4RU, 0181 695 6000. Called: Oct 1990, Inner Temple, LLB (So'ton)

Goldsworth *John Graham*
Goldsworth Chambers, 1st Floor, 10-11 Gray's Inn Square, London, WC1R 5JD. Called: Nov 1965, Middle Temple

Goldsworthy *Ian Francis* QC (1992)
Recorder, 23 Essex Street, London, WC2R 3AS. Called: Nov 1968, Inner Temple

Goldsworthy *Lieutenant Peter Jarvis RN*
The Wardroom, HMS Fearless, BFPO 283, M 0467 494 869. Called: July 1993, Inner Temple, B Eng (Hons, Bris)

Gollop *Advocate Julian Clive*
Advocate Royal Ct Jersey & Crown Advocate, Crills, PO Box 72, 44 Esplanade, St Helier, Jersey, C I JE4 8PN, 01534 611055, Fax: 01534 611066. Called: July 1983, Gray's Inn, BA (Hons)

Gomez *Cosmas Stephen*
Called: Nov 1994, Inner Temple, BA (Lond)

Gomez *David Jide* •
Called: Oct 1995, Lincoln's Inn, MA (Hons)(Oxon), LLM, Dip in Law

Gomez *Miss Monique Vanessa Ann*
Office of Attorney General, 4th, 5th & 6th Floors, Post Office Building, East Hill Street,P.O.Box N3007, Nassau, N.P. Bahamas, 809 32221141, Fax: 809 3222555, and Member Bahamas Bar. Called: July 1988, Lincoln's Inn, LLB (Hons) (Lond)

Goncalves *Miss Elaine Laura*
Isola & Isola, Suite 23, Portland House, Glacis Road, 78363, Fax: 78699, and Member Gibraltar Bar. Called: Nov 1995, Middle Temple, LLB (Hons)

Gong *Chin Nam*
Called: July 1995, Middle Temple, LLB (Hons) (Hull)

Gonsalves-Sabola *Miss Mary Margaret*
Registered Associate, McKinney Bancroft & Hughes, Nassau, Bahamas, McKinney, Bancroft & Hughes, Counsel & Attorneys-at-Law, No 4 George Street, Mareva House, Nassau, (242) 322 4195, Fax: (242) 328 2520, and Member Jamaica. Called: Nov 1994, Gray's Inn, LLB, LLM

Gooch *Alan Lucas*
Clerk to Justices. Called: June 1957, Middle Temple

Gooch *Ian Edward* •
A Bilbrough & Co, 50 Leman Street, London E1 8HQ, 0171 772 8000, Fax: 0171 772 8200. Called: Nov 1989, Inner Temple, LLB

Goodchild *Graham Stuart* •
Head of Legal Section (Northern Office), Charity Commission, Northern Office, 20 Kings Parade, Queens Dock, Liverpool L3 4DQ, 0151 703 1538. Called: July 1966, Lincoln's Inn

Goodchild John Cadbury
Called: July 1973, Middle Temple, BA
(Hons) Law, Southampton

Goodfellow Stephen John
Called: Nov 1997, Middle Temple, BSc
(Hons)(Bris)

Goodier John Stuart •
Senior Crown Prosecutor. Called: Oct 1992,
Middle Temple, MA (Oxon)

Goodman David Roderick
Deputy Clerk to the Justices, Stafford
Magistrates Court, The Court House, South
Walls, Stafford ST16 3DW, 01785 223144,
Fax: 01785 58508. Called: Nov 1983, Gray's
Inn, DML

Goodwill John Francis
Chief Legal Counsel, Coutts & Co Group.,
Coutts Private Banking, Talstrasse 59, Zurich
CH-8022, Switzerland, 01-214-54 59, Fax:
01-214-55 63, Also Inn of Court G.
Called: Nov 1974, Lincoln's Inn, MA
(Hons)(Oxon)

Goodyear Damon John
Thurleigh MK44 2DB, 01234 771983.
Called: May 1997, Middle Temple, BSc
(Hons)(Denelm), MSc

Gooi Hsiao-Leung
Called: July 1995, Lincoln's Inn, LLB (Hons)

Goom Ms Sarah Louise •
Grade 7 Lawyer, Lord Chancellor's
Department, Royal Courts of Justice, Strand,
London, 0171 936 6517, Fax: 0171 936
6900. Called: Nov 1992, Inner Temple, BA
(Kent), MPhil (Cantab)

Gopalakrishnan Dinagaran
Called: Nov 1996, Lincoln's Inn, LLB
(Hons)(Lond)

Gopaul Miss Dorothea Mohinee
Called: July 1990, Lincoln's Inn, LLB

Gordon Alexander George
Clifford Chance, 200 Aldersgate Street,
London EC1A 4JJ. Called: Feb 1995,
Lincoln's Inn, BA (Hons)

Gordon Asher Karleel •
Office of the Building Society, Ombudsman,
Millbank Tower, Millbank, London
SW1P 4XS, 0171 931 0044, Fax: 0171 931
8485. Called: Feb 1989, Middle Temple,
LLM (Wales), BA

Gordon David •
Halifax Building Society, Trinity Road,
Halifax, West Yorkshire HX1 2RG, 01422
333333 Ext 33238, Fax: 01422 333453.
Called: July 1984, Middle Temple, LLB
[Manc], M Phil [Manc]

Gordon Duncan Silvester
Called: Nov 1957, Gray's Inn, MA (Oxon)

Gordon Graeme Andrew
Eversheds, Cloth Hall Court, Washington,
Leeds, 0113 2430391. Called: July 1984,
Gray's Inn, MA (Oxon)

Gordon Ian Jason
Called: Oct 1994, Lincoln's Inn, BA (Hons),
BCL

Gordon Joseph Isaac
50 Redhill Drive, Withdean, Brighton, East
Sussex BN1 5FL, 01273 551618. Called: July
1957, Gray's Inn, LLB, FCIArb

Gordon Mrs Sophia Ira Geraldine
Mayer, Brown & Platt, Bucklersbury House,
3 Queen Victoria Street, London EC4N 8EN,
0171 246 6200, Fax: 0171 329 4465, and
Member India Bar West Bengal Bar.
Called: Nov 1994, Inner Temple, AB
(Wellesley), MBA (Cantab)

Gordon Mrs Vanessa Maria Juliet
Maxine
7 Edwardes Square, London W8 6HE.
Called: July 1970, Gray's Inn, LLB
(Hons)(Lond), A.K.C.

Gore Mark
Called: July 1947, Inner Temple, MA
(Oxon), FCIArb

Gorman Mark
Called: Nov 1996, Gray's Inn, LLB

Gornall Mark Andrew •
Crown Prosecutor, Crown Prosecution
Service, 2nd Floor, Prudential House,
Topping Street, Blackpool FY1 3AB.
Called: July 1987, Middle Temple, LLB
(Hons) Lancaster

Gornall Paul
Called: July 1991, Middle Temple, BSC
(Edin), Dip Law

Gorner Jason
Called: Oct 1994, Gray's Inn, LLB (Hons)
(Law with, French Law) (Leeds)

Gorringe Mathew David •
Tax Consultant at Coopers & Lybrand.
Called: Feb 1995, Middle Temple, BSc
(Hons)(E.Anglia), MSc (Kent), CPE
(Coventry)

Gort Miss Jill Christina •
p/t Chairman of VAT Tribunal Commission,
Member Criminal Cases Review
Commission, Value Added Tax Tribunals,
Lord Chancellors Department, 15/19
Bedford Avenue, London EC1B 3AS, 0171
631 4242. Called: July 1977, Gray's Inn, BA
(Sussex)

Gosalia Miss Amita Ashok
Enron Europe Limited, Four Millbank,
London SW1P 3ET, 0171 316 5466.
Called: Oct 1991, Inner Temple, LLB (Lond)

Gosland Daniel Emrys
Called: Mar 1996, Gray's Inn, MA

Goss Kenneth Jack •
Principal Crown Prosecutor, Priory Gate,
Union Street, Maidstone, Kent, 01622
686425. Called: Nov 1985, Gray's Inn

Goswell Joseph Ahosu
Called: Nov 1997, Middle Temple, LLB
(Hons)(Lond)

Goudie William Henry MC
24 Nimala Street, Rosny, Tasmania 7018,
0102 442326, Formerly Solicitor England
(1938) Barrister & Solicitor Tasmania
(1972). Called: July 1952, Gray's Inn

Gough Mark
Called: Oct 1997, Lincoln's Inn, LLB
(Hons)(Luton)

Goulandris Miss Atalanta Eugenia
13 King's Bench Walk, 1st Floor, Temple,
London, EC4Y 7EN. Called: Nov 1985,
Middle Temple, BA (Lond), Dip law

Gould Miss Ciaran Amy
Called: Nov 1996, Gray's Inn, LLB (Wales)

Gould David Richard Statham
Called: July 1995, Gray's Inn, BSc

Gour Miss Bharati
Called: July 1996, Lincoln's Inn, LLB
(Hons)(Lond)

Gouriet Gerald William
3 Raymond Buildings, Gray's Inn, London,
WC1R 5BH. Called: July 1974, Inner
Temple, BMus (Lond)

Gouthro William Christopher
Associate, McKinney, Bancroft, & Hughes,
Chambers, Mareva House, 4 George Street,
P.O.Box N3937 Nassau, 809 322 4195, Fax:
809 356 2713, and Member Bahamas.
Called: July 1996, Middle Temple, LLB
(Hons)(Lond)

Govindan Sathees Kumar
Called: July 1996, Lincoln's Inn, LLB
(Hons)(E.Lond)

Govindasamy Balasunderam
Called: Nov 1994, Middle Temple, LLB
(Lond)

Govindasamy Paul Elangovan •
Senior Crown Prosecutor, CPS (London),
Solar House, 1-9 Romford Road, Stratford,
London E15 4LJ, and Member Singapore
Bar. Called: July 1983, Lincoln's Inn, BA

Gowings James Richard Humphrey
Called: Nov 1973, Lincoln's Inn, MA (Oxon)

Goyder Miss Joanna Ruth
Barrister working for Linklaters & Paines,
Brussels, Linklaters & Paines, 47-51 Rue du
Luxembourg, 1050 Brussels, 32 2 513 7800,
Fax: 32 2 513 2583, and Member Flemish
Bar of Brussels. Called: Nov 1987, Lincoln's
Inn, MA (Cantab), Licence Speciale,
(Brussels), LLM (Florence)

Gracie Malcolm Reeves
12th Floor, Wentworth Chambers, 180
Phillip Street, Sydney, New South Wales, 61
29 232 4293, Fax: 61 29 221 7183, and
Member New South Wales, Victoria,
Queensland, Northern Territory, Australian
Capital Territory. New South Wales Bar.
Called: July 1992, Lincoln's Inn, BA, LLB
(Hons)

Grady Paul Damien
District Auditor, Audit Commission,
Nicholson House, Lime Kiln Close, Stoke
Gifford, Bristol BS12 6SU, 0117 923 6757,
Fax: 0117 979 4100. Called: Nov 1996,
Lincoln's Inn, LLB (Hons)(Warw)

Graffy Miss Colleen Patricia
Director of Pepperdine Univ, 9 Gough
Square, London, EC4A 3DE. Called: Oct
1991, Middle Temple, BA, MA, Dip Law

Graham *Miss Adena Rozanne*
Called: Nov 1994, Gray's Inn, LLB

Graham *Mrs Alana Nicole* •
Cliford Chance, 200 Aldersgate Street,
London. Called: Nov 1993, Lincoln's Inn, BA
(Hons), LLB (Hons, Brunel)

Graham *Alexander Donald* •
Manager, Legal Services, General Accident
Life Services, 2 Rougier Street, York
YO1 1HR, 01904 452400, Fax: 01904
452696. Called: Feb 1975, Inner Temple,
LLB

Graham *Miss Ann Marie*
Court Clerk, Chesterfield Magistrates Court,
c/o The Court House, West Bars,
Chesterfield S40 1AE. Called: Nov 1991,
Middle Temple, LLB Hons (Cardiff)

Graham *Jeremy John Mason* •
Deputy Clerk to the Justices (Legal)
Gateshead Magistrates' Court. Called: Nov
1984, Gray's Inn, LLB (Manch)

Graham *Sir Peter KCB* QC (1990)
Consultant to J Hassan & Partners, Gibraltar,
Le Petit Chateau, La Vallette, 87190 Magnac
Level, Also Inn of Court L. Called: June
1958, Gray's Inn, MA, LLM (Cantab)

Graham *Stewart David* QC (1977)
6 Grosvenor Lodge, Dennis Lane, Stanmore,
Middlesex HA7 4JE, 0181 954 3783.
Called: Feb 1957, Middle Temple

Graham *Mrs Susan Elizabeth*
Principal Court Clerk, Kingston Magistrates
Court, 19 High Street, Kingston upon
Thames, Surrey KT1 1JW, 0181 546 5603,
Fax: 0181 547 3551. Called: Feb 1985,
Gray's Inn

Graham *Mrs Veronica Joo Lee*
Thrings and Long Solicitors, Midland Bridge,
Bath BA1 2HQ, Fax: 01225 448494.
Called: Nov 1994, Gray's Inn, LLB

Graham-Dixon *Anthony Philip* QC
(1973)
31 Hereford Square, London SW7 4NB,
0171 370 1902, Fax: 0171 373 5912.
Called: Feb 1956, Inner Temple, MA (Oxon)

Graham-Wells *Miss Alison Christine* •
Called: July 1992, Inner Temple

Grainger *John Andrew* •
Assistant Legal Adviser, Foreign &
Commonwealth Office, Legal Advisers, King
Charles Street, London SW1A 2AH.
Called: July 1981, Lincoln's Inn, BA
(Cantab), BA, BCL (Oxon)

Grange *Hugh* •
Legal Adviser, retired, c/o Legal Secretariat
to the, Law Officers, Attorney General's
Chambers, 9 Buckingham Gate, London
SW1E 6JP, and Member Northern Ireland
Bar. Called: Nov 1973, Gray's Inn, MA, LLB
(Dublin)

Grange-Bennett *Derek Francis Dupre*
VRD •
Legal Adviser, Glenburn, Insurance Brokers,
Oaks House, 16-22 West Street, Epsom,
Surrey KT18 7RQ, 01372 727271, Fax:
01372 747574. Called: June 1949, Inner
Temple, MA (Oxon)

Grant *Professor Alan*
Chair, First Nations Resources Negotiations
Ontario, Fraser Grant Associates, P O Box
275, Eureka, Nova Scotia Bok 1BO, 902-923-
2866, Fax: 902-923-2755, and Member
Ontario Bar. Called: Nov 1970, Inner
Temple, LLB (Lond)

Grant *Andrew*
J.P., White Lodge, Courtenay Avenue,
London N6 4LR, 0181 348 1555.
Called: Nov 1968, Inner Temple

Grant *Miss Angela Marie*
Called: Nov 1997, Lincoln's Inn, LLB
(Hons)(Dunelm)

Grant *Miss Berenice Anne*
Called: July 1990, Inner Temple, LLB
(Warw)

Grant *Ian Edward*
Called: May 1994, Middle Temple, LLB
(Hons)

Grant *James Alexander*
Spring Bank, Sutton Valence, Nr Maidstone,
Kent ME17 3BT. Called: Nov 1979, Inner
Temple, MA (Cantab), RIBA, FCIArb.

Grant *Miss Julie*
Called: Nov 1991, Middle Temple, BSc Hons
(Manch), MA, Dip Law

Grant-Whyte *Graham Denoon*
and Member South Africa. Called: July 1963,
Gray's Inn, MA, LLB (Cantab)

Grantham *David Adrian*
Called: Feb 1994, Gray's Inn, LLB (Lond)

Granville *Steven James*
Despacho Gil-Robles, Velazquez 3, Piso 2,
Madrid 28001, 435-8678/435 5377.
Called: Nov 1991, Gray's Inn, LLB (Leics)

Graves *Mrs Sheila May* •
Company Secretary, Urenco Limited, 18
Oxford Road, Marlow, Bucks SL7 2NL,
01628 486941, Fax: 01628 475867.
Called: July 1988, Inner Temple, LLB (Hons)

Gray *Angus John*
Muckamore Cottage, 53 West Farm Avenue,
Ashtead, Surrey KT21 2JZ. Called: Nov
1972, Gray's Inn, BSc, CChem, MRSC

Gray *Mrs Jennifer Jane*
2 Temple Gardens, Temple, London, EC4Y
9AY. Called: Nov 1988, Middle Temple, BA
(Manch), Dip Law (City)

Gray *Professor Kevin John*
Professor of Law, University of Cambridge.
Fellow of Trinity College, Cambridge,
Trinity College, Cambridge CB2 1TQ,
(0223) 338400, Fax: (0223) 338564.
Called: July 1993, Middle Temple, MA, Ph.D
& LL.D, (Cantab), DCL (Oxon)

Gray *Mark Julian*
Called: Nov 1996, Gray's Inn, B.Eng
(L'pool), B.Eng (L'pool)

Gray *Dr Peter*
76 The Street, Newnham, Nr Sittingbourne,
Kent ME9 0LL. Called: Oct 1992, Middle
Temple, B.Sc (St Andrews), Ch.B (Manch),
Diploma in Law, MRCGP

Gray *Lt Cdr Robert Stanley RN* •
SFLA FOSF, 2-6 The Parade, HM Naval Base,
Portsmouth, Hants PO1 3LR, 01705 726519,
Fax: 01705 726614. Called: Oct 1992,
Middle Temple, BSc (Econ)(Wales),
Common Professional, Examination

Grayson *Mrs Myra Wendy JP* •
p/t Chairman Social Security Disability
Appeal Tribunals, 3rd Floor Flat, 1 Brick
Court, Temple, London EC4Y 9BY, 0171
583 6207, Also Inn of Court Middle (1961)..
Called: Feb 1952, Gray's Inn, LLB

Grayson *Mrs Shamini Nainappan* •
Senior Crown Prosecutor. Called: Nov 1988,
Middle Temple, LLB (Leeds)

Grayson *Stephen Arthur* •
Senior Principal Legal Officer, DTI Solicitors
Office, INV L S (P), 10 Victoria Street,
London SW1H 0NN, 0171 215 3150, Fax:
0171 215 3235. Called: Nov 1990, Inner
Temple, BA

Grazebrook *Donald McDonald Dennis*
Durley
Honorary Life President International
Nuclear Law Association (AIDN/INLA).
Called: Feb 1952, Lincoln's Inn, LLB (Lond)

Greaves *David William*
Legal Counsel, SITA, 26 Chemin de Joinville,
1216 Cointrin, Geneva, 41.22.710.0112,
Fax: 41.22.710.0166. Called: Feb 1990,
Gray's Inn, LLB (So'ton)

Grech *Leslie Francis*
Villa Grech-Mifsud, Mosta, Malta MST O6,
432071 243946, Fax: 414458, and Member
Malta Bar. Called: June 1944, Gray's Inn

Grech *Miss Maria Penelope Christine*
Called: July 1996, Inner Temple, LLB
(Wolverhampton)

Green *Miss Amanda Jane*
Hunter & Hunter, Attorneys at Law, 3
Verulam Buildings, London, WC1R 5NT.
Called: Oct 1990, Middle Temple, BA
(Cantab)

Green *Andrew William Nightingale* •
Legal & Administration Director,
Amalgamated Metal Corporation plc, 55
Bishopsgate, London EC2N 3AH, 0171 626
4521, Fax: 0171 623 6015. Called: Feb 1960,
Gray's Inn

Green *Miss Carol Laura Nancy*
Called: Nov 1994, Lincoln's Inn, LLB
(Hons)(Bucks)

Green *Cyril*
44 High Haden Road, Cradley Heath, West
Midlands B64 7PJ, 0121 550 1099.
Called: Feb 1958, Middle Temple, LLB, FCIS

Green *David Michael* •
Legal Adviser, Guardian Royal Exchange, Services Limited, One Aldgate, London EC3N 1RE, 0171 369 3966, Fax: 0171 369 3981. Called: Nov 1987, Middle Temple, LLB (Hons)

Green *Jason Brian*
Advocates Collas Day & Rowland, Manor Place, St Peter Port, Guernsey GY1 4EW, 01481 723191, Fax: 01481 711880, and Member Guernsey Bar. Called: July 1996, Inner Temple, LLB (W.Eng)

Green *Mrs Karen Patricia*
Box 1460, Mendocino, CA 95460, U.S.A., 707 937 3960, Fax: 707 937 5861, and Member California, USA. Called: May 1990, Middle Temple, LLB (Cardiff)

Green *Mrs Miranda Odofuorkor*
Senior Court Clerk, Victoria Law Courts, Corporation Street, Birmingham, West Midlands B4 6QA, 0121 235 4798, Fax: 0121 236 7837. Called: Nov 1983, Gray's Inn, BA

Green *Robert Alan*
Court Clerk, Stevenage Court Office, Bayley House, Sish Lane, Old Town, Stevenage, 01438 730429. Called: Nov 1990, Gray's Inn, BSc (Econ) (Cardiff)

Greenald *Miss Miriam Ruth*
Called: Oct 1996, Inner Temple, LLB (Dunelm)

Greenald *Timothy Alexander* •
Lawyer, Which? Ltd, Castlemead, Gascoyne Way, Hertford X SG14 1LH, 01992 822 828. Called: Mar 1996, Middle Temple, LLB (Hons)

Greenberg *Daniel Isaac* •
Senior Assistant Parliamentary Counsel, Office of the Parliamentary, Counsel, 36 Whitehall, London SW1, 0171 210 3000. Called: July 1987, Lincoln's Inn, BA (Cantab)

Greene *Richard Joseph Eugene*
and Member Northern Ireland 1 Gray's Inn Square, Ground Floor, London, WC1R 5AA. Called: Nov 1990, Middle Temple, MA (Cantab)

Greenhalgh *Stephen John Edwin* •
Legal Team Leader, Personal Investment Authority, 1 Canada Square, Canary Wharf, London E14 5AZ, 0171 538 8860, Fax: 0171 418 9300. Called: July 1977, Inner Temple, LLB (London)

Greenhill *John William*
Justices' Clerk, Inner London Magistrates', Courts Service, 65 Romney Street, London SW1P 3RD. Called: Nov 1972, Middle Temple

Greenidge *Douglas Burton*
Attorney-at-Law, Barbados and the West Indies, Bonnetts, Brittons Hill, St Michael, Barbados, 4360001, and Member Barbados Bar Association. Called: Nov 1982, Gray's Inn, LLB (Lond)

Greenland *Mrs Sheridan Dawn*
Deputy Clerk to the Justices, Surrey Magistrates Court Comm, Chief Executive's Office, Court House, London Road, Dorking, Surrey RH4 1SX, 01306 885544, Fax: 01306 877447. Called: July 1982, Inner Temple, LLB

Greenrod *Mrs Barbara* •
Senior Solicitor, Hampshire County Council, The Castle, Winchester SO23 8UJ, 01962 847377. Called: Feb 1974, Inner Temple, LLB

Greensmith *David*
Clerk to the Justices, The Courthouse, P O Box 8, Town Meadows, Rochdale OL16 1AR, 01706 352442. Called: July 1981, Gray's Inn, BA, D.M.S, MIMgt, MIPD, MBA

Greenwood *Miss Fiona Caroline*
10 King's Bench Walk, Ground Floor, Temple, London, EC4Y 7EB. Called: Nov 1986, Gray's Inn, LLB, Dip in Law

Greenwood *Geoffrey William* •
Crown Prosecutor, Crown Prosecution Service, Heron House, Houghoumont Avenue, Crosby, Merseyside. Called: July 1979, Lincoln's Inn, BA (Nottm)

Greenwood *George Edward*
39 Bell Lane, London E1 7LU. Called: July 1973, Inner Temple, LLB

Greenwood *Mrs Sarah Elizabeth Ewule* •
Assistant Solicitor, West Lancashire District, Council, P O Box 16, 52 Derby Street, Ormskirk, Lancashire L39 2DF, 01695 585026, Fax: 01695 585082. Called: July 1975, Lincoln's Inn, BA (Hons)

Greeves *Miss Susan Patricia* •
Crown Prosecutor, Crown Prosecution Service, 4/5 South Parade, Wakefield WF1 1LR. Called: Oct 1990, Inner Temple, LLB

Gregory *Ms Ann Marie*
Called: Nov 1994, Middle Temple, LLB (Hons)

Gregory *Michael Anthony OBE*
Beam Ends, Dipley Common, Hartley Wintney, Hook, Hampshire RG27 8JS, 01252 842559, Fax: 01252 845698. Called: July 1952, Middle Temple, LLB

Gregory *Michael Raymond*
Called: Oct 1996, Middle Temple, BA (Hons)(Lond), CPE (Westminster)

Grenade-Nurse *Mrs Florabelle*
and Member Trinidad & Tobago. Called: July 1990, Lincoln's Inn, M.Phil (Lond), Dip, Law, LLM (Lond), LLB, (Lond), BSc (Econ)

Gretton *Ms Joanne Claire*
Called: Nov 1997, Inner Temple, LLB (Exon)

Grew *Miss Michelle Robyn* •
Director of Compliance, Lehman Brothers Limited, One Broadgate, London EC2M 7HA, 0171 379 2843. Called: Oct 1991, Middle Temple, LLB (Hons)

Grewal *Jarnel Singh*
66 Gunnersbury Avenue, Ealing, London W5 4HA. Called: Nov 1981, Gray's Inn, BA, ATII

Grey *John Egerton CB*
51 St Peter's Road, West Mersea, Colchester, Essex CO5 8LL, 01206 383007. Called: June 1954, Inner Temple, MA. BCL

Grey *The Hon Jolyon Kenneth Alnwick*
Consultant & p/t Adjudicator, Immigration Appeals, Messrs Sedgwick, Detert,, Moran & Arnold, 5 Lloyds Avenue, London EC3N 3AX, 0171 929 1829, Fax: 0171 929 1808. Called: Nov 1968, Inner Temple, MA (Cantab)

Grief *Professor Nicholas John*
Head of School of Finance & Law, Bournemouth University, Dorset House, Talbot Campus, Fern Barrow, Poole, Dorset BH12 5BB, 01202 524111, Fax: 01202 595261. Called: Mar 1996, Gray's Inn, BA, PhD (Kent)

Grier *Warren*
Court Clerk, Sunderland Magistrates Court, Gilbridge Avenue, Sunderland SR1 3AP, 0191 5141621, Fax: 0191 5658564. Called: Nov 1989, Inner Temple, LLB (Newc)

Grieve *(William) Percival QC (1962)*
Recorder, 32 Gunterstone Road, London W14 9BU, 0171 603 0376, Also Inn of Court I and Member Hong Kong Bar. Called: June 1938, Middle Temple, MA (Cantab)

Griffin *Miss Charlotte Louise*
Called: Oct 1995, Lincoln's Inn, BA (Hons), B.Arch (Manc), CPE (Manc)

Griffith *Edward QPM,*
Called: Feb 1965, Gray's Inn

Griffith *Gavan*
QC Australia, and Member Victoria Bar Essex Court Chambers, 24 Lincoln's Inn Fields, London, WC2A 3ED. Called: Nov 1969, Lincoln's Inn, LLB (Mel)

Griffiths *Bryn Lloyd*
Fleet Chambers, Mitre House, 44-46 Fleet Street, London, EC4Y 1BN. Called: Apr 1989, Inner Temple, LLB

Griffiths *David Huw*
Called: May 1997, Gray's Inn, LLB (Exon)

Griffiths *Miss Dawn Christine*
Associate, Conyers Dill & Pearman, Clarendon House, Church Street, Hamilton HM 11, (441) 295 1422, Fax: (441) 292 4720, and Member Bermuda Bar. Called: May 1995, Lincoln's Inn, LLB (Hons)

Griffiths *Mr Huw David*
Compliance Consultant, Flat 3, 26 Woodstock Road, Croydon, Surrey CR0 1JR, 0181 680 8614. Called: Nov 1992, Inner Temple, LLB

Griffiths *John Calvert CMG* QC (1972)
Recorder, Des Voeux Chambers, 10/F Bank
of East Asia Bldg, 10 Des Voeux Road
Central, 2526-3071, Fax: 2810-5287, and
Member Brunei Bars Hong Kong Bar Brick
Court Chambers, 15/19 Devereux Court,
London, WC2R 3JJ. Called: June 1956,
Middle Temple, MA (Cantab)

Griffiths *Jonathan Morris*
Compliance & Administration Director,
0171 724 0049. Called: July 1975, Middle
Temple, LLB(Lond)

Griffiths *Ms Judith*
Called: Nov 1995, Gray's Inn, LLB (Wales)

Griffiths *Mark Peter* •
Crown Prosecutor, Crown Prosecution
Service, Brunswick Court, Brunswick Street,
Oldham, Greater Manchester. Called: Nov
1986, Lincoln's Inn, LLB (Leeds)

Griffiths *Robert Norton* •
Senior Crown Prosecutor, Crown
Prosecution Service, First Floor, Oxford
House, Oxford Road, Bournemouth, Dorset
BH8 8HA, 01202 296917, Fax: 01202
556513. Called: July 1988, Middle Temple,
LLB (Hons) (Reading)

Griffiths *Robert Ray*
Called: Oct 1995, Lincoln's Inn, LLB
(Hons)(Leeds)

Griggs *Mrs Cecile Beatrice Jeanne*
Court Clerk, Croydon Magistrates' Court,
Barclay Road, Croydon, Surrey CR9 3NG,
0181 686 8680, Fax: 0181 680 9801.
Called: Nov 1988, Lincoln's Inn, BA
(Sydney), LLB (Lond), MA

Grimshaw *David* •
Senior Legal Adviser, Conoco (UK) Limited,
Park House, 116 Park Street, London
W1Y 4NN, 0171 408 6000, Fax: 0171 408
6466. Called: Nov 1975, Middle Temple, BA
(Cantab) MA, (Business Law)

Grimshaw *Gary Leo*
Called: Mar 1998, Inner Temple, LLB (Leeds)

Grindrod *Mark Adrian*
Called: July 1987, Lincoln's Inn, BA (Sussex)
Dip Law

Griswood *Miss Lisa Claire*
Healthcare Consultant, Hogg Robinson
Financial Services, 110 Fenchurch Street,
London EC3M 5JJ. Called: Oct 1995, Middle
Temple, LLB (Hons)

Grohs *Miss Sibylle Dietlinde* •
European Commission, Enviroment
Directorate (DGXI). Called: Feb 1993,
Middle Temple, LLB (Hons)(Lond)

Grose *Robert John*
Called: Apr 1991, Middle Temple, LLB
(Hons)

Gross *Richard Stephen*
Called: Oct 1992, Middle Temple, LL.B
(Hons)

Ground *The Hon Mr Justice Richard
William OBE*
Puisne Judge, Supreme Court of Bermuda,
c/o Supreme Court, 21 Parliament Street,
Hamilton HM12, 441 292 1350, Fax: 441
236 8183, QC Cayman Islands. Called: July
1975, Gray's Inn, BA (Oxon)

Grounds *Christopher Malcolm*
501 Man Yee Bldg, 60-68 Des Voeux Road,
Central, Hong Kong, and Member Hong
Kong Bar 1 Gray's Inn Square, Ground
Floor, London, WC1R 5AA. Called: Feb
1977, Inner Temple, LLB

Grove *John Alexander Richard*
2 Mitre Ct Bldgs, 2nd Floor, Temple,
London, EC4Y 7BX. Called: Nov 1963,
Lincoln's Inn

Grundy *Ms Stephanie Christine* •
Legal Advisor, H M Treasury, Parliament
Street, London SW1. Called: July 1983,
Middle Temple, MA, BCL

Gubbay *Mrs Joyce Bolissa*
Called: July 1972, Middle Temple, BA

Guch *Miss Karen Anne*
Shook Lin & Bok, 19th Floor, Arab-Malaysian
Building, Jalan Raja Chulan, 50200 Kuala
Lumpur, 00 603 2558596/20117888, Fax:
00 603 2555673. Called: Nov 1996,
Lincoln's Inn, LLB (Hons)(Lond), LLM
(Hons)(Cantab)

Guedes *Lawrence*
Legal Advisor (Computer Law/Commercial/
Corporate). Called: Oct 1992, Gray's Inn,
LLB, LLM

Guha Thakurta *Sujoy*
Called: Nov 1996, Middle Temple, LLB
(Hons)(Hull)

Gui *Ms Karen Phek-Inn*
Legal Assistant, Wong Meng Meng &
Partners, 80 Raffles Place, [H]58-01 UOB
Plaza, 65 5327488, Fax: 65 5325711, and
Member Singapore Bar. Called: July 1993,
Gray's Inn, LLB

Gul-Mohamed *Mohamed*
Peter Low tang & Partners, Advocates &
Solicitors, 15A Smith Street, 227 6206, Fax:
227 4861. Called: Nov 1995, Lincoln's Inn,
LLB (Hons)

Gulleford *Dr Kenneth Arnold*
Company Secretary Professional Solutions &
Services Ltd, 26 Wakelin Chase, Ingatestone,
Essex CM4 9HH, Formerly Senior Lecturer
in Law. Called: Nov 1991, Lincoln's Inn, LLB
(Hons) (Birm), PhD (Birm)

Gulliford *Jonathan Robert*
Called: Nov 1992, Middle Temple, LLB
(Hons), LLM

Gumbel *Rev Nicholas Glyn Paul*
Called: July 1977, Middle Temple, MA
(Cantab) MA(Oxon)

Gunasekera *Miss Kuda Liyanage Don
Manuja*
286 Bullers Road, Colombo 7, Sri Lanka,
716011. Called: Feb 1994, Lincoln's Inn, LLB
(Hons), LLM, Dip Business, Administration

Gunning *Alastair John Alan Bond*
and Member Bermuda Bar. Called: Nov
1961, Lincoln's Inn, MA (Oxon)

Gunning *James John MBE*
Alnor House, 23-25 The Green, Wye, Nr
Ashford, Kent TN25 5AJ, 01233 812 771,
Fax: 01233 812 771. Called: June 1956,
Inner Temple, MA

Gupta *Ms Rajita Sharma*
Denton Hall, 5 Chancery Lane, London
EC4A 1Bu, 0171 242 1212/320 6852, Fax:
0171 320 6068, Member of the Bombay Bar
Association and Member Indian Bar.
Called: July 1992, Inner Temple, BSc
(Bombay), LLB (Bombay), LLM (London)

Guttman *Professor Egon*
American University Washington US Dept of
State Advisory Com. on Private International
Law. American Law Institute. American Bar
Association. Federal Bar Association., 930
Clintwood Drive,, Silver Spring, Maryland,
20902, USA, 301 649 5739/202 274 4213,
Fax: 202 274 4130. Called: May 1952,
Middle Temple, LLM

Guy *Ian Leslie* •
Senior Lawyer, Legal Services Department,
Neath Port Talbot, County Borough Council,
Civic Centre, Port Talbot SA13 1PJ, 01639
763365, Fax: 01639 763370. Called: Nov
1988, Gray's Inn, BA (Hons), FRSA

Guzman *Miss Gillian Maria*
Attias & Levy, Suites 1 & 3, 3 Irish Place,
72150, Fax: 74986, and Member Gibraltar
Bar. Called: Nov 1994, Middle Temple, LLB
(Hons)(Wales)

Gwee *Boon Kim*
11 Lothian Terrace, Singapore 456784,
Republic of Singapore, 4424652, and
Member Singapore Bar. Called: July 1994,
Middle Temple, LLB (Hons)(L'pool)

Haberbeck *Andreas*
Abbas F.Ghazzawi Law Firm, P.O.Box 2335,
Jeddah 21451, 966 2 6654646, Fax: 966 2
6659155. Called: Nov 1981, Gray's Inn, LLB,
LLM

Hadik *Andrew John William Michael* •
Branch Crown Prosecutor, Crown
Prosecution Service, Camberwell Branch,
2nd Floor,The Cooperage, Gainsford Street,
London SE1 2NG, 0171 357 7010, Fax: 0171
962 0902. Called: Nov 1980, Middle
Temple, BA, MA (Lond)

Hadjimanoli *Miss Marina*
Lawyer, P O Box 1358, Limassol, 05-367535,
Fax: 05-372072, and Member Cyprus Bar.
Called: Nov 1995, Lincoln's Inn, LLB (Hons)

Hadjipetrou *Leonidas*
00-357-2-422166, and Member Cyprus Bar.
Called: Nov 1995, Lincoln's Inn, LLB (Hons),
LLM (Lond)

Hadjisimou *Miss Androulla Sotiris*
Called: Mar 1998, Inner Temple, LLB
(Keele)

Hadley *Richard Mark Andrew*
Called: Oct 1997, Gray's Inn, BA (Wolves)

Haffenden Mrs Rebekah Ruth ●
Principal Legal Officer, HM Customs &
Excise, New King's Beam House, 22 Upper
Ground, London SE1 9PJ. Called: July 1987,
Lincoln's Inn, LLB

Hagan Philip Ashley Thorpe ●
Crown Prosecutor, Crown Prosecution
Service, York Street, Leicester. Called: July
1975, Inner Temple, BA (Keele)

Hagenmeyer Moritz Wilhelm
4 Paper Bldgs, Ground Floor, Temple,
London, EC4Y 7EX. Called: July 1995, Inner
Temple, Doctorate in Law, (Hamburg), CPE
(City)

Hager Miss Sarah Jane
Called: July 1986, Gray's Inn, LLB

Haggis Robert Arthur ●
Director RV Chemicals Ltd, Company
Secretary HPG Industrial Coatings 4 R's
Limited - Chairman Company Secretary:
Kalle Nalo Limited. Hoechst International
Services HI Serv Limited, Hoechst UK
Limited, Hoechst House, Salisbury Road,
Hounslow, Middlesex TW4 6JH, 0181 754
3399, Fax: 0171 570 5809. Called: Nov
1980, Gray's Inn, BA Hons

Haigh John ●
Group Corporate Lawyer & Company
Secretary, Kalon Group Plc, Huddersfield
Road, Birstall, Batley, W Yorks WF17 9XA,
01924 477201, Fax: 01924 470950.
Called: Nov 1976, Lincoln's Inn, BA Hons

Hailes Ms Susan Dulcie Luisa
Called: Oct 1995, Inner Temple, MA
(Cantab), CPE

Haines Michael John
6 Priory Farm, Inner Road, St Clements,
Jersey JE2 6GP, 01534 854412. Called: July
1995, Gray's Inn, LLB

Haines William Michael
Old School House, Colwinston, Cowbridge,
Vale of Glamorgan CF71 7NL, 01656
654330. Called: Feb 1960, Gray's Inn, MA
(Oxon)

Hajamaideen Shamim Fyaz Bin
Called: July 1997, Middle Temple, LLB
(Hons)

Hajarnis Miss Aditi
Called: July 1995, Lincoln's Inn, LLB (Hons)

Haji Abdul Hamid Muhammad Zainidi
and Member Brunei Bar. Called: July 1996,
Lincoln's Inn, LLB (Hons)(Manch)

Haji Anuar Fathan
Legal Counsel, Attorney General's
Chambers, Ministry of Law, Bandar Seri
Begawan, Brunei 2690, (6732) 244872, Fax:
(6732) 223100. Called: July 1995, Lincoln's
Inn, LLB (Hons)

Haji Ismail Miss Norismizan
Called: Nov 1996, Lincoln's Inn, LLB (Hons)

Haji Mohammed Miss Mazlin Haslinda
Called: Nov 1995, Lincoln's Inn, LLB (Hons)

Haji Sahlan Miss Shahida
Called: Nov 1995, Lincoln's Inn, LLB (Hons)

Hajjar Miss Fountoun Taj
Legal Advisor, Sookias & Sookias Sol, 3rd
Floor, Clarebell House, 6 Cork Street,
London W1X 1PB, 0171 465 8000, Fax:
0171 465 8001. Called: Nov 1993, Inner
Temple, BA (Washington), BA (Cantab)

Hakimi Miss Hasrina
Called: Oct 1997, Gray's Inn, LLB (Notts)

Haldane Mrs Sally Anne ●
Principal Crown Prosecutor, Crown
Prosecution Service, St Georges House,
Lever Street, Wolverhampton, 01902 870900,
Fax: 01902 352017, Also Inn of Court L.
Called: July 1983, Inner Temple, BA (Hons)

Hale Miss Catherine Margaret
Called: Feb 1995, Middle Temple, LLB
(Hons)(Warws)

Hales Christopher James ●
Lawyer Grade 7, Treasury Solicitor's, Queen
Anne's Chambers, 28 Broadway, London
SW1H 9JS, 0171 210 3000, Fax: 0171 222
6006. Called: Nov 1979, Gray's Inn, BA

Halhead Thomas Edmund
Called: Nov 1960, Lincoln's Inn

Hall Amory Jocelyn Arnold ●
Legal Advisor, Huddersfield Magistrates
Court, Justice Clerks Office, The Court
House, P.O.Box B37, Civic Centre,
Huddersfield HD1 2NH, 01 484 423552.
Called: Nov 1992, Inner Temple, LLB
(Lancs)

Hall Edmund Charles Douglas ●
Crown Prosecution Service, Highbury
Branch, 1-9 Romford Road, Stratford,
London, 0181 534 6601. Called: Oct 1993,
Middle Temple, BA (Hons)(Newc), CPE
(City)

Hall Eric Michael ●
Principal Crown Prosecutor Prosecution
Team Leader, Crown Prosecution Service,
Marlborough St Section, 2nd Floor, Portland
House, Stag Place, Victoria, London
SW1E 5BH, 0171 915 5821. Called: Nov
1986, Lincoln's Inn, Dip Mag Law

Hall mrs Lorraine Mary
Senior Court Clerk, Mansfield Magistrates
Court, Rosemary Street, Mansfield,
Nottinghamshire NG19 6EE, 01623 451500,
Fax: 01623 451648. Called: Feb 1988, Gray's
Inn, Diploma in Magister-, ial Law, Diploma
Law

Hall Miss Margaret Anne
Called: July 1982, Inner Temple, BA

Hall Mark Kevin ●
Called: Nov 1990, Lincoln's Inn, LLB (Hons),
BCL

Hall Matthew Ronald Vickery
Called: Oct 1990, Middle Temple, BA
(Oxon)

Hall Mrs Rosemary
Called: June 1964, Inner Temple

Hall Stephen ●
Called: July 1983, Lincoln's Inn, BA(Cardiff)

Hall Miss Victoria Jayne
Called: Mar 1996, Gray's Inn, LLB (Leeds)

Hall-Jones Stephen David ●
Called: July 1973, Middle Temple, LLB
(Hons) (Manch)

Hall-Paterson Wayne
Called: Mar 1998, Gray's Inn, LLB

Hallam Nigel Edwin
Clerk to the Justices, Derby and Soith
Derbyshire, Magistrates Court, The Court
House, Derwent Street, Derby DE1 2EP,
01332 292 100, Fax: 01332 293 459.
Called: July 1987, Gray's Inn, Diploma
Magistrate's, Court Law, DMS, MIMgt, MCI
NVQ Level, 5 in Senior Mgmnt

Hallam Mrs Susan ●
Part-time Court Clerk, Bolton Magistrates',
Courts Committee, PO Box 24, Civic
Centre, Bolton BL1 1QX, 01204 522244,
Fax: 01204 364373. Called: Feb 1987,
Lincoln's Inn, Dip M Law, (Manchester)

Halliday Christopher Martin Jonathan
Called: Nov 1997, Gray's Inn, LLB, LLM
(Nott'm)

Halliday David Ross
Called: Mar 1996, Inner Temple, LLB
(Wolverhampton)

Halliday Ian Nicolas ●
Senior Crown Prosecutor, Crown
Prosecution Service, Fox Talbot House,
Bellinger Close, Chippenham, Wilts.
Called: Nov 1989, Lincoln's Inn, LLB (Leeds)

Halloran Ms Catherine Mary
Called: Nov 1996, Lincoln's Inn, LLB
(Hons)(Lancs)

Halpern Leonard Isaac
Linwood, Warren Rd, Fairlight, Hastings, E
Sussex TN35 4AN, 01424 813424.
Called: Apr 1947, Middle Temple, LLB
(Lond)

Ham Nicholas Treharne
Called: Oct 1997, Middle Temple, BA
(Hons)(Bris)

Hambley Ms Elizabeth ●
Treasury Solicitor, Queen Anne's Chambers,
28 Broadway, London SW1H 9JS, 0171 210
3000. Called: Nov 1992, Inner Temple, LLB
(Warw)

Hamblin Miss Susan Caroline ●
Senior Publishing Editor, John Wiley & Sons
LTD, 42 Leinster Gardens, London W2 3AN,
0171 298 3832, Fax: 0171 262 5093.
Called: Nov 1990, Lincoln's Inn, LLB (Wales)

Hambly Hedley Maurice
Called: Nov 1960, Gray's Inn

Hambrook Ronald Vivian
136 Waxwell Lane, Pinner, Middlesex
HA5 3ES, Also Member of M. Called: Nov
1953, Gray's Inn, LLB, DGA

Hamed Joseph Mohamed Joseph
1 Crown Office Row, Ground Floor,
Temple, London, EC4Y 7HH. Called: July
1982, Middle Temple, LLB (Lond), BA

Hamid Miss Simea
Called: Nov 1997, Lincoln's Inn, LLB (HOns)

Hamill *Miss Elaine* •
Called: July 1979, Gray's Inn, LLB (L'pool), A.C.I.B

Hamill *Michael Garvin* •
Senior Legal Adviser, Deutsche Morgan Grenfell, 133 Houndsditch, London EC3A 7DX, 0171 545 4061. Called: Nov 1989, Inner Temple, LLB (Hons)

Hamilton *James Frederick Hume EDS, CBE*
Acting Chairman,Kenya Law Reform Commission, Kenya Law Reform Commission, Maendeleo House, 8th Floor, Monrovia Street,, PO Box 34999, Nairobi Kenya, Nairobi 220888/9, and Member Kenya Bar. Called: Jan 1938, Gray's Inn, MA (Cantab)

Hamilton *Miss Laura*
Slaughter & May, 35 Basinghall Street, London EC2V 5DB, 0171 600 1200. Called: Nov 1987, Lincoln's Inn, BA (Lond) Dip Law, (City)

Hamilton *Patrick Joseph Martin*
Clerk to the Justices Justices Chief Executive, Uxbridge Magistrates Court, The Court House, Harefield Road, Uxbridge, Middlesex UB8 1PQ, 01895 208401, Fax: 01895 274280. Called: July 1980, Gray's Inn, MA (Oxon)

Hamilton *Mrs Penelope Ann*
Chartered Tax Adviser Partner, VAT Division, Coopers & Lybrand, 1 Embankment Place, London WC2N 6NN, 0171 213 5895, Fax: 0171 213 4607. Called: July 1972, Gray's Inn, LLB (Hons) (Bristol), FTII

Hamilton *Simon Austin*
Called: Oct 1992, Lincoln's Inn, BA(Hons), LLM

Hamilton Sugden *Miss Meredith Theresa* •
Managing Director, Hamilton Advisory Services Ltd, 7th Floor, Sir John Moores' Building, 100 Old Hall Street, Liverpool L3 9QJ, 0151 236 0510, Fax: 0151 255 0675. Called: Nov 1969, Gray's Inn

Hamilton-Kane *Nicholas John*
Legal Adviser, Hong Kong & Shanghai Banking, Corporation Limited, 1 Queen's Road Central. Called: July 1985, Inner Temple, LLB (Bristol)

Hamilton-White *Miss Jane Elizabeth* •
Senior Crown Prosecutor, Crown Prosecution Service, Hawkins House, Pynes Hill, Rydon Lane, Exeter, Devon EX2 5SS, 01392 422555, Fax: 01392 422111. Called: Nov 1990, Inner Temple, BA (Queensland), BA Law (Hons)

Hamlyn Williams *Philip Leslie Anstee* •
Diocesan Secretary, The Lincoln Diocesan Trust and, Board of Finance Ltd, The Old Palace, Lincoln LN2 1PU, 01522 529241, Fax: 01522 512717. Called: Apr 1978, Lincoln's Inn, FCA, ATII

Hamm *Roderick Norman Lewis*
p/t Chairman: Lancashire Valuation Tribunal. Called: Feb 1954, Lincoln's Inn, MA

Hammersley *Bryan James* •
Treasury Solicitor, Treasury Solicitor's Dept, Dept of Transport Outstation, 2 Marsham Street, London SW1, 0171 276 3799. Called: June 1970, Middle Temple

Hammerton *Ms Gillian Margaret Felicity*
1 Pump Court, Lower Ground Floor, Temple, London, EC4Y 7AB. Called: Nov 1973, Gray's Inn, BSc,LLB

Hammond *Michael John* •
Senior Crown Prosecutor, Crown Prosecution Service, 50 Ludgate Hill, London EC4M 7EX. Called: Oct 1991, Inner Temple, BSc, CPE

Hammond *Miss Tracey Ann*
Deputy Chief Clerk, Inner London Magistrates, Courts Service, SW Magistrates' Court, Lavender Hill, London SW11. Called: Feb 1989, Gray's Inn, LLB (Lond)

Hamon *Francis Charles*
Deputy Bailiff Royal Court of Jersey, La Maison Du Sud, Rue De La Piece Mauger, Trinity, Jersey, 01534 863199. Called: Nov 1966, Middle Temple

Hamon *Kenneth George*
Woodside, Shinfield Roadn, Shinfield, Reading, Berks RG2 9BE. Called: July 1972, Gray's Inn

Hampshire *Mrs Ann Christine* •
Principal Crown Prosecutor, Crown Prosecution Service, Hawkins House, Pynes Hill, Rydon Lane, Exeter, Devon EX2 5SS, 01392 422555, Fax: 01392 422111. Called: Nov 1983, Gray's Inn, LLB (Sheff)

Hampson *Miss Francoise Jane*
Called: Nov 1996, Lincoln's Inn, LLB (Hons)

Hampson *Graham William*
c/o Quin & Hampson, Barristers & Attorneys at Law, PO Box 1348 Georgetown, Grand Cayman, Cayman Islands, 809 9494123, Fax: 809 9494647, Former solicitor and Member Cayman Islands Bar. Called: Feb 1992, Middle Temple, LLB (Hon) (Notts)

Hampson *Michael David* •
Company Secretary, RMC Group plc, RMC House, Coldharbour Lane, Thorpe, Egham, Surry TW20 8TD, 01932 568833, Fax: 01932 568933. Called: July 1985, Middle Temple, LLB (Cardiff)

Hampson *Rodney*
Clerk to the Justices, Sefton Magistrates, Courts Committee, The Law Courts, Albert Road, Southport PR9 0LJ, 01704 534141, Fax: 01704 500226. Called: Nov 1982, Gray's Inn, LLB (Lond)

Hampton *Gordon ED*
P O Box 19, Pebble Beach, California, 408 625 1876, Fax: 408 625 1876, Former Solicitor and Member Hong Kong Bar. Called: July 1985, Middle Temple, BL (St Andrews)

Hampton *John*
Recorder, 37 Park Square, Leeds, LS1 2NY. Called: July 1952, Inner Temple, LLB

Hamzah *Miss Hazleena*
Called: Nov 1996, Lincoln's Inn, LLB (Hons)(Bris)

Hamzah *Miss Nor Raviah Adliza*
Called: Oct 1996, Lincoln's Inn, LLB (Hons)

Han *Miss Chin June*
Called: Mar 1997, Lincoln's Inn, BSc (Hons), CPE

Han *Miss Chin May*
Called: July 1996, Lincoln's Inn, LLB (Hons)(Sheff)

Han *Hean Juan*
Called: July 1996, Inner Temple, LLB (Lond)

Han *Teck Kwong*
Called: July 1995, Middle Temple, LLB (Hons)

Hanam *Andrew John*
Blk 350, Woodlands Ave 3, 11-99. Called: Nov 1996, Middle Temple, LLB (Hons)

Hancox *Chief Justice (Retd) Alan Robin Winston CBE, EGH*
Attorney General of St Helena and it's Dependencies, Government of St Helena, Legal & Lands Department, Essex House, Jamestown, 00 290 2270, Fax: 00 290 2454, Fellow Chartered Institute of Arbitrators Formerly a Solicitor and Member Kenya. Called: July 1954, Gray's Inn

Handmaker *Jeffrey David*
Lawyers for Human Rights, 730 Van Erkom Bldg, 217 Pretorius St, Pretoria 0002, +27 12 21 21 35, Fax: +27 12 32 56 318. Called: July 1995, Inner Temple, LLB (Newc), LLM (Lond)

Hands *Mrs Maryvonne Edith*
Tax Consultant General Commissioner of Taxation, Browne Jacobson, 44 Castle Gate, Nottingham NG1 6EA, 0115 9500055, Fax: 0115 9475246. Called: July 1974, Inner Temple, MA (Oxon), ATII

Hangchi *Kevin*
Called: July 1997, Middle Temple, BSc (Hons)

Hankers *Miss Julia Anne*
Principal Legal Advisor, Bedfordshire Magistrates Court, The Court House, Stuart Street, Luton, Beds LU1 5BL, 01582 402333, Fax: 01582 24852. Called: Jan 1985, Gray's Inn

Hanlon *Keith George*
33 Bedford Row, London, WC1R 4JH. Called: Nov 1979, Gray's Inn, LLB, MSc, BSc, F.I.Mech.E, FIEE,C.Eng, A.C.I.Arb

Hanna *Ms Elizabeth Colette* •
Called: Feb 1994, Lincoln's Inn, LLB (Hons)

Hannibal *Martin Charles* •
School of Law, Staffordshire University,
College Road, Stoke on Trent ST4 2DE,
01782 573407, Fax: 01782 294335.
Called: May 1988, Lincoln's Inn, BA (Hons),
LLM

Hanratty *Miss Judith Christine* •
Company Secretary, The British Petroleum
Company PLC, The British Petroleum Co
plc, Britannic House, 1 Finsbury Circus,
London EC2M 7BA, 0171 496 4244, Fax:
0171 496 4678, and Member Victoria Bar
New Zealand Bar. Called: Feb 1987, Inner
Temple, LLB, LLM

Hanson *Derrick George*
Bridgend, Deepdale Bridge, Patterdale,
Cumbria CA11 ONS, 017684 82345.
Called: July 1952, Lincoln's Inn, LLM, FCIB

Hanson *Ian Lawrence* •
Executive Vice President, EMI Records
Limited, 43 Brook Green, London W6 7EF,
0171 605 5407, Fax: 0171 605 5069.
Called: Feb 1989, Inner Temple, LLB, MBA

Hanson *Robert Edward*
Called: Oct 1996, Lincoln's Inn, BA
(Hons)(Hudders)

Happe *Dominic Peter Alexander*
Called: Nov 1993, Gray's Inn, BA

Happold *Matthew Charles Edmund*
Called: Nov 1995, Middle Temple, BA
(Hons), MSc, MA (Oxon)

Haq *Miss Tasneem Rehana*
Called: Nov 1996, Middle Temple, BA
(Hons)(Kecle)

Haque *Md Nizamul*
Legal Adviser, 4 Carpenter House, Burgess
Street, London E14 7BB, 0171 515 0400/
0181 640 3331/0181 543 3111, Fax: 0181
543 0033, and Member Bangladesh Bar.
Called: Mar 1997, Lincoln's Inn, LLB
(Hons)(Dhaka), LLB (Hons), LLM, (Lond)

Haque *Mohammed Azharul*
Called: May 1997, Inner Temple, B.Com
(Bangladesh), LLB (Lond)

Haque *Muhammed Luthful*
Called: Oct 1997, Lincoln's Inn, BA (Hons)

Harben *Paul Ralph*
Jersey Solicitor, Crill Canavan, La Chasse
Chambers, La Chasse, St Helier, Channel
Islands, 0534 888933, Fax: 0534 887040.
Called: Oct 1993, Middle Temple, LLB
(Hons)(Kingston)

Harbert *Ms Anna Katherine* •
Legal Adviser, Imperial Chemical Industries,
Plc, Wexham Road, Slough, Berks, 01753
877338. Called: July 1980, Inner Temple, BA
(Hons), Diploma in, Intellectural, Property
Law

Hardcastle *Ian Martin*
01604 470161. Called: Nov 1995, Gray's
Inn, LLB (Leeds), LLM, (Lond), MBA,
(Bradford)

Harden *Brian George*
14 Badger's Meadow, Pwllmeyric,
Chepstow, Gwent NP6 6UE. Called: Nov
1966, Inner Temple, BSc (Bris)

Harding *Edward James*
Clerk to the Justices, Gwent Magistrates
Court, 2nd Floor, Gwent House, Gwent
Square, Cwnbran, Gwent NP44 1PL, 01633
862112, Fax: 01633 868944. Called: Nov
1984, Middle Temple, Dip Law

Harding *Geoffrey Nathaniel Augustine
A*
Called: July 1994, Lincoln's Inn, BA (Hons)

Harding *Kenneth*
01423 886380. Called: Nov 1970, Gray's Inn

Harding *Malvin Adebayo Julian*
Legal Consultant, Harding & Co, Legal
Consultants, South Bank House, Black
Prince Road, London SE1 7SJ, 0171 582
9708/735 8171, Fax: 0171 735 1555.
Called: Oct 1990, Middle Temple, LLB
(Hons) (Lond), BSc (Econ) (Hons)

Harding *Miss Patricia Yvette*
Hodges Chambers, The Valley, P.O.Box 840,
Anguilla, 264 497 3793, Fax: 264 497 2863,
and Member Anguilla Bar (Eastern
Caribbean States). Called: July 1980, Middle
Temple, BA

Hardman *Miss Eryl Wendy*
Called: Oct 1997, Middle Temple, LLB
(Hons)(B'ham)

Hardwick *Malcolm Rodger QC*
QC NSW & ACT Bar and Member Barrister
and Solicitor for Supreme Ct Papua New
Guinea. Called: Nov 1950, Inner Temple,
MA (Oxon)

Hardy *Benedict*
Called: Oct 1995, Inner Temple, BA (Keele),
MA (Bris)

Hardy *David Peter*
Deputy Chief Clerk, Clerkenwell Magistrates
Court, 78 King's Cross Road, London
WC1X 5QS, 0171 278 6571, Fax: 0171 633
3662. Called: Nov 1987, Gray's Inn

Hardy *Richard Evelyn Whittelle*
Japonica Cottage, 205 Stanley Road,
Twickenham TW2 5NW, 0181 977 5611.
Called: July 1974, Inner Temple, BA, MSc
(Lond), FCA, MBA

Hardyman *Matthew James*
Called: Oct 1997, Lincoln's Inn, BA
(Hons)(Brunel)

Hare *Ivan Charles*
Fellow & Director of Studies in Law, Trinity
College, Cambridge CB2 1TQ, 01223
338420, Fax: 01223 338564. Called: Oct
1991, Gray's Inn, LLB (Lond), BCL (Oxon),
LLM (Harvard), MA (Cantab)

Harffey *Robert*
120A Abbeville Road, London SW4 9LU,
0831 728245. Called: Nov 1986, Middle
Temple, BA

Harington *Sir Nicholas John Bt* •
Legal Adviser ECGD, ECGD, 2 Exchange
Tower, Harbour Exchange Square, London
E14 9GS, 0171 512 7862, Fax: 0171 572
7052. Called: July 1969, Inner Temple, MA
(Oxon)

Hariri *Arham Rahimy*
Called: Nov 1997, Lincoln's Inn, LLB
(Hons)(L'pool)

Harkins *Mrs Sheila*
Called: Nov 1995, Lincoln's Inn, LLB
(Hons)(Wales)

Harley *David William* •
Senior Crown Prosecutor, Crown
Prosecution Service, Seaton House, 62
Wellington Street, Stockport, Cheshire.
Called: July 1988, Middle Temple, LLB
(Hons)

Harling *Peter John*
Clerk to the Justices, Lancashire Magistrates
Courts, Commitee, Penine Magistrates
Courts, P O Box 64, Burnley BB10 2NQ,
01282 610032, Fax: 01282 610034.
Called: July 1980, Gray's Inn, Dip Law

Harling *Russell James* •
Thomas R Miller & Sons, International
House, Creechurch Lane, London
EC3A 5BA, 0171 283 4646. Called: Apr
1991, Gray's Inn, BA (Oxford)

Harlow *Mrs Irma Sylvia*
Called: Nov 1971, Lincoln's Inn, BA, Dip
Ed(Leeds)

Harlow *Mrs Nirmala*
Called: Nov 1974, Lincoln's Inn

Harman *Andrew Michael* •
Casework Lawyer, Crown Prosecution
Service, 50 Ludgate Hill, London EC4, 0171
273 1230, Fax: 0171 329 8171. Called: July
1983, Gray's Inn, BA

Harman *Lady Katherine Frances
Goddard*
Called: July 1960, Inner Temple

Harmer *Donald Leonard*
Called: Nov 1979, Lincoln's Inn, Dip Arch
(Leics), RIBA

Harmes *Stephen Douglas* •
Senior Crown Prosecutor, CPS Cardiff, Pearl
Assurance House, Greyfriars Road, Cardiff
CF1 3PL, 01222 378201 Ext 168, Fax: 01222
373596. Called: Oct 1993, Gray's Inn, B.Sc
(Econ, Wales)

Harms *Anthony David*
Called: Nov 1997, Middle Temple, BA
(Hons)(Manch), LLB (Hons)(City)

Harold *Miss Caroline Grace* •
Lawyer, The Office of the Solicitor, Dept of
Social Security, London South Area Lawyers,
Office, Sutherland House, 29-37 Brighton
Road, Sutton SM2 5AN, 0181 652 6500.
Called: July 1993, Inner Temple, LLB

Haron *Miss Hidayati*
Called: Nov 1997, Lincoln's Inn, LLB (Hons)

Haron *Miss Maria*
Called: July 1994, Lincoln's Inn, LLB (Hons)

Haron Kamar *Miss Haslinda*
Managing Director, and Member Malaysia.
Called: July 1996, Lincoln's Inn, LLB
(Hons)(Notts)

Harper *Mrs Belinda Margaret*
Trainee Recruitment Consultant. Called: Oct
1993, Lincoln's Inn, BSc (Hons)(Leeds),
Zoology, Dip Law, (B'ham)

Harper *John Charles VRD*
Also Inn of Court L. Called: Nov 1946, Inner
Temple, LLB (Lond)

Harper *Miss Lisa-Jane*
Called: Oct 1996, Lincoln's Inn, BSc
(Hons)(St Andr), Dip in Law (City)

Harper *Mrs Sandra Elizabeth Lillian*
Called: July 1985, Middle Temple, BA
(Soton)

Harper *Mrs Vivian* •
Senior Crown Prosecutor, Crown
Prosecution Service, 1st Floor, Coniston
House, District 4, Washington, Tyne & Wear
NE38 7RN. Called: Oct 1990, Gray's Inn, BA

Harraj *Mohammad Raza Hayat*
Called: Nov 1995, Lincoln's Inn, BA (Hons),
LLB (Hons) (Leics)

Harre *Mr Justice George Elliott*
Chief Justice, Grand Court, P.O. Box 495,
George Town, Grand Cayman, (345) 949
4296, Fax: (345) 949-1049. Called: Feb
1954, Middle Temple, MA

Harries *Miss Janet Mary*
Principal Court Clerk, Magistrates Court,
Fitzalan Place, Cardiff, South Glamorgan
CF2 1RZ, 01222 463040, Fax: 01222
460264. Called: July 1978, Gray's Inn, LLB
(Hons), MBA

Harrigan *Patrick Bernard*
Employee Relations Consultant, School
Croft, off Church Lane, ADEL, Leeds
LS16 8DE. Called: Nov 1982, Gray's Inn, LLB

Harrington *Mrs Elaine* •
Legal Advisor, Sema Group UK Limited,
3300 Solihull Parkway, Birmingham Business
Park, Birmingham B37 7TQ, 0121 627 5500,
Fax: 0121 627 5313. Called: Nov 1996,
Gray's Inn, LLB, ACIS

Harrington *Joseph Francis*
Called: Nov 1997, Inner Temple, BA
(Cantab)

Harris *Mrs Alyson* •
Senior Crown Prosecutor, Crown
Prosecution Service, Froomsgate House,
Rupert Street, Bristol, Avon BS1 2PS, 0117
9273093, and Member Hong Kong Bar.
Called: July 1979, Middle Temple, LLB
(B'ham)

Harris *Colin*
3 St Leonards Terrace, London SW3 4QA,
0171 730 8746, Fax: 0171 824 8320.
Called: June 1956, Inner Temple, MA
(Cantab)

Harris *Daniel Alexander*
and Member Cayman Islands. Called: Oct
1995, Lincoln's Inn, LLB (Hons)(Sussex)

Harris *David*
Called: Oct 1997, Lincoln's Inn, BSc
(Hons)(Lond)

Harris *Miss Elizabeth Mary*
Called: Mar 1996, Inner Temple, LLB

Harris *Graham Anthony*
Crown Prosecutor Hong Kong 7 Stone
Bldgs, 1st Floor, Lincoln's Inn, London,
WC2A 3SZ. Called: Nov 1975, Middle
Temple, LLB

Harris *John David* •
Senior Crown Prosecutor, Crown
Prosecution Service, Provincial House, 140
Victoria Street, Grimsby. Called: Nov 1981,
Inner Temple, LLB

Harris *Martin John*
Legal Advisor, Essex Magistrates' Court
Cmtte, The Court House, Victoria Avenue,
Southend on Sea, Essex SS2 6EU, 01702
348491. Called: July 1984, Lincoln's Inn, BA

Harris *Michael Joseph George*
Formerly a Solicitor. Called: July 1970,
Middle Temple, MA (Oxon)

Harris *Neil Charles* •
Head of Legal Affairs Company Secretary,
Shire Pharmaceuticals Group, plc,, East
Anton, Andover, Hants SP1D 5RG, 01264
333455, Fax: 01264 334657. Called: July
1984, Middle Temple, BA (Hons)

Harris *Professor Neville Stuart*
Professor of Law, School of Law, Liverpool
John Moores, University, Liverpool, 0151
231 2000, Fax: 0151 231 3935. Called: Feb
1993, Gray's Inn, LLB, LLM, Ph.D (Sheff)

Harris *Paul*
1 Gray's Inn Square, 1st Floor, London,
WC1R 5AG. Called: Feb 1976, Lincoln's Inn,
MA Hons [Oxon]

Harris *Peter Graham* •
Head of Family Law & Procedure Division,
Lord Chancellor's Department, Trevelyan
House, Great Peter Street, London SW1.
Called: Nov 1973, Inner Temple

Harris *Peter Michael* •
Official Solicitor to the Supreme Court, The
Official Solicitor, 81 Chancery Lane, London
WC2A 1DD, 0171 911 7116, Fax: 0171 911
7105. Called: Nov 1971, Gray's Inn

Harris *Rupert William* •
Steamship Mutual Underwriting, Association
Limited, 39 Bell Lane, Aquatical House,
London E1 7LU, 0171 247 5490 Ext 463,
Fax: 0171 377 2912. Called: Oct 1993,
Lincoln's Inn, LLB (Hons)(Bris)

Harris *Miss Sally Fiona* •
Principal Legal Officer, Office of the
Solicitor, Dept of Social Security, Dept, of
Health, 48 Carey Street, London WC2A 2LS,
0171 412 1262, Fax: 0171 412 1499.
Called: July 1986, Inner Temple, LLB (Hull)

Harris *William Barclay QC (1961)*
Moatlands, Vowels Lane, East Grinstead,
Sussex RH19 4LL, 01342 810 228.
Called: Jan 1937, Inner Temple, MA
(Cantab)

Harrison *Mrs Angela Marjorie*
South Lawn, Eastcote High Rd, Pinner,
Middx HA5 2HJ, 0181 866 5416.
Called: Nov 1961, Gray's Inn

Harrison *Ms Anne Denise* •
Advisory Counsel, Environment Agency,
King's Meadow House, King's Meadow
Road, Reading RG1 8DQ, 0118 953 5000,
Fax: 0118 950 9440. Called: May 1992,
Inner Temple, LLB

Harrison *Carl Matthew*
Called: Nov 1997, Gray's Inn, LLB (Wales)

Harrison *Mrs Caroline Anne* •
Court Clerk, Norwich Magistrates Court,
Bishopsgate, Norwich NR3 1UP, 01603
632421, Fax: 01603 663263. Called: Oct
1992, Lincoln's Inn, LLB(Hons)

Harrison *Christopher Robert* •
Lawyer, Ministry of Agriculture,, Fisheries
and Food, 55 Whitehall, London SW1A 2EY,
0171 270 8312. Called: July 1975, Middle
Temple, LLB (Hons)

Harrison *Clive Osler*
Called: Mar 1997, Inner Temple, LLB
(Wales)

Harrison *Gordon William*
Called: Oct 1996, Inner Temple, LLB
(Reading)

Harrison *Dr Graeme*
Called: Mar 1997, Inner Temple, MA
(Oxon), DPhil (Oxon)

Harrison *Mrs Hazel Kathleen* •
Lawyer, Ministry of Agriculture,, Fisheries
and Food, 55 Whitehall, London SW1A 2EY,
0171 270 8337. Called: July 1981, Lincoln's
Inn, LLB (Hons)

Harrison *Miss Jane Emily*
Called: Nov 1996, Inner Temple, BSc
(L'pool)

Harrison *Michael John* •
Assistant Legal Advisor, Ministry of Defence,
Room 0182, Main Building, White Hall,
London SW1A 2HB, 0171 218 1933.
Called: Oct 1994, Middle Temple, MA
(Hons)(Cantab)

Harrison *Neil Richard*
Called: Nov 1997, Lincoln's Inn, LLB
(Hons)(Leics)

Harrison *Nigel Jeffrey* •
Crown Prosecutor, Crown Prosecution
Service, 2nd Floor, Calder House, St James
Street, Burnley, Lancashire BB11 1XG.
Called: Nov 1985, Gray's Inn, LLB(Sheffield)

Harrison *Robert*
Called: Nov 1995, Inner Temple, LLB
(L'Pool)

Harrison *Mrs Rosalynde Victoria* •
Assistant Corporate Counsel, Gillette
Management Inc, Great West Road,
Isleworth, Middlesex TW7 5NP, 0181 560
1234, Fax: 0181 568 4082. Called: July
1981, Middle Temple, BA

Harrison *Rupert Knight*
12 Clarendon Road, London W11 3AB, 0171
452 2861. Called: July 1982, Middle Temple,
LLB (Lond), LLM (Lond)

Harrison *Mrs Teresa Frances Helen* •
Assistant Solicitor, Town Hall, The
Burroughs, Hendon, London NW4 4BG, Fax:
0181 359 2680. Called: Nov 1992, Middle
Temple, LLB (Hons)

Harrison *Trevor Kenneth* •
Group Legal Adviser, Tramp Group Ltd,
Wells House, 15-17 Elmfield Road, Bromley,
Kent BR1 1LT, 0181 290 6722, Fax: 0181
464 7508. Called: July 1978, Inner Temple,
LLB

Harrison-Hall *Rupert Andrew James*
44a Hazelbourne Road, London SW12 9NS,
0181 675 6648. Called: Oct 1991, Inner
Temple, LLB (Bucks), Dip Agriculture,
(MRAC)

Harrold *Nicholas James*
Called: Mar 1998, Lincoln's Inn, LLB
(Hons)(Leics)

Harsham *Joseph Amin*
Dep Chief Clerk to the Justices, 3 Briar
Road, Pollards Hill, Norbury, London
SW16 4LT, 0171 703 0909/0181 764 5480,
Fax: 0171 708 3318, and Member Guyana
Bar. Called: July 1969, Inner Temple, LLB
Lond, MBIM

Harshaw *Paul Andrew*
Suite 349, 48 Par-la-Ville Road, Hamilton HM
11. Called: May 1997, Lincoln's Inn, LLB
(Hons)

Hart *Miss Jane Elizabeth Sarah*
Called: Nov 1995, Inner Temple, BA, CPE

Hart *John Richard Samuel TD*
Townsend Farm House, Over Wallop,
Stockbridge, Hampshire SO20 8HU, 01264
782 227, Fax: 01264 782 379. Called: June
1955, Middle Temple, FCIS

Hart *Peter Martin* •
Deputy Insurance Ombudsman, Insurance
Ombudsman Bureau, City Gate One, 135
Park Street, London SE1 9EA, 0171 928
4488, Fax: 0171 928 7478. Called: Nov
1975, Lincoln's Inn, BA (Cantab)

Hart *Robert William*
Called: June 1961, Inner Temple, BA
(Cantab)

Hart *Timothy George*
Bailhache Labesse, Advocates & Solicitors,
14/16 Hill Street, St Helier, Jersey, 01534
888777, Fax: 01534 888778, and Member
Jersey Bar. Called: Feb 1995, Gray's Inn, BA
(Oxon)

Hartley *Christopher John* •
Prosecution Team Leader, Crown
Prosecution Service, Humber, Greenfield
House, 32 Scotland Street, Sheffield S3 7DQ.
Called: July 1987, Inner Temple, BA (Hons)
(Kent)

Hartridge *Miss Juliet Claire* •
Principal Legal Officer, The Dept. of Social
Security, New Court, 48 Carey Street,
London WC2A 2LS, 0171 412 1597, Fax:
0171 412 1220. Called: Oct 1993, Lincoln's
Inn, LLB (Hons)(Lond)

Hartshorne *John Trevor*
Lecturer in Law, University of Leicester,
Faculty of Law, University Road, Leicester
LE1 7RH, 0116 252 2363, Fax: 0116 252
5023. Called: Oct 1993, Inner Temple, LLB
(Exon), LLM (Leics)

Harty *Mrs Eily Imogen Mary*
Part-time Chairman Social Security Appeal
Tribunals, The Thatched House, Littleworth
Avenue, Esher, Surrey KT10 9PB.
Called: Nov 1977, Middle Temple, MA
(Oxon)

Harty *Martin John* •
European Legal & Compliance Director,
Fidelity Brokerage Services, Kingswood
Place, Tadworth, Surrey KT20 6RB, 01737
836328, Fax: 01737 837337. Called: July
1976, Middle Temple, MA (Oxon), ACIArb

Harvey *Ms Alison Roma*
Called: Nov 1994, Inner Temple, BA
(Oxon), M.Litt/D.Phil (Oxon), MA (Leic)

Harvey *Christopher*
Russell & DuMoulin, 2100-1075 W Georgia
St, Vancouver V6E 3G2, 604 631 3131, Fax:
604 631 3232, QC British Columbia Bar and
Member British Columbia Bar. Called: July
1968, Middle Temple, BA (Mcgill), Dip Law,
LLM, PhD (Lond)

Harvey *Mrs Leah*
28 Rodway Road, London SW15 5DS, 0181
788 9778, Justice of the Peace, Inner
London, South Central Division 1965-1989.
Called: July 1972, Gray's Inn, Dip
Criminology

Harvey *Peter CB*
Called: June 1948, Lincoln's Inn, MA, BCL
(Oxon)

Harvey *Richard Derek* •
Region Manager, Legal (Europe Russia,
Africa, Middle East), BHP Petroleum
Limited, Devonshire House, Picadilly,
London W1X 6AQ, 0171 408 7055, Fax:
0171 408 7095. Called: July 1976, Lincoln's
Inn, BSc, MSc, CEng, MIChem E

Harvey Wood *Andrew James*
Camp Lodge, The Camp, Near Stroud,
Gloucs GL6 7EW. Called: Nov 1965, Inner
Temple

Harwood *Matthew Nicholas*
Called: July 1974, Gray's Inn, LLB

Harwood *Miss Susan Mary
Josephine* •
Legal Officer Grade 7, Criminal Injuries
Compensation, Board, Whittington House,
19 Alfred Place, London WC1E 7LG, 0171
355 6802, Fax: 0171 436 0804. Called: Nov
1988, Middle Temple, BA (Keele)

Hasan *Miss Jamila Zehra*
Freelance Journalist. Called: May 1993, Inner
Temple, LLB (Southbank), LLM (Lond)

Hasan *Mohammed Ziaul*
Called: Mar 1997, Gray's Inn, LLB (Lond)

Hashim *Miss Zaheera*
Legal Assistant, M/S Haq & Namazie
Partnership, 20 Cecil Street, [H]22-03, (65)
4386604, Fax: (65) 4387383, and Member
Singapore Bar. Called: July 1995, Middle
Temple, LLB (Hons), BA

Haskins *Mrs Felicity Jane*
Partner, F Haskins & Co, College Chambers,
3 St James' Street, St Peter Port, Guernsey,
01481 721316, Fax: 01481 721317,
Advocate of Royal Court of Guernsey.
Called: Nov 1989, Inner Temple, LLB (Lond)

Haslam *Miss Emily*
Lecturer, University of Wales, Deaprtment
of Law, Hugh Owen Building, Penglais,
Aberysthyth, Dyfed SY23 3DY, 01970
622712, Fax: 01970 622729. Called: Nov
1995, Middle Temple, LLB (Hons), LLM

Hassan *Miss Fleur Judith Sol*
Called: Nov 1996, Middle Temple, LLB
(Hons)

Hassan *Miss Haslina*
Called: July 1995, Middle Temple, LLB
(Hons) (Kent)

Hassan *Robin Anthony* •
Junior Counsel, British Sky Broadcasting Ltd,
Grant Way, Isleworth, Middlesex TW7 5QD,
0171 705 3387, Fax: 0171 705 3254.
Called: Nov 1994, Inner Temple, LLB
(Essex)

Hassan *Toper*
Called: July 1989, Middle Temple, BA
(Sussex), LLM (Lond)

Hassett *Professor Patricia*
Syracuse College of Law, Syracuse, New
York 13244, United States of America, 315
443 2535, Fax: 315 443 4141, US Supreme
Court and Member New York Bar.
Called: Nov 1992, Inner Temple, BA, LLB,
LLM, Proff at Law

Hatcher *Mark*
Head of Public Affairs Consultancy Head of
Public Affairs, Coopers & Lybrand, Coopers
& Lybrand, Management Consultancy, 1
Embankment Place, London WC2N 6NN,
0171 213 4714, Fax: 0171 213 1893, Also L
1982 Inns of Court. Called: Nov 1978,
Middle Temple, MA (Oxon), FRSA

Hatfield *Mrs Linda*
Called: July 1974, Middle Temple, MA
(Cantab)

Hatfield-Hadjiioannou *Mrs Ruth
Elizabeth*
Christos M Georgiades &, Telemachos M
Georgiades Advoc., 22 25th March Street,
P.O.Box 85, Paphos, and Member Cyprus
Bar. Called: Nov 1986, Gray's Inn, LLB
(Nott'm)

Hattersley *Lt Cdr Jonathan Peter
George RN* •
Called: Nov 1984, Gray's Inn, LLB (Hons)

Hatton *Miss Theresa Jacqueline*
Called: Mar 1998, Lincoln's Inn, LLB
(Hons)(Derby)

Haugstad *Miss Annelise Charlotte* ●
Called: Nov 1996, Lincoln's Inn, BA
(Hons)(Keele)

Havard *Dr John David Jayne CBE*
1 Wilton Square, London N1 3DL, 0171 383
6095, Fax: 0171 383 6195, Hon Sec
Commonwealth Medical Assoc Secretary
BMA 1979-89. Called: July 1954, Middle
Temple, MA, MD, LLM (Cantab), FRCP
(Lond)

Havard *Nigel George*
Called: Mar 1998, Gray's Inn, BA

Havelock *Martin John*
Group Personnel Director: Oxford
University Press, Oxford University Press,
Great Clarendon Street, Oxon OX2 6DP,
01865 267611, Fax: 01865 267612.
Called: Nov 1977, Gray's Inn, MA (Oxon)

Havers *John Kingsley OBE*
QC Belize (1966) QC Gibraltar (1972), The
Glebe Cottage, Woolfardisworthy, Nr
Crediton, Devon EX17 4RX, 01363 866484,
Senior Magistrate British Indian Ocean
Territory. Called: Feb 1952, Inner Temple,
MA,BCL

Haw *Miss Judith Mary* ●
East Court, Shipton-By-Beningbrough, York
YO6 1AR. Called: July 1973, Gray's Inn

Hawa *Miss Nayla*
Al Tamimi & Company, P.O.Box 9275,
Dubai, 009714 317090, Fax: 009714
3613177. Called: Oct 1994, Middle Temple,
LLB (Hons)(Lond)

Haward *Mrs Linda Ruth*
Jacksons Solicitors, Queens Square,
Middlesbrough. Called: July 1994, Lincoln's
Inn, LLB (Hons) (Essex)

Hawe *Miss Cathleen Margaret* ●
Senior Principal Legal Officer, HM Customs
& Excise, New King's Beam House, 22
Upper Ground, London SE1 9PJ, 0171 865
5135, Fax: 0171 865 5248. Called: Nov
1972, Gray's Inn

Hawken *Simon Charles*
Called: July 1977, Middle Temple, MA

Hawker *Miss Susan Rachel Louise* ●
Called: Nov 1994, Lincoln's Inn, BA (Hons),
CPE (Sussex)

Hawkes *Miss Audrey* ●
Principal Crown Prosecutor, Crown
Prosecution Service, Portland House, Stag
Place, London SW1, 0171 915 5700.
Called: July 1983, Inner Temple, LLB (Lond)

Hawkes *Ms Gillian*
Called: Oct 1997, Gray's Inn, LLB (Lond)

Hawkes *Terence Arthur*
8 Dale Drive, Holmer, Hereford HR4 9RF.
Called: July 1962, Gray's Inn

Hawkins *Miss Alison*
Called: Nov 1978, Gray's Inn, BA

Hawkins *Andrew Stehen Lindsay*
Director of Policy & PR, London Chamber
of Commerce, & Industry, 33 Queen Street,
London EC4P 1AP, 0171 203 1898, Fax:
0171 203 1920. Called: July 1995, Gray's
Inn, MA (St Andrews)

Hawkins *Nicholas John MP*
Parliamentary Private Secretary MOD, then
DNH, House of Commons, Westminster,
London SW1A OAA, 0171 219 6329, Fax:
0171 219 2754/2693, Verulam Chambers,
Peer House, 8-14 Verulam Street, Gray's Inn,
London, WC1X 8LZ. Called: Nov 1979,
Middle Temple, MA (Oxon),ACIArb, Assoc
IPS

Hawkins *Commander Nicholas Simon
RN* ●
Naval Prosecuting Authority, Jervis Block,
HMS Nelson, Queen Street, Portsmouth,
Hants PO1 3HH, 01705 726218. Called: Oct
1991, Inner Temple, MA (Oxon), Dip Law

Hawkins *Richard George Plume*
International Environment Consultant, Eden
Hall, Kelso, Roxburghshire TD5 7QD, 01890
830666, Fax: 01890 830667. Called: Nov
1954, Inner Temple, MA (Oxon)

Hawks *James Edward*
Called: Nov 1996, Gray's Inn, LLB (Bris)

Haworth *Paul George* ●
Senior Crown Prosecutor, Crown
Prosecution Service, 1st Floor,Solar House,
1-9 Romford Road, Stratford, London
E15 4LJ, 0181 534 6601, Fax: 0181 519
5479. Called: May 1985, Lincoln's Inn, BA
(Hons)

Haworth *Thomas*
Senior Court Clerk, Hull Magistrates Court,
31 Lairgate, Beverley, North Humberside,
01482 881264. Called: Feb 1991, Gray's Inn,
LLB (Hull)

Hawthorne *Mrs Caroline Jane*
Called: Oct 1994, Lincoln's Inn, LLB (Hons)

Hawthorne *Michael Eliot*
Called: Nov 1994, Lincoln's Inn, LLB
(Hons)(Lond)

Hawtin *Ian Alexander* ●
Company Secretary, The Boots Company
Plc, Head Office, 1 Thane Road West,
Nottingham NG2 3AA, 0115 9687092, Fax:
0115 9687152. Called: July 1967, Gray's Inn,
MA (Oxon)

Hay *David John Mackenzie*
General Editor, Major Works, Malayan Law
Journal Sdn Bhd, 10th Floor, Hamzah
Kwong Hing, No 1 Leboh Ampang, 50100
Kuala Lumpur, 60 3 232 1218, Fax: 60 3
238 7073. Called: July 1977, Inner Temple,
MA (Edin), MA, LLM, (Cantab)

Hay *Miss Eleanor Frances Margaret*
Called: Nov 1996, Lincoln's Inn, LLB (Hons)

Haycock *Mrs Anne* ●
Legal Adviser to Social Services,Berkshire.
Called: Nov 1986, Gray's Inn, Dip.Mag.Law

Haycock *Jonathan Allan*
Called: Oct 1996, Middle Temple, B.Sc.
(Hons)

Hayden *Matthew Simon*
Called: Oct 1994, Gray's Inn, LLB

Haydock *James William*
Clerk to the Justices, Wigan Magistrates'
Court, Darlington Street, Wigan WN1 1DW,
01942 405405, Fax: 01942 405444.
Called: Feb 1984, Inner Temple, DML

Haydon *Hilary Risdon*
Also Inn of Court I. Called: June 1961,
Gray's Inn, MA (Cantab)

Haye *Miss Cinderella*
Called: Nov 1982, Lincoln's Inn, BA (Hons)

Hayes *John Patrick*
Called: Nov 1993, Inner Temple, BA

Hayford *Miss Jane Helene*
Called: Oct 1997, Gray's Inn, LLB (Bucks)

Hayley *Mrs Angela Judith*
and Member Brunei Bar 1975. Called: July
1973, Inner Temple, LLB Hons (Bristol)

Haynes *Gregory Laurence Warwick*
Called: Nov 1997, Inner Temple, LLB
(Wales)

Haythorne *Eric George*
Legal Advisor-Private Sector Development,
Senior Counsel, Legal Dept, The World
Bank, 1818 H Street, N.W., Washington,
D.C. 20433, (202)458-0014, Fax: (202)522-
1592, and Member Ontario, Canada Paris,
France. Called: July 1973, Inner Temple, BA
(Cantab), MA (Cantab), BA (Hons)(Queen's),
LLB(Dalhousie), Doc de L'Universite, (Paris)

Hayward *Peter Allan*
St Peter's College, Oxford OX1 2DL.
Called: Nov 1958, Lincoln's Inn, MA
(Cantab) MA, (Oxon)

Haywood *Keith Brett*
Called: Oct 1996, Gray's Inn, LLB (Anglia)

Hayzelden *John Eastcott CBE*
Ofwat Thames Customers Service
Committee, Uplands, 39 Mortimer Hill,
Tring, Herts HP23 5JB. Called: Nov 1968,
Middle Temple, MA

Hazarika *Loona*
Campaign Manager, Burton Group., London
Correspondent The Sentinel, Burton Group
(Home Shopping), 32 Haymarket, London
SW1Y 4TP. Called: Mar 1997, Inner Temple,
MA (Cantab)

Hazelden *John Winston WKhM* ●
European General Counsel, The Risk
Advisory Group Ltd, Russell Square, 10-12
Russell Square, London WC1B 5EH, 0171
578 0000, Fax: 0171 578 7855. Called: July
1975, Middle Temple

Hazell *Dirk Nicholas Downing* ●
6 Deepdale, Wimbledon Common, London
SW19 5EZ, 0181 946 8486, Fax: 0181 946
8486. Called: July 1978, Middle Temple, MA
(Cantab)

Hazell *Laurence Paul*
York Chambers, 14 Toft Green, York, YO1
1JT. Called: Nov 1984, Gray's Inn, BA Hons
PhD (Dunelm)

Hazewindus *Frank Sieger* •
Intellectual Property Lawyer, Shell
International Petroleum Co Ltd, Shell
Centre, London SE1 7NA, 0171 934 4379,
Fax: 0171 934 6627, and Member Holland
Bar. Called: Nov 1982, Middle Temple, LLB
(Utrecht), LLM (Univ Chicago), Dip Law
(City)

Head *David Mark*
Called: Oct 1990, Lincoln's Inn, BSC (Hons)
(Essex), MSC (Reading), Dip Law (City)

Head *John Kenneth*
1 Woodfield Gardens, Highcliffe,
Christchurch, Dorset BH23 4QA, 01425
273594. Called: Feb 1965, Lincoln's Inn, LLB
(Lond)

Headen *Miss Margaret Bernice*
Clerk to the Justices, Clerk to the Justices',
Barbican Way, Bearland, Gloucester
GL1 2JH, 01452 426152. Called: Nov 1970,
Gray's Inn

Heagney *Ms Caroline Ann*
Called: Oct 1995, Gray's Inn, LLB

Heal *James Arthur David*
Consultant in Judicial Administration
Associate Fellow of the Society for
Advanced Legal Studies, Wroxham, 12
Oakfield Road, Ashtead, Surrey KT21 2RE,
01372 274003, Fax: 01372 278369.
Called: Jan 1951, Middle Temple, LLB
(Lond)

Healy *Miss Angela Maria*
Called: Mar 1997, Lincoln's Inn, LLB (Hons)

Healy *John Pascal*
Arbitrator, Tara, Waterfall Road,
Bishoptown, Cork, 353 21 371562, Fax: 353
21 371562, Kings Inn, Dublin and Member
Southern Ireland Bar. Called: Feb 1982,
Middle Temple, ACIArb

Healy *Ms Margaret Virginia*
Called: Nov 1996, Gray's Inn, BA (Open),
MA (Sussex)

Healy-Pratt *James Simon* •
Legal Adviser, British Aviation Insurance
Grp, Fitzwilliam House, 10 St Mary Avenue,
London EC3A 8EQ, 0171 369 2244, Fax:
0171 369 2820. Called: Oct 1991, Gray's
Inn, BA (Durham), LLM (Lond UCL), Cert.
Air Law

Heap *Michael James*
Justices' Chief Executive, South Wales,
Committee Offices, 47 Charles Street,
Cardiff CF1 4ED, 01222 300250, Fax: 01222
300240. Called: July 1975, Middle Temple,
MBA

Hearn *Steven Maxwell* •
Crown Prosecutor, Crown Prosecution
Service, King's Road, Kymberley Road,
Harrow, Middlesex HA1 1YH, 0181 424
8688, Fax: 0181 424 9134. Called: Nov
1992, Inner Temple, LLB, LLM

Hearne *Mrs Jennifer Christina*
Called: Nov 1977, Inner Temple

Heath *Philip James*
Deputy District Secretary, Local & Public
Authority Unit, Lawrence Graham Solicitors,
190 Strand, London WC2R 1JN, 0171 379
0000, Fax: 0171 379 6854. Called: Nov
1988, Gray's Inn, LLB, MA, F.R.S.A.

Heather *Miss Catherine Ann* •
Senior Crown Prosecutor, Crown
Prosecution Service, Fox Talbot House,
Bellinger Close, Malmesbury Road,
Chippenham, Wiltshire ON15 1BN, 01249
443 443, Fax: 01249 440 800. Called: Oct
1992, Gray's Inn, BA (Dunlem)

Heatley *Richard Jonathon* •
Senior Crown Prosecutor, Crown
Prosecution Service, 3rd Floor, Portland
House, Stag Place, Victoria, London
SW1E 5BH, 0171 915 5875. Called: Nov
1989, Inner Temple, LLB (Oxon), LLM
(Lond)

Heatly *Derek William George*
14 Lenamore Park, Jordanstown, Co Antrim.
Called: Nov 1975, Lincoln's Inn, LLB,BSc
(Econ), B.Comm.Sc

Heaton *Richard Nicholas* •
Grade 6, Legal Secretariat to the, Law
Officers, 9 Buckingham Gate, London
SW1E 6JP. Called: July 1988, Inner Temple,
BA (Oxon)

Hebblethwaite *Ms Sandra Louise* •
Acting Bracnh Crown Prosecutor, Crown
Prosecution Section, 2-4 City Gates,
Southgate, Chichester, West Sussex
PO19 2DJ, 01243 776851, Fax: 01243
784316. Called: Nov 1986, Gray's Inn, LLB
(Brunel)

Hedge *Leslie Joseph*
5 Evendons Lane, Wokingham, Berks
RG41 4AA. Called: June 1955, Gray's Inn,
LLB (Lond)

Hedley-Dent *Mrs Gloria* •
Senior Civil Service, Legal Dept, Department
of the, Environment, Transport and, the
Regions, Eland House, 2 Bressenden Place,
London SW1E 5DU, 0171 890 4819.
Called: July 1970, Inner Temple, BA
(Dunelm)

Hee *Miss Cher Sun*
7 Jalan Cahaya 6, Taman Salak Selatan,
57100 Kuala Lumpur, (603) 957 3693, Fax:
(603) 957 3695. Called: July 1995, Middle
Temple, LLB (Hons)

Hee *Rev Kim San Vincent*
66 The Greenway, Colindale, London
NW9 5AP, 0181 200 4873, Fax: 0181 200
4873. Called: Nov 1989, Gray's Inn, LLB
(Lond), GG (USA), FGA (GB), LLM (Lond)

Heenan *Miss Rachael Ann Georgina* •
Solicitors Department, Co-operative
Insurance Limited, Miller Street, Manchester
H60 0AL, 0161 837 5162, Fax: 0161 837
5889. Called: Nov 1995, Middle Temple, LLB
(Hons), LLM

Heffernan *John Francis*
City Editor, Yorkshire Post 1985/93, Prime
Warden 1996/97 Worshipful Company of
Basketmakers., 1 Fern Dene, Templewood,
London W13 8AN, 0181 997 6868.
Called: Nov 1954, Inner Temple, BCom
(Hons)

Heggs *Oliver Geoffrey*
Called: Nov 1987, Middle Temple, LLB
(Lond)

Heim *Mathew Jacques*
Called: Oct 1993, Lincoln's Inn, BA
(Hons)(Bris), MA (Exon), CPE (Stafford)

Hein *Raymond Marie Marc*
Thomas More Chambers, 52 Carey Street,
Lincoln's Inn, London, WC2A 2JB.
Called: July 1979, Gray's Inn

Heine *Ms Eleanor Louise*
Sedgwick, Detert, Moran &, Arnold, 5
Lloyds Avenue, London EC3N 3AX, 0171
929 1829, Fax: 0171 929 1808, and Member
New York Bar. Called: Nov 1995, Inner
Temple, BA (Pennsylvania), LLB

Helfrecht *William John*
Head of Litigation, Ian Boxall & Co, CIBC
Financial Centre, P O Box 1234, George
Town, Grand Cayman, Cayman Islands,
(345) 949 9876, Fax: (345) 949 9877, and
Member Cayman Islands. Called: Nov 1978,
Middle Temple, MA (Oxon)

Heller *Miss Claire Andrea*
6 Cascade Avenue, London N10 3PU, 0181
883 1041. Called: Nov 1992, Inner Temple,
BA (Exon), CPE

Hellier *Ms Sarah Jane Elizabeth*
Called: Nov 1994, Inner Temple, BA, CPE
(City)

Hellings *Ms Suzan Marion* •
Hellings Morgan Associates, House No 5,
Bisney View, 47-49 Bisney Road, Pokfulam,
Hong Kong, 2855 1428, Fax: 2855 1510.
Called: July 1981, Middle Temple, LLB
(Hons), FCIArb

Hellman *Stephen Geoffrey*
Paget-Brown, Quin & Hampson, Harbour
Centre, Third Floor, P.O.Box 1348, Grand
Cayman, Cayman Islands, 00 1 809 949
4123, Fax: 00 1 809 949 4647. Called: July
1988, Inner Temple, BA (Oxon), Dip Law

Hemming *Martin John* •
Assistant Treasury Solicitor, Treasury Legal
Adviser, HM Treasury, Parliament Street,
London SW1P 3AG, 0171 270 1664.
Called: July 1972, Gray's Inn, MA (Cantab),
LLM (Lond)

Hemming *Miss Susan Jane* •
Acting Principal Crown Prosecutor, Crown
Prosecution Service, Justinian House,
Spitfire Way, Ermine Business Park,
Huntingdon Cambs PE18 6XY, 01480
432333, Fax: 01480 432404. Called: July
1988, Middle Temple, LLB (Hons) (Wales)

Hemmings *Liam*
Called: Nov 1996, Inner Temple, LLB
(Huddersfield)

Hendrickson *Miss Christine*
Called: Nov 1982, Inner Temple, LLB (UCL)

Hendry *Ian Duncan CMG* •
Legal Counsellor, Foreign & Commonwealth
Office, King Charles Street, London
SW1A 2AH, 0171 270 3041. Called: July
1971, Gray's Inn, LLB, LLM

Heng *Clive Boon Howe*
Managing Director of an Investment Holding
Company, 17 Leedon Road, Wilmer Park,
3244 553, Fax: 65 3244 552, and Member
Singapore Bar. Called: July 1976, Lincoln's
Inn, LLB (Hons) (Lond)

Heng *Hui Tek*
Commissioner for Oaths, Heng & Rada, 1
North Bridge Road, 30-05 High Street
Centre, 3389800, Fax: 3392328, Advocate &
Solicitor, Singapore. Called: July 1984,
Lincoln's Inn, LLB (Warwick), M.Phil
(Cantab)

Henley *Mrs Margaret Edith Mary*
Court Clerk, Walsall Magistrates Court,
Stafford Street, Walsall, West Midlands
WS2 8HA, 01922 38222, Fax: 01922 35657.
Called: Oct 1990, Middle Temple, BSc
(Hons)

Henley *Mark Simon*
Called: Oct 1996, Middle Temple, BA
(Hons)(Oxon)

Henley-Price *Julian Kendall* •
Legal Counsel, Rothmans of Pall Mall
(Intn'l), Oxford Road, Aylesbury, Bucks
WD1 1QH, 01296 335000. Called: Feb 1994,
Gray's Inn, LLB (Lond), Maitrise es Droit,
(Paris)

Henning *Miss Caroline Ann*
Hill Dickenson Davis Campbell, Pearl
Assurance House, Derby Square, Liverpool
L2 9XL, 0151 236 5400, Fax: 0151 236
2175. Called: Nov 1993, Middle Temple, BA
(Hons)(Oxon), CPE, MA (Oxon)

Henry *Ian Leroy* •
Employment Solicitor, London Borough of
Hackney, Legal Services Directorate, 298
Mare Street, Hackney, London E8 1HE, and
Member Jamaica Bar. Called: July 1983,
Middle Temple, BA

Henry *Philip Ivan* •
Assistant Director, Serious Fraud Office, Elm
House, 10-16 Elm Street, London WC1X 0BJ,
and Member Antigua Bar Northern Ireland
Bar. Called: Nov 1979, Gray's Inn, BA

Henry *Miss Winsome Hyacinth*
Appointed Stipendary Magistrate, Montego
Bay, Jamaica. Staple Inn Chambers, 1st
Floor, 9 Staple Inn, Holborn, London, WC1V
7QH. Called: Nov 1979, Middle Temple, BA

Heppel *Kenneth Henry*
The Cottage, Bishops Itchington,
Leamington Spa, Warks CV33 0QB, 01926
612463, Fax: 01926 612463. Called: Nov
1960, Middle Temple, LLB, LLM

Heptonstall *Miss Emma Victoria*
Called: Nov 1997, Gray's Inn, LLB (Keele)

Herbert *Piers Marinel*
also Inn of Court G. Called: Feb 1960, Inner
Temple, MA (Oxon)

Herbert Young *Nicholas Anthony*
Lecturer in Law, Department of Law,
University College of Wales, Hugh Owen
Building, Penglais, Aberystwyth, Dyfed
SY23 3DY, 01970 622712, Fax: 01970
622729. Called: May 1988, Middle Temple,
LLB (Hons) Lond, LLM (Hons) Lond

Herbst *Jonathan Raymond Selbey* •
Called: Nov 1992, Gray's Inn, BA (Exon)

Heritage *John Langdon CB*
Chairman, Chesham Bldg Society, C/O
Chesham Building Society, 12 Market
Square, Chesham, Bucks HP5 1ER, 01494 72
5165, Fax: 01494 72 5165. Called: Feb 1956,
Middle Temple, MA (Oxon)

Herling *Dr David Andrew*
Law Department, City University,
Northampton Square, London EC1V 0HB,
0171 477 8301, Fax: 0171 477 8578.
Called: Oct 1991, Gray's Inn, BA, MA, D.Phil
(Oxon,)

Hermele *Daniel Stephen*
Called: Oct 1994, Lincoln's Inn, BSc (Hons),
MA (Bris)

Hermon *Richard Alexander Gower* •
Senior Legal Assistant, Lord Chancellor's
Department, Selborne House, 54/60 Victoria
Street, London SW1E 6QB. Called: Nov
1977, Inner Temple, MA

Hernandez *Christian*
Called: Nov 1995, Middle Temple, LLB
(Hons)

Heron *Ronald*
Called: July 1957, Middle Temple, MA
(Cantab)

Heron *Ms Sarah Katherine* •
Ministry of Agriculture, Fisheries & Food, 55
Whitehall, London SW1A 2EY, 0171 270
8727, Fax: 0171 270 8096. Called: Oct
1991, Middle Temple, BSc Hons (Manch),
Dip Law

Hesford *Stephen MP*
38 Young Street, Manchester, M3 3FT.
Called: Nov 1981, Gray's Inn, BSc (Bradford)

Hesse-Djabatey *Mrs Leonora Akousa
Kwakua*
P.O.Box 128, Tradefair Site, Accra, Ghana,
665915, and Member Ghana. Called: Nov
1988, Gray's Inn, LLB (Lond)

Hession *Martin Niall*
Called: Nov 1991, Lincoln's Inn, LLB (Hons)
(Dublin), LLM

Hesslewood *Mrs Josephine Florence*
Called: Mar 1996, Gray's Inn, LLB (Lond)

Hetherington *Sir Thomas Chalmers
KCB,CBE,TD QC (1978)*
Rosemount, Mount Pleasant Road, Lingfield,
Surrey RH7 6BH, 01342 833923. Called: Nov
1952, Inner Temple

Hewitson *Miss Melanie Jayne*
Called: Oct 1996, Middle Temple, LLB
(Hons)(Lond)

Hewitt *John Allan*
Called: Feb 1993, Middle Temple, BA
(Hons), LLM

Hext *Miss Carole Anne* •
Crown Prosecutor, Crown Prosecution
Service, 32 Scotland Street, Sheffield
S3 7DQ, 0114 2912000. Called: Oct 1993,
Inner Temple, LLB (Hons)(Leic)

Hext *Christopher John Richard* •
Senior Crown Prosecutor, Crown
Prosecution Service, County House, County
Square, 100 New London Road, Chelmsford,
Essex CM2 0RG, 01245 252939, Fax: 01245
494710. Called: July 1986, Lincoln's Inn,
LLB

Hey *Peter Wilson*
59 Rue Porte Poitevine, 37600 Loches, 02
47 59 10 04. Called: June 1948, Inner
Temple, MA, LLB (Cantab)

Heybrook *Miss Rose Catherine*
Called: Oct 1993, Inner Temple, MA
(Cantab)

Heycock *David Huw* •
CPS Inter-Agency Projects Manager, Crown
Prosecution Service, 50 Ludgate Hill,
London EC4M 7EX, 0171 273 8058, Fax:
0171 273 8016. Called: Feb 1982, Middle
Temple, LLB (Lond), MPhil (Cantab), Dip
Psyc (Wales)

Heyman *Allan KCD QC (1969)*
Cand Jur Master of Law Univ of
Copenhagen June 1947 Arbitrator
Arbitrator, 1 New Square, Lincoln's Inn,
London WC2A 3SA, 0171 405 0884/
01394450 298, Fax: 0171 831 6109/
01394450 298, Also Inn of Court L Knight
Commander of Dannebrog (Danish).
Called: June 1951, Middle Temple, MA
(Copenhagen)

Heywood *Eric* •
Senior Crown Prosecutor, CPS
(G.Manchester Area), PO Box 377, 8th
Floor,Sunlight House, Quay Street,
Manchester M60 3LU, 0161 837 7402.
Called: Feb 1988, Gray's Inn

Heywood *Dr Linda Jane*
Family Planning, Instructing Doctor,
Fornham End, Sheepwash Bridge, Fornham
All Saints, Bury St Edmunds, Suffolk
IP28 6JJ, 01284 769772. Called: Oct 1993,
Inner Temple, MB, ChB (University, of
Leeds Medical, School), CPE, MFFP

Hibbert *Arthur John* •
Principal Crown Prosecutor, Crown
Prosecution Service, Greenfield House, 32
Scotland Street, Sheffield, South Yorkshire
S3 7DQ, 0114 2912000. Called: May 1984,
Middle Temple, BA (Manch)

Hickey *Desmond Paul*
Called: Mar 1998, Gray's Inn, BA (Dublin)

Hickey *Julian James Bernard*
Called: Oct 1995, Inner Temple, LLB (Lond),
LLM (Lond)

Hickman *Ms Jane* •
Principal Legal Officer, Metropolitan Police
Sols Dept, Wellington House, 67-73
Buckingham Gate, London SW1. Called: Nov
1983, Gray's Inn, BA (Lond), Dip Law

Hicks *Ms Barbara Helen*
Chairman of the Webb Consumer Council..
Called: July 1995, Gray's Inn, LLB
(Glamorgan)

Hicks *Miss Lisa Marie*
Zarak Macrae Brenner, 37 Sun Street,
London EC2M 2PY, 0171 377 0510, Fax:
0171 247 5174. Called: Nov 1991, Inner
Temple, LLB (So'ton)

Hickson *Miss Fabiola Annaliese
Amelia* •
Called: Nov 1992, Inner Temple, LLB

Hiew *Miss Fatimah Yen Won*
Called: Mar 1998, Lincoln's Inn, LLB (Hons)

Higgins *Richard CBE* •
Legal Consultant, Dept of Trade & Industry,
10-18 Victoria Street, London SW1H ONN.
Called: Nov 1955, Inner Temple, B.C.L., MA

Higgins *Dame Rosalyn DBE* QC
(1986)
Member of the International Court of
Justice, The Hague. Called: Nov 1975, Inner
Temple, MA LLB (Cantab), JSD (Yale), LLM,
LLD (Hons) (Paris)

Higgs *Conrad Clephane*
South School Lane, Back Salina, Grand Turk,
Turks & Caicos Islands, (809) 946 1320, and
Member Turks & Caicos Bar. Called: Nov
1995, Middle Temple, BA (Hons)(W.Indies),
MSc (B'ham)

Higham *Cdr Michael Bernard Shepley
RN*
Grand Secretary, United Grand Lodge of
England, Freemasons' Hall, Great Queen
Street, London WC2B 5AZ, 0171 831 9811,
Fax: 0171 831 6021. Called: July 1968,
Middle Temple

Highman *Mark Gideon*
Called: Feb 1993, Gray's Inn, BA

Hill *Alastair Malcolm* QC (1982)
Recorder Lawyer, Crown Prosecution
Service, Police Division, 10 Furnival Street,
London EC4A 1PE. Called: May 1961, Gray's
Inn, BA (Oxon)

Hill *David Lewis* •
Legal Adviser, Willis Corroon Group plc, 10
Trinity Square, London EC3P 3AX, 0171 481
7161, Fax: 0171 481 7183. Called: Oct
1992, Middle Temple, MA (Cantab)

Hill *Jeffrey Paul*
Called: Mar 1997, Gray's Inn, LLB (Staff)

Hill *John Arthur*
Clerk to the Justices for Blackpool, Fylde &
Wyre, Management & Training Centre, P O
Box 717, Weind House, Park Hill Road,
Garstang PR3 1EY, 01995 601596, Fax:
01995 601776. Called: July 1965, Gray's Inn

Hill *Richard Aubrey*
Legal Assistant, McKenna & Co, Mitre
House, 160 Aldersgate Street, London
EC1A 4DD, 0171 606 9000, Fax: 0171 606
9100. Called: Nov 1992, Middle Temple, BA
(Hons), Dip in Law

Hill *Miss Susan Enid Clare* •
Principal Legal Officer, Office of the
Solicitor DHSS, SOL A1, Room 420512, New
Court, 48 Carey Street, London WC2A 2LS,
0171 412 1260, Fax: 0171 412 1394.
Called: Oct 1992, Gray's Inn, MA (Oxon)

Hillas *Miss Samantha*
Called: Oct 1996, Inner Temple, LLB (Hull)

Hillier *Gerald Cyril* •
Crown Prosecution Service, Winston
Churchill Avenue, Portsmouth PO1 2PJ.
Called: July 1978, Middle Temple, BA
(Manch), LLB (Lond)

Hillman *Michael John Timothy*
Called: Nov 1995, Inner Temple, LLB

Hilton *George* •
Company Secretary, Lloyd Thompson Group
Plc, Beaufort House, 15 St Botolph Street,
London EC3A 7LT, 0171 247 2345, Fax:
0171 247 4488. Called: July 1976, Inner
Temple, BA

Hilton *Miss Lindsey Isobel*
Mitre House Chambers, Mitre House, 44
Fleet Street, London, EC4Y 1BN. Called: Nov
1988, Gray's Inn, LLB

Hinchliffe *Peter Michael* •
Senior Lawyer, GEC plc, 1 Stanhope Gate,
London W1A 1EH, 0171 493 8484, Fax:
0171 491 0752. Called: July 1982, Lincoln's
Inn, LLB

Hind *Mrs Nirmala*
Called: July 1994, Lincoln's Inn, LLB (Hons)

Hindle *Leon Miller*
Called: Mar 1997, Inner Temple, LLB (Leeds)

Hindley *Mrs Brenda Mary*
Part-time Chairman Tribunals, 6 Longworth
Drive, Maidenhead, Berks SL6 8XA, 01628
777668, Fax: 01628 30167. Called: Nov
1962, Lincoln's Inn, LLB

Hingorani *Jeevan*
Pacific Chambers, 1301 Dina House, 11
Duddell Street, Central, 521 5544, Fax: 524
5912, and Member West Indies Bar.
Called: Feb 1977, Gray's Inn, BA (Hons)

Hingston *Ms Theresa Clothilde*
1 Gray's Inn Square, 1st Floor, London,
WC1R 5AG. Called: July 1978, Inner Temple

Hinton *Ian Hughes VRD*
25 Glebelands, Bidborough, Tunbridge
Wells, Kent TN3 OUQ, 01892 529604.
Called: May 1957, Gray's Inn, MA (Oxon),
MIMgt

Hippe *Ms Birgit*
Called: Oct 1994, Middle Temple, LLB
(Hons)(Lond)

Hirschfeld *Charl Benno*
Barrister of the High Court of New Zealand
(1984) and in the Ferderal Republic of
Germany (1992). Called: July 1990, Inner
Temple, LLB, LLM (Auckland)

Hirst *Miss Abigale Louise*
Called: Nov 1997, Gray's Inn, BA (Leeds)

Hirst *Alastair John*
Arbitrator, 72 Northumberland Street,
Edinburgh EH3 6JG, 031 556 5324, Fax: 031
557 5338, and Member Sultanate of Oman.
Called: Nov 1971, Inner Temple, MA
(Cantab), FCIArb

Hirst *Karl Douglas* •
Criminal Cases Review Comm., Alpha
Tower, Suffolk Street, Queensway,
Birmingham B1 1TT, 0121 633 1800.
Called: Oct 1997, Inner Temple, LLB
(Lancaster)

Hirtenstein *Anthony Trevor* •
Senior Legal Assistant, Department of the
Environment, 2 Marsham Street, London
SW1P 3EB. Called: July 1969, Gray's Inn, MA
(Oxon)

Hiscock *Miss Olive Gladys*
Called: July 1985, Inner Temple, Dip Law

Hitchings *Paul Barrington Knowles* •
Group Legal Adviser, Eagle Star Holdings
Plc, 60 St Mary Axe, London EC3A 8JQ,
0171 929 1111, Fax: 0171 626 0311.
Called: July 1968, Gray's Inn, BA (Oxon)

Hj Mat *Yaackub*
Legal Advisor, Batu 34, Kampong Baru
Myalas, 77100 Asahan, Melaka, 06-5229689.
Called: Mar 1997, Lincoln's Inn, LLB (Hons),
LLM (Wales)

Hj Md Noor *Zulkhairi*
Called: Nov 1996, Lincoln's Inn, LLB (Hons)

Ho *Ms Adaline See Yin*
Called: July 1997, Inner Temple, LLB (Lond)

Ho *Miss Annie Yin Yin*
Called: Nov 1994, Lincoln's Inn, LLB
(Hons)(Lond)

Ho *Miss Elaine Kit Yee*
Called: July 1994, Lincoln's Inn, LLB (Hons)

Ho *Kam Tim*
Called: Nov 1993, Lincoln's Inn, LLB (Hons,
Lond)

Ho *Kenneth Boon Kuan*
Called: July 1996, Lincoln's Inn, LLB
(Hons)(Notts)

Ho *Miss Kim Foong*
Sim Hill Tan & Wong, 4 Shenton Way, 14-
07/12, Shing Kwan House, Singapore 0106,
65 2200035, Fax: 65 2240693, and Member
Singapore Bar. Called: July 1994, Middle
Temple, BA (Hons)(Keele)

Ho *Miss Melissa Yee Ling*
Called: July 1994, Middle Temple, LLB
(Hons)(Brunel)

Ho *Sammy Wai Chuen*
Called: Nov 1997, Inner Temple, BSc (Hong
Kong), LLB (Lond)

Ho *Shi King*
Called: Oct 1996, Middle Temple, LLB
(Hons)

Ho *Miss Shok Heng*
60 Taman Merlin, 43000 Kajang, Selangor,
Malaysia, 00603-8364779. Called: July 1995,
Middle Temple, LLB (Hons)

Ho *Tzin Wen*
Called: July 1994, Middle Temple, BA
(Hons)(Keele)

Hoare *Miss Joanna* •
Criminal Appeal Office, Royal Courts of
Justice, Strand, London WC2A 2LL, 0171
936 6475, Fax: 0171 936 6900. Called: Nov
1982, Gray's Inn, LLB Warw

Hoare *John Michael*
54 Westminster Gardens, Marsham Street,
London SW1P 4JG, 0171 834 4950, Fax:
0171 828 2230. Called: Feb 1955, Inner
Temple, MA [Cantab]

Hoare Temple *Piers Howard*
3 Serjeants Inn, London, EC4Y 1BQ.
Called: July 1972, Middle Temple

Hobbs *Miss Patricia Joan*
Called: Nov 1995, Inner Temple, LLB (Kent)

Hobday *Miss Natasha Anne*
Clifford Chance, 200 Aldersgate, London
EC1A 4JJ, 0171 600 1000, Fax: 0171 600
5555. Called: Oct 1991, Middle Temple, LLB
Hons (Exon)

Hobson *Miss Sally Anne* •
Senior Crown Prosecutor. Called: Apr 1991,
Inner Temple, LLB, LLM

Hock *Lee Kay*
Called: July 1991, Gray's Inn, B.Soc.Sci
(Keele)

Hockey *Gordon Andrew* •
Secretary to the Statutory Committee of the
Pharmaceutica Society, Royal
Pharmaceutical Society, of Great Britain, 1
Lambeth High Street, London SE1 7JN, 0171
735 9141, Fax: 0171 735 7629. Called: Feb
1995, Lincoln's Inn, BSc (Manc)

Hocking *Stephen John*
Called: Nov 1994, Inner Temple, BA
(Oxon), CPE (City)

Hockman *David Philip*
Polygram International, Music Publishing
Limited, 8 St James's Square, London
SW1Y 4JU, 0171 747 4000, Fax: 0171 747
4467. Called: May 1972, Inner Temple, LLB

Hodder *Andrew Charles*
Called: Oct 1997, Gray's Inn, LLB (Wales),
MBA (Lond)

Hodge *Alistair Blackwood*
Called: Nov 1997, Inner Temple, LLB (Bris)

Hodges *Mark Cameron QGM*
RAC Legal Services, P.O.Box 700, Great
Park Road, Almondsbury, Bristol BS12 4QP,
0117 9441515. Called: Nov 1992, Lincoln's
Inn, LLB (Hons)

Hodgetts *Glen*
Called: Nov 1995, Inner Temple, LLB
(Lancs)

Hodgson *John James TD,* •
Head of Legal Services, Broxbourne
Borough Council, Bishops College,
Churchgate, Cheshunt, Herts EN8 9XQ,
01992 631921 Ext 2712, Fax: 01992
639391. Called: June 1955, Gray's Inn,
MA,Law Society Final

Hodgson *Mrs Margaret* •
Lord Chancellor's Department, Selborne
House, 54-60 Victoria Street, London
SW1 6QW. Called: July 1978, Gray's Inn, BA

Hodgson *Nicholas* •
Grade 6 (Legal), Lord Chancellor's
Department, Selborne House, 54-60 Victoria
Street, London SW1E 6QB, 0171 210 0714,
Fax: 0171 210 0746. Called: July 1976,
Middle Temple, MA (Oxon)

Hodson *Miss Loveday Cerys*
Called: July 1997, Gray's Inn, LLB (Warwick)

Hoe *Cheah Seng*
Legal Assistant, and Member Malaysia.
Called: Nov 1996, Lincoln's Inn, LLB
(Hons)(Sheff)

Hoe *Miss Chee May*
Called: July 1997, Middle Temple, LLB
(Hons), LLM, (L'pool)

Hoffman *David John* •
General Counsel, Oracle Corporation UK
Limited, Oracle Centre, The Ring, Bracknell,
Berkshire RG12 1BW. Called: Feb 1991,
Inner Temple, LLB (Manch)

Hogan *Miss Catherine Anne*
Called: Nov 1997, Gray's Inn, LLB (L'pool),
LLM (L'pool)

Hogan *Miss Emma Jane*
Called: Oct 1996, Middle Temple, BA
(Hons)(Oxon), CPE (City)

Hogarth *Adrian John* •
Deputy Parliamentary Counsel, Office of the
Parliamentary, Counsel, 36 Whitehall,
London SW1A 2AY, 0171 210 6646.
Called: July 1983, Inner Temple, IT, MA,
LLM (Cantab)

Hoh *Miss Gigi Anne*
3451308, Fax: 3451182. Called: July 1995,
Middle Temple, LLB (Hons)

Hohler *Miss Camilla Clare* •
47 Sutton Square, Urswick Road, London
E9 6EQ. Called: Nov 1994, Middle Temple,
BA (Hons)

Holden *David Thomas* •
Arab Banking Corporation, International
Bank PLC, 1-5 Moorgate, London EC2R 6AB.
Called: Oct 1991, Lincoln's Inn, MA
(Cantab)

Holden *Dr Hazel Diane*
Called: Feb 1995, Gray's Inn, B.Sc (St
Andrews), Ph.D (St Andrews)

Holden *Philip Anthony*
Called: Oct 1994, Lincoln's Inn, LLB
(Hons)(Northum)

Holden *Richard Thomas JP*
South Acre, Barlow, Blaydon on Tyne, Tyne
& Wear NE21 6JU, 01207 544331.
Called: Nov 1978, Lincoln's Inn, BSc, MSc
(Dunelm), LLB (Lond), MA, Dip Ed
(Dunelm), C.Chem,MRSC, C.Phy, M.Inst.P

Holder *Jonathan Alfred* •
Senior Lawyer, BBC Worldwide Limited,
Wood Lane, London W12, 0181 576 2308.
Called: July 1980, Middle Temple, BA Leeds

Holderness *David Alan* •
Crown Prosecutor, Crown Prosecution
Service, 4-5 South Parade, Wakefield, West
Yorkshire WF1 1LR, 01924 290620.
Called: Nov 1991, Lincoln's Inn, BA (Hons)

Holdsworth *Robert Drewry*
Called: July 1979, Gray's Inn, MA (Cantab)

Holland *Damian Paul* •
Principal Crown Prosecutor, Crown
Prosecution Service, Sceptre House, 7-9
Castle Street, Luton, Beds, 01582 404808,
Fax: 01582 400642. Called: Nov 1986,
Middle Temple, LLB(Manch)

Holland *Miss Debra Joanne*
Called: Oct 1996, Lincoln's Inn, LLB
(Hons)(Leic)

Holland *Richard David* •
Legal Manager, Crewe Magistrates Court,
Civic Centre, Crewe, Cheshire CW1 2DT,
01270 256221, Fax: 01270 589357.
Called: Nov 1987, Gray's Inn, Dip Magisteral
Law, Common Professional, Examination
Law

Holland-Elliott *Dr Kevin*
Chief Medical Adviser, The Chaucer
Hospital, Knackington Roasd, Canterbury,
Kent CT4 7AR, 01227 455466, Health &
Safety/Medico-Legal Opinion. Called: May
1996, Middle Temple, MB.ChB, MFOM,
MRCGP, MIOSH

Hollick *Cllr Peter Nugent*
Bedfordshire Police Authority Bedfordshire
Probation Board, 1 Carlisle Close,
Dunstable, Beds LU6 3PH, 01582 662821,
Fax: 01582 476619. Called: July 1973,
Middle Temple, JP,LLB (Hons)(B'ham),
MEd,FCollP

Holliday *Miss Valerie Anne*
Called: Nov 1994, Middle Temple, LLB
(Hons)

Hollins *Lt Cdr Rupert Patrick RN* •
Naval Barrister, 01329 832047. Called: Oct
1995, Gray's Inn, MA (Oxon)

Hollis *Daniel Ayrton QC (1968)*
Called: Nov 1949, Middle Temple, MA
(Oxon)

Holloway *Brian Spencer Charles*
Legal Adviser, James R Knowles, 53 Bedford
Square, London WC1. Called: Nov 1987,
Gray's Inn, LLB (Lond), CEng, FICE, FCIArb,
MSc (Const Law)

Holloway *David John*
Called: July 1996, Gray's Inn, BA (Cantab)

Holloway *Ms Jean*
Court Clerk, Richmond Upon Thames Mag Crt, Richmond Magistrates Court, Parkshot, Richmond, Surrey TW9 2RF, 0181 948 2101, Fax: 0181 322 2628. Called: July 1983, Gray's Inn, BA (Hons)

Holmback *Dr Ulf Aake Olof*
Svartmangatan 27, S-111 29 Stockholm, 0046 8218129, and Member Sweden Bar. Called: July 1979, Gray's Inn, JUR DR (Uppsala)

Holmberg *Miss Loretta Vanessa*
Called: July 1996, Middle Temple, LLB (Hons)(Wales)

Holmes *Carl Stanley* •
Principal Crown Prosecutor, Crown Prosecution Service, 1-9 Romford Road, Stratford, 0181 534 6601 Ext 215. Called: July 1986, Lincoln's Inn, B.A.

Holmes *Sir Maurice Andrew*
The Limes, Felsted, Nr Dunmow, Essex CH6 5HB. Called: June 1948, Gray's Inn

Holt *Jason Brian*
Police Station Representative, Stevens Solicitors, Fitzgerald House, Suterland Rd, Longton, Stoke on Trent, Staffordshire ST3 1HH, 01782 343353, Fax: 01782 599321. Called: Oct 1996, Middle Temple, LLB (Hons)(B'ham)

Holt *Peter Alexander*
C/O Langley & Co, 199 Bishopsgate, London EC2M 3TY, 0171 814 6637, Fax: 0171 814 6604. Called: Mar 1996, Inner Temple, LLB (Teeside)

Holter *Michael Rolf*
Wilmer, Cutler & Pickering, 4 Carlton Gardens, Pall Mall, London SW1Y 5AA, 0171 872 1000, Fax: 0171 839 3537. Called: Nov 1988, Lincoln's Inn, BA Hons (Cantab)

Hon *Chi Keung*
Called: Nov 1994, Middle Temple, LLB (Hons)

Hon *Omar Adam*
Called: Nov 1996, Middle Temple, LLB (Hons)

Honey *Damian James Bartholemew*
Holman Fenwick & Willan, Marlow House, Lloyds Avenue, London EC3N 3AL, 0171 488 2300, Fax: 0171 481 0316. Called: Nov 1994, Inner Temple, LLB (Sheff)

Honeyball *Dr Simon Eric*
Head of Department of Law, University of Exeter 1993-1995 Senior Lecturer in Law, Chilton Barton, Chilton, Stockleigh Pomeroy, Nr Crediton EX17 4AQ, 01363 866198, Fax: 01363 263196. Called: July 1996, Middle Temple, LLB (Hons), PhD (B'ham), ARCM

Hong *Aeron Yea Chun*
(60) 3 7743063, and Member Malaysian Bar. Called: Oct 1995, Middle Temple, LLB (Hons)

Hoo *Alan*
16th Floor, Malahon Centre, 10-12 Stanley Street, Central, 852-28686155, Fax: 852-28106795, Queen's Counsel in Hong Kong and Member Hong Kong Bar. Called: Nov 1973, Middle Temple, LLB (Lond)

Hoo *Miss Lina*
Called: Nov 1997, Lincoln's Inn, LLB (Hons)(L'pool)

Hoo *Miss Sheau Peng*
Called: Oct 1993, Middle Temple, BA (Hons)

Hood *Ms Rachel Dene Serena*
and Member Attorney at Law, California. Called: July 1976, Middle Temple, MA Hons [Cantab]

Hood *Miss Rosalind Emily* •
Court Clerk, Secretariat Offices, Court House, London Road, Dorking, Surrey, 01306 885544. Called: Nov 1986, Gray's Inn

Hoodless *Neil Gordon* •
Senior Crown Prosecutor, Crown Prosecution Service, 5th Floor, St Peters House, Gower Street, Derby DE1, 01332 621600. Called: Nov 1989, Middle Temple, LLB(Hons)(Essex)

Hooker *Miss Louise Jane*
Called: Nov 1993, Gray's Inn, LLB

Hoon *Geoffrey William MP*
House of Commons, King Charles House, Standard Hill, Nottingham, NG1 6FX. Called: July 1978, Gray's Inn, MA (Cantab)

Hooper *Brian Michael* •
Grade 6 Senior Principal, Dept of Trade & Industry, 10-18 Victoria Street, London SW1H 0NN, 0171 215 3020. Called: July 1971, Middle Temple

Hooper *Graham Boucher*
Clerk to the Justices, Leicestershire Magistrates' Ct, The Court House, Woodgate, Loughborough LE11 2XB, 01509 215715, Fax: 01509 261714. Called: July 1984, Lincoln's Inn, LLB

Hoosen *Abdul Aziz*
113 New Henry House, 10 Ice House Street, Central, 852 8770087, Fax: 852 25246202, and Member Hong Kong Bar. Called: Nov 1974, Gray's Inn, BA (McGill)

Hope *Jacques Derek*
Called: Nov 1952, Gray's Inn, LLB (Manch)

Hope *John Richard*
Deputy Clerk to the Justices, Chief Executive Wiltshire MCC, 43/55 Milford Street, Salisbury SP1 2BP, 0722 333225, Fax: 0722 413395. Called: Nov 1980, Gray's Inn

Hope *Ms Karen Andrea*
Called: Nov 1997, Gray's Inn, BA

Hopkin *Ms Jean Winifred*
01298 872327, and Member Hong Kong Bar. Called: July 1987, Lincoln's Inn, BA

Hopkins *Anthony*
Called: Oct 1997, Middle Temple, LLB (Hons)(Kingston)

Hopkins *Christopher Neil*
Called: Oct 1995, Gray's Inn, BA

Hopkins *Nicholas Martin*
Called: July 1984, Middle Temple, LLB (Bucks)

Hopper *Martyn John* •
The Securities & Investments, Board, Gavrelle House, 2-14 Bunhill Row, London EC1Y 8RA, 0171 638 1240, Fax: 0171 382 5997. Called: Nov 1991, Middle Temple, BA Hons (Oxon), LLM (Lond)

Hopwell *Mark David*
Called: Oct 1997, Lincoln's Inn, LLB (Hons)(Derby)

Hopwood *Miss Sandra Margaret*
Called: July 1985, Gray's Inn, LLB

Horan *Shaun Patrick Robert*
Called: Nov 1995, Inner Temple, LLB (Soton)

Horn *Mark Phillip Malcolm* •
International Aluminium and Steel Analyst, T Hoare & Co, 4th Floor, Cannon Bridge, 25 Dowgate Hill, London EC4R 2YA, 0171 220 7001, Fax: 0171 929 1836. Called: Nov 1993, Lincoln's Inn, BA, BA (Hons) & MA, (Rhodes S.A.), LLB, (Lond), Dip in Bus, Admin, MSI (Dip)

Horn *Miss Shirley Ann*
Senior Legal Adviser, Secretariat Offices, The Court House, Tufton Street, Ashford, Kent TN23 1QS, 01233 663204, Fax: 01233 663206. Called: Feb 1987, Middle Temple, BA (Hons) (Kent)

Hornby *Mrs Elizabeth Jane*
Consultant, Elizabeth Hornby & Associates, 30 Welford Place, Wimbledon, London SW19 5AJ, 0181 944 1004, Fax: 0181 944 1004. Called: July 1988, Gray's Inn, LLB (Notts), M.Phil (Cantab)

Horne *Brian Joseph* •
Principal Crown Prosecutor, Crown Prosecution Service, 2nd Floor, Portland House, Stag Place, Victoria, London SW1E 5BH. Called: Nov 1986, Inner Temple, LLB (PCL), LLM (Lond)

Horne *John Newport*
Senior Executive, The General Council of the Bar, 3 Bedford Row, London WC1R 4DB, 0171 242 0082, Fax: 0171 831 9217. Called: Nov 1972, Gray's Inn, BCL

Horne *Miss Zhinga Arlette*
Legal Advisor, Phillips & Williams, Middle Street, P O Box 262, St Vincent, (809) 456 1390 or 456 1580, Fax: (809) 456 2344, and Member St Vincent & the Grenadines Bar. Called: Oct 1995, Middle Temple, LLB (Hons), LLM (Cantab), LLM, IMLI (Malta)

Horseman *Richard Thomas*
Called: Nov 1995, Gray's Inn, BA (St.Louis), LLB

Horsford *Cyril Edward Sheehan CVO*
Clerk to Bar Disciplinary Tribunal, 32 Prairie Street, London SW8 3PP. Called: Feb 1953, Inner Temple, MA (Cantab)

Horsington *Simon* •
Fidelity Investments Services, Oakhill House, 130 Tonbridge Road, Hildenborough, Tonbridge, Kent TN11 9DZ, 01732 777473, 20 Britton Street, 1st Floor, London, EC1M 5NQ. Called: July 1978, Gray's Inn

Horton *Daniel Edmund*
Level 62, MCL Centre, Martin's Place, Sydney, NSW 2000 Australia, QC Sydney Brick Court Chambers, 15/19 Devereux Court, London, WC2R 3JJ. Called: July 1985, Middle Temple, LLB (Sydney)

Horton-Strachan *Mrs Arlene Patricia*
Called: Nov 1995, Gray's Inn, BSc (W.Indies), LLB (Lond)

Hosein *Miss Aisling Tara Philomena* •
Called: Nov 1990, Middle Temple, LLB (W Indies)

Hosein *Faarees Fayaz*
39 Richmond Street, PO Box 1003, Port of Spain, Trinidad W.I., 623-2695/8303, Fax: 623-8303, Attorney-at-Law, Supreme Court of Trinidad & Tobago (Admitted October 1988), Attorney-at-Law, Supreme Court of Barbados (Admitted May 1991). Called: July 1988, Lincoln's Inn, LLB (Hons) (Dundee)

Hosking *Emile John*
London Rent Assessment Panel, 99 Priory Road, London NW6 3NL. Called: Nov 1976, Lincoln's Inn, LLB, LLM (Lond), MSc, FCIArb ARICS

Hoskins *Nicholas John*
46 Par-La-Ville Road, Hamilton HM11, Bermuda, (441) 296 0253, Fax: (441) 296 0809, and Member Bermuda. Called: Nov 1992, Middle Temple, LLB (Hons, Bucks)

Hossain *Miss Lolita Lamis*
Called: July 1997, Lincoln's Inn, LLB (Hons)(LSE)

Hotchen *Miss Jennifer Marie Anne*
Deputy Chief Clerk, Inner London Magistrates', Courts Service, 65 Romney Street, London SW1 3RD. Called: July 1985, Middle Temple, BA (Keele)

Hotham *Anthony TD*
Called: Nov 1971, Middle Temple

Hough *Mrs Alison Jayne*
Called: July 1997, Lincoln's Inn, LLB (Hons)(Lond)

Houghton *Anthony Kenneth*
Des Voeux Chambers, 10/F Bank of East Asia Bldg, 10 Des Voeux Road Central, 2526-3071, Fax: 2810 5287/5309/0274, and Member Hong Kong Bar. Called: Nov 1988, Gray's Inn, LLB (Lond), ARICS, AHKIS,FCI Arb

Houghton *Edward John Willoughby*
Justices' Clerk, Fixed Penalty Clerk for Inner London. London Parking Adjudicator, Marylebone Magistrates Court, 181 Marylebone Road, London NW1 5QS, 0171 706 1261, Fax: 0171 724 9884. Called: July 1975, Gray's Inn, MA (Cantab)

Houghton-Jones *Mrs Gaynor*
Justices Clerk, Inner London Magistrates', Courts Service, 65 Romney Street, London SW1P 3RD, 0171 799 3072. Called: Nov 1971, Gray's Inn, LLB (Wales)

Hourican *James Kevin*
4903 Island View Street, Oxnard, CA 93035, 011-1-805-984447922, Major, United States Marine Corps Reserve and Member Pennsylvania Bar California Bar. Called: Feb 1994, Gray's Inn, BA JD (Pittsburgh)

House *Christopher* •
Assistant Treasury Solicitor, Dept of Education/Employment, Queen Anne's Chambers, 28 Broadway, London SW1H 9JS. Called: Nov 1976, Lincoln's Inn, LLB (Lond)

Housego *Nigel William*
Manager, Legal Dept, Hambro Legal Protection Ltd, Stephenson Road, Colchester, Essex CO4 4QR, 0990 234500, Fax: 0990 234508. Called: Nov 1989, Lincoln's Inn, LLB

How *Chi Hoong Nicholas*
Called: July 1996, Middle Temple, LLB (Hons)(Bris)

How *Miss Su Fen*
Called: July 1997, Lincoln's Inn, LLB (Hons)(Wales)

Howard *David*
Called: Mar 1996, Gray's Inn, LLB (Wales)

Howard *Ian Charles*
Called: Feb 1958, Middle Temple, MA

Howard *Miss Jane Anna*
Called: Mar 1998, Middle Temple, LLB (Hons)

Howard *Michael MP QC* (1982)
Recorder, 4 Breams Buildings, London, EC4A 1AQ. Called: Nov 1964, Inner Temple, BA, LLB (Cantab)

Howard *Ms Rebecca Alexandra*
Employment Litigator, Rowley Ashworth Solicitors, 247 The Broadway, Wimbledon, London SW19 1SE, 0181 543 2277, Fax: 0181 543 0143. Called: Oct 1991, Middle Temple, BSc

Howard *Robin Ivan*
Called: July 1976, Gray's Inn, Associate of the, ICAEW

Howard *Dr Timothy John*
Called: May 1996, Gray's Inn, B.Med.Sci, B.M.B.S, (Nottingham)

Howe *Allen*
2 Orchard Drive, Whitchurch, Cardiff, S Glamorgan CF4 2AE, 01222 626626. Called: Nov 1953, Middle Temple

Howe *Peter Charles* •
Company Secretary, Professional Services, (Life & Pensions) Limited, Allied Dunbar Centre, Station Road, Swindon SN1 1EL, 01793 514514, Fax: 01793 513076. Called: July 1974, Gray's Inn, LLB

Howe of Aberavon *Lord PC,CH QC* (1965)
House of Lords, London SW1A 0PW, 0171 236 0137. Called: Feb 1952, Middle Temple, MA, LLB (Cantab)

Howell *Lt Col David Malcom OBE*
Chief Military Legal Advisor GOC Hong Kong. Called: July 1973, Lincoln's Inn, LLB (Hons)

Howells *Ian David* •
Legal Advisor, Sema Group plc, 3300 Solihull Parkway, Birmingham Business park, Birmingham B37 7YQ, 0121 627 5411, Fax: 0121 627 5334. Called: July 1989, Middle Temple, LLB

Howse *Miss Patricia Geraldine* •
Legal Unit (HO-4), Bank of England, Threadneedle Street, London EC2R 8AH, 0171 601 4367, Fax: 0171 601 3865. Called: Nov 1972, Gray's Inn, LLB

Hoyle *Dr Robert*
Called: Nov 1996, Inner Temple, MA (Cantab), MSc (Bris), MA, Dphil (Oxon)

Huang *Miss Lianne*
Financial Analyst, Bankers Trust Company, (65) 331 4798. Called: July 1997, Gray's Inn, LLB (Bristol)

Hubbard *Miss Rosemary Sylvia* •
Legal Adviser, The Brewers & Licensed, Retailers Association, 42 Portman Square, London W1H 0BB, 0171 486 4831, Fax: 0171 935 3991. Called: July 1974, Inner Temple, LLB

Hubbick *Mrs Elizabeth Anne JP,*
Associate, Bacon & Woodrow, St Olaf House, London Bridge City, London SE1 2PE, 0171 716 7434, Fax: 0171 716 7144. Called: July 1986, Lincoln's Inn, BA (Dunelm), Dip Law (PCL)

Hudgson *Ms Fiona Jane*
Garrett & Co Solicitors, Abbots House, Abbey Street, Reading RG1 3BD, 0118 949 0000, Fax: 0118 949 0049, Former Solicitor. Called: Feb 1995, Middle Temple, LLB, BSc (Melbourne)

Hudson *Alastair Scott*
Lecturer in Law, Kings College University of London, Legal Affairs, Policy Advisor Labour Party. Called: Oct 1991, Lincoln's Inn, LLB (Hons) (Lond), LLM (Hons)(Lond)

Hudson *Miss Emma Ceril* •
Community Care Lawyer Senior Lawyer, London Borough of Lewisham. Called: Nov 1992, Inner Temple, LLB (Hons)

Hudson *Frank Michael Stanislaus*
Former Recorder of the Crown Court. Called: June 1961, Middle Temple, BA

Hudson Davies *Gwilym Ednyfed*
2 King's Bench Walk, 1st Floor, Temple, London, EC4Y 7DE. Called: July 1975, Gray's Inn, MA (Oxon)

Huebner *Michael Denis CB* •
Chief Executive of the Court Service,
Deputy Clerk of the Crown in Chancery,
The Court Service, Southside, 105 Victoria
Street, London SW1 6QT. Called: Nov 1965,
Gray's Inn, BA

Huggett *Miss Clare Lesley*
Called: Nov 1987, Lincoln's Inn, LLB
(Bristol)

Huggins *Adrian Armstrong*
Temple Chambers, 16th Floor, One Pacific
Place, 88 Queensway, 852 2523 2003, Fax:
852 2523 6343, QC (Hong Kong) and
Member Hong Kong Bar. Called: Nov 1975,
Gray's Inn, MA (Cantab), LLM

Huggins *Anthony Arthur*
Hayes Barton, Betchworth, Surrey RH3 7DF,
01737 842648. Called: Feb 1959, Middle
Temple

Hugh-Jones *Michael Gwyn*
C/O Victorian Bar, 205 William Street,
Melbourne, Victoria 3000, 03 9608 7111,
Barrister & Solicitor, High Court of Australia
& Supreme Court of Victoria. and Member
Victoria Bar. Called: July 1970, Lincoln's Inn

Hughes *Alan John* •
Head of Prosecutions (Manchester), H M
Customs & Excise, Solicitor's Office, Ralli
Quays West, 3 Stanley Street, Salford
M60 9LB, 0161 827 0553, Fax: 0161 827
0550. Called: Nov 1971, Middle Temple

Hughes *Anthony Pelham Cotton*
Coopers & Lybrand, 1 Embankment Place,
London WC2N 6NN, 0171 213 5466, Fax:
0171 213 2418. Called: Nov 1975, Inner
Temple, MA,ATII

Hughes *Barry Michael* •
Assistant Chief Crown Prosecuter, Crown
Prosecution Service, Portland House, Stag
Place, Victoria, London SW1E 5BH, 0171
915 5775. Called: Nov 1983, Middle
Temple, LLB (Sheff)

Hughes *Charles Michael*
Yewlands, Penton Grafton, Nr Andover,
Hants SP11 0RR, 01264 772330. Called: Jan
1937, Middle Temple

Hughes *Clarence Albert Fitzgerald*
and Member Guyana & Grenada Bars
Cloisters, 1st Floor, Temple, London, EC4Y
7AA. Called: Feb 1958, Inner Temple, LLB

Hughes *David Gordon*
Called: Oct 1997, Middle Temple, BA
(Hons)(Wolves), CPE (Glamorgan)

Hughes *David Martin* •
Senior Crown Prosecutor, Crown
Prosecution Service, 4 Artillery Row,
London SW1. Called: Nov 1984, Gray's Inn,
LLB

Hughes *Gareth Bryn* •
Chief Advocate, Westminster City Council,
City Hall, 64 Victoria Street, London SW1.
Called: Nov 1984, Lincoln's Inn, LLB
(Cardiff)

Hughes *Geoffrey Tudor*
Called: May 1955, Gray's Inn, MA (Oxon)

Hughes *Miss Gwyneth Elizabeth* •
Grade 7 Lawyer, Treasury Solicitor's Dept,
28 Broadway, London SW1H 9JS.
Called: Nov 1992, Lincoln's Inn, BA (Hons)

Hughes *MrS Helen Sian* •
Senior Crown Prosecutor, Crown
Prosecution Service, 1-9 Romford Road,
Stratford, London E15, 0181 534 6601, Fax:
0181 519 9690. Called: Oct 1993, Inner
Temple, BSc (Lond), CPE

Hughes *Jonathan Patrick*
Solomon, Zauderer, Ellenhorn,, Frisher &
Sharp, 45 Rockefeller Plaza, New York, NY
10111, (212) 424 0728, Fax: (212) 956
4068, and Member New York Bar.
Called: Nov 1983, Middle Temple, LLB
(Sheff)

Hughes *Mrs Merril* •
Principal Crown Prosecutor, Crown
Prosecution Service, 4-6 Prebendal Court,
Oxford Road, Aylesbury, Buckinghamshire.
Called: July 1984, Lincoln's Inn, LLB

Hughes *Miss Olwen Catherine*
Principle Assistant, Wrexham Magistrates'
Court, Bodhyfryd, Wrexham, Clwyd, 01978
291855, Fax: 01978 358213. Called: Feb
1988, Gray's Inn, LLB (Wales)

Hughes *Paul Laurence*
Called: Oct 1995, Middle Temple, LLB
(Hons)

Hughes *Miss Paula Jeffryne Denise* •
Crown Prosecutor, Crown Prosecution
Service, Devon/Cornwall at Exeter.
Called: Nov 1983, Gray's Inn, BA(York), Dip
Law

Hughes *Miss Sally Catherine*
Solicitor, Scott-Moucrieff, Harbour &,
Sinclair, 49/51 Farringdon Road, London
EC1M 3JB, 0171 242 4114, Fax: 0171 242
3605. Called: Oct 1992, Middle Temple,
BA(Hons)(Lond)

Hughes *Miss Susan Ann* •
Senior Crown Prosecutor Part Time Lecturer
in Adult Education, Crown Prosecution
Service, Cambia House, Merthyd Tydfil
Industrial, Estate, Pentrebach, Merthyd
Tydfil CF48 4X. Called: Nov 1982, Gray's
Inn, LLB (Leeds)

Hughes *Miss Suzy Belinda* •
Legal Counsel, Central & Eastern Europe, A
T & T Capital Limited, 66 Buckingham Gate,
London SW1E 6AU, 0171 411 4800, Fax:
0171 411 5032. Called: Nov 1991, Lincoln's
Inn, LLB (Hons) (Manch)

Hughes Ferrari *Mrs Margaret Hazell*
Hughes & Cummings, P.O. Box 32, Saint
Vincent & The Grenadines, 809 456 1954/
1711, Fax: 809 457 2768, and Member Saint
Vincent and The Grenadines Bar.
Called: July 1990, Lincoln's Inn, LLB (Lond)

Hughes-O'Flanagan *Mrs Margaret
Winifred* •
Legal Advisor, Bank of Ireland, 36 Queen
Street, London EC4R 1BN, 0171 236 2000,
Fax: 0171 634 3102. Called: Feb 1981,
Lincoln's Inn, MA, LLB (Dublin), DEA (Paris)

Hugill *Miss Cheryl Dawn* •
Senior Principal Legal Officer, Solicitors
Office, HM Customs & Excise, New Kings
Beam House, 22 Upper Ground, London
SE1 9PJ, 0171 865 5187. Called: Nov 1979,
Gray's Inn, LLB (Lond)

Hugill *John QC (1976)*
Recorder (retired 1996), 45 Hardman Street,
Manchester M3 3HA, 01260 224 368, Fax:
01260 224 703. Called: Feb 1954, Middle
Temple, MA (Cantab)

Hui *Wai Chun Sammy*
1318 Princes Building, Chater Road, Central,
2526 8128, Fax: 2526 8500, and Member
Hong Kong Bar. Called: July 1991, Lincoln's
Inn, LLB (Hons)

Hui *Miss Ying Ying*
Called: Nov 1996, Gray's Inn, LLB

Huka *Mrs Geraldine Oghenenyorbe*
Called: July 1981, Middle Temple, LLB, LLM

Hulme *Mrs Susan Anne* •
Deputy Arbitration Officer, Arbitration Unit,
Southwark Council, East House, London
SE5 8QB, 0171 525 7483, Fax: 0171 525
7422, Pioneered Concept and Practice of
Pupillage in a Law Centre. Called: Oct 1994,
Middle Temple, BSc (Hons), LLB (Hons),
ARCS (Lond)

Humberstone *Miss Sarah Georgina*
4 King's Bench Walk, Ground/First Floor,
Temple, London, EC4Y 7DL. Called: Nov
1984, Gray's Inn, LLB (Bristol)

Humby *Lee Richard*
Called: Mar 1997, Middle Temple, LLB
(Hons)

Hume *Miss Elizabeth Anna* •
Legal Officer, Welsh Office, Crown
Buildings, Cathays Park, Cardiff CF1 3NQ.
Called: Nov 1983, Gray's Inn, LL.B (Wales)

Humphrey *Captain David Roger RN* •
Chief Naval Judge Advocate/ Recorder.
Called: July 1975, Middle Temple

Humphrey *Miss Tanya Clare*
Called: Nov 1997, Middle Temple, LLB
(Hons)(Exon)

Humphreys *David Charlton*
P/t Chairman Property Investment
Company. Called: Jan 1948, Inner Temple,
MA (Oxon)

Humphreys *Gordon David Thomas*
21 Boulevard Pierre Dupong, L-1430
Luxembourg, Luxembourg, 352 44 65 64,
Fax: 352 44 65 64, and Member Belgium
Bar. Called: Nov 1986, Middle Temple, LLB
(Bucks), LLM (UWIST), Licence speciale en,
droit Economique, (Univ de Liege)

Humphreys *Nicholas Bruce* •
Lecturer in Law, Bower Cotton, 36
Whitefriars Street, London EC4Y 8DH, 0171
353 3040. Called: Oct 1994, Lincoln's Inn,
LLB (Hons), LLM (Lond)

Humphries *Neil Thomas*
Called: Nov 1993, Lincoln's Inn, LLB (Hons)

Humphryes *Miss Gail Kay* •
Consultant - Special Projects Securities &
Futures Commissio Hong Kong. Called: July
1983, Middle Temple, BA Kent

Hungerford-Welch *Peter John* •
Senior Lecturer (I.C.S.L.), Inns of Court
school of Law, 4 Gray's Inn Place, London
WC1R 5DX, 0171 404 5787, Fax: 0171 831
4188. Called: July 1984, Inner Temple, LLB
(Hull)

Hunt *Miss Angela Elizabeth*
Called: Nov 1996, Lincoln's Inn, LLB
(Hons)(Leeds)

Hunt *Mrs Melinda Rose* •
Justices Clerks Assistant, The Courthouse,
Victoria AvenuE, Southend-on-Sea Essex,
01702 3488491. Called: Nov 1994, Middle
Temple, LLB (Hons), Dip Law

Hunt *Paul David* •
Principal Legal Officer, Harborough District
Council, Adam & Eve Street, Market
Harborough, Leics LE16 7AG, 01858
410000, Fax: 01858 462766. Called: July
1985, Lincoln's Inn, BA

Hunt *Richard Henry*
Registrar High Court of Justice in
Bankruptcy. Chief Registrar 1981-1984, 2
Woodland Close, Ingatestone, Essex
CM4 9SR, 01277 352328. Called: Jan 1936,
Middle Temple, MA (Oxon)

Hunt *Ronald Frank*
25 Worlds View, Abelia Street, Somerset
West 7130, Cape, 8553860. Called: July
1967, Inner Temple

Hunt *Miss Victoria Mary*
Called: Oct 1993, Middle Temple, BA
(Hons))Leic

Hunter *Mrs Johanis Mariam* •
Lawyer Grade 7, Court of Criminal appeal,
Royal Court of Justice, The Strand, London,
0171 936 6098. Called: Oct 1990, Lincoln's
Inn, LLB (Brunel)

Huq *Faheemul*
Called: Nov 1997, Lincoln's Inn, LLB
(Wolver'ton)

Huq *Rafique-ul*
Head of Chambers, Huq & Company, 47/1
Purana Paltan, Dhaka, Bangladesh, 955 2196
or 955 5953, Fax: 956 2434, Senior
Advocate, Supreme Court of Bangladesh and
Member Bangladesh Bar Association.
Called: Nov 1962, Lincoln's Inn, MA, LLB

Huque *Mrs Daliah Shah*
In House Barrister, J H Nathan & Co, 21
Dudden Hill Lane, London NW10.
Called: Feb 1974, Lincoln's Inn

Hurhangee *Ashley*
Called: Mar 1997, Lincoln's Inn, LLB (Hons)

Husain *Farrukh Najeeb*
Called: July 1996, Inner Temple, LLB, LLM
(Lond)

Husain *Maqbool Asker* •
Senior Crown Prosecutor, Crown
Prosecution Service, 8th Floor, Prospect
House, 81 Station Road, Croydon.
Called: Nov 1985, Lincoln's Inn, BA

Husain *Rehan*
Called: Nov 1996, Lincoln's Inn, LLB
(Hons)(Leeds)

Husain-Naviatti *Miss Robina*
Called: Nov 1997, Lincoln's Inn, BA (Hons)

Huskinson *Mrs Pennant Elfrida
Lascelles*
Called: May 1972, Inner Temple

Hussain *Asam*
Called: Nov 1996, Lincoln's Inn, Bsc
(Hons)(City)

Hussain *Miss Dheena*
Called: July 1997, Lincoln's Inn, LLB (Hons)

Hussain *Karamat*
Called: July 1996, Lincoln's Inn, LLB (Hons)

Hussain *Tariq Parvez*
Legal Advisor/Advocate, Alan Petherbridge
& Co, Solicitors/Advocates, 1st Floor, 10
Piece Hallyard, Bradford, 01274 724114,
Fax: 01274 724161. Called: Nov 1991,
Lincoln's Inn, LLB (Hons)

Hutchinson of Lullington *Lord* QC
(1961)
House of Lords, London SW1. Called: June
1939, Middle Temple, MA (Oxon)

Hutley *Robert Neil*
Justices' Chief Executive, Justices' Chief
Executive Unit, Vivian House, Newham
Quay, Truro, Cornwall TR1 2DP, 01872
271873, Fax: 01872 271859. Called: Feb
1976, Middle Temple, LLB (Lond)

Huxtable *Mrs Alison Jane* •
Head of Legal & Commercial. Called: July
1983, Gray's Inn, LLB Hons (Manc)

Hyams *David Ian* •
Vice President, Commercial and Legal
Affairs, Fujitsu ICL Computers Ltd, Lovelace
Road, Bracknell, Berks RG12 8SN, 01344
475000. Called: July 1981, Middle Temple,
LLB [Lond]

Hyde *David Austin*
Called: Nov 1997, Lincoln's Inn, BA
(Hons)(Lancs)

Hyder *Stuart Henry* •
Senior Counsel, Chevron UK Ltd, 2 Portman
Street, London W1H 0AN, 0171 487 8828,
Fax: 0171 487 8905. Called: July 1974,
Lincoln's Inn, MA (Cantab) MBA

Hynes *Dermott Francis*
Brandon Lodge, New Ross, Co. Wexford,
Ireland, 0151 425005. Called: July 1963,
Inner Temple, LLM, LLB (Lond)

Iacovides *Petros*
Libra Housa, 21 P Catelaris Str, P O Box
5001, Nicosia, Cyprus, 02 46 67 66, Fax: 02
44 87 77, and Member Cyprus Bar.
Called: Feb 1994, Gray's Inn, B.Soc.Sc
(Keele)

Ian *Lim Teck Soon*
Called: Nov 1997, Inner Temple, LLB (Lond)

Ibbotson *David James*
Bedell & Orston, Normandy House, Greville
Street, St Helier, Jersey, 814814, Fax:
814815. Called: Mar 1996, Middle Temple,
LLB (Hons)(Wales)

Ibrahim *Miss Hasnah*
Legal Counselor, DPP at the Attorney
General's Chambers of law, Brunei,
Darussalam, Attorney General's Chambers,
Bandar Seri Begawan, 2016 Negara, Brunei,
Darussalam. Called: July 1994, Lincoln's Inn,
LLB (Hons)

Ibrahim *Ian*
Called: Oct 1997, Middle Temple, BSc
(Hons), MSc, Dip in Law (Plymou)

Ibrahim *Sarfraz* •
Senior Crown Prosecutor, Crown
Prosecution Service, Froomsgate House,
Rupert Street, Bristol, Avon BS1 2PS, 0117
9273093, Fax: 0117 9230697. Called: July
1982, Gray's Inn, LLB (Lond)

Ibrahim *Miss Shadida*
Called: July 1993, Lincoln's Inn, LLB (Hons)

Idan *Lionel*
Called: Mar 1996, Middle Temple, LLB
(Hons)

Idrees *Rasheed*
Advocate, Haidermota & Co, 303-305 Kashif
Centre, Sharea Faisal, Karachi 75530,
519226/5662589/5133714, Fax: 5662583/
58770761, and Member Pakistan Bar.
Called: Nov 1994, Inner Temple, LLB (Lond)

Idris *Miss Kemi Rashida* •
Office of the Solicitor. Called: Feb 1995,
Lincoln's Inn, LLB (Hons)(Bris)

Idris *Miss Norazlina*
and Member Malaysia Bar. Called: July 1994,
Lincoln's Inn, LLB (Hons)

Iles *Colin John*
Clerk to the Justices, Secretariat Offices,
The Courthouse, Tufton Street, Ashford,
Kent TN23 1QS, 01233 663203, Fax: 01233
663206. Called: Nov 1984, Middle Temple

Iles *Trevor Anthony*
4 Lansdown Close, Banbury, Oxon
OX16 9LH, 01295 254345. Called: Nov
1983, Middle Temple, M.Soc.Sc, DML, Dip,
Law

Illingworth *Graham*
16 Bromwich House, 45 Howson Terrace,
Richmond Hill, Richmond, Surrey
TW10 6RU, 0181 940 4655. Called: Feb
1964, Gray's Inn

Ilyas *Daud* •
Legal Advisor, European Bank for
Reconstruction & Development, 5
Whittingstall Road, London SW6 4EA, 0171
736 5137, Fax: 0171 371 7242, Advocate,
Supreme Court of Pakistan. Called: Nov
1959, Gray's Inn, BCL, MA (Oxon)

Ilyas *Gheias Uddin Azam*
Called: Mar 1996, Middle Temple, B.Sc
(Hons)(Leeds)

Ilyas Shaiba
Called: Mar 1998, Lincoln's Inn, LLB
(Hons)(Herts)

Impey Gerald Lawrence
Nigerian Bar Council (1964) Chief Editor
Lawtel, The Ashlish, 2 Close Famman, Port
Erin, Isle of Man IM9 6BJ, 01624 835548/
833550, Fax: 01624 624344/835551/
834022, and Member Nigerian Bar.
Called: July 1954, Middle Temple

Ina Miss Eucharia Asari •
Legal Adviser, DAS Legal Expenses
Insurance, Company Limited, DAS House,
Quay Side, Temple Back, Bristol BS1 6NH.
Called: Nov 1992, Inner Temple, LLB (E.
Lond), LLM (Cantab)

Ing Noel Denis CBE
37 Anthony Close, Colchester CO4 4LD.
Called: June 1958, Lincoln's Inn, MA (Oxon)

Ingham Charles Neill •
Assistant Chief Crown Prosecutor CPS
Anglia Part-time Industrial Tribunal
Chairman (London Health Region), Crown
Prosecution Service, Queen's House, 58
Victoria Street, St Albans, Herts AL1 3HZ,
01727 818104, Fax: 01727 833144, and
Member Hong Kong Bar. Called: Nov 1972,
Inner Temple, BA (Lond)

Inglese Anthony Michael Christopher •
Deputy Treasury Solicitor, Treasury
Solicitors Dept, Queen Annes Chambers, 28
Broadway, London SW1H 9JS. Called: Nov
1976, Gray's Inn, MA, LLB

Inglewood The Rt Hon Lord D.L.
Hutton-in-the Forest, Penrith, Cumbria
CA11 9TH, 017684 84500, Fax: 017684
84571. Called: July 1975, Lincoln's Inn, MA
(Cantab), ARICS

Inglis George Grant Gordon Otto
Called: Oct 1991, Inner Temple, BSc
(Dunelm), LLB (Bucks)

Ingman Miss Ruth Margaret
Called: Feb 1992, Inner Temple, LLB

Ingram Jamie Andrew •
Business Affairs Assistant, Sony Psygnosis,
Napier Court, Stephenson Way, Wavetree
Technology Park, Liverpool L13 1HD, 0151
2823000, Fax: 0151 2823001. Called: Oct
1994, Middle Temple, LLB (Hons)

Ingram Philip John
Called: Nov 1996, Lincoln's Inn, LLB (Hons)

Innes Thomas John Stanley
64 Monnow Street, Monmouth, Gwent
NP5 3EN, 01600 2372. Called: Nov 1982,
Middle Temple, BA (Oxon)

Insole Roy William
The Garden House, Smeeth, Ashford, Kent
TN25 6SP, 0130 381 3011, Fax: 0130 381
4313. Called: Nov 1974, Inner Temple

Ioannides Mrs Eleni
Chr.Sozou 2, Flat 206, Nicosia, 357 2
473558/ 474533, Fax: 357 2 475692, and
Member Cyprus Bar. Called: Nov 1961,
Middle Temple

Ip Kwai Hong
Called: Oct 1995, Lincoln's Inn, LLB
(Hons)(Lond)

Ip Tak Keung
603 Ruttonjee House, 11 Duddell Street,
Central, 2868 1249, Fax: 2868 0368, and
Member Hong Kong Bar Singapore Bar
Barrister of the Australian Capital Terrritory.
Called: July 1985, Gray's Inn, LLB (Bucks)
B.Soc.Sc, LLM (LSE),ACIArb, Dip (Chinese
Law)

Irani Miss Simone
Contracts Administrator (Hewlett-Packard,
Singapore), 3 Pandan Valley, [H] 16-313,
4699286/4677276, Fax: 4633209.
Called: Nov 1995, Middle Temple, LLB
(Hons)

Ireland Sidney Harold
01753 663684. Called: Nov 1979, Middle
Temple, B Com (Hons), BSC (Hons)

Irvine Norman Forrest QC (1973)
11 Upland Park Road, Oxford OX2 7RU,
01865 513570, Formerly a
Solicitor,Scotland. Called: Nov 1955, Gray's
Inn, BL (Glasgow)

Irving Ms Frances Margaret
Called: July 1996, Gray's Inn, MA
(Edinburgh)

Isa Amir Yahaya
Called: July 1997, Middle Temple, BA
(Hons)(Keele)

Isaac Miss Elma Gene
Called: Nov 1997, Lincoln's Inn, LLB (Hons)

Isaac Tito Shane
Legal Assistant Member of the panel of
Mediators, 111 North Bridge Road, [H]23-
01, Peninsula Plaza, Singapore 0617, (065)
3382251, Fax: (065) 3381818, and Member
Singapore Bar. Called: Nov 1994, Gray's Inn,
LLB (Leeds)

Isaacs Miss Deborah Jane •
Contoller of Legal Services, London
Weekend Television Ltd, South Bank
Television Centre, London SE1 9LT, 0171
261 3586, Fax: 0171 928 7825. Called: Nov
1987, Lincoln's Inn, MA (Oxon) Dip Law

Ishak Miss Irma Norris
Called: Nov 1997, Lincoln's Inn, LLB
(Hons)(Wales)

Ishaque Miss Shabnam
Called: Oct 1996, Lincoln's Inn, BSc
(Hons)(Lond), CPE

Isherwood John Denys
Director of Development, PT Fajar
Surashakti, Samudera Indonesia Building,
Jalan Let.S. Parman Kav 35, Jakarta 11480,
Jakarta 5307877, Fax: Jakarta 5482567.
Called: Nov 1986, Gray's Inn, Bsc(Eng)
MBA, CEng, Eur Ing, FICE, FIArb

Isherwood Malcolm Oliver •
Principal Crown Prosecutor, Crown
Prosecution Service, 2nd Floor, Red Rose
House, Lancaster Road, Preston, Lancashire
PR1 1ER. Called: Nov 1980, Gray's Inn, BA

Islam Abdul Kashem Muhammad
Fakrul
Called: May 1997, Gray's Inn, BSS, MSS
(Dhaka), LLB (Hertfordshire)

Islam Aminul Ruhul
Called: Oct 1997, Lincoln's Inn, LLB
(E.London)

Islam Misbahul
5 Nottingwood House, Clarendon Road,
London W11. Called: Nov 1977, Lincoln's
Inn, MA, MSc, Dip M, DIA

Islam Zaglul
Called: Nov 1995, Lincoln's Inn, BSc (Hons)
(Wales)

Ismail Abdul Rashid
Called: July 1994, Lincoln's Inn, LLB (Hons)

Ismail Miss Fariza
Called: July 1994, Lincoln's Inn, LLB (Hons)

Ismail Miss Shahin
Called: Nov 1993, Lincoln's Inn, LLB (Hons)

Ismail Miss Zarina
Called: Nov 1997, Middle Temple, LLB
(Hons)

Israeli Guy
2 Derech Haganim St, Kfar Shmaryahu
46910, and Member Israel. Called: Oct 1994,
Lincoln's Inn, LLB (Hons)(Bucks), LLM (LSE)

Issa Khoda-Baksh Mahmood Ibreh
Called: Nov 1996, Inner Temple, LLB (Lond)

Ivamy Mrs Christine Ann Frances
7 Egliston Mews, London SW15 1AP, 0181
785 6718. Called: Nov 1968, Gray's Inn, MA
(Hons)

Ives Terence John
Superintendent, Hertfordshire Constabulary,
County H.Q., Welwyn Garden City, Herts,
01707 331177. Called: July 1990, Middle
Temple, MA (Cantab)

Iyer Mrs Rukmani Tiru Krishna
114A Newlands Road, Newlands,
Wellington, (64-4) 4773191, Fax: (64-4)
4773191. Called: July 1995, Gray's Inn, LLB
(Lond)

Izzard Miss Heidi Louise
Called: Nov 1996, Lincoln's Inn, BSc
(Hons)(Surrey)

Izzuddin Miss Izzaty
Called: July 1995, Inner Temple, LLB (Sheff)

Jaafar Miss Jafisah
Called: July 1992, Lincoln's Inn, BA (Hons)
(Kent)

Jaafar Sallehudin
Messrs Yeow & Salleh, Suite 6.02, 6th Floor,
Wisma MCA, Jalan Ampang, 50450 Kuala
Lumpur, 03 2623833, Fax: 03 2613833, and
Member Malaysia Bar. Called: Nov 1992,
Lincoln's Inn, LLB (Hons)(Sheff)

Jaafar-Thani Dzuhairi
Called: Nov 1996, Middle Temple, LLB
(Nott'm)

Jabbar Miss Sk. Jenwfa Khanom
Called: Mar 1997, Lincoln's Inn, LLB
(Hons)(Lond)

Jackson *Andrew Richard* ●
Grade 6 Lawyer, Serious Fraud Office, Elm House, 10-16 Elm Street, London WC1X OBJ, 0171 239 7139. Called: July 1987, Gray's Inn, LLB (Warwick)

Jackson *Calvin Leigh Raphael*
Head of Strategic Compensation Consulting, Watson Wyatt Partners, 21 Tothill Street, London SW1H 9LL, 0171 222 8033, Fax: 0171 222 9182. Called: July 1975, Lincoln's Inn, LLB,LLM (Lon), MPhil [Cantab]

Jackson *Ms Carol* ●
Crown Prosecution Service, 'D' Division, Manchester, 0161 908 2682. Called: Oct 1994, Inner Temple, BA (Essex), CPE (Lond)

Jackson *Professor David Cooper*
Immigration Appeal Tribunal, 231 Strand, London WC2. Called: Feb 1957, Inner Temple

Jackson *Miss Helen Elizabeth*
Called: Nov 1975, Middle Temple, MA (Hons), LLB

Jackson *James Alexander Heitz*
Called: Nov 1995, Inner Temple, BSc (Bris), MA (Lond), CPE

Jackson *Lee Anthony*
Caseworker, Refugee Legal Centre, Sussex House, 39-45 Bermondsey Street, London SE1 3XF, 0171 827 5362, Fax: 0171 378 1979. Called: Oct 1995, Lincoln's Inn, LLB (Hons)(Lond)

Jackson *Ms Madeleine Annette* ●
Acquisition Editor, Sweet and Maxwell Ltd, South Quay Plaza, 183 Marsh Wall, London E14 9FT, 0171 538 8686, Fax: 0171 538 8625, and Member Israel Bar. Called: Nov 1983, Middle Temple, BA Hons Law (Nott'm)

Jackson *Marc Richard Steen* ●
Called: Nov 1992, Middle Temple, LLB (Hons)(Hull)

Jackson *Mark Adrian* ●
Principal Crown Prosecutor, Crown Prosecution Service, 3rd Floor, Portland House, Stag Place, London SW1. Called: July 1986, Lincoln's Inn, LLB

Jackson *His Honour Peter Brierley*
Dep Chief Clerk ILMCS 1980-89 Registrar of Court of Appeal & Chief Clerk of the Grand Court 1989-93, Stipendary Magistrate 1993 to date., Magistrate's Chambers, Judicial Department, P.O. Box 495, George Town, Grand Cayman, 081 809 949 5151/4296, Fax: 081 809 949 9856. Called: July 1979, Gray's Inn, MA (Cantab), Dip in Crim.[Lond], FBIM, Teaching Cert in F.E

Jackson *Philip David Martin*
Lecturer in Law, Commercial Dispute Mediator, Flat 2, 73 Shooters Hill Road, Blackheath, London SE3 7HU, 0181 293 4210. Called: Nov 1995, Inner Temple, BSc (York), CPE (Lond)

Jackson *Ronald* ●
Legal Director & Company Secretary, LEP International Worldwide, Limited, Charles Stuart House, Epsom, Surrey KT17 4QP, 01372 812181, Fax: 01372 817397. Called: July 1975, Gray's Inn, LLB (Lond)

Jackson *Miss Samantha Jane*
Called: Nov 1996, Middle Temple, LLB (Hons), LLM

Jackson *Stephen Malcolm*
Bristol Claims & Property, Consultants, 27 Westbury Road, Westbury-On-Trym, Bristol BS9 3AX, 0117 9624665, Fax: 0117 9744701. Called: July 1975, Gray's Inn, LLB

Jackson *Mrs Tara Veronica* ●
Company Secretary. Called: July 1988, Middle Temple, LLB

Jackson *Warner*
Called: Feb 1991, Lincoln's Inn, LLB

Jackson-Lipkin *The Hon Mr Justice Miles Henry KCLJ, JP, QC,*
Arbitrator and Consultant M.L.C.I.A., (852) 2838 1838, Fax: (852) 2891 6993, and Member Hong Kong Bar New South Wales Bar. Called: June 1951, Middle Temple, FCIArb, CArb (Canada)

Jacob *Miss Cynty*
Called: Oct 1995, Middle Temple, LLB (Hons)

Jacob *George Ramkissoon*
Called: July 1994, Lincoln's Inn

Jacob *Peter Leo* ●
Lord Chancellor's Dept, Southside, 105 Victoria Street, London SW1E 6QT. Called: July 1974, Middle Temple

Jacobs *Miss Leonie Kathleen Jennie T'Sahai*
and Member St Vincent & The Grenadines Bar. Called: July 1995, Middle Temple, LLB (Hons)

Jacobs *Richard*
Arbitrator, American Arbitration Assoc, British Columbia Int'l Commercial Arbitration Centre, Suite 201, 1010 Harris Ave, Bellingham, Washington 98225, (360) 671 3116, Fax: (360) 671 6116, U.S. Immigration & Naturalization Law and Member California & Washington. Called: July 1978, Lincoln's Inn, LLB (Lond), NCA Certified, Mediator

Jacobs *Miss Susan Jane* ●
Crown Prosecutor, Crown Prosecution Service, The Cooperage, 8 Gainsford Street, London SE1 2NG. Called: Nov 1988, Gray's Inn, BA

Jacobs *Timothy Julian*
Called: Oct 1995, Middle Temple, BA (Hons)

Jacobsen *Miss Anne Marie Elisabeth*
Ledbury Cottage, Lebury Road, Reigate, Surrey RH2 9HN, 01737 249100, Former Deputy Charity Commissioner. Called: Nov 1950, Gray's Inn, BA (Hons) (Cantab)

Jacomb *Sir Martin Wakefield*
142 Holborn Bars, London EC1N 2NH. Called: Nov 1955, Inner Temple, MA

Jaganathan *Jagan Persath s/o*
Called: Nov 1996, Lincoln's Inn, LLB (Hons)(Wolv'ton)

Jaganathan *Miss Shanti*
Called: Nov 1996, Lincoln's Inn, LLB (Hons)(Leics)

Jaggers *Desmond* ●
Principal Crown Prosecutor, Crown Prosecution Service, Birmingham Branch 1, Colmore Gate, 2 Colmore Row, Birmingham B3 2QA, 0121 629 7200, Fax: 0121 629 7335. Called: July 1974, Inner Temple, LLB

Jaggi *Deepak* ●
Senior Legal Officer, The Office of the Solicitor, of Inland Revenue, Somerset House (East Wing), The Strand, London WC2R 1LB, 0171 438 7259, Fax: 0171 438 6246. Called: Nov 1977, Middle Temple, BA (Oxon)

Jagmohan *Ms Judith*
Called: Nov 1993, Middle Temple, BA (Hons)(Keele), LLM (Nott'm)

Jailani *Bin Shariff*
Called: July 1994, Lincoln's Inn, LLB (Hons)

Jalan *Prateek*
7th Floor, 233/5 Acharya J.C. Bose Road, Calcutta 700020, India, (91-33) 2475990/402549, Fax: (91-33) 401727, and Member India Bar. Called: July 1993, Inner Temple, BA (Delhi), BA (Cantab), LLM (Michigan)

Jalleh *Ms Mayleen Ann*
Law Lecturer LLM (Cantab), University of the West of, England, Frenchay Campus, Coldharbour Lane, Bristol BS16 1QY, 0117 9656261, and Member Malaysia Bar New York Bar. Called: July 1986, Lincoln's Inn, LLB (Hons) Warwick

Jamal *Miss Damaris Dorothy* ●
Crown Prosecutor, Crown Prosecution Service, 2nd Floor, Kings House, Kymberley Road, Harrow, Middlesex, 0181 424 8688. Called: July 1989, Gray's Inn, BA [Dunelm]

Jamaluddin *Miss Jasmin Hussain Jamalatiff*
Called: July 1994, Lincoln's Inn, LLB (Hons, Bucks)

Jamaludin *Miss Aini Hayati*
Advocate & Solicitor, High Court of Malaya, Messrs Lee Hishammuddin, Advocate & Solicitors, 16th Floor, Wisma Hla, Jalan Raja Chulan, 50200 Kuala Lumpur, (6-03) 2011681, Fax: (6-03) 2011714/2011746, and Member Malaysia Bar. Called: July 1995, Inner Temple, LLB (Nott)

James *Andrew John* ●
PNG Legal Adviser, GPT Ltd, Edge Lane, Liverpool L7 9NW, 0151 254 4340, Fax: 0151 254 3326. Called: July 1983, Gray's Inn, BA

James *Mrs Anita Mary* •
Senior Principal Legal Officer, Solicitor &
Legal Adviser's, Officer, Department of the,
Environment, Transport & the, Regions,
Gland House, Bressender Place, London
SW1E 5DU, 0171 890 4756, Fax: 0171 890
4752. Called: July 1974, Middle Temple, BA
Hons

James *Arnold Victor* •
Office of the Social Security,
Commissioners, Harp House, 83 farringdon
Street, London EC4A 4DH, 0171 353 3145.
Called: Nov 1991, Inner Temple, BSc, Dip
Law

James *Basil*
Presiding Special Commissioner of Income
Tax 1983. Called: June 1940, Lincoln's Inn,
MA (Cantab)

James *Brian Wardell CBE,*
Called: Feb 1961, Middle Temple, LLB
(Lond)

James *Mrs Clare*
Called: Mar 1996, Lincoln's Inn, LLB
(Hons)(Leics)

James *David John*
Called: May 1996, Gray's Inn, LLB

James *David Madoc* •
Legal Adviser (Grade 6), Dept of Trade &
Industry, 10-18 Victoria Street, London
SW1H ONN, 0171 215 3050, Fax: 0171 215
3141. Called: July 1973, Lincoln's Inn

James *Frederick Nicholas* •
Group Legal Adviser, Burmah Castrol Plc,
Burmah Castrol House, Pipers Way,
Wiltshire SN3 1RE, 01793 452500, Fax:
01793 618162. Called: July 1977, Inner
Temple

James *Miss Gloria Magdalen*
Blk 170, [H]02-865, Yishun Ave 7, pgr:
93062380/7530014, and Member Singapore.
Called: July 1995, Lincoln's Inn, LLB (Hons)

James *Miss Jacquelinne Agnes*
Gomez Building, High Street, St John's, P O
Box 1519, 268 462 4468/9, Fax: 268 462
0327, and Member Antigua Bar Barbuda Bar.
Called: Nov 1995, Lincoln's Inn, LLB
(Hons)(Leeds)

James *John Maxwell*
11 Broadmead Green, Thorpe End,
Norwich, Norfolk NR13 5DE. Called: June
1948, Lincoln's Inn, LLB (Lond)

James *Ms Julie* •
Assistant Director of Legal & Administrative
Services, City & County of Swansea, County
Hall, Swansea SA1 3SN, 01792 636012, Fax:
01792 636340. Called: July 1983, Gray's Inn,
BA Sussex

James *Leslie*
Called: Nov 1951, Gray's Inn, BA, LLB, FCIT

James *Miss Mabel Nirmala*
Legal Assistant, 64 Jalan 2/27C, Section 5,
Wang 59 MAJU, 53300 Kuala Lumpur, 03-
4118391. Called: July 1996, Lincoln's Inn,
LLB (Hons), LLM (Wolves)

James *Mark David*
Lecturer, Manchester Metropiltan Uni.,
School of Law, Hatersage Road, Manchester
M13 0JA, 0161 247 2432, Fax: 0161 224
0893. Called: Nov 1994, Lincoln's Inn, LLB
(Hons)(Leeds)

James *Miss Nilakrisna Isnarti*
Prins & Co, 24 LRG Kinabalu 1, Luyang PH
7, Jalan Kolam, 88300 Kota Kinabalu, Sabah,
(6088) 262858, Fax: (6088) 238808, and
Member Malaysia Bar Sabah Bar Sarawak
Bar. Called: Oct 1994, Lincoln's Inn, LLB
(Hons)(Hull), LLM (Lond)

James *Roger Ivor Rendall*
Baker & McKenzie, Hutchinson House, 14th
Floor, 10 Harcourt Road, Central, (852)
2846 2426, Fax: (852) 2845 0476, and
Member New York Bar (1990). Called: July
1988, Lincoln's Inn, LLB (Hons)

James *Miss Suzanne Margaret*
17 Downs Court Road, Purley, Surrey
CR8 1BE. Called: July 1985, Gray's Inn, BA
(Cantab), BA (Lond)

Jameson *Andrew Charles* •
Royal Naval Officer, c/o Office of the Chief
Naval, Judge Advocate, Royal Naval College,
Greenwich, London SE10 9NN, 0181 858
2154. Called: Oct 1993, Middle Temple, LLB
(Hons)(Newc)

Jameson *Gary Antony*
Called: Mar 1997, Lincoln's Inn, LLB (Hons)

Jamieson *Andrew* •
Legal Adviser/Director, I.T.I.M. Ltd,
International House, 26 Creechurch Lane,
London EC3A 5BA, 0171 338 0150, Fax:
0171 338 0151. Called: July 1985, Middle
Temple, BA (Lond), Dip Law, ACI Arb

Jamieson *Miss Cara*
Called: Oct 1994, Lincoln's Inn, LLB
(Hons)(Lond)

Jamieson *Maurice*
Assigned Defence Counsel to the
International Tribunal on war crimes in the
former Yugoslavia., and Member Scotland.
Called: July 1997, Middle Temple, LLB
(Hons)

Jamil *Zahid Usman*
Called: July 1997, Gray's Inn, LLB (Lond)

Jani *Miss Jamie*
Called: Oct 1995, Inner Temple, LLB (Lond)

Janner of Braunstone *Lord QC*
(1971)
Chairman, Parliamentary Employment Select
Committee 1992-96, House of Lords,
London SW1A 2PW, 0171 222 2863, Fax:
0171 222 2864. Called: July 1954, Middle
Temple, MA (Cantab), PhD (Hon)

Janusz *Mrs Frances Miriam* •
Principal Crown Prosecutor, Crown
Prosecution Service, 2 Bedford Park,
Croydon, Surrey CR0 2AP. Called: July 1979,
Lincoln's Inn, BA (Reading)

Jap *Ms Chee Miau*
Called: Nov 1971, Gray's Inn, LLB (Lond)

Jardine *Dr Francis Stephen John* •
Company/Commercial Lawyer, Morgan
Grenfell Asset, Management Limited, 20
Finsbury Circus, London EC2M 1NB, 0171
545 3348. Called: July 1996, Gray's Inn, BSc,
D.Phil (Sussex), LLB, LLM (London), C Eng,
MIM, ACIS, FCCA, MIM, MIMgt

Jarman *David A E JP*
Justice of the Peace, Surrey. Called: July
1969, Inner Temple

Jarraw *Colin Tarang*
Called: July 1996, Inner Temple, LLB
(Northumbria), M.Phil (Cantab)

Jarrett *Mrs Evelyne Blake Chinedum*
Legal Officer, 10 Springett House, St
Matthews Road, Brixton Hill, London
SW2 1NG. Called: Mar 1996, Middle
Temple, BA (Nigeria), LLB (Hons) (Lond),
MA (B'ham)

Jarrett *Miss Stephanie Ann*
Called: Oct 1990, Lincoln's Inn, LLB (Lond)

Jarvis *Julian Ross*
Called: Oct 1995, Inner Temple, LLB
(Sussex)

Jat *Sew Tong*
Temple Chambers, 1607 One Pacific Place,
88 Queensway, Hong Kong, 852 2523 2003,
Fax: 852 2810 0302, and Member Hong
Kong Singapore Bar. Called: July 1988,
Gray's Inn, LLB (LSE),BCL(Oxon)

Javali *Kirit Sharat*
Called: Oct 1996, Gray's Inn, BA (Delhi),
LLB (Leeds)

Jayadevan *Jayaperakash*
Called: Nov 1997, Lincoln's Inn, LLB (Hons)

Jayakumar *Miss Shalita*
and Member Singapore Bar. Called: July
1995, Middle Temple, LLB (Hons)

Jeddere-Fisher *Arthur Joseph*
Called: June 1949, Inner Temple

Jee *Fabian Soo Chen*
Called: Nov 1996, Gray's Inn, BA (Keele)

Jee *Mrs Jane Angela*
Division Manager, Mondex International Ltd,
47-53 Cannon Street, London EC4M 5SQ,
0171 557 5129, Fax: 0171 557 5329, nee
HAZLEWOOD. Called: July 1977, Inner
Temple, LLB Hons (Exon), Dip (Indus Relat
&, Personnel Manag)

Jeffrey *David Abbott*
Business Consultant, Cahill, Foxton,
Alnwick, Northumberland NE66 3BB, 01665
830553. Called: July 1960, Lincoln's Inn,
LLB, FCIS, C.Inst.M

Jeffrey *Sean Peter*
Called: July 1995, Middle Temple, BA
(Hons) (Oxon)

Jeffreys *Mrs Michelle Joy*
Senior Court Clerk, Nottingham Magistrates'
Court, Carrington Street, Nottingham
NG2 1EE, 0115 955 8111, Fax: 0115 955
8131. Called: July 1980, Gray's Inn, LLB
(B'ham)

Jeffreys *Miss Rosemary Anne* •
Legal Adviser. Consitution Secretariat,
Cabinet Office, 70 Whitehall, London
SW1A 2AS, 0171 270 6093. Called: July
1978, Gray's Inn, LLB(Bristol), LLM [Lond]

Jeffries *William Anthony*
Chief Executive, Victoria Law Courts,
Corporation Street, Birmingham, 0121 212
6612, Fax: 0121 212 6766. Called: Nov
1979, Gray's Inn, MBA

Jeganathan *Miss Michelle Frances*
21 Shangri La Walk, 65 452 1733, Fax: 65
458 5486, and Member Singapore Bar.
Called: July 1996, Inner Temple, LLB (Hull)

Jelf *Simon Edward* •
Research Assistant (Company/Commercial),
The Law Commission, Conquest House, 37-
38 John Street, London WC1N 2BQ, 0171
453 1291. Called: Oct 1996, Gray's Inn, LLB
(E.Anglia)

Jellie *Miss Violet Hilary*
Called: Nov 1958, Gray's Inn

Jelly *Fullerton McWilliam*
Called: July 1984, Middle Temple, BSc
(Belfast),CEng, MICE, FIMgt

Jenking-Rees *Mark* •
Principal Legal Officer, Department of Social
Security, New Court, 48 Carey Street,
London WC2. Called: May 1987, Lincoln's
Inn, LLB

Jenkins *Arthur Bernard*
46 Court Hill, Sanderstead, Surrey CR2 9NA.
Called: Nov 1959, Lincoln's Inn, LLB, FCII

Jenkins *Miss Glynys Ceri* •
Senior Principal Legal Officer, HM Customs
& Excise, 22 Upper Ground, London
SE1 9PJ, 0171 865 5210, Fax: 0171 865
5022. Called: July 1974, Gray's Inn, LLB

Jenkins *Paul Christopher* •
Legal Adviser, Dept for Culture, Media &
Sport, Treasury Solicitor's Dept, Queen
Anne's Chambers, 28 Broadway, London
SW1H 9JS, 0171 210 3256/3278, Fax: 0171
210 3448. Called: July 1977, Middle Temple,
LLB

Jenkins *Miss Sarah Valerie*
Called: Oct 1994, Middle Temple, LLB
(Hons)(Leeds)

Jenkinson *Daniel Thomas*
Compliance Officer, Natwest Life, Trinity
Quay, Avon Street, Bristol B52 OYY, 0117
9404715, Fax: 0117 9404807. Called: July
1981, Middle Temple, BA Hons

Jennings *Miss Anita*
Called: Nov 1994, Inner Temple, LLB
(Middx)

Jennings *Mrs Caroline Patricia*
Deputy Clerk to the Justices Assistant
Training Officer, Northamptonshire
Magistrates, Court, Regents Pavillion,
Summerhouse Road, Moulton Park,
Northampton NN3 1AS, 01604 497036, Fax:
01604 497010. Called: July 1989, Middle
Temple, Dip Law, Dip Mag Law, Dip
Management Stud

Jennings *Derek Geoffrey*
30 Onslow Avenue, Cheam, Surrey
SM2 7EB, 0181 642 7517. Called: May 1949,
Gray's Inn, MA, LLB (Cantab)

Jennings *Mrs Gina Anne*
Freshfields, 65 Fleet Street, London
EC4Y 1HS, 0171 832 7202, Fax: 0171 832
7518. Called: July 1980, Gray's Inn, LLB
(Bris)

Jennings *Mark*
25 Waldgrave Road, Wavertree, Liverpool
L15 7JL, 0151 722 9806. Called: Oct 1995,
Gray's Inn, LLB

Jennings *Michael Stuart* •
Called: Oct 1994, Gray's Inn, BA

Jennings *Ms Sally Jane* •
Racal Group Services Limited, Richmond
Court, 309 Fleet Road, Fleet, Hants
GU13 8BU. Called: Oct 1991, Middle
Temple, BA Hons, Dip Law, LLM (Lond)

Jensen *Paul*
James R Knowles Ltd, Wardle House, King
Street, Knutsford, Cheshire WA16 6PD,
01565 654666, Fax: 01565 755009.
Called: July 1979, Lincoln's Inn, FRICS,
F.C.IArb

Jeram *Miss Kirti*
Called: Nov 1996, Gray's Inn, LLB
(Newcastle)

Jerram *Nelson Richard Joseph*
Paterson & Co Solicitors, Clent Chambers,
Barnsley Hall Drive, Birmingham Road,
Bromsgrove, Worcestershire B61 0ED,
01527 577715, Fax: 01527 577716.
Called: Nov 1980, Gray's Inn, Dip Law

Jessel *Robin Richard*
Called: June 1953, Lincoln's Inn

Jhogasundram *Miss Jayanthi*
Called: July 1995, Lincoln's Inn, LLB (Hons)

Jimdar *Roger Michael* •
Principal Legal Officer, HM Customs &
Excise, New King's Beam House, 22 Upper
Ground, London SE1 9PJ, 0171 865 5983,
and Member Trinidad & Tobago Bar.
Called: Nov 1986, Lincoln's Inn, LLB (Lond)

Jinadu *Mr Justice Yaya Abiodun
Olatunde*
Formerly; Deputy Team Clerk of Lagos;
Crown Counsel, Treasury Counsel, Deputy
Solicitor- General of Nigeria, 2 Redwoods,
Alton Road, Roehampton, London
SW15 4NL, 0181 788 3192, High Court
Judge, formerly of Lagos State. Called: July
1954, Middle Temple, LLB (Lond)

Jinu *Ms Feona*
Legal Assistant, Messrs JNLS Associates, Lot
22, Block D, Damai Plaza Phase 111, Damai
Reservoir Road, 88300 Kota Kinabalu,
Sabah, (88) 212117, Fax: (88) 238866, and
Member Borneo Bar. Called: May 1990,
Gray's Inn, LL.B., LLM

Joad *Miss Nicola Ward* •
Senior Principal Legal Officer, HM Customs
& Excise, New Kings Beam House, 22
Upper Ground, London SE1 9PJ. Called: Nov
1983, Middle Temple, LLB (Lond)

Joannou *Miss Emily Pia*
Le Quatorze, 14 Gorey Pier, St Martin,
Jersey JE3 6EW, 01534 853392, Fax: 01534
853392. Called: Oct 1996, Gray's Inn, BA
(Keele), LLM

Jobes *Mrs Jharna* •
Crown Prosecution Service, 50 Ludgate Hill,
London EC4M 7EX. Called: July 1982,
Middle Temple, BA

Joel *Dan*
Advocate & Notary, Joel & Joel, P.O.B.
1671, Tel Aviv 61015, 4 Rothschild
Boulevard, 66881 Tel-Aviv, Israel, 013 65
8317, and Member Israeli Bar 2 Hare Court,
Ground Floor, Temple, London, EC4Y 7BH.
Called: Nov 1967, Inner Temple

Joels *Harold*
Also Inn of Court I. Called: Nov 1954,
Gray's Inn, MA LLB (Cantab)

Joelson *Stephen Laurance Robert*
and Member California Bar Hardwicke
Building, New Square, Lincoln's Inn,
London, WC2A 3SB. Called: Nov 1980,
Gray's Inn, LLB (Reading)

Johal *Sudeep Singh*
Called: Oct 1996, Gray's Inn, LLB (Lond)

Johansen *Piers Charles Christian*
Called: Nov 1995, Middle Temple, BA
(Hons)(Dunelm)

Johari *Miss Lindahyni*
Called: July 1997, Lincoln's Inn, LLB
(Hons)(L'pool)

John *Jeevan Noel*
Called: Nov 1997, Middle Temple, BA
(Hons)(Keele)

John *Jeffrey*
Called: July 1996, Lincoln's Inn, LLB (Hons)

John *Miss Louise*
Clifford Chance, 200 Aldersgate Street,
London EC1A 4JJ, 0171 600 1000, Fax: 0171
600 5555. Called: July 1989, Inner Temple,
LLB

John *Simon Paul*
Called: July 1996, Lincoln's Inn, BA
(Hons)(Wales)

John *Thomas Huw*
Called: Oct 1997, Middle Temple, LLB
(Hons)(Lond), BSc (Lond)

John-Charles *Lee* •
Lawyer, Treasury Solicitors, Queen Anne's
Chambers, 28 Broadway, London SW1H 9JS,
0171 210 3446, Fax: 0171 222 3410.
Called: Nov 1985, Lincoln's Inn, LLB (Hons)

Johnatty *Malcom*
P.O.Box 146, Port of Spain, Trinidad &
Tobago, 1-809-665-6173, and Member
Trinidad & Tobago Bar. Called: July 1994,
Inner Temple, BSc (West Indies), LLB
(Lond)

Johns *Alain*
c/o Messrs John & Co, No 7500A Beech
Road, [H]14-302 The Plaza, 294 3150/ 296
2975, Fax: 291 4662, and Member
Singapore. Called: July 1995, Middle
Temple, LLB (Hons)

Johnson *Ms Annette Rose-Marie* •
Tax Specialist, Grant Thornton
International, Melton Street, Euston Square,
London NW1, 0171 383 5100 ext2642, Fax:
0171 383 4052. Called: Nov 1988, Inner
Temple, LLB (W Indies), LLM (York Uni
Can)

Johnson *Anthony Lesroy*
Called: July 1995, Lincoln's Inn, LLB (Hons)

Johnson *Babatunde* •
Commercial Director, Adecco, Adecco
House, Elstree Way, Borehamwood,
Herfordshire WD6 1HY, 0181 236 5346,
Fax: 0181 905 2541. Called: July 1989, Inner
Temple, BA, Dip Law

Johnson *Mrs Catherine Anne*
Called: Feb 1978, Lincoln's Inn, BA, MA
(Oxon)

Johnson *Craig Rothwell*
01242 511009. Called: Nov 1995, Gray's
Inn, BSc (Hons), Dip Law, PGCE

Johnson *Edward Thomas Darren*
Called: Nov 1995, Inner Temple, LLB
(L'pool)

Johnson *Miss Gillian Sheila* •
Legal Adviser, DSS, Solicitor's Office, New
Court, 48 Carey Street, London WC2A 2LS.
Called: July 1965, Gray's Inn, LLB

Johnson *Lenworth Walter*
Maundy Building, 29A St Mary's Street, St
John's, Antigua, 268 460 9714, Fax: 268 460
9715, and Member Antigua, Barbuda.
Called: Nov 1996, Inner Temple, LLB
(Wolverh'ton)

Johnson *Lindsay Charles Whitley*
Called: Oct 1997, Inner Temple, BSc
(Brunel)

Johnson *Miss Melanie Jane*
Called: Oct 1993, Middle Temple, MA
(Hons)(Oxon), CPE (City)

Johnson *Miss Nancy Alexander Miller*
Called: July 1993, Middle Temple, LLB
(Hons)

Johnson *Nicholas Guy* •
Deutsche Morgan Grenfell, 6-8 Bishopsgate,
London EC2. Called: Nov 1993, Inner
Temple, BA (Oxon), CPE

Johnson *Ms Nicola Lorraine*
Called: Oct 1997, Gray's Inn, BSc (Manc)

Johnson *Richard Francis*
Called: Oct 1996, Gray's Inn, LLB (Lond)

Johnson *Mrs Sandra*
Bridge Gap, Main Street, Linton, Wetherby,
W Yorks LS22 4HT. Called: Feb 1977,
Middle Temple, LLB, MA

Johnston *Dr Alexandra Kate* •
Board Advocates, Criminal Injuries Board,
Morley House, 26-30 Holborn Viaduct,
London EC1A 2JQ. Called: Oct 1993, Inner
Temple, MB ChB (University, of Leicester
Medical, School), Specialist, Diploma in
Tort, CPE

Johnston *David Ian*
Called: Oct 1994, Lincoln's Inn, LLB
(Hons)(Leeds)

Johnston *Frank* •
Legal Advisor, Leeds City Council.
Called: Oct 1995, Inner Temple, LLB (Sheff)

Johnston *James Scott* •
Legal Services Manager, Dept of Central
Services, Legal Services Division, Darlington
Borough Council, Town Hall, Darlington
DL1 5QT, 01325 388232, Fax: 01325
388333. Called: Oct 1990, Lincoln's Inn, LLB
(Hons)

Johnston *John Douglas Hartley*
Assistant Editor, Simon's Tax Cases,
Butterworths, Halsbury House, 35 Chancery
Lane, London WC2A 1EL, 0171 400 2500.
Called: July 1962, Lincoln's Inn, MA, LLB,
LLM (Harvard), PHD (Cambridge)

Johnston *John Leslie Kerr*
de Zoete & Bevan Ltd, Ebbgate House, 2
Swan Lane, London EC4R 3TS, 0171 623
2323. Called: Nov 1980, Lincoln's Inn, LLB
(Lond)

Johnston *Kenneth Barry*
Level 3, Landcorp House, 101 Lambton
Quay, P.O.Box 5058, Wellington, 471 2727,
Fax: 499 4620, and Member New Zealand
Bar. Called: May 1988, Middle Temple, LLB,
DIP H.R.M.

Johnston *Lindsay Alexander
McLennan*
Legal Advisor, 46 Cedars Drive, Walton,
Stone, Staffordshire ST15 0BB, 01785
819202, Fax: 01785 819202. Called: Nov
1996, Lincoln's Inn, LLB (Hons), LLM, BSc,
ACIArb

Johnston *Mark*
Rue De L'Epargne 10 BTE 7, 1000-Bruxelles,
Belgium, 00 322 223 2785, Member of
King's Inn, Dublin and Member Southern
Ireland Bar. Called: July 1988, Middle
Temple, BCL (U.C.D), BL (Kings Inns)

Johnstone *James Burke*
Treleaver, Coverack, Cornwall TR12 6SF,
0374 44 5020. Called: Nov 1994, Lincoln's
Inn, BA (Hons)

Johnstone *Roy Harvey OBE*
26 Maplin Close, London N21 1NB, 0181
360 3764. Called: Jan 1949, Gray's Inn, LLB

Jones *Adrian Richard Hope* •
Steamship Mutual Underwriting, Association
(Bermuda) Limited. Called: Nov 1994, Inner
Temple, BA (Durham), MA (York), CPE
(Lond)

Jones *Miss Alison Louise*
23 Essex Street, London, WC2R 3AS.
Called: Nov 1988, Inner Temple, BA
(Manch)

Jones *Andrew John*
Attorney at Law, Cayman Is Panel member,
American Arbitration Association, Maples
and Calder, P.O. Box 309 GT, Grand
Cayman, Cayman Islands, 345 949 8066,
Fax: 345 949 8080, and Member Cayman
Islands. Called: Nov 1973, Inner Temple,
MA (Cantab)

Jones *Mrs Anjette Nadine*
20 Queensway Quay, 00 350 40730, Fax: 00
350 73315, and Member Gibraltar Bar.
Called: Oct 1992, Inner Temple, LLB

Jones *Anthony Charles Frederick
Norm*
Called: July 1970, Inner Temple, BA

Jones *Brian Edward*
Called: Oct 1994, Middle Temple, LLB
(Hons)

Jones *Mrs Carmel Margaret Anne*
Principal Court Clerk, Ealing Magistrates'
Court, Green Man Lane, West Ealing,
London W13, 0181 579 9311. Called: Nov
1970, Inner Temple

Jones *Ms Catrin Helen* •
Litigation Lawyer, London Borough of
Richmond, Legal Services, Civic Centre, 44
York Street, Twickenham TW1 3BZ, 0181
891 7142. Called: Nov 1994, Lincoln's Inn,
LLB (Hons)(Lanc)

Jones *Daniel Owen Malcolm* •
Legal Assistant. Called: Nov 1995, Middle
Temple, BA (Hons), LLM

Jones *Darius Wilmoth*
Called: July 1997, Lincoln's Inn, LLB (Hons)
(Lond)

Jones *Dominic Clive*
Morgan Stanley & Co, International, 25
Cabot Square, London E14 4QA, 0171 425
8689, Fax: 0171 425 8971, and Member
French Bar. Called: July 1987, Middle
Temple, LLB (Bristol)

Jones *Mrs Doris Jean*
56 Grove Park Terrace, Chiswick, London
W4 3QE, 0181 994 2241. Called: Jan 1948,
Lincoln's Inn, MA (Oxon)

Jones *Edward John*
Clerk to the Justices, The Court House,
Stafford Street, Walsall, West Midlands
WS2 8HA, 01922 38222, Fax: 01922 35657.
Called: July 1982, Gray's Inn, Dip Law

Jones *Gareth Alun* •
Commercial Operative, British Telecom,
Stadium House, Cardiff, 01222 229064.
Called: Oct 1997, Middle Temple, LLB
(Hons)(Lond)

Jones *Glynmor Richard*
Called: Feb 1960, Gray's Inn, BSc, MICE

Jones *Grant Meredith*
Called: Nov 1996, Middle Temple, LLB
(Hons)

Jones *Haydn Peter*
NatWest Markets, Old Billingsgate Market, 16 Lower Thames Street, London EC3R 6AA, 0171 264 6136, Fax: 0171 264 8566. Called: Oct 1995, Inner Temple, M.Eng (Manc), CPE (City), AMIEE

Jones *Miss Hilary Jean*
Silwood House, Runnymede Close, Gateacre, Woolton, Liverpool L25 5JU. Called: June 1951, Middle Temple, LLB

Jones *Huw Gruffydd*
Hopkins Williams Shaw, 110 Kennington Road, London SE11 6RE, 0171 582 4662, Fax: 0171 735 0719. Called: Nov 1993, Middle Temple, BA (Hons)(Kent), MA, (Lond), CPE

Jones *Ian Harvey* •
Asst Director of Resources (Legal & Admin) Oadby & Wigston B.C., Oadby & Wigston Brgh Council, Council Offices, Station Road, Wigston, Leicestershire LE18 2DR, 0116 288 8961, Fax: 0116 288 7828. Called: Oct 1993, Inner Temple, MA (Oxon)

Jones *Miss Jacqueline Margarete*
Called: Feb 1995, Gray's Inn, B.Sc, LLB (Wales), M.Phil (Wales)

Jones *James William*
Legal Manager Production Sales & Marketing, Powergen PLC, Westwood Business Park, Coventry CV4 8LG, 01203 424000. Called: Feb 1989, Middle Temple, LLB

Jones *Mrs Jane Margaret*
Called: July 1980, Inner Temple, MA (Cantab), LL.M

Jones *The Hon Jeffrey Richard CBE*
Chief Justice, Bradley Cottage, Holt, Wilts BA14 6QE, 01225 782004, and Member Kiribati Nigerian Bar. Called: July 1954, Middle Temple, MA Oxon

Jones *Miss Joanne Claire*
Court Clerk, Lancashire Magistrates Court, Preston. Called: July 1997, Middle Temple, LLB (Hons)

Jones *John Edward* •
Assistant Solicitor, Corporation of Lloyd's, One Lime Street, London EC3M 7HA, 0171 327 635, Fax: 0171 327 5502. Called: July 1973, Middle Temple, LL.B [Lond]

Jones *John Nicholas*
Justices' Chief Exec/Justices' Clerk, Justices' Chief Executive's, Office, The Courthouse, Worcester Road, Ledbury, Hertfordshire HR8 3QL, 01531 634658. Called: July 1977, Gray's Inn, LLB, MIPD

Jones *Jonathan Guy* •
Legal Adviser, Legal Secretariat to the Law, Officers, Attorney General's Chambers, 9 Buckingham Gate, London SW1E 6JP, 0171 828 7155, Fax: 0171 828 0593. Called: July 1985, Middle Temple, BA (Durham)

Jones *Mrs Jorina Mary* •
Area Manager, Dept of Social Security, Solicitors Office, Room 515, Sutherland House, 29 Brighton Road, Sutton, Surrey SM2 5AN, 0181 652 6500, Fax: 0181 652 6397. Called: July 1986, Middle Temple, BA (Hons)

Jones *Dr Karen Patricia Nievergelt* •
Legal Adviser, Country Landowners' Assoc., 16 Belgrave Square, London SW1X 8PX, 0171 460 7952. Called: Nov 1995, Middle Temple, BSc (Hons)(Wales), Ph.D (Cantab)

Jones *Ms Kathrine Margaret* •
Legal Advisor, Leeds City Council, Civic Hall, Leeds LS1 1UR, 0113 224 3263, Fax: 0113 247 4729. Called: Nov 1995, Gray's Inn, BA (Hons)

Jones *Miss Kathryn Anne* •
Senior Crown Prosecutor, Crown Prosecution Service, Cae Banc, Tanerdy, Carmarthen, Dyfed, 01267 237779. Called: July 1992, Middle Temple, LLB (Hons)

Jones *Kelvin McAllister*
Called: Oct 1995, Inner Temple, LLB

Jones *Miss Kristin Francesca Deirdre* •
Lawyer, Department of Trade & Industry, Solicitor's Office, Investigations & Enforcement, Directorate, 10-18 Victoria St, London SW1H 0NN, 0171 215 3161, Fax: 0171 215 3223. Called: July 1984, Inner Temple, LLB (Nottm)

Jones *Marc Paul*
Called: Mar 1997, Gray's Inn, BA (Oxon)

Jones *Michael Scott*
Advocates Library, Parliament House, Edinburgh EH1 1RF, 0131 226 5071, Fax: 0131 226 3642, Queen's Counsel in Scotland (1989) and Member Scottish Bar. Called: July 1987, Lincoln's Inn, LLB (Dundee)

Jones *Lieutenant Colonel Neil James Henry* •
SO1 Prosecutions Germany, Army Prosecuting Authority, (Germany), Block 3, Rochdale Barracks, BFPO 39, 0049 521 9254 469/0049 521 2399 243, Fax: 0049 521 9254 472. Called: Nov 1978, Gray's Inn, LLB Newc

Jones *Paul*
Called: Oct 1994, Gray's Inn, BA (Manch)

Jones *Peter Michael*
Legal Manager, Warrington Magistrates' Court, Winmarleigh Street, Warrington WA1 1PB, 01925 253136. Called: Nov 1987, Middle Temple, LLB

Jones *Philip*
Called: Nov 1993, Lincoln's Inn, BA (Hons)

Jones *Reginald Lewis*
69 Ashley Gdns, Ambrosden Avenue, London SW1P 1QG. Called: June 1948, Lincoln's Inn

Jones *Roger Kenneth* •
Secretary, Cooperative Wholesale Soc. Ltd, PO Box 53, New Century House, Manchester M60 4ES, 0161 834 1212, Fax: 0161 833 1383. Called: Feb 1977, Gray's Inn, BA Hons (Econ)

Jones *Ms Sharon Maria* •
Principal Legal Adviser. Called: July 1981, Middle Temple, LLB(Lond)

Jones *Ms Sian Elizabeth*
Deputy Clerk to the Justices, Wrexham Maelor & Berwyn, Magistrates Court, Law Courts, Bodhyfrd, Wrexham, Clwyd LL12 7BP, 01978 291855, Fax: 01978 358213. Called: July 1981, Lincoln's Inn, LLB (Hons), DMS

Jones *Simon Alexander*
Called: Nov 1994, Inner Temple, BSC (Bris), Dip Law (Lond)

Jones *Simon David* •
Legal Adviser, Royal Borough of Kensington &, Chelsea, The Town Hall, London W8 7NX, 0171 361 2194, Fax: 0171 361 3488. Called: Nov 1985, Gray's Inn, LLB (Sheffield)

Jones *Miss Susan Ann*
Legal Advisor. Called: July 1987, Lincoln's Inn, LLB (Hons)

Jones *Mrs Susan Eleanor*
Principal Court Clerk Deputy Stipendiary Magistrate, Victoria Law Courts, Corporation Street, Birmingham, West Midlands, 0121 212 6676, Fax: 0121 212 6613. Called: July 1972, Lincoln's Inn, LLB (Sheff)

Jones *Miss Susan Heather* •
Senior Court Clerk, Hertfordshire Magistrates', Courts Committee, The Register Office Block, County Hall, Hertford, Hertfordshire SG13 8DF, 01727 816823, Fax: 01727 816829. Called: Nov 1985, Lincoln's Inn, BA

Jones *Mrs Vanessa* •
Manager, Coopers & Lybrand, 1 Embankment Place, London WC2N 6NN, 0171 213 2753, Fax: 0171 213 2117. Called: Nov 1984, Gray's Inn, LLB (Hons)

Jones *Miss Verity Gill*
Part time Parking Adjudicator, 71 Mapledene Road, London E8 3JW, 0171 275 8327. Called: July 1986, Inner Temple, LLB London

Jones-Crawford *Mrs Shaaron*
179 Dawlish Avenue, Toronto, Ontario M4N1H6, 416 485 3410, Fax: 416 485 3329. Called: July 1990, Lincoln's Inn, LLB

Jong *Miss Ling*
Called: Nov 1996, Lincoln's Inn, LLB (Hons)(Hull)

Joo *Miss Connie Mei Ling*
Legal Adviser, and Member Malaysia Bar. Called: Nov 1990, Middle Temple, LLB (Lond)

Joof *Miss Amie*
Called: Nov 1997, Lincoln's Inn, LLB (Hons)(Warw)

Joomratty *Mohammud Massood*
Called: Nov 1995, Gray's Inn, LLB

Joon *Ms Loy Siew*
Called: Nov 1996, Inner Temple, LLB (Lond)

Jopling *John Lindsay*
7 Chamberlain Street, London NW1 8XB,
0171 722 3710, Fax: 0171 722 3959, also
Inn of Court L. Called: July 1960, Inner
Temple, MA (Oxon)

Jopling *Norman*
Called: Nov 1978, Middle Temple, LLB
(Lond), ACIS

Jordan *Christopher Nigel*
Deputy Clerk to the Justices & Deputy
Clerk to the Magistrates' Courts Committee,
Ealing Magistrates Court Cmtte, Green Man
Lane, London W13 9EN, 0181 579 9311,
Fax: 0181 840 9492. Called: July 1978,
Middle Temple, MA (Oxon)

Jordan *Nigel Alan* •
Legal Adviser, Griffin Services Limited,
Royton House, 14 George Road, Edgbaston,
Birmingham B15 1NT, 0121 455 2732, Fax:
0121 455 2770. Called: July 1982, Gray's
Inn, LLB (Lond), ACIB

Jordan *Miss Sarah Louise* •
Called: Nov 1995, Inner Temple, LLB
(Notts)

Jordan *Victor Charles*
43 Cornwall Road, Cheam, Surrey SM2 6DU,
0181 642 2635. Called: June 1959, Gray's
Inn, LLB, F.I.O.S.H.

Jordan *Victor Frederick John*
8 Gresham Way, Wimbledon Park, London
SW19 8ED. Called: Feb 1968, Middle
Temple, MA, LLM (Cantab)

Jorro *Peter Antonio Raimo*
Called: Nov 1986, Lincoln's Inn, LLB (Hons)
(LSE)

Josef *Miss Rozanna Jacqueline*
10 Jalan 4L, Ampang Jaya, 68000 Ampang,
Selangor DE, 03 456 9401, Fax: 65 475
8665, and Member Malaysia. Called: Nov
1994, Inner Temple, LLB (Bris)

Joseph *Eugene Roy*
Suite 2.10, 2nd Floor, Wisma Mirama, Jalan
Wisma Putra, 50460 Kuala Lumpur, West
Malaysia, 03-2432395, Fax: 03-2440827/
2448760, and Member Malaysia Bar.
Called: July 1996, Lincoln's Inn, LLB
(Hons)(Lond)

Joseph *Leslie QC (1978)*
Devereux Chambers, Devereux Court,
London, WC2R 3JJ. Called: Nov 1952,
Middle Temple, LLB

Joseph *Miss Margaret Mary*
Called: July 1996, Middle Temple, LLB
(Hons)(Lond)

Joseph *Vincent*
Called: July 1996, Lincoln's Inn, LLB
(Hons)(Lond)

Joseph-Njoku *Uche Christian*
Called: Mar 1998, Lincoln's Inn, LLB (Hons)

Josephson *Ms Diana Hayward*
Principal Deputy Assistant Secreatary of the
Navy (Installations and Environment) US
Department of Defense, 1000 Navy
Pentagon, Washington D.C. 20350-1000,
703 693 4527, and Member District of
Columbia Bar. Called: June 1959, Gray's Inn,
BA,MA (Hons) (Oxon), M Comp.

Joshi *Rajendra Jugatray* •
Crown Prosecution Service, Headquarters,
50 Ludgate Hill, London EC4M 7EX, 0171
273 8318, Fax: 0171 329 8165, Diplome de
l'Institut International de Droits de
l'Homme. Called: Nov 1983, Inner Temple,
BA (Hons)

Joshi *Sunit Kishor*
Called: Nov 1997, Lincoln's Inn, LLB
(Hons)(Nott'm)

Joshua *Julian Mathic* •
Directorate-General for Competition,
Commission of the, European Communities,
200 Rue de la Loi, 1049 Brussels, 295 5519,
Fax: 299 0880. Called: Nov 1969, Middle
Temple, MA (Cantab)

Joslin *Mrs Elizabeth Anne* •
Principal Crown Prosecutor, Crown
Prosecution Service, Solar House, 1-9
Romford Road, Stratford, London E15 4LJ,
0181 534 6601. Called: July 1984, Lincoln's
Inn, LLB (Hons) (Lond), AKC

Jospeh Xavier *Annou Anselm*
Called: Nov 1996, Lincoln's Inn, LLB
(HOns)(Lond)

Jouanneau *Mrs Angela* •
Senior Crown Prosecutor, Crown
Prosecution Service, Priory Gate, 29 Union
Gate, Maidstone. Called: Nov 1987, Gray's
Inn

Jouhal *Sukhraj* •
Litigation Co-ordinator, Anglo Group Plc, c/
o Woodchester Credit Lyonnai,
Woodchester House, Selsdon Way, London
E14 9HA, 0171 712 4467, Fax: 0171 712
4462. Called: Nov 1996, Inner Temple, LLB
(Lond)

Jowett *Edward Ian* •
Director of Legal Affairs, European Credit
Operations, Ford of Europe Inc, The Drive,
Warley, Brentwood, Essex CM13 3AR,
01277 224400. Called: Nov 1955, Middle
Temple, MA, BCL

Jowitt *Justin Samuel*
Allen & Overy, 1 New Change, London
EC4N 9QQ. Called: Nov 1993, Middle
Temple, BA (Hons)(Oxford)

Joyce *Mrs Eva Margaret Bridget*
Anglia Polytechnic University, Dept of Law,
Victoria Road South, Chelmsford CM1 1LL,
01245 493131. Called: Oct 1990, Lincoln's
Inn, BA (Kent)

Joyce *John Gerald McEwan*
Ballaig Hse, Comrie, Crieff, Perthshire
PH7 4JX, 017646 70261. Called: Nov 1964,
Inner Temple, BL

Joynes *Matthew Robert*
Pinsent Curtis Solicitors, 41 Park Square,
Leeds LS1 2NS, 0113 244 5000. Called: Oct
1994, Inner Temple, BSc (Hon)(Econ), MA
(Belgium)

Jublee *Cilve Clive*
P.O.Box 21206, 88769 Luyang, Sabah, 088
231111, Fax: 088 233122, and Member
Advocate & Solcitor, Sabah. Called: July
1995, Middle Temple, LLB (Hons) (Warw)

Judge *Mrs Ruth Patricia*
Teacher of Modern Languages Deputy Head
of Department, London Borough of Harrow.
Called: Oct 1993, Gray's Inn, BA (Leic), MA
(Cantab)

Judge *Ms Sophie Tallulah* •
Senior Crown Prosecutor, Crown
Prosecution Service, 17th Floor, Tolworth
Tower, Ewell Road, Surbiton, Surrey
KT6 7DS, 0181 399 5171, Fax: 0181 390
3474. Called: Nov 1990, Inner Temple, LLB

Julian *Gareth Wynn* •
Lawyer, Crown Prosecution Service, 50
Ludgate Hill, London EC4Y 7EX. Called: July
1980, Gray's Inn, LLB (Warw), FRSA

Jump *Michael Edward Pearson*
Formerly a Solicitor, Formerly 24 Old Bldgs,
Lincoln's Inn. Called: June 1964, Lincoln's
Inn

Jung *Moo-Kyung*
Called: July 1996, Middle Temple, BA
(Hons)(Seoul), LLM (Warw), CPE (B'ham)

Jupe *Mrs Patricia Lorna*
Called: July 1958, Gray's Inn

Jusoh *Sufian Bin*
Skrine & Co, 2nd Floor, Straits Trading
Building, 4 Leboh Pasar, 50050 Kuala
Lumpur Malaysia, (60) (3) 2945111, Fax:
(60) (3) 2934327, and Member Malaysia Bar.
Called: Nov 1992, Lincoln's Inn, LLB
(Hons)(Wales)

Kaburise *Professor John Bonaventure
Kubongpwa*
Professorship of Public Law, Department of
Public Law, Faculty of Law, University of
Durban-Westville, Private Bag X54001,
Durban 4000, (031) 820 9111, Fax: (031)
820 2848, Solicitor Papua New Guinea and
Member Papua New Guinea Bar. Called: July
1988, Middle Temple, LLB (Hons) (Ghana),
LLM (Pennsylvannia)

Kahar Bador *Rizal*
Called: Nov 1997, Lincoln's Inn, BA
(Hons)(Oxon)

Kahmei *Miss Chee*
Called: Nov 1994, Inner Temple, LLB (Lond)

Kaim-Caudle *Peter Robert*
Emeritus Professor of Social Policy,
Beechwood, Princes Street, Durham
DH1 4RP, 0191 3864768, Fax: 0191
3744743. Called: Nov 1956, Lincoln's Inn

Kainyah *Miss Rosalind Nana Emela*
0171 465 7200. Called: July 1988, Gray's
Inn, BA (Ghana), LLB (Lond), LLM (Lond)

Kaleniuk *Nicholas George*
Called: Nov 1992, Inner Temple, LLB
(L'pool)

Kalis *Dirk Hems*
14 Westfield Road, Lymington, Hampshire
SO41 3PY, 01590 679542, Fax: 01590
679486. Called: Nov 1968, Inner Temple,
MA (Cantab)

Kalpanath Singh *Miss Rina*
Kalpanath & Co, 101-A Upper Cross Street,
[H]12-17 Peoples Part Centre, Singapore
0105, 533 4833, Fax: 532 7408, and
Member Singapore Bar. Called: July 1994,
Middle Temple, LLB (Hons)(Warw)

Kalra *Kasturi*
Kalra & Co, 304 High Road, Leyton, London
E10 5PW, 0181 539 0123. Called: Nov 1985,
Lincoln's Inn, MA, LLB

Kam *Aubeck Tse Tsuen*
Called: July 1993, Lincoln's Inn, LLB (Hons)

Kam *Chin Khoon*
Called: Nov 1993, Middle Temple, BA
(Hons)

Kam-Chuen *Cheung*
and Member Hong Kong Bar. Called: July
1996, Inner Temple, LLB (Wolverhampton),
MBA (Leic)

Kamalanathan *Selva Kumaran*
and Member Malaysia Bar. Called: July 1994,
Lincoln's Inn, LLB (Hons), LLM (Malaya)

Kamara *Miss Lanla Fatma*
Basma & Macaulay Solicitors, 21 Charlotte
Street, P O Box 83, Freetown, 232 22
222798, Fax: 232 22 224248. Called: July
1995, Lincoln's Inn, LLB (Hons), LLM (Sheff)

Kamaruddin *Kamarul Hisham*
Called: May 1995, Gray's Inn, LLB

Kamaruddin *Miss Siti Ardila*
Called: Nov 1992, Gray's Inn, BA (Keele)

Kamaruzaman *Miss Zuwita*
Called: July 1994, Lincoln's Inn, LLB (Hons)

Kamaruzzaman *Ms Intan Zubaidah*
and Member Malaysia. Called: Feb 1994,
Inner Temple, LLB (Hull), MBA, (Lond), DIC

Kammitsi *Miss Lefkothea*
Associate, C/O George L Savvides & Co, 1
Glafkos Str, 1085 Nicosia, 02-422355, Fax:
02-421819, and Member Cyprus Bar.
Called: July 1990, Middle Temple, BSocSc
(Keele)

Kan *Miss Caroline Yuen Oi*
M/s Harry Elias & Partners, 79 Robinson
Road [H]16-03, CPF Building, Singapore
0106. Called: Nov 1987, Middle Temple,
LLB(Hons) London, BA(Hons) McMaster

Kanagalingam *Miss Sharini Prema*
Legal Officer, Communications & Satellite
Services, 91 Jalan Telawi, Bangsar Baru,
59100 Kuala Lumpur, Malaysia, 03 253
0933, Fax: 03 794 2000 EXT 218 (0), and
Member Malaysia Bar. Called: July 1991,
Inner Temple, LLB (Notts)

Kanagarajan *Veluthevar*
Ambassador, The Ministry of Foreign Affairs,
Raffles City 06-00, 250 North Bridge Road,
Singapore, 179101, 336 1177, Fax: 339
4330. Called: Nov 1977, Lincoln's Inn, LLB
(Lond)

Kanagavijayan *Nadarajan*
Called: Nov 1996, Inner Temple, BA
(Singpaore), LLB, LLM (Lond)

Kandola *Miss Gurinder*
Senior Court Clerk, Walsall Magistrates
Court, Stafford Street, Walsall WS2 8HA,
01922 38222, Fax: 01922 35657.
Called: May 1984, Middle Temple

Kanfer *George Thomas*
GM Industrial Supply Co Ltd, Victoria Hse,
Bloomsbury Sq, London WC1B 4DH, 0171
242 7553, Fax: 0171 242 5850. Called: Feb
1981, Lincoln's Inn, MA (Cantab), MSc, MBA

Kang *Colin Seng Kok*
Called: Nov 1997, Middle Temple, LLB
(Hons)(Bucks)

Kangeson *Miss Gowri R.*
Called: Oct 1997, Gray's Inn, LLB
(Glamorgan)

Kanthosamy *Rajendran*
Called: July 1996, Middle Temple, LLB
(Hons)(Lond)

Kanu *Allieu Ibrahim Badara*
Called: May 1984, Middle Temple, BA
(Ealing), MA (Prague), MSc (Southampton)

Kanyerezi *Timothy Masembe*
Mugerwa & Matovu Advocates, 3rd Floor,
Diamond Trust Bldg, Plot 17/19 Kampala
Road, PO Box 7166, Kampala, 256 41
343859,259920,255431, Fax: 256 41
259992, and Member Ugandan Bar.
Called: July 1992, Inner Temple, LLB (Lond)

Kapetaniou *Miss Phani*
Called: Mar 1996, Lincoln's Inn, LLB
(Hons)(Leics)

Kaplan *Neil*
Arbitrator, S. 1601,Bank of East Asia Bldg,
10 Des Vouex Road, Central, Hong Kong,
(852) 2869 6301, Fax: (852) 2869 6372, QC
(Hong Kong) and Member Hong Kong Bar
New York Victoria Australia. Called: Feb
1965, Inner Temple, LLB (Lond) FCIArb

Kapri *Miss Zuhra Jabeen*
Called: Nov 1996, Lincoln's Inn, LLB (Hons)

Kapur *Ravi Krishan*
Called: July 1997, Lincoln's Inn, B.Com
(Hons), (Calcutta), LLB, (Hons)(Leeds)

Karan-Appukutten *Shubakaran* •
Senior Crown Prosecutor, Crown
Prosecution Service, Richmond & Kingston
Branch, 18th Floor, Tolworth Tower,
Surbiton KT6 7DS, 0181 399 5171.
Called: Feb 1991, Lincoln's Inn, LLB (Warw)

Karia *Chirag*
Gray Cary Ware & Friedenrich, 400
Hamilton Avenue, Palo Alto, CA 94301-
1825, (650) 833 2147, Fax: 9650) 327 3699,
and Member The State Bar of California.
Called: Nov 1988, Lincoln's Inn, BA
(Hons)(Cantab), MA (Hons)(Cantab), LLM

Karim *Khurram*
Called: May 1997, Lincoln's Inn, LLB (Hons)

Karim *Shaikh Saleem*
Called: Oct 1996, Middle Temple, LLB
(Hons)(Essex)

Karlin *Ms Fiona Elizabeth Joy*
Fiona Karlin Corporate, Services, Sheraton
House, Castle Park, Cambridge CB3 OAX,
01223 300960, Fax: 01223 300942.
Called: July 1982, Gray's Inn, MA (Cantab),
FCIArb

Karpinski *(Charles) Jan* •
Head of Legal & Compliance, Bristol & West
plclding Soc., PO Box 27, Broad Quay,
Bristol, Avon BS99 7AX, 0117 9432553, Fax:
0117 9291115. Called: Nov 1976, Middle
Temple, BA. [Oxon]

Karupiah *Jegathesean*
Called: Oct 1995, Gray's Inn, BA

Karuppen *Miss Nagesvary*
Called: Oct 1996, Gray's Inn, LLB (Lond)

Karuppiah *Kalidass s/o*
Called: Nov 1996, Inner Temple, LLB (Lond)

Karuppiah *Sathinathan*
Legal Assistant, Tan Lian Ker & Company, 2
Havelock Road [H] 07-10, Apollo Centre, 65
532 7117. Called: July 1996, Lincoln's Inn,
LLB (Hons), LLM (Sussex)

Karydes *Marios Andrea*
P.O.Box 77086, GR 175, 10 Athens, 01-
4116942, Fax: 01-4179221, and Member
Piraeus Bar Association. Called: July 1971,
Inner Temple, Athens University, Law
Degree

Kasim *Ms Siti Zabedah*
Called: Nov 1997, Gray's Inn, LLB

Kassim *Miss Noor Sukhairiyani*
Called: Nov 1997, Lincoln's Inn, LLB
(Hons)(B'ham)

Kassim *Ms Shishila Surya*
01245 514489, and Member Malaysia Bar.
Called: Feb 1993, Gray's Inn, LLB (Nott')

Kat *Nigel Louis Ian*
and Member Hong Kong Bar 2 King's Bench
Walk, 1st Floor, Temple, London, EC4Y
7DE. Called: Nov 1977, Middle Temple, LLB

Katan *Miss Deborah Rachel* •
HM Customs & Excise, Solicitors Office, 22
Upper Ground, London SE1 9PJ, 0171 620
1313. Called: Nov 1983, Middle Temple, BA
Hons

Kathriaratchi *Miss Shaminka*
Called: Nov 1997, Lincoln's Inn, LLB
(Hons)(Keele)

Katsapaou *Miss Chrystalla*
Called: May 1995, Inner Temple, LLB
(Sussex)

Kattan *William Victor*
Legislative Draftsman, Attorney General's
Chambers, Grand Turk, Turk & Caicos
Islands, (809)946 2096/2882, Fax: (809)946
2588. Called: May 1973, Gray's Inn, LLB,LLM
(Lond)

Kaur *Miss Balbir*
Called: July 1995, Middle Temple, LLB
(Hons) (Lond)

Kaur *Miss Baltej*
Called: July 1995, Middle Temple, LLB
(Hons)

Kaur *Miss Daljit*
Called: July 1997, Lincoln's Inn, LLB (Hons)

Kaur *Miss Devinder*
Called: July 1995, Lincoln's Inn, LLB (Hons)

Kaur *Miss Har Sharon*
Called: July 1990, Middle Temple, LLB
(Lond)

Kaur *Miss Jagdish* •
Crown Prosecution Service, 2nd Floor, The
Cooperage, Gainsford Street, London SE1.
Called: Nov 1988, Middle Temple, LLB
(L'pool)

Kaur *Miss Jasvendar*
Called: July 1995, Middle Temple, LLB
(Hons)

Kaur *Miss Kuldip*
Called: Nov 1994, Lincoln's Inn, LLB
(Hons)(Lond)

Kaur *Miss Kulwinder* •
Legal Officer, Salisbury District Council, The
Council Offices, Bourne Hill, Salisbury
SP1 3UZ, 01722 434233. Called: July 1984,
Middle Temple, BA Dip Law

Kaur *Miss Mejindarpal*
Called: July 1989, Lincoln's Inn, LLB (Lond),
LLM (Lond)

Kaur *Mrs Paramjit*
Called: July 1996, Lincoln's Inn, LLB
(Hons)(Lond)

Kaur *Miss Ravinder*
Called: Oct 1994, Lincoln's Inn, LLB
(Hons)(Bucks)

Kaur *Miss Sangreet* •
Legal Advisor. Called: July 1990, Lincoln's
Inn, LLB (Wales)

Kaur *Miss Sharanjit*
and Member Singapore Bar. Called: July
1995, Middle Temple, LLB (Hons)

Kaur *Ms Upbinder Sunita*
14 Mules Place, Macarthur ACT 2904,
Singapore, (061)(02)62919971, and Member
Singapore. Called: July 1994, Middle
Temple, LLB (Hons)(Newc)

Kaur Jaswant Singh *Miss Sharan*
Called: July 1997, Middle Temple, LLB
(Hons)(Wales)_

Kavanagh *Daniel Antony* •
Called: Nov 1988, Lincoln's Inn, BA Hons,
Dip Law

Kavanagh *Kevin* •
Principal Crown Prosecutor, Crown
Prosecution Service, Princes Court, 34 York
Road, Leicester LE1 5TU, 0116 2549333.
Called: July 1983, Gray's Inn, B.A.

Kaw *Miss Seok Hien*
and Member Singapore Bar. Called: Nov
1994, Gray's Inn, BA (Keele)

Kawa *Miss Lois Anita*
Called: Nov 1997, Lincoln's Inn, BA
(Hons)(Luton)

Kawaley *Ian Rowe Chukudinka*
Head of Insolvency and Corporate
Resource, Acting Manager, c/o Milligan
Whyte & Smith, Bermuda Commercial Bank
Bldg, 44 Church Street, Hamilton HM1Z,
(441) 295 4294, Fax: (441) 295 1348,
Member of the Bermuda Bar Council (1992)
and Member Bermuda Bar. Called: July
1978, Middle Temple, LLB (Liverpool), LLM
(LSE)

Kay *Graham* •
Principal Court Clerk, Hereford &
Worcester, Magistrates' Courts Committee.
Called: Nov 1985, Gray's Inn, BA

Kay *John Lawrence* •
Manager - Business Legal Services, Imperial
Chemical Industries, PLC, PO Box 90,
Wilton, Middlesborough, Cleveland
TS90 8JE, 01642 454144, Fax: 01642
432971. Called: July 1973, Middle Temple,
LLB, LLM (Lond)

Kay *Ms Sylvia Mary* •
Legal Adviser, DERA, A1 Building,
Farnborough, Hants GU14 0LX, UK.
Called: Nov 1969, Gray's Inn, LLB (B'ham)

Kaya *Hussein Ahmet* •
Senior Principal Legal Officer, Department
of Trade & Industry, Solicitors Office, 10-18
Victoria Street, London SW1H 0NN, 0171
215 3444, Fax: 0171 215 3141. Called: July
1977, Gray's Inn, LLB (Lond), LLM (Lond)

Kaye *David Grahame* •
Legal Adviser, Wakefield Magistrates Court,
Cliff Parade, Wakefield, West Yorkshire
WF1 2TW, 01924 303460, Fax: 01924
303465. Called: Nov 1989, Gray's Inn, DML

Kaye *Jeremy Robin* •
Company Secretary, Secure Trust Group Plc,
Royex House, Aldermanbury Square,
London EC2V 7HR, 0171 600 3831, Fax:
0171 626 7041. Called: July 1962, Inner
Temple, MA (Oxon), FCIS

Kaye *Professor Peter*
Department of Law, University of Wales
Swansea, Singleton Park, Swansea SA2 8PP,
01792 295831/3, Fax: 01792 295855.
Called: Oct 1994, Gray's Inn, LLB, AKC,
LLM, Ph.D, (Lond)

Kaye *Ms Siana*
Called: Nov 1994, Inner Temple, BA (Lond),
CPE (City)

Kazantzis *Ms Miranda Elizabeth*
Called: Feb 1993, Middle Temple, BA (Hons)
(Oxon), Dip in Law

Kazzora *John Wycliffer*
and Member Uganda Bar Chancery
Chambers, 1st Floor Offices, 70/72
Chancery Lane, London, WC2A 1AB.
Called: June 1958, Middle Temple

Kearney *Robert Michael*
Called: Nov 1996, Inner Temple, LLB

Kearns *James Anthony*
Called: July 1997, Middle Temple, BA
(Hons), Dip Law

Kearns *Kevin Patrick*
Called: July 1992, Lincoln's Inn, BA (L'Pool),
LLB, (Lond), MA (S'field)

Kedge *Miss Natalie Louise*
Called: Oct 1993, Middle Temple, BA
(Hons)(Lond), CPE

Kee *Chuin Liang Alvyn*
Called: Nov 1997, Lincoln's Inn, LLB (Hons),
(Wolver'ton)

Kee *Ju-Ven*
Called: July 1994, Middle Temple, BA
(Hons)(Cantab)

Kee *Peter William*
and Member Papua New Guinea.
Called: July 1983, Middle Temple, BA
(Oxon)

Keegan *Brian McMurrough*
Called: Mar 1998, Lincoln's Inn, LLB
(Hons)(Leics)

Keelan *Miss Emma Louise*
Called: Mar 1997, Gray's Inn, LLB (Wales)

Keen *Mrs Patricia*
"Laujan", Ashton Road, Siddington,
Cirencester, Glos GL7 6HD, 01285 654978.
Called: July 1985, Gray's Inn, Dip Law

Keenan *Miss Claudia Louise* •
General Counsel, Premier Oil plc, 23 Lower
Belgrave Street, London SW1W 0NR, 0171
730 1111, Fax: 0171 730 4696. Called: July
1986, Middle Temple, LLB

Keene *Gareth John* •
Director/International Counsel, GAMIDA for
Life BV, Marten Meesweg 51, 3068 AV
Rotterdam, The Netherlands, 010 31 20
5497777, Fax: 010 31 20 6610654.
Called: May 1966, Gray's Inn, MA, LLM
(Cantab)

Keery *Neil William*
Called: Oct 1997, Gray's Inn, LLB (Belfast)

Keeton *Darren*
Called: Oct 1994, Lincoln's Inn, LLB
(Hons)(E.Ang)

Keir *James Dewar QC (1980)*
Chairman Proffessional Committee, Royal
College of Speech & Language Therapists,
The Crossways, 1 High Street, Dormansland,
Lingfield, Surrey RH7 6PU, 01342 834621.
Called: Nov 1949, Inner Temple, MA

Kelaart *Ms Jennifer Rosanne Sabina*
Lecturer in Law - University of Colombo -
Sri Lanka, 12/2A Tickell Road, Colombo 8,
(94-1) 696623, Fax: (94-1) 422768.
Called: Nov 1995, Inner Temple, LLB
(Lond), LLM (Syd)

Kellam *James Antony Plenderleith* ●
Senior Crown Prosecutor, CPS (Thames Branch), Portland House, Stag Place, Victoria, London, 0171 915 5820, Fax: 0171 915 5811. Called: Nov 1991, Inner Temple, LLB (South)

Kelleher *Miss Catherine*
Called: July 1979, Middle Temple, BA, M Phil(Lond)

Kelleher *Dr John Daniel*
Partner, Olsen Backhurst & Dorey, Eaton House, 9 Seaton Place, St Helier, Jersey JE2 3QL, 01534 888900, Fax: 01534 887744, Advocate of the Royal Court of Jersey (1995). Jersey Law Society. and Member Jersey Bar. Called: Oct 1991, Middle Temple, BA Hons (Warw), Dip Law (Lond), PhD (Warw), Certificat De, Juridiques Francaise

Kelley *Simon Sukhdeep*
Called: Nov 1996, Lincoln's Inn, LLB (Hons)(Cardiff), LLM (Tulane), Dip. (Ship) Law, (Lond)

Kellock *James Donald* ●
Grade 5 Lawyer, Serious Fraud Office, Elm House, 10-16 Elm Street, London WC1X OBJ, Fax: 0717 239 7115. Called: Nov 1979, Inner Temple, MA (Cantab)

Kellow *Ian Robert* ●
Director and General Counsel, ING Barings, 60 London Wall, London EC2M 5TQ, 0171 767 6060. Called: July 1982, Inner Temple, MBA, LLB

Kelly *Andrew Mark* ●
Prosecuting Solicitor, HM Customs & Excise, New King's Beam House, 22 Upper Ground, London SE1. Called: July 1985, Inner Temple, LLB

Kelly *Bernard Anthony* QC (1991)
Part Time Chairman of Industrial Tribunals, Northbrook, 32 Fairmile Lane, Cobham, Surrey KT11 2DQ, 01932 867811, Fax: 01932 867811. Called: July 1957, Gray's Inn, MA (Cantab)

Kelly *Mrs Carys Lindsay*
Deputy Chief Clerk, Inner London Magistrates', Courts Service, 65 Romney Street, London SW1P 3RD. Called: July 1982, Gray's Inn, LLB (B'ham)

Kelly *Christopher Andrew*
Clayton UtZ, Solicitors & Attorneys, Levels 27-35, 1 O'Connell Street, Sydney NSW 2000. Called: Nov 1993, Middle Temple, LLB (Hons)(Lond)

Kelly *David*
40/30 M6 Bangrateuk, Mooban Ladaporn, Sampran 73210, Nakhon Pathom, 00 662 441 0545, Fax: 00 662 441 0527. Called: Feb 1962, Inner Temple, MA (Oxon)

Kelly *Eamonn*
Called: Oct 1997, Inner Temple, BA (Cork), LLB (South Bank)

Kelly *Mrs Henrietta* ●
Chairman,London Rent Assessment Panel,Chairman Leashold Valuation Tribunal. Called: Feb 1960, Middle Temple, LLB

Kelly *John Denis Ryan*
Director, United Nations, 23 Avenue de Bude, CH-1202 Geneva, Geneva 733-79-13. Called: Jan 1943, Inner Temple, MA (Oxon)

Kelly *Mark Frank*
Called: Nov 1997, Gray's Inn, LLB

Kelly *Miss Mary Josephine* ●
Senior Crown Prosecutor, Crown Prosecution Service, South Parade, Wakefield WF1 1LR, Wakefield 290620. Called: Nov 1986, Gray's Inn, BSc, Dip Law

Kelly *Mrs Maureen Elizabeth*
Deputy Chief Clerk, Inner London Magistrates', Courts Service, 65 Romney Street, London SW1P 3RD. Called: Nov 1988, Gray's Inn, BA (Lond)

Kelly *Philip James*
Barrister of Ireland. Called: May 1996, Middle Temple, BA, MSc (Dublin)

Kelly *Shaw Martin*
Called: Oct 1997, Middle Temple, BA (Hons)(Lond)

Kelly *Ms Tara Jane*
Legal Advisor, Derby & South Derbyshire, Magistrates' Court, The Court House, Derwent Street, Derby DE1 2EP, (01332) 292100, Fax: (01332) 293459. Called: Oct 1992, Gray's Inn, LLB, LLM

Kelso *Donald Iain Junor*
Called: Nov 1995, Lincoln's Inn, BA (Hons)

Kelvin *Carl George Leslie Steven* ●
Senior Crown Prosecutor, Crown Prosecution Service, Southern Branch, The Cooperage, Gainsford Street, London SE1 2NG. Called: Nov 1988, Middle Temple, LLB (Hons), LLM (Lond)

Kemp *David Ashton McIntyre* QC (1973)
and Member Hong Kong, Gibraltar, Malaysia & Kenya Bars Monckton Chambers, 4 Raymond Buildings, Gray's Inn, London, WC1R 5BP. Called: Nov 1948, Inner Temple, BA (Cantab), FCIArb

Kendall *Mark Noel* ●
Principal Crown Prosecutor. Called: Nov 1987, Inner Temple, LLB (So'ton)

Kendrew *Miss Elizabeth Anne Hamilton*
Called: July 1997, Middle Temple, BA (Hons)(Cantab)

Keng *Miss Wan Ling*
Called: July 1995, Lincoln's Inn, LLB (Hons)

Kennedy *Andrew George* ●
Legal Advisor, Lloyds Registrar of Shipping, 71 Fenchurch Street, London EC3M 4BS, 0171 423 2439, Fax: 0171 709 9166. Called: July 1987, Middle Temple, BA (Kent)

Kennedy *Hugh Paul*
Bencher Inn of Court N Ireland Past Chairman Bar Council of N.I., Past Treasurer, Inn of Court of N.I., Bar Library, Royal Courts of Justice, Chichester Street, Belfast, 0232 241523, Fax: 0232 231850, QC (N Ireland) SC Republic of Ireland. Called: Nov 1990, Gray's Inn, BA,LLB (Belfast)

Kennedy *Ian McColl*
University College, Department of Law, London, 2 Hare Court, Ground Floor, Temple, London, EC4Y 7BH. Called: July 1974, Inner Temple, LLB, LLM

Kennedy *John Brendan* ●
Crown Prosecutor, Crown Prosecution Service, Trafalgar House, 2 Bedford Park, Croydon, Surrey. Called: July 1987, Lincoln's Inn, LLB (B'ham)

Kennedy *Michael Joseph*
Called: Nov 1991, Middle Temple, LLB Hons (Manch)

Kennedy *Thomas Alastair Plunkett*
Head of Information Office, Court of Justice of the, European Communities, L 2925, 352-4303 3355, Fax: 352-4303 2500. Called: Nov 1975, Gray's Inn, LLB

Kennon *Andrew Rowland*
Parliamentary Adviser, Cabinet Office, Cabinet Office, 70 Whitehall, London SW1. Called: July 1979, Gray's Inn, MA (Cantab)

Kenny *Miss Bernadette Joan* ●
Lord Chancellors Department, Trevelyan House, 30 Great Peter Street, London SW1P 2BY. Called: July 1979, Lincoln's Inn, LLB (Hons)

Kenny *Judge Harvey*
and Member Southern Ireland Bar. Called: Feb 1982, Middle Temple, BCL (Nat Univ, Ireland), ACIArB

Kent *Gordon Peter Selim Mehmet*
Called: Feb 1995, Gray's Inn, LLB (Lond)

Kent *Graham Edward* ●
Senior Principal Legal Officer, Department of Social Security, New Court, 48 Carey Street, London WC2A 2LS. Called: July 1975, Gray's Inn, MA (Oxon), M.Jur[Man]

Kent *Mr. Graham Gregory*
International Securities & Capital Markets, Simmons & Simmons, 21 Wilson Street, London EC2M 2TX, 0171 628 2020, Fax: 0171 628 2070. Called: Oct 1995, Gray's Inn, LLB

Kent *Philip Anthony* ●
Lawyer (Grade 5), Ministry of Agriculture,, Fisheries and Food, 55 Whitehall, London SW1A 2EY, 0171 270 8399, Fax: 0171 270 8270. Called: July 1977, Gray's Inn, LLB (Lond)

Kentish *Mrs Louise Anne*
Associate, J A Hassan & Partners, 57/63 Line Wall Road, 00 350 79000, Fax: 00 350 71966, and Member Gibraltar. Called: Nov 1996, Middle Temple, BA (Hons)

Kenton *Simon Timothy*
26 Melina Road, London W12 9HZ, 0181
749 8658. Called: Feb 1993, Gray's Inn, LLB

Kenyon-Jackson *Mrs Carolyn*
Called: July 1990, Middle Temple, BA
(Hons), CPE

Kenyon-Vaughan *David*
Called: Mar 1998, Lincoln's Inn, LLB
(Hons)(Staffs)

Keogh *Andrew William* •
Called: Nov 1994, Inner Temple, LLB (Sheff)

Keogh *Miss Sonia Elizabeth*
Called: July 1995, Gray's Inn, LLB (Lond)

Keoy *Soo Khim*
Called: July 1997, Gray's Inn, LLB

Kerr *Ms Clare Patricia* •
Criminal Appeal Office, Royal Courts of
Justice, London WC1R, 0171 936 6725.
Called: Nov 1995, Middle Temple, BA
(Hons)

Kerr *Donald TD*
32 Downs Road, Epsom, Surrey KT18 5JD,
01372 724744. Called: Nov 1946, Gray's
Inn, BA Com(Manch)

Kerr *Miss Elizabeth Ann Scott*
Called: Mar 1997, Lincoln's Inn, LLB
(Hons)(L'pool)

Kerr *John Stuart*
Called: Nov 1995, Inner Temple, MA (Edin),
CPE

Kerrigan *Mrs Greer Sandra* •
Legal Director, Solicitor's Office, Dept of,
Social Security,Dept of Health, New Court,
Carey Street, London WC2A 2LS, 0171 412
1341, Fax: 0171 412 1583, and Member
Trinidad & Tobago. Called: July 1971,
Middle Temple

Kershaw *Nicholas John*
Ogier & Le Masurier, Pirouet House, Union
Street, St Helier, Jersey, Channel Islands,
01534 504000, Fax: 01534 35328, and
Member New South Wales Bar Jersey Bar.
Called: May 1988, Middle Temple, LLB
(Hons) London

Kershaw *Dr Steven*
Called: Oct 1997, Lincoln's Inn, BSc
(Hons)(Bris)

Kesavapany *Muralitherapany*
Called: Nov 1995, Middle Temple, LLB
(Hons)(Lond)

Kessel *Ms Joanna Nicolle*
Television Reporter/Director. Called: Oct
1993, Middle Temple, BA (Hons)(Sussex)

Kesselman *Rabbi Neville* •
Senior Crown Prosecutor, London Area,
Kings House, Kymberley Road, Harrow,
Middlesex HA1 1YH, 0181 424 8688, Fax:
0181 424 9134, Formerly a Solicitor.
Called: July 1970, Gray's Inn

Kew *Michael Deslie*
Called: Nov 1967, Inner Temple, LLB (Lond)

Keymer *Robert Michael*
Called: Nov 1995, Inner Temple, LLB
(Lancs)

Khairuddin *Miss Fateh Hanum*
Called: July 1996, Lincoln's Inn, BA
(Hons)(Keele)

Khakhar *Miss Ketki*
Called: Nov 1975, Middle Temple, BA

Khambatta *Sam Pirosha QC (1946)*
5 St Margaret's Close, Horstead, Norfolk
NR12 7ER, Also Inn of Court G International
Law Assoc 1952-1987 and Member India Bar
Nigeria Bar. Called: June 1929, Middle
Temple

Khan *Abdul Shakoor*
Called: Nov 1997, Lincoln's Inn, BA
(Peshawar), LLB (Hons) (Leeds)

Khan *Ms Amira Farhat*
Called: Nov 1994, Inner Temple, BA
(Middx), CPE (Lond)

Khan *Averroes Aldeboran Karam* •
Principal Legal Officer, HM Customs &
Excise, New Kings Beam House, 22 Upper
Ground, London SE1 9PJ, and Member
Trinidad & Tobago Bar. Called: Nov 1986,
Lincoln's Inn, MA (Cantab)

Khan *Inayat Ullah* •
Director, Southampton Racial Equality,
Council, 12 Palmerston Road, Southampton
SO14 1LL, 01703 229646, Fax: 01703
337467, and Member Punjab Bar Council.
Called: Nov 1980, Lincoln's Inn, LLB
(Leeds), BA, Dip in Law

Khan *Karim Asad Ahmad*
Legal Advisor, Office of the Prosecutor,
United Nations, International, Criminal
Tribunal, 1 Churchill Plein, 2517JA, Den
Haag, 0031 70 4165353, Fax: 0031 70
4165325. Called: Oct 1992, Lincoln's Inn,
LLB(Hons)(Lond), AKC (Lond), Dip Int Rel
(Nice)

Khan *Miss Mahreen Aziz*
Called: Nov 1994, Inner Temple, BA
(Cantab)

Khan *Mirazul Hossain*
Called: Nov 1997, Lincoln's Inn, LLB
(Hons)(Lond)

Khan *Mohamed Amjad*
Called: May 1992, Lincoln's Inn, LLB (Hons)

Khan *Muhammed Mustafizur Rahman*
Called: Nov 1997, Lincoln's Inn, BSS
(Hons)(Dhaka), LLB (Hons)

Khan *Miss Nadine Miriam*
Called: May 1995, Lincoln's Inn, LLB (Hons)

Khan *Nicholas Paul* •
Legal Adviser, Legal Service, Commission of
European Communities, 200 Rue de la Loi,
1049 Brussels, Belgium, 010 322 295 4137,
Fax: 010 322 296 5965. Called: July 1983,
Inner Temple, LLB Soton

Khan *Miss Noshaba Sarfaraz*
Called: Nov 1997, Middle Temple, LLB
(Hons)(Lond)

Khan *Miss Roshan Ara*
Called: Feb 1994, Middle Temple, LLB
(Hons)(Lond)

Khan *Shafi*
01582 598394, Advocate of the High Court
of Pakistan. Called: Feb 1994, Lincoln's Inn,
BA (Punjab), MA (Karachi), LLB (Hons,
Brunel)

Khan *Sirdar Ejaz*
10a Civil Lines, Rawalpindi, Pakistan, (010)
9251 564346, and Member Punjab Bar.
Called: July 1993, Lincoln's Inn, BA (Hons)

Khan *Tariq Ali*
Called: Nov 1996, Lincoln's Inn, LLB (Hons)

Khan *Miss Yasmin*
Called: Oct 1996, Lincoln's Inn, LLB
(Hons)(Lond)

Khan *Miss Zoe Yasmin* •
5 King Street Cloisters, Clifton Walk,
London W6 0GY. Called: Oct 1993, Middle
Temple, MA (Cantab)

Khanna *Nechal Chand*
Called: July 1997, Middle Temple, LLB
(Hons)

Kharran *Miss Devi Samantha*
Called: July 1994, Lincoln's Inn, LLB (Hons)

Khasru *Najrul Islam*
Court Clerk, Waltham Forest Magistrates',
Court, 1 Farnan Avenue, Walthamstow
E17 4NX, 0181 527 8000, Fax: 0181 527
9063. Called: July 1988, Inner Temple, LLB

Khattak *Aurang Zeb* •
Senior Crown Prosecutor, Crown
Prosecution Service, Dale House, Dale End,
Birmingham B5, 233-3133. Called: Apr 1989,
Gray's Inn, LLB (Hons)

Khaw *Ms Claire Kuen Hui*
Called: Nov 1997, Gray's Inn, LLB
(Kingston)

Khaw *Miss Gim Hong*
27 Jalan Bijaksana, Taman Century, 80250
Johor Bahru, Johor, Malaysia, 07 3342753,
and Member Singapore Bar. Called: July
1994, Middle Temple, LLB (Hons), ACCA

Khaw *Kenneth Jin Teck*
Called: July 1993, Middle Temple, LLB
(Hons, Bris), ACA

Khaw *Oliver Kar Heng*
Called: July 1997, Middle Temple, LLB
(Hons)

Khong *Miss Gilliam Li Shen*
Called: July 1997, Middle Temple, LLB
(Hons)(Nott'm)

Khong *Yu Cheong*
Called: July 1994, Lincoln's Inn, LLB (Hons,
Lond)

Khoo *Gavin Lay Keong*
Called: July 1997, Middle Temple, LLB
(Hons)(Wales)

Khoo *Kay Kwan*
Called: Nov 1997, Lincoln's Inn, LLB
(Hons)(Wales)

Khoo *Melvin Lay Jin*
Called: Nov 1993, Middle Temple, LLB
(Hons)(Bucks)

Khoo *Per-Ern*
Called: July 1993, Middle Temple, LLB (Hons)(Hull)

Khoo *Miss Selkie*
Called: Nov 1997, Middle Temple, LLB (Hons)(Leics)

Khoo *Miss Su Sen*
Called: July 1996, Middle Temple, LLB (Hons)(Glamorg)

Khor *Gerald Guan Yu*
Called: Nov 1996, Gray's Inn, BA (Keele)

Khor *Wee Siong*
and Member Singapore Bar. Called: July 1996, Lincoln's Inn, LLB (Hons)(Hull)

Khubber *Ranjiv*
Called: Nov 1994, Middle Temple, BA (Hons) (Kent), MA (Sussex)

Kiddle *John Otto OBE*
Keeper's Cottage, Privett, Alton, Hants GU34 3PF, Privett 217. Called: Feb 1958, Lincoln's Inn

Kidwell *Raymond Incledon QC (1968)*
Recorder. Called: Nov 1951, Gray's Inn, MA, BCL (Oxon)

Kieran *Brian Laurence*
P.O.Box 2071, General Post Office, (852) 2501 0471, Fax: (852) 2592 7086, and Member Jamaica Bar Hong Kong Bar. Called: July 1968, Gray's Inn, LLB, DIP Air, FBIS

Kilby *Edwin Philip* •
Grade 6 (Legal), Lord Chancellor's Dept, Selborne House, 54-60 Victoria Street, London SW1E 6QW, 0171 210 0740, Fax: 0171 210 0746. Called: July 1980, Inner Temple

Kilby *James Richard* •
Lawyer, Charity Commission, The Deane, Tangier, Taunton, Somerset TA1 4A. Called: Nov 1979, Inner Temple, BA Hons (Oxon)

Kilgarriff *Patrick Herbert* •
Treasury Solicitor's Dept, Queen Anne's Chambers, 28 Broadway, London SW1H 9JS. Called: Nov 1986, Gray's Inn, BSc, Dip Law

Kilic *Mrs Meena Barathi*
Called: Feb 1992, Lincoln's Inn, LLB (Hons) (Wales), BA (Singapore)

Killerby *Miss Joan Margaret*
Head of the Private &, International Law Division, Council of Europe, Strasbourg Cedex, 03 88 41 22 10, Fax: 03 88 41 27 94. Called: Nov 1967, Inner Temple, doc de Univ d'Aix-, Marseille

Killick *Marcus Charles*
Head of Banking Supervision, Cayman Island Monetary Auth, P.O.Box 10052 APO, Georgetown, Grand Cayman, Cayman Islands IM99 1DT, (345) 949 1839, Fax: (345) 949 2532, and Member New York Bar. Called: July 1989, Gray's Inn, LLB (Leeds)

Kilpatrick *Miss Lisa*
Called: Nov 1995, Gray's Inn, BA (Manch)

Kim *Theodore Joseph*
37 Store Street, London WC1E 7BS, Fax: (44) 171-636 5550. Called: Nov 1995, Lincoln's Inn, BSc (Hons)(Econ), MSc (Econ)

Kinahan *Mrs Ann*
Joint Manager of Bromley Citizens Advice Bureau, 83 Tweedy Road, Bromley BR1 1RG, 0181 464 0599. Called: Nov 1981, Inner Temple, LLB

Kinch *Alec Anthony CBE*
36 Greenways, Beckenham, Kent BR3 3NG, 0181 658 2298, Fax: 0181 663 0737. Called: Nov 1951, Middle Temple, MA (Oxon)

Kindell *James William*
Company Secretary, Company Secretarial Department, Price Waterhouse, No 1 London Bridge, London SE1 9QL, 0171 939 3000/939 5019, Fax: 0171 403 5265/939 4173. Called: Nov 1992, Middle Temple, B.Sc (Hons, City), Dip in Law, LLM (Surrey)

Kindred *Frank Paul* •
26 Offley Road, London SW9, 0171 735 1444. Called: July 1985, Gray's Inn, BSc (Lond), MSc, (Dunelm)

King *Alesdair Martin James* •
Crown Prosecutor, Crown Prosecution Service, 4,5,6 & 7 Prebended Court, Oxford Road, Aylesbury, Bucks HP19 3EY, 01296 436441, Fax: 01296 88664. Called: Oct 1991, Gray's Inn, LLB (Essex)

King *Frank Rowland*
Cherries, 26 Druid Stoke Avenue, Stoke Bishop, Bristol BS9 1DD. Called: July 1970, Gray's Inn, LLB (Lond)

King *Geoffrey William*
Group Secretary, Guinness PLC, 39 Portman Square, London W1H OEE, 0171 486 0288, Fax: 0171 878 4388. Called: May 1968, Gray's Inn, LLB, AKC, FCIS, FInst M

King *Miss Jacqueline Doreen*
Court Clerk, Richmond Upon Thames Mags Crt, Parkshot, Richmond, Surrey TW9 2RF, 0181 948 2101, Fax: 0181 332 2628. Called: Feb 1983, Middle Temple

King *James Charles*
Called: Oct 1996, Inner Temple, LLB (Soton)

King *Mrs Joyce Belinda*
Deputy Clerk to the Justices, Wiltshire Magistrates Court, 43-55 Milford Street, Salisbury SP1 2BP, 01722 333225, Fax: 01722 413395. Called: July 1985, Gray's Inn

King *Miss Juliet Ann*
Called: Feb 1995, Inner Temple, LLB (Soton)

King *Michael Bruce*
1 Gray's Inn Square, 1st Floor, London, WC1R 5AG. Called: July 1971, Gray's Inn

King *Paul John*
Graham Thompson & Co, Sasson House, Shirley Street, Victoria Avenue, P.O.Box N272, Nassau, (242) 322 4130, Fax: (242) 328 1069, and Member Bahamas. Called: July 1996, Middle Temple, LLB (Hons)(Soton), BA (Hons)(Miami)

King *Peter Andrew*
Member of the Northern Ireland Forum, Bar Library, Royal Courts of Justice, P O Box 414, Chichester Street, Belfast BT1 3JP, 01232 562354, Fax: 01232 231850, and Member Northern Ireland Bar. Called: Nov 1993, Gray's Inn, LLB (Manch)

King *Robert George Cecil* •
Part-time Chairman (SSAT/DAT) Tribunals. Called: Nov 1965, Lincoln's Inn

King *Simon David* •
Claims Executive, A Bilbrough & Co Ltd, 50 Leman Street, London E1 8HQ, 0171 772 8000, Fax: 0171 772 8200. Called: Oct 1991, Inner Temple, BA (Dunelm), CPE

Kingsbury *Miss Carol Jayne*
Allen & Overy Solicitors, One New Change, London EC4M 9QQ, 0171 330 3000, Fax: 0171 330 9999. Called: July 1984, Middle Temple, MA (Cantab)

Kingsbury *Lt Cdr James Arthur Timothy RN* •
Directorate of Defence Programming, Defence programmes - CP5a, Ministry of Defence, Room 4304, Main Building, Whitehall, London SW1A 2HB. Called: July 1989, Middle Temple, BSc, Dip Law

Kingsbury *Simon Anthony*
Called: Nov 1996, Gray's Inn, LLB (Sussex)

Kingsdown *Lord KG*
Torry Hill, Sittingbourne, Kent ME9 0SP, 01795 830 258, Fax: 01795 830 243. Called: July 1954, Inner Temple

Kingsmill *Miss Elizabeth* •
Lord Chancellor's Department, Criminal Appeal Office, Royal Courts of Justice, The Strand, London WC2A 2LL, 0171 936 6140, Fax: 0171 936 6900. Called: July 1985, Lincoln's Inn, LLB(Lond)

Kinnear *David Thomas Alexander*
Director Credit Suisse, First Boston Corporation, 212 325 7029, Fax: 212 325 9177. Called: July 1989, Middle Temple, LLB (Manch)

Kinnell *Ian QC (1987)* •
Arbitrator, Woodside House, The Maypole, Monmouth NP5 3QH, 01600 713077, Fax: 01600 772880. Called: July 1967, Gray's Inn

Kinoshi *John Ayoola*
Legal Advisor (Legal Private Practitioner), 5 Kinoshi St, Abeokuta, Nigeria, Also Inn of Court I and Member Nigerian Bar. Called: Nov 1972, Lincoln's Inn

Kinsman *Ms Fiona Jane* •
Legal Adviser, DSS, The Solicitor's Office, Room 516 New Court, 48 Carey Street, London WC2A 2LS, 0171 412 1489, Fax: 0171 412 1523. Called: July 1989, Lincoln's Inn, BA (Kent), Dip French Law, LLM (Lond)

Kiplagat *Miss Betty Jepkoech*
Called: Nov 1996, Middle Temple, LLB (Hons)

Kiralfy *Professor Albert Roland*
Retired Professor of Law, c/o School of
Law, King's College, Strand, London.
Called: Jan 1947, Gray's Inn, PhD, LLM, LLB

Kirk *Alexander Frederick*
Bailache Labesse Trustees Ltd, Piermont
House, 33-35 Pier Road, St Helier, Jersey
JE1 1BD, (44) 534 888777. Called: June
1949, Middle Temple, MA (Oxon)

Kirkham *Miss Karen Lesley* •
Acting Director of Legal Affairs, Building
Employers, Confederation, 82 New
Cavendish Street, London W1M 8AD, 0171
580 5588. Called: Nov 1988, Middle
Temple, MA (Oxon)

Kirkham *Keith* •
Principal Crown Prosecutor, Crown
Prosecution Service, Unicentre, Lords Walk,
Preston, Lancashire PR1 1DH, 01772
555015. Called: Feb 1985, Middle Temple

Kirkham-Smith *Mrs Marjorie Anne* •
Senior Crown Prosecutor, CPS, 4-12 Queen
Anne's Gate, London SW1H 9AZ.
Called: July 1981, Middle Temple, BA
(Hons)

Kirkman *Patrick John* •
Legal Advisor, The West of England Ship,
Owners Insurance Services Ltd, 224-226
Tower Bridge Road, London SE1 2UP, 0171
716 6015, Fax: 0171 716 6111. Called: Nov
1990, Middle Temple, MA (St Andrew's),
Dip Law (City)

Kirkpatrick *Gavin Waring* •
Crown Prosecution Service, 10 Furnival St,
London EC4A 1PE. Called: Nov 1981, Middle
Temple, BA (Hons)

Kirsop *Ms Sara Jane*
Called: Nov 1997, Inner Temple, BSc
(So'ton)

Kitchin *Ms Hilary Judith*
Local Government Information, Unit, 1-5
Bath Street, London EC1V 9QQ, 0171 608
1051, Former Solicitor 4 Brick Court,
Ground Floor, Temple, London, EC4Y 9AD.
Called: Nov 1987, Lincoln's Inn, BA (Sussex)

Klausner *Isidor* •
Stancroft Trust Limited, Bride House, 20
Bride Lane, London EC4Y 8DX, 0171 583
3808, Fax: 0171 583 5912. Called: Nov
1981, Middle Temple, LLM, DRS EC
[Rotterdam]

Klein *Miss Miriam-Xenia*
Financial Advisor, City Financial Partners,
Russell Square House, London WC1B 5EH,
0171 323 2828, Fax: 0171 436 0304.
Called: July 1997, Lincoln's Inn, LLB (Hons),
LLM

Klein *Silviu Thomas Rudolf* •
Director of Legal Affairs, Specialist
Engineering, Contractors Group, ESCA
House, 34 Palace Court, Bayswater,London
W2 4JG, 0171 229 2488, Fax: 0171 727
9268. Called: Nov 1979, Middle Temple, LLB
(Hons) (Lond)

Klouda *Thomas Joseph* •
Senior Crown Prosecutor, Crown
Prosecution Service, CPS Yorkshire,
Wakefield Branch Office, 4-5 South Parade,
Wakefield WF1 1LR. Called: Nov 1980,
Middle Temple, BA, LLB (Leeds)

Knapman *Mrs Lynne Geraldine* •
Head of Crown Office and Deputy Registrar
of Criminal Appeals, Lord Chancellor's
Department, Crown Office/Criminal Appeal,
Royal Courts of Justice, The Strand, London
WC2A, 0171 936 6454, Fax: 0171 936 6276.
Called: July 1973, Middle Temple, LLB
(Hons) Lond

Knapper *Don* •
Crown Prosecution Service, Blackburn
House, Midway, Newcastle-under-Lyme,
Staffordshire. Called: Oct 1992, Gray's Inn,
B.Sc

Kneller *Sir Alister Alister Walter Arthur
Ernest*
15 Summersdale Court, The Drive, Lavant
Road, Chichester, West Sussex PO19 4RF,
01243 528408, Knight Bachelor.
Called: June 1953, Gray's Inn, MA (Hons)
(Cantab), LLM (Hons) (Cantab)

Kneller *Miss Karen Belinda* •
Crown Prosecutor, Crown Prosecution
Service, Crown House, Winston Churchill
Avenue, Portsmouth, 01705 752004, Fax:
01705 753390. Called: Nov 1993, Inner
Temple, BA (L'pool), LLB (Lond)

Knight *Miss Amanda*
26C Browning Street, London SE17 1LU,
0171 703 1178. Called: Oct 1994, Gray's
Inn, BA

Knight *David Alan*
Chairman of Barnsbury Housing Association,
Member of Member Investment Property
Forum Investment Property Forum, Member
of British Property Forum European Forum,
Lovell White Durrant, 65 Holborn Viaduct,
London EC1A 2DY, 0171 236 0066, Fax:
0171 248 4212. Called: Nov 1983, Inner
Temple, BA (Hons)

Knight *Ms Judith* •
Devon County Council, County Hall,
Topsham Road, Exeter, Devon, 01752
382000. Called: Oct 1991, Lincoln's Inn, LLB
(Hons) (Notts)

Knight *Nigel Merley* •
Principal Crown Prosecutor, Crown
Prosecution Service, PO Box 229, Horsham,
West Sussex RH12 1YB, 01403 272923.
Called: July 1984, Gray's Inn, LLB (E Anglia)

Knight *Miss Tracey Ann*
Called: Oct 1997, Lincoln's Inn, LLB
(Hons)(Oxon), LLM (E.Anglia)

Knorpel *Henry CB QC (1988)*
Conway, 32 Sunnybank, Epsom, Surrey
KT18 7DX, 01372 721394. Called: Jan 1947,
Inner Temple, BCL, MA (Oxon)

Knott *Miss Judith Mary* •
Principal Crown Prosecutor, Crown
Prosecution Service, 8th Floor, Sunlight
House, Quay Street, Manchester M60 3LU,
0161 626 6238, Fax: 0161 835 2663.
Called: July 1980, Inner Temple, LL.B. (Hull)

Knowles *Miss Adrianna Desiree*
and Member Bahamas Bar. Called: July 1997,
Lincoln's Inn, LLB (Hons), LLM

Knowles *Mrs Christina Jane* •
Grade 6 (Legal), Dept of Trade & Industry,
Room 120, 10-18 Victoria Street, London
SW1, Fax: 0171 215 3141. Called: July 1980,
Inner Temple

Knowles *James Roger*
53 Bedford Square, London WC1B 3DP,
0171 580 3536, Fax: 0171 436 4860.
Called: Nov 1971, Lincoln's Inn,
FRICS,FCIArb

Knowles *Mrs Patricia Katharine* •
Grade 6, Department of the Environment, 2
Marsham Street, London SW1P 3EB.
Called: Oct 1971, Gray's Inn

Knowles *Peter Francis Arnold C.B.* •
Parliamentary Counsel, Parliamentary
Counsel Office, 36 Whitehall, London
SW1A 2AY. Called: July 1971, Gray's Inn,
MA (Oxon)

Knowles *Philip Jonathan*
Justices' Clerk, The Magistrates Court,
Walton Street, Aylesbury, Bucks HP21 7QZ,
01296 338959, Fax: 01296 338960.
Called: July 1982, Gray's Inn, LLB (Lond),
DMS

Knox *Miss Heather Elizabeth* •
Legal Adviser, Premier Consolidated,
Oilfields plc, 23 Lower Belgrave Street,
London SW1W 0NR. Called: Nov 1976,
Gray's Inn

Knox *Terry Daniel*
Called: Oct 1996, Middle Temple, LLB
(Hons) (Lond)

Knox-Hooke *Zaccheaus Aubrey*
Called: Oct 1991, Inner Temple, BSc, LLB
(Lond), LLM (Lond)

Ko *Hiu Fung*
Called: Nov 1997, Lincoln's Inn, LLB (Hons)

Ko *Justin King Sau*
806 Wheelock House, 20 Pedder Street,
Central, Hong Kong, 852 25220209, Fax:
852 28450720, and Member Hong-Kong
Bar. Called: July 1993, Lincoln's Inn, LLB
(Hons, B'ham)

Kobani *Kenneth Bie*
Called: Nov 1994, Inner Temple, BA, MA
(Keele)

Koe *Miss Kian Fei*
Called: July 1996, Middle Temple, LLB
(Hons)(Lond)

Koenig *Michel*
Legal Adviser to French Embassy &
Consulate General, 4 Essex Court, Temple,
London, EC4Y 9AJ. Called: Nov 1953,
Middle Temple

Koenigsberger *Carl Wolfgang*
Called: Feb 1958, Gray's Inn, BA

Koh *Miss Aileen Geok Pin*
Called: July 1995, Middle Temple, LLB
(Hons)

Koh *Chia Ling*
Called: July 1997, Middle Temple, LLB
(Hons)(Lond)

Koh *Darren Ngiap Thiam*
Procter & Gamble Far East Inc., 17 Koyo-
cho Naka 1-chome, Higashinada-ku, Kobe
658-0032, 078 845 2344, Fax: 078 845
6900. Called: July 1989, Lincoln's Inn, LLB
(Buck), ACA, ATII

Koh *Gerald Teck Hock*
Called: Mar 1996, Middle Temple, LLB
(Hons)

Koh *Hua Hong*
Block 758 [H]09-131, Choa Chu Kang North
5, Singapore 680758, 065 766 2016/065 337
6368, Fax: 065 337 2425, Full Name is Koh
Hua Hong alias Koh Dar Eng. Called: July
1994, Lincoln's Inn, LLB (Hons), FCCA

Koh *Miss Jean Bee Khim*
Called: Oct 1996, Middle Temple, LLB
(Hons)(Lond)

Koh *Miss Joanna Wei Ser*
Called: July 1997, Middle Temple, LLB
(Hons)(Exon)

Koh *Kok Shen*
Called: Oct 1995, Middle Temple, LLB
(Hons)

Koh *Miss Lee Tze*
Called: July 1995, Lincoln's Inn, LLB (Hons)

Koh *Miss Maisie Su-Mei*
and Member Singapore. Called: July 1995,
Middle Temple, LLB (Hons)

Koh *Sam Mong Poo*
Block 817, Tampines Street 81, [H] 04-588,
65 7892048, and Member Member of the
Singapore Bar. Called: July 1996, Middle
Temple, LLB (Hons)(Wolves)

Koh *Miss Selena Lay Na*
Called: Nov 1996, Middle Temple, LLB
(Hons)(Bucks)

Koh *Siew Hui*
Called: July 1995, Lincoln's Inn, LLB (Hons)

Koh *Sim Teck*
Called: May 1994, Middle Temple, LLB
(Hons)

Koh *Terence Kah Hoe*
Called: Oct 1995, Middle Temple, LLB
(Hons)

Koh *Terence Sebastian Ker Siang*
Called: July 1996, Middle Temple, LLB
(Hons)(Bris)

Kok *Miss Aik Wan*
Called: Nov 1996, Lincoln's Inn, LLB
(Hons)(So'ton)

Kok *Lak Hin*
Called: July 1995, Lincoln's Inn, LLB (Hons)

Kok *Miss Meng Wei*
Called: July 1995, Lincoln's Inn, LLB
(Hons)(Leeds)

Kok *Ms Yoke Kieng*
Called: Nov 1996, Gray's Inn, LLB

Konecki *Andrew Anthony*
Called: Nov 1991, Lincoln's Inn, LLB (Hons)

Kong *Chi Man*
Called: Nov 1997, Middle Temple, B.Soc.Sci
(Hong Kong)

Kong *Miss Jennifer Lee Jean*
Advocate & Solicitor in a Legal Firm, and
Member Sabah Bar Malaysia Bar. Called: Nov
1992, Lincoln's Inn, BA (Hons)(Nott'm)

Kong *Kelvin Wen Wai*
Called: July 1989, Lincoln's Inn, LLB (Newc)

Kong *Miss Seh Ping*
Called: July 1995, Middle Temple, LLB
(Hons)

Konotey-Ahulu *Dawid Konotey-Adade*
Director, Natwest Markets Ltd, 135
Bishopsgate, London EC2M 3UR, 0171 334
1780, Fax: 0171 375 5060. Called: Nov
1987, Lincoln's Inn, LLB Hons

Konstam *Michael John*
Legal Adviser, A & L Goodbody Solicitors,
Pinnacle House, 23-26 St Dunstan's Hill,
London EC3R 8HL, 0171 929 2425, Fax:
0171 489 9677. Called: July 1981, Gray's
Inn, MA (Cantab)

Koo *John*
Called: Feb 1993, Lincoln's Inn, LLB (Hons)

Kooi *Tock Ken*
Called: July 1996, Lincoln's Inn, LLB
(Hons)(Lond)

Koon *Keen Hoong*
Called: July 1996, Gray's Inn, LLB (Exeter)

Kor *Darren Yit Meng*
Called: July 1996, Lincoln's Inn, LLB
(Hons)(Warw)

Kor *Don Shiang Hua*
and Member Malaysia Bar. Called: July 1994,
Middle Temple, BA (Hons)(Manc)

Koroma *Saidu Abdulai* •
Senior Crown Prosecuter, Crown
Prosecution Service, 4 Artillery Row,
London SW1P 1RZ, 0171 976 5699, Fax:
0171 233 2039. Called: Feb 1987, Gray's
Inn, BSc Econ Hons (Lond), Dip Law

Korpal *Miss Bendna*
Called: Nov 1997, Lincoln's Inn, BA (Hons)

Kothari *Raj Motilal*
Called: Oct 1996, Inner Temple, LLB (Lond),
CPE (Oxon)

Kotun *Chief Lateef Olakunle*
Legal Adviser & Consultant, 14 Westhorpe
Gardens, Hendon, London NW4 1TU, 0181
203 5053, and Member Nigerian Bar.
Called: Feb 1962, Inner Temple

Kotwal *Ebrahim Mohammad OBE,JP*
Called: Feb 1962, Middle Temple

Koul *Ms Priyanka*
Called: Nov 1997, Inner Temple, LLB (Kent)

Kountouri-Tapiero *Ms Elena*
Called: Nov 1996, Inner Temple, LLB
(Lond), Maitrise in French, Law (Paris)

Koutouroussi *Miss Galatia*
Called: Nov 1995, Lincoln's Inn, LLB (Hons)
(Kent)

Kowlessur *Miss Nita*
4 Temple Road, Epsom, Surrey KT19 8HA.
Called: July 1995, Gray's Inn, BA (Keele),
Dip Law

Kramer *Ian Lewis*
and Member California Bar. Called: Nov
1996, Lincoln's Inn, BA, MA (Oxon), JD
(Columbia)

Kratz *Peter Charles*
Called: Feb 1952, Gray's Inn

Kreling *Paul Alexander Julian* •
Senior Legal Officer, Inland Revenue,
Solicitors' Office, Somerset House, Strand,
London WC2R 1LB, 0171 438 6747, Fax:
0171 438 6246. Called: Nov 1989, Inner
Temple, LLB (Exon)

Kremner *Jonathan*
8721 Bay Pointe Drive, Tampa, Florida
33615, USA 813 884 8841, Fax: USA 813
639 9716, and Member New York.
Called: July 1984, Inner Temple, MA (Law),
BA (Hons), Dip Law

Krishna *Miss Maheswari Rani*
and Member Malaysia. Called: July 1995,
Lincoln's Inn, LLB (Hons)

Krishnan *Elengovan*
Block 661, Buffalo Road, 11-29 Singapore
210661. Called: July 1993, Middle Temple,
LLB (Hons, Hull)

Krishnan *Miss Shubhaa*
Called: Nov 1997, Lincoln's Inn, LLB
(Hons)(Lond)

Krishnasamy *Siva Sambo*
S Bala & Associates, Advocates & Solicitors,
135 Cecil Street, [H]08-02, LKN Building,
225 5277, Fax: 225 2498, and Member
Singapore Bar. Called: July 1995, Lincoln's
Inn, LLB (Hons)

Krofah *Miss Rosemary*
44 Clifton Road, Finchley, London N3 2AR.
Called: July 1995, Middle Temple, LLB
(Hons)

Kron *Michael* •
Head of Rules of Court & Regulations
Division. Joint Secretary to Lord Woolfs
Inquiry, Lord Chancellors Department,
Selborne House, 54-60 Victoria Street,
London SW1E 6QT, 0171 210 0729, Fax:
0171 210 0725. Called: July 1975, Lincoln's
Inn

Krrishnan *Ms Seethalkshmi P S*
Called: July 1997, Lincoln's Inn, LLB
(Hons)(Lond)

Ku *Miss Pui Fong*
and Member Hong Kong Bar. Called: Nov
1991, Gray's Inn, LLB (Lond)(Hon), A.C.I.S.

Kua *Miss Lay Theng*
Called: July 1997, Middle Temple, LLB
(Hons)(Leics)

Kuan *Anthony Chee Kee*
Called: Nov 1996, Lincoln's Inn, LLB (Hons)

Kudiabor *Cyril Fui*
0181 858 2776. Called: Nov 1996, Inner
Temple, BA (Kent), LLM (Lond)

Kuen *Paul Yong Wei*
Called: July 1995, Inner Temple, LLB (Lond)

Kulasegaran *Miss Aneeta*
Advocate (Practising), M/S Ranjit Thomas &
Kula, No 24, Jalan 12/13, 46200 Petaling
Jaya, Selangor Darul Ehsan, 00 60 3
7542269, Fax: 00 60 3 7542321, and
Member Malaysia Bar. Called: Nov 1992,
Middle Temple, LLB (Hons, E.Anglia)

Kullar *Mrs Richenda Margaret*
Senior Assistant Lawyer, Alliance &
Leicester plc, Carlton Park, Narborough,
Leicester LE9 5XX, 0116 200 4149.
Called: Feb 1993, Gray's Inn, LLB

Kumar *KV Sudeep*
and Member Singapore Bar. Called: July
1994, Inner Temple, LLB (Lond)

Kumar *Mazumdar Swapan*
Called: Nov 1996, Lincoln's Inn, LLB
(Hons)(Lond)

Kumar *Rajesh*
Called: Nov 1997, Middle Temple, LLB
(Hons)(Newcas)

Kumar *Miss Sharika*
Called: July 1996, Lincoln's Inn, LLB
(Hons)(Lond)

Kumar *Vishnu*
Called: July 1995, Middle Temple, LLB
(Hons)

Kumarasamy *Pathmanathan*
Called: Nov 1996, Gray's Inn, LLB (Wales)

Kunjuraman *Dharmendra*
Called: Nov 1996, Middle Temple, LLB
(Hons)(Nott'm)

Kunjuraman *Miss Previtha*
Called: July 1996, Middle Temple, LLB
(Hons)(Wolves)

Kunzlik *Professor Peter Forster*
The Nottingham Law School, The
Nottingham Trent Universit, Burton Street,
Nottingham, Bradford NG1 4BU, 0115 948
8418, Paradise Square Chambers, 26
Paradise Square, Sheffield, S1 2DE.
Called: July 1983, Inner Temple, MA, LLM
(Cantab)

Kuok *David Han Peh*
Called: July 1997, Lincoln's Inn, LLB
(Hons)(Wales)

Kuok *Miss Pearl Ming Yew*
Legal Advisor, Allen & Gledhill, 36 Robinson
Road [H]18-01, City House, Singaopre 0106,
65 2251611, Fax: 65 2233787, and Member
Singapore Bar. Called: July 1992, Middle
Temple, LLB (Hons) (Lond)

Kuppusamy *Mahendran*
Block 136, Bukit Batok West Avenue 6,
[H]08-509, 5690464. Called: July 1996,
Middle Temple, LLB (Hons)(Lond), LLM
(Lond)

Kwa *Miss Su-Lin*
Called: July 1995, Inner Temple, LLB (Lond)

Kwan *Pang Moon*
Called: Mar 1998, Gray's Inn, LLB (Lond)

Kwan Pang *Mrs Maying*
Called: Nov 1996, Lincoln's Inn, LLB
(Hons)(Wales)

Kwek *Julian Choon Yeow*
Legal Assistant, Haridas Ho & Partners, 24
Raffles Place, Clifford Centre [H]18-00, 65-
5332323, Fax: 65-5337029, and Member
Singapore Bar. Called: July 1995, Middle
Temple, LLB (Hons)

Kwek *Kevin Yiu Wing*
Legal Assistant, M/S Shook Lin & Bok, 1
Robinson Road, [H]18-00 Aia Tower,
Singapore 048542, Singapore, (65) 5351944,
Fax: (65) 5358577, and Member Singapore
Bar. Called: July 1994, Middle Temple, BA
(Hons)(Keele)

Kwok *Lester Chi-Hang JP*
30th Floor, Wing On House, 71 Des Voeux
Road, Central, (852) 2523 4091, Fax: (852)
2868 0118, Associate Member of the Hong
Kong Bar Association. Called: Nov 1975,
Gray's Inn, BA (Stanford)

Ky *Ms Tania Kim*
Called: July 1977, Middle Temple, LLB
(Lond)

Kyle *David William*
Chief Crown Prosecutor, CPS Central
Casework. Called: July 1973, Inner Temple,
BA (Cantab)

Kyle *Miss Samantha Ann Wilcock*
Called: Oct 1995, Inner Temple, BA
(Dunelm)

Kyprianou *Menelaos Michael*
Law Office of Michael, Kyprianou &
Associates, P.O.Box 8765, Stassinos Court,
Stassinos Avenue, Nicosia, 02 360800, Fax:
02 467880, and Member Cyprus Bar.
Called: Nov 1994, Middle Temple, LLB
(Hons)

La Niece *Jeremy Peter Babington* •
Head of Prosecutions, The Securities and
Futures, Authority Limited, Cottons Centre,
Cottons Lane, London SE1 2QB, 0171 378
5689, Fax: 0171 378 0591. Called: Nov
1973, Middle Temple, LLB

Labesse *Advocate Jacques Pierre*
Piermont Hse, 33 Pier Rd, St Helier, Jersey,
0534 888777, Fax: 0534 888778.
Called: July 1957, Inner Temple, MA (Oxon)

Lack *Daniel*
Consultant (of Counsel), Lindenfeld,
Grumbach, 78 Rue du Rhone, 1204 Geneva,
(41-22) 311 38 11, Fax: (41-22) 781 17 38,
Registered as Foreign Lawyer Geneva Bar.
Called: Nov 1955, Middle Temple, MA
(Oxon)

Lack *Jeremy*
Attorney, Becton Dickinson Europe, 5
Chemin Des Sources, B.P.37, 38241 Meylan
Cedex, (+33) 7641 6801, Fax: (+33) 7641
6800, Admitted to various US Federal Courts
& the US CAFC Registered U.S. Patent
Attorney, Reg No 35, 813 Patent &
Trademark Office. and Member New York
State Bar (1990). Called: Nov 1989, Middle
Temple, BA (Oxon), Law &, Physiological,
Sciences

Lack *Paul Vernon*
Called: Oct 1993, Lincoln's Inn, LLB (Hons)

Ladimeji *Waliu Dele*
Called: Nov 1995, Middle Temple, BA
(Hons)(Anglia), MA (Cantab)

Ladlow *Mrs Loraine Lesley*
Senior Court Clerk, North & East
Hertfordshire, Magistrates' Court, Bayley
House, Sish Lane, Stevenage SG1 3SS, 01438
730438, Fax: 01438 730413. Called: Nov
1993, Gray's Inn, BA

Lai *Miss Amy Hur-Ling*
Called: July 1995, Lincoln's Inn, LLB (Hons)

Lai *Miss Fui Sim*
16 Lorong Kemaris 4, Bukit Bandaraya,
Bangsar, 59100 Kuala Lumpur, 03 2561243.
Called: July 1995, Lincoln's Inn, LLB (Hons)

Lai *Miss Iy Lee*
Court Clerk, Cambridgeshire Magistrates',
Courts Committee, Bridge Street,
Peterborough, Cambs PE1 1ED, 01733
63971, Fax: 01733 313749. Called: July
1989, Middle Temple, BSoc Sci [Keele]

Lai *Kwok Seng*
Called: Nov 1995, Lincoln's Inn, LLB (Hons)

Lai *Philippe*
Called: July 1997, Lincoln's Inn, MSc, CPE

Lai *Miss Sheau Wei*
Called: July 1997, Middle Temple, LLB
(Hons)(Hull)

Lai *Stanley Tze Chang*
Flat 10, Redwood Lodge, Pinehurst, Grange
Road, Cambridge CB3 9AR, 01223-364034,
Fax: 01223-572054, and Member Singapore
Bar. Called: Nov 1993, Lincoln's Inn, LLB
(Hons, Leic), LLM (Hons)(Cantab)

Lai *Ms Tsang Ka*
Called: Nov 1997, Inner Temple, BA (Hong
Kong), LLB (Lond)

Lai Pat Fong *Miss Josee*
Tax Adviser, and Member Mauritian Bar.
Called: Nov 1987, Gray's Inn, LLB (Lond),
AKC, ACA, ATII

Laidlaw *Stuart Robert* •
Crown Prosecutor, Crown Prosecution
Service, Croydon Branch, Trafalgar House, 2
Bedford Prk, Croydon. Called: Feb 1989,
Inner Temple, LLB (B'ham)

Laing *Adrian Charles* •
Director of Legal Affairs, Harper-Collins
Publishers, 77/85 Fulham Palace Road,
Hammersmith, London W6 8JB, 0181 307
4665, Fax: 0181 307 4668. Called: Nov
1979, Inner Temple, LLB (Exon)

Laing *Hugh Charles Desmond*
The Rectory, Toppesfield, Essex CO9 4DQ, 01787 237 924. Called: Nov 1976, Inner Temple

Laing *Miss Paula Ulander*
Called: Oct 1991, Inner Temple, MA (Hons)(Lond)

Lake *Andrew Peter*
Called: Nov 1995, Inner Temple, BA (York), CPE (City)

Lakeman *Advocate Christopher Gerard Pellow*
Associate, Olsen Backhurst & Dorey, Eaton House, 9 Seaton Place, St Helier, Jersey JE2 3QL, +44 (0) 01534 888900, Fax: +44 (0) 01534 887744/55, Formerly Ecrivain (Jersey 1994) Advocate of the Royal Court of Jersey (1995) Jersey Law Society and Member Jersey Bar. Called: Nov 1991, Middle Temple, BA Hons (Kent), Diplome de Droit, Francais (Paris XI)

Laken *Mrs Elaine Anne*
Clerk to the North Avon Justices, Bristol Magistrates Court, Nelson Street, Bristol, 01454 310505. Called: July 1978, Inner Temple

Lakin *Mrs Deborah Rachel*
Court Clerk, Kingston Magistrates Court, 19-23 High Street, Kingston, Surrey KT1 1JW, 0181 546 5603, Fax: 0181 547 3551. Called: Nov 1992, Inner Temple, LLB (Hons)

Lakin *Mark Anthony●*
Crown Prosecutor, Crown Prosecution Service, Gemini Centre, 88 New London Road, Chelmsford, Essex CM2 0BR, 01245 252939, Fax: 01245 490476. Called: July 1986, Gray's Inn, LLB

Lall *Tersaim*
Chartered Management Accountan, Shariz Sdn BHD, No 39B Jalan SS 3/29, Taman University, 47300 Petaling Jaya, Selangor Darul, Ehsan, 00 603 7761641, Fax: 00 603 7766818, and Member Malaysia. Called: July 1996, Gray's Inn, Dip Law

Lam *Chee On*
Called: July 1997, Lincoln's Inn, LLB (Hons)(Lond)

Lam *Edward Chung Weng*
Legal Assistant, Alban Tay Mahtani & de Silva, 105 Cecil Street, [H]13-00 The Octagon, 65-534 5266, Fax: 65-223 8762, and Member Singapore Bar. Called: July 1992, Middle Temple, LLB (Hons) (E.Ang)

Lam *Jen Yii*
Called: July 1996, Middle Temple, LLB (Hons)(Warw)

Lam *Ken Chung Simon*
1103 Prince's Building, Central, 25220066, Fax: 28450851, and Member Australian Capital Territory Hong Kong Bar. Called: July 1989, Middle Temple, BSc, LLB (Buck)

Lam *Osmond Kwok Fai*
and Member Hong Kong Bar. Called: Feb 1988, Inner Temple, LLB (Manch), LLM (Lond)

Lam *Stephen Sui Lung OBE, JP*
Director of Administration & Development, Department of Justice, Hong Kong, 4th Floor, High Block, Queensway Government Offices, 66 Queensway, 2867 2160, Fax: 2869 0720. Called: Feb 1986, Gray's Inn, BSocSc, LLB

Lam *Steven Kuet Keng*
Lecturer at Law/Tutor Singapore Institute of Commerc, Apt Blk 121, [H] 01-81, Bishan St 12, S 570121, Singapore, and Member Singapore. Called: July 1995, Middle Temple, LLB (Hons)

Lam *Tin Sing*
Called: Nov 1994, Middle Temple, LLB (Hons)

Lamba *Sanjay*
Called: Nov 1994, Gray's Inn, LLB (Bris)

Lambert *Nigel Acheson Drummond●*
Assistant Treasury Solicitor, Legal Adviser's Office, Dept for Education and, Employment, Caxton House, Tothill Street, London SW1H 9NF, 0171 273 5909, Fax: 0171 273 5605. Called: July 1975, Middle Temple, LLB (Belfast), LLM (Lond)

Lamblin *Miss Claire Therese Helene*
European Bank for, Reconstruction Development, 1 Exchange Square, London EC2A 2EH, and Member New York (1995). Called: July 1992, Inner Temple, LLB (Lond), MA (Sorbonne,Paris), LLM (Cambs), MPA (Harvard)

Lammy *David Lindon*
Howard Rice, Nemerovski, Canady, Falk & Rabkin, Three Embarcadero Center, 7th Floor, San Francisco 941114065, 001 415 434 1600, and Member California Bar. Called: Feb 1995, Lincoln's Inn, LLB (Hons)(Lond)

Lampard *Miss Kathryn Felice*
1 New Square, Ground Floor, Lincoln's Inn, London, WC2A 3SA. Called: Nov 1984, Middle Temple, BA (Exon), Dip Law (City)

Lan *Ms Sin Cynthia Mei*
Called: Nov 1997, Inner Temple, BA (LSE)

Lancaster *Kenneth Alan*
Called: July 1995, Lincoln's Inn, LLM (Lond), FCA, ACIArb

Lancaster *Miss Rosemary Ann*
Called: Nov 1984, Inner Temple, LLB (PCL), LLM (Lond)

Lanch *David*
Langdale, Regal Way, Kenton, Harrow, Middlesex HA3 0RX, 0181 907 9388. Called: July 1987, Lincoln's Inn, BA, MA M.LITT (Oxon), FCA, Dip Law

Landau *Frederic Moses*
Ex-Chairman, Sunday Trading Trib, 5 Langford Close, London NW8 0LN, 0171 328 1145, Rights and Duties, Transport Undertakings (Pitmans). Called: May 1928, Gray's Inn, LLB (Lond)

Landau *Lady Pamela Ann*
Called: Nov 1985, Gray's Inn, LLB (Lond)

Landick *Pierre Stanley*
Ogier & Le Masurier, Pirouet House, Union Street, St Helier, Jersey, Channel Islands JE4 9WG, 01534 504000, Fax: 01534 35328, and Member Advocate of the Royal Court of Jersey. Called: Feb 1989, Lincoln's Inn, LLB

Landman *Rowland Harold*
Director of Companies, 17 Harley Street, London WIN IDA, 0171 935 0106, Fax: 0171 255 1039. Called: May 1936, Middle Temple, MA (Cantab)

Lane *John Robert Benjamin*
Frommer Lawrence & Haug LLP, 745 Fifth Avenue, New York, NY 10151, 212 588 0800, Fax: 212 588 0500, and Member New York Bar Washington DC Bar. Called: Nov 1989, Middle Temple, BA

Lane *Nicholas John Graham*
Called: Mar 1997, Gray's Inn, BA (Cantab)

Lane *Miss Nyree Victoria●*
First American Title Insurance, Company (UK) Ltd, Broxbournebury Mansion, White Stubbs Lane, Broxbourne, Herfordshire EN10 7AF. Called: Oct 1994, Middle Temple, LLB (Hons)(Bucks)

Lane *Paul Timothy*
Legal Adviser, Eastbourne & Hailsham Mags Crt, Old Orchard Road, Eastbourne BN21 4UN, 01323 727518. Called: Oct 1993, Inner Temple, LLB

Lane *William*
87 New Henry House, 10 Ice House Street, Hong Kong, 522 5494, 22 Old Bldgs, Lincoln's Inn, London, WC2A 3UJ. Called: July 1971, Gray's Inn, FRICS, FCIArb., QC Hong Kong

Lang *Lawrence Fatt Khim*
Called: July 1996, Middle Temple, LLB (Hons)(Wolves)

Langdon *Miss Penelope Jane*
Acting Senior Deputy Chief Clerk, Inner London Magistrates', Courts Service, 65 Romney Street, London W1. Called: May 1981, Inner Temple, LLB (Cardiff)

Langley *Mrs Patricia Virginia●*
Departmental Lawyer, New Court, Carey St, London WC2A 2L, 0171 972 1300, Fax: 0171 412 1523. Called: July 1978, Gray's Inn, LLB (Wales), LLM (Lond)

Langridge *Ms Natalie Katherine*
Estidio Interjuridico S.L., Estudio legaly Tributario, Edificio IVC, Arturo Soria, 245, 28033 Madrid, (341) 359 7679, Fax: (341) 345 5373, and Member Madrid. Called: Nov 1992, Middle Temple, BA (Hons, Kent)

Langrish *Mrs Sally●*
Assistant Legal Adviser, Foreign & Commonwealth Office, King Charles Street, London SW1, 0171 270 1478, Fax: 0171 270 2280. Called: Apr 1991, Middle Temple, LLB (Hons)

Langsdale *Miss Jane*
Called: Nov 1989, Inner Temple, BA, Dip Law (City)

E

Langton *Miss Sara Louise* ●
Head of Legal & Business Affairs,
Concorgence Productions Ltd, 10-12 Crown
Street, London W3 8SB, 0181 993 3666.
Called: Nov 1997, Middle Temple, BA
(Hons)

Langwallner *David Johann Herbert*
and Member Irish Bar. Called: Feb 1993,
Gray's Inn, BA (Dublin), LLM

Larder *Graham Charles*
Loss Adjuster, Thomas Howell
Group(S.A.)(PTY), GF Office Park,
Grosvenor Road, Bryanston, 2021, (011) 463
5900, Fax: (011) 463 5920. Called: Nov
1974, Middle Temple, LLB

Larkin *James Alan* QC (1992) ●
Director, Aon CIA Trade Finance, 13
Grosvenor Place, London SW1X 7HH, 0171
253 3550, Fax: 0171 235 4397. Called: Nov
1974, Middle Temple, BA

Lass *Jonathan Marc*
Called: Mar 1998, Gray's Inn, LLB (Lond)

Latham *Matthew John Richard*
Called: Nov 1997, Lincoln's Inn, LLB
(Hons)(Leics)

Latimer *Mrs Ai-Yuen*
5/61 Wyralla Avenue, Epping 2121, Sydney
NSW, 02 9868 5773, and Member Malaysia.
Called: July 1994, Middle Temple, LLB
(Hons)(Reading)

Latimer *Miss Karen Elaine* ●
Crown Prosecutor, Solar House, 1-9
Romford Road, Stratford, London E15.
Called: Nov 1990, Inner Temple, LLB

Latimer *Raymond Raj*
5/61 Wyralla Avenue, Epping 2121, Sydney
NSW, 02 9868 5773. Called: July 1994,
Middle Temple, LLB (Hons)(Reading)

Latto *Paul Stuart*
Called: Oct 1996, Inner Temple, BA (Oxon),
CPE

Lau *Cecil Ning Kiang*
Called: July 1995, Lincoln's Inn, LLB (Hons)

Lau *Miss Cheh Meng Patricia*
Called: July 1995, Middle Temple, LLB
(Hons)

Lau *Miss Chew Mee*
Called: Nov 1996, Lincoln's Inn, LLB
(Hons)(L'pool)

Lau *Dennis Yee Meng*
Iza Ng Yeoh & Kit, Advocates & Solicitors,
19th Floor, Bangunan Dato, Zainal, 23 Jalan
Melaka, 50100 Kuala Lumpur Malaysia, 03
2986066, Fax: 03 2982593. Called: July
1995, Lincoln's Inn, LLB (Hons)

Lau *Dr James Chi Wang*
Flat 3A, Block 8 29, Braemar Hill Road,
Hong Kong, 852-8930332, Fax: 852-
8380011. Called: July 1992, Gray's Inn, LLB
(Lond), PhD (Lond), MSc (Manch), LLM
(Hong Kong), MBA, MICE, MIStructE, Ceng

Lau *Miss Jean Aye Lin*
Called: July 1996, Lincoln's Inn, LLB (Hons)

Lau *Miss Julia Pui G*
Room 1432, Prince's Building, 10 Chater
Road, Central, 252 40151, Fax: 281 01731,
and Member Hong Kong. Called: Nov 1994,
Gray's Inn, BSc (Hong Kong), LLB

Lau *Lee Sing Edward*
Legal Adviser/Assistant General Manager,
See Hua Daily News/The Borneo, Post/
Sinhua Evening News, PO Box 20, 96007
Sibu,Sarawak, E Malaysia, 084 332055, Fax:
084 321255, and Member Sarawak Bar
Malaysia Bar. Called: July 1988, Lincoln's
Inn, LLB (Hons) (Manch), LLM (Hons)
(Lond)

Lau *Miss Man Sai*
[H]07-07 Derby Court, 5 Derbyshire Road,
(65) 355 1507, Fax: (65) 222 2521, and
Member Singapore Bar. Called: Oct 1995,
Middle Temple, LLB (Hons)

Lau *Miss Mei Lyn*
No 6, SS1/13A, Kampung Tunku, Petaling
Jaya, 47300 Selangor Malaysia, 03 7760610.
Called: July 1994, Middle Temple, LLB
(Hons)(Kent)

Lau *Robert Chun Keong*
M/S Rashid & Lee, 6th Floor, 56 Jalan
Tuanku, Abdul Rahman, 50100 Kuala
Lumpur, 60 3 2938155 Ext 333, Fax: 60-3-
2939566, and Member Malaysia Bar.
Called: Oct 1991, Gray's Inn, LLB (Warwick)

Lau *Teik Soon*
Called: July 1996, Lincoln's Inn, LLB
(Hons)(Lond)

Lau *Tiew Kung*
Called: July 1996, Lincoln's Inn, LLB
(Hons)(Lond)

Lau *Wai Hin*
Called: Nov 1997, Lincoln's Inn, BSc
(eng)(Hons)(Hong, Kong), CPE (Manch)

Lau *William John*
Merchant Banker, C/O HSBC Investment
Bank, Asia Ltd, Level 15, 1 Queen's Road,
Central, (852) 28418888, Fax: (852)
28455654, and Member Hong Kong Bar.
Called: July 1990, Lincoln's Inn, LLB
(B'ham), ACCA, AHKSA

Lau *Miss Winnie Yee Wan*
Called: Nov 1997, Middle Temple, BSc
(Hons)(Lond)

Lau *Miss Yin Fong*
Called: Nov 1997, Middle Temple, LLB
(Hons)(Lond)

Lau *Yun Tseng*
Lau Yun Tseng & Co Advocates, No 17c,
Jalan Kai Peng, Off Jalan Tuanku Osman,
96000 Sibu, Sarawak, 084 319886, Fax: 084
349886, and Member Malaysian Bar.
Called: July 1994, Lincoln's Inn, LLB (Hons)

Laubi *Anthony Henry Alfred*
Flat 4, 52 Onslow Gardens, London
SW7 3QA, 0171 373 0533, Fax: 0171 982
2256. Called: July 1988, Gray's Inn, LLB

Laughton *Denis Sidney*
The Red Hse, Sandpits Lane, Penn, High
Wycombe, Bucks HP10 8HD, 01494
813182. Called: June 1949, Gray's Inn, MA,
LLB (Cantab)

Laurance *Miss Julie Astrid Marina
Salicath*
Gammel and Kershaw, 38 St Mary Avenue,
London, 0171 621 0777. Called: Nov 1995,
Gray's Inn, LLB (Bucks)

Lavender *Michael David* ●
Legal Adviser, United Dominions Trust Ltd,
Holbrook House, 116 Cockfosters Road,
Cockfosters, Barnet, Herts EN4 0DY, 0181
447 2299, Fax: 0181 447 2604. Called: Nov
1986, Lincoln's Inn, LLB (Birmingham)

Lavin *Miss Mary Mandie Jane* ●
Director of Professional Conduct at UKCC,
UKCC, 23 Portland Place, London W1N 4JT,
0171 333 6548, Fax: 0171 333 6536.
Called: Oct 1993, Middle Temple, LLB
(Hons)(Lond)

Lavin *Miss Sarah Joy*
Called: Nov 1996, Gray's Inn, BA (Keele)

Law *Cheok Maan*
Legal Advisor, Rm 301, 3rd Floor, No 44
Jalan Pudu, 55100 Kuala Lumpur, 03
2381231, Fax: 03 2329430. Called: July
1994, Middle Temple, BA (Hons)(Cantab)

Law *Ms Cheok Yin*
Top Floor, See Woh Building, 90 Jalan
Pudu, 55100 Kuala Lumpur, Malaysia, (603)
2381231, Fax: (603) 2329430, and Member
Malaysian Bar. Called: July 1993, Middle
Temple, BA (Hons)(Cantab)

Law *Chun Keat*
Called: July 1997, Middle Temple, LLB
(Hons)

Law *Miss Jee Wei*
Called: July 1996, Middle Temple, LLB
(Hons)(Lond)

Law *Robert*
Office of the Minister of, State for Justice &,
Constitutional Affairs, P O Box 7272,
Kampala, 430431, 3 Temple Gardens, 2nd
Floor, Temple, London, EC4Y 9AU.
Called: July 1987, Middle Temple, BA, Dip
Law, FRGS

Law *Miss Yuk-Ching*
Called: Nov 1997, Middle Temple, BA
(Hons)

Lawless *Ms Jacqueline*
Called: Mar 1997, Inner Temple, BA
(Westminster), Dip In Law (City)

Lawrence *Bernard Hilary*
Called: Nov 1996, Gray's Inn, LLB (Warw)

Lawrence *Eloghosa Stephen*
Called: Feb 1994, Middle Temple, LLB
(Hons)(Lond)

Lawrence *Miss Kerry Joy*
Ogier & Le Masurier, P O Box 404, Pirouet
House, Union Street, St Helier, Jersey
JE4 9WG, 01534 504000, Fax: 01534 35328.
Called: Nov 1995, Inner Temple, MA
(Oxon), CPE (Lond), BA (Hons)

E

Lawrence *Stuart John* •
Legal Officer in Prosecutions Division, H M
Customs & Excise, New King's Beam
House, 22 Upper Ground, London SE1 9PJ,
0171 865 5170, Fax: 0171 865 5248.
Called: Nov 1994, Inner Temple, BA
(Swansea), CPE (Bournemouth)

Lawrey *Keith*
Justice of Peace Member Social Security
Appeals Tribunal Panel. Called: July 1972,
Gray's Inn, JP, LLB, MSc Econ, FCIS,
FCOLLP, MA

Laws *Stephen Charles CB* •
Parliamentary Counsel, Office of the
Parliamentary, Counsel, 36 Whitehall,
London SW1, 0171 210 6648, Fax: 0171 210
6632. Called: Feb 1973, Middle Temple, LLB

Lawson *Martin Jeffery*
Legal Advisor, Hambro Legal Protection Ltd,
Hambro House, Stephenson Road,
Colchester, Essex CO4 4QR, 0990 234500,
Fax: 0990 234508. Called: Feb 1994,
Lincoln's Inn, LLB (Hons, Essex), DMS

Lawson *Miss Nicola Jane* •
Assistant Group Chief Legal Adviser, Lloyds
TSB Group plc, Legal Dept, 71 Lombard St,
London EC3P 3BS, 0171 356 1200, Fax:
0171 929 1654. Called: July 1978, Middle
Temple, BA (Oxon)

Lawton *(John) Philip QC (1981)*
Formerly a Solicitor, 12 Abbotts, 129 Kings
Road, Brighton, Sussex BN1 2FA.
Called: May 1971, Lincoln's Inn, MA, LLM
(Cantab)

Lawunmi *Miss Doyin Margaret* •
Principal Legal Officer, Inland Revenue,
Solicitor's Office (East Wing), Somerset
House, Strand, London WC2A 1LB.
Called: Nov 1984, Inner Temple, BA, LLM

Lay *Mrs Teresa Christine*
Called: Nov 1993, Inner Temple, LLB
(So'ton)

Laycock *Miss Ann*
The Corn Exchange, 5th Floor, Fenwick
Street, Liverpool, L2 7QS. Called: July 1980,
Gray's Inn, LLB (L'pool)

Layman *Mrs Anne Valaire* •
Acting Senior Solicitor, London Borough of
Camden, Legal Services, Town Hall, Euston
Road, London NW1 2RU, 0171 860 5588,
Fax: 0171 860 5649, and Member Trinidad
& Tobago Bar. Called: Nov 1987, Middle
Temple, LLB (LSE)

Layton *Mr John Michael George*
94 The Broadway, Thorpe Bay, Southend
On Sea, Essex SS1 3HH, 01702 587834, Fax:
01702 587834. Called: Nov 1978, Middle
Temple, BSC (Dunelm), BA (Lond)

Le Cocq *Timothy John*
Partner - Litigation Group, Ogier & Le
Masurier, P O Box 404, Pirouet House,
Union Street, St Helier, Jersey JE4 8WZ,
01534 504370, Fax: 01534 35328, Advocate
of the Royal Court of Jersey and Member
Jersey Bar. Called: July 1981, Inner Temple,
BA (Hons)(Keele)

Le Feuvre *Miss Dorothy Mary*
Deputy Clerk to the Justices,
Cambridgeshire Magistrates Crt, Windsor
House, Anderson Centre, Spitfire Close,
Huntingdon PE18 6XY, 01480 414455, Fax:
01480 123220. Called: Feb 1987, Gray's Inn,
LLB

Le Marchant *Piers Alfred* •
Legal Counsel, Lehman Brothers Int
(Europe), 1 Broadgate, London EC3, 0171
260 2944. Called: Nov 1987, Inner Temple,
LLB (Lond)

Le Pichon *Mrs Doreen*
Judge of the High Cout, High Court, (852)
2825 4430, Fax: (852) 2869 0640, and
Member Hong Kong Bar New York Bar.
Called: Nov 1969, Lincoln's Inn, BA, BCL
(Oxon)

Le Poidevin *Nicholas*
Advocates Babbe Le Poidevin, Allez P O Box
612, Hirzel Court, St Peter Port, Guernsey,
Channel Islands, 01481 710585, Fax: 01481
712245, and Member Royal Court of
Guernsey. Called: Nov 1986, Gray's Inn, MA
(Oxon), PhD (RVC Lond), C.Biol

Le Quesne *David Fisher*
Vibert & Valpy, 8 Duhamel Place, St Helier,
Jersey JE2 4XA, 0534 888666, Fax: 0534
888555, Advocate of the Royal Ct of Jersey.
Secretary of the Jersey Law Society.
Called: Nov 1976, Inner Temple, LLB

Le Sueur *Andrew Philip*
Lecturer in Laws, University College,
London, Faculty of Laws, University College
London, Bentham House, Endsleigh
Gardens, London WC1H OEG, 0171 391
1417, Fax: 0171 387 9597. Called: July
1987, Middle Temple, LLB (Lond)

Lea *Lady Gerry Valerie* •
Senior Court Clerk, West Suffolk
Magistrates' Crt, Shire Hall, Honey Hill, Bury
St Edmunds, Suffolk IP33 1HF, 01284
352300, Fax: 01284 352345. Called: Nov
1969, Gray's Inn

Leach *Ernest Terrance*
Trem-Y-Garn, Park Road, Barmouth,
Gwynedd LL42 1PH, 01341 281364.
Called: Feb 1960, Gray's Inn, LLB, F.C.I Arb,
FRICS

Leach *Miss Judith Vanessa*
Called: Nov 1994, Inner Temple, LLB

Leach *Miss Sandra Elizabeth*
Assistant Deputy Justice's Clerk, West Kent
Magistrates Court, Secretariat Offices, The
Courthouse, Tufton Street, Ashford, Kent,
01233 663203. Called: Apr 1986, Middle
Temple, LLB (Hons)

Leach-Smith *Mrs Caryn Gail* •
Senior Crown Prosecutor, Crown
Prosecution Service, St Georges House,
Lever Street, Wolverhampton WV2 1EZ,
01902 870900. Called: July 1988, Lincoln's
Inn, LLB (Hons)

Leader *Peter George Frederick*
Tankards, Ockham, Woking, Surrey
GU23 6NQ, 01483 225178, Fax: 01483
211505, Barrister and Solicitor of the
Supreme Court of New Zealand. Called: July
1954, Lincoln's Inn

Lean *Vincent Edward*
Case Review Manager, CCRC, Alpha Tower,
Suffolk Street, Queensway, Birmingham
B1 1TT, 0121 6331853. Called: Oct 1992,
Lincoln's Inn, LLB(Hons)(Leeds)

Leasor *Miss Julia*
Called: Mar 1997, Lincoln's Inn, LLB (Hons)

Leat *Ian Ralph*
Called: Oct 1993, Middle Temple, BSc
(Hons)

Leathem *Ms Patricia Elton*
Called: Nov 1979, Inner Temple, AB Magna
Cum Laude, MSc, LLM

Leathley *David Jonathan* •
Senior Crown Prosecutor, Crown
Prosecution Service, Pearl Assurance House,
20th Floor, Greyfriars Road, Cardiff
CF1 3PL, 378 201 Ext 126. Called: July
1980, Lincoln's Inn, LLB (Hons)(B'ham)

Lebus *Timothy Andrew*
Bankers Trust Company, 1 Appold Street,
Broadgate, London EC2A 2HE, 0171 982
2500, Fax: 0171 982 2281, and Member
New York State Bar. Called: Nov 1973,
Gray's Inn, MA (Cantab)

Leck *Andy Kwang Hwee*
c/o Messrs Wong & Leow, 1 Temasek
Avenue 27-01, Millenia Tower, 65 338 1888,
Fax: 65 337 5100, and Member Singapore
Bar. Called: July 1992, Gray's Inn, LLB
(Bristol)

Ledwidge *Francis Andrew*
Called: Oct 1990, Gray's Inn, MA (Oxon)

Lee *Ms Alison Jayne* •
Lawyer (Grade 7), Mental Health Act
Commissioner, Charity Commission,
Woodfield House, Tanger, Taunton,
Somerset TA4 1BL, 01823 345000.
Called: July 1988, Middle Temple, LLB

Lee *Audley Martin Dowell*
Director, Ocean P & I Services Ltd, Ocean
House, Waterloo Lane, Chelmsford, Essex
CM1 1BD, 01245 703600, Fax: 01245
703879. Called: July 1968, Gray's Inn, MA,
ACII

Lee *Brian Ying Wah*
Company Secretary, 51 Sixth Crescent, 65
4690892, Fax: 65 4697554, and Member
Advocate & Solicitor Singapore. Called: July
1995, Middle Temple, LLB (Hons)

Lee *Chai Seng*
Called: Nov 1994, Lincoln's Inn, LLB
(Hons)(Leeds)_

Lee *Chau Ee*
Called: July 1995, Middle Temple, LLB
(Hons)

Lee *Chau Yee*
M/S Chor Pee Anwarul & Co, Unit 10.01, Level 10, Wisma LKN, 49 Jalan Wong Ah Fook, 80000 Johor Bahru, 607 2234733, Fax: 607 2234734, and Member Malaysia Bar. Called: July 1995, Lincoln's Inn, LLB (Hons)

Lee *Chee Hong*
Called: Nov 1996, Middle Temple, LLB (Hons)(Lond)

Lee *Miss Cheryl Siew Fung*
Called: July 1995, Middle Temple, LLB (Hons) (Hull)

Lee *Miss Chiek Chuin*
Called: July 1996, Middle Temple, LLB (Hons)(Notts)

Lee *Miss Chin Theng*
Legal Officer, No 74, Jalan 11/3N, Subang Jaya, 47620 Petaling Jaya, Selangor, 03-737 6846, and Member Malaysian Bar. Called: July 1996, Lincoln's Inn, LLB (Hons)(Lond)

Lee *David Ken Hwa*
Called: July 1997, Middle Temple, LLB (Hons)

Lee *Miss Deanna Maria*
Called: Mar 1997, Middle Temple, BSc (Florida), LLB (Hons) (L'pool)

Lee *Dennis Preston*
S.V.P. & C.F.O. Mechala Group Jamaica Limited, Mechala Group Jamiaca Limited, 7/9 Harbour Street, Kingston, Jamaica, 92-26670, Fax: 92-20256, and Member Jamaica. Called: July 1988, Lincoln's Inn, BSc (Hons) (Lond), MBA (California)

Lee *Desmond Boon Teck*
Called: July 1996, Lincoln's Inn, LLB (Hons)(Leeds)

Lee *Edward Adam Michael*
Consultant and Trust Coordinator Non Executive Director, Crediton Minerals Plc Secretary, Inverforth Charitable Trust, Matthews Wrightson, Charitable Trust, The Farm, Northington, Alresford, Hampshire SO24 9TH, 01962 73 2205, Fax: 01962 73 2205. Called: June 1964, Middle Temple, MA (Oxon), FCIB

Lee *Miss Elaine Yu Lian*
Called: July 1997, Lincoln's Inn, LLB (Hons)(Lond), LLM (Lond)

Lee *Eng Seng*
Chew, Tan & Lim, Advocates & Solicitors, 51-20 A Menara BHL Bank, 10050 Penang, 04-2281998, Fax: 04-2281367 & 04-2285521, and Member Malaysia Bar. Called: July 1995, Lincoln's Inn, LLB (Hons)

Lee *Eugene*
Called: July 1997, Lincoln's Inn, LLB (Hons)

Lee *Han Meng*
Called: July 1996, Lincoln's Inn, LLB (Hons)(Lond)

Lee *Mrs Helen*
Called: Nov 1992, Lincoln's Inn, LLB (Hons)

Lee *Dr Helen Ho-Yan*
Securities and Futures Comm, 12/F Edinburgh Tower, The Landmark, Central Hong Kong, 28409246, Fax: 25217929, Hong Kong Barrister. Called: Nov 1989, Middle Temple, LLB, LLM M Soc Sc, PhD

Lee *Miss Hong*
84 Jalan Daud, [H]12-03 Windy Heights, Singapore 1441, 7465086, Fax: 7465973. Called: July 1995, Lincoln's Inn, LLB (Hons) (Wales)

Lee *James Kim-Keung BH (St John)*
Reg Architect (Hong Kong) Chief Inspector Ryl Hong Kong Aux Police Force.Personal Asst to Commandant of Ryl Hong Kong Aux Police. Div Vice-President St John's Ambulance Brigade. Vice-President Director & Hon Sec of Lions Club. Dist Gov of Interact Cl, 1323A Prince's Building, 10 Chater Road, Central, Hong Kong, (852) 252-66182, Fax: (852) 252-66011, and Member Hong Kong Bar. Called: Feb 1992, Gray's Inn, B.Arch (Hong Kong), BA (Arch Studies), (Hong Kong), LLB, (Hons)(Lond), RIBA, ARAIA, HKIA, ACIArb, AHKCIArb, Dip in, Chinese Law

Lee *Jason Chong*
Called: July 1994, Middle Temple, LLB (Hons)(Brunel)

Lee *Miss Jeanette Tsui Ling*
and Member Singapore Bar. Called: Nov 1993, Middle Temple, LLB (Hons)(Lond)

Lee *Jonathan Joshua* •
Manager, Legal Affairs, Enterprise Oil plc, Grand Buildings, Trafalgar Square, London WC2N 5EJ, 0171 925 4000, Fax: 0171 925 4321. Called: July 1974, Middle Temple, LLB

Lee *Jonathan Kuan Yee*
60-3-2823916, Fax: 60-3-2825687. Called: July 1996, Middle Temple, LLB (Hons)(Bris)

Lee *Miss June Hsiao Tsun*
Called: Nov 1992, Middle Temple, LLB (Hons, Hull)

Lee *Keat Chee*
Called: Oct 1996, Lincoln's Inn, LLB (Hons)(L'pool)

Lee *Khai*
256 Jalan Utara, 11700 Gelugor, Penang, Malaysia, 04 6579757, and Member Malaysia Bar. Called: July 1993, Lincoln's Inn, LLB (Hons, N'ham)

Lee *Kim Meng David*
Called: July 1997, Gray's Inn, LLB (Notts)

Lee *Kok Chew*
Called: July 1997, Lincoln's Inn, LLB (Hons)(LSE)

Lee *Miss Krista Chui Lan*
Called: Nov 1996, Lincoln's Inn, BA (Hons)(Oxon)

Lee *Ms Kuan Wei*
Called: July 1997, Gray's Inn, LLB (Sheff)

Lee *Miss Lai Lee Lily*
Called: Nov 1996, Gray's Inn, LLB

Lee *Miss Lynette Kwok Foeng*
P K Wong & Advani, 20 Raffles Place, [H] 12-03 Ocean Towers, Singapore 048620, 538 1822, Fax: 538 1838, and Member Singapore Bar. Called: July 1994, Middle Temple, LLB (Hons)(Newc)

Lee *Martin John* •
Principal Assistant - Family, Leeds Magistrates' Court, P O Box, Westgate, Leeds LS1 3JP, 0113 245 9653, Fax: 0113 244 7400. Called: Nov 1987, Lincoln's Inn, LLB (Hons)(Manc), DMS, Assoc I.P.D.

Lee *Miss Mary Chung Ching*
Szetu & Associates, 95 Lorong Ikan Lais, off Jalan Mat Salleh, 88100 Tanjung Aru, P.O.Box 319, 88858 Tanjung Aru, Kota Kinaba, 088 221125/233558, Fax: 088 237543, Advocate of the High Court in Sabah & Sarawak in the State of Sabah (Malaysia). Called: July 1996, Lincoln's Inn, BSc (Hons), MSc (Hons) (Leeds), Dip in Law

Lee *Miss Melanie Anne*
Called: July 1997, Middle Temple, LLB (Hons)

Lee *Min Kin*
8 Nim Drive, Seletar Hills, Singapore 2880, 00 65 4812024. Called: July 1993, Inner Temple, LLB (Warw)

Lee *Miss Noushi*
Called: July 1997, Lincoln's Inn, LLB (Hons)(Leeds)

Lee *Miss Nyet Fah*
Called: July 1996, Middle Temple, LLB (Hons)(Lond)

Lee *Pak Chau*
Called: Mar 1997, Middle Temple, BSc (Hons)(L'pool), MSc (B'ham)

Lee *Miss Pamela Wing Haan*
1E Villa Monte Rosa, 12/F, 41A Stubbs Road, and Member Hong Kong Bar Melbourne. Called: July 1966, Inner Temple

Lee *Paul Richard* •
Senior Attorney - AT&T Uk, Basking Ridge, Kettlewell Close, Horsell, Woking, Surrey GU21 4HY, 01483 715359, Fax: 01483 727412. Called: Feb 1990, Gray's Inn, LLB [Lanc]

Lee *Miss Pauline Aileen*
and Member Malaysia Bar. Called: July 1995, Middle Temple, LLB (Hons) (Wales)

Lee *Peter Kong Chung*
c/o Messrs Lee & Associates, Advocates & Solicitors, P.O. Box 12604, 88829 Kota Kinabalu, Sabah, 088 215262, Fax: 088 217892, Sabah Bar, The Sabah Law Association. Called: July 1988, Lincoln's Inn, LLB (Hons) (Bucks)

Lee *Miss Pin Pin*
Called: Nov 1995, Middle Temple, LLB (Hons)

Lee *Miss Rachel Yim Kuan*
Called: July 1994, Middle Temple, LLB (Hons)(Lond)

Lee *Raphael Khong Wen*
IVI 19 UK Building, 5 Shenton Way,
2200666 (065), and Member Singapore Bar.
Called: Nov 1994, Middle Temple, LLB
(Hons)

Lee *Richard Ian Jeremy*
Called: Nov 1995, Inner Temple, LLB
(L'pool), LLM (Dunelm)

Lee *Miss Seow Ser*
Called: July 1996, Middle Temple, LLB
(Hons)(Leeds)

Lee *Miss Siew Mui*
Called: July 1996, Lincoln's Inn, LLB
(Hons)(Lond)

Lee *Miss Siew Peng*
Called: Feb 1995, Middle Temple, LLB
(Hons)(Lond)

Lee *Mrs Siew See* •
Legal Manager, Zepter International (UK)
Ltd, Unit 23, Shield Drive, West Cross
Centre, Brentford TW8 9EX, 0181 847 3619,
Fax: 0181 847 3618. Called: July 1993,
Gray's Inn, LLB (Hons)

Lee *Miss Simone*
Called: July 1995, Middle Temple, LLB
(Hons) (Bris)

Lee *Ms Su-Lin*
and Member Singapore Bar. Called: July
1990, Gray's Inn, LLB (Manch)

Lee *Miss Sue Chien*
Called: July 1997, Middle Temple, LLB
(Hons)(Warw)

Lee *Teck Hock*
Called: Mar 1998, Lincoln's Inn, LLB
(Hons)(Leics)

Lee *Tin Yan*
Called: July 1994, Middle Temple, LLB
(Hons)(Lond)

Lee *Towk Boon*
Called: July 1995, Lincoln's Inn, LLB (Hons)

Lee *Tzu Voon*
P O Box 20269, Pejabat Pos Luyang, 88759
Kota Kinabalu, Sabah, 6 088 224820, Fax: 6
088 219046. Called: Nov 1994, Lincoln's
Inn, LLB (Hons)(Lond)

Lee *Miss Vanessa Jayne*
Called: Oct 1995, Inner Temple, LLB
(Huddersfield)

Lee *Miss Victoria Jane* •
Commissioning Editor - Law, Oxford
University Press, Great Clarendon Street,
Oxford OX2 6DP, 01865 556767.
Called: Nov 1994, Lincoln's Inn, LLB
(Hons)(Lond)

Lee *Wei Chiang*
Called: Oct 1997, Gray's Inn, LLB (Lancs)

Lee *Wei Yung*
Senior Investigating Officer, Legal Assistant
(Litigation - Insurance, Contract, Shipping)
Senior Officer, Singapore Police Force
(PNS), B 873 Yishun St 81, 03-167, 535
0550, Fax: 438 0550, and Member
Singapore Bar. Called: July 1991, Middle
Temple, LLB (Hons) (Warw)

Lee *Miss Wendy Hsiao Wen*
and Member Singapore Bar. Called: July
1993, Middle Temple, LLB (Hons)

Lee *Miss Wendy Su Lin*
Called: July 1995, Middle Temple, LLB
(Hons) (Hull)

Lee *Yi Chung*
Called: Nov 1996, Middle Temple, LLB
(Hons)(Hull)

Lee *Yih Leang*
Called: July 1995, Lincoln's Inn, LLB (Hons)

Lee *Miss Yoke Har*
Called: July 1994, Middle Temple, LLB
(Hons)(Lond)

Lee *Mr Yuen Wai*
16 Raffles Quay, [H]36-00, (65) 322 1479,
Fax: (65) 234 2621, and Member Singapore
Bar. Called: July 1993, Lincoln's Inn, LLB
(Hons, Sheff)

Leece *Patrick Richard James*
Called: Oct 1993, Lincoln's Inn, LLB
(Hons)(Leic)

Leeder *Miss Lynne Angela* •
Senior Legal Officer (B1), Tax Simplication
Project Team, South West Bush House, The
Strand, London WC2B 4RO, 0171 438 7568,
Fax: 0171 438 7959. Called: July 1985,
Lincoln's Inn, MA [Cantab]

Lees *Alan James*
Called: Nov 1952, Gray's Inn, MA, LLB
(Edin)

Lees *Alastair Richard*
Called: Feb 1995, Inner Temple, BA
(Durham)

Lees *David Slater*
Principal Court Clerk, Victoria Law Courts,
Corporation Street, Birmingham B4 6QA,
0121 212 6607. Called: July 1984, Middle
Temple, BA

Lees *Gordon Clifford*
Clerk to the Justices, North Yorkshire
Magistrates', Courts Committee, The Law
Courts, Clifford Street, York YO1 1RE,
01904 615200, Fax: 01904 615201.
Called: July 1979, Gray's Inn, BA, Dip Law

Lees *Rear Admiral Rodney Burnett* •
Director General Naval Personnel, Strategy
& Plans MOD, 01705 727100. Called: July
1976, Gray's Inn

Lefcoe *Miss Karen Vivian*
Called: Oct 1997, Middle Temple, LLB
(Hons)(City)

Lefton *Nigel Spencer* •
Assistant Solicitor, Attorney General's
Chambers, 9 Buckingham Gate, London
SW1, 828 1553. Called: Nov 1979, Inner
Temple

Legg *Miss Christina Marie*
Called: Oct 1997, Middle Temple, LLB
(Hons)(Bournem)

Legg *Sir Thomas Stuart KCB, QC*
(1990) •
Permanent Secretary to the Lord Chancellor
and Clerk of the Crown in Chancery, Lord
Chancellor's Department, House of Lords,
London SW1A 0PW. Called: Feb 1960, Inner
Temple, MA, LLM

Leigh *Miss Camilla Anne*
Called: July 1984, Lincoln's Inn, MA
(Cantab)

Leigh *Geoffrey JP*
14 Gresley Court, Little Heath, Potters Bar,
Herts EN6 1LF, 01707 647162. Called: Nov
1959, Gray's Inn, MA, FCIS

Leigh-Morgan *Miss Tonia Lesley
Winson*
Called: Nov 1996, Lincoln's Inn, LLB (Hons)

Leigh-Smith *Alfred Nicholas Hardstaff*
Clerk to the Justices, Cambridgeshire
Magistrates' Ct, The Court House, Lion
Yard, Cambridge CB2 3NA, 01223 314311,
Fax: 01223 355237. Called: Nov 1976,
Lincoln's Inn, LLB (Leeds)

Leighton *Miss Alison Margaret*
Compensation Manager, Dresdner Kleinwort
Benson, 20 Fenchurch Street, London
EC3P 3DB, 0171 623 8000. Called: Oct
1990, Middle Temple, LLB, LLM (Tax Law),
ATT ATII

Leighton *Paul Robert*
Senior Quantity Surveyor. Legal Advisor.,
Turner & Townsend Contract, Services, 1
Clinton Terrace, Derby Road, Nottingham
NG7 1LY, 0115 947 0997, Fax: 0115 947
5679. Called: July 1997, Middle Temple, BSc
(Hons), ARICS

Leith *Daniel*
Called: Nov 1995, Inner Temple, LLB (Exon)

Lekic *Milo*
5 Septembra 68, Surdulica 17530, Serbia
Yugoslavia, 38 1 17 85 22 1. Called: Nov
1975, Gray's Inn, LLB (Belgrade), LLB
(Exon)

Lemkey *Miss Jennifer Anne*
Called: July 1987, Middle Temple, MA
(Cantab)

Lemon *Guy Robert* •
Assistant Legal Adviser to Chief Constable,
Thames Valley Police HQ, Oxford Road,
Kidlington, Oxford OX5 2NX, 01865
846676. Called: Nov 1995, Inner Temple,
LLB (B'ham)

Leng *Chua Kee*
Called: Nov 1997, Inner Temple, B.Acc
(Singapore), LLB (Lond)

Leng *Mrs Jacqueline Mary*
Called: Nov 1996, Middle Temple, LLB
(Hons)

Leng *Miss Lai Yoke*
Associate, Zaid Ibrahim & Co, 12th Floor,
Menara Bank, Pembangunan, Jalan Sultan
Ismail, 50250 Kuala Lumpur, 603 2926688,
Fax: 603 2981632, and Member Bar of
Malaysia. Called: July 1993, Inner Temple,
LLB (Nott'm)

Lenihan *Martin* •
Legal Adviser, Legal Dept, John Laing PLC, Page Street, Mill Hill, London NW7 2ER. Called: July 1983, Middle Temple, BA, LL.M [Lond], ACI Arb

Lenygon *Mr Bryan Norman*
Company Director General Comm of Income Tax, Highfield, Bells Yew Green, East Sussex TN3 9AP, 01892 750343, Fax: 01892 750609. Called: Nov 1976, Gray's Inn, MA, LLB, FCA, FCIS, ATII

Leon *Kwong Wing*
35 Dunearn Close, (65) 466 0285, Fax: (65) 466 0285, and Member Singapore. Called: Nov 1995, Gray's Inn, LLB (Wales)

Leon *Miss Le Lyn*
Called: Nov 1995, Gray's Inn, LLB (Wales)

Leonard *Ms Catherine Martine* •
Senior Crown Prosecutor, Crown Prosecution Service, Riverpark House, The High Road, Wood Green, London N22, 0181 888 8889 Ext 306, Fax: 0181 888 0746. Called: Nov 1990, Middle Temple, BA (Oxon)

Leonard *Eamonn Benedict Knightley*
E102, Hermann-Ehlers-Hans, Martinsburg 29, 49078 Osnabruck, Germany (0541) 41599. Called: Nov 1992, Inner Temple, BA (Dunelm), LLM (Osnabruck)

Leonard *Hywel*
One Harbour Place, P.O. Box 3239, Tampa, Florida 33601, 813 223 7000, Fax: 813 229 4133, and Member Florida. Called: July 1974, Gray's Inn, LLB (Wales), JD [Florida State]

Leonard *Miss Julia Adella*
Called: Nov 1996, Gray's Inn, BBA (Puerto Rico), LLM (Manch)

Leonard-Morgan *Scott*
Called: Oct 1996, Middle Temple, LLB (Hons)(Lond)

Leone *Miss Sidonie Lisa Maria*
Called: Feb 1991, Lincoln's Inn, Diploma in Law (PCL)

Leong *Miss Bik Yoke*
Called: July 1994, Lincoln's Inn, LLB (Hons, Leic)

Leong *Miss Chee Sian*
Called: Oct 1994, Middle Temple, LLB (Hons)(Wales)

Leong *Miss Chee Wei*
Called: Nov 1995, Middle Temple, LLB (Hons)(Hull)

Leong *Miss Cherly Suet Mei*
Called: Nov 1997, Lincoln's Inn, LLB (Hons)(Leics)

Leong *Miss Constance Choy Leng*
and Member Singapore. Called: July 1996, Middle Temple, LLB (Hons)(Lond), BA (Singapore)

Leong *Gary Tat Hau* •
Senior Crown Prosecutor, Crown Prosecution Service, Portland House, Stag Place, London SW1E 5BH, 0171 915 5840. Called: July 1990, Gray's Inn, LLB (Lond)

Leong *Miss Isabelle May Yue*
Called: July 1997, Middle Temple, LLB (Hons)(Sheff)

Leong *Miss Jacqueline Pamela*
1531 Prince's Building, Chater Road, (852) 2523-2899, Fax: (852) 2840-0786, QC Hong Kong and Member Hong Kong, Victoria, New South Wales Singapore Bar. Called: July 1970, Inner Temple

Leong *Miss Joycelyn Wai Keng*
Called: July 1991, Lincoln's Inn, LLB (Hons) (East An)

Leong *Kee Han*
Called: Nov 1996, Lincoln's Inn, LLB (Hons)

Leong *Kwok Yan*
12th Floor, Menara Bank Pembangunan, Jalan Sultan Ismail, 50250 Kuala Lumpur, 03 292 6688, Fax: 07 298 1632, and Member Malaysia. Called: July 1992, Lincoln's Inn, LLB (Hons) (Lond)

Leong *Miss Li Lian*
Called: Nov 1995, Gray's Inn, LLB

Leong *Miss Lynette Su-Mein*
Legal Assistant, 15a Jalan Jarak, and Member Singapore Bar. Called: July 1994, Middle Temple, BA (Hons)(Keele)

Leong *Michael Kim Seng*
Called: Nov 1997, Middle Temple, BA (Singapore), LLB (Hons)(Lond)

Leong *Miss Nu-Yen Mireille*
Called: Nov 1997, Lincoln's Inn, LLB (Hons)(Leeds)

Leong *Miss Pat Lynn*
Called: July 1992, Lincoln's Inn, LLB (Hons) (Exon)

Leong *Miss Sue Lynn*
Called: Nov 1995, Middle Temple, BA (Hons)(Keele)

Leong *Tat Kee*
Legal Assistant, 109 Spottiswood Park, [H]16-81, Singapore 0208, 2215404. Called: Nov 1991, Middle Temple, LLB Hons (Lond Ext)

Leong *Why Kong*
Braddell Brothers, 1 Colombo Court, [H]06-30, (65) 3366032, Fax: (65) 3366042, and Member Singapore. Called: July 1995, Gray's Inn, LLB (Lond)

Leontiou *Gregory*
504 Libra House, 21 P Caterlaris Street, P O Box 5001, Nicosia, Cyprus, 02-466 766, Fax: 02-448 777, 02-452 052, and Member Cyprus Bar. Called: Nov 1994, Lincoln's Inn, BA (Hons)(Manc)

Leow *Miss Christabel Tze Hoon*
Called: July 1994, Middle Temple, LLB (Hons)(Wales)

Leow *Miss Fui Fui*
Called: July 1995, Middle Temple, LLB (Hons) (Wales)

Leow *Michael Yung Fuong*
Robert W H Wang & Woo, 9 Temasek Boulevard [H]14-01, Suntec Tower 2, 336 0123, Fax: 332 1480, and Member Singapore Bar. Called: July 1992, Gray's Inn, LLB, LLM (Lond)

Leskin *Ian Paul* •
Assistant. Called: Feb 1991, Inner Temple, BA (Lanc), Dip Law (PCL)

Leslie *Craig Raymond*
Called: Oct 1996, Middle Temple, LLB (Hons)(Lond)

Lesser *Miss Janis Erica*
Senior Deputy Chief Clerk, Inner London Magistrates', Courts Service, 3rd Floor, North West Wing, Bush House, Aldwych, London WC2B 4PJ. Called: Nov 1970, Inner Temple

Lester *Alan Nicholas* •
Employment Lawyer, John Lewis plc, 171 Victoria Street, London SW1E 5NN, 0171 592 6287, Fax: 0171 592 6566. Called: July 1984, Inner Temple, MA (Oxon)

Lester *Lady Catherine Elizabeth Debora*
Immigration Adjudicator, Special Adjudicator, 38 Half Moon Lane, London SE24 9HU, 0171 733 2964, Fax: 0171 737 7282. Called: Nov 1969, Lincoln's Inn, MA, LLB (Cantab), LLM (Harvard)

Letemendia *Dr Miren Argi* •
Grade 6 Legal Adviser, Dept of Transport, Transport Advisory Division, 2 Marsham Street, London SW1P 3EB, 0171 276 4894, Fax: 0171 276 6755. Called: Nov 1973, Middle Temple, BA (Hons)

Leung *Michael Hung Kuk*
1002 Chekiang First Bank, 1 Duddell Street, Central, 2521 7317, Fax: 2845 0654, and Member Hong Kong Bar. Called: Nov 1993, Gray's Inn, LLB (Lond)

Leung *Paul Hei Ming*
Called: Nov 1997, Middle Temple, B.Eng (Hons)(NSW, Australia)

Leung *Richard Wai-Keung*
Des Voeux Chambers, 10/F Bank of East Asia, Building, 10 Des Voeux Road, Central, 852 2526 3071, Fax: 852 2810 5287, and Member Hong Kong Bar. Called: July 1994, Inner Temple, MA (Lancs), LLB

Leung *Siu Ying*
and Member Hong Kong Bar. Called: Nov 1992, Gray's Inn, B Arch (Newc), LLB (Lond)

Leung *Sun So*
Called: Nov 1989, Gray's Inn, LLB [Lond]

Leung *Tak Yin*
and Member Hong Kong Bar. Called: July 1995, Middle Temple, LLB (Hons)

Leung *Wai Man R*
16/F One Pacific Place, 88 Queensway, 852 25233003, Fax: 852 28100302, and Member Hong Kong Bar. Called: Feb 1992, Gray's Inn, BA (Hong Kong), LLB (Lond)

Leung *Yew Kwong*
Chief Legal Officer, Inland Revenue
Authority of, Singapore Law Division, 55
Newtown Road, Revenue House, 00656
3512022, Fax: 00656 3512077, Advocate &
Solicitor (Singapore). Called: Nov 1989,
Lincoln's Inn, LLB, BSc (Lond), MSc
(Reading), MBA (Singapore)

Leung *Miss Yuet Ngor*
Called: Oct 1996, Middle Temple, BSc
(Hons)(HongKong), CPE (Manc)

Levene *Mordecai*
1 Temple Gardens, London EC4, 0181 203
2234, Fax: 0181 203 2234. Called: Jan 1937,
Lincoln's Inn, LLB

Levene *Richard William Osborne* •
Principal Team Leader, Crown Prosecution
Service, 2nd Floor' Froomsgate House,
Rupert Street, Bristol, Avon BS1 2PS, 0117
9273093 x350, Fax: 0117 9230697.
Called: July 1982, Gray's Inn, BA (Law) Kent

Levene *Stanley Anthony Jack*
Former Solicitor. Called: Feb 1993, Middle
Temple

Lever *Mrs Andrina Gay Richards*
Managing Director, Suite 2308, 965 Bay
Street, Toronto, Ontario M55 2A3, 416 920
5114, Fax: 416 920 6764, and Member
Victoria Bar Australia Bar. Called: July 1980,
Gray's Inn, BA, BA (Hons)

Lever *Jeremy Frederick* QC (1972)
Dean, All Souls College, Oxford Chairman,
Oftel Advisory Body on Fair Trading in
Telecommunications; Chairman, Performing
Right Society Appeals Panel, 26 John Street,
London WC1N 2BL, 0171 831 0351, Fax:
0171 405 1675, QC Northern Ireland and
Member Northern Ireland Bar. Called: Nov
1957, Gray's Inn, MA (Oxon)

Levin *Andrew Paul* •
Principal Crown Prosecutor Prosecution
Team Leader, Crown Prosecution Service,
3rd Floor, King's House, Kymberley Road,
Harrow, Middlesex HA1 1YH, 0181 424
8688 X 287, Fax: 0181 424 9157.
Called: July 1984, Middle Temple, BA
(Hons)

Levin *David Samuel*
Owen Dixon Chambers, 205 William St,
Melbourne 3000, 61 39608 7043, Fax: 61
39608 8729, and Member Victoria,
Australian Capital Territory, Tasmania, New
South Wales, Northern Territory, South
Australia New South Wales Bar South
Australia Bar. Called: July 1972, Middle
Temple, MA (Cantab)

Levine *Ms Iona Jayne* •
Senior Legal Adviser, HSBC Holdings Plc, 10
Lower Thames Street, London EC3R 6AE,
0171 260 9736, Fax: 0171 260 0303.
Called: Feb 1982, Lincoln's Inn

Levine *Joshua Mark*
Called: Nov 1994, Inner Temple, LLB
(Soton), LLM (Lond)

Levins *Thomas Arthur* •
Senior Crown Prosecutor, Crown
Prosecution Service, Harrow Branch, 2nd
Floor, Kings House, Kymberley Road,
Harrow, Middlesex HA1 1YH, 0181 424
8688, Fax: 0181 424 9134. Called: Nov
1988, Middle Temple, LLB

Levitt *Matthew Charles*
Called: Feb 1992, Middle Temple, BA (Hon),
BCL (Oxon)

Lew *Miss Chen Chen*
Called: July 1996, Lincoln's Inn, LLB (Hons)

Lewer *Ms Helen Jeannette*
Deputy Clerk to the Justices, Brent
Magistrates Court, Church End, 448 High
Road, London NW10 2DZ, 0181 451 7111.
Called: Nov 1993, Inner Temple, BA (Lond),
CPE (City)

Lewin *Miss Maurine Joy*
Senior Deputy Chief Clerk, Inner London
Magistrates', Courts Service, 3rd Floor,
North West Wing, Bush House, Aldwych,
London WC2B 4PJ, 0171 436 8600, Fax:
0171 436 5239. Called: July 1982, Middle
Temple, MA (Sheffield), BA (Hons)

Lewis *Alexandre Xavier Pierre* •
Legal Service, European Commission, Rue
de la Loi, 200, 1049 Brussels, Belgium, and
Member Paris Bar. Called: July 1983, Middle
Temple, LLB (Lond), Maitrise en Droit, DEA
Droit Prive

Lewis *Miss Ann Molyneux OBE*
Past President,Royal Pharmaceutical Society
of Great Britain 1994/6, Timberscombe, 58
Wynnstay Lane, Marford, Nr Wrexham,
Clwyd LL12 8LH. Called: July 1980, Gray's
Inn, LLB (Lond) Hon DSc, FRPharmS

Lewis *The Hon Antony Thomas*
Chairman: Powys Health Care NHS Trust,
The Skreen, Erwood, Builth Wells, Powys
LD2 3SJ. Called: Nov 1971, Inner Temple,
LLM

Lewis *Brandon Keith*
Called: Oct 1997, Inner Temple, LLB
(Buckingham)

Lewis *Miss Caroline Daphne*
Training Officer, Inner London Magistrates',
Courts Service, 65 Romney Street, London
SW1P 3RD, 0171 799 3332. Called: Nov
1975, Middle Temple, MA (Oxon)

Lewis *Ms Catrin Eluned* •
Hackney Law Centre, 236-238 Mare Street,
London E8 1HE. Called: Nov 1991, Middle
Temple, BA (Hons)(Lond), Dip Law

Lewis *Cenio Elwin* •
Legal Officer, High Commission for Eastern,
Caibbean States, 10 Kensington Court,
London W8 5DL, 0171 937 9522, Fax: 0171
937 5514. Called: Apr 1978, Lincoln's Inn,
LLB, LLM (Lond), MA

Lewis *Charles Eliot* •
Legal Adviser, Department of Trade &
Industry, Room 118, 10 Victoria Street,
London SW1H 0NN, 0171 215 5000.
Called: Nov 1986, Gray's Inn, MA,
PhD(Cantab)

Lewis *Mrs Clare*
Deputy Chief Court Clerk, Camberwell
Green Magistrates, D'Eynsford Road,
London SE5, 0171 7030 0909. Called: July
1988, Lincoln's Inn, LLB (Hons) (Lond), BA
(Hons)

Lewis *Miss Coleen Bekere*
Called: July 1997, Inner Temple, BA (West
Indies), Dip in Law (Exon)

Lewis *Miss Danielle Soraya*
Called: Nov 1995, Lincoln's Inn, LLB (Hons)

Lewis *Edwin*
Called: Nov 1997, Lincoln's Inn, LLB (Hons)

Lewis *Humphrey John Nigel*
St Mary's Chambers, 50 High Pavement,
Lace Market, Nottingham, NG1 1HW.
Called: Nov 1953, Gray's Inn, MA, LLB
(Cantab)

Lewis *Miss Jacqueline Ann*
Clifford Chance, 200 Aldersgate Street,
London EC1A 4JJ, 0171 600 1000 Ext 8697,
Fax: 0171 600 5555. Called: Oct 1992,
Lincoln's Inn, BSc(Hons)(Bris), Dip Law

Lewis *Mrs Lesley*
38 Whitelands Hse, Cheltenham Terrace,
London SW3 4QY. Called: Nov 1956,
Lincoln's Inn, MA [Lond]

Lewis *Miss Linda Catherine*
Called: Feb 1990, Inner Temple, BSc
(Surrey), LLM

Lewis *Linton Aron*
Offshore Finance Inspector, P.O.Box 1407,
Queen's Drive, St Vincent & The
Grenadines, 1 809 456 2577, Fax: 1 809 456
5372, and Member St VIncent & The
Grenadines. Called: July 1996, Gray's Inn,
MA (Bristol), ACCA

Lewis *Mrs Pauline Grace*
Legal Adviser, McDonald's Restaurants
Limited, 11-59 High Road, East Finchley,
London N2 8AW, 0181 883 6400, Fax: 0181
442 1379. Called: Nov 1984, Lincoln's Inn,
LLB (Hons)

Lewis *Philip Stephen* •
Serious Fraud Office, Elm House, 10-16 Elm
Street, London WC1X OBI. Called: July
1981, Gray's Inn, BA, MA Dip L

Lewis *Robyn*
Former Solicitor. Called: Nov 1997, Gray's
Inn, LLB (Wales)

Lewis *Lieutenant Colonel Roger David
OBE* •
Legal Officer, Army Prosecution Authority,
RAF Uxbridge, Middlesex UB10 0XE.
Called: Nov 1983, Lincoln's Inn, LLB Lond

Lewis *Stephen John*
Called: Feb 1992, Lincoln's Inn, LLB (Honss)

Lewis *Miss Susan Ann*
Called: July 1997, Lincoln's Inn, LLB
(Hons)(L'pool), LLM (L'Pool)

Lewis-Jones *Robert Kevin*
Called: Oct 1996, Middle Temple, BA (Hons)
(Kingston), Dip Law

E

Lewis-Nunn *Howard*
Capsticks Solicitors, 77-83 Upper Richmond Road, London SW15 2TT. Called: Nov 1994, Inner Temple, LLB (E.Anglia)

Lewis-Ruttley *Miss Hilary Jane* •
Jt Director of Studies (Int & Prof Training Unit) and Research Fellow, Inst of Advanced Legal Studies (Lond), Institute of Advanced, Legal Studies, Charles Clore House, 17 Russell Square, London WC1B 5DR, 0171 637 1731, Fax: 0171 580 9613 or 436 8824. Called: July 1980, Inner Temple, BA

Leyland *Mrs Sheila Margaret*
Called: Nov 1970, Inner Temple, LLB

Li *Ms Cynthia Sun-Ming*
1318 Prince's Building, 10 Chater Road, Central, Hong Kong, (852) 2526 8128, Fax: (852) 2526 8500, and Member Hong Kong Bar. Called: July 1994, Inner Temple, BA (Canada), LLB

Li *Miss Gladys Veronica*
2507 Edinburgh Tower, The Landmark, 15 Queen's Road Central, 25-2 17188, Fax: 2810 1823, QC (Hong Kong) and Member Hong Kong Bar. Called: Feb 1971, Lincoln's Inn, MA (Cantab)

Li-Ann *Ms Cheong*
Called: July 1994, Inner Temple, LLB (Nott'm)

Lian *Miss Alice Meng Li*
Called: July 1996, Lincoln's Inn, LLB (Hons)(Herts)

Liao *Martin Cheung-Kong*
61 New Henry House, 10 Ice House Street, Central, Hong Kong, 2522 5121, and Member Hong Kong Bar Singapore Bar. Called: July 1984, Lincoln's Inn, BSc (Econ), LLM, Dip Law

Liban *Stefan Ryszard*
Called: Mar 1998, Middle Temple, MSc (Poland)

Libbish *Simon Lyndsey Darren* •
High Risk Unit, Credit & Risk, First Direct, Millshaw Park Lane, Leeds LS98 1FD, 0113 2766729, Fax: 0113 2766531. Called: Nov 1993, Inner Temple, LLB

Licata *Joseph*
Bench Legal Adviser, Northampton Magistrates Court3, Regents Pavilion, Summerhouse Road, Moulton Park, Northampton NN3 1AS, 01604 497000, Fax: 01604 497010; 497020. Called: July 1981, Middle Temple, BA (Hons), MBA

Licht *Mrs Judith*
Called: Nov 1971, Lincoln's Inn

Liew *Bernard Jin Yang*
Assistant Manager, Neptune Orient Lines Limited, 456 Alexandra Road [H]06-00, Nol Building, Singapore 119962, (65) 3715381, Fax: (65) 2731697, and Member Singapore Bar. Called: July 1989, Gray's Inn, LLB (Bucks)

Liew *Miss Lan-Hing*
Called: July 1995, Middle Temple, B.Sc (Hons), LLB (Hons)

Liew *Miss Siew Ling*
Called: July 1997, Lincoln's Inn, LLB (Hons)

Liew *Sunny Siew Pang*
Liew Hazalina, No 286 Lafite Apartments, Jalan SS 17/1G, 47500 Petaling Jaya, Selangor, 732 7668, Fax: 732 6188, and Member Malaysia Bar. Called: July 1993, Gray's Inn, LLB (Brunel)

Liew-Mouawad *Mrs Joyce Huey*
Lecturer, Holborn College, Holborn College, 200 Greyhound Road, London W14 9RY, 0171 385 3377, Fax: 0171 381 3377. Called: May 1995, Middle Temple, LLB (Hons) (Lond)

Lightbourn *Miss Sandra Jean*
Called: July 1997, Lincoln's Inn, LLB (Hons)

Lightfoot *Miss Kathryn Louise*
Called: Feb 1991, Middle Temple, LLB (Manch)

Lillycrop *David Peter* •
General Counsel & Group Secretary, TI Group plc, Lambourn Court, Abingdon, Oxon OX14 1UH, 01235 555570/01235 540133, Fax: 01235 555818/01235 554216. Called: July 1978, Middle Temple, LLB (Exon), FIMgt

Lillywhite *David Victor* •
Legal Advisor and Compliance Manager, National Provident Institution, 55 Calverley Road, Tunbridge Wells, Kent TN1 2UE, 01892 705314, Fax: 01892 705614. Called: Nov 1980, Middle Temple, LLB

Lim *Miss Ai Leen*
Legal Executive Officer, Malaysian Derivatives Clearing, House, 4th Floor, Citypoint, Dayabumi Complex, 50050 Kuala Lumpur, 60 3 294 5070, Fax: 60 3 294 5040, and Member Malaysia Bar. Called: Oct 1992, Middle Temple, LL.B (Hons, B'ham)

Lim *Miss Angelina Swee Peng*
Called: July 1994, Lincoln's Inn, LLB (Hons)

Lim *Miss Bee San*
Called: Nov 1994, Middle Temple, LLB (Hons)

Lim *Miss Choi Ming*
and Member Singapore Bar. Called: July 1995, Middle Temple, LLB (Hons)

Lim *Chong Fong*
Partner, Azman Davidson & Co, Advocates & Solicitors, Suite 13.03, Menara Tan & Tan, 207 Jalan Tun Razak, 50400 Kuala Lumpur Malaysia, 603 264 0200, Fax: 603 264 0280, and Member Malaysia Bar. Called: July 1995, Middle Temple, LLB (Hons), BSc, (Bldg)(Hons), ARICS, ACIArb

Lim *Choon How*
Called: Nov 1996, Lincoln's Inn, LLB (Hons)(Lond)

Lim *Christopher Su Heng*
Legal Assistant (Corporate Affairs), Suite 16.01, 16th Floor, Wisma Nusantara, Jalan Punchak, 50050 Kuala Lumpur, 0603 203 3541, Fax: 0603 203 3542, and Member Malaysia Bar. Called: July 1996, Lincoln's Inn, LLB (Hons)(Bris)

Lim *Miss Cynthia Siew Leng*
Legal Assistant, Messrs Iza Ng Yeoh & Kit, 19th Floor, Bangunan, Dato, Zainal, Jalan Melaka, 50100 Kuala Lumpur, 2986066, Fax: 2982593, and Member Malaysia Bar. Called: July 1992, Lincoln's Inn, LLB (Hons) (Lond)

Lim *Fung Peen*
Called: Nov 1995, Middle Temple, LLB (Hons)

Lim *Miss Gek Hoon*
Called: July 1996, Lincoln's Inn, LLB (Hons)(Lond)

Lim *George Chee Huat*
Called: July 1997, Middle Temple, LLB (Hons)(Lond)

Lim *Ms Goon Lwee*
Group Financial Controller. Called: July 1996, Inner Temple, LLB (Lond)

Lim *Miss Grace Siew Hua*
Called: July 1994, Lincoln's Inn, LLB (Hons)

Lim *Miss Helen Bek Yun*
P.O.Box 2773, 90731 Sandakan, Sabah, Advocate of the High Court in Sabah & Sarawak, Malaysia Advocate of the Supreme Court of Brunei, Darussalam. Called: July 1995, Lincoln's Inn, LLB (Hons)(Leeds)

Lim *Miss Heliz Hsien Ling*
Called: Nov 1997, Lincoln's Inn, LLB (Hons)(E.Lond)

Lim *Miss Hui Min*
51 Dyson Road, 2551868, Fax: 2519078. Called: July 1996, Lincoln's Inn, BA (Oxon), BCL

Lim *Miss Hui Ting*
Called: Nov 1996, Lincoln's Inn, LLB (Hons) (Sheff)

Lim *Miss Hwee Bin*
Called: July 1996, Lincoln's Inn, LLB (Hons)

Lim *Miss Jacqueline Hui Erh*
9F Three Exchange Square, 8 Connaught Place, Central, 852 2840 1282, Fax: 852 2840 0515. Called: Oct 1994, Middle Temple, LLB (Hons)(Bris), LLM (Bris)

Lim *Miss Jane Chen*
Called: Nov 1997, Lincoln's Inn, LLB (Hons)(Bucks)

Lim *Miss Jeanne Tsze Ye*
Called: Nov 1992, Middle Temple, LLB (Hons, Lond)

Lim *Miss Jessica Hai Ean*
Called: July 1997, Lincoln's Inn, LLB (Hons)

Lim *Miss Julie Siu Yen*
Called: July 1997, Middle Temple, LLB (Hons)(Lond)

Lim *Miss Karen Um-Chai Hui Lin*
Legal Officer, Oversea-Chinese Banking, Corporation Limited, 65 China Street, [H]08-00, OCBC Centre, 5306143, Fax: 5352335. Called: Nov 1995, Middle Temple, LLB (Hons)

Lim *Karl Adrian*
Called: Oct 1995, Inner Temple, LLB (Exon)

Lim *Miss Kay Li Deborah*
Called: July 1997, Middle Temple, LLB
(Hons)(Nott'm)

Lim *Kelvin Kuan Chin*
Called: July 1994, Lincoln's Inn, LLB (Hons)

Lim *Kong Yuk*
Called: Nov 1996, Middle Temple, LLB
(Hons)(Wales)

Lim *Kuok Sim Edwin*
Legal Advisor, 42 Jalan Permai, Robson
Heights, Kuala Lumpur 50460, (603)
2742234. Called: Nov 1995, Gray's Inn, LLB
(Wales), LLM (Bris)

Lim *Lay Hor*
Pupillage in Chambers, M.P.Raja, E.T. Low
& Tan, Room 304, 3rd Floor, Wisma Tah
peh, No 86 Jalan Masjid India 50100, Kuala
Lumpur, 03 293 4293. Called: July 1997,
Middle Temple, LLB (Hons)(Lond)

Lim *Miss Lee Hoon*
Called: July 1995, Lincoln's Inn, LLB (Hons)

Lim *Miss Li Lian*
and Member Singapore Bar. Called: Nov
1992, Middle Temple, LLB (Hons, Sheff)

Lim *Miss Li Lin*
Called: July 1996, Middle Temple, LLB
(Hons)(Lanc)

Lim *Miss Liau Yan*
Called: July 1997, Lincoln's Inn, LLB
(Hons)(Kent)

Lim *Miss Lorinne May-Suan*
Called: July 1994, Lincoln's Inn, LLB (Hons)

Lim *Mark Chin Hian*
Called: Nov 1996, Middle Temple, BA
(Hons)

Lim *Miss Michele Hwee Ling*
Called: July 1995, Middle Temple, LLB
(Hons) (Hull)

Lim *Miss Michele Kythe Beng Sze*
Called: Nov 1992, Middle Temple, LLB
(Hons)

Lim *Ms Nyuk Yun*
Called: July 1997, Inner Temple, BSc

Lim *Perry Che-How*
Called: July 1994, Middle Temple, LLB
(Hons)(Wales)

Lim *Miss Ping*
Called: Nov 1997, Lincoln's Inn, LLB
(Hons)(Lond)

Lim *Miss Puay Yuen*
Called: July 1995, Middle Temple, LLB
(Hons) (Wales)

Lim *Miss Pui Keng*
Called: July 1997, Lincoln's Inn, LLB
(Hons)(Leics)

Lim *Ralph Howard U Wei*
Called: July 1995, Lincoln's Inn, LLB (Hons)

Lim *Raymond Kuan Yew*
Blk 34 [H]02-218, Jalan Bahagia, Singapore
320034, 2547821, and Member Singapore
Bar. Called: July 1995, Lincoln's Inn, LLB
(Hons)

Lim *Richard Teck Hock*
Advocate & Solicitor of the Supreme Court
of Singapore, Blk 94 Henderson Road,
[H]09-270 Singapore 150094, (65) 2762011,
and Member Singapore. Called: July 1995,
Lincoln's Inn, LLB (Hons)

Lim *Seng Sheoh*
Called: Nov 1994, Middle Temple, BA
(Hons) (Kent)

Lim *Miss Sharon Yen Li*
Chooi & Company, Penthouse, Mine
Building, Jalan Bukit Nanas, 50250 Kuala
Lumpur, and Member Malaysia. Called: July
1995, Lincoln's Inn, LLB (Hons)

Lim *Miss Siew Ming*
Called: July 1996, Lincoln's Inn, LLB
(Hons)(Sheff)

Lim *Miss Siew Peng*
Called: July 1996, Lincoln's Inn, BA
(Hons)(Keele)

Lim *Miss Siew Symn*
c/o Messrs Abdullah,Ooi & Chan, Suite 17-
03, 17th Floor, MCB Plaza, 6 Cangkat Raja
Chulan, 50200 Kuala Lumpur Malaysia, 603
2324293, Fax: 603 2301644, Advocate &
Solicitor of the High Court of Malaya.
Called: Nov 1992, Gray's Inn, LLB (So'ton)

Lim *Miss Sim Yi*
Called: July 1995, Gray's Inn, LLB

Lim *Siu Yin Jeffrey*
Called: July 1997, Gray's Inn, LLB (Bris)

Lim *Song Chia*
First Vice President, Pt Bank Ekspor Impor
Indonesia Singapore Branch, (65) 439 5680,
Fax: (65) 532 0206. Called: Nov 1996,
Lincoln's Inn, LLB (Hons)(Lond)

Lim *Stephen Yew Huat*
15th/16th Floors, Bank of China Building, 4
Battery Road, 535 3600, Fax: 538 8598,
Advocate & Solicitor of Supreme Court of
Singapore and Member Singapore.
Called: July 1992, Middle Temple, LLB
(Hons) LSe, LLM (Columbia)

Lim *Miss Su-ching*
Messrs Ramdas & Wong, 6 Shenton Way,
[H] 25-06 DBS Building Tower 2, Singapore
068809, 65 220 1121, Fax: 65 225 9152/65
225 9153, and Member Singapore Bar.
Called: July 1992, Middle Temple, LLB
(Hons) (E.Ang)

Lim *Miss Su-Fen*
Drew & Napier, 20 Raffles Place, [H]17-00
Ocean Towers, Singapore 048620, (65) 535
0733, Fax: (65) 535 4864, and Member
Singapore Bar. Called: Nov 1994, Middle
Temple, LLB (Hons)

Lim *Miss Su-Lynn*
Drew & Napier, 20 Raffles Place, [H] 17.00
Ocean Towers, 535 0733, Fax: 532 7149,
and Member Singapore Bar. Called: July
1995, Middle Temple, LLB (Hons) (Hull)

Lim *Swee Tee*
Called: July 1996, Middle Temple, BSc
(Singapore), LLB (Hons)(Wolves)

Lim *Tanguy Yuteck*
Chor Pee & Partners, 50 Raffles Place, 18th
Floor, Singapore Land, Tower, Singapore
048623, 4355726, Fax: 5363155.
Called: Nov 1993, Middle Temple, LLB
(Hons)(Wales)

Lim *Tchuang Cheio Tchwonyoson*
Legal Assistant, Rodyk & Davidson, 9 Raffles
Place, [H]55-01 Republic Plaza, 65-2252626,
Fax: 65-2251838, and Member Singapore
Bar. Called: July 1993, Middle Temple, LLB
(Hons)(Lond)

Lim *Tiong-Piow*
Called: July 1995, Lincoln's Inn, LLB (Hons)

Lim *Tuck Sum*
Called: July 1996, Lincoln's Inn, LLB
(Hons)(Lond)

Lim *Wye Hon*
Called: July 1996, Middle Temple, LLB
(Hons)(Leic)

Lim *Yang Hsing Leslie*
Called: July 1995, Middle Temple, LLB
(Hons)(Kent)

Lim *Yek Lai*
Called: July 1996, Lincoln's Inn, LLB (Hons)

Lim *Miss Yen-Hui*
Called: July 1997, Gray's Inn, LLB (Bristol)

Lim *Miss Yoon Cheng Audrey*
Justices' Law Clerk - Supreme Court of
Singapore, Supreme Court, St Andrew's
Road, Singapore 0617, 3323918, Fax:
3379450. Called: July 1994, Middle Temple,
BA (Hons)(Cantab)

Lin *Miss Diaan-Yi*
Called: July 1996, Lincoln's Inn, BA (Hons)

Lin *Feng*
Called: Nov 1997, Middle Temple, LLB
(Fudan), LLM (Victoria)

Lindblom *Mrs Fiona Margaret*•
N M Rothschild & Sons, New Court, St
Swithins Lane, London EC4P 4DU, 0171 280
5000, Fax: 0171 929 5239, Also Inn of
Court L. Called: July 1989, Inner Temple, BA
(Oxon)

Lindsay *Miss Alison*
Barrister of Ireland. Called: May 1996,
Middle Temple, BA (Hons)(Dublin), BL
(King's Inn)

Lindsay *Alistair David*
Allen & Overy Solicitors. Called: Oct 1993,
Inner Temple, BA

Line *Matthew*
Called: Oct 1997, Lincoln's Inn, LLB
(Hons)(L'pool)

Linehan *Miss Maxine Therese*
Called: Nov 1996, Gray's Inn, LLB (Lond)

Lines *Paul Francis*
Managing Director, Widney plc, Willowbank
House, Oxford Road, Uxbridge, Middlesex
UB 1UL, 01895 819340, Fax: 01895 819341.
Called: Nov 1969, Middle Temple, LLB
(So'ton)

E

Lines *Richard* •
Highways Agency, Room 11/19, St
Christopher House, Southwark Street,
London SE1 0TE, 0171 921 4658, Fax: 0171
921 4060. Called: Feb 1965, Gray's Inn, MA
(Oxon)

Ling *Miss Carolyn Dora Li-Hsing*
Called: Nov 1989, Middle Temple, LLB
(Newc), LLM (Lond)

Ling *Chun Wai*
Called: July 1996, Lincoln's Inn, LLB
(Hons)(Lond)

Ling *Clarence Louis Li-Tien*
ATMD, 39 Robinson Road, [H] 07-01,
Robinson Point, (65) 5345266, Fax: (65)
2238762, and Member Singapore.
Called: Nov 1995, Lincoln's Inn, LLB (Hons)
(Leics), BSc (Chem.emph, Biochem)

Ling *Hee Keat*
54 Jalan Setiabakti 8, Bukit Damansara,
50490 Kuala Lumpur, Malaysia, 03 2530257,
Fax: 03 2531520. Called: July 1995,
Lincoln's Inn, LLB (Hons)

Ling *Miss Jing Jinn*
M/S Battenberg & Talma Advocat, 4, 1st
Floor, Jalan Song Thian, Cheok, Kuching,
Sarawak, 082 253277, Fax: 082 420430,
Advocate & Solicitor of Singapore Advocate
of Sarawak. Called: July 1994, Middle
Temple, LLB (Hons)(Manc)

Ling *Miss Jocettta Ching Tse*
Called: July 1995, Lincoln's Inn, LLB (Hons)

Ling *Leong Hui*
Called: July 1996, Inner Temple, LLB (Lond)

Ling *Peter Liong Ing*
Regional General Counsel, BP Asia Pacific
Pte. Ltd, 396 Alexander Road, [H]18-01, BP
Tower, (65) 371 8701, Fax: (65) 371 8797.
Called: Nov 1969, Lincoln's Inn

Ling *Ms Sharon Hea Mei*
Called: Oct 1997, Inner Temple, LLB
(Brunel)

Ling *Tien Wah*
Legal Assistant, M/S Helen Yeo & Partners,
11 Collyer Quay [H]12-01, The Arcade,
2251040, Fax: 2221345, and Member
Singapore Bar Malaysia Bar. Called: Nov
1990, Lincoln's Inn, LLB (Leeds)

Ling *Miss Wei Lin*
Called: July 1996, Lincoln's Inn, LLB
(Hons)(Leeds)

Linkins *Mark Harold* •
Principal Crown Prosecutor, Crown
Prosecution Service, Mayfield House,
Mayfield Drive, London Road, Shrewsbury
SY2 6PE, 01743 235726, Fax: 01743
240455. Called: Nov 1986, Gray's Inn

Linnett *Mrs Lynn Marie*
Court Clerk, Northampton Magistrates
Court, Regents Pavilion, Summerhouse
Road, Moulton Park, Northampton
NN3 1AS, 01604 497000, Fax: 01604
497010. Called: Nov 1986, Gray's Inn, Dip
Law

Linsey *Mrs Pamela Christine* •
The Lord Chancellor's Dept, Selborne
House, Victoria Street, London SW1.
Called: July 1988, Lincoln's Inn, LLB (Hons)
(Essex)

Linton *Miss Georgina Charmaine* •
Corporate Counsel European Region, Jacobs
Engineering Ltd, Croydon, Surrey, 0181 688
4477, Fax: 0181 667 0852. Called: July
1985, Middle Temple, LLB (Hons)

Linton *Miss Sara Geraldine* •
Assistant Solicitor Grade 5, HM Customs &
Excise, The Solicitor's Office, New Kings
Beam House, 22 Upper Ground, London
SE1 9PJ. Called: Nov 1970, Inner Temple

Lintott *George David*
Squirrels Chase, Gully Rd, Seaview, Isle of
Wight PO34 5BZ, 01983 612749.
Called: July 1957, Middle Temple, BSc
Econ(Lond), FCIS

Lio *Chee Yeong*
Called: Nov 1996, Middle Temple, LLB
(Hons)(Lond)

Liow *Henny Woon Loong*
Khattar Wong & Partners, 80 Raffles Place,
[H] 25-01, UOB Plaza 1, 535 6844, Fax: 534
1090, and Member Singapore. Called: July
1994, Lincoln's Inn, LLB (Hons)

Lippell *Miss Sabrina Rose*
Management & Training Consultant.
Business Development Consultant to the
Institute of Personnel & Development.,
01705 631574, Fax: 01705 631574.
Called: Oct 1994, Lincoln's Inn, BSc
(Hons)(Soton), CPE (Lond)

Lipscomb *Mrs Marina Lynn* •
Group Solicitor Public Relations Officer. Bar
Association for Local Government and the
Public Service, Milton Keynes Council, Civic
Offices, 1 Saxon Gate East, Milton Keynes
MK9 3HG, 01908 252478, Fax: 01908
252600. Called: Nov 1987, Gray's Inn, BSc
Econ (Hons), Dip Law

Lipskier-Curtis *Mrs Sylvie*
Called: Oct 1990, Gray's Inn, BA (Kent), MA
(France)

Lipworth *Sir Sydney* QC (1993)
Master of the Bench Deputy Chairman,
National Westminster Bank PLC Chairman,
Zeneca Group Plc, 41 Lothbury, London
EC2P 2BP, 0171 726 1225, Fax: 0171 726
1038, and Member South Africa Bar.
Called: Oct 1991, Inner Temple, B.Com LLB

Lis *Miss Jacqueline Mary* •
Crown Prosecutor. Called: July 1985,
Lincoln's Inn, BA, Dip Law

Lister *Ms Theresa Ann Alice* •
Senior Crown Prosecutor, Crown
Prosecution Service, 5-6 Prebendal Court,
Oxford Road, Aylesbury HP19 3EY, 01296
436441. Called: May 1990, Lincoln's Inn,
LLB (Hons)

Little *Andrew Paul*
Called: July 1996, Middle Temple, LLB
(Hons)

Little *Miss Claire*
Called: Oct 1997, Gray's Inn, LLB (Hull)

Little *Robert Edward*
Little Heavegate, Crowborough, East Sussex
TN6 1TU, 01892 652035. Called: Feb 1955,
Gray's Inn, LLM, FCIS

Littlewood *Mrs Helen Elizabeth*
Deputy Clerk to the Justices, Harrow
Magistrates', Courts Committee, PO Box
164, Rosslyn Crescent, Harrow HA1 2JY,
0181 427 5146. Called: July 1980, Gray's
Inn, BA (Nott'm)

Litton *Henry Denis OBE*
Permanent Judge of the Court of Final
Appeal, Court of Final Appeal, 1 Battery
Path, 852-2123-0012, Fax: 852-2524-3991,
Hong Kong QC. Called: June 1959, Gray's
Inn, MA (Oxon)

Litvin *Mark Ian*
Called: Feb 1993, Middle Temple, BA (Hons)
(Oxon)

Liu *Kee Yong*
Called: July 1996, Middle Temple, LLB
(Hons)(Hull)

Liu *Owen Heng Su*
Called: Nov 1997, Lincoln's Inn, LLB
(Hons)(Manch)

Liu *Sern Yang*
Called: Nov 1996, Gray's Inn, LLB

Liu *Zhipeng*
Called: July 1996, Middle Temple, LLB
(Hons)(Notts)

Livesey *Miss Julia Mary*
Stipendiary Magistrate in Hong Kong, 2
King's Bench Walk, 1st Floor, Temple,
London, EC4Y 7DE. Called: Nov 1974,
Gray's Inn, BA

Livingstone *Philip Martin*
Vibert & Valpy, 8 Duhamel Place, St Helier,
Jersey, 01534 888666, Fax: 01534 888555,
Advocate of the Royal Court of Jersey.
Called: July 1987, Middle Temple, LLB (Hull)

Livingstone *Reuben*
Called: Nov 1995, Inner Temple, BA, MA
(Lond), LLB (Lond), LLM (Lond)

Llewellyn *David Alexander Wilson*
Called: Mar 1998, Inner Temple, MA
(Cantab)

Llewellyn *Howard Neil* •
Legal Adviser to Chief Constable and
Director of Legal Services, Cambridgeshire
Constabulary, Headquarters,
Hinchingbrooke Park, Huntingdon
PE18 8NP, 01480 456111, Fax: 01480
422297. Called: July 1982, Middle Temple,
BA (Hons)(Law)

Llewellyn-Lloyd *Edward John*
Chief Executive, Close Brothers Corporate,
Finance Limited, 12 Appold Street, London
EC2A 2AA. Called: Nov 1984, Inner Temple,
BA (Oxon)

Lloyd *Daniel Rhys*
Called: Nov 1996, Inner Temple, BA (Wales)

Lloyd *David Gareth Beechey*
Called: Mar 1996, Gray's Inn, BA (Dunelm)

Lloyd *John Desmond* ●
Senior Crown Prosecutor, Crown
Prosecution Service, South Glamorgan
Branch, 19th,20th & 21st Floor, Pearl
Assurance House, Greyfriars Road, Cardiff
CF1 3PL. Called: Nov 1987, Gray's Inn, LLB
(Wales)

Lloyd *Miss Marisa Rachel*
Ford & Warren Solicitors, Westgate Point,
Westgate, Leeds LS1 2AX, 0113 243 6601.
Called: Nov 1994, Inner Temple, BA (Essex),
CPE (Glamorgan)

Lloyd *Michael Gordon*
Rua do Norte 18,20, 1200 Lisbon, 00 351 1
343 3762, Fax: 00 351 1 343 3762.
Called: Nov 1967, Gray's Inn, MA (Oxon)

Lloyd *Reginald William*
Litigation Clerk, Morgan Jones & Pett
Solicitors, St George's Road, Great
Yarmouth, Norfolk. Called: Nov 1993,
Lincoln's Inn, CPE, LLM (Wales)

Lloyd *Rupert Charles*
26 Lancaster Mews, London W2.
Called: Nov 1990, Lincoln's Inn, MA (Oxon),
Dip Law (PCL)

Lloyd *Mrs Susan Helen* ●
President of the London Rent Assessment
Panel Member of the Broadcasting Standards
Commission. Governor of the Expert
Witness Institute, London Rent Assessment
Panel, Newlands House, 37-40 Berners
Street, London W1P 4BP, 0171 446 7700.
Called: July 1965, Middle Temple

Lloyd-Eley *John* QC (1970)
Recorder. Called: Jan 1951, Middle Temple,
MA, BA (Oxon)

Lloyd-Nesling *Miss Tracey Norma
Beatrice* ●
Senior Crown Prosecutor, Crown
Prosecution Service, Mayfield House,
Mayfield Drive, London Road, Shrewsbury
SY2 6PE, 01743 235726, Fax: 01743
240455. Called: July 1988, Middle Temple,
LLB (Hons) (Bucks)

Lloyd-Williams *Miss Mairwen Cecelia*
67 Paxton Road, Chiswick, London
W4 2QT, 0181 747 3217, Fax: 0181 747
3217. Called: Oct 1995, Lincoln's Inn, LLB
(Hons)(Lond), BSc (Hons)

Lo *Miss Phyllis Set Fui*
Called: July 1996, Middle Temple, LLB
(Hons)(Bris)

Lo *Pui Yin*
1001 Far East Finance Centre, 16 Harcourt
Road, Hong Kong, (852) 2866 8233, Fax:
(852) 2866 3932, and Member Hong Kong
Bar. Called: July 1992, Inner Temple, LLB
(LSE)

Lobo *Anthony Finton* KSG
8 Jaquets Court, North Cray Rd, Bexley,
Kent DA5 3NF, 01322 524436. Called: Nov
1958, Lincoln's Inn, BA, LLB, Dip Law,
(International)

Lock *Alex Richard*
Called: Oct 1996, Inner Temple, LLB
(Wales)

Lock *David Anthony* MP
7 Fountain Court, Steelhouse Lane,
Birmingham, B4 6DR. Called: Nov 1985,
Gray's Inn, MA (Cantab), DipL

Locke *Geoffrey Norman Wanstall*
Deputy Stipendiary Magistrate. Called: Nov
1970, Gray's Inn

Locke *William George* ●
Office of the Public Defender, Alameda
County Court House, 1225 Fallon Street,
Oakland, California 94612 U.S.A., 1 510 272
6600, Fax: 1 510 271 5149, and Member
California, USA Bar, US District Court,
Northern District of California Bar.
Called: Nov 1989, Inner Temple, BA (Notre
Dame), MA (Indiana), JD (California)

Lockey *Mrs Barbara Louise*
Called: July 1987, Lincoln's Inn, LLB (Hons)

Lockley *Peter Jonathan*
Called: Mar 1998, Lincoln's Inn, BA
(Hons)(Oxon)

Loebl *Ms Daphne Miriam*
Wilde Sapte, 1 Fleet Place, London
EC4M 7WS, 0171 46 7000. Called: July
1985, Middle Temple, MA (Cantab)

Loft *Laurence*
Clerk to the Justices, P O Box No 717
Weind House, Park Hill Road, Garstang,
Lancashire PR3 1EY, 01995 601596, Fax:
01995 601776. Called: July 1981, Gray's Inn

Logan *Cecil Corbett Malcolm*
Galleries, Harewood End, Hereford HR2 8JT,
01989 730226. Called: Nov 1934, Gray's
Inn, TD, MA (Oxon)

Logan *David Preston*
Senior Government Counsel - Department
of Justices, Appearing on behalf of the
Hong Kong Special Administrative Region of
China in the Hong Kong Courts,
Department of Justice, Queensway
Government Offices, 66 Queensway, 852
2867 2041, Fax: 852 2869 0062, and
Member Hong Kong Bar. Called: July 1983,
Inner Temple, LLB (Sheff)

Loh *Miss Annabelle Li Kien*
Called: July 1997, Middle Temple, LLB
(Hons)(Lond)

Loh *Benjamin Tse Min*
Called: July 1996, Middle Temple, LLB
(Hons)(Hull)

Loh *Miss Christina Huey Shya*
Called: July 1997, Lincoln's Inn, LLB
(Hons)(Leeds)

Loh *Miss Jennifer May Ying*
Called: July 1996, Lincoln's Inn, LLB
(Hons)(Cardiff)

Loh *Miss Julia Su Khoon*
Called: Oct 1991, Gray's Inn, BA (Oxon)

Loh *Lik Peng*
Called: July 1997, Middle Temple, LLB
(Hons)(Sheff)

Loh *Ms Lynette Moon Lan*
Called: Nov 1997, Inner Temple, LLB (Leics)

Loh *Miss May*
Justices' Law Clerk, Supreme Court, St
Andrew's Road, (65) 332 4026, Fax: (65)
337 9450, and Member Singapore Bar.
Called: July 1996, Middle Temple, LLB
(Hons)(Kent)

Loh *Miss Melissa Yuet Meng*
Called: Nov 1997, Lincoln's Inn, LLB (Hons)

Loh *Miss Mui Leng*
Called: Nov 1993, Gray's Inn, LLB

Loh *Nigel Lin Kwang*
Called: July 1995, Middle Temple, LLB
(Hons) (Leic)

Loh *Shu Hon*
Called: July 1993, Middle Temple, LLB
(Hons)

Loh *Miss Siau Joe*
Called: July 1996, Gray's Inn, LLB (West of
England

Loh *Wei Leong*
Called: Nov 1996, Gray's Inn, LLB (L'pool),
LLM (Lond)

Loh *Ms Yee Mun*
Called: July 1994, Lincoln's Inn, LLB (Hons,
Warw), LLM (Warw)

Loh *Ms Yun Ping*
Graduate Trainee in DCB Bank. Called: July
1995, Gray's Inn, B.Soc.Sci (Keele)

Loi *Dhillon Chia Wei*
Fax: 065 280 4930. Called: July 1996,
Lincoln's Inn, LLB (Hons)

Loi *Miss Laurel Thanh Moi*
Called: July 1994, Lincoln's Inn, BA (Hons,
Keele)

Loi *Miss Lay Hong*
Called: Nov 1992, Gray's Inn, LLB (Lond)

Loizides *Miss Vicky*
The Chanteclair House, 2 Sophoulis Street,
P.O.Box 1646, Nicosia, Cyprus, (357) (2)
444391, Fax: (357) (2) 451620, and Member
Cyprus Bar. Called: Nov 1993, Gray's Inn,
LLB (Bris)

Loke *Adrian Weng Hong*
Legal Assistant, Messrs Rodyk & Davidson, 9
Raffles Place, Republic Plaza, [H]55-01 &
[H]56-01, 225 2626, Fax: 225 1838.
Called: July 1995, Middle Temple, LLB
(Hons)

Loke *Miss Moon Cee*
Called: July 1997, Lincoln's Inn, LLB
(Hons)(Manch)

Loke *Siew Meng*
Partner, 42 Everton Road [H]17-02, Asia
Gardens, Singapore 0208, 2204980, Fax:
5364748, and Member Singapore Bar.
Called: Nov 1990, Lincoln's Inn, LLB (Lond),
AIBA, LLM (Lond), CDAF, B.Sc (Est Man)
Hons, (S'pore)

Lomax Ian Stuart
Clerk to the Justices/ Justices' Chief
Executive, City Magistrate'sCourt, Crown
Square, Manchester M60 1PR, 0161 832
7272, Fax: 061 834 2198. Called: May 1977,
Gray's Inn, MSoc.Sc., LLB, FIMgt, MIPD

Loming James Ih-wuen
No 37 (1st Floor), BDA- Shahida Centre,
Abang Galau Road, 97000 Bintulu, Sarawak,
086 331991, Fax: 086 338339, and Member
Sabah Bar Sarawak Bar. Called: Oct 1992,
Middle Temple, LL.B (Hons)

Londors Mrs Wendy Pamela
Legal Adviser, Hambro Legal Protection,
Hambro House, Stephenson Road,
Colchester CO4 4QR, 0990 234500, Fax:
0990 234508. Called: Feb 1994, Lincoln's
Inn, LLB (Hons)

Loney Keith Edward
Called: Nov 1972, Lincoln's Inn, LLB, FCA,
LLM (Lond)

Long Miss Lorinda Joanne ●
International Finance & Legal, Dept, Banque
Paribasl Markets, 10 Harewood Avenue,
London NW1 6AA, 0171 595 2438, Fax:
0171 595 5094. Called: Nov 1988, Middle
Temple, Dip in PET Law

Long Miss Lynette Li-Shen
Called: July 1994, Middle Temple, LLB
(Hons)(Bris)

Long Mervyn Tan Chye
Called: July 1994, Inner Temple, LLB (Lond)

Long Patrick
United Nations Consultant Fellow of Irish
Institute of Secretaries (FIIS), Law Library,
Four Courts, Dublin 7, Ireland, 8214397,
Fax: 8215297, Barrister of King's Inn.
Called: Nov 1994, Middle Temple, Dip Law

Longley His Honour Judge
District Judge's Chambers, Wan Chai Law
Courts, Wan Chai Tower 1, 12 Harbour
Road, 2582 4425, Fax: 2824 1641, and
Member Hong Kong Bar. Called: Nov 1970,
Lincoln's Inn, MA (Oxon)

Lonie Miss Anne Morag
Account Manager, J Walter Thompson, 40
Berkley Square, London W1X 6AD, 0171
499 4040. Called: Nov 1994, Gray's Inn, LLB

Loo Miss Bernice Ming Nee
and Member Singapore Bar. Called: July
1995, Lincoln's Inn, LLB (Hons)

Loo Miss Ee-Ling
Called: July 1997, Lincoln's Inn, LLB (Hons)

Loo Miss Hwee Fang
Called: July 1997, Gray's Inn, LLB (Sheff)

Loo Miss Josephine Yi
Sole Proprieter; M/S Josephine Loo & Co,
1606 Bayshore Park, Pearl Tower, Bayshore
Road, Singapore 1646, 4486114
(Residence), and Member Singapore Bar.
Called: July 1994, Lincoln's Inn, LLB (Hons)

Loo Miss Peggy Chee Hoon
and Member Malaysia Bar. Called: Nov 1990,
Gray's Inn, LLB (Lond)

Loo Miss Peh Fern
Called: Nov 1997, Lincoln's Inn, LLB
(Hons)(Warw)

Looi Miss Lai Kiew
Link Tower 1, Unit 11-03, The Bayshore, 24
Bayshore Road, 2778483, Fax: 2763774.
Called: July 1994, Middle Temple, LLB
(Hons)(Lond)

Looker Roger Frank William
Director, Rea Brothers ltd Chairman, RPS
Plc Member Financial Reporting Review
Panel, Norwood Farmhouse, Cobham,
Surrey KT11 1BS, 01932 862531.
Called: Feb 1978, Lincoln's Inn, LLB

Loong Gee Yung
Assistant to the Head of Legal Affairs.,
Finance & Leasing Association, Upper
Grosvenor Street, London W1X 9PB.
Called: July 1992, Inner Temple, LLB (Manc)

Lopez Carlos Ramon
Called: Nov 1995, Lincoln's Inn, BA (Hons)

Lord Nicholas Jeffrey
Deputy Clerk to the Justices, Cornwall
Magistrates', Courts Committee, Justices'
Clerks' Office, County Hall, Truro TR1 3HQ,
01872 74075, Fax: 01872 76227. Called: Feb
1986, Gray's Inn, Dip Law

Lothian Miss Lisa Amanda ●
Tax Accountant, Coopers & Lybrand,
Central Business Exchange, Midsummer
Boulevard, Central Milton Keynes MK9 2DF,
01908 690064. Called: Oct 1997, Lincoln's
Inn, LLB (Hons)(Keele)

Loughlin Ms Paula Mary
Called: Nov 1988, Lincoln's Inn, LLB Hons
(Lond), LLM (Lond)

Loughrey James Terence John ●
Legal Adviser, Siemens Group Services
Limited, Siemens House, Oldbury, Bracknell,
Berkshire RG12 8FZ, 01344 396104.
Called: July 1979, Inner Temple, LLB (Hull)

Lourdesamy Gerard Samuel Vijayan
No 546 Jalan 17/15, 46400 Petaling Jaya,
Selangor, and Member Malaysia Bar.
Called: July 1992, Lincoln's Inn, LLB (Hons)
(Leeds)

Loustau-Lalanne Bernard Michel
and Member Member Seychelles Bar.
Called: July 1969, Middle Temple

Love Miss Deborah Jane
Called: Nov 1995, Gray's Inn, LLB (Manch)

Love Miss Kathy Lee ●
Senior Legal Adviser, Shell International
B.V., LSOP/1 Postbus 162, NL-2501 AN The
Hague, 00 31 70 377 47 96, Fax: 00 31 70
377 67 90, and Member California, US
Federal. Called: Nov 1977, Gray's Inn, BA,
LLM [Cantab]

Lovell Harold Earl Edmund
P O Box 20, 29 Redcliffe Street, St John's,
268 462 1136, Fax: 268 462 8980, and
Member Antigua Bar Monserrat Bar Barbuda
Bar. Called: July 1987, Middle Temple, BA
(W.Indies), LLB, M.Jur (B'ham)

Lovett Miss Linda Marie ●
Area Lawyer, D.S.S., Office of the Solicitor,
Warwick House, Wade Lane, Leeds, 0113
220 7221, Fax: 0113 244 4435. Called: Nov
1994, Inner Temple, LLB (Westminster)

Low Miss Anisah Suyuti
Called: July 1995, Lincoln's Inn, LLB (Hons)

Low Mrs Cheng Mooi ●
Senior Crown Prosecutor. Called: Nov 1990,
Lincoln's Inn, LLB (Buck'ham)

Low Dr Cheng Teong
Oral Surgeon, 111 Taman Sia Her Yam,
85000 Segamat Johor, 07 931 2042, Fax: 07
931 2042. Called: Nov 1996, Lincoln's Inn,
LLB (Hons)(Lond), BDS (Singapore)

Low Miss Chi Cheng
Advocate & Solicitor, Lim Kian Leong & Co,
Suite 1802 18th Floor, Wisma Hamzah-
Kwong Hing, No 1 Leboh Ampang, 50100
Kuala Lumpur, 2301440, 2301441, Fax:
2388039, and Member Malaysia Bar.
Called: July 1991, Middle Temple, LLB
(Hons) (Leics)

Low Chwan Yiing Dennis
Called: Nov 1996, Lincoln's Inn, LLB
(Nott'm)

Low Denis Kheng Yin
Called: Nov 1997, Middle Temple, LLB
(Hons)

Low Miss Geok Ping
Called: July 1997, Lincoln's Inn, LLB (Hons)

Low Hun Kiat
Legal Executive, Olympic Industries Bhd,
Level 23,Plaza Raja Chulan, No 8 Jlan Raja
Chulan, 50200 Kuala Lumpur, 03 2323993,
Fax: 03 2323996, Bar Council Malaysia
(Advocate & Solicitor of High Court of
Malaya). Called: July 1995, Middle Temple,
LLB (Hons)

Low Jeng Kiat Timothy Aeron
Called: July 1996, Middle Temple, LLB
(Hons)(Wolves)

Low Keng Siong
Called: Nov 1997, Lincoln's Inn, LLB
(Hons)(Lond)

Low Miss Lynette
Legal Assistant, c/o M/S Allen & Gledhill,
[H] 18-01 City House, 36 Robinson Road,
Singapore, (65) 4207964, Fax: (65)
2254950/2250062, and Member Singapore
Bar. Called: Nov 1993, Middle Temple, LLB
(Hons)

Low Miss Peck Yin
Called: July 1996, Lincoln's Inn, LLB (Hons)

Low Miss Peng Peng
Called: July 1996, Lincoln's Inn, LLB
(Hons)(Wales)

Low Ms Polly Ann ●
Principal Lawyer, Islington Council, Chief
Executive's Department, Town Hall, Upper
Street, London N1 2UD, 0171 477 1234,
Fax: 0171 477 3243. Called: Nov 1990,
Middle Temple, LLB (Cardiff)

Low *Reginald Heng Chuan*
Called: Nov 1997, Middle Temple, LLB
(Hons)(Leics)

Low *Tak Fatt*
Called: Oct 1994, Gray's Inn, LLB (Warw)

Low *Wan Kwong*
Block 157, BT Batok Street 11, [H]01-200,
561 6334, Fax: 561 6334. Called: Nov 1996,
Middle Temple, LLB (Hons)

Low *Miss Wee Jee*
Called: July 1995, Lincoln's Inn, LLB (Hons)

Low *Willin*
Called: July 1997, Gray's Inn, LLB (Notts)

Lowans *Benjamin Anthony*
Called: Mar 1997, Gray's Inn, LLB (Sheff)

Lowdon *Christopher Ian*
Called: Oct 1994, Lincoln's Inn, LLB
(Hons)(Plymouth)

Lowe *Mrs Jane*
Legal Adviser, Basingstoke Magistrates
Court, Court House, London Street,
Basingstoke, 01252 366000. Called: Oct
1992, Gray's Inn, BA (Kent)

Lowe *Professor Nigel Vaughan*
St John's Chambers, Small Street, Bristol,
BS1 1DW. Called: Nov 1972, Inner Temple,
LLB

Lowe *Philip Raymond* •
Senior Crown Prosecutor, Crown
Prosecution Service, Mayfield House,
Mayfield Drive, London Road, Shrewsbury
SY2 6PE, 01743 235726, Fax: 01743
240455. Called: July 1986, Middle Temple,
LLB Wolverhampton

Lowe *Roger*
15 Winckley Square, Preston, PR1 3JJ.
Called: July 1984, Inner Temple, LLB (Sheff)

Lowndes *Miss Joanna Bridin*
Called: Mar 1997, Gray's Inn, BA (Manch)

Lowndes *Ms Melanie Louise Anne* •
World Service Lawyer, BBC World Service
Legal Dept, Bush House, G21 NW, P O Box
76, Strand, London WC2B 4PH, 0171 557
2697, Fax: 0171 240 6254. Called: July
1988, Inner Temple, BA (Sussex)

Lowndes *William David* •
Goldman Sachs International, Limited, 140
Fleet Street, London EC4A 2BJ, 0171 774
5018, Fax: 0171 774 1475. Called: July
1985, Middle Temple, BA (Lond)

Lowther *Ms Joanna Clayre*
Patent & Trade Mark Agent, W. H. Beck
Greener & Co, 7 Stone Buildings, Lincoln's
Inn, London WC2A 3SZ, 0171 405 0921.
Called: July 1996, Lincoln's Inn, BSc
(Hons)(Lond), ARCS, Dip in Law, Cert of,
Intellectual, Property.

Lowy *Mrs Julienne Katrine*
24 Old Bldgs, Ground Floor, Lincoln's Inn,
London, WC2A 3UJ. Called: July 1986,
Middle Temple, BA (Oxon) Dip Law, (City)

Loyal *Miss Jasbir* •
Director of Legal/HR Services, PPP/
Columbia Healthcare Ltd, Wellington Place,
London NW8 9L8, 0171 586 5959, Fax:
0171 483 5151. Called: July 1984, Inner
Temple, LLB, LLM

Loynes *Mrs Kate Julia* •
Lawyer (Legal Services, Social Services
Team), Kent County Council, Countyhall,
Maidstone, Kent ME14 1XQ, 01622 694413.
Called: Oct 1994, Lincoln's Inn, LLB (Hons)

Lu *Miss Su Lian*
Called: July 1996, Middle Temple, BA
(Hons)(Cantab)

Lubin *Dean Jonathon*
Called: Oct 1994, Gray's Inn, BA

Lucey *John Joseph*
Called: May 1996, Middle Temple, BCL
(Cork), LLM, (Cork), BL (King's, Inn)

Luck *John Michael*
Called: Mar 1998, Gray's Inn, LLB
(Kingston), LLM

Luckham *Kai Anthony*
Teacher of Law, Shena Simon College,
Whitworth Street, Manchester M1 3HB,
0161 236 3418. Called: Nov 1991, Inner
Temple, LLB

Lugar-Mawson *His Hon Judge Gareth
John*
Deputy Chairman, Town Planning Appeal
Board (Hong Kong) Honorary Lecturer in
the Department of Professional Legal
Education, University of Hong Kong &
Consultant to the Faculty of Law in
Advocacy, High Court, 38 Queensway, 852
2825 4316, Fax: 852 2869 0640, Former
Solicitor (England & Wales and Hong Kong
Judge of the District Court of Hong Kong
and Deputy Judge of the High Court of
Hong Kong and Member Hong Kong Bar.
Called: July 1985, Middle Temple, LLB
(Lond), FCIArb

Lui *Simon Kin Man*
Called: Nov 1997, Gray's Inn, BSc (Hong
Kong)

Luis *Gerard Andrew*
Senior Legal Executive, Measat Broadcast
Network Syst., All Asia Broadcast Centre,
Technology Park Malaysia, Lebuhraya
Puchong - SG BESI, 57000 Kuala Lumpur, 60
3 583 6688, Fax: 60 3 583 6875, Advocate
& Solicitor (Malaysia). Called: July 1991,
Lincoln's Inn, LLB (Hons) (Lond), LLM
(Lond)

Luk *King Yip*
Called: Nov 1997, Middle Temple, BS.Sc
(Hons)(Hong, Kong)

Lum *Miss May Lee Chan*
10 Kensington Park Drive, [H]18-03,
2857352. Called: July 1995, Middle Temple,
BA (Hons)(Keele)

Lumb *Keith Simon Martin* •
Crown Prosecutor, Crown Prosecution
Service, 3rd Floor, Beaumont House,
Cliftonville, Northampton NN1 5BE.
Called: Nov 1979, Gray's Inn

Lumm *David*
Assistant Deputy Justices' Clerk, Magistrates'
Courts Brent, Church End, 448 High Road,
London NW10 2DZ, 0181 451 7111, Fax:
0181 451 2040. Called: Nov 1987, Gray's
Inn

Lung *Dr Francois Ka-Kui*
Director. Called: Nov 1992, Inner Temple,
Bsc (Hong Kong), DPhil (Leeds),Master, in
Mgtmt, LLB (Lond)

Lunn *Miss Christine Nicola*
Court Clerk, Wimbledon Magistrates' Court,
The Law Courts, Alexandra Road,
Wimbledon, London SW19 7JP, 0181 946
8622. Called: Nov 1992, Lincoln's Inn, LLB
(Hons)

Lunn *Christopher Simon* •
Specialist Derivatives Lawyer, J.P.Morgan
Securities Limited, P.O.Box 161, 60 Victoria
Embankment, London EC4Y 0JP, 0171 325
4384, Fax: 0171 325 8205. Called: Nov
1995, Gray's Inn, LLB (Lond)

Lunt *Mark Antony* •
Senior Crown Prosecutor, Crown
Prosecution Service, (Staffordshire &
Warwickshire), Newbold Terrace,
Leamington Spa, Warwickshire, 01926
450131. Called: Nov 1984, Inner Temple,
LLB (Manchester)

Lunzer *Raphael Alan*
19 Old Buildings, Lincoln's Inn, London,
WC2A 3UP. Called: Feb 1962, Inner Temple,
BSc (Lond)

Lupton *Charles Stephen Douglas* •
Vice President, Legal Services, AGCO Ltd,
P.O.Box 62, Banner Lane, Coventry
CV4 9GF, 01203 531285, Fax: 01203
531398. Called: July 1970, Gray's Inn, LLB

Luthi *Charles Christian Rolf*
Secretary, Chartered Institute of Arbitrators
Bermuda Branch, c/o Conyers, Dill &
Pearman, Clarendon House, Church Street,
Hamilton, Bermuda, (441) 295 1422, Fax:
(441) 295 4720, and Member Bermuda.
Called: Feb 1993, Middle Temple, BA
(Hons)(Oxon)

Lutter *Mrs Susan*
Deputy Clerk to the Justices, Chief
Executive & Clerk to MCC, Berkeley House,
Walton Street, Aylesbury, Bucks HP21 7QG,
01296 383058, Fax: 01296 383436.
Called: July 1978, Gray's Inn, LLB, DMS

Luttrell *Dr Steven Richard Rankin*
Church Cottage, Grovely Wood, Great
Wishford, Salisbury, Wiltshire SP3 4SQ.
Called: Oct 1992, Lincoln's Inn, MB ChB
BSc(Glas), Dip Law, MRCP

Lycourgou *Miss Olive*
Called: July 1997, Gray's Inn, LLB (Middx)

Lydiate *Peter William Henry*
Clerk to the Justices, Magistrates Courts
Brent, Church End, 448 High Road, London
NW10 2DZ, 0181 451 7111, Fax: 0181 451
2040. Called: July 1974, Middle Temple, LLB

Lynch *Bernard Gerard*
Project Manager, B und P, Bavcoordination
UND, Projektsteuerung GMBH, Hauptstrasse
24, 48712 Gescher, Germany, 02542 5099.
Called: Nov 1995, Lincoln's Inn, LLB
(Hons)(Lond)

Lynch *Michael John*
Lecturer and Researcher, 9 Suckling Green
Lane, Codsall, Wolverhampton WV8 2BL,
01902 843471, Fax: 01902 843471.
Called: Nov 1994, Middle Temple, MA, LLB

Lynch *Miss Selena Ruth*
Full-time Coroner, Former Solicitor.
Called: May 1992, Middle Temple

Lyne *Godfrey John* •
Assistant Parliamentary Counsel, Office of
the Parliamentary, Counsel, 36 Whitehall,
London SW1A 2AY, 0171 210 6626, Fax:
0171 210 6632. Called: July 1987, Middle
Temple, MA (Cantab)

Lyon *Mrs Jacqueline Anne* •
Called: Feb 1988, Inner Temple, LLB (Hons)

Lyons *Mrs Anne Rebecca JP*
27 Manor Crescent, Surbiton, Surrey
KT5 8LG, 0181 399 1452. Called: June
1964, Gray's Inn, LLB

Lyons *Mrs Ruth* •
Lawyer Grade 6, Dept of Trade & Industry,
10-18 Victoria Street, London SW1, 0171
215 3523. Called: Nov 1981, Middle Temple

Lyster *Miss Grania Mary*
Called: Nov 1992, Inner Temple, MA
(Cantab), Dip Law

Lythgoe *Stuart Graham Silvester* •
Called: July 1982, Gray's Inn, LLB (Bristol)

M'Bai *Ousman*
Called: Oct 1996, Lincoln's Inn, LLB
(Hons)(Leeds)

Ma *Geoffrey Tao-Li*
Temple Chambers, Unit 1607-1612, One
Pacific Place, 88 Queensway, 5-2 32003,
Fax: 5-8 100302, and Member Hong Kong
Bar Brick Court Chambers, 15/19 Devereux
Court, London, WC2A 3JJ. Called: July 1978,
Gray's Inn, LLB(Birmingham)

Ma *Miss Pin Yen*
Called: Nov 1997, Lincoln's Inn, LLB
(Hons)(Leeds)

Ma *Dr Siu Yung Alan*
Odebrecht - SLP Engineering, c/o Tenenge
(UK) Holdings Ltd, 197 Knightsbridge,
London SW7 1RB, 0171 225 3393, Fax:
0171 225 3133. Called: Nov 1993, Lincoln's
Inn, BSc (Hons, Warw), PhD (Warw), CEng,
MICE, MBCS, FCIArb

Maarof *Miss Norzaimah*
Called: Nov 1993, Inner Temple, LLB
(So'ton)

MacArthur *Ian Stewart*
Called: Nov 1995, Inner Temple, B.Acc
(Glasgow), CPE (Lond)

Macaulay *Neil David* •
Prininpal Legal Officer, 0171 865 5044,
Fax: 0171 865 4875. Called: Nov 1990,
Lincoln's Inn, LLB

Macaulay *Roderick Hugh Russell* •
Senior Crown Prosecutor, Crown
Prosecution Service, Headquarters, 50
Ludgate Hill, London EC4. Called: July 1989,
Inner Temple, BA, Dip Law

MacCormick *Prof Donald Neil FBA
FRSE*
Regius Professor of Public Law, Littleton
Chambers, 3 King's Bench Walk North,
Temple, London, EC4Y 7HR. Called: July
1971, Inner Temple, Jur Dr Lc (Uppsala),
LLD (Edinburgh), MA, (Oxon), MA
(Glasgow)

MacCrindle *Robert Alexander QC*
(1963)
and Member Hong Kong Bar Essex Court
Chambers, 24 Lincoln's Inn Fields, London,
WC2A 3ED. Called: Feb 1952, Gray's Inn,
LLB (Cantab) LLB, (Lond)

MacCrone *Miss Roberta*
Clerk to the Justices, The Law Courts,
Castle Hill Avenue, Folkestone, Kent
CT20 2DH, 01303 851371, Fax: 01303
220512. Called: Nov 1975, Inner Temple,
LLB

MacDaid *Miss Moira Majella*
Called: July 1985, Gray's Inn, BA (Hons)

MacDiarmid *Ross*
Senior Relationship Manager, ING Bank, 15
Kiseleff Boulevard, Sector 1, Bucharest, 00
401 222 1600, Fax: 00 401 222 1401.
Called: Nov 1982, Inner Temple, BSc
(Reading) Hons, ARICS, Dip Law

Macdonald *Alasdair Neil Gray*
Called: Oct 1994, Gray's Inn, BA (Cantab)

Macdonald *Donald Gordon*
Called: Oct 1995, Lincoln's Inn, BA
(Hons)(Lond)

Macdonald *Duncan Hamish*
8 Horse barrack Lane, 00 350 50254/(Spain)
00 34 52 838806, and Member Gibraltar
Bar, St Helena. Called: Oct 1992, Middle
Temple, LL.B (Hons)

Macdonald *Miss Morag CBE*
Company Secretary, Ardshiel, Gwydyr Road,
Crief, Perthshire PH7 4BS. Called: July 1974,
Inner Temple, LLB (Hons), BA

Macdonald *Miss Patricia Margaret
Jean*
Thomas More Chambers, 52 Carey Street,
Lincoln's Inn, London, WC2A 2JB.
Called: Nov 1979, Inner Temple, LLB (Hull)

Macdonald *Roderick Francis*
QC of Scotland and Member Scotland.
Called: July 1997, Inner Temple, LLB
(Glasgow)

MacDonald *Ms Sarah Jane*
Called: Nov 1994, Inner Temple, BA (Lond),
CPE (Lond)

Mace *Andrew James*
Called: Oct 1997, Lincoln's Inn, LLB
(Hons)(Wales)

Machado *Miss Thushani Vincentia
Michele*
Called: Nov 1997, Lincoln's Inn, LLB (Lond)

Maciejowski *Mrs Mara Georgina* •
Senior Crown Prosecutor. Called: Nov 1990,
Inner Temple, BA, MA (Lond)

Maciel *Miss Kareena*
Called: July 1994, Lincoln's Inn, LLB (Hons)

MacInnes *Colin Charles* •
Senior Crown Prosecutor, Crown
Prosecution Service, County House, New
London Road, Chelmsford, Essex.
Called: Nov 1989, Inner Temple, LLB

MacIver *Anthony Digby Duffus*
Faculty of Advocates, Advocates Library,
Parliament House, Edinburgh EH1 1RF,
0131 226 2881, Fax: 0131 225 3642,
Standing Junior Counsel for Scottish
Charities Office and Member Scottish Bar.
Called: Apr 1991, Lincoln's Inn, LLB (Hons)
(Edin)

Mackelvie Jutsum *Miss Jane
Margaret Louise*
47 Moreton Place, London SW1V 2NL, 0171
821 6410. Called: Oct 1995, Gray's Inn, B.Sc
(Wales), MSc (Lond), DIC, Dip Law, FGS

Mackender *Richard Philip*
Called: Oct 1997, Gray's Inn, LLB (Wales)

MacKenzie *Miss Cailin Catriona
Elizabeth*
Called: Nov 1992, Lincoln's Inn, LLB
(Hons)(Lond), Maitrise (Paris)

MacKenzie *Miss Catherine Patricia*
Commonwealth Scholar & Lecturer in Law,
Australian National University, Faculty of
Law, Australian National University,
Canberra ACT 0200, 612 6279 8446/6249
3482, Fax: 612 6249 0103, Solicitor of ACT
and Member State Bars of Queensland, New
South Wales, Australian Capital Territories,
High Court of Australia. Called: May 1995,
Inner Temple, BA, MA, Dip Law

MacKenzie *Miss Judith-Anne* •
Legal Adviser, Legal Services Directorate,
Dept of Trade & Industry, 10 Victoria
Street, London SW1H 0NN, 0171 215 3268,
Fax: 0171 215 3271. Called: July 1987,
Lincoln's Inn, LLB, LLM (Univ Lond), AKC

Mackenzie *Robert Sutherland*
308 Windsor Road, Oldham, Lancashire
OL8 4HA, 0161 624 2698. Called: Mar 1996,
Gray's Inn, BA (Hons)(U.C.L.), M.S.I. (Dip)

Mackenzie of Mornish *Captain John
Hugh Munro*
President of SEET plc, Mortlake Hse,
Vicarage Rd, London SW14 8RU, 0171 580
7557, Fax: 0181 878 1065, Harmsworth
Law. Called: June 1950, Middle Temple, MA
(Hons, Oxon), FRSA, CBIM

MacKenzie Ross *David*
113-114 New Henry House 11/F, 10 Ice
House Street, Central, 852 877 0087, Fax:
852 524 6202, and Member Hong Kong,
SAR China Victoria (Australia). Called: Nov
1962, Gray's Inn, MA (Cantab)

Mackenzie-Williams *Barry James George*
"Wenlock Edge", 6 Earlsdon Road, St Johns, Worcester WR2 4PF, 01905 748 018. Called: Feb 1994, Inner Temple, BA, MA (Cantab), CEng, MIEE

Mackesy *Ms Tertia Elizabeth* •
Crown Prosecutor, Crown Prosecution Service, The Cooperage, Gainsford Street, London SE1 2NG, 0171 962 2784, Fax: 0171 962 0902. Called: Nov 1993, Inner Temple, BA, CPE (City)

Mackey *Miss Sarah Margaret*
Called: Oct 1997, Lincoln's Inn, BA (Hons)

Mackiggan *Keith Sinclair*
Called: Oct 1996, Lincoln's Inn, BA (Hons)(Cantab)

Mackley *David John*
Called: Oct 1997, Lincoln's Inn, BA (Hons)(Wales)

Maclean *Andrew Donald*
Called: Nov 1995, Inner Temple, LLB (B'ham), M.St (Oxon)

MacLennan *Ms Alison*
Called: Nov 1996, Gray's Inn, LLB (Reading)

Maclennan *John Gordon*
Called: Oct 1995, Lincoln's Inn, LLB (Hons)(Newc)

Maclennan *The Rt Hon Robert Adam Ross DC MP*
House of Commons, London SW1A OAA, 0171 219 6553, Fax: 0171 219 4846. Called: May 1962, Gray's Inn, MA (Oxon), LLB (Cantab)

Macleod *Francis Roderick* •
Chief Executive, Foundation, 55/57 Owen Street, Hereford HR1 2JQ, 01432 264777, Fax: 01432 264888. Called: Nov 1978, Inner Temple, MA (Oxon)

MacNamara *Miss Jillian* •
Principal Crown Prosecutor, CPS Brent Harrow Uxbridge Bch, 3rd Floor, Kings House, Kymberley Road, Harrow, Middlesex HA1 1YH, 0181 424 8688. Called: Feb 1987, Gray's Inn, LLB (Nott)

Macnaughton *Alistair David* •
Director, Legal Services & Company Secretary, Hill Samuel Life Assurance Ltd, NLA Tower, 12-16 Addiscombe Road, Croydon CR9 6BP, 0181 662 3266. Called: Nov 1986, Middle Temple, BSc (Wales), MA

Macrae *Mrs Anne Glover*
Called: Nov 1989, Inner Temple, B.Arch (Glas), Dip Law (City), R.I.B.A, ACIArb

Maddan *Archie Gracie* •
London Borough of Enfield. Called: Nov 1993, Gray's Inn, BA (Dunelm)

Madhani *Mohamed Ali Kassamali*
Mohamed Madhani & Co Advocates, P O Box 48539, Nairobi, Kenya, 254 2 228255/229233, Fax: 254 2 230896, and Member Kenya. Called: July 1980, Lincoln's Inn, LLB, FCII

Madhub *Oomeshwarnath Beny*
Called: July 1991, Middle Temple, LLB (Hons) (Warw)

Madigan *Mrs Patricia Josephine*
Barrister of Ireland. Called: Nov 1995, Middle Temple, BL (King's Inn)

Madnani *Ms Veena*
Called: Nov 1980, Lincoln's Inn, MA (Bus.Law)

Magee *Miss Rosemary*
Called: May 1997, Lincoln's Inn, BA (Hons)

Magennis *Bernard James Joseph*
Rossglass, Downpatrick, Co Down, 01396 842082, and Member Southern Ireland Bar. Called: Oct 1994, Middle Temple, BA, BL

Maggs *Ian Lorne*
Appt 1, 28 Campard Grove, Stoke Newington, London N16 0XB, 0181 442 4458. Called: Nov 1996, Inner Temple, BSc (York), Dip Law (City)

Maggs *Stuart Peter*
Called: May 1997, Lincoln's Inn, LLB (Hons)(Lond)

Magill *Kevin Diarmuid*
Called: Oct 1995, Gray's Inn, BA (Kent)

Magimay *Miss Anita Shoba*
and Member Malaysian Bar. Called: July 1996, Lincoln's Inn, LLB (Hons)

Magne *Dominic Loic Christopher*
Called: Mar 1996, Gray's Inn, BA

Maguire *Dermot Gerard*
Called: Nov 1995, Gray's Inn, BSc, LLB

Maguire *Miss Lindsay Jane* •
County Secretary's Dept(Legal), West Sussex County Council, County Hall, Chichester, West Sussex PO19 1RH. Called: Nov 1981, Gray's Inn, BA (Hons)

Maguire *Patrick Robert*
M H Cockell & Ptnrs, Room 776, Lloyds, Lime Street, London EC3M 7DQ, 0171 327 3487, Fax: 01284 789 509. Called: July 1973, Inner Temple, MA (Cantab), FCII

Maguire *Richmond Edmund*
Called: Nov 1978, Inner Temple, BA

Magyar *Nicholas* •
Legal Adviser, The Treasury Solicitor, Queen Anne's Chambers, 28 Broadway, London SW1H 9JS. Called: July 1986, Inner Temple, LLB (So'ton)

Mah *Miss Catherine Siok Hean*
Called: July 1988, Gray's Inn, LLB (Bristol)

Mah *Cheong Fatt*
Called: July 1997, Middle Temple, LLB (Hons)(Lond)

Mahan *Anil Kumar*
Called: Nov 1992, Inner Temple, LLB (B'ham)

Maharaj *Miss Lou-Ann*
Called: Nov 1991, Gray's Inn, LLB (W Indies), LLM

Maharaj *Miss Saveeta*
Called: Oct 1993, Inner Temple, BA, LLM

Mahatantila *Duleep Rohan*
Executive, Development Finance Corporation of Ceylon. Called: Nov 1988, Middle Temple, BA, Dip Law

Mahendra *Dr Bala*
37 Jessel House, Judd Street, London WC1H 9NU, 0171 833 8321, Fax: 0171 833 8321. Called: Oct 1993, Gray's Inn, LLB (Lond)

Mahendran *Miss Jyeshta*
Called: Nov 1995, Lincoln's Inn, BSc (Hons)(Keele)

Mahendran *Miss Sonia*
Called: July 1995, Middle Temple, LLB (Hons)(Warw)

Mahmood *Asad*
Called: Mar 1996, Lincoln's Inn, LLB (Hons)

Mahmood *Mario Bin*
Called: Nov 1996, Middle Temple, LLB (Hons)

Mahmood *Miss Samira*
Called: Nov 1995, Lincoln's Inn, LLB (Hons)

Mahmood *Shiraz*
Called: Nov 1992, Middle Temple, BA (Hons, Herts)

Mahmud *Miss Ishrat*
Called: Mar 1997, Lincoln's Inn, LLB (Hons)

Mahmud *Ms Sahia*
Called: July 1996, Lincoln's Inn

Mahomed *Ismail*
Doughty Street Chambers, 11 Doughty Street, London, WC1N 2PG. Called: July 1984, Gray's Inn

Mahoney *Paul John* •
Deputy Registrar, European Court of Human Rights, Council of Europe, 67 075 Strasbourg Cedex, 03 88 41 23 93, Fax: 03 88 41 27 91. Called: Nov 1971, Inner Temple, MA, LLM

Mahoney *Miss Sarah Ann*
Called: Oct 1996, Middle Temple, LLB (Hons)(Wales)

Mahy *Ms Helen Margaret*
Group General Counsel & Commercial Manager, Babcock International Group, PLC, Badminton Court, Church Street, Amersham, Bucks HP7 0DD, 01494 727296, Fax: 01494 721909. Called: July 1982, Middle Temple, LLB (Hons) (Manch)

Maiden *Andrew Simon Kelly*
Called: Oct 1996, Middle Temple, LLB (Hons)(Lond)

Maidment *Richard John Haylock*
c/o Clerk B, Owen Dixon Chambers, 205 William Street, Melbourne, Victoria 3000, 039 608 7049, Fax: 039 608 8485, and Member Victorian Bar New South Wales Bar. Called: Nov 1971, Gray's Inn, LLM

Maillis II *Alexander Pericles*
Called: July 1997, Lincoln's Inn, LLB (Hons)(Wales)

E

Main *Ms Angela Patricia*
Texas Instruments Singapore, Legal Department, 990 Bendemeer Road, (65) 390 7627, Fax: (65) 390 7064. Called: July 1997, Lincoln's Inn, BA, MA (Auckland), Dip in Journalism, (Cantab)

Mair *Mrs Margaret Mary Plowden* ●
Lawyer, Dept of Social Security, New Court, Carey Street, London WC2. Called: Nov 1977, Inner Temple, MA (Oxon)

Maitland *Richard John*
Called: Mar 1997, Gray's Inn, LLB (L'pool)

Maitland *Roger Dundas* ●
Senior Legal Assistant, Lord Chancellor's Department, The Law Commission, Conquest House, 37-38 John Street, London WC1N 2BQ. Called: Nov 1965, Gray's Inn

Maizels *Miss Heather Jill*
Barclays Private Bank Limited, Executive Director, Barclays Private Bank Limited, 59 Grosvenor Street, London W1X 9DA, 0171 487 2000, Fax: 0171 487 2042. Called: July 1977, Inner Temple, MA (Cantab)

Majid *Dr Amir Ali*
Part time Immigration Adjudicator Reader in Law Member of the Disability Appeal Tribunal, Dept of Law, London Guildhall University, 84 Moorgate, London EC2M 6SQ, 0171 320 1507, Fax: 0181 925 9577. Called: Nov 1980, Lincoln's Inn, BA, LLB,LLM (Lond), DCL

Majiyagbe *Jonathan Babatunde*
J B Majiyagbe & Co, Barristers Solicitors &, Notaries Public, 4 Human Rights Avenue, P.O.Box 726, Kano, 064 631261/064 644171, Fax: 064 647146, Senior Advocate of Nigeria and Member Nigerian Bar. Called: Nov 1964, Middle Temple, LLB (Lond)

Majumdar *Soumya Kanti* ●
Senior Crown Prosecutor, Crown Prosecution Service, Central Casework, 50 Ludgate Hill, London EC4M 7EX, 0171 273 1310, Fax: 0171 273 1325. Called: Nov 1988, Lincoln's Inn, LLB Hons

Mak *Andrew Yip Shing*
Room 1432, Prince's Building, Central, 25 2 40151, Fax: 28 101731, and Member Hong Kong, Australia, Singapore. Called: July 1988, Lincoln's Inn, BSc, MBA (Hong Kong), LLB, LLM (Lond) ACIS, Dip Dev Studies, (Cantab), ACIArb

Mak *Chi Biu*
Contract Advisor, Flat 3B, Block 29, Greenwood Terrace, 26-28 Sui Wo Road, Sha Tin, Hong Kong, 852 2601 6587, Fax: 852 2577 3562, and Member Hong Kong Bar. Called: Nov 1992, Gray's Inn, BSc (Eng)(Hong Kong), LLB (Lond), MICE, MIStructE, FCIArb

Mak *Miss Mabel Min-Theng*
Called: July 1997, Gray's Inn, LLB (Bris)

Mak *Miss Rosanna Tsui Shan*
Called: Nov 1997, Gray's Inn, LLB (Lond)

Makele *Ibrahim Daniel* ●
Legal Counsel - International, Financial Insurance Group Ltd, Vantage West, Great West Road, Brentford, Middlesex TW8 9AG, 0181 380 3064, Fax: 0181 380 3065. Called: Nov 1992, Inner Temple, BA (Sussex), LLM (Bris)

Makkan *Shamshuddin* ●
Senior Crown Prosecutor, Crown Prosecution Service, Sunlight House, 8th Floor, Quay Street, Manchester M60 3LU, 0161 837 7402/908 2600, Fax: 0161 835 2663. Called: Feb 1987, Lincoln's Inn, LLB Hons

Malaiyandi Chettiar *Kamalarajan*
36 Robinson Road, [H] 18-01 City House, 420 7693, Fax: 224 8210, and Member Singapore Bar. Called: Nov 1995, Middle Temple, LLB (Hons)

Maland *David*
Called: Nov 1986, Gray's Inn, MA(Oxon)

Male *Christopher*
Part time President of Mental Health Review Tribunal., Part Time Chairman Social Security Appeals Tribunal, "Conifers", 34 Morview Road, Widegates, Nr Looe, Cornwall PL13 1QE, (01503) 240525. Called: July 1979, Gray's Inn, DML

Malik *Ahmed Yar*
Called: Nov 1987, Gray's Inn, BA (Keele)

Malik *Ijaz Ahamed* ●
Senior Crown Prosecutor, Crown Prosecution Service, Croydon/Branch Office, Trafalgar House, 2 Bedford Park, Croydon CR0 2AP, 0181 686 6033, Fax: 0181 681 3382. Called: Nov 1982, Gray's Inn, LLB

Malik *Tahir*
and Member Advocate of the Kenyan Bar. Called: June 1951, Gray's Inn, MAE

Malik *Miss Yasmin Munir*
Called: Nov 1993, Lincoln's Inn, LLB (Hons)

Malins *Stephen John*
Deputy Clerk to the Justices, The Court House, Friars Walk, Lewes, East Sussex BN7 2PG, 01273 486455, Fax: 01273 486470. Called: Nov 1981, Middle Temple, LLB(Lond)

Malkin *Captain Henry Charles CBE RN*
West Cottage, Cromer, Norfolk NR27 9EF, 01263 513335. Called: Jan 1950, Inner Temple, MA

Mallett *Laurence Edwin*
Legal Adviser, BP Oil Europe, Legal Department, Les Quatre, Bras, Chaussee de Malines 455, 1950 Kraainem, 32 2 766 3849, Fax: 32 2 766 3828. Called: May 1969, Middle Temple, LLB

Malley *Brian Malcolm* ●
Legal Advisor, Flyde Clerkship, P.O.Box 27, Chapel Street, Blackpool FY1 5RH, 01253 757000, Fax: 01253 757024. Called: May 1983, Gray's Inn

Mallia *Steven Joseph*
Called: Nov 1996, Inner Temple, BA (Nott'm)

Malpass *Roger Ernest* ●
Principal Crown Prosecutor., Crown Prosecution Service, St George's House, Lever Street, Wolverhampton WV2 1EZ, 01384 230471, Fax: 01384 236301. Called: Feb 1983, Middle Temple, BA, Dip Mag Law

Mamun *Abdullah Al*
Admiralty Chambers, Barristers, Advocates &, Notaries, 53 Dit Extension Rd, Naya Paltan, Mothijheel, 834327 (W) 319870 (H), and Member Bangladesh Bar. Called: July 1994, Lincoln's Inn, LLB (Hons), BA (Hons), MA

Mandal *Paritosh*
and Member Southern Ireland Bar. Called: June 1941, Middle Temple

Mandal *Miss Ruma*
Legal Consultant with United Nations High Commission for Refugees, Geneva/London. Called: Oct 1994, Inner Temple, MA (Cantab)

Mander *Ms Verinder Kaur*
Called: Nov 1996, Middle Temple, LLB (Hons)

Manecksha *Ms Ferina Pervez*
Editorial Executive, Computine, IT Publications SDN BHD, Balai Berita Level 2, 31 Jalan Riong, 59000 Kuala Lumpur, 603 282 2022 x 118, Fax: 603 282 0097/8214. Called: July 1995, Inner Temple, LLB (Northumbria)

Mangat *Arvinder Singh*
Called: Nov 1996, Inner Temple, BA (Oxon)

Manickam *Ms Kasturibai*
Called: July 1997, Lincoln's Inn, LLB (Hons)

Manickam *Vengetraman*
34 Jalan Dinding, Lim Garden, 30100 Ipoh, Perak Malaysia, 05 5275305, and Member Malaysia. Called: July 1995, Lincoln's Inn, LLB (Hons)

Mann *Peter* ●
Crown Prosecutor, Crown Prosecution Service, London. Called: July 1986, Middle Temple, LLB (Manch)

Manning *James Robert*
Called: Nov 1993, Gray's Inn, B.Sc (Bris)

Manning *Julian Henry*
Called: Nov 1995, Lincoln's Inn, BSc (Hons)(Manch)

Manning *Mrs Sharon Ann* ●
Deputy Clerk to the Justices, Secretariat Offices, The Court House, London Road, Dorking RG64 1SX. Called: May 1988, Gray's Inn

Mannish *Martin*
Called: July 1996, Lincoln's Inn, BA (Hons)

Mansell *Mrs Deborah Anne*
Technical Advisor to the Institute of Credit Management (Pro Bono). Called: Nov 1994, Middle Temple, BA (Hons), MICM (Grad)

Mansell *Jason Francis Guy* ●
Senior Crown Prosecutor, Crown
Prosecution Service, Central Casework, CPS
National HQ, Ludgate Hill, London, 0171
273 8000. Called: Oct 1991, Lincoln's Inn,
LLB (Hons) (Birm)

Mansfield *The Earl of*
Called: Feb 1958, Inner Temple

Mansfield *Miss Gillian*
Called: Oct 1994, Lincoln's Inn, BA
(Hons)(Warw), CPE (Leeds)

Mansi *Miss Luisa Margaret*
Called: Oct 1997, Lincoln's Inn, LLB
(Hons)(Oxon)

Mansoor *Miss Parveen*
Called: Oct 1996, Inner Temple, LLB
(B'ham)

Mansor *Maritz*
Blk 2, Marina Vista, 04-73, 0065 4487992,
Fax: 0065 2434904. Called: July 1994,
Lincoln's Inn, LLB (Hons)

Maples *John Craddock MP*
Economic Secretary to the Treasury (90/92)
Shadow Secretary of State for Health 97-,
House of Commons, London SW1, 0171 219
5495, Former MP (83/92) MP for Stratford
on Avon 97-. Called: July 1965, Inner
Temple, MA (Cantab)

Mapondera *Miss Dulcie Tsitsi*
Called: Nov 1987, Middle Temple, LLB, LLM
(LSE), MBA (Warwick)

Marballie *Anthony*
Magistrates Clerk, Inner London Magistrates
Court, Horseferry Road, Magistrates Court,
70 Horseferry Road, London SW1P 2AX,
0171 233 2000. Called: Nov 1994, Lincoln's
Inn, LLB (Hons)(Lond)

Marchant *Percy Faredoon*
Ex Local Councillor 1990-94 London
Borough of Merton, 0171 521 2658, Fax:
0171 521 2551, and Member India Bar.
Called: July 1988, Lincoln's Inn, LLB (Hons)
(LSE)

Marcou *Miss Mary-Ann*
Counsel for the Republic of Cyprus,
Attorney General's Attorney Office, Nicosia,
Cyprus, The Law Office of the Republic, of
Cyprus, Apellis Str, Nicosia, and Member
Cyprus Bar. Called: Nov 1993, Gray's Inn,
LLB (Sheff), LLM (Cantab)

Marcus *Miss Michelle*
Called: Nov 1976, Gray's Inn

Marenah *Miss Kirsten Tiyana Clare*
Called: Nov 1997, Middle Temple, LLB
(Hons)(B'ham)

Marett *Dr Warwick Paul*
20 Barrington Road, Stoneygate, Leicester
LE2 2RA, 0116 2703392. Called: July 1993,
Gray's Inn, BA (Bris), BA (CNAA), MA
(Cantab), BScEcon, (Lond), BCom (Lond),
PhD (Lond), ACIArb

Mariappan *Mogan*
Nor'Ain Mogan & Manoharan, 72b Ting 1,
Jalan Melati, 28400 Mentakab, Pahang
Darulmakmur, 09-2782290/2784131, Fax:
09-2782293, and Member Malaysia Bar.
Called: July 1993, Inner Temple, LLB
(Lancs), AFF.A.I.I.

Marican *Abdul Rahim*
Called: May 1996, Lincoln's Inn, LLB (Hons)
(Lond)

Marican *Mrs Bee Bee Sultan*
Called: July 1995, Lincoln's Inn, LLB (Hons)

Marimuthu *Jeeva Kumar*
Called: Nov 1997, Lincoln's Inn, LLB (Hons)

Marimuthu *Miss Meera*
Called: Nov 1997, Lincoln's Inn, LLB
(Hons)(Herts)

Marimuttu *Jeyan T M*
Messrs Teo Marimuttu & Ptnrs, P O Box No
10869, 88809 Kota Kinabalu, Sabah,
Malaysia, 088 252997/252998, Fax: 088
252889, and Member Malaysia Bar.
Called: Nov 1992, Gray's Inn, LLB
(Buckingham), MI Mgt

Markar *Mrs Fathima Faiza*
Called: Mar 1998, Lincoln's Inn, LLB (Lond)

Markey *Ms Anne King*
Called: July 1995, Inner Temple, LLB

Markey *Miss Eileen Elizabeth*
Called: Nov 1994, Lincoln's Inn, LLB
(Hons)(Warw)

Markey *Mrs Mo Lan Maureen*
"The Limes", High Street, Broadwinsor,
Beaminster, Dorset DT8 3QP, 01308
868101, Fax: 01308 868101, and Member
Hong Kong Bar. Called: Nov 1988, Gray's
Inn, BSocSc, MSocSc, LLB (Lond)

Marks *Miss Clementine Medina*
46/48 Essex Street, London, WC2R 3GH.
Called: Oct 1992, Middle Temple, BA
(Hons), Diploma in Law

Marks *Stuart David* ●
Legal Dept, Office of the Rail Regulator, 1
Waterhouse Square, 138-142 Holborn,
London EC1N 2ST, 0171 282 2146, Fax:
0171 282 2040. Called: July 1982, Gray's
Inn, LLB (Lond)

Marland *Ross Crispian* ●
Consultant, Maxwell Marland & Associates,
84 East Hill, Wandsworth, London
SW18 2HG, 0181 874 5964, Fax: 0181 488
7487. Called: Nov 1975, Inner Temple, LLM
(Lond), MRAes, AIA, MRIN, Dip Air Law

Marlow *Mrs Patricia* ●
Senior Crown Prosecutor, Crown
Prosecution Service, Bournemouth Branch
Office, 1st Floor, Oxford House, Oxford
Road, Bournemouth BH8 8HA. Called: Nov
1988, Middle Temple, BA

Marnham *Mrs Michelle Joanne*
Called: Nov 1994, Inner Temple, LLB
(Essex)

Marrache *Benjamin John Samuel*
Fortress House, Gibraltar, 00 350 79918/
74901, Fax: 00 350 74042\73315.
Called: Nov 1988, Inner Temple, LLB, LLM
(LSE)

Marreco *Anthony*
Called: Jan 1941, Inner Temple

Marriner *Mrs Elaine*
Assistant Company Secretary, The Morgan
Crucible Company, plc, Morgan House,
Madeira Walk, Windsor, Berkshire SL4 1EP,
01753 837000, Fax: 01753 868194.
Called: Feb 1992, Middle Temple, LLB
(Hons), FCIS

Marriott *Alan Ogilvie*
Clerk to the Justices, Kent Magistrates
Courts Comm.,, The Magistrates Courts,
Broad Street, Canterbury, Kent CT1 2UE,
01227 454731, Fax: 01227 457727.
Called: July 1971, Inner Temple

Marriott *Ian Leslie* ●
Local Authority Lawyer, C/O City
Secretary's Dept, Coventry City Council,
Council House, Coventry CV1 1NH, 01203
833085, Fax: 01203 833070. Called: Nov
1984, Middle Temple, LLB (Nott'm)

Marsden *Miss Marion Jean*
Called: Nov 1996, Gray's Inn, BA (Leeds)

Marsh *Miss Claie June*
Called: Nov 1997, Lincoln's Inn, LLB
(Hons)(Manch)

Marsh *Norman Stayner CBE QC*
(1967)
Law Commissioner 1965-78, Wren House,
13 North Side, Clapham Common, London
SW4, 0171 622 2865. Called: Apr 1937,
Middle Temple, MA BCL (Oxon)

Marshall *Adam*
Pitmans Solicitors, 47 Castle Street, Reading,
Berkshire RG1 7SR, 01734 580224.
Called: Nov 1995, Lincoln's Inn, LLB (Hons)

Marshall *Albert Simon Obiri*
Called: Nov 1995, Middle Temple, LLB
(Hons), LLM

Marshall *Mrs Alison Jean*
Principal Legal Adviser, Derbyshire County
Council, Clerk to the Justices, Derwent
Street, Derby, 01332 292100, Fax: 01332
293459. Called: Nov 1987, Inner Temple,
LLB (Leic)

Marshall *Andrew Francis*
164a Fleet Road, Fleet, Hampshire
GU13 8BA, 01252 810265. Called: May
1996, Gray's Inn, BA (L'pool)

Marshall *Andrew George*
Clerk to the Justices, Justices Clerk's Office,
55 Wade Street, Lichfield, Staffs WS13 6HW,
01543 264124, Fax: 01543 258701.
Called: July 1978, Gray's Inn

Marshall *Christopher Allen*
Called: Nov 1968, Inner Temple, MA, LLB
(Cantab)

Marshall Ms Joanna Tamar
Legal Adviser, Norton Rose, Kempson House, Camomile Street, London EC3A 7AN, 0171 444 2531. Called: Nov 1990, Middle Temple, BA (Cantab), Dip European Law, Bruges

Marshall Mrs Katherine Jane
Legal Team Manager, Berkshire & Oxfordshire, Magistrates Courts Committee, Easby House, Northfield End, Henley, Oxon RG9 2NB, 01491 412720, Fax: 01491 412762. Called: July 1983, Inner Temple, MA (Cantab)

Marshall Miss Kathryn Louise
Called: Oct 1992, Lincoln's Inn, LLB(Hons)

Marshall Sir Roy CBE
Kirk House, Kirk Croft, Cottingham, East Yorkshire HU16 4AU, 01482 847413, Fax: 01482 847413, and Member Barbados Bar Jamaican Bar. Called: Jan 1947, Inner Temple, MA, PhD, LLD (Hon), D.Litt (Hon)

Marshall Ms Susan Elizabeth
Bursar, Exeter College, Oxford OX1 3DP, 01865 279649, Fax: 01865 279630. Called: Nov 1978, Middle Temple, MA

Marshall William Roberts QC (H.K.), SC
Legal Consultant, Hong Kong SAR Government of China, Department of Justice, Queensway Government Office, 3rd Floor, High Block, 66 Queensway, Hong Kong, 852 2867 2092, Fax: 852 2869 0670, and Member Hong Kong Bar Victoria Bar. Called: Nov 1968, Inner Temple, MA (Glas) LLB (Lond)

Marshall Bain Miss Lydia Esther
Called: Mar 1998, Lincoln's Inn, LLB (Hons)

Marson Mrs Patricia Ann
Runsley, Whitney-on-Wye, Hereford HR3 6EQ. Called: Nov 1980, Middle Temple, LLB (Leeds)

Marston Dr Geoffrey
Fellow of Sidney Sussex College Lecturer in Law, University of Cambridge, Sidney Sussex College, Cambridge CB2 3HU, 01223 338800, Fax: 01223 338884. Called: July 1993, Middle Temple, LLB (Hons), LLM &, Ph.D

Martin Sir Bruce QC (1977)
Called: Feb 1960, Middle Temple, LLB (L'pool)

Martin Christopher Leonard •
Company Secretary, Avon Rubber Plc, Manvers House, Kingston Road, Bradford-on-Avon, Wilts BA15 1AA, 01225 861100, Fax: 01225 861195. Called: Feb 1967, Gray's Inn, LLB (Nott'm)

Martin Dennis James
Justices' Chief Executive, 15 Newland, Lincoln LN1 1XE, 01522 514200. Called: Nov 1978, Gray's Inn, B.A.

Martin Edward James
Called: July 1983, Lincoln's Inn

Martin Mrs Elizabeth Anne •
Principal Crown Prosecutor, Crown Prosecution Service, CPS Humber, Greenfield House, 39 Scotland Street, Sheffield S3 7DQ, 0114 291 2000. Called: Nov 1984, Middle Temple, LLB (Hons)

Martin Gerard •
Senior Crown Prosecutor, Crown Prosecution Service, Solar House, 1-9 Romford House, Stratford, London E15 4LJ, 0181 534 6601, Fax: 0181 522 1236. Called: July 1986, Gray's Inn, LLB (Lond)

Martin Henry
3 Westmount Park, Newtownards, Northern Ireland BT23 4BP, 01247 819809. Called: July 1971, Inner Temple, LLB, FCA

Martin Nigel Gregory
Barrister of Northern Ireland. Called: May 1994, Middle Temple, LLB (Hons)

Martin Peter David Acheson
Legal Adviser, Mello Hollis Jones & Martin, Reid House, 31 Church Street, Hamilton HM 13, (809) 292 1345, Fax: (809) 292 9151, and Member Bermuda Bar. Called: Nov 1983, Gray's Inn, LLB (Manch)

Martin Miss Rachael Christina
Called: Nov 1991, Inner Temple, BA (Sussex)

Martin Robert Marshall
Called: July 1978, Gray's Inn

Martin Miss Susannah Nicole
Called: Oct 1996, Inner Temple, LLB (Bris)

Martin Mrs Thelma Lynne
Called: July 1976, Inner Temple

Martin Cdr. Timothy Frederick Wilkins RN •
Cdr RNSS, HMS Raleigh, Torpoint, Cornwall PL11 2PD. Called: July 1985, Gray's Inn, LLB (Cardiff)

Martine Giselle Clare
Shearsby House, Shearsby, Leicestershire LE17 6PN, 0116 2478644, Fax: 0116 2478057. Called: July 1977, Middle Temple, BA

Martyn Peter Leyshon
Called: Nov 1950, Lincoln's Inn, LLB (Lond)

Martyn Tristram Ralph
Pauntley, 13 Upland Rd, Eastbourne, East Sussex BN20 8EN, 01323 723642, Hon.Fellow, College of Estate Management. Called: Nov 1965, Middle Temple, LLB, DipEd (Lond)

Maryan-Green Neville Ayton
77 bis Avenue de Bieteul, 75015 Paris, France, and Member Paris Bar. Called: Nov 1963, Middle Temple, BA LLB (Cantab)

Masemola Nathaniel Mashilo
P.O.Box 576, Gallo Manor 2052, Sandton, Johannesburg, (011) 804 5341, Fax: (011) 804 3579, and Member Botswana & Zambia Bars South Africa Bar. Called: June 1964, Gray's Inn, BA LLB (SA), LLB (Lond), UED (Rhodes), FILGAZ (Zambia)

Mashhadi Ahsan Hussain
Lecturer in Law, City & Islington College, 45 Courtney Road, Colliers Wood, London SW19 2EE, 0181 544 0347. Called: July 1980, Lincoln's Inn, LLB (Hons), LLM (Lond), Cert Ed (Dist)

Mason James Stephen CB, •
Counsel to the Speaker, House of Commons, Counsel, London SW1A 0AA, 0171 219 3776. Called: Oct 1958, Middle Temple, MA, BCL

Mason Revd. Nigel James
The Church Flat, Wilbury Road, Hove, East Sussex BN3 3PB. Called: Nov 1987, Inner Temple, Dip Law

Mason Philip Jude •
Assistant Director (Legal), Norwich City Council, St Peters Street, Norwich, Norfolk. Called: July 1975, Gray's Inn, BA

Mason Stephen Charles Winston
Director, Legal Education, Ivel Meads Legal Education Ltd, 19A Church Street, Langford, Biggleswade, Bedfordshire SG18 9QT, 01462 701098, Fax: 01462 701098. Called: Nov 1988, Middle Temple, BA (Hons), MA, LLM, PGCE (FE)

Masood Syed Aaamir
Called: Nov 1997, Lincoln's Inn, BSc (Hons)(LSE)

Massam Arthur David Wright •
80a Westbury Road, Finchley, London N12 7PD, 0181 446 1037. Called: Nov 1968, Inner Temple, LLB (Lond), FRPharmS

Masselis Maria
Called: Oct 1997, Lincoln's Inn, LLB (Hons)(Manc)

Massey Peregrine Tatton Eyre
Director, Thomas Miller & Co Ltd, Thomas Miller & Co Ltd, International House, 26 Creechurch Lane, London EC3A 5BA, 0171 283 4646, Fax: 0171 621 1782. Called: Nov 1975, Middle Temple, MA (Cantab)

Massias Isaac Clive
Massias & Partners, 117 Main Street, P.O.Box 213, 40888, Fax: 40999, and Member Gibraltar Bar. Called: Nov 1986, Middle Temple, LLB (Hons)

Massias Miss Victoria Stella
Massias & Partners, 117 Main Street, P.O.Box 213, 40888, Fax: 40999, and Member Gibraltar Bar. Called: Nov 1989, Middle Temple, LLB Hons (Lond), LLM (Lond)

Mat Rasip Miss Mariza Azen
Zain & Co, 6th Floor, Bangunan Dato', Zainal, 23 Jalan Melaka, 50100 Kuala Lumpur, 03-2986255, Fax: 2986969, and Member Malaysian Bar. Called: July 1994, Lincoln's Inn, LLB (Hons)

Matharu Jitinder Singh •
Principal Crown Prosecutor, Crown Prosecution Service, Colmore Gate, 2 Colmore Row, Birmingham B3 2QA, 0121 629 7200, Fax: 0121 629 7335. Called: July 1981, Inner Temple

Mather *Miss Alison Elisabeth*
Called: Oct 1997, Lincoln's Inn, BA (Hons)

Mather *Steven James*
Called: Oct 1997, Middle Temple, B.Ed (Hull), Dip in Law (Kingston

Mathialahan *K*
Called: July 1996, Middle Temple, LLB (Hons)(Leic)

Mathivaranam *Rueben*
Azman, Davidson & Co, Suite 13-03 13th Floor, Menara Tan & Tan, 207 Jalan Tun Razak, 50400 Kuala Lumpur Malaysia, (03) 2640200, Fax: (03) 2640280, and Member Malaysia Bar Australia Bar. Called: Nov 1989, Lincoln's Inn, BA (Kent)

Mathurasingh *Steve*
Called: Mar 1997, Lincoln's Inn, LLB (Hons)(Wolv'ton)

Matthews *Charles Howard* •
Woodhouse, Idsworth, Horndean, Hampshire, PO8 0AN, 01705 413276, and Member Supreme Court of New South Wales. Called: July 1976, Middle Temple, BSc (Eng), C Eng, MIEE

Matthews *Miss Keirumetse Seipelo Thandeka* •
Called: July 1982, Middle Temple, BA

Matthews *Mrs Margaret Louise*
Lecturer, Exeter College. Called: July 1988, Middle Temple, LLB (Hons) (Lond)

Matthews *Paul Justin*
Called: Nov 1993, Gray's Inn, BA (Sheff)

Matthews *Paul William*
Called: Nov 1996, Lincoln's Inn, LLB (Hons)(L'pool)

Matthias *Mrs Sarah Elizabeth*
Called: Nov 1988, Middle Temple, MA (Oxon)

Maude *Miss Victoria Viola*
Called: Oct 1995, Middle Temple, LLB (Hons)

Maurice *Jack* •
Head of Ethical Standards, Institute of Chartered, Accountants in England & Wales, Gloucester House, 399 Silbury Boulevard, Central Milton Keynes MK9 2HL, 01908 248264, Fax: 01908 231858. Called: May 1957, Gray's Inn, MA [Cantab]

Mawdsley *David John*
Called: Nov 1995, Gray's Inn, BA, LLB

Maxwell *Anthony Michael Lockhart*
Gesnaire, Le Petit Val, Alderney GY9 3UX, 01481 823889, Fax: 01481 824319. Called: Nov 1985, Middle Temple, LLB (Lond),MRIN, MRAeS, Cert Air & Space Law, (UCL)

May *James Nicholas Welby*
Director General, UK Offshore Operators Assoc, 3 Hans Crescent, London SW1X 0LN, 0171 589 5255, Fax: 0171 589 8961. Called: July 1974, Lincoln's Inn, BSc

Maycock *Miss Tania Jane*
Called: Nov 1993, Inner Temple, BA, CPE

Maydon *Gary*
Masons Solicitors, 30 Aylesbury Solicitors, London EC1R 0ER, 0171 490 6207, Fax: 0171 490 2545, Partnership Secretary, Masons Solicitors. Called: July 1996, Middle Temple, LLB (Hons)(Lond), FCIS, FCIB, FFA

Mayer *Mrs Jane Carolyn Stafford* •
Principal Crown Prosecutor, Crown Prosecution Service, 2nd Floor, Blackburn House, The Midway, Newcastle-U-Lyme, Staffs. Called: Nov 1966, Lincoln's Inn, LLB (B'ham)

Mayer *Mrs Nancy Elaine* •
Senior Lawyer, HM Customs & Excise, Ralli Quays West, Stanley Street, Salford, Manchester M60 9LB, 0161 839 7839. Called: Nov 1983, Middle Temple, LLB (Nott'm)

Mayers *Miss Maferne Telene*
Called: Nov 1997, Gray's Inn, LLB (Wolver'ton)

Mayhew of Twysden *The Rt Hon Lord PC QC (1972)*
House of Lords, London SW1A 0PW, 1 Temple Gardens, 1st Floor, Temple, London, EC4Y 9BB. Called: June 1955, Middle Temple, MA (Oxon)

Mayhew-Arnold *Michael Charles John*
Director, Henry Ansbacker & Co Limited, One Mitre Square, London EC3A 5AN. Called: Nov 1983, Inner Temple, LLB (Hons) (So'ton)

Maynard *Michael John* •
Senior Principal Legal Officer, Treasury Solicitors Dept, Queen Anne's Chambers, 28 Broadway, London, 0171 210 3041. Called: July 1984, Middle Temple, BA (Hons)

Mayne *Miss Caroline Margaret* •
Head of Litigation Team, Lloyds of London, 1 Lime Street, London EC3, 0171 327 6955, Fax: 0171 327 5502. Called: Nov 1984, Inner Temple, LLB Hons (Leics)

Mazda *Rohinten Daddy*
Deputy Justices' Clerk, Inner London Magistrates', Courts Service, Romney Street, London SW1P 3RD, 0171 799 3332, Fax: 0171 799 3072. Called: Nov 1972, Inner Temple

Mazlan *Azri Sani*
Called: Nov 1995, Gray's Inn, LLB (Wales)

Mazzawi *Prof Musa Elias*
Lane House, Mortimer, Reading, Berks RG7 3PP, 01189 332897, Fax: 01189 331501. Called: Nov 1950, Gray's Inn, LLM, PhD (Lond)

Mbanefo *Thomas Chuba*
and Member Nigerian Bar. Called: July 1988, Gray's Inn, LLB (Warwick), LLM (Lond), BL (Nigeria)

Mbiti *John Maithya*
Apt 320, 240 Mercer Street, New York 10012, (212) 443 5208. Called: Oct 1996, Lincoln's Inn, LLB (Hons)(Lond)

McAleer *Dominic Alphonsus*
Called: Nov 1989, Gray's Inn, BA [Oxon]

McAleer *James Joseph*
Former Police Officer. Called: Oct 1997, Middle Temple, BA (Hons)(Oxon)

McArdle *Eamonn Terence*
The Bar Library, Royal Courts of Justice, Chichester Street, Belfast BT1 3JP, 01232 241523, Fax: 01232 231850, and Member Northern Ireland. Called: Oct 1996, Inner Temple, BA (East Anglia), CALS (Belfast)

McArdle *Kevin Edward* •
Legal Officer, Merck Sharp & Dohme Limited, Hertford Road, Hoddesdon, Hertfordshire EN11 9BU, 01992 452509, Fax: 01992 470189. Called: Nov 1989, Middle Temple, BSc, LLB

McAvock *Captain Gabrielle* •
55 Temple Chambers, Temple Avenue, London, EC4Y 0HP. Called: Oct 1994, Lincoln's Inn, LLB (Hons)(Lond)

McBride *Martin Peter*
Called: Oct 1994, Lincoln's Inn, LLB (Hons)(Plymouth)

McCabe *Adrian Thomas*
Called: May 1994, Inner Temple, BA, LLB

McCabe *Matthew Mel* •
Acting Assistant Branch Crown Prosecutor, Crown Prosecution Service, 3rd Floor, Government Blgs, Bromyard Avenue, Acton, London W3 7AY. Called: Nov 1973, Lincoln's Inn, LLB (Cantab)

McCabe *Robert Stuart*
Tax Consultant, Sony, 25 Golden Square, London W1R 6LU, 0171 533 1481, Fax: 0171 533 1488. Called: Nov 1988, Inner Temple, BA (Dunelm), ACA, ATII

McCahon *David John* •
Grade 6, Legal Advisers Branch, Home Office, 50 Queen Annes Gate, London SW1H 9AT, 0171 273 2532. Called: July 1988, Middle Temple, LLB (Hons) (Reading), LLM (Cantab)

McCance *John Neill*
Brook Farm, Bramley Road, Silchester, Reading, Berks RG7 2LJ, 01256 881383, Fax: 01256 880985. Called: July 1952, Inner Temple, MA (Oxon)

McCandlish *John Gordon*
Former Solicitor. Called: Oct 1995, Gray's Inn

McCann *Miss Mary Brigid*
Called: July 1995, Gray's Inn, BA (Middx)

McCarroll *John Michael*
Called: Oct 1997, Gray's Inn, LLB (Wales)

McCarthy *Miss Mary Patricia Nodlaig*
Irish Barrister, and Member Southern Ireland Bar. Called: Feb 1988, Inner Temple, BL, LLB (Dublin)

McCartin *John*
Called: Nov 1989, Inner Temple, BA (Kent)

McCartney *Miss Tanya Cecile*
Called: July 1995, Lincoln's Inn, LLB (Hons)

• Barristers in employment

McCartney, *Miss Clarise Yvette*
Yvette McCartney Chambers, Wilmacs Pharmacy Building, No 55 Collins Avenue, P.O.Box G.T. 2830, Nassau, N.P., 242 328 6725/326 4620, Fax: 242 328 6725, and Member Bahamas. Called: Nov 1992, Inner Temple, LLB (Wales)

McCleave *Miss Ingrid Anne*
Called: Oct 1995, Lincoln's Inn, LLB (Hons)

McClellan *Anthony CBE*
Formerly Principal Legal Advisor, European Commission, Brussels.. Called: Nov 1958, Inner Temple

McClelland *Ms Sara Louise* •
The Home Office, 50 Queen Anne's Gate, London SW1H 9AT. Called: Nov 1992, Middle Temple, BA (Hons) & BCL, (Oxon)

McCloskey *Conor Martin*
Called: Oct 1996, Inner Temple, LLB (N. Lond)

McCombie-Lawrence *Miss Alison Maria*
Called: Nov 1993, Inner Temple, LLB

McConomy *Paul*
Called: July 1997, Inner Temple, LLB (Leics)

McCormac *Kevin Francis*
Justices' Chief Executive, West Sussex Magistrates, West Sussex Magistrates Courts, Sussex Chambers, 5 Liverpool Terrace, Worthing, West Sussex BN11 1TA, 01903 232218, Fax: 01903 214778. Called: July 1974, Gray's Inn, MA (Oxon)

McCrory *Miss Amanda Jayne*
Called: May 1996, Inner Temple, LLB

McCrudden *Dr John Christopher*
Fellow, Lincoln College, Oxford Reader in Law, Oxford University, Lincoln College, Oxford OX1 3DR, (01865) 279772, Fax: (01865) 279802. Called: May 1996, Gray's Inn, LLB (Belfast), LLM (Yale), MA (Oxon), D.Phil (Oxon)

McCullough *Miss Denise Susanne*
6 Ballycastle Road, Newtownards, Co.Down, N.Ireland BT22 2AY, 01247 815737, Member of the Honorable Society of the Inn of Court of Northern Ireland and Member Northern Ireland Bar. Called: Nov 1992, Lincoln's Inn, BA (Hons)(Belfast), CPE

McCully *Alvin Jeffrey*
Called: July 1997, Middle Temple, LLB (Hons)

McDonagh *Peter Martin Michael* •
Prosecution Team Leader, Crown Prosecution Service, Northamptonshire Branch, Level 3, Beaumont House, Cliftonville, Northampton NN1 5BE, 01604 230220, Fax: 01604 232081. Called: July 1981, Inner Temple, LLB

McDonald *Adrian Clive*
Called: Feb 1995, Inner Temple, BA, LLM (Edin)

McDonald *David*
Deputy Clerk to the Justices, Bedford Magistrates Court, Shire Hall, St Paul's Square, Bedford MK40 1SQ, 01234 359422, Fax: 01234 354515. Called: Nov 1985, Gray's Inn, Diploma Mag Law, Diploma in, Management Studies

McDonald *Miss Eileen Rebecca*
Called: Feb 1993, Inner Temple, LLB (Wolver'ton)

McDonald *Miss Gail Marie*
Osborne Clarke, 50 Queen Charlotte Street, Bristol BS1 4HE, 0117 984 5300, Fax: 0117 925 9798. Called: July 1986, Middle Temple, LLB (B'ham)

McDonald *Miss Julie Anne Marie*
Called: Nov 1996, Gray's Inn, LLB (Kent)

McDonald *Lawrence Patrick*
Called: Oct 1996, Inner Temple, LLB (Lond)

McDonald *Ms Susan Michelle* •
Legal Advisor, Sun Life Assurance Society, 107 Cheapside, London EC2V 0DU, 0171 606 7788. Called: Nov 1993, Lincoln's Inn, BA (Hons), LLM

McDonnell *Captain Scott* •
Directorate of Army Legal, Services, Trenchard Lines, Upavon, Pewsey, Wiltshire SN9 6BE. Called: Oct 1994, Middle Temple, BA (Hons), CPE (Bournemouth)

McDougall *Ian Paul*
Called: Oct 1997, Lincoln's Inn, BA (Hons)(Hull)

McDowell *Major Thomas Bleakley*
Chairman The Irish Times Ltd, St Thomas, Whitechurch, County Dublin 16, and Member Southern Ireland Bar. Called: June 1951, Gray's Inn, LLB

McElhatton *Miss Ita Louise Patricia*
Flat 4, 103 Blackheath Park, London SE3 0EH. Called: Nov 1993, Gray's Inn, B.Sc (Salford)

McEneny *Greg Martin* •
Legal Advisor, UBS Limited, 100 Liverpool Street, London EC2M 2RH, 0171 901 7557, Fax: 0171 901 3910. Called: Nov 1995, Middle Temple, BA (Hons)(Sheff), Dip Law

McEntee *Francis Richard* •
Senior Crown Prosecutor, Crown Prosecution Service, Calder House, St James's Street, Burnley, Lancashire. Called: July 1987, Inner Temple, LLB

McEvedy *Miss Flora Helen*
Called: Oct 1995, Inner Temple, LLB (City), BA (Oxon)

McEwen *Miss Ruth Elizabeth* •
Legal Adviser Grade 7, DSS, New Court, 48 Carey Street, London WC2A 2LS, 0171 412 1492, Fax: 0171 412 1523. Called: Oct 1992, Middle Temple, MA (Hons, St.Andrews, Diploma in Law(City)

McFarlane *Miss Marcia Pamela* •
Lawyer. Called: Feb 1990, Lincoln's Inn, LLB Hons

McFarlane *Miss Susan Joyce* •
Legal Adviser, West Merchant Bank Ltd, 33/36 Gracechurch Street, London EC3V 0AX, 0171 623 8711, Fax: 0171 626 1610, Postgraduate Certificate in Corporate & Investment Law. Called: Nov 1985, Gray's Inn, LLB (Manc), LLM (Lond)

McGary *Miss Raedene*
Called: Feb 1995, Middle Temple, LLB (Hons)(Lond), BA

McGee *Miss Kathryn C* •
Oxfordshire County Council, New Road, Oxford. Called: Nov 1978, Middle Temple, BA (Sussex)

McGee *Terence Alfred Francis*
27 Brabourne Rise, Beckenham, Kent BR3 6SQ, 0181 658 3674, Fax: 0181 658 2770. Called: Nov 1959, Gray's Inn, LLB, FCIS

McGibbon *Eric John Wallace* •
Legal Adviser, The Post Office, Legal Department, Impact House, 2 Edridge Road, Croydon CR9 1PJ, 0181 681 9025, Fax: 0181 681 9220. Called: July 1978, Gray's Inn, LLB (Lond)

McGibbon *Miss Susanna Justine* •
Legal Adviser. Called: Nov 1990, Lincoln's Inn, LLB (Sheff)

McGill *John Gerard Antony*
Called: July 1992, Lincoln's Inn, LLB (Hons), Bsc ACIArb

McGinty *Kevin Charles Patrick* •
Legal Adviser, Legal Secretariat to the Law, Officers, 9 Buckingham Gate, London SW1E 6JP, 0171 828 7155. Called: July 1982, Gray's Inn, BA

McGirl *Barry John* •
Lawyer, CPS (Midlands), St George's House, Lever Street, Wolverhampton WV2 1EZ, 01902 870900, Fax: 01902 871570. Called: July 1974, Gray's Inn, BA (Oxon)

McGonigal *Miss Rachel*
Called: Oct 1991, Lincoln's Inn, BA (Hons), Dip Law

McGowan *James Hugh Menzies*
Admiralty Chambers, 1405 Tower 11, Admiralty Centre, 2527 3082, Fax: 2529 8226, and Member Hong Kong Bar. Called: July 1979, Middle Temple, BA (Nott'm), Dip Comm Law (HK)

McGrath *John Paul Francis*
Called: Nov 1994, Middle Temple, MA (Hons)

McGrath *John Thomas*
Gandangara, Oxley Drive, Mittagong, New South Wales 2575, +61 2 9221 1199, Fax: +61 416 990 405, Former Executive Legal Assistant to Chief Justice Federal Court of Australia 1982-85 and Member New South Wales Bar. Called: Apr 1991, Lincoln's Inn, BA, LLB, BEc (Sydney), LLM, (Euro Law)(Lond)

McGrath *Ms Sarah Linda*
Tax Partner, Deloitte Touche Tohmatsu, Deloitte Touche Tohmatsu, 26th Floor, Wing on Centre, 111 Connaught Road, (852) 28521095, Fax: (852) 25434647. Called: Feb 1990, Lincoln's Inn, B.Soc.Sc [Hong Kong], LLB Hons [Lond]

McGrenaghan *Aidan Edward*
Called: July 1997, Lincoln's Inn, LLB (Hons)(Lond)

McGuinness *Robin Michael*
Called: Oct 1995, Gray's Inn, B.Sc

McHaffie *Malcolm Bruce* •
Senior Crown Prosecutor, Crown Prosecution Service, Bow Street Branch, 3rd Floor, Portland House, Stag Place, London SW1E 5BH, 0171 915 5700, Fax: 0171 915 5850. Called: Oct 1991, Lincoln's Inn, LLB (Hons) (Birm)

McHale *Henry*
Called: Nov 1969, Inner Temple, MA (Cantab)

McHenry *Brian Edward* •
Senior Civil Service Lawyer., Currently Solicitor to the North Wales Tribunal of Inquiry into Child Abuse, Treasury Solicitors Department, Queen Anne's Chambers, 28 Broadway, London SW1, 0171 210 3000. Called: July 1976, Middle Temple, MA (Oxon)

McHugo *Christopher Benedict* •
Taxation Manager, Assoc of British Insurers, 51 Gresham Street, London EC2V 7HQ, 0171 600 3333, Fax: 0171 696 8999. Called: Nov 1978, Middle Temple, MA (Oxon),FCA

McIlroy *Mrs Rosemary* •
Senior Crown Prosecutor, Crown Prosecution Service, 1-2 York Place, Scarborough, North Yorkshire, 01723 500206. Called: July 1981, Lincoln's Inn, LLB (Hons)(Leeds)

McInnes *Richard Bishop*
24 Heritage Way, Cleveleys FY5 3BD. Called: July 1971, Middle Temple, MA

McIntyre *David John Christopher* •
Assistant Solicitor, HM Customs & Excise, New King's Beam House, Upper Ground, London SE1. Called: July 1976, Gray's Inn, LLB (Lond)

McKay *Howard Miles*
Called: May 1995, Inner Temple, LLB

McKee *Richard Anthony*
Eldon Chambers, Fourth Floor, 30/32 Fleet Street, London, EC4Y 1AA. Called: Oct 1991, Inner Temple, MA (Cantab), MA (Lond)

McKenna *Ms Mariead Maria* •
Senior Lawyer, PHH Europe plc, PHH Centre, Windmill Hill, Whitehill Way, Swindon SN5 9YT, 01793 884424, Fax: 01793 886056, Irish Barrister. Called: July 1992, Gray's Inn, BCL

McKenny *Simon Edward*
James R Knowles, Wardle House, King Street, Knutsford, Cheshire WA16 6PD, 01565 654666, Fax: 01565 755009. Called: Feb 1991, Lincoln's Inn, BSc, LLB (Lond), ARICS, ACIArb

McKenzie *Mrs Dulcibel Edna Jenkins*
89 Cornwall Gardens, London SW7 4AX, 0171 5847674/01243 512411, Fax: 0171 5847674. Called: July 1967, Lincoln's Inn, BA, DIP Ed (Lond)

McKeon *Ms Caroline*
1 Pump Court, Lower Ground Floor, Temple, London, EC4Y 7AB. Called: Nov 1983, Inner Temple, BA

McKeown *Miss Jennifer*
Called: Oct 1994, Gray's Inn, LLB, LLM

McKevitt *Miss Una Frances*
Legal Adviser, Wilde Sapte Solicitors, 1 Fleet Place, London EC4M 7WS, 0171 246 7000, Fax: 0171 246 7777. Called: Oct 1995, Inner Temple, LLB (Manc)

McKibbin *Robert*
29 Brookfield, Weald Hall Lane, Thornwood, Epping, Essex CM16 6NG, 01992 560 348, Chartered Architect. Called: July 1997, Middle Temple, BSc (Belfast), MSc (Lond), RIBA, FCIArb

McKie *Miss Suzanne Elizabeth*
Fox Williams, City Gate House, 39-45 Finsbury Square, London EC2A 1UU, 0171 628 2000, Fax: 0171 628 2100. Called: Nov 1991, Inner Temple, LLB (Notts)

McLachlan *Ewan* •
Senior Crown Prosecutor, Crown Prosecution Service, Windsor House, 10 Manchester Road, Bradford, 01274 742530. Called: July 1984, Gray's Inn, LLB (Leeds)

McLachlan *Paul Robert*
Called: Oct 1996, Middle Temple, BA (Hons)(Oxon), CPE (Westminster)

McLachlan *Stuart Munro* •
Senior Crown Prosecutor, 2 Bedford Park, Croydon CR0 2AP, 9 King's Bench Walk, Ground Floor, Temple, London, EC4Y 7DX. Called: July 1982, Gray's Inn, LL.B(Nottingham)

McLaughlin *Richard*
Chairman, Bar Council (NI) 1994-1996, Bar Library, P.O.Box 414, Royal Courts of Justice, Chichester Street, Belfast BT1 3JP, 01232 660283, Fax: 01232 667399, QC 1985 (N.Ireland)(Called 1971) and Member Bar of N.Ireland (1971) King's Inn,Dublin (1978) and Bar of N.S.W. Australia 1992. Called: Nov 1974, Gray's Inn, LLB, F.C.I.Arb

McLean *Mrs Helen Lavinia Freda Allen*
The Gnomon, Cuttinglye Rd, Crawley Down, West Sussex RH10 4LR, 01342 712432. Called: Nov 1951, Middle Temple, MA (Oxon)

McLean *Patrick Joseph*
Highgarth, Town Hill, Lingfield, Surrey RH7 6AG, 01342 832574. Called: June 1938, Inner Temple

McLean *Miss Suzanne Victoria* •
Director of legal Affairs and Company Secretary, Biocompatibles International, Frensham House, Farnham Business Park, Weydon Lane, Farnham, Surrey GU9 8QL. Called: July 1979, Gray's Inn, BA

McLeish *Ms Jennifer Kerr*
Called: Oct 1993, Gray's Inn, BA

McLeish *Robin*
Deputy Provacy Commissioner for Personal Data, Office of the Privacy, Commissioner for Personal Data, Unit 2001, 20/F Office Tower, Convention Plaza, 1 Harbour Rd, Wanchai, (852) 2877 7128. Called: Oct 1997, Gray's Inn, MA

McLeod *Ms Geraldine Fiona*
Called: July 1981, Inner Temple, BSc, MA

McLoughlin *Miss Catherine Mary* •
Office of the Solicitor, DSS/DH, New Court, 48 Carey Street, London WC2A 2LS, 0171 962 8000, Fax: 0171 412 1227. Called: Nov 1994, Middle Temple, BA (Oxon), M.Phil (Cantab)

McLoughlin *Ms Joan* •
Grade 6, Health and Safety Executive, Rose Court, 2 Southwark Bridge, London SE1 9HS, 0171 717 6000. Called: Nov 1984, Middle Temple, BSc,MSc, Dip Law

McLoughlin *Sean Francis*
Called: Oct 1996, Gray's Inn, BSc (Lond)

McLusky *Nigel John Cooper*
Recorder, Kerris Vean, Old Church Road, Mawnan, Falmouth TR11 5HX. Called: Nov 1960, Middle Temple, LLB

McLusky *Torquil Corbett*
Called: Nov 1994, Inner Temple, BA (Lond), CPE (Wolverhampton)

McMahon *Miss Jacynta Elizabeth Mary*
Called: Nov 1994, Middle Temple, BA (Hons)

McMahon *Richard James*
Legislative Draftsman, States of Guernsey, St James' Chambers, Guernsey GY1 2PA, 01481 723355, Fax: 01481 725439. Called: Nov 1986, Middle Temple, LLB (L'pool), LLM (Cantab)

McMaster *Stuart Charles*
Called: July 1996, Gray's Inn, BA,BCL (Oxon)

McMath *Miss Clare Mary Astrid*
Deloitte & Touche, Hill House, 1 Little New Street, London EC4A 3TR, 0171 303 4195, Fax: 0171 583 8517. Called: Oct 1992, Lincoln's Inn, BA (Hons) ATII

McMenemy *Simon John*
Assistant, Allen & Overy Solcitors, One New Change, London EC4M 9QQ, 0171 330 3000. Called: Oct 1995, Inner Temple, LLB (Lond)

McMinnies *Stephen Mark*
1B Cloudesley Place, Islington, London N1 0JA, 0171 833 9382 Mobile telephone 0956 104517. Called: Nov 1996, Gray's Inn, LLB (Hons)(Lond)

McMorrow *Ms Grainne*
and Member Irish Bar July 1985 New South
Wales Australia, Sydney. Called: July 1989,
Middle Temple, BA (Hons), LLB (Hons), BL

McMullan *Miss Adele Maree*
Legal Clerk, Levi & Co Solicitors, First Floor
Deacon House, Seacroft Avenue, Leeds
LS14. Called: Nov 1996, Middle Temple, LLB
(Hons)(Lancs)

McMurdie *Donald Charles*
St Andrews's Cottage, Kingsmead, Ewhurst
Road, Cranleigh, Surrey GU6 7TA, 01483
271603. Called: Feb 1963, Gray's Inn, LLB

McNamara *Miss Rosemary Cardus*
Called: Oct 1994, Gray's Inn, BA

McNaught *Peter Godfrey* •
Crown Prosecution Service, 8th Floor,
Sunlight House, Quay Street, Manchester
M60 3LU, 0161 837 7402, Fax: 0161 835
2663. Called: July 1982, Middle Temple,
LL.B (B'ham)

McNeill *George Kenneth*
Called: Oct 1997, Inner Temple, LLB
(Middlesex)

McNerney *Kevin John* •
Royal College of Nursing, Raven House, 81
Clarendon Road, Leeds LS2 9PJ, 0113 244
4725, Fax: 0113 234 3641. Called: Nov
1992, Inner Temple, BA, Dip in Law

McNicholas *Christopher John*
St Mary's Rectory, 4/5 Eldon Street, London
EC2M 7LS, 0171 247 8390, Fax: 0171 375
0094. Called: Nov 1995, Lincoln's Inn, LLB
(Hons), ACIB

McQuaid *Miss Paula*
Called: Oct 1993, Middle Temple, LLB
(Hons)

McRandal *Mrs Pauline Mary*
10 Fairlawns, Saval Park Road, Dalkey, Co
Dublin, 2856078, Fax: 2856078, and
Member Southern Ireland Bar. Called: July
1988, Middle Temple, BL (Kings Inns)

Mcshane *Ms Anne Mary Sylvia*
University College, Dublin. Called: July
1989, Gray's Inn, BA

McVey *Ms Najma* •
Legal Officer, HM Customs & Excise, New
Kings Beam House, 22 Upper Ground,
London SE1 9PJ, 0171 865 5820, Fax: 0171
865 5502. Called: July 1993, Lincoln's Inn,
BSc (Glasgow), LLB (Hons)

McVitie *Miss Justine*
Called: Nov 1995, Inner Temple, LLB (Lond)

McWilliams *Sir Francis*
Chairman C.E.B.R., Bartlett House, 9-12
Basinghall Street, London EC2V 5NS, 0171
600 6661, Fax: 0171 600 6671, 1 Atkin
Building, Gray's Inn, London, WC1R 5AT.
Called: July 1978, Lincoln's Inn, BSc Eng, C.
(Eng), FICE

Md Sidik *Miss Norazmah*
A.Renggonathan & Co, 345-A Taman Melaka
Raya, 75000 Melaka, Malaysia, Fax: 249276.
Called: July 1994, Lincoln's Inn, LLB (Hons)

Mead *Geoffrey Hugh*
Called: Nov 1993, Lincoln's Inn, BA (Hons),
BCL

Mead *Larry Frederick*
57 Cavendish Way, Mickleover, Derby,
Derbyshire DE3 5BL, 01332 518397.
Called: July 1977, Lincoln's Inn, LLB (Lond)

Meade *Barrie Norman QC*
Solicitor General, Attorney General's
Chambers, Global House, 43 Church Street,
Hamilton HM 12, Bermuda, 809 292 2463,
Fax: 809 292 3608, Commander Brother of
the Order of St John Queens Counsel
(Bermuda 1996) and Member Bermuda.
Called: July 1981, Inner Temple, LLB (Lond),
ACIArb

Meade *Stephen John*
Called: Nov 1997, Middle Temple, LLB
(Hons)(Manch)

Meadows *Ian James*
Called: Mar 1996, Lincoln's Inn, LLB (Hons),
LLM, (E.Anglia)

Meager *Miss Karen Margaret* •
Crown Prosecution Service, C/O 50 Ludgate
Hill, London EC4M 7EX. Called: Oct 1992,
Inner Temple, MA (Cantab), CPE

Meah *Ashook*
Called: May 1997, Gray's Inn, BA (Lond),
MA (Essex)

Meakin *Ian Leonard*
Arbitrator, Megevand, Grosjean, Revaz &,
Associes, 1 Rue Etienne - Dumont, Case
Postale 3487, 1211 Geneva 3, 0041 22 312
11 61, Fax: 0041 22 312 11 63. Called: Oct
1991, Gray's Inn, BD, AKC, Dip Law,
ACIArb

Meakin *Robert Grant*
Lawyer Qualified Sub Editor, Simmons &
Simmons, 21 Wilson Street, London
EC2M 2TX, 0171 628 2020, Fax: 0171 628
2070. Called: Nov 1987, Gray's Inn, LLB,
LLM

Mear *Miss Lynn* •
Legal Adviser, Solicitor's Office, Dept of
Tade & Industry, 10 Victoria Street, London
SW1H 0NN, 0171 215 3000. Called: July
1981, Gray's Inn, LLB

Mecenero *Ms Nicole*
Called: Nov 1995, Middle Temple, LLB
(Hons)

Medcalf *Jonathan Paul*
Called: Nov 1994, Inner Temple, LLB
(Soton)

Medlock *Andrew Hewitt* •
Legal & Company & Commercial Secretary,
Mitsui Babcock Energy Limited, 11 The
Boulevard, Crawley, West Sussex
RH10 1UX, 01293 584974, Fax: 01293
584190. Called: Nov 1969, Middle Temple,
LLB

Medwynter *Philip Edward* •
Prosecution Team Leader, C/O Crown
Prosecution Service, Marylebone West
London Branch, 4 Artillery Row, London
SW1P 1RZ. Called: Nov 1982, Middle
Temple, LLB (Hons)

Meechan *Hugh Lawrence*
10 Barnsdale Close, Gt. Easton LE16 8SQ.
Called: July 1984, Inner Temple, BA (Lond)
Dip Law

Meek *Ian Kingsley*
Winding Wood House, Kintbury,
Hungerford, Berkshire RG17 9RN, 01488
658957, and Member Malaysia Bar
Singapore Bar. Called: Jan 1950, Inner
Temple, MA (Oxon)

Meeke *Colin Wilson* •
Senior Crown Prosecutor, Crown
Prosecution Service, Fox Talbot House,
Bellinger Close, Malmesbury Road,
Chippenham SN15 1BN, 01249 443443,
Fax: 01249 440800. Called: July 1983,
Gray's Inn, BA Leics

Meeres *Mrs Nicola Jane*
Called: Nov 1988, Gray's Inn, BA

Meeson *Michael Anthony* •
Commercial Work, LLoyds of London, 0171
327 5526, Fax: 0171 327 5858. Called: Nov
1978, Middle Temple, MBIM, MBA

Meharia *Miss Vineeta*
Called: July 1997, Gray's Inn, LLB (Lond)

Mehta *Ismail* •
Head of Legal & Compliance Department.,
The Bank of, Tokyo-Mitsubishi Limited, 12-
15 Finsbury Circus, London EC2M 7BT,
0171 577 1295, Fax: 0171 577 1299.
Called: Nov 1984, Gray's Inn, LLB
(Hons)(Lond)

Mehta *Mrs Krushavali*
Principal Court Clerk, Trafford Magistrates'
Court, P O Box 13, Ashton Lane, Sale
M33 1UP, 0161 976 3333, Fax: 0161 962
4333. Called: July 1980, Gray's Inn, B.A.

Mehta *Sharad Navnitlal*
Called: Nov 1959, Middle Temple

Mehta *Mrs Smita Durgesh*
Called: Nov 1982, Gray's Inn, BA

Mei *Miss Chee Yin*
and Member Malaysia Bar. Called: July 1991,
Gray's Inn, LLB (Warwick)

Meigh *Andrew Patrick*
Called: Oct 1995, Lincoln's Inn, BA
(Hons)(Leeds), Dip in Law (Covent)

Melhuish-Hancock *Simon* •
Senior Legal Adviser, British Steel plc, 9
Albert Embankment, London SE1 7SN, 0171
820 7393, Fax: 0171 582 5776. Called: July
1981, Gray's Inn, LLB

Melling *Gerard Philip* •
Deputy General Manager, Legal Dept Mitsui
& Co Uk PLC, Mitsui & Co UK Plc, 20 Old
Bailey, London EC4M 7QQ, 0171 822 0543,
Fax: 0171 248 5075. Called: Nov 1980,
Gray's Inn, LLB (Lond), Dip Eur Int,
(Amsterdam)

Mellish *George Harvey*
Called: Oct 1995, Gray's Inn, B.Sc

Mello *Michael Joseph JP*
Justice of Supreme Court of Bermuda,
Mello, Hollis, Jones & Martin, Reid House,
31 Church Street, Hamilton, HM FX, (441)
292 1345, Fax: (441) 292 2277, QC
Bermuda (1990) and Member Bermuda Bar
10 Old Square, Ground Floor, Lincoln's Inn,
London, WC2A 3SU. Called: July 1972,
Gray's Inn, BA

Melnick *Miss Judith Ann*
Senior Deputy Chief Clerk, Inner London &
City Family, Proceedings Courts, 59-65
Wells Street, London W1A 3AE, 0171 323
1649. Called: July 1979, Middle Temple, LLB
(Lond)

Melville-Brown *Ms Penelope Gillian* •
Naval Barrister, Commander, Staff of
Directorate of Naval, Manning, Old Naval
Academy, HM Naval Base, Portsmouth,
Hants PO1 3NA. Called: July 1989, Gray's
Inn, BA, DipLaw, PGCE

Melvin *James Warren*
Called: Nov 1997, Inner Temple, LLB (South
Bank)

Mendonca *Mrs Judith Mary*
Called: Nov 1989, Middle Temple, LLB

Menezes *Justin Carl*
Wilmer, Cutler & Pickering, Rue de la Loi
15, B-1040 Brussels, (32) (2) 2854900, Fax:
(32) (2) 2854949, and Member Belgium.
Called: Oct 1995, Lincoln's Inn, LLB
(Hons)(Sheff)

Menon *Mrs Deborah Damayanthi*
Called: Nov 1995, Inner Temple, LLB (Herts)

Menon *Sree Govind*
Called: July 1996, Lincoln's Inn, LLB
(Hons)(Lond)

Menon *Miss Sumytra*
Called: Nov 1993, Lincoln's Inn, LLB (Hons,
B'ham)

Mensah *Mrs Grace*
00 223 21 22 4260, Fax: 00 233 21 23
2262. Called: Nov 1995, Lincoln's Inn, LLB
(Hons)(Lond)

Mensah *Miss Lorraine Sonia Louise*
Called: Oct 1997, Gray's Inn, LLB (L'pool)

Menzies *Robert Anthony*
Corporate Legal Adviser, Greystones, 1
North Court, Nettleham, Lincoln LN2 2XJ,
01522 754287, Fax: 01522 595515.
Called: July 1978, Middle Temple, F.C.I.S,
F.C.IArb

Mercer *Ms Amanda* •
Senior Crown Prosecutor, Crown
Prosecution Service, Tolworth Tower,
Surbiton, Surrey KT6 7DS. Called: July 1986,
Inner Temple, LLB

Mercer *Anthony Michael TD,*
Senior Court Clerk, Ashton Under Lyne Mag
Crt, Manchester Road, Ashton-u-Lyne,
Manchester OL7 0BG, 0161 330 2023.
Called: Feb 1989, Middle Temple, LLB
(Hons), DMS

Merchant *Liaquat Habib*
Called: Nov 1991, Gray's Inn, BA, LLB
(Bombay)

Meredith *Jack Edward*
Called: Nov 1996, Lincoln's Inn, LLB
(Hons)(Herts)

Meredith *Stephen Paul*
Called: Oct 1995, Lincoln's Inn, LLB
(Hons)(Wales)

Meredith-Hardy *Michael Francis*
Chairman - Immigration Adjud Chairman
Appeal Board High Court Examiner.
Tribunal Chairman., Radwell Mill, Baldock,
Herts SG7 5ET. Called: Nov 1951, Inner
Temple

Merican *Megat Suffian*
Called: July 1996, Lincoln's Inn, LLB (Hons)

Merrien *Alan Martin*
Litigation Assistant, Ozanne Van Leuven
Perrot &, Evans, 1 Le Marchant Street, St
Peter Port, Guernsey, Channel Islands, 0481
723466, Fax: 0481 727935, and Member
Guernsey Bar. Called: Feb 1992, Inner
Temple, LLB (So'ton)

Merrills *Jon Vernon*
Parkdale House, Peveril Drive, The Park,
Nottingham. Called: Feb 1986, Middle
Temple, B.Pharm; BA, BA(Law)

Merriman *Huw William*
Called: Oct 1996, Inner Temple, BA
(Dunelm)

Merritt *Miss Hazel Anne*
Called: Oct 1992, Gray's Inn, BA

Mertcan *Erol*
Called: Nov 1996, Gray's Inn, LLB, LLM
(LSE)

Mesenas *Miss May Lucia*
Deputy Public Prosecutor State Counsel
(Singapore), Attorney General's Chambers, 1
Coleman Street, [H]10-00 The Adelphi, (65)
3325940, Fax: (65) 3390286/4355100.
Called: July 1995, Middle Temple, LLB
(Hons)

Messeter *Mrs Ulanta Ann* •
Court Clerk, Bromley Magistrates Court,
Court House, South Street, Bromley, Kent
BR1 3RD, 0181 4666621, Fax: 0181
4666214. Called: Apr 1991, Gray's Inn, LLB,
B.Ed

Metcalf *Richard James*
Called: Nov 1992, Lincoln's Inn, LLB (Hons)

Metcalfe *Miss Jacqueline Nellie*
Granby, 27 Godstone Road, Purley, Surrey
CR8 2AN, 0181 660 4588. Called: June
1948, Inner Temple

Metcalfe *Noel Percy*
Law Reporter,Editor Criminal Appeal
Reports, 4 Field Court, Gray's Inn, London,
WC1R 5EA. Called: July 1952, Inner Temple,
MA (Cantab)

Metson *Nicholas Richard*
Called: Oct 1996, Inner Temple, LLB
(Dunelm)

Mews *Corin James Stuart*
Called: Oct 1997, Lincoln's Inn, BA (Hons),
LLM

Meyer *Ellis Raymond*
Snr Advoc Sup Ct Ind, 24 Shirehall Close,
London NW4 2QP, 0181 202 9031, and
Member Calcutta Bar. Called: June 1938,
Gray's Inn, BA Hons (Calcutta)

Meyrick *George William Owen*
Called: Mar 1997, Lincoln's Inn, BA (Hons)

Mian *Ms Sminah*
Cambell Hooper Solicitors, 35 Old Queen
Street, London SW1H 9JD, 0171 222 9070.
Called: Oct 1995, Inner Temple, LLB
(Newcastle)

Michael *Michael CBE* •
Senior Civil Servant, H.M. Customs and
Excise, Solicitor's Office, New King's Beam
House, 22 Upper Ground, London SE1 9PJ,
0171 865 5205, Fax: 0171 865 5194.
Called: Nov 1969, Inner Temple

Michaelides *Miss Christiana Kyriacou*
Kyriacos Th Michaelides Law, Offices, P O
Box 1548, Crete Str 2, Nicosia 135, Cyprus,
02 473751/465995, Fax: 02 451878, and
Member Cyprus Bar. Called: Nov 1992,
Middle Temple, LLB (Hons, Lond)

Michaelides *Miss Dina*
Legal Advisor in the Shipping Finance
Department, Chrysses Demetriades & Co,
Fortuna Court, Block B, 2nd F, 284 Arch.
Makarios III Avenue, P.O.Box 132, Limasol
3601, 00357 5 362424, Fax: 00357 5
370055. Called: Nov 1996, Middle Temple,
LLB (Hons)(Warw), LLM (So'ton)

Michaelides *Nicos R.*
P O Box 86, 3600 Limassol, 00357 5363742,
and Member Cyprus Bar. Called: Nov 1995,
Middle Temple, LLB (Hons)

Michaelides *Renos Kyriacou*
Advocate & Legal Advisor, Crete Street No2,
PO Box 1548, Nicosia, Cyprus, 357-2
473751/465995, Fax: 357-2 451878, and
Member Cyprus Bar. Called: Nov 1988,
Middle Temple, LLB (Lond)

Michell *Charles Henry Wroughton*
1 Gray's Inn Square, 1st Floor, London,
WC1R 5AG. Called: July 1978, Lincoln's Inn

Middleton *Miss Anne*
610 North 32nd Avenue, Hollywood, Florida
33021. Called: July 1970, Gray's Inn

Middleton *Christopher Edward*
Called: Oct 1997, Middle Temple, BSc
(Hons)(Kingston), MA (Lond), CPE (Lond)

Middleton *Miss Emma Louise*
Called: Nov 1996, Lincoln's Inn, BA(Jnt
Hons)(Dunelm)

Middleton *Timothy John* •
Deputy Legal Adviser, Home Office, 50
Queen Anne's Gate, London SW1H 9AT,
0171 273 3098, Fax: 0171 273 4075.
Called: July 1977, Gray's Inn, MA (Oxon)

Midha *Om Parkash*
Called: July 1967, Inner Temple

Mier *Andrew Stanley*
Grade 5 Branch Head Sols A 3, 59
Shaftesbury Road, London N19 4QW, 0171
272 6577. Called: July 1973, Middle Temple,
LLB (Lond)

Mifsud *Simon Paul*
Legal Advisor, S Mifsu & Sons Ltd, 311
Republic Street, Valletta - VLT 04, 00 356
232211, Fax: 00 356 240097. Called: Nov
1992, Inner Temple, LLB, LLM(Buckingham)

Mijatovic *Djura*
Called: July 1997, Middle Temple, LLB
(Hons)

Milburn *Hugh Charles*
Called: Mar 1997, Inner Temple, BA
(Manch)

Miles *Miss Alice Cecile Vernor*
Called: Nov 1994, Inner Temple, BA
(Soton), CPE (City)

Miles *Eric Charles* OBE
Thornhill, Redlands Lane, Ewshot, Farnham,
Surrey GU10 5AS. Called: Nov 1962, Gray's
Inn, FRAeS

Miles *William Frank*
Clerk to the Justices, Berkshire &
Oxfordshire, Magistrates Courts Committee,
Easby House, Northfield End, Henley, Oxon
RG9 2NB, 01491 412720, Fax: 01491
412762. Called: July 1976, Gray's Inn, LLB
(Lond)

Miles-Kingston *Mrs Janice Victoria*
Called: Nov 1996, Gray's Inn, BA (Sheff)

Milford *Mark Geoffrey*
Bank for International, Settlements,
Centralbahnplatz 2, CH-4002 Basle, 41 61
2809736, Fax: 41 61 2809112, and Member
New York. Called: Oct 1991, Lincoln's Inn,
LLB (Hons) (Lond), Maitrise (Paris)

Millar *Alexander David Wharton*
Called: Nov 1995, Inner Temple, BA
(Cantab), LLM (Illinois, USA)

Millar *David Bruce*
Called: Nov 1975, Inner Temple, MA (Oxon)

Millar-Parker *Miss Yvonne*
Called: May 1993, Inner Temple, LLB
(Reading)

Millbrook *Miss Alexandra Maria* •
Lawyer Grade 7, Lord Chancellor's
Department, Civil Appeals Office, Royal
Courts of Justice, Strand, London
WC2A 2LL, 0171 936 6738, Fax: 0171 936
6810. Called: July 1987, Middle Temple, BA
(Hons) (Oxon), Dip Law

Milledge *Peter Neil* •
Assistant Director of Legal Services,
Solicitor's Office DHSS, New Court, 48
Carey Street, London WC2A 2LS, 0171 412
1473, Fax: 0171 412 1227. Called: July
1977, Middle Temple, LLB (Lond)

Miller *Andrew Paul*
Macfarlanes Solicitors, 10 Norwich Street,
London EC4Y 1BD. Called: Nov 1995, Inner
Temple, BA (Oxon)

Miller *Miss Anna Belinda*
Called: Nov 1996, Inner Temple, BA
(Sussex)

Miller *Anthony Frederick Charles*
31 Cotsford Avenue, New Malden, Surrey
KT3 5EU. Called: June 1956, Gray's Inn,
BSc, LLB

Miller *Mrs Diana Susan* •
Company Legal Adviser Director
(Compliance), Legal & General Assurance,
Society Ltd, Legal & General House, St
Monica's Road, Kingswood, Tadworth,
Surrey KT20 6EU, 01737 370370, Fax:
01737 376240. Called: July 1980, Gray's Inn,
LLB

Miller *Miss Jaine Caroline* •
Legal Adviser, Lasmo Plc, 100 Liverpool
Street, London EC2M 2BB, 0171 945 4544.
Called: Mar 1996, Lincoln's Inn, LLB (Hons)

Miller *James Edward*
Called: Oct 1995, Middle Temple, LLB
(Hons) (Bris), LLM

Miller *John William*
Called: July 1976, Middle Temple

Miller *Justin Hayden*
Called: Oct 1994, Gray's Inn, BA (Keele)

Miller *Mrs Lynne*
Barrister of South Africa. Called: Apr 1991,
Middle Temple, BA (South Africa), LLb
(South Africa)

Miller *Mrs Maureen Patricia*
Called: Oct 1997, Middle Temple, BA
(Hons)(Lond), LLB (Lond)

Miller *Michael Christopher*
Called: Nov 1995, Middle Temple, LLB
(Hons)(Leeds)

Miller *Nathaniel Thomas*
Called: Oct 1994, Middle Temple, BA
(Hons)(Cantab)

Miller *Robert Ormiston*
Called: July 1987, Inner Temple, BA (Oxon)
Dip Law

Miller *Ronald Kinsman* CB
Part-time Chairman of VAT Tribunals, 4
Liskeard Close, Chislehurst, Kent BR7 6RT.
Called: Nov 1953, Gray's Inn

Miller *Miss Sophie Jane*
Paradise House, Granchester Street,
Newnham Village, Cambridge CB3 9HY,
01223 766118. Called: Oct 1993, Lincoln's
Inn, MA (Hons, Cantab), Diploma in Law

Miller *Stephen David*
Called: Oct 1996, Gray's Inn, LLB (Staffs),
MA (Keele)

Miller *Mrs Yvonne Ann*
Legal Advisor, 9 Cassis Drive, 65 466 2792.
Called: Nov 1985, Inner Temple,
LLB(B'ham), LLM (Cantab)

Millett *Timothy Patrick*
Legal Adviser for Administrative Affairs,
Court of Justice of the, European
Communities L-2925, (00352) 43031, Fax:
(00352) 4303-2600. Called: Nov 1975,
Gray's Inn, MA (Oxon)

Millhouse *Mrs Susan Mary*
Called: Nov 1996, Gray's Inn, BA (N.Wales),
LLB (E. Anglia)

Milligan *Scott Gregor* •
Dept of Trade and Industry, 10 Victoria
Street, London SW1H 0NN, 0171 215 5000,
Fax: 0171 215 3221. Called: July 1975,
Middle Temple, MA (Oxon)

Millin *Mrs Leslie Marilyn*
Capsticks, 77/83 Upper Richmond Road,
London SW15 2TT, 0181 780 2211, Fax:
0181 780 1141. Called: Nov 1988, Gray's
Inn, LLB (Reading)

Millington *Trevor John* •
Senior Principal Legal Officer, HM Customs
& Excise, New King's Beam House, 22
Upper Ground, London SE1 9PJ, 0171 865
5819, Fax: 0171 865 5902. Called: July
1981, Middle Temple, LLB (Wales)

Mills *Miss Andrea Elaine Susan* •
Called: Oct 1991, Lincoln's Inn, LLB (Hons)

Mills *Dame Barbara Jean Lyon* QC
(1986) •
Director of Public Prosecutions, Crown
Prosecution Service, 50 Ludgate Hill,
London EC4M 7EX, 0171 273 3000, QC,
Northern Ireland 23 Essex Street, London,
WC2R 3AS. Called: July 1963, Middle
Temple, MA (Oxon)

Mills *George Arthur Charles* •
Case Controller, Serious Fraud Office,
Serious Fraud Office, Elm House, 10-16 Elm
Street, London WC1X OBJ, 0171 239 7061,
Fax: 0171 833 2443. Called: Nov 1987,
Inner Temple, LLB (So'ton), LLM (Lond),
M.Phil (Cantab)

Mills *Ms Janet*
Called: Mar 1996, Inner Temple, LLM
(Harvard, USA), BA (Hons)

Mills *John* OBE QC (1962)
Greenleas, Highleigh, Chichester, Sussex
PO20 7NP, 01243 641396, Also Inn of
Court L. Called: June 1938, Middle Temple,
MA (Cantab)

Mills *Mrs Julie Ann*
Deputy Clerk to the Justices, Bath &
Wansdyke Magistrates', Court,, North Parade
Road, Bath, Avon BA1 5AF, 01225 463281,
Fax: 01225 420255. Called: July 1986, Inner
Temple

Mills *Leopold Nathaniel* JP
Secretary to the Cabinet, PO Box HM 287,
Hamilton HMAX, 441 292 5501, Fax: 441
292 8397, and Member Bermuda Bar.
Called: Nov 1988, Middle Temple, LLB
(Bucks)

Mills *Michael John Patrick*
Hatten Asplin Glenny, 90 Orsett Road,
Grays, Essex RM17 5ER, 01375 374851, Fax:
01375 374332, Solicitor of the Supreme
Court of England & Wales. Called: Oct 1992,
Inner Temple, BA (Hons)

Mills Peter John
Manager of Legal & Corporate Services, The
Court House, Lichfield Road, Sutton
Coldfield B74 2NS, 0121 354 7777, Fax:
0121 355 0547. Called: Nov 1983, Gray's
Inn, BA

Mills Richard Sinclair
EC Harris, 7-12 Tavistock Square, London
WC1H 9LX, 0171 387 8431, Fax: 0171 380
0493. Called: July 1994, Lincoln's Inn, LLB
(Hons), BSc, ARICS

Mills Miss Sarah Jane
Called: Oct 1995, Lincoln's Inn, LLB
(Hons)(Leic)

Mills Miss Susan Elizabeth
Called: Mar 1998, Lincoln's Inn, LLB
(Hons)(L'pool)

Millward Mrs Lisa Sarah Liat
7 Purcell Close, Tewin Wood, Hertfordshire
AL6 0NN, 01438 798 3391/01727 868686,
Fax: 01727 858 888. Called: Nov 1996,
Lincoln's Inn, LLB (Hons)(Lond)

Milner Miss Lesley •
17th Floor, Tolworth Tower, Surbiton,
Surrey KT6 7DS, 399-5171, Fax: 390-3474.
Called: Feb 1992, Middle Temple, BA (Hon)
(Lond), LLB (Hons) (Lond)

Milner Nicholas Emmanuel
Called: Mar 1996, Gray's Inn, MA
(Edinburgh)

Mimmack Andrew Elstob
Clerk to the Justices, South Devon
Magistrates', Courts, The Court House,
Union Street, Torquay, Devon TQ1 4BP,
01803 298683, Fax: 01803 291425.
Called: July 1973, Inner Temple, LLB, MSc

Minchin Brian Patrick John
Called: June 1959, Gray's Inn, MA (Cantab)

Minichiello Miss Andrea Rose
New Court, Temple, London, EC4Y 9BE.
Called: July 1988, Inner Temple, BA (Wales)

Minns Miss Tracy Jane
Senior Legal Worker, Acton for Victims of
Medical, Accidents, Bank Chambers, 1
London Road, Forest Hill, London SE23 3JP,
0181 291 2793. Called: Nov 1991, Gray's
Inn, MA (Oxon)

Minta Ms Lucia
Darshan Singh & Co, No 18-A, Lebuh Pantai,
(Beach Street), 10300 Pulau Pinang, 0106 04
2611820, Fax: 0106 04 2627476, Master in
Tropical Health of the University of
Queensland, Australia. Called: July 1997,
Lincoln's Inn, BSc (Hons)(Salford)

Mirpuri Miss Sunita
Former Solicitor. Called: Nov 1996, Inner
Temple, BA (Kent)

Misick Miss Yvette Denise
McLean Mcnally, McLean Building, P O Box
62, 2001 Leeward Highway, Providenciales,
809 946 4277. Called: July 1996, Lincoln's
Inn, LLB (Hons)(Leeds)

Mistlin Trevor
Former Solicitor. Called: Nov 1996,
Lincoln's Inn, BSc (Hons)(Notts)

Mistry Mrs Chandraprabha •
Senior Crown Prosecutor, Crown
Prosecution Service, St Albans Branch,
Queens House, 58 Victoria Street, St Albans
AL1 3HZ. Called: July 1976, Inner Temple

Mitcalf Richard James •
Principal Crown Prosecutor Prosecution
Team Leader, Crown Prosecution Service,
7th Floor South, Royal Liver Buildings,
Water Street, Liverpool L3 1HN, 0151 236
7575. Called: July 1983, Gray's Inn, BA
(Hons)

Mitchell Mrs (Sarah) Felicity Jane •
Legal Officer, The Office of the Banking,
Ombudsman, 70 Gray's Inn Road, London
WC1, 0171 404 9944. Called: Oct 1992,
Middle Temple, BA (Hons), Dip in Law

Mitchell Alistair Stephen Fabian
Called: Oct 1997, Middle Temple, LLB

Mitchell Anthony Geoffrey Fulton
Called: Feb 1959, Gray's Inn, LLB

Mitchell David John
Called: Oct 1995, Lincoln's Inn, BSc
(Hons)(Lond), LLB (Hons)(City)

Mitchell Harry QC (1987)
Part-time Immigration Adjudicator Trustee,
The Migraine Trust Chairman, Sarsen
Housing Assoc, The Mount, Brook Street,
Great Bedwyn, Marlborough, Wilts SN8 3LZ,
01672 870898. Called: July 1968, Gray's Inn,
BA,FCIS

Mitchell John Winterburn •
Principal Crown Prosecutor, Crown
Prosecution Service, Crosstrend House, 10A
Newport, Loncoln LN1 3DF, 01522 512800,
Fax: 01522 515700. Called: Nov 1984,
Gray's Inn

Mitchell Jonathan
Called: Mar 1998, Inner Temple, BA (Open
Uni)

Mitchell Mrs Karen Joy •
Principle Assistant - Legal, Bolton
Magistrates Court, P O Box 24, The Courts,
Civic Centre, Bolton BL1 1QX, 01204
522244, Fax: 01204 364373. Called: Nov
1982, Gray's Inn

Mitchell Paul Martin Selby
Deputy Clerk to the Justices, The
Secretariat, The Court House, Friars Walk,
Lewes, East Sussex BN7 2PE, 01273 486455.
Called: Nov 1986, Gray's Inn

Mitchell Ms Victoria Grant
Wilde Sapte, 1 Fleet Place, London
EC4Y 7NS. Called: Nov 1988, Middle
Temple, LLB (B'ham)

Mitchels David Lloyd
0171 405 8828, Fax: 0171 405 6680, and
Member Seychelles Bar 14 Tooks Court,
Cursitor St, London, EC4A 1LB. Called: Nov
1970, Lincoln's Inn, LLB (Lond)

Mitchiner James Patrick
Called: Oct 1996, Middle Temple, BSc
(Hons)(Lond), Dip in Law (Notts)

Mitchinson Mr Robert Charles
Glovers, Whites Lane, Little Leighs,
Chelmsford CM3 1PA, 01245 362472, Fax:
01245 362472. Called: Nov 1969, Gray's
Inn, ACIS, FIMgt

Mitha Abdulsultan Alibhai
32 Hawkwood Place NW, Calgary Alberta,
Calgary, Alberta T3G 1X6, 403 239 7427.
Called: July 1972, Inner Temple, MA

Mitra Joydeep
Called: July 1994, Middle Temple, LLB
(Hons)(Lond)

Mitra Siddhartha
Called: July 1991, Lincoln's Inn, LLB (Hons)

Mittelholzer Neville Arthur
Called: Nov 1967, Middle Temple

Mittelstadt David Joseph
The Thompson Corporation, Metro Center,
One Staton Place, Stamford CT 06902, (203)
328 9457, and Member Massachusettss
(USA) US Tax Court. Called: Feb 1989,
Lincoln's Inn, MA (Cantab), JD (Chicago)

Miyajima Miss Mitsue
8 Welbeck Street, London W1M 7PB.
Called: July 1997, Lincoln's Inn, BA (Japan),
CPE, LLDip (Wolves)

Moal Ms Suja
Called: Nov 1997, Inner Temple, LLM
(S'ton)

Mobsby Mrs Sheilah Innes
Called: Feb 1965, Middle Temple, LLB
(Exon)

Mochun Dr Wolodymyr
11 Seely Road, Nottingham NG7 7NU,
Pharmacist. Called: Nov 1992, Inner
Temple, BSc, LLB, PhD, MSc, (M.I.P.L), LLM

Mockett Graham Andrew
Principal Court Clerk, Feltham Magistrates
Court, Hanworth Road, Feltham, Middlesex
TW13 5AG, 0181 751 3727, Fax: 0181 844
1779. Called: July 1989, Middle Temple, Dip
Law, Dip Mag Law, Diploma in,
Management Studies, (DMS)

Mockett John Vere Brooke
Called: Feb 1958, Gray's Inn, MA (Oxon)

Moe Mr Justice Henry Stanley Rawle
Justice of the Supreme Court, Eastern
Caribbean, High Court of Justice, Antigua &
Barbuda, P.O.Box 1722, St John's, Antigua,
462 0039, Attorney at Law, Barbados and
Member Barbados. Called: Nov 1970,
Lincoln's Inn, BA (Hons) Durham, PG Dip
Ed, FCI, MBIM, ACIS, LLM (Leic)

Moffat Alexander Peter
Called: Nov 1985, Lincoln's Inn

Moh Yong Alan Chee Chuen
Called: Nov 1995, Middle Temple, LLB
(Hons)

Mohamad Salleh Miss Aldila
Called: Oct 1994, Middle Temple, LLB
(Hons)(Bris)

Mohamed Miss Elina
Called: July 1994, Lincoln's Inn, LLB (Hons)

E

Mohamed Haniffa *Seeni Syed Ahamed Kabeer*
Called: July 1996, Middle Temple, LLB (Hons)(Lond)

Mohamed Hashim *Abdul Rasheed*
Legal Advisor, Blk 602, Yishun St 61, [H]06-359, Singapore 2776, 0065 7523574, Advocate & Solicitor of the Supreme Court of Singapore. Called: July 1993, Lincoln's Inn, LLB (Hons)

Mohamed Shafie *Jamil*
Called: Feb 1994, Lincoln's Inn, BA (Hons), Dip in Law

Mohamed Yakub *Mohamed Ibrahim*
Block 138, Bishan Street 12, 05-460, 2589772. Called: July 1996, Middle Temple, LLB (Hons)(Lond)

Mohamedi *Miss Reena* •
Ince & Co, Knollys House, 11 Byward Street, London EC3R 5EN, 0171 623 2011, Fax: 0171 623 3225. Called: July 1987, Middle Temple, BA (Cantab) BS (USA), Georgetown Uni

Mohammad Taha *Zamri*
Called: July 1997, Lincoln's Inn, LLB (Hons)

Mohammed *Asif*
Called: July 1997, Lincoln's Inn, BA (Hons)(Swansea)

Mohammed *Miss Mardzlinda*
Called: May 1995, Lincoln's Inn, LLB (Hons)

Mohan *Mrs Mankalam*
Called: July 1994, Middle Temple, LLB (Lond), B.Sc (Singapore)

Mohd Ali *Miss Nor Hasliza*
Legal Assistant, Mohd Ali & Co, Advocates & Solicitors, No 105 Jalan Telawi, Bangsar Baru, 59100 Kuala Lumpur, 00 603 2842276, Fax: 00 603 2842273, and Member Malaysia Bar. Called: July 1995, Lincoln's Inn, LLB (Hons)

Mohd Amin *Haji Mohammed*
Called: Oct 1993, Middle Temple, LLB (Hons), LLM, BA (Hons), CertEdu

Mohd Ibrahim Zain *Miss Rosdena*
Called: July 1997, Middle Temple, LLB (Hons)(Nott'm)

Mohd Kalok *Miss Azlina Yati*
Called: July 1996, Lincoln's Inn, LLB (Hons)(Notts)

Mohd Khalil *Miss Mas Aryani*
Called: July 1996, Middle Temple, LLB (Hons)(Keele), BA (Hons)(Keele)

Mohd Naim *Miss Farah Wahidah*
Wan Haron Sukri & Nordin, Advocates & Solcitors, No 64-2 Jalan 2A/27A, Seksyen 1, Bandar Baru Wangsa, Maju, 53300 Setapak, Kuala Lumpur, 603 4112611, Fax: 603 4112622, Advocate & solicitor (Malaysia) and Member Malaysia Bar. Called: July 1993, Lincoln's Inn, LLB (Hons), LLM (Lond)

Mohd Radzi *Miss Nonee Ashirin*
Called: July 1997, Lincoln's Inn, LLB (Hons)

Mohd Saffian *Miss Azlin*
Called: July 1996, Lincoln's Inn, LLB (Hons)

Mohd Said *Miss Norhafiza*
Legal Assistant, Messrs 12a Ng Yeoh & Kit, 19th Floor, Bangunan Dato, Zainal 23 Jalan Melaka 50100, Kuala Lumpur, 01-06-03 2986066, Fax: 01-06-03-2982593, and Member Malaysian Bar. Called: July 1995, Middle Temple, LLB (Hons) (Wales)

Mohindra *Dr Raj Kumar*
Currently Practising Doctor, 89 Albion Road, Hounslow, Middlesex TW3 3RS. Called: Oct 1991, Inner Temple, MA Hons (Cantab), BM Bch (Oxon), MRCP (UK)

Mohipp *H. Anthony*
Called: July 1957, Middle Temple

Mok *Miss Ida Yin Leng*
Called: Nov 1995, Middle Temple, LLB (Hons)

Mok *Ignatius Yann Shi*
16 Jalan ATI-ATI, Taman Perdana, 83000 Batu Pahat, Johor, 00-6007-4318694, and Member Malaysia Bar. Called: July 1996, Lincoln's Inn, LLB (Hons)(Lond)

Mok *Miss Karen Yu-Yen*
Called: July 1996, Inner Temple, LLB (Hull)

Mok *Miss Wai Mun*
56-H King's Road, Singapore 268118, 466 1703, Advocate & Solicitor of the Supreme Court of Singapore. Called: July 1994, Middle Temple, LLB (Hons)(B'ham)

Mok *Yick-Fan Danny*
Chief Engineer, Hong Kong Government, c/o Works Branch, 11/F Murray Building, Garden Road, Hong Kong, (852) 28482045, Fax: (852) 25371961. Called: Feb 1994, Gray's Inn, BSc (Eng), MBA (CUHK), MSocSc (Hong Kong), LLB (Lond), LLM (Lond)

Mok *Yiu Fai*
Called: July 1995, Gray's Inn, LLB (Wales)

Mokal *Sardar Rizwaan Jameel*
Called: Nov 1997, Gray's Inn, BSc (Punjab), LLB (Lond)

Mokhtiar *Baldev Singh*
Called: Nov 1995, Middle Temple, LLB (Hons)(Keele)

Mokty *Miss Mazita*
Called: July 1995, Lincoln's Inn, LLB (Hons)

Molla *Abdur Razzaq*
and Member Bangladesh Bar. Called: Nov 1970, Inner Temple, BA, LLB

Molloy *Colin Vincent* •
Principal Crown Prosecutor, Crown Prosecution Service, St Johns House, Union Street, Dudley DY2 8PP, 01384 230471. Called: Feb 1985, Middle Temple, BA

Molloy *Ms Karen Rose*
Called: May 1996, Gray's Inn, LLB (Belfast)

Moloney *Miss Louise Claire*
ILMCS, 65 Romney Street, London SW1P 3RD. Called: Nov 1988, Gray's Inn, BA

Monaghan *Neill Roderick* •
Principal Legal Officer, H M Customs & Excise, New Kings Beam House, 22 Upper Ground, London SE1 9PJ, 0171 865 5803, Fax: 0171 865 5987. Called: July 1979, Lincoln's Inn, LLB (Newc)

Monaghan *Peter John*
Bench Legal Adviser, Dorset Magistrates' Court, The Law Courts, Park Road, Poole, Dorset BH15 2RH, 01305 783891. Called: Feb 1986, Middle Temple, Dip Mag Law, DMS MIMgt

Monaghan *Miss Sarah Jane*
Called: Feb 1995, Inner Temple, BA (Keele), CPE

Monah *Miss Helen Anne*
Called: Nov 1996, Lincoln's Inn, LLB (Hons)(Lond)

Monk *Miss Sheryl Jane* •
Called: Nov 1996, Gray's Inn, BA (Nott'm)

Monk *Thomas John*
Legal Director, Company Secretary. Called: July 1976, Middle Temple, LLB

Monnington *Bruce Gilbert*
Country Landowners Assoc., 16 Belgrave Square, London SW1X 8PQ, 0171 235 0511. Called: July 1989, Inner Temple, MA (City), Dip EU Law (Lond)

Monro *Miss Vijaya* •
Senior Crown Prosecutor, Crown Prosecution Service, St Peter's House, Gower Street, Derby, 01332 621600. Called: May 1990, Lincoln's Inn, BA (Hons)

Montador *Adrien Francis*
Legal Advisor, The Court House, Elmleigh Road, Havant PO9 2AL, 01252 366083, Fax: 01256 811447. Called: May 1987, Lincoln's Inn, LLB (Dundee)

Montague *Major John Charles*
Peamore Cottage, Alphington, Exeter EX2 9SJ, 01392 832606. Called: Nov 1972, Inner Temple, AMICE

Monteil *Dr Rene Leon*
Former Lecturer at the University of the West Indies, The National Gas Company of, Trinidad & Tobago, Goodrich Bay Road, Point Lisas, Trinidad, 1-809 636 4662, Fax: 1-809 636 2905. Called: July 1987, Middle Temple, BSc, PhD (Lond), MA (Law) (City), FRSC, C.Chem

Monteiro *James Patrick*
Called: Nov 1995, Lincoln's Inn, LLB (Hons)

Monterio *Miss Cheryl Ann*
Partner, Bajwa & Co, No 4 Shenton Way, [H]08-07 Shing Kwan House, (65) 227 5293, Fax: (65) 227 3780, and Member Singapore. Called: Nov 1994, Middle Temple, LLB (Hons)

Montgomery *Ms Laura Louise* •
Company Secretary, L L Briggs Limited, Three Mill Island, Three Mill Lane, London E3 3DZ, 0181 980 3000, Fax: 0181 980 4544. Called: Nov 1992, Gray's Inn, LLB (Westminster)

Moo *Chee Leong*
No 18-1 Changkat Bukit Bintang, (Hicks Road), 50200 Kuala lumpur, 2432128, Fax: 2433919, and Member Malaya Bar. Called: July 1995, Middle Temple, LLB (Hons) (Lond)

Moody *John David*
Trainee Solicitor, Simons & Simons, 21 Wilson Street, London, 0171 825 3530. Called: Oct 1996, Middle Temple, BA (Hons), LLM (Lond)

Moolla *Umer Faruque*
Called: Nov 1994, Gray's Inn, LLB

Moorby *Idris James*
Justices' Chief Executive, Weind House P O Box 717, Parkhill Road, Garstang, Lancs PR3 1EY, 01995 601596, Fax: 01995 601776. Called: Nov 1979, Gray's Inn, BA, MBA

Moore *Alan*
Justices' Clerk, Justices' Clerk's Office, The Court House, Station Road, Brough HU15 1DY, 01724 281100. Called: Nov 1981, Inner Temple

Moore *Miss Caroline Mary Phyllis*
Accredited CEDR Mediator, Lovell White Durrant, 65 Holborn Viaduct, London EC1A 2DY, 0171 236 0066, Fax: 0171 248 4212. Called: July 1977, Middle Temple, BA (Oxon)

Moore *Christopher Peter-John* •
Assistant Lawyer, Dow Jones Markets Limited, Winchmore House, 15 Fetter Lane, London EC4A 1BR, 44 171 832 9506, Fax: 44 171 583 3900. Called: Oct 1995, Middle Temple, B.Sc (Hons) (Dunelm), Grad Inst P

Moore *Colin*
28 Orchard Court, St Chad's Road, Leeds LS16 5QS, 0113 274 0900, Fax: 0113 274 0900. Called: Nov 1967, Gray's Inn

Moore *Derek Edmund*
20 Sussex Street, London SW1V 4RW, 0171 834 5286. Called: July 1957, Gray's Inn, MA

Moore *Dominique Jean*
Called: Oct 1996, Inner Temple, BA (Cantab)

Moore *Dudley John*
Law Lecturer, Bellerbys College, 44 Cromwell Road, Hove, Sussex, 01273 723911. Called: Oct 1996, Middle Temple, BA (Hons)(Sussex)

Moore *Eric Frank*
Senior Crown Prosecutor (Retired). Called: Nov 1976, Lincoln's Inn, LLB (Lond)

Moore *Geoffrey*
Called: July 1965, Gray's Inn

Moore *George Crawford Jackson*
Attorney, Citzens Building, Suite 812, 105 S. Narcissus Avenue, West Palm Beach, Florida 33401, (561) 833 9000, Fax: (561) 833 9990, and Member Florida, Jamaica, Turks & Caicos Islands, British Virgin Islands, Grenada, Montserrat, St Lucia and Antigua. Called: July 1970, Inner Temple, BA, BPhil, MA, (Cantab) LLB, LLM

Moore *Mrs Gillian Patricia*
Court Clerk, The Law Courts, Alexandra Road, Wimbledon, London SW19 7JP, 0181 946 8622, Fax: 0181 946 7030. Called: Nov 1982, Gray's Inn

Moore *Mrs Karen Marie*
Called: Nov 1992, Middle Temple, LLB (Hons)

Moore *Kevin Ryland* •
Deputy Clerk to the Justices, Redbridge Magistrates Court, 850 Cranbrook Road, Ilford, Essex IG6 IHW, 0181 498 8902, Fax: 0181 550 2181. Called: July 1983, Lincoln's Inn, Dip Law (Mag), Adv.Dip P.T.D., M.I.Mgt

Moore *Matthew James* •
Bureau LEO 5A53, Legal Service, European Parliamemt, 89-113 Rue Belliard, B-1047 Bruxelles. Called: Nov 1989, Inner Temple, BA (Kent)

Moore *Miss Nicola Jean* •
Flight Lieutenant - RAF, RAF Innsworth, Gloucestershire. Called: Nov 1993, Lincoln's Inn, LLB (Hons, Bris)

Moore *Mrs Patricia Margaret Waring JP*
Kirklands, West Street, Odiham, Hook, Hants RG29 1NT, 01256 703085. Called: May 1953, Inner Temple, LLB

Moore *Philip Anthony* •
Senior Crown Prosecutor, Crown Prosecution Service, The Cooperage, 6 Gainsford Street, London SE1 2NS. Called: July 1971, Gray's Inn, BA

Moore *Richard John*
Called: Oct 1992, Lincoln's Inn, BA(Hons)

Moore *Robert Dennis* •
International Legal Manager, Enterprise Oil Plc, Grand Buildings, Trafalgar Square, London WC2N 5EJ, 0171 925 4000, Fax: 0171 925 4606. Called: July 1981, Middle Temple, BA (Hons)

Moore *Rowland Peter*
Kirklands, West Street, Odiham, Hook, Hants RG29 1NT, 01256 703085. Called: July 1952, Lincoln's Inn, LLB

Moore-Williams *Miss Anne Elizabeth* •
Law Commission, Conquest House, 37/38 John Street, Theobalds Road, London WC1N 2BQ, 0171 453 1220, Fax: 0171 453 1297, and Member Czech Republic Bar. Called: Oct 1992, Inner Temple, BA (Keele), LLM (Lond)

Moorhouse *Brendon Scott* •
Senior Crown Prosecutor, Crown Prosecution Service, 2nd Floor, Froomsgate House, Rupert Street, Bristol BS1 2QS, 0117 9273093, Fax: 0117 9230697. Called: Nov 1992, Middle Temple, LLB (Hons)

Moosajee *Mrs Aliya Khanum*
Called: July 1987, Middle Temple, LLB (Lond), LLM (LSE)

Moosdeen *Miss Munira*
2108 Melbourne Plaza, No 33 Queen's Road Central, 25239775, Fax: 28452464. Called: July 1984, Lincoln's Inn, LLB, PCLL

Mootoo *Jason Kelvin*
Called: Nov 1995, Gray's Inn, LLB (Kent), LLM

Moran *Ms Elena Roberta* •
BBC White City, 201 Wood Lane, London W12 7TS, 0181 752 4053, Fax: 0181 752 5080. Called: Nov 1989, Inner Temple, LLB, LLM (UCL)

Moran *Mr. John Michael*
Called: Nov 1995, Inner Temple, BA (Oxon), LLM (California)

Moran *Patrick Michael*
Called: Oct 1997, Inner Temple, LLB (Birmingham)

More *Miss Gillian Catherine* •
Advice on Individual Rights, in Europe (The AIRE Centre), 74 Eurolink Business Centre, 49 Effra Road, London SW2 1BZ. Called: Nov 1996, Middle Temple, BA (Hons)(Kent), LLM (Canada)

Moreira *John Robert*
Called: Nov 1997, Gray's Inn, BA

Moreno *Mrs Yvonne Laraine* •
Principal Crown Prosecutor Team Leader, Crown Prosecution Service, Kings House, 3rd Floor, Kymberley Road, Harrow on the Hill, Middlesex HA1 1YH, 0181 424 8688 Ext 301. Called: Nov 1974, Gray's Inn, LLB (Hons), M/C, Dip in Criminology, (Cantab)

Moreton *Mrs Kirsty Leigh*
Called: Nov 1996, Gray's Inn, LLB (Wales)

Morey *Mrs Deborah Ann*
Called: Oct 1997, Middle Temple, LLB (Hons)(Lond)

Morgan *Ceri Richards*
18 Bowham Avenue, Bridgend, Mid Glamorgan CF31 3PA, 01656 667294. Called: Nov 1982, Gray's Inn, LLB (Lond), M.C.I.E.H., M.I.O.S.H.

Morgan *Charles Lawrence* •
Legal & Negotiations Manager, LASMO Plc, 101 Liverpool Street, London EC2, 0171 892 9707, and Member California, USA. Called: Feb 1977, Middle Temple, MA (Oxon)

Morgan *Miss Chloe Rebecca*
Babbe, Le Poidevin, Allez, Wirzel Court, P O Box 612, St Peter Port, Guernsey, 01481 710585, Fax: 01481 712245, and Member Guernsey Bar. Called: July 1995, Inner Temple, LLB

Morgan *Miss Diana Mary*
Called: Nov 1976, Gray's Inn, BA (Hons), Post-, Graduate Diploma in, Language Studies

Morgan *Lieut.Commander Eric Wilfred DSC, RN*
Hollows, Matterdale, Penrith, Cumbria CA11 0LD, 017684 82315. Called: Jan 1950, Lincoln's Inn, MA (Oxon), Master Mariner

Morgan *Glyn James*
Called: Nov 1947, Middle Temple, MA (Cantab)

Morgan *Miss Gwyneth Anne Rhoda*
Called: July 1977, Gray's Inn, BA [Oxon]

Morgan *John Vincent Lyndon*
Orchard House, The Way, Reigate, Surrey RH2 0LB, 01737 247071. Called: Feb 1960, Gray's Inn, MA (Oxon)

Morgan *Mrs Marilynne Ann CB* •
The Solicitor to the Dept of Social Security & the Dept of Health., Dept of Social security, Dept of Health, New Court, 48 Carey Street, London WC2A 2LS, 0171 412 1404, Fax: 0171 412 1501. Called: Nov 1972, Middle Temple, BA (Lond)

Morgan *Miss Marlene Marilyn* •
Legal Officer, Inland Revenue, Solicitors Office, Somerset House, The Strand, London WC2R 1LB, 0171 438 6669. Called: July 1989, Lincoln's Inn, LLB

Morgan *Rhys Gareth*
Called: Nov 1995, Inner Temple, BA (Swansea), CPE (Wolves)

Morgan *Robert James Marcello* •
Senior Consultant, Hellings Morgan Associates, No 5, Bisney View, 47-49 Bisney Road, Pokfulam, Hong Kong, +852 2855 1428/2819 5792, Fax: +852 2855 1510. Called: Feb 1980, Gray's Inn, BA (Hons), LLM, FCIArb, FHKIArb, FSIArb, AMAE

Morgan *Miss Shelagh Elizabeth*
2 Crown Office Row, 2nd Floor, Temple, London, EC4Y 7HJ. Called: June 1964, Middle Temple, LLB

Morgan *Simon Halvor*
Called: Feb 1995, Lincoln's Inn, LLB (Hons)

Morkel *Richard Pierre*
Called: Nov 1994, Gray's Inn, LLB (Bris)

Morley *Alistair Eric* •
Called: Nov 1991, Middle Temple, BA Hons (Lond), MPhil (Oxon)

Morley *Miss Joanne Louise* •
Lawyer (Prosecutions), Solicitors Office, H M Customs & Excise, New Kings Beam House, 22 Upper Ground, London SE1, 0171 620 1313. Called: Feb 1995, Inner Temple, BA (Oxon)

Morrell *Neil Edward Sheperd*
Called: Nov 1995, Lincoln's Inn, LLB (Hons)

Morris *Arthur Rowland*
Called: Nov 1997, Gray's Inn, BSc (Econ) (LSE), MA (Ed)

Morris *Mrs Helen Elizabeth* •
Crown Prosecution Service, 7th Floor, Liver Building, Pier Head, Liverpool, Former Solicitor. Called: Nov 1996, Gray's Inn, LLB (Lond)

Morris *John Cameron*
Scottish Advocate, Queens Counsel, Advocates Library, Parliament House, Edinburgh, 0131 226 5071, Temporary Sheriff (Scotland) Queen's Counsel (Scotland). Called: July 1990, Inner Temple, LLB (Strathclyde)

Morris *Ms Karen Anne*
European Counsel- Vice President, Chubb Insurance Company of, Europe S.A., 16 Avenue de Matignan, Paris, 331/45.61.73.68, Fax: 331/45.61.41.62. Called: Nov 1986, Gray's Inn, MA (Edin), Dip Law, (City), LLM (Univ of, Lond)

Morris *Nicholas Guy Ussher*
Woodfield House, Oxford Road, Clifton, Hampden, Oxon OX14 3EW, 01865 407149, Fax: 01865 407149. Called: July 1970, Middle Temple, MA (Oxon)

Morris *Paul Derek*
Called: Oct 1996, Inner Temple, LLB (Lancs)

Morris *Paul Xavier* •
Legal Adviser, Lloyds of London, Legal Services Department, 1958 Building, Lime Street, London EC3M 7HA, 0171 327 6672, Fax: 0171 327 5502. Called: Nov 1993, Middle Temple, MA (Cantab)

Morris *William John* •
Commercial Union Assurance, Company plc, Room 113, Institute of London, Underwriters, 49 Leadenhall St, London EC3A 2BE, 0171 283 7500. Called: May 1996, Middle Temple, LLB (Hons), LLM (Dunelm)

Morris-Marsham *Mrs Margaret Lindelia*
Legal Adviser, Coopers & Lybrand, 1 Embankment Place, London WC2N 6NN, 0171 583 5000, Fax: 0171 213 2463. Called: Nov 1967, Lincoln's Inn

Morrison *Sheriff Nigel Murray Paton QC*
Sheriff of Lothian and Borders at Edinburgh, 9 India Street, Edinburgh EH3 6HA, 031 225 2807, Fax: 031 225 5688, and Member Scottish Bar. Called: Nov 1972, Inner Temple

Morrison *Philip William*
Called: Nov 1956, Gray's Inn, LLB

Morse *Miss Beverley Anne*
Senior Deputy Chief Clerk, Inner London Magistrates', Courts Service, 65 Romney Street, London SW1P 3RD, 0171 799 3332, Fax: 0171 799 3072. Called: July 1978, Gray's Inn, LLM (Cantab), Cert Crim (Lond)

Morse *Nicholas Stephen*
Called: Oct 1997, Lincoln's Inn, LLB (Hons)(Lond)

Morsingh *Miss Wern Li*
Called: July 1996, Gray's Inn, LLB (London)

Mortimer *John Clifford CBE QC (1966)*
1 Dr Johnson's Bldgs, Ground Floor, Temple, London, EC4Y 7AX. Called: Jan 1948, Inner Temple, BA

Mortimer *Jonathan*
Called: Oct 1996, Gray's Inn, BA (Dunelm), LLM (Cantab)

Morton *Michael Quentin*
Deputy Clerk to the Justices', The Court House, Tufton Street, Ashford, Kent TN23 1QS, 01233 663204, Fax: 01233 663206. Called: July 1979, Lincoln's Inn, BA (Lond), DMS

Morton *Mrs Sheelagh Alice* •
Prosecution Team Leader, CPS (Derby), 5th Floor, St Peter's House, Gower Street, Derbyshire DE1 1SB, 01332 621 600. Called: Nov 1980, Inner Temple, LLB (Hull),MA

Morton *Thomas*
Called: Oct 1995, Inner Temple, BSc (Lond), CPE

Moscrop *John James* •
Crown Prosecutor, Crown Prosecution Service, 4-5 Ralli Court, West Riverside, Salford, Manchester, 0161 834 8551. Called: July 1983, Middle Temple, BA (Manch) LLB(Hull), M Phil (Salford), Dip Lib Studs (Bel), PhD (Leic)

Moses *Eric George Rufus CB*
Broome Cottage, Castle Hill, Nether Stowey, Bridgwater, Somerset TA5 1NB. Called: Jan 1938, Middle Temple

Mosko *Nicholas Terry*
Called: Nov 1995, Middle Temple, LLB (Hons)

Moss *Jeremy Paul*
Senior Court Lawyer, Cambridge Magistrates Court, The Court House, Lion Yard, Cambridge CB2 3NA, 01223 314311, Fax: 01223 355237. Called: Nov 1989, Inner Temple, LLB

Moss *Mitchell James* •
VAT Consultant, Ernest & Young, Becket House, 1 Lambeth Palace Road, London SE1. Called: Feb 1992, Gray's Inn, BA (Oxon)

Moss *Paul David*
Legal Adviser, P O Box N-9932, Nassau, 1-242 32-65084, Fax: 1-242 32-80541, and Member Bahamas Bar. Called: July 1995, Lincoln's Inn, LLB (Hons), BA, TEP

Moss *Mrs Sandra Marie* •
Competition Consultant, C. I. P. F. A, 3 Robert Street, London WC2N 6BH, 0171 543 5600. Called: Oct 1993, Gray's Inn, LLB (Anglia)

Mott *Matthew John Spencer* •
Company Secretary & Legal Adviser, William Hill Organization, Greenside House, 50 Station Road, Wood Green, London N22 4TP, 0181 918 3600, Fax: 0181 918 3726. Called: July 1983, Gray's Inn, LLB FCIS

Mottram *Paul Richard* •
Legal Advisor to the Sunday Mirror, MGN Ltd, 1 Canada Square, Canary Wharf, London E14 5AP, 0171 293 3934. Called: Nov 1995, Middle Temple, LLB (Hons)

Motts *Miss Kirsteen*
Called: Nov 1996, Lincoln's Inn, BA (Hons)

Moulden *Simon Peter*
Called: Oct 1995, Inner Temple, LLB (Leic)

Moule *Justin Daniel*
Called: Nov 1995, Inner Temple, LLB (Lond)

• Barristers in employment

Mount David Richard •
Legal Advisor/Head of Claims, Tamoil
Shipping Limited, Leconfield House, Curzon
Street, London W1Y 7FB, 0171 344 5650.
Called: Nov 1973, Inner Temple

Moustras Andrew Thomas
Legal Assistant to Jersey Advocates, Philip
Sinel & Co, P O Box 595, 8 Wests Centre, St
Helier, Jersey, 01534 35407. Called: Nov
1995, Inner Temple, BA (Wales)

Mouton Marc Phillippe
Called: Oct 1995, Inner Temple, LLB (Exon)

Moutou Lewis Toussaint
10 Georges Guibert Street, Port-Louis,
Mauritius, 230 2085153, Fax: 230
28338678/230 210 7888, and Member
Mauritius Bar. Called: Apr 1975, Middle
Temple

Mowbray Anthony Leighton •
Senior Crown Prosecutor, Crown
Prosecution Service, Heritage House,
Fishermans Wharf, Grimsby DN31 1SY,
01472 240170, Fax: 01472 240756.
Called: Nov 1983, Middle Temple, LLB
(Wales)

Moxom John Matthew Cameron
"Pannells", Belchamp St Paul, Sudbury,
Suffolk CO10 7BS, 01787 277410, Also Inn
of Court G. Called: July 1968, Inner Temple,
MA (Cantab)

Moylan Ms Pauline Mary •
Metropolitan Wigan, Borough Solicitor's
Department, New Town Hall, Library Street,
Wigan WN1 1YN, 01942 244991 x 2567,
Fax: 01942 827093, and Member New
South Wales. Called: Nov 1995, Gray's Inn,
LLB

Mubarak Syed
03-2981128/2986036, Fax: 603-2913816.
Called: Nov 1995, Lincoln's Inn, LLB (Hons),
LLM, (Lond), FCCA, FCIS

Muda Ms Shamsiah Haji
Called: July 1994, Inner Temple, LLB

Muehl Miss Ruth Anna
Untere Feldstrasse 2, 81675 Munchen,
Germany, 089 475707. Called: Feb 1960,
Gray's Inn

Mufti Sohail Imran
Called: Nov 1995, Inner Temple, LLB (Lond)

Mughal Mrs Sahzadi Bilqiis
Legal Adviser & Assistant, 135 Mornington
Crescent, Cranford, Hounslow, Middlesex
TW8 9SU, 0181 759 2003, Fax: 0181 759
2005. Called: Nov 1995, Lincoln's Inn, LLB
(Hons)

Muhammad Nor Hisham Haji
Called: Nov 1995, Gray's Inn, LLB (Sheff),
LLM

Muharrem Ahmet Nedjati
Principal Court Clerk, Magistrates Courts
Committee, The Court House, 1 Farnan
Avenue, Walthamstow, London E17 4NX,
0181 527 8000, Fax: 0181 527 9063.
Called: July 1963, Gray's Inn

Mukherjee Abhijeet
Called: Feb 1995, Middle Temple, LLB
(Hons)(Lond)

Mukhi Miss Anna-Kumkum
18 Palalce Gardens Terrace, London
W8 4RP, 0171 727 4787, Fax: 0171 460
2050. Called: Feb 1994, Gray's Inn, BA
(Bris)

Mulcahy Michael Edward Joseph
Ruben
and Member King's Inn. Called: Mar 1998,
Middle Temple, BA (Dublin)

Mulhern John Joseph
Justices' Clerk, Inner London Magistrates',
Courts Service, 65 Romney Street, London
SW1P 3RD. Called: July 1974, Middle
Temple, LLB (Lond)

Mulholland John Peter Patrick
New Cottage, Painswick, Gloucestershire
GL6 6UA, 01452 812960, Fax: 01452
812960, also Inn of Court L and Member
Irish Republic Bar. Called: Nov 1969, Middle
Temple, BA, ACIArb, MRAC

Mulholland Michael Joseph
Called: Nov 1997, Inner Temple, BA (Hull)

Mullan James Anthony
Called: Feb 1995, Lincoln's Inn, BA (Hons)

Mullen Miss Emily-Jane
Called: Oct 1997, Gray's Inn, BA

Mullholland Mrs Gillian Lesley •
Senior Crown Prosecutor, Crown
Prosecution Service, Tudor House,
Manchester Road, Bradford, West Yorkshire.
Called: Nov 1971, Inner Temple, LLB, BSc
(Econ)

Mullins Bruce Ashley
Registered Foreign Resident Lawyer, P O
Box 200, Jewel Beach, Postal Code 134,
Muscat, Sultanate of Oman, (968) 607725,
Fax: (968) 607724, and Member Hong Kong
Bar Ministry of Justice, Awqaf & Islamic
Affairs, Sultanate of Oman.. Called: July
1980, Lincoln's Inn, B.Sc (Hons)(Wales)

Mullins Miss Lorraine Pamela •
Team Leader, IMRO, Broadwalk House, 6
Appold Street, London EC2A 2AA.
Called: July 1981, Gray's Inn, BA (Oxon)

Mulreany James Vivian
Senior Deputy Chief Clerk, Inner London
Magistrates', Courts Service, 65 Romney
Street, London SW1 3RD, 0171 799 3332,
Fax: 0171 799 3072. Called: Nov 1974,
Gray's Inn, MA (Oxon)

Mulvenna Miss Glenis Beverley •
Senior Legal Advisor, Glaxo Wellcome PLC,
Glaxo Wellcome House, Berkeley Avenue,
Greenford, Middlesex UB6 ONN, 0171 493
4060. Called: July 1983, Inner Temple, LLB
(Bris)

Mun Tien Shoong
Called: July 1993, Middle Temple, LLB
(Hons)

Munden Paul Alexanda JP
Business Adviser Justice of the Peace, 15
Woodlands Avenue, Wanstead, London
E11 3RA, 0171 354 6400, Fax: 0171 704
2565. Called: Oct 1996, Inner Temple, LLB
(Lond)

Muniandy Ms Anjalli
Called: July 1996, Inner Temple, LLB (Lond)

Munro Christopher Hamish
Called: Oct 1997, Gray's Inn, BA

Munro Ranald Torquil Ian •
Counsel UK & Ireland, Chubb Insurance
Company of, Europe, 106 Fenchurch Street,
London EC3M 5JB, 0171 867 5555, Solicitor.
Called: July 1986, Gray's Inn, BA (Hons),
Dip Law

Munro Miss Susan Lesley
Called: Oct 1997, Middle Temple, BA
(Hons)(Lond), CPE (Manc)

Munsaf Waheed
Called: Nov 1996, Lincoln's Inn, LLB (Hons)

Munshi Muhammed Biplob Islam
Called: July 1997, Lincoln's Inn, LLB (Hons)
(Middx)

Muntakim Mohammad Abdul
Called: Nov 1996, Lincoln's Inn, LLB
(Wolv'ton)

Munton Miss Jean Margaret
Deputy clerk to the Justices for the Isle of
Wight, Magistrate's Clerk's Office, Quay
Street, Isle of Wight PO30 5BB, 01983
524244. Called: July 1983, Middle Temple,
BA (Hons), DMS

Munu Miss Neneh Hawa
Called: July 1997, Inner Temple, LLB
(Leeds), LLM (LSE)

Murdie Alan David
Called: Nov 1988, Lincoln's Inn, LLB

Murdoch-De Silva Mrs Constance
Arlene •
Senior Crown Prosecutor, Crown
Prosecution Service, Thames/Marlborough
St Branch, 2nd Floor, Portland House, Stag
Place, London SW1E 5BH, 0171 915 5912,
Fax: 0171 915 5795. Called: Nov 1989,
Middle Temple, BA, LLB (Lond)

Mure Kenneth Nisbet QC
Advocates Library, Parliament House,
Edinburgh EH1 1RF, 0131 226 5071, QC in
Scotland. Called: July 1990, Gray's Inn, LLB
(Glas), MA (Glas), F.T.I.I.

Murgatroyd Christopher George
Called: Nov 1989, Middle Temple, BA Hons
(Oxon)

Murley Ms Jenny •
Officer - Enforcement, Lloyds Chambers, 1
Portsoken Street, London E1 8BT, 0171 390
5515, Fax: 0171 480 5846. Called: July
1982, Lincoln's Inn, BA (Hons), LLM

Murphy Francis Patrick •
Senior Crown Prosecutor, Crown
Prosecution Service, Fox Talbot House,
Bellington Close, Malmesbury Road,
Chippenham, Wilts SN15 1BN, 01249 443
443. Called: Nov 1976, Middle Temple, BA

Murphy *Paul William*
Called: Oct 1997, Middle Temple, MA
(Oxon), CPE (Lond)

Murphy *Professor Peter William*
Trustee of the American Inns of Court
Foundation, Professor of Law, South Texas
College of Law, 1303 San Jacinto, Houston,
Texas 77002, 713-646 1849, Fax: 713 659
2217, Master of Bench, American Inn of
Court XV and Member California Bar Texas
Bar. Called: July 1968, Middle Temple, MA,
LLB

Murphy *Pierre Eric*
Law Offices of Pierre Murphy, Suite 260,
2445 M Street N.W., Washington D.C.
20037, (202) 872 1679, Fax: (202) 872
1725, and Member District of Columbia,
Wisconsin. Called: July 1979, Lincoln's Inn,
LLB, JD

Murray *Alastair James*
Called: Nov 1957, Middle Temple

Murray *Archibald Russell*
38 Gallow Hill, Peebles, Borders EH45 9BG,
01721 721095. Called: Feb 1963, Lincoln's
Inn, BA (Dunelm)

Murray *Miss Christine Maria*
Principal Assistant, Buckinghamshire
Magistrates', Court Committee, Berkeley
House, Walton Street, Aylesbury,
Buckinghamshire HP21 7QG, 01296 82371,
Fax: 01296 26347. Called: Oct 1992, Gray's
Inn, LL.B

Murray *Miss Fiona Mary*
Called: Nov 1995, Middle Temple, LLB
(Hons)

Murray *Iain Patrick Joseph*
Automobile Association Legal Advisor, A A
Legal Dept, Lambert House, Stockport Road,
Cheadle, Cheshire SK8 2DY, 0161 488
7505, Fax: 0161 488 7260. Called: Nov
1993, Middle Temple, LLB (Hons)

Murray *Miss Jean Lennox* •
Principal Legal Officer, The Treasury
Solicitor, Queen Anne's Chambers, 28
Broadway, London SW1H 9JS. Called: Oct
1992, Middle Temple, LL.B (Hons, Lond)

Murray *Keiron James*
Called: Oct 1997, Middle Temple, LLB
(Hons)(Sheff)

Murray *Michael*
1 Denbigh Close, Chislehurst, Kent
BR7 5EB. Called: June 1953, Gray's Inn

Murray *Richard Kennett*
Deputy Coroner,City of L'pool, Flat 10, The
Outlook, Riverside, Hightown, Merseyside
L38 OBU, 0151 929 2282. Called: June
1950, Middle Temple, LLB (Lond)

Murray *Richard Petrocokino Dalrymple*
Called: Oct 1993, Inner Temple, BA, CPE

Murray *Miss Virginia Louise*
C/O Professor I K Rokas, 25 Boukourestiou
St, Athens, 9 Bedford Row, London, WC1R
4AZ. Called: Oct 1991, Middle Temple, MA
Hons (Cantab)

Murray-Walker *Miss Lynette Ruth*
Called: Oct 1994, Lincoln's Inn, LLB
(Hons)(Leic)

Murrin *Mrs Denise Selby* •
Magistrates Court Clerk, Magistrates Court,
7c High Street, Barnet, Herts EN5 5UE.
Called: Nov 1993, Inner Temple, LLB
(So'ton)

Murugaiyan *Sivakumar Vivekanandan*
Member,Singapore Institute of Arbitrators
(MSIArb), 1 Colombo Court, [H]07-23,
Singapore 179742, 338 3996, Fax: 338
5993, Advocate & Solicitor of the Supreme
Court of Singapore and Member Australian
Capital Territory, High Court of Australia.
Called: July 1988, Lincoln's Inn, LLB (Hons)
(Lond)

Murugason *Ranjit*
Investment Banker, 0171 286 4387, Fax:
0171 286 4387. Called: July 1989, Middle
Temple, LLB (Lond), BCL, (Oxon)

Murugasu *Miss Chitrakala*
Called: July 1995, Middle Temple, LLB
(Hons)

Musaala Mukasa *Miss Christine Rose
Miranda* •
Grade 7 Lawyer, Treasury Solicitor's, Queen
Anne's Chambers, 28 Broadway, London
SW1H 9JS. Called: Nov 1985, Gray's Inn,
LLB

Musaret *Miss Shaheen* •
Legal Advisor, Lancashire County Council,
Trading Standards Dept, 55 Guildhall Street,
Preson PR1 3NU, (01772) 263574, Mayoress
of Hyndburn. Called: Nov 1991, Lincoln's
Inn, LLB (Hons)

Musari *Sadari Bin*
Advocate & Solicitor, 256 Upper Thomson
Road, 4532501, Fax: 7360102, and Member
Singapore. Called: July 1994, Inner Temple,
LLB

Musariri *Miss Blessing Concilia
Ropafadzo*
Called: July 1997, Middle Temple, LLB
(Hons)(Wolv'ton), MA

Musselwhite *Harry Thomas*
Deputy College & Medical School Secretary,
United Medical and Dental, Schools of Guy's
& St Thomas's, Hospitals, Lambeth Palace
Road, London SE1 7EH, 0171 928 9292 Ext
2546, Fax: 0171 922 8254. Called: July
1983, Gray's Inn, BA (Lond), FKC

Mussenden *Larry Devron*
PO Box HM 2186, Hamilton HMJX, and
Member Bermuda Bar. Called: Oct 1995,
Gray's Inn, B.Sc (Canada), MA (USA), LLB
(Kent)

Musson *Anthony Joseph*
Called: Oct 1997, Middle Temple, BA
(Hons)(Cantab), MA (Lancs), Ph.D (Cantab)

Mustakas *Dr George*
150 Minories, London EC3N 1LS, 0171 264
2110, Fax: 0171 264 2107, Attorney &
Counselor at Law (USA) and Member
Louisiana Bar, Federal Bar (USA). Called: Oct
1994, Middle Temple, BA (Louisiana), JD
(Tulane), LLM (Europa, Institute Edinburgh)

Muthu *Muthuraman*
Called: Oct 1996, Gray's Inn, LLB (Sheff)

Muthukrishan *Nedumaran*
Legal Assistant, M/S Ong Teck Gee &
Partners, No 10 Anson Road, International
Plaza, 31-04/05, 2216622, Fax: 2259168,
and Member Singapore Bar. Called: Nov
1994, Lincoln's Inn, LLB (Hons)(Bucks)

Muthupalaniyappan *Yegappan*
Legal Adviser, Raja Devan & Associates,
Advocates & Solicitors, Suites 8.03 and 8.04,
8th Floor, Wisma Lal Doshi, 135 Jalan
Tuanku Abdul Rahman 50100, (03)
2938378/8682, Fax: (03) 2938050, and
Member Malaysia. Called: Oct 1996,
Lincoln's Inn, LLB (Hons), LLM (Staffs),
UPg.Dip (Staffs)

Muthusamy *Panirselvam s/o*
Called: July 1997, Lincoln's Inn, LLB
(Hons)(Lond)

Muthusamy *Ms Santhi*
Called: Nov 1995, Inner Temple, LLB
(Bucks)

Muttitt *Andrew*
Called: Nov 1994, Lincoln's Inn, BA
(Hons)(Leeds), Dip Law (City), LLM
(Nottingham)

Muttukumaru *Christopher Peter
Jayantha* •
Assistant Treasury Solicitor Appointed the
Secretary to the Lord Justice Scott's Inquiry
into the Export of Defence Equipment &
Dual use Goods to Iraq: November 1992,
Deputy Legal Adviser, (General &
International), Ministry of Defence, Room 3/
37, Metropole Building, Nortumbeeland
Avenue WC2N 5BL, 0171 218 9451.
Called: Nov 1974, Gray's Inn, MA (Oxon)

Mutucumarara *Mrs Liyange
Sugunawathi*
7 Balmuir Gardens, London SW15, 0181 788
9311. Called: June 1964, Gray's Inn

Myers *John Richard*
Called: Oct 1996, Gray's Inn, BA (Cantab),
LLM (Harvard)

Myers *Stephen Paul* •
Grade 6 Lawyer, Serious Fraud Office, Elm
House, 10-16 Elm Street, London WC1X 0BJ.
Called: July 1980, Middle Temple, BA
(Essex)

Myles *Charles Rory*
Called: May 1996, Gray's Inn, BA (Bris)

Mylona *Miss Sofi C*
Called: Nov 1996, Lincoln's Inn, LLB
(Hons)(Leics)

Mylvaganam *(Miceal) Joseph (Tharmasothy)* •
Head of Legal Affairs, Channel One T.V. Ltd, 60 Charlotte Street, London W1P 2AX, and Member Hong Kong Bar. Called: July 1989, Inner Temple, BSc (Hons)(E.Ang), Dip Law, LLM (Lond)(I.P)

N'dow *Saidou Abdoulie*
Called: Mar 1998, Inner Temple, LLB (Middx)

Nabi *Muhammed Ghulam*
Called: July 1971, Lincoln's Inn, BA, LLB

Nabi *Miss Nighat Sultana*
Called: Nov 1997, Lincoln's Inn, LLB (Hons)(Lond)

Nabijou *Dr Sharifeh*
Called: Oct 1996, Inner Temple, BSc (Leeds), MSc DIC, PhD (Lond), CPE

Nadarajah *Ranjan Errol*
Called: Nov 1995, Inner Temple, LLB (Lond)

Nadarajah *Miss Sumithra*
Called: July 1997, Lincoln's Inn, LLB (Hons)(L'pool)

Nadarajah *Mrs Tapashi* •
Senior Crown Prosecutor, Crown Prosecution Service, Queen's House, 58 Victoria Street, St Albans AL1 3HZ, 01727 818100, Fax: 01727 833144. Called: Nov 1989, Inner Temple, LLB

Nadarajan *Mrs Kanakavalli*
Called: July 1997, Lincoln's Inn, LLB (Hons)

Nadasan *Dinesh*
25 Telok Blangah Crescent, [H]06-77, 2739619. Called: July 1996, Middle Temple, LLB (Hons)(Lond)

Nadchatiram *Thiruchelva Segaram*
Called: July 1996, Inner Temple, LLM (Cantab), LLB (Lond)

Nagaraja *Maniam*
Called: July 1997, Middle Temple, LLB (Hons)(Lond)

Nagaraw *Samyraw*
Called: Nov 1997, Lincoln's Inn, LLB (Hons)

Nagel *William*
10 Ely Place, London EC1N 6TY, 0171 242 9636, Fax: 0171 430 0990. Called: June 1949, Lincoln's Inn, LLB (Hons)

Nagra *Kashmir*
Called: Oct 1994, Gray's Inn, BSc

Nagreh *Miss Ranmeet Kaur*
Called: July 1996, Lincoln's Inn, LLB (Hons)(Sheff)

Nahar *Miss Lutfun*
Called: Nov 1997, Lincoln's Inn, LLB (Hons)(Lond)

Naik *Miss Sonali* •
Immigration Lawyer, Tower Hamlets Law Centre, 341 Commercial Road, London E1 2PS, 0171 791 0741, Fax: 0171 702 7301. Called: Nov 1991, Middle Temple, BA Hons (Oxon)

Nainappan *Shane*
Lot 2224/18, Taman Tanjung Gemuk, 71000 Port Dickson, Negeri Semilan, Malaysia, and Member Malaysia Bar. Called: Nov 1994, Middle Temple, LLB (Hons)

Nainby-Luxmoore *James Victor Chave*
Called: July 1985, Gray's Inn, BA

Nair *Miss Heama Latha*
Called: Nov 1996, Lincoln's Inn, LLB (Hons)(Lond)

Nair *Kesavan*
Partner, M P D Nair & Co, [H]12-15 International Plaza, 10 Anson Road, Singapore 0207, 2218800, Fax: 2240667, Supreme Court of Singapore and Member Canberra, Australian Capital Territory. Called: Nov 1990, Middle Temple, LLB M.S.I.Arb

Nair *Miss Maala*
Block 209, Tampines Street 21, [H]08-1335, Singapore 520209, and Member Singapore. Called: July 1995, Middle Temple, LLB (Hons)

Nair *Miss Namarath Sudha*
and Member Singapore Bar, Malaysian Bar. Called: Feb 1994, Lincoln's Inn, LLB (Hons, Lond)

Nair *Prakesh*
Called: July 1996, Middle Temple, LLB (Hons)(Lond)

Nair *Miss Sharmila*
M P D Nair & Co, [H]12-15 International Plaza, 10 Anson Road, 221-8800, Fax: 224-0667, and Member Singapore Bar. Called: July 1995, Middle Temple, LLB (Hons)

Nair *Miss Sulojana*
Called: Oct 1997, Middle Temple, LLB (Hons) (Lond)

Nair *Vijayan*
Block 7 Kim Tian Place, [H]19-59, Singapore 0316, 2743439. Called: Nov 1990, Lincoln's Inn, BA (Singapore), LLB (Lond)

Naismith *Dr William Edwin Fraser*
Called: July 1978, Middle Temple, BSc, PhD (Glas),

Nalpon *Zero Geraldo Mario*
Called: Feb 1993, Gray's Inn, LLB (Hull)

Namakula *Ms Ritah Harriet*
Called: Nov 1997, Inner Temple, LLB (Lond)

Namasivayam *Ramesh*
Called: July 1996, Lincoln's Inn, LLB (Hons)(Lond)

Namasivayam *Srinivasan s/o*
Called: July 1997, Lincoln's Inn, LLB (Hons)(Lond)

Nandwani *Manoj Prakash*
Advocate & Solicitor, 12 Mount Echo Park, 2353536, Fax: 7351210. Called: July 1996, Middle Temple, LLB (Hons)(Lond)

Nannini *Antony Joel Peter*
Called: Oct 1995, Lincoln's Inn, LLB (Hons)(Lond), LLM (Lond)

Napal *Raj*
20 Britton Street, 1st Floor, London, EC1M 5NQ. Called: Nov 1981, Middle Temple, LLB (Hons)(Leeds)

Napper *Miss Miranda Fleur* •
Solicitor's Office, H M Customs & Excise, New King's Beam House, 22 Upper Ground, London SE1 9PJ. Called: Oct 1993, Lincoln's Inn, LLB (Hons)(B'ham)

Naqvi *Ms Syeda Shazia Haider*
Called: Mar 1998, Gray's Inn, LLB (LSE)

Narayan *Miss Janise*
Called: Nov 1989, Middle Temple, LLB

Narayanan *Nicholas Jeyaraj*
Called: July 1997, Inner Temple, LLB

Narayanan *Palaniappan*
Called: May 1996, Inner Temple, BA (Madras, India), LLM (Lond)

Narayanan *Miss Shalini*
Called: July 1994, Lincoln's Inn, LLB (Hons)

Narayanasamy *Miss Subashini d/o*
Block 152, Lorong 2, Toa Payoh, [H]11-450, 3531272. Called: Nov 1996, Lincoln's Inn, LLB (Hons)(Lond)

Nardell *Gordon Lawrence* •
Assistant Parliamentary Counsel, Parliamentary Counsel Office, 36 Whitehall, London SW1A 2AY, 0171 210 0959, Fax: 0171 210 6632, Former Solicitor. Called: Nov 1995, Inner Temple, LLB (Hons)(Leeds)

Nardi *Riccardo Angelo* •
Head of Legal Services/Company Secretary, The Association of British, Travel Agents, 55-57 Newman Street, London W1P 4AH, 0171 307 1910, Fax: 0171 631 4623. Called: Nov 1989, Middle Temple, LLB (Lanc)

Naritomi *Nobukata*
13th Floor, Urbannet Ohtemachi Bldg, Ohtemachi 2-2-2, Chiyoda-ku, Tokyo, 03 3231 0101, Fax: 03 3231 0102, and Member Daiichi Tokyo Bar Association. Called: July 1972, Lincoln's Inn, LL.B (Tokyo)

Narwal *Miss Jaswant Kaur* •
Senior Crown Prosecutor, Crown Prosecution Service, 4 Artillery Row, Victoria, London SW1P 1RZ, 0171 976 5699, Fax: 0171 233 2043. Called: Nov 1993, Inner Temple, BA (Lancs), CPE

Nash *Ms Susan Joyce*
14 Tooks Court, Cursitor St, London, EC4A 1LB. Called: July 1979, Gray's Inn, B Ed (Sussex) LLM

Nasim *Asim-Bin*
Orr Dignam & Co, State Life Bldg No 1.B, I.I. Chundrigai Road, Karachi, 2416003/ 2421761, Fax: 2416571. Called: Nov 1994, Lincoln's Inn, LLB (Hons)(Lond)

Nasir *Khaled Jahal Nasir*
Called: Nov 1991, Lincoln's Inn, BA (Hons) (Cambs)

Nasir *Syed Azfar Ali*
Called: July 1997, Lincoln's Inn, LLB (Hons)

Nasser *Ms Amatul-Shafi* •
Grade 7 (Lawyer), The Treasury Solicitor,
Queen Anne's Chambers, 28 Broadway,
London SW1H 9JS, 0171 210 3501.
Called: Nov 1988, Lincoln's Inn, LLB Hons

Nasser *Mrs Anne Kathleen*
Legal Adviser/Court Clerk, Barking
Magistrates' Court, East Street, Barking,
Essex IG11 8EW, 0181 594 5311, Fax: 0181
594 4297. Called: July 1990, Middle Temple,
LLB, LLM (Lond)

Nath *Rakesh* •
Legal Counsel, Rhone-Poulenc Chemicals
Ltd, Oak House, Reeds Crescent, Watford
WD1 1QH, 01923 201 515, Fax: 01923 201
931, and Member Mauritius Bar. Called: July
1985, Inner Temple, LLB (Lond)

Nathan *Dr Kathirgamar Veeragathy
Sinnath*
Int Comm Lawyer/Arbitrator, Studio Legale
Nathan, Viale Mazzini 12, 35035 Mestrino
(PD), 049 9002326, Fax: 049 9002313.
Called: July 1971, Middle Temple, EurIng
BSc BSc (Eng), LLB (Leeds)LLM(Kent), Phd
in Law, (Lond)

Nattan *David Charles*
Principal Court Clerk, Tameside Magistrates'
Court, Manchester Road, Ashton-u-Lyne
0L7 0BG, 0161 330 2023, Fax: 0161 343
1498. Called: Feb 1989, Inner Temple, BA
(Leeds)

Natverlal *Deepak*
Apt Blk 1 [H]09-27, Jalan Pasar Baru, and
Member Singapore Bar. Called: July 1995,
Lincoln's Inn, LLB (Hons)

Naughten *John Peter*
Called: Oct 1995, Lincoln's Inn, LLB
(Hons)(Lond)

Naughton *John Stuart*
Legal Director, Red Eye Software, Ardeen
House, Marine Terrace, Dun Laoghaire,
County Dublin, 00 3531 230 2561, Fax: 00
3531 230 2561. Called: Oct 1993, Gray's
Inn, LLB (Hons)(Wales)

Naughton *Miss Regina Marian* •
Principal Crown Prosecutor, Crown
Prosecution Service, Portland Place, 4th
Floor, Stag Place, London SW1, 0171 915
5700, Fax: 0171 915 5965. Called: July
1980, Gray's Inn, LLB (Brunel)

Navaratnam *Sivarajan*
Called: July 1997, Lincoln's Inn, LLB (Hons)

Navarro *Miss Rebecca*
Called: Nov 1995, Inner Temple, LLB
(Cardiff)

Nawbatt *Lalchand* •
Branch Crown Prosecutor, 10 Victoria
Street, London SW1H 0NN, 0181 534 6601.
Called: July 1972, Middle Temple, LLB
(Hons)(Lond)

Nayar *David*
and Member Singapore Bar. Called: July
1992, Gray's Inn, LLB (Lond)

Nayee *Mrs Manjula Dullabhbhai* •
Called: Nov 1988, Gray's Inn, LLB (Lond)

Nazar *Boaz*
M/S Laycock & Ong, 41 Bukit Pasoh Road,
533 9115, Fax: 533 2206, and Member
Singapore Bar. Called: July 1993, Lincoln's
Inn, LLB (Hons)

Nazeer *Malik Mohammed*
Arbitrator, Khair Court, 67 Inverness
Terrace, Bayswater, London W2 3JT, and
Member Pakistan Bar. Called: May 1993,
Lincoln's Inn, LLB (Hons)

Nazmi *Saiful*
Called: July 1996, Lincoln's Inn, LLB
(Hons)(Notts)

Ncube *Ms Elizabeth Betty*
Managing Director, Global Legal
Immigration, Consultancy, Suite 114,
Queensway House, 275-281 High Street,
Stratford, London E15 2TF, 0181 534 2229,
Fax: 0181 534 2229. Called: Oct 1994,
Lincoln's Inn, BA (Hons), LLB (Lond)

Neafsey *Giles Edward*
Called: Oct 1995, Gray's Inn, LLB (Wales)

Needham *Christopher Eric* •
Senior Legal Adviser Group Legal
Department, Royal & Sun Alliance
Insurance, Group., P O Box 30, New Hall
Place, Old Hall Street, Liverpool L69 3HS,
0151 239 4170, Fax: 0151 239 3342.
Called: Nov 1974, Middle Temple, LLB

Neil *Miss Susan Deborah* •
Senior Principle Legal Officer, HM Customs
& Excise, New King's Beam House, 22
Upper Ground, London SE1 9PJ, 0171 865
5930, Fax: 0171 865 5022. Called: Nov
1986, Inner Temple, LLB (Soton)

Neilly *Miss Heather Robina*
Cayman Islands Law School, Tower
Building, George Town, Grand Cayman.
Called: Oct 1990, Middle Temple, BSc
(Aston), LLB (Lond), MPhil (Ulster)

Neilson *Robert Rowan Cochrane*
Called: Nov 1947, Inner Temple, MA
(Cantab)

Nell *Adam Edward O'Neill*
Called: Nov 1995, Gray's Inn, BA

Nelson *Desmond Montague*
Called: Nov 1975, Gray's Inn, LLB

Nelson *Mrs Paula Miriam* •
Company Secretary & Head of Legal
Department, Nestle UK Ltd, St George's
House, Croydon, Surrey CR9 1NR, 0181 667
5648, Fax: 0181 667 5775, Solicitor Nigeria
and Member Nigerian Bar. Called: July 1973,
Gray's Inn, LLB

Nelson *Robert Charles James*
Deputy Chairman, Stanley Gibbons
Holdings, Deputy Chairman, Bushield Alloys
Limited, Chairman, Britannic Group PLC,
Director, Armourglass Limited, Room 77,
London Fruit Exchange, BrushField Street,
London E1 6EP, 0171 377 9784, Fax: 0171
377 9839. Called: June 1959, Middle
Temple, BA juris(Oxon)

Nelson *Robin Stuart* •
Principal Crown Prosecutor, Crown
Prosecution Service, 2nd Floor, Portland
House, Stag Place, Victoria, London
SW1E 5BH, 0171 915 5797, Fax: 0171 915
5811. Called: Nov 1983, Middle Temple, BA,
LLM

Neo *Miss Shien Ching*
Called: Mar 1998, Lincoln's Inn, LLB
(Hons)(Lond)

Neocleous *Elias Andrea*
Neocleous House, 199 Makarios III Avenue,
P.O.Box 613, Limassol, 357 5 362818, Fax:
357 5 359262, and Member Cyprus Bar.
Called: May 1993, Inner Temple, BA (Oxon)

Neocleous *Ms Olympia*
Called: Nov 1997, Inner Temple, LLB
(Lond), MSc, (Lond)

Neofytou *Thomas*
Called: Oct 1996, Lincoln's Inn, LLB
(Hons)(Hudders)

Neoh *Ang Wei*
Messrs Mohd Noor & S Y Lee, Room 110,
First Floor,, Asia Life Building, 45-B Jalan
Tun Sambanthan, 30000 Ipoh, Perak, (05)
2543589, Fax: (05) 2542611, and Member
Malaya Bar. Called: July 1995, Lincoln's Inn,
LLB (Hons), LLM (Lond)

Neoh *Anthony Francis*
13th Floor, 10 Queen's Road, Central, Hong
Kong, 5 2 23365, Fax: 810 1872, QC Hong
Kong 1990 and Member Hong Kong Bar 2
Mitre Ct Bldgs, 2nd Floor, Temple, London,
EC4Y 7BX. Called: July 1976, Gray's Inn

Neoh *Miss Hong Sean*
Raja Eleena Sielo Ang & Tan, Suite 2003,
20th Floor, Plaza See Hoy Chan, Jalan Raja
Chulan, 50250 Kuala Lumpur, 2322411, and
Member Malaysia Bar. Called: July 1996,
Lincoln's Inn, LLB (Hons)(Leeds)

Neoh *Ms Sue Lynn*
Legal Assistant, Helen Yeo & Partners, 11
Collyer Quay, [H]12-01 The Arcade, 422
1622, Fax: 222 1345, and Member
Singapore Bar. Called: Oct 1990, Gray's Inn,
LLB LLM

Neophytou *Miss Anna*
Called: Nov 1994, Gray's Inn, LLB (Wales)

Nesbitt *Alexander Owain Peter*
Called: Oct 1995, Lincoln's Inn, BA
(Hons)(Oxon)

Nesbitt *Lawrence Kenneth*
Called: Oct 1996, Gray's Inn, LLB

Nesbitt *Richard Law*
Member of the Committee on Court
Practice and Procedure in Ireland, 2 Arran
Square, Arran Quay, Dublin 7, 8733344,
Fax: 8733737, Senior Counsel, The Bar of
Ireland Oct 1993 and Member Northern
Ireland Bar Bar of Ireland. Called: May 1987,
Middle Temple, TCD

Nettelton *John Marcus* •
Manager Commercial, Hardy Oil & Gas plc,
10 Great George Street, London SW1P 3AE,
0171 470 2262, Fax: 0171 470 2300.
Called: Nov 1986, Middle Temple, BA

Neville *James Richard*
Specialist Reports (Editor), Butterworths &
Co, Halsbury House, 35 Chancery Lane,
London WC2A 1EL, 0171 400 2500, Fax:
0171 400 2559, and Member Southern
Ireland. Called: Nov 1991, Lincoln's Inn,
BCL (Cork), BL (Dublin)

Neville *Miss Karen Wendy*
Called: Nov 1986, Inner Temple, LLB

Nevshehir-Owen *Miss Carolyn
Elisabeth* •
Director, NDN Owen Ltd, 39A Smallgate,
Beccles, Suffolk NR34 9AE, 01508 548613,
Fax: 01508 548613. Called: Nov 1990, Inner
Temple, BA, ACIArb, FLAND Inst

Newbold *Dr Anne Lorraine Elsie* •
Legal Director,, The Nikko Bank (UK) PLC,
Nikko House, 17/21 Godliman Street,
London EC4V 5NB, 0171 528 7070.
Called: Nov 1990, Lincoln's Inn, LLB, PhD
(Lond)

Newcombe *Richard Allan* •
Branch Crown Prosecutor, Crown
Prosecution Service, Ealing/Hounsow
Branch, 2nd Floor, Kings House, Kymberley
Road, Harrow, Middlesex HA3 1YH, 0181
424 8688, Fax: 0181 424 9134. Called: July
1979, Middle Temple, LLB (Bris)

Newell *Christopher William Paul* •
Director of Casework Evaluation and Chief
Inspector, Crown Prosecution Service, 50
Ludgate Hill, London EC4M 7EX, 0171 273
1226, Fax: 0171 329 8167. Called: July
1973, Middle Temple, LLB

Newell *Michael Harold Banks*
Commissioner for Affidavits, Notary Public,
Migration Agent, Michael Newell & Co,
Barristers Solicitors & Notaries, 225 Oxford
Street, Leederville WA 6007, 61 8
94432888, Fax: 61 8 94441871, Barrister
and Solicitor W Australia 1980 Member of
the Professional Conduct Committee of The
Law Society of Western Australia Barrister
and Solicitor High Court of Australia 1984.
Called: July 1965, Middle Temple, LLB

Newey *Miss Rachel Anne*
Senior Legal Adviser, Berkshire Magistrates
Court, Easby House, Northfield End, Henley-
on-Thames, Oxfordshire RG9 2NB, 01491
412720, Fax: 01491 412762. Called: Oct
1993, Middle Temple, LLB (Hons)(Lanc)

Newman *Miss Erica Rachel*
Warner Cranston Solicitors, Pickfords
Wharf, Clink Street, London SE1 9DG, 0171
403 2900, Fax: 0171 403 4221. Called: Nov
1994, Inner Temple, BA (Oxon)

Newman *Paul*
Edwards Geldard, Dumfries House,
Dumfries Place, Cardiff CF1 4YF, 01222
238239, Fax: 01222 237268. Called: Nov
1982, Gray's Inn, MA (Cantab), Dip Law,
(City), ACIArb

Newman *Peter David*
Called: Nov 1995, Middle Temple, LLB
(Hons)(Essex)

Newman *Miss Susan Alexandra*
Court Clerk, Cambridgeshire Magistrates',
Courts, The Court House, Lion Yard,
Cambridge CB2 3NA, 01223 314311, Fax:
01223 355237. Called: July 1980, Lincoln's
Inn

Newman *Mrs Veronica*
University of Glamorgan, Pontypridd, Mid
Glamorgan CF37 1DL. Called: Nov 1984,
Gray's Inn, BA DipLaw

Newman-Chalk *Geoffrey*
101 Mount View Road, Hornsey, London,
N4 4JH, 0181 340 1649. Called: Oct 1992,
Gray's Inn, BA, ATC, Post Cert, RA, Dip
Law, FRSA

Newton *Andrew Charles*
Called: Nov 1997, Inner Temple, LLB
(Lancs)

Newton *Clive Trevor CB*
Called: Nov 1969, Middle Temple, LLB,
FCCA

Newton *Miss Jessica Clare* •
Assistant Parliamentary Counsel. Called: Oct
1994, Gray's Inn, BA (Bris)

Ng *Miss Audrey Su Yin*
Called: July 1997, Lincoln's Inn, LLB
(Hons)(Lond)

Ng *Bock Hoh*
Called: Nov 1991, Gray's Inn, LLB (E Ang)

Ng *Daryll Richard*
Called: July 1996, Middle Temple, LLB
(Hons)(Notts)

Ng *David Wai Cheong*
Called: Mar 1998, Lincoln's Inn, LLB
(Hons)(Lond)

Ng *Desmond Tiong Keng*
Called: Nov 1997, Middle Temple, LLB
(Hons)(Hull)

Ng *Miss Eileen*
Called: July 1995, Lincoln's Inn, LLB (Hons)

Ng *Miss Foong Meng*
Messrs Shook Lin & Bok, 20th Floor, Arab-
Malaysian, Building, 55 Jln Raja Chulan,
50200 Kuala Lumpur, (603) 2011788, Fax:
(603) 2011775/2011778/2011779, and
Member Malaysian Bar. Called: July 1994,
Lincoln's Inn, LLB (Hons, Leeds)

Ng *Miss Hwee Lee*
Called: Nov 1995, Middle Temple, LLB
(Hons)(Kent)

Ng *Kenneth Lien Shen*
Called: July 1995, Middle Temple, LLB
(Hons) (Hull)

Ng *Kim Tean*
Legal Counsel, Blk 331, [H]14-225 Bukit
Batok, Street 33, 65 9 6651538, and
Member Singapore Bar. Called: July 1995,
Middle Temple, LLB (Hons), B.Eng

Ng *Mr Kin Keung*
Called: July 1994, Middle Temple, LLB
(Hons)(Lond)

Ng *Miss Ling Li*
Legal Assistant, John Koh & Co, 8 Robinson
Road, [H]12-00 Casco Building, (65)
5389880, Fax: (65) 5382221, and Member
Malaysia Bar. Called: July 1992, Lincoln's
Inn, LLB (Hons) (Lond), LLM (Lond)

Ng *Miss Lyn*
Called: July 1992, Middle Temple, BA
(Hons) (Oxon)

Ng *Maurice Kar-Fai*
Called: July 1994, Gray's Inn, LLB
(Glamorgan), LLM (Bristol)

Ng *Miss Pei Chun*
Called: July 1997, Middle Temple, LLB
(Hons)(Leics)

Ng *Robert Chee Siong*
17 Mt. Cameron Road, The Peak, (852)
2734-8383, Fax: 2369 8471. Called: July
1975, Middle Temple

Ng *Seng Chan*
Called: July 1996, Inner Temple, BA,
BSocSC, BA (Lond)

Ng *Miss Shoo Cheng*
Called: Nov 1996, Lincoln's Inn, LLB
(Hons)(Lond)

Ng *Siew Hoong*
Called: July 1997, Middle Temple, LLB
(Hons)(Lond)

Ng *Miss Sonia Win-Yen*
Called: July 1996, Lincoln's Inn, LLB
(Hons)(So'ton)

Ng *Stephen Shiu Chi*
Called: July 1997, Middle Temple, LLB
(Hons)

Ng *Miss Su Hing*
Called: Nov 1997, Lincoln's Inn, LLB (Hons)

Ng *Sze Meng*
Called: July 1996, Middle Temple, LLB
(Hons)(Lond)

Ng *Timothy Wai Keong*
Called: Nov 1995, Gray's Inn, LLB (Bucks)

Ng *Miss Wendy Yee Cheng*
Called: July 1996, Inner Temple, LLB
(Bristol)

Ng *Miss Yee Yung*
Called: Nov 1993, Gray's Inn, B.Sc, B.Com,
(Melbourne), LLB, (Lond)

Ngeh *Anthony Koh Seh*
Called: July 1997, Lincoln's Inn, LLB
(Hons)(Wales)

Ngoo *Miss Ping Chue*
Quantity Surveyor. Called: Nov 1991, Middle
Temple, LLB (Hons) (Lond), BSc (Reading)

Ngooi *Chiu-Ing*
Associate, Baker & Mckenzie, 1 Temasek
Avenue [H]27-01, Millenia Tower, 65 338
1888, Fax: 65 337 5100, and Member
Australian Capital Territory Malaysia Bar.
Called: July 1991, Lincoln's Inn, BA
(Oxford)

Niblett *Ramon John*
Called: Nov 1979, Gray's Inn

Nicholas *Arthur Leary*
14 Elmete Drive, Roundhay, Leeds, West
Yorks LS8 2LA. Called: Nov 1956, Middle
Temple, MA (Oxon), DipEd

Nicholas *Ms Christina Michalina de
Weld*
Called: Nov 1997, Inner Temple, BA
(Warsaw, Poland)

Nicholls *James William*
Called: Nov 1997, Middle Temple, BA
(Hons)(Kent)

Nicholls *Michael John* ●
Principal Crown Prosecutor, Crown
Prosecution Service, Sedgemore House,
Deane Gate Avenue, Taunton, Somerset
TA1 2UH, 01823 442422. Called: July 1978,
Gray's Inn, LLB (Nott'm)

Nicholson *Andrew David*
Director of Legal Services, Wimbledon
Magistrates' Court, The Law Courts,
Alexandra Road, London SW19 7JP, 0181
946 8622. Called: July 1987, Inner Temple,
BA (Oxon)

Nicholson *Edward Graves*
Called: Nov 1993, Middle Temple, BA
(Hons)(Lanc), CPE

Nicholson *John* ●
Manches & Co, Aldwych House, 81
Aldwych, London WC2B 4RP, 0171 404
4433, Fax: 0171 404 1838. Called: Nov
1994, Middle Temple, MA

Nicholson *Paul Andrew*
Eatons Solicitors, The Old Library, 34A
Darley Street, Bradford, BD1 3LH, 01274
728 327, Fax: 01274 305 056. Called: Oct
1992, Lincoln's Inn, LLB(Hons)

Nicks *Marvin* ●
Lawyer Grade 7, Intervention Board, Kings
House, 33 Kings Road, Reading RG1 3YD,
01734 531522, Fax: 01734 531230.
Called: May 1971, Gray's Inn, MA (Oxon)

Nicol *Stuart Henry David*
Called: Nov 1994, Lincoln's Inn, LLB
(Hons)(Lond)

Nicolaou *Miss Athena Maria*
Advocate, Andreas Georghadjis & Co,
Apollo Court, Office 101, 232 Makarios III
Avenue, P.O.Box 6777, Limassol, 00357 5
353554, Fax: 00357 5 354414, and Member
Cyprus. Called: Nov 1995, Middle Temple,
LLB (Hons), LLM

Nicoletti *Gian-Lorenzo*
10 Hillside Avenue, Exeter EX4 4NW.
Called: July 1994, Inner Temple, LLB
(Warwick)

Nicolle *Jason Paul St John*
Called: Nov 1995, Inner Temple, BA
(Oxon), CPE

Nicolle *William John Alles* ●
Manager, Tax Policy, Esso UK Plc, Esso
House, Victoria Street, London SW1E 5JW,
0171 245 2954, Fax: 0171 245 2542.
Called: July 1971, Gray's Inn, BA, AKC

Niekirk *Paul Henry*
40 Rectory Avenue, High Wycombe, Bucks
HP13 6HW, 01494 527200. Called: June
1956, Gray's Inn, MA

Nield *Jason Paul*
Called: Oct 1996, Lincoln's Inn

Nightingale *Andrew John*
Called: Nov 1987, Inner Temple, LLB (Lond)

Nightingale *John Stuart*
Secretary, The Converts' Aid Society, 20
Beaumont Buildings, Oxford OX1 2LL,
01865 53536. Called: Nov 1985, Middle
Temple, BA (Lond)

Nijabat *Miss Reedah Zahra*
Called: Nov 1997, Lincoln's Inn, LLB (Hons),
LLM (Lond).

Nijar *Miss Belinder Kaur*
Called: July 1997, Middle Temple, LLB
(Hons)(Lond)

Nijar *Navinder Singh*
Called: July 1994, Lincoln's Inn, LLB (Hons)

Niklas *Miss Elizabeth Anne*
Legal Advisor, Merrill Lynch Asset
Management, L.P., P.O.Box 9011, Princeton,
New Jersey 08543-90119, 609-282-3275,
Fax: 609-282-0724. Called: Nov 1995, Middle
Temple, BA (Cincinnati), Dip in Law

Ning *Ms Lam Shiao*
Called: July 1996, Inner Temple, LLB (Hull)

Niraiselvan *Kumaravellu*
Messers Bannir & Associates, [H] 13-12
Peoples Park Centre, 101A Upper Cross
Street, Singapore 0105, 5330622, Fax:
5355397. Called: July 1995, Lincoln's Inn,
LLB (Hons)

Niven *Laurence*
Tax Partner, 36 Main Street, Great Glen,
Leicester LE8 9GG, 0116 259 3349, Fax:
0116 259 3349. Called: July 1975, Gray's
Inn, LLB, ACA

Nixon *Miss Abigail Lisa Barbara* ●
Crown Prosecutor, Crown Prosecution
Service, Buckinghamshire Branch, 4,5,6 & 7
Prebendal Court, Oxford Road, Aylesbury,
Bucks HP19 3EY. Called: Oct 1991, Inner
Temple, BA (Dunelm)

Nixon *Anthony Michael*
Called: July 1979, Middle Temple, MA
(Cantab),FCIArb, CEDR Accredited,
Mediator

Nixon *Miss Paulette Pamela*
Called: July 1997, Lincoln's Inn, LLB (Hons)

Niyazi *Ihsan*
Principal Legal Adviser, Haringey Magistrates
Court, The Court house, Bishops Road,
Archway Road, Highgate, London N6 4HS,
0181 340 3472, Fax: 0181 348 3343.
Called: July 1973, Middle Temple

Njie *Omar Momodou Musa*
78 Wellington Street, Banjul, The Gambia,
00 220 229819, Fax: 00 220 229347, and
Member Gambia Bar. Called: Oct 1991,
Middle Temple, BA Hons (E Anglia)

Noakes *Christopher*
Part Time Chairman of Tribunal. Called: Nov
1972, Gray's Inn

Noble-Mathews *Dr Priscilla Mary O St
J*
Lovehill Cottage, Trotton, Petersfield,
Hampshire GU31 5ER, 01730 816583, Fax:
01730 816583. Called: Feb 1953, Middle
Temple, BM (Soton), Dip PALL MED, Dip
IMC (RCS ED)

Nock *Reginald Stanley*
Deloitte & Touche, Hill House, Little New
Street, London EC4A 3TR, 0171 303 4242,
Fax: 0171 303 4778. Called: Nov 1968,
Lincoln's Inn, LLB, LLM (Lond), FTII

Noel *Lynton Cosmas*
Called: Nov 1976, Middle Temple, LLB
(Lond)

Nonis *Darren Anthonio Marino*
Blk 936, Tampines Ave 5, [H] 06-101.
Called: July 1996, Inner Temple, LLB (Lond),
Dip.M (MCIM)

Noone *Stephen Anthony*
Called: July 1997, Inner Temple, BA (Oxon)

Norcross *Miss Sarah Ann*
Called: Oct 1990, Gray's Inn, LLB (Lond)

Nordin *Norazali Bin*
Called: Nov 1997, Lincoln's Inn, LLB
(Hons)(Nott'm)

Norfolk *Miss Bridget Jane* ●
Crown Prosecutor, Crown Prosecution
Service, 3 Clifton Mews, Clifton Hill,
Brighton, East Sussex BN1 3HR. Called: July
1989, Middle Temple, LLB [Leic]

Norman *Mrs Helen Elizabeth*
Lecturer in Law, Faculty of Law, University
of Bristol, Wills Memorial Building, Queens
Road, Bristol BS8 1RJ, 0117 9288245, Fax:
0117 9251870. Called: Nov 1973, Gray's
Inn, LLB,LLM

Norrell *Gregory Gordon*
Called: July 1980, Middle Temple, LLB

Norris *Charles John* ●
Grade 6, Solicitors Office, Dept of Trade &
Industry, 1 Palace Road, London SW1, 0171
238 3236. Called: July 1986, Lincoln's Inn,
LLB, LLM (Cardiff)

Norris *Graham Kenneth*
Clerk to the Justices & Justices Chief
Executive, Stratford Magistrates' Court, The
Court House, 389-397 High Street, Stratford,
London E15 4SB, 0181 522 5000, Fax: 0181
519 9214. Called: Nov 1974, Gray's Inn,
B.Tech (Hons)

Norris *Dr James Alfred*
Non-Executive Director, Dist Health
Commission 1990-96; Norfolk County
Councillor 1997, 25 West End, Northwold,
Norfolk IP26 5LE, 01366 728296, Fax:
01366 728059. Called: July 1975, Middle
Temple, MA, PhD (Cantab)

Norris *Richard*
Director, Customer Care Solutions, Logica Inc., 32 Hartwell Avenue, Lexington, MA 01273, 00 1 617 476 8132, Fax: 00 1 617 476 8010. Called: July 1979, Inner Temple, LLB (So'ton), ACMA

North *David Michael* •
Assistant Solicitor, HM Customs & Excise, New King's Beam House, 22 Upper Ground, London SE1, 0171 865 5235. Called: July 1974, Middle Temple

North *Dr Peter Machin CBE, FBA* QC (1993)
Vice-Chancellor, University of Oxford. Principal of Jesus College, Oxford Master of the Bench, Jesus College, Oxford OX1 3DW, 01865 279701, Fax: 01865 279696. Called: May 1992, Inner Temple, BA (Oxon), MA (Oxon), BCL (Oxon), DCL (Oxon)

North *Simon Timothy* •
Principal Crown Prosecutor, Crown Prosecution Service, Sceptre House, 7-9 Castle Street, Luton, Beds LU1 3AJ, 01582 404808, Fax: 01582 400642. Called: Nov 1984, Gray's Inn, BA

Northage *Mark Jason* •
Senior Crown Prosecutor, Barrister & Solicitor Australia. Called: Nov 1992, Gray's Inn, LLB, BSc Econ (Australia)

Northfield *Miss Jane Anne*
Hazelwood Farm, Doghurst Lane, Chipstead, Surrey CR5 3PL. Called: Oct 1994, Inner Temple, BA (Hons)(Keele)

Northway *Ms Nicola Jane*
Allen & Overy Solicitors, 9 Cheapside, London EC2V 6AD. Called: Nov 1989, Middle Temple, LLB (Hons), LLM

Norton *Paul Andrew James Edward*
Deputy Chief Clerk, Inner London Magistrates', Courts Service, Old Street Magistrates' Court, 335 Old Street, London EC1. Called: Apr 1989, Inner Temple, LLB (Leeds)

Norton *Mrs Roswitha*
Called: July 1979, Lincoln's Inn, LLB (Lond)

Nottage *D. Sean*
Associate, Graham, Thompson & Co, Graham Thompson & Co, Sassoon House, P.O.Box N272, Nassau, U.S.A. 02110, (809) 322 4130, Fax: (809) 328 1069, and Member Massachusetts, Commonwealth of the Bahamas. Called: Nov 1993, Middle Temple, LLB (Hons)(Bucks), JD (Suffolk Uni, Law, School, Boston, Massachuetts)

Nottidge *Oliver Richard*
Deputy Director, Recruitment & Placement Division - UN, Apt 5D, 176 E.71st Street, New York, NY 10021-5159, (212) 936 0565. Called: Feb 1958, Middle Temple, BA, MA (Cantab)

Nottridge *Robin Ernest* •
Director of Training for Justices and Legal Staff, Leicestershire Magistrates', Courts Committee, 674 Melton Road, Thurmaston, Leicester LE4 8BB, 0116 264 0922, Fax: 0116 269 2369. Called: June 1961, Middle Temple, BA

Nowak *Miss Karen Elizabeth*
Called: Nov 1976, Inner Temple, LLB and Member Hong Kong Bar. Called: July 1969, Middle Temple, LLB (Exon), F.C.I.Arb

Nunns *Malcolm Reeve Mark MC*
and Member Hong Kong Bar. Called: July 1969, Middle Temple, LLB (Exon), F.C.I.Arb

Nursaw *Sir James KCB* QC (1988) •
Called: Nov 1955, Middle Temple, MA, LLB (Cantab)

Nurse *Lewitt Carter* •
Called: Oct 1990, Inner Temple, LLB (W Indies), LLM (Lond)

Nursimloo *Kumaraswamy*
Called: Nov 1993, Lincoln's Inn, LLB (Hons)

Nussle *Miss Sophie Juliette Suzanne*
Called: Feb 1994, Middle Temple, BA (Hons)(Oxon), CPE (City)

Nutley *Dr Peter Graham*
Bishops Park Health Centre, Bishops Stortford, Herts CM23 4DA, 01279 755057. Called: July 1984, Middle Temple, BA, MB, BS, LRCP, MRCS,DCH, DRCOG,MFPM

Nwanodi *Antony Chidi Kojo Ezihuo* •
Grade 7 (L) Principal Legal Officer, Treasury Solicitors Department, Queen Anne's Chambers, 28 Broadway, London SW1H 9JS. Called: Nov 1987, Gray's Inn, BA (Keele), LLB, (Buck)

Nyhan *Miss Norah Maria*
Called: Mar 1996, Lincoln's Inn, LLB (Hons)(Sheff)

Nylander *Leslie Arthur*
Called: Oct 1992, Gray's Inn, LLB, LLM

O'Brien *Miss Alison Joy* •
Group Legal Adviser, Hambro Countrywide PLC, Kingsgate, 1 King Edward Road, Brentwood, Essex CM14 4HG, 01277 264466, Fax: 01277 217916. Called: Nov 1993, Inner Temple, MA (Cantab)

O'Brien *James Gerard*
P O Box 2424, Law Library, Four Courts, Dublin 7, 8720622, Fax: 8720455, and Member Southern Ireland Bar. Called: July 1988, Middle Temple, BL (King's Inn)

O'Brien *Nicholas William Wattebot*
Called: Nov 1996, Lincoln's Inn, BA (Hons)(Oxon)

O'Brien *Paul Anthony* •
Company Secretary, 20 Parkfield Road South, Didsbury, Manchester M20 0DH, 0161 434 9721. Called: July 1981, Inner Temple, MA (Oxon)

O'Brien *Peter Arthur*
18a Carlisle Avenue, St Albans, Herts AL3 5LU, 01727 851941, Fax: 01727 851941. Called: Nov 1992, Inner Temple, BA (New Zealand), Dip in Law

O'Callaghan *John Anthony*
Called: Nov 1988, Gray's Inn, LLB (Lond)

O'Connell *David James Oliver* •
Senior Crown Prosecutor, Crown Prosecution Service, 4 Artillery Row, London SW1, 0171 976 5699. Called: July 1988, Gray's Inn

O'Connell *Eamon Francis*
Called: Nov 1977, Middle Temple, LLB (Warwick), LLM (Lond)

O'Connor *Miss Julie Elizabeth* •
Senior Crown Prosecutor, Crown Prosecution Service, 5-10 St Chad's Court, Rochdale, Greater Manchester OL16 1XA, 01706 352 434. Called: July 1980, Gray's Inn, BA

O'Connor *Michael Patrick* •
Deputy Master QBD. High Court Arbitrator, The Questor Consultancy Group, Tailours, Windmill Way, Much Haddham, Herts SG10 6BH, 01279 842721, Fax: 01279 842721. Called: Nov 1973, Middle Temple, LLB (Lond), FCIArb

O'Connor *Miss Sharon Noelle*
Called: Nov 1995, Lincoln's Inn, BSc (Hons)

O'Connor *Stephen Robert William* •
Police Officer, Metropolitan Police, New Scotland Yard, London SW1P 4AN, 0171 230 1212. Called: Nov 1996, Inner Temple, BSc (L'pool)

O'Culachain *Maoiliosa Seosamh*
Human Resources Manager, Telecom Eirann PLC, St Stephen's Green West, Dublin 2, 00 3531 701 5560, Fax: 00 3531 671 4255. Called: Feb 1995, Lincoln's Inn, BA (Hons), LLB (Hons)(Galway)

O'Dair *David Richard Frazer*
Lecturer, University College of London, Bentham House, 4-8 Endsleigh Gardens, London WC1H 0EG, 0171 391 1454, Fax: 0171 387 8057. Called: Nov 1987, Gray's Inn, MA, BCL (Oxon)

O'Donnell *Everard Jeffrey Echlin*
Called: July 1976, Gray's Inn, MSc

O'Donnell *Michael Antony Jude*
Called: Mar 1997, Gray's Inn, BSc (Bris)

O'Donnell *Peter John* •
Senior Crown Prosecutor. Called: July 1983, Middle Temple, BA (Hons)

O'Donoghue *Miss Margaret Mary* •
Called: Nov 1986, Gray's Inn, MA (London), BA (Sheffield)

O'Donoghue *Michael Gerard* •
Paddington Law Centre, 439 Harrow Road, London W10 4RE, 0181 960 3155, Fax: 0181 968 0417. Called: July 1993, Lincoln's Inn, LLM, BA

O'Donovan *Morgan Teige Gerald*
Farrer & Company Solicitors, 66 Lincoln's Inn Fields, London WC2A 3LH, 0171 242 2022, Fax: 0171 831 9748. Called: Nov 1985, Middle Temple, MA (Cantab)

O'Donovan *Patrick Anthony Hopkins*
Maritime Arbitrator, Churcham House, 1
Bridgeman Road, Teddington, Middlesex
TW11 8DR, 0181 977 3666, Fax: 0181 977
3052. Called: Nov 1976, Middle Temple, MA
(Cantab), FCI Arb

O'Donovan *Ronan Daniel James*
Called: Nov 1995, Lincoln's Inn, BA
(Hons)(Nott'm)

O'Donovan *Sean*
Barrister of Ireland. Called: May 1996,
Middle Temple, BA (Cork), BL (King's Inn)

O'Driscoll *Denis Patrick*
Called: Nov 1997, Inner Temple, BSc
(L'pool), LLB (Lond), ARICS

O'Driscoll *Miss Karen Margaret Helen*
Courthouse Chambers, 27/29 Washington
Street, Cork, 00 353 21 275151, Fax: 00 353
21 272821, Barrister of Ireland. Called: May
1997, Middle Temple, BCL (Cork), M.Litt
(Dublin)

O'Dubhghaill *Feargal Padraig*
Barrister of Ireland. Called: May 1996,
Middle Temple, BCL (Cork), BL (King's Inn)

O'Flynn *Miss Elisabeth Nuala* •
Legal Director, Dept of Trade & Industry, 10
Victoria Street, London SW1H ONN, 0171
215 3473, Fax: 0171 215 3471. Called: Feb
1965, Inner Temple, LLB (Lond)

O'Grady *Miss Eileen Joyce* •
Editor, Law Reporter Managing Editor,
Thomson Tax Ltd, Paradise Street, Oxford
OX1 1LD, 01865 261 430, Fax: 01865 261
404/0181 998 0501. Called: Nov 1976,
Lincoln's Inn, LLB

O'Halloran *Mark Anthony*
General Counsel, Tokyo Electron Europe
Ltd, Premiere House, Betts Way, Crawley,
West Sussex RH10 2GB, 01293 655897, Fax:
01293 655870. Called: Nov 1995, Inner
Temple, LLB (Essex)

O'Hare *Miss Jane Anne Josephine
Mary*
Deputy Chairman Oxfordshire Health
Authority Discipline Committee (Part Time).
Called: Nov 1977, Gray's Inn, LLB (Newc)

O'Kane *Michael Colin* •
Called: Nov 1992, Middle Temple, LLB
(Hons)

O'Kelly *Donal Francis*
Criminal Bar Association Family Law Bar
Association, "Different Strokes", Sir Walter
Scott House, 2 Broadway Market, London
E8 4QJ, 0171 249 6645, Fax: 0171 249
6645. Called: July 1973, Inner Temple, LLB

O'Leary *Miss Carol-Ann*
Called: July 1982, Middle Temple, LLB
(Lond)

O'Leary *Miss Fiona Kieran Margaret*
Called: Apr 1978, Inner Temple

O'Leary *Shaun Vincent Patrick* •
Assistant Director Chartered Insurer, Allied
Dunbar, Allied Dunbar Centre, Station Road,
Swindon, Wilts SN6 1EL, 01793 514 514.
Called: July 1979, Inner Temple, LLB
(Manch), A.C.I.I

O'Malley *Eamon Augustine*
Called: Mar 1997, Middle Temple

O'Neill *Aidan Mark*
ADvocates Library, Parliament House,
Edinburgh EH1 1RF, 0131 226 5071, Fax:
0131 225 3642, Member of the Faculty of
Advocates, Scotland (July 1987) and
Member Scotland Bar. Called: July 1996,
Inner Temple, LLB (Edinburgh), LLM
(Sydney), LLM (Florence)

O'Neill *Ms Elizabeth Helen* •
Lord Chancellor's Department, Criminal
Appeal Office, Royal Courts of Justice, The
Strand, London WC2. Called: Nov 1984,
Middle Temple

O'Neill *Miss Elizabeth Marie*
Called: Nov 1996, Middle Temple, LLB
(Hons)(Dublin), BCL (Oxon)

O'Neill *Ms Heather June*
336 West End Ave, New York, N.Y., and
Member New York State Bar. Called: Oct
1992, Inner Temple, LLB(Hons)

O'Neill *Mrs Joanne*
Legal Aid Board, Area Office 15, Cavern
Walks, 8 Mathew Street, Liverpool L2 6RE,
0151 236 8371. Called: Feb 1995, Lincoln's
Inn, LLB (Hons)(L'pool)

O'Neill *Miss June*
Called: Nov 1997, Lincoln's Inn, LLB
(Hons)(Lond)

O'Reilly *Michael Anthony Joseph* •
Legal Advisor, Kvaerner Construction Group
Lt, Maple Cross House, Denham Way, Maple
Cross, Rickmansworth, Herts WD3 2SW,
01923 776666. Called: Oct 1997, Inner
Temple, BSc, CPE

O'Riordan *Miss Catherine Nuala* •
Assistant Parliamentary Counsel,
Parliamentary Counsel Office, 36 Whitehall,
London SW1. Called: Nov 1989, Middle
Temple, MA (Oxon),BCL

O'Riordan *Dennis Thomas Delcaron* •
Legal Counsel, Sumitomo Finance
International, Temple Court, 11 Queen
Victoria Street, London EC4N 4UQ, 0171
842 3000, Fax: 0171 840 3271. Called: Oct
1993, Inner Temple, LLB (Hons), MA (Lon)

O'Riordan *Mrs Miriam Bernadette*
Courthouse Chambers, 27-9 Washington
Street, Cork, (021) 277563, Fax: (021)
277563, Member Cork & Munster
Circuit,Republic of Ireland Barrister at Law,
Kings Inn Dublin and Member Southern
Ireland Bar. Called: Feb 1982, Middle
Temple, BCL Cork

O'Rourke *Raymond John*
Stanbrook & Hooper, European Community
Lawyers, Rue du Taciturne 42, 1000
Brussels, (32-2) 230 50 59, Fax: (32-2) 230
57 13. Called: Nov 1995, Gray's Inn, BA, MA
(Dublin), LLB (Lond)

O'Sullivan *Miss Lorraine Anne*
Courthouse Chambers, 27/29 Washington
Street, Cork, 0044 353 21 276186, Fax:
(021) 272821, Barrister of Ireland.
Called: May 1996, Middle Temple, BCL
(Cork), BL (King's Inn)

O'Sullivan *Patrick John*
Property Adviser, Assignments International
Ltd, 14 Old Square, Lincoln's Inn, London
WC2A 3UB, 0171 447 1278, Fax: 0171 447
1279. Called: July 1982, Lincoln's Inn, BA

O'Sullivan *Miss Rosalind Mary*
Called: Mar 1998, Middle Temple, LLB
(Hons)(Lond)

O'Sullivan *Sean Denis*
Called: Oct 1995, Middle Temple, B.Sc
(Hons)(Wales), Dip in Law

O'Toole *Miss Ellie*
Called: Mar 1998, Gray's Inn, LLB (Not'ham)

Oakes *Miss Sheila Gwendoline*
Principal Legal Adviser, Derbyshire
Magistrates, Courts Committee, West Bank
House, Albion Road, Chesterfield,
Derbyshire S40 1UQ, 01246 220008, Fax:
01246 231196. Called: July 1990, Middle
Temple, LLB

Oakley-White *Olivier Philip*
Called: Feb 1995, Gray's Inn, BA (Oxon)

Oates *Laurence Campbell* •
Director, Lord Chancellor's Magistrates'
Courts Group, Lord Chancellor's Dept,
Selborne House, 54-60 Victoria Street,
London SW1E 6QW, 0171 210 8809.
Called: July 1968, Middle Temple, LLB

Oberholzer *Dr Gerhard*
Called: Oct 1994, Inner Temple, LLB
(S.Africa), PhD (Cantab), CPE

Obonyo *Miss Caroline Amony*
Called: Oct 1996, Middle Temple, LLB
(Hons)(Anglia)

Oddie *Ms Rosamund Juliet*
Called: Oct 1990, Middle Temple, BA
(Oxon), Dip Law

Oderberg *Keith John*
South China Chambers, Room 1101, 16
Harcourt Road, 01852 5282378, Fax: 01852
5201512, and Member Hong Kong Bar
Victorian Bar 2 King's Bench Walk, 1st
Floor, Temple, London, EC4Y 7DE.
Called: July 1990, Middle Temple, LLB, BA
(Melbourne)

Odilibe *Miss Amanda Ifeoma*
Called: Nov 1992, Middle Temple, LLB
(Hons)

Odim *Edward Usim*
Called: Nov 1995, Middle Temple, BA
(Hons), Dip in, Law

Oduba *Olujimi Olajide*
8/57 Drayton Gardens, London SW10 9RU, 0171 353 5492, Fax: 0171 244 6819, and Member Nigerian Bar. Called: Nov 1971, Gray's Inn, LLB Hons (Lond)

Oei *Miss Carolyn Jane*
81 Langford Court, Langford Place, 22 Abbey Road, London NW8 9DP, and Member Singapore Bar. Called: July 1995, Gray's Inn, LLB (Lond)

Oei *Miss Mona*
Called: Nov 1993, Lincoln's Inn, LLB (Hons)

Oei *Su Chi Ian*
Called: July 1997, Middle Temple, LLB (Hons)(Lond)

Ofokansi *Emmanuel Nwalie*
Member - Inst of Professional Managers and Specialists, Formerly Deputy Chief Clerk to the Justices - Inner London Magistrates' Court Service.. Called: July 1967, Lincoln's Inn

Ogborne *Nigel John* •
Prosecution Team Leader, CPS, Prebendal Court, 4-7 Oxford Road, Aylesbury, Bucks HP19 3EY, 01296 436441, Fax: 01296 88664. Called: Nov 1985, Gray's Inn, BA

Ogle *Michael Burton*
Skerraton, Buckfastleigh, Devon TQ11 0NB, 01364 642232, Fax: 01364 644282. Called: Feb 1956, Inner Temple, MA

Oh *Miss Carolyn Li Lin*
Ghazi & Lim, No 10-1 Bishop Street, 10200 Penang, Malaysia, 01 06 04 633 688, Fax: 01 06 04 2634 188, and Member Malaysia Bar. Called: July 1994, Middle Temple, LLB (Hons)(Kent)

Oh *Douglas Kim Chuan*
Called: July 1996, Lincoln's Inn, LLB (Hons)(Lond)

Oh *Madam Kim Heoh*
95 Yuk Tong Ave, 4691266 (R) 2235221 (O), Fax: 22335229, and Member Advocate & Solicitor of Supreme Court, Singapore. Called: July 1993, Middle Temple, LLB (Hons)

Ohene-Kontoh *Kenneth*
Lecturer in Law, 111 Knoll Drive, Styvechale, Coventry CV3 5DE. Called: Nov 1975, Middle Temple, LLB (Lond), MBIM

Ohiullah *Muhammad*
Called: July 1997, Inner Temple, LLB (So'ton)

Ohonbamu *Miss Fleur Izogie Carmen*
Called: Nov 1997, Lincoln's Inn, LLB (Hons)(Lond)

Ojo *Chief Samuel Ladosu*
Hon Citizen of Louisville, Kentucky State, U.S.A. and Member Nigerian Bar. Called: Nov 1962, Lincoln's Inn, MSc, LLB (Lond), LLM (Leic)

Ojukwu *Mrs Mary Ada* •
Called: Oct 1993, Lincoln's Inn, BA (Hons), MSc

Okara *Kemela Oduoboye Olisaeloka* •
Solicitor & Advocate, 0181 731 9393, Fax: 0181 731 9393, and Member Nigeria. Called: Feb 1989, Gray's Inn, LLB

Okaru *Paul Newton Chinedu*
Called: Nov 1996, Lincoln's Inn, LLB (Hons)(LSE)

Okereke *Mrs Florence Chinyere*
Freelance Legal Assistant, 0181 357 8316, and Member Nigeria Bar. Called: Oct 1996, Middle Temple, LLB (Hons) (Bucks)

Okhai *Miss Zeenat Kassam*
Called: Oct 1996, Gray's Inn, LLB (Kent)

Okine *Miss Julie Anne*
Called: Oct 1996, Lincoln's Inn, LLB (Hons)(Lond)

Okorefe *Miss Nancy Emuobo*
Called: Nov 1992, Middle Temple, LLB (Hons)

Okoro *James Derek*
Called: Oct 1997, Gray's Inn, LLB (Lond)

Okosi *Miss Felicia Nkechi Bernadette*
Tenancy Relation Officer, London Borough of Croydon, Housing Department, Taberner House, Park Lane, Croydon CR9 1DN. Called: Feb 1994, Inner Temple, LLB (Wales)

Okosi *Miss Frances Chineze*
Called: Oct 1995, Gray's Inn, LLB

Okpaluba *Johnson Chukwuemeka*
Called: Nov 1992, Inner Temple, LLB, LLM (Lond)

Okubajo *Miss Olufunmilayo Olukemi* •
Crown Prosecutor, Crown Prosecutor Service, 4 Artillery Row, Victoria, London SW1, 0171 976 5699, Fax: 0171 630 9250. Called: Oct 1994, Gray's Inn, BA (Nigeria), CPE (Middx)

Okunlola *Oluwaremilekun Oluwatoyin*
Deputy Chief Clerk, Student of the New York State Bar. Called: July 1989, Lincoln's Inn, LLB (Hons)

Olaide *Fatai Adeleke*
38 Lynn Road, Clapham South, London SW12 9LA, 0171 498 0467 or 0958 317 233. Called: Nov 1996, Inner Temple, LLB

Oldfield *Ian John Frank Robert*
Called: Nov 1996, Inner Temple, LLB (Bris)

Oldknow *Christopher James*
Called: Oct 1995, Middle Temple, B.Sc (Hons)

Oliver *Mrs Judy Dorothy*
Freelance Consultant, 33 St. James's Road, Gravesend, Kent DA11 0HF, 01474 323707, Fax: 01474 331674. Called: Feb 1980, Lincoln's Inn, BA, FIPM

Oliver *Miss Lindsey Frances*
Called: July 1977, Middle Temple, BA

Oliver *Mrs Marcia Frances* •
Britvic Soft Drinks Limited, Britvic House, Broomfield Road, Chelmsford CM1 1TU, (01245) 261871, Fax: (01245) 346983. Called: Nov 1984, Middle Temple, LLB (Hons)(Lond)

Oliver *Dr Peter John* •
Member, Legal Service, Legal Service, European Commission, Rue de Loi 200, 1049 Brussels, 296 63 39, Fax: 296 43 08. Called: Nov 1977, Middle Temple, BA (Cantab), Licence Speciale, en Droit Europeen, (Brussels), PhD [Cantab]

Ollerenshaw *Michael Frederic*
Eighteen Carlton Crescent, Southampton, SO15 2XR. Called: Feb 1969, Gray's Inn

Ollivry *Guy Marie*
105 Chancery House, Port-Louis, Mauritius, (230) 2123083/2129906, Fax: (203) 2128799, QC Mauritius 1987 and Member Mauritius Bar. Called: July 1957, Gray's Inn

Olphin *Albert Edward Laurence*
Foxes Meadow, 12 Daisy Lane, Alrewas, Staffs DE13 7EW, 01283 790185. Called: May 1958, Lincoln's Inn, LLB

Olsen *Mrs Jeraine Dickin* •
p/t Commissioner on the Mental Health Act Commission. Called: July 1969, Gray's Inn

Olver *Graham Dudley* •
Legal & Contracts Director, GEC ALSTHOM Limited, Investment Projects Depart, P O Box 115, Mill Road, Rugby CV21 1ZN, 01788 545300, Fax: 01788 535305. Called: Nov 1985, Gray's Inn, BA (Warw)

Omar *Miss Nurul Akmar*
Called: Nov 1994, Lincoln's Inn, LLB (Hons)(L'pool)

Omar *Paul Johan*
Flat 3, 25 Holland Road, Hove, Sussex BN3 1JF, (01273) 739921, and Member Malaysia Bar. Called: Oct 1990, Gray's Inn, LLB (Exeter), LLM (Sussex)

Omar *Miss Uzianna*
Called: July 1994, Lincoln's Inn, LLB (Hons)

Omezie *Anthony Nwabudike*
Chancery Chambers, 1st Floor Offices, 70/72 Chancery Lane, London, WC2A 1AB. Called: Nov 1991, Lincoln's Inn, LLB (Hons), LLM

Omideyi *Mrs Christina Ayinke* •
Housing Lawyer, Lonodn Borough of Lambeth, Town Hall, Brixton SW1 1RW, 0171 926 2384, Fax: 0171 926 2361. Called: July 1987, Lincoln's Inn, LLB

Omotosho *Mrs Olalekan Kuburat*
Deputy Chief Clerk, Inner London Magistrates', Courts Service, 3rd Floor, North West Wing, Bush House, Aldwych, London SE15 5QF. Called: Nov 1989, Gray's Inn, LLB Hons (Lond), Post.Dip. Management, Studies

Onafowokan *Miss Oluwayinka Taiwo*
Called: Nov 1994, Middle Temple, LLB (Hons)

Ong *Basil Kah Liang*
and Member Singapore Bar. Called: July 1993, Middle Temple, LLB (Hons)(Lond)

Ong *Boon Kiat*
Called: Nov 1995, Lincoln's Inn, LLB (Hons) (Lond)

E

Ong *Chee Huan*
Legal Assistant, 32 Jalan Setiabakti 8, Bukit
Damansara, 50490 Kuala Lumpur, 010 60 3
2541842, and Member Malaysia Bar.
Called: July 1995, Lincoln's Inn, LLB (Hons)

Ong *Chee Kiam*
Deputy Chief Clerk, Inner London
Magistrates', Courts Service, 65 Romney
Street, London SW1P 3RD. Called: July
1988, Lincoln's Inn, LLB (Hons) (Lond), MA
(City)

Ong *Cheong Wei*
Called: July 1994, Middle Temple, LLB
(Hons)(Lond)

Ong *Miss Chih-Ching*
and Member Singapore Bar. Called: Nov
1992, Gray's Inn, LLB (Buckingham)

Ong *Miss Ellen Mei Luan*
Called: July 1997, Middle Temple, LLB
(Hons)

Ong *Eng Tuan*
Loh Eben Ong & Partners, 112 Middle Road
[H] 07-00, Midland House, (65) 338 1810,
Fax: (65) 338 7678, and Member Singapore
Bar. Called: July 1991, Gray's Inn, LLB

Ong *Miss Geik Khuan*
Called: Nov 1992, Middle Temple, LLB
(Hons)

Ong *Ivan Ban Phing*
Hamzah & Ong Advocates, 13, 1st Floor,
Jalan P Ramlee, 93400 Kuching, P.O.Box
1543, 93730 Kuching, 082 246876, Fax: 082
247217. Called: July 1989, Middle Temple,
LLB [Essex]

Ong *Miss Janaine Jo Lin*
Called: July 1997, Middle Temple, LLB
(Hons)(Hull)

Ong *Miss Jo-Ann Wei-Syn*
Called: July 1997, Lincoln's Inn, LLB
(Hons)(Sheff)

Ong *Kenneth Heng Heng*
Called: Nov 1996, Middle Temple, LLB
(Hons)(Bucks)

Ong *Lee Woei*
Called: Nov 1993, Lincoln's Inn, LLB (Hons),
LLM (Exon)

Ong *Miss Lu-Yi*
Called: Nov 1996, Middle Temple, LLB
(Hons)(Lond)

Ong *Ms May Anne*
Called: July 1994, Middle Temple, BA
(Hons)(Cantab)

Ong *Miss May Li Karen*
Called: July 1997, Middle Temple, LLB
(Hons)(Kent)

Ong *Miss Melita Sue Chen*
Called: July 1997, Lincoln's Inn, LLB (Hons)

Ong *Miss Ming Suan*
Messrs Raja Eleena,Siew,Ang & Tan, Suite
20.03 20th Floor, Plaza See Hoy Chan, Jalan
Raja, Chulan, 50200 Kuala Lumpur Malaysia,
03 2322411, Fax: 03 2301613, and Member
Malaysia Bar. Called: July 1991, Lincoln's
Inn, LLB (Hons) (Warwick)

Ong *Peng Boon*
Partner, (65) 3232320, Fax: (65) 2213211,
and Member Singapore Bar. Called: Feb
1994, Middle Temple, LLB (Hons)(Lond)

Ong *Miss Rita Lee Hiang*
Called: July 1994, Middle Temple, LLB
(Hons)(Lond)

Ong *Seng Hoong*
Called: July 1994, Lincoln's Inn, LLB (Hons)

Ong *Miss Sharon Get-Jin*
Called: July 1993, Inner Temple, BA

Ong *Miss Sharon Si Hsien* •
Counsel, Rank Xerox Limited, Parkway,
Marlow, Buckinghamshire SL7 1YL, 01628
890000. Called: July 1987, Middle Temple,
BSc, MSc (Lond), Dip Law (City)

Ong *Miss Shirley*
Called: July 1994, Lincoln's Inn, LLB (Hons)

Ong *Sim Ho*
Senior Officer (Tax Interpretations &
Treaties), Inland Revenue Authority of,
Singapore, Fullerton Building, Singapore,
065-7856932, Bachelor of Accountancy Co-
Author, Goods & Services Tax-Law &
Practice, Butterworths 1995.. Called: July
1995, Lincoln's Inn, LLB (Hons), BAcc
(Hons)(S'pore)

Ong *Sin Qui*
Member Criminal Law Advisory Committee,
P.O.Box 2670, Robinson Road, (65)
5339115, Fax: (65) 5332206, Advocate &
Solicitor, Singapore and Member Singapore
Bar. Called: Nov 1974, Middle Temple, MA
(Cantab)

Ong *Miss Su Mei*
Called: Oct 1996, Middle Temple, LLB
(Hons)(Notts), LLM (Lond)

Ong *Miss Su-Lin Vivienne*
Called: Nov 1996, Middle Temple, LLB
(Hons)(Kent)

Ong *Miss Suzanna Ann-Francesca*
Called: July 1996, Lincoln's Inn, LLB
(Hons)(Bris)

Ong *Teng Kok*
Called: July 1997, Lincoln's Inn, LLB (Hons)

Ong *Teng Ping*
Public Accountant of Malaysian Institute of
Accountants, Paul Ong & Associates, 7th
Floor, Bangunan Yee Seng, No 15 Jalan Raja
Chulan, 50200 Kuala Lumpur, 03 2321562,
Fax: 603 2327260, and Member Malaysian
Bar. Called: July 1995, Lincoln's Inn, LLB
(Hons), FCCA, ATII, PA

Ong *Theng Soon*
Called: July 1997, Lincoln's Inn, LLB
(Hons)(Leeds)

Ong *Miss Wee En*
Called: July 1997, Lincoln's Inn, LLB
(Hons)(Wales)

Ong *Miss Yin Ee*
Abu Talib Shahrom & Zahari, Advocates &
Solicitors, 43-1 Jalan Desa, 58100 Kuala
Lumpur, (603) 780 4494, Fax: (603) 784
5434. Called: July 1997, Middle Temple, LLB
(Hons)

Ong *Yu En*
Allen & Gledhill, 36 Robinson Road, [H] 18-
01 City House, Singapore 068877, 65
4207755, Fax: 65 2233787, and Member
Singapore Bar. Called: July 1994, Middle
Temple, LLB (Hons)(Hull)

Onn *Shaharuddin*
Shahruddin, Arida & Assoc., (Advocates &
Solicitors), No 116-1C, 1st Floor, Jalan Loke
Yew, 55200 Kuala Lumpur Malaysia, 03-
2222264/2217012, Fax: 603 2222632, and
Member Malaysia Bar. Called: May 1993,
Lincoln's Inn, LLB (Hons)

Onuma-Elliott *Mrs Nkolika Anne* •
Senior Crown Prosecutor, Kings House,
Kymberly Road, Harrow, Middlesex HA1,
0181 424 8688, and Member Law School
Nigeria. Called: Oct 1992, Inner Temple,
LLB, LLM (Lond)

Ooi *David Chai Lee*
Called: July 1994, Lincoln's Inn, LLB (Hons)

Ooi *Peng Cuan*
Called: July 1996, Lincoln's Inn, LLB
(Hons)(Lond)

Oon *Miss Diana Bee Lin*
Called: July 1995, Middle Temple, BA
(Hons)

Oon *Wee Phing*
Called: Nov 1996, Middle Temple, LLB
(Hons)(Lond)

Oppenheimer *Mrs Nicola Anne* •
Principal Establishment & Finance Officer,
Cabinet Office, Queen's Chambers, 28
Broadway, London SW1, 0171 210 0300.
Called: July 1972, Middle Temple, LLB

Opstad *Christopher Thorleif*
Called: July 1975, Lincoln's Inn, MA (Oxon)
MPhil, (Lond)

Oram *Miss Deborah Ruth*
Legal Advisor, Wragge & Co Solicitors, 55
Colmore Row, Birmingham B3 2AS, 0121
233 1000, Fax: 0171 210 3171. Called: Oct
1991, Lincoln's Inn, LLB (Hons)

Orange *John Robert Wellwood*
Chief Executive, Manor House, Tot Hill,
Fornham All Saints, Bury St Edmunds,
Suffolk IP28 6LD. Called: Nov 1966, Gray's
Inn, BA Hons (Dublin)

Orange *Stephen Michael*
160 Aldersgate Street, LondoN EC1A 4DD,
0171 367 3000, Fax: 0171 367 2000.
Called: Mar 1997, Inner Temple, LLB
(Nott'm)

Ordish *Mrs Judith*
Senior Court Clerk, Nottinghamshire Mags
Court, Carrington Street, Nottingham
NG2 1EE, 0115 955 8111, Fax: 0115 955
8131. Called: Nov 1983, Inner Temple, BA,
MBA

Orgill *Mrs Deborah Jean*
Called: Oct 1997, Lincoln's Inn, LLB
(Hons)(B'Ham)

Orkin *Edmond Leonard*
41 Elliot Road, London NW4 3DS, 0181 203
7077, Fax: 0181 202 7077. Called: Nov
1950, Middle Temple, LLB (Lond)

Orme *John Richard*
Called: Feb 1995, Lincoln's Inn, BSc
(Hons)(Lond), PhD, Dip in Law (City)

Orme *Simon Timothy* •
Senior Crown Prosecutor, Crown
Prosecution Service, United House,
Piccadilly, York YO1 1SQ, 01904 456684.
Called: July 1986, Inner Temple, BSc (Econ)

Ormsby *Miss Carol-Anne Rose*
Called: Nov 1993, Middle Temple, LLB
(Natal), CPE (Bris)

Orphanou *Vrahimis Antoniou*
Called: Nov 1971, Lincoln's Inn

Orr *Miss Patricia*
Called: Nov 1995, Lincoln's Inn, BA (Hons)

Orrell *John Edward*
Called: Nov 1957, Gray's Inn, BA (Oxon)

Ortega *Mark Benjamin*
12 Jalan Anak Patong, Singapore 489328,
(65) 4458691, and Member Singapore Bar.
Called: July 1995, Middle Temple, LLB
(Hons)

Osborne *Andrew James* •
Group Legal Adviser, Camelot Group Plc,
Tolpit Lane, Watford WD1 8RN, 01923
425104, Fax: 01923 425006. Called: Feb
1984, Gray's Inn, LLB (Reading)

Osborne *Miss Antoinette Marie-
Therese*
Called: Nov 1996, Inner Temple, BA (Lond),
LLB (Lond)

Osborne *Miss Christine Louise* •
Professional Services, (Life & Pensions)
Limited, Allied Dunbar Centre, Swindon
SN1 1EL, 01793 514514. Called: Nov 1995,
Gray's Inn, B.Comm (B'ham)

Osborne *Ms Clare Elizabeth Ann* •
Legal Advisor, Allied Dunbar Assurance PLC,
Allied Dunbar Centre, Swindon SN1 1EL,
01793 514514. Called: Nov 1994, Middle
Temple, BA (Hons)

Osborne *Clive Maxwell Lawton* •
Department of Trade & Industry, 10 Victoria
Street, London SW1, 0171 215 3263, Fax:
0171 215 3242. Called: Nov 1978, Gray's
Inn, MA (Oxon)

Osborne *Miss Jennifer Janet* •
Joint Council for the Welfare, 115 Old
Street, London EC1V 9JR, 0171 251 8708,
Fax: 0171 251 8707. Called: Nov 1992,
Lincoln's Inn, LLB (Hons)

Osborne *Miss Nicola Frances* •
Solicitor's Office, East Wing, Somerset
House, Strand, London WC2R 1LB, 0171
438 6111, Fax: 0171 438 6246. Called: Nov
1994, Lincoln's Inn, LLB (Hons)(Anglia)

Osiecki *Desmond*
Called: Nov 1996, Middle Temple, LLB
(Hons)

Osman *Miss Nishet*
Called: July 1995, Middle Temple, LLB
(Hons)

Osner *Nigel Ralph* •
Law Ommission Report, (Backlog) Project,
Lord Chancellor's Department, Selbourne
House, 54-60 Victoria Street,London SW1,
0171 210 8860. Called: July 1971, Inner
Temple, LLB

Osofsky *Mrs Lisa Kate*
American Attorney. Called: Nov 1997,
Middle Temple, BA (Amherst), JD (Harvard)

Osoria *Miss Paulette Barbara*
The Grand Bahama Port, Authority Limited,
P O Box F.42666, Freeport, Grand Bahama,
242 352 6611 Ext 2242, Fax: 242 352 4568.
Called: July 1997, Gray's Inn, BSc (Ontario),
LLB (Bucks)

Ossei *Mrs Vida Afua Sarpong*
Called: July 1996, Inner Temple, LLB

Oster *Norman Howard*
7 Etzion Street, Ramat Gan 52383, 03
5743834, Fax: 03 6776942, 9 Gough Square,
London, EC4A 3DE. Called: Feb 1954,
Middle Temple

Othman *Adil*
Called: Nov 1994, Lincoln's Inn, LLB
(Hons)(Notts)

Otieno *John Rowland* •
Principal Legal Officer, The Solicitor's
Office, Health & Safety Executive, Rose
Court, 2 Southwark Bridge, London
SE1 9NS, 0171 717 6912, Fax: 0171 717
6661. Called: July 1979, Lincoln's Inn, LLB
(Hons), LLM (Lond)

Ottaway *Bradley John Charles*
Called: Feb 1994, Lincoln's Inn, BA (Hons,
Toronto), MA (Lond), LLB (Hons, Lond)

Otty *Neville John*
Corporate Pensions Technical Manager, 74
Elm Grove Road, Barnes, London SW13 0BS,
0181 878 1646. Called: Nov 1962, Gray's
Inn, APMI

Oultram *Jonathan Richard Gerard* •
Senior Crown Prosecutor, Crown
Prosecution Service, Windsor House, 10
Manchester Road, Bradford, 01274 742530,
Fax: 01274 870640. Called: Nov 1988,
Middle Temple, LLB

Outhwaite *Brian* •
Senior Crown Prosecutor. Called: Nov 1988,
Lincoln's Inn, LLB Hons (Leeds)

Ouzounian *Dickran Aram*
General Manager, Dickran Ouzounian & Co
Ltd, PO Box 1567, Nicosia, Cyprus, 02
353053, Fax: 02 350536. Called: Nov 1988,
Inner Temple, LLB

Oven *Patrick Jerome* •
Principal Crown Prosecutor, Crown
Prosecution Service, One Onslow Street,
Guildford GU1 4YA, 01483 882600, Fax:
01483 882603/4. Called: Nov 1984, Gray's
Inn, LLB (Manch)

Overton *Martin John* •
Company/Commercial Lawyer, Ernst &
Young, Becket House, 1 Lambeth Palace
road, London SE1 7EU. Called: July 1987,
Lincoln's Inn, LLB.

Ow *Tan Cheng*
Called: Nov 1996, Lincoln's Inn, LLB
(Hons)(Lond)

Owaisi *Asaduddin*
Called: May 1995, Lincoln's Inn, LLB (Hons)

Owen *Christopher Henry*
Called: Feb 1963, Inner Temple

Owen *David Paul*
Deputy Justices Clerk, Trafford Magistrates'
Court, The Court House, Ashton Lane, Sale
M33 1UP, 0161 976 3333, Fax: 0161 962
4333. Called: Nov 1983, Gray's Inn, BA

Owen *Ms Elen Mai* •
Senior Crown Prosecutor, Crown
Prosecution Service, Haes y Ffynon, Penrhos
Road, Bangor, North Wales, 01248 373151,
Fax: 01248 373150. Called: Nov 1985,
Gray's Inn, LLB (Lond)

Owen *Miss Elizabeth Jane* •
Group Legal Adviser, Aon UK Holdings Ltd,
Law Division, 8 Devonshire Square, London
EC2M 4PL, 0171 623 5500, Fax: 0171 972
9862. Called: July 1978, Middle Temple, MA
(Oxon)

Owen *Gerald Victor QC (1969)*
also Inn of Court I 1969. Called: June 1949,
Gray's Inn, MA (Cantab) LLB, (Lond)

Owen *Mrs Mary Lisa Hacon* •
Senior Commercial Lawyer Cadbury
Schweppes plc and Company Secretary
Trebor Bassett Ltd, Cadbury Schweppes Plc,
Legal Department, Franklin House,
Bournville, Birmingham B30 2NB,
0121 698 4813, Fax: 0121 459 0383.
Called: July 1972, Gray's Inn

Owen *Miss Susanna Wynne*
Lecturer in Law, Law School, University of
East London, 0181 590 7722 Ext 2192, Fax:
0181 599 5122. Called: July 1988, Lincoln's
Inn, BA (Hons) (Oxon), Dip Law

Owen *Miss Tracy Rebecca* •
Institute of Chartered, Accountants,
Gloucester House, 399 Silbury Boulevard,
Central Milton Keynes MK9 2HL, 01908
248271, Fax: 01908 691165. Called: July
1984, Middle Temple

Owen *William John*
Neuadd Deg, 31 Bronwydd Road,
Carmarthen, Dyfed SA31 2AL, 01267
236437, Fax: 01267 236437. Called: June
1949, Lincoln's Inn

Owen *Xhuanelado Walave Durage*
Called: July 1994, Inner Temple, LLB (Lond)

Owen Hughes *Archibald*
First National Building, 2nd Floor, 24
Fenwick Street, Liverpool, L2 7NE.
Called: Nov 1940, Gray's Inn, LLM

Owens *Gareth Richard* ●
Principal Legal Officer, West Wiltshire District, Council, Bradley Road, Trowbridge, Wiltshire BA14 ORD, 01225 770310, Fax: 01225 761053. Called: Nov 1993, Gray's Inn, LLB (Wales)

Owusu-Afriyie *John*
Advisor, and Member Ghana Bar.
Called: July 1963, Inner Temple, BL

Owusu-Afriyie *Samuel Osei*
Nimoh & Co Solicitors, 92 Coldharbour Lane, London SE5 9PU. Called: Nov 1992, Middle Temple, LLB (Hons, Lond)

Owusu-Tevie *Ms Alberta Elizabeth* ●
Chief Solicitor, Town Hall, The Burroughs, Hendon NW4 4BG, 0181 359 2517, Fax: 0181 359 2680. Called: July 1984, Inner Temple, BA

Oxley *Miss Denise Eudene*
Apt 411, Cabrillo Square, 1399 Ninth Avenue, San Diego, California 92101, (619) 486 2957. Called: Oct 1993, Lincoln's Inn, LLB (Hons)(Lond)

Oyediji *Chief Ademola Olushola*
New Tower Centre, 181 Tower Bridge Road, London SE1 2EU, 0171 357 0445/ 0171 378 9506, Fax: 0171 357 0288, and Member Nigeria. Called: July 1997, Lincoln's Inn, LLB (Hons)(Lond), LLM (Lagos), BL

Oyetunde *Ms Margaret Oyeronke*
Called: Oct 1994, Gray's Inn, LLB

Pacifico *Adam Louis*
Called: Nov 1991, Inner Temple, LLB

Pacifico *Miss Stephanie Lizbeth*
Called: July 1982, Gray's Inn, BA

Padamakavander *Miss Kavija Padama*
Legal Assistant, 1304-K Lorong Bentara, Jalan Teluk Wanjah 05200, Alor Setar, Kedah, Malaysia, 04 7313310, and Member Malaysia Bar. Called: July 1994, Middle Temple, LLB (Hons)(Brunel)

Paddock *Richard Christopher* ●
Director of Lands Advisory, Government Property Lawyers, Riverside Chambers, Castle Street, Tangier, Taunton, Somerset TA1 4AP, 01823 345276, Fax: 01823 345330. Called: July 1979, Lincoln's Inn, LLB (Manch)

Padfield *Guy Lawrence Notton*
Called: Oct 1995, Inner Temple, MA (Cantab), M.Phil (Oxon), CPE

Page *Matthew Charles* ●
Senior Assistant Lawyer, Cambridge City Council, The Guildhall, Cambridge CB2 3QJ. Called: Feb 1986, Middle Temple, MA (Oxon), MSc, ACI Arb

Page *Miss Sarah Elizabeth* ●
Senior Crown Prosecutor, CPS (Oxfordshire Branch), The Courtyard, Lombard Street, Abingdon, Oxon OX14 5SE, 01235 555678. Called: July 1989, Inner Temple, LLB (Hons)

Paget-Brown *Ian*
West Wind Building, Harbour Drive, Box 2197, Grand Cayman, 809-949-4904, Fax: 809-949-7920, and Member Washington, Virginia, Colorado Bar Cayman Islands Bar 5 Paper Bldgs, Ground Floor, Temple, London, EC4Y 7HB. Called: July 1968, Lincoln's Inn, LLB (Lond)

Paglar *Miss Constance Margaret*
Called: Nov 1996, Inner Temple, LLB (Lond)

Pagni *Marco Patrick Anthony*
European Legal Director, McDonald's Development Company, Ltd, 178-180 Edgware Road, London W2 2DS, 0171 402 6677, Fax: 0171 723 2818. Called: Feb 1988, Middle Temple, MA, BCL (Oxon)

Pah *Miss Yvonne Li-Ean*
15a Jalan Wu Lean Teh, Ipoh Garden South, 31400 Ipoh, Perak, Malaysia, 60-5-5475521. Called: July 1995, Middle Temple, LLB (Hons)

Paige *Richard Mark*
Called: Oct 1997, Middle Temple, BA (Hons)(Oxon)

Pain *Kevin Mark*
Called: Oct 1995, Gray's Inn, BA

Pakenham-Walsh *John CB* QC (1992) ●
Standing Counsel to the General Synod of the Church of England, Crinken, Weydown Road, Haslemere, Surrey GU27 1DS, 01428 642033. Called: June 1951, Lincoln's Inn, MA (Oxon)

Pakrooh *Ramin*
Called: Mar 1996, Lincoln's Inn, LLB (Hons)

Pal *Partha Sarathi*
and Member India Bar. Called: May 1994, Gray's Inn, BA (Cantab)

Palaniveloo *S P Muthuveloo*
Called: Nov 1994, Lincoln's Inn, LLB (Hons)(Herts)

Palaniyappan *Allagarsamy s/o*
Called: Nov 1996, Lincoln's Inn, LLB (Hons)(Lond)

Palas *Miss Esme*
Called: Nov 1996, Gray's Inn, LLB (Bris)

Palin *Henry* ●
Regional Lawyer, Department of Social Security, Government Buildings, St Agnes Road, Galbalfa, Cardiff, 01222 586749, Fax: 01222 586080. Called: Nov 1971, Gray's Inn, LLB

Pallister *Neil* ●
Senior Crown Prosecutor, Crown Prosecution Service, A, 136 Sandyford Road, Newcastle Upon Tyne, Tyne & Wear. Called: July 1982, Lincoln's Inn, LLB (Hull)

Palmer *Adrian Jeremy*
18 Heads Road, Donvale 3111, Melbourne, Victoria, 61 3 873 5650. Called: Nov 1978, Middle Temple, MA, LLM, Dip Comp, Sci (Cantab)

Palmer *Mrs Ann*
Principal Court Clerk, Leicester Magistrates' Court, 674 Melton Road, Thurmaston, Leicester LE4 8BB, 0116 2692369. Called: July 1988, Middle Temple, BA (Hons)

Palmer *Dr Roy Newberry*
Secretary and Medical Director, The Medical Protection Society, 33 Cavendish Square, London W1M 0PS, 0171 399 1300, Fax: 0171 399 1367. Called: Feb 1977, Middle Temple, MB, BS, MRCS, LRCP, DObstRCOG, LLB

Palmes *Peter Manfred Jerome*
Called: Jan 1948, Inner Temple

Pan *Wai Liong*
Blk 704 [H]11-137, Pasir Ris Drive 10, 5842476. Called: July 1996, Middle Temple, LLB (Hons)(Wolves)

Panagopoulos *Dr Panayotis Constantinou*
8 Merlin Steet No 8, 10671 Athens, 362 3 930, Fax: 30- 1-3628.566, and Member Athens Bar. Called: Nov 1951, Gray's Inn, LLB, BSc, LLD, (Athens)

Panayides *Ioannis*
Finance & Legal Advisor, P O Box 4682, 3726 Limassol, 00 357 5 586876. Called: Nov 1992, Middle Temple, LLB (Hons)(Lond), M.I.C.S., F.C.M.A.

Pang *Chesper-Joghne*
Called: Mar 1997, Lincoln's Inn, LLB (Hons)(Lond)

Pang *Wai-Cheung*
Winstan & Co Solicitors, 72/74 Notting Hill Gate, London W11 3HT, 0171 727 5675, Fax: 0171 221 1211. Called: May 1992, Lincoln's Inn, BSc (Hon), Dip Associateship, Dip Law

Pannirselvam *Miss Priya*
Called: Nov 1997, Lincoln's Inn, LLB (Hons)(Nott'm)

Panoo *Sunil Singh*
Called: July 1996, Middle Temple, LLB (Hons)(Lond)

Pao *Felix Ho Ming*
Consultant Editor of the Hong Kong Law Digest, 87 New Henry House, 10 Ice House Street, Hong Kong, 2522 5494, Fax: 2810 4677, and Member Hong Kong Bar Australia Bar. Called: Apr 1991, Gray's Inn, LLB, PCLL

Paonessa *Miss Laura Alexandria*
Called: Oct 1993, Middle Temple, BA (Hons)(Manc)

Papachan *Gopalan Krishnan*
Called: Nov 1990, Gray's Inn, BSc, Dip Law

Papacosta *Miss Ismini Andrea*
Called: Nov 1996, Gray's Inn, LLB (Lond), LLM (E.Anglia)

Papadopulos *Nicholas Charles*
Called: Oct 1990, Middle Temple, BA (Cantab), Dip Law (City)

Paphiti *Anthony Steven*
Chief Legal Officer, Commander, Army Prosecuting Authority, (Germany), Rochdale Barracks, British Forces Post Office 39. Called: Nov 1975, Inner Temple, LLB (Leeds)

Paradysz *Roger John* •
Principal Crown Prosecutor, Crown Prosecution Service, 23rd Floor, Portland House, Stag Place, London SW1. Called: Nov 1985, Gray's Inn, BA (Hons) (Trent)

Parasie *Ms Gudrun*
European Legal Advice (ELA) Service, 0181 888 0216. Called: Oct 1994, Middle Temple, LLB (Hons)(Lond)

Parasram *Miss Isabelle Amanda* •
General Practice Adviser-Legal Services, British Dental Association, 64 Wimpole Street, London W1M 8AL, 0171 935 0875, Fax: 0171 486 0855. Called: Oct 1995, Gray's Inn, LLB (Hons)

Parfitt *Mrs Ifeyinwa Maureen* •
Senior Crown Prosecutor, Crown Prosecution Service, 5th Floor, Riverpark House, 225 High Road, Wood Green, London N22, 0181 888 8889. Called: July 1983, Lincoln's Inn, BA

Parhar *Miss Sunita Sonya*
50 Raffles Place, 18th Floor, Singapore Land Tower, 2201911, Fax: 2244118, Kelvin Chia Partnership and Member Singapore Bar. Called: Nov 1995, Lincoln's Inn, LLB (Hons)(Lond)

Parikh *Romesh Chandra*
8 Shackleton Road, Southall, Middlesex UB1 2JA. Called: Nov 1975, Middle Temple

Paris *Mrs Susan Jill*
Called: Nov 1979, Lincoln's Inn, BA (Hons)

Park *Mrs Deborah Jane*
32 Birchwood Avenue, London N10 3BE. Called: Nov 1994, Inner Temple, BA (Lond), CPE (Middx)

Parker *Christopher Ian* •
Director, Legal Services, Digital Equipment Co Ltd, Digital Park, Imperial Way, Worton Grange, Reading RG2 OTL, 01734 203850, Fax: 01734 202390. Called: July 1977, Gray's Inn, LLB

Parker *Christopher John Gorrill*
Talltrees, 197 Newport, Lincoln LN1 3DX, 01522 526534. Called: July 1984, Inner Temple, LLB (Newcastle)

Parker *Miss Danya Larissa*
Called: July 1997, Middle Temple, LLB (Hons)

Parker *Miss Fern*
Called: Oct 1995, Lincoln's Inn, BA (Hons)(Bris), Dip in Law (City)

Parker *George Brian*
alos Inn of Court L. Called: Nov 1934, Middle Temple, MA, LLB (Cantab)

Parker *Miss Janice Teresa*
Deputy Chief Clerk, Inner London & City Family, Proceedings Court, 59-65 Wells Street, London W1A 3AE. Called: July 1981, Lincoln's Inn, LLB (Lond)

Parker *Mark Laurence*
Called: July 1983, Inner Temple, MA (Hons)(Cantab)

Parker *Nigel Denis* •
Legal Adviser to Dependent Territories. Regional Secretariat, Bridgetown, Foreign & Commonwealth Office, (Bridgetown), King Charles Street, London SW1A 2AH, 1 246 436 6694, Fax: 1 246 430 0168. Called: July 1985, Middle Temple, MA (Cantab)

Parker *Oliver John* •
Lord Chancellor's Department, Trevelyan House, Great Peter Street, London SW1. Called: Nov 1977, Inner Temple

Parker *Robert Stewart* •
Parliamentary Counsel, Office of The Parliamentary Counsel, 36 Whitehall, London SW1A 2AY, 0171 210 6611, also Inn of Court L. Called: July 1975, Middle Temple, MA (Oxon), M.I.Mgt

Parker *Stephen Albert* •
The Home Office, Room 806, Queen Annes's Gate, London SW1H 9AD, 0171 273 2768. Called: July 1982, Lincoln's Inn, MA, LLB (Cantab)

Parker *Miss Susan Annette*
Called: July 1975, Gray's Inn, LLB (Lond)

Parkes *Bruce Winfield*
Company Secretary, 'Littlefields', Lea Lane, Little Braxted, Witham, Essex CM8 3XA. Called: Nov 1953, Middle Temple, LLB (Lond)

Parkes *David John*
Called: Nov 1969, Middle Temple

Parkin *Ms Victoria Howell*
Sweet & Maxwell, 100 Avenue Road, London NW3 3PF, 0171 393 7000, Fax: 0171 393 7010. Called: Nov 1994, Inner Temple, LLB (Soton)

Parkins *Miss Diane Julie* •
Barrister, Bedfordshire County Council, County Hall, Bedford MK42 9AP, 01234 228802, Fax: 01234 228125. Called: Feb 1986, Gray's Inn

Parkinson *Mrs Dorren Patricia* •
Lord Chancellor's Department, Criminal Appeal Office, Royal Courts of Justice, The Strand, London WC2A 2LL. Called: Feb 1973, Inner Temple

Parkinson *Stephen Lindsay* •
Head of Sols A1 Branch, Dept of Trade & Industry, Ashdown House, 123 Victoria Street, London SW1, 0171 215 6644. Called: July 1980, Lincoln's Inn, LLB (Lond)

Parmar *Karam Singh*
Legal Associate, Lee & Lee, Level 19, UIC Building, 5 Shenton Way, 00 65 22 00 666, Fax: 00 65 22 19 712, and Member Singapore Bar. Called: Nov 1992, Middle Temple, B.Eng (Singapore), LLB (Hons, Lond)

Parnell *Christopher Charles* •
Director, The Lantern Corporation., Adviser to the Russian Securities Commission and Member of the Arbitration Panel, 52 Addington Square, London SE5 7LB, 0171 701 8315, Fax: 0171 703 4209. Called: Nov 1979, Lincoln's Inn, LLB (Hons)

Parnell King *Mrs Sarah Lorraine*
Called: July 1996, Middle Temple, LLB (Hons)(Soton)

Parr-Ferris *Benedict Joseph George*
Called: Nov 1996, Middle Temple, LLB (Hons)

Parrack *Miss Jane Elizabeth*
Called: July 1978, Lincoln's Inn, LLB (Lond)

Parrish *Mrs Melanie Jane* •
Crown Prosecution Service, Portland House, London SW1. Called: Nov 1992, Middle Temple, BA (Hons)

Parry *Dr Anthony*
Director, British Aerospace, 227 Rue De La Loi, 1040 Brussels, Belgium, 010 322 2800300, Fax: 010 322 2800375. Called: Feb 1971, Middle Temple, BA (Cantab), MA, PhD

Parry *Mrs Deborah* •
Legal Advisor, Preston Magistrates' Court, Lawson Street, Preston, 01772 208000. Called: Feb 1994, Inner Temple, LLB (Lancs)

Parry *Hubert Brian*
Called: Nov 1997, Middle Temple, LLB (Hons)(Lond)

Parry *Jacques Henri* •
Head of Criminal Law Team, Law Commission, Conquest House, 37-38 John Street, Theobalds Road, London WC1N 2BQ. Called: July 1975, Middle Temple, BCL,MA

Parry *Miss Margaret Helen*
Justices' Clerk & Clerk to the Licensing Justices, Thames Division Justice's Clerkto the Inner London Youth Courts., West London Magistrates' Court, 181 Talgarth Road, London W6 8DN, 0181 741 1234, Fax: 0181 741 0808. Called: July 1974, Gray's Inn, LLB (Lond)

Parry *Philip Christopher*
Russell & Russell Solicitors, 7-13 Wood Street, Bolton BL1 1EE, 01204 399299, Fax: 01204 389223. Called: Oct 1995, Lincoln's Inn, LLB (Hons)(Sheff)

Parsell *Richard Alan* •
Senior Crown Prosecutor, Crown Prosecution Service, Teeside Branch, Crown House, Linthorpe Road, Middlesborough, Cleveland TS1 1TX, 01642 230444, Fax: 01642 253224. Called: July 1975, Gray's Inn, LLB (B'ham)

Parsey *Richard Leveson Moreland ISO*
40 Eastbury Avenue, Northwood, Middlesex HA6 3LN, 01923 821484. Called: Nov 1954, Inner Temple, M.A.

Parslow *Carl Geoffrey*
Ogier & Le Masurier, P.O.Box 404, Pirouet
House, Union Street, St Helier, Jersey,
01534 504177, Fax: 01534 619632.
Called: Oct 1996, Middle Temple, LLB
(Hons)(Plymouth)

Parson *Peter John* •
Principal Crown Prosecutor, Crown
Prosecution Service, Artillery House,
Heritage Way, Droitwich, Worcestershire.
Called: Nov 1976, Middle Temple, BA
(Oxon)

Parsons *David Robert Kingdon*
Lovell White Durrant Solicitor, 65 Holborn
Viaduct, London EC1A 2DY, 0171 236 0066,
Fax: 0171 248 4212. Called: July 1985,
Middle Temple, MA (Cantab)

Parsons *Thomas Alan CB*
11 Northiam Street, Pennethorne Place,
London E9 7HX, 0181 986 0930. Called: Jan
1950, Middle Temple, LLB

Partridge *Ms Elizabeth Ann* •
Senior Court Clerk, West Glamorgan
Magistrates', Courts Committee, Grove
Place, Swansea, West Glamorgan SA1 5DB,
01792 655171, Fax: 01792 651066.
Called: July 1989, Gray's Inn, LLB [So'ton]

Partridge *Graham David* •
Senior Crown Prosecutor, Crown
Prosecution Service, London Branch,
Prospect West, Croydon, Surrey. Called: Feb
1991, Gray's Inn, LLB (Lond)

Partridge *Richard Jack*
Called: Oct 1997, Inner Temple, LLB
(Manchester)

Partridge *William George*
Deputy Clerk to the Justices, Berkshire &
Oxfordshire, Magistrates' Court Service,
Easby House, Henley, Oxon. Called: Feb
1984, Middle Temple, Dip in Magisterial,
Law (Bris), M.Soc.Sci

Parwani *Miss Sharon Sheela*
Called: Nov 1995, Lincoln's Inn, LLB
(Hons)(Lond)

Pascoe *Eric Kenneth*
Calenick House, Calenick, Truro, Cornwall
TR3 6AA, 01872 272128. Called: Nov 1958,
Middle Temple, FCIB

Pascoe *Michael Peter*
Justice's Clerk, West Central Division of
Inner London, Inner London Magistrates',
Courts Service, Clerkenwell Magistrates'
Court, 78 King's Cross Road, London
WC1X 9QJ, 0171 278 6541, Fax: 0171 837
4526. Called: Feb 1966, Middle Temple

Pasha *Miss Dua Sultan*
Called: July 1996, Lincoln's Inn, LLB (Hons)

Passfield *Miss Zoe Victoria*
Called: Nov 1995, Inner Temple, LLB
(Lancs)

Passi *Pradeep Kumar*
Freelance Researcher/Employed, 01772
254527. Called: Nov 1993, Inner Temple,
LLB (Manch), LLM (Lancs)

Patel *Alpesh Bipin*
Company Director, Melina Court, Melina
Place, St John's Wood, Lonodn NW8 9SB,
0171 280 6718, Fax: 0171 286 6718.
Called: Nov 1993, Lincoln's Inn, LLB (Hons),
A.K.C., BA (Oxford)

Patel *Mayoor* •
Legal Advisor, Lombard Bank Limited,
Lombard House, 339 Southbury Road,
Enfield, Middlesex EN1 1TW, 0181 344
5811, Fax: 0181 344 5601. Called: Feb 1989,
Inner Temple, LLM (Lond), LLB (Hons)

Patel *Pravin Mahendra*
Called: July 1978, Middle Temple, BA

Patel *Sheriyar*
Called: Oct 1996, Gray's Inn, B.Sc (City),
LLB

Paterson *Alex Norman* •
Company Secretary & Lawyer, Oscar Faber
Plc, Marlborough House, Upper
Marlborough Road, St Albans, Herts
AL1 3UT, 0181 784 5784. Called: Feb 1958,
Gray's Inn, LLB

Paterson *Gerald Dudley*
Chairman of a European Patent Office Board
of Appeal, Erhardstrasse 27, 8000 Munich 2,
089 23990, Fax: 089 23994465. Called: July
1966, Gray's Inn, MA (Oxon)

Paterson *Richard Christopher* •
Crown Prosecutor, Crown Prosecution
Service, Norfolk Branch, CPS Anglia, Haldin
House, Old Bank of England Court, Queen
Street, Norwich NR2 4SX. Called: Nov 1994,
Middle Temple, BA (Hons)(Lancs)

Pathumanathan *Miss Kaushala*
Called: Nov 1996, Lincoln's Inn, LLB
(Hons)(Leics)

Patmore *Miss Janet Adelza*
Deputy Registrar, Supreme Court of
Jamaica, Supreme Court of Judicature of,
Jamaica, Public Building E, 134 Tower
Street, Kingston, (809) 922 8300, Fax: (809)
967 0669, and Member Jamaica. Called: July
1992, Middle Temple, LLB (Hons)

Paton *Ewan William*
Called: Oct 1996, Inner Temple, BA (Oxon)

Paton *Michael Lennox*
Devonshire House, Queen Street, P.O.Box
N4875, Nassau, 242 328 0563, Fax: 242 328
0566, and Member Bahamas Bar. Called: July
1991, Lincoln's Inn, BSc (USA), Dip Law,
CPA (USA)

Patra *Biswa Nath*
MA, BCom, 1-5 Nant Road, London
NW2 2AL, 0181 209 1112, Fax: 0181 458
3207. Called: July 1965, Inner Temple

Patrick *Sheriff Gail*
Sheriff, Kirkcaldy, Fife, ADVOCATE, 13
Succoth Place, EDINBURGH EH12 6BJ, 031
346 1883, Fax: 031 346 0004, and Member
Scottish Bar. Called: Nov 1990, Lincoln's
Inn, MA (St A's), LLB (Edin)

Patrick *Miss Joanne Penelope* •
Crown Prosecution Service, Princes Court,
34 York Street, Leicester LE1 5TU, 0116
2549333, Fax: 0116 2550855. Called: July
1992, Middle Temple, BA (Hons), Dip Law

Patten *Mrs Mary Lavender St Leger*
Called: Feb 1969, Gray's Inn, BA (Oxon)

Patterson *Brent James* •
Parker & Pickles, Richmond House,
Richmond Terrace, Blackburn BB1 7BQ,
01254 682424, Fax: 01254 682400.
Called: Nov 1991, Inner Temple, LLB

Patterson *Miss Carina Jane*
Called: Nov 1997, Gray's Inn, LLB (Derby)

Patterson *Lloyd Roy*
Called: Mar 1997, Lincoln's Inn, LLB (Hons)

Patterson *Miss Margaret Elizabeth* •
The Legal Adviser, Home Office. Called: July
1973, Middle Temple, LLB (lond)

Pattie *The Rt Hon Sir Geoffrey Edwin
PC*
GEC PLC, 1 Stanhope Gate, London
W1A 1EH, 0171 493 8484. Called: Nov
1964, Gray's Inn, MA

Pattinson *John Ernest* •
Principal Legal Officer, HM Customs &
Excise, The Solicitors Office, 22 Upper
Ground, London SE1, 0171 865 5189, Fax:
0171 865 5987, Also Inn of Court I.
Called: Nov 1983, Middle Temple, LLB

Paul *Miss Cynthia*
Called: July 1997, Lincoln's Inn, LLB
(Hons)(Reading)

Pawson *Kenneth Vernon Frank*
Haggas Hall, Weeton, Nr Leeds, North
Yorkshire LS17 0BH, 01423 734200, Fax:
01423 734731. Called: June 1949, Gray's
Inn, MA

Paxton *Paul*
Head Plantiff Personal Injury Shoosmiths &
Harrison. Chairman Berkshire Medical Legal
Society, Stewarts, 63 Lincoln's Inn Fields,
London WC2A 3LW, 0171 242 6462, Fax:
0171 831 6843. Called: Nov 1993, Middle
Temple, BSc (Hons)(Lough)

Payne *Alan Patrick*
Called: Nov 1996, Middle Temple, LLB
(Hons)(LSE)

Payne *Miss Helen Margaret*
Consultant to the Oriel Group Practice,
Masons, 30 Aylesbury Street, London
EC1R 0ER, 0171 490 4000, Fax: 0171 490
6309. Called: July 1987, Gray's Inn, LLB,
MSc

Payne *Jonathan Edward*
Called: Oct 1997, Gray's Inn, BSc (Wales)

Payton *Miss Keima*
Fee Earner, Chadwyck-Healey & Co Sols, 4
Brabant Court, Philpot Lane, London
EC3M 8AD, 0171 623 2002, Fax: 0171 623
2003. Called: Nov 1994, Lincoln's Inn, LLB
(Hons)

Peach *Neville Eric*
4 Pondfield Road, Hayes, Kent BR2 7HS, 0181 462 4745. Called: Feb 1960, Gray's Inn, ACII

Peacock *Kenneth Samuel*
Called: May 1994, Middle Temple, LLB (Hons)

Peacock *Miss Natasha Valerie* •
Legal Services Officer, National Mutual Life, Assurance Society, The Priory, Hitchin, Herts SG5 2DW. Called: Oct 1995, Gray's Inn, LLB (Hons)

Peaker *Marcus Timothy George*
Meis Limited, 34 Paradise Road, Richmond, Surrey TW9 1SE. Called: July 1994, Lincoln's Inn, MA

Pearl *Bernard* •
p/t Chairman Medical Appeal, Disability Appeal Tribunal Mental Health Review Tribunals, 4 Kidderpore Avenue, London NW3 7SP, 0171 435 1081. Called: Nov 1970, Gray's Inn, BDS (Lond), LDS. RCS, ENG., BA (OU), Dip, Soc (Lond), Dip F.O.

Pearmain *Advocate Susan Ann*
Advocate, Notary Public. Partner in Bedell & Cristin, Former Acting Batonnier, Bedell & Cristin, PO Box 75, One the Forum, Grenville Street, St Helier, Jersey JE4 8PP, 01534 814814, Fax: 01534 814815, and Member Jersey. Called: Nov 1971, Middle Temple

Pearman *Miss Jo-Dina Michelle*
Crown Counsel, Attorney General's Chambers, Global House, 43 Church Street, Hamilton, 292 2463, Fax: 292 3608. Called: July 1994, Lincoln's Inn, LLB (Hons)

Pearman *Peter Appleby Scott*
Associate, Conyers Dill & Pearman, Clarendon House, Church Street, Hamilton, 441 295 1422, Fax: 441 292 4720, and Member Bermuda Bar. Called: July 1995, Middle Temple, LLB (Hons), BA

Pearn *Ms Shirley Linda*
Called: Nov 1997, Inner Temple, LLB (Kent)

Pearse *Miss Christine Anne*
Director, ABS Riste Management Price Waterhouse, Price Waterhouse, 32 London Bridge Street, London SE1 9SY, 0171 939 3934, Fax: 0171 939 3276. Called: Oct 1996, Inner Temple, LLB (L'pool), ACA

Pearson *Edward Stuart*
Visiting Professor - Cranfield University, 2 Flowton Grove, Harpenden, Herts AL5 2J2, 01582 713163. Called: July 1965, Gray's Inn, BA (Hons), B.SC, (Econ), LLM, Ph.D

Pearson *Peter Roderick Prescott* •
Crown Prosecutor, Crown Prosecution Service, C/O 50 Ludgate Hill, LondoN EC4M 7EX. Called: July 1972, Middle Temple, LLB (Lond)

Pearson *Mrs Vivienne Mary* •
Senior Crown Prosecutor, Crown Prosecution Service, Priory Gate, Starne Court, Union Street, Maidstone, Kent, 01622 686425. Called: July 1982, Middle Temple, B.A.

Peat *Richard Colin* •
Enforcement Counsel, Investment Management, Regulatory Organisation, Lloyds Chambers, 1 Portsoken Street, London E1 8BT, 0171 390 5000. Called: Oct 1993, Gray's Inn, BA

Peckham *Stephen John*
Deputy Clerk to the Justices, Swindon Magistrates' Court, Princes Street, Swindon, Wiltshire SN1 2JB, 01793 527281, Fax: 01793 488525. Called: July 1989, Gray's Inn

Peddie *Jonathan Peter*
Corporate & Industrial Litigation Department of Clifford Chance, Clifford Chance, 200 Aldersgate Street, London EC1A 4JJ, 0171 600 1000, Fax: 0171 600 5555. Called: Nov 1994, Inner Temple, BA (Soton), CPE (City)

Pedlar *Samuel James*
Woodley, 7 Wychbury, Fox Hollies Road, Sutton Coldfield, West Midlands B76 1BY, 0121 351 7124, Fax: 0121 351 7124. Called: July 1952, Lincoln's Inn, MA

Pedropillai *Ms Corinne Damayanthi*
Called: Oct 1992, Gray's Inn, LL.B (Leic)

Peel *Mrs Victoria Sarah*
Called: Nov 1990, Inner Temple, BSc (Edin), Dip Law (City)

Peers *Benedict Giles Frederick*
Called: Mar 1998, Middle Temple, BA (Hons)(Exon)

Pegg *Captain Jason Geoffrey*
HQ 4th Division, Legal Branch, BFPO 15. Called: Oct 1994, Gray's Inn, LLB (Anglia)

Peh *Khaik Kew*
Called: Nov 1996, Lincoln's Inn, LLB (Hons)(Warw)

Peh *Miss Natalie Suan Wan*
Called: July 1995, Gray's Inn, LLB (Bris)

Peh *Miss Xiao-Shan*
Called: July 1996, Lincoln's Inn, LLB (Hons)(LSE)

Pek *Miss Chin-Choo*
Called: July 1996, Lincoln's Inn, LLB (Hons)(Sheff)

Pelekanos *Michalis*
Pelekanos & Co, Advocate & Legal Consultants, P.O.Box 2124, Larnaca, 4 657272, Fax: 4 653531, and Member Cyprus. Called: Nov 1996, Gray's Inn, LLB (Kent)

Pelekanou *Miss Elena*
Evagorou & Arch Makarios 111, Ave, Mitsis Building 3, 1st Floor Office 111, P O Box 1633, Nicosia, Cyprus, 00-357-2447400, Fax: 00-357-2443939, and Member Cyprus Bar. Called: Nov 1995, Lincoln's Inn, LLB (Hons)(So'ton)

Pelham *Paul Nicolas David*
24 Frognal Lane, London NW3 7DT, 0171 431 5298, Fax: 0171 431 5384, Also Lincoln's Inn May 1971. Called: July 1969, Gray's Inn, MA (Oxon)

Pemberton *Miss Brenda*
Called: July 1988, Lincoln's Inn, LLB (Hons)

Pemberton *Miss Frances Sandys*
Called: Nov 1991, Middle Temple, LLB (Hons)

Pemberton *Kenneth Leonard*
Called: July 1995, Inner Temple, BSc (Soton), CPE (Hong Kong)

Pendley *Mrs Beryl Elizabeth*
0171 370 6955, Fax: 0171 244 7596. Called: Nov 1994, Inner Temple, LLB

Pendley *James Ian*
KPMG Corporate Finance, 8 Salisbury Square, London EC4Y 8BB, 0171 311 8539, Fax: 0171 311 8252. Called: Oct 1992, Inner Temple, BSc (Finance), MA (Law)

Pendower *John Edward Hicks*
Rosemary, Promenade de Verdun, Purley, Surrey CR8 3LN. Called: July 1972, Inner Temple, MB, BS, FRCS

Penfold *Ronald Dean*
4 Livingstone Court, Christchurch Lane, Barnet, Herts EN5 4PL, 0181 449 6854. Called: Nov 1949, Lincoln's Inn, LLB (Lond)

Pengiran Tengah *Miss Dayangku Siti Nurbani*
Called: Nov 1994, Lincoln's Inn, LLB (Hons)(Lond)

Penhale *Ms Deborah Jane*
Court Clerk, Cardiff Magistrate's Court, Fitzalan Place, Cardiff, 01222 463040. Called: Feb 1994, Inner Temple, BA (Kent)

Penketh *Steven James*
Called: Nov 1995, Inner Temple, BA (Lond), CPE

Pennell *Mrs Lindsay Alexandra*
Called: Nov 1994, Inner Temple, LLB (Wales)

Penry *John Richard Phelps*
Scholar of Worcester College. Called: July 1960, Inner Temple, MA (Oxon)

Pepper *Ivan William*
Justice's Clerk, Woolwich Magistrates' Court, Market Street, London SE18 6QY, 0181 855 8518. Called: Nov 1963, Middle Temple

Pera *Mrs Mary*
Boxted Hall, Colchester, Essex CO4 5TJ. Called: Jan 1948, Lincoln's Inn

Peralta *Paul Charles Philip*
and Member Gibraltar Bar. Called: Oct 1994, Middle Temple, LLB (Hons)(Lond)

Percival *Richard Allighan* •
Special Cases/Research Lawyer, Criminal Appeal Office, Royal Courts of Justice, Strand, London WC2A 2LL, 0171 936 5070, Fax: 0171 936 6900. Called: Oct 1992, Gray's Inn, MA (Oxon)

Pereira *Ms Sanchia Rachael*
Called: Oct 1997, Inner Temple, LLB (Sussex)

Perkins *John Beaumont*
21 Crossby Close, Alkrington, Middleton, Manchester M24 1NU. Called: July 1968, Gray's Inn, LLB (Lond)

Perkins *Miss Marianne Yvette*
Called: Mar 1997, Gray's Inn, LLB (Lond), LLM (Lond)

Perkins *Michael*
Called: Oct 1994, Gray's Inn, BA, MA (Keele)

Perkins *Richard Charles* •
Legal Director, Department of Trade & Industry, 10 Victoria Street, London SW1H 0NN, 0171 215 3257, Fax: 0171 215 3480. Called: Nov 1972, Inner Temple, MA (Oxon)

Permanand *Miss Radha*
Called: July 1996, Lincoln's Inn, LLB (Hons)(LSE)

Perrett *Anthony James* •
Legal Advisor & Assistant Registrar of Friendly Societies, Registry of Friendly Societies, Victory House, 30-34 Kingsway, London WC2B 6ES, 0171 663 5000/5180, Fax: 0171 269 9820, Legal Advisor Building and Friendly Societies Commissions. Called: July 1972, Lincoln's Inn, CEng, MIEE, BA Hons

Perrins *Mrs Victoria Patricia*
Called: Oct 1996, Lincoln's Inn, LLB (Hons)

Perrot *Roger Allen*
Ozanne's, 1 Le Marchant Street, St Peter Port, Guernsey CI, 0481723466, Fax: 0481727935, and Member Guernsey Bar. Called: Nov 1974, Inner Temple, BSc (Lond), FCIArb

Perry *Gary Stephen* •
Principal Crown Prosecutor, Crown Prosecution Service, 27 St Leonards Road, Eastbourne, East Sussex BN21 3NN. Called: July 1989, Middle Temple, LLB (Leic)

Perry *Hugh Stanley*
Elm House, Coxwold, York YO6 4AB, 01347 868354, Fax: 01347 868390. Called: July 1957, Gray's Inn, BA, LLB

Pert *Mrs Vivien Victoria* •
Branch Crown Prosecutor, Crown Prosecution Service, The Cooperage, Gainsford St, London SE1. Called: Nov 1970, Gray's Inn, LLB

Perumal *Miss Krisna Kumari*
Called: Nov 1996, Middle Temple, LLB (Hons)(Lond)

Perumal *Vasantha Kumar*
Called: Nov 1993, Gray's Inn, LLB (Lond)

Perveen *Ms Usmat*
Called: Nov 1995, Lincoln's Inn, BSc (Hons)

Petasis *Andreas*
Called: Nov 1997, Inner Temple, LLB (Lancs)

Peters *David Edward Oluremi*
Senior Court Clerk, Berkeley House, Walton Street, Aylesbury, Bucks HP21 7QG, 0126 383058, Fax: 01296 383436. Called: Apr 1978, Lincoln's Inn

Peters *Mrs Emma-Kate* •
Legal Officer, Army Prosecuting Authority, RAF Uxbridge, Middlesex. Called: Oct 1991, Lincoln's Inn, LLB (Hons)

Peters *Francis Raymond*
Residinza Platani, Via G Di Vittorio 4, 27020 Travaco, Siccomario Pv, 382 499827, Fax: 382 499827. Called: Feb 1955, Inner Temple, MA (Oxon)

Petersen *Andrew Vincent*
Called: Oct 1997, Lincoln's Inn, LLB (Hons)(Wales)

Petri-Kassapi *Mrs Rona Vrahimi*
Legal Advisor, 89 Kennedy Avenue, Off 201, P O Box 6624, Nicosia, Cyprus, 357-2-379210, Fax: 357-2-379212, and Member Cyprus Bar. Called: May 1993, Gray's Inn, LLB (E.Anglia), LLM (Lond)

Pettican *Kevin*
Warner Cranston, Pickfords Wharf, London, 0171 403 2900. Called: Nov 1994, Inner Temple, BA, BCL (Oxon)

Pettinger *Stephen James*
Called: Nov 1997, Gray's Inn, BA

Pettit *Sean*
Called: Oct 1997, Inner Temple, LLB (LSE)

Petty *Christopher Roger William* •
Legal Director, Zeneca Pharmaceuticals, Alderley Park, Macclesfield, Cheshire SK10 4TF, 01625 512591, Fax: 01625 585618. Called: Nov 1976, Middle Temple, MA (Cantab)

Petty *George Oliver*
(510) 528-1721, Fax: (510) 528-9180, and Member State Bar of California. Called: Apr 1986, Middle Temple, BA, LLB (U, California)

Pg Hj Mohammad *Miss Dk Hajah Siti Rahmah*
Called: Nov 1995, Lincoln's Inn, LLB (Hons)

Phan *Miss Catherine Pui Lin*
Called: Nov 1997, Lincoln's Inn, LLB (Hons)(Lond)

Phang *Miss Sweet Lee*
Called: Nov 1994, Lincoln's Inn, LLB (Hons)(Lond), BSc (Australia)

Phelan *Ms Kristina Claudia* •
Lawyer, KPMG, P O Box 486, 1 Puddle Dock, London EC4V 3PD, 0171 311 2641, Fax: 0171 311 2114. Called: Oct 1995, Middle Temple, BA (Hons), Dip Law

Phelan *Miss Patricia Jean*
Threeburnford, Oxon, Lauder, Berwickshire TD2 6PU, 01578 750615. Called: July 1977, Gray's Inn, MA (Cantab)

Philip *Manalil Mathew*
Chittumala House, Veerbhadra Gardens, Pattom, Trivandrum - 4, TRIVANDRUM INDIA 446628, Member Indian Law Inst, Indian Inst Public Admin Advocate of the Kerala (India) Bar and Member India Bar. Called: July 1962, Lincoln's Inn, MA (Mysore)

Philip *Paul Gerard*
Called: Nov 1997, Lincoln's Inn, LLB (Hons)

Phillimore *Miss Sarah Victoria* •
Grade 7 Lawyer, Lord Chancellor's Dept, Selborne House, 54-60 Victoria Street, London SW1E 6QW, 0171 210 8500, Fax: 0171 210 1477. Called: Oct 1994, Lincoln's Inn, LLB (Hons)(Lond)

Phillipps *Miss Karen Shirley*
2 King's Bench Walk, 1st Floor, Temple, London, EC4Y 7DE. Called: July 1980, Gray's Inn, BA

Phillips *Mrs Anne Margaret* •
Senior Crown Prosecutor, Crown Prosecution Service, Woolwich/Bexley Branch, The Cooperage, 8 Gainsford Street, London SE1 2NG, 0171 357 7010, Fax: 0171 962 0903. Called: July 1988, Middle Temple, LLB (Hons), LLM

Phillips *Bleddyn Glynne Leyshon*
Clifford Chance (Solicitors), 200 Aldersgate Street, London EC1, 0171 600 1000, Fax: 0171 600 5555. Called: July 1978, Gray's Inn, BCL, LLB, AKC

Phillips *Miss Claudette* •
Senior Crown Prosecutor, Crown Prosecution Service, Greenwich/Bexley Branch, 2nd Floor, The Cooperage, Gainsford Street, London SE1 2NG, 0171 357 7010, Fax: 0171 962 0903. Called: Nov 1991, Middle Temple, BA Hons (Kent)

Phillips *Colin Andrew* •
VAT Consultant, Price Waterhouse, No 1 London Bridge, London SE1 9QL, 0171 939 3000. Called: Nov 1995, Gray's Inn, LLB (Wales)

Phillips *Mrs Elaine Margaret*
Called: Oct 1997, Gray's Inn, BA

Phillips *Fraser Guy*
Called: Nov 1996, Gray's Inn, LLB (Swansea)

Phillips *Lady Hazel Bradbury JP*
Fountain Court, Temple, London EC4Y 9DH, 0171 353 7356/1878, Also Inn of Court G. Called: June 1948, Inner Temple, LLB

Phillips *Mrs Henrike Deborah*
Called: Oct 1992, Lincoln's Inn, LLB(Hons)

Phillips *Howard Michael* •
Crown Prosecutor, Crown Prosecution Service, Oxford House, Leeds. Called: Nov 1991, Inner Temple, LLB (Reading)

Phillips *Mark David* •
Crown Prosecutor. Called: Apr 1991, Middle Temple, BSc Econ (Hons)

Phillips *Michael Roland* •
Called: Oct 1994, Lincoln's Inn, LLB (Hons)

Phillips *Norman Robert*
The White Cottage, 26 Stirling Road, Burley in Wharfedale, Ilkley, West Yorkshire LS29 7LH, 01943 864 818. Called: July 1965, Gray's Inn, LLB (Lond)

Phillips *Rhodri Jonathan Humphrey V*
Company Secretary, 3 Coopers Lane, Cowbridge, South Glamorgan, 01446 774861. Called: Feb 1990, Inner Temple, MA (Cantab)

Phillips *Roger Michael*
Non Executive Director, Thameside
Community Healthcare NHS Trust.,
Thurrock Community Hospital, Long Lane,
Grays RM16 2PX, 01375 390044, Fax:
01375 364468. Called: Nov 1983, Gray's
Inn, BA

Phillips *Miss Rowena Jane*
Senior Legal Adviser, Berkshire Magistrates'
Crt, Easby House, Northfield End, Henley on
Thames, Oxon RG9 2NB, 01491 412720,
Fax: 01491 412762. Called: Nov 1989,
Gray's Inn

Philliskirk *Ian* •
The Solicitor's Office, Welsh Office, Cathays
Park, Cardiff CF1 3NQ. Called: Nov 1993,
Lincoln's Inn, LLB

Philp *David Hugh* •
36 Ashbury Road, London SW11 5UN, 0171
350 1494, Fax: 0171 350 1494. Called: July
1973, Middle Temple, MA (Oxon)

Philpott *Mrs Deirdre Patricia Mary* •
Senior Crown Prosecutor, Crown
Prosecution Service, Eaton Court, Oxford
Road, Reading. Called: July 1976, Gray's Inn,
LLB (Lond)

Philpott *John Philip*
Called: Oct 1997, Lincoln's Inn, LLB
(Hons)(Westmins)

Phipps *Matthew Llewelyn*
Eversheds, Fitzalan House, Fitzalan Road,
Cardiff CF2 1XZ, 01222 471147. Called: May
1992, Lincoln's Inn, BA (Hons) (Reading),
Dip Law

Phipps *Piers Anthony Constantine H*
Managing Director of Hoopoe Finance
Limited, Trerose Manor, Mawnan, Falmouth,
Cornwall, 0171 292 5420, Fax: 0171 292
5435. Called: Apr 1986, Inner Temple

Photis *Andrew David*
Deputy Clerk to the Justices, Newham
Magistrates' Court, The Court House, 389-
397 High Street, Stratford, London E15 4SB,
0181 522 5000, Fax: 0181 519 9214.
Called: July 1982, Middle Temple, Dip Law
(Lond), DMS

Phua *Charles Cheng Sye*
Called: July 1994, Lincoln's Inn, LLB (Hons)
(Sheff)

Phua *Chung Ann Robert*
Called: July 1997, Lincoln's Inn, LLB
(Hons)(Leeds)

Phua *Miss Karen Jin Sim*
Called: July 1996, Middle Temple, LLB
(Hons)(Warw)

Phua *Pao Ann*
Called: July 1996, Middle Temple, BA
(Hons)(Cantab)

Piatt *Andrew*
Solicitor, Dibb Lupton Alsop Solicitors, 101
Barbirolli Square, Manchester M2 3DL, 0161
235 4024, Fax: 0161 235 4125. Called: July
1987, Gray's Inn, LLB (Soton) (Hons)

Picardo *Mr Fabian Raymond*
Gibraltar Bar Council (Committee Member),
Gibraltar Bar Council, 57/63 Line Wall Road,
Gibraltar, 00 350 79000, Fax: 00 350 71966,
and Member Gibraltar Bar. Called: Oct 1994,
Middle Temple, BA (Hons)(Oxon)

Piccolo *Vaughan*
Called: Nov 1994, Inner Temple, BA
(Cantab)

Pickard *Henry Francis*
17 Grangewood Court, Otley Road, Leeds
LS16 6ED. Called: Feb 1973, Gray's Inn, LLB,
MA (Cantab), M.S.I.

Pickering *Mrs Jane Margaret* •
Grade 7 Legal, Lord Chancellor's
Department, Criminal Appeal Office, Royal
Courts of Justice, Strand WC2A 2LL, 0171
936 7406. Called: July 1971, Inner Temple

Pickering *Miss Lorna Blanche* •
Senior Crown Prosecutor, Crown
Prosecution Service, Inner London Branch.
Called: Nov 1990, Inner Temple, BA (Hons)
(L'pool), Dip Law (City)

Pickett *Ian Jeffrey*
Former Police Officer. Called: Oct 1997,
Middle Temple, BA (Hons)(Salford), CPE
(Lond)

Pickett *Mrs Jennifer Wynne* •
Trade Marks Manager, Chanel Limited,
Queens Way, Croydon, Surrey CR9 4DL,
0181 688 7131, Fax: 0181 688 0012.
Called: July 1985, Inner Temple, LLB
(Cardiff)

Pickup *David Francis William* •
Solicitor for the Customs & Excise, New
Kings Beam House, 22 Upper GrounD,
London SE1 9PJ, 0171 865 5121, Fax: 0171
865 4820, and Member Gibraltar.
Called: Nov 1976, Lincoln's Inn, LLB (Lond)

Pierce *Raymond John Joseph*
Flat D, 10/F, University Heights, 42-44
Kotewell Road, (0852) 2813 7827, Fax:
(0852) 9106 0054, and Member Hong Kong
Bar. Called: Feb 1995, Gray's Inn, LLB
(Lond)

Piercy *Anthony Hart GM*
"The Birches", Little Holme Road, Walpole
Cross Keys, Kings Lynn PE34 4EW, 01843
581810. Called: Nov 1978, Lincoln's Inn,
LLB (Lond)

Pierpoint *Mrs Louise Marie* •
Senior Crown Prosecutor, Crown
Prosecution Service, Rossmore House, 10
Newbold Terrace, Leamington Spa.
Called: July 1979, Gray's Inn, LLB (Leic)

Pierre-Louis *Paul* •
H M Customs & Excise, New Kings Beam
House, 22 Upper Ground, London SE1.
Called: July 1981, Lincoln's Inn, BA (Hons)

Pigford *Jonathan Robert*
Called: Nov 1995, Middle Temple, LLB
(Hons)

Pigott *Mrs Margaret Louise* •
Head of Judicial Appointments Division
1(Job Share) Grade 5, Lord Chancellor's
Department, Selborne House, 54/60 Victoria
Street, London SW1E 6QB. Called: Nov
1973, Middle Temple, MA

Pikett *Christopher* •
Company Secretary General Manager Legal
Affairs, 3M United Kingdom PLC, 3M House,
PO Box No 1, Bracknell, Berkshire
RG12 1JU, 01344 858565, Fax: 01344
858553. Called: Nov 1975, Middle Temple,
LLB (Hons, Soton)

Pikis *Michael G*
12 Promitheos Str, Pelekanos Court 21,
Office 401, 1065 Nicosia Cyprus, 02
476838, Fax: 02 476631, and Member
Cyprus Bar. Called: Nov 1994, Gray's Inn,
LLB (Hons)

Pilbrow *David Gordon*
15/F Printing House, 6 Duddell Street, Hong
Kong, 852 25212616, Fax: 852 28450260,
Former Solicitor and Member Hong Kong
Bar. Called: July 1989, Middle Temple, BA
[Oxon]

Pilcher *Ms Rebecca Charlotte*
C/O The Garden House, Steventon,
Basingstoke, Hampshire, and Member
Northern Ireland Bar. Called: Nov 1994,
Middle Temple, MA

Pilcher *William Edgar*
Called: Nov 1996, Lincoln's Inn, LLB
(Hons)(Bucks)

Pilkington *Aubrey Alfred St John*
Acting Justices Clerk, Lincolnshire
Magistrates', Courts Committee, 15
Newland, Lincoln LN1 1XG, 01522 514200,
Fax: 01522 514200. Called: Nov 1982,
Middle Temple, LLB (Brunel), DMS (Notts)

Pilkington *Lionel Alexander* •
Senior Crown Prosecutor, Crown
Prosecution Service, The Cooperage, 8
Gainsford Street, London SE1 2NE, 0171
357 7010/962 2785, Fax: 0171 962 0902.
Called: Nov 1974, Inner Temple, BA

Pillai *Gopinath*
Called: July 1995, Lincoln's Inn, LLB (Hons)

Pillai *Pradeep G*
Called: July 1997, Middle Temple, LLB
(Hons)

Pillai *Prakash*
Called: July 1995, Middle Temple, LLB
(Hons)

Pillai *Miss Sharmini*
Messrs Tan Eng Choong & Co, Jalan Yap
Ahloy, Kuala Lumpur, and Member
Malaysian Bar (July 1995). Called: July 1994,
Middle Temple, LLB (Hons)(Lond)

Pillai *Ms Smeetha* •
Crown Prosecution Service, Kings House,
Kymberley Road, Harrow, Middlesex.
Called: July 1988, Gray's Inn, LLB (London)

Pillans *Mrs Diana Kerin*
Programme Manager College of Graduate &
Professional Studies, Thames Valley
University, St Mary's Road, Ealing, London
W5, 0181 579 5000, Fax: 0181 231 2307.
Called: July 1985, Gray's Inn, BSc (Lond),
LL.B

Pilling *Miss Cynthia Dorothy*
Called: Nov 1959, Gray's Inn, LLB (Hons)

Pilling *David James*
33b Willoughby Park Road, Tottenham,
London N17 0RR, 0181 801 7950.
Called: Feb 1992, Gray's Inn, LLB

Pimm *Geoffrey Leonard*
Royal Courts of Justice, Strand, London
WC2A 2LL, Goldsworth Chambers, 1st
Floor, 10-11 Gray's Inn Square, London,
WC1R 5JD. Called: Feb 1952, Gray's Inn

Pincott *Mrs Antoinette Jean Marie*
Chartered Accountant, Grant Thornton,
Grant Thornton House, Melton Street,
Euston Square, London NW1 2EP, 0171 728
2672, Fax: 0171 353 4035. Called: Feb 1991,
Middle Temple, LLB (Reading), ACA

Pinfold *Martin Franks* •
The Serious Fraud Office, Elm House, 10-16
Elm Street, London WC1X 0BJ. Called: July
1981, Middle Temple, LLB (London)

Ping *Miss Lim Yoke*
Legal Assistant, 37 Jalan 5/66, Bukit Gasing
46000, Petaling Jaya, Selangor, 03-7958833,
Fax: 03-7928833, and Member Malaysia Bar.
Called: July 1993, Inner Temple, LLB
(Nott'm)

Ping *Ms Wong Yuen*
Called: July 1994, Inner Temple, LLB

Pinion *Mrs Deborah*
Deputy Chief Clerk, 625 Romney Street,
London SW1. Called: Oct 1992, Gray's Inn,
LLB (Lancs)

Pinsolle *Philippe*
c/o Shearman & Sterling, 114 avenue des
Champs Elysees, 75008 Paris, France, (33) 1
53 89 70 00, Fax: (33) 1 53 89 70 70, and
Member Paris Bar. Called: July 1995, Gray's
Inn, Maitrise En Droit, (Paris), M.Juris
(Oxon),Essec

Pinson *Barry QC (1973)*
804 Hood House, Dolphin Square, London
SW1V 3NL, 0171 798 8450, Fax: 0171 834
9881. Called: Nov 1949, Gray's Inn, LLB

Pirbhai Zamin *Miss Iram*
Called: May 1997, Middle Temple, LLB
(Hons)

Pirie *Nicholas Frederick Francis*
Fellow of the Chartered Institute of
Arbitrators, Garden Chambers, 5th Floor, 10
Queen's Road Central, 2525-0221, Fax:
2845-2441, and Member Hong Kong Bar 2-3
Gray's Inn Square, Gray's Inn, London,
WC1R 5JH. Called: Nov 1971, Inner Temple,
LLB (Hons)

Pirzada *Syed Sharifuddin*
Attorney General of Pakistan, Press Centre,
Sharirah-E-Attaturk, Karachi - 1, Pakistan,
and Member Pakistan Bar. Called: Feb 1981,
Lincoln's Inn

Pishias *Yiannis*
Called: Nov 1997, Lincoln's Inn, LLB
(Hons)(Warw)

Pitblado *Alastair Bruce* •
Department of Trade & Industry, Legal
Services Directorate B, 10 Victoria Street,
London SW1H 0NN, 0171 215 3433, Fax:
0171 215 3520. Called: July 1974, Middle
Temple

Pitman *Miss Frances Mary*
Mourant Du Feu & Jeune, Advocates,
Solicitors &, Notaries Public, 22 Grenville
Street, St Helier, Jersey JE4 8PX, 01534
609000, Fax: 01534 609333. Called: Oct
1995, Lincoln's Inn, LLB (Hons)(Bucks)

Pitt *Daniel Crawford* •
Wandsworth Borough Council, London
SW18 2PU. Called: Oct 1995, Inner Temple,
BSc (Bath), CPE

Pitt *Mrs Georgina*
Senior Court Clerk, Law Courts, North
Street, Wolverhampton WV1 1RA, 01902
773151, Fax: 01902 27875. Called: Nov
1984, Gray's Inn, BA (Joint Hons)

Pitt *Nigel Christopher*
1 Crown Office Row, Ground Floor,
Temple, London, EC4Y 7HH. Called: July
1976, Middle Temple, BA (Oxon)

Pitto *Charles John*
Attorney General's Chambers, 17 Town
Range, Gibraltar, (010350) 70723, and
Member Gibraltar Bar. Called: Nov 1994,
Inner Temple, CPE (Wolverhampton), BA
(Newc)

Plant *Dr Glen*
20 Essex Street, London, WC2R 3AL.
Called: July 1985, Inner Temple, MA
(Oxon), Ph.D (Lond), MA (USA)

Platt *The Hon Mr Justice Harold Grant*
Justice of the Sup CT,Uganda, Supreme
Court of Uganda, P O Box 6679, Kampala,
270 362/3. Called: Feb 1952, Middle Temple

Platt *Robert Fetherston*
Curtis Davis Garrard Solicitor, Lancaster
House, Northumberland House, Staines
TW19 7LN, 0181 400 2400, Fax: 0181 400
2420. Called: Oct 1993, Lincoln's Inn, BA
(Hons)

Platt *Steven*
Clerk to the Justices, Clerk to the Justices,
Justices Clerks Office, Bury Magistrates
Court, Tenters Street, Bury BL9 0HX, 0161
764 3358, Fax: 0161 763 1190. Called: Feb
1986, Middle Temple, BA, DML

Platt *Terence Frederick* •
Legal Advisor, Kent County Council, Legal
Services Department, County Hall,
Maidstone, Kent ME14 1XQ, 01622 671411,
Fax: 01622 694266. Called: Nov 1977,
Middle Temple

Pliskin *Miss Melanie Clare* •
Prosecution Team Leader, Crown
Prosecution Service, 3rd Floor, Black Horse
House, Leigh Road, Eastleigh,Hants.
Called: Nov 1985, Lincoln's Inn, BA, LLM
(S'oton), MA (S'oton)

Plume *John Trevor*
Called: June 1936, Gray's Inn, LAM, RTPI

Plummer *Paul* •
Crown Prosecution Service, Eaton Court,
112 Oxford Road, Reading RG1 7LL.
Called: Feb 1986, Middle Temple, Dip Mag
Law, Dip Law

Plunkett *Oliver*
Called: Nov 1997, Middle Temple, LLB
(Hons)(Kingston)

Png *Cheong-Ann*
Advocate & Solicitor Supreme Court of
Singapore, Institute of Advanced Legal,
Studies, University of London, Charles Clore
House, 17 Russell Square, London
WC1H 2AB, 0171 837 8888 Ext 2519, Fax:
0171 837 9321. Called: July 1996, Gray's
Inn, LLB (London)

Poh *Ban Chuan*
Called: July 1993, Lincoln's Inn, LLB (Hons)

Pohjola *Ms Satu Heidi*
Rovastintie, 1 20 c, 03400 Vihti, 358 9
2247699, Fax: 358 9 2249041. Called: Oct
1995, Middle Temple, LLB (Hons), MAG.IUR

Poi *Melvin Chew-Yeun*
Called: July 1994, Lincoln's Inn, LLB (Hons)

Pok *Miss Abby Say Lin*
Called: Nov 1996, Middle Temple, LLB
(Hons)(Leics)

Pok *John Li-Wen*
Called: Nov 1993, Middle Temple, LLB
(Hons)(Lond)

Pokkan Vasu *Rakesh*
Called: July 1996, Middle Temple, LLB
(Hons)(Lond)

Polaine *Martin Daniel* •
Senior Case Lawyer, Crown Proscution
Service, Solar House, 1-9 Romford Road,
Stratford, London E15 4LJ, 0181 534 6601,
Fax: 0181 519 9690. Called: July 1988,
Gray's Inn, BA (Manc), DIP.LAW (The City,
Univ)

Polding *Richard John* •
Senior Manager, Business & Legal Affairs, V2
Music Group Limited, 131 Molland Park
Avenue, London W11 4UT, 0171 603 2652,
Fax: 0171 603 4796. Called: July 1985, Inner
Temple, LLB Hons (L'pool)

Poles *George Christian Harry*
Called: Nov 1991, Middle Temple, BA Hons
(Oxon)

Pollard *Bernard CB* •
Clerk to the Commissioners, General
Commissioners, of Income Tax, (Blackheath
Division). Called: July 1968, Middle Temple,
BA, BSC Econ

Pollard *Mrs Lynn Annette* •
Crown Prosecutor, CPS (Coventry Branch), Hertford House, Hertford Street, Coventry, Warwickshire CV1 1LS. Called: July 1967, Lincoln's Inn

Polledri *Miss Elisabetta* •
Legal Adviser, Treasury Solicitors Department, Queen Anne's Chambers, 28 The Broadway, London SW1H 9JS, 0171 218 0714. Called: July 1989, Lincoln's Inn, LLB

Pollock *Adam Alexander Brewis*
113 Moore Park Road, London SW6 4PS, 0171 375 6529. Called: July 1982, Gray's Inn, LLB (Hons)

Pollock *Desmond Thomas Campbell*
Called: Feb 1952, Inner Temple, LLB Hons (Lond)

Pollock *Miss Julia Mary* •
Legal Adviser, Country Landowners Association, 16 Belgrave Square, London SW1X 8PQ, 0171 235 0511, Fax: 0171 235 4696. Called: Nov 1984, Lincoln's Inn, LLB (Hons)

Polsom-Jenkins *Keith* •
Commercial Union Plc, 13th Floor, St Helens, 1 Undershaft, London EC3P 3DQ, 0171 283 7500. Called: July 1971, Inner Temple, LLB

Pomeroy *Toby*
Called: Mar 1997, Lincoln's Inn, LLB (Hons)

Pomson *David Seymour*
16 Prothero Gardens, London NW4 3SL, 0181 203 3364, Fax: 0181 203 7651. Called: Nov 1955, Middle Temple, MA (Oxon)

Ponnambalam *Gajendrakumar Gangaser*
Called: Nov 1997, Lincoln's Inn, LLB (Hons)(Lond)

Ponnusamy *Miss Grace Malathy d/o*
Called: July 1997, Lincoln's Inn, LLB (Hons)(Lond)

Ponnusamy *Waytha Moorthy*
30/1226 3rd Mile, Jalan Rasah, 70300 Seremban, and Member Advocate Solicitor of the High Court of Malaya. Called: Nov 1994, Lincoln's Inn, LLB (Hons)(Lond)

Pontin *Benjamin*
Called: Nov 1996, Inner Temple, BA, MA (Warw), LLM (Lond)

Pool *Mrs Lucie Antoinette*
State Counsel, Dept of Legal Affairs, P O Box 58, National House, Victoria, Mahe, 00 248 38300, Fax: 225063. Called: Nov 1995, Lincoln's Inn, LLB (Hons)

Poole *Frederick Thomas*
The Old Rectory, Landbeach, Cambridge CB4 4ED, 01223 861408, Fax: 01223 441276. Called: July 1966, Lincoln's Inn, MA, LLB(Cantab)

Poole *Mrs Jill*
Law Lecturer, Cardiff Law School, University of Wales, Cardiff, PO Box 427 Museum Avenue, Cardiff CF1 1XD, 01222 874367, Fax: 01222 874097. Called: Feb 1992, Lincoln's Inn, LLB (Hons) (Reading), LLM (Bristol), Commercial Law, ACIArb

Poole *Michael George*
David & Levene & Co, Ashley House, 235-239 High Road, Wood Green, London N22, 0181 881 7777, Fax: 0181 889 6395. Called: Nov 1993, Inner Temple, LLB (Notts)

Poon *Mr Lik Hang Herman*
801 Yip Fung Building, 2-12 D'Aguilar Street, Central, Hong Kong, and Member Hong Kong Bar. Called: Nov 1992, Inner Temple, LLB (Reading)

Poopalaratnam *Miss Shamini d/o*
Called: Nov 1996, Lincoln's Inn, LLB (Hons)(Lond)

Pooran *Miss Priya Nandita*
Called: Nov 1997, Gray's Inn, LLB, LLM (LSE)

Poostchi *Miss Banafsheh*
Called: Nov 1996, Lincoln's Inn, BA (Hons)(Oxon)

Poots *Laurence James*
House No 6, Harmony Heights, No 5 Hang Lok Lane, Shatin, 26666033, Fax: 26677662, and Member Hong Kong Bar Australia Bar. Called: Nov 1990, Gray's Inn, LLB (Lond), MIMgt

Pope *George Philip*
6 Chyngton Way, Seaford, E Sussex BN25 4JA, 01323 898 603. Called: July 1970, Gray's Inn, DMA

Pope *Jeremy David*
New Zealand Solicitor (1963), Transparency International, (TI), Otto-sulr Allee 97-99, D-10585 Berlin, +49 30 343 8200, Fax: +49 30 343 82044, and Member New Zealand Bar. Called: Nov 1993, Inner Temple, LLB (N.Zealand)

Pope *Miss Lorna Ann*
Deputy Chief Clerk, Inner London Magistrates, Courts Service, 65 Romney Street, London SW1P 3RD. Called: Nov 1978, Lincoln's Inn, BA

Pope *Miss Lucy Anne*
Trade Marks Adviser, Clifford Chance, 200 Aldersgate Street, London EC1A 4JJ, 0171 600 1000. Called: Nov 1992, Middle Temple, LLB (Hons, B'ham)

Porter *Miss Elaine Margaret* •
Legal Adviser, UBS Asset Management London, Ltd, 14 Triton Court, London, 0171 901 5257. Called: July 1987, Middle Temple, LLB

Porter *Gordon John*
9 Bromham Mill, Giffard Park, Milton Keynes MK14 5QP, 01908 612 892. Called: Nov 1962, Gray's Inn, LLB (Lond)

Porter *Miss Jane Elizabeth*
Court Clerk, Manchester City Magistrates', Court, Crown Square, Manchester M60 1PR, 0161 832 7272, Fax: 0161 832 5421. Called: Nov 1988, Middle Temple, BA Hons

Porter *Mark Alexander* •
Sema Group UK Limited, Norcliffe House, Station Road, Wilmslow, Cheshire SK9 1BU. Called: July 1982, Lincoln's Inn, LLB (Hons)

Porter *Stephen David* •
Legal Adviser, British Telecom, 2-12 Gresham Street, London EC2V 7AG, 0171 356 8488, Fax: 0171 356 3719. Called: Feb 1992, Lincoln's Inn, LLB (Hons)

Portland *Miss Brender*
Called: Nov 1997, Middle Temple, LLB (Hons)

Posner *Robert* •
Assistant Controller of Legal Services. Hon Sec. Assoc for Barristers in local Govt and Public Service, London Borough of Bexley, Bexley Civic Offices, Broadway, Bexleyheath, Kent DA6 7LB, 0181 303 7777, Fax: 0181 301 2661, and Member Victoria Bar Queensland Bar. Called: July 1981, Lincoln's Inn, BA (Hons)

Pote *Mrs Tracey Ann Candlish* •
Court Clerk, Ipswich Magistrates Court, Elm Street, Ipswich, Suffolk IP1 2AP, 01473 217261, Fax: 01473 231249. Called: Nov 1991, Gray's Inn, BA (Hons)

Potter *Miss Alison Lisa*
4 Pump Court, Temple, London, EC4Y 7AN. Called: Feb 1987, Middle Temple, MA (Oxon)

Potter *Donald Charles* QC (1972)
Pump Court Tax Chambers, 16 Bedford Row, London WC1R 4ED, 0171 414 8080, also Inn of Court L and Member Northern Ireland Bar Pump Court Tax Chambers, 16 Bedford Row, London, WC1R 4EB. Called: Nov 1948, Middle Temple, LLB

Potter *Miss Felicite MBE*
Gapperies, West Porlock, Somerset TA24 8NX, 01643 862497. Called: June 1951, Lincoln's Inn

Potter *Raymond CB*
p/t President, South Western Rent Assessment Panel. Called: Nov 1971, Inner Temple

Potts *Richard Vivian*
Corporate Finance - Associate Director, Panmure Gordon & Co Limited, New Broad Street House, 35 New Broad Street, London EC2M 1NH, 0171 638 4010, Fax: 0171 588 5297. Called: July 1982, Middle Temple, BA, MSI

Potts *Stephen George*
Called: Oct 1997, Inner Temple, BSC (City), BSc (London), CPE (Wolverhampton)

Pourgourides *Evangelos*
P.O.Box 4137, Limassol, (00357) 5 346634, Fax: (00357) 5 346633, Practising Barrister in Cyprus and Member Cyprus. Called: July 1997, Lincoln's Inn, LLB (Hons)(Leics)

E

Povall Ms Kathryn Elizabeth
c/o Overseas Liaison Office, Allen & overy,
One New Change, London EC4M 9QQ.
Called: Oct 1991, Lincoln's Inn, LLB (Hons)
(New)

Povey Jonathan Micheal
Called: Oct 1996, Gray's Inn, LLB (Wales),
LLM (Cantab)

Powar Mrs Sabina Ayesha
Legal Adviser, The Law Courts, Alexandra
Road, London SW19 7JP, 0181 946 8622.
Called: Nov 1986, Middle Temple, LLB

Powell Miss Alison Louise
2 Crown Office Row, 2nd Floor, Temple,
London, EC4Y 7HJ. Called: July 1982, Inner
Temple, LLB (Manch)

Powell Glyn Stephen •
Crown Prosecutor, Crown Prosecution
Service, 2nd Floor, Kings House, Kymberley
Road, Harrow, Middlesex HA1 1YH, 0181
424 8688, Fax: 0181 429 9134. Called: Oct
1993, Middle Temple, LLB (Hons)(Lond)

Powell Guy Storer
Bedell & Cristin, Normandy House,
Grenville Street, St Helier, Jersey, 01534
872949. Called: Nov 1982, Middle Temple,
LLB

Powell Ian George •
Legal Adviser, Bass plc, 20 North Audley
Street, London W1Y 1WE, 0171 409 8419,
Fax: 0171 409 8526. Called: July 1983, Inner
Temple, LLB (Sheff)

Powell Mrs Josephine •
Crown Prosecutor, Crown Prosecution
Service, Fylde & North Lancs, Prudential.
House, Topping Street, Blackpool, Lancaster
PR1 1ER, 01772 556886. Called: Nov 1987,
Middle Temple, LLB (UCL), M.Phil

Powell Richard Arthur Gayler •
Court Clerk, Exeter & E Devon Magistrates,
The Court House, Heavitree Road, Exeter,
Devon, 01392 270081, Fax: 01392 420913.
Called: July 1989, Middle Temple, LLB
(Hons), LLM

Powell Miss Tracey Ann •
Crown Prosecutor, Crown Prosecution
Service, The Courtyard, Lombard Street,
Abingdon, Oxfordshire OX14 5SE, 01235
555678, Fax: 01235 554144. Called: Nov
1989, Middle Temple, BA (Hons) (Sheff),
Dip in Law

Power Ms Alexia Clare •
Senior Crown Prosecutor, Crown
Prosecution Service, Tower Hill, City & Old
Street, Branch Office, The Cooperage, 8
Gainsford St, London SE1 2NG, 0171 357
7010, Fax: 0171 962 0905. Called: Oct
1992, Gray's Inn, BSc (Hons)(Surrey)

Power Miss Kathryn Mary •
Government Lawyer, Criminal Appeal
Office, Royal Courts of Justice, Strand,
London WC2A 2LL, 0171 936 6875.
Called: Oct 1991, Inner Temple, LLB (Exon)

Poxon Philip Edward •
Legal Counsel, Brown & Root, Wellheads
Place, Wellheads Industrial Estate, Dyce,
Aberdeen AB21 7GB, 01244 778332, Fax:
01224 777710. Called: July 1985, Lincoln's
Inn, LLB (Newc)

Prabhakaran Miss Prasanna T.V.
Called: July 1996, Middle Temple, LLB
(Hons)(Lond)

Prabhu Miss Warsha Rewati Sudhakar
Called: Nov 1997, Lincoln's Inn, BA
(Hons)(Cantab)

Prager Ms Sarah Jane
Called: Oct 1997, Inner Temple, LLB
(Nottingham)

Prasad Henry Durga
90 Ingleton Road, London N18 2RT, 0181
292 9984, and Member Guyana, Bermuda.
Called: July 1965, Middle Temple

Pratt Miss Chinique Elmega
Called: Nov 1997, Gray's Inn, BA (Windsor,
Canada), LLB (Kent)

Pratt Derek Norman •
Senior Civil Servant, HM Customs & Excise,
Solicitor's Office, New King's Beam House,
London SE1 9PJ, 0171 865 5144, Fax: 0171
865 5822. Called: July 1971, Gray's Inn, LLB

Pratt Miss Olivia Deloris
and Member Bahamas. Called: Nov 1996,
Gray's Inn, LLB (Buckingham)

Pratt Miss Sara Caroline
Called: Oct 1996, Inner Temple, LLB
(N'ham)

Pratt Simon Derek •
Financial Director Group Company
Secretary, Aureus Leisure Group Ltd, 22
High Street, Leicester LE1 5YN, 0116
2511229. Called: July 1981, Lincoln's Inn,
BA Hons (Durham), M.B.A [Leics]

Pratt Timothy Jean Geoffrey CB
Old Vicarage, Radwinter, Saffron Waldon,
Essex CB10 2SN, 01799 599507. Called: Feb
1959, Middle Temple, MA

Premaraj Belden
Sivananthan, Suite 253-4, 4th Floor, 253
Jalan Tun Sambanthan, 50470 Kuala
Lumpur, 2738273, Fax: 2739273, and
Member Malaysia Bar. Called: Nov 1993,
Lincoln's Inn, LLB (Hons, L'pool)

Prendiville Rice Irwin •
Legal Advisor, Vlasov Group, "Aigue
Marine", 24 avenue de Fontvieille, P.O.Box
628, MC 98018 MONACO cedex, 92 05 10
10, Fax: 92 05 94 12. Called: July 1981,
Gray's Inn

Prentice Ms Dorothy May •
Crown Prosecutor, Crown Prosecution
Service, First Floor, Oxford House, Oxford
Road, Bournemouth BH8 8HA. Called: Nov
1983, Lincoln's Inn, BA

Prentice Edward Arthur Gerald
Advocate of Royal Court of Guernsey,
Notary Public Notary Public, Ozannes
Advocates, 1 le Marchant Street, St Peter
Port, Guernsey, 01481 723466, Fax: 01481
714571. Called: Nov 1983, Inner Temple,
LLB (Lond)

Prentis Mrs Victoria Mary Boswell •
The Treasury Solicitor, Queen Anne's
Chambers, 28 Broadway, London SW1H 9JS,
0171 210 3090. Called: Oct 1995, Middle
Temple, BA (Hons)

Preston Alan David •
Registry of Friendly Societies, Victory
House, 30-34 Kingsway, London WC2B 6ES,
0171 663 5192, Fax: 0171 269 9812.
Called: May 1972, Gray's Inn, LLM

Preston Geoffrey Averill
Called: June 1950, Gray's Inn

Pretzell Andreas Erich Joachim
Called: Oct 1997, Middle Temple, LLB
(Hons)(Brunel), LLM (Lond)

Prew James Martin
Enviromental Claims Manager, Commercial
Union Assurance, St Helens, 1 Undershaft,
London EC3P 3DQ, 0171 283 7500, Fax:
0171 662 1025. Called: Nov 1976, Lincoln's
Inn, LLB (Lond), FCII

Price Anthony John •
Group Legal Director Secretary, Bartle Bogle
Hegarty Ltd, 60 Kingly Street, London
W1R 3DS, 0171 734 1677, Fax: 0171 437
3666. Called: July 1983, Gray's Inn, BA Hons

Price Mrs Caroline Sarah •
Legal Adviser Grade 5, The Home Office, 50
Queen Anne's Gate, London SW1H 9AT.
Called: July 1970, Gray's Inn, LLB

Price David Allan
Managing Director - International Division,
21 Hallside Park, Knutsford, Cheshire
WA16 8NQ. Called: Feb 1991, Lincoln's Inn,
BSc (Hons), LLB, FRICS, Dip Arb, FCIArb

Price Mrs Huma Sabih
Called: Nov 1991, Inner Temple, LLB

Price John Philip
Director General, Dairy Industry Federation,
19 Cornwall Terrace, London NW1 4QP,
0171 486 7244, Fax: 0171 487 4734.
Called: July 1974, Inner Temple, MA, B Phil
(Oxon)

Price Jonathan Nicholas
Deputy Clerk to the Justices, Northampton
Magistrates' Court, Regents Pavillion,
Summerhouse Road, Moulton Park,
Northampton NN3 6AS, 01604 497033, Fax:
01604 497010. Called: Nov 1989, Inner
Temple, LLB (B'ham), MBA (B'ham)

Price Ms Kim Elizabeth •
Senior Lawyer, Cheltenham & Gloucester
Plc, Barnet Way, Barnwood, Gloucester
GL4 7RL, 01452 375547, Fax: 01452
375570. Called: Nov 1982, Gray's Inn, LLB

Price *Miss Pauline Beryl* ●
Senior Crown Prosecutor, Crown
Prosecution Service, St John's House, Union
Street, Dudley, W Midlands, 01384 230471.
Called: Nov 1985, Middle Temple, BA
(Hons)

Price *Thomas Leolin Alfred*
Called: Oct 1994, Middle Temple, BA
(Hons)(Oxon)

Price *Toby David*
Called: Mar 1997, Lincoln's Inn, LLB
(Hons)(Warw)

Price *Miss Victoria*
In-House Counsel, Linder Myers Solicitors,
45 Cross Street, Manchester, 0161 832
6972, Fax: 0161 834 0718. Called: Oct
1993, Gray's Inn, BA (Sussex), Dip Law
(Staff)

Priddis *Simon James*
Legal Officer, Cleary, Gottlieb, Steen &,
Hamilton, Rue de la Loi, 1040 Bruxelles, 00
32 2 287 21 74. Called: Oct 1995, Lincoln's
Inn, BA (Hons), LLM

Pridham *Miss Laura Rebecca*
Called: Oct 1997, Gray's Inn, LLB
(Glamorgan)

Priest *Andrew Jonathan*
Called: Nov 1994, Inner Temple, BA (Oxon)

Priest *Mrs Jacqueline Ann*
York Chambers, 14 Toft Green, York, YO1
1JT. Called: July 1973, Inner Temple, LLB

Prince *Oscar Peter* ●
Company Lawyer, RMC Group plc, RMC
House, Coldharbour Lane, Thorpe, Egham,
Surrey TW20 8TD, 01932 568833, Fax:
01932 568933. Called: Nov 1966, Gray's Inn

Prince *Raymond Andrew* ●
Department of Law, London Borough of
Harrow, PO Box 2, Civic Centre, Station
Road,, Harrow, Middlesex HA1 2UH.
Called: July 1985, Lincoln's Inn, BA

Pringle *Robert Henry Becker*
Barristers' Chambers, Allendale Square, 77
St George's Terrace, Perth WA 6000, (08)
9220 0444, Fax: (08) 9325 9008/9111, QC
Western Australia. Called: Nov 1978, Gray's
Inn, BA, LLB

Prinn *Edmund Charles*
Called: Oct 1997, Middle Temple, BA, LLB
(City)

Pritchard *Anthony Paul*
Called: Nov 1992, Inner Temple, LLB

Pritchard *Mr. John Bertram*
Called: Oct 1995, Inner Temple, LLB (Kent)

Proctor *Adrian Francis*
Financial Advisor, 0161 236 7885.
Called: Mar 1996, Inner Temple, BA
(Honours)

Proctor *Miss Carmel Gail* ●
BUPA, Anchorage Quay, Salford Quay,
Manchester M5 2XL, 0161 931 5586.
Called: Oct 1997, Lincoln's Inn, LLB
(Hons)(Manc)

Proctor *Charles Robert*
Cumbria Social Services, Civic Centre,
Rickergate, Carlisle CA3 8QQ, 01228
607025. Called: July 1980, Lincoln's Inn, BA
(Dunelm), MA (Hull)

Prosser *John Rogers*
Editor - Accounting & Business, ACCA, 29
Lincoln's Inn Fields, London WC2A 3EE,
0171 396 5734, Fax: 0171 396 5741.
Called: July 1975, Middle Temple, LLB

Pryer *David*
Clerk to the Justices Justices' Chief
Executive, Northumberland Magistrates',
Courts Committee, PO Box 16, Law Courts,
Bedlington, Northumberland NE22 5PQ,
01670 531100, Fax: 01665 510247.
Called: Nov 1982, Gray's Inn, MIMgt

Pryer *Eric John CB*
"Sprangewell", Poles Lane, Thundridge,
Ware, Herts SG12 0SQ, 01920 462595, Fax:
01920 463212. Called: Nov 1957, Gray's
Inn, BA (Hons), Hon Assc Member RICS

Pryer *Mrs Julia Mary* ●
Crown Prosecution Service, (Leics/
Northants), 50 Ludgate Hill, London
EC4M 7EX. Called: Feb 1986, Middle
Temple, BA

Psaila *Ms Tara Antonia Maria*
Called: Mar 1998, Gray's Inn, LLB., BCL
(Cork), LLM (Lond)

Psillidou *Miss Kathryn Andreou*
Called: Nov 1994, Gray's Inn, LLB

Pugh *Clive Anthony*
Called: Oct 1994, Lincoln's Inn, LLB
(Hons)(Lond)

Pugh *Denzil Anthony* ●
Barrier House, Barrier Road, Chatham, Kent
ME4 4SG. Called: July 1980, Gray's Inn

Pullin *Miss Samantha Joan*
Called: Oct 1996, Middle Temple, LLB
(Hons)(Wales)

Pulsford-Harris *Miss Dorothy Ann* ●
Senior Crown Prosecutor, Crown
Prosecution Service, Haldin House, Old
Bank of England Court, Queen Street,
Norwich, Norfolk NR2 4SX, 01603 666491,
Fax: 01603 617989. Called: Nov 1988,
Middle Temple, LLB (E Anglia)(Hons)

Pumphrey *Mrs Lyn Susan*
Court Clerk, Hounslow Magistrates' Court,
Justices' Clerk's Office, Market Place,
Brentford, Middlesex TW8 8EN, 0181 568
9811. Called: May 1994, Lincoln's Inn, BA
(Hons, Hull), LLB (Hons), Dip Ed

Pung *Miss So Ken*
NO 68 Jalan Seri Cheras 6A, Taman Seri
Cheras, BT 9 1/2 Cheras, 43200 BT 9
Cheras, Selangor Malaysia. Called: July 1995,
Inner Temple, LLB

Purcell *John Thomas*
Senior Lecturer in Law, School of Law,
University of Westminster, Red Lion Square,
London WC1R 4SR, 0171 911 5000 ext
2513, Fax: 0171 911 5152. Called: July
1987, Lincoln's Inn, LLB

Purchas *James Alexander Francis*
Called: Oct 1997, Inner Temple, BA
(Cantab), CPE (City)

Purnell *Miss Marcia Ann*
Le Logis de Souvigne, 79800 Souvigne, 49
76 25 03, Fax: 49 76 25 03. Called: Nov
1983, Gray's Inn, BA LLM PhD

Purse *Alfred Turnbull*
8 Wellesford Close, Banstead, Surrey
SM7 2HL, 01737 355804. Called: Nov 1942,
Gray's Inn, LLB, FCIS

Purse *Hugh Robert Leslie*
Part Time Chairman of Industrial Tribunals,
The Industrial Tribunal, 44 Broadway,
Stratford, London E15 1XH. Called: Feb
1964, Gray's Inn, LLB (Lond)

Purshotamdas *Prakash*
Legal Assistant, Azman Soh & Murugaiyan, 1
Columbo Court, 07-23, Singapore 179742,
338 3996, Fax: 338 5993, and Member
Singapore Bar. Called: July 1994, Lincoln's
Inn, LLB (Hons)

Purves *Michael Neil* ●
Principal Legal Officer, HM Customs &
Excise, Solicitors Office, 22 Upper Ground,
London SE1 9PJ, 0171 865 5153, Fax: 0171
865 5194. Called: July 1989, Inner Temple,
LLB (Lond)

Purves *Robert Frederick*
and Member New South Wales Bar 36
Bedford Row, London, WC1R 4JH.
Called: July 1973, Middle Temple, BA, LLB

Purvis *Andrew John* ●
Compliance Officer. Called: Feb 1993,
Gray's Inn, Bsc (Econ)(Wales), FCII

Purvis *Ian Bremmer* ●
Senior Legal Adviser & General Counsel,
Age Concern England, Astral House, 1268
London Road, London SW16 4ER, 0181 679
8000, Fax: 0181 679 6069. Called: Nov
1960, Inner Temple, BA (Law) (So'ton)

Purvis *Julian*
Called: Nov 1997, Lincoln's Inn, BA (Hons),
MA (Oxon), LLB (Hons)

Purvis *Stephen Harald* ●
Manager, North of England Protecting &,
Indemnity Association Ltd, The Quayside,
Newcastle Upon Tyne NE1 3DU, 0191 232
5221, Fax: 0191 261 0540. Called: Nov
1984, Middle Temple, BA

Pushparasah *Miss Thevarani*
Called: July 1996, Lincoln's Inn, LLB (Hons)

Pustam *Miss Helen Denise*
Senior Court Clerk, Berkeley House, Walton
Street, Aylesbury, Bucks HP21 7QG, 01296
383058, Fax: 01296 383436. Called: Oct
1992, Lincoln's Inn, LLB(Hons)

Puxon *Mrs Christine Margaret QC*
(1982)
Medical Legal Consultant, 19 Clarence Gate
Gardens, London NW1 6AY, 0171 723
7922, Fax: 0171 258 1038, also Gray's Inn
1965. Called: Feb 1954, Inner Temple, MB,
CHB, MRCS, LRCP, MD, FRCOG

E

Pye *James Edward Kensey* •
Group Legal Adviser, Vendome Luxury
Group PLC, 27 Knightsbridge, London
SW1X 7YB, 0171 838 8500, Fax: 0171 838
8555. Called: July 1972, Gray's Inn, LLB

Pyfrom *Basil Lorraine*
Called: July 1997, Inner Temple, LLB
(Dunelm)

Pym *Michael John* •
In-house Counsel, Cognos Limited, Westerly
Point, Market Street, Bracknell, Berkshire
RG12 1QB, 01344 707 789, Fax: 01344 707
703. Called: Nov 1986, Gray's Inn,
LLB(Sheff)

Pyrgou *Mrs Melina*
Partner, Chr P Kinanis & Co, Annis
Komninis 29A, P.O.Box 2303, Nicosia,
Cyprus, 00357 2 456486, Fax: 00357 2
362777, and Member Cyprus Bar
Association. Called: Nov 1995, Gray's Inn,
B.Soc.Sci (Keele)

Qadri *Adnan Abdullah Shafqat*
Called: July 1995, Middle Temple, LLB
(Hons)

Qayyum *Abdul*
Village Bhuttian Mohra, Tehsil-Gujar-Khan,
Dist, Rawalpindi. Called: May 1982, Gray's
Inn, BA, LLb

Qazi *Faysal Ali*
Called: Mar 1997, Lincoln's Inn, LLB (Hons)

Quah *Chiang Fu*
Called: July 1994, Lincoln's Inn, LLB (Hons)

Quaife *Ramsay Justin Malin*
Called: Oct 1995, Middle Temple, BA (Hons)

Quain *Paul Andrew*
Called: Nov 1997, Middle Temple, BA
(Hons)(Hull)

Quek *Miss Bee Choo*
1 Park Road, [H] 04-04 People's Park
Complex, 5336077, Fax: 5342339, and
Member Singapore Bar. Called: Nov 1995,
Lincoln's Inn, LLB (Hons)

Quek *Miss Gwang Hwa*
Called: July 1996, Lincoln's Inn, LLB (Hons)

Quek *Miss Karen Chia-Huei*
Legal Assistant, Company Secretary, 36
Robinson Road, [H] 18-01, City House, 065
420 7653, Fax: 065 224 8210, and Member
Singapore Bar. Called: July 1995, Lincoln's
Inn, LLB (Hons)

Quek *Miss Karen Tzun Tjin*
Called: July 1997, Gray's Inn, LLB

Quek *Miss Sue Yian*
Called: Oct 1997, Middle Temple, LLB
(Hons)(Brunel)

Quenby *Richard Alan*
Called: July 1985, Inner Temple, BA

Quickfall *Frank*
Called: Nov 1959, Gray's Inn, LLB

Quinlan *Kevin Joseph* •
Senior Legal Advisor, Securities & Futures
Authority, Cottons Centre, Cottons Lane,
London SE1 2QB, 0171 378 9000.
Called: Feb 1995, Gray's Inn, LLB (L'pool)

Quinlan *Michael John Maxwell*
Director of Stamp Duty, Coopers &
Lybrand, 1 Embankment Place, London
WC2N 6NN, 0171 213 5836, Fax: 0171 213
2440, and Member Australia Bar. Called: July
1992, Middle Temple, LLB, LLM

Quinn *Anthony Paschal*
Law Library, Four Courts, Dublin 7, Ireland,
0001 8720622/8254811, Fax: 0001
8721455/720031, Barrister, Kings Inn
Dublin Also Inn of Court M and Member
Northern Ireland Bar. Called: July 1990,
Lincoln's Inn, MA, DipPbl, ADM (Dub, Dip
Lgl Studies, (Kings Inns), FCIArb, Dip Intnl
Arb, Dip Arb Law, B.COMM

Quinn *Stuart John* •
Cleveland Magistrates Courts, Committee,
Teeside Law Courts, Victoria Square,
Middlesborough, Cleveland TS1 2AS, 01642
240301, Fax: 01642 224010. Called: Oct
1990, Gray's Inn, BSc, LLM

Quinn *Miss Tamara Jane*
Called: Oct 1995, Lincoln's Inn, BA
(Hons)(Lond)

Quinn-Smith *Duncan Niall*
Called: Oct 1995, Inner Temple, LLB (Bris)

Qureshi *Adnan Aslam*
Called: Nov 1994, Gray's Inn, LLB (Middx)

Qureshi *Azra Perveen* •
Crown Prosecutor, Crown Prosecution
Service, Queen's House, 58 Victoria Street,
St Albans, Herts Al1 3HZ, and Member
Pakistan Bar. Called: Nov 1983, Lincoln's
Inn, LLB (Hons)

Qureshi *Miss Yasmin* •
Senior Crown Prosecutor, Crown
Prosecution Service, Kings House, 2nd
Floor, Kymberley Road, Harrow, Middlesex
HA1 1YH, 0181 424 8688 X 204.
Called: Nov 1985, Lincoln's Inn, BA (Hons)
(Lond), LLM (Lond)

Qureshi *Ms Zainab Bilal*
Called: July 1997, Inner Temple, BA
(Sussex)

Rabin *Anthony Leon Philip*
Called: July 1978, Middle Temple, LLB, FCA

Raby *Edward Menashi*
01865 341694. Called: Nov 1967, Inner
Temple, BA

Rackow *Patrick Joseph William*
Called: Nov 1992, Inner Temple, MA
(St.Andrews), Dip in Law

Radakin *Antony David*
Called: Mar 1996, Middle Temple, LLB
(Hons)

Radcliffe *George Whiteley*
18 Bladon Drive, Belfast BT9 5JL.
Called: July 1985, Inner Temple, MA
(Oxon), FCA

Radcliffe *Miss Penelope Jane*
Capsticks, 77/83 Upper Richmond Road,
London SW15 2TT, 0181 780 4716, Fax:
0181 780 4728. Called: Oct 1992, Middle
Temple, BA (Hons, Dumelm), Diploma in
Law(City)

Radford *Patrick Vaughan CBE, MC,
TD, DL*
Langford Hall, Newark, Notts NG23 7RS,
01636 76802. Called: Nov 1954, Gray's Inn,
FCIS

Radin *Alang Iskandar*
2A Lorong Ara kiri 3, Bangsar Lucky
Gardens, 59100 Kuala Lumpur, 03 2580331/
7567929, Fax: 03 2536331, and Member
Malaysia. Called: Oct 1995, Middle Temple,
BA (Hons)

Radon *Mrs Joyce*
Flat 2, 188 Kennington Lane, (Entrance
Cardigan Street), London SE11 5DL, 0171
735 1574. Called: July 1976, Inner Temple

Radway *Jonathan Mark*
Justices' Chief Executive, Justices' Chief
Executive, Hertfordshire Magistrates, Court
Service, Register Office Block, County Hall,
Hertford SG13 8DF, 01992 556544.
Called: July 1977, Middle Temple, LLB
(Lond), MIMgt

Rae *Alexander* •
Senior Principal Legal Officer, Legal
Department, Ministry of Agriculture, 55
Whitehall, London SW1A 2EY, 0171 270
8227, Fax: 0171 270 8295. Called: July
1978, Inner Temple, BA (Dunelm)

Rae *Ian Andrew* •
Legal Advisor, Provident Mutual Life,
Assurance Association, Six Hills Way,
Stevenage, Herts SG1 2ST, 01438 732755,
Fax: 01438 732415. Called: Nov 1986,
Middle Temple, LLB, MBA, DIC

Rafiq *Nabil*
Called: Mar 1998, Middle Temple, LLB
(Hons)(Brunel)

Rafn *Jamie George*
Called: Oct 1996, Lincoln's Inn, BA
(Hons)(Oxon)

Ragnauth *Miss Portia Uranie* •
Crown Prosecutor, Crown Prosecution
Service, 23rd Floor, Portland House, Stag
Place, London SW1E 5BH. Called: July 1985,
Lincoln's Inn, LLB

Rahim *Miss Anisah Binte Abdul*
Advocate & Solicitor, 55 Market Street,
Sinsov Building, [H]08-01, 65-5383177, and
Member Singapore Bar. Called: July 1995,
Middle Temple, LLB (Hons)

Rahman *Andaleeve*
Called: Mar 1998, Lincoln's Inn, LLB
(Hons)(Wolv'ton)

Rahman *Mian Habibur*
and Member Bangladesh, Dhaka Barrister's
Common Law Chambers, 57 Whitechapel
Road, Aldgate East, London, E1 1DU.
Called: Nov 1972, Lincoln's Inn, MSc, LLB
(Dhaka)

Rahman *Qazi Abdur*
Called: Nov 1977, Gray's Inn, BA, BL, MA
Business Law

Rahming *Andre Joseph*
Called: July 1995, Gray's Inn, LLB (Lond)

Rai *Yogesh Kumar*
Called: Nov 1995, Middle Temple, BA (Hons)

Raja *Anil Jayantilal* •
BUPA, Anchorage Quay, Salford Quays, Manchester M5 2XL, 0161 931 5616. Called: Mar 1996, Gray's Inn, LLB (Lond)

Raja *Miss Fozia Naz* •
In-house Lawyer, SPS (Software Products, Services Limited), 19-20 The Broadway, Regent House, Woking, Surrey GU21 5AP. Called: Nov 1994, Inner Temple, LLB (Hull)

Raja *Nomaam Akram*
Called: July 1997, Gray's Inn, LLB

Raja *Abdul Rashid Miss Raja Rozmin*
Called: Nov 1996, Middle Temple, LLB(Hons)(Glamorgan)

Raja *Alang Petra Miss Raja Nor Azwa*
Yeo, Tan, Hoon & Tee, Advocates & Solicitors, Rooms 704-705, 7th Floor, Asis Life Building, Jalan Segget, 80000 Johor, 607 2233768, Fax: 607 2244882, and Member Malaysia. Called: July 1995, Gray's Inn, LLB (Kent)

Rajah *Tharuma*
Called: July 1993, Lincoln's Inn, LLB (Hons)

Rajan *Sanjiv Kumar*
Called: July 1997, Middle Temple, LLB (Hons)(Leics)

Rajanathan *John Victor Stanislaus*
28 Cromer Road, Leyton, London E10 6JA, 0181 539 5140. Called: Nov 1970, Middle Temple, BSc Econ(Lond)

Rajaratnam *Miss Indira*
and Member Advocate & Solicitor of the High Court of Malaya. Called: Nov 1995, Lincoln's Inn, BA (Hons)(Kent)

Rajasingham *Rajanathan*
18 Cunningham Avenue, Guildford, Surrey GU1 2PE, 01483 562852, QC (Belize) and Member Sri Lankan Bar. Called: July 1957, Lincoln's Inn, MA, LLB (Cantab)

Rajendran *Miss Kalyani*
Called: July 1997, Middle Temple, LLB (Hons)(Leics)

Rajendran *Kumaresan*
Called: July 1996, Middle Temple, LLB (Hons)(Lond)

Rajendran *M S*
Called: Nov 1997, Lincoln's Inn, LLB (Hons)(Lond)

Rajgopal *Miss Uthra Devi*
Called: Mar 1998, Inner Temple, LLB (Not'ham)

Rajvinder Singh
Legal Assistant, 53 Jalan Air Duson, Setapak, 53200 Kuala Lumpur, and Member Malaysia Bar. Called: July 1994, Lincoln's Inn, LLB (Hons, Lond)

Rajwani *Ms Vandana*
Flat 2-B Kam Fai Mansions, 68a Macdonnell Road, (852) 28575089, Fax: (852) 28681652, and Member Hong Kong Bar. Called: July 1996, Lincoln's Inn, BA

Ralston *Peter Saintjohn*
Called: May 1997, Gray's Inn, LLB (Liverpool)

Ramachandran *A J*
Apt Block 38, Upper Boon Keng Road, [H]04-2406, Singapore 380038, Republic of Singapore, 7488072 (H)/2209344, Fax: 2257827, and Member Singapore Bar. Called: July 1994, Lincoln's Inn, LLB (Hons), B.Sc (Singapore)

Ramachandran *Miss Deepa*
Called: Nov 1997, Lincoln's Inn, LLB (Hons)(Nott'm)

Ramachandran *Raj Sativale*
Sativale & Associates, 6-1 Jalan SS15/8B, Subang Jaya, 47500, Petaling Jaya, Selangor Malaysia, 03 733 8787, Fax: 03 733 1103. Called: Feb 1990, Middle Temple, LLM, Dip Law, MCIT, MICS

Ramachandran *Sathish*
No 6 Tepian Tunku, Bukit Tunku, 50480 Kuala Lumpur, 603 6512989, Fax: 603 6510850, and Member Malaysia. Called: July 1993, Middle Temple, LLB (Hons)(Kent)

Ramagge *James George*
28 Irish Town, P O Box 15, (350) 72020, Fax: (350) 72270, and Member Gibraltar Bar. Called: Oct 1994, Middle Temple, LLB (Hons)(Lond)

Ramakrishnan *Miss Sharmila*
Called: Feb 1994, Lincoln's Inn, LLB (Hons, Wales)

Ramalingam *Paramasivam*
Called: July 1996, Lincoln's Inn, LLB (Hons)(Lond)

Ramanathan *Miss Shsmini*
Called: Nov 1994, Lincoln's Inn, LLB (Hons)(Lond)

Ramason *Raji*
Called: July 1996, Middle Temple, LLB (Hons)(Wolves)

Rambridge *Rene Charles*
Called: Nov 1997, Middle Temple, LLB (Hons)

Ramdin *Ashvinsingh*
Called: May 1994, Lincoln's Inn, LLB (Hons)

Ramful *Jugdeo* •
Assistant Solicitor, and Member Mauritius Bar. Called: Nov 1984, Lincoln's Inn, BA

Ramiah *Sivaraja*
Called: July 1996, Lincoln's Inn, LLB (Hons)(Lond)

Ramlogan *Anand*
113 Ben-Lomond Village, Williamsville P.O., Trinidad, 809-650-0536, Fax: 809 658 0350, and Member Trinidad & Tobago. Called: July 1995, Middle Temple, LLB (West Indies), LLM (Lond), Dip (Law), LEC

Ramnarace *William Taij Bhowan* •
Principal Crown Prosecutor, Crown Prosecution Service, 3rd Floor, Kymberley Road, Harrow, Middlesex, 0181 248 5738. Called: Nov 1979, Lincoln's Inn, BA (Hons) LAW

Ramsahoye *Fenton Harcourt Wilworth*
Doughty Street Chambers, 11 Doughty Street, London, WC1N 2PG. Called: Feb 1953, Lincoln's Inn

Ramsay *Alexander William*
15 Brunswick Gardens, London W8 4AS, 0171 727 6282, Fax: 0171 460 0871. Called: Nov 1955, Gray's Inn, MA,

Ramsay *Miss Cheryl Diana*
Called: Oct 1997, Inner Temple, LLB, MA (Brunel)

Ramsden *Dr William Michael* •
Whitehead Woodwards & Co, 26 Talbot Road, Blackpool, Lancashire BT1 1NJ. Called: Oct 1992, Lincoln's Inn, LLB(Hons), Ph.D,LL.D

Ramsewak *Miss Premila*
Called: July 1996, Lincoln's Inn, LLB (Hons)

Ramsey *Miss Jane* •
Head of Legal Services, Legal Services, London Borough of Merton, Civic Centre, Morden, 0181 545 4015, Fax: 0181 543 7126. Called: July 1989, Middle Temple, BA Hons, MSc

Ranai *Ashok Kimar Mahadev*
Skrine & Co, No 4, Leboh Pasar Besar, Straits Trading Building, 50050 Kuala Lumpur, 603 2945111, Fax: 603 2934327, Advocate & Solicitor, High Court of Malaya and Member Malaysian Bar. Called: Nov 1995, Gray's Inn, LLB (Wales)

Ranasinha *Mrs Ranmini Manisha*
Called: July 1993, Middle Temple, MA (Hons)(Oxon), LLM (Lond)

Ranauta *Miss Manvinder Kaur*
Called: May 1997, Gray's Inn, LLB (Glamorgan)

Randhawa *Ravinderpal Singh*
Bernard, Rada, Barker and, Pauline Chen, Advocates & Solicitors, 1 Colombo Court, [H]07-30, 336 1717, Fax: 339 9782/339 4991, and Member Singapore. Called: July 1995, Middle Temple, LLB (Hons) (Wales)

Randle *Alexander Toby*
Called: Nov 1994, Lincoln's Inn, BA (Hons)(Lond)

Randle *Ms Christine Annjeanette*
Dunn, Cox, Orrett & Ashenheim, 48 Duke Street, Kingston, Jamaica, West Indies, (809) 922 1500, Fax: (809) 922 9002, and Member Jamaica Bar. Called: Oct 1994, Gray's Inn, LLB

Rangan *Krishnan Harihara Kastthuri*
Principal, National Maritime Academy, Singapore, 48 Pemimpan Place, Singapore 2057, (65) 354 0786 (Res), Fax: (65) 7582321. Called: July 1994, Lincoln's Inn, B.Sc, BE, LLB (Lond), First Class Engineer, (Motor)

Rankin *Glynn* •
Principal Crown Prosecutor, Crown Prosecution Service, 2nd Floor, Windsor Hse, Pepper Street, Chester CH1 1TD. Called: Feb 1983, Middle Temple, LLB

Rapson Ms Isabel Frances •
Called: Oct 1995, Gray's Inn, BA (Hull), MA (UEA), Dip Law

Rasaiah Ms Santha Geraldine •
Head of Legal and Editorial Affairs, The Newspaper Society, Bloomsbury House, Bloomsbury Square, 74-77 Great Russell Street, London WC1B 3DA, 0171 636 7014, Fax: 0171 631 5119. Called: July 1983, Middle Temple, BA (Oxon)

Rasanayagam Miss Marlene Sunita
Called: July 1996, Middle Temple, LLB (Hons)(Bucks)

Rashid Khurram
Called: Nov 1997, Lincoln's Inn, LLB (Hons)

Rashid Miss Naz Parveen
Called: July 1994, Lincoln's Inn, LLB (Hons)

Rashid Miss Yasmin
Called: Mar 1996, Lincoln's Inn, LLB (Hons)

Rasiah Sanjeev Kumar
Serine & Co, (Advocates & Solicitors), No % Leboh Pasar Besar, 50050 Kuala Lumpur, Malaysia, and Member Malaysia Bar. Called: July 1994, Middle Temple, LLB (Hons)(Hull)

Ratcliffe Simon Timothy James
Called: Oct 1997, Gray's Inn, BA (Anglia)

Ratcliffe Steven James •
Lincolnshire County Council, (Legal Division), 13 The Avenue, Lincoln, Lincs LN1 1YP, 01522 552114, Fax: 01522 552138. Called: Nov 1984, Gray's Inn, LLB (Hons), Warwick

Ratnasingham Rajasingham
Called: July 1996, Lincoln's Inn, LLB (Hons)

Ratti Ms Alison Julie
Oakleigh, Wernffrwd, Gower, Swansea SA4 3TY, 01792 851599, Fax: 01792 850056. Called: Nov 1991, Gray's Inn, BA (Oxon)

Rauf Miss Neetasha
Called: July 1995, Lincoln's Inn, LLB (Hons), LLM

Raut Viveka
Called: May 1994, Inner Temple, LLB, MSc

Raval AnilKumar Harish •
Compliance Manager, Henderson Administration Group, Plc, 3 Finsbury Avenue, London EC2M 2PA, 0171 410 4786, Fax: 0171 377 5742. Called: Oct 1991, Lincoln's Inn, MA (Hons) (Cantab)

Ravi Arumugam
Block 551, Pasir Ris Street 51, [H]08-97, and Member Singapore Bar. Called: July 1995, Lincoln's Inn, LLB (Hons)

Ravindran Miss Subithra
Called: July 1994, Lincoln's Inn, LLB

Rawat Mrs Ismet Parveen •
Crown Prosecutor, Crown Prosecution Service, The Cooperage, Gainsford Street, London SE1, 0171 962 2701. Called: Nov 1992, Inner Temple, BA (Hons)

Rawlins Christopher Stuart
Assistant Recorder. Called: Feb 1957, Gray's Inn

Rawlins Jeremy John •
Senior Crown Prosecutor, CPS, 2 King Edward Street, Nottingham NG1 1EL. Called: Nov 1982, Middle Temple, LLB (Hons)

Rawlinson Iain David
P.O.Box 25011, Awali, 973 826003, Fax: 973 537637. Called: Oct 1994, Lincoln's Inn, BA (Hons)(Durham)

Rawlinson Jonathan James Charles
Called: Oct 1997, Lincoln's Inn, BA (Hons)(Leeds)

Rawlinson William CBE
11 King's Bench Walk, Temple, London EC4Y 7EQ, 0171 632 8500, Fax: 0171 583 9123/3690, 11 King's Bench Walk, Temple, London, EC4Y 7EQ. Called: Jan 1939, Inner Temple, MA

Rawlinson of Ewell The Rt Hon Lord PC,KB QC (1959)
Honorary Recorder Kingston- upon-Thames Hon Fellow US College of Trial Lawyers, House of Lords, London SW1, Hon Fellow Christ's College Cambridge QC Northern Ireland (1971) and Member American Bar. Called: Nov 1946, Inner Temple

Ray Gaur Gopal
Legal Consultant Legal Advisor/Evaluator, Sang Health Affairs, King Fahad National Guard, Hospital, P.O. Box 22490, Riyadh 11426, (KSA) 1 252 0088, Fax: (KSA) 1 252 0088, Advocate, Supreme Court of India and Member West Bengal Bar. Called: July 1973, Lincoln's Inn, BCom, FCIArb

Ray John Betson
"Pond Acre", Malthouse Lane, West Ashling, Chichester, West Sussex PO18 8DX. Called: Feb 1956, Inner Temple, MA (Oxon)

Ray Miss Lapita
Called: July 1997, Lincoln's Inn, LLB (Hons)(Leeds)

Rayne Jason Edward
Called: July 1997, Gray's Inn, LLB (Middx)

Rayner Ms Catherine Elizabeth •
Housing Lawyer/Employment, South Islington Law Centre, 131-132 Upper Street, Islington, London N1. Called: Nov 1988, Gray's Inn, LLB

Rayner Christopher Glenn
Senior Legal Adviser, Colchester Magistrates' Court, Stanwell House, Stanwell Street, Colchester CO2 7DL, 01206 563057, Fax: 01206 42933. Called: Feb 1977, Middle Temple, LLB

Rayner Miss Donna Frances •
Principal Crown Prosecutor, Crown Prosecution Service, Riverpark House, 225 High Road, Wood Green, London N22, 0181 888 8889, Fax: 0181 888 0746. Called: Nov 1988, Gray's Inn, BA (Hons)

Rayner Miss Jacqueline
Senior Court Clerk, Sutton Coldfield Mag Court, The Court House, Lichfield Road, Sutton Coldfield B74 2NG, 0121 354 7777, Fax: 0121 355 0547. Called: Nov 1991, Gray's Inn, LLB

Raywood Caleb
Called: Oct 1995, Inner Temple, LLB (Essex), LLM

Raza Khurram
Called: Nov 1995, Lincoln's Inn, LLB (Hons)

Razzaque Miss Jona
Called: Nov 1997, Lincoln's Inn, LLM (Lond)

Rea James •
Police Legal Adviser, Devon & Cornwall Constabulary, Police Headquarters, Middlemoor, Exeter, Devon EX2 7HQ, 01392 52101 Ext 22863, Fax: 01392 452765. Called: July 1978, Gray's Inn, BA

Rea Luigi Orlando Anthony
Garden Flat, 14 Grantham Street, Dublin 8, 0001 4781105, Fax: 0001 4781105, and Member Southern Ireland Bar. Called: July 1982, Middle Temple, BA (Dublin)

Rea Robert Kevin
The Bar Library, Royal Courts of Justice, Chichester Street, Belfast, (01232) 562438, and Member Northern Ireland. Called: Mar 1996, Gray's Inn, LLB, LLM (Int'l &, European)

Read Miss Pauline Anne
Called: May 1979, Inner Temple, LLB (Hons) (Leeds), Dip Public Admin, (Manch)

Reading Timothy Mark Lucas •
Manager, Legal BP Shipping Ltd, BP Shipping Limited, Breakspear Park, Breakspear Way, Hemel Hempstead, Herts HP2 4UL, 01442 225536, Fax: 01442 225855. Called: July 1981, Lincoln's Inn, MA (Oxon)

Record Miss Suzannah Jane
Called: Nov 1997, Gray's Inn, BSc (Kent)

Reddin Lieutenant Colonel David Gordon MBE •
Directorate of Army Legal Svcs, Ministry of Defence, Trenchard Lines, Upauon, Wiltshire SN9 6BE. Called: Nov 1982, Gray's Inn, LLB (Hons) (L'pool)

Reddy Miss Challa Anudita •
Legal Officer, H M Customs & Excise, New Kings Beam House, 22 Upper Ground, London SE1, 0171 865 5109, Fax: 0171 865 5197. Called: Nov 1993, Inner Temple, BSc (Lond), CPE (City)

Redfearn Charles •
Legal Adviser, General Counsel's Office, Export Credits Guarantee Dept, P.O.Box 2200, 2 Exchange Tower, Harbour Exchange Square, London E14 9GS, 0171 512 7177, Fax: 0171 512 7052. Called: Nov 1986, Lincoln's Inn, BA, Dip Law

Redman *Graham Frederick*
Assistant Grand Secretary United Grand
Lodge of England, 60 Great Queen Street,
London WC2B 5AZ, 0171 831 9811, Fax:
0171 831 6021. Called: July 1974, Middle
Temple, MA (Oxon)

Redman *Martin David*
Legal Adviser, Old School, Piddinghoe,
Newhaven, Sussex BN9 9AP, 01273 514768.
Called: Nov 1969, Inner Temple

Redman *Paul Darren* •
Havering Magistrates Court, The Court
House, Main Road, Romford, Essex
RM1 3BH. Called: July 1994, Lincoln's Inn,
MA

Redman *Stephen Michael* •
Unum Limited, Milton Court, Dorking,
Surrey RH4 3LZ, 01306 887766, Fax: 01306
887504. Called: July 1986, Lincoln's Inn, BA

Redpath *John Scott*
Called: Oct 1996, Middle Temple, BA (Hons)
MA (Hons), (Lond) D.Phil (Oxon)

Redpath *Ms Lara Catherine* •
Crown Prosecution Service, Brent Section,
3rd Water, King's House, Kymberly Road,
Harrow HA1 1YH, 0181 424 8688 Ext 270.
Called: Feb 1994, Lincoln's Inn, BA
(Hons)(Oxon)

Reece *Alan Charles* •
Director of Negotiations, Kerr McGee Oil
(UK) PLC, 75 Davies Street, London
W1Y 1FA, 0171 872 9700, Fax: 0171 493
2672. Called: July 1974, Lincoln's Inn

Reed *Ms Jane Elizabeth* •
Called: Nov 1986, Middle Temple, BA
(Oxon) DipLing, Dip Law

Reed *Mrs Marie Gabrielle* •
Principal Crown Prosecutor Prosecution
Team Leader, Crown Prosecution Service,
Kings House, Kymberley Road, Harrow,
Middlesex HA1 1YH, 0181 424 8688, Fax:
0181 424 9134. Called: Nov 1972, Gray's
Inn, LLB

Rees *Miss Nerys Wyn*
Called: Oct 1997, Gray's Inn, LLB (Wales)

Rees *Mrs Patricia Anne*
Called: Oct 1995, Inner Temple, BSc
(Australia), CPE (Lond)

Rees *Miss Penelope* •
Senior Crown Prosecutor, Crown
Prosecution Service, 24 South Gate,
Chichester CF1 3PL, 01222 378201.
Called: July 1985, Gray's Inn, BA
(Hons)(E.Anglia)

Rees *The Rt Hon Lord Peter Wynford
Innes PC, QC* (1969)
Called: Feb 1953, Inner Temple, MA
(Hons)(Oxon)

Rees *Roland Vaughan* •
4 The Close, Richmond, Surrey TW9 4QW,
0181 876 2948. Called: Nov 1966, Middle
Temple, LLB

Rees *Thomas Lionel* •
Lord Chancellor's Department, Criminal
Appeal Office, Law Courts, The Strand,
London WC2A 2LL, 0171 936 6606.
Called: Nov 1968, Middle Temple, MA, LLM
(Cantab)

Rees *William Patrick Charles*
Deputy Justice's Clerk, Inner London
Magistrates', Courts Service, 65 Romney
Street, London SW1. Called: Nov 1974,
Middle Temple, LLB (Lond)

Reese *Dr Alan John Morris TD, JP*
9 Hopping Lane, Canonbury, London
N1 2NU, 0171 226 2088. Called: Nov 1955,
Middle Temple, MD (Lond), FRCPath

Reeve *Robert Arthur*
Called: Nov 1975, Middle Temple, BA, FCIS

Reeves *Christopher David*
Lecturer (BVC), The College of Law, 14
Store Street, Bloomsbury, London
WC1E 7DE, 0171 291 1200. Called: Oct
1992, Lincoln's Inn, LLB(Hons)(Sheff)

Reeves *Christopher Patrick*
Called: July 1993, Inner Temple, BA (E.
Anglia), Dip. in Law

Reeves *Mrs Mary* •
Civil Servant. Called: Oct 1994, Middle
Temple, BA (Hons), CPE (Middx)

Regal *Richard Neill*
Technical Manager, International Federation
of, Accountants, 114 West 42nd Street,
Suite 2410, New York 10036, 001 212 302
5952. Called: July 1997, Inner Temple, BA
(L'pool), MBA (Kingston), FCA, ATII

Regan *Gerald Thomas*
Called: Nov 1993, Middle Temple, BA
(Hons)(Leeds), CPE (City)

Regan *Matthew James*
I T & Management Consultant, Metro
Consulting, 11 Carteret Street, London
SW1H 9DL, 0171 222 2526, Fax: 0171 222
2527. Called: Mar 1996, Middle Temple, BA
(Hons)

Reggiori *Miss Brenda Clare* •
Inspector, Crown Prosecution Service, CPS
Inspectorate, 50 Ludgate Hill, London
EC4M 7EX, 0171 273 1286, Fax: 0171 273
8194. Called: Nov 1970, Middle Temple, LLB
(Lond), LLM

Regnart *Horace*
Cleveland Chambers, 63-65 Borough Road,
Middlesbrough, Cleveland, TS1 3AA.
Called: July 1985, Gray's Inn, LLB (Newc)

Rehman *Miss Ghulam Sakina*
Called: July 1994, Lincoln's Inn, LLB (Hons)

Reid *Ms Claire Fiona*
Called: July 1995, Inner Temple, LLB (Lond)

Reid *George Alan* •
Called: July 1972, Lincoln's Inn, MA, Ph.D
(Cantab)

Reid *Horace Deighton*
Called: July 1975, Lincoln's Inn, LLB (Lond)

Reid *James Gordon*
Standing Junior Scottish Office,
Environment Dept 1986 to 1993,
Advocatess Library, Parliament House,
Edinburtgh, Scotland EH1 1RF, 031 226
5071, Fax: 031 225 3642, QC Scotland 1993
and Member Scottish Bar 1 Atkin Building,
Gray's Inn, London, WC1R 5AT. Called: Apr
1991, Inner Temple, LLB (Edin), F.C.I.Arb

Reid *Kiron John Cuchulain*
Lecturer in Law, Faculty of Law, University
of Liverpool, Liverpool L69 3BX, 0151 794
2801, Fax: 0151 794 2884. Called: Nov
1994, Inner Temple, LLB (Bris)

Reid *Mrs Mary Helene Theresa* •
Team Leader, Crown Prosecution Service,
One Onslow Street, Guildford, Surrey
GU1 4YA, 01483 882600, Fax: 01483
882603/4. Called: Nov 1982, Middle
Temple, LLB (Hons)

Reilly *Miss Clare* •
Legal Officer, The Office of the Investment,
Ombudsman, 6 Frederick's Place, London
EC2R 8BT, 0171 796 3065. Called: Feb
1988, Inner Temple, MA, LLM

Reilly *Thomas Edward Martin*
Called: Nov 1996, Lincoln's Inn, LLB (Hons)

Rein *Dr Andrew Paul*
12 Mavor Close, Woodstock, Oxon
OX7 1YL, (0993) 811121. Called: Nov 1992,
Middle Temple, BA (Hons), MA, B.Phil &
D.Phil

Relan *Vershal*
Called: Oct 1997, Gray's Inn, LLB (L'pool)

Rendell *Antoine Mark John*
Principal Court Clerk, Bristol Magistrates
Court, P O Box 107, Nelson Street, Bristol,
Avon BS99 7BJ, 0117 9435100. Called: Nov
1987, Gray's Inn, LLB (Reading)

Rendell-Reynolds *Charles James
Samuel*
Called: Mar 1997, Lincoln's Inn, LLB (Hons)

Renee *Mrs Karen Anne*
Called: Oct 1992, Lincoln's Inn, LLB(Hons)

Renganathan *Nandakumar*
Legal Assistant Advocate & Solicitor, 1
Colombo Court, [H]09-05, 3362626, Fax:
3388001, and Member Singapore.
Called: Nov 1993, Lincoln's Inn, LLB (Hons,
Sheff)

Rengasamy *Rama Krishnan*
Called: July 1997, Lincoln's Inn, LLB (Hons)

Rennell *Nigel John Nicholas* •
Bench Legal Adviser, The Law Courts, Park
Road, Poole, Dorset BH15 2RH, 01202
721650, Fax: 01202 745309. Called: Nov
1990, Lincoln's Inn, BA (Hons)

Rennie *Mrs Brenda Dawn*
Called: July 1985, Inner Temple, LLB (Lond)

Rennie *John Alistair QPM*
Also Inn of Court L. Called: July 1974, Inner
Temple

Renouf *Mark Philip*
22 Grenville Street, St Helier, Jersey
JE4 8PX, (01534) 609000. Called: Oct 1994,
Middle Temple, LLB (Hons)(Lond)

Renton *The Rt Hon Lord PC KBE TD*
QC (1954)
Bencher. Treasurer 1979. Chairman,
Committee on Preparation of Legislation.
President, Statute Law Society, 16 Old
Bldgs, Lincoln's Inn, London WC2A 3TL,
0171 242 8986, Hon.Fellow:
Univ.College,Oxon Member of Royal
Commission on the Constitution 1971-73.
Called: Jan 1933, Lincoln's Inn, MA, BCL

Renton *David Malcolm Alexander*
Called: Nov 1997, Gray's Inn, LLB

Rentrop *Timm Ulrich Wilhelm*
Square Marguerite 1/49, B-1000 Bruxelles,
322 733 1236. Called: Nov 1991, Inner
Temple, MA (Oxon), Licence Speciale en,
Droit Europeen

Renwick *John* •
Called: Feb 1987, Middle Temple, LLB

Restano *John Ernest*
Called: Nov 1994, Middle Temple, LLB
(Hons)

Retnam *Rajah*
and Member Singapore Bar. Called: Feb
1993, Gray's Inn, LLB (Buckingham)

Reyes *Dr Anselnio Francisco Trinidad*
and Member Hong Kong Bar. Called: Nov
1985, Inner Temple, MA, LLM,
PhD(Cantab), BA (Harv)

Reyes *John Bernard*
Stagnetto & Co, 186 Main Street, 350
73530/75783, Fax: 71431, and Member
Gibraltar. Called: Nov 1996, Middle Temple,
BA (Hons)

Reyes *Stephen Edward* •
Called: Nov 1991, Gray's Inn, BA

Reynolds *Basil John*
50 The Avenue, Cheam, Sutton, Surrey
SM2 7QE, 0181 642 2324. Called: Nov 1953,
Gray's Inn

Reynolds *Steven* •
Clerk to the Justices, Devon Magistrates'
Courts Cmte, County Hall, Topsham Road,
Exeter, Devon EX2 4QD, 01392 70081, Fax:
01392 420913. Called: Feb 1981, Middle
Temple, LLB (Hull), MBA, Dip M

Reza *Abu Mohammad Manzur Ahsan*
Called: Nov 1995, Lincoln's Inn, LLB
(Hons)(Dhaka), LLM (Dhaka), LLM (Lond)

Rhodes *Richard William*
12 Avenue Peschier, 1206 Geneva, (022)
3463775. Called: Feb 1958, Inner Temple,
MA (Oxon)

Rhodes *Steven Marc* •
Liberty RE, Corn Exchange, 55 Mark Lane,
London EC3R 7NE, 0171 661 9000, Fax:
0171 903 7720. Called: Oct 1991, Lincoln's
Inn, BD, AKC, Dip L

Riach *Miss Emma Simone*
Arthur Andersen International, 41 Rue Ybry,
92200 Neuilly-Sur-Seine, Paris, (331) 55 61
1076, Fax: (331) 55 61 1515. Called: Oct
1994, Lincoln's Inn, LLB (Hons)(Lond)

Riaz *Mohammad Iftikhar Uddin*
Associate, Rizvi Isa Kabraji, 517-518 Clifton
Centre, DC-1 Block 5, Clifton, Karachi
75600, Pakistan, (92-21) 587 2879, Fax: (92-
21) 587 0014, and Member Pakistan Bar.
Called: July 1994, Inner Temple, BA, CPE,
MA

Riaz *Zahir*
Called: Mar 1997, Gray's Inn, LLB (LSE), LLB
(Cantab)

Ribeiro *Roberto Alexandre Vieira*
Member Hong Kong Law Reform
Commission Member Operations Review
Committee, Independent Commision
Against Corruption., Temple Chambers,
16th Floor, One Pacific Place, 88
Queensway, 00 852 5232033/25263263,
Fax: 00 852 5232033/281003021, QC Hong
Kong 1990 and Member Hong Kong Bar
Singapore Bar 4 Essex Court, Temple,
London, EC4Y 9AJ. Called: July 1978, Inner
Temple, LLM (Lond) LLB

Rich *Christopher Paul Donald*
Advocate, Barings (Guernsey) Ltd, Arnold
House, St Julians Avenue, St Peter Port,
Guernsey, Supreme Court of the Northern
Territory, Australia and Member Royal Court
of Guernsey. Called: Nov 1988, Gray's Inn,
LLB (Soton)

Rich *Gordon Ian* •
Musicians' Union, 60/62 Clapham Road,
London SW9 OJJ, 0171 582 5566, Fax: 0171
582 9805. Called: Nov 1960, Gray's Inn, MA

Rich *Mrs Marion Constance* •
Director of Legal & Contractual Affairs and
Company Secretary, The British
Constructional, Steelwork Association
Limited, 4 Whitehall, Westminster, London
SW1A 2ES, 0171 839 8566, Fax: 0171 976
1634. Called: Nov 1978, Middle Temple

Richard *Solomon Asoka*
Called: July 1994, Lincoln's Inn, BA (Econs),
MA (Econs), LLB (Wales)

Richards *Alun*
Deputy Clerk to the Justices,
Cambridgeshire Magistrates' Ct, Lion Yard,
Cambridge CB2 3NA, 01223 314311, Fax:
01223 355237. Called: Nov 1985, Middle
Temple, LLB

Richards *Huw Joseph*
Principal Court Clerk, Waltham Forest
Magistrates Crt, The Court House, 1 Farnan
Avenue, Walthamstow, London E17 4NX,
0181 531 3121, Fax: 0181 527 9063.
Called: Nov 1986, Gray's Inn

Richards *Jefry Loyd*
01902 750497. Called: July 1978, Gray's Inn,
LLB, MBA

Richards *John Hesketh Rigby* •
Principal Administrator European
Commission, European Commission, (BEL
28, 4/54), Rue de la Loi 200, B-1049
Brussels, Belgium, 010322 2354397.
Called: July 1974, Gray's Inn, LLB

Richards *Ms Julia*
Called: July 1994, Gray's Inn, LLB
(Glamorgan), P.G.C.E.

Richards *Keith David* •
Head of Consumer Affairs, ABTA, 68-71
Newman Street, London W1P 4AH, 0171
637 2444, Fax: 0171 631 4623. Called: July
1985, Middle Temple, BA (Kent)

Richards *Miss Sara Elizabeth*
and Member Isle of Man Bar (1984).
Called: July 1981, Inner Temple, LLB

Richardson *Frank Cameron* •
Principal Crown Prosecutor, Crown
Prosecution Service, Black Horse House, 8-
10 Leigh Road, Eastleigh, Hants SO50 4FH,
01703 614622. Called: July 1981, Inner
Temple, BSc (Hons), Dip Law

Richardson *John Philip*
Called: Nov 1976, Gray's Inn

Richardson *Michael Alan*
Called: Oct 1995, Middle Temple, BA
(Hons), Dip in Law, MA, AKC

Richardson *Philip Martin* •
Legal Services Manager, Rugby Borough
Council, Town Hall, Rugby CV21 2LB,
01788 533533, Fax: 01788 533577.
Called: July 1988, Lincoln's Inn, LLB (Hons)
(Leics)

Richardson *Professor Sam Scruton*
AO,CBE
Law Revision Commissioner, Northern
States of Nigeria. Vice President Britain
Australia Society., The Malt Hse, Wylye,
Warminster, Wilts BA12 0QP, 01985 248
348. Called: May 1960, Lincoln's Inn, MA,
LLD

Richardson *Miss Sheila Frances*
Called: July 1979, Middle Temple, MA
(Cantab)

Richardson *Miss Shelagh Barbara*
Called: Oct 1996, Middle Temple, LLB
(Hons) (Manch)

Richings *Francis Gordon SC*
908 Salmon Grove Chambers, 407 Smith
Street, Durban 4001, (031)3018694, Fax:
(031)3056420, Advocate of South Africa and
Member Lesotho Bar. Called: May 1992,
Middle Temple, BA,LLB (Cape Town), M
Phil (Cantab)

Richmond *David Andrew*
Court Clerk, Northampton Magistrate's
Court, Moulton Park, Regents Pavilion,
Summerhouse Road, Northampton
NN3 6AS, 0604 49700. Called: Nov 1992,
Inner Temple, LLB

Richmond *Martyn*
Called: Nov 1997, Gray's Inn, BA
(Newcastle), LLB (Lond)

Ricketts *Pascal John*
Called: Feb 1962, Inner Temple, MA, FCIS

Riddell *Christopher William*
Called: Oct 1992, Lincoln's Inn, BSc(Hons)(Lond), Dip Law(Lond)

Rideout *Dr Roger William*
255 Chipstead Way, Woodmansterne, Surrey SM7 3JW, 01737 52033. Called: Apr 1964, Gray's Inn, LLB, Ph.D

Rider *Professor Barry Alexander Kenneth*
Professor of Law and Director of the Institute of Advanced Legal Studies, University of London & Fellow of Jesus College, Cambridge, Fellow in Law, Jesus College, Cambridge CB5 8BL, 01223 339339. Called: Feb 1979, Inner Temple, LLB, PhD (Lond), MA, PhD (Cantab), LLD

Ridgway *Philip* ●
Senior Manager, Deloitte & Touche, 1 Little New Street, London EC4A 3TR, 0171 303 3434, Fax: 0171 303 4778. Called: July 1986, Middle Temple, BA, LLM(Cantab)

Ridzuan *Shahril Ridza*
c/o Zain & Co, 6th Floor, Bangunan Dato Zainal, 23 Jalan Melaka, 50100 Kuala Lumpur Malaysia, 03 2986255, Fax: 03 2986969, and Member Malaysia Bar. Called: July 1994, Middle Temple, BA (Hons)(Cantab), BCL (Oxon)

Rigby *Jonathan David*
Legal Associate, Cameron MCkennaHewitt, Sceptre Court, 40 Tower Hill, London EC3N 4BB, 0171 702 2345, Fax: 0171 702 2303. Called: Oct 1995, Middle Temple, BA (Hons)

Rigby *Raynard Sherman*
McKinney, Bancroft & Hughes, Mareva House, 4 George Street, P.O.Box N 3937, Nassau. Called: July 1995, Gray's Inn, BA (Ontario), LLB (Leeds)

Riggs *Miss Rachel*
Assistant Solicitor, Nelsons Solicitors, Pennine House, 8 Stanford Street, Nottingham, 0115 958 6262. Called: Oct 1994, Lincoln's Inn, LLB (Hons)(Leic)

Riglia *Enzo* ●
Senior Court Clerk, Barnet, 13 Calder Avenue, Perivale, Greenford, Middlesex UB6 8JQ, 0181 997 5027. Called: May 1990, Inner Temple, LLB

Riley *Mrs Alison Claire* ●
Principal Crown Prosecutor, Crown Prosecution Service, 50 Ludgate Hill, London EC4M 7EX, 0171 273 1240, Fax: 0171 329 8171. Called: July 1981, Middle Temple, BA (Hons)

Riley *James Edward*
Called: Nov 1995, Inner Temple, LLB

Riley *Philip Duncan* ●
Senior Crown Prosecutor, Crown Prosecution Service, 2 Aalborg Square, Lancaster LA1 1GG, 01524 847676. Called: July 1981, Inner Temple, BA

Riley *Richard Patrick*
Called: Oct 1997, Gray's Inn, BA (Kent)

Riley *Mrs Susan Peta Lonsdale* ●
Legal Advisor. Called: Nov 1976, Middle Temple, LLB (London)

Ring *Thomas Joseph*
Clerk to the Justices, Havering Mag Court Committee, The Court House, Main Road, Romford, Essex RM1 3BH, 01708 771771, Fax: 01708 771721. Called: Nov 1987, Inner Temple, LLB

Ringguth *John Stephen* ●
Assistant Chief Crown Prosecutor, Central Casework, Crown prosecution Service, 50 Ludgate Hill, London EC4M 7EX, 0171 273 8335, Fax: 0171 329 8167. Called: July 1974, Gray's Inn, LLB

Rioda *Carlo Mark*
Called: May 1993, Middle Temple, LLB (Hons)(B'ham)

Ripman *Peter Hugo M.C.*
Called: June 1947, Inner Temple, MA (Cantab)

Rippengal *Derek CB QC (1980)* ●
Counsel to the Chairman of Committees, Chairman of Comittees Office, House of Lords, London SW1A 0PW, 0171 219 3211, Fax: 0171 219 2571. Called: June 1953, Middle Temple, MA

Rippon *Simon John*
Called: Nov 1996, Gray's Inn, BA (Lond)

Rivlin *Paul Denis*
6 Bishopsgate, London EC2N 4DA, 0171 545 2111, Fax: 0171 545 2092. Called: Nov 1995, Middle Temple, BA (Hons), FCMA, MCT

Riza *Ms Sheila Shule Antoinette* ●
Legal Officer, Claims Manager, M.E Warrington & Others, Syndicate 1239, Lloyd's of London, 1 Lime Street, London EC3M 7HA, 0171 265 0071, Fax: 0171 481 1631. Called: July 1982, Gray's Inn, BA Law, A.C.I.I

Roath *Mrs Josephine Elizabeth Mary*
Lincolns, Boyatt Lane, Eastleigh, Hampshire SO50 4IJ, 01703 252727. Called: July 1981, Middle Temple, LLB (Hons), MA

Robb *Ms Cairo Anne Reyner*
Research Associate at the Research Centre for International Law, Cambridge. Called: Oct 1993, Middle Temple, MA (Hons)(Cantab), LIC.Spec.Dr Eur, (Brussels)

Robb *John Edmund Boulton*
Called: Mar 1998, Gray's Inn, BA (Oxon)

Robb *Lt Cdr RN Louis Joseph*
Scottish Advocate. Called: June 1964, Inner Temple

Robbins *Miss Emelita Ann*
12 Clarence Road, London N15 5BB, 0181 245 4839. Called: Oct 1995, Middle Temple, LLB (Hons)

Robbins *Ms Kelly*
Called: Nov 1995, Middle Temple, BA (Hons)

Robert *Leslie Gregory*
Called: July 1995, Lincoln's Inn, LLB (Hons)

Roberts *Miss Andrea*
Called: Oct 1994, Middle Temple, BA (Hons)(Oxon)

Roberts *Mrs Anne P*
Called: July 1982, Gray's Inn, BA (Hons), Dip Droit Francais

Roberts *Christopher Andrew*
Clerk to the Justices, Justices' Clerk's Office, The Court House, Old Bury Road, Thetford, Norfolk IP24 3AQ, 01842 754941, Fax: 01842 766068. Called: July 1980, Gray's Inn

Roberts *Colin*
HM Diplomatic Service. Called: Nov 1986, Inner Temple, MA (Cantab), Dip Law (City), ACIArb

Roberts *Craig* ●
Home Office Presenting Officer, Home Office Presenting, Officers Unit, 3rd & 4th Floors, Feltham Green, 21-47 High St, Feltham, Middlesex TW13 4AG, 0181 957 3228, Fax: 0181 957 3259. Called: Nov 1994, Lincoln's Inn, LLB (Hons), LLM, (Lond), MRIN

Roberts *Miss Emma Charlotte* ●
Cazenove & Co, 12 TokenHouse Yard, London, 0171 588 2828. Called: Nov 1996, Middle Temple, BA (Hons)(Manch)

Roberts *Graham Martin*
Senior Lecturer, Dept of Management &, Professional Development, London Guildhall University, 84 Moorgate, London EC2M 6SQ, 0171 320 1581, Fax: 0171 320 1585. Called: July 1982, Middle Temple, BA (Kent)

Roberts *Howard Vincent* ●
Senior Principal Legal Officer, Department of Social Security, New Court, 48 Carey Street, London WC2A 2LS, 0171 412 1591, Fax: 0171 412 1440. Called: July 1972, Middle Temple, LLB

Roberts *Mrs Jane Carol*
Called: Nov 1996, Inner Temple, BA (Oxon), MA (Kent), LLB (City)

Roberts *Mrs Marian*
Assistant Director (Professional Practice & Training), National Family Mediator, NFM, 9 Tavistock Place, London WC1H 9SN, 0171 383 5993, Fax: 0171 383 5994. Called: July 1979, Gray's Inn, BA, PGrad.Dip, (Social Studies)

Roberts *Paul Lachal* ●
European Commission, Rue de la Loi 200, B-1049 Brussels, Belgium, 32 2 2954385, Fax: 32 2 2956451, and Member New South Wales Bar. Called: Oct 1992, Gray's Inn, BA (Tasmania), LL.B (Australian, National Uni.)

Roberts *Miss Sarah*
Called: Oct 1991, Middle Temple, LLB (Hons)

Roberts *Simon David*
Finnegan, Henderson, Farabow, Garret & Dunner, 1300 Eye Street, NW [H]700, Washington DC, 20005-3315, 001 202 408 4000, Fax: 001 202 408 4400, and Member New York State Bar US Patent Bar. Called: Nov 1991, Gray's Inn, BSc, BA (Exon)

Roberts *Miss Stella*
Justices' Chief Executive, Berkshire & Oxfordshire, Magistrates' Courts' Committee, Easby House, Northfield End, Henley on Thames, Oxon RG9 2NB, 01491 412720, Fax: 01491 412762. Called: Feb 1984, Lincoln's Inn, MIPD, MIMgt

Roberts *Stephen Gwilym* •
Court Clerk, North Wales Magistrates Court, 11 Rhiw Road, Colwyn Bay, Conwy LL29 7TE, 01492 534 550. Called: Nov 1987, Gray's Inn, LL.B.(Cardiff)

Roberts *Walter*
30 Bartholomew Street, Hythe, Kent CT21 5BT, 01303 267492. Called: July 1963, Middle Temple, FCIS

Robertshaw *Alan Stuart*
Called: Oct 1997, Middle Temple, LLB (Lond)

Robertson *Mrs Elaine Emmett*
Appletree House, Burnthouse Lane, Whickham NE16 5AS, 0191 488 6027, Fax: 0191 488 6027, and Member Hong Kong Bar Dec 1987. Called: Nov 1977, Gray's Inn, BA (Hon)

Robertson *John*
44 Willoughby Road, London NW3 1RU, 0171 435 4907. Called: Nov 1961, Lincoln's Inn, LLB

Robinski *Miss Zofia Teresa*
Called: Feb 1995, Middle Temple, BA (Hons)(Bris), CPE (City)

Robinson *Anthony Jonathan Kent*
Called: July 1995, Gray's Inn, LLB, M.Phil (Wales)

Robinson *David Edward* •
Crown Prosecution Service, Crown Prosecution Service, The Court Yard, Lombard Street, Abingdon, Oxon OX14 5SE, 01235 555678. Called: Oct 1993, Gray's Inn, BSc (So'ton)

Robinson *David Francis* •
Director & Secretary, Robinson & Sons Ltd, Wheat Bridge, Chesterfield, Derbyshire S40 1YE, 01246 220022, Fax: 01246 209517. Called: Nov 1963, Inner Temple, BA [Oxon]

Robinson *Miss Emma Millicent* •
Principal Legal Officer Area Lawyer, Office of the Solicitor, London South Area Lawyers, Sutherland House, Brighton Rd, Sutton, Surrey, 0181 652 6500, Fax: 0181 652 6400. Called: May 1995, Inner Temple, BA, CPE

Robinson *Miss Justine Victoria*
Associate Solicitor in Private Practice, Messrs Marron Dodds Solicitors, 32 Friar Lane, Leicester LE1 5RA, 0116 2628596, Fax: 0116 2518322. Called: Nov 1990, Middle Temple, BA (Hons)(Kent), M Phil (Cantab)

Robinson *Mrs Letchumy*
Called: July 1975, Inner Temple

Robinson *Professor Mary Terese Winifred*
SC Ireland 1980 and Member Southern Ireland Bar 2 Hare Court, Ground Floor, Temple, London, EC4Y 7BH. Called: July 1973, Middle Temple, BA (Dublin), LLB (Dublin)

Robinson *Mrs Maura Frances*
Called: Oct 1992, Lincoln's Inn, BA, LLB (Hons)

Robinson *Paul Anthony* •
Principle Crown Prosecutor, Crown Prosecution Service, Headquarters, 50 Ludgate Hill, London EC4M 7EX, 0171 273 1353, Fax: 0171 329 8164. Called: Nov 1985, Middle Temple, LLB

Robinson *Miss Penelope Therese*
Called: Nov 1986, Gray's Inn, BSc (Cardiff)

Robinson *Raymund Francis*
Called: Nov 1968, Gray's Inn

Robinson *Steven Andrew* •
Prosecution Team Leader, Crown Prosecution Service, Coniston House, Washington, Tyne and Wear, 0191 417 0079. Called: Nov 1985, Gray's Inn, BA

Robinson *Miss Tina* •
Legal Adviser, Ministry of Defence, Room 4107, Main Building, Whitehall, London SW1A 2HB. Called: July 1989, Inner Temple, LLB (Lanc), LLM (Leics)

Robinson *Wendel Glenroy*
Called: Nov 1997, Inner Temple, LLB (Lond)

Robless *Miss Sharon Marie*
Called: July 1994, Middle Temple, LLB (Hons)(Notts)

Robson *Andrew John* •
General Counsel and Company Secretary, PHH Europe PLC, PHH Centre, Windmill Hill, Whitehill Way, Swindon SN5 6PZ, 01793 884424, Fax: 01793 886056. Called: July 1985, Inner Temple, LLB(Nott'm)

Robson *Cameron James Elliot*
Called: Oct 1993, Lincoln's Inn, LLB (Hons)(Wolver), BA (Oxon), LLM (L'pool)

Robson *Hugh Wallace*
Called: Nov 1992, Middle Temple, BA (Oxon), MA (Warw), Diploma in Law

Robson *John Christian* •
Prosecution Team Leader, Crown Prosecution Service, First Floor, The Cooperage, Gainsford Street, London SE1, 0171 962 2625, Fax: 0171 962 0906. Called: Nov 1987, Inner Temple, MA [Carleton], BA [Lond], Dip in Law

Rocca *Christian Manuel*
Isola & Isola, Suite 23, Portland House, Gibraltar, 78363, Fax: 78990, and Member Gibraltar Bar. Called: Oct 1994, Inner Temple, LLB

Rocca *Terence Joseph*
Attorney-General's Chambers, 17 Town Range, Gibraltar, 010 350 78882, Fax: 010 350 79891, and Member Gibraltar Bar. Called: Oct 1993, Middle Temple, LLB (Hons)(Kingston)

Rochat-Spechter *Mrs Alison Jean*
Associate (Foreign Lawyer), Secretan, Troyanov and Partners, 2 Rue Charles - Bonnet, P.O.Box 189, 1211 Geneva 12, Switzerland, (41) 22 789 7000, Fax: (41) 22 789 7070. Called: Oct 1993, Gray's Inn, LLB (Buck'm)

Roche *Mrs Barbara Maureen MP*
Member of Parliament, House of Commons, London SW1, 0171 219 3000. Called: July 1977, Middle Temple, BA (Oxon)

Roche *Michael Anthony* •
Assistant Land Registrar H M Land Registry, Telford District Land Registry, Parkside Court, Hall Park Way, Telford, Shropshire TF3 4LR, 01952 290355. Called: July 1973, Gray's Inn

Rodaway *Miss Deborah Jackson*
Martin Murray & Associates, Solicitors, 138 High Street, Yiewsley, West DraytoN, Middlesex UB7 7BD, 01895 431332. Called: July 1997, Gray's Inn, BSc (Lond)

Rodrigo *Jayanath Avindra Gian*
Called: Feb 1994, Gray's Inn, LLB (Warwick)

Rodriguez *Stuart James*
Called: Mar 1997, Middle Temple, LLB (Hons), MA (Leeds)

Rodwell *Christopher John*
Called: Nov 1997, Middle Temple, BA (Hons)

Roe *Jeremy James*
Downe Farm, Hartland, Woking, Bideford, North Devon, 01237 441210. Called: July 1972, Lincoln's Inn, LLB, AIB

Rogers *Anthony Gerrard Vernede*
11th Floor, Southern Cross Building, cnr Victoria St East & High St, Auckland 1, 093733 196, Fax: 09 3774850, PO Box 1771, Auckland, and Member New Zealand Bar New South Wales Bar 6 King's Bench Walk, Ground Floor, Temple, London, EC4Y 7DR. Called: Feb 1986, Inner Temple, LLM (Hons), (U Auckland)

Rogers *Anthony Gordon Justice*
High Court Judge, Hong Kong, Supreme Court, Queensway, 852 28254332, Fax: 852 25523327, Former Chairman Hong Kong Bar Association, QC Hong Kong Bar Association. Called: Nov 1969, Gray's Inn

Rogers *Christopher John Edwin* •
The Old Blue School, Lower Square, Isleworth, Middlesex TW7 6RL. Called: Nov 1981, Gray's Inn, MA (Cantab)

Rogers *Mrs Deborah Elizabeth* ●
Principal Crown Prosecutor, Crown
Prosecution Service, Pearl Assurance House,
20th Floor, Greyfriars Road, Cardiff
CF1 3PL. Called: July 1983, Lincoln's Inn,
BA

Rogers *Ms Francesca*
Ashnurst Morris Crisp, Broadwalk House, 5
Appold Street, London EC2. Called: Nov
1996, Inner Temple, BA (Lond)

Rogers *Kevin Patrick* ●
Prosecution Team Leader, Crown
Prosecution Service, C/O 50 Ludgate Hill,
London EC4M 7EX. Called: Nov 1985,
Middle Temple

Rogers *Michael* ●
Legal Director, Harrods Limited, 85-137
Brompton Road, Knightsbridge, London
SW1X 7XL, 0171 225 5735, Fax: 0171 225
5906. Called: Nov 1974, Gray's Inn, LLB

Rogers *Michael Richard*
Law Chambers, World Trade Centre,
P.O.Box 896, 1215 Geneva 15, +44 22 788
0551, Fax: +44 22 788 1502. Called: Feb
1972, Inner Temple, F.C.I.S., A.C.I.I

Rogers *Raymond Alexander*
Deputy Clerk to the Justices, Doncaster
Magistrates' Court, PO Box 49, The Law
Courts, College Road, Doncaster DN1 3HT,
01302 366711, Fax: 01302 340323.
Called: Nov 1978, Gray's Inn, BA

Rogers *Richard John*
Called: Nov 1994, Lincoln's Inn, LLB
(Hons)(Sheff)

Rogers *Simon John* ●
Principal Legal Officer, Office of the
Solicitor, Dept of Health & Social, Security,
New Court, 48 Carey Street, London3
WC2A 2LS, 0171 412 1475. Called: May
1994, Gray's Inn, BA

Rogers *Stephen Thomas*
Law Lecturer (Freelance). Called: Nov 1968,
Gray's Inn, LLB

Rogers *Stephen Urban*
Legal Adviser, Lot 8359, Mukim of Batu,
Batu 8,, Jalan Batu Caves, 68100 Batu Caves,
Selangor. Called: May 1988, Gray's Inn, BSc
(Leeds), M Jur (B'ham)

Rogerson *Paul* ●
Chief Legal Officer, Leeds City Council,
Legal Services, Civic Hall, Leeds LS1 1UR,
0113 2474414, Fax: 0113 2474651.
Called: Feb 1971, Gray's Inn, LLB, MA
(Econ)

Rohit *Miss Lina*
Called: May 1997, Gray's Inn, BA
(Middlesex), LLM (Leicester)

Rokison *Kenneth Stuart* QC (1976)
20 Essex Street, London, WC2R 3AL.
Called: Feb 1961, Gray's Inn, BA (Cantab)

Ronan *Michael Marc*
Called: Mar 1998, Lincoln's Inn, LLB
(Hons)(Thames)

Rook *Ms Susanne Elizabeth*
Called: May 1994, Lincoln's Inn, LLB (Hons)

Roopra *Ravinder Singh* ●
Legal Adviser, Hambro Legal Protection Ltd,
Hambro House, Stephenson Road,
Colchester, Essex CO4 4QR, 0990 234500,
Fax: 0990 234508. Called: Oct 1996,
Lincoln's Inn, LLB (Hons)(Wolves)

Roper *Frank Spencer Duncan* ●
Senior Legal Adviser, British Gas plc, 5th
Floor, Heron House, 322 High Holborn,
London WC1V 7PW. Called: Nov 1975,
Middle Temple, LLB

Roscoe *John Gareth* ●
Legal Adviser, The Legal Adviser, British
Broadcasting Corp, Broadcasting House,
Room 1057, Portland Place, London
W1A 1AA, 0171 765 4375, Fax: 0171 765
4381. Called: Nov 1972, Gray's Inn,
LLB(Lond)

Roscoe *Nicholas Charles Marshall* ●
Legal Adviser, Sedgwick, Sedgwick House,
Sedgewick Centre, London E1 8DX, 0171
377 3456, Fax: 0171 377 3199. Called: Nov
1990, Middle Temple, BA (Manch), Dip Law
(City)

Rose *Andrew Wyness*
Called: Nov 1968, Gray's Inn, MA, LLB
(Cantab)

Rose *Dr Christopher Philip*
Called: Oct 1995, Gray's Inn, B.Sc, MC
(Canada), MA (Oxon)

Rose *Craig Mark*
Legal Editor of Commerical Lawyer.
Called: Nov 1994, Lincoln's Inn, BA
(Hons)(Bris), Ph.D

Rose *Martin John* ●
Group Legal & Compliance Director, Smith
& Williamson Investment, Management
Limited, No 1 Riding House Street, London
W1A 3AS, 0171 637 5377, Fax: 0171 631
0741. Called: July 1979, Middle Temple, LLB

Rose *Martyn Craig*
Called: July 1972, Inner Temple

Rose *Miss Vivien Judith* ●
Lawyer (Grade 6), Tresurer's Solicitor's
Dept, Queen Anne's Chambers, 28
Broadway, London SW1H 9JS. Called: July
1984, Gray's Inn, MA (Cantab) BCL Oxon

Rosell *Mrs Tracey Allison Grosser*
Dolphin House, St Peter's Street,
Winchester, Hampshire SO23 8BW, 01962
829888, Fax: 01962 829777. Called: Nov
1987, Middle Temple, LLB, ATT, Assoc IPD

Rosen *Jonathan Leon*
Called: Nov 1996, Gray's Inn, BSc, LLB
(Lond)

Rosenberg *Robert Alan*
Called: July 1983, Gray's Inn, BA (Hons),
MSc

Ross *Ms Alison*
Senior Court Clerk, Ealing Magistrates'
Court, Green Man Lane, Ealing, London
W13 OSD, 0181 579 9311, Fax: 0181 579
2985. Called: July 1982, Middle Temple, BA
(Hons)

Ross *Miss Alison Mary*
Called: Nov 1992, Middle Temple, LLB
(Hons)

Ross *David*
Director, Company Secretary. Called: Mar
1996, Gray's Inn, BA (York), ACIS

Ross *Keith James*
Tutor, University of Canberra Law School,
10 Roper Place, Chifley ACT 2606, 0262
816748, and Member Barrister & Solicitor
Papau New Guinea, Australian Capital
Territory, Federal Court, Solicitor, New
South Wales New South Wales Bar Solicitor,
New South Wales. Called: July 1967,
Lincoln's Inn, LLB

Ross *Martin Christopher Jude* ●
Principal Court Clerk, North East & Surrey
Mag's Crt, The Law Courts, Knowle Green,
Staines, Middlesex TW18 1XR, 01784
459261, Fax: 01784 466257. Called: Nov
1976, Gray's Inn

Ross *Ms Nicola Jane*
Called: Oct 1992, Middle Temple, BA (Hons)

Ross *Stephen David*
Senior Legal Adviser, Staffordshire
Magistrates Crt, P O Box 428, Leek,
Staffordshire ST13 5ST, 01538 372858.
Called: Nov 1990, Inner Temple, LLB

Ross *Miss Susan Janet* ●
Legal Adviser, Crown Prosecution Service,
50 Ludgate Hill, London EC4M 7EX, 0171
273 8315, Fax: 0171 273 8431. Called: July
1985, Middle Temple, LLB (Warwick)

Rossiter *Derek Trevor*
Hon.President of P.T.M.G, The Wall House,
31a Cottenham Park Road, London
SW20 0RX, 0181 946 8564, Fax: 0181 944
0062. Called: Nov 1968, Middle Temple, BA

Roudette *Miss Wendy Shirley*
Called: July 1996, Inner Temple, BA (Lond),
CPE

Rover *Jan-Hendrik Manfred*
Legal Adviser, Visiting Fellow King's College
London, Centre of European Law, and
Member Munich Bar. Called: Mar 1996,
Middle Temple, LLM (LSE)

Rowan *Michael Anthony* ●
Principal Lawyer, North Somerset Council,
Town Hall, Legal Dept, Weston-super-Mare,
North Somerset BS23 4XE, 01934 634946,
Fax: 01934 418194. Called: Nov 1992, Inner
Temple, LLB

Rowbottom *Stephen Peter*
Clerk to the Gateshead Justices, Gateshead
Magistrates, Courts Committee, P O Box 26,
Warwick Street, Gateshead, Tyne & Wear
NE8 1DT, 0191 477 5821, Fax: 0191 478
7825. Called: Feb 1983, Gray's Inn, LLB,
MBA

Rowland *Edward Anthony Powys
Lance*
25a Holland Park Gardens, London W11,
0171 912 0952, Fax: 0171 912 0952.
Called: May 1992, Middle Temple, BA
(Durham), MA (Durham), Dip Law, LLM
(Lond)

E

Rowland *Mrs Marjorie Susan*
Hollywood, Tokers Green, S Oxon
RG4 9EB, 01734 723107. Called: Nov 1975,
Inner Temple

Rowland *Robert Todd*
Part-time Chairman, Value Added Tax
Tribunals, The Periwinkle, 25 Back Lane,
South Luffenham, Rutland LE15 8NQ, 01780
721 520, QC. N Ireland Retired County
Court Judge in Northern Ireland and
Member Northern Ireland Bar. Called: July
1989, Lincoln's Inn, LLB (Belfast)

Rowlands *Ian Richard*
5 Clifton Terrace, The Mumbles, Swansea
SA3 4EJ, 0410 037062. Called: Nov 1986,
Middle Temple, BSc (Econ)(Hons)

Rowlands *Oscar Thomas* •
Legal Adviser, Group Technology &
Operations, Standard Chartered Bank, 1
Aldermanbury Square, London EC1M 4DB,
0171 280 7500. Called: Nov 1990, Inner
Temple, MSc (Wales)

Roy *Duncan*
Called: Oct 1997, Gray's Inn, BSc
(Econ)(Wales)

Roy *John Scott* •
Legal Adviser, Royal Bank of Scotland, 29
Gresham Street, London EC2V 7HM, 0171
615 5588, Fax: 0171 726 2338. Called: Feb
1991, Inner Temple, LLB (Lond)

Roy *Ms Shapna* •
Legal Adviser, Balfour Beatty International,
Marlowe House Station Road, Sidcup, Kent
DA15 7AU, 0181 300 3355, Fax: 0181 308
5140, and Member Malaysian Bar.
Called: Nov 1995, Lincoln's Inn, LLB (Hons),
CLP

Roy *Stefan Alexander Hiren*
Called: May 1996, Gray's Inn, LLB

Royce *Mrs Rosemary Elizabeth*
Called: Nov 1976, Lincoln's Inn

Royce-Lewis *Ms Christine Alison* •
Vice President Senior Legal Adviser, Visa
International Service, Association, PO Box
253, London W8 5TE, 0171 937 8111, Fax:
0171 937 3390. Called: Nov 1982, Middle
Temple, BA MSc (Wales)

Roycroft *Andrew Alan*
Called: Nov 1993, Gray's Inn, LLB (Bris)

Royle *Charles Fanshawe*
Called: Oct 1997, Lincoln's Inn, BSc (Hons),
Dip in law (City)

Royle *John Hardy Layton*
24 Beaconsfield Road, Claygate, Esher,
Surrey KT10 0PW. Called: June 1937, Inner
Temple, MA (Cantab)

Rozain *Miss Roz Mawar*
54 Setiabakit 9, Bukit Damansara, 50490
Kuala Lumpur, 00603 2551179, and
Member Malaysian Bar. Called: July 1995,
Lincoln's Inn, LLB (Hons)

Ruane *James FitzGerald*
Called: Nov 1994, Middle Temple, BA
(Hons)

Ruane *Miss Mairead Mary*
Called: Nov 1991, Gray's Inn, BCL (Dub)

Rubin *Mohideen M P Haja*
Member of Appeal Board Singapore Syariah
Court. Called: July 1987, Middle Temple,
LLB

Ruck Keene *Benjamin Charles*
Bursar-Corpus Christi College Oxford JP
(Oxfordshire), Mill Hill, Brandsby, York
YO6 4RQ. Called: July 1971, Gray's Inn, BA
(York), MA (Oxon)

Rudd *David Eric* •
Legal Services Manager, Salford Magistrates
Court, The Court House, Bexley Square,
Salford M3 6DJ, 0161 834 9457, Fax: 0161
839 1806. Called: July 1981, Inner Temple,
LLB (Hull)

Rudeloff *Walter*
4 King's Bench Walk, Ground/First Floor,
Temple, London, EC4Y 7DL. Called: Oct
1990, Middle Temple, BA, LLM (Lond)

Rudoff *Stephen Frederick* •
Business Affairs Executive. Called: July 1979,
Middle Temple, LLB (B'ham)

Rudolf *Nathaniel David*
8 The Oaks, Woodside Avenue, London
N12 8AR, 0181 446 5571, Fax: 0181 556
5571. Called: Nov 1996, Middle Temple, LLB
(Hons)(Warw)

Rudralingham *Miss Sharadamani*
Legal Executive, Electronic Data
Interchange (M) SDN BHD, 15 Jalan Telok
Gadon G, 41200 Kelang, Selangor, (603)
2536676, Fax: (603) 2537767, and Member
Malaysia. Called: Nov 1992, Inner Temple,
LLB, LLM (Lond)

Ruff *Ms Anne Russell*
Principal Lecturer in Law Head of CPE
Course, Middlesex University, The
Burroughs, London NW4 4BT, 0181 362
5000, Fax: 0181 202 1539. Called: July
1989, Gray's Inn, LLB (Lond), LLM (Lond)

Ruffin *William Haywood*
Attorney of the United States and Member
Pennsylvania, New York & North Carolina
Bars 11 Stone Bldgs, 1st Floor, Lincoln's
Inn, London, WC2A 3TG. Called: July 1972,
Inner Temple, BA, JD

Rufford *John George* •
Principal Legal Officer, DTI Investigation
and, Enforcement Directorate, 10 Victoria
Street, London SW1H 0NN, 0171 215 5000,
Fax: 0171 215 6894, Currently on
Appointment as DTI Inspector. Called: Nov
1986, Middle Temple, LLB (Leeds)

Rufus-Isaacs *The Lord Alexander
Gerald*
Recorder, 1 Gray's Inn Square, Ground
Floor, London, WC1R 5AA. Called: Nov
1982, Middle Temple, BA (Oxon)

Rugarabamu *Ms Donata Mary* •
Chief Project Officer (Legal), Ground Floor
Flat, 36 Sinclair Road, London W14 0NH,
0171 603 5025, Fax: 0171 603 5025.
Called: July 1992, Lincoln's Inn, MA (Hons)

Rumgay *Peter Nicholas*
Senior Quantity Surveyor, 199 West Park
Drive West, Roundhay, Leeds, Yorks
LS8 2BE. Called: Mar 1996, Gray's Inn, B.Sc,
Dip Law, ARICS

Rundle *Mrs Christina Marie*
Havengarth, Fore Street, West Canal, Nr
Yeovil BA22 7QW. Called: Nov 1994,
Lincoln's Inn, BSc (Hons)(Exon), CPE
(Bournemouth)

Rupasinghe *Miss Anouchka Charmini*
Called: Nov 1996, Lincoln's Inn, LLB
(Hons)(E.Anglia)

Rush *Anthony John*
Called: Feb 1993, Lincoln's Inn, BCL

Rushford *Anthony Redfern CMG,
C.StJ FRSA*
46 Lower Sloane Street, London SW1W 8BP,
0171 730 4714, Formerly a Solicitor (1944-
57). Called: Nov 1983, Inner Temple, MA,
LLM (Cantab)

Rushton *Ms Elizabeth Lisa*
Amin & Co, The Bon Marche Centre, 444
Brixton Road, London SW9 8EJ, 0171 737
5050, Fax: 0171 274 6561. Called: Nov
1991, Inner Temple, LLB

Rushton *Miss Marilyn*
4a Carey Mansions, Rutherford Street,
Westminster, London SW1P 2LT, 0171 828
3954. Called: Nov 1992, Inner Temple, MSC,
LLB, MA

Rushton-Turner *John Martin* •
Legal Adviser, Nat West Capital Markets,
135 Bishopsgate, London EC2M, 0171 375
5454, Fax: 0171 334 1004, and Member
New York Bar. Called: Oct 1991, Middle
Temple, LLB Hons, ACA

Russell *Miss Carron-Ann*
0956 545448/ 0171 831 5344, Fax: 0171
242 7799, Opinion Writing & Drafting in
Contract Law, Cavendish Press 1996. and
Member Jamaican Bar. Called: July 1986,
Middle Temple, LLB (Hons)(W.Indies), LLM
(Hons)(Lond), BA (Hons)(Sussex), PGCE
(Oxon)

Russell *Christopher Corbet*
Assistant Recorder, 20 Essex Street, London,
WC2R 3AL. Called: July 1973, Middle
Temple, MA (Oxon)

Russell *Mrs Fiona McLean* •
Principal Crown Prosecutor, CPS,
Headquarters, 50 Ludgate Hill, London
EC4M 7EX, 0171 273 8000. Called: Nov
1978, Gray's Inn, BA

Russell *Geoffrey David* •
Legal Advisor, Nottinghamshire County
Council, Loughborough Road, West
Bridgford, Nottingham NG2 7QP, 01159
773111, Fax: 01159 9455131. Called: July
1997, Inner Temple, LLB (Nott'm)

Russell *Mrs Gillian*
Senior Court Clerk, Milton Keynes
Magistrates' Crt, 301 Silbury Boulevard,
Witan Gate East, Milton Keynes, Bucks
MK9 2AJ, 01908 684901, Fax: 01908
684904. Called: July 1986, Gray's Inn, BA
(Hons)

Russell *Nicholas Ogilvy Hunter*
Called: Nov 1996, Gray's Inn, LLB (Sussex)

Russell *Miss Susan McCarrison*
3 Serjeants Inn, London, EC4Y 1BQ, 0171
353 5537. Called: Nov 1972, Middle Temple

Russell *Miss Veena Maya* •
Legal Advisor, CSO Valuations AG, 17
Charterhouse Street, London EC1N 6RA,
0171 404 4444/430 3040, Fax: 0171 430
3445. Called: July 1976, Gray's Inn, LLB
(Lond)

Russell-Hargreaves *Barry*
Called: Nov 1988, Middle Temple, LLB

Rutherford *Mrs Hazel Linda*
Called: Oct 1997, Gray's Inn, BA

Ryan *Alexander Cameron Cranston*
Called: July 1972, Inner Temple, BA

Ryan *Miss Catherine Mary*
Called: Oct 1997, Middle Temple, LLB
(Hons)(Lond)

Ryan *Miss Hilary Margaret* •
Crown Prosecution Service, Trafalgar
House, 2 Bedford Park, Croydon CR0 2AP,
0181 686 6033. Called: Feb 1990, Inner
Temple, LLB (Hons)

Ryan *Mark Richard*
Part Time Lecturer in Law at Coventry
University, 64 Cliffe Way, Warwick,
Warwickshire CV34 5JG. Called: Feb 1993,
Gray's Inn, BA (Ulster), MA (City), Cert Ed
(Cardiff)

Ryan *Martin Philip* •
Principal Crown Prosecutor T.L., Crown
Prosecution Service, The Cooperage, 8
Gainsford Street, London SE1, 0171 357
7010, Fax: 0171 962 0905. Called: Feb 1978,
Lincoln's Inn, BA Hons

Ryan *William Charles*
81 Antrim Mansions, Antrim Road, London
NW3 4XL, 0171 722 7492. Called: July
1989, Lincoln's Inn, LLB (Dub)

Ryan *William Fabian*
Associate of the Royal Institution of
Chartered Surveyors. Called: Mar 1998,
Inner Temple, BSc (Dublin), Dip Law
(Thames)

Ryb *Miss Samantha Danielle* •
Called: Oct 1993, Middle Temple, LLB
(Hons)(Lond)

Ryder *Derek* •
2 Kimbrose Way, Gloucester G4 2DB.
Called: May 1988, Gray's Inn

Rylands *Keith William* •
Principal Crown Prosecutor, Crown
Prosecution Service, County House, County
Square, 100 New London Road, Chelmsford,
Essex CM2 0BR, 01245 252939, Fax: 01245
490476. Called: July 1979, Middle Temple,
LL.B (Lond)

Rynd *Dr Aaron James*
Spier Harben, Barristers & Solicitors, Suite
1000, Dominion House, 665-8 Street S.W.,
Calgary, Alberta T2P 3K7, 403 263 5130,
Fax: 403 264 9600, and Member Alberta,
Canada. Called: July 1976, Lincoln's Inn, BA,
PHd

Saadi *Mir Abdul Wares*
Called: Nov 1996, Lincoln's Inn, LLB
(Hons)(Lond)

Sabben-Clare *Mrs Geraldine Mary*
Part-time Teacher of Law at Winchester
College, Mental Health Act "Manager"
General Commissioner for Income Tax,
Witham Close, 62 Kingsgate Street,
Winchester, Hants SO23 9PF, 01962
865832. Called: July 1966, Gray's Inn, LLB
(Lond)

Sachdeva *Akash*
Called: Mar 1997, Lincoln's Inn, LLB (Hons)

Sachdeva *Sanjiv*
Business Consultant, Governor Wyggeston
& Queen Elizabeth I Sixth Form College,
Leicester, 758 Hanowrth Road, Richmond,
Middlesex TW4 5NU, 0171 971 8845.
Called: Nov 1991, Inner Temple, LLB
(Lond)(Hons)

Sachs *Mrs Anne Marie* •
Department of Trade & Industry, Solicitors
Department, 10-18 Victoria Street, London
SW1H 0NN. Called: July 1978, Gray's Inn,
MA (Cantab), LLM (Lond)

Sadat *Omar*
Called: Nov 1997, Lincoln's Inn, LLB
(Hons)(Lond), LLM (Cantab)

Sadd *Robert Clive* •
Crown Prosecutor, CPS Suffolk Branch,
Saxon House, 1 Cromwell Square, Ipswich
IP1 1TS, 01473 230332. Called: Oct 1990,
Inner Temple, LLB (Reading)

Sadheura *Dr Mohinder Kumar*
Called: Mar 1998, Middle Temple, BSc
(Hons), MBBS, MRCGP (Royal London,
Hospital Medical, College)

Sadhwani *Kamlesh Arjan*
Room 1405, Tower II, Admiralty Centre, 18
Harcourt Road, 25273082, Fax: 25298226,
and Member Hong Kong Bar. Called: July
1995, Lincoln's Inn, BA (Hons)

Sadjadi-Nourani *Mrs Leila*
Law Offices of Foley, Lardner, Weissburg &
Aronson, 2029 Century Park East, 36th
Floor, Los Angeles CA 90067, 310-975 7853,
Fax: 310-557 8475, and Member California
Bar. Called: Nov 1990, Gray's Inn, LLB
(Hons)

Saga *Miss Regina V*
Called: Nov 1997, Lincoln's Inn, LLB (Hons)
LLM

Sagar *Miss Nadia*
Called: Nov 1997, Middle Temple, LLB
(Hons)

Sagayam *Miss Martina*
Called: Oct 1995, Gray's Inn, LLB

Sagayam *Miss Selina Shanti*
Simmons & Simmons, 21 Wilson Street,
London EC2M 2TX, 0171 628 2020, Fax:
0171 628 2070. Called: Oct 1993, Gray's
Inn, LLB (Hons), LLM (Lond)

Sage *Miss Melanie Jane* •
Senor Crown Prosecutor, Queens House, 58
Victoria Street, St Albans, Hertfordshire
AL1 3HZ, 01727 818 100. Called: July 1984,
Lincoln's Inn, LLB (Hons) (B'ham)

Sahu *Mark*
Called: Nov 1995, Middle Temple, LLB
(Hons) (Leeds)

Said *Miss Farah Shireen Mohamed*
Called: July 1997, Gray's Inn, LLB (Lond)

Said *Miss Shaesta*
Called: July 1994, Middle Temple

Sainer *Alan Philip* •
Senior Legal Officer, Solicitor's Office,
Inland Revenue, Somerset House, Strand,
London WC2R 1LB, 0171 438 6765.
Called: Nov 1974, Lincoln's Inn, MA
(Cantab)

Sakhrani *Miss Anisha*
Called: July 1996, Lincoln's Inn, LLB (Hons)

Sakhrani *Arjan Heera*
SC Hong Kong and Member Hong Kong Bar
3 Verulam Buildings, London, WC1R 5NT.
Called: Feb 1968, Lincoln's Inn

Sakhrani *Sanjay Arjan*
503 Dina House, Ruttonsee Centre, 11
Duddell Street, Central, Hong Kong, 2525
9083, Fax: 2877 0051, and Member Hong
Kong Bar. Called: July 1995, Lincoln's Inn,
BA, LLB (Hons)(Lond)

Sale *Martin Ronald*
Justices Chief Executive, Norfolk Magistrates
Court, Service, 4 Barton Way, Carrow Road,
Norwich NR1 1DL, 01603 219223, Fax:
01603 219227. Called: Nov 1982, Gray's
Inn, DML

Salehkon *Ramli Bin*
Kertar & Co, Advocates & Solicitors, 133
New Bridge Road, [H] 17-04, Chinatown
Point, (65) 5366266, Fax: (65) 5366533.
Called: Nov 1995, Middle Temple, LLB
(Hons)(Lond), BA (Singapore)

Sales *Harry Brimelow MBE*
Formerly a Solicitor. Called: Apr 1975, Inner
Temple, LLM (Manch)

Salisbury *Derek John Brian*
Lugwardine Court, Hereford HR1 4AE.
Called: Feb 1957, Gray's Inn, MA (Cantab)

Sallehuddin *Mohamed Nasri*
Called: July 1995, Gray's Inn, LLB (Wales)

Salmon *Ms Christine* •
Grade 7, Law Commisson, Conquest House, 37/38 John Street, Theobalds Road, London WC1, 0171 453 1232. Called: Nov 1989, Gray's Inn, MA (Oxon) Dip Law

Salmon *Rudolf Archibald*
PO Box 143, 50 Main Street, St Anne's Bay, Jamaica, 0101 809 972 2423, and Member Jamaican Bar Southsea Chambers, PO Box 148, Southsea, Portsmouth, Hampshire, PO5 2TU. Called: Nov 1965, Lincoln's Inn

Salmond *Giles Menzies* •
Principal Legal Officer (Grade 7), H M Customs & Excise, New King's Beam House, 22 Upper Ground, London SE1 9BJ, 0171 865 5462, Fax: 0171 865 5248. Called: Oct 1992, Inner Temple, LLB (Hull)

Salmons *Miss Caroline Louise*
Called: Nov 1995, Middle Temple, BA (Hons) (Kent)

Salomon *William Henry*
Deputy Chairman, Rea Brothers Group Plc, Rea Brothers Group Plc, Alderman's House, Alderman's Walk, London EC2M 3XR, 0171 623 1155, Fax: 0171 626 3446. Called: July 1986, Inner Temple, MA, LLB

Saltissi *Miss Kathleen Dorothy* •
Principal Legal Officer, HM Customs & Excise, New King's Beam House, 22 Upper Ground, London SE1. Called: July 1985, Inner Temple, BA, MSR, SRR

Salvi *Miss Sharmila Vijay*
Called: Nov 1997, Lincoln's Inn, BSc (Hons)(Lond)

Sam *Miss Lisa Hui Min*
Legal Assistant, Donaldson & Burkinshaw, 24 Raffles Place [H] 15-00, Clifford Centre, 5339422, Fax: 5337806/5330809, and Member Singapore Bar. Called: July 1996, Inner Temple, LLB (Kent)

Sambei *Miss Arvinder Kaur* •
Principal Crown Prosecutor, Crown Prosecution Service, 50 Ludgate Hill, London EC4M 7EX. Called: July 1985, Gray's Inn, BA (Kent)

Samimi *Miss Maryam*
Called: July 1994, Middle Temple, BA (Hons), LLM (Lond)

Saminathan *Miss Vignaswari*
Called: Nov 1995, Middle Temple, LLB (Hons)(Sheff)

Samnadda *Ms Julie Karen* •
Grade 7 Lawyer, D.T.I., 10-18 Victoria Street, London SW1H ONN. Called: Nov 1986, Middle Temple

Samnakay *Mrs Minaxi Saeed*
and Member Kenyan Bar. Called: Nov 1989, Inner Temple, BA (Nairobi), LLB

Sample *Miss Jacquelyn* •
Crown Prosecutor, Crown Prosecution Service, Yorkshire Area Office, 6th Floor, Ryedale Building, Piccadilly, York YO1 1NS, 01904 610726, Fax: 01904 610394. Called: Feb 1994, Inner Temple, BA, CPE

Sampson *Alistair Hubert*
103 Clifton Hill, London NW8, 0171 624 6483. Called: June 1955, Gray's Inn, BA (Cantab)

Sampson *Jonathan Charles Hiaulme*
Called: Oct 1996, Inner Temple, BA (Herts)

Sampson *William Stuart TD* •
London Area Grade 6 Special Casework Lawyer, Crown Prosecution Service, London Area, 5th Floor, Portland House, Victoria, London SW1E 5BH, 0171 915 5882, Fax: 0171 915 5897. Called: July 1974, Inner Temple, LLB

Samuel *Adam Wilfred*
14C Adamson Road, London NW3 3HR, 0171 586 1938, Fax: 0171 586 1938, and Member New York. Called: July 1983, Inner Temple, BA (Oxon), LLM (Boston), ACI Arb, FPC

Samuel *Edwin Douglas Lincoln*
Called: Mar 1998, Inner Temple, BA (Oxon)

Samuel *Miss Shanti Loraine*
Called: Nov 1996, Inner Temple, LLB (Hull)

Samuel *Mrs Vimala*
Called: Nov 1990, Lincoln's Inn, LLB (Lond)

Samuels *Miss Carla Simone*
Called: Oct 1996, Lincoln's Inn, BA (Hons)(Oxon)

Samuels *Darren Scott* •
Board Advocate, Criminal Injuries Compensation, Board, Morley House, 26-30 Holborn Viaduct, London EC1A 2JQ, 0171 842 6800. Called: Oct 1992, Middle Temple, BA (Hons)(York), Dip Law

Samuelson *Neville Anthony Wylie*
The Manor Hse, Totteridge, London N20, 0181 445 1330, Fax: 0181 446 0944. Called: Nov 1950, Inner Temple

Samupfonda *Ms Evis* •
London Borough of Southwark. Called: Nov 1992, Inner Temple, LLB

Samwell-Smith *Mrs Rosemary Sheila* •
Law Lecturer, Council of Legal Education, The Inns of Court, School of Law, Gray's Inn PLace, London WC1R. Called: Nov 1986, Gray's Inn, LLB, LLM (Lond)

Sanchez *Mrs Karin Louise*
Management & Service Co Ltd, P.O.Box F 42544, Freeport, 242 352 7063, Fax: 242 352 3932, and Member Bahamas. Called: July 1996, Lincoln's Inn, LLB (Hons)

Sandelson *Neville Devonshire*
Dep Circuit Judge & Asst Recorder 1977-1985. Called: Nov 1946, Inner Temple, MA (Cantab)

Sanders *Oliver Tschanz* •
Treasury Solicitor's Dept, Queen Anne's Chambers, 28 Broadway, London SW1H 9JS, 0171 210 3080, Fax: 0171 210 3001. Called: July 1995, Inner Temple, LLB (Lond), BCL (Oxon)

Sanderson *Mrs Bronwen Jane*
Called: Nov 1996, Lincoln's Inn, LLB (Hons)(Manch)

Sanderson *Miss Katie Alison*
Called: Nov 1996, Gray's Inn, LLB (Sheff)

Sandhu *Miss Sandip*
Called: Nov 1997, Gray's Inn, LLB (East Lond)

Sandhu *Sarbrinder Singh*
Called: July 1994, Middle Temple, LLB (Hons)(Wales)

Sandhu *Miss Viviene Kaur*
m/s Kumar & Loh, Advocates & Solicitors, 51 Anson Road [H] 10-53, Anson Centre, 225 6362, Fax: 225 9690. Called: Nov 1996, Middle Temple, LLB (Hons)(L'pool)

Sandiford-Austin *Miss Allison Joanne*
Called: Mar 1996, Middle Temple, B.Sc (Hons)

Sandilands *Richard James* •
Company Secretary, Abbey National Treasury, Services plc, Abbey House, Baker Street, London NW1 6XL, 0171 204 1000, Fax: 0171 612 4581. Called: July 1995, Lincoln's Inn, BA (Hons)

Sangam *Paul Stephen Jason* •
Legal Affairs Advisor, 42-46 St Lukes Mews, London W11 1DG, 0171 211 5101, Fax: 0171 211 3374. Called: Oct 1996, Inner Temple, LLB (Westminster)

Sangha *Ranbir Singh*
Called: July 1995, Lincoln's Inn, BA (Hons)

Sanitt *Adam Franklin* •
Associate, Bucklersbury House, 3 Queen Victoria Street, London EC4N 8EL, 0171 246 6200, Fax: 0171 329 4465. Called: Oct 1995, Lincoln's Inn, MA (Cantab), BCL (Oxon)

Sankar *Ramphal*
Principal Court Clerk, Enfield Magistrates' Court, Lordship Lane, Tottenham, London N17 6RT, 0181 808 5411. Called: Nov 1971, Lincoln's Inn

Sankaran *Chandrakandan*
Called: July 1995, Lincoln's Inn, LLB (Hons)

Sankey *Rohan Ashwin*
17 Jalan 14/37, 46100 Petaling Jaya, Selangor, 03 2911511, Fax: 03 2929105, and Member Malaysia. Called: July 1994, Middle Temple, LLB (Hons)(Bris)

Sansam *Miss Heather Rosemary*
Senior Legal Manager, Warley Magistrates Court, Oldbury Ringway, Oldbury, Warley B69 4JN, 0121 511 2222, Fax: 0121 5448492. Called: July 1981, Gray's Inn, LLB

Sansom *Nicholas* •
Thomas Miller & Co, International House, 26 Creechurch Lane, London EC3, 0171 283 4646. Called: Nov 1978, Inner Temple, LLB (Lond)

Sarfraz *Miss Ayesha*
Called: Nov 1995, Gray's Inn, BA (Punjab), LLB (Dunelm)

Sarkar *Rakhal Chandra*
50 Cleveleys Road, Hackney, London E5 9JN, 0181 806 7027. Called: Nov 1978, Inner Temple, MA

Sarkar *Shib Sankar*
21/2 Gora Chand Road, Calcutta-700014, 009133-244-8778, Senior Advocate of the Supreme Court of India. Called: May 1997, Lincoln's Inn, MA, LLB (Calcutta), FCI Arb (Lond)

Sarkaria *Mrs Neelam* •
Senior Crown Prosecutor, Crown Prosecution Service, Harrow Branch, Kings House, Kymberley Road, Harrow, Middlesex, 0181 424 8688, Fax: 0181 424 9157. Called: Nov 1988, Gray's Inn, BA Hons

Sarony *Neville Leslie*
Recorder, Advocate Supreme Court of Nepal and Member Hong Kong Bar New Court Chambers, 5 Verulam Buildings, Gray's Inn, London, WC1R 5LY. Called: June 1964, Gray's Inn, LLB (Lond), LSE

Sarwan *Mahabir*
Deputy Chief Clerk, Inner London Magistrates', Courts Service, 65 Romney Street, London SW1P 3RD, and Member Trinidad & Tobago. Called: July 1969, Middle Temple

Sarwar *(Ali) Nabeel*
Adjunct Faculty, Lahore Business School (LUMS) Lecturer at the Civil Services Academy, Lahore, Advocate, Lahore High Court, Pakistan. Called: July 1989, Middle Temple, MA (Cantab)

Sarwar *Ms Firdus Akhtar*
Called: Nov 1997, Lincoln's Inn, LLB (Hons)(Derby)

Sasegbon *Daniel Afolabi Olanrewaju*
Called: Nov 1996, Gray's Inn, LLB (Lond), LLM (Lond), MPhil (Lond)

Sathiasingam *Miss Lynette Shakunthala*
(65) 481 3113. Called: July 1995, Middle Temple, LLB (Hons)

Satkuru-Granzella *Mrs Sheamala*
Project/Research Officer, The Malaysian Timber Council, 24 Old Queen Street, London SW1H 9HP, 0171 222 8188, Fax: 0171 222 8884. Called: July 1993, Inner Temple, LLB, LLM

Saujani *Vijesh*
Called: May 1997, Lincoln's Inn, LLB (Hons)

Saul *Anthony Joseph* •
Senior Legal Adviser, Statoil (UK) Limited, Statoil House, 11 Regent Street, London SW1Y 4ST. Called: Feb 1989, Middle Temple, LLB

Saul *Guy Patrick Selwyn* •
Crown Prosecutor, Crown Proseution Service, North London Area, 2nd Floor,Kings House, Kymberley Road, Harrow,Middlesex HA1 1YH, 0181 424 8688 Ext 286, Fax: 0181 424 9157. Called: Nov 1980, Lincoln's Inn, BA

Saunders *Mrs Alison Margaret* •
Grade 6 Inspector, Crown Prosecution Service, 50 Ludgate Hill, London EC4M 7EX, 0171 273 8171, Fax: 0171 329 8166. Called: Nov 1983, Inner Temple, LLB (Leeds)

Saunders *Denis*
Company Director, TI Group plc, 50 Curzon Street, London W1Y 7PN, 0171 499 9131, Fax: 0171 493 6533. Called: Feb 1958, Gray's Inn, MA, LLM

Saunders *Edward Philip Morton*
Called: Nov 1992, Middle Temple, B.Mus (Hons)

Saunders *Miss Emma Charlotte* •
Appeals Caseworker, Arden Chambers, 27 John Street, London, WC1N 2BL. Called: Nov 1994, Gray's Inn, BA (Sheff), CPE (Manch)

Saunders *Miss Harriet Mary Elizabeth*
Called: Oct 1995, Gray's Inn, LLB

Saunt *Ms Linda Patricia* •
Principal Crown Prosecutor, Crown Prosecution Service, 50 Ludgate Hill, London EC4M 7EX, 0171 273 1300, Fax: 0171 273 1325. Called: Nov 1986, Inner Temple, MA (Cantab)

Saunthararajah *Miss Vaani*
Called: Nov 1993, Middle Temple, LLB (Hons)(Warwick)

Savage *Dr Andrew William George*
Medical Pratitioner, Minstrel Cottage, Westmill, Herts SG9 9LL, 01763 271636. Called: Nov 1993, Lincoln's Inn, MBBS (Medicine), Dip Law

Savage *David James*
12a Knot House, 3 Brewery Square, London SE1 2LF, 0171 403 2416. Called: Nov 1994, Middle Temple, BA (Hons)

Savage *Stephen Richard*
Clerk to the Justices, Maidstone Sevenoaks, Tonbridge & Malling, Tunbridge Wells & Cranbrook, Kent Magistrates Court, The Court House, Tufton Street, Ashford, Kent TN23 1QS, 01233 663204. Called: Nov 1976, Middle Temple, LLB, MBA

Saveriades *Marios Kyriacou*
Iris House, John Kennedy Str, Office 740B, Limassol, Cyprus, (05) 366767, Fax: 4745 JUSTLAW, and Member Cyprus Bar. Called: Feb 1995, Lincoln's Inn, LLB (Hons)(Leic)

Saville *Thomas William*
Called: Oct 1995, Lincoln's Inn, LLB (Hons)(Northum)

Savin *Charles Timothy*
Called: Nov 1962, Gray's Inn, BSc, FRSC, C.Chem, MIPD

Savvides *George Loukis*
Managing Partner, 1st, 2nd & 4th Floor, Omega Court, 4 Rigas Fereos Street, P.O.Box 4098, 3720 Limmassol, 357 5 376886, Fax: 357 5 374930. Called: July 1983, Middle Temple, LLB (Hons)(Exon), ACIArb

Saw *Miss Hooi Lee*
Called: July 1997, Lincoln's Inn, LLB (Hons)(Wales)

Saw *Leon Eng Tiong*
Called: July 1995, Lincoln's Inn, LLB (Hons)

Saw *Miss Lily* •
Crown Prosecution Service, 4 Artillery Row, Victoria, London SW1P 1RZ, 0171 976 5699. Called: Feb 1987, Middle Temple, LLB (Newc), LLM

Saw *Seang Kuan*
80 Robinson Road, [H]17-02, Singapore 068898, 2228008, Fax: 2228001, and Member Singapore Bar. Called: July 1996, Middle Temple, BA (Hons)(Cantab)

Sawtell-Fearn *Ms Jane Elizabeth*
Called: Oct 1997, Gray's Inn, LLB (De Montfort)

Sawyer *Ms Katrine Mary*
Called: Nov 1996, Middle Temple, BA (Hons)(Oxon)

Sayers *Michael Warwick* •
The Secretary, Law Commission, Conquest House, 37/38 John Street, Theobalds Road, London WC1N 2BQ, 0171 411 1250, Fax: 0171 411 1297. Called: July 1967, Middle Temple

Sayers *Ms Veronica Margaret*
Legal Assistant, Law Officer's Department, Morier House, Halkett Place, St Helier, Jersey, 01534 502200. Called: Nov 1997, Inner Temple, BSc (Open Uni), LLB (So'ton)

Scarborough *Dominic Philip*
Called: Nov 1995, Middle Temple, BA (Hons)

Sceeny *Mark David*
Squire & Co Solicitors, 49-52 St John's Square, London EC1V 4JL, 0171 490 3444, Fax: 0171 524 4087/4115. Called: Oct 1995, Gray's Inn, LLB

Schapira *Lawrence*
0171 267 3925. Called: Nov 1984, Gray's Inn, BA (Keele)

Schenck *Mrs Susan Jean* •
Senior Crown Prosecutor, Crown Prosecution Service, 7th Floor, Liver Buildings, Liverpool, Merseyside. Called: July 1981, Gray's Inn, BA (Hons)

Scheurer *Vincent Stuart*
Called: Nov 1994, Lincoln's Inn, BA (Hons)(Oxon)

Schimming-Chase *Miss Esi Malaika*
Called: Oct 1994, Middle Temple, LLB (Hons)(Coventry)

Schinis *Miss Theodoti A*
Assiciate Advocate, P.L.Cacoyannis & Co, B, Rigas Feros Street, Libra Chambers, Limassol, P.O. Box 122, (357) 5 363154. Called: Nov 1997, Lincoln's Inn, LLB (Hons)(Leics)

Schmiegelow *Ian Lunn*
46 Catherine Place, London SW1E 6HL, 0171 233 7440, Fax: 0171 233 7442. Called: July 1967, Inner Temple, MA (Cantab)

Schofield *Peter Graham* •
Senior Legal Adviser, EEF, Broadway House, Tothill Street, London SW1H 9NQ, 0171 222 7777, Fax: 0171 222 2782. Called: Feb 1988, Lincoln's Inn, BA (Hons) Durham

Scholefield *Miss Jane Elizabeth* •
Senior Crown Prosecutor, Crown Prosecution Service, 18th Floor, Tolworth Tower, Ewell Road, Surbiton, Surrey KT6 7DS, 399 5171. Called: Oct 1991, Middle Temple, BSc, Dip Law

Schoneveld *Frank Robert*
Legal Counsel (Europe), Attorney General's Department, Robert Garrar Offices, National Circuit, ACY 2600, 61 2 6250 5515, Fax: 61 2 6250 5910, and Member Australia Bar 2 Harcourt Bldgs, Ground Floor/Left, Temple, London, EC4Y 9DB. Called: May 1992, Inner Temple, B.Jurisprudence, LLB (Australia), Dip Eur Law (Neth)

Schroder *Miss Hildegard Katharina* •
Law Lecturer, Colchester Institute, Sheepen Road, Colchester. Called: Nov 1983, Inner Temple, BA

Schumacher *Tobias*
Called: Nov 1997, Middle Temple, LLB (Hons)

Schwartzman *Ivor Walter*
Supreme Court Judge, 300 Innes Chambers, Johannesburg, South Africa, and Member South Africa Bar Swaziland Bar. Called: May 1988, Lincoln's Inn, BA, LLB (Rand)

Schwarz *Dr Heinz OMS*
P O Box 3089, Parklands 2121, (2711) 286 1115, Fax: (2711) 784 9976, Former Ambassador of South Africa to the United States of America, Dr of Humane Letters (Honoris Causa). Called: Nov 1961, Inner Temple, BA, LLB, D.Phil, (Hon Causa),

Schwarzschild *Maimon*
1 Gray's Inn Square, 1st Floor, London, WC1R 5AG. Called: May 1987, Lincoln's Inn, BA, JD Columbia Univ

Schwehr *Ms Belinda Zoe*
Rowe & Maw, 20 Black Friars Lane, London EC4V 6HD, 0171 248 4282, Fax: 0171 248 2009. Called: Feb 1985, Middle Temple, LLM, LLB (Hons)(Lond)

Science *Benjamin David*
12 Morritt Avenue, Halton, Leeds, Yorkshire LS15 7EP, 0113 2946805. Called: Oct 1993, Gray's Inn, LLB (Leeds), MSc

Scipio *Miss Mona Kathleen*
Deputy Chief Clerk, Inner London Magistrates', Courts Service, Highbury Magistrtates' Court, 51 Holloway Road, London N7. Called: Nov 1970, Middle Temple, LLB (Lond)

Scoon *Leo Rennie* •
Principal Legal Officer, Office of the Solicitor, Department of Social Security, New Court, 48 Carey Street, London WC2A 2LS, 0171 412 1498, Fax: 0171 412 1220. Called: Feb 1986, Inner Temple, LL.B.

Scordis *Kyriacos*
P O Box 533, 30 Karpenisi Street, The Business Forum, Nicosia, (357) 2 843000, Fax: (357) 2 375227, and Member Cyprus Bar. Called: Nov 1994, Lincoln's Inn, LLB (Hons), LLM (Lond)

Scott *Professor Adam TD*
Professorial Fellow, St Andrews Management Institute, Hon Lecturer, School of Economics and Management, University of St Andrews, 19 Blackheath Park, Blackheath, London SE3 9RW, 0181 852 3286, Fax: 0181 852 6247. Called: Nov 1972, Inner Temple, MA (Oxon), MSc, (City), CEng, FIEE, FRSA

Scott *Miss Charlene Annette*
Crown Counsel (Criminal), Attorney General's Chambers, Global House, 43 Church Street, Hamilton HM 12, 441 292 2463, Fax: 441 292 3608. Called: Nov 1986, Inner Temple, BA, MSc (New York), LLB (Essex)

Scott *David Gidley*
High Court Bankruptcy Registrar (1984-96), 45 Benslow Lane, Hitchin, Herts SG4 9RE, 01462 434391, also Inn of Court L. Called: June 1951, Middle Temple, MA, LLM (Cantab)

Scott *Mrs Fusun*
Called: Nov 1988, Inner Temple, BA (Lond), Dip in Law

Scott *Howard David Ashley*
Called: May 1996, Lincoln's Inn, BA (Hons)

Scott *Mr Ian Richard*
Called: Nov 1995, Gray's Inn, LLB (Melbourne), PhD

Scott *Miss Josephine Sarah*
Called: May 1997, Middle Temple, LLB (Hons), LLM (Lond)

Scott *Miss Karen*
Called: Nov 1997, Middle Temple, BSc (Hons)(Reading), LLB (Hons)

Scott *Kenneth Leslie*
K L Scott Associates, Chartered Quantity Surveyors, Central Chambers, Eldon Street, Barnsley S Yorks, 01226 201342, Fax: 01226 294632. Called: May 1988, Middle Temple, LLB (Hons), Dip.Arb, FRICS, FCIOB, FCIArb

Scott *Miss Kristine*
Employment Advisor, Rickerby Watterson Solicitors, Ellenborough House, Wellington Street, Cheltenham GL50 1YO, 01242 224422, Fax: 01242 518428. Called: Nov 1992, Inner Temple, LLB

Scott *Miss Rachael Elizabeth* •
Senior Crown Prosecutor, Froomgate House, Rupert Street, Bristol, Avon, 0117 9273093. Called: July 1989, Inner Temple, LLB(Hons)

Scott *Mrs Sandra Louise*
Called: July 1997, Gray's Inn, LLB (Lanc), BEd, MEd

Scott *Trevor Pierre* •
Called: Oct 1996, Gray's Inn, LLB (Anglia)

Scott-Lynch *Miss Andrea Georgina*
Called: Oct 1996, Inner Temple, LLB (East Anglia)

Scott-Wilson *Christopher John* •
Principal Legal Adviser, Guinness Plc, 39 Portman Square, London W1H 9HB, 0171 486 0288, Fax: 0171 486 0279. Called: July 1982, Middle Temple, BSc

Scrantom *Timothy Dillon*
Goldsworth Chambers, 1st Floor, 10-11 Gray's Inn Square, London, WC1R 5JD. Called: Feb 1995, Gray's Inn, BA (Stetson, USA), JD (Georgia, USA), LLM

Scrase *Thomas Davis*
24 Castle Street, Buckingham MK18 1BP, 01280 823073, Fax: 01280 823774. Called: Feb 1953, Middle Temple, LLB (Lond)

Screeche-Powell *Miss Genevieve Bernadette Faith*
Called: Oct 1997, Gray's Inn, BA (Warks)

Scruton *Professor Roger Vernon*
Called: Feb 1978, Inner Temple

Scudamore *Jeremy Richard*
Principe de Vergara, 261-5 C, (34) 91 4577262, and Member Madrid Bar. Called: Nov 1982, Middle Temple, BA (Hons) (Exeter)

Scudder *Mrs Laura Jean* •
Senior Court Clerk (part time), Havering Magistrates', Courts Committee, The Courthouse,Main Raod, Romford, Essex RM1 3BH, 01708 771771, Fax: 01708 771777. Called: Nov 1984, Gray's Inn

Scudder *Peter Alan* •
Court Clerk, Redbridge Magistrates', Court Committee, 850 Cranbrook Road, Barkingside, Essex IG6 1HW, 0181 551 4461. Called: July 1983, Gray's Inn, LLB

Scully *Gerard*
22 Richmond Park, Monkstown, County Dublin, 00 3531 670 1818, Fax: 00 3531 829 0283. Called: Nov 1996, Middle Temple, BA (Dublin), MA (Lond)

Seagroatt *Conrad QC (1983)*
Formerly Solicitor of the Supreme Court. 3 Fountain Court, Steelhouse Lane, Birmingham, B4 6DR. Called: Apr 1970, Gray's Inn, MA (Oxon)

Seah *Miss Chui Ling Engelyn*
Called: July 1994, Middle Temple, LLB (Hons)(Lond)

Seah *Miss Ee Leng*
Called: July 1995, Lincoln's Inn, LLB (Hons)

Seah *Miss Heww Ying Melina*
Called: Nov 1995, Middle Temple, LLB (Hons)

Seah *Miss Lu Sean*
Called: July 1996, Gray's Inn, LLB (Warwick)

Seah *Miss Suat Eng*
and Member Singapore Bar. Called: July 1994, Lincoln's Inn, BSc (Econ) (Hons)

Sealy *Richard Campbell* •
Crown Prosecutor, Crown Prosecution
Service, No 3 Bankside, Crosfield Street,
Warrington, Cheshire. Called: July 1981,
Lincoln's Inn, BA (Hons)

Searle *Ms Frances Anne*
Deputy Chief Clerk, Inner London Mag Crt
Service, 65 Romney Street, London
SW1P 3RD, 0171 799 3332. Called: Nov
1979, Gray's Inn, BA (Hons) (Lond)

Searle *Jason Ario Xavier* •
Advocate, Peninsula Business Services,
Limited, Stamford House, 361/365 Chapel
Street, Manchester M3 5JY, 0161 834 2773,
Fax: 0161 839 2700. Called: Oct 1993,
Middle Temple, LLB (Hons)

Searle *Miss Lyndsey Anne* •
VAT Consultant & Litigator, Deloitte &
Touche, Hill House, 1 Little New Street,
London EC4A 3TR, 0171 303 3565.
Called: Oct 1995, Middle Temple, B.Sc

Searle *Richard Nathan* •
Called: Oct 1995, Middle Temple, BA (Hons)

Sears *The Hon Mr Justice*
Commioner of the Supreme Crt of Brunei,
Justice of the High Court of Hong Kong.
Vice Chairman Judge's Forum., The High
Court, 38 Queensway, 8254433, Fax:
8690640. Called: Feb 1957, Gray's Inn, MA
(Cantab)

Seaton *Ian Christopher Norman*
Accounts Director, Citigate Communications
Ltd, 26 Finsbury Square, London EC2, 0171
282 8000, Fax: 0171 282 8010. Called: Apr
1975, Middle Temple, LLB (Hons) (Bris)

Sebastos *George*
Called: Oct 1994, Lincoln's Inn, LLB
(Hons)(Lond)

Seben *Ivan Michael* •
Legal Advisor, 35 Church Street, Saffron
Walden, Essex CB10 1JQ, 01799 522576,
Fax: 01799 513067. Called: May 1953, Inner
Temple

Sebom *Polycarp Teo*
and Member Sarawak Bar. Called: Oct 1991,
Inner Temple, BA, LLB (Hull), ACIS, ATII

Seculer *Mrs Joy Rosina* •
Lawyer, Welsh Office Office, Welsh Office,
Civic Centre, Cardiff CF1. Called: Nov 1983,
Middle Temple

Seculer-Faber *Anthony Roy*
Clerk to the Justices, Vale of Glamorgan
Magistrates, Court, Thompson Street, Barry
CF63 4SX, 01268 293129, Fax: 01268
293187. Called: Nov 1985, Middle Temple,
B.Sc (Cardiff)

See *Ben Sin*
Called: July 1997, Lincoln's Inn, LLB
(Hons)(Lond)

See *David Thiam Soon*
Called: Nov 1997, Middle Temple, LLB
(Hons)(Reading)

See *Eng Teong*
Called: July 1996, Lincoln's Inn, LLB
(Hons)(Lond)

See *Ms Esther Lay Lin*
Legal Adviser, Messrs Cheang & Ariff, 39
Court, 39 Jalan Yap Kwan Seng, 50450
Kuala Lumpur, 03 2610803, Fax: 03
2614475, and Member Malaysia. Called: July
1995, Middle Temple, LLB (Hons)

See *Miss Guat Har*
Senior Assistant, Messrs Shearn Delamore &
Co, 6th Floor,Wisma Penang Gdn, No.42
Jalan Sultan Ahmad Shah, 10050 Penang
Malaysia, 04-2267062/2266664899, Fax: 04-
2275166, and Member Malaysia Bar.
Called: July 1989, Middle Temple, BA, LLB
(Bucks)

See *Hans Han-E*
2355501, Fax: 5363622, and Member
Singapore. Called: July 1995, Middle
Temple, LLB (Hons) (Hull)

See Tho *Miss Ving Mei*
Called: July 1995, Middle Temple, LLB
(Hons) (Hull)

Seely *Richard Evelyn*
33 Upper Park Road, London NW3 2UL.
Called: Nov 1961, Gray's Inn

Seevaratnam *Harichandran*
0181 445 9101. Called: May 1960, Gray's
Inn

Seevaratnam *Miss Nathalie Mallikai*
Called: Oct 1994, Inner Temple, LLB
(Bucks)

Sefton *David Graeme Fennick*
Called: Nov 1995, Middle Temple, BA
(Hons), BCL

Segal *Mrs Jill Patricia*
39 Cathcart Road, London SW10 9JG, 0171
352 0730, Fax: 0171 352 7309. Called: July
1974, Gray's Inn

Segbefia *Alex Percival* •
Senior Crown Prosecutor, Crown
Prosecution Service, 2nd Floor, Kings
House, Kimberley Road, Harrow, Middx
HA1 1YH, 0181 424 8688, Fax: 0181 424
9157. Called: Nov 1988, Inner Temple, LLB
(Essex)

Sehrawat *Sahib Ram* •
District Land Registrar, Portsmouth District
Land, Registry, St Andrews Court,, St
Michaels Rd, Portsmouth, Hants PO1 2JH,
01705 768800, Fax: 01705 768768, and
Member India Bar. Called: July 1979, Middle
Temple, BA, LLB

Seitler *Anthony Julian*
Called: Nov 1995, Gray's Inn, BA

Sekarajasekaran *Miss Sharmila*
Called: Nov 1996, Middle Temple, BA
(Hons)(Keele)

Sekhon *Gurmit Singh*
Called: Nov 1988, Lincoln's Inn, LLB Hons

Selby *Andrew Robert Vincent*
Called: Nov 1997, Gray's Inn, BA

Seligman *Edgar*
Harry B. Sands & Co, Chambers, 50 Shirley
Street, P O Box N-624, Nassau, Bahamas, 1-
(809) 322-2670, Fax: 1-(809) 323-8914, and
Member Bahamas. Called: Oct 1992, Gray's
Inn, MA (Dublin), Dip Law

Seller *Timothy John*
Called: May 1997, Lincoln's Inn, BA
(Hons)(Dunelm)

Sellers *Geoffrey Bernard CB,* •
Parliamentary Counsel, Parliamentary
Counsel Office, 36 Whitehall, London
SW1A 2AY. Called: July 1971, Gray's Inn,
MA, BCL

Sells *Peter Charles*
c/o Azema Sells, Aldwych House, 81
Aldwych, London WC2B 4HN, 0171 836
7993, Fax: 0171 836 3882, and Member
Avocat a la Cour de Paris. Called: Nov 1976,
Inner Temple, MA (Cantab), A.C.I.,Arb

Selvakumar *MIss Shiela*
Called: July 1997, Lincoln's Inn, LLB (Hons)

Selvan *Kaniamuthan s/o Thiruvida*
Called: Nov 1997, Lincoln's Inn, LLB (Hons)

Selvaraj *Steven*
Called: Nov 1996, Gray's Inn, LLB (Lond)

Selvarajah *Miss Pushpaleela*
Called: Feb 1995, Lincoln's Inn, LLB
(Hons)(Lond)

Selvarajan *Balamurugan*
Called: Nov 1997, Lincoln's Inn, LLB
(Hons)(Wolv)

Selvaratnam *Joseph* •
Crown Prosecution Service, Buckingham
Branch Office, 4,5 & 6 Prebendal Court,
Oxford Road, Aylesbury HP19 3RY, 01296
436441, Fax: 01296 88664. Called: Nov
1990, Gray's Inn, LLB (Bristol), LLM (Lond)

Selwyn *Norman*
Chairman SSAT, Immigration Adjudictor, 14
Blythe Way, Solihull, West Midlands
B91 3EY, 0121 705 3330. Called: Feb 1961,
Gray's Inn, LLM, Dip Econ (Oxon)

Semmence *Matthew Herbert*
Called: Nov 1995, Middle Temple, LLB
(Hons)

Sen *Ms Lisa*
6 Southern Avenue, Maharani Bagh, New
Delhi 110065, India, 00-91-11-6910545, and
Member India Bar. Called: July 1995, Gray's
Inn, BA, MA (New York), LLB (Lond)

Sen *Raj Ratna*
149/IC Rash Behari Avenue, Calcutta,
700029, (033) 464-3601/464 2651.
Called: July 1994, Gray's Inn, BA (Calcutta),
LLB (Leeds)

Sen *Miss Sheila Ruth*
Called: July 1974, Inner Temple, LLB (Lond),
MJur (Manc)

Senathipathy *Miss Renuka*
Called: July 1994, Lincoln's Inn, LLB (Hons)

Seng *Joo How*
Secretary(Town Council)HDB. Called: Nov 1991, Middle Temple, BSc Hons (Econ), LLB Hons (Lond Ext), ARICS,ACIS

Sengupta *Miss Amgana*
Called: July 1995, Inner Temple, LLB (Lond)

Sentance *Joseph Richard Pattison* •
Crown Prosecutor, Crown Prosecution Service, 1st Floor, The Cooperage, Gainsford Street, London SE1 2NG. Called: Nov 1986, Inner Temple, BA(Cantab)

Seow *Miss Deanna Yim Ling*
Called: July 1994, Middle Temple, LLB (Hons)(Bris)

Seow *John Hwang Seng*
Called: July 1995, Middle Temple, LLB (Hons)

Serghides *Miss Lydia Gabrielle*
Called: July 1997, Gray's Inn, LLB (Kent)

Serjeant *David John* •
Assistant Legal Adviser, BBC, British Broadcasting Corp., Room 1055, Broadcasting House, Portland Place, London W1A 1AA. Called: Nov 1973, Middle Temple, LLB

Sessions *Paul Mark*
Thomas Miller & Co Ltd, International House, 26 Creechurch Lane, London EC3A 5BA, 0171 204 2211, Fax: 0171 204 2102. Called: Feb 1991, Inner Temple, BA (Lond), LLM

Seth *Mrs Prabha*
Called: July 1993, Middle Temple, LLB (Hons)(Lond)

Setty *Miss Padmini*
Called: Nov 1996, Gray's Inn, LLB

Sevasamy *Shankar Angammah*
Called: July 1996, Middle Temple, LLB (Hons)(Lond)

Seward *Guy William* QC (1982)
Stocking Lane Cottage, Ayot St Lawrence, Welwyn, Herts AL6 9BW, 01438 820 259. Called: June 1956, Inner Temple, IRRV

Seward *Robert Canton* •
47 Kingstown Street, London NW1 8JP. Called: July 1971, Inner Temple, MA (Oxon)

Seyan *Balbir* •
Aylesbury Crown Pros Service, 4,5 and 6 Prebendal Court, Oxford Road, Aylesbury, Buckinghamshire HP19 3EY, 01296 436441, Fax: 01296 88664. Called: July 1984, Inner Temple, BA

Seymour *Christopher Roger* RD
Justices Chief Executive & Clerk to the Justices, Wolverhampton Magistrates', Courts, Law Courts, North Street, Wolverhampton WV1 1RA, 01902 773151, Fax: 01902 27875. Called: July 1972, Gray's Inn

Seymour *Dr Colin Brian*
and Member King's Inn (Dublin). Called: May 1996, Lincoln's Inn, PhD (Dublin)

Seymour *David* •
Legal Secretary to the Law Offices, Attorney General Chambers, 9 Buckingham Gate, London SW1E 6JP, 0171 828 1968, Fax: 0171 233 9206, and Member Northern Ireland 1997. Called: July 1975, Gray's Inn, MA (Oxon), LLB (Cantab)

Shadid *Miss Lina Ali*
Afridi & Angell, Legal Consultants, P.O.Box 9371, Dubai, 00971 4 883900, Fax: 00971 4 883979. Called: July 1996, Lincoln's Inn, LLB (Hons)(Lond)

Shadwick *Mark Jonathan Henry*
Called: Oct 1997, Middle Temple, LLB (Hons)(Guildhal)

Shafiq *Imran*
Called: Nov 1997, Lincoln's Inn, LLB (Hons), LLM (Georgetown)

Shafiq *Mohammad*
Called: Nov 1996, Lincoln's Inn, LLB (Hons)(Lond)

Shah *Aly Abbas*
Called: July 1994, Lincoln's Inn, LLB (Hons), LLM (Bucks)

Shah *Ms Bhavini Jayakant*
Called: July 1994, Middle Temple, LLB (Hons)(Lond)

Shah *Ms Fatima* •
Head of Legal Affairs, Gotaas-Larsen Ltd, 105 Victoria Street, London SW1E 6QJ, 0171 828 7822, Fax: 0171 834 2259. Called: Nov 1987, Gray's Inn, LLB (Hons)

Shah *Miss Rukhsana Anjum* •
Senior Principal Legal Officer, HM Customs & Excise, New King's Beam House, Upper Ground, London SE1. Called: July 1976, Middle Temple

Shah *Sattar* •
Senior Crown Prosecutor, Crown Prosecution Service, Special Casework Unit, Portland House, Stag Place, Victoria, London SW1. Called: Nov 1989, Lincoln's Inn, LLB (B'ham), B.Ed, MBA

Shah *Miss Sheilja Harsukhlal* •
Legal Advisor, Department of Trade & Industry, 10 Victoria Street, London SW1H 0ET. Called: Oct 1994, Middle Temple, LLB (Hons), LLM (Lond)

Shah *Shuaib Mohammed*
Called: Nov 1994, Inner Temple, BA (Lond)

Shah *Syed Fasih Asghar*
Called: Nov 1995, Lincoln's Inn, BA, LLB (Punjab), LLM (Edinburgh)

Shah *Syed Najaf Hussain*
Advisor to Punjab Cooperative Board for Liquidation, Najaf Shah & Co, Opp Punjab Bar Council Blds, 13 Fane Road, Lahore, Pakistan, 042 7244888/7248088, Fax: 042 7230808/5721008, and Member Lahore High Court Bar,Lahore,Pakistan. Called: July 1989, Lincoln's Inn, BA (Punjab), LLB (Buck), LLM (Lond)

Shah *Tajamal Hussain* •
Legal Adviser, ECGD, 2 Exchange Tower, Harbour Exchange Square, Docklands, London, 0171 512 7854. Called: Nov 1989, Lincoln's Inn, LLB, LLM

Shah-Kazemi *Mrs Sonia Nourin Gul*
Senior Lecturer in Law, University of Westminster, Faculty of Law, 4 Red Lion Street, London WC1R 4SR, 0171 911 5153, Fax: 0171 911 5152. Called: Nov 1988, Lincoln's Inn, LLB Hons

Shahar-Martin *Mrs Norshila* •
Senior Crown Prosecutor, Crown Prosecution Service, 5th Floor, River Park House, 225 High Road, Wood Green, London N22 4HQ, 0181 888 8889, Fax: 0181 888 0746. Called: Nov 1988, Lincoln's Inn, LLB (Lond)

Shahrim *Ms Azlina*
Called: Nov 1996, Gray's Inn, LLB (Warw)

Shahruddin Leong *Miss Julianna*
Called: July 1994, Lincoln's Inn, LLB (Hons)

Shaik Hussain *Miss Khatijah*
Messrs Achan & Co, Advocates & Solicitors, No 12-C, Jalan SS 3/33, Talman University 47300, Petaling Jaya, Selangor Darul Ehsan, 03-7773622/7773042, and Member Malaysian Bar. Called: July 1993, Lincoln's Inn, LLB (Hons, Manch)

Shaikh *Zaher Abduz*
Called: Nov 1997, Gray's Inn, B.Com (Bangladesh), LLB

Shakesby *David John*
Called: Oct 1996, Inner Temple, LLB

Sham *Chun Hung*
and Member Hong Kong Bar. Called: Feb 1992, Gray's Inn, BSc (Hong Kong), LLB (Lond), C.Biol (UK)

Sham *Ms Rachel Fung-Ying* •
Solicitor, Redbridge Magistrates Court, 850 Cranbrook Road, Barkingside, Essex IG6 1HW, 0181 551 4461. Called: Nov 1986, Lincoln's Inn, LLB (Hons)

Shamel *Ms Linda Jusuf Zain* •
Principal Crown Prosecutor, Crown Prosecution Service, 5th Floor, River Park House, Wood Green, London N22. Called: Nov 1984, Middle Temple, LLB, MA (Juris)

Shammah *Miss Diane*
Called: Apr 1964, Middle Temple, LLB

Shamsuddin *Miss Heidi*
Called: Nov 1997, Lincoln's Inn, LLB (Hons)(Nott'm)

Shamsuddin *Shamsuflan B* •
Legal Adviser, Shell UK Limited, Shell-Mex House, Strand, London WC2R 0DX, 0171 257 3539, Fax: 0171 257 3441. Called: July 1990, Middle Temple, LLB (B'ham)

Shankar *Renganathan*
Called: July 1995, Middle Temple, LLB (Hons)

Shanmugaguru *Miss Shanthini*
Called: Oct 1997, Gray's Inn, LLB (Lond)

Shanmuganathan *Indran*
Called: July 1996, Lincoln's Inn, LLB (Hons)(Leics)

Sharbawi *Miss Zuraini*
Called: Nov 1994, Lincoln's Inn, LLB (Hons)(Lond)

Shardin *Miss Emilda*
Called: July 1994, Lincoln's Inn, LLB (Hons)

Sharif *Hussain Nawaz*
Called: Nov 1996, Lincoln's Inn, LLB (Hons)(LSE)

Sharif *Raja* •
In House Counsel, Guardian Dr Ltd, Benchmark House, St George's Business Centre, 203 Brooklands Road, Weybridge, Surrey KT13 0RH. Called: Nov 1992, Gray's Inn, LLB (Hull), LLM (Notts)

Shariff *Navroz*
Called: May 1990, Inner Temple, LL.B. (Lond)

Sharifi *Ms Neda*
Called: Nov 1991, Lincoln's Inn, LLB (Hons) (Lond)

Sharma *Miss Aneeta*
Called: Nov 1991, Lincoln's Inn, LLB (Hons)

Sharma *Rajesh Dutt*
Called: July 1996, Gray's Inn, BA (Keele)

Sharpe *Mrs Sally*
Crown Advocate, Law Officers' Department, Royal Court House, St Helier, Jersey JE1 1DD, 01534 502200, Fax: 01534 502299, Advocate of the Royal Court of Jersey (1992). Called: July 1988, Middle Temple, BA (OU), LLB (Hons) (Lond)

Sharpe *Miss Susan Clare*
Law Officers' Department, Royal Court House, Royal Square, Jersey JE1 1DD, 01534 502200, Fax: 01534 502299. Called: Oct 1992, Middle Temple, BA (Hons)

Sharpe *Mrs Susan Elizabeth* •
Director of Legal Services, Royal Pharmaceutical Society, of Great Britain (RPSGB), 1 Lambeth High Street, London SE1 7JN, 0171 735 9141, Fax: 0171 735 7629. Called: Nov 1972, Gray's Inn, LLB

Sharples *Ignatius Brian*
Chartered Surveyor, Francis Taylor Bldg, 3rd Floor, Temple, London, EC4Y 7BY. Called: Nov 1986, Lincoln's Inn, LLB (Hons, E.Anglia)

Sharples *John Michael*
Called: Nov 1992, Inner Temple, LLB (Hons)

Sharples *Dr Kenneth Strang*
LEA rep on governing bodies of local colleges & schools Legal Adviser, 26 London Court, London Road, Headington, Oxford OX3 7SL. Called: Jan 1951, Gray's Inn, LLM, MSc, PhD(Manch), DJur (Amsterdam), DU (Brussels), C.Chem, FRSC

Sharples *Miss Lesley-Anne*
Called: Oct 1997, Lincoln's Inn, LLB (Hons)

Sharples *Paul James*
Called: Feb 1994, Middle Temple, BA (Hons)(Oxon), MA

Sharples *Simon Andrew*
Called: July 1987, Inner Temple, BA (Kent), Dip Law, LLM

Sharpling *Miss Drusilla Hope* •
Chief Crown Prosecutor, Central Casework, Crown Prosecution Service, 50 Ludgate Hill, London EC4M 7EX. Called: July 1987, Gray's Inn, LLB (B'ham)

Shatz *Anthony*
Called: Oct 1995, Lincoln's Inn, LLB (Hons)(Lond)

Shaw *Colin Don CBE*
Called: Feb 1960, Inner Temple, MA

Shaw *Gabriele*
Called: Mar 1998, Inner Temple, BA (Lond), LLM (Manch)

Shaw *George Bernard*
Called: Oct 1997, Inner Temple, LLB (London)

Shaw *Dr Gordon Wallace*
206 Nelson House, Dolphin Square, London SW1V 3LX, 0171 798 5742, and Member American Bar Association. Called: Nov 1955, Gray's Inn, PhD, LLB, FCII

Shaw *Ian Douglas* •
Senior Crown Prosecutor, Crown Prosecution Service, St Peters House, Gower Street, Derby DE1 1SB, 01332 621615, Fax: 01332 621698. Called: Nov 1991, Middle Temple, BSc (Hons)

Shaw *John Martin* •
Legal Adviser, NPI, National Provident House, Tunbridge Wells, Kent TN1 2UE, 01892 515151, Fax: 01892 705843. Called: Nov 1992, Lincoln's Inn, LLB (Hons

Shaw *Jonathan Leonard Maukes*
Central Chambers, 1505 Bank of America Tower, 12 Harcourt Road, Central, Hong Kong, 852 845 1909, Fax: 852 868 1965, and Member Hong Kong Bar. Called: Nov 1978, Gray's Inn, FCIArb, LLM

Shaw *Justin Edward Magnus*
Called: Nov 1992, Lincoln's Inn, BA (Hons), Dip in Law

Shaw *Ms Nicola Jane Duckworth*
Martins Building, Water Street, Liverpool, L2 3SP. Called: Oct 1992, Lincoln's Inn, BA(Hons)(Leeds), CPE

Shaw *Peter Vernon Hugh*
Called: Nov 1993, Lincoln's Inn, BA (Hons)

Shaw *Mrs Sandra Nan Demby* •
Commercial & Legal Manager, LASMO North Sea PLC, 101 Bishopsgate, London EC2M 3XH, 0171 892 9712, Fax: 0171 892 9793, and Member Florida Bar. Called: Nov 1987, Gray's Inn, BA (New Orleans), Juris Doctorate, (Florida)

Shaw *Terence John* •
Legal Correspondent, Daily Telegraph, 1 Canada Square, London E14 5DT, 0171 538 5000 DL 6498, Fax: 0171 538 7842. Called: Nov 1961, Gray's Inn, MA (Cantab)

Shawcross *Rt Hon Lord GBE QC* (1939)
60 Victoria Embankment, London EC4Y OJP, 0171 325 5133, Fax: 0171 325 8195, Honorary Chairman of the Bar Council.. Called: May 1925, Gray's Inn, LLM,LLD

Shawkat *Miss Tasnim* •
Assistant Lawyer, Surrey County Council, County Hall, Kingston Upon Thames KT1 2DN, 0181 541 9259, Fax: 0181 541 9005. Called: Oct 1991, Inner Temple, LLB (Brunel)

Shea *Nicholas James*
Called: Oct 1993, Middle Temple, BA (Hons)(Oxon), Dip in Law (City)

Shear *Elliot Marc*
Called: Oct 1996, Inner Temple, LLB (Hons)(Leeds)

Shedden *Colonel Robert Charles TD*
Chief Clerk, Clerkenwell Magistrates Court, 78 King's Cross Road, London WC1X 9QJ, 0171 278 6541, Fax: 0171 833 3662. Called: July 1979, Gray's Inn

Sheehan *Mrs Jayne Mary*
Senior Legal Adviser, Harlow Magistrates Court, South Gate, The High, Harlow, Essex CM20 1HH, 01279 425108, Fax: 01279 450522. Called: July 1989, Middle Temple, LLB Hons

Sheehan *Richard Anthony Padraig*
Director; HSBC Gibbs Ltd Chairman: GHC Financial Institutions Insurance Services Ltd, 50 Cadogan Place, London SW1, 0171 247 5433. Called: July 1973, Gray's Inn, MA, A.C.I.I

Sheikh *Fazle Noor Taposh*
Called: Nov 1997, Lincoln's Inn, LLB (Hons)

Sheinfield *Miss Anne Harriet* •
Manager, Legal Affairs, Sony Music Entertainment (UK), Ltd, 10 Great MarlborougH Street, LondoN W1V 2LP. Called: Nov 1990, Middle Temple, Dip Law (City), MA (Cantab)

Sheldrick *Andrew William*
3 Radford Court, Princeton Junction, New Jersey, 08550-2218, 609 799 5719, Fax: 609 799 9170, and Member New York Bar. Called: July 1979, Gray's Inn, MA (Cantab), MCL(George, Washington Univ)

Sheldrick *Benjamin Charles Patrick*
D J Webb & Co, 43 Berkeley Square, Mayfair, London W1X 5DB, 0171 499 3009, Fax: 0171 499 3004. Called: Oct 1994, Lincoln's Inn, BA (Hons)(Lond)

Shell *Ms Sally Louise* •
Head of Business Affairs, Wall to Wall Television Ltd, 8-9 Spring Place, Kentish Town, London NW5 3ER, 0171 485 7424, Fax: 0171 267 5292. Called: July 1989, Gray's Inn, LLB (Lanc)

Shelley *Ms Catherine Jean*
Parliamentary Officer, Church Action on Poverty. Called: Oct 1990, Lincoln's Inn, LLM (Cantab), MA (Cantab)

Shelley *Dr Frederick Charles*
7-27 Heathside, Avalon, Poole, Dorset
BH14 8HT, 01202 707510. Called: Nov
1976, Gray's Inn, MB BS FRCA DA

Shenton *Alan Newman*
Partner, c/o Ernst & Young, Apex Plaza,
Reading RG1 1YE, 01189 500611, Fax:
01189 507744. Called: Nov 1985, Gray's
Inn, LLB(Warwick), FCA, ATII

Shephard *Mrs Carole* •
Company Secretary, Rank Xerox Ltd, The
Parkway, Marlow, Bucks SL7 1YL, 01628
890000, and Member New York Bar.
Called: July 1979, Middle Temple, LLB
(Lond)

Shephard *Ms Judith Catherine* •
Crown Prosecution Service, Severn/Thames
Area, Buckinghamshire Branch, 4-7
Prebendal Court, Oxford Rd, Aylesbury,
Bucks HP19 3EY, 0296 436441. Called: July
1989, Gray's Inn, LLB [Lond], AKC [Lond]

Shepheard *Huw Owen*
Compliance Manager, Insinger Trust (Jersey)
Ltd, P O Box 546, 28-30 The Parade, St
Helier, Jersey JE4 8XY, 01534 636211, Fax:
01534 636215. Called: July 1982, Gray's Inn,
LLB (Hons)

Shepherd *Mrs Amanda Robin*
Called: Nov 1992, Middle Temple, LLB
(Hons)

Shepherd *Miss Joanne Elizabeth*
Called: Oct 1993, Inner Temple, BA, CPE

Shepherd *Miss Johanna Kate*
Public Relations Consultant, Declavy Public
Relations, 3 Northington Street, London
WC1N 2JE, 0171 404 3244, Fax: 0171 404
3233. Called: Oct 1995, Lincoln's Inn, LLB
(Hons)(Lond)

Shepherd *Ms Judith Elizabeth*
Called: Oct 1996, Lincoln's Inn, LLB
(Hons)(Derby)

Sheppard *Miss Caroline Diana
Burnell* •
Chief Adjudicator, Chief Adjudicator,
Parking Committee for London, New
Zealand House, 80 Haymarket, London
SW1Y 4TE, 0171 747 4700, Fax: 0171 747
4848. Called: Nov 1974, Gray's Inn

Sheppard *Samuel Edward Hugh* •
Senior Crown Prosecutor, CPS (London),
Bow Street/Clerkenwell Branch, Portland
House 3rd Floor, Stag Place, London
SW1E 5BH, 0171 915 5700, Fax: 0171 915
5850. Called: July 1976, Gray's Inn

Sheppard *Miss Susannah George
Fullerton* •
Lawyer, Ministry of Agriculture,, Fisheries &
Food, 53 Whitehall, London SW1A 2EY,
0171 270 8349, Fax: 0171 270 8270.
Called: Nov 1994, Lincoln's Inn, BA
(Hons)(Oxon)

Sher *Christopher* •
12A High Street, Slough, Berkshire SL1 1EE,
01753 535577, Fax: 01753 535770.
Called: Nov 1993, Gray's Inn, BA

Shergill *Miss Usha Sita* •
Senior Crown Prosecutor, Crown
Prosecution Service, North London Area,
Harrow Branch 2nd Floor, Kings
House,Kymberley Road, Harrow,Middlesex
HA1 1YH, 0181 424 8688, Fax: 0181 424
9134. Called: July 1984, Gray's Inn, BA
(Hons)(Law)

Sheridan *Brian Dominic George*
Called: Oct 1994, Inner Temple, LLB (Lond),
LLM (Lond)

Sheridan *Iain Douglas*
Called: Nov 1997, Inner Temple, BA (Staffs),
MSc (LSE)

Sherlock *Peter Anthony*
Clerk to the Justices/Justices Chief
Executive, Calderdale P.S.D., Justices'
Clerk's Office, PO Box 32, Harrison Road,
Halifax HX1 2AN, 01422 360695, Fax:
01422 347874. Called: Apr 1986, Middle
Temple, Dip in Magisterial, Law

Sherlock *Miss Samatha Frances*
Pollonais & Blanc, 62 Sackville Street, Port
of Spain, Trinidad, 623-5461, Fax: 625-8415,
and Member Trinidad & Tobago Bar.
Called: July 1995, Gray's Inn, LLB (Warks)

Sherrard *Michael David QC (1968)*
Director of Middle Temple Advocacy, Also
Inn of Court I. Called: June 1949, Middle
Temple, LLB (Lond), F.R.S.A.

Sherratt *Peter Robert* •
Legal Director, Board Director & Company
Secretary, Lehman Brothers Group, 1
Broadgate, London EC2M 7HA, 0171 260
3132, Fax: 0171 260 2882. Called: July
1985, Inner Temple, BA (Oxon), LLM
(Cantab)

Sheth *Pranlal CBE*
Company Secretary Executive Director -
Legal Div, 70 Howberry Road, Edgware,
Middlesex HA8 6SY, 0181 952 2413, Fax:
0181 952 5332. Called: July 1962, Lincoln's
Inn, F.Inst.M., F.Inst.D.

Shewaram *Ms Harsha*
Called: Nov 1995, Middle Temple, BA
(Hons)(Manch)

Shi *Miss Xiao-Cong*
Legal Assistant, 5 Chancery Lane, Clifford's
Inn, London EC4A 1BU, 0171 320 6886,
Fax: 0171 320 6070. Called: July 1994,
Lincoln's Inn, LLB (Hons), BA (Hons)

Shiacolas *Menelaos*
Called: Nov 1995, Lincoln's Inn, LLB
(Hons)(Kent), LLM

Shields *Mrs Janice Rhian*
Called: Oct 1993, Inner Temple, LLB
(Manch)

Shields *Leslie Stuart QC (1970)*
Recorder, Devereux Chambers, Devereux
Court, London, WC2R 3JJ. Called: Jan 1948,
Middle Temple, BA (Oxon)

Shin *Miss Su Wen*
and Member Hong Kong. Called: July 1996,
Lincoln's Inn, LLB (Hons)(LSE)

Shine *Miss Clare Camilla*
37 Rue Erlanger, 75016 Paris, France, (33 1)
46 51 90 11, Fax: (33 1) 46 51 90 11.
Called: Nov 1988, Middle Temple, BA
(Oxon), Dip Law (Central), D.E.A. (Paris)

Shiner *David Colin* •
Legal Advisor, Suffolk County Council, St
Helen Court, County Hall, Ipswich IP4 2JS,
01473 264147, Fax: 01473 214549.
Called: Nov 1990, Middle Temple, BSc
(Hons)

Shipman *Anthony Michael*
Called: July 1992, Middle Temple, BA
(Hons) (Bristol), LLB (Hons) (Lond)

Shivaprasad *Suvarna Sudarshan*
5 South Side, Stamford Brook, London
W6 0XY, Attorney at Law, Republic of
Trinidad & Tobago and Member Trinidad &
Tobago Bar. Called: Nov 1987, Lincoln's
Inn, BA (Canada), LLB (Lond), LLM (Lond)

Shoderu *Ms Aderonke Olayinka*
Senior Lecturer Commercial & Int'l Law,
The Business School, Stapleton House,
University of North London, 277-281
Holloway Road, London N7 8HN, 0171 607
2789, Fax: 0171 852 8871. Called: July
1997, Lincoln's Inn, BA (Hons)

Shorts *Edwin Michael*
Called: Nov 1989, Lincoln's Inn, MA (Dub),
Dip Law

Shoulders *Paul*
Deputy Clerk to the Justices, Lincolnshire
Magistrates Court, 358 High Street, Lincoln
LN5 7QA, 01522 528218, Fax: 01522
560139. Called: Feb 1988, Middle Temple,
Dip Mag Law, Dip Law, Dip in Management,
Studies

Shour *Miss Rima Fouad*
Called: July 1988, Gray's Inn, LLB (LSE)

Shrimplin *Miss Katherine Anne* •
Grade 6, Dept of Trade & Industry,
Solicitor's Office, Legal Services:
Prosecutions, Room 423, 10-18 Victoria
Street, London SW1H 0NN, 0171 215 3203,
Fax: 0171 215 3235. Called: July 1984,
Middle Temple, LLB (Lond)

Shroff *Cyrus* •
Principal Crown Prosecutor, Crown
Prosecution Service, 1st Floor, County
House, 100 New London Road, Chelmsford,
Essex CM2 0RG, 01245 252939, Fax: 01245
490476. Called: July 1983, Gray's Inn, BA

Shroff *Mrs Kaiser Deepak*
P O Box 250, Penta Court, Borehamwood,
Herts WD6 1DW. Called: July 1988,
Lincoln's Inn, LLB, LLM (Hons), Bombay,
BSc (Hons) Baroda

Shropshire *Miss Alison Elizabeth
Mary* •
Employment Law & Policy Adviser, BAA Plc,
Group Personnel Dept, Heathrow Point,
234 Bath Road, Harlington, Middlesex
UB3 5AP, 0181 745 7342. Called: Nov 1979,
Lincoln's Inn, BA (CNAA),LLM (Lond)

Shucksmith *Thomas Sykes*
Shucksmith & Co., Consulting Actuaries, Lincoln House, Nutley Lane, Reigate, Surrey RH2 9HP, 01737 222011, Fax: 01737 222130. Called: July 1977, Lincoln's Inn, MA (Cantab), FIA, F.P.M.I

Shukla *Ms Vina*
Davis Polk & Wardwell, 450 Lekington Avenue, New York NY 10017, (212) 450 4291, Fax: (212) 450 4800, and Member New York. Called: Nov 1992, Gray's Inn, MA (Cantab), BCL

Shulman *Mark Bernard* •
Litigation Group Leader, Legal Services, Kent County Council, County Hall, Maidstone, Kent ME14 1XQ, 01622 694394. Called: July 1981, Middle Temple

Shum *Cheuk Yum*
24th Floor, Shum Tower, 268 Des Voeux Road, Sheung Wan, (852)2805 2730, Fax: (852)2851 2266, and Member Hong Kong Bar. Called: June 1959, Middle Temple, LLB (Lond)

Shum *Ka Hei*
Called: July 1996, Middle Temple, BSSc (Hons), (Hong Kong), CPE (Staffs)

Shuster *Robert Anthony* •
Senior Crown Prosecutor (p/t) Senior Lecturer Inns of Court School of law Independent Member Central Rail Users Consultative Committee, Crown Prosecution Service, Beaumont House, Cliftonville, Northampton NN1 5BE, 01604 230220, Fax: 01604 232081, Council of Legal Education, Inns of Court School of Law, 39 Eagle Street, London, 0171 404 5787. Called: July 1988, Middle Temple, LLB (Hons), BA

Sia *Edmund Wei Keong*
Called: July 1996, Lincoln's Inn, LLB (Hons)(Warw)

Sia *Miss Pebble Huei-Chieh*
Called: July 1996, Middle Temple, LLB (Hons)(Lond)

Siah *Miss Karen Wei Kuan*
Called: Nov 1996, Middle Temple, LLB (Hons)(Sheff)

Siak *Miss Diane Chi-Yi*
Messrs Allen & Gledhill, 36 Robinson Road, [H]18-01 City House, Singapore 068877, (65) 225 1611, Fax: (65) 224 1574, and Member Singapore Bar. Called: July 1994, Middle Temple, BA (Hons)(Oxon)

Siani *Paul Anthony* •
Company Director, 304 St Pauls Road, London N1 2LH, 0171 359 3669. Called: May 1997, Inner Temple, LLB (Wales)

Sibbles *Miss Geraldine Jane*
Legal Team Manager, Bradford Magistrates' Court, City Courts, The Tyrls, Bradford, W Yorkshire BD1 1JL, 01274 390111, Fax: 01274 391731. Called: Nov 1979, Gray's Inn

Siddondo *Miss Camilla Dorothy Adhiambo*
Called: July 1995, Lincoln's Inn, LLB (Hons)

Sidhu *Miss Anup Kaur*
Called: Mar 1998, Lincoln's Inn, B.Econ (Australia), LLB (Hons)(Lond), LLM (Lond)

Sidhu *Bhupinder Kaur*
Called: Mar 1998, Gray's Inn, BA (Leics), LL.B., LLM (Bucks)

Sidhu *Ms Citran Sheila Sarjit*
Called: Nov 1994, Gray's Inn, LLB

Sidhu *Mr Daljit Singh*
M/S Y H Goh & Co, 101 Upper Cross Street, [H]05-40 People's Park Centre, Singapore 0105, 535 9022/535 6641, Fax: 538 4313, and Member Singapore Bar. Called: July 1990, Middle Temple, LLB (Lond)

Sidhu *Ravi* •
Senior Crown Prosecutor, Crown Prosecution Service, Eaton Court, Oxford Road, Reading, Berkshire. Called: Feb 1988, Inner Temple, LLB (Lancaster)

Sidhu *Sarjeet Singh*
Messrs Gill & Tang, Room 228, 2nd Floor, Campbell Complex, jalan Dang Wangi, 50100 Kuala Lumpur Malaysia, 03 2924266, Fax: 03 2910413, and Member Malaysian Bar. Called: Nov 1992, Gray's Inn, LLB (So'ton)

Siew *Miss Anne Eee Peng*
Called: Nov 1995, Lincoln's Inn, LLLB (Hons), LLM (Dunelm)

Siew *Miss Li-Lian*
Legal Advisor, M/S K M Chye & Partners, Advocates & Solicitors, 6th Floor, UBN Tower, Letter Box 163, Jalan P Ramlee, 50250 Kuala Lumpur, (603) 2388055, Fax: (603) 2019300, and Member Malaysia. Called: July 1995, Lincoln's Inn, BCL

Siew *Miss Yvonne*
Called: Nov 1997, Lincoln's Inn, LLB (Hons)(Wales)

Silcock *Ian Peter*
Called: Oct 1997, Middle Temple, LLB (Hons)(Lond)

Silman *Stephen Anthony*
Director, Barclays Private Bank Limited, 59 Grosvenor Street, London W1X 9DA, 0171 487 2000, Fax: 0171 487 2040. Called: Nov 1974, Middle Temple, MA (Oxon)

Silver *Richard Norman*
Legal Advisor, Alway Associates, Howard House, The Runway, South Ruislip, Middlesex HA4 6SG, 0181 842 0028, Fax: 0181 842 0003. Called: July 1997, Gray's Inn, LLB (Lond), ADBM, MCIOB

Silvera *Wayne Delano*
Clayton Morgan & Co, 59 Church Street, Kingston, Montego Bay, (876) 952 1800/979 1733, Fax: (876) 952 1514, and Member Jamaican. Called: July 1996, Lincoln's Inn, LLB (Hons), BSc (Hons)

Silvester *John Darragh Mostyn*
Advocate of High Court - Kenya, Uganda & Tanzania, Lenana Forest Centre, Ngong Road, P O Box 24397, Nairobi, 254 2 567515/566970, Fax: 254 2 564945. Called: June 1958, Inner Temple, MA (Hons) (Oxon), ACIA (Lond)

Silwaraju *Miss Hemalatha*
Called: July 1997, Middle Temple, LLB (Hons)(Wales)

Sim *Miss Annabelle Seu Cheun*
Called: July 1997, Lincoln's Inn, LLB (Hons)(Leics)

Sim *Chee Siong*
Called: Nov 1995, Middle Temple, LLB (Hons)

Sim *Geoffrey Poh Leong*
c/o Mesrs. Sandhu & Co, Suites 6, 7 & 8, 5th Floor, Badiah Complex, Kim 2, Jalan Tutong, 673 2 220783, Fax: 673 2 241237. Called: July 1993, Lincoln's Inn, LLB (Hons)

Sim *Hwang Hwa*
Called: July 1995, Lincoln's Inn, LLB (Hons)

Sim *Miss Hwee Ai*
Called: July 1994, Middle Temple, LLB (Hons)(Lond)

Sim *Mrs Lai Yin*
Blk 13, Holland Avenue, [H]07-62, 7605729. Called: July 1994, Lincoln's Inn, LLB (Hons)

Sim *Miss Lay Bee*
Messrs Shahriza,Varegheeses &, Chandran, No 119a Jalan Gasing, 1st Floor, Petaling Jaya 46000, Selangor, Malaysia, 03 7565299/ 177, Fax: 03 7572655, and Member Malaysia Bar. Called: July 1992, Inner Temple, LLB

Sim *Miss Sok Nee*
Called: Nov 1997, Lincoln's Inn, LLB (Hons)(Wales)

Sim *Miss Sok See*
Chorpee Anwarul & Co, Suite 8-16-6 Level 16, Menara Olympia, 8 Jalan Raja Chulan, 50200 Kuala Lumpur, 010603 2022566, Fax: 010603 2022577, and Member Malaysia Bar. Called: July 1994, Lincoln's Inn, LLB (Hons)

Sim *Yuan Meng*
Called: July 1994, Lincoln's Inn, LLB (Hons)

Simmance *Alan James Francis*
Route De Mucelle, 01630 Challex, 04 (50) 563511, and Member Kenya Bar. Called: July 1957, Inner Temple, BA, FCIS, FIM

Simmonds *Andrew John* •
Arthur Young, Rolls House, 7 Rolls Buildings, Fetter Lane, London EC4A 1NH, 0171 831 7130, Fax: 0171 405 2147. Called: Nov 1986, Gray's Inn, LLB(Hons)

Simmonds *John Andrew*
Court Clerk, Manchester City Magistrates, Court, Crown Square, Manchester M60 1PR, 0161 832 7272, Fax: 0161 832 5421. Called: Nov 1991, Inner Temple, LLB (Manch)

Simmons *Everard Barclay*
Called: Mar 1997, Gray's Inn, LLB (Kent)

Simmons *Mrs Patterson Carr*
Principal Lecturer in Law, Middlesex University, The Burroughs, London NW4 4BT, 0181 362 5000, Fax: 0181 202 1539. Called: July 1983, Gray's Inn, MA, LLB, LLM

E

Simmons *Ronald*
Burley Gate, 54 Coggeshall Road, Earls Colne, Essex CO6 2JR, 01787 222715. Called: July 1966, Inner Temple, LLB, FCII

Simms *Miss Sonia Angela*
Called: Nov 1993, Middle Temple, BSc (Hons), Dip in Law (City)

Simon *Miss Dale Inez* •
Crown Prosecutor, Crown Prosecution Service, 1/9 Romford Road, Stratford, London E15, 0181 534 6601. Called: Nov 1986, Inner Temple, LLB

Simons *Charles*
Flat 8, 16 THe Ridgeway, Enfield, Middlesex EN2 8QH, 0181 367 5731. Called: Nov 1950, Inner Temple, PH.D,BSc

Simons *Gary Peter*
Called: Nov 1995, Gray's Inn, BA (Keele),MA (Lond), MA (E.Anglia)

Simpson *Professor Alfred William Brian*
36 High Street, Wingham, Canterbury, Kent CT3 1AB, 01227 720 979. Called: Oct 1994, Gray's Inn, MA, F.B.A., F.A.A.A.S., DCL

Simpson *Anthony Maurice Herbert TD*
Avenue Michel-Ange 57, 1000 Brussels, Belgium, (00 322) 7364219, Fax: (00 322) 7339404, European Civil Servant. Called: Feb 1961, Inner Temple, MA, LLM

Simpson *Miss Carol Monica*
Called: Mar 1998, Gray's Inn, LLB (Thames)

Simpson *Charles James Geraint*
C/O J A Hassan & Partners, 57-63 Line Wall Road, 00 350 79000, Fax: 00 350 79166, and Member Gibraltar Bar. Called: Oct 1996, Middle Temple, BA (Hons)(B'ham), CPE (Westminster)

Simpson *Mrs Christine Ffoulkes* •
Legal Advisor, Pioneer LDCE Ltd, Pioneer House, Hollybush Hill, Stoke Poges SL2 4QP. Called: Nov 1993, Inner Temple, LLB

Simpson *Francis*
40 Weare Court, Baltic Wharf, Bristol BS1 6XF, 0117 927 6668. Called: Nov 1976, Middle Temple, BSc, MCIOB

Simpson *Miss Lydia Caron*
Called: Feb 1993, Lincoln's Inn, LLB, A.T.I.I.

Simpson *Mark Banner*
Called: July 1994, Inner Temple, LLB (Manch)

Simpson *Robert Laver* •
Hewlett-Packard Limited, Cain Road, Bracknell, Berkshire RG12 1HN, 01 344 362214, Fax: 01 344 362224. Called: July 1974, Middle Temple, LLB (Hons)

Simpson *Robert Thompson* •
Crown Prosecution Service, 1-9 Romford Road, Stratford, London E15. Called: Nov 1986, Inner Temple, LLB (Manch)

Simpson *Robin Muschamp Garry QC (1971)*
Called: June 1951, Middle Temple, MA (Cantab)

Simpson *William Peter*
and Member Advocat of Royal Court of Guernsey 11 King's Bench Walk, 1st Floor, Temple, London, EC4Y 7EQ. Called: July 1980, Lincoln's Inn, LLB (Leeds)

Sin *Miss Charlotte Minng Minng*
Called: July 1996, Middle Temple, LLB (Hons)(Hull)

Sin *Miss Li Lian*
Called: July 1996, Lincoln's Inn, LLB (Hons)(Sheff)

Sin *Pui Wah*
Called: Nov 1997, Middle Temple, BSc (Hons,Hong Kong)

Sinai *Ali Reza*
Called: July 1997, Gray's Inn, LLB, LLM, Diplome d'Etudes, Juridiques (Strasbo)

Sinanan *Travers Selden* •
and Member Trinidad & Tobago Bar Association. Called: Nov 1982, Lincoln's Inn, BA Hons

Singaram *Miss Kalai Selvi*
Called: July 1994, Lincoln's Inn, LLB (Hons)

Singh *Ajinderpal*
Called: July 1996, Middle Temple, LLB (Hons)(Leeds)

Singh *Andel*
Messrs Pictons, 13 Town Square, Stevenage, Herts SG1 !BP, 01438 350711, Fax: 01438 359255. Called: July 1987, Middle Temple, LLB

Singh *Mrs Anjali*
Called: July 1994, Gray's Inn, LLB (Bucks)

Singh *Ms Ann-Marie Valerie* •
Asprey Plc, 165-169 New Bond Street, London W1Y 0AR, 0171 493 6767, Fax: 0171 918 8086. Called: July 1986, Gray's Inn, LLB

Singh *Bhajanvir*
and Member Singapore Bar. Called: July 1994, Lincoln's Inn, LLB (Sheff)

Singh *David Hardatt* •
18 Sydney Road, West Ealing, London W13 9EY, 0181 840 0083. Called: Feb 1965, Lincoln's Inn

Singh *Gurcharanjit Dewan*
Called: July 1996, Lincoln's Inn, LLB (Hons)(Lond)

Singh *Gurdeep Sekhon*
Partner, Blk 110 Potong Pasir Avenue 1, [H]06-620, (65) 5383611 (Office), Fax: (65) 5383708, and Member Australia Bar Singapore Bar. Called: Nov 1990, Lincoln's Inn, LLB (Hons) (Wales)

Singh *Herbans*
Called: Nov 1997, Lincoln's Inn, LLB (Hons)(Lond)

Singh *Jagjit Richard* •
Legal Counsel, Lehman Brothers Limited, 1 Broadgate, London EC2M 7HA, 0171 260 2748, Fax: 0171 260 2882. Called: Nov 1994, Gray's Inn, BA

Singh *Jispal*
Called: July 1997, Lincoln's Inn, LLB (Hons)(Lond)

Singh *Kertar*
Called: Feb 1994, Middle Temple, LLB (Hons)(Wolves)

Singh *Kirindeep*
Called: July 1996, Middle Temple, LLB (Leeds)

Singh *Kirpal*
Advocate & Solicitor, Messrs Kalamohan & Kirpal, 101 Cecil Street, Tong Eng Building, [H] 08-07, (65) 227 9377, Fax: (65) 227 8098, and Member Singapore Bar. Called: July 1994, Lincoln's Inn, LLB (Hons)

Singh *Kuldip*
Naidu Ng & Partners, 1 Colombo Court, [H]05-04, 65 3365115, Fax: 65 339610. Called: Nov 1995, Middle Temple, LLB (Hons)(Lond)

Singh *Mrs Kumud* •
Senior Crown Prosecutor, Crown Prosection Service, Priory Gate, Maidstone. Called: Nov 1987, Inner Temple, LLB (Hons), LLM

Singh *Mohan s/o Gurdial Singh*
Block 52, Apt No 04-299, Lengkok Bahru, Singapore 150052, 4727479. Called: July 1995, Lincoln's Inn, LLB (Hons)

Singh *Mohan s/o Kernal Singh*
Called: Nov 1995, Lincoln's Inn, LLB (Hons)(Lond)

Singh *Rajesh Kumar*
Called: Nov 1996, Gray's Inn, BA (Cantab)

Singh *Rajindar*
Block 250, Tampines Street 21, [H]10-520, Singapore 1852, 7810273. Called: Feb 1994, Middle Temple, LLB (Hons)(Lond)

Singh *Rajindar*
Called: July 1994, Lincoln's Inn, LLB (Hons)

Singh *Ranbir*
Called: Oct 1997, Middle Temple, LLB (Hons)(Oxon)

Singh *Ranjit*
Called: July 1993, Middle Temple, LLB (Hons)

Singh *Sarindar*
Called: Nov 1996, Lincoln's Inn, LLB (Hons)

Singh *Sarjeet*
Called: July 1992, Middle Temple, LLB (Hons) (Lond)

Singh *Satwant*
Called: Nov 1995, Middle Temple, LLB (Hons)

Singh *Deo Gobind*
Called: July 1995, Lincoln's Inn, LLB (Hons)

Siohn *Daniel Asher*
Called: May 1997, Inner Temple, BA, LLM, MA (Leeds)

Siow *Miss Hua Lin*
Called: Nov 1995, Middle Temple, LLB (Hons)(Hull)

Siow *Kim Leong*
Called: Nov 1996, Middle Temple, LLB
(Hons)

Siraj *Naeem Mohamed*
Dibb Lupton Alsop, 117 The Headrow,
Leeds LS1 5JX, 0113 2412635, Fax: 0113
2431260. Called: July 1993, Inner Temple,
LLB (Hons)

Sircar *Muhammad Jamiruddin*
Senior Council, Supreme Court Bar, Room
41, Dhaka, Bangladesh, 8802 896883,
Member of Parliament Bangladesh and
Member Supreme Court of Bangladesh.
Called: Nov 1967, Lincoln's Inn, MA, LL.B

Sissoho *Edrisa Mansajang*
Called: Mar 1998, Lincoln's Inn, LLB (Hons)

Sisson-Pell *Mrs Jane Alison* •
Senior Crown Prosecutor, Crown
Prosecution Service, 4-5 South Parade,
Wakefield, 01924 290620, Fax: 01924
369360. Called: July 1984, Lincoln's Inn, BA
(Hons)

Sivagnanam *Rutheran*
Shearn Delamore & Co, No 2 Benteng,
50050 Kuala Lumpur, 2300644, Fax:
2385625, and Member Malaysia. Called: Nov
1994, Lincoln's Inn, LLB (Hons)(Leeds)

Sivagnanaratnam *Sivananthan*
Partner (Since 1/7/97), Messrs Drew &
Napier, 20 Raffles Place, [H]17-00 Ocean
Towers, Singapore 048620, 65 5350733,
Fax: 65 5330694/5330693, Advocate &
Solicitor in Singapore (May 1992)0 and
Member Singapore Bar. Called: July 1991,
Middle Temple, LLB (Hons) (Lond)

Sivalingam *Miss Seetha*
Called: Nov 1996, Middle Temple, LLB
(Hons)(Lond)

Sivaloganathan *Miss Damita Devi*
Called: July 1995, Lincoln's Inn, LLB (Hons)

Sivapiragasam *Miss Rani Christina*
Pernas Otis Elevator Co, Son BHD, 2 Medan
Setia 2, Plaza Damansara, Bukit Damansara,
50490, 03 2554811, Fax: 03 2559684, and
Member Malaysia Bar. Called: Feb 1993,
Lincoln's Inn, LLB (Buck'ham), LLM
(Buck'ham)

Sivasankar *Chelliah*
42 Jalan Bintang, Taman Westpool, Ipoh,
Perak, 05-5489451, Fax: 05-5497311,
Advocate and Solicitor, High Court of
Malaya and Member Malaysian Bar.
Called: Nov 1993, Gray's Inn, LLB

Sivasubramaniam *Miss Kavitha*
Called: Nov 1997, Lincoln's Inn, LLB (Hons)

Sivasubramaniam *Sivaruban*
Called: July 1996, Lincoln's Inn, LLB (Hons)

Sivell *Colin Peter* •
Head of Legal Services, Chief Executive,
Brentwood Council Offices, Brentwood,
Essex CM15 8AY. Called: July 1979, Inner
Temple

Skeen *Colin Jeffrey* •
Group Secretary, The Automobile
Association, Norfolk House, Priestley Road,
Basingstoke, Hants RG24 9NY, 01256
493060. Called: July 1975, Inner Temple,
LLB (Lond)

Skelcher *Gary Stephen* •
Corporate Commercial Adviser, Thames
Water PLC, Commercial Services Group,
Blake House, Manor Farm, Reading, 01734
236689. Called: Mar 1996, Middle Temple,
LLB (Hons)

Skellett *Rupert William Nicholas*
Called: Nov 1996, Gray's Inn, BA (Cantab),
LLB (City)

Skemp *Mrs Sandra Pauline CB*
997 Finchley Road, London NW11 7HB,
0181 455 7335, Fax: 0181 458 2164.
Called: June 1964, Middle Temple, MA, BCL

Skinner *Conor William Richard* •
Senior Legal Adviser, B G plc (International,
Downstream), 100 Thames Valley Park
Drive, Reading, Berkshire RG6 1PT, 0118
929 3697, Pepys' Chambers, 17 Fleet Street,
London, EC4Y 1AA. Called: Nov 1979,
Gray's Inn, MA

Skinner *Miss Sarah Elizabeth*
Called: Nov 1994, Lincoln's Inn, LLB
(Hons)(Lond)

Skyrme *Sir Thomas Charles
KCVO,CB,CBE,TD,DL*
Called: Jan 1935, Inner Temple, MA

Slack *Jason*
Colemans Solicitors, Elisabeth House, 16 St
Peter's Square, Manchester M2 3DF, 0161
228 7393, Fax: 0161 228 7509. Called: Oct
1995, Lincoln's Inn, LLB (Hons)(Anglia)

Slade *Miss Shelagh Patricia* •
Senior Legal Counsel, Oracle Corporation
UK Limited, Oracle Parkway, Thames Valley
Park, Reading, Berkshire RG6 1RA, 0118924
0000, Fax: 0118924 3717. Called: Nov 1985,
Inner Temple, LLB (Lond), LLM (Can

Sladen *Michael*
10 Little Lane, Ely, Cambridge CB6 1AZ.
Called: Feb 1963, Lincoln's Inn, LLB, FCIB

Slaney *Miss Louise Pauline* •
Wiltshire County Council, Chief Executive's
Office, County Hall, Trowbridge, Wiltshire
BA14 8JN, 01225 713062. Called: Nov 1990,
Inner Temple, LLB (Exon)

Slater *Miss Alison Fiona*
Called: Nov 1996, Middle Temple, LLB
(Leics)

Slattery *Peter Anthony*
6 Wonford House, Heath Drive, Walton on
the Hill, Tadworth, Surrey KT20 7QL, 01737
814086, Fax: 01737 814086. Called: July
1957, Middle Temple

Slaughter *Miss Ingrid Elizabeth* •
Assistant Legal Adviser, General Synod of
the Church of, England, Church House,
Great Smith Street, London SW1P 3NZ,
0171 340 0208, Fax: 0171 233 2660.
Called: July 1969, Gray's Inn, LLB (Lond)

Slegg *Kevin Andrew* •
Quantity Surveyor, Project Manager, Drake
& Reynolds, The Old Mill, Mill Lane,
Godalming, Surrey GU7 1EY, 01483 425744,
Fax: 01483 426936. Called: Nov 1996,
Middle Temple, BSc, LLB (Hons), ARICS

Sloma *Albert Abraham*
Ad Hoc Consultant to the Sloma Partnership
UK and Gibraltar, PO Box 555, Gibraltar,
350 79385, Fax: 350 79385. Called: July
1963, Gray's Inn, B.Sc (Eng), FICE, LMRTPI,
FGIS

Smagh *Jerrinder Singh*
Called: Nov 1997, Middle Temple, LLB
(Hons)

Small *Miss Elizabeth Anne*
K.P.M.G. Peat Marwick, 1 Puddledock,
London EC1, 0171 236 8000. Called: Feb
1991, Lincoln's Inn, LLB

Smals *Rufus Alexander Ogilvie* •
Head of Legal Dept., Chairman CBI
Competition Panel, GKN plc, P.O. Box 55,
Ipsley House, Ipsley Church Lane, Redditch,
Worcs B98 OTL, 01527 517715, Fax: 01527
533470. Called: Nov 1973, Middle Temple,
MA (Cantab) Dip Euro, Integration,
(Amsterdam)

Smedley *George Roscoe Relph
Boleyne*
Garden House, Whorlton, Barnard Castle,
Co Durham DL12 8XQ, 01833 627381, also
Inn of Court L. Called: May 1965, Inner
Temple, LLB (Lond)

Smedley *Nicholas Keith*
North Yorkshire Police, Police Station,
North Park Road, Harrogate, North
Yorkshire, (0423) 505541, Fax: (0423)
539313. Called: Nov 1990, Inner Temple,
LLB (Lond)

Smele *Jeffrey Stephen*
External Affairs Executive, Rio Tinto plc, 6
St. James's Square, London SW1Y 4LD, 0171
753 2458, Fax: 0171 3753 2309. Called: July
1995, Middle Temple, B.Met (Hons), C.Eng,
LLB (Hons), M.I.M

Smith *Miss Abigail Jill*
Called: Oct 1996, Inner Temple, LLB (City)

Smith *Alexander Gordon*
334 Walton Road, East Molesey, Surrey
KT8 2JD. Called: July 1980, Gray's Inn, BSc,
PhD, FGS

Smith *Miss Amelie Jane* •
Assistant Contracts Manager, Litton Marine
Systems B.V., U.K. Branch, Burlington
House, 118 Burlington Road, New Malden,
Surrey KT3 4NR, 0181 942 2464/7833 Ext
3851, Fax: 0181 949 1273. Called: Nov
1992, Lincoln's Inn, LLB (Hons)(B'ham)

Smith *Mrs Angela Rosemary*
Senior Court Clerk, Grimsby Magistrates'
Court, The Law Courts, Victoria Street,
Grimsby, North East Lincs DN31 1RD,
01472 320444, Fax: 01472 320440.
Called: July 1986, Middle Temple, BA
(Dunelm)

Smith *Professor Anthony Terry Hanmer*
Deputy Chairman of Cambridge Law Faculty Board Professor of Criminal and Public Laws, Gonville & Caius College, Cambridge CB2 1TA, 01223 332 449, Fax: 01223 332 456, Fellow of Gonville & Caius College, Cambridge and Member New Zealand Bar. Called: May 1992, Middle Temple, PhD (Cantab), LLM (Cantuar)(New, Zealand)

Smith *Benjamin Michael*
Called: Oct 1997, Inner Temple, LLB (Bristol)

Smith *Carl Neville* •
Health Safety & Environmental Advisor, P & O Road Tanks Ltd, Station House, Stanford New Road, Altrincham, Cheshire WA14 1ER, 0161 928 4884, Fax: 0161 926 9613. Called: Nov 1990, Inner Temple, LLB

Smith *Ms Carol Marie*
Called: Nov 1997, Inner Temple, LLB (Lond)

Smith *Miss Charmaine Natasha*
Called: July 1997, Gray's Inn, BA (Canada), LLB (Lond)

Smith *Cornelius Leo*
Legal Assistant, 14 Fairholme Road, West Kensington, London W14 9JX, 0171 381 8083. Called: July 1974, Inner Temple, BCL

Smith *Miss Damask Mary*
Called: July 1997, Middle Temple, LLB (Hons)

Smith *David Martin*
Director, Jacob White (Packaging) Ltd, Unit F, Riverside Industrial, Estate, Riverside Way, Dartford, Kent DA1 5BY. Called: July 1981, Inner Temple, LLB (Wales), ACIS

Smith *David McLeod*
Called: Oct 1996, Inner Temple, LLB (City)

Smith *Derek Owen*
7 Dartmouth Row, London SE10 8AW, 0181 692 1463. Called: Nov 1962, Inner Temple, MA (Cantab)

Smith *Duncan Graeme* •
Legal Officer, Serious Fraud House, 3rd Floor, Elm House, 10-16 Elm Street, London WC1X OBJ, 0171 239 7355, Fax: 0171 713 7708. Called: July 1989, Gray's Inn, LLB (Hons) (Lanc), Dip E.I. (Amsterdam)

Smith *Mrs Eirlys Morven Sheena Lloyd*
Part Time Chairman Social Security Appeal Tribunal, Disabilites Tribunal, Advocates Library, Parliament House, Parliament Square, Edinburgh, Scotland, 0131 226 5071, Scottish Advocate. Called: Apr 1991, Middle Temple, LLB (Edin)

Smith *Geoffrey*
Arbitrator Expert Witness Adjudicator, Conciliator, BP13, 78113 Bourdonne, 134871746, Fax: 134871751. Called: Feb 1995, Middle Temple, BSc (Loughborough), LLDip, CDipAF, CEng, FICE, ACIArb

Smith *Graham Stuart*
Deputy Clerk to the Justices, Tameside Magistrates' Courts, Henry Square, Ashton under Lyne, Tameside OL6 7TP, 0161 330 2023, Fax: 0161 343 1498. Called: July 1973, Gray's Inn, LLB (Lond), DMS, MA

Smith *Grant Ian Graham*
Called: Mar 1998, Gray's Inn, LLB (Leeds)

Smith *Dr Harry*
65 Meriden Road, Hampton in Arden, Solihull, West Midlands B92 OBS, and Member Victoria Bar. Called: Nov 1957, Gray's Inn, BA, LLB, MA, PhD

Smith *James Arthur*
Trainee Accountant, Coopers & Lybrand, 1 Embankment Place, London, 0171 583 5000. Called: Oct 1994, Inner Temple, LLB (Hons)(E.Ang)

Smith *Jeffrey Prowse*
37 Alderbrook Road, Solihull, W Midlands B91 1NW. Called: June 1951, Inner Temple, MA

Smith *Jeremy James Russell*
Director, Local Government International, Bureau, 35 Great Smith Street, London SW1P 3BJ, 0171 664 3100, Fax: 0171 664 3128. Called: July 1969, Lincoln's Inn, BA (Cantab)

Smith *Miss Jessica Clare* •
Employed Barrister, Advises the Chief,Adjudication Officer, Dept of Health & Social, Security, New Court, 48 Carey Street, London WC2A 2LS, 0171 412 1372, Fax: 0171 412 1220. Called: Oct 1992, Middle Temple, BA (Hons, Dunelm), Diploma in Law

Smith *Leslie William*
Called: Mar 1997, Inner Temple, BA, CPE

Smith *Miss Lisa Imogen* •
Called: Oct 1994, Lincoln's Inn, LLB (Hons)(Lond)

Smith *Miss Lorna Marie*
Called: Oct 1997, Middle Temple, BA (Hons)(Lond), CPE (Manc)

Smith *Miss Louise Anne*
Tax Consultant, KPMG, Heritage Court, 41 Athol Street, Douglas, 01624 681000. Called: Nov 1994, Lincoln's Inn, LLB (Hons)

Smith *Mrs Marisa*
Called: July 1982, Middle Temple, BA (Exon)

Smith *Mark Andrew*
Called: Feb 1995, Lincoln's Inn, BSc (Salford), LLB (Hons)(Manc)

Smith *Mark Winton* •
Legal Adviser to the Certification Officer for Trade Unions & Employers' Associations, Solicitor's Office, Department of Trade & Industry, 10 Victoria Street, London SW1H ONN, 0171 215 3326, Fax: 0171 215 3141. Called: July 1982, Middle Temple, BA (Dunelm)

Smith *Martin Lloyd*
Rowe & Maw, 20 Blackfriars Lane, London EC4V 6HD, 0171 248 4282. Called: Oct 1996, Middle Temple, BA (Hons) (Oxon)

Smith *Mrs Mary Edwina Elizabeth*
Called: July 1980, Lincoln's Inn, LLB

Smith *Miss Mary-Emma*
Called: Nov 1991, Inner Temple, MA (Cantab), Dip Law

Smith *Matthew James* •
Barlow, Lyde & Gilbert. Called: Oct 1993, Middle Temple, BA (Hons)(Oxon)

Smith *Miss Megan Emma*
Called: Oct 1994, Lincoln's Inn, LLB (Hons)(Wales)

Smith *Dr Michael Robert* •
Grade 7 Lawyer, Dept of the Environment, Transport & the Regions, Zone 8/F8 Eland House, Bressenden Place, London SW1P 3EB, 0171 890 4785, Fax: 0171 890 4782. Called: Nov 1987, Gray's Inn, MA, PhD (Cantab), Dip Law (City)

Smith *Michael Steven* •
Legal Adviser, Yoshiko Records, Great Westwood, Old House Lane, Kings Langley, Hertfordshire WD4 9AD, 01923 261545. Called: Oct 1995, Middle Temple, BA (Hons)

Smith *Miss Monica Frances*
Called: Oct 1996, Inner Temple, LLB (Lond)

Smith *Murray Lorne*
Essex Court Chambers, 24 Lincoln's Inn Fields, London, WC2A 3ED. Called: May 1990, Middle Temple, LL.B., LL.M.

Smith *Mr. Neal Trevor*
Called: Oct 1996, Inner Temple, LLB (Buck'ham)

Smith *The Hon Mr Justice Neville Leroy*
Member of Bars of Barbados and the Bahamas Justice of the Supreme Court of the Bahamas Formerly a solicitor of England and of Barbados. Called: July 1991, Lincoln's Inn

Smith *Dr Peter Michael*
Faculty of Law, Amory Building, Rennes Drive, Exeter EX4 4RJ, 0392 263263, Fax: 0392 263196. Called: Feb 1993, Lincoln's Inn, LLB & Ph.D (Sheff)

Smith *Peter Stanley* •
Consultant, Old Gold Script Services, An Cala House, 10 Kingsfold Close, Billingshurst, West Sussex RH14 9HG, 01403 782853, Fax: 01403 782796. Called: July 1980, Middle Temple, LLB (Hons)

Smith *Peter Vivian Henworth CB*
Legal Advisor to the Broadcasting Standards Council, Likabula, 14 St Albans Road, Clacton on Sea, Essex CO15 6BA, 01255 422053. Called: Feb 1953, Lincoln's Inn, MA, BCL (Oxon)

Smith *Ralph Clovis Henniker*
Called: Jan 1949, Gray's Inn, MA

Smith *Richard Vernon*
Director of Marketing (UK) Ltd, Onyx UK
Ltd, Onyx House, Mile End Road, London
E3, 0181 983 1000. Called: Nov 1977,
Middle Temple, BSc Econ

Smith *Roger Paul Radford FRGS*
Chairman, Who Cares? Trust Deputy
Chairman, Hounslow Police Consultative
Committee Financial Correspondent
Counsel Magazine Since 1996, Radford
Smith Financial, Services Limited, 46
Chiswick High Road, London W4 1SZ, 0181
995 8351, Fax: 0181 995 2488. Called: July
1975, Middle Temple, LLB (Lond)

Smith *Ronald Henry*
Part-time Chairman Independent Tribunal
Service, 22 High Oaks, Southgate, Crawley,
W Sussex RH11 8PJ, 01293 527373.
Called: June 1955, Gray's Inn, LLB

Smith *Mrs Sara Margaret* •
Senior Crown Prosecutor, 7 Denwick
Terrace, Tynemouth, Tyne & Wear
NE30 2SG, 0191 296 3489. Called: Nov
1982, Gray's Inn, BA

Smith *Miss Sarah Anne*
c/o Callenders & Co, One Millars Court,
P.O.Box 7117, Nassau, Bahamas, 809 322
2511, Fax: 809 326 7666, and Member
Bahamas. Called: Oct 1994, Middle Temple,
LLB (Hons)(Bucks)

Smith *Sean Michael*
Called: Oct 1994, Gray's Inn, LLB

Smith *Stephen Vernon* •
Branch Crown Prosecutor, Crown
Prosecution Service, 2nd Floor, Blackburn
House, Midway, Newcastle-under Lyme
ST5 1TB. Called: Nov 1969, Inner Temple,
LLB (Lond)

Smith *Timothy Paul*
Deputy Chief Clerk, Inner London
Magistrates', Courts Service, Greenwich
Magistrates' Court, 9-10 Blackheath Road,
London SE10 8PG. Called: July 1983, Middle
Temple, BA (Lond) BSc, (Hull) Dip Law,
LLM (Lond), MSC (Lond)

Smith *William Harold*
Called: Nov 1994, Middle Temple, LLB
(Hons)

Smith-Hughes *Miss Alexandra Marika
Niki* •
Senior Legal Assistant, Crown Prosecution
Service, 50 Ludgate Hill, London EC4M 7EX,
0171 273 8361, Fax: 0171 273 8450.
Called: July 1975, Inner Temple, LLB (Leeds)

Smith-Jones *John Anthony*
Clerk to the Justices, Dyfed Magistrates
Courts, 4/5 Quay Street, Carmathen, Dyfed
SA31 3JT, 01267 221658, Fax: 01267
221812. Called: Feb 1987, Gray's Inn

Smithard *Ms Jane Caroline
Grantham* •
Company Secretary & Legal Counsel, Micro
Focus Ltd, 26 West St, Newbury, Berks,
01635 32646, Fax: 01635 33966.
Called: July 1982, Middle Temple, BA Hons,
FCI Arb

Smithburn *Professor John Eric*
Notre Dame Law School, Notre Dame,
Indiana 46556, U.S.A, 219 631 5865, and
Member Indiana Bar, USA 1 Mitre Ct Bldgs,
Ground Floor, Temple, London, EC4Y 7BS.
Called: July 1989, Middle Temple, BS, MA,
JD

Smithers *Miss Amelia Frances Otway*
CH-6921 Vico Morcote, Switzerland, 41-91-
9961692, Fax: 41-91-9961692, and Member
Turks & Caicos Islands Bar. Called: Oct
1991, Inner Temple, BA (Lond), Dip Law

Smithies *Miss Emma Claire*
Called: Nov 1997, Middle Temple, BSc
(Hons)(Herts)

Smouha *Derrick Maurice*
32 Chemin des Crets-de-Champel, 1206
Geneva, (00) 41 22/347 05 18, Fax: (00) 41
22/346 15 16. Called: Nov 1962, Lincoln's
Inn, MA (Cantab)

Smout *Mrs Ann Susan*
Called: July 1988, Gray's Inn, BA (Lond)

Smyth *John Jackson QC (1979)*
Director of Zambesi Ministries, PO Box CH
210, Chisipite, Harare, 490561, Fax: 494127.
Called: July 1965, Inner Temple, MA, LLB
(Cantab)

Smyth *Mrs Philippa Jane*
Kersey's Solicitors, 32 Lloyd Avenue,
Ipswich, Suffolk IP1 3HD, 01473 213311,
Fax: 01473 257739. Called: May 1995,
Lincoln's Inn, LLB (Hons)

Snell *John Bernard*
Managing Director, Romney Hythe &,
Dymchurch Railway, New Romney, Kent
TN28 8PL, 01797 362353, Fax: 01797
363591. Called: Nov 1971, Lincoln's Inn, BA
(Oxon)

Soanes *Marcus Robert*
Lecturer at the ICSL. Called: Oct 1991,
Lincoln's Inn, BA (Hons), MA (Lond), Dip
Law

Soar *Kiran*
Called: Oct 1997, Inner Temple, LLB (Lond)

Soar *Miss Rebecca Jane*
Called: Nov 1996, Gray's Inn, LLB (Nott'm)

Sodha *Babubhai Nanjibhai*
Senior Court Clerk, Bradford Magistrates'
Cts Comm, The Tyrls, Bradford, W
Yorkshire BD1 1JL, 01274 390111, Fax:
01274 391731. Called: Nov 1964, Inner
Temple

Sofat *Sushil Kumar Baburam* •
Regulatory Control Consultant Legal Adviser
BPCA. Legal Advisor SFHT, 44 Greenacres,
Leverstock Green, Hemel Hempstead, Herts
HP2 4NA, 01442 257579, Fax: 01442
257579. Called: July 1960, Lincoln's Inn,
BSc Hons, BSc Tech, C.Chem, F.R.S.C

Sofowora *Mrs Paula Bolanle*
Called: Oct 1993, Inner Temple, BA
(Nigeria), LLB (Lond)

Soh *Miss Diana Wei Yi*
Called: July 1995, Middle Temple, LLB
(Hons) (Warw)

Solomon *Daniel Iestyn* •
Crown Prosecution Service, River Park
House, 225 High Road, Woodgreen, London
N22 4HQ. Called: Oct 1996, Gray's Inn, BA
(Oxon)

Solomon *Steven Jack Sido Feller*
3 Briary Close, Fellows Road, London
NW3 3JZ, 0171 586 8156. Called: July 1978,
Gray's Inn, LLB (Belfast) MSc, (Lond), MSI

Somen *Michael Lewis*
Commissioner for Oaths Notary Public,
Hamilton Harrison & Matthews, ICEA
Building, Kenyatta Avenue, P.O. Box 30333,
Nairobi Kenya, 254 2 330870, Fax: 254 2
222318, Advocate High Court of Kenya and
Member Kenya. Called: Feb 1961, Gray's
Inn, MA (Oxon)

Somerville *Andrew Alexander*
KPMG Peat Marwick, 1 Puddle Dock,
Blackfriars, London EC4V, 0171 311 2583,
Fax: 0171 311 2902. Called: Oct 1993,
Lincoln's Inn, MA (Hons)(Edin), Dip in Law
(Lond)

Somerville *Miss Rachel*
Called: Mar 1996, Lincoln's Inn, LLB (Hons)

Somu *Retana Vellu Palani*
Called: July 1995, Gray's Inn, LLB (Lond)

Soo *Kok Loong*
M/S Peter Lo & Co, Chartered Bank
Chambers, P O Box 683, 90707 Sandakan,
Sabah, Malaysia, (089) 216222, Fax: (089)
271080, and Member Advocate of the High
Court in Sabah & Sarawak, Malaysia.
Called: Nov 1992, Inner Temple, BA (Keele)

Soo *Kwok Leung*
1320 Prince's Building, Central, Hong Kong,
and Member Hong Kong Bar. Called: July
1995, Gray's Inn, BSc (Hong Kong), LLB
(Lond), C.Eng, MIStractE, MICE, MHKIE,
RPE, ACIArb

Soo *Ms Sheagan*
Messrs Soo Thien Ming &, Nashrah, No 1,
1st Floor, Jalan SS2/55, 47300 Petaling, Jaya,
03-7748763, Fax: 03-7744314. Called: July
1995, Gray's Inn, LLB (Middx)

Soo *Miss Wai Leng*
Called: July 1995, Lincoln's Inn, LLB (Hons)

Soon *Eric Boon Teck*
Called: July 1994, Lincoln's Inn, LLB (Hons)

Soon *Miss Vivienne Wen Pin*
Called: July 1995, Lincoln's Inn, LLB (Hons)

Soosai *Joseph Arokianathan* •
Senior Court Clerk, Havering Magistrates'
Court, The Court House, Main Road,
Romford, Essex RM1 3BH, 01708 771741,
Fax: 01708 47947. Called: July 1987,
Lincoln's Inn, BA (Hons)

Soquar *Miss Ruta Woldehaimanot*
Called: July 1997, Inner Temple, LLB
(Dunelm)

Soraya *Ms Raja Eileen*
Called: Oct 1994, Inner Temple, LLB (Lond)

Sotunde Miss Marie-Therese Olufunmilayo Ngo •
Associate Director, Tokyo-Mitsubishi Intl plc, 6 Broadgate, London EC2M 2AA, 0171 577 2813, Fax: 0171 782 9145. Called: July 1988, Middle Temple, BA (Hons) (Essex)

Southcombe Alan Melville
Called: July 1983, Gray's Inn, BA (Leic)

Southern Raymond Joseph
Called: Oct 1997, Middle Temple, LLB (Hons)(Leeds)

Southworth Miss Jean May QC (1973)
Part Time Chairman, Police Discipline & Misuse of Drugs Act Appeal Committee. Called: Feb 1954, Gray's Inn, MA (Oxon)

Souza-Lewis Malcolm Jason •
Snr Lecturer Maritime Law, London Guildhall University, 84 Moorgate, London EC2M 8SQ, 0171 320 1000. Called: July 1986, Inner Temple, MA, B.Sc, Master Mariner

Sowemimo Miss Efunike Kofoworola Aduni
Called: July 1994, Middle Temple, LLB (Hons)(Bucks), LLM (Lond)

Sower Mrs Patricia Ann •
Crown Prosecutor, Crown Prosecution Service, St Georges House, Lever Road, Wolverhampton, West Midlands. Called: Nov 1986, Middle Temple, LLB (Wolv)

Sowerby Ms Helen Jane
Called: Nov 1994, Middle Temple, BA (Hons)

Sparks Ms Paula Denise
Called: Oct 1994, Gray's Inn, LLB

Speak Richard Gibson •
Legal Negotiator, Barclays De Zoete Wedd, Legal Ebbgate House, 2 Swan Lane, London EC3R 3TS, 0171 775 6752. Called: Nov 1992, Inner Temple, LLB

Spear Christopher Mark
201-140 King Street, Peterborough, Ontario, Canada K93 728, 705-7412144, Fax: 705-7412712, and Member Ontario, Canada. Called: July 1981, Middle Temple, BA, Dip Law, LLB

Speck Christopher John •
BT Group Commerciasl Contracts, St Martins House, Britannia Street, Leeds LS12 2DZ, 0113 246 6115, Fax: 0113 246 6142. Called: Oct 1996, Lincoln's Inn, BSc (Hons)(Manc)

Speck Jonathan Paul
Messrs Mourant du Feu & Jeune, Advocates & Solicitors, 18 Grenville Street, St Helier, Jersey,Channel Islands, 01534 609000, Fax: 01534 609333, and Member Jersey Eighteen Carlton Crescent, Southampton, SO15 2XR. Called: Nov 1990, Middle Temple, LLB (Exon)

Speed David Mervyn
Clerk to the Justices, Bristol Magistrates' Court, P.O.Box 107, Nelson Street, Bristol BS99 7BJ, 0117 943 5100. Called: Nov 1976, Middle Temple, MA (Oxon)

Speed Sir Robert CB QC (1963)
6 Upper Culham, Wargrave, Reading, Berkshire RG10 8NR, 01491 574271. Called: Jan 1928, Inner Temple, MA

Spence Lt Cdr Andrei Barry RN •
Royal Naval Officer, SLA to FOST, Grenville Block, HMS Drake, Devonport, Plymouth PL2 2BG. Called: Oct 1993, Middle Temple, BSc (Hons)(Aston), CPE (Lond)

Spence Joseph Desmond
51 Stradbroke Grove, Buckhurst Hill, Essex IG9 5PE. Called: Nov 1982, Middle Temple, LLB

Spencer Ms Alison Heather
Mills & Reeves Solicitors, Francis House, 112 Hills Road, Cambridge CB2 1PH, 01223 364422, Fax: 01223 355848. Called: Nov 1995, Middle Temple, BA (Hons)(York)

Spencer Antony Francis Newman
Called: Oct 1993, Middle Temple, BSc (Hons)(Newc)

Spencer Miss Francoise Mary •
Solicitor's Office, Division E, Dept of Trade & Industry, 1 Palace Street, London SW1E 5HE, 0171 238 3676, Fax: 0171 238 3452. Called: Feb 1993, Gray's Inn, LLB, Diplome de Hautes, Etudes Europeannes, (Droit), Bruges

Spencer Mrs Geraldine Erica •
Senior Crown Prosecutor, Crown Prosecution Service, The Cooperage, Gainsford Street, London SE1 2NG. Called: Nov 1968, Gray's Inn

Spencer Dr Jane Patricia
Fellow & College Lecturer in Law, Churchill College, Cambridge CB3 ODS, 01223 336170. Called: July 1979, Inner Temple, MA, Dip Law, PhD

Spencer Miss Janet Elizabeth
Deputy Clerk to the Justices, North Sefton Magistrates Court, The Law Courts, Albert Road, Southport PR9 OLJ, 01704 534141, Fax: 01704 500226. Called: July 1983, Gray's Inn, D.M.L., D.M.S.

Spencer Mrs Margaret Elizabeth
President of Guernsey International Legal Ass., Wilde & Co Trustees Ltd, Pollet House, Lower Pollet, Guernsey, Channel Islands GY1 4EA, 01481 726446, Fax: 01481 711156. Called: Feb 1989, Gray's Inn

Spencer Miss Maureen Cecilia
Law Clerk, Patton Boggs LLP, 2550 M Street NW, Washington DC 20037, 001 202 457 6000, Fax: 001 202 457 6315. Called: Oct 1994, Gray's Inn, BA, LLM

Spencer Mrs Maureen Patricia
Senior Lecturer in Law, School of Law, The Burrows, Hendon, London NW4 4BT. Called: July 1989, Inner Temple, BA (Oxon), Dip Law, LLM (Lond)

Spencer Simeon
Legal Consultant. Called: Mar 1997, Inner Temple, LLB (Sussex), LLM (Lond)

Sperry Miss Sandra Denise
Called: Oct 1996, Inner Temple, BSc (Soton), CPE (Lond)

Spicer David Leslie •
Assistant County Secretary, County Secretary's Dept, Legal Services, Friary Chambers, 26/34 Friar Lane, Nottingham NG1 6DQ, 0115 9243010, Fax: 0115 9243020. Called: July 1973, Gray's Inn, LLB

Spicer Rupert Nicholas Bullen
15th Fl Printing House, 6 Duddell Street, Central, 852 2 5 212616, Fax: 852 2 8 450260, and Member Hong Kong Bar. Called: Nov 1980, Lincoln's Inn, BSc (Dunelm), Diplaw

Spilsbury Miss Jane Helen •
Principle Legal Officer, New King's Beam House, 22 Upper Ground, London SE1. Called: Nov 1984, Gray's Inn, BA Hons

Spina Miss Naomi Angela
Called: Nov 1994, Middle Temple, BA (Hons)

Spink Jonathan Howard
Fagus House, Castlegate, Pickering, North Yorkshire YO18 7AX, 01751 473413. Called: Nov 1991, Gray's Inn, BSc (Lond), MSc (Lond), PGCE (Lond)

Spokes John Arthur Clayton QC (1973)
p/t Chairman Data Protn Trib. Called: June 1955, Gray's Inn

Spong Alan Michael •
Principal Crown Prosecutor, Crown Prosecution Service, Riding Gate House, 37 Old Dover Road, Canterbury, Kent CT1 3JG, 01227 451144, Fax: 01227 456368. Called: July 1979, Lincoln's Inn, LLB (Lond)

Spooner Mrs Karen Margaret •
Clerk to the Justices, North Worcestershire Mag's Crt, Grove Street, Redditch, Worcs B98 8DB, 01527 591035, Fax: 01527 64580. Called: Nov 1984, Middle Temple, LLB

Sprigge William Liddon •
Legal Advisor, Office of Gas Supply, Stockley House, 130 Wilton Road, London SW1V 1LQ, 0171 932 1670, Fax: 0171 932 1600. Called: July 1976, Lincoln's Inn, BSc, ACIS

Spring Anthony John
19 Laburnham Court, 124 Robin Hood Lane, Sutton, Surrey SM1 2SE. Called: Nov 1963, Gray's Inn

Spyrou George Andrew Rankin
Chairman, Airship Management Services Ltd, 12 Richmond Hill Road, Greenwich CT 06831, 203 625 0071, Fax: 203 625 0065. Called: Nov 1980, Inner Temple, AB (Harvard), MA, LLB (Cantab)

Squire Stuart James
Winchester House School, Brackley, Northants NN13 7AZ, 01280 703580. Called: Nov 1994, Middle Temple, BA (Hons)

Sram Iqbal Singh
Called: Oct 1996, Lincoln's Inn, M.B, CH.B (Manc), CPE

Sreenevasan Gopal
and Member Malaysia. Called: Nov 1993, Middle Temple, LLB (Hons)(Warwick)

Sreenivasan *Rajesh*
94 Jalan Angin Laut, Singapore 1648, 00 65
5453851, and Member Singapore Bar.
Called: July 1993, Middle Temple, LLB
(Hons)

St John *Miss Jeanette Sandra*
Civil Servant. Called: Oct 1991, Middle
Temple, BA (Open Univ), LLB Hons (Lond
Ext)

Stacey *Daniel Thomas*
Called: Nov 1996, Gray's Inn, BA (Oxon)

Stack *Malcolm Brian*
Called: Nov 1995, Inner Temple, BA (Hull),
CPE (Northumbria)

Stadnik *Miss Nina*
Principal Court Clerk, Leicestershire
Magistrates' Ct, The Court House,
Woodgate, Loughborough, 01509 215715.
Called: Nov 1986, Inner Temple, BA

Staff *Marcus Richard*
Employed Barrister, Brunschwig Wittmer,
13, Quai de L'ile, 1211 Geneva 11, 4122
781 33 22, Fax: 4122 781 31 00,
International Commercial Arbitration Law.
Called: Nov 1994, Inner Temple, BA (York)

Staheli *Mrs Rebecca* ●
Legal Advisor, Office of Fair Trading, Field
House, 15-22 Breams Buildings, London
EC4A 1PR, 0171 269 8896, Fax: 0171 269
8830. Called: Nov 1989, Middle Temple, BA
(Cantab)

Staley *Miss Helen Elizabeth*
Called: Mar 1997, Lincoln's Inn, LLB
(Hons)(Hull)

Stamford *Miss Susan Deborah*
Called: Oct 1997, Middle Temple, LLB
(Hons)(Lond)

Stanbrook *Dr Ivor Robert*
Called: May 1960, Inner Temple, BSc
(Econ), Ph.D.

Stancliffe *David*
Called: Nov 1995, Middle Temple, LLB
(Hons)(Kent)

Standfast *Mrs Heidi* ●
Principal Crown Prosecutor, Crown
Prosecution Service, Windsor House, 10
Manchester Road, Bradford BD5 0QH,
01274 742530, Fax: 01274 370640.
Called: July 1980, Gray's Inn, BA
(Hons)(Sheff)

Stanek *Mrs Susan Alexandra*
Woodperry Farm, Woodperry, Oxford
OX33 1AH. Called: Nov 1972, Middle
Temple

Stanford *Tony James*
Called: Nov 1996, Lincoln's Inn, LLB
(Hons)(Lond)

Stanley *Dr Christopher John*
Quintin Hogg Research Fellow in Law &
Social Theory, School of Law, University of
Westminster, 4 Red Lion Square, London
WC1R 4AR, 0171 911 5000. Called: Apr
1986, Gray's Inn, LLB, Ph.D

Stanley *Oliver Duncan*
Company Chairman, 5 The Park, London
NW11 7SR. Called: Nov 1963, Middle
Temple, MA (Oxon)

Stanley *Simon Hugh Francis*
Corporate Public Affairs Consultant. Former
Legal Policy Assistant to Paul Boateng M.P.,
Bruce Naughton Wade, Public Affairs
Management, Consultants, Enterprise House,
59/65 Upper Ground, London SE1 9PQ,
0171 620 1113, Fax: 0171 401 8319.
Called: Nov 1993, Lincoln's Inn, BA
(Hons)(Dunelm), Dip in Law (City)

Stanley *Miss Sybella Jane*
Called: Nov 1984, Lincoln's Inn, MA (Oxon)

Stanojlovic *Miss Mara Ellena*
Called: Nov 1992, Inner Temple, LLB (Lond)

Stansfield *Miss Jane* ●
Principle Crown Prosecutor, Crown
Prosecution Service, 3-5 Lumley Avenue,
Skegness. Called: July 1986, Lincoln's Inn,
LLB Business Law

Stansfield *John Oliver*
Called: July 1952, Gray's Inn, MA (Oxon)

Stansfield *Robert Harvey*
Bexhill Citizens Advice Bureau, 38 Sackville
Road, Bexhill-on-Sea, East Sussex TN39 3JE,
01424 215055. Called: Nov 1991, Inner
Temple, BSc (Eng), Dip Law

Stanton *Miss Alexandra Victoria*
Assistant, Sinclair, Roche & Temperley,
Royex House, Aldermanbury Square,
London EC2Y 7LE, 0171 452 4000, Fax:
0171 452 4001. Called: Nov 1993, Middle
Temple, BA (Hons)(Cantab) MA, Licence
Speciale Eu, Droit Europeen

Stanton *Miss Margaret Judith*
Westbourne, 21 Station Rd, Princes
Risborough, Aylesbury, Bucks HP27 9DE.
Called: July 1966, Gray's Inn, BA (Hons)

Stanway-Mayers *Martin Victor
James* ●
BP Gas, D'Arcy House, 146 Queen Victoria
Street, London EC4V BY, 0171 579 7504,
Fax: 0171 579 7776. Called: July 1976,
Middle Temple, LLB (Lond)

Stanyer *Simon Michael*
Called: Nov 1992, Inner Temple, LLB
(Leeds)

Stapleton *Adam*
3 Temple Gardens, 3rd Floor, Temple,
London, EC4Y 9AU. Called: Nov 1985,
Gray's Inn, BA (Cantab) Dip Law

Stapleton *David Alan*
Called: Nov 1997, Inner Temple, BSc

Stapleton *Giles William* ●
Commercial Lawyer, Legal & Compliance
Department, UBS Asset Management, Triton
Court, 14 Finsbury Sq, London EC2A 1PD,
0171 901 5000. Called: Nov 1994, Lincoln's
Inn, LLB (Hons)(Hull)

Starke *Professor Joseph Gabriel QC*
Legal Counsel, Prof of Humanitarian Law,
San Remo Italy 1974. Member Panel of Int
Arbitrators, Int Court of Justice, The Hague
Formerly, member in a legal capacity of
League of Nations Secretariat, Geneva 1935-
1940, 2 Kemp Close, Swinger Hill, Phillip,
Canberra, ACT 2606, (02) 6286 2278, QC
Australia 1961, Vinerian Law Scholar,
Oxford 1934. Called: June 1939, Inner
Temple, BA, LLB (Hons), BCL (Hons)(Oxon)

Starling *Keith*
Deputy Clerk to the Justices, Tewkesbury
Magistrates' Court, Gander Lane,
Tewkesbury, Gloucestershire GL20 5TR,
01684 294632, Fax: 01684 274596.
Called: Nov 1983, Gray's Inn, LLB,Dip Law

Stavrou *Stavros*
60 Dighenis Akritas Avenue, PO Box 6620,
Nicosia, Cyprus, 00357 2 756932, Fax:
00357 2 757693, and Member Cyprus Bar.
Called: Nov 1993, Gray's Inn, LLB (Sheff)

Steadman *Mark John*
The Faculty Office of the, Archbishop of
Canterbury, Lee Bolton & Lee, 1 The
Santuary, Westminster, London SW1P 3JT,
0171 222 5381, Fax: 0171 222 7502.
Called: Oct 1996, Inner Temple, LLB (Soton)

Stearns *Ms Elizabeth Jane Elford*
Called: Oct 1997, Inner Temple, BDS, MBBS,
CPE (London)

Steel *Commander David George RN* ●
Commander, Royal Navy. Fleet Legal &
Personnel. Officer. 0, Commander-in-Chief
Fleet, Northwood Headquarters,
Northwood, Middlesex HA6 3HP, 01923
837157, Fax: 01923 837090. Called: July
1988, Middle Temple, BA (Hons) (Dunelm)

Steel *Henry CMG,OBE*
Called: June 1951, Lincoln's Inn, BA (Oxon)

Steel *Mrs Marianne Valentine*
Swindon Hall, Swindon Village, Cheltenham,
Glos GL51 9QR. Called: June 1950, Gray's
Inn, LLB (Wales)

Steel *Nicholas Peter Robin*
Called: Oct 1993, Middle Temple, BA (Hons)

Steel *Simon Arthur*
Simpson. Thacher & Bartlett, 425 Lexington
Avenue, New York, NY 10017-3954, 001
212 455 3789, Fax: 001 212 455 2502, and
Member New York. Called: Feb 1992,
Lincoln's Inn, MA (Hons) (Cambs), LLM
(Chicago)

Steel *Stephen Paul* ●
Crown Prosecution Service, C/O 50 Ludgate
Hill, London EC4M 7EX. Called: Nov 1985,
Lincoln's Inn, BSc, Dip Law

Steen *Anthony David MP*
2 Hare Court, Ground Floor, Temple,
London, EC4Y 7BH. Called: May 1962,
Gray's Inn

Steen *Simon Edward Melle*
Legal Adviser, UK Retailing, Gosschalks
Solicitors, Queen's Gardens, Hull, HU1 3DZ,
01482 590290. Called: Nov 1989, Middle
Temple, BA (Hons)

● Barristers in employment

Steer *Miss Joanne Monica*
Called: Oct 1995, Lincoln's Inn, LLB
(Hons)(Exon)

Steiner *William Anthony Frederick Paul*
27 Cavendish Avenue, Cambridge CB1 4UP, 01223 247131. Called: Nov 1942, Gray's Inn, MA (Cantab), LLM (Lond), FLA, Dipl.Kons

Stephens *James Ross*
Called: Nov 1994, Middle Temple, BA (Hons)

Stephens-Ofner *John Alfred*
Judge on the Board of Appeals of the European Patent Organ. Organisation, Lersnerstrasse 5 A, 85579 Neubiberg. Called: Nov 1966, Middle Temple, MA (Oxon)

Stephenson *Anthony Mark*
Called: Nov 1997, Gray's Inn, LLB

Stephenson *Miss Stephanie Joy*
Called: July 1970, Gray's Inn, LLB,AKC

Stephenson *Sydney Dingaan*
Called: Nov 1996, Middle Temple, LLB (Hons)(Lond)

Stephenson *Thomas* •
Town Clerk, Leicester City Council, New Walk Centre, Welford Place, Leicester LE1 6ZG, 0116 252 6300, Fax: 0116 254 3668. Called: July 1976, Middle Temple, BSc, Cert. Ed

Stephenson-Burton *Ian*
Called: Oct 1994, Inner Temple, BSc (Sheff), MPhil (Cantab), CPE (Lond)

Sterling *Miss Valerie* •
Legal Officer, Leeds City Council, Selectapost 2, Civic Hall, Leeds LS1 1UR. Called: July 1981, Gray's Inn, LLB

Stern *Miss Elizabeth*
Called: Oct 1994, Lincoln's Inn, LLB (Hons)(Lond)

Stern *George Jerome Albert*
6 Eton Court, Shepherds Hill, London N6 5AF, 0181 340 0214, Fax: 0181 348 6586. Called: Nov 1994, Middle Temple, MA, BSc, Msc, F.S.S.

Stesin *Mrs Vasantha*
Solicitor, 6 Amber Close, Brighton, Victoria 3186, (03) 9596 0697, and Member Australian Capital Territory Victoria, Singapore Bar. Called: Nov 1990, Lincoln's Inn, LLB (Wales), LLM (Lond)

Stevens *Clyde Robert*
Called: July 1978, Middle Temple, LLB (Hons) Leicester, ADPTD (Homerton)

Stevens *Robert Bocking*
Essex Court Chambers, 24 Lincoln's Inn Fields, London, WC2A 3ED. Called: Feb 1956, Gray's Inn, MA, BCL (Oxon), LLM

Stevens *Robert Hedley*
Fellow & Tutor in Law, Lady Margaret Hall, Oxford OX2 6QA, 01865 274289. Called: Nov 1992, Gray's Inn, BA (Oxon), BCL (Oxon)

Stevenson *Heon Lindsay Stuart*
C/O 12 Fern Road, Storrington, West Sussex RH20 4LW. Called: May 1994, Gray's Inn, MA

Stevenson *Miss Isabel Emma* •
Lawyer (Grade 6). Called: Nov 1985, Inner Temple, LLB

Stevenson *John Michael*
Tower Bridge Court, 224 Tower Bridge Road, London SE1 2UP, 0171 716 6000, Fax: 0171 716 6104. Called: July 1967, Middle Temple

Steward *Derek John*
Little Thatch, Mill Lane, Bradford Abbas, Sherborne, Dorset DT9 6RH, 01835 427111. Called: Feb 1973, Inner Temple, LDSRCS, DDPH

Stewart *Allan Keith*
Called: July 1954, Middle Temple, MA (Oxon)

Stewart *Andrew William* •
Grade 6, Solicitor's Office, Dept of Trade & Industry, 10-18 Victoria Street, London SW1H 0NN, 0171 215 3446, Fax: 0171 215 3503. Called: July 1983, Middle Temple, BA Hons {Oxon}

Stewart *Seymour George*
Called: Nov 1995, Middle Temple, BA (Hons)(Kent)

Stewart *Mrs Victoria Joy*
Called: Feb 1990, Inner Temple, LLB

Stewart-Richardson *Alastair Lucas Graham*
Called: Nov 1952, Inner Temple, MA (Cantab)

Stibbs *Michael John Parker*
Senior Court Clerk, Solihull Magistrates Court, Homer Road, Solihull, Birmingham B91 3RD, 0121 705 8101, Fax: 0121 711 2045. Called: Nov 1982, Middle Temple, BA

Stickings *Miss Sian Rosemary*
Devereux Chambers, Devereux Court, London, WC2R 3JJ. Called: Nov 1983, Inner Temple, MA (Oxon)

Stimpson *Miss Natasha*
Called: Nov 1993, Inner Temple, LLB (Leic)

Stirling *Andrew Fraser* •
Senior Crown Prosecutor, Crown Prosecution Service, 2nd Floor, King Willam House, Market Place, Kingston upon Hull. Called: July 1985, Lincoln's Inn, LLB (Hons) (B'ham)

Stivadoros *Paul George*
Chairman Bar Assoc.for Local Government and the Public Service, 23 Wentworth Way, Bletchley, Milton Keynes MK3 7RW, 01908 370887, and Member Cyprus Bar. Called: Nov 1962, Gray's Inn, LLB (Lond)

Stockdale *James Arthur Fitzroy*
Called: July 1972, Gray's Inn

Stocks *Neil Richard* •
Head of the Legal Department, SBC Warburg, Swiss Bank House, 1 High Timber Street, London EC4Y, 0171 711 2804, Fax: 0171 711 2364. Called: July 1978, Middle Temple, B.Sc (Lond)

Stockton *Miss Fay*
Called: July 1976, Lincoln's Inn, LLB

Stockton *John Paul* •
Director of Tribunal Operation, The Court Service, Southside, 105 Victoria Street, London SW1E 6QT, 0171 210 1890, Fax: 0171 210 1893. Called: Nov 1974, Middle Temple, BA (Oxon)

Stokes *Stanley William*
Clerk to the Justices/Justices Chief Executive, Doncaster Magistrates', Courts Committee, P O Box 49, College Road, Doncaster DN1 3HT, 01302 366711, Fax: 01302 340323. Called: Nov 1985, Gray's Inn

Stomberg *Miss Christina-Caroline*
Called: Oct 1992, Gray's Inn, MA (St.Andrews Scot)

Stone *Andrew Mark*
Called: May 1997, Lincoln's Inn, LLB (Hons)(Derby)

Stone *Ms Frances Julia*
Lecturer in Medical Law & Ethics, Department of Biomedical, Science & Biomedical Ethics, The Medical School, University of Birmingham, Edgbaston, Birmingham B15 2TT, 0121 414 3616, Fax: 0121 414 6979. Called: July 1987, Middle Temple, LLB(Hons) (Manc), MA

Stone *Miss Gillian*
Called: July 1997, Middle Temple, LLB (Nott'm)

Stone *Julian Anthony*
Called: July 1997, Gray's Inn, LLB

Stone *Miss Penelope Helen* •
Called: Nov 1984, Gray's Inn

Stoneham *Ms Nicole Holly Marie*
Attorney General's Chambers, Global House, 43 Church Street, Hamilton HM 12, (809) 292 2463, Fax: (809) 292 3608, and Member Bermuda Bar. Called: Nov 1992, Gray's Inn, BA, LLB

Stoplar *David Jonathan Aron* •
Assistant Legal Adviser, Civil Aviation Authority, CAA House, 45-59 Kingsway, London WC2B 6TE, 0171 832 5417, Fax: 0171 832 6635. Called: July 1982, Gray's Inn, LLB (Lond)

Storey *Mrs Bernadette* •
Senior Crown Prosecutor, Crown Prosecution Service, Crown House, Winston Churchill Avenue, Portsmouth, Hampshire PO12 2PJ, 01705 752004. Called: Feb 1990, Lincoln's Inn, LLB Hons

Storey *Ms Elizabeth Anne*
Called: Apr 1991, Gray's Inn, BA (Sydney), LLB

Storr *Philip Leonard*
Crown Counsel to the Government of Bermuda, P.O.Box HM 2653, Hamilton, HMKX, Bermuda, (809) 296 1807, Fax: (809) 292 3608, Former Solicitor (1958) and Member Bermuda 46/48 Essex Street, London, WC2R 3GH. Called: Nov 1990, Inner Temple, MA

Storrs-Fox *Jonathan Storrs*
Former Solicitor. Called: Feb 1993, Gray's Inn, LLB (Hull)

Stout *Geoffrey Hamer VRD*
4 Greenlands, Tattenhall, Chester CH3 9QY, 01829 70461. Called: Nov 1982, Gray's Inn, LLB (Lond), LDS (Man

Strachan *Jeremy Alan Watkin* •
Executive Director, Glaxo Wellcome plc, Flaxo Wellcome House, Berkeley Avenue, Greenford, Middlesex UB6 0NN, 0171 493 4060, Fax: 0181 966 8330. Called: Nov 1969, Inner Temple, MA (Cantab), LLB

Strachan *Ms Mary Jane*
Called: Nov 1991, Inner Temple, LLB (Hons)

Strachan *William Arthur Watkin*
Silver Birches, Blockley Road, North Wembley, Middx HA0 3LL, 0181 904 8539, and Member Jamaica. Called: June 1959, Inner Temple, DMA, LLB (Lond), FCIS, F.I.Mgt

Stranaghan *Miss Patricia Ann* •
Legal Advisor, G E Capital Equipment Finance, Limited, Capital House, 3 Bond Street, Bristol BS1 3LA, 0117 929 8899. Called: Nov 1984, Lincoln's Inn, LLB (Hons)

Stratford *Jonathan Charles*
Bailhouse, Labesse, P O Box 207, St Helier, Jersey, and Member Jersey Bar. Called: Oct 1995, Gray's Inn, LLB

Strauss *Dr Herman*
New Zealand Barrister & Solicitor, Flat 2A, 88A Salamanca Road, Wellington 5, 4727455. Called: Nov 1951, Lincoln's Inn

Straw *John Whitaker MP*
MP for Blackburn, House Of Commons, London, SW1, 0171 219 5477, Fax: 0171 219 6694. Called: July 1972, Inner Temple, LLB

Straw *Miss Louise Victoria*
Burton Copeland Solicitors, Royal London House, 196 Deansgate, Manchester M3 3NE, 0161 834 7374. Called: Nov 1987, Gray's Inn, LLB (L'pool)

Stripp *Ian Robert*
Police Officer Detective Superintendent, Leicestershire Constabulary, Police Headquarters, St Johns, Enderby, PO Box 999, Leicestershire, 0116 2482511, Fax: 0116 2484127. Called: Nov 1993, Middle Temple, LLB (Hons)

Strong *Richard Neville*
Solicitors Law Stationery, Society Ltd, Oyez House, PO Box 55, 7 Spa Road, London SE16 3QQ. Called: July 1991, Inner Temple, LLM (Lond), LLB, DMS

Strong *Samuel Jonathan*
Called: Feb 1995, Middle Temple, LLB (Hons)(Bucks)

Struggles *Jonathan Michael*
Called: Oct 1997, Gray's Inn, LLB (Bris)

Stuart *Mrs Margaret Ann*
Called: Nov 1990, Lincoln's Inn, LLB (Essex)

Stuart-Moore *Michael QC (1990)*
Judge of the High Court, Hong Kong, Supreme Court. Called: July 1966, Middle Temple

Stubbs *Matthew James* •
Grade 7 Lawyer, Health & Safety Executive, Rose Court, 2 Southwark Bridge, London SE1 9HS, 0171 717 6668. Called: July 1989, Inner Temple, LLB [Exon]

Stubbs *Michael James*
Business Affairs Attorney, DreamWorks, 10 Universal City Plaza, Building 10, Universal City, California 91608 U.S.A, 818 7336000, Fax: 818 7336194. Called: Oct 1993, Gray's Inn, LLB (Buck'ham)

Stuber *Mrs Ruth Henrietta*
Court Clerk, Harrow Magistrates', Courts Committee, PO Box 164, Rossyln Crescent, Harrow HA1 2JY, 0181 427 5146. Called: Feb 1963, Gray's Inn

Stuckey *Derek Richard*
3 Dr Johnson's Bldgs, Ground Floor, Temple, London, EC4Y 7BA. Called: May 1949, Gray's Inn, MA, BCL (Oxon)

Stutt *Colin Richard Hamilton* •
Legal Adviser, Legal Aid Board Head Office, 85 Gray's Inn Road, London WC1X 8AA, 0171 813 1000, Fax: 0171 813 8631. Called: July 1985, Inner Temple, MA (Cantab)

Styles *Peter Richard* •
Vice-President, European Government Affairs, Enron Capital & Trade Resource, Four Millbank, London SW1P 3ET, 0171 316 5480, Fax: 0171 316 5391, 1996-7 Chairman of Bar Association for Commerce Finance & Industry. Called: July 1978, Inner Temple, MA (Cantab)

Stylianou *Miss Eleni Byron*
Called: Nov 1994, Gray's Inn, LLB (Lond)

Subraa
Called: Nov 1996, Lincoln's Inn, LLB (Hons)

Subramaniam *Bhaskar S*
In House Barrister, Mathis Solicitors, 231-232 Elephant & Castle, Shopping Centre, London SE1 6TE, 0171 277 0306. Called: July 1997, Middle Temple, LLB (Hons)(Lond), MA (Lond)

Subramaniam *Miss Pushpakantha*
Legal Officer/Advisor, Level 40, Menara Lion, No 165 Jalan Ampang, P O Box 12485, 50780 Kuala Lumpur, 03-4677868, Fax: 03-4666546, and Member Malaysia Bar. Called: Nov 1994, Inner Temple, LLB (Hons)(Lond)

Subramaniam *Miss Sumitra R*
Called: July 1996, Middle Temple, LLB (Hons)(Wales)

Subramaniam *Eliatamby Nathan*
Called: July 1995, Middle Temple, LLB (Hons), LLM

Sudin *Miss Suhana*
Called: Nov 1995, Lincoln's Inn, LLB (Hons)

Sugden *Paul Birkby*
Ogier & Le Masurier, Pirouet House, Union Street, St Helier, Jersey JE4 8WZ, 01534 504000, Fax: 01534 35328, and Member Jersey Bar. Called: July 1983, Lincoln's Inn, BA,ACIB

Sugden *Richard Alexander*
Called: Oct 1997, Gray's Inn, BSc (Middx)

Sugrue *Miss Clare Veronica* •
Director, Legal & Business Affairs, Islands Records Ltd, 22 St Peters Square, London W6 9NW, 0181 910 3287, Fax: 0181 910 3218. Called: Nov 1985, Middle Temple, LLB(Lond)

Sugunaretnam *Miss Yogarani*
Called: Mar 1996, Middle Temple, LLB (Hons)(Lond)

Suhara *Miss Binte Mohd Said*
603 9583857, Fax: 603 9583859. Called: Nov 1996, Lincoln's Inn, LLB (Hons)(Lond)

Sukul *Ganesh Shankar*
G & S Law Offices, Suite 15, 14 Cathedral Road, Cardiff, South Wales CF1 9LJ, 01222 660163, Fax: 01222 664891. Called: July 1982, Gray's Inn, BA

Sukul *Ms Kheemelia*
Called: Oct 1997, Inner Temple, LLB (Lond)

Sukul *Mrs Sitalakshmi*
G & S Law Offices, Suite 15, 14 Cathedral Road, Cardiff, South Wales CF1 9LJ, 01222 660163, Fax: 01222 664891. Called: Nov 1982, Lincoln's Inn, BA (Hons)

Sulehria *Mrs Carol Joan*
Principal Assistant, Ealing Magistrates' Court, Green Man Lane, London W13 OSD, 0181 579 9311, Fax: 0181 579 2985. Called: Nov 1974, Middle Temple, LLB (Lond)

Sulek *Ms Joanna Elizabeth Maria*
Called: Oct 1994, Gray's Inn, MA, LLB (Leeds)

Sullivan *David Douglas Hooper QC (1975)*
Called: Nov 1951, Inner Temple, MA, BCL

Sullivan *Mrs Debra* •
Trade Marks Adviser, BATMark Limited, Export House, Cawsey Way, Woking, Surrey GU21 1YB, 01483 759967, Fax: 01483 759982. Called: July 1988, Lincoln's Inn, LLB (Hons) (Lond), Maitrise En Droit, (Sorbonne)

Sultan *Hamid*
Legal Assistant, M/S Khattar Wong & Partners, 80 Raffles Place, [H]25-01 UOB Plaza 1, \ingapore 0104, 5356844, Fax: 5351606, and Member Singapore Bar. Called: July 1994, Lincoln's Inn, LLB (Hons)

Sum *Chin Liang*
Called: July 1995, Lincoln's Inn, LLB (Hons)

Summerfield *Henry Jacob Isidore*
Camden Mediation Services Management
Committee Member, 38 Hillfield Court,
London NW3 4BJ, 0171 209 1379, Also Inn
of Court I. Called: Apr 1948, Gray's Inn, BA
(Cantab), ACIArb

Summerlin *Mrs Sara Hill* •
Crown Prosecutor, Crown Prosecution
Service, Hull Branch Office, King William
House, Market Place, Kingston Upon Hull
HU1 1RS, 01482 228816, Fax: 01482
587275. Called: Oct 1993, Gray's Inn, B.Sc

Summers *Gary*
Magrath & Co, 52/54 Maddox Street,
London W1R 9PA, 0171 495 3003, Formerly
a Solicitor. Called: Nov 1985, Gray's Inn, BA

Sumner *Miss Michaela Simone*
Associate, Graham Thompson & Co,
P.O.Box N272, Nassau N.P, 00 1 242 322
4130, Fax: 00 1 242 328 1069, and Member
Bahamas. Called: July 1997, Middle Temple,
LLB (Hons)

Sundaram *Subramanian*
Advocate & Solicitor in the Republic of
Singapore. Called: Nov 1993, Middle
Temple, LLB (Hons)(Lond)

Sundararaj *Miss Aneeta Rajah*
60 4 7310049. Called: Nov 1996, Middle
Temple, LLB (Hons)(Wales)

Sundram-Selvadurai *Mrs Naomi* •
Medical Protection Society, 33 Cavendish
Square, London W1M 0PS. Called: Oct 1990,
Lincoln's Inn, LLB

Sunkin *Maurice Simon*
1 Pump Court, Lower Ground Floor,
Temple, London, EC4Y 7AB. Called: July
1975, Middle Temple, LLM

Sunnassee *Atmanand*
Lecturer. Called: Nov 1988, Lincoln's Inn,
MSc (LSE), BA, Dip Law

Sunner *Navtej Singh*
Called: Oct 1994, Lincoln's Inn, LLB
(Hons)(Wolves)

Sunner *Miss Sundip Kaur*
Called: Nov 1997, Middle Temple, LLB
(Hons)(Hull)

Supaiyah *Dravida Maran*
Called: Mar 1998, Lincoln's Inn, LLB (Hons)

Suppayan *Miss Malarkodi*
Called: Nov 1995, Lincoln's Inn, LLB (Hons)

Suppayya *Gogulakannan s/o*
Called: July 1997, Lincoln's Inn, LLB
(Hons)(Lond)

Suppiah *Arul*
Called: Nov 1997, Middle Temple, LLB
(Hons)(Lond)

Suppiah *Krishnamurthi*
Called: July 1996, Middle Temple, LLB
(Hons)(Lond)

Suppiah *Sarasvathy*
Called: July 1997, Lincoln's Inn, LLB
(Hons)(Leeds)

Supramaniam *Ramesh*
Called: July 1996, Middle Temple, LLB
(Hons)(Lond)

Suresh *Veloo*
Called: July 1994, Lincoln's Inn, LLB (Hons,
Lond)

Sureshan *T. Kulasingam*
Called: July 1996, Middle Temple, LLB
(Hons)(Lond)

Surjit *Miss Belinda Kaur*
Called: Nov 1997, Lincoln's Inn, LLB
(Hons)(Thames)

Surman *Giles Mark*
Called: Nov 1997, Gray's Inn, BSc (Wales)

Surman *Peter John*
Judge of the Supreme Court, Fiji 1 Temple
Gardens, 1st Floor, Temple, London, EC4Y
9BB. Called: July 1974, Gray's Inn

Surridge *Mr. Robert Conway*
J Keith Pack & Co, World Trade Centre, 8
Exchange Quay, Salford, Manchester, 0161
789 8272, Fax: 0161 789 8285. Called: Mar
1996, Gray's Inn, LLB

Sutcliffe *Miss Katrina Jane Stuart*
Recruitment Consultant for Legal
Appointments, Quarry Dougall, 37-41
Bedford Row, London WC1R 4JH, 0171 405
6062, Fax: 0171 831 6394. Called: Nov
1994, Lincoln's Inn, LLB (Hons)(Kingston)

Sutherland *Reginald Francis*
Eastbourne, Sussex. Called: Jan 1927, Middle
Temple

Sutherland *Robert David*
Deputy Chief Clerk, Inner London
Magistrates', Courts Service, 65 Romney
Street, London SW1P 3RD. Called: July
1985, Lincoln's Inn, LLB

Suttill *Brian*
Assistant Law Draftsman, 52 Huntsman
Lane, Stamford Bridge, York YO4 1ET,
01759 372 896, Fax: 01759 372 896, and
Member Hong Kong Bar York Chambers, 14
Toft Green, York, YO1 1JT. Called: Nov
1970, Gray's Inn, LLB (Leeds), Dip L.D.
(Ottawa), ACI Arb

Sutton *Andre John*
Called: Nov 1994, Middle Temple, LLB
(Hons)

Sutton *Mrs Joyah Junella*
P.O.Box 534, Main Street, Charlestown,
Nevis, 00 1 869 469 5158/1326, Fax: 00 1
869 469 5834, and Member St Kitts &
Nevis. Called: July 1993, Middle Temple,
LLB (Hons), BA, LEC, ACIArb

Suvvaru *Miss Sonali Rao*
Called: July 1997, Gray's Inn, BA, LLB

Svoboda *Marek John Julian*
Neklauova 14, 128 00 Prague 2, 0042 2
2185 5001/5, Fax: 0042 2 2185 5055, and
Member Czech Bar. Called: July 1986,
Lincoln's Inn, MA (Cantab), MSc (Lond)

Swabey *John Charles Merttins*
Legal Advisor/Company Secretary, JJB
Consultancy Services Ltd, 27 High Street,
Shaftesbury, Dorset S77 7JE, 0171 792 1618.
Called: Nov 1974, Gray's Inn

Swaffield *Mrs Helen Linda*
Pinsent Curtis, 3 Colmore Circus,
Birmingham B4 6BH. Called: July 1988,
Lincoln's Inn, LLB (Hons) (Leics), Dip D'et
Jur FR

Swain *Barry* •
Senior Crown Prosecutor, Crown
Prosecution Service, 32 Scotland Street,
Sheffield S3 7DQ, 0114 291 2062, Fax: 0114
291 2050. Called: July 1989, Inner Temple,
LLB (Hons) (Sheff)

Swain *Miss Hadassah Annette*
Bain & Co, P O Box F-44533, Freeport,
Grand Bahama, (242) 352 5971, Fax: (242)
352 6075, and Member Bahamas Bar.
Called: July 1997, Gray's Inn, LLB (Lond)

Swainson *Mrs Jill Marguerite* •
Principal Legal Officer, Department of Social
Security, New Court, 48 Carey Street,
London WC2A 2LS. Called: Feb 1970, Gray's
Inn, BA

Swainson *John Honeyman* •
Grade 5, Solicitor's Office, DSS, New Court,
Carey Street, London WC2A 2LS, 0171 412
1355, Fax: 0171 412 1513. Called: July
1966, Lincoln's Inn, BA (Hull)

Swami *Miss Sobana*
c/o Hillborne & Co, No 1 Colombo Court,
[H]09-01, 3362882, Fax: 3362886, and
Member Singapore. Called: July 1996,
Middle Temple, LLB (Hons)

Swan *Ms Pauline Mary*
Called: Mar 1998, Gray's Inn, LLB (Lond)

Swan *Stephen Andrew John* •
Health & Safety Executive, Solicitor's Office,
Rose Court, 2 Southwark Bridge, London
SE1 9HS, 0171 717 6659, Fax: 0171 717
6661. Called: July 1983, Lincoln's Inn, LLB
(Hons)(Lond), LLM (Lond)

Swan *Rev Thomas Hugh Winfield*
24 Chiefs Street, Ely, Cambridge CB6 1AT,
01353 668452. Called: June 1951, Lincoln's
Inn, MA (Oxon)

Swannell *Robert William Ashburnham*
Vice-Chairman - J Henry Schroder & Co
Limited, 120 Cheapside, London EC2V 6DS,
0171 658 6000, Fax: 0171 658 6459.
Called: Nov 1976, Lincoln's Inn, FCA

Swartz *Bruce Carlton*
U.S. Department of Justice, Criminal
Division, Washington DC 20530, 202-514-
9906, Fax: 202-514-9412, and Member
United States of America. Called: July 1997,
Middle Temple, BA, JD (Yale)

Swayne *Christopher David George*
Called: Feb 1983, Inner Temple, MA (Oxon)

Swee *Colin Lay Keong*
24 Jalan Ladang, Palm Grove, Klang,
Selangor 41200, Malaysia, 60 3 3326200,
and Member Malaysia Bar. Called: Nov 1993,
Lincoln's Inn, LLB (Hons, Sheff)

• Barristers in employment

Sweeney *James Peter*
Eversheds, Milburn House, Dean Street, Newcastle upon Tyne NE1 1NP, 0191 261 1661, Fax: 0191 261 8270. Called: Nov 1989, Inner Temple, LLB (Hons)

Sweeney *Thomas Gerard* •
Principal Crown Prosecutor, CPS (G.Manchester Area), PO Box 377, 8th Floor,Sunlight House, Quay Street, Manchester M60 3LU, 0161 837 7402. Called: Feb 1988, Gray's Inn

Sweeney-Baird *Mrs Magarita*
Lecturer, Birmingham Business School, University of Birmingham (p/t) & Queen Mary & Westfield College Law School University of London (p/t), 225 Leigh Hunt Drive, Southgate, London N14 6DS, 0181 447 9392. Called: July 1989, Middle Temple, LLB [Glas], LLM [Harvard]

Sweeting *Miss Margaret Francis*
Called: Oct 1996, Lincoln's Inn, LLB (Hons)(Notts), MA (Lond)

Sweeting *Roy William Mark*
Called: Nov 1997, Lincoln's Inn, LLB (Hons)

Sweeting *Miss Valerie Frances*
Called: Mar 1998, Lincoln's Inn, BA (Econ)(Canada), Dip Law (Westmister)

Swersky *Abraham Jowel*
18 Church Avenue, Pinner, Middlesex HA5 5JQ, 0181 868 0156, Fax: 0181 868 0156, SC of South Africa and Member South Africa. Called: Nov 1996, Lincoln's Inn, B.Comm(Witwatersrand,), LLB (S.Africa)

Swetenham *Richard Clement*
European Commission, L-2920, 00 352 4301 32400, Fax: 00 352 4301 33190. Called: Nov 1974, Middle Temple, BA (Oxon)

Swift *Christopher Richard* •
Legal Adviser, Office of Fair Trading, Field House, 15-25 Bream's Buildings, London EC4A 1PR. Called: Nov 1972, Middle Temple, MA, LLB (Cantab)

Swift *David Bernard*
44 Jacksons Lane, Highgate, London N6 5SX, 0181 348 2154, Fax: 0181 348 4287. Called: Nov 1955, Gray's Inn, MA (Cantab)

Swift *John Anthony* QC (1981)
Office of the Rail Regulator, 1 Waterhouse Square, 138-142 Holborn, London EC1N 2ST, 0171 282 2020, Fax: 0171 282 2041. Called: Nov 1965, Inner Temple, MA (Oxon)

Sy *Choon Yen*
Called: July 1996, Inner Temple, LLB (Manchester)

Syed *Abdur Razzaque*
77 Cecil Avenue, Barking, Essex IG11 9TG, 0181 220 9479. Called: July 1971, Inner Temple, BA, LLB

Syed *Mohammed Hussain*
and Member Pakistan Bar. Called: Nov 1989, Lincoln's Inn, BA (Oxon), Dip Law (City)

Syed *Nayleem Ahmed* •
Legal & Business Affairs Manager, Coalition Recordings/Warner, Music International, Electric Lighting Station, London W8 5DP, 0171 591 5900, Fax: 0171 591 5999. Called: May 1995, Lincoln's Inn, LLB (Hons), LLM, Dip Law

Syed *Yahya*
26 Maria Avenue, 241 1883/5338188, Fax: 533 6100, Advocate & Solicitor, Supreme Court, Singapore Commissioner for Oaths and Member Singapore Bar. Called: July 1981, Inner Temple

Syed Abdullah *Syed Faisal*
Called: Nov 1994, Lincoln's Inn, LLB (Hons)(Sheff)

Syed Abu Bakar *Miss Sharifah Mazwin*
Called: July 1993, Lincoln's Inn, BA (Hons)

Syed-Mohamed *Miss Sharifah Saeedah*
Khairuddin, Ngiam & Tan, Advocates & Solicitors, Lot 16.03, 16th Floor, Wisma, Nusantara, Jalan Punchak off, Jalan P Ramlee, 50250 Kuala Lumpur, 6 03 2382388/2305081, Fax: 6 03 2301994, and Member Malaysia Bar. Called: July 1995, Gray's Inn, LLB (E.Anglia)

Sykes *Martin Howard*
129 Millgate, Selby, N Yorkshire YO8 0LL, 01757 702826. Called: May 1973, Middle Temple, MA (Oxon)

Sykes *Richard John Davies*
Legal Adviser, Nestle S.A., Avenue Nestle 55, 1800 Vevey, Switzerland, 021 924 3429. Called: July 1981, Gray's Inn, BA, LLM

Symeonidou *Miss Eleni*
Called: Nov 1997, Lincoln's Inn, LLB (Hons)(Lond)

Symes *Ms Mary Elizabeth*
Called: July 1977, Lincoln's Inn

Symington *James Richard* •
Legal Officer Legal Adviser, Foreign & Commonwealth Office, London SW1A 2AH, 0171 270 0745, Fax: 0171 270 3536. Called: Nov 1991, Middle Temple, MA Econ (Edin), CPE, Dip in Law

Symington *Noel Ian*
1 Asserton Cottages, Berwick St James, Salisbury, Wilts SP3 4TY, 01722 790785, Fax: 01722 782356. Called: Nov 1993, Inner Temple, BA, CPE

Symonds *Robert Stephen*
Called: Nov 1995, Gray's Inn, LLB (Warw)

Symons *Miss April Naomi Wallace*
120 Grove End Gardens, London NW8 9LR. Called: June 1953, Inner Temple, MA (Oxon)

Synmoie *Ms Lorrayne* •
Crown Prosecutor, Rossmore House, 10 Newbold Terrace, Leamington Spa CV32 4EA, 01926 450277. Called: July 1991, Lincoln's Inn, LLB (Hons) (Hull)

Synnott *Terence James*
Group Secretary at DSR Group Director/ Company Secretary at Keele Consultants, Bank House, 21 Market Street, Edenfield, Via Bury, Lancashire BL0 0JQ, 01706 821190, Fax: 01604 765798. Called: July 1989, Lincoln's Inn, BA Hons (Keele)

Szagun *Miss Teresa Ewa*
Clerk to the Magistrates, Justices Training Office & Legal Trainer Essex., Basildon Magistrates' Court, Great Oaks, Basildon, Essex SS14 1EH, 01268 293129, Fax: 01268 293187. Called: Nov 1985, Middle Temple, BA (Hons), Dip Law

Sze *Ge Pek*
Called: Nov 1996, Middle Temple, LLB (Hons)(Lond)

Sze-Ling *Miss Shum*
Called: Nov 1993, Inner Temple, LLB, LLM

Szell *Patrick John* •
Head of the International Environmental Law Division, Dept of the Environment,, Transport and the Regions, Eland House, Bressenden Place, London SW1E 5DU, 0171 890 4820, Fax: 0171 890 4804. Called: Nov 1966, Inner Temple, MA, LLB (Dub)

Szeto *Benjamin*
Called: July 1997, Lincoln's Inn, LLB (Hons)

Sziklai *Mrs Siew Fong*
738 S.E. 8th St, Ocala FL 34471, (352) 620 8033. Called: July 1995, Middle Temple, LLB (Hons)

Tabbush *Simon James* •
Lord Chancellor's Department, Selborne House, 54-60 Victoria Street, London SW1E 6QW, 0171 210 0734, Fax: 0171 210 0725. Called: July 1979, Middle Temple, MA (Oxon)

Tack *Geoffrey Joel* •
Principal Legal Officer, Solicitor's Office, HM Customs and Exise, New King's Beam House, 22 Upper Ground, London SE1 9PJ, 0171 620 1313. Called: Feb 1989, Lincoln's Inn, LLB(Hons)

Tackie *Abraham Nokwei*
Senior Lecturer, Middlesex University, Faculty of Business Studies, and Management, Middlesex, Business School, Law School, The Burroughs, London NW4 4BT, 0181 362 5000, Fax: 0181 202 1539. Called: Nov 1983, Middle Temple, BA (Hons)(Law), LLM, RMN

Taggart *Anthony Francis*
Called: June 1955, Lincoln's Inn, LLB (Lond)

Taggart *Patrick Joseph*
Royal Courts of Justice, Belfast, and Member Northern Ireland Bar. Called: Mar 1997, Gray's Inn, LLB

Tai *Cheh Seak*
Called: July 1997, Lincoln's Inn, LLB (Hons)(Lond)

Tailby *Christopher Russell*
Price Waterhouse, Cornwall Court, 19 Cornwall Street, Birmingham B3 2DT, 0121 200 3000, Fax: 0121 200 2464. Called: Nov 1971, Inner Temple

Tait *Ms Arabella Elizabeth Connel Cargill*
Faculty of Advocates, Advocates Library, Parliament House, Edinburgh, Scotland EH1, and Member Scottish Bar. Called: Oct 1993, Inner Temple, BA, LLM

Tait *Ms Helen*
Called: Oct 1997, Inner Temple, BA (Wolverhampton), CPE

Takla *Ms Joanna Antoine*
Called: Oct 1997, Inner Temple, BA (Westminster)

Talib *Miss Muna Mohamad*
Called: Nov 1996, Lincoln's Inn, LLB (Hons)(Lond)

Tallents *Anthony Alan* ●
Senior Legal Adviser, British Steel plc, 9 Albert Embankment, London, SE1 7SN, 0171 820 7339, Fax: 0171 582 5776. Called: Nov 1970, Gray's Inn, LLB Hons, MBA

Tam *Chee Jack*
Called: Nov 1997, Lincoln's Inn, LLB (Hons)(Lond)

Tam *Miss Winnie Wan-Chi*
and Member Hong Kong Bar Australia Bar 8 New Square, Lincoln's Inn, London, WC2A 3QP. Called: Feb 1988, Middle Temple, LLB (Hons) Hong Kong

Tamlyn *Alexander*
Dibb Lupton Alsop, 125 London Wall, London. EC2Y 5AE, 0171 796 6185, Fax: 0171 600 1727. Called: July 1988, Lincoln's Inn, LLB (Hons) (Cardiff)

Tampion *Andrew Neil* ●
113 Main Street, Higham On The Hill, Nr Nuneaton, Warwickshire CV13 6AJ, 01455 212022. Called: May 1988, Lincoln's Inn, BA (Hons) Keele

Tan *Adrian Chong Jin*
Called: July 1995, Middle Temple, LLB (Hons)

Tan *Miss Ai Ling Joanna*
Called: July 1996, Middle Temple, LLB (Hons)(Kent)

Tan *Miss Ai Tin*
Called: Nov 1996, Lincoln's Inn, LLB (Hons)(Lond)

Tan *Aik Yong*
Called: July 1994, Lincoln's Inn, LLB (Hons)

Tan *Miss Alison Geck-Chin*
Legal Assistant, c/o Drew & Napier, 20 Raffles Place, Singapore 048620, (65) 535 0733, Fax: JURES RS 21361, and Member Singapore Bar. Called: July 1994, Lincoln's Inn, BA (Hons)

Tan *Ms Anastasia Pei Pei*
Chew, Tan & Lim, Asia Insurance Building, No 1 China Street, 10200 Penang, West Malaysia, and Member Malaysia Bar. Called: July 1994, Gray's Inn, LLB (Lond)

Tan *Andrew Pheng Lock*
Called: July 1994, Middle Temple, LLB (Hons)(Lond)

Tan *Aylwin Wee En*
065 2543513. Called: July 1997, Middle Temple, BA (Hons)(Kent)

Tan *Bak Leng*
Called: July 1997, Lincoln's Inn, LLB (Hons)(Leics)

Tan *Beng Lok Edwin*
Legal Counsel, Sembawang Marine & Logistic, Ltd, 6639244, and Member Singapore Bar. Called: July 1995, Middle Temple, LLB (Hons) (Lond)

Tan *Bernard E Wei*
Called: July 1997, Lincoln's Inn, LLB (Hons)

Tan *Boon Chiang PPA, BBM*
Director of General Magnetics Ltd., 75 Shelford Road, 4622914, Fax: 4622924. Called: Nov 1954, Lincoln's Inn, LL.B, Dip.Arts

Tan *Boon Khai*
Justices's Law Clerk, Supreme Court, Singapore, 10 Palm Drive, Singapore 456490, 4483600. Called: July 1996, Lincoln's Inn, LLB (Hons)(Notts)

Tan *Brian Yang Seng*
Called: Nov 1996, Middle Temple, LLB (Hons)(Lond)

Tan *Chee Siang*
Called: Nov 1995, Middle Temple, LLB (Hons)

Tan *Miss Cheng Foong*
Called: July 1996, Middle Temple, LLB (Hons)(Leic)

Tan *Chia Loong*
Called: July 1995, Middle Temple, LLB (Hons) (Kent)

Tan *Miss Chin Chin*
Called: July 1997, Middle Temple, LLB (Hons)(Wales)

Tan *Chin Tee*
Called: July 1996, Middle Temple, LLB (Hons)(Sheff)

Tan *Miss Choo Lye*
Called: July 1994, Lincoln's Inn, LLB (Hons)

Tan *Choo Teck*
Kington & Tan, Advocates & Solicitors, Suite 6, 4th Floor, Wisma Ann Koai, 67 Jalan Ampang, Kuala Lumpur 50450, 03 238 2128, Fax: 03 201 2272, and Member Malaysia Bar. Called: Nov 1992, Lincoln's Inn, LLB (Hons)(Lond)

Tan *Miss Christine Mai Yean*
Called: July 1997, Lincoln's Inn, LLB (Hons)(Wales)

Tan *Chuan Thye*
Hon Secretary, Committee on Legal Education & Studies, Singapore Academy of Law, M/S Allen & Gledhill, 36 Robinson Road [H]18-01, City House, Singapore 068877, 225 1611, Fax: 224 8210, and Member Singapore Bar. Called: July 1990, Middle Temple, BA (Oxon)

Tan *Chun Hou*
Called: July 1997, Lincoln's Inn, LLB (Hons)(Lond)

Tan *Clarence Keng Loon*
and Member Singapore. Called: Nov 1995, Lincoln's Inn, LLB (Hons) (Leeds)

Tan *Colin Teck-Ee*
Called: July 1997, Middle Temple, BA (Hons)

Tan *Dennis Lip Fong*
9 Temasek Boulevard, [H]17 - 01, Suntec Tower 2, 3367727, Fax: 3360110, and Member Singapore. Called: July 1996, Middle Temple, LLB (Hons)(Notts)

Tan *Miss Diana Mei-Ying*
Advocate & Solicitor of Singapore. Called: July 1992, Lincoln's Inn, LLB (Hons)

Tan *Dominic Dwayne Kok Heng*
18th Floor Shell Tower, 50 Raffles Place, Singapore, 048623, 2201911, Fax: 2244118, and Member Singapore Bar. Called: July 1992, Lincoln's Inn, LLB (Hons) (Bucks), LLM (London)

Tan *Edmund Yen Kuan*
Merchant Banker, Project Finance, N M Rothschild & Sons Ltd, The Exchange, 20 Cecil Street, [H]09-00, Singapore 0104, 65 535 8311, Fax: 65 535 9109. Called: Nov 1992, Middle Temple, LLB (Hons, Lond), MBA (City)

Tan *Miss Emily Jee Neo*
and Member Malaysia. Called: July 1996, Lincoln's Inn, LLB (Hons), BEc (Hons), MBA (Hons), LLM (Hons)

Tan *Ernest Peng Ern*
43 Mayflower Place, (0065) 459 0367, Fax: (0065) 452 0260, and Member Singapore Bar. Called: July 1996, Lincoln's Inn, LLB (Hons)(Leeds), LLM (Cantab), ACIArb

Tan *Miss Esther*
Magistrates' Court Clerk, Norwich Magistrates' Court, Bishopgate, Norwich, Norfolk NR3 1UP, 01603 632421 ext 219, Fax: 0603 663263. Called: Nov 1990, Middle Temple, LLB (Buck'ham)

Tan *Miss Esther Ai Ping*
44 Richards Avenue, 2885943, and Member Singapore. Called: July 1994, Lincoln's Inn, LLB (Hons)

Tan *Eu Gin*
Called: July 1996, Middle Temple, LLB (Hons)(Hull)

Tan *Gerald Eng Chan*
Called: July 1996, Gray's Inn, LLB (Wales)

Tan *Hee Liang*
Tan See Swan & Co, Advocates & Solicitors, No 1 Park Road [H]04-49, People's Park Complex, Singapore 0105, 5351442/5324036/5344252, Fax: 5333609, and Member Singapore Bar. Called: July 1988, Inner Temple, B Soc Sc (Keele), LLM (Singapore)

Tan *Heok Ping Joshua*
Called: Nov 1996, Middle Temple, LLB (Hons)(Keele)

Tan *Hock Boon David*
Block 718, Hougang Avenue 2, [H]04-313, 65-2886011. Called: Nov 1996, Gray's Inn, LLB

Tan *Miss Hsiao Ling*
Called: July 1996, Middle Temple, LLB (Hons)(Warw)

Tan *Miss Hui Mei*
Legal Assistant, M/S Drew & Napier, 20 Raffles Place [H]17-00, Ocean Towers, 2803136 (Resid), Fax: 2803958, and Member Singapore Bar. Called: July 1995, Middle Temple, LLB (Hons)

Tan *Miss Hui Tsing*
Called: July 1995, Middle Temple, LLB (Hons)

Tan *Miss Ivy*
26 Sennett Avenue, S 467034, (065) 2448556. Called: July 1997, Gray's Inn, LLB

Tan *Miss Jacqueline*
Called: Nov 1996, Middle Temple, LLB (Hons)(Sheff)

Tan *James Chee Hau*
Justices' Law Clerk, Singapore Supreme Court, C/O HSBC Investment Bank Asia, Level 15, 1 Q.R.C., and Member Singapore Bar. Called: July 1993, Middle Temple, BA (Hons)

Tan *Miss Jeannie*
and Member Singapore Bar. Called: July 1993, Lincoln's Inn, LLB (Hons)

Tan *Jonanthan See Leh*
Called: July 1996, Lincoln's Inn, LLB (Hons)(Lond)

Tan *Ms June Sooi Ee*
Box 225, Tanjung Aru 89458, Kota Kinabalu, Sabah, Malaysia, 088 221262, Fax: 088 218043, and Member Sabah, Malaysia. Called: July 1994, Lincoln's Inn, LLB (Hons)

Tan *Kay Kian*
Called: July 1995, Middle Temple, LLB (Hons)

Tan *Kee Tay*
Called: Nov 1997, Lincoln's Inn, LLB (Hons)(Lond)

Tan *Kelvin David Sia Khoon*
Called: Nov 1996, Middle Temple, LLB (Hons)(Hull)

Tan *Kelvin Miang Ser*
Legal Officer(Judiciary), The Subordinate Courts of the Republic of Singapore, 180 Tai Keng Gardens. Called: July 1996, Lincoln's Inn, LLB (Hons)(Leeds), ACIArb, ASIArb

Tan *Khee Guan*
and Member Malaysia Bar. Called: July 1992, Middle Temple, LLB (Hons) (Leeds)

Tan *Kheng-Guan*
Called: Nov 1996, Middle Temple, BA (Hons)(Keele)

Tan *Kian Yuap*
and Member Malaysia. Called: July 1996, Lincoln's Inn, LLB (Hons)(Lond)

Tan *Miss Kim Suan*
Called: Nov 1996, Middle Temple, LLB (Hons)(Lond)

Tan *Kok Siang*
and Member Singapore Bar. Called: Apr 1991, Gray's Inn, LLB, MSIArb

Tan *Kong Yam*
Kadir, Tan & Ramli, 8th Floor, Sufuan Tower, 80 Jalan Ampang, 50450 Kuala Lumpur, 6 03 2382888, Fax: 6 03 2388431, and Member Malaysia Bar. Called: July 1996, Lincoln's Inn, LLB (Hons), LLM (LSE)

Tan *Kwong Ming Gerald*
Called: Nov 1994, Lincoln's Inn, LLB (Hons)(Lond)

Tan *Lai An*
C/O Tan & Lee, Advocates & Solicitors, Suite 2.04 2nd Level, Wisma MBF 37c Jalan Meldrum, 80000 Johor Bahru, Johor, (607) 2239259, Fax: (607) 2239142, and Member Malaysia Bar. Called: July 1989, Lincoln's Inn, LLB (Lond)

Tan *Miss Lai Tee*
Called: Nov 1997, Lincoln's Inn, LLB (Hons)(Leeds)

Tan *Laren Kian Seng*
Called: July 1994, Lincoln's Inn, LLB (Hons)

Tan *Dr Lauren Guet Lan*
Regional Legal Counsel, 1 Temasek Avenue, Millenia Tower, 23rd Floor, (65) 4322100, Fax: (65) 4322169, and Member Singapore Bar. Called: Nov 1993, Middle Temple, LLB (Hons), PH.D (B'ham)

Tan *Miss Lay Keng*
Called: Feb 1994, Inner Temple, LLB (Essex)

Tan *Miss Lay Khim*
Called: July 1996, Middle Temple, LLB (Hons)(Bris)

Tan *Leroy Kok Heng*
Called: Nov 1996, Middle Temple, LLB (Hons)

Tan *Miss Lip Sim*
Called: July 1997, Middle Temple, LLB (Hons)(Lond)

Tan *Miss Lu Gim*
Allen & Gledhill, 36 Robinson Road [H]18-01, City House, Singapore 0106, 2251611, Fax: 2254950, and Member Singapore Bar. Called: Nov 1991, Lincoln's Inn, BA (Hons) (Kent)

Tan *Lye Huat*
Called: Nov 1997, Middle Temple, LLB (Hons)(Lond)

Tan *Mark Jin Leong*
LLB (Hons)(Notts). Called: July 1996, Middle Temple

Tan *Miss May Yee*
Called: Nov 1997, Middle Temple, LLB (Hons)

Tan *Miss Mei-Yen*
Called: July 1995, Middle Temple, LLB (Hons) (Warw)

Tan *Miss Michelle Ai Ling*
Called: Mar 1997, Middle Temple, LLB (Hons)(Bris)

Tan *Ms Michelle Su May*
Called: July 1995, Middle Temple, LLB (Hons)

Tan *Miss Oi Peng*
Called: Nov 1994, Inner Temple, LLB (Kent)

Tan *Miss Peck Yen*
Called: July 1997, Lincoln's Inn, LLB (Hons) (Lond)

Tan *Miss Ping Ying*
and Member Malaysia. Called: July 1996, Inner Temple, LLB (Wolverhampton), MA

Tan *Miss Poh Hua*
Called: July 1995, Lincoln's Inn, LLB (Hons)

Tan *Miss Reina Chui-Lin*
Called: Nov 1997, Gray's Inn, LLB (Nott'm)

Tan *Richard Seng Chew*
Called: Nov 1996, Inner Temple, LLB (Lond)

Tan *Miss See Peng*
Called: July 1994, Lincoln's Inn, LLB (Hons) (Leic)

Tan *Miss Selene Ling Ling*
c/o Allen & Gledhill, 36 Robinson Road, [H]18-01 City House, 4207632, Fax: 2241574, and Member Singapore. Called: July 1994, Middle Temple, LLB (Hons)(B'ham)

Tan *Miss Sharon Suyin*
Called: July 1996, Lincoln's Inn, LLB (Hons)(Lond)

Tan *Miss Sheh-Lynn*
and Member Malaysia Bar. Called: July 1991, Middle Temple, LLB (Hons) (Wales)

Tan *Miss Sherain Ai Seok*
Called: Mar 1997, Lincoln's Inn, LLB (Hons)(Lond)

Tan *Miss Shirley Ching Ping*
Harry Ellas & Partners, 79 Robinson Road, [H]16-03 CPF Building, Singapore 068897, 2235006, Fax: 2262360, and Member Singapore Bar. Called: July 1994, Middle Temple, LLB (Hons)(Newc), LLM (Lond)

Tan *Miss Siew Siew*
Called: July 1997, Gray's Inn, LLB (Bris)

Tan *Miss Siew Wai*
and Member Singapore Bar. Called: July 1992, Lincoln's Inn, LLB (Hons) (Bucks)

Tan *Miss Siew Yung*
Called: July 1997, Lincoln's Inn, LLB (Hons)

Tan *Sin Oon*
Justices' Law Clerk, Supreme Court of Singapore, St Andrews Road, Singapore 178957. Called: July 1995, Middle Temple, LLB (Hons) (Bris)

Tan *Miss Soek Phee*
Called: July 1996, Middle Temple, LLB (Hons)(Wales)

Tan *Stanley Richard Sia Kong*
Called: July 1995, Inner Temple, LLB

Tan *Miss Sue Ann*
Called: July 1997, Lincoln's Inn,
LLB(Hons)(Wales)

Tan *Ms Sui Lin*
and Member Singapore Bar. Called: July
1991, Middle Temple, BA (Hons) (Cambs)

Tan *Miss Suzanne Sie Gek*
Called: Nov 1996, Lincoln's Inn, LLB
(Hons)(Bucks)

Tan *Miss Swee Lin Corrine*
Called: July 1997, Gray's Inn, LLB (Bristol)

Tan *Miss Tammy*
Called: July 1996, Middle Temple, LLB
(Hons)(Lond)

Tan *Teck Howe*
Called: July 1996, Lincoln's Inn, BA (Hons)

Tan *Teck Kiong*
Called: Nov 1997, Lincoln's Inn, LLB
(Hons)(Thames.V)

Tan *Tee Poon*
Unit 12, Blue Bay Apartments, Valley Road,
Halls Head WA 6210, Australia. Called: Feb
1963, Middle Temple, BDS (Malaya)

Tan *Teng Ta Benedict*
Called: July 1997, Middle Temple, LLB
(Hons)

Tan *Terence Li-Chern*
Messrs Wong Partnership, 80 Raffles Place,
[H] 58-01 UOB Plaza 1, (65) 539 7503, Fax:
(65) 532 5722, and Member Singapore Bar.
Called: July 1995, Inner Temple, LLB (Kent)

Tan *Tian Luh*
Called: July 1996, Lincoln's Inn, LLB
(Hons)(B'ham)

Tan *Tiong Hian*
Called: July 1994, Lincoln's Inn, LLB (Hons)

Tan *Tuan Wee*
Called: Nov 1995, Middle Temple, LLB
(Hons)

Tan *Miss Valerie Whei Tet*
Called: July 1995, Middle Temple, BA
(Hons)

Tan *Miss Wei Mann Germaine*
Called: Nov 1997, Lincoln's Inn, LLB (Hons)

Tan *Miss Wei-Lyn*
Called: July 1995, Middle Temple, LLB
(Hons)

Tan *Winston Kheng Huang*
Called: July 1997, Lincoln's Inn, LLB (Hons)

Tan *Woon Chay*
Figueiredo & Co Solicitors, Berkeley House,
3rd Floor, 73 Upper Richmond Road,
Putney, London SW15 2SZ, 0181 877 3844,
Fax: 0181 877 0556. Called: July 1991, Inner
Temple, BA (Kent)

Tan *Miss Yang Wah*
Called: July 1997, Lincoln's Inn, LLB
(Hons)(Lond)

Tan *Miss Yeun Fui*
Skrine & Co, Straits Trading Building, 4
Leboh Pasar Besar, 50050 Kuala Lumpur, 03-
2945111, Fax: 03-2934327, and Member
Malaysia Bar. Called: July 1994, Lincoln's
Inn, LLB (Hons)

Tan *Yew Hwee*
Called: Nov 1997, Middle Temple, B.Soc.Sc
(Hons), (Singapore), LLB, (Lond)

Tan *Miss Ying Hui*
Called: Nov 1978, Gray's Inn, BA, (Lond)

Tan *Miss Ying Wee*
Called: July 1995, Middle Temple, LLB
(Hons)

Tanaka *Ms Diana Tei*
0171 286 7089, and Member Eastern &
Southern Districts of New York (Federal)
USA, First Circuit (Federal) USA,
Massachusetts District Court (Federal) USA,
New York Washington DC & Massachusetts
State Bar (USA). Called: Nov 1988, Middle
Temple, BA [Harvard], JD [Harvard], LLM
[Georgetown]

Tang *Miss Ai Leen*
Called: Mar 1998, Middle Temple, LLB
(Hons)(B'ham)

Tang *Edmund Ming-Wai*
Called: Nov 1994, Gray's Inn, LLB (Lond)

Tang *Ms Fong Har*
Advocate & Solicitor of the Supreme Court
of Singapore and Member Singapore Bar.
Called: July 1990, Inner Temple, LLB (Hons)
Singapore

Tang *Jay Son*
Called: July 1997, Lincoln's Inn, LLB
(Hons)(Lond)

Tang *Kenneth Wai Loong*
80 Chay Yan Street, [H] 02-08, Singapore
160080, Singapore, 2231513, Fax: 7487936.
Called: Nov 1993, Middle Temple, LLB
(Hons)(Newc), LLM (London)

Tang *Kwong Leung*
and Member Hong Kong Bar. Called: Feb
1992, Gray's Inn, B.Soc.Sc (Hong Kong),
MSW (Hong Kong), MSc (LSE),LLB (Lond),
LLM (Cantab), Ph.D (Berkley)

Tang *Michael Vee Mun*
Called: July 1995, Lincoln's Inn, LLB (Hons)

Tang *Quin Choy*
Called: July 1997, Middle Temple, LLB
(Hons)(Lond)

Tang *Ms Suet Yean*
and Member Malaysia. Called: July 1993,
Lincoln's Inn, LLB (Hons)

Tangavellu *Resebalingam*
Called: July 1995, Lincoln's Inn, LLB (Hons)

Tank *Rajnikant*
Called: Mar 1996, Inner Temple, LLB (LSE)

Tankel *David*
Director, New Bridge Street Consultants, 20
Little Britain, London EC1A 7DH, 0171 282
3030, Fax: 0171 282 0011. Called: July
1983, Middle Temple, BA (Manch), Dip Law

Tanner *Mrs Elizabeth Anne* •
Legal Advisor, National Farmers Union
(LISS), Station Road, Hampshire GU33 7AR,
01730 893 723. Called: Nov 1994, Inner
Temple, LLB (Swansea)

Tanner *Dr Mark*
Senior Registrar in Psychiatry, Royal London
Hospital, Whitechapel, London E1 1BB.
Called: Nov 1986, Middle Temple, MB, BCh,
Dip Law, MRC Psych

Tanner *Paul Martyn Roger*
Called: Oct 1996, Inner Temple, BA (Oxon),
CPE (Lond)

Tanner *Peter Christopher*
5 West View Close, Colchester CO4 4SP,
01206 844577, Fax: 01206 844577.
Called: Feb 1990, Gray's Inn, LLB [Essex]

Tantam *Mark Andrew Howard*
Partner, Forensic Services, Deloitte &
Touche, Chartered Accountants, Hill House,
1 Little New Street, London EC4A 3TR,
0171 936 3000, Fax: 0171 936 2638.
Called: July 1982, Inner Temple, MA (Oxon)

Tappin *Douglas Owen* •
Island Records Limited, 22 St Peters Square,
London W6 9NW. Called: Oct 1993,
Lincoln's Inn, LLB (Hons)(Lond)

Tarling *Mrs Angela Bernadette Hardie*
Called: Oct 1990, Gray's Inn, LLB (Hons),
MA

Tarling *Miss Karen Joan* •
Essex County Council, Legal Services,
County Hall, Chelmsford, Essex, 01245
42211 Ext 20404, Fax: 01245 346994.
Called: July 1991, Gray's Inn, LLB

Tarling *Richard David* •
Assistant Director, Trade Indemnity plc, 1
Canada Square, London E14 5DX, 0171 860
2753, Fax: 0171 729 7682. Called: Nov
1976, Gray's Inn, LLB, ACIS.

Tate *William John* •
Deputy Parliamentary Commissioner for
Administration, Office of the Parliamentary,
Commissioner for, Administration, Church
House, Great Smith Street, London
SW1P 3BW. Called: July 1974, Gray's Inn,
LLB

Tatham *Allan Francis*
Called: Oct 1992, Gray's Inn, BA (Dunelm),
BCL (Dunelm)

Tattersall *Bruce*
Called: Oct 1997, Middle Temple, MA
(Edinburgh), CPE (Westminster)

Tawiah *James Kofi* •
Legal Adviser, 8 Bernwood House, Seven
Sister Road, Woodbery Down, London
N4 2RU, 0181 802 4065, Fax: 0171 690
5404, and Member Ghana Bar. Called: May
1960, Lincoln's Inn, LLB(London)

Tay *Miss April Glenys*
Called: Nov 1996, Lincoln's Inn, LLB
(Hons)(Lond)

Tay *Ms Dorothy*
18 Sin Ming Walk [H] 02-03, Bishan Park
Condominium, Singapore 575569, 65
4531567, and Member Singapore Bar.
Called: July 1993, Middle Temple, LLB
(Hons)(Lond)

Tay *Miss Elaine Ling Yan*
Called: July 1997, Middle Temple, LLB
(Hons)

Tay *Eng Kwee*
Called: July 1994, Lincoln's Inn, LLB (Hons)

Tay *Francis Chien Thuan*
Called: Oct 1994, Middle Temple, LLB
(Hons)(Kent)

Tay *Miss Hwee Hua*
and Member Singapore Bar. Called: Nov
1995, Middle Temple, LLB (Lond)

Tay *Miss Jin Keng*
Called: Nov 1995, Middle Temple, LLB
(Hons)(Lond)

Tay *Lai Eng*
Called: Nov 1996, Lincoln's Inn, LLB (Hons)

Tay *Miss Li Shing*
Called: July 1997, Gray's Inn, LLB (Bris)

Tay *Miss Sock Kheng*
Called: July 1996, Lincoln's Inn, LLB
(Hons)(Lond)

Tay *Wee Chong*
Called: July 1994, Lincoln's Inn, LLB (Hons)

Tay *Miss Yien Ling Daisy*
Called: July 1994, Middle Temple, LLB
(Hons)(Lond)

Taye *Miss Lynette Wei Ching*
Called: July 1997, Lincoln's Inn, LLB
(Hons)(Nott'm)

Tayler *Mrs Keri* •
Southampton City Council, Southbrook
Rise, 4-8 Millbrook Road East, Southampton
SO15 1YG, 01703 833213, Fax: 01703
833217. Called: Feb 1995, Inner Temple,
LLB (Soton)

Taylerson *Anthony William Finlay*
Called: Apr 1951, Lincoln's Inn, MA (Oxon)

Taylor *Miss Anne Bridget*
Deputy Chief Clerk, Inner London & City
Family, Proceedings Court, 59/65 Wells
Street, London W1A 3AE, 0171 323 1649,
Fax: 0171 636 0617. Called: July 1976,
Middle Temple, LLB

Taylor *Arthur Rodney* •
Senior Pensions Lawyer, General Accident
Life, Pensions Legal, Six Hills Way,
Stevenage, Herts SG1 2ST, 01438 732716.
Called: Nov 1966, Middle Temple

Taylor *Christopher Paul* •
Litigation Counsel, Enviroment Agency,
Kingfisher House, Goldhay Way, Orton
Goldhay, Peterborough PE2 5ZR, 01733
464434, Fax: 01733 464487, 7 New Square,
Lincoln's Inn, London, WC2A 3QS.
Called: Oct 1990, Lincoln's Inn, LLB (Hons)

Taylor *Miss Diana Folland*
Allen & Overy Solicitors, One New Charge,
London EC4M 9QQ. Called: Nov 1970,
Gray's Inn

Taylor *Miss Helga June*
Chavasse Court Chambers, 2nd Floor,
Chavasse Court, 24 Lord Street, Liverpool,
L2 1TA. Called: Nov 1952, Gray's Inn, LLB
(L'pool)

Taylor *Howard*
Bench Legal Adviser, Northamptonshire
Mags Court, Magistrates Court Office,
Regents Pavilion, Summerhouse Road,
Moulton Park, Northampton NN3 6AS,
01604 497001. Called: May 1988, Gray's Inn

Taylor *Howard Robert Frank*
Called: Nov 1995, Inner Temple, LLB (Lond)

Taylor *Ian Russell*
Called: Mar 1998, Gray's Inn, MA (Cantab)

Taylor *James Edward*
R D Black & Co, 31 Old Jewry, London
EC2R 8DQ, 0171 600 8282, Fax: 0171 600
8228, and Member Bar of Western Australia.
Called: July 1986, Inner Temple, LLB
Nottingham

Taylor *Ms Judith Hannah*
Called: Nov 1994, Inner Temple, LLB
(Lond), LLB (Hons)

Taylor *Michael John* •
Deputy General Counsel, 1 Queen Caroline
Street, London W6 9BN, 0181 600 1010,
Fax: 0181 741 0851. Called: Feb 1986,
Gray's Inn, BA

Taylor *Peter John Bernard*
Called: Nov 1997, Inner Temple, MBE, FICE,
FCIArb, CE

Taylor *Peter John Frederick*
Consultant & Construction Law Advisor, 28
Great Pulteney Street, Bath BA2 4BU, 01225
483583, Fax: 01225 315164, Included on
FIDIC & ICE List of Arbitrators. Called: Nov
1979, Middle Temple, C.Eng, FIStrE.FHKIE,
FCIArb

Taylor *Peter William Edward* QC
(1981)
also Lincoln's Inn 17 Old Bldgs, Ground
Floor, Lincoln's Inn, London, WC2A 3UP.
Called: Nov 1946, Inner Temple, MA

Taylor *Richard Graham*
Called: Oct 1992, Gray's Inn, BA (Hons),
MBA, Dip Law

Taylor *Ross Clyde*
Called: July 1984, Gray's Inn, LLB (Lond)

Taylor *Simon Mark* •
Legal Advisor, Cable & Wireless
Communication, 26 Red Lion Square,
London WC1R 4HQ, 0171 528 2167, Fax:
0171 528 2039. Called: Nov 1987, Gray's
Inn, BA (Oxon), License Speciale en, droit
Europeen, (Brussels)

Taylor *Simon Peter James*
Called: Nov 1997, Inner Temple, LLB
(Middx)

Taylor *Lieutenant Commander
Stephen John*
Called: Oct 1996, Middle Temple, BA (Hons)
(York)

Taylor *Miss Susan Mary Edith* •
Branch Crown Prosecution, Central
Confiscation Branch., Crown Prosecution
Service, Central Casework, Central
Confiscations Branch, 50 Ludgate Hill,
London EC4M 7EX, 0171 273 1308, Fax:
0171 273 1325. Called: July 1980, Middle
Temple, LLB (Leeds)

Taylor *Miss Teresa Dawn*
Called: Nov 1994, Gray's Inn, LLB

Taylor *Timothy John*
Called: Nov 1953, Gray's Inn

Taylor *Ms Wendy Rutledge*
Associate Reinsurance Counsel, Risk
Enterprise Management Ltd, 59 Maiden
Lane, New York, New York 10038, 212
5306944, Fax: 212 5306997, and Member
State of New Jersey Bar. Called: July 1987,
Lincoln's Inn, BA, H.Dip. Pers.Man, Dip
Law, JD

Taylor of Warwick *Lord*
9 Gough Square, London, EC4A 3DE.
Called: Feb 1978, Gray's Inn, BA
(Hons)(Keele)

Taylor-Carroll De Mueller *Mrs Athena
Robina*
General Counsel, Action on Smoking &
Health, Washington D.C.1984-1996, 2904
Viceroy Avenue, Forestville, Maryland
20747, and Member US Sup Ct, US Ct of
App(DC Cir),US Dist Ct (DC), Dist of
Columbia Ct of Appeals. Called: July 1952,
Lincoln's Inn, MA,LLB (Cantab), JD, LLM
(Miami)

Teah *Mrs Jacqueline Mooi Hua* •
Called: Feb 1992, Lincoln's Inn, LLB (Hons),
LLM

Teasdale *Jonathan Paul*
Legal Consultant, Bunkers Solicitors, 7 The
Drive, Hove, East Sussex BN3 3JS, 01273
329797, Fax: 01273 324082, Past Vice
Chairman Bar Assoc for Local Govt &
Public Service. Past Chairman Joint Practice
Management Working Party. Member
Administration Law Bar Association..
Called: July 1977, Inner Temple, LLB,
ACIArb, FRSA, Legal Associate RTPI

Teather *Mrs Maureen*
Legal Advisor, Derbyshire Magistrates'
Court, P O Box 11, The Court House, West
Bars, Chesterfield S40 1AE, 01246 278171,
Fax: 01246 276344. Called: May 1992, Inner
Temple, LLB

Teck *Tan Yew*
Called: Mar 1998, Gray's Inn, LLB (Lond)

Tee *Miss Clare Antoinette*
and Member Guernsey Bar. Called: Nov
1995, Inner Temple, LLB (Manc)

Tee *Miss Dawn Pei Sze*
Called: July 1996, Lincoln's Inn, LLB (Hons)
(Notts)

E

Tee *Miss En Peng*
Called: July 1997, Lincoln's Inn, LLB
(Hons)(Lond)

Tee *Kien Moon*
Called: July 1994, Lincoln's Inn, LLB (Hons)

Tee *Ling Zhi*
Called: Nov 1997, Lincoln's Inn, LLB (Hons)

Tegally *Mrs Assilla Bibi*
Called: Oct 1992, Lincoln's Inn, LLB(Hons)

Teh *Miss Ee-Von*
Called: July 1997, Middle Temple, LLB
(Hons)(Leics)

Teh *Miss Hong Koon*
Called: Nov 1997, Lincoln's Inn, LLB
(Hons)(E.Lond)

Teh *John Teong Beng*
Called: Nov 1995, Middle Temple, LLB
(Hons)(Wales)

Teh *Ms Julie Chooi Gan*
Partner, Dorairaj, Low & Teh, Wisman
AMGM, 1st Floor, No 57 Jalan Hang Lekiu,
50100 Kuala Lumpur, 03 2011136, Fax: 03
2010113, and Member Malaysia Bar.
Called: Nov 1992, Gray's Inn, LLB (Lond)

Teh *Khang Suon*
Legal Assistant (Practising Lawyer), c/o
Azalina Chan & Chia, Advocates & Solictors,
Lot 716, 7th Floor, Wisma, Cosway, 88 Jalan
Raja Chulan, 50200 Kuala Lumpur, 603
2488625, Fax: 603 2411913. Called: Nov
1996, Gray's Inn, LLB (Sheff)

Teh *Lawrence Kee Wee*
C/O Rodyk & Davidson, 9 Raffles Place,
[H]55-00 Republic Plaza, 65 225 2626, Fax:
65 225 1838, and Member Singapore Bar.
Called: Nov 1992, Inner Temple, LLB (Lond)

Teh *Lip Jin*
Legal Assistant, and Member Malaysia Bar.
Called: July 1994, Gray's Inn, BA (Kent)

Teh *Miss Mui Kim*
Advocate & Solicitor, 1 Queensway [H]14-
65, Fax: 334 3623, and Member Singapore
Bar. Called: July 1995, Middle Temple, LLB
(Hons)

Teh *Miss Wee Tee*
Called: July 1995, Middle Temple, LLB
(Hons) (Wales)

Teh *Miss Yuen Ting*
Called: July 1997, Lincoln's Inn, LLB
(Hons)(Nott'm)

Tehal *Tanvir*
Called: Nov 1996, Middle Temple, LLB
(Hons)

Telemaque *Marc Timothy*
Called: May 1993, Gray's Inn, LLB
(Buckinghamshi)

Telfer *Miss Fredelinda Jane*
Project Manager, Paradoc /GP Care, The
Lawson Practice, St Leonards, London
N1 5LZ, 0171 739 9701. Called: Feb 1995,
Middle Temple, Dip in Stage, Management,
LLB (Hons)(Lond)

Telford *Ms Venous*
Called: Oct 1996, Gray's Inn, BA, MSc
(Indiana), LLB (Kent)

Telling *Arthur Edward*
Called: June 1949, Inner Temple, MA
(Oxon)

Tempest *Alistair Mark*
Called: Oct 1997, Middle Temple, LLB
(Hons)(Lond)

Tempest *Leonard*
Deputy Clerk to the Justices for
Leicestershire's Northern Divisions,
Leicestershire Magistrates Crt, 674 Melton
Road, Thurmaston, Leicester LE4 8BB,
01162 640920, Fax: 01162 692369.
Called: Feb 1987, Gray's Inn, DML, DMS,
M.A.(Mgmt), 0

Temple *Matthew*
Called: Nov 1992, Inner Temple, LLB (Hons)

Teng *Hin Fatt*
Block 128, Lorong Ah Soo, [H]12-314,
Singapore 1953. Called: Nov 1993, Lincoln's
Inn, LLB (Hons, Lond)

Teng *Miss Joanna*
Legal Assistant, Salina, Lim Kim Chuan &
Co, Advocates & Solcitors, No 28-c Lorong
Abu Siti, 10400 Penang, 228 2089, Fax: 228
2093, and Member Malaysia. Called: July
1995, Lincoln's Inn, LLB (Hons)

Teng *Mrs Whee Tin* •
Court Clerk, Harrow Magistrates', Courts
Committee, PO Box 164, Rosslyn Crescent,
Harrow HA1 2JY, 0181 427 5146.
Called: July 1986, Lincoln's Inn

Tengara *Miss Mestika*
Called: Nov 1996, Lincoln's Inn, LLB
(Hons)(Kent)

Tengku Ismail *Miss Tengku Ida Adura*
Legal Assistant (Advocate & Solicitor), Lloyd
Fernando & Razak, Suite 1203, 12th Floor,
Wisma Hangsam, No 1 Jalan Hang Lekir,
50000 Kuala Lumpur, 603 2308036, Fax:
603 2320312, and Member High Court of
Malaya. Called: July 1996, Lincoln's Inn, LLB
(Hons)(Notts)

Teo *Miss Bee Leay*
99 Sunset Way, Singapore 2159, 4691221,
Fax: 4663583, and Member New York State
Bar. Called: July 1993, Middle Temple, LLB
(Hons, Kent), LLM (Boston, USA)

Teo *Chee Kang*
Called: July 1994, Lincoln's Inn, LLB (Hons,
Lond)

Teo *Miss Deav-Tieng*
Called: Nov 1995, Middle Temple, LLB
(Hons)(Lond)

Teo *Eu Jin Nicholas*
Called: July 1996, Middle Temple, LLB
(Hons)(Leic)

Teo *Eugene Weng Kuan*
Assistant Registrar, Supreme Court, City
Hall, St Andrews Road. Called: July 1995,
Middle Temple, LLB (Hons) (Hull)

Teo *Francis Teng Siu*
Called: Nov 1996, Lincoln's Inn, LLB
(Hons)(Lond)

Teo *Miss Geok Yen*
Called: Nov 1994, Middle Temple, LLB
(Hons)

Teo *Miss Hwee Ping*
55 Market Street, 08-01 Sinsov Building,
Singapore 0104, 538 3177, Fax: 532 5554,
and Member Singapore Bar. Called: Nov
1991, Gray's Inn, BA (Kent)

Teo *Miss Josephine Siew Ing*
Called: July 1995, Middle Temple, LLB
(Hons) (Hull)

Teo *Miss May May* •
Lawyer (Grade 7), Office of the Social
Security, & Child Support Commissioners,
Harp House, 33-86 Farringdon Street,
London EC4A 4DH, 0171 353 5145, Fax:
0171 936 2171. Called: July 1989, Middle
Temple, LLB

Teo *Miss Yi-Ling*
Called: Nov 1996, Middle Temple, LLB
(Hons)(L'pool)

Teoh *Ms Gim See*
Called: Nov 1996, Lincoln's Inn, BA
(Hons)(E.Anglia)

Terry *James* •
Principal Crown Prosecutor, Crown
Prosecution Service, Saxon House, 1
Cromwell Square, Ipswich, Suffolk IP1 1TS,
01473 230332, Fax: 01473 231 377.
Called: Nov 1981, Gray's Inn, LLB

Terry *Mrs Jennifer* •
Principal Crown Prosecutor, Crown
Prosecution Service, 50 Ludgate Hill,
London EC4, 0171 273 8305, Fax: 0171 329
8166. Called: Nov 1973, Inner Temple, MSc,
LLB, Dip Soc Ad

Tester *John William Nielson* •
Assistant Secretary (Legal), Solicitors Office,
HM Customs & Excise, New King's Beam
House, 22 Upper Ground, London SE1 9PJ,
0171 865 5212, Fax: 0171 865 5022.
Called: July 1980, Gray's Inn, LLB (B'ham)

Tetsola *Miss Augustina* •
Crown Prosecutor, Crown Prosecution
Service, 3 Clifton Mews, Clifton Hill,
Brighton, East Sussex. Called: July 1988,
Lincoln's Inn, LLB (Hons) (Essex)

Teuten *Miss Julie Helen* •
Compliance, National Westminster Bank Plc,
27 Leadenhall Street, London EC3A 1AA,
0171 920 1641, Fax: 0171 920 6740.
Called: Nov 1990, Middle Temple, LLB

Tevlin *Aidan Matthew* •
Prosecution Team Leader, Crown
Prosecution Service, Justinian House,
Spitfire Close, Ermine Business Park,
Huntingdon Cambs PE18 6XY, 01480
432333. Called: July 1980, Gray's Inn, LLB
(Leic),MA, MPhil (CNAA)

Tew *Lieutenant Commander John Philip RN* •
Command Legal Adviser, Flag Officer Naval Aviation, Command Legal Adviser, Flag Officer Naval Aviation, FONA HQ, Yeovil, Somerset BA22 8HL, 01935 455503, Fax: 01935 455844. Called: Oct 1993, Lincoln's Inn, BA (Hons), LLM

Tey *Tsun Hang*
Called: July 1995, Gray's Inn, LLB

Thacker *Charles Malcom Belford*
Notary Public, Messrs Vibert & Valpy, Advocates, 8 Duhamel Place, St Helier, Jersey JE2 4XA, 0534 888666, Fax: 0534 888555, and Member Jersey Bar. Called: Nov 1970, Lincoln's Inn, MA (Hons)

Thai *Jiin Peir*
No 46B Lorong Ismail, 81000 Kulain, Johor, 07 6624732/3/6625057, Fax: 07 6624639, and Member Malaysia Bar. Called: Nov 1993, Lincoln's Inn, LLB (Hons)

Thain *Derek Anthony Teague MBE*
Hon Director, European Union Council Secretariat, Woodlands, Bishop's Down Park Rd, Tunbridge Wells, Kent TN4 8XR, 01892 526372. Called: Nov 1963, Inner Temple

Thakar *Miss Rina Rajendra*
Called: July 1997, Gray's Inn, LLB (Warwick)

Thakkar *Mrs Sapna Niranjan*
The Northwood Law Practice, 17 The Broadway, Joel Street, Northwood Hills HA6 1NU. Called: Oct 1993, Middle Temple, LLB (Hons)

Thakrar *Miss Bijal*
Called: July 1996, Middle Temple, LLB (Hons)(Lond), LLM (Keele)

Thalben-Ball *John Michael*
51 Lodge Close, Stoke D'Abernon, Cobham, Surrey KT11 2SQ, 01932 863995. Called: Nov 1958, Middle Temple, MA (Cantab)

Tham *Miss Melissa Lyn-li*
Called: July 1995, Middle Temple, LLB (Hons)

Tham *Soong Meng Edwin*
Associate, Allen & Overy Legal Services, Moscow, Dmitrovskiy Pereulok, 9, 103031 Moscow, 7 501 258 3111, Fax: 7 501 258 3113, and Member New York Bar. Called: July 1989, Middle Temple, LLB [Nott'm]

Tham *Miss Swee Hiong*
Senior Planner, Overseas Chinese Banking Corp, 65 Chulia Street, 5357222/5302929. Called: July 1995, Middle Temple, LLB (Hons)

Thampuran *Miss Sandhia*
and Member Singapore Bar. Called: July 1995, Middle Temple, LLB (Hons)

Thanarajoo *Miss Frances Angeline*
Called: July 1994, Lincoln's Inn, LLB (Hons)

Thanki *Mrs Catherine Jane Margaret*
Called: Nov 1988, Lincoln's Inn, BA (Durham)

Thatcher *Miss Nichola Jane* •
Principal Legal Officer, Metropolitan Police Service, New Scotland Yard, Broadway, London SW1H OBG, 0171 230 7339, Fax: 0171 230 7209. Called: Nov 1992, Inner Temple, LLB (Hons)

Thatcher *Roger Francis* •
Senior Crown Prosecutor, Formerly a solicitor. Called: Feb 1977, Gray's Inn, Dip Criminology

Thavalou *Rajah Kulan*
Called: Nov 1996, Middle Temple, LLB (Hons) (Lond), MA (Guildhall)

The *Miss Diana Hui Ling*
Legal Assistant Advocate & Solictor, 7 Temasek Boulevard, [H]15-01, Suntec Tower One, (065) 4566501/3375822, Fax: (065) 3372932, and Member Singapore. Called: July 1996, Middle Temple, LLB (Hons)(Bris)

Theaker *Ms Michele Lorraine*
Called: Oct 1997, Inner Temple, LLB (Reading)

Theodorides *Miss Melita-Despina*
Called: Mar 1997, Lincoln's Inn, LLB (Leics)

Theseira *Joseph Dominic*
Palakrishnan & Partners, Advocates & Solicitors, 1 Colombo Court, [H]07-13/14/15a, 3382294, Fax: 3391400, and Member Singapore Bar. Called: Nov 1991, Middle Temple, LLB (Hons) (Lond)

Thew *Mrs Stephanie Mary* •
Clerk to the Justices, The Magistrates Court, Elm Street, Ipswich, Suffolk IP1 2AP, 01473 217261, Fax: 01473 231249. Called: July 1973, Middle Temple, LLB

Thiagarajah *Miss Thanuja*
Called: July 1996, Lincoln's Inn, LLB (Hons)(Lond)

Thiagarajan *Anand*
and Member Singapore Bar. Called: July 1995, Lincoln's Inn, LLB (Hons)

Thinathayalan *Suppiah*
Called: July 1996, Inner Temple, LLB,LLM (Lond)

Thio *Miss Jean Puay Jin*
Called: July 1997, Lincoln's Inn, LLB (Hons)(Lond)

Thirumaney *Miss Manimala*
Called: Nov 1996, Lincoln's Inn, LLB (Hons)

Thng *Miss Hwei Lin*
Called: July 1993, Middle Temple, LLB (Hons)

Thomas *Alan David*
Called: Oct 1996, Inner Temple, LLB (Lancs)

Thomas *Ms Belinda Jane* •
Government Lawyer, Investigations & Enforcement Directorate, Dept. Trade & Industry, Dept of Trade & Industry, 419 Victoria Buildings, 10 Victoria Street, London SW1H 0NN, 0171 215 3214. Called: Oct 1991, Middle Temple, BA Hons (B'ham), Dip Law

Thomas *Ms Cheryl Diane*
Called: Oct 1997, Inner Temple, LLB (Hull)

Thomas *Miss Christina* •
Portsmouth City Council. Called: Feb 1994, Inner Temple, LLB (Wales)

Thomas *Miss Christine Margaret Mary*
Law Lecturer, Mitre House Chambers, Mitre House, 44 Fleet Street, London, EC4Y 1BN. Called: Oct 1991, Inner Temple, LLB (Hons)

Thomas *David John*
Called: Nov 1996, Gray's Inn, BA, MPhil (Nott'm)

Thomas *Hugh Vivian* •
Senior Attorney, Merrill Lynch Europe Plc, Ropemaker Place, 25 Ropemaker Street, London EC2Y 9LY, 0171 867 4451, Fax: 0171 867 4818. Called: Nov 1986, Lincoln's Inn, LLB

Thomas *Ian Geoffrey*
Aviation Insurance Underwriter, Robert Malatier Limited, 8-11 Lime Street, London EC3M 7AA, 0171 623 4524, Fax: 0171 623 3648. Called: Nov 1991, Middle Temple, LLB,(Lond) FCII, ACIS

Thomas *Miss Janet Elfrida*
Called: Nov 1994, Gray's Inn, BA (Lancs)

Thomas *Jason Richard*
Called: Oct 1996, Lincoln's Inn, BA (Hons)(Lond), LLB (Hons)(City)

Thomas *John*
34B Bayshore Road, The Bayshore, Tower 2b [H]18-02, 65-2452040, Law Society of Singapore. Called: Oct 1993, Gray's Inn, BA, B.Soc.Sci (Hons), (Singapore), LLB, (Manch)

Thomas *Norman Edgar ERD*
Sun Holm, 51 Cranford Avenue, Littleham Cross, Exmouth, Devon EX8 2QF, 01395 264802. Called: Nov 1956, Lincoln's Inn, BSc[Eng],MIEE, CEng

Thomas *Miss Sarah Jane* •
Masons' & Co, 30 Aylesbury Street, London EC1R OER. Called: Oct 1990, Gray's Inn, BA (Oxon)

Thomasson *Miss Claire Margaret Mary* •
Senior Crown Prosecutor, Crown Prosecution Service, Cuthbert House, All Saints Office Centre, Newcastle Upon Tyne, 0191 232 6602. Called: Oct 1991, Gray's Inn, BA (Hons)

Thomlinson *Peter Robert* •
Legal Advisor, Mitsubishi Electric Europe B.V, Travellers Lane, Hatfield, Herts AL10 8XB, 01707 276100, Fax: 01707 278525, and Member Northern Ireland Bar. Called: July 1981, Lincoln's Inn, BA, LLM

Thompson *Miss Alison Mary*
Gilt Chambers, Hong Kong, 866 8233, Fax: 866 3932, and Member Hong Kong Bar. Called: July 1986, Middle Temple, BSc, LLB

Thompson *Dennis*
8 Rue des Belles Filles, 1299 Crans, 022 7761687, Fax: 022 7767303, LI (ad eundem). Called: Jan 1939, Inner Temple, MA (Cantab), FCIArb (Ret'd)

Thompson *Mrs Diana Elizabeth*
La Hure, Rue des Cambrees, Torteral, Guerney GY8 0LD, 0481 65831, Fax: 0481 66160, and Member Royal Court of Guernsey. Called: Nov 1990, Inner Temple, LLB

Thompson *Miss Elizabeth*
Called: Mar 1997, Middle Temple, LLB (Hons)(E.Lond)

Thompson *Miss Elizabeth Joyce*
Called: July 1968, Middle Temple, BA (Hons)

Thompson *Gilbert Anselm*
McKinney, Bancroft & Hughes, P.O. Box F-40437, Freeport, (242) 352 7425-7, Fax: (242) 352 7214, and Member Bahamas Bar (September 1996). Called: July 1996, Gray's Inn, BA (Canada), LLB (Buck)

Thompson *James Kwasi*
Associate Attorney, James R Thompson & Company, Suite 31A, Kipling Building, P.O.Box F 42912, Freeport, GB, Bahamas, (242) 352 7451 2, Fax: (242) 352 7453, and Member Bahamas. Called: July 1997, Middle Temple, LLB (Hons)

Thompson *John David*
Inspector into suspected insider dealing under Financial Services Act 1986, Ballyrawer House, Carrowdore, Co Down BT22 2HZ, 01247 861478, Fax: 01247 861095, QC (Northern Ireland) and Member Northern Ireland Bar Republic of Ireland Bar. Called: Nov 1992, Gray's Inn, LLB (Belfast)

Thompson *Kenneth Manour*
Called: Nov 1995, Gray's Inn, BA (W.Indies), LLB (Lond)

Thompson *Miss Lillian Amorella Elizabeth*
42 Rockford Ave, Daly City, CA 94015, U.S.A.. Called: Nov 1993, Inner Temple, LLB (Lond)

Thompson *Miss Lindsey Claire*
Called: Nov 1995, Gray's Inn, LLB (Notts)

Thompson *Mrs Paula Mary*
Called: July 1989, Middle Temple, LLB [Lond]

Thompson *Peter Kenneth James* QC (1997)
Called: Feb 1961, Lincoln's Inn, MA, LLB

Thompson *Miss Samantha*
Called: Mar 1996, Gray's Inn, B.Sc

Thompson *Miss Sharyn Anne* •
Senior Crown Prosecutor, Crown Prosecution Service, Hawkins House, Pynes Hill, Exeter, Devon EX2 5SS, 01392 422555, Fax: 01392 422111. Called: July 1975, Inner Temple, LLB

Thompson *Thomas TD*
Construction disputes Consultant/Arbitrator, Garth House, Evening Hill, Thursby, Carlisle CA5 6PU, 01228 710688. Called: June 1958, Middle Temple, MA (Oxon), ACIArb

Thompson *William John*
Called: Feb 1977, Inner Temple, MA, LLB (Lond)

Thompson Alabi-Isama *Mrs Elizabeth*
LLB (Hons)(Bucks) BA (Canada). Called: Nov 1994, Lincoln's Inn

Thomson *Eric Matheson*
Called: Feb 1957, Gray's Inn, BA

Thomson *James Smith*
Gilt Chambers, Room 1001, Far East Finance Centre, 16 Harcourt Road, Central Hong Kong, 866 8233, Fax: 866 3932, and Member Hong Kong Bar. Called: July 1983, Lincoln's Inn, BA (Kent)

Thomson *Malcolm George*
Chairman Natioanl Health Services Tribunal (Scotland), 12 Succoth Avenue, Edinburgh EH12 6BT, 0131 337 4911, Fax: 0131 337 9100, QC Scotland. Called: Apr 1991, Lincoln's Inn, LLB (Edin)

Thomson *Neil Clarke*
Des Voeux Chambers, 10/F Bank of East Asia Bldg, 10 Des Voeux Road, Central, Hong Hong, 2526 3071, Fax: 2810 5287, and Member Hong Kong Bar. Called: Nov 1994, Gray's Inn, BA, LLM, FTIHK

Thomson *Peter*
Director General, Chartered Institute of, Purchasing & Supply, Easton House, Easton on the Hill, Stamford, Lincs PE9 3NZ, 01780 756777, Fax: 01780 751610. Called: May 1966, Middle Temple, MA (Oxon)

Thomson *Ronald Christopher*
Called: Apr 1986, Gray's Inn, BA (Hons), FRICS, ACIArb.

Thong *Ms Jessie Yuen Siew*
Legal Assistant, Rodyk and Davidson, 9 Raffles Place, [H] 55-01, 2252626, Fax: 2257511, and Member Singapore Bar. Called: Apr 1991, Gray's Inn, BA, LLM

Thong *Miss Yen Hwa*
Court Clerk, Court House, Oldbury Ringway, Oldbury, Warley, West Midlands B69 4JN, 0121 511 2222, Fax: 0121 544 8492, and Member Malaysia Bar. Called: July 1982, Lincoln's Inn, LLB (Law)

Thorley *Giles Alexander* •
Director, Principal Finance, Nomura International Plc, 1 St Martins Le Grand, London EC1A 4NP, 0171 521 2000, Fax: 0171 521 2189. Called: Oct 1990, Inner Temple, LLB (Lond)

Thorn *Miss Sheryl Lorraine*
Court Clerk, Norwich Magistrates Court, The Court House, Bishopgate, Norwich, Norfolk NR3 1UP, 01603 632421, Fax: 01603 663263. Called: Oct 1994, Inner Temple, LLB (E.Anglia)

Thorndycraft *Mr. Jason Victor Francis*
Called: July 1995, Inner Temple, LLB, LLM

Thorne-Johnson *Mrs Mary Ann*
Called: Nov 1987, Lincoln's Inn, LLB (Hons) (Lond)

Thornton *Miss Justine*
Called: Feb 1994, Lincoln's Inn, BA (Hons)

Thorpe *Harry* •
Juriscommerce Securities Ltd, 32-36 Bath Road, Hounslow TW3 3EF, 0114 233 2683, Fax: 0114 233 2683. Called: Feb 1965, Middle Temple, MA (Oxon)

Thorpe *The Rt Hon John Jeremy*
2 Orme Square, London W2 4RS, 0171 727 8175, Fax: 0171 792 5950. Called: Feb 1954, Inner Temple, MA (Oxon), LLB (Hons)(Exon)

Thorpe *Richard David*
Called: Nov 1997, Lincoln's Inn, LLB (Hons)(Nott'm)

Thrower *Miss Alexandra Katherine*
Called: Oct 1997, Middle Temple, LLB (Hons)(Keele)

Thrussell *Graham*
Called: Nov 1983, Inner Temple, LLB (Reading)

Ti *Miss Chin Ming*
Paul Cheah & Associates, 3a Lorong Raja Bot, Klang, 03 344300, Fax: 03 3444301, and Member Malaysia Bar. Called: Nov 1994, Lincoln's Inn, LLB (Hons)(Hull)

Tiah *Miss Ee Laine*
Advocate & Solcitor, Lee Hishammuddin, Advocates & Solicitors, 16th Floor, Wisma HLA, 50200 Kuala Lumpur, 03 2011681, Fax: 03 2011714, and Member Malaysia. Called: July 1996, Middle Temple, LLB (Hons)(Kent)

Tiang *Michael Ming Tee*
Called: July 1997, Middle Temple, LLB (Hons)(Wales)

Tibbitts *Mrs Susan Lesley Marilyn* •
Senior Attorney, Hewlett Packard Ltd, Cain Road, Amen Corner, Bracknell, Berkshire, 01344 362212, Fax: 01344 362224. Called: Nov 1977, Lincoln's Inn, LLB

Tibbo *Miss Heather Dorothy*
Messrs Ogier & Le Masurier, P O Box 404, Pirouet House, Union Street, St Helier, Jersey JE4 9WG, 01534 504000, Fax: 01534 35328, and Member Advocate of the Royal Court of Jersey. Called: Nov 1989, Middle Temple, LLB

Tickner *Ms Karen Sara* •
Hammersmith & Fulham, Legal Services, Town Hall, King Street, Hammersmith W6 9JU, 0181 748 3020, and Member New York. Called: Nov 1992, Middle Temple, LLB (Hons, Manch), BCL (Oxon)

Tilley *Miss Joy Elizabeth*
Called: Nov 1994, Middle Temple, BA (Hons), MA (Sheff,)

Tillson *Mrs Judith Anne*
Called: Nov 1994, Lincoln's Inn, BA (Hons)(York), CPE (Notts)

Timmins *Andrew James*
Legal Adviser, Airsys ATM Limited, Oakcroft Road, Chessington, Surrey KT9 1QZ, 0181 391 6168, Fax: 0181 391 6335, Solicitor (Admitted Sept 1996). Called: July 1985, Gray's Inn, MA (Oxon), LLB

Timms *Howard Maurice Wainwright*
Swepstone Walsh, 9 Lincoln's Inn Fields, London. Called: Nov 1992, Inner Temple, LLB (So'ton)

Timms *Neil Richard Frederick Charles*
Maples & Calder, PO Box 309, George Town, Grand Cayman, 001 809949 8066, Fax: 001 809949 8080, and Member Cayman Bar. Called: Nov 1974, Inner Temple, MA (Cantab)

Timothis *Miss Alison*
Called: Nov 1995, Lincoln's Inn, LLB (Hons)

Timothy *Miss Sonia Agnes*
Assistant Counsel Commonwealth of the Bahamas, P.O.Box N3007, (242) 322 1141, Fax: (242) 322 2255. Called: July 1996, Lincoln's Inn, LLB (Hons)

Timson *Corin James*
Called: Nov 1994, Inner Temple, BA (B'ham), CPE (City)

Ting *Shu Kiong*
Called: July 1997, Lincoln's Inn, LLB (Hons)(Leeds)

Ting *Shu Leong*
Legal Adviser, Messrs Jayasuriya Kah & Co, Room 207, 2nd Floor, Wisma Sabah, P.O.Box 11350, 88815 Kota Kinabalu, Sabah, 088 242311 (W)/ 211742 (H), Fax: 088 231250, and Member Sabah. Called: July 1995, Lincoln's Inn, LLB (Hons)

Ting *Ms Sui Ing*
Called: July 1996, Lincoln's Inn, LLB (Hons)

Ting *Tiew Hee*
Called: Nov 1994, Lincoln's Inn, LLB (Hons)(Wales)

Tingle *John Harold*
Reader in Health Law, Nottingham Law School, Nottingham Trent University, Burton Street, Nottingham NG8 5AY, 0115 9486045. Called: Nov 1979, Gray's Inn, BA, Cert Ed., MEd

Tiong *Hok Chiun*
and Member Advocate of the High Court in Sabah & Sarawak, Malaysia. Called: July 1996, Lincoln's Inn, LLB (Hons)(Leeds)

Tippet *Vice Admiral Sir Anthony Sanders KCB,CIMgt*
Chairman, Funding Agency for Schools., Meadow Court, 95 Morton Lane, East Morton, Keighley, West Yorkshire BD20 5RP, 01274 510712, Fax: 01274 510 807. Called: Apr 1959, Gray's Inn, Hon FICH, Hon FSBU

Tippet *Simon John* •
Manager, Corporate Affairs, Renault UK Limited, Denham Lock, Widewater Place, Moorhall Road, Harefield, Middlesex UB9 6RT, 01895 827660, Fax: 01895 827681. Called: July 1989, Gray's Inn, BA (Hull), Dip Law (CLP)

Tipping *John Alfred*
Called: Nov 1992, Lincoln's Inn, BSc (Lond), LLB (Hons), FCA

Titchener *Alan John* •
Legal Advisor, Willis Corroon Group Plc, Ten Trinity Square, London EC3P 3AX, 0171 481 7021, Fax: 0171 481 7183. Called: Feb 1990, Lincoln's Inn, LLB Hons [Leeds]

Tiwari *Sean* •
Global Derivatives, Legal Adviser, Union Bank of Switzerland, 100 Liverpool Street, London EC2M 2RH. Called: Nov 1993, Inner Temple, BA (Oxon), Dip Law

Tiwary *Miss Anuradha*
Called: July 1996, Lincoln's Inn, LLB (Hons) (Lond)

Toal *Kieran Michael*
Called: Mar 1998, Gray's Inn, LLB (Sheff)

Tobias *Douglas Guedella*
South Africa 031 301 1196, Fax: South Africa 031 301 2138, Barrister of South Africa. Called: July 1991, Middle Temple, B Com (Cape Town), Dip Juris (Witwaters, -rand), LLB (Natal), LLM (Natal)

Tobitt *Ms Linda Jean*
Called: Oct 1997, Inner Temple, LLB (Wolverhampton)

Todd *Mrs (Joan) Hilary*
Court Clerk, Surrey Magistrates Courts Comm, Secretariat Offices, Court House, London Road, Dorking, Surrey RH4 1SX, 01306 885544. Called: Nov 1967, Middle Temple

Todd *Arnold James III*
Called: Mar 1998, Gray's Inn, BA (Ontario), LLB (Lond)

Todd *Miss Judith Ann*
Senior Lawyer. Called: Feb 1960, Gray's Inn, LLB

Todd *Mark Rutherford* •
Crown Prosecutor, Crown Prosecution Service, 1st Floor, Oxford House, Oxford Road, Bournemouth, Dorset BH8 8HA. Called: Apr 1986, Gray's Inn

Todd *Ms Susan Margaret*
Called: Nov 1991, Gray's Inn, BA (Cantab), MA (Sussex)

Todhunter *Stephen Edward*
ILMCS, 65 Romney Street, London SW1P 3RD. Called: Apr 1989, Lincoln's Inn, LLB (Lanc)

Toft *Nigel Timothy* •
Law Department, London Guildhall University, 84 Moorgate, London EC2, 0171 320 1000. Called: Nov 1974, Inner Temple, LL.M (Lond)

Toh *Miss Beng Suan*
Called: July 1995, Lincoln's Inn, LLB (Hons)

Toh *Jason Su Jin*
Ho Wong & Partners, 46 Tras Street, 2250271, Fax: 2250272, and Member Singapore Bar. Called: July 1995, Middle Temple, LLB (Hons)

Toh *Lean Seng*
Called: July 1997, Lincoln's Inn, LLB (Hons)(Lond)

Toh *Miss May Ching Jenny*
Messrs Toh Chin & Co, Advocates & Solicitors, No 21, 1st Floor, Jalan Dato, Abdul Rahman, 70000 Seremban, N.Sembilan, (06) 7635058/5059, Fax: (06) 7624308, and Member Malaysia. Called: Oct 1996, Lincoln's Inn, LLB (Hons)(Leic)

Toh *Miss Su Fen*
Called: July 1996, Lincoln's Inn, LLB (Hons)(Lond)

Tok *Miss Audrey*
Legal Assistant, M/S Allan & Gledhill, Unit 18.01 18th Floor, Public Bank Tower, 80000 Johor Bahru, (07) 2244422, Fax: (07) 2248718, and Member Malaysian Bar. Called: Nov 1994, Gray's Inn, BA (Kent)

Tok *Miss Julie Chwee Hwei*
Called: July 1995, Lincoln's Inn, LLB (Hons)

Tokunbo *Khamisi Mawuli*
Principal Crown Counsel, Attorney General's Chambers, Global House, 43 Church Street, Hamilton 5-24, Bermuda, 809 292 2463, Fax: 809 292 3608. Called: Nov 1988, Inner Temple, BA (Ohio), LLB (Lond)

Tolan *Anthony* •
General Manager, Legal Services Department, Hitachi Europe Limited, Whitebrook Park, Lower Cookham Road, Maidenhead, Berkshire SL6 8YA, 01628 585000, Fax: 01628 585380. Called: Nov 1974, Lincoln's Inn, BA

Tolia *Miss Dina Arun*
Called: July 1996, Lincoln's Inn, BA (Hons)(Warw)

Tolland *Ms Anne Marie*
Senior Court Clerk, South Somerset Magistrates Crt, Law Courts, Petters Way, Yeovil, Somerset BA20 1SW, 01278 452182, Fax: 01278 453667. Called: July 1988, Lincoln's Inn, LLB (Hons) Sheffield

Toman *Mrs Maria* •
Assistant Company Secretary Member of Board of Visitors, HM YOI/RC Reading, YWCA of Great Britain, Clarendon House, 52 Cornmarket Street, Oxford OX1 3EJ, Fax: 01865 204805. Called: Nov 1972, Inner Temple, LLB, MA

Toman *Vincent* •
Robin Thompson & Partners, Wentworth House, Eastern Avenue, Gantshill, Ilford, Essex IG2 6NH, 0181 554 2263, Fax: 0181 518 4819. Called: Nov 1988, Inner Temple, LLB (Shef)

Tomlin *Miss Adele Lisa*
Called: Oct 1996, Inner Temple, LLB (Warw)

Tomlinson *Bernard Thomas Bertram*
33 Palatine Road, London N16. Called: Nov 1954, Inner Temple, MSc (Lond), ARCS

Tompkinson *Miss Catherine Mary* •
Senior Principal Legal Officer, HM Customs & Excise, Solicitor's Office, New King's Beam House, 22 Upper Ground, London SE1 9PJ. Called: Feb 1985, Middle Temple, BA (Hons) (Lond), Dip Law

Tong *Mrs Ah Pooi*
Fin d'Elez, 1261 Le Muids, (022) 366 4606,
Fax: (022) 366 4606. Called: Nov 1988,
Lincoln's Inn, LLB (Lond)

Tong *Kington Kum Loong*
Partner, Suite 6, 4th Floor, Wisma Ann Koai,
67 Jalan Ampang, 50450 Kuala Lumpur, 03-
2382128, Fax: 03-2012272, and Member
Malaysian Bar. Called: July 1992, Gray's Inn,
LLB (Lond)

Tong *Raymond Wei Min*
C/O Shook Lin & Bok, 1 Robinson Road,
[H]18-00 A1A Tower, 65-4394895, Fax: 65-
5358577, and Member Singapore Bar.
Called: Nov 1991, Middle Temple, LLB Hons
(Nott'm)

Tong *Ronny Ka Wah*
16th Floor, Temple Chambers, One Pacific
Place, 88 Queensway, 00 852 5232033, Fax:
00 852 8100302, QC Hong Kong and
Member Singapore Bar 4 Essex Court,
Temple, London, EC4Y 9AJ. Called: Nov
1974, Middle Temple, BCL (Oxon) LLB (HK)

Tong *Miss Tricia Min Wei*
43 Nim Green, and Member Singapore Bar.
Called: July 1996, Lincoln's Inn, LLB
(Hons)(Lond)

Tonge *Andrew*
Civil Litigator, Birchall Blackburn Solcitors,
Crystal House, Birley Street, Preston, 01772
561663. Called: Oct 1995, Inner Temple,
LLB (Sheff)

Tooley *Michael Philip* •
Crown Prosecutor, Crown Prosecution
Service, 32 Scotland Street, Sheffield
S1 2EH, 0114 2761601, Fax: 0114 2761735.
Called: Nov 1982, Gray's Inn, LLB (Reading)

Toon *Anthony Douglas*
Deputy Clerk to the Justices, Hampshire
Magistrates Court, The Court House,
Elmleigh Road, Havant, Hampshire
PO9 2AL, 01705 492024, Fax: 01705
475356. Called: Nov 1982, Gray's Inn,
D.M.S.

Torode *Mark Andrew*
Called: Oct 1995, Inner Temple, LLB
(Sussex)

Torrance *Guy DCP*
Court Clerk Chairman of Opera by
Charabanc trading as "Opera By Charabanc"
Limited, Stockport Magistrates', Courts
Committee, PO Box 155, Edward Street,
Stockport SK1 3NF, 0161 477 2020 Ext
2107, Fax: 0161 474 1115. Called: Nov
1988, Middle Temple, LLB (LSE)

Torrington *John Raymond Lyon*
7 Hythe Place, New Gate Park, Sandwich,
Kent CT13 0RB, 01304 615076. Called: Nov
1962, Gray's Inn

Touche Arends *Mrs Susan Ruth*
Steraloids Inc, P O Box 85, Newport, Rhode
Island 02840, 401 848 5422, Fax: 401 848
5638. Called: Nov 1991, Gray's Inn, BFA
(Canada), Dip in, Law, Professional,
Certification, (Education)

Towler *Mrs Alison* •
Deputy Fleet Legal and Personnel Officer,
DFLPO & SLA FOSM, Commander in Chief
Fleet, Northwood, Middlesex HA6 3HP,
01923 837 138, Fax: 01923 837 090.
Called: Oct 1995, Gray's Inn, B.Sc (Wales)

Townley *Miss Lynne*
Called: Oct 1996, Middle Temple, LLB
(Hons), LLM (B'ham)

Townsend *Peter Maurice*
Clerk to the Justices, Powys Magistrates'
Court Comm, The Court House, Back Lane,
Newtown, Powys SY16 2NJ, 01686 627150,
Fax: 01686 628304. Called: July 1980,
Gray's Inn

Tracey *Andrew John*
Called: July 1996, Gray's Inn, B.Ed, MA
(Reading), LLB

Tracey *Ms Gerardine Anne*
Called: Oct 1992, Lincoln's Inn, LLB(Hons)

Tracey *Gerrard*
Called: Oct 1997, Gray's Inn, LLB (L'pool)

Tracey *Simon William*
Litigation Department, Titmuss Sainer
Dechert, 2 Serjeant's Inn, London
EC4Y 1LT, 0171 583 5353, Fax: 0171 353
3683. Called: Mar 1996, Middle Temple, BA
(Hons), MA (Cantab)

Tranter *Gavin Andrew*
Called: Oct 1996, Middle Temple, BA (Hons)
(Cantab)

Traynor *Miss Julie*
High Point Europe Limited, 6 Gold Top 5,
Newport, Gwent NP9 4PG, 01633 244404,
Fax: 01633 244753. Called: Nov 1993,
Lincoln's Inn, BSC (Cmnd), LLB, ARICS,
ACIArb

Treanor *Stephen John*
Called: Oct 1997, Gray's Inn, BSc (Notts)

Trefgarne *The Hon Mary Elizabeth* •
Assistant Director (Legal), Office of the
Solicitor to the, the Departments of Health,
and Social Security, New Court, Carey
Street, London WC2A 2LS, 0171 412 1371,
Fax: 0171 412 1440. Called: Nov 1971,
Gray's Inn

Tregilgas-Davey *Captain Marcus Ian* •
Army Legal Services Advocate. Called: Feb
1993, Gray's Inn, LLB (Southampton), LLM
(Cantab)

Treherne *Miss Victoria Margaret* •
Company Secretary, Cater Allen Holdings
PLC, 20 Birchin Lane, London EC3V 9DJ,
0171 623 2070, Fax: 0171 623 3606.
Called: July 1979, Gray's Inn, LLB (Hons)

Tremlett *Mrs Iona Alison*
35 Brockenhurst Gardens, Mill Hill, London
NW7 2JY, 0181 959 0400. Called: Jan 1950,
Gray's Inn, BA, LLB (Manch), LLM (Lond)

Trenhaile *John Stevens*
Called: July 1972, Middle Temple, MA
(Oxon)

Trenton *Anthony Eric*
Associate, Taylor Joynson Garrett,
Carmelite, 50 Victoria Embankment,
Blackfriars, London EC4Y 0DX, 0171 353
1234, Fax: 0171 936 2666. Called: Oct
1993, Inner Temple, MA, CPE

Trew *John Alistair*
Called: Nov 1997, Inner Temple, BA
(Leeds), MICS, (Lond)

Triay *Louis Bernard*
Louis W Triay & Partners, Suite C, 2nd
Floor, Regal House, Queensway, 00 350
79423, Fax: 00 350 71405, and Member
Gibraltar Bar. Called: July 1989, Middle
Temple, LLB [Lond]

Trinder *Jeremy Alexander*
Called: Oct 1996, Lincoln's Inn, LLB
(Hons)(Lond)

Trivess-Smith *Mrs Veronica*
Called: Oct 1995, Middle Temple, LLB
(Hons)

Trounson *Richard Noy*
Lawyer, Dibb Lupton Alsop, 125 London
Wall, London EC2Y 5AE, 0171 796 6318,
Fax: 0171 796 6588. Called: Nov 1975,
Lincoln's Inn, MA (Oxon)

Trueman *Scott Andrew*
Called: Oct 1996, Middle Temple, LLB
(Hons)(Manc)

Truss *Mrs Maureen* •
Principal Crown Prosecutor, Crown
Prosecution Service, 9th Floor, RAS House,
Alencon Link, Basingstoke, 01256 466722,
Fax: 01256 840268. Called: July 1975, Inner
Temple

Tsang *David Kwok Kei*
Des Voeux Chambers, 10/F Bank of East
Asia Bldg, 10 Des Voeux Road Central,
Hong Kong, (852) 2526 3071, Fax: (852)
2810 5287, and Member Hong Kong Bar
Attorney at Law of the Peoples Republic of
China. Called: July 1994, Middle Temple,
BSc(Hons)(Hong Kong), CPE (Manc), FRICS,
ACIArb

Tsang *Miss Jennifer Chiu Chun*
1501 Two Pacific Place, 88 Queensway,
Hong Kong, (852) 2840 1130, Fax: (852)
2810 0612, and Member Hong Kong Bar.
Called: July 1994, Middle Temple, LLB
(Hons)(Bris)

Tsang *Dr Lincoln Ling Hong* •
Principal Officer, Medicine Control Agency,
Department of Health, 1 Nine Elms Lane,
London SW8 5NQ. Called: Nov 1995, Inner
Temple, B.Pharm (Lond), PhD (B'ham), LLB
(Lond)

Tsang *Siu Wah*
Mei Foo Sun Chuen, 99c Broadway, 6/F,
Kowloon, (852) 2785 7628, Fax: (852) 2785
7628, and Member Ontario. Called: Nov
1988, Middle Temple, LLB (Lond)

Tse *Hayson Ka Sze*
Government Counsel, Hong Kong
Government, Department of Justice,
Queensway Government Office,
Queensway, Hong Kong, 2867 2211, and
Member Hong Kong Bar. Called: July 1995,
Lincoln's Inn, LLB (Hons), Dip Chinese Law

Tse *Sammy Lai*
Called: Nov 1997, Middle Temple, LLB
(Hons)

Tselingas *Charalambos Christophorou*
Called: Nov 1997, Lincoln's Inn, LLB
(Hons)(Leics)

Tsirides *Alexandros*
Called: Nov 1997, Lincoln's Inn, LLB (Hons)

Tsui *Chi Keung Wilfred*
Called: May 1996, Gray's Inn, BSc (Lond),
MBA (Hong Kong), MHA(New South Wales)

Tsui *Cho Man*
Called: Mar 1998, Middle Temple, BSc
(Hons)(HongKong)

Tsui *Kwok Wah Peter*
Engineer, and Member Hong Kong Bar.
Called: Nov 1994, Gray's Inn, B.Eng, M.Eng,
LLB, MICE, MHKIE, ACIArb

Tubb *Mrs Elizabeth Janet Mary* •
Group Legal Adviser, Legal & General
Group Plc, Temple Court, 11 Queen
Victoria Street, London EC4N 4TP, 0171
528 6375, Fax: 0171 528 6229. Called: Nov
1989, Middle Temple, LLB (Hons)

Tubbs *Mrs Julie Dawn*
Called: Oct 1995, Gray's Inn, BA (Warw),
LLB

Tuberi *Iniasi Vodo*
Legal Officer, P O Box 2034, Government
Buildings, Suva, and Member Fiji Bar.
Called: July 1993, Inner Temple, Dip. in
Education, BEd (USP), LLB (So'ton)

Tuck *Gordon Charles*
Called: Feb 1955, Gray's Inn, LLB

Tucker *Miss Clare Elizabeth* •
Principal Crown Prosecutor, Crown
Prosecution Service, The Courtyard,
Lombard Street, Abingdon, Oxon OX13 5SE,
01235 555678. Called: July 1982, Gray's Inn,
LLB

Tucker *Mrs Lorraine Jean* •
Principal Crown Prosecutor, Crown
Prosecution Service, Haldin House, Old
Bank Of, England Crt, Queen Street,
Norwich, Norfolk NR2 4SX, 01603 666491,
Fax: 01603 617989. Called: Nov 1982,
Middle Temple, BA

Tudor *Anthony David* •
The Chartered Insurance, Institute, 20
Aldermanbury, London EC2V 7HY, 0171
606 3835, Fax: 0171 726 0131. Called: Feb
1983, Lincoln's Inn, BA (Exon), LLB (Lond)

Tudor *Miss Carol*
Called: Oct 1996, Inner Temple, LLB (Manc)

Tuite *Michael Donald*
Barrister of Ireland. Called: Nov 1996,
Lincoln's Inn, BCL (Dublin), LLM (Cantab)

Tullo *Mrs Carol*
Controller, Her Majesty's Stationary Office.
Queen's Printer. Deputy Director, Cabinet
Office., St Clements House, 2-16 Colegate,
Norwich NR3 1BQ, 01603 723012, Fax:
01603 723018. Called: July 1977, Inner
Temple, LLB (Hons)

Tulloch *Mrs Gloria Veronica* •
Court Clerk, Bexley Magistrates Court,
Norwich Place, Bexleyheath, Kent
DA6 7NB, 0181 304 5211 X 128.
Called: Nov 1987, Middle Temple, LLB
(London)

Tully *John James*
Called: Oct 1995, Middle Temple, LLB
(Hons)

Tun *Alan* •
Compliance Officer, Banque Paribas,
Compliance Department, 10 Harewood
Avenue, London NW1 6AA, 0171 595 2000,
Fax: 0171 595 255. Called: July 1984, Inner
Temple, BSc (Notts), LLB (Lond)

Tung *Dr Wai Kit*
M.B.B.S.(Hong Kong), and Member Hong
Kong Bar. Called: July 1992, Gray's Inn,
M.B.BS, LLB (Lond), FRCS (Edinburgh)

Tung *Yau Ming*
Director, James R Knowles (Hong Kong)Ltd,
1111 Wing On Centre, 111 Connaught Road
Central, Hong Kong, (852) 25422818, Fax:
(852) 25414648, Chartered Quantity
Surveyor and Member Hong Kong Bar.
Called: July 1992, Middle Temple, BSc (QS)
(Hons), LLM, ARICS, AHKIS, ACIArb, MA
Cost E

Tupper *Stephen Charles Preiswerk*
and Member New York Bar. Called: Nov
1982, Middle Temple, LLB

Turfitt *Richard James Grenville* •
Casual Legal Officer, Dept of Social Security,
Block 2, Cannon Park, London, 0171 972
3795. Called: Oct 1993, Middle Temple, LLB
(Hons)(Kingston)

Turnbull *Graham Walter*
Forbes Chambers, 185 Elizabeth Street,
Sydney 2000, 02-93907777, Formerly a
Solicitor of the Supreme Court of New
South Wales and Member New South Wales
Bar 3 Hare Court, 1st Floor, Temple,
London, EC4Y 7BJ. Called: July 1990, Gray's
Inn, BA, LLB

Turnbull *Mrs Linda Angela*
Called: Mar 1998, Lincoln's Inn, LLB
(Northumbria)

Turner *Alan Richard*
Legal Adviser, The British Petroleum Co Plc,
Britannic House, Finsbury Circus, London
EC2M 7BA, 0171 496 4000, Fax: 0171 496
4630. Called: July 1992, Inner Temple, LLB
(Hons) (Lond), BSc (Hons) (Wales)

Turner *Christopher*
Called: Nov 1992, Inner Temple, LLB

Turner *Lady Deborah*
Legal Consultant, Hope House, Maidford,
Towcester, Northants NN12 8HU, 01327
860997, Fax: 01327 860997. Called: Feb
1964, Gray's Inn, MA (Hons) (Cantab), LLM
(Warwick)

Turner *John Charles*
4 Brookside Manor, 240 Leigh Road,
Wimborne, Dorset BH21 2BZ, 01202
840502. Called: Nov 1989, Gray's Inn, LLB
[Lond], DPA

Turner *Miss Katy-Marie*
Clifford Chance, 200 Aldersgate Street,
London EC1A 4JJ, 0171 600 1000, Fax: 0171
600 5555. Called: Oct 1993, Gray's Inn, LLB
(B'ham)

Turner *Marcus Philip Robert*
Head of Legal Affairs, Amsterdam based
Record & Music Publishing Co, Roadrunner
International BV, Bijdorp 2, 1182 M2,
Amsterdam, ++ 31 20 65 66 670, Fax: ++
31 20 64 06 126. Called: Nov 1991, Middle
Temple, LLB Hons (Lond)

Turner *Nigel Stuart*
Called: Nov 1990, Gray's Inn, LLB
(Hons)(B'ham)

Turner *Mrs Rhonda Natalie* •
Legal Advisor, Focus Housing Association
Ltd, Daimler House, Paradise Circus,
Birmingham B1 2BJ, 0121 687 5035, Fax:
0121 687 5123. Called: Nov 1984, Middle
Temple, BA(Hons)

Turner *Miss Rowena M* •
Legal Manager, Panasonic UK Limited,
Panasonic House, Willoughby Road,
Bracknell, Berkshire RG12 8FP, 01344
853599, Fax: 01344 853727. Called: Nov
1996, Lincoln's Inn, LLB (Hons)(Lond)

Turner *Mrs Shalimar Wilhelmina
Varuna*
and Member Trinidad & Tobago Bar.
Called: July 1985, Lincoln's Inn, BSc
Zoology (Lond), Dip Law, GRAD, ICSA

Turner-Samuels *David Jessel* QC
(1972)
and Member Trinidad & Tobago Bar
Cloisters, 1st Floor, Temple, London, EC4Y
7AA. Called: May 1939, Middle Temple

Turnill *James Lindsay* •
Crown Prosecutor, Crown Prosecution
Service, London Area, Horseferry Road
Branch, Portland House, Stag Place, London
SW1E 5BH. Called: Nov 1989, Middle
Temple, BA Hons [York], Dip in Law

Turquet *Mrs Susan Jane* JP
Part-Time Chairman SSAT Tribunal, Parking
Adjudicator, Member of the Parole Board.
Called: July 1966, Inner Temple, LLB, AKC

Tuxford *Miss Emma-Jane* •
Senior Crown Prosecutor, Crown
Prosecution Service, Burnley Branch Office,
2nd Floor, Calder House, St James Street,
Burnley, Lancashire BB11 1XC, 01282
412298 X 172, Fax: 01282 458097.
Called: Nov 1991, Middle Temple, LLB
(Hons)

Tweeddale *Andrew Gavin*
Called: Feb 1992, Inner Temple, LLB
(Reading), MSc, Dip Arb

Tweeddale *Mrs Keren Danielle*
Eldon Chambers, Fourth Floor, 30/32 Fleet
Street, London, EC4Y 1AA. Called: Oct
1991, Lincoln's Inn, BA (Hons) (Lond)

Twort *Alastair Crampton* •
Senior Principal Legal Officer, Lord
Chancellor's Department, Royal Courts of
Justice, The Strand, London WC2A 2LL.
Called: July 1971, Inner Temple, LLB

Twycross-Hills *Ms Lorna Jane* •
Securities & Investment Board, 2-14 Bunhill
Row, London EC1, Eldon Chambers, Fourth
Floor, 30/32 Fleet Street, London, EC4Y
1AA. Called: Feb 1991, Gray's Inn, BA
(Lond), LLB (Warw), ALCM

Tyler *Christopher Robin* •
Special Verications Assistant (Trade Marks),
BAT, Export House, Cawsey Way, Woking,
Surrey GU21 1YB, 01483 792385, Fax:
01483 792581. Called: Oct 1994, Middle
Temple, LLB (Hons), M.Sc (Lond), MBCS

Tyrer *Mrs Monica Jane JP*
Senior Lecturer in Law Thames Valley
University, Randall's Cottage, Lower Road,
Loosley Row, Princes Risborough, Bucks
HP27 ONU. Called: Nov 1973, Inner
Temple, LLB, MA

Tyrrell *Simon James Walter* •
Legal Adviser, Lloyd's of London, One Lime
Street, London EC3M 7HA, 0171 623 7100,
Fax: 0171 623 8236. Called: Feb 1989,
Middle Temple, BA (Hons)

Ubhi *Miss Navjit Kaur*
Called: Feb 1994, Middle Temple, LLB
(Hons)

Uddin *Syed Afsor Hasan*
Called: May 1997, Lincoln's Inn, LLB
(Hons)(Lond)

Uddin *Syed Afzal Hasan*
Called: Mar 1996, Lincoln's Inn, LLB (Hons)

Uden *Martin David*
C/o FCO, King Charles St, London
SW1A 2AH. Called: July 1977, Inner Temple,
LLB

Udeze *Ufondu Karuiki* •
Called: Oct 1995, Inner Temple, LLB
(Plymouth)

Uff *Keith* •
Faculty of Law, Univ of Birmingham, PO
Box 363, Birmingham, B15 2TT, 0121 414
3344, Fax: 0121 414 3971. Called: Nov
1969, Gray's Inn, MA, BCL (Oxon)

Ullaganathan *Krishnasamy Velu
Archary*
Called: July 1993, Lincoln's Inn, LLB (Hons)

Umar *Miss Hajh Sarimah Haji*
Legal Assistant, Abrahams, Davidson & Co,
Room 516, 5th Floor Plaza, Athirah, Jln
Kubah Makan, Diraja, B.S.B. 2682, Brunei.
Called: Nov 1993, Gray's Inn, LLB

Umezuruike *Israel Nzeako*
Principal Counsel, Umezuruike &
Associates, Umez Chambers, 58 Pound
Road, PO Box 1677, Aba Abia State, 082-
221315, Fax: 082-221315, Senior Advocate
of Nigeria (SAN) and Member Nigerian Bar.
Called: Nov 1964, Inner Temple, LLB (Lond)

Umoren *Ms Aniekan* •
Called: July 1983, Lincoln's Inn, BA (Hons)
Law, MA

Underhill *Gareth Adam* •
Called: Oct 1995, Lincoln's Inn, LLB
(Hons)(Huddersf)

Underwood *Geoffrey Edward*
Sixth Floor, Wentworth Selborne Chambers,
180 Phillip Street, Sydney NSW 2000,
(0011) 612 235 0140, Fax: (0011) 612 221
5604, Former Solicitor and Member Victoria
Bar, Queensland Bar, Northern Territory Bar
Australian Capital Territory Bar, Western
Australia Bar New South Wales Bar.
Called: July 1995, Middle Temple, B.Comm
(Queensland), LLB (Queensland), LLM
(London)

Unerman *Ms Sandra Diane* •
Grade 3, Department of the Environment,,
Transport & the Regions, Eland House,
Floor 8/F6, Bressenden Place, London
SW1E 5DU. Called: July 1973, Inner Temple,
BA

Ung *Eu-Chung*
Duval & Stachenfeld LLP, 575 Madison
Avenue, Suite 1006, New York, NY 10022,
(212) 605 0104, and Member New York
(1994). Called: July 1990, Lincoln's Inn, LLB
(Lond) 1989, LLM (Fordham) 1991, JD
(Georgetown) 1994

Ung *Miss Monin*
Clifford Chance, 30th Floor, Jardine House,
One Connaught Place, (852) 28258809, Fax:
(852) 28690067, and Member Singapore Bar
Hong Kong Law Society. Called: July 1993,
Gray's Inn, LLB (Brunel)

Unwin *Paul Charles*
Called: July 1968, Middle Temple, LLB
(Hons)

Upadhyaya *Miss Kanaklata Bhaskerrai*
Called: Oct 1997, Middle Temple, LLB
(Hons)(Lond)

Urquhart *Miss Jane Abigail*
Maxwell Batley, 27 Chancery Lane, London
WC2A 1PA. Called: Nov 1994, Middle
Temple, BA (Hons)

Urquhart *Miss Mhairi Christine* •
Principal Crown Prosecutor, Crown
Prosecution Service, The Cooperage, 8
Gainsford Street, Bermondsey, London
SE1 1NG, 0171 962 2761, Fax: 0171 962
0902. Called: Nov 1984, Gray's Inn, LLB
(B'ham)

Usher *Professor John Anthony*
Called: Nov 1993, Lincoln's Inn, LLB (Hons)

Usher *Richard Ian*
Head of Group Legal Dept., A Meredith
Jones & Co Ltd, Yorkshire House, 18 Chapel
Street, Liverpool L3 9AG, 0151 236 3563,
Fax: 0151 236 6699. Called: Oct 1996,
Gray's Inn, LLB, LLM (Sheff)

Uthayachanran *B*
Called: July 1993, Middle Temple, LLB
(Hons)(Lond)

Uttley *Stephen Edward* •
Senior Crown Prosecutor, Crown
Prosecution Service, Windsor House, 10
Manchester Road, Bradford BD5 0QH,
01274 742530. Called: Apr 1986, Inner
Temple, BA (Hons)

Uwemedimo *David Brian Okuma* •
Campbell Hooper, 35 Old Queen Street,
London SW1H 9JD, 0171 222 9070, Fax:
0171 222 5591. Called: July 1986, Lincoln's
Inn, BA, LLB

Vacy-Ash *Charles Gilbert* •
Manager Legal Affairs, Europe Ford Motor
Company Limited Assistant Company
Secretary; Ford Motor Company Limited
Senior Attorney, Office of the General
Counsel; Jaguar Cars Limited, Ford Motor
Company Ltd, Eagle Way, Brentwood, Essex
CM13 3BW, 01277 253000, Fax: 01277
252676, Jaguar Cars Limited, Browns Lane,
Allesley, Coventry CV5 9DR Tel. 01203
202114 Fax. 01203 407150. Called: Nov
1972, Middle Temple, Dip, Management,
Studies

Vagg *Ms Irene Juliette*
Called: Oct 1995, Gray's Inn, BA (Ghana)

Vahey *Philip Thomas Anthony*
Clerk to the Justices, The Law Courts, P O
Box 199, Christchurch Road, West Sussex
BN11 1JE, 01903 210981, Fax: 01903
820074. Called: Nov 1986, Inner Temple,
MBA

Vaines *Peter Stephen*
J.P., Brebner Allen & Trapp, Chartered
Accountants, The Quadrangle, 180 Wardour
Street, London W1V 3AA, 0171 734 2244,
Fax: 0171 287 5315. Called: July 1989,
Middle Temple, FCA, ATII

Vaizey *The Hon Edward Henry Butler*
Called: Oct 1993, Middle Temple, BA
(Hons)(Oxon), CPE (City)

Valansot *Miss Christiane* •
Legal Advisor, First Boston, One Cabot
Square, London E14 4QR, 0171 888 8939,
Fax: 0171 888 4251. Called: Nov 1989,
Middle Temple, BA

Vale *Anthony Charles Howard*
Pepper, Hamilton & Scheetz, 3000 Two
Logan Sq, Philadelphia, PA 19103 USA, 215
981 4502, Fax: 215 981 4750, and Member
Pennsylvania (1978). Called: Nov 1974,
Inner Temple, LLB

Valera *Miss Elizabeth* •
Senior Crown Prosecutor, Crown
Prosecution Service, 1-9 Romford Road,
Solar House, Stratford, London E8, 0181 534
6601, Fax: 0181 519 9690. Called: Oct
1991, Middle Temple, BA Hons (Kent)

Vallat Sir Francis Aime GBE, KCMG QC (1961)
Called: Jan 1935, Gray's Inn, BA,LLB (Cantab)

Vallera Giovanni
Called: Oct 1996, Lincoln's Inn, LLB (Hons)(Cardiff)

Valles Jaime Albert
Called: Oct 1992, Middle Temple, LLM (Lond), LLB (Lancaster)

Valley Stanley John
11 Park Row, Farnham, Surrey GU9 7JH, 01252 715840. Called: July 1966, Middle Temple

Van Der Stoep David Floris
Le Panorama, 57 Rue Grimaldi, MC-98000, 377 9310 6311, Fax: 377 9310 6313. Called: Nov 1970, Gray's Inn, Dip Law

Van Hagen Anthony Frederick William
Avocat a la Cour, Cabinet Van Hagen, 6 Avenue George V, Paris 75008, 01 47200064, Fax: 01 47202509, and Member French Bar. Called: Nov 1975, Lincoln's Inn, BA (Hons) Law

van Leuven Advocate John Nikolas
Ozannes, 1 Le Marchant Street, St Peter Port, Guernsey, 0481 723466, Fax: 0481 727935/714571/714653. Called: Nov 1970, Inner Temple, MA (Cantab), ACIArb

Vandermeer Arnold Roy QC (1978)
Recorder. Called: Feb 1955, Gray's Inn, LLB (Lond)

Vangadasalam Suriamurthi
Called: Nov 1997, Middle Temple, LLB (Hons)(Lond)

Vantyghem Julien Darren
Legal Adviser to the Justices, Oxford, Thame & Henley, Magistrates' Court, The Court House, P O Box 37, Spedwell Street, Oxford OX1 1RZ, (0865) 815922, Fax: (0865) 243730. Called: Oct 1992, Inner Temple, LLB

Vanular Mrs Sonia Audrey
12 Route Des Ciappes, F O 6500 Menton, 33 4 935873516. Called: Feb 1957, Gray's Inn

Varela Miss Anna
Called: Nov 1996, Middle Temple, BA (Hons), Dip Law

Varghese Joseph
Varghese & Co, 112 East Coast Road, [H] 03-33 Katong Mall, 3444989, Fax: 3444419, and Member Singapore Bar. Called: July 1994, Lincoln's Inn, LLB (Hons)

Varley James Robert Kenrick
Called: Nov 1997, Lincoln's Inn, BA (Hons)(Keele)

Varma Satya Narayan
44 Alanthus Close, Lee Green, London SE12 8RE, 0181 852 0317. Called: Feb 1963, Gray's Inn, ACIArb, Cert Ed

Varney Philip
Called: Oct 1996, Middle Temple, B.Ed (Brighton), M.Sc (Staffs)

Varughese Miss Sucy
9 Dilali Road, City Beach, Western Australia WA 6015, (09) 385 9552. Called: Oct 1993, Lincoln's Inn, LLB (Hons)(Bucks)

Vassis Mrs Stacy Gemma Mary
Called: Nov 1986, Middle Temple, BA, DipEd. (W. Aust), Dip Law

Vasu Rajasekharan
Called: Nov 1996, Middle Temple, LLB (Hons)

Vasudevan Dhanaraj
Called: July 1996, Middle Temple, LLB (Hons)(Lond)

Vaswani Mrs Hardevi
and Member Singapore. Called: Nov 1995, Middle Temple, LLB (Hons)

Vaudin D'Imecourt Charles
and Member Mauritian Bar 10 King's Bench Walk, Ground Floor, Temple, London, EC4Y 7EB. Called: Nov 1971, Gray's Inn

Vaughan Beverley Seymour Tyrone
Called: July 1978, Gray's Inn, MA, tcd

Vaughan-Brown Ms Janine Nicolle Gemini
Called: Mar 1996, Gray's Inn, LLB (Dunelm)

Vaughan-Davies Geoffrey
"Ardmore", 13 Norfolk Avenue, Sanderstead, South Croydon, Surrey CR2 8AT, 0181 657 1449. Called: June 1953, Inner Temple, MA (Cantab)

Vaz Keith Anthony Standish MP
144 Uppingham Road, Leicester LE5 OQF, 0116 2768834, Fax: 0116 2460677, Former Solicitor. Called: Nov 1990, Gray's Inn, MA (Cantab)

Veen Andrew Tavis
In-House Counsel (Commercial Litigation), Fenwick & Co, 125 High Holborn, London WC1V 6QA, 0171 404 5474, Fax: 0171 831 5695. Called: Nov 1993, Middle Temple, BA (Jnt Hons)

Veerasamy Miss Sarojini Muthusamy
Called: Nov 1997, Lincoln's Inn, LLB (Hons)

Veits Peter John
Clerk to the Justices, Lincolnshire Magistrates Crt, The Court House, 358 High Street, Lincoln LN5 7QA, 01522 528218, Fax: 01522 560139. Called: Oct 1985, Gray's Inn

Veljovic Mark
Called: Nov 1996, Middle Temple, LLB (Hons)(Lond)

Vellani Badaruddin Fatehali
Vellani & Vellani, 810-820 Muhammadi Hse, 8th Floor, I.I. Chundrigar Rd, Karachi 0225, Pakistan. Called: July 1982, Middle Temple, BSc Diplaw

Vellani Fatehali Walimohammad
Vellani & Vellani, 810-820 Muhammadi Hse 8th, I.I. Chundrigar Road, Karachi 74000, Pakistan, 2414021, Fax: 2419874. Called: Feb 1956, Middle Temple

Velupillai Miss Vijayalatha
Abdul Raman Saad & Assoc, No 240 A & B, Taman Melaka Raya, 75000 Jalan Taman, Melaka, 06 2821446, and Member Malaysia Bar. Called: Nov 1994, Middle Temple, LLB (Hons)

Velusamy Miss Santha Devi
Called: Nov 1996, Gray's Inn, LLB (Lond)

Venables Miss Claire Rosemary
Called: Oct 1995, Lincoln's Inn, BA (Hons)(Newc), CPE (York)

Vencatachellum Ms Glenda Roxande
Called: Oct 1996, Middle Temple, LLB (Hons) (Keele)

Vengadasalam Mrs Pakkia Letchumi
Called: Nov 1995, Lincoln's Inn, LLB (Hons)

Vengadesan Miss Joanne Jayanti
Called: July 1996, Middle Temple, LLB (Notts)

Vening-Richards Mrs Hilary Jane •
Senior Crown Prosecutor, Crown Prosecution Service, Princes Court, York Road, Leicester, 0116 2549333. Called: Nov 1990, Middle Temple, BA

Venkata Rajoo Miss Sheila Devi
Called: Nov 1995, Lincoln's Inn, LLB (Hons)

Venkatasami Kris •
Senior Crown Prosecutor, Crown Prosecution Service, Thames/Marl Street Branch, Portland House, Stag Place, Victoria, London SW1E, 0171 915 5700. Called: July 1989, Lincoln's Inn, LLB (Hons), MA

Venn John Kenneth
124 Young Street, Hamilton, Ontario, Canada L8N 1V6, (905) 522 9116, Fax: 9905) 529 5112, and Member Upper Canada. Called: July 1971, Middle Temple, M.A (Oxon), M.B.A (Warwick)

Venn Mark Austin •
Lawyer, Credit Suisse Financial Produc, One Cabot Square, London E14 4QS, 0171 888 2000, Fax: 0171 888 2772. Called: Nov 1991, Middle Temple, MA Hons (Cantab)

Venn Robert Denis
Called: July 1983, Middle Temple, LLB Lond

Venne Roger Andre •
Deputy Secretary of Commissions, Lord Chancellor's Department, Selbourne House, 54-60 Victoria Street, London SW1E 6QW, 0171 210 8986, Fax: 0171 210 0660. Called: July 1972, Gray's Inn

Ventrella Antonio •
Called: July 1978, Lincoln's Inn, LLB (Sheff)

Venturi Gary Anthony
Called: Oct 1996, Middle Temple, LLB (Hons)(City)

Venturino Miss Anna Maria Alfonsina
Called: Mar 1998, Middle Temple, BA (Hons)

Venugopal *Vijayan*
Shearn Delamore & Co, 7th Floor, Wisma Hamzah Kwong - Hing, No 1 Leboh Ampang, 50100 Kuala Lumpur, 03 2300644, Fax: 03 2385625, and Member Malaysia Bar. Called: July 1993, Middle Temple, LLB (Hons)

Vercoe *John Christopher William*
Baker & McKenzie, 8th Floor, 155 Abai Avenue, Almaty. Called: Nov 1973, Gray's Inn, LLB(Lond)

Verghese-Dipple *Mrs Mary*
In-House Lawyer, European Bank for, Reconstruction & Development, One Exchange Square, London EC2A 2EH. Called: Nov 1991, Lincoln's Inn, LLB (Hons), MA Business Law

Verghis *Mrs Kathryn Mary*
Principal Court Clerk, Justices' Clerks Office, Hanworth Road, Feltham, Middlesex TW13 5AG, 0181 890 4811, Fax: 0181 844 1779. Called: Nov 1985, Inner Temple, LLB

Verghis *Mathew* •
Senior Legal Officer, The Inland Revenue, Solicitor's Office, Somerset House, The Strand, London WC2R 1LB, 0171 438 7083, Fax: 0171 438 6246, and Member Malaysia Bar. Called: Nov 1984, Inner Temple, LLB

Vernon *Ms Helen Sara Jane*
Called: Oct 1995, Inner Temple, BA, CPE

Vesin-Samnadda *Mrs Indrani Veronica*
Credit Suisse Private Banking, P O Box 500, CH-1211 Geneva, 41 22 391 34 66, Fax: 41 22 391 38 77, Entitled to practice in Caricom States Currently practising in Switzerland. and Member Trinidad and Tobago Bar. Called: July 1992, Middle Temple, LLB (Hons) (Exeter)

Vessey *Miss Gloria Clare*
Called: Oct 1996, Middle Temple, BA, MA (Lond), CPE

Vethanayagam *Maria Stanislas*
Called: Nov 1996, Middle Temple, LLB (Hons)(Lond)

Vickers *Andrew Robert*
Clerk to the Justices Justices Chief Executive Kingston Upon Thames Petty Sessions Area., Kingston Upon Thames Court, 19 High Street, Kingston Upon Thames, Surrey KT1 1JW, 0181 546 5603, Fax: 0181 974 5612. Called: Nov 1987, Gray's Inn, BA (Lond)

Vickers *Paul Andrew* •
Company Secretary and Group Legal Director, Mirror Group PLC, One Canada Square, Canary Wharf, London E14 5AP, 0171 293 3359, Fax: 0171 293 3360. Called: July 1983, Inner Temple, LLB (soton)

Vickery *Mrs Maeve Teresa* •
Group Employment Advisor, United news & Media plc, Ludgate House, 245 Blackfriars Road, London SE1 9UY, 0171 921 5000. Called: Oct 1994, Middle Temple, BA (Hons)(B'ham), Dip in Law (City)

Victor-Mazeli *Miss Jacqueline*
Called: Nov 1997, Middle Temple, LLB (Hons)(Leeds)

Vigar *Miss Amanda Adele*
Robson Rhodes, Cambridge. Called: Nov 1987, Inner Temple, LLB (Reading), ACA, ATII

Vij *Arvind Kumar*
139 Cavenagh Road, [H]12-02 Town Apt, Singapore 0922, 65 -7360820, Fax: 65-7360820. Called: July 1995, Middle Temple, LLB (Hons), BBA (Hons)

Vijh *Naveen Kumar*
Group Legal Adviser, Berwin Leighton, Adelaide House, London Bridge, London EC4R 9HA, 0171 623 3144, Fax: 0171 623 4416. Called: Nov 1995, Inner Temple, LLB (Lond)

Villiers *Miss Theresa Anne*
Lecturer, King's College London, Strand, London WC2R 2LS, 0171 836 5454, Fax: 0171 873 2465, 5 New Square, 1st Floor, Lincoln's Inn, London, WC2A 3RJ. Called: Nov 1992, Inner Temple, LLB (Hons, Bris), BCL (Oxon)

Vincent-Emery *Ms Bobbie Maureen Mary* •
Senior Crown Prosecutor, Youth Branch, CPS, The Cooperage, Gainsford St, London SE1 2NG, 0171 962 2369. Called: July 1984, Middle Temple, BA

Vinestock *Mrs Jacqueline Marion*
Called: Oct 1995, Lincoln's Inn, MA (Edinburgh), CPE (Notts)

Virgo *Graham John*
Fellow in Law Lecturer University of Cambs, Downing College, Cambridge CB2 1DQ, 01223 334856. Called: July 1989, Lincoln's Inn, MA (Cantab), BCL (Oxon)

Virk *Hari Singh*
Called: Oct 1993, Middle Temple, BA (Hons)(Kent)

Vizard *Miss Diana Jane* •
Head of Statutory & Commercial Legal Affairs, British Broadcasting Corp, Room 3664, White City, 201 Wood Lane, London W12 7TS, 0181 752 5523/5742. Called: Nov 1977, Middle Temple

Voliotis *Seraphim*
Called: Oct 1995, Lincoln's Inn, BA (Hons), MA, PhD (Cantab)

Von Achten *Miss Susan Jane*
Called: Oct 1992, Lincoln's Inn, LLB (Hons)(Sheff)

Von Pokorny *Thomas Laszlo*
01905 355221, and Member New Zealand Hong Kong Bar. Called: Feb 1959, Middle Temple, LLB

Von Wachter *Lady Victoria Nora Cressida*
Godington Farm, Godington, Bicester, Oxon OX6 9AF, 01869 277562, Fax: 01869 277762. Called: July 1997, Gray's Inn, BSc, M Phil (Soton), LLB

Voo *Miss Mui Ching Cheryl*
7 Pemimpin Place, 65-2581213, Fax: 65-4539160. Called: July 1997, Gray's Inn, LLB (Lond)

Voon *Miss Meng Lye*
Blk 66 [H]02-339, Commonwealth Drive, Singapore 140066, 4730146. Called: July 1995, Lincoln's Inn, LLB (Hons)

Voon *Richard Chee Fatt*
Called: Nov 1996, Lincoln's Inn, LLB (Hons)(Bucks)

Vos *Andrew Mitchell* •
UK Group Legal Adviser, Sema Group UK Ltd, Fulcrum House, 2 Killick Street, London N1 9AZ, 0171 830 4213, Fax: 0171 830 4206. Called: July 1978, Gray's Inn, MA Hons (Cantab)

Vose *Martin*
Principal Court Clerk, City of London Magistrates', Courts Committee, No.1 Queen Victoria Street, London EC4M 4XY, 0171 260 1185, Fax: 0171 260 1493. Called: July 1983, Inner Temple, LLB(Hons) Kings Coll, London

Vout *Andrew Paul*
Called: Nov 1995, Gray's Inn, LLB (Warw)

Vrahimis *Laris*
Chr. Sozou 2, Flat 206, Nicosia, Cyprus, 357 2 473558, Fax: 357 2 475692, and Member Cyprus Bar. Called: May 1994, Middle Temple, LLB (Hons)

Vung *Peter Yin Sing*
Called: July 1996, Middle Temple, BA (Hons)(Keele)

Waddington *Lord QC (1971)*
Recorder, 2 Pump Court, 1st Floor, Temple, London, EC4Y 7AH. Called: June 1951, Gray's Inn, BA

Wade *David Anthony*
Arbitrator: Insurance, Financial Services, Solicitors Panels, Professional Negligence, SFA & ABTA, Roman Way, Benenden, Kent TN17 4ES, 01580 241873, Fax: 01580 241395. Called: Feb 1959, Inner Temple, FCI Arb

Wade *Mrs Vyvienne Yvonne Alexandra* •
Group Legal Director, Jardine Lloyd Thompson Group, Plc, Jardine House, 6 Crutched Friars, London EC3N 2HT, 0171 528 4151, Fax: 0171 528 4432. Called: July 1984, Inner Temple, LLB (Hons)(Reading)

Wadham *Vivian Anthony*
p/t Chairman of Social Security Appeals Tribunals, Rose Farm, Barton, Malpas, Cheshire SY14 7HU, 01829 782 396, Fax: 01829 782 107, and Member Barrister & Solicitor, Victoria, Australia Advocate of Brunei Darus Salam. Called: June 1955, Gray's Inn, MA (Oxon)

Wagner *Miss Juliette Gabrielle*
Called: Mar 1996, Gray's Inn, LLB

Wagstaff *David St John Rivers*
Called: July 1954, Lincoln's Inn, MA, LLB (Cantab)

Wagstaff *Matthew Edward* ●
Legal Officer, H M Customs & Excise, New Kings Beam House, 22 Upper Ground, London SE1 9PJ, 0171 865 5427, Fax: 0171 865 5461. Called: Oct 1993, Lincoln's Inn, LLB (Hons)(E.Ang)

Wah *Ronald Wong Soon*
Called: July 1995, Middle Temple, LLB (Hons), LLM (Lond)

Waheed *Erum Junade*
Called: Nov 1995, Gray's Inn, LLB

Wahi *Miss Shelina Razaly*
Called: July 1996, Lincoln's Inn, LLB (Hons)(Bris)

Wahyuni *Faizal*
Called: July 1994, Lincoln's Inn, LLB (Hons)

Wainwright *Richard Barry*
Principal Legal Adviser, Commission of the European Communities, 200 Rue de La Loi, 1049 Brussels, Belgium, 02 295 3807, Fax: 02 295 2486. Called: July 1965, Middle Temple, BA (Oxon)

Waite *Kiril*
Called: Nov 1997, Gray's Inn, LLB (Lond)

Waite *William Francis* ●
European Regional Counsel and Head of Corporate Investigations Board Member - American Corporate Counsel Association - Europe, Kroll Associates UK Ltd, 25 Saville Row, London W1X 0AL, 0171 396 0000, Fax: 0171 396 9966. Called: Nov 1984, Middle Temple, LLB (E Anglia), LLM

Wakefield *Gavin Jonathan* ●
Legal Advisor, Dun & Bradstreet Ltd, Holmers Farm Way, High Wycombe, Bucks HP12 4UL, 01494 423413, Fax: 01494 423551. Called: Oct 1992, Inner Temple, LLB (Warw)

Wakefield *James Alan George* ●
The Lawyers Christian, Fellowship, 97 High Road, Beeston, Nottingham NG9 2LH, 0115 9255335, Fax: 0115 9431222. Called: Nov 1993, Lincoln's Inn, BA (Hons, Keele)

Wakeford *Geoffrey Michael Montgomery OBE*
Mercers' Hall, Ironmonger Lane, London EC2V 8HE, 0171 726 4991. Called: Feb 1961, Gray's Inn, MA, LLB (Cantab)

Wakeham *Mrs Jane Elizabeth*
Company Secretary, Surrey Roll Leaf Ltd, Castleham Road, St Leonards on Sea, East Sussex TN38 9NS, 01424 775769, Fax: 01424 775769. Called: Nov 1984, Middle Temple, LLB (Lond)

Wakerley *John Charles OBE*
Senior Vice President, Director & General Counsel - USA, SmithKline Beecham Corporation, One Franklin Plaza, P O Box 7929, Philadelphia, PA 19101-7929, (215) 751 5844, Fax: (215) 751 5132, and Member New York Bar. Called: May 1960, Gray's Inn, LLB

Walder *Kenneth James Mowbray* ●
Legal Director, British Airways plc, 109a Onslow Square, London SW7 3LU, 0181 562 5880, Fax: 0181 562 5621. Called: July 1966, Gray's Inn

Waldon *Bernard Samuel*
Called: July 1966, Gray's Inn, MA [Cantab]

Waldron *Miss Kay* ●
Legal Adviser/Representive, West Glamorgan County Council, County Hall, Swansea, 01792 471111. Called: Nov 1989, Inner Temple, LLB

Walford *Justin Hugh* ●
Legal Advisor, Legal Department, Express Newspapers Plc, 245 Blackfriars Road, London SE1 9UX, 0171 922 7785, Fax: 0171 922 7967. Called: July 1981, Inner Temple, BA Hons (Sussex)

Walker *Andrew Viersen* ●
Crown Prosecution Service, Brighton, Sussex. Called: Nov 1987, Inner Temple, BA, Dip Law (City)

Walker *Miss Clare Louise*
Employment & Employee Adviser, Deloitte & Touche, Hill House, Little New Street, London EC4. Called: Oct 1995, Middle Temple, BA (Hons)

Walker *David*
Called: Mar 1998, Lincoln's Inn, BA (Hons)(Oxon), CPE (Northumbria)

Walker *Miss Debra Dorothy*
Deputy Chief Clerk, Inner London Magistrates', Courts Service, 65 Romney Street, London SW1P 3RD, 0171 799 3332. Called: May 1990, Inner Temple, LLB

Walker *Francis Norman*
Called: Nov 1947, Middle Temple, MA

Walker *Miss Hazel Louise* ●
Company Secretary & Director of Legal Services, Southern Electric plc, Southern Electric House, Westacott Way, Littlewick Green, Maidenhead, Berks SL6 3QB, 01628 822166. Called: Nov 1982, Gray's Inn, BA (Hons)

Walker *Miss Jessica Louise Helen*
Called: Nov 1996, Middle Temple, BA (Hons)

Walker *Miss Jill Christine Vezey* ●
Senior Legal Assistant, Lord Chancellor's Department, Office of Social Security, Commissioners, Harp House, 83-86 Farringdon Street, London EC4A 4BL, 0171 353 5145, Fax: 0171 936 2171. Called: Nov 1970, Middle Temple, LLB (Hons, Lond)

Walker *Miss Muriel Maud Florence Goldsmith*
10 The Meadows, West Rainton, Houghton-Le-Spring, Tyne & Wear DH4 6NP. Called: May 1936, Lincoln's Inn

Walker *Murray*
Assistant Branch Secretary & Compliance Officer, Assicurazioni Generali Spa, United Kingdom Branch, 117 Fenchurch Street, London EC3M 5DY, 0171 488 0733, Fax: 0171 481 0745. Called: Nov 1985, Lincoln's Inn, LLB Hons [Reading]

Walker *Peter Maxwell* ●
Vice President-Finance, E.C. Datacom Limited, Linburn House, 342 Kilburn High Road, London NW6 2QJ, 0171 624 6054, Fax: 0171 372 7087. Called: July 1977, Lincoln's Inn, LLB (Lond), FFA, FIAB, MISM

Walker *Robert Greenhalgh*
12 Wilfred Street, Hamilton. Called: July 1972, Lincoln's Inn

Walker *Mrs Wei Hong*
14 Claremont Park, Finchley, London N3 1TH, 0181 522 5000, Fax: 0181 519 9214. Called: July 1988, Lincoln's Inn, BA (Hons) Newcastle, Dip Law

Walker *William Henry*
Called: Feb 1961, Gray's Inn, LLB (Lond)

Walker *William Stuart O.B.E.*
Chairman; Cayman Islands Planning Appeals Tribunal, Chairman; Caledonian Bank & Trust Company Ltd, Dep. Chairman; British Caymanian Insurance Company Ltd, W S Walker & Company, P O Box 265G, Caledonian House, Grand Cayman, (345)949-0100, Fax: (345)949-7886, Attorney-at-Law Cayman Islands Notary Public, Cayman Islands. Called: June 1950, Inner Temple, MA (Cantab)

Walklate *Mrs Rebecca Christine*
Legal Advisor, 31 Middlewich Road, Sandbach, Cheshire CW11 9DW, 01270 762521, Fax: 01270 764795. Called: July 1995, Inner Temple, LLB (Staffs)

Walkling *Miss Helen Kay*
Called: Nov 1995, Lincoln's Inn, LLB (Hons)

Wall *Ian Laurence*
Called: Nov 1994, Inner Temple, LLB

Wallace *Alasdair Willaim McKinnon* ●
Deputy Head, Legal Advice & Litigation Division, Lord Chancellor's Department, Legal Adviser's Group, Selborne House, London SW1E 6QW. Called: July 1985, Gray's Inn, MA, LLM

Wallace *Miss Janet Mary* ●
6 Agar Street, London WC2N 4HR. Called: Nov 1963, Middle Temple

Wallace *John Francis Newlyn* ●
Court Clerk, Richmond Magistrates Court, Parkshot, Richmond, Surrey, 0181 948 2101. Called: July 1989, Gray's Inn, BA (Hons) Law

Wallace *Philip Christopher* ●
Investment Management, Regulatory Organisation, Lloyds Chambers, 1 Portsoken Street, London E1 8BT, 0171 390 5717, Fax: 0171 480 5846. Called: Nov 1994, Gray's Inn, BA (Exon)

Wallbank *Gerhard Henry Anthony*
and Member New Zealand. Called: Nov 1990, Lincoln's Inn, LLB, LLM (UCL)

Walledge *Christopher Rowan*
The Magistrates' Court, Union Street, Torquay, Devon TQ1 2BP, 01803 298683, Fax: 01803 291425. Called: Feb 1995, Inner Temple, LLB (Exeter)

Wallington *Andrew David* •
Senior Crown Prosecutor, Crown
Prosecution Service, Bristol Branch, 2nd
Floor, Froomsgate House, Rupert Street,
Bristol BS1 2QJ, 0117 9273093. Called: Nov
1993, Inner Temple, BA, CPE

Wallis *Dominic Laurence Carden*
Called: Nov 1992, Gray's Inn, BA

Wallis *Mrs Sarah Elizabeth*
Called: Nov 1997, Middle Temple, BA
(Hons)

Wallis *Timothy James*
Legal & Tax Adviser, Messrs Kingston Smith,
Devonshire House, 60 Goswell Road,
London EC1M 7AD, 0171 566 4000, Fax:
0171 566 4010. Called: July 1979, Gray's
Inn, BA

Walmsley *Peter Matthew*
Called: Nov 1995, Middle Temple, LLB
(Hons)

Walsh *Bernard David James TD*
The Old Rectory, Burgate, Diss, Norfolk
IP22 1QD, 01379 783278. Called: Nov 1952,
Inner Temple

Walsh *Darren Stephen*
Called: Oct 1997, Inner Temple, LLB
(Staffordshire)

Walsh *Ms Elizabeth* •
Grade 6, Registry of Friendly Societies, 15
Great Marlborough Street, London
W1V 2AX, 0171 494 6558. Called: July
1987, Gray's Inn, BA (Hons)(Cantab), LLM

Walsh *Francis*
Carraroe, 1 Polefield Road, Blackley,
Manchester M9 6FN, 0161 740 5788.
Called: July 1972, Lincoln's Inn, LLB, LLM
(Lond), FCA, FCCA, FCMA, FCIS, FTII

Walsh *Graham*
Called: Nov 1992, Inner Temple, BChD LDS
(Leeds), LLB (Leeds)

Walsh *Gregory Francis Andrew* •
Legal Adviser, Royal Insurance plc, P.O.Box
30, New Hall Place, Liverpool L69 3HS,
0151 239 4775, Fax: 0151 239 3360.
Called: Feb 1991, Lincoln's Inn, LLB (L'pool)

Walsh *Ms Greta Margaret Breda* •
C/O Crown Prosecution Service, 50 Ludgate
Hill, London EC4M 7EX. Called: Nov 1986,
Middle Temple, BCL (Dub)

Walsh *Mrs Margaret Josephine*
91 Whitebarn Road, Churchtown, Dublin
14, 00 3531 2981346, Barrister of Ireland.
Called: May 1995, Middle Temple, BL
(King's Inn)

Walsh *Ms Patricia Mary*
Osborne Clarke Solicitors, 6-9 Middle Street,
London EC1A 7JA, 0171 634 1684, Fax:
0171 600 0155. Called: Oct 1992, Inner
Temple, LLB (S'ton), LLM (Leics)

Walters *Miss Dinah Mary* •
Crown Prosecution Service, County House,
County Square, New London Road,
Chelmsford, Essex CM2 0RG, 01245
252939, Fax: 01245 490476. Called: Nov
1981, Gray's Inn, LLB (B'ham)

Walters *Sir Donald*
Chairman Llandough Hospital &
Community NHS Trust, Llandough Hospital,
Penlan Road, Penarth CF64 2XX, 01222
711711, Fax: 01222 712843. Called: Nov
1946, Inner Temple, LLB

Walters *Jeannot-Michel*
Called: Nov 1997, Middle Temple, LLB
(Hons)

Walters *Mrs Kathryn Ann* •
p/t Court Clerk. Called: Nov 1981, Gray's
Inn, BSc

Walters *Kevin Frank*
Justices' Clerk Southampton & New Forest
Magistrates' Courts, Hampshire Magistrates
Court, Committee, The Court House,
Elmleigh Road, Havant, Hants PO9 2AL,
01703 635911, Fax: 01703 233882.
Called: July 1975, Inner Temple, MA FCIS
FIPD

Walters *Richard Fraser* •
Assistant Solicitor, The Inland Revenue,
Solicitor's Office, Somerset House (East
Wing), The Strand, London WC2R 1LB,
0171 438 7286, Fax: 0171 438 6246.
Called: Nov 1977, Inner Temple, LLB
(Hons), MA, Dip in EC Law

Walton *Andrew David* •
Vice President & Legal Counsel, Morgan
Stanley, 25 Cabot Square, London E14 4QA,
0171 425 8908, Fax: 0171 425 8971.
Called: Nov 1986, Inner Temple, BA,LLM

Walton *Derek Antony Ruffel* •
Assistant Legal Adviser, Foreign &
Commonwealth Office, King Charles Street,
London SW1A 2AH, 0171 270 3055, Fax:
0171 270 2767. Called: Nov 1989, Lincoln's
Inn, MA, LLM (Cantab)

Walton *Jeremy Paul*
Contributor to Atkin's Court Forms, Ritch &
Connolly, Attorneys at Law, P.O.Box 1994,
Grand Cayman, 001 345 949 7366, Fax: 001
345 949 8652, and Member Cayman Islands
Bar. Called: Nov 1995, Lincoln's Inn, BA
(Hons)

Walton *John Lawson* •
Evington Corporation, Ltd, Evington House,
Smalldale, Bradwell, Hope Valley S33 9JQ,
01433 621599, Fax: 01433 621544.
Called: Nov 1970, Gray's Inn

Wan *Azli Kuzaini*
Called: Nov 1995, Lincoln's Inn, LLB (Hons)

Wan *Kai Chee*
Called: July 1997, Lincoln's Inn, LLB
(Hons)(Lond)

Wan *Mrs Sally Elizabeth*
Lawyer. Called: Oct 1991, Middle Temple,
BSc (Brunel) (Hons), MBA, DipM

Wan *Ms Shuk Fong Polly*
Senior Government Counsel, Department of
Justice, Hong Kong, 6/F High Block,
Queensway Government Offices, 66
Queensway, 28672302, Fax: 28451609, and
Member Hong Kong Bar. Called: Nov 1993,
Gray's Inn, LLB

Wan *Miss Teh Leok*
2193-A Lorong Kampung Pisang, Alor Setar,
05100 Kedah, Malaysia, 0604 7330837, and
Member Malaysia Bar. Called: July 1995,
Inner Temple, LLB (Soton)

Wan Hussin *Wan Fairuz*
Called: July 1995, Middle Temple, BA
(Hons) (Keele)

Wan Mohd Noor *Wan Annuar*
Called: Nov 1995, Lincoln's Inn, LLB (Hons)

Wanduragala *Miss Louise-Marie
Randini*
21 Holden Road, North Finchley, London
N12 8HP, 0181 445 4614, and Member
Gibraltar Bar. Called: Nov 1984, Gray's Inn,
LLB (Aberystwyth)

Wang *John Shing Chun*
52 Kampong Chantek, (65) 4668928.
Called: July 1996, Middle Temple, BA
(Hons)(Cantab)

Wang *Peter Kai-Hung*
Called: July 1995, Middle Temple, B.Sc, M.Sc
(Toronto), LLB (Hons), LLM, (Wales)

Wang *Sui Sang*
Called: Nov 1991, Lincoln's Inn, LLB (Hons)
(L'Pool)

Wang *Tziak-Chuen*
Called: Feb 1995, Gray's Inn, BA
(Manchester)

Warburton *John Kenneth CBE*
35 Hampshire Drive, Birmingham B15 3NY,
0121 454 6764, Formerly Director General,
Birmingham Chamber of Commerce &
Industry. Called: Feb 1977, Gray's Inn, MA,
Cedr Accredited, Mediator

Warburton *Paul Richard*
Called: Mar 1998, Lincoln's Inn, LLB (Hons)

Ward *Andrew Robert*
Called: Oct 1997, Lincoln's Inn, BA (Hons)

Ward *Anthony Desborough*
Called: Oct 1994, Gray's Inn, MA, MSc

Ward *Benjamin William*
Editor in Chief. American Language Review.
Publisher Arch Law., 8383 Wilshire
Boulevard, Suite 360, Beverley Hills,
California 90211, 213 658 7620, Fax: 213
658 7530. Called: Nov 1994, Gray's Inn, BA
(Manch), MA (Lond)

Ward *Mr Brian Stanley*
Nottingham Law School, Nottingham Trent
University, Nottingham, 0115 9418418, Fax:
0115 9486489. Called: Feb 1988, Lincoln's
Inn, BA (Hons) Keele, PGCE

Ward *Miss Claire* •
Principal Crown Prosecutor. Called: July
1985, Lincoln's Inn, LLB (Hons)

Ward *Eoin Francis*
Company Lawyer, Kindle Banking Systems,
East Point Business Park, Dublin 3 Ireland,
353 1 68554555, Fax: 353 1 8554550, and
Member Irish Bar (King's Inn). Called: July
1988, Middle Temple, BCL (Dublin), AITI,
(Dublin), Dip, European Law(Dublin)

Ward *George Arthur*
38 Arlington Square, London N1 7DP.
Called: July 1973, Inner Temple, BA

Ward *Ian Robert* •
Legal Adviser, Ministry of Defence, Room
4107, Main Building, Whitehall, London
SW1A 2HB. Called: Nov 1981, Middle
Temple, BA LLB (Cantab), LLM (UBC)

Ward *Squadron Leader John Harold*
Half Acre, Ampney Crucis, Cirencester, Glos
GL7 5RY, 01285 851323. Called: July 1946,
Inner Temple

Ward *Marcus Daniel Wright* •
Business Development Manager, The
Princes Trust, 227a City Road, London,
0171 251 2696 ext 107. Called: Oct 1996,
Lincoln's Inn, LLB (Hons)(Newc)

Ward *Peter Graham*
Director of Corporate Services, Victoria Law
Courts, Corporation Street, Birmingham
B4 6QA, 0121 212 6622, Fax: 0121 236
7837. Called: Nov 1987, Lincoln's Inn, LLB,
DMS

Ward *Ms Susan Mary* •
General Counsel P/t Immigration Appeals
Adjudicator & Special Adjudicator, APACS,
Mercury House, Triton Court, 14 Finsbury
Square, London EC2A 1BR, 0171 711 6216,
Fax: 0171 711 6276, Barrister of NSW &
High Court of Australia and Member New
South Wales Bar. Called: July 1976, Inner
Temple, LLB (Bristol) (Hons), Dip M

Ware *Michael John CB QC (1988)*
Chairman, Meat Hygiene Appeals Tribunal
for England & Wales, 12 Hill Road,
Haslemere, Surrey GU27 2JN, 01428
644699. Called: Feb 1955, Middle Temple,
BA, LLB

Wareham *Gerard* •
Crown Prosecutor, Crown Prosecution
Service, Portland House, Stag Place,
Victoria, London SW1E 5BH. Called: July
1988, Gray's Inn, BA

Wareham *Mrs Tracey Anne* •
Prosecution Team Leader, Crown
Prosecution Service, Queen's House,
Victoria Street, St Albans AL1, 01727
818100. Called: Nov 1987, Gray's Inn, LLB
(Wales)

Warhurst *Keith*
Called: July 1996, Gray's Inn, LLB

Waring *Thomas*
Called: Feb 1965, Gray's Inn

Warland *Christian Geoffery Lougheed*
Clifford Chance, 200 Aldersgate Street,
London EC1A 4JJ, 0171 600 1000, Fax: 0171
600 5555. Called: Nov 1993, Middle
Temple, BA (Hons)(Exon), CPE

Warman *Andrew Cecil James* •
Crown Prosecutor, Crown Prosecution
Service, Bromfield House, Ellice Way,
Wrexham Technology Park, Wrexham,
Clwyd, 01978 312002, Fax: 01978 311960.
Called: Feb 1994, Inner Temple, BSc
(Wales), CPE

Warner *David Alexander*
Called: Oct 1996, Gray's Inn, LLB

Warnford-Davis *John David*
Hill Barn, Hailey, Ipsden, Wallingford, Oxon
OX10 6AD, 01491 681655. Called: Nov
1954, Gray's Inn

Warnsby *Grant Darren*
Called: May 1997, Lincoln's Inn, BA
(Hons)(Keele)

Warren *James*
Called: Nov 1996, Middle Temple, BSc
(Econ)(Wales)

Warren *John Benton* •
Principal Crown Prosecutor, Crown
Prosecution Service, Fifth Floor, Chartist
Tower, Dock Street, Newport, Gwent
NP9 1DW. Called: Nov 1978, Gray's Inn,
LLB (Soton)

Warrick *Paul Terence Philip* •
Law Office of Paul Warrick, 7 Hobury
Street, London SW10 OJD, 0171 795 1122,
Fax: 0171 351 3245. Called: July 1972, Inner
Temple, BL

Warwick *Kevin*
Called: Oct 1995, Middle Temple, LLB
(Hons)

Wasley *Julian Mark*
Called: Oct 1996, Lincoln's Inn, LLB
(Hons)(Wales)

Wass *Andrew Paul*
Called: July 1986, Middle Temple, BA
(Notts) Dip Law, (City)

Wasserson *Rodney Bernard*
Deputy Chief Clerk, Inner London
Magistrates', Courts Service, 65 Romney
Street, London SW1P 3RD. Called: Nov
1970, Lincoln's Inn, BA (Rhodes), LLB
(Edin)

Waters *Conrad Alexis*
Senior Credit Analyst, Bank of Tokyo -
Mitsubishi, The Bank of Tokyo - Mitsubishi,
limited, Finsbury Circus House, 12-15
Finsbury Circus, London EC2M 7BT, 0171
577 1228, Fax: 0171 577 1234. Called: Nov
1989, Gray's Inn, LLB (L'pool), ACIB

Waters *Jonathan Roy* •
UK Legal Advisor & Queens Moat House
plc. Employment Law Consul. Law
Lecturer., Queens Moat Houses plc, Queens
Court, 9-17 Eastern Road, Romford, Essex
RM1 3NG, 01708 730522, Fax: 01708
762691, Association of Law Teachers
Employment Lawyers Association.
Called: Nov 1990, Lincoln's Inn, LLB (Hons),
ACIarb, LLM

Waterson *Roger Stephen* •
Assistant Solicitor, The Inland Revenue,
Solicitor's Office, Somerset House, The
Strand, London WC2R 1LB, 0171 438 7118,
Fax: 0171 438 6246. Called: Nov 1968,
Gray's Inn, BA, BCL {oxon}

Watherston *John Anthony Charles* •
Head, International & Common Law
Services Division, Lord Chancellor's
Department, Selborne House, 54-60 Victoria
Street, London SW1E 6QW. Called: Nov
1967, Inner Temple, MA

Watkin *Tegwyn Thomas Herbert*
Gwynda, Ffordd Henllan, Nr Trefnant, St
Asaph, Clwyd LL17 OBT, 01745 730342.
Called: Nov 1968, Lincoln's Inn, ACIB

Watkins *Mrs Beverley Anne* •
Senior Crown Prosecutor, RAS House,
Alencon Link, Basingstoke. Called: July
1982, Gray's Inn, BA

Watkins *Dr Owen David* •
Securities & Investments Board, Gavrelle
House, 2-14 Bunhill Row, London
EC1Y 8RA, 0171 638 1240, Fax: 0171 382
5900. Called: July 1986, Lincoln's Inn, MA,
D.Phil (Oxon), MA (City)

Watkins *Paul John* •
Senior Lawyer, I.P.E., International House, 1
St Katherine's Way, London E1 9UN, 0171
481 0643, Fax: 0171 481 8485. Called: Nov
1986, Middle Temple, LLB (Manc)

Watson *Andrew Robert James*
Called: Nov 1982, Lincoln's Inn, LLB MA
(Sheffield), Dip Soc Admin

Watson *Andrew Simon*
Called: Oct 1997, Lincoln's Inn, BA
(Hons)(Leeds), CPE (Northumbria)

Watson *Anthony*
Associate, Institute of Investment
Management and Research, Cedar Hse, 50
The Street, Manuden, Bishop's Stortford,
Herts CM23 1DJ. Called: Nov 1976,
Lincoln's Inn, BSc (Econ)

Watson *Bernard Gerald* •
Police Inspector, Surrey Police, Mount
Brown, Sandy Lane, Guildford GU3 1HG,
01483 571212, Former Police Officer.
Called: Oct 1997, Middle Temple, LLB
(Hons)(Kingston)

Watson *Miss Deborah Jane* •
Crown Prosecution Service, Essex Area
Office, 2nd Floor, County House, 100 New
London Road, Chelmsford, Essex CM2 ORG,
01245 252939. Called: Oct 1992, Inner
Temple, LLB

Watson *Ms Deidre Mary Watson* •
Assistant Company Secretary, Shell UK
Limited, Shell-Mex House, Strand, London
WC2R ODX, 0171 257 1861, Fax: 0171 257
3441. Called: Nov 1996, Inner Temple, BA
(Lond), MBA, FCIS

Watson *Duncan Allen*
Called: Oct 1997, Inner Temple, BA (Wales),
CPE

Watson *Graham*
Called: Oct 1996, Lincoln's Inn, LLB
(Hons)(Newc)

Watson *Ms Isobel Mary* •
Senior Principal Legal Officer, Department
of the Environment, 2 Marsham Street,
London SW1P 3EB. Called: July 1975,
Middle Temple, LLB

E

Watson *James*
Called: Nov 1996, Lincoln's Inn, BA (Hons)(Sheff)

Watson *Marc Clive*
Called: Nov 1993, Inner Temple, LLB (Hull)

Watson *Nicholas Bruce*
Clerk to the Justices, Leicester Magistrates' Ct, P.O.Box 1, Pocklingtons Walk, Leicester LE1 9BE, 0116 255 3666, Fax: 0116 254581. Called: July 1986, Gray's Inn, LLB, LLM

Watson *Roy Stuart*
Senior Legal Adviser, Berkshire Magistrates' Court, Easby House, Northfield End, Henley-on-Thames, Oxon RG9 2NB, 01491 412720, Fax: 01491 412762. Called: Feb 1993, Gray's Inn, BA

Watson *Miss Zillah Mary*
Called: Nov 1994, Gray's Inn, BA

Watt *James Muir OBE*
47 Fort Street, Ayr KA7 1DH, 01292 203102. Called: Jan 1935, Inner Temple, MA (Oxon), MA (Glas), Hon Assoc RICS, FAAV

Watt *John Gillie McArthur QC*
Temporary Sheriff, Advocates' Library, Parliament House, Edinburgh, 303 456 1548, Fax: 303 456 1548, Scottish Advocate, QC Scotland 1992 and Member Colorado Bar. Called: Feb 1992, Middle Temple, LLB (Edin)

Watters *Charles Patrick •*
Group Secretary and General Counsel, Allied Colloids Group plc, P.O.Box 38, Bradford, West Yorkshire BD12 0JZ, 01274 417000. Called: July 1981, Middle Temple, LLB (Hons)

Watters *Simon Barry*
Practitioner - Federal & High Court of Australia, P O Box X 2291, Perth, Western Australia 6001, 08-9264 1750, Fax: 08-9264 1455, Former Solicitor and Member Western Australia Bar, Federal High Court of Australia Tasmania Bar. Called: July 1992, Gray's Inn, BA, LLB

Watts *Mrs Alison*
Clerk to the Justices, Derbyshire Magistrates' Court, The Court House, West Bars, Chesterfield, Derbyshire S40 1AE, 01246 278171, Fax: 01246 276344. Called: July 1984, Inner Temple

Watts *Ronald*
79 Great King Street, Edinburgh, Scotland EH3 6RN, 0131 557 4474. Called: June 1964, Gray's Inn, LLB (Nott), LLM (Cantab), BD (Edin)

Watts *Trevor Robert*
Chateau Du Seuil, Cerons 33720, France, 00 33 56271156, Fax: 00 33 56272879. Called: Nov 1979, Lincoln's Inn, FRVA, FSVA, Winemaker

Wayman *Mrs Anne Elizabeth*
Principal Court Clerk, Sutton Magistrates Court, Shotfield, Wallington, Surrey SM6 0JA, 0181 770 5939, Fax: 0181 770 5959. Called: Nov 1987, Gray's Inn, D.M.L.

Wayman *Miss Caroline Ann*
Called: Mar 1998, Middle Temple, LLB (Hons)

Weatherhead *Miss Louise*
Called: Oct 1997, Lincoln's Inn, BA (Hons)(Sheff)

Weaver *Oliver QC (1985)*
also Inn of Court L Erskine Chambers, 30 Lincoln's Inn Fields, Lincoln's Inn, London, WC2A 3PF. Called: Feb 1965, Middle Temple, MA, LLM (Cantab)

Weaver *Miss Ouida Marjorie*
Human Resources Manager, Manpower plc, International House, 66 Chiltern Street, London W1M 1PR, 0171 224 6688, Fax: 0171 935 6611. Called: July 1983, Lincoln's Inn, BA (Washington) LLB, (Lond)

Webb *David Royston •*
Consultant, Harrods Holdings Plc, 13 Buckingham Hse, Courtlands, Sheen Road, Richmond, Surrey TW10 5AX, 0171 409 2963, Fax: 0171 491 2472. Called: May 1973, Lincoln's Inn, LLB, ACIS

Webb *Ian Christopher*
Justices' Chief Executive, Cheshire Magistrates Courts, Committee, PWB House, Middlewich Road, Sandbach Cheshire CW11 1HY, 01270 760344, Fax: 01270 760594. Called: July 1979, Gray's Inn, BA

Webb *Miss Kelly*
Called: Oct 1993, Lincoln's Inn, LLB (Hons)(Lond)

Webb *Malcolm George John*
Kelsters Cottage, Hugus, Near Truro, Cornwall TR3 6EQ, (01872) 560696. Called: July 1972, Middle Temple, FFA,ACIS

Webb *Robert Craig*
Called: Oct 1993, Lincoln's Inn, BA (Hons)(Notts)

Webb *Mrs Susan Pamela*
14 Hanson Close, London SW14 7SH, 0181 392 2801, Fax: 0181 392 2801. Called: Oct 1995, Middle Temple, LLB (Hons)

Webber *Andrew John*
Called: Feb 1994, Middle Temple, LLB (Hons)(Lond)

Webber *David Malcolm T.D.*
Part Time Chairman of Medical Appeal Tribunal and Disability Appeal Tribunal. Called: Nov 1955, Gray's Inn, MA (Cantab)

Webster *Colin Peter •*
Legal Team Manager, The Court House, Speedwell Street, Oxford OX1 1RZ, 01865 815922/815938 (direct line), Fax: 01865 243730. Called: Nov 1987, Middle Temple, Dip Mag Law, DMS

Webster *Ms Gail Louise*
4 Brick Court, Ground Floor, Temple, London, EC4Y 9AD. Called: July 1981, Gray's Inn

Webster *Ms Mandy Patricia*
Called: May 1993, Lincoln's Inn, BA (Hons, Keele), ACIS

Webster *Peter*
Called: Nov 1994, Lincoln's Inn, LLB (Hons)

Wedderburn *Miss Kim •*
UK Legal Counsel, J.D.Edwards (UK) Limited, Oxford Road, Stokenchurch, High Wycombe, Bucks HP14 3AD, 01494 682700, Fax: 01494 682699. Called: Nov 1991, Middle Temple, LLB (Hons)

Wee *Miss Adeline Ai Lin*
Called: July 1995, Middle Temple, BA (Hons) (Keele)

Wee *Aloysius Meng Seng*
105 Cecil Street, [H]10-02 The Octagon, 5352077, Fax: 5333969, and Member Singapore Bar. Called: Oct 1994, Middle Temple, BA (Hons)(Kent)

Wee *Desmond Guan Oei*
Called: July 1995, Middle Temple, LLB (Hons)

Wee *Gerald Martin Ee Ming*
Called: Nov 1996, Middle Temple, LLB (Hons)(L'pool)

Wee *Jee Pin*
Legal Assistant, Rodyk & Davidson, Six Battery [H]38-01, Singapore 0104, (65) 225 2626, Fax: (65) 225 7511/225 1838, Advocate & Solicitor the Supreme Court of Singapore. Called: July 1992, Middle Temple, LLB (Hons) (Hull)

Wee *Miss Nicole Fiona Sue-Ren*
Called: July 1995, Lincoln's Inn, LLB (Hons)

Wee *Miss Vivienne Chui Ling*
Apt Blk 222, Tampines Street 24, [H] 10-96, 065 7830102, Fax: 065 7830102. Called: July 1991, Middle Temple, LLB (Hons) (Bucks)

Wee *Miss Ying Ling Beverly*
Called: July 1995, Gray's Inn, LLB

Wee Ewe Lay *Laurence John*
No 2 Ewart Park, 65 5345155, Fax: 65 5342622, Avocate & Solicitor of the Supreme Court of Singapore. Called: July 1982, Middle Temple, LLB (Hons)

Wee Inn *The Hon. Mr Roland Sagrah*
State Assemblyman, State Legislative Assembly Sarawak, Malaysia, M/S David Allan Sagah & Teng, Advocates, Lot 196, Sublot 4, 1st Floor, Jalan Kulas, Satok CDT 3045, 93990 Kuching, 082-232739, Fax: 082-251831, Advocate & Solicitor of the High Court of Sabah & Sarawak Malaysia. and Member Sarawak Bar. Called: July 1980, Gray's Inn, LLB (Hons Lond)

Weeden-Padgham *Miss Louise Anne •*
Senior Crown Prosecutor, Crown Prosecution Service, Saxon House, 1 Cromwell Square, Ipswich, Suffolk IP1 1TS, 01473 230332, Fax: 01473 231377. Called: Nov 1987, Inner Temple, LLB

Weedon *Simon John*
Called: Oct 1994, Gray's Inn, LLB

Weekes *Thomas Charles*
Called: Oct 1995, Inner Temple, BA (Oxon), CPE (City)

Weeks *Stephen Thomas* ●
Company Secretary, Freemans PLC, 139 Clapham Road, London SW99 0HR, 0171 820 2336, Fax: 0171 820 2796. Called: July 1978, Lincoln's Inn, MA (Cantab)

Wehlau *Mrs Caroline Ann*
Called: July 1983, Inner Temple, LLB (Soton)

Wei *Miss Hui Yen*
Called: July 1996, Gray's Inn, BA (Keele), MBA (London)

Weinberg *Mrs Jose Letitia*
Special Adjudicator Immigration p/t, Elm Green Cottage, Drinkstone, Nr Bury St Edmunds, Suffolk IP30 9TN, 01449 737 640. Called: July 1963, Middle Temple

Weir *Alan Anthony*
Northern Ireland Barrister. Called: Nov 1996, Gray's Inn, BSc, MSc (Belfast)

Weir *Miss Heather Anne* ●
Senior Crown Prosecutor, Crown Prosecution Service, Leeds Branch Office, Oxford House, Oxford Row, Leeds LS1 3BE, 0113 2454590. Called: July 1989, Gray's Inn, LLB Hons

Weir *Ms Rachel Sian Shapland*
Called: Nov 1991, Inner Temple, MA(Cantab)

Weir *Richard Stanton*
10 Fort Gate, Newhaven, East Sussex BN9 9DR, 01273 516851. Called: Nov 1957, Inner Temple, MA (Oxon)

Welch *Bryan James* ●
Legal Director, Department of Trade and Industry, Dept of Trade & Industry, Room 201, 10 Victoria Street, London SW1H 0NN, 0171 215 3460, Fax: 0171 215 3520. Called: July 1975, Inner Temple, MA (Cantab)

Welch *Nicholas Randall*
Called: Oct 1994, Gray's Inn, BA, LLB

Welling *Robert David* ●
Senior Crown Prosecutor, Crown Prosecution Service, Avonbridge House, Bath Road, Chippenham, Wiltshire SN15 2BB, 01249 659622, Fax: 01249 659722. Called: Nov 1989, Lincoln's Inn, LLB

Wells *Anthony Francis Michael* ●
Crown Prosecution Service, Princes Court, 34 York Road, Leicester LE1 5TU, 0116 2549333, Fax: 0116 2550855. Called: Nov 1968, Gray's Inn, MA (Oxon)

Wells *Commander Anthony Roland*
P.O. Box 2102, The Plains, Middleburg 20118, 703-253 5048, Fax: 703-253 5049. Called: Nov 1980, Lincoln's Inn, MA (Dunelm), MSc, PhD (Lond)

Wells *Ronald Michael* ●
North Herts College, Cambridge Road, Hitchin, Herts, 01462 422882. Called: Apr 1989, Gray's Inn, BA, LLB (Lond), LLM

Wells *Ms Stephanie Jane*
Called: Nov 1997, Inner Temple, BA (La Troube, Australia), LLB, (Reading)

Wells-Carmona *Ms Sandra Anne*
Notary Public, Callenders & Co, P O Box F.40132, Freeport, Grand Bahama, 809 352-7458, Fax: 809 352-4000, and Member Bahamas Bar. Called: July 1994, Inner Temple, BA, LLB (Hons)

Wells-Thorpe *Rupert Sebastian*
Called: Nov 1997, Inner Temple, LLB (Wolver'ton)

Welsh *Miss Amanda Jane*
00 301 451 4452, Fax: 00 301 451 4452. Called: Nov 1992, Gray's Inn, LLB (Leeds)

Welsh *Malcolm James MacGregor*
Called: Oct 1996, Gray's Inn, BSc (Lond)

Wendon *John Mark* ●
Divisional Director Area Counsel Europe, Letterland Limited, 33 New Road, Barton, Cambridgeshire CB3 7AY, 01223 26 2781, Fax: 01223 26 4126. Called: Nov 1975, Middle Temple, MA (Cantab)

Werbicki *Mrs Anne Vivien* ●
Grade 6 Lawyer, Ministry of Agriculture,, Fisheries and Food, Legal Dept, 55 Whitehall, London SW1A 2EY, 0171 270 8257, Fax: 0171 270 8096, and Member Gibraltar Bar. Called: Feb 1981, Gray's Inn, LLB (Bris)

Werhun *John* ●
Senior Crown Prosecutor, Crown Prosecution Service, Sunlight House, 5th Floor, Quay Street, Manchester, 0161 908 2696, Fax: 0161 869 2663. Called: July 1982, Gray's Inn, BA (Law)

Werrett *Miss Melanie Gertrude* ●
Principal Crown Prosecutor, Crown Proecution Service, Gemini Centre, 88 New London Road, Chelmsford, Essex CM2 0BR, 01245 252939, Fax: 01245 490476. Called: July 1979, Gray's Inn

Wesel *Thomas*
Called: Nov 1993, Middle Temple, LLB (Hons)(Lond)

Wessels *Mattheus Hendrikus*
Iustitia Chambers, Aliwal Street, Bloemfontein 9301, Republic of South Africa, 051 303567, Fax: 051 474228, Senior Counsel, South Africa Member: Orange Free State Society of Advocates and Member South African Bar Lesotho Bar 28 St John Street, Manchester, M3 4DJ. Called: Oct 1993, Gray's Inn, B.Iuris, LLB

West *Andrew Peter* ●
Crown Prosecutor, Crown Prosecution Service, 2nd Floor, Portland House, Stag Place, London SW1E 5BH, 0171 915 5912, Fax: 0171 915 5795. Called: Nov 1995, Gray's Inn, BA

West *Christopher John* ●
Solicitor to HM Land Registry, HM Land Registry, 32 Lincoln's Inn Fields, London WC2A 3PH, 0171 917 5994, Fax: 0171 917 5966. Called: July 1966, Lincoln's Inn

West *David John Courtney* ●
Head of Legal Services, Hunting - Brae Ltd, A.W.E., Aldermaston, Reading RG7 4PR, 01734 825095, Fax: 01734 815320. Called: July 1977, Middle Temple, LLB (Hons)

West *Mrs Julie Amanda* ●
Sedgwick Noble Lowndes Ltd, P.O.Box 144, Norfolk House, Wellesley Road, Croydon CR3 3EB, 0181 686 2466, Fax: 0181 681 1458. Called: Nov 1984, Middle Temple, BA (Hons)

Westbrook *Simon Nicholas*
15/Floor Printing House, 6 Duddell Street, Central, (852) 2521 2616, Fax: (852) 2845 0260, and Member Hong Kong Bar. Called: July 1973, Inner Temple, LLB, FCIArb

Westcott *Richard Henry*
Deputy Chairman, Fairview New Homes plc, Non-Exec Director TBI plc.. Called: July 1978, Lincoln's Inn, FCA,FTII,ACIB

Westlake *George Alan*
Called: Oct 1992, Lincoln's Inn, BA(Hons)(Bris), Dip in Law

Westoll *James K.St.J,DL*
Dykeside, Longtown, Carlisle, Cumbria CA6 5ND, 01228 791 235. Called: July 1952, Lincoln's Inn, MA (Hons), LLD

Weston *Miss Sarah Dawn* ●
Bench Legal Adviser, Dorset Magistrates Courts, Law Courts, Park Road, Poole, Dorset BH15 2RJ, 0202 743309, Fax: 0202 711999. Called: July 1985, Gray's Inn, LLB (Manchester), DMS, MBA

Wetherfield *Ms Alison Clare* ●
Associate, Warner Cranston, Warner Cranston, Pickfords'Wharf, Clink Street, London SE1 9DG, 0171 403 2900, Fax: 0171 403 4221, and Member New York. Called: May 1996, Middle Temple, BA (Hons)(Cantab)

Weyers *Jacek Witold*
Juris Angliae Scientia, Warsaw University, The White House, Gotherington Lane, Cheltenham, Gloucester GL52 4EN, 01242 678283, Fax: 01242 678283. Called: Nov 1956, Gray's Inn, LLB, MIWSP

Whale *Stephen John Trehane*
Clerk to the Justices, Brecknock and Radnorshire, Magistrates' Clerks Office, Captains Walk, Brecon, Powys LD3 7HS, 01874 622993, Fax: 01874 622441. Called: Feb 1986, Gray's Inn, MBA, Dip (Mag Law)

Wharam *Alan Neville*
Called: Nov 1953, Inner Temple, MA (Cantab)

Whatham *Stephen Benjamin* ●
Senior Crown Prosecutor, Heron House, Houghamont Avenue, Crosby, Merseyside L22 0LL. Called: Nov 1990, Inner Temple, LLB

E

Whatnell *Mrs Helen Mary*
1407 Azalea Bend, Sugar Land TX 77479, 281 343 7569, Fax: 281 343 6019. Called: Nov 1993, Inner Temple, LLB

Whattam *Charles Barrie*
Called: Oct 1996, Lincoln's Inn, BA (Hons)(Portsm), Dip in Law (Westmin)

Wheater *Miss Jennifer Clare*
Called: Nov 1995, Inner Temple, BA (Dunelm)

Wheeldon *Stuart Lawrence Verner* •
Principal Crown Prosecutor, CPS, 4-12 Queen Anne's Gate, London SW1H 9AZ. Called: Feb 1988, Lincoln's Inn, LLB

Wheeler *John Gerald Patrick*
Templar House, Don Road, St Helier, Jersey, 0534 500300, Fax: 0534 500350, Advocate of the Royal Court of Jersey. Called: July 1978, Inner Temple, BA

Wheeler *Miss Philippa Ruth*
Hewlett Packard GMBH, Postfach 1430, D 71003 Boeblingen, 49 7031 14 3169, Fax: 49 7031 14 3812. Called: July 1988, Inner Temple, LLB

Wheldon *Miss Caroline Anne*
Called: Nov 1992, Inner Temple, BA, Dip in Law (City)

Wheldon *Miss Juliet Louise CB QC (1997)* •
Legal Administrator to the Home Office, Home Office, 4-12 Queen Anne's Gate, London SW1, 0171 273 2681. Called: July 1975, Gray's Inn, MA (Oxon)

Whelon *Charles Patrick Clavell*
Recorder. Called: Nov 1954, Middle Temple

Whetcombe *Timothy Howard Arundel* •
Legal Adviser, Lloyds Bank Plc, Private Banking & Financial, Services Division, Capital Hse, 1/5 Perrymount Rd, Haywards Heath W.Sussex, 01444 459144. Called: July 1987, Lincoln's Inn, LLB (Lond)

Whincup *Miss Catherine Elizabeth* •
Crown Prosecutor, C/O CPS Headquarters, 50 Ludgate Hill, London EC4M 7EX, 0171 273 8000. Called: Nov 1987, Middle Temple, LLB

Whipham *Thomas Henry Martin CBE*
Also Inn of Court M. Called: Jan 1949, Lincoln's Inn

Whipp *Roger Donald* •
Legal Adviser, British Airways Plc, Speedbird House, Heathrow Airport (London), Hounslow, Middlesex TW6 2JA, 0181 562 3602, Fax: 0181 562 3323. Called: July 1987, Lincoln's Inn, LLB (Hons)

Whisson-Eastwick *Kevin Paul* •
CPS (Norfolk Branch), Haldin House, Old Bank of England Court, Queen Street, Norwich, Norfolk NR2 4SX. Called: Nov 1989, Middle Temple, BA Hons, Dip in Law

Whiston *Ms Teresa*
Called: July 1997, Inner Temple, LLB

Whitaker *Anthony Cowburn OBE* •
P/t Chairman Immigration Appeal Tribunal, 36 Doddington Grove, Kennington, London SE17 3TT, Fax: 0171 793 8851. Called: June 1958, Gray's Inn, BA

White *Miss Amanda Ashley*
Called: Nov 1995, Inner Temple, LLB (Middx)

White *Andrew Mark*
Court Clerk, The Law Courts, Northway, Scarborough YO12 7AE, 01723 354258, Fax: 01723 353250. Called: Nov 1986, Gray's Inn, BA (Kent)

White *Miss Catherine Rose*
Deputy Clerk to the Justices, 4/5 Quay Street, Carmarthen, Dyfed SA31 3JT, 01267 221658, Fax: 01267 221812. Called: July 1977, Gray's Inn, LLB

White *Charles David* •
Crown Prosecutor, Crown Prosecution Service, Queens House, 58 Victoria Street, St Albans AL1 3HQ, 01727 818100, Fax: 01727 851080. Called: May 1988, Inner Temple, LLB (Hull)

White *Christopher Bevis Eve OBE*
Called: Nov 1972, Inner Temple, MA

White *David John* •
Senior Crown Prosecutor, 4 Highbury Crescent, London N5 1RN, 0171 609 9151, Fax: 0171 607 4793. Called: Nov 1978, Gray's Inn, LLB

White *David Malcolm*
Clerk to the Justices & Chief Executive, Sheffield Magistrates' Court, Castle Street, Sheffield S3 8LU, 0114 276 0760, Fax: 0114 272 0129. Called: July 1976, Middle Temple, LLB, MSc, MIMgt

White *Miss Esther Ceridwen* •
Called: Nov 1991, Gray's Inn, MA (Oxon)

White *Iain Charles* •
Senior Crown Prosecutor, Crown Prosecution Service, Avon Office, Level 1, Froomsgate House, Rupert Street, Bristol BS1 2QJ. Called: July 1986, Middle Temple, MA (Hons) (Cantab)

White *Ian Robert* •
Company Secretary/In House Lawyer, Gartmore Investment Management, Gartmore House, 16-18 Monument Street, London, 0171 940 5743, Fax: 0171 638 3468. Called: Nov 1989, Inner Temple, BA (Bris), Dip Law (City)

White *Ms Jennifer Susan* •
Legal Adviser, The Electricity Association, 30 Millbank, London, SW1P 4RD, 0171 963 5932, Fax: 0171 630 6186. Called: July 1970, Middle Temple, LLB

White *Jeremy Barry* •
Senior Lawyer, KPMG Tax Advisers, P.O.Box 486, 1 Puddle Dock, London EC4V 3PD, 0171 311 1000, Fax: 0171 311 2943. Called: July 1976, Gray's Inn, LLB

White *Martin Stephen*
Called: July 1973, Middle Temple, BA (Cantab)

White *Paul Murray*
11 King's Bench Walk, 1st Floor, Temple, London, EC4Y 7EQ. Called: July 1975, Lincoln's Inn, BA (Cantab)

White *Miss Rachel*
Watson Wyatt Partners, Park Gate, 21 Tothill Street, London SW1H 9LL, 0171 222 8033, Fax: 0171 222 9182. Called: July 1974, Gray's Inn

White *Richard Charles* •
Called: Nov 1983, Gray's Inn, BA

Whitehead *Miss Claire Helen*
Called: May 1997, Lincoln's Inn, BA (Hons)

Whitehead *Daniel James*
Ashurst Morris Crisp, Broadwalk House, Appold Street, London EC2A 2HA, 0171 972 7192, Fax: 0171 972 7990. Called: Oct 1995, Middle Temple, BA (Hons)(Keele)

Whitehouse *Christopher*
Called: Nov 1997, Gray's Inn, LLB (E.Anglia)

Whitehouse *John Frederic*
Woodstock, Marlow Road, Abbotsbrook, Bourne End, Bucks SL8 5NU, 01628 522898. Called: Nov 1958, Inner Temple, LLB

Whitehouse *Martin* •
Principal Crown Prosecutor, Crown Prosecution Service, 3rd Floor, Solar House, 1-9 Romford Road, Stratford, London E15 4LJ, 0181 534 6601 x309, Fax: 0181 522 1236. Called: Feb 1985, Middle Temple, LLB

Whiteley *Charles Stuart*
Called: Nov 1995, Gray's Inn, BA

Whiteside *Mrs Nilkanthi Maharanee* •
Legal Advisor, City of Salford Magistrates Ct, The Court House, Bexley Square, Salford M3 6DJ, 0161 834 9457, Fax: 0161 839 1806. Called: Feb 1990, Middle Temple, LLB Hons

Whitesides *Keith Robert MBE*
Director (Investor Relations), (0115) 9687031, Fax: (0115) 9687151. Called: Nov 1972, Gray's Inn, MPhil, LLB ACII

Whiting *David Justin* •
In-House Legal, THe BPA Group, 18-20 St John Street, London EC1M 4AY, 0171 251 5657, Fax: 0171 251 5658. Called: May 1995, Lincoln's Inn, BA (Hons), CPE

Whitlock *Miss Charlotte Angela*
Called: July 1983, Gray's Inn, BA

Whitmore *David*
Called: Nov 1995, Middle Temple, BA (Hons)

Whitney *David Roy*
Called: Mar 1998, Gray's Inn, LLB (W'hampton)

Whittaker *Brian Paul* •
Branch Crown Prosecutor, Branch Crown Prosecutor, Bromfield House, Wrexham Technology Park, Wrexham, Clwyd LL13 7YW, 01978 312002 X 301, Fax: 01978 311960. Called: July 1977, Gray's Inn, BA Hons

Whittaker *Ian Dorien Geoffrey* •
H M Customs & Excise, Solicitor's Office,
New Kings Beam House, 22 Upper Ground,
London SE1 9PJ, 22 Albion Place,
Northampton, NN1 1UD. Called: Oct 1994,
Inner Temple, MA (Oxon), CPE

Whittaker *Rodney Martin* •
Associate General Counsel, SmithKline
Beecham plc, One New Horizons Court,
Brentford, Middlesex TW8 9EP, 0181 975
2052, Fax: 0181 975 2070. Called: July
1971, Inner Temple, MA (Oxon)

Whittaker *Dr Simon John*
Fellow, St John's College, Oxford, St John's
College, Oxford OX1 3JP, 01865 277300,
Fax: 01865 277435. Called: Nov 1987,
Lincoln's Inn, BCL MA DPhil (Oxon)

Whitting *Mrs Emma Elizabeth* •
Queen Anne's Chambers, 28 Broadway,
London SW1H 9JS. Called: Nov 1991, Inner
Temple, MA (Oxon), Dip Law

Whitworth *Peter Ernest*
Dorchester House, 5 Dorchester Drive,
London SE24 0DQ, 0171 733 2978, Also L &
I Inns Court. Called: July 1946, Middle
Temple, BA

Whitworth *Simon William Battams*
Legal Consultant, O'Higgins 1085, (1686)
Hurlingham, Provincia Buenos Aires, 54 1
662 8216, Fax: 54 1 662 8216. Called: July
1974, Inner Temple, MA (Cantab)

Whomersley *Christopher Adrian* •
Legal Counsellor, Foreign & Commonwealth
Office, King Charles Street, London SW1.
Called: Nov 1980, Middle Temple, LLB
(LSE), LLM (Cantab)

Wicken *Ronald Edward* •
Principal Assistant, Dudley Magistrates
Court, The Inhedge, Dudley, West Midlands,
01384 455200. Called: Nov 1984, Inner
Temple

Wickens *Simon*
Called: Mar 1998, Lincoln's Inn, BA (Hons)

Wickrama-Sekera *Miss Yasoda*
Legal Officer, Department of Fair Trading, 1
Fitzwilliam Street, New South Wales 2150,
02 9895 0643, Fax: 02 9635 5247, and
Member New South Wales Bar Australia Bar.
Called: Oct 1994, Lincoln's Inn, LLB
(Hons)(Lond), MA (Brunel)

Wickremasinghe *Mrs Jayanthi
Abhayaratne* •
Crown Prosecutor, Crown Prosecution
Service, Priory Gate, 29 Union Street,
Maidstone, Kent, 01622 686425. Called: July
1975, Lincoln's Inn, BA

Widjaja *Prawiro*
Called: July 1994, Middle Temple, BA
(Hons)(Cantab)

Wienholdt *Barry*
Well Bank Cottage, Over Peover, Knutsford,
Cheshire WA16 8UW, 01625 861488.
Called: July 1970, Gray's Inn

Wightman *Paul Edward*
Called: May 1996, Middle Temple, LLB
(Hons)

Wightwick *Ian Richard MC*
49 Molyneux Street, London W1H 5HW,
0171 262 9085. Called: June 1959, Inner
Temple, MA

Wignall *Julian David*
Chief Executive, City of London
Magistrates', Courts, 1 Queen Victoria
Street, London EC4N 4XY, 0171 332 1820/
1828, Fax: 0171 332 1493. Called: July
1975, Middle Temple, LLB, M.B.A.

Wignall *Miss Natalie Elizabeth* •
Legal Adviser, Legal Department, GPT Ltd,
Edge Lane, Liverpool L7 9NW, 0151 254
3769, Fax: 0151 254 3326. Called: Oct
1992, Lincoln's Inn, LLB(Hons)

Wigoder *Lord QC (1966)*
Called: Nov 1946, Gray's Inn, MA (Oxon)

Wijeyaratne *Miss Sonali Arundhini* •
Legal & Business Affairs, Guild
Entertainment, Kent House, 14-17 Market
Place, Great Titchfield Street, London
W1N 8AR, 0171 323 5151. Called: Nov
1986, Middle Temple, BA (Oxon)

Wikeley *Professor Nicholas John*
p/t Chairman,Social Security Appeal
Tribunals & Disability Appeal Tribunals,
Faculty of Law, The University, Highfield,
Southampton SO17 1BJ, 01703 593416, Fax:
01703 593024. Called: July 1981, Gray's Inn,
MA (Cantab)

Wilcox *Lawrence Gaywood*
Called: Oct 1996, Lincoln's Inn, LLB
(Hons)(Exon)

Wilcox *Stephen John* •
Senior Principal, Lord Chancellor's
Department, Selborne House, 54-60 Victoria
Street, London SW1E 6QW, 0171 210 0718,
Fax: 0171 210 0725. Called: July 1972,
Gray's Inn, LLB

Wilde *James Richard*
Called: Jan 1935, Middle Temple

Wilde *Ralph Garfield*
Called: Oct 1997, Middle Temple, LLB
(Hons)(Lond), CPE (City)

Wiles *Philip George* •
Group LegaL Adviser, Sun Life Assurance
Society Plc, 107 Cheapside, London
EC2V 6DU, 0171 606 7788, Fax: 0171 378
1865. Called: Nov 1982, Gray's Inn

Wilfred Jr *Bode*
Called: Nov 1997, Middle Temple, LLB
(Hons)(Sheff), LLM (Dundee)

Wilkes *Miss Jayne Denise* •
Crown Prosecution Service, The Old
Barracks, Sandon Road, Grantham
NG32 9AS, (01476) 70585, Fax: (01476)
590857. Called: Nov 1991, Inner Temple,
LLB

Wilkins *Adrian Mark*
Called: Oct 1992, Gray's Inn, LL.B (L'pool),
MSc (Stirling)

Wilkins *Nigel Granville* •
Principal Crown Prosecutor, Crown
Prosecution Service, Friars House, Manor
House Drive, Coventry CV1 2TE. Called: Feb
1974, Inner Temple, LLB

Wilkins *Richard Leslie*
Called: Mar 1996, Middle Temple, BA
(Hons)

Wilkinson *Mrs Ann Elizabeth* •
Called: July 1988, Inner Temple, LLB
(Soton)

Wilkinson *James Leo* •
Senior Counsel, Smithkline Beecham Plc,
One New Horizons Court, Brentford,
Middlesex TW8 9EP, 0181 975 2058, Fax:
0181 975 2071. Called: July 1972, Middle
Temple, MR Pharm S

Wilks *Miss Elizabeth*
Called: Nov 1997, Gray's Inn, LLB

Wilks *Ian*
Called: Oct 1996, Middle Temple, LLB
(Hons) (Sheff)

Willers *Peter Alan*
Legal Director, Ballagawne Farm, Baldrine,
0624 661662, Fax: 0624 661663.
Called: Nov 1973, Middle Temple, MA
(Cantab)

Willetts *Andrew Philip*
Called: Nov 1997, Inner Temple, BSc
(Wales)

Willey *Stuart Christopher* •
Head of Legal Services, Personal Investment
Authority, Limited, 7th Floor, 1 Canada
Square, Canary Wharf E14 5AZ, 0171 538
8860, Fax: 0171 418 9300. Called: May
1979, Middle Temple, B.A. (York)

Williams *Alexander Steuart*
12 King's Bench Walk, Temple, London,
EC4Y 7EL. Called: Oct 1994, Lincoln's Inn,
BA (Hons)(Oxon), Dip in Law (City)

Williams *Miss Ameeta Chandra*
Called: Nov 1995, Middle Temple, LLB
(Hons)(Sheff)

Williams *Mrs Annie Yoke Yean Chew*
Called: Nov 1992, Middle Temple, LLB
(Hons)

Williams *Miss April Nicole*
Called: Nov 1996, Inner Temple, BA
(Canada), BA (Keele)

Williams *Mrs Beverley*
Senior Court Clerk - Part time, Victoria Law
Courts, Corporation Street, Birmingham
B4 6QA, 0121 212 6612, Fax: 0121 212
6766. Called: Feb 1985, Middle Temple, BA

Williams *Carl David*
Called: Nov 1994, Inner Temple, LLB
(Essex)

Williams *Ms Caroline*
5 Cool Na Mara, Marine Terrace,
Dunlaoghaire, Co Dublin, 00353 12842770,
Fax: 00353 12842770, Barrister of King's
Inn. Called: Nov 1994, Middle Temple

E

Williams *Cecil Alfred*
Called: July 1997, Gray's Inn, BA (West Indies), MSc (Bradford), LLB (Lond)

Williams *Charles Edouard Vaughan* •
Directorate General for, Competition, Commission of the European, Communities, Rue de la loi 200, B-1049 Brussels. Called: Nov 1990, Middle Temple, BA (Oxon), DAES (Bruges)

Williams *David Edward Huw*
Legal Consultant, 7 Hertford Street, London W1Y 8LP, 0171 355 1886, Fax: 0171 355 1887. Called: Nov 1977, Lincoln's Inn

Williams *David John*
10e Thorney Crescent, Morgans Walk, London SW11 3TR, 0171 223 9059. Called: Jan 1939, Inner Temple, MA (Oxon)

Williams *David Michael* •
Lawyer Fraud London Division, Crown Prosecution Service, Headquarters, 50 Ludgate Hill, London EC4M 7EX, 0171 273 1338. Called: July 1972, Inner Temple, LLB (Manch), MBA

Williams *Miss Elaine Denise* •
Director, Transferry Shipping Co Ltd, Transferry House, Southend Arterial Road, Hornchurch, Essex RM11 3UT, 01708 452500, Fax: 01708 456218. Called: July 1982, Gray's Inn, BA (Kent), LLM (Lond, M.B.A (Warw), F.Inst.D.

Williams *Francis Joseph*
Called: Nov 1984, Inner Temple, BA, PGCE

Williams *Huw David* •
The Environment Agency, Rio House, Waterside Drive, Aztec West, Almondsbury, Bristol BS12 4UD, 01454 624022, Fax: 01454 624010. Called: July 1988, Inner Temple, BA (Cantab), Dip Law

Williams *Jonathan Steuart*
Senior Crown Prosecutor Magistrate of the NSW Local Court, Magistrates' Chambers, Level 5, Downing Centre, 143-147 Liverpool Street, Sydney, NSW 2000, 02 9664 2924, and Member Australian Capital Territory New South Wales Bar. Called: May 1990, Lincoln's Inn, Dip Law, Dip Crim, LLM

Williams *Miss Julie Ann* •
Lawyer, Department of Trade & Industry, 10 Victoria Street, London SW1H 0NN, 0171 215 3230, Fax: 0171 215 3235. Called: Nov 1990, Middle Temple, LLB (Warw)

Williams *Leon Norman*
1 Mitre Ct Bldgs, Ground Floor, Temple, London, EC4Y 7BS. Called: May 1943, Gray's Inn

Williams *Llewelyn Jones*
4 Raphael Avenue, Brackla, Bridgend CF31 2AU, 01656 647477. Called: July 1983, Gray's Inn

Williams *Michael James John* •
Group Legal Counsel, SubC Offshore Limited, Greenweel Base, Greenwell Road, Tullos, Aberdeen AB12 3AX. Called: Feb 1990, Gray's Inn, LLB, MA

Williams *Miss Michele Donna* •
Financial Services Authority, Gavrelle House, 2-14 Bunhill Row, London EC1Y 8RA, 0171 638 1240, Fax: 0171 382 5906. Called: Nov 1980, Lincoln's Inn, LLB (Hons), FCIArb

Williams *Miss Natasha Louise* •
Company Lawyer, JC Decaux UK Ltd, Uniti Goldhawk Ind Est, 2A Brackenbury Road, London W6 0BA, 0181 746 1000, Fax: 0181 749 2046. Called: Oct 1995, Gray's Inn, LLB

Williams *Nicholas William Edwin* •
Legal Advisor to the Magistrates (Court Clerk), Telford Magistrates Court, Telford Square, Malinsgate, Telford, Shropshire TF3 4HX, 01952 204500, Fax: 01952 204554. Called: Nov 1994, Inner Temple, LLB (Soton)

Williams *Paul Richard* •
Legal Advisor, Banque Nationale de Paris, London Branch, 8-13 King William Street, London EC4P 4HS, 0171 548 9511, Fax: 0171 548 9387. Called: Nov 1984, Middle Temple, BA (Hons)(B'ham), Dip Law (Lond)

Williams *Ray Anthony*
Called: May 1996, Lincoln's Inn, LLB (Hons) (Warw)

Williams *Richard David*
Bircham & Co Solicitors, 1 Dean Farrar Street, Westminster, London Sw1H 0DY, 0171 222 8044. Called: Oct 1993, Gray's Inn, MA

Williams *Richard Mark St.John*
Called: Oct 1997, Gray's Inn, BA (Dunelm)

Williams *Commander Robert Evan RN* •
DNSC/C2, Room 215a, Victory Building, HM Naval Base, Portsmouth PO1 3LR, 01705 727252, Fax: 01705 727112. Called: July 1981, Gray's Inn, LLB

Williams *Miss Rosemarie Maud Josephine* •
and Member Attorney at Law, Guyana. Called: July 1978, Middle Temple, BA (Kent), LLM (Lond)

Williams *Ms Rowan Elaine*
Bench Legal Adviser, Eastbourne & Hailsham, Magistrates Court, The Law Courts, Old Orchard Road, Eastbourne, East Sussex BN21 4UN, 01323 727518, Fax: 01323 649372. Called: July 1981, Middle Temple

Williams *Miss Samantha* •
Senior Crwon Prosecutor. Called: Oct 1992, Lincoln's Inn, LLB(Hons)(Wales)

Williams *Ms Samantha Tracey*
Called: Nov 1997, Lincoln's Inn, LLB (Hons)(Middx)

Williams *Miss Sara*
Called: Oct 1996, Lincoln's Inn, LLB (Hons)(Wales)

Williams *Simon Peter* •
HM Customs & Excise, Ralli Quays, 3 Stanley Street, Salford, Manchester M60 9LA. Called: Nov 1993, Lincoln's Inn, LLB (Hons)

Williams *Stephen John*
Called: Nov 1977, Middle Temple, LLB (Hons)(Lond)

Williams *Terence John*
Called: Nov 1992, Gray's Inn

Williams *Thomas Anthony John* •
Senior Crown Prosecutor, Crown Prosecution Service, Seven Thames Area, Berkshire Branch Office, Eaton Court, 112 Oxford Road, Reading RG1 7LL, 01734 503771, Fax: 01734 508192. Called: Nov 1983, Gray's Inn, LLB (wales)

Williams *Miss Victoria Anna*
Called: Mar 1998, Middle Temple, BSc (Hons)(Lond)

Williams of Mostyn *Lord* QC (1978)
Recorder Deputy High Court Judge, also Inns of Court I & L and Member Northern Ireland Bar Irish Bar. Called: Feb 1965, Gray's Inn, MA, LLM(Cantab)

Williamson *Ms Jacqueline*
and Member Scottish Bar. Called: Feb 1995, Inner Temple, LLB, LLM (Lond)

Williamson *Mrs Judith Nicola*
Grove House, Semley, Shaftesbury, Dorset SP7 9AP, 01747 830389. Called: Nov 1978, Inner Temple

Williamson *Kris*
Legal Adviser, Daniel & CIA, Trade Mark & Patent Attorneys, Avenida Republica da Chile, 230/60 Andor, Rio de Janeiro, CEP 20070-001, RJ, 005521 224 4212, Fax: 005521 224 3344. Called: Nov 1993, Middle Temple, BA (Hons)(Leic), LLB (Hons)(Lond)

Williamson *Mrs Romi Wai Ming*
30b Century Tower, 1 Tregunter Path, 25222884, and Member Hong Kong Bar. Called: Nov 1994, Middle Temple, BA (Econ)(Australia)

Williamson *Miss Rosemary Anne* •
Principal Assistant, Buckinghamshire County Council, County Hall, Aylesbury, Bucks, 0296 82371, Fax: 0296 26347. Called: Feb 1979, Middle Temple, BA (Lond)

Williamson *Stephen Ellis*
The Corner, 1a Glen Iris Ave, Canterbury, Kent CT2 8HW. Called: Jan 1951, Inner Temple, MA (Cantab)LLB

Willimsky *Miss Sonya Margaret*
Emplyed Corporate/Commercial Lawyer, Haarmann, Hemmelrath & Partner, Martin Luther Plate 26, 40212 Dusseldorf, 00 49 211 8399 0, Fax: 00 49 211 8399 133. Called: Nov 1996, Lincoln's Inn, LLB (Hons)(Lond)

Willis-Jones *William Mark* •
European Legal Counsel, Armstrong World Industries, Armstrong House, 38 Market Square, Uxbridge, Middlesex UB8 1NG, 01895 202045, Fax: 01895 256869. Called: Nov 1982, Middle Temple, BSc (Lond) Dip Law

• Barristers in employment

Willits *Ms Joanne Cresswell*
Lecturer in Law, University of North Umbria at, Newcastle, Law Department, Sutherland Building, Newcastle Upon Tyne NE1 8ST, 0191 227 3466. Called: Nov 1993, Gray's Inn, LLB (L'pool)

Willmer *John Franklin* QC (1967)
Arbitrator: Wreck Commissioner, 7 King's Bench Walk, Ground Floor, Temple, London, EC4Y 7DS. Called: Feb 1955, Inner Temple, MA (Oxon)

Willmer *Paul Richard*
Principal Court Clerk, Humberside Magistrates Court, 31 Lairgate, Beverley HU17 8EP, 01482 881264. Called: Feb 1989, Gray's Inn, LLB (Hull)

Willmin *Mrs Rosalind Dawn* •
Senior Crown Prosecutor, Crown Prosecution Service, 4/6 Prebendal Court, Oxford Road, Aylesbury, Buckinghamshire, 01296 436441. Called: Nov 1984, Middle Temple, Dip Magisterial Law

Willmore *Ms Christine Joan*
3 Church Farm Close, Yate, Bristol BS17 5BZ, 01454 311777, Fax: 01454 311777. Called: July 1979, Inner Temple, LLB (Bris)

Wills *Jeffrey*
Court Clerk, Manchester City, Magistrates' Court, Crown Square, Manchester M60 1PR, 0161 832 7272, Fax: 0161 832 5421. Called: Nov 1991, Gray's Inn, Dip Law, CPE, Cert, in Training &, Development, Dip., Nebs.M.

Willson *John* •
Legal Adviser, The Yasuda Trust & Banking, Company Limited, 1 Liverpool Street, London EC2M 7NH, 0171 628 5721. Called: July 1978, Lincoln's Inn

Wilne *Richard James*
Called: July 1996, Middle Temple, BA (Hons)(Durham)

Wilson *Adam Richard*
SFA (Registered Representive), Teather & Greenwood, 12-20 Camomile Street, London EC3A 7NN, 0171 426 9510, Fax: 0171 929 0900, Private Client Stockbroker. Called: Nov 1994, Gray's Inn, BA (Essex), Dip Law, Dip Fin, ALLMR, MSI

Wilson *Alan Paul*
Senior Law Lecturer Consumer & Contract Law, University of East London, Longbridge Road, Dagenham, London, Essex RM8 2AS, 0181 590 7722, Fax: 0181 590 7799, Formerly of the Consumers Association. Called: May 1983, Gray's Inn, LLB (L'pool), LLM (Lond)

Wilson *Miss Anne Christine* •
Senior Legal Adviser, 3i plc, 91 Waterloo Road, London SE1 8XP, 0171 928 3131. Called: Nov 1970, Gray's Inn, LL.B

Wilson *Arthur William Darragh*
Called: July 1957, Inner Temple, MA (Cantab)

Wilson *Calvin Egbert Junior*
and Member Trinidad & Tobago Bar. Called: Nov 1988, Lincoln's Inn, LLB (Lond), LLM (LSE)

Wilson *Miss Caroline Ann* •
Legal Adviser, Berkshire & Oxfordshire Magistrates' Courts' Committee, Bracknell Magistrates' Court, Town Square, Bracknell, Berks, 01344 425051. Called: Oct 1993, Inner Temple, LLB (Northumbria)

Wilson *Mrs Christine Elisabeth*
Legal Team Manager, Berkshire & Oxfordshire Mag's, Court's Committee, Easby House, Northfield End, Henley on Thames, Oxfordshire RG9 2NB, 01491 412720, Fax: 01491 412762. Called: July 1974, Inner Temple, LLB

Wilson *Mrs Faye Claudette* •
Crown Prosecutor, Crown Prosecution Service, 8th Floor, Prospect West, 81 Station Road, Croydon, Surrey. Called: Nov 1983, Lincoln's Inn, BSc.Soc, LLB (W Indies), LLM (Lond)

Wilson *Gareth William*
J R Jones Solicitors, 56a The Mall, Ealing Broadway, London W5 3TA, 0181 566 2595, Fax: 0181 579 4288. Called: Feb 1986, Lincoln's Inn, LLM (Cantab), BA

Wilson *Gavin Bruce*
2/12 Abercorn Place, London NW8 9XP, 0171 286 3045. Called: Nov 1976, Gray's Inn, BSc (Hons), C.Eng,MICE

Wilson *George Richard Roland*
Called: Oct 1996, Middle Temple, BSc (Hons)(Lond), CPE (City)

Wilson *Graham James*
33 Boulevard Grande-Duchesse, Charlotte, Luxembourg L-1331, 252740, Fax: 252741, Gray's Inn Chambers, 3rd Floor, Gray's Inn, London, WC1R 5JA. Called: July 1975, Gray's Inn, LLB (Lond)

Wilson *Miss Hilary Margaret* •
Legal Adviser, Kvaerner Construction Group Lt, Maple Cross House, Denham Way, Maple Cross, Rickmansworth, Herts WD3 2SW, 01923 776666, Fax: 01923 423864. Called: Nov 1974, Gray's Inn, MA (Cantab)

Wilson *Mrs Hilda*
7 Acacia Gardens, London NW8 6RH, 0171 722 7809, Fax: 0171 722 7809, also Inn of Court M & L. Called: Nov 1953, Gray's Inn, BA

Wilson *John*
365 Dam Street, Colombo 12, 94 1 324579 or 94 1 446954, Fax: 94 1 446954. Called: Oct 1996, Lincoln's Inn, LLB (Hons)(Lond), Maitrise en Droit, Francais (Paris)

Wilson *John Frederick*
Constitutional Advisor, C/O Parliamentary Counsel, Office, Parliament Buildings, Vuya Road, Suva, Fiji. Called: July 1966, Inner Temple, BA (Oxon)

Wilson *Julian* •
Lawyer, Durham County Council, County Hall, Durham DH1 5UL, (0191) 386 4411. Called: Oct 1994, Middle Temple, BSc (Hons)(York), CPE (Northumbria)

Wilson *Kenneth*
42 Hawthylands Road, Hailsham, East Sussex BN27 1EY, 01323 840966. Called: Nov 1957, Middle Temple, LLB

Wilson *Leslie Arnold*
Called: Nov 1974, Inner Temple, BA

Wilson *Mark John* •
Senior Principal Legal Officer, Department of Social Security, Department of Health, New Court, 48 Carey Street, London WC2A 2LS, 0171 412 1234, Fax: 0171 412 1227. Called: Apr 1991, Lincoln's Inn, LLB (Hons)

Wilson *Michael Alexander* •
Editor, Butterworth, Halsbury House, 35 Chancery Lane, London WC2A 1EL, 0171 400 2688. Called: Oct 1994, Inner Temple, BA, CPE (Coventry)

Wilson *Michael J. H.*
Clerk to the Justices, Huddersfield Magistrates' Crt, Civic Centre, Huddersfield, 01484 423552. Called: Nov 1975, Inner Temple, LLM

Wilson *Peter Julian*
Called: Oct 1995, Middle Temple, BA (Hons)

Wilson *Richard Colin*
Called: Oct 1996, Middle Temple, LLB (Hons)(Sheff)

Wilson *Mrs Shelley Anne* •
Senior Crown Prosecutor, Crown Prosecution Service, Justinian House, Spitfire Close, Ermine Bus Pk, Huntington, Cambs. Called: Nov 1987, Inner Temple, BA (Kent)

Wilson *Terence John* •
Head of Legal Department, Panic Link PLC, Control Sortation Centre, Melbourne Road, Lount, Leicestershire LE67 1PL, 01530 411111, Fax: 01530 41191. Called: Nov 1982, Lincoln's Inn, LLB (Leics)

Wilson *Miss Vanessa Gay*
Legal & Business Affairs Executive, United Broadcasting &, Enertainment, Ludgate House, 245 Blackfriars Road, London SE1 9UY, 0171 579 4418, Fax: 0171 579 4438. Called: Oct 1992, Middle Temple, LLB (Hons)

Wilson *Ms Victoria Anne* •
Legal Services, London Borough of Camden, Town Hall, Judd Street, London WC1H 9LP, 0171 278 4444, Fax: 0171 860 5671. Called: Nov 1994, Inner Temple, BA, CPE (Notts)

Wilson *The Hon William Edward Alexander* •
Dept of Environment Legal Dept Harkness Fellowship 1996/97. Called: Nov 1978, Middle Temple, LLM

Wilson Appukuttan *Joy*
Messrs Kitson Foong &, Associates, No 75B Jalan Dato Haji Eusoff, Damai Complex, Off Jalan Ipoh, 50400 Kuala Lumpur, 603 4436797/603-4428411, Fax: 603-4429297, Advocate & Solicitor and Member Malaysia Bar Singapore Bar. Called: Nov 1989, Middle Temple, LLB Hons (Lond)

Wilson Thomas *Robert* •
Legal Chemical Engineering Officer; International Legal Consultant, Head of Legal Affairs &, Company Secretary, GTL Int'l, Ltd, Bay Chambers, West Bute Street, Cardiff CF1 6HG, 01222 454 864, Fax: 01222 454 865. Called: July 1977, Inner Temple, BSC (Hons)

Wilton *Stephen Barsley* •
Senior Court Clerk, Magistrates' Courts, PO Box 97, Westgate, Leeds LS1 3JP, 0113 2459653, Fax: 0113 2444700. Called: May 1976, Middle Temple, LLB (Lond)

Winckless *Michael Louis John*
1430 Prince's Building, Central, (852) 2525 7388, Fax: (852) 2525 3930, and Member Hong Kong Bar. Called: July 1994, Middle Temple, BSc (Hons), MBA

Winckley *Peter Frederick*
J Chandler & Co (Buckfast) Ltd, Abbey House, Peterborough Road, London SW6 3BP, 0171 736 2185, Fax: 0171 736 4503. Called: July 1989, Gray's Inn, LLB [Wales]

Windsor *Miss Ann Victoria*
Called: Nov 1969, Inner Temple, LLB (Lond), LLM (Lond)

Winfield *Miss Georgina Mary* •
Crown Prosecutor, Crown Prosecution Service, 17th Floor, Tolworth Tower, Surbiton, Surrey. Called: Nov 1989, Middle Temple, LLB Hons

Winfield *Miss Sarah* •
Legal Officer, Metropolitian Police, Solicitor's Department, New Scotland Yard, Broadway, London SW1H 0BG, 0171 230 7242, Fax: 0171 230 7209. Called: Oct 1990, Inner Temple, LLB (Hons)(Exon)

Wingfield-Digby *Kenelm Edward*
Called: Oct 1996, Inner Temple, BSc (City), CPE (Westminster)

Wingrove *Roderick Stephen Fontannaz*
73 Elgin Crescent, London W11 2JE, 0171 727 5722, Fax: 0171 229 8907. Called: Nov 1973, Middle Temple, MA (Cantab)

Winkley *Julian Patrick* •
Senior Lawyer, HM Customs & Excise, Solicitor's Office, Ralli Quays, 3 Stanley Street, Salford M60 9LB, 0161 827 0500, Fax: 0161 827 0551. Called: Nov 1983, Middle Temple, BA

Winny *Ms Elspeth Margaret*
Called: Nov 1996, Lincoln's Inn, LLB (Hons)(Lond)

Winship *Peter Thomas* •
Principal Crown Prosecutor (Team Leader), Crown Prosecution Service, Kings House, Kymberly Road, Harrow, Middlesex HA1, 0171 424 8688, Fax: 0171 424 9134. Called: Nov 1988, Gray's Inn, MA (St Andrews)

Winter *Rex Alexander*
Called: Oct 1997, Lincoln's Inn, CPE (Northumbria)

Wise *Curt Nicolas* •
Principal Crown Prosecutor, Crown Prosecution Service, 50 Ludgate Hill, London EC4M 7EX, 0171 273 8120. Called: Nov 1983, Middle Temple, BA, LLM

Wiseheart *Malcolm Boyd*
Special Master, Property Appraisal Adjustment Board, 2840 Southwest Third Avenue, Miami, Florida 33129, 305 285 1222, Fax: 305 858 4864, and Member Florida & Washington DC Bars Jamaica & Trinidad & Tobago Bars. Called: Feb 1970, Gray's Inn, MA (Cantab) JD, (Florida) BA (Yale)

Witcombe *Richard Joshua*
Called: Oct 1997, Lincoln's Inn, LLB (Hons)(Coventry), LLM (Lond)

Witham *Simon* •
Senior Legal Adviser, Gallaher Limited, Member's Hill, Brooklands Road, Weybridge, Surrey, 01932 859777, Fax: 01932 832570. Called: Nov 1987, Gray's Inn, LLB

Withey *Richard Leslie*
Called: Oct 1996, Inner Temple, LLB

Withington *Neil Robert* •
British American Tobacco, Millbank, Knowle Green, Staines, Middlesex TW18 1DY, 01784 460400, Fax: 01784 448570. Called: July 1981, Middle Temple, MA (Oxon) B.C.L.

Wittering *Robin*
Herbert Smith, Exchange House, Primrose Street, London EC2A 2HS, 0171 374 8000, Fax: 0171 496 0043. Called: Nov 1995, Lincoln's Inn, BA, LLM

Wolstenholme *Christopher Donald Humphreys*
Senior Deputy Chief Clerk, Inner London Magistrates', Courts Service, 65 Romney Street, London SW1P 3RD, 0171 799 3332, Fax: 0171 799 3072. Called: Nov 1971, Middle Temple, MA (Cantab)

Womersley *Walter Giro*
41 Tennyson Avenue, Harrogate, North Yorkshire HG1 3LE, 01423 563442. Called: Nov 1994, Gray's Inn, LLB (Warw)

Womersley-Smith *Howard Anthony*
Called: Nov 1996, Inner Temple, LLB (Plymouth)

Wong *Adrian Kwai Ming*
Called: July 1997, Lincoln's Inn, LLB (Hons)(Leeds)

Wong *Alex Li Kok*
Called: July 1997, Middle Temple, LLB (Hons)

Wong *Miss Angela Mo Yen*
Called: Nov 1996, Gray's Inn, LLB

Wong *Miss Annie Sook Cheng*
Called: Nov 1997, Middle Temple, LLB (Hons)(Lond)

Wong *Chak Yan*
Called: Nov 1997, Middle Temple, BSc (Hons,Hong Kong)

Wong *Chao-Wai*
Associate, Hong Kong Institute of Arbitrators Ltd, CNAC Group Building, 13th Flr, 10 Queens Road C, Central, Hong Kong, 28101008, Fax: 25960945, and Member Hong Kong Bar. Called: Nov 1991, Inner Temple, LLB, LLM, MA, MIL, ACIArb

Wong *Miss Cheryl Pooi Leng*
Called: July 1996, Lincoln's Inn, LLB (Hons)(Lond)

Wong *Chi Wing John*
Called: Nov 1997, Middle Temple, LLB (Hons)

Wong *Chin Wun Wilfred*
Called: Oct 1992, Middle Temple, LLB(Hons), LLM(Lond)

Wong *Miss Denise Chin Wuen*
Called: July 1996, Lincoln's Inn, LLB (Hons)(Bris)

Wong *Eden Yi Dung*
Called: Nov 1997, Gray's Inn, B.Com (Melbourne), LLB (Lond)

Wong *Mrs Fung Kwai*
065 5660812. Called: July 1995, Middle Temple, LLB (Hons)

Wong *Miss Grace Teck Lian*
Called: July 1996, Lincoln's Inn, LLB (Hons)(Leics)

Wong *Hong Wai*
Legal Assistant, c/o Cheang & Ariff, Advocates & Solicitors, 39 Court, No 39 Jalan Yap Kwan, Seng, 50450, Kuala Lumpur Malaysia, 03 2610803, Fax: 03 2621533. Called: Nov 1992, Gray's Inn, LLB (Hull)

Wong *Miss I-Lin Petula*
Called: Nov 1995, Gray's Inn, LLB (Lond)

Wong *James Seow Boon*
Called: Nov 1996, Middle Temple, LLB (Hons)(Bucks)

Wong *James Yuen Weng*
Called: July 1996, Lincoln's Inn, LLB (Hons)(Nott's)

Wong *John Sing Kiu*
Called: Nov 1994, Middle Temple, B.Sc, LLB (Hons)

Wong *Joseph Tai Nang*
Called: July 1984, Gray's Inn, LLB, MA (Social, Science)

Wong *Kah Hui*
Called: Nov 1995, Lincoln's Inn, LLB (Hons)

Wong *Kean Li*
Called: July 1995, Middle Temple, BA (Hons)

Wong *Kee Them*
Called: Nov 1997, Lincoln's Inn, LLB (Hons)

Wong *Kelvin Weng Wah*
and Member Singapore Bar. Called: July 1995, Middle Temple, LLB (Hons), ACIArb

Wong *Miss Ket Yee*
Called: July 1997, Middle Temple, LLB (Hons)(B'ham)

Wong *Kwee Hoi*
Called: Nov 1997, Lincoln's Inn, LLB (Hons)

Wong *Kwok Fai*
Called: Nov 1996, Middle Temple, LLB (Hons)(Lond)

Wong *Miss Li Chien*
Called: Nov 1996, Middle Temple, BA (Hons)(Kent)

Wong *Li Fei*
Called: July 1997, Lincoln's Inn, LLB (Hons)

Wong *Mark Kuan Meng*
P.K.Wong & Advani, 20 Raffles Place, [H]12-03 Ocean Towers, Singapore 0104, 65 5381822, Fax: 65 5381838, and Member Singapore Bar. Called: Nov 1992, Middle Temple, LLB (Hons, Hull)

Wong *Dr Melvin*
Fax: (852) 26987403, and Member Hong Kong Bar. Called: July 1997, Gray's Inn, Pharm.D, LLB (Lond)

Wong *Ming Fung*
Called: July 1997, Middle Temple, BA (Hons)

Wong *Nai Chee*
No 25 Lorong Hang Jebat, 75200 Melaka, 010606 2825105, Fax: 010606 2848004, and Member Malaysia Bar. Called: July 1994, Middle Temple, LLB (Hons)(Hull)

Wong *Pak Heung*
3rd Floor, Fook Shing Court, 50 Wyndham Street, 852 2523 3450, and Member Supreme Court of Hong Kong Supreme Court of Australian Capital Territory. Called: July 1966, Inner Temple

Wong *Miss Pei-Ling*
37 Lorong Maa'rof, Bangsar Park, 59000 Kuala Lumpur, 03 2836193. Called: July 1996, Lincoln's Inn, LLB (Hons)

Wong *Raymond Kwai Sang*
Called: Nov 1996, Middle Temple, LLB (Hons)(HongKong)

Wong *Richard T W*
Room 1205-6 New World Tower, Tower 1, 16-18 Queens Road Central, Central, 25211388, Fax: 28451738, Barrister of the Supreme Court of the Australian Capital Territory(Dec 1990) and Member Hong Kong Bar. Called: Nov 1986, Inner Temple, LLB (Lond), PCLL (HK)

Wong *Miss Rita Kee Ning*
Called: July 1996, Lincoln's Inn

Wong *Ronny Fook*
SC Hong Kong and Member Hong Kong Bar 3 Verulam Buildings, London, WC1R 5NT. Called: Nov 1970, Lincoln's Inn, LLB (Hull)

Wong *Miss Rosaline Wing Yue*
and Member Hong Kong. Called: July 1993, Middle Temple, LLB (Hons)(Lond)

Wong *Miss Shou Ning*
Called: Nov 1996, Middle Temple, LLB (Hons)(Kent)

Wong *Ms Shou Sien*
Raja Darryl & Loh, 18th Floor, Wisma Sime Darby, Jln Raja Laut, 50350 Kuala Lumpur, Malaysia, 603-2949999, Fax: 603 2933823, and Member Malaysia Bar. Called: Feb 1994, Middle Temple, LLB (Hons)(Kent), LLM (Lond)

Wong *Miss Siew Mei*
Called: July 1997, Middle Temple, LLB (Hons)(Wales)

Wong *Sin Yee*
BBA, CPE. Called: July 1994, Gray's Inn

Wong *Miss Sook Ling*
Shooklin & Bok, Advocates & Solicitors, 1 Robinson Road, [H]18-00 AIA Tower, Singapore 099310, (65) 535 1944, Fax: (65) 535 8577, and Member Singapore Bar. Called: July 1994, Inner Temple, LLB

Wong *Soon Chee*
Called: July 1997, Lincoln's Inn, LLB (Hons)(Lond)

Wong *Sow Wei*
and Member Advocate & Solicitor of the High Court of Malaya. Called: July 1996, Lincoln's Inn

Wong *Stephen Yee Onn*
Called: July 1994, Lincoln's Inn, LLB (Hons)

Wong *Miss Su-Mene*
Called: July 1995, Middle Temple, LLB (Hons)

Wong *Miss Sui Ching Janet*
Called: Nov 1997, Middle Temple, BA (Hons)(Hong Kong)

Wong *Wai Ip*
17 Gerrard Street, London WC1V 8HB, 44 0171 301 8881, Fax: 44 0171 301 8801, and Member Hong Kong. Called: July 1997, Lincoln's Inn, LLB (Hons), BSc (Hons), MSc, MScDPM, MA, ACCA, ACIArb, ACIB, MCIPS, MCIM, MIMgt, MACS, MIEEE

Wong *Wai Keong*
and Member Malaysia. Called: Nov 1995, Lincoln's Inn, LLB (Hons)(Lond)

Wong *Wee Kok*
Called: Nov 1996, Lincoln's Inn, LLB (Hons)(Wales)

Wong *Miss Weng Ho* •
Trade Mark Associate, D Young & Co, 10 Staple Inn, London WC1. Called: July 1987, Gray's Inn, LLB (Lond), LLM (Lond)

Wong *Miss Weng Yuen* •
Senior Crown Prosecutor, Crown Prosecution Service, 3rd Floor, King's House, Kymberley Road, Harrow, Middlesex, 0181 424 8688, Fax: 0181 424 9157. Called: July 1990, Middle Temple, LLB (Brunel)

Wong *Winston Paul Chi-Huang*
Legal Assistant, Suite 12-02, 12th Floor, Menara Pelangi, Jalan Kuning, 80400 Johor Bahru, Joor Malaysia, 010 60 7 3342266, Fax: 010 60 7 3344708, and Member Malaysia Bar. Called: Nov 1994, Middle Temple, BA (Hons), LLM, (Singapore)

Wong *Yew Kit*
and Member Singapore. Called: July 1995, Middle Temple, LLB (Hons)

Wong *Yun Wah Gordon*
Pacific Chambers, 901 Dina House, Rutterjee Centre, 11 Duddell Street, Central, (852) 2521 5544, Fax: (852) 2524 5912, and Member Hong Kong Bar. Called: July 1996, Lincoln's Inn, LLB (Hons)(Leeds)

Woo *Hubert Iu-Kwok*
New World Tower, Room 602, 18 Queen's Road Central, Hong Kong, 2525 7007, Fax: 2845 2001, and Member Hong Kong Bar. Called: Feb 1992, Gray's Inn, BSc (Hong Kong), LLB (Lond), MICE,FCIArb

Woo *Miss Siew Khim*
Senior Bank Officer, Blk 623, Bukit Batok Central, [H]03-680, 7786740. Called: Nov 1993, Middle Temple, LLB (Hons)(Lond)

Woo *Wei Kwang*
Called: July 1997, Lincoln's Inn, LLB (Hons)(Leeds)

Wood *Allan William*
Arbitrator, James R Knowles, Wardle House, King Street, Knutsford, Cheshire WA16 6PD, 01565 654666, Fax: 01565 755009. Called: Mar 1996, Lincoln's Inn, BSc (Sheff), Dip Law, C Eng, MICE, FCIArb

Wood *Andrew Nigel Marquis* •
Principal Court Clerk, Barnet Magistrates Court, 7c High Street, Barnet, Herts, 0181 441 9042. Called: Nov 1991, Lincoln's Inn, LLB (Hons) (Hull)

Wood *Miss Caroline Sarah*
Called: Mar 1998, Gray's Inn, LLB (W'hampton)

Wood *Christopher Douglas*
Called: May 1997, Lincoln's Inn, BSc (Hons)

Wood *Christopher Martin*
Called: Oct 1997, Gray's Inn, BSc (L'pool)

Wood *Wing Commander Christopher Nigel Wiley* •
Legal Services, RAF Prosecuting Authority, HQ PTC RAF Innsworth, Gloucester GL3 1EZ, 01452 712612, Fax: 01452 510829. Called: July 1977, Middle Temple, MA (Cantab)

Wood *Miss Emily Bridget Ellen*
Called: Mar 1998, Lincoln's Inn, LLB (Hons)(Wales)

Wood *Miss Gaynor Ellen* •
Legal Adviser, Banque Nationale de Paris, Interest rate Derivatives, Legal Department, 8-13 King William Street, London EC4P 4HS, 0171 548 9413, Fax: 0171 772 9655. Called: Nov 1994, Gray's Inn, LLB

Wood *James Maitland* ●
Crown Prosecution Service, Crown
Prosecution Service, Colemore Gate, 2
Colemore Row, Birmingham B3 2QA, 0121
629 7200. Called: Nov 1989, Lincoln's Inn,
LLB (Wales)

Wood *Mrs Janine Suzanne Dean* ●
Called: July 1983, Inner Temple, BA

Wood *Sir John Crossley*
Judicial Studies Board (Tribunals
Committee), Queen's Chambers, 5 John
Dalton Street, Manchester, M2 6ET.
Called: June 1950, Gray's Inn, LLB, LLM
(Manch)

Wood *Karl Bradwell*
Called: Feb 1994, Middle Temple, LLB
(Hons)(Anglia)

Wood *Miss Katherine Alice*
Called: Oct 1997, Middle Temple, LLB
(Hons)(Lond)

Wood *Kelvin John* ●
Principal Crown Prosecutor, Crown
Prosecution Service, Crown House, Winston
Churchill Avenue, Portsmouth, Hants,
01705 752004. Called: Nov 1985, Middle
Temple, MA (Cantab)

Wood *Michael Charles CMG* ●
Deputy Legal Adviser at the Foreign &
Commonwealth Office, Foreign &
Commonwealth Office, Legal Advisers, King
Charles Street, London SW1A 2AH, 0171
270 3061, Fax: 0171 270 2280. Called: Nov
1968, Gray's Inn, MA, LLB

Wood *Miss Priscilla Jane*
Called: Nov 1973, Middle Temple, BA, MLitt
(Edin)

Wood *Miss Rachel*
Called: Nov 1997, Gray's Inn, LLB (Lond)

Wood *Richley William* ●
Senior Crown Prosecutor, Crown
Prosecution Service, Westway House,
Westway Road, Weymouth, Dorset.
Called: Nov 1980, Lincoln's Inn, BA (Hons)

Wood *Mrs Sarah Ann* ●
Director/Company Secretary Re-Waste
Group plc Director,ECO Europe Director/
Co Secretary Sear Green Cone Ltd,
Cockshoot Farm, West Wycombe, High
Wycombe, Buckinghamshire HP14 3AR,
01494 443329 or 01 494 564004, Fax:
01494 442194. Called: July 1989, Inner
Temple, BA, MI Infsci, F InstD, M.Inst WM

Woodhead *Mrs Sarah Elizabeth* ●
Called: Nov 1991, Inner Temple, LLB

Woodhead *Simon Andrew*
Eversheds, Holland Court, The Close,
Norwich NR1 4DX, 01603 272727, Fax:
01603 610535. Called: Oct 1990, Lincoln's
Inn, LLB (E.Anglia)

Woodhouse *Antony James*
Davies Arnold Cooper, 6-8 Bouverie Street,
London EC4Y 8DD, 0171 936 2222, Fax:
0171 936 2020. Called: Oct 1993, Lincoln's
Inn, BA (Hons)

Woodhouse *John Sidney Lister VRD*
Brooklyn, Kelsall, Tarporley, Cheshire
CW6 0QB, 01829 751462. Called: June
1949, Gray's Inn, MA (Cantab)

Woodhouse *Nigel Martin*
Called: Nov 1997, Gray's Inn, LLB (Anglia)

Woodhouse *Richard Francis* ●
H.M.Senior Planning Inspector, Department
of the Environment, Tollgate House,
Houlton Street, Bristol BS2 9DJ. Called: July
1962, Inner Temple, MA (Cantab)

Woodhull *Miss Anuita*
Called: May 1997, Inner Temple, LLB (Lond)

Wooding *Mrs Anne Marie*
Called: Mar 1997, Gray's Inn, LLB (Nott'm)

Woodings *David Jon* ●
Senior Crown Prosecutor. Called: Oct 1992,
Lincoln's Inn, BA(Hons)(Lancaster),
LLB(Hons)(Lond), LLM (Sussex)

Woodman *Paul Norman* ●
Legal Adviser with the Ministry of Defence,
MOD (PE) Legal Advisers, MOD Abbey
Wood [H]120, P O Box 702, Bristol BS12,
0117 91 32641, Fax: 0117 91 30965.
Called: Oct 1991, Inner Temple, LLB (Hull)

Woods *Alex*
"Nightingales", Birch, Colchesterr, Essex
CO2 0NA, 01206 330325. Called: July 1996,
Inner Temple, BA (Lond), CPE

Woods *Miss Lynn*
Called: Feb 1965, Middle Temple, MA
(Oxon)

Woods *Miss Rachael Helen* ●
Crown Prosecution Service, 8th Floor,
Sunlight House, Quay Street, Manchester,
0161 837 7440. Called: Oct 1992, Gray's
Inn, LL.B

Woods *Sidney Wilfred*
Bramley Mill, Mill Lane, Bramley, Guildford,
Surrey GU5 0HW. Called: June 1951, Gray's
Inn, LLB, BCom (Hons)

Woodward *Mrs Georgina*
Legal Adviser, Hampshire Magistrates Court,
The Court house, Elmleigh Road, Havant,
Hants PO9 2AL, 01705 492024, Fax: 01705
475356. Called: May 1983, Gray's Inn, LLB
(Manch)

Woodward *Mrs Sarah Elizabeth Ann*
Legal Adviser, Bedfordshire Mag Crts
Comm, Shire Hall, 3 St Paul's Square,
Bedford, 01234 359422. Called: Nov 1988,
Gray's Inn, BA

Woodworth *Miss Michelle Elizabeth*
Called: July 1996, Middle Temple, LLB
(Hons)(Lond)

Woodyatt *Mrs Valerie Anne*
Called: Nov 1972, Inner Temple, LLM

Woogara *Ranjitsingh*
Called: Nov 1994, Middle Temple, BA, LLB

Wooldridge *Ms Deborah*
Called: Mar 1997, Gray's Inn, BA (B'ham),
LL Dip

Wooler *Stephen John* ●
Deputy Legal Secretary, Legal Secretariat to
the Law, Officers, Attorney General's
Chambers, 9 Buckingham Gate, London
SW1 6JP, 0171 828 1721, Fax: 0171 828
0593. Called: Nov 1969, Gray's Inn, LLB
(Lond)

Woolf *John Moss CB*
West Lodge, 113 Marsh Lane, Stanmore,
Middx HA7 4TH, 0181 952 1373.
Called: June 1948, Lincoln's Inn

Woolfe *Steven Marcus*
Associate Company, Commercial Financial
Services Law., Taylor Joynson Garrett,
Carmelite, 50 Victoria Embankment,
Blackfriars, LondoN EC4Y 0DK, 0171 353
1234, Fax: 0171 936 2666. Called: Oct
1992, Inner Temple, LLB (Hons)

Woolhouse *Oliver Duncan Campbell*
Called: Nov 1996, Inner Temple, LLB (Leics)

Woolhouse *Ms Sarita Patil*
Assistant Solicitor, Herbert Smith, Exchange
House, Primrose Street, London EC2A 2HS,
0171 374 8000, Fax: 0171 496 0043, and
Member India Bar. Called: Nov 1994, Inner
Temple, M.Phil (Cantab)

Woollcombe *James Humphrey
George*
Called: Feb 1955, Inner Temple, MA, BCL
Hons [Oxon]

Woolley *David John Llewellyn*
Called: May 1987, Gray's Inn, LLB, FCII, FTII

Woolley *Mrs Diana Rosemary* ●
Group Company Secretary, Diversified
Agency, Services Limited, 239 Old
Marylebone Road, London NW1 5QT, 0171
298 7000, Fax: 0171 724 8292. Called: July
1962, Gray's Inn, LLB

Woolley *Edward Timothy Starbuck*
c/o The Court of Final Appeal, 1 Battery
Park, 2123 0017, Fax: 2121 0300, Registrar,
Court of Final Appeal and Member Hong
Kong Bar, Australian Bar. Called: July 1968,
Middle Temple

Wootton *Miss Nicola Jane Dawn* ●
Coventry Magistrates' Court, Little Park
Street, Coventry. Called: July 1995, Middle
Temple, BA (Hons)

Wootton *Toby Giles Denis*
Called: Oct 1997, Middle Temple, LLB
(Hons), (De Montfort)

Workman *Andrew John* ●
Senior Principal Court Clerk, Liverpool
Magistrates Court, Committee, Liverpool
Magistrates Court, 107 Dale Street,
Liverpool L2 2JQ, 0151 236 5871, Fax: 0151
231 5594. Called: Feb 1994, Gray's Inn, LLB

Wormald-Cripps *Darren William* ●
Legal Counsel (Fixed Income Capital
Markets Division), Lehman Brothers
International, One Broadgate, Broadgate
Circle, London EC2M 7HA, 0171 260 2085,
Fax: 0171 260 2882. Called: Nov 1995,
Lincoln's Inn, LLB (Hons)(Essex)

Worrell *Gavin Jon Francis* ●
Called: Nov 1994, Middle Temple, BA
(Hons)

Worsfold *Miss Priscilla Anne* ●
Principal Crown Prosecutor (Team Leader),
Crown Prosecution Service, Broadlands
House, Staplers Road, Newport, Isle of
Wight PO30 2HY, 01983 528309, Fax:
01983 521808. Called: July 1975, Gray's Inn

Worsley *Miss Jane Fay*
97 East Hill, London SW18 2QD, 0181 875
0781. Called: Feb 1995, Inner Temple, CPE
(Middx), FIBMS

Worsley *John Bertrand*
Furlong Hse, West Furlong Lane,
Hurstpierpoint, Sussex BN6 9QA, 01273
833320. Called: July 1954, Inner Temple,
MA, LLB (Cantab)

Worthington *Robert Edward*
Called: Oct 1996, Gray's Inn, BSc (Leeds)

Wrack *Robert Nicholas*
Called: Mar 1997, Inner Temple, MA, LLB,
(Cantab)

Wragg *Jonathan Robert* ●
Locum Civil Litigation Barrister, Legal
Services Department, The Town Hall, King
Street, Hammersmith, London, 0181 748
9736. Called: Nov 1995, Gray's Inn, BA
(Hull)

Wray *Nigel Duncan Andrew*
Appeals Worker. European Lobbyist, Free
Tibet Campaign., Joint Council for the
Welfare, of Immigrants, 115 Old Street,
London EC1V 9JR, 0171 251 8706 Ext 206,
Fax: 0171 251 8707. Called: Feb 1993,
Gray's Inn, MA (St Andrews), Dip Law
(City)

Wreford *John Bertram*
01732 456439. Called: July 1954, Gray's Inn,
FCII

Wrench *Benjamin James* ●
Compliance Assistant, Refco Overseas
Limited, Europe House, East Smithfield,
London EC1 9AA. Called: Nov 1995,
Lincoln's Inn, LLB (Hons)(Exon)

Wright *Alexander*
Called: Nov 1997, Inner Temple, LLB
(Manch)

Wright *Alistair Charles*
Furnival Chambers, 32 Furnival Street,
London, EC4A 1JQ. Called: Nov 1992,
Gray's Inn, LLB (Hons)

Wright *Mrs Angela* ●
Librarian & Information Officer, Fishburn
Boxer, 60 Strand, London WC2N 5LR, 0171
925 2884, Fax: 0171 486 3256. Called: Oct
1993, Inner Temple, MA (Cantab)

Wright *Brendan Paul*
Called: Feb 1995, Gray's Inn, BA (Cantab)

Wright *Miss Charlotte Helen Mary*
Legal Adviser. Called: Nov 1991, Middle
Temple, LLB Hons (Leic)

Wright *Mrs Lesley Ann*
Legal Adviser, The Court House, Tufton
Street, Ashford, Kent TN23 1QS, 01233
663203, Fax: 01233 663206. Called: Nov
1986, Lincoln's Inn, BA

Wright *Mrs Moira Elynwy*
Faculty of Law, University of Birmingham,
Edgbaston, Birmingham B15 2TT.
Called: July 1989, Gray's Inn, LLB [Wales],
BCL [Oxon]

Wright *Robert Pickering* ●
Lord Chancellor's Department,
Headquarters, Selborne House, 54-60
Victoria Street, London SW1E 6QW, 0171
210 8810. Called: Nov 1986, Lincoln's Inn,
LLB

Wright *Robin*
Clerk to the Justices & Justices Chief
Executive, Barking & Dagenham
Magistrates, Courts Committee, The Court
House, East Street, Barking,Essex IG11 8EW,
0181 594 5311, Fax: 0181 594 4297.
Called: July 1980, Gray's Inn, DML, DMS

Wright *Mrs Rosalind* ●
Director, Serious Fraud Office, Elm House,
10-16 Elm Street, London WC1X 0BJ, 0171
239 7272, Fax: 0171 837 1689, Member
International Bar Association. Called: June
1964, Middle Temple, LLB (Hons)

Wright *Lt Cdr Stuart Hugh RN* ●
Called: Oct 1995, Middle Temple, BA (Hons)

Wright *Ms Teresa Jane*
Called: Nov 1996, Lincoln's Inn, LLB
(Hons)(Herts)

Wrobel *Brian John Robert Karen*
Honorary Legal Adviser Parliamentary
Human Rights Group, Also Inn of Court G
and Member Atty at Law California, USA
Supreme Court Bar. Called: Nov 1973,
Lincoln's Inn, LLM (Lond)

Wrzesien *Thomas James*
Called: Oct 1995, Lincoln's Inn, LLB (Lond)

Wu *Chi Sing*
Called: Nov 1995, Gray's Inn, LLB (Lond)

Wu *Chun Shing*
Flat A, 3/F, Tower 6, Metro City, 1 Wan
Hang Road, Tseung Kwan O, N.T., (00 852)
2695 0252, Fax: (00 852) 2695 0252, and
Member Hong Kong. Called: Nov 1996,
Gray's Inn, LLB (Lond)

Wu *Mrs Lorna Shui Wan*
p/t Small Claims Adjudicator of Hong Kong
Judiciary, 1002 Chekiang Bank Centre, 1
Duddell Street, 5 25217317, Fax: 852 5
28450654, and Member Hong Kong &
Singapore Bars. Called: Nov 1982, Inner
Temple, LLB, Dip in Chinese Law, ACIArb

Wu *Roderick Kam Fun*
1002 Chekiang First, Bank Centre, 1
Duddell Street, Central, 5 25217317, Fax:
852 5 28450654, and Member Hong
Kong,Victorian & Singapore Bars.
Called: July 1980, Inner Temple, LLB, Dip in
Chinese Law, ACIArb

Wun *Rizwi*
Company Secretary. Sembawang
Engineering & Construction PTE Ltd, and
Member Singapore. Called: July 1992, Gray's
Inn, LLB (Lond)

Wyatt *Murat William*
18 Sheridan Lodge, Chase Side, Southgate,
London N14 4RJ. Called: Oct 1996,
Lincoln's Inn, LLB (Hons)(Lond)

Wyles *Miss Rhona Irene*
Managing Director Director: IBC Group plc,
IBC UK Conferences Limited, Gilmoora
House, 57-61 Mortimer Street, London
W1N 8JX, 0171 637 4383, Fax: 0171 631
3214. Called: July 1973, Inner Temple, BA
(Jt Hons)

Wylie *Alexander Featherstonhaugh*
Advocates Library, Parliament House,
Edinburgh, Lothian EH1 1RF, 0131 226
2881 (Clerk), Fax: 0131 225 3642, QC,
Formerly a Scottish Solicitor and Member
Scottish Bar. Called: Nov 1990, Lincoln's
Inn, LLB (Edin), FCI Arb

Wylie-Otte *Ms Regan*
Legal Adviser, 3 Um Kallek, L-5369
Schuttrange. Called: Feb 1978, Middle
Temple, MA, LLM

Wyllie *Alistair*
Simmons & Simmons, 71 Connell Crescent,
Ealing, London W5 3BH, 0171 628 2020,
Fax: 0171 628 2070. Called: Feb 1989, Inner
Temple, LLB (Dundee), LLM (Cantab)

Wyman *Miss Ann Elizabeth*
Called: July 1974, Gray's Inn, LLB

Wynn Davies *Arthur Geraint* ●
Legal Manager, Telegraph Group Limited, 1
Canada Square, Canary Wharf, London
E14 5DT, 0171 538 6220, Fax: 0171 538
7838. Called: Nov 1971, Middle Temple, LLB
(Wales)

Wynn Davies *Ms Patricia Margaret*
Political Correspondent,The Independent
Independent, 40 City Road, London
EC1Y 2DB, 0171 334 0078, Fax: 0171 334
0082. Called: July 1982, Gray's Inn, BA

Wynne *Michael Williams*
Called: July 1979, Gray's Inn, MA (Cantab)

Wynne-Griffiths *David Peter*
Group Legal Auditor, ARC Ltd, Ivy Cottage,
Kingsdown, Corsham, Wilts SN13 8AZ,
01225 742904, Fax: 01225 742904.
Called: Feb 1955, Gray's Inn, MA (Cantab)

Xie *Miss Janice Zhao Shan*
and Member Singapore Bar. Called: July
1994, Lincoln's Inn, LLB (Hons)

Xu *Daniel Atticus*
Called: Nov 1997, Middle Temple, LLB
(Hons)(Lond)

Yale *Andrew Charles John*
Called: Mar 1998, Inner Temple, BA
(Kingston), MA (Washington), CPE (Lond)

E

Yam *Jeffrey Pei Tseng*
Messrs Rodyk & Davidson, 9 Raffles Place, [H]55-01, Republic Plaza, 65 5399254, Fax: 65 2251838. Called: July 1996, Middle Temple, LLB (Hons)(Wales)

Yan *Keen Wah Stephen*
19 Highgate Crescent, 65-5614048 (R) 65-7320021 (O), Fax: 65-5614048, and Member Singapore Bar. Called: May 1994, Gray's Inn, LLB

Yang *Miss Caroline Yuen Tsyr*
Legal Advisor. Called: July 1992, Middle Temple, LLB (Hons) (Lond)

Yap *Miss Adeline Bee-Yen*
Partner, Azri Chuah & Yap, No 22-3 (Third Floor), Jalan Sri Hartamas 8, Taman Sri Hartamas, 50480 Kuala Lumpur, 603 6512714/6512784/6531105, Fax: 603 6531078, and Member Malaysia Bar. Called: July 1992, Middle Temple, LLB (Hons) (Manch)

Yap *Benjamin Soon Tat*
Godwin & Co, 1 Robinson Road, [H] 20-02 AIA Tower, Singapore 048542, (065) 5338313, Fax: (065) 5331113, and Member Singapore. Called: Nov 1994, Middle Temple, LLB (Hons)

Yap *Miss Camilla Tee Neo*
Called: Nov 1995, Lincoln's Inn, LLB (Hons)

Yap *Miss Grace Mei Wan*
Legal Assistant, Albar Zulkifly & Yap, 17th Floor, Menara Sabre, & Lorong P Ramlee, 50200 Kuala Lumpur, 01-06-03-2388228, Fax: 01-06-03-2041913, and Member Malaysia Bar. Called: July 1991, Middle Temple, LLB (Notts)

Yap *Miss Hsu-Lyn*
Called: July 1997, Lincoln's Inn, LLB (Hons)(Nott'm)

Yap *Miss Huey Hoong*
Called: July 1996, Lincoln's Inn, LLB (Hons)

Yap *Miss Hui Lu*
Advocate & Solicitor, Messrs Lee Hishammuddin, Solicitors & Advocates, 16th Floor, Wisma HLA, Jalan Raja Chulan, 50200 Kuala Lumpur, (603) 2011681 x 173, Fax: (603) 2011746, and Member Malaysia. Called: July 1994, Middle Temple, LLB (Hons)(Bris), LLM (Hons)(Lond)

Yap *Miss Janice Bee Hong*
Called: July 1997, Lincoln's Inn, LLB (Hons)(Leeds)

Yap *Miss Juliana Chin Choo*
B-3258, Taman Tunas, 25300 Kuantan, Pahang Darulmakmur, Malaysia. Called: July 1995, Inner Temple, LLB (Lond)

Yap *Keng Siong*
Called: July 1996, Lincoln's Inn, LLB (Hons)

Yap *Miss Lai-Lian*
Called: Nov 1996, Lincoln's Inn, LLB (Hons)(Herts)

Yap *Miss Lareina Chu Han*
Legal Assistant, [H]02-01, Amica Block, The Beaumont, 147 Devonshire Road, 733-9923, and Member Supreme Court of Brunei Darussalam Singapore Bar. Called: Nov 1988, Middle Temple, LLB (Brunel), LLM (Lond)

Yap *Miss Lay Hoon*
Called: July 1996, Lincoln's Inn, LLB (Hons)(Leeds)

Yap *Miss Lay Kuan*
Called: Nov 1997, Middle Temple, LLB (Hons)

Yap *Miss Lisa*
Called: Nov 1996, Middle Temple, LLB (Hons)(Kent)

Yap *Miss Luna-Whye Tzu*
22 Lorong K, Telok Kurau [H]03-01, Wen Yuan Court, 065-2276206, Fax: 065-2274861, and Member Singapore Bar. Called: July 1994, Middle Temple, LLB (Hons)

Yap *Miss Lynette*
Called: Nov 1996, Lincoln's Inn, LLB (Hons)(Lond)

Yap *Miss Pett Chin*
Called: Nov 1996, Lincoln's Inn, LLB (Hons)(Leics)

Yap *Richard Hoong Keng* •
Senior Crown Prosecutor, Crown Prosecution Service, Queen's House, 58 Victoria Street, St Albans, Herts AL1 3HZ, 01727 818100, Fax: 01727 851080. Called: July 1985, Lincoln's Inn, BA

Yap *Miss Shirley Mae-Yen*
Called: July 1996, Lincoln's Inn, LLB (Hons)

Yap *Miss Vicky Lan Hiang*
Called: July 1995, Inner Temple, LLB (Warw)

Yap *Vincent Leng Khim*
Called: July 1997, Lincoln's Inn, LLB (Hons)

Yap *Yew Inn*
Called: July 1995, Gray's Inn, LLB (Lond)

Yap *Yin-Soon*
Allen & Gledhill, 36 Robinson Road, [H]18-01 City House, Singapore 0106, 225 1611, Fax: 221 3726, Advocate & Solicitor of the Supreme Court of Singapore. Called: July 1993, Middle Temple, LLB (Hons, Exon), LLM

Yardley *Robert Huw* •
Senior Crown Prosecutor, Crown Prosecution Service, 5th Floor, Chartist Tower, Upper Dock Street, Newport, Gwent NP9 1DW, 01633 241024, Fax: 01633 842953. Called: Oct 1990, Gray's Inn, LLB

Yardy *Keith Stuart* •
Senior Crown Prosecutor, Crown Prosecution Service, Priory Gate, 29 Union Street, Maidstone, Kent ME14 1PT, 01622 686425. Called: July 1988, Inner Temple, LLB (Lond)

Yasin *Saladin Mohd.*
No 3 Jalan 4/3F, 40000 Shah Alam, Selangor, Malaysia. Called: July 1993, Gray's Inn, LLB

Yassin *Miss Aishah Saleema*
Called: Nov 1993, Inner Temple, LLB (Hons), LLM (Notts)

Yates *Miss Lindsay Anne*
The Vicarage, 292 Thorney Leys, Witney, Oxon OX8 7YP, 01993 773281. Called: Nov 1992, Inner Temple, MA (Cantab), Dip Th

Yau *Wai-Leong*
Advocate & Solicitor, Chan & Associates, Standard Chartered Bank Chamb., 21-27 Jalan Dato Maharaja Lela, 30000 Ipoh, 605 2545293, Fax: 605 2534091, and Member Malaysia. Called: July 1996, Lincoln's Inn, LLB (Hons)(Leeds)

Yeap *Miss Su-Lynn*
6B Jalan Brown, 10350 Penang, Malaysia, (04) 226 6916, Fax: (04) 323 5093, and Member Malaysia Bar. Called: Nov 1991, Inner Temple, LLB (Hull)

Yearwood *Martin Edmund*
31 La Estancia Drive, PO Box 3239, Diego Martin, Trinidad, 632-8223. Called: Nov 1971, Lincoln's Inn, BSc

Yeates *Stephen Robert* •
Crown Prosecuter, Crown Prosecution Service, 2nd Floor, Froomsgate House, Rupert Street, Bristol BS1 2QJ, 0117 9273093. Called: Nov 1992, Middle Temple, BA (Hons, Wales)

Yeats *Liam James*
Stagnetto & Co, 186 Main Street, and Member Gibraltar. Called: Mar 1997, Middle Temple, LLB (Hons)

Yee *Miss Eileen Khor Kit*
Called: July 1995, Middle Temple, LLB (Hons)

Yee *Jackie Keen Meng*
Called: July 1995, Lincoln's Inn, LLB (Hons)

Yee *Mei Ken*
Called: July 1997, Lincoln's Inn, LLB (Hons)(Wales)

Yeen *Chong Foo*
Lim Seong Chun & Co, No 11, Jalan Panglima, 30000 Ipoh, Perak, (05) 2413655, Fax: (05) 2550194. Called: July 1997, Inner Temple, LLB (Sheff)

Yek *Nai Hui*
24 Newton Road, [H]07-01 Surrey Tower. Called: Oct 1993, Middle Temple, LLB (Hons, Hull)

Yelloly *Christopher John*
Part-time Immigration Appeals Ajudicator. Called: Nov 1964, Middle Temple

Yen *Heng Teng*
Called: Nov 1996, Middle Temple, LLB (Hons)(Hull)

Yen-Yen *Ms Lee Amelia*
Called: Nov 1997, Inner Temple, LLB, LLM (Lond)

Yeo *Miss Charmaine Swan Mei*
Called: Nov 1994, Middle Temple, LLB
(Hons) (Hull)

Yeo *Miss Chiew Pin*
Called: Nov 1997, Lincoln's Inn, LLB
(Hons)(Wales)

Yeo *Clayton Jack* •
Senior Crown Prosecutor, Crown
Prosecution Service, 29th Floor, Portland
House, Stag Place, London SW1E 5BH.
Called: Nov 1988, Gray's Inn, BA, MA
(Manitoba), LLB (Lond)

Yeo *Jih Shian*
Called: July 1993, Gray's Inn, BA

Yeo *Ms Marianne Mei-Lin*
5B Sea & Sky Court, 92 Stanley Main Street,
Stanley, 852 28131788, Fax: 852 28132086,
and Member Malaysia Bar. Called: July 1982,
Inner Temple, BSc (Manch), Diplaw

Yeo *Raymond Khee Chye*
Called: July 1996, Lincoln's Inn, LLB
(Hons)(Lond)

Yeo *Ronald*
Called: Feb 1993, Lincoln's Inn, LLB (Hons)

Yeo *Roy Kan Kiang*
Advocate & Solicitor of the Supreme of
Singapore. Called: July 1994, Middle
Temple, LLB (Hons)(Bris)

Yeo *Sia Eng*
Called: Oct 1997, Middle Temple, LLB
(Hons)(Lond)

Yeo *Miss Siok Kiang Fiona*
Called: July 1996, Middle Temple, LLB
(Hons)(Hull)

Yeo *Ms Sok Huang*
5 Peck Hay Road, [H]09-OO Peck Hay View,
Singapore 0922, 7334868, Advocate &
Solicitor of the Supreme Court of Singapore.
Called: July 1992, Gray's Inn, LLB (Brist)

Yeo *Willie Sie Keng*
and Member Singapore Bar. Called: July
1995, Lincoln's Inn, LLB (Hons)

Yeo *Miss Yee Ling*
Called: July 1997, Gray's Inn

Yeoh *Miss Daryl*
Chan & Associates, Advocates & Solicitors,
Standard Chartered Bk Chambers, 21-27
Jalan Dato Maharja Lela, 30000 Ipoh, Perak
Malaysia. Called: July 1995, Lincoln's Inn,
LLB (Hons)

Yeoh *Gary Cheng Lee*
Legal Advisor, 7th Floor, Bangunan Kassim
Chan, 3 Cangkat Raja Chulan, P O Box
11151, 50736 Kuala Lumpur, 2320711, Fax:
2300585, and Member Malaysia Bar.
Called: May 1994, Lincoln's Inn, LLB (Hons)

Yeoh *Miss Geraldine Poh Im*
Advocate & Solicitor, 7th Floor, 3 Changkat
Raja Chulan, 50200 Kuala Lumpur, P.O.Box
11151, 50736 Kuala Lumpur Malaysia, 03
2320711, Fax: 03 2304746/2300585, and
Member Malaysia Bar. Called: Nov 1991,
Lincoln's Inn, LLB (Hons)(Reading), LLM

Yeoh *Miss Grace Chee Leng*
Advocate and Solcitor, High Court of Malaya
and Member Malaysia Bar. Called: Nov 1990,
Lincoln's Inn, LLB (East Anglia)

Yeoh *Miss Huei-Keng*
Called: July 1997, Lincoln's Inn, LLB (Hons)

Yeoh *Leonard Soon Beng*
Called: July 1995, Lincoln's Inn, LLB (Hons)

Yeoh *Miss Melissa Ann Lin*
Called: Nov 1997, Middle Temple, LLB
(Hons)(Nott'm)

Yeoh *Nigel Lian Chuan*
Called: July 1993, Lincoln's Inn, LLB (Hons)

Yeoh *Miss Wai Ling*
Called: July 1996, Lincoln's Inn, LLB
(Hons)(Warw)

Yeoman *Howard Victor*
Associate Lecturer in Law - Open University.
Called: Nov 1995, Gray's Inn, BA, Dip Law

Yeow *Miss Ping Lin*
State Counsel, Attorney General's
Chambers, 1 Coleman Street [H]10-00, The
Aldelphi, Singapore 0617, 3361411 (065),
Fax: 3390286, and Member Singapore Bar.
Called: July 1993, Middle Temple, BA (Hons,
Bris)

Yerrell *Miss Nicola Jane*
Legal Service, European Commission,
Avenue des Nerviens, 105, B-1040 Bruxelles,
+32 2 295 1969, Fax: +32 2 296 5972.
Called: Oct 1993, Middle Temple, BA
(Hons)(Oxon), Licence Special en, Droit
Europeen, Brussels

Yeung *Miss Lai Sheung*
and Member Hong Kong Bar. Called: May
1994, Middle Temple, LLB (Hons)

Yeung *Sunny Kwong*
Called: Nov 1997, Inner Temple, BA, B.Arch
(Hong, Kong)

Yeung *Yiu Wing*
Called: Nov 1995, Middle Temple, BSc, MSc
& MBA, (Hong Kong)

Yew *Andrew*
Called: Mar 1997, Lincoln's Inn, LLB

Yew *Mrs Lily*
Called: July 1985, Lincoln's Inn, BSc
(Detroit) LLB, (Lond)

Yik *Miss Sara Synn Yi*
Legal Counsel, Jurong Town Corporation,
301 Jurong Town Hall Road, Singapore
591001, 65 5688293, Fax: 65 5651977, and
Member Singapore Bar. Called: July 1995,
Middle Temple, LLB (Hons)

Yilman *Hussein Djahit*
11 Mahmout Pasha Street, PO Box 556,
Lefkosa, Mersin 10, 90392-2271646/
2272406, Fax: 90392-2288154, Retired
District Court President Overseas Expert on
Turkish Law and Member Cyprus Bar.
Called: Feb 1962, Gray's Inn, LLB (Istanbul)

Yin *Michael Chi-Ming*
10/F New Henry House, 10 Ice House
Street, and Member Hong Kong. Called: Nov
1993, Lincoln's Inn, LLB (Hons)(Bris), LLM
(Bris)

Yin *Yip Shee*
70 St Thomas Walk, [H] 07-70 Pheonix
Court, 732 0758. Called: Nov 1996, Inner
Temple, BA (Dunelm)

Ying *Wan Chong*
Flat 20G, Fu Dat Court, 32 Fortress Hill
Road, 887 8552, Fax: 858 4575. Called: Nov
1990, Gray's Inn, BScEng (HK), MSc (LSE),
LLB (Lond)

Yip *Mrs Aik Hooi*
Principle Legal Adviser, Newham
Magistrates', Court Committee, 389-397
High Street, Stratford, London E15 4SB,
0181 522 5000, Fax: 0181 519 9214.
Called: July 1985, Lincoln's Inn, BA (Sussex)

Yip *Allan Kai-Lun*
Called: Oct 1995, Middle Temple, BA (Hons)

Yip *Kwok Ching*
Senior Solicitor, Official Receiver's Office,
Hong Kong Government, Official Receiver's
Office, 11/F1 Queensway Government,
Offices, 66 Queensway, and Member Hong
Kong Bar. Called: Nov 1988, Gray's Inn, LLB
(Lond), BSocSc, MSocSc (Hong Kong), ACIS,
MCIT

Yiu *Kam Hung*
Called: Nov 1994, Middle Temple, B.Soc.Sc
(Hons)

Yo-Hann *Tan*
Called: July 1997, Inner Temple, LLB (Kent),
LLM (Lond)

Yogarajah *Miss Anusuya*
Called: July 1994, Inner Temple, BBA, LLB

Yogarajah *Miss Yoga Sharmini*
Legal Assistant, 66 Medway Drive,
Serangoon Garden Estate, Singapore, 1955,
2836271, and Member Singapore Bar.
Called: July 1989, Middle Temple, BA, LLB
(Lond)

Yong *Alvin Sze Lung*
Called: Nov 1996, Gray's Inn, LLB

Yong *Christopher Shu Wei*
Called: July 1994, Middle Temple, LLB
(Hons)(Hull)

Yong *Miss Fook-Tai*
Called: Nov 1995, Middle Temple, LLB
(Hons)

Yong *Miss Janet Hway Ming*
Legal Assistant, Shook Lin & Bok, 20th
Floor, Arab-Malaysian Bld, 55 Jalan Raja
Chulan, 50200 Kuala Lumpur, (03)
2011788, and Member Malaya Bar.
Called: July 1995, Lincoln's Inn, LLB (Hons),
LLM

Yong *Miss Jocelyn*
Called: Nov 1992, Lincoln's Inn, LLB
(Hons)(Lond)

E

Yong Sek-Cheong
Malayan Law Journal, 3rd Floor, Wisma
Bandar, No 18, Jalan Tuanku Abdul,
Rahman, Kuala Lumpur 50100, 291 7273,
Fax: 291 6440, and Member Malaysia Bar.
Called: Oct 1992, Gray's Inn, BA (Kent)

Yong Miss Siew Lee Magdalene
Blk 408, [H]12-433, Pasir Ris Drive 6,
Singapore 510408, 5820103. Called: July
1995, Middle Temple, LLB (Hons)

Yong Vincent Wai Bun
Called: July 1996, Lincoln's Inn, LLB (Hons)

Yonge William James George Rowley
S J Berwin & Co, 222 Gray's Inn Road,
London WC1X 8HB, 0171 533 2222, Fax:
0171 533 2000. Called: July 1989, Middle
Temple, BA Hons (Dunelm)

Yongo Thomas
Associate Legal Officer, United Nations
Environment, Programme, Secretariat of the,
Convention on Biological, Diversity, 393 St-
Jacques, Suite 300,Montreal,Quebec
H2Y IN9, (514) 288 2220, Fax: (514) 288
6588. Called: Nov 1994, Gray's Inn, BA
(Michigan), Diploma(Cantab), LLB (Kent),
LLM (Lond)

Yoon Ming Sun
Legal Assistant (Advocate & Solicitor), 10
Lorong Derumun, Damansara Heights,
50490 Kuala Lumpur, 03 255 8307, Fax: 03
255 8307, and Member Malaysia.
Called: Nov 1995, Middle Temple, LLB
(Hons), MSc (So'ton)

Yoong Weng Leong
21 Jalan 5/4, 46000 Petaling Jaya, Selangor,
West Malaysia, and Member Malaysia Bar.
Called: Nov 1992, Lincoln's Inn, BA
(Hons)(Keele)

York John Graham
Latimer Cottage, 2 Orchard Court, Church
Street, Nr Farnham, Surrey. Called: June
1956, Middle Temple, MA, LLM (Cantab)

Yoshinaga Junichiro
Legal Advisor, Corporate Business
Development. Sony Corp, Corporate
Business Development, Sony Corp, 6-7-35
Kitashinagawa, Shinagawa, Tokyo, Japan
141, 03 5448 2564, Fax: 03 5448 4248.
Called: July 1994, Lincoln's Inn, BA (Econ)
(Hons), Dip Law

You Miss Lou Yuh
Called: July 1997, Lincoln's Inn, LLB
(Hons)(Lond)

Youell Christopher James ●
Senior Crown Prosecutor, Crown
Prosecution Service, Haldin House, Queen
Street, Norwich, Norfolk NR2 4SX, 01603
666491. Called: Feb 1991, Gray's Inn, LLB

Young Miss Ai Peng
Called: Nov 1997, Lincoln's Inn, LLB (Hons)

Young Andrew David ●
Crown Prosecutor, Crown Prosecution
Service, 11A Princes Street, Stafford
ST16 2EU, 01785 223511, Fax: 01785
223577. Called: July 1986, Gray's Inn, MA
(Cantab)

Young Andrew Paul ●
Deloitte & Touche, VAT Customs Litigation
&, Senior-in-house Counsel, Hill House, 1
Little New Street, London EC4A 3TR, 0171
303 3398, Fax: 0171 303 4780. Called: Oct
1992, Lincoln's Inn, LLB(Hons), BSc

Young Barry ●
The Red House, Heckington, Lincs
NG34 9QU, 01529 460205, Fax: 01529
461144. Called: Nov 1968, Inner Temple,
F.P.M.I

Young Christopher John Deans
Called: Oct 1997, Middle Temple, BA
(Hons)(Leeds), CPE (Lond)

Young Dr David Reginald
Managing Director Oxford Analytica, Oxford
Analytica, 5 Alfred Street, Oxford OX1 4EH,
01865 343202, Fax: 01865 242018, and
Member New York and District of
Columbia, USA. Called: July 1965, Inner
Temple, BA (Oxon), MA (Oxon), D.Phil
(Oxon), LLB, (Cornell), BS, (Wheaton)

Young Edwin Briden John
Consultant. Called: Nov 1977, Lincoln's Inn,
MA (Cantab)

Young Jeffrey Sinclair
Justices' Chief Executive Justices Clerk,
Magistrates' Courts, Market Street,
Newcastle Upon Tyne NE1 6UR, 0191 232
7326, Fax: 0191 221 0025. Called: Feb 1973,
Middle Temple, LLB

Young Michael James
Called: Oct 1994, Inner Temple, BA
(Cantab), BCL (Oxon)

Young Mrs Patricia Nuckchin
Barrister - Family Law Dept, Frankins
Solicitors, 390 Silbury Court, Silbury
Boulevard, Milton Keynes MK9 2LY, 01908
660966. Called: May 1997, Lincoln's Inn,
LLB (Hons)(Lond)

Young Peter John
and Member New York. Called: Oct 1995,
Lincoln's Inn, LLB (Hons)(Bucks), LLM
(Cantab)

Young Miss Sarah Joanna
Called: Oct 1992, Middle Temple, BA (Hons,
Manch), Diploma in Law

Young Simon Jonathan
Civil & Commercial Litigation, Bedell &
Cristin, One the Forum, St Helier, Jersey
JE4 8PP, 01534 814814, Fax: 01534 814815,
and Member Jersey Bar. Called: Oct 1991,
Middle Temple, LLB Hons (Buck'ham),
F.I.B.M.S.

Young Stuart Richard
8 Wainwright Street, St Clair, Trinidad,
(868) 628 4558. Called: July 1997, Gray's
Inn, LLB (Notts)

Younger Ms Brynn Leadbitter
Called: Nov 1994, Gray's Inn, BA (Dumelm)

Youngman Brian John
Orchard Rise, Priory Close, East Budleigh,
Devon EX9 7EZ, 01395 444015, Fax: 01395
444015. Called: June 1953, Gray's Inn, LLB
(Lond)

Yousef Mrs Naseem
Called: Mar 1997, Lincoln's Inn, LLB (Hons)

Yousuf Miss Farah
Assistant Deputy Justices Clerk, Magistrates'
Courts Brent, Church End, 448 High Road,
London NW10 2DZ, 0181 451 7111, Fax:
0181 451 2040. Called: July 1985, Lincoln's
Inn, BA

Yu Denis Gordon Quok Chung
Called: July 1982, Lincoln's Inn, BA (Oxon)

Yu-Min Ms Ng Adeline
Called: July 1997, Inner Temple, LLB (LSE)

Yue Jonathan Tin-Kong
Flat D, 15th Floor, Block One, Pokfulam
Gardens, Pokfulam Hong Kong, Supreme
Court of Hong Kong. Called: Nov 1994,
Middle Temple, BA (Hons)

Yung Shing Jit
Legal Assistant, M/S Haridass Ho & Partners,
24 Raffles Place, [H]18-00 Clifford Centre,
Singapore, 048621, 65-5332323, Fax: 65-
5331579, and Member Singapore Bar.
Called: July 1990, Middle Temple, LLB (Hull)

Yusoff Yusrin Faidz
Legal Assistant, 34 Jalan SS21/44, Damansara
Utama, 47400 Petaling Jaya, Selangor, 03
7171210, and Member Malaysia. Called: July
1996, Lincoln's Inn, LLB (Hons), MBA

Yusuf Ismail
Called: Nov 1992, Lincoln's Inn, LLB (Hons)

Yusuf Miss Kartini
17-27-1 Majestic Tower, Mont' Kiara Palma,
Jln Mont Kiara, Jln 1/40c, 50480 Kuala
Lumpur, (03) 2533127. Called: May 1995,
Lincoln's Inn, BA (Hons), LLB (Hons), LLM

Zabihi Miss Tanya ●
Lawyer, Legal Services Division, County
Hall, Surrey County Council, Kingston upon
Thames, 0181 541 9125, Fax: 0181 541
9005. Called: Nov 1988, Gray's Inn, LLB

Zachariadou Miss Anthie Philippou
14 Mnasiadou Street, Nicosia, 003572
475047, Fax: 003572 467532. Called: Feb
1995, Lincoln's Inn, LLB (Hons)(Lond)

Zacharias Dr Peter Lindsay
Consultant Occupational Physician,
Ardinamar, 4 Budworth Close, Oxton,
Birkenhead L43 9TJ, 0151 652 6894, Fax:
0151 670 1633. Called: July 1973, Middle
Temple, MA, MB, ChB, MFOM, DIH

Zackon Israel Terence ●
Secretary to Lord Chancellor's Advisory
Committee On Legal Education and
Conduct, Lord Chancellor's Advisory,
Committee on Legal Education, and
Conduct, 8th Floor, Millbank Tower,
Millbank SW1P 4QU, 0171 217 4296.
Called: Nov 1978, Inner Temple, BA (Oxon)

Zadra-Symes Mrs Lynda Julie
Knobbe Martens Olson & Bear, 620
Newport Center Drive, Newport Beach
CA 92660, 00 1 714 760 0404, Fax: 00 1
714 760 9502, and Member California Bar.
Called: Nov 1989, Inner Temple, LLB

Zafar *Ms Yasmeen*
Wakefields, Devon House, 171-177 Great Portland Street, London W1N 5FD, 0171 436 2151, Fax: 0171 636 5035. Called: Nov 1993, Lincoln's Inn, MA (Oxon), LLM

Zafer *Mohammed Abu*
Called: Mar 1997, Gray's Inn, MCom (Dhaka), LLB (Lond)

Zaharudin *Miss Faten Aina*
Called: July 1997, Lincoln's Inn, LLB (Hons)(Nott'm)

Zaidin *Miss Zalita*
Called: Nov 1992, Lincoln's Inn, LLB (Hons) (Warw)

Zain-Yusuf *Miss Shazlin*
Called: July 1995, Lincoln's Inn, LLB (Hons)

Zainal *Ms Suriawati*
Called: July 1994, Lincoln's Inn, LLB (Hons)

Zainal *Miss Zerenewati*
Called: July 1994, Lincoln's Inn, LLB (Hons)

Zainol-Abidin *Miss Adlina Hasni*
Partner, Messrs Chin Eng Adlina & Lim, Advocate & Solicitors, Suite 1-1, Burmah House, Jalan Burmah, 10350 Penang, (04) 229 4725, Fax: (04) 229 4728, and Member Malaysia. Called: July 1994, Gray's Inn, BSc (Denver), LLB (Wales)

Zaki *Ms Sara*
Credit Lyonnais Rouse Ltd, Broadwalk House, 5 Appold Street, London EC2A 2DA, 0171 214 6586, Fax: 0171 638 0401. Called: May 1997, Lincoln's Inn, BA (Hons)(Lond)

Zam Zam *Mrs Asiah*
Called: Nov 1996, Lincoln's Inn, LLB (Hons)(Lond)

Zaman *Mrs Sajada* •
Senior Solicitor, Stockport Metropolitan, Borough Council, Town Hall, Edward Street, Stockport, Cheshire, 0161 474 3247. Called: Nov 1985, Lincoln's Inn, BA

Zammit *Ms Frances Ann*
Called: Oct 1993, Inner Temple, LLB

Zawoda-Martin *Justin Raphael*
Legal Counsel and Chief of Staff., Coutts Group, Talstrasse 59, P O Box CH-8022, Zurich, +41 1 214 5580, Fax: +41 1 214 5563. Called: Oct 1994, Middle Temple, BA (Hons)(Lond), CPE (City)

Zeffman *Michael* •
Senior Principal Legal Officer, HM Customs & Excise, Solicitor's Office, New King's Beam House, 22 Upper Ground, London SE1 9PJ. Called: July 1977, Gray's Inn, LLB (Lond)

Zellick *Professor Graham John*
Principal, Professor of Law, Vice-Chancellor, Senate House, University of London, London WC1E 7HU, 0171 636 4752, Fax: 0171 580 3605, 3 Verulam Buildings, London, WC1R 5NT. Called: Nov 1992, Middle Temple, BA (Hons), MA & PhD, (Cantab), CIMgt,FRSA, FInstD, FRSM, Hon FSALS

Zinner *Peter Anthony* •
Principal Crown Prosecutor, Crown Prosecution Service, London Area, 4th Floor, Portland House, London SW1E 5BH, 0171 915 5700, Roll of Solicitors for England and Wales. Called: Nov 1983, Middle Temple, BA (Hons)

Zollner *Roland Louis* •
Senior Crown Prosecutor, CPS Mersey North, Heron House, Hougoumont Avenue, Crosby, Merseyside L22 0LL, 0151 920 8711, Fax: 0151 920 8233. Called: July 1978, Middle Temple, BA

Zombory-Moldovan *Peter Paul* •
Squire & Co, 49-52 St John's Street, London EC1V 4JL, 0171 490 3444, Fax: 0171 250 4087. Called: Oct 1995, Middle Temple, BA (Hons), MA

Zornoza *Simon*
Vice President and Counsel, Legal Division - Securities Op, State Street Bank & Trust Co, 1776 Heritage Drive, North Quincy, MA 02171, (617) 985 9271, Fax: (617) 985 4000, and Member New York Bar, District of Columbia Bar. Called: July 1983, Inner Temple, LLB (B'ham), Diplome, d'Etudes Juridiques, Francaises

Zoumaras *Miss Anna*
Called: Oct 1997, Gray's Inn, LLB (Sheff)

Zuberi *Miss Danish*
Called: Nov 1995, Gray's Inn, LLB (Wales)

Zugg *Julian Michael*
Called: July 1996, Inner Temple, LLB (Bucks)

Zulkifli *Miss Zurisafina*
Called: July 1997, Lincoln's Inn, LLB (Hons)

Zwennes *Charles William Leopold Bartel*
Called: Nov 1995, Gray's Inn, LLB (Kent)

Zymanczyk-Tedder *Miss Bozenna Zofia Zuzanna*
Senior Court Clerk, Nottingham Magistrates' Court, Carrington Street, Nottingham NG2 1EE, 0115 955 8111, Fax: 0115 955 8139. Called: July 1982, Middle Temple, BSc (Lond)

Individual Barristers Overseas

This section lists barristers who are based overseas. Barristers are listed alphabetically by surname and details include their membership of other Bars where appropriate, date of call to the Bar, their Inn of Court and academic qualifications.

F

F

Abd. Karim *Miss Ida Hanani*
Called: July 1994, Lincoln's Inn, LLB (Hons)

Abdul Ghafor *Miss Siti Norishan*
51 Jalan Madewa, Jalan Tutong, Bandar Seri
Begawan 2688, 00673 (2) 651732.
Called: July 1996, Lincoln's Inn, LLB (Hons)
(LSE)

Abdul Hamid *Miss Muslin*
Called: July 1993, Middle Temple, LLB
(Hons, Warw)

Abdul Jabid *Miss Soraya*
Called: Nov 1995, Lincoln's Inn, LLB (Hons)

Abdul Kadir *Rizal*
Shell Malaysia Ltd, Legal Department,
Bangunan Shell, Off Jalan Semantan,
P.O.Box 11027, 50732 Kuala Lumpur, 60 - 3
- 2512891, Fax: 60 - 3 - 2512732.
Called: Nov 1993, Lincoln's Inn, LLB (Hons,
Leic)

Abdul Karim *Miss Yasmeen*
Called: July 1997, Lincoln's Inn, LLB
(Hons)(Lond)

Abdul Majid Khan *Miss Sabriya*
and Member Malaysia Bar. Called: Nov 1992,
Lincoln's Inn, LLB (Hons)(Sheff)

Abdul Malek *Faisal Ramza*
Called: July 1995, Middle Temple, LLB
(Hons)

Abdul Rahman *Mrs Ramzidah*
Called: Mar 1998, Lincoln's Inn, LLB (Hons)

Abdul Rashid *Miss Zaidatul Mazwin*
Called: Nov 1996, Lincoln's Inn, LLB
(Hons)(Manch)

Abdul Shukor *Miss Shazwan*
Called: July 1996, Lincoln's Inn, LLB
(Hons)(Sheff)

Abdullah *Arshad*
BAP 35-C, Cantonment Plaza, Sadmar Road,
Peshawar, N W F P, 00 92 91 285 277, Fax:
00 92 91 285 277, and Member Pakistan.
Called: Nov 1996, Lincoln's Inn, LLM (Staff),
MA (Pakistan)

Abdullah *Miss Azleena*
Called: Nov 1997, Gray's Inn, LLB (Bris)

Abdullah *Miss Hajah Pauziah*
Called: July 1996, Lincoln's Inn, LLB
(Hons)(Kent)

Abdulrahim *Miss Nor Rejina*
(603) 253 4852, Fax: (603) 253 4537.
Called: July 1997, Lincoln's Inn, LLB
(Hons)(Kent)

Abedi *Ali Abbas Welayat Husain*
Abbas F.Ghazzawi Law Firm, P O Box 2335,
Jeddah 21451, (+9662) 6654646, Fax:
(+9662) 6659155, and Member New York.
Called: Nov 1988, Middle Temple, LLB
(Lond), LLM (NY)

Abu Bakar *Mustaffa*
Called: July 1996, Lincoln's Inn, LLB
(Hons)(L'pool)

Abu Bakar *Miss Nor'ain Binte*
Called: July 1996, Middle Temple, LLB
(Hons)(Lond)

Acton-Bond *Jonathan Edward*
and Member Hong Kong Bar. Called: July
1971, Gray's Inn, BA

Adaikalasamy *Miss Jeyanthy*
Called: Nov 1997, Lincoln's Inn, LLB
(Hons)(N'Castle)

Adamidou *Miss Effie*
P.O.Box 1211, Nicosia, Cyprus, 357 2
318995, Fax: 357 2 314869, and Member
Cyprus Bar. Called: Feb 1993, Middle
Temple, LLB (Hons)(Leic), Dip in Shipping
Law, (UCL)

Adderley *Miss Paula Anne Lilith*
Graham Thompson & Co, P O Box N272,
Nassau, 242 322 4130, Fax: 242 328 1069,
and Member Bahamas Bar. Called: July 1997,
Middle Temple, BA (Hons)

Adimoolam *Anpualagan*
Called: July 1996, Middle Temple, LLB
(Hons)(Lond)

Advani *Ajay Jiwat*
Called: July 1997, Middle Temple, LLB
(Hons)(Nott'm)

Aepli *Peter Andrew*
16 A, Chemin du Grand Communal, CH-
1222 Vesenaz, Geneva, (41 22) 855 07 23,
Fax: (41 22) 855 07 24. Called: July 1974,
Inner Temple

Ahmad *Adi Satria*
Called: Nov 1994, Lincoln's Inn, LLB
(Hons)(Wales)

Ahmad *Azlin*
Called: July 1996, Gray's Inn, LLB (Warwick)

Ahmad *Mohd Faizal*
Called: July 1994, Lincoln's Inn, LLB (Hons,
Leeds)

Ahmad *Miss Sahia*
Called: Nov 1994, Lincoln's Inn, LLB
(Hons)(Lond)

Ahmad *Miss Sakinah*
Called: Nov 1997, Middle Temple, LLB
(Hons)(Lond)

Ahmed *Miss Ayla*
Rizvi, Isa & Co, 517/518 Clifton Centre, DC
- 1, Block 5, Clifton, Karachi 75600,
(92)(21) 570727. Called: July 1997,
Lincoln's Inn, LLB (Hons)(Lond), LLM
(Cantab)

Ahmed *Sultan Tanvir*
and Member Punjab Bar. Called: Nov 1996,
Lincoln's Inn, BA (Punjab), LLB (Bucks)

Ahyow *Miss Dorothee Paola Cathie*
Called: Nov 1996, Lincoln's Inn, BSc
(Hons)(Wales), Dip Law

Akbar *Ms Ruby*
4 Shenton Way, [H]21-03A, 2240100, Fax:
2276002, and Member Singapore.
Called: July 1992, Gray's Inn, LLB (Brist)

Akel *Richard Livingstone*
Richard L Akel,Attorney at Law, 151
Meeting Street, Suite 600, Charleston S.C.
29401, U.S.A., 803.720.9142, Fax:
803.577.7513, American Trial Lawyers
Association, Trial Lawyers' Associations of
Washington DC & California & South
Carolina American Bar Association.
International Bar Association U.S.Supreme
Court, U.S. Courts of Appeal for District of
Columbia and 3rd, 4th, 5th. Called: July
1992, Lincoln's Inn, LLB (Hons, N.Z.), LLM
(Cantab), Dip., of Trial Advocacy, (U.S.)

Akhand *Shahnawaz*
Called: Nov 1996, Lincoln's Inn, LLB
(Hons)(Lond)

Akiwumi *Christopher Stephen Akilano*
Daly & Figgis Advocates, P O Box 40034,
8th Floor, Lonrho House, Standard Street,
Nairobi, Kenya, 336332/1, Fax: 334892, and
Member Kenya. Called: Nov 1992, Lincoln's
Inn, BA (Rhode Island), LLB (Hons)(Bucks),
Dip Law (Kenya)

Akosile *Adeleke Jacob*
Called: Mar 1997, Lincoln's Inn, LLB (Hons)

Al-Attas *Syed Reza Helmy*
and Member Malaysia Bar. Called: Oct 1994,
Lincoln's Inn, LLB (Hons)(Sheff)

Alam *Kazi Mohammad Tanjibul*
Called: Nov 1997, Lincoln's Inn, LLB
(Hons)(Lond)

Albury *Ms Candia Aubyn Patricia*
Called: July 1994, Inner Temple, LLB (Keele)

Alexander-Jack *Mrs Juliana Marie*
Mello,Hollis,Jones & Martin, Reid House,
Church Street, Hamilton, Bermuda, (441)
292 1345, Fax: (441) 292 2277, and
Member Bermuda Bar. Called: Oct 1994,
Inner Temple, BA (California), BA (Oxon)

Alexandrou *Miss Maria*
Called: Mar 1996, Gray's Inn, LLB (East
Anglia)

Ali *Muhammad Imman*
Lee Khan & Associates, City Heart Suit [H]
5/7, Naya Paltan (4th Floor), V.I.P. Road,
Motijheel, Dhaka - 1000, 88-02- 865412/
933508, Fax: 88-02- 865412, and Member
Dhaka Supreme Court Bar. Called: July
1978, Inner Temple, BA, LLM

Ali *Sham Shudin*
Called: July 1994, Lincoln's Inn, LLB (Hons)

Aling *Miss Jenny Li Ting Chin*
Called: July 1995, Middle Temple, LLB
(Hons)

Allen *Andrew Clifford*
Called: Nov 1996, Gray's Inn, LLB (Hull)

Allen *Harold Davis*
Called: July 1995, Middle Temple, LLB
(Hons)

Allen *Miss Tawanna Cherrel*
Called: July 1995, Gray's Inn, BA (Ottawa),
LLB (Hull)

Allgrove *Jeffrey William*
Unilever United States, 390 Park Avenue, New York, NY 10022 USA. Called: July 1976, Lincoln's Inn, LLB, FCCA

Ameen *Mahmud Riad*
Called: Mar 1998, Lincoln's Inn, LLB (Hons)(Lond)

Ameer *Mohammed Ameen Chezard*
Called: July 1996, Middle Temple, LLB (Hons)(Lond)

Amin *Omar Kemal Shaikh Mohamed*
Nairobi Hilton, Mama Ngina Street, P O Box 25241, Nairobi, Kenya, 254 (2) 334000, Fax: 254 (2) 339462, and Member Kenya Bar. Called: Nov 1991, Lincoln's Inn, LLB (Hons) (Bucks)

Amin *Salah-El-Din Mohamed*
First Floor, Nairobi Hilton Building, P O Box 25241, Nairobi, 254-2-242443/254-2-48453, Advocate of the High Court of Kenya. Called: Oct 1993, Lincoln's Inn, LLB (Hons)(Bucks)

Anahory *Moses Jacob*
138 Main Street, Gibraltar, 78804/79000, Fax: 71966, and Member Gibraltar Bar. Called: Oct 1994, Middle Temple, LLB (Hons)(Middx)

Anandakrishna *Thiagu*
Called: Nov 1997, Middle Temple, LLB (Hons)(Manch)

Anastassiou *Miss Maria Andreas*
Called: July 1997, Gray's Inn, LLB (Lond)

Anderson *Miss Maxanne Javita*
Called: May 1997, Lincoln's Inn, LLB (Hons)(Kent), BA (Atlanta)

Andreou *Andreas*
8 Rigas Fereos Str, Libra Chambers, 3095 Limassol, 00357 5 363154, Fax: 00357 5 342887, and Member Cyprus Bar. Called: Nov 1995, Lincoln's Inn, LLB (Hons)(Leic)

Andrews *Robert Craig*
Admiralty centre, 1405 Tower 2, 18 Harcourt Road, 00852 25273082, Fax: 00852 25298226, and Member Hong Kong Bar. Called: May 1971, Middle Temple, BA

Ang *Miss Alexia Hui Tsun*
Called: July 1997, Middle Temple, LLB (Hons)

Ang *Andrew Lye Whatt*
Called: July 1996, Middle Temple, LLB (Hons)(Leic)

Ang *Cheng Yong*
Blk 503 *03-233, Pasir Ris Street 52, Singapore 1851, Singapore, 583-3559, Fax: 583-3559, and Member Singapore Bar. Called: July 1991, Gray's Inn, LLB (Hons) (Lond), ACII, LM(Lond)

Ang *Kah Soon*
Messrs Gregory Chan, Tam Moo &, Ang, M2-D-6 Jalan Pandan Indah 4/6, Pahdan Indah, 55100 Kuala Lumpur, 603-4943186, Fax: 603-4948186, and Member Malaysia Bar. Called: July 1994, Middle Temple, LLB (Hons)(Lond)

Ang *Khoon Cheong*
c/o Messrs C P Ang & Co, 18 Lebuh Kampung Benggali, 12000 Butterworth, Penang, 04 3313009, Fax: 04 3328115, and Member Malaysia. Called: July 1995, Middle Temple, LLB (Hons) (Wales)

Ang *Miss Kim Noi*
Called: July 1995, Middle Temple, LLB (Hons)

Ang *Miss Ru-Lin*
Called: July 1997, Middle Temple, LLB (Hons)(Nott'm)

Ang *Miss Sue Khoon*
and Member Malaysia Bar. Called: July 1994, Middle Temple, LLB (Hons)(Bris)

Ang *Miss Valerie Freda Mei-Ling*
Messrs Derrick, Ravi & Partner, 133 New Bridge Road, [H]16-03/04 Chinatown Point, Singapore 059413, 538 1300, Fax: 538 1311, and Member Singapore Bar. Called: July 1994, Middle Temple, LLB (Hons)(Hull)

Ang *Wen Po Andrew*
Called: July 1997, Gray's Inn, LLB (Notts)

Ang *Woon Kherk*
Called: July 1996, Lincoln's Inn, LLB (Hons)

Angelides *Savvas*
Called: Nov 1997, Gray's Inn, LLB

Annanth *Mrs Parvathi*
Called: Nov 1996, Middle Temple, LLB (Hons)

Antao *Mrs Alexia Gertrude*
355b Romford Road, Forest Gate, London E7 8AA, 0181 519 8658, and Member Seychelles Bar. Called: May 1996, Inner Temple, LLB (Hons)(Lond), LLM (LSE)

Anuar *Miss Ifa Mutiara*
Called: Nov 1997, Lincoln's Inn, LLB (Hons)(Nott'm)

Anuar *Miss Zeti Azita*
Called: Nov 1997, Lincoln's Inn, LLB (Hons)(Warw)

Anwar *Miss Fatema*
Called: Nov 1997, Lincoln's Inn, LLB (Hons) (Lond)

Appaduray *Miss Nina Urmilla*
Called: July 1996, Middle Temple, LLB (Hons)(Lond)

Armstrong *Henry Napier DL*
Called: June 1961, Inner Temple, BA

Arrowsmith *Christopher John*
Mann & Partners, 20 Finch Road, Douglas, Isle of Man IM1 2PS, 01624 622221, Fax: 01624 627222, Partner and Member Manx Bar. Called: Oct 1990, Gray's Inn, LLB (Hons) (Brunel)

Asghar *Miss Shermine*
Called: July 1997, Lincoln's Inn, LLB (Hons)(City)

Asher *Peter John*
5 Garth Road, Kingston 8, Jamaica, West Indies, and Member Jamaican Bar. Called: July 1994, Lincoln's Inn, LLB (Hons), BA

Ashhab *Bazul*
Called: July 1997, Lincoln's Inn, LLB (Hons)(Lond)

Ashraf *Ms Leila*
Called: July 1995, Gray's Inn, LLB (E.Anglia)

Ashraf *Miss Nida*
Called: July 1996, Lincoln's Inn, BA (Hons)(Kent)

Aslam *Miss Sharen*
Block 554, [H] 11-219, Bedok North Street 3, Singapore 460554, 2436057. Called: July 1995, Middle Temple, LLB (Hons)

Asnani *Shankar Ram Pohumall*
197 Taman Star (Lorong 4), 93150 Kuching, Sarawak, Malaysia, 245421, Fax: 255758. Called: July 1995, Middle Temple, LLB (Hons) (Wales)

Attaur-Rehman *Ahmad*
Orr Dignam & Co Advocates, 3 Street 32 F-8/1, Islamabad, Pakistan, 260517/253086/260518, Fax: 260653, and Member Lahore High Court Bar. Called: Nov 1993, Lincoln's Inn, LLB (Hons), LLM

Attygalle *Miss Amila Sita*
Called: July 1996, Lincoln's Inn, LLB (Hons)(LSE)

Au *Cheen Kuan*
Called: July 1995, Middle Temple, LLB (Hons)

Au *Seng Heng*
Called: Mar 1996, Middle Temple, LLB (Hons)

Au *Tony Thye Chuen*
111 North Bridge Road, [H]22-04, Singapore 0617, 4338102, Fax: 3395436. Called: July 1995, Lincoln's Inn, LLB (Hons)

Au Yong *Miss Pei Yi*
Called: July 1996, Lincoln's Inn, LLB (Hons)(Sheff)

Aussant *Mrs Jill Amaryllis*
Council of the European Union, Legal Dept, Rue de la Loi 175, 1049 Bruxelles, Belgium, 02 285 7919, Fax: 285 6743. Called: Nov 1966, Inner Temple, MA (Cantab), LLB

Austin *Christopher Bound*
Bedell & Cristin, Advocates & Notaries Public, P.O.Box 75, One The Forum, Grenville Street, St Helier, Jersey JE4 8PP, 01534 814814, Fax: 01534 814815. Called: May 1996, Inner Temple, LLB (Hons)

Avraamides *Nicos*
10 Mylinae Str, Off 22, Nicosia, 766156 or 766157, Fax: 766123. Called: Nov 1995, Middle Temple, LLB (Hons)(Hull)

Aw *Dominic Kian-Wee*
DKH Management & Sdn Bhd, 20th Floor, Mewara Multi, Purpose, 8 Jalan Munshi Abdullah, 50100 Kuala Lumpur, 603 2982611, Fax: 603 2928112, and Member Malaysia Bar. Called: July 1992, Middle Temple, LLB (Hons) (Hull)

Ayaduray *Jeyapalan*
Called: July 1997, Lincoln's Inn, LLB (Hons)(Lond)

Ayres *Andrew John*
Court Place, St Peter Port, Guernsey,
Channel Islands, (01481) 723191, Fax:
(01481) 711880/711881, and Member
Guernsey Bar. Called: Nov 1992, Inner
Temple, LLB (Warw)

Aziz *Imran*
Called: July 1997, Lincoln's Inn, LLB (Lond),
LLM (Lond)

Aziz *Miss Miriam*
Mommsentrabe 47, 10629 Berlin.
Called: July 1994, Inner Temple, LLB
(Manch)

Aziz *Munir Mydin Abdul*
8 Jalan Desa Ria, Taman Desa, 58100 Kuala
Lumpur, 00 603 7803766. Called: July 1997,
Lincoln's Inn, BA (Hons)

Aziz *Miss Noor Afizah*
Called: Oct 1992, Middle Temple, BA (Hons)

Aziz *Miss Noraini*
Khattar Wong & Partners, 80 Raffles Place
[H]25-01, Plaza 1, and Member Singapore.
Called: Nov 1993, Gray's Inn, LLB, LLM

Aziz *Miss Tengku Azrina Bt Raja Abdul*
Called: July 1997, Lincoln's Inn, BA (Hons)

Azlan *Miss Nor Azrini*
Called: July 1995, Lincoln's Inn, BA (Hons)

Azopardi *The Hon Keith MHA*
213 Rosia Plaza, Rosia Bay, (350) 50294,
Fax: (350) 71143, and Member Gibraltar
Bar. Called: Nov 1990, Middle Temple, BA
(Keele)

Babalola *Chief Emmanuel Afe*
and Member Nigerian Bar. Called: July 1963,
Lincoln's Inn, B.Sc (Econ)(Lond), LLB
(Hons)(Lond), B.L

Bacik *Ms Ivana Catherine Alexis*
Law School, Trinity College, Dublin 6, 608
2299, Fax: 677 0449, Member of King's
Inns, Dublin and Member Southern Ireland
Bar. Called: Nov 1992, Middle Temple, LLB,
LLM

Badaruddin *Nabil Daraina*
Attorney General's Chambers, Jalan Tutong,
Bandar Seri, Begawan 2016, Brunei,
(673)(2)227959. Called: Nov 1996, Lincoln's
Inn, LLB (Hons)(Bucks)

Bahadursingh *Ravi Ananta*
2 Main Street, New Amsterdam, Berbice,
(592) 3 2841, and Member Guyana Bar.
Called: Nov 1995, Gray's Inn, LLB (Dublin)

Bahrin *Awangku Izad-Ryan*
Skrine & Co, 303B Wisma Jaya, 406A Jalan
Pemancha, Bandar Seri Begawan 2085,
Brunei, 23 29 46/48, Fax: 23 29 49, and
Member Brunei Darussalam. Called: Nov
1994, Lincoln's Inn, BA (Hons)(Keele)

Bahrin *Miss Dayangku Nina Jasmine*
Called: Mar 1998, Lincoln's Inn, LLB
(Hons)(E.Anglia)

Bainbridge *Garth Tristan Athelstan*
Ozannes, 1 Le Marchant St, St Peter Port4,
Guernsey, 01481 723466, Fax: 01481
727935/720378, and Member Guernsey Bar.
Called: Nov 1978, Gray's Inn, LLB

Bajaj *Harpal Singh*
Called: Nov 1997, Middle Temple, LLB
(Hons)(Lond)

Bakar *Miss Falisa Abu*
Called: July 1996, Gray's Inn, LLB
(Manchester)

Bakar *Mohamad Husini*
Brunei Shell Petroleum Company, Sendirian
Berhad, Seria 7082, Brunei, Darussalam, 673
3 373375, Fax: 673 3 373996, and Member
Supreme Court of Brunei. Called: July 1994,
Lincoln's Inn, BA (Hons) (Keele)

Bal *Miss Karen Kaur*
Called: July 1995, Inner Temple, LLB
(Northumbria)

Balasamy *Kasturi Kesveren*
Kas & Co, Advocates & Solicitors, 19b
Wisma Chye Hin, Jalan Sultain Idris, Shah
Ipoh 30,000, 241 4635, Fax: 241 5776, and
Member Malaysia Bar. Called: July 1994,
Lincoln's Inn, LLB (Hons)

Balen *Miss Bernadette*
and Member Singapore. Called: Nov 1993,
Lincoln's Inn, LLB (Hons)

Balendra *Miss Natasha Thiruni Jayasekara*
Called: July 1994, Lincoln's Inn, LLB (Hons)

Balfour *James Selby*
Called: Nov 1997, Inner Temple, BA

Balia *Miss Sabwati Shukrin*
Called: July 1996, Lincoln's Inn, LLB
(Hons)(Soton)

Banerji *Ratnanko*
Called: July 1994, Inner Temple, LLB

Bapu *David Salim*
P O Box 1042, Blantyre, Malawi, (265)
624820, Fax: (265) 622105, and Member
Malawi Bar. Called: Nov 1991, Gray's Inn,
LLB (Wales), LLM (Lond)

Barit *Ms Georgette De Stefanis*
Appleby, Spurling & Kempe, 41 Cedar
Avenue, Hamilton, 441 295 7563, and
Member Bermuda Bar. Called: Feb 1995,
Middle Temple, MBA, BA, CPE (City), Dip
Law

Barlen *Miss Catherine Veronica*
Lovell White Durrant, Avenue Louise 523,
Boite 24, 1050 Brussels, 00 32 2 647 0660,
Fax: 00 32 2 647 1124. Called: Oct 1990,
Inner Temple, BA (Oxon), Dip Law, LLM EC
Law (Bruges)

Baron *Miss Francis Althea*
Called: July 1995, Middle Temple, LLB
(Hons)

Barrett *Richard*
and Member Northern Ireland Bar Southern
Ireland Bar. Called: Feb 1988, Middle
Temple, BCL, LLB (Ireland), LLM (Lond)

Barretto *Ruy Octavio*
Temple Chambers, 16/F One Pacific Place,
88 Queensway, 5-2 32003, Fax: 8 100302,
and Member New South Wales Bar Hong
Kong Bar. Called: Nov 1974, Middle
Temple, LLB (Lond), AKC

Basah *Miss Nashah*
Called: Mar 1998, Middle Temple, LLB
(Hons)(Staffs)

Bastos G Martin *Philip John*
Dorsey & Whitney LLP, 35 Square de
Meeus, B-100 Brussels, (32-2) 5044611, Fax:
(32-2) 5044646. Called: Nov 1993, Gray's
Inn, LLB (Essex), DEA (France)

Batuk *Sanjay*
Called: Oct 1997, Middle Temple, LLB
(Hons)(Wales)

Baudains *Martyn*
Called: Mar 1998, Gray's Inn, LLB
(W'hampton)

Bay *Miss Chern Chieh*
Called: July 1995, Middle Temple, LLB
(Hons)

Beel *Robert William Trevor*
Called: May 1996, Gray's Inn, LLB (Lond)

Belle *Mrs Berthalee Louise*
Called: Oct 1997, Gray's Inn, BA (Ohio), LLB
(Leeds)

Benest *David John*
Bailache Labesse, 14/16 Hill Street, St
Helier, Jersey JE2 3ZB, 01534 888777, Fax:
01534 888778. Called: Nov 1995, Inner
Temple, BA (Sussex)

Benest *Frederick John*
Called: July 1996, Middle Temple

Benest *Miss Nina Sophie Hacquoil*
Bois & Bois, 2 Bond Street, P.O.Box 429, St
Helier, Jersey JE4 5QR, 01534 601010, Fax:
01534 601011. Called: July 1996, Middle
Temple, LLB (Hons)(Kent)

Beng *Miss Li-Sher*
Called: July 1996, Middle Temple, BA
(Hons)(Notts)

Bensadon *Mrs Janine Yvette*
Called: Oct 1994, Lincoln's Inn, LLB
(Hons)(Hudders)

Benzaquen *Joseph Pinhas*
350 78534, Fax: 350 73201, and Member
Gibraltar Bar. Called: July 1992, Middle
Temple, LLB (Hons)

Benzaquen *Rafael Jacob*
Legislation Support Unit, 13 Town Range, +
(350) 41821, Fax: + (350) 41822.
Called: July 1995, Middle Temple, LLB
(Hons), Maitre en Droit, (Paris)

Berkeley-Hill *Michael Amar Samuel*
Squadron Ellenoff Plesent &, Sheinfeld LLP,
551 Fifth Avenue, New York, NY 10176-
0001, 00 1 212 661 6500, Fax: 00 1 212
697 6686. Called: Oct 1994, Middle Temple,
LLB (Hons)(Lond), AKC (Lond), LLM (Lond)

Bernacchi *Brook Antony OBE JP*
1103 Prince's Building, Central, 5 2 20066,
Fax: 8 450851, QC, Hong Kong. Called: Jan
1943, Middle Temple, FCIArb

Bhar *Miss Sherina*
Called: Nov 1997, Lincoln's Inn, LLB (Hons)

Bhimjee *Anwar Ali*
244 Juanita Way, San Francisco, California
94127, (415) 242 1734, Chartered
Accountant. Called: July 1965, Lincoln's Inn,
MA, FCA, LLB

Bhola *Miss Susan*
Supreme Court of Trinidad & Tobago.
Called: Nov 1993, Lincoln's Inn, LLB (Hons,
Buck'ham)

Biesmans *John Robert*
European Parliament, Rue Belliard 97, 1040
Brussels, 02 284 30 26, Fax: 02 231 11 83/
02 284 9877. Called: July 1979, Middle
Temple, MA (Oxon), LLB (Cantab) LLM

Binder *Miss Naveen Kaur*
Called: July 1995, Middle Temple, LLB
(Hons)

Binet *Miss Francoise Charlotte*
Called: Mar 1998, Lincoln's Inn, LLB (Hons),
LLM, (Bucks)

Binns *Miss Quinell Maria*
Called: Nov 1997, Lincoln's Inn, LLB (Hons)

Birt *Michael Cameron St John*
Law Officer's Department, Royal Court
House, Jersey JE1 1DD, 0534 502200, Fax:
0534 502299, QC 1995 and Member Jersey
Bar 9 Bedford Row, London, WC1R 4AZ.
Called: Nov 1970, Middle Temple, MA
(Cantab)

Birtwistle *Daniel James*
Called: July 1996, Middle Temple, LLB
(Hons)(Wales)

Black *James Walter* QC (1979)
Edmund Barton Chambers, Level 44 MLC
Centre, Martin Place, Sydney 2000, 02 9220
6100, Fax: 02 9232 3949, and Member
Australian Capitol Territory New South
Wales Bar. Called: Feb 1964, Middle
Temple, MA (Cantab)

Black *Julian Neil*
Called: Oct 1995, Lincoln's Inn, LLB
(Hons)(Leic)

Blackburn *Mrs Diana Jeanette*
P O Box 748, Belgrave, Victoria 3160, and
Member New Zealand Bar. Called: Nov
1991, Middle Temple, BA Hons (Kent),
ACIArb, AArbInz

Blackman *Colin*
Wharf Cable, 8/F Wharf Cable Tower, 9 Hoi
Shing Road, Tsuen Wan, 2112 6222, Fax:
2112 7824. Called: July 1988, Gray's Inn,
BSc (Lond), MSc (Reading), C Phys

Blackshaw *Miss Gail*
Called: Oct 1997, Middle Temple, BSc
(Hons)(Bris), CPE

Bodden *Truman Murray OBE*
Truman Bodden & Co, P O Box 1796,
Anderson Square Building, Grand Cayman,
British West Indies, 809 949 7555, Fax: 809
949 8492, and Member Cayman Islands.
Called: July 1969, Inner Temple, ACIB, FFA,
FICM, FCI, MBIM, ACIArB, FBSC, LLB
(Hons) (Lond)

Bodruddoza *Md*
Hall Room, No 3, Supreme Court Bar
Association, Building, Dhaka-1000,
Bangladesh, Chamber 45/Kha, New Eskaton
2nd Floor, Dhaka, 88-02-9340080, and
Member Bangladesh Bar Council Dhaka Bar.
Called: Nov 1995, Lincoln's Inn, LLB
(Hons)(Lond), LLB (Hons)(Banglade), LLM
(Bangladesh)

Bogaert *Peter Willy Luc*
Kunstlaan 44, 1040 Brussel, 32-2-5495230,
Fax: 32-2-5021598, and Member Brussels
Bar. Called: May 1995, Gray's Inn, Licenciaat
in de, Rechten, BA

Boh *Miss Wah Boon*
Called: July 1996, Middle Temple, LLB
(Hons)(Glamorg)

Bolton *Miss Sally Margaret*
and Member Manx Bar. Called: July 1988,
Gray's Inn, BA (E Anglia), Dip Law

Bolton *Miss Susan Anne*
Called: Oct 1997, Gray's Inn, BA
(Edinburgh)

Bon *Edmund*
Called: July 1997, Lincoln's Inn, LLB
(Hons)(Lond)

Boo *Moh Cheh*
Called: July 1994, Lincoln's Inn, LLB (Hons)

Boon *Swan Ngee*
Called: Nov 1994, Middle Temple, LLB
(Hons)

Borge *Paul Louis Anthony*
Called: Mar 1998, Gray's Inn, BA (Derby)

Boss *Miss Bernadette Carmel*
Dept of Defence - Army, Defence Centre
Melbourne, Victoria Barracks, St Kilda Road,
Melbourne 3006, 00 617 364 4455, and
Member Queensland Bar. Called: Oct 1992,
Middle Temple, B.Sc (Hons, Lond), Diploma
in Law

Bossino *Damon James*
Suite C, 2nd Floor, Regal House,
Queensway, 010 350 79423, Fax: 010 350
71405, and Member Gibraltar. Called: Nov
1995, Middle Temple, LLB (Hons)

Bossino *Stephen Richard*
2 Hadfield House, P.O.Box 659, Library
Street, Gibraltar, 74998/73316, Fax: 73074,
and Member Gibraltar. Called: Oct 1994,
Lincoln's Inn, LLB (Hons)(Leic)

Bostwick *Ms Janet Lissette Racquel*
Bostwick & Bostwick, Attorneys at Law, 50
George Street, PO Box N-1605, Nassau N.P.,
(809) 322 2039/2038, Fax: (809) 328 2521,
and Member Bahamas Bar Association.
Called: July 1996, Gray's Inn, BA (McGill,
Canada), LLB (Buckingham)

Bostwick *John Henry*
Called: Nov 1995, Gray's Inn, BA (Keele)

Bowers *Miss Deborah*
Alberton Richelieu & Associate, P.O.Box
2130, Gros-Islet, St Lucia, 001 758 4524515,
Fax: 001 758 4523329, and Member St
Lucia. Called: July 1997, Middle Temple, LLB
(Hons)(Lond)

Boyle *Miss Jane Kerr*
Via S Martino E Solferino 90, Padova, (049)
65 40 58. Called: Feb 1992, Middle Temple,
MA (Lond), LLB (Hons)

Boyle *Dr John Charles*
Kvaerner PLC, 55/F Central Plaza, 18
Harbour Road, Wanchai, (852) 28681100,
Fax: (852) 28681522. Called: July 1974,
Lincoln's Inn, B.Sc, PhD, C.Eng, M.I.C.E

Boyton *David Rex*
Flat 4-H, Ventris Court, 15 Ventris Road,
(832) 2521 5544, Fax: (832) 2524 5912, and
Member Hong Kong. Called: July 1997,
Gray's Inn, BA (Newc), LLB (Lond), LLM
(Lond)

Brady *Kevin Joseph*
47 Hervey Close, Finchley, London N3 O6H.
Called: July 1984, Gray's Inn, BA (Belfast)
LLB, (Lond)

Bramwell *Philip Nicholas*
DDV Telecommunications, Strategy,
Woluwe Garden, Woluwedal 26,65, 1932
Brussels, 00 322 715 0930, Fax: 00 322 715
0931. Called: Nov 1983, Lincoln's Inn, BA
(Hons)

Brandon *Michael*
P O Box 200, 1291 Commugny, Vaud, 0041
22 776 14 00/776 15 00, Fax: 0041 22 776
55 18. Called: Nov 1952, Inner Temple, MA,
LLM (Cantab), MA (Yale), FCIArb

Brankin *Sean-Paul*
Called: Oct 1993, Lincoln's Inn, BA (Hons),
LLM (Virginia)

Bridge *Mrs Anabelle Jane*
Le Haugard, La Ville de l'Eglise, St Ouen,
Jersey JE3 2LR, 01534 482671, Fax: 01534
481675. Called: Nov 1981, Gray's Inn, LLB
(Nott'm)

Bridge *Mark David*
3395 Cadboro Bay Road, Victoria, BC,
Canada V8R 5K4, 604-592 9457, and
Member British Columbia. Called: July 1992,
Lincoln's Inn, LLB (Canada), BSc (Canada),
LLM (Lond)

Bridgeford *William Andrew Macrae*
Crills, 44 The Esplanade, St Helier, Jersey,
Channel Islands, 01534 873521, Advocate of
the Royal Court of Jersey. Called: July 1986,
Middle Temple, LLB (Dundee) MPhil,
(Cantab)

Bristol *Anthony Fitzgerald Le Varrie*
Called: Oct 1997, Gray's Inn, BSc (West
Indies)

Bristol *James Anthony Louis*
Henry, Henry & Bristol, P.O.Box 386, St.
Georges, Grenada, 809 440 2500/2809, Fax:
809 440 4128, and Member Grenada,
Trinidad & Tobago, St Lucia, Barbados.
Called: July 1989, Middle Temple, LLB

Britton *His Honour Judge Ian Robert*
The Law Courts, Harbour Road, Wan Chai,
5824106, Formerly a Solicitor admitted
1965. Called: May 1977, Inner Temple

Brodie *Philip Hope*
Advocates Library, Parliament House,
Edinburgh, Scotland EH1 1RF, 031 226
5071, Fax: 031 225 3642, Scottish Advocate
Queens Counsel, Scotland. Called: Nov
1991, Lincoln's Inn, LLB (Hons) (Edin), LLM
Virginia

Brown *Eric Crichton*
Advocate's Library, Parliment House,
Edinburgh, Scotland EH1 1RF, 0131 226
5071, Fax: 0131 225 3642, and Member
Scottish Bar. Called: Nov 1990, Lincoln's
Inn, LLB (Hons) (Edin)

Brunton *Captain Ian Arthur Joseph*
6 La Boiselle Road, La Baja, St Joseph,
Trinidad, West Indies, 868-645 5693, Fax:
868-662 4822, and Member Trinidad &
Tobago Bar Antigua Bar Bermuda Bar.
Called: July 1990, Lincoln's Inn, LLB (Lond)

Buchanan *Mrs Charissa Siew-Fong*
Messrs Rodyk & Davidson, 9 Raffles Place
[H]55-01, Republic Plaza, Singapore 048619,
(65) 5399247/22552626, Fax: (65) 2251838
& 2257511, and Member Singapore Bar.
Called: July 1993, Inner Temple, LLB
(Hons)(Notts)

Buchanan *Mark Philip*
Called: Nov 1991, Inner Temple, LLB

Bukhari *Syed Mustafa Ali*
Called: July 1997, Lincoln's Inn, LLB
(Hons)(Lond)

Bull *Cavinder*
Drew & Napier, 20 Raffles Place, Ocean
Towers [H]17-00, (65) 535 0733, Fax: (65)
532 7149, and Member Singapore Bar, New
York. Called: July 1993, Gray's Inn, BA
(Oxon), LLM (Harv)

Burger *Schalk Frederick*
621 Innes Chambers, Pritchard Street,
Johannesburg, 11-333 8903, Fax: 11-333
0626, and Member Johannesburg Bar;
Senior Counsel Cape Town; Senior Counsel.
Called: Feb 1990, Lincoln's Inn, B.Comm,
LLB, (Stellenbosch), LLM (Lond)

Burke *John Stewart*
Called: Oct 1994, Gray's Inn, BA

Burney *Ali Hasan*
Called: Nov 1997, Lincoln's Inn, BA
(Hons)(Tennessee)

Burrell *The Hon Mr Justice Michael
Peter*
Supreme Court, Queensway, Hong Kong,
28254316, Fax: 28495494, and Member
Hong Kong Bar. Called: July 1971, Inner
Temple, MA (Cantab)

Burrows *Miss Tameka Shevone*
Attorney Generals Office, P.O.Box N3007,
Nassau N.P., and Member Bahamas.
Called: July 1997, Middle Temple, LLB
(Hons)

Burton *Ralph Dennis*
Graham Miller Carvallo SA, Argentina, Av
Cordoba 836 (Office 1304), (1054) Buenos
Aires, Argentina, 00 54 1 393 3209/6539,
Fax: 00 54 1 393 6242. Called: Nov 1985,
Inner Temple, BA (Oxon)

Bury *Miss Claire Louise*
Rue de la Loi 200, 1040 Brussels, 00 32 2
296 0499, Fax: 00 32 2 295 2483.
Called: July 1988, Middle Temple, LLB
(Hons) (Lond)

Butler *Miss Bernadette Mae Evelyn*
Called: July 1995, Lincoln's Inn, LLB (Hons)

Butler *Miss Jacinda Pomona*
Called: Nov 1995, Gray's Inn, LLB (Lond)

Butler *Truman Kirkland*
Called: July 1996, Middle Temple, LLB
(Hons)(Wolves)

Butterfield *Toby Michael John*
Kay Collyer & Boose LLP, One Dag
Hammarskjold Plaza, New York, NY 10017-
2299, USA, (212) 940 8369, Fax: (212) 755
0921, and Member New York. Called: July
1989, Lincoln's Inn, BA (Oxon), LLM (Int'l)

Butterworth *Miss Pamela*
Called: Nov 1995, Middle Temple, LLB
(Hons)(Dundee)

Bywater *Andre Edward*
85 Broadmead, Tunbridge Wells, Kent
TN2 5NW, 01892 542335. Called: Oct 1993,
Middle Temple, MA (Sussex), BA (Hull), BA
(Cantab)

Cahalan *Michael James*
and Member Northern Ireland Bar.
Called: July 1996, Middle Temple, CPE,
B.S.Sc, M.Sc (Belfast)

Caldwell *Miss Marion Allan*
Advocates' Library, Parliament, House,
Parliament Square, Edinburgh EH1 1RF,
0131 226 5071, Scottish Advocate.
Called: July 1991, Inner Temple, LLB
(Aberdeen), Dip Law P (Glasgow)

Callaghan *Valentine Edward*
Guillermo Golding Abogados S.L,
Bethencourt Alfonso, 33-3o, 38002 Santa
Cruz De Tenerife, 24 12 85/38 40 17, Fax:
24 25 27/37 03 78, King's Inns. Called: Nov
1979, Lincoln's Inn, MA, BCL (Dub), Post
Grad Dip Eu Law

Callender *Jason Colin*
Callenders & Co, One Millars Court, PO Box
N-7117, Nassau, 809 322 2511, Fax: 809
326 7666, and Member Bahamas Bar (1996).
Called: July 1996, Middle Temple, LLB
(Hons)(Soton)

Callender *Sean Bradley*
P O Box N-7117, Nassau, Bahamas, (809)
322 2511, Fax: (809) 326 7666, and
Member Bahamas Bar. Called: Nov 1994,
Lincoln's Inn, LLB (Kent)

Calvert-Lee *Miss Georgina Eliza Jane*
Sonnenschein, Nath & Rosenthal, 8000
Sears Tower, Chicago, Illinois 60606, (USA)
312 876 8964, Fax: (USA) 312 876 7934.
Called: Oct 1993, Middle Temple, MA
(Hons)(Oxon), CPE (City)

Campbell *Andrew Neil*
Called: Nov 1988, Middle Temple, BA
(Cantab)

Campbell *Charles Grigor Gordon*
45 Avenue Montaigne, 75008 Paris, 0147-23-
64-82, Fax: 0147-23-37-74, Avocat in France
and Member Paris Bar. Called: Feb 1965,
Gray's Inn, BA (Cantab), Cert Comm Mkt
Law, (Paris)

Campbell *Miss Michelle Yvonne*
P.O. Box N-9180, Nassau, (809) 393 5551,
Fax: (809) 393 5116, and Member Member
of the Bar of the Commonwealth of The
Bahamas. Called: July 1996, Inner Temple,
LLB (Lond)

Campos *Miss Helen*
Called: July 1994, Middle Temple, LLB
(Hons)(Lond)

Campos *Miss Pamela Jennifer*
Called: Nov 1996, Middle Temple, LLB
(Hons)(Wales)

Canepa *James Silvio*
Called: May 1996, Inner Temple, LLB (Lond)

Cargill *Miss Marie*
P O Box SS-5569, Nassau, Bahamas.
Called: Nov 1993, Gray's Inn, BA, MBA, LLB

Cariou *Marcel Robert*
Les Queux, Ruette Des Effards, Castel,
Guernsey. Called: Nov 1987, Gray's Inn,
LLB(Hons)

Carpenter *Richard John*
Called: July 1981, Gray's Inn, BSc

Carr *Miss Chelon Marie*
Lennox Paton, Devonshire House, Queens
Street, P O Box N-4875, Nassau, (809) 328
0563, Fax: (809) 328 0566, and Member
Bahamas Bar. Called: July 1996, Lincoln's
Inn, LLB (Hons)(Leeds)

Carter *Robert James*
Shell International B.V., Carel Van
Bylandtlaan 30, 2501 An The Hague, 31
(0)70 377 1822, Fax: 31 (0) 70 377 6141.
Called: July 1995, Inner Temple, BSc
(Leeds), CPE (Notts)

Cartwright *Mrs Monique Ruth*
and Member Bahamas. Called: July 1994,
Lincoln's Inn, LLB (Hons, Bris), LLM (LSE)

Casey *Miss Niamh Ann*
Called: Nov 1993, Middle Temple, BCL, LLM

Ch'ng *Frank Eng Hing*
Called: July 1995, Middle Temple, LLB
(Hons)

Ch'ng *Miss Li-Ling*
Called: July 1996, Lincoln's Inn, LLB
(Hons)(Lond)

Chacko *Miss Grace*
Called: Feb 1994, Lincoln's Inn, LLB (Hons)

Chadwick *Neville*
Attorney General's Chambers, Private Bag 62, Francistown, 212 342, Fax: 213 402, Advocate of the High Court of Botswana. Called: July 1972, Middle Temple, BA, LLM (Lond)

Chai *Hean Leong*
Called: July 1996, Lincoln's Inn, LLB (Hons)(Lond)

Chai *Jen Chiew*
Called: Nov 1994, Middle Temple, LLB (Hons) (Sheff)

Chai *Miss Yoke Peng*
Called: July 1995, Lincoln's Inn, LLB (Hons)

Chair *Yong Huang Adrian*
Called: July 1996, Gray's Inn, LLB (Leicester)

Chan *Allan Chun Hwee*
Called: July 1996, Middle Temple, LLB (Hons)(Lond)

Chan *Miss Amanda Yuk Ying*
Called: July 1996, Middle Temple, LLB (Hons)(Wolves)

Chan *Bo Ching*
Called: July 1995, Gray's Inn, LLB, LLM (Lond)

Chan *Ms Charmaine Poh Meng*
Called: July 1997, Gray's Inn, LLB (Notts)

Chan *Che Bun Anderson*
Called: Nov 1997, Gray's Inn, LLB, LLM (Lond), LLM (Deakin, Australia)

Chan *Chee Choong*
Called: Nov 1997, Lincoln's Inn, LLB (Hons)

Chan *Miss Ching Fan*
Room B, 12/F, Yee Cheung Mansion, Lei King Wan, Sai Wan Ho, (852) 2535 6251, Fax: (852) 2539 5416, and Member Hong Kong Bar. Called: July 1996, Middle Temple, BA (Hons)(Hong Kong), CPE (Manc)

Chan *Ms Christine Mei-An*
Messrs Khattar Wong & Partners, 80 Raffles Place, [H]25-01 UOB Plaza 1, 65-5356844 65-5314022, Fax: 65-5351030. Called: Nov 1994, Middle Temple, LLB (Hons)

Chan *David Ming Onn*
Called: July 1996, Middle Temple, LLB (Hons)(Lond)

Chan *Mrs Dora Kit Ho*
and Member Hong Kong. Called: July 1996, Middle Temple, BSc (Hons)(Lond), MSc (City), CPE (Manc)

Chan *Eu Gene*
Called: Nov 1996, Middle Temple, LLB (Hons)

Chan *Miss Evelyn Lillian Swee Lian*
12 Lorong Taman Pantai 6, Bukit Pantai, 59100 Kuala Lumpur, Malaysia, 603-2821636. Called: July 1995, Lincoln's Inn, LLB (Hons)

Chan *Miss Fiona Foong Ling*
Called: July 1996, Lincoln's Inn, LLB (Hons)(Leics)

Chan *Fu Kit Brian*
and Member Hong Kong Bar. Called: July 1996, Gray's Inn, LLB (Wolverhampton)

Chan *Hing Wai*
and Member Hong Kong Bar. Called: July 1990, Gray's Inn, B.Pharm (Brad), MRPharmS, LLB (Lond)

Chan *Hock Keng*
Called: July 1993, Middle Temple, LLB (Hons, Bris)

Chan *Hon Wan Edwin*
Department of Building & Real, Estate, Hong Kong Polytechnic Uni, Hung Hom, Kowloon, Hong Kong, (HK) 27665800, Fax: (HK) 27645131, and Member Hong Kong Bar. Called: July 1993, Inner Temple, BA, Dip. Arch., MA, LLB, RIBA, ACIArb, Pg.D Prc law

Chan *Ms Ifan*
Temple Chambers, 1607-1612 One Pacific Place, 88 Queensway, 852 25232003, Fax: 852 28179326, and Member Hong Kong Bar. Called: July 1996, Inner Temple, BA, CPE

Chan *Ka Sing Louise*
Called: Nov 1997, Inner Temple, LLB, LLM

Chan *Miss Keng Yean*
Called: Nov 1997, Lincoln's Inn, LLB (Hons)(L'pool)

Chan *Kia Khuang*
Called: July 1996, Middle Temple, LLB (Hons)(Bris)

Chan *Kong Meng Lawrence*
Called: July 1997, Middle Temple, LLB (Hons)(Keele)

Chan *Kun Ming*
Called: Nov 1994, Middle Temple, LLB (Hons)

Chan *Kwai Chun Charles*
and Member Hong-Kong Bar. Called: July 1993, Gray's Inn, B.BA, LLB

Chan *Kwok-Chun*
Called: Nov 1997, Gray's Inn, LLB (Lond), BSc, MSc, (Hong Kong)

Chan *Miss Lin Wai Ruth*
Called: July 1995, Gray's Inn, LLB (Bris)

Chan *Miss Lin-Mei*
Called: July 1996, Lincoln's Inn, LLB (Hons)(Lond)

Chan *LLoyd Kah Seng*
Called: July 1996, Middle Temple, LLB (Hons)(Lond)

Chan *Miss Michelle Geraldine Chui-Wah*
20 Cecil Street, [H]25-02 to 05, The Exchange, (65) 534 1711, Fax: (65) 534 3331, and Member Singapore Bar. Called: Nov 1993, Middle Temple, LLB (Hons)(B'ham)

Chan *Ming-Ki*
and Member Barrister, Supreme Court of Hong Kong. Called: Oct 1995, Middle Temple, LLB (Hons), LLM

Chan *Nicholas Kei Cheong*
Orrick, Herrington & Sutcliffe, 10 Collyer Quay, [H]23-08 Ocean Building, Singapore 049315, (65) 538 6116, Fax: (65) 538 0606, and Member Singapore Bar. Called: Feb 1993, Inner Temple, MA (Cantab)

Chan *Pat Lun*
Des Voeux Chambers, 10th Floor, Bank of East Asia Building, 10 Des Voeux Road, Central, (852) 2526 3071, Fax: (852) 2810 5287, and Member Hong Kong Bar. Called: July 1994, Lincoln's Inn, BA (Hons)

Chan *Peter Chi-Kwan*
604 Cosmos Bldg, 8-11 Lan Kwai Fong, D'Aguilar St, 852 25230858, Fax: 852 28684673, and Member Hong Kong Bar. Called: Nov 1965, Middle Temple

Chan *Miss Pik Dzee*
Called: July 1995, Middle Temple, LLB (Hons)

Chan *Miss Shui Ping Peggy*
Called: July 1997, Middle Temple, LLB (Hons)(Lond)

Chan *Miss Suk-Wai Winsome*
Room 545, High Block, Queensway Government Offices, Admiralty, (852) 28672231, Fax: (852) 25368423. Called: Nov 1994, Gray's Inn, BA (Hong Kong)

Chan *Tak Pun*
Called: Nov 1997, Gray's Inn, BSc (Hong Kong)

Chan *Thomas Chun Yee*
Called: Oct 1995, Middle Temple, LLB (Hons)

Chan *Wa Shing*
Called: Nov 1994, Middle Temple, B.Sc (Hons)

Chan *Wing-Cheong*
5 Cluny Hill, Singapore 1025, Republic of Singapore, 468 1188, and Member Singapore Bar New York Bar. Called: July 1991, Gray's Inn, BA, LLM (Cornell)

Chan *Yee Kwong*
Called: Mar 1998, Middle Temple, LLB (Hons)(Lond)

Chan *Miss Yew Ping*
J5, 2nd Floor, Bangunan Khas, Lorong 8/1E, 46050 petaling Jaya, Selangor, Malaysia, 03 7552466, Fax: 603 7552405, and Member Malaysia Bar. Called: Nov 1994, Lincoln's Inn, LLB (Hons)(Lond)

Chan *Yoong Heng*
Called: July 1997, Lincoln's Inn, LLB (Hons)(Lond)

Chandrakesan *Prabakaran*
Called: Mar 1998, Middle Temple, LLB (Hons)

Chandranayagam *Daniel Masillamaney*
Called: July 1997, Gray's Inn, LLB (Glamorgan)

Chang *Chi Hoong*
Called: July 1995, Lincoln's Inn, LLB (Hons)

Chang *Choon Chuen Kevin*
PVD-2 G-08 Jln Perdana 2/1, Pandan
Perdana, 55300 Kuala Lumpur, Malaysia,
603-9826722. Called: July 1994, Lincoln's
Inn, LLB (Hons)

Chang *Miss Jo-Anne*
Called: Nov 1996, Lincoln's Inn, LLB
(Hons)(Lond), AKC Diploma

Chang *Kin Hui*
Called: Nov 1995, Middle Temple, BA
(Hons)

Chang *Miss Laura Vun Tzin*
Called: Nov 1992, Lincoln's Inn, LLB (Hons)

Changaroth *Anil M*
Lim & Lim, 63 Market Street, [H]13-03/05,
Tat Lee Bank Building, Singapore 048942,
5358626, Fax: 5356736, and Member
Singapore Bar. Called: Nov 1993, Middle
Temple, LLB (Hons)(Bucks)

Chao *Bernard Wee Chun*
J S Yeh & Company, 133 New Bridge Road,
[H]18-03/04/05 Chinatown Point, 065 533
1188, Fax: 065 535 0388, and Member
Singapore. Called: July 1993, Lincoln's Inn,
LLB (Hons)

Chao *Miss Elaine Wen Su*
Drew & Napier, 20 Raffles Place, [H]17-00,
Ocean Towers, (65) 531 2496, Fax: (65)
532 7149, and Member Singapore.
Called: July 1996, Middle Temple, LLB
(Hons)(Lond)

Chapman *Christopher Scott*
Buddle Findlay, P O Box 2694, 1 Willis
Street, Wellington, 00 644 499 4242, Fax:
00 644 499 4141, Barrister & Solicitor, High
Court of New Zealand (1983) Formerly a
solicitor of the Supreme court and Member
New Zealand Bar. Called: July 1980, Inner
Temple, BSc, LLM (Vic, Wellington)

Chapman *James Charles Begg-
Hempton*
P O Box 1234 GT, Grand Cayman, 345 949
9876, Fax: 345 949 9877, and Member
Cayman Islands. Called: Nov 1987, Inner
Temple, LLM, MA (Cantab), BSc, BA

Chapman *Richard Kenneth*
2 Route De La Cascade, 78110 Le Vesinet,
00 33 1 34801234, Fax: 00 33 1 34801263.
Called: Nov 1976, Lincoln's Inn, FCA

Charalambous *Andreas*
Called: Nov 1997, Gray's Inn, LLB (Sheff)

Charitonos *Miss Panayiota Costa*
Called: Nov 1995, Middle Temple, LLB
(Hons)

Chau *Miss Catherine Siew Ping*
40 Luyang Phase 4, Jalan Kijang, 88100
Koya Kinabalu, Sabah, and Member
Advocate, Sabah Bar. Called: Nov 1991,
Gray's Inn, BA (Hons) (Kent), LLM (Lond)

Chau *Kwok Leung Raymond*
Called: Oct 1997, Middle Temple, BSc
(Hons)(Lond)

Chau *Philip*
South China Chambers, 16 Harcourt Road,
Far East Finance Centre, Room 1101, 2528
2378, Fax: 2520 1512, and Member Hong
Kong Bar. Called: May 1995, Inner Temple,
LLB

Chaudhri *Ferhan Munir*
Called: Nov 1995, Lincoln's Inn, LLB
(Hons)(Warw)

Chaudhry *Muhammad Alfaz*
Called: Nov 1997, Lincoln's Inn, BA, LLB
(Punjab), LLM (Lond)

Chay *Miss Kum Yoon*
Block 68, Dakota Crescent [H]12-600, 346
2990. Called: July 1996, Middle Temple, LLB
(Hons)(Leeds)

Che *Shu Fai*
Called: Nov 1992, Lincoln's Inn, LLB (Hons)

Cheah *Peng Kun*
Called: July 1995, Middle Temple, LLB
(Hons) (Wales)

Cheah *Sau Voon*
Messrs Mohd Noor & SY Lee, Room 110, 1st
Floor, Asia Life Building, 45-B Jalan Tun
Sambanthan, 30000 Ipoh, Perak, 05
2543589/9823, Fax: 05 2542611, and
Member Malaysia. Called: Nov 1995, Middle
Temple, LLB (Hons)

Cheah *Soo Chuan*
Called: July 1995, Lincoln's Inn, LLB (Hons)

Cheah *Tien Eu*
Called: July 1996, Lincoln's Inn, LLB
(Hons)(Leeds)

Cheah *Mrs Wai Mun*
and Member Singapore Bar. Called: July
1986, Lincoln's Inn, BA (Kent)

Cheam *Miss Phaik Ling*
Nordin Hamid & Co, 9th Floor, Campbell
Complex, Jalan DanG Wangi, 50100 Kuala
Lumpur, 03-2944677, Fax: 03-2944418, and
Member Malaysia Bar. Called: July 1992,
Middle Temple, LLB (Hons) (Leics)

Chechatwala *Shabbir Ismail*
Called: July 1997, Middle Temple, LLB
(Hons)(Keele)

Chedumbarum Pillay *Neil
Radhakrishna*
Called: July 1997, Middle Temple, LLB
(Hons)(Wales)

Chee *Miss Julie Suk-Yuen*
Called: Nov 1996, Gray's Inn, LLB (LSE), MA
(Lond)

Chee *Yew Chung*
Ling Koh & Partners, 7500a Beach Road, 04-
332/333 The Plaza, Int ++ (65) 2953335,
Fax: Int ++ (65) 2950102, and Member
Singapore Bar. Called: July 1996, Inner
Temple, LLB (Hull)

Cheesman *William James*
Northern Constabulary, Police
Headquarters, Inverness, 01463 720300.
Called: Nov 1990, Lincoln's Inn, LLB (Lond)

Chelliah *Kumarendran*
Called: July 1995, Middle Temple, LLB
(Hons)

Chen *Mian Kuang*
Messrs Raja, Darryl & Loh, 18th Floor,
Wisma Sime Darby, Jalan Raja Laut, 50350,
Kuala Lumpur, (Malaysia) 03 2949999, and
Member Malaysia Bar. Called: July 1995,
Lincoln's Inn, LLB (Hons)

Cheng *Alvin Sun Cheok*
7th Floor, Maybank Chambers, 2 Battery
Road, 3366533, Fax: 3370906, and Member
Singapore Bar. Called: Nov 1993, Lincoln's
Inn, LLB (Hons)

Cheng *Miss Angelina Tan*
Called: July 1996, Middle Temple, LLB
(Hons)(Kent)

Cheng *Francis Ming Bun*
Called: Nov 1994, Middle Temple, LLB
(Hons)

Cheng *Glenn Li Huei*
Called: Nov 1995, Middle Temple, LLB
(Hons)(Wales)

Cheng *Hock Hua*
Called: Oct 1993, Middle Temple, LLB
(Hons)(Lond)

Cheng *Kim Kuan*
Billy Ng Chua & Partners, Advocates &
Solicitors, No 17 Upper Circular Road,
[H]02-01, 5366382, Fax: 5366387, and
Member Singapore. Called: July 1996,
Middle Temple, BA (Hons)(Keele)

Cheng *Miss Kitty Kit Yee*
c/o Legal Service Division, Legislative
Council Secretaria, 8 Jackson Road, Central,
Hong Kong, 8699209, Fax: 8775029, and
Member Hong Kong Bar Australian Capital
Territory Bar. Called: Apr 1991, Gray's Inn,
LLB, PCLL, MIL

Cheng *Miss Mai*
Measat Broadcast Network SDN, BHD, All
Asia Broadcast Centre, Lebuhraya Puchong -
SG Besi, Bukit Jalil, Kuala Lumpur, 603-
5836688, Fax: 603-5836872, and Member
Malaysia Bar. Called: July 1993, Middle
Temple, LLB (Hons)(Lond)

Cheng *Miss Patricia May Li*
M/S C C Choo & Co, Suite D33 & D34, 3rd
Floor, Pekeliling Plaza, Jalan Tun Razak,
50400 Kuala Lumour, 603 4411481, Fax:
603 4411481, and Member Malaysia Bar.
Called: July 1995, Middle Temple, LLB
(Hons)

Cheng *Peter Ong Lip*
and Member Malaysia Bar. Called: Nov 1995,
Inner Temple, LLB (Lond)

Cheng *Tak Ying*
Called: Nov 1996, Middle Temple, LLB
(Hons)

Cheng *Miss Teresa Chin Pei*
Called: July 1994, Middle Temple, LLB
(Hons)(Sheff)

F

Cheng *Miss Wei Lin*
Toh Tan & Partners, Advocates & Solicitors, 79 Robinson Road, [H] 21-03, CPF Building, 225 6446, Fax: 225 2356, and Member Singapore Bar. Called: July 1993, Lincoln's Inn, LLB (Hons, Bris)

Cheng *Miss Wei Min*
Called: Nov 1995, Middle Temple, LLB (Hons)

Cheng *Miss Yen Lin*
and Member Singapore Bar. Called: July 1993, Lincoln's Inn, LLB (Hons, L'pool)

Cheng *Miss Yvonne Wai Sum*
2B Goldson Place, 11 Shouson Hill Road West, Deep Water Bay, and Member Hong Kong Bar. Called: July 1996, Gray's Inn, BA (Oxon)

Cheok *Robin Van Kee*
Abrahams, Davidson & Co, Room 516, 5th Floor, Plaza Athirah, Jalan Kubah Makam Diraja, Bandar Seri Begawan, Brunei Darussala, 673 2 242840, Fax: 673 2 242836, and Member Brunei Darussalam. Called: July 1995, Inner Temple, LLB (Essex)

Cheong *Chin Min*
Called: July 1996, Middle Temple, LLB (Hons)(Lond)

Cheong *Goh Boon Wilfred*
Apt Block 75, Whampoa Drive, [H]10-368, Singapore 320075, Republic of Singapore, 5365334/98277457, Fax: 5365134, and Member Supreme Court of Australian Capital Territory, Supreme Court of Brunei Darrussalam Singapore Bar Supreme Court of Singapore. Called: Nov 1990, Lincoln's Inn, LLb (Lond) (Hons)

Cheong *Miss Seok Wah*
7500 Beach Road, [H] 07-301 The Plaza, 65 2985755, Fax: 65 2988390, and Member Singapore Bar. Called: July 1993, Middle Temple, LLB (Hons, Bris)

Cheong *Miss Whye Mun*
Called: July 1995, Lincoln's Inn, LLB (Hons)

Cheong *Yuk Leung*
and Member Malaysian Bar. Called: July 1996, Lincoln's Inn, LLB (Hons)(Warw)

Chern *Aik Hua*
and Member Singapore Bar. Called: July 1992, Lincoln's Inn, LLB (Hons) (Lond)

Chern *Miss Chyi Ching*
15 Tagore Avenue, Singapore 787650, Republic of Singapore, and Member Singapore Bar. Called: July 1994, Lincoln's Inn, LLB (Hons)

Chesney *George Cecil TD*
Bar Library, Royal Courts of Justice, Chichester Street, Belfast, N Ireland, 0232 241523, Fax: 0232 231850, and Member Northern Ireland Bar. Called: May 1988, Middle Temple, LLB (Hons) Bristol

Cheung *Adonis Kam Wing*
Suite 401, Printing House, 6 Duddell Street, Central, 852 2526 0888, Fax: 852 2869 8320, and Member Hong Kong Bar. Called: July 1994, Inner Temple, LLB

Cheung *K-John*
7208 Queenston Court, Burnaby, B.C. V5A 3M4, (604) 299 8193, Fax: (604) 299 8365, and Member British Columbia Law Society (Canada), Canada, Hong Kong & Victoria (Availraila) Bars Hong Kong Bar. Called: July 1973, Lincoln's Inn, BSc, LLB, JD, Dip Comp Law, Dip Ch Law

Cheung *Miss Kuan Swan*
Called: Nov 1994, Middle Temple, BA in Law & Econ, (Joint Hons)

Cheung *Miss Man Ching*
Called: Nov 1996, Lincoln's Inn, LLB (Hons)

Cheung *Man To Raymond*
Called: Nov 1997, Lincoln's Inn, Postgraduate Diploma, In Law

Cheung *Sir Oswald Victor CBE, LLD*
New Henry House, 10th Floor, 10 Ice House Street, 2524-2156, Fax: 2810-5656, QC Hong Kong. Called: Jan 1950, Lincoln's Inn, MA (Oxon)

Cheung *Phei Chiet*
Called: July 1994, Gray's Inn, BA, LLM

Cheung *Miss Tania Su Li*
Called: July 1995, Lincoln's Inn, LLB (Hons)

Chew *Miss Chin Yean*
Called: Nov 1996, Lincoln's Inn, LLB (Hons)(Kent)

Chew *Eng Ghee*
Messrs P S Ranjan & Co, Advocates & Solicitors, 12th Floor MUI Plaza, Jalan P Ramlee, 50250 Kuala Lumpur, 03 2489200, Fax: 03 2423758, and Member Malaysia Bar. Called: Nov 1992, Lincoln's Inn, LLB (Hons)

Chew *Hew Wearn*
Called: Nov 1997, Lincoln's Inn, LLB (Hons)(Sheff)

Chew *Kei-Jin*
9 Battery Road, Straits Trading Building, [H]15-00, Singapore 049910, 65 5322271, Fax: 65 5352975, and Member Singapore Bar. Called: July 1993, Middle Temple, BA (Cantab), MA (Cantab)

Chew *Kok Liang*
2 Jalan SS 20/22, Damansara Utama, 47400 Petaling Jaya, Selangor, Malaysia, 03 7180095, and Member Malaysia Bar. Called: July 1991, Inner Temple, BSc Econ (Wales), LLM (Leic), Dip in Shariah Law &, Practice (IIU)

Chew *Kok Liang*
Called: May 1994, Middle Temple, LLB (Hons)

Chew *Kok Wye*
Called: Nov 1997, Middle Temple, BA (Hons)(Kent)

Chew *Kwee-San*
Advocate & Solicitor of the Supreme Court in Singapore. Called: July 1994, Middle Temple, LLB (Hons)(Notts)

Chew *Miss Lynette Mei Lin*
4 Shenton Way, [H]15-07 Shing Kwan House, 220 6888, Fax: 223 1736, and Member Singapore. Called: July 1995, Lincoln's Inn, LLB (Hons)

Chew *Miss Mong Fei Vivian*
Called: Nov 1997, Middle Temple, LLB (Hons)(Lond)

Chew *Miss Pitt Har*
and Member Malaysia Bar. Called: July 1992, Lincoln's Inn, LLB (Hons) (Lanc)

Chew *Miss Soo San*
Messrs Tang & Yoges, 8b Jalan Raja Haroun, 43000 Kajang, Selangor Darul Ehsan, 60-3-8376510, Fax: 60-3-8376515, and Member Malaysia Bar. Called: July 1992, Middle Temple, LLB (Hons) (Warw)

Chew *Yee Teck Eric*
Blk 113, Clementi Street 13, [H]06-25, 8728562. Called: July 1997, Gray's Inn, LLB (Sheff), ACIArb

Chhabra *Sunit*
Called: July 1997, Lincoln's Inn, LLB (Hons)(Lond)

Chhabra *Vinit*
Called: July 1996, Middle Temple, LLB (Hons)(Lond)

Chia *Boon Teck*
5 Shenton Way, UIC Building, Level 19, 2200666/3295322 (Direct), Fax: 2219712, and Member Singapore Bar. Called: July 1994, Lincoln's Inn, LLB (Hons)

Chia *Miss Corrinne Ee-Lynn*
Port of Singapore Authority, 460 Alexandra Road, PSA Building, (65) 279 4049, Fax: (65) 279 5811, and Member Singapore. Called: Nov 1994, Lincoln's Inn, LLB (Hons)(Lond)

Chia *Miss En-Lin*
151 Cavenagh Road, [H]09-159, 0065 7340697/7384245. Called: Nov 1996, Gray's Inn, LLB (Nott'm)

Chia *Miss Gillian Hsu-Lien*
Called: July 1997, Gray's Inn, LLB (Bris)

Chia *Miss Jeanette Shau Ken*
Called: July 1996, Lincoln's Inn, LLB (Hons)(Leeds)

Chia *Peng Chuang*
Block 7, Teck Whye Avenue [H]04-102, Singapore 680007, 7647753, and Member Singapore Bar. Called: Nov 1993, Middle Temple, LLB (Hons)(Lond), BSc (Hons), ARICS

Chia *Soo Michael*
Called: July 1997, Middle Temple, LLB (Hons)

Chia *Yau Hoong*
Called: July 1994, Lincoln's Inn, LLB (Hons)

Chiah *Miss Yoke Li*
Called: July 1997, Lincoln's Inn, LLB (Hons)(Wales)

Chiang *Pak Chien*
17 Goldhill Drive, (65) 3520821, and Member Singapore. Called: Nov 1995, Middle Temple, LLB (Hons)

Chiang *Wee Sean*
Called: July 1995, Middle Temple, LLB (Hons)

Chiang *Miss Wen-Shan*
and Member Singapore Bar. Called: July 1990, Gray's Inn, LLB (Leic)

Chibwana *Enock Daniel Alfred*
Ministry of Justice, P/B 333, Lilongwe 3, 782411. Called: Feb 1994, Gray's Inn, LLB, LLM

Chien *Hoe Yong*
Lippo Securities Ltd, 2302 Lippo Tower, Lippo Centre, 89 Queensway, Central, Hong Kong, 25337434/28457711, Fax: 25337435. Called: Nov 1988, Middle Temple, LLB (Lanc), ACA, HKSA

Chieng *Miss Stephanie Lun Tying*
Awang Lai & Co Advocates, Lots 432 & 434, 2nd Floor, Jalan Bendahara, 98000 Miri, Sarawak, Malaysia, 085-416688, Fax: 085-416684, and Member Sarawak Bar. Called: July 1995, Inner Temple, LLB (Kent)

Chiew *Ean Vooi*
Called: July 1997, Middle Temple, LLB (Hons)(Leeds)

Chijner *David*
Called: Oct 1993, Inner Temple, Diplome de Droit, Francais (Paris), BA (Kent), LLM (European, University Institut)

Chin *Miss Beatrice Choon Hwa*
Chooi & Co, Penthouse, Bangunan Ming, Jalan Bukit Nanas, 50250 Kuala Lumpur, Malaysia, 03-2327344, Fax: 03-2382915/03-2380708, and Member Malaysia Bar. Called: July 1994, Lincoln's Inn, LLB (Hons)

Chin *Chee Chien*
No 20 Jalan SS 21/32, Damansara Utama, 47400 Petaling Jaya, Selangor Darul Ehsan, 603-716-9285, Fax: 603-716-9287, and Member Malaysian Bar. Called: Nov 1993, Gray's Inn, LLB

Chin *Miss Emily Mei Fong*
and Member Singapore Bar. Called: July 1990, Gray's Inn, LLB,ICSA.GRAD

Chin *Hein Choong*
Called: July 1995, Lincoln's Inn, LLB (Hons)

Chin *Miss Jia Huey*
7-4 Lorong Teratai 4, Off Jalan Haji Jaib, 84000 Muar, Johor, Malaysia, 06 921367, Fax: 03 2301768, and Member Malaysia Bar. Called: July 1992, Lincoln's Inn, LLB (Hons), LLM

Chin *Julian Ye-Fung*
Asia Pulp & Paper Co Ltd, 1 Maritime Square, [H]10-01 (Lobby 13), World Trade Centre, (65) 2729288, Fax: (65) 3749388, and Member Singapore Bar. Called: July 1992, Middle Temple, LLB (Hons) (Leics)

Chin *Keith Hsiun*
C/O Yong Wong & Chin Advocates, 1st Floor, Bangunan Chin Fook, Lot 382 South Yu Seng Road, P O Box 736 98007 Miri, Sarawak, 085 414348, Fax: 085 415602, and Member Brunei Darrusalam (High Court of Brunei) Malaya (Kuala Lumpur Bar). Called: July 1995, Lincoln's Inn, LLB (Hons) (Sheff)

Chin *Miss Mye-Ling*
and Member High Court of Malaya. Called: Nov 1994, Middle Temple, LLB

Chin *Miss Oi Jean*
123 Jalan SS22/37, Damansara Jaya, 47400 Petaling Jaya, Selangor, (60)(3) 7189 232. Called: Nov 1995, Lincoln's Inn, LLB (Hons), LLM

Chin *Miss Pek Khen*
Called: July 1994, Middle Temple, LLB (Hons)(Lond)

Chin *Miss Pheik Lin Elaine*
Called: Nov 1997, Lincoln's Inn, LLB (Hons)

Chin *Miss Pik Khiun*
M/S Kean Chye & Sivalingam, 42 Jalan Medan Ipoh 6, Bandar Baru Medan Ipoh, 31400 Ipoh, Perak, 05-545 6010, Fax: 05-545 6359, and Member High Court of Malaya. Called: July 1995, Lincoln's Inn, LLB (Hons)

Chin *Miss Tze Jin*
Called: July 1996, Lincoln's Inn, LLB (Hons) (Kent)

Chin *Tze Jone*
Called: July 1995, Middle Temple, LLB (Hons)

Chin *Yuen Fong*
Called: Nov 1995, Middle Temple, BA (Hons)(Keele)

Chin *Miss Yvonne Mei Oy*
Called: Nov 1989, Lincoln's Inn, LLB, LLM (Lond)

Ching *Miss Fiona Pui Yeng*
and Member Singapore. Called: July 1994, Middle Temple, LLB (Hons)(Notts)

Ching *Kim Chuah*
Called: Nov 1994, Middle Temple, LLB (Hons)

Ching *Leonard Tchi Pang*
Called: Nov 1994, Middle Temple, LLB (Hons)

Chiok *Beng Piow*
724 Bedok Reservoir Road, [H]06-5232 Singapore 470724, 065 449 3121, and Member Singapore Bar. Called: July 1993, Middle Temple, LLB (Hons)

Chionh *Miss Mavis Sze-Chyi*
Called: July 1993, Middle Temple, BA (Hons)

Chisholm *Miss Marcela*
Glasgow Caledonian University, Dept of Law and Public Admin, Cowcaddens Road, Glasgow G4 OBA, 041 331 3427, Fax: 041 331 3798. Called: July 1991, Gray's Inn, JUDr (Prague), LLM (Manch)

Chitthu *Arut*
Called: July 1995, Middle Temple, LLB (Hons)

Chiu *Hsu-Hwee*
and Member Singapore. Called: July 1995, Middle Temple, LLB (Hons) (Hull)

Chiu *Kwok Kit*
C/O Hong Kong Inland Revenue, Appeals Section, 36/F Wanchai Tower 3, 5 Gloucester Road, Hong Kong, 852 2594 5038, Fax: 852 2877 1131. Called: Nov 1990, Lincoln's Inn, LLB (Lond), LLM, (Lond), LLB (Peking), MCom, FCCA, AHKSA, CPA (Aust), Graduate, Diploma in Taxation

Chiu *Michael Kai Ting*
Called: Nov 1996, Middle Temple, LLB (Hons), MA (Hull)

Chiu *Paul Hung Shun*
Room 1931, Swire House, 11 Chater Road, Central, Hong Kong, (852) 2522 9168, Fax: (852) 2845 2072, Barrister & Solicitor Supreme Court and High Court of Australian Capital Territory and Barrister of Supreme Court of Hong Kong and Member Australia Bar Hong Kong Bar. Called: Nov 1971, Middle Temple

Chiu *Ms Yong Yong*
Called: July 1997, Lincoln's Inn, LLB (Hons)(Lond)

Chng *Miss Angeline Kim-Ann*
3 Astrid Hill, Singapore 269926, 65-4697011, Fax: 65-4697012. Called: July 1995, Middle Temple, LLB (Hons)

Cho *Chi-kong*
10/F, 2 Murray Road, Central, Hong Kong, 28264397, Fax: 25626912, Barrister Supreme Court of Hong Kong and Member Canberra, Australia. Called: Nov 1989, Lincoln's Inn, LLB (Lond)

Choa *Brendon Sn-Yien*
133 New Bridge Road, China Point [H]15-09, 5382687, Fax: 5380287, Advocate & Solicitor Supreme Court of Singapore and Member Singapore. Called: July 1991, Inner Temple, BA (Sussex)

Choa *Miss Deborah Deb-Bie*
Messrs Lee Choon Wan & Co, No 12, Lorong Dungun, Damansara Heights, 50490 Kuala Lumpur, 03 2530078, Fax: 03 2541750, and Member Malaysian Bar. Called: July 1994, Lincoln's Inn, LLB (Hons)

Choh *Irving Thian Chee*
No 9 Jalan Rengkam, Singapore 537566, 65 3361878, Fax: 65 2242270, and Member Singapore Bar. Called: July 1993, Middle Temple, LLB (Hons)(Bucks)

Choi *Sheung Kong*
Called: Nov 1997, Lincoln's Inn, LLB (Hons)(Lond)

Chok *Miss Ketty Li Ket*
Called: July 1997, Middle Temple, LLB (Hons)(Wales)

Chong *Miss Ann Ching*
Called: July 1997, Middle Temple, LLB (Hons)(Leics)

Chong *Avery Soon Yong*
Called: July 1996, Inner Temple, LLB (Warwick)

Chong *Miss Boon Chin*
Called: July 1997, Lincoln's Inn, LLB (Hons)(Leics)

Chong *Miss Chee Er*
20 Margoliouth Road, (+65) 732 2603, Fax:
(+65) 261 7075. Called: Nov 1994, Middle
Temple, LLB (Hons) (Warw), MBA

Chong *Chi On*
Called: Nov 1997, Lincoln's Inn, LLB (Hons)

Chong *Christopher Fook Choy*
Called: July 1993, Lincoln's Inn, LLB (Hons, Bris)

Chong *Miss Fiona Yeo-Peen*
Called: July 1993, Lincoln's Inn, LLB (Hons)

Chong *Gerald Siak Yen*
20 Malacca Street [H]05-00, Malacca Centre,
Singapore 048979, (65) 536 5369, Fax: (65)
536 5811, and Member Singapore Bar.
Called: Nov 1994, Middle Temple, BA (Joint Hons)

Chong *Miss Jia Ling*
Called: July 1996, Lincoln's Inn, LLB (Hons)

Chong *Kah Heng*
Called: July 1996, Gray's Inn, LLB (Leicester)

Chong *Karl Shang Chin*
Called: July 1994, Middle Temple, LLB (Hons)

Chong *Kenneth Yun Kien*
c/o Chin Lau Wong & Foo, A818, 8th Floor,
Wisma Merdeka, 88000 Kota Kinablau,
Sabah, 088 238111, Fax: 088 238222, and
Member Sabah. Called: July 1993, Lincoln's
Inn, LLB (Hons, Leeds)

Chong *Kuok Peng*
Called: July 1997, Lincoln's Inn, LLB
(Hons)(Exon)

Chong *Miss Mae Shan*
35 Jelutong Villas, Lorong Jelutong Kanan,
Damansara Heights, 50490 Kuala Lumpur,
254 8111. Called: July 1996, Middle Temple,
BA (Hons)(Cantab)

Chong *Mark Choong Weng*
Called: July 1996, Lincoln's Inn, LLB
(Hons)(Lond)

Chong *Miss May Yean*
Called: July 1996, Lincoln's Inn, LLB
(Hons)(Wales)

Chong *Michael Wai Yen*
Called: Mar 1998, Middle Temple, LLB
(Hons)(Keele)

Chong *Miss Su Ping Cecilia*
Called: July 1997, Middle Temple, LLB
(Hons)(Hull)

Chong *Victor Thien Loi*
Called: July 1995, Middle Temple, BA
(Hons) (Keele)

Choo *Miss Audrey Pao Lin*
Called: Nov 1997, Lincoln's Inn, LLB
(Nott'm)

Choo *Miss Josephine Poh Hua*
Called: Nov 1996, Middle Temple, LLB
(Hons)(Lond)

Choo *Raymond Choon Sheng*
and Member Singapore. Called: Nov 1995,
Middle Temple, LLB (Hons)(Hull), LLM
(King's College, Lond)

Choo *Miss Yuin*
Called: July 1996, Lincoln's Inn, LLB
(Hons)(Leeds)

Choong *Allen Ching Yet*
Called: Nov 1997, Lincoln's Inn, LLB
(Hons)(Lond)

Choong *Miss Kartina Abdullah*
Called: July 1995, Lincoln's Inn, LLB (Hons)

Chou *Sean Yu*
Messrs Wong Partnership, 80 Raffles Place,
[H]58-01, UOB Plaza 1, Singapore 0106, 532
7488, Fax: (65) 532 5722, and Member
Singapore Bar. Called: July 1993, Middle
Temple, LLB (Hons, Bris)

Chow *Miss Ee-Chin*
Fong & Ng Solicitors, 7th Floor, China
Building, 29 Queen's Road Central, Central,
852 28484848, Fax: 852 28452995, and
Member Malaysia Bar. Called: July 1994,
Gray's Inn, LLB (Reading)

Chow *Miss Fung Kwan*
Called: Oct 1997, Middle Temple, BSc
(Hong Kong), CPE (Hong Kong)

Chow *Kenneth Charn Ki*
11/F Flat G, Skyline Mansion, 51 Conduit
Road, Hong Kong, 25212555, Fax:
28691527, Formerly Solicitor. Called: May
1988, Middle Temple, LLB (Hons), LLM
(London)

Chow *Kenneth Kok Wee*
Called: July 1995, Lincoln's Inn, LLB (Hons)

Chow *Kenny Yin Wo*
Flat 12h, Braemar Terrace, 1 Pak Fuk Road,
28950025, Fax: 28950025, and Member
Supreme Court of the Australia Capital
Territory. Called: July 1990, Gray's Inn, LLB
(Lond)

Chow *Miss Lai Yin*
Called: July 1994, Lincoln's Inn, LLB (Hons)

Chow *Miss Letty Yu Shu*
and Member Hong Kong Bar. Called: Nov
1985, Lincoln's Inn, LLB

Chow *Miss Min Wei*
Called: July 1995, Middle Temple, LLB
(Hons) (Hull)

Chow *Miss Nona Swee Li*
Called: Nov 1997, Lincoln's Inn, LLB
(Hons)(Wales)

Chow *Wai Lun*
Called: Nov 1997, Gray's Inn, BSc
(Eng)(Hong Kong), Diplome d'ingenieur,
(Ecole Nationale des, Treavaux Publics)

Chowdhury *Khaled Hamid*
Asfia House, Road 36, House 13, Ghulshan,
Dhaka 1212, 880 2 885872/017525542, Fax:
880 2 885736, and Member Dhaka,
Bangladesh. Called: July 1995, Lincoln's Inn,
LLB (Hons), MA (Legal Studies), LLM (Int'l
Bus Law), (KCL)

Chowdhury *Md Moinal Islam*
and Member Bangladesh Bar. Called: Nov
1994, Lincoln's Inn, BA (Hons), MA, LLB
(Dhaka), LLB (Hons)

Choy *Montague Wing Kin*
Called: July 1997, Lincoln's Inn, LLB
(Hons)(L'pool)

Christofides *Miss Etta*
Called: Feb 1993, Gray's Inn, LLB (Anglia),
LLM

Chrysanthou *Nicos*
4 Demosthenes Str, P.O.Box 1762, 1513
Nicosia, (3572) 447443, Fax: (3572)
472075, and Member Cyprus. Called: Nov
1996, Inner Temple, LLB (Lond), LLM
(So'ton)

Chrysostomides *Mrs Eleni*
Dr K Chrysostomides & Co, PO Box 2119, 1
Lambousa Street, Nicosia, 448 278, Fax: 02
451391. Called: Nov 1973, Gray's Inn, LLB

Chu *Chung Keung*
Called: Nov 1996, Middle Temple, LLB
(Hons)

Chu *Miss Yuen Yee*
Called: July 1995, Middle Temple, LLB
(Hons)

Chu *Miss Yvonne Siok Teang*
Suite 2, Montagu Pavilion, 10 Queensway,
Gibraltar, 45467/40824, Fax: 45467/40931,
and Member Gibraltar Bar. Called: Nov
1993, Gray's Inn, LLB (Manch)

Chua *Boon Thien*
Called: July 1994, Lincoln's Inn, LLB (Hons)

Chua *Miss Cynthia Cher Lan*
and Member Singapore Bar. Called: July
1995, Middle Temple, LLB (Hons)

Chua *Miss Geok Hong*
Called: Nov 1995, Middle Temple, LLB
(Hons)

Chua *Miss Grace Hwee Bin*
and Member Malaysia Bar. Called: Nov 1992,
Lincoln's Inn, LLB (Hons)(Wales)

Chua *Miss Huey Sian*
M/S Chooi & Company, Penthouse, Ming
Building PH-O1, Jalan Bukit Nanas, 50200
Kuala Lumpur, 03 2327344, and Member
Malaysia. Called: July 1996, Lincoln's Inn,
LLB (Hons)(Sheff)

Chua *Miss Hui Peng*
and Member Malaysian Bar. Called: July
1995, Middle Temple, LLB (Hons)

Chua *Kok Wan*
Called: July 1995, Middle Temple, B.Ec, LLB

Chua *Miss Lay Kuang*
Called: Nov 1994, Middle Temple, B.Pharm
(Hons)

Chua *Miss Lik Teng*
Yeo-Leong & Peh, 20 McCallum Street, 12-
03, Asia Chambers, Singapore, 65 2238168,
Fax: 65 2207888, Advocate & Solicitor of
the Supreme Court of Singapore.
Called: July 1992, Middle Temple, LLB
(Hons) LSe

Chua *Lincoln*
579 L Lorong Utama 6, Air Keroh Heights,
75450 Malacca, West Malaysia, 06 326860,
and Member Malaysia Bar. Called: July 1992,
Inner Temple, LLB

Chua *Miss Lucianna Mei Ling*
2 Ridgewood Close, [H]05-02, Himiko Court, and Member Singapore. Called: July 1996, Middle Temple, LLB (Hons)(Sheff)

Chua *Miss Siew Gaik*
Called: July 1996, Lincoln's Inn, BA (Hons)

Chua *Miss Soo Fon*
Called: July 1995, Lincoln's Inn, LLB (Hons)

Chua *Miss Suzanie May-Li*
501-1155 Mainland Street, Vancouver V6B 5P2, (604) 6828231, Fax: (604) 6828231, International Bar Association, Chartered Accountant (ICAEW) Honorary Legal Scholar (Centre for Int'l Legal Studies) and Member Singapore Bar. Called: July 1988, Gray's Inn, LLB Hons (Bris)

Chua *Tze Wei*
Called: July 1990, Gray's Inn, LLB(Bris), BCL (Oxon)

Chua *Miss Yak Hoon*
15 N Kang Choo Bin Road, Singapore 548285. Called: July 1991, Middle Temple, LLB (Hons) (Lond)

Chuah *Miss Hooi Bien*
Called: July 1997, Middle Temple, LLB (Hons)(Leics)

Chuah *Jern Ern*
Shearn Delamore & Co, 7th Floor, Wisma Hamzah, Kwong-Hing, 2 Leboh Ampang, 50100 Kuala Lumpur, 2300644 (0603), Fax: 2386525, and Member Malaysia Bar. Called: July 1993, Lincoln's Inn, LLB (Hons, N'ham)

Chuah *Miss Sheena Sze Ching*
Called: July 1997, Middle Temple, LLB (Hons)

Chuah *Miss Yean Ping*
Messrs Shook Lin & Bok, Advocates & Solicitors, 20th Floor, Arab - Malaysian, Building, 55 Jalan Raja Chulan, 50200 Kuala Lumpur, 03 2011788, Fax: 03 2011778/779/ 775, and Member Malaysia. Called: July 1996, Lincoln's Inn, LLB (Hons)(Leics)

Chuang *Miss Effie Twan Phey*
Called: Nov 1997, Lincoln's Inn, LLB (Hons)(Leeds)

Chuang *Keng Chiew*
2 Battery Road, Maybank Chambers, 7th Floor, 3366533, Fax: 3370906. Called: July 1996, Middle Temple, LLB (Hons)(Lond)

Chui *Miss Yee Mei Ivy*
Called: July 1996, Middle Temple, LLB (Hons)(Wales)

Chularojmontri *Prathan*
Called: July 1995, Gray's Inn, LLB (Wales)

Chun *Lim Whei*
Called: Nov 1997, Inner Temple, LLB (Lond)

Chung *Kee Ying*
and Member Hong Kong Bar Supreme Court of the Australian Capital Territory. Called: Nov 1990, Gray's Inn, LLB (Lond)

Chung *Miss Rebecca Wan-Yi*
64 Jalan Lembah Thomson, 4544266, Fax: 4544766, and Member Singapore Bar. Called: Nov 1992, Middle Temple, LLB (Hons, Hull)

Chung *Yiu Ming*
26d South Bay Towers, 59 South Bay Road, (852) 25769090, and Member Hong Kong Bar. Called: July 1991, Lincoln's Inn, BSc (Hons), Dip Law (City Uni), ACIArb, FRICS, FHKIS

Chwee *Han Sin*
Called: Nov 1995, Middle Temple, LLB (Hons)

Clark *Dr Margaret Lynda*
Advocates Library, Parliament Square, Edinburgh, Scotland, 031 226 2881, QC Scotland and Member Scottish Bar. Called: July 1988, Inner Temple, PhD (Edinburgh), LLB (St Andrews)

Clarke *Andrew Terence*
Mobil Power Inc., [H] 10-00 Winsland House, 3 Killiney Road, 65 739 5574, Fax: 65 739 5640. Called: July 1982, Middle Temple, MA (Cantab)

Clarke *Dominic Tobias*
40 King Street West, Suite 2100, Toronto M5H 3C2, (416) 869 5300, Fax: (416) 360 8877, and Member Ontario Bar. Called: July 1988, Middle Temple, MA, LLM (Cantab)

Clarke *Mrs Maria Anne*
11a Craigleith Drive, Edinburgh EH4 3HR, and Member Scottish Bar. Called: Apr 1991, Inner Temple, LLB (Glasgow), BA (Hons) Open

Clarke *Miss Petra Cecilia*
and Member Trinidad & Tobago Bar. Called: Nov 1989, Middle Temple, BA, Dip Int. Law

Cleare *Miss Camille Amanda*
Called: Nov 1997, Gray's Inn, LLB (Kent)

Clifford *Nigel Robert Leslie*
Admitted as Attorney-at-Law Cayman Islands. Called: July 1973, Middle Temple, LLB (Hons)

Coakley *Miss Jamaine*
Called: July 1994, Lincoln's Inn, LLB (Hons, Manch)

Coast-Powell *Mrs Susan Mary*
Cater Allen Trust Co Ltd, 01534 828000. Called: Nov 1994, Middle Temple, LLB (Hons), TEP

Codrai *Christian Augustus*
Legal Services, I.F.A.D. of the United Nations, 107 Via Del Serafico, 00142 Roma, (396) 5459 2457, Fax: (396) 504-3463. Called: Nov 1979, Inner Temple, LLB,LLM

Coelho *Oswaldo Gerardo*
Rua Garrett 21, PO Box 91, 8600 Lagos, 82 762408, Fax: 82 767258, and Member Portugal. Called: Nov 1979, Lincoln's Inn, MA (Hons) (Bombay), Licentiate in Law, (Lisbon)

Coffey *Paul Michael Matthew*
Law Library, Four Courts, Dublin, Republic of Ireland, 720622, Fax: 722254, King's Inns (Dublin) and Member Southern Ireland Bar. Called: Feb 1988, Middle Temple, BCL (Ireland), LLM (Dublin

Coghlan *Christopher David Francis*
5/F 10 Queen's Road, Central, (852) 2525 0221, Fax: (852) 2845 2441, and Member Hong Kong Bar. Called: Nov 1972, Inner Temple, BCL

Cohen *Ms Susan Elizabeth*
Polygram Pty Ltd, 3 Munn Reserve, Millers Point, Sydney 2000, N.S.W. Australia, (02) 9207 0519, Fax: (02) 9241 1497. Called: July 1981, Gray's Inn, LLB (B'ham),MA

Colclough *Mrs Leslie Ann*
Lobosky & Lobosky, P O Box N-7123, Nassau, (242) 323 1317, Fax: (242) 323 1318, and Member Bahamas Bar. Called: Nov 1996, Lincoln's Inn, LLB (Hons)(Bucks)

Colebrook *Miss Ashlar Shikell*
and Member Bahamas Bar, Sept 1996. Called: July 1996, Lincoln's Inn, BBA (Miami), MA (Bris)

Collie *Ellison Isaac*
Michael A Dean & Co, 94 Dowdeswell Street, P O Box N7521, Nassau, 809 322 3997, Fax: 809 325 3345, Counsel and Attorney-at-Law and Member Bahamas Bar Association. Called: July 1996, Lincoln's Inn, CPE (City)

Collins *Ruaidhri Jolyon McCracken*
Called: Oct 1994, Middle Temple, BA (Hons)(Cantab), LLM (Lond)

Collins *Miss Sara Jane*
W S Walker & Co, P O Box 26SGT, Grand Cayman, 1-809-949-0100, Fax: 1-809-949-7886, and Member Cayman Islands Bar. Called: July 1995, Lincoln's Inn, LLB (Hons)

Collu *Miss Melissa*
Called: Oct 1997, Middle Temple, BA (Hons)(Notts), CPE (Lond)

Colombo *Kevin Joseph*
Called: Mar 1996, Gray's Inn, LLB

Colquitt *Robert Ian*
Dickinson Cruickshank & Co, Advocates, 33-37 Athol Street, Douglas, Isle of Man IM1 1LB, 01624 673391, Fax: 01624 620992. Called: July 1995, Inner Temple, LLB

Commissiong *Miss Mira Elisabet*
(809) 457 1293, Fax: (809) 456 2696. Called: July 1997, Lincoln's Inn, LLB (Hons)(City)

Compton *Petrus*
Attorney General's Chambers, Erdiston Place, Mandel Street, Castries, St Lucia, 758 45 23622/23772, Fax: 758 45 36315, Eastern Caribbean Supreme Court. Called: July 1992, Gray's Inn, BA, LLB, LLM (Lond)

Concisom *Miss Audry*
Concisom & Co, 2 Jalan Seenivasagam, 30450 Ipoh, Perak, and Member Malaysia Bar. Called: Nov 1996, Middle Temple, LLB (Hons)

Conlon *Benjamin Vincenzo Rosario*
Conlon Law Offices, P.O.Box 937, Keene Road, Elizabethtown, New York 12932-0937, 00 1 (518) 873 6887, Fax: 00 1 (518) 873 6897, US. Supreme Court, US. Court of Appeals for 2nd, 3rd and 9th Circuits, US. District Courts for Northern, Southern, Eastern and Western Districts of New York. US. District Court of Vermont, US. Tax Court, US Court of International Trade and Member New. Called: Nov 1975, Gray's Inn, LLB (Hons)

Conlon *Mrs Loraine*
Conlon Law Offices, Keene Road, Elizabethtown, New York 12932-0937, (518) 873 6887, Fax: (518) 873 6897, Essex County Bar Assoc 1 Crown Office Row, 2nd Floor, Temple, London, EC4Y 7HH. Called: Nov 1977, Gray's Inn

Connolly *Oliver Joseph*
and Member Ireland. Called: July 1997, Middle Temple, LLB (Hons)(Dublin)

Constantinidou *Ms Eleni Adoni*
P.O.Box 897, Larnaca, Cyprus, 04-620400, Fax: 04-620860, and Member Cyprus Bar. Called: July 1992, Lincoln's Inn, LLB (Hons) (Leics)

Constantinou *Miss Maria*
Called: Feb 1994, Lincoln's Inn, LLB (Hons)

Conti *John Patrick*
Conti, 17 Circular Road, Douglas, Isle of Man IM1 1AF, 01624 670003, Fax: 01624 612281, Member International Bar Association and Member Isle of Man Bar. Called: Nov 1988, Inner Temple, LLB (Wales)

Coomaraswamy *Punch*
Judge's Chambers, Supreme Court. Called: Feb 1956, Lincoln's Inn, LLB (Nottm)

Coope *Simon Paul*
547 Pacific Street, Brooklyn, NY 11217, (718) 875 1355, and Member New York State Bar. Called: Oct 1991, Middle Temple, LLB Hons

Coriat *Christopher Archibald*
Coriats Trustees, Bristol House, PO Box 171, Providenciales, Turks & Caicos Islands, +1 649 946 4800, Fax: +1 649 946 4850, Attorney at Law, Turks & Caicos Islands and Member Turks & Caicos Islands. Called: July 1977, Lincoln's Inn, TEP

Corke *Donald Stevenson*
Advocates Library, Parliament House, Edinburgh EH1 1RF, 0131 226 5071, Fax: 0131 225 3642, and Member Scottish Bar. Called: July 1995, Middle Temple, BA (Cape Town), LLB (Witwatersrand)

Coroneos *Miss Georgina*
B Logothetidis 23, Athens 115-24, 6928040, Fax: 6928040. Called: Oct 1996, Middle Temple, BA (Hons) (Keele)

Corrigan *Anthony John QC*
15/F Printing House, 6 Duddell Street, Central, 25212 616, Fax: 28450260. Called: July 1962, Gray's Inn, LLB

Cort *Dr Leon Errol*
Chambers, 44 Church Street, PO Box 260, St John's, Antigua, 809 462 5232, Fax: 809 462 5234, Eastern Caribbean. Called: Nov 1990, Middle Temple, B Comm, MA, PhD (Canada), MA (Oxon)

Cort *Miss Sharon May*
Called: Nov 1997, Middle Temple, LLB (Hons)

Cosma *Miss Maria*
Called: Oct 1994, Middle Temple, LLB (Hons)(Reading)

Cotsen *Stuart Hugh*
15/F Printing House, 6 Duddell Street, Central, Hong Kong, 25212616, Fax: 28450260, Formerly Solicitor of the Supreme Court of England & Wales and Member Australia Bar Hong Kong Bar Victoria Bar New South Wales Bar. Called: Apr 1986, Middle Temple

Coucouni *Miss Dimitria*
Called: Mar 1996, Lincoln's Inn, LLB (Hons)(Leics)

Course *Ms Lindy*
and Member Hong Kong Bar. Called: July 1994, Middle Temple, BA (Hons)(Lanc), CPE (Manc)

Coutts *Thomas Gordon QC*
6 Heriot Row, Edinburgh, Scotland EH3 6HU, 0131 556 3042, Fax: 0131 556 3042, A Scottish Advocate and Member Scottish Bar. Called: July 1995, Lincoln's Inn, MA, LLB, FCI(Arb)

Cox *Miss Charise Felicia Vanessa*
Higgs & Johnson Chambers, 83 Sandringham House, Shirley Street, Nassau, Bahamas, 1-809-32-28571-9, Fax: 1-809-32-87727, and Member Bahamas Bar. Called: July 1991, Lincoln's Inn, BA (Hons)(Cant), LLM (Lond)

Cox *David Rupert Fenwick*
Called: July 1970, Middle Temple, MA

Cox *Ms Iona Maxine*
Called: Nov 1997, Lincoln's Inn, LLB (Hons)

Crabbe *The Hon Mr Justice Vincent Cyril Richard Arthur C CV*
Faculty of Law, University of The West Indies, Cave Hill Campus, Bridgetown, (246) 417 4236, Fax: (246) 424 1788. Called: Feb 1955, Inner Temple, LLD

Crawford *Marcel Christopher*
Called: June 1964, Lincoln's Inn

Crean *Ms Catherine*
Law Library, P.O. Box 2424, Four Courts, Dublin 7, 0103531 720 622, Fax: 0103531 722 254, and Member Irish Bar. Called: May 1982, Middle Temple, BA, HDE, LLB, ALCM

Crichlow *Carl Ulrick*
Middle Chambers, Cr Crichlow's Alley & Maidens, Lane, Roebuck Street, Bridgetown, Barbados W I, 246 427 8191, Fax: 246 427 8213, and Member Barbados Bar Association,Barbados,West Indies. Called: July 1987, Middle Temple, BSc (Boston), LLB, (Lond), FCCA, LLM (Lond)

Crossley *Anthony Dominic*
Reinsurance Australia Corp Ltd, Level 41, Tower Building, Australia Square, 264 George Street, Sydney 2000, New South Wales, Australia, 9247 6565, Fax: 9252 1614. Called: Nov 1977, Lincoln's Inn, LLB (Lond), ACA

Crowley *Dale Michael*
Maples & Calder, P O Box 309, Cayman Islands, (345) 949 8066, Fax: (345) 949 8080, and Member Attorney-at-Law, Cayman Islands. Called: July 1996, Middle Temple, LLB (Hons)(L'pool)

Cubbon *John Edward*
Called: Oct 1993, Middle Temple, BA (Hons)(Oxon), MSc, B Phil

Cubitt Sowden *Patrick Flinn*
44 The Esplanade, St Helier, Jersey JE2 3QB, 01534 871415, Fax: 01534 872699, Advocate of Royal Court of Jersey Notary Public and Member Jersey Bar. Called: Nov 1960, Middle Temple

Cucchi *Frederick*
Via F. Civinini, 111, 00197 Rome, 39-6, 8085460, Fax: 39-6-8072793. Called: Nov 1978, Middle Temple, MA (Oxon)

Culbard *Ms Karen Cecilia*
Inn Chambers, "Inga Lodge", Pinfold Street, Bridgetown, Barbados, (246) 427-7192, Fax: (246) 429-2771, and Member Barbados Bar. Called: Nov 1994, Inner Temple, LLB (W.Indies), LLM (Lond), CPE (Lond)

Cully *Ms Louise Dorothy*
Called: Nov 1994, Inner Temple, LLB (Belfast)

Cumberbatch *Miss Sherrylyn Kathlean*
Called: July 1997, Middle Temple, LLB (Hons)

Cushen *Mrs Helen Margaret*
Crills, 44 Esplanade, St Helier, Jersey JE4 8PZ, (0) 534 611055, Fax: (0) 534 611066, and Member Jersey Bar. Called: Nov 1993, Middle Temple, BA (Hons)(Lond), MA (Kent), CPE (City)

Cushen *Peter Roy*
Crills, P.O. Box No 72, 44 Esplanade, St Helier, Jersey JE4 8PN, 01534 611055, Fax: 01534 611066, Admitted to the Jersey Bar (Oct 1984) and Member Jersey Bar. Called: July 1981, Inner Temple, LLB (Soton)

D'Cruz *Rodney Gerard*
Called: July 1994, Lincoln's Inn, LLB (Hons)

Da Costa *Christopher Luis Athaide*
43 Jalan Jambu Ayer, Singapore 2158, 00 65 4692170, and Member Singapore Bar. Called: July 1993, Inner Temple, LLB

Daly *The Hon Francis Lenton*
Judges Chambers District Court, Cairns, Queensland, 070 528904, Fax: 070 515173. Called: June 1961, Gray's Inn, LLB (Lond)

Dang *Miss Lee Boon*
Called: July 1997, Middle Temple, LLB (Hons)

Dangerfield *Jeremy George Bubb*
3P-300 Roslyn Road, Winnipeg, Manituba R3L0H4, (204) 453-8340, QC Canada and Member Manituba Bar. Called: Nov 1983, Gray's Inn, BSc,LLM (Manitoba)

Danker *Miss Geralyn Germaine*
34 Jalan Chelagi, 542 6684. Called: July 1995, Middle Temple, LLB (Hons)

Danou *Miss Georgia*
The Cyprus Popular Bank Ltd, Popular Bank Building, 154 Limassol Avenue, P O Box 2032 CY-1598, Nicosia, 02 81 1187, Fax: 02 81 1492, and Member Cyprus Bar. Called: Feb 1991, Lincoln's Inn, LLB (Leic), LLM (Lond)

Darley *Miss Gillian Elizabeth Anne*
O'Connor & Company, European Lawyers, rue de Spa 30, 1000 Brussels, (0032) 2 285 46 85, Fax: (0032) 2 285 46 90. Called: July 1981, Inner Temple, LLB (Lond), AKC

Darr *Miss Amber*
Called: July 1997, Lincoln's Inn, BA (Pennsylvania), CPE

Darville *Miss Camille Diane*
Called: July 1995, Gray's Inn, BA (Soc)(Ontario), LLB (Leeds)

Darwyne *Michael Thurston*
Overseas Company Registration, Agents Ltd, Companies House, Tower Street, Ramsey, 01624 816 800, Fax: 01624 816 300, and Member Hong Kong Bar Fiji Bar New York Bar. Called: July 1969, Inner Temple, MA, BCL (Oxon), LLM (Harvard)

Daswani *Jeevan*
Attorney General Chambers, 17 Town Range, Gibraltar, 78882, Fax: 79891. Called: Nov 1994, Middle Temple, LLB (Hons)

Dato Haji Abdul Razak *Miss Rahayu*
02-61025 3, and Member Brunei Bar. Called: July 1994, Lincoln's Inn, LLB (Hons) (Manch)

Dato Hj Abdul Rahman *Mohd Rozaiman*
Attorney General Chambers, Ministry of Law, B.S.B., Brunei, Darussalam 2016, 6732 244872 Ext 174, Fax: 6732 222720, and Member Brunei Bar. Called: July 1995, Lincoln's Inn, LLB (Hons), LLM (Exeter)

Dato Hj Zaidan *Miss Hanariza*
Called: Nov 1997, Lincoln's Inn, LLB (Hons)(Wales)

Davidson *Alasdair Michael*
Dempsey & Company, Caribbean Place, P.O.Box 97, Leeward Highway, Providenciales, Turks & Caicos Islands, 00 649 94 64344, Fax: 00 649 94 65464, and Member Turks & Caicos Islands. Called: Oct 1992, Gray's Inn, LL.B (Newc)

Davidson *Neil Forbes*
Advocates' Library, Parliament House, Edinburgh EH1 1RF, 031 226 5071, Fax: 031 220 4440, QC (Scotland) and Member Scottish Bar. Called: May 1990, Inner Temple, B.A. (Stirl), M.Sc. (Brad), LL.B.& LL.M. (Edin)

Davies *Dr Gillian*
European Patent Office, DG III, Erhardtstrasse 27, D-80298 Munich, Germany, 4989 2399 3230, Fax: 4989 2399 4460, Chairman, Technical Board of Appeal and Member, Enlarged Board of Appeal, EPO. Called: Nov 1961, Lincoln's Inn, Ph.D

Davis *Andrew Raj*
Called: July 1997, Lincoln's Inn, LLB (Hons)(Nott'm), LLM (Nott'm)

Davis *Peter Andrew*
S G Archibald, Archibald Andersen Association, d'Avocats, 41 rue Ybry, 92576 Newilly-sur-seine, 331 55 61 12 69, Fax: 331 55 61 15 15. Called: Oct 1994, Lincoln's Inn, LLB (Hons)(Leic)

Davis *Miss Susan Lynn*
Called: Mar 1998, Gray's Inn, LLB (Bucks)

Dawson *Miss Anne Diana*
Called: July 1996, Middle Temple, LLB (Hons)(Lond)

Daya-Winterbottom *Trevor*
Chapman Tripp Sheffield Young, Level 35, Coopers & Lybrand Tower, 23-29 Albert Street, Auckland, 00 64 9 357 9000, Fax: 00 64 9 357 9099, and Member Barrister & Solicitor of the High Court of New Zealand (Admitted November 1996). Called: Nov 1985, Lincoln's Inn, BA (Hons), Diplome de Droit, International et De, Droit Compares des, Droits de l'Homme, MA, Legal Associate of, the Royal Town, Planning Institute, FRSA, Affiliate Member of, the New Zealand, Planning Institute

De Berti *Giovanni*
De Berti & Jacchia, Foro Buonaparte 20, 20121 Milano, 39- 2-725541, Fax: 39- 2-72554600, and Member Italy Bar. Called: Nov 1970, Gray's Inn

de Bruir *Rory*
Law Library, Four Courts, Dublin 7, 045 521881, Fax: 045 521881, and Member Southern Ireland Bar Northern Ireland Bar. Called: Oct 1992, Middle Temple, Diploma in Legal, Studies (Kings Inns), Dip US Army Command, & General Staff, College, Commission, Irish Army, BL, FCIArb

De Cruz *Miss Clares*
24 Raffles Place, [H]18-00 Clifford Centre, 533 2323, Fax: 533 1579, and Member Singapore Bar. Called: July 1995, Middle Temple, LLB (Hons), BA (Singapore)

De Rozario *Miss Lynette Rita*
Called: Nov 1992, Middle Temple, BA (Hons, Kent)

De Silva *Miss Natasha Esther*
Called: July 1997, Middle Temple, LLB (Hons)(Warw)

De Silva *Suren Charitha*
Called: July 1996, Gray's Inn, LLB (Wales)

De Souza *Miss Vanessa-Anne*
Straits Tradine Building, 9 Battery Road, [H]15-00, (65) 5322271, Fax: (65) 5352475, and Member Singapore. Called: July 1996, Middle Temple, LLB (Hons)(Leeds)

De Ste Croix *Miss Emma Rebecca*
Ogier & Le Masurier, P O Box 404, Pirouet House, Union Street, St Helier, Jersey, Channel Islands, 01534 504000, Fax: 01534 35328. Called: May 1995, Inner Temple, LLB

Dean *Ms Margaret*
Called: Nov 1992, Middle Temple, B.Sc (Hons, Wales)

Deeny *Donnell Justin JP*
Bar Library, Royal Courts of Justice, Belfast, 0232 241523/323243, Fax: 0232 231850, QC Northern Ireland Senior Counsel Republic of Ireland and Member Northern Ireland Bar. Called: July 1986, Middle Temple, BA Dublin

Delaney *Barry Douglas*
P O Box 36, Orchasrd Point. Called: Oct 1993, Inner Temple, LLB (Lond)

Delip Singh *Tara Singh*
Called: Nov 1995, Lincoln's Inn, LLB (Hons)

Demetriades *Demetris*
P.O.Box 47, 8100 Pafos, 06-232689, 235755, Fax: 06-2322313, and Member Cyprus Bar. Called: Nov 1994, Gray's Inn, LLB

Demetriou *Antonis*
Called: Oct 1996, Gray's Inn, LLB (Kent)

Demetriou *Miss Elina*
Called: Nov 1995, Lincoln's Inn, LLB (Hons) (So'ton)

Dendroff *Jason Peter*
Called: Nov 1993, Middle Temple, LLB (Hons)(Lond)

Deo *Jagdeep Singh*
C/O Karpal Singh & Co, 17 Green Hall, 10200 Penang, Malaysia, 04 2638543/2639558, Fax: 04 2630461, and Member Malaysia Bar. Called: July 1993, Gray's Inn, LLB (Warw)

DeSilva *Miss Joanne*
Morgan, Lewis & Badans LLP, 80 Raffles Place, [H]14-20 UOB Plaza 2, (010) (65) 438 2188, Fax: (010) (65) 230 7100, and Member Singapore Bar. Called: Oct 1992, Gray's Inn, BA

Dessain *Anthony James*
Bedell & Cristin, P.O. Box 75, One the Forum, Grenville Street, St Helier,Jersey JE4 8PP, 01534 814814, Fax: 01534 814815. Called: July 1974, Middle Temple, LLB

Devendarajah *Vivekananda*
Called: July 1995, Middle Temple, LLB (Hons) (Wales)

Deverell *William Shirley*
Kaplan & Stratton, Advocates, PO Box 40111, Nairobi, Kenya, 335 333, Fax: 340 827, and Member Advocate of the High Court of Kenya. Called: Nov 1961, Gray's Inn, BA

Dhaniram *Mahendranath*
5 Gordon Street (North), San Fernando, Trinidad, (809) 652 6806, Fax: (809) 652 6806, and Member Trinidad & Tobago Bar. Called: Feb 1994, Gray's Inn, LLB (Lond), LLM (Lond), LEC (Trinidad &, Tobago)

Dharsan *Miss Kiranjit Kaur*
Called: July 1997, Middle Temple, LLB (Hons)(Lond)

Dhillon *Gurmit Singh*
Called: Nov 1996, Lincoln's Inn, LLB (Hons)

Dhillon *Gursharan Singh*
Called: Nov 1996, Middle Temple, LLB (Hons)(Leeds)

Dhillon *Surinder Singh*
Chua Dhillon Tan & Partners, 71 Robinson Road, [H]03-03, 32332320, Fax: 2213211, and Member Singapore Bar. Called: Nov 1991, Lincoln's Inn, LLB (Hons) (Lond)

Dickson *Donald John Kurt*
L'Ardailler, 87230 Bussiere-Galant, France, (+33) 05 55 78 85 77, Fax: (+33) 05 55 78 85 33. Called: Nov 1966, Inner Temple, LLB (Leeds)

Dilbert *Miss Sophia Armanda*
Called: July 1996, Middle Temple, LLB (Hons)(L'pool)

Dixon *Keith Owen*
Ogier & Le Masurier, Pirouet Chambers, Union Street, St Helier, Jersey, Channel Islands, 01534 504000, Fax: 01534 35238, and Member Jersey Bar. Called: May 1994, Middle Temple, MA (Hons)

Doherty *John*
Barrister of Ireland. Called: Nov 1995, Middle Temple, BL (King's Inn)

Don *Brendan Robert*
Called: July 1994, Middle Temple, LLB (Hons)(Leic), LLM (Boston)

Dorai Raj *Dinesh Pragasam*
Called: Nov 1995, Middle Temple, LLB (Hons)(Wales)

Doraisamy *Raghunath Ramachandran*
Called: Nov 1997, Middle Temple, LLB (Hons)(Nott'm)

Dorey *Sir Graham Martyn*
The Bailiff's Chambers, Royal Court, Guernsey, 0481 726161, Fax: 0481 713861, Former Solicitor and Member Member of the Jersey Court of Appeal. Called: Feb 1992, Gray's Inn, BA (Bristol)

Dorsett *Kenred Michael Ansara*
Providence Consulting Group, P.O.Box N-1527, Nassau, (240) 394 0886, Fax: (240) 394 0573, and Member Bahamas Bar. Called: July 1995, Middle Temple, BA (Hons) (Keele)

Downes *Ms Christine Beverley*
Monplaisir & Co, Floissac Building, Brazil Street, PO Box 256, Castries, St Lucia, 809-45 22837/22803, Fax: 32358, and Member St Lucian Bar. Called: Nov 1989, Gray's Inn, BA, LLB (Lond)

Drahaman *Ms Cirami Mastura*
Called: Nov 1996, Gray's Inn, LLB (Lond)

Driu *Miss Sera Palu*
The Ministry of Justice, Attorney General's Chambers, Rogorogoivuda House, Lautoka, 679 667710, Fax: 679 668077, and Member The Fiji Bar. Called: July 1995, Inner Temple, LLB (Wolverhampton)

Du Toit *Dr Emma Jeanne*
300 Innes Chambers, 84 Pritchard Street, Johannesburg 2001, +27 11 337 2370, Fax: +27 11 333 8425, and Member Johannesburg Bar. Called: Nov 1995, Middle Temple, BA, M.Phil, D.Phil

Dudley *Anthony Edward*
Called: Nov 1989, Middle Temple, LLB Hons [Hull]

Duffett *Peter Lionel*
c/o Allianz Shanghai, Representative Office, 707 Office Complex, Hotel Equatorial Shangai, 65 Yanan Xi Lu, Shanghai 2000040, 0086 21 6248 8148, Fax: 0086 21 6248 8240. Called: Feb 1980, Middle Temple, MA, FIA, FCCA, FCII

Dukes *Christopher James Noel*
Yolaw Trust & Corporate, Services Limited, P O Box 415, Templar House, Don Road, St Helier, Jersey JE4 8WH, 01534 500419, Fax: 01534 500450. Called: July 1983, Middle Temple, LLB

Duncan *Benjamin Paul*
Scotland Europa, 35 Square de Meeus, B-1040, Brussels, (32-2) 502 50 28, Fax: (32-2) 502 51 56. Called: Oct 1990, Lincoln's Inn, LLB (Lanc), LLM (Edin)

Duncan *Delroy*
Messrs Trott & Duncan, 1st Floor, Sea Venture, Building 19, Parliament Street, Hamilton, 441 295 7444, Fax: 441 295 6600, and Member Bermuda. Called: Nov 1984, Gray's Inn, MA, LLB, FCIArb

Duncan *Miss Marjorie Camille*
Called: Mar 1996, Gray's Inn, BA (West Indies), LLB (Lond)

Duncanson *Beryn Sigurd*
Called: Mar 1997, Gray's Inn, BA (Toronto), LLB (Bucks)

Dunham *Michael John*
29 Spring Street, Sandringham, Victoria, 9 336 1917, Fax: 9 320 4178, and Member Australia Bar. Called: Nov 1980, Middle Temple, Master Mariner

Dunne *Ms Lynn Noelle*
Called: Oct 1997, Inner Temple, BA (Cantab)

Dunnett *Denzil Roderick Rawcliffe*
L-2950 Luxembourg, 352 43791, Fax: 352 437704. Called: Nov 1970, Middle Temple, MA (Oxon)

Duraipandi *Miss Ganaselvarani*
M.N.Swami & Yap, No 1 North Bridge Road, [H]18-05 High Street Centre, 3361677, Fax: 3371737, and Member Singapore Bar. Called: Feb 1994, Lincoln's Inn, LLB (Hons, Lond)

Dusun *Marcus*
Called: Nov 1996, Lincoln's Inn, LLB (Hons)(Lond)

Dwan *Francis Eugene*
The Law Library, The Four Courts, Inns Quay, Dublin 7, 00 353 1 702 3925, Fax: 00 353 1 872 0455, Barrister of Ireland. Called: Mar 1996, Middle Temple, BA (Hons), BL (Kings Inn)

Dykes *Jonathan Hugh Elwand Maxwell*
P.O.Box 1407, Queen's Drive, London WC1X 8NF, 0171 404 5566, Fax: 0171 404 2244. Called: Nov 1994, Inner Temple, LLB (Lond), ACCA

Dykes *Philip John*
Suite 1517-1522, Two Pacific Place, Queensway, 2810 7222, Fax: 2845 0439, Queen's Counsel (Hong Kong 1997), Senior Counsel, (1997) and Member Hong Kong Bar. Called: July 1977, Lincoln's Inn, BA (Oxon)

Edgar *Effrem Owen*
Edgar & Co Chambers, P.O.Box 500, Castries, St Lucia, 758 452 2405, Fax: 758 451 8979, and Member East Caribbean Supreme Court (St Lucia). Called: July 1995, Lincoln's Inn, BA (Hons), LLM

Edmonds *Mrs Mary Xue-Ying*
Called: Nov 1996, Lincoln's Inn, LLB (Hons)(Lond)

Edmondson *James Douglas*
Called: Oct 1997, Gray's Inn, BA, MBA (Belfast)

Ee *Miss Annie Yeok Leng*
Called: Mar 1998, Lincoln's Inn, LLB (Hons)(Keele)

Efrem *Mrs Eleni Andreas*
District Court of Larnaca, Larnaca, 04 630531. Called: July 1990, Gray's Inn, LLB (E Ang), LLM (Lond)

Ehamparam *Santhirasegaram*
Called: July 1995, Inner Temple, LLB

Ekins *Charles Wareing*
25 Park Square, Leeds, LS1 2PW. Called: July 1980, Gray's Inn, LLB (Leeds)

Elkinson *Jeffrey Philip*
Conyers Dill & Pearman, Clarendon House, Church Street, Hamilton HM CX, 809 295 1422, Fax: 809 292 4720, and Member Southern Ireland (1978) Hong Kong (1985), New South Wales, Australia (1985), New York (1987), Bermuda (1989) New York (1987) and Bermuda (1989) Bars. Called: Feb 1982, Middle Temple, BL, MA, LLB, FCIArb

Elliott *Sebastion Michael Garcia*
Called: Oct 1996, Lincoln's Inn, BA (Hons)(Essex), Dip in Law (City)

Ellis *Edward David*
Lot 2809, Church Avenue, Brooklyn, New York 11226, and Member Guyana Bar New York Bar. Called: July 1979, Lincoln's Inn, BA

Ellul *Marc Xavier*
Suite 7, Hadfield House, Library Street, 00 (350) 70921, Fax: 00 (350) 74969, and Member Gibratar. Called: Nov 1993, Inner Temple, BA (Hons)(Cardiff)

Eng *Ms Audrey Cher Hwee*
Messrs Drew & Napier, 20 Raffles Place,
[H]17-00 Ocean Towers, Fax: 65 535 0733,
Advocate & Solicitor of the Supreme Court
of the Republic of Singapore. Called: July
1993, Gray's Inn, LLB (Leeds)

Enser *Miss Juliette Corinne*
Weil, Gotshal and Manges LLP, 81 Avenue
Louise, P.O.Box 9-10, 1050 Brussels, 00 32
2 543 7484. Called: Oct 1991, Inner
Temple, BA (Oxon), Dip EC LAW

Ephraim *Miss Pamela*
Called: July 1997, Middle Temple, LLB
(Hons)(Lond)

Er *Miss Joanna Wuan Sher*
Called: July 1995, Lincoln's Inn, LLB (Hons)

Ern *Lai Daryl Chee*
Called: July 1997, Inner Temple, LLB (Lond)

Eronen *Mrs Gonul*
Supreme Court, Lefkosa, TRNC, 90 392
2273690, Fax: 90 392 2286001. Called: Nov
1975, Gray's Inn

Erotocritou *Miss Elena*
Called: Nov 1996, Lincoln's Inn, LLB
(Hons)(Leics)

Erotokritou *Miss Christianna A*
A.P.Erotokritou & Co, Advocate, P.O.Box
2154, Nicosia, 357 2 452466. Called: Nov
1997, Lincoln's Inn, LLB (Hons)

Erriah *Ramdeo*
Called: Nov 1995, Gray's Inn, LLB (Lond)

Erskine *Thomas Ralph CB*
Office of the Legislative Csl., Parliament
Bldgs, Stormont, Belfast, Northern Ireland
BT4 3SW. Called: Feb 1962, Gray's Inn, LLB

Eshun *Yaw Fenyi*
Called: July 1995, Lincoln's Inn, BA (Hons)
(Ghana)

Etican *Ramsay Roy*
Called: July 1997, Lincoln's Inn, LLB
(Hons)(Hull)

Evangelou *Miss Theano Alexandros*
Called: July 1995, Gray's Inn, LLB (Lond)

Evans *Guy St John*
World Trade Organisation, Geneva.
Called: Nov 1992, Inner Temple, BA
(Hons)(Kent), MA (Bruges)

Everett-Heath *Miss Catharine Rose*
Called: Nov 1989, Lincoln's Inn, MA
(Cantab)

Evie *Mrs Georgiou Antoniou*
Supreme Court, Nicosia, 02-302391, and
Member Cyprus Bar. Called: Nov 1995,
Gray's Inn, LLB (Leic), LLM

Eyton *Mrs Nik Mariah Zainab*
Abdullah A Rahman & Co, Suite 1803, 18th
Floor, Wisma Hamzah-Kwong, No 1 Leboh
Ampang, 50100 Kuala Lumpur, Fellow,
Institute of Legal Executives and Member
Malaysia Bar. Called: July 1971, Lincoln's
Inn, LLB

Faal *Dr Edirissa Mohammad Omar*
222 S.Harbor Blvd, Suite 830, Anaheim,
California 92805, 714 502 1900, Fax: 714
502 1909, Attorney at Law(USA) and
Member Bar of U.S. Supreme Court,
California Bar, Indiana Bar. Called: July
1992, Middle Temple, BSc, Dr of Juris
Prudence

Faherty *Miss Mary*
and Member Irish Bar. Called: Nov 1996,
Middle Temple, BA, LLB (Galway), BL
(King's Inn)

Faidz *Miss Saliza*
Called: July 1994, Lincoln's Inn, LLB (Hons,
Sheff)

Fair *James Dale*
29154 Jefferson Ct, St Clair Shores,
Michigan 48081, 810 415 0625, Fax: 810
294 1811, and Member State of Kansas USA.
Called: Nov 1980, Lincoln's Inn, AB
(Princeton), MA, (Oxon) JD (Stanford)

Fairey *Hamish Webster*
Called: Nov 1997, Lincoln's Inn, LLB (Hons)

Fan *Edward*
and Member Hong Kong. Called: July 1997,
Inner Temple, BDS (Lond), MGDSRCS
(Edinburgh), Dip.F.Od (LHMC), LLB
(Westminster)

Fan *Miss Yuen Chi Edwina*
Called: July 1995, Middle Temple, LLB
(Hons)

Farid *Ms Fuzet*
2 Lorong Abang Haji Openg 3, Taman Tun
Dr Ismail, 60000 Kuala Lumpur, 603-718
2198, Fax: 603-201 4257, and Member
Malaysia Bar. Called: July 1993, Middle
Temple, BA (Hons)

Fennelly *Nial (Michael Patrick)*
84 Rue du Kirchberg, L-1858 Luxembourg,
Senior Counsel, Ireland (1978) and Member
Southern Ireland Bar Northern Ireland Bar.
Called: July 1988, Middle Temple, MA
(Dublin)

Ferguson *Miss Joyann Louise*
Called: Nov 1997, Gray's Inn, BA, MA
(Morgan State,) LLB (Bucks)

Ferguson *Samuel William*
Barrister in N Ireland Employed barrister.
Called: July 1991, Gray's Inn, LLB (Belfast)

Fernandez *Christopher*
and Member Singapore. Called: Nov 1994,
Middle Temple, LLB (Hons)

Fernandez *James*
Called: July 1996, Lincoln's Inn, LLB
(Hons)(Lond)

Fields *Mrs Fiona Catharine*
Ogier & le Masurier, Pirouet House, Union
Street, St Helier, Jersey JE4 9WG, 01534
504000, Fax: 01534 35328. Called: Nov
1984, Middle Temple, BA (Kent)

Finch *Paul John*
and Member Australia, California and New
York Bars 2 Field Court, Gray's Inn,
London, WC1R 5BB. Called: Nov 1990,
Lincoln's Inn, LLB, B.Comm (NSW)

Findlay *The Hon Mr Justice James
Kerr OBE*
Supreme Court, Queensway, 2825 432534,
Fax: 2523 4253, Formerly a Solicitor
(Scotland) QC Hong Kong and Member
Zimbabwe Bar Victoria Bar Hong Kong Bar.
Called: May 1985, Inner Temple, LLB
(Lond), FCIA

Finigan *John Patrick*
Qatar National Bank SAQ, P O Box 1000,
Doha, 00974 430240, Fax: 00974 438349.
Called: July 1980, Lincoln's Inn, FCIB, ACIS,
FRSA, MSI

Finnegan *Joseph Gerald*
Ardara, Killarney Road, Bray, Co Wicklow,
2868 108, Fax: 2867 306. Called: Nov 1986,
Middle Temple, BCL LLB (Dublin)

Fisher *Michael John*
Called: July 1992, Gray's Inn, LLB (Manch),
MA (Brunel)

Fitzgerald *Tyrone Leon Easton*
Called: July 1995, Lincoln's Inn, LLB (Hons)

Fitzpatrick *David*
1001 Far East Finance Centre, 16 Harcourt
Road, Central, Hong Kong, 28668233, Fax:
28663932, Barrister of Hong Kong Barrister
& Solicitor of Supreme Court of Victoria.
Called: July 1992, Middle Temple, MA
(Cambs)

Fitzpatrick *Mark John*
Scottish Advocate. Called: July 1991,
Lincoln's Inn, BA (Oxon), MA (Oxon)

Fitzsimons *Eoghan Patrick*
Law Library, Four Courts, Dublin 7, Ireland,
01 8720622, Fax: 01 8720455, S.C.(Ireland)
and Member Southern Ireland Bar New
South Wales Bar. Called: Feb 1986, Middle
Temple, BCL (U C Dublin), LLM (Yale),
Doct de l'Univ, (Paris)

Fletcher *Peter Grey*
Charlotte House Nassau, P.O.Box N3950,
Nassau NP, 809 322 2871, Fax: 809 322
2874, and Member Commonwealth of the
Bahamas. Called: Nov 1992, Lincoln's Inn,
LLB (Hons)(E Anglia)

Flood *Miss Sarah-Lucy*
1 809 453 6966, Fax: 1 809 452 5655,
Minister for Health, Human Services Family
Affairs, Women's Affairs. Called: July 1995,
Lincoln's Inn, LLB (Hons), MP

Floyd *Robert Hamilton*
22-24 Boulevard Alexander 111, 06400
Cannes, 00 334 93 43 93 55, Fax: 00 334 93
43 40 26. Called: Nov 1971, Middle Temple,
LLM (Lond)

Fock *Miss Yin Ling*
Called: July 1996, Middle Temple, LLB
(Hons)(Bris)

Fogarty *Paul*
The Bar Library, Four Courts, Dublin 7,
Ireland, 283 3513/677 8373, Fax: 677 8375,
and Member Southern Ireland Bar.
Called: May 1988, Middle Temple, BCL
(Dublin), BA, BL (Kings Inn), ACIArb

Fong *Miss Cornelia Siew Ping*
13 Crichton Close, Singapore 557990, 0065
2888365, and Member Singapore Bar.
Called: July 1994, Inner Temple, LLB
(Nott'm)

Fong *Miss Gwendolyn Teen-Li*
Messrs Shook Lin & Bok, 1 Robinson Road,
AIA Tower, [H]18-00, and Member
Singapore. Called: July 1995, Middle
Temple, LLB (Hons)(Hull)

Fong *Kelvin Kai Tong*
325k Bukit Timah Road, Singapore 259714,
(65) 2355120, Fax: (65) 2353500.
Called: July 1996, Middle Temple, LLB
(Hons)(Newc)

Fong *Philip Yeng Fatt*
Messrs Harry Elias & Partners, No 79
Robinson Road, [H]16-03, Singapore 06, 65-
2235006 Ext 359, Fax: 65-2270281, and
Member Singapore Bar. Called: July 1994,
Inner Temple, LLB (Lond), B.Econs (Hons)

Fong *Ms Shin Ni*
Called: Nov 1997, Lincoln's Inn, LLB
(Hons)(Sheff)

Fong *Miss Yuke Ching*
Called: July 1994, Lincoln's Inn, LLB (Hons)

Foo *Ms Chiew Eng*
479 River Valley Road, [H]13-07, Valley
Park. Called: July 1996, Inner Temple, LLB
(Lond)

Foo *Miss Fiona Wei Ling*
Called: July 1997, Lincoln's Inn, LLB (Lond)

Foo *Frederick Kong Tuck*
Called: July 1996, Lincoln's Inn, LLB
(Hons)(Lond)

Foo *Miss Jon-Hui Amanda*
Khattar Wong & Partners, 80 Raffles Place,
[H]25-01 UOB Plaza 1, Singapore 048624,
535 6844, Fax: 533 0585, and Member
Singapore Bar. Called: Oct 1990, Gray's Inn,
LLB (Lond), LLM (Lond), AKC

Foo *Ms Li Mei*
27 Jalan Telawi 8, Bangsar Baru, 59100
Kuala Lumpur, 09 7474 653. Called: July
1996, Lincoln's Inn, LLB (Hons)(Cardiff)

Foo *Say Tun*
Messrs David Lim & Partners, Advocates &
Solicitors, 50 Raffles Place, [H]17-01
Singapore Land Tower, Singapore 048623,
65 532 2122, Fax: 65 532 0122, and
Member Malaysia Bar Singapore Bar.
Called: Nov 1991, Middle Temple, LLB Hons
(E Ang)

Foo *Yong Teng*
Called: Nov 1995, Lincoln's Inn, LLB (Hons)

Forde *Dr Michael Patrick*
33 Mountainview Rd, Dublin 6, 00353 14
978349, Fax: 00353 14 966835, King's Inn,
Dublin (1984), Senior Counsel (1995) and
Member Southern Ireland Bar. Called: Nov
1987, Middle Temple, BA, LLB (Dublin),
LLM (Brussels), PhD (Cantab)

Foreman *Mrs Marguerite Alyce*
Seaton & Foreman, Chambers P O Box 82,
Central Street, Basseterre, St Kitts, (809) 465
9292, Fax: (809) 465 7373, and Member
Saint Christopher & Nevis. Called: Oct 1991,
Inner Temple, MA (Edin), LLB (Hons),
D.M.S.

Forsyth *Alistair James Menteith*
O.St.J.
Ethie Castle, By Arbroath, Angus DD11 5SP,
01241 830458, Fax: 01241 830477, Also Inn
of Court L and Member Scottish Bar.
Called: July 1990, Inner Temple, MTh (St
Andrews), LLB (Buck), LLB,
(Edinburgh),FSA.Scot, DipLp (Edinburgh),
ACII, Chartered, Insurance Practioner

Forsyth *Iain Grant*
C.P.V.O., PO Box 2141, F-40921 ANgers,
Cedex 02. Called: Feb 1988, Inner Temple,
LLB (Notts)

Foy *Miss Agnes*
Barrister of Ireland. Called: Nov 1996,
Middle Temple, BA (Dublin), BL (King's
Inn)

Francis *Benedict Peter Beauchamp*
The Ackerson Group, 1275 Pennsylvania
Avenue, N.W., Suite 1100, Washington DC
20004-2417, 001 202 628 1100, Fax: 001
202 628 0242, and Member New York.
Called: Nov 1989, Lincoln's Inn, MA (Edin),
Dip Law (City), LLM (USA)

Francis *Miss Bridget Cecile*
Called: Nov 1997, Gray's Inn, LLB (Lond),
LLM

Francis *Ms Charmaine*
Called: July 1995, Middle Temple, LLB
(Hons)

Francis *Derek Roy Lebert*
Advocates' Library, Parliament House,
Edinburgh, Scottish Advocate. Called: Feb
1991, Lincoln's Inn, LLB (Edin)

Francis *Miss Kenrah Nicole Philippa*
Chancery Law Associates, P.O.Box N-8199,
Nassau, 1-242 356 6108, Fax: 1-242 356
6109, and Member Bahamas. Called: July
1996, Lincoln's Inn, LLB (Hons)(Reading)

Frederick *Richard*
[H] 13 Bridge Street, Castries, St. Lucia,
West Indies, 809 451 7773, Fax: 809 451
7373, and Member St Lucia Bar. Called: July
1994, Lincoln's Inn, BSc (Hons)

Frias *Miss Cristina Samantha*
Called: Mar 1997, Middle Temple, BA
(Hons)

Frida *Miss Samantha*
Called: July 1996, Lincoln's Inn, LLB
(Hons)(Leeds)

Froomkin *Saul Morten*
Mello,Hollis,Jones & Martin, Reid House, 31
Church Street, PO Box HM 1564,
Hamilton,Bermuda, 441-292 1345, Fax: 441-
292 2277, QC (Canada & Bermuda) and
Member Canada, Bermuda, Anguilla.
Called: Apr 1989, Middle Temple, LLB, LLM
(Manitoba), FCIArb

Fuchs *Miss Iris*
Called: Oct 1997, Middle Temple, LLB
(Hons)(Lond), BA (New York)

Fuller *Nicolas Alan*
Called: July 1995, Middle Temple, LLB
(Hons)

Fulthorpe *Mrs Elizabeth Clare*
Sutton Associates, 60 Avenue de Wagram,
75017 Paris, 331 4440 0232/46681 0159,
Fax: 331 4440 0232/46681 0159.
Called: Nov 1974, Gray's Inn, LLB Hons

Fung *Miss Catherine Shuk Yin*
Department of Justice, Queensway Govt
Offices, 66 Queensway, 28672356, Fax:
28690236, and Member Australian Capital
Territory, 1988 & Northern Territory,
Australia 1991 Australia Bar Hong Kong Bar.
Called: July 1987, Middle Temple, BA
(Manitoba) LLB, (Bucks)

Fung *Daniel Richard JP*
4th Floor, High Block, Queensway
Government Offices, 66 Queensway, (852)
2867 2003, Fax: (852) 2501 0371, Q.C.,
S.C., Hong Kong and Member Victoria,
Australian Capital Territory Bar Hong Kong
Bar. Called: Nov 1975, Middle Temple, LLB
LLM

Fung *Eugene Ting Sek*
Temple Chambers, 16/F One Pacific Place,
88 Queensway, (852) 2523 2003, Fax: (852)
2810 0302, and Member Hong Kong.
Called: Mar 1997, Lincoln's Inn, BA
(Cantab), LLM, (Cantab)

Fung *Miss Lucille Yun Sim*
A2-19 Evergreen Villa, 43 Stubbs Road, and
Member Brunei, and Victoria Bars Hong
Kong Bar New South Wales. Called: July
1960, Middle Temple, BA, MCI Arb

Fung *Patrick Chee Yuen*
and Member Singapore Bar. Called: July
1992, Middle Temple, LLB (Hons) (Leics)

Fung *Patrick Pak-Tung*
10/F, New Henry House, 10 Ice House
Street, Central, (852) 2524 2156, Fax: (852)
2810 5656, Queen's Counsel 1995 (Hong
Kong) and Member Hong Kong Bar.
Called: Nov 1968, Inner Temple, LLB
(Lond), FCI Arb

Gaik *Miss Anne Ooi*
Called: July 1994, Middle Temple, LLB
(Hons)(Sheff)

Gajadhar *Jerome*
Called: Nov 1996, Lincoln's Inn, BA, MA
(Ontario), LLM (Leeds)

Gallagher *Miss Grace Marie Walsh*
Called: Nov 1997, Lincoln's Inn, BA, LLB
(Galway), BL (King's Inn)

Gallagher *Martin John*
No 1 Arran Square, Arran Quay, Dublin 7,
872 5908, Fax: 872 8963, Senior Counsel.
Called: Nov 1981, Middle Temple, BA,
FCIArb

Gan *Mr David Chern Ning*
7601218. Called: Nov 1992, Middle Temple,
LLB (Hons, B'ham), LLM (Southampton)

Gan *Gerry Kian Koon*
Called: July 1997, Middle Temple, LLB (Hons)

Gan *Miss Huey Piin*
C/O M/S Gulam & Wong, Advocates & Solicitors, Suite 1103-1106, 11th Floor, 15 Jalan Gereja, 80100 Johor, West Malaysia, 07-2246851/2 2245963, Fax: 07-2246854 2245460. Called: July 1994, Lincoln's Inn, LLB

Gan *Miss Jui Chui*
Called: July 1995, Lincoln's Inn, LLB (Hons)

Gan *Miss Sye Ni*
Called: July 1997, Lincoln's Inn, LLB (Hons)(Wales)

Gan *Miss Yee Min*
Called: July 1995, Middle Temple, LLB (Hons)

Gandy *Geoffrey Harold*
Montell Polyolefins, Centro Ricerche "G Natta", P.Le G Donegani 12, 44100 Ferrara, 00 39 532 468205, Fax: 00 39 532 467675. Called: Feb 1963, Inner Temple, MA, LLM (Cantab)

Ganesan *Anandan*
Called: July 1996, Middle Temple, LLB (Hons)(Bris)

Ganesan *Miss Susila*
Called: July 1995, Lincoln's Inn, LLB (Hons)

Ganeson *Miss Visahini*
Called: July 1995, Lincoln's Inn, LLB (Hons)

Gangadharan *Miss Prasanna Devi*
Called: Nov 1996, Middle Temple, LLB (Hons)(Lond)

Garland *Peter William*
1501, Two Pacific Place, 88 Queensway, 852-28401130, Fax: 852-28100612, QC (Hong Kong 1995), SC (Hong Kong 1997), Supreme Court of the Australian Capital Territory, High Court of Australia and Member Hong Kong Bar. Called: Nov 1978, Middle Temple

Gau *Miss Susan*
Called: July 1996, Lincoln's Inn, LLB (Hons)(Hull)

Gaudin *James Harman*
Called: Nov 1996, Middle Temple, LLB (Hons)

Gauntlett *Jeremy John SC*
1114 Huguenot Chambers, 40 Queen Victoria St, Cape Town, South Africa, 249340, Fax: 245666, Senior Counsel, South Africa, Lesotho & Namibia. Called: May 1994, Gray's Inn, BA, LLB, BCL

Gavaloo *Miss Vedna*
Called: Nov 1995, Lincoln's Inn, LLB (Hons)

Geer *David John Granville*
European Human Rights, Foundation, Avenue Michelange 70, Brussels 1049, (322) 732 6653, Fax: (322) 7346831. Called: Nov 1988, Middle Temple, BA (Cantab), Dip Law, LLM

Genkatharan *Mrs Kala Malar*
Called: Mar 1998, Middle Temple, LLB (Hons)(Lond)

George *Miss Caroline Mary*
Called: Nov 1996, Lincoln's Inn, LLB (Hons)

George *Rynholdt*
Group 500, Innes Chambers, P.O.Box 1073, Johannesburg 2000, (2711) 337 4355, Fax: (2711) 333 1602, and Member Johannesburg Bar. Called: July 1996, Lincoln's Inn, LLB (Hons), BA(Hon), (Oxon)

Georgiadis *Byron Nicholas*
P.O.Box 42851, Nairobi, Kenya, Nairobi 882319/884037, Fax: 884037, and Member Kenya Bar Seychelles Bar. Called: Nov 1951, Inner Temple, MA (Oxon), MCA Arb

Georgiou *Miss Chloe*
Called: Nov 1997, Gray's Inn, LLB (Leics)

Georgis Taylor *Miss Vivian*
Peter I Foster & Associates, 35 Jeremie Street, Castries, 758 4531100, Fax: 758 4524940, and Member St Lucia. Called: Nov 1995, Middle Temple, LLB (Hons)

Gevisser *Antony James*
12 Montrose Road, Hurlingham, Sandton 2196, South Africa, 0171 730 9371, Fax: 011 7831317, and Member Johannesburg Bar. Called: Nov 1993, Gray's Inn, BA, LLB (Cape)

Ghandinesen *Kanarasan*
Called: July 1995, Lincoln's Inn, LLB (Hons)

Ghani *Ahmad Shukri Abdul*
Called: Nov 1997, Gray's Inn, LLB (Wales)

Ghani *Miss Marianne Antoinette*
00 60 88 218667/218663, Fax: 00 60 88 239627, and Member Sabah & Sarawak, Malaysia. Called: Oct 1995, Gray's Inn, LLB

Ghosh *Dhruba*
Called: July 1995, Lincoln's Inn, LLB (Hons)

Gibbons *John Thomas*
Law Library, Four Courts, Inns Quay, Dublin 7, 01 872 0622, Barrister of Ireland and Member Kings Inn, Dublin. Called: Nov 1991, Middle Temple, BL (Dublin), BE, (NUI), DIP. LScEng, FIEI, FCIArb, LAM, RTPI

Gibson *Kenyatta Mboya*
Called: July 1994, Lincoln's Inn, LLB (Hons, Bucks)

Gibson *Mrs Mavis Dorothy*
Called: Nov 1965, Lincoln's Inn

Gilbert *Miss Dionne*
Crill Canavan, La Chasse Chambers, La Chasse, St Helier, Jersey, 01534 888933, Fax: 01534 887040. Called: July 1996, Inner Temple, LLB (Bucks)

Gilbert *Ms Lorianne Darnelle*
Called: Nov 1994, Gray's Inn, BA (USA), LLB

Gill *The Honourable Lord*
Court of Session, Parliament House, Edinburgh EH1 1RQ, 0131 225 2595, Fax: 0131 225 8213. Called: Apr 1991, Lincoln's Inn, MA (Glas), LLB (Glas), PH.D (Edinburgh)

Gill *Amarick Singh*
Called: Mar 1998, Middle Temple, LLB (Hons)

Gill *Jagjit Singh*
Chinese Chambers of Commerce, & Industry Building, 47 Hill Street, [H]04-03, 3382622, Fax: 3392386, and Member Singapore. Called: July 1996, Lincoln's Inn, LLB (Hons)(Lond)

Gill *Zaminder Singh*
No 87 Beach Road, [H]04-01 Chye Sing Building, 3387225, Fax: 3388815, and Member Singapore. Called: Nov 1993, Middle Temple, LLB (Hons)(Lanc)

Gillard *The Hon Mr Justice Eugene William*
Judges' Chambers, Supreme Court of Victoria, 210 William Street, Melbourne, Vic.3000, (03) 9603 6222, Fax: (03) 9670 8408, QC (Australia) and Member Victorian, Tasmania, New South Wales, Queensland 4 Stone Bldgs, Ground Floor, Lincoln's Inn, London, WC2A 3XT. Called: Feb 1991, Gray's Inn, LLB (Melbourne)

Gillespie *Brian David*
2 Glenvar Park, Blackrock, Co. Dublin, 2882887, Fax: 720455, and Member Southern Ireland Bar. Called: July 1989, Middle Temple, MA [Dub], MAI [Dub], B Comm [Dub], FIEE

Girvin *Miss Cecelia Ann*
Called: Nov 1994, Middle Temple, LLB (Hons)

Gittings *Daniel John*
South China Morning Post, 29/F Dorset House, 979 King's Road, + 852 28653584, Fax: + 852 28653464, and Member High Court of Hong Kong. Called: July 1997, Gray's Inn, MA

Glitzenhirn-Augustin *Mrs Natalie Elaine*
P O Box 1695, Castries, Fax: (758) 451 8409, and Member St Lucia Bar Association. Called: July 1996, Middle Temple, BA (Hons)(Warw), CPE

Gnanapragasam *Miss Christina Olivia*
Called: Nov 1997, Middle Temple, LLB (Hons)(Wales)

Go *Tiong Siew*
Called: July 1997, Lincoln's Inn, LLB (Hons)

Goddard *David John*
Chapman Tripp Sheffield Young, Barristers & Solicitors, P O Box 993, Wellington, 64 4 499 5999, Fax: 64 4 472 7111, Barrister & Solicitor of the High Court of New Zealand. Called: July 1988, Lincoln's Inn, BA (Hons) (Victoria), BA (Oxon)

Goddard *Peter Andrew George*
ATC Trustees (BVI) Limited, P O Box 933, Road Town Tortola, (809) 494 6122, Fax: (809) 494 6124, Formerly a solicitor. Called: Nov 1987, Middle Temple, LLB (Wales)

Goh *Aik Leng*
Goh Aik Leng & Partners, No 50A Temple Street, 065 222 6330, Fax: 065 222 4262, and Member Singapore Bar. Called: Nov 1991, Middle Temple, LLB Hons (Buck'm)

Goh *Boon Yee*
Called: July 1996, Middle Temple, LLB (Hons)(Lond)

Goh *Miss Christina Choy Boon*
Block 7, Teck Whye Ave [H]04-102, Singapore 680007, 7647753. Called: July 1995, Middle Temple, LLB (Hons)(Lond), BSC (Est Mg+)(Hons)

Goh *Chuan Huat*
Called: July 1996, Middle Temple, LLB (Hons)(Lond)

Goh *Hoon Huar*
Called: July 1996, Middle Temple, LLB (Hons)(Notts)

Goh *Miss Hui Nee*
Called: Nov 1996, Lincoln's Inn, BA (Hons)(Keele)

Goh *Miss Joan Penn Nee*
Called: July 1996, Lincoln's Inn, LLB (Hons)(Wales)

Goh *Joseph Chye Hock*
Blk 146 Pasir Ris Street 11, [H] 02-61 Singapore 510146, (65) 5840843, and Member Singapore Bar. Called: Nov 1994, Middle Temple, LLB (Hons)

Goh *Miss Justine Soo Hsien*
Called: Nov 1997, Gray's Inn, LLB (LSE)

Goh *Kien Ping*
Called: Nov 1993, Lincoln's Inn, LLB (Hons)

Goh *Lam Chuan*
Called: May 1994, Middle Temple, LLB (Hons)

Goh *Laurence Eng Yau*
47 Saraca Road, Singapore 807392, Republic of Singapore, 4822285/ 3240727, Fax: 4841060/ 3240703, Advocate & Solicitor, Singapore and Member Singapore Bar. Called: July 1989, Lincoln's Inn, LLB (Hons)(Lond)

Goh *Li Kian*
Called: July 1995, Middle Temple, LLB (Hons)

Goh *Miss Li Peen*
546 Ang Mo Kio Avenue 10, [H]03-2252, Singapore 560546, 65 4578225, and Member Singapore Bar. Called: July 1994, Gray's Inn, LLB (Lond)

Goh *Miss Li Yen*
17 Thomson View, Singapore 2057, (65) 455 4883, and Member Singapore Bar. Called: July 1994, Middle Temple, BA (Hons)(Oxon)

Goh *Miss Maxine Whui Min*
Called: Nov 1995, Middle Temple, LLB (Hons)(Hull)

Goh *Miss Pricilla May Lih*
2175-J Taman Tunku Habsah, 05100, Alor Setar, Kedah, 04 7317154, Fax: 04 7311375, and Member Malaysia Bar. Called: July 1995, Lincoln's Inn, LLB (Hons)

Goh *Miss Sen Fong*
Called: July 1995, Lincoln's Inn, BA (Hons)

Goh *Seng Leong Christopher*
Harry Elias & Partners, 9 Raffles Place, [H]12-00 Republic Plaza, 535 0550, Fax: 438 0550, and Member Singapore. Called: July 1996, Middle Temple, LLB (Hons)(Lond)

Goh *Miss Susan Hui San*
Called: July 1992, Lincoln's Inn, LLB (Hons)(Notts)

Goh *Miss Swee Hua Phylina*
Called: July 1997, Middle Temple, LLB (Hons)(Lond)

Goh *Miss Wei Lin*
Called: Nov 1994, Lincoln's Inn, LLB (Hons)(Sheff)

Goh *Miss Yolande Hui Lynn*
Called: July 1996, Lincoln's Inn, LLB (Hons)

Goins *Ms Debra Lynn*
Bermuda Monetary Authority, Burnaby House, 26 Burnaby Street, Hamilton, 441 295 5278, Fax: 441 292 7471, and Member Bermuda. Called: Nov 1996, Inner Temple, LLB (Lond)

Golamaully *Abdus Samad*
Called: Nov 1995, Lincoln's Inn, LLB (Hons)

Goldie *Gainneos Jacob*
Messrs Yusoff Shamsuddin &, Partners, 5th Floor, Straits Trading, Building No 4 Lebow Pasar, Besar 50050, Kuala Lumpur Malaysia, 03 2938244, Fax: 03 2938381, and Member Malaysia Bar. Called: Nov 1992, Middle Temple, LLB (Hons)

Golding *Ms Jane Lindsey*
Brosio Casati e Associati, Corso Vittorio Emanuele II, 68, 10121 Torino, 00 39 11 5155300, Fax: 00 39 11 541018. Called: Nov 1989, Lincoln's Inn, LLB (Lond), Maitrise (Paris)

Goldsmith *Immanuel*
Smart & Biggar, 439 University Avenue, Suite 1500, Box 111, Toronto, Ontario, 416 593 5514, Fax: 416 591 1690, and Member Ontario Bar. Called: Jan 1950, Middle Temple, LLB

Gollop *Advocate Julian Clive*
Crills, PO Box 72, 44 Esplanade, St Helier, Jersey, C I JE4 8PN, 01534 611055, Fax: 01534 611066. Called: July 1983, Gray's Inn, BA (Hons)

Gomez *Cosmas Stephen*
Called: Nov 1994, Inner Temple, BA (Lond)

Gomez *Miss Monique Vanessa Ann*
Office of Attorney General, 4th, 5th & 6th Floors, Post Office Building, East Hill Street,P.O.Box N3007, Nassau, N.P. Bahamas, 809 32221141, Fax: 809 3222555, and Member Bahamas Bar. Called: July 1988, Lincoln's Inn, LLB (Hons) (Lond)

Goncalves *Miss Elaine Laura*
Isola & Isola, Suite 23, Portland House, Glacis Road, 78363, Fax: 78699, and Member Gibraltar Bar. Called: Nov 1995, Middle Temple, LLB (Hons)

Gong *Chin Nam*
Called: July 1995, Middle Temple, LLB (Hons) (Hull)

Gonsalves-Sabola *Miss Mary Margaret*
McKinney, Bancroft & Hughes, Counsel & Attorneys-at-Law, No 4 George Street, Mareva House, Nassau, (242) 322 4195, Fax: (242) 328 2520, and Member Jamaica. Called: Nov 1994, Gray's Inn, LLB, LLM

Goodwill *John Francis*
Coutts Private Banking, Talstrasse 59, Zurich CH-8022, Switzerland, 01-214-54 59, Fax: 01-214-55 63, Also Inn of Court G. Called: Nov 1974, Lincoln's Inn, MA (Hons)(Oxon)

Gooi *Hsiao-Leung*
Called: July 1995, Lincoln's Inn, LLB (Hons)

Gopalakrishnan *Dinagaran*
Called: Nov 1996, Lincoln's Inn, LLB (Hons)(Lond)

Gour *Miss Bharati*
Called: July 1996, Lincoln's Inn, LLB (Hons)(Lond)

Gouthro *William Christopher*
McKinney, Bancroft, & Hughes, Chambers, Mareva House, 4 George Street, P.O.Box N3937 Nassau, 809 322 4195, Fax: 809 356 2713, and Member Bahamas. Called: July 1996, Middle Temple, LLB (Hons)(Lond)

Govindan *Sathees Kumar*
Called: July 1996, Lincoln's Inn, LLB (Hons)(E.Lond)

Govindasamy *Balasunderam*
Called: Nov 1994, Middle Temple, LLB (Lond)

Gowings *James Richard Humphrey*
Called: Nov 1973, Lincoln's Inn, MA (Oxon)

Goyder *Miss Joanna Ruth*
Linklaters & Paines, 47-51 Rue du Luxembourg, 1050 Brussels, 32 2 513 7800, Fax: 32 2 513 2583, and Member Flemish Bar of Brussels. Called: Nov 1987, Lincoln's Inn, MA (Cantab), Licence Speciale, (Brussels), LLM (Florence)

Gracie *Malcolm Reeves*
12th Floor, Wentworth Chambers, 180 Phillip Street, Sydney, New South Wales, 61 29 232 4293, Fax: 61 29 221 7183, and Member New South Wales, Victoria, Queensland, Northern Territory, Australian Capital Territory. New South Wales Bar. Called: July 1992, Lincoln's Inn, BA, LLB (Hons)

Graham *Sir Peter KCB QC (1990)*
Le Petit Chateau, La Vallette, 87190 Magnac Level, Also Inn of Court L. Called: June 1958, Gray's Inn, MA, LLM (Cantab)

Grant *Professor Alan*
Fraser Grant Associates, P O Box 275,
Eureka, Nova Scotia Bok 1BO, 902-923-2866,
Fax: 902-923-2755, and Member Ontario
Bar. Called: Nov 1970, Inner Temple, LLB
(Lond)

Granville *Steven James*
Despacho Gil-Robles, Velazquez 3, Piso 2,
Madrid 28001, 435-8678/435 5377.
Called: Nov 1991, Gray's Inn, LLB (Leics)

Greaves *David William*
SITA, 26 Chemin de Joinville, 1216 Cointrin,
Geneva, 41.22.710.0112, Fax:
41.22.710.0166. Called: Feb 1990, Gray's
Inn, LLB (So'ton)

Grech *Miss Maria Penelope Christine*
Called: July 1996, Inner Temple, LLB
(Wolverhampton)

Green *Miss Amanda Jane*
Hunter & Hunter, Attorneys at Law, 3
Verulam Buildings, London, WC1R 5NT.
Called: Oct 1990, Middle Temple, BA
(Cantab)

Green *Miss Carol Laura Nancy*
Called: Nov 1994, Lincoln's Inn, LLB
(Hons)(Bucks)

Green *Jason Brian*
Advocates Collas Day & Rowland, Manor
Place, St Peter Port, Guernsey GY1 4EW,
01481 723191, Fax: 01481 711880, and
Member Guernsey Bar. Called: July 1996,
Inner Temple, LLB (W.Eng)

Green *Mrs Karen Patricia*
Box 1460, Mendocino, CA 95460, U.S.A.,
707 937 3960, Fax: 707 937 5861, and
Member California, USA. Called: May 1990,
Middle Temple, LLB (Cardiff)

Greenidge *Douglas Burton*
Bonnetts, Brittons Hill, St Michael, Barbados,
4360001, and Member Barbados Bar
Association. Called: Nov 1982, Gray's Inn,
LLB (Lond)

Grenade-Nurse *Mrs Florabelle*
and Member Trinidad & Tobago. Called: July
1990, Lincoln's Inn, M.Phil (Lond), Dip,
Law, LLM (Lond), LLB, (Lond), BSc (Econ)

Griffiths *Miss Dawn Christine*
Conyers Dill & Pearman, Clarendon House,
Church Street, Hamilton HM 11, (441) 295
1422, Fax: (441) 292 4720, and Member
Bermuda Bar. Called: May 1995, Lincoln's
Inn, LLB (Hons)

Griffiths *John Calvert CMG QC (1972)*
Des Voeux Chambers, 10/F Bank of East
Asia Bldg, 10 Des Voeux Road Central,
2526-3071, Fax: 2810-5287, and Member
Brunei Bars Hong Kong Bar Brick Court
Chambers, 15/19 Devereux Court, London,
WC2R 3JJ. Called: June 1956, Middle
Temple, MA (Cantab)

Gross *Richard Stephen*
Called: Oct 1992, Middle Temple, LL.B
(Hons)

Ground *The Hon Mr Justice Richard
William OBE*
c/o Supreme Court, 21 Parliament Street,
Hamilton HM12, 441 292 1350, Fax: 441
236 8183, QC Cayman Islands. Called: July
1975, Gray's Inn, BA (Oxon)

Guch *Miss Karen Anne*
Shook Lin & Bok, 19th Floor, Arab-Malaysian
Building, Jalan Raja Chulan, 50200 Kuala
Lumpur, 00 603 2558596/20117888, Fax:
00 603 2555673. Called: Nov 1996,
Lincoln's Inn, LLB (Hons)(Lond), LLM
(Hons)(Cantab)

Guha Thakurta *Sujoy*
Called: Nov 1996, Middle Temple, LLB
(Hons)(Hull)

Gui *Ms Karen Phek-Inn*
Wong Meng Meng & Partners, 80 Raffles
Place, [H]58-01 UOB Plaza, 65 5327488,
Fax: 65 5325711, and Member Singapore
Bar. Called: July 1993, Gray's Inn, LLB

Gul-Mohamed *Mohamed*
Peter Low tang & Partners, Advocates &
Solicitors, 15A Smith Street, 227 6206, Fax:
227 4861. Called: Nov 1995, Lincoln's Inn,
LLB (Hons)

Gunasekera *Miss Kuda Liyanage Don
Manuja*
286 Bullers Road, Colombo 7, Sri Lanka,
716011. Called: Feb 1994, Lincoln's Inn, LLB
(Hons), LLM, Dip Business, Administration

Guttman *Professor Egon*
930 Clintwood Drive,, Silver Spring,
Maryland, 20902, USA, 301 649 5739/202
274 4213, Fax: 202 274 4130. Called: May
1952, Middle Temple, LLM

Guzman *Miss Gillian Maria*
Attias & Levy, Suites 1 & 3, 3 Irish Place,
72150, Fax: 74986, and Member Gibraltar
Bar. Called: Nov 1994, Middle Temple, LLB
(Hons)(Wales)

Gwee *Boon Kim*
11 Lothian Terrace, Singapore 456784,
Republic of Singapore, 4424652, and
Member Singapore Bar. Called: July 1994,
Middle Temple, LLB (Hons)(L'pool)

Haberbeck *Andreas*
Abbas F.Ghazzawi Law Firm, P.O.Box 2335,
Jeddah 21451, 966 2 6654646, Fax: 966 2
6659155. Called: Nov 1981, Gray's Inn, LLB,
LLM

Hadjimanoli *Miss Marina*
P O Box 1358, Limassol, 05-367535, Fax: 05-
372072, and Member Cyprus Bar.
Called: Nov 1995, Lincoln's Inn, LLB (Hons)

Hadjipetrou *Leonidas*
00-357-2-422166, and Member Cyprus Bar.
Called: Nov 1995, Lincoln's Inn, LLB (Hons),
LLM (Lond)

Hager *Miss Sarah Jane*
Called: July 1986, Gray's Inn, LLB

Haines *Michael John*
6 Priory Farm, Inner Road, St Clements,
Jersey JE2 6GP, 01534 854412. Called: July
1995, Gray's Inn, LLB

Hajamaideen *Shamim Fyaz Bin*
Called: July 1997, Middle Temple, LLB
(Hons)

Hajarnis *Miss Aditi*
Called: July 1995, Lincoln's Inn, LLB (Hons)

Haji Abdul Hamid *Muhammad Zainidi*
and Member Brunei Bar. Called: July 1996,
Lincoln's Inn, LLB (Hons)(Manch)

Haji Anuar *Fathan*
Attorney General's Chambers, Ministry of
Law, Bandar Seri Begawan, Brunei 2690,
(6732) 244872, Fax: (6732) 223100.
Called: July 1995, Lincoln's Inn, LLB (Hons)

Haji Ismail *Miss Norismizan*
Called: Nov 1996, Lincoln's Inn, LLB (Hons)

Haji Mohammed *Miss Mazlin Haslinda*
Called: Nov 1995, Lincoln's Inn, LLB (Hons)

Haji Sahlan *Miss Shahida*
Called: Nov 1995, Lincoln's Inn, LLB (Hons)

Hakimi *Miss Hasrina*
Called: Oct 1997, Gray's Inn, LLB (Notts)

Halliday *Christopher Martin Jonathan*
Called: Nov 1997, Gray's Inn, LLB, LLM
(Nott'm)

Hamilton *James Frederick Hume
EDS, CBE*
Kenya Law Reform Commission, Maendeleo
House, 8th Floor, Monrovia Street,, PO Box
34999, Nairobi Kenya, Nairobi 220888/9,
and Member Kenya Bar. Called: Jan 1938,
Gray's Inn, MA (Cantab)

Hamilton-Kane *Nicholas John*
Hong Kong & Shanghai Banking,
Corporation Limited, 1 Queen's Road
Central. Called: July 1985, Inner Temple,
LLB (Bristol)

Hamon *Francis Charles*
La Maison Du Sud, Rue De La Piece Mauger,
Trinity, Jersey, 01534 863199. Called: Nov
1966, Middle Temple

Hampson *Graham William*
c/o Quin & Hampson, Barristers &
Attorneys at Law, PO Box 1348
Georgetown, Grand Cayman, Cayman
Islands, 809 9494123, Fax: 809 9494647,
Former solicitor and Member Cayman
Islands Bar. Called: Feb 1992, Middle
Temple, LLB (Hon) (Notts)

Hamzah *Miss Hazleena*
Called: Nov 1996, Lincoln's Inn, LLB
(Hons)(Bris)

Han *Miss Chin June*
Called: Mar 1997, Lincoln's Inn, BSc (Hons),
CPE

Han *Miss Chin May*
Called: July 1996, Lincoln's Inn, LLB
(Hons)(Sheff)

Han *Hean Juan*
Called: July 1996, Inner Temple, LLB (Lond)

Han *Teck Kwong*
Called: July 1995, Middle Temple, LLB
(Hons)

Hanam *Andrew John*
Blk 350, Woodlands Ave 3, 11-99.
Called: Nov 1996, Middle Temple, LLB
(Hons)

Handmaker *Jeffrey David*
Lawyers for Human Rights, 730 Van Erkom
Bldg, 217 Pretorius St, Pretoria 0002, +27
12 21 21 35, Fax: +27 12 32 56 318.
Called: July 1995, Inner Temple, LLB
(Newc), LLM (Lond)

Hangchi *Kevin*
Called: July 1997, Middle Temple, BSc
(Hons)

Haq *Miss Tasneem Rehana*
Called: Nov 1996, Middle Temple, BA
(Hons)(Keele)

Haque *Mohammed Azharul*
Called: May 1997, Inner Temple, B.Com
(Bangladesh), LLB (Lond)

Harben *Paul Ralph*
Crill Canavan, La Chasse Chambers, La
Chasse, St Helier, Channel Islands, 0534
888933, Fax: 0534 887040. Called: Oct
1993, Middle Temple, LLB (Hons)(Kingston)

Harding *Miss Patricia Yvette*
Hodges Chambers, The Valley, P.O.Box 840,
Anguilla, 264 497 3793, Fax: 264 497 2863,
and Member Anguilla Bar (Eastern
Caribbean States). Called: July 1980, Middle
Temple, BA

Hariri *Arham Rahimy*
Called: Nov 1997, Lincoln's Inn, LLB
(Hons)(L'pool)

Harkins *Mrs Sheila*
Called: Nov 1995, Lincoln's Inn, LLB
(Hons)(Wales)

Haron *Miss Hidayati*
Called: Nov 1997, Lincoln's Inn, LLB (Hons)

Haron *Miss Maria*
Called: July 1994, Lincoln's Inn, LLB (Hons)

Haron Kamar *Miss Haslinda*
and Member Malaysia. Called: July 1996,
Lincoln's Inn, LLB (Hons)(Notts)

Harraj *Mohammad Raza Hayat*
Called: Nov 1995, Lincoln's Inn, BA (Hons),
LLB (Hons) (Leics)

Harre *Mr Justice George Elliott*
Grand Court, P.O. Box 495, George Town,
Grand Cayman, (345) 949 4296, Fax: (345)
949-1049. Called: Feb 1954, Middle Temple,
MA

Harshaw *Paul Andrew*
Suite 349, 48 Par-la-Ville Road, Hamilton HM
11. Called: May 1997, Lincoln's Inn, LLB
(Hons)

Hart *Timothy George*
Bailhache Labesse, Advocates & Solicitors,
14/16 Hill Street, St Helier, Jersey, 01534
888777, Fax: 01534 888778, and Member
Jersey Bar. Called: Feb 1995, Gray's Inn, BA
(Oxon)

Harvey *Christopher*
Russell & DuMoulin, 2100-1075 W Georgia
St, Vancouver V6E 3G2, 604 631 3131, Fax:
604 631 3232, QC British Columbia Bar and
Member British Columbia Bar. Called: July
1968, Middle Temple, BA (Mcgill), Dip Law,
LLM, PhD (Lond)

Hasan *Mohammed Ziaul*
Called: Mar 1997, Gray's Inn, LLB (Lond)

Hashim *Miss Zaheera*
M/S Haq & Namazie Partnership, 20 Cecil
Street, [H]22-03, (65) 4386604, Fax: (65)
4387383, and Member Singapore Bar.
Called: July 1995, Middle Temple, LLB
(Hons), BA

Haskins *Mrs Felicity Jane*
F Haskins & Co, College Chambers, 3 St
James' Street, St Peter Port, Guernsey,
01481 721316, Fax: 01481 721317,
Advocate of Royal Court of Guernsey.
Called: Nov 1989, Inner Temple, LLB (Lond)

Hassan *Miss Fleur Judith Sol*
Called: Nov 1996, Middle Temple, LLB
(Hons)

Hassan *Miss Haslina*
Called: July 1995, Middle Temple, LLB
(Hons) (Kent)

Hassett *Professor Patricia*
Syracuse College of Law, Syracuse, New
York 13244, United States of America, 315
443 2535, Fax: 315 443 4141, US Supreme
Court and Member New York Bar.
Called: Nov 1992, Inner Temple, BA, LLB,
LLM, Proff at Law

Hatfield-Hadjiioannou *Mrs Ruth
Elizabeth*
Christos M Georgiades &, Telemachos M
Georgiades Advoc., 22 25th March Street,
P.O.Box 85, Paphos, and Member Cyprus
Bar. Called: Nov 1986, Gray's Inn, LLB
(Nott'm)

Hawa *Miss Nayla*
Al Tamimi & Company, P.O.Box 9275,
Dubai, 009714 317090, Fax: 009714
3613177. Called: Oct 1994, Middle Temple,
LLB (Hons)(Lond)

Hay *David John Mackenzie*
Malayan Law Journal Sdn Bhd, 10th Floor,
Hamzah Kwong Hing, No 1 Leboh Ampang,
50100 Kuala Lumpur, 60 3 232 1218, Fax:
60 3 238 7073. Called: July 1977, Inner
Temple, MA (Edin), MA, LLM, (Cantab)

Haythorne *Eric George*
Senior Counsel, Legal Dept, The World
Bank, 1818 H Street, N.W., Washington,
D.C. 20433, (202)458-0014, Fax: (202)522-
1592, and Member Ontario, Canada Paris,
France. Called: July 1973, Inner Temple, BA
(Cantab), MA (Cantab), BA (Hons)(Queen's),
LLB(Dalhousie), Doc de L'Universite, (Paris)

Healy *John Pascal*
Tara, Waterfall Road, Bishoptown, Cork,
353 21 371562, Fax: 353 21 371562, Kings
Inn, Dublin and Member Southern Ireland
Bar. Called: Feb 1982, Middle Temple,
ACIArb

Hee *Miss Cher Sun*
7 Jalan Cahaya 6, Taman Salak Selatan,
57100 Kuala Lumpur, (603) 957 3693, Fax:
(603) 957 3695. Called: July 1995, Middle
Temple, LLB (Hons)

Helfrecht *William John*
Ian Boxall & Co, CIBC Financial Centre, P O
Box 1234, George Town, Grand Cayman,
Cayman Islands, (345) 949 9876, Fax: (345)
949 9877, and Member Cayman Islands.
Called: Nov 1978, Middle Temple, MA
(Oxon)

Hellman *Stephen Geoffrey*
Paget-Brown, Quin & Hampson, Harbour
Centre, Third Floor, P.O.Box 1348, Grand
Cayman, Cayman Islands, 00 1 809 949
4123, Fax: 00 1 809 949 4647. Called: July
1988, Inner Temple, BA (Oxon), Dip Law

Heng *Clive Boon Howe*
17 Leedon Road, Wilmer Park, 3244 553,
Fax: 65 3244 552, and Member Singapore
Bar. Called: July 1976, Lincoln's Inn, LLB
(Hons) (Lond)

Heng *Hui Tek*
Heng & Rada, 1 North Bridge Road, 30-05
High Street Centre, 3389800, Fax: 3392328,
Advocate & Solicitor, Singapore. Called: July
1984, Lincoln's Inn, LLB (Warwick), M.Phil
(Cantab)

Hernandez *Christian*
Called: Nov 1995, Middle Temple, LLB
(Hons)

Hesse-Djabatey *Mrs Leonora Akousa
Kwakua*
P.O.Box 128, Tradefair Site, Accra, Ghana,
665915, and Member Ghana. Called: Nov
1988, Gray's Inn, LLB (Lond)

Hiew *Miss Fatimah Yen Won*
Called: Mar 1998, Lincoln's Inn, LLB (Hons)

Higgs *Conrad Clephane*
South School Lane, Back Salina, Grand Turk,
Turks & Caicos Islands, (809) 946 1320, and
Member Turks & Caicos Bar. Called: Nov
1995, Middle Temple, BA (Hons)(W.Indies),
MSc (B'ham)

Hingorani *Jeevan*
Pacific Chambers, 1301 Dina House, 11
Duddell Street, Central, 521 5544, Fax: 524
5912, and Member West Indies Bar.
Called: Feb 1977, Gray's Inn, BA (Hons)

Hirschfeld *Charl Benno*
Barrister of the High Court of New Zealand
(1984) and in the Ferderal Republic of
Germany (1992). Called: July 1990, Inner
Temple, LLB, LLM (Auckland)

Hirst *Alastair John*
72 Northumberland Street, Edinburgh
EH3 6JG, 031 556 5324, Fax: 031 557 5338,
and Member Sultanate of Oman. Called: Nov
1971, Inner Temple, MA (Cantab), FCIArb

Hj Mat *Yaackub*
Batu 34, Kampong Baru Myalas, 77100
Asahan, Melaka, 06-5229689. Called: Mar
1997, Lincoln's Inn, LLB (Hons), LLM
(Wales)

Hj Md Noor *Zulkhairi*
Called: Nov 1996, Lincoln's Inn, LLB (Hons)

Ho *Ms Adaline See Yin*
Called: July 1997, Inner Temple, LLB (Lond)

Ho *Miss Annie Yin Yin*
Called: Nov 1994, Lincoln's Inn, LLB (Hons)(Lond)

Ho *Miss Elaine Kit Yee*
Called: July 1994, Lincoln's Inn, LLB (Hons)

Ho *Kam Tim*
Called: Nov 1993, Lincoln's Inn, LLB (Hons, Lond)

Ho *Kenneth Boon Kuan*
Called: July 1996, Lincoln's Inn, LLB (Hons)(Notts)

Ho *Miss Kim Foong*
Sim Hill Tan & Wong, 4 Shenton Way, 14-07/12, Shing Kwan House, Singapore 0106, 65 2200035, Fax: 65 2240693, and Member Singapore Bar. Called: July 1994, Middle Temple, BA (Hons)(Keele)

Ho *Miss Melissa Yee Ling*
Called: July 1994, Middle Temple, LLB (Hons)(Brunel)

Ho *Sammy Wai Chuen*
Called: Nov 1997, Inner Temple, BSc (Hong Kong), LLB (Lond)

Ho *Shi King*
Called: Oct 1996, Middle Temple, LLB (Hons)

Ho *Miss Shok Heng*
60 Taman Merlin, 43000 Kajang, Selangor, Malaysia, 00603-8364779. Called: July 1995, Middle Temple, LLB (Hons)

Ho *Tzin Wen*
Called: July 1994, Middle Temple, BA (Hons)(Keele)

Hock *Lee Kay*
Called: July 1991, Gray's Inn, B.Soc.Sci (Keele)

Hoe *Cheah Seng*
and Member Malaysia. Called: Nov 1996, Lincoln's Inn, LLB (Hons)(Sheff)

Hoe *Miss Chee May*
Called: July 1997, Middle Temple, LLB (Hons), LLM, (L'pool)

Hoh *Miss Gigi Anne*
3451308, Fax: 3451182. Called: July 1995, Middle Temple, LLB (Hons)

Holliday *Miss Valerie Anne*
Called: Nov 1994, Middle Temple, LLB (Hons)

Holmback *Dr Ulf Aake Olof*
Svartmangatan 27, S-111 29 Stockholm, 0046 8218129, and Member Sweden Bar. Called: July 1979, Gray's Inn, JUR DR (Uppsala)

Holmberg *Miss Loretta Vanessa*
Called: July 1996, Middle Temple, LLB (Hons)(Wales)

Hon *Chi Keung*
Called: Nov 1994, Middle Temple, LLB (Hons)

Hon *Omar Adam*
Called: Nov 1996, Middle Temple, LLB (Hons)

Hong *Aeron Yea Chun*
(60) 3 7743063, and Member Malaysian Bar. Called: Oct 1995, Middle Temple, LLB (Hons)

Hoo *Alan*
16th Floor, Malahon Centre, 10-12 Stanley Street, Central, 852-28686155, Fax: 852-28106795, Queen's Counsel in Hong Kong and Member Hong Kong Bar. Called: Nov 1973, Middle Temple, LLB (Lond)

Hoo *Miss Lina*
Called: Nov 1997, Lincoln's Inn, LLB (Hons)(L'pool)

Hoo *Miss Sheau Peng*
Called: Oct 1993, Middle Temple, BA (Hons)

Hoosen *Abdul Aziz*
113 New Henry House, 10 Ice House Street, Central, 852 8770087, Fax: 852 25246202, and Member Hong Kong Bar. Called: Nov 1974, Gray's Inn, BA (McGill)

Horne *Miss Zhinga Arlette*
Phillips & Williams, Middle Street, P O Box 262, St Vincent, (809) 456 1390 or 456 1580, Fax: (809) 456 2344, and Member St Vincent & the Grenadines Bar. Called: Oct 1995, Middle Temple, LLB (Hons), LLM (Cantab), LLM, IMLI (Malta)

Horseman *Richard Thomas*
Called: Nov 1995, Gray's Inn, BA (St.Louis), LLB

Horton-Strachan *Mrs Arlean Patricia*
Called: Nov 1995, Gray's Inn, BSc (W.Indies), LLB (Lond)

Hosein *Faarees Fayaz*
39 Richmond Street, PO Box 1003, Port of Spain, Trinidad W.I., 623-2695/8303, Fax: 623-8303, Attorney-at-Law, Supreme Court of Trinidad & Tobago (Admitted October 1988), Attorney-at-Law, Supreme Court of Barbados (Admitted May 1991). Called: July 1988, Lincoln's Inn, LLB (Hons) (Dundee)

Hoskins *Nicholas John*
46 Par-La-Ville Road, Hamilton HM11, Bermuda, (441) 296 0253, Fax: (441) 296 0809, and Member Bermuda. Called: Nov 1992, Middle Temple, LLB (Hons, Bucks)

Hossain *Miss Lolita Lamis*
Called: July 1997, Lincoln's Inn, LLB (Hons)(LSE)

Houghton *Anthony Kenneth*
Des Voeux Chambers, 10/F Bank of East Asia Bldg, 10 Des Voeux Road Central, 2526-3071, Fax: 2810 5287/5309/0274, and Member Hong Kong Bar. Called: Nov 1988, Gray's Inn, LLB (Lond), ARICS, AHKIS,FCI Arb

Hourican *James Kevin*
4903 Island View Street, Oxnard, CA 93035, 011-1-805-984447922, Major, United States Marine Corps Reserve and Member Pennsylvania Bar California Bar. Called: Feb 1994, Gray's Inn, BA JD (Pittsburgh)

How *Chi Hoong Nicholas*
Called: July 1996, Middle Temple, LLB (Hons)(Bris)

How *Miss Su Fen*
Called: July 1997, Lincoln's Inn, LLB (Hons)(Wales)

Howell *Lt Col David Malcom OBE*
Called: July 1973, Lincoln's Inn, LLB (Hons)

Huang *Miss Lianne*
Bankers Trust Company, (65) 331 4798. Called: July 1997, Gray's Inn, LLB (Bristol)

Huggins *Adrian Armstrong*
Temple Chambers, 16th Floor, One Pacific Place, 88 Queensway, 852 2523 2003, Fax: 852 2523 6343, QC (Hong Kong) and Member Hong Kong Bar. Called: Nov 1975, Gray's Inn, MA (Cantab), LLM

Hughes *Jonathan Patrick*
Solomon, Zauderer, Ellenhorn,, Frisher & Sharp, 45 Rockefeller Plaza, New York, NY 10111, (212) 424 0728, Fax: (212) 956 4068, and Member New York Bar. Called: Nov 1983, Middle Temple, LLB (Sheff)

Hughes Ferrari *Mrs Margaret Hazell*
Hughes & Cummings, P.O. Box 32, Saint Vincent & The Grenadines, 809 456 1954/1711, Fax: 809 457 2768, and Member Saint Vincent and The Grenadines Bar. Called: July 1990, Lincoln's Inn, LLB (Lond)

Hui *Wai Chun Sammy*
1318 Princes Building, Chater Road, Central, 2526 8128, Fax: 2526 8500, and Member Hong Kong Bar. Called: July 1991, Lincoln's Inn, LLB (Hons)

Hui *Miss Ying Ying*
Called: Nov 1996, Gray's Inn, LLB

Humphreys *Gordon David Thomas*
21 Boulevard Pierre Dupong, L-1430 Luxembourg, Luxembourg, 352 44 65 64, Fax: 352 44 65 64, and Member Belgium Bar. Called: Nov 1986, Middle Temple, LLB (Bucks), LLM (UWIST), Licence speciale en, droit Economique, (Univ de Liege)

Huq *Faheemul*
Called: Nov 1997, Lincoln's Inn, LLB (Wolver'ton)

Huq *Rafique-ul*
Huq & Company, 47/1 Purana Paltan, Dhaka, Bangladesh, 955 2196 or 955 5953, Fax: 956 2434, Senior Advocate, Supreme Court of Bangladesh and Member Bangladesh Bar Association. Called: Nov 1962, Lincoln's Inn, MA, LLB

Hurhangee *Ashley*
Called: Mar 1997, Lincoln's Inn, LLB (Hons)

Husain *Rehan*
Called: Nov 1996, Lincoln's Inn, LLB (Hons)(Leeds)

Hussain *Miss Dheena*
Called: July 1997, Lincoln's Inn, LLB (Hons)

Iacovides *Petros*
Libra Housa, 21 P Catelaris Str, P O Box 5001, Nicosia, Cyprus, 02 46 67 66, Fax: 02 44 87 77, and Member Cyprus Bar. Called: Feb 1994, Gray's Inn, B.Soc.Sc (Keele)

Ian *Lim Teck Soon*
Called: Nov 1997, Inner Temple, LLB (Lond)

Ibbotson *David James*
Bedell & Orston, Normandy House, Greville Street, St Helier, Jersey, 814814, Fax: 814815. Called: Mar 1996, Middle Temple, LLB (Hons)(Wales)

Ibrahim *Miss Hasnah*
Attorney General's Chambers, Bandar Seri Begawan, 2016 Negara, Brunei, Darussalam. Called: July 1994, Lincoln's Inn, LLB (Hons)

Ibrahim *Miss Shadida*
Called: July 1993, Lincoln's Inn, LLB (Hons)

Idrees *Rasheed*
Haidermota & Co, 303-305 Kashif Centre, Sharea Faisal, Karachi 75530, 519226/ 5662589/5133714, Fax: 5662583/58770761, and Member Pakistan Bar. Called: Nov 1994, Inner Temple, LLB (Lond)

Idris *Miss Norazlina*
and Member Malaysia Bar. Called: July 1994, Lincoln's Inn, LLB (Hons)

Ioannides *Mrs Eleni*
Chr.Sozou 2, Flat 206, Nicosia, 357 2 473558/ 474533, Fax: 357 2 475692, and Member Cyprus Bar. Called: Nov 1961, Middle Temple

Ip *Tak Keung*
603 Ruttonjee House, 11 Duddell Street, Central, 2868 1249, Fax: 2868 0368, and Member Hong Kong Bar Singapore Bar Barrister of the Australian Capital Territory. Called: July 1985, Gray's Inn, LLB (Bucks) B.Soc.Sc, LLM (LSE),ACIArb, Dip (Chinese Law)

Irani *Miss Simone*
3 Pandan Valley, [H] 16-313, 4699286/ 4677276, Fax: 4633209. Called: Nov 1995, Middle Temple, LLB (Hons)

Irving *Ms Frances Margaret*
Called: July 1996, Gray's Inn, MA (Edinburgh)

Isa *Amir Yahaya*
Called: July 1997, Middle Temple, BA (Hons)(Keele)

Isaac *Miss Elma Gene*
Called: Nov 1997, Lincoln's Inn, LLB (Hons)

Isaac *Tito Shane*
111 North Bridge Road, [H]23-01, Peninsula Plaza, Singapore 0617, (065) 3382251, Fax: (065) 3381818, and Member Singapore Bar. Called: Nov 1994, Gray's Inn, LLB (Leeds)

Ishak *Miss Irma Norris*
Called: Nov 1997, Lincoln's Inn, LLB (Hons)(Wales)

Ismail *Abdul Rashid*
Called: July 1994, Lincoln's Inn, LLB (Hons)

Ismail *Miss Fariza*
Called: July 1994, Lincoln's Inn, LLB (Hons)

Ismail *Miss Zarina*
Called: Nov 1997, Middle Temple, LLB (Hons)

Israeli *Guy*
2 Derech Haganim St, Kfar Shmaryahu 46910, and Member Israel. Called: Oct 1994, Lincoln's Inn, LLB (Hons)(Bucks), LLM (LSE)

Issa *Khoda-Baksh Mahmood Ibreh*
Called: Nov 1996, Inner Temple, LLB (Lond)

Iyer *Mrs Rukmani Tiru Krishna*
114A Newlands Road, Newlands, Wellington, (64-4) 4773191, Fax: (64-4) 4773191. Called: July 1995, Gray's Inn, LLB (Lond)

Izzuddin *Miss Izzaty*
Called: July 1995, Inner Temple, LLB (Sheff)

Jaafar *Miss Jafisah*
Called: July 1992, Lincoln's Inn, BA (Hons) (Kent)

Jaafar *Sallehudin*
Messrs Yeow & Salleh, Suite 6.02, 6th Floor, Wisma MCA, Jalan Ampang, 50450 Kuala Lumpur, 03 2623833, Fax: 03 2613833, and Member Malaysia Bar. Called: Nov 1992, Lincoln's Inn, LLB (Hons)(Sheff)

Jaafar-Thani *Dzuhairi*
Called: Nov 1996, Middle Temple, LLB (Nott'm)

Jackson *His Honour Peter Brierley*
Magistrate's Chambers, Judicial Department, P.O. Box 495, George Town, Grand Cayman, 081 809 949 5151/4296, Fax: 081 809 949 9856. Called: July 1979, Gray's Inn, MA (Cantab), Dip in Crim.[Lond], FBIM, Teaching Cert in F.E

Jackson-Lipkin *The Hon Mr Justice Miles Henry KCLJ, JP, QC,*
(852) 2838 1838, Fax: (852) 2891 6993, and Member Hong Kong Bar New South Wales Bar. Called: June 1951, Middle Temple, FCIArb, CArb (Canada)

Jacobs *Richard*
Suite 201, 1010 Harris Ave, Bellingham, Washington 98225, (360) 671 3116, Fax: (360) 671 6116, U.S. Immigration & Naturalization Law and Member California & Washington. Called: July 1978, Lincoln's Inn, LLB (Lond), NCA Certified, Mediator

Jaganathan *Jagan Persath s/o*
Called: Nov 1996, Lincoln's Inn, LLB (Hons)(Wolv'ton)

Jaganathan *Miss Shanti*
Called: Nov 1996, Lincoln's Inn, LLB (Hons)(Leics)

Jailani *Bin Shariff*
Called: July 1994, Lincoln's Inn, LLB (Hons)

Jalan *Prateek*
7th Floor, 233/5 Acharya J.C. Bose Road, Calcutta 700020, India, (91-33) 2475990/ 402549, Fax: (91-33) 401727, and Member India Bar. Called: July 1993, Inner Temple, BA (Delhi), BA (Cantab), LLM (Michigan)

Jamaluddin *Miss Jasmin Hussain*
Jamalatiff
Called: July 1994, Lincoln's Inn, LLB (Hons, Bucks)

Jamaludin *Miss Aini Hayati*
Messrs Lee Hishammuddin, Advocate & Solicitors, 16th Floor, Wisma Hla, Jalan Raja Chulan, 50200 Kuala Lumpur, (6-03) 2011681, Fax: (6-03) 2011714/2011746, and Member Malaysia Bar. Called: July 1995, Inner Temple, LLB (Nott)

James *Miss Gloria Magdalen*
Blk 170, [H]02-865, Yishun Ave 7, pgr: 93062380/7530014, and Member Singapore. Called: July 1995, Lincoln's Inn, LLB (Hons)

James *Miss Jacquelinne Agnes*
Gomez Building, High Street, St John's, P O Box 1519, 268 462 4468/9, Fax: 268 462 0327, and Member Antigua Bar Barbuda Bar. Called: Nov 1995, Lincoln's Inn, LLB (Hons)(Leeds)

James *Miss Mabel Nirmala*
64 Jalan 2/27C, Section 5, Wang S9 MAJU, 53300 Kuala Lumpur, 03-4118391. Called: July 1996, Lincoln's Inn, LLB (Hons), LLM (Wolves)

James *Miss Nilakrisna Isnarti*
Prins & Co, 24 LRG Kinabalu 1, Luyang PH 7, Jalan Kolam, 88300 Kota Kinabalu, Sabah, (6088) 262858, Fax: (6088) 238808, and Member Malaysia Bar Sabah Bar Sarawak Bar. Called: Oct 1994, Lincoln's Inn, LLB (Hons)(Hull), LLM (Lond)

James *Roger Ivor Rendall*
Baker & McKenzie, Hutchinson House, 14th Floor, 10 Harcourt Road, Central, (852) 2846 2426, Fax: (852) 2845 0476, and Member New York Bar (1990). Called: July 1988, Lincoln's Inn, LLB (Hons)

Jamieson *Maurice*
and Member Scotland. Called: July 1997, Middle Temple, LLB (Hons)

Jamil *Zahid Usman*
Called: July 1997, Gray's Inn, LLB (Lond)

Jarraw *Colin Tarang*
Called: July 1996, Inner Temple, LLB (Northumbria), M.Phil (Cantab)

Jarrett *Miss Stephanie Ann*
Called: Oct 1990, Lincoln's Inn, LLB (Lond)

Jat *Sew Tong*
Temple Chambers, 1607 One Pacific Place, 88 Queensway, Hong Kong, 852 2523 2003, Fax: 852 2810 0302, and Member Hong Kong Singapore Bar. Called: July 1988, Gray's Inn, LLB (LSE),BCL(Oxon)

Javali *Kirit Sharat*
Called: Oct 1996, Gray's Inn, BA (Delhi), LLB (Leeds)

Jayadevan *Jayaperakash*
Called: Nov 1997, Lincoln's Inn, LLB (Hons)

Jayakumar *Miss Shalita*
and Member Singapore Bar. Called: July 1995, Middle Temple, LLB (Hons)

Jee *Fabian Soo Chen*
Called: Nov 1996, Gray's Inn, BA (Keele)

Jeganathan *Miss Michelle Frances*
21 Shangri La Walk, 65 452 1733, Fax: 65
458 5486, and Member Singapore Bar.
Called: July 1996, Inner Temple, LLB (Hull)

Jhogasundram *Miss Jayanthi*
Called: July 1995, Lincoln's Inn, LLB (Hons)

Jinu *Ms Feona*
Messrs JNLS Associates, Lot 22, Block D,
Damai Plaza Phase 111, Damai Reservoir
Road, 88300 Kota Kinabalu, Sabah, (88)
212117, Fax: (88) 238866, and Member
Borneo Bar. Called: May 1990, Gray's Inn,
LL.B., LLM

Johari *Miss Lindahyni*
Called: July 1997, Lincoln's Inn, LLB
(Hons)(L'pool)

John *Jeevan Noel*
Called: Nov 1997, Middle Temple, BA
(Hons)(Keele)

John *Jeffrey*
Called: July 1996, Lincoln's Inn, LLB (Hons)

Johnatty *Malcom*
P.O.Box 146, Port of Spain, Trinidad &
Tobago, 1-809-665-6173, and Member
Trinidad & Tobago Bar. Called: July 1994,
Inner Temple, BSc (West Indies), LLB
(Lond)

Johns *Alain*
c/o Messrs John & Co, No 7500A Beech
Road, [H]14-302 The Plaza, 294 3150/ 296
2975, Fax: 291 4662, and Member
Singapore. Called: July 1995, Middle
Temple, LLB (Hons)

Johnson *Anthony Lesroy*
Called: July 1995, Lincoln's Inn, LLB (Hons)

Johnson *Lenworth Walter*
Maundy Building, 29A St Mary's Street, St
John's, Antigua, 268 460 9714, Fax: 268 460
9715, and Member Antigua, Barbuda.
Called: Nov 1996, Inner Temple, LLB
(Wolverh'ton)

Johnston *Kenneth Barry*
Level 3, Landcorp House, 101 Lambton
Quay, P.O.Box 5058, Wellington, 471 2727,
Fax: 499 4620, and Member New Zealand
Bar. Called: May 1988, Middle Temple, LLB,
DIP H.R.M.

Johnston *Mark*
Rue De L'Epargne 10 BTE 7, 1000-Bruxelles,
Belgium, 00 322 223 2785, Member of
King's Inn, Dublin and Member Southern
Ireland Bar. Called: July 1988, Middle
Temple, BCL (U.C.D), BL (Kings Inns)

Jones *Andrew John*
Maples and Calder, P.O. Box 309 GT, Grand
Cayman, Cayman Islands, 345 949 8066,
Fax: 345 949 8080, and Member Cayman
Islands. Called: Nov 1973, Inner Temple,
MA (Cantab)

Jones *Mrs Anjette Nadine*
20 Queensway Quay, 00 350 40730, Fax: 00
350 73315, and Member Gibraltar Bar.
Called: Oct 1992, Inner Temple, LLB

Jones-Crawford *Mrs Shaaron*
179 Dawlish Avenue, Toronto, Ontario
M4N1H6, 416 485 3410, Fax: 416 485 3329.
Called: July 1990, Lincoln's Inn, LLB

Jong *Miss Ling*
Called: Nov 1996, Lincoln's Inn, LLB
(Hons)(Hull)

Joof *Miss Amie*
Called: Nov 1997, Lincoln's Inn, LLB
(Hons)(Warw)

Joon *Ms Loy Siew*
Called: Nov 1996, Inner Temple, LLB (Lond)

Josef *Miss Rozanna Jacqueline*
10 Jalan 4L, Ampang Jaya, 68000 Ampang,
Selangor DE, 03 456 9401, Fax: 65 475
8665, and Member Malaysia. Called: Nov
1994, Inner Temple, LLB (Bris)

Joseph *Eugene Roy*
Suite 2.10, 2nd Floor, Wisma Mirama, Jalan
Wisma Putra, 50460 Kuala Lumpur, West
Malaysia, 03-2432395, Fax: 03-2440827/
2448760, and Member Malaysia Bar.
Called: July 1996, Lincoln's Inn, LLB
(Hons)(Lond)

Joseph *Miss Margaret Mary*
Called: July 1996, Middle Temple, LLB
(Hons)(Lond)

Joseph *Vincent*
Called: July 1996, Lincoln's Inn, LLB
(Hons)(Lond)

Josephson *Ms Diana Hayward*
1000 Navy Pentagon, Washington D.C.
20350-1000, 703 693 4527, and Member
District of Columbia Bar. Called: June 1959,
Gray's Inn, BA,MA (Hons) (Oxon), M Comp.

Jospeh *Xavier Annou Anselm*
Called: Nov 1996, Lincoln's Inn, LLB
(HOns)(Lond)

Jublee *Cilve Clive*
P.O.Box 21206, 88769 Luyang, Sabah, 088
231111, Fax: 088 233122, and Member
Advocate & Solcitor, Sabah. Called: July
1995, Middle Temple, LLB (Hons) (Warw)

Jung *Moo-Kyung*
Called: July 1996, Middle Temple, BA
(Hons)(Seoul), LLM (Warw), CPE (B'ham)

Jusoh *Sufian Bin*
Skrine & Co, 2nd Floor, Straits Trading
Building, 4 Leboh Pasar, 50050 Kuala
Lumpur Malaysia, (60) (3) 2945111, Fax:
(60) (3) 2934327, and Member Malaysia Bar.
Called: Nov 1992, Lincoln's Inn, LLB
(Hons)(Wales)

Kaburise *Professor John Bonaventure
Kubongpwa*
Department of Public Law, Faculty of Law,
University of Durban-Westville, Private Bag
X54001, Durban 4000, (031) 820 9111, Fax:
(031) 820 2848, Solicitor Papua New
Guinea and Member Papua New Guinea
Bar. Called: July 1988, Middle Temple, LLB
(Hons) (Ghana), LLM (Pennsylvannia)

Kahar *Bador Rizal*
Called: Nov 1997, Lincoln's Inn, BA
(Hons)(Oxon)

Kahmei *Miss Chee*
Called: Nov 1994, Inner Temple, LLB (Lond)

Kalpanath *Singh Miss Rina*
Kalpanath & Co, 101-A Upper Cross Street,
[H]12-17 Peoples Part Centre, Singapore
0105, 533 4833, Fax: 532 7408, and
Member Singapore Bar. Called: July 1994,
Middle Temple, LLB (Hons)(Warw)

Kam *Aubeck Tse Tsuen*
Called: July 1993, Lincoln's Inn, LLB (Hons)

Kam *Chin Khoon*
Called: Nov 1993, Middle Temple, BA
(Hons)

Kam-Chuen *Cheung*
and Member Hong Kong Bar. Called: July
1996, Inner Temple, LLB (Wolverhampton),
MBA (Leic)

Kamalanathan *Selva Kumaran*
and Member Malaysia Bar. Called: July 1994,
Lincoln's Inn, LLB (Hons), LLM (Malaya)

Kamaruddin *Kamarul Hisham*
Called: May 1995, Gray's Inn, LLB

Kamaruddin *Miss Siti Ardila*
Called: Nov 1992, Gray's Inn, BA (Keele)

Kamaruzaman *Miss Zuwita*
Called: July 1994, Lincoln's Inn, LLB (Hons)

Kamaruzzaman *Ms Intan Zubaidah*
and Member Malaysia. Called: Feb 1994,
Inner Temple, LLB (Hull), MBA, (Lond), DIC

Kammitsi *Miss Lefkothea*
C/O George L Savvides & Co, 1 Glafkos Str,
1085 Nicosia, 02-422355, Fax: 02-421819,
and Member Cyprus Bar. Called: July 1990,
Middle Temple, BSocSc (Keele)

Kan *Miss Caroline Yuen Oi*
M/s Harry Elias & Partners, 79 Robinson
Road [H]16-03, CPF Building, Singapore
0106. Called: Nov 1987, Middle Temple,
LLB(Hons) London, BA(Hons) McMaster

Kanagalingam *Miss Sharini Prema*
91 Jalan Telawi, Bangsar Baru, 59100 Kuala
Lumpur, Malaysia, 03 253 0933, Fax: 03 794
2000 EXT 218 (0), and Member Malaysia
Bar. Called: July 1991, Inner Temple, LLB
(Notts)

Kanagarajan *Veluthevar*
The Ministry of Foreign Affairs, Raffles City
06-00, 250 North Bridge Road, Singapore,
179101, 336 1177, Fax: 339 4330.
Called: Nov 1977, Lincoln's Inn, LLB (Lond)

Kanagavijayan *Nadarajan*
Called: Nov 1996, Inner Temple, BA
(Singpaore), LLB, LLM (Lond)

Kang *Colin Seng Kok*
Called: Nov 1997, Middle Temple, LLB
(Hons)(Bucks)

Kangeson *Miss Gowri R.*
Called: Oct 1997, Gray's Inn, LLB
(Glamorgan)

Kanthosamy *Rajendran*
Called: July 1996, Middle Temple, LLB
(Hons)(Lond)

F

Kanyerezi *Timothy Masembe*
Mugerwa & Matovu Advocates, 3rd Floor,
Diamond Trust Bldg, Plot 17/19 Kampala
Road, PO Box 7166, Kampala, 256 41
343859,259920,255431, Fax: 256 41
259992, and Member Ugandan Bar.
Called: July 1992, Inner Temple, LLB (Lond)

Kapetaniou *Miss Phani*
Called: Mar 1996, Lincoln's Inn, LLB
(Hons)(Leics)

Kaplan *Neil*
S. 1601,Bank of East Asia Bldg, 10 Des
Vouex Road, Central, Hong Kong, (852)
2869 6301, Fax: (852) 2869 6372, QC
(Hong Kong) and Member Hong Kong Bar
New York Victoria Australia. Called: Feb
1965, Inner Temple, LLB (Lond) FCIArb

Kapri *Miss Zuhra Jabeen*
Called: Nov 1996, Lincoln's Inn, LLB (Hons)

Kapur *Ravi Krishan*
Called: July 1997, Lincoln's Inn, B.Com
(Hons), (Calcutta), LLB, (Hons)(Leeds)

Karia *Chirag*
Gray Cary Ware & Friedenrich, 400
Hamilton Avenue, Palo Alto, CA 94301-
1825, (650) 833 2147, Fax: 9650) 327 3699,
and Member The State Bar of California.
Called: Nov 1988, Lincoln's Inn, BA
(Hons)(Cantab), MA (Hons)(Cantab), LLM

Karim *Shaikh Saleem*
Called: Oct 1996, Middle Temple, LLB
(Hons)(Essex)

Karupiah *Jegathesean*
Called: Oct 1995, Gray's Inn, BA

Karuppiah *Kalidass s/o*
Called: Nov 1996, Inner Temple, LLB (Lond)

Karuppiah *Sathinathan*
Tan Lian Ker & Company, 2 Havelock Road
[H] 07-10, Apollo Centre, 65 532 7117.
Called: July 1996, Lincoln's Inn, LLB (Hons),
LLM (Sussex)

Karydes *Marios Andrea*
P.O.Box 77086, GR 175, 10 Athens, 01-
4116942, Fax: 01-4179221, and Member
Piraeus Bar Association. Called: July 1971,
Inner Temple, Athens University, Law
Degree

Kasim *Ms Siti Zabedah*
Called: Nov 1997, Gray's Inn, LLB

Kassim *Miss Noor Sukhairiyani*
Called: Nov 1997, Lincoln's Inn, LLB
(Hons)(B'ham)

Kattan *William Victor*
Attorney General's Chambers, Grand Turk,
Turk & Caicos Islands, (809)946 2096/2882,
Fax: (809)946 2588. Called: May 1973,
Gray's Inn, LLB,LLM (Lond)

Kaur *Miss Balbir*
Called: July 1995, Middle Temple, LLB
(Hons) (Lond)

Kaur *Miss Baltej*
Called: July 1995, Middle Temple, LLB
(Hons)

Kaur *Miss Daljit*
Called: July 1997, Lincoln's Inn, LLB (Hons)

Kaur *Miss Devinder*
Called: July 1995, Lincoln's Inn, LLB (Hons)

Kaur *Miss Jasvendar*
Called: July 1995, Middle Temple, LLB
(Hons)

Kaur *Miss Kuldip*
Called: Nov 1994, Lincoln's Inn, LLB
(Hons)(Lond)

Kaur *Mrs Paramjit*
Called: July 1996, Lincoln's Inn, LLB
(Hons)(Lond)

Kaur *Miss Sharanjit*
and Member Singapore Bar. Called: July
1995, Middle Temple, LLB (Hons)

Kaur *Ms Upbinder Sunita*
14 Mules Place, Macarthur ACT 2904,
Singapore, (061)(02)62919971, and Member
Singapore. Called: July 1994, Middle
Temple, LLB (Hons)(Newc)

Kaur Jaswant Singh *Miss Sharan*
Called: July 1997, Middle Temple, LLB
(Hons)(Wales)_

Kaw *Miss Seok Hien*
and Member Singapore Bar. Called: Nov
1994, Gray's Inn, BA (Keele)

Kawa *Miss Lois Anita*
Called: Nov 1997, Lincoln's Inn, BA
(Hons)(Luton)

Kawaley *Ian Rowe Chukudinka*
c/o Milligan Whyte & Smith, Bermuda
Commercial Bank Bldg, 44 Church Street,
Hamilton HM1Z, (441) 295 4294, Fax: (441)
295 1348, Member of the Bermuda Bar
Council (1992) and Member Bermuda Bar.
Called: July 1978, Middle Temple, LLB
(Liverpool), LLM (LSE)

Kee *Ju-Ven*
Called: July 1994, Middle Temple, BA
(Hons)(Cantab)

Keegan *Brian McMurrough*
Called: Mar 1998, Lincoln's Inn, LLB
(Hons)(Leics)

Keery *Neil William*
Called: Oct 1997, Gray's Inn, LLB (Belfast)

Kelaart *Ms Jennifer Rosanne Sabina*
12/2A Tickell Road, Colombo 8, (94-1)
696623, Fax: (94-1) 422768. Called: Nov
1995, Inner Temple, LLB (Lond), LLM (Syd)

Kelleher *Dr John Daniel*
Olsen Backhurst & Dorey, Eaton House, 9
Seaton Place, St Helier, Jersey JE2 3QL,
01534 888900, Fax: 01534 887744,
Advocate of the Royal Court of Jersey
(1995). Jersey Law Society. and Member
Jersey Bar. Called: Oct 1991, Middle
Temple, BA Hons (Warw), Dip Law (Lond),
PhD (Warw), Certificat De, Juridiques
Francaise

Kelly *Christopher Andrew*
Clayton UtZ, Solicitors & Attorneys, Levels
27-35, 1 O'Connell Street, Sydney
NSW 2000. Called: Nov 1993, Middle
Temple, LLB (Hons)(Lond)

Kelly *Philip James*
Barrister of Ireland. Called: May 1996,
Middle Temple, BA, MSc (Dublin)

Keng *Miss Wan Ling*
Called: July 1995, Lincoln's Inn, LLB (Hons)

Kennedy *Hugh Paul*
Bar Library, Royal Courts of Justice,
Chichester Street, Belfast, 0232 241523,
Fax: 0232 231850, QC (N Ireland) SC
Republic of Ireland. Called: Nov 1990,
Gray's Inn, BA,LLB (Belfast)

Kennedy *Thomas Alastair Plunkett*
Court of Justice of the, European
Communities, L 2925, 352-4303 3355, Fax:
352-4303 2500. Called: Nov 1975, Gray's
Inn, LLB

Kenny *Judge Harvey*
and Member Southern Ireland Bar.
Called: Feb 1982, Middle Temple, BCL (Nat
Univ, Ireland), ACIArB

Kentish *Mrs Louise Anne*
J A Hassan & Partners, 57/63 Line Wall
Road, 00 350 79000, Fax: 00 350 71966,
and Member Gibraltar. Called: Nov 1996,
Middle Temple, BA (Hons)

Keoy *Soo Khim*
Called: July 1997, Gray's Inn, LLB

Kershaw *Nicholas John*
Ogier & Le Masurier, Pirouet House, Union
Street, St Helier, Jersey, Channel Islands,
01534 504000, Fax: 01534 35328, and
Member New South Wales Bar Jersey Bar.
Called: May 1988, Middle Temple, LLB
(Hons) London

Kesavapany *Muralitherapany*
Called: Nov 1995, Middle Temple, LLB
(Hons)(Lond)

Khairuddin *Miss Fateh Hanum*
Called: July 1996, Lincoln's Inn, BA
(Hons)(Keele)

Khan *Karim Asad Ahmad*
Office of the Prosecutor, United Nations,
International, Criminal Tribunal, 1 Churchill
Plein, 2517JA, Den Haag, 0031 70 4165353,
Fax: 0031 70 4165325. Called: Oct 1992,
Lincoln's Inn, LLB(Hons)(Lond), AKC
(Lond), Dip Int Rel (Nice)

Khan *Mirazul Hossain*
Called: Nov 1997, Lincoln's Inn, LLB
(Hons)(Lond)

Khan *Muhammed Mustafizur Rahman*
Called: Nov 1997, Lincoln's Inn, BSS
(Hons)(Dhaka), LLB (Hons)

Khan *Sirdar Ejaz*
10a Civil Lines, Rawalpindi, Pakistan, (010)
9251 564346, and Member Punjab Bar.
Called: July 1993, Lincoln's Inn, BA (Hons)

Khaw *Miss Gim Hong*
27 Jalan Bijaksana, Taman Century, 80250
Johor Bahru, Johor, Malaysia, 07 3342753,
and Member Singapore Bar. Called: July
1994, Middle Temple, LLB (Hons), ACCA

Khaw *Kenneth Jin Teck*
Called: July 1993, Middle Temple, LLB
(Hons, Bris), ACA

Khaw *Oliver Kar Heng*
Called: July 1997, Middle Temple, LLB
(Hons)

Khong *Miss Gilliam Li Shen*
Called: July 1997, Middle Temple, LLB
(Hons)(Nott'm)

Khong *Yu Cheong*
Called: July 1994, Lincoln's Inn, LLB (Hons,
Lond)

Khoo *Gavin Lay Keong*
Called: July 1997, Middle Temple, LLB
(Hons)(Wales)

Khoo *Kay Kwan*
Called: Nov 1997, Lincoln's Inn, LLB
(Hons)(Wales)

Khoo *Melvin Lay Jin*
Called: Nov 1993, Middle Temple, LLB
(Hons)(Bucks)

Khoo *Per-Ern*
Called: July 1993, Middle Temple, LLB
(Hons)(Hull)

Khoo *Miss Selkie*
Called: Nov 1997, Middle Temple, LLB
(Hons)(Leics)

Khoo *Miss Su Sen*
Called: July 1996, Middle Temple, LLB
(Hons)(Glamorg)

Khor *Gerald Guan Yu*
Called: Nov 1996, Gray's Inn, BA (Keele)

Khor *Wee Siong*
and Member Singapore Bar. Called: July
1996, Lincoln's Inn, LLB (Hons)(Hull)

Kieran *Brian Laurence*
P.O.Box 2071, General Post Office, (852)
2501 0471, Fax: (852) 2592 7086, and
Member Jamaica Bar Hong Kong Bar.
Called: July 1968, Gray's Inn, LLB, DIP Air,
FBIS

Kilic *Mrs Meena Barathi*
Called: Feb 1992, Lincoln's Inn, LLB (Hons)
(Wales), BA (Singapore)

Killerby *Miss Joan Margaret*
Head of the Private &, International Law
Division, Council of Europe, Strasbourg
Cedex, 03 88 41 22 10, Fax: 03 88 41 27
94. Called: Nov 1967, Inner Temple, doc de
Univ d'Aix-, Marseille

Killick *Marcus Charles*
Cayman Island Monetary Auth, P.O.Box
10052 APO, Georgetown, Grand Cayman,
Cayman Islands IM99 1DT, (345) 949 1839,
Fax: (345) 949 2532, and Member New
York Bar. Called: July 1989, Gray's Inn, LLB
(Leeds)

King *Paul John*
Graham Thompson & Co, Sasson House,
Shirley Street, Victoria Avenue, P.O.Box
N272, Nassau, (242) 322 4130, Fax: (242)
328 1069, and Member Bahamas.
Called: July 1996, Middle Temple, LLB
(Hons)(Soton), BA (Hons)(Miami)

King *Peter Andrew*
Bar Library, Royal Courts of Justice, P O
Box 414, Chichester Street, Belfast BT1 3JP,
01232 562354, Fax: 01232 231850, and
Member Northern Ireland Bar. Called: Nov
1993, Gray's Inn, LLB (Manch)

Kinnear *David Thomas Alexander*
212 325 7029, Fax: 212 325 9177.
Called: July 1989, Middle Temple, LLB
(Manch)

Kinoshi *John Ayoola*
5 Kinoshi St, Abeokuta, Nigeria, Also Inn of
Court I and Member Nigerian Bar.
Called: Nov 1972, Lincoln's Inn

Kiplagat *Miss Betty Jepkoech*
Called: Nov 1996, Middle Temple, LLB
(Hons)

Knowles *Miss Adrianna Desiree*
and Member Bahamas Bar. Called: July 1997,
Lincoln's Inn, LLB (Hons), LLM

Ko *Hiu Fung*
Called: Nov 1997, Lincoln's Inn, LLB (Hons)

Ko *Justin King Sau*
806 Wheelock House, 20 Pedder Street,
Central, Hong Kong, 852 25220209, Fax:
852 28450720, and Member Hong-Kong
Bar. Called: July 1993, Lincoln's Inn, LLB
(Hons, B'ham)

Koe *Miss Kian Fei*
Called: July 1996, Middle Temple, LLB
(Hons)(Lond)

Koh *Miss Aileen Geok Pin*
Called: July 1995, Middle Temple, LLB
(Hons)

Koh *Chia Ling*
Called: July 1997, Middle Temple, LLB
(Hons)(Lond)

Koh *Darren Ngiap Thiam*
Procter & Gamble Far East Inc., 17 Koyo-
cho Naka 1-chome, Higashinada-ku, Kobe
658-0032, 078 845 2344, Fax: 078 845
6900. Called: July 1989, Lincoln's Inn, LLB
(Buck), ACA, ATII

Koh *Gerald Teck Hock*
Called: Mar 1996, Middle Temple, LLB
(Hons)

Koh *Hua Hong*
Block 758 [H]09-131, Choa Chu Kang North
5, Singapore 680758, 065 766 2016/065 337
6368, Fax: 065 337 2425, Full Name is Koh
Hua Hong alias Koh Dar Eng. Called: July
1994, Lincoln's Inn, LLB (Hons), FCCA

Koh *Miss Jean Bee Khim*
Called: Oct 1996, Middle Temple, LLB
(Hons)(Lond)

Koh *Miss Joanna Wei Ser*
Called: July 1997, Middle Temple, LLB
(Hons)(Exon)

Koh *Kok Shen*
Called: Oct 1995, Middle Temple, LLB
(Hons)

Koh *Miss Lee Tze*
Called: July 1995, Lincoln's Inn, LLB (Hons)

Koh *Miss Maisie Su-Mei*
and Member Singapore. Called: July 1995,
Middle Temple, LLB (Hons)

Koh *Sam Mong Poo*
Block 817, Tampines Street 81, [H] 04-588,
65 7892048, and Member Member of the
Singapore Bar. Called: July 1996, Middle
Temple, LLB (Hons)(Wolves)

Koh *Miss Selena Lay Na*
Called: Nov 1996, Middle Temple, LLB
(Hons)(Bucks)

Koh *Siew Hui*
Called: July 1995, Lincoln's Inn, LLB (Hons)

Koh *Sim Teck*
Called: May 1994, Middle Temple, LLB
(Hons)

Koh *Terence Kah Hoe*
Called: Oct 1995, Middle Temple, LLB
(Hons)

Koh *Terence Sebastian Ker Siang*
Called: July 1996, Middle Temple, LLB
(Hons)(Bris)

Kok *Miss Aik Wan*
Called: Nov 1996, Lincoln's Inn, LLB
(Hons)(So'ton)

Kok *Lak Hin*
Called: July 1995, Lincoln's Inn, LLB (Hons)

Kok *Miss Meng Wei*
Called: July 1995, Lincoln's Inn, LLB
(Hons)(Leeds)

Kok *Ms Yoke Kieng*
Called: Nov 1996, Gray's Inn, LLB

Kong *Chi Man*
Called: Nov 1997, Middle Temple, B.Soc.Sci
(Hong Kong

Kong *Miss Jennifer Lee Jean*
and Member Sabah Bar Malaysia Bar.
Called: Nov 1992, Lincoln's Inn, BA
(Hons)(Nott'm)

Kong *Kelvin Wen Wai*
Called: July 1989, Lincoln's Inn, LLB (Newc)

Kong *Miss Seh Ping*
Called: July 1995, Middle Temple, LLB
(Hons)

Konotey-Ahulu *Dawid Konotey-Adade*
Natwest Markets Ltd, 135 Bishopsgate,
London EC2M 3UR, 0171 334 1780, Fax:
0171 375 5060. Called: Nov 1987, Lincoln's
Inn, LLB Hons

Kooi *Tock Ken*
Called: July 1996, Lincoln's Inn, LLB
(Hons)(Lond)

Koon *Keen Hoong*
Called: July 1996, Gray's Inn, LLB (Exeter)

Kor *Darren Yit Meng*
Called: July 1996, Lincoln's Inn, LLB
(Hons)(Warw)

Kor *Don Shiang Hua*
and Member Malaysia Bar. Called: July 1994,
Middle Temple, BA (Hons)(Manc)

Koutouroussi *Miss Galatia*
Called: Nov 1995, Lincoln's Inn, LLB (Hons)
(Kent)

Kremner *Jonathan*
8721 Bay Pointe Drive, Tampa, Florida
33615, USA 813 884 8841, Fax: USA 813
639 9716, and Member New York.
Called: July 1984, Inner Temple, MA (Law),
BA (Hons), Dip Law

Krishna *Miss Maheswari Rani*
and Member Malaysia. Called: July 1995,
Lincoln's Inn, LLB (Hons)

Krishnan *Elengovan*
Block 661, Buffalo Road, 11-29 Singapore
210661. Called: July 1993, Middle Temple,
LLB (Hons, Hull)

Krishnan *Miss Shubhaa*
Called: Nov 1997, Lincoln's Inn, LLB
(Hons)(Lond)

Krishnasamy *Siva Sambo*
S Bala & Associates, Advocates & Solicitors,
135 Cecil Street, [H]08-02, LKN Building,
225 5277, Fax: 225 2498, and Member
Singapore Bar. Called: July 1995, Lincoln's
Inn, LLB (Hons)

Krrishnan *Ms Seethalkshmi P S*
Called: July 1997, Lincoln's Inn, LLB
(Hons)(Lond)

Ku *Miss Pui Fong*
and Member Hong Kong Bar. Called: Nov
1991, Gray's Inn, LLB (Lond)(Hon), A.C.I.S.

Kua *Miss Lay Theng*
Called: July 1997, Middle Temple, LLB
(Hons)(Leics)

Kuan *Anthony Chee Kee*
Called: Nov 1996, Lincoln's Inn, LLB (Hons)

Kuen *Paul Yong Wei*
Called: July 1995, Inner Temple, LLB (Lond)

Kulasegaran *Miss Aneeta*
M/S Ranjit Thomas & Kula, No 24, Jalan 12/
13, 46200 Petaling Jaya, Selangor Darul
Ehsan, 00 60 3 7542269, Fax: 00 60 3
7542321, and Member Malaysia Bar.
Called: Nov 1992, Middle Temple, LLB
(Hons, E.Anglia)

Kumar *KV Sudeep*
and Member Singapore Bar. Called: July
1994, Inner Temple, LLB (Lond)

Kumar *Mazumdar Swapan*
Called: Nov 1996, Lincoln's Inn, LLB
(Hons)(Lond)

Kumar *Rajesh*
Called: Nov 1997, Middle Temple, LLB
(Hons)(Newcas)

Kumar *Miss Sharika*
Called: July 1996, Lincoln's Inn, LLB
(Hons)(Lond)

Kumar *Vishnu*
Called: July 1995, Middle Temple, LLB
(Hons)

Kumarasamy *Pathmanathan*
Called: Nov 1996, Gray's Inn, LLB (Wales)

Kunjuraman *Dharmendra*
Called: Nov 1996, Middle Temple, LLB
(Hons)(Nott'm)

Kunjuraman *Miss Previtha*
Called: July 1996, Middle Temple, LLB
(Hons)(Wolves)

Kuok *David Han Peh*
Called: July 1997, Lincoln's Inn, LLB
(Hons)(Wales)

Kuok *Miss Pearl Ming Yew*
Allen & Gledhill, 36 Robinson Road [H]18-
01, City House, Singaopre 0106, 65
2251611, Fax: 65 2233787, and Member
Singapore Bar. Called: July 1992, Middle
Temple, LLB (Hons) (Lond)

Kuppusamy *Mahendran*
Block 136, Bukit Batok West Avenue 6,
[H]08-509, 5690464. Called: July 1996,
Middle Temple, LLB (Hons)(Lond), LLM
(Lond)

Kwa *Miss Su-Lin*
Called: July 1995, Inner Temple, LLB (Lond)

Kwan *Pang Moon*
Called: Mar 1998, Gray's Inn, LLB (Lond)

Kwan Pang *Mrs Maying*
Called: Nov 1996, Lincoln's Inn, LLB
(Hons)(Wales)

Kwek *Julian Choon Yeow*
24 Raffles Place, Clifford Centre [H]18-00,
65-5332323, Fax: 65-5337029, and Member
Singapore Bar. Called: July 1995, Middle
Temple, LLB (Hons)

Kwek *Kevin Yiu Wing*
M/S Shook Lin & Bok, 1 Robinson Road,
[H]18-00 Aia Tower, Singapore 048542,
Singapore, (65) 5351944, Fax: (65)
5358577, and Member Singapore Bar.
Called: July 1994, Middle Temple, BA
(Hons)(Keele)

Kwok *Lester Chi-Hang JP*
30th Floor, Wing On House, 71 Des Voeux
Road, Central, (852) 2523 4091, Fax: (852)
2868 0118, Associate Member of the Hong
Kong Bar Association. Called: Nov 1975,
Gray's Inn, BA (Stanford)

Kyprianou *Menelaos Michael*
Law Office of Michael, Kyprianou &
Associates, P.O.Box 8765, Stassinos Court,
Stassinos Avenue, Nicosia, 02 360800, Fax:
02 467880, and Member Cyprus Bar.
Called: Nov 1994, Middle Temple, LLB
(Hons)

Labesse *Advocate Jacques Pierre*
Piermont Hse, 33 Pier Rd, St Helier, Jersey,
0534 888777, Fax: 0534 888778.
Called: July 1957, Inner Temple, MA (Oxon)

Lack *Daniel*
Lindenfeld, Grumbach, 78 Rue du Rhone,
1204 Geneva, (41-22) 311 38 11, Fax: (41-
22) 781 17 38, Registered as Foreign Lawyer
Geneva Bar. Called: Nov 1955, Middle
Temple, MA (Oxon)

Lack *Jeremy*
Becton Dickinson Europe, 5 Chemin Des
Sources, B.P.37, 38241 Meylan Cedex, (+33)
7641 6801, Fax: (+33) 7641 6800, Admitted
to various US Federal Courts & the US CAFC
Registered U.S. Patent Attorney, Reg No 35,
813 Patent & Trademark Office. and
Member New York State Bar (1990).
Called: Nov 1989, Middle Temple, BA
(Oxon), Law &, Physiological, Sciences

Lai *Miss Amy Hur-Ling*
Called: July 1995, Lincoln's Inn, LLB (Hons)

Lai *Miss Fui Sim*
16 Lorong Kemaris 4, Bukit Bandaraya,
Bangsar, 59100 Kuala Lumpur, 03 2561243.
Called: July 1995, Lincoln's Inn, LLB (Hons)

Lai *Kwok Seng*
Called: Nov 1995, Lincoln's Inn, LLB (Hons)

Lai *Miss Sheau Wei*
Called: July 1997, Middle Temple, LLB
(Hons)(Hull)

Lai *Ms Tsang Ka*
Called: Nov 1997, Inner Temple, BA (Hong
Kong), LLB (Lond)

Lakeman *Advocate Christopher
Gerard Pellow*
Olsen Backhurst & Dorey, Eaton House, 9
Seaton Place, St Helier, Jersey JE2 3QL, +44
(0) 01534 888900, Fax: +44 (0) 01534
887744/55, Formerly Ecrivain (Jersey 1994)
Advocate of the Royal Court of Jersey
(1995) Jersey Law Society and Member
Jersey Bar. Called: Nov 1991, Middle
Temple, BA Hons (Kent), Diplome de Droit,
Francais (Paris XI)

Lall *Tersaim*
Shariz Sdn BHD, No 39B Jalan SS 3/29,
Taman University, 47300 Petaling Jaya,
Selangor Darul, Ehsan, 00 603 7761641,
Fax: 00 603 7766818, and Member Malaysia.
Called: July 1996, Gray's Inn, Dip Law

Lam *Chee On*
Called: July 1997, Lincoln's Inn, LLB
(Hons)(Lond)

Lam *Edward Chung Weng*
Alban Tay Mahtani & de Silva, 105 Cecil
Street, [H]13-00 The Octagon, 65-534 5266,
Fax: 65-223 8762, and Member Singapore
Bar. Called: July 1992, Middle Temple, LLB
(Hons) (E.Ang)

Lam *Jen Yii*
Called: July 1996, Middle Temple, LLB
(Hons)(Warw)

Lam *Ken Chung Simon*
1103 Prince's Building, Central, 25220066,
Fax: 28450851, and Member Australian
Capital Territory Hong Kong Bar.
Called: July 1989, Middle Temple, BSc, LLB
(Buck)

Lam *Osmond Kwok Fai*
and Member Hong Kong Bar. Called: Feb
1988, Inner Temple, LLB (Manch), LLM
(Lond)

Lam *Stephen Sui Lung OBE, JP*
4th Floor, High Block, Queensway
Government Offices, 66 Queensway, 2867
2160, Fax: 2869 0720. Called: Feb 1986,
Gray's Inn, BSocSc, LLB

Lam *Steven Kuet Keng*
Apt Blk 121, [H] 01-81, Bishan St 12, S
570121, Singapore, and Member Singapore.
Called: July 1995, Middle Temple, LLB
(Hons)

Lam *Tin Sing*
Called: Nov 1994, Middle Temple, LLB
(Hons)

Lammy *David Lindon*
Howard Rice, Nemerovski, Canady, Falk &
Rabkin, Three Embarcadero Center, 7th
Floor, San Francisco 941114065, 001 415
434 1600, and Member California Bar.
Called: Feb 1995, Lincoln's Inn, LLB
(Hons)(Lond)

Lan *Ms Sin Cynthia Mei*
Called: Nov 1997, Inner Temple, BA (LSE)

Lancaster *Kenneth Alan*
Called: July 1995, Lincoln's Inn, LLM (Lond),
FCA, ACIArb

Landick *Pierre Stanley*
Ogier & Le Masurier, Pirouet House, Union
Street, St Helier, Jersey, Channel Islands
JE4 9WG, 01534 504000, Fax: 01534 35328,
and Member Advocate of the Royal Court of
Jersey. Called: Feb 1989, Lincoln's Inn, LLB

Lane *John Robert Benjamin*
Frommer Lawrence & Haug LLP, 745 Fifth
Avenue, New York, NY 10151, 212 588
0800, Fax: 212 588 0500, and Member New
York Bar Washington DC Bar. Called: Nov
1989, Middle Temple, BA

Lang *Lawrence Fatt Khim*
Called: July 1996, Middle Temple, LLB
(Hons)(Wolves)

Langridge *Ms Natalie Katherine*
Estidio Interjuridico S.L., Estudio legaly
Tributario, Edificio IVC, Arturo Soria, 245,
28033 Madrid, (341) 359 7679, Fax: (341)
345 5373, and Member Madrid. Called: Nov
1992, Middle Temple, BA (Hons, Kent)

Langwallner *David Johann Herbert*
and Member Irish Bar. Called: Feb 1993,
Gray's Inn, BA (Dublin), LLM

Larder *Graham Charles*
Thomas Howell Group(S.A.)(PTY), GF
Office Park, Grosvenor Road, Bryanston,
2021, (011) 463 5900, Fax: (011) 463 5920.
Called: Nov 1974, Middle Temple, LLB

Latimer *Mrs Ai-Yuen*
5/61 Wyralla Avenue, Epping 2121, Sydney
NSW, 02 9868 5773, and Member Malaysia.
Called: July 1994, Middle Temple, LLB
(Hons)(Reading)

Latimer *Raymond Raj*
5/61 Wyralla Avenue, Epping 2121, Sydney
NSW, 02 9868 5773. Called: July 1994,
Middle Temple, LLB (Hons)(Reading)

Lau *Cecil Ning Kiang*
Called: July 1995, Lincoln's Inn, LLB (Hons)

Lau *Miss Cheh Meng Patricia*
Called: July 1995, Middle Temple, LLB
(Hons)

Lau *Miss Chew Mee*
Called: Nov 1996, Lincoln's Inn, LLB
(Hons)(L'pool)

Lau *Dennis Yee Meng*
Iza Ng Yeoh & Kit, Advocates & Solicitors,
19th Floor, Bangunan Dato, Zainal, 23 Jalan
Melaka, 50100 Kuala Lumpur Malaysia, 03
2986066, Fax: 03 2982593. Called: July
1995, Lincoln's Inn, LLB (Hons)

Lau *Dr James Chi Wang*
Flat 3A, Block 8 29, Braemar Hill Road,
Hong Kong, 852-8930332, Fax: 852-
8380011. Called: July 1992, Gray's Inn, LLB
(Lond), PhD (Lond), MSc (Manch), LLM
(Hong Kong), MBA, MICE, MIStructE, Ceng

Lau *Miss Jean Aye Lin*
Called: July 1996, Lincoln's Inn, LLB (Hons)

Lau *Miss Julia Pui G*
Room 1432, Prince's Building, 10 Chater
Road, Central, 252 40151, Fax: 281 01731,
and Member Hong Kong. Called: Nov 1994,
Gray's Inn, BSc (Hong Kong), LLB

Lau *Lee Sing Edward*
See Hua Daily News/The Borneo, Post/
Sinhua Evening News, PO Box 20, 96007
Sibu,Sarawak, E Malaysia, 084 332055, Fax:
084 321255, and Member Sarawak Bar
Malaysia Bar. Called: July 1988, Lincoln's
Inn, LLB (Hons) (Manch), LLM (Hons)
(Lond)

Lau *Miss Man Sai*
[H]07-07 Derby Court, 5 Derbyshire Road,
(65) 355 1507, Fax: (65) 222 2521, and
Member Singapore Bar. Called: Oct 1995,
Middle Temple, LLB (Hons)

Lau *Robert Chun Keong*
M/S Rashid & Lee, 6th Floor, 56 Jalan
Tuanku, Abdul Rahman, 50100 Kuala
Lumpur, 60 3 2938155 Ext 333, Fax: 60-3-
2939566, and Member Malaysia Bar.
Called: Oct 1991, Gray's Inn, LLB (Warwick)

Lau *Teik Soon*
Called: July 1996, Lincoln's Inn, LLB
(Hons)(Lond)

Lau *Tiew Kung*
Called: July 1996, Lincoln's Inn, LLB
(Hons)(Lond)

Lau *Wai Hin*
Called: Nov 1997, Lincoln's Inn, BSc
(eng)(Hons)(Hong, Kong), CPE (Manch)

Lau *William John*
C/O HSBC Investment Bank, Asia Ltd, Level
15, 1 Queen's Road, Central, (852)
28418888, Fax: (852) 28455654, and
Member Hong Kong Bar. Called: July 1990,
Lincoln's Inn, LLB (B'ham), ACCA, AHKSA

Lau *Miss Winnie Yee Wan*
Called: Nov 1997, Middle Temple, BSc
(Hons)(Lond)

Lau *Miss Yin Fong*
Called: Nov 1997, Middle Temple, LLB
(Hons)(Lond)

Lau *Yun Tseng*
Lau Yun Tseng & Co Advocates, No 17c,
Jalan Kai Peng, Off Jalan Tuanku Osman,
96000 Sibu, Sarawak, 084 319886, Fax: 084
349886, and Member Malaysian Bar.
Called: July 1994, Lincoln's Inn, LLB (Hons)

Law *Cheok Maan*
Rm 301, 3rd Floor, No 44 Jalan Pudu, 55100
Kuala Lumpur, 03 2381231, Fax: 03
2329430. Called: July 1994, Middle Temple,
BA (Hons)(Cantab)

Law *Ms Cheok Yin*
Top Floor, See Woh Building, 90 Jalan
Pudu, 55100 Kuala Lumpur, Malaysia, (603)
2381231, Fax: (603) 2329430, and Member
Malaysian Bar. Called: July 1993, Middle
Temple, BA (Hons)(Cantab)

Law *Chun Keat*
Called: July 1997, Middle Temple, LLB
(Hons)

Law *Miss Jee Wei*
Called: July 1996, Middle Temple, LLB
(Hons)(Lond)

Law *Miss Yuk-Ching*
Called: Nov 1997, Middle Temple, BA
(Hons)

Lawrence *Bernard Hilary*
Called: Nov 1996, Gray's Inn, LLB (Warw)

Lawrence *Miss Kerry Joy*
Ogier & Le Masurier, P O Box 404, Pirouet
House, Union Street, St Helier, Jersey
JE4 9WG, 01534 504000, Fax: 01534 35328.
Called: Nov 1995, Inner Temple, MA
(Oxon), CPE (Lond), BA (Hons)

Le Cocq *Timothy John*
Ogier & Le Masurier, P O Box 404, Pirouet
House, Union Street, St Helier, Jersey
JE4 8WZ, 01534 504370, Fax: 01534 35328,
Advocate of the Royal Court of Jersey and
Member Jersey Bar. Called: July 1981, Inner
Temple, BA (Hons)(Keele)

Le Pichon *Mrs Doreen*
High Court, (852) 2825 4430, Fax: (852)
2869 0640, and Member Hong Kong Bar
New York Bar. Called: Nov 1969, Lincoln's
Inn, BA, BCL (Oxon)

Le Poidevin *Nicholas*
Advocates Babbe Le Poidevin, Allez P O Box
612, Hirzel Court, St Peter Port, Guernsey,
Channel Islands, 01481 710585, Fax: 01481
712245, and Member Royal Court of
Guernsey. Called: Nov 1986, Gray's Inn, MA
(Oxon), PhD (RVC Lond), C.Biol

Le Quesne *David Fisher*
Vibert & Valpy, 8 Duhamel Place, St Helier,
Jersey JE2 4XA, 0534 888666, Fax: 0534
888555, Advocate of the Royal Ct of Jersey.
Secretary of the Jersey Law Society.
Called: Nov 1976, Inner Temple, LLB

Leck *Andy Kwang Hwee*
c/o Messrs Wong & Leow, 1 Temasek
Avenue 27-01, Millenia Tower, 65 338 1888,
Fax: 65 337 5100, and Member Singapore
Bar. Called: July 1992, Gray's Inn, LLB
(Bristol)

Lee *Brian Ying Wah*
51 Sixth Crescent, 65 4690892, Fax: 65
4697554, and Member Advocate & Solicitor
Singapore. Called: July 1995, Middle
Temple, LLB (Hons)

Lee *Chai Seng*
Called: Nov 1994, Lincoln's Inn, LLB
(Hons)(Leeds)_

Lee *Chau Ee*
Called: July 1995, Middle Temple, LLB
(Hons)

Lee *Chau Yee*
M/S Chor Pee Anwarul & Co, Unit 10.01,
Level 10, Wisma LKN, 49 Jalan Wong Ah
Fook, 80000 Johor Bahru, 607 2234733,
Fax: 607 2234734, and Member Malaysia
Bar. Called: July 1995, Lincoln's Inn, LLB
(Hons)

Lee *Miss Cheryl Siew Fung*
Called: July 1995, Middle Temple, LLB
(Hons) (Hull)

Lee *Miss Chiek Chuin*
Called: July 1996, Middle Temple, LLB
(Hons)(Notts)

Lee *Miss Chin Theng*
No 74, Jalan 11/3N, Subang Jaya, 47620
Petaling Jaya, Selangor, 03-737 6846, and
Member Malaysian Bar. Called: July 1996,
Lincoln's Inn, LLB (Hons)(Lond)

Lee *David Ken Hwa*
Called: July 1997, Middle Temple, LLB
(Hons)

Lee *Miss Deanna Maria*
Called: Mar 1997, Middle Temple, BSc
(Florida), LLB (Hons) (L'pool)

Lee *Dennis Preston*
Mechala Group Jamiaca Limited, 7/9
Harbour Street, Kingston, Jamaica, 92-
26670, Fax: 92-20256, and Member Jamaica.
Called: July 1988, Lincoln's Inn, BSc (Hons)
(Lond), MBA (California)

Lee *Desmond Boon Teck*
Called: July 1996, Lincoln's Inn, LLB
(Hons)(Leeds)

Lee *Miss Elaine Yu Lian*
Called: July 1997, Lincoln's Inn, LLB
(Hons)(Lond), LLM (Lond)

Lee *Eng Seng*
Chew, Tan & Lim, Advocates & Solicitors,
51-20 A Menara BHL Bank, 10050 Penang,
04-2281998, Fax: 04-2281367 & 04-
2285521, and Member Malaysia Bar.
Called: July 1995, Lincoln's Inn, LLB (Hons)

Lee *Eugene*
Called: July 1997, Lincoln's Inn, LLB (Hons)

Lee *Han Meng*
Called: July 1996, Lincoln's Inn, LLB
(Hons)(Lond)

Lee *Dr Helen Ho-Yan*
Securities and Futures Comm, 12/F
Edinburgh Tower, The Landmark, Central
Hong Kong, 28409246, Fax: 25217929,
Hong Kong Barrister. Called: Nov 1989,
Middle Temple, LLB, LLM M Soc Sc, PhD

Lee *Miss Hong*
84 Jalan Daud, [H]12-03 Windy Heights,
Singapore 1441, 7465086, Fax: 7465973.
Called: July 1995, Lincoln's Inn, LLB (Hons)
(Wales)

Lee *James Kim-Keung BH (St John)*
1323A Prince's Building, 10 Chater Road,
Central, Hong Kong, (852) 252-66182, Fax:
(852) 252-66011, and Member Hong Kong
Bar. Called: Feb 1992, Gray's Inn, B.Arch
(Hong Kong), BA (Arch Studies), (Hong
Kong), LLB, (Hons)(Lond), RIBA, ARAIA,
HKIA, ACIArb, AHKCIArb, Dip in, Chinese
Law

Lee *Jason Chong*
Called: July 1994, Middle Temple, LLB
(Hons)(Brunel)

Lee *Miss Jeanette Tsui Ling*
and Member Singapore Bar. Called: Nov
1993, Middle Temple, LLB (Hons)(Lond)

Lee *Jonathan Kuan Yee*
60-3-2823916, Fax: 60-3-2825687.
Called: July 1996, Middle Temple, LLB
(Hons)(Bris)

Lee *Miss June Hsiao Tsun*
Called: Nov 1992, Middle Temple, LLB
(Hons, Hull)

Lee *Keat Chee*
Called: Oct 1996, Lincoln's Inn, LLB
(Hons)(L'pool)

Lee *Khai*
256 Jalan Utara, 11700 Gelugor, Penang,
Malaysia, 04 6579757, and Member Malaysia
Bar. Called: July 1993, Lincoln's Inn, LLB
(Hons, N'ham)

Lee *Kim Meng David*
Called: July 1997, Gray's Inn, LLB (Notts)

Lee *Kok Chew*
Called: July 1997, Lincoln's Inn, LLB
(Hons)(LSE)

Lee *Ms Kuan Wei*
Called: July 1997, Gray's Inn, LLB (Sheff)

Lee *Miss Lai Lee Lily*
Called: Nov 1996, Gray's Inn, LLB

Lee *Miss Lynette Kwok Foeng*
P K Wong & Advani, 20 Raffles Place, [H]
12-03 Ocean Towers, Singapore 048620,
538 1822, Fax: 538 1838, and Member
Singapore Bar. Called: July 1994, Middle
Temple, LLB (Hons)(Newc)

Lee *Miss Mary Chung Ching*
Szetu & Associates, 95 Lorong Ikan Lais, off
Jalan Mat Salleh, 88100 Tanjung Aru,
P.O.Box 319, 88858 Tanjung Aru, Kota
Kinaba, 088 221125/233558, Fax: 088
237543, Advocate of the High Court in
Sabah & Sarawak in the State of Sabah
(Malaysia). Called: July 1996, Lincoln's Inn,
BSc (Hons), MSc (Hons) (Leeds), Dip in Law

Lee *Miss Melanie Anne*
Called: July 1997, Middle Temple, LLB
(Hons)

Lee *Min Kin*
8 Nim Drive, Seletar Hills, Singapore 2880,
00 65 4812024. Called: July 1993, Inner
Temple, LLB (Warw)

Lee *Miss Noushi*
Called: July 1997, Lincoln's Inn, LLB
(Hons)(Leeds)

Lee *Miss Nyet Fah*
Called: July 1996, Middle Temple, LLB
(Hons)(Lond)

Lee *Pak Chau*
Called: Mar 1997, Middle Temple, BSc
(Hons)(L'pool), MSc (B'ham)

Lee *Miss Pauline Aileen*
and Member Malaysia Bar. Called: July 1995,
Middle Temple, LLB (Hons) (Wales)

Lee *Peter Kong Chung*
c/o Messrs Lee & Associates, Advocates &
Solicitors, P.O. Box 12604, 88829 Kota
Kinabalu, Sabah, 088 215262, Fax: 088
217892, Sabah Bar, The Sabah Law
Association. Called: July 1988, Lincoln's Inn,
LLB (Hons) (Bucks)

Lee *Miss Pin Pin*
Called: Nov 1995, Middle Temple, LLB
(Hons)

Lee *Miss Rachel Yim Kuan*
Called: July 1994, Middle Temple, LLB
(Hons)(Lond)

Lee *Raphael Khong Wen*
IVI 19 UK Building, 5 Shenton Way,
2200666 (065), and Member Singapore Bar.
Called: Nov 1994, Middle Temple, LLB
(Hons)

Lee *Miss Seow Ser*
Called: July 1996, Middle Temple, LLB
(Hons)(Leeds)

Lee *Miss Siew Mui*
Called: July 1996, Lincoln's Inn, LLB
(Hons)(Lond)

Lee *Miss Siew Peng*
Called: Feb 1995, Middle Temple, LLB
(Hons)(Lond)

Lee *Miss Simone*
Called: July 1995, Middle Temple, LLB
(Hons) (Bris)

Lee *Ms Su-Lin*
and Member Singapore Bar. Called: July
1990, Gray's Inn, LLB (Manch)

Lee *Miss Sue Chien*
Called: July 1997, Middle Temple, LLB
(Hons)(Warw)

Lee *Teck Hock*
Called: Mar 1998, Lincoln's Inn, LLB
(Hons)(Leics)

Lee *Tin Yan*
Called: July 1994, Middle Temple, LLB
(Hons)(Lond)

Lee *Towk Boon*
Called: July 1995, Lincoln's Inn, LLB (Hons)

Lee *Tzu Voon*
P O Box 20269, Pejabat Pos Luyang, 88759
Kota Kinabalu, Sabah, 6 088 224820, Fax: 6
088 219046. Called: Nov 1994, Lincoln's
Inn, LLB (Hons)(Lond)

Lee *Wei Chiang*
Called: Oct 1997, Gray's Inn, LLB (Lancs)

Lee *Wei Yung*
B 873 Yishun St 81, 03-167, 535 0550, Fax:
438 0550, and Member Singapore Bar.
Called: July 1991, Middle Temple, LLB
(Hons) (Warw)

Lee *Miss Wendy Hsiao Wen*
and Member Singapore Bar. Called: July
1993, Middle Temple, LLB (Hons)

Lee *Miss Wendy Su Lin*
Called: July 1995, Middle Temple, LLB
(Hons) (Hull)

Lee *Yi Chung*
Called: Nov 1996, Middle Temple, LLB
(Hons)(Hull)

Lee *Yih Leang*
Called: July 1995, Lincoln's Inn, LLB (Hons)

Lee *Miss Yoke Har*
Called: July 1994, Middle Temple, LLB
(Hons)(Lond)

Lee *Mr Yuen Wai*
16 Raffles Quay, [H]36-00, (65) 322 1479,
Fax: (65) 234 2621, and Member Singapore
Bar. Called: July 1993, Lincoln's Inn, LLB
(Hons, Sheff)

Leigh-Morgan *Miss Tonia Lesley Winson*
Called: Nov 1996, Lincoln's Inn, LLB (Hons)

Leng *Chua Kee*
Called: Nov 1997, Inner Temple, B.Acc
(Singapore), LLB (Lond)

Leng *Miss Lai Yoke*
Zaid Ibrahim & Co, 12th Floor, Menara
Bank, Pembangunan, Jalan Sultan Ismail,
50250 Kuala Lumpur, 603 2926688, Fax:
603 2981632, and Member Bar of Malaysia.
Called: July 1993, Inner Temple, LLB
(Nott'm)

Leon *Kwong Wing*
35 Dunearn Close, (65) 466 0285, Fax: (65)
466 0285, and Member Singapore.
Called: Nov 1995, Gray's Inn, LLB (Wales)

Leon *Miss Le Lyn*
Called: Nov 1995, Gray's Inn, LLB (Wales)

Leonard *Eamonn Benedict Knightley*
E102, Hermann-Ehlers-Hans, Martinsring 29,
49078 Osnabruck, Germany (0541) 41599.
Called: Nov 1992, Inner Temple, BA
(Dunelm), LLM (Osnabruck)

Leonard *Hywel*
One Harbour Place, P.O. Box 3239, Tampa,
Florida 33601, 813 223 7000, Fax: 813 229
4133, and Member Florida. Called: July
1974, Gray's Inn, LLB (Wales), JD [Florida
State]

Leonard *Miss Julia Adella*
Called: Nov 1996, Gray's Inn, BBA (Puerto
Rico), LLM (Manch)

Leong *Miss Bik Yoke*
Called: July 1994, Lincoln's Inn, LLB (Hons,
Leic)

Leong *Miss Chee Sian*
Called: Oct 1994, Middle Temple, LLB
(Hons)(Wales)

Leong *Miss Chee Wei*
Called: Nov 1995, Middle Temple, LLB
(Hons)(Hull)

Leong *Miss Cherly Suet Mei*
Called: Nov 1997, Lincoln's Inn, LLB
(Hons)(Leics)

Leong *Miss Constance Choy Leng*
and Member Singapore. Called: July 1996,
Middle Temple, LLB (Hons)(Lond), BA
(Singapore)

Leong *Miss Isabelle May Yue*
Called: July 1997, Middle Temple, LLB
(Hons)(Sheff)

Leong *Miss Jacqueline Pamela*
1531 Prince's Building, Chater Road, (852)
2523-2899, Fax: (852) 2840-0786, QC Hong
Kong and Member Hong Kong, Victoria,
New South Wales Singapore Bar. Called: July
1970, Inner Temple

Leong *Miss Joycelyn Wai Keng*
Called: July 1991, Lincoln's Inn, LLB (Hons)
(East An)

Leong *Kee Han*
Called: Nov 1996, Lincoln's Inn, LLB (Hons)

Leong *Kwok Yan*
12th Floor, Menara Bank Pembangunan,
Jalan Sultan Ismail, 50250 Kuala Lumpur, 03
292 6688, Fax: 07 298 1632, and Member
Malaysia. Called: July 1992, Lincoln's Inn,
LLB (Hons) (Lond)

Leong *Miss Li Lian*
Called: Nov 1995, Gray's Inn, LLB

Leong *Miss Lynette Su-Mein*
15a Jalan Jarak, and Member Singapore Bar.
Called: July 1994, Middle Temple, BA
(Hons)(Keele)

Leong *Michael Kim Seng*
Called: Nov 1997, Middle Temple, BA
(Singapore), LLB (Hons)(Lond)

Leong *Miss Nu-Yen Mireille*
Called: Nov 1997, Lincoln's Inn, LLB
(Hons)(Leeds)

Leong *Miss Pat Lynn*
Called: July 1992, Lincoln's Inn, LLB (Hons)
(Exon)

Leong *Miss Sue Lynn*
Called: Nov 1995, Middle Temple, BA
(Hons)(Keele)

Leong *Tat Kee*
109 Spottiswood Park, [H]16-81, Singapore
0208, 2215404. Called: Nov 1991, Middle
Temple, LLB Hons (Lond Ext)

Leong *Why Kong*
Braddell Brothers, 1 Colombo Court, [H]06-
30, (65) 3366032, Fax: (65) 3366042, and
Member Singapore. Called: July 1995, Gray's
Inn, LLB (Lond)

Leontiou *Gregory*
504 Libra House, 21 P Caterlaris Street, P O
Box 5001, Nicosia, Cyprus, 02-466 766, Fax:
02-448 777, 02-452 052, and Member
Cyprus Bar. Called: Nov 1994, Lincoln's Inn,
BA (Hons)(Manc)

Leow *Miss Christabel Tze Hoon*
Called: July 1994, Middle Temple, LLB
(Hons)(Wales)

Leow *Miss Fui Fui*
Called: July 1995, Middle Temple, LLB
(Hons) (Wales)

Leow *Michael Yung Fuong*
Robert W H Wang & Woo, 9 Temasek
Boulevard [H]14-01, Suntec Tower 2, 336
0123, Fax: 332 1480, and Member
Singapore Bar. Called: July 1992, Gray's Inn,
LLB, LLM (Lond)

Leung *Michael Hung Kuk*
1002 Chekiang First Bank, 1 Duddell Street,
Central, 2521 7317, Fax: 2845 0654, and
Member Hong Kong Bar. Called: Nov 1993,
Gray's Inn, LLB (Lond)

Leung *Paul Hei Ming*
Called: Nov 1997, Middle Temple, B.Eng
(Hons)(NSW, Australia)

Leung *Richard Wai-Keung*
Des Voeux Chambers, 10/F Bank of East
Asia, Building, 10 Des Voeux Road, Central,
852 2526 3071, Fax: 852 2810 5287, and
Member Hong Kong Bar. Called: July 1994,
Inner Temple, MA (Lancs), LLB

Leung *Siu Ying*
and Member Hong Kong Bar. Called: Nov
1992, Gray's Inn, B Arch (Newc), LLB
(Lond)

Leung *Sun So*
Called: Nov 1989, Gray's Inn, LLB [Lond]

Leung *Tak Yin*
and Member Hong Kong Bar. Called: July
1995, Middle Temple, LLB (Hons)

Leung *Wai Man R*
16/F One Pacific Place, 88 Queensway, 852
25232003, Fax: 852 28100302, and Member
Hong Kong Bar. Called: Feb 1992, Gray's
Inn, BA (Hong Kong), LLB (Lond)

Leung *Yew Kwong*
Inland Revenue Authority of, Singapore Law
Division, 55 Newtown Road, Revenue
House, 00656 3512022, Fax: 00656
3512077, Advocate & Solicitor (Singapore).
Called: Nov 1989, Lincoln's Inn, LLB, BSc
(Lond), MSc (Reading), MBA (Singapore)

Leung *Miss Yuet Ngor*
Called: Oct 1996, Middle Temple, BSc
(Hons)(HongKong), CPE (Manc)

Lever *Mrs Andrina Gay Richards*
Suite 2308, 965 Bay Street, Toronto, Ontario
M55 2A3, 416 920 5114, Fax: 416 920 6764,
and Member Victoria Bar Australia Bar.
Called: July 1980, Gray's Inn, BA, BA (Hons)

F

Levin *David Samuel*
Owen Dixon Chambers, 205 William St,
Melbourne 3000, 61 39608 7043, Fax: 61
39608 8729, and Member Victoria,
Australian Capital Territory, Tasmania, New
South Wales, Northern Territory, South
Australia New South Wales Bar South
Australia Bar. Called: July 1972, Middle
Temple, MA (Cantab)

Lewis *Edwin*
Called: Nov 1997, Lincoln's Inn, LLB (Hons)

Lewis *Miss Linda Catherine*
Called: Feb 1990, Inner Temple, BSc
(Surrey), LLM

Lewis *Linton Aron*
P.O.Box 1407, Queen's Drive, St Vincent &
The Grenadines, 1 809 456 2577, Fax: 1
809 456 5372, and Member St VIncent &
The Grenadines. Called: July 1996, Gray's
Inn, MA (Bristol), ACCA

Li *Ms Cynthia Sun-Ming*
1318 Prince's Building, 10 Chater Road,
Central, Hong Kong, (852) 2526 8128, Fax:
(852) 2526 8500, and Member Hong Kong
Bar. Called: July 1994, Inner Temple, BA
(Canada), LLB

Li *Miss Gladys Veronica*
2507 Edinburgh Tower, The Landmark, 15
Queen's Road Central, 25-2 17188, Fax:
2810 1823, QC (Hong Kong) and Member
Hong Kong Bar. Called: Feb 1971, Lincoln's
Inn, MA (Cantab)

Li-Ann *Ms Cheong*
Called: July 1994, Inner Temple, LLB
(Nott'm)

Lian *Miss Alice Meng Li*
Called: July 1996, Lincoln's Inn, LLB
(Hons)(Herts)

Liao *Martin Cheung-Kong*
61 New Henry House, 10 Ice House Street,
Central, Hong Kong, 2522 5121, and
Member Hong Kong Bar Singapore Bar.
Called: July 1984, Lincoln's Inn, BSc (Econ),
LLM, Dip Law

Liew *Bernard Jin Yang*
Neptune Orient Lines Limited, 456
Alexandra Road [H]06-00, Nol Building,
Singapore 119962, (65) 3715381, Fax: (65)
2731697, and Member Singapore Bar.
Called: July 1989, Gray's Inn, LLB (Bucks)

Liew *Miss Lan-Hing*
Called: July 1995, Middle Temple, B.Sc
(Hons), LLB (Hons)

Liew *Miss Siew Ling*
Called: July 1997, Lincoln's Inn, LLB (Hons)

Liew *Sunny Siew Pang*
Liew Hazalina, No 286 Lafite Apartments,
Jalan SS 17/1G, 47500 Petaling Jaya,
Selangor, 732 7668, Fax: 732 6188, and
Member Malaysia Bar. Called: July 1993,
Gray's Inn, LLB (Brunel)

Lightbourn *Miss Sandra Jean*
Called: July 1997, Lincoln's Inn, LLB (Hons)

Lim *Miss Ai Leen*
Malaysian Derivatives Clearing, House, 4th
Floor, Citypoint, Dayabumi Complex, 50050
Kuala Lumpur, 60 3 294 5070, Fax: 60 3
294 5040, and Member Malaysia Bar.
Called: Oct 1992, Middle Temple, LL.B
(Hons, B'ham)

Lim *Miss Angelina Swee Peng*
Called: July 1994, Lincoln's Inn, LLB (Hons)

Lim *Miss Bee San*
Called: Nov 1994, Middle Temple, LLB
(Hons)

Lim *Miss Choi Ming*
and Member Singapore Bar. Called: July
1995, Middle Temple, LLB (Hons)

Lim *Chong Fong*
Azman Davidson & Co, Advocates &
Solicitors, Suite 13.03, Menara Tan & Tan,
207 Jalan Tun Razak, 50400 Kuala Lumpur
Malaysia, 603 264 0200, Fax: 603 264 0280,
and Member Malaysia Bar. Called: July 1995,
Middle Temple, LLB (Hons), BSc,
(Bldg)(Hons), ARICS, ACIArb

Lim *Choon How*
Called: Nov 1996, Lincoln's Inn, LLB
(Hons)(Lond)

Lim *Christopher Su Heng*
Suite 16.01, 16th Floor, Wisma Nusantara,
Jalan Punchak, 50050 Kuala Lumpur, 0603
203 3541, Fax: 0603 203 3542, and Member
Malaysia Bar. Called: July 1996, Lincoln's
Inn, LLB (Hons)(Bris)

Lim *Miss Cynthia Siew Leng*
Messrs Iza Ng Yeoh & Kit, 19th Floor,
Bangunan, Dato, Zainal, Jalan Melaka, 50100
Kuala Lumpur, 2986066, Fax: 2982593, and
Member Malaysia Bar. Called: July 1992,
Lincoln's Inn, LLB (Hons) (Lond)

Lim *Fung Peen*
Called: Nov 1995, Middle Temple, LLB
(Hons)

Lim *Miss Gek Hoon*
Called: July 1996, Lincoln's Inn, LLB
(Hons)(Lond)

Lim *George Chee Huat*
Called: July 1997, Middle Temple, LLB
(Hons)(Lond)

Lim *Ms Goon Lwee*
Called: July 1996, Inner Temple, LLB (Lond)

Lim *Miss Grace Siew Hua*
Called: July 1994, Lincoln's Inn, LLB (Hons)

Lim *Miss Helen Bek Yun*
P.O.Box 2773, 90731 Sandakan, Sabah,
Advocate of the High Court in Sabah &
Sarawak, Malaysia Advocate of the Supreme
Court of Brunei, Darussalam. Called: July
1995, Lincoln's Inn, LLB (Hons)(Leeds)

Lim *Miss Heliz Hsien Ling*
Called: Nov 1997, Lincoln's Inn, LLB
(Hons)(E.Lond)

Lim *Miss Hui Min*
51 Dyson Road, 2551868, Fax: 2519078.
Called: July 1996, Lincoln's Inn, BA (Oxon),
BCL

Lim *Miss Hui Ting*
Called: Nov 1996, Lincoln's Inn, LLB (Hons)
(Sheff)

Lim *Miss Hwee Bin*
Called: July 1996, Lincoln's Inn, LLB (Hons)

Lim *Miss Jacqueline Hui Erh*
9F Three Exchange Square, 8 Connaught
Place, Central, 852 2840 1282, Fax: 852
2840 0515. Called: Oct 1994, Middle
Temple, LLB (Hons)(Bris), LLM (Bris)

Lim *Miss Jane Chen*
Called: Nov 1997, Lincoln's Inn, LLB
(Hons)(Bucks)

Lim *Miss Jeanne Tsze Ye*
Called: Nov 1992, Middle Temple, LLB
(Hons, Lond)

Lim *Miss Jessica Hai Ean*
Called: July 1997, Lincoln's Inn, LLB (Hons)

Lim *Miss Julie Siu Yen*
Called: July 1997, Middle Temple, LLB
(Hons)(Lond)

Lim *Miss Karen Um-Chai Hui Lin*
Oversea-Chinese Banking, Corporation
Limited, 65 China Street, [H]08-00, OCBC
Centre, 5306143, Fax: 5352335. Called: Nov
1995, Middle Temple, LLB (Hons)

Lim *Miss Kay Li Deborah*
Called: July 1997, Middle Temple, LLB
(Hons)(Nott'm)

Lim *Kelvin Kuan Chin*
Called: July 1994, Lincoln's Inn, LLB (Hons)

Lim *Kong Yuk*
Called: Nov 1996, Middle Temple, LLB
(Hons)(Wales)

Lim *Kuok Sim Edwin*
42 Jalan Permai, Robson Heights, Kuala
Lumpur 50460, (603) 2742234. Called: Nov
1995, Gray's Inn, LLB (Wales), LLM (Bris)

Lim *Lay Hor*
M.P.Raja, E.T. Low & Tan, Room 304, 3rd
Floor, Wisma Tah peh, No 86 Jalan Masjid
India 50100, Kuala Lumpur, 03 293 4293.
Called: July 1997, Middle Temple, LLB
(Hons)(Lond)

Lim *Miss Lee Hoon*
Called: July 1995, Lincoln's Inn, LLB (Hons)

Lim *Miss Li Lian*
and Member Singapore Bar. Called: Nov
1992, Middle Temple, LLB (Hons, Sheff)

Lim *Miss Li Lin*
Called: July 1996, Middle Temple, LLB
(Hons)(Lanc)

Lim *Miss Liau Yan*
Called: July 1997, Lincoln's Inn, LLB
(Hons)(Kent)

Lim *Miss Lorinne May-Suan*
Called: July 1994, Lincoln's Inn, LLB (Hons)

Lim *Mark Chin Hian*
Called: Nov 1996, Middle Temple, BA
(Hons)

Lim *Miss Michele Hwee Ling*
Called: July 1995, Middle Temple, LLB
(Hons) (Hull)

Lim *Miss Michele Kythe Beng Sze*
Called: Nov 1992, Middle Temple, LLB
(Hons)

Lim *Perry Che-How*
Called: July 1994, Middle Temple, LLB
(Hons)(Wales)

Lim *Miss Puay Yuen*
Called: July 1995, Middle Temple, LLB
(Hons) (Wales)

Lim *Miss Pui Keng*
Called: July 1997, Lincoln's Inn, LLB
(Hons)(Leics)

Lim *Ralph Howard U Wei*
Called: July 1995, Lincoln's Inn, LLB (Hons)

Lim *Raymond Kuan Yew*
Blk 34 [H]02-218, Jalan Bahagia, Singapore
320034, 2547821, and Member Singapore
Bar. Called: July 1995, Lincoln's Inn, LLB
(Hons)

Lim *Richard Teck Hock*
Blk 94 Henderson Road, [H]09-270
Singapore 150094, (65) 2762011, and
Member Singapore. Called: July 1995,
Lincoln's Inn, LLB (Hons)

Lim *Seng Sheoh*
Called: Nov 1994, Middle Temple, BA
(Hons) (Kent)

Lim *Miss Sharon Yen Li*
Chooi & Company, Penthouse, Mine
Building, Jalan Bukit Nanas, 50250 Kuala
Lumpur, and Member Malaysia. Called: July
1995, Lincoln's Inn, LLB (Hons)

Lim *Miss Siew Ming*
Called: July 1996, Lincoln's Inn, LLB
(Hons)(Sheff)

Lim *Miss Siew Peng*
Called: July 1996, Lincoln's Inn, BA
(Hons)(Keele)

Lim *Miss Siew Symn*
c/o Messrs Abdullah,Ooi & Chan, Suite 17-
03, 17th Floor, MCB Plaza, 6 Cangkat Raja
Chulan, 50200 Kuala Lumpur Malaysia, 603
2324293, Fax: 603 2301644, Advocate &
Solicitor of the High Court of Malaya.
Called: Nov 1992, Gray's Inn, LLB (So'ton)

Lim *Miss Sim Yi*
Called: July 1995, Gray's Inn, LLB

Lim *Siu Yin Jeffrey*
Called: July 1997, Gray's Inn, LLB (Bris)

Lim *Song Chia*
(65) 439 5680, Fax: (65) 532 0206.
Called: Nov 1996, Lincoln's Inn, LLB
(Hons)(Lond)

Lim *Stephen Yew Huat*
15th/16th Floors, Bank of China Building, 4
Battery Road, 535 3600, Fax: 538 8598,
Advocate & Solicitor of Supreme Court of
Singapore and Member Singapore.
Called: July 1992, Middle Temple, LLB
(Hons) LSe, LLM (Columbia)

Lim *Miss Su-ching*
Messrs Ramdas & Wong, 6 Shenton Way,
[H] 25-06 DBS Building Tower 2, Singapore
068809, 65 220 1121, Fax: 65 225 9152/65
225 9153, and Member Singapore Bar.
Called: July 1992, Middle Temple, LLB
(Hons) (E.Ang)

Lim *Miss Su-Fen*
Drew & Napier, 20 Raffles Place, [H]17-00
Ocean Towers, Singapore 048620, (65) 535
0733, Fax: (65) 535 4864, and Member
Singapore Bar. Called: Nov 1994, Middle
Temple, LLB (Hons)

Lim *Miss Su-Lynn*
Drew & Napier, 20 Raffles Place, [H] 17.00
Ocean Towers, 535 0733, Fax: 532 7149,
and Member Singapore Bar. Called: July
1995, Middle Temple, LLB (Hons) (Hull)

Lim *Swee Tee*
Called: July 1996, Middle Temple, BSc
(Singapore), LLB (Hons)(Wolves)

Lim *Tanguy Yuteck*
Chor Pee & Partners, 50 Raffles Place, 18th
Floor, Singapore Land, Tower, Singapore
048623, 4355726, Fax: 5363155.
Called: Nov 1993, Middle Temple, LLB
(Hons)(Wales)

Lim *Tchuang Cheio Tchwonyoson*
Rodyk & Davidson, 9 Raffles Place, [H]55-01
Republic Plaza, 65-2252626, Fax: 65-
2251838, and Member Singapore Bar.
Called: July 1993, Middle Temple, LLB
(Hons)(Lond)

Lim *Tiong-Piow*
Called: July 1995, Lincoln's Inn, LLB (Hons)

Lim *Tuck Sum*
Called: July 1996, Lincoln's Inn, LLB
(Hons)(Lond)

Lim *Wye Hon*
Called: July 1996, Middle Temple, LLB
(Hons)(Leic)

Lim *Yang Hsing Leslie*
Called: July 1995, Middle Temple, LLB
(Hons)(Kent)

Lim *Yek Lai*
Called: July 1996, Lincoln's Inn, LLB (Hons)

Lim *Miss Yen-Hui*
Called: July 1997, Gray's Inn, LLB (Bristol)

Lim *Miss Yoon Cheng Audrey*
Supreme Court, St Andrew's Road,
Singapore 0617, 3323918, Fax: 3379450.
Called: July 1994, Middle Temple, BA
(Hons)(Cantab)

Lin *Miss Diaan-Yi*
Called: July 1996, Lincoln's Inn, BA (Hons)

Lin *Feng*
Called: Nov 1997, Middle Temple, LLB
(Fudan), LLM (Victoria)

Lindsay *Miss Alison*
Barrister of Ireland. Called: May 1996,
Middle Temple, BA (Hons)(Dublin), BL
(King's Inn)

Ling *Miss Carolyn Dora Li-Hsing*
Called: Nov 1989, Middle Temple, LLB
(Newc), LLM (Lond)

Ling *Chun Wai*
Called: July 1996, Lincoln's Inn, LLB
(Hons)(Lond)

Ling *Clarence Louis Li-Tien*
ATMD, 39 Robinson Road, [H] 07-01,
Robinson Point, (65) 5345266, Fax: (65)
2238762, and Member Singapore.
Called: Nov 1995, Lincoln's Inn, LLB (Hons)
(Leics), BSc (Chem.emph, Biochem)

Ling *Hee Keat*
54 Jalan Setiabakti 8, Bukit Damansara,
50490 Kuala Lumpur, Malaysia, 03 2530257,
Fax: 03 2531520. Called: July 1995,
Lincoln's Inn, LLB (Hons)

Ling *Miss Jing Jinn*
M/S Battenberg & Talma Advocat, 4, 1st
Floor, Jalan Song Thian, Cheok, Kuching,
Sarawak, 082 253277, Fax: 082 420430,
Advocate & Solicitor of Singapore Advocate
of Sarawak. Called: July 1994, Middle
Temple, LLB (Hons)(Manc)

Ling *Miss Jocettta Ching Tse*
Called: July 1995, Lincoln's Inn, LLB (Hons)

Ling *Leong Hui*
Called: July 1996, Inner Temple, LLB (Lond)

Ling *Peter Liong Ing*
BP Asia Pacific Pte. Ltd, 396 Alexander
Road, [H]18-01, BP Tower, (65) 371 8701,
Fax: (65) 371 8797. Called: Nov 1969,
Lincoln's Inn

Ling *Tien Wah*
M/S Helen Yeo & Partners, 11 Collyer Quay
[H]12-01, The Arcade, 2251400, Fax:
2221345, and Member Singapore Bar
Malaysia Bar. Called: Nov 1990, Lincoln's
Inn, LLB (Leeds)

Ling *Miss Wei Lin*
Called: July 1996, Lincoln's Inn, LLB
(Hons)(Leeds)

Lio *Chee Yeong*
Called: Nov 1996, Middle Temple, LLB
(Hons)(Lond)

Liow *Henny Woon Loong*
Khattar Wong & Partners, 80 Raffles Place,
[H] 25-01, UOB Plaza 1, 535 6844, Fax: 534
1090, and Member Singapore. Called: July
1994, Lincoln's Inn, LLB (Hons)

Litton *Henry Denis OBE*
Court of Final Appeal, 1 Battery Path, 852-
2123-0012, Fax: 852-2524-3991, Hong Kong
QC. Called: June 1959, Gray's Inn, MA
(Oxon)

Liu *Kee Yong*
Called: July 1996, Middle Temple, LLB
(Hons)(Hull)

Liu *Owen Heng Su*
Called: Nov 1997, Lincoln's Inn, LLB
(Hons)(Manch)

Liu *Sern Yang*
Called: Nov 1996, Gray's Inn, LLB

Liu *Zhiping*
Called: July 1996, Middle Temple, LLB
(Hons)(Notts)

Livingstone *Philip Martin*
Vibert & Valpy, 8 Duhamel Place, St Helier,
Jersey, 01534 888666, Fax: 01534 888555,
Advocate of the Royal Court of Jersey.
Called: July 1987, Middle Temple, LLB (Hull)

Lloyd *Michael Gordon*
Rua do Norte 18,20, 1200 Lisbon, 00 351 1
343 3762, Fax: 00 351 1 343 3762.
Called: Nov 1967, Gray's Inn, MA (Oxon)

Lo *Miss Phyllis Set Fui*
Called: July 1996, Middle Temple, LLB
(Hons)(Bris)

Lo *Pui Yin*
1001 Far East Finance Centre, 16 Harcourt
Road, Hong Kong, (852) 2866 8233, Fax:
(852) 2866 3932, and Member Hong Kong
Bar. Called: July 1992, Inner Temple, LLB
(LSE)

Logan *David Preston*
Department of Justice, Queensway
Government Offices, 66 Queensway, 852
2867 2041, Fax: 852 2869 0062, and
Member Hong Kong Bar. Called: July 1983,
Inner Temple, LLB (Sheff)

Loh *Miss Annabelle Li Kien*
Called: July 1997, Middle Temple, LLB
(Hons)(Lond)

Loh *Benjamin Tse Min*
Called: July 1996, Middle Temple, LLB
(Hons)(Hull)

Loh *Miss Christina Huey Shya*
Called: July 1997, Lincoln's Inn, LLB
(Hons)(Leeds)

Loh *Miss Jennifer May Ying*
Called: July 1996, Lincoln's Inn, LLB
(Hons)(Cardiff)

Loh *Miss Julia Su Khoon*
Called: Oct 1991, Gray's Inn, BA (Oxon)

Loh *Lik Peng*
Called: July 1997, Middle Temple, LLB
(Hons)(Sheff)

Loh *Ms Lynette Moon Lan*
Called: Nov 1997, Inner Temple, LLB (Leics)

Loh *Miss May*
Supreme Court, St Andrew's Road, (65) 332
4026, Fax: (65) 337 9450, and Member
Singapore Bar. Called: July 1996, Middle
Temple, LLB (Hons)(Kent)

Loh *Miss Melissa Yuet Meng*
Called: Nov 1997, Lincoln's Inn, LLB (Hons)

Loh *Miss Mui Leng*
Called: Nov 1993, Gray's Inn, LLB

Loh *Nigel Lin Kwang*
Called: July 1995, Middle Temple, LLB
(Hons) (Leic)

Loh *Shu Hon*
Called: July 1993, Middle Temple, LLB
(Hons)

Loh *Miss Siau Joe*
Called: July 1996, Gray's Inn, LLB (West of
England

Loh *Wei Leong*
Called: Nov 1996, Gray's Inn, LLB (L'pool),
LLM (Lond)

Loh *Ms Yee Mun*
Called: July 1994, Lincoln's Inn, LLB (Hons,
Warw), LLM (Warw)

Loh *Ms Yun Ping*
Called: July 1995, Gray's Inn, B.Soc.Sci
(Keele)

Loi *Dhillon Chia Wei*
Fax: 065 280 4930. Called: July 1996,
Lincoln's Inn, LLB (Hons)

Loi *Miss Laurel Thanh Moi*
Called: July 1994, Lincoln's Inn, BA (Hons,
Keele)

Loi *Miss Lay Hong*
Called: Nov 1992, Gray's Inn, LLB (Lond)

Loizides *Miss Vicky*
The Chanteclair House, 2 Sophoulis Street,
P.O.Box 1646, Nicosia, Cyprus, (357) (2)
444391, Fax: (357) (2) 451620, and Member
Cyprus Bar. Called: Nov 1993, Gray's Inn,
LLB (Bris)

Loke *Adrian Weng Hong*
Messrs Rodyk & Davidson, 9 Raffles Place,
Republic Plaza, [H]55-01 & [H]56-01, 225
2626, Fax: 225 1838. Called: July 1995,
Middle Temple, LLB (Hons)

Loke *Miss Moon Cee*
Called: July 1997, Lincoln's Inn, LLB
(Hons)(Manch)

Loke *Siew Meng*
42 Everton Road [H]17-02, Asia Gardens,
Singapore 0208, 2204980, Fax: 5364748,
and Member Singapore Bar. Called: Nov
1990, Lincoln's Inn, LLB (Lond), AIBA, LLM
(Lond), CDAF, B.Sc (Est Man) Hons, (S'pore)

Loming *James Ih-wuen*
No 37 (1st Floor), BDA- Shahida Centre,
Abang Galau Road, 97000 Bintulu, Sarawak,
086 331991, Fax: 086 338339, and Member
Sabah Bar Sarawak Bar. Called: Oct 1992,
Middle Temple, LL.B (Hons)

Long *Miss Lynette Li-Shen*
Called: July 1994, Middle Temple, LLB
(Hons)(Bris)

Long *Mervyn Tan Chye*
Called: July 1994, Inner Temple, LLB (Lond)

Long *Patrick*
Law Library, Four Courts, Dublin 7, Ireland,
8214397, Fax: 8215297, Barrister of King's
Inn. Called: Nov 1994, Middle Temple, Dip
Law

Longley *His Honour Judge*
District Judge's Chambers, Wan Chai Law
Courts, Wan Chai Tower 1, 12 Harbour
Road, 2582 4425, Fax: 2824 1641, and
Member Hong Kong Bar. Called: Nov 1970,
Lincoln's Inn, MA (Oxon)

Loo *Miss Bernice Ming Nee*
and Member Singapore Bar. Called: July
1995, Lincoln's Inn, LLB (Hons)

Loo *Miss Ee-Ling*
Called: July 1997, Lincoln's Inn, LLB (Hons)

Loo *Miss Hwee Fang*
Called: July 1997, Gray's Inn, LLB (Sheff)

Loo *Miss Josephine Yi*
1606 Bayshore Park, Pearl Tower, Bayshore
Road, Singapore 1646, 4486114
(Residence), and Member Singapore Bar.
Called: July 1994, Lincoln's Inn, LLB (Hons)

Loo *Miss Peggy Chee Hoon*
and Member Malaysia Bar. Called: Nov 1990,
Gray's Inn, LLB (Lond)

Loo *Miss Peh Fern*
Called: Nov 1997, Lincoln's Inn, LLB
(Hons)(Warw)

Looi *Miss Lai Kiew*
Link Tower 1, Unit 11-03, The Bayshore, 24
Bayshore Road, 2778483, Fax: 2763774.
Called: July 1994, Middle Temple, LLB
(Hons)(Lond)

Lourdesamy *Gerard Samuel Vijayan*
No 546 Jalan 17/15, 46400 Petaling Jaya,
Selangor, and Member Malaysia Bar.
Called: July 1992, Lincoln's Inn, LLB (Hons)
(Leeds)

Lovell *Harold Earl Edmund*
P O Box 20, 29 Redcliffe Street, St John's,
268 462 1136, Fax: 268 462 8980, and
Member Antigua Bar Monserrat Bar Barbuda
Bar. Called: July 1987, Middle Temple, BA
(W.Indies), LLB, M.Jur (B'ham)

Low *Miss Anisah Suyuti*
Called: July 1995, Lincoln's Inn, LLB (Hons)

Low *Dr Cheng Teong*
111 Taman Sia Her Yam, 85000 Segamat
Johor, 07 931 2042, Fax: 07 931 2042.
Called: Nov 1996, Lincoln's Inn, LLB
(Hons)(Lond), BDS (Singapore)

Low *Miss Chi Cheng*
Lim Kian Leong & Co, Suite 1802 18th
Floor, Wisma Hamzah-Kwong Hing, No 1
Leboh Ampang, 50100 Kuala Lumpur,
2301440, 2301441, Fax: 2388039, and
Member Malaysia Bar. Called: July 1991,
Middle Temple, LLB (Hons) (Leics)

Low *Chwan Yiing Dennis*
Called: Nov 1996, Lincoln's Inn, LLB
(Nott'm)

Low *Denis Kheng Yin*
Called: Nov 1997, Middle Temple, LLB
(Hons)

Low *Miss Geok Ping*
Called: July 1997, Lincoln's Inn, LLB (Hons)

Low *Hun Kiat*
Olympic Industries Bhd, Level 23,Plaza Raja
Chulan, No 8 Jlan Raja Chulan, 50200 Kuala
Lumpur, 03 2323993, Fax: 03 2323996, Bar
Council Malaysia (Advocate & Solicitor of
High Court of Malaya). Called: July 1995,
Middle Temple, LLB (Hons)

Low *Jeng Kiat Timothy Aeron*
Called: July 1996, Middle Temple, LLB
(Hons)(Wolves)

Low *Keng Siong*
Called: Nov 1997, Lincoln's Inn, LLB
(Hons)(Lond)

Low *Miss Lynette*
c/o M/S Allen & Gledhill, [H] 18-01 City
House, 36 Robinson Road, Singapore, (65)
4207964, Fax: (65) 2254950/2250062, and
Member Singapore Bar. Called: Nov 1993,
Middle Temple, LLB (Hons)

Low *Miss Peck Yin*
Called: July 1996, Lincoln's Inn, LLB (Hons)

Low *Miss Peng Peng*
Called: July 1996, Lincoln's Inn, LLB
(Hons)(Wales)

Low *Reginald Heng Chuan*
Called: Nov 1997, Middle Temple, LLB
(Hons)(Leics)

Low *Tak Fatt*
Called: Oct 1994, Gray's Inn, LLB (Warw)

Low *Wan Kwong*
Block 157, BT Batok Street 11, [H]01-200,
561 6334, Fax: 561 6334. Called: Nov 1996,
Middle Temple, LLB (Hons)

Low *Miss Wee Jee*
Called: July 1995, Lincoln's Inn, LLB (Hons)

Low *Willin*
Called: July 1997, Gray's Inn, LLB (Notts)

Lu *Miss Su Lian*
Called: July 1996, Middle Temple, BA
(Hons)(Cantab)

Lucey *John Joseph*
Called: May 1996, Middle Temple, BCL
(Cork), LLM, (Cork), BL (King's, Inn)

Lugar-Mawson *His Hon Judge Gareth John*
High Court, 38 Queensway, 852 2825 4316,
Fax: 852 2869 0640, Former Solicitor
(England & Wales and Hong Kong Judge of
the District Court of Hong Kong and
Deputy Judge of the High Court of Hong
Kong and Member Hong Kong Bar.
Called: July 1985, Middle Temple, LLB
(Lond), FCIArb

Lui *Simon Kin Man*
Called: Nov 1997, Gray's Inn, BSc (Hong Kong)

Luis *Gerard Andrew*
Measat Broadcast Network Syst., All Asia
Broadcast Centre, Technology Park
Malaysia, Lebuhraya Puchong - SG BESI,
57000 Kuala Lumpur, 60 3 583 6688, Fax:
60 3 583 6875, Advocate & Solicitor
(Malaysia). Called: July 1991, Lincoln's Inn,
LLB (Hons) (Lond), LLM (Lond)

Luk *King Yip*
Called: Nov 1997, Middle Temple, BS.Sc
(Hons)(Hong, Kong)

Lum *Miss May Lee Chan*
10 Kensington Park Drive, [H]18-03,
2857352. Called: July 1995, Middle Temple,
BA (Hons)(Keele)

Luthi *Charles Christian Rolf*
c/o Conyers, Dill & Pearman, Clarendon
House, Church Street, Hamilton, Bermuda,
(441) 295 1422, Fax: (441) 295 4720, and
Member Bermuda. Called: Feb 1993, Middle
Temple, BA (Hons)(Oxon)

Lynch *Bernard Gerard*
B und P, Bavcoordination UND,
Projektsteuerung GMBH, Hauptstrasse 24,
48712 Gescher, Germany, 02542 5099.
Called: Nov 1995, Lincoln's Inn, LLB
(Hons)(Lond)

M'Bai *Ousman*
Called: Oct 1996, Lincoln's Inn, LLB
(Hons)(Leeds)

Ma *Miss Pin Yen*
Called: Nov 1997, Lincoln's Inn, LLB
(Hons)(Leeds)

Maarof *Miss Norzaimah*
Called: Nov 1993, Inner Temple, LLB
(So'ton)

MacDiarmid *Ross*
ING Bank, 15 Kiseleff Boulevard, Sector 1,
Bucharest, 00 401 222 1600, Fax: 00 401
222 1401. Called: Nov 1982, Inner Temple,
BSc (Reading) Hons, ARICS, Dip Law

Macdonald *Duncan Hamish*
8 Horse barrack Lane, 00 350 50254/(Spain)
00 34 52 838806, and Member Gibraltar·
Bar, St Helena. Called: Oct 1992, Middle
Temple, LL.B (Hons)

Macdonald *Roderick Francis*
QC of Scotland and Member Scotland.
Called: July 1997, Inner Temple, LLB
(Glasgow)

Machado *Miss Thushani Vincentia Michele*
Called: Nov 1997, Lincoln's Inn, LLB (Lond)

MacKenzie *Miss Cailin Catriona Elizabeth*
Called: Nov 1992, Lincoln's Inn, LLB
(Hons)(Lond), Maitrise (Paris)

MacKenzie *Miss Catherine Patricia*
Faculty of Law, Australian National
University, Canberra ACT 0200, 612 6279
8446/6249 3482, Fax: 612 6249 0103,
Solicitor of ACT and Member State Bars of
Queensland, New South Wales, Australian
Capital Territories, High Court of Australia.
Called: May 1995, Inner Temple, BA, MA,
Dip Law

MacKenzie Ross *David*
113-114 New Henry House 11/F, 10 Ice
House Street, Central, 852 877 0087, Fax:
852 524 6202, and Member Hong Kong,
SAR China Victoria (Australia). Called: Nov
1962, Gray's Inn, MA (Cantab)

Madhani *Mohamed Ali Kassamali*
Mohamed Madhani & Co Advocates, P O
Box 48539, Nairobi, Kenya, 254 2 228255/
229233, Fax: 254 2 230896, and Member
Kenya. Called: July 1980, Lincoln's Inn, LLB,
FCII

Madhub *Oomeshwarnath Beny*
Called: July 1991, Middle Temple, LLB
(Hons) (Warw)

Madigan *Mrs Patricia Josephine*
Barrister of Ireland. Called: Nov 1995,
Middle Temple, BL (King's Inn)

Magennis *Bernard James Joseph*
Rossglass, Downpatrick, Co Down, 01396
842082, and Member Southern Ireland Bar.
Called: Oct 1994, Middle Temple, BA, BL

Magimay *Miss Anita Shoba*
and Member Malaysian Bar. Called: July
1996, Lincoln's Inn, LLB (Hons)

Mah *Miss Catherine Siok Hean*
Called: July 1988, Gray's Inn, LLB (Bristol)

Mah *Cheong Fatt*
Called: July 1997, Middle Temple, LLB
(Hons)(Lond)

Maharaj *Miss Lou-Ann*
Called: Nov 1991, Gray's Inn, LLB (W
Indies), LLM

Mahatantila *Duleep Rohan*
Called: Nov 1988, Middle Temple, BA, Dip
Law

Mahendran *Miss Jyeshta*
Called: Nov 1995, Lincoln's Inn, BSc
(Hons)(Keele)

Mahendran *Miss Sonia*
Called: July 1995, Middle Temple, LLB
(Hons)(Warw)

Mahmood *Mario Bin*
Called: Nov 1996, Middle Temple, LLB
(Hons)

Mahmud *Miss Ishrat*
Called: Mar 1997, Lincoln's Inn, LLB (Hons)

Mahmud *Ms Sahia*
Called: July 1996, Lincoln's Inn

Maidment *Richard John Haylock*
c/o Clerk B, Owen Dixon Chambers, 205
William Street, Melbourne, Victoria 3000,
039 608 7049, Fax: 039 608 8485, and
Member Victorian Bar New South Wales
Bar. Called: Nov 1971, Gray's Inn, LLM

Maillis II *Alexander Pericles*
Called: July 1997, Lincoln's Inn, LLB
(Hons)(Wales)

Main *Ms Angela Patricia*
Texas Instruments Singapore, Legal
Department, 990 Bendemeer Road, (65) 390
7627, Fax: (65) 390 7064. Called: July 1997,
Lincoln's Inn, BA, MA (Auckland), Dip in
Journalism, (Cantab)

Majiyagbe *Jonathan Babatunde*
J B Majiyagbe & Co, Barristers Solicitors &,
Notaries Public, 4 Human Rights Avenue,
P.O.Box 726, Kano, 064 631261/064
644171, Fax: 064 647146, Senior Advocate
of Nigeria and Member Nigerian Bar.
Called: Nov 1964, Middle Temple, LLB
(Lond)

Mak *Andrew Yip Shing*
Room 1432, Prince's Building, Central, 25 2
40151, Fax: 28 101731, and Member Hong
Kong, Australia, Singapore. Called: July
1988, Lincoln's Inn, BSc, MBA (Hong Kong),
LLB, LLM (Lond) ACIS, Dip Dev Studies,
(Cantab), ACIArb

Mak *Chi Biu*
Flat 3B, Block 29, Greenwood Terrace, 26-28 Sui Wo Road, Sha Tin, Hong Kong, 852 2601 6587, Fax: 852 2577 3562, and Member Hong Kong Bar. Called: Nov 1992, Gray's Inn, BSc (Eng)(Hong Kong), LLB (Lond), MICE, MIStructE, FCIArb

Mak *Miss Mabel Min-Theng*
Called: July 1997, Gray's Inn, LLB (Bris)

Mak *Miss Rosanna Tsui Shan*
Called: Nov 1997, Gray's Inn, LLB (Lond)

Malaiyandi Chettiar *Kamalarajan*
36 Robinson Road, [H] 18-01 City House, 420 7693, Fax: 224 8210, and Member Singapore Bar. Called: Nov 1995, Middle Temple, LLB (Hons)

Mallett *Laurence Edwin*
BP Oil Europe, Legal Department, Les Quatre, Bras, Chaussee de Malines 455, 1950 Kraainem, 32 2 766 3849, Fax: 32 2 766 3828. Called: May 1969, Middle Temple, LLB

Mamun *Abdullah Al*
Admiralty Chambers, Barristers, Advocates &, Notaries, 53 Dit Extension Rd, Naya Paltan, Mothijheel, 834327 (W) 319870 (H), and Member Bangladesh Bar. Called: July 1994, Lincoln's Inn, LLB (Hons), BA (Hons), MA

Manecksha *Ms Ferina Pervez*
IT Publications SDN BHD, Balai Berita Level 2, 31 Jalan Riong, 59000 Kuala Lumpur, 603 282 2022 x 118, Fax: 603 282 0097/8214. Called: July 1995, Inner Temple, LLB (Northumbria)

Manickam *Ms Kasturibai*
Called: July 1997, Lincoln's Inn, LLB (Hons)

Manickam *Vengetraman*
34 Jalan Dinding, Lim Garden, 30100 Ipoh, Perak Malaysia, 05 5275305, and Member Malaysia. Called: July 1995, Lincoln's Inn, LLB (Hons)

Mansor *Maritz*
Blk 2, Marina Vista, 04-73, 0065 4487992, Fax: 0065 2434904. Called: July 1994, Lincoln's Inn, LLB

Mapondera *Miss Dulcie Tsitsi*
Called: Nov 1987, Middle Temple, LLB, LLM (LSE), MBA (Warwick)

Marcou *Miss Mary-Ann*
The Law Office of the Republic, of Cyprus, Apellis Str, Nicosia, and Member Cyprus Bar. Called: Nov 1993, Gray's Inn, LLB (Sheff), LLM (Cantab)

Mariappan *Mogan*
Nor'Ain Mogan & Manoharan, 72b Ting 1, Jalan Melati, 28400 Mentakab, Pahang Darulmakmur, 09-2782290/2784131, Fax: 09-2782293, and Member Malaysia Bar. Called: July 1993, Inner Temple, LLB (Lancs), AFF.A.I.I.

Marican *Abdul Rahim*
Called: May 1996, Lincoln's Inn, LLB (Hons) (Lond)

Marican *Mrs Bee Bee Sultan*
Called: July 1995, Lincoln's Inn, LLB (Hons)

Marimuthu *Jeeva Kumar*
Called: Nov 1997, Lincoln's Inn, LLB (Hons)

Marimuthu *Miss Meera*
Called: Nov 1997, Lincoln's Inn, LLB (Hons)(Herts)

Marimuttu *Jeyan T M*
Messrs Teo Marimuttu & Ptnrs, P O Box No 10869, 88809 Kota Kinabalu, Sabah, Malaysia, 088 252997/252998, Fax: 088 252889, and Member Malaysia Bar. Called: Nov 1992, Gray's Inn, LLB (Buckingham), MI Mgt

Markar *Mrs Fathima Faiza*
Called: Mar 1998, Lincoln's Inn, LLB (Lond)

Markey *Ms Anne King*
Called: July 1995, Inner Temple, LLB

Marrache *Benjamin John Samuel*
Fortress House, Gibraltar, 00 350 79918/74901, Fax: 00 350 74042\73315. Called: Nov 1988, Inner Temple, LLB, LLM (LSE)

Marshall *William Roberts QC (H.K.), SC*
Department of Justice, Queensway Government Office, 3rd Floor, High Block, 66 Queensway, Hong Kong, 852 2867 2092, Fax: 852 2869 0670, and Member Hong Kong Bar Victoria Bar. Called: Nov 1968, Inner Temple, MA (Glas) LLB (Lond)

Martin *Nigel Gregory*
Barrister of Northern Ireland. Called: May 1994, Middle Temple, LLB (Hons)

Martin *Peter David Acheson*
Mello Hollis Jones & Martin, Reid House, 31 Church Street, Hamilton HM 13, (809) 292 1345, Fax: (809) 292 9151, and Member Bermuda Bar. Called: Nov 1983, Gray's Inn, LLB (Manch)

Maryan-Green *Neville Ayton*
77 bis Avenue de Bieteul, 75015 Paris, France, and Member Paris Bar. Called: Nov 1963, Middle Temple, BA LLB (Cantab)

Masemola *Nathaniel Mashilo*
P.O.Box 576, Gallo Manor 2052, Sandton, Johannesburg, (011) 804 5341, Fax: (011) 804 3579, and Member Botswana & Zambia Bars South Africa Bar. Called: June 1964, Gray's Inn, BA LLB (SA), LLB (Lond), UED (Rhodes), FILGAZ (Zambia)

Masood *Syed Aaamir*
Called: Nov 1997, Lincoln's Inn, BSc (Hons)(LSE)

Massias *Isaac Clive*
Massias & Partners, 117 Main Street, P.O.Box 213, 40888, Fax: 40999, and Member Gibraltar Bar. Called: Nov 1986, Middle Temple, LLB (Hons)

Massias *Miss Victoria Stella*
Massias & Partners, 117 Main Street, P.O.Box 213, 40888, Fax: 40999, and Member Gibraltar Bar. Called: Nov 1989, Middle Temple, LLB Hons (Lond), LLM (Lond)

Mat Rasip *Miss Mariza Azen*
Zain & Co, 6th Floor, Bangunan Dato', Zainal, 23 Jalan Melaka, 50100 Kuala Lumpur, 03-2986255, Fax: 2986969, and Member Malaysian Bar. Called: July 1994, Lincoln's Inn, LLB (Hons)

Mathialahan *K*
Called: July 1996, Middle Temple, LLB (Hons)(Leic)

Mathiavaranam *Rueben*
Azman, Davidson & Co, Suite 13-03 13th Floor, Menara Tan & Tan, 207 Jalan Tun Razak, 50400 Kuala Lumpur Malaysia, (03) 2640200, Fax: (03) 2640280, and Member Malaysia Bar Australia Bar. Called: Nov 1989, Lincoln's Inn, BA (Kent)

Maxwell *Anthony Michael Lockhart*
Gesnaire, Le Petit Val, Alderney GY9 3UX, 01481 823889, Fax: 01481 824319. Called: Nov 1985, Middle Temple, LLB (Lond),MRIN, MRAeS, Cert Air & Space Law, (UCL)

Mayers *Miss Maferne Telene*
Called: Nov 1997, Gray's Inn, LLB (Wolver'ton)

Mayhew-Arnold *Michael Charles John*
Henry Ansbacker & Co Limited, One Mitre Square, London EC3A 5AN. Called: Nov 1983, Inner Temple, LLB (Hons) (So'ton)

Mazlan *Azri Sani*
Called: Nov 1995, Gray's Inn, LLB (Wales)

Mbiti *John Maithya*
Apt 320, 240 Mercer Street, New York 10012, (212) 443 5208. Called: Oct 1996, Lincoln's Inn, LLB (Hons)(Lond)

McAleer *James Joseph*
Former Police Officer. Called: Oct 1997, Middle Temple, BA (Hons)(Oxon)

McArdle *Eamonn Terence*
The Bar Library, Royal Courts of Justice, Chichester Street, Belfast BT1 3JP, 01232 241523, Fax: 01232 231850, and Member Northern Ireland. Called: Oct 1996, Inner Temple, BA (East Anglia), CALS (Belfast)

McCartney *Miss Tanya Cecile*
Called: July 1995, Lincoln's Inn, LLB (Hons)

McCartney, *Miss Clarise Yvette*
Yvette McCartney Chambers, Wilmacs Pharmacy Building, No 55 Collins Avenue, P.O.Box G.T. 2830, Nassau, N.P., 242 328 6725/326 4620, Fax: 242 328 6725, and Member Bahamas. Called: Nov 1992, Inner Temple, LLB (Wales)

McCullough *Miss Denise Susanne*
6 Ballycastle Road, Newtownards, Co.Down, N.Ireland BT22 2AY, 01247 815737, Member of the Honorable Society of the Inn of Court of Northern Ireland and Member Northern Ireland Bar. Called: Nov 1992, Lincoln's Inn, BA (Hons)(Belfast), CPE

McCully *Alvin Jeffrey*
Called: July 1997, Middle Temple, LLB (Hons)

McDowell *Major Thomas Bleakley*
St Thomas, Whitechurch, County Dublin 16, and Member Southern Ireland Bar.
Called: June 1951, Gray's Inn, LLB

McGowan *James Hugh Menzies*
Admiralty Chambers, 1405 Tower 11, Admiralty Centre, 2527 3082, Fax: 2529 8226, and Member Hong Kong Bar.
Called: July 1979, Middle Temple, BA (Nott'm), Dip Comm Law (HK)

McGrath *John Thomas*
Gandangara, Oxley Drive, Mittagong, New South Wales 2575, +61 2 9221 1199, Fax: +61 416 990 405, Former Executive Legal Assistant to Chief Justice Federal Court of Australia 1982-85 and Member New South Wales Bar. Called: Apr 1991, Lincoln's Inn, BA, LLB, BEc (Sydney), LLM, (Euro Law)(Lond)

McGrath *Ms Sarah Linda*
Deloitte Touche Tohmatsu, 26th Floor, Wing on Centre, 111 Connaught Road, (852) 28521095, Fax: (852) 25434647.
Called: Feb 1990, Lincoln's Inn, B.Soc.Sc [Hong Kong], LLB Hons [Lond]

McGrenaghan *Aidan Edward*
Called: July 1997, Lincoln's Inn, LLB (Hons)(Lond)

McLaughlin *Richard*
Bar Library, P.O.Box 414, Royal Courts of Justice, Chichester Street, Belfast BT1 3JP, 01232 660283, Fax: 01232 667399, QC 1985 (N.Ireland)(Called 1971) and Member Bar of N.Ireland (1971) King's Inn,Dublin (1978) and Bar of N.S.W. Australia 1992.
Called: Nov 1974, Gray's Inn, LLB, F.C.I.Arb

McLeish *Robin*
Office of the Privacy, Commissioner for Personal Data, Unit 2001, 20/F Office Tower, Convention Plaza, 1 Harbour Rd, Wanchai, (852) 2877 7128. Called: Oct 1997, Gray's Inn, MA

McMahon *Richard James*
St James' Chambers, Guernsey GY1 2PA, 01481 723355, Fax: 01481 725439.
Called: Nov 1986, Middle Temple, LLB (L'pool), LLM (Cantab)

McRandal *Mrs Pauline Mary*
10 Fairlawns, Saval Park Road, Dalkey, Co Dublin, 2856078, Fax: 2856078, and Member Southern Ireland Bar. Called: July 1988, Middle Temple, BL (Kings Inns)

Mcshane *Ms Anne Mary Sylvia*
University College, Dublin. Called: July 1989, Gray's Inn, BA

Md Sidik *Miss Norazmah*
A.Renggonathan & Co, 345-A Taman Melaka Raya, 75000 Melaka, Malaysia, Fax: 249276.
Called: July 1994, Lincoln's Inn, LLB (Hons)

Meade *Barrie Norman QC*
Attorney General's Chambers, Global House, 43 Church Street, Hamilton HM 12, Bermuda, 809 292 2463, Fax: 809 292 3608, Commander Brother of the Order of St John Queens Counsel (Bermuda 1996) and Member Bermuda. Called: July 1981, Inner Temple, LLB (Lond), ACIArb

Meakin *Ian Leonard*
Megevand, Grosjean, Revaz &, Associes, 1 Rue Etienne - Dumont, Case Postale 3487, 1211 Geneva 3, 0041 22 312 11 61, Fax: 0041 22 312 11 63. Called: Oct 1991, Gray's Inn, BD, AKC, Dip Law, ACIArb

Meharia *Miss Vineeta*
Called: July 1997, Gray's Inn, LLB (Lond)

Mei *Miss Chee Yin*
and Member Malaysia Bar. Called: July 1991, Gray's Inn, LLB (Warwick)

Menezes *Justin Carl*
Wilmer, Cutler & Pickering, Rue de la Loi 15, B-1040 Brussels, (32) (2) 2854900, Fax: (32) (2) 2854949, and Member Belgium.
Called: Oct 1995, Lincoln's Inn, LLB (Hons)(Sheff)

Menon *Mrs Deborah Damayanthi*
Called: Nov 1995, Inner Temple, LLB (Herts)

Menon *Sree Govind*
Called: July 1996, Lincoln's Inn, LLB (Hons)(Lond)

Mensah *Mrs Grace*
00 223 21 22 4260, Fax: 00 233 21 23 2262. Called: Nov 1995, Lincoln's Inn, LLB (Hons)(Lond)

Meredith *Jack Edward*
Called: Nov 1996, Lincoln's Inn, LLB (Hons)(Herts)

Merican *Megat Suffian*
Called: July 1996, Lincoln's Inn, LLB (Hons)

Merrien *Alan Martin*
Ozanne Van Leuven Perrot &, Evans, 1 Le Marchant Street, St Peter Port, Guernsey, Channel Islands, 0481 723466, Fax: 0481 727935, and Member Guernsey Bar.
Called: Feb 1992, Inner Temple, LLB (So'ton)

Mesenas *Miss May Lucia*
Attorney General's Chambers, 1 Coleman Street, [H]10-00 The Adelphi, (65) 3325940, Fax: (65) 3390286/4355100. Called: July 1995, Middle Temple, LLB (Hons)

Michaelides *Miss Christiana Kyriacou*
Kyriacos Th Michaelides Law, Offices, P O Box 1548, Crete Str 2, Nicosia 135, Cyprus, 02 473751/465995, Fax: 02 451878, and Member Cyprus Bar. Called: Nov 1992, Middle Temple, LLB (Hons, Lond)

Michaelides *Miss Dina*
Chrysses Demetriades & Co, Fortuna Court, Block B, 2nd F, 284 Arch. Makarios III Avenue, P.O.Box 132, Limasol 3601, 00357 5 362424, Fax: 00357 5 370055. Called: Nov 1996, Middle Temple, LLB (Hons)(Warw), LLM (So'ton)

Michaelides *Nicos R.*
P O Box 86, 3600 Limassol, 00357 5363742, and Member Cyprus Bar. Called: Nov 1995, Middle Temple, LLB (Hons)

Michaelides *Renos Kyriacou*
Crete Street No2, PO Box 1548, Nicosia, Cyprus, 357-2 473751/465995, Fax: 357-2 451878, and Member Cyprus Bar.
Called: Nov 1988, Middle Temple, LLB (Lond)

Middleton *Miss Anne*
610 North 32nd Avenue, Hollywood, Florida 33021. Called: July 1970, Gray's Inn

Mifsud *Simon Paul*
S Mifsu & Sons Ltd, 311 Republic Street, Valletta - VLT 04, 00 356 232211, Fax: 00 356 240097. Called: Nov 1992, Inner Temple, LLB, LLM(Buckingham)

Milford *Mark Geoffrey*
Bank for International, Settlements, Centralbahnplatz 2, CH-4002 Basle, 41 61 2809736, Fax: 41 61 2809112, and Member New York. Called: Oct 1991, Lincoln's Inn, LLB (Hons) (Lond), Maitrise (Paris)

Miller *Michael Christopher*
Called: Nov 1995, Middle Temple, LLB (Hons)(Leeds)

Miller *Mrs Yvonne Ann*
9 Cassis Drive, 65 466 2792. Called: Nov 1985, Inner Temple, LLB(B'ham), LLM (Cantab)

Millett *Timothy Patrick*
Court of Justice of the, European Communities L-2925, (00352) 43031, Fax: (00352) 4303-2600. Called: Nov 1975, Gray's Inn, MA (Oxon)

Mills *Leopold Nathaniel JP*
PO Box HM 287, Hamilton HMAX, 441 292 5501, Fax: 441 292 8397, and Member Bermuda Bar. Called: Nov 1988, Middle Temple, LLB (Bucks)

Minta *Ms Lucia*
Darshan Singh & Co, No 18-A, Lebuh Pantai, (Beach Street), 10300 Pulau Pinang, 0106 04 2611820, Fax: 0106 04 2627476, Master in Tropical Health of the University of Queensland, Australia. Called: July 1997, Lincoln's Inn, BSc (Hons)(Salford)

Mirpuri *Miss Sunita*
Former Solicitor. Called: Nov 1996, Inner Temple, BA (Kent)

Misick *Miss Yvette Denise*
McLean Mcnally, McLean Building, P O Box 62, 2001 Leeward Highway, Providenciales, 809 946 4277. Called: July 1996, Lincoln's Inn, LLB (Hons)(Leeds)

Mitha *Abdulsultan Alibhai*
32 Hawkwood Place NW, Calgary Alberta, Calgary, Alberta T3G 1X6, 403 239 7427.
Called: July 1972, Inner Temple, MA

Mitra *Joydeep*
Called: July 1994, Middle Temple, LLB (Hons)(Lond)

Mitra *Siddhartha*
Called: July 1991, Lincoln's Inn, LLB (Hons)

F

Mittelstadt *David Joseph*
The Thompson Corporation, Metro Center,
One Staton Place, Stamford CT 06902, (203)
328 9457, and Member Massachusettss
(USA) US Tax Court. Called: Feb 1989,
Lincoln's Inn, MA (Cantab), JD (Chicago)

Moal *Ms Suja*
Called: Nov 1997, Inner Temple, LLM
(S'ton)

Mockett *John Vere Brooke*
Called: Feb 1958, Gray's Inn, MA (Oxon)

Moe *Mr Justice Henry Stanley Rawle*
High Court of Justice, Antigua & Barbuda,
P.O.Box 1722, St John's, Antigua, 462 0039,
Attorney at Law, Barbados and Member
Barbados. Called: Nov 1970, Lincoln's Inn,
BA (Hons) Durham, PG Dip Ed, FCI, MBIM,
ACIS, LLM (Leic)

Moh Yong *Alan Chee Chuen*
Called: Nov 1995, Middle Temple, LLB
(Hons)

Mohamad Salleh *Miss Aldila*
Called: Oct 1994, Middle Temple, LLB
(Hons)(Bris)

Mohamed *Miss Elina*
Called: July 1994, Lincoln's Inn, LLB (Hons)

Mohamed Haniffa *Seeni Syed
Ahamed Kabeer*
Called: July 1996, Middle Temple, LLB
(Hons)(Lond)

Mohamed Hashim *Abdul Rasheed*
Blk 602, Yishun St 61, [H]06-359, Singapore
2776, 0065 7523574, Advocate & Solicitor
of the Supreme Court of Singapore.
Called: July 1993, Lincoln's Inn, LLB (Hons)

Mohamed Shafie *Jamil*
Called: Feb 1994, Lincoln's Inn, BA (Hons),
Dip in Law

Mohamed Yakub *Mohamed Ibrahim*
Block 138, Bishan Street 12, 05-460,
2589772. Called: July 1996, Middle Temple,
LLB (Hons)(Lond)

Mohammad Taha *Zamri*
Called: July 1997, Lincoln's Inn, LLB (Hons)

Mohammed *Miss Mardzlinda*
Called: May 1995, Lincoln's Inn, LLB (Hons)

Mohan *Mrs Mankalam*
Called: July 1994, Middle Temple, LLB
(Lond), B.Sc (Singapore)

Mohd Ali *Miss Nor Hasliza*
Mohd Ali & Co, Advocates & Solicitors, No
105 Jalan Telawi, Bangsar Baru, 59100 Kuala
Lumpur, 00 603 2842276, Fax: 00 603
2842273, and Member Malaysia Bar.
Called: July 1995, Lincoln's Inn, LLB (Hons)

Mohd Ibrahim Zain *Miss Rosdena*
Called: July 1997, Middle Temple, LLB
(Hons)(Nott'm)

Mohd Kalok *Miss Azlina Yati*
Called: July 1996, Lincoln's Inn, LLB
(Hons)(Notts)

Mohd Khalil *Miss Mas Aryani*
Called: July 1996, Middle Temple, LLB
(Hons)(Keele), BA (Hons)(Keele)

Mohd Naim *Miss Farah Wahidah*
Wan Haron Sukri & Nordin, Advocates &
Solicitors, No 64-2 Jalan 2A/27A, Seksyen 1,
Bandar Baru Wangsa, Maju, 53300 Setapak,
Kuala Lumpur, 603 4112611, Fax: 603
4112622, Advocate & solicitor (Malaysia)
and Member Malaysia Bar. Called: July 1993,
Lincoln's Inn, LLB (Hons), LLM (Lond)

Mohd Radzi *Miss Nonee Ashirin*
Called: July 1997, Lincoln's Inn, LLB (Hons)

Mohd Saffian *Miss Azlin*
Called: July 1996, Lincoln's Inn, LLB (Hons)

Mohd Said *Miss Norhafiza*
Messrs 12a Ng Yeoh & Kit, 19th Floor,
Bangunan Dato, Zainal 23 Jalan Melaka
50100, Kuala Lumpur, 01-06-03 2986066,
Fax: 01-06-03-2982593, and Member
Malaysian Bar. Called: July 1995, Middle
Temple, LLB (Hons) (Wales)

Mok *Miss Ida Yin Leng*
Called: Nov 1995, Middle Temple, LLB
(Hons)

Mok *Ignatius Yann Shi*
16 Jalan ATI-ATI, Taman Perdana, 83000
Batu Pahat, Johor, 00-6007-4318694, and
Member Malaysia Bar. Called: July 1996,
Lincoln's Inn, LLB (Hons)(Lond)

Mok *Miss Karen Yu-Yen*
Called: July 1996, Inner Temple, LLB (Hull)

Mok *Miss Wai Mun*
56-H King's Road, Singapore 268118, 466
1703, Advocate & Solicitor of the Supreme
Court of Singapore. Called: July 1994,
Middle Temple, LLB (Hons)(B'ham)

Mok *Yick-Fan Danny*
c/o Works Branch, 11/F Murray Building,
Garden Road, Hong Kong, (852) 28482045,
Fax: (852) 25371961. Called: Feb 1994,
Gray's Inn, BSc (Eng), MBA (CUHK),
MSocSc (Hong Kong), LLB (Lond), LLM
(Lond)

Mok *Yiu Fai*
Called: July 1995, Gray's Inn, LLB (Wales)

Mokal *Sardar Rizwaan Jameel*
Called: Nov 1997, Gray's Inn, BSc (Punjab),
LLB (Lond)

Mokty *Miss Mazita*
Called: July 1995, Lincoln's Inn, LLB (Hons)

Molloy *Ms Karen Rose*
Called: May 1996, Gray's Inn, LLB (Belfast)

Monteil *Dr Rene Leon*
The National Gas Company of, Trinidad &
Tobago, Goodrich Bay Road, Point Lisas,
Trinidad, 1-809 636 4662, Fax: 1-809 636
2905. Called: July 1987, Middle Temple,
BSc, PhD (Lond), MA (Law) (City), FRSC,
C.Chem

Monteiro *James Patrick*
Called: Nov 1995, Lincoln's Inn, LLB (Hons)

Monterio *Miss Cheryl Ann*
Bajwa & Co, No 4 Shenton Way, [H]08-07
Shing Kwan House, (65) 227 5293, Fax:
(65) 227 3780, and Member Singapore.
Called: Nov 1994, Middle Temple, LLB
(Hons)

Moo *Chee Leong*
No 18-1 Changkat Bukit Bintang, (Hicks
Road), 50200 Kuala lumpur, 2432128, Fax:
2433919, and Member Malaya Bar.
Called: July 1995, Middle Temple, LLB
(Hons) (Lond)

Moore *George Crawford Jackson*
Citzens Building, Suite 812, 105 S. Narcissus
Avenue, West Palm Beach, Florida 33401,
(561) 833 9000, Fax: (561) 833 9990, and
Member Florida, Jamaica, Turks & Caicos
Islands, British Virgin Islands, Grenada,
Montserrat, St Lucia and Antigua.
Called: July 1970, Inner Temple, BA, BPhil,
MA, (Cantab) LLB, LLM

Moosdeen *Miss Munira*
2108 Melbourne Plaza, No 33 Queen's Road
Central, 25239775, Fax: 28452464.
Called: July 1984, Lincoln's Inn, LLB, PCLL

Moreira *John Robert*
Called: Nov 1997, Gray's Inn, BA

Morgan *Miss Chloe Rebecca*
Babbe, Le Poidevin, Allez, Wirzel Court, P O
Box 612, St Peter Port, Guernsey, 01481
710585, Fax: 01481 712245, and Member
Guernsey Bar. Called: July 1995, Inner
Temple, LLB

Morris *John Cameron*
Queens Counsel, Advocates Library,
Parliament House, Edinburgh, 0131 226
5071, Temporary Sheriff (Scotland) Queen's
Counsel (Scotland). Called: July 1990, Inner
Temple, LLB (Strathclyde)

Morris *Ms Karen Anne*
Chubb Insurance Company of, Europe S.A.,
16 Avenue de Matignan, Paris, 331/
45.61.73.68, Fax: 331/45.61.41.62.
Called: Nov 1986, Gray's Inn, MA (Edin),
Dip Law, (City), LLM (Univ of, Lond)

Morrison *Sheriff Nigel Murray Paton
QC*
9 India Street, Edinburgh EH3 6HA, 031 225
2807, Fax: 031 225 5688, and Member
Scottish Bar. Called: Nov 1972, Inner
Temple

Morsingh *Miss Wern Li*
Called: July 1996, Gray's Inn, LLB (London)

Mosko *Nicholas Terry*
Called: Nov 1995, Middle Temple, LLB
(Hons)

Moss *Paul David*
P O Box N-9932, Nassau, 1-242 32-65084,
Fax: 1-242 32-80541, and Member Bahamas
Bar. Called: July 1995, Lincoln's Inn, LLB
(Hons), BA, TEP

Moustras *Andrew Thomas*
Philip Sinel & Co, P O Box 595, 8 Wests
Centre, St Helier, Jersey, 01534 35407.
Called: Nov 1995, Inner Temple, BA (Wales)

Moutou *Lewis Toussaint*
10 Georges Guibert Street, Port-Louis,
Mauritius, 230 2085153, Fax: 230
28338678/230 210 7888, and Member
Mauritius Bar. Called: Apr 1975, Middle
Temple

Mubarak *Syed*
03-2981128/2986036, Fax: 603-2913816.
Called: Nov 1995, Lincoln's Inn, LLB (Hons),
LLM, (Lond), FCCA, FCIS

Muda *Ms Shamsiah Haji*
Called: July 1994, Inner Temple, LLB

Muhammad *Nor Hisham Haji*
Called: Nov 1995, Gray's Inn, LLB (Sheff),
LLM

Mulcahy *Michael Edward Joseph Ruben*
and Member King's Inn. Called: Mar 1998,
Middle Temple, BA (Dublin)

Mullins *Bruce Ashley*
P O Box 200, Jewel Beach, Postal Code 134,
Muscat, Sultanate of Oman, (968) 607725,
Fax: (968) 607724, and Member Hong Kong
Bar Ministry of Justice, Awqaf & Islamic
Affairs, Sultanate of Oman.. Called: July
1980, Lincoln's Inn, B.Sc (Hons)(Wales)

Mun *Tien Shoong*
Called: July 1993, Middle Temple, LLB
(Hons)

Muniandy *Ms Anjalli*
Called: July 1996, Inner Temple, LLB (Lond)

Muntakim *Mohammad Abdul*
Called: Nov 1996, Lincoln's Inn, LLB
(Wolv'ton)

Mure *Kenneth Nisbet QC*
Advocates Library, Parliament House,
Edinburgh EH1 1RF, 0131 226 5071, QC in
Scotland. Called: July 1990, Gray's Inn, LLB
(Glas), MA (Glas), F.T.I.I.

Murphy *Professor Peter William*
Professor of Law, South Texas College of
Law, 1303 San Jacinto, Houston, Texas
77002, 713-646 1849, Fax: 713 659 2217,
Master of Bench, American Inn of Court XV
and Member California Bar Texas Bar.
Called: July 1968, Middle Temple, MA, LLB

Murphy *Pierre Eric*
Law Offices of Pierre Murphy, Suite 260,
2445 M Street N.W., Washington D.C.
20037, (202) 872 1679, Fax: (202) 872
1725, and Member District of Columbia,
Wisconsin. Called: July 1979, Lincoln's Inn,
LLB, JD

Murray *Keiron James*
Called: Oct 1997, Middle Temple, LLB
(Hons)(Sheff)

Murugaiyan *Sivakumar Vivekanandan*
1 Colombo Court, [H]07-23, Singapore
179742, 338 3996, Fax: 338 5993, Advocate
& Solicitor of the Supreme Court of
Singapore and Member Australian Capital
Territory, High Court of Australia.
Called: July 1988, Lincoln's Inn, LLB (Hons)
(Lond)

Murugasu *Miss Chitrakala*
Called: July 1995, Middle Temple, LLB
(Hons)

Musari *Sadari Bin*
256 Upper Thomson Road, 4532501, Fax:
7360102, and Member Singapore.
Called: July 1994, Inner Temple, LLB

Musariri *Miss Blessing Concilia Ropafadzo*
Called: July 1997, Middle Temple, LLB
(Hons)(Wolv'ton), MA

Mussenden *Larry Devron*
PO Box HM 2186, Hamilton HMJX, and
Member Bermuda Bar. Called: Oct 1995,
Gray's Inn, B.Sc (Canada), MA (USA), LLB
(Kent)

Muthu *Muthuraman*
Called: Oct 1996, Gray's Inn, LLB (Sheff)

Muthukrishan *Nedumaran*
M/S Ong Teck Gee & Partners, No 10
Anson Road, International Plaza, 31-04/05,
2216622, Fax: 2259168, and Member
Singapore Bar. Called: Nov 1994, Lincoln's
Inn, LLB (Hons)(Bucks)

Muthupalaniyappan *Yegappan*
Raja Devan & Associates, Advocates &
Solicitors, Suites 8.03 and 8.04, 8th Floor,
Wisma Lal Doshi, 135 Jalan Tuanku Abdul
Rahman 50100, (03) 2938378/8682, Fax:
(03) 2938050, and Member Malaysia.
Called: Oct 1996, Lincoln's Inn, LLB (Hons),
LLM (Staffs), UPg.Dip (Staffs)

Muthusamy *Panirselvam s/o*
Called: July 1997, Lincoln's Inn, LLB
(Hons)(Lond)

Muthusamy *Ms Santhi*
Called: Nov 1995, Inner Temple, LLB
(Bucks)

Mylona *Miss Sofi C*
Called: Nov 1996, Lincoln's Inn, LLB
(Hons)(Leics)

Nabi *Miss Nighat Sultana*
Called: Nov 1997, Lincoln's Inn, LLB
(Hons)(Lond)

Nadarajah *Miss Sumithra*
Called: July 1997, Lincoln's Inn, LLB
(Hons)(L'pool)

Nadarajan *Mrs Kanakavalli*
Called: July 1997, Lincoln's Inn, LLB (Hons)

Nadasan *Dinesh*
25 Telok Blangah Crescent, [H]06-77,
2739619. Called: July 1996, Middle Temple,
LLB (Hons)(Lond)

Nadchatiram *Thiruchelva Segaram*
Called: July 1996, Inner Temple, LLM
(Cantab), LLB (Lond)

Nagaraja *Maniam*
Called: July 1996, Middle Temple, LLB
(Hons)(Lond)

Nagaraw *Samyraw*
Called: Nov 1997, Lincoln's Inn, LLB (Hons)

Nagreh *Miss Ranmeet Kaur*
Called: July 1996, Lincoln's Inn, LLB
(Hons)(Sheff)

Nahar *Miss Lutfun*
Called: Nov 1997, Lincoln's Inn, LLB
(Hons)(Lond)

Nair *Miss Heama Latha*
Called: Nov 1996, Lincoln's Inn, LLB
(Hons)(Lond)

Nair *Kesavan*
M P D Nair & Co, [H]12-15 International
Plaza, 10 Anson Road, Singapore 0207,
2218800, Fax: 2240667, Supreme Court of
Singapore and Member Canberra, Australian
Capital Territory. Called: Nov 1990, Middle
Temple, LLB M.S.I.Arb

Nair *Miss Maala*
Block 209, Tampines Street 21, [H]08-1335,
Singapore 520209, and Member Singapore.
Called: July 1995, Middle Temple, LLB
(Hons)

Nair *Miss Namarath Sudha*
and Member Singapore Bar, Malaysian Bar.
Called: Feb 1994, Lincoln's Inn, LLB (Hons,
Lond)

Nair *Prakesh*
Called: July 1996, Middle Temple, LLB
(Hons)(Lond)

Nair *Miss Sharmila*
M P D Nair & Co, [H]12-15 International
Plaza, 10 Anson Road, 221-8800, Fax: 224-
0667, and Member Singapore Bar.
Called: July 1995, Middle Temple, LLB
(Hons)

Nair *Miss Sulojana*
Called: Oct 1997, Middle Temple, LLB
(Hons) (Lond)

Nair *Vijayan*
Block 7 Kim Tian Place, [H]19-59, Singapore
0316, 2743439. Called: Nov 1990, Lincoln's
Inn, BA (Singapore), LLB (Lond)

Nalpon *Zero Geraldo Mario*
Called: Feb 1993, Gray's Inn, LLB (Hull)

Namasivayam *Ramesh*
Called: July 1996, Lincoln's Inn, LLB
(Hons)(Lond)

Namasivayam *Srinivasan s/o*
Called: July 1997, Lincoln's Inn, LLB
(Hons)(Lond)

Nandwani *Manoj Prakash*
12 Mount Echo Park, 2353536, Fax:
7351210. Called: July 1996, Middle Temple,
LLB (Hons)(Lond)

Nannini *Antony Joel Peter*
Called: Oct 1995, Lincoln's Inn, LLB
(Hons)(Lond), LLM (Lond)

Narayanan *Nicholas Jeyaraj*
Called: July 1997, Inner Temple, LLB

Narayanan *Palaniappan*
Called: May 1996, Inner Temple, BA
(Madras, India), LLM (Lond)

Narayanan *Miss Shalini*
Called: July 1994, Lincoln's Inn, LLB (Hons)

Narayanasamy *Miss Subashini d/o*
Block 152, Lorong 2, Toa Payoh, [H]11-450,
3531272. Called: Nov 1996, Lincoln's Inn,
LLB (Hons)(Lond)

Naritomi *Nobukata*
13th Floor, Urbannet Ohtemachi Bldg,
Ohtemachi 2-2-2, Chiyoda-ku, Tokyo, 03
3231 0101, Fax: 03 3231 0102, and Member
Daiichi Tokyo Bar Association. Called: July
1972, Lincoln's Inn, LL.B (Tokyo)

F

Nasim *Asim-Bin*
Orr Dignam & Co, State Life Bldg No 1.B, I.I. Chundrigai Road, Karachi, 2416003/2421761, Fax: 2416571. Called: Nov 1994, Lincoln's Inn, LLB (Hons)(Lond)

Nasir *Syed Azfar Ali*
Called: July 1997, Lincoln's Inn, LLB (Hons)

Nathan *Dr Kathirgamar Veeragathy Sinnath*
Studio Legale Nathan, Viale Mazzini 12, 35035 Mestrino (PD), 049 9002326, Fax: 049 9002313. Called: July 1971, Middle Temple, EurIng BSc BSc (Eng), LLB (Leeds)LLM(Kent), Phd in Law, (Lond)

Natverlal *Deepak*
Apt Blk 1 [H]09-27, Jalan Pasar Baru, and Member Singapore Bar. Called: July 1995, Lincoln's Inn, LLB (Hons)

Naughton *John Stuart*
Red Eye Software, Ardeen House, Marine Terrace, Dun Laoghaire, County Dublin, 00 3531 230 2561, Fax: 00 3531 230 2561. Called: Oct 1993, Gray's Inn, LLB (Hons)(Wales)

Navaratnam *Sivarajan*
Called: July 1997, Lincoln's Inn, LLB (Hons)

Nayar *David*
and Member Singapore Bar. Called: July 1992, Gray's Inn, LLB (Lond)

Nazar *Boaz*
M/S Laycock & Ong, 41 Bukit Pasoh Road, 533 9115, Fax: 533 2206, and Member Singapore Bar. Called: July 1993, Lincoln's Inn, LLB (Hons)

Nazmi *Saiful*
Called: July 1996, Lincoln's Inn, LLB (Hons)(Notts)

Neilly *Miss Heather Robina*
Cayman Islands Law School, Tower Building, George Town, Grand Cayman. Called: Oct 1990, Middle Temple, BSc (Aston), LLB (Lond), MPhil (Ulster)

Neo *Miss Shien Ching*
Called: Mar 1998, Lincoln's Inn, LLB (Hons)(Lond)

Neocleous *Elias Andrea*
Neocleous House, 199 Makarios III Avenue, P.O.Box 613, Limassol, 357 5 362818, Fax: 357 5 359262, and Member Cyprus Bar. Called: May 1993, Inner Temple, BA (Oxon)

Neocleous *Ms Olympia*
Called: Nov 1997, Inner Temple, LLB (Lond), MSc, (Lond)

Neoh *Ang Wei*
Messrs Mohd Noor & S Y Lee, Room 110, First Floor,, Asia Life Building, 45-B Jalan Tun Sambanthan, 30000 Ipoh, Perak, (05) 2543589, Fax: (05) 2542611, and Member Malaya Bar. Called: July 1995, Lincoln's Inn, LLB (Hons), LLM (Lond)

Neoh *Miss Hong Sean*
Raja Eleena Sielo Ang & Tan, Suite 2003, 20th Floor, Plaza See Hoy Chan, Jalan Raja Chulan, 50250 Kuala Lumpur, 2322411, and Member Malaysia Bar. Called: July 1996, Lincoln's Inn, LLB (Hons)(Leeds)

Neoh *Ms Sue Lynn*
Helen Yeo & Partners, 11 Collyer Quay, [H]12-01 The Arcade, 422 1622, Fax: 222 1345, and Member Singapore Bar. Called: Oct 1990, Gray's Inn, LLB LLM

Neophytou *Miss Anna*
Called: Nov 1994, Gray's Inn, LLB (Wales)

Nesbitt *Richard Law*
2 Arran Square, Arran Quay, Dublin 7, 8733344, Fax: 8733737, Senior Counsel, The Bar of Ireland Oct 1993 and Member Northern Ireland Bar Bar of Ireland. Called: May 1987, Middle Temple, TCD

Newell *Michael Harold Banks*
Michael Newell & Co, Barristers Solicitors & Notaries, 225 Oxford Street, Leederville WA 6007, 61 8 94432888, Fax: 61 8 94441871, Barrister and Solicitor W Australia 1980 Member of the Professional Conduct Committee of The Law Society of Western Australia Barrister and Solicitor High Court of Australia 1984. Called: July 1965, Middle Temple, LLB

Ng *Miss Audrey Su Yin*
Called: July 1997, Lincoln's Inn, LLB (Hons)(Lond)

Ng *Bock Hoh*
Called: Nov 1991, Gray's Inn, LLB (E Ang)

Ng *Daryll Richard*
Called: July 1996, Middle Temple, LLB (Hons)(Notts)

Ng *David Wai Cheong*
Called: Mar 1998, Lincoln's Inn, LLB (Hons)(Lond)

Ng *Desmond Tiong Keng*
Called: Nov 1997, Middle Temple, LLB (Hons)(Hull)

Ng *Miss Eileen*
Called: July 1995, Lincoln's Inn, LLB (Hons)

Ng *Miss Foong Meng*
Messrs Shook Lin & Bok, 20th Floor, Arab-Malaysian, Building, 55 Jln Raja Chulan, 50200 Kuala Lumpur, (603) 2011788, Fax: (603) 2011775/2011778/2011779, and Member Malaysian Bar. Called: July 1994, Lincoln's Inn, LLB (Hons, Leeds)

Ng *Miss Hwee Lee*
Called: Nov 1995, Middle Temple, LLB (Hons)(Kent)

Ng *Kenneth Lien Shen*
Called: July 1995, Middle Temple, LLB (Hons) (Hull)

Ng *Kim Tean*
Blk 331, [H]14-225 Bukit Batok, Street 33, 65 9 6651538, and Member Singapore Bar. Called: July 1995, Middle Temple, LLB (Hons), B.Eng

Ng *Mr Kin Keung*
Called: July 1994, Middle Temple, LLB (Hons)(Lond)

Ng *Miss Ling Li*
John Koh & Co, 8 Robinson Road, [H]12-00 Casco Building, (65) 5389880, Fax: (65) 5382221, and Member Malaysia Bar. Called: July 1992, Lincoln's Inn, LLB (Hons) (Lond), LLM (Lond)

Ng *Miss Lyn*
Called: July 1992, Middle Temple, BA (Hons) (Oxon)

Ng *Maurice Kar-Fai*
Called: July 1994, Gray's Inn, LLB (Glamorgan), LLM (Bristol)

Ng *Miss Pei Chun*
Called: July 1997, Middle Temple, LLB (Hons)(Leics)

Ng *Robert Chee Siong*
17 Mt. Cameron Road, The Peak, (852) 2734-8383, Fax: 2369 8471. Called: July 1975, Middle Temple

Ng *Seng Chan*
Called: July 1996, Inner Temple, BA, BSocSC, BA (Lond)

Ng *Miss Shoo Cheng*
Called: Nov 1996, Lincoln's Inn, LLB (Hons)(Lond)

Ng *Siew Hoong*
Called: July 1997, Middle Temple, LLB (Hons)(Lond)

Ng *Miss Sonia Win-Yen*
Called: July 1996, Lincoln's Inn, LLB (Hons)(So'ton)

Ng *Stephen Shiu Chi*
Called: July 1997, Middle Temple, LLB (Hons)

Ng *Miss Su Hing*
Called: Nov 1997, Lincoln's Inn, LLB (Hons)

Ng *Sze Meng*
Called: July 1996, Middle Temple, LLB (Hons)(Lond)

Ng *Timothy Wai Keong*
Called: Nov 1995, Gray's Inn, LLB (Bucks)

Ng *Miss Wendy Yee Cheng*
Called: July 1996, Inner Temple, LLB (Bristol)

Ng *Miss Yee Yung*
Called: Nov 1993, Gray's Inn, B.Sc, B.Com, (Melbourne), LLB, (Lond)

Ngeh *Anthony Koh Seh*
Called: July 1997, Lincoln's Inn, LLB (Hons)(Wales)

Ngoo *Miss Ping Chue*
Called: Nov 1991, Middle Temple, LLB (Hons) (Lond), BSc (Reading)

Ngooi *Chiu-Ing*
Baker & Mckenzie, 1 Temasek Avenue [H]27-01, Millenia Tower, 65 338 1888, Fax: 65 337 5100, and Member Australian Capital Territory Malaysia Bar. Called: July 1991, Lincoln's Inn, BA (Oxford)

Nicolaou *Miss Athena Maria*
Andreas Georghadjis & Co, Apollo Court, Office 101, 232 Makarios III Avenue, P.O.Box 6777, Limassol, 00357 5 353554, Fax: 00357 5 354414, and Member Cyprus. Called: Nov 1995, Middle Temple, LLB (Hons), LLM

Nijar *Miss Belinder Kaur*
Called: July 1997, Middle Temple, LLB (Hons)(Lond)

Nijar *Navinder Singh*
Called: July 1994, Lincoln's Inn, LLB (Hons)

Niklas *Miss Elizabeth Anne*
Merrill Lynch Asset Management, L.P., P.O.Box 9011, Princeton, New Jersey 08543-90119, 609-282-3275, Fax: 609-282-0724. Called: Nov 1995, Middle Temple, BA (Cincinnati), Dip in Law

Ning *Ms Lam Shiao*
Called: July 1996, Inner Temple, LLB (Hull)

Niraiselvan *Kumaravellu*
Messers Bannir & Associates, [H] 13-12 Peoples Park Centre, 101A Upper Cross Street, Singapore 0105, 5330622, Fax: 5355397. Called: July 1995, Lincoln's Inn, LLB (Hons)

Nixon *Miss Paulette Pamela*
Called: July 1997, Lincoln's Inn, LLB (Hons)

Njie *Omar Momodou Musa*
78 Wellington Street, Banjul, The Gambia, 00 220 229819, Fax: 00 220 229347, and Member Gambia Bar. Called: Oct 1991, Middle Temple, BA Hons (E Anglia)

Nonis *Darren Anthonio Marino*
Blk 936, Tampines Ave 5, [H] 06-101. Called: July 1996, Inner Temple, LLB (Lond), Dip.M (MCIM)

Nordin *Norazali Bin*
Called: Nov 1997, Lincoln's Inn, LLB (Hons)(Nott'm)

Norris *Richard*
Logica Inc., 32 Hartwell Avenue, Lexington, MA 01273, 00 1 617 476 8132, Fax: 00 1 617 476 8010. Called: July 1979, Inner Temple, LLB (So'ton), ACMA

Nottage *D. Sean*
Graham Thompson & Co, Sassoon House, P.O.Box N272, Nassau, U.S.A. 02110, (809) 322 4130, Fax: (809) 328 1069, and Member Massachuetts, Commonwealth of the Bahamas. Called: Nov 1993, Middle Temple, LLB (Hons)(Bucks), JD (Suffolk Uni, Law, School, Boston, Massachusetts)

O'Brien *James Gerard*
P O Box 2424, Law Library, Four Courts, Dublin 7, 8720622, Fax: 8720455, and Member Southern Ireland Bar. Called: July 1988, Middle Temple, BL (King's Inn)

O'Culachain *Maoiliosa Seosamh*
Telecom Eirann PLC, St Stephen's Green West, Dublin 2, 00 3531 701 5560, Fax: 00 3531 671 4255. Called: Feb 1995, Lincoln's Inn, BA (Hons), LLB (Hons)(Galway)

O'Donnell *Everard Jeffrey Echlin*
Called: July 1976, Gray's Inn, MSc

O'Donovan *Sean*
Barrister of Ireland. Called: May 1996, Middle Temple, BA (Cork), BL (King's Inn)

O'Driscoll *Miss Karen Margaret Helen*
Courthouse Chambers, 27/29 Washington Street, Cork, 00 353 21 275151, Fax: 00 353 21 272821, Barrister of Ireland. Called: May 1997, Middle Temple, BCL (Cork), M.Litt (Dublin)

O'Dubhghaill *Feargal Padraig*
Barrister of Ireland. Called: May 1996, Middle Temple, BCL (Cork), BL (King's Inn)

O'Neill *Aidan Mark*
ADvocates Library, Parliament House, Edinburgh EH1 1RF, 0131 226 5071, Fax: 0131 225 3642, Member of the Faculty of Advocates, Scotland (July 1987) and Member Scotland Bar. Called: July 1996, Inner Temple, LLB (Edinburgh), LLM (Sydney), LLM (Florence)

O'Neill *Ms Heather June*
336 West End Ave, New York, N.Y., and Member New York State Bar. Called: Oct 1992, Inner Temple, LLB(Hons)

O'Neill *Miss June*
Called: Nov 1997, Lincoln's Inn, LLB (Hons)(Lond)

O'Riordan *Mrs Miriam Bernadette*
Courthouse Chambers, 27-9 Washington Street, Cork, (021) 277563, Fax: (021) 277563, Member Cork & Munster Circuit,Republic of Ireland Barrister at Law, Kings Inn Dublin and Member Southern Ireland Bar. Called: Feb 1982, Middle Temple, BCL Cork

O'Rourke *Raymond John*
Stanbrook & Hooper, European Community Lawyers, Rue du Taciturne 42, 1000 Brussels, (32-2) 230 50 59, Fax: (32-2) 230 57 13. Called: Nov 1995, Gray's Inn, BA, MA (Dublin), LLB (Lond)

O'Sullivan *Miss Lorraine Anne*
Courthouse Chambers, 27/29 Washington Street, Cork, 0044 353 21 276186, Fax: (021) 272821, Barrister of Ireland. Called: May 1996, Middle Temple, BCL (Cork), BL (King's Inn)

Oei *Miss Carolyn Jane*
81 Langford Court, Langford Place, 22 Abbey Road, London NW8 9DP, and Member Singapore Bar. Called: July 1995, Gray's Inn, LLB (Lond)

Oei *Miss Mona*
Called: July 1993, Lincoln's Inn, LLB (Hons)

Oei *Su Chi Ian*
Called: July 1997, Middle Temple, LLB (Hons)(Lond)

Oh *Miss Carolyn Li Lin*
Ghazi & Lim, No 10-1 Bishop Street, 10200 Penang, Malaysia, 01 06 04 633 688, Fax: 01 06 04 2634 188, and Member Malaysia Bar. Called: July 1994, Middle Temple, LLB (Hons)(Kent)

Oh *Douglas Kim Chuan*
Called: July 1996, Lincoln's Inn, LLB (Hons)(Lond)

Oh *Madam Kim Heoh*
95 Yuk Tong Ave, 4691266 (R) 2235221 (O), Fax: 22335229, and Member Advocate & Solicitor of Supreme Court, Singapore. Called: July 1993, Middle Temple, LLB (Hons)

Ollivry *Guy Marie*
105 Chancery House, Port-Louis, Mauritius, (230) 2123083/2129906, Fax: (203) 2128799, QC Mauritius 1987 and Member Mauritius Bar. Called: July 1957, Gray's Inn

Omar *Miss Nurul Akmar*
Called: Nov 1994, Lincoln's Inn, LLB (Hons)(L'pool)

Omar *Miss Uzianna*
Called: July 1994, Lincoln's Inn, LLB (Hons)

Ong *Basil Kah Liang*
and Member Singapore Bar. Called: July 1993, Middle Temple, LLB (Hons)(Lond)

Ong *Boon Kiat*
Called: Nov 1995, Lincoln's Inn, LLB (Hons) (Lond)

Ong *Chee Huan*
32 Jalan Setiabakti 8, Bukit Damansara, 50490 Kuala Lumpur, 010 60 3 2541842, and Member Malaysia Bar. Called: July 1995, Lincoln's Inn, LLB (Hons)

Ong *Cheong Wei*
Called: July 1994, Middle Temple, LLB (Hons)(Lond)

Ong *Miss Chih-Ching*
and Member Singapore Bar. Called: Nov 1992, Gray's Inn, LLB (Buckingham)

Ong *Miss Ellen Mei Luan*
Called: July 1997, Middle Temple, LLB (Hons)

Ong *Eng Tuan*
Loh Eben Ong & Partners, 112 Middle Road [H] 07-00, Midland House, (65) 338 1810, Fax: (65) 338 7678, and Member Singapore Bar. Called: July 1991, Gray's Inn, LLB

Ong *Miss Geik Khuan*
Called: Nov 1992, Middle Temple, LLB (Hons)

Ong *Ivan Ban Phing*
Hamzah & Ong Advocates, 13, 1st Floor, Jalan P Ramlee, 93400 Kuching, P.O.Box 1543, 93730 Kuching, 082 246876, Fax: 082 247217. Called: July 1989, Middle Temple, LLB [Essex]

Ong *Miss Janaine Jo Lin*
Called: July 1997, Middle Temple, LLB (Hons)(Hull)

Ong *Miss Jo-Ann Wei-Syn*
Called: July 1997, Lincoln's Inn, LLB (Hons)(Sheff)

Ong *Kenneth Heng Heng*
Called: Nov 1996, Middle Temple, LLB (Hons)(Bucks)

Ong *Lee Woei*
Called: Nov 1993, Lincoln's Inn, LLB (Hons), LLM (Exon)

Ong *Ms May Anne*
Called: July 1994, Middle Temple, BA (Hons)(Cantab)

Ong *Miss May Li Karen*
Called: July 1997, Middle Temple, LLB (Hons)(Kent)

Ong *Miss Melita Sue Chen*
Called: July 1997, Lincoln's Inn, LLB (Hons)

Ong *Miss Ming Suan*
Messrs Raja Eleena,Siew,Ang &, Tan, Suite 20.03 20th Floor, Plaza See Hoy Chan, Jalan Raja, Chulan, 50200 Kuala Lumpur Malaysia, 03 2322411, Fax: 03 2301613, and Member Malaysia Bar. Called: July 1991, Lincoln's Inn, LLB (Hons) (Warwick)

Ong *Peng Boon*
(65) 3232320, Fax: (65) 2213211, and Member Singapore Bar. Called: Feb 1994, Middle Temple, LLB (Hons)(Lond)

Ong *Miss Rita Lee Hiang*
Called: July 1994, Middle Temple, LLB (Hons)(Lond)

Ong *Seng Hoong*
Called: July 1994, Lincoln's Inn, LLB (Hons)

Ong *Miss Sharon Get-Jin*
Called: July 1993, Inner Temple, BA

Ong *Miss Shirley*
Called: July 1994, Lincoln's Inn, LLB (Hons)

Ong *Sim Ho*
Inland Revenue Authority of, Singapore, Fullerton Building, Singapore, 065-7856932, Bachelor of Accountancy Co-Author, Goods & Services Tax-Law & Practice, Butterworths 1995.. Called: July 1995, Lincoln's Inn, LLB (Hons), BAcc (Hons)(S'pore)

Ong *Sin Qui*
P.O.Box 2670, Robinson Road, (65) 5339115, Fax: (65) 5332206, Advocate & Solicitor, Singapore and Member Singapore Bar. Called: Nov 1974, Middle Temple, MA (Cantab)

Ong *Miss Su-Lin Vivienne*
Called: Nov 1996, Middle Temple, LLB (Hons)(Kent)

Ong *Miss Suzanna Ann-Francesca*
Called: July 1996, Lincoln's Inn, LLB (Hons)(Bris)

Ong *Teng Kok*
Called: July 1997, Lincoln's Inn, LLB (Hons)

Ong *Teng Ping*
Paul Ong & Associates, 7th Floor, Bangunan Yee Seng, No 15 Jalan Raja Chulan, 50200 Kuala Lumpur, 03 2321562, Fax: 603 2327260, and Member Malaysian Bar. Called: July 1995, Lincoln's Inn, LLB (Hons), FCCA, ATII, PA

Ong *Theng Soon*
Called: July 1997, Lincoln's Inn, LLB (Hons)(Leeds)

Ong *Miss Wee En*
Called: July 1997, Lincoln's Inn, LLB (Hons)(Wales)

Ong *Miss Yin Ee*
Abu Talib Shahrom & Zahari, Advocates & Solicitors, 43-1 Jalan Desa, 58100 Kuala Lumpur, (603) 780 4494, Fax: (603) 784 5434. Called: July 1997, Middle Temple, LLB (Hons)

Ong *Yu En*
Allen & Gledhill, 36 Robinson Road, [H] 18-01 City House, Singapore 068877, 65 4207755, Fax: 65 2233787, and Member Singapore Bar. Called: July 1994, Middle Temple, LLB (Hons)(Hull)

Onn *Shaharuddin*
Shahruddin, Arida & Assoc., (Advocates & Solicitors), No 116-1C, 1st Floor, Jalan Loke Yew, 55200 Kuala Lumpur Malaysia, 03-2222264/2217012, Fax: 603 2222632, and Member Malaysia Bar. Called: May 1993, Lincoln's Inn, LLB (Hons)

Ooi *David Chai Lee*
Called: July 1994, Lincoln's Inn, LLB (Hons)

Ooi *Peng Cuan*
Called: July 1996, Lincoln's Inn, LLB (Hons)(Lond)

Oon *Miss Diana Bee Lin*
Called: July 1995, Middle Temple, BA (Hons)

Oon *Wee Phing*
Called: Nov 1996, Middle Temple, LLB (Hons)(Lond)

Orme *John Richard*
Called: Feb 1995, Lincoln's Inn, BSc (Hons)(Lond), PhD, Dip in Law (City)

Ortega *Mark Benjamin*
12 Jalan Anak Patong, Singapore 489328, (65) 4458691, and Member Singapore Bar. Called: July 1995, Middle Temple, LLB (Hons)

Osman *Miss Nishet*
Called: July 1995, Middle Temple, LLB (Hons)

Osofsky *Mrs Lisa Kate*
American Attorney. Called: Nov 1997, Middle Temple, BA (Amherst), JD (Harvard)

Osoria *Miss Paulette Barbara*
The Grand Bahama Port, Authority Limited, P O Box F.42666, Freeport, Grand Bahama, 242 352 6611 Ext 2242, Fax: 242 352 4568. Called: July 1997, Gray's Inn, BSc (Ontario), LLB (Bucks)

Othman *Adil*
Called: Nov 1994, Lincoln's Inn, LLB (Hons)(Notts)

Ouzounian *Dickran Aram*
Dickran Ouzounian & Co Ltd, PO Box 1567, Nicosia, Cyprus, 02 353053, Fax: 02 350536. Called: Nov 1988, Inner Temple, LLB

Ow *Tan Cheng*
Called: Nov 1996, Lincoln's Inn, LLB (Hons)(Lond)

Owaisi *Asaduddin*
Called: May 1995, Lincoln's Inn, LLB (Hons)

Owen *Xhuanelado Walave Durage*
Called: July 1994, Inner Temple, LLB (Lond)

Oxley *Miss Denise Eudene*
Apt 411, Cabrillo Square, 1399 Ninth Avenue, San Diego, California 92101, (619) 486 2957. Called: Oct 1993, Lincoln's Inn, LLB (Hons)(Lond)

Padamakavander *Miss Kavija Padama*
1304-K Lorong Bentara, Jalan Teluk Wanjah 05200, Alor Setar, Kedah, Malaysia, 04 7313310, and Member Malaysia Bar. Called: July 1994, Middle Temple, LLB (Hons)(Brunel)

Paglar *Miss Constance Margaret*
Called: Nov 1996, Inner Temple, LLB (Lond)

Pagni *Marco Patrick Anthony*
McDonald's Development Company, Ltd, 178-180 Edgware Road, London W2 2DS, 0171 402 6677, Fax: 0171 723 2818. Called: Feb 1988, Middle Temple, MA, BCL (Oxon)

Pah *Miss Yvonne Li-Ean*
15a Jalan Wu Lean Teh, Ipoh Garden South, 31400 Ipoh, Perak, Malaysia, 60-5-5475521. Called: July 1995, Middle Temple, LLB (Hons)

Paige *Richard Mark*
Called: Oct 1997, Middle Temple, BA (Hons)(Oxon)

Palaniveloo *S P Muthuveloo*
Called: Nov 1994, Lincoln's Inn, LLB (Hons)(Herts)

Palaniyappan *Allagarsamy s/o*
Called: Nov 1996, Lincoln's Inn, LLB (Hons)(Lond)

Palas *Miss Esme*
Called: Nov 1996, Gray's Inn, LLB (Bris)

Palmer *Adrian Jeremy*
18 Heads Road, Donvale 3111, Melbourne, Victoria, 61 3 873 5650. Called: Nov 1978, Middle Temple, MA, LLM, Dip Comp, Sci (Cantab)

Pan *Wai Liong*
Blk 704 [H]11-137, Pasir Ris Drive 10, 5842476. Called: July 1996, Middle Temple, LLB (Hons)(Wolves)

Panagopoulos *Dr Panayotis Constantinou*
8 Merlin Steet No 8, 10671 Athens, 362 3 930, Fax: 30- 1-3628.566, and Member Athens Bar. Called: Nov 1951, Gray's Inn, LLB, BSc, LLD, (Athens)

Panayides *Ioannis*
P O Box 4682, 3726 Limassol, 00 357 5 586876. Called: Nov 1992, Middle Temple, LLB (Hons)(Lond), M.I.C.S., F.C.M.A.

Pang *Chesper-Joghne*
Called: Mar 1997, Lincoln's Inn, LLB (Hons)(Lond)

Pannirselvam *Miss Priya*
Called: Nov 1997, Lincoln's Inn, LLB (Hons)(Nott'm)

Panoo Sunil Singh
Called: July 1996, Middle Temple, LLB
(Hons)(Lond)

Pao Felix Ho Ming
87 New Henry House, 10 Ice House Street,
Hong Kong, 2522 5494, Fax: 2810 4677,
and Member Hong Kong Bar Australia Bar.
Called: Apr 1991, Gray's Inn, LLB, PCLL

Papachan Gopalan Krishnan
Called: Nov 1990, Gray's Inn, BSc, Dip Law

Papacosta Miss Ismini Andrea
Called: Nov 1996, Gray's Inn, LLB (Lond),
LLM (E.Anglia)

Paphiti Anthony Steven
Commander, Army Prosecuting Authority,
(Germany), Rochdale Barracks, British
Forces Post Office 39. Called: Nov 1975,
Inner Temple, LLB (Leeds)

Parhar Miss Sunita Sonya
50 Raffles Place, 18th Floor, Singapore Land
Tower, 2201911, Fax: 2244118, Kelvin Chia
Partnership and Member Singapore Bar.
Called: Nov 1995, Lincoln's Inn, LLB
(Hons)(Lond)

Parker Miss Danya Larissa
Called: July 1997, Middle Temple, LLB
(Hons)

Parmar Karam Singh
Lee & Lee, Level 19, UIC Building, 5
Shenton Way, 00 65 22 00 666, Fax: 00 65
22 19 712, and Member Singapore Bar.
Called: Nov 1992, Middle Temple, B.Eng
(Singapore), LLB (Hons, Lond)

Parnell King Mrs Sarah Lorraine
Called: July 1996, Middle Temple, LLB
(Hons)(Soton)

Parslow Carl Geoffrey
Ogier & Le Masurier, P.O.Box 404, Pirouet
House, Union Street, St Helier, Jersey,
01534 504177, Fax: 01534 619632.
Called: Oct 1996, Middle Temple, LLB
(Hons)(Plymouth)

Parwani Miss Sharon Sheela
Called: Nov 1995, Lincoln's Inn, LLB
(Hons)(Lond)

Pasha Miss Dua Sultan
Called: July 1996, Lincoln's Inn, LLB (Hons)

Pathumanathan Miss Kaushala
Called: Nov 1996, Lincoln's Inn, LLB
(Hons)(Leics)

Patmore Miss Janet Adelza
Supreme Court of Judicature of, Jamaica,
Public Building E, 134 Tower Street,
Kingston, (809) 922 8300, Fax: (809) 967
0669, and Member Jamaica. Called: July
1992, Middle Temple, LLB (Hons)

Paton Michael Lennox
Devonshire House, Queen Street, P.O.Box
N4875, Nassau, 242 328 0563, Fax: 242 328
0566, and Member Bahamas Bar. Called: July
1991, Lincoln's Inn, BSc (USA), Dip Law,
CPA (USA)

Patrick Sheriff Gail
ADVOCATE, 13 Succoth Place, EDINBURGH
EH12 6BJ, 031 346 1883, Fax: 031 346
0004, and Member Scottish Bar. Called: Nov
1990, Lincoln's Inn, MA (St A's), LLB (Edin)

Paul Miss Cynthia
Called: July 1997, Lincoln's Inn, LLB
(Hons)(Reading)

Pearmain Advocate Susan Ann
Bedell & Cristin, PO Box 75, One the
Forum, Grenville Street, St Helier, Jersey
JE4 8PP, 01534 814814, Fax: 01534 814815,
and Member Jersey. Called: Nov 1971,
Middle Temple

Pearman Miss Jo-Dina Michelle
Global House, 43 Church Street, Hamilton,
292 2463, Fax: 292 3608. Called: July 1994,
Lincoln's Inn, LLB (Hons)

Pearman Peter Appleby Scott
Conyers Dill & Pearman, Clarendon House,
Church Street, Hamilton, 441 295 1422,
Fax: 441 292 4720, and Member Bermuda
Bar. Called: July 1995, Middle Temple, LLB
(Hons), BA

Peh Khaik Kew
Called: Nov 1996, Lincoln's Inn, LLB
(Hons)(Warw)

Peh Miss Natalie Suan Wan
Called: July 1995, Gray's Inn, LLB (Bris)

Peh Miss Xiao-Shan
Called: July 1996, Lincoln's Inn, LLB
(Hons)(LSE)

Pek Miss Chin-Choo
Called: July 1996, Lincoln's Inn, LLB
(Hons)(Sheff)

Pelekanos Michalis
Pelekanos & Co, Advocate & Legal
Consultants, P.O.Box 2124, Larnaca, 4
657272, Fax: 4 653531, and Member
Cyprus. Called: Nov 1996, Gray's Inn, LLB
(Kent)

Pelekanou Miss Elena
Evagorou & Arch Makarios 111, Ave, Mitsis
Building 3, 1st Floor Office 111, P O Box
1633, Nicosia, Cyprus, 00-357-2447400, Fax:
00-357-2443939, and Member Cyprus Bar.
Called: Nov 1995, Lincoln's Inn, LLB
(Hons)(So'ton)

Pemberton Kenneth Leonard
Called: July 1995, Inner Temple, BSc
(Soton), CPE (Hong Kong)

Pengiran Tengah Miss Dayangku Siti
Nurbani
Called: Nov 1994, Lincoln's Inn, LLB
(Hons)(Lond)

Peralta Paul Charles Philip
and Member Gibraltar Bar. Called: Oct 1994,
Middle Temple, LLB (Hons)(Lond)

Permanand Miss Radha
Called: July 1996, Lincoln's Inn, LLB
(Hons)(LSE)

Perrot Roger Allen
Ozanne's, 1 Le Marchant Street, St Peter
Port, Guernsey CI, 0481723466, Fax:
0481727935, and Member Guernsey Bar.
Called: Nov 1974, Inner Temple, BSc
(Lond), FCIArb

Perumal Miss Krisna Kumari
Called: Nov 1996, Middle Temple, LLB
(Hons)(Lond)

Perumal Vasantha Kumar
Called: Nov 1993, Gray's Inn, LLB (Lond)

Petasis Andreas
Called: Nov 1997, Inner Temple, LLB
(Lancs)

Petri-Kassapi Mrs Rona Vrahimi
89 Kennedy Avenue, Off 201, P O Box
6624, Nicosia, Cyprus, 357-2-379210, Fax:
357-2-379212, and Member Cyprus Bar.
Called: May 1993, Gray's Inn, LLB (E.Anglia),
LLM (Lond)

Petty George Oliver
(510) 528-1721, Fax: (510) 528-9180, and
Member State Bar of California. Called: Apr
1986, Middle Temple, BA, LLB (U,
California)

Pg Hj Mohammad Miss Dk Hajah Siti
Rahmah
Called: Nov 1995, Lincoln's Inn, LLB (Hons)

Phan Miss Catherine Pui Lin
Called: Nov 1997, Lincoln's Inn, LLB
(Hons)(Lond)

Phang Miss Sweet Lee
Called: Nov 1994, Lincoln's Inn, LLB
(Hons)(Lond), BSc (Australia)

Phillips Mrs Henrike Deborah
Called: Oct 1992, Lincoln's Inn, LLB(Hons)

Phua Charles Cheng Sye
Called: July 1994, Lincoln's Inn, LLB (Hons)
(Sheff)

Phua Chung Ann Robert
Called: July 1997, Lincoln's Inn, LLB
(Hons)(Leeds)

Phua Miss Karen Jin Sim
Called: July 1996, Middle Temple, LLB
(Hons)(Warw)

Phua Pao Ann
Called: July 1996, Middle Temple, BA
(Hons)(Cantab)

Picardo Mr Fabian Raymond
Gibraltar Bar Council, 57/63 Line Wall Road,
Gibraltar, 00 350 79000, Fax: 00 350 71966,
and Member Gibraltar Bar. Called: Oct 1994,
Middle Temple, BA (Hons)(Oxon)

Pierce Raymond John Joseph
Flat D, 10/F, University Heights, 42-44
Kotewell Road, (0852) 2813 7827, Fax:
(0852) 9106 0054, and Member Hong Kong
Bar. Called: Feb 1995, Gray's Inn, LLB
(Lond)

Pikis Michael G
12 Promitheos Str, Pelekanos Court 21, Office 401, 1065 Nicosia Cyprus, 02 476838, Fax: 02 476631, and Member Cyprus Bar. Called: Nov 1994, Gray's Inn, LLB (Hons)

Pilbrow David Gordon
15/F Printing House, 6 Duddell Street, Hong Kong, 852 25212616, Fax: 852 28450260, Former Solicitor and Member Hong Kong Bar. Called: July 1989, Middle Temple, BA [Oxon]

Pilcher William Edgar
Called: Nov 1996, Lincoln's Inn, LLB (Hons)(Bucks)

Pillai Gopinath
Called: July 1995, Lincoln's Inn, LLB (Hons)

Pillai Pradeep G
Called: July 1997, Middle Temple, LLB (Hons)

Pillai Prakash
Called: July 1995, Middle Temple, LLB (Hons)

Pillai Miss Sharmini
Messrs Tan Eng Choong & Co, Jalan Yap Ahloy, Kuala Lumpur, and Member Malaysian Bar (July 1995). Called: July 1994, Middle Temple, LLB (Hons)(Lond)

Ping Miss Lim Yoke
37 Jalan 5/66, Bukit Gasing 46000, Petaling Jaya, Selangor, 03-7958833, Fax: 03-7928833, and Member Malaysia Bar. Called: July 1993, Inner Temple, LLB (Nott'm)

Ping Ms Wong Yuen
Called: July 1994, Inner Temple, LLB

Pinsolle Philippe
c/o Shearman & Sterling, 114 avenue des Champs Elysees, 75008 Paris, France, (33) 1 53 89 70 00, Fax: (33) 1 53 89 70 70, and Member Paris Bar. Called: July 1995, Gray's Inn, Maitrise En Droit, (Paris), M.Juris (Oxon),Essec

Pirie Nicholas Frederick Francis
Garden Chambers, 5th Floor, 10 Queen's Road Central, 2525-0221, Fax: 2845-2441, and Member Hong Kong Bar 2-3 Gray's Inn Square, Gray's Inn, London, WC1R 5JH. Called: Nov 1971, Inner Temple, LLB (Hons)

Pirzada Syed Sharifuddin
Press Centre, Sharirah-E-Attaturk, Karachi - 1, Pakistan, and Member Pakistan Bar. Called: Feb 1981, Lincoln's Inn

Pishias Yiannis
Called: Nov 1997, Lincoln's Inn, LLB (Hons)(Warw)

Pitman Miss Frances Mary
Mourant Du Feu & Jeune, Advocates, Solicitors &, Notaries Public, 22 Grenville Street, St Helier, Jersey JE4 8PX, 01534 609000, Fax: 01534 609333. Called: Oct 1995, Lincoln's Inn, LLB (Hons)(Bucks)

Pitto Charles John
Attorney General's Chambers, 17 Town Range, Gibraltar, (010350) 70723, and Member Gibraltar Bar. Called: Nov 1994, Inner Temple, CPE (Wolverhampton), BA (Newc)

Platt The Hon Mr Justice Harold Grant
Supreme Court of Uganda, P O Box 6679, Kampala, 270 362/3. Called: Feb 1952, Middle Temple

Png Cheong-Ann
Institute of Advanced Legal, Studies, University of London, Charles Clore House, 17 Russell Square, London WC1H 2AB, 0171 837 8888 Ext 2519, Fax: 0171 837 9321. Called: July 1996, Gray's Inn, LLB (London)

Poh Ban Chuan
Called: July 1993, Lincoln's Inn, LLB (Hons)

Pohjola Ms Satu Heidi
Rovastintie, 1 20 c, 03400 Vihti, 358 9 2247699, Fax: 358 9 2249041. Called: Oct 1995, Middle Temple, LLB (Hons), MAG.IUR

Poi Melvin Chew-Yeun
Called: July 1994, Lincoln's Inn, LLB (Hons)

Pok Miss Abby Say Lin
Called: Nov 1996, Middle Temple, LLB (Hons)(Leics)

Pok John Li-Wen
Called: Nov 1993, Middle Temple, LLB (Hons)(Lond)

Pokkan Vasu Rakesh
Called: July 1996, Middle Temple, LLB (Hons)(Lond)

Ponnambalam Gajendrakumar Gangaser
Called: Nov 1997, Lincoln's Inn, LLB (Hons)(Lond)

Ponnusamy Miss Grace Malathy d/o
Called: July 1997, Lincoln's Inn, LLB (Hons)(Lond)

Ponnusamy Waytha Moorthy
30/1226 3rd Mile, Jalan Rasah, 70300 Seremban, and Member Advocate Solicitor of the High Court of Malaya. Called: Nov 1994, Lincoln's Inn, LLB (Hons)(Lond)

Pool Mrs Lucie Antoinette
Dept of Legal Affairs, P O Box 58, National House, Victoria, Mahe, 00 248 38300, Fax: 225063. Called: Nov 1995, Lincoln's Inn, LLB (Hons)

Poon Mr Lik Hang Herman
801 Yip Fung Building, 2-12 D'Aguilar Street, Central, Hong Kong, and Member Hong Kong Bar. Called: Nov 1992, Inner Temple, LLB (Reading)

Poopalaratnam Miss Shamini d/o
Called: Nov 1996, Lincoln's Inn, LLB (Hons)(Lond)

Pooran Miss Priya Nandita
Called: Nov 1997, Gray's Inn, LLB, LLM (LSE)

Poots Laurence James
House No 6, Harmony Heights, No 5 Hang Lok Lane, Shatin, 26666033, Fax: 26677662, and Member Hong Kong Bar Australia Bar. Called: Nov 1990, Gray's Inn, LLB (Lond), MIMgt

Portland Miss Brender
Called: Nov 1997, Middle Temple, LLB (Hons)

Pourgourides Evangelos
P.O.Box 4137, Limassol, (00357) 5 346634, Fax: (00357) 5 346633, Practising Barrister in Cyprus and Member Cyprus. Called: July 1997, Lincoln's Inn, LLB (Hons)(Leics)

Povall Ms Kathryn Elizabeth
c/o Overseas Liaison Office, Allen & overy, One New Change, London EC4M 9QQ. Called: Oct 1991, Lincoln's Inn, LLB (Hons) (New)

Powell Guy Storer
Bedell & Cristin, Normandy House, Grenville Street, St Helier, Jersey, 01534 872949. Called: Nov 1982, Middle Temple, LLB

Prabhakaran Miss Prasanna T.V.
Called: July 1996, Middle Temple, LLB (Hons)(Lond)

Pratt Miss Chinique Elmega
Called: Nov 1997, Gray's Inn, BA (Windsor, Canada), LLB (Kent)

Pratt Miss Olivia Deloris
and Member Bahamas. Called: Nov 1996, Gray's Inn, LLB (Buckingham)

Premaraj Belden
Sivananthan, Suite 253-4, 4th Floor, 253 Jalan Tun Sambanthan, 50470 Kuala Lumpur, 2738273, Fax: 2739273, and Member Malaysia Bar. Called: Nov 1993, Lincoln's Inn, LLB (Hons, L'pool)

Prentice Edward Arthur Gerald
Ozannes Advocates, 1 le Marchant Street, St Peter Port, Guernsey, 01481 723466, Fax: 01481 714571. Called: Nov 1983, Inner Temple, LLB (Lond)

Pringle Robert Henry Becker
Barristers' Chambers, Allendale Square, 77 St George's Terrace, Perth WA 6000, (08) 9220 0444, Fax: (08) 9325 9008/9111, QC Western Australia. Called: Nov 1978, Gray's Inn, BA, LLB

Psaila Ms Tara Antonia Maria
Called: Mar 1998, Gray's Inn, LLB., BCL (Cork), LLM (Lond)

Psillidou Miss Kathryn Andreou
Called: Nov 1994, Gray's Inn, LLB

Pung Miss So Ken
NO 68 Jalan Seri Cheras 6A, Taman Seri Cheras, BT 9 1/2 Cheras, 43200 BT 9 Cheras, Selangor Malaysia. Called: July 1995, Inner Temple, LLB

Purnell Miss Marcia Ann
Le Logis de Souvigne, 79800 Souvigne, 49 76 25 03, Fax: 49 76 25 03. Called: Nov 1983, Gray's Inn, BA LLM PhD

Purshotamdas *Prakash*
Azman Soh & Murugaiyan, 1 Columbo Court, 07-23, Singapore 179742, 338 3996, Fax: 338 5993, and Member Singapore Bar. Called: July 1994, Lincoln's Inn, LLB (Hons)

Pushparasah *Miss Thevarani*
Called: July 1996, Lincoln's Inn, LLB (Hons)

Pyfrom *Basil Lorraine*
Called: July 1997, Inner Temple, LLB (Dunelm)

Pyrgou *Mrs Melina*
Chr P Kinanis & Co, Annis Komninis 29A, P.O.Box 2303, Nicosia, Cyprus, 00357 2 456486, Fax: 00357 2 362777, and Member Cyprus Bar Association. Called: Nov 1995, Gray's Inn, B.Soc.Sci (Keele)

Qayyum *Abdul*
Village Bhuttian Mohra, Tehsil-Gujar-Khan, Dist, Rawalpindi. Called: May 1982, Gray's Inn, BA, LLb

Qazi *Faysal Ali*
Called: Mar 1997, Lincoln's Inn, LLB (Hons)

Quah *Chiang Fu*
Called: July 1994, Lincoln's Inn, LLB (Hons)

Quek *Miss Bee Choo*
1 Park Road, [H] 04-04 People's Park Complex, 5336077, Fax: 5342339, and Member Singapore Bar. Called: Nov 1995, Lincoln's Inn, LLB (Hons)

Quek *Miss Gwang Hwa*
Called: July 1996, Lincoln's Inn, LLB (Hons)

Quek *Miss Karen Chia-Huei*
36 Robinson Road, [H] 18-01, City House, 065 420 7653, Fax: 065 224 8210, and Member Singapore Bar. Called: July 1995, Lincoln's Inn, LLB (Hons)

Quek *Miss Karen Tzun Tjin*
Called: July 1997, Gray's Inn, LLB

Quek *Miss Sue Yian*
Called: Oct 1997, Middle Temple, LLB (Hons)(Brunel)

Quinn *Anthony Paschal*
Law Library, Four Courts, Dublin 7, Ireland, 0001 8720622/8254811, Fax: 0001 8721455/720031, Barrister, Kings Inn Dublin Also Inn of Court M and Member Northern Ireland Bar. Called: July 1990, Lincoln's Inn, MA, DipPbl, ADM (Dub, Dip Lgl Studies, (Kings Inns), FCIArb, Dip Intnl Arb, Dip Arb Law, B.COMM

Qureshi *Ms Zainab Bilal*
Called: July 1997, Inner Temple, BA (Sussex)

Radin *Alang Iskandar*
2A Lorong Ara kiri 3, Bangsar Lucky Gardens, 59100 Kuala Lumpur, 03 2580331/7567929, Fax: 03 2536331, and Member Malaysia. Called: Oct 1995, Middle Temple, BA (Hons)

Rahim *Miss Anisah Binte Abdul*
55 Market Street, Sinsov Building, [H]08-01, 65-5383177, and Member Singapore Bar. Called: July 1995, Middle Temple, LLB (Hons)

Rahman *Andaleeve*
Called: Mar 1998, Lincoln's Inn, LLB (Hons)(Wolv'ton)

Rahming *Andre Joseph*
Called: July 1995, Gray's Inn, LLB (Lond)

Raja *Nomaam Akram*
Called: July 1997, Gray's Inn, LLB

Raja Abdul Rashid *Miss Raja Rozmin*
Called: Nov 1996, Middle Temple, LLB(Hons)(Glamorgan)

Raja Alang Petra *Miss Raja Nor Azwa*
Yeo, Tan, Hoon & Tee, Advocates & Solictors, Rooms 704-705, 7th Floor, Asis Life Building, Jalan Segget, 80000 Johor, 607 2233768, Fax: 607 2244882, and Member Malaysia. Called: July 1995, Gray's Inn, LLB (Kent)

Rajah *Tharuma*
Called: July 1993, Lincoln's Inn, LLB (Hons)

Rajan *Sanjiv Kumar*
Called: July 1997, Middle Temple, LLB (Hons)(Leics)

Rajaratnam *Miss Indira*
and Member Advocate & Solicitor of the High Court of Malaya. Called: Nov 1995, Lincoln's Inn, BA (Hons)(Kent)

Rajendran *Miss Kalyani*
Called: July 1997, Middle Temple, LLB (Hons)(Leics)

Rajendran *Kumaresan*
Called: July 1996, Middle Temple, LLB (Hons)(Lond)

Rajendran *M S*
Called: Nov 1997, Lincoln's Inn, LLB (Hons)(Lond)

Rajvinder Singh
53 Jalan Air Duson, Setapak, 53200 Kuala Lumpur, and Member Malaysia Bar. Called: July 1994, Lincoln's Inn, LLB (Hons, Lond)

Rajwani *Ms Vandana*
Flat 2-B Kam Fai Mansions, 68a Macdonnell Road, (852) 28575089, Fax: (852) 28681652, and Member Hong Kong Bar. Called: July 1996, Lincoln's Inn, BA

Ramachandran *A J*
Apt Block 38, Upper Boon Keng Road, [H]04-2406, Singapore 380038, Republic of Singapore, 7488072 (H)/2209344, Fax: 2257827, and Member Singapore Bar. Called: July 1994, Lincoln's Inn, LLB (Hons), B.Sc (Singapore)

Ramachandran *Miss Deepa*
Called: Nov 1997, Lincoln's Inn, LLB (Hons)(Nott'm)

Ramachandran *Raj Sativale*
Sativale & Associates, 6-1 Jalan SS15/8B, Subang Jaya, 47500, Petaling Jaya, Selangor Malaysia, 03 733 8787, Fax: 03 733 1103. Called: Feb 1990, Middle Temple, LLM, Dip Law, MCIT, MICS

Ramachandran *Sathish*
No 6 Tepian Tunku, Bukit Tunku, 50480 Kuala Lumpur, 603 6512989, Fax: 603 6510850, and Member Malaysia. Called: July 1993, Middle Temple, LLB (Hons)(Kent)

Ramagge *James George*
28 Irish Town, P O Box 15, (350) 72020, Fax: (350) 72270, and Member Gibraltar Bar. Called: Oct 1994, Middle Temple, LLB (Hons)(Lond)

Ramakrishnan *Miss Sharmila*
Called: Feb 1994, Lincoln's Inn, LLB (Hons, Wales)

Ramalingam *Paramasivam*
Called: July 1996, Lincoln's Inn, LLB (Hons)(Lond)

Ramanathan *Miss Shsmini*
Called: Nov 1994, Lincoln's Inn, LLB (Hons)(Lond)

Ramason *Raji*
Called: July 1996, Middle Temple, LLB (Hons)(Wolves)

Ramdin *Ashvinsingh*
Called: May 1994, Lincoln's Inn, LLB (Hons)

Ramiah *Sivaraja*
Called: July 1996, Lincoln's Inn, LLB (Hons)(Lond)

Ramlogan *Anand*
113 Ben-Lomond Village, Williamsville P.O., Trinidad, 809-650-0536, Fax: 809 658 0350, and Member Trinidad & Tobago. Called: July 1995, Middle Temple, LLB (West Indies), LLM (Lond), Dip (Law), LEC

Ramsewak *Miss Premila*
Called: July 1996, Lincoln's Inn, LLB (Hons)

Ranai *Ashok Kimar Mahadev*
Skrine & Co, No 4, Leboh Pasar Besar, Straits Trading Building, 50050 Kuala Lumpur, 603 2945111, Fax: 603 2934327, Advocate & Solicitor, High Court of Malaya and Member Malaysian Bar. Called: Nov 1995, Gray's Inn, LLB (Wales)

Randhawa *Ravinderpal Singh*
Bernard, Rada, Barker and, Pauline Chen, Advocates & Solicitors, 1 Colombo Court, [H]07-30, 336 1717, Fax: 339 9782/339 4991, and Member Singapore. Called: July 1995, Middle Temple, LLB (Hons) (Wales)

Randle *Ms Christine Annjeanette*
Dunn, Cox, Orrett & Ashenheim, 48 Duke Street, Kingston, Jamaica, West indies, (809) 922 1500, Fax: (809) 922 9002, and Member Jamaica Bar. Called: Oct 1994, Gray's Inn, LLB

Rangan *Krishnan Harihara Kastthuri*
48 Pemimpan Place, Singapore 2057, (65) 354 0786 (Res), Fax: (65) 7582321. Called: July 1994, Lincoln's Inn, B.Sc, BE, LLB (Lond), First Class Engineer, (Motor)

Rasanayagam *Miss Marlene Sunita*
Called: July 1996, Middle Temple, LLB (Hons)(Bucks)

Rashid *Khurram*
Called: Nov 1997, Lincoln's Inn, LLB (Hons)

Rashid *Miss Naz Parveen*
Called: July 1994, Lincoln's Inn, LLB (Hons)

Rasiah *Sanjeev Kumar*
Serine & Co, (Advocates & Solicitors), No %
Leboh Pasar Besar, 50050 Kuala Lumpur,
Malaysia, and Member Malaysia Bar.
Called: July 1994, Middle Temple, LLB
(Hons)(Hull)

Ratnasingham *Rajasingham*
Called: July 1996, Lincoln's Inn, LLB (Hons)

Rauf *Miss Neetasha*
Called: July 1995, Lincoln's Inn, LLB (Hons),
LLM

Ravi *Arumugam*
Block 551, Pasir Ris Street 51, [H]08-97, and
Member Singapore Bar. Called: July 1995,
Lincoln's Inn, LLB (Hons)

Ravindran *Miss Subithra*
Called: July 1994, Lincoln's Inn, LLB

Rawlinson *Iain David*
P.O.Box 25011, Awali, 973 826003, Fax:
973 537637. Called: Oct 1994, Lincoln's
Inn, BA (Hons)(Durham)

Ray *Gaur Gopal*
Sang Health Affairs, King Fahad National
Guard, Hospital, P.O. Box 22490, Riyadh
11426, (KSA) 1 252 0088, Fax: (KSA) 1 252
0088, Advocate, Supreme Court of India and
Member West Bengal Bar. Called: July 1973,
Lincoln's Inn, BCom, FCIArb

Ray *Miss Lapita*
Called: July 1997, Lincoln's Inn, LLB
(Hons)(Leeds)

Raza *Khurram*
Called: Nov 1995, Lincoln's Inn, LLB (Hons)

Razzaque *Miss Jona*
Called: Nov 1997, Lincoln's Inn, LLM (Lond)

Rea *Luigi Orlando Anthony*
Garden Flat, 14 Grantham Street, Dublin 8,
0001 4781105, Fax: 0001 4781105, and
Member Southern Ireland Bar. Called: July
1982, Middle Temple, BA (Dublin)

Rea *Robert Kevin*
The Bar Library, Royal Courts of Justice,
Chichester Street, Belfast, (01232) 562438,
and Member Northern Ireland. Called: Mar
1996, Gray's Inn, LLB, LLM (Int'l &,
European)

Regal *Richard Neill*
International Federation of, Accountants,
114 West 42nd Street, Suite 2410, New
York 10036, 001 212 302 5952. Called: July
1997, Inner Temple, BA (L'pool), MBA
(Kingston), FCA, ATII

Renganathan *Nandakumar*
1 Colombo Court, [H]09-05, 3362626, Fax:
3388001, and Member Singapore.
Called: Nov 1993, Lincoln's Inn, LLB (Hons,
Sheff)

Rengasamy *Rama Krishnan*
Called: July 1997, Lincoln's Inn, LLB (Hons)

Renouf *Mark Philip*
22 Grenville Street, St Helier, Jersey
JE4 8PX, (01534) 609000. Called: Oct 1994,
Middle Temple, LLB (Hons)(Lond)

Rentrop *Timm Ulrich Wilhelm*
Square Marguerite 1/49, B-1000 Bruxelles,
322 733 1236. Called: Nov 1991, Inner
Temple, MA (Oxon), Licence Speciale en,
Droit Europeen

Restano *John Ernest*
Called: Nov 1994, Middle Temple, LLB
(Hons)

Retnam *Rajah*
and Member Singapore Bar. Called: Feb
1993, Gray's Inn, LLB (Buckingham)

Reyes *Dr Anselnio Francisco Trinidad*
and Member Hong Kong Bar. Called: Nov
1985, Inner Temple, MA, LLM,
PhD(Cantab), BA (Harv)

Reyes *John Bernard*
Stagnetto & Co, 186 Main Street, 350
73530/75783, Fax: 71431, and Member
Gibraltar. Called: Nov 1996, Middle Temple,
BA (Hons)

Reza *Abu Mohammad Manzur Ahsan*
Called: Nov 1995, Lincoln's Inn, LLB
(Hons)(Dhaka), LLM (Dhaka), LLM (Lond)

Riach *Miss Emma Simone*
Arthur Andersen International, 41 Rue Ybry,
92200 Neuilly-Sur-Seine, Paris, (331) 55 61
1076, Fax: (331) 55 61 1515. Called: Oct
1994, Lincoln's Inn, LLB (Hons)(Lond)

Riaz *Mohammad Iftikhar Uddin*
Rizvi Isa Kabraji, 517-518 Clifton Centre,
DC-1 Block 5, Clifton, Karachi 75600,
Pakistan, (92-21) 587 2879, Fax: (92-21) 587
0014, and Member Pakistan Bar. Called: July
1994, Inner Temple, BA, CPE, MA

Riaz *Zahir*
Called: Mar 1997, Gray's Inn, LLB (LSE), LLB
(Cantab)

Rich *Christopher Paul Donald*
Barings (Guernsey) Ltd, Arnold House, St
Julians Avenue, St Peter Port, Guernsey,
Supreme Court of the Northern Territory,
Australia and Member Royal Court of
Guernsey. Called: Nov 1988, Gray's Inn, LLB
(Soton)

Richings *Francis Gordon SC*
908 Salmon Grove Chambers, 407 Smith
Street, Durban 4001, (031)3018694, Fax:
(031)3056420, Advocate of South Africa and
Member Lesotho Bar. Called: May 1992,
Middle Temple, BA,LLB (Cape Town), M
Phil (Cantab)

Richmond *Martyn*
Called: Nov 1997, Gray's Inn, BA
(Newcastle), LLB (Lond)

Riddell *Christopher William*
Called: Oct 1992, Lincoln's Inn,
BSc(Hons)(Lond), Dip Law(Lond)

Ridzuan *Shahril Ridza*
c/o Zain & Co, 6th Floor, Bangunan Dato
Zainal, 23 Jalan Melaka, 50100 Kuala
Lumpur Malaysia, 03 2986255, Fax: 03
2986969, and Member Malaysia Bar.
Called: July 1994, Middle Temple, BA
(Hons)(Cantab), BCL (Oxon)

Rigby *Raynard Sherman*
McKinney, Bancroft & Hughes, Mareva
House, 4 George Street, P.O.Box N 3937,
Nassau. Called: July 1995, Gray's Inn, BA
(Ontario), LLB (Leeds)

Robb *Lt Cdr RN Louis Joseph*
Scottish Advocate. Called: June 1964, Inner
Temple

Robert *Leslie Gregory*
Called: July 1995, Lincoln's Inn, LLB (Hons)

Roberts *Simon David*
Finnegan, Henderson, Farabow, Garret &
Dunner, 1300 Eye Street, NW [H]700,
Washington DC, 20005-3315, 001 202 408
4000, Fax: 001 202 408 4400, and Member
New York State Bar US Patent Bar.
Called: Nov 1991, Gray's Inn, BSc, BA
(Exon)

Robinson *Wendel Glenroy*
Called: Nov 1997, Inner Temple, LLB (Lond)

Robless *Miss Sharon Marie*
Called: July 1994, Middle Temple, LLB
(Hons)(Notts)

Rocca *Christian Manuel*
Isola & Isola, Suite 23, Portland House,
Gibraltar, 78363, Fax: 78990, and Member
Gibraltar Bar. Called: Oct 1994, Inner
Temple, LLB

Rocca *Terence Joseph*
Attorney-General's Chambers, 17 Town
Range, Gibraltar, 010 350 78882, Fax: 010
350 79891, and Member Gibraltar Bar.
Called: Oct 1993, Middle Temple, LLB
(Hons)(Kingston)

Rochat-Spechter *Mrs Alison Jean*
Secretan, Troyanov and Partners, 2 Rue
Charles - Bonnet, P.O.Box 189, 1211
Geneva 12, Switzerland, (41) 22 789 7000,
Fax: (41) 22 789 7070. Called: Oct 1993,
Gray's Inn, LLB (Buck'm)

Rodrigo *Jayanath Avindra Gian*
Called: Feb 1994, Gray's Inn, LLB (Warwick)

Rodriguez *Stuart James*
Called: Mar 1997, Middle Temple, LLB
(Hons), MA (Leeds)

Rogers *Anthony Gerrard Vernede*
11th Floor, Southern Cross Building, cnr
Victoria St East & High St, Auckland 1,
093733 196, Fax: 09 3774850, PO Box
1771, Auckland, New Zealand and Member
New Zealand Bar New South Wales Bar 6
King's Bench Walk, Ground Floor, Temple,
London, EC4Y 7DR. Called: Feb 1986, Inner
Temple, LLM (Hons), (U Auckland)

Rogers *Anthony Gordon Justice*
Supreme Court, Queensway, 852 28254332,
Fax: 852 25523327, Former Chairman Hong
Kong Bar Association, QC Hong Kong Bar
Association. Called: Nov 1969, Gray's Inn

Rogers *Michael Richard*
Law Chambers, World Trade Centre, P.O.Box 896, 1215 Geneva 15, +44 22 788 0551, Fax: +44 22 788 1502. Called: Feb 1972, Inner Temple, F.C.I.S., A.C.I.I

Rogers *Stephen Urban*
Lot 8359, Mukim of Batu, Batu 8,, Jalan Batu Caves, 68100 Batu Caves, Selangor. Called: May 1988, Gray's Inn, BSc (Leeds), M Jur (B'ham)

Rose *Dr Christopher Philip*
Called: Oct 1995, Gray's Inn, B.Sc, MC (Canada), MA (Oxon)

Ross *Keith James*
10 Roper Place, Chifley ACT 2606, 0262 816748, and Member Barrister & Solicitor Papau New Guinea, Australian Capital Territory, Federal Court, Solicitor, New South Wales New South Wales Bar Solicitor, New South Wales. Called: July 1967, Lincoln's Inn, LLB

Rozain *Miss Roz Mawar*
54 Setiabakit 9, Bukit Damansara, 50490 Kuala Lumpur, 00603 2551179, and Member Malaysian Bar. Called: July 1995, Lincoln's Inn, LLB (Hons)

Ruane *Miss Mairead Mary*
Called: Nov 1991, Gray's Inn, BCL (Dub)

Rubin *Mohideen M P Haja*
Called: July 1987, Middle Temple, LLB

Rupasinghe *Miss Anouchka Charmini*
Called: Nov 1996, Lincoln's Inn, LLB (Hons)(E.Anglia)

Ryan *William Fabian*
Associate of the Royal Institution of Chartered Surveyors. Called: Mar 1998, Inner Temple, BSc (Dublin), Dip Law (Thames)

Rynd *Dr Aaron James*
Spier Harben, Barristers & Solicitors, Suite 1000, Dominion House, 665-8 Street S.W., Calgary, Alberta T2P 3K7, 403 263 5130, Fax: 403 264 9600, and Member Alberta, Canada. Called: July 1976, Lincoln's Inn, BA, PHd

Saadi *Mir Abdul Wares*
Called: Nov 1996, Lincoln's Inn, LLB (Hons)(Lond)

Sadat *Omar*
Called: Nov 1997, Lincoln's Inn, LLB (Hons)(Lond), LLM (Cantab)

Sadhwani *Kamlesh Arjan*
Room 1405, Tower II, Admiralty Centre, 18 Harcourt Road, 25273082, Fax: 25298226, and Member Hong Kong Bar. Called: July 1995, Lincoln's Inn, BA (Hons)

Sadjadi-Nourani *Mrs Leila*
Law Offices of Foley, Lardner, Weissburg & Aronson, 2029 Century Park East, 36th Floor, Los Angeles CA 90067, 310-975 7853, Fax: 310-557 8475, and Member California Bar. Called: Nov 1990, Gray's Inn, LLB (Hons)

Saga *Miss Regina V*
Called: Nov 1997, Lincoln's Inn, LLB (Hons) LLM

Sagayam *Miss Martina*
Called: Oct 1995, Gray's Inn, LLB

Said *Miss Farah Shireen Mohamed*
Called: July 1997, Gray's Inn, LLB (Lond)

Said *Miss Shaesta*
Called: July 1994, Middle Temple

Sakhrani *Miss Anisha*
Called: July 1996, Lincoln's Inn, LLB (Hons)

Sakhrani *Sanjay Arjan*
503 Dina House, Ruttonsee Centre, 11 Duddell Street, Central, Hong Kong, 2525 9083, Fax: 2877 0051, and Member Hong Kong Bar. Called: July 1995, Lincoln's Inn, BA, LLB (Hons)(Lond)

Salehkon *Ramli Bin*
Kertar & Co, Advocates & Solicitors, 133 New Bridge Road, [H] 17-04, Chinatown Point, (65) 5366266, Fax: (65) 5366533. Called: Nov 1995, Middle Temple, LLB (Hons)(Lond), BA (Singapore)

Sallehuddin *Mohamed Nasri*
Called: July 1995, Gray's Inn, LLB (Wales)

Sam *Miss Lisa Hui Min*
Donaldson & Burkinshaw, 24 Raffles Place [H] 15-00, Clifford Centre, 5339422, Fax: 5337806/5330809, and Member Singapore Bar. Called: July 1996, Inner Temple, LLB (Kent)

Saminathan *Miss Vignaswari*
Called: Nov 1995, Middle Temple, LLB (Hons)(Sheff)

Samnakay *Mrs Minaxi Saeed*
and Member Kenyan Bar. Called: Nov 1989, Inner Temple, BA (Nairobi), LLB

Samuel *Miss Shanti Loraine*
Called: Nov 1996, Inner Temple, LLB (Hull)

Samuel *Mrs Vimala*
Called: Nov 1990, Lincoln's Inn, LLB (Lond)

Sanchez *Mrs Karin Louise*
Management & Service Co Ltd, P.O.Box F 42544, Freeport, 242 352 7063, Fax: 242 352 3932, and Member Bahamas. Called: July 1996, Lincoln's Inn, LLB (Hons)

Sandhu *Sarbrinder Singh*
Called: July 1994, Middle Temple, LLB (Hons)(Wales)

Sandhu *Miss Viviene Kaur*
m/s Kumar & Loh, Advocates & Solicitors, 51 Anson Road [H] 10-53, Anson Centre, 225 6362, Fax: 225 9690. Called: Nov 1996, Middle Temple, LLB (Hons)(L'pool)

Sangha *Ranbir Singh*
Called: July 1995, Lincoln's Inn, BA (Hons)

Sankaran *Chandrakandan*
Called: July 1995, Lincoln's Inn, LLB (Hons)

Sankey *Rohan Ashwin*
17 Jalan 14/37, 46100 Petaling Jaya, Selangor, 03 2911511, Fax: 03 2929105, and Member Malaysia. Called: July 1994, Middle Temple, LLB (Hons)(Bris)

Sarfraz *Miss Ayesha*
Called: Nov 1995, Gray's Inn, BA (Punjab), LLB (Dunelm)

Sarkar *Shib Sankar*
21/2 Gora Chand Road, Calcutta-700014, 009133-244-8778, Senior Advocate of the Supreme Court of India. Called: May 1997, Lincoln's Inn, MA, LLB (Calcutta), FCI Arb (Lond)

Sarony *Neville Leslie*
Advocate Supreme Court of Nepal and Member Hong Kong Bar New Court Chambers, 5 Verulam Buildings, Gray's Inn, London, WC1R 5LY. Called: June 1964, Gray's Inn, LLB (Lond), LSE

Sarwar *(Ali) Nabeel*
Advocate, Lahore High Court, Pakistan. Called: July 1989, Middle Temple, MA (Cantab)

Sathiasingam *Miss Lynette Shakunthala*
(65) 481 3113. Called: July 1995, Middle Temple, LLB (Hons)

Saunthararajah *Miss Vaani*
Called: Nov 1993, Middle Temple, LLB (Hons)(Warwick)

Saveriades *Marios Kyriacou*
Iris House, John Kennedy Str, Office 740B, Limassol, Cyprus, (05) 366767, Fax: 4745 JUSTLAW, and Member Cyprus Bar. Called: Feb 1995, Lincoln's Inn, LLB (Hons)(Leic)

Savvides *George Loukis*
1st, 2nd & 4th Floor, Omega Court, 4 Rigas Fereos Street, P.O.Box 4098, 3720 Limmassol, 357 5 376886, Fax: 357 5 374930. Called: July 1983, Middle Temple, LLB (Hons)(Exon), ACIArb

Saw *Miss Hooi Lee*
Called: July 1997, Lincoln's Inn, LLB (Hons)(Wales)

Saw *Leon Eng Tiong*
Called: July 1995, Lincoln's Inn, LLB (Hons)

Saw *Seang Kuan*
80 Robinson Road, [H]17-02, Singapore 068898, 2228008, Fax: 2228001, and Member Singapore Bar. Called: July 1996, Middle Temple, BA (Hons)(Cantab)

Sayers *Ms Veronica Margaret*
Law Officer's Department, Morier House, Halkett Place, St Helier, Jersey, 01534 502200. Called: Nov 1997, Inner Temple, BSc (Open Uni), LLB (So'ton)

Schimming-Chase *Miss Esi Malaika*
Called: Oct 1994, Middle Temple, LLB (Hons)(Coventry)

Schinis *Miss Theodoti A*
P.L.Cacoyannis & Co, B, Rigas Feros Street, Libra Chambers, Limassol, P.O. Box 122, (357) 5 363154. Called: Nov 1997, Lincoln's Inn, LLB (Hons)(Leics)

Schoneveld *Frank Robert*
Attorney General's Department, Robert Garrar Offices, National Circuit, ACY 2600, 61 2 6250 5515, Fax: 61 2 6250 5910, and Member Australia Bar 2 Harcourt Bldgs, Ground Floor/Left, Temple, London, EC4Y 9DB. Called: May 1992, Inner Temple, B.Jurisprudence, LLB (Australia), Dip Eur Law (Neth)

Schwartzman *Ivor Walter*
300 Innes Chambers, Johannesburg, South Africa, and Member South Africa Bar Swaziland Bar. Called: May 1988, Lincoln's Inn, BA, LLB (Rand)

Schwarz *Dr Heinz OMS*
P O Box 3089, Parklands 2121, (2711) 286 1115, Fax: (2711) 784 9976, Former Ambassador of South Africa to the United States of America, Dr of Humane Letters (Honoris Causa). Called: Nov 1961, Inner Temple, BA, LLB, D.Phil, (Hon Causa),

Scordis *Kyriacos*
P O Box 533, 30 Karpenisi Street, The Business Forum, Nicosia, (357) 2 843000, Fax: (357) 2 375227, and Member Cyprus Bar. Called: Nov 1994, Lincoln's Inn, LLB (Hons), LLM (Lond)

Scott *Miss Charlene Annette*
Attorney General's Chambers, Global House, 43 Church Street, Hamilton HM 12, 441 292 2463, Fax: 441 292 3608. Called: Nov 1986, Inner Temple, BA, MSc (New York), LLB (Essex)

Scudamore *Jeremy Richard*
Principe de Vergara, 261-5 C, (34) 91 4577262, and Member Madrid Bar. Called: Nov 1982, Middle Temple, BA (Hons) (Exeter)

Seah *Miss Chui Ling Engelyn*
Called: July 1994, Middle Temple, LLB (Hons)(Lond)

Seah *Miss Ee Leng*
Called: July 1995, Lincoln's Inn, LLB (Hons)

Seah *Miss Heww Ying Melina*
Called: Nov 1995, Middle Temple, LLB (Hons)

Seah *Miss Lu Sean*
Called: July 1996, Gray's Inn, LLB (Warwick)

Seah *Miss Suat Eng*
and Member Singapore Bar. Called: July 1994, Lincoln's Inn, BSc (Econ) (Hons)

Sears *The Hon Mr Justice*
The High Court, 38 Queensway, 8254433, Fax: 8690640. Called: Feb 1957, Gray's Inn, MA (Cantab)

Sebom *Polycarp Teo*
and Member Sarawak Bar. Called: Oct 1991, Inner Temple, BA, LLB (Hull), ACIS, ATII

See *Ben Sin*
Called: July 1997, Lincoln's Inn, LLB (Hons)(Lond)

See *David Thiam Soon*
Called: Nov 1997, Middle Temple, LLB (Hons)(Reading)

See *Eng Teong*
Called: July 1996, Lincoln's Inn, LLB (Hons)(Lond)

See *Ms Esther Lay Lin*
Messrs Cheang & Ariff, 39 Court, 39 Jalan Yap Kwan Seng, 50450 Kuala Lumpur, 03 2610803, Fax: 03 2614475, and Member Malaysia. Called: July 1995, Middle Temple, LLB (Hons)

See *Miss Guat Har*
Messrs Shearn Delamore & Co, 6th Floor,Wisma Penang Gdn, No.42 Jalan Sultan Ahmad Shah, 10050 Penang Malaysia, 04-2267062/2266664899, Fax: 04-2275166, and Member Malaysia Bar. Called: July 1989, Middle Temple, BA, LLB (Bucks)

See *Hans Han-E*
2355501, Fax: 5363622, and Member Singapore. Called: July 1995, Middle Temple, LLB (Hons) (Hull)

See Tho *Miss Ving Mei*
Called: July 1995, Middle Temple, LLB (Hons) (Hull)

Sekarajasekaran *Miss Sharmila*
Called: Nov 1996, Middle Temple, BA (Hons)(Keele)

Seligman *Edgar*
Harry B. Sands & Co, Chambers, 50 Shirley Street, P O Box N-624, Nassau, Bahamas, 1-(809) 322-2670, Fax: 1-(809) 323-8914, and Member Bahamas. Called: Oct 1992, Gray's Inn, MA (Dublin), Dip Law

Selvakumar *Miss Shiela*
Called: July 1997, Lincoln's Inn, LLB (Hons)

Selvan *Kaniamuthan s/o Thiruvida*
Called: Nov 1997, Lincoln's Inn, LLB (Hons)

Selvaraj *Steven*
Called: Nov 1996, Gray's Inn, LLB (Lond)

Selvarajah *Miss Pushpaleela*
Called: Feb 1995, Lincoln's Inn, LLB (Hons)(Lond)

Selvarajan *Balamurugan*
Called: Nov 1997, Lincoln's Inn, LLB (Hons)(Wolv)

Sen *Ms Lisa*
6 Southern Avenue, Maharani Bagh, New Delhi 110065, India, 00-91-11-6910545, and Member India Bar. Called: July 1995, Gray's Inn, BA, MA (New York), LLB (Lond)

Sen *Raj Ratna*
149/IC Rash Behari Avenue, Calcutta, 700029, (033) 464-3601/464 2651. Called: July 1994, Gray's Inn, BA (Calcutta), LLB (Leeds)

Senathipathy *Miss Renuka*
Called: July 1994, Lincoln's Inn, LLB (Hons)

Seng *Joo How*
Called: Nov 1991, Middle Temple, BSc Hons (Econ), LLB Hons (Lond Ext), ARICS,ACIS

Sengupta *Miss Amgana*
Called: July 1995, Inner Temple, LLB (Lond)

Seow *Miss Deanna Yim Ling*
Called: July 1994, Middle Temple, LLB (Hons)(Bris)

Seow *John Hwang Seng*
Called: July 1995, Middle Temple, LLB (Hons)

Serghides *Miss Lydia Gabrielle*
Called: July 1997, Gray's Inn, LLB (Kent)

Sevasamy *Shankar Angammah*
Called: July 1996, Middle Temple, LLB (Hons)(Lond)

Seymour *Dr Colin Brian*
and Member King's Inn (Dublin). Called: May 1996, Lincoln's Inn, PhD (Dublin)

Shadid *Miss Lina Ali*
Afridi & Angell, Legal Consultants, P.O.Box 9371, Dubai, 00971 4 883900, Fax: 00971 4 883979. Called: July 1996, Lincoln's Inn, LLB (Hons)(Lond)

Shafiq *Imran*
Called: Nov 1997, Lincoln's Inn, LLB (Hons), LLM (Georgetown)

Shah *Aly Abbas*
Called: July 1994, Lincoln's Inn, LLB (Hons), LLM (Bucks)

Shah *Ms Bhavini Jayakant*
Called: July 1994, Middle Temple, LLB (Hons)(Lond)

Shah *Syed Najaf Hussain*
Najaf Shah & Co, Opp Punjab Bar Council Blds, 13 Fane Road, Lahore, Pakistan, 042 7244888/7248088, Fax: 042 7230808/5721008, and Member Lahore High Court Bar,Lahore,Pakistan. Called: July 1989, Lincoln's Inn, BA (Punjab), LLB (Buck), LLM (Lond)

Shahruddin Leong *Miss Julianna*
Called: July 1994, Lincoln's Inn, LLB (Hons)

Shaik Hussain *Miss Khatijah*
Messrs Achan & Co, Advocates & Solicitors, No 12-C, Jalan SS 3/33, Talman University 47300, Petaling Jaya, Selangor Darul Ehsan, 03-7773622/7773042, and Member Malaysian Bar. Called: July 1993, Lincoln's Inn, LLB (Hons, Manch)

Shaikh *Zaher Abduz*
Called: Nov 1997, Gray's Inn, B.Com (Bangladesh), LLB

Sham *Chun Hung*
and Member Hong Kong Bar. Called: Feb 1992, Gray's Inn, BSc (Hong Kong), LLB (Lond), C.Biol (UK)

Shamsuddin *Miss Heidi*
Called: Nov 1997, Lincoln's Inn, LLB (Hons)(Nott'm)

Shankar *Renganathan*
Called: July 1995, Middle Temple, LLB (Hons)

Shanmuganathan *Indran*
Called: July 1996, Lincoln's Inn, LLB (Hons)(Leics)

Sharbawi *Miss Zuraini*
Called: Nov 1994, Lincoln's Inn, LLB (Hons)(Lond)

Shardin *Miss Emilda*
Called: July 1994, Lincoln's Inn, LLB (Hons)

Sharif *Hussain Nawaz*
Called: Nov 1996, Lincoln's Inn, LLB
(Hons)(LSE)

Sharpe *Mrs Sally*
Law Officers' Department, Royal Court
House, St Helier, Jersey JE1 1DD, 01534
502200, Fax: 01534 502299, Advocate of
the Royal Court of Jersey (1992).
Called: July 1988, Middle Temple, BA (OU),
LLB (Hons) (Lond)

Sharpe *Miss Susan Clare*
Law Officers' Department, Royal Court
House, Royal Square, Jersey JE1 1DD, 01534
502200, Fax: 01534 502299. Called: Oct
1992, Middle Temple, BA (Hons)

Shaw *Jonathan Leonard Maukes*
Central Chambers, 1505 Bank of America
Tower, 12 Harcourt Road, Central, Hong
Kong, 852 845 1909, Fax: 852 868 1965,
and Member Hong Kong Bar. Called: Nov
1978, Gray's Inn, FCIArb, LLM

Sheikh *Fazle Noor Taposh*
Called: Nov 1997, Lincoln's Inn, LLB (Hons)

Sheldrick *Andrew William*
3 Radford Court, Princeton Junction, New
Jersey, 08550-2218, 609 799 5719, Fax: 609
799 9170, and Member New York Bar.
Called: July 1979, Gray's Inn, MA (Cantab),
MCL(George, Washington Univ)

Shepheard *Huw Owen*
Insinger Trust (Jersey) Ltd, P O Box 546, 28-
30 The Parade, St Helier, Jersey JE4 8XY,
01534 636211, Fax: 01534 636215.
Called: July 1982, Gray's Inn, LLB (Hons)

Sherlock *Miss Samatha Frances*
Pollonais & Blanc, 62 Sackville Street, Port
of Spain, Trinidad, 623-5461, Fax: 625-8415,
and Member Trinidad & Tobago Bar.
Called: July 1995, Gray's Inn, LLB (Warks)

Shiacolas *Menelaos*
Called: Nov 1995, Lincoln's Inn, LLB
(Hons)(Kent), LLM

Shields *Mrs Janice Rhian*
Called: Oct 1993, Inner Temple, LLB
(Manch)

Shin *Miss Su Wen*
and Member Hong Kong. Called: July 1996,
Lincoln's Inn, LLB (Hons)(LSE)

Shine *Miss Clare Camilla*
37 Rue Erlanger, 75016 Paris, France, (33 1)
46 51 90 11, Fax: (33 1) 46 51 90 11.
Called: Nov 1988, Middle Temple, BA
(Oxon), Dip Law (Central), D.E.A. (Paris)

Shukla *Ms Vina*
Davis Polk & Wardwell, 450 Lekington
Avenue, New York NY 10017, (212) 450
4291, Fax: (212) 450 4800, and Member
New York. Called: Nov 1992, Gray's Inn,
MA (Cantab), BCL

Shum *Cheuk Yum*
24th Floor, Shum Tower, 268 Des Voeux
Road, Sheung Wan, (852)2805 2730, Fax:
(852)2851 2266, and Member Hong Kong
Bar. Called: June 1959, Middle Temple, LLB
(Lond)

Shum *Ka Hei*
Called: July 1996, Middle Temple, BSSc
(Hons), (Hong Kong), CPE (Staffs)

Sia *Edmund Wei Keong*
Called: July 1996, Lincoln's Inn, LLB
(Hons)(Warw)

Sia *Miss Pebble Huei-Chieh*
Called: July 1996, Middle Temple, LLB
(Hons)(Lond)

Siah *Miss Karen Wei Kuan*
Called: Nov 1996, Middle Temple, LLB
(Hons)(Sheff)

Siak *Miss Diane Chi-Yi*
Messrs Allen & Gledhill, 36 Robinson Road,
[H]18-01 City House, Singapore 068877,
(65) 225 1611, Fax: (65) 224 1574, and
Member Singapore Bar. Called: July 1994,
Middle Temple, BA (Hons)(Oxon)

Siddondo *Miss Camilla Dorothy
Adhiambo*
Called: July 1995, Lincoln's Inn, LLB (Hons)

Sidhu *Miss Anup Kaur*
Called: Mar 1998, Lincoln's Inn, B.Econ
(Australia), LLB (Hons)(Lond), LLM (Lond)

Sidhu *Mr Daljit Singh*
M/S Y H Goh & Co, 101 Upper Cross Street,
[H]05-40 People's Park Centre, Singapore
0105, 535 9022/535 6641, Fax: 538 4313,
and Member Singapore Bar. Called: July
1990, Middle Temple, LLB (Lond)

Sidhu *Sarjeet Singh*
Messrs Gill & Tang, Room 228, 2nd Floor,
Campbell Complex, jalan Dang Wangi,
50100 Kuala Lumpur Malaysia, 03 2924266,
Fax: 03 2910413, and Member Malaysian
Bar. Called: Nov 1992, Gray's Inn, LLB
(So'ton)

Siew *Miss Anne Eee Peng*
Called: Nov 1995, Lincoln's Inn, LLLB
(Hons), LLM (Dunelm)

Siew *Miss Li-Lian*
M/S K M Chye & Partners, Advocates &
Solicitors, 6th Floor, UBN Tower, Letter Box
163, Jalan P Ramlee, 50250 Kuala Lumpur,
(603) 2388055, Fax: (603) 2019300, and
Member Malaysia. Called: July 1995,
Lincoln's Inn, BCL

Siew *Miss Yvonne*
Called: Nov 1997, Lincoln's Inn, LLB
(Hons)(Wales)

Silvera *Wayne Delano*
Clayton Morgan & Co, 59 Church Street,
Kingston, Montego Bay, (876) 952 1800/979
1733, Fax: (876) 952 1514, and Member
Jamaican. Called: July 1996, Lincoln's Inn,
LLB (Hons), BSc (Hons)

Silvester *John Darragh Mostyn*
Lenana Forest Centre, Ngong Road, P O Box
24397, Nairobi, 254 2 567251/566970, Fax:
254 2 564945. Called: June 1958, Inner
Temple, MA (Hons) (Oxon), ACIA (Lond)

Silwaraju *Miss Hemalatha*
Called: July 1997, Middle Temple, LLB
(Hons)(Wales)

Sim *Miss Annabelle Seu Cheun*
Called: July 1997, Lincoln's Inn, LLB
(Hons)(Leics)

Sim *Chee Siong*
Called: Nov 1995, Middle Temple, LLB
(Hons)

Sim *Geoffrey Poh Leong*
c/o Mesrs. Sandhu & Co, Suites 6, 7 & 8,
5th Floor, Badiah Complex, Kim 2, Jalan
Tutong, 673 2 220783, Fax: 673 2 241237.
Called: July 1993, Lincoln's Inn, LLB (Hons)

Sim *Hwang Hwa*
Called: July 1995, Lincoln's Inn, LLB (Hons)

Sim *Miss Hwee Ai*
Called: July 1994, Middle Temple, LLB
(Hons)(Lond)

Sim *Mrs Lai Yin*
Blk 13, Holland Avenue, [H]07-62, 7605729.
Called: July 1994, Lincoln's Inn, LLB (Hons)

Sim *Miss Lay Bee*
Messrs Shahriza,Varegheeses &, Chandran,
No 119a Jalan Gasing, 1st Floor, Petaling
Jaya 46000, Selangor, Malaysia, 03 7565299/
177, Fax: 03 7572655, and Member Malaysia
Bar. Called: July 1992, Inner Temple, LLB

Sim *Miss Sok Nee*
Called: Nov 1997, Lincoln's Inn, LLB
(Hons)(Wales)

Sim *Miss Sok See*
Chorpee Anwarul & Co, Suite 8-16-6 Level
16, Menara Olympia, 8 Jalan Raja Chulan,
50200 Kuala Lumpur, 010603 2022566, Fax:
010603 2022577, and Member Malaysia Bar.
Called: July 1994, Lincoln's Inn, LLB (Hons)

Sim *Yuan Meng*
Called: July 1994, Lincoln's Inn, LLB (Hons)

Simmons *Everard Barclay*
Called: Mar 1997, Gray's Inn, LLB (Kent)

Simpson *Anthony Maurice Herbert TD*
Avenue Michel-Ange 57, 1000 Brussels,
Belgium, (00 322) 7364219, Fax: (00 322)
7339404, European Civil Servant.
Called: Feb 1961, Inner Temple, MA, LLM

Sin *Miss Charlotte Minng Minng*
Called: July 1996, Middle Temple, LLB
(Hons)(Hull)

Sin *Miss Li Lian*
Called: July 1996, Lincoln's Inn, LLB
(Hons)(Sheff)

Sin *Pui Wah*
Called: Nov 1997, Middle Temple, BSc
(Hons,Hong Kong)

Singaram *Miss Kalai Selvi*
Called: July 1994, Lincoln's Inn, LLB (Hons)

Singh *Ajinderpal*
Called: July 1996, Middle Temple, LLB
(Hons)(Leeds)

Singh *Bhajanvir*
and Member Singapore Bar. Called: July
1994, Lincoln's Inn, LLB (Sheff)

Singh *Gurcharanjit Dewan*
Called: July 1996, Lincoln's Inn, LLB
(Hons)(Lond)

Singh *Gurdeep Sekhon*
Blk 110 Potong Pasir Avenue 1, [H]06-620, (65) 5383611 (Office), Fax: (65) 5383708, and Member Australia Bar Singapore Bar. Called: Nov 1990, Lincoln's Inn, LLB (Hons) (Wales)

Singh *Herbans*
Called: Nov 1997, Lincoln's Inn, LLB (Hons)(Lond)

Singh *Jispal*
Called: July 1997, Lincoln's Inn, LLB (Hons)(Lond)

Singh *Kertar*
Called: Feb 1994, Middle Temple, LLB (Hons)(Wolves)

Singh *Kirindeep*
Called: July 1996, Middle Temple, LLB (Leeds)

Singh *Kirpal*
Messrs Kalamohan & Kirpal, 101 Cecil Street, Tong Eng Building, [H] 08-07, (65) 227 9377, Fax: (65) 227 8098, and Member Singapore Bar. Called: July 1994, Lincoln's Inn, LLB (Hons)

Singh *Kuldip*
Naidu Ng & Partners, 1 Colombo Court, [H]05-04, 65 3365115, Fax: 65 339610. Called: Nov 1995, Middle Temple, LLB (Hons)(Lond)

Singh *Mohan s/o Gurdial Singh*
Block 52, Apt No 04-299, Lengkok Bahru, Singapore 150052, 4727479. Called: July 1995, Lincoln's Inn, LLB (Hons)

Singh *Mohan s/o Kernal Singh*
Called: Nov 1995, Lincoln's Inn, LLB (Hons)(Lond)

Singh *Rajindar*
Block 250, Tampines Street 21, [H]10-520, Singapore 1852, 7810273. Called: Feb 1994, Middle Temple, LLB (Hons)(Lond)

Singh *Rajindar*
Called: July 1994, Lincoln's Inn, LLB (Hons)

Singh *Ranjit*
Called: July 1993, Middle Temple, LLB (Hons)

Singh *Sarindar*
Called: Nov 1996, Lincoln's Inn, LLB (Hons)

Singh *Sarjeet*
Called: July 1992, Middle Temple, LLB (Hons) (Lond)

Singh *Satwant*
Called: Nov 1995, Middle Temple, LLB (Hons)

Singh Deo *Gobind*
Called: July 1995, Lincoln's Inn, LLB (Hons)

Siow *Miss Hua Lin*
Called: Nov 1995, Middle Temple, LLB (Hons)(Hull)

Siow *Kim Leong*
Called: Nov 1996, Middle Temple, LLB (Hons)

Sircar *Muhammad Jamiruddin*
Supreme Court Bar, Room 41, Dhaka, Bangladesh, 8802 896883, Member of Parliament Bangladesh and Member Supreme Court of Bangladesh. Called: Nov 1967, Lincoln's Inn, MA, LL.B

Sissoho *Edrisa Mansajang*
Called: Mar 1998, Lincoln's Inn, LLB (Hons)

Sivagnanam *Rutheran*
Shearn Delamore & Co, No 2 Benteng, 50050 Kuala Lumpur, 2300644, Fax: 2385625, and Member Malaysia. Called: Nov 1994, Lincoln's Inn, LLB (Hons)(Leeds)

Sivagnanaratnam *Sivananthan*
Messrs Drew & Napier, 20 Raffles Place, [H]17-00 Ocean Towers, Singapore 048620, 65 5350733, Fax: 65 5330694/5330693, Advocate & Solicitor in Singapore (May 1992)0 and Member Singapore Bar. Called: July 1991, Middle Temple, LLB (Hons) (Lond)

Sivalingam *Miss Seetha*
Called: Nov 1996, Middle Temple, LLB (Hons)(Lond)

Sivaloganathan *Miss Damita Devi*
Called: July 1995, Lincoln's Inn, LLB (Hons)

Sivapiragasam *Miss Rani Christina*
Pernas Otis Elevator Co, Son BHD, 2 Medan Setia 2, Plaza Damansara, Bukit Damansara, 50490, 03 2554811, Fax: 03 2559684, and Member Malaysia Bar. Called: Feb 1993, Lincoln's Inn, LLB (Buck'ham), LLM (Buck'ham)

Sivasankar *Chelliah*
42 Jalan Bintang, Taman Westpool, Ipoh, Perak, 05-5489451, Fax: 05-5497311, Advocate and Solicitor, High Court of Malaya and Member Malaysian Bar. Called: Nov 1993, Gray's Inn, LLB

Sivasubramaniam *Miss Kavitha*
Called: Nov 1997, Lincoln's Inn, LLB (Hons)

Sivasubramaniam *Sivaruban*
Called: July 1996, Lincoln's Inn, LLB (Hons)

Skinner *Miss Sarah Elizabeth*
Called: Nov 1994, Lincoln's Inn, LLB (Hons)(Lond)

Smagh *Jerrinder Singh*
Called: Nov 1997, Middle Temple, LLB (Hons)

Smith *Miss Charmaine Natasha*
Called: July 1997, Gray's Inn, BA (Canada), LLB (Lond)

Smith *Geoffrey*
BP13, 78113 Bourdonne, 134871746, Fax: 134871751. Called: Feb 1995, Middle Temple, BSc (Loughborough), LLDip, CDipAF, CEng, FICE, ACIArb

Smith *Miss Louise Anne*
KPMG, Heritage Court, 41 Athol Street, Douglas, 01624 681000. Called: Nov 1994, Lincoln's Inn, LLB (Hons)

Smith *The Hon Mr Justice Neville Leroy*
Member of Bars of Barbados and the Bahamas Justice of the Supreme Court of the Bahamas Formerly a solicitor of England and of Barbados. Called: July 1991, Lincoln's Inn

Smith *Miss Sarah Anne*
c/o Callenders & Co, One Millars Court, P.O.Box 7117, Nassau, Bahamas, 809 322 2511, Fax: 809 326 7666, and Member Bahamas. Called: Oct 1994, Middle Temple, LLB (Hons)(Bucks)

Smithers *Miss Amelia Frances Otway*
CH-6921 Vico Morcote, Switzerland, 41-91-9961692, Fax: 41-91-9961692, and Member Turks & Caicos Islands Bar. Called: Oct 1991, Inner Temple, BA (Lond), Dip Law

Smouha *Derrick Maurice*
32 Chemin des Crets-de-Champel, 1206 Geneva, (00) 41 22/347 05 18, Fax: (00) 41 22/346 15 16. Called: Nov 1962, Lincoln's Inn, MA (Cantab)

Smyth *John Jackson QC (1979)*
PO Box CH 210, Chisipite, Harare, 490561, Fax: 494127. Called: July 1965, Inner Temple, MA, LLB (Cantab)

Soh *Miss Diana Wei Yi*
Called: July 1995, Middle Temple, LLB (Hons) (Warw)

Somen *Michael Lewis*
Hamilton Harrison & Matthews, ICEA Building, Kenyatta Avenue, P.O. Box 30333, Nairobi Kenya, 254 2 330870, Fax: 254 2 222318, Advocate High Court of Kenya and Member Kenya. Called: Feb 1961, Gray's Inn, MA (Oxon)

Somu *Retana Vellu Palani*
Called: July 1995, Gray's Inn, LLB (Lond)

Soo *Kok Loong*
M/S Peter Lo & Co, Chartered Bank Chambers, P O Box 683, 90707 Sandakan, Sabah, Malaysia, (089) 216222, Fax: (089) 271080, and Member Advocate of the High Court in Sabah & Sarawak, Malaysia. Called: Nov 1992, Inner Temple, BA (Keele)

Soo *Kwok Leung*
1320 Prince's Building, Central, Hong Kong, and Member Hong Kong Bar. Called: July 1995, Gray's Inn, BSc (Hong Kong), LLB (Lond), C.Eng, MIStractE MICE, MHKIE, RPE, ACIArb

Soo *Ms Sheagan*
Messrs Soo Thien Ming & Nashrah, No 1, 1st Floor, Jalan SS2/55, 47300 Petaling, Jaya, 03-7748763, Fax: 03-7744314. Called: July 1995, Gray's Inn, LLB (Middx)

Soo *Miss Wai Leng*
Called: July 1995, Lincoln's Inn, LLB (Hons)

Soon *Eric Boon Teck*
Called: July 1994, Lincoln's Inn, LLB (Hons)

Soon *Miss Vivienne Wen Pin*
Called: July 1995, Lincoln's Inn, LLB (Hons)

Soraya *Ms Raja Eileen*
Called: Oct 1994, Inner Temple, LLB (Lond)

Spear *Christopher Mark*
201-140 King Street, Peterborough, Ontario, Canada K93 728, 705-7412144, Fax: 705-7412712, and Member Ontario, Canada. Called: July 1981, Middle Temple, BA, Dip Law, LLB

Spencer *Mrs Margaret Elizabeth*
Wilde & Co Trustees Ltd, Pollet House, Lower Pollet, Guernsey, Channel Islands GY1 4EA, 01481 726446, Fax: 01481 711156. Called: Feb 1989, Gray's Inn

Spencer *Miss Maureen Cecilia*
Patton Boggs LLP, 2550 M Street NW, Washington DC 20037, 001 202 457 6000, Fax: 001 202 457 6315. Called: Oct 1994, Gray's Inn, BA, LLM

Spicer *Rupert Nicholas Bullen*
15th Fl Printing House, 6 Duddell Street, Central, 852 2 5 212616, Fax: 852 2 8 450260, and Member Hong Kong Bar. Called: Nov 1980, Lincoln's Inn, BSc (Dunelm), Diplaw

Spyrou *George Andrew Rankin*
12 Richmond Hill Road, Greenwich CT 06831, 203 625 0071, Fax: 203 625 0065. Called: Nov 1980, Inner Temple, AB (Harvard), MA, LLB (Cantab)

Sreenevasan *Gopal*
and Member Malaysia. Called: Nov 1993, Middle Temple, LLB (Hons)(Warwick)

Sreenivasan *Rajesh*
94 Jalan Angin Laut, Singapore 1648, 00 65 5453851, and Member Singapore Bar. Called: July 1993, Middle Temple, LLB (Hons)

Staff *Marcus Richard*
Brunschwig Wittmer, 13, Quai de L'ile, 1211 Geneva 11, 4122 781 33 22, Fax: 4122 781 31 00, International Commercial Arbitration Law. Called: Nov 1994, Inner Temple, BA (York)

Stavrou *Stavros*
60 Dighenis Akritas Avenue, PO Box 6620, Nicosia, Cyprus, 00357 2 756932, Fax: 00357 2 757693, and Member Cyprus Bar. Called: Nov 1993, Gray's Inn, LLB (Sheff)

Steel *Simon Arthur*
Simpson. Thacher & Bartlett, 425 Lexington Avenue, New York, NY 10017-3954, 001 212 455 3789, Fax: 001 212 455 2502, and Member New York. Called: Feb 1992, Lincoln's Inn, MA (Hons) (Cambs), LLM (Chicago)

Stephens-Ofner *John Alfred*
Lersnerstrasse 5 A, 85579 Neubiberg. Called: Nov 1966, Middle Temple, MA (Oxon)

Stesin *Mrs Vasantha*
6 Amber Close, Brighton, Victoria 3186, (03) 9596 0697, and Member Australian Capital Territory Victoria, Singapore Bar. Called: Nov 1990, Lincoln's Inn, LLB (Wales), LLM (Lond)

Stoneham *Ms Nicole Holly Marie*
Attorney General's Chambers, Global House, 43 Church Street, Hamilton HM 12, (809) 292 2463, Fax: (809) 292 3608, and Member Bermuda Bar. Called: Nov 1992, Gray's Inn, BA, LLB

Stratford *Jonathan Charles*
Bailhouse, Labesse, P O Box 207, St Helier, Jersey, and Member Jersey Bar. Called: Oct 1995, Gray's Inn, LLB

Stuart-Moore *Michael QC (1990)*
Supreme Court. Called: July 1966, Middle Temple

Stubbs *Michael James*
DreamWorks, 10 Universal City Plaza, Building 10, Universal City, California 91608 U.S.A, 818 7336000, Fax: 818 7336194. Called: Oct 1993, Gray's Inn, LLB (Buck'ham)

Stylianou *Miss Eleni Byron*
Called: Nov 1994, Gray's Inn, LLB (Lond)

Subraa
Called: Nov 1996, Lincoln's Inn, LLB (Hons)

Subramaniam *Miss Pushpakantha*
Level 40, Menara Lion, No 165 Jalan Ampang, P O Box 12485, 50780 Kuala Lumpur, 03-4677868, Fax: 03-4666546, and Member Malaysia Bar. Called: Nov 1994, Inner Temple, LLB (Hons)(Lond)

Subramaniam *Miss Sumitra R*
Called: July 1996, Middle Temple, LLB (Hons)(Wales)

Subramaniam Eliatamby *Nathan*
Called: July 1995, Middle Temple, LLB (Hons), LLM

Sudin *Miss Suhana*
Called: Nov 1995, Lincoln's Inn, LLB (Hons)

Sugden *Paul Birkby*
Ogier & Le Masurier, Pirouet House, Union Street, St Helier, Jersey JE4 8WZ, 01534 504000, Fax: 01534 35328, and Member Jersey Bar. Called: July 1983, Lincoln's Inn, BA,ACIB

Sugunaretnam *Miss Yogarani*
Called: Mar 1996, Middle Temple, LLB (Hons)(Lond)

Suhara *Miss Binte Mohd Said*
603 9583857, Fax: 603 9583859. Called: Nov 1996, Lincoln's Inn, LLB (Hons)(Lond)

Sultan *Hamid*
M/S Khattar Wong & Partners, 80 Raffles Place, [H]25-01 UOB Plaza 1, \ingapore 0104, 5356844, Fax: 5351606, and Member Singapore Bar. Called: July 1994, Lincoln's Inn, LLB (Hons)

Sum *Chin Liang*
Called: July 1995, Lincoln's Inn, LLB (Hons)

Sumner *Miss Michaela Simone*
Graham Thompson & Co, P.O.Box N272, Nassau N.P, 00 1 242 322 4130, Fax: 00 1 242 328 1069, and Member Bahamas. Called: July 1997, Middle Temple, LLB (Hons)

Sundaram *Subramanian*
Advocate & Solicitor in the Republic of Singapore. Called: Nov 1993, Middle Temple, LLB (Hons)(Lond)

Sundararaj *Miss Aneeta Rajah*
60 4 7310049. Called: Nov 1996, Middle Temple, LLB (Hons)(Wales)

Supaiyah *Dravida Maran*
Called: Mar 1998, Lincoln's Inn, LLB (Hons)

Suppayan *Miss Malarkodi*
Called: Nov 1995, Lincoln's Inn, LLB (Hons)

Suppayya *Gogulakannan s/o*
Called: July 1997, Lincoln's Inn, LLB (Hons)(Lond)

Suppiah *Arul*
Called: Nov 1997, Middle Temple, LLB (Hons)(Lond)

Suppiah *Krishnamurthi*
Called: July 1996, Middle Temple, LLB (Hons)(Lond)

Suppiah *Sarasvathy*
Called: July 1997, Lincoln's Inn, LLB (Hons)(Leeds)

Suresh *Veloo*
Called: July 1994, Lincoln's Inn, LLB (Hons, Lond)

Sureshan *T. Kulasingam*
Called: July 1996, Middle Temple, LLB (Hons)(Lond)

Surjit *Miss Belinda Kaur*
Called: Nov 1997, Lincoln's Inn, LLB (Hons)(Thames)

Surman *Giles Mark*
Called: Nov 1997, Gray's Inn, BSc (Wales)

Suttill *Brian*
52 Huntsman Lane, Stamford Bridge, York YO4 1ET, 01759 372 896, Fax: 01759 372 896, and Member Hong Kong Bar York Chambers, 14 Toft Green, York, YO1 1JT. Called: Nov 1970, Gray's Inn, LLB (Leeds), Dip L.D. (Ottawa), ACI Arb

Sutton *Mrs Joyah Junella*
P.O.Box 534, Main Street, Charlestown, Nevis, 00 1 869 469 5158/1326, Fax: 00 1 869 469 5834, and Member St Kitts & Nevis. Called: July 1993, Middle Temple, LLB (Hons), BA, LEC, ACIArb

Suvvaru *Miss Sonali Rao*
Called: July 1997, Gray's Inn, BA, LLB

Svoboda *Marek John Julian*
Neklauova 14, 128 00 Prague 2, 0042 2 2185 5001/5, Fax: 0042 2 2185 5055, and Member Czech Bar. Called: July 1986, Lincoln's Inn, MA (Cantab), MSc (Lond)

Swain *Miss Hadassah Annette*
Bain & Co, P O Box F-44533, Freeport, Grand Bahama, (242) 352 5971, Fax: (242) 352 6075, and Member Bahamas Bar. Called: July 1997, Gray's Inn, LLB (Lond)

Swami *Miss Sobana*
c/o Hillborne & Co, No 1 Colombo Court, [H]09-01, 3362882, Fax: 3362886, and Member Singapore. Called: July 1996, Middle Temple, LLB (Hons)

Swartz *Bruce Carlton*
U.S. Department of Justice, Criminal
Division, Washington DC 20530, 202-514-
9906, Fax: 202-514-9412, and Member
United States of America. Called: July 1997,
Middle Temple, BA, JD (Yale)

Swee *Colin Lay Keong*
24 Jalan Ladang, Palm Grove, Klang,
Selangor 41200, Malaysia, 60 3 3326200,
and Member Malaysia Bar. Called: Nov 1993,
Lincoln's Inn, LLB (Hons, Sheff)

Sweeting *Roy William Mark*
Called: Nov 1997, Lincoln's Inn, LLB (Hons)

Swetenham *Richard Clement*
European Commission, L-2920, 00 352 4301
32400, Fax: 00 352 4301 33190. Called: Nov
1974, Middle Temple, BA (Oxon)

Sy *Choon Yen*
Called: July 1996, Inner Temple, LLB
(Manchester)

Syed *Yahya*
26 Maria Avenue, 241 1883/5338188, Fax:
533 6100, Advocate & Solicitor, Supreme
Court, Singapore Commissioner for Oaths
and Member Singapore Bar. Called: July
1981, Inner Temple

Syed Abdullah *Syed Faisal*
Called: Nov 1994, Lincoln's Inn, LLB
(Hons)(Sheff)

Syed Abu Bakar *Miss Sharifah
Mazwin*
Called: July 1993, Lincoln's Inn, BA (Hons)

Syed-Mohamed *Miss Sharifah
Saeedah*
Khairuddin, Ngiam & Tan, Advocates &
Solicitors, Lot 16.03, 16th Floor, Wisma,
Nusantara, Jalan Punchak off, Jalan P
Ramlee, 50250 Kuala Lumpur, 6 03
2382388/2305081, Fax: 6 03 2301994, and
Member Malaysia Bar. Called: July 1995,
Gray's Inn, LLB (E.Anglia)

Sykes *Richard John Davies*
Nestle S.A., Avenue Nestle 55, 1800 Vevey,
Switzerland, 021 924 3429. Called: July
1981, Gray's Inn, BA, LLM

Symeonidou *Miss Eleni*
Called: Nov 1997, Lincoln's Inn, LLB
(Hons)(Lond)

Sze *Ge Pek*
Called: Nov 1996, Middle Temple, LLB
(Hons)(Lond)

Sze-Ling *Miss Shum*
Called: Nov 1993, Inner Temple, LLB, LLM

Szeto *Benjamin*
Called: July 1997, Lincoln's Inn, LLB (Hons)

Sziklai *Mrs Siew Fong*
738 S.E. 8th St, Ocala FL 34471, (352) 620
8033. Called: July 1995, Middle Temple, LLB
(Hons)

Taggart *Patrick Joseph*
Royal Courts of Justice, Belfast, and Member
Northern Ireland Bar. Called: Mar 1997,
Gray's Inn, LLB

Tai *Cheh Seak*
Called: July 1997, Lincoln's Inn, LLB
(Hons)(Lond)

Tait *Ms Arabella Elizabeth Connel
Cargill*
Faculty of Advocates, Advocates Library,
Parliament House, Edinburgh, Scotland EH1,
and Member Scottish Bar. Called: Oct 1993,
Inner Temple, BA, LLM

Talib *Miss Muna Mohamad*
Called: Nov 1996, Lincoln's Inn, LLB
(Hons)(Lond)

Tam *Chee Jack*
Called: Nov 1997, Lincoln's Inn, LLB
(Hons)(Lond)

Tan *Adrian Chong Jin*
Called: July 1995, Middle Temple, LLB
(Hons)

Tan *Miss Ai Ling Joanna*
Called: July 1996, Middle Temple, LLB
(Hons)(Kent)

Tan *Miss Ai Tin*
Called: Nov 1996, Lincoln's Inn, LLB
(Hons)(Lond)

Tan *Aik Yong*
Called: July 1994, Lincoln's Inn, LLB (Hons)

Tan *Miss Alison Geck-Chin*
c/o Drew & Napier, 20 Raffles Place,
Singapore 048620, (65) 535 0733, Fax:
JURES RS 21361, and Member Singapore
Bar. Called: July 1994, Lincoln's Inn, BA
(Hons)

Tan *Ms Anastasia Pei Pei*
Chew, Tan & Lim, Asia Insurance Building,
No 1 China Street, 10200 Penang, West
Malaysia, and Member Malaysia Bar.
Called: July 1994, Gray's Inn, LLB (Lond)

Tan *Andrew Pheng Lock*
Called: July 1994, Middle Temple, LLB
(Hons)(Lond)

Tan *Aylwin Wee En*
065 2543513. Called: July 1997, Middle
Temple, BA (Hons)(Kent)

Tan *Bak Leng*
Called: July 1997, Lincoln's Inn, LLB
(Hons)(Leics)

Tan *Beng Lok Edwin*
Sembawang Marine & Logistic, Ltd,
6639244, and Member Singapore Bar.
Called: July 1995, Middle Temple, LLB
(Hons) (Lond)

Tan *Bernard E Wei*
Called: July 1997, Lincoln's Inn, LLB (Hons)

Tan *Boon Khai*
10 Palm Drive, Singapore 456490, 4483600.
Called: July 1996, Lincoln's Inn, LLB
(Hons)(Notts)

Tan *Brian Yang Seng*
Called: Nov 1996, Middle Temple, LLB
(Hons)(Lond)

Tan *Chee Siang*
Called: Nov 1995, Middle Temple, LLB
(Hons)

Tan *Miss Cheng Foong*
Called: July 1996, Middle Temple, LLB
(Hons)(Leic)

Tan *Chia Loong*
Called: July 1995, Middle Temple, LLB
(Hons) (Kent)

Tan *Miss Chin Chin*
Called: July 1997, Middle Temple, LLB
(Hons)(Wales)

Tan *Chin Tee*
Called: July 1996, Middle Temple, LLB
(Hons)(Sheff)

Tan *Miss Choo Lye*
Called: July 1994, Lincoln's Inn, LLB (Hons)

Tan *Choo Teck*
Kington & Tan, Advocates & Solicitors,
Suite 6, 4th Floor, Wisma Ann Koai, 67 Jalan
Ampang, Kuala Lumpur 50450, 03 238
2128, Fax: 03 201 2272, and Member
Malaysia Bar. Called: Nov 1992, Lincoln's
Inn, LLB (Hons)(Lond)

Tan *Miss Christine Mai Yean*
Called: July 1997, Lincoln's Inn, LLB
(Hons)(Wales)

Tan *Chuan Thye*
M/S Allen & Gledhill, 36 Robinson Road
[H]18-01, City House, Singapore 068877,
225 1611, Fax: 224 8210, and Member
Singapore Bar. Called: July 1990, Middle
Temple, BA (Oxon)

Tan *Chun Hou*
Called: July 1997, Lincoln's Inn, LLB
(Hons)(Lond)

Tan *Clarence Keng Loon*
and Member Singapore. Called: Nov 1995,
Lincoln's Inn, LLB (Hons) (Leeds)

Tan *Colin Teck-Ee*
Called: July 1997, Middle Temple, BA
(Hons)

Tan *Dennis Lip Fong*
9 Temasek Boulevard, [H]17 - 01, Suntec
Tower 2, 3367727, Fax: 3360110, and
Member Singapore. Called: July 1996,
Middle Temple, LLB (Hons)(Notts)

Tan *Miss Diana Mei-Ying*
Advocate & Solicitor of Singapore.
Called: July 1992, Lincoln's Inn, LLB (Hons)

Tan *Dominic Dwayne Kok Heng*
18th Floor Shell Tower, 50 Raffles Place,
Singapore, 048623, 2201911, Fax: 2244118,
and Member Singapore Bar. Called: July
1992, Lincoln's Inn, LLB (Hons) (Bucks),
LLM (London)

Tan *Edmund Yen Kuan*
N M Rothschild & Sons Ltd, The Exchange,
20 Cecil Street, [H]09-00, Singapore 0104,
65 535 8311, Fax: 65 535 9109. Called: Nov
1992, Middle Temple, LLB (Hons, Lond),
MBA (City)

Tan *Miss Emily Jee Neo*
and Member Malaysia. Called: July 1996,
Lincoln's Inn, LLB (Hons), BEc (Hons), MBA
(Hons), LLM (Hons)

Tan *Ernest Peng Ern*
43 Mayflower Place, (0065) 459 0367, Fax: (0065) 452 0260, and Member Singapore Bar. Called: July 1996, Lincoln's Inn, LLB (Hons)(Leeds), LLM (Cantab), ACIArb

Tan *Miss Esther Ai Ping*
44 Richards Avenue, 2885943, and Member Singapore. Called: July 1994, Lincoln's Inn, LLB (Hons)

Tan *Eu Gin*
Called: July 1996, Middle Temple, LLB (Hons)(Hull)

Tan *Gerald Eng Chan*
Called: July 1996, Gray's Inn, LLB (Wales)

Tan *Hee Liang*
Tan See Swan & Co, Advocates & Solicitors, No 1 Park Road [H]04-49, People's Park Complex, Singapore 0105, 5351442/5324036/5344252, Fax: 5333609, and Member Singapore Bar. Called: July 1988, Inner Temple, B Soc Sc (Keele), LLM (Singapore)

Tan *Heok Ping Joshua*
Called: Nov 1996, Middle Temple, LLB (Hons)(Keele)

Tan *Hock Boon David*
Block 718, Hougang Avenue 2, [H]04-313, 65-2886011. Called: Nov 1996, Gray's Inn, LLB

Tan *Miss Hsiao Ling*
Called: July 1996, Middle Temple, LLB (Hons)(Warw)

Tan *Miss Hui Mei*
M/S Drew & Napier, 20 Raffles Place [H]17-00, Ocean Towers, 2803136 (Resid), Fax: 2803958, and Member Singapore Bar. Called: July 1995, Middle Temple, LLB (Hons)

Tan *Miss Hui Tsing*
Called: July 1995, Middle Temple, LLB (Hons)

Tan *Miss Ivy*
26 Sennett Avenue, S 467034, (065) 2448556. Called: July 1997, Gray's Inn, LLB

Tan *Miss Jacqueline*
Called: Nov 1996, Middle Temple, LLB (Hons)(Sheff)

Tan *James Chee Hau*
C/O HSBC Investment Bank Asia, Level 15, 1 Q.R.C., and Member Singapore Bar. Called: July 1993, Middle Temple, BA (Hons)

Tan *Miss Jeannie*
and Member Singapore Bar. Called: July 1993, Lincoln's Inn, LLB (Hons)

Tan *Jonanthan See Leh*
Called: July 1996, Lincoln's Inn, LLB (Hons)(Lond)

Tan *Ms June Sooi Ee*
Box 225, Tanjung Aru 89458, Kota Kinabalu, Sabah, Malaysia, 088 221262, Fax: 088 218043, and Member Sabah, Malaysia. Called: July 1994, Lincoln's Inn, LLB (Hons)

Tan *Kay Kian*
Called: July 1995, Middle Temple, LLB (Hons)

Tan *Kee Tay*
Called: Nov 1997, Lincoln's Inn, LLB (Hons)(Lond)

Tan *Kelvin David Sia Khoon*
Called: Nov 1996, Middle Temple, LLB (Hons)(Hull)

Tan *Kelvin Miang Ser*
180 Tai Keng Gardens. Called: July 1996, Lincoln's Inn, LLB (Hons)(Leeds), ACIArb, ASIArb

Tan *Khee Guan*
and Member Malaysia Bar. Called: July 1992, Middle Temple, LLB (Hons) (Leeds)

Tan *Kheng-Guan*
Called: Nov 1996, Middle Temple, BA (Hons)(Keele)

Tan *Kian Yuap*
and Member Malaysia. Called: July 1996, Lincoln's Inn, LLB (Hons)(Lond)

Tan *Miss Kim Suan*
Called: Nov 1996, Middle Temple, LLB (Hons)(Lond)

Tan *Kok Siang*
and Member Singapore Bar. Called: Apr 1991, Gray's Inn, LLB, MSIArb

Tan *Kong Yam*
Kadir, Tan & Ramli, 8th Floor, Sufuan Tower, 80 Jalan Ampang, 50450 Kuala Lumpur, 6 03 2382888, Fax: 6 03 2388431, and Member Malaysia Bar. Called: July 1996, Lincoln's Inn, LLB (Hons), LLM (LSE)

Tan *Kwong Ming Gerald*
Called: Nov 1994, Lincoln's Inn, LLB (Hons)(Lond)

Tan *Lai An*
C/O Tan & Lee, Advocates & Solicitors, Suite 2.04 2nd Level, Wisma MBF 37c Jalan Meldrum, 80000 Johor Bahru, Johor, (607) 2239259, Fax: (607) 2239142, and Member Malaysia Bar. Called: July 1989, Lincoln's Inn, LLB (Lond)

Tan *Miss Lai Tee*
Called: Nov 1997, Lincoln's Inn, LLB (Hons)(Leeds)

Tan *Laren Kian Seng*
Called: July 1994, Lincoln's Inn, LLB (Hons)

Tan *Dr Lauren Guet Lan*
1 Temasek Avenue, Millenia Tower, 23rd Floor, (65) 4322100, Fax: (65) 4322169, and Member Singapore Bar. Called: Nov 1993, Middle Temple, LLB (Hons), PH.D (B'ham)

Tan *Miss Lay Keng*
Called: Feb 1994, Inner Temple, LLB (Essex)

Tan *Miss Lay Khim*
Called: July 1996, Middle Temple, LLB (Hons)(Bris)

Tan *Leroy Kok Heng*
Called: Nov 1996, Middle Temple, LLB (Hons)

Tan *Miss Lip Sim*
Called: July 1997, Middle Temple, LLB (Hons)(Lond)

Tan *Miss Lu Gim*
Allen & Gledhill, 36 Robinson Road [H]18-01, City House, Singapore 0106, 2251611, Fax: 2254950, and Member Singapore Bar. Called: Nov 1991, Lincoln's Inn, BA (Hons) (Kent)

Tan *Lye Huat*
Called: Nov 1997, Middle Temple, LLB (Hons)(Lond)

Tan *Mark Jin Leong*
Called: July 1996, Middle Temple

Tan *Miss May Yee*
Called: Nov 1997, Middle Temple, LLB (Hons)

Tan *Miss Mei-Yen*
Called: July 1995, Middle Temple, LLB (Hons) (Warw)

Tan *Miss Michelle Ai Ling*
Called: Mar 1997, Middle Temple, LLB (Hons)(Bris)

Tan *Ms Michelle Su May*
Called: July 1995, Middle Temple, LLB (Hons)

Tan *Miss Peck Yen*
Called: July 1997, Lincoln's Inn, LLB (Hons) (Lond)

Tan *Miss Ping Ying*
and Member Malaysia. Called: July 1996, Inner Temple, LLB (Wolverhampton), MA

Tan *Miss Poh Hua*
Called: July 1995, Lincoln's Inn, LLB (Hons)

Tan *Miss Reina Chui-Lin*
Called: Nov 1997, Gray's Inn, LLB (Nott'm)

Tan *Richard Seng Chew*
Called: Nov 1996, Inner Temple, LLB (Lond)

Tan *Miss See Peng*
Called: July 1994, Lincoln's Inn, LLB (Hons) (Leic)

Tan *Miss Selene Ling Ling*
c/o Allen & Gledhill, 36 Robinson Road, [H]18-01 City House, 4207632, Fax: 2241574, and Member Singapore. Called: July 1994, Middle Temple, LLB (Hons)(B'ham)

Tan *Miss Sharon Suyin*
Called: July 1996, Lincoln's Inn, LLB (Hons)(Lond)

Tan *Miss Sheh-Lynn*
and Member Malaysia Bar. Called: July 1991, Middle Temple, LLB (Hons) (Wales)

Tan *Miss Sherain Ai Seok*
Called: Mar 1997, Lincoln's Inn, LLB (Hons)(Lond)

Tan *Miss Shirley Ching Ping*
Harry Ellas & Partners, 79 Robinson Road, [H]16-03 CPF Building, Singapore 068897, 2235006, Fax: 2262360, and Member Singapore Bar. Called: July 1994, Middle Temple, LLB (Hons)(Newc), LLM (Lond)

F

Tan *Miss Siew Siew*
Called: July 1997, Gray's Inn, LLB (Bris)

Tan *Miss Siew Wai*
and Member Singapore Bar. Called: July 1992, Lincoln's Inn, LLB (Hons) (Bucks)

Tan *Miss Siew Yung*
Called: July 1997, Lincoln's Inn, LLB (Hons)

Tan *Sin Oon*
Supreme Court of Singapore, St Andrews Road, Singapore 178957. Called: July 1995, Middle Temple, LLB (Hons) (Bris)

Tan *Miss Soek Phee*
Called: July 1996, Middle Temple, LLB (Hons)(Wales)

Tan *Stanley Richard Sia Kong*
Called: July 1995, Inner Temple, LLB

Tan *Miss Sue Ann*
Called: July 1997, Lincoln's Inn, LLB(Hons)(Wales)

Tan *Ms Sui Lin*
and Member Singapore Bar. Called: July 1991, Middle Temple, BA (Hons) (Cambs)

Tan *Miss Suzanne Sie Gek*
Called: Nov 1996, Lincoln's Inn, LLB (Hons)(Bucks)

Tan *Miss Swee Lin Corrine*
Called: July 1997, Gray's Inn, LLB (Bristol)

Tan *Miss Tammy*
Called: July 1996, Middle Temple, LLB (Hons)(Lond)

Tan *Teck Howe*
Called: July 1996, Lincoln's Inn, BA (Hons)

Tan *Teck Kiong*
Called: Nov 1997, Lincoln's Inn, LLB (Hons)(Thames.V)

Tan *Teng Ta Benedict*
Called: July 1997, Middle Temple, LLB (Hons)

Tan *Terence Li-Chern*
Messrs Wong Partnership, 80 Raffles Place, [H] 58-01 UOB Plaza 1, (65) 539 7503, Fax: (65) 532 5722, and Member Singapore Bar. Called: July 1995, Inner Temple, LLB (Kent)

Tan *Tian Luh*
Called: July 1996, Lincoln's Inn, LLB (Hons)(B'ham)

Tan *Tiong Hian*
Called: July 1994, Lincoln's Inn, LLB (Hons)

Tan *Tuan Wee*
Called: Nov 1995, Middle Temple, LLB (Hons)

Tan *Miss Valerie Whei Tet*
Called: July 1995, Middle Temple, BA (Hons)

Tan *Miss Wei Mann Germaine*
Called: Nov 1997, Lincoln's Inn, LLB (Hons)

Tan *Miss Wei-Lyn*
Called: July 1995, Middle Temple, LLB (Hons)

Tan *Winston Kheng Huang*
Called: July 1997, Lincoln's Inn, LLB (Hons)

Tan *Miss Yang Wah*
Called: July 1997, Lincoln's Inn, LLB (Hons)(Lond)

Tan *Miss Yeun Fui*
Skrine & Co, Straits Trading Building, 4 Leboh Pasar Besar, 50050 Kuala Lumpur, 03-2945111, Fax: 03-2934327, and Member Malaysia Bar. Called: July 1994, Lincoln's Inn, LLB (Hons)

Tan *Yew Hwee*
Called: Nov 1997, Middle Temple, B.Soc.Sc (Hons), (Singapore), LLB, (Lond)

Tan *Miss Ying Wee*
Called: July 1995, Middle Temple, LLB (Hons)

Tang *Miss Ai Leen*
Called: Mar 1998, Middle Temple, LLB (Hons)(B'ham)

Tang *Edmund Ming-Wai*
Called: Nov 1994, Gray's Inn, LLB (Lond)

Tang *Ms Fong Har*
Advocate & Solicitor of the Supreme Court of Singapore and Member Singapore Bar. Called: July 1990, Inner Temple, LLB (Hons) Singapore

Tang *Jay Son*
Called: July 1997, Lincoln's Inn, LLB (Hons)(Lond)

Tang *Kenneth Wai Loong*
80 Chay Yan Street, [H] 02-08, Singapore 160080, Singapore, 2231513, Fax: 7487936. Called: Nov 1993, Middle Temple, LLB (Hons)(Newc), LLM (London)

Tang *Kwong Leung*
and Member Hong Kong Bar. Called: Feb 1992, Gray's Inn, B.Soc.Sc (Hong Kong), MSW (Hong Kong), MSc (LSE),LLB (Lond), LLM (Cantab), Ph.D (Berkley)

Tang *Michael Vee Mun*
Called: July 1995, Lincoln's Inn, LLB (Hons)

Tang *Quin Choy*
Called: July 1997, Middle Temple, LLB (Hons)(Lond)

Tang *Ms Suet Yean*
and Member Malaysia. Called: July 1993, Lincoln's Inn, LLB (Hons)

Tangavellu *Resebalingam*
Called: July 1995, Lincoln's Inn, LLB (Hons)

Tay *Miss April Glenys*
Called: Nov 1996, Lincoln's Inn, LLB (Hons)(Lond)

Tay *Ms Dorothy*
18 Sin Ming Walk [H] 02-03, Bishan Park Condominium, Singapore 575569, 65 4531567, and Member Singapore Bar. Called: July 1993, Middle Temple, LLB (Hons)(Lond)

Tay *Miss Elaine Ling Yan*
Called: July 1997, Middle Temple, LLB (Hons)

Tay *Eng Kwee*
Called: July 1994, Lincoln's Inn, LLB (Hons)

Tay *Francis Chien Thuan*
Called: Oct 1994, Middle Temple, LLB (Hons)(Kent)

Tay *Miss Hwee Hua*
and Member Singapore Bar. Called: Nov 1995, Middle Temple, LLB (Lond)

Tay *Miss Jin Keng*
Called: Nov 1995, Middle Temple, LLB (Hons)(Lond)

Tay *Lai Eng*
Called: Nov 1996, Lincoln's Inn, LLB (Hons)

Tay *Miss Li Shing*
Called: July 1997, Gray's Inn, LLB (Bris)

Tay *Miss Sock Kheng*
Called: July 1996, Lincoln's Inn, LLB (Hons)(Lond)

Tay *Wee Chong*
Called: July 1994, Lincoln's Inn, LLB (Hons)

Tay *Miss Yien Ling Daisy*
Called: July 1994, Middle Temple, LLB (Hons)(Lond)

Taye *Miss Lynette Wei Ching*
Called: July 1997, Lincoln's Inn, LLB (Hons)(Nott'm)

Taylor *Ms Wendy Rutledge*
Risk Enterprise Management Ltd, 59 Maiden Lane, New York, New York 10038, 212 5306944, Fax: 212 5306997, and Member State of New Jersey Bar. Called: July 1987, Lincoln's Inn, BA, H.Dip. Pers.Man, Dip Law, JD

Taylor-Carroll De Mueller *Mrs Athena Robina*
2904 Viceroy Avenue, Forestville, Maryland 20747, and Member US Sup Ct, US Ct of App(DC Cir),US Dist Ct (DC), Dist of Columbia Ct of Appeals. Called: July 1952, Lincoln's Inn, MA,LLB (Cantab), JD, LLM (Miami)

Teck *Tan Yew*
Called: Mar 1998, Gray's Inn, LLB (Lond)

Tee *Miss Clare Antoinette*
and Member Guernsey Bar. Called: Nov 1995, Inner Temple, LLB (Manc)

Tee *Miss Dawn Pei Sze*
Called: July 1996, Lincoln's Inn, LLB (Hons)(Notts)

Tee *Miss En Peng*
Called: July 1997, Lincoln's Inn, LLB (Hons)(Lond)

Tee *Kien Moon*
Called: July 1994, Lincoln's Inn, LLB (Hons)

Tee *Ling Zhi*
Called: Nov 1997, Lincoln's Inn, LLB (Hons)

Teh *Miss Ee-Von*
Called: July 1997, Middle Temple, LLB (Hons)(Leics)

Teh *Miss Hong Koon*
Called: Nov 1997, Lincoln's Inn, LLB (Hons)(E.Lond)

Teh *John Teong Beng*
Called: Nov 1995, Middle Temple, LLB (Hons)(Wales)

Teh *Ms Julie Chooi Gan*
Dorairaj, Low & Teh, Wisman AMGM, 1st Floor, No 57 Jalan Hang Lekiu, 50100 Kuala Lumpur, 03 2011136, Fax: 03 2010113, and Member Malaysia Bar. Called: Nov 1992, Gray's Inn, LLB (Lond)

Teh *Khang Suon*
c/o Azalina Chan & Chia, Advocates & Solictors, Lot 716, 7th Floor, Wisma, Cosway, 88 Jalan Raja Chulan, 50200 Kuala Lumpur, 603 2488625, Fax: 603 2411913. Called: Nov 1996, Gray's Inn, LLB (Sheff)

Teh *Lawrence Kee Wee*
C/O Rodyk & Davidson, 9 Raffles Place, [H]55-00 Republic Plaza, 65 225 2626, Fax: 65 225 1838, and Member Singapore Bar. Called: Nov 1992, Inner Temple, LLB (Lond)

Teh *Lip Jin*
and Member Malaysia Bar. Called: July 1994, Gray's Inn, BA (Kent)

Teh *Miss Mui Kim*
1 Queensway [H]14-65, Fax: 334 3623, and Member Singapore Bar. Called: July 1995, Middle Temple, LLB (Hons)

Teh *Miss Wee Tee*
Called: July 1995, Middle Temple, LLB (Hons) (Wales)

Teh *Miss Yuen Ting*
Called: July 1997, Lincoln's Inn, LLB (Hons)(Nott'm)

Telemaque *Marc Timothy*
Called: May 1993, Gray's Inn, LLB (Buckinghamshi)

Teng *Hin Fatt*
Block 128, Lorong Ah Soo, [H]12-314, Singapore 1953. Called: Nov 1993, Lincoln's Inn, LLB (Hons, Lond)

Teng *Miss Joanna*
Salina, Lim Kim Chuan & Co, Advocates & Solicitors, No 28-c Lorong Abu Siti, 10400 Penang, 228 2089, Fax: 228 2093, and Member Malaysia. Called: July 1995, Lincoln's Inn, LLB (Hons)

Tengara *Miss Mestika*
Called: Nov 1996, Lincoln's Inn, LLB (Hons)(Kent)

Tengku Ismail *Miss Tengku Ida Adura*
Lloyd Fernando & Razak, Suite 1203, 12th Floor, Wisma Hangsam, No 1 Jalan Hang Lekir, 50000 Kuala Lumpur, 603 2308036, Fax: 603 2320312, and Member High Court of Malaya. Called: July 1996, Lincoln's Inn, LLB (Hons)(Notts)

Teo *Miss Bee Leay*
99 Sunset Way, Singapore 2159, 4691221, Fax: 4663583, and Member New York State Bar. Called: July 1993, Middle Temple, LLB (Hons, Kent), LLM (Boston, USA)

Teo *Chee Kang*
Called: July 1994, Lincoln's Inn, LLB (Hons, Lond)

Teo *Eu Jin Nicholas*
Called: July 1996, Middle Temple, LLB (Hons)(Leic)

Teo *Eugene Weng Kuan*
Supreme Court, City Hall, St Andrews Road. Called: July 1995, Middle Temple, LLB (Hons) (Hull)

Teo *Francis Teng Siu*
Called: Nov 1996, Lincoln's Inn, LLB (Hons)(Lond)

Teo *Miss Geok Yen*
Called: Nov 1994, Middle Temple, LLB (Hons)

Teo *Miss Hwee Ping*
55 Market Street, 08-01 Sinsov Building, Singapore 0104, 538 3177, Fax: 532 5554, and Member Singapore Bar. Called: Nov 1991, Gray's Inn, BA (Kent)

Teo *Miss Josephine Siew Ing*
Called: July 1995, Middle Temple, LLB (Hons) (Hull)

Teo *Miss Yi-Ling*
Called: Nov 1996, Middle Temple, LLB (Hons)(L'pool)

Teoh *Ms Gim See*
Called: Nov 1996, Lincoln's Inn, BA (Hons)(E.Anglia)

Tey *Tsun Hang*
Called: July 1995, Gray's Inn, LLB

Thacker *Charles Malcom Belford*
Messrs Vibert & Valpy, Advocates, 8 Duhamel Place, St Helier, Jersey JE2 4XA, 0534 888666, Fax: 0534 888555, and Member Jersey Bar. Called: Nov 1970, Lincoln's Inn, MA (Hons)

Thai *Jiin Peir*
No 46B Lorong Ismail, 81000 Kulain, Johor, 07 6624732/3/6625057, Fax: 07 6624639, and Member Malaysia Bar. Called: Nov 1993, Lincoln's Inn, LLB (Hons)

Thakar *Miss Rina Rajendra*
Called: July 1997, Gray's Inn, LLB (Warwick)

Tham *Miss Melissa Lyn-li*
Called: July 1995, Middle Temple, LLB (Hons)

Tham *Soong Meng Edwin*
Allen & Overy Legal Services, Moscow, Dmitrovskiy Pereulok, 9, 103031 Moscow, 7 501 258 3111, Fax: 7 501 258 3113, and Member New York Bar. Called: July 1989, Middle Temple, LLB [Nott'm]

Tham *Miss Swee Hiong*
Overseas Chinese Banking Corp, 65 Chulia Street, 5357222/5302929. Called: July 1995, Middle Temple, LLB (Hons)

Thampuran *Miss Sandhia*
and Member Singapore Bar. Called: July 1995, Middle Temple, LLB (Hons)

Thanarajoo *Miss Frances Angeline*
Called: July 1994, Lincoln's Inn, LLB (Hons)

The *Miss Diana Hui Ling*
7 Temasek Boulevard, [H]15-01, Suntec Tower One, (065) 4566501/3375822, Fax: (065) 3372932, and Member Singapore. Called: July 1996, Middle Temple, LLB (Hons)(Bris)

Theodorides *Miss Melita-Despina*
Called: Mar 1997, Lincoln's Inn, LLB (Leics)

Theseira *Joseph Dominic*
Palakrishnan & Partners, Advocates & Solicitors, 1 Colombo Court, [H]07-13/14/15a, 3382294, Fax: 3391400, and Member Singapore Bar. Called: Nov 1991, Middle Temple, LLB (Hons) (Lond)

Thiagarajah *Miss Thanuja*
Called: July 1996, Lincoln's Inn, LLB (Hons)(Lond)

Thiagarajan *Anand*
and Member Singapore Bar. Called: July 1995, Lincoln's Inn, LLB (Hons)

Thinathayalan *Suppiah*
Called: July 1996, Inner Temple, LLB,LLM (Lond)

Thio *Miss Jean Puay Jin*
Called: July 1997, Lincoln's Inn, LLB (Hons)(Lond)

Thirumaney *Miss Manimala*
Called: Nov 1996, Lincoln's Inn, LLB (Hons)

Thng *Miss Hwei Lin*
Called: July 1993, Middle Temple, LLB (Hons)

Thomas *John*
34B Bayshore Road, The Bayshore, Tower 2b [H]18-02, 65-2452040, Law Society of Singapore. Called: Oct 1993, Gray's Inn, BA, B.Soc.Sci (Hons), (Singapore), LLB, (Manch)

Thompson *Miss Alison Mary*
Gilt Chambers, Hong Kong, 866 8233, Fax: 866 3932, and Member Hong Kong Bar. Called: July 1986, Middle Temple, BSc, LLB

Thompson *Mrs Diana Elizabeth*
La Hure, Rue des Cambrees, Torteral, Guerney GY8 0LD, 0481 65831, Fax: 0481 66160, and Member Royal Court of Guernsey. Called: Nov 1990, Inner Temple, LLB

Thompson *Gilbert Anselm*
McKinney, Bancroft & Hughes, P.O. Box F-40437, Freeport, (242) 352 7425-7, Fax: (242) 352 7214, and Member Bahamas Bar (September 1996). Called: July 1996, Gray's Inn, BA (Canada), LLB (Buck)

Thompson *James Kwasi*
James R Thompson & Company, Suite 31A, Kipling Building, P.O.Box F 42912, Freeport, GB, Bahamas, (242) 352 7451 2, Fax: (242) 352 7453, and Member Bahamas. Called: July 1997, Middle Temple, LLB (Hons)

Thompson *John David*
Ballyrawer House, Carrowdore, Co Down BT22 2HZ, 01247 861478, Fax: 01247 861095, QC (Northern Ireland) and Member Northern Ireland Bar Republic of Ireland Bar. Called: Nov 1992, Gray's Inn, LLB (Belfast)

Thompson *Kenneth Manour*
Called: Nov 1995, Gray's Inn, BA (W.Indies), LLB (Lond)

F

Thompson *Miss Lillian Amorella Elizabeth*
42 Rockford Ave, Daly City, CA 94015, U.S.A.. Called: Nov 1993, Inner Temple, LLB (Lond)

Thompson Alabi-Isama *Mrs Elizabeth*
Called: Nov 1994, Lincoln's Inn

Thomson *James Smith*
Gilt Chambers, Room 1001, Far East Finance Centre, 16 Harcourt Road, Central Hong Kong, 866 8233, Fax: 866 3932, and Member Hong Kong Bar. Called: July 1983, Lincoln's Inn, BA (Kent)

Thomson *Neil Clarke*
Des Voeux Chambers, 10/F Bank of East Asia Bldg, 10 Des Voeux Road, Central, Hong Kong, 2526 3071, Fax: 2810 5287, and Member Hong Kong Bar. Called: Nov 1994, Gray's Inn, BA, LLM, FTIHK

Thong *Ms Jessie Yuen Siew*
Rodyk and Davidson, 9 Raffles Place, [H] 55-01, 2252626, Fax: 2257511, and Member Singapore Bar. Called: Apr 1991, Gray's Inn, BA, LLM

Ti *Miss Chin Ming*
Paul Cheah & Associates, 3a Lorong Raja Bot, Klang, 03 344300, Fax: 03 3444301, and Member Malaysia Bar. Called: Nov 1994, Lincoln's Inn, LLB (Hons)(Hull)

Tiah *Miss Ee Laine*
Lee Hishammuddin, Advocates & Solicitors, 16th Floor, Wisma HLA, 50200 Kuala Lumpur, 03 2011681, Fax: 03 2011714, and Member Malaysia. Called: July 1996, Middle Temple, LLB (Hons)(Kent)

Tiang *Michael Ming Tee*
Called: July 1997, Middle Temple, LLB (Hons)(Wales)

Tibbo *Miss Heather Dorothy*
Messrs Ogier & Le Masurier, P O Box 404, Pirouet House, Union Street, St Helier, Jersey JE4 9WG, 01534 504000, Fax: 01534 35328, and Member Advocate of the Royal Court of Jersey. Called: Nov 1989, Middle Temple, LLB

Timms *Neil Richard Frederick Charles*
Maples & Calder, PO Box 309, George Town, Grand Cayman, 001 809949 8066, Fax: 001 809949 8080, and Member Cayman Bar. Called: Nov 1974, Inner Temple, MA (Cantab)

Timothis *Miss Alison*
Called: Nov 1995, Lincoln's Inn, LLB (Hons)

Timothy *Miss Sonia Agnes*
P.O.Box N3007, (242) 322 1141, Fax: (242) 322 2255. Called: July 1996, Lincoln's Inn, LLB (Hons)

Ting *Shu Kiong*
Called: July 1997, Lincoln's Inn, LLB (Hons)(Leeds)

Ting *Shu Leong*
Messrs Jayasuriya Kah & Co, Room 207, 2nd Floor, Wisma Sabah, P.O.Box 11350, 88815 Kota Kinabalu, Sabah, 088 242311 (W)/ 211742 (H), Fax: 088 231250, and Member Sabah. Called: July 1995, Lincoln's Inn, LLB (Hons)

Ting *Ms Sui Ing*
Called: July 1996, Lincoln's Inn, LLB (Hons)

Ting *Tiew Hee*
Called: Nov 1994, Lincoln's Inn, LLB (Hons)(Wales)

Tiong *Hok Chiun*
and Member Advocate of the High Court in Sabah & Sarawak, Malaysia. Called: July 1996, Lincoln's Inn, LLB (Hons)(Leeds)

Tiwary *Miss Anuradha*
Called: July 1996, Lincoln's Inn, LLB (Hons) (Lond)

Tobias *Douglas Guedella*
South Africa 031 301 1196, Fax: South Africa 031 301 2138, Barrister of South Africa. Called: July 1991, Middle Temple, B Com (Cape Town), Dip Juris (Witwaters, -rand), LLB (Natal), LLM (Natal)

Todd *Arnold James III*
Called: Mar 1998, Gray's Inn, BA (Ontario), LLB (Lond)

Toh *Miss Beng Suan*
Called: July 1995, Lincoln's Inn, LLB (Hons)

Toh *Jason Su Jin*
Ho Wong & Partners, 46 Tras Street, 2250271, Fax: 2250272, and Member Singapore Bar. Called: July 1995, Middle Temple, LLB (Hons)

Toh *Lean Seng*
Called: July 1997, Lincoln's Inn, LLB (Hons)(Lond)

Toh *Miss May Ching Jenny*
Messrs Toh Chin & Co, Advocates & Solicitors, No 21, 1st Floor, Jalan Dato, Abdul Rahman, 70000 Seremban, N.Sembilan, (06) 7635058/5059, Fax: (06) 7624308, and Member Malaysia. Called: Oct 1996, Lincoln's Inn, LLB (Hons)(Leic)

Toh *Miss Su Fen*
Called: July 1996, Lincoln's Inn, LLB (Hons)(Lond)

Tok *Miss Audrey*
M/S Allan & Gledhill, Unit 18.01 18th Floor, Public Bank Tower, 80000 Johor Bahru, (07) 2244422, Fax: (07) 2248718, and Member Malaysian Bar. Called: Nov 1994, Gray's Inn, BA (Kent)

Tok *Miss Julie Chwee Hwei*
Called: July 1995, Lincoln's Inn, LLB (Hons)

Tokunbo *Khamisi Mawuli*
Attorney General's Chambers, Global House, 43 Church Street, Hamilton 5-24, Bermuda, 809 292 2463, Fax: 809 292 3608. Called: Nov 1988, Inner Temple, BA (Ohio), LLB (Lond)

Tolia *Miss Dina Arun*
Called: July 1996, Lincoln's Inn, BA (Hons)(Warw)

Tong *Mrs Ah Pooi*
Fin d'Elez, 1261 Le Muids, (022) 366 4606, Fax: (022) 366 4606. Called: Nov 1988, Lincoln's Inn, LLB (Lond)

Tong *Kington Kum Loong*
Suite 6, 4th Floor, Wisma Ann Koai, 67 Jalan Ampang, 50450 Kuala Lumpur, 03-2382128, Fax: 03-2012272, and Member Malaysian Bar. Called: July 1992, Gray's Inn, LLB (Lond)

Tong *Raymond Wei Min*
C/O Shook Lin & Bok, 1 Robinson Road, [H]18-00 A1A Tower, 65-4394895, Fax: 65-5358577, and Member Singapore Bar. Called: Nov 1991, Middle Temple, LLB Hons (Nott'm)

Tong *Miss Tricia Min Wei*
43 Nim Green, and Member Singapore Bar. Called: July 1996, Lincoln's Inn, LLB (Hons)(Lond)

Touche Arends *Mrs Susan Ruth*
Steraloids Inc, P O Box 85, Newport, Rhode Island 02840, 401 848 5422, Fax: 401 848 5638. Called: Nov 1991, Gray's Inn, BFA (Canada), Dip in, Law, Professional, Certification, (Education)

Tracey *Andrew John*
Called: July 1996, Gray's Inn, B.Ed, MA (Reading), LLB

Tracey *Ms Gerardine Anne*
Called: Oct 1992, Lincoln's Inn, LLB(Hons)

Triay *Louis Bernard*
Louis W Triay & Partners, Suite C, 2nd Floor, Regal House, Queensway, 00 350 79423, Fax: 00 350 71405, and Member Gibraltar Bar. Called: July 1989, Middle Temple, LLB [Lond]

Tsang *David Kwok Kei*
Des Voeux Chambers, 10/F Bank of East Asia Bldg, 10 Des Voeux Road Central, Hong Kong, (852) 2526 3071, Fax: (852) 2810 5287, and Member Hong Kong Bar Attorney at Law of the Peoples Republic of China. Called: July 1994, Middle Temple, BSc(Hons)(Hong Kong), CPE (Manc), FRICS, ACIArb

Tsang *Miss Jennifer Chiu Chun*
1501 Two Pacific Place, 88 Queensway, Hong Kong, (852) 2840 1130, Fax: (852) 2810 0612, and Member Hong Kong Bar. Called: July 1994, Middle Temple, LLB (Hons)(Bris)

Tsang *Siu Wah*
Mei Foo Sun Chuen, 99c Broadway, 6/F, Kowloon, (852) 2785 7628, Fax: (852) 2785 7628, and Member Ontario. Called: Nov 1988, Middle Temple, LLB (Lond)

Tse *Hayson Ka Sze*
Hong Kong Government, Department of Justice, Queensway Government Office, Queensway, Hong Kong, 2867 2211, and Member Hong Kong Bar. Called: July 1995, Lincoln's Inn, LLB (Hons), Dip Chinese Law

Tse *Sammy Lai*
Called: Nov 1997, Middle Temple, LLB (Hons)

Tselingas *Charalambos Christophorou*
Called: Nov 1997, Lincoln's Inn, LLB
(Hons)(Leics)

Tsirides *Alexandros*
Called: Nov 1997, Lincoln's Inn, LLB (Hons)

Tsui *Chi Keung Wilfred*
Called: May 1996, Gray's Inn, BSc (Lond),
MBA (Hong Kong), MHA(New South Wales)

Tsui *Cho Man*
Called: Mar 1998, Middle Temple, BSc
(Hons)(HongKong)

Tsui *Kwok Wah Peter*
and Member Hong Kong Bar. Called: Nov
1994, Gray's Inn, B.Eng, M.Eng, LLB, MICE,
MHKIE, ACIArb

Tuberi *Iniasi Vodo*
P O Box 2034, Government Buildings, Suva,
and Member Fiji Bar. Called: July 1993,
Inner Temple, Dip. in Education, BEd (USP),
LLB (So'ton)

Tuite *Michael Donald*
Barrister of Ireland. Called: Nov 1996,
Lincoln's Inn, BCL (Dublin), LLM (Cantab)

Tung *Dr Wai Kit*
and Member Hong Kong Bar. Called: July
1992, Gray's Inn, M.B.BS, LLB (Lond), FRCS
(Edinburgh)

Tung *Yau Ming*
James R Knowles (Hong Kong)Ltd, 1111
Wing On Centre, 111 Connaught Road
Central, Hong Kong, (852) 25422818, Fax:
(852) 25414648, Chartered Quantity
Surveyor and Member Hong Kong Bar.
Called: July 1992, Middle Temple, BSc (QS)
(Hons), LLM, ARICS, AHKIS, ACIArb, MA
Cost E

Turner *Marcus Philip Robert*
Roadrunner International BV, Bijdorp 2,
1182 M2, Amsterdam, ++ 31 20 65 66 670,
Fax: ++ 31 20 64 06 126. Called: Nov 1991,
Middle Temple, LLB Hons (Lond)

Turner *Nigel Stuart*
Called: Nov 1990, Gray's Inn, LLB
(Hons)(B'ham)

Ullaganathan *Krishnasamy Velu
Archary*
Called: July 1993, Lincoln's Inn, LLB (Hons)

Umar *Miss Hajh Sarimah Haji*
Abrahams, Davidson & Co, Room 516, 5th
Floor Plaza, Athirah, Jln Kubah Makan,
Diraja, B.S.B. 2682, Brunei. Called: Nov
1993, Gray's Inn, LLB

Umezuruike *Israel Nzeako*
Umezuruike & Associates, Umez Chambers,
58 Pound Road, PO Box 1677, Aba Abia
State, 082-221315, Fax: 082-221315, Senior
Advocate of Nigeria (SAN) and Member
Nigerian Bar. Called: Nov 1964, Inner
Temple, LLB (Lond)

Underwood *Geoffrey Edward*
Sixth Floor, Wentworth Selborne Chambers,
180 Phillip Street, Sydney NSW 2000,
(0011) 612 235 0140, Fax: (0011) 612 221
5604, Former Solicitor and Member Victoria
Bar, Queensland Bar, Northern Territory Bar
Australian Capital Territory Bar, Western
Australia Bar New South Wales Bar.
Called: July 1995, Middle Temple, B.Comm
(Queensland), LLB (Queensland), LLM
(London)

Ung *Eu-Chung*
Duval & Stachenfeld LLP, 575 Madison
Avenue, Suite 1006, New York, NY 10022,
(212) 605 0104, and Member New York
(1994). Called: July 1990, Lincoln's Inn, LLB
(Lond) 1989, LLM (Fordham) 1991, JD
(Georgetown) 1994

Ung *Miss Monin*
Clifford Chance, 30th Floor, Jardine House,
One Connaught Place, (852) 28258809, Fax:
(852) 28690067, and Member Singapore Bar
Hong Kong Law Society. Called: July 1993,
Gray's Inn, LLB (Brunei)

Upadhyaya *Miss Kanaklata Bhaskerrai*
Called: Oct 1997, Middle Temple, LLB
(Hons)(Lond)

Usher *Professor John Anthony*
Called: Nov 1993, Lincoln's Inn, LLB (Hons)

Uthayachanran *B*
Called: July 1993, Middle Temple, LLB
(Hons)(Lond)

Vagg *Ms Irene Juliette*
Called: Oct 1995, Gray's Inn, BA (Ghana)

Vale *Anthony Charles Howard*
Pepper, Hamilton & Scheetz, 3000 Two
Logan Sq, Philadelphia, PA 19103 USA, 215
981 4502, Fax: 215 981 4750, and Member
Pennsylvania (1978). Called: Nov 1974,
Inner Temple, LLB

Van Der Stoep *David Floris*
Le Panorama, 57 Rue Grimaldi, MC-98000,
377 9310 6311, Fax: 377 9310 6313.
Called: Nov 1970, Gray's Inn, Dip Law

Van Hagen *Anthony Frederick William*
Cabinet Van Hagen, 6 Avenue George V,
Paris 75008, 01 47200064, Fax: 01
47202509, and Member French Bar.
Called: Nov 1975, Lincoln's Inn, BA (Hons)
Law

van Leuven *Advocate John Nikolas*
Ozannes, 1 Le Marchant Street, St Peter
Port, Guernsey, 0481 723466, Fax: 0481
727935/714571/714653. Called: Nov 1970,
Inner Temple, MA (Cantab), ACIArb

Vangadasalam *Suriamurthi*
Called: Nov 1997, Middle Temple, LLB
(Hons)(Lond)

Varghese *Joseph*
Varghese & Co, 112 East Coast Road, [H]
03-33 Katong Mall, 3444989, Fax: 3444419,
and Member Singapore Bar. Called: July
1994, Lincoln's Inn, LLB (Hons)

Varughese *Miss Sucy*
9 Dilali Road, City Beach, Western Australia
WA 6015, (09) 385 9552. Called: Oct 1993,
Lincoln's Inn, LLB (Hons)(Bucks)

Vasu *Rajasekharan*
Called: Nov 1996, Middle Temple, LLB
(Hons)

Vasudevan *Dhanaraj*
Called: July 1996, Middle Temple, LLB
(Hons)(Lond)

Vaswani *Mrs Hardevi*
and Member Singapore. Called: Nov 1995,
Middle Temple, LLB (Hons)

Vaughan *Beverley Seymour Tyrone*
Called: July 1978, Gray's Inn, MA, tcd

Veerasamy *Miss Sarojini Muthusamy*
Called: Nov 1997, Lincoln's Inn, LLB (Hons)

Vellani *Badaruddin Fatehali*
Vellani & Vellani, 810-820 Muhammadi Hse,
8th Floor, I.I. Chundrigar Rd, Karachi 0225,
Pakistan. Called: July 1982, Middle Temple,
BSc Diplaw

Vellani *Fatehali Walimohammad*
Vellani & Vellani, 810-820 Muhammadi Hse
8th, I.I. Chundrigar Road, Karachi 74000,
Pakistan, 2414021, Fax: 2419874.
Called: Feb 1956, Middle Temple

Velupillai *Miss Vijayalatha*
Abdul Raman Saad & Assoc, No 240 A & B,
Taman Melaka Raya, 75000 Jalan Taman,
Melaka, 06 2821446, and Member Malaysia
Bar. Called: Nov 1994, Middle Temple, LLB
(Hons)

Vengadasalam *Mrs Pakkia Letchumi*
Called: Nov 1995, Lincoln's Inn, LLB (Hons)

Vengadesan *Miss Joanne Jayanti*
Called: July 1996, Middle Temple, LLB
(Notts)

Venkata Rajoo *Miss Sheila Devi*
Called: Nov 1995, Lincoln's Inn, LLB (Hons)

Venn *John Kenneth*
124 Young Street, Hamilton, Ontario,
Canada L8N 1V6, (905) 522 9116, Fax:
9905) 529 5112, and Member Upper
Canada. Called: July 1971, Middle Temple,
M.A (Oxon), M.B.A (Warwick)

Venugopal *Vijayan*
Shearn Delamore & Co, 7th Floor, Wisma
Hamzah Kwong - Hing, No 1 Leboh
Ampang, 50100 Kuala Lumpur, 03 2300644,
Fax: 03 2385625, and Member Malaysia Bar.
Called: July 1993, Middle Temple, LLB
(Hons)

Vercoe *John Christopher William*
Baker & McKenzie, 8th Floor, 155 Abai
Avenue, Almaty. Called: Nov 1973, Gray's
Inn, LLB(Lond)

Vesin-Samnadda *Mrs Indrani Veronica*
Credit Suisse Private Banking, P O Box 500, CH-1211 Geneva, 41 22 391 34 66, Fax: 41 22 391 38 77, Entitled to practice in Caricom States Currently practising in Switzerland. and Member Trinidad and Tobago Bar. Called: July 1992, Middle Temple, LLB (Hons) (Exeter)

Vij *Arvind Kumar*
139 Cavenagh Road, [H]12-02 Town Apt, Singapore 0922, 65 -7360820, Fax: 65-7360820. Called: July 1995, Middle Temple, LLB (Hons), BBA (Hons)

Voliotis *Seraphim*
Called: Oct 1995, Lincoln's Inn, BA (Hons), MA, PhD (Cantab)

Voo *Miss Mui Ching Cheryl*
7 Pemimpin Place, 65-2581213, Fax: 65-4539160. Called: July 1997, Gray's Inn, LLB (Lond)

Voon *Miss Meng Lye*
Blk 66 [H]02-339, Commonwealth Drive, Singapore 140066, 4730146. Called: July 1995, Lincoln's Inn, LLB (Hons)

Voon *Richard Chee Fatt*
Called: Nov 1996, Lincoln's Inn, LLB (Hons)(Bucks)

Vrahimis *Laris*
Chr. Sozou 2, Flat 206, Nicosia, Cyprus, 357 2 473558, Fax: 357 2 475692, and Member Cyprus Bar. Called: May 1994, Middle Temple, LLB (Hons)

Vung *Peter Yin Sing*
Called: July 1996, Middle Temple, BA (Hons)(Keele)

Wah *Ronald Wong Soon*
Called: July 1995, Middle Temple, LLB (Hons), LLM (Lond)

Wahi *Miss Shelina Razaly*
Called: July 1996, Lincoln's Inn, LLB (Hons)(Bris)

Wahyuni *Faizal*
Called: July 1994, Lincoln's Inn, LLB (Hons)

Wainwright *Richard Barry*
Commission of the European Communities, 200 Rue de La Loi, 1049 Brussels, Belgium, 02 295 3807, Fax: 02 295 2486. Called: July 1965, Middle Temple, BA (Oxon)

Wakerley *John Charles OBE*
SmithKline Beecham Corporation, One Franklin Plaza, P O Box 7929, Philadelphia, PA 19101-7929, (215) 751 5844, Fax: (215) 751 5132, and Member New York Bar. Called: May 1960, Gray's Inn, LLB

Walker *William Stuart O.B.E.*
W S Walker & Company, P O Box 265G, Caledonian House, Grand Cayman, (345)949-0100, Fax: (345)949-7886, Attorney-at-Law Cayman Islands Notary Public, Cayman Islands. Called: June 1950, Inner Temple, MA (Cantab)

Walsh *Mrs Margaret Josephine*
91 Whitebarn Road, Churchtown, Dublin 14, 00 3531 2981346, Barrister of Ireland. Called: May 1995, Middle Temple, BL (King's Inn)

Walters *Jeannot-Michel*
Called: Nov 1997, Middle Temple, LLB (Hons)

Walton *Jeremy Paul*
Ritch & Connolly, Attorneys at Law, P.O.Box 1994, Grand Cayman, 001 345 949 7366, Fax: 001 345 949 8652, and Member Cayman Islands Bar. Called: Nov 1995, Lincoln's Inn, BA (Hons)

Wan *Azli Kuzaini*
Called: Nov 1995, Lincoln's Inn, LLB (Hons)

Wan *Kai Chee*
Called: July 1997, Lincoln's Inn, LLB (Hons)(Lond)

Wan *Ms Shuk Fong Polly*
6/F High Block, Queensway Government Offices, 66 Queensway, 28672302, Fax: 28451609, and Member Hong Kong Bar. Called: Nov 1993, Gray's Inn, LLB

Wan *Miss Teh Leok*
2193-A Lorong Kampung Pisang, Alor Setar, 05100 Kedah, Malaysia, 0604 7330837, and Member Malaysia Bar. Called: July 1995, Inner Temple, LLB (Soton)

Wan Hussin *Wan Fairuz*
Called: July 1995, Middle Temple, BA (Hons) (Keele)

Wan Mohd Noor *Wan Annuar*
Called: Nov 1995, Lincoln's Inn, LLB (Hons)

Wang *John Shing Chun*
52 Kampong Chantek, (65) 4668928. Called: July 1996, Middle Temple, BA (Hons)(Cantab)

Wang *Peter Kai-Hung*
Called: July 1995, Middle Temple, B.Sc, M.Sc (Toronto), LLB (Hons), LLM, (Wales)

Wang *Sui Sang*
Called: Nov 1991, Lincoln's Inn, LLB (Hons) (L'Pool)

Ward *Eoin Francis*
Kindle Banking Systems, East Point Business Park, Dublin 3 Ireland, 353 1 68554555, Fax: 353 1 8554550, and Member Irish Bar (King's Inn). Called: July 1988, Middle Temple, BCL (Dublin), AITI, (Dublin), Dip, European Law(Dublin)

Warwick *Kevin*
Called: Oct 1995, Middle Temple, LLB (Hons)

Watt *John Gillie McArthur QC*
Advocates Library, Parliament House, Edinburgh, 303 456 1548, Fax: 303 456 1548, Scottish Advocate, QC Scotland 1992 and Member Colorado Bar. Called: Feb 1992, Middle Temple, LLB (Edin)

Watters *Simon Barry*
P O Box X 2291, Perth, Western Australia 6001, 08-9264 1750, Fax: 08-9264 1455, Former Solicitor and Member Western Australia Bar, Federal High Court of Australia Tasmania Bar. Called: July 1992, Gray's Inn, BA, LLB

Watts *Trevor Robert*
Chateau Du Seuil, Cerons 33720, France, 00 33 56271156, Fax: 00 33 56272879. Called: Nov 1979, Lincoln's Inn, FRVA, FSVA, Winemaker

Wee *Miss Adeline Ai Lin*
Called: July 1995, Middle Temple, BA (Hons) (Keele)

Wee *Aloysius Meng Seng*
105 Cecil Street, [H]10-02 The Octagon, 5352077, Fax: 5333969, and Member Singapore Bar. Called: Oct 1994, Middle Temple, BA (Hons)(Kent)

Wee *Desmond Guan Oei*
Called: July 1995, Middle Temple, LLB (Hons)

Wee *Gerald Martin Ee Ming*
Called: Nov 1996, Middle Temple, LLB (Hons)(L'pool)

Wee *Jee Pin*
Rodyk & Davidson, Six Battery [H]38-01, Singapore 0104, (65) 225 2626, Fax: (65) 225 7511/225 1838, Advocate & Solicitor the Supreme Court of Singapore. Called: July 1992, Middle Temple, LLB (Hons) (Hull)

Wee *Miss Vivienne Chui Ling*
Apt Blk 222, Tampines Street 24, [H] 10-96, 065 7830102, Fax: 065 7830102. Called: July 1991, Middle Temple, LLB (Hons) (Bucks)

Wee *Miss Ying Ling Beverly*
Called: July 1995, Gray's Inn, LLB

Wee Ewe Lay *Laurence John*
No 2 Ewart Park, 65 5345155, Fax: 65 5342622, Avocate & Solicitor of the Supreme Court of Singapore. Called: July 1982, Middle Temple, LLB (Hons)

Wee Inn *The Hon. Mr Roland Sagrah*
M/S David Allan Sagah & Teng, Advocates, Lot 196, Sublot 4, 1st Floor, Jalan Kulas, Satok CDT 3045, 93990 Kuching, 082-232739, Fax: 082-251831, Advocate & Solicitor of the High Court of Sabah & Sarawak Malaysia. and Member Sarawak Bar. Called: July 1980, Gray's Inn, LLB (Hons Lond)

Wei *Miss Hui Yen*
Called: July 1996, Gray's Inn, BA (Keele), MBA (London)

Weir *Alan Anthony*
Northern Ireland Barrister. Called: Nov 1996, Gray's Inn, BSc, MSc (Belfast)

Wells *Commander Anthony Roland*
P.O. Box 2102, The Plains, Middleburg 20118, 703-253 5048, Fax: 703-253 5049. Called: Nov 1980, Lincoln's Inn, MA (Dunelm), MSc, PhD (Lond)

Wells-Carmona *Ms Sandra Anne*
Callenders & Co, P O Box F.40132,
Freeport, Grand Bahama, 809 352-7458,
Fax: 809 352-4000, and Member Bahamas
Bar. Called: July 1994, Inner Temple, BA,
LLB (Hons)

Welsh *Miss Amanda Jane*
00 301 451 4452, Fax: 00 301 451 4452.
Called: Nov 1992, Gray's Inn, LLB (Leeds)

Westbrook *Simon Nicholas*
15/Floor Printing House, 6 Duddell Street,
Central, (852) 2521 2616, Fax: (852) 2845
0260, and Member Hong Kong Bar.
Called: July 1973, Inner Temple, LLB,
FCIArb

Whatnell *Mrs Helen Mary*
1407 Azalea Bend, Sugar Land TX 77479,
281 343 7569, Fax: 281 343 6019.
Called: Nov 1993, Inner Temple, LLB

Wheeler *John Gerald Patrick*
Templar House, Don Road, St Helier, Jersey,
0534 500300, Fax: 0534 500350, Advocate
of the Royal Court of Jersey. Called: July
1978, Inner Temple, BA

Wheeler *Miss Philippa Ruth*
Hewlett Packard GMBH, Postfach 1430, D
71003 Boeblingen, 49 7031 14 3169, Fax:
49 7031 14 3812. Called: July 1988, Inner
Temple, LLB

Whitmore *David*
Called: Nov 1995, Middle Temple, BA
(Hons)

Widjaja *Prawiro*
Called: July 1994, Middle Temple, BA
(Hons)(Cantab)

Willers *Peter Alan*
Ballagawne Farm, Baldrine, 0624 661662,
Fax: 0624 661663. Called: Nov 1973, Middle
Temple, MA (Cantab)

Williams *Miss Ameeta Chandra*
Called: Nov 1995, Middle Temple, LLB
(Hons)(Sheff)

Williams *Miss April Nicole*
Called: Nov 1996, Inner Temple, BA
(Canada), BA (Keele)

Williams *Ms Caroline*
5 Cool Na Mara, Marine Terrace,
Dunlaoghaire, Co Dublin, 00353 12842770,
Fax: 00353 12842770, Barrister of King's
Inn. Called: Nov 1994, Middle Temple

Williams *Cecil Alfred*
Called: July 1997, Gray's Inn, BA (West
Indies), MSc (Bradford), LLB (Lond)

Williams *Jonathan Steuart*
Magistrates' Chambers, Level 5, Downing
Centre, 143-147 Liverpool Street, Sydney,
NSW 2000, 02 9664 2924, and Member
Australian Capital Territory New South
Wales Bar. Called: May 1990, Lincoln's Inn,
Dip Law, Dip Crim, LLM

Williamson *Kris*
Daniel & CIA, Trade Mark & Patent
Attorneys, Avenida Republica da Chile, 230/
60 Andor, Rio de Janeiro, CEP 20070-001,
RJ, 005521 224 4212, Fax: 005521 224
3344. Called: Nov 1993, Middle Temple, BA
(Hons)(Leic), LLB (Hons)(Lond)

Williamson *Mrs Romi Wai Ming*
30b Century Tower, 1 Tregunter Path,
25222884, and Member Hong Kong Bar.
Called: Nov 1994, Middle Temple, BA
(Econ)(Australia)

Willimsky *Miss Sonya Margaret*
Haarmann, Hemmelrath & Partner, Martin
Luther Plate 26, 40212 Dusseldorf, 00 49
211 8399 0, Fax: 00 49 211 8399 133.
Called: Nov 1996, Lincoln's Inn, LLB
(Hons)(Lond)

Wilson *John Frederick*
C/O Parliamentary Counsel, Office,
Parliament Buildings, Vuya Road, Suva, Fiji.
Called: July 1966, Inner Temple, BA (Oxon)

Wilson Appukuttan *Joy*
Messrs Kitson Foong &, Associates, No 75B
Jalan Dato Haji Eusoff, Damai Complex, Off
Jalan Ipoh, 50400 Kuala Lumpur, 603
4436797/603-4428411, Fax: 603-4429297,
Advocate & Solicitor and Member Malaysia
Bar Singapore Bar. Called: Nov 1989, Middle
Temple, LLB Hons (Lond)

Winckless *Michael Louis John*
1430 Prince's Building, Central, (852) 2525
7388, Fax: (852) 2525 3930, and Member
Hong Kong Bar. Called: July 1994, Middle
Temple, BSc (Hons), MBA

Winny *Ms Elspeth Margaret*
Called: Nov 1996, Lincoln's Inn, LLB
(Hons)(Lond)

Wiseheart *Malcolm Boyd*
2840 Southwest Third Avenue, Miami,
Florida 33129, 305 285 1222, Fax: 305 858
4864, and Member Florida & Washington
DC Bars Jamaica & Trinidad & Tobago Bars.
Called: Feb 1970, Gray's Inn, MA (Cantab)
JD, (Florida) BA (Yale)

Wong *Adrian Kwai Ming*
Called: July 1997, Lincoln's Inn, LLB
(Hons)(Leeds)

Wong *Alex Li Kok*
Called: July 1997, Middle Temple, LLB
(Hons)

Wong *Miss Angela Mo Yen*
Called: Nov 1996, Gray's Inn, LLB

Wong *Miss Annie Sook Cheng*
Called: Nov 1997, Middle Temple, LLB
(Hons)(Lond)

Wong *Chak Yan*
Called: Nov 1997, Middle Temple, BSc
(Hons,Hong Kong)

Wong *Chao-Wai*
CNAC Group Building, 13th Flr, 10 Queens
Road C, Central, Hong Kong, 28101008,
Fax: 25960945, and Member Hong Kong
Bar. Called: Nov 1991, Inner Temple, LLB,
LLM, MA, MIL, ACIArb

Wong *Miss Cheryl Pooi Leng*
Called: July 1996, Lincoln's Inn, LLB
(Hons)(Lond)

Wong *Chi Wing John*
Called: Nov 1997, Middle Temple, LLB
(Hons)

Wong *Miss Denise Chin Wuen*
Called: July 1996, Lincoln's Inn, LLB
(Hons)(Bris)

Wong *Eden Yi Dung*
Called: Nov 1997, Gray's Inn, B.Com
(Melbourne), LLB (Lond)

Wong *Mrs Fung Kwai*
065 5660812. Called: July 1995, Middle
Temple, LLB (Hons)

Wong *Miss Grace Teck Lian*
Called: July 1996, Lincoln's Inn, LLB
(Hons)(Leics)

Wong *Hong Wai*
c/o Cheang & Ariff, Advocates & Solicitors,
39 Court, No 39 Jalan Yap Kwan, Seng,
50450, Kuala Lumpur Malaysia, 03 2610803,
Fax: 03 2621533. Called: Nov 1992, Gray's
Inn, LLB (Hull)

Wong *Miss I-Lin Petula*
Called: Nov 1995, Gray's Inn, LLB (Lond)

Wong *James Seow Boon*
Called: Nov 1996, Middle Temple, LLB
(Hons)(Bucks)

Wong *James Yuen Weng*
Called: July 1996, Lincoln's Inn, LLB
(Hons)(Nott's)

Wong *John Sing Kiu*
Called: Nov 1994, Middle Temple, B.Sc, LLB
(Hons)

Wong *Kah Hui*
Called: Nov 1995, Lincoln's Inn, LLB (Hons)

Wong *Kean Li*
Called: July 1995, Middle Temple, BA
(Hons)

Wong *Kee Them*
Called: Nov 1997, Lincoln's Inn, LLB (Hons)

Wong *Kelvin Weng Wah*
and Member Singapore Bar. Called: July
1995, Middle Temple, LLB (Hons), ACIArb

Wong *Miss Ket Yee*
Called: July 1997, Middle Temple, LLB
(Hons)(B'ham)

Wong *Kwee Hoi*
Called: Nov 1997, Lincoln's Inn, LLB (Hons)

Wong *Kwok Fai*
Called: Nov 1996, Middle Temple, LLB
(Hons)(Lond)

Wong *Miss Li Chien*
Called: Nov 1996, Middle Temple, BA
(Hons)(Kent)

Wong *Li Fei*
Called: July 1997, Lincoln's Inn, LLB (Hons)

Wong *Mark Kuan Meng*
P.K.Wong & Advani, 20 Raffles Place, [H]12-03 Ocean Towers, Singapore 0104, 65 5381822, Fax: 65 5381838, and Member Singapore Bar. Called: Nov 1992, Middle Temple, LLB (Hons, Hull)

Wong *Dr Melvin*
Fax: (852) 26987403, and Member Hong Kong Bar. Called: July 1997, Gray's Inn, Pharm.D, LLB (Lond)

Wong *Ming Fung*
Called: July 1997, Middle Temple, BA (Hons)

Wong *Nai Chee*
No 25 Lorong Hang Jebat, 75200 Melaka, 010606 2825105, Fax: 010606 2848004, and Member Malaysia Bar. Called: July 1994, Middle Temple, LLB (Hons)(Hull)

Wong *Pak Heung*
3rd Floor, Fook Shing Court, 50 Wyndham Street, 852 2523 3450, and Member Supreme Court of Hong Kong Supreme Court of Australian Capital Territory. Called: July 1966, Inner Temple

Wong *Miss Pei-Ling*
37 Lorong Maa'rof, Bangsar Park, 59000 Kuala Lumpur, 03 2836193. Called: July 1996, Lincoln's Inn, LLB (Hons)

Wong *Raymond Kwai Sang*
Called: Nov 1996, Middle Temple, LLB (Hons)(HongKong)

Wong *Richard T W*
Room 1205-6 New World Tower, Tower 1, 16-18 Queens Road Central, Central, 25211388, Fax: 28451738, Barrister of the Supreme Court of the Australian Capital Territory(Dec 1990) and Member Hong Kong Bar. Called: Nov 1986, Inner Temple, LLB (Lond), PCLL (HK)

Wong *Miss Rita Kee Ning*
Called: July 1996, Lincoln's Inn

Wong *Miss Rosaline Wing Yue*
and Member Hong Kong. Called: July 1993, Middle Temple, LLB (Hons)(Lond)

Wong *Miss Shou Ning*
Called: Nov 1996, Middle Temple, LLB (Hons)(Kent)

Wong *Ms Shou Sien*
Raja Darryl & Loh, 18th Floor, Wisma Sime Darby, Jln Raja Laut, 50350 Kuala Lumpur, Malaysia, 603-2949999, Fax: 603 2933823, and Member Malaysia Bar. Called: Feb 1994, Middle Temple, LLB (Hons)(Kent), LLM (Lond)

Wong *Miss Siew Mei*
Called: July 1997, Middle Temple, LLB (Hons)(Wales)

Wong *Sin Yee*
Called: July 1994, Gray's Inn

Wong *Miss Sook Ling*
Shooklin & Bok, Advocates & Solicitors, 1 Robinson Road, [H]18-00 AIA Tower, Singapore 099310, (65) 535 1944, Fax: (65) 535 8577, and Member Singapore Bar. Called: July 1994, Inner Temple, LLB

Wong *Soon Chee*
Called: July 1997, Lincoln's Inn, LLB (Hons)(Lond)

Wong *Sow Wei*
and Member Advocate & Solicitor of the High Court of Malaya. Called: July 1996, Lincoln's Inn

Wong *Stephen Yee Onn*
Called: July 1994, Lincoln's Inn, LLB (Hons)

Wong *Miss Su-Mene*
Called: July 1995, Middle Temple, LLB (Hons)

Wong *Miss Sui Ching Janet*
Called: Nov 1997, Middle Temple, BA (Hons)(Hong Kong)

Wong *Wai Keong*
and Member Malaysia. Called: Nov 1995, Lincoln's Inn, LLB (Hons)(Lond)

Wong *Wee Kok*
Called: Nov 1996, Lincoln's Inn, LLB (Hons)(Wales)

Wong *Winston Paul Chi-Huang*
Suite 12-02, 12th Floor, Menara Pelangi, Jalan Kuning, 80400 Johor Bahru, Joor Malaysia, 010 60 7 3342266, Fax: 010 60 7 3344708, and Member Malaysia Bar. Called: Nov 1994, Middle Temple, BA (Hons), LLM, (Singapore)

Wong *Yew Kit*
and Member Singapore. Called: July 1995, Middle Temple, LLB (Hons)

Wong *Yun Wah Gordon*
Pacific Chambers, 901 Dina House, Rutterjee Centre, 11 Duddell Street, Central, (852) 2521 5544, Fax: (852) 2524 5912, and Member Hong Kong Bar. Called: July 1996, Lincoln's Inn, LLB (Hons)(Leeds)

Woo *Hubert Iu-Kwok*
New World Tower, Room 602, 18 Queen's Road Central, Hong Kong, 2525 7007, Fax: 2845 2001, and Member Hong Kong Bar. Called: Feb 1992, Gray's Inn, BSc (Hong Kong), LLB (Lond), MICE,FCIArb

Woo *Miss Siew Khim*
Blk 623, Bukit Batok Central, [H]03-680, 7786740. Called: Nov 1993, Middle Temple, LLB (Hons)(Lond)

Woo *Wei Kwang*
Called: July 1997, Lincoln's Inn, LLB (Hons)(Leeds)

Woodworth *Miss Michelle Elizabeth*
Called: July 1996, Middle Temple, LLB (Hons)(Lond)

Woolley *Edward Timothy Starbuck*
c/o The Court of Final Appeal, 1 Battery Park, 2123 0017, Fax: 2121 0300, Registrar, Court of Final Appeal and Member Hong Kong Bar, Australian Bar. Called: July 1968, Middle Temple

Wu *Chi Sing*
Called: Nov 1995, Gray's Inn, LLB (Lond)

Wu *Chun Shing*
Flat A, 3/F, Tower 6, Metro City, 1 Wan Hang Road, Tseung Kwan O, N.T., (00 852) 2695 0252, Fax: (00 852) 2695 0252, and Member Hong Kong. Called: Nov 1996, Gray's Inn, LLB (Lond)

Wu *Mrs Lorna Shui Wan*
1002 Chekiang Bank Centre, 1 Duddell Street, 5 25217317, Fax: 852 5 28450654, and Member Hong Kong & Singapore Bars. Called: Nov 1982, Inner Temple, LLB, Dip in Chinese Law, ACIArb

Wu *Roderick Kam Fun*
1002 Chekiang First, Bank Centre, 1 Duddell Street, Central, 5 25217317, Fax: 852 5 28450654, and Member Hong Kong,Victorian & Singapore Bars. Called: July 1980, Inner Temple, LLB, Dip in Chinese Law, ACIArb

Wun *Rizwi*
and Member Singapore. Called: July 1992, Gray's Inn, LLB (Lond)

Wylie-Otte *Ms Regan*
3 Um Kallek, L-5369 Schuttrange. Called: Feb 1978, Middle Temple, MA, LLM

Xie *Miss Janice Zhao Shan*
and Member Singapore Bar. Called: July 1994, Lincoln's Inn, LLB (Hons)

Xu *Daniel Atticus*
Called: Nov 1997, Middle Temple, LLB (Hons)(Lond)

Yam *Jeffrey Pei Tseng*
Messrs Rodyk & Davidson, 9 Raffles Place, [H]55-01, Republic Plaza, 65 5399254, Fax: 65 2251838. Called: July 1996, Middle Temple, LLB (Hons)(Wales)

Yan *Keen Wah Stephen*
19 Highgate Crescent, 65-5614048 (R) 65-7320021 (O), Fax: 65-5614048, and Member Singapore Bar. Called: May 1994, Gray's Inn, LLB

Yang *Miss Caroline Yuen Tsyr*
Called: July 1992, Middle Temple, LLB (Hons) (Lond)

Yap *Miss Adeline Bee-Yen*
Azri Chuah & Yap, No 22-3 (Third Floor), Jalan Sri Hartamas 8, Taman Sri Hartamas, 50480 Kuala Lumpur, 603 6512714/6512784/6531105, Fax: 603 6531078, and Member Malaysia Bar. Called: July 1992, Middle Temple, LLB (Hons) (Manch)

Yap *Benjamin Soon Tat*
Godwin & Co, 1 Robinson Road, [H] 20-02 AIA Tower, Singapore 048542, (065) 5338313, Fax: (065) 5331113, and Member Singapore. Called: Nov 1994, Middle Temple, LLB (Hons)

Yap *Miss Camilla Tee Neo*
Called: Nov 1995, Lincoln's Inn, LLB (Hons)

Yap *Miss Grace Mei Wan*
Albar Zulkifly & Yap, 17th Floor, Menara Sabre, & Lorong P Ramlee, 50200 Kuala Lumpur, 01-06-03-2388228, Fax: 01-06-03-2041913, and Member Malaysia Bar. Called: July 1991, Middle Temple, LLB (Notts)

Yap *Miss Hsu-Lyn*
Called: July 1997, Lincoln's Inn, LLB
(Hons)(Nott'm)

Yap *Miss Huey Hoong*
Called: July 1996, Lincoln's Inn, LLB (Hons)

Yap *Miss Hui Lu*
Messrs Lee Hishammuddin, Solicitors &
Advocates, 16th Floor, Wisma HLA, Jalan
Raja Chulan, 50200 Kuala Lumpur, (603)
2011681 x 173, Fax: (603) 2011746, and
Member Malaysia. Called: July 1994, Middle
Temple, LLB (Hons)(Bris), LLM
(Hons)(Lond)

Yap *Miss Janice Bee Hong*
Called: July 1997, Lincoln's Inn, LLB
(Hons)(Leeds)

Yap *Miss Juliana Chin Choo*
B-3258, Taman Tunas, 25300 Kuantan,
Pahang Darulmakmur, Malaysia. Called: July
1995, Inner Temple, LLB (Lond)

Yap *Keng Siong*
Called: July 1996, Lincoln's Inn, LLB (Hons)

Yap *Miss Lai-Lian*
Called: Nov 1996, Lincoln's Inn, LLB
(Hons)(Herts)

Yap *Miss Lareina Chu Han*
[H]02-01, Amica Block, The Beaumont, 147
Devonshire Road, 733-9923, and Member
Supreme Court of Brunei Darussalam
Singapore Bar. Called: Nov 1988, Middle
Temple, LLB (Brunel), LLM (Lond)

Yap *Miss Lay Hoon*
Called: July 1996, Lincoln's Inn, LLB
(Hons)(Leeds)

Yap *Miss Lay Kuan*
Called: Nov 1997, Middle Temple, LLB
(Hons)

Yap *Miss Lisa*
Called: Nov 1996, Middle Temple, LLB
(Hons)(Kent)

Yap *Miss Luna-Whye Tzu*
22 Lorong K, Telok Kurau [H]03-01, Wen
Yuan Court, 065-2276206, Fax: 065-
2274861, and Member Singapore Bar.
Called: July 1994, Middle Temple, LLB
(Hons)

Yap *Miss Lynette*
Called: Nov 1996, Lincoln's Inn, LLB
(Hons)(Lond)

Yap *Miss Pett Chin*
Called: Nov 1996, Lincoln's Inn, LLB
(Hons)(Leics)

Yap *Miss Shirley Mae-Yen*
Called: July 1996, Lincoln's Inn, LLB (Hons)

Yap *Miss Vicky Lan Hiang*
Called: July 1995, Inner Temple, LLB
(Warw)

Yap *Vincent Leng Khim*
Called: July 1997, Lincoln's Inn, LLB (Hons)

Yap *Yin-Soon*
Allen & Gledhill, 36 Robinson Road, [H]18-
01 City House, Singapore 0106, 225 1611,
Fax: 221 3726, Advocate & Solicitor of the
Supreme Court of Singapore. Called: July
1993, Middle Temple, LLB (Hons, Exon),
LLM

Yasin *Saladin Mohd.*
No 3 Jalan 4/3F, 40000 Shah Alam,
Selangor, Malaysia. Called: July 1993, Gray's
Inn, LLB

Yau *Wai-Leong*
Chan & Associates, Standard Chartered Bank
Chamb., 21-27 Jalan Dato Maharaja Lela,
30000 Ipoh, 605 2545293, Fax: 605
2534091, and Member Malaysia. Called: July
1996, Lincoln's Inn, LLB (Hons)(Leeds)

Yeap *Miss Su-Lynn*
6B Jalan Brown, 10350 Penang, Malaysia,
(04) 226 6916, Fax: (04) 323 5093, and
Member Malaysia Bar. Called: Nov 1991,
Inner Temple, LLB (Hull)

Yearwood *Martin Edmund*
31 La Estancia Drive, PO Box 3239, Diego
Martin, Trinidad, 632-8223. Called: Nov
1971, Lincoln's Inn, BSc

Yeats *Liam James*
Stagnetto & Co, 186 Main Street, and
Member Gibraltar. Called: Mar 1997, Middle
Temple, LLB (Hons)

Yee *Miss Eileen Khor Kit*
Called: July 1995, Middle Temple, LLB
(Hons)

Yee *Jackie Keen Meng*
Called: July 1995, Lincoln's Inn, LLB (Hons)

Yee *Mei Ken*
Called: July 1997, Lincoln's Inn, LLB
(Hons)(Wales)

Yeen *Chong Foo*
Lim Seong Chun & Co, No 11, Jalan
Panglima, 30000 Ipoh, Perak, (05) 2413655,
Fax: (05) 2550194. Called: July 1997, Inner
Temple, LLB (Sheff)

Yek *Nai Hui*
24 Newton Road, [H]07-01 Surrey Tower.
Called: Oct 1993, Middle Temple, LLB
(Hons, Hull)

Yen *Heng Teng*
Called: Nov 1996, Middle Temple, LLB
(Hons)(Hull)

Yen-Yen *Ms Lee Amelia*
Called: Nov 1997, Inner Temple, LLB, LLM
(Lond)

Yeo *Miss Charmaine Swan Mei*
Called: Nov 1994, Middle Temple, LLB
(Hons) (Hull)

Yeo *Miss Chiew Pin*
Called: Nov 1997, Lincoln's Inn, LLB
(Hons)(Wales)

Yeo *Jih Shian*
Called: July 1993, Gray's Inn, BA

Yeo *Ms Marianne Mei-Lin*
5B Sea & Sky Court, 92 Stanley Main Street,
Stanley, 852 28131788, Fax: 852 28132086,
and Member Malaysia Bar. Called: July 1982,
Inner Temple, BSc (Manch), Diplaw

Yeo *Raymond Khee Chye*
Called: July 1996, Lincoln's Inn, LLB
(Hons)(Lond)

Yeo *Ronald*
Called: Feb 1993, Lincoln's Inn, LLB (Hons)

Yeo *Roy Kan Kiang*
Advocate & Solicitor of the Supreme of
Singapore. Called: July 1994, Middle
Temple, LLB (Hons)(Bris)

Yeo *Sia Eng*
Called: Oct 1997, Middle Temple, LLB
(Hons)(Lond)

Yeo *Miss Siok Kiang Fiona*
Called: July 1996, Middle Temple, LLB
(Hons)(Hull)

Yeo *Ms Sok Huang*
5 Peck Hay Road, [H]09-OO Peck Hay View,
Singapore 0922, 7334868, Advocate &
Solicitor of the Supreme Court of Singapore.
Called: July 1992, Gray's Inn, LLB (Brist)

Yeo *Willie Sie Keng*
and Member Singapore Bar. Called: July
1995, Lincoln's Inn, LLB (Hons)

Yeo *Miss Yee Ling*
Called: July 1997, Gray's Inn

Yeoh *Miss Daryl*
Chan & Associates, Advocates & Solicitors,
Standard Chartered Bk Chambers, 21-27
Jalan Dato Maharja Lela, 30000 Ipoh, Perak
Malaysia. Called: July 1995, Lincoln's Inn,
LLB (Hons)

Yeoh *Gary Cheng Lee*
7th Floor, Bangunan Kassim Chan, 3
Cangkat Raja Chulan, P O Box 11151, 50736
Kuala Lumpur, 2320711, Fax: 2300585, and
Member Malaysia Bar. Called: May 1994,
Lincoln's Inn, LLB (Hons)

Yeoh *Miss Geraldine Poh Im*
7th Floor, 3 Changkat Raja Chulan, 50200
Kuala Lumpur, P.O.Box 11151, 50736 Kuala
Lumpur Malaysia, 03 2320711, Fax: 03
2304746/2300585, and Member Malaysia
Bar. Called: Nov 1991, Lincoln's Inn, LLB
(Hons)(Reading), LLM

Yeoh *Miss Huei-Keng*
Called: July 1997, Lincoln's Inn, LLB (Hons)

Yeoh *Leonard Soon Beng*
Called: July 1995, Lincoln's Inn, LLB (Hons)

Yeoh *Miss Melissa Ann Lin*
Called: Nov 1997, Middle Temple, LLB
(Hons)(Nott'm)

Yeoh *Nigel Lian Chuan*
Called: July 1993, Lincoln's Inn, LLB (Hons)

Yeoh *Miss Wai Ling*
Called: July 1996, Lincoln's Inn, LLB
(Hons)(Warw)

F

Yeow *Miss Ping Lin*
Attorney General's Chambers, 1 Coleman Street [H]10-00, The Aldelphi, Singapore 0617, 3361411 (065), Fax: 3390286, and Member Singapore Bar. Called: July 1993, Middle Temple, BA (Hons, Bris)

Yerrell *Miss Nicola Jane*
Legal Service, European Commission, Avenue des Nerviens, 105, B-1040 Bruxelles, +32 2 295 1969, Fax: +32 2 296 5972. Called: Oct 1993, Middle Temple, BA (Hons)(Oxon), Licence Special en, Droit Europeen, Brussels

Yeung *Miss Lai Sheung*
and Member Hong Kong Bar. Called: May 1994, Middle Temple, LLB (Hons)

Yeung *Sunny Kwong*
Called: Nov 1997, Inner Temple, BA, B.Arch (Hong, Kong)

Yeung *Yiu Wing*
Called: Nov 1995, Middle Temple, BSc, MSc & MBA, (Hong Kong)

Yew *Mrs Lily*
Called: July 1985, Lincoln's Inn, BSc (Detroit) LLB, (Lond)

Yik *Miss Sara Synn Yi*
Jurong Town Corporation, 301 Jurong Town Hall Road, Singapore 591001, 65 5688293, Fax: 65 5651977, and Member Singapore Bar. Called: July 1995, Middle Temple, LLB (Hons)

Yin *Michael Chi-Ming*
10/F New Henry House, 10 Ice House Street, and Member Hong Kong. Called: Nov 1993, Lincoln's Inn, LLB (Hons)(Bris), LLM (Bris)

Yin *Yip Shee*
70 St Thomas Walk, [H] 07-70 Pheonix Court, 732 0758. Called: Nov 1996, Inner Temple, BA (Dunelm)

Ying *Wan Chong*
Flat 20G, Fu Dat Court, 32 Fortress Hill Road, 887 8552, Fax: 858 4575. Called: Nov 1990, Gray's Inn, BScEng (HK), MSc (LSE), LLB (Lond)

Yip *Kwok Ching*
Official Receiver's Office, 11/F1 Queensway Government, Offices, 66 Queensway, and Member Hong Kong Bar. Called: Nov 1988, Gray's Inn, LLB (Lond), BSocSc, MSocSc (Hong Kong), ACIS, MCIT

Yiu *Kam Hung*
Called: Nov 1994, Middle Temple, B.Soc.Sc (Hons)

Yo-Hann *Tan*
Called: July 1997, Inner Temple, LLB (Kent), LLM (Lond)

Yogarajah *Miss Anusuya*
Called: July 1994, Inner Temple, BBA, LLB

Yogarajah *Miss Yoga Sharmini*
66 Medway Drive, Serangoon Garden Estate, Singapore, 1955, 2836271, and Member Singapore Bar. Called: July 1989, Middle Temple, BA, LLB (Lond)

Yong *Alvin Sze Lung*
Called: Nov 1996, Gray's Inn, LLB

Yong *Christopher Shu Wei*
Called: July 1994, Middle Temple, LLB (Hons)(Hull)

Yong *Miss Fook-Tai*
Called: Nov 1995, Middle Temple, LLB (Hons)

Yong *Miss Janet Hway Ming*
Shook Lin & Bok, 20th Floor, Arab-Malaysian Bld, 55 Jalan Raja Chulan, 50200 Kuala Lumpur, (03) 2011788, and Member Malaya Bar. Called: July 1995, Lincoln's Inn, LLB (Hons), LLM

Yong *Miss Jocelyn*
Called: Nov 1992, Lincoln's Inn, LLB (Hons)(Lond)

Yong *Sek-Cheong*
Malayan Law Journal, 3rd Floor, Wisma Bandar, No 18, Jalan Tuanku Abdul, Rahman, Kuala Lumpur 50100, 291 7273, Fax: 291 6440, and Member Malaysia Bar. Called: Oct 1992, Gray's Inn, BA (Kent)

Yong *Miss Siew Lee Magdalene*
Blk 408, [H]12-433, Pasir Ris Drive 6, Singapore 510408, 5820103. Called: July 1995, Middle Temple, LLB (Hons)

Yong *Vincent Wai Bun*
Called: July 1996, Lincoln's Inn, LLB (Hons)

Yongo *Thomas*
United Nations Environment, Programme, Secretariat of the, Convention on Biological, Diversity, 393 St-Jacques, Suite 300,Montreal,Quebec H2Y IN9, (514) 288 2220, Fax: (514) 288 6588. Called: Nov 1994, Gray's Inn, BA (Michigan), Diploma(Cantab), LLB (Kent), LLM (Lond)

Yoon *Ming Sun*
10 Lorong Derumun, Damansara Heights, 50490 Kuala Lumpur, 03 255 8307, Fax: 03 255 8307, and Member Malaysia. Called: Nov 1995, Middle Temple, LLB (Hons), MSc (So'ton)

Yoong *Weng Leong*
21 Jalan 5/4, 46000 Petaling Jaya, Selangor, West Malaysia, and Member Malaysia Bar. Called: Nov 1992, Lincoln's Inn, BA (Hons)(Keele)

Yoshinaga *Junichiro*
Corporate Business Development, Sony Corp, 6-7-35 Kitashinagawa, Shinagawa, Tokyo, Japan 141, 03 5448 2564, Fax: 03 5448 4248. Called: July 1994, Lincoln's Inn, BA (Econ) (Hons), Dip Law

You *Miss Lou Yuh*
Called: July 1997, Lincoln's Inn, LLB (Hons)(Lond)

Young *Miss Ai Peng*
Called: Nov 1997, Lincoln's Inn, LLB (Hons)

Young *Simon Jonathan*
Bedell & Cristin, One the Forum, St Helier, Jersey JE4 8PP, 01534 814814, Fax: 01534 814815, and Member Jersey Bar. Called: Oct 1991, Middle Temple, LLB Hons (Buck'ham), F.I.B.M.S.

Young *Stuart Richard*
8 Wainwright Street, St Clair, Trinidad, (868) 628 4558. Called: July 1997, Gray's Inn, LLB (Notts)

Yu *Denis Gordon Quok Chung*
Called: July 1982, Lincoln's Inn, BA (Oxon)

Yu-Min *Ms Ng Adeline*
Called: July 1997, Inner Temple, LLB (LSE)

Yue *Jonathan Tin-Kong*
Flat D, 15th Floor, Block One, Pokfulam Gardens, Pokfulam Hong Kong, Supreme Court of Hong Kong. Called: Nov 1994, Middle Temple, BA (Hons)

Yung *Shing Jit*
M/S Haridass Ho & Partners, 24 Raffles Place, [H]18-00 Clifford Centre, Singapore, 048621, 65-5332323, Fax: 65-5331579, and Member Singapore Bar. Called: July 1990, Middle Temple, LLB (Hull)

Yusoff *Yusrin Faidz*
34 Jalan SS21/44, Damansara Utama, 47400 Petaling Jaya, Selangor, 03 7171210, and Member Malaysia. Called: July 1996, Lincoln's Inn, LLB (Hons), MBA

Yusuf *Miss Kartini*
17-27-1 Majestic Tower, Mont' Kiara Palma, Jln Mont Kiara, Jln 1/40c, 50480 Kuala Lumpur, (03) 2533127. Called: May 1995, Lincoln's Inn, BA (Hons), LLB (Hons), LLM

Zachariadou *Miss Anthie Philippou*
14 Mnasiadou Street, Nicosia, 003572 475047, Fax: 003572 467532. Called: Feb 1995, Lincoln's Inn, LLB (Hons)(Lond)

Zadra-Symes *Mrs Lynda Julie*
Knobbe Martens Olson & Bear, 620 Newport Center Drive, Newport Beach CA 92660, 00 1 714 760 0404, Fax: 00 1 714 760 9502, and Member California Bar. Called: Nov 1989, Inner Temple, LLB

Zafer *Mohammed Abu*
Called: Mar 1997, Gray's Inn, MCom (Dhaka), LLB (Lond)

Zaharudin *Miss Faten Aina*
Called: July 1997, Lincoln's Inn, LLB (Hons)(Nott'm)

Zaidin *Miss Zalita*
Called: Nov 1992, Lincoln's Inn, LLB (Hons) (Warw)

Zain-Yusuf *Miss Shazlin*
Called: July 1995, Lincoln's Inn, LLB (Hons)

Zainal *Ms Suriawati*
Called: July 1994, Lincoln's Inn, LLB (Hons)

Zainal *Miss Zerenewati*
Called: July 1994, Lincoln's Inn, LLB (Hons)

Zainol-Abidin *Miss Adlina Hasni*
Messrs Chin Eng Adlina & Lim, Advocate & Solicitors, Suite 1-1, Burmah House, Jalan Burmah, 10350 Penang, (04) 229 4725, Fax: (04) 229 4728, and Member Malaysia. Called: July 1994, Gray's Inn, BSc (Denver), LLB (Wales)

Zam Zam *Mrs Asiah*
Called: Nov 1996, Lincoln's Inn, LLB (Hons)(Lond)

Zawoda-Martin *Justin Raphael*
Coutts Group, Talstrasse 59, P O Box CH-
8022, Zurich, +41 1 214 5580, Fax: +41 1
214 5563. Called: Oct 1994, Middle Temple,
BA (Hons)(Lond), CPE (City)

Zornoza *Simon*
Legal Division - Securities Op, State Street
Bank & Trust Co, 1776 Heritage Drive,
North Quincy, MA 02171, (617) 985 9271,
Fax: (617) 985 4000, and Member New
York Bar, District of Columbia Bar.
Called: July 1983, Inner Temple, LLB
(B'ham), Diplome, d'Etudes Juridiques,
Francaises

Zuberi *Miss Danish*
Called: Nov 1995, Gray's Inn, LLB (Wales)

Zulkifli *Miss Zurisafina*
Called: July 1997, Lincoln's Inn, LLB (Hons)

F

Languages/Barristers'
Clerks/A-Z Chambers

Index of Languages Spoken

This section provides an index of languages spoken by chambers and individual barristers. The languages are listed alphabetically, as are chambers and individuals.

All chambers in this section have an expanded entry in *Part C Chambers by Location* and all individual barristers in this section have an expanded entry in *Part D Individual Barristers in Private Practice*.

G

G

AFRIKAANS

Equity Chambers
Fountain Court
2 Garden Court
1 Gray's Inn Square
Littman Chambers

ARABIC

Equity Chambers
One Essex Court
Foster, Charles Andrew
Gray's Inn Chambers
1 Gray's Inn Square Chambers of the Baroness Scotland of Asthal QC
1 Gray's Inn Square
One Hare Court
Keating Chambers
2 Paper Buildings
3 Paper Buildings
3 Raymond Buildings

BENGALI

Equity Chambers
1 Gray's Inn Square Chambers of the Baroness Scotland of Asthal QC
9 King's Bench Walk
Mitre Court Chambers
Singh, Balbir

BRITISH SIGN LANGUAGE

Doughty Street Chambers

CANTONESE

One Essex Court
King's Bench Chambers
13 King's Bench Walk
MacKillop, Norman Malcolm
2 Paper Buildings

CHINESE

Essex Court Chambers
Chambers of Norman Palmer
Peel Court Chambers

CZECH

Doughty Street Chambers
Sovereign Chambers

DANISH

4 Paper Buildings

DUTCH

Blackstone Chambers (formerly known as 2 Hare Court)
Chancery House Chambers
1 Crown Office Row
4 Essex Court
2 Garden Court
3 Hare Court
Lamb Building
Littman Chambers
Monckton Chambers
13 Old Square

(cont.)
Oriel Chambers
4 Paper Buildings
1 Pump Court
3 Raymond Buildings

FARSI

Hardwicke Building

FINNISH

Blackstone Chambers (formerly known as 2 Hare Court)

FRENCH

Adejumo, Mrs Hilda Ekpo
Arden Chambers
29 Bedford Row Chambers
5 Bell Yard
9–12 Bell Yard
Blackstone Chambers (formerly known as 2 Hare Court)
Bracton Chambers
4 Breams Buildings
4 Brick Court
4 Brick Court
4 Brick Court, Chambers of Anne Rafferty QC
17 Carlton Crescent
Cathedral Chambers (Jan Wood Independent Barristers' Clerk)
Central Chambers
Chancery House Chambers
Cobden House Chambers
College Chambers
Cotter, Miss Sara Elizabeth
Chambers of Mr Peter Crampin QC
1 Crown Office Row
1 Crown Office Row
Two Crown Office Row
Crown Office Row Chambers
Devereux Chambers
Doggart, Piers Graham
Doughty Street Chambers
3 Dr Johnson's Buildings
Dr Johnson's Chambers
Eighteen Carlton Crescent
Elleray, Anthony John
Enterprise Chambers
Equity Chambers
One Essex Court
One Essex Court
4 Essex Court
Essex Court Chambers
20 Essex Street
35 Essex Street
39 Essex Street
Exchange Chambers
Farrar's Building
Fenners Chambers
Chambers of Norman Palmer
4 Field Court
Foster, Charles Andrew
Fountain Court
3 Fountain Court
5 Fountain Court
2nd Floor, Francis Taylor Building
Furnival Chambers
2 Garden Court
Goldsmith Building

(cont.)
Goodbody, Peter James
9 Gough Square
Gough Square Chambers
Gray's Inn Chambers
Gray's Inn Chambers
1 Gray's Inn Square Chambers of the Baroness Scotland of Asthal QC
1 Gray's Inn Square
2-3 Gray's Inn Square
4-5 Gray's Inn Square
Guildford Chambers
Gun Cuninghame, Julian Arthur
Chambers of John Hand QC
1 Harcourt Buildings
2 Harcourt Buildings
2 Harcourt Buildings
Harcourt Chambers
Hardwicke Building
1 Hare Court
One Hare Court
3 Hare Court
Harrow-on-the-Hill Chambers
Henderson, Launcelot Dinadan James
Hockman, Stephen Alexander
Hodgkinson, Tristram Patrick
Chambers of James Hunt QC
John Street Chambers
Jones, Timothy Arthur
Kavanagh, Giles Wilfred Conor
Keating Chambers
40 King Street
King's Bench Chambers
One King's Bench Walk
4 King's Bench Walk
6 King's Bench Walk
8 King's Bench Walk
9 King's Bench Walk
11 King's Bench Walk
12 King's Bench Walk
13 King's Bench Walk
Kolodziej, Andrzej Jozef
Kramer, Stephen Ernest
Lamb Building
Legh-Jones, Piers Nicholas
Littleton Chambers
Littman Chambers
The Chambers of Adrian Lyon
Maidstone Chambers
Martins Building
Merchant Chambers
Michael, Simon Laurence
1 Middle Temple Lane
1 Mitre Court Buildings
Mitre Court Chambers
Mitre House Chambers
Monckton Chambers
New Court
New Court
New Court Chambers
New Court Chambers
1 New Square
8 New Square
12 New Square
Newcombe, Andrew Bennett
Newman, Miss Catherine Mary No. 6
Oakley, Tony
22 Old Buildings
Twenty-Four Old Buildings

(cont.)
9 Old Square
11 Old Square
13 Old Square
Old Square Chambers
Oriel Chambers
Ough, Dr Richard Norman
2 Paper Buildings
2 Paper Buildings
3 Paper Buildings
3 Paper Buildings
4 Paper Buildings
4 Paper Buildings
5 Paper Buildings
Park Court Chambers
30 Park Square
37 Park Square
Parkin, Jonathan
Peel Court Chambers
Pitt-Payne, Timothy Sheridan
Portsmouth Barristers' Chambers
Chambers of John L Powell QC
1 Pump Court
Pump Court Chambers
4 Pump Court
5 Pump Court
Queen Elizabeth Building
Queen Elizabeth Building
Queen's Chambers
1 Raymond Buildings
3 Raymond Buildings
5 Raymond Buildings
3 Serjeants' Inn
Serle Court Chambers
Shepherd, Philip Alexander
Sheridan, Maurice Bernard Gerard
Sheridan, Norman Patrick
Silverleaf, Michael
Slade, Miss Elizabeth Ann
3-4 South Square
11 South Square
Southern, Professor David Boardman
Sovereign Chambers
St James's Chambers
28 St John Street
St Paul's House
St Philip's Chambers
Stanbrook & Henderson
3 Stone Buildings
5 Stone Buildings
9 Stone Buildings
Stone, Gregory
199 Strand
1 Temple Gardens
2 Temple Gardens
3 Temple Gardens
Thomas More Chambers
14 Tooks Court
Trace, Anthony John
Turner, Jonathan David Chattyn
3 Verulam Buildings
West, Mark
Wilberforce Chambers
Wilson, Alastair James Drysdale
9 Woodhouse Square
Woolley, David Rorie
York Chambers

GERMAN

29 Bedford Row Chambers
5 Bell Yard

(cont.)
3-4 South Square
Sovereign Chambers
St Paul's House
St Philip's Chambers
Stanbrook & Henderson
5 Stone Buildings
2 Temple Gardens
14 Tooks Court
3 Verulam Buildings

JAPANESE

Blackstone Chambers (formerly
  known as 2 Hare Court)
2 Harcourt Buildings
4 King's Bench Walk
Monckton Chambers
3 New Square
30 Park Square
Stanbrook & Henderson
199 Strand

KRIO

1 Gray's Inn Square
3 Hare Court

MALAY

4 Brick Court
1 Gray's Inn Square

MANDARIN

4 Brick Court
Chambers of Norman Palmer
1 Gray's Inn Square Chambers of
  the Baroness Scotland of Asthal
  QC
Littleton Chambers
Peel Court Chambers
3-4 South Square
199 Strand

MARATHI

2 Paper Buildings

NEPALI

New Court Chambers

NORWEGIAN

Blackstone Chambers (formerly
  known as 2 Hare Court)
40 King Street

POLISH

35 Essex Street
Chambers of James Hunt QC
Kolodziej, Andrzej Jozef
Littman Chambers
Merchant Chambers
2 Paper Buildings
5 Raymond Buildings

PORTUGUESE

Blackstone Chambers (formerly
  known as 2 Hare Court)
1 Crown Office Row
Enterprise Chambers
4 Essex Court

(cont.)
Furnival Chambers
Hardwicke Building
King's Bench Chambers
One King's Bench Walk
12 King's Bench Walk
13 King's Bench Walk
4 Paper Buildings
Stanbrook & Henderson
3 Stone Buildings
3 Verulam Buildings

PUNJABI

Central Chambers
Equity Chambers
2 Garden Court
Gray's Inn Chambers
1 Gray's Inn Square
Chambers of John Hand QC
Chambers of James Hunt QC
9 King's Bench Walk
Mitre House Chambers
2 Paper Buildings
5 Paper Buildings
1 Pump Court
Singh, Balbir
Sovereign Chambers
St Philip's Chambers
York Chambers

RUSSIAN

9-12 Bell Yard
Blackstone Chambers (formerly
  known as 2 Hare Court)
4 Brick Court
Chambers of Norman Palmer
Fountain Court
Hardwicke Building
Littman Chambers
Martins Building
New Court
Newcombe, Andrew Bennett
13 Old Square
4 Paper Buildings
Queen Elizabeth Building
St James's Chambers
3 Verulam Buildings

SERBO-CROAT

Chambers of Norman Palmer
Furnival Chambers
3 Hare Court
Chambers of James Hunt QC
Mitre Court Chambers

SINHALA

2 Garden Court
Mitre House Chambers

SPANISH

29 Bedford Row Chambers
9-12 Bell Yard
Blackstone Chambers (formerly
  known as 2 Hare Court)
Bracton Chambers
4 Brick Court
4 Brick Court
4 Brick Court, Chambers of Anne
  Rafferty QC

(cont.)
1 Crown Office Row
1 Crown Office Row
Crown Office Row Chambers
Doughty Street Chambers
Dr Johnson's Chambers
Enterprise Chambers
One Essex Court
4 Essex Court
Essex Court Chambers
20 Essex Street
39 Essex Street
Chambers of Norman Palmer
5 Fountain Court
Furnival Chambers
2 Garden Court
Gray's Inn Chambers
1 Gray's Inn Square Chambers of
  the Baroness Scotland of Asthal
  QC
1 Gray's Inn Square
4-5 Gray's Inn Square
Chambers of John Hand QC
1 Harcourt Buildings
2 Harcourt Buildings
Hardwicke Building
1 Hare Court
Chambers of James Hunt QC
Keating Chambers
One King's Bench Walk
4 King's Bench Walk
6 King's Bench Walk
11 King's Bench Walk
12 King's Bench Walk
Lamb Building
Littman Chambers
Merchant Chambers
Mitre Court Chambers
Mitre House Chambers
New Court Chambers
8 New Square
Oakley, Tony
Twenty-Four Old Buildings
9 Old Square
11 Old Square
Old Square Chambers
2 Paper Buildings
3 Paper Buildings
4 Paper Buildings
4 Paper Buildings
5 Paper Buildings
Peel House Chambers
Chambers of John L Powell QC
1 Pump Court
4 Pump Court
Queen Elizabeth Building
Queen Elizabeth Building
1 Raymond Buildings
3-4 South Square
St James's Chambers
28 St John Street
St Philip's Chambers
Stanbrook & Henderson
3 Stone Buildings
5 Stone Buildings
7 Stone Buildings
1 Temple Gardens
2 Temple Gardens
Thomas More Chambers
14 Tooks Court
3 Verulam Buildings
9 Woodhouse Square

SWAHILI

Equity Chambers
1 Gray's Inn Square
9 King's Bench Walk
Trace, Anthony John

SWEDISH

Blackstone Chambers (formerly
  known as 2 Hare Court)

TURKISH

4 King's Bench Walk
Mitre House Chambers
14 Tooks Court

URDU

29 Bedford Row Chambers
9-12 Bell Yard
Blackstone Chambers (formerly
  known as 2 Hare Court)
4 Brick Court
Central Chambers
3 Dr Johnson's Buildings
Equity Chambers
4 Field Court
Fountain Chambers
2 Garden Court
Gray's Inn Chambers
1 Gray's Inn Square
Chambers of John Hand QC
Hardwicke Building
1 Hare Court
Chambers of James Hunt QC
40 King Street
8 King's Bench Walk
9 King's Bench Walk
No. 6
Park Court Chambers
1 Pump Court
5 Pump Court
Singh, Balbir
Sovereign Chambers
St Paul's House
Thomas More Chambers
14 Tooks Court
9 Woodhouse Square

WELSH

4 Brick Court, Chambers of Anne
  Rafferty QC
Dr Johnson's Chambers
Exchange Chambers
Farrar's Building
Chambers of Norman Palmer
Goldsmith Building
3 Hare Court
13 Old Square
33 Park Place
Peel House Chambers
Chambers of John L Powell QC
St Philip's Chambers
9 Stone Buildings

YORUBA

Adejumo, Mrs Hilda Ekpo
Gray's Inn Chambers

G

Qualified Members of the Institute of Barristers' Clerks

This section lists all qualified members of the Institute of Barristers' Clerks. The listings are divided into four sections: Senior Clerks, Junior Clerks, Senior Associates and Junior Associates. The information in Part H was supplied by the Institute of Barristers' Clerks. The year of qualification, if supplied, is shown in brackets. Management Committee Members and Executive Committee Members are identified by the following symbols:

* Management Committee Member
** Executive Committee Member

H

SENIOR CLERKS

Alden, Philip
(1990) Colleton Chambers, Colleton
Crescent, Exeter EX2 4DG, DX: 8330, Tel:
01392 274898

Aldridge, Kevin
(1979) 3 Temple Gardens, Temple, EC4Y
9AU, LDE: 485, Tel: 0171 353 9297

Appleyard, Neil
Broadway House Chambers, 9 Bank
Street, Bradford BD1 1TW, DX: 11746
Bradford, Tel: 01274 722560

Armstrong, Gordon
(1978) 4 Essex Court, Temple, EC4Y 9AP,
LDE: 292, Tel: 0171 797 7970

Arter, John
2 Pump Court, Temple, EC4Y 7AH, LDE:
290, Tel: 0171 353 5597

Austin, Alan
(1993) 11 Stone Buildings, Lincoln's Inn,
WC2A 3TG, LDE: 314, Tel: 0171 404 5055

Austin, David
(1976) Rope Walk Chambers,
Nottingham, DX: 10060, Tel: 01159
472581

Austin, M. (Trevor)
Verulam Chambers, Peer House, 8/14
Verulam Street, WC1X, 8LZ, LDE: 436, Tel:
0171 813 2400

Ballard, Paul
(1979) 1 Hare Court, Temple, EC4Y 7BE,
LDE: 0065, Tel: 0171 353 3171

Barrow, Adrian
(1979) 6 Pump Court, Temple, EC4Y 7AR,
LDE: 409, Tel: 0171 583 6013

Bayliss, Richard
3 New Square, Lincoln's Inn, WC2A 3RS,
LDE: 384, Tel: 0171 405 5577

Beazley, Roy
8 New Square, Lincoln's Inn, WC2A 3QP,
LDE: 311, Tel: 0171 306 0102

Berry, Christopher
11 Stone Buildings, Lincoln's Inn, WC2A
3TG, LDE: 1022, Tel: 0171 831 6381

Blaney, Arthur
11 King's Bench Walk, Temple, EC4Y 7EQ,
LDE: 389, Tel: 0171 353 3337

Bowker, John
11 Bolt Court, London EC4A 3DQ, LDE:
0022, Tel: 0171 353 2300

Breadmore, Gordon
Gray's Inn Chambers, Gray's Inn, WC1R
5JA, LDE: 0074, Tel: 0171 404 1111

Brewer, Alan
22 Old Buildings, Lincoln's Inn, WC2A
3UJ, LDE: 201, Tel: 0171 831 0222

Bridgman, Barry
10 Essex Street, Outer Temple, WC2R 3AA,
LDE: 1045, Tel: 0171 240 6981

Brooks, Norman
(1976) 4 King's Bench Walk, Temple,
EC4Y 7DL, LDE: 383, Tel: 0171 353 6832

Brown, William
(1978) 40 King Street, Manchester M2 6BA,
DX: 718188 MAN 3, Tel: 0161 832 9082

Bryant, Stuart
5 Paper Buildings, Temple, EC4Y 7HB,
LDE: 365, Tel: 0171 583 6117

Butchard, Robin
2 Fountain Court, Birmingham B4 6DR,
DX: 16071 Birm , Tel: 0121 236 3882

Butler, David
5 Stone Buildings, Lincoln's Inn, WC2A
3XT, LDE: 304, Tel: 0171 242 6201

Butler, Deryk
1 Hare Court, Temple, EC4Y 7BE, LDE:
444, Tel: 0171 353 3982

Butler, Ronald
3 Raymond Buildings, Gray's Inn, WC1R
5BH, LDE: 237, Tel: 0171 831 3833

Calver, Neil
Warwick House Chambers, Gray's Inn,
WC1R 5DJ, LDE: 1001, Tel: 0171 430 2323

Call, John
8 New Square, Lincoln's Inn, WC2A 3QP,
LDE: 379, Tel: 0171 405 4321

Charlick, John
3 Paper Buildings, Temple, EC4Y 7EU,
LDE: 1024, Tel: 0171 583 8055

Chessis, Clark
1 Serjeants' Inn, London, EC4Y 1LL, LDE:
364, Tel: 0171 353 9901

Clark, Michael
2 Field Court, Gray's Inn, WC1R 5BB, LDE:
457, Tel: 0171 405 6114

**Clayton, Barry
9 Old Square, Lincoln's Inn, WC2A 3SR,
LDE: 301, Tel: 0171 405 9471
(Chancery Secretary)

Clewley, Mark
Falcon Chambers, Falcon Court, EC4Y
1AA, LDE: 408, Tel: 0171 353 2484

Clinnick, Paul
Gray's Inn Chambers, Gray's Inn, WC1R
5JA, LDE: 0074, Tel: 0171 404 1111

Collier, Alan
2 Harcourt Buildings, Temple, EC4Y 9DB,
LDE: 402, Tel: 0171 353 8415

Collison, Peter
25 Byron Street, Manchester M3 4PF, DX:
18156 MAN, Tel: 0161 834 8468

Conner, Alan
King's Bench Walk Chambers, Wellington
House, 175 HoLDE:nhurst Rd,
Bournemouth BH8 8DQ, DX: 7617
Bournemouth, Tel: 01202 250025

Conner, William
New Court Chambers, 5 Verulam Bldgs,
WC1R 5LY, LDE: 363, Tel: 0171 831 9500

Cook, Colin
2 Garden Court, Temple, EC4Y 9BL, LDE:
34, Tel: 0171 353 1633

Coomber, Simon
New Court, Temple, EC4Y 9BE, LDE: 420,
Tel: 0171 797 8999

Corrigan, Michael
4th Floor, 4 Brick Court, Temple, EC4Y
9AD, LDE: 491, Tel: 0171 797 8910

Creathorn, Teresa
Deans Court Chambers, Manchester M3
3HA, DX: 18155, Tel: 0161 834 4097

Davies, Hugh
(1988) 30 Park Place, Cardiff CF1 3BA,
DX: 50756, Tel: 01222 398421

Davies, Dennis
(1988)

Dean, Michael
(1988) 5 Essex Court, Temple, EC4Y 9AH,
LDE: 1048, Tel: 0171 583 2825

Dear, David
(1988) 1 King's Bench Walk, Temple,
EC4Y 7DB, LDE: 20, Tel: 0171 583 6266

Diggles, S.
68 Quay Street, Manchester M3 3BL, DX:
14350, Tel: 0161 834 7000

Doe, Christopher
1 Essex Court, Temple, EC4Y 9AR, LDE:
371, Tel: 0171 936 3030

Dorsett, Arthur
169 Temple Chambers, Temple Avenue,
EC4, LDE: 348, Tel: 0171 583 7644

Down, Barry
(1977)

Driscoll, Robin
2 Paper Buildings, Temple, EC4, LDE:
494, Tel: 0171 936 2611

Edmiston, James
3 Temple Gardens, EC4Y 9AU, LDE: 427,
Tel: 0171 353 7884

Effeny, Wayne
(1984) 2/3 College Place, Southampton
SO1 2FB, DX: 38533, Tel: 01703 230338

Elder, Malcolm
(1976)

Elliott, Geoffrey
6 Park Square, Leeds LS1 2LW, DX: 26402
Leeds, Tel: 0113 245 9763

Ellis, Barry
1 Hare Court, Temple, EC4Y 7BE, LDE:
0065, Tel: 0171 353 3171

Eves, Michael
(1975) 4 Brick Court, 1st Floor, Temple,
EC4Y 9AD, LDE: 453, Tel: 0171 583 8455

*Farrell, Michael
(1978) 18 St John Street, Manchester M3
4EA, DX: 728854, Tel: 0161 278 1800

Foss, Marc
(1984) 8 King's Bench Walk, Temple,
EC4Y 7DU, LDE: 195, Tel: 0171 797 8888

Gallogly, Lawrence
(1976) Phoenix Chambers, 47A Bedford
Row, WC1R 4LR, LDE: 78, Tel: 0171 404
7888

Garstang, David
6 King's Bench Walk, Temple, EC4Y 7DR,
LDE: 26, Tel: 0171 583 0410

Gibbs, Michael
(1988) 11 New Square, Lincoln's Inn, WC2A 3QB, LDE: 319, Tel: 0171 831 0081

**Goddard, David
(1976) 4 Stone Buildings, Lincoln's Inn, WC2A 3XT, LDE: 385, Tel: 0171 242 5524 (Vice-Chairman)

Goldsmith, Stuart
(1976) 1 Atkin Building, Gray's Inn, WC1R 5BQ, DX: 1033, Tel: 0171 404 0102

Goodger, Gary
(1980) Lamb Buildings, Temple, EC4, LDE: 1038, Tel: 0171 797 7788

**Graham, Stephen
4 Breams Buildings, London EC4A 1AQ, LDE: 1042, Tel: 0171 353 5835 (Chairman)

*Gray, Michael
5/7 Harrington Street, Liverpool L2 9QA, DX: 14225, Tel: 0151 236 4321

Green, Paul
(1982) Tindall Chambers, Chelmsford CM1 1SW, DX: 3358, Tel: 01245 267742

Greenaway, Michael
Queen Elizabeth Building, Temple, EC4Y 9BS, LDE: 482, Tel: 0171 583 5766

Grief, David
(1976) Essex Court Chambers, EC4Y 9AJ, LDE: 320, Tel: 0171 813 8000

Griffiths, Martin
(1978) 199 Strand, London WC2R 1DR, LDE: 322, Tel: 0171 379 9779

Grisdale, Neil
(1976) 20 North John Street, Liverpool L2 9RL, DX: 14220, Tel: 0151 236 6757

**Gutteridge, John
(1983) 32 Furnival Street, EC4A 1JQ, LDE: 72, Tel: 0171 405 3232

Hallett, C.J.
Thomas More Chambers, 51/52 Carey Street, WC2A 2JB, LDE: 90, Tel: 0171 404 7000

**Hannibal, Michael
(1977)Erskine Chambers, 30 Lincoln's Inn Fields, WC2A 3PF, LDE: 308, Tel: 0171 242 5532

Hawes, Julian
Brick Court Chambers, Devereux Court, WC2, LDE: 302, Tel: 0171 583 0777

Hayfield, C.
1 Fountain Court, Birmingham B4 6DR, DX: 16077 B'ham, Tel: 0121 236 5721

Hogg, Ian
(1991) Hamilton House, 1 Temple Ave, EC4Y 0HA, LDE: 416, Tel: 0171 353 4212

Hopgood, Nicholas
36 Essex Street, London WC2 3AB, LDE: 148, Tel: 0171 413 0353

Hoskins, Peter

Hyatt, Bernie
(1988) 7 King's Bench Walk, Temple, EC4Y 7DS, LDE: 239, Tel: 0171 583 0404

Hyde, Nicholas
St John's Chambers, Small Street, Bristol BS1 1DW, DX: 78138, Tel: 0117 921 3456

James, Christopher
(1988) 4 Field Court, WC1R 5EA, LDE: 483, Tel: 0171 440 6900

Jeffery, Gary
(1988) 6 King's Bench Walk, Temple, EC4Y 7EQ, LDE: 471, Tel: 0171 353 4931

Jenkins, Derek
(1988) 35 Essex Street, Temple, WC2R 3AR, LDE: 351, Tel: 0171 353 6381

Jones, Michael
15 Winkley Square, Preston PR1 3JJ, DX: 17110, Tel: 01772 252828

Kaye, Roberta
3 St Andrew Street, Plymouth, Devon PL1 2AH, DX: 8290, Tel: 01752 661659

Kay, Jonathan
3 East Pallant, Chichester, PO19 1TR, DX: 30303, Tel: 01243 784538

Kennedy, John
Wilberforce Chambers, Hull HU1 1NE, DX: 11940, Tel: 01482 23264

Kilbey, Alan
Farrars Building, Temple, EC4Y 7DB, LDE: 406, Tel: 0171 583 9241

King, Robert
Peel House, 5/7 Harrington Street, Liverpool L2 9QA, DX: 14225, Tel: 0151 236 4321

Knight, Lynda
17 Carlton Crescent, Southampton SO9 5AL, DX: 49663, Tel: 01703 639001

Laking, John
Oriel Chambers, 14 Water St, Liverpool L2 8TD, DX: 14106, Tel: 0151 236 7191

Lee, Warren
1 New Square, Lincoln's Inn, WC2A 3SA, LDE: 295, Tel: 0171 405 0884

Lister, Graham
4 Raymond Buildings, Gray's Inn, WC1R 5BP, LDE: 257, Tel: 0171 405 7211

*Lister, John
17 Old Buildings, Lincoln's Inn, WC2A 3UP, LDE: 300, Tel: 0171 405 9653

Logan, Graeme
1 King's Bench Walk, Temple, EC4Y 7DB, LDE: 360, Tel: 0171 353 8436

Luff, Alan
8 Stone Bldgs, WC2A 3TA, LDE: 216, Tel: 0171 831 9881

Maloney, Miss C.
8 Fountain Court, Birmingham B4 6DR, DX: 16078 Bir, Tel: 0121 236 5514

McDaid, Anthony
(1988) 5 Fountain Court, Birmingham B4 6DR, DX: 16705, Tel: 0121 236 5771

Markham, John
2 Mitre Court, Temple, EC4Y 7BX, LDE: 0023, Tel: 0171 353 1553

Markham, Timothy
5 Pump Court, Temple, EC4Y 7AP, LDE: 497, Tel: 0171 353 2532

Martin, Michael
Cloisters, Temple, EC4Y 7AA, LDE: 452, Tel: 0171 583 0303

Maryon, Elton
Devereux Chambers, Devereux Court, Temple, WC2R 3JJ, LDE: 349, Tel: 0171 353 7534

Maskew, Jonathan
(1988) 3 Fountain Court, Birmingham B4 6DR, DX: 16079, Tel: 0121 236 2286

McCombe, Carolyn
4 Pump Court, Temple, EC4Y 7AN, LDE: 303, Tel: 0171 353 2656

McLaren, Fraser
East Anglian Chambers, Colchester CO1 1PY, DX: 3611, Tel: 01206 573401

Merry-Price, Roger
3 Gray's Inn Place, Gray's Inn, WC1R 5EA, LDE: 331, Tel: 0171 831 8441

Monham, Philip
11 King's Bench Walk, Temple, EC4Y 7EQ, LDE: 368, Tel: 0171 583 0610

**Monksfield, Celia
Goldsmith Building, Temple EC4Y 7BL, LDE: 376, Tel: 0171 353 6802 (Treasurer)

Moore, John
13 Old Square, Lincoln's Inn, WC2A 3UA, LDE: 326, Tel: 0171 404 4800

Moore, Kevin
(1979)5 Bell Yard, London WC2A 2JR, LDE: 400, Tel: 0171 333 8811

Moore, Richard
Guildford Chambers, Guildford GU1 4LY, DX: 97863, Tel: 01483 39131

*Neeld, Rodney
4 Fountain Court, Birmingham B4 6DR, DX: 16074, Tel: 0121 236 3476

Newcomb, John
(1983)2 Crown Office Row, Temple, EC4Y 7HJ, LDE: 344, Tel: 0171 797 8100

Nicholls, Martyn
(1980) 11 South Square, Gray's Inn, WC1, LDE: 433, Tel: 0171 405 1222

*Nixon, Peter
Assize Court Chambers, Bristol BS1 1DE, DX: 78134, Tel: 0117 926 4587

Oliver, Ken
Francis Taylor Buildings, Temple, EC4Y 7BY, LDE: 46, Tel: 0171 353 2182

**Owen, Christopher
9 Bedford Row, WC1R 4AZ, LDE: 347, Tel: 0171 242 3555 (Common Law Secretary)

Packman, Barry

Page, Leslie
4/5 Gray's Inn Square, Gray's Inn, WC1R 5AY, LDE: 1029, Tel: 0171 404 5252

Palmer, Neil
(1984) 20 Essex Street, London WC2R 3AL, LDE: 0009, Tel: 0171 583 9294

Parker, David

Petchey, Clive
(1984) 12 New Square, Lincoln's Inn, WC2A 3SW, LDE: 366, Tel: 0171 405 3808

Pithers, Jason
3-4 South Square, Gray's Inn, WC1R 5HP, LDE: 338, Tel: 0171 696 9900

Phipps, John
1 Crown Office Row, Temple, EC4Y 7HH, LDE: 226, Tel: 0171 797 7111

Pickles, Jack
28 St John Street Chambers, Manchester M3 4DJ, DX: 728861, Tel: 0161 834 8418

**Poulter, Martin
36 Bedford Row, London, WC1R 4JH, LDE: 360, Tel: 0171 421 8000

*Price, Michael
Queen Elizabeth Building, Temple, EC4Y 9BS, LDE: 340, Tel: 0171 353 7181

Pyne, John
(1991) 1 Middle Temple Lane, Temple, EC4, LDE: 464, Tel: 0171 583 0659

Ralphs, Robert
1 Essex Court, Temple, EC4Y 9AR, LDE: 430, Tel: 0171 583 2000

Reed, Gary (1980)
9/12 Bell Yard, WC2N 3ED, LDE: 390, Tel: 0171 400 1800

Regan, John
Gray's Inn Chambers, London WC1R 5JA, LDE: 352, Tel: 0171 242 2642

Rogers, Graham
Crown Square Chambers, Manchester M3 3HA, DX: 14326, Tel: 0161 833 9801

*Riley, Hugh
2 Crown Office Row, Temple, EC4Y 7HJ, LDE: 1041, Tel: 0171 797 8000

Riordan, Matthew

Rugg, John

Ryan, Michael
27 New Walk, Leicester LE1 6TE, DX: 10872, Tel: 01162 559144

*Salt, Nicholas
(1977) 3 Serjeant's Inn, London EC4Y 1BQ, LDE: 421, Tel: 0171 353 5537

Salter, John

Sampson, Paul
4 Brick Court, Temple, EC4Y 9AD, LDE: 404, Tel: 0171 797 7766

Scothern, David
10/11 Gray's Inn Square, Gray's Inn, WC1, LDE: 484, Tel: 0171 405 2576

Segal, Robert
29 Bedford Row, London WC1R 4HE, LDE: 1044, Tel: 0171 831 2626

Shrubsall, Paul
1 Essex Street, Temple, EC4Y 9AR, LDE: 430, Tel: 0171 583 2000

Skelton, Frank
3 Temple Gardens, London EC4Y 9AU, LDE: 485, Tel: 0171 353 7884

Slater, Stephen
(1983) 25 Park Square (West), Leeds LS1 2PW, DX: 16408, Tel: 0113 245 1841

Smith, Alan
1 Crown Office Row, Temple, EC4Y 7HH, LDE: 1020, Tel: 0171 797 7500

*Smith, Martin
2 Hare Court, Temple, EC4Y 7BH, LDE: 281, Tel: 0171 583 1770

Stammers, Alan
5 Paper Buildings, Temple, EC4Y 7HB, LDE: 415, Tel: 0171 583 9275

Stinton, Linda
(1984) 7 King's Bench Walk, Temple, EC44Y 7DS, LDE: 239, Tel: 0171 583 0404

Strong, Michael

Taylor, John
Old Square Chambers, 1 Verulam Bldgs, Gray's Inn, LDE: 1046, Tel: 0171 831 0801

Terry, Neil
(1995) Barton Mill House, Canterbury, CT1 1BP, DX: 5342, Tel: 01227 764899

Thomas, Joanne
(1992) 2 Paper Buildings, Temple, EC4Y 7ET, LDE: 210, Tel: 0171 936 2613

Townsend, Gregory
17 Carlton Crescent, Southampton SO9 5AL, DX: 49663, Tel: 01703 320320

Tracy, Andrea
Arden Chambers, 59 Fleet Street, EC4Y 1JU, LDE: 29, Tel: 0171 353 3132

Treherne, Ivor
Queen Elizabeth Building, Temple, EC4Y 9BS, LDE: 339, Tel: 0171 797 7837

Ward, Stephen
South Western Chambers, Taunton, TA1 1SH, DX: 32146, Tel: 01823 331919

Watts, Michael
2 Harcourt Buildings, Temple, EC44Y 9DB, LDE: 489, Tel: 0171 353 2112

Weaver, Andrew
Lincoln House, Manchester, M2 5EL, DX: 14338, Tel: 0161 832 57Tel: 01

*Whinnett, Robin
21 Whitefriars, Chester CH1 1NJ, DX: 19979, Tel: 01244 323070

White, John
2 Harcourt Buildings, Temple, EC4Y 9DB, LDE: 1039, Tel: 0171 583 9020

Wilson, David
50 High Pavement, Nottingham NG1 1HN, DX: 10036, Tel: 01602 503503

Woods, Robert
(1984) 2 Mitre Court Bldgs, Temple, EC4Y 7BX, LDE: 0032, Tel: 0171 583 1380

Wright, Peter
Young Street Chambers, 38 Young Street, Manchester M3 3FT, DX: 25583 Man 5, Tel: 0161 835 3938

JUNIOR CLERKS

Allen, Elizabeth
(1976) Gray's Inn Chambers, Gray's Inn, WC1, LDE: 352, Tel: 0171 242 2642

Allen, Perry
(1992) 9 Bedford Row, WC1R, LDE: 347, Tel: 0171 242 3555

Ansell, Richard
(1988) 3 Gray's Inn Place, Gray's Inn, WC1, LDE: 331, Tel: 0171 831 8441

Barker, Tracy
(1992) 3 Serjeants Inn, London EC4, LDE: 421, Tel: 0171 353 5537

Barnes, Andrew
(1979) 6 King's Bench Walk, Temple, EC4, LDE: 26, Tel: 0171 583 0410

Barnes, David
1 Atkin Building, Gray's Inn, WC1, LDE: 1033, Tel: 0171 404 0201

Bateman, Garfield
3 Stone Buildings, Lincoln's Inn, WC2, LDE: 317, Tel: 0171 242 4937

Belford, Carol
10 King's Bench Walk, Temple, EC4, LDE: 294, Tel: 0171 353 2501

Bennett, Mark
18 Red Lion Court, London, EC4A 3EB, LDE: 478, Tel: 0171 520 6000

Biggerstaff, Sam
Essex Court Chambers, 24 Lincoln's Inn Fields, WC2A 3ED, LDE: 320, Tel: 0171 813 8000

Bocock, Robert
(1994) 2 Harcourt Buildings, Temple, EC4, LDE: 1039, Tel: 0171 583 9020

Boutwood, Simon
(1994) 2 Harcourt Buildings, Temple, EC4, LDE: 1039, Tel: 0171 583 9020

Branchflower, Rich
(1993) 2 Hare Court, Temple, EC4Y 7BH, LDE: 281, Tel: 0171 583 1770

Broom, Christopher
(1987) 2/3 Gray's Inn Square, WC1R 5JH, LDE: 316, Tel: 0171 242 4986

Burnell, Philip
(1992) 4 King's Bench Walk, Temple, EC4, LDE: 1050, Tel: 0171 353 3581

Burton, Russell J.
(1995) 17 Old Buildings, Lincoln's Inn, WC2A 3UP, LDE: 300, Tel: 0171 831 1621

Carver, Paul S.
(1992) 9 Old Square, Lincoln's Inn, WC2, LDE: 305, Tel: 0171 405 4682

Clark, Janet
Francis Taylor Buildings, Temple, EC4Y 7BY, LDE: 441, Tel: 0171 353 7768

Clark, Nick
(1995) 1 Atkin Buildings, Gray's Inn, WC1R 5BQ, LDE: 1033, Tel: 0171 404 0102

---

* Management Committee Member   ** Executive Committee Member

Clark, Stephen
1st Floor, 3 Paper Buildings, Temple, EC4Y 7EU, LDE: 1024, Tel: 0171 583 8055

Collins, Ian
(1977) 3 Raymond Buildings, Gray's Inn, WC1R 5BH, LDE:, Tel: 0171 831 3833

Connor, Paul
(1992) Gray's Inn Chambers, Gray's Inn, WC1, LDE: 352, Tel: 0171 242 2642

Cornell, Mark
(1988) 1 Paper Buildings, Temple, EC4, LDE: 332, Tel: 0171 353 3728

Cox, Geoffrey

Coyne, Alistair
(1990) Littleton Chambers, Temple, EC4, LDE: 1047, Tel: 0171 797 8600

Davis, Spencer

Dixon, Christopher
(1987) 25 Park Square, Leeds LS1 2PW, DX: 26408, Tel: 0113 2457841

* Doyle, Jason
(1990) 4 Stone Buildings, Lincoln's Inn, WC2, LDE: 385, Tel: 0171 242 5524

Easton, Andrew
(1987) Park Court Chambers, Leeds LS1 2QH, DX: 26401, Tel: 0113 433277

Fantham, Danny
(1988) 3 Pump Court, Temple, EC4, LDE: 362, Tel: 0171 353 0711

Farrell, Chris
(1990) Farrars Building, Temple, EC4, LDE: 406, Tel: 0171 585 9241

Ferrigno, Joe
(1987) 24 Lincoln's Inn Fields, WC1A 3ED, LDE: 320, Tel: 0171 813 8000

Flanagan, Paul
(1988) 20/23 Holborn, EC1N 2JD, LDE: 336, Tel: 0171 242 8508

Fleming, Matthew
(1988) 7 Fountain Court, Birmingham B4 6DR, DX: 16073, Tel: 0121 233 3282

Gant, Judy
(1991) 35 Essex St, WC2R 3AR, LDE: 351, Tel: 0171 353 6381

Garrett, Neil
12 New Square, Lincoln's Inn, WC2, LDE: 366, Tel: 0171 405 3808

Gilbert, Richard
Francis Taylor Buildings, Temple EC4Y, LDE: 46, Tel: 0171 797 7250

Ginty, Jacqueline
(1994) 1 Essex Court, Temple, EC4, LDE: 430, Tel: 0171 583 2000

Goldsmith, Philip
(1980) 10 Essex Street, Outer Temple, WC2, LDE: 1045, Tel: 0171 240 6981

Gray, Mary
(1978) 1 Essex Court, Temple, EC4, LDE: 430, Tel: 0171 583 2000

Griffin, Colin

(1988) 40 King Street, Manchester M2 6BA, DX: 718188, Tel: 0161 832 9082

Grove, Tom
(1987) 2 Temple Gardens, Temple, EC4, LDE: 134, Tel: 0171 583 6041

Hamilton, Nicholas
(1990) 2 Crown Office Row, Temple, EC4, LDE: 344, Tel: 0171 797 8100

Harwood, John
(1988) 11 Bolt Court, EC4A 3DQ, LDE: 0022, Tel: 0171 353 2300

Hawes, Adrian
(1990) 5 Bell Yard, WC2A 2JE, LDE: 400, Tel: 0171 585 1770

Hewitt, David
(1988) Hollins Chambers, 64 Bridge Street, Manchester, M3 3BA, DX: 14327, Tel: 0161 835 3451

Hill, Nicholas
(1991) Essex Court Chambers, Lincoln's Inn Fields, LDE: 320, Tel: 0171 813 8000

Hobbs, Russell
King Charles House, Standard Hill, Nottingham, DX: 10042, Tel: 0121 236 5771

Hodkinson, Denise
(1995) Derby Square Chambers, Liverpool L2 1TS, DX: 14213, Tel: 0151 709 4222

Holland, Clifford
(1992) Devereux Chambers, Devereux Court, WC2, LDE: 349, Tel: 0171 353 7534

Housden, Jason
(1992) Hardwicke Bldg, 3 New Square Lincoln's Inn, WC2, LDE: 393, Tel: 0171 242 2523

Jennings, Paul
(1986) 5 Stone Buildings, Lincoln's Inn, WC2, LDE: 304, Tel: 0171 242 6201

Johnson, Lee
3 Serjeants Inn, London EC4Y 1BQ, LDE: 421, Tel: 0171 353 5537

Jones, Nigel
(1988) Essex Court Chambers, Lincoln's Inn, WC1A 3ED, LDE: 320, Tel: 0171 813 8000

Kaplan, Michael
4/5 Gray's Inn Square, WC1R, LDE: 1029, Tel: 0171 404 5252

Kilbey, John
4 Bell Yard, WC2, LDE: 400, Tel: 0171 333 8811

Land, Lynne
(1984) 199 Strand, London WC2, LDE: 322, Tel: 0171 379 9770

Lay, Michael
(1992) 4 Paper Buildings, Temple, EC4Y 7EX, LDE: 1035, Tel: 0171 583 0816

Lee, Brian
(1980) 20 Essex Court, Temple, EC4, LDE: 0009, Tel: 0171 583 9294

Livesey, Graham
9 St Johns Street, Manchester M3 3HA, DX: 14326, Tel: 0161 955 9000

Lombardi, Franco
(1994) 24 Old Buildings, Lincoln's Inn, WC2, LDE: 386, Tel: 0171 242 2744

Madden, Timothy
1 King's Bench Walk, Temple, EC4Y 7DB, LDE: 360, Tel: 0171 353 8436

Marquis, Peter
Queen Elizabeth Building, Temple, EC4, LDE: 482, Tel: 0171 583 5766

McCarron-Child, Nicholas
10 Essex Street, Outer Temple, WC2, LDE: 1045, Tel: 0171 240 6981

Mitchell, Kevin
Hardwicke Bldgs, 3 New Square, Lincoln's Inn, WC2, LDE: 393, Tel: 0171 242 2523

Moore, Andrew
(1988) 4 Raymond Buildings, Gray's Inn, WC1, LDE: 257, Tel: 0171 405 7211

Morley, Stephen
(1988) Queen Elizabeth Building, Temple, EC4, LDE: 339, Tel: 0171 797 7837

Munday, Paul
(1984) 2 Harcourt Buildings, Temple, EC4, LDE: 402, Tel: 0171 353 8415

Munton, John
(1997) 10 Essex Street, London WC2R 3AA, LDE: 1045, Tel: 0171 240 6981

Nicholls, Clive
(1987) 5 New Square, Lincoln's Inn, WC2, LDE: 272, Tel: 0171 404 0404

Norton, Gary
(1988) 1 Harcourt Buildings, Temple, EC4, LDE: 417, Tel: 0171 353 9421

**Odiam, Alan
(1990) 3 Paper Buildings, Temple, EC4, LDE: 1024, Tel: 0171-583-8055
(Education Secretary)

Oliver, Gary
2 Hare Court, Temple, EC4, LDE: 281, Tel: 0171 583 1770

Oliver, Michael
(1979) 1 Crown Office Row, Temple, EC4, LDE: 212 , Tel: 0171 583 9292

O'Mullane, Paul
(1988) Lamb Building, Temple, EC4Y 7AB, LDE: 418, Tel: 0171 797 8300

Parkinson, Nick
(1994 5 King's Bench Walk, Temple, EC4Y 7DN, LDE: 478, Tel: 0171 797 7600

Partridge, David
(1988) 2 Fountain Court, Birmingham B4 6DR, DX: 16071, Tel: 0121 236-3882

Perry, Ben
Essex Court Chambers, 24 Lincoln's Inn Fields, WC2A 3ED, LDE: 320, Tel: 0171 813 8000

Perry, Simon
Brick Court Chambers, Devereux Court, WC2, LDE: 302, Tel: 0171 583 0777

Phelan, Sean
(1975) Phoenix Chambers, 47A, Bedford Row, WC1R 4LR, Tel: 0171 404 7888

Phipps, Alan
24 The Ropewalk, Nottingham NG1 5EF, DX: 10060, Tel: 0115 947 2581

Phipps, Matthew
(1988) 1Crown Office Row, Temple, EC4, LDE: 1020, Tel: 0171 797 7500

Phipps, Michael
(1988) 39 Essex Street, London, WC2R 3AT, LDE: 298, Tel: 0171 583 1111

Piner, Gregory
Hardwicke Bldgs, New Square Lincoln's Inn, WC2, LDE: 393, Tel: 0171 242 2523

Powell, Haydn
(1982) 1 New Square, Lincoln's Inn, WC2, LDE: 295, Tel: 0171 405 0884

Price, Stephen
(1978) 33 Park Place, Cardiff, CF1 3BA, DX: 50755 Cardiff 2, Tel: 01222 233313

Pringle, Stuart
4 St Peters Street, Winchester, SO23 8BW, DX: 2507, Tel: 01962 868884

Rankin, Louis
(1991) Fenners Chambers, 3 Madingley Road, Cambridge, CB3 0EE, DX: 5809 Cambridge 1, Tel: 01223 368761

Rayner, Howard
1988) 1 Garden Court, Temple, EC4, LDE: 1034, Tel: 0171 797 7900

Read, Paul
(1988) New Court Chambers, 5 Verulam Bldgs, WC1R 5LY, LDE: 363, Tel: 0171 831 9500

Reade, Christopher
(1988) Erskine Chambers, 30 Lincoln's Inn Fields, WC2, LDE: 308, Tel: 0171 242 5532

Redmond, Declan
(1987) 8 New Square, Lincoln's Inn, WC2A, 3QS, LDE: 311, Tel: 0171 306 0102

Reece, Paul
(1991) 4 Stone Buildings, Lincoln's Inn, WC2, LDE: 385, Tel: 0171 242 5524

Richardson, Paul
32, Furnival Street, London EC4A 1JQ, LDE: 72, Tel: 0171 405 3232

Ridley, Clive
(1995)6 Fountain Court, Steelhouse Lane, Birmingham, DX: 16076, Tel: 0121 233 3282

Robson, Hadyn
(1988) 3 Temple Gardens, Temple, EC4, LDE: 485, Tel: 0171 353 9297

Ronan, Christopher
(1988)28 St John Street, Manchester M3 4EA, DX: 72886, Tel: 0161 834 8418

Rowe, Maureen
(1993) St John's Chambers, Bristol BS1 1DW, DX: 78138, Tel: 01272 213456

Sabini, Dominic
(1993) 2 Crown Office Row, EC4Y 7HJ, LDE: 1041, Tel: 0171 797 8000

Sale, Matthew
(1992) 11 Stone Buildings, Lincoln's Inn, WC2, LDE: 314, Tel: 0171 404 5055

Shiakallis, A.
11 Stone Buildings, Lincoln's Inn, WC2A 3TG, LDE: 1022, Tel: 0171 831 6381

Simpkin, Mark
(1991) Brick Court Chambers, 15-19 Devereux Court, WC2R 3JJ, LDE: 302, Tel: 0171 583 0777

Smith, David
(1991) 39 Essex Street, London WC2, LDE: 298, Tel: 0171 583 1111

Smith, Francis
11 South Square, Gray's Inn, WC1, LDE: 433, Tel: 0171 405 1222

Smith, Lloyd
(1975) Hardwicke Blgs, New Square, Lincoln's Inn, WC2A, LDE: 393, Tel: 0171 242 2523

Southworth, Helen
Peel House, Harrington Street, Liverpool 2, DX: 14227, Tel: 0151 236 0718

Strong, Clifford
(1992) 1 Middle Temple Lane, Temple, EC4, LDE: 464, Tel: 0171 583 0659

Stubbs, Michael
(1988) 40 King Street, Manchester B2 6BA, DX: 718188, Tel: 0161 832 9082

Stubbs, Susan
(1988)Manchester House Chambers, 18-22 Bridge Street, Manchester, DX: 718153 Manchester 3, Tel: 0161 834 7007

Swallow, Mark
(1983) Erskine Chambers, 30 Lincoln's Inn Fields, WC2, LDE: 308, Tel: 0171 242 5532

Taylor, Judith
(1988) Assize Court Chambers, Bristol BS1 1DE, DX: 78134, Tel: 0117 926 587

Thompson, Paul
(1980) 14 Water Street, Liverpool L2 8TD, DX: 14106, Tel: 0151 236 7191

Walker, John
(1992)4 Essex Court, Temple, EC4Y 9AJ, LDE: 292, Tel: 0171 797 7970

Wall, Stephen
(1979) 1 Hare Court, Temple, EC4, LDE: 444, Tel: 0171 353 5324

Walter, Mark
(1987) 1 Paper Buildings, Temple, EC4, LDE: 80, Tel: 0171 583 7355

West, Samantha
(1995) Lamb Buildings, Temple, EC4Y 7AS, LDE: 1038, Tel: 0171 797 7788

Winders, Ann
(1990) 1 Serjeants Inn, Fleet Street, London EC4, LDE: 364, Tel: 0171 353 9901

SENIOR CLERK ASSOCIATED MEMBERS

Ackerley, Neville

Adams, Alistair
Mitre Court Chambers, Temple, EC4Y 7BP, LDE: 449, Tel: 0171 353 9394

Ashton, Steven
(1987) 1 Gray's Inn Square, WC1R 5AA, LDE: 238, Tel: 0171 405 8946

Barber, David
3 Pump Court, Temple, EC4, LDE: 362, Tel: 0171 353 0711

Barrett, Graham
33 Park Place, Cardiff CF1 3BA, DX: 50755 Cardiff 2, Tel: 01222 233313

Beaumont, Kevin
14 Toft Green, York YD1 1JT, DX: 61517, Tel: 01904 620048

Bell, Brian
33 Broad Chare, Newcastle Upon Tyne NE1 3DQ, DX: 61001, Tel: 0191 232 0541

Biswas, Savanah
New Bailey Chambers, Preston PR1 2QT, DX: 710050, Tel: 01772 258087

Boardman, Ian
17 Bedford Row, WC1R 4EB, LDE: 370, Tel: 0171 353 0711

Brinning, David
32 Park Place, Cardiff CF1 3BA, DX: 50769, Tel: 01222 397364

Brown, Kim J.
Lion Court, Chancery Lane, WC2A 1SJ, LDE: 98, Tel: 0171 404 6565

Burrow, Ian
2 Pump Court, Temple, EC4Y 9AB, LDE: 109, Tel: 0171 353 4341

Campbell, Alastair
Merchant Chambers, 1 North Parade, Parsonage Gardens, Manchester M3 2NH, DX: 14319 M'ster 1, Tel: 0161 839 7070

Coia, Julian
Godolphin Chambers, 50 Castle Street, Truro, TR1 3AF, DX: 81233, Tel: 01872 76312

Collis, Steven
10 Park Square, Leeds LS1, DX: 26412 Leeds 1, Tel: 0113 245 5438

Connor, Nigel
39 Essex Street, London WC2R 3AT, LDE: 298, Tel: 0171 583 1111

Cooke, Paul
17 Charlton Crescent, Southampton, SO15 2XR, DX: 96877, Tel: 01703 639001

Cubley, Colin
2nd Floor, Chavasse Court, Liverpool L2 1TA, DX: 14223, Tel: 0151 707 1191

Currie, Donald
John Street, Chambers, 2 John Street, WC1R 2HJ, LDE: 1000, Tel: 0171 242 1911

Cuttle, Karen
Parsonage Chambers, 3 The Parsonage, Manchester M3 2H, Tel: 0161 833 1996, DX: 718183 Manchester 3

Daniell, Joy
33 Southernhay East, Exeter EX1 1NX, DX: 8353, Tel: 01392 55777

Davies, Andrew
Chartland Chambers, Cherry Tree Lane, Great Houghton, Northants NN4 7AT, DX: 12408 Northampton 1, Tel: 01604 700524

Davis, Robert
Maidstone Chambers, 33 Earl Street, Maidstone, ME14 1PF, DX: 51982 Maidstone 2, Tel: 01622 688592

Day, Anthony
12 Kings Bench Walk, Temple, EC4Y 7EL, LDE: 1037, Tel: 0171 583 0811

Doe, Christopher
Walnut House, 63 St David's Hill, Exeter, EX4 4DW, DX: 115582Exeter St David's, Tel: 01392 79751

Donovan, James
1 Crown Office Row, Temple, EC4, LDE: 212, Tel: 0171 583 9292

Dooley, Leslie
33 King St Chambers, Manchester M3 3PW, DX: 18160, Tel: 0161 834 4364

Douglas, David
Littleton Chambers, 3 KBW, EC4Y 7HR, LDE: 1047, Tel: 0171 797 8600

Duane, Patrick
2 Dr Johnson's Bldgs, Temple, EC4Y 7BY, LDE: 429, Tel: 0171 353 4716

Duric, David
1 High Pavement, Nottingham NG1 1HF, DX: 10168, Tel: 0115 941 8218

Edmonds, James
22 Albion Place, Northampton, NN1 1UD, DX: 12464, Tel: 01604 36271

Evers, Stephen
3 Paper Buildings, Temple, EC4Y, LDE: 337, Tel: 0171 353 6208

Farrow, Peter J.

Finney, Roy
Exchange Chambers, Pearl Assurance House, Derby Square, Liverpool L2 9XX, DX: 14207, Tel: 0151 236 7747

Freeman, Stephen
All Saints Chambers, Bristol BS1 2HP, DX: 7870 Bristol, Tel: 0117 921 1966

Grant, Trace
7 Stone Buildings, Lincoln's Inn, WC2A 3SZ, LDE: 1007, Tel: 0171 242 0961

Grimmer, John
3 Hare Court, Temple, EC4Y 7BJ, LDE: 17, Tel: 0171 353 7561

Grimshaw, C.
St Pauls House, 25 Park Square, Leeds LS1 2ND, DX: 26410, Tel: 0113 245 5866

Groom, Sean
53 North Hill, Colchester, Essex CO1 1PY, DX: 3611, Tel: 01206 572756

Gunner, Mary
Earl Street Chambers, Broughton House, 33 Earl Street, Maidstone, ME14 1PF, DX: 4844 Maidstone 1, Tel: 01622 671222

Handley, Thomas
Exchange Chambers, Derby Square, Liverpool L2 9XX, DX: 14207, Tel: 0151 236 7747

Hands, Colin
9-12 Trinity Chase, Newcastle Upon Tyne, DX: 61185, Tel: 0191 232 1927

Harris, Michael
6 Fountain Court, Birmingham B4 6DR, DX: 16076, Tel: 0121 233 3282

Hart, Martin
2 Grays Inn Square, London, WC1R 5JH, LDE: 316, Tel: 0171 242 4986

Hewitt, Dorothy
Guildhall Chambers, Bristol BS1 2HG, DX: 7823, Tel: 0117 9273366

Hubbard, John
3 Dr Johnson's Building, Temple, EC4Y 7BA, LDE: 1009, Tel: 0171 353 4854

Hutchins, Andrew
Francis Taylor Buildings, Temple, EC4Y, LDE: 211, Tel: 0171 353 9942

Hutt, Carey
2 New Street, Leicester LE1 5NA, DX: 10849 Leicester l, Tel: 0116 2625906

Islin, Graham
3 Gray's Inn Square, Gray's Inn, WC1R 5AH, LDE: 1043, Tel: 0171 831 2311

Janes, Mrs Kim
5 Raymond Bldgs, Gray's Inn, WC1R 5BP, LDE: 1054, Tel: 0171 242 2902

Jones, Stuart
14 Castle Street, Liverpool L2 YLS, DX: 14176, Tel: 0151 236 4421

Kelly, Peter
Lamb Buldings, Temple, EC4Y 7AS, LDE: 418, Tel: 0171 797 8300

Kemp, Roy
Park Court Chambers, Leeds LS1 2QH, DX: 26401, Tel: 0113 243 3277

Kettle, Graham
16 Bedford Row, London WC1R 4EB, LDE: 312, Tel: 0171 414 8080

Kilgallon, John
Martins Buildings, Liverpool L2 3SP, DX: 14232, Tel: 0151 236 4919

Kyprian, Lee
10 Kings Bench Walk, Temple, EC4Y, LDE: 24, Tel: 0171 353 7742

Lewis, Julie
Becket Chambers, 17 New Dover Rd, Canterbury, DX: 5330, Tel: 01227 786331

McSweeney, Christopher
9 Old Square, WC2A, LDE: 305, Tel: 0171 405 4682

Marsh, Anthony
7 Stone Buildings, Lincoln's Inn, WC2A 3SZ, LDE: 335, Tel: 0171 405 3886

Maw, Geoffrey
1 Raymond Buildings, Gray's Inn, WC2R 5BZ, LDE: 16, Tel: 0171 430 1234

Maynard, William
Coleridge Chambers, Birmingham B4 6RG, DX: 23503, Tel: 0121 233 3303

Miller, Gerald
Francis Taylor Buildings, 2nd Floor, Temple, EC4Y 7BY, LDE: 211, Tel: 0171 353 9942

Moore, Keith
2 Pump Court, Temple, EC4Y 7AH, LDE: 290, Tel: 0171 353 5597

Morrison Jacq
Victory House, 7 Belle Vue Terrace, Portsmouth PO5 3AT, DX: 2239, Tel: 01705 831292

Moss, Robert
Peel House, 5-7 Harrington Street, Liverpool L2 9XN, DX: 14227, Tel: 0151 236 0718

Mylchreest, Terry
5 John Dalton Street, Manchester M2 6ET, DX: 18182, Tel: 0161 834 6875

Nagle, Keith
11 Old Square, Lincoln's Inn, WC2A 3TS, LDE: 1031, Tel: 0171 430 0341

O'Connor, Sandra
Lancaster Buildings, 77 Deansgate, Manchester, M3 2BW, DX: 14488 Manchester 2, Tel: 0161 661 4444

Palmer, Andrew
3 Stone Buildings, Lincoln's Inn, WC2A 3XL, LDE: 317, Tel: 0171 242 4937

Plowman, Keith
10 Old Square, Lincoln's Inn, WC2A 3SU, LDE: 306, Tel: 0171 405 0758

Poulton, Joanna
9 Gough Square, EC4A 3DE, LDE: 439, Tel: 0171 353 5371

Rainbird, Walter
86 St Helens Rd, Swansea SA1 4BQ, DX: 39554, Tel: 01792 652988

Rotherham, Geoffrey
King Charles House, Standard Hill, Notts, DX: 10042, Tel: 0115 941 8851

Simpson, Michelle

Skinner, David
Waldorf House, Cooper Street, Manchester M2 2FW, DX: 715637 Manchester 2, Tel: 0161 236 1840

Smith, Stephen
4 Paper Buildings, Temple, EC4Y 7EB, LDE: 1036, Tel: 0171 353 3366

Springham, Mark
3 Madingley Road, Cambridge CB3 0EE, DX: 5809, Tel: 01223 68761

Stapley, Joanne
25-27 Castle Street Liverpool L2 4TA, DX: 14224, Tel: 0151 227 5661

Summerell, Zena
Theatre House, Percival Road, Clifton, Bristol BS8 3LE, Tel: 0117 974 1553

Thiele, Teresa
Manchester House Chambers, 18-22 Bridge Street, Manchester, M3 3BZ, DX: 718153 Manchester 3, Tel: 0161 834 7007

Thorne, Jeremy
Gower Chambers, 53 Mansel Street, Swansea SA1 5TD, DX: 5295, Tel: 01792-644466

Thwaites, Tristan,
Guildhall Chambers, Portsmouth PO1 2DE, DX: 2225, Tel: 01705 75240

Trotter, Andrew
Equity Chambers, Suite 110, Gazette Building, 168 Corporation Street, Birmingham B4 6TF, DX: 23531 Birmingham 3, Tel: 0121 233 2100

Waller, Donald
45 Hardman Street, Manchester M3 3HA, DX: 14320, Tel: 0161 832 3791

Watts, Chris
11 Old Square, Lincoln's Inn, WC2A 3TS, LDE: 164, Tel: 0171 242 5022

Wells, Anthony
Hardwicke Building, New Square Lincoln's Inn WC2A 3SB, LDE: 393, Tel: 0171 242 2523

Weekes, Bob
6-7 Gough Square, London EC4A 3DE, LDE: 476, Tel: 0171 353 0924

Weston, Allan
Derby Square Chambers, Liverpool L2 1TS, DX: 14213, Tel: 0151 709 4222

Wheeler, Brian
2 Harcourt Buildings, Temple, EC4Y 9DB, LDE: 373, Tel: 0171 353 6961

Whitman, Peter
8 King Street, Manchester M2 6AQ, DX: 14354, Tel: 0161 834 9560

Willmore, Keith
Trinity Chambers, 140 New London Road, Chelmsford CM2 0AW, DX: 89725 Chelmsford 2, Tel: 01245 605040

Witcomb, Clive
7 Fountain Court, Steelhouse Lane, B'ham B4 6DR, DX: 16073, Tel: 0121 236 8531

Wood, Janice
No. 5, 2nd Floor, 15 Castle Street, Exeter EX4 3PT, DX: 122699, Tel: 01392 210900

Woodcock, John
1 Brick Court, Temple, EC4Y 9BY, LDE: 468, Tel: 0171 353 8845

Wright, Paul
Regency Chambers, 18 Cowgate, Peterborough PE1 1NA, DX: 12349 Peterborough 1, Tel: 01733 315215

JUNIOR CLERK ASSOCIATED MEMBERS

Addis, Frances
2 Hare Court, Temple, EC4Y 2BH, LDE: 281, Tel: 0171 583 1770

Adlam, Andrew
3 Raymond Buildings, Gray's Inn, WC1, LDE: 237, Tel: 0171-831-3833

Alexander, Michael
Arden Chambers, 59 Fleet Street, EC4Y 1JU, LDE: 29, Tel: 0171 353 3132

Allen, Justin
199 Strand, WC2R 1DR, LDE: 322, Tel: 0171 379 9779

Ambrose, Daphne
5 Paper Buildings, Temple, EC4, LDE: 415, Tel: 0171 583 9275

Anderson, Deborah
Littleton Chambers, Temple, EC4, LDE: 1047, Tel: 0171 797 8600

Armstrong, Anthony
Enterprise Chambers, 9 Old Square, WC2A 3SR, LDE: 301, Tel: 0171 405 4682

Armstrong, S. K.
20 Essex Street, WC2R 3AL, LDE: 0009, Tel: 0171 583 9294

Archer, Matthew
22 Old Buildings, Lincoln's Inn, WC2A 3UJ, LDE: 201, Tel: 0171 831 0222

Ashton, Lucy
Westgate Chambers, 144 High Street, Lewes, E Sussex BN7 1XT, DX: 50250 Lewes 2, Tel: 01275 480510

Atkins, Tony
Francis Taylor Buildings, Temple, EC4Y 7BY, LDE: 46, Tel: 0171 797 7250

Baldwin, Scott
Hollins Chambers, 64A Bridge St, M3 3BA, DX: 14327 Manchester, Tel: 0161 835 3451

Barnes, Jayne
4 King's Bench Walk, Temple, EC4, LDE: 1050, Tel: 0171 353 3581

Barratt, Timothy
East Anglian Chambers, 57 London Street, Norwich NR2 1HL, DX: 5213 Norwich l, Tel: 01603 617351

Barrow, David
199 Strand, WC2R 1DR, LDE: 322, Tel: 0171 379 9779

Barrow, Kevin
5 Bell Yard, WC2A 2JR, LDE: 400, Tel: 0171 333 8811

Barrow, Ryan
Q E B, Temple, London EC4Y 9BS, LDE: 339, Tel: 0171 797 7837

Baum, Perry
7 Stone Buildings, Lincoln's Inn, WC2A 3SZ, LDE: 1007, Tel: 0171 242 0961

Bennetts, Angharad
Francis Taylor Bldgs, Temple, EC4Y 7BY, LDE: 441, Tel: 0171 353 7768

Bingham, David
3 New Square, WC2A 3RS, LDE: 384, Tel: 0171 405 5577

Binnie, Mark
3 Gray's Inn Place, WC1R 5EA, LDE: 331, Tel: 0171 831 8441

Bird, Paul
199 Strand, WC2R 1DR, LDE: 322, Tel: 0171 379 9779

Bisland John
13 Old Square, Lincoln's Inn, WC2, LDE: 326, Tel: 0171 404 4800

Blanchard, Conrad
2 Gray's Inn Square, WC1R 5AA, LDE: 43, Tel: 0171 242 0328

Braithwaite, Denise
3 Temple Gardens, Temple, EC4Y 9AU, LDE: 0064, Tel: 0171 583 1155

Briggs, Graham
Francis Taylor Bldgs, Temple, EC4Y 7BY, LDE: 211, Tel: 0171 353 9924

Briton, Andrew
2 Harcourt Buildings, Temple, EC4Y 9DB, LDE: 489, Tel: 0171 353 8339

Broadbent, Matthew
8 New Square, Lincoln's Inn, WC2A, LDE: 311, Tel: 0171 306 0102

Bromage, Philip
6 Park Square, Leeds, LS1 2LW, DX: 26402, Tel: 0113 245 9763

Brown, Justin
1 New Square, Lincoln's Inn, WC2, LDE: 295, Tel: 0171 405 0884

Broom, Stephen
Essex Court Chambers, 24 Lincoln's Inn Fields WC2A 3ED, LDE: 320, Tel: 0171 813 8000

Bryant, Gary
5 Fountain Court, Birmingham, DX: 16075, Tel: 0121 606 0500

Bryant, Robert
4 King's Bench Walk, Temple, EC4Y 7DL, LDE: 1050, Tel: 0171 353 3581

Bryant, Nicholas
4 Breams Buildings, EC4A 1AQ, LDE: 1042, Tel: 0171 353 5835

Burgess, Tony
14 Tooks Court, Cursitor Street, EC4A 1LB, LDE: 68, Tel: 0171 405 8828

Burrows, Andrew
5 Verulam Bldgs, Grays Inn, WC2R 5NT, LDE: 363, Tel: 0171 831 9500

Butchard, Matthew
9 Bedford Row, WC1R 4DB, LDE: 347, Tel: 0171 242 3555

Butcher, Sophie
2 Crown Office Row, Temple, EC4Y 7HJ, LDE: 1041, Tel: 0171 797 8000

Byrne, Michael
Goldsmith Building, Temple, EC4Y 7BL, LDE: 435, Tel: 0171 353 6802

Cade, Richard
36 Bedford Row, London, WC1R 4JH, LDE: 360, Tel: 0171 421 8000

Cadwallader, Lee
1/Flr, Refuge Assn House, Derby Square, Liverpool L2 1TS, DX: 14213, Tel: 0151 709 4222

Call, Andrew
1 New Square, Lincoln's Inn, WC2A, LDE: 295, Tel: 0171 405 0884

Carter, Vincent
11 Old Square, Lincoln's Inn, WC2A 3TS, LDE: 1031, Tel: 0171 430 0341

Carter, Andrea
Godolphin Chambers, 50 Castle Street, Truro TR1 3AF, DX: 81233, Tel: 01872 76312

Cavanagh, Sarah
Deans Court Chambers, Cumberland House, Crown Square, Manchester M3 3HA, DX: 718155 Manchester 3, Tel: 0161 834 4097

Charlick, Neil

Christie, Susan
1 Gray's Inn Square, WC1R 5AA, LDE: 1013, Tel: 0171 405 8946

Clarke, Addeline
2 New Street, Leicester, LE1 5NA, DX: 17404 Leics 3, Tel: 0116 262 5906

Clarke, Lisa
177 Corporation Street, Birmingham, DX: 23520 Bir 3, Tel: 0121 236 9900

Clayton, David
11 Stone Bldgs, Lincoln's Inn, WC2A 3TG, LDE: 314, Tel: 0171 404 5055

Clent, Victoria
Northampton Chambers, NN1 1UD, DX: 12464 Northampton 1, Tel: 01604 36271

Cockram, Lee
4 Stone Buildings, Lincoln's Inn WC2A 3XT, LDE: 385, Tel: 0171 242 5524

Colley, Martin
13 Old Square, Lincoln's Inn, WC2A, 3UA, LDE: 326, Tel: 0171 404 4800

Collings, Janet
9 Bedford Row, London, WC1R 4AZ, LDE: 347, Tel: 0171 242 3555

Colloff, Graham
6 Pump Court, Temple, EC4Y, 7AR, LDE: 293, Tel: 0171 797 8400

Conway, Kirstie
2 Mitre Court Buildings, Temple, EC4Y, LDE: 0032, Tel: 0171 583 1380

Cooklin, Paul
3 Gray's Inn Place, Gray's Inn, WC1R 5EA, LDE: 331, Tel: 0171 831 8441

Cooper, John
12 KBW, Temple, EC4Y 7EL, LDE: 1037, Tel: 0171 583 0811

Coote, Daniel
1 Temple Gardens, EC4Y 9BB, LDE: 382, Tel: 0171 583 1315

Costa, James
3/4 South Square, Gray's Inn, WC1R 5HP, DX: 338, Tel: 0171 696 9900

Cowling, C.
St Paul's Chambers, 23 Park Square South, Leeds LS1 2ND, DX: 26410, Tel: 0113 245 5866

Cowup, Julie
Furnival Chambers, 32 Furnival Street, EC4A 1TQ, LDE: 72, Tel: 0171 405 3232

Creighton, David
29 Bedford Row, London, WC1R 4HE, LDE: 1044, Tel: 0171 831 2626

Cross, Nichola
Bridge Street Chambers, 72 Bridge Street, Manchester, DX: 14307, Tel: 0161 834 8468

Cue, Jonathan
14 Gray's Inn Square, WC1R 5JP, LDE: 399, Tel: 0171 242 0858

Curtis, Alan
10 King's Bench Walk, EC4Y 7EB, LDE: 24, Tel: 0171 353 7742

Cutler, Lee
12 Gray's Inn Square, London WC1R 5JP, LDE: 0055, Tel: 0171 404 4866

Darvell, Mark
Gray's Inn Chambers, 5th Floor, WC1R 5JA, LDE: 0074, Tel: 0171 404 1111

Dawson, Colin
9 Old Square, Lincoln's Inn, WC2A 3SR, LDE: 305, Tel: 0171 405 4862

Day, Ann
4 Breams Buildings, EC4A 1AQ, LDE: 1042, Tel: 0171 353 5835

Davidson, Alastair
1 Essex Court, Temple, EC4Y 9AR, LDE: 430, Tel: 0171 583 2000

Dear, Christopher

De Rose, Ann
3 Temple Gardens, Temple, EC4Y 9AU, Tel: 0171 353 7884

Donaghey, Sylvia
1 & 2 Plowden Bldgs, Temple, EC4Y 9BU, LDE: 0020, Tel: 0171 583 0808

Douglas, Marie
35 Essex Street, WC2R 3AR, LDE: 351, Tel: 0171 353 6381

Downey, Alan
11 Old Square, Lincoln's Inn, WC2A 3TS, LDE: 1031, Tel: 0171 430 0341

Driscoll, Sarah

Duckett, Andrew
Farrars Bldgs, Temple, EC4Y 7BD, LDE: 406, Tel: 0171 583 9241

Dyer, Justin
1 Gray's Inn Square, Gray's Inn WC1R 5AA, LDE: 1013, Tel: 0171 405 8946

Eadie, Christine
5 Paper Buildings, London EC4Y 7HB, LDE: 367, Tel: 0171 353 5638

East, Nigel
7 Park Place, Cardiff CF1 3TN, DX: 50757, Tel: 01222 382731

Edwards, Elizabeth
Angel Chambers, 94 Walter Road, Swansea SM1 5QA, DX: 39566 Swansea, Tel: 01792 464623

Emmings, Christopher
6 King's Bench Walk, London EC4Y 7DR, LDE: 26, Tel: 0171 583 0410

Essex, Mark
6 King's Bench Walk, Temple, EC4Y 7DR, LDE: 26, Tel: 0171 583 0410

Essex, Michael
2 King's Bench Walk, Temple, EC4Y 7DE, LDE: 1032, Tel: 0171 353 1746

Evans, Jeffrey
Iscoed Chambers, 86 St Helen's Rd Swansea SA1 4BQ, DX: 39554, Tel: 01792 652988

Evans, Nicholas
12 King's Bench Walk, Temple, EC4Y 7EL, LDE: 1037, Tel: 0171 583 0811

Eze, Gregory
Horizon Chambers, 95A Chancery Lane, WC2A 1DT, LDE: 275, Tel: 0171 242 2440

Fairburn, Timothy
3 New Square, Lincoln's Inn, WC2A 3RS, LDE: 454, Tel: 0171 405 1111

Falconer, Charlotte
1 Atkin Building, Gray's Inn, WC1R 5AT, LDE: 1033, Tel: 0171 404 0102

Farrow, Garry
9 Gough Square, EC4A 3DE, DX: 439 Chancery Lane, Tel: 0171 353 5371

Fawole, Dele
Suite 1, 2nd Floor, Gray's Inn Chambers, WC1R, LDE: 442, Tel: 0171 405 7011

Ferrison, Chris
1 Garden Court, Temple, EC4Y 9BL, LDE: 1034, Tel: 0171 797 7900

Filby, Martin
2 Pump Court, Temple, EC4Y 7AH, LDE: 290, Tel: 0171 353 5597

Finney, Roy
Exchange Chambers, Pearl Assurance House, Derby Square, Liverpool, L2 9XX, DX: 14207 Liverpool, Tel: 0151 236 7747

Fletcher, Paul
Guildhall Chambers, 23 Broad Street, Bristol BS1 2HG, DX: 7823, Tel: 0117 927 3366

Foreman, Dean
4/5 Gray's Inn Square, Gray's Inn, WC1R 5AY, LDE: 1029, Tel: 0171 404 5252

Fowler, Richard
7 Fountain Court, Birmingham, DX: 16073 Birmingham, Tel: 0121 236 8531

Francis, Stephen
Falcon Chambers, Falcon Court, EC4Y 1AA, LDE: 408, Tel: 0171 353 2484

Frankland, Andrew
Devereux Chambers, London, WC2R 3JJ, LDE: 349, Tel: 0171 353 7534

Franks, Davie
36 Bedford Row, Gray's Inn, WC1R 4JH, LDE: 360, Tel: 0171 421 8000

Freak, Rhonda
Goldsmith Chambers, Goldsmith Building, EC4Y 7BL, LDE: 376, Tel: 0171 353 6802

Frewin, Gregory
2 Crown Office Row, Temple, EC4Y 7HJ, LDE: 344, Tel: 0171 797 8100

Friend, P.W.
Farrars Building, Temple, EC4Y 7BD, LDE: 406, Tel: 0171 583 9241

Friend, Kara
John Street, Chambers, 2 John Street, WC1N 2HJ, LDE: 1000, Tel: 0171 242 1911

Fullilove S. (Jay)
4 Breams Buildings, EC4A 2AQ, LDE: 1042, Tel: 0171 430 1221

Gallagher, Nathan
5 Fountain Court, Steelhouse Lane, Birm B4 6DR, DX: 16075, Tel: 0121 606 0500

Garstang, Neil
9 Gough Square, London, EC4A, LDE: 439, Tel: 0171 353 5371

Gibbons, Matthew
Deans Court Chambers, Manchester, DX: 718155, Tel: 0161 834 4097

Gibbs, Stewart
4 Pump Court, Temple, EC4Y 7AN, LDE: 303, Tel: 0171 353 2656

Gidaree, Sandra
2 Crown Office Row, Temple, EC4Y 7HJ, LDE: 344, Tel: 0171 797 8100

Gilbert, Michelle
5 Stone Buildings, Lincoln's Inn WC2A, LDE: 304, Tel: 0171 242 6201

Gilbert, Susan
Priory Chambers, 2 Fountain Court, Birmingham B4 6DR, DX: 16071, Tel: 0121 236 3882

Gillespie-Bell, Sylvia
King Charles House, Nottingham NG1 6FX, DX: 10042, Tel: 0115 941 8851

Gilson, John
2 Harcourt Buildings, Temple, EC4, LDE: 1039, Tel: 0171 583 9020

***Goodrham, Jayne**
5 Pump Court, Temple, EC4Y 7AP, LDE: 497, Tel: 0171 353 2532

Gould, Sean
16/17 Wellington Square, Hastings, TN34 1PB, DX: 7062 Hastings, Tel: 01424 432105

Gray, Joanna
3 Madingley Rd, Cambridge, CB2 0EE, DX: 5809 Cambridge, Tel: 01223 368761

Griggs, Pauline
Francis Taylor Buildings, Temple, EC4Y 7BY, LDE: 46, Tel: 0171 797 7250

Grimwood, Rachel
9 Baker Street, Middlesbrough, DX: 60591 M bro, Tel: 01642 873873

Haigh, Joanne
55 Temple Chambers, Temple EC4Y 0HP, LDE: 260, Tel: 0171 353 7400

Haley, Nicholas
15 Winkley Square, Preston PR1 3JJ, DX: 17110, Tel: 01772 252828

Hall, Andrew
5 Paper Building EC4Y 7HB, LDE: 415, Tel: 0171 583 9275

Hall, Stuart
10 Kings Bench Walk, Temple, EC4Y 7EB, LDE: 294, Tel: 0171 353 2501

Hammond, John
18 St John Street, Manchester, M3 4EA, DX: 728854, Tel: 0161 834 9843

Hammond, Paul
Lamb Building, Temple, EC4Y 7AS, LDE: 1038, Tel: 0171 797 7788

Harding, Mark
4 Brick Court, Temple, EC4Y 9AD, LDE: 453, Tel: 0171 583 8455

Harding Michael,
Albion Chambers, Broad Street, Bristol BS1 1DR, DX: 7822, Tel: 0117 927 2144

Harris, Lian
50 High Pavement, Nottingham NG1 1HW, DX: 10036, Tel: 0115 959 3503

Harris, Paul
1 Garden Court, Temple, EC4Y 9BL, LDE: 1034, Tel: 0171 797 7900

Harrison, Mark
17 Carlton Crescent, Southampton SO9 5AL, DX: 96875, Tel: 01703 320320

Harwood-Stammer, D.

Haslam, David
18 St John Street, Manchester M3 4EA, DX: 728854 Man 4, Tel: 0161 278 1800

Hayns, Deborah
6-7 Gough Square, EC4A 3DE, LDE: 476, Tel: 0171 353 0924

Heath, Mark
3 Verulam Buildings, WC1R 5NT, LDE: 331, Tel: 0171 831 8441

Heyhirst, Bridget
St Paul's House, 23 Park Square South, Leeds LS1 2ND, DX: 26410, Tel: 0113 245 5866

Hill, Anthony Tyler
Old Square Chambers, 1 Verulam Bldgs, WC1R 5LQ, LDE: 1046, Tel: 0171 831 0891

Hill, Dorothea
Suite 1, 2nd Floor, Gray's Inn Chambers, WC1R, LDE: 442, Tel: 0171 405 7011

Hobson, Matthew
Pump Court Tax Chambers, 16 Bedford Row WC1R 4EB, LDE: 312, Tel: 0171 414 8080

Hockney, David
4 Raymond Bldgs, Gray's Inn, WC1R 5BP, LDE: 257, Tel: 0171 405 7211

Hockney, Nicholas
1 Hare Court, Temple, EC4Y 7BE, LDE: 0065, Tel: 0171 353 3171

Hodges, Kelly
27 New Walk, Leicester, LE1, DX: 10872 Leics 1, Tel: 0116 255 9144

Holden, Pauline
Lincoln House Chambers, 1 Brazenose Street, Deansgate, Manchester M3, DX: 14338 Manchester 1, Tel: 0161 832 5301

Holland, Edward
4 King's Bench Walk, EC4, LDE: 422, Tel: 0171 353 0478

Hood, Clare
1 Hare Court, Temple, EC4Y 7BE, LDE: 0065, Tel: 0171 353 3171

Hooson, Stacey
Refuge House, Derby Square, Lord Street, Liverpool, DX: 14213, Tel: 0151 709 4222

Hopkins, Annie
2 Crown Office Row, EC4, LDE: 1041, Tel: 0171 797 8000

Houchin, Terry
Field Court Chambers, 3 Field Court, Gray'sInn, WC1R, LDE: 136, Tel: 0171 404 7474

Howdle, Colin
1 Fountain Court, Steelhouse Lane, Birmingham, DX: 16077, Tel: 0121 236 5721

Hughton, Michelle
14 Tooks Court, Cursitor Street, EC4A 1JY, LDE: 68, Tel: 0171 405 8828

Hunt, Mary
5 King's Bench Walk, Temple, EC4Y 7DN, LDE: 478, Tel: 0171 797 7600

Hunt, Carl
5 Fountain Court, Steelhouse Lane, Birmingham, DX: 16075, Tel: 0121 606 0500

Hyde, Janet
33 Broad Chare, Newcastle Upon Tyne NE1 3OQ, DX: 61001, Tel: 0191 232 0541

Irons, Luke
Enterprise Chambers, 9 Old Square, WC2A 3SR, LDE: 301, Tel: 0171 405 9471

Jackson, Daniel

Jarvis, Neil
2 Crown Office Row, Temple, EC4Y 7HJ, LDE: 1041, Tel: 0171 797 8000

Jennings, Marc
2 Paper Buildings, Temple, EC4Y 7ET, LDE: 494, Tel: 0171 936 2611

Johns, Eddie
7 Kings Bench Walk, Temple, EC4Y 7DS, LDE: 239, Tel: 0171 583 0404

Johnson, Graham
199 Strand, London WC2R 1DR, LDE: 322, Tel: 0171 379 9778

Johnson, Susan
199 Strand, London, WC2R 1DR, LDE: 322, Tel: 0171 379 9778

Jones, Dale
5 Paper Buildings, Temple, EC4Y 7HB, LDE: 365, Tel: 0171 583 6117

Jones, Daniel
1 Atkin Building, Gray's Inn, WC1R 5AT, LDE: 1033, Tel: 0171 404 1033

Jolly Kathryn
New Court Chambers, 5 Verulam Bldgs WC1R 5LY, LDE: 363, Tel: 0171 831 9500

Jones, Georgina
6 Fountain Court, Steelhouse Lane, Birmingham B4 6DR, DX: 16076, Tel: 0121 233 3282

H

Jones, Matthew
2 Garden Court, Temple, EC4Y 9BL, LDE: 34, Tel: 0171 353 1633

Kelley, Nicola
9 King's Bench Walk, Temple, EC4Y, LDE: 472, Tel: 0171 353 7202

Kelly, Kevin
13 King's Bench Walk, Temple, EC4Y 7EN, LDE: 359, Tel: 0171 353 7204

Kelly, Shona
7 Stone Buildings, Lincoln's Inn WC2A 3SZ, LDE: 335, Tel: 0171 405 3886

Kelly, Lisa
St John's Chambers, Small Street, Bristol, BS1 1DW, DX: 78138, Tel: 0117 921 3456

Kempston, Julie
2 Mitre Court Bldgs, Temple, EC4Y 7BX, LDE: 0023, Tel: 0171 353 1353

Kesbey, Jack
9 Bedford Row, London, WC1R 4AZ, LDE: 347, Tel: 0171 242 3555

Kesby, Matthew
24 Lincoln's Inn Fields, WC1A 3ED, LDE: 320, Tel: 0171 813 8000

Kilbey, Michael
4 Paper Buildings, Temple, EC4Y 7EX, LDE: 1036, Tel: 0171 353 3366

Kirby, Mark
Essex Court, Chambers, 24 Lincoln's Inn Fields, WC2A 3ED, LDE: 320, Tel: 0171 813 8000

Kitchen, Ian
1 Middle Temple Lane, EC4Y 9AA, LDE: 464, Tel: 0171 583 0659

Krogulec, Anthony
King Charles House, Standard Hill, Notts, DX: 10042, Tel: 0115 947 2581

Lamba, Raj Krishan
3 Gray's Inn Place, WC1R 5EA, LDE: 331, Tel: 0171 831 8441

Lambert, Katie
1 Essex Court, Temple, EC4Y 9AR, LDE: 430, Tel: 0171 583 2000

Lane, Christopher
24 Old Buildings, WC2A 3UJ, LDE: 307, Tel: 0171 404 0946

Lane, Wendy
2 Harcourt Buildings, EC4Y 9DB, LDE: 1039, Tel: 0171 583 9020

Laverty, Paul
5 John Dalton Street, Manchester, M2 6ET, DX: 718182, Tel: 0161 834 6875

Lawrence, Stephen
12 Gray's Inn Square, WC1R 5JP, LDE: 0055, Tel: 0171 404 4866

Lea, David
8 King Street, Manchester M2 6AQ, DX: 14354 Man, Tel: 0161 834 9560

Leahy, Paul
New Court, Temple, EC4Y 9BE, LDE: 0018, Tel: 0171 583 5123

Leech, Martin
8 King Street, Manchester, M2 6AQ, DX: 14354 Man, Tel: 0161 834 9560

Lashmar, Ben
4 Stone Buildings, Lincoln's Inn, WC2A, LDE: 385, Tel: 0171 242 5524

Lewis, Jenny
Crown Office Row Chambers, Brighton BN1 1WH, DX: 36670, Tel: 01273 625626

Liddon, Anthony
8 New Square, Lincoln's Inn, WC2A 3QP, LDE: 379, Tel: 0171 405 4321

Longhurst, Dominic
18 St. John Street, Manchester, M3 4EA, DX: 728854 Man4, Tel: 0161 278 1800

Love, Andrew
5 Raymond Buildings, Gray's Inn, WC1R, LDE: 1054, Tel: 0171 242 2902

Luckman, Justin
3 Fountain Court, Steelhouse Lane, Birmingham B4 6DR, DX: 16079, Tel: 0121 236 5854

Lumley, Melanie
58 Kingsgate St, Manchester M2 6DE, DX: 710297, Tel: 0161 831 7477

Mace, David
1 Brick Court, Temple, EC4Y 9BY, LDE: 468, Tel: 0171 353 8845

Makepiece, Emma
10 Kings Bench Walk, Temple, EC4Y 7EB, LDE: 294, Tel: 0171 353 25Tel: 01

Malcolmson, Ang
40 King Street, Chester, CH1 2AH, DX: 22154 Chester, Tel: 01244 323886

Maloney, Rosemary
8 Fountain Court, Birmingham, DX: 15078, Tel: 0121 236 5514

Mansell, Mark
4 Fountain Court, Birmingham, B4 6DR, DX: 16074, Tel: 0121 236 3476

Marsh, Darin
32 Furnival Street, EC4A 1JQ, LDE: 72, Tel: 0171 405 3232

Marsh, Iain

Marshall, Lisa
24 The Ropewalk, Nottingham, NG1 5EF, DX: 10060 Nottm 17, Tel: 0115 947 2581

May, Kay
17 Carlton Crescent, Southampton SO15 2XR, DX: 96875, Tel: 01703 320320

McBlain, Alexis
9 King's Bench Walk, Temple, EC4Y, LDE: 472, Tel: 0171 353 7202

McCarthy, Kevin
3 Temple Gardens, EC4Y, LDE: 0008, Tel: 0171 353 0853

McCourt, Kevin
1 Paper Buildings, Temple, EC4Y 7EP, LDE: 80, Tel: 0171 583 7355

McCrone, Steven
1 Mitre Court Bldgs, Temple, EC4Y 7BS, LDE: 342, Tel: 0171 797 7070

McCusker, Paul
5 Essex Court, Temple, EC4Y 9AH, LDE: 1048, Tel: 0171 410 2000

McDermott, Gail
Rational House, 64 Bridge Street, Manchester M3 3BN, DX: 14338, Tel: 0161 832 5701

McDonald, David
1 King's Bench Walk, Temple, EC4Y 7DB, LDE: 20, Tel: 0171 583 6266

McGrath, Michelle
33 Bedford Row, London WC1R 4JH, LDE: 75, Tel: 0171 242 6476

McHugh, Neil
3rd Floor, Peel House, 5-7 Harrington Street, Liverpool, L2 9NX, DX: 14227 Liverpool, Tel: 0151 234 0718

McKay, Fiona
Young Street Chambers, 38 Young Street, Manchester M3 3FT, DX: 25583 Manchester 5, Tel: 0161 833 0489

McKenna, Toni
4 Field Court, Gray's Inn, WC1R, LDE: 483, Tel: 0171 440 6900

McKimm, William
3 Temple Gardens, Temple, EC4Y 9AU, LDE: 0073, Tel: 0171 583 0010

Meade, William
Old Square Chambers, 3 Verulam Bldgs, WC1R 5LQ, LDE: 1046, Tel: 0171 831 0801

Melli, Yvonne
All Saints Chambers, Bristol, DX: 7870 Bristol, Tel: 0117 921 1966

Miller, Jonathan
2 Crown Office Row, Temple, EC4Y 7HJ, LDE: 344, Tel: 0171 797 8100

Milsom, Pavel
2 Crown Office Row, EC4Y 7HJ, LDE: 1041, Tel: 0171 797 8000

Milton, Daren
36 Essex Street, WC2R 3AS, LDE: 148, Tel: 0171 353 3533

Mo, George
4 Brick Court, Temple, EC4Y 9AD, LDE: 404, Tel: 0171 797 7766

Moles, Annette
St Johns Chambers, Small Street, Bristol BS1 1DW, DX: 78138 Bristol, Tel: 0117 9213456

Monaghan, Daniel
40 King Street, Manchester, M2 6BA, DX: 718188, Tel: 0161 832 9082

Monks, John
1 Atkin Buildings, WC1R 5BQ, LDE: 1033, Tel: 0171 404 0102

Money, Moira
Park Court Chambers, 40 Park Cross Street, Leeds LS1 2QH, DX: 26401, Tel: 0113 243 3277

Morrissey, Anthony
9 St John Street, Manchester M3 4DN, DX: 14326 Man, Tel: 0161 955 9000

Mott, Stanley
1 Middle Temple Lane, EC4Y 9AA, LDE: 464, Tel: 0171 583 0659

Newton, Mark
7 Stone Buildings, Lincoln's Inn WC2A 3SZ, LDE: 335, Tel: 0171 405 3886

Nicholl, Vincent
5 Paper Buildings, Temple, EC4Y 7HB, LDE: 365, Tel: 0171 583 6117

Nickless, Julia

Norman, Daniel
East Anglian Chambers, 52 North Hill, Colchester CO11PY, DX: 3611, Tel: 01206 572756

Nunn, Alex
Goldsmith Chambers, Goldsmith Bldgs, EC4Y 7BL, LDE: 376, Tel: 0171 353 6802

O'Brien, D.
Goldsmith Building, Temple, EC4Y 7BL, LDE: 435, Tel: 0171 353 7881

O'Rourke, Brendon
4 Brick Court, Temple, EC4Y, 9AD, LDE: 404, Tel: 0171 797 7766

O'Sullivan, Geraldine
16 Bedford Row, WC1R 4EB, LDE: 312, Tel: 0171 414 8080

Outen, Paul
4 Brick Court, 1st Flr, Temple, EC4Y 9AD, LDE: 453, Tel: 0171 583 8455

Parham, Donna
55 Temple Chambers, Temple Ave, EC4Y, LDE: 260, Tel: 0171 353 7400

Parr, Steven
Thomas More Chambers, 51/52 Carey St, WC2A 2JB, LDE: 90, Tel: 0171 404 7000

Passmore, Bonita
Albion Chambers, Broad St, Bristol BS1 1DR, DX: 7822, Tel: 0117 927 2144

Patrick, Richard
39 Essex Street, London, WC2R 3AT, LDE: 298, Tel: 0171 583 1111

Payne, Samantha

Peck, Dennis
Enterprise Chambers, 9 Old Square, Lincoln's Inn, WC2A 3SR, LDE: 301, Tel: 0171 405 9471

Penson, David
2 Hare Court, Temple, EC4Y 7BH, LDE: 281, Tel: 0171 583 1770

Penson, Stephen
11 King's Bench Walk, Temple, EC4Y 7EQ, LDE: 368, Tel: 0171 583 0610

Peters, Brian
3 Temple Gardens, Temple, EC4Y 9AU, LDE: 0008, Tel: 0171 353 0853

Peto, Nicholas
31/33 Broad Chare Chambers, Newcastle-Upon-Tyne NE1 3DQ, DX: 61001, Tel: 0191 232 0541

Phillips, David J.
2 KBW, Temple, London EC4Y 7DE, LDE: 1032, Tel: 0171 353 1746

Phillips-Griffiths, Phil
30 Park Place, Cardiff, CF1 3BA, DX: 50756, Tel: 01222 398421

*Pickersgill, Joanne
36 Bedford Row, London, WC1R 4JH, LDE: 360, Tel: 0171 421 8000

Pike, James
5 Bell Yard, London, WC2, LDE: 400, Tel: 0171 333 8811

Pocock, Susie
39 Essex Street, London WC2R 3AT, LDE: 298, Tel: 0171 583 1111

Polhill, Benjamin
1 Serjeants Inn, Temple EC4Y 1LL, LDE: 364, Tel: 0171 353 9901

Powell, Michael E.
4 Fountain Court, Steelhouse Lane B4 6DR, DX: 16074, Tel: 0121 236 3476

Poyser, A.
13 Old Square, Lincoln's Inn, WC2A 3UA, LDE: 1025, Tel: 0171 242 6105

Poyser, David
5 Verulam Buildings, WC1R, LDE: 363, Tel: 0171 831 9500

Price, Stephen
25 Byrom Street, Manchester, M3 4PF, DX: 718156, Tel: 0161 834 5238

Price, Steven J.
2/3 College Place, London Rd, SO1 2FB, DX: 38533, Tel: 01703 230338

Pringle, Stuart
4 St. Peter Street, Winchester, SO23 8BW, DX: 2507, Tel: 01962 868884

Pullam, Stuart
2/3 Gray's Inn Square, London, WC1R 5JH, LDE: 316, Tel: 0171 242 4986

Rankin, Lewis
2 Hare Court, Temple, EC4Y 7BH, LDE: 281, Tel: 0171 583 1770

Reding, S.
2 Gray's Inn Square, Gray's Inn, WC1R 5AA, LDE: 43, Tel: 0171 242 0328

Regan, Mark
4/5 Gray's Inn Square, Gray's Inn, WC1R 5AY, LDE: 1029, Tel: 0171 404 5252

Reynolds, Conrad
Deans Court Chambers, Crown Square, Manchester M3 3HA, DX: 718155, Tel: 0161 834 4097

Ritchie, Stuart
39 Essex Street, London, WC2, LDE: 298, Tel: 0171 583 1111

Robinson, Mark
21 Whitefriars, Chester CH1 1NZ, DX: 19979, Tel: 01244 323070

Robinson, Francis
3 Temple Gardens, 2nd Flr, Temple, EC4Y 9AU, LDE: 0064, Tel: 0171 583 1155

Robinson, Jonathan
24-26 Lincoln's Inn Fields, WC2A 3ED, LDE: 320, Tel: 0171 813 8000

Robinson, Paul

Robinson, Simon
19 Old Buildings, Lincoln's Inn, WC2, LDE: 397, Tel: 0171 405 2001

Rogers, Maxine
Queen Elizabeth Building, EC4Y, LDE: 340, Tel: 0171 353 7181

Rogers, Janet
Redhill Chambers, Seloduct House, Station Road, Redhill RH1 1NF, DX: 100203 Redhill, Tel: 01737 780781

Roukin, Jason
5 Bell Yard, WC2A 2JR, LDE: 400, Tel: 0171 333 8811

Royal, Leigh
Deans Court Chambers, Manchester, M3 3HA, DX: 718188 Man 3, Tel: 0161 834 4097

Rycroft, Timothy
Essex Court Chambers, 24 Lincoln's Inn Fields, WC2A 3ED, LDE: 320, Tel: 0171 813 8000

Sansom, Carol
50 High Pavement, Nottingham NG1 1HW, DX: 10036, Tel: 0115 950 3503

Salisbury, Emma
Lamb Chambers, Temple, EC4Y, LDE: 418, Tel: 0171 797 8300

Savage, Jason
2 Temple Gardens, EC4Y 9AY, LDE: 134, Tel: 0171 583 6041

Schofield, Marc
10 Old Square, Lincoln's Inn WC2A 3SU, LDE: 306, Tel: 0171 405 0758

Schultz, Jean P.
4 Field Court, Gray's Inn, WC1R 5EA, LDE: 483, Tel: 0171 440 6900

Secrett, Martin
Queen Elizabeth Building, EC4, LDE: 340, Tel: 0171 353 7181

Sellen, Stuart
Thomas More Building, 51/2 Carey Street, Lincoln's Inn, LDE: 90, Tel: 0171 404 7000

Silverman, Philip
5 Pump Court, Temple, EC4Y 7AP, LDE: 497, Tel: 0171 353 2532

Simpson, Vivien

Sizer, John
5 Raymond Buildings, Gray's Inn, WC1R 5BP, LDE: 1054, Tel: 0171 242 2902

Slattery, Simon
4 Pump Court, Temple, EC4Y 7AN, LDE: 303, Tel: 0171 353 2656

Smillie, Danny
Wilberforce Chambers, 8 New Square, WC2A 3QP, LDE: 311, Tel: 0171 306 0102

Smith, Ann
Park Court Chambers, 40 Park Cross Street, Leeds LS1 2QH, DX: 26401, Tel: 0113 243 3277

Sommerville, Stephen
6 Pump Court, Temple, EC4Y 7AR, LDE: 409, Tel: 0171 583 6013

Speller, Gregory
South Western Chambers, 12 Middle Street, Taunton, DX: 32146, Tel: 01823 331919

Squires, Kevin
1 Serjeants Inn, Temple, EC4Y 1NH, LDE: 440, Tel: 0171 583 1355

Stanhope, Darren
Francis Taylor Bldg, Temple, EC4Y 7BY, LDE: 441, Tel: 0171 797 8999

Stickels, Gareth
40 King Street, Chester, DX: 22154 Chester Northgate, Tel: 01244 323886

Storer, Alison
Refuge House, Derby Square, Liverpool 2, DX: 14213, Tel: 0151 709 4222

Strachan, Thomas
Claremont Chambers, 26 Waterloo Street, Wolverhampton, WV1 4BL, DX: 10455 Wolverhampton 1, Tel: 01902 426222

Street, Gary
13 Old Square, Lincoln's Inn, WC2A 3UA, LDE: 326, Tel: 0171 404 4800

Swann, Christopher
18 St John Street, Manchester M3 4EA, DX:728854 Man 4, Tel: 0161 278 1800

Swile, Robert
5th Floor, Gray's Inn Chambers, Grey's Inn, WC1R 5JA, LDE: 0074, Tel: 0171 404 1111

Tansley, Philip
2 Field Court, Gray's Inn, WC1R 5BB, LDE: 457, Tel: 0171 405 6114

Tidiman, Cheri
Littleton Chambers, 3 KBW, EC4Y 7HR, LDE: 1047, Tel: 0171 797 8600

Tindale, Eleanore
3 Hare Court, Temple, EC4Y 7BJ, LDE: 17, Tel: 0171 353 7561

Thorne, Kris
Iscoed Chambers, 86 St Helen's Rd, Swansea, DX: 39554 Swansea l, Tel: 01792 652988

Thornton, Kathryn
2nd Flr, Francis Taylor Buildings, Temple, EC4Y 7BY, LDE: 211, Tel: 0171353 9942

Tong, Tanya
2-3 Grays Inn Square, Grays Inn, WC1R 5JH, LDE: 316, Tel: 0171 242 4986

Toole, Russell

Townsend, Mark
5 New Square, Lincoln's Inn, WC2A 3RJ, LDE: 272, Tel: 0171 404 0404

Tulett, Peter
4 Breams Buildings, London, EC4A 1AQ, LDE: 1042, Tel: 0171 353 5835

Turner, E.
5th Floor, Gray's Inn Chambers, WC1A 5JA, LDE: 0074, Tel: 0171 404 1111

Vella, Rita
7 Stone Buildings, 1st Flr, Lincoln's Inn WC2A 3SZ, LDE: 1007, Tel: 0171 242 0961

Venables, Duncan
Lamb Building, Temple, EC4Y 7AS, LDE: 418, Tel: 0171 797 8300

Venables, Paul
5 Paper Buildings, Temple, EC4Y 7HB, LDE: 367, Tel: 0171 353 5638

Ventura, Gary
11 New Square, Lincoln's Inn, WC2A 3QB, LDE: 319, Tel: 0171 831 0081

Vile, Richard
1 Middle Temple Lane, Temple, EC4Y 9AA, LDE: 464, Tel: 0171 583 0659

Wadden, Clair
14 Small Street, Bristol, BS1 1DE, DX: 78134 Bristol, Tel: 0117 926 4587

Wakeling, Lee
14 Tooks Court, Cursitor Street, EC4A 1LB DE 68, Tel: 0171 405 8828

Wall, Carl
4 Pump Court, Temple, EC4Y 7AN, LDE: 303, Tel: 0171 353 2656

Wallace, Emma
2 Gray's Inn Square, WC1R 2AA, LDE: 43, Tel: 0171 242 0328

Wallis, Daniel
1 Pump Court, Temple, EC4Y 7AB, LDE: 109, Tel: 0171 353 4341

Ward, David

Waterman, Simon
Hardwicke Bldg, New Square, WC2A 3SB, LDE: 393, Tel: 0171 242 2523

Watson, Sarah
3 Paper Buildings, Temple, EC4, LDE: 0071, Tel: 0171 797 7000

Webb, Garrin
Ropewalk Chambers, 14 The Ropewalk, Nottingham, NG1 5EF, DX: 10060 Nottingham, Tel: 0115 947 2581

Wedderburn, Everton
36 Bedford Row, WC1R, LDE: 360, Tel: 0171 421 8000

Wheeler, Timothy
2 Harcourt Buildings, Temple, EC4Y, 9DB, LDE: 373, Tel: 0171 353 6961

Whitaker, Steven
13 Old Square, Lincoln's Inn, WC2A 3UA, LDE: 1025, Tel: 0171 242 6105

Whitford, William
Queen Elizabeth Building, Temple, EC4Y 9BS, LDE: 482, Tel: 0171 583 5766

Wigley, Simon
4 Paper Buildings, Temple, EC4Y 7EX, LDE: 1036, Tel: 0171 353 3 366

Wiggs, Robert
1 Atkin Buildings, Grays Inn, WC1R 5BQ, LDE: 1033, Tel: 0171 404 0102

Wildish, Matthew
Thornwood House, 102 New London Road, Chelmsford CM12, DX: 89706 Chelmsford 2, Tel: 01245 280880

Wilkes, Emma
1st Floor, 1 Brick Court, Temple, EC4Y 9BY, LDE: 468, Tel: 0171 353 8845

Wilkinson, Danny
Fountain Court, Temple, EC4Y 9DH, LDE: 5, Tel: 0171 583 3335

Williams, Emlyn

Williams, Alister J.
3 New Square, Lincoln's Inn, WC2A 3RS, LDE: 384, Tel: 0171 405 5577

Williams, Gary
1 Fountain Court, Steelhouse Lane, Birm B4 6DR, DX: 16077, Tel: 0121 236 5721

Williams, Guy
3 Gray's Inn Square, WC1R 5AH, LDE: 1043, Tel: 0171831 2311

Williams, A. Keith

Williams, Martin
3/4 South Square, Gray's Inn, WC1R 5HP, LDE: 338, Tel: 0171 696 9900

Williams, Paula
Essex Court Chambers, London WC2A 3ED, LDE: 320, Tel: 0171 813 8000

Williams, Sandra
33 Park Place, Cardiff CF1 3BA, DX: 50755 Cardiff 2, Tel: 01222 233313

Willicombe, Richard
1 Middle Temple Lane, EC4Y 9AA, LDE: 464, Tel: 0171 583 0659

Wood, Debbie
10 Old Square, Lincoln's Inn, WC2A 3SU, LDE: 306, Tel: 0171 405 0758

Woodbridge, Daniel
3 Serjeants Inn, EC4Y 1BQ, LDE: 421, Tel: 0171 353 5537

Woods, Danny
4 Brick Court, Temple, EC4Y, LDE: 453, Tel: 0171 583 8455

Wright, Seb
11 Stone Buildings, Lincoln's Inn, WC2A 3TG, LDE: 1022, Tel: 0171 831 6381

Wright, Clare
3 Pump Court, Temple, EC4Y 7AJ, LDE: 362, Tel: 0171 353 0711

Wright, Sarah
Kenworthy Buildings, 83 Bridge Street, Manchester, M3 2RF, DX: 718200 Manchester 3, Tel: 0161 832 4036

A–Z Index of Chambers

This section lists all the chambers from *Part C Chambers by Location* alphabetically with the Part C page reference.

I

A

A K Chambers 19 Headlands Drive, Hull, East Yorkshire HU13 0JP 01482 641180 .... C24

Abbey Chambers PO Box 47, 47 Ashurst Drive, Shepperton, Middlesex TW17 0LD 01932 560913 .... C212

ACHMA Chambers 44 Yarnfield Square, Clayton Road, London SE15 5JD 0171 639 7817 .... C40

Acre Lane Neighbourhood Chambers 30A Acre Lane, London SW2 5SG 0171 274 4400 .... C40

Chambers of Ibrahim Addoo Bloxworth Villa, 38 Delafield Road, London SE7 7NP 0181 244 3555 .... C40

Advolex Chambers 70 Coulsdon Road, Coulsdon, Surrey CR5 2LB 0181 763 2345 .... C20

3 Aisby Drive Doncaster DN11 0YY 01302 866495 ...... C20

Alban Chambers 27 Old Gloucester Street, London WC1N 3XX 0171 419 5051 .... C40

Albany Chambers 91 Kentish Town Road, London NW1 8NY 0171 485 5736/38 .... C40

Albion Chambers Broad Street, Bristol BS1 1DR 0117 9272144 .... C12

22 Albion Place Northampton NN1 1UD 01604 636271 .... C202

1 Alfred Street Oxford OX1 4EH 01865 793736 .... C205

All Saints Chambers 9/11 Broad Street, Bristol BS1 2HP 0117 921 1966 .... C12

Chambers of Andrew Campbell QC 10 Park Square, Leeds LS1 2LH 0113 245 5438 .... C25

Angel Chambers 94 Walter Road, Swansea, West Glamorgan SA1 5QA 01792 464623/464648 .... C215

54 Anne Way Ilford, Essex IG6 2RL 0181 501 4311 .... C25

Chambers of James Apea 11 Helix Road, London SW2 2JR 0181 244 5545 .... C40

1 Appleton Road Fareham, Hampshire PO15 5QH 01329 847711 .... C23

Arbitration Chambers 22 Willes Road, London NW5 3DS 0171 267 2137 .... C40

Arcadia Chambers P O Box 16674, 18 Kensington Court, London W8 5DW 0171 938 1285 .... C41

Arden Chambers 27 John Street, London WC1N 2BL 0171 242 4244 .... C42

1 Argyle Road Wolverhampton WV2 4NY 01902 561047 .... C219

Chambers of Dr Michael Arnheim 101 Queen Alexandra Mansions, Judd Street, London WC1H 9DP 0171 833 5093 .... C42

Assize Court Chambers 14 Small Street, Bristol BS1 1DE 0117 926 4587 .... C12

3 Athol Street Douglas, Isle of Man 01624 897 420 .... C20

Atkin Chambers 1 Atkin Building, London WC1R 5AT 0171 404 0102 .... C43

Avondale Chambers 2 Avondale Avenue, London N12 8EJ 0181 445 9984 .... C43

B

Baker Street Chambers 9 Baker Street, Middlesbrough, Cleveland TS1 2LF 01642 873873 .... C197

Bank House Chambers Old Bank House, Sheffield S1 2EL 0114 275 1223 .... C212

Barclay Chambers 2a Barclay Road, London E11 3DG 0181 558 2289/925 0688 .... C43

17a Barclay Road London E17 9JH 0181 521 3112 .... C43

Barnard's Inn Chambers Halton House, 20-23 Holborn, London EC1N 2JD 0171 242 8508 .... C43

Barnstaple Chambers c/o Glebe Cottage, Winkleigh, Devon EX19 8ED 0183 783763 .... C219

Barristers' Common Law Chambers 57 Whitechapel Road, London E1 1DU 0171 375 3012 .... C44

Becket Chambers 17 New Dover Road, Canterbury, Kent CT1 3AS 01227 786331 .... C15

Bedford Chambers The Clock House, 2 Bedford Street, Bedford, Bedfordshire MK45 2NB 0870 733 7333 .... C3

9 Bedford Row London WC1R 4AZ 0171 242 3555 ...... C44

17 Bedford Row London WC1R 4EB 0171 831 7314 ..... C44

33 Bedford Row London WC1R 4JH 0171 242 6476 ...... C44

Chambers of James Hunt QC 36 Bedford Row, London WC1R 4JH 0171 421 8000 .... C45

48 Bedford Row London WC1R 4LR 0171 430 2005 ..... C46

29 Bedford Row Chambers Bedford Row, London WC1R 4HE 0171 831 2626 .... C47

5 Bell Yard London WC2A 2JR 0171 333 8811 .... C48

9–12 Bell Yard London WC2A 2LF 0171 400 1800 .... C49

Bell Yard Chambers 116-118 Chancery Lane, London WC2A 1PP 0171 306 9292 .... C50

Belmarsh Chambers 20 Warland Road, London SE18 2EU 0181 316 7322 .... C50

Beresford Chambers 21 King Street, Luton, Bedfordshire LU1 2DW 01582 429111 .... C184

Berkeley Chambers 52 High Street, Henley-in-Arden, Warwickshire B95 5AN 01564 795546 .... C24

4 Bingham Place London W1M 3FF 0171 486 5347/ 071 487 5910 .... C50

Blackstone Chambers (formerly known as 2 Hare Court) Blackstone House, London EC4 0171 583 1770 .... C50

Chambers of Richard Bloomfield 2 Lansdowne Place, Newcastle Upon Tyne NE3 1HR 0191 285 4664 .... C198

11 Bolt Court London EC4A 3DQ 0171 353 2300 .... C51

Bond Street Chambers Standbrook House 2-5 Old Bond Street, London W1X 3TB 01932 342951 .... C51

Chambers of Karen R Boyes P.O.Box 458, Northampton NN6 9ZT 01604 882942 .... C202

23 Bracken Gardens London SW13 9HW 0181 748 4924 .... C51

Bracton Chambers 95a Chancery Lane, London WC2A 1DT 0171 242 4248 .... C52

4 Breams Buildings London EC4A 1AQ 0171 353 5835/ 430 1221 .... C52

Brentwood Chambers Denton, North Yorkshire LS29 0HE 01943 817230 .... C20

1 Brick Court 1st Floor, London EC4Y 9BY 0171 353 8845 .... C53

4 Brick Court London EC4Y 9AD 0171 797 8910 .... C53

4 Brick Court Ground Floor, London EC4Y 9AD 0171 797 7766 .... C54

4 Brick Court, Chambers of Anne Rafferty QC 1st Floor, London EC4Y 9AD 0171 583 8455 .... C54

Brick Court Chambers 7-8 Essex Street, London WC2R 3LD 0171 379 3550 .... C55

Bridewell Chambers 2 Bridewell Place, London EC4V 6AP 0171 797 8800 .... C56

Britton Street Chambers 20 Britton Street, 1st Floor, London EC1M 5NQ 0171 608 3765 .... C56

Broad Chare 33 Broad Chare, Newcastle upon Tyne NE1 3DQ 0191 232 0541 .... C198

Broadway House Chambers 9 Bank Street, Bradford BD1 1TW 01274 722560 .... C11

Bromley Chambers 39 Durham Road, Bromley, Kent BR2 0SN 0181 325 0863 .... C14

517 Bunyan Court London EC2Y 8DH 0171 638 5076 .. C56

Byrom Street Chambers 25 Byrom Street, Manchester
M3 4PF 0161 829 2100 .... C185

C

Camberwell Chambers 66 Grove Park, London SE5 8LF
0171 274 0830 .... C57

4 Camden Place Preston, Lancashire PR1 3JL
01772 828300 .... C209

16a Campden Hill Court Campden Hill Road, London
W8 7HS 0171 937 3492 .... C57

17 Carlton Crescent Southampton, Hampshire SO15 2XR
01703 320320 .... C213

Carmarthen Chambers 30 Spilman Street, Carmarthen,
Dyfed SA31 1LQ 01267 234410 .... C17

146 Carshalton Park Road Carshalton, Surrey SM5 3SG
0181 773 0531 .... C17

Castle Chambers Court House, Taylor's Yard, Bristol
BS1 2EY 0117 934 9833 .... C12

25–27 Castle Street 25–27 Castle Street, 1st Floor,
Liverpool, Merseyside L2 4TA 0151 227 5661/5666/
236 5072 .... C34

19 Castle Street Chambers Liverpool, Merseyside L2 4SX
0151 236 9402 .... C34

**Cathedral Chambers (Jan Wood Independent Barristers'
Clerk)** 15 Castle Street, Exeter, Devon EX4 3PT
01392 210900 .... C22

Cathedral Chambers Milburn House, Dean Street,
Newcastle upon Tyne NE1 1LE 0191 232 1311 .... C199

Cathedral Chambers, Ely P O Box 24, Ely, Cambridgeshire
CB6 1SL 01353 666775 .... C21

Central Chambers Greg's Buildings, 1 Booth Street,
Manchester M2 4DU 0161 833 1774 .... C186

Chancery Chambers 1st Floor Offices, 70/72 Chancery
Lane, London WC2A 1AB 0171 405 6879/6870 .... C57

Chancery House Chambers 7 Lisbon Square, Leeds
LS1 4LY 0113 244 6691 .... C26

74 Chancery Lane First Floor, London WC2A 1AA
0171 430 0667 .... C57

95A Chancery Lane London WC2A 1DT
0171 405 3101 .... C57

70 Charlecote Drive Nottingham NG8 2SB
0115 928 8901 .... C203

Chartlands Chambers 3 St Giles Terrace, Northampton
NN1 2BN 01604 603322 .... C202

Chavasse Court Chambers 2nd Floor, Chavasse Court, 24
Lord Street, Liverpool, Merseyside L2 1TA
0151 707 1191 .... C35

19 Chestnut Drive Pinner, Middlesex HA5 1LX
0181 866 7603/933 2382 .... C207

Chichester Chambers 12 North Pallant, Chichester, West
Sussex PO19 1TQ 01243 784538 .... C19

140 Cholmeley Road Reading, Berkshire RG1 3LR
01189 676318 .... C210

Flat 4, Churston Mansions Churston Mansions, 176 Gray's
Inn Road, London WC1R 4DB 0171 837 1596 .... C57

Clapham Chambers 21-25 Bedford Road, London SW4 7SH
0171 978 8482/642 5777 .... C57

Claremont Chambers 26 Waterloo Road, Wolverhampton
WV1 4BL 01902 426222 .... C220

Clavenes Chambers 46 Stag Lane, Edgware, Middlesex
HA8 5JY 0181 931 2648 .... C21

Cleveland Chambers 63-65 Borough Road, Middlesbrough,
Cleveland TS1 3AA 01642 226036 .... C197

Clock Chambers 78 Darlington Street, Wolverhampton
WV1 4LY 01902 313444 .... C220

Cloisters 1 Pump Court, London EC4Y 7AA
0171 827 4000 .... C57

The Clove Hitch High Street, Bristol BS17 1UG
01454 228243 .... C12

Cobden House Chambers 19 Quay Street, Manchester
M3 3HN 0161 833 6000/6001 .... C187

Coleridge Chambers Citadel, 190 Corporation Street,
Birmingham B4 6QD 0121 233 3303 .... C3

College Chambers 19 Carlton Crescent, Southampton,
Hampshire SO15 2ET 01703 230338 .... C213

21 Colless Road London N15 4NR 0181 365 1706 .... C57

Colleton Chambers Colleton Crescent, Exeter, Devon
EX2 4DG 01392 274898 .... C22

Colleton Chambers 22 The Crescent, Taunton, Somerset
TA1 4EB 01823 324252 .... C217

Commonwealth Chambers 354 Moseley Road, Birmingham
B12 9AZ 0121 446 5732 .... C3

The Corn Exchange Chambers 5th Floor, Fenwick Street,
Liverpool, Merseyside L2 7QS 0151 227 1081/5009 .... C35

62 Cortworth Road Sheffield S11 9LP 0114 236 0988 . C212

The Courts 8 Abbotsleigh Road, London SW16 1SP
0181 769 6243 .... C58

Chambers of Mr Peter Crampin QC 11 New Square,
Lincoln's Inn, London WC2A 3QB 0171 831 0081 .... C58

21 Craven Road Kingston-Upon-Thames, Surrey KT2 6LW
0181 974 6799 .... C25

Crayshott House Woodlands Road, West Byfleet, Surrey
KT14 6JW 01932 342951 .... C217

Cromwell-Ayeh-Kumi Chambers 1st Floor Suite, 119
Cricklewood Broadway, London NW2 3JG
0181 450 6620 .... C58

1 Crown Office Row Ground Floor, London EC4Y 7HH
0171 797 7500 .... C58

1 Crown Office Row 2nd Floor, London EC4Y 7HH
0171 797 7111 .... C59

1 Crown Office Row 3rd Floor, Temple, London EC4Y 7HH
0171 583 9292 .... C60

Two Crown Office Row Ground Floor, London EC4Y 7HJ
0171 797 8100 .... C60

Crown Office Row Chambers Blenheim House, 120 Church
Street, Brighton, Sussex BN1 1WH 01273 625625 .... C11

Crystal Chambers 25A Cintra Park, London SE19 2LH
0181 402 5801 .... C61

D

Chambers of Joseph Dalby First Floor, No 28 St Stephens
Road, Winchester SO22 6DE 01962 886555 .... C218

66 Daubeney Road London E5 0EF 0181 985 3030 .... C61

Chambers of Timothy Deal First Floor, 5 Eastbrook Road,
London SE3 8BP 0181 856 8738 .... C61

Deans Court Chambers Cumberland House, Crown Square,
Manchester M3 3HA 0161 834 4097 .... C188

Deans Court Chambers 41-43 Market Place, Preston,
Lancashire PR1 1AH 01772 555163 .... C209

334 Deansgate Manchester M3 4LY 0161 834 3767 .... C188

Chambers of Melanie den Brinker West House Town Row,
Rotherfield, East Sussex TN6 3QU 01892 783505 .... C211

Derby Square Chambers Merchants Court, Liverpool
L2 1TS 0151 709 4222 .... C35

Devereux Chambers Devereux Court, London WC2R 3JJ
0171 353 7534 .... C61

Devizes Chambers 11 High Street, Devizes, Wiltshire
SN10 5PY 01380 724896 .... C20

Devon Chambers 3 St Andrew Street, Plymouth, Devon
PL1 2AH 01752 661659 .... C207

Doughty Street Chambers 11 Doughty Street, London
WC1N 2PG 0171 404 1313 .... C63

1 Dr Johnson's Buildings Ground Floor, London EC4Y 7AX
0171 353 9328 .... C64

3 Dr Johnson's Buildings Ground Floor, London EC4Y 7BA
0171 353 4854 .... C65

Dr Johnson's Chambers Two Dr Johnson's Buildings,
London EC4Y 7AY 0171 353 4716 .... C65

Dr Johnson's Chambers The Atrium Court, Apex Plaza,
Reading, Berkshire RG1 1AX 01189 254221 .... C210

Chambers of Stewart Dunn 93 Millview Drive, Tynemouth,
North Shields NE30 2QJ 0191 258 0520 .... C217

Durham Barristers' Chambers 27 Old Elvet, Durham City
DH1 3HN 0191 386 9199 .... C21

E

Earl Street Chambers 47 Earl Street, Maidstone, Kent
ME14 1PD 01622 671222 .... C185

East Anglian Chambers 52 North Hill, Colchester, Essex
CO1 1PY 01206 572756 .... C20

East Anglian Chambers Gresham House, 5 Museum Street,
Ipswich, Suffolk IP1 1HQ 01473 214 481 .... C25

East Anglian Chambers 57 London Street, Norwich,
Norfolk NR2 1HL 01603 617351 .... C202

Eastbourne Chambers 15 Hyde Gardens, Eastbourne, East
Sussex BN21 4PR 01323 642102/416466 .... C21

Eastern Chambers Badgers Bottom, Dysons Wood Lane,
Oxford RG4 9EY 0118 972 3722 .... C205

2 Eastwood Road London E18 1BW 0181 491 0980 ..... C66

Eaton House 1st Floor, 4 Eaton Road, Poole, Dorset
BH13 6DG 01202 766301/768068 .... C208

43 Eglantine Road London SW18 2DE 0181 874 3469 .. C66

Eighteen Carlton Crescent Southampton, Hampshire
SO15 2XR 01703 639001 .... C214

Eldon Chambers Fourth Floor, 30/32 Fleet Street, London
EC4Y 1AA 0171 353 4636 .... C66

197 Ellesmere Road London NW10 1LG
0181 208 1663 .... C66

61 Elm Grove Sutton, Surrey SM1 4EX 0181 643 9714 C215

Enfield Chambers 1st Floor, Refuge House, 9-10 River Front,
Enfield, Middlesex EN2 3SZ 0181 364 5627 .... C21

Enterprise Chambers 38 Park Square, Leeds LS1 2PA
0113 246 0391 .... C26

Enterprise Chambers 9 Old Square, London WC2A 3SR
0171 405 9471 .... C66

Enterprise Chambers 65 Quayside, Newcastle upon Tyne
NE1 3DS 0191 222 3344 .... C199

Equity Barristers' Chambers 50 Claude Road, London
E10 6ND 0181 558 8336 .... C67

Equity Chambers 153A Corporation Street, Birmingham,
West Midlands B4 6PH 0121 233 2100 .... C3

Erskine Chambers 30 Lincoln's Inn Fields, London
WC2A 3PF 0171 242 5532 .... C67

One Essex Court Ground Floor, London EC4Y 9AR
0171 583 2000 .... C68

One Essex Court London EC4Y 9AR 0171 936 3030 .... C69

4 Essex Court Temple, London EC4Y 9AJ
0171 797 7970 .... C69

5 Essex Court 1st Floor, London EC4Y 9AN
0171 410 2000 .... C70

Essex Court Chambers 24 Lincoln's Inn Fields, London
WC2A 3ED 0171 813 8000 .... C71

Essex House Chambers Essex House, 375-377 Stratford
High Street, London E15 4QZ 0181 536 1077 .... C72

20 Essex Street 20 Essex Street, London WC2R 3AL
0171 583 9294 .... C72

23 Essex Street London WC2R 3AS 0171 413 0353 ...... C73

35 Essex Street London WC2R 3AR 0171 353 6381 ...... C73

39 Essex Street London WC2R 3AT 0171 832 1111 ...... C74

Chambers of Geoffrey Hawker 46 Essex Street, London
WC2R 3GH 0171 583 8899 .... C75

Eurolawyer Chambers PO Box 3621, London N7 0BQ
0171 607 0075 .... C75

Exchange Chambers Pearl Assurance House, Derby Square,
Liverpool, Merseyside L2 9XX 0151 236 7747 .... C36

F

Falcon Chambers Falcon Court, London EC4Y 1AA
0171 353 2484 .... C76

3 & 4 Farnham Hall Saxmundham, Suffolk IP17 1LB
01728 602758 .... C211

Farrar's Building London EC4Y 7BD 0171 583 9241 ..... C76

Fenners Chambers 3 Madingley Road, Cambridge CB3 0EE
01223 368761 .... C14

Fenners Chambers 8-12 Priestgate, Peterborough PE1 1JA
01733 562030 .... C206

Chambers of Norman Palmer 2 Field Court, London
WC1R 5BB 0171 405 6114 .... C77

4 Field Court London WC1R 5EA 0171 440 6900 .... C78

Field Court Chambers 2nd Floor, 3 Field Court, London
WC1R 4EP 0171 404 7474 .... C79

19 Figtree Lane Sheffield S1 2DJ 0114 2759708/
2738380 .... C212

First National Chambers 2nd Floor, 24 Fenwick Street,
Liverpool, Merseyside L2 7NE 0151 236 2098 .... C36

Fleet Chambers Mitre House, 44-46 Fleet Street, London
EC4Y 1BN 0171 936 3707 .... C79

Forest House Chambers 15 Granville Road, London
E17 9BS 0181 925 2240 .... C79

Fountain Chambers Cleveland Business Centre, 1 Watson
Street, Middlesbrough, Cleveland TS1 2RQ
01642 217037 .... C197

Fountain Court London EC4Y 9DH 0171 583 3335 .... C79

1 Fountain Court Steelhouse Lane, Birmingham, West
Midlands B4 6DR 0121 236 5721 .... C4

3 Fountain Court Steelhouse Lane, Birmingham, West
Midlands B4 6DR 0121 236 5854 .... C4

4 Fountain Court Birmingham B4 6DR 0121 236 3476 .... C5

5 Fountain Court Steelhouse Lane, Birmingham, West
Midlands B4 6DR 0121 606 0500 .... C5

6 Fountain Court Steelhouse Lane, Birmingham, West
Midlands B4 6DR 0121 233 3282 .... C7

8 Fountain Court Steelhouse Lane, Birmingham, West
Midlands B4 6DR 0121 236 5514 .... C7

9 Fountains Way Wakefield, West Yorkshire WF1 4TQ
01924 378631 .... C217

Francis Taylor Building Ground Floor, London EC4Y 7BY
0171 353 7768/2711 .... C80

2nd Floor, Francis Taylor Building 2nd Floor, Francis
Taylor Building, London EC4Y 7BY 0171 353 9942 .... C80

Francis Taylor Bldg 3rd Floor, London EC4Y 7BY
0171 797 7250 .... C81

Frederick Place Chambers 9 Frederick Place, Bristol
BS8 1AS 0117 9738667 .... C12

Furnival Chambers 32 Furnival Street, London EC4A 1JQ
0171 405 3232 .... C81

Fyfield Chambers Field Cottage, Southrop, Gloucestershire
GL7 3NT 01367 850304 .... C214

G

Chambers of Davina Gammon Ground Floor, 103 Walter
Road, Swansea SA1 5QS 01792 480770 .... C215

One Garden Court Family Law Chambers London
EC4Y 9BJ 0171 797 7900 .... C82

2 Garden Court London EC4Y 9BL 0171 353 1633 .... C83

The Garden House 14 New Square, London WC2A 3SH
0171 404 6150 .... C84

1 Garfield Road London SW11 5PL 0171 228 1137 .... C84

Godolphin Chambers 50 Castle Street, Truro, Cornwall
TR1 3AF 01872 276312 .... C217

243A Goldhurst Terrace 2nd Floor, London NW6 3EP
0171 625 8455 .... C84

2 Goldingham Avenue Loughton, Essex IG10 2JF
0181 502 4247 .... C184

Goldsmith Building 1st Floor, Temple, London EC4Y 7BL
0171 353 7881 .... C84

Goldsmith Chambers Ground Floor, Goldsmith Building,
London EC4Y 7BL 0171 353 6802/3/4/5 .... C85

Goldsworth Chambers 11 Gray's Inn Square, First Floor,
London WC1R 5JD 0171 405 7117 .... C86

9 Gough Square London EC4A 3DE 0171 353 5371 ...... C86

Gough Square Chambers 6-7 Gough Square, London
EC4A 3DE 0171 353 0924 .... C87

Gower Chambers 57 Walter Road, Swansea, West
Glamorgan SA1 5PZ 01792 644466 .... C215

34 Graham Road London N15 3NL 0181 889 7671 .... C88

Granary Chambers 4 Glenleigh Park Road, Bexhill-on-Sea,
East Sussex TN39 4EH 01424 733008 .... C3

Gray's Inn Chambers 1st Floor, Gray's Inn Chambers,
London WC1R 5JA 0171 831 5344 .... C88

Gray's Inn Chambers London WC1R 5JA
0171 404 1111 .... C88

**1 Gray's Inn Square, Chambers of the Baroness
Scotland of Asthal QC** 1 Gray's Inn Square, London
WC1R 5AG 0171 405 3000 .... C89

1 Gray's Inn Square Ground Floor, London WC1R 5AA
0171 405 8946 .... C90

2-3 Gray's Inn Square 2-3 Gray's Inn Square, London
WC1R 5JH 0171 242 4986 .... C91

2 Gray's Inn Square Chambers Gray's Inn Square, London
WC1R 5AA 0171 242 0328/405 1317 .... C93

3 Gray's Inn Square Ground Floor, London WC1R 5AH
0171 520 5600 .... C93

4-5 Gray's Inn Square Ground Floor, London WC1R 5AY
0171 404 5252 .... C94

6 Gray's Inn Square London WC1R 5AZ
0171 242 1052 .... C96

Gray's Inn Square 8 Gray's Inn Square, London WC1R 5AZ
0171 242 3529 .... C96

10 - 11 Gray's Inn Square 2nd Floor, 10-11 Gray's Inn
Square, London WC1R 5JD 0171 405 2576 .... C97

14 Gray's Inn Square London WC1R 5JP
0171 242 0858 .... C97

Gray's Inn Tax Chambers 3rd Floor, Gray's Inn Chambers,
London WC1R 5JA 0171 242 2642 .... C97

100E Great Portland Street London W1N 5PD
0171 636 6323 .... C98

Greenway Sonning Lane, Sonning-on-Thames, Berkshire
RG4 6ST 0118 969 2484 .... C213

Chambers of Helen Grindrod QC 1st Floor, 95a Chancery
Lane, London WC2A 2JG 0171 404 4777 .... C98

Guildford Chambers Stoke House, Leapale Lane, Guildford,
Surrey GU1 4LY 01483 539131 .... C23

Guildhall Chambers 23 Broad Street, Bristol BS1 2HG
0117 9273366 .... C13

Guildhall Chambers Portsmouth Prudential Buildings, 16
Guildhall Walk, Portsmouth, Hampshire PO1 2DE
01705 752400 .... C208

Chambers of Beverley Gutteridge 36 Dunmore Road,
London SW20 8TN 0181 947 0717 .... C98

H

Hampshire Chambers Malton House, 24 Hampshire
Terrace, Portsmouth, Hampshire PO1 2QF
01705 826636 .... C208

Chambers of John Hand QC 9 St John Street, Manchester
M3 4DN 0161 955 9000 .... C188

Harbour Court Chambers 11 William Price Gardens,
Fareham, Hampshire PO16 7PD 01329 827828 .... C23

1 Harcourt Buildings London EC4Y 9DA 0171 353 9421/
0375 .... C98

2 Harcourt Buildings Ground Floor, London EC4Y 9DB
0171 583 9020 .... C99

2 Harcourt Buildings 1st Floor, London EC4Y 9DB
0171 353 2112/2817 .... C101

2 Harcourt Buildings Temple, London EC4Y 9DB
0171 353 8415 .... C101

Harcourt Chambers 2 Harcourt Buildings, London
EC4Y 9DB 0171 353 6961/7 .... C102

Harcourt Chambers Churchill House, 3 St Aldate's
Courtyard, Oxford OX1 1BN 01865 791559 .... C205

Hardwicke Building New Square, London WC2A 3SB
0171 242 2523 .... C103

1 Hare Court Ground Floor, London EC4Y 7BE
0171 353 3982/5324 .... C105

One Hare Court 1st Floor, London EC4Y 7BE
0171 353 3171 .... C105

3 Hare Court 1st Floor, London EC4Y 7BJ
0171 353 7561 .... C107

Chambers of Harjit Singh 2 Middle Temple Lane, Ground
Floor, London EC4Y 9AA 0171 353 1356 .... C107

23 Harries Road Hayes, Middlesex UB4 9DD
0181 841 8236 .... C24

Harrow-on-the-Hill Chambers 60 High Street, Harrow on
the Hill, Middlesex HA1 3LL 0181 423 7444 .... C108

Helions Chambers Pilgrims' Waye, Camps Road, Haverhill,
Suffolk CB9 7AS 01440 730523 .... C24

Herons Rest Parkham Lane, Brixham, Devon TQ5 9JR
01803 882293 .... C14

Hickstead Cottage Brighton Road, Hickstead, West Sussex
RH17 5NU 01444 881182 .... C24

No. 1 High Pavement Chambers Nottingham NG1 1HF
0115 941 8218 .... C203

Higher Combe Hawkcombe, Minehead, Somerset TA24 8LP
01643 862722 .... C198

10 Highlever Road London W10 6PS 0181 969 8514 .. C108

Chambers of Paul Hogben 199 Kingsworth Road, Ashford,
Kent TN23 6NB 01233 645805 .... C3

Holborn Chambers 6 Gate Street, London WC2A 3HP
0171 242 6060 .... C108

Horizon Chambers 95a Chancery Lane, London WC2A 1DT
0171 242 2440 .... C108

I

India Buildings Chambers India Buildings, Water Street, Liverpool, Merseyside L2 0XG 0151 243 6000 .... C37

International Law Chambers ILC House 77/79 Chepstow Road, London W2 5QR 0171 221 5684/5/4840 .... C108

Iscoed Chambers 86 St Helen's Road, Swansea, West Glamorgan SA1 4BQ 01792 652988/9/330 .... C215

J

John Pugh's Chambers 3rd Floor 14 Castle Street, Liverpool L2 0NE 0151 236 5415 .... C37

John Street Chambers 2 John Street, London WC1N 2HJ 0171 242 1911 .... C109

Justice Court Chambers 75 Kendal Road, London NW10 1JE 0181 830 7786 .... C109

K

Keating Chambers 10 Essex Street, London WC2R 3AA 0171 544 2600 .... C109

Kenworthy's Chambers 83 Bridge Street, Manchester M3 2RF 0161 832 4036 .... C189

King Charles House Standard Hill, Nottingham NG1 6FX 0115 941 8851 .... C204

40 King Street Chester CH1 2AH 01244 323886 .... C18

40 King Street Manchester M2 6BA 0161 832 9082 ..... C189

65-67 King Street Leicester LE1 6RP 0116 2547710 ...... C33

8 King Street Chambers 8 King Street, Manchester M2 6AQ 0161 834 9560 .... C190

58 King Street Chambers 1st Floor, Kingsgate House, 51-53 South King Street, Manchester M2 6DE 0161 831 7477 .... C191

King's Bench Chambers 175 Holdenhurst Road, Bournemouth, Dorset BH8 8DQ 01202 250025 .... C10

King's Bench Chambers 32 Beaumont Street, Oxford OX1 2NP 01865 311066 .... C205

King's Bench Chambers 115 North Hill, Plymouth PL4 8JY 01752 221551 .... C207

One King's Bench Walk London EC4Y 7DB 0171 936 1500 .... C110

2 King's Bench Walk Ground Floor, London EC4Y 7DE 0171 353 1746 .... C111

4 King's Bench Walk Ground/1st Floor, London EC4Y 7DL 0171 822 8822 .... C111

4 King's Bench Walk 2nd Floor, London EC4Y 7DL 0171 353 3581 .... C112

6 King's Bench Walk Ground Floor, London EC4Y 7DR 0171 583 0410 .... C113

6 King's Bench Walk London EC4Y 7DR 0171 353 4931/ 583 0695 .... C113

S Tomlinson QC 7 King's Bench Walk, London EC4Y 7DS 0171 583 0404 .... C114

8 King's Bench Walk London EC4Y 7DU 0171 797 8888 .... C114

9 King's Bench Walk Ground Floor, London EC4Y 7DX 0171 353 7202/3909 .... C115

The Chambers of Mr Ali Mohammad Azhar 9 King's Bench Walk (Lower Ground South), London EC4Y 7DX 0171 353 9564 (4 lines) C115

10 King's Bench Walk Ground Floor, London EC4Y 7EB 0171 353 7742 .... C116

10 King's Bench Walk 1st Floor, London EC4Y 7EB 0171 353 2501 .... C116

11 King's Bench Walk 3 Park Court, Park Cross Street, Leeds LS1 2QH 0113 2971 200 .... C27

11 King's Bench Walk London EC4Y 7EQ 0171 632 8500 .... C116

11 King's Bench Walk 1st Floor, London EC4Y 7EQ 0171 353 3337/8 .... C117

12 King's Bench Walk London EC4Y 7EL 0171 583 0811 .... C118

13 King's Bench Walk Temple, London EC4Y 7EN 0171 353 7204 .... C119

Chambers of Lord Campbell of Alloway QC 2 King's Bench Walk Chambers, London EC4Y 7DE 0171 353 9276 .... C119

8 King's Bench Walk North 1 Park Square East, Leeds LS1 2NE 0113 2439797 .... C27

King's Chambers 5a Gildredge Road, Eastbourne, East Sussex BN21 4RB 01323 416053 .... C21

King's Chambers 49a Broadway, London E15 4BW C120

10 Kingsfield Avenue Harrow, Middlesex HA2 6AH 0181 427 8709/081 248 4943 .... C24

Kingsway Chambers 88 Kingsway, London WC2B 6AA 07000 653529 .... C120

L

Lamb Building Ground Floor, London EC4Y 7AS 0171 797 7788 .... C120

Lamb Chambers Lamb Building, Elm Court, London EC4Y 7AS 0171 797 8300 .... C121

8 Lambert Jones Mews London EC2Y 8DP 0171 638 8804 .... C121

29a Lambs Conduit Street London WC1N 3NG 0171 831 9907 .... C121

Lancaster Building Chambers 77 Deansgate, Manchester M3 2BW 0161 661 4444 .... C191

21 Lauderdale Tower London EC2Y 8BY 0171 920 9308 .... C121

10 Launceston Avenue Reading, Berkshire RG4 6SW 01189 479548 .... C210

Lavenham Chambers Rookery Farm, Near Lavenham, Suffolk CO10 0BJ 01787 248247 .... C198

Law Chambers 2nd Floor, 5 Cardiff Road, Luton, Bedfordshire LU1 1PP 01582 431352 or 0958 674785 ... C184

Leone Chambers 72 Evelyn Avenue, London NW9 0JH 0181 931 1712 .... C121

Chambers of Nigel Ley Second Floor, South Gray's Inn Chambers, London WC1R 5JA 0171 831 7888 .... C121

Library Chambers First Floor, Gray's Inn Chambers, London WC1R 5JA 0171 404 6500 .... C122

Lincoln House Chambers 5th Floor, Lincoln House, Manchester M2 5EL 0161 832 5701 .... C192

Lion Court Chancery House, 53-64 Chancery Lane, London WC2A 1SJ 0171 404 6565 .... C122

Littleton Chambers 3 King's Bench Walk North, London EC4Y 7HR 0171 797 8600 .... C122

Littman Chambers 12 Gray's Inn Square, London WC1R 5JP 0171 404 4866 .... C123

114 Liverpool Road London N1 0RE 0171 226 9863 ... C124

Lloyds House Chambers 3rd Floor, 18 Lloyds House, Manchester M2 5WA 0161 839 3371 .... C192

235 London Road London TW1 1ES 0181 892 5947 ... C124

20 Lorne Park Road Bournemouth, Dorset BH1 1JN 01202 292102 .... C10

Luton Bedford Chambers C/O Mr Alex Reid, 15 Holly Park Road, London N11 3HB 0181 361 9024/0181 444 6337 C124

The Chambers of Adrian Lyon 14 Castle Street, Liverpool, Merseyside L2 0NE 0151 236 4421/8240/6757 .... C37

M

Chambers of Ian Macdonald QC Waldorf House, 2nd Floor, 5 Cooper Street, Manchester M2 2FW 0161 236 1840 .... C192

Maidstone Chambers Broughton House, 33 Earl Street, Maidstone, Kent ME14 1PF 01622 688592 .... C185

Manchester House Chambers 18–22 Bridge Street, Manchester M3 3BZ 0161 834 7007 .... C193

5 Marney Road London SW11 1ES 0171 978 4492 ...... C124

Martins Building Water Street, Liverpool, Merseyside L2 3SP 0151 236 5818/4919 .... C38

Melbury House 55 Manor Road, Leicester LE2 2LL 0116 2711848 .... C33

Mendhir Chambers 38 Priest Avenue, Wokingham, Berkshire RG40 2LX 0118 9771274 .... C219

Merchant Chambers 1 North Parade, Parsonage Gardens, Manchester M3 2NH 0161 839 7070 .... C193

Mercury Chambers Mercury House, 33-35 Clarendon Road, Leeds LS2 9NZ 0113 234 2265 .... C27

Merriemore Cottage Nr Rugby, Warwickshire CV23 8BB 01788 891832 .... C204

1 Middle Temple Lane London EC4Y 9AA 0171 583 0659 (12 lines) C124

2 Middle Temple Lane 3rd Floor, London EC4Y 9AA 0171 583 4540 .... C125

1a Middle Temple Lane Ground Floor, London EC4Y 9AA 0171 353 8815 .... C125

Middlesex Chambers Suite 3 & 4, Stanley House, Stanley Avenue, Wembley, Middlesex HA0 4SB 0181 902 1499 . C217

Milburn House Chambers 'A' Floor, Milburn House, Newcastle upon Tyne NE1 1LE 0191 230 5511 .... C199

6-8 Mill Street Maidstone, Kent ME15 6XH 01622 688094 .... C185

10 Millfields Road London E5 OSB 0181 986 8059 ...... C125

Milton Keynes Chambers 27 Broad Street, Milton Keynes, N Buckinghamshire MK16 0AN 01908 217857 .... C198

Chambers of Lesley Mitchell Stapleton Lodge, 71 Hamilton Road, Brentford, Middlesex TW8 0QJ 0181 568 2164 ...... C11

1 Mitre Court Buildings London EC4Y 7BS 0171 797 7070 .... C125

2 Mitre Court Buildings 1st Floor, London EC4Y 7BX 0171 353 1353 .... C126

2 Mitre Court Buildings 2nd Floor, London EC4Y 7BX 0171 583 1380 .... C127

Mitre Court Chambers 3rd Floor, Mitre Court, London EC4Y 7BP 0171 353 9394 .... C127

Mitre House Chambers Mitre House, 44 Fleet Street, London EC4Y 1BN 0171 583 8233 .... C128

Monckton Chambers 4 Raymond Buildings, London WC1R 5BP 0171 405 7211 .... C129

26 Morley Avenue Chesterfield S40 4DA 01246 234790 C19

Chambers of Christopher J Morrison 5 Gladeside, Chessington, Surrey KT9 2JQ C18

Mottingham Barrister's Chambers 43 West Park, London SE9 4RZ 0181 857 5565 .... C129

N

Chambers of Dr Jamal Nasir 1st Floor, 2 Stone Buildings, London WC2A 3RH 0171 405 3818/9 .... C129

Neston Home Chambers 42 Greenhill, Corsham, Wiltshire SN13 9SQ 01225 811909 .... C216

New Bailey Chambers 10 Lawson Street, Preston, Lancashire PR1 2QT 01772 258 087 .... C209

New Chambers 3 Sadleir Road, St Albans, Hertfordshire AL1 2BL 0966 212126 .... C214

New Court London EC4Y 9BE 0171 583 5123 .... C130

New Court 1st Floor, London EC4Y 9BE 0171 797 8999 .... C130

New Court Chambers 168 Corporation Street, Suite 200, Gazette Building, Birmingham, West Midlands B4 6TZ 0121 693 6656 .... C8

New Court Chambers 5 Verulam Buildings, London WC1R 5LY 0171 831 9500 .... C131

New Court Chambers 3 Broad Chare, Newcastle upon Tyne NE1 3DQ 0191 232 1980 .... C200

1 New Square Ground Floor, London WC2A 3SA 0171 405 0884/5/6/7 .... C131

3 New Square Lincoln's Inn, London WC2A 3RS 0171 405 1111 .... C132

Chambers of Lord Goodhart QC 3 New Square, Lincoln's Inn, London WC2A 3RS 0171 405 5577 .... C132

5 New Square 1st Floor, London WC2A 3RJ 0171 404 0404 .... C132

7 New Square London WC2A 3QS 0171 430 1660 .... C133

8 New Square London WC2A 3QP 0171 405 4321 ...... C134

Chambers of John Gardiner QC 11 New Square, London WC2A 3QB 0171 242 4017 .... C135

12 New Square London WC2A 3SW 0171 419 1212 .... C135

2 New Street Leicester LE1 5NA 0116 262 5906 .... C34

New Walk Chambers 27 New Walk, Leicester LE1 6TE 0116 2559144 .... C34

Newport Chambers 12 Clytha Park Road, Newport, Gwent NP9 47L 01633 267403/255855 .... C201

No. 6 Barristers Chambers, 6 Park Square, Leeds LS1 2LW 0113 245 9763 .... C28

North London Chambers 14 Keyes Road, London NW2 3XA 0181 208 4651 .... C136

Northeastern Law Chambers The Chocolate Factory, B305 Clarendon Road / Western Road, London N22 6UN 0181 881 3890 .... C136

7 Norwich Street Cambridge CB2 1ND 07000 226584 ... C15

O

Octagon House 19 Colegate, Norwich, Norfolk NR3 1AT 01603 623186 .... C203

Odogor Chambers 14 Cairns Road, London SW11 1ES C136

Chambers of Joy Okoye Suite 1, 2nd Floor, Grays Inn Chambers, London WC1R 5JA 0171 405 7011 .... C137

17 Old Bldgs Ground Floor, London WC2A 3UP 0171 405 9653 .... C137

19 Old Buildings London WC2A 3UP 0171 405 2001 .. C137

22 Old Buildings London WC2A 3UJ 0171 831 0222 ... C138

Twenty-Four Old Buildings Ground Floor, London WC2A 3UJ 0171 404 0946 .... C138

24 Old Buildings 1st Floor, London WC2A 3UJ 0171 242 2744 .... C139

Old Colony House 6 South King Street, Manchester M2 6DQ 0161 834 4364 .... C193

9 Old Square Ground Floor, London WC2A 3SR 0171 405 4682 .... C139

The Chambers of Leolin Price CBE, QC 10 Old Square, Lincoln's Inn, London WC2A 3SU 0171 405 0758/ 242 5002 .... C140

11 Old Square Ground Floor, London WC2A 3TS 0171 242 5022 .... C141

11 Old Square Ground Floor, London WC2A 3TS 0171 430 0341 .... C141

12 Old Square 1st Floor, London WC2A 3TX
0171 404 0875 .... C142

13 Old Square London WC2A 3UA 0171 404 4800 ...... C142

Old Square Chambers Hanover House, 47 Corn Street,
Bristol BS1 1HT 0117 927 7111 .... C13

Old Square Chambers 1 Verulam Buildings, London
WC1R 5LQ 0171 269 0300 .... C144

Oriel Chambers 14 Water Street, Liverpool, Merseyside
L2 8TD 0151 236 7191 .... C38

The Outer Temple Room 26, London WC2R 1BQ
0171 353 4647 .... C144

4 Overdale Road Leicester LE2 3YH 0116 2883930 .... C34

90 Overstrand Mansions Prince of Wales Drive, London
SW11 4EU 0171 622 7415 .... C145

Oxdale 2 Hoby Road, Melton Mowbray, Leics LE14 3PE
01664 434787 .... C196

P

Pall Mall Chambers Executive House, 40A Young Street,
Manchester M3 3FT 0161 832 3373/4 .... C193

One Paper Buildings Ground Floor, London EC4Y 7EP
0171 583 7355 .... C145

1 Paper Buildings 1st Floor, London EC4Y 7EP
0171 353 3728/4953 .... C145

2 Paper Buildings London EC4Y 7ET 0171 353 0933 C145

2 Paper Buildings 1st Floor, London EC4Y 7ET
0171 936 2611 (10 lines) C146

2 Paper Buildings, Basement North London EC4Y 7ET
0171 936 2613 .... C147

3 Paper Buildings Ground Floor, London EC4Y 7EU
0171 797 7000 .... C147

3 Paper Buildings 1st Floor, London EC4Y 7EU
0171 583 8055 .... C148

3 Paper Bldgs 2nd Floor, London EC4Y 7EU
0171 353 6208 .... C149

4 Paper Buildings Ground Floor, London EC4Y 7EX
0171 353 3366/583 7155 .... C149

4 Paper Buildings 1st Floor, London EC4Y 7EX
0171 583 0816 .... C150

5 Paper Bldgs Lower Ground Floor, London EC4Y 7HB
0171 353 5638 .... C151

5 Paper Buildings Ground Floor, London EC4Y 7HB
0171 583 9275 .... C151

5 Paper Buildings 1st Floor, London EC4Y 7HB
0171 583 6117 .... C151

Paradise Square Chambers 26 Paradise Square, Sheffield
S1 2DE 0114 273 8951 .... C212

39 Park Avenue Mitcham, Surrey CR4 2ER
0181 648 1684 .... C198

Park Court Chambers 16 Park Place, Leeds LS1 1SJ
0113 243 3277 .... C28

Park Lane Chambers 19 Westgate, Leeds LS1 2RU
0113 228 5000 .... C29

The Chambers of Philip Raynor QC 5 Park Place, Leeds
LS1 2RU 0113 242 1123 .... C29

9 Park Place 9 & 10 Park Place, Cardiff CF1 3DP
01222 382731 .... C16

30 Park Place Cardiff CF1 3BA 01222 398421 .... C16

32 Park Place Cardiff CF1 3BA 01222 397364 .... C17

33 Park Place Cardiff CF1 3BA 01222 233313 .... C17

30 Park Square Leeds LS1 2PF 0113 243 6388 .... C30

37 Park Square Leeds LS1 2NY 0113 243 9422 .... C30

39 Park Square Leeds LS1 2NU 0113 2456633 .... C30

Parsonage Chambers 5th Floor, 3 The Parsonage,
Manchester M3 2HW 0161 833 1996 .... C193

12 Paxton Close Richmond, Surrey TW9 2AW
0181 940 5895 .... C211

Peel Court Chambers 45 Hardman Street, Manchester
M3 3PL 0161 832 3791 .... C194

Peel House Chambers Ground Floor, Peel House, 5-7
Harrington Street, Liverpool, Merseyside L2 9QA
0151 236 4321 .... C39

Pembroke House 18 The Crescent, Leatherhead, Surrey
KT22 8EE 01372 376160/376493 .... C25

Pendragon Chambers 124 Walter Road, Swansea, West
Glamorgan SA1 5RG 01792 411188 .... C216

Pepys' Chambers 17 Fleet Street, London EC4Y 1AA
0171 936 2710 .... C152

Perivale Chambers 15 Colwyn Avenue, Perivale, Middlesex
UB6 8JY 0181 998 1935/081 248 0246 .... C206

Phoenix Chambers First Floor, Gray's Inn Chambers,
London WC1R 5JA 0171 404 7888 .... C152

Plowden Buildings London EC4Y 9BU
0171 583 0808 .... C152

Plowden Buildings 1 Jesmond Dene Terrace, Newcastle
upon Tyne NE2 2ET 0191 281 2096 .... C200

21 Portland Road Clarendon Park, Leicester LE2 3AB
0116 2706235 .... C34

Portsmouth Barristers' Chambers Victory House, 7
Bellevue Terrace, Portsmouth, Hampshire PO5 3AT
01705 831292 .... C208

Chambers of John L Powell QC 2nd Floor, 2 Crown Office
Row, London EC4Y 7HJ 0171 797 8000 .... C153

Primrose Chambers 5 Primrose Way, Alperton, Middlesex
HA0 1DS 0181 998 1806 .... C3

Prince Henry's Chambers 17 Fleet Street, London
EC4Y 1AA 0171 353 1183/1190 .... C154

Priory Chambers 2 Fountain Court, Birmingham B4 6DR
0121 236 3882/1375 .... C8

Pulteney Chamber 14 Johnstone Street, Bath, Somerset
BA2 4DH 01225 465667 .... C3

1 Pump Court London EC4Y 7AB 0171 583 2012/
353 4341 .... C154

2 Pump Court 1st Floor, London EC4Y 7AH
0171 353 5597 .... C155

Pump Court Chambers Upper Ground Floor, 3 Pump
Court, London EC4Y 7AJ 0171 353 0711 .... C156

4 Pump Court Temple, London EC4Y 7AN 0171 353 2656/
9 .... C157

5 Pump Court Ground Floor, London EC4Y 7AP
0171 353 2532 .... C158

Chambers of Kieran Coonan QC 6 Pump Court, Ground
Floor & Lower Ground Floor, London EC4Y 7AR
0171 583 6013/2510 .... C158

6 Pump Court 1st Floor, London EC4Y 7AR
0171 797 8400 .... C159

Pump Court Chambers 1st Floor, 5 Temple Chambers,
Temple Street, Swindon, Wiltshire SN1 1SQ
01793 539899 .... C216

Pump Court Chambers 31 Southgate Street, Winchester
SO23 9EE 01962 868161 .... C218

Pump Court Tax Chambers 16 Bedford Row, London
WC1R 4EB 0171 414 8080 .... C159

Q

Queen Elizabeth Building Ground Floor, London EC4Y 9BS
0171 353 7181 (12 lines) C160

Queen Elizabeth Building Hollis Whiteman Chambers, London EC4Y 9BS 0171 583 5766 .... C160

Queen Elizabeth Bldg 2nd Floor, London EC4Y 9BS 0171 797 7837 .... C161

Queen's Chambers 5 John Dalton Street, Manchester M2 6ET 0161 834 6875/4738 .... C194

R

The Ralek 66 Carshalton Park Road, Carshalton, Surrey SM5 3SS 0181 669 1777 .... C18

189 Randolph Avenue London W9 1DJ 0171 624 9139 .... C161

1 Raymond Buildings London WC1R 5BH 0171 430 1234 .... C161

3 Raymond Buildings London WC1R 5BH 0171 831 3833 .... C162

5 Raymond Buildings 1st Floor, London WC1R 5BP 0171 242 2902 .... C162

18 Red Lion Court (off Fleet Street), London EC4A 3EB 0171 520 6000 .... C163

Redhill Chambers Seloduct House, 30 Station Road, Redhill, Surrey RH1 1NF 01737 780781 .... C211

Regency Chambers Sheraton House, Castle Park, Cambridge CB3 0AX 01223 301517 .... C15

Regency Chambers Cathedral Square, Peterborough PE1 1XW 01733 315215 .... C207

Regent Chambers 29 Regent Road, Stoke-on-Trent ST1 3BT 01782 286666 .... C215

Resolution Chambers Oak Lodge, 55 Poolbrook Road, Malvern, Worcestershire WR14 3JN 01684 561279 .... C185

Richmond Green Chambers Greyhound House, 23-24 George Street, Richmond-upon-Thames, Surrey TW9 1HY 0181 940 1841 .... C211

20 Richmond Way 1st Floor, London W12 8LY 0181 749 2004 .... C163

Ridgeway Chambers 6 The Ridgeway, London NW11 8TB 0181 455 2939 .... C163

Roehampton Chambers 30 Stoughton Close, London SW15 4LS 0181 788 1238 .... C163

Ropewalk Chambers 24 The Ropewalk, Nottingham NG1 5EF 0115 947 2581 .... C204

27 Rose Grove Bury, Greater Manchester BL8 2UJ 0161 763 4739 .... C14

Rosemont Chambers 26 Rosemont Court, Rosemont Road, London W3 9LS 0181 992 1100 .... C164

Rougemont Chambers 15 Barnfield Road, Exeter, Devon EX1 1RR 01392 410471 .... C22

Rowchester Chambers 4 Rowchester Court, Whittall Street, Birmingham B4 6DH 0121 233 2327/2361951 .... C8

"Rydal Mount" 164 Heaton Moor Road, Stockport, Cheshire SK4 4HS 0161 432 8875 .... C214

S

Sackville Chambers Sackville Place, 44-48 Magdalen Street, Norwich, Norfolk NR3 1JU 01603 613516 .... C203

2 Salvia Gardens Perivale, Middlesex UB6 7PG 0181 997 9905 .... C206

Sedan House Stanley Place, Chester CH1 2LU 01244 320480/348282 .... C18

No 1 Serjeants' Inn Fleet Street, London EC4Y 1LL 0171 415 6666 .... C164

1 Serjeants' Inn 4th Floor, London EC4Y 1NH 0171 583 1355 .... C164

3 Serjeants' Inn London EC4Y 1BQ 0171 353 5537 ..... C165

Serle Court Chambers Thirteen Old Square, London WC2A 3UA 0171 242 6105 .... C166

20 Sewardstone Gardens London E4 7QE 0181 524 3054 .... C166

26 Shaftesbury Road Coventry, Warwickshire CV5 6FN 01203 677337 .... C20

Somersett Chambers 52 Bedford Row, London WC1R 4LR 0171 404 6701 .... C166

2 South Avenue Cleverley, Lancashire BFY5 1JY C19

3–4 South Square London WC1R 5HP 0171 696 9900 C167

11 South Square 2nd Floor, London WC1R 5EU 0171 405 1222 .... C168

South Western Chambers Melville House, 12 Middle Street, Taunton, Somerset TA1 1SH 01823 331919 .... C217

Southernhay Chambers 33 Southernhay East, Exeter, Devon EX1 1NX 01392 255777 .... C23

Southsea Chambers PO Box 148, Portsmouth, Hampshire PO5 2TU 01705 291261 .... C209

Sovereign Chambers 25 Park Square, Leeds LS1 2PW 0113 245 1841/2/3 .... C31

Spon Chambers 13 Spon Street, Coventry, Warwickshire CV1 3BA 01203 632977 .... C20

85 Springfield Road Birmingham B14 7DU 0121 444 2818 .... C8

11 St Bernards Road Slough, Berkshire SL3 7NT 01753 553806/817989 .... C212

St George's Chambers 32/33 Foregate Street, Worcester WR1 1EE 0345 413635 .... C220

St Ive's Chambers 9 Fountain Ct, Birmingham B4 6DR 0121 236 0863/0929 .... C8

St James's Chambers 68 Quay Street, Manchester M3 3EJ 0161 834 7000 .... C194

18 St John Street Manchester M3 4EA 0161 278 1800 C195

24A St John Street Manchester M3 4DF 0161 833 9628 .... C195

28 St John Street Manchester M3 4DJ 0161 834 8418 C196

St John's Chambers Small Street, Bristol BS1 1DW 0117 921 3456/929 8514 .... C13

St John's Chambers One High Elm Drive, Hale Barns, Cheshire WA15 0JD 0161 980 7379 .... C24

St John's Chambers 2 St John's Street, Manchester M3 4DT 0161 832 1633 .... C196

St Mary's Chambers 50 High Pavement, Nottingham NG1 1HW 0115 950 3503 .... C204

St Paul's House 5th Floor, 23 Park Square South, Leeds LS1 2ND 0113 245 5866 .... C32

4 St Peter Street Winchester SO23 8BW 01962 868 884 .... C219

St Philip's Chambers Fountain Court, Steelhouse Lane, Birmingham, West Midlands B4 6DR 0121 246 7000 .... C8

Stanbrook & Henderson 2 Harcourt Buildings, Ground Floor, London EC4Y 9DB 0171 353 0101 .... C168

Staple Inn Chambers 1st Floor, 9 Staple Inn, London WC1V 7QH 0171 242 5240 .... C169

Chambers of Elizabeth Steventon 50 Firle Road, Brighton, Sussex BN2 2YH 01273 670394 .... C12

3 Stone Buildings Ground Floor, London WC2A 3XL 0171 242 4937/405 8358 .... C170

4 Stone Buildings Ground Floor, London WC2A 3XT 0171 242 5524 .... C171

5 Stone Buildings London WC2A 3XT 0171 242 6201 C171

7 Stone Buildings Ground Floor, London WC2A 3SZ 0171 405 3886/242 3546 .... C172

7 Stone Buildings 1st Floor, London WC2A 3SZ
0171 242 0961 .... C173

8 Stone Buildings London WC2A 3TA 0171 831 9881   C173

9 Stone Buildings London WC2A 3NN
0171 404 5055 .... C173

11 Stone Buildings London WC2A 3TG
+44 (0)171 831 6381 .... C174

Stour Chambers Barton Mill House, Barton Mill Road,
Canterbury, Kent CT1 1BP 01227 764899 .... C15

199 Strand London WC2R 1DR 0171 379 9779 .... C174

Sussex Chambers 9 Old Steine, Brighton BN1 1FJ
01273 607953 .... C12

Swan House P.O.Box 8749, London W13 9WQ
0181 998 3035 .... C175

T

16 Tatnell Road London SE23 1JY 0181 699 3818 .... C175

Temple Chambers Rooms 111/112, 3/7 Temple Avenue,
London EC4Y 0HP 0171 583 1001 (2 lines) C175

199B Temple Chambers 3-7 Temple Avenue, London
EC4Y 0DB 0171 583 8008 .... C175

55 Temple Chambers Temple Avenue, London EC4Y 0HP
0171 353 7400 .... C175

169 Temple Chambers Temple Avenue, London EC4Y 0DA
0171 583 7644 .... C176

Temple Fields Hamilton House, 1 Temple Avenue, London
EC4Y 0HA 0171 353 4212 .... C176

1 Temple Gardens 1st Floor, London EC4Y 9BB
0171 353 0407/583 1315 .... C176

2 Temple Gardens London EC4Y 9AY 0171 583 6041   C177

3 Temple Gardens Lower Ground Floor, London EC4Y 9AU
0171 353 3102/5/9297 .... C178

3 Temple Gardens 2nd Floor, London EC4Y 9AU
0171 583 1155 .... C179

3 Temple Gardens 3rd Floor, London EC4Y 9AU
0171 353 0832 .... C179

3 Temple Gardens 3rd Floor, London EC4Y 9AU
0171 583 0010 .... C179

3 Temple Gardens (North) Fifth Floor, London EC4Y 9AU
0171 353 0853/4/7222 .... C179

3 Temple Gardens Tax Chambers 1st Floor, London
EC4Y 9AU 0171 353 7884 .... C179

The Thames Chambers Wickham House, 10 Cleveland
Way, London E1 4TR 0171 790 7377 .... C179

Theatre House Percival Road, Bristol BS8 3LE
0117 974 1553 .... C13

Thetford Lodge Farm Brandon, Suffolk IP27 0TU
01842 813132 .... C11

Thomas More Chambers More House, 51-2 Carey Street,
Lincoln's Inn, London WC2A 2JB 0171 404 7000 .... C179

29 Gwilliam Street Bristol BS3 4LT 0117 966 8997 .... C13

Thornwood House 102 New London Road, Chelmsford,
Essex CM2 0RG 01245 280880 .... C18

Tindal Chambers 3/5 New Street, Chelmsford, Essex
CM1 1NT 01245 267742 .... C18

Tindal Chambers 3 Waxhouse Gate, St Albans, Herts
AL5 4DU 01727 843383 .... C214

Tollgate Mews Chambers 113 Tollgate Road, Tollgate
Mews, London E6 4JY 0171 511 1838 .... C180

14 Tooks Court Cursitor Street, London EC4A 1LB
0171 405 8828 .... C180

Tower Hamlets Barristers Chambers First Floor, 45 Brick
Lane, London E1 6PU 0171 247 9825 .... C181

Tower Hamlets Barristers Chambers 37B Princelet Street,
London E1 5LP 0171 377 8090 .... C181

Trafalgar Chambers 53 Fleet Street, London EC4Y 1BE
0171 583 5858 .... C181

Trinity Chambers 140 New London Road, Chelmsford,
Essex CM2 0AW 01245 605040 .... C18

Trinity Chambers 9-12 Trinity Chare, Newcastle upon Tyne
NE1 3DF 0191 232 1927 .... C201

Twin Firs P.O.Box 32, Pontyclun, South Wales CF72 9BY
01443 229850 .... C208

U

Chambers of Mohammed Hashmot Ullah 72 Brick Lane,
London E1 6RL 0171 377 0119 .... C181

45 Ullswater Crescent London SW15 3RG
0181 546 9284 .... C181

V

Veritas Chambers 33 Corn Street, Bristol BS1 1HT
0117 930 8802 .... C14

3 Verulam Buildings London WC1R 5NT
0171 831 8441 .... C182

Verulam Chambers Peer House, 8-14 Verulam Street,
London WC1X 8LZ 0171 813 2400 .... C183

Victoria Chambers 3rd Floor, 177 Corporation Street,
Birmingham B4 6RG 0121 236 9900 .... C10

136B Vine Lane Uxbridge, Middlesex UB10 0BQ
01895 270221 .... C217

W

Walnut House 63 St David's Hill, Exeter, Devon EX4 4DW
01392 279751 .... C23

23 Warham Road Sevenoaks, Kent TN14 5PF
01959 522325 .... C212

Warwick House Chambers 8 Warwick Court, Gray's Inn,
London WC1R 5DJ 0171 430 2323 .... C183

Watford Chambers 74 Mildred Avenue, Watford,
Hertfordshire WD1 7DX 01923 220553 .... C217

52 Wembley Park Drive Wembley, Middlesex HA9 8HB
0181 902 5629 .... C217

1 Wensley Avenue Woodford Green, Essex IG8 9HE
0181 505 9259 .... C220

Wessex Chambers 48 Queens Road, Reading, Berkshire
RG1 4BD 0118 956 8856 .... C211

West Lodge Farm Wrotham Road, Meopham, Kent
DA13 0QG 01474 812280 .... C197

243 Westbourne Grove London W11 2SE
0171 229 3819 .... C183

28 Western Road Oxford OX1 4LG 01865 204911 ...... C206

Westgate Chambers 16-17 Wellington Square, Hastings, East
Sussex TN34 1PB 01424 432105 .... C24

Westgate Chambers 144 High Street, Lewes, East Sussex
BN7 1XT 01273 480510 .... C34

Westgate Chambers 67a Westgate Road, Newcastle upon
Tyne NE1 1SG 0191 261 4407/232 9785 .... C201

Westgate Chambers 4 Copse Close, Northwood, Middlesex
HA6 2XG 01923 823671 .... C202

Westleigh Chambers Westleigh Wiltown, Langport,
Somerset TA10 0JE 01458 251261 .... C25

7 Westmeath Avenue Leicester LE5 6SS 0116 2412003   C34

Westminster Chambers 3 Crosshall Street, Liverpool
L1 6DQ 0151 236 4774 .... C39

White Friars Chambers 21 White Friars, Chester CH1 1NZ
01244 323070 .... C19

Wilberforce Chambers 7 Bishop Lane, Hull HU1 1PA
01482 323 264 .... C24

Wilberforce Chambers 8 New Square, London WC2A 3QP
0171 306 0102 .... C183

Chambers of Derek Willmott 8 Links Crescent, Romney
Marsh, Kent TN29 0RS 01303 87 3899 .... C211

7 Wilton Road Redhill, Surrey RH1 6QR
01737 760264 .... C211

15 Winckley Square Preston, Lancashire PR1 3JJ
01772 252 828 .... C210

Windsor Barristers' Chambers Windsor
01753 648899 .... C219

Windsor Chambers 2 Penuel Lane, Pontypridd, Mid
Glamorgan, South Wales CF37 4UF 01443 402067 .... C208

39 Windsor Road London N3 3SN 0181 349 9194 ...... C184

10 Winterbourne Grove Weybridge, Surrey KT13 0PP
0181 941 3939 .... C217

9 Woodhouse Square 9 Woodhouse Square, Leeds LS3 1AD
0113 245 1986 .... C32

66 Worthington Road Kingston, Surrey KT6 .... C25

Wynne Chambers 1 Wynne Road, London SW9 0BB
0171 737 7266 .... C184

Y

York Chambers 14 Toft Green, York YO1 6JT
01904 620 048 .... C220

York House Borough Road, Middlesbrough, Cleveland
TS1 2HJ 01642 213000 .... C198

Young Street Chambers 38 Young Street, Manchester
M3 3FT 0161 833 0489 .... C196

I